2018 Harris New York Manufacturers Directory

Exclusive Provider of
Dun & Bradstreet Library Solutions

dun & bradstreet

Published January 2018 next update January 2019

WARNING: Purchasers and users of this directory may not use this directory to compile mailing lists, other marketing aids and other types of data, which are sold or otherwise provided to third parties. Such use is wrongful, illegal and a violation of the federal copyright laws.

CAUTION: Because of the many thousands of establishment listings contained in this directory and the possibilities of both human and mechanical error in processing this information, Mergent Inc. cannot assume liability for the correctness of the listings or information on which they are based. Hence, no information contained in this work should be relied upon in any instance where there is a possibility of any loss or damage as a consequence of any error or omission in this volume.

Publisher
Mergent Inc.
444 Madison Ave
New York, NY 10022

©Mergent Inc All Rights Reserved
2018 Mergent Business Press
ISSN 1080-2614
ISBN 978-1-68200-802-7

TABLE OF CONTENTS

Summary of Contents & Explanatory Notes 4
User's Guide to Listings 6

Geographic Section
County/City Cross-Reference Index 9
Firms Listed by Location City 13

Standard Industrial Classification (SIC) Section
SIC Alphabetical Index 701
SIC Numerical Index 703
Firms Listed by SIC 705

Alphabetic Section
Firms Listed by Firm Name 879

Product Section
Product Index 1097
Firms Listed by Product Category 1121

SUMMARY OF CONTENTS

Number of Companies 17,548
Number of Decision Makers 44,293
Minimum Number of Employees 5

EXPLANATORY NOTES

How to Cross-Reference in This Directory

Sequential Entry Numbers. Each establishment in the Geographic Section is numbered sequentially (G-0000). The number assigned to each establishment is referred to as its "entry number." To make cross-referencing easier, each listing in the Geographic, SIC, Alphabetic and Product Sections includes the establishment's entry number. To facilitate locating an entry in the Geographic Section, the entry numbers for the first listing on the left page and the last listing on the right page are printed at the top of the page next to the city name.

Source Suggestions Welcome

Although all known sources were used to compile this directory, it is possible that companies were inadvertently omitted. Your assistance in calling attention to such omissions would be greatly appreciated. A special form on the facing page will help you in the reporting process.

Analysis

Every effort has been made to contact all firms to verify their information. The one exception to this rule is the annual sales figure, which is considered by many companies to be confidential information. Therefore, estimated sales have been calculated by multiplying the nationwide average sales per employee for the firm's major SIC/NAICS code by the firm's number of employees. Nationwide averages for sales per employee by SIC/NAICS codes are provided by the U.S. Department of Commerce and are updated annually. All sales—sales (est)—have been estimated by this method. The exceptions are parent companies (PA), division headquarters (DH) and headquarter locations (HQ) which may include an actual corporate sales figure—sales (corporate-wide) if available.

Types of Companies

Descriptive and statistical data are included for companies in the entire state. These comprise manufacturers, machine shops, fabricators, assemblers and printers. Also identified are corporate offices in the state.

Employment Data

This directory contains companies with 5 or more employees in the manufacturing industry. The employment figure shown in the Geographic Section includes male and female employees and embraces all levels of the company: administrative, clerical, sales and maintenance. This figure is for the facility listed and does not include other plants or offices. It should be recognized that these figures represent an approximate year-round average. These employment figures are broken into codes A through G and used in the Product and SIC Sections to further help you in qualifying a company. Be sure to check the footnotes on the bottom of pages for the code breakdowns.

Standard Industrial Classification (SIC)

The Standard Industrial Classification (SIC) system used in this directory was developed by the federal government for use in classifying establishments by the type of activity they are engaged in. The SIC classifications used in this directory are from the 1987 edition published by the U.S. Government's Office of Management and Budget. The SIC system separates all activities into broad industrial divisions (e.g., manufacturing, mining, retail trade). It further subdivides each division. The range of manufacturing industry classes extends from two-digit codes (major industry group) to four-digit codes (product).

For example:

Industry Breakdown	Code	Industry, Product, etc.
*Major industry group	20	Food and kindred products
Industry group	203	Canned and frozen foods
*Industry	2033	Fruits and vegetables, etc.

*Classifications used in this directory

Only two-digit and four-digit codes are used in this directory.

Arrangement

1. The **Geographic Section** contains complete in-depth corporate data. This section is sorted by cities listed in alphabetical order and companies listed alphabetically within each city. A County/City Index for referencing cities within counties precedes this section.

> IMPORTANT NOTICE: It is a violation of both federal and state law to transmit an unsolicited advertisement to a facsimile machine. Any user of this product that violates such laws may be subject to civil and criminal penalties, which may exceed $500 for each transmission of an unsolicited facsimile. Mergent Inc. provides fax numbers for lawful purposes only and expressly forbids the use of these numbers in any unlawful manner.

2. The **Standard Industrial Classification (SIC) Section** lists companies under approximately 500 four-digit SIC codes. An alphabetical and a numerical index precedes this section. A company can be listed under several codes. The codes are in numerical order with companies listed alphabetically under each code.

3. The **Alphabetic Section** lists all companies with their full physical or mailing addresses and telephone number.

4. The **Product Section** lists companies under unique Harris categories. An index preceding this section lists all product categories in alphabetical order. Companies can be listed under several categories.

USER'S GUIDE TO LISTINGS

GEOGRAPHIC SECTION

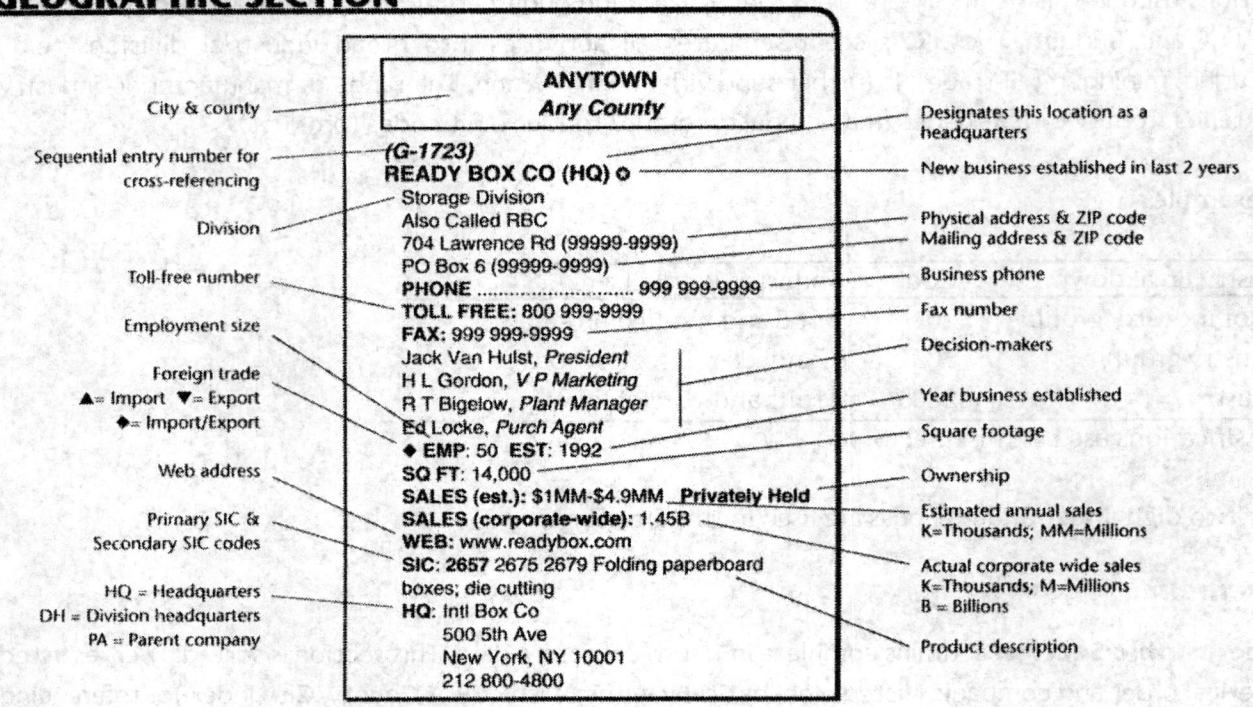

SIC SECTION

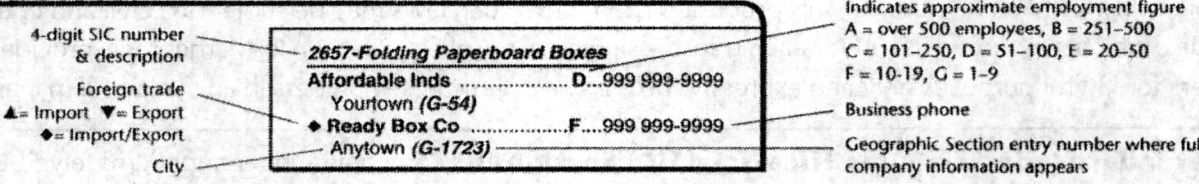

ALPHABETIC SECTION

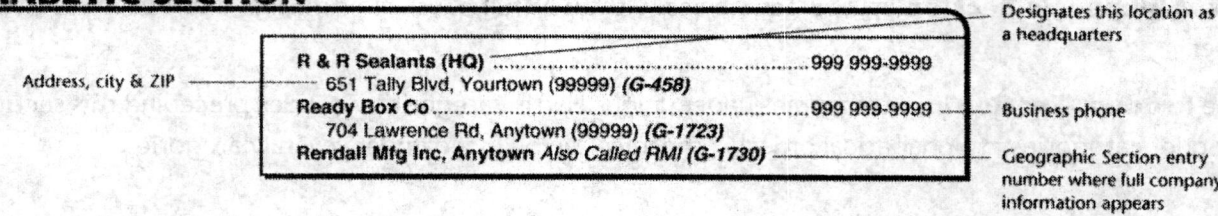

PRODUCT SECTION

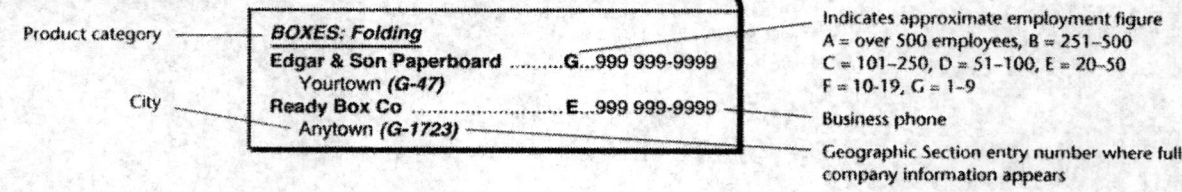

GEOGRAPHIC SECTION
Companies sorted by city in alphabetical order
In-depth company data listed

STANDARD INDUSTRIAL CLASSIFICATIONS
Alphabetical index of classifcation descriptions
Numerical index of classifcation descriptions
Companies sorted by SIC product groupings

ALPHABETIC SECTION
Company listings in alphabetical order

PRODUCT INDEX
Product categories listed in alphabetical order

PRODUCT SECTION
Companies sorted by product and manufacturing service classifications

New York
County Map

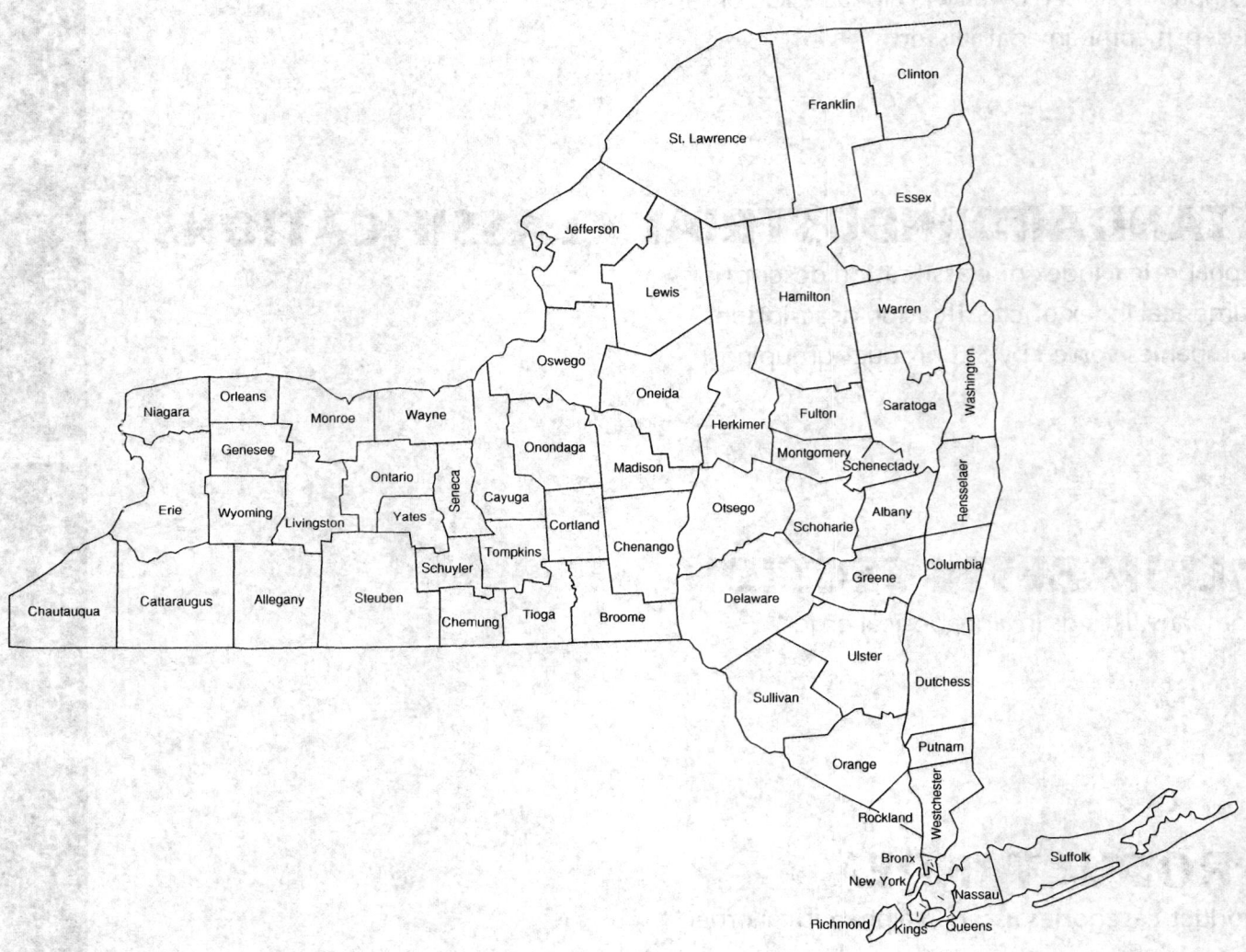

COUNTY/CITY CROSS-REFERENCE INDEX

Albany
City	Entry #
Albany	(G-30)
Alcove	(G-175)
Altamont	(G-208)
Coeymans	(G-3770)
Cohoes	(G-3771)
Colonie	(G-3845)
Delmar	(G-4269)
East Berne	(G-4405)
Feura Bush	(G-5180)
Glenmont	(G-5682)
Green Island	(G-5871)
Guilderland	(G-5924)
Latham	(G-7377)
Medusa	(G-8318)
Menands	(G-8395)
Ravena	(G-14033)
Selkirk	(G-15376)
Slingerlands	(G-15499)
South Bethlehem	(G-15536)
Troy	(G-16239)
Voorheesville	(G-16538)
Watervliet	(G-16702)
Westerlo	(G-17071)

Allegany
City	Entry #
Alfred	(G-196)
Alfred Station	(G-198)
Almond	(G-206)
Angelica	(G-376)
Belmont	(G-841)
Bolivar	(G-1156)
Canaseraga	(G-3391)
Cuba	(G-4094)
Fillmore	(G-5183)
Friendship	(G-5466)
Scio	(G-15342)
Wellsville	(G-16774)

Bronx
City	Entry #
Bronx	(G-1250)

Broome
City	Entry #
Binghamton	(G-881)
Castle Creek	(G-3445)
Chenango Bridge	(G-3623)
Conklin	(G-3889)
Deposit	(G-4299)
Endicott	(G-4802)
Endwell	(G-4840)
Johnson City	(G-7122)
Kirkwood	(G-7257)
Vestal	(G-16461)
Whitney Point	(G-17248)
Windsor	(G-17294)

Cattaraugus
City	Entry #
Allegany	(G-201)
Cattaraugus	(G-3464)
Delevan	(G-4260)
Ellicottville	(G-4654)
Franklinville	(G-5378)
Freedom	(G-5387)
Gowanda	(G-5763)
Hinsdale	(G-6450)
Kill Buck	(G-7195)
Limestone	(G-7472)
Little Valley	(G-7534)
Machias	(G-8023)
Olean	(G-13155)
Portville	(G-13892)
Randolph	(G-14029)
Salamanca	(G-15125)
South Dayton	(G-15539)

Cayuga
City	Entry #
Auburn	(G-475)
Aurora	(G-528)
Cato	(G-3453)
Genoa	(G-5602)
King Ferry	(G-7198)
Locke	(G-7595)
Moravia	(G-8656)
Port Byron	(G-13762)
Scipio Center	(G-15343)
Weedsport	(G-16772)

Chautauqua
City	Entry #
Ashville	(G-423)
Bemus Point	(G-842)
Brocton	(G-1248)
Cassadaga	(G-3442)
Clymer	(G-3758)
Dunkirk	(G-4356)
Ellington	(G-4658)
Falconer	(G-4896)
Findley Lake	(G-5185)
Forestville	(G-5340)
Fredonia	(G-5381)
Frewsburg	(G-5462)
Gerry	(G-5604)
Irving	(G-6807)
Jamestown	(G-7003)
Kennedy	(G-7182)
Lakewood	(G-7310)
Mayville	(G-8246)
Portland	(G-13891)
Ripley	(G-14147)
Sheridan	(G-15422)
Sherman	(G-15423)
Silver Creek	(G-15469)
Sinclairville	(G-15473)
Westfield	(G-17073)

Chemung
City	Entry #
Big Flats	(G-879)
Chemung	(G-3621)
Elmira	(G-4682)
Elmira Heights	(G-4721)
Horseheads	(G-6596)
Millport	(G-8515)
Pine City	(G-13577)
Pine Valley	(G-13583)
Wellsburg	(G-16773)

Chenango
City	Entry #
Afton	(G-8)
Bainbridge	(G-553)
Earlville	(G-4384)
Greene	(G-5880)
Mount Upton	(G-8700)
New Berlin	(G-8826)
Norwich	(G-13037)
Oxford	(G-13388)
Sherburne	(G-15411)
South Otselic	(G-15555)

Clinton
City	Entry #
Au Sable Forks	(G-474)
Champlain	(G-3565)
Chazy	(G-3589)
Keeseville	(G-7166)
Mooers	(G-8654)
Mooers Forks	(G-8655)
Peru	(G-13550)
Plattsburgh	(G-13677)
Rouses Point	(G-15065)
Saranac	(G-15161)

Columbia
City	Entry #
Ancram	(G-375)
Canaan	(G-3359)
Chatham	(G-3585)
Copake	(G-3913)
Copake Falls	(G-3914)
Germantown	(G-5603)
Ghent	(G-5620)
Hudson	(G-6630)
Kinderhook	(G-7196)
Livingston	(G-7587)
Philmont	(G-13565)
Stottville	(G-15803)
Stuyvesant	(G-15804)
Stuyvesant Falls	(G-15805)
Valatie	(G-16390)

Cortland
City	Entry #
Cincinnatus	(G-3681)
Cortland	(G-4033)
Homer	(G-6543)
Marathon	(G-8115)
Mc Graw	(G-8252)

Delaware
City	Entry #
Arkville	(G-409)
Bloomville	(G-988)
Davenport	(G-4105)
Delhi	(G-4262)
Halcottsville	(G-5927)
Hancock	(G-5984)
Hobart	(G-6451)
Margaretville	(G-8123)
Masonville	(G-8137)
Sidney	(G-15457)
Stamford	(G-15643)
Walton	(G-16568)

Dutchess
City	Entry #
Amenia	(G-218)
Barrytown	(G-619)
Beacon	(G-776)
Clinton Corners	(G-3748)
Dover Plains	(G-4338)
Fishkill	(G-5187)
Hopewell Junction	(G-6574)
Hyde Park	(G-6771)
Lagrangeville	(G-7278)
Millbrook	(G-8510)
Millerton	(G-8514)
Pawling	(G-13473)
Pine Plains	(G-13581)
Pleasant Valley	(G-13742)
Poughkeepsie	(G-13904)
Poughquag	(G-13957)
Red Hook	(G-14041)
Rhinebeck	(G-14067)
Staatsburg	(G-15637)
Stanfordville	(G-15647)
Stormville	(G-15801)
Wappingers Falls	(G-16586)
Wassaic	(G-16622)
Wingdale	(G-17296)

Erie
City	Entry #
Akron	(G-17)
Alden	(G-176)
Amherst	(G-221)
Angola	(G-378)
Blasdell	(G-954)
Bowmansville	(G-1168)
Buffalo	(G-2802)
Chaffee	(G-3560)
Cheektowaga	(G-3590)
Clarence	(G-3682)
Clarence Center	(G-3699)
Colden	(G-3797)
Collins	(G-3840)
Depew	(G-4272)
Derby	(G-4306)
East Amherst	(G-4386)
East Aurora	(G-4390)
East Concord	(G-4407)
Eden	(G-4597)
Elma	(G-4659)
Getzville	(G-5607)
Glenwood	(G-5718)
Grand Island	(G-5764)
Hamburg	(G-5941)
Holland	(G-6507)
Kenmore	(G-7173)
Lackawanna	(G-7268)
Lake View	(G-7303)
Lancaster	(G-7321)
North Collins	(G-12942)
Orchard Park	(G-13271)
Springville	(G-15630)
Tonawanda	(G-16154)
Wales Center	(G-16559)
West Falls	(G-16876)
West Seneca	(G-16967)
Williamsville	(G-17258)

Essex
City	Entry #
Crown Point	(G-4093)
Elizabethtown	(G-4640)
Jay	(G-7088)
Lake Placid	(G-7297)
Lewis	(G-7452)
Mineville	(G-8573)
Ray Brook	(G-14037)
Ticonderoga	(G-16146)
Upper Jay	(G-16327)
Westport	(G-17096)
Willsboro	(G-17288)
Wilmington	(G-17290)

Franklin
City	Entry #
Akwesasne	(G-29)
Burke	(G-3292)
Chateaugay	(G-3584)
Hogansburg	(G-6453)
Malone	(G-8036)
Moira	(G-8581)
Saranac Lake	(G-15162)
Tupper Lake	(G-16300)

Fulton
City	Entry #
Broadalbin	(G-1239)
Gloversville	(G-5719)
Johnstown	(G-7138)
Mayfield	(G-8244)
Northville	(G-13036)

Genesee
City	Entry #
Alexander	(G-190)
Batavia	(G-621)
Bergen	(G-843)
Byron	(G-3295)
Corfu	(G-3975)
East Bethany	(G-4406)
Le Roy	(G-7427)
Oakfield	(G-13083)
Pavilion	(G-13472)
Stafford	(G-15640)

Greene
City	Entry #
Athens	(G-463)
Cairo	(G-3296)
Catskill	(G-3454)
Coxsackie	(G-4082)
Durham	(G-4378)
East Durham	(G-4409)
Elka Park	(G-4643)
Greenville	(G-5902)
Hannacroix	(G-5991)
Palenville	(G-13423)
Prattsville	(G-13961)
Round Top	(G-15064)
Surprise	(G-15832)

Hamilton
City	Entry #
Lake Pleasant	(G-7301)
Speculator	(G-15587)

Herkimer
City	Entry #
Dolgeville	(G-4329)
Frankfort	(G-5358)
Herkimer	(G-6324)
Ilion	(G-6778)
Jordanville	(G-7160)
Little Falls	(G-7520)
Middleville	(G-8508)
Mohawk	(G-8575)
Newport	(G-12814)
Old Forge	(G-13152)
Poland	(G-13757)
Van Hornesville	(G-16455)
West Winfield	(G-16986)

Jefferson
City	Entry #
Adams	(G-2)
Adams Center	(G-4)
Alexandria Bay	(G-194)
Brownville	(G-2797)
Cape Vincent	(G-3410)
Carthage	(G-3435)
Clayton	(G-3710)
Dexter	(G-4308)
Felts Mills	(G-5175)
Fort Drum	(G-5345)
Great Bend	(G-5798)
Henderson	(G-6313)

COUNTY/CITY CROSS-REFERENCE

	ENTRY #		ENTRY #		ENTRY #		ENTRY #		ENTRY #
La Fargeville	(G-7262)	Fultonville	(G-5491)	**New York**		Memphis	(G-8394)	**Oswego**	
Philadelphia	(G-13564)	Nelliston	(G-8820)	New York	(G-9004)	Nedrow	(G-8818)	Bernhards Bay	(G-857)
Three Mile Bay	(G-16145)	Palatine Bridge	(G-13421)	**Niagara**		North Syracuse	(G-12957)	Central Square	(G-3542)
Watertown	(G-16655)	Saint Johnsville	(G-15118)	Barker	(G-611)	Skaneateles	(G-15476)	Cleveland	(G-3718)
Woodville	(G-17383)	Sprakers	(G-15601)	Burt	(G-3294)	Skaneateles Falls	(G-15489)	Constantia	(G-3906)
Kings		**Nassau**		Gasport	(G-5570)	Solvay	(G-15528)	Fulton	(G-5467)
Brooklyn	(G-1510)	Albertson	(G-155)	Lewiston	(G-7453)	Syracuse	(G-15864)	Hannibal	(G-5992)
Lewis		Atlantic Beach	(G-467)	Lockport	(G-7596)	Tully	(G-16297)	Lacona	(G-7277)
Beaver Falls	(G-789)	Baldwin	(G-557)	Middleport	(G-8454)	**Ontario**		Mexico	(G-8430)
Castorland	(G-3450)	Bayville	(G-775)	Newfane	(G-12811)	Bloomfield	(G-975)	Oswego	(G-13353)
Croghan	(G-4084)	Bellmore	(G-809)	Niagara Falls	(G-12817)	Canandaigua	(G-3363)	Parish	(G-13439)
Harrisville	(G-6014)	Bethpage	(G-860)	North Tonawanda	(G-12970)	Clifton Springs	(G-3739)	Phoenix	(G-13567)
Lowville	(G-7963)	Carle Place	(G-3411)	Ransomville	(G-14032)	Farmington	(G-5155)	Pulaski	(G-13962)
Lyons Falls	(G-8004)	Cedarhurst	(G-3482)	Sanborn	(G-15140)	Fishers	(G-5186)	Sandy Creek	(G-15159)
Livingston		East Meadow	(G-4438)	Wilson	(G-17291)	Geneva	(G-5582)	Williamstown	(G-17257)
Avon	(G-535)	East Norwich	(G-4464)	Youngstown	(G-17548)	Hall	(G-5940)	**Otsego**	
Caledonia	(G-3302)	East Rockaway	(G-4487)	**Oneida**		Honeoye	(G-6551)	Cherry Valley	(G-3624)
Conesus	(G-3874)	Elmont	(G-4728)	Ava	(G-529)	Manchester	(G-8084)	Colliersville	(G-3839)
Dansville	(G-4101)	Farmingdale	(G-4932)	Barneveld	(G-613)	Naples	(G-8810)	Cooperstown	(G-3909)
Geneseo	(G-5579)	Floral Park	(G-5197)	Blossvale	(G-991)	Oaks Corners	(G-13088)	Edmeston	(G-4635)
Hemlock	(G-6287)	Franklin Square	(G-5369)	Boonville	(G-1158)	Phelps	(G-13552)	Fly Creek	(G-5317)
Lakeville	(G-7305)	Freeport	(G-5388)	Camden	(G-3340)	Seneca Castle	(G-15381)	Milford	(G-8509)
Leicester	(G-7442)	Garden City	(G-5506)	Chadwicks	(G-3558)	Shortsville	(G-15456)	Morris	(G-8660)
Lima	(G-7464)	Garden City Park	(G-5553)	Clayville	(G-3712)	Victor	(G-16482)	Oneonta	(G-13193)
Livonia	(G-7590)	Glen Cove	(G-5621)	Clinton	(G-3742)	**Orange**		Richfield Springs	(G-14074)
Mount Morris	(G-8695)	Glen Head	(G-5645)	Deansboro	(G-4109)	Bullville	(G-3289)	Schenevus	(G-15336)
Nunda	(G-13059)	Great Neck	(G-5799)	Forestport	(G-5338)	Central Valley	(G-3547)	Unadilla	(G-16310)
Piffard	(G-13573)	Greenvale	(G-5897)	Holland Patent	(G-6513)	Chester	(G-3625)	West Burlington	(G-16874)
Retsof	(G-14064)	Hempstead	(G-6288)	Marcy	(G-8121)	Cornwall	(G-4006)	**Putnam**	
York	(G-17521)	Hewlett	(G-6330)	Mc Connellsville	(G-8251)	Cornwall On Hudson	(G-4013)	Brewster	(G-1203)
Madison		Hicksville	(G-6342)	New Hartford	(G-8846)	Florida	(G-5217)	Carmel	(G-3426)
Canastota	(G-3392)	Inwood	(G-6789)	New York Mills	(G-12740)	Goshen	(G-5746)	Cold Spring	(G-3787)
Cazenovia	(G-3469)	Island Park	(G-6817)	Oriskany	(G-13328)	Greenwood Lake	(G-5916)	Garrison	(G-5569)
Chittenango	(G-3659)	Jericho	(G-7094)	Oriskany Falls	(G-13342)	Harriman	(G-5993)	Mahopac	(G-8025)
De Ruyter	(G-4106)	Lawrence	(G-7416)	Remsen	(G-14052)	Highland Falls	(G-6437)	Patterson	(G-13462)
Hamilton	(G-5970)	Levittown	(G-7445)	Rome	(G-14832)	Highland Mills	(G-6438)	Putnam Valley	(G-13989)
Morrisville	(G-8661)	Lido Beach	(G-7461)	Sangerfield	(G-15160)	Huguenot	(G-6682)	**Queens**	
Munnsville	(G-8795)	Locust Valley	(G-7659)	Sauquoit	(G-15228)	Middletown	(G-8458)	Arverne	(G-421)
Oneida	(G-13177)	Long Beach	(G-7667)	Sherrill	(G-15426)	Monroe	(G-8582)	Astoria	(G-428)
Wampsville	(G-16574)	Lynbrook	(G-7971)	Stittville	(G-15784)	Montgomery	(G-8627)	Bayside	(G-757)
West Edmeston	(G-16875)	Manhasset	(G-8087)	Taberg	(G-16100)	Mountainville	(G-8793)	Bayside Hills	(G-773)
Monroe		Massapequa	(G-8206)	Utica	(G-16328)	New Hampton	(G-8842)	Bellerose	(G-805)
Brockport	(G-1242)	Massapequa Park	(G-8218)	Vernon	(G-16456)	New Windsor	(G-8974)	Cambria Heights	(G-3331)
Churchville	(G-3663)	Merrick	(G-8415)	Vernon Center	(G-16460)	Newburgh	(G-12769)	College Point	(G-3798)
East Rochester	(G-4472)	Mineola	(G-8520)	Waterville	(G-16700)	Otisville	(G-13369)	Corona	(G-4014)
Fairport	(G-4849)	New Hyde Park	(G-8859)	Westernville	(G-17072)	Pine Bush	(G-13575)	Douglaston	(G-4334)
Gates	(G-5576)	North Baldwin	(G-12921)	Westmoreland	(G-17091)	Pine Island	(G-13580)	East Elmhurst	(G-4410)
Hamlin	(G-5973)	North Bellmore	(G-12931)	Whitesboro	(G-17220)	Port Jervis	(G-13803)	Elmhurst	(G-4671)
Henrietta	(G-6314)	Oceanside	(G-13090)	Yorkville	(G-17539)	Rock Tavern	(G-14809)	Far Rockaway	(G-4926)
Hilton	(G-6443)	Old Bethpage	(G-13145)	**Onondaga**		Salisbury Mills	(G-15139)	Floral Park	(G-5215)
Honeoye Falls	(G-6553)	Old Westbury	(G-13153)	Baldwinsville	(G-563)	Slate Hill	(G-15496)	Flushing	(G-5227)
Mendon	(G-8412)	Oyster Bay	(G-13390)	Brewerton	(G-1199)	Southfields	(G-15580)	Forest Hills	(G-5324)
North Chili	(G-12940)	Plainview	(G-13605)	Bridgeport	(G-1234)	Sparrow Bush	(G-15586)	Fresh Meadows	(G-5451)
Penfield	(G-13521)	Port Washington	(G-13818)	Camillus	(G-3349)	Sugar Loaf	(G-15824)	Glen Oaks	(G-5654)
Pittsford	(G-13584)	Rockville Centre	(G-14816)	Cicero	(G-3670)	Tuxedo Park	(G-16306)	Glendale	(G-5657)
Rochester	(G-14175)	Roosevelt	(G-15027)	Clay	(G-3709)	Unionville	(G-16326)	Hollis	(G-6520)
Rush	(G-15070)	Roslyn	(G-15040)	De Witt	(G-4108)	Walden	(G-16549)	Howard Beach	(G-6625)
Scottsville	(G-15355)	Roslyn Heights	(G-15049)	East Syracuse	(G-4517)	Warwick	(G-16608)	Jackson Heights	(G-6921)
Spencerport	(G-15589)	Sea Cliff	(G-15363)	Elbridge	(G-4636)	Washingtonville	(G-16620)	Jamaica	(G-6926)
Webster	(G-16737)	Seaford	(G-15365)	Fabius	(G-4848)	West Point	(G-16959)	Kew Gardens	(G-7186)
West Henrietta	(G-16897)	South Hempstead	(G-15553)	Fayetteville	(G-5171)	Westtown	(G-17097)	Laurelton	(G-7412)
Montgomery		Syosset	(G-15833)	Jamesville	(G-7077)	**Orleans**		Little Neck	(G-7529)
Amsterdam	(G-333)	Uniondale	(G-16311)	Jordan	(G-7158)	Albion	(G-164)	Long Island City	(G-7675)
Canajoharie	(G-3360)	Valley Stream	(G-16423)	Kirkville	(G-7254)	Holley	(G-6515)	Maspeth	(G-8139)
Esperance	(G-4846)	Wantagh	(G-16576)	La Fayette	(G-7265)	Kendall	(G-7171)	Middle Village	(G-8442)
Fonda	(G-5320)	West Hempstead	(G-16880)	Liverpool	(G-7535)	Lyndonville	(G-7994)	Oakland Gardens	(G-13086)
Fort Plain	(G-5356)	Westbury	(G-16988)	Manlius	(G-8101)	Medina	(G-8298)	Ozone Park	(G-13401)
		Williston Park	(G-17285)	Marcellus	(G-8117)			Queens Village	(G-13990)
		Woodbury	(G-17303)						
		Woodmere	(G-17328)						

COUNTY/CITY CROSS-REFERENCE

City	ENTRY #
Rego Park	(G-14043)
Richmond Hill	(G-14077)
Ridgewood	(G-14109)
Rockaway Beach	(G-14810)
Rockaway Park	(G-14812)
Rosedale	(G-15036)
Saint Albans	(G-15110)
South Ozone Park	(G-15556)
South Richmond Hill	(G-15558)
Springfield Gardens	(G-15629)
Sunnyside	(G-15825)
Whitestone	(G-17227)
Woodhaven	(G-17324)
Woodside	(G-17334)

Rensselaer
City	ENTRY #
Averill Park	(G-530)
Berlin	(G-854)
Castleton On Hudson	(G-3446)
Cropseyville	(G-4085)
Eagle Bridge	(G-4380)
East Greenbush	(G-4420)
Hoosick Falls	(G-6566)
Nassau	(G-8816)
Petersburg	(G-13551)
Poestenkill	(G-13752)
Rensselaer	(G-14053)
Stephentown	(G-15778)
Troy	(G-16245)
Valley Falls	(G-16422)
West Sand Lake	(G-16960)
Wynantskill	(G-17394)

Richmond
City	ENTRY #
Staten Island	(G-15649)

Rockland
City	ENTRY #
Airmont	(G-10)
Blauvelt	(G-963)
Chestnut Ridge	(G-3651)
Congers	(G-3875)
Garnerville	(G-5566)
Haverstraw	(G-6261)
Hillburn	(G-6441)
Monsey	(G-8601)
Nanuet	(G-8797)
New City	(G-8828)
Nyack	(G-13061)
Orangeburg	(G-13238)
Palisades	(G-13425)
Pearl River	(G-13476)
Piermont	(G-13572)
Pomona	(G-13758)
Sloatsburg	(G-15502)
Spring Valley	(G-15602)
Stony Point	(G-15794)
Suffern	(G-15806)
Tallman	(G-16101)
Tappan	(G-16102)
Thiells	(G-16137)
Tomkins Cove	(G-16153)
Valley Cottage	(G-16400)
West Haverstraw	(G-16878)
West Nyack	(G-16940)

Saratoga
City	ENTRY #
Ballston Lake	(G-578)
Ballston Spa	(G-588)
Burnt Hills	(G-3293)
Clifton Park	(G-3719)
Corinth	(G-3979)
Galway	(G-5498)
Gansevoort	(G-5499)
Greenfield Center	(G-5889)
Hadley	(G-5926)
Halfmoon	(G-5930)
Malta	(G-8051)
Mechanicville	(G-8255)
Middle Grove	(G-8437)
Rexford	(G-14065)
Rock City Falls	(G-14807)
Round Lake	(G-15061)
Saratoga Springs	(G-15168)
Schuylerville	(G-15340)
South Glens Falls	(G-15545)
Stillwater	(G-15781)
Waterford	(G-16630)

Schenectady
City	ENTRY #
Alplaus	(G-207)
Delanson	(G-4257)
Duanesburg	(G-4349)
Glenville	(G-5716)
Niskayuna	(G-12910)
Pattersonville	(G-13471)
Rotterdam Junction	(G-15059)
Schenectady	(G-15256)
Scotia	(G-15345)

Schoharie
City	ENTRY #
Central Bridge	(G-3507)
Charlotteville	(G-3583)
Cobleskill	(G-3759)
Howes Cave	(G-6629)
Middleburgh	(G-8452)
Richmondville	(G-14101)
Schoharie	(G-15338)
Sharon Springs	(G-15404)
Sloansville	(G-15501)
Warnerville	(G-16599)

Schuyler
City	ENTRY #
Beaver Dams	(G-788)
Burdett	(G-3290)
Cayuta	(G-3467)
Hector	(G-6282)
Montour Falls	(G-8648)
Odessa	(G-13129)
Rock Stream	(G-14808)
Watkins Glen	(G-16718)
Wayne	(G-16736)

Seneca
City	ENTRY #
Fayette	(G-5170)
Interlaken	(G-6785)
Lodi	(G-7665)
Ovid	(G-13370)
Romulus	(G-14869)
Seneca Falls	(G-15382)
Waterloo	(G-16646)

St. Lawrence
City	ENTRY #
Brasher Falls	(G-1171)
Canton	(G-3406)
Childwold	(G-3658)
Cranberry Lake	(G-4083)
Gouverneur	(G-5757)
Hammond	(G-5974)
Madrid	(G-8024)
Massena	(G-8225)
Norfolk	(G-12914)
North Lawrence	(G-12951)
Norwood	(G-13058)
Ogdensburg	(G-13130)
Potsdam	(G-13894)
South Colton	(G-15537)
Star Lake	(G-15648)
Waddington	(G-16542)

Steuben
City	ENTRY #
Addison	(G-5)
Arkport	(G-408)
Avoca	(G-534)
Bath	(G-653)
Campbell	(G-3357)
Canisteo	(G-3405)
Corning	(G-3982)
Hammondsport	(G-5975)
Hornell	(G-6586)
Lindley	(G-7519)
Painted Post	(G-13415)
Wayland	(G-16733)
Woodhull	(G-17327)

Suffolk
City	ENTRY #
Amagansett	(G-217)
Amityville	(G-273)
Aquebogue	(G-383)
Babylon	(G-541)
Bay Shore	(G-663)
Bayport	(G-749)
Bellport	(G-819)
Blue Point	(G-993)
Bohemia	(G-996)
Brentwood	(G-1172)
Bridgehampton	(G-1230)
Brightwaters	(G-1237)
Brookhaven	(G-1504)
Calverton	(G-3314)
Center Moriches	(G-3489)
Centereach	(G-3494)
Centerport	(G-3500)
Central Islip	(G-3508)
Cold Spring Harbor	(G-3792)
Commack	(G-3848)
Copiague	(G-3915)
Coram	(G-3964)
Cutchogue	(G-4097)
Deer Park	(G-4110)
Dix Hills	(G-4311)
East Hampton	(G-4425)
East Islip	(G-4437)
East Moriches	(G-4449)
East Northport	(G-4452)
East Patchogue	(G-4466)
East Quogue	(G-4469)
East Setauket	(G-4494)
East Yaphank	(G-4593)
Eastport	(G-4596)
Edgewood	(G-4602)
Farmingville	(G-5167)
Great River	(G-5869)
Greenlawn	(G-5890)
Greenport	(G-5894)
Halesite	(G-5928)
Hampton Bays	(G-5982)
Hauppauge	(G-6026)
Holbrook	(G-6455)
Holtsville	(G-6525)
Huntington	(G-6685)
Huntington Station	(G-6730)
Islandia	(G-6824)
Islip	(G-6845)
Islip Terrace	(G-6854)
Jamesport	(G-7002)
Kings Park	(G-7199)
Lake Grove	(G-7290)
Lake Ronkonkoma	(G-7302)
Lindenhurst	(G-7474)
Lloyd Harbor	(G-7593)
Manorville	(G-8110)
Mastic	(G-8234)
Mastic Beach	(G-8236)
Mattituck	(G-8238)
Medford	(G-8264)
Melville	(G-8319)
Middle Island	(G-8438)
Montauk	(G-8623)
Moriches	(G-8659)
Mount Sinai	(G-8696)
Nesconset	(G-8821)
North Babylon	(G-12918)
Northport	(G-13025)
Oakdale	(G-13074)
Patchogue	(G-13440)
Peconic	(G-13494)
Port Jeff STA	(G-13786)
Port Jefferson	(G-13797)
Quogue	(G-14028)
Ridge	(G-14103)
Riverhead	(G-14149)
Ronkonkoma	(G-14873)
Sag Harbor	(G-15103)
Sagaponack	(G-15109)
Saint James	(G-15113)
Sayville	(G-15232)
Selden	(G-15369)
Setauket	(G-15398)
Shelter Island	(G-15408)
Shirley	(G-15434)
Smithtown	(G-15503)
Sound Beach	(G-15535)
Southampton	(G-15562)
Southold	(G-15581)
Speonk	(G-15599)
Stony Brook	(G-15787)
Wading River	(G-16543)
Wainscott	(G-16548)
Water Mill	(G-16625)
West Babylon	(G-16786)
West Islip	(G-16932)
West Sayville	(G-16962)
Westhampton	(G-17085)
Westhampton Beach	(G-17087)
Wyandanch	(G-17384)
Yaphank	(G-17400)

Sullivan
City	ENTRY #
Barryville	(G-620)
Bethel	(G-858)
Callicoon	(G-3312)
Cochecton	(G-3765)
Ferndale	(G-5176)
Harris	(G-5997)
Hurleyville	(G-6769)
Jeffersonville	(G-7092)
Kauneonga Lake	(G-7165)
Liberty	(G-7458)
Livingston Manor	(G-7588)
Long Eddy	(G-7674)
Monticello	(G-8642)
Narrowsburg	(G-8814)
Roscoe	(G-15034)
South Fallsburg	(G-15542)
Thompsonville	(G-16138)
Wht Sphr Spgs	(G-17250)
Woodridge	(G-17333)

Tioga
City	ENTRY #
Berkshire	(G-852)
Candor	(G-3403)
Lockwood	(G-7658)
Nichols	(G-12909)
Owego	(G-13375)
Richford	(G-14076)
Spencer	(G-15588)
Waverly	(G-16724)

Tompkins
City	ENTRY #
Dryden	(G-4344)
Freeville	(G-5447)
Groton	(G-5918)
Ithaca	(G-6856)
Lansing	(G-7373)
Trumansburg	(G-16290)

Ulster
City	ENTRY #
Accord	(G-1)
Bearsville	(G-787)
Bloomington	(G-987)
Boiceville	(G-1155)
Ellenville	(G-4646)
Gardiner	(G-5560)
High Falls	(G-6426)
Highland	(G-6430)
Kerhonkson	(G-7183)
Kingston	(G-7206)
Lake Katrine	(G-7294)
Marlboro	(G-8135)
Milton	(G-8516)
Mount Marion	(G-8692)
New Paltz	(G-8918)
Rifton	(G-14144)
Saugerties	(G-15207)
Shokan	(G-15455)
Stone Ridge	(G-15785)
Tillson	(G-16152)
Ulster Park	(G-16308)
Wallkill	(G-16561)
Wawarsing	(G-16732)
West Hurley	(G-16931)
Woodstock	(G-17377)

Warren
City	ENTRY #
Bakers Mills	(G-556)
Bolton Landing	(G-1157)
Brant Lake	(G-1170)
Chestertown	(G-3649)
Glens Falls	(G-5685)
Lake George	(G-7286)
Lake Luzerne	(G-7296)
North Creek	(G-12949)
Queensbury	(G-14001)
Silver Bay	(G-15468)
Warrensburg	(G-16600)

Washington
City	ENTRY #
Argyle	(G-406)
Cambridge	(G-3332)
Cossayuna	(G-4081)
Fort Ann	(G-5344)
Fort Edward	(G-5347)
Granville	(G-5789)
Greenwich	(G-5904)
Hampton	(G-5981)
Hartford	(G-6015)
Hudson Falls	(G-6669)
Middle Granville	(G-8431)
Salem	(G-15137)

COUNTY/CITY CROSS-REFERENCE

	ENTRY #		ENTRY #		ENTRY #		ENTRY #		ENTRY #
Whitehall	(G-17217)	Armonk	(G-410)	Irvington	(G-6808)	Rye	(G-15079)	Castile	(G-3444)

Wayne

		Baldwin Place	(G-562)	Jefferson Valley	(G-7090)	Rye Brook	(G-15096)	Gainesville	(G-5497)
Clyde	(G-3749)	Bedford	(G-791)	Katonah	(G-7161)	Scarsdale	(G-15245)	Java Village	(G-7087)
Lyons	(G-7997)	Bedford Hills	(G-796)	Larchmont	(G-7375)	Sleepy Hollow	(G-15497)	North Java	(G-12950)
Macedon	(G-8006)	Briarcliff Manor	(G-1229)	Mamaroneck	(G-8055)	Somers	(G-15531)	Perry	(G-13545)
Marion	(G-8124)	Bronxville	(G-1499)	Mohegan Lake	(G-8577)	South Salem	(G-15559)	Portageville	(G-13890)
Newark	(G-12748)	Buchanan	(G-2799)	Montrose	(G-8652)	Tarrytown	(G-16108)	Silver Springs	(G-15472)
North Rose	(G-12952)	Chappaqua	(G-3578)	Mount Kisco	(G-8663)	Thornwood	(G-16139)	Warsaw	(G-16604)
Ontario	(G-13217)	Cortlandt Manor	(G-4072)	Mount Vernon	(G-8701)	Tuckahoe	(G-16293)	Wyoming	(G-17395)
Palmyra	(G-13430)	Cross River	(G-4086)	New Rochelle	(G-8928)	Valhalla	(G-16391)		
Red Creek	(G-14038)	Croton Falls	(G-4087)	North Salem	(G-12955)	Waccabuc	(G-16541)	**Yates**	
Savannah	(G-15231)	Croton On Hudson	(G-4088)	Ossining	(G-13344)	White Plains	(G-17100)		
Sodus	(G-15525)	Dobbs Ferry	(G-4324)	Peekskill	(G-13497)	Yonkers	(G-17426)	Branchport	(G-1169)
Walworth	(G-16571)	Eastchester	(G-4594)	Pelham	(G-13513)	Yorktown Heights	(G-17522)	Dresden	(G-4342)
Williamson	(G-17251)	Elmsford	(G-4741)	Pleasantville	(G-13744)			Dundee	(G-4351)
Wolcott	(G-17298)	Harrison	(G-5998)	Port Chester	(G-13765)	**Wyoming**		Himrod	(G-6448)
		Hartsdale	(G-6016)	Pound Ridge	(G-13958)	Arcade	(G-386)	Penn Yan	(G-13529)
Westchester		Hastings On Hudson	(G-6022)	Purchase	(G-13970)	Attica	(G-470)	Rushville	(G-15078)
Ardsley	(G-402)	Hawthorne	(G-6265)	Purdys	(G-13988)	Bliss	(G-974)		

GEOGRAPHIC SECTION

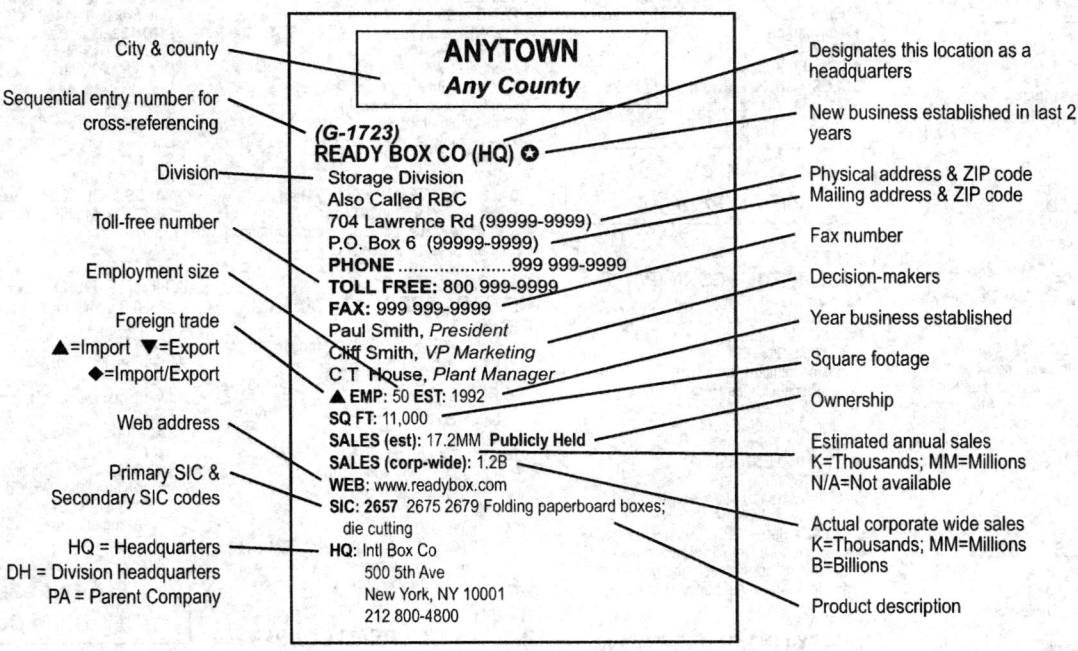

See footnotes for symbols and codes identification.
- This section is in alphabetical order by city.
- Companies are sorted alphabetically under their respective cities.
- To locate cities within a county refer to the County/City Cross Reference Index.

IMPORTANT NOTICE: It is a violation of both federal and state law to transmit an unsolicited advertisement to a facsimile machine. Any user of this product that violates such laws may be subject to civil and criminal penalties which may exceed $500 for each transmission of an unsolicited facsimile. Harris InfoSource provides fax numbers for lawful purposes only and expressly forbids the use of these numbers in any unlawful manner.

Accord
Ulster County

(G-1)
VIC DEMAYOS INC
4967 Us Highway 209 (12404-5723)
P.O. Box 253 (12404-0253)
PHONE.....................845 626-4343
Fax: 845 626-3335
Vic De Mayo, President
Eugene De Mayo, President
EMP: 6 EST: 1964
SQ FT: 4,000
SALES (est): 225K Privately Held
SIC: 3111 5941 Accessory products, leather; sporting goods & bicycle shops

Adams
Jefferson County

(G-2)
BENJAMIN PRINTING INC
Also Called: Minuteman Press
60 E Church St (13605-1103)
PHONE.....................315 788-7922
Fax: 315 788-8103
Charles Adams, President
Michael Biolsi, General Mgr
Vitusa Adams, Vice Pres
EMP: 14
SQ FT: 4,000
SALES (est): 1.1MM Privately Held
WEB: www.benjaminprinting.com
SIC: 2752 Commercial printing, lithographic

(G-3)
GREAT LAKES CHEESE NY INC
23 Phelps St (13605-1096)
PHONE.....................315 232-4511
Fax: 315 232-4055
Gary Vanic, Ch of Bd
Hans Epprecht, President
John Epprecht, Vice Pres
Tracy Stuckey, Purch Dir
Tim Elmer, Manager
EMP: 79
SQ FT: 88,000
SALES (est): 19.2MM
SALES (corp-wide): 1.6B Privately Held
WEB: www.greatlakescheese.com
SIC: 2022 Cheese, natural & processed
PA: Great Lakes Cheese Co., Inc.
17825 Great Lakes Pkwy
Hiram OH 44234
440 834-2500

Adams Center
Jefferson County

(G-4)
R G KING GENERAL CONSTRUCTION
Also Called: Kings Quarry
13018 County Route 155 (13606-3104)
PHONE.....................315 583-3560
Ronald King, President
Bill King, Vice Pres
EMP: 5
SALES (est): 462K Privately Held
SIC: 1442 Construction sand & gravel

Addison
Steuben County

(G-5)
CRAWFORD PRINT SHOP INC
6120 Herrington Rd (14801-9235)
PHONE.....................607 359-4970
Adam Crawford, President
EMP: 5
SALES (est): 220K Privately Held
WEB: www.crawfordsprintshop.com
SIC: 2752 Color lithography

(G-6)
FICS INC
25 Community Dr (14801-1140)
P.O. Box 328, Painted Post (14870-0328)
PHONE.....................607 359-4474
Fax: 607 359-4478
Shawn E Smith, President
Michael Harold, Corp Secy
Steve E Boyer, Vice Pres
EMP: 20
SQ FT: 4,000
SALES (est): 6.2MM Privately Held
WEB: www.fics.cc
SIC: 3625 Alternators & generators, rebuilding & repair; generators

(G-7)
HES INC
6303 Symonds Hill Rd (14801-9564)
PHONE.....................607 359-2974
John J Crane, President
Paula Spencer, Office Mgr
EMP: 8
SQ FT: 10,000
SALES: 450K Privately Held
SIC: 3621 3599 Electric motor & generator parts; machine shop, jobbing & repair

Afton
Chenango County

(G-8)
BABYSAFE USA LLC
251 County Road 17 (13730-3111)
PHONE.....................877 367-4141
Sagi Ben-Dov, Mng Member
Ron Berry, Manager
Mary Rosario, Manager
Jamie Baciuska,
Lynn Baciuska,
▲ EMP: 5
SQ FT: 8,000
SALES: 235K Privately Held
SIC: 3944 Baby carriages & restraint seats

(G-9)
COBRA OPERATING INDUSTRIES LLC
37 Main St (13730-3164)
PHONE.....................607 639-1700
Barbara A Wagner,
Richard W Wagner,
EMP: 6
SALES (est): 400K Privately Held
SIC: 3441 Fabricated structural metal

Airmont
Rockland County

(G-10)
901 D LLC
360 Route 59 Ste 3 (10952-3416)
P.O. Box 615, Tallman (10982-0615)
PHONE..................................845 369-1111
Fax: 845 369-0531
Serge Seguin, *CEO*
Frank Duvergne, *General Mgr*
Francois Duvergne, *COO*
Aldric Seguin, *Exec VP*
Fred Sainclvier, *Project Engr*
EMP: 48
SALES (est.): 13.4MM
SALES (corp-wide): 32.5MM **Privately Held**
WEB: www.901d.com
SIC: 3499 8711 3812 3679 Aerosol valves, metal; engineering services; search & navigation equipment; antennas, receiving; computer terminals, monitors & components
PA: Graycliff Partners, Lp
500 5th Ave Fl 47
New York NY 10110
212 300-2900

(G-11)
ART ESSENTIALS OF NEW YORK (PA)
25 Church Rd (10952-4108)
P.O. Box 38, Tallman (10982-0038)
PHONE..................................845 368-1100
Bella Jacobs, *President*
Arnold A Jacobs, *Shareholder*
EMP: 2
SQ FT: 1,400
SALES: 1MM **Privately Held**
WEB: www.artessentialsofnewyork.com
SIC: 2499 Decorative wood & woodwork

(G-12)
DRT LABORATORIES LLC
331 Spook Rock Rd (10901-5319)
PHONE..................................845 547-2034
Ronit Arginteanu,
EMP: 5
SALES (est) 556K **Privately Held**
SIC: 2844 2834 Cosmetic preparations; druggists' preparations (pharmaceuticals)

(G-13)
HANDY LAUNDRY PRODUCTS CORP (PA)
382 Route 59 Ste 318 (10952-3422)
PHONE..................................800 263-5973
Edward Pinkesz, *President*
Aron Braun, *Principal*
Shlome Masri, *Office Mgr*
▲ EMP: 6
SALES (est) 456.5K **Privately Held**
SIC: 2392 Laundry, garment & storage bags

(G-14)
JOMAR INDUSTRIES INC
382 Route 59 Ste 352 (10952-3484)
P.O. Box 379, Monsey (10952-0379)
PHONE..................................845 357-5773
Fax: 845 357-5119
Alan Marks, *President*
Jonathan Marks, *Vice Pres*
▲ EMP: 20
SQ FT: 4,000
SALES (est): 1.6MM **Privately Held**
WEB: www.jomarindustries.com
SIC: 3993 2395 5961 2759 Advertising novelties; art needlework: made from purchased materials; gift items, mail order; commercial printing

(G-15)
MINTED GREEN INC
85 Regina Rd (10952-4527)
PHONE..................................845 458-1845
Chaim Rosenberg, *Ch of Bd*
EMP: 6
SQ FT: 1,200
SALES: 2.8MM **Privately Held**
SIC: 3942 5092 5945 Dolls & stuffed toys; toys & games; toys & games

(G-16)
PRINCETON SCIENCES
386 Route 59 Ste 402 (10952-3411)
PHONE..................................845 368-1214
Todd Hoffman,
EMP: 7
SQ FT: 1,000
SALES (est) 327.4K **Privately Held**
SIC: 2833 Vitamins, natural or synthetic: bulk, uncompounded

Akron
Erie County

(G-17)
AAKRON RULE CORP (PA)
8 Indianola Ave (14001-1199)
P.O. Box 418 (14001-0418)
PHONE..................................716 542-5483
Fax: 585 542-5789
Danielle Robillard, *Ch of Bd*
Devin Piscitelli, *Vice Pres*
Angel Alicea, *Plant Mgr*
George Vancleef, *Opers Mgr*
Jean Taylor, *Purch Mgr*
◆ EMP: 150 EST: 1967
SQ FT: 16,000
SALES (est): 41.6MM **Privately Held**
WEB: www.aakronline.com
SIC: 2499 3993 3952 3951 Rulers & rules, wood; paint sticks, wood; signs & advertising specialties; lead pencils & art goods; pens & mechanical pencils

(G-18)
COUNTY LINE STONE CO INC
4515 Crittenden Rd (14001-9517)
P.O. Box 150 (14001-0150)
PHONE..................................716 542-5435
Fax: 585 542-5442
John Buyers Jr, *Vice Pres*
Bruce M Buyers, *Vice Pres*
Wendy Seabo, *Admin Sec*
EMP: 30
SQ FT: 20,000
SALES (est): 4.2MM **Privately Held**
SIC: 1429 5032 Sandstone, crushed & broken-quarrying; asphalt mixture

(G-19)
FORD GUM & MACHINE COMPANY INC (PA)
18 Newton Ave (14001-1099)
P.O. Box 330 (14001-0330)
PHONE..................................716 542-4561
Fax: 585 542-4610
George H Stege, *Ch of Bd*
Robert A R Clouston, *Ch of Bd*
George H Stege, *Ch of Bd*
George Stege, *President*
Luela Lo, *General Mgr*
▲ EMP: 100 EST: 1913
SQ FT: 125,000
SALES (est): 59.7MM **Privately Held**
WEB: www.fordgum.com
SIC: 2067 5441 Chewing gum; candy

(G-20)
G & S FARM & HOME INC
Also Called: Agway
13550 Bloomingdale Rd (14001-9801)
P.O. Box 214 (14001-0214)
PHONE..................................716 542-9922
Gregg Brown, *President*
Sue Brown, *Admin Sec*
EMP: 6
SQ FT: 6,000
SALES (est): 1.1MM **Privately Held**
SIC: 2879 5261 Agricultural chemicals; arsenates, arsenites (formulated); nurseries & garden centers

(G-21)
IGNITER SYSTEMS INC
12600 Clarence Center Rd (14001-9749)
PHONE..................................716 542-5511
John Davis, *President*
EMP: 20
SQ FT: 90,000
SALES (est): 1.6MM **Privately Held**
WEB: www.ignitersystems.com
SIC: 3567 Heating units & devices, industrial: electric

(G-22)
NIAGARA LABEL COMPANY INC
12715 Lewis Rd (14001-9668)
P.O. Box 90 (14001-0090)
PHONE..................................716 542-3000
Fax: 585 542-2608
Michael C Witmarsh, *CEO*
Marjorie Witmarsh, *Corp Secy*
Connie Ribbeck, *Prdtn Mgr*
Chris Whitmarsh, *Sales Mgr*
Tina Lemley, *Accounts Mgr*
▲ EMP: 17
SQ FT: 5,000
SALES (est): 3MM **Privately Held**
WEB: www.niagaralabel.com
SIC: 2754 2759 Labels: gravure printing; labels & seals: printing

(G-23)
NIAGARA SPECIALTY METALS INC
12600 Clarence Center Rd (14001-9749)
P.O. Box 280 (14001-0280)
PHONE..................................716 542-5552
Fax: 585 542-5555
Robert F Shabala Jr, *President*
Julie Majka, *General Mgr*
Timothy Gelnett, *Vice Pres*
Bob Shabala, *Financial Exec*
Ray Ferington, *Sales Staff*
◆ EMP: 37
SQ FT: 110,000
SALES (est): 13.4MM **Privately Held**
WEB: www.nsm-ny.com
SIC: 3312 Hot-rolled iron & steel products

(G-24)
PERRYS ICE CREAM COMPANY INC
1 Ice Cream Plz (14001-1031)
PHONE..................................716 542-5492
Fax: 716 542-2544
Robert Denning, *President*
Brian Perry, *Exec VP*
Diane Austin, *Vice Pres*
Jim Marshall, *Manager*
Paul Zilliox, *Manager*
▲ EMP: 300
SQ FT: 135,000
SALES (est): 71.2MM **Privately Held**
SIC: 2024 5145 Ice cream & frozen desserts; snack foods

(G-25)
RE-AL INDUSTRIAL CORP
Also Called: D & E Industrial
5391 Crittenden Rd (14001-9598)
P.O. Box 37, Newfane (14108-0037)
PHONE..................................716 542-4556
Fax: 585 542-4558
Richard Bottom, *President*
EMP: 8
SQ FT: 8,000
SALES: 700K **Privately Held**
WEB: www.d-eind.com
SIC: 3535 1796 Conveyors & conveying equipment; machinery installation

(G-26)
STRIPPIT INC (DH)
Also Called: L V D
12975 Clarence Center Rd (14001-1371)
PHONE..................................716 542-5500
Fax: 585 542-5957
John Lesebbre, *President*
James C Blackstone, *Vice Pres*
Pam Halchishak, *Vice Pres*
John J Quigley, *Vice Pres*
Bruce Turner, *Vice Pres*
◆ EMP: 200
SQ FT: 255,000
SALES (est): 63.9MM
SALES (corp-wide): 68.1K **Privately Held**
SIC: 3542 3544 3549 3545 Machine tools, metal forming type; special dies, tools, jigs & fixtures; metalworking machinery; machine tool accessories
HQ: L.V.D. Company Nv
Nijverheidslaan 2
Wevelgem 8560
564 305-11

(G-27)
WHITING DOOR MFG CORP (PA)
113 Cedar St (14001-1038)
P.O. Box 388 (14001-0388)
PHONE..................................716 542-5427
Fax: 716 542-5947
Donald J Whiting, *Ch of Bd*
Chris Ericksen, *Area Mgr*
Michael Winter, *Area Mgr*
Steve Shelby, *Vice Pres*
Bob Stoll, *Vice Pres*
▼ EMP: 330 EST: 1953
SQ FT: 371,000
SALES (est): 128MM **Privately Held**
SIC: 3714 Motor vehicle parts & accessories

(G-28)
WHITING DOOR MFG CORP
13550 Bloomingdale Rd (14001-9801)
PHONE..................................716 542-3070
Fax: 585 542-1658
Craig Smith, *Plant Mgr*
Michael Whiting, *Manager*
Joe Lukasiewizod, *Info Tech Dir*
EMP: 60
SALES (corp-wide): 128MM **Privately Held**
SIC: 3493 Coiled flat springs
PA: Whiting Door Mfg Corp
113 Cedar St
Akron NY 14001
716 542-5427

Akwesasne
Franklin County

(G-29)
OHSERASE MANUFACTURING LLC
26 Eagle Dr (13655)
P.O. Box 1221 (13655-1221)
PHONE..................................518 358-9309
Justin Tarbell, *Vice Pres*
▲ EMP: 23
SALES (est): 3MM **Privately Held**
SIC: 3999 Barber & beauty shop equipment

Albany
Albany County

(G-30)
ACCESSIBLE BATH TECH LLC
6 Albright Ave (12203-4802)
PHONE..................................518 937-1518
Craig La Londe, *President*
EMP: 15
SALES: 950K **Privately Held**
SIC: 3999 Manufacturing industries

(G-31)
ACCUPRINT (PA)
2005 Western Ave Ste 1 (12203-5073)
PHONE..................................518 456-2431
Donald Blais, *Owner*
EMP: 6
SALES (est): 538.8K **Privately Held**
SIC: 2752 Commercial printing, lithographic

(G-32)
ADIRONDACK SPCLTY ADHSIVES INC
4258 Albany St (12205-4614)
P.O. Box 13283 (12212-3283)
PHONE..................................518 869-5736
Fax: 518 869-3584
Jerald Casey, *President*
Debra Stoecker, *Controller*
Phil Desnoyers, *Systems Staff*
EMP: 15
SQ FT: 7,500
SALES (est): 3.5MM **Privately Held**
WEB: www.adktapes.com
SIC: 2891 Adhesives

GEOGRAPHIC SECTION

Albany - Albany County (G-56)

(G-33)
AIRGAS INC
84 Karner Rd (12205-4730)
PHONE.................518 690-0068
Lester Mackey, *Branch Mgr*
F Gay Dunn, *Co-Mgr*
EMP: 14
SALES (corp-wide): 163.9MM **Privately Held**
SIC: 2813 Oxygen, compressed or liquefied; nitrogen; argon
HQ: Airgas, Inc.
259 N Radnor Chester Rd # 100
Radnor PA 19087
610 687-5253

(G-34)
ALBANY ASP & AGGREGATES CORP
101 Dunham Dr (12202-2106)
PHONE.................518 436-8916
Frederick M Stutzman, *President*
Philip Carnevale, *Vice Pres*
Eugene D Hallock III, *Vice Pres*
John Stutzman, *Vice Pres*
Ray Lohrebsa, *Director*
EMP: 20 **EST:** 1948
SQ FT: 10,000
SALES (est): 4.3MM
SALES (corp-wide): 12.7MM **Privately Held**
SIC: 2951 Asphalt paving mixtures & blocks
PA: Hudson River Construction Co., Inc.
101 Dunham Dr
Albany NY 12202
518 434-6677

(G-35)
ALBANY CATHOLIC PRESS ASSOC
Also Called: EVANGELIST, THE
40 N Main Ave Ste 2 (12203-1481)
PHONE.................518 453-6688
Fax: 518 453-6793
James Breig, *Principal*
Bishop Hubbard, *Principal*
Stephanie Zebrowski, *Manager*
Barbra Oliver, *Manager*
EMP: 9
SQ FT: 10,000
SALES: 1MM **Privately Held**
SIC: 2711 8661 Newspapers: publishing only, not printed on site; religious organizations

(G-36)
ALBANY ENGNERED COMPOSITES INC
455 Patroon Creek Blvd (12206-5003)
P.O. Box 1907 (12201-1907)
PHONE.................518 445-2200
Brian Coffenberry, *President*
James Shea, *Treasurer*
Charles J Silva Jr, *Admin Sec*
EMP: 12
SALES (est): 1.8MM **Privately Held**
SIC: 2269 Chemical coating or treating of narrow fabrics

(G-37)
ALBANY LETTER SHOP INC
16 Van Zandt St Ste 20 (12207-1448)
P.O. Box 1003 (12201-1003)
PHONE.................518 434-1172
Fax: 518 434-6261
EMP: 6
SQ FT: 2,900
SALES (est): 41.6K **Privately Held**
SIC: 2752 Offset Printing

(G-38)
ALBANY MOLECULAR RESEARCH INC
21 Corporate Cir (12203-5154)
PHONE.................518 512-2234
James Boyer, *Senior VP*
Michael Pettersson, *Vice Pres*
Kathryn Saybe, *Purch Agent*
Kim Blattner, *Manager*
Jason Byra, *Manager*
EMP: 6
SALES (corp-wide): 77.1MM **Privately Held**
SIC: 2836 8731 Biological products, except diagnostic; commercial physical research
HQ: Albany Molecular Research, Inc.
26 Corporate Cir
Albany NY 12203
518 512-2000

(G-39)
ALBANY MOLECULAR RESEARCH INC (HQ)
Also Called: Amri
26 Corporate Cir (12203-5121)
P.O. Box 15098 (12212-5098)
PHONE.................518 512-2000
Fax: 518 464-0289
William S Marth, *President*
Vijay Batra, *Managing Dir*
George Svokos, *COO*
Margalit Fine, *Exec VP*
Milton Boyer, *Senior VP*
▲ **EMP:** 277
SQ FT: 159,000
SALES: 570.4MM
SALES (corp-wide): 77.1MM **Privately Held**
SIC: 2836 8731 Biological products, except diagnostic; biotechnical research, commercial

(G-40)
ALBANY MTAL FBRCATION HOLDINGS
67 Henry Johnson Blvd (12210-1413)
PHONE.................518 463-5161
Fax: 518 426-4232
Dave Warzek, *Principal*
EMP: 7 **EST:** 2008
SALES (est): 1.1MM **Privately Held**
SIC: 3499 Fabricated metal products

(G-41)
ALBANY STUDENT PRESS INC
Also Called: A S P
1400 Washington Ave Cc329 (12222-0100)
PHONE.................518 442-5665
Carey Qeen, *Manager*
EMP: 30
SALES: 12.4MM **Privately Held**
SIC: 2711 2741 Newspapers; miscellaneous publishing

(G-42)
ALL-LIFTS INCORPORATED
27-39 Thatcher St (12207-5016)
PHONE.................518 465-3461
Fax: 518 465-0342
Steven R Dewey, *President*
Patrick Dewey, *Vice Pres*
Beth Wilson, *Accountant*
Brian Dewey, *Marketing Staff*
Jannes Scott, *Manager*
EMP: 25 **EST:** 1966
SQ FT: 12,400
SALES (est): 6.7MM **Privately Held**
WEB: www.all-lifts.com
SIC: 3496 2298 5063 Miscellaneous fabricated wire products; chain, welded; slings, rope; electrical construction materials

(G-43)
ALO ACQUISITION LLC (DH)
26 Corporate Cir (12203-5121)
PHONE.................518 464-0279
Thomas E D'Ambra, *Ch of Bd*
EMP: 4
SALES (est): 96.2MM
SALES (corp-wide): 77.1MM **Privately Held**
SIC: 2833 5122 8733 Medicinals & botanicals; drugs & drug proprietaries; research institute
HQ: Albany Molecular Research, Inc.
26 Corporate Cir
Albany NY 12203
518 512-2000

(G-44)
AMERICAN BOILER TANK WLDG INC
53 Pleasant St (12207-1385)
PHONE.................518 463-5012
Fax: 518 463-5087
William A Novak, *President*
Bill Engel, *Buyer*
Patrick Griffin, *Project Engr*
Paul Engel, *Manager*
Brenda Longe, *Manager*
EMP: 20 **EST:** 1936
SQ FT: 30,000
SALES: 5MM **Privately Held**
WEB: www.americanboiler.com
SIC: 3443 Fabricated plate work (boiler shop)

(G-45)
ARCY PLASTIC LAMINATES INC (PA)
555 Patroon Creek Blvd (12206-5007)
PHONE.................518 235-0753
Robert Cecucci, *Asst Sec*
EMP: 40 **EST:** 1952
SQ FT: 31,000
SALES (est): 4.3MM **Privately Held**
SIC: 2541 Counter & sink tops

(G-46)
ARDENT MILLS LLC
Cargill
101 Normanskill St (12202-2155)
PHONE.................518 447-1700
Jim Hess, *Sales Staff*
Cody Meyers, *Manager*
Karen Horton, *Executive*
EMP: 100
SALES (corp-wide): 658.9MM **Privately Held**
WEB: www.cargill.com
SIC: 2041 0723 Flour & other grain mill products; flour milling custom services
PA: Ardent Mills, Llc
1875 Lawrence St Ste 1400
Denver CO 80202
800 851-9618

(G-47)
ART & UNDERSTANDING INC
Also Called: A & U America's Aids Magazine
25 Monroe St Ste 205 (12210-2744)
PHONE.................518 426-9010
David Waggoner, *Director*
EMP: 7
SALES (est): 690K **Privately Held**
SIC: 2721 Magazines: publishing only, not printed on site

(G-48)
BACKYARD FENCE INC
4204 Albany St (12205-4508)
PHONE.................518 452-9496
Fax: 518 456-4568
Gerald Haley, *President*
EMP: 12
SALES: 1.2MM **Privately Held**
SIC: 3499 Barricades, metal

(G-49)
BARKER STEEL LLC
126 S Port Rd (12202-1087)
P.O. Box 800, Coeymans (12045-0800)
PHONE.................518 465-6221
Fax: 518 465-6224
John Gradoni, *Sales Mgr*
Duane Miller, *Sales Staff*
Gary Wolfe, *Sales Staff*
David Legenbauer, *Branch Mgr*
Scott Henricks, *Branch Mgr*
EMP: 20
SALES (corp-wide): 122.1MM **Privately Held**
WEB: www.barker.com
SIC: 3449 8742 3441 Bars, concrete reinforcing; fabricated steel; management consulting services; fabricated structural metal
PA: Barker Steel Llc
55 Sumner St Ste 1
Milford MA 01757
508 473-8484

(G-50)
BEN WEITSMAN OF ALBANY LLC
300 Smith Blvd (12202-1090)
PHONE.................518 462-4444
Heather Davison, *Office Mgr*
Adam Weitsman, *Mng Member*
Stephnen Green,
Daniel Innarella,
Joel Root,
EMP: 22 **EST:** 2013
SALES: 21MM
SALES (corp-wide): 139MM **Privately Held**
SIC: 3559 3341 Recycling machinery; copper smelting & refining (secondary)
PA: Weitsman Shredding, Llc
1 Recycle Dr
Owego NY 13827
607 687-7777

(G-51)
BENWAY-HAWORTH-LWLR-LACOSTA HE
Also Called: Hearing Aid Office, The
21 Everett Rd (12205-1437)
PHONE.................518 432-4070
Fax: 518 432-4070
Robert Lacosta, *President*
EMP: 12
SQ FT: 2,000
SALES (est): 1.4MM **Privately Held**
SIC: 3842 5999 Hearing aids; hearing aids

(G-52)
BEST PALLET & CRATE LLC
22 Railroad Ave (12205-5727)
PHONE.................518 438-2945
Neil Manasse,
EMP: 6
SALES (est): 836.2K **Privately Held**
SIC: 2448 Wood pallets & skids

(G-53)
BIMBO BAKERIES
78 N Manning Blvd (12206-2294)
PHONE.................518 463-2221
Joe Rebholtz, *Principal*
EMP: 16
SALES (est): 2.6MM **Privately Held**
SIC: 2051 Bread, cake & related products

(G-54)
BIMBO BAKERIES USA INC
40 Fuller Rd (12205-5122)
PHONE.................518 489-4053
Mike Totaro, *Area Mgr*
Ralph Lysorgorski, *Regl Sales Mgr*
EMP: 18 **Privately Held**
WEB: www.gwbakeries.com
SIC: 2051 Bread, cake & related products
HQ: Bimbo Bakeries Usa, Inc
255 Business Center Dr # 200
Horsham PA 19044
215 347-5500

(G-55)
BULLEX INC (DH)
Also Called: Bullex Digital Safety
20 Corporate Cir Ste 3 (12203-5153)
PHONE.................518 689-2023
Ryan O Donnell, *CEO*
Joe Careccia, *Regl Sales Mgr*
Damien Pinto-Martin, *Manager*
Jane Tezze, *Manager*
Tom Rossi,
▲ **EMP:** 10
SALES (est): 13.5MM
SALES (corp-wide): 96.6MM **Privately Held**
WEB: www.bullexsafety.com
SIC: 3569 8748 Firefighting apparatus; safety training service
HQ: Lion Training Resources Group, Inc.
7200 Poe Ave Ste 400
Dayton OH 45414
937 898-1949

(G-56)
BULLEX INC
Also Called: Bullex Digital Safety
20 Corporate Cir Ste 3 (12203-5153)
PHONE.................518 689-2023
Thomas Roffi, *Branch Mgr*
EMP: 50
SALES (corp-wide): 96.6MM **Privately Held**
WEB: www.bullexsafety.com
SIC: 3999 Fire extinguishers, portable
HQ: Bullex, Inc.
20 Corporate Cir Ste 3
Albany NY 12203
518 689-2023

Albany - Albany County (G-57)

(G-57)
CALLANAN INDUSTRIES INC (DH)
8 Southwoods Blvd Ste 4 (12211-2554)
P.O. Box 15097 (12212-5097)
PHONE..................518 374-2222
Fax: 518 374-2222
Jonas Havens, *President*
Kevin D Browne, *Safety Dir*
Bryan Francett, *Plant Mgr*
Peter Skelly, *Credit Mgr*
Kaitlyn Bessey, *Accountant*
▲ **EMP:** 205
SQ FT: 24,000
SALES (est): 117.4MM
SALES (corp-wide): 28.6B **Privately Held**
WEB: www.callanan.com
SIC: 3272 2951 Concrete products, precast; asphalt paving mixtures & blocks

(G-58)
CAPITAL REGION WKLY NEWSPAPERS
Also Called: Advertiser
645 Albany Shaker Rd (12211-1158)
P.O. Box 1450, Clifton Park (12065-0806)
PHONE..................518 877-7160
Fax: 518 877-7824
Patrick Smith, *President*
EMP: 29
SQ FT: 4,000
SALES (est): 1.3MM **Privately Held**
SIC: 2711 Newspapers, publishing & printing

(G-59)
CAPITOL CITY SPECIALTIES CO
10 Burdick Dr (12205-1467)
PHONE..................518 486-8935
Michael Campagna, *Principal*
EMP: 8 **EST:** 2013
SALES (est): 759.3K **Privately Held**
SIC: 2099 Peanut butter

(G-60)
CHAMPLAIN HUDSON POWER EX INC
600 Broadway Fl 3 (12207-2235)
PHONE..................518 465-0710
John Douglas, *CEO*
Donald Jensson, *President*
Scott Hargreaves, *CFO*
Nancy Clarke, *Director*
Sara Rong, *Coordinator*
EMP: 7
SQ FT: 500
SALES (est): 540K **Privately Held**
SIC: 3568 Power transmission equipment

(G-61)
CHAPMAN STAINED GLASS STUDIO
212 Quail St (12203-1223)
PHONE..................518 449-5552
Fax: 518 449-5594
Philip H Morgan, *President*
P Keith Morgan, *Vice Pres*
EMP: 7
SQ FT: 15,000
SALES (est): 430K **Privately Held**
SIC: 3231 1793 Stained glass: made from purchased glass; glass & glazing work

(G-62)
CHARLES FREIHOFER BAKING CO
1 Prospect Rd (12206-2229)
PHONE..................518 463-2221
Fax: 518 438-7721
Peter Rollins, *President*
Richard M Lee Jr, *Vice Pres*
Eileen Connor, *Accounting Mgr*
EMP: 8
SALES (est): 720K **Privately Held**
SIC: 2499 Bakers' equipment, wood

(G-63)
CIMLINE INC
21 Railroad Ave (12205-5951)
PHONE..................518 880-4073
Rick Stone, *Owner*
Brandon Beltran, *Sales Executive*
EMP: 6
SALES (corp-wide): 263.9MM **Privately Held**
SIC: 3531 Road construction & maintenance machinery
HQ: Cimline, Inc.
2601 Niagara Ln N
Minneapolis MN 55447
763 557-1982

(G-64)
CLEAR VIEW BAG COMPANY INC
5 Burdick Dr (12205-1405)
P.O. Box 11160 (12211-0160)
PHONE..................518 458-7153
Fax: 518 458-1401
William J Romer, *Ch of Bd*
Deborah S Romer, *Vice Pres*
Len Smith, *QC Mgr*
Todd Romer, *Human Res Mgr*
Angie Fullam, *Sales Executive*
EMP: 156 **EST:** 1957
SQ FT: 45,000
SALES (est): 27.9MM **Privately Held**
WEB: www.clearviewbag.com
SIC: 3081 2673 Polyethylene film; bags: plastic, laminated & coated

(G-65)
CMC-KUHNKE INC
1060 Brdwy (12204)
PHONE..................518 694-3310
Fax: 518 694-3311
Heinz Grossjohann, *President*
Alex Grossjohann, *Vice Pres*
Edward L Shively, *Technical Mgr*
Eric Mooberry, *Regl Sales Mgr*
Nathan Zerrahn, *Sales Staff*
EMP: 12
SQ FT: 10,000
SALES (est): 2.2MM **Privately Held**
SIC: 3411 Food & beverage containers

(G-66)
CMP INDUSTRIES LLC (PA)
Also Called: Ticonium Division
413 N Pearl St (12207-1311)
PHONE..................518 434-3147
Fax: 518 434-1288
Walter Piepro, *Mfg Staff*
Greg Smith, *Engineer*
Ed Civiok, *CFO*
Devon Howe, *Mng Member*
Chris Hamilton, *Consultant*
◆ **EMP:** 40 **EST:** 1889
SQ FT: 90,000
SALES (est): 8.3MM **Privately Held**
WEB: www.cmpindustry.com
SIC: 3843 Dental equipment & supplies

(G-67)
CMP INDUSTRIES LLC
Also Called: Nobilium
413 N Pearl St (12207-1311)
PHONE..................518 434-3147
William Regan, *Branch Mgr*
EMP: 5
SALES (corp-wide): 8.3MM **Privately Held**
WEB: www.cmpindustry.com
SIC: 3843 Dental laboratory equipment
PA: Cmp Industries Llc
413 N Pearl St
Albany NY 12207
518 434-3147

(G-68)
COACH INC
120 Washington Avenue Ext # 57 (12203-6442)
PHONE..................518 456-5657
Erik Brandl, *Marketing Staff*
James Levy, *Branch Mgr*
Marina Skouras, *Manager*
Esther Silberstein, *Admin Asst*
EMP: 5
SALES (corp-wide): 4.4B **Publicly Held**
SIC: 3171 Women's handbags & purses
PA: Coach, Inc.
10 Hudson Yards
New York NY 10001
212 594-1850

(G-69)
COCA-COLA BOTTLING CO OF NY
38 Warehouse Row (12205-5757)
PHONE..................518 459-2010
Dwayne St Claire, *COO*
Dwayne St Clair, *Opers Mgr*
Julie Francis, *Sales/Mktg Mgr*
Mike Richardson, *Human Res Mgr*
Tony Perichilli, *Telecom Exec*
EMP: 11
SALES (corp-wide): 41.8B **Publicly Held**
SIC: 2086 5149 Bottled & canned soft drinks; groceries & related products
HQ: The Coca-Cola Bottling Company Of New York Inc
2500 Windy Ridge Pkwy Se
Atlanta GA 30339
770 989-3000

(G-70)
COCCADOTTS INC
1179 Central Ave (12205-5436)
PHONE..................518 438-4937
Rachel Dott, *Owner*
Luke Dott, *Treasurer*
EMP: 11
SALES (est): 982K **Privately Held**
SIC: 2051 Cakes, bakery: except frozen

(G-71)
COMMERCEHUB INC (PA)
201 Fuller Rd Fl 6 (12203-3621)
PHONE..................518 810-0700
Fax: 518 810-0701
Richard N Baer, *Ch of Bd*
Francis Poore, *President*
Richard Jones, *Exec VP*
Bill Kong, *Exec VP*
Kathleen Conley, *Senior VP*
EMP: 7 **EST:** 1997
SQ FT: 49,500
SALES: 87.6MM **Publicly Held**
SIC: 7372 Prepackaged software

(G-72)
DAVIES OFFICE REFURBISHING INC (PA)
40 Loudonville Rd (12204-1513)
PHONE..................518 426-7188
Fax: 518 449-4036
William E Davies, *President*
Evelyn Davies, *Vice Pres*
Bob Rowe, *Transptn Dir*
Sue Risler, *Finance Mgr*
Patrick Doody, *Natl Sales Mgr*
▲ **EMP:** 125
SQ FT: 96,000
SALES (est): 41.9MM **Privately Held**
WEB: www.daviesoffice.com
SIC: 2522 7641 Office furniture, except wood; office furniture repair & maintenance

(G-73)
DIGITAL PAGE LLC
75 Benjamin St (12202-1137)
PHONE..................518 446-9129
Eugene R Spada II,
EMP: 11
SQ FT: 2,000
SALES (est): 174.4K **Privately Held**
SIC: 2791 Typesetting

(G-74)
DYNAMIC SCREENPRINTING
12 Vatrano Rd (12205-3404)
PHONE..................518 487-4256
Jeff Serge, *Mng Member*
EMP: 9
SALES (est): 829.3K **Privately Held**
SIC: 2261 Screen printing of cotton broadwoven fabrics

(G-75)
EASY BOOK PUBLISHING INC
260 Osborne Rd Ste 3 (12211-1856)
PHONE..................518 459-6281
Nydia Russum, *President*
John Russum, *Vice Pres*
EMP: 6
SQ FT: 1,500
SALES (est): 622.5K **Privately Held**
WEB: www.easy-book.net
SIC: 2741 Directories: publishing only, not printed on site

(G-76)
EDP RENEWABLES NORTH AMER LLC
1971 Western Ave 230 (12203-5066)
PHONE..................518 426-1650
Patrick Doyle, *Branch Mgr*
EMP: 8
SALES (corp-wide): 2.7B **Privately Held**
SIC: 3621 Windmills, electric generating
HQ: Edp Renewables North America Llc
808 Travis St Ste 700
Houston TX 77002
713 265-0350

(G-77)
EMPIRE AIR SPECIALTIES INC
40 Kraft Ave (12205-5428)
PHONE..................518 689-4440
Fax: 518 689-4442
Robert J Miner, *President*
Rebecca Miner, *Treasurer*
EMP: 35
SQ FT: 5,500
SALES (est): 5.4MM **Privately Held**
SIC: 3444 Sheet metalwork

(G-78)
ENGINEERED MOLDING TECH LLC
Also Called: Emt
59 Exchange St (12205-3326)
PHONE..................518 482-2004
Todd Eteffe, *CEO*
Carrie Eteffe, *Manager*
Michael Pandori,
EMP: 16
SQ FT: 5,000
SALES: 2MM **Privately Held**
SIC: 3089 Molding primary plastic

(G-79)
FASTSIGNS
1593 Central Ave (12205-2457)
PHONE..................518 456-7446
Fax: 518 869-1808
James Pritchard, *Principal*
EMP: 10
SALES (est): 1.1MM **Privately Held**
SIC: 3993 Signs & advertising specialties

(G-80)
FINGERPRINT AMERICA INC
1843 Central Ave (12205-4796)
P.O. Box 12542 (12212-2542)
PHONE..................518 435-1609
Fax: 518 435-1507
Chris Migliaro, *President*
EMP: 6
SQ FT: 3,000
SALES (est): 814.7K **Privately Held**
WEB: www.fingerprintamerica.com
SIC: 3999 Fingerprint equipment

(G-81)
FORT ORANGE PRESS INC
11 Sand Creek Rd (12205-1442)
PHONE..................518 489-3233
Fax: 800 950-7117
Robert F Witko, *Ch of Bd*
Frank P Witko, *Ch of Bd*
Michael P Witko, *President*
Jamie Dickinson, *Vice Pres*
William Dorsman, *Vice Pres*
EMP: 37 **EST:** 1905
SQ FT: 33,000
SALES (est): 11.4MM **Privately Held**
WEB: www.fortorangepress.com
SIC: 2752 2791 Commercial printing, offset; typesetting

(G-82)
GENERAL ELECTRIC COMPANY
11 Anderson Dr (12205-1401)
PHONE..................518 459-4110
Gabe Davis, *Project Mgr*
James Miner, *Safety Mgr*
Christopher Bouch, *Opers Staff*
Kyle Badeau, *Engineer*
David Ebbing, *Engineer*
EMP: 50
SQ FT: 1,680

GEOGRAPHIC SECTION

Albany - Albany County (G-108)

SALES (corp-wide): 123.6B **Publicly Held**
SIC: 3629 7694 Electronic generation equipment; electric motor repair
PA: General Electric Company
41 Farnsworth St
Boston MA 02210
617 443-3000

(G-83)
GREENBUSH TAPE & LABEL INC
40 Broadway Unit 31 (12202-1174)
P.O. Box 1488 (12201-1488)
PHONE..................................518 465-2389
Fax: 518 465-5781
Alfred Chenot, *Corp Secy*
James Chenot, *Vice Pres*
EMP: 35 EST: 1966
SQ FT: 75,000
SALES (est): 4.4MM **Privately Held**
WEB: www.greenbushlabel.com
SIC: 2759 2672 Labels & seals: printing; coated & laminated paper

(G-84)
HANES SUPPLY INC
156 Railroad Ave Ste 3 (12205-5773)
PHONE..................................518 438-0139
Fax: 518 438-5343
Bill Kenny, *Manager*
Kevin Sitterly, *Manager*
EMP: 26
SALES (corp-wide): 108.4MM **Privately Held**
SIC: 3315 Wire & fabricated wire products
PA: Hanes Supply, Inc.
55 James E Casey Dr
Buffalo NY 14206
716 826-2636

(G-85)
HEARST CORPORATION
Capital Newspaper Div
645 Albany Shaker Rd (12211-1158)
P.O. Box 15000 (12212-5000)
PHONE..................................518 454-5694
Tony Pallone, *Editor*
Lisa Stevens, *Editor*
Kurt M Vantosky, *Senior VP*
David P White, *Vice Pres*
George Hearst, *Vice Pres*
EMP: 550
SALES (corp-wide): 6.4B **Privately Held**
WEB: www.hearstcorp.com
SIC: 2721 2752 2711 Periodicals: publishing only; commercial printing, lithographic; newspapers
PA: The Hearst Corporation
300 W 57th St Fl 42
New York NY 10019
212 649-2000

(G-86)
HOCKEY FACILITY
830 Albany Shaker Rd (12211-1054)
PHONE..................................518 452-7396
Fax: 518 452-5408
Paul Hebert, *Manager*
EMP: 5
SALES (est): 494.1K **Privately Held**
SIC: 2329 Hockey uniforms: men's, youths' & boys'

(G-87)
HOEHN INC
Also Called: Hoehn.us
159 Chestnut St (12210-1905)
PHONE..................................518 463-8900
James G Hoehn Jr, *President*
Melissa Nigro, *Vice Pres*
EMP: 15
SALES: 1.6MM **Privately Held**
WEB: www.hoehn.com
SIC: 2339 2389 Women's & misses' accessories; men's miscellaneous accessories

(G-88)
HP HOOD LLC
9 Norman Dr (12205-4721)
PHONE..................................518 218-9097
EMP: 299
SALES (corp-wide): 1.7B **Privately Held**
SIC: 2026 Fluid milk

PA: Hp Hood Llc
6 Kimball Ln Ste 400
Lynnfield MA 01940
617 887-8441

(G-89)
ION OPTICS INC
Also Called: Cosmo Optics
75 Benjamin St (12202-1137)
PHONE..................................518 339-6853
Brian Sebastian, *Principal*
EMP: 13
SALES (est): 1MM **Privately Held**
SIC: 3229 Lens blanks, optical

(G-90)
ISIMULATE LLC
90 State St Ste 700 (12207-1707)
PHONE..................................877 947-2831
Bobby Sied, *General Mgr*
EMP: 5
SQ FT: 1,000
SALES: 500K **Privately Held**
SIC: 7372 Educational computer software

(G-91)
JASON LADANYE GUITAR PIANO & H
605 Park Ave (12208-3217)
PHONE..................................518 527-3973
Jason Ladanye, *Owner*
EMP: 50
SALES (est): 90.9K **Privately Held**
SIC: 3931 Harmonicas

(G-92)
JOHNSON CONTROLS INC
130 Railroad Ave (12205-5701)
PHONE..................................518 694-4822
John Desare, *Manager*
EMP: 9 **Privately Held**
SIC: 2531 Seats, automobile
HQ: Johnson Controls, Inc.
5757 N Green Bay Ave
Milwaukee WI 53209
414 524-1200

(G-93)
KAL-HARBOUR INC
Also Called: Harbour Roads
11 Villa Rd (12204-2213)
P.O. Box 4087 (12204-0087)
PHONE..................................518 266-0690
Laura Harbour, *President*
EMP: 10
SALES (corp-wide): 1.9MM **Privately Held**
WEB: www.harbourroads.com
SIC: 2951 Asphalt paving mixtures & blocks
PA: Kal-Harbour Inc
21 Arch St
Watervliet NY 12189
518 266-0690

(G-94)
KING ROAD MATERIALS INC (DH)
Also Called: King Paving
8 Southwoods Blvd (12211-2554)
P.O. Box 15097 (12212-5097)
PHONE..................................518 381-9995
Fax: 518 374-1721
Donald E Fane, *President*
EMP: 35 EST: 1959
SQ FT: 2,552
SALES (est): 20.9MM
SALES (corp-wide): 28.6B **Privately Held**
SIC: 2951 Asphalt & asphaltic paving mixtures (not from refineries)

(G-95)
KING ROAD MATERIALS INC
Cordell Rd (12212)
P.O. Box 12699 (12212-2699)
PHONE..................................518 382-5354
Mellissa Bennett, *Principal*
EMP: 15
SALES (corp-wide): 28.6B **Privately Held**
SIC: 3273 Ready-mixed concrete
HQ: King Road Materials, Inc.
8 Southwoods Blvd
Albany NY 12211
518 381-9995

(G-96)
KOEPPELS KUSTOM KITCHENS INC
16 Van Rensselaer Rd (12205-1413)
PHONE..................................518 489-0092
Fax: 518 489-0363
Carl J Koeppel Jr, *President*
EMP: 5
SQ FT: 4,500
SALES (est): 520K **Privately Held**
SIC: 2541 1751 Counter & sink tops; cabinet building & installation

(G-97)
KRONOS INCORPORATED
16 Sage Est Ste 206 (12204-2241)
PHONE..................................518 459-5545
Frank Shipp, *Manager*
EMP: 36
SALES (corp-wide): 1.4B **Privately Held**
WEB: www.kronos.com
SIC: 7372 Prepackaged software
HQ: Kronos Incorporated
900 Chelmsford St
Lowell MA 01851
978 250-9800

(G-98)
LIDS CORPORATION
131 Colonie Ctr Spc 429 (12205-2751)
PHONE..................................518 459-7060
Dinelle Jackson, *Manager*
EMP: 5
SALES (corp-wide): 2.8B **Publicly Held**
WEB: www.hatworld.com
SIC: 2253 Hats & headwear, knit
HQ: Lids Corporation
7555 Woodland Dr
Indianapolis IN 46278

(G-99)
M&G DURAVENT INC
10 Jupiter Ln (12205-4947)
PHONE..................................518 463-7284
EMP: 20 **Privately Held**
SIC: 3444 Metal ventilating equipment
HQ: M&G Duravent, Inc.
877 Cotting Ct
Vacaville CA 95688
707 446-1786

(G-100)
MCD METALS LLC
20 Corporate Cir Ste 2 (12203-5175)
PHONE..................................518 456-9694
Kevin Gleason, *President*
Jacek Wozniak, *Opers Mgr*
EMP: 11
SALES (est): 734.5K **Privately Held**
SIC: 3499 Shims, metal

(G-101)
MECHANICAL TECHNOLOGY INC (PA)
Also Called: MTI
325 Washington Avenue Ext (12205-5581)
PHONE..................................518 218-2550
Fax: 518 533-2201
David C Michaels, *Ch of Bd*
Frederick W Jones, *President*
EMP: 29 EST: 1961
SQ FT: 17,400
SALES: 7MM **Publicly Held**
SIC: 3829 Stress, strain & flaw detecting/measuring equipment; vibration meters, analyzers & calibrators

(G-102)
MOMENTIVE PRFMCE MTLS HOLDINGS
Also Called: Momentive Prfmce Mtls Holdings
22 Corporate Woods Blvd (12211-2374)
PHONE..................................518 533-4600
Bradley J Bell, *Ch of Bd*
Mark Brammer, *Exec VP*
Douglas Johns, *Exec VP*
David Rusinko, *Vice Pres*
Nick Wilhelm, *Purch Mgr*
EMP: 9270
SALES (est): 614.7K **Privately Held**
SIC: 2869 3479 Silicones; coating of metals with silicon
PA: Hexion Holdings Llc
180 E Broad St
Columbus OH 43215

(G-103)
MOTOROLA SOLUTIONS INC
251 New Karner Rd (12205-4627)
PHONE..................................518 869-9517
EMP: 142
SALES (corp-wide): 5.7B **Publicly Held**
SIC: 3663 Mfg Communication Equipment
PA: Motorola Solutions, Inc.
1303 E Algonquin Rd
Schaumburg IL 60661
847 576-5000

(G-104)
MTI INSTRUMENTS INC
325 Washington Ave 3 (12206-3012)
PHONE..................................518 218-2550
Fax: 518 218-2506
Kevin G Lynch, *Principal*
Don Welch, *Engineer*
Matt Denoncour, *Electrical Engi*
Rick Jones, *Controller*
Maribel Lape, *Sales Staff*
EMP: 10
SALES (est): 5.2MM
SALES (corp-wide): 7MM **Publicly Held**
WEB: www.mtiinstruments.com
SIC: 3829 8731 Stress, strain & flaw detecting/measuring equipment; vibration meters, analyzers & calibrators; commercial research laboratory; engineering laboratory, except testing; energy research
PA: Mechanical Technology Incorporated
325 Washington Avenue Ext
Albany NY 12205
518 218-2550

(G-105)
NATURES BOUNTY CO
120 Wash Ave Ext Ste 110 (12203-0302)
PHONE..................................518 452-5813
Michael Austin, *Manager*
EMP: 19 **Publicly Held**
SIC: 2833 Vitamins, natural or synthetic: bulk, uncompounded
HQ: The Nature's Bounty Co
2100 Smithtown Ave
Ronkonkoma NY 11779
631 200-2000

(G-106)
NEW YORK PRESS & GRAPHICS INC
12 Interstate Ave (12205-5319)
PHONE..................................518 489-7089
Fax: 518 489-8232
David J Goldstein, *CEO*
Adam Goldstein, *Vice Pres*
Gail Wilty, *Opers Mgr*
Daniel Goldstein, *CFO*
EMP: 16
SQ FT: 13,000
SALES (est): 2.4MM **Privately Held**
WEB: www.nypressandgraphics.com
SIC: 2752 Commercial printing, lithographic

(G-107)
NEWKIRK PRODUCTS INC (HQ)
15 Corporate Cir (12203-5177)
PHONE..................................518 862-3200
Fax: 518 862-3399
Raymond Newkirk, *CEO*
Peter Newkirk, *President*
Kassie Scholz, *Assistant VP*
James B Salada, *Vice Pres*
John J Graham, *CFO*
EMP: 240
SQ FT: 135,000
SALES (est): 28.9MM
SALES (corp-wide): 1.5B **Publicly Held**
WEB: www.newkirk.com
SIC: 2731 Pamphlets: publishing & printing
PA: Dst Systems, Inc.
333 W 11th St
Kansas City MO 64105
816 435-1000

(G-108)
NEWSPAPER TIMES UNION
Also Called: Capitol Newspaper
645 Albany Shaker Rd (12211-1158)
P.O. Box 15000 (12212-5000)
PHONE..................................518 454-5676
David White, *President*
On April, *Publisher*
George R Hearst, *Vice Pres*

Janet Reynolds, *Opers Mgr*
Dan Couto, *Opers Staff*
EMP: 12
SALES (est): 690K **Privately Held**
WEB: www.saratogasignature.com
SIC: 2711 Newspapers, publishing & printing

(G-109)
NINE PIN CIDERWORKS LLC
929 Broadway (12207-1305)
PHONE..................................518 449-9999
Alejandro Del Peral, *Mng Member*
EMP: 10 **EST:** 2013
SALES (est): 828.5K **Privately Held**
SIC: 2099 Cider, nonalcoholic

(G-110)
NORTHEAST COMMERCIAL PRTG INC (PA)
Also Called: Eastern Offset
1237 Central Ave Ste 3 (12205-5328)
PHONE..................................518 459-5047
Fax: 518 459-5048
Anthony Mosca, *President*
EMP: 7
SQ FT: 4,000
SALES (est): 854K **Privately Held**
WEB: www.northeastcommercial.com
SIC: 2752 Commercial printing, offset

(G-111)
NORTHEASTERN AIR QUALITY INC
730 3rd St (12206-2007)
PHONE..................................518 857-3641
Robert Kelley, *President*
Russell Hilton, *Opers Mgr*
Dan Guay, *Technician*
EMP: 12
SALES: 5MM **Privately Held**
SIC: 1389 Testing, measuring, surveying & analysis services

(G-112)
ORACLE AMERICA INC
Also Called: Sun Microsystems
7 Southwoods Blvd Ste 1 (12211-2526)
PHONE..................................518 427-9353
Frank Wickham, *Systs Engr*
Leslie Woodin, *Sales/Mktg Mgr*
Tom Karpowitz, *Technical Staff*
EMP: 52
SALES (corp-wide): 37.7B **Publicly Held**
SIC: 3571 Minicomputers
HQ: Oracle America, Inc.
500 Oracle Pkwy
Redwood City CA 94065
650 506-7000

(G-113)
OTIS ELEVATOR COMPANY
20 Loudonville Rd Ste 1 (12204-1509)
PHONE..................................518 426-4006
Fax: 518 426-1101
Dorothy Mynahan, *Branch Mgr*
EMP: 33
SALES (corp-wide): 57.2B **Publicly Held**
WEB: www.otis.com
SIC: 3534 Elevators & equipment
HQ: Otis Elevator Company
1 Carrier P
Farmington CT 06032
860 674-3000

(G-114)
OUR DAILY EATS LLC
10 Burdick Dr Ste 1 (12205-1457)
PHONE..................................518 810-8412
EMP: 12
SALES (est): 1.8MM **Privately Held**
SIC: 2068 Mfg Salted/Roasted Nuts/Seeds

(G-115)
PATRICK RYANS MODERN PRESS
1 Colonie St (12207-2434)
PHONE..................................518 434-2921
Fax: 518 434-2954
Michael Ryan, *President*
Patrick Ryan, *Vice Pres*
EMP: 10 **EST:** 1946
SQ FT: 6,000
SALES (est): 1MM **Privately Held**
WEB: www.modernpress.com
SIC: 2752 2759 2791 Commercial printing, offset; letterpress printing; typesetting

(G-116)
PBR GRAPHICS INC
20 Railroad Ave Ste 1 (12205-5785)
PHONE..................................518 458-2909
Fax: 518 458-7118
Robert Cullum Jr, *President*
Robert G Cullum Sr, *Vice Pres*
Barbara Cullum, *Treasurer*
EMP: 9
SQ FT: 11,000
SALES: 920K **Privately Held**
SIC: 2759 Laser printing

(G-117)
PENGUIN RANDOM HOUSE LLC
80 State St (12207-2541)
PHONE..................................212 366-2377
David Shanks, *CEO*
EMP: 200
SALES (corp-wide): 17.9B **Privately Held**
SIC: 2731 5942 Book publishing; book stores
HQ: Penguin Random House Llc
1745 Broadway
New York NY 10019
212 782-9000

(G-118)
PETERSONS NELNET LLC
3 Columbia Cir Ste 205 (12203-5158)
PHONE..................................609 896-1800
Randi Tobin, *Manager*
EMP: 220
SALES (corp-wide): 1.2B **Publicly Held**
WEB: www.culinaryschools.com
SIC: 2731 2741 Textbooks: publishing & printing; miscellaneous publishing
HQ: Peterson's Nelnet, Llc
3 Columbia Cir Ste 205
Albany NY 12203
609 896-1800

(G-119)
PHARMACEUTIC LABS LLC
15 Walker Way (12205-4945)
PHONE..................................518 608-1060
Ernesto Samuel, *CEO*
Raleigh Hamilton, *CFO*
Amy Milani PHD, *Marketing Staff*
John Mather, *Director*
Melissa Stefko, *Director*
▲ **EMP:** 14
SALES (est): 2.4MM **Privately Held**
SIC: 2834 Pharmaceutical preparations

(G-120)
PHYLJOHN DISTRIBUTORS INC
Also Called: Gillette Creamery
6 Interstate Ave (12205-5309)
PHONE..................................518 459-2775
Richard H Gillette, *Supervisor*
EMP: 10
SALES (corp-wide): 32.8MM **Privately Held**
WEB: www.gillettecreamery.com
SIC: 2024 Ice cream & frozen desserts
PA: Phyljohn Distributors, Inc.
47 Steves Ln
Gardiner NY 12525
845 419-0900

(G-121)
PIEDMONT PLASTICS INC
4 Access Rd (12205-4744)
PHONE..................................518 724-0563
Dawn Carden, *Principal*
EMP: 8
SALES (corp-wide): 165.8MM **Privately Held**
SIC: 2295 Resin or plastic coated fabrics
PA: Piedmont Plastics, Inc.
5010 W Wt Harris Blvd
Charlotte NC 28269
704 597-8200

(G-122)
PINE BUSH PRINTING CO INC
2005 Western Ave (12203-7016)
PHONE..................................518 456-2431
Don Blais, *President*
EMP: 7
SALES (est): 684.8K **Privately Held**
SIC: 2752 Commercial printing, lithographic

(G-123)
PRAXAIR INC
116 Railroad Ave (12205-5789)
PHONE..................................518 482-4360
EMP: 20
SALES (corp-wide): 10.5B **Publicly Held**
SIC: 2813 Industrial gases
PA: Praxair, Inc.
10 Riverview Dr
Danbury CT 06810
203 837-2000

(G-124)
PRINTING RESOURCES INC
Also Called: The Printing Company
100 Fuller Rd Ste 1 (12205-5760)
PHONE..................................518 482-2470
Fax: 518 482-2567
Darcy Harding, *President*
Denise Harris, *Cust Svc Dir*
EMP: 20
SQ FT: 15,000
SALES (est): 2MM **Privately Held**
SIC: 2759 2791 2789 2752 Commercial printing; typesetting; bookbinding & related work; commercial printing, lithographic

(G-125)
R & J SHEET METAL DISTRS INC
Also Called: R and J Sheet Metal
119 Sheridan Ave (12210-2426)
PHONE..................................518 433-1525
Robert Gardner, *President*
EMP: 6
SALES (est): 892.1K **Privately Held**
SIC: 3441 Fabricated structural metal

(G-126)
R R DONNELLEY & SONS COMPANY
Moore Graphics Services
4 Executive Park Dr Ste 2 (12203-3717)
PHONE..................................518 438-9722
Fax: 518 489-7080
Joe Benoit, *Manager*
EMP: 100
SALES (corp-wide): 6.9B **Publicly Held**
WEB: www.moore.com
SIC: 2759 Screen printing
PA: R. R. Donnelley & Sons Company
35 W Wacker Dr Ste 3650
Chicago IL 60601
312 326-8000

(G-127)
RAFF ENTERPRISES
12 Petra Ln Ste 6 (12205-4973)
PHONE..................................518 218-7883
Sean Raff, *Owner*
EMP: 9
SALES (est): 876K **Privately Held**
SIC: 2511 China closets

(G-128)
RATIONAL RETENTION LLC (PA)
Also Called: Rational Enterprises
2 Tower Pl Ste 13 (12203-3726)
PHONE..................................518 489-3000
Bob Thayer, *Accountant*
William W Duker, *Mng Member*
EMP: 30
SALES (est): 2MM **Privately Held**
SIC: 7372 7374 Prepackaged software; data processing & preparation

(G-129)
RATIONAL RETENTION LLC
2 Tower Pl Ste 13 (12203-3726)
PHONE..................................518 489-3000
Michael McCreary, *Branch Mgr*
EMP: 5
SALES (corp-wide): 2MM **Privately Held**
SIC: 7372 Prepackaged software
PA: Rational Retention, Llc
2 Tower Pl Ste 13
Albany NY 12203
518 489-3000

(G-130)
REM PRINTING INC
55 Railroad Ave (12205-5947)
PHONE..................................518 438-7338
Paul Remmert, *President*
Matthew Remmert, *VP Sales*
EMP: 6
SQ FT: 5,000
SALES: 600K **Privately Held**
WEB: www.remprinting.com
SIC: 2752 Commercial printing, lithographic

(G-131)
SARATOGA TRUNK AND FURNITURE
Also Called: Tomorrow Group, The
5 Macaffer Dr (12204-1207)
PHONE..................................518 463-3252
Ronald Richardson, *President*
David Tamburelli, *Exec VP*
Sheila Richardson, *Admin Sec*
▲ **EMP:** 15 **EST:** 1924
SQ FT: 20,000
SALES: 1MM **Privately Held**
SIC: 3499 Novelties & giftware, including trophies

(G-132)
SCARANO BOAT BUILDING INC
194 S Port Rd (12202-1075)
PHONE..................................518 463-3401
John S Scarano, *President*
William Hubert, *Controller*
EMP: 45
SALES: 950K **Privately Held**
WEB: www.scaranoboat.com
SIC: 3731 Shipbuilding & repairing

(G-133)
SCARANO BOATBUILDING INC
194 S Port Rd (12202-1075)
PHONE..................................518 463-3401
John Scarano, *President*
Rick Scarano, *Vice Pres*
EMP: 27
SQ FT: 90,000
SALES (est): 4.3MM **Privately Held**
SIC: 3732 Boat building & repairing

(G-134)
SMITHS GAS SERVICE INC
Also Called: J and M Schwarz
5 Walker Way Ste 1 (12205-4953)
PHONE..................................518 438-0400
John Schwarz, *President*
EMP: 5
SALES (est): 522.4K **Privately Held**
SIC: 3494 Plumbing & heating valves

(G-135)
SOMML HEALTH LLC
43 New Scotland Ave Mc25 (12208-3412)
PHONE..................................518 880-2170
David B Wood, *Owner*
Kurt Lozier, *Principal*
David Wood, *Mng Member*
EMP: 5 **EST:** 2015
SQ FT: 200
SALES (est): 128.9K **Privately Held**
SIC: 7372 Prepackaged software

(G-136)
STANLEY PAPER CO INC
1 Terminal St (12206-2283)
PHONE..................................518 489-1131
Fax: 518 453-2603
Matthew Jasinski II, *President*
Pearl Jasinski, *Corp Secy*
EMP: 11 **EST:** 1942
SQ FT: 6,000
SALES (est): 2.4MM **Privately Held**
SIC: 2679 5113 Conduits, fiber (pressed pulp): from purchased material; industrial & personal service paper

(G-137)
STEIN FIBERS LTD (PA)
4 Computer Dr W Ste 200 (12205-1630)
PHONE..................................518 489-5700
Fax: 518 489-5713
Sidney J Stein III, *Ch of Bd*
Peter J Spitalny, *President*
Rich Lachiusa, *Transptn Dir*
Allen Greenberg, *CFO*

GEOGRAPHIC SECTION

Albertson - Nassau County (G-162)

Allen Greenburg, *CFO*
◆ EMP: 18
SQ FT: 4,600
SALES: 266.9MM **Privately Held**
WEB: www.steinfibers.com
SIC: 2824 Polyester fibers

(G-138)
STOP N SHOP LLC
911 Central Ave Ste 149 (12206-1350)
PHONE..................518 512-9657
Efasto Bowl, *Mng Member*
EMP: 6
SALES (est): 135.3K **Privately Held**
SIC: 7372 Business oriented computer software

(G-139)
SUPPLY TECHNOLOGIES (NY) (DH)
80 State St (12207-2541)
PHONE..................212 966-3310
Jack Laufer, *CEO*
Samuel Laufer, *President*
Frank Negron, *Asst Controller*
▲ EMP: 18 EST: 1953
SQ FT: 10,000
SALES (est): 11.4MM
SALES (corp-wide): 1.2B **Publicly Held**
SIC: 3452 3599 5072 3451 Bolts, metal; rivets, metal; washers, metal; screws, metal; machine shop, jobbing & repair; bolts; rivets; washers (hardware); screws; screw machine products
HQ: Supply Technologies Llc
6065 Parkland Blvd Ste 1
Cleveland OH 44124
440 947-2100

(G-140)
TECHNICAL WLDG FABRICATORS LLC
27 Thatcher St (12207-5052)
PHONE..................518 463-2229
Fax: 518 462-1360
Carol Boyer,
EMP: 10
SALES (est): 1.4MM **Privately Held**
SIC: 3315 Welded steel wire fabric

(G-141)
TEL TECHNOLOGY CENTER AMER LLC (DH)
255 Fuller Rd Ste 244 (12203-3663)
PHONE..................512 424-4200
Fax: 518 292-4300
Hiroshi Takenaka, *President*
▲ EMP: 27
SALES (est): 4.5MM
SALES (corp-wide): 7B **Privately Held**
SIC: 3674 Semiconductors & related devices
HQ: Tokyo Electron U.S. Holdings, Inc.
2400 Grove Blvd
Austin TX 78741
512 424-1000

(G-142)
THERMOAURA INC
132b Railroad Ave Ste B (12205-5701)
PHONE..................518 813-4997
Rutvik J Mehta, *President*
Richard Frederick, *COO*
Theodorine Borca-Tasciuk, *Director*
Ganpati Ramanath, *Director*
EMP: 11
SQ FT: 4,800
SALES: 500K **Privately Held**
SIC: 3674 Wafers (semiconductor devices)

(G-143)
TOKYO ELECTRON AMERICA INC
255 Fuller Rd Ste 214 (12203-3604)
PHONE..................518 292-4200
Fax: 518 320-1985
Bruce Altemus, *Engineer*
Norman Jacobson, *Engineer*
Aelan Mosden, *Engineer*
Chris Krammer, *Branch Mgr*
Anton Devilliers, *Manager*
EMP: 9

SALES (corp-wide): 7B **Privately Held**
WEB: www.telusa.com
SIC: 3826 Electrolytic conductivity instruments
HQ: Tokyo Electron America, Inc.
2400 Grove Blvd
Austin TX 78741
512 424-1000

(G-144)
U ALL INC
9 Interstate Ave (12205-5320)
PHONE..................518 438-2558
Fax: 518 438-7282
James Holodak, *President*
Stephanie Marion, *Purchasing*
Peggy Holodak, *Controller*
Tina Benson, *Sales Mgr*
Robert White, *Sales Mgr*
EMP: 25
SQ FT: 10,000
SALES (est): 3.4MM **Privately Held**
WEB: www.allu.com
SIC: 2759 2395 5199 2396 Screen printing; embroidery & art needlework; advertising specialties; automotive & apparel trimmings

(G-145)
UCC GUIDE INC (PA)
Also Called: Ernst Publishing Co
99 Washington Ave (12210-2822)
PHONE..................518 434-0909
Gregory E Teal, *CEO*
Jan Clark, *Vice Pres*
Kathryn Teal, *Vice Pres*
Liz Kelly, *Research*
John Duff, *Manager*
EMP: 10
SQ FT: 4,000
SALES (est): 2.6MM **Privately Held**
WEB: www.ernstinfo.com
SIC: 2741 Miscellaneous publishing

(G-146)
ULTREPET LLC
136c Fuller Rd (12205)
PHONE..................781 275-6400
M Scott Mellen, *President*
Carol C Forman, *Principal*
David B Spencer, *Chairman*
Leigh A Peritz, *Vice Pres*
Paul C Zordan, *Vice Pres*
▲ EMP: 65
SALES (est): 13.4MM
SALES (corp-wide): 51.9MM **Privately Held**
SIC: 3559 Plastics working machinery
PA: Wte Corporation
7 Alfred Cir
Bedford MA 01730
781 275-6400

(G-147)
UNIVERSITY AT ALBANY
Also Called: College Nnoscale Science Engrg
257 Fuller Rd (12203-3613)
PHONE..................518 437-8686
Fax: 518 437-8687
Laura Babcock, *Assistant VP*
Sara Brenner, *Assistant VP*
Diana L Dumesnil, *Assistant VP*
Diana Dumesnil, *Assistant VP*
Steven Novak, *Assistant VP*
EMP: 28 **Privately Held**
SIC: 3674 9411 Semiconductors & related devices;
HQ: University At Albany
1400 Washington Ave
Albany NY 12222
518 442-3300

(G-148)
UTC FIRE SEC AMERICAS CORP INC
10 Walker Way Ste 3 (12205-4964)
PHONE..................518 456-0444
EMP: 54
SALES (corp-wide): 57.2B **Publicly Held**
SIC: 3669 Burglar alarm apparatus, electric
HQ: Utc Fire & Security Americas Corporation, Inc.
8985 Town Center Pkwy
Lakewood Ranch FL 34202

(G-149)
VERTICAL LAX INC
20 Corporate Cir Ste 4 (12205-5157)
PHONE..................518 669-3699
Curt Styres, *CEO*
Paul Gait, *President*
Lewis Staats, *Treasurer*
Kelly Anderson, *Accountant*
▲ EMP: 7 EST: 2010
SALES (est): 632.2K **Privately Held**
SIC: 3949 7389 Sporting & athletic goods;

(G-150)
WEST END IRON WORKS INC
4254 Albany St (12205-4684)
PHONE..................518 456-1105
Fax: 518 456-1335
Eric R Frey, *President*
EMP: 5 EST: 1890
SQ FT: 9,000
SALES (est): 460K **Privately Held**
SIC: 3446 Architectural metalwork

(G-151)
WILD WORKS INCORPORATED
30 Railroad Ave (12205-5721)
PHONE..................716 891-4197
William C Smith, *CEO*
EMP: 6
SALES (est): 536.4K **Privately Held**
SIC: 2891 Adhesives & sealants

(G-152)
XEROX CORPORATION
80 State St Ste 3 (12207-2603)
PHONE..................518 434-6543
Gabriela Baron, *President*
Randy Burrows, *President*
Craig Freeman, *Vice Pres*
Robert Hellewell, *Vice Pres*
Karl Sobylak, *Opers Staff*
EMP: 50
SALES (corp-wide): 10.7B **Publicly Held**
WEB: www.xerox.com
SIC: 3861 Photographic equipment & supplies
PA: Xerox Corporation
201 Merritt 7
Norwalk CT 06851
203 968-3000

(G-153)
YS METAL
54 Dott Ave (12205-5321)
PHONE..................518 512-5275
Mike Bondari, *Principal*
EMP: 7
SALES (est): 689.8K **Privately Held**
SIC: 3399 Primary metal products

(G-154)
ZELA INTERNATIONAL CO
13 Manor St (12207-3008)
PHONE..................518 436-1833
Fax: 518 436-1533
Ike Sukljian, *President*
Cristina Samuels, *VP Sales*
▲ EMP: 25
SQ FT: 60,000
SALES (est): 2.2MM **Privately Held**
WEB: www.zela.com
SIC: 2844 5122 Toilet preparations; cosmetics

Albertson
Nassau County

(G-155)
BRAUN INDUSTRIES INC
Also Called: Braun Brush Company
43 Albertson Ave (11507-2102)
PHONE..................516 741-6000
Fax: 516 741-6299
Max W Cheney, *Ch of Bd*
Lance W Cheney, *President*
Adam Czerniawski, *Vice Pres*
Jerilyn Leis, *Cust Mgr*
Peter Lassen, *Business Dir*
▲ EMP: 20 EST: 1875
SQ FT: 15,000
SALES (est): 3.3MM **Privately Held**
WEB: www.brush.com
SIC: 3991 Brooms & brushes

(G-156)
BURT MILLWORK CORPORATION
85 Fairview Dr (11507-1007)
PHONE..................718 257-4601
Fax: 718 649-4398
Eli Gordon, *President*
Seymour Gordon, *Vice Pres*
Bruce Gordon, *Admin Sec*
▲ EMP: 22
SQ FT: 42,500
SALES (est): 5.4MM **Privately Held**
SIC: 2431 Doors, wood; door shutters, wood; windows, wood

(G-157)
DAIGE PRODUCTS INC
1 Albertson Ave Ste 3 (11507-1444)
PHONE..................516 621-2100
Fax: 516 621-1916
I M Harris, *President*
EMP: 15
SQ FT: 3,500
SALES (est): 3.1MM **Privately Held**
WEB: www.daige.com
SIC: 3555 Printing trades machinery

(G-158)
GEMSON GRAPHICS INC
820 Willis Ave Ste 2c (11507-1979)
PHONE..................516 873-8400
Emanuel Manicone, *Chairman*
EMP: 5
SALES (est): 854.4K **Privately Held**
SIC: 2752 2759 Commercial printing, offset; flexographic printing

(G-159)
PATSY STROCCHIA & SONS IRON WO
Also Called: Strocchia Iron Works
175 I U Willets Rd Ste 4 (11507-1342)
PHONE..................516 625-8800
Fax: 718 349-2852
Ralph J Strocchia, *Ch of Bd*
Leonard D Strocchia, *Vice Pres*
Michaelann Rago, *Office Mgr*
Michael Anne, *Manager*
Ralph Strocchia Jr, *Admin Sec*
▲ EMP: 18 EST: 1922
SALES: 3.2MM **Privately Held**
SIC: 3441 Fabricated structural metal

(G-160)
PAYA PRINTING OF NY INC
87 Searingtown Rd (11507-1125)
PHONE..................516 625-8346
Fax: 516 625-9658
Mohammad Samii, *President*
EMP: 5
SQ FT: 1,000
SALES (est): 482.9K **Privately Held**
SIC: 2754 2752 Commercial printing, gravure; commercial printing, lithographic

(G-161)
PELLA CORPORATION
Also Called: Pella Window Door
77 Albertson Ave Ste 2 (11507-2127)
PHONE..................516 385-3622
Shanade Alton, *Branch Mgr*
EMP: 316
SALES (corp-wide): 1.9B **Privately Held**
SIC: 2431 Windows, wood
PA: Pella Corporation
102 Main St
Pella IA 50219
641 621-1000

(G-162)
PELLA CORPORATION
Also Called: Pella Window Door
77 Albertson Ave Ste 2 (11507-2127)
PHONE..................516 385-3622
EMP: 316
SALES (corp-wide): 663.7MM **Privately Held**
SIC: 2431 Mfg Millwork
PA: Pella Corporation
102 Main St
Pella IA 50219
641 621-1000

Albertson - Nassau County (G-163)

(G-163)
SHRITEC CONSULTANTS INC
91 Searingtown Rd (11507-1125)
PHONE..................516 621-7072
Rathi Raja, *President*
Venkat Raja, *Vice Pres*
EMP: 9
SALES: 1.7MM **Privately Held**
SIC: 7372 Prepackaged software

Albion
Orleans County

(G-164)
ALBION-HOLLEY PENNYSAVER INC
Also Called: Lake Country Media
170 N Main St (14411-1063)
P.O. Box 231 (14411-0231)
PHONE..................585 589-5641
Fax: 585 589-1239
Karen Sawicz, *President*
Gary Hill, *Editor*
Kevin Weese, *Sales Staff*
Brad London, *Sales Associate*
Susan Cook, *Graphic Designe*
EMP: 48
SQ FT: 22,000
SALES (est): 6.8MM **Privately Held**
SIC: 2791 2711 2741 Typesetting; job printing & newspaper publishing combined; miscellaneous publishing

(G-165)
AUSTIN INDUSTRIES INC (PA)
3871 Oak Orchard Rd (14411-9536)
PHONE..................585 589-1353
Alan Austin, *President*
Vernon Carl Austin, *Vice Pres*
Denise Austin, *Treasurer*
Simeon O Terry, *Program Mgr*
Tim Gregg, *Info Tech Dir*
EMP: 7
SQ FT: 7,200
SALES (est): 931.1K **Privately Held**
SIC: 3542 5085 Machine tools, metal forming type; welding supplies; industrial tools

(G-166)
CDL MANUFACTURING INC
15661 Telegraph Rd (14411)
PHONE..................585 589-2533
Kaz Laszewski, *President*
Steve Chiruck, *Vice Pres*
EMP: 5
SQ FT: 8,000
SALES (est): 662.1K **Privately Held**
WEB: www.cclmfg.com
SIC: 3599 Machine shop, jobbing & repair

(G-167)
EAGLE HARBOR SAND & GRAVEL INC
4780 Eagle Harbour Rd (14411)
PHONE..................585 798-4501
Paul D Pass, *President*
Tom Diamonte, *Vice Pres*
EMP: 5
SALES (est): 323K **Privately Held**
SIC: 1442 Construction sand mining; gravel mining

(G-168)
FREEZE-DRY FOODS INC
111 West Ave Ste 2 (14411-1500)
PHONE..................585 589-6399
Fax: 585 589-6402
Alasdair Grant, *CEO*
Karen Richardson, *President*
Andy Rose, *Plt & Fclts Mgr*
Anna Marie Clif, *Controller*
▲ EMP: 40
SALES (est): 6.6MM
SALES (corp-wide): 525.3K **Privately Held**
WEB: www.freeze-dry.com
SIC: 2038 Frozen specialties
PA: Freeze-Dry Foods Limited
2916 South Sheridan Way Suite 300
Oakville ON L6J 7
905 844-1471

(G-169)
J PAHURA CONTRACTORS
415 East Ave (14411-1620)
PHONE..................585 589-5793
James Pahura, *Owner*
EMP: 5
SALES (est): 210K **Privately Held**
SIC: 2951 Asphalt paving mixtures & blocks

(G-170)
ORLEANS PALLET COMPANY INC
227 West Ave (14411-1520)
PHONE..................585 589-0781
Shawn R Malark, *President*
EMP: 11
SQ FT: 65,000
SALES: 954K **Privately Held**
SIC: 2448 Pallets, wood

(G-171)
PENASACK MACHINE COMPANY INC
49 Sanford St (14411-1117)
P.O. Box 396 (14411-0396)
PHONE..................585 589-7044
Fax: 585 589-0046
Gerard Damore, *Ch of Bd*
Jeffrey Kinser, *Engineer*
Nancy Cole, *Accounts Mgr*
Jessica Tobin, *Manager*
EMP: 40 EST: 1967
SQ FT: 35,000
SALES (est): 7.2MM **Privately Held**
SIC: 3444 Sheet metal specialties, not stamped

(G-172)
RS AUTOMATION
Also Called: Richard Stacey Rs Automation
4015 Oak Orchard Rd (14411-9326)
PHONE..................585 589-0199
Richard Stacey, *Owner*
Christina Farabella, *Purchasing*
Dawn Stacey, *Clerk*
EMP: 17
SQ FT: 12,000
SALES (est): 4.6MM **Privately Held**
SIC: 3441 5084 Fabricated structural metal; industrial machinery & equipment

(G-173)
SAINT-GOBAIN ADFORS AMER INC
14770 East Ave (14411-9709)
PHONE..................585 589-4401
Ron Paeth, *Facilities Mgr*
Michele Guzman, *Human Res Mgr*
Joel Allen, *Branch Mgr*
Wendy Moriarty, *Personnel Assit*
EMP: 52
SALES (corp-wide): 185.8MM **Privately Held**
SIC: 2297 Nonwoven fabrics
HQ: Saint-Gobain Adfors America, Inc.
1795 Baseline Rd
Grand Island NY 14072
716 775-3900

(G-174)
WOODSIDE GRANITE INDUSTRIES (PA)
Also Called: Brigden Memorials
13890 Ridge Rd W (14411-9160)
PHONE..................585 589-6500
Fax: 585 589-4221
Leo Lacroix, *President*
Mickey Babcock, *Office Mgr*
▲ EMP: 3
SQ FT: 1,500
SALES (est): 1.2MM **Privately Held**
SIC: 3272 5999 Grave markers, concrete; gravestones, finished

Alcove
Albany County

(G-175)
NEW YORK QUARRIES INC
305 Rte 111 (12007)
PHONE..................518 756-3138
Fax: 518 756-8000
Nancy O'Brien, *President*
▲ EMP: 15
SQ FT: 1,200
SALES: 1.5MM **Privately Held**
WEB: www.newyorkquarries.com
SIC: 3281 1411 Cut stone & stone products; limestone, dimension-quarrying

Alden
Erie County

(G-176)
AGRI SERVICES CO
13899 North Rd (14004-9779)
PHONE..................716 937-6618
James Guarino, *Owner*
EMP: 5
SALES (est): 125K **Privately Held**
SIC: 3714 5531 Automotive wiring harness sets; truck equipment & parts

(G-177)
ALDEN AURORA GAS COMPANY INC
Also Called: Reserve Gas Company
13441 Railroad St (14004-1389)
P.O. Box 207 (14004-0207)
PHONE..................716 937-9484
Edward Harris, *Ch of Bd*
James C Gorom, *President*
Paul Tryanowski, *Treasurer*
Jacqueline Harris, *Shareholder*
Bernice Rosenbloom, *Shareholder*
EMP: 8
SQ FT: 1,200
SALES (est): 566.7K **Privately Held**
SIC: 1381 Drilling oil & gas wells

(G-178)
BENNETT MANUFACTURING CO INC
13315 Railroad St (14004-1390)
PHONE..................716 937-9161
Fax: 716 937-3137
Steven L Yellen, *Ch of Bd*
Richard D Yellen, *Vice Pres*
Susan Wessel, *Purch Agent*
Robert Cowing, *Purchasing*
Toby F Yellen, *Treasurer*
▲ EMP: 150
SQ FT: 100,000
SALES (est): 32.3MM **Privately Held**
WEB: www.bennettmfg.com
SIC: 3441 2842 Fabricated structural metal; specialty cleaning, polishes & sanitation goods

(G-179)
D J CROWELL CO INC
2815 Town Line Rd (14004-9676)
PHONE..................716 684-3343
Fax: 716 684-3345
David C Bressette, *President*
Jeffrey Minotti, *Vice Pres*
EMP: 6 EST: 1900
SQ FT: 6,000
SALES: 500K **Privately Held**
SIC: 3599 Machine shop, jobbing & repair

(G-180)
DUNDAS-JAFINE INC
11099 Broadway St (14004-9517)
PHONE..................716 681-9690
Fax: 716 681-0011
Debbie Patterson, *General Mgr*
James Feldmeyer, *Mfg Staff*
Bill Szajn, *CFO*
Colleen Ference, *Human Resources*
Dave Rockwell, *Natl Sales Mgr*
EMP: 50
SALES (corp-wide): 7.3MM **Privately Held**
WEB: www.dundasjafine.com
SIC: 3585 3564 3444 Heating equipment, complete; air conditioning equipment, complete; blowers & fans; sheet metalwork
PA: Dundas Jafine Inc
80 West Dr
Brampton ON L6T 3
905 450-7200

(G-181)
GAMMA NORTH CORPORATION
13595 Broadway St (14004-9736)
PHONE..................716 902-5100
Matthew Baum, *President*
James Mitchell, *President*
Elliot Kracko, *Chairman*
Juan J Alpizar, *Senior VP*
Jose M Rodriguez, *Senior VP*
EMP: 50 EST: 2012
SALES (est): 9.3MM **Privately Held**
SIC: 3442 Store fronts, prefabricated, metal

(G-182)
HUBCO INC
2885 Commerce Dr (14004-8538)
PHONE..................716 683-5940
Craig Huber, *President*
Paul Huber, *Vice Pres*
Mark Richardson, *Info Tech Mgr*
▲ EMP: 5
SQ FT: 6,000
SALES (est): 856.6K **Privately Held**
WEB: www.hubcopads.com
SIC: 3569 Assembly machines, non-metalworking

(G-183)
INTEGER HOLDINGS CORPORATION
Also Called: Greatbatch Medical
11900 Walden Ave (14004-9706)
PHONE..................716 937-5100
Fax: 716 937-5333
Ed Voboril, *Chairman*
Scott Bowers, *Engineer*
Stan Bystrak, *Engineer*
Jeffrey Grisante, *Engineer*
Kerstin Hokanson, *Engineer*
EMP: 23
SALES (corp-wide): 1.3B **Publicly Held**
SIC: 3675 Electronic capacitors
PA: Integer Holdings Corporation
2595 Dallas Pkwy Ste 310
Frisco TX 75034
214 618-5243

(G-184)
PHELINGER TOOL & DIE CORP
1254 Town Line Rd (14004-9672)
PHONE..................716 685-1780
Fax: 716 685-9306
Gordon Phelinger, *President*
Scott Phelinger, *Vice Pres*
EMP: 7
SQ FT: 1,000
SALES (est): 1MM **Privately Held**
WEB: www.phelingertool.com
SIC: 3544 Special dies & tools; jigs & fixtures

(G-185)
RESERVE GAS COMPANY INC
13441 Railroad St (14004-1338)
P.O. Box 207 (14004-0207)
PHONE..................716 937-9484
Sterlin Harris, *CEO*
James C Gorom, *President*
EMP: 8
SQ FT: 3,200
SALES (est): 1MM **Privately Held**
SIC: 1311 Natural gas production

(G-186)
SDR TECHNOLOGY INC
1613 Lindan Dr (14004-1113)
PHONE..................716 583-1249
Charles Chauncey, *President*
EMP: 5
SALES (est): 381.2K **Privately Held**
SIC: 3663 Radio & TV communications equipment

(G-187)
TURBOPRO INC
1284 Town Line Rd (14004-9672)
PHONE..................716 681-8651
Joseph Bantle, *President*
Brenda Bantle, *Vice Pres*
Mike Wittmeyer, *Chief Engr*
EMP: 4
SALES (est): 1MM **Privately Held**
SIC: 3563 Air & gas compressors

(G-188)
UNITED RBOTIC INTEGRATIONS LLC
2781 Town Line Rd (14004-9676)
PHONE..................................716 683-8334
John M Lass, *President*
William Penney, *Treasurer*
Michelle M Berger, *Admin Sec*
Paul Barker,
Melvin Bernhard,
EMP: 5
SALES (est): 530K Privately Held
WEB: www.unitedpmr.com
SIC: 3535 Robotic conveyors

(G-189)
WEISBECK PUBLISHING PRINTING
Also Called: Alden Advertiser
13200 Broadway St (14004-1313)
PHONE..................................716 937-9226
Leonard A Weisbeck Jr, *President*
EMP: 5 **EST:** 1948
SQ FT: 1,748
SALES (est): 421.1K Privately Held
WEB: www.aldenadvertiser.com
SIC: 2711 Newspapers, publishing & printing; job printing & newspaper publishing combined

Alexander
Genesee County

(G-190)
LENAPE ENERGY INC (PA)
Also Called: Leape Resources,
9489 Alexander Rd (14005-9795)
PHONE..................................585 344-1200
Fax: 585 344-3283
John Holko, *President*
Amy Holko, *Vice Pres*
Pat Sanders, *Office Mgr*
Jack Crooks, *Supervisor*
EMP: 2
SQ FT: 3,200
SALES (est): 1MM Privately Held
WEB: www.lenaperesources.com
SIC: 1381 1389 1382 4923 Drilling oil & gas wells; haulage, oil field; gas compressing (natural gas) at the fields; oil & gas exploration services; gas transmission & distribution

(G-191)
LENAPE RESOURCES INC
9489 Alexander Rd (14005-9795)
PHONE..................................585 344-1200
John Holko, *President*
Amy Holko, *Vice Pres*
EMP: 10
SALES: 1MM Privately Held
WEB: www.lenaperesources.com
SIC: 1382 4923 Oil & gas exploration services; gas transmission & distribution
PA: Lenape Energy Inc
    9489 Alexander Rd
    Alexander NY 14005
    585 344-1200

(G-192)
P & D EQUIPMENT SALES LLC
10171 Brookville Rd (14005-9783)
PHONE..................................585 343-2394
Josh Raines,
Brian Raines,
Dennis Raines,
Mark Raines,
Paul Raines,
EMP: 5
SALES (est): 592.3K Privately Held
SIC: 3523 Barn, silo, poultry, dairy & livestock machinery

(G-193)
RICHARD BAUER LOGGING
3936 Cookson Rd (14005-9718)
PHONE..................................585 343-4149
Richard Bauer, *Owner*
EMP: 5
SALES (est): 292.4K Privately Held
SIC: 2411 Logging camps & contractors

Alexandria Bay
Jefferson County

(G-194)
THOUSAND ISLANDS PRINTING CO
Also Called: Thousand Islands Sun
45501 St Rt 12 (13607)
PHONE..................................315 482-2581
Fax: 315 482-6315
Jeanne Roy Snow, *President*
William F Roy, *Vice Pres*
Helethea Roy, *Treasurer*
EMP: 9 **EST:** 1901
SQ FT: 3,250
SALES (est): 633.6K Privately Held
SIC: 2711 Job printing & newspaper publishing combined

(G-195)
THOUSAND ISLANDS WINERY LLC
43298 Seaway Ave Ste 1 (13607-2141)
PHONE..................................315 482-9306
Fax: 315 482-9302
Roxy Raymo, *General Mgr*
Steven J Conaway,
Erika Conaway,
EMP: 22
SQ FT: 4,771
SALES (est): 3.3MM Privately Held
WEB: www.thousandislandswinery.com
SIC: 2084 Wines

Alfred
Allegany County

(G-196)
CS MANUFACTURING LIMITED
56 S Main St (14802-1317)
PHONE..................................607 587-8154
Edward Fan, *Principal*
EMP: 50
SALES (est): 2.4MM Privately Held
SIC: 3312 3089 3324 Pipes, iron & steel; stainless steel; forgings, iron & steel; injection molding of plastics; commercial investment castings, ferrous

(G-197)
SAXON GLASS TECHNOLOGIES INC
200 N Main St Ste 114 (14802-1000)
P.O. Box 575 (14802-0575)
PHONE..................................607 587-9630
Arun Varshneya, *President*
Darshana Varshneya, *Vice Pres*
EMP: 10
SQ FT: 4,500
SALES (est): 1.2MM Privately Held
WEB: www.saxonglass.com
SIC: 3211 Strengthened or reinforced glass

Alfred Station
Allegany County

(G-198)
ASK CHEMICALS HI-TECH LLC
6329 Rte 21 (14803)
P.O. Box 788, Alfred (14802-0788)
PHONE..................................607 587-9146
Truett Sweeting, *Managing Dir*
Edward Holzlein, *Plant Mgr*
Jeannie Cartwright, *Purch Mgr*
Paul Bronson, *Plant Engr*
Rick Glenn, *Controller*
▲ **EMP:** 100
SALES (est): 15.3MM Privately Held
SIC: 3297 Nonclay refractories

(G-199)
BUFFALO CRUSHED STONE INC
638 State Route 244 (14803-9766)
P.O. Box 38 (14803-0038)
PHONE..................................607 587-8102
Fax: 607 587-8004
Douglas Drake, *Manager*
EMP: 9
SALES (corp-wide): 651.9MM Privately Held
SIC: 1442 Construction sand mining; gravel mining
HQ: Buffalo Crushed Stone, Inc.
    500 Como Park Blvd
    Buffalo NY 14227
    716 826-7310

(G-200)
NORTHERN TIMBER HARVESTING LLC
6042 State Route 21 (14803-9641)
P.O. Box 30, Society Hill SC (29593-0030)
PHONE..................................585 233-7330
Adam Ricci,
EMP: 11
SQ FT: 10,000
SALES: 2.9MM Privately Held
SIC: 2411 Logging

Allegany
Cattaraugus County

(G-201)
ALLEGANY LAMINATING AND SUPPLY
158 W Main St (14706-1235)
PHONE..................................716 372-2424
Charles Cousins, *President*
Wanda Cousins, *Corp Secy*
Athena Silluzio, *Admin Sec*
Kimberly Roth, *Clerk*
EMP: 5
SQ FT: 8,300
SALES (est): 460K Privately Held
SIC: 2541 3088 Table or counter tops, plastic laminated; partitions for floor attachment, prefabricated: wood; cabinets, except refrigerated: show, display, etc.: wood; tubs (bath, shower & laundry), plastic

(G-202)
E F LIPPERT CO INC
4451 S Nine Mile Rd (14706-9790)
PHONE..................................716 373-1100
Fax: 585 373-1100
Mary Stayer, *President*
Tom Stayer, *Vice Pres*
Bryan Howard, *Manager*
Cinda Warner, *Admin Sec*
EMP: 13 **EST:** 1945
SQ FT: 500
SALES (est): 725.7K Privately Held
SIC: 1442 5261 Common sand mining; gravel mining; sod; top soil

(G-203)
HANSON AGGREGATES EAST LLC
4419 S Nine Mile Rd (14706-9790)
PHONE..................................716 372-1574
EMP: 6
SALES (est): 326.8K Privately Held
SIC: 3272 Mfg Concrete Products

(G-204)
I & S OF NY INC
4174 Route 417 (14706-9787)
P.O. Box 380 (14706-0380)
PHONE..................................716 373-7001
Frank Steven, *President*
Mary Stephens, *Manager*
EMP: 10
SQ FT: 6,000
SALES (est): 1.5MM Privately Held
SIC: 1389 Servicing oil & gas wells

(G-205)
POTTER LUMBER CO INC
3786 Potter Rd (14706-9410)
P.O. Box 10 (14706-0010)
PHONE..................................716 373-1260
Fax: 716 373-1297
Robert G Potter, *President*
Theodore Potter, *Vice Pres*
Mary Frances Potter, *Treasurer*
Lucy Benson, *Admin Sec*
EMP: 40 **EST:** 1910
SQ FT: 700
SALES (est): 5.7MM Privately Held
SIC: 2421 2426 Sawmills & planing mills, general; hardwood dimension & flooring mills

Almond
Allegany County

(G-206)
HANSON AGGREGATES NEW YORK LLC
Also Called: Hanson Ready Mix Concrete
546 Clark Rd (14804)
PHONE..................................607 276-5881
Jeffrey Feenaughty, *Manager*
EMP: 5
SALES (corp-wide): 16B Privately Held
SIC: 3271 Concrete block & brick
HQ: Hanson Aggregates New York Llc
    8505 Freport Pkwy Ste 500
    Irving TX 75063

Alplaus
Schenectady County

(G-207)
INDUSTRIAL HANDLING SVCS INC
209 Alplaus Ave (12008-1014)
P.O. Box 2922, Glenville (12325-0922)
PHONE..................................518 399-0488
Fax: 518 399-0491
Michael F Coffey, *President*
EMP: 9
SQ FT: 1,598
SALES (est): 1,000K Privately Held
SIC: 3531 Cranes

Altamont
Albany County

(G-208)
ALFRED B PARELLA
Also Called: Latham Seamless Gutters
20 Reservoir Rd (12009-3230)
P.O. Box 448 (12009-0448)
PHONE..................................518 872-1238
Fax: 518 872-9777
Alfred B Parella, *President*
EMP: 5
SALES: 400K Privately Held
SIC: 3444 Gutters, sheet metal

(G-209)
ALTAMONT SPRAY WELDING INC
133 Lewis Rd (12009-3220)
PHONE..................................518 861-8870
Fax: 518 861-7212
Mark C Schrowang, *President*
Sandra E Schrowang, *Vice Pres*
EMP: 9
SQ FT: 9,000
SALES (est): 730K Privately Held
WEB: www.altamontspraywelding.com
SIC: 3599 Machine shop, jobbing & repair

(G-210)
INDIAN LADDER FARMSTEAD BREWER
287 Altamont Rd (12009-3542)
PHONE..................................518 577-1484
Dietrich Gehring,
EMP: 5
SQ FT: 875
SALES (est): 185.3K Privately Held
SIC: 2082 Beer (alcoholic beverage)

(G-211)
INOVA LLC
6032 Depot Rd (12009-4313)
P.O. Box 644 (12009-0644)
PHONE..................................866 528-2804
Jerry Blackwell, *General Mgr*
Guy Bucey, *Manager*
Heheher Curris, *Manager*

Altamont - Albany County (G-212)

Loren Sherman,
▲ **EMP:** 5
SQ FT: 39,000
SALES (est): 3.6MM **Privately Held**
SIC: 2511 2599 2531 Bed frames, except water bed frames: wood; hotel furniture; school furniture

(G-212)
INOVA LLC
6032 Depct Rd (12009-4313)
P.O. Box 644 (12009-0644)
PHONE.................................518 861-3400
EMP: 15
SALES (est): 2.5MM **Privately Held**
SIC: 2599 Mfg Furniture/Fixtures

(G-213)
MET WELD INTERNATIONAL LLC
5727 Ostrander Rd (12009-4209)
PHONE.................................518 765-2318
Fax: 518 765-2310
William M Mc Grath, *Plant Mgr*
Kevin Shaw, *Engineer*
Jay Terry, *Engineer*
Betty Hill, *Bookkeeper*
Jim Kuba, *Financial Analy*
EMP: 70
SQ FT: 55,000
SALES (est): 19.8MM
SALES (corp-wide): 87MM **Privately Held**
WEB: www.metweldintl.com
SIC: 3498 Fabricated pipe & fittings
PA: Gavial Holdings, Inc.
    1435 W Mccoy Ln
    Santa Maria CA 93455
    805 614-0060

(G-214)
REMARKABLE LIQUIDS LLC
6032 Depot Rd (12009-4313)
P.O. Box 122, Guilderland Center (12085-0122)
PHONE.................................518 861-5351
Jared Kingsley,
EMP: 70 **EST:** 2011
SALES (est): 13.1MM **Privately Held**
SIC: 2082 Beer (alcoholic beverage)

(G-215)
ROBERT PIKCILINGIS
Also Called: Candy Kraft
2575 Western Ave (12009-9488)
PHONE.................................518 355-1860
Robert Pikcilingis, *Owner*
EMP: 10
SQ FT: 4,000
SALES (est): 974.8K **Privately Held**
SIC: 2064 2066 Chocolate candy, except solid chocolate; chocolate & cocoa products

(G-216)
RSB ASSOCIATES INC
Also Called: Bruno Associates
488 Picard Rd (12009-3519)
P.O. Box 14825, Albany (12212-4825)
PHONE.................................518 281-5067
Robert S Bruno Sr, *President*
Sean Bruno, *Vice Pres*
EMP: 11 **EST:** 2006
SQ FT: 4,000
SALES: 650K **Privately Held**
SIC: 3554 Die cutting & stamping machinery, paper converting

Amagansett
Suffolk County

(G-217)
COSMETICS PLUS LTD
Also Called: Pixy Dust
23 Deep Wood Ln (11930)
PHONE.................................516 768-7250
Rose Evangelista, *President*
EMP: 8
SQ FT: 10,000
SALES (est): 579.5K **Privately Held**
SIC: 3942 Dolls & stuffed toys

Amenia
Dutchess County

(G-218)
CASCADE MOUNTAIN WINERY & REST
835 Cascade Rd (12501)
PHONE.................................845 373-9021
William Wetmore, *President*
EMP: 10 **EST:** 1972
SALES (est): 680K **Privately Held**
SIC: 2084 5812 Wines; eating places

(G-219)
GREY HOUSE PUBLISHING INC (PA)
4919 Route 22 (12501-5585)
P.O. Box B, Millerton (12546-0640)
PHONE.................................518 789-8700
Fax: 518 789-0556
Richard H Gottlieb, *Ch of Bd*
Leslie Mackenzie, *Publisher*
David Garoogian, *Editor*
Katie Keeran, *Editor*
Leslie McKenzie, *Vice Pres*
EMP: 26
SALES (est): 6.1MM **Privately Held**
WEB: www.greyhouse.com
SIC: 2741 2731 Miscellaneous publishing; book publishing

(G-220)
TIA LATTRELL
13 Powder House Rd (12501-5517)
PHONE.................................845 373-9494
Tia Lattrell, *Owner*
Frederic Latrell, *Owner*
EMP: 5
SALES (est): 322.9K **Privately Held**
SIC: 2024 Ice cream & frozen desserts

Amherst
Erie County

(G-221)
3G GRAPHICS LLC
7138 Transit Rd (14221-7214)
PHONE.................................716 634-2585
Robert Ganz,
EMP: 6
SQ FT: 5,000
SALES: 350K **Privately Held**
SIC: 2752 Commercial printing, lithographic

(G-222)
AIRSEP CORPORATION
Airsep Commercial Products Div
260 Creekside Dr Ste 100 (14228-2075)
PHONE.................................716 691-0202
EMP: 100
SALES (corp-wide): 1.1B **Publicly Held**
SIC: 3569 Mfg Oxygen Generators
HQ: Airsep Corporation
    401 Creekside Dr
    Amherst NY 14228
    716 691-0202

(G-223)
ALLIED MOTION SYSTEMS CORP (DH)
Also Called: Hathaway Process Instrmentation
495 Commerce Dr Ste 3 (14228-2311)
PHONE.................................716 691-5868
Ronald Meyer, *President*
Herbert Franson, *Controller*
Tracy Montford, *Human Res Dir*
Chester Clarridge, *Bd of Directors*
EMP: 15
SQ FT: 13,000
SALES (est): 2.2MM
SALES (corp-wide): 6.2B **Publicly Held**
SIC: 3825 Electrical power measuring equipment
HQ: Qualitrol Company Llc
    1385 Fairport Rd
    Fairport NY 14450
    586 643-3717

(G-224)
ALLIED MOTION TECHNOLOGIES INC (PA)
495 Commerce Dr Ste 3 (14228-2311)
PHONE.................................716 242-8634
Fax: 716 242-8638
Richard S Warzala, *Ch of Bd*
Burcu Karpuz, *Managing Dir*
Florian Meister, *Managing Dir*
Matteo Snidero, *Managing Dir*
Sylvia Wisniwski, *Managing Dir*
▲ **EMP:** 165
SQ FT: 6,000
SALES: 245.8MM **Publicly Held**
WEB: www.alliedmotion.com
SIC: 3621 3825 Motors & generators; rotary converters (electrical equipment); function generators

(G-225)
ALLSAFE TECHNOLOGIES INC
290 Creekside Dr (14228-2031)
PHONE.................................716 691-0400
Fax: 716 691-0404
James Pokornowski, *President*
Mary Koteras, *Opers Mgr*
Robert P Pokornowski, *Treasurer*
Sally Ditzel, *Accounting Mgr*
Christine Blackburn, *Marketing Staff*
▲ **EMP:** 65
SQ FT: 35,000
SALES (est): 13.5MM **Privately Held**
WEB: www.allsafe.com
SIC: 3089 2759 Identification cards, plastic; commercial printing

(G-226)
AMERICAN BUSINESS FORMS INC
3840 E Robinson Rd # 249 (14228-2001)
PHONE.................................716 836-5111
Larry Zavadil, *Branch Mgr*
EMP: 32
SALES (corp-wide): 325MM **Privately Held**
SIC: 2752 Commercial printing, lithographic
PA: American Business Forms, Inc.
    31 E Minnesota Ave
    Glenwood MN 56334
    320 634-5471

(G-227)
AMERICAN PRECISION INDS INC (HQ)
Also Called: Basco
45 Hazelwood Dr (14228-2224)
PHONE.................................716 691-9100
Fax: 716 691-9181
James W Bingel, *CEO*
Brian Buzzard, *Engineer*
◆ **EMP:** 200 **EST:** 1946
SQ FT: 106,800
SALES (est): 233.5MM
SALES (corp-wide): 16.8B **Publicly Held**
WEB: www.apischmidtbretten.com
SIC: 3677 3621 3625 3443 Coil windings, electronic; inductors, electronic; motors & generators; electromagnetic clutches or brakes; heat exchangers: coolers (after, inter), condensers, etc.; condensers, steam; separators, industrial process: metal plate
PA: Danaher Corporation
    2200 Penn Ave Nw Ste 800w
    Washington DC 20037
    202 828-0850

(G-228)
AMHERST STNLESS FBRICATION LLC
60 John Glenn Dr (14228-2118)
PHONE.................................716 691-7012
Fax: 716 691-8202
Gerald J Bogdan, *President*
Joseph B Huber, *Corp Secy*
Jim Mazur, *Engineer*
Christopher Bogdan, *Project Engr*
Mike Huber, *Manager*
▼ **EMP:** 40 **EST:** 1945
SQ FT: 35,000
SALES (est): 7.5MM
SALES (corp-wide): 9.4MM **Privately Held**
WEB: www.avinsfab.com
SIC: 3443 Tanks, lined: metal plate
PA: General Oil Equipment Co., Inc.
    60 John Glenn Dr
    Amherst NY 14228
    716 691-7012

(G-229)
BEKAERT CORPORATION
Also Called: Advanced Coating Technologies
6000 N Bailey Ave Ste 9 (14226-5102)
PHONE.................................716 830-1321
Chandra Venkatraman, *Branch Mgr*
EMP: 20
SALES (corp-wide): 378.8MM **Privately Held**
WEB: www.bekaert.com
SIC: 3315 Wire & fabricated wire products; fencing made in wiredrawing plants
HQ: Bekaert Corporation
    1395 S Marietta Pkwy Se 500-100
    Marietta GA 30067
    770 421-8520

(G-230)
BFC PRINT NETWORK INC (PA)
455 Commerce Dr Ste 6 (14228-2313)
PHONE.................................716 838-4532
John Crainer, *President*
Nancy Zabka, *Treasurer*
Marlene Wirth, *Sales Executive*
EMP: 1
SQ FT: 5,800
SALES (est): 1.2MM **Privately Held**
WEB: www.bfcprintnetwork.com
SIC: 2759 Business forms: printing

(G-231)
BIRDAIR INC (HQ)
65 Lawrence Bell Dr # 100 (14221-7094)
PHONE.................................716 633-9500
Fax: 716 633-9850
Mitsuo Sugimoto, *President*
Kimberly Boeheime, *General Mgr*
Jerry Lisowski, *Vice Pres*
Eiichi Okamoto, *Vice Pres*
Benoit Fauchon, *Engineer*
▲ **EMP:** 60 **EST:** 1956
SQ FT: 20,000
SALES (est): 12.3MM
SALES (corp-wide): 328.8MM **Privately Held**
SIC: 3448 Prefabricated metal buildings
PA: Taiyo Kogyo Corporation
    4-8-4, Kikawahigashi, Yodogawa-Ku
    Osaka OSK 532-0
    663 063-008

(G-232)
CCA HOLDING INC
300 Corporate Pkwy (14226-1207)
PHONE.................................716 446-8800
Edward Bredniak, *President*
William F Sullivan, *Vice Pres*
◆ **EMP:** 245
SALES (est): 11.6MM **Privately Held**
SIC: 3313 Ferroalloys

(G-233)
CENTER FOR INQUIRY INC (PA)
Also Called: Councel For Sclar Hmnism Cscop
3965 Rensch Rd (14228-2743)
P.O. Box 664, Buffalo (14226-0664)
PHONE.................................716 636-4869
Paul Kurtz, *President*
Chris Mooney, *Pub Rel Dir*
Nora Hurley, *Producer*
Nicole Scott, *Assoc Editor*
Michael Rupp, *Database Admin*
EMP: 15
SALES (est): 3.8MM **Privately Held**
WEB: www.centerforinquiry.net
SIC: 2721 Magazines: publishing only, not printed on site

(G-234)
CHART INDUSTRIES INC
Also Called: Airsep
260 Creekside Dr Ste 100 (14228-2047)
PHONE.................................716 691-0202
Ravi Bansal PHD, *CEO*
EMP: 25

GEOGRAPHIC SECTION

Amherst - Erie County (G-259)

SALES (corp-wide): 859.1MM **Publicly Held**
SIC: 3569 Generators: steam, liquid oxygen or nitrogen
PA: Chart Industries, Inc.
   1 Infinity Corp Ctr Dr # 300
   Cleveland OH 44125
   440 753-1490

(G-235)
COLUMBUS MCKINNON CORPORATION
Also Called: C M
470 John Jmes Adubon Pkwy (14228-1142)
PHONE....................716 689-5400
Linda Riggi, *General Mgr*
Kathleen Butler, *Commissioner*
EMP: 100
SALES (corp-wide): 637.1MM **Publicly Held**
WEB: www.cmworks.com
SIC: 3536 Hoists, cranes & monorails
PA: Columbus Mckinnon Corporation
   205 Crosspoint Pkwy
   Getzville NY 14068
   716 689-5400

(G-236)
CRANE EQUIPMENT & SERVICE INC (HQ)
140 John Jmes Adubon Pkwy (14228-1183)
PHONE....................716 689-5400
Jena Buer, *President*
Karen L Howard, *CFO*
Rakesh A Jobanputra, *Treasurer*
Linda Wrobel, *Manager*
Timothy R Harvey, *Admin Sec*
EMP: 3 EST: 1997
SQ FT: 3,000
SALES (est): 30MM
SALES (corp-wide): 637.1MM **Publicly Held**
WEB: www.broussardla.com
SIC: 3531 Crane carriers
PA: Columbus Mckinnon Corporation
   205 Crosspoint Pkwy
   Getzville NY 14068
   716 689-5400

(G-237)
DELPHI AUTOMOTIVE LLP
Also Called: Delphi Amherst Test Operations
4326 Ridge Lea Rd (14226)
PHONE....................716 438-4886
EMP: 5 **Privately Held**
SIC: 3714 Motor vehicle parts & accessories
PA: Delphi Automotive Llp
   Courteney Road
   Gillingham

(G-238)
ENHANCED TOOL INC
90 Pineview Dr (14228-2120)
PHONE....................716 691-5200
Fax: 716 691-0109
Michael Emmert, *CEO*
David M Healey, *Vice Pres*
Pat Healey, *Manager*
EMP: 20
SQ FT: 6,000
SALES (est): 3.7MM **Privately Held**
WEB: www.enhancedtool.com
SIC: 3544 Special dies & tools

(G-239)
ESM GROUP INC (DH)
Also Called: E S M
300 Corporate Pkwy 118n (14226-1207)
PHONE....................716 446-8914
Gregory P Marzec, *Ch of Bd*
William F Sullivan, *Exec VP*
Charles A Zak, *Exec VP*
◆ EMP: 15 EST: 1988
SQ FT: 15,000
SALES (est): 36.1MM
SALES (corp-wide): 241.5MM **Privately Held**
WEB: www.esmgroup.com
SIC: 2819 Industrial inorganic chemicals
HQ: Skw Stahl-Metallurgie Gmbh
   Rathausplatz 11
   Unternewkirchen 84579
   863 462-7203

(G-240)
ESM II INC (DH)
300 Corporate Pkwy 118n (14226-1258)
PHONE....................716 446-8888
Fax: 716 446-8911
Charles F Wright, *President*
John Tobias, *VP Mktg*
Troy Kislak, *Manager*
Michael Mohan, *Manager*
▲ EMP: 50
SALES (est): 10.8MM
SALES (corp-wide): 241.5MM **Privately Held**
SIC: 3549 Metalworking machinery
HQ: Esm Group Inc.
   300 Corporate Pkwy 118n
   Amherst NY 14226
   716 446-8914

(G-241)
ESM SPECIAL METALS & TECH INC
300 Corporate Pkwy 118n (14226-1207)
PHONE....................716 446-8914
Hartmut Meyer-Grnow, *CEO*
Sandyee Whipple, *Principal*
EMP: 20
SALES (est): 2.7MM **Privately Held**
SIC: 2819 Industrial inorganic chemicals

(G-242)
GENERAL OIL EQUIPMENT CO INC (PA)
60 John Glenn Dr (14228-2118)
PHONE....................716 691-7012
Fax: 716 691-7990
Gerald Bogdan, *Ch of Bd*
Joseph B Huber, *President*
Bob Gladwell, *Purch Mgr*
Jim Mazur, *Engineer*
Christopher Bogdan, *Project Engr*
EMP: 50
SQ FT: 34,000
SALES (est): 9.4MM **Privately Held**
WEB: www.goe-avins.com
SIC: 3625 5084 7699 3443 Electric controls & control accessories, industrial; oil refining machinery, equipment & supplies; industrial machinery & equipment repair; tanks, lined: metal plate

(G-243)
GROVER CLEVELAND PRESS INC
2676 Sweet Home Rd (14228-2128)
PHONE....................716 564-2222
Fax: 716 691-6766
Michael Degen, *President*
Tom Degen, *Vice Pres*
EMP: 10
SQ FT: 12,800
SALES (est): 2MM **Privately Held**
WEB: www.groverclevelandpress.com
SIC: 2752 2759 Commercial printing, lithographic; photo-offset printing; letterpress printing; embossing on paper

(G-244)
I-EVOLVE TECHONOLOGY SERVICES (PA)
501 John James Audubon Pk (14228-1143)
PHONE....................801 566-5268
Dan Larkin, *President*
Heidi Fischer, *VP Admin*
Joshua Randle, *Vice Pres*
Dave Blaszak, *Opers Mgr*
Nathan Brozyna, *Engineer*
EMP: 12
SALES (est): 5.9MM **Privately Held**
SIC: 3433 Solar heaters & collectors

(G-245)
INTERNATIONAL IMAGING MTLS INC (PA)
Also Called: Iimak
310 Commerce Dr (14228-2396)
PHONE....................716 691-6333
Fax: 716 691-1133
Douglas Wagner, *CEO*
Richard Marshall, *Ch of Bd*
Susan R Stamp, *Senior VP*
Rick Johnson, *Engineer*
Margo Bendetti, *Controller*
◆ EMP: 587
SQ FT: 250,000

(G-246)
INTRI-CUT INC
90 Pineview Dr (14228-2120)
PHONE....................716 691-5200
Fax: 716 691-5344
Ronald Janson, *President*
EMP: 12
SQ FT: 6,000
SALES: 1.6MM **Privately Held**
WEB: www.intri-cut.com
SIC: 3544 Special dies & tools

(G-247)
LIBERTY DISPLAYS INC
4230b Ridge Lea Rd # 110 (14226-1063)
PHONE....................716 743-1757
Dean Rainer, *President*
EMP: 30
SQ FT: 57,000
SALES: 5MM **Privately Held**
SIC: 3999 Forms: display, dress & show

(G-248)
MAHLE INDSTRBETEILIGUNGEN GMBH
Also Called: Delphi-T Compressor Engrg Ctr
4236 Ridge Lea Rd (14226-1016)
PHONE....................716 319-6700
Tim Skinner, *Manager*
EMP: 75 **Privately Held**
SIC: 3563 Air & gas compressors
HQ: Mahle Industriebeteiligungen Gmbh
   Pragstr. 26-46
   Stuttgart
   711 501-0

(G-249)
MAHLE INDUSTRIES INCORPORATED
4236 Ridge Lea Rd (14226-1016)
PHONE....................248 735-3623
EMP: 14 **Privately Held**
SIC: 3714 Motor vehicle parts & accessories
HQ: Mahle Industries, Incorporated
   23030 Mahle Dr
   Farmington Hills MI 48335
   248 305-8200

(G-250)
MOTIVAIR CORPORATION
85 Woodridge Dr (14228-2221)
PHONE....................716 691-9222
Fax: 716 689-0073
Graham Whitmore, *President*
Dan Arnold, *Opers Mgr*
Kevin Werely, *Regl Sales Mgr*
Jeffrey Barnes, *Manager*
Randy Partin, *Manager*
▲ EMP: 20
SQ FT: 25,000
SALES (est): 6.1MM **Privately Held**
SIC: 3585 3443 Air conditioning condensers & condensing units; separators, industrial process: metal plate

(G-251)
NEXSTAR HOLDING CORP
Also Called: PHASE IL MARKETING DBA
275 Northpointe Pkwy (14228-1895)
PHONE....................716 929-9000
Fax: 716 929-9090
Gary Robinson, *President*
Richard S Elliott, *Vice Pres*
Danny Jayes, *Production*
Paula Bednarz, *Admin Asst*
EMP: 5
SALES (est): 1MM **Privately Held**
SIC: 3564 Filters, air: furnaces, air conditioning equipment, etc.

(G-252)
NK MEDICAL PRODUCTS INC (PA)
80 Creekside Dr (14228-2027)
PHONE....................716 759-7200
Fax: 716 759-0700
Norman V Kurlander, *President*
Joseph Manzella, *Manager*
▲ EMP: 5
SQ FT: 1,600
SALES (est): 1.2MM **Privately Held**
WEB: www.nkmedicalproducts.com
SIC: 2514 2599 Cribs: metal; hospital beds

(G-253)
NOVUM MEDICAL PRODUCTS INC
80 Creekside Dr (14228-2027)
PHONE....................716 759-7200
Joe Mandella, *President*
Jennifer Cappello, *Manager*
▲ EMP: 10
SALES (est): 1MM **Privately Held**
SIC: 2514 2599 Cribs: metal; hospital beds

(G-254)
OERLIKON BLZERS CATING USA INC
6000 N Bailey Ave Ste 9 (14226-5102)
PHONE....................716 270-2228
EMP: 40
SALES (corp-wide): 2.3B **Privately Held**
SIC: 3479 Coating of metals & formed products
HQ: Oerlikon Balzers Coating Usa Inc.
   1475 E Wdfield Rd Ste 201
   Schaumburg IL 60173
   847 619-5541

(G-255)
OERLIKON BLZERS CATING USA INC
6000 N Bailey Ave Ste 9 (14226-5102)
PHONE....................716 270-2228
EMP: 40
SALES (corp-wide): 2.3B **Privately Held**
SIC: 3479 Coating of metals & formed products
HQ: Oerlikon Balzers Coating Usa Inc.
   1475 E Wdfield Rd Ste 201
   Schaumburg IL 60173
   847 619-5541

(G-256)
OERLIKON METCO (US) INC
6000 N Bailey Ave (14226-5102)
PHONE....................716 270-2228
Dan Wisniewski, *Branch Mgr*
EMP: 8
SALES (corp-wide): 2.3B **Privately Held**
SIC: 3399 Powder, metal
HQ: Oerlikon Metco (Us) Inc.
   1101 Prospect Ave
   Westbury NY 11590
   516 334-1300

(G-257)
ONY BIOTECH INC
1576 Sweet Home Rd (14228-2710)
PHONE....................716 636-9096
Fax: 716 636-3942
Edmund Egan, *President*
Bill Ferguson, *CFO*
Judy Wetter, *Accounting Mgr*
Lynn Hlavaty, *Manager*
Curt Mancuso, *Director*
EMP: 26
SQ FT: 8,000
SALES (est): 5.8MM **Privately Held**
WEB: www.ony.com
SIC: 2834 Pharmaceutical preparations

(G-258)
ORIGINAL CRUNCH ROLL FCTRY LLC
90 Sylvan Pkwy (14228-1109)
PHONE....................716 402-5030
Zachary Bohn, *President*
EMP: 5 EST: 2016
SALES (est): 181K **Privately Held**
SIC: 2013 Frozen meats from purchased meat

(G-259)
PROMETHEUS BOOKS INC
59 John Glenn Dr (14228-2197)
PHONE....................716 691-2158
Paul Kurtz, *President*
Jonathan Kurtz, *Vice Pres*
Mary Read, *Human Resources*
Lynette Nisbet, *Mktg Dir*
Steven Mitchell, *Manager*

Amherst - Erie County (G-260)

▲ EMP: 30
SQ FT: 28,000
SALES (est): 3.4MM **Privately Held**
WEB: www.prometheusbooks.com
SIC: 2731 Book publishing

(G-260)
SAINT-GBAIN ADVNCED CRMICS LLC
Boron Nitride Div
168 Creekside Dr (14228-2037)
PHONE.................................716 691-2000
Dawn Bell, *Prdtn Mgr*
William Hil, *Manager*
Mary Corb, *Manager*
Linda A Broderick, *Administration*
Michael Rogers, *Maintence Staff*
EMP: 50
SALES (corp-wide): 185.8MM **Privately Held**
WEB: www.hexoloy.com
SIC: 3291 Abrasive products
HQ: Saint-Gobain Advanced Ceramics Llc
   23 Acheson Dr
   Niagara Falls NY 14303

(G-261)
SIEMENS INDUSTRY INC
85 Northpointe Pkwy (14228-1886)
PHONE.................................716 568-0983
EMP: 87
SALES (corp-wide): 89.6B **Privately Held**
SIC: 3822 Air conditioning & refrigeration controls
HQ: Siemens Industry, Inc.
   1000 Deerfield Pkwy
   Buffalo Grove IL 60089
   847 215-1000

(G-262)
STERLING UNITED INC
Also Called: Sommer
6030 N Bailey Ave Ste 1 (14226-1000)
P.O. Box 374, Clarence Center (14032-0374)
PHONE.................................716 835-9290
Fax: 716 871-9085
John Giblin, *Ch of Bd*
EMP: 7
SALES (est): 994.7K **Privately Held**
SIC: 2752 Commercial printing, lithographic

(G-263)
SUITE SOLUTIONS INC
100 Corporate Pkwy # 338 (14226-1200)
PHONE.................................716 929-3050
Alan Perlmuter, *President*
Richard Wolney, *CFO*
Dennis Malinowski, *E-Business*
Kathleen Morabito, *MIS Staff*
Edward F O'Gara, *Bd of Directors*
EMP: 25
SALES (est): 1.1MM **Privately Held**
SIC: 7372 7371 Prepackaged software; custom computer programming services

(G-264)
SYNERGY TOOLING SYSTEMS INC (PA)
287 Commerce Dr (14228-2302)
PHONE.................................716 834-4457
Richard E Morrison Jr, *President*
EMP: 35
SQ FT: 20,000
SALES (est): 4.8MM **Privately Held**
SIC: 3544 Special dies, tools, jigs & fixtures

(G-265)
TARGETPROCESS INC (PA)
1325 Millersport Hwy (14221-2932)
P.O. Box 1845 (14226-7845)
PHONE.................................877 718-2617
Michael Dubakov, *President*
Andrey Mihailenko, *Vice Pres*
Vladimir Shumskij, *Manager*
Benjamin Ryan, *Consultant*
David Hart, *Director*
EMP: 10
SALES (est): 827.5K **Privately Held**
SIC: 7372 Prepackaged software

(G-266)
THOMSON INDUSTRIES INC (PA)
45 Hazelwood Dr (14228-2224)
PHONE.................................716 691-9100
Dan Daniel, *CEO*
Brian Buzzard, *Engineer*
Michael Dolpp, *VP Sales*
EMP: 10
SALES (est): 6.3MM **Privately Held**
SIC: 3585 Heating equipment, complete

(G-267)
TRANSCONTINENTAL PRINTING GP
300 International Dr # 200 (14221-5781)
PHONE.................................716 626-3078
Louis J Continelli, *Branch Mgr*
EMP: 5
SALES (corp-wide): 716.8MM **Privately Held**
SIC: 2752 Commercial printing, lithographic
PA: Imprimeries Transcontinental 2005 S.E.N.C
   1 Place Ville-Marie Bureau 3315
   Montreal QC H3B 3
   514 954-4000

(G-268)
TRI-METAL INDUSTRIES INC
100 Pineview Dr (14228-2120)
PHONE.................................716 691-3323
Fax: 716 691-3327
Donald Chatwin Jr, *President*
Jerry Stetter, *Foreman/Supr*
Brian McCracken, *Purchasing*
Douglas B Chatwin, *Treasurer*
EMP: 38 EST: 1960
SQ FT: 33,000
SALES (est): 2MM **Privately Held**
SIC: 3444 Sheet metalwork

(G-269)
UFC BIOTECHNOLOGY
1576 Sweet Home Rd # 225 (14228-2710)
PHONE.................................716 777-3776
Levent Cosan, *Technology*
EMP: 9
SALES (est): 1.8MM **Privately Held**
SIC: 2835 Microbiology & virology diagnostic products

(G-270)
ULTRA-SCAN CORPORATION
4240 Ridge Lea Rd Ste 10 (14226-1083)
PHONE.................................716 832-6269
John K Schneider, *President*
Stephen Gojevic, *Design Engr*
David C Horan, *Admin Sec*
EMP: 11
SQ FT: 12,600
SALES (est): 2MM **Privately Held**
WEB: www.ultra-scan.com
SIC: 3575 Computer terminals, monitors & components

(G-271)
WATSON BOWMAN ACME CORP
95 Pineview Dr (14228-2121)
PHONE.................................716 691-8162
Fax: 716 691-9239
Markus Burri, *President*
Jim Weglarski, *Project Engr*
Mike Turchiarelli, *Finance Dir*
Greg Ross, *Manager*
Rick Patterson, *Director*
▼ EMP: 100
SALES (est): 31.8MM
SALES (corp-wide): 60.8B **Privately Held**
WEB: www.wbacorp.com
SIC: 3441 2899 3568 Expansion joints (structural shapes), iron or steel; concrete curing & hardening compounds; power transmission equipment
HQ: Basfin Corporation
   100 Park Ave
   Florham Park NJ 07932
   973 245-6000

(G-272)
WELCOME MAGAZINE INC
4511 Harlem Rd (14226-3803)
PHONE.................................716 839-3121
Fax: 716 839-1187
Julie Kianof More, *President*
Margaret Ashley, *Manager*
Julie Kianof, *Manager*
EMP: 10
SQ FT: 500
SALES (est): 1MM **Privately Held**
WEB: www.welcome-magazine.com
SIC: 2721 Magazines: publishing only, not printed on site

Amityville
Suffolk County

(G-273)
A & G PRECISION CORP
680 Albany Ave (11701-1123)
PHONE.................................631 957-5613
Fax: 631 957-8722
Gus Georgopoulos, *President*
Nick Georgopoulos, *Vice Pres*
EMP: 15
SALES (est): 1.5MM **Privately Held**
SIC: 3599 Machine shop, jobbing & repair

(G-274)
ACRAN SPILL CONTAINMENT INC (PA)
599 Albany Ave (11701-1140)
PHONE.................................631 841-2300
John Deangelo, *President*
EMP: 8
SALES (est): 846.7K **Privately Held**
SIC: 2655 Containers, liquid tight fiber: from purchased material

(G-275)
ANCON GEAR & INSTRUMENT CORP (PA)
29 Seabro Ave (11701-1201)
PHONE.................................631 694-5255
Fax: 516 694-5056
Joseph Markiewicz, *President*
Ed Markiewicz, *Vice Pres*
Micheal Chapman, *Manager*
EMP: 18
SQ FT: 6,000
SALES (est): 2.5MM **Privately Held**
WEB: www.ancongear.com
SIC: 3599 Machine shop, jobbing & repair

(G-276)
BIGNAME COMMERCE LLC ◯
5300 New Horizons Blvd (11701-1145)
PHONE.................................631 693-1070
Seth Newman,
EMP: 95 EST: 2017
SALES (est): 3.2MM **Privately Held**
SIC: 2679 Converted paper products

(G-277)
CALICO COTTAGE INC
210 New Hwy (11701-1116)
PHONE.................................631 841-2100
Fax: 516 841-2401
Mark Wurzel, *President*
Mark L Wurzel, *President*
David A Sank, *Exec VP*
Larry Wurzel, *Vice Pres*
Lawrence J Wurzel, *Vice Pres*
▼ EMP: 50
SQ FT: 45,000
SALES (est): 15.4MM **Privately Held**
WEB: www.calicocottage.com
SIC: 2064 Candy & other confectionery products

(G-278)
CALPAC INCORPORATED
44 Seabro Ave (11701-1202)
PHONE.................................631 789-0502
Fax: 631 789-0586
Pierre Lintault, *President*
EMP: 10
SQ FT: 11,000
SALES (est): 1MM **Privately Held**
SIC: 3086 2653 Packaging & shipping materials, foamed plastic; display items, corrugated: made from purchased materials

(G-279)
CASUAL HOME WORLDWIDE INC
Also Called: Prefered Directors Share
38 William St (11701-2916)
PHONE.................................631 789-2999
Fax: 631 789-2970
Ming Chiang, *CEO*
Su O Chiang, *Vice Pres*
Su Chiang, *Vice Pres*
Fang Chiang, *Treasurer*
▲ EMP: 6
SALES (est): 612.5K **Privately Held**
SIC: 2759 Imprinting

(G-280)
CONTINENTAL INSTRUMENTS LLC (HQ)
Also Called: Continental Access
355 Bayview Ave (11701-2801)
PHONE.................................631 842-9400
Fax: 631 842-9135
Bob Weinstein, *Opers Staff*
Richard Soloway, *Mng Member*
Richard Tare, *Manager*
John Banks,
EMP: 34
SQ FT: 90,000
SALES (est): 3.1MM
SALES (corp-wide): 87.3MM **Publicly Held**
SIC: 3625 Control equipment, electric
PA: Napco Security Technologies, Inc.
   333 Bayview Ave
   Amityville NY 11701
   631 842-9400

(G-281)
CONTROL RESEARCH INC
Also Called: Cri Graphic
385 Bayview Ave Unit C (11701-2801)
PHONE.................................631 225-1111
Robert Slomkowski, *President*
Sheryl Young, *Office Mgr*
EMP: 5 EST: 1963
SQ FT: 10,000
SALES (est): 597.5K **Privately Held**
WEB: www.stageresearch.com
SIC: 2759 2395 Screen printing; embroidery & art needlework

(G-282)
CRAFTMASTER FLAVOR TECHNOLOGY
23 Albany Ave (11701-2829)
PHONE.................................631 789-8607
Fax: 631 789-2721
Thomas Massetti, *President*
Ellen McDonald, *Vice Pres*
Joseph Massetti, *Treasurer*
EMP: 10
SQ FT: 4,000
SALES (est): 1.4MM **Privately Held**
SIC: 2869 2087 Flavors or flavoring materials, synthetic; extracts, flavoring

(G-283)
DANIEL DEMARCO AND ASSOC INC
25 Greene Ave (11701-2943)
PHONE.................................631 598-7000
Fax: 631 598-1140
Daniel Demarco, *Ch of Bd*
Danielle Jahn, *Bookkeeper*
Lyn Setffek, *Manager*
Mike Smith, *Director*
EMP: 35
SALES (est): 8.9MM **Privately Held**
WEB: www.danieldemarco.com
SIC: 3429 1751 2499 Cabinet hardware; cabinet building & installation; decorative wood & woodwork

(G-284)
EDO LLC (HQ)
Also Called: Edo Corporation
1500 New Horizons Blvd (11701-1130)
PHONE.................................631 630-4000
Charles Greene, *CEO*
Joseph Cangelosi, *General Mgr*
Lawrence Schwartz, *Principal*
Jon A Anderson, *Senior VP*
Frank W Otto, *Senior VP*
◆ EMP: 9 EST: 1925
SQ FT: 6,000

SALES (est): 965MM
SALES (corp-wide): 5.9B Publicly Held
WEB: www.nycedo.com
SIC: 3812 3728 3663 3679 Search & navigation equipment; sonar systems & equipment; warfare counter-measure equipment; detection apparatus: electronic/magnetic field, light/heat; military aircraft equipment & armament; countermeasure dispensers, aircraft; research & dev by manuf., aircraft parts & auxiliary equip; antennas, transmitting & communications; satellites, communications; electronic crystals; piezoelectric crystals
PA: Harris Corporation
  1025 W Nasa Blvd
  Melbourne FL 32919
  321 727-9100

(G-285)
EDO LLC
1500 New Horizons Blvd (11701-1130)
PHONE..................631 630-4200
James Smith, *President*
Joseph Canova, *Business Mgr*
Peter Martin, *Vice Pres*
EMP: 1000
SALES (corp-wide): 5.9B Publicly Held
SIC: 3825 3812 3761 3699 Instruments to measure electricity; search & navigation equipment; guided missiles & space vehicles; electrical equipment & supplies; radio & TV communications equipment
HQ: Edo Llc
  1500 New Horizons Blvd
  Amityville NY 11701
  631 630-4000

(G-286)
EDO LLC
1500 New Horizons Blvd (11701-1130)
PHONE..................631 630-4000
Joseph Canova, *Business Mgr*
Milo Hyde, *Vice Pres*
Peter Martin, *Vice Pres*
Ed Blasko, *Engineer*
Glenn Umstetter, *Engineer*
EMP: 123
SALES (corp-wide): 5.9B Publicly Held
WEB: www.nycedo.com
SIC: 3625 Control equipment, electric
HQ: Edo Llc
  1500 New Horizons Blvd
  Amityville NY 11701
  631 630-4000

(G-287)
G MARKS HDWR LIQUIDATING CORP
Also Called: Marks USA
333 Bayview Ave (11701-2801)
PHONE..................631 225-5400
Fax: 631 225-6136
George Marks, *President*
Donna Gallagher, *Purch Mgr*
Florin Mirica, *Engineer*
Bert Weichselbaum, *Finance Mgr*
Dave Koogler, *Business Dir*
EMP: 90 EST: 1977
SQ FT: 35,000
SALES (est): 14MM
SALES (corp-wide): 87.3MM Publicly Held
WEB: www.marksusa.com
SIC: 3429 Locks or lock sets
PA: Napco Security Technologies, Inc.
  333 Bayview Ave
  Amityville NY 11701
  631 842-9200

(G-288)
GKN AEROSPACE MONITOR INC
1000 New Horizons Blvd (11701-1138)
PHONE..................562 619-8558
Fax: 631 957-0179
Daniele Cagnatel, *CEO*
Kevin L Cummings, *Ch of Bd*
Fran Novak, *President*
David Maguire, *General Mgr*
Paul Kowack, *Vice Pres*
▲ **EMP:** 275 EST: 1947
SQ FT: 238,000

SALES (est): 89.6MM
SALES (corp-wide): 10.8B Privately Held
WEB: www.monair.com
SIC: 3728 3769 Aircraft assemblies, sub-assemblies & parts; guided missile & space vehicle parts & auxiliary equipment
PA: Gkn Plc
  Po Box 55
  Redditch WORCS B98 0
  152 751-7715

(G-289)
GRAND KNITTING MILLS INC (PA)
7050 New Horizons Blvd # 1 (11701-1179)
PHONE..................631 226-5000
Fax: 631 226-8336
▲ **EMP:** 40 EST: 1910
SQ FT: 35,000
SALES (est): 2.9MM Privately Held
SIC: 2361 5137 Mfg Girl/Youth Dresses/Blouses Whol Women's/Child's Clothing

(G-290)
HABCO CORP
Also Called: Habco Sales
41 Ranick Dr E (11701-2844)
PHONE..................631 789-1400
Herb Auleta, *CEO*
Steven Auleta, *President*
Philip Auleta, *Vice Pres*
▲ **EMP:** 50
SQ FT: 19,175
SALES: 9MM Privately Held
SIC: 2022 Processed cheese

(G-291)
HART SPECIALTIES INC
Also Called: New York Eye
5000 New Horizons Blvd (11701-1143)
P.O. Box 9003 (11701-9003)
PHONE..................631 226-5600
Fax: 631 226-5884
Arthur Jankolovits, *Ch of Bd*
Shannon Johnson, *Vice Pres*
Lucy Korn, *Vice Pres*
Shannon Melendez, *Vice Pres*
Jan Phillips, *Vice Pres*
◆ **EMP:** 70
SQ FT: 25,000
SALES (est): 21.6MM Privately Held
WEB: www.newyorkeye.net
SIC: 3827 5995 Optical instruments & apparatus; optical goods stores

(G-292)
HELGEN INDUSTRIES INC
Also Called: De Santis Holster and Lea Gds
431 Bayview Ave (11701-2638)
PHONE..................631 841-6300
Fax: 631 841-6320
Gene De Santis, *Ch of Bd*
Helen De Santis, *Vice Pres*
Stacey Falek, *Manager*
▲ **EMP:** 125
SQ FT: 14,000
SALES (est): 20.5MM Privately Held
WEB: www.desantisholster.com
SIC: 3199 3172 Holsters, leather; personal leather goods

(G-293)
HI-TECH PHARMACAL CO INC (HQ)
Also Called: Hi-Tech Pharmacal - An Akorn
369 Bayview Ave (11701-2801)
PHONE..................631 789-8228
Fax: 631 789-8429
David S Seltzer, *President*
Gary M April, *President*
April Caccavale, *Counsel*
April Polikoff, *Counsel*
Kamel Egbaria, *Exec VP*
▲ **EMP:** 237
SALES (est): 101.7MM
SALES (corp-wide): 1.1B Publicly Held
WEB: www.hitechpharm.com
SIC: 2834 Pharmaceutical preparations
PA: Akorn, Inc.
  1925 W Field Ct Ste 300
  Lake Forest IL 60045
  847 279-6100

(G-294)
IMC TEDDY FOOD SERVICE
Also Called: Sefi Fabricator
50 Ranick Dr E (11701-2822)
P.O. Box 338 (11701-0338)
PHONE..................631 789-8881
Rasik Patel, *Partner*
Madelin Fernandez, *Purch Agent*
Joan Brent, *Bookkeeper*
Joe Campbell, *Sales Mgr*
EMP: 48 EST: 1956
SALES (est): 6.6MM Privately Held
WEB: www.imcteddy.com
SIC: 3589 Commercial cooking & food-warming equipment

(G-295)
INNOGENIX INC
8200 New Horizons Blvd (11701-1152)
PHONE..................631 450-4704
Manish Potti, *President*
EMP: 10
SALES (est): 493.3K Privately Held
SIC: 2834 Pharmaceutical preparations

(G-296)
INTERSTATE WOOD PRODUCTS INC
Also Called: Interstate Wood & Vinyl Pdts
1084 Sunrise Hwy (11701-2526)
PHONE..................631 842-4488
Fax: 516 842-4345
Jennifer Cerullo, *CEO*
John Hokanson, *Manager*
EMP: 25
SQ FT: 8,500
SALES (est): 3.6MM
SALES (corp-wide): 29.7MM Privately Held
SIC: 2499 5031 3496 1799 Fencing, wood; fencing, wood; miscellaneous fabricated wire products; fence construction
PA: Amendola Industries, Inc.
  1084 Sunrise Hwy
  Amityville NY 11701
  631 842-4427

(G-297)
ISLAND LITE LOUVERS INC
35 Albany Ave (11701-2828)
PHONE..................631 608-4250
Kristin Hill, *Ch of Bd*
Joe Serbo, *Manager*
EMP: 25
SALES (est): 3.6MM Privately Held
WEB: www.islandlitelouver.com
SIC: 3648 Reflectors for lighting equipment: metal

(G-298)
JAXSON ROLLFORMING INC
145 Dixon Ave Ste 1 (11701-2836)
PHONE..................631 842-7775
Fax: 631 842-7791
Alexander Trink, *President*
▲ **EMP:** 37
SALES (est): 8MM Privately Held
WEB: www.jaxsonrollforming.com
SIC: 3446 5031 Fences, gates, posts & flagpoles; partitions & supports/studs, including accoustical systems; molding, all materials

(G-299)
JEFFREY JOHN
Also Called: Creative Compositions
25 Elm Pl (11701-2815)
PHONE..................631 842-2850
John Jeffrey, *Owner*
EMP: 6
SALES (est): 370K Privately Held
SIC: 2499 Decorative wood & woodwork

(G-300)
KABCO PHARMACEUTICALS INC
2000 New Horizons Blvd (11701-1137)
PHONE..................631 842-3600
Fax: 516 842-6008
Abu Kabir, *Ch of Bd*
Saiful Kibria, *President*
Mohammad Hassan, *QA Dir*
Amir Hossain, *QC Mgr*
Miran Noor, *Cust Mgr*
▲ **EMP:** 4

SQ FT: 30,000
SALES (est): 1.6MM Privately Held
WEB: www.kabco.org
SIC: 2834 Vitamin preparations

(G-301)
KDO INDUSTRIES INC
32 Ranick Dr W (11701-2825)
PHONE..................631 608-4612
Lucelle Del Rosaio, *CEO*
George Koenig, *Vice Pres*
EMP: 7
SQ FT: 10,000
SALES (est): 1.5MM Privately Held
SIC: 3441 Fabricated structural metal

(G-302)
KEY CAST STONE COMPANY INC
113 Albany Ave (11701-2632)
PHONE..................631 789-2145
Fax: 631 920-5422
Filippo Pedalino, *President*
John Gonzalez, *Treasurer*
Carmelo Cicero, *Admin Sec*
▲ **EMP:** 20 EST: 1958
SQ FT: 20,000
SALES (est): 3MM Privately Held
WEB: www.keycaststone.com
SIC: 3272 Precast terrazo or concrete products; steps, prefabricated concrete; sills, concrete

(G-303)
KLEER-FAX INC
750 New Horizons Blvd (11701-1130)
PHONE..................631 225-1100
Elias Cruz, *CEO*
Louis Nigro, *President*
Larry Campbell, *Opers Mgr*
Dan Smith, *Safety Mgr*
Hank Cartabuke, *Technology*
▼ **EMP:** 97
SQ FT: 50,000
SALES (est): 24.2MM Privately Held
WEB: www.kleer-fax.com
SIC: 2678 2677 3089 5943 Stationery products; envelopes; extruded finished plastic products; office forms & supplies; die-cut paper & board

(G-304)
LAMBRO INDUSTRIES INC (PA)
115 Albany Ave (11701-2632)
P.O. Box 367 (11701-0367)
PHONE..................631 842-8088
Fax: 516 842-8083
Shiv Anand CPA, *Ch of Bd*
Angela Candreva, *Bookkeeper*
Ira Shuldman, *Sales Dir*
▲ **EMP:** 100
SQ FT: 56,000
SALES (est): 18.5MM Privately Held
WEB: www.lambro.net
SIC: 3444 Ventilators, sheet metal

(G-305)
LEMODE CONCEPTS INC
19 Elm Pl (11701-2815)
PHONE..................631 841-0796
Robert Tolda, *President*
Bob Tolda, *President*
Susan Tolda, *Vice Pres*
EMP: 6
SALES (est): 430K Privately Held
WEB: www.lemodeconcepts.com
SIC: 2511 Kitchen & dining room furniture

(G-306)
LYNMAR PRINTING CORP
8600 New Horizons Blvd (11701-1154)
PHONE..................631 957-8500
Lou Dilorenzo, *President*
Anthony Lisanti, *Vice Pres*
EMP: 8
SQ FT: 8,000
SALES: 1MM Privately Held
WEB: www.lynmarprinting.com
SIC: 2752 Commercial printing, offset

(G-307)
M & D MILLWORK LLC
178 New Hwy (11701-1117)
PHONE..................631 789-1439
Darren Winter,
Marek Zaleski,

Amityville - Suffolk County (G-308) GEOGRAPHIC SECTION

EMP: 10
SQ FT: 14,000
SALES (est): 1.6MM Privately Held
SIC: 2431 Millwork

(G-308)
MADJEK INC
185 Dixon Ave (11701-2840)
PHONE..................631 842-4475
R Freemar, Vice Pres
Robert Cummings, Project Mgr
Fred Ianacci, Project Mgr
Barbara Oneil, Purchasing
Philip Erickson, Engineer
▲ EMP: 85
SALES (est): 14.4MM Privately Held
WEB: www.madjek.com
SIC: 2541 Store fixtures, wood

(G-309)
MAGNIFLOOD INC
7200 New Horizons Blvd (11701-1150)
PHONE..................631 226-1000
Fax: 631 226-4444
Kenneth Greene, President
Anita Greere, Admin Sec
▲ EMP: 20 EST: 1977
SQ FT: 27,500
SALES (est): 4.7MM Privately Held
WEB: www.magniflood.com
SIC: 3646 Commercial indusl & institutional electric lighting fixtures

(G-310)
MASSAPQUA PRCSION MCHINING LTD
30 Seabro Ave (11701-1202)
PHONE..................631 789-1485
Fax: 631 789-1798
Richard Beleski, President
EMP: 9
SQ FT: 7,000
SALES: 1.9MM Privately Held
SIC: 3599 Machine shop, jobbing & repair

(G-311)
MEGA CABINETS INC
51 Ranick Dr E (11701-2821)
PHONE..................631 789-4112
Fax: 516 789-8394
Anthony Griffo, President
Arthur Griffo, Vice Pres
Alice Braun, Bookkeeper
EMP: 25
SQ FT: 20,000
SALES: 1.4MM Privately Held
WEB: www.megacabinets.com
SIC: 2434 5031 Wood kitchen cabinets; vanities, bathroom: wood; kitchen cabinets

(G-312)
MERLIN PRINTING INC
215 Dixon Ave (11701-2832)
PHONE..................631 842-6666
Steven Vid, President
Mike Giardina, President
Jill Sisco, Prd'n Mgr
Irene Post, Controller
Julia Kezer, Asst Controller
EMP: 35 EST 1963
SQ FT: 14,200
SALES: 9MM Privately Held
WEB: www.merlinprinting.com
SIC: 2759 7336 Commercial printing; newspapers: printing; graphic arts & related design

(G-313)
NAPCO SECURITY TECH INC (PA)
333 Bayview Ave (11701-2801)
PHONE..................631 842-9400
Fax: 631 789-9292
Richard L Soloway, Ch of Bd
Michael Carrieri, Senior VP
Jorge Hevia, Senior VP
Byron Thurmond, Vice Pres
Kevin S Buche, Treasurer
◆ EMP: 1013
SQ FT: 90,000

SALES: 87.3MM Publicly Held
WEB: www.napcosecurity.com
SIC: 3669 3699 3429 1731 Emergency alarms; fire alarm apparatus, electric; security control equipment & systems; door locks, bolts & checks; safety & security specialization; systems software development services

(G-314)
NATURAL ORGANICS LABORATORIES
Also Called: Universal Proteins
9500 New Horizons Blvd (11701-1155)
PHONE..................631 957-5600
Gerald Kessler, President
Heather Fairman, QC Mgr
Nancy Devera, Research
Liz Mendoza, Manager
Greg Madden, Maintence Staff
EMP: 500
SALES (est): 72.8MM Privately Held
SIC: 2834 2087 Vitamin preparations; flavoring extracts & syrups

(G-315)
NEW BUSINESS SOLUTIONS INC
Also Called: Nbs
31 Sprague Ave (11701-2618)
PHONE..................631 789-1500
Michele Ruggeri, CEO
George J Ruggeri, President
Michael Filangeri, Project Mgr
Marleny Huggins, Bookkeeper
Gregory Pfaff, Sales Staff
▲ EMP: 28
SALES (est): 5.7MM Privately Held
WEB: www.newbusinesssolutions.com
SIC: 2542 2541 7389 Fixtures: display, office or store: except wood; store & office display cases & fixtures; window trimming service

(G-316)
OFFICIAL OFFSET CORPORATION
8600 New Horizons Blvd (11701-1183)
PHONE..................631 957-4606
Fax: 631 957-4606
Benjamin Paulino, Ch of Bd
Frank Paulino, Vice Pres
Philene Abraham, Prdtn Mgr
Mary Paulino, Admin Sec
▼ EMP: 20 EST: 1957
SQ FT: 20,000
SALES: 4.5MM Privately Held
WEB: www.officialoffset.com
SIC: 2752 2791 Commercial printing, offset; typesetting

(G-317)
OIL AND LUBRICANT DEPOT LLC
Also Called: Oil Depot, The
61 Ranick Dr S (11701-2823)
PHONE..................718 258-9220
Steven Krausman, Mng Member
Jeffrey Sanet, Manager
EMP: 10 EST: 2011
SALES (est): 1.8MM Privately Held
SIC: 2992 Lubricating oils & greases

(G-318)
OIL SOLUTIONS INTL INC
35 Mill St (11701-2819)
PHONE..................631 608-8889
Dennis Traina, Chairman
EMP: 7
SALES (est): 146.1K Privately Held
SIC: 2911 Oils, lubricating

(G-319)
P & M LLC
Also Called: Sefi Fabricators
50 Ranick Dr E (11701-2822)
P.O. Box 338 (11701-0338)
PHONE..................631 842-2200
Fax: 516 842-2203
Tony Cabrera, Sales Mgr
Rasik Patel, Mng Member
Tom Zebrowski, Associate
EMP: 46 EST: 1997
SQ FT: 17,000

SALES (est): 9.3MM Privately Held
SIC: 3556 Food products machinery

(G-320)
PAULIN INVESTMENT COMPANY
8600 New Horizons Blvd (11701-1154)
PHONE..................631 957-8500
Ben M Paulino, Owner
EMP: 27
SALES (est): 2.9MM Privately Held
SIC: 2759 Commercial printing

(G-321)
PEPSI BOTTLING VENTURES LLC
Also Called: Pepsico
550 New Horizons Blvd (11701-1139)
PHONE..................631 226-9000
Fax: 631 226-4233
Carl Cariffunior, General Mgr
Stephen Ernst, Executive
EMP: 40
SALES (corp-wide): 2.2B Privately Held
SIC: 2086 Carbonated soft drinks, bottled & canned
HQ: Pepsi Bottling Ventures Llc
4141 Parklake Ave Ste 600
Raleigh NC 27612
919 865-2300

(G-322)
PORTFAB LLC
Also Called: Wenig Company, The
45 Ranick Dr E (11701-2821)
PHONE..................718 542-3600
Luz Ruiz, Bookkeeper
William Friedman, Mng Member
Rosemarie Friedman,
EMP: 32
SQ FT: 38,000
SALES: 5.2MM Privately Held
WEB: www.portfab.com
SIC: 3441 Fabricated structural metal

(G-323)
PRECISION SIGNSCOM INC
Also Called: Precision Engraving Company
243 Dixon Ave (11701-2830)
PHONE..................631 842-5060
Fax: 516 842-0064
Michael Anzalone, Ch of Bd
Gary Anzalone, Vice Pres
Kathy Winter, Asst Controller
EMP: 51
SQ FT: 23,500
SALES (est): 8MM Privately Held
SIC: 3993 Signs & advertising specialties

(G-324)
SARAGA INDUSTRIES CORP
Also Called: Lenco
690 Albany Ave Unit D (11701-1199)
PHONE..................631 842-4049
Fax: 516 842-3908
Robert Saraga, President
Pat Hermel, Office Mgr
EMP: 6
SQ FT: 4,000
SALES (est): 988K Privately Held
WEB: www.lencocoolers.com
SIC: 3443 Heat exchangers, condensers & components

(G-325)
STEIN INDUSTRIES INC
22 Sprague Ave (11701-2634)
PHONE..................631 789-2222
Fax: 631 789-8888
Stuart Stein, President
Jared Stein, COO
Andrew Stein, Vice Pres
Andrew Jinks, Manager
Jane McCaffrey, Manager
EMP: 40 EST: 1937
SQ FT: 30,000
SALES (est): 5.8MM Privately Held
WEB: www.steinindustries.com
SIC: 2541 Wood partitions & fixtures

(G-326)
STRUCTURED 3D INC
188 Dixon Ave (11701-2812)
PHONE..................346 704-2614
Mitchell Proux, President
EMP: 5

SALES (est): 190.4K Privately Held
SIC: 2759 Commercial printing

(G-327)
SUNDIAL BRANDS LLC
11 Ranick Dr S (11701-2823)
PHONE..................631 842-8800
Richelieu Dennis, CEO
Nyema Tudman, President
Pernell Cezar, Regional Mgr
Cyrus Dennis, Senior VP
Bonnie Beer, Vice Pres
▲ EMP: 215
SALES (est): 84.7MM Privately Held
SIC: 2844 Toilet preparations

(G-328)
SUNDIAL FRAGRANCES & FLAVORS
11 Ranick Dr S (11701-2823)
PHONE..................631 842-8800
Fax: 631 842-4444
Richelieu Dennis, CEO
Nyema S Tubman, Ch of Bd
Mary Dennis, Treasurer
EMP: 24
SQ FT: 50,000
SALES (est): 7.8MM Privately Held
WEB: www.nhexec.com
SIC: 2869 5122 Perfumes, flavorings & food additives; perfumes

(G-329)
SUNDIAL GROUP LLC
Also Called: Sundial Creations
11 Ranick Dr S (11701-2823)
PHONE..................631 842-8800
Marry Dennis, CEO
Dennis Richelieu, CEO
Roberta Kaznocha, President
Richard Gallucci, Senior VP
Christine Williams, Research
EMP: 40
SQ FT: 50,000
SALES (est): 18.8MM Privately Held
SIC: 2844 Toilet preparations; perfumes & colognes

(G-330)
TOPIDERM INC (PA)
5200 New Horizons Blvd (11701-1189)
PHONE..................631 226-7979
Burt Shaffer, Ch of Bd
Eric Stern, VP Opers
Bob Arnaiz, Prdtn Mgr
Carol Donaldson, Purch Mgr
Alice Dorschler, Purch Mgr
▲ EMP: 106
SALES (est): 39.7MM Privately Held
SIC: 2834 Pharmaceutical preparations; cosmetic preparations

(G-331)
TOPIX PHARMACEUTICALS INC (PA)
5200 New Horizons Blvd (11701-1189)
PHONE..................631 226-7979
Fax: 631 226-8588
Burt Shaffer, President
Marie Hughes, Controller
Judy Kehelenbeck, Human Res Mgr
Jody Manganiello, Human Resources
Joe Ragosta, VP Sales
▲ EMP: 300
SALES (est): 50.9MM Privately Held
WEB: www.topixpharm.com
SIC: 2834 Pharmaceutical preparations

(G-332)
TRITON BUILDERS INC
645 Broadway Ste T (11701-2118)
PHONE..................631 841-2534
Stacy Guercia-Baldea, President
EMP: 20
SQ FT: 2,000
SALES: 6MM Privately Held
SIC: 3441 Fabricated structural metal

Amsterdam
Montgomery County

(G-333)
AMSTERDAM PRINTING & LITHO INC
Go Promos
166 Wallins Corners Rd (12010-1817)
PHONE...................................518 842-6000
Melissa Santamaria, *Admin Mgr*
EMP: 15
SALES (corp-wide): 4.3B Privately Held
WEB: www.amsterdamprinting.com
SIC: 3993 2752 2761 Advertising novelties; commercial printing, lithographic; manifold business forms
HQ: Amsterdam Printing & Litho, Inc.
    166 Wallins Corners Rd
    Amsterdam NY 12010
    518 842-6000

(G-334)
AMSTERDAM PRINTING & LITHO INC
Baldwin Cooke
166 Wallins Corners Rd (12010-1817)
PHONE...................................518 842-6000
Melissa Santamaria, *Admin Mgr*
EMP: 49
SALES (corp-wide): 4.3B Privately Held
WEB: www.amsterdamprinting.com
SIC: 3993 2752 2761 Advertising novelties; commercial printing, lithographic; manifold business forms
HQ: Amsterdam Printing & Litho, Inc.
    166 Wallins Corners Rd
    Amsterdam NY 12010
    518 842-6000

(G-335)
BECKMANN CONVERTING INC (PA)
14 Park Dr (12010-5340)
P.O. Box 390 (12010-0390)
PHONE...................................518 842-0073
Klaus Beckmann, *CEO*
Peter Piusz, *Vice Pres*
Ray Hart, *Opers Staff*
Gale Daley, *QA Dir*
Chuck Gerardi, *Engineer*
▲ EMP: 40
SQ FT: 100,000
SALES (est): 5.5MM Privately Held
WEB: www.beckmannconverting.com
SIC: 2295 2262 Leather, artificial or imitation; fire resistance finishing: manmade & silk broadwoven

(G-336)
BEECH-NUT NUTRITION COMPANY (DH)
1 Nutritious Pl (12010-8105)
PHONE...................................518 839-0300
Jeffrey Boutelle, *President*
Tami Colby, *Editor*
Shen-Youn Chang, *Vice Pres*
Mark Mocko, *Buyer*
Katherine Dougherty, *QA Dir*
◆ EMP: 295
SALES (est): 130.4MM
SALES (corp-wide): 1.2B Privately Held
SIC: 2032 Baby foods, including meats: packaged in cans, jars, etc.
HQ: Hero Ag
    Karl Roth-Strasse 8
    Lenzburg AG
    628 855-111

(G-337)
BRETON INDUSTRIES INC (PA)
1 Sam Stratton Rd (12010)
PHONE...................................518 842-3030
Fax: 518 842-1031
Alfred Damofal, *CEO*
Peter A Lewis, *Senior VP*
G Eric Lewis, *Vice Pres*
G Richard Lewis, *Treasurer*
EMP: 96
SQ FT: 55,000
SALES (est): 15.7MM Privately Held
WEB: www.bretonindustries.com
SIC: 2394 2399 3443 2295 Canvas & related products; canvas awnings & canopies; canvas covers & drop cloths; shades, canvas: made from purchased materials; aprons, breast (harness); fabricated plate work (boiler shop); coated fabrics, not rubberized; narrow fabric mills

(G-338)
CAPITOL CUPS INC
1030 Riverfront Ctr (12010-4616)
PHONE...................................518 627-0051
Robert S Abrams, *President*
John Belfance Jr, *COO*
Robert N Sawyer, *CFO*
Robert L Thompson, *Controller*
EMP: 26
SQ FT: 10,000
SALES (est): 4.4MM Privately Held
WEB: www.capitolcups.com
SIC: 3089 Cups, plastic, except foam

(G-339)
CAPITOL PLASTIC PRODUCTS INC
1030 Riverfront Ctr (12010-4616)
P.O. Box 710 (12010-0710)
PHONE...................................518 627-0051
Robert Abrams, *Principal*
▼ EMP: 210
SALES (est): 9.2MM
SALES (corp-wide): 114.6MM Privately Held
SIC: 3085 Plastics bottles
PA: Cv Holdings, Llc
    1030 Riverfront Ctr
    Amsterdam NY 12010
    518 627-0051

(G-340)
COBLESKILL RED E MIX & SUPPLY (PA)
Also Called: Cobleskill Concrete Ready Mix
774 State Highway 5s (12010-7668)
PHONE...................................518 234-2015
John Tesiero, *President*
Carol Whelly, *Admin Sec*
EMP: 10
SQ FT: 15,000
SALES (est): 16.4MM Privately Held
SIC: 3273 Ready-mixed concrete

(G-341)
CRANESVILLE BLOCK CO INC (PA)
Also Called: Cranesville Ready-Mix
1250 Riverfront Ctr (12010-4602)
PHONE...................................518 684-6154
John A Tesiero III, *Ch of Bd*
Elizabeth Tesiero, *Corp Secy*
Joe Nolan, *Opers Mgr*
Rj Kumpitsch, *Purchasing*
Robert Tousaw, *Sales Mgr*
▲ EMP: 45 EST: 1947
SALES (est): 45.4MM Privately Held
SIC: 3271 3273 5211 Blocks, concrete or cinder: standard; ready-mixed concrete; concrete & cinder block; cement; masonry materials & supplies

(G-342)
CSP TECHNOLOGIES INC (HQ)
1031 Riverfront Ctr (12010)
PHONE...................................518 627-0051
Robert Abrams, *CEO*
Bob Thompson, *Controller*
Laurie Gomula, *Accountant*
▲ EMP: 45
SALES (est): 10MM
SALES (corp-wide): 114.6MM Privately Held
SIC: 3089 Plastic processing
PA: Cv Holdings, Llc
    1030 Riverfront Ctr
    Amsterdam NY 12010
    518 627-0051

(G-343)
ELECTRIC CITY CONCRETE CO INC (HQ)
774 State Highway 5s (12010-7668)
PHONE...................................518 887-5560
John A Tesiero Jr, *President*
Carol Whelly, *Vice Pres*
Anthony Zarrelli, *Manager*
EMP: 25 EST: 1977
SALES (est): 1.5MM
SALES (corp-wide): 45.4MM Privately Held
SIC: 3273 Ready-mixed concrete
PA: Cranesville Block Co., Inc.
    1250 Riverfront Ctr
    Amsterdam NY 12010
    518 684-6154

(G-344)
EMBASSY MILLWORK INC
3 Sam Stratton Rd (12010-5243)
PHONE...................................518 839-0965
Michael Caruso, *President*
EMP: 12
SALES (est): 1.1MM Privately Held
SIC: 2421 Planing mill, independent: except millwork

(G-345)
FIBER GLASS INDUSTRIES INC (PA)
Also Called: Fgi
69 Edson St (12010-5247)
PHONE...................................518 842-4000
Fax: 518 842-4408
John Menzel, *CEO*
Mike Lanham, *President*
Ken Weiss, *Engineer*
James Farnan, *Controller*
Kathy Griffin, *Sales Mgr*
◆ EMP: 75 EST: 1957
SQ FT: 60,000
SALES (est): 31.1MM Privately Held
SIC: 2221 Fiberglass fabrics; glass broad-woven fabrics

(G-346)
FIBER GLASS INDUSTRIES INC
1 Homestead Pl (12010)
PHONE...................................518 843-3533
Bob Grant, *Branch Mgr*
EMP: 73
SALES (corp-wide): 31.1MM Privately Held
SIC: 2221 Fiberglass fabrics
PA: Fiber Glass Industries, Inc.
    69 Edson St
    Amsterdam NY 12010
    518 842-4000

(G-347)
FULMONT READY-MIX COMPANY INC (PA)
774 State Highway 5s (12010-7668)
PHONE...................................518 887-5560
Fax: 518 887-2561
Elizabeth Tesiero, *President*
John Tesiero III, *Vice Pres*
EMP: 50 EST: 1947
SALES (est): 1.1MM Privately Held
SIC: 3273 Ready-mixed concrete

(G-348)
GLENS FALLS READY MIX INC (HQ)
774 State Highway 5s (12010-7668)
PHONE...................................518 793-1695
Elizabeth Tesiero, *President*
John Tesiero III, *Vice Pres*
EMP: 1
SALES (est): 1MM
SALES (corp-wide): 1.1MM Privately Held
SIC: 3273 Ready-mixed concrete
PA: Fulmont Ready-Mix Company Inc
    774 State Highway 5s
    Amsterdam NY 12010
    518 887-5560

(G-349)
GREAT ADIRONDACK YARN COMPANY
950 County Highway 126 (12010-6287)
PHONE...................................518 843-3381
Patti Subik, *Owner*
Paul Subik, *Vice Pres*
EMP: 10
SALES: 400K Privately Held
SIC: 2281 2253 5949 5199 Natural & animal fiber yarns, spun; sweaters & sweater coats, knit; sewing & needlework; yarns

(G-350)
HYPERBARIC TECHNOLOGIES INC
1 Sam Stratton Rd (12010-5243)
P.O. Box 69 (12010-0069)
PHONE...................................518 842-3030
Peter Lewis, *President*
Richard Lewis, *CFO*
EMP: 2
SQ FT: 5,000
SALES (est): 3.6MM Privately Held
SIC: 3443 Chambers & caissons

(G-351)
J H BUHRMASTER COMPANY INC
Also Called: Amsterdam Oil Heat
164 W Main St (12010-3130)
PHONE...................................518 843-1700
Donald L Hosier, *Sales/Mktg Mgr*
EMP: 8
SALES (corp-wide): 10.8MM Privately Held
SIC: 3567 Industrial furnaces & ovens
PA: J. H. Buhrmaster Company, Inc.
    421 Sacandaga Rd
    Scotia NY 12302
    518 382-0260

(G-352)
KAPSTONE CONTAINER CORPORATION
28 Park Dr (12010-5340)
PHONE...................................518 842-2450
G Robertshaw, *Mfg Staff*
Linda Ruback, *Personnel*
Eugene C Mowry Jr, *Sales Mgr*
Paul Robbens, *Sales Staff*
Edward H Poulin, *Manager*
EMP: 60
SALES (corp-wide): 3B Publicly Held
SIC: 2411 2674 2621 2631 Wooden logs; shipping & shopping bags or sacks; kraft paper; container board; boxes, corrugated: made from purchased materials; boxes, solid fiber: made from purchased materials
HQ: Kapstone Container Corporation
    1601 Blairs Ferry Rd Ne
    Cedar Rapids IA 52402
    319 393-3610

(G-353)
KC TAG CO
108 Edson St (12010-7213)
PHONE...................................518 842-6666
Kevin Collins, *Ch of Bd*
EMP: 8
SALES (est): 1.1MM Privately Held
SIC: 3089 Plastics products

(G-354)
KEEP AMERICA BEAUTIFUL INC
Also Called: For A Safer America
1 Prospect St (12010-3637)
P.O. Box 229 (12010-0229)
PHONE...................................518 842-4388
Anna Podolec, *Branch Mgr*
EMP: 6
SALES (corp-wide): 9MM Privately Held
WEB: www.kab.org
SIC: 3993 Advertising novelties
PA: Keep America Beautiful, Inc.
    1010 Washington Blvd 22-1
    Stamford CT 06901
    203 659-3000

(G-355)
LOSURDO FOODS INC
78 Sam Stratton Rd (12010-5244)
PHONE...................................518 842-1500
Fax: 518 842-1594
Maria Hammill, *Branch Mgr*
EMP: 25
SALES (corp-wide): 100.9MM Privately Held
WEB: www.losurdofoods.com
SIC: 2041 Doughs & batters

Amsterdam - Montgomery County (G-356)

PA: Losurdo Foods, Inc.
20 Owens Rd
Hackensack NJ 07601
201 343-6680

(G-356)
MHXCO FOAM COMPANY LLC
120 Edsor St (12010-7213)
P.O. Box 579 (12010-0579)
PHONE................518 843-8400
Stephen Trembley, Mng Member
EMP: 14
SQ FT: 10,000
SALES: 3MM Privately Held
SIC: 3069 Foam rubber

(G-357)
MILLER PRINTING & LITHO INC
97 Guy Park Ave (12010-3225)
PHONE................518 842-0001
Fax: 518 842-6397
Scott Miller, President
Eben Miller, Vice Pres
EMP: 6
SQ FT: 9,000
SALES (est): 914.7K Privately Held
SIC: 2752 Commercial printing, offset

(G-358)
MILNOT HOLDING CORPORATION
1 Nutritious Pl (12010-8105)
PHONE................518 839-0300
EMP: 5
SALES (est): 502.2K
SALES (comp-wide): 1.2B Privately Held
SIC: 2099 Food preparations
HQ: Hero Ag
Karl Roth-Strasse 8
Lenzburg AG
628 855-111

(G-359)
MOHAWK FABRIC COMPANY INC
96 Guy Park Ave (12010-3241)
P.O. Box 587 (12010-0587)
PHONE................518 842-3090
Fax: 518 842-3095
Gregory Needham, President
Dominic Wade, Principal
Blaine Harvey, Plant Mgr
EMP: 15 EST: 1922
SQ FT: 35,000
SALES (est): 4.4MM Privately Held
WEB: www.mohawkfabric.com
SIC: 2258 Lace & warp knit fabric mills

(G-360)
MOHAWK RESOURCES LTD
65 Vrooman Ave (12010-5321)
P.O. Box 110 (12010-0110)
PHONE................518 842-1431
Fax: 518 842-1289
Steven Perlstein, President
Andrea Baldomar, General Mgr
Nancy Rogers, Business Mgr
Pamela Smith, Hum Res Coord
Buck Gasner, Sales Mgr
▲ EMP: 70
SQ FT: 55,000
SALES (est): 40.9MM Privately Held
WEB: www.mohawklifts.com
SIC: 3536 Hoists

(G-361)
MOHAWK SIGN SYSTEMS INC
5 Dandreano Dr (12010-5253)
P.O. Box 966, Schenectady (12301-0966)
PHONE................518 842-5303
Fax: 518 842-5306
James Gryzbowski, President
Neal Dill, Vice Pres
Neale Dill, Vice Pres
Bettina Grzybowski, Vice Pres
Loureen Hingle, Manager
EMP: 30
SQ FT: 10,000
SALES: 2.5MM Privately Held
WEB: www.mohawksign.com
SIC: 3993 Signs, not made in custom sign painting shops

(G-362)
NATIONWIDE TARPS INCORPORATED (PA)
Also Called: NTI Global
50 Willow St (12010-4219)
P.O. Box 189 (12010-0189)
PHONE................518 843-1545
Fax: 518 843-0828
Stephen Raeburn, Ch of Bd
Anita Raeburn, Vice Pres
Barbara Salie, Human Res Mgr
▲ EMP: 75
SQ FT: 195,000
SALES (est): 16MM Privately Held
WEB: www.ntiglobal.com
SIC: 3081 2821 2394 2392 Polyethylene film; plastics materials & resins; canvas & related products; household furnishings; solar cells

(G-363)
NORTH E RGGERS ERECTORS NY INC
178 Clizbe Ave (12010-2935)
PHONE................518 842-6377
Fax: 518 842-7248
Scott Egan, President
Michael Egan, Vice Pres
Charles Egan, Treasurer
Lynn Clough, Admin Sec
Thomas Egan, Admin Sec
EMP: 40
SQ FT: 6,000
SALES (est): 7.7MM Privately Held
SIC: 3441 Fabricated structural metal

(G-364)
NORTHEASTERN WATER JET INC
4 Willow St (12010-4219)
PHONE................518 843-4988
Lenny Laporte, President
David Siiss, General Mgr
Andre Laporte, Vice Pres
Laport Lenny, Administration
EMP: 18
SQ FT: 176,000
SALES (est): 3.8MM Privately Held
WEB: www.newj.com
SIC: 3545 Cutting tools for machine tools

(G-365)
NOTEWORTHY INDUSTRIES INC
Also Called: Noteworthy Company, The
336 Forest Ave (12010-2723)
P.O. Box 490 (12010-0490)
PHONE................800 866-8317
Fax: 518 842-2662
Anthony Constantino, President
Elsa Buseck, President
Tim Gralewski, General Mgr
John P Colangelo, Vice Pres
Nicholas Costantino, Vice Pres
▲ EMP: 148 EST: 1971
SQ FT: 400,000
SALES: 18MM Privately Held
WEB: www.noteworthy.com
SIC: 2673 2679 Bags: plastic, laminated & coated; paper products, converted

(G-366)
POWER AND COMPOSITE TECH LLC
Also Called: P C T
200 Wallins Corners Rd (12010-1819)
PHONE................518 843-6825
Robert Mylott, CEO
Phil Day, Managing Dir
Joseph Day, Vice Pres
Bill Pabis, Vice Pres
Fabio Tucci, Vice Pres
▲ EMP: 90
SQ FT: 55,000
SALES (est): 24.6MM Privately Held
WEB: www.pactinc.com
SIC: 3621 Electric motor & generator parts
PA: Thayer Capital Partners, L.P.
1455 Penn Ave Nw Ste 350
Washington DC 20004

(G-367)
RAYCO OF SCHENECTADY INC
4 Sam Stratton Rd (12010)
PHONE................518 212-5113
Fax: 518 843-8317

Ed Legere, President
Michael Kilgallen, Managing Prtnr
Janis Legere, Vice Pres
EMP: 13
SQ FT: 6,000
SALES (est): 1.7MM Privately Held
SIC: 3471 Electroplating of metals or formed products; polishing, metals or formed products

(G-368)
SARATOGA HORSEWORKS LTD
57 Edson St (12010-5238)
P.O. Box 549 (12010-0549)
PHONE................518 843-6756
Fax: 518 843-5057
Michael Libertucci, President
Adrienne Libertucci, Corp Secy
Jordan Casey, Manager
EMP: 25
SQ FT: 15,000
SALES (est): 1.2MM Privately Held
WEB: www.horseworks.com
SIC: 2399 Horse & pet accessories, textile

(G-369)
TAYLOR
166 Wallins Corners Rd (12010-1817)
PHONE................518 954-2832
Shirley McAuliff, Human Res Mgr
Ron Baker, Manager
Ashleigh A Simeone, Technology
William Rocas, Prgrmr
EMP: 6
SALES (est): 239.3K Privately Held
SIC: 2752 Commercial printing, lithographic

(G-370)
TONCHE TIMBER LLC
3959 State Highway 30 (12010-6509)
PHONE................845 389-3489
Ronald Cohen, Owner
EMP: 6 EST: 2007
SALES (est): 398.1K Privately Held
SIC: 2411 Timber, cut at logging camp

(G-371)
TRI-VILLAGE PUBLISHERS INC
Also Called: Recorder, The
1 Venner Rd (12010-5617)
PHONE................518 843-1100
Fax: 518 843-1338
Sidney Lafavour, Publisher
Elizabeth Mangle, Sls & Mktg Exec
Charles Tobey, Controller
John Deneuville, Loan Officer
Bob Engle, Manager
EMP: 60
SALES (est): 3.4MM Privately Held
WEB: www.recordernews.com
SIC: 2711 Newspapers

(G-372)
UNIVERSAL CUSTOM MILLWORK INC
3 Sam Stratton Rd (12010-5243)
PHONE................518 330-6622
Fax: 518 843-6622
Stephen R Chapman, Ch of Bd
Jeffrey W Pahl, Vice Pres
Robert Chapman, Finance
Lisa Gizara, Manager
Kelly Shaw, Manager
EMP: 60
SQ FT: 50,000
SALES (est): 6.9MM Privately Held
WEB: www.ucmillwork.com
SIC: 2431 Millwork

(G-373)
VIDA-BLEND LLC
1430 State Highway 5s (12010-8184)
PHONE................518 627-4138
Freddy Luna, Mng Member
Edward Pragliabento, Mng Member
Michael Pragliabento, Mng Member
Levon Schilling, Lab Dir
EMP: 20 EST: 2013
SALES (est): 3.4MM Privately Held
SIC: 2834 Vitamin, nutrient & hematinic preparations for human use

(G-374)
WILLIAM J KLINE & SON INC (PA)
Also Called: Hamilton County News
1 Venner Rd (12010-5617)
PHONE................518 843-1100
Sidney Lefavour, President
Kevin McClary, Publisher
Bill Brzezicki, Business Mgr
John Deneuville, Finance
Bruce Lefavour, Manager
EMP: 80 EST: 1878
SQ FT: 30,000
SALES (est): 4.3MM Privately Held
SIC: 2711 2752 Newspapers; commercial printing, lithographic

Ancram
Columbia County

(G-375)
SCHWEITZER-MAUDUIT INTL INC
2424 Route 82 (12502-5414)
P.O. Box 10 (12502-0010)
PHONE................518 329-4222
Chet Potash, Buyer
Gary Kennedy, Manager
Dorothea Hotaling, Executive
EMP: 135 Publicly Held
SIC: 2141 2111 2621 Tobacco stemming & redrying; cigarettes; cigarette paper
PA: Schweitzer-Mauduit International, Inc.
100 N Point Ctr E Ste 600
Alpharetta GA 30022

Angelica
Allegany County

(G-376)
ANGELICA FOREST PRODUCTS INC
54 Closser Ave (14709-8746)
P.O. Box 685 (14709-0685)
PHONE................585 466-3205
Fax: 585 466-3411
David Chamberlain, Principal
EMP: 9
SALES (est): 1.1MM Privately Held
SIC: 2421 Sawmills & planing mills, general

(G-377)
ANGELICA SPRING COMPANY INC
99 West Ave (14709-8713)
P.O. Box 681 (14709-0681)
PHONE................585 466-7892
William Geoppner, President
EMP: 17
SQ FT: 4,400
SALES (est): 3.2MM Privately Held
WEB: www.angelicaspringcompany.com
SIC: 3493 3496 Coiled flat springs; flat springs, sheet or strip stock; miscellaneous fabricated wire products

Angola
Erie County

(G-378)
ADVANCED ASSEMBLY SERVICES INC
35 S Main St (14006-1517)
PHONE................716 217-8144
Tim Kosmowski, President
Ra Kosmowski, Vice Pres
EMP: 6 EST: 2000
SQ FT: 5,000
SALES (est): 1MM Privately Held
WEB: www.advancedassemblyservices.com
SIC: 3083 Plastic finished products, laminated

GEOGRAPHIC SECTION

(G-379)
ANGOLA PENNYSAVER INC
19 Center St (14006-1305)
PHONE.................................716 549-1164
Fax: 716 549-1611
Daniel Guest, *President*
EMP: 12 EST: 1922
SQ FT: 5,950
SALES (est): 1MM **Privately Held**
SIC: 2711 Newspapers: publishing only, not printed on site

(G-380)
GOYA FOODS INC
Also Called: Goya Foods Great Lakes
200 S Main St (14006-1534)
P.O. Box 152 (14006-0152)
PHONE.................................716 549-0076
Robert J Drago Sr, *Principal*
Greg Drago, *Opers Staff*
Cynthia Badama, *Human Res Dir*
John Cortes, *Supervisor*
EMP: 75
SALES (corp-wide): 867.1MM **Privately Held**
SIC: 2033 2032 2035 2034 Canned fruits & specialties; canned specialties; pickles, sauces & salad dressings; dehydrated fruits, vegetables, soups; poultry slaughtering & processing
PA: Goya Foods, Inc.
350 County Rd
Jersey City NJ 07307
201 348-4900

(G-381)
POLYTEX INC
1305 Eden Evans Center Rd (14006-8839)
PHONE.................................716 549-5100
Jacob H Ilioha, *President*
Jennifer Forgens, *Clerk*
▲ EMP: 100
SQ FT: 8,000
SALES (est): 5.9MM **Privately Held**
SIC: 2221 Fiberglass fabrics

(G-382)
TX RX SYSTEMS INC
8625 Industrial Pkwy (14006-9692)
PHONE.................................716 549-4700
Fax: 716 549-4772
David J Hessler, *Ch of Bd*
Wayne Newman, *General Mgr*
Anthony Delgobbo, *Plant Mgr*
Michael Fetto, *Engineer*
Ken Pokigo, *Engineer*
▲ EMP: 115 EST: 1976
SQ FT: 31,000
SALES (est): 22.5MM **Privately Held**
WEB: www.txrx.com
SIC: 3669 Intercommunication systems, electric
PA: Bird Technologies Group Inc
30303 Aurora Rd
Solon OH 44139

Aquebogue
Suffolk County

(G-383)
ALTAIRE PHARMACEUTICALS INC
311 West Ln (11931)
P.O. Box 849 (11931-0849)
PHONE.................................631 722-5988
Fax: 631 722-9683
Teresa Sawaya, *President*
Al Sawaya, *President*
Joseph Sawaya, *Vice Pres*
Kelly Jeffries, *Admin Sec*
▲ EMP: 130
SALES (est): 26.8MM **Privately Held**
SIC: 2834 Pharmaceutical preparations

(G-384)
CRESCENT DUCK FARM INC
10 Edgar Ave (11931)
P.O. Box 500 (11931-0500)
PHONE.................................631 722-8700
Fax: 631 722-5324
Douglas H Corwin, *President*
Douglas Corwin, *Vice Pres*
Jeffrey Corwin, *Treasurer*
Blake Corwin, *Manager*
Janet Wedel, *Admin Sec*
▼ EMP: 50 EST: 1959
SQ FT: 6,000
SALES (est): 8.2MM **Privately Held**
SIC: 2015 4222 2011 Ducks, processed: fresh; refrigerated warehousing & storage; meat packing plants

(G-385)
PAUMANOK VINEYARDS LTD
1074 Main Rd Rte 25 (11931)
P.O. Box 741 (11931-0741)
PHONE.................................631 722-8800
Fax: 631 722-5110
Charles Massoud, *President*
Ursula Massoud, *Vice Pres*
Ej Cory, *Sales Staff*
Thomas Matthews, *Info Tech Dir*
▲ EMP: 20
SQ FT: 9,000
SALES (est): 2.5MM **Privately Held**
WEB: www.paumanok.com
SIC: 2084 Wines; wine cellars, bonded: engaged in blending wines

Arcade
Wyoming County

(G-386)
AMERICAN PRECISION INDS INC
Surface Mounted Devices Div
95 North St (14009-9196)
P.O. Box 38 (14009-0038)
PHONE.................................585 496-5755
Fax: 585 496-5072
Steve Chandler, *Plant Mgr*
Kevin Heffler, *Branch Mgr*
EMP: 100
SALES (corp-wide): 16.8B **Publicly Held**
WEB: www.apischmidtbretten.com
SIC: 3677 Coil windings, electronic; inductors, electronic
HQ: American Precision Industries Inc.
45 Hazelwood Dr
Amherst NY 14228
716 691-9100

(G-387)
API HEAT TRANSFER INC
A P I Airtech Division
91 North St (14009-9196)
PHONE.................................585 496-5755
Jack Bellomo, *President*
Rudolph Kristich, *Div Sub Head*
Mike Williams, *Vice Pres*
Jason Williams, *Buyer*
Bob Mladenovic, *Engineer*
EMP: 200
SQ FT: 85,000
SALES (corp-wide): 465.8MM **Privately Held**
WEB: www.apiheattransfer.com
SIC: 3443 Heat exchangers: coolers (after, inter), condensers, etc.
HQ: Api Heat Transfer Inc.
2777 Walden Ave Ste 1
Buffalo NY 14225
716 684-6700

(G-388)
BATAVIA ENCLOSURES INC
636 Main St (14009-1037)
PHONE.................................585 344-1797
Toll Free:..................................877 -
Fax: 585 344-1503
Leonard Roberto, *President*
EMP: 6
SQ FT: 10,000
SALES (est): 1MM **Privately Held**
WEB: www.bataviaenclosures.com
SIC: 3444 Sheet metalwork

(G-389)
BLISS MACHINE INC
260 North St (14009-1206)
P.O. Box 145 (14009-0145)
PHONE.................................585 492-5128
Fax: 585 492-5166
William Kanner, *President*
Randy Kanner, *Vice Pres*
Nichole Kanner, *Manager*
EMP: 18
SQ FT: 9,500
SALES (est): 3.6MM **Privately Held**
WEB: www.blissmachine.net
SIC: 3599 Machine shop, jobbing & repair

(G-390)
BRAUEN CONSTRUTION
1087 Chaffee Rd (14009-9779)
PHONE.................................585 492-0042
Fax: 585 492-0042
Floyd Brauen, *President*
EMP: 7 EST: 1983
SQ FT: 16,000
SALES (est): 1.1MM **Privately Held**
WEB: www.brauenmillwork.com
SIC: 2431 Woodwork, interior & ornamental

(G-391)
DEVIN MFG INC
40 Edward St (14009-1012)
P.O. Box 97 (14009-0097)
PHONE.................................585 496-5770
William A Devin, *President*
Anne Devin, *Vice Pres*
Erica Smith, *Purchasing*
Erica Bigos, *Admin Sec*
▼ EMP: 17 EST: 1959
SQ FT: 17,400
SALES (est): 3.1MM **Privately Held**
WEB: www.devinmfg.com
SIC: 3599 3537 3494 3949 Machine shop, jobbing & repair; engine stands & racks, metal; valves & pipe fittings; target shooting equipment; targets, archery & rifle shooting

(G-392)
EMKAY TRADING CORP
Also Called: Emkay Bordeaux
58 Church St (14009-1117)
P.O. Box 174 (14009-0174)
PHONE.................................585 492-3800
Fax: 585 492-3700
Cathy Golman, *Branch Mgr*
EMP: 30
SQ FT: 51,500
SALES (corp-wide): 1.9MM **Privately Held**
WEB: www.emkaytrading.org
SIC: 2022 2026 Cheese, natural & processed; cream, sweet
PA: Emkay Trading Corp
250 Clearbrook Rd Ste 127
Elmsford NY 10523
914 592-9000

(G-393)
GM PALMER INC
51 Edward St (14009-1012)
P.O. Box 343 (14009-0343)
PHONE.................................585 492-2990
Fax: 585 492-2991
Greg Palmer, *President*
Mary Palmer, *Corp Secy*
Mary Keenan, *Manager*
◆ EMP: 15
SQ FT: 47,500
SALES (est): 10MM **Privately Held**
SIC: 2421 Fuelwood, from mill waste

(G-394)
GOWANDA - BTI LLC
Also Called: CHIPTEK
7426a Tanner Pkwy (14009-9758)
PHONE.................................716 492-4081
Thomas Norsen, *Controller*
Don McElheny, *President*
EMP: 66
SALES (est): 7.6MM **Privately Held**
SIC: 3677 Electronic coils, transformers & other inductors

(G-395)
J A YANSICK LUMBER CO INC
16 Rule Dr (14009-1019)
PHONE.................................585 492-4312
Fax: 585 492-4663
James Yansick, *President*
Ken Buckley, *Opers Staff*
Scott Holmes, *Controller*
EMP: 30 EST: 1966
SQ FT: 1,979
SALES (est): 3.1MM **Privately Held**
SIC: 2421 2426 Lumber: rough, sawed or planed; hardwood dimension & flooring mills

(G-396)
MAPLE GROVE CORP
Also Called: Maple Grove and Enterprises
7075 Route 98 (14009-9756)
P.O. Box 156 (14009-0156)
PHONE.................................585 492-5286
Phillip M Hobin, *Ch of Bd*
Rachel Bookmiller, *COO*
Ted Hobin Jr, *Vice Pres*
Jen Hobin, *CFO*
Michelle Hobin, *Admin Sec*
EMP: 25
SQ FT: 1,200
SALES (est): 4.9MM **Privately Held**
SIC: 7692 7213 Welding repair; coat supply

(G-397)
NEIGHBOR TO NEIGHBOR NEWS INC
Also Called: Arcade Herald
223 Main St (14009-1209)
PHONE.................................585 492-2525
Fax: 716 492-2667
Grant Hamilton, *President*
Judy Kessler, *Advt Staff*
EMP: 9
SQ FT: 1,200
SALES (est): 360K **Privately Held**
SIC: 2711 Newspapers: publishing only, not printed on site

(G-398)
NEW EAGLE SILO CORP
7648 Hurdville Rd (14009-1021)
PHONE.................................585 492-1300
Fax: 585 492-4029
Leonard Johnson, *President*
EMP: 8 EST: 1967
SQ FT: 6,000
SALES: 400K **Privately Held**
SIC: 3531 Cement silos (batch plant)

(G-399)
STEEL & OBRIEN MFG INC
274 Rte 98 S (14009)
PHONE.................................585 492-5800
Bryan Wells, *President*
Pete Beyette, *Vice Pres*
Michael Lovelace, *Vice Pres*
Scott Wells, *Vice Pres*
Jim Maiorano, *Purch Agent*
▲ EMP: 72
SQ FT: 55,000
SALES (est): 15.9MM **Privately Held**
WEB: www.steelobrien.com
SIC: 3494 3492 Valves & pipe fittings; fluid power valves & hose fittings

(G-400)
TPI ARCADE INC
7888 Route 98 (14009-9601)
PHONE.................................585 492-0122
Fax: 585 492-0169
Jack Pohlman, *Ch of Bd*
Gerald Byrne, *Chairman*
Traci Hemmerlin, *Controller*
EMP: 75
SALES (est): 16.2MM
SALES (corp-wide): 557.2MM **Privately Held**
WEB: www.tpicast.com
SIC: 3363 Aluminum die-castings
PA: Ligon Industries, Llc
1927 1st Ave N Ste 500
Birmingham AL 35203
205 322-3302

(G-401)
WHATS NEXT MANUFACTURING INC
4 Rule Dr (14009-1019)
PHONE.................................585 492-1014
Fax: 585 492-1018
Brad Countryman, *President*
Deborah Fields, *Purch Mgr*
EMP: 20
SQ FT: 20,000
SALES (est): 2MM **Privately Held**
SIC: 3944 Games, toys & children's vehicles

Ardsley
Westchester County

(G-402)
ACORDA THERAPEUTICS INC (PA)
420 Saw Mill River Rd (10502-2605)
PHONE.................914 347-4300
Fax: 914 347-4560
Ron Cohen, *President*
David Lawrence, *Principal*
Tierney Saccavino, *Exec VP*
Denise J Duca, *Senior VP*
Tara Stevens, *Vice Pres*
▲ EMP: 250
SQ FT: 138,000
SALES: 519.6MM **Publicly Held**
WEB: www.acorda.com
SIC: 2834 8731 2836 Drugs acting on the central nervous system & sense organs; biotechnical research, commercial; biological products, except diagnostic

(G-403)
ADVANCED COMM SOLUTIONS
38 Ridge Rd (10502-2226)
PHONE.................914 693-5076
EMP: 5
SALES: 900K **Privately Held**
SIC: 3663 Mfg Radio/Tv Communication Equipment

(G-404)
IRTRONICS INSTRUMENTS INC
132 Forest Blvd (10502-1031)
PHONE.................914 693-6291
Fax: 914 693-6291
John Jenkofsky, *President*
EMP: 10
SQ FT: 1,200
SALES: 870K **Privately Held**
SIC: 3822 3355 3672 Temperature sensors for motor windings; aluminum wire & cable; printed circuit boards

(G-405)
SUPRESTA US LLC (DH)
420 Saw Mill River Rd (10502-2605)
PHONE.................914 674-9434
Peggy Viehweger, *CEO*
Thomas Emignanelli, *CFO*
Andrew Schemick, *Finance Dir*
Charlotte Jurg, *Credit Mgr*
Pasqual Zottela, *Manager*
▼ EMP: 21
SALES (est) 25.2MM
SALES (corp-wide): 5.6B **Privately Held**
SIC: 2899 Fire retardant chemicals
HQ: Icl Performance Products Lp
622 Emerson Rd Ste 500
Saint Louis MO 63141
314 983-7500

Argyle
Washington County

(G-406)
ADIRONDACK PLAS & RECYCL INC (PA)
453 County Route 45 (12809-3514)
PHONE.................518 746-9212
Fax: 518 638-3951
John Aspland, *CEO*
John S Clair, *Manager*
◆ EMP: 21
SQ FT: 125,000
SALES (est): 5.2MM **Privately Held**
SIC: 3089 3559 Plastic processing; recycling machinery

(G-407)
ADIRONDACK SCENIC INC
Also Called: Adirondack Studios
439 County Route 45 Ste 1 (12809-3514)
PHONE.................518 638-8000
Fax: 518 638-8238
David Thomas Lloyd, *CEO*
Louis Allen, *Vice Pres*
Stephen Detmer, *Project Mgr*
Patrick Tynan, *Foreman/Supr*
Richard Mahaney, *Opers Staff*
▲ EMP: 100
SQ FT: 128,000
SALES: 180MM **Privately Held**
WEB: www.adirondackscenic.com
SIC: 2599 Factory furniture & fixtures

Arkport
Steuben County

(G-408)
HP HOOD LLC
25 Hurlbut St (14807-9706)
P.O. Box 474 (14807-0474)
PHONE.................607 295-8134
Stephen Lally, *QC Dir*
Freeman Covert, *Manager*
EMP: 100
SQ FT: 5,184
SALES (corp-wide): 1.7B **Privately Held**
WEB: www.hphood.com
SIC: 2026 2099 2022 Cottage cheese; cream, sour; yogurt; food preparations; cheese, natural & processed
PA: Hp Hood Llc
6 Kimball Ln Ste 400
Lynnfield MA 01940
617 887-8441

Arkville
Delaware County

(G-409)
CATSKILL MOUNTAIN PUBLISHING
Also Called: Catskill Mountain News
43414 State Hwy 28 (12406)
PHONE.................845 586-2601
Fax: 845 586-3266
Richard D Sanford, *President*
Laurie Sanford, *Vice Pres*
Linda Schebesta, *Manager*
James Krueger, *Director*
Jenny Rosenzweig, *Director*
EMP: 11 EST: 1903
SALES (est): 881.7K **Privately Held**
WEB: www.catskillmountainnews.com
SIC: 2711 Newspapers; publishing only, not printed on site

Armonk
Westchester County

(G-410)
ARUMAI TECHNOLOGIES INC (PA)
175 King St (10504-1606)
PHONE.................914 217-0038
P Stephen Lamont, *CEO*
David J Colter, *CTO*
Gregory B Thagard, *CTO*
EMP: 12
SALES (est): 652.1K **Privately Held**
SIC: 7372 Prepackaged software

(G-411)
IBM WORLD TRADE CORPORATION (HQ)
1 New Orchard Rd Ste 1 (10504-1722)
PHONE.................914 765-1900
Fax: 914 499-6007
Virginia M Rometty, *CEO*
Asif Samad, *Partner*
Hoonmeng Ong, *General Mgr*
Val Rahmani, *General Mgr*
Robert Zapfel, *General Mgr*
EMP: 8
SQ FT: 417,000
SALES: 35.8B
SALES (corp-wide): 79.9B **Publicly Held**
WEB: www.Inn.com
SIC: 3577 3571 7377 7379 Computer peripheral equipment; electronic computers; computer rental & leasing; computer related maintenance services

PA: International Business Machines Corporation
1 New Orchard Rd Ste 1
Armonk NY 10504
914 499-1900

(G-412)
INTERNATIONAL BUS MCHS CORP
Also Called: IBM
1 New Orchard Rd Ste 1 (10504-1722)
PHONE.................914 345-5219
Fax: 914 499-7534
Sid Singh, *Managing Dir*
Stephen Ward, *Senior VP*
Rod Smith, *Vice Pres*
Deborah Hilfman, *Project Mgr*
Liz Mendenhall, *Project Mgr*
EMP: 23
SALES (corp-wide): 79.9B **Publicly Held**
SIC: 7372 Prepackaged software
PA: International Business Machines Corporation
1 New Orchard Rd Ste 1
Armonk NY 10504
914 499-1900

(G-413)
INTERNATIONAL BUS MCHS CORP
Also Called: IBM
20 Old Post Rd (10504-1314)
PHONE.................914 499-2000
Fax: 914 499-2188
David Leftwich, *General Mgr*
Andrew J Decustai, *Vice Pres*
Jim Gregory, *Vice Pres*
Ted Hoff, *Vice Pres*
Nancy Lewis, *Manager*
EMP: 50
SALES (corp-wide): 79.9B **Publicly Held**
WEB: www.ibm.com
SIC: 7372 Prepackaged software
PA: International Business Machines Corporation
1 New Orchard Rd Ste 1
Armonk NY 10504
914 499-1900

(G-414)
JINGLEBELL INC
Also Called: JINGLENOG DBA
190 Byram Lake Rd (10504-1509)
PHONE.................914 219-5395
Melissa Byrne, *President*
▲ EMP: 6 EST: 2008
SALES: 200K **Privately Held**
SIC: 3229 3231 7389 Christmas tree ornaments, from glass produced on-site; Christmas tree ornaments: made from purchased glass; design services

(G-415)
MAIN STREET CONNECT LLC
Also Called: Daily Voice
200 Business Park Dr # 209 (10504-1719)
PHONE.................203 803-4110
Kathryn Desilva, *Sales Dir*
Carll Tucker,
EMP: 11 EST: 2012
SALES (est): 760.9K **Privately Held**
SIC: 2711 Newspapers, publishing & printing

(G-416)
PRODUCTION RESOURCE GROUP LLC (PA)
Also Called: Prg Integrated Solutions
200 Business Park Dr # 109 (10504-1751)
PHONE.................877 774-7088
Jeremiah Harris, *CEO*
Stephan Paridaen, *President*
John Hovis, *COO*
Steven Greenberg, *Exec VP*
Robert Manners, *Exec VP*
▲ EMP: 100
SQ FT: 140,000
SALES (est): 384.7MM **Privately Held**
WEB: www.prg.com
SIC: 3999 7922 Theatrical scenery; equipment rental, theatrical; lighting, theatrical

(G-417)
SUMMIT COMMUNICATIONS
28 Half Mile Rd (10504-1306)
PHONE.................914 273-5504
Russell Dekker, *Owner*
EMP: 6
SALES (est): 283.9K **Privately Held**
SIC: 2741 Miscellaneous publishing

(G-418)
SURGICAL DESIGN CORP
Also Called: S D C
3 Macdonald Ave (10504-1935)
PHONE.................914 273-2445
Fax: 914 273-2691
William Banko MD, *President*
Stanislava Banko, *Corp Secy*
Clara Santos, *Purchasing*
EMP: 15
SQ FT: 10,000
SALES (est): 2.4MM **Privately Held**
WEB: www.surgical.com
SIC: 3841 3851 3827 Surgical instruments & apparatus; instruments, microsurgical: except electromedical; ophthalmic goods; optical instruments & lenses

(G-419)
TRINITY PACKAGING CORPORATION (HQ)
357 Main St (10504-1717)
PHONE.................914 273-4111
Fax: 914 273-4715
John H Freund, *CEO*
Peter Freund, *President*
Tim Shiley, *Plant Mgr*
Tom Walters, *Opers Staff*
Jacob Schreiber, *QA Dir*
▲ EMP: 18
SQ FT: 9,000
SALES (est): 152.1MM
SALES (corp-wide): 1.2B **Privately Held**
SIC: 2673 2679 Plastic bags: made from purchased materials; paper products, converted
PA: Proampac Llc
12025 Tricon Rd
Cincinnati OH 45246
513 671-1777

(G-420)
VISANT SECONDARY HOLDINGS CORP (DH)
357 Main St (10504-1808)
PHONE.................914 595-8200
Fax: 914 595-8239
Marie Hlavaty, *Senior VP*
Paul B Carousso, *Vice Pres*
James Denkus, *Manager*
EMP: 30
SALES (est): 831.7MM
SALES (corp-wide): 13.2B **Publicly Held**
SIC: 2741 Yearbooks: publishing & printing
HQ: Visant Holding Corp.
3601 Minnesota Dr Ste 400
Minneapolis MN 55435
914 595-8200

Arverne
Queens County

(G-421)
ARMOUR BEARER GROUP INC
Also Called: 2fish 5loaves Comminty Pantry
424 Beach 65th St (11692-1440)
PHONE.................646 812-4487
Clinton Nixon, *President*
EMP: 5 EST: 2014
SALES (est): 234.8K **Privately Held**
SIC: 2099 Food preparations

(G-422)
DARRELL MITCHELL
Also Called: D.A.M. Construction, Company
704 Beach 67th St (11692-1314)
PHONE.................646 659-7075
Darrell Mitchell, *Owner*
EMP: 5

▲ = Import ▼ = Export
◆ = Import/Export

SALES (est): 175.1K **Privately Held**
SIC: **1389** 1799 8741 8742 Construction, repair & dismantling services; construction site cleanup; construction management; construction project management consultant

Ashville
Chautauqua County

(G-423)
CASTELLI AMERICA LLC
5151 Fairbanks Rd (14710-9796)
PHONE..................................716 782-2101
Jay Arcata, *Branch Mgr*
EMP: 80
SALES (corp-wide): 367.4MM **Privately Held**
HQ: Castelli America, Llc
    277 Fairfield Rd Ste 208
    Fairfield NJ 07004
    973 227-0002
SIC: **2022** Cheese, natural & processed

(G-424)
CHAUTAUQUA MACHINE SPC LLC
1880 Open Meadows Rd (14710-9793)
PHONE..................................716 782-3276
Fax: 716 782-4801
Dave Hishman, *Engineer*
Dennis Furlow,
EMP: 10
SQ FT: 8,000
SALES (est): 750K **Privately Held**
SIC: **3441** 7692 Fabricated structural metal; automotive welding

(G-425)
CHAUTQUA PRCSION MACHINING INC
1287 Hunt Rd (14710-9612)
PHONE..................................716 763-3752
Jeff Christie, *President*
Craig Lassinger, *Engineer*
Mary Ann Attard, *Administration*
EMP: 12
SALES (est): 1.7MM **Privately Held**
SIC: **3599** Machine shop, jobbing & repair

(G-426)
FAIRBANK RECONSTRUCTION CORP
Also Called: Fairbank Farms
5151 Fairbanks Rd (14710-9796)
PHONE..................................800 628-3276
Fax: 716 782-2900
Ronald G Allen, *CEO*
Rick Fahle, *President*
A Joseph Fairbank, *Vice Pres*
Brenda L Fahe, *Treasurer*
Robert Anderson, *Director*
EMP: 90
SQ FT: 100,000
SALES (est): 11.1MM **Privately Held**
WEB: www.fairbankfarms.com
SIC: **2011** 2013 Meat packing plants; sausages & other prepared meats
PA: Afa Group Inc.
    860 1st Ave Ste 9a
    King Of Prussia PA 19406

(G-427)
THAYER TOOL & DIE INC
1718 Blckvlle Watts Flts (14710-9538)
PHONE..................................716 782-4841
Fax: 716 782-3261
John Thayer, *President*
Jennifer Henry, *Office Mgr*
EMP: 15
SQ FT: 5,000
SALES: 577.6K **Privately Held**
SIC: **3544** Special dies & tools

Astoria
Queens County

(G-428)
4 OVER 4COM INC
1941 46th St (11105-1101)
PHONE..................................718 932-2700
Taso Panagiotopoulos, *President*
Elizabeth Salazar, *Prdtn Mgr*
EMP: 6
SALES (est): 660K **Privately Held**
SIC: **2759** Post cards, picture: printing

(G-429)
AKI CABINETS INC
2636 2nd St (11102-4130)
PHONE..................................718 721-2541
Mujo Todic, *Ch of Bd*
Gloria Henderson, *Principal*
▲ EMP: 22
SALES (est): 2.6MM **Privately Held**
SIC: **2434** Wood kitchen cabinets

(G-430)
ALPS PROVISION CO INC
2270 45th St (11105-1336)
PHONE..................................718 721-4477
Fax: 718 956-4050
Giulio Sottovia, *President*
Leonardo Castorina, *Vice Pres*
Remo Tozzi, *Treasurer*
EMP: 27 EST: 1928
SQ FT: 12,500
SALES (est): 4.1MM **Privately Held**
WEB: www.alpsinstyle.com
SIC: **2013** 5143 5147 Sausages & other prepared meats; cheese; meats, fresh

(G-431)
COMFORT WAX INCORPORATED
3174 Steinway St Fl 5 (11103-3909)
PHONE..................................718 204-7028
Fei Qinhua, *Owner*
EMP: 11
SALES (est): 1.2MM **Privately Held**
SIC: **2842** Wax removers

(G-432)
D & S SUPPLIES INC
2067 21st St (11105-3507)
PHONE..................................718 721-5256
Paul Melky, *President*
EMP: 17
SALES (est): 1.2MM **Privately Held**
SIC: **3679** Electronic loads & power supplies

(G-433)
D-LITE DONUTS
4519 Broadway (11103-1625)
PHONE..................................718 626-5953
George Kaparakos, *Owner*
EMP: 5
SALES (est): 150K **Privately Held**
SIC: **2051** Doughnuts, except frozen

(G-434)
DF MAVENS INC
2420 49th St (11103-1017)
PHONE..................................347 813-4705
Malcolm Stogo, *Principal*
WEI Lo, *Assistant*
EMP: 20 EST: 2013
SALES (est): 970K **Privately Held**
SIC: **2024** Ice cream & frozen desserts

(G-435)
DIGITAL BREWERY LLC
3537 36th St Ste 4 (11106-1347)
PHONE..................................646 665-2106
Humayun Rashid,
Amaln Das,
EMP: 6 EST: 2015
SALES (est): 283K **Privately Held**
SIC: **2759** 7372 Commercial printing; prepackaged software

(G-436)
ECONOMY PUMP & MOTOR REPAIR
3652 36th St (11106-1304)
PHONE..................................718 433-2600
Fax: 718 433-2296
Elsie Domagala, *President*
EMP: 6
SALES (est): 540K **Privately Held**
SIC: **3433** 3585 3586 5999 Heating equipment, except electric; heat pumps, electric; compressors for refrigeration & air conditioning equipment; measuring & dispensing pumps; motors, electric

(G-437)
ELECTROTECH SERVICE EQP CORP
2450 46th St (11103-1008)
PHONE..................................718 626-7700
Joseph Amendalara, *CEO*
Jerry Magnotta, *Purchasing*
Larisa Shafir, *Engineer*
George Krokondelas, *Financial Exec*
Bob Strayer, *Sales Mgr*
EMP: 46
SQ FT: 15,000
SALES (est): 19.1MM **Privately Held**
SIC: **3613** 5731 Switchgear & switchboard apparatus, except instruments; consumer electronic equipment

(G-438)
EMPIRE METAL FINISHING INC
2469 46th St (11103-1007)
PHONE..................................718 545-6700
Fax: 718 932-0300
Michael Vetrone, *President*
Lisa Vetrone, *Vice Pres*
EMP: 30 EST: 1922
SQ FT: 5,000
SALES (est): 2.9MM **Privately Held**
SIC: **3471** 3499 3449 Gold plating; fire- or burglary-resistive products; miscellaneous metalwork

(G-439)
EXQUISITE GLASS & STONE INC
3117 12th St (11106-4801)
PHONE..................................718 937-9266
Fax: 718 473-4808
Buz Vaultz, *President*
EMP: 5
SQ FT: 900
SALES (est): 500K **Privately Held**
SIC: **3231** Decorated glassware: chipped, engraved, etched, etc.

(G-440)
FAME CONSTRUCTION INC
2388 Brklyn Queens Expy W (11103-1023)
PHONE..................................718 626-1000
Michael Andreou, *President*
Kosta Savelibis, *Manager*
EMP: 50
SQ FT: 1,700
SALES (est): 4.9MM **Privately Held**
SIC: **1389** Construction, repair & dismantling services

(G-441)
HEAT AND FROST INSLATRS & ASBS
Also Called: Insulators Local 12
3553 24th St (11106-4416)
PHONE..................................718 784-3456
Fax: 718 784-8357
Nino Grgas, *President*
Matt Aracich, *President*
Al Wassell, *President*
Sal Gargiulo, *Corp Secy*
EMP: 6
SQ FT: 500
SALES: 11.8MM **Privately Held**
WEB: www.asbestosworkers.com
SIC: **3644** 8399 Insulators & insulation materials, electrical; community chest

(G-442)
HELLAS STONE INC
3344 9th St (11106-4902)
PHONE..................................718 545-4716
Esdavros Cayioulis, *CEO*
▲ EMP: 5
SALES (est): 505.2K **Privately Held**
SIC: **2514** Kitchen cabinets: metal

(G-443)
INTER CRAFT CUSTOM FURNITURE
1431 Astoria Blvd (11102-3691)
PHONE..................................718 278-2573
Chipiv Savva, *President*
EMP: 9
SALES (est): 840K **Privately Held**
SIC: **2511** Wood household furniture

(G-444)
KEYSTONE ELECTRONICS CORP (PA)
3107 20th Rd (11105-2017)
PHONE..................................718 956-8900
Fax: 718 956-9040
Richard David, *President*
Jim Magnuson, *General Mgr*
Joe Roosenblum, *General Mgr*
Bob Hubert, *Mfg Staff*
Al Berger, *Senior Buyer*
▲ EMP: 126
SQ FT: 40,000
SALES (est): 19.9MM **Privately Held**
WEB: www.keyelco.com
SIC: **3678** Electronic connectors

(G-445)
LEMODE PLUMBING & HEATING
3455 11th St (11106-5011)
PHONE..................................718 545-3336
Angelo Lemodetis, *Owner*
EMP: 30
SALES (est): 4.7MM **Privately Held**
SIC: **3494** Plumbing & heating valves

(G-446)
LENS LAB EXPRESS SOUTHERN BLVD
3097 Steinway St Ste 301 (11103-3820)
PHONE..................................718 626-5184
Fax: 718 626-5405
Jeffery Nesses, *President*
EMP: 7
SALES (est): 925.8K **Privately Held**
SIC: **3851** 5048 Ophthalmic goods; ophthalmic goods

(G-447)
MELITA CORP
3330 14th St (11106-4624)
PHONE..................................718 392-7280
Emanuel Darmanin, *Ch of Bd*
Joann Atek, *COO*
Jack Darmanin, *VP Prdtn*
Michelle D' Oleivra, *Purchasing*
Michael Cassar, *CFO*
EMP: 201
SQ FT: 44,000
SALES (est): 40.8MM **Privately Held**
SIC: **2051** 5411 Bread, cake & related products; grocery stores

(G-448)
MODERN ART FOUNDRY INC
Also Called: Jeffrey Spring Modern Art
1870 41st St (11105-1025)
PHONE..................................718 728-2030
Fax: 718 267-0819
Robert Spring, *President*
Jeffrey Spring, *Vice Pres*
Mary Jo Bursig, *Controller*
▲ EMP: 30
SQ FT: 14,000
SALES (est): 5MM **Privately Held**
WEB: www.modernartfoundry.com
SIC: **3366** 3446 Castings (except die): bronze; architectural metalwork

(G-449)
NIEBYLSKI BAKERY INC
2364 Steinway St (11105-1913)
PHONE..................................718 721-5152
Anthony Niebylski, *President*
Rose Niebylski, *Vice Pres*
EMP: 7
SALES: 500K **Privately Held**
SIC: **2051** 5461 Bakery: wholesale or wholesale/retail combined; bakeries

Astoria - Queens County (G-450)

(G-450)
NY PHRMACY COMPOUNDING CTR INC
3715 23rd Ave (11105-1993)
PHONE.....................201 403-5151
Wesam Abdrabouh, *President*
EMP: 5 EST: 2014
SALES (est): 549.5K **Privately Held**
SIC: 2834 Pharmaceutical preparations

(G-451)
OMNICARE ANESTHESIA PC (PA)
3636 33rd St Ste 211 (11106-2329)
PHONE.....................718 433-0044
Evans Crevecoeur MD, *Ch of Bd*
Gina Duva, *Principal*
Michelle Vega, *Administration*
EMP: 23
SALES (est): 4.9MM **Privately Held**
SIC: 3841 Anesthesia apparatus

(G-452)
QCR EXPRESS CORP
2565 23rd St Apt 3d (11102-3393)
PHONE.....................888 924-5888
Oscar Bayona, *President*
Veronica Bayona, *Vice Pres*
EMP: 6
SALES: 1.2MM **Privately Held**
SIC: 3993 Signs & advertising specialties

(G-453)
RAGO FOUNDATIONS LLC
Also Called: Fago Shapewear
1815 27th Ave (11102-3744)
PHONE.....................718 728-8436
Fax: 718 728-8465
Steven H Chernoff, *General Mgr*
Georgiana Petrobono, *Bookkeeper*
Kieran Hohammed, *Manager*
Justin Cherroff,
▼ EMP: 96 EST: 1944
SALES (est): 10.5MM **Privately Held**
WEB: www.agoshapewear.com
SIC: 2342 Foundation garments, women's

(G-454)
ROSENWACH TANK CO INC (PA)
Also Called: Rosenwach Group, The
4302 Ditmars Blvd (11105-1337)
PHONE.....................212 972-4411
Fax: 718 482-0661
Andrew Rosenwach, *Ch of Bd*
Wallace Rosenwach, *Principal*
George Vassiliades, *Principal*
Alice Rosenwach, *Treasurer*
Robert Obus, *Admin Sec*
EMP: 35 EST: 1945
SQ FT: 23,000
SALES (est): 18MM **Privately Held**
SIC: 2449 3443 2531 Tanks, wood: coopered; fabricated plate work (boiler shop); public building & related furniture

(G-455)
SINGLECUT BEERSMITHS LLC
1933 37th St (11105-1118)
PHONE.....................718 606-0788
Rich Bueceta, *Mng Member*
EMP: 14 EST: 2012
SALES (est): 1.2MM **Privately Held**
SIC: 3556 Brewers' & maltsters' machinery

(G-456)
SITECRAFT INC
Also Called: Rosenwach Tank Co
4302 Ditmars Blvd (11105-1337)
PHONE.....................718 729-4900
Andrew Rosenwach, *President*
Al Seabra, *Opers Staff*
Wallace Rosenwach, *Director*
EMP: 5
SQ FT: 10,000
SALES (est): 791.4K
SALES (corp-wide): 18MM **Privately Held**
SIC: 2511 Wood lawn & garden furniture
PA: Rosenwach Tank Co. Inc.
    4302 Ditmars Blvd
    Astoria NY 11105
    212 972-4411

(G-457)
SPONGEBATH LLC
2334 28th St Apt 2r (11105-2877)
PHONE.....................917 475-1347
Matthew Flannery, *Mng Member*
Tod Maitland, *Mng Member*
EMP: 6
SQ FT: 2,200
SALES: 2MM **Privately Held**
SIC: 2842 Disinfectants, household or industrial plant

(G-458)
STEINWAY AWNING II LLC (PA)
Also Called: Steinway Awnings
4230 24th St (11101-4608)
PHONE.....................718 729-2965
Fax: 718 729-2968
Cuzana Michalovicoug, *Executive*
EMP: 6
SQ FT: 4,000
SALES: 300K **Privately Held**
SIC: 2394 5999 Awnings, fabric: made from purchased materials; canopies, fabric: made from purchased materials; awnings

(G-459)
VSHIP CO
3636 33rd St Ste 207 (11106-2329)
PHONE.....................718 706-8566
Vindu Koil, *President*
Ali Siddiqui, *Manager*
◆ EMP: 12 EST: 2000
SALES (est): 1.1MM **Privately Held**
SIC: 3443 Containers, shipping (bombs, etc.): metal plate

(G-460)
WAINLAND INC
2460 47th St (11103-1010)
PHONE.....................718 626-2233
Fax: 718 626-9222
Donald Wainland, *President*
Mark Wainland, *Vice Pres*
Neil Wainland, *Vice Pres*
Amel Mustajbasic, *Purch Mgr*
Karin Kovi, *Manager*
▲ EMP: 45
SALES (est): 8.9MM **Privately Held**
WEB: www.wainlands.com
SIC: 3645 3444 Residential lighting fixtures; sheet metalwork

(G-461)
WHITE COFFEE CORP
1835 38th St (11105-1076)
PHONE.....................718 204-7900
Fax: 718 956-6836
Carole White, *Ch of Bd*
Al Gaviria, *President*
Jonathan White, *Exec VP*
Gregory White, *Vice Pres*
John Bosco, *Opers Mgr*
▲ EMP: 85 EST: 1939
SALES (est): 32.9MM **Privately Held**
SIC: 2095 5149 Coffee roasting (except by wholesale grocers); tea

(G-462)
YOYO LIP GLOSS INC
2438 47th St (11103-1010)
PHONE.....................718 357-6304
Angie Parlionas, *Principal*
Margarita Parlionas, *CFO*
▲ EMP: 10
SQ FT: 25,000
SALES: 1.3MM **Privately Held**
SIC: 2844 Cosmetic preparations

Athens
Greene County

(G-463)
NORTHEAST TREATERS INC
796 Schoharie Tpke (12015-4306)
PHONE.....................518 945-2660
Frank Crowe, *Manager*
EMP: 25
SALES (corp-wide): 17MM **Privately Held**
WEB: www.netreaters.com
SIC: 2491 Wood preserving
PA: Northeast Treaters, Inc.
    201 Springfield Rd
    Belchertown MA 01007
    413 323-7811

(G-464)
NORTHEAST TREATERS NY LLC
796 Schoharie Tpke (12015-4306)
PHONE.....................518 945-2660
Fax: 518 945-2662
Joan Lamotte, *Office Mgr*
David A Reed, *Mng Member*
Douglas C Elder,
Charles Geiger,
Henry G Page Jr,
EMP: 20
SQ FT: 884
SALES (est): 1.7MM **Privately Held**
WEB: www.otda.state.ny.us
SIC: 2491 Wood preserving

(G-465)
PECKHAM INDUSTRIES INC
Uninn St (12015)
PHONE.....................518 945-1120
John R Peckham, *Branch Mgr*
EMP: 5
SALES (corp-wide): 200.6MM **Privately Held**
SIC: 2951 Asphalt paving mixtures & blocks
PA: Peckham Industries, Inc.
    20 Haarlem Ave Ste 200
    White Plains NY 10603
    914 949-2000

(G-466)
PECKHAM MATERIALS CORP
2 Union St Ext (12015-1298)
PHONE.....................518 945-1120
Mark Libruk, *Terminal Mgr*
Joe Widermuth, *Manager*
Art Coe, *Manager*
Joe Wildermith, *Manager*
EMP: 20
SQ FT: 242
SALES (corp-wide): 200.6MM **Privately Held**
SIC: 2951 Asphalt paving mixtures & blocks
HQ: Peckham Materials Corp
    20 Haarlem Ave Ste 200
    White Plains NY 10603
    914 686-2045

Atlantic Beach
Nassau County

(G-467)
ANCHOR COMMERCE TRADING CORP
53 Dutchess Blvd (11509-1223)
P.O. Box 238 (11509-0238)
PHONE.....................516 881-3485
Meryl P Benin, *President*
EMP: 6 EST: 1976
SALES (est): 266.2K **Privately Held**
SIC: 3714 3533 2819 3823 Motor vehicle parts & accessories; oil field machinery & equipment; industrial inorganic chemicals; computer interface equipment for industrial process control

(G-468)
HORIZON APPAREL MFG INC
115 Bayside Dr (11509-1608)
PHONE.....................516 361-4878
Mark Hassin, *President*
Bonnie Hassin, *Vice Pres*
▲ EMP: 5
SQ FT: 800
SALES: 25MM **Privately Held**
SIC: 2211 Apparel & outerwear fabrics, cotton

(G-469)
SMALL BUSINESS ADVISORS INC
2005 Park St (11509-1235)
PHONE.....................516 374-1387
Joseph Gelb, *President*
Dawson Vandam, *Manager*
Barbara Goetz Gelb, *Shareholder*
EMP: 10
SALES (est): 465.8K **Privately Held**
SIC: 2721 8721 Periodicals; accounting, auditing & bookkeeping

Attica
Wyoming County

(G-470)
ATTICA MILLWORK INC
71 Market St (14011-1023)
P.O. Box 118 (14011-0118)
PHONE.....................585 591-2333
Fax: 585 591-3240
Kevin Demars, *President*
Justin Papucci, *Vice Pres*
Doug Houghton, *Opers Staff*
Thomas Wackenheim, *Shareholder*
▲ EMP: 19 EST: 1945
SQ FT: 65,000
SALES (est): 3MM **Privately Held**
WEB: www.atticamillwork.com
SIC: 2431 Moldings, wood: unfinished & prefinished

(G-471)
ATTICA PACKAGE COMPANY INC
45 Windsor St (14011-1208)
P.O. Box 295 (14011-0295)
PHONE.....................585 591-0510
Fax: 585 591-3655
Douglas W Domes, *President*
Brittany Gadd, *Office Mgr*
Barbara Schmidt, *Administration*
EMP: 10 EST: 1917
SQ FT: 16,000
SALES (est): 870K **Privately Held**
SIC: 2411 5199 5211 Logging; sawdust; millwork & lumber

(G-472)
HLW ACRES LLC
Also Called: Hlw Acres Poultry Processing
1727 Exchange Street Rd (14011-9627)
PHONE.....................585 591-0795
Hermann Weber, *Owner*
EMP: 9
SALES (est): 548.4K **Privately Held**
SIC: 2015 Poultry slaughtering & processing

(G-473)
PRECISION FABRICATION LLC
40 S Pearl St (14011-1207)
PHONE.....................585 591-3449
Donald McCulloch, *Owner*
EMP: 5
SALES: 530K **Privately Held**
SIC: 3444 3448 Sheet metalwork; prefabricated metal components

Au Sable Forks
Clinton County

(G-474)
COLD SPRING GRANITE COMPANY
Lake Placid Granite Co
Hc 9 Box N (12912)
P.O. Box 778 (12912-0778)
PHONE.....................518 647-8191
Fax: 518 647-8340
Rick Barber, *Manager*
EMP: 27
SALES (corp-wide): 317.5MM **Privately Held**
WEB: www.granitemountainstonedesign.com
SIC: 1411 Granite, dimension-quarrying
PA: Cold Spring Granite Company Inc
    17482 Granite West Rd
    Cold Spring MN 56320
    320 685-3621

Auburn
Cayuga County

▲ = Import ▼ = Export ◆ = Import/Export

GEOGRAPHIC SECTION

Auburn - Cayuga County (G-498)

(G-475)
4M PRECISION INDUSTRIES INC
4000 Technology Park Blvd (13021-9030)
PHONE..................................315 252-8415
Fax: 315 253-9611
Margaret Morin, *President*
Daniel Morin, *Vice Pres*
Allen Morin, *Purchasing*
Megan Byrne, *Sales Staff*
Stephen C Morin, *Shareholder*
EMP: 43
SQ FT: 55,000
SALES (est): 11.1MM **Privately Held**
WEB: www.4mprecision.com
SIC: 3469 Metal stampings

(G-476)
AAI ACQUISITION LLC
70 Wright Cir (13021-3159)
P.O. Box 870 (13021-0870)
PHONE..................................800 333-0519
Gerry Dicunzolo, *CEO*
EMP: 100
SALES (est): 433.2K
SALES (corp-wide): 32.2MM **Privately Held**
SIC: 7694 Motor repair services
PA: Power-Flo Technologies, Inc.
  270 Park Ave
  New Hyde Park NY 11040
  516 812-6800

(G-477)
AUBURN CUSTOM MILLWORK INC
Also Called: SLC
4022 Technology Park Blvd (13021-9014)
PHONE..................................315 253-3843
Fax: 315 258-8613
Christopher Colella, *President*
Sherry Colella, *Manager*
EMP: 8
SALES (est): 1.3MM **Privately Held**
SIC: 2431 2541 Millwork; cabinets, lockers & shelving

(G-478)
AUBURN FOUNDRY INC
15 Wadsworth St (13021-2257)
P.O. Box 715 (13021-0715)
PHONE..................................315 253-4441
Fax: 315 253-5918
David Boglione, *President*
Nicholas Boglione, *Vice Pres*
Denise Boglione, *Admin Sec*
EMP: 17 EST: 1947
SQ FT: 60,000
SALES (est): 1.7MM **Privately Held**
WEB: www.auburnfoundry.com
SIC: 3321 Gray & ductile iron foundries; gray iron castings

(G-479)
AUBURN PUBLISHING CO
Also Called: Citizen , The
25 Dill St (13021-3605)
PHONE..................................315 253-5311
Fax: 315 253-6031
Richard J Emanuel, *President*
Jeremy Boyer, *Editor*
David Wilcox, *Editor*
Deborah Feeley, *Sales Staff*
John Micglire Jr, *Adv Dir*
EMP: 85
SALES (est): 5.4MM
SALES (corp-wide): 614.3MM **Publicly Held**
SIC: 2711 Newspapers: publishing only, not printed on site
HQ: Lee Publications, Inc.
  201 N Harrison St Ste 600
  Davenport IA 52801
  563 383-2100

(G-480)
AUBURN TANK & MANUFACTURING CO
Also Called: Atco EZ Dock
24 Mcmaster St (13021-2442)
P.O. Box 488 (13021-0488)
PHONE..................................315 255-2788
Fax: 315 253-9239
Carl Weber, *President*
April Amodei, *Safety Mgr*
Charles Masters, *Sales Mgr*
Kristy Weber, *Office Mgr*
EMP: 14
SQ FT: 12,000
SALES (est): 2.2MM **Privately Held**
WEB: www.auburntank.com
SIC: 3444 Sheet metalwork

(G-481)
AUBURN VACUUM FORMING CO INC
40 York St (13021-1251)
P.O. Box 489 (13021-0489)
PHONE..................................315 253-2440
Fax: 315 253-2203
Martin Pelchat, *President*
Jack Hutson, *Sls & Mktg Exec*
Paul Pucek, *CFO*
EMP: 19
SQ FT: 71,000
SALES: 2.1MM
SALES (corp-wide): 3.2MM **Privately Held**
SIC: 3563 Vacuum (air extraction) systems, industrial
PA: Plastique M.P. Inc
  250 Rue Gouin
  Richmond QC J0B 2
  819 826-5921

(G-482)
AVSTAR FUEL SYSTEMS INC
15 Brookfield Pl (13021-2209)
PHONE..................................315 255-1955
EMP: 6
SALES (est): 670.7K **Privately Held**
SIC: 2869 Fuels

(G-483)
BIMBO BAKERIES USA INC
11 Corcoran Dr (13021-2213)
PHONE..................................315 253-9782
Bill Bos, *Plant Mgr*
EMP: 100
SQ FT: 28,668 **Privately Held**
SIC: 2051 Breads, rolls & buns
HQ: Bimbo Bakeries Usa, Inc
  255 Business Center Dr # 200
  Horsham PA 19044
  215 347-5500

(G-484)
BLAIR CNSTR FABRICATION SP
13 Brae Ridge Rd (13021-9672)
PHONE..................................315 253-2321
Fax: 315 253-2302
Blair Longo, *President*
EMP: 6
SQ FT: 6,000
SALES (est): 632.1K **Privately Held**
SIC: 3599 Machine shop, jobbing & repair

(G-485)
BO-MER PLASTICS LLC
13 Pulaski St (13021-1105)
PHONE..................................315 252-7216
Thomas R Herbert, *President*
Robin Axton, *Office Mgr*
▼ EMP: 46 EST: 2001
SQ FT: 44,000
SALES (est): 10.5MM **Privately Held**
WEB: www.bo-mer.com
SIC: 3089 Thermoformed finished plastic products; plastic processing

(G-486)
BROOK NORTH FARMS INC
89 York St (13021-1135)
P.O. Box 1239, Weedsport (13166-1239)
PHONE..................................315 834-9390
Fax: 315 834-9675
Carolyn Kyle, *CEO*
Peter Kyle, *President*
▲ EMP: 12
SALES (est): 2.1MM **Privately Held**
WEB: www.northbrookfarms.com
SIC: 2515 3496 5083 Mattresses & bedsprings; mats & matting; dairy machinery & equipment

(G-487)
CIERRA INDUSTRIES INC
491 Grant Avenue Rd (13021-8204)
PHONE..................................315 252-6630
F Paul Vanderpool, *President*
▲ EMP: 11
SQ FT: 4,000
SALES (est): 2.2MM **Privately Held**
SIC: 3568 Power transmission equipment

(G-488)
COPPER JOHN CORPORATION
173 State St (13021-1841)
PHONE..................................315 258-9269
Fax: 315 258-0529
Douglas A Springer, *President*
Eric Springer, *Vice Pres*
▲ EMP: 19
SQ FT: 11,000
SALES (est): 1.9MM **Privately Held**
WEB: www.copperjohn.com
SIC: 3949 Archery equipment, general

(G-489)
CURRIER PLASTICS INC
101 Columbus St (13021-3101)
PHONE..................................315 255-1779
Fax: 315 255-6643
John Currier, *Ch of Bd*
Massimo A Leone, *President*
Ron Ringleben, *President*
Tom Maloney, *Business Mgr*
James E Currier, *Vice Pres*
▲ EMP: 99
SQ FT: 60,000
SALES (est): 25.6MM **Privately Held**
WEB: www.currierplastics.com
SIC: 3089 Injection molding of plastics

(G-490)
DAIKIN APPLIED AMERICAS INC
Also Called: Applied Terminal Systems
4900 Technology Park Blvd (13021-8592)
PHONE..................................315 253-2771
Fax: 315 253-5181
Steve Henry, *Vice Pres*
Mary Currier, *Facilities Mgr*
Jeff Cusyck, *Engineer*
Albert Eldik, *Engineer*
Michael Holahan, *Engineer*
EMP: 55
SALES (corp-wide): 17.9B **Privately Held**
SIC: 3585 3822 3564 3561 Heating & air conditioning combination units; auto controls regulating residntl & coml environmt & applncs; blowers & fans; pumps & pumping equipment; fabricated pipe & fittings
HQ: Daikin Applied Americas Inc.
  13600 Industrial Pk Blvd
  Minneapolis MN 55441
  763 553-5330

(G-491)
DEWITT PLASTICS INC
28 Aurelius Ave (13021-2231)
PHONE..................................315 255-1209
David M Hess, *President*
Traci Kowal, *Marketing Staff*
▲ EMP: 11 EST: 1972
SALES (est): 2.7MM **Privately Held**
WEB: www.dewittplastics.com
SIC: 2821 Plasticizer/additive based plastic materials

(G-492)
EMCOM INC
Also Called: Electomechanical Componets
62 Columbus St Ste 4 (13021-3161)
PHONE..................................315 255-5300
Fax: 315 255-5311
Endy China, *President*
Joseph Reding, *President*
Tony Pongipat, *Vice Pres*
Debra Johnston, *Materials Mgr*
Joseph D'Urso, *Production*
▲ EMP: 100
SQ FT: 10,000
SALES (est): 36.8MM **Privately Held**
WEB: www.em-com.com
SIC: 3699 Electrical equipment & supplies

(G-493)
FINGER LAKES LEA CRAFTERS LLC
Also Called: Auburn Leathercrafters
42 Washington St (13021-2479)
PHONE..................................315 252-4107
Fax: 315 252-4734
Anita Dungey, *President*
Alan Dungey, *Vice Pres*
▼ EMP: 15
SQ FT: 13,000
SALES: 1.2MM **Privately Held**
WEB: www.auburndirect.com
SIC: 3199 Dog furnishings: collars, leashes, muzzles, etc.: leather

(G-494)
FIRST PRESBYTERIAN CHURCH
112 South St (13021-4891)
PHONE..................................315 252-3861
Gerald Rife Jr, *Pastor*
EMP: 6
SALES (est): 500.9K **Privately Held**
SIC: 3281 Cut stone & stone products

(G-495)
FLP GROUP LLC
301 Clark St (13021-2236)
PHONE..................................315 252-7583
Greg Kanane, *President*
Joseph Mirabito, *Production*
Gerard Mirabito Jr, *Executive*
Kathy Feocco, *Administration*
Rex Dean, *Recruiter*
EMP: 11 EST: 1928
SQ FT: 20,000
SALES (est): 1.7MM
SALES (corp-wide): 3.9MM **Privately Held**
WEB: www.fingerlakespress.com
SIC: 2752 2791 2789 2759 Commercial printing, offset; typesetting; bookbinding & related work; commercial printing; automotive & apparel trimmings
PA: Kinaneco., Inc.
  2925 Milton Ave
  Syracuse NY 13209
  315 468-6201

(G-496)
GEN-WEST ASSOCIATES LLC
101 Columbus St (13021-3121)
PHONE..................................315 255-1779
Louri Hapkins, *Principal*
Pat Craine, *Accountant*
EMP: 5
SALES (est): 569.3K **Privately Held**
SIC: 3089 Injection molding of plastics

(G-497)
GOULDS PUMPS INCORPORATED
1 Goulds Dr (13021-3134)
PHONE..................................315 258-4949
Fax: 315 252-9713
Solly Durado, *Branch Mgr*
Kathy Dewaele, *Admin Asst*
EMP: 338
SALES (corp-wide): 2.4B **Publicly Held**
SIC: 3561 5084 Pumps & pumping equipment; industrial pumps & parts; pumps, oil well & field; pumps, domestic: water or sump; industrial machinery & equipment
HQ: Goulds Pumps Llc
  240 Fall St
  Seneca Falls NY 13148
  315 568-2811

(G-498)
HAMMOND & IRVING INC (PA)
254 North St (13021-1129)
PHONE..................................315 253-6265
Fax: 315 253-3136
Edward Gallager, *President*
Edward C Gallagher, *Exec VP*
Barbara Zach, *Treasurer*
Crystal Reyes, *Sales Staff*
Mary Vanacore, *Sales Staff*
▲ EMP: 76
SQ FT: 20,000

Auburn - Cayuga County (G-499)

SALES (est): 14.8MM **Privately Held**
WEB: www.hammond-irving.com
SIC: 3463 Nonferrous forgings

(G-499)
INTERNATIONAL FIRE-SHIELD INC
194 Genesee St (13021-3360)
P.O. Box 7305 (13022-7305)
PHONE..........................315 255-1006
Fax: 315 255-2765
Patrick D Bumpus, CEO
George Murray, Ch of Bd
Jean Graves, Vice Pres
EMP: 12
SALES (est): 1.4MM **Privately Held**
WEB: www.nyfs.com
SIC: 2899 Fire retardant chemicals

(G-500)
ITT LLC
Also Called: ITT Water Technology
1 Goulds Dr (13021-3134)
PHONE..........................315 258-4904
Jim Jones, Engineer
Louis Juliano, Branch Mgr
Amy Bergan, Manager
Scott Liscum, Manager
EMP: 58
SALES (corp-wide): 2.4B **Publicly Held**
SIC: 3625 Control equipment, electric
HQ: Itt Llc
   1133 Westchester Ave N-100
   White Plains NY 10604
   914 641-2000

(G-501)
JACOBS PRESS INC
87 Columbus St (13021-3121)
P.O. Box 580 (13021-0580)
PHONE..........................315 252-4861
Fax: 315 253-3618
Michael K Trapani, President
Pat Nation, Sales Staff
Laura Posecznick, Business Dir
Molly Trapani, Admin Sec
Marsha Bell, Graphic Designe
EMP: 10 EST: 1915
SQ FT: 7,228
SALES: 1.1MM **Privately Held**
WEB: www.jacobspress.com
SIC: 2752 Commercial printing, offset

(G-502)
JOHN G RUBINO INC
Also Called: Gleason-Avery
45 Aurelius Ave (13021-2249)
PHONE..........................315 253-7396
Fax: 315 253-8344
John G Rubino, CEO
John Rubino, President
▲ EMP: 30
SQ FT: 32,000
SALES: 4.8MM **Privately Held**
WEB: www.geasonavery.com
SIC: 3621 3566 Motors, electric; speed changers, drives & gears

(G-503)
JOHNSTON PRECISION INC
7 Frank Smith St (13021-1145)
PHONE..........................315 253-4181
Fax: 315 253-4188
Theodore Johnston, President
EMP: 5
SQ FT: 2,400
SALES (est): 568.1K **Privately Held**
SIC: 3599 Machine & other job shop work

(G-504)
LOLLIPOP TREE INC
181 York St (13021-9009)
PHONE..........................845 471-8733
Laurie V Lynch, Ch of Bd
Robert Lynch, President
Denise Birch, Accountant
EMP: 20
SQ FT: 18,200
SALES (est): 2.6MM **Privately Held**
WEB: www.lollipoptree.com
SIC: 2045 2033 2099 2035 Prepared flour mixes & doughs; preserves, including imitation: in cans, jars, etc.; food preparations; pickles, sauces & salad dressings

(G-505)
MACK STUDIOS DISPLAYS INC
5500 Technology Park Blvd (13021-8555)
P.O. Box 917 (13021-0917)
PHONE..........................315 252-7542
Fax: 315 252-5786
Peter Maciulewicz, CEO
Christine Lockrow, Business Mgr
Dan Fleischman, Accountant
Sabina Coppola, Manager
EMP: 45
SQ FT: 125,000
SALES: 10.9MM **Privately Held**
WEB: www.mackstudios.com
SIC: 3999 Advertising display products

(G-506)
MATTEO & ANTONIO BARTOLOTTA
Also Called: Bartolotta Furniture
282 State St (13021-1144)
PHONE..........................315 252-2220
Fax: 315 252-9251
Matteo Bartolotta, President
EMP: 10 EST: 1976
SQ FT: 4,000
SALES (est): 1MM **Privately Held**
SIC: 2512 2521 2434 Upholstered household furniture; wood office furniture; wood kitchen cabinets

(G-507)
NEW HOPE MILLS INC
181 York St (13021-9009)
PHONE..........................315 252-2676
Fax: 315 497-0810
Dale E Weed, President
David J Weed, Vice Pres
Mamie Weed, Marketing Staff
EMP: 12
SQ FT: 11,500
SALES (est): 1.1MM **Privately Held**
WEB: www.newhopemills.com
SIC: 2045 0723 Pancake mixes, prepared: from purchased flour; flour milling custom services

(G-508)
NEW HOPE MILLS MFG INC (PA)
181 York St (13021-9009)
PHONE..........................315 252-2676
Douglas Weed, CEO
Dale Weed, President
Dana Weed, Office Mgr
EMP: 50
SQ FT: 30,000
SALES (est): 8MM **Publicly Held**
SIC: 2051 5461 Bakery products, partially cooked (except frozen); bakeries

(G-509)
NUCOR STEEL AUBURN INC
25 Quarry Rd (13021-1146)
P.O. Box 2008 (13021-1077)
PHONE..........................315 253-4561
Fax: 315 253-5377
Mary E Slate, General Mgr
Dave Smith, General Mgr
Dan Dimicco, Chairman
Luke Scott, Safety Mgr
Dan Dygert, Buyer
▲ EMP: 290 EST: 2001
SQ FT: 300,000
SALES (est): 130.2MM
SALES (corp-wide): 16.2B **Publicly Held**
WEB: www.nucorauburn.com
SIC: 3312 Blast furnaces & steel mills
PA: Nucor Corporation
   1915 Rexford Rd Ste 400
   Charlotte NC 28211
   704 366-7000

(G-510)
OWENS-BROCKWAY GLASS CONT INC
7134 County House Rd (13021-5901)
PHONE..........................315 258-3211
Judy Johnson, Purchasing
Steven Gabel, Manager
EMP: 210
SALES (corp-wide): 6.7B **Publicly Held**
SIC: 3221 Glass containers
HQ: Owens-Brockway Glass Container Inc.
   1 Michael Owens Way
   Perrysburg OH 43551
   567 336-8449

(G-511)
PRINTERY
55 Arterial W (13021-2730)
PHONE..........................315 253-7403
Fax: 315 253-0590
Pam Flaherty, Owner
EMP: 5
SALES (est): 190K **Privately Held**
SIC: 2261 Screen printing of cotton broad-woven fabrics

(G-512)
R P M INDUSTRIES INC
Also Called: RPM Displays
26 Aurelius Ave (13021-2212)
PHONE..........................315 255-1105
Fax: 315 252-1167
Roger P Mueller, President
David Hess, Vice Pres
Beatrice Hess, Accounting Mgr
Martin Lynch, Asst Treas
Roy P Mueller, VP Sales
▲ EMP: 50 EST: 1925
SQ FT: 60,000
SALES (est): 49.2K **Privately Held**
WEB: www.rpmdisplays.com
SIC: 3089 5046 2499 Boxes, plastic; plastic hardware & building products; mannequins; shoe trees

(G-513)
ROBINSON CONCRETE INC (PA)
Also Called: Vitale Ready Mix Concrete
3486 Franklin Street Rd (13021-9348)
PHONE..........................315 253-6666
Fax: 315 252-7595
Michael Vitale Jr, President
Norman Chirco, Counsel
Vincent Vitale, Vice Pres
Tim Brigden, Manager
Paul F Vitale, Admin Sec
EMP: 50 EST: 1865
SQ FT: 2,500
SALES (est): 24MM **Privately Held**
SIC: 3273 3272 1442 Ready-mixed concrete; concrete products, precast; construction sand & gravel

(G-514)
SCHOTT CORPORATION
Also Called: Fiber Optics Schott America
62 Columbus St (13021-3167)
PHONE..........................315 255-2791
Hinz Keiser, Plant Mgr
EMP: 64 **Privately Held**
SIC: 3229 3827 3674 Pressed & blown glass; optical instruments & lenses; semi-conductors & related devices
HQ: Schott Corporation
   555 Taxter Rd Ste 470
   Elmsford NY 10523
   914 831-2200

(G-515)
SIGN GUYS LLC
67 Franklin St (13021-2154)
PHONE..........................315 253-4276
Thomas Shayler, Mng Member
EMP: 5
SALES: 220K **Privately Held**
SIC: 3993 Signs & advertising specialties

(G-516)
SIMPLEX MANUFACTURING CO INC
105 Dunning Ave (13021-4403)
P.O. Box 279 (13021-0279)
PHONE..........................315 252-7524
Fax: 315 252-0980
Robert C Merritt, President
Richard C Merritt, Vice Pres
Dan Bird, Marketing Staff
EMP: 19
SQ FT: 25,000
SALES (est): 3.1MM **Privately Held**
WEB: www.simplexco.com
SIC: 3469 Metal stampings

(G-517)
SPECTRUM MICROWAVE INC
Also Called: API Technologies Corp
23 N Division St (13021-2357)
PHONE..........................315 253-6241
Richard Southworth, President
Walt Gorden, Manager
EMP: 22
SALES (corp-wide): 303.2MM **Privately Held**
WEB: www.idt.com
SIC: 3679 Microwave components
HQ: Spectrum Microwave, Inc.
   8061 Avonia Rd
   Fairview PA 16415
   814 474-4300

(G-518)
SUNNYCREST INC (PA)
58 Prospect St (13021-1699)
PHONE..........................315 252-7214
Fax: 315 252-7859
Robert Atkinson, President
William Atkinson, Vice Pres
Ron Shortsleeve, Finance Mgr
Eleanor Atkinson, Admin Sec
EMP: 30 EST: 1969
SQ FT: 53,000
SALES (est): 4.4MM **Privately Held**
WEB: www.sunnycrest.com
SIC: 3272 7261 Concrete products, precast; funeral service & crematories

(G-519)
T SHORE PRODUCTS LTD
Also Called: Shore Products Co
5 Eagle Dr (13021-8695)
PHONE..........................315 252-9174
Fax: 315 252-9174
Thomas H Tutt II, President
Marlene Tutt, Vice Pres
EMP: 6
SQ FT: 8,500
SALES: 800K **Privately Held**
SIC: 3536 3448 5461 Hoists; boat lifts; docks: prefabricated metal; bakeries

(G-520)
TARO MANUFACTURING COMPANY INC
114 Clark St (13021-3325)
PHONE..........................315 252-9430
Fax: 315 252-9431
Mario Buttaro, President
Mark Buttaro, Vice Pres
Steve Buttaro, Vice Pres
Roxanne Foster, Manager
▲ EMP: 19
SQ FT: 17,000
SALES (est): 3MM **Privately Held**
WEB: www.taromfg.com
SIC: 3621 3694 3678 Rotors, for motors; ignition apparatus & distributors; electronic connectors

(G-521)
TOWPATH MACHINE CORP
31 Allen St (13021-9004)
PHONE..........................315 252-0112
Fax: 315 255-1580
Patricia Hanford, President
George Hanford, Treasurer
EMP: 7
SQ FT: 3,000
SALES: 500K **Privately Held**
WEB: www.towpathmachine.com
SIC: 3599 Machine shop, jobbing & repair

(G-522)
TRW AUTOMOTIVE INC
TRW Manufacturing
2150 Crane Brook Dr (13021-9516)
PHONE..........................315 255-3311
Larry Trent, Branch Mgr
Robert Nearpass, Systems Analyst
EMP: 300 **Privately Held**
SIC: 3469 3714 Metal stampings; motor vehicle parts & accessories
HQ: Trw Automotive Inc.
   12025 Tech Center Dr
   Livonia MI 48150
   734 855-2600

GEOGRAPHIC SECTION

(G-523)
TRW AUTOMOTIVE US LLC
Also Called: T R W Automotive
2150 Crane Brook Dr (13021-9516)
PHONE...................315 255-3311
Fax: 315 253-8747
David Cunningham, *Engineer*
Mark Ingianni, *Manager*
Jeffrey Hohman, *Manager*
EMP: 250 **Privately Held**
WEB: www.trw.mediaroom.com
SIC: **3469** Metal stampings
HQ: Trw Automotive U.S. Llc
   12001 Tech Center Dr
   Livonia MI 48150
   734 855-2600

(G-524)
UFP NEW YORK LLC (HQ)
Also Called: Universal Forest Products
11 Allen St (13021-9004)
PHONE...................315 253-2758
Ralph Gschwind, *Principal*
EMP: 20
SALES (est): 2MM
SALES (corp-wide): 3.2B **Publicly Held**
WEB: www.ufpinc.com
SIC: **2439** Trusses, wooden roof
PA: Universal Forest Products, Inc.
   2801 E Beltline Ave Ne
   Grand Rapids MI 49525
   616 364-6161

(G-525)
VOLPI MANUFACTURING USA CO INC
5 Commerce Way (13021-8557)
PHONE...................315 255-1737
Fax: 315 255-1202
Max Kunz, *CEO*
Scott Kittelberger, *COO*
Jennifer Ross, *Buyer*
James Casasanta, *Engineer*
Richard Cincotta, *Engineer*
◆ EMP: 38
SQ FT: 37,000
SALES (est): 6.4MM **Privately Held**
WEB: www.volpiusa.com
SIC: **3229** Glass fiber products
HQ: Volpi Ag
   Wiesenstrasse 33
   Schlieren ZH
   447 324-343

(G-526)
WEAVER MACHINE & TOOL CO INC
44 York St (13021-1136)
PHONE...................315 253-4422
Fax: 315 253-0058
Victor Ianno, *President*
Susan Garrigan, *Prdtn Mgr*
Charles Fitzgerald, *Data Proc Exec*
Joe Artman, *Officer*
EMP: 15
SQ FT: 26,000
SALES (est): 3.1MM **Privately Held**
WEB: www.weavermachine.com
SIC: **3599** Machine shop, jobbing & repair

(G-527)
XYLEM INC
1 Goulds Dr (13021-3134)
PHONE...................315 258-4949
Sally Dorado, *Branch Mgr*
Lucas Fisher, *Manager*
Tom Flood, *Admin Asst*
EMP: 150 **Publicly Held**
SIC: **3561** Pumps & pumping equipment
PA: Xylem Inc.
   1 International Dr
   Rye Brook NY 10573

Aurora
Cayuga County

(G-528)
MACKENZIE-CHILDS LLC (PA)
3260 State Route 90 (13026-9769)
PHONE...................315 364-6118
Fax: 315 364-8075
Lee Feldman, *CEO*
Tony Ciccone, *Purch Mgr*
Julie Schneider, *Buyer*
Howard Cohen, *CFO*
Sheila Grinnelo, *Human Resources*
◆ EMP: 150
SQ FT: 70,000
SALES (est): 41.3MM **Privately Held**
WEB: www.mackenzie-childs.com
SIC: **3263** 2512 2511 Cookware, fine earthenware; upholstered household furniture; wood household furniture

Ava
Oneida County

(G-529)
ROBERT W STILL
Also Called: Ava Wood Products
11755 State Route 26 (13303)
PHONE...................315 942-5594
Robert Still, *Owner*
Nick Calogero, *Accountant*
EMP: 16
SALES: 1.2MM **Privately Held**
SIC: **2411** Logging

Averill Park
Rensselaer County

(G-530)
518 PRINTS LLC
1548 Burden Lake Rd Ste 4 (12018-2818)
P.O. Box 632 (12018-0632)
PHONE...................518 674-5346
Jesse Brust, *Owner*
EMP: 6
SALES (est): 661.2K **Privately Held**
SIC: **2752** Commercial printing, lithographic

(G-531)
CAPITAL REG WKLY NEWSPPR GROUP
Also Called: Advertiser, The
29 Sheer Rd (12018-4722)
P.O. Box 70 (12018-0070)
PHONE...................518 674-2841
Fax: 518 674-8680
Charles Hug, *Principal*
Alyson Regan, *Principal*
Karen Demis, *Manager*
EMP: 10
SALES (est): 850K **Privately Held**
SIC: **2721** Periodicals: publishing only

(G-532)
GARMENT CARE SYSTEMS LLC
Also Called: Laura Star Service Center
50 Blue Heron Dr (12018-4601)
PHONE...................518 674-1826
James E Wells, *Mng Member*
▲ EMP: 6
SALES (est): 654.5K **Privately Held**
WEB: www.garmentcaresystems.com
SIC: **3499** Ironing boards, metal

(G-533)
L J VALENTE INC
8957 Ny Highway 66 (12018-5822)
PHONE...................518 674-3750
Fax: 518 674-3228
Anthony Valente, *President*
Steve A Valente, *Vice Pres*
EMP: 8
SALES (est): 1.4MM **Privately Held**
SIC: **2421** Building & structural materials, wood

Avoca
Steuben County

(G-534)
HAINES EQUIPMENT INC
20 Carrington St (14809-9766)
PHONE...................607 566-8531
Fax: 607 566-2240
Patricia Haines, *President*
Jack Stewart, *Sales Executive*
EMP: 50
SQ FT: 50,000
SALES (est): 9.6MM **Privately Held**
WEB: www.hainesequipment.com
SIC: **3523** 3565 3556 3535 Farm machinery & equipment; packaging machinery; food products machinery; conveyors & conveying equipment; tire cord & fabrics

Avon
Livingston County

(G-535)
B & B PRECISION MFG INC (PA)
310 W Main St (14414-1150)
P.O. Box 279 (14414-0279)
PHONE...................585 226-6226
Gerald Macintyre, *President*
Steve Megliore, *Plant Supt*
Lawrence Bailey, *Treasurer*
Shelly Guerin, *Accounts Mgr*
EMP: 28 EST: 1976
SQ FT: 15,900
SALES (est): 3.2MM **Privately Held**
WEB: www.bbprecision.com
SIC: **3545** Precision measuring tools

(G-536)
BARILLA AMERICA NY INC
100 Horseshoe Blvd (14414-1164)
PHONE...................585 226-5600
Kirk Trofholz, *Principal*
Tj Dioguardi, *Controller*
▲ EMP: 121
SALES (est): 18.7MM **Privately Held**
SIC: **2099** Packaged combination products: pasta, rice & potato
HQ: Barilla America Inc.
   885 Sunset Ridge Rd
   Northbrook IL 60062

(G-537)
KRAFT HEINZ FOODS COMPANY
140 Spring St (14414-1153)
PHONE...................585 226-4400
Fax: 585 226-4306
Steve Vanderbilt, *Production*
Jeff McMindes, *Purchasing*
Kenneth Rowe, *Engineer*
Greg Manning, *Manager*
Sarah Barnes, *Manager*
EMP: 450
SALES (corp-wide): 26.4B **Publicly Held**
WEB: www.kraftfoods.com
SIC: **2038** 2099 Whipped topping, frozen; food preparations
HQ: Kraft Heinz Foods Company
   1 Ppg Pl Ste 3200
   Pittsburgh PA 15222
   412 456-5700

(G-538)
MONROE INDUSTRIES INC
5611 Tec Dr (14414-9562)
PHONE...................585 226-8230
Fax: 585 538-2911
John C Webster, *President*
Cary Holdsworth, *Director*
EMP: 8
SALES (est): 720K **Privately Held**
SIC: **3281** Marble, building: cut & shaped

(G-539)
PENNY LANE PRINTING INC
Also Called: Penny Express
1471 Rte 15 (14414)
P.O. Box 340 (14414-0340)
PHONE...................585 226-8111
Steven Harrison, *President*
Kimberly Dougherty, *Vice Pres*
Gina Doran, *Manager*
Jennifer Howe, *Manager*
EMP: 54
SQ FT: 25,000
SALES: 4.5MM **Privately Held**
SIC: **2759** 7319 Commercial printing; distribution of advertising material or sample services

(G-540)
STAR HEADLIGHT LANTERN CO INC (PA)
455 Rochester St (14414-9503)
PHONE...................585 226-9500
Fax: 585 226-2029
Christopher D Jacobs, *Ch of Bd*
Christopher D Jacobs, *President*
David W Jacobs, *President*
Debra Blaszkow, *General Mgr*
Gary Starks, *Opers Spvr*
◆ EMP: 146
SQ FT: 85,000
SALES (est): 31.6MM **Privately Held**
WEB: www.star1889.com
SIC: **3648** 3669 Strobe lighting systems; railroad signaling devices, electric

Babylon
Suffolk County

(G-541)
A C J COMMUNICATIONS INC
Also Called: Beacon
65 Deer Park Ave Ste 2 (11702-2820)
PHONE...................631 587-5612
Fax: 631 587-0198
Carolyn James, *Principal*
◆ EMP: 15
SALES (est): 87.5K **Privately Held**
SIC: **2711** Newspapers: publishing only, not printed on site

(G-542)
ADVANCED COATING TECHNIQUES
313 Wyandanch Ave (11704-1501)
PHONE...................631 643-4555
Fax: 631 643-1412
Anthony Gaitan, *President*
Maria Gaitan, *Corp Secy*
EMP: 20
SQ FT: 50,000
SALES (est): 2.4MM **Privately Held**
WEB: www.advancedcoatingtech.com
SIC: **3479** Galvanizing of iron, steel or end-formed products

(G-543)
BEDROCK LANDSCAPING MTLS CORP (PA)
Also Called: Bedrock Plus
454 Sunrise Hwy (11704-5906)
PHONE...................631 587-4950
David Cannetti, *President*
EMP: 9
SALES (est): 781.8K **Privately Held**
WEB: www.bedrockmaterial.com
SIC: **3291** Abrasive buffs, bricks, cloth, paper, stones, etc.

(G-544)
EAST PENN MANUFACTURING CO
790 Railroad Ave (11704-7820)
PHONE...................631 321-7161
Fax: 631 321-6611
Timothy Dunn, *Principal*
EMP: 6
SALES (corp-wide): 2.4B **Privately Held**
SIC: **3999** Barber & beauty shop equipment
PA: East Penn Manufacturing Co.
   102 Deka Rd
   Lyon Station PA 19536
   610 682-6361

(G-545)
EDM MFG
141 John St Ste 600 (11702-2945)
PHONE...................631 669-1966
Dariusz Mejer, *Chairman*
EMP: 8
SALES (est): 801K **Privately Held**
SIC: **3999** Manufacturing industries

(G-546)
JEWELERS MACHINIST CO INC
400 Columbus Ave (11704-5599)
PHONE...................631 661-5020
Raymond Pawloski, *President*
John Pawloski, *Vice Pres*

Babylon - Suffolk County (G-547)

GEOGRAPHIC SECTION

Kathleen Pawloski, *Admin Sec*
EMP: 7 **EST:** 1946
SQ FT: 3,000
SALES (est): 1MM **Privately Held**
WEB: www.threadgrind.com
SIC: 3599 Machine shop, jobbing & repair

(G-547)
M C PACKAGING CORPORATION
Also Called: M C Packaging Corp Plant
300 Governor Ave (11704-1900)
PHONE..................................631 643-3763
EMP: 40
SALES (corp-wide): 22.9MM **Privately Held**
SIC: 2679 5113 2759 2657 Mfg Converted Paper Prdt Whol Indstl/Svc Paper Commercial Printing Mfg Folding Paperbrd Box Mfg Corrugated/Fiber Box
PA: M C Packaging Corporation
200 Adams Blvd
Farmingdale NY 11735
631 414-7840

(G-548)
NSJ GROUP LTD
Also Called: Edible Arragement
80 W Main St Ste A (11702-3442)
PHONE..................................631 893-9300
Jason Varach, *Managing Prtnr*
Lindsey Ohland, *Manager*
EMP: 11
SALES (est): 624K **Privately Held**
SIC: 3999 Artificial flower arrangements

(G-549)
PHARMAVANTAGE LLC
15 Lakeland Ave (11702-1409)
PHONE..................................631 321-8171
Susan Capie, *Managing Dir*
▲ **EMP:** 6 **EST:** 2000
SALES (est): 584.9K **Privately Held**
SIC: 2834 Druggists' preparations (pharmaceuticals)

(G-550)
PREMIER SYSTEMS LLC
41 John St Ste 6 (11702-2932)
PHONE..................................631 587-9700
Joseph Pegno,
EMP: 6
SALES (est): 670K **Privately Held**
SIC: 3679 Electronic circuits

(G-551)
PREMIUM PROCESSING CORP
30 Kittiwake Ln (11702-4215)
PHONE..................................631 232-1105
Keith Schmict, *President*
EMP: 52
SQ FT: 30,000
SALES (est): 654.9K **Privately Held**
SIC: 2834 Vitamin preparations

(G-552)
WOLTERS KLUWER US INC
400 W Main St Ste 244 (11702-3009)
PHONE..................................631 517-8060
Thomas A Lesica, *President*
Bill O'Brien, *Director*
EMP: 30
SALES (corp-wide): 4.5B **Privately Held**
SIC: 2731 Books: publishing only
HQ: Wolters Kluwer United States Inc.
2700 Lake Cook Rd
Riverwoods IL 60015
847 580-5000

Bainbridge
Chenango County

(G-553)
SHEHAWKEN ARCHERY CO INC
40 S Main St (13733-1216)
P.O. Box 187 (13733-0187)
PHONE..................................607 967-8333
Fax: 607 967-2828
EMP: 12
SQ FT: 17,000
SALES (est): 720K **Privately Held**
SIC: 3949 Mfg Archery Equipment

(G-554)
TRIMAC MOLDING SERVICES
13 Pruyn St (13733-1155)
P.O. Box 176 (13733-0176)
PHONE..................................607 967-2900
Linda Pickwick, *Partner*
Harold Pickwick, *Partner*
EMP: 9
SQ FT: 60,000
SALES (est): 1.1MM **Privately Held**
WEB: www.trimacmolding.com
SIC: 3089 Injection molding of plastics

(G-555)
UPTURN INDUSTRIES INC
2-4 Whitney Way (13733)
PHONE..................................607 967-2923
Mike Horoszewski, *CEO*
Donna L Enck, *CEO*
Tomas Mahar, *Business Mgr*
Sharon Delello, *Manager*
Kelly Lanten, *Manager*
▲ **EMP:** 31
SQ FT: 12,000
SALES (est): 5.1MM **Privately Held**
WEB: www.upturnindustries.com
SIC: 3599 Machine shop, jobbing & repair

Bakers Mills
Warren County

(G-556)
CHAD PIERSON
Also Called: Chad Pierson Logging & Trckg
Chad Pierson (12811)
P.O. Box 29 (12811-0029)
PHONE..................................518 251-0186
Chad Pierson, *President*
Melissa Pierson, *Bookkeeper*
EMP: 7
SQ FT: 5,600
SALES (est): 701K **Privately Held**
SIC: 2411 Logging

Baldwin
Nassau County

(G-557)
ELLIQUENCE LLC
2455 Grand Ave (11510-3556)
PHONE..................................516 277-9000
Fax: 516 277-9023
Anthony Carone, *Controller*
Paul Thau, *Controller*
Alan Ellman, *Mng Member*
Jackie Weber, *Manager*
▲ **EMP:** 19
SALES (est): 3.2MM **Privately Held**
SIC: 3841 Surgical & medical instruments

(G-558)
JAL SIGNS INC
Also Called: Sign-A-Rama
540 Merrick Rd (11510-3439)
PHONE..................................516 536-7280
Fax: 516 536-1687
Agnes Lidner, *President*
Jim Lindner, *Manager*
James Lidner, *Admin Sec*
EMP: 10 **EST:** 1999
SALES (est): 1.3MM **Privately Held**
SIC: 3993 Signs & advertising specialties

(G-559)
NOTICIA HISPANOAMERICANA INC
53 E Merrick Rd Ste 353 (11510)
PHONE..................................516 223-5678
Cinthia Diaz, *Owner*
Silvana Diaz, *Publisher*
Jeovanny Mata, *Director*
▲ **EMP:** 30
SALES (est): 913.4K **Privately Held**
SIC: 2711 Newspapers

(G-560)
ROSE FENCE INC
345 Sunrise Hwy (11510)
PHONE..................................516 223-0777
Scott Rose, *Branch Mgr*

EMP: 10
SALES (corp-wide): 20.2MM **Privately Held**
WEB: www.rosefence.com
SIC: 2499 5211 3496 3315 Fencing, wood; fencing; miscellaneous fabricated wire products; steel wire & related products
PA: Rose Fence, Inc.
345 W Sunrise Hwy
Freeport NY 11520
516 223-0777

(G-561)
TECHNICAL PACKAGING INC
2365 Milburn Ave (11510-3349)
P.O. Box 504 (11510-0504)
PHONE..................................516 223-2300
Fax: 516 223-0025
Don Romig, *President*
James Kane, *Vice Pres*
Maureen Romig, *Sales Mgr*
EMP: 15
SALES (est): 3MM **Privately Held**
WEB: www.technicalpackaging.com
SIC: 2653 2441 3053 3086 Corrugated & solid fiber boxes; packing cases, wood: nailed or lock corner; packing materials; packaging & shipping materials, foamed plastic; packaging materials; corrugated & solid fiber boxes

Baldwin Place
Westchester County

(G-562)
GOODWILL INDS OF GREATER NY
80 Route 6 Unit 605 (10505-1033)
PHONE..................................914 621-0781
Herbert Wright, *Principal*
EMP: 138
SALES (corp-wide): 117.3MM **Privately Held**
SIC: 3999 Barber & beauty shop equipment
PA: Goodwill Industries Of Greater New York Inc
421 27th Ave
Astoria NY 11102
718 728-5400

Baldwinsville
Onondaga County

(G-563)
2 ELEMENTS REAL EST LLC
33 Water St (13027-2320)
PHONE..................................315 635-4662
EMP: 5
SALES (est): 115.4K **Privately Held**
SIC: 2819 Elements

(G-564)
ACME SIGNS OF BALDWINSVILLE
3 Marble St (13027-2918)
PHONE..................................315 638-4865
Dennis Sick, *Owner*
EMP: 6
SALES (est): 276.4K **Privately Held**
SIC: 3993 4226 Signs & advertising specialties; special warehousing & storage

(G-565)
ADVANCED RECOVERY & RECYCL LLC
3475 Linda Ln (13027-9217)
PHONE..................................315 450-3301
Byron Tietjen, *President*
Peter Stockmann,
EMP: 10
SALES (est): 667.5K **Privately Held**
SIC: 2611 Pulp mills, mechanical & recycling processing

(G-566)
ANHEUSER-BUSCH LLC
2885 Belgium Rd (13027-2797)
P.O. Box 200 (13027-0200)
PHONE..................................315 638-0365
Fax: 315 635-4404
Howard Triche, *General Mgr*
Chris Lukaczyk, *Area Mgr*
Luis Joo, *Vice Pres*
Stephen McMorick, *Plant Mgr*
Sue Alexander, *Project Mgr*
EMP: 162 **Privately Held**
WEB: www.hispanicbud.com
SIC: 2082 Beer (alcoholic beverage)
HQ: Anheuser-Busch, Llc
1 Busch Pl
Saint Louis MO 63118
314 632-6777

(G-567)
CAPCO MARKETING
Also Called: Gourmet Connection
8417 Oswego Rd 177 (13027-8813)
P.O. Box 1727, Cicero (13039-1727)
PHONE..................................315 699-1687
Kirk Capece, *Owner*
EMP: 10
SALES (est): 453.3K **Privately Held**
WEB: www.capcomarketing.com
SIC: 2721 5812 Magazines: publishing & printing; eating places

(G-568)
FRIEDEL PAPER BOX & CONVERTING
7596 Rania Rd (13027-9399)
PHONE..................................315 437-3325
Nadim Jabaji, *President*
Douglas Andrews, *Manager*
EMP: 7
SALES (est): 1MM **Privately Held**
SIC: 2652 3554 Setup paperboard boxes; die cutting & stamping machinery, paper converting

(G-569)
GIOVANNI FOOD CO INC (PA)
8800 Sixty Rd (13027-1235)
PHONE..................................315 457-2373
Louis J Dement, *Vice Pres*
Tim Budd, *Plant Mgr*
Richard G Latimer, *Plant Mgr*
John Dunn, *Production*
Katie Weber, *Purch Mgr*
◆ **EMP:** 70
SQ FT: 25,000
SALES (est): 13.9MM **Privately Held**
WEB: www.giovannifoods.com
SIC: 2033 Tomato products: packaged in cans, jars, etc.

(G-570)
INDIAN SPRINGS MFG CO INC
2095 W Genesee Rd (13027-8649)
P.O. Box 469 (13027-0469)
PHONE..................................315 635-6101
Fax: 315 635-7473
Maurice J Ferguson, *CEO*
Shawn Ferguson, *President*
Robert Wolniak, *General Mgr*
Donna Miner, *Bookkeeper*
Beth White, *Info Tech Dir*
EMP: 18 **EST:** 1946
SQ FT: 9,000
SALES (est): 4.9MM **Privately Held**
WEB: www.indiansprings.com
SIC: 2812 3599 Chlorine, compressed or liquefied; machine & other job shop work

(G-571)
METROPOLITAN SIGNS INC (PA)
3760 Patchett Rd (13027-9454)
P.O. Box 3062, Liverpool (13089-3062)
PHONE..................................315 638-1448
Fax: 315 638-1509
David R Razzante, *President*
EMP: 7 **EST:** 1970
SQ FT: 4,000
SALES: 600K **Privately Held**
WEB: www.metropolitansigns.com
SIC: 3993 Signs & advertising specialties

(G-572)
PAPERWORKS INDUSTRIES INC
2900 Mclane Rd (13027-1319)
PHONE..................................913 621-0922

GEOGRAPHIC SECTION

Ronald Jenkins, *Principal*
EMP: 10 **EST:** 2013
SALES (est): 1.2MM
SALES (corp-wide): 17.6B **Privately Held**
SIC: 3999 2671 Barber & beauty shop equipment; packaging paper & plastics film, coated & laminated
HQ: Ros-Mar Litho Inc
 19500 Av Clark-Graham
 Baie-D'urfe QC H9X 3
 514 694-2178

(G-573)
PATIENT PORTAL TECH INC (PA)
8276 Willett Pkwy Ste 200 (13027-1328)
PHONE 315 638-2030
Brian Kelly, *CEO*
John O'Mara, *President*
Thomas Hagan, *CFO*
Kevin Kelly, *Director*
EMP: 19
SALES (est): 7.1MM **Publicly Held**
WEB: www.gambinoapparel.com
SIC: 7372 Prepackaged software

(G-574)
SPECIALIZED PACKG GROUP INC (DH)
Also Called: Paperworks
2900 Mclane Rd (13027-1319)
PHONE 315 638-4355
Carlton Highsmith, *Chairman*
Elizabeth Emig-Rosekrans, *Finance*
▲ **EMP:** 2
SALES (est): 48.3MM
SALES (corp-wide): 17.6B **Privately Held**
SIC: 2653 2657 Corrugated & solid fiber boxes; folding paperboard boxes

(G-575)
SPECIALIZED PACKG RADISSON LLC
8800 Sixty Rd (13027-1235)
PHONE 315 638-4355
Robert Gariepy, *COO*
Basciano Leo, *Plant Mgr*
Elizabeth Emig-Rosekrans, *Finance*
Brenda Chapman, *Human Res Dir*
Tom Saylor, *Sales Executive*
EMP: 150 **EST:** 1998
SALES (est): 37.3MM
SALES (corp-wide): 17.6B **Privately Held**
SIC: 2653 2657 Boxes, solid fiber: made from purchased materials; folding paperboard boxes
HQ: The Specialized Packaging Group Inc
 2900 Mclane Rd
 Baldwinsville NY 13027
 315 638-4355

(G-576)
SSAC INC
8242 Loop Rd (13027-1391)
PHONE 800 843-8848
Fax: 315 638-0333
EMP: 21
SALES (est): 3.3MM **Privately Held**
SIC: 3625 Mfg Relays/Industrial Controls

(G-577)
SYRASOFT LLC
6 Canton St (13027-2300)
PHONE 315 708-0341
Fax: 315 708-0819
Thomas Gardener, *Partner*
EMP: 10
SALES (est): 1MM **Privately Held**
WEB: www.syrasoft.com
SIC: 7372 7371 Prepackaged software; custom computer programming services

Ballston Lake
Saratoga County

(G-578)
ASTRO CHEMICAL COMPANY INC
3 Mill Rd (12019-2022)
P.O. Box 1250 (12019-0250)
PHONE 518 399-5338
Fax: 518 399-8859
Duane A Ball, *Ch of Bd*
Jay Arnold, *Manager*
▲ **EMP:** 20
SQ FT: 24,000
SALES (est): 5.7MM **Privately Held**
WEB: www.astrochemical.com
SIC: 2821 Epoxy resins

(G-579)
BENNETT STAIR COMPANY INC
1021 State Route 50 (12019-1915)
PHONE 518 384-1554
Fax: 518 384-1555
Dave Bennett, *President*
EMP: 8
SQ FT: 2,800
SALES: 650K **Privately Held**
SIC: 2431 Staircases, stairs & railings

(G-580)
CBM FABRICATIONS INC
15 Westside Dr (12019-2025)
PHONE 518 399-8023
Fax: 518 399-8064
Charles B McCormack II, *Ch of Bd*
Margaret Spoonogle, *Administration*
EMP: 30
SQ FT: 8,100
SALES (est): 8.4MM **Privately Held**
WEB: www.cbmfab.com
SIC: 3441 7692 3599 3444 Fabricated structural metal; welding repair; machine shop, jobbing & repair; sheet metalwork

(G-581)
LAKESIDE CIDER MILL FARM INC
336 Schauber Rd (12019-2104)
PHONE 518 399-8359
Fax: 518 399-6907
Richard Pearce, *President*
Jeffrey Pearce, *Vice Pres*
EMP: 8 **EST:** 1944
SQ FT: 5,000
SALES (est): 1MM **Privately Held**
SIC: 2099 5812 5431 Cider, nonalcoholic; eating places; vegetable stands or markets

(G-582)
MERCURY PEN COMPANY INC
245 Eastline Rd (12019-1810)
PHONE 518 899-9653
Fax: 518 899-9657
Jody Gentilesco, *President*
▲ **EMP:** 7 **EST:** 1946
SQ FT: 5,000
SALES: 216.6K **Privately Held**
WEB: www.mercurypen.com
SIC: 3951 Ball point pens & parts; penholders & parts; pencils & pencil parts, mechanical

(G-583)
MTS SYSTEMS CORPORATION
30 Gleneagles Blvd (12019-1014)
PHONE 518 899-2140
EMP: 116
SALES (corp-wide): 650.1MM **Publicly Held**
SIC: 3829 Measuring & controlling devices
PA: Mts Systems Corporation
 14000 Technology Dr
 Eden Prairie MN 55344
 952 937-4000

(G-584)
NORTHEAST TONER INC
26 Walden Gln Fl 2 (12019-9234)
PHONE 518 899-5545
Gail Trietiak, *President*
Paul Trietiak, *Vice Pres*
EMP: 7
SALES (est): 800K **Privately Held**
SIC: 3955 Print cartridges for laser & other computer printers

(G-585)
SIXNET LLC
331 Ushers Rd Ste 14 (12019-1546)
P.O. Box 767, Clifton Park (12065-0767)
PHONE 518 877-5173
Fax: 518 877-8346
Steve Schoenberg, *CEO*
Stuart Eaton, *Vice Pres*
Rake W Jiang, *Vice Pres*
Mark Loperano, *Opers Staff*
Michael Mokay, *Engineer*
EMP: 80
SQ FT: 20,000
SALES (est): 12.3MM
SALES (corp-wide): 1.6B **Privately Held**
WEB: www.sixnetio.com
SIC: 3823 Computer interface equipment for industrial process control
HQ: Red Lion Controls, Inc.
 20 Willow Springs Cir
 York PA 17406
 717 767-6961

(G-586)
SIXNET HOLDINGS LLC
331 Ushers Rd Ste 10 (12019-1546)
PHONE 518 877-5173
Jason Koeferl, *Marketing Staff*
Hilton Nicholson,
Jason Koeserl, *Administration*
▲ **EMP:** 5
SALES (est): 7.9MM
SALES (corp-wide): 1.6B **Privately Held**
SIC: 3823 Industrial instrmnts msrmnt display/control process variable
PA: Spectris Plc
 Heritage House
 Egham TW20
 178 447-0470

(G-587)
TJB SUNSHINE ENTERPRISES
6 Redwood Dr (12019-2631)
PHONE 518 384-6483
Tom Brundige, *President*
EMP: 14
SALES (est): 1MM **Privately Held**
SIC: 2842 Window cleaning preparations

Ballston Spa
Saratoga County

(G-588)
ADVANCED COMFORT SYSTEMS INC
Also Called: ACS
12b Commerce Dr (12020-3631)
PHONE 518 884-8444
Fax: 518 884-8411
Roger M Kerr, *President*
Kitty Stake, *Manager*
EMP: 10
SALES (est): 1.9MM **Privately Held**
WEB: www.advancedcomfortsys.com
SIC: 7372 1742 Application computer software; insulation, buildings

(G-589)
ALBATROS NORTH AMERICA INC
Also Called: Sepsa North America
6 Mccrea Hill Rd (12020-5515)
PHONE 518 381-7100
John Hanrahan, *CEO*
Nicholas Fuster, *President*
William D Kolberg, *Finance*
▲ **EMP:** 45
SQ FT: 36,000
SALES (est): 12.2MM
SALES (corp-wide): 538.3MM **Privately Held**
WEB: www.sepsa.es
SIC: 3679 3699 Static power supply converters for electronic applications; security control equipment & systems
HQ: Albatros SI
 Calle De Albatros (Pol Ind La Estaci),
 7 - 9
 Pinto 28320
 914 957-000

(G-590)
ALLYTEX LLC
540 Acland Blvd (12020-3074)
PHONE 518 376-7539
Alison Arakelian,
EMP: 5
SALES (est): 345.1K **Privately Held**
SIC: 2311 Men's & boys' suits & coats

(G-591)
BURNT HILLS FABRICATORS INC
318 Charlton Rd B (12020-3412)
P.O. Box 2, Burnt Hills (12027-0002)
PHONE 518 885-1115
Fax: 518 885-0526
James Fantauzzi, *President*
EMP: 15
SQ FT: 7,000
SALES (est): 1.8MM **Privately Held**
SIC: 3441 Fabricated structural metal

(G-592)
DIGITAL IMAGING TECH LLC
425 Eastline Rd D (12020-3617)
PHONE 518 885-4400
Fax: 518 885-4423
Michael Marino, *Mng Member*
Richard Siciliano,
EMP: 6
SQ FT: 5,000
SALES: 1MM **Privately Held**
WEB: www.digimtech.com
SIC: 2752 Commercial printing, lithographic

(G-593)
DIT PRINTS INCORPORATED
Also Called: Digital Imiging Technologies
425 Eastline Rd Ste D (12020-3617)
PHONE 518 885-4400
Deborah Libratore Le Blanc, *President*
Paul Le Blanc, *General Mgr*
EMP: 5
SQ FT: 2,400
SALES (est): 426.9K **Privately Held**
SIC: 2759 Commercial printing

(G-594)
DURA-MILL INC
Also Called: Newco Products Division
16 Stonebreak Rd (12020)
PHONE 518 899-2255
Fax: 518 899-7869
Richard J Walrath, *President*
David Walrath, *Vice Pres*
Suzanne Walrath, *Accounting Mgr*
EMP: 33
SALES (est): 8MM **Privately Held**
WEB: www.duramill.com
SIC: 3545 5085 Cutting tools for machine tools; industrial supplies; abrasives; bearings, bushings, wheels & gears; industrial wheels

(G-595)
GLOBALFOUNDRIES US INC
107 Hermes Rd (12020-4534)
PHONE 408 462-3900
Jason Cargin, *Engineer*
Aaron Sinnott, *Engineer*
James Depasquale, *Finance Mgr*
Norman Armour, *Branch Mgr*
Al Frank, *Manager*
EMP: 19
SALES (corp-wide): 8.5B **Privately Held**
SIC: 3369 3674 Nonferrous foundries; integrated circuits, semiconductor networks, etc.
HQ: Globalfoundries U.S. Inc.
 2600 Great America Way
 Santa Clara CA 95054

(G-596)
GREAT AMERICAN AWNING & PATIO
43 Round Lake Rd (12020)
PHONE 518 899-2300
Frank Rasalik, *President*
EMP: 15
SALES (est): 1.2MM **Privately Held**
SIC: 3271 Blocks, concrete: chimney or fireplace

(G-597)
HARVEST TECHNOLOGIES INC
36 Featherfoil Way (12020-4371)
PHONE 518 899-7124
Donna Morris, *Partner*
Turk Ellis, *Partner*
EMP: 2
SALES: 2MM **Privately Held**
SIC: 2611 Pulp manufactured from waste or recycled paper

Ballston Spa - Saratoga County (G-598)

(G-598)
JOHNSON CONTROLS INC
339 Brownell Rd (12020-3705)
PHONE..................518 884-8313
David Bardsley, *Branch Mgr*
EMP: 95 Privately Held
SIC: 2531 Seats, automobile
HQ: Johnson Controls, Inc.
5757 N Green Bay Ave
Milwaukee WI 53209
414 524-1200

(G-599)
LANE ENTERPRISES INC
825 State Route 67 (12020-3604)
PHONE..................518 885-4385
M J Cathers, *Branch Mgr*
EMP: 20
SALES (corp-wide): 70.5MM Privately Held
WEB: www.lanepipe.com
SIC: 3444 3449 Pipe, sheet metal; miscellaneous metalwork
PA: Lane Enterprises, Inc.
3905 Hartzdale Dr Ste 514
Camp Hill PA 17011
717 761-8175

(G-600)
LEMANS CORPORATION
Also Called: Drag Specialties
10 Mccrea Hill Rd (12020-5515)
PHONE..................518 885-7500
Mike Cornell, *Manager*
▲ EMP: 9
SALES (corp-wide): 662.8MM Privately Held
SIC: 3714 Acceleration equipment, motor vehicle
PA: Lemans Corporation
3501 Kennedy Rd
Janesville WI 53545
608 758-1111

(G-601)
MAGSOFT CORPORATION
2715 State Route 9 # 102 (12020-5306)
PHONE..................518 877-8390
Sheppard Salon, *President*
Brenda Beard, *General Mgr*
Philippe F Wendling, *Exec VP*
EMP: 9
SQ FT: 3,500
SALES: 840K
SALES (corp-wide): 1.6B Publicly Held
WEB: www.magsoft-flux.com
SIC: 7372 7371 Prepackaged software; computer software development & applications
PA: Altair Engineering Inc.
1820 E Big Beaver Rd
Troy MI 48083
248 614-2400

(G-602)
MERIDIAN MANUFACTURING INC
27 Kent St Ste 103a (12020-1543)
PHONE..................518 885-0450
Paul Michael, *President*
Robin Guarino, *Vice Pres*
EMP: 7
SQ FT: 8,100
SALES (est): 1.1MM Privately Held
SIC: 3599 Machine shop, jobbing & repair

(G-603)
MESSENGER PRESS
1826 Amsterdam Rd (12020-3323)
P.O. Box 376 (12020-0376)
PHONE..................518 885-9231
Ed Bellamy, *Owner*
EMP: 8
SALES (est): 460K Privately Held
SIC: 2752 7336 Lithographic Commercial Printing/Commercial Art/Graphic Design

(G-604)
NORTH AMERICAN SVCS GROUP LLC (HQ)
Also Called: North American Service Group
1240 Saratoga Rd (12020-3500)
PHONE..................518 885-1820
Fax: 518 885-7638
Frank Zilka, *President*
Rick Matteson, *General Mgr*
Will Hearn, *Regional Mgr*
Tim Zilka, *COO*
Matthew Greene, *Project Mgr*
EMP: 15
SQ FT: 40,000
SALES (est): 5.6MM Privately Held
SIC: 3443 1799 Cryogenic tanks, for liquids & gases; service station equipment installation, maintenance & repair

(G-605)
NORTHWIND GRAPHICS
2453 State Route 9 (12020-4407)
PHONE..................518 899-9651
Steve Richardson, *Owner*
EMP: 5
SQ FT: 3,500
SALES (est): 420.9K Privately Held
SIC: 2759 Screen printing

(G-606)
PREMIUM BLDG COMPONENTS INC
831 Rt 67 Bldg 46 (12020)
PHONE..................518 885-0194
John Buyaskas, *Principal*
EMP: 20
SALES (corp-wide): 7.1MM Privately Held
SIC: 3713 Truck & bus bodies
PA: Premium Building Components, Inc.
527 Queensbury Ave
Queensbury NY 12804
518 792-0189

(G-607)
SAND HILL INDUSTRIES INC
Also Called: T-Shirt Graphics
12 Grove St (12020-1814)
PHONE..................518 885-7991
Fax: 518 885-8068
Dennis Albright, *President*
Eileen Albright, *Vice Pres*
EMP: 6
SQ FT: 10,000
SALES (est): 560K Privately Held
WEB: www.t-shirtgraphics.com
SIC: 2759 2395 2752 3081 Screen printing; embroidery & art needlework; commercial printing, offset; unsupported plastics film & sheet

(G-608)
SPECIALTY SILICONE PDTS INC
Also Called: SSP
3 Mccrea Hill Rd (12020-5511)
PHONE..................518 885-8826
Fax: 518 885-4682
Daniel Natarelli, *CEO*
Randall Putnam, *President*
Paul Decaprio, *COO*
Patricia S Babbie, *Senior VP*
Ned REO, *Senior VP*
▲ EMP: 45
SQ FT: 37,000
SALES (est): 12.2MM Privately Held
WEB: www.sspinc.com
SIC: 2869 2822 3714 2992 Silicones; silicone rubbers; motor vehicle parts & accessories; lubricating oils & greases

(G-609)
STEWARTS PROCESSING CORP (PA)
2907 State Route 9 (12020-4201)
P.O. Box 435, Saratoga Springs (12866-0435)
PHONE..................518 581-1200
Gary C Dake, *Ch of Bd*
Michael Cocca, *Treasurer*
David Farr, *Asst Treas*
Lanyel Brandon, *Manager*
Erica Maree, *Manager*
EMP: 85
SALES: 59.1MM Privately Held
SIC: 2026 2024 2086 Fluid milk; ice cream & ice milk; soft drinks: packaged in cans, bottles, etc.

(G-610)
WINDOW TECH SYSTEMS INC
15 Old Stonebreak Rd (12020-4900)
P.O. Box 2260 (12020-8260)
PHONE..................518 899-9000
Fax: 518 899-4104
David L Bangert, *President*
Dave Bangert, *President*
Tracy Carpenter, *Manager*
Tracy Mason, *Admin Asst*
EMP: 22 EST: 1952
SQ FT: 30,000
SALES (est): 4.8MM Privately Held
WEB: www.windowtechsystems.net
SIC: 3442 3089 Screens, window, metal; windows, plastic

Barker
Niagara County

(G-611)
ATLANTIC TRANSFORMER INC
1674 Quaker Rd (14012-9616)
P.O. Box 276 (14012-0276)
PHONE..................716 795-3258
Fax: 716 795-3101
John Khorrami, *President*
EMP: 10
SQ FT: 8,500
SALES: 400K Privately Held
WEB: www.mgs4u.com
SIC: 3677 Electronic transformers

(G-612)
JT PRECISION INC
8701 Haight Rd (14012-9630)
PHONE..................716 795-3860
Jeff Thuman Sr, *President*
Brian Rakfeldt, *General Mgr*
Richard Meyers, *Principal*
Sarah Munn, *Principal*
Cristine O'Keefe, *Officer*
EMP: 34
SALES: 3MM Privately Held
SIC: 3714 Motor vehicle engines & parts

Barneveld
Oneida County

(G-613)
JET SEW CORPORATION
8119 State Route 12 (13304-2105)
PHONE..................315 896-2683
Edward Wiehl, *President*
EMP: 15
SQ FT: 65,000
SALES: 550K Privately Held
WEB: www.jetsew.com
SIC: 3599 Custom machinery

(G-614)
METAL PARTS MANUFACTURING INC
119 Remsen Rd (13304-2407)
PHONE..................315 831-2530
Fax: 315 831-2397
William Noeth, *President*
Paul Lopus, *Admin Sec*
EMP: 5
SQ FT: 3,000
SALES: 375K Privately Held
WEB: www.mpminc.net
SIC: 3599 Machine shop, jobbing & repair

(G-615)
MOHAWK ELECTRO TECHNIQUES INC
7677 Cameron Hill Rd (13304-1917)
PHONE..................315 896-2661
Fax: 315 896-2954
Lee Broomfield, *President*
Fred Ingo, *Vice Pres*
Mike Locke, *Manager*
Kathy Hite, *Officer*
EMP: 90
SQ FT: 5,000
SALES (est): 10MM Privately Held
SIC: 3677 Coil windings, electronic; electronic transformers

(G-616)
ROLLING STAR MANUFACTURING INC
125 Liberty Ln (13304-2537)
P.O. Box 471 (13304-0471)
PHONE..................315 896-4767
Fax: 315 896-5055
Jamie R Servello, *President*
Dean Beck, *Vice Pres*
Melissa Parzych, *Manager*
EMP: 20
SQ FT: 2,728
SALES (est): 3.8MM Privately Held
WEB: www.customizedtrailers.com
SIC: 3799 Trailers & trailer equipment

(G-617)
SAMPO INC
Also Called: Donmaar Enterprises
119 Remsen Rd (13304-2407)
P.O. Box 109, Rome (13442-0109)
PHONE..................315 896-2606
Brian Butts, *President*
EMP: 23
SQ FT: 12,038
SALES (est): 2MM Privately Held
WEB: www.sampoinc.com
SIC: 3949 2298 Fishing equipment; cordage & twine

(G-618)
SQUARE STAMPING MFG CORP
108 Old Remsen Rd (13304)
PHONE..................315 896-2641
Fax: 315 896-2734
David Allen, *President*
Dan Hart, *General Mgr*
Edward Allen III, *Treasurer*
Jeffrey Gouger, *Treasurer*
Beth McGovern, *Office Mgr*
EMP: 35 EST: 1926
SQ FT: 25,000
SALES (est): 7MM Privately Held
WEB: www.squarestamping.com
SIC: 3469 Stamping metal for the trade

Barrytown
Dutchess County

(G-619)
STATION HILL OF BARRYTOWN
120 Station Hill Rd (12507-5018)
PHONE..................845 758-5293
Fax: 845 758-8163
George Quasha, *President*
Susan Quasha, *Vice Pres*
Siu Yuen, *Marketing Staff*
EMP: 6
SALES (est): 423.6K Privately Held
SIC: 2731 5961 Book publishing; book club, mail order; record &/or tape (music or video) club, mail order

Barryville
Sullivan County

(G-620)
N A R ASSOCIATES INC
128 Rte 55 (12719)
P.O. Box 233 (12719-0233)
PHONE..................845 557-8713
Fax: 845 557-6770
Nick A Roes, *President*
Nancy Bennett, *Vice Pres*
EMP: 6
SALES (est): 537.5K Privately Held
WEB: www.nickroes.com
SIC: 2731 Book publishing

Batavia
Genesee County

(G-621)
ALICIA F HERDLEIN
Also Called: Extreme Streetwear
5450 E Main Street Rd (14020-9625)
PHONE..................585 344-4411
Herdlein F Alicia, *Owner*
Alicia Herdlein, *Owner*
EMP: 5
SALES: 500K Privately Held
SIC: 2759 Screen printing

GEOGRAPHIC SECTION — Batavia - Genesee County (G-645)

(G-622)
ALPINA FOODS INC
5011 Agpark Dr W (14020-3446)
PHONE..................855 886-1914
Carlos Mejia, *Principal*
EMP: 13
SALES (est): 1.7MM **Privately Held**
SIC: 2023 Dry, condensed, evaporated dairy products
PA: Alpina Productos Alimenticios S A
   Via Briceno Sopo Kilometro 3
   Sopo

(G-623)
AMADA TOOL AMERICA INC
4 Treadeasy Ave Ste A (14020-3010)
PHONE..................585 344-3900
Hitoshi Iizuka, *President*
Michael Guerin, *Corp Secy*
Don Grower, *Manager*
▲ EMP: 55
SQ FT: 50,000
SALES (est): 9.4MM
SALES (corp-wide): 2.4B **Privately Held**
SIC: 3544 Special dies & tools
HQ: Amada North America, Inc
   7025 Firestone Blvd
   Buena Park CA 90621

(G-624)
AUTOMOTIVE LLC
4320 Federal Dr (14020-4104)
PHONE..................248 728-8642
Douglas Delgrosso, *CEO*
EMP: 15
SALES (est): 2MM
SALES (corp-wide): 1.3B **Privately Held**
WEB: www.automotivecorporation.com
SIC: 3465 Body parts, automobile: stamped metal
HQ: Chassix, Inc.
   300 Galleria Ofcntr # 501
   Southfield MI 48034
   248 728-8642

(G-625)
BATAVIA PRESS LLC
3817 W Main Street Rd (14020-9402)
PHONE..................585 343-4429
Becky Almeter, *Partner*
Robert Hodgins,
EMP: 32
SALES (est): 1.5MM **Privately Held**
SIC: 2752 7389 2759 Business form & card printing, lithographic; document embossing; engrossing: diplomas, resolutions, etc.; invitation & stationery printing & engraving; security certificates: engraved

(G-626)
BILL SHEA ENTERPRISES INC
Also Called: Deluxe Machine & Tool Co
8825 Alexander Rd (14020-9581)
PHONE..................585 343-2284
Fax: 585 343-0480
William Shea, *President*
Ken Lowell, *General Mgr*
Steven Shea, *Vice Pres*
EMP: 2
SQ FT: 20,000
SALES (est): 1.1MM **Privately Held**
WEB: www.trojanloaders.com
SIC: 3599 Machine shop, jobbing & repair

(G-627)
BRACH MACHINE INC
4814 Ellicott Street Rd (14020-3420)
PHONE..................585 343-9134
Fax: 585 343-1292
William H Brach, *President*
Nancy E Brach, *Vice Pres*
▲ EMP: 12
SQ FT: 15,000
SALES (est): 1.7MM **Privately Held**
WEB: www.brachmachine.com
SIC: 3469 Machine parts, stamped or pressed metal

(G-628)
CHAPIN INTERNATIONAL INC
700 Ellicott St (14020-3744)
P.O. Box 549 (14021-0549)
PHONE..................585 343-3140
Andris K Chapin, *Ch of Bd*
James W Campbell, *President*
James Grant, *Vice Pres*
William Kegler, *Materials Mgr*
Greg Klein, *Engineer*
◆ EMP: 225
SQ FT: 710,000
SALES (est): 24.7MM
SALES (corp-wide): 50.1MM **Privately Held**
SIC: 3499 3524 3085 3563 Aerosol valves, metal; lawn & garden equipment; plastics bottles; air & gas compressors
PA: Chapin Manufacturing, Inc
   700 Ellicott St Ste 3
   Batavia NY 14020
   585 343-3140

(G-629)
CHAPIN MANUFACTURING INC (PA)
700 Ellicott St Ste 3 (14020-3794)
P.O. Box 549 (14021-0549)
PHONE..................585 343-3140
Fax: 585 344-1775
James W Campbell, *Ch of Bd*
Andris K Chapin, *Ch of Bd*
James Grant, *Vice Pres*
Robert C Mathis, *Vice Pres*
Lorie Anderson, *Purch Agent*
◆ EMP: 220
SQ FT: 710,000
SALES (est): 50.1MM **Privately Held**
WEB: www.chapinmfg.com
SIC: 3499 3524 3085 3563 Aerosol valves, metal; lawn & garden equipment; plastics bottles; air & gas compressors; spraying outfits: metals, paints & chemicals (compressor); spreaders, fertilizer

(G-630)
CONSOLIDATED CONTAINER CO LLC
Also Called: Liquitane
14 Hall St (14020-3216)
PHONE..................585 343-9351
Fax: 585 343-0086
Bob Henry, *Facilities Mgr*
Michael Campbell, *Manager*
Robert Henri, *Manager*
Sharon Cummings, *Office Admin*
James Cervi, *Executive*
EMP: 15
SALES (corp-wide): 13.1B **Publicly Held**
WEB: www.ccellc.com
SIC: 3089 Plastic containers, except foam
HQ: Consolidated Container Company, Llc
   3101 Towercreek Pkwy Se
   Atlanta GA 30339
   678 742-4600

(G-631)
COUNTRY FOLKS
123 N Spruce St (14020-2611)
PHONE..................585 343-9721
Patrick Berg, *Principal*
EMP: 5
SALES (est): 196.4K **Privately Held**
SIC: 2711 Newspapers

(G-632)
DAIRY FARMERS AMERICA INC
Also Called: Muller Quaker Dairy
5140 Agi Business Pk Dr W (14020)
PHONE..................585 409-2200
Rick Smith, *Branch Mgr*
EMP: 156
SALES (corp-wide): 13.5B **Privately Held**
SIC: 2023 Dried & powdered milk & milk products
PA: Dairy Farmers Of America, Inc.
   1405 N 98th St
   Kansas City KS 66111
   816 801-6455

(G-633)
EXIDE TECHNOLOGIES
Also Called: Exide Batteries
4330 Commerce Dr (14020-4102)
PHONE..................585 344-0656
Sam Manuele, *Sales/Mktg Mgr*
Deborah Cravatta, *Manager*
Michael Ellis, *Supervisor*
EMP: 9
SALES (corp-wide): 2.4B **Privately Held**
WEB: www.exideworld.com
SIC: 3691 Lead acid batteries (storage batteries)
PA: Exide Technologies
   13000 Deerfield Pkwy # 200
   Milton GA 30004
   678 566-9000

(G-634)
FONTRICK DOOR INC
9 Apollo Dr (14020-3001)
PHONE..................585 345-6032
Fax: 585 345-6033
Michael J Fontaine, *CEO*
Jacob Mingle, *Engineer*
Judy Brown, *Bookkeeper*
EMP: 30
SQ FT: 26,000
SALES (est): 5.2MM **Privately Held**
WEB: www.fontrickdoor.com
SIC: 2431 1751 Doors & door parts & trim, wood; cabinet building & installation

(G-635)
FRITO-LAY NORTH AMERICA INC
8063 Kelsey Rd (14020-9433)
PHONE..................585 343-5456
Keith Matteson, *Branch Mgr*
EMP: 20
SALES (corp-wide): 62.8B **Publicly Held**
WEB: www.fritolay.com
SIC: 2096 Potato chips & similar snacks
HQ: Frito-Lay North America, Inc.
   7701 Legacy Dr
   Plano TX 75024

(G-636)
GENESEE PRECISION INC
4300 Commerce Dr (14020-4102)
PHONE..................585 344-0385
Robert Shepard, *President*
Patricia Vincent, *Corp Secy*
Gregory Almeter, *Vice Pres*
Patty Drew, *Admin Asst*
▲ EMP: 43
SQ FT: 24,000
SALES (est): 4.1MM **Privately Held**
SIC: 3544 3089 Special dies, tools, jigs & fixtures; injection molding of plastics

(G-637)
GEORGIA-PACIFIC CORRUGARED LLC
Also Called: Majic Corrugated Inc
4 Etreadeasy Ave (14020)
PHONE..................585 343-3800
Fax: 585 343-5236
Andrew Perkins, *Manager*
EMP: 65
SALES (est): 9.4MM
SALES (corp-wide): 27.8B **Privately Held**
WEB: www.gp.com
SIC: 2611 Pulp manufactured from waste or recycled paper
HQ: Georgia-Pacific Llc
   133 Peachtree St Ne # 4810
   Atlanta GA 30303
   404 652-4000

(G-638)
GRAHAM CORPORATION (PA)
20 Florence Ave (14020-3318)
PHONE..................585 343-2216
Fax: 585 343-1097
James J Malvaso, *Ch of Bd*
James R Lines, *President*
Alan E Smith, *Vice Pres*
Michele Engle, *Buyer*
Ken Salphine, *Engineer*
◆ EMP: 368
SQ FT: 45,000
SALES: 91.7MM **Publicly Held**
WEB: www.graham-mfg.com
SIC: 3563 3585 3443 Vacuum pumps, except laboratory; compressors for refrigeration & air conditioning equipment; condensers, refrigeration; heat exchangers, condensers & components; heat exchangers, plate type; heat exchangers: coolers (after, inter), condensers, etc.

(G-639)
HEATH MANUFACTURING COMPANY
Also Called: Heath Outdoors Products
700 Ellicott St (14020-3744)
PHONE..................800 444-3140
EMP: 6
SALES (corp-wide): 50.1MM **Privately Held**
SIC: 2048 Bird food, prepared
HQ: Heath Manufacturing Company
   140 Mill St Ste A
   Coopersville MI 49404
   616 997-8181

(G-640)
HODGINS ENGRAVING CO INC
3817 W Main Street Rd (14020-9402)
PHONE..................585 343-4444
Fax: 585 343-0412
Robert Hodgins, *President*
Elaine Skoczylas, *Purch Agent*
Becky Hodgins, *Cust Mgr*
Kathleen Dixson, *Comms Mgr*
Becky Almeter, *Manager*
◆ EMP: 70
SQ FT: 36,000
SALES (est): 13MM **Privately Held**
WEB: www.hodginsengraving.com
SIC: 3555 3953 Printing trades machinery; marking devices

(G-641)
INTERSTATE CHEMICAL CO INC
4 Treadeasy Ave (14020-3089)
PHONE..................585 344-2822
Fax: 585 344-2608
Mark Shea, *Sales Staff*
Jeff Heverly, *Branch Mgr*
Jeff Heverley, *Executive*
EMP: 11
SQ FT: 72,000
SALES (corp-wide): 349MM **Privately Held**
WEB: www.interstatechemical.com
SIC: 2819 Industrial inorganic chemicals
PA: Interstate Chemical Company, Inc.
   2797 Freedland Rd
   Hermitage PA 16148
   724 981-3771

(G-642)
LICKITY SPLITS
238 East Ave (14020-2704)
PHONE..................585 345-6091
Fred Hamilton, *Partner*
Craig Hargrades, *Partner*
EMP: 8
SALES (est): 508K **Privately Held**
SIC: 2024 Ice cream & frozen desserts

(G-643)
MONDELEZ GLOBAL LLC
Also Called: Nabisco
4303 Federal Dr (14020-4105)
PHONE..................585 345-3300
Phil Barter, *Branch Mgr*
Anthony Del Duca, *Maintence Staff*
EMP: 9 **Publicly Held**
SIC: 2099 5141 Food preparations; groceries, general line
HQ: Mondelez Global Llc
   3 Parkway N Ste 300
   Deerfield IL 60015
   847 943-4000

(G-644)
N Y WESTERN CONCRETE CORP
638 E Main St (14020-2812)
PHONE..................585 343-6850
Fax: 585 343-8440
Joseph Penepent, *President*
Eugene Penepent, *Vice Pres*
Vincent Penepent, *Treasurer*
Jeanne Penepent, *Manager*
EMP: 5 EST: 1950
SQ FT: 2,000
SALES (est): 1.3MM **Privately Held**
SIC: 3273 Ready-mixed concrete

(G-645)
O-AT-KA MILK PRODUCTS COOP INC (PA)
700 Ellicott St (14020-3744)
P.O. Box 718 (14021-0718)
PHONE..................585 343-0536
Fax: 585 343-4473
Robert Hall, *CEO*
Herbert Nobles, *Ch of Bd*
Mac McCampbell, *COO*
Dan Wolf, *COO*

Batavia - Genesee County (G-646)

Clyde Rutherford, *Vice Pres*
◆ **EMP:** 277 **EST:** 1956
SQ FT: 205,000
SALES: 500.1MM **Privately Held**
WEB: www.oatkamilk.com
SIC: 2023 2021 2026 Concentrated skim milk; evaporated milk; dried nonfat milk; creamery butter; fluid milk

(G-646)
PINNACLE MANUFACTURING CO INC
56 Harvester Ave (14020-3357)
P.O. Box 1446 (14021-1446)
PHONE.................................585 343-5664
Fax: 585 344-3099
Kim Kisiel, *President*
Kevin Kisiel, *Vice Pres*
Luis Pulviro, *Plant Mgr*
Kevin Bishoff, *Foreman/Supr*
Kelly Boyle, *QC Mgr*
▲ **EMP:** 25
SQ FT: 35,000
SALES (est): 6.1MM **Privately Held**
WEB: www.pinnaclemanufacturing.com
SIC: 3363 3364 Aluminum die-castings; zinc & zinc-base alloy die-castings

(G-647)
SEVEN SPRINGS GRAVEL PDTS LLC
8479 Seven Springs Rd (14020-9632)
PHONE.................................585 343-4336
Mike Doyle
Carmen Pariso,
EMP: 6
SALES (est): 570K **Privately Held**
SIC: 1442 Gravel mining

(G-648)
STRONG FORGE & FABRICATION
20 Liberty St (14020-3208)
P.O. Box 803 (14021-0803)
PHONE.................................585 343-5251
Mitchell Strong, *President*
Debbie Buchinger, *Manager*
Brian Delillo, *Manager*
EMP: 37
SALES (est): 7.2MM **Privately Held**
WEB: www.strongforge.com
SIC: 3599 Machine shop, jobbing & repair

(G-649)
SUMMIT LUBRICANTS INC
4d Treadeasy Ave (14020-3010)
P.O. Box 966 (14021-0966)
PHONE.................................585 815-0798
Fax: 585 344-4302
Ronald Krol, *President*
Brian Caputi, *Accountant*
Anne Nelson, *Human Res Mgr*
Donna Kurek, *Manager*
Danielle Brinkman, *Administration*
▲ **EMP:** 47
SQ FT: 50,000
SALES (est): 13.9MM
SALES (corp-wide): 746.6MM **Publicly Held**
WEB: www.summitlubricants.com
SIC: 2911 Greases, lubricating
PA: Quaker Chemical Corporation
901 E Hector St
Conshohocken PA 19428
610 832-4000

(G-650)
TOMPKINS METAL FINISHING INC
6 Apollo Dr (14020-3002)
PHONE.................................585 344-2600
Allen C Tompkins, *President*
John Tompkins, *Vice Pres*
Bill Schuler, *Safety Mgr*
Jim McCarrick, *QC Mgr*
Dan Peashey, *Info Tech Mgr*
EMP: 80
SALES (est): 16.2MM **Privately Held**
SIC: 3559 Metal finishing equipment for plating, etc.

(G-651)
TRACO MANUFACTURING INC
4300 Commerce Dr (14020-4102)
PHONE.................................585 343-2434
Fax: 585 343-2881
Tracy Jachimowicz, *President*
Daniel Jachimowicz, *Vice Pres*
Dave Morrill, *Mfg Staff*
Gary Buchholz, *Regl Sales Mgr*
Vince Pilletteri, *Sales Engr*
EMP: 5
SQ FT: 16,500
SALES (est): 582K **Privately Held**
WEB: www.tracomfg.com
SIC: 2542 Partitions & fixtures, except wood

(G-652)
VISUAL IMPACT GRAPHICS INC
653 Ellicott St Ste 6 (14020-3746)
P.O. Box 236, Byron (14422-0236)
PHONE.................................585 548-7118
Fax: 585 548-7139
Tom Chapell, *President*
EMP: 6
SALES (est): 497.9K **Privately Held**
WEB: www.visualimpactonline.com
SIC: 3993 Signs & advertising specialties

Bath
Steuben County

(G-653)
BABCOCK CO INC
36 Delaware Ave (14810-1607)
PHONE.................................607 776-3341
Mark McConnell, *President*
J Ward McConnell, *Chairman*
EMP: 25
SQ FT: 107,000
SALES (est): 4.9MM **Privately Held**
SIC: 2499 Ladders, wood

(G-654)
BOMBARDIER TRNSP HOLDINGS USA
7940 State Route 415 (14810-7571)
PHONE.................................607 776-4791
Carl Drum, *Branch Mgr*
EMP: 60
SALES (corp-wide): 16.3B **Privately Held**
SIC: 3441 8711 3799 3585 Fabricated structural metal; engineering services; cars, off-highway: electric; refrigeration & heating equipment; electrical apparatus & equipment; electrical equipment & supplies
HQ: Bombardier Transportation (Holdings) Usa Inc.
1501 Lebanon Church Rd
Pittsburgh PA 15236
412 655-5700

(G-655)
CLARK SPECIALTY CO INC
7185 State Route 54 (14810-9502)
PHONE.................................607 776-3193
Fax: 607 569-3694
James L Presley, *Ch of Bd*
Thomas Presley, *Vice Pres*
Robert Schuck, *Plant Mgr*
Gene Patterson, *Opers Staff*
Robert Abbey, *Purch Mgr*
EMP: 37 **EST:** 1946
SQ FT: 90,000
SALES (est): 6.2MM **Privately Held**
WEB: www.clarkspecialty.com
SIC: 2542 3444 Telephone booths: except wood; sheet metalwork

(G-656)
GATEHOUSE MEDIA LLC
Also Called: Steuben Courier Advocate
10 W Steuben St (14810-1512)
PHONE.................................607 776-2121
Fax: 607 776-3967
Karen Causer, *Manager*
EMP: 7
SQ FT: 3,700
SALES (corp-wide): 1.2B **Publicly Held**
WEB: www.gatehousemedia.com
SIC: 2711 Newspapers: publishing only, not printed on site
HQ: Gatehouse Media, Llc
175 Sullys Trl Ste 300
Pittsford NY 14534
585 598-0030

(G-657)
HANGER PRSTHETCS & ORTHO INC
47 W Steuben St (14810-1540)
PHONE.................................607 776-8013
Erico Webster, *General Mgr*
EMP: 7
SALES (corp-wide): 451.4MM **Publicly Held**
SIC: 3842 Orthopedic appliances
HQ: Hanger Prosthetics & Orthotics, Inc.
10910 Domain Dr Ste 300
Austin TX 78758
512 777-3800

(G-658)
KEELER SERVICES
47 W Steuben St Ste 4 (14810-1540)
PHONE.................................607 776-5757
Fax: 607 776-5777
Mathew Keeler, *Owner*
EMP: 6
SQ FT: 6,270
SALES (est): 412.1K **Privately Held**
SIC: 3585 Heating & air conditioning combination units

(G-659)
KNIGHT STTLEMENT SAND GRAV LLC
7291 County Route 15 (14810-8245)
P.O. Box 191 (14810-0191)
PHONE.................................607 776-2048
Fax: 607 776-2691
Tom Roye, *Controller*
Bryan Dickson,
Brett Dickson,
L Jay Dickson,
EMP: 38
SQ FT: 9,408
SALES (est): 6.3MM **Privately Held**
SIC: 1442 Gravel mining

(G-660)
LANE ENTERPRISES INC
Also Called: Lane Metal Products
16 May St (14810-9716)
PHONE.................................607 776-3366
Fax: 607 776-3899
Richard A Walter, *Manager*
EMP: 10
SQ FT: 18,416
SALES (corp-wide): 70.5MM **Privately Held**
WEB: www.lanepipe.com
SIC: 3443 Culverts, metal plate
PA: Lane Enterprises, Inc.
3905 Hartzdale Dr Ste 514
Camp Hill PA 17011
717 761-8175

(G-661)
PHILIPS ELEC N AMER CORP
Philips Lighting
7265 State Route 54 (14810-9586)
PHONE.................................607 776-3692
Fax: 607 776-3892
Ken Greenwood, *Engineer*
Tom Mason, *Engineer*
Gerry Greaney, *Project Engr*
Alexander Dunaevsky, *Senior Engr*
Mike Schaffner, *Electrical Engi*
EMP: 110
SALES (corp-wide): 25.9B **Privately Held**
WEB: www.usa.philips.com
SIC: 3645 3641 Residential lighting fixtures; electric lamps
HQ: Philips North America Llc
3000 Minuteman Rd Ms1203
Andover MA 01810
978 659-3000

(G-662)
SMART SYSTEMS INC
320 E Washington St (14810-1323)
P.O. Box 158, Bohemia (11716-0158)
PHONE.................................607 776-5380
Fax: 607 776-5383
Marven Smith, *President*
EMP: 20
SALES (est): 2.2MM **Privately Held**
WEB: www.smartsystemsinc.org
SIC: 3711 5012 Snow plows (motor vehicles), assembly of; truck bodies

Bay Shore
Suffolk County

(G-663)
A AND K MACHINE AND WELDING
20 Drexel Dr (11706-2202)
P.O. Box 713, Deer Park (11729-0713)
PHONE.................................631 231-2552
Fax: 631 231-1616
Kenneth Melin, *President*
EMP: 5
SQ FT: 6,000
SALES (est): 300K **Privately Held**
SIC: 3599 1799 5046 Machine & other job shop work; custom machinery; welding on site; commercial cooking & food service equipment

(G-664)
ABS TALKX INC
34 Cleveland Ave (11706-1223)
PHONE.................................631 254-9100
Ron Bregman, *President*
Chuck Hedge, *Opers Staff*
EMP: 8
SQ FT: 7,300
SALES (est): 890K **Privately Held**
SIC: 3661 5999 4813 Telephones & telephone apparatus; telephone equipment & systems; voice telephone communications

(G-665)
ADEPTRONICS INCORPORATED
Also Called: Ziptswitch
281 Skip Ln Ste C (11706-1215)
PHONE.................................631 667-0659
EMP: 6
SALES: 850K **Privately Held**
SIC: 3625 Mfg Relays/Industrial Controls

(G-666)
AIR INDUSTRIES MACHINING CORP
1460 5th Ave (11706-4147)
PHONE.................................631 968-5000
Fax: 631 968-5775
Anthony Fabbo, *General Mgr*
Kerry Lamarca, *Purch Agent*
Denise Pilaccio, *Purch Agent*
Michael Recca, *CFO*
Gary Settoducato, *Manager*
▲ **EMP:** 172
SQ FT: 76,000
SALES (est): 31.4MM
SALES (corp-wide): 66.9MM **Publicly Held**
SIC: 3728 Aircraft parts & equipment
PA: Air Industries Group
3609 Motor Pkwy Ste 100
Hauppauge NY 11788
631 881-4920

(G-667)
ALL STAR CARTS & VEHICLES INC
1565 5th Industrial Ct B (11706-3434)
PHONE.................................631 666-5581
Fax: 631 666-1319
Steven Kronrad, *President*
Robert Conrad, *Vice Pres*
Gregory Kronrad, *Vice Pres*
Robert Kronrad, *Vice Pres*
Syed Zadi, *Accountant*
EMP: 51
SQ FT: 25,000
SALES (est): 8.7MM **Privately Held**
WEB: www.allstarcarts.com
SIC: 2599 3792 3444 2451 Carts, restaurant equipment; travel trailers & campers; sheet metalwork; mobile homes

(G-668)
ALTEC DATACOM LLC
70 Corbin Ave Ste I (11706-1039)
PHONE.................................631 242-2417
Fax: 631 242-2475
John Andreala, *Office Mgr*
Abraham Mendez,
Teresa Mendez,
EMP: 8
SQ FT: 1,500

GEOGRAPHIC SECTION
Bay Shore - Suffolk County (G-695)

SALES (est): 867.1K **Privately Held**
SIC: **3679** Harness assemblies for electronic use: wire or cable

(G-669)
AMERICAN PRIDE FASTENERS LLC
195 S Fehr Way (11706-1207)
PHONE.................................631 940-8292
Lynda Zacpal, *President*
George W Hughes III, *Vice Pres*
Nicholas Zacpal, *QC Mgr*
Kathy Sheirdan, *Controller*
Anthony Manno, *Sales Mgr*
▲ EMP: 20
SQ FT: 10,000
SALES: 4.2MM **Privately Held**
SIC: **3965** **3452** **5085** Fasteners; bolts, nuts, rivets & washers; fasteners & fastening equipment

(G-670)
ANTENNA & RADOME RES ASSOC (PA)
15 Harold Ct (11706-2220)
P.O. Box 113, Old Bethpage (11804-0113)
PHONE.................................631 231-8400
Fax: 631 434-1116
Florence Isaacson, *President*
EMP: 50
SQ FT: 20,000
SALES (est): 21.7MM **Privately Held**
WEB: www.arra.com
SIC: **3679** Microwave components

(G-671)
ARTISTIC IRONWORKS INC
94 Saxon Ave (11706-7005)
PHONE.................................631 665-4285
Rick Portera, *President*
EMP: 8
SQ FT: 5,500
SALES (est): 973.6K **Privately Held**
SIC: **3446** **3312** **2431** Stairs, fire escapes, balconies, railings & ladders; rails, steel or iron; staircases, stairs & railings

(G-672)
ASTRO ELECTROPLATING INC
171 4th Ave (11706-7303)
PHONE.................................631 968-0656
Neil Weinstein, *CEO*
Leonard Seid, *Vice Pres*
Jennifer Calderone, *Human Resources*
Chris Myers, *Manager*
EMP: 36
SALES (est): 5.1MM **Privately Held**
SIC: **3471** Electroplating of metals or formed products

(G-673)
BAIRD MOLD MAKING INC
195 N Fehr Way Ste C (11706-1234)
PHONE.................................631 667-0322
Fax: 631 667-0324
John Baird, *President*
Henry Quintin, *Vice Pres*
▲ EMP: 6
SQ FT: 3,000
SALES (est): 823.4K **Privately Held**
SIC: **3089** Molding primary plastic; injection molding of plastics

(G-674)
BFG MARINE INC
200 Candlewood Rd (11706-2217)
PHONE.................................631 586-5500
Glenn Burgos, *President*
Kevin Kohn, *General Mgr*
Ellis W Konkel III, *Vice Pres*
EMP: 16 EST: 1959
SQ FT: 20,000
SALES (est): 2.6MM **Privately Held**
WEB: www.bfgmarine.com
SIC: **3429** **5085** Marine hardware; industrial supplies

(G-675)
BIMBO BAKERIES USA INC
30 Inez Dr (11706-2204)
PHONE.................................203 531-2311
James Montgomery, *Branch Mgr*
EMP: 50 **Privately Held**
WEB: www.englishmuffin.com
SIC: **2051** Doughnuts, except frozen; cakes, bakery: except frozen; pies, bakery: except frozen
HQ: Bimbo Bakeries Usa, Inc
255 Business Center Dr # 200
Horsham PA 19044
215 347-5500

(G-676)
BIMBO FOODS BAKERIES INC (DH)
Also Called: Bimbo Bakeries USA
40 Harold Ct (11706-2220)
PHONE.................................631 273-6000
▲ EMP: 150
SQ FT: 600,000
SALES (est): 2B
SALES (corp-wide): 13B **Privately Held**
WEB: www.gwbakeries.com
SIC: **2051** Mfg Bread/Related Products
HQ: Bimbo Bakeries Usa, Inc
255 Business Center Dr # 200
Horsham PA 19044
215 347-5500

(G-677)
BONDY PRINTING CORP
Also Called: Sir Speedy
267 W Main St (11706-8319)
PHONE.................................631 242-1510
Fax: 631 666-0979
William Bondy Jr, *President*
Donna Bondy, *Vice Pres*
EMP: 5
SALES (est): 864.3K **Privately Held**
SIC: **2752** **2791** **2789** **2759** Commercial printing, lithographic; typesetting; bookbinding & related work; commercial printing; automotive & apparel trimmings

(G-678)
CABLE MANAGEMENT SOLUTIONS INC
Also Called: Jette Group
291 Skip Ln (11706-1206)
PHONE.................................631 674-0004
Fax: 631 674-0010
Roger Jette, *President*
Denise Facquet, *Mktg Dir*
Bob Renz, *Executive*
▲ EMP: 30
SQ FT: 3,500
SALES (est): 7.1MM **Privately Held**
WEB: www.snaketray.com
SIC: **3496** Miscellaneous fabricated wire products

(G-679)
CCS MACHINERY INC
2175 Union Blvd (11706-8016)
PHONE.................................631 968-0900
Mark Wilenkin, *Ch of Bd*
EMP: 14 EST: 2001
SALES (est): 2.4MM **Privately Held**
SIC: **3531** Construction machinery

(G-680)
CENTURY METAL PARTS CORP
230 S Fehr Way (11706-1208)
PHONE.................................631 667-0800
Fax: 631 667-0802
Frank Swierzbin, *President*
Thomas Larkin, *IT/INT Sup*
EMP: 25
SQ FT: 17,000
SALES (est): 4MM **Privately Held**
SIC: **3663** **3451** Antennas, transmitting & communications; screw machine products

(G-681)
CHEM-TEK SYSTEMS INC
Also Called: Moldedtanks.com
208 S Fehr Way (11706-1208)
P.O. Box 222, Nesconset (11767-0222)
PHONE.................................631 253-3010
Shawn Sprague, *President*
EMP: 10
SQ FT: 4,000
SALES (est): 1.1MM **Privately Held**
SIC: **3089** Plastic & fiberglass tanks

(G-682)
CLAD METAL SPECIALTIES INC
1516 5th Industrial Ct (11706-3402)
PHONE.................................631 666-7750
Denise Marcoccia, *Exec VP*
Dominick Bodami, *Vice Pres*
Karen Gerkey, *Finance*
Richard Bodami, *Sales Staff*
EMP: 19
SQ FT: 13,500
SALES (est): 3.9MM **Privately Held**
WEB: www.cladmetal.com
SIC: **3479** Bonderizing of metal or metal products; aluminum coating of metal products

(G-683)
COLONIAL LABEL SYSTEMS INC
Also Called: Colonial Rapid
50 Corbin Ave Ste L (11706-1047)
P.O. Box 812, Deer Park (11729-0976)
PHONE.................................631 254-0111
Ron Afzelius, *President*
EMP: 25
SALES (est): 4.1MM **Privately Held**
SIC: **2759** Commercial printing

(G-684)
COLONIE PLASTICS CORP
188 Candlewood Rd (11706-2219)
PHONE.................................631 434-6969
Fax: 631 434-6984
Paul Gurbatri, *President*
Laura Arzeno, *Controller*
Louie Passi, *Manager*
▲ EMP: 130
SQ FT: 11,500
SALES (est): 17.9MM **Privately Held**
WEB: www.colonieplastics.com
SIC: **3089** Injection molded finished plastic products

(G-685)
COLORFULLY YOURS INC
11 Grant Ave (11706-1007)
PHONE.................................631 242-8600
Fax: 631 242-8664
Joseph Lindner, *President*
Deborah Lindner, *Vice Pres*
EMP: 10
SQ FT: 5,000
SALES (est): 1.2MM **Privately Held**
WEB: www.colorfullyyours.com
SIC: **2752** Commercial printing, offset

(G-686)
COMMAND COMPONENTS CORPORATION
6 Cherry St (11706-7325)
PHONE.................................631 666-4411
Fax: 631 666-4422
Jerry Sukman, *President*
EMP: 8
SQ FT: 3,000
SALES (est): 1.2MM **Privately Held**
WEB: www.commandcomponents.com
SIC: **3643** Electric connectors

(G-687)
CYNCAL STEEL FABRICATORS INC
225 Pine Aire Dr (11706-1147)
PHONE.................................631 254-5600
Cynthia Callahan, *Owner*
Martha Gray, *Admin Asst*
EMP: 12
SALES (est): 1.2MM **Privately Held**
SIC: **3441** Fabricated structural metal

(G-688)
D K P WOOD RAILINGS & STAIRS
1971 Union Blvd (11706-7956)
PHONE.................................631 665-8656
Dmitri Onishchuk, *President*
EMP: 11
SALES (est): 1.2MM **Privately Held**
SIC: **2431** Stair railings, wood

(G-689)
DAVID PEYSER SPORTSWEAR INC (PA)
Also Called: Weatherproof
90 Spence St (11706-2230)
P.O. Box 9171 (11706-9171)
PHONE.................................631 231-7788
Fax: 631 435-8018
Paul Peyser, *President*
Irwin Peyser, *Corp Secy*
Irwin Hosea, *Vice Pres*
Hunter McMillan, *Vice Pres*
Alan Peyser, *Vice Pres*
▲ EMP: 260 EST: 1948
SQ FT: 110,000
SALES (est): 56.5MM **Privately Held**
WEB: www.mvsport.com
SIC: **2329** Men's & boys' sportswear & athletic clothing

(G-690)
DECAL TECHNIQUES INC
40 Corbin Ave Ste I (11706-1048)
PHONE.................................631 491-1800
Fax: 631 491-1816
Eugene P Snyder, *President*
Terry Lomanto, *Vice Pres*
Helen Rider, *Admin Sec*
EMP: 8 EST: 1979
SQ FT: 4,000
SALES (est): 600K **Privately Held**
WEB: www.decaltech.com
SIC: **2752** Decals, lithographed; posters, lithographed

(G-691)
DEER PARK SAND & GRAVEL CORP
145 S 4th St (11706-1200)
PHONE.................................631 586-2323
David Ciardullo, *President*
Joe Ciardullo, *Vice Pres*
EMP: 20
SQ FT: 4,000
SALES (est): 3.6MM **Privately Held**
SIC: **3273** **5032** Ready-mixed concrete; gravel; sand, construction

(G-692)
DEJAH ASSOCIATES INC
Also Called: Dejah Enterprises
1515 5th Industrial Ct (11706-3430)
PHONE.................................631 265-2185
Fax: 631 744-4560
Raymond Dejah, *President*
Loretta Temkin, *Office Mgr*
EMP: 20
SQ FT: 24,000
SALES: 4.5MM **Privately Held**
SIC: **2542** Office & store showcases & display fixtures

(G-693)
DELTA POLYMERS INC
130 S 2nd St (11706-1036)
PHONE.................................631 254-6240
Razia Rana, *President*
Riasat Rana, *Vice Pres*
Shazia Rana, *Manager*
EMP: 8
SQ FT: 10,000
SALES (est): 1.5MM **Privately Held**
WEB: www.deltapolymers.com
SIC: **2851** **1752** Epoxy coatings; floor laying & floor work

(G-694)
DURO DYNE MACHINERY CORP
81 Spence St (11706-2206)
P.O. Box 9117 (11706-9117)
PHONE.................................631 249-9000
Milton Hinden, *CEO*
Randall Hinden, *President*
Joe Auriemmo, *Vice Pres*
Carole D'Agosta, *Vice Pres*
Carole Dagosta, *Vice Pres*
◆ EMP: 40 EST: 1952
SQ FT: 25,000
SALES (est): 10MM
SALES (corp-wide): 126.3MM **Privately Held**
SIC: **3585** Air conditioning equipment, complete; heating equipment, complete
PA: Dyne Duro National Corp
81 Spence St
Bay Shore NY 11706
631 249-9000

(G-695)
DURO DYNE NATIONAL CORP (PA)
81 Spence St (11706-2206)
P.O. Box 9117 (11706-9117)
PHONE.................................631 249-9000
Randall Hinden, *President*
Charlie Larocca, *Plant Supt*

Bay Shore - Suffolk County (G-696)

Bob Ramotor, *Plant Mgr*
Tina Scheuer, *Mfg Spvr*
Steve Friedstein, *CFO*
▲ EMP: 125
SQ FT: 35,000
SALES (est) 126.3MM **Privately Held**
SIC: 3585 Air conditioning equipment, complete; heating equipment, complete

(G-696)
E F IRON WORKS & CONSTRUCTION
241 N Fehr Way Ste 3 (11706-1233)
PHONE.................................631 242-4766
Fax: 631 242-6873
Ed Frage, *President*
EMP: 6
SALES: 390K **Privately Held**
WEB: www.efiron.com
SIC: 3446 1799 Architectural metalwork; ornamental metal work

(G-697)
EMPIRE INDUSTRIAL SYSTEMS CORP (PA)
40 Corbin Ave (11706-1048)
PHONE.................................631 242-4619
Shali Roufberg, *President*
Rosemarie Price, *Office Mgr*
EMP: 10
SQ FT: 7,500
SALES (est): 1.1MM **Privately Held**
SIC: 3443 1711 7699 3441 Boilers: industrial, power, or marine; industrial vessels, tanks & containers; boiler & furnace contractors; boiler repair shop; fabricated structural metal

(G-698)
FENIX FURNITURE CO
Also Called: Mica America
35 Drexel Dr (11706-2235)
PHONE: (11706-2235) 631 273-3500
Fax: 631 273-3572
Jared Fenigstein, *President*
Sol Portnoy, *Vice Pres*
EMP: 30
SQ FT: 24,000
SALES (est): 3.4MM **Privately Held**
SIC: 2511 Wood household furniture

(G-699)
FRED M LAWRENCE CO INC (PA)
45 Drexel Dr (11706-2201)
PHONE.................................718 786-7227
Vincent Lanci, *President*
▲ EMP: 25
SQ FT: 22,000
SALES (est) 2.5MM **Privately Held**
WEB: www.photoframes.net
SIC: 2499 Picture & mirror frames, wood

(G-700)
GBV PROMOTIONS INC
44 Drexel Dr (11706-2202)
PHONE.................................631 231-7300
Richard Goldstein, *President*
Allan Goldstein, *Manager*
Marilyn Goldstein, *Admin Sec*
EMP: 11 EST: 1960
SQ FT: 3,000
SALES: 1.4MM **Privately Held**
SIC: 2752 Commercial printing, offset

(G-701)
GNY EQUIPMENT LLC
20 Drexel Dr (11706-2202)
PHONE.................................631 667-1010
Bill Peil, *President*
Kathy James, *Office Mgr*
Louis Colon, *Manager*
Charlie Creamer, *Manager*
Megan Peil, *Manager*
▲ EMP: 10
SQ FT: 20,000
SALES (est): 1.8MM **Privately Held**
WEB: www.gnyequipment.com
SIC: 3728 5084 5082 Refueling equipment for use in flight, airplane; pumps & pumping equipment; contractors' materials

(G-702)
HARBOR WLDG & FABRICATION CORP
208 S Fehr Way (11706-1208)
PHONE.................................631 667-1880
Fax: 631 242-2441
Joseph Awing, *President*
EMP: 11
SQ FT: 5,400
SALES: 1.8MM **Privately Held**
SIC: 3449 Bars, concrete reinforcing: fabricated steel

(G-703)
INNOVATIVE JEWELRY INC (PA)
Also Called: Fiora Italy
5 Inez Dr (11706-2203)
PHONE.................................718 408-8950
Abraham Rowe, *Vice Pres*
▲ EMP: 4
SQ FT: 3,000
SALES: 4MM **Privately Held**
SIC: 3911 Bracelets, precious metal

(G-704)
INTER MOLDS INC
26 Cleveland Ave (11706-1223)
PHONE.................................631 667-8580
Fax: 631 667-8581
Victor Goncalves, *President*
Francisco Silva, *Vice Pres*
Douglas Cooper, *Treasurer*
Mario Santiago, *Admin Sec*
EMP: 6
SQ FT: 5,000
SALES (est): 766.6K **Privately Held**
WEB: www.intermolds.com
SIC: 3544 Forms (molds), for foundry & plastics working machinery

(G-705)
INTERFACE PRODUCTS CO INC
215 N Fehr Way Ste C (11706-1209)
PHONE.................................631 242-4605
George Miller, *President*
Mary Ann Harrell, *Office Mgr*
EMP: 8
SQ FT: 2,125
SALES (est): 770K **Privately Held**
SIC: 3534 Elevators & equipment

(G-706)
ISLIP MINITURE GOLF
500 E Main St (11706-8502)
PHONE.................................631 940-8900
Mike Flemming,
EMP: 8
SALES (est): 355.8K **Privately Held**
SIC: 3999 Miniatures

(G-707)
JERRY CARDULLO IRON WORKS INC
Also Called: Cardullo, J Iron Works
101 Spence St (11706-2208)
PHONE.................................631 242-8881
Fax: 631 242-4326
Jerry Cardullo, *President*
EMP: 12
SQ FT: 3,000
SALES (est): 880K **Privately Held**
SIC: 3446 Architectural metalwork

(G-708)
LAMINATED WINDOW PRODUCTS INC
211 N Fehr Way (11706-1203)
PHONE.................................631 242-6883
Ismael Santiago, *President*
EMP: 10
SQ FT: 4,000
SALES: 800K **Privately Held**
SIC: 2391 2394 Draperies, plastic & textile: from purchased materials; shades, canvas: made from purchased materials

(G-709)
LANWOOD INDUSTRIES INC
Also Called: Fred Lawrence Co
45 Drexel Dr (11706-2201)
PHONE.................................718 786-3000
EMP: 30
SQ FT: 25,000

SALES (est): 193.4K **Privately Held**
SIC: 2499 2782 Mfg Wood Products Mfg Blankbooks/Binders

(G-710)
LASTICKS AEROSPACE INC
35 Washington Ave Ste E (11706-1027)
PHONE.................................631 242-8484
Fax: 631 242-8485
Guy T Russo, *President*
Keith Johns, *Vice Pres*
Steve Rizzi, *Purchasing*
Denise Walker, *Manager*
Gregory Nasta, *Software Dev*
EMP: 14
SQ FT: 5,000
SALES (est): 2.9MM **Privately Held**
WEB: www.lasticksaero.com
SIC: 3599 Machine shop, jobbing & repair

(G-711)
LEXAN INDUSTRIES INC
Also Called: Struthers Electronics
15 Harold Ct (11706-2220)
PHONE.................................631 434-7586
Fax: 631 434-7589
Florence Isaacson, *President*
Daniel Richardson, *General Mgr*
Daniel Gibbons, *Div Sub Head*
Roberta Simmons, *Purchasing*
Jayme Sohnis, *Manager*
EMP: 19
SQ FT: 11,000
SALES (est): 1.3MM **Privately Held**
SIC: 3679 3825 Microwave components; test equipment for electronic & electrical circuits

(G-712)
M F L B INC
Also Called: S D S of Long Island
7 Grant Ave (11706-1007)
PHONE.................................631 254-8300
Frank Baubille, *Vice Pres*
Michael Cafiero, *Admin Sec*
EMP: 13
SQ FT: 2,500
SALES: 450K **Privately Held**
WEB: www.mflb.com
SIC: 3677 Electronic coils, transformers & other inductors

(G-713)
MARKS CORPEX BANKNOTE CO (PA)
1440 5th Ave (11706-4149)
PHONE.................................631 968-0277
Fax: 631 968-0397
Henri Bertuch, *Principal*
Rhoda Bertuch, *Treasurer*
Linda Newton, *Administration*
EMP: 8
SQ FT: 12,000
SALES (est): 1MM **Privately Held**
WEB: www.corpexnet.com
SIC: 2752 5085 Commercial printing, lithographic; industrial supplies

(G-714)
MBA ORTHOTICS INC
60 Corbin Ave Unit 60g (11706-1046)
PHONE.................................631 392-4755
Andrea Tamayo, *President*
EMP: 5 EST: 2015
SALES: 300K **Privately Held**
SIC: 3131 Sole parts for shoes

(G-715)
MILEX PRECISION INC
66 S 2nd St Ste G (11706-1000)
PHONE.................................631 595-2393
Fax: 631 595-1907
Aeric Misko, *President*
Dagmar Misko, *Vice Pres*
EMP: 14
SQ FT: 4,000
SALES: 1.5MM **Privately Held**
SIC: 3728 3599 Aircraft parts & equipment; machine shop, jobbing & repair

(G-716)
MINICO INDUSTRIES INC
66a S 2nd St Ste A (11706)
PHONE.................................631 595-1455
Fax: 631 595-1620
Nicholas Chonis, *President*

Constantine Chonis, *Vice Pres*
Michael Chonis, *Treasurer*
EMP: 9
SQ FT: 4,500
SALES (est): 1MM **Privately Held**
WEB: www.minicoindustries.com
SIC: 3089 Injection molding of plastics

(G-717)
MV CORP INC
Also Called: M V Sport
88 Spence St Ste 90 (11706-2229)
P.O. Box 9171 (11706-9171)
PHONE.................................631 273-8020
Joshua Peyser, *Ch of Bd*
Alan Peyser, *Principal*
Paul Peyser, *Principal*
Phil Potash, *Opers Mgr*
Joe Rodriguez, *Warehouse Mgr*
▲ EMP: 150
SQ FT: 40,000
SALES (est): 16.5MM
SALES (corp-wide): 59.9MM **Privately Held**
WEB: www.mvsport.com
SIC: 2311 2262 2759 2339 Men's & boys' suits & coats; screen printing: manmade fiber & silk broadwoven fabrics; screen printing; women's & misses' outerwear
PA: David Peyser Sportswear, Inc.
    88 Spence St
    Bay Shore NY 11706
    631 231-7788

(G-718)
NASSAU SUFFOLK BRD OF WOMENS
145 New York Ave (11706-3209)
PHONE.................................631 666-8835
Cris McNamara, *President*
EMP: 50
SALES (est): 1.7MM **Privately Held**
SIC: 2387 Apparel belts

(G-719)
NEW YORK GOURMET COFFEE INC
204 N Fehr Way Ste C (11706-1229)
PHONE.................................631 254-0076
Douglas Robinson, *President*
Deborah Robinson, *Vice Pres*
EMP: 5
SALES: 500K **Privately Held**
SIC: 2095 Roasted coffee

(G-720)
PLATINUM CARTING CORP
1806 Carleton Ave (11706-1632)
PHONE.................................631 649-4322
Carol Key, *President*
Zed Key, *Treasurer*
EMP: 15
SALES (est): 1.3MM **Privately Held**
SIC: 3639 Garbage disposal units, household

(G-721)
POLY SCIENTIFIC R&D CORP
70 Cleveland Ave (11706-1282)
PHONE.................................631 586-0400
John J Caggiano, *Ch of Bd*
John H Arnold, *Exec VP*
Joseph Caggiano, *Vice Pres*
Delio Dicuffa, *Manager*
Cory Gabe, *Executive*
EMP: 40 EST: 1969
SQ FT: 22,000
SALES (est): 8.8MM **Privately Held**
WEB: www.polyrnd.com
SIC: 2869 5169 2819 Industrial organic chemicals; chemicals & allied products; industrial inorganic chemicals

(G-722)
POLYCAST INDUSTRIES INC
130 S 2nd St (11706-1036)
PHONE.................................631 595-2530
Razia Rana, *President*
Riasat Rana, *Vice Pres*
EMP: 5
SQ FT: 100,000

GEOGRAPHIC SECTION

Bay Shore - Suffolk County (G-747)

SALES: 1MM Privately Held
SIC: 3679 2992 2891 2821 Electronic circuits; lubricating oils & greases; adhesives & sealants; plastics materials & resins

(G-723)
PRECISION METALS CORP
221 Skip Ln (11706-1206)
PHONE..................631 586-5032
Thomas J Figlozzi, Ch of Bd
Anna Maria Figlozzi, Corp Secy
Tony Figlozzi, Vice Pres
Carol Nudelman, Admin Sec
EMP: 45
SQ FT: 16,000
SALES (est): 13MM Privately Held
WEB: www.precisionmetalscorp.com
SIC: 3441 3599 3444 Fabricated structural metal; machine & other job shop work; sheet metalwork

(G-724)
PRESTIGELINE INC
5 Inez Dr (11706-2203)
P.O. Box 100 (11706-0703)
PHONE..................631 273-3636
Scott Roth, President
Randy Gaumer, Division Mgr
Stuart Goldstein, Senior VP
Kenneth Golden, Vice Pres
▲ EMP: 82
SQ FT: 150,000
SALES (est): 11.1MM Privately Held
WEB: www.prestigelineinc.com
SIC: 3645 5063 Residential lighting fixtures; lighting fixtures, residential

(G-725)
PROTO MACHINE INC
60 Corbin Ave Ste D (11706-1046)
PHONE..................631 392-1159
James Bailey, President
Eric Lindskog, Vice Pres
EMP: 11
SQ FT: 3,600
SALES: 1.2MM Privately Held
SIC: 3599 Machine shop, jobbing & repair

(G-726)
R G FLAIR CO INC
199 S Fehr Way (11706-1207)
PHONE..................631 586-7311
Fax: 631 586-7316
Gerhard Raible, President
Dieter Thole, Corp Secy
Soraya Rodrigues, Senior VP
Martin Sievers, Vice Pres
Chris Thole, Manager
▲ EMP: 22
SQ FT: 13,000
SALES (est): 3.9MM Privately Held
WEB: www.rgflair.com
SIC: 3469 3915 Metal stampings; jewelers' materials & lapidary work

(G-727)
RAN MAR ENTERPRISES LTD
143 Anchor Ln (11706-8121)
PHONE..................631 666-4754
Melvin Small, President
EMP: 12
SQ FT: 13,000
SALES (est): 1.4MM Privately Held
SIC: 2891 Adhesives

(G-728)
RASJADA ENTERPRISES LTD
1337 Richland Blvd (11706-5415)
PHONE..................631 242-1055
Ronald C Cusano Jr, President
EMP: 12
SQ FT: 15,000
SALES: 2MM Privately Held
SIC: 2541 Cabinets, except refrigerated: show, display, etc.: wood

(G-729)
RFN INC
40 Drexel Dr (11706-2202)
PHONE..................516 764-5100
Alex Treyger, President
EMP: 18
SQ FT: 28,000
SALES: 1.5MM Privately Held
SIC: 2759 8742 Commercial printing; marketing consulting services

(G-730)
RINALDI PRECISION MACHINE
Also Called: R P M
60 Corbin Ave Ste F (11706-1046)
PHONE..................631 242-4141
Fax: 631 242-4422
Angelo Rinaldi, President
EMP: 10
SQ FT: 1,700
SALES (est): 1.5MM Privately Held
SIC: 3599 Machine shop, jobbing & repair

(G-731)
RIT PRINTING CORP
250 N Fairway (11706)
PHONE..................631 586-6220
Fax: 631 586-6247
Anthony Buono, President
Maria Brown, Manager
EMP: 10
SQ FT: 8,000
SALES (est): 1.5MM Privately Held
WEB: www.ritprinting.com
SIC: 2752 2759 Commercial printing, lithographic; commercial printing

(G-732)
ROCKET TECH FUEL CORP
20 Corbin Ave (11706-1004)
PHONE..................516 810-8947
Richard Miller, President
Derek Sidebottom, Vice Pres
Joseph Silhan, Vice Pres
EMP: 10 EST: 2004
SQ FT: 1,800
SALES: 90MM Privately Held
SIC: 1311 Crude petroleum & natural gas

(G-733)
ROMAN STONE CONSTRUCTION CO
85 S 4th St (11706-1210)
PHONE..................631 667-0566
Fax: 631 667-0617
Thomas Montalbine, President
Ken Rymer, General Mgr
Layne Urbas, Treasurer
Richard Benz, Sales Mgr
Ryan Camberdella, Sales Mgr
EMP: 45 EST: 1903
SQ FT: 25,000
SALES (est): 9.3MM Privately Held
WEB: www.romanstoneco.com
SIC: 3272 Pipe, concrete or lined with concrete

(G-734)
ROSSITER & SCHMITT CO INC
220 S Fehr Way (11706-1208)
PHONE..................516 937-3610
Richard Shapiro, Chairman
David Shapiro, Assistant VP
EMP: 5
SALES: 1MM Privately Held
SIC: 3991 Brushes, household or industrial

(G-735)
ROYAL WINDOWS MFG CORP
Also Called: Royal Windows and Doors
1769 5th Ave Unit A (11706-1735)
PHONE..................631 435-8888
Fax: 631 435-8899
Solomos Hajicharalambous, Ch of Bd
George Efthymiou, Treasurer
Tim Efthymio, Controller
Efthymios Efthymiou, Controller
Solon Efthymiou, Manager
EMP: 27
SQ FT: 60,000
SALES (est): 4.4MM Privately Held
WEB: www.royalwindow.com
SIC: 2431 5031 1751 Windows, wood; doors, wood; doors & windows; window & door (prefabricated) installation

(G-736)
RUBIES COSTUME COMPANY INC
Also Called: Collegeville Imagineering
158 Candlewood Rd (11706-2219)
PHONE..................631 777-3300
EMP: 100
SALES (corp-wide): 464.8MM Privately Held
SIC: 2389 7299 Mfg Costumes
PA: Rubie's Costume Company, Inc.
12008 Jamaica Ave
Richmond Hill NY 11418
718 846-1008

(G-737)
RUBIES COSTUME COMPANY INC
Also Called: Rubie's Distribution Center
1 Holloween Hwy (11706-1633)
PHONE..................631 951-3688
Fax: 631 951-3723
Marc Beige, Manager
EMP: 120
SALES (corp-wide): 428MM Privately Held
SIC: 2389 7299 Costumes; costume rental
PA: Rubie's Costume Company, Inc.
12008 Jamaica Ave
Richmond Hill NY 11418
718 846-1008

(G-738)
SIW INC
271 Skip Ln (11706-1206)
PHONE..................631 888-0130
Lisa Gurcan, President
Dominic Amorosa, Vice Pres
▲ EMP: 12
SQ FT: 11,500
SALES (est): 1.9MM Privately Held
SIC: 3449 Bars, concrete reinforcing: fabricated steel

(G-739)
STANDARD INDUSTRIAL WORKS INC
271 Skip Ln (11706-1206)
PHONE..................631 888-0130
Fax: 631 888-0133
Paul Spotts, President
Lisa Gurcan, Software Dev
EMP: 10
SQ FT: 11,800
SALES: 700K Privately Held
SIC: 3444 Sheet metalwork

(G-740)
SUFFOLK COPY CENTER INC
Also Called: Suffolk Printing
26 W Main St (11706-8383)
PHONE..................631 665-0570
Fax: 631 665-0403
William Beitch, President
Florence Beitch, Corp Secy
Charles Beitch, Vice Pres
EMP: 6 EST: 1971
SQ FT: 4,000
SALES (est): 947.6K Privately Held
WEB: www.suffolkprinting.com
SIC: 2752 Commercial printing, offset

(G-741)
SUMMIT MANUFACTURING LLC (HQ)
Also Called: Summit Plastics
100 Spence St (11706-2231)
PHONE..................631 952-1570
Louis Marinello, President
◆ EMP: 7 EST: 2015
SALES (est): 6MM
SALES (corp-wide): 48.6MM Privately Held
SIC: 3089 Plastic containers, except foam
PA: Array Canada Inc
45 Progress Ave
Scarborough ON M1P 2
416 299-4865

(G-742)
SUMNER INDUSTRIES INC
Also Called: Ateco Products
309 Orinoco Dr (11706-7111)
PHONE..................631 666-7290
Fax: 631 666-1424
Jonathan Sumner, President
Danny Deprospo, Manager
Yewa Sawicka, Manager
▼ EMP: 15 EST: 1935
SQ FT: 10,000
SALES (est): 3.2MM Privately Held
SIC: 3728 Aircraft parts & equipment

(G-743)
TAPE-IT INC
233 N Fehr Way (11706-1203)
PHONE..................631 243-4100
Fax: 631 243-4326
Arnold Rabinowitz, President
Lorie Amuro, Human Res Mgr
Alex Aguirre, Sales Mgr
Scott Rabinowitz, Marketing Staff
Arnold Robinwitz, Director
◆ EMP: 50
SQ FT: 55,000
SALES (est): 14.8MM Privately Held
WEB: www.tapeit.com
SIC: 2672 5113 5122 Tape, pressure sensitive: made from purchased materials; pressure sensitive tape; drugs, proprietaries & sundries

(G-744)
TENSATOR INC
Also Called: Tensator Group
260 Spur Dr S (11706-3917)
P.O. Box 400 (11706-0779)
PHONE..................631 666-0300
Alan McPherson, CEO
Ben Gale, CEO
James Baker, General Mgr
David Cohen, Business Mgr
William Goebel, Business Mgr
▲ EMP: 94
SQ FT: 81,000
SALES (est): 25.7MM
SALES (corp-wide): 39.2MM Privately Held
WEB: www.lawrencemetal.com
SIC: 3446 Ornamental metalwork
HQ: Tensator Group Limited
Unit 7 Danbury Court
Milton Keynes BUCKS MK14
190 868-4600

(G-745)
TROJAN METAL FABRICATION INC (PA)
Also Called: Trojan Powder Coating
2215 Union Blvd (11706-8015)
PHONE..................631 968-5040
Fax: 631 968-5939
Carl Troiano, CEO
James Dunne, Counsel
Keith Rein, Vice Pres
Dora Simpson, Prdtn Mgr
Kerry Nelson, Director
EMP: 50
SQ FT: 80,000
SALES (est): 6.6MM Privately Held
WEB: www.trojanpowder.com
SIC: 3479 Coating of metals & formed products

(G-746)
ULTIMATE STYLES OF AMERICA
27 Garfield Ave Unit A (11706-1052)
PHONE..................631 254-0219
David Goldstein, President
EMP: 12
SQ FT: 4,000
SALES (est): 1.3MM Privately Held
SIC: 2499 5712 Kitchen, bathroom & household ware: wood; cabinet work, custom

(G-747)
VIATECH PUBG SOLUTIONS INC
1440 5th Ave (11706-4149)
PHONE..................631 968-8500
Fax: 631 968-8830
Alyssa Graziano, Prdtn Mgr
Sophia Cario, Purch Agent
Louise Gore, Finance Mgr
Tom Bergenholtz, VP Sales
Lauren Clemens, Accounts Mgr
EMP: 48
SALES (corp-wide): 93.9MM Privately Held
SIC: 2752 7389 Commercial printing, offset; lithographing on metal; subscription fulfillment services: magazine, newspaper, etc.
PA: Viatech Publishing Solutions, Inc.
11935 N Stemmons Fwy
Dallas TX 75234
214 827-8151

Bay Shore - Suffolk County (G-748)

(G-748)
WOOD TALK
Also Called: Woodtalk Stairs & Rails
203 N Fehr Way Ste C (11706-1235)
PHONE............................631 940-3085
Fax: 631 940-1631
Scott Braun, *Principal*
EMP: 5
SALES (est): 487.2K **Privately Held**
SIC: **2431** Staircases, stairs & railings

Bayport
Suffolk County

(G-749)
CARE ENTERPRISES INC
435 Renee Dr (11705-1237)
PHONE............................631 472-8155
Lina Torre, *Vice Pres*
EMP: 6
SALES: 650K **Privately Held**
SIC: **3822** Air conditioning & refrigeration controls

(G-750)
CGW CORP (PA)
102 S Gillette Ave (11705-2239)
PHONE............................631 472-6600
Fax: 631 472-3521
George Werner, *President*
EMP: 7
SALES: 800K **Privately Held**
WEB: www.cgwcorp.com
SIC: **3825** Network analyzers

(G-751)
CHIMNEY DOCTORS AMERICAS CORP
738a Montauk Hwy (11705-1621)
PHONE............................631 868-3586
Nicole Newberg, *President*
EMP: 5
SQ FT: 500
SALES (est): 227.5K **Privately Held**
SIC: **3259** 3271 3272 1799 Clay chimney products; blocks, concrete: chimney or fireplace; fireplace & chimney material: concrete; prefabricated fireplace installation

(G-752)
JOHNSON MANUFACTURING CO
326 3rd Ave (11705-1316)
PHONE............................631 472-1184
David Johnson Sr, *Owner*
EMP: 7
SQ FT: 5,000
SALES: 350K **Privately Held**
SIC: **3089** Plastic processing

(G-753)
NATURES BOUNTY CO
Capsuleworks
10 Vitamin Dr (11705-1115)
PHONE............................631 200-2000
Jeff Johnston, *Technical Staff*
EMP: 14 **Publicly Held**
SIC: **2833** Medicinals & botanicals
HQ: The Nature's Bounty Co
2100 Smithtown Ave
Ronkonkoma NY 11779
631 200-2000

(G-754)
PLASTIC SOLUTIONS INC
158 Schenck Ave (11705)
PHONE............................631 234-9013
AVI Ben-Basset, *Ch of Bd*
Amanda Vassallo, *Manager*
EMP: 32
SALES (est): 4.6MM **Privately Held**
SIC: **3089** 3544 Plastic containers, except foam; special dies, tools, jigs & fixtures

(G-755)
STICKERSHOPCOM INC
Also Called: Labels, Stickers and More
582 Middle Rd (11705-1900)
PHONE............................631 563-4323
Stacy Ianson, *CEO*
EMP: 5
SALES (est): 718.7K **Privately Held**
SIC: **2679** 5999 3993 2759 Tags & labels, paper; banners, flags, decals & posters; letters for signs, metal; poster & decal printing & engraving

(G-756)
WENNER BREAD PRODUCTS INC (PA)
33 Rajon Rd (11705-1101)
PHONE............................800 869-6262
Fax: 631 563-6546
Richard R Wenner, *CEO*
Lawrence L Wenner, *Senior VP*
Daniel Wenner, *Vice Pres*
John J Wenner, *Vice Pres*
William W Wenner Jr, *Vice Pres*
▲ EMP: 314 EST: 1975
SQ FT: 140,000
SALES (est): 127.7MM **Privately Held**
WEB: www.wenner-bread.com
SIC: **2051** 2053 5461 Bread, all types (white, wheat, rye, etc): fresh or frozen; frozen bakery products, except bread; bakeries

Bayside
Queens County

(G-757)
A & G FOOD DISTRIBUTORS LLC
21610 47th Ave Apt 3b (11361-3412)
PHONE............................917 939-3457
Rocco Macri, *President*
▲ EMP: 3 EST: 2009
SALES: 1.5MM **Privately Held**
SIC: **2032** Italian foods: packaged in cans, jars, etc.

(G-758)
A AND K GLOBAL INC
3312 208th St (11361-1319)
PHONE............................718 412-1876
Darrow Wu, *General Mgr*
EMP: 67 EST: 2008
SALES (est): 4.4MM **Privately Held**
SIC: **3651** Home entertainment equipment, electronic
PA: Dongguan Naifan Packing Engineering Co., Ltd.
Datang Village, Dalingshan Town
Dongguan
769 827-8410

(G-759)
A T A BAGEL SHOPPE INC
Also Called: Bagel Club
20814 Cross Island Pkwy (11360-1187)
PHONE............................718 352-4948
Anthony Lombardo, *President*
EMP: 5
SALES (est): 270K **Privately Held**
SIC: **2051** 5812 5461 Bagels, fresh or frozen; eating places; bagels

(G-760)
ABSOLUTE FITNESS US CORP
21337 39th Ave Ste 322 (11361-2071)
PHONE............................732 979-8582
Salvatore Naimo, *CEO*
Dina Destafano, *Director*
EMP: 100
SALES (est): 4.7MM **Privately Held**
SIC: **3949** Sporting & athletic goods

(G-761)
ALEXANDER POLAKOVICH
Also Called: Minuteman Press
4235 Bell Blvd (11361-2863)
PHONE............................718 229-6200
Fax: 718 229-0485
Alexander Polakovich, *Owner*
EMP: 6
SQ FT: 2,000
SALES (est): 340K **Privately Held**
SIC: **2752** Commercial printing, lithographic

(G-762)
BAGEL CLUB INC
20521 35th Ave (11361-1245)
PHONE............................718 423-6106
Rosa Lombardo, *President*
EMP: 13
SALES (est): 1.5MM **Privately Held**
SIC: **2051** Bagels, fresh or frozen

(G-763)
CANAAN PRINTING INC
20007 46th Ave (11361-3018)
PHONE............................718 729-3100
Fax: 718 729-3159
Sang Miung Kim, *President*
EMP: 10 EST: 1980
SQ FT: 5,000
SALES (est): 840K **Privately Held**
WEB: www.canaanprinting.com
SIC: **2752** Commercial printing, offset

(G-764)
DADA GROUP US INC
22104 67th Ave Apt B (11364-2628)
PHONE............................631 888-0818
Zhiqian Zhang, *President*
▲ EMP: 4
SALES: 3MM **Privately Held**
SIC: **2386** Garments, leather

(G-765)
FREEMAN TECHNOLOGY INC
2355 Bell Blvd Apt 2h (11360-2051)
PHONE............................732 829-8345
Tim Freeman, *President*
John Yin, *Project Mgr*
EMP: 20 EST: 2012
SQ FT: 1,500
SALES: 2MM **Privately Held**
SIC: **3829** Measuring & controlling devices
PA: Freeman Technology Limited
1 Miller Court
Tewkesbury GLOS

(G-766)
G PESSO & SONS INC
20320 35th Ave (11361-1110)
PHONE............................718 224-9130
Gidon Pesso, *Principal*
EMP: 7
SALES (est): 494.2K **Privately Held**
SIC: **2024** Ice cream & frozen desserts

(G-767)
KASTOR CONSULTING INC
3919 218th St (11361-2331)
PHONE............................718 224-9109
Greg Manaris, *President*
EMP: 9 EST: 1995
SALES (est): 780K **Privately Held**
WEB: www.kastor.com
SIC: **7372** Prepackaged software

(G-768)
NATIONAL PROSTHETIC ORTHOT
21441 42nd Ave Ste 3a (11361-2963)
PHONE............................718 767-8400
Fax: 718 423-8708
Fernando Perez, *President*
Sibia Perez, *Manager*
EMP: 9
SQ FT: 1,500
SALES (est): 900K **Privately Held**
SIC: **3842** Limbs, artificial; braces, orthopedic

(G-769)
SCHNEPS PUBLICATIONS INC (PA)
Also Called: Forest Hills Courier
3815 Bell Blvd Ste 38 (11361-2058)
PHONE............................718 224-5863
Fax: 718 224-5441
Victoria A Schneps, *President*
Katrina Medoff, *Editor*
Joshua Schneps, *Vice Pres*
Keith Fiocca, *Accounts Exec*
Bob Brennan, *Sales Executive*
EMP: 35
SALES (est): 5.6MM **Privately Held**
SIC: **2711** Newspapers

(G-770)
UL CORP
3812 Corporal Stone St # 2 (11361-2141)
PHONE............................201 203-4453
Hyung Ho Kim, *President*
EMP: 8
SALES: 1.2MM **Privately Held**
SIC: **3953** Marking devices

(G-771)
URBAN RACERCOM
21333 39th Ave (11361-2091)
PHONE............................718 279-2202
Jackie Yi, *Principal*
Bob Hernandez, *Editor*
Eri Magara, *Opers Staff*
Vivian Chin, *Production*
Jacob Leveton, *Marketing Staff*
EMP: 5
SALES (est): 610.3K **Privately Held**
SIC: **2721** Periodicals: publishing only

(G-772)
VF IMAGEWEAR INC
333 Pratt Ave (11359-1119)
PHONE............................718 352-2363
Martin Soto, *Manager*
Paul G Policarpio, *Administration*
EMP: 21
SALES (corp-wide): 12B **Publicly Held**
WEB: www.vfsolutions.com
SIC: **2311** 2326 2339 Men's & boys' uniforms; work uniforms; women's & misses' outerwear
HQ: Vf Imagewear, Inc.
545 Marriott Dr Ste 200
Nashville TN 37214
615 565-5000

Bayside Hills
Queens County

(G-773)
CAPTURE GLOBA INTEG SOLUT INC
21214 48th Ave (11364-1204)
PHONE............................718 352-0579
Harry Pateroulakis, *President*
EMP: 8 EST: 2003
SALES: 1MM **Privately Held**
SIC: **3577** Magnetic ink & optical scanning devices

(G-774)
CATHAY GLOBAL CO INC
Also Called: Vactronics
5815 215th St (11364-1839)
PHONE............................718 229-0920
Fu Geng, *President*
Janet Jiang, *Vice Pres*
EMP: 6 EST: 1991
SQ FT: 2,000
SALES (est): 406.5K **Privately Held**
SIC: **3699** Electrical equipment & supplies

Bayville
Nassau County

(G-775)
PLURIBUS PRODUCTS INC
1 Overlook Ave (11709-2113)
PHONE............................718 852-1614
Fax: 718 852-4575
Peter V Martino, *President*
John V Martino, *Purchasing*
Michael Racconova, *Manager*
Sabrina Stabile, *Manager*
EMP: 32 EST: 1966
SQ FT: 50,000
SALES (est): 4.5MM **Privately Held**
SIC: **2531** 2449 3341 Public building & related furniture; wood containers; secondary nonferrous metals

Beacon
Dutchess County

(G-776)
ARCHITECTURAL GLASS INC
71 Maple St Apt 2 (12508-2034)
PHONE............................845 831-3116
Fax: 845 831-3321
Michael Benzer, *President*
Jennifer Smith, *Vice Pres*

EMP: 10
SQ FT: 8,000
SALES (est): 550K Privately Held
WEB: www.glasstiles.com
SIC: 3229 Glassware, art or decorative

(G-777)
CHEMPRENE INC
483 Fishkill Ave (12508-1251)
P.O. Box 471 (12508-0471)
PHONE..................................845 831-2800
Fax: 845 831-4639
John Nicoletti, *President*
Motria Iverson, *Accounts Mgr*
Debbie Tibido, *MIS Dir*
▲ EMP: 110
SQ FT: 200,000
SALES (est): 38.5MM Privately Held
WEB: www.chemprene.com
SIC: 3496 3069 3535 2295 Conveyor belts; rubberized fabrics; rubber hardware; conveyors & conveying equipment; coated fabrics, not rubberized; investment holding companies, except banks
HQ: Ammeraal Beltech International Beheer B.V.
    Comeniusstraat 8
    Alkmaar
    725 751-212

(G-778)
CHEMPRENE HOLDING INC
483 Fishkill Ave (12508-1251)
PHONE..................................845 831-2800
Jami Goud, *Ch of Bd*
Paul Hamilton, *President*
▲ EMP: 180
SALES (est): 19.8MM Privately Held
SIC: 3496 3069 3535 2295 Conveyor belts; rubberized fabrics; rubber hardware; conveyors & conveying equipment; coated fabrics, not rubberized

(G-779)
DOREL HAT CO (PA)
1 Main St (12508)
PHONE..................................845 831-5231
Fax: 845 831-0481
Salvatore Cumella, *CEO*
Ramon Moreno, *Vice Pres*
EMP: 30
SQ FT: 28,000
SALES (est): 1.6MM Privately Held
WEB: www.aldohats.com
SIC: 2353 Hats, caps & millinery; hats, trimmed: women's, misses' & children's

(G-780)
FCR LLC
Also Called: Recommunity
508 Fishkill Ave (12508-1255)
PHONE..................................845 926-1071
EMP: 8 Privately Held
SIC: 2611 Pulp manufactured from waste or recycled paper
HQ: Fcr, Llc
    809 W Hill St Ste B
    Charlotte NC 28208
    704 332-1603

(G-781)
HUDSON VALLEY CHOCOLATIER INC (PA)
Also Called: Alps Sweet Shop
269 Main St (12508-2735)
PHONE..................................845 831-8240
Sally Craft, *President*
Terry Craft, *Vice Pres*
EMP: 14
SALES (est): 1.8MM Privately Held
WEB: www.alpssweetshop.com
SIC: 2064 5441 Candy & other confectionery products; candy

(G-782)
MECHTRONICS CORPORATION (PA)
511 Fishkill Ave (12508-1253)
PHONE..................................845 231-1400
Fax: 914 989-2726
Richard J Fellinger, *Ch of Bd*
Anthony Squitieri, *President*
Keith Arndt, *Vice Pres*
Tony Siragusa, *Project Mgr*
Kim Perrin, *Engineer*
▲ EMP: 190 EST: 1944
SQ FT: 20,000
SALES (est): 27.6MM Privately Held
WEB: www.mech-tronics.com
SIC: 3993 Displays, paint process

(G-783)
MECHTRONICS CORPORATION
511 Fishkill Ave (12508-1253)
PHONE..................................845 831-9300
Richard Fellinger, *Branch Mgr*
EMP: 40
SALES (corp-wide): 27.6MM Privately Held
WEB: www.mech-tronics.com
SIC: 3993 2542 2653 Displays, paint process; fixtures: display, office or store: except wood; corrugated boxes, partitions, display items, sheets & pad
PA: Mechtronics Corporation
    511 Fishkill Ave
    Beacon NY 12508
    845 231-1400

(G-784)
METAL CONCEPTS
9 Hanna Ln 12 (12508-2868)
PHONE..................................845 592-1863
Herman Roggeman, *Owner*
Jan Roggeman, *Co-Owner*
EMP: 3
SALES (est): 1.5MM Privately Held
SIC: 3441 Fabricated structural metal

(G-785)
SIEGFRIEDS CALL INC
20 Kent St 109 (12508-2042)
PHONE..................................845 765-2275
Scott H Bacon, *Partner*
Andrea Bacon, *Officer*
EMP: 6
SALES (est): 133.1K Privately Held
SIC: 3931 Brass instruments & parts

(G-786)
TIGA HOLDINGS INC
74 Dennings Ave (12508-3624)
PHONE..................................845 838-3000
Gary Santagata, *President*
Timothy Hochberj, *Vice Pres*
Michael J Siciliano, *Director*
EMP: 24
SQ FT: 2,300
SALES (est): 2.3MM Privately Held
WEB: www.tigallc.com
SIC: 3911 Jewelry, precious metal

Bearsville
Ulster County

(G-787)
LIFELINK MONITORING CORP (PA)
3201 Route 212 (12409-5224)
PHONE..................................845 336-2098
Fax: 845 679-7938
Arthur G Avedisian, *President*
John K Holland, *Chairman*
EMP: 15 EST: 1994
SQ FT: 25,000
SALES (est): 1.1MM Privately Held
WEB: www.llmi.com
SIC: 2835 In vitro & in vivo diagnostic substances

Beaver Dams
Schuyler County

(G-788)
M & H RESEARCH AND DEV CORP
Also Called: M&H Soaring
471 Post Creek Rd (14812-9124)
P.O. Box 368, Big Flats (14814-0368)
PHONE..................................607 734-2346
Claude M Sullivan, *President*
Hinz Weissembuehler, *Principal*
Karen Schlosser, *Vice Pres*
EMP: 6
SALES (est): 450K Privately Held
WEB: www.mandhsoaring.com
SIC: 3721 Gliders (aircraft)

Beaver Falls
Lewis County

(G-789)
INTERFACE PERFORMANCE MTLS
9635 Main St (13305)
PHONE..................................315 346-3100
Fax: 315 346-3286
John Tabolt, *Principal*
EMP: 15
SALES (est): 407.5K Privately Held
SIC: 2679 Paper products, converted

(G-790)
OMNIAFILTRA LLC
9567 Main St (13305)
P.O. Box 410 (13305-0410)
PHONE..................................315 346-7300
Fax: 315 346-7301
Gino Fronzoni, *President*
Jill Bush, *CFO*
Michele Moore, *Financial Exec*
Patty Flint, *Accounts Mgr*
Vicky Miller, *Director*
▼ EMP: 35
SALES (est): 9.5MM Privately Held
SIC: 2621 Paper mills

Bedford
Westchester County

(G-791)
BEDFORD WDWRK INSTLLATIONS INC
200 Pound Ridge Rd (10506-1243)
PHONE..................................914 764-9434
EMP: 6
SALES (est): 440K Privately Held
SIC: 2493 Mfg Reconstituted Wood Products

(G-792)
JSD COMMUNICATIONS INC
Also Called: Remodeling News
10 Colonel Thomas Ln (10506-1521)
P.O. Box 911 (10506-0911)
PHONE..................................914 588-1841
James F Duffy, *President*
EMP: 13
SALES: 500K Privately Held
WEB: www.remodelingconnection.com
SIC: 2721 Magazines: publishing only, not printed on site

(G-793)
LESANNE LIFE SCIENCES LLC
47 Brook Farm Rd (10506-1309)
PHONE..................................914 234-0860
Robert J Beckman,
Robert Beckman,
EMP: 5
SALES: 300K Privately Held
SIC: 2835 In vitro & in vivo diagnostic substances

(G-794)
TORY ELECTRIC
641 Old Post Rd (10506-1218)
PHONE..................................914 292-5036
EMP: 7
SALES (est): 174.6K Privately Held
SIC: 3699 Electrical equipment & supplies

(G-795)
WALCO LEATHER CO INC
5 Banks Farm Rd (10506-1914)
PHONE..................................212 243-2244
Fax: 212 989-2766
Monroe Jay Chaikin, *President*
Rosalie Tenzer, *Director*
EMP: 50
SQ FT: 15,000
SALES (est): 6.4MM Privately Held
SIC: 3111 3199 3172 2512 Specialty leathers; leather belting & strapping; personal leather goods; upholstered household furniture; apparel belts

Bedford Hills
Westchester County

(G-796)
BEDFORD PRECISION PARTS CORP
290 Adams St (10507-1910)
P.O. Box 357 (10507-0357)
PHONE..................................914 241-2211
Fax: 914 241-3063
Daniel L Kleinman, *President*
Paul Kleinman, *Chairman*
Evalyn S Kleinman, *Corp Secy*
David Kleinman, *Vice Pres*
Robert Kleinman, *Vice Pres*
EMP: 35
SQ FT: 14,000
SALES (est): 4.5MM Privately Held
WEB: www.bedfordprecision.com
SIC: 3993 3563 Signs & advertising specialties; spraying outfits: metals, paints & chemicals (compressor)

(G-797)
CUSTOM SPORTSWEAR CORP
Also Called: Sportswear Unlimited
375 Adams St (10507-2001)
PHONE..................................914 666-9200
Adam Giardina, *President*
Gene King, *Production*
Len Schlangel, *CFO*
Helen Bowers, *Program Mgr*
Ryria Singer, *Administration*
EMP: 5 EST: 1988
SQ FT: 6,000
SALES (est): 500K Privately Held
WEB: www.sptunl.com
SIC: 2759 5136 Screen printing; uniforms, men's & boys'

(G-798)
DAVID HOWELL PRODUCT DESIGN
Also Called: David Howell & Company
405 Adams St (10507-2066)
PHONE..................................914 666-4080
David Howell, *President*
Gina L Nuccetelli, *District Mgr*
Jeanne M May, *Marketing Staff*
Susan Howell, *Admin Sec*
EMP: 20
SQ FT: 6,000
SALES: 2MM Privately Held
WEB: www.davidhowell.com
SIC: 3911 Jewelry, precious metal

(G-799)
DISPERSION TECHNOLOGY INC
364 Adams St (10507-2048)
PHONE..................................914 241-4777
Andre Dukhin, *President*
EMP: 4
SQ FT: 3,000
SALES: 2MM Privately Held
SIC: 3829 Measuring & controlling devices

(G-800)
EYEGLASS SERVICE INDUSTRIES
Also Called: Vision World
777 Bedford Rd (10507-1504)
PHONE..................................914 666-3150
Patricia Ausiello, *CEO*
EMP: 5
SALES (corp-wide): 7.1MM Privately Held
WEB: www.visionworld.com
SIC: 3841 5995 Surgical & medical instruments; opticians
PA: Eyeglass Service Industries Inc
    420 Sunrise Hwy
    Lynbrook NY 11563
    516 561-3937

Bedford Hills - Westchester County (G-801)   GEOGRAPHIC SECTION

(G-801)
MALCON INC
405 Adams St (10507-2066)
P.O. Box 463 (10507-0463)
PHONE..................914 666-7146
Fax: 914 666-7842
Peter Malavenda, *President*
Frances Malavenda, *Corp Secy*
EMP: 18
SQ FT: 15,000
SALES (est): 439.6K *Privately Held*
WEB: www.malcon.com
SIC: 3823 Panelboard indicators, recorders & controllers: receiver

(G-802)
PRODUCTION MILLING COMPANY
364 Adams St Ste 5 (10507-2047)
PHONE..................914 666-0792
Frank G Servidio, *President*
EMP: 5
SQ FT: 1,900
SALES (est): 495K *Privately Held*
SIC: 3599 Machine shop, jobbing & repair

(G-803)
RAINBEAU RIDGE FARM
49 Davids Way (10507-2531)
PHONE..................914 234-2197
Lisa Schwartz, *Owner*
Karen Sabath, *Partner*
Mark Schwartz, *Co-Owner*
Ron Brooks, *Manager*
Isaac Jahns, *Manager*
EMP: 9
SQ FT: 6,000
SALES (est): 443.3K *Privately Held*
SIC: 2022 8299 Cheese, natural & processed educational services

(G-804)
WATER TREATMENT SERVICES INC
Also Called: Water Treatment Svce
395 Adams St (10507-2001)
PHONE..................914 241-2261
Fax: 914 241-2517
Frank Maknocta, *President*
EMP: 7
SALES: 425K *Privately Held*
SIC: 3589 Water treatment equipment, industrial

Bellerose
Queens County

(G-805)
ADVANTEX SOLUTIONS INC
24845 Jericho Tpke (11426-1912)
PHONE..................718 278-2290
Giovanni Natale, *President*
Antonio Sferrazz, *Vice Pres*
Danielle Haselton, *Administration*
EMP: 6
SALES (est): 1MM *Privately Held*
SIC: 3822 Temperature controls, automatic

(G-806)
LEIGH SCOTT ENTERPRISES INC
Also Called: Minuteman Press
24802 Union Tpke (11426-1837)
PHONE..................718 343-5440
Fax: 718 343-2329
Scott Levine, *President*
EMP: 6
SALES (est): 550K *Privately Held*
WEB: www.minutemanbellrose.com
SIC: 2752 279 Commercial printing, lithographic; typesetting

(G-807)
RITNOA INC
24019 Jamaica Ave Fl 2 (11426-1054)
PHONE..................212 660-2148
Shabbir Khan, *President*
EMP: 38 EST: 2006
SQ FT: 12,000
SALES (est): 3 MM *Privately Held*
SIC: 7372 Business oriented computer software

(G-808)
ZINNIAS INC
24520 Grand Central Pkwy 4l (11426-2712)
PHONE..................718 746-8551
▲ EMP: 12
SQ FT: 3,800
SALES: 1.4MM *Privately Held*
SIC: 2369 2361 Girls And Childrens Outerwear, Nec, Nsk

Bellmore
Nassau County

(G-809)
ARNOLD TAYLOR PRINTING INC
2218 Brody Ln (11710-5102)
PHONE..................516 781-0564
Fax: 212 822-4822
Carey Platt, *President*
EMP: 5 EST: 1963
SALES (est): 350K *Privately Held*
SIC: 2752 Commercial printing, offset

(G-810)
BANNER TRANSMISSION & ENG CO
Also Called: Banner Transmissions
2765 Broadway (11710-5612)
P.O. Box 90 (11710-0757)
PHONE..................516 221-9459
Fax: 516 221-0813
Clifforddwin Hettinger, *President*
Christopher B Sweeny, *Admin Sec*
EMP: 10
SQ FT: 4,500
SALES (est): 1.2MM *Privately Held*
WEB: www.bannertransmission.com
SIC: 3714 7539 Transmissions, motor vehicle; automotive repair shops

(G-811)
BELLMORE STEEL PRODUCTS CORP
2282 Bellmore Ave (11710-5627)
P.O. Box 825 (11710-0825)
PHONE..................516 785-9667
Fax: 516 785-9631
Glenn S Suskind, *Ch of Bd*
EMP: 16
SQ FT: 3,000
SALES (est): 2.6MM *Privately Held*
SIC: 3443 Fabricated plate work (boiler shop)

(G-812)
CLPA EMBROIDERY
2635 Pettit Ave (11710-3630)
PHONE..................516 409-0002
Fax: 516 409-2049
Joseph Clabby, *Owner*
EMP: 5 EST: 2001
SALES (est): 250.8K *Privately Held*
SIC: 2395 Art needlework: made from purchased materials

(G-813)
DECAL MAKERS INC
2477 Merrick Rd (11710-5751)
PHONE..................516 221-7200
Fax: 516 221-7229
Audrey J Hastingscooper, *President*
Leslie A Hastings-Bensi, *Corp Secy*
Mark Harris, *Vice Pres*
Linda Hennessy, *Vice Pres*
Matthew Hennessy, *Plant Mgr*
EMP: 25 EST: 1923
SALES (est): 2.3MM *Privately Held*
SIC: 2752 3993 2396 Decals, lithographed; name plates: except engraved, etched, etc.: metal; automotive & apparel trimmings

(G-814)
METRO CITY GROUP INC
2283 Bellmore Ave (11710-5623)
PHONE..................516 781-2500
Carlos Jaramillo, *President*
EMP: 4
SALES: 4.5MM *Privately Held*
SIC: 3423 1711 Plumbers' hand tools; carpenters' hand tools, except saws: levels, chisels, etc.; plumbing contractors

(G-815)
PAPERWORLD INC
3054 Lee Pl (11710-5034)
PHONE..................516 221-2702
Carol Grubman, *President*
▲ EMP: 37
SALES (est): 7.3MM *Privately Held*
SIC: 2679 2675 Adding machine rolls, paper: made from purchased material; die-cut paper & board

(G-816)
RUSH GOLD MANUFACTURING LTD
Also Called: G R M
2400 Merrick Rd (11710-3821)
PHONE..................516 781-3155
Harold Lazar, *President*
Shirley Lazar, *Admin Sec*
▲ EMP: 74
SQ FT: 10,000
SALES: 5MM *Privately Held*
SIC: 3499 3961 Novelties & giftware, including trophies; costume jewelry

(G-817)
SALISBURY SPORTSWEAR INC
2523 Marine Pl (11710-5107)
PHONE..................516 221-9519
Herbert Margolis, *President*
EMP: 50
SALES (est): 3MM *Privately Held*
SIC: 2339 Sportswear, women's

(G-818)
SPEEDY SIGN A RAMA USA INC
Also Called: Sign-A-Rama
2956 Merrick Rd (11710-5760)
PHONE..................516 783-1075
Fax: 516 783-4708
Michael Bolz, *President*
Stanley Swanson, *CFO*
EMP: 5
SALES (est): 389.3K *Privately Held*
SIC: 3993 Signs & advertising specialties

Bellport
Suffolk County

(G-819)
50+ LIFESTYLE
146 S Country Rd Ste 4 (11713-2530)
PHONE..................631 286-0058
Hon Frank C Trotta, *President*
Frank C Trotta, *Owner*
Mary Alice Graham, *Finance*
Tim Edwards, *Sales Executive*
Janine Murphy, *Admin Asst*
EMP: 8
SALES: 750K *Privately Held*
SIC: 2711 Newspapers

(G-820)
ABLE ELECTRONICS INC
18 Sawgrass Dr (11713-1549)
PHONE..................631 924-5386
Fax: 631 924-5389
Loraine Leverock, *CEO*
Elizabeth Padrazo, *Chairman*
Ann Konon, *Vice Pres*
Kenneth Levebrock, *Vice Pres*
Cody Valentin, *Sales Mgr*
EMP: 10
SQ FT: 995
SALES: 3.1MM *Privately Held*
SIC: 3674 Semiconductors & related devices

(G-821)
AVS LAMINATES INC
Also Called: Steigercraft
99 Bellport Ave (11713-2106)
PHONE..................631 286-2136
Alan Steiger, *President*
John Manarte, *Vice Pres*
William Rufer, *Vice Pres*
Mark Harak, *Controller*
▲ EMP: 25
SQ FT: 20,800
SALES: 5.3MM *Privately Held*
WEB: www.steigercraft.com
SIC: 3732 Fishing boats: lobster, crab, oyster, etc.: small

(G-822)
C HOWARD COMPANY INC
1007 Station Rd (11713-1552)
PHONE..................631 286-7940
Fax: 631 286-7947
EMP: 9 EST: 1934
SQ FT: 10,000
SALES (est): 520K *Privately Held*
SIC: 2064 Mfg Candy/Confectionery

(G-823)
CRAZ WOODWORKING ASSOC INC
24 Sawgrass Dr (11713-1549)
PHONE..................631 205-1890
Peter Craz, *President*
Steve Lineberger, *Office Mgr*
EMP: 12
SQ FT: 12,000
SALES (est): 1.8MM *Privately Held*
SIC: 2499 Decorative wood & woodwork

(G-824)
EASTERN PRECISION MACHINING
11 Farber Dr Ste I (11713-1500)
PHONE..................631 286-4758
Norbert G Schreiber, *President*
Annmarie Schreiber, *Vice Pres*
EMP: 5
SQ FT: 6,000
SALES (est): 653.8K *Privately Held*
WEB: www.easternprecisionmachining.com
SIC: 3728 3599 Aircraft parts & equipment; machine shop, jobbing & repair

(G-825)
EDGE DISPLAY GROUP ENTP INC
35 Sawgrass Dr Ste 2 (11713-1577)
PHONE..................631 498-1373
Philip J Zellner, *President*
▼ EMP: 10
SALES (est): 1MM *Privately Held*
SIC: 3993 Displays & cutouts, window & lobby

(G-826)
FIREWORKS BY GRUCCI INC
20 Pinehurst Dr (11713-1573)
PHONE..................631 286-0088
Phil Grucci, *President*
Felix Grucci Jr, *President*
Donna Butler, *Vice Pres*
◆ EMP: 30
SQ FT: 6,000
SALES (est): 7.1MM *Privately Held*
SIC: 2899 Flares, fireworks & similar preparations

(G-827)
HEINECK ASSOCIATES INC
28 Curtis Ave (11713-1120)
PHONE..................631 207-2347
Andrew Heineck, *President*
EMP: 6 EST: 2000
SALES: 500K *Privately Held*
SIC: 7372 Prepackaged software

(G-828)
K INDUSTRIES INC (PA)
1107 Station Rd Ste 5a (11713-1562)
P.O. Box 542 (11713-0542)
PHONE..................631 897-2125
Victor Schneider, *President*
EMP: 5
SQ FT: 10,000
SALES: 1MM *Privately Held*
SIC: 3443 Tanks, standard or custom fabricated: metal plate

(G-829)
MAEHR INDUSTRIES INC
14 Sawgrass Dr (11713-1549)
PHONE..................631 924-1661
Michael Maehr, *President*
EMP: 6
SQ FT: 5,000
SALES (est): 760K *Privately Held*
WEB: www.maehr.com
SIC: 3469 3599 Machine parts, stamped or pressed metal; machine shop, jobbing & repair

GEOGRAPHIC SECTION

(G-830)
MCKEON ROLLING STL DOOR CO INC (PA)
44 Sawgrass Dr (11713-1549)
PHONE..........................631 803-3000
Joseph J McKeon, *President*
Magid S Shata, *Managing Dir*
David L Dodge, *Vice Pres*
Ashraf Gomaa, *Vice Pres*
Jean Elizer, *Purchasing*
▲ **EMP:** 48 **EST:** 1986
SALES (est): 7.5MM Privately Held
SIC: 3442 Metal doors; rolling doors for industrial buildings or warehouses, metal; fire doors, metal

(G-831)
MOTION MESSAGE INC
22 Sawgrass Dr Ste 4 (11713-1571)
PHONE..........................631 924-9500
William Sheridan, *President*
Irene Sheridan, *Admin Sec*
EMP: 10
SQ FT: 12,000
SALES (est): 1.1MM Privately Held
SIC: 3993 Electric signs

(G-832)
OPTISOURCE INTERNATIONAL INC
Also Called: Nu-Chem Laboratories
40 Sawgrass Dr Ste 1 (11713-1564)
PHONE..........................631 924-8360
Daryl Squicciarini, *President*
Anthony Zanghi, *Project Mgr*
Roseann Ullman, *Accounting Mgr*
Charlene Friend, *Sales Mgr*
Wendy Schneider, *Sales Mgr*
▲ **EMP:** 30
SQ FT: 30,000
SALES: 13MM
SALES (corp-wide): 938.9MM Privately Held
WEB: www.1-800-optisource.com
SIC: 3851 Lens coating, ophthalmic
HQ: Essilor Laboratories Of America, Inc.
13515 N Stemmons Fwy
Dallas TX 75234
972 241-4141

(G-833)
ORE-LUBE CORPORATION
Also Called: Orelube
20 Sawgrass Dr (11713-1549)
PHONE..........................631 205-0030
Fax: 631 205-9797
Robert Silverstein, *President*
Stan Steckler, *General Mgr*
Fritz Louif, *Warehouse Mgr*
Donna Klempka, *Office Mgr*
Debbie Desprel, *Manager*
▲ **EMP:** 15 **EST:** 1958
SQ FT: 15,000
SALES (est): 3.7MM Privately Held
WEB: www.orelube.com
SIC: 2992 Lubricating oils & greases

(G-834)
PALLETS R US INC
555 Woodside Ave (11713-1220)
PHONE..........................631 758-2360
Nicholas Sorge, *Ch of Bd*
Thomas Sorge, *Vice Pres*
Joyce Sorge, *Financial Exec*
EMP: 50
SQ FT: 10,000
SALES (est): 11.4MM Privately Held
SIC: 2448 Pallets, wood

(G-835)
PINPOINT SYSTEMS INTL INC (PA)
10 Pinehurst Dr (11713-1573)
PHONE..........................631 775-2100
William Silhan, *President*
Joe Reisinger, *Vice Pres*
Bruce Barlowe, *Buyer*
Tom Hicks, *Controller*
Michael McIntire, *Director*
EMP: 100
SALES (est): 8.5MM Privately Held
WEB: www.destdirect.com
SIC: 3699 Electrical equipment & supplies

(G-836)
POLYMAG INC
685 Station Rd Ste 2 (11713-1697)
PHONE..........................631 286-4111
Fax: 631 286-0607
Devineni Ratnam, *President*
Lou Gunn, *Manager*
Dev Ranam, *Manager*
▲ **EMP:** 20
SQ FT: 15,000
SALES (est): 2.9MM Privately Held
WEB: www.polymaginc.com
SIC: 3499 Magnets, permanent: metallic

(G-837)
PYROTECHNIQUE BY GRUCCI INC (PA)
Also Called: Starlight Properties
20 Pinehurst Dr (11713-1573)
PHONE..........................540 639-8800
Fax: 631 286-9036
Felix P Grucci, *President*
Donna Butler Grucci, *Vice Pres*
Chris Carlino, *Opers Staff*
Felix J Grucci Jr, *CFO*
John Grennan, *Controller*
▼ **EMP:** 30
SQ FT: 8,000
SALES (est): 14.9MM Privately Held
WEB: www.grucci.com
SIC: 2899 Flares, fireworks & similar preparations

(G-838)
THEGO CORPORATION
Also Called: Acme Marine Hoist
2 Mooring Dr (11713-2810)
PHONE..........................631 776-2472
EMP: 5 **EST:** 1948
SQ FT: 11,500
SALES: 1MM Privately Held
SIC: 3536 Mfg Marine Hoists

(G-839)
TORINO INDUS FABRICATION INC
4 Pinehurst Dr (11713-1573)
PHONE..........................631 509-1640
Maria Passanante, *President*
Joseph Passanante, *Vice Pres*
EMP: 9
SALES (est): 417.9K Privately Held
SIC: 3441 Building components, structural steel

(G-840)
TORINO INDUSTRIAL INC
Also Called: Torino Industrial Fabrication
4 Pinehurst Dr (11713-1573)
PHONE..........................631 509-1640
Vincent Sette, *Ch of Bd*
Keith Passanante, *Vice Pres*
Maria Passanante, *Treasurer*
Palmina Sette, *Shareholder*
EMP: 13
SQ FT: 10,000
SALES (est): 2.4MM Privately Held
WEB: www.torinoindustrial.com
SIC: 3449 Bars, concrete reinforcing: fabricated steel

Belmont
Allegany County

(G-841)
SUIT-KOTE CORPORATION
5628 Tuckers Corners Rd (14813-9604)
PHONE..........................585 268-7127
EMP: 79
SALES (corp-wide): 226MM Privately Held
SIC: 2911 Asphalt or asphaltic materials, made in refineries
PA: Suit-Kote Corporation
1911 Lorings Crossing Rd
Cortland NY 13045
607 753-1100

Bemus Point
Chautauqua County

(G-842)
LAKESIDE INDUSTRIES INC
Also Called: Point Industrial
2 Lakeside Dr (14712-9310)
P.O. Box 9130 (14712-0913)
PHONE..........................716 386-3031
Fax: 716 386-5428
Roy Benson, *CEO*
Brad Benson, *President*
Timothy Benson, *Vice Pres*
EMP: 10
SQ FT: 2,000
SALES: 950K Privately Held
SIC: 3599 Amusement park equipment

Bergen
Genesee County

(G-843)
DIEHL DEVELOPMENT INC
Also Called: Diehl Sand & Gravel
5922 N Lake Rd (14416-9507)
PHONE..........................585 494-2920
Fax: 585 494-2920
Keith Diehl, *President*
EMP: 5
SQ FT: 500
SALES (est): 1.6MM Privately Held
SIC: 1442 Gravel mining

(G-844)
GT INNOVATIONS LLC
7674 Swamp Rd (14416-9352)
PHONE..........................585 739-7659
Fax: 585 293-2826
Daniel Grastorf, *Owner*
EMP: 5
SALES (est): 684.5K Privately Held
SIC: 3444 Concrete forms, sheet metal

(G-845)
GUTHRIE HELI-ARC INC
6276 Clinton Street Rd (14416-9738)
PHONE..........................585 548-5053
Fax: 716 434-2662
Will Guthrie, *President*
EMP: 8
SQ FT: 4,500
SALES (est): 715K Privately Held
SIC: 7692 Welding repair

(G-846)
K2 PLASTICS INC
8210 Buffalo Rd (14416-9444)
PHONE..........................585 494-2727
Klaus Kremmin II, *President*
Carol Zaccour, *Manager*
EMP: 5
SALES (est): 829.4K Privately Held
WEB: www.k2plasticsinc.com
SIC: 3089 Molding primary plastic

(G-847)
LEWIS & MYERS INC (PA)
Also Called: LMI
7307 S Lake Rd (14416-9357)
PHONE..........................585 494-1410
Fax: 585 494-1436
Lawrence Lewis, *President*
Rebecca Taylor, *General Mgr*
EMP: 4
SQ FT: 33,000
SALES (est): 1.7MM Privately Held
WEB: www.lmipacking.com
SIC: 3086 Plastics foam products

(G-848)
LIBERTY PUMPS INC
7000 Appletree Ave (14416-9446)
PHONE..........................800 543-2550
Fax: 585 494-1839
Charles E Cook, *Principal*
Robyn Brookhart, *Business Mgr*
Allan Davis, *Vice Pres*
Rebecca Evangelista, *Vice Pres*
Gary Volk, *Vice Pres*
◆ **EMP:** 130 **EST:** 1965
SQ FT: 120,000
SALES: 96.1MM Privately Held
WEB: www.libertypumps.com
SIC: 3561 Pumps, domestic: water or sump

(G-849)
MILLERS MILLWORKS INC
Also Called: Millers Presentation Furniture
29 N Lake Ave (14416-9528)
P.O. Box 175 (14416-0175)
PHONE..........................585 494-1420
Greg Lumb, *President*
Kathleen Dunlap, *Office Mgr*
Michelle Yoffee, *Office Admin*
EMP: 20 **EST:** 1996
SQ FT: 6,192
SALES (est): 2.1MM Privately Held
WEB: www.millersmillwork.com
SIC: 2521 Wood office furniture

(G-850)
ODYSSEY CONTROLS INC
6256 Clinton Street Rd (14416-9738)
P.O. Box 613 (14416-0613)
PHONE..........................585 548-9800
Danie T Harmon Jr, *Ch of Bd*
EMP: 6
SALES (est): 974.7K Privately Held
SIC: 3613 Control panels, electric

(G-851)
SCOMAC INC
8629 Buffalo Rd (14416)
P.O. Box 455 (14416-0455)
PHONE..........................585 494-2200
Fax: 585 494-2300
Lawrence Scott, *President*
EMP: 12
SQ FT: 12,000
SALES (est): 1.9MM Privately Held
WEB: www.scomac.com
SIC: 3545 Diamond dressing & wheel crushing attachments

Berkshire
Tioga County

(G-852)
TIOGA HARDWOODS INC (PA)
12685 State Route 38 (13736-1930)
P.O. Box 195 (13736-0195)
PHONE..........................607 657-8686
Fax: 607 687-9439
Kevin Gillette, *President*
Randy Bowers, *Vice Pres*
Scott Snyder, *Vice Pres*
Chad Cotterill, *Sales Staff*
▼ **EMP:** 1
SQ FT: 20,000
SALES (est): 4.5MM Privately Held
WEB: www.tiogahardwoods.com
SIC: 2861 Hardwood distillates

(G-853)
TREIMAN PUBLICATIONS CORP
12724 State Route 38 (13736-1911)
PHONE..........................607 657-8473
Fax: 607 657-8505
Dov Trieman, *President*
EMP: 5
SALES (est): 287.1K Privately Held
SIC: 2741 Miscellaneous publishing

Berlin
Rensselaer County

(G-854)
COWEE FOREST PRODUCTS INC
28 Taylor Ave (12022-7740)
PHONE..........................518 658-2233
William Stallkamp, *President*
Tara Fisher, *General Mgr*
Arthur Bogen, *Vice Pres*
▲ **EMP:** 20 **EST:** 1898
SQ FT: 100,000
SALES: 2MM Privately Held
WEB: www.cowee.com
SIC: 2499 Novelties, wood fiber; carved & turned wood

Berlin - Rensselaer County (G-855)

(G-855)
GREEN RENEWABLE INC
28 Taylor Ave (12022-7740)
PHONE..................518 658-2233
Sean M Gallivan, *President*
Todd Tierney, *General Mgr*
EMP: 40
SALES (est): 194.8K Privately Held
SIC: 2499 Clothespins, wood

(G-856)
MILANESE COMMERCIAL DOOR LLC
28 Taylor Ave (12022-7740)
P.O. Box 560 (12022-0560)
PHONE..................518 658-0398
Brian Milanese, *Principal*
EMP: 10 EST: 2007
SALES (est): 1.4MM Privately Held
SIC: 3442 5031 Metal doors; door frames, all materials

Bernhards Bay
Oswego County

(G-857)
MCINTOSH BOX & PALLET CO INC
741 State Route 49 (13028)
P.O. Box 76 (13028-0076)
PHONE..................315 675-8511
Fax: 315 675-3068
Brian Cole, *Opers Mgr*
Michael Milson, *Branch Mgr*
EMP: 60
SALES (corp-wide): 26.9MM Privately Held
WEB: www.mcintoshbox.com
SIC: 2448 2441 Pallets, wood; nailed wood boxes & shook
PA: Mcintosh Box & Pallet Co., Inc.
5864 Pyle Dr
East Syracuse NY 13057
315 446-9350

Bethel
Sullivan County

(G-858)
ALEXY ASSOCIATES INC
86 Jim Stephenson Rd (12720)
PHONE..................845 482-3000
Fax: 845 482-3040
Cornelius Alexy, *President*
James Alexy, *Systems Mgr*
Sharon Alexy, *Admin Sec*
EMP: 20 EST: 1974
SALES: 200K Privately Held
WEB: www.aaultrasoniccleaners.com
SIC: 3699 7629 Cleaning equipment, ultrasonic, except medical & dental; electronic equipment repair

(G-859)
CAMPANELLIS POULTRY FARM INC
4 Perry Rd (12720)
PHONE..................845 482-2222
Anthony Campanelli, *Owner*
EMP: 5
SALES: 1.7MM Privately Held
SIC: 2015 Poultry slaughtering & processing

Bethpage
Nassau County

(G-860)
A & M LITHO INC
4 Hunt Pl (11714-6411)
PHONE..................516 342-9727
Anna Laperuta, *President*
EMP: 25
SALES: 2.5MM Privately Held
SIC: 2752 Commercial printing, offset

(G-861)
ABBLE AWNING CO INC
313 Broadway Ste 315 (11714-3003)
PHONE..................516 822-1200
Thomas Catalano, *President*
John Catalano, *Vice Pres*
EMP: 9
SQ FT: 2,400
SALES: 500K Privately Held
WEB: www.abbleawning.com
SIC: 2394 Awnings, fabric: made from purchased materials; canopies, fabric: made from purchased materials

(G-862)
AC MOORE INCORPORATED
3988 Hempstead Tpke (11714-5603)
PHONE..................516 796-5831
Fax: 516 796-5852
EMP: 5
SALES (corp-wide): 546.1MM Privately Held
SIC: 2499 5023 Mfg Wood Products Whol Homefurnishings
HQ: A.C. Moore Incorporated
130 A C Moore Dr
Berlin NJ 08009
856 768-4930

(G-863)
AGUA ENERVIVA LLC
15 Grumman Rd W Ste 1300 (11714-5029)
PHONE..................516 597-5440
Michael Venuti, *President*
Carol Dollard, *COO*
Thomas Reynolds, *Finance*
John Borelli, *Marketing Staff*
EMP: 12
SALES (est): 1.4MM Privately Held
SIC: 2087 Beverage bases, concentrates, syrups, powders & mixes

(G-864)
BRUNSCHWIG & FILS LLC (HQ)
245 Central Ave (11714-3922)
PHONE..................800 538-1880
Carlos Anderson, *Credit Mgr*
Peter Smith,
Brusnchwig Fils, *Representative*
▲ EMP: 15
SALES (est): 26.8MM
SALES (corp-wide): 388.8MM Privately Held
SIC: 2329 2211 Ski & snow clothing: men's & boys'; upholstery, tapestry & wall coverings: cotton
PA: Kravet Inc.
225 Cent Ave S
Bethpage NY 11714
516 293-2000

(G-865)
DOCTOR PAVERS
2 Mack Pl (11714-4722)
PHONE..................516 342-6016
Roberto A Mendonca, *Owner*
EMP: 5
SALES (est): 286.1K Privately Held
SIC: 2951 Asphalt paving mixtures & blocks

(G-866)
EVENT JOURNAL INC
700 Hicksville Rd (11714-3471)
PHONE..................516 470-1811
Dawn Strain, *President*
Marisa Kerby, *Opers Staff*
William Frank, *Client Mgr*
Laura Kaplan, *Marketing Staff*
Catherine Kaczmarczyk, *Creative Dir*
EMP: 9
SALES (est): 518.6K Privately Held
SIC: 2711 Newspapers, publishing & printing

(G-867)
GRUMMAN FIELD SUPPORT SERVICES
S Oyster Bay Rd (11714)
PHONE..................516 575-0574
Ed Sax, *Principal*
Brian Boyer, *Vice Pres*
Tony Miller, *Finance*
EMP: 70

SALES (est): 11.7MM Publicly Held
WEB: www.sperry.ngc.com
SIC: 3721 8731 Aircraft; commercial physical research
HQ: Northrop Grumman Systems Corporation
2980 Fairview Park Dr
Falls Church VA 22042
703 280-2900

(G-868)
HOWE MACHINE & TOOL CORP
236 Park Ave (11714-3709)
PHONE..................516 931-5687
Fax: 516 931-5717
Paul Howe, *President*
Ryan Howe, *Vice Pres*
Sue Howe, *Manager*
Jacquelin Castagna, *Admin Asst*
EMP: 11 EST: 1953
SQ FT: 11,500
SALES: 11.5MM Privately Held
WEB: www.howemachine.com
SIC: 3724 Aircraft engines & engine parts

(G-869)
KREON INC
999 S Oyster Bay Rd # 105 (11714-1041)
PHONE..................516 470-9522
Thomas Mindt, *CEO*
Darin Fowler, *President*
Christina Sewkaran, *Administration*
▲ EMP: 5
SALES (est): 1MM Privately Held
SIC: 3641 Electric lamps
HQ: Kreon Nv
Industrieweg-Noord 1152
Opglabbeek 3660
898 197-80

(G-870)
LOGIC CONTROLS INC
Also Called: Bematech
999 S Oyster Bay Rd (11714-1038)
PHONE..................516 248-0400
Fax: 516 248-0443
Juliet Derby, *President*
Waldimir Alvarez, *Principal*
Breann Murray, *Business Mgr*
Wladimir Alvarez, *VP Sls/Mktg*
Paul Cagnard, *Controller*
◆ EMP: 33
SQ FT: 10,000
SALES (est): 7.4MM Privately Held
WEB: www.logiccontrols.com
SIC: 3578 Accounting machines & cash registers; cash registers; point-of-sale devices; registers, credit account
HQ: Bematech Industria E Comercio De Equipamentos Eletronicos S/A.
Av. Rui Barbosa 2.529
Sao Jose Dos Pinhais PR 83055

(G-871)
MARK DRI PRODUCTS INC
999 S Oyster Bay Rd # 312 (11714-1042)
PHONE..................516 484-6200
Fax: 516 484-6279
Charles Reichmann, *CEO*
Andre Reichmann, *President*
Lynn Paugh, *COO*
Mickey Ciranni, *Purch Mgr*
Cathy Williams-Owen, *Controller*
▲ EMP: 200
SQ FT: 54,000
SALES (est): 23.5MM Privately Held
WEB: www.drimark.com
SIC: 3951 5112 Markers, soft tip (felt, fabric, plastic, etc.); pens &/or pencils

(G-872)
MELMONT FINE PRINGNG/GRAPHICS
6 Robert Ct Ste 24 (11714-1415)
P.O. Box 395, Old Bethpage (11804-0395)
PHONE..................516 939-2253
Angela Melledy, *President*
EMP: 6
SALES: 150K Privately Held
SIC: 2711 7389 Newspapers, publishing & printing; printing broker

(G-873)
MLS SALES
226 10th St (11714-1703)
PHONE..................516 681-2736

Mary Lafauci, *Owner*
EMP: 6
SALES: 120K Privately Held
SIC: 3679 Electronic components

(G-874)
NORTHROP GRUMMAN CORPORATION
660 Grumman Rd W (11714)
PHONE..................703 280-2900
Wesley G Bush, *Branch Mgr*
EMP: 702 Publicly Held
SIC: 3812 Search & navigation equipment
PA: Northrop Grumman Corporation
2980 Fairview Park Dr
Falls Church VA 22042

(G-875)
NORTHROP GRUMMAN SYSTEMS CORP
925 S Oyster Bay Rd (11714-3582)
PHONE..................516 575-0574
Fax: 516 575-7428
Michael Gross, *General Mgr*
Dominic Anton, *Project Mgr*
John Munyak, *Technical Mgr*
Thomas Chyczewski, *Research*
Paul Buckley, *Engineer*
EMP: 1659 Publicly Held
WEB: www.sperry.ngc.com
SIC: 3721 8731 Aircraft; commercial physical research
HQ: Northrop Grumman Systems Corporation
2980 Fairview Park Dr
Falls Church VA 22042
703 280-2900

(G-876)
PACS SWITCHGEAR LLC (PA)
1211 Stewart Ave (11714-1601)
PHONE..................516 465-7100
Neil Minihane, *CEO*
Larry Bloom, *CFO*
Glen Ring, *Controller*
EMP: 9
SALES (est): 5MM Privately Held
SIC: 3613 Switchgear & switchboard apparatus

(G-877)
RAIN CATCHERS SEAMLESS GUTTERS
39 Park Ln (11714-5226)
PHONE..................516 520-1956
Robert Dambrosio, *CEO*
EMP: 5
SALES (est): 420.5K Privately Held
SIC: 3272 Floor slabs & tiles, precast concrete

(G-878)
WILSONART INTL HOLDINGS LLC
999 S Oyster Bay Rd # 3305 (11714-1038)
PHONE..................516 935-6980
Fax: 516 935-6875
Greg Martino, *Manager*
EMP: 20
SALES (corp-wide): 7.7B Privately Held
WEB: www.wilsonart.com
SIC: 2821 2541 Plastics materials & resins; table or counter tops, plastic laminated
HQ: Wilsonart International Holdings Llc
10501 Mw Hk Podgen Loop
Temple TX 76503
254 207-7000

Big Flats
Chemung County

(G-879)
REYNOLDS MANUFACTURING INC
3298 State Rte 352 (14814)
PHONE..................607 562-8936
Kasandra Reynolds, *Ch of Bd*
Terri Fitzpatrick, *Purchasing*
Paula White-Arcovio, *Accounts Mgr*
Kristi Hackrd, *Administration*
EMP: 17

SQ FT: 11,000
SALES (est): 3.9MM **Privately Held**
SIC: 3444 3469 Sheet metalwork; machine parts, stamped or pressed metal

(G-880)
X-GEN PHARMACEUTICALS INC (PA)
300 Daniel Zenker Dr (14814)
P.O. Box 445 (14814-0445)
PHONE..................................607 562-2700
Fax: 607 562-2760
Susan E Badia, *Ch of Bd*
Robin Liles, *Vice Pres*
Tony Dowd, *Safety Mgr*
Catherine Liles, *Treasurer*
Steve Eller, *Marketing Mgr*
EMP: 3
SQ FT: 53,000
SALES (est): 4.4MM **Privately Held**
SIC: 2834 Pharmaceutical preparations

Binghamton
Broome County

(G-881)
A-LINE TECHNOLOGIES INC
197 Corporate Dr (13904-3214)
PHONE..................................607 772-2439
Fax: 607 772-2439
Alex Boyce, *President*
Frank J Boyce, *Vice Pres*
Tucker Williams, *Manager*
EMP: 10
SQ FT: 10,000
SALES: 1.1MM **Privately Held**
SIC: 3714 3599 Motor vehicle transmissions, drive assemblies & parts; machine shop, jobbing & repair

(G-882)
ALL AMERICAN BUILDING
109 Crestmont Rd (13905-3951)
PHONE..................................607 797-7123
Douglas E Hamm, *Owner*
EMP: 8
SALES (est): 728.2K **Privately Held**
SIC: 3448 Prefabricated metal buildings

(G-883)
ALL SPEC FINISHING INC
219 Clinton St (13905-2236)
PHONE..................................607 770-9174
Fax: 607 770-9174
Anthony Milasi, *President*
Dennis Smith, *President*
Seth Blood, *Finance Other*
Shirley Milasi, *Admin Sec*
EMP: 50
SQ FT: 80,000
SALES (est): 5.6MM **Privately Held**
WEB: www.allspecfinishing.com
SIC: 3479 7699 Painting, coating & hot dipping; painting of metal products; plastics products repair

(G-884)
AMERICAN QUALITY TECHNOLOGY
6 Emma St (13905-2508)
PHONE..................................607 777-9488
Gary Crounse, *President*
Jerome Luchuk, *CFO*
EMP: 12
SALES: 980K **Privately Held**
SIC: 3672 3679 3825 Printed circuit boards; electronic circuits; instruments to measure electricity

(G-885)
AMETEK INC
33 Lewis Rd Ste 6 (13905-1045)
PHONE..................................607 763-4700
Ed Scott, *Engineer*
Greg Shepherd, *Engineer*
Robert Glydon, *Finance Mgr*
Kevin McLoughlin, *Comptroller*
Robert Hyland, *Branch Mgr*
EMP: 68
SALES (corp-wide): 3.8B **Publicly Held**
SIC: 3621 Motors & generators

PA: Ametek, Inc.
1100 Cassatt Rd
Berwyn PA 19312
610 647-2121

(G-886)
ARNOLD-DAVIS LLC
Also Called: Harris Assembly Group
187 Indl Pk Dr (13904)
PHONE..................................607 772-1201
Thomas Davis, *CEO*
Michael Querry, *Engineer*
Kenneth Tinklepaugh, *Engineer*
David Arnold, *President*
David Martin, *VP Finance*
▲ **EMP:** 125
SQ FT: 30,000
SALES (est): 28.7MM **Privately Held**
WEB: www.harrisasm.com
SIC: 3679 Harness assemblies for electronic use; wire or cable

(G-887)
BARRETT PAVING MATERIALS INC
14 Brandywine St (13901-2203)
P.O. Box 2368 (13902-2368)
PHONE..................................607 723-5367
Bill Lallier, *Facilities Mgr*
Craig Scovell, *Facilities Mgr*
Gary Hoyt, *Manager*
EMP: 6
SQ FT: 1,144
SALES (corp-wide): 77.1MM **Privately Held**
WEB: www.barrettpaving.com
SIC: 2951 1442 Asphalt paving mixtures & blocks; construction sand & gravel
HQ: Barrett Paving Materials Inc.
3 Becker Farm Rd Ste 307
Roseland NJ 07068
973 533-1001

(G-888)
BINGHAMTON BURIAL VAULT CO INC
1114 Porter Ave (13901-1688)
PHONE..................................607 722-4931
Brian Abbey, *President*
Janet Evenson, *Vice Pres*
EMP: 14
SQ FT: 10,000
SALES (est): 2MM **Privately Held**
SIC: 3272 Steps, prefabricated concrete; burial vaults, concrete or precast terrazzo

(G-889)
BINGHAMTON KNITTING CO INC
11 Alice St (13904-1587)
P.O. Box 1646 (13902-1646)
PHONE..................................607 722-6941
Fax: 607 722-4621
Douglas W Hardler, *President*
Lee Sherwood, *Prdtn Mgr*
Craig Hardler, *Shareholder*
Julia Sherwood, *Admin Sec*
▲ **EMP:** 20
SQ FT: 23,200
SALES (est): 1.1MM **Privately Held**
WEB: www.brimwick.com
SIC: 2253 2258 Knit outerwear mills; sweaters & sweater coats, knit; lace & warp knit fabric mills

(G-890)
BINGHAMTON PRECAST & SUP CORP
18 Phelps St (13901-1858)
PHONE..................................607 722-0334
Fax: 607 722-0496
Jay Abbey, *Ch of Bd*
EMP: 50
SALES (est): 10.5MM **Privately Held**
WEB: www.binghamtonprecast.com
SIC: 3272 Pipe, concrete or lined with concrete

(G-891)
BINGHAMTON SIMULATOR CO INC
Also Called: B S C
151 Court St (13901-3529)
PHONE..................................607 321-2980
Fax: 607 722-6504
John Matthews, *CEO*

E Terry Lewis, *President*
Robin Laabs, *Principal*
Joe Vilasi, *Business Mgr*
Greg Stanton, *COO*
▲ **EMP:** 40
SQ FT: 14,000
SALES (est): 5.9MM **Privately Held**
WEB: www.bsc.com
SIC: 3571 3577 7699 7373 Electronic computers; graphic displays, except graphic terminals; aircraft & heavy equipment repair services; systems integration services; electrical equipment & supplies

(G-892)
BOCES BUSINESS OFFICE
Also Called: Broom Tioga Boces
435 Glenwood Rd (13905-1699)
PHONE..................................607 763-3300
Sandra Ruffo, *President*
Callie Kavleski, *Engineer*
Donna Balles, *Accountant*
Alan Slocum, *Cust Mgr*
Valerie Vavra, *Manager*
EMP: 19
SALES (est): 2.2MM **Privately Held**
SIC: 2761 Continuous forms, office & business

(G-893)
BOKA PRINTING INC
12 Hall St (13903-2114)
PHONE..................................607 725-3235
Bob Carr, *Principal*
EMP: 7 **EST:** 2013
SALES (est): 931.9K **Privately Held**
SIC: 2752 Commercial printing, lithographic

(G-894)
BRAND BOX USA LLC
1 Chamberlain St (13904-1314)
PHONE..................................607 584-7682
EMP: 6
SALES (est): 569.1K **Privately Held**
SIC: 2653 Corrugated & solid fiber boxes

(G-895)
BSC ASSOCIATES LLC
151 Court St (13901-3502)
PHONE..................................607 321-2980
Greg Stanton, *Branch Mgr*
Troy Jannison, *Manager*
Barry Wolf, *Systs Prg Mgr*
Barbara Blincoe,
EMP: 19
SALES: 1.5MM **Privately Held**
SIC: 3699 Flight simulators (training aids), electronic

(G-896)
BW ELLIOTT MFG CO LLC
11 Beckwith Ave (13901-1726)
P.O. Box 773 (13902-0773)
PHONE..................................607 772-0404
Fax: 607 772-0431
Richard Allbritton, *CEO*
George Scherer, *President*
Cyril Macinka, *COO*
Dan Tasker, *QA Dir*
Ken Palmer, *Engineer*
▲ **EMP:** 295
SQ FT: 250,000
SALES (est): 101.8MM
SALES (corp-wide): 1.1B **Publicly Held**
WEB: www.elliottmfg.com
SIC: 3568 3492 3531 Power transmission equipment; shafts, flexible; joints, swivel & universal, except aircraft & automotive; control valves, fluid power; hydraulic & pneumatic; construction machinery
PA: Actuant Corporation
N86w12500 Westbrook Xing
Menomonee Falls WI 53051
262 293-1500

(G-897)
C H THOMPSON COMPANY INC
69-93 Eldredge St (13902)
PHONE..................................607 724-1094
Fax: 607 724-6990
Stacy Cacialli, *President*
Thomas Talerico, *President*
Stacy Schraeder, *Vice Pres*
Joseph Talerico, *CFO*
Mary Ciatiak, *Office Mgr*

EMP: 65
SQ FT: 75,000
SALES (est): 8.7MM **Privately Held**
SIC: 3471 2396 3479 Anodizing (plating) of metals or formed products; automotive & apparel trimmings; painting, coating & hot dipping

(G-898)
CMP ADVNCED MECH SLTNS NY LLC
Also Called: Cmp New York
90 Bevier St (13904-1020)
PHONE..................................607 352-1712
Damon Snyder, *General Mgr*
Steven Zimmerman, *Mng Member*
Larry Farr, *Manager*
EMP: 1
SALES (est): 1.1MM
SALES (corp-wide): 364.8K **Privately Held**
SIC: 3824 Mechanical & electromechanical counters & devices
PA: Cmp Ams (International) Limitee
1241 Rue Des Cascades
Chateauguay QC J6J 4
450 691-5510

(G-899)
CREATIVE ORTHOTICS PROSTHETICS
65 Pennsylvania Ave 207 (13903-1651)
PHONE..................................607 771-4672
Thomas Kirk PHD, *CEO*
David Sicklis, *Manager*
Sheryl Price, *Director*
EMP: 9
SALES (corp-wide): 451.4MM **Publicly Held**
SIC: 3842 5999 Limbs, artificial; orthopedic & prosthesis applications
HQ: Creative Orthotics & Prosthetics, Inc.
1300 College Ave Ste 1
Elmira NY 14901
607 734-7215

(G-900)
CROWLEY FOODS INC (HQ)
93 Pennsylvania Ave (13903-1645)
PHONE..................................800 637-0019
John Kaned, *President*
Lynn Wordsworth, *Manager*
▼ **EMP:** 31 **EST:** 1904
SALES (est): 198.6MM
SALES (corp-wide): 1.7B **Privately Held**
WEB: www.crowleyfoods.com
SIC: 2026 2024 Fluid milk; fermented & cultured milk products; yogurt; cottage cheese; ice cream & frozen desserts
PA: Hp Hood Llc
6 Kimball Ln Ste 400
Lynnfield MA 01940
617 887-8441

(G-901)
CRYSTA-LYN CHEMICAL COMPANY
Also Called: Clearweld
6 Emma St (13905-2508)
PHONE..................................607 296-4721
Frank Goreleski, *President*
Bradly Galusha, *Vice Pres*
▲ **EMP:** 8
SQ FT: 12,000
SALES (est): 1.4MM **Privately Held**
WEB: www.crystalyn.com
SIC: 3699 Laser welding, drilling & cutting equipment

(G-902)
D D & L INC
Also Called: E D I Window Systems
3 Alice St (13904-1502)
P.O. Box 2949 (13902-2949)
PHONE..................................607 729-9131
Fax: 607 772-1855
David P Smith, *President*
Richard Smith, *Vice Pres*
EMP: 17
SQ FT: 15,120
SALES (est): 1.7MM **Privately Held**
SIC: 3442 5211 Window & door frames; door & window products

Binghamton - Broome County (G-903)

(G-903)
DBASE LLC
31 Front St (13905-4703)
P.O. Box 617, Oxford (13830-0917)
PHONE..................607 729-0234
Fax: 607 729-3830
Robert Thompson, *Principal*
Cheryl Thompson, *Controller*
Paul McGee, *Sales Dir*
Alonda Manzer, *Cust Mgr*
Martin Kay, *CTO*
EMP: 8 EST: 2011
SALES (est): 795.4K Privately Held
SIC: 7372 Application computer software

(G-904)
DOT TOOL CO INC
131 Nowlan Rd (13901-1693)
PHONE..................607 724-7001
Fax: 607 773-1446
Gary Braman, *President*
EMP: 5
SQ FT: 3,004
SALES (est): 695.2K Privately Held
WEB: www.dottoolco.com
SIC: 3544 3444 Special dies, tools, jigs & fixtures; sheet metalwork

(G-905)
ECK PLASTIC ARTS INC
87 Prospect Ave (13901-2616)
PHONE..................607 722-3227
Fax: 607 722-3081
Robert L Eck Jr, *President*
Chris Figures, *Opers Mgr*
Mark Bowers, *Info Tech Mgr*
▲ EMP: 25
SQ FT: 30,000
SALES (est): 5.9MM Privately Held
WEB: www.eckplastics.com
SIC: 3089 Plastic processing; injection molded finished plastic products

(G-906)
ELECTRO FORM CORP
128 Bevier St (13904-1094)
PHONE..................607 722-6404
Fax: 607 724-5184
Auguste Mathey Jr, *President*
Donna Kadaronak, *Office Mgr*
Donna Jadarondak, *Admin Sec*
Bonnie Johnson, *Admin Sec*
EMP: 11
SQ FT: 6,000
SALES (est): 1.3MM Privately Held
SIC: 3544 Special dies & tools

(G-907)
EMS TECHNOLOGIES INC
71 Frederick St (13901-2563)
PHONE..................607 723-3676
Clarence Hotchkiss, *Ch of Bd*
Mark Hotchkiss, *President*
Robert Phillips, *President*
Tom Costello, *Principal*
Joanne Delanoy, *Engineer*
EMP: 40
SQ FT: 36,000
SALES (est): 10.2MM
SALES (corp-wide): 11.1MM Privately Held
WEB: www.emstech.com
SIC: 3629 Electronic generation equipment
PA: Nelson Holdings Ltd
71 Frederick St
Binghamton NY 13901
607 772-1794

(G-908)
ENJOY CITY NORTH INC
Also Called: Save Around
31 Front St (13905-4703)
P.O. Box 2399 (13902-2399)
PHONE..................607 584-5061
Luke Stanton, *President*
Eric Hinkle, *Business Mgr*
Jessica Nurczynski, *Production*
Wendy Hickin, *Accountant*
Ray Stanton, *Sales Staff*
EMP: 64
SALES: 5.9MM Privately Held
SIC: 2741 Miscellaneous publishing

(G-909)
FELCHAR MANUFACTURING CORP (HQ)
Also Called: Norwich Manufacturing Division
196 Corporate Dr (13904-3295)
PHONE..................607 723-3106
Fax: 607 723-4084
Jonathan Miller, *President*
Vince Bungo, *Vice Pres*
Steve Cole, *Vice Pres*
Mike Carr, *Plant Mgr*
Ron Sternberg, *Plant Mgr*
▲ EMP: 650
SQ FT: 40,000
SALES (est): 146.2MM
SALES (corp-wide): 399.1MM Privately Held
WEB: www.felchar.com
SIC: 3678 3089 3621 Electronic connectors; injection molding of plastics; motors & generators
PA: Shop Vac Corporation
2323 Reach Rd
Williamsport PA 17701
570 326-0502

(G-910)
FRATELLIS LLC
Also Called: New Horizons Bakery
20 Campbell Rd (13905-4304)
PHONE..................607 722-5663
Anthony Roma, *Principal*
Mary Roma, *Mng Member*
EMP: 21
SQ FT: 23,000
SALES (est): 850K Privately Held
SIC: 2051 2053 5142 5149 Bread, cake & related products; frozen bakery products, except bread; croissants, frozen; bakery products, frozen; bakery products

(G-911)
FRITO-LAY NORTH AMERICA INC
10 Spud Ln (13904-3299)
PHONE..................607 775-7000
Fax: 607 775-3567
Pat Zimmer, *Safety Mgr*
Frank Armetta, *Mfg Spvr*
Thomas Brown, *Mfg Staff*
Brian Stringer, *Opers-Prdtn-Mfg*
Paula Kellum, *Purchasing*
EMP: 85
SQ FT: 4,906
SALES (corp-wide): 62.8B Publicly Held
WEB: www.fritolay.com
SIC: 2096 2099 Potato chips & other potato-based snacks; food preparations
HQ: Frito-Lay North America, Inc.
7701 Legacy Dr
Plano TX 75024

(G-912)
G J C LTD INC
Also Called: Wilson Electroplating
6 Emma St (13905-2508)
PHONE..................607 770-4500
Fax: 607 770-9117
Gary Crounse, *President*
Olin Russell, *Mng Officer*
EMP: 24
SQ FT: 30,000
SALES (est): 2.2MM Privately Held
SIC: 3471 Electroplating & plating

(G-913)
GLOWA MANUFACTURING INC
6 Emma St (13905-2508)
PHONE..................607 770-0811
Fax: 607 770-0950
Jerry Glowa, *President*
Karen Glowa, *Vice Pres*
William Pomeroy, *Shareholder*
EMP: 47
SQ FT: 10,000
SALES (est): 5.3MM Privately Held
SIC: 3577 Computer peripheral equipment

(G-914)
GOLUB CORPORATION
Also Called: Price Chopper Pharmacy 234
33 Chenango Bridge Rd (13901-1233)
PHONE..................607 235-7240
EMP: 99
SALES (corp-wide): 3.4B Privately Held
SIC: 3751 Motorcycles & related parts
PA: The Golub Corporation
461 Nott St
Schenectady NY 12308
518 355-5000

(G-915)
HANGER PRSTHETCS & ORTHO INC
65 Pennsylvania Ave (13903-1651)
PHONE..................607 771-4672
EMP: 7
SALES (corp-wide): 451.4MM Publicly Held
SIC: 3842 Limbs, artificial
HQ: Hanger Prosthetics & Orthotics, Inc.
10910 Domain Dr Ste 300
Austin TX 78758
512 777-3800

(G-916)
HP HOOD LLC
Also Called: Crowley Foods
93 Pennsylvania Ave (13903-1645)
PHONE..................607 772-6580
Joe Cervantes, *Senior VP*
Jeff Wager, *Director*
EMP: 1660
SALES (corp-wide): 1.7B Privately Held
WEB: www.hphood.com
SIC: 2026 2024 Fluid milk; fermented & cultured milk products; yogurt; cottage cheese; ice cream & frozen desserts
PA: Hp Hood Llc
6 Kimball Ln Ste 400
Lynnfield MA 01940
617 887-8441

(G-917)
I 3 MANUFACTURING SERVICES INC
100 Eldredge St (13901-2631)
PHONE..................607 238-7077
James T Matthews, *President*
Paul Marra, *Controller*
Michelle Elderd, *Admin Sec*
EMP: 5
SALES (est): 349.2K Privately Held
SIC: 3672 Printed circuit boards

(G-918)
I3 ASSEMBLY LLC
100 Eldredge St (13901-2631)
PHONE..................607 238-7077
James Matthews, *President*
Paul Marra, *Controller*
Roger Billings, *Supervisor*
EMP: 70 EST: 2015
SQ FT: 185,000
SALES (est): 10.3MM
SALES (corp-wide): 108.2MM Privately Held
SIC: 3679 Harness assemblies for electronic use: wire or cable
PA: I3 Electronics, Inc.
100 Eldredge St
Binghamton NY 13901
607 238-7077

(G-919)
I3 ELECTRONICS INC (PA)
100 Eldredge St (13901-2631)
PHONE..................607 238-7077
Jim Matthews Jr, *President*
Pierre Lavignette, *Business Mgr*
John Snyder, *Opers Mgr*
James Thornton, *Opers Staff*
Matthew Coppola, *Production*
EMP: 139 EST: 2013
SALES (est): 108.2MM Privately Held
SIC: 3672 Printed circuit boards

(G-920)
IHD MOTORSPORTS LLC
Also Called: Independence Harley-Davidson
1152 Upper Front St (13905-1119)
PHONE..................979 690-1669
James E Booth, *Mng Member*
EMP: 15 EST: 2014
SQ FT: 15,000
SALES (est): 2.6MM Privately Held
SIC: 3751 2396 Motorcycles & related parts; motorcycle accessories; automotive & apparel trimmings

(G-921)
ILLINOIS TOOL WORKS INC
33 Lewis Rd (13905-1048)
PHONE..................607 770-4945
Ron Skeeles, *General Mgr*
EMP: 20
SALES (corp-wide): 13.6B Publicly Held
SIC: 3444 Metal housings, enclosures, casings & other containers
PA: Illinois Tool Works Inc.
155 Harlem Ave
Glenview IL 60025
847 724-7500

(G-922)
INSULATING COATINGS CORP
27 Link Dr Ste D (13904-3208)
PHONE..................607 723-1727
Tony Loup, *Manager*
EMP: 11
SALES (corp-wide): 9.8MM Privately Held
WEB: www.insulatingcoatings.com
SIC: 2851 Paints & allied products
PA: Insulating Coatings Corp.
956 S Us Highway 41
Inverness FL 34450
352 344-8741

(G-923)
IPP ENERGY LLC
Also Called: Transalta
22 Charles St (13905-2268)
PHONE..................607 773-3307
Richard Langhammer, *President*
Doug Haglund, *Vice Pres*
Gary Hart, *Treasurer*
Elizabeth J Osler, *Admin Sec*
EMP: 5
SQ FT: 19,640
SALES (est): 353.9K Privately Held
WEB: www.transalta.com
SIC: 1311 Natural gas production

(G-924)
IVI SERVICES INC
Also Called: Indian Valley
5 Pine Camp Dr (13904-3109)
PHONE..................607 729-5111
Wayne A Rozen, *CEO*
Chuck Hutton, *Natl Sales Mgr*
◆ EMP: 72 EST: 1940
SQ FT: 250,000
SALES (est): 13.8MM Privately Held
WEB: www.iviindustries.com
SIC: 2299 4225 4953 2673 Bagging, jute; general warehousing; recycling, waste materials; bags: plastic, laminated & coated; textile bags; broadwoven fabric mills, manmade

(G-925)
JANE LEWIS
Also Called: Sun Valley Printing
82 Castle Creek Rd (13901-1004)
PHONE..................607 722-0584
Fax: 607 723-7741
Jane Lewis, *Owner*
David A Lewis, *Co-Owner*
Janet Ingraham, *Office Mgr*
EMP: 6
SQ FT: 2,400
SALES: 250K Privately Held
SIC: 2752 2791 2789 Commercial printing, lithographic; typesetting; bookbinding & related work

(G-926)
JOHNSON OUTDOORS INC
Eureka Tents
625 Conklin Rd (13903-2700)
P.O. Box 966 (13902-0966)
PHONE..................607 779-2200
Tom Poplawski, *Engineer*
William Kelly, *Branch Mgr*
Suzanne Lewis-Mott, *Manager*
EMP: 175
SALES (corp-wide): 433.7MM Publicly Held
SIC: 2394 2393 5091 5941 Tents: made from purchased materials; knapsacks, canvas: made from purchased materials; camping equipment & supplies; camping equipment; canoe & kayak dealers; sporting & athletic goods

▲ = Import ▼ = Export
◆ = Import/Export

GEOGRAPHIC SECTION
Binghamton - Broome County (G-953)

PA: Johnson Outdoors Inc.
555 Main St
Racine WI 53403
262 631-6600

(G-927)
JONES HUMDINGER
204 Hayes Rd (13905-5918)
PHONE.....................607 771-6501
Steve Kallfelz, *Owner*
EMP: 15
SALES: 180K Privately Held
SIC: 2024 Ice cream & frozen desserts

(G-928)
LABRADOR STONE INC
11 Dutchess Rd (13901-1411)
PHONE.....................570 465-2120
EMP: 7 EST: 2010
SALES (est): 912.6K Privately Held
SIC: 1429 7389 Crushed & broken stone;

(G-929)
LEO P CALLAHAN INC
229 Lwer Stlla Ireland Rd (13905)
PHONE.....................607 797-7314
Fax: 607 797-3538
James Callahan, *President*
EMP: 10 EST: 1960
SQ FT: 1,600
SALES (est): 1MM Privately Held
SIC: 2796 Color separations for printing

(G-930)
MECHANICAL PWR CONVERSION LLC
Also Called: E&M Power
6 Emma St (13905-2508)
PHONE.....................607 766-9620
David Eddy, *President*
William Peterson, *Vice Pres*
EMP: 12
SQ FT: 10,000
SALES: 5MM Privately Held
WEB: www.eandmpower.com
SIC: 3679 Electronic loads & power supplies

(G-931)
MELLEM CORPORATION
Also Called: Goldsmith
31 Lewis St Ste 1 (13901-3018)
PHONE.....................607 723-0001
Gina McHugh, *President*
▲ EMP: 10
SQ FT: 750
SALES (est): 1.6MM Privately Held
SIC: 3911 5944 Jewelry, precious metal; jewelry, precious stones & precious metals

(G-932)
METAL FAB LLC
13 Spud Ln (13904-3210)
PHONE.....................607 775-3200
Fax: 607 775-3233
Janet Beal, *Mng Member*
Rick Simon,
Eugene Taren,
EMP: 5
SQ FT: 9,500
SALES: 857K Privately Held
SIC: 3441 Fabricated structural metal

(G-933)
MORO CORPORATION
Also Called: Titchener Iron Works Division
23 Griswold St (13904-1511)
PHONE.....................607 724-4391
Fax: 607 724-3439
Wendy Coman, *Accountant*
Douglas Wilcox, *Branch Mgr*
EMP: 25
SQ FT: 7,368
SALES (corp-wide): 65.4MM Publicly Held
WEB: www.mcgregorindustries.com
SIC: 3446 Architectural metalwork
PA: Moro Corporation
994 Old Eagle School Rd # 1000
Wayne PA 19087
484 367-0300

(G-934)
MS MACHINING INC
Also Called: Mechanical Specialties Co
2 William St (13904-1418)
PHONE.....................607 723-1105
Fax: 607 772-6805
Eugene Mazza, *President*
Jo Ann Risley, *Office Mgr*
EMP: 9 EST: 1956
SQ FT: 10,000
SALES (est): 1.4MM Privately Held
SIC: 3544 3599 Special dies & tools; custom machinery; machine shop, jobbing & repair

(G-935)
NELSON HOLDINGS LTD (PA)
71 Frederick St (13901-2529)
PHONE.....................607 772-1794
Clarence Hotchkiss Jr, *Ch of Bd*
Mark Hotchkiss, *President*
Frederick Hotchkiss, *Vice Pres*
EMP: 1 EST: 1875
SQ FT: 180,000
SALES (est): 11.1MM Privately Held
SIC: 3679 5261 7699 Electronic circuits; lawn & garden equipment; lawn mower repair shop

(G-936)
NIELSEN HARDWARE CORPORATION (PA)
Also Called: Nielsen/Sessions
71 Frederick St (13901-2529)
P.O. Box 773 (13902-0773)
PHONE.....................607 821-1475
Fax: 607 821-1476
Gary Oliveira, *Vice Pres*
Don Conant, *Purchasing*
Sonia Pelletier Moore, *CFO*
Candie Mirch, *Sales Staff*
Wassef Moukalled, *Director*
▲ EMP: 25
SQ FT: 40,000
SALES (est): 3.7MM Privately Held
WEB: www.nielsensessions.com
SIC: 3429 Manufactured hardware (general)

(G-937)
PARLOR CITY PAPER BOX CO INC
2 Eldredge St (13901-2600)
P.O. Box 756 (13902-0756)
PHONE.....................607 772-0600
Fax: 607 772-0806
David L Culver, *Ch of Bd*
Bruce Culver, *Vice Pres*
Maryanne Bebla, *Manager*
EMP: 56
SQ FT: 140,000
SALES (est): 13MM Privately Held
WEB: www.pghcitypaper.com
SIC: 2653 2652 Corrugated & solid fiber boxes; setup paperboard boxes

(G-938)
PETER PAPASTRAT
Also Called: A A P C O Screen Prntng/Sprtwr
193 Main St (13905-2619)
P.O. Box 285 (13905-0285)
PHONE.....................607 723-8112
Peter Papastrat, *Owner*
EMP: 5
SQ FT: 6,000
SALES (est): 326.2K Privately Held
SIC: 2759 5699 Screen printing; customized clothing & apparel

(G-939)
R M S MOTOR CORPORATION
41 Travis Dr (13904-2822)
PHONE.....................607 723-2323
Fax: 607 723-8165
Michael Jimenez, *President*
Ruth Rusiloski, *Vice Pres*
EMP: 13 EST: 1962
SQ FT: 10,000
SALES (est): 1.4MM Privately Held
SIC: 3621 Motors, electric

(G-940)
RB CONVERTING INC
28 Track Dr (13904-2717)
PHONE.....................607 777-1325
Paul Haslett, *Branch Mgr*
EMP: 5
SALES (corp-wide): 11.1MM Privately Held
SIC: 2679 Paper products, converted
HQ: Rb Converting, Inc.
12855 Valley Branch Ln
Dallas TX 75234
800 543-7690

(G-941)
REYNOLDS BOOK BINDERY LLC
37 Milford St (13904-1615)
PHONE.....................607 772-8937
Fax: 607 772-0152
EMP: 11
SQ FT: 15,000
SALES (est): 720K Privately Held
SIC: 2789 Book Bindery Company

(G-942)
ROCKWELL COLLINS SIMULATION
31 Lewis Rd (13905-1005)
PHONE.....................607 352-1298
Ronald Fitzpatrick, *General Mgr*
Robert Wuestner, *Managing Dir*
Frank Carl, *Opers Mgr*
Scott Evans, *Engineer*
Peter Kumpon, *Engineer*
EMP: 67 Publicly Held
SIC: 3699 Electronic training devices
HQ: Rockwell Collins Simulation & Training Solutions Llc
400 Collins Rd Ne
Cedar Rapids IA 52498

(G-943)
S L C INDUSTRIES INCORPORATED
63 Barlow Rd (13904-2722)
P.O. Box 116, Kirkwood (13795-0116)
PHONE.....................607 775-2299
Fax: 607 775-2785
Art Boyle, *President*
Adam Milligan, *General Mgr*
Michael Prozeralik, *Treasurer*
Thomas O Milligan, *Admin Sec*
EMP: 10
SQ FT: 20,000
SALES (est): 910K Privately Held
WEB: www.slcindustries.com
SIC: 2759 Commercial printing

(G-944)
SENSOR & DECONTAMINATION INC
Also Called: S D I
892 Powderhouse Rd (13903-7104)
P.O. Box 132 (13903-0132)
PHONE.....................301 526-8389
Barry R Jones, *President*
David Doetschman, *Corp Secy*
EMP: 10
SALES (est): 710K Privately Held
WEB: www.sensoranddecon.com
SIC: 2842 7389 Specialty cleaning preparations;

(G-945)
SOUTHERN TIER PLASTICS INC
Kirkwood Industrial Park (13902)
P.O. Box 2015 (13902-2015)
PHONE.....................607 723-2601
Fax: 607 772-9881
John Gwyn, *CEO*
Joyce Gray, *President*
Douglas Gray, *Treasurer*
Holly Geiser, *Controller*
Barbara Gwyn, *Admin Sec*
▲ EMP: 72
SQ FT: 30,000
SALES (est): 15.6MM Privately Held
WEB: www.southerntierplastics.com
SIC: 3089 Injection molding of plastics

(G-946)
SUNY AT BINGHAMTON
Also Called: School of Management
Vestal Pkwy E (13901)
PHONE.....................607 777-2316
Gary Roodman, *Dean*
EMP: 73 Privately Held

SIC: 2731 8221 9411 Books: publishing only; university; administration of educational programs;
HQ: Suny At Binghamton
4400 Vestal Pkwy
Binghamton NY 13902
607 777-2000

(G-947)
SURESCAN CORPORATION
Also Called: X1000
100 Eldredge St (13901-2631)
PHONE.....................607 321-0042
James J McNamara Jr, *Ch of Bd*
John Percival, *President*
EMP: 23
SALES (est): 5.7MM Privately Held
WEB: www.surescaneds.com
SIC: 3844 X-ray apparatus & tubes

(G-948)
TCMF INC
Also Called: C.H.thompson Finishing
69-93 Eldredge St (13901)
PHONE.....................607 724-1094
George Morgan, *President*
Charles Morgan, *Vice Pres*
Trevor Morgan, *Admin Sec*
EMP: 75
SALES: 3.7MM Privately Held
SIC: 3471 2759 Plating & polishing; commercial printing

(G-949)
TJ POWDER COATERS LLC
24 Broad St (13904-1017)
PHONE.....................607 724-4779
Fax: 607 724-4655
Jim Foran, *Owner*
EMP: 7
SQ FT: 7,500
SALES (est): 885.9K Privately Held
SIC: 3479 Coating of metals with plastic or resins

(G-950)
TOTAL DISPLAY SOLUTIONS INC
1429 Upper Front St (13901-1151)
PHONE.....................607 724-9999
Pete Gulick, *CFO*
Richard Stahlman, *Administration*
EMP: 15
SQ FT: 18,000
SALES: 1.5MM Privately Held
SIC: 2541 Store & office display cases & fixtures

(G-951)
TRI CITY HIGHWAY PRODUCTS INC
111 Bevier St (13904-1013)
PHONE.....................607 722-2967
Fax: 607 722-3469
Martin A Galasso Jr, *CEO*
Warner Hodydon, *Opers Mgr*
EMP: 30
SQ FT: 2,500
SALES (est): 5.2MM Privately Held
SIC: 2951 1442 Asphalt paving mixtures & blocks; construction sand & gravel

(G-952)
VIRTUSPHERE INC
7 Hillside Ave (13903-2025)
PHONE.....................607 760-2207
Nourakhmed Latypov, *CEO*
Nurulla Latypov, *President*
EMP: 11
SALES: 150K Privately Held
SIC: 7372 Educational computer software

(G-953)
WESTCODE INCORPORATED
2226 Airport Rd (13905-5912)
PHONE.....................607 766-9881
Fax: 607 766-9868
Edward J Widdowson, *CEO*
EMP: 25
SALES (corp-wide): 15.9MM Privately Held
WEB: www.westcodeus.com
SIC: 3743 Railroad equipment

PA: Westcode Incorporated
3 Dickinson Dr Ste 100
Chadds Ford PA 19317
610 738-1200

Blasdell
Erie County

(G-954)
B F G ELCPLTG AND MFG CO
3949 Jeffrey Blvd (14219-2334)
P.O. Box 825, Hamburg (14075-0825)
PHONE..................................716 362-0888
Fax: 716 649-5649
Minta Marie, *CEO*
EMP: 32
SALES (est): 231.8K **Privately Held**
SIC: 3999 Manufacturing industries

(G-955)
BUFFALLO SPORTS INC
3840 Mckinley Pkwy (14219-3006)
PHONE..................................716 826-7700
David Westfall, *President*
EMP: 6
SQ FT: 4,000
SALES (es): 450.4K **Privately Held**
SIC: 3949 Sporting & athletic goods

(G-956)
EVERLASTING MEMORIES
3701 Mckinley Pkwy # 210 (14219-2695)
PHONE..................................716 833-1111
Dennis Field, *Owner*
EMP: 6
SALES (est): 284.1K **Privately Held**
SIC: 2335 Wedding gowns & dresses

(G-957)
RAPISTAK CORPORATION
2025 Electric Ave (14219-1045)
PHONE..................................716 822-2804
Nathan Paulorek, *CEO*
EMP: 7
SALES (est): 1.8MM **Privately Held**
WEB: www.rapistak.com
SIC: 3531 Dozers, tractor mounted: material moving

(G-958)
REPUBLIC STEEL INC
Also Called: Lackawanna Hot Rolled Plant
3049 Lake Shore Rd (14219-1447)
PHONE..................................716 827-2800
Tom Tyrrell, *Branch Mgr*
William Kilinskas, *Technician*
EMP: 360 **Privately Held**
SIC: 3312 Blast furnaces & steel mills
HQ: Republic Steel Inc.
2633 8th St Ne
Canton OH 44704
330 438-5435

(G-959)
SAMUEL SON & CO INC
250 Lake Ave Ste 3 (14219-1500)
PHONE..................................716 856-6500
Don Clark, *Branch Mgr*
EMP: 8
SALES (corp-wide): 1.7B **Privately Held**
SIC: 3312 Blast furnaces & steel mills
HQ: Samuel Son & Co. Inc.
4334 Walden Ave
Lancaster NY 14086

(G-960)
SOTEK INC
3590 Jeffrey Blvd (14219-2390)
PHONE..................................716 821-5961
Fax: 716 821-5965
John E Maurer, *President*
Michael Maurer, *Vice Pres*
Jim Carroll, *Opers Mgr*
Ann Skummer, *Accounting Mgr*
Ann Schumael, *Accountant*
▲ **EMP:** 52
SQ FT: 45,000
SALES (est): 9.3MM **Privately Held**
WEB: www.sotek.com
SIC: 3599 Machine shop, jobbing & repair

(G-961)
TRANSCO RAILWAY PRODUCTS INC
Milestrip Rd (14219)
P.O. Box 1968, Buffalo (14219-0168)
PHONE..................................716 824-1219
Fax: 716 825-1108
Tom Jakubowski, *Manager*
EMP: 23
SALES (corp-wide): 104.3MM **Privately Held**
SIC: 3743 Railroad equipment, except locomotives
HQ: Transco Railway Products Inc.
200 N La Salle St # 1550
Chicago IL 60601
312 427-2818

(G-962)
VALENTI DISTRIBUTING
84 Maple Ave (14219-1624)
PHONE..................................716 824-2304
John Valenti, *Principal*
EMP: 7
SALES (est): 21.4K **Privately Held**
SIC: 2064 Candy & other confectionery products

Blauvelt
Rockland County

(G-963)
AERCO INTERNATIONAL INC (HQ)
100 Oritani Dr (10913-1022)
PHONE..................................845 580-8000
James F Dagley, *President*
Fred Depuy, *Vice Pres*
Bree McQuillan, *Vice Pres*
Lou Vorsteveld, *Vice Pres*
Karen Defranco, *Opers Mgr*
▲ **EMP:** 153
SQ FT: 150,000
SALES (est): 44.9MM
SALES (corp-wide): 1.4B **Publicly Held**
WEB: www.aerco.com
SIC: 3443 3492 Heat exchangers, plate type; heat exchangers: coolers (after, inter), condensers, etc.; boilers: industrial, power, or marine; control valves, fluid power: hydraulic & pneumatic
PA: Watts Water Technologies, Inc.
815 Chestnut St
North Andover MA 01845
978 688-1811

(G-964)
CWS POWDER COATINGS COMPANY LP
2234 Bradley Hill Rd # 12 (10913-1014)
PHONE..................................845 398-2911
Fax: 845 398-2912
Cws Powder Coatings, *Partner*
Victoria Phillips, *Controller*
Jonathan Abrams, *Director*
▲ **EMP:** 9
SQ FT: 2,500
SALES (est): 2.4MM
SALES (corp-wide): 73.1MM **Privately Held**
SIC: 3399 Powder, metal
HQ: Cws Powder Coatings Gmbh
Katharinenstr. 61
Duren 52353
242 198-30

(G-965)
ERT SOFTWARE INC
4 Pine Glen Dr (10913-1150)
PHONE..................................845 358-5721
Roman Tenenbaum, *President*
EMP: 5
SALES (est): 1.5MM **Privately Held**
WEB: www.alivest.com
SIC: 7372 Prepackaged software

(G-966)
K-BINET INC
624 Route 303 (10913-1170)
PHONE..................................845 348-1149
Fax: 845 620-0666
Jay Kim, *President*
Ann Degli, *Admin Sec*
EMP: 8 **EST:** 2001
SALES (est): 680K **Privately Held**
SIC: 2434 Wood kitchen cabinets

(G-967)
LIGHTING N BEYOND LLC
628 Ste 303 (10913)
P.O. Box 539, Spring Valley (10977-0539)
PHONE..................................718 669-9142
Mike Oberlander,
EMP: 5
SQ FT: 6,000
SALES (est): 150K **Privately Held**
SIC: 3648 Lighting equipment

(G-968)
RBHAMMERS CORP
Also Called: Heatherdell RB Hammers
500 Bradley Hill Rd (10913-1134)
PHONE..................................845 353-5042
Richard Tegtmeier, *President*
Derrick Ternvillo, *Accountant*
Ann Glasthal, *Office Mgr*
◆ **EMP:** 10
SQ FT: 1,500
SALES (est): 7.4MM **Privately Held**
SIC: 3546 Hammers, portable: electric or pneumatic, chipping, etc.

(G-969)
RYAN PRINTING INC
300 Corporate Dr Ste 6 (10913-1162)
PHONE..................................845 535-3235
Fax: 845 353-8740
Al Ryan, *President*
Jeff Fay, *Sales Mgr*
EMP: 26
SQ FT: 35,000
SALES (est): 5.1MM **Privately Held**
SIC: 2752 Commercial printing, lithographic

(G-970)
SWIVELIER COMPANY INC
Also Called: Point Electric Div
600 Bradley Hill Rd Ste 3 (10913-1171)
PHONE..................................845 353-1455
Fax: 845 353-1512
Michael I Schwartz, *President*
I Schucker, *Sales Staff*
Carol Zane, *Sales Staff*
Louis M Cafarchio, *Admin Sec*
EMP: 27
SQ FT: 125,000
SALES (est): 10.3MM **Privately Held**
WEB: www.swivelier.com
SIC: 3646 3645 3643 Commercial industl & institutional electric lighting fixtures; residential lighting fixtures; current-carrying wiring devices

(G-971)
TAPPAN WIRE & CABLE INC (HQ)
100 Bradley Pkwy (10913-1012)
P.O. Box 4000, Carrollton GA (30112-5050)
PHONE..................................845 353-9000
Fax: 845 353-9315
Stuart W Thorn, *Ch of Bd*
Darren Krych, *President*
Mike Luterzo, *Vice Pres*
Jerry Rosen, *CFO*
Michael Dougher, *Controller*
▲ **EMP:** 189 **EST:** 1978
SQ FT: 180,000
SALES (est): 46.5MM
SALES (corp-wide): 3.5B **Privately Held**
WEB: www.tappanwire.com
SIC: 3315 3643 3357 Wire & fabricated wire products; current-carrying wiring devices; nonferrous wiredrawing & insulating
PA: Southwire Company, Llc
1 Southwire Dr
Carrollton GA 30119
770 832-4242

(G-972)
TRI-SEAL HOLDINGS INC
900 Bradley Hill Rd (10913-1163)
PHONE..................................845 353-3300
Paul Young, *Ch of Bd*
Diane Schweitzer, *Owner*
F Patrick Smith, *Chairman*
Shevman Smith, *Accounts Mgr*
Kevin Baker, *Manager*
EMP: 63 **EST:** 1946
SQ FT: 58,000
SALES (est): 9.1MM
SALES (corp-wide): 1.1B **Privately Held**
WEB: www.tri-seal.com
SIC: 3081 2821 Packing materials, plastic sheet; plastics materials & resins
PA: Tekni-Plex, Inc.
460 E Swedesford Rd # 3000
Wayne PA 19087
484 690-1520

(G-973)
VITS INTERNATIONAL INC
200 Corporate Dr (10913-1119)
PHONE..................................845 353-5000
Fax: 845 353-7759
Deirdre Ryder, *President*
John Friedl, *Plant Mgr*
Nina Shapiro, *Office Mgr*
Kim Markovich, *Director*
◆ **EMP:** 40
SQ FT: 22,000
SALES (est): 20MM **Privately Held**
WEB: www.vitsamerica.com
SIC: 3555 Printing trades machinery

Bliss
Wyoming County

(G-974)
FIVE CORNERS REPAIR INC
6653 Hardys Rd (14024-9714)
PHONE..................................585 322-7369
Jason Sampson, *President*
Scott Lester, *Vice Pres*
EMP: 12
SALES (est): 950K **Privately Held**
SIC: 3441 Fabricated structural metal

Bloomfield
Ontario County

(G-975)
BENJAMIN SHERIDAN CORPORATION (DH)
7629 State Route 5 And 20 (14469-9210)
PHONE..................................585 657-6161
Ken D'Arcy, *President*
George Ribbert, *Div Sub Head*
Rhonda Emmons, *Manager*
Hal Parker, *Director*
Kathy Chapman, *Executive*
EMP: 5
SQ FT: 224,000
SALES (est): 9.3MM
SALES (corp-wide): 978.3MM **Publicly Held**
SIC: 3484 3482 Small arms; pellet & BB guns; pellets & BB's, pistol & air rifle ammunition
HQ: Crosman Corporation
7629 State Route 5 And 20
Bloomfield NY 14469
585 657-6161

(G-976)
BRISTOL METALS INC
7817 State Route 5 And 20 (14469-9352)
PHONE..................................585 657-7665
Edward Gilligan, *President*
Kelly Gilligan, *Corp Secy*
Kecia Donnelly, *Executive Asst*
EMP: 10
SQ FT: 15,000
SALES (est): 1.4MM **Privately Held**
SIC: 3441 Fabricated structural metal

(G-977)
CARVER CREEK ENTERPRISES INC
2524 Cannan Rd (14469-9655)
PHONE..................................585 657-7511
Fax: 585 657-1175
Donald Dean, *President*
Thomas Dean, *Vice Pres*
EMP: 5
SQ FT: 1,764
SALES (est): 647K **Privately Held**
WEB: www.carvercreekent.com
SIC: 2511 Wood household furniture

GEOGRAPHIC SECTION

(G-978)
COMMODORE MACHINE CO INC
26 Maple Ave (14469-9228)
PHONE.....................585 657-6916
Fax: 585 657-6400
George Brandoon, *Ch of Bd*
▲ EMP: 17 EST: 1970
SALES (est): 2.9MM Privately Held
SIC: 3089 Trays, plastic

(G-979)
COMMODORE PLASTICS LLC
26 Maple Ave (14469-9228)
PHONE.....................585 657-7777
George Braddon III, *President*
Jeffrey Braddon, *Vice Pres*
Justin Grant, *Opers Mgr*
Fritz Seager, *Prdtn Mgr*
Suzanne Wright, *Production*
▲ EMP: 50
SQ FT: 35,000
SALES (est): 16.9MM Privately Held
SIC: 3089 Plastic processing
PA: 26-28 Maple Avenue, Inc.
   26 Maple Ave
   Bloomfield NY 14469
   585 657-7777

(G-980)
CROSMAN CORPORATION (DH)
7629 State Route 5 And 20 (14469-9210)
PHONE.....................585 657-6161
Fax: 585 657-5407
Robert Beckwith, *CEO*
Lloyd Heise, *Vice Pres*
Dan Maier, *Vice Pres*
David Swanson, *Vice Pres*
Dan Schultz, *VP Opers*
▲ EMP: 29
SQ FT: 224,000
SALES (est): 18.7MM
SALES (corp-wide): 978.3MM Publicly Held
WEB: www.crosman.com
SIC: 3484 3482 3563 Pellet & BB guns; pellets & BB's, pistol & air rifle ammunition; shot, steel (ammunition); air & gas compressors
HQ: Cbcp Acquisition Corp.
   60 One Wilton Rd Fl 2
   Westport CT 06880
   203 221-1703

(G-981)
ELAM SAND & GRAVEL CORP (PA)
8222 State Route 5 And 20 (14469-9567)
P.O. Box 65, West Bloomfield (14585-0065)
PHONE.....................585 657-8000
Fax: 585 657-6575
Joseph Spezio, *President*
Ritamarie Dreimiller, *Vice Pres*
EMP: 35 EST: 1892
SQ FT: 9,000
SALES (est): 7.4MM Privately Held
SIC: 1442 Construction sand mining

(G-982)
FURNITURE DOCTOR INC
7007 State Route 5 And 20 (14469-9322)
P.O. Box 519 (14469-0519)
PHONE.....................585 657-6941
Fax: 585 657-6751
Thomas Baker, *President*
Marfa Baker, *Corp Secy*
Stacey Conley, *Finance Mgr*
EMP: 9
SQ FT: 16,000
SALES (est): 770K Privately Held
WEB: www.thefurnituredoctoronline.com
SIC: 2511 2514 5712 5021 Wood household furniture; metal household furniture; furniture stores; furniture; reupholstery & furniture repair; interior decorating

(G-983)
GULLO MACHINE & TOOL INC
4 E Main St (14469-9334)
P.O. Box 273 (14469-0273)
PHONE.....................585 657-7318
Fax: 585 657-4463
Nancy Gullo, *President*
EMP: 10
SQ FT: 15,000
SALES: 500K Privately Held
SIC: 3599 Machine shop, jobbing & repair

(G-984)
TERPHANE HOLDINGS LLC (DH)
2754 W Park Dr (14469-9385)
PHONE.....................585 657-5800
Dan Roy, *General Mgr*
Richard Composto, *Plant Mgr*
Frank J Shutter, *Maint Spvr*
Linda Wilson, *Purch Mgr*
Renan Bergmann,
▼ EMP: 7
SALES (est): 16.7MM
SALES (corp-wide): 830.7MM Publicly Held
SIC: 2821 5199 Plastics materials & resins; packaging materials
HQ: Tredegar Film Products Corporation
   1100 Boulders Pkwy # 200
   North Chesterfield VA 23225
   804 330-1000

(G-985)
TERPHANE INC
2754 W Park Dr (14469-9385)
PHONE.....................585 657-5800
Renan Bergmann, *CEO*
Roy Danis, *General Mgr*
Frank Shutter, *COO*
Francisco Cavalcanti, *Plant Mgr*
Richard Compasto, *Plant Mgr*
◆ EMP: 52
SQ FT: 100,000
SALES (est): 16.7MM
SALES (corp-wide): 830.7MM Publicly Held
WEB: www.terphane.com
SIC: 2821 Polyesters
HQ: Terphane Holdings Llc
   2754 W Park Dr
   Bloomfield NY 14469

(G-986)
VELMEX INC
7550 State Route 5 And 20 (14469-9389)
PHONE.....................585 657-6151
Fax: 585 657-6153
Mitchel Evans, *President*
Evans Mitchel, *Project Engr*
Alayne Evans, *Treasurer*
Joseph Mehring, *Controller*
Alice Miller, *Accounts Mgr*
EMP: 32
SQ FT: 15,500
SALES: 5.8MM Privately Held
WEB: www.velmex.com
SIC: 3545 Machine tool attachments & accessories

Bloomington
Ulster County

(G-987)
COBRA SYSTEMS INC
2669 New York 32 (12411)
PHONE.....................845 338-6675
Michael V Pavlov, *President*
▼ EMP: 10
SQ FT: 2,400
SALES (est): 1.6MM Privately Held
WEB: www.cobracoil.com
SIC: 3496 Barbed wire, made from purchased wire

Bloomville
Delaware County

(G-988)
ED BEACH FOREST MANAGEMENT
2042 Scott Rd (13739-1203)
PHONE.....................607 538-1745
Edwin R Beach, *Principal*
EMP: 6
SALES (est): 512.3K Privately Held
SIC: 2411 Logging

(G-989)
G HAYNES HOLDINGS INC
Also Called: Catskill Castings Co
51971 State Highway 10 (13739-2242)
P.O. Box 752 (13739-0752)
PHONE.....................607 538-1160
Fax: 607 538-1160
George Haynes, *President*
Tracy Kinch, *Office Mgr*
EMP: 9
SQ FT: 3,500
SALES (est): 350K Privately Held
WEB: www.catskillcastings.com
SIC: 3543 Foundry patternmaking

(G-990)
GREENE BRASS & ALUM FNDRY LLC
51971 State Highway 10 (13739-2242)
P.O. Box 752 (13739-0752)
PHONE.....................607 656-4204
Thomas Dodd, *Mng Member*
George Heynes,
EMP: 7
SALES: 1.1MM Privately Held
SIC: 3334 3363 7389 Primary aluminum; aluminum die-castings;

Blossvale
Oneida County

(G-991)
BLUEBAR OIL CO INC
8446 Mill Pond Way (13308)
PHONE.....................315 245-4328
Fax: 315 245-2160
David Link, *President*
EMP: 11
SQ FT: 2,000
SALES (est): 1MM Privately Held
SIC: 1389 5983 5172 Oil field services; fuel oil dealers; gasoline; fuel oil

(G-992)
ORCHARD HILL MCH & TL CO INC
2855 State Route 49 (13308-3127)
PHONE.....................315 245-0015
William Zorn, *President*
Sandra Zorn, *Vice Pres*
EMP: 7
SALES: 86.2K Privately Held
SIC: 3599 Machine shop, jobbing & repair

Blue Point
Suffolk County

(G-993)
DEER PK STAIR BLDG MLLWK INC
51 Kennedy Ave (11715-1009)
P.O. Box 107 (11715-0107)
PHONE.....................631 363-5000
Fax: 631 363-2167
Michael Souto, *President*
Annette Andriano, *Manager*
Leita Souto, *Admin Sec*
EMP: 45 EST: 1950
SQ FT: 30,000
SALES (est): 7.9MM Privately Held
WEB: www.deerparkstairs.com
SIC: 2431 5211 5031 Stair railings, wood; staircases & stairs, wood; lumber products; cabinets, kitchen; kitchen cabinets

(G-994)
NOCHEM PAINT STRIPPING INC
32 Bergen Ln (11715-2111)
PHONE.....................631 563-2750
Gilbert H Kelley, *President*
Stephen Kelley, *Vice Pres*
EMP: 5
SALES (est): 531.3K Privately Held
SIC: 2851 7699 7532 1799 Paint removers; boat repair; body shop, automotive; paint & wallpaper stripping

(G-995)
SPECIALTY INK CO INC (PA)
Also Called: Aero Brand Inks
40 Harbour Dr (11715-1421)
P.O. Box 778, Deer Park (11729-0778)
PHONE.....................631 586-3666
Fax: 631 586-3874
Gary Werwa, *President*
▲ EMP: 16 EST: 1934
SQ FT: 15,000
SALES (est): 1.7MM Privately Held
WEB: www.specialtyink.com
SIC: 2899 3953 2893 Ink or writing fluids; pads, inking & stamping; printing ink

Bohemia
Suffolk County

(G-996)
A P MANUFACTURING
21 Floyds Run (11716-2155)
PHONE.....................909 228-3049
Jane P Sobota, *Owner*
EMP: 7
SALES (est): 340.7K Privately Held
SIC: 3599 Industrial machinery

(G-997)
ABACO STEEL PRODUCTS INC
1560 Locust Ave (11716-2194)
PHONE.....................631 589-1800
Fax: 631 589-1197
Kenneth Podd, *President*
Jennifer Rivera, *Bookkeeper*
EMP: 4 EST: 1972
SQ FT: 10,000
SALES (est): 1.2MM Privately Held
WEB: www.abacosteel.com
SIC: 2542 2541 Shelving, office & store: except wood; partitions for floor attachment, prefabricated: except wood; cabinets, lockers & shelving

(G-998)
ABLE ENVIRONMENTAL SERVICES
1599 Ocean Ave (11716-1947)
PHONE.....................631 567-6585
Fax: 631 567-9390
Faith Barnard, *President*
EMP: 5
SALES (est): 550K Privately Held
SIC: 1382 Oil & gas exploration services

(G-999)
ABSOLUTE MANUFACTURING INC
Also Called: Absolute Engineering Company
210 Knickerbocker Ave (11716-3175)
PHONE.....................631 563-7466
Val Palzzynski, *President*
Helene Strafford, *Manager*
EMP: 8
SQ FT: 5,000
SALES: 1MM Privately Held
SIC: 3599 Machine shop, jobbing & repair

(G-1000)
ACCURATE MARINE SPECIALTIES
2200 Artic Ave (11716-2414)
PHONE.....................631 589-5502
Gary Lucas, *President*
Chip Watkins, *Corp Secy*
EMP: 6
SQ FT: 5,900
SALES (est): 959.8K Privately Held
SIC: 7694 5541 Motor repair services; marine service station

(G-1001)
ACE CNTRACTING CONSULTING CORP
Also Called: Island Chimney Service
515 Johnson Ave (11716-2671)
PHONE.....................631 567-4752
Marc Jagerman, *President*
EMP: 9
SALES (est): 829.2K Privately Held
SIC: 3271 Blocks, concrete: chimney or fireplace

Bohemia - Suffolk County (G-1002) — GEOGRAPHIC SECTION

(G-1002)
ACE MOLDING & TOOL INC
51 Floyds Run (11716-2155)
PHONE.....................631 567-2355
Americo Carnaxide, *President*
EMP: 5
SALES: 40K **Privately Held**
SIC: 3089 Molding primary plastic

(G-1003)
ADVANCED CYBER SECURITY CORP
3880 Veterans Memorial Hw (11716-1038)
PHONE.....................866 417-9155
Daniel Delgiorno, *CEO*
EMP: 20
SALES (est): 1MM **Privately Held**
SIC: 7372 Prepackaged software; operating systems computer software

(G-1004)
AEROSPACE LIGHTING CORPORATION (DH)
355 Knickerbocker Ave (11716-3103)
PHONE.....................631 563-6400
Fax: 631 563-8781
Werner Lieberherr, *President*
Thomas P McCaffrey, *Senior VP*
Sean Crome, *Vice Pres*
Wayne R Exton, *Vice Pres*
Steve Scover, *Vice Pres*
EMP: 100 EST: 1987
SQ FT: 60,000
SALES (est): 17MM **Publicly Held**
SIC: 3647 5063 Aircraft lighting fixtures; electrical apparatus & equipment
HQ: B/E Aerospace, Inc.
  1400 Corporate Center Way
  Wellington FL 33414
  561 791-5000

(G-1005)
AGRIUM ADVANCED TECH US INC
165 Orville Dr (11716-2508)
PHONE.....................631 286-0598
Ada Dundor, *Branch Mgr*
EMP: 11
SALES (corp-wide): 13.6B **Privately Held**
SIC: 2873 Nitrogenous fertilizers
HQ: Agrium Advanced Technologies (U.S.) Inc.
  2915 Rocky Mountain Ave # 400
  Loveland CO 80538

(G-1006)
AID WOOD WORKING
1555 Ocean Ave Ste C (11716-1933)
PHONE.....................631 244-7768
Rick Olveri, *Owner*
EMP: 10
SALES (est): 830.8K **Privately Held**
SIC: 2499 Wood products

(G-1007)
ALL AMERICAN AWARDS INC
Also Called: All American Uniform
331 Knickerbocker Ave (11716-3134)
PHONE.....................631 567-2025
Fax: 631 567-3953
Frank Coppola, *President*
Jean Coppola, *Vice Pres*
Julie Gotell, *Frdtn Mgr*
Gina Fecile, *Office Mgr*
Dominic Coppola, *Manager*
EMP: 11
SQ FT: 10,000
SALES (est): 830K **Privately Held**
SIC: 3914 5699 5199 2395 Trophies; uniforms & work clothing; advertising specialties; embroidery & art needlework

(G-1008)
ALL COUNTY BLOCK & SUPPLY CORP
899 Lincoln Ave (11716-4105)
P.O. Box 502 11716-0502)
PHONE.....................631 589-3675
Fax: 631 472-6690
Robert Affenita, *Mktg Dir*
Ken Walker, *Mktg Dir*
EMP: 5
SALES (est): 1.1MM **Privately Held**
WEB: www.allcountyblock.com
SIC: 3271 Concrete block & brick

(G-1009)
ALL ISLAND BLOWER & SHTMTL
1585 Smithtown Ave Unit C (11716-2406)
PHONE.....................631 567-7070
Fax: 631 567-6505
Brian Levine, *President*
Brian Higgins, *President*
Micheal Higgins, *Opers Mgr*
EMP: 10
SQ FT: 4,000
SALES: 1MM **Privately Held**
SIC: 3444 Sheet metalwork

(G-1010)
AMPLITECH INC
620 Johnson Ave Ste 2 (11716-2658)
PHONE.....................631 521-7738
Fax: 631 521-7871
Fawad Maqbool, *CEO*
Ewa Polubiak, *Production*
Don Sartorius, *QC Mgr*
Louisa Sanfratello, *CFO*
Carol Klemm, *Finance*
EMP: 8
SQ FT: 5,500
SALES: 1.2MM **Privately Held**
WEB: www.amplitechinc.com
SIC: 3663 Microwave communication equipment

(G-1011)
AMPLITECH GROUP INC
620 Johnson Ave (11716-2649)
PHONE.....................631 521-7831
Fawad Maqbool, *CEO*
Louisa Sanfratello, *CFO*
EMP: 6 EST: 2002
SALES: 2MM **Privately Held**
SIC: 3651 3663 Amplifiers: radio, public address or musical instrument; microwave communication equipment

(G-1012)
ANDREA ELECTRONICS CORPORATION (PA)
620 Johnson Ave Ste 1b (11716-2636)
PHONE.....................631 719-1800
Fax: 631 719-1998
Douglas J Andrea, *Ch of Bd*
Stephan Auguste, *Electrical Engi*
Corisa L Guiffre, *CFO*
Gary Jones, *Director*
▲ EMP: 9 EST: 1934
SQ FT: 3,000
SALES: 3.5MM **Publicly Held**
WEB: www.andreaelectronics.com
SIC: 3651 3663 3577 Microphones; mobile communication equipment; computer peripheral equipment

(G-1013)
APEX SIGNAL CORPORATION
110 Wilbur Pl (11716-2402)
PHONE.....................631 567-1100
Fax: 631 981-1823
William Forman, *President*
Wayne Grandner, *COO*
David Dayton, *Planning Mgr*
Patty Angelos, *Manager*
EMP: 90
SALES (est): 10.5MM
SALES (corp-wide): 43.9MM **Privately Held**
SIC: 3669 5065 Traffic signals, electric; electronic parts & equipment
PA: North Atlantic Industries, Inc.
  110 Wilbur Pl
  Bohemia NY 11716
  631 567-1100

(G-1014)
ARCHIMEDES PRODUCTS INC
21 Floyds Run (11716-2155)
PHONE.....................631 589-1215
Fax: 631 589-1216
Jane Sobota, *President*
Mike Kielcewski, *Supervisor*
EMP: 8
SQ FT: 6,000
SALES (est): 760K **Privately Held**
WEB: www.cncarch.com
SIC: 3599 Machine shop, jobbing & repair

(G-1015)
ARLAN DAMPER CORPORATION
1598 Lakeland Ave (11716-2198)
PHONE.....................631 589-7431
Fax: 631 589-7558
Albert A Sapio, *President*
Valerie Cooper, *Office Mgr*
Gina Marx, *Executive*
EMP: 25 EST: 1961
SQ FT: 6,400
SALES (est): 4.8MM **Privately Held**
SIC: 3444 Sheet metalwork

(G-1016)
AUTOMOTIVE FILTERS MFG INC
80a Keyland Ct A (11716-2656)
PHONE.....................631 435-1010
Manny Hadad, *General Mgr*
◆ EMP: 13
SQ FT: 14,000
SALES: 3.2MM **Privately Held**
SIC: 3714 7538 5013 3564 Filters: oil, fuel & air, motor vehicle; general automotive repair shops; automotive supplies & parts; filters, air: furnaces, air conditioning equipment, etc.

(G-1017)
B & H PRECISION FABRICATORS
95 Davinci Dr (11716-2601)
PHONE.....................631 563-9620
Fax: 631 563-9658
Dan Barthelomew, *President*
Deborah Barthelomew, *Vice Pres*
Jared Bartholomew, *VP Opers*
Kathy Ott, *Manager*
Debbie Bartholomew, *Officer*
EMP: 15
SQ FT: 3,500
SALES: 1MM **Privately Held**
SIC: 3444 Sheet metalwork

(G-1018)
B/E AEROSPACE INC
355 Knickerbocker Ave (11716-3103)
PHONE.....................631 563-6400
Amin J Khoury, *Ch of Bd*
EMP: 29 **Publicly Held**
SIC: 2531 3728 3647 Seats, aircraft; aircraft parts & equipment; aircraft lighting fixtures
HQ: B/E Aerospace, Inc.
  1400 Corporate Center Way
  Wellington FL 33414
  561 791-5000

(G-1019)
B/E AEROSPACE INC
355 Knickerbocker Ave (11716-3103)
PHONE.....................631 589-0877
Steve Scover, *Vice Pres*
Vincent Cipolla, *Electrical Engi*
Peggy Knapp, *Manager*
Elaine Frank, *Admin Asst*
Gail Reissig, *Admin Asst*
EMP: 230 **Publicly Held**
SIC: 2531 Seats, aircraft
HQ: B/E Aerospace, Inc.
  1400 Corporate Center Way
  Wellington FL 33414
  561 791-5000

(G-1020)
BETA TRANSFORMER TECH CORP (DH)
40 Orville Dr Ste 2 (11716-2529)
PHONE.....................631 244-7393
Fax: 631 244-8893
Terrance M Paradie, *CEO*
Vincent Buffa, *President*
Nicholas Ocasio, *QA Dir*
Owen A Hayes Jr, *QC Mgr*
Frank Battaglia, *Engineer*
EMP: 31
SQ FT: 30,000
SALES: 5.2MM
SALES (corp-wide): 3.1B **Publicly Held**
WEB: www.bttc-beta.com
SIC: 3677 Electronic transformers
HQ: Data Device Corporation
  105 Wilbur Pl
  Bohemia NY 11716
  631 567-5600

(G-1021)
BGA TECHNOLOGY LLC
116 Wilbur Pl (11716-2402)
PHONE.....................631 750-4600
Fax: 631 218-1579
Michael Cody, *President*
Ralph Prescott, *Vice Pres*
Jayanth Kygonhalli, *CTO*
Bill Kaspar, *Director*
EMP: 17
SALES (est): 3.2MM **Privately Held**
SIC: 3674 8734 Semiconductors & related devices; testing laboratories

(G-1022)
BMG PRINTING AND PROMOTION LLC
170 Wilbur Pl Ste 700 (11716-2416)
PHONE.....................631 231-9200
Paulette Desimone, *Principal*
John L Melillo,
EMP: 8
SALES: 50K **Privately Held**
SIC: 2761 3993 2732 2752 Manifold business forms; signs & advertising specialties; pamphlets: printing & binding, not published on site; commercial printing, offset; promotional printing, lithographic

(G-1023)
BROCKYN CORPORATION
Also Called: Amax Industrial Products
606 Johnson Ave Ste 31 (11716-2688)
P.O. Box 577, East Islip (11730-0577)
PHONE.....................631 244-2770
Glen Heller, *President*
Tony Englin, *Vice Pres*
Tony England, *Manager*
EMP: 10
SQ FT: 3,500
SALES (est): 1MM **Privately Held**
WEB: www.amaxindustrial.com
SIC: 2869 Industrial organic chemicals

(G-1024)
BULLITT MOBILE LLC
Also Called: Bullitt Group
80 Orville Dr Ste 100 (11716-2505)
PHONE.....................631 424-1749
Theresa Cangialosi, *Vice Pres*
Janelle Stoner, *Vice Pres*
Adriene Ohare, *Accounts Mgr*
Martin Hanwright, *CTO*
EMP: 56
SQ FT: 1,200
SALES (est): 5.4MM
SALES (corp-wide): 165.7MM **Privately Held**
SIC: 3663 Cellular radio telephone
HQ: Bullitt Mobile Limited
  One Valpy Valpy Street
  Reading BERKS RG1 1
  118 958-0449

(G-1025)
C & C DUPLICATORS INC
220 Knickerbocker Ave # 1 (11716-3181)
PHONE.....................631 244-0800
Fax: 631 244-0807
Frank Carroll Jr, *President*
Frank Carroll Sr, *Vice Pres*
EMP: 30
SQ FT: 11,000
SALES (est): 3.7MM **Privately Held**
SIC: 3652 7389 Magnetic tape (audio): prerecorded; printing broker

(G-1026)
C & H MACHINING INC
281 Knickerbocker Ave (11716-3103)
PHONE.....................631 582-6737
Cliff W Havel, *President*
Phillip A Russo, *Vice Pres*
EMP: 13
SQ FT: 6,000
SALES: 1.3MM **Privately Held**
SIC: 3599 Machine shop, jobbing & repair

(G-1027)
C & M CIRCUITS INC
50 Orville Dr (11716-2548)
PHONE.....................631 589-0208
Fax: 631 589-1247
Charles Gwynn, *Ch of Bd*
John Lindy, *Administration*
EMP: 24

▲ = Import ▼ = Export
◆ = Import/Export

GEOGRAPHIC SECTION

Bohemia - Suffolk County (G-1053)

SQ FT: 7,500
SALES (est): 1.7MM **Privately Held**
SIC: 3629 Electronic generation equipment

(G-1028)
CERTIFIED PRCSION MCHINING INC
70 Knickerbocker Ave # 4 (11716-3166)
PHONE..................631 244-3671
Michael Staib, *President*
James Turano, *Vice Pres*
EMP: 6
SQ FT: 8,000
SALES (est): 784.2K **Privately Held**
SIC: 3599 Machine shop, jobbing & repair

(G-1029)
CHOCOLATE BY DESIGN INC
660 Sycamore Ave (11716-3513)
PHONE..................631 737-0082
Fax: 631 737-0188
Richard Motlin, *President*
Ellen Motlin, *Corp Secy*
EMP: 5 EST: 1979
SQ FT: 5,000
SALES (est): 542.6K **Privately Held**
WEB: www.chocolatebydesigninc.com
SIC: 2066 Chocolate & cocoa products

(G-1030)
CLIMATRONICS CORP (HQ)
606 Johnson Ave Ste 28 (11716-2419)
PHONE..................541 471-7111
Thomas Pottberg, *President*
Joann Pottberg, *Corp Secy*
David W Gilmore, *Vice Pres*
James Riley Loftin, *CFO*
EMP: 14
SQ FT: 16,500
SALES (est): 1.2MM
SALES (corp-wide): 23.7MM **Privately Held**
WEB: www.climatronics.com
SIC: 3829 Meteorological instruments
PA: Met One Instruments, Inc.
  1600 Nw Washington Blvd
  Grants Pass OR 97526
  541 471-7111

(G-1031)
CLINTRAK CLINICAL LABELING S (PA)
Also Called: Eagle Business Systems
2800 Veterans Hwy (11716-1002)
PHONE..................888 479-3900
Bob Scarth, *General Mgr*
Kevin Greenwood, *Mfg Dir*
Brianne Teemsma, *Project Mgr*
Jamie Pieron, *Opers Mgr*
Joe Macdougall, *Opers Staff*
▲ EMP: 55
SQ FT: 45,000
SALES (est): 10.1MM **Privately Held**
WEB: www.clintrak.com
SIC: 2754 Letter, circular & form: gravure printing

(G-1032)
CMB WIRELESS GROUP LLC (PA)
116 Wilbur Pl (11716-2402)
PHONE..................631 750-4700
Joseph Lucania, *CEO*
Rich Meigh, *Exec VP*
Vincent Vivolo Jr, *Exec VP*
James McGuirk, *Vice Pres*
Frank Pipolo, *Vice Pres*
▲ EMP: 280
SALES (est): 43.9MM **Privately Held**
SIC: 3663 Mobile communication equipment

(G-1033)
CMS HEAT TRANSFER DIVISION INC
273 Knickerbocker Ave (11716-3103)
PHONE..................631 968-0084
Chris Mauro, *President*
Steve White, *Vice Pres*
Lisa White, *Manager*
Marek Dolat, *Admin Sec*
EMP: 20
SQ FT: 16,000
SALES (est): 5.9MM **Privately Held**
WEB: www.cmsheattransfer.com
SIC: 3443 Finned tubes, for heat transfer; heat exchangers, plate type

(G-1034)
COLOR CRAFT FINISHING CORP
30 Floyds Run Ste A (11716-2212)
PHONE..................631 563-3230
Fax: 631 563-3298
Angelo Zegarelli, *President*
EMP: 10
SALES (est): 1.1MM **Privately Held**
SIC: 3089 3479 Painting of metal products; coloring & finishing of plastic products

(G-1035)
COS TEC MANUFACTURING CORP
Also Called: K C Technical Services
390 Knickerbocker Ave # 1 (11716-3123)
PHONE..................631 589-7170
Fax: 631 589-7196
Guy A Cosmo, *President*
Elizabeth Cosmo, *Vice Pres*
▲ EMP: 7
SQ FT: 11,000
SALES (est): 500K **Privately Held**
SIC: 2678 Stationery products

(G-1036)
COTTONWOOD METALS INC
1625 Sycamore Ave Ste A (11716-1728)
PHONE..................646 807-8674
Christopher Smith, *Chairman*
Jim Carter, *Manager*
EMP: 20 EST: 2011
SQ FT: 15,000
SALES (est): 2.2MM **Privately Held**
SIC: 3441 Fabricated structural metal

(G-1037)
COVERGRIP CORPORATION
30 Aero Rd (11716-2902)
PHONE..................855 268-3747
John Barry, *President*
▲ EMP: 5 EST: 2011
SALES (est): 800K **Privately Held**
WEB: www.covergrip.com
SIC: 2394 Canvas covers & drop cloths

(G-1038)
CRAFT-TECH MFG CORP
1750 Artic Ave (11716-2423)
PHONE..................631 563-4949
Fax: 631 563-4711
Joseph Desantis, *CEO*
Ralph Desantis Jr, *Vice Pres*
Ralph Desantis Sr, *Treasurer*
Steve Taylor, *Office Mgr*
EMP: 7 EST: 1978
SQ FT: 19,500
SALES (est): 840K **Privately Held**
SIC: 3444 Casings, sheet metal

(G-1039)
CREATIVE METAL FABRICATORS
360 Knickerbocker Ave # 13 (11716-3124)
PHONE..................631 567-2266
Fax: 631 589-3924
Richard W Donovan, *President*
Liz King, *Bookkeeper*
EMP: 7
SQ FT: 8,500
SALES (est): 600K **Privately Held**
SIC: 3446 Architectural metalwork

(G-1040)
CROWNLITE MFG CORP
1650 Sycamore Ave Ste 24 (11716-1900)
PHONE..................631 589-9100
William Siegel, *President*
EMP: 30 EST: 1948
SQ FT: 57,600
SALES (est): 4.1MM **Privately Held**
SIC: 3646 3645 Commercial indusl & institutional electric lighting fixtures; residential lighting fixtures

(G-1041)
CUSTOM DESIGN METALS INC
1612 Locust Ave Ste C (11716-2100)
PHONE..................631 563-2444
Fax: 631 589-9198
Robert Lyon, *President*
Richard Mellace, *Vice Pres*
EMP: 5
SQ FT: 7,500
SALES (est): 576.1K **Privately Held**
SIC: 3446 Railings, bannisters, guards, etc.: made from metal pipe

(G-1042)
CUSTOM HOUSE ENGRAVERS INC
Also Called: Village Plaquesmith, Ththe
104 Keyland Ct (11716-2656)
PHONE..................631 567-3004
Fax: 631 567-3019
Terry McLean, *President*
Terry Mc Lean, *Principal*
Brian McLean, *Vice Pres*
▲ EMP: 6
SQ FT: 3,200
SALES (est): 1MM **Privately Held**
SIC: 2796 3089 3479 Engraving platemaking services; engraving of plastic; etching & engraving

(G-1043)
CYGNUS AUTOMATION INC
1605 9th Ave (11716-1202)
PHONE..................631 981-0909
Fax: 631 981-1294
Sharon Dietrich, *President*
John Alessandro, *Vice Pres*
Mark Salerno, *Vice Pres*
Christian Dietrich, *Admin Sec*
EMP: 20
SQ FT: 6,000
SALES (est): 2.5MM **Privately Held**
SIC: 3629 3672 5063 Electronic generation equipment; printed circuit boards; wire & cable

(G-1044)
D & I FINISHING INC
1560 Ocean Ave Ste 7 (11716-1951)
PHONE..................631 471-3034
Danny Guerrier, *President*
Barbara Guerrier, *General Mgr*
EMP: 6
SQ FT: 4,500
SALES (est): 400K **Privately Held**
SIC: 3479 1721 3471 Painting of metal products; painting & paper hanging; finishing, metals or formed products

(G-1045)
DATA DEVICE CORPORATION (DH)
105 Wilbur Pl (11716-2426)
PHONE..................631 567-5600
Fax: 631 567-6357
Terrance M Paradie, *CEO*
Vincent Buffa, *President*
Charles Frazer, *President*
Frank Bloomfield, *Vice Pres*
Tammy Huml, *Vice Pres*
▲ EMP: 320
SQ FT: 104,000
SALES (est): 128MM
SALES (corp-wide): 3.1B **Publicly Held**
WEB: www.ddc-web.com
SIC: 3577 3674 3677 Data conversion equipment, media-to-media: computer; modules, solid state; electronic transformers
HQ: Ilc Industries, Llc
  105 Wilbur Pl
  Bohemia NY 11716
  631 567-5600

(G-1046)
DAVIS AIRCRAFT PRODUCTS CO INC
1150 Walnut Ave Ste 1 (11716-2168)
P.O. Box 525 (11716-0525)
PHONE..................631 563-1500
Fax: 631 563-1117
Bruce T Davis, *CEO*
Douglas Davis, *Vice Pres*
Jill Davis, *Vice Pres*
Judy Bender, *Purchasing*
Jason Kuhlken, *Purchasing*
▲ EMP: 143 EST: 1967
SQ FT: 30,000
SALES (est): 32.5MM **Privately Held**
WEB: www.davisaircraftproducts.com
SIC: 3724 3728 Aircraft engines & engine parts; aircraft parts & equipment

(G-1047)
DAVIS RESTRAINT SYSTEMS INC
1150 Walnut Ave (11716-2196)
PHONE..................631 563-1500
Bruce Davis, *President*
EMP: 11
SQ FT: 2,000
SALES: 1.2MM **Privately Held**
SIC: 2399 Seat belts, automobile & aircraft

(G-1048)
DAYTON T BROWN INC (PA)
Also Called: D T B
1175 Church St (11716-5014)
PHONE..................631 589-6300
Fax: 631 589-3648
Dayton T Brown Jr, *Ch of Bd*
Richard Dunne, *President*
Dan Malore, *General Mgr*
Tom Volpe, *Business Mgr*
Steve Marini, *Senior VP*
EMP: 276 EST: 1950
SQ FT: 250,000
SALES (est): 74MM **Privately Held**
WEB: www.daytontbrown.com
SIC: 3444 2741 8731 8734 Sheet metal specialties, not stamped; technical manuals: publishing only, not printed on site; technical papers: publishing only, not printed on site; engineering services; testing laboratories; measuring & controlling devices

(G-1049)
DEALER-PRESSCOM INC
1595 Smithtown Ave Ste A (11716-2418)
PHONE..................631 589-0434
Fax: 631 589-4449
Michael Endelson, *Principal*
William Ronnan, *Principal*
EMP: 7
SALES (est): 710K **Privately Held**
SIC: 2752 7334 Commercial printing, offset; photocopying & duplicating services

(G-1050)
DEJAY LITHO INC
230 Knickerbocker Ave (11716-3140)
PHONE..................631 319-6916
Fax: 212 262-5140
Jay Levine, *President*
Tyler Rubin, *Vice Pres*
EMP: 15 EST: 1963
SQ FT: 13,000
SALES: 3MM **Privately Held**
WEB: www.dejaylitho.com
SIC: 2752 Commercial printing, offset

(G-1051)
DELTA LOCK COMPANY LLC
366 Central Ave (11716-3105)
PHONE..................631 238-7035
▲ EMP: 12
SALES (est): 2MM **Privately Held**
SIC: 3429 Locks or lock sets

(G-1052)
DENTON ADVERTISING INC
1650 Sycamore Ave Ste 28 (11716-1731)
PHONE..................631 586-4333
Fax: 631 586-7851
Dennis Dornan, *President*
Robert Dornan, *Managing Dir*
Patty Lyons, *Admin Sec*
EMP: 12
SQ FT: 8,000
SALES: 1.4MM **Privately Held**
WEB: www.dentonadvertising.com
SIC: 2752 Lithographing on metal; advertising posters, lithographed

(G-1053)
DEROSA FABRICATIONS INC
250 Knickerbocker Ave (11716-3112)
PHONE..................631 563-0640
Fax: 631 563-1070
Tony Derosa, *President*
Lorry Derosa, *Vice Pres*
EMP: 20
SQ FT: 12,500

Bohemia - Suffolk County (G-1054)

GEOGRAPHIC SECTION

SALES (est): 2.3MM Privately Held
SIC: 3599 Machine shop, jobbing & repair

(G-1054)
DESIGN WORKS CRAFT INC (PA)
70 Orville Dr Ste 1 (11716-2547)
PHONE..................................631 244-5749
Fax: 631 244-6138
Susan Goldsmith, Ch of Bd
Daniel Knopp, President
Mike Giuliano, Human Resources
▲ EMP: 9
SQ FT: 24,500
SALES (est): 5.1MM Privately Held
WEB: www.designworkscrafts.com
SIC: 3944 Craft & hobby kits & sets

(G-1055)
EAGLE TELEPHONICS INC
3880 Veterans Mem Hwy (11716-1038)
PHONE..................................631 471-3600
Fax: 631 471-6595
Richard J Riccoboni, Ch of Bd
Don H Coleman, COO
Alexander Nenger, Exec VP
Frederic H Chapus, Vice Pres
Paul Neumann, Data Proc Exec
EMP: 15
SQ FT: 10,000
SALES (est): 3.3MM Privately Held
WEB: www.eagletelephonics.com
SIC: 3661 5794 Telephones & telephone apparatus; patent owners & lessors

(G-1056)
EASTERN COLOR STRIPPING INC
Also Called: Eastern Color Imaging
666 Lanson St (11716-3427)
PHONE..................................631 563-3700
Fax: 631 563-5085
Michael Catera, President
Laura Catera, Admin Sec
EMP: 10 EST: 1975
SQ FT: 3,000
SALES (est): 1.1MM Privately Held
WEB: www.easterncolor.com
SIC: 2796 7335 Color separations for printing; color separation, photographic & movie film

(G-1057)
EASTERN EXTERIOR WALL
869 Lincoln Ave (11716-4105)
PHONE..................................631 589-3880
Steven Boyce, Engineer
Charlie Bona, Manager
EMP: 20
SALES (corp-wide): 146.7MM Privately Held
SIC: 2452 Prefabricated wood buildings
HQ: Wall Eastern Exterior Systems Inc
    645 Hamilton St Ste 300
    Allentown PA 18101
    610 868-5522

(G-1058)
EDO LLC
Also Called: Edo Crprtion-Fiber Science Div
5852 Johnson Ave (11716)
PHONE..................................631 218-1413
Fax: 631 218-3505
Weily Tung, Branch Mgr
EMP: 17
SALES (corp-wide): 5.9B Publicly Held
SIC: 3825 Instruments to measure electricity
HQ: Edo Llc
    1500 New Horizons Blvd
    Amityville NY 11701
    631 630-4000

(G-1059)
EELE LABORATORIES LLC
50 Orville Dr (11716-2548)
PHONE..................................631 244-0051
Fax: 631 244-0053
Karlheinz Strob, President
N Wayne Bailey, Vice Pres
Kris Volven, CFO
Gina Sansivero, Marketing Staff
Paul Gasteiger, Director
EMP: 16 EST: 2000
SQ FT: 14,000
SALES: 500K Privately Held
WEB: www.eele.com
SIC: 3827 Optical instruments & lenses

(G-1060)
EL-GEN LLC
7 Shirley St Unit 1 (11716-1735)
PHONE..................................631 218-3400
Gerard Verbiar, Treasurer
Roy J Mc Keen, President
EMP: 5
SQ FT: 7,500
SALES (est): 400K Privately Held
WEB: www.elgenmfg.com
SIC: 2023 Dietary supplements, dairy & non-dairy based

(G-1061)
ELAN UPHOLSTERY INC
120b Wilbur Pl Ste B (11716-2404)
PHONE..................................631 563-0650
Fax: 631 563-0652
Alan Fogg, President
Ann Fogg, President
EMP: 10
SQ FT: 7,500
SALES (est): 1MM Privately Held
SIC: 2512 7641 Upholstered household furniture; upholstery work

(G-1062)
ELECTRO ALLOY RECOVERY INC
Also Called: Electro Waste Systems
130 Knickerbocker Ave M (11716-3171)
PHONE..................................631 879-7530
John Wellman, President
EMP: 8
SQ FT: 15,000
SALES: 2MM Privately Held
SIC: 3339 Gold refining (primary); platinum group metal refining (primary)

(G-1063)
FORERUNNER TECHNOLOGIES INC (PA)
1430 Church St Unit A (11716-5028)
PHONE..................................631 337-2100
Jim Wallace, President
Michael Viola, Vice Pres
Ba S Viola, Human Res Dir
▲ EMP: 45
SQ FT: 8,000
SALES (est): 17.1MM Privately Held
SIC: 3661 7371 4813 4899 Telephone & telegraph apparatus; computer software development & applications; telephone communication, except radio; data communication services; electronic parts & equipment; communication services

(G-1064)
FOSTER - GORDON MANUFACTURING
55 Knickerbocker Ave G (11716-3131)
PHONE..................................631 589-6776
Fax: 631 589-5353
Jonathan Gordon, President
Pat Sharp, Manager
EMP: 8
SQ FT: 9,000
SALES (est): 949K Privately Held
SIC: 2789 2782 Bookbinding & related work; blankbooks & looseleaf binders

(G-1065)
FURNITURE BY CRAFTMASTER LTD
1595 Ocean Ave Ste A9 (11716-1962)
PHONE..................................631 750-0658
Michael Ruggiero, President
Donna Agate, Corp Secy
EMP: 5
SQ FT: 3,600
SALES (est): 622.1K Privately Held
SIC: 2521 2512 Wood office furniture; upholstered household furniture

(G-1066)
GABRIELLA IMPORTERS INC (PA)
481 Johnson Ave Ste D (11716-2608)
PHONE..................................212 579-3945
Jacques Azoulay, President
▲ EMP: 4

SALES (est): 2MM Privately Held
SIC: 2084 Wines

(G-1067)
GE AVIATION SYSTEMS LLC
1000 Macarthur Mem Hwy (11716)
P.O. Box 1000 (11716-0999)
PHONE..................................631 467-5500
Fax: 631 467-5510
Kathleen Moosmueller, General Mgr
Brett Rowles, Manager
Frank Komornik, Director
William Collins,
EMP: 250
SALES (corp-wide): 123.6B Publicly Held
SIC: 3728 Aircraft parts & equipment
HQ: Ge Aviation Systems Llc
    1 Neumann Way
    Cincinnati OH 45215
    513 243-2000

(G-1068)
GFH ORTHOTIC & PROSTHETIC LABS
Also Called: Hutnick Rehab
161 Keyland Ct (11716-2621)
PHONE..................................631 467-3725
Glenn F Hutnick, Ch of Bd
Kathleen Ciano, Admin Sec
EMP: 5 EST: 1979
SALES (est): 609.6K Privately Held
SIC: 3842 Limbs, artificial; braces, orthopedic

(G-1069)
GLENN WAYNE WHOLESALE BKY INC
Also Called: Glenn Wayne Bakery
1800 Artic Ave (11716-2443)
PHONE..................................631 289-9200
Glenn Alessi, Ch of Bd
Wayne Stelz, President
Coleen Goehle, Manager
Dominic Seruggio, Manager
EMP: 85
SQ FT: 15,000
SALES (est): 19MM Privately Held
WEB: www.glennwayne.com
SIC: 2051 Bread, cake & related products

(G-1070)
GLOBAL PAYMENT TECH INC (PA)
Also Called: Gpt
170 Wilbur Pl Ste 600 (11716-2433)
PHONE..................................631 563-2500
Fax: 631 563-2630
Andre Soussa, Ch of Bd
William McMahon, President
Hal Chayrch, Vice Pres
Richard Soussa, Vice Pres
Dennys Noriega, Opers Staff
▲ EMP: 25
SQ FT: 25,550
SALES (est): 11.8MM Publicly Held
WEB: www.gptx.com
SIC: 3581 Mechanisms & parts for automatic vending machines

(G-1071)
HW SPECIALTIES CO INC
210 Knickerbocker Ave B (11716-3175)
PHONE..................................631 589-0745
Fax: 631 589-0739
Kevin Anderson, President
Fred Wichelman, Vice Pres
EMP: 18
SQ FT: 2,500
SALES (est): 1.4MM Privately Held
SIC: 3599 Machine shop, jobbing & repair

(G-1072)
ILC HOLDINGS INC (HQ)
105 Wilbur Pl (11716-2426)
PHONE..................................631 567-5600
Clifford P Lane, CEO
EMP: 9 EST: 1966
SALES (est): 128MM
SALES (corp-wide): 3.1B Publicly Held
SIC: 3674 Semiconductors & related devices

PA: Transdigm Group Incorporated
    1301 E 9th St Ste 3000
    Cleveland OH 44114
    216 706-2960

(G-1073)
ILC INDUSTRIES LLC (DH)
Also Called: I L C
105 Wilbur Pl (11716-2426)
PHONE..................................631 567-5600
Fax: 631 567-7358
Clifford P Lane, CEO
Roy Heyder, Senior Engr
Ken Sheedy, CFO
Nancy Henzel, Accountant
Jerry Kessler, Product Mgr
▲ EMP: 18 EST: 2010
SQ FT: 150,000
SALES (est): 128MM
SALES (corp-wide): 3.1B Publicly Held
WEB: www.ilcindustries.com
SIC: 3674 Semiconductors & related devices
HQ: Ilc Holdings, Inc.
    105 Wilbur Pl
    Bohemia NY 11716
    631 567-5600

(G-1074)
INTELLIGENT TRAFFIC SYSTEMS
140 Keyland Ct Unit 1 (11716-2646)
PHONE..................................631 567-5994
Joseph Battista, President
Karen Battista, Admin Sec
EMP: 8
SQ FT: 3,200
SALES: 400K Privately Held
SIC: 3669 Signaling apparatus, electric

(G-1075)
J PERCOCO INDUSTRIES INC
Also Called: Mjs Woodworking
1546 Ocean Ave Ste 4 (11716-1938)
PHONE..................................631 312-4572
Jerolamo Percoco, President
EMP: 8
SQ FT: 15,000
SALES: 1MM Privately Held
SIC: 2511 2434 2431 Wood household furniture; wood kitchen cabinets; millwork

(G-1076)
JAMES D RUBINO INC
20 Jules Ct Ste 5 (11716-4106)
PHONE..................................631 244-8730
James D Rubino, President
EMP: 24
SALES (est): 3MM Privately Held
SIC: 3499 Fabricated metal products

(G-1077)
JANCO PRESS INC
20 Floyds Run (11716-2154)
PHONE..................................631 563-3003
Fax: 631 563-9475
Maurice Janco, President
Florence Janco, Vice Pres
Seth Janco, Vice Pres
EMP: 15
SQ FT: 10,000
SALES: 4MM Privately Held
SIC: 2754 2759 Labels: gravure printing; labels & seals: printing; embossing on paper

(G-1078)
JEROME STVENS PHRMCUTICALS INC
Also Called: Jsp
60 Davinci Dr (11716-2633)
PHONE..................................631 567-1113
Fax: 631 567-1189
Ronald Steinlauf, Chairman
EMP: 15
SQ FT: 20,000
SALES (est): 4.6MM Privately Held
SIC: 2834 Pharmaceutical preparations

(G-1079)
JOKA INDUSTRIES INC
65 Knickerbocker Ave A (11716-3160)
PHONE..................................631 589-0444
Fax: 631 589-0817
Nick Prignano, Chairman
Roger Chabra, Manager

GEOGRAPHIC SECTION

Bohemia - Suffolk County (G-1106)

Bibi Latiff, *Manager*
▲ EMP: 22
SQ FT: 15,000
SALES (est): 4.4MM Privately Held
WEB: www.jokaindustries.com
SIC: 3721 Aircraft

(G-1080)
JOLIN MACHINING CORP
1561 Smithtown Ave (11716-2409)
PHONE..................................631 589-1305
Fax: 631 589-1318
John Lutjen, *President*
EMP: 12
SQ FT: 7,000
SALES (est): 1.9MM Privately Held
SIC: 3599 Machine shop, jobbing & repair

(G-1081)
JONATHAN LORD CORP
87 Carlough Rd Unit A (11716-2921)
PHONE..................................631 563-4445
Fax: 631 563-8505
Carole Kentrup, *Co-President*
Kathleen Dancik, *Co-President*
EMP: 12
SQ FT: 8,000
SALES (est): 970K Privately Held
WEB: www.jonathanlord.com
SIC: 2051 2052 Bread, cake & related products; cakes, bakery: except frozen; cookies & crackers

(G-1082)
K C TECHNICAL SERVICES INC
390 Knickerbocker Ave # 1 (11716-3123)
PHONE..................................631 589-7170
Guy Cosmo, *President*
Elizabeth Cosmo, *Vice Pres*
EMP: 7
SQ FT: 12,700
SALES (est): 800K Privately Held
WEB: www.kctecserv.com
SIC: 3565 Packaging machinery

(G-1083)
KENTRONICS INC
140 Keyland Ct Unit 1 (11716-2646)
PHONE..................................631 567-5994
Robert W Davis, *President*
Joseph Battista, *Vice Pres*
EMP: 5
SQ FT: 3,200
SALES (est): 406K Privately Held
WEB: www.kentronics.net
SIC: 3669 Highway signals, electric

(G-1084)
L & J INTERIORS INC
35 Orville Dr Ste 3 (11716-2533)
PHONE..................................631 218-0838
Fax: 631 218-0380
Jerry Esquibel, *President*
Leon Esquibel, *Vice Pres*
Liz Vanderbilt, *Manager*
EMP: 8
SALES (est): 870K Privately Held
WEB: www.ljinteriors.com
SIC: 2541 1742 Store fixtures, wood; drywall

(G-1085)
LABEL MAKERS INC
170 Wilbur Pl Ste 100 (11716-2451)
PHONE..................................631 319-6329
Craig Becker, *President*
Teri Nolan, *Credit Mgr*
Babra Michkana, *Office Mgr*
Adel Altman, *Systems Analyst*
EMP: 20
SQ FT: 8,000
SALES (est): 3.1MM Privately Held
WEB: www.labelmakersinc.com
SIC: 2672 Adhesive papers, labels or tapes: from purchased material

(G-1086)
LED LUMINA USA LLC
116 Wilbur Pl (11716-2402)
PHONE..................................631 750-4433
Christina Bonlarron, *CFO*
John Bonlarron, *Mng Member*
James McGuirk, *Manager*
▲ EMP: 1
SALES: 1MM Privately Held
SIC: 3229 Bulbs for electric lights

(G-1087)
LEETECH MANUFACTURING INC
105 Carlough Rd Unit C (11716-2914)
PHONE..................................631 563-1442
Fred Vasta, *President*
Jolleen Ogallagher, *Administration*
EMP: 5
SALES (est): 480K Privately Held
SIC: 3599 Machine shop, jobbing & repair

(G-1088)
LEIDEL CORPORATION (PA)
Also Called: Pentaplastics
95 Orville Dr (11716-2501)
PHONE..................................631 244-0900
Fax: 631 694-7876
Warren H Leidel, *Ch of Bd*
Roger D Leidel, *President*
Susan Barrisich, *Manager*
Abe Weisfelner, *Director*
EMP: 26 EST: 1902
SQ FT: 14,000
SALES: 5.9MM Privately Held
WEB: www.leidelcorp.com
SIC: 3089 Injection molded finished plastic products; molding primary plastic

(G-1089)
LOGITEK INC
110 Wilbur Pl (11716-2402)
PHONE..................................631 567-1100
William Forman, *CEO*
Debby Klaus, *Controller*
Patty Angelos, *Administration*
EMP: 90 EST: 1969
SALES: 20MM
SALES (corp-wide): 43.9MM Privately Held
WEB: www.naii.com
SIC: 3679 3825 3812 3674 Electronic circuits; instruments to measure electricity; search & navigation equipment; semiconductors & related devices; relays & industrial controls
PA: North Atlantic Industries, Inc.
110 Wilbur Pl
Bohemia NY 11716
631 567-1100

(G-1090)
LONG ISLANDS BEST INC
1650 Sycamore Ave Ste 4b (11716-1731)
PHONE..................................855 542-3785
John Bosco, *President*
EMP: 7
SALES: 119K Privately Held
SIC: 2741 Telephone & other directory publishing

(G-1091)
LOUGHLIN MANUFACTURING CORP
1601 9th Ave (11716-1202)
PHONE..................................631 585-4422
Fax: 631 585-4518
Martin Loughlin, *President*
Kathy Loughlin, *Manager*
EMP: 14 EST: 1970
SQ FT: 5,000
SALES (est): 2.5MM Privately Held
SIC: 3599 Machine shop, jobbing & repair

(G-1092)
LSC PERIPHERALS INCORPORATED
415 Central Ave Ste F (11716-3118)
PHONE..................................631 244-0707
Fax: 631 244-0794
Frank Villa, *President*
Roger Strolin, *Vice Pres*
EMP: 4
SQ FT: 4,000
SALES: 1.5MM Privately Held
SIC: 3577 Computer peripheral equipment

(G-1093)
LUCAS DENTAL EQUIPMENT CO INC
360 Knickerbocker Ave # 4 (11716-3124)
PHONE..................................631 244-2807
Fax: 718 789-3819
Richard Lucas, *Ch of Bd*
Joyce Lucas, *President*
David Lichtman, *Exec Dir*
EMP: 14 EST: 1930
SQ FT: 20,000
SALES (est): 1.9MM Privately Held
SIC: 3843 Dental equipment

(G-1094)
MAGELLAN AEROSPACE NY INC
25 Aero Rd (11716-2901)
PHONE..................................631 589-2440
Fax: 631 589-2767
David Grynberg, *Mfg Staff*
Lee Pappas, *Mfg Staff*
Francis Dorsey, *Engineer*
John Mansfield, *Financial Exec*
Jerry Myszka, *Manager*
EMP: 250
SALES (corp-wide): 742.4MM Privately Held
SIC: 3599 3728 5088 Machine shop, jobbing & repair; aircraft parts & equipment; aircraft equipment & supplies
HQ: Magellan Aerospace, New York, Inc.
9711 50th Ave
Corona NY 11368
718 699-4000

(G-1095)
MAGNAWORKS TECHNOLOGY INC
36 Carlough Rd Unit H (11716-2905)
PHONE..................................631 218-3431
Stan Stromski, *Director*
EMP: 7
SALES (est): 623K Privately Held
WEB: www.magnaworkstechnology.com
SIC: 3499 Magnets, permanent: metallic

(G-1096)
MALHAME PUBLS & IMPORTERS INC
Also Called: Regina Press
180 Orville Dr Unit A (11716-2546)
PHONE..................................631 694-8600
Robert Malhame, *President*
George E Malhame, *President*
Robert E Malhame, *Treasurer*
Barbara Ryan, *Manager*
▲ EMP: 22
SALES (est): 3.9MM Privately Held
WEB: www.malhame.com
SIC: 2731 5049 Books: publishing only; religious supplies

(G-1097)
MASS MDSG SELF SELECTION EQP
35 Orville Dr Ste 2 (11716-2533)
PHONE..................................631 234-3300
Fax: 631 234-3676
Stephen D Jaha, *Ch of Bd*
Bob Panagos, *Vice Pres*
Richard Benardes, *Sales Executive*
Stephanie Friscia, *Manager*
▲ EMP: 20 EST: 1961
SQ FT: 4,000
SALES (est): 3.4MM Privately Held
WEB: www.masmerch.com
SIC: 2542 1751 Partitions & fixtures, except wood; store fixture installation

(G-1098)
MCGUIGAN INC
Also Called: Concept Components
210 Knickerbocker Ave (11716-3175)
PHONE..................................631 750-6222
Fax: 631 563-4675
James W McGuigan, *Ch of Bd*
Mike Potuczo, *Plant Mgr*
Helene Stradford, *Manager*
EMP: 25
SQ FT: 9,000
SALES (est): 6.2MM Privately Held
WEB: www.mcguigan.com
SIC: 3566 3599 3724 Gears, power transmission, except automotive; custom machinery; aircraft engines & engine parts

(G-1099)
MED SERVICES INC
100 Knickerbocker Ave C (11716-3127)
PHONE..................................631 218-6450
Steven Cortese, *President*
Stefani Katz, *Senior VP*
EMP: 55
SQ FT: 1,800
SALES: 155MM Privately Held
SIC: 3845 7699 Electromedical equipment; medical equipment repair, non-electric

(G-1100)
MONARCH METAL FABRICATION INC
1625 Sycamore Ave Ste A (11716-1728)
PHONE..................................631 563-8967
James Carter, *President*
Rosemary Noll, *Administration*
▼ EMP: 8
SQ FT: 17,000
SALES (est): 1.4MM Privately Held
WEB: www.monarchmetal.com
SIC: 3441 3444 Fabricated structural metal; sheet metalwork

(G-1101)
MPE GRAPHICS INC
Also Called: Milburn Printing
120 Wilbur Pl Ste A (11716-2440)
PHONE..................................631 582-8900
Fax: 631 582-8995
Keith Quinn, *President*
Lisa Quinn, *Manager*
EMP: 11 EST: 2004
SQ FT: 5,000
SALES (est): 1.4MM Privately Held
SIC: 2759 Commercial printing

(G-1102)
MTWLI PRECISION CORP
1605 Sycamore Ave Unit B (11716-1734)
PHONE..................................631 244-3767
Thelma Walerstein, *President*
EMP: 5
SQ FT: 2,100
SALES: 200K Privately Held
SIC: 3549 Metalworking machinery

(G-1103)
NATURES BOUNTY (NY) INC
90 Orville Dr (11716-2521)
PHONE..................................631 567-9500
EMP: 10 Publicly Held
SIC: 2834 Vitamin preparations
HQ: Nature's Bounty Inc.,
2100 Smithtown Ave
Ronkonkoma NY 11779
631 580-6137

(G-1104)
NEW KIT ON THE BLOCK
100 Knickerbocker Ave K (11716-3127)
PHONE..................................631 757-5655
Fax: 631 757-5680
Lee Holcomb, *President*
John Burke, *Managing Dir*
Margaret Courtemancke, *Office Mgr*
EMP: 5
SQ FT: 4,000
SALES (est): 369.2K Privately Held
WEB: www.thenewkitontheblock.com
SIC: 3993 5099 Signs & advertising specialties; signs, except electric

(G-1105)
NEWPORT BUSINESS SOLUTIONS INC
61 Keyland Ct (11716-2654)
PHONE..................................631 319-6129
Gina Lanzillotta, *President*
Brendan Primus, *Manager*
Lynn Stillwell-Marks, *Manager*
Catherine Fairburn, *Director*
George Feinman, *Director*
EMP: 18 EST: 2010
SALES (est): 2.2MM Privately Held
SIC: 2759 3555 5045 Commercial printing; promotional printing; printing trades machinery; printers, computer

(G-1106)
NORTH ATLANTIC INDUSTRIES INC (PA)
110 Wilbur Pl (11716-2402)
PHONE..................................631 567-1100
William Forman, *President*
Lino Massafra, *Vice Pres*
Edward Doepp, *Plant Mgr*
Eddie Gonzalez, *Facilities Mgr*
Deborah L Klaus, *Controller*
EMP: 115

Bohemia - Suffolk County (G-1107)

SQ FT: 30,000
SALES: 43.9MM **Privately Held**
SIC: 3825 Instruments to measure electricity

(G-1107)
NORTHROCK INDUSTRIES INC
31 Crossway E (11716-1204)
PHONE.................................631 924-6130
Brian F Robertson, *President*
Alan Browning, *Treasurer*
Eric Rueb, *Admin Sec*
▲ EMP: 21
SQ FT: 12,000
SALES (est): 3.5MM **Privately Held**
WEB: www.northrockindustries.com
SIC: 3559 Concrete products machinery

(G-1108)
NYCON DIAMOND & TOOLS CORP
55 Knickerbocker Ave (11716-3120)
PHONE.................................855 937-6922
John Pierpaoli, *President*
Sean Johnson, *Accounting Mgr*
EMP: 7
SQ FT: 2,000
SALES (est): 313.1K **Privately Held**
SIC: 3559 Concrete products machinery

(G-1109)
OLD WORLD MOULDINGS INC
821 Lincoln Ave (11716-4103)
PHONE.................................631 563-8660
Fax: 631 563-8815
Alan D Havranek, *President*
EMP: 8
SQ FT: 20,000
SALES: 2.4MM **Privately Held**
WEB: www.oldworldmouldings.com
SIC: 2431 Moldings, wood: unfinished & prefinished

(G-1110)
PACKAGING DYNAMICS LTD
35 Carlough Rd Ste 2 (11716-2913)
PHONE.................................631 563-4499
Daniel Lehmann, *CEO*
Eric Lehmann, *President*
Darrin Tosh, *Prdtn Mgr*
Ann Lange, *Office Mgr*
Pat Lehmann, *Admin Sec*
◆ EMP: 15
SALES (est): 3.5MM **Privately Held**
SIC: 3565 Packaging machinery

(G-1111)
PASSUR AEROSPACE INC
35 Orville Dr Ste 1 (11716-2533)
PHONE.................................631 589-6800
G S Beckwith Gilbert, *Ch of Bd*
James T Barry, *President*
Keith Wichman, *President*
Bruce N Whitman, *Chairman*
James A Cole, *Senior VP*
EMP: 6
SQ FT: 3,000
SALES: 1.7MM **Privately Held**
SALES (corp-wide): 14.8MM **Publicly Held**
WEB: www.passur.com
SIC: 3671 Cathode ray tubes, including rebuilt
PA: Passur Aerospace, Inc.
  1 Landmark Sq Ste 1900
  Stamford CT 06901
  203 622-4086

(G-1112)
PDA PANACHE CORP
Also Called: P D A Panache
70 Knickerbocker Ave # 7 (11716-3151)
P.O. Box 577, Bellport (11713-0577)
PHONE.................................631 776-0523
Paul Schiller, *President*
Lynn Schiller, *Vice Pres*
EMP: 5
SALES (est): 580K **Privately Held**
WEB: www.pdapanache.com
SIC: 3577 5941 5112 Input/output equipment, computer; sporting goods & bicycle shops; pens &/or pencils

(G-1113)
PERVI PRECISION COMPANY INC
220 Knickerbocker Ave # 1 (11716-3181)
PHONE.................................631 589-5557
Fax: 631 589-7637
Carlos Perez, *Owner*
EMP: 6
SQ FT: 4,100
SALES (est): 888K **Privately Held**
SIC: 3469 3599 Machine parts, stamped or pressed metal; machine shop, jobbing & repair

(G-1114)
POWER CONNECTOR INC
140 Wilbur Pl Ste 4 (11716-2400)
PHONE.................................631 563-7878
Fax: 631 563-6482
Andrew S Linder, *President*
Arlene R Linder, *Vice Pres*
Peter Spadaro, *Opers Staff*
Joan Saracino, *Controller*
▲ EMP: 30
SQ FT: 32,000
SALES (est): 8.8MM **Privately Held**
SIC: 3678 Electronic connectors

(G-1115)
PRECISION ASSEMBLY TECH INC
Also Called: P.A.t
160 Wilbur Pl Ste 500 (11716-2437)
PHONE.................................631 699-9400
Lorraine Caruso, *Principal*
Russell Gulotta, *Chairman*
Thomas Gulotta, *Vice Pres*
Michael Kellwick, *Manager*
Lorraine Caurso, *Administration*
▲ EMP: 50
SQ FT: 25,000
SALES (est): 16.6MM **Privately Held**
WEB: www.pat-inc.com
SIC: 3679 Electronic circuits; harness assemblies for electronic use: wire or cable

(G-1116)
PRECISION CHARTS INC
Also Called: PCI
130 Wilbur Pl Dept Pc (11716-2404)
P.O. Box 456 (11716-0456)
PHONE.................................631 244-8295
Barry Spencer, *President*
Michael Lesh, *General Mgr*
Peggy Easparro, *Manager*
▲ EMP: 25
SQ FT: 30,000
SALES (est): 5.3MM **Privately Held**
WEB: www.pcicharts.com
SIC: 2621 Book, bond & printing papers

(G-1117)
PRIMOPLAST INC
1555 Ocean Ave Ste E (11716-1933)
PHONE.................................631 750-0680
Eugene Ruoff, *President*
William Hayes, *Admin Sec*
EMP: 12
SQ FT: 1,000
SALES: 950K **Privately Held**
SIC: 3089 3531 Injection molded finished plastic products; construction machinery attachments

(G-1118)
PRO TORQUE
Also Called: J Rivera
1440 Church St (11716-5027)
PHONE.................................631 218-8700
Joseph Rivera, *President*
Susan Rivera, *Vice Pres*
Lynn Dimino, *CFO*
Lorrie Rivera, *Manager*
EMP: 25
SQ FT: 165,000
SALES: 1.7MM **Privately Held**
WEB: www.jrivera.com
SIC: 3714 Motor vehicle transmissions, drive assemblies & parts

(G-1119)
PROJECTOR LAMP SERVICES LLC
120 Wilbur Pl Ste C (11716-2440)
PHONE.................................631 244-0051
Santa Maria Scalza, *Accounting Mgr*
Barbara Trezza, *Accounting Mgr*
Paul Gasteiger,
EMP: 15
SALES (est): 2.4MM **Privately Held**
SIC: 3648 Reflectors for lighting equipment: metal

(G-1120)
PROTEX INTERNATIONAL CORP
Also Called: Securax
366 Central Ave (11716-3105)
PHONE.................................631 563-4250
David Wachsman, *CEO*
William Azzoli, *Electrical Engi*
Kevin Boyle, *CFO*
Patricia Voigt, *Accounts Mgr*
Arthur Varga, *Mktg Dir*
▲ EMP: 75
SQ FT: 34,000
SALES (est): 13MM **Privately Held**
WEB: www.protex-intl.com
SIC: 3699 Security control equipment & systems

(G-1121)
QUEUE SOLUTIONS LLC
250 Knickerbocker Ave (11716-3112)
PHONE.................................631 750-6440
Richard Prigg, *President*
EMP: 10
SALES: 5MM **Privately Held**
SIC: 2387 Apparel belts

(G-1122)
REPELLEM CONSUMER PDTS CORP
Also Called: Ecosmartplastics
1626 Locust Ave Ste 6 (11716-2159)
PHONE.................................631 273-3992
Terry Feinberg, *President*
EMP: 10
SALES (est): 29.2K **Privately Held**
SIC: 2673 2392 Trash bags (plastic film): made from purchased materials; tablecloths: made from purchased materials

(G-1123)
ROAD CASES USA INC
1625 Sycamore Ave Ste A (11716-1728)
PHONE.................................631 563-0633
Lucille Maielna, *Office Mgr*
EMP: 20
SALES (est): 106.3K **Privately Held**
SIC: 3523 Farm machinery & equipment

(G-1124)
S G NEW YORK LLC (PA)
Also Called: Pennysaver News
2950 Vtrans Mem Hwy Ste 1 (11716-1030)
PHONE.................................631 665-4000
Fax: 631 580-7748
Richard Megenedy Jr,
Murray Rossby,
EMP: 33
SQ FT: 4,000
SALES (est): 5.9MM **Privately Held**
SIC: 2741 2711 Shopping news: publishing & printing; newspapers, publishing & printing

(G-1125)
SCIENTIFIC INDUSTRIES INC (PA)
80 Orville Dr Ste 102 (11716-2505)
PHONE.................................631 567-4700
Fax: 631 567-5896
Joseph G Cremonese, *Ch of Bd*
Helena R Santos, *President*
Robert P Nichols, *Admin Sec*
▲ EMP: 33 EST: 1954
SQ FT: 19,000
SALES: 8.1MM **Publicly Held**
WEB: www.scind.com
SIC: 3821 Shakers & stirrers

(G-1126)
SECURITY DYNAMICS INC
Also Called: Sdi Cable
217 Knickerbocker Ave (11716-3132)
PHONE.................................631 392-1701
Huihua Wang, *Ch of Bd*
William Wang, *President*
Lillian Chen, *General Mgr*
▲ EMP: 12
SQ FT: 3,000
SALES (est): 2.7MM **Privately Held**
SIC: 3699 Security devices

(G-1127)
SELECT CONTROLS INC
45 Knickerbocker Ave # 3 (11716-3119)
PHONE.................................631 567-9010
Fax: 631 567-9013
Robert Ufer, *President*
Diane Morris, *Corp Secy*
Tom Morris, *Opers Mgr*
Joe Cardimone, *Opers Staff*
Art Nintsel, *Engineer*
EMP: 32
SQ FT: 2,500
SALES (est): 5.7MM **Privately Held**
WEB: www.select-controls.com
SIC: 3823 3625 8711 3613 Industrial flow & liquid measuring instruments; industrial electrical relays & switches; consulting engineer; switchgear & switchboard apparatus

(G-1128)
SG-TEC LLC
1520 Ocean Ave (11716-1916)
PHONE.................................631 750-6161
William Feldman, *Mng Member*
Harold Goettlich,
EMP: 4
SQ FT: 1,200
SALES: 2MM **Privately Held**
SIC: 2891 5072 Epoxy adhesives; screws

(G-1129)
SHAR-MAR MACHINE COMPANY
1648 Locust Ave Ste F (11716-2156)
PHONE.................................631 567-8040
Fax: 631 567-8042
Myron Rubin, *Owner*
EMP: 5
SQ FT: 3,200
SALES (est): 439.3K **Privately Held**
SIC: 3599 Machine shop, jobbing & repair

(G-1130)
SHORT RUN FORMS INC
171 Keyland Ct (11716-2621)
PHONE.................................631 567-7171
Fax: 631 567-4550
Steven Looney, *President*
Andrew Boccio, *Senior VP*
Robert Stumpo, *Vice Pres*
Jerry Gagliardo, *Foreman/Supr*
Jan Merritt, *Accountant*
EMP: 60
SQ FT: 17,000
SALES (est): 9MM **Privately Held**
WEB: www.shortrunforms.com
SIC: 2759 5943 Business forms: printing; office forms & supplies

(G-1131)
SIEMENS INDUSTRY INC
50 Orville Dr Ste 2 (11716-2548)
PHONE.................................631 218-1000
Fax: 631 218-1009
Tim Krauskopf, *Vice Pres*
Kristin Kehyaian, *QA Dir*
Cassandra Kocsis, *QC Mgr*
Juan Morillo, *Engineer*
Denise Carroll, *Financial Analy*
EMP: 115
SALES (corp-wide): 89.6B **Privately Held**
WEB: www.sibt.com
SIC: 3823 Temperature measurement instruments, industrial
HQ: Siemens Industry, Inc.
  1000 Deerfield Pkwy
  Buffalo Grove IL 60089
  847 215-1000

(G-1132)
SMART HIGH VOLTAGE SOLUTIONS
390 Knickerbocker Ave # 6 (11716-3123)
P.O. Box 5135, Hauppauge (11788-0001)
PHONE.................................631 563-6724
Kevin R Smith, *President*
Hersh Ochakovski, *Exec VP*
▼ EMP: 16
SQ FT: 1,825
SALES: 2.5MM **Privately Held**
SIC: 3542 High energy rate metal forming machines

GEOGRAPHIC SECTION

(G-1133)
SPECTRUM CRAFTS INC
Also Called: Janlynn Corporation, The
70 Orville Dr Ste 1 (11716-2547)
PHONE..................................631 244-5749
Daniel Knopp, *President*
EMP: 26 **EST:** 2013
SALES (est): 141.6K
SALES (corp-wide): 5.1MM **Privately Held**
SIC: 3944 Craft & hobby kits & sets
PA: Design Works Craft Inc.
  70 Orville Dr Ste 1
  Bohemia NY 11716
  631 244-5749

(G-1134)
STRUCTURAL INDUSTRIES INC
2950 Veterans Memorial Hw (11716-1030)
PHONE..................................631 471-5200
Stanley Hirsch, *CEO*
Jamie Hirsch, *President*
Cliff Burger, *Exec VP*
Judy Hirsch, *Vice Pres*
Judy Vietheer, *CFO*
▲ **EMP:** 180 **EST:** 1966
SQ FT: 70,000
SALES (est): 25.4MM **Privately Held**
WEB: www.structuralindustries.com
SIC: 2499 3089 3499 Picture & mirror frames, wood; plastic processing; picture frames, metal

(G-1135)
SURF-TECH MANUFACTURING CORP
80 Orville Dr Ste 115 (11716-2538)
PHONE..................................631 589-1194
Fax: 631 589-1629
Richard Eggert, *President*
EMP: 12
SQ FT: 8,000
SALES (est): 2.3MM **Privately Held**
WEB: www.surftechmfg.com
SIC: 3672 5045 Printed circuit boards; computers, peripherals & software

(G-1136)
SYMBOL TECHNOLOGIES LLC
110 Orville Dr (11716-2506)
PHONE..................................631 738-2400
Ron Goldman, *Branch Mgr*
EMP: 15
SALES (corp-wide): 3.5B **Publicly Held**
WEB: www.symbol.com
SIC: 3577 Computer peripheral equipment
HQ: Symbol Technologies, Llc
  1 Zebra Plz
  Holtsville NY 11742
  631 737-6851

(G-1137)
SYNCO CHEMICAL CORPORATION
24 Davinci Dr (11716-2631)
P.O. Box 405 (11716-0405)
PHONE..................................631 567-5300
Fax: 631 567-5359
Sal A Randisi, *President*
Bill Reilly, *General Mgr*
Patrick E Malloy II, *Vice Pres*
◆ **EMP:** 50
SQ FT: 18,000
SALES (est): 10.9MM **Privately Held**
WEB: www.super-lube.com
SIC: 2842 Specialty cleaning, polishes & sanitation goods

(G-1138)
T R P MACHINE INC
35 Davinci Dr Ste B (11716-2666)
PHONE..................................631 567-9620
Patrick Price, *President*
Roger Price, *Principal*
Thomas Price, *Vice Pres*
Michelle Weiss, *Controller*
EMP: 25
SQ FT: 8,500
SALES (est): 4.1MM **Privately Held**
WEB: www.trpmachine.com
SIC: 3599 Machine & other job shop work; machine shop, jobbing & repair

(G-1139)
TEMRICK INC
1605 Sycamore Ave Unit B (11716-1734)
PHONE..................................631 567-8860
Fax: 631 567-1361
Trevor Glausen Jr, *President*
Melissa Glausen, *Vice Pres*
EMP: 5
SQ FT: 5,000
SALES: 550K **Privately Held**
SIC: 3599 7389 Machine shop, jobbing & repair; grinding, precision: commercial or industrial

(G-1140)
TEXTURE PLUS INC
1611 Lakeland Ave (11716-2190)
PHONE..................................631 218-9200
Katrina Vassar, *Manager*
Paul Kampe,
Brian Kampe,
EMP: 40
SQ FT: 16,000
SALES (est): 7.2MM **Privately Held**
WEB: www.foamvisions.com
SIC: 2952 Siding materials

(G-1141)
TOUCH ADJUST CLIP CO INC
1687 Roosevelt Ave (11716-1428)
PHONE..................................631 589-3077
Fax: 631 589-7489
Richard Haug Sr, *President*
Richard C Haug, *President*
Frank Grande, *Plant Mgr*
▲ **EMP:** 9
SQ FT: 10,000
SALES: 1.3MM **Privately Held**
WEB: www.touchadjustclip.com
SIC: 3915 Jewelers' materials & lapidary work

(G-1142)
TREO INDUSTRIES INC
Also Called: Genie Fastener Mfg Co
35 Carlough Rd Ste 1 (11716-2913)
PHONE..................................631 737-4022
Thomas W Blank, *Ch of Bd*
Tim Blank, *President*
Donald Blank, *Vice Pres*
Eugenia Blank, *Treasurer*
Corine Duffy, *Bookkeeper*
EMP: 7
SQ FT: 8,000
SALES (est): 957.7K **Privately Held**
SIC: 3452 Bolts, nuts, rivets & washers

(G-1143)
TRIAD COUNTER CORP
1225 Church St (11716-5014)
PHONE..................................631 750-0615
Frank Simone, *President*
Peter Amari, *Vice Pres*
Kirk Ibsen, *Treasurer*
EMP: 20
SQ FT: 20,000
SALES (est): 2.8MM **Privately Held**
SIC: 2541 5031 1799 Counter & sink tops; kitchen cabinets; kitchen & bathroom remodeling

(G-1144)
TRIANGLE RUBBER CO INC
50 Aero Rd (11716-2909)
PHONE..................................631 589-9400
Fax: 631 589-9403
Thomas Barresi, *President*
Joseph Barresi Jr, *Vice Pres*
Ann Taylor, *Manager*
▲ **EMP:** 25
SQ FT: 13,000
SALES (est): 4.1MM **Privately Held**
WEB: www.trianglerubber.com
SIC: 3069 5085 3061 Hard rubber & molded rubber products; rubber goods, mechanical; mechanical rubber goods

(G-1145)
TRIPAR MANUFACTURING CO INC
1620 Ocean Ave Ste 1 (11716-1930)
PHONE..................................631 563-0855
John M McNamara, *President*
EMP: 7
SQ FT: 8,000

SALES: 1.3MM **Privately Held**
SIC: 3444 3599 Sheet metalwork; machine shop, jobbing & repair

(G-1146)
TRIPLE POINT MANUFACTURING
1371 Church St Ste 6 (11716-5026)
PHONE..................................631 218-4988
Fax: 631 218-4999
Bernard Lichtenberger, *President*
Karl Zorn, *Vice Pres*
Paul Jessen, *Purchasing*
Erwin Stropagel, *Treasurer*
EMP: 7
SQ FT: 4,000
SALES: 671K **Privately Held**
WEB: www.tpmny.com
SIC: 3451 3599 Screw machine products; machine & other job shop work

(G-1147)
TUSK MANUFACTURING INC
1371 Church St Ste 1 (11716-5026)
PHONE..................................631 567-3349
Fax: 631 567-3348
Edmund F Zorn, *President*
Karl Zorn, *Vice Pres*
Kevin Zorn, *Vice Pres*
EMP: 21 **EST:** 1979
SQ FT: 8,000
SALES: 2.2MM **Privately Held**
WEB: www.tuskmfg.com
SIC: 3812 Search & navigation equipment

(G-1148)
UNITED DATA FORMS INC
500 Johnson Ave Ste B (11716-2709)
P.O. Box 363 (11716-0363)
PHONE..................................631 218-0104
Fax: 631 218-0209
Louis Giangaspro, *President*
Wayne Silverman, *Treasurer*
EMP: 12 **EST:** 1997
SQ FT: 10,000
SALES: 3MM **Privately Held**
SIC: 2621 Business form paper

(G-1149)
UNITED MACHINING INC
1595 Smithtown Ave Ste D (11716-2418)
PHONE..................................631 589-6751
Corey Vercellone, *President*
EMP: 6
SALES: 430K **Privately Held**
SIC: 3599 Machine shop, jobbing & repair

(G-1150)
UPTEK SOLUTIONS CORP
130 Knickerbocker Ave A (11716-3171)
Rural Route 130-A Knic (11716)
PHONE..................................631 256-5565
Lin Xu, *President*
Jeffrey Tian, *Vice Pres*
EMP: 13 **EST:** 2012
SALES (est): 2.1MM **Privately Held**
SIC: 3826 3699 Laser scientific & engineering instruments; laser systems & equipment

(G-1151)
VJ TECHNOLOGIES INC (PA)
Also Called: Vjt
89 Carlough Rd (11716-2903)
PHONE..................................631 589-8800
Fax: 631 589-8992
Vijay Alreia, *Chairman*
Jeffrey Ackerman, *Engineer*
Boris Soyfer, *Engineer*
Birgit Franz, *Senior Engr*
Anand Krishan, *Controller*
◆ **EMP:** 35
SQ FT: 30,000
SALES (est): 0 **Privately Held**
SIC: 3844 3812 3829 X-ray apparatus & tubes; search & detection systems & instruments; nuclear radiation & testing apparatus

(G-1152)
VYTEK INC
271 Knickerbocker Ave (11716-3103)
PHONE..................................631 750-1770
Joan Crisafulli, *President*
EMP: 10

SALES (est): 1.2MM **Privately Held**
SIC: 3599 7539 Machine shop, jobbing & repair; machine shop, automotive

(G-1153)
WEMCO CASTING LLC
20 Jules Ct Ste 2 (11716-4106)
PHONE..................................631 563-8050
Fax: 631 563-8054
Sharen Fenchel, *Owner*
EMP: 70
SQ FT: 2,000
SALES (est): 9.6MM **Privately Held**
WEB: www.wemcocastingllc.com
SIC: 3369 Nonferrous foundries

(G-1154)
Z WORKS INC
1395 Lakeland Ave Ste 10 (11716-3318)
PHONE..................................631 750-0612
Zoltan Mata, *Owner*
Katalin Gergely, *Owner*
EMP: 5 **EST:** 2001
SALES (est): 502.2K **Privately Held**
WEB: www.z-works.com
SIC: 3544 Special dies, tools, jigs & fixtures

Boiceville
Ulster County

(G-1155)
STUCKI EMBROIDERY WORKS INC (PA)
Also Called: Am-Best Emblems
Rr 28 Box W (12412)
PHONE..................................845 657-2308
Fax: 845 657-2860
Murray Fenwick, *President*
Ilse Fenwick, *Corp Secy*
Arthur Stucki, *Vice Pres*
Emily Oppimitti, *Sales Staff*
EMP: 18 **EST:** 1924
SQ FT: 17,000
SALES (est): 2.3MM **Privately Held**
SIC: 2395 Swiss loom embroideries; emblems, embroidered

Bolivar
Allegany County

(G-1156)
KLEIN CUTLERY LLC
Also Called: Scissor Online
7971 Refinery Rd (14715-9605)
PHONE..................................585 928-2500
Fax: 585 928-9739
Wayne J West,
▲ **EMP:** 60
SQ FT: 18,000
SALES (est): 8.4MM **Privately Held**
WEB: www.scissorsonline.com
SIC: 3421 Scissors, hand; shears, hand

Bolton Landing
Warren County

(G-1157)
NORTHERN LIFTS ELEVATOR CO LLC (PA)
45 Indian Brook Hollow Rd (12814-3813)
P.O. Box 1117 (12814-1117)
PHONE..................................518 644-2831
Jennifer Jackson, *Accounting Mgr*
Shirley Tennent,
EMP: 8
SALES (est): 1.5MM **Privately Held**
SIC: 3534 Elevators & moving stairways; elevators & equipment; escalators, passenger & freight

Boonville
Oneida County

(G-1158)
3B TIMBER COMPANY INC
8745 Industrial Dr (13309-4845)
P.O. Box 761 (13309-0761)
PHONE..............315 942-6580
Fax: 315 942-4332
Mark S Bourgeois, *President*
Gary S Bourgeois, *Vice Pres*
Janet F Bourgeois, *Treasurer*
EMP: 19
SQ FT: 5,400
SALES (est): 1.5MM **Privately Held**
SIC: 2411 Poles, wood: untreated; posts, wood: hewn, round or split; piling, wood: untreated; wood chips, produced in the field

(G-1159)
BAILEY BOONVILLE MILLS INC
123 Mill St (13309-1115)
P.O. Box 257 (13309-0257)
PHONE..............315 942-2131
Delbert C Bailey, *President*
Sue Cain, *Office Mgr*
EMP: 7 EST: 1968
SALES (est): 721.6K **Privately Held**
SIC: 2048 5999 Prepared feeds; feed & farm supply

(G-1160)
BAILLIE LUMBER CO LP
189 West St (13309-1000)
P.O. Box 154 (13309-0154)
PHONE..............315 942-5284
Arnold Levensailor, *Manager*
EMP: 40
SALES (corp-wide): 300.9MM **Privately Held**
WEB: www.baillie.com
SIC: 2421 Sawmills & planing mills, general
PA: Baillie Lumber Co., L.P.
    4002 Legion Dr
    Hamburg NY 14075
    800 950-2850

(G-1161)
BOONVILLE HERALD INC
Also Called: Boonville Hrald Adrndack Turist
105 E Schuyler St (13309-1103)
PHONE..............315 942-4449
Joe Kelly, *President*
EMP: 7
SALES (est): 316.6K **Privately Held**
SIC: 2711 Newspapers: publishing only, not printed on site

(G-1162)
BOONVILLE MANUFACTURING CORP
13485 State Route 12 (13309-3530)
P.O. Box 301 (13309-0301)
PHONE..............315 942-4368
Fax: 315 942-4367
Randy Anderson, *President*
Cheryl Tarasek, *Bookkeeper*
EMP: 7
SQ FT: 8,000
SALES (est): 951.5K **Privately Held**
SIC: 3053 Gaskets & sealing devices

(G-1163)
C J LOGGING EQUIPMENT INC
Also Called: CJ Motor Sports
8730 Industrial Dr (13309-4828)
P.O. Box 661 (13309-0661)
PHONE..............315 942-5431
Mark S Bourgeois, *Ch of Bd*
J Yates Hudson, *President*
Robert Martin Calfee III, *Chairman*
Gary S Bourgeois, *Vice Pres*
Linda Bourgeois, *Treasurer*
▲ EMP: 25
SALES (est): 8.5MM **Privately Held**
WEB: www.cjlogequip.com
SIC: 3531 Logging equipment

(G-1164)
NORTHERN FOREST PDTS CO INC
9833 Crolius Dr (13309-5001)
PHONE..............315 942-6955
Jeffrey Crolius, *President*
Jay Crolius, *Vice Pres*
EMP: 7
SQ FT: 2,800
SALES (est): 530K **Privately Held**
SIC: 2431 2499 Millwork; decorative wood & woodwork

(G-1165)
PRESERVING CHRSTN PUBLICATIONS (PA)
12614 State Route 46 (13309-4353)
P.O. Box 221 (13309-0221)
PHONE..............315 942-6617
Gerard Maicher, *President*
John Parrot, *Admin Sec*
EMP: 8
SQ FT: 6,300
SALES: 252.7K **Privately Held**
WEB: www.pcpbooks.com
SIC: 2731 Book publishing

(G-1166)
QUALITY DAIRY FARMS INC
Also Called: Mercer's Dairy
13584 State Route 12 (13309-3532)
PHONE..............315 942-2611
Dalton Givens, *President*
Jackie Karpinski, *Manager*
Ruth Migneery, *Shareholder*
▼ EMP: 24
SQ FT: 9,600
SALES (est): 4.3MM **Privately Held**
SIC: 2024 Ice cream & frozen desserts

(G-1167)
S M S C INC
Also Called: Central Adirondack Textiles
101 Water St (13309-1327)
PHONE..............315 942-4394
Fax: 315 942-4394
Chad Shoemaker, *Principal*
EMP: 6 EST: 2008
SALES (est): 588.4K **Privately Held**
SIC: 3321 Cooking utensils, cast iron

Bowmansville
Erie County

(G-1168)
PRECISION DENTAL CERAMICS OF B
5204 Genesee St (14026-1038)
PHONE..............716 681-4133
James Mantzanis, *President*
EMP: 11
SQ FT: 2,298
SALES: 700K **Privately Held**
SIC: 3843 Dental equipment & supplies

Branchport
Yates County

(G-1169)
HUNT COUNTRY VINEYARDS
4021 Italy Hill Rd (14418-9615)
PHONE..............315 595-2812
Fax: 315 595-2835
Art Hunt, *Owner*
Joyce Hunt, *Owner*
James Alsina, *Marketing Staff*
Bonnie Barney, *Manager*
David Mortensen, *Manager*
EMP: 25
SQ FT: 2,256
SALES (est): 800K **Privately Held**
WEB: www.huntcountryvineyards.com
SIC: 2084 Wines, brandy & brandy spirits

Brant Lake
Warren County

(G-1170)
GAR WOOD CUSTOM BOATS
20 Duell Hill Rd (12815-2026)
PHONE..............518 494-2966
Thomas Turcotte, *Mng Member*
EMP: 8
SALES (est): 740K **Privately Held**
WEB: www.garwoodcustomboats.com
SIC: 3732 Boat building & repairing

Brasher Falls
St. Lawrence County

(G-1171)
TRI-TOWN PACKING CORP
Helena Rd (13613)
P.O. Box 387, Winthrop (13697-0387)
PHONE..............315 389-5101
Fax: 315 389-5106
John Liberty, *President*
Thomas Liberty, *President*
Jeff Liberty, *Vice Pres*
EMP: 15
SQ FT: 5,300
SALES: 1MM **Privately Held**
WEB: www.adirondacksmokedmeats.com
SIC: 2011 5147 Meat packing plants; meats & meat products

Brentwood
Suffolk County

(G-1172)
ALLIED AERO SERVICES INC
506 Grand Blvd (11717-7902)
PHONE..............631 277-9368
Larry Soech, *President*
Steven Leonard, *Vice Pres*
EMP: 6
SALES (est): 449.2K **Privately Held**
SIC: 3295 Minerals, ground or treated

(G-1173)
APPLAUSE COATING LLC
8b Grand Blvd (11717-5117)
PHONE..............631 231-5223
Fax: 631 231-5565
Barbara Pinto, *Mng Member*
EMP: 11
SALES: 750K **Privately Held**
SIC: 3479 Coating of metals & formed products

(G-1174)
B & J DELIVERS INC
70 Emjay Blvd Bldg D (11717-3327)
P.O. Box 634 (11717-0633)
PHONE..............631 524-5550
Linda Marquez, *Owner*
EMP: 5
SALES (est): 496.9K **Privately Held**
SIC: 3537 Industrial trucks & tractors

(G-1175)
BECKS CLASSIC MFG INC
50 Emjay Blvd Ste 7 (11717-3300)
PHONE..............631 435-3800
Fax: 631 868-8282
Warren Beck, *CEO*
Steven Beck, *President*
Mary Closen, *Manager*
EMP: 100
SQ FT: 60,000
SALES (est): 11.6MM **Privately Held**
SIC: 2399 2341 2322 2676 Diapers, except disposable: made from purchased materials; panties: women's, misses', children's & infants'; underwear, men's & boys': made from purchased materials; sanitary paper products

(G-1176)
CUBITEK INC
95 Emjay Blvd Ste 2 (11717-3330)
PHONE..............631 665-6900
Daniel Hartman, *President*
Peter Hartman, *Vice Pres*
Judy Hartman, *Treasurer*
▼ EMP: 15
SQ FT: 500
SALES: 3.1MM **Privately Held**
SIC: 3599 Machine shop, jobbing & repair

(G-1177)
DATAGRAPHIC BUSINESS SYSTEMS
79 Emjay Blvd (11717-3323)
PHONE..............516 485-9069
Fax: 516 485-0544
Glenn M Schuster, *President*
EMP: 6
SQ FT: 3,000
SALES (est): 1.2MM **Privately Held**
WEB: www.datagraphicdesign.com
SIC: 2621 5943 Business form paper; office forms & supplies

(G-1178)
DELSUR PARTS
112 Pheasant Cir (11717-5047)
PHONE..............631 630-1606
Carlos Fuentes, *Owner*
EMP: 5
SALES: 150K **Privately Held**
SIC: 3556 Food products machinery

(G-1179)
DORMITORY AUTHORITY - STATE NY
998 Crooked Hill Rd # 26 (11717-1019)
PHONE..............631 434-1487
Fax: 631 434-1488
Terry McGowan, *Director*
EMP: 8
SALES (corp-wide): 2.1B **Privately Held**
SIC: 3599 Pump governors, for gas machines
PA: Dormitory Authority - State Of New York
    515 Broadway Ste 100
    Albany NY 12207
    518 257-3000

(G-1180)
EXPRESS CONCRETE INC
1250 Suffolk Ave (11717-4507)
PHONE..............631 273-4224
Bruno Palmieri, *President*
Mario Palmieri, *Office Mgr*
EMP: 6
SQ FT: 3,000
SALES (est): 706.5K **Privately Held**
SIC: 3272 Concrete products

(G-1181)
I MEGLIO CORP
151 Alkier St (11717-5135)
PHONE..............631 617-6900
Barbara Khanat, *President*
David Suarez, *Vice Pres*
EMP: 30
SQ FT: 65,000
SALES: 67MM **Privately Held**
SIC: 2431 5031 Millwork; millwork

(G-1182)
INTERSTATE LITHO CORP
151 Alkier St (11717-5135)
PHONE..............631 232-6025
Fax: 631 273-8504
Henry Becker, *President*
Richard Becker, *Vice Pres*
EMP: 100 EST: 1975
SQ FT: 100,000
SALES (est): 8.3MM **Privately Held**
SIC: 2752 2791 2789 Commercial printing, lithographic; typesetting; bookbinding & related work

(G-1183)
INTERSTATE WINDOW CORPORATION
Also Called: Mannix
345 Crooked Hill Rd Ste 1 (11717-1020)
PHONE..............631 231-0800
Fax: 631 231-0571
Robert Salzer, *President*
Paul Greenstein, *Vice Pres*
Sue Hausner, *Vice Pres*
Daniel Monosson, *Vice Pres*
Maria Juarez, *Human Res Dir*

GEOGRAPHIC SECTION

▲ EMP: 100
SQ FT: 51,000
SALES (est): 30.7MM **Privately Held**
WEB: www.mannixwindows.com
SIC: 3442 Metal doors, sash & trim

(G-1184)
J & A USA INC
335 Crooked Hill Rd (11717-1041)
PHONE.....................631 243-3336
Fax: 631 243-3339
Yunho Kim, *President*
Sidney Park, *CFO*
◆ EMP: 9
SQ FT: 15,000
SALES (est): 1.7MM **Privately Held**
WEB: www.jausa.com
SIC: 3999 Barber & beauty shop equipment

(G-1185)
KENNEY MANUFACTURING DISPLAYS
Also Called: Kenny Mfg
12 Grand Blvd (11717-5117)
PHONE.....................631 231-5563
Fax: 631 231-5821
Robert Kenney Jr, *President*
Michael Kenney, *Vice Pres*
Carolann Kenney, *Admin Sec*
EMP: 11
SQ FT: 7,500
SALES (est): 1.7MM **Privately Held**
WEB: www.kenneydisplays.com
SIC: 3089 3578 Plastic containers, except foam; point-of-sale devices

(G-1186)
LAURICELLA PRESS INC
Also Called: Imperial Color
81 Emjay Blvd (11717-3329)
PHONE.....................516 931-5906
Arthur Lauricella, *President*
Marc Lauricella, *Vice Pres*
EMP: 20
SALES: 500K **Privately Held**
SIC: 2759 Commercial printing

(G-1187)
LLOYDS FASHIONS INC (PA)
335 Crooked Hill Rd (11717-1041)
P.O. Box 1162, Syosset (11791-0489)
PHONE.....................631 435-3353
Lloyd Goldberg, *President*
Rita Goldberg, *Vice Pres*
▲ EMP: 58 EST: 1958
SQ FT: 22,000
SALES: 2.6MM **Privately Held**
SIC: 2353 2253 5137 Millinery; shawls, knit; women's & children's clothing

(G-1188)
MARKETSHARE LLC
90 Cain Dr (11717-1265)
PHONE.....................631 273-0598
Nancy Mantell, *Principal*
Steven Zaken, *Co-Owner*
Monique Greene, *Manager*
EMP: 5
SALES (est): 380K **Privately Held**
SIC: 2752 3991 Playing cards, lithographed; toothbrushes, except electric

(G-1189)
MICHBI DOORS INC
Also Called: Open & Shut Doors
75 Emjay Blvd (11717-3323)
PHONE.....................631 231-9050
Fax: 631 231-9040
Michelle Biancurli, *President*
Doug Hommel, *Vice Pres*
Suzanne Mutone, *Vice Pres*
Craig Gough, *Project Mgr*
Christopher Biancurli, *CFO*
EMP: 56 EST: 1981
SQ FT: 30,000
SALES (est): 8.6MM **Privately Held**
WEB: www.michbidoors.com
SIC: 2431 3231 3442 Millwork; products of purchased glass; metal doors, sash & trim

(G-1190)
PLASTIRUN CORPORATION
70 Emjay Blvd Bldg A (11717-3394)
PHONE.....................631 273-2626

Fax: 631 273-7644
Jack Elyahouzadeh, *President*
Jacob Y Lavi, *Treasurer*
◆ EMP: 35 EST: 1982
SQ FT: 51,000
SALES (est): 13.8MM **Privately Held**
WEB: www.plastirun.com
SIC: 2656 2621 Straws, drinking: made from purchased material; towels, tissues & napkins: paper & stock

(G-1191)
SLEEPY HOLLOW CHIMNEY SUP LTD
85 Emjay Blvd (11717-3323)
PHONE.....................631 231-2333
Fax: 631 231-2364
Fred Schukal, *President*
Stephen Schukal, *VP Opers*
Jeff Steffensen, *Office Mgr*
▲ EMP: 14
SQ FT: 9,000
SALES (est): 3.6MM **Privately Held**
WEB: www.bellfiresusa.com
SIC: 3229 Chimneys, lamp: pressed or blown glass

(G-1192)
STRATEGIC PHARMA SERVICES INC
58 Bradley St (11717-3417)
PHONE.....................631 231-5424
Susan Camean, *CEO*
EMP: 10
SALES (est): 993.3K **Privately Held**
SIC: 2834 Pharmaceutical preparations

(G-1193)
T S O GENERAL CORP
81 Emjay Blvd Unit 1 (11717-3329)
P.O. Box 552 (11717-0552)
PHONE.....................631 952-5320
Kirk Malandrakis, *President*
Monica Cura, *Manager*
EMP: 20
SQ FT: 30,000
SALES: 2MM **Privately Held**
WEB: www.tsogen.com
SIC: 2759 Commercial printing

(G-1194)
THURO METAL PRODUCTS INC (PA)
21-25 Grand Blvd N (11717)
PHONE.....................631 435-0444
Fax: 631 435-0293
Albert Thuro, *Ch of Bd*
David Thuro, *President*
Louis Krieger, *General Mgr*
Carolyn Thuro, *Corp Secy*
David Harrison, *Safety Mgr*
▲ EMP: 40 EST: 1971
SQ FT: 25,000
SALES (est): 12.2MM **Privately Held**
WEB: www.thurometal.com
SIC: 3451 3545 Screw machine products; machine tool attachments & accessories

(G-1195)
UNIWARE HOUSEWARE CORP
120 Wilshire Blvd Ste B (11717-8333)
PHONE.....................631 242-7400
Lily Hsu, *President*
Roger Hsu, *Vice Pres*
▲ EMP: 20
SALES (est): 3.4MM **Privately Held**
SIC: 3634 Electric housewares & fans

(G-1196)
US NONWOVENS CORP (PA)
100 Emjay Blvd (11717-3322)
PHONE.....................631 952-0100
Fax: 631 952-0200
Shervin Mehdizadeh, *CEO*
Samuel Mehdizadeh, *Ch of Bd*
Rody Mehdizadeh, *COO*
Michael Pischel, *CFO*
Alan Wolsky, *Credit Mgr*
◆ EMP: 600
SALES (est): 228.8MM **Privately Held**
WEB: www.usnonwovens.com
SIC: 2842 Specialty cleaning, polishes & sanitation goods

(G-1197)
USA FOIL INC
70 Emjay Blvd Bldg C (11717-3327)
PHONE.....................631 234-5252
Joseph Phami, *President*
Akhtar Gadi, *President*
Kami Youssi, *Vice Pres*
Deborah Joseph, *Manager*
▲ EMP: 20
SQ FT: 12,000
SALES (est): 3.7MM **Privately Held**
SIC: 3353 Aluminum sheet, plate & foil

(G-1198)
V E POWER DOOR CO INC
140 Emjay Blvd (11717-3322)
P.O. Box 663, Commack (11725-0663)
PHONE.....................631 231-4500
Fax: 631 231-4274
James Lanzarone, *CEO*
Philip Lanzarone, *President*
Evelyn Semar, *Corp Secy*
Susan Cruz, *Vice Pres*
Edward Lanzarone, *Vice Pres*
▲ EMP: 40
SQ FT: 23,000
SALES (est): 10.3MM **Privately Held**
SIC: 3699 Door opening & closing devices, electrical

Brewerton
Onondaga County

(G-1199)
AE FUND INC
Also Called: Frigo Design
5860 Mckinley Rd (13029-9691)
PHONE.....................315 698-7650
Fax: 315 698-7859
Eric J Gantley, *President*
Anthony Verdi, *Exec VP*
Allan Issacs, *Vice Pres*
EMP: 30
SQ FT: 15,000
SALES (est): 6.6MM **Privately Held**
WEB: www.frigodesign.com
SIC: 3632 Refrigerator cabinets, household: metal & wood

(G-1200)
GEORDIE MAGEE UPHL & CANVAS
Also Called: Magee Canvas & Trailer Sales
Weber Rd (13029)
P.O. Box 656 (13029-0656)
PHONE.....................315 676-7679
Fax: 315 676-2655
Geordie H Magee, *President*
Patty Arnoel, *Bookkeeper*
EMP: 6
SQ FT: 4,400
SALES: 1.1MM **Privately Held**
WEB: www.mageetrailers.com
SIC: 2211 5999 Canvas; canvas products

(G-1201)
IRENE CERONE
Also Called: Brewerton Special Tee's
9600 Brewerton Rd (13029-8798)
P.O. Box 670 (13029-0670)
PHONE.....................315 668-2899
Fax: 315 676-3010
Michael Cerone, *Owner*
Irene Cerone, *Co-Owner*
Sue Finley, *Office Mgr*
EMP: 7
SALES (est): 594.8K **Privately Held**
SIC: 2396 Screen printing on fabric articles

(G-1202)
ROBINSON CONCRETE INC
7020 Corporate Park Dr (13029)
PHONE.....................315 676-4662
Michael J Vitale, *Principal*
EMP: 10
SALES (corp-wide): 24MM **Privately Held**
SIC: 3273 Ready-mixed concrete
PA: Robinson Concrete, Inc.
3486 Franklin Street Rd
Auburn NY 13021
315 253-6666

Brewster
Putnam County

(G-1203)
AAAAAR ORTHOPEDICS INC
141 Main St (10509-1476)
PHONE.....................845 278-4938
Fax: 845 838-0967
Elizabeth Hawkins, *President*
Richard Dipompo, *Vice Pres*
EMP: 5
SALES (est): 360K **Privately Held**
SIC: 3842 Limbs, artificial

(G-1204)
ADVANCED PRECISION TECHNOLOGY
577 N Main St Ste 7 (10509-1240)
PHONE.....................845 279-3540
Fax: 845 278-0754
Olaf Brauer, *President*
Christine Brauer, *Vice Pres*
EMP: 10
SQ FT: 6,800
SALES (est): 1.1MM **Privately Held**
SIC: 3444 3341 Sheet metalwork; secondary nonferrous metals

(G-1205)
AKZO NOBEL FUNCTIONAL CHEM LLC
281 Fields Ln (10509-2676)
PHONE.....................845 276-8200
Terry Busch, *HR Admin*
Ton B Chner, *Branch Mgr*
EMP: 88
SALES (corp-wide): 15B **Privately Held**
SIC: 2869 Industrial organic chemicals
HQ: Akzo Nobel Functional Chemical, Llc
525 W Van Buren St # 1600
Chicago IL 60607
312 544-7000

(G-1206)
ALLIANCE CONTROL SYSTEMS INC
577 N Main St Ste 9 (10509-1240)
PHONE.....................845 279-4430
Doug Homberg, *President*
▲ EMP: 8
SALES (est): 943.6K **Privately Held**
SIC: 3629 Electronic generation equipment

(G-1207)
AMPRO INTERNATIONAL INC
30 Coventry Ln (10509-4808)
PHONE.....................845 278-4910
Fax: 845 279-9753
Floyd Pircio, *President*
Laura Arone, *Admin Sec*
EMP: 2
SQ FT: 1,000
SALES: 1MM **Privately Held**
SIC: 3679 Antennas, receiving

(G-1208)
BASE SYSTEMS INC
Also Called: Tower Computers
1606 Route 22 (10509-4014)
PHONE.....................845 278-1991
Lee Seacord, *President*
Linda Seacord, *Vice Pres*
EMP: 2
SQ FT: 3,000
SALES: 2MM **Privately Held**
SIC: 7372 5045 Prepackaged software; computer software

(G-1209)
BLACK & DECKER (US) INC
Also Called: Powers Fasteners
2 Powers Ln (10509-3633)
PHONE.....................914 235-6300
William Taylor, *Branch Mgr*
EMP: 375
SALES (corp-wide): 11.4B **Publicly Held**
SIC: 3546 Power-driven handtools
HQ: Black & Decker (U.S.) Inc.
1000 Stanley Dr
New Britain CT 06053
860 225-5111

Brewster - Putnam County (G-1210)

(G-1210)
BREWSTER TRANSIT MIX CORP (PA)
31 Fields Ln (10509-3507)
P.O. Box 410 (10509-0410)
PHONE..................................845 279-3738
Fax: 845 279-6506
Ted Petrillo, *President*
James Harahan, *Division Mgr*
Henry Paparazzo, *Vice Pres*
Curtis McGann, *Admin Sec*
▲ EMP: <5
SQ FT: 1,000
SALES (est): 5.2MM **Privately Held**
SIC: 3273 5032 Ready-mixed concrete; gravel; sand, construction

(G-1211)
BREWSTER TRANSIT MIX CORP
Fields Ln (10509)
P.O. Box 410 (10509-0410)
PHONE..................................845 279-3738
Jeff Chattin, *General Mgr*
EMP: 35
SALES (corp-wide): 5.2MM **Privately Held**
SIC: 3273 Ready-mixed concrete
PA: Brewster Transit Mix Corp
    31 Fields Ln
    Brewster NY 10509
    845 279-3738

(G-1212)
DAIRY CONVEYOR CORP (PA)
38 Mount Ebo Rd S (10509-4005)
P.O. Box 411 (10509-0411)
PHONE..................................845 278-7878
Fax: 845 278-7305
Gary Freudenberg, *President*
Roland Debald, *Vice Pres*
Karl Horberg, *CFO*
Pete Debalc, *Treasurer*
Peter Debald, *Treasurer*
▲ EMP: 86 EST: 1954
SQ FT: 68,000
SALES (est): 36.2MM **Privately Held**
SIC: 3535 7699 Conveyors & conveying equipment; industrial machinery & equipment repair

(G-1213)
DESIGN A SIGN OF PUTNAM INC
Also Called: Design-A-Sign
1456 Route 22 Ste A102 (10509-4352)
PHONE..................................845 279-5328
Pam Caesar, *President*
EMP: 6
SQ FT: 1,250
SALES (est): 460K **Privately Held**
SIC: 3993 Signs & advertising specialties

(G-1214)
DUNMORE CORPORATION
3633 Danbury Rd (10509-4516)
PHONE..................................845 279-5061
Fax: 845 279-5231
Donald Cregar, *Prdtn Mgr*
John Finger, *Prdtn Mgr*
Laurie Delbalzo, *Human Resources*
Jen King, *Personnel*
Terry Jones, *Manager*
EMP: 75
SQ FT: 49,432
SALES (corp-wide): 62MM **Privately Held**
WEB: www.dunmore.com
SIC: 2621 3081 2672 Paper mills; plastic film & sheet; coated & laminated paper
PA: Dunmore Corporation
    145 Wharton Rd
    Bristol PA 19007
    215 781-8895

(G-1215)
ELSAG NORTH AMERICA LLC
7 Sutton Pl Ste A (10509-3537)
PHONE..................................877 773-5724
Nate Maloney, *VP Mktg*
EMP: 5
SALES (corp-wide): 6.3MM **Privately Held**
SIC: 3829 Photogrammetrical instruments
PA: Elsag North America Llc
    205 Creek Ridge Rd Ste H
    Greensboro NC 27406
    336 379-7135

(G-1216)
FEYEM USA INC
7 Sutton Pl (10509-3536)
PHONE..................................845 363-6253
Palma Settini, *President*
Rudy Settini, *Manager*
EMP: 5
SALES (est): 202.9K **Privately Held**
SIC: 2329 2331 Men's & boys' sportswear & athletic clothing; women's & misses' blouses & shirts

(G-1217)
HIPOTRONICS INC (HQ)
1650 Route 22 (10509-4013)
P.O. Box 414 (10509-0414)
PHONE..................................845 279-8091
Fax: 845 279-2467
Timothy H Powers, *CEO*
Richard Davies, *President*
Jeff Brown, *Vice Pres*
Reinold Grob, *Vice Pres*
Charles Consalvo, *Opers Mgr*
▲ EMP: 115 EST: 1962
SQ FT: 90,000
SALES (est): 30.5MM
SALES (corp-wide): 3.5B **Publicly Held**
WEB: www.hipotronics.com
SIC: 3825 3679 3829 3677 Instruments to measure electricity; test equipment for electronic & electric measurement; power supplies, all types: static; measuring & controlling devices; electronic coils, transformers & other inductors; electronic capacitors; semiconductors & related devices
PA: Hubbell Incorporated
    40 Waterview Dr
    Shelton CT 06484
    475 882-4000

(G-1218)
HUDSON MACHINE WORKS INC
Also Called: H M W
30 Branch Rd (10509-4522)
PHONE..................................845 279-1413
Fax: 845 279-7220
Daniel R Ferguson, *Ch of Bd*
Michael Ferguson, *General Mgr*
Jennifer Ferguson, *Vice Pres*
Glenn Moss, *CFO*
Nancy Dally, *Mktg Dir*
EMP: 110
SQ FT: 25,000
SALES (est): 18.8MM **Privately Held**
WEB: www.hudsonmachine.com
SIC: 3743 Railroad equipment

(G-1219)
LAMOTHERMIC CORP
391 Route 312 (10509-2328)
PHONE..................................845 278-6118
Amos Noach, *Ch of Bd*
Gideon Noach, *Vice Pres*
Carol Smith, *Manager*
Taylor Seymour, *Director*
EMP: 97
SQ FT: 42,000
SALES (est): 12MM **Privately Held**
WEB: www.lamothermic.com
SIC: 3369 Castings, except die-castings, precision

(G-1220)
MATERION ADVANCED MATERIALS
42 Mount Ebo Rd S (10509-4005)
PHONE..................................800 327-1355
Raymond Chan, *Branch Mgr*
EMP: 6
SALES (corp-wide): 969.2MM **Publicly Held**
SIC: 3339 Primary nonferrous metals
HQ: Materion Advanced Materials Technologies And Services Inc.
    2978 Main St
    Buffalo NY 14214
    800 327-1355

(G-1221)
MATERION BREWSTER LLC
42 Mount Ebo Rd S (10509-4005)
P.O. Box 1950 (10509-8950)
PHONE..................................845 279-0900
Jon Ciccone, *Purch Mgr*
Robert Greco, *Controller*
Pamela Every, *Accountant*
Richard Fager, *Mng Member*
Tim Baxter, *Manager*
▲ EMP: 75
SQ FT: 36,000
SALES (est): 26.4MM
SALES (corp-wide): 969.2MM **Publicly Held**
WEB: www.puretechinc.com
SIC: 3499 3674 Friction material, made from powdered metal; semiconductors & related devices
HQ: Materion Advanced Materials Technologies And Services Inc.
    2978 Main St
    Buffalo NY 14214
    800 327-1355

(G-1222)
MIGGINS SCREW PRODUCTS INC
66 Putnam Ave (10509-1114)
PHONE..................................845 279-2307
Fax: 845 279-2602
Merle Delfay, *President*
John H Miggins, *President*
Merle Delsay, *Post Master*
▲ EMP: 9 EST: 1946
SQ FT: 2,500
SALES (est): 1MM **Privately Held**
SIC: 3451 Screw machine products

(G-1223)
PARACO GAS CORPORATION
4 Joes Hill Rd (10509-5323)
PHONE..................................845 279-8414
Jim Mc Ginty, *Principal*
EMP: 7
SALES (corp-wide): 214.3MM **Privately Held**
SIC: 1321 Propane (natural) production
PA: Paraco Gas Corporation
    800 Westchester Ave S604
    Rye Brook NY 10573
    800 647-4427

(G-1224)
PEDIFIX INC
281 Fields Ln (10509-2676)
PHONE..................................845 277-2850
Fax: 845 277-2851
Dennis Case, *President*
Jon Case, *Vice Pres*
Richard Ovadek, *Purchasing*
Caroline Bochnia, *Executive*
▲ EMP: 25
SQ FT: 15,000
SALES (est): 4.9MM **Privately Held**
WEB: www.pedifix.com
SIC: 3144 3143 Orthopedic shoes, women's; orthopedic shoes, men's

(G-1225)
PRE CYCLED INC
1689 Route 22 (10509-4022)
P.O. Box 341 (10509-0341)
PHONE..................................845 278-7611
Daniel Horkan, *President*
Carol Horkan, *Vice Pres*
EMP: 5
SQ FT: 3,000
SALES (est): 887.9K **Privately Held**
WEB: www.pre-cycled.com
SIC: 2752 Commercial printing, lithographic

(G-1226)
TRAFFIC LANE CLOSURES LLC
3620 Danbury Rd (10509-4507)
P.O. Box 726 (10509-0726)
PHONE..................................845 228-6100
Fax: 845 278-5450
Ralph M Rosenfeld, *General Mgr*
Jason Rosenfeld, *Opers Mgr*
Teri Godfrey, *Mng Member*
Ralph Rosenfeld, *Mng Member*
Mellisa Erreich, *Manager*
EMP: 9
SQ FT: 3,800
SALES (est): 1.5MM **Privately Held**
WEB: www.trafficlaneclosures.com
SIC: 3669 Highway signals, electric

(G-1227)
UNILOCK NEW YORK INC (HQ)
51 International Blvd (10509-2343)
PHONE..................................845 278-6700
Fax: 845 278-6788
Edward Bryant, *President*
Sean O' Lary, *General Mgr*
Lyle Selk, *General Mgr*
Glenn Wiley, *General Mgr*
Joseph Kerr, *Vice Pres*
▲ EMP: 8
SALES (est): 11.5MM **Privately Held**
WEB: www.unilock.com
SIC: 3281 5211 3272 3271 Paving blocks, cut stone; paving stones; concrete products; concrete block & brick; asphalt paving mixtures & blocks

(G-1228)
VISTALAB TECHNOLOGIES INC
2 Geneva Rd (10509-2340)
PHONE..................................914 244-6226
Richard Scordato, *Ch of Bd*
Jeffrey E Calhoun, *Vice Pres*
Edward Flynn, *CFO*
Christine Boccia, *Accountant*
David Metrena, *VP Sales*
▲ EMP: 34
SQ FT: 25,000
SALES (est): 8.5MM **Privately Held**
SIC: 3821 Pipettes, hemocytometer

Briarcliff Manor
Westchester County

(G-1229)
THALLE INDUSTRIES INC (PA)
51 Route 100 (10510-1441)
PHONE..................................914 762-3415
Gregg J Pacchiana, *Ch of Bd*
Glenn Pacchiana, *Principal*
George Pacchiana, *Corp Secy*
Jeff Manganello, *Vice Pres*
Marco Pereira, *Opers Staff*
EMP: 35
SQ FT: 720
SALES (est): 4.5MM **Privately Held**
SIC: 2951 3281 Asphalt paving mixtures & blocks; stone, quarrying & processing of own stone products

Bridgehampton
Suffolk County

(G-1230)
BRIDGEHAMPTON STEEL & WLDG INC
Also Called: A and D Maintenance
27 Foster Ave (11932)
P.O. Box 19 (11932-0019)
PHONE..................................631 537-2486
John Parry, *President*
Suzanne Parry, *Vice Pres*
EMP: 10
SQ FT: 3,000
SALES (est): 1.2MM **Privately Held**
SIC: 3443 1799 Fabricated plate work (boiler shop); welding on site

(G-1231)
COMERFORD HENNESSY AT HOME INC
Also Called: Comerford Collection
2442 Main St (11932)
P.O. Box 44 (11932-0044)
PHONE..................................631 537-6200
Fax: 631 725-5226
Karen Comerford, *President*
Michael Hennessy, *Vice Pres*
EMP: 5
SQ FT: 1,500
SALES (est): 584.1K **Privately Held**
SIC: 2511 Wood household furniture

(G-1232)
IRON HORSE GRAPHICS LTD
112 Maple Ln (11932)
PHONE..................................631 537-3400
Fax: 631 537-3424
Grover Gatewood, *President*

GEOGRAPHIC SECTION

Bronx - Bronx County (G-1257)

EMP: 9
SQ FT: 2,200
SALES: 782.1K **Privately Held**
SIC: 2752 2759 Offset & photolithographic printing; commercial printing

(G-1233)
SAGAPONACK SAND & GRAVEL CORP (PA)
Also Called: Keith Grimes
Haines Path (11932)
P.O. Box 964, Montauk (11954-0801)
PHONE..................631 537-2424
Fax: 631 537-2911
Keith Grimes, *President*
Susan Grimes, *Vice Pres*
EMP: 20
SALES: 403K **Privately Held**
SIC: 1442 Common sand mining; gravel mining

Bridgeport
Onondaga County

(G-1234)
POWER GNERATION INDUS ENGS INC
8927 Tyler Rd (13030-9727)
PHONE..................315 633-9389
Mike Verdow, *President*
EMP: 18
SALES (est): 2.4MM **Privately Held**
SIC: 3621 Power generators

(G-1235)
ROBERT M VAULT
1360 Lestina Beach Rd (13030-9722)
PHONE..................315 243-1447
Robert M Vault, *Principal*
EMP: 5 EST: 2013
SALES (est): 365.6K **Privately Held**
SIC: 3272 Burial vaults, concrete or pre-cast terrazzo

(G-1236)
SYRACUSE LETTER COMPANY INC
Also Called: Lettergraphics
1179 Oak Ln (13030-9779)
PHONE..................315 476-8328
Fax: 315 476-1818
Nancy Osborn, *President*
David L Osborn, *Chairman*
Bill Davidson, *Vice Pres*
Joh Davidson, *Controller*
▲ EMP: 15
SQ FT: 24,500
SALES (est): 1.7MM **Privately Held**
SIC: 2759 7331 7389 Promotional printing; direct mail advertising services; coupon redemption service

Brightwaters
Suffolk County

(G-1237)
ALLEN FIELD CO INC
256 Orinoco Dr Ste A (11718-1823)
PHONE..................631 665-2782
Fax: 631 756-0436
Andrew Franzone, *CEO*
Andrew Franzone Jr, *Ch of Bd*
David Kassel, *Ch of Bd*
Harry Goodman, *Vice Pres*
▲ EMP: 12 EST: 1945
SQ FT: 20,000
SALES: 6MM **Privately Held**
WEB: www.allenfield.com
SIC: 3089 Handles, brush or tool: plastic; injection molded finished plastic products

(G-1238)
UNLIMITED INDUSTRIES INC
234 Orinoco Dr (11718-1822)
PHONE..................631 666-9483
Joseph Leone, *President*
EMP: 8
SALES (est): 1MM **Privately Held**
SIC: 3999 Manufacturing industries

Broadalbin
Fulton County

(G-1239)
BROADALBIN MANUFACTURING CORP
Also Called: BMC
8 Pine St (12025-3128)
P.O. Box 398 (12025-0398)
PHONE..................518 883-5313
Fax: 518 883-5320
James C Stark, *President*
Michael Deuel, *President*
Mike Deuel, *Vice Pres*
Karen Deuel, *Manager*
Beverly Reed, *Asst Mgr*
EMP: 23 EST: 1970
SQ FT: 8,000
SALES (est): 4.2MM **Privately Held**
SIC: 3599 7692 1761 Machine shop, jobbing & repair; welding repair; sheet metalwork

(G-1240)
EMVI INC
Also Called: Emvi Chocolate
111 Bellen Rd Ste 2 (12025-2101)
PHONE..................518 883-5111
Irina Gelman, *Principal*
EMP: 5
SALES (est): 459.9K **Privately Held**
SIC: 2066 Chocolate

(G-1241)
GL & RL LOGGING INC
713 Union Mills Rd (12025-1988)
PHONE..................518 883-3936
George Lee, *President*
EMP: 15
SALES (est): 1.1MM **Privately Held**
SIC: 2411 Logging: timber, cut at logging camp

Brockport
Monroe County

(G-1242)
CUSTOM SERVICE SOLUTIONS INC
1900 Transit Way (14420-3006)
PHONE..................585 637-3760
Paul Guglielmi, *CEO*
Diana Petranek, *CFO*
Tiffany Petranek, *Office Mgr*
Earl Luce, *Technical Staff*
Dallas Wadsworth, *Technical Staff*
EMP: 6
SQ FT: 4,200
SALES: 1.4MM **Privately Held**
WEB: www.customservicesolutions.com
SIC: 3545 Machine tool accessories

(G-1243)
HAMILTON MARKETING CORPORATION
5211 Lake Rd S (14420-9753)
PHONE..................585 395-0678
Edward Hamilton, *President*
EMP: 5
SQ FT: 5,000
SALES (est): 513.6K **Privately Held**
SIC: 3825 Microwave test equipment

(G-1244)
HAMLIN BOTTLE & CAN RETURN INC
3423 Redman Rd (14420-9478)
PHONE..................585 259-1301
Andriy Basisty, *President*
EMP: 7
SALES: 240K **Privately Held**
SIC: 2611 Pulp mills, mechanical & recycling processing

(G-1245)
JETS LEFROIS CORP
Also Called: Jets Lefrois Foods
56 High St (14420-2058)
PHONE..................585 637-5003

Fax: 585 637-2855
Duncan Tsay, *President*
Rosalinc Tsay, *Vice Pres*
EMP: 6 EST: 1910
SQ FT: 6,000
SALES (est): 626K **Privately Held**
SIC: 2033 2035 Barbecue sauce: packaged in cans, jars, etc.; relishes, vinegar

(G-1246)
RHEINWALD PRINTING CO INC
Also Called: Tri County Advertiser
15 Main St (14420-1901)
PHONE..................585 637-5100
Fax: 585 637-0111
Sally Abrams Becht, *President*
EMP: 15 EST: 1956
SQ FT: 3,000
SALES (est): 1MM **Privately Held**
SIC: 2741 2752 2711 Shopping news: publishing & printing; commercial printing, lithographic; newspapers

(G-1247)
ROCK IROQUOIS PRODUCTS INC
5251 Sweden Walker Rd (14420-9716)
PHONE..................585 637-6834
Fax: 585 637-4475
Chris Pangrizio, *Manager*
EMP: 20
SALES (corp-wide): 28.6B **Privately Held**
SIC: 1429 Dolomitic marble, crushed & broken-quarrying
HQ: Iroquois Rock Products Inc.
1150 Penfield Rd
Rochester NY 14625
585 381-7010

Brocton
Chautauqua County

(G-1248)
CARBON GRAPHITE MATERIALS INC
Also Called: Cgm
115 Central Ave (14716-9771)
PHONE..................716 792-7979
Ryan Walker, *President*
▲ EMP: 9
SALES (est): 2.2MM **Privately Held**
SIC: 3624 Carbon & graphite products

(G-1249)
JAMESTOWN PLASTICS INC (PA)
8806 Highland Ave (14716-9791)
P.O. Box U (14716-0680)
PHONE..................716 792-4144
Fax: 716 792-4154
Jay J Baker, *Ch of Bd*
Brandy Smith, *QC Mgr*
James Barry, *Engineer*
Romaine Hohenstein, *Accountant*
Dale Akin, *Manager*
EMP: 50
SQ FT: 87,000
SALES (est): 15.3MM **Privately Held**
WEB: www.jamestownplastics.com
SIC: 3089 Plastic containers, except foam

Bronx
Bronx County

(G-1250)
527 FRANCO BAKERY CORPORATION
Also Called: Caribe Bakery
527 E 138th St (10454-4971)
PHONE..................718 993-4200
Franco Guillermo, *President*
EMP: 5
SALES (est): 332.8K **Privately Held**
SIC: 2051 Bread, cake & related products

(G-1251)
872 HUNTS POINT PHARMACY INC
872 Hunts Point Ave (10474-5402)
PHONE..................718 991-3519

EMP: 7
SALES (est): 631.6K **Privately Held**
SIC: 2834 Mfg Pharmaceutical Preparations

(G-1252)
A & L DOORS & HARDWARE LLC
375 E 163rd St Frnt 2 (10451-4391)
PHONE..................718 585-8400
Pinches Herman, *Manager*
Leo Lichstein,
EMP: 14
SQ FT: 16,000
SALES (est): 2.3MM **Privately Held**
WEB: www.urban-architectural-interiors.com
SIC: 3442 3429 7699 Metal doors; window & door frames; locks or lock sets; locksmith shop

(G-1253)
A & L SHTMTL FABRICATIONS CORP
1243 Oakpoint Ave (10474-6803)
PHONE..................718 842-1600
Fax: 718 842-2597
Anatoly Lekhter, *President*
Marat Golnick, *Vice Pres*
Boris Gitelson, *Engineer*
Howard Schultz, *Accountant*
Margarita Martinez, *Manager*
EMP: 45
SQ FT: 37,500
SALES (est): 10MM **Privately Held**
WEB: www.aandlsheetmetal.com
SIC: 3444 Sheet metalwork

(G-1254)
A L EASTMOND & SONS INC (PA)
Also Called: Easco Boiler
1175 Leggett Ave (10474-6246)
PHONE..................718 378-3000
Fax: 718 378-4560
Arlington Leon Eastmond, *Chairman*
EMP: 80 EST: 1914
SQ FT: 50,000
SALES (est): 14MM **Privately Held**
WEB: www.easco.com
SIC: 3443 7699 7629 Boilers: industrial, power, or marine; boiler repair shop; electrical repair shops

(G-1255)
A&S REFRIGERATION EQUIPMENT
557 Longfellow Ave (10474-6913)
PHONE..................718 993-6030
Alexander Savinon, *President*
EMP: 5
SALES: 98K **Privately Held**
SIC: 3585 Refrigeration & heating equipment

(G-1256)
A-1 TRANSITMIX INC
431 E 165th St Frnt 1 (10456-6644)
PHONE..................718 292-3200
Fax: 718 292-3255
Sal Gelso, *President*
Frankie Gentile, *Vice Pres*
EMP: 12
SQ FT: 25,000
SALES (est): 2MM **Privately Held**
SIC: 3273 Ready-mixed concrete

(G-1257)
A1 INTERNATIONAL HEAT TREATING
905 Brush Ave (10465-1810)
P.O. Box 93, Valhalla (10595-0093)
PHONE..................718 863-5552
Fax: 718 792-6902
Peter Palmero, *President*
John Palmero, *Vice Pres*
Theresa Palmero, *Manager*
EMP: 5
SQ FT: 2,000
SALES (est): 480K **Privately Held**
SIC: 3398 Metal heat treating

Bronx - Bronx County (G-1258) GEOGRAPHIC SECTION

(G-1258)
ABOVE THE REST BAKING CORP
531-533 Bryant Ave (10474)
PHONE.....................718 313-9222
Natalie Dermanin, *President*
Alan Carpanini, *Controller*
EMP: 60 EST: 2016
SQ FT: 12,000
SALES: 7MM Privately Held
SIC: 2051 Bakery: wholesale or wholesale/retail combined

(G-1259)
AC AIR COOLING CO INC
Also Called: Air Conditioning
1637 Stillwell Ave (10461-2216)
PHONE.....................718 933-1011
Cac Dong Bui, *President*
Deonarine Booknarain, *Vice Pres*
Maritza Ma os, *Manager*
EMP: 15
SALES (est): 1.9MM Privately Held
SIC: 3585 Air conditioning units, complete: domestic or industrial

(G-1260)
ACA QUALITY BUILDING PDTS LLC
1322 Garrison Ave (10474-4710)
PHONE.....................718 991-2423
Rubin Goldklang, *Manager*
EMP: 25
SALES (corp-wide): 4.3MM Privately Held
SIC: 3446 Partitions & supports/studs, including accoustical systems
PA: Aca Quality Building Products Llc
   920 Longfellow Ave
   Bronx NY 10474
   718 991-2423

(G-1261)
ACE DROP CLOTH CANVAS PDTS INC
Also Called: Ace Drop Cloth Co
4216 Park Ave (10457-4201)
PHONE.....................718 731-1550
Fax: 718 299-5122
Jerry Mathios, *President*
Adam Mathios, *Vice Pres*
David Mathios, *Vice Pres*
Marc Mathios, *Vice Pres*
▲ EMP: 31
SQ FT: 35,000
SALES (est): 1.3MM Privately Held
WEB: www.acedropcloth.com
SIC: 2299 2326 2394 2393 Fibers, textile: recovery from textile mill waste & rags; work pants; work shirts: men's, youths' & boys'; cloth, drop (fabric): made from purchased materials; textile bags; socks

(G-1262)
ACE FIRE DOOR CORP
4000 Park Ave (10457-7318)
PHONE.....................718 901-0001
Fax: 718 294-1304
Aharon Blum, *President*
Joseph Strulovich, *Vice Pres*
Irving Bauer, *Treasurer*
EMP: 20
SQ FT: 20,000
SALES (est): 4MM Privately Held
SIC: 3442 2431 Fire doors, metal; doors, wood

(G-1263)
ACME AWNING CO INC
435 Van Nest Ave (10460-2876)
PHONE.....................718 409-1881
Fax: 718 824-3571
Lawrence Loiacono, *President*
Jay Loiacono, *Vice Pres*
Peggy Zeaphey, *Bookkeeper*
Trent Weideman, *Sales Associate*
EMP: 15 EST: 1924
SQ FT: 25,000
SALES: 1MM Privately Held
WEB: www.acmeawn.com
SIC: 2394 3089 5039 5999 Awnings, fabric: made from purchased materials; awnings, fiberglass & plastic combination; awnings, awnings

(G-1264)
ADDEO BAKERS INC
2372 Hughes Ave (10458-8148)
PHONE.....................718 367-8316
Fax: 718 295-8746
Lawrence Addeo, *President*
EMP: 12
SQ FT: 2,300
SALES (est): 730K Privately Held
SIC: 2051 5461 Bread, all types (white, wheat, rye, etc): fresh or frozen; bread

(G-1265)
ADVANCED CMPT SFTWR CONSULTING
2236 Pearsall Ave (10469-5436)
PHONE.....................718 300-3577
Mohammad Ziauddin, *President*
EMP: 5
SALES: 241.7K Privately Held
SIC: 7372 Prepackaged software

(G-1266)
AIR WAVE AIR CONDITIONING CO
Also Called: AC Air Cooling Company
1637 Stillwell Ave (10461-2216)
PHONE.....................212 545-1122
Fax: 212 365-4731
Cac Bui, *President*
William Saferstein, *President*
EMP: 20
SQ FT: 20,000
SALES (est): 4.8MM Privately Held
WEB: www.airwaveac.com
SIC: 3564 Filters, air: furnaces, air conditioning equipment, etc.

(G-1267)
ALBA FUEL CORP
2135 Wllmsbrdge Rd Fl 2 (10461)
PHONE.....................718 931-1700
Esad Kukaj, *President*
EMP: 5
SALES (est): 910.8K Privately Held
SIC: 1389 Oil field services

(G-1268)
ALBERT MENIN INTERIORS LTD
2417 3rd Ave Fl 3 (10451-6339)
PHONE.....................212 876-3041
Fax: 212 876-4536
Emil Shikh, *President*
Clara Silva, *Manager*
EMP: 12
SQ FT: 1,500
SALES (est): 1.2MM Privately Held
WEB: www.albertmenin.com
SIC: 2519 5023 5713 5714 Household furniture, except wood or metal: upholstered; carpets; draperies; carpets; draperies

(G-1269)
ALLIED METAL SPINNING CORP
1290 Viele Ave (10474-7133)
PHONE.....................718 893-3300
Fax: 718 589-5780
Arlene Saunders, *Ch of Bd*
▲ EMP: 60
SQ FT: 80,000
SALES (est): 10.7MM Privately Held
WEB: www.alliedmetalusa.com
SIC: 3469 Cooking ware, except porcelain enamelled

(G-1270)
ALLWAY TOOLS INC
1255 Seabury Ave (10462-5534)
PHONE.....................718 792-3636
Brent Swenson, *President*
EMP: 100
SALES (est): 6.2MM
SALES (corp-wide): 12.9MM Privately Held
SIC: 3423 3425 Hand & edge tools; saw blades & handsaws
HQ: Linzer Products Corp.
   248 Wyandanch Ave
   West Babylon NY 11704
   631 253-3333

(G-1271)
ALSTROM CORPORATION
1408 Seabury Ave (10461-3691)
PHONE.....................718 824-4901
Fax: 718 409-3605
Decklan Power, *President*
Philip Larosa, *Vice Pres*
Philip Rosa, *Vice Pres*
Zhanna Mayzelshteyn, *Project Mgr*
Alex Fayershteyn, *Engineer*
▲ EMP: 20 EST: 1939
SQ FT: 10,000
SALES (est): 4.5MM Privately Held
WEB: www.alstromcorp.com
SIC: 3585 Evaporative condensers, heat transfer equipment

(G-1272)
ALTYPE FIRE DOOR CORP
886 E 149th St (10455-5012)
PHONE.....................718 292-3500
Harold Halman, *President*
Douglas Halamn, *Corp Secy*
Gary Halman, *Vice Pres*
Aneda Rivera, *Manager*
EMP: 5
SQ FT: 12,000
SALES (est): 766.6K Privately Held
WEB: www.altypefiredoor.com
SIC: 3442 Fire doors, metal

(G-1273)
AMERICAN REFUSE SUPPLY INC
Also Called: American Hose & Hydralics
521 Longfellow Ave (10474-6913)
PHONE.....................718 893-8157
Tim Butler, *Manager*
EMP: 7
SALES (corp-wide): 2.1MM Privately Held
SIC: 3714 3562 Motor vehicle parts & accessories; ball & roller bearings
PA: American Refuse Supply Inc
   700 21st Ave
   Paterson NJ 07513
   973 684-3225

(G-1274)
ANASIA INC
1175 Jerome Ave (10452-3331)
PHONE.....................718 588-1407
Victor Florencio, *President*
EMP: 5
SALES (est): 451.7K Privately Held
SIC: 2671 Packaging paper & plastics film, coated & laminated

(G-1275)
ANHEUSER-BUSCH COMPANIES LLC
510 Food Center Dr (10474-7047)
PHONE.....................718 589-2610
Nelson Jamel, *President*
Barbara Muliero, *Purch Dir*
Liz Montenegro, *Financial Exec*
Daniel Chelladurai, *Sales Mgr*
Dave Anderson, *VP Mktg*
EMP: 7 Privately Held
SIC: 2082 3411 Beer (alcoholic beverage); aluminum cans
HQ: Anheuser-Busch Companies, Llc
   1 Busch Pl
   Saint Louis MO 63118
   314 632-6777

(G-1276)
ATLAS COATINGS CORP
820 E 140th St (10454-1904)
PHONE.....................718 402-2000
Michael Landau, *President*
Stephan Landau, *Vice Pres*
EMP: 64
SQ FT: 25,000
SALES (est): 5.9MM Privately Held
SIC: 2893 Printing ink

(G-1277)
AURA DETERGENT LLC (PA)
1811 Mayflower Ave (10461-4103)
PHONE.....................718 824-2162
John Poppola, *Mng Member*
EMP: 11
SALES (est): 5MM Privately Held
SIC: 2841 Soap & other detergents

(G-1278)
BACO ENTERPRISES INC (PA)
1190 Longwood Ave (10474-5714)
P.O. Box 740487 (10474-0009)
PHONE.....................718 589-6225
Fax: 718 991-6647
Barry L Cohen, *President*
David Cohen, *VP Opers*
Scott Boyer, *Manager*
Jeannette Origazano, *Manager*
▲ EMP: 80
SQ FT: 60,000
SALES (est): 22.6MM Privately Held
WEB: www.bacoent.com
SIC: 3449 3452 Bars, concrete reinforcing: fabricated steel; bolts, metal

(G-1279)
BANDIT INTERNATIONAL LTD
600 E 132nd St (10454-4639)
PHONE.....................718 402-2100
Albert Berkner, *President*
Sophie Berkner, *Vice Pres*
EMP: 15
SQ FT: 50,000
SALES (est): 1.1MM Privately Held
SIC: 2329 2339 5136 5137 Men's & boys' sportswear & athletic clothing; sportswear, women's; sportswear, men's & boys'; women's & children's sportswear & swimsuits

(G-1280)
BEEHIVE PRESS INC
3742 Boston Rd (10469-2633)
P.O. Box 409 (10469-0409)
PHONE.....................718 654-1200
Fax: 718 653-4272
Roger Denhoff, *President*
Peter Kirkel, *Vice Pres*
EMP: 7 EST: 1927
SQ FT: 4,500
SALES: 1.2MM Privately Held
WEB: www.beehivepress.com
SIC: 2752 2791 Commercial printing, offset; typesetting

(G-1281)
BEL ART INTERNATIONAL
Also Called: Scala Furniture Industries NY
600 E 132nd St (10454-4639)
PHONE.....................718 402-2100
Fax: 718 402-2351
Albert Berkner, *President*
Sophie Berkner, *Vice Pres*
EMP: 25 EST: 1964
SQ FT: 50,000
SALES (est): 1.9MM Privately Held
SIC: 2511 Wood household furniture

(G-1282)
BELMET PRODUCTS INC (PA)
1350 Garrison Ave (10474-4807)
PHONE.....................718 542-8220
Fred Collins, *President*
Angelo Demauro, *Vice Pres*
John Collins, *Opers Mgr*
Sal Monteleone, *Sales Mgr*
Paul Norton, *Business Dir*
EMP: 48 EST: 1919
SQ FT: 39,000
SALES (est): 2.8MM Privately Held
WEB: www.belmetproducts.com
SIC: 3469 3312 Stamping metal for the trade; blast furnaces & steel mills

(G-1283)
BIMBO BAKERIES USA INC
5625 Broadway Frnt 2 (10463-5548)
PHONE.....................718 601-1561
EMP: 5
SALES (corp-wide): 13.7B Privately Held
SIC: 2051 Mfg Bread/Related Products
HQ: Bimbo Bakeries Usa, Inc
   255 Business Center Dr # 200
   Horsham PA 19044
   215 347-5500

(G-1284)
BMS DESIGNS INC
1385 Seabury Ave (10461-3629)
PHONE.....................718 828-5792
Henry Mazzoni, *President*
▲ EMP: 30
SALES (est): 2MM Privately Held
SIC: 2335 Bridal & formal gowns

GEOGRAPHIC SECTION
Bronx - Bronx County (G-1313)

(G-1285)
BONK SAM UNFORMS CIVILIAN CAP
Also Called: Sam Bonk Uniform
131 Rose Feiss Blvd Fl 2 (10454-3662)
PHONE..................................718 585-0665
Fax: 718 402-3498
Sarah Bonk, *President*
Harry Bonk, *General Mgr*
Rachel B Jones, *Vice Pres*
Robert Striedl, *Treasurer*
Judy Bonk, *Manager*
EMP: 50 **EST:** 1963
SQ FT: 18,000
SALES (est): 5.4MM **Privately Held**
SIC: 2353 Uniform hats & caps

(G-1286)
BORGATTIS RAVIOLI EGG NOODLES
632 E 187th St (10458)
PHONE..................................718 367-3799
Mario John Borgatti, *President*
Christopher Borgatti, *Vice Pres*
EMP: 5
SQ FT: 500
SALES: 500K **Privately Held**
WEB: www.borgattis.com
SIC: 2098 2032 Noodles (e.g. egg, plain & water), dry; ravioli: packaged in cans, jars, etc.

(G-1287)
BRANDT EQUIPMENT LLC
Also Called: Brandt Industries
4461 Bronx Blvd (10470-1407)
PHONE..................................718 994-0800
Fax: 718 325-7905
Abe Reich,
Kathleen Rice, *Admin Asst*
EMP: 9
SQ FT: 10,000
SALES: 1.5MM **Privately Held**
WEB: www.brandtind.com
SIC: 2599 3843 Hospital furniture, except beds; dental equipment

(G-1288)
BRONX NEW WAY CORP
113 E Kingsbridge Rd (10468-7510)
PHONE..................................347 431-1385
Adel Maflahi, *Principal*
EMP: 6
SALES (est): 459.1K **Privately Held**
SIC: 3643 Outlets, electric: convenience

(G-1289)
BUILDING MANAGEMENT ASSOC INC
998 E 167th St Ofc (10459-2054)
PHONE..................................718 542-4779
Fax: 718 328-6850
Jaime Diaz, *Manager*
EMP: 36
SALES (corp-wide): 11.8MM **Privately Held**
SIC: 3822 Building services monitoring controls, automatic
PA: Building Management Associates, Inc.
885 Bruckner Blvd
Bronx NY 10459
718 617-2800

(G-1290)
CARIB PRINTS LTD
752 E 137th St (10454-3403)
P.O. Box 153 (10456-0153)
PHONE..................................646 210-2863
Vernon Andre, *Owner*
EMP: 10
SQ FT: 15,000
SALES: 50K **Privately Held**
SIC: 2759 Screen printing

(G-1291)
CASA REDIMIX CONCRETE CORP
886 Edgewater Rd (10474-4906)
PHONE..................................718 589-1555
Fax: 718 842-0443
Lucy Figueroa, *Principal*
EMP: 13
SALES (est): 2.2MM **Privately Held**
SIC: 3273 Ready-mixed concrete

(G-1292)
CEC ELEVATOR CAB CORP
540 Manida St (10474-6818)
PHONE..................................718 328-3632
Carlos Vanga Sr, *President*
Rakesh Rampersaud, *Purch Agent*
Carlos Vanga Jr, *CFO*
Helen Kim, *Controller*
Sonia Rivas, *Accountant*
EMP: 65
SQ FT: 30,000
SALES (est): 16.1MM **Privately Held**
WEB: www.cecelevator.com
SIC: 3534 7699 Elevators & equipment; elevators: inspection, service & repair

(G-1293)
CENTER SHEET METAL INC
1371 E Bay Ave (10474-7025)
PHONE..................................718 378-4476
Fax: 718 893-7223
Maureen O'Connor, *CEO*
Victor Gany, *President*
Peter Pappas Jr, *Exec VP*
Dennis M Appel Jr,
EMP: 150
SQ FT: 45,000
SALES (est): 23.5MM **Privately Held**
SIC: 3444 Sheet metalwork

(G-1294)
CENTURY SYSTEMS LTD
485 W 246th St (10471-3331)
PHONE..................................718 543-5991
Jack Jakubowicz, *Owner*
EMP: 7
SQ FT: 500
SALES (est): 803.2K **Privately Held**
WEB: www.centurysystems.com
SIC: 3699 Security devices

(G-1295)
CFS ENTERPRISES INC
Also Called: CFS Steel Company
650 E 132nd St (10454-4603)
PHONE..................................718 585-0500
Fax: 718 993-8079
James R Melvin Jr, *Ch of Bd*
EMP: 20
SQ FT: 40,000
SALES (est): 4.7MM
SALES (corp-wide): 35.8MM **Privately Held**
WEB: www.cfssteel.com
SIC: 3315 Wire & fabricated wire products
PA: Re-Steel Supply Company, Inc.
2000 Eddystone Indus Park
Eddystone PA 19022
610 876-8216

(G-1296)
CGSI GROUP LLC
3835 Sedgwick Ave (10463-4452)
PHONE..................................516 986-5503
Shannon Herdricks, *Principal*
EMP: 12
SQ FT: 1,000
SALES (est): 624.6K **Privately Held**
SIC: 3731 Drilling & production platforms, floating (oil & gas)

(G-1297)
CHARLES H BECKLEY INC (PA)
749 E 137th St (10454-3402)
PHONE..................................718 665-2218
Fax: 718 402-3386
Theodore W Marschke, *President*
Charles L Beckley, *Principal*
Ken Marschke, *Marketing Staff*
▲ **EMP:** 18 **EST:** 1932
SQ FT: 12,000
SALES (est): 2.1MM **Privately Held**
WEB: www.chbeckley.com
SIC: 2515 2511 Box springs, assembled; mattresses & foundations; wood household furniture

(G-1298)
CHRONICLE
3468 Wilson Ave Apt 2b (10469-2325)
PHONE..................................347 969-7281
Lindsey Beharry, *Principal*
EMP: 7 **EST:** 2015
SALES (est): 94.4K **Privately Held**
SIC: 2711 Newspapers

(G-1299)
CIBAO MEAT PRODUCTS INC
630 Saint Anns Ave (10455-1404)
PHONE..................................718 993-5072
Fax: 718 993-5638
Heinz Vieluf, *CEO*
Lutzi V Isidor, *President*
Julio G Isidor, *General Mgr*
Edgar Soto, *Vice Pres*
Maria Sandner, *Manager*
▲ **EMP:** 55
SQ FT: 6,000
SALES (est): 13MM **Privately Held**
WEB: www.cibaomeat.com
SIC: 2013 Sausages from purchased meat

(G-1300)
CITY EVOLUTIONARY
336 Barretto St (10474-6718)
PHONE..................................718 861-7585
Matt Tan, *General Mgr*
EMP: 8
SALES (est): 546.6K **Privately Held**
SIC: 3449 Bars, concrete reinforcing: fabricated steel

(G-1301)
CITY JEANS INC
845 White Plins Rd Frnt 1 (10473)
PHONE..................................718 239-5353
Kyle Christianson, *Owner*
EMP: 5
SALES (corp-wide): 35.8MM **Privately Held**
SIC: 2329 Men's & boys' sportswear & athletic clothing
PA: City Jeans Inc
1515 132nd St Fl 2nd
College Point NY 11356
718 359-2489

(G-1302)
COCA-COLA REFRESHMENTS USA INC
977 E 149th St (10455-5090)
PHONE..................................718 401-5200
Fax: 718 292-1848
Tom Druell, *Sales & Mktg St*
Gary Battaglya, *Manager*
EMP: 20
SALES (corp-wide): 41.8B **Publicly Held**
WEB: www.cokecce.com
SIC: 2086 5149 Bottled & canned soft drinks; groceries & related products
HQ: Coca-Cola Refreshments Usa, Inc.
2500 Windy Ridge Pkwy Se
Atlanta GA 30339
770 989-3000

(G-1303)
COLOR CARTON CORP
341 Canal Pl (10451-6091)
PHONE..................................718 665-0840
Nicholas F Loprinzi, *President*
Vincent Loprinzi, *Corp Secy*
Nicholas V Loprinzi, *Vice Pres*
Jimmy Martinelli, *Warehouse Mgr*
Debbie Loprinzi, *Manager*
▲ **EMP:** 60 **EST:** 1960
SQ FT: 90,000
SALES: 7.7MM **Privately Held**
WEB: www.colorcarton.com
SIC: 2752 2653 2657 Commercial printing, offset; corrugated & solid fiber boxes; folding paperboard boxes

(G-1304)
COLUMBIA POOL ACCESSORIES INC
111 Bruckner Blvd (10454-4514)
PHONE..................................718 993-0389
Fax: 718 993-8323
▲ **EMP:** 5
SALES (est): 504K **Privately Held**
SIC: 3585 Mfg Refrigeration/Heating Equipment

(G-1305)
COMPLETE FIBER SOLUTIONS INC
1459 Bassett Ave (10461-2309)
PHONE..................................718 828-8900
Victor Desantis, *Principal*
Josh Brite, *Principal*
Chris Richard, *Principal*
EMP: 8
SALES (est): 161K **Privately Held**
SIC: 3357 3229 1731 Fiber optic cable (insulated); fiber optics strands; fiber optic cable installation

(G-1306)
CORAL MANAGEMENT CORP
Also Called: Total Machine and Welding
923 Bryant Ave (10474-4701)
PHONE..................................718 893-9286
EMP: 5
SALES: 320K **Privately Held**
SIC: 3449 Mfg Misc Structural Metalwork

(G-1307)
COVINGTON SOUND
2705 Kingsbridge Ter (10463-7456)
PHONE..................................646 256-7486
Velma Harris, *Owner*
EMP: 6
SALES: 570K **Privately Held**
SIC: 3651 Speaker systems

(G-1308)
CUMMINS INC
890 Zerega Ave (10473-1122)
PHONE..................................718 892-2400
Joanne Bastin, *Credit Mgr*
Shannon Vicks, *Sales Staff*
Marshall Lomazow, *Branch Mgr*
Melinda Schultz, *Manager*
EMP: 343
SALES (corp-wide): 17.5B **Publicly Held**
WEB: www.cummins.com
SIC: 3519 Internal combustion engines
PA: Cummins Inc.
500 Jackson St
Columbus IN 47201
812 377-5000

(G-1309)
CUSTOM 101 PRINTS INC
3601 Bronxwood Ave (10469-1143)
PHONE..................................718 708-4425
Anthony Matthews, *CEO*
EMP: 10
SQ FT: 2,000
SALES: 300K **Privately Held**
SIC: 2759 Screen printing

(G-1310)
D B F ASSOCIATES
Also Called: August Graphics
1150 E 156th St (10474-6227)
PHONE..................................718 328-0005
Fax: 718 328-1123
Bruce Feldman, *President*
Debra Bashore, *Assistant VP*
EMP: 8
SALES: 460K **Privately Held**
WEB: www.dbfassociates.com
SIC: 2759 Screen printing

(G-1311)
D W HABER & SON INC
825 E 140th St (10454-1930)
PHONE..................................718 993-6405
Fax: 718 585-0726
Robert H Haber, *President*
David Haber, *Vice Pres*
▲ **EMP:** 25
SQ FT: 40,000
SALES (est): 4MM **Privately Held**
WEB: www.habersilver.com
SIC: 3914 Silversmithing; holloware, plated (all metals)

(G-1312)
DA ELECTRIC
6 E Clarke Pl (10452-7501)
PHONE..................................347 270-3422
Damal Dudley, *Owner*
EMP: 45
SALES (est): 4MM **Privately Held**
SIC: 3699 Electrical equipment & supplies

(G-1313)
DALE PRESS INC
Also Called: Riverdale Press, The
5676 Riverdale Ave # 311 (10471-2138)
PHONE..................................718 543-6200
Fax: 718 548-4038
Bernard L Stein, *President*
Richard L Stein, *Vice Pres*
EMP: 25

Bronx - Bronx County (G-1314)

SQ FT: 2,500
SALES (est): 1.5MM Privately Held
WEB: www.riverdalepress.com
SIC: 2711 Newspapers: publishing only, not printed on site

(G-1314)
DAYTON INDUSTRIES INC
1350 Garrison Ave (10474-4807)
PHONE.................................718 542-8144
Fax: 718 793-2758
J Fred Collins, *CEO*
Milovan Petrovic, *QC Dir*
Barbara Agovino, *Human Resources*
Hector Medina, *Prgrmr*
▲ **EMP:** 45 **EST:** 1980
SQ FT: 45,000
SALES (est): 11.9MM Privately Held
WEB: www.daytonind.com
SIC: 3469 3442 Stamping metal for the trade; metal doors, sash & trim

(G-1315)
DELBIA DO COMPANY INC (PA)
2550 Park Ave (10451-6014)
PHONE.................................718 585-2226
Fax: 718 665-7922
Daryl Do, *Vice Pres*
Jerry Chow *Vice Pres*
▲ **EMP:** 9
SQ FT: 8,000
SALES (est): 1.6MM Privately Held
SIC: 2087 2844 Flavoring extracts & syrups; perfumes, natural or synthetic

(G-1316)
DELBIA DO COMPANY INC
11 Canal Pl (10451-6009)
PHONE.................................718 585-2226
Delbia Do, *Branch Mgr*
EMP: 13
SALES (corp-wide): 1.6MM Privately Held
SIC: 2844 2087 Toilet preparations; flavoring extracts & syrups
PA: Delbia Do Company Inc.
2550 Park Ave
Bronx NY 10451
718 585-2226

(G-1317)
DELICIOSO COCO HELADO INC
849 Saint Anns Ave (10456-7633)
PHONE.................................718 292-1930
Fax: 718 292-1243
Alfred Thiebaud, *President*
Lois Thiebaud, *Bookkeeper*
Sophia Thiebaud, *Admin Sec*
EMP: 15
SQ FT: 20,000
SALES (est): 2.4MM Privately Held
SIC: 2024 5451 Ice cream, bulk; ice cream (packaged)

(G-1318)
DOMENICK DENIGRIS INC (PA)
1485 Bassett Ave (10461-2309)
PHONE.................................718 823-2264
Fax: 718 823-5765
Donald Denigris, *President*
◆ **EMP:** 50
SQ FT: 4,000
SALES (est): 6.8MM Privately Held
SIC: 3281 Monument or burial stone, cut & shaped

(G-1319)
DOMINIC DE NIGRIS INC
3255 E Tremon Ave Frnt (10461-5790)
PHONE.................................718 597-4460
Dominic De Nigris, *President*
Dan A De Nigris *Vice Pres*
Dan C De Nigris, *Admin Sec*
EMP: 30
SQ FT: 2,910
SALES (est): 2.7MM Privately Held
SIC: 3281 1411 Monuments, cut stone (not finishing or lettering only); dimension stone

(G-1320)
DOYLE-HILD SAILMAKERS
225 Fordham St (10464)
PHONE.................................718 885-2255
Mark Ploch, *Owner*
EMP: 8
SALES (est): 360K Privately Held
SIC: 2394 Sails: made from purchased materials

(G-1321)
DRYVE LLC
4515 Waldo Ave (10471-3933)
PHONE.................................646 279-3648
Erika Boyer,
EMP: 5 **EST:** 2016
SALES (est): 130.5K Privately Held
SIC: 2741 Miscellaneous publishing

(G-1322)
DUFOUR PASTRY KITCHENS INC
251 Locust Ave (10454-2004)
PHONE.................................718 402-8800
Fax: 718 402-7002
EMP: 24
SALES (est): 3.7MM Privately Held
SIC: 2038 2053 Mfg Frozen Specialties Mfg Frozen Bakery Products

(G-1323)
DUN-RITE SPCLIZED CARRIERS LLC
1561 Southern Blvd (10460-5602)
PHONE.................................718 991-1100
Brett Deutsch, *Vice Pres*
Carl Panepinto, *Warehouse Mgr*
Dominick Conetta, *Opers Staff*
Anthony Conetta, *VP Finance*
Dawn Rao, *Mktg Dir*
EMP: 12
SALES: 1MM Privately Held
SIC: 3536 Hoists, cranes & monorails

(G-1324)
E & J IRON WORKS INC
801 E 136th St (10454-3546)
PHONE.................................718 665-6040
Gerhard Teicht, *President*
Edmund Teicht, *General Mgr*
EMP: 20
SQ FT: 22,000
SALES (est): 3.7MM Privately Held
SIC: 3446 Architectural metalwork; gates, ornamental metal; railings, prefabricated metal; fire escapes, metal

(G-1325)
E H HURWITZ & ASSOCIATES
3000 Kingsbridge Ave (10463-5101)
PHONE.................................718 884-3766
EMP: 9 **EST:** 1978
SALES (est): 720K Privately Held
SIC: 7372 Prepackaged Software Services

(G-1326)
EASCO BOILER CORP
1175 Leggett Ave (10474-6294)
PHONE.................................718 378-3000
Arlington Leon Eastmond, *Ch of Bd*
Leon Eastmond, *President*
Emil Stranzl, *Plant Mgr*
Bequn Pong, *Engineer*
Ben Sosin, *Engineer*
EMP: 30
SQ FT: 15,000
SALES (est): 6.5MM Privately Held
SIC: 3567 Heating units & devices, industrial: electric

(G-1327)
EDWARD C LYONS COMPANY INC
Also Called: E C Lyons
3646 White Plains Rd Frnt (10467-5717)
PHONE.................................718 515-5361
Gary Owens, *President*
Cheryl Owens, *Vice Pres*
EMP: 7 **EST:** 1958
SQ FT: 5,000
SALES (est): 500K Privately Held
WEB: www.eclyons.com
SIC: 3423 Engravers' tools, hand

(G-1328)
EDWARD C MULLER CORP
Also Called: Edward C. Lyons
3646 White Plains Rd Frnt (10467-5717)
PHONE.................................718 881-7270
Fax: 718 515-7790
Gary Owens, *President*
Cheryl D Owens, *Vice Pres*
EMP: 15 **EST:** 1898
SQ FT: 3,600
SALES: 700K Privately Held
SIC: 3423 Engravers' tools, hand

(G-1329)
EDWARDS GRAPHIC CO INC
3801 Hudson Manor Ter 4s (10463-1105)
PHONE.................................718 548-6858
Fax: 718 796-2255
Jackie Ginsberg, *President*
Ed Edwards, *Vice Pres*
Paula Mack, *Sales Staff*
EMP: 5
SALES (est): 424.8K Privately Held
SIC: 2752 Commercial printing, lithographic

(G-1330)
ENDRES KNITWEAR CO INC
3020 Jerome Ave (10468-1333)
PHONE.................................718 933-8687
Adam Endres, *President*
Ann Endres, *Corp Secy*
EMP: 5
SQ FT: 10,000
SALES (est): 367.4K Privately Held
SIC: 2253 Sweaters & sweater coats, knit; skirts, knit

(G-1331)
EVE SALES CORP
945 Close Ave (10473-4906)
PHONE.................................718 589-6800
Stuart Gale, *President*
Larry Leffler, *Vice Pres*
◆ **EMP:** 13
SQ FT: 22,000
SALES (est): 3MM Privately Held
WEB: www.evesales.com
SIC: 2032 Mexican foods: packaged in cans, jars, etc.

(G-1332)
FELIX STORCH INC (PA)
Also Called: Summit Appliances
770 Garrison Ave (10474-5603)
PHONE.................................718 893-3900
Fax: 718 328-5069
Paul Storch, *President*
Susan Storch, *Corp Secy*
Stephen Ross, *Vice Pres*
Mark Weingarten, *Opers Mgr*
Duane Santos, *Finance Mgr*
◆ **EMP:** 122 **EST:** 1969
SQ FT: 100,000
SALES (est): 32.9MM Privately Held
WEB: www.summitappliance.com
SIC: 3632 Household refrigerators & freezers

(G-1333)
FIDAZZEL INC
2280 Olinville Ave # 409 (10467-7806)
PHONE.................................917 557-3860
Erick Wright, *CEO*
Melissa Colbourne, *Admin Sec*
EMP: 6
SALES (est): 225.6K Privately Held
SIC: 2741 Miscellaneous publishing

(G-1334)
FINEST CC CORP
3111 E Tremont Ave (10461-5705)
PHONE.................................917 574-4525
Larry Derasmo, *President*
EMP: 6
SQ FT: 1,000
SALES (est): 249.8K Privately Held
SIC: 3471 Electroplating of metals or formed products

(G-1335)
FIVE ISLANDS PUBLISHING INC
Also Called: Fire Island News
8 Fort Charles Pl (10463-6705)
PHONE.................................631 583-5345
Shawn Beqaj, *President*
Nicole Pressly, *Treasurer*
EMP: 10
SQ FT: 1,000
SALES (est): 460K Privately Held
SIC: 2711 Newspapers

(G-1336)
FLAIR DISPLAY INC
3920 Merritt Ave (10466-2502)
PHONE.................................718 324-9330
Fax: 718 994-4174
Eugene Dilorenzo, *President*
Chris Dilorenzo, *Vice Pres*
Raymond Hand, *Vice Pres*
Betty Hood, *Assistant*
▲ **EMP:** 60 **EST:** 1953
SQ FT: 50,000
SALES (est): 8.5MM Privately Held
WEB: www.flairdisplay.com
SIC: 3993 Signs & advertising specialties; displays & cutouts, window & lobby; displays, paint process

(G-1337)
FOAM PRODUCTS INC
360 Southern Blvd (10454-1711)
PHONE.................................718 292-4830
Karen Ippolito, *President*
Frank Ippolito, *Vice Pres*
Jim Wink, *VP Sales*
EMP: 20
SQ FT: 32,000
SALES (est): 4.6MM Privately Held
SIC: 3069 3086 Foam rubber; insulation or cushioning material, foamed plastic

(G-1338)
FOUR SASONS MULTI-SERVICES INC
3525 Decatur Ave Apt 2k (10467-1729)
PHONE.................................347 843-6262
Gabriel Gomez, *CEO*
Juan Carlos, *Office Mgr*
EMP: 5
SQ FT: 100
SALES (est): 428.1K Privately Held
SIC: 2842 Specialty cleaning preparations

(G-1339)
FRA-RIK FORMICA FABG CO INC
1464 Blondell Ave Fl 2 (10461-2688)
PHONE.................................718 597-3335
Philip De Candido, *President*
Frank Maiore, *Vice Pres*
EMP: 9 **EST:** 1965
SQ FT: 5,000
SALES (est): 962.5K Privately Held
SIC: 2434 3299 Wood kitchen cabinets; mica products

(G-1340)
FUEL WATCHMAN SALES & SERVICE
Also Called: Full Timer
364 Jackson Ave (10454-1698)
P.O. Box 202, Garden City (11530-0202)
PHONE.................................718 665-6100
Benjamin Strysko, *President*
Tom Strysco, *Vice Pres*
Joan Strysko, *Admin Sec*
EMP: 10 **EST:** 1944
SALES (est): 1.7MM Privately Held
SIC: 3822 3669 Auto controls regulating residntl & coml environmt & applncs; smoke detectors

(G-1341)
G & O EQUIPMENT CORP
1211 Oakpoint Ave (10474-6701)
PHONE.................................718 218-7844
Donato Sammarco, *President*
Phil Seltzer, *Exec VP*
EMP: 5
SQ FT: 1,000
SALES (est): 880.7K Privately Held
SIC: 3824 Fluid meters & counting devices

(G-1342)
G&J GRAPHICS INC
Also Called: Bronx Design Group, The
2914 Westchester Ave (10461-4504)
PHONE.................................718 409-9874
Fax: 718 931-0717
Geri Sciortino, *President*
John Sciortino, *Vice Pres*
Ann M Papanagnostou, *Graphic Designe*
EMP: 7
SQ FT: 3,100
SALES (est): 894.2K Privately Held
WEB: www.bronxdesign.com
SIC: 2759 Commercial printing

GEOGRAPHIC SECTION
Bronx - Bronx County (G-1368)

(G-1343)
GARY PLASTIC PACKAGING CORP (PA)
Also Called: Garyline
1340 Viele Ave (10474-7134)
PHONE..................................718 893-2200
Fax: 718 860-7002
Gary Hellinger, *Ch of Bd*
Richard Hellinger, *President*
Gustavo That, *Opers Mgr*
Gianna Morea, *Purchasing*
Harold King, *CFO*
◆ **EMP:** 395 **EST:** 1962
SQ FT: 300,000
SALES (est): 68.3MM **Privately Held**
WEB: www.plasticboxes.com
SIC: 3089 Plastic containers, except foam

(G-1344)
GENERAL FIRE-PROOF DOOR CORP
913 Edgewater Rd (10474-4930)
PHONE..................................718 893-5500
Fax: 718 893-1770
Aaron Szabo, *President*
Rubin Kuszel, *Vice Pres*
EMP: 50 **EST:** 1921
SALES (est): 7.5MM **Privately Held**
SIC: 3442 Fire doors, metal

(G-1345)
GENERAL GALVANIZING SUP CO INC (PA)
652 Whittier St Fl Mezz (10474-6194)
PHONE..................................718 589-4300
Fax: 718 589-4738
Anthony Visentin, *President*
Tarek Elgendy, *Engineer*
Edith Jenkins, *Bookkeeper*
Tony Visentin, *Personnel Exec*
EMP: 37 **EST:** 1935
SQ FT: 10,000
SALES (est): 5.4MM **Privately Held**
SIC: 3471 5085 Electroplating & plating; fasteners & fastening equipment

(G-1346)
GLOBUS CORK INC
741 E 136th St (10454-3410)
PHONE..................................347 963-4059
Fax: 718 742-7265
Jen Biscoe, *Vice Pres*
▲ **EMP:** 11
SALES (est): 1.5MM **Privately Held**
WEB: www.globuscork.com
SIC: 2499 Tiles, cork

(G-1347)
GOLDEN GLOW COOKIE CO INC
Also Called: Cookie Factory
1844 Givan Ave (10469-3155)
PHONE..................................718 379-6223
Fax: 718 379-4417
Rose Florio, *President*
Joan Florio, *Vice Pres*
Salvatore Florio Jr, *Vice Pres*
EMP: 20
SQ FT: 15,000
SALES (est): 3.1MM **Privately Held**
SIC: 2051 2052 Bread, cake & related products; cookies

(G-1348)
GOODO BEVERAGE COMPANY
Also Called: Coco Rico Southeast
1801 Boone Ave (10460-5101)
PHONE..................................718 328-6400
Fax: 718 328-7002
Kersia Corporation, *Partner*
Steven Kucerak, *Principal*
Jose Regalado, *Sales Mgr*
George Deyarca, *Manager*
Domiciano Diaz, *Manager*
▲ **EMP:** 18 **EST:** 1942
SQ FT: 53,000
SALES (est): 4.4MM **Privately Held**
WEB: www.good-o.com
SIC: 2086 Carbonated soft drinks, bottled & canned

(G-1349)
GOURMET GURU INC
1123 Worthen St (10474-6223)
P.O. Box 706, Keene NH (03431-0706)
PHONE..................................718 842-2828
Fax: 718 425-9860
Jeff Lichtenstein, *President*
Brandon Lee, *Vice Pres*
Kim Lichtenstein, *CFO*
Yang Yong, *Controller*
Mou Myint, *Accountant*
▲ **EMP:** 50
SALES (est): 17.2MM **Publicly Held**
WEB: www.gourmetguru.com
SIC: 2099 Food preparations
PA: United Natural Foods, Inc.
313 Iron Horse Way
Providence RI 02908

(G-1350)
GRAPHIC PRINTING
2376 Jerome Ave (10468-6401)
PHONE..................................718 701-4433
Joao Oliveira, *Owner*
EMP: 5
SALES (est): 218.7K **Privately Held**
SIC: 2759 Publication printing

(G-1351)
GRUBER DISPLAY CO INC
3920g Merritt Ave (10466-2502)
PHONE..................................718 882-8220
Fax: 718 392-0071
Jay Merkel, *President*
Ralph Merkel, *General Mgr*
EMP: 15
SQ FT: 10,000
SALES: 750K **Privately Held**
SIC: 2759 Screen printing

(G-1352)
H W WILSON COMPANY INC
950 University Ave (10452-4297)
P.O. Box 602, Ipswich MA (01938-0602)
PHONE..................................718 588-8635
Fax: 800 590-1617
F Dixon Brooke Jr, *President*
J David Walker, *President*
Clifford Thompson, *Editor*
Tim Collins, *Vice Pres*
Rose Fragola-Jones, *Manager*
EMP: 450
SQ FT: 150,000
SALES (est): 24.2MM
SALES (corp-wide): 1.8B **Privately Held**
WEB: www.hwwilson.com
SIC: 2721 2731 Periodicals: publishing & printing; books: publishing & printing
HQ: Ebsco Publishing, Inc.
10 Estes St
Ipswich MA 01938
978 356-6500

(G-1353)
HAT ATTACK INC (PA)
Also Called: Hat Attack I Bujibaja
4643 Bullard Ave Ste A (10470-1415)
PHONE..................................718 994-1000
Fax: 718 324-0519
William Gedney, *President*
Barbara J Gedney, *Vice Pres*
◆ **EMP:** 20
SQ FT: 11,000
SALES: 5MM **Privately Held**
WEB: www.hatattack.com
SIC: 3111 2353 Bag leather; hats, caps & millinery

(G-1354)
HB ARCHITECTURAL LIGHTING INC
862 E 139th St (10454-1909)
PHONE..................................347 851-4123
Howard Baldinger, *President*
Edison Alulema, *Purch Mgr*
Chris Hartmann, *Engineer*
Michele Sonsini, *Marketing Mgr*
▲ **EMP:** 40
SQ FT: 7,000
SALES (est): 7.7MM **Privately Held**
WEB: www.hblightinginc.com
SIC: 3648 Lighting equipment

(G-1355)
HEALTHEE ENDEAVORS INC
3565c Boston Rd (10469-2500)
P.O. Box 690159 (10469-0761)
PHONE..................................718 653-5499
Junior Blake, *President*
Jennifer Blake, *Vice Pres*
Julian Reynolds, *Administration*
EMP: 7 **EST:** 1985
SALES: 400K **Privately Held**
SIC: 2833 Vitamins, natural or synthetic: bulk, uncompounded

(G-1356)
HEAT-TIMER CORPORATION
Also Called: Heat-Timer Service
79 Alexander Ave Ste 36a (10454-4428)
PHONE..................................212 481-2020
Fax: 212 684-5444
John Winston, *Manager*
EMP: 30
SALES (corp-wide): 7.7MM **Privately Held**
WEB: www.heat-timer.com
SIC: 3824 1711 7623 Controls, revolution & timing instruments; heating & air conditioning contractors; refrigeration service & repair
PA: Heat-Timer Corporation
20 New Dutch Ln
Fairfield NJ 07004
973 575-4004

(G-1357)
HEATING & BURNER SUPPLY INC
479 Walton Ave (10451-5337)
PHONE..................................718 665-0006
Bob Broker, *President*
Terrance Broker, *Vice Pres*
EMP: 7
SQ FT: 10,000
SALES (est): 1.8MM **Privately Held**
WEB: www.heatingandburner.com
SIC: 3822 5063 Auto controls regulating residntl & coml environmt & applncs; motors, electric

(G-1358)
HENDRICKSON CUSTOM CABINETRY
132 Saint Anns Ave Fl 2 (10454-4600)
PHONE..................................718 401-0137
Fax: 718 401-0153
Felix Hendrickson, *President*
Mike Krall, *COO*
Lisa Hendrickson, *Vice Pres*
Kevin Swinderman, *Corp Comm Staff*
EMP: 10
SQ FT: 8,000
SALES (est): 627.3K **Privately Held**
WEB: www.hccco.com
SIC: 2434 Wood kitchen cabinets

(G-1359)
HIGH RIDGE NEWS LLC
5818 Broadway (10463-4105)
PHONE..................................718 548-7412
Atul Patel, *Owner*
EMP: 5
SALES (est): 268.4K **Privately Held**
SIC: 2711 Newspapers, publishing & printing

(G-1360)
IDEAL SIGNS INC
538 Wales Ave (10455-4510)
PHONE..................................718 292-9196
Fax: 718 292-9196
Yeudy Diaz, *President*
EMP: 5
SQ FT: 3,000
SALES (est): 396.1K **Privately Held**
SIC: 3993 Signs & advertising specialties

(G-1361)
IMPERIAL DAMPER & LOUVER CO
907 E 141st St (10454-2009)
PHONE..................................718 731-3800
Fax: 718 731-4920
Brad Mattes, *President*
Tom Tulley, *Vice Pres*
Myrna Garcia, *Prdtn Mgr*
Matt Kranz, *Engineer*
Aida Rivera, *Office Mgr*
EMP: 35
SQ FT: 16,500
SALES (est): 6.6MM **Privately Held**
WEB: www.imperialdamper.com
SIC: 3444 3446 Metal ventilating equipment; louvers, ventilating

(G-1362)
INDEX INCORPORATED
415 Concord Ave (10455-4801)
PHONE..................................440 632-5400
Elias Wexler, *President*
Tom McCartney, *General Mgr*
Roy Keech, *General Mgr*
Tim K McCartney, *Manager*
EMP: 13
SQ FT: 3,500
SALES (est): 1.4MM **Privately Held**
WEB: www.zerointernational.com
SIC: 3052 Rubber & plastics hose & beltings
HQ: Schlage Lock Company, Llc
11819 N Pennsylvania St
Carmel IN 46032
317 810-3700

(G-1363)
INDUSTRIAL PAPER TUBE INC
1335 E Bay Ave (10474-6992)
PHONE..................................718 893-5000
Fax: 718 378-0055
Howard Kramer, *President*
John Costello, *Vice Pres*
EMP: 19
SQ FT: 50,000
SALES (est): 3.2MM **Privately Held**
WEB: www.mailingtubes-ipt.com
SIC: 3089 2655 Closures, plastic; tubes, for chemical or electrical uses: paper or fiber

(G-1364)
INFORM STUDIO INC
480 Austin Pl Frnt E (10455-5023)
PHONE..................................718 401-6149
Patrick Eck, *President*
Emad Ebrahim, *Vice Pres*
EMP: 10
SQ FT: 7,000
SALES (est): 1.7MM **Privately Held**
SIC: 2431 Interior & ornamental woodwork & trim

(G-1365)
INNOVA INTERIORS INC
780 E 134th St Fl 2 (10454-3527)
PHONE..................................718 401-2122
Leon Mace Natenzon, *President*
EMP: 20
SALES (est): 1.2MM **Privately Held**
SIC: 2499 1751 Decorative wood & woodwork; carpentry work

(G-1366)
IWEB DESIGN INC
1491 Metro Ave Ste 3i (10462)
PHONE..................................805 243-8305
John Horne, *CEO*
Jon Jaskiel, *Vice Pres*
EMP: 10
SALES (est): 460K **Privately Held**
SIC: 3577 Encoders, computer peripheral equipment

(G-1367)
JAB CONCRETE SUPPLY CORP
1465 Bronx River Ave (10472-1001)
P.O. Box 1223 (10472-0965)
PHONE..................................718 842-5250
Carmine Valente, *President*
EMP: 30 **EST:** 1994
SALES (est): 2.3MM **Privately Held**
SIC: 3272 Concrete products

(G-1368)
JEM THREADING SPECIALTIES INC
1059 Washington Ave (10456-6636)
P.O. Box 491, Lake Peekskill (10537-0491)
PHONE..................................718 665-3341
Fax: 718 292-0020
Michael Rottenkolber, *President*
John Rottenkolber, *Vice Pres*
Maria Vazqezi, *Manager*
EMP: 5
SQ FT: 17,500
SALES (est): 652.8K **Privately Held**
SIC: 3965 3354 3452 Fasteners; rods, extruded, aluminum; bolts, metal

Bronx - Bronx County (G-1369)

(G-1369)
JENNA CONCRETE CORPORATION
1465 Bronx River Ave (10472-1001)
PHONE..................718 842-5250
Fax: 718 589-3446
Carmine Valente, *President*
Denny Lijlage, *Office Mgr*
Anthony Valente, *Manager*
EMP: 30
SQ FT: 1,000
SALES (est): 5.8MM **Privately Held**
SIC: 3272 3273 3271 Concrete products; ready-mixed concrete; concrete block & brick

(G-1370)
JENNA HARLEM RIVER INC
1465 Bronx River Ave (10472-1001)
PHONE..................718 842-5997
Carmine Valente, *President*
EMP: 5
SQ FT: 1,000
SALES (es): 454.9K **Privately Held**
SIC: 3272 3273 3271 Concrete products; ready-mixed concrete; concrete block & brick

(G-1371)
JOHN LANGENBACHER CO INC
888 Longfellow Ave (10474-4804)
PHONE..................718 328-0141
Fax: 718 542-2005
Harry Boyd, *President*
William Boyd, *President*
Larry Scherer, *Exec VP*
William Hudspeth, *CFO*
EMP: 50 **EST:** 1907
SQ FT: 100,000
SALES (est): 4.6MM **Privately Held**
SIC: 2431 5712 Millwork; custom made furniture, except cabinets

(G-1372)
JPMORGAN CHASE BANK NAT ASSN
Also Called: White Plains Rd & E 211th St
3514 White Plains Rd (10467-5706)
PHONE..................718 944-7964
EMP: 6
SALES (corp-wide): 105.4B **Publicly Held**
SIC: 3578 Automatic teller machines (ATM)
HQ: Jpmorgan Chase Bank, National Association
1111 Polaris Pkwy
Columbus OH 43240
614 436-3055

(G-1373)
KD DIDS INC (PA)
Also Called: K D Dance
140 E 144th St (10451-5434)
PHONE..................718 402-2012
Fax: 718 402-2013
David Lee, *President*
EMP: 2
SQ FT: 6,000
SALES (est): 4.5MM **Privately Held**
WEB: www.kddance.com
SIC: 2253 5961 Shirts (outerwear), knit; fitness & sporting goods, mail order

(G-1374)
KEMET PROPERTIES LLC
1179 W 224th St (10466-5834)
PHONE..................718 654-8079
Douglas Malcolm, *Principal*
EMP: 5
SALES (est): 588.5K **Privately Held**
SIC: 3675 Electronic capacitors

(G-1375)
KENMAR SHIRTS INC (PA)
1415 Blondell Ave (10461-2622)
PHONE..................718 824-3880
Fax: 718 823-4233
Mark Greene, *President*
Karen Greene, *Corp Secy*
Irwin Haberman, *Vice Pres*
EMP: 20
SQ FT: 8,000
SALES (est): 1.7MM **Privately Held**
WEB: www.kenmarshirts.com
SIC: 2759 5136 5137 2396 Screen printing; men's & boys' clothing; women's & children's clothing; automotive & apparel trimmings

(G-1376)
KICKS CLOSET SPORTSWEAR INC
1031 Southern Blvd Frnt 2 (10459-3435)
PHONE..................347 577-0857
Ismail Abadi, *President*
EMP: 6 **EST:** 2014
SQ FT: 1,800
SALES: 2.7MM **Privately Held**
SIC: 2329 3149 2339 Men's & boys' sportswear & athletic clothing; athletic shoes, except rubber or plastic; women's & misses' athletic clothing & sportswear

(G-1377)
KIRSCHNER BRUSH LLC
Also Called: Kbc
605 E 132nd St Frnt 3 (10454-4638)
PHONE..................718 292-1809
Fax: 718 292-1899
Israel Kirschner,
▲ **EMP:** 15 **EST:** 1939
SQ FT: 20,000
SALES: 900K **Privately Held**
SIC: 3991 Paint brushes

(G-1378)
KNJ FABRICATORS LLC
4341 Wickham Ave (10466-1809)
PHONE..................347 234-6985
Krishnadatt N Joe,
EMP: 10
SQ FT: 4,000
SALES: 900K **Privately Held**
SIC: 3441 Fabricated structural metal

(G-1379)
L & D MANUFACTURING CORP
Also Called: D & L Manufacturing
366 Canal Pl Frnt (10451-5911)
PHONE..................718 665-5226
Larry Weisel, *President*
Leon Weisel, *Vice Pres*
EMP: 6
SALES (est): 624.9K **Privately Held**
SIC: 2599 Restaurant furniture, wood or metal

(G-1380)
L A S REPLACEMENT PARTS INC
1645 Webster Ave (10457-8096)
P.O. Box 873 (10457-0873)
PHONE..................718 583-4700
Fax: 718 294-0661
Alan Siegel, *President*
Lloyd Siegel, *Corp Secy*
EMP: 10 **EST:** 1946
SQ FT: 10,000
SALES (est): 1.3MM **Privately Held**
WEB: www.lasparts.com
SIC: 3432 1711 Plumbing fixture fittings & trim; plumbing, heating, air-conditioning contractors

(G-1381)
LA PRIMA BAKERY INC (PA)
765 E 182nd St (10460-1140)
PHONE..................718 584-4442
Fax: 718 584-7521
Sal Attina, *President*
Rocco Attina, *Vice Pres*
EMP: 19
SQ FT: 18,000
SALES (est): 1.1MM **Privately Held**
SIC: 2051 Bread, all types (white, wheat, rye, etc): fresh or frozen

(G-1382)
LEADER SHEET METAL INC
759 E 133rd St 2 (10454-3425)
PHONE..................347 271-4961
Jenny Dashevsky, *President*
EMP: 18
SALES (est): 3.4MM **Privately Held**
SIC: 3444 Sheet metalwork

(G-1383)
LEGACY USA LLC
Also Called: Legacy Manufacturing
415 Concord Ave (10455-4801)
PHONE..................888 383-3330
Jacob Wexler, *Mng Member*
EMP: 15 **EST:** 2016
SQ FT: 20,000
SALES: 700K **Privately Held**
SIC: 2891 Adhesives & sealants

(G-1384)
LEMON BROTHERS FOUNDATION INC
Also Called: Not For Profit Chari
23b Debs Pl (10475-2575)
PHONE..................347 920-2749
Mohammed Rahman, *Principal*
EMP: 15
SALES: 24K **Privately Held**
SIC: 3999 Education aids, devices & supplies

(G-1385)
LENS LAB
2124 Bartow Ave (10475-4615)
PHONE..................718 379-2020
Janet Bennis, *Manager*
Maria Ortiz, *Manager*
EMP: 6
SALES (est): 266.2K **Privately Held**
SIC: 3851 Ophthalmic goods

(G-1386)
LINDA CAMPBELL
Also Called: Campbell's Print Shop
4420 Richardson Ave (10470-1545)
PHONE..................718 994-4026
Linda Campbell, *Owner*
EMP: 7 **EST:** 1998
SALES (est): 349.4K **Privately Held**
SIC: 2759 Circulars: printing

(G-1387)
LINO PRESS INC
652 Southern Blvd (10455-3637)
PHONE..................718 665-2625
Franklin Nunez, *Owner*
EMP: 20
SALES (est): 1.2MM **Privately Held**
SIC: 2741 Miscellaneous publishing

(G-1388)
M J M TOOLING CORP
Also Called: Sutter Machine Tool and Die
1059 Washington Ave (10456-6636)
PHONE..................718 292-3590
John Rottenkolber, *President*
Michael Rottenkolber, *Treasurer*
EMP: 9
SALES (est): 1.1MM **Privately Held**
SIC: 3544 Special dies & tools

(G-1389)
MARATHON ENTERPRISES INC
Also Called: House O'Weenies
787 E 138th St (10454-1989)
PHONE..................718 665-2560
Fax: 718 292-0610
Allan Thoreson, *Manager*
EMP: 60
SALES (corp-wide): 25.1MM **Privately Held**
WEB: www.sabrett.com
SIC: 2013 Frankfurters from purchased meat
PA: Marathon Enterprises, Inc.
9 Smith St
Englewood NJ 07631
201 935-3330

(G-1390)
MARINE BOILER & WELDING INC
1428 Sheridan Expy (10459-2106)
PHONE..................718 378-1900
William Falco, *President*
Thomas Falco, *Vice Pres*
EMP: 12
SQ FT: 5,000
SALES (est): 1MM **Privately Held**
SIC: 3443 1799 Boiler & boiler shop work; welding on site

(G-1391)
MARS FASHIONS INC
780 E 134th St Fl 5 (10454-3527)
PHONE..................718 402-2200
Rafael Sanchez, *President*
Sam Mann, *Treasurer*
Stuart Mann, *Admin Sec*
EMP: 50
SQ FT: 25,000
SALES: 756.9K **Privately Held**
SIC: 2339 2253 Women's & misses' athletic clothing & sportswear; knit outerwear mills

(G-1392)
MASON TRANSPARENT PACKAGE INC
1180 Commerce Ave (10462-5506)
PHONE..................718 792-6000
Fax: 718 823-7279
Richard Cole, *President*
Ellen Cole, *Vice Pres*
Kevin O'Connell, *Vice Pres*
Sylvia A Cole, *Admin Sec*
EMP: 30 **EST:** 1947
SQ FT: 25,000
SALES (est): 3.8MM **Privately Held**
WEB: www.masontransparent.com
SIC: 2671 2673 2673 Plastic film, coated or laminated for packaging; plastic bags: made from purchased materials; commercial printing

(G-1393)
MATERIALS DESIGN WORKSHOP
830 Barry St (10474-5707)
PHONE..................718 893-1954
Fax: 718 842-1122
Eugene Black, *President*
David Black, *Vice Pres*
Avelin Ramiez, *Administration*
EMP: 14 **EST:** 1973
SQ FT: 11,000
SALES (est): 2.1MM **Privately Held**
SIC: 2521 Wood office furniture; cabinets, office: wood

(G-1394)
MENU SOLUTIONS INC
4510 White Plains Rd (10470-1609)
PHONE..................718 575-5160
Irwin Joel Borracas, *CEO*
Praful Pandya, *Controller*
▲ **EMP:** 75 **EST:** 1996
SALES (est): 3.2MM **Privately Held**
WEB: www.menucovers.biz
SIC: 2759 Commercial printing

(G-1395)
MERCURY LOCK AND DOOR SERVICE
529 C Wortham St (10474)
PHONE..................718 542-7048
Howard Levine, *President*
EMP: 29
SALES (est): 2.8MM **Privately Held**
SIC: 3442 Fire doors, metal

(G-1396)
METALLINE FIRE DOOR CO INC (PA)
4110 Park Ave (10457-6017)
PHONE..................718 583-2320
Fax: 718 294-5681
Lydia Rodriguez, *President*
William Rodriguez, *Vice Pres*
EMP: 20
SQ FT: 12,500
SALES (est): 4.7MM **Privately Held**
SIC: 3442 5072 Fire doors, metal; window & door frames; hardware

(G-1397)
METALWORKS INC
1303 Herschell St (10461-3622)
PHONE..................718 319-0011
Michael Josephs, *Ch of Bd*
Jeff Dynhas, *Vice Pres*
John Single, *Production*
Jeff Dyzenhaus, *Sales Staff*
Denise Joseph, *Admin Sec*
EMP: 30
SQ FT: 15,000

GEOGRAPHIC SECTION

Bronx - Bronx County (G-1425)

SALES (est): 3.6MM **Privately Held**
SIC: 3446 Architectural metalwork

(G-1398)
METROPOLITAN SIGN & RIGGIN
330 Casanova St (10474-6708)
PHONE.....................718 231-0010
Dave Wehmeier, *President*
Tamara Kelly, *Manager*
EMP: 5
SALES (est): 523.9K **Privately Held**
SIC: 3993 Signs & advertising specialties

(G-1399)
MIL & MIR STEEL PRODUCTS CO
1210 Randall Ave (10474-6399)
PHONE.....................718 328-7596
Fax: 718 328-7913
William Miraglia, *President*
EMP: 6 EST: 1958
SQ FT: 5,000
SALES: 350K **Privately Held**
SIC: 3537 Lift trucks, industrial: fork, platform, straddle, etc.

(G-1400)
MILLENNIUM RMNFCTRED TONER INC
7 Bruckner Blvd (10454-4411)
PHONE.....................718 585-9887
Fax: 718 585-7445
Frank Garcia, *President*
Charles Baker, *Senior VP*
EMP: 11
SALES (est): 920K **Privately Held**
WEB: www.mrtoners.com
SIC: 2893 Printing ink

(G-1401)
MILLER BLAKER INC
620 E 132nd St (10454-4603)
PHONE.....................718 665-3930
Cliff Blaker, *Ch of Bd*
Lee Miller, *Senior VP*
Rabin Ramcharan, *Vice Pres*
Ernie Pitone, *Project Mgr*
Rachel Lime, *Purch Agent*
▲ EMP: 100
SQ FT: 50,000
SALES (est): 15.8MM **Privately Held**
WEB: www.millerblaker.com
SIC: 2431 2521 Interior & ornamental woodwork & trim; wood office furniture

(G-1402)
MISS GRIMBLE ASSOCIATES INC
Also Called: Grimble Bakery
909 E 135th St (10454-3611)
PHONE.....................718 665-2253
Errol Bier, *President*
Craig Bier, *Sales Mgr*
EMP: 12
SQ FT: 15,000
SALES (est): 720K **Privately Held**
WEB: www.missgrimble.com
SIC: 2051 Bakery: wholesale or wholesale/retail combined

(G-1403)
MODULAR MEDICAL CORP
1513 Olmstead Ave (10462-4254)
PHONE.....................718 829-2626
Fax: 718 430-0914
Jeffery S Offner, *President*
Peter Wachs, *Vice Pres*
EMP: 30
SQ FT: 30,000
SALES (est): 1.3MM **Privately Held**
SIC: 3841 Surgical & medical instruments

(G-1404)
MONA SLIDE FASTENERS INC (PA)
Also Called: Mona Belts
4510 White Plains Rd (10470-1609)
PHONE.....................718 325-7700
Fax: 718 324-7222
Joel Barrocas, *President*
Mona Barrocas, *Vice Pres*
▲ EMP: 50 EST: 1944
SQ FT: 30,000
SALES (est): 10.8MM **Privately Held**
SIC: 3965 Buttons & parts

(G-1405)
MONARCH ELECTRIC PRODUCTS INC
Also Called: Vicron Electronic Mfg
4077 Park Ave Fl 5 (10457-7310)
PHONE.....................718 583-7996
Fax: 718 299-9121
▲ EMP: 6 EST: 1946
SQ FT: 5,000
SALES (est): 500K **Privately Held**
SIC: 3643 Mfg Fluorescent Starting Switches

(G-1406)
MONTE PRESS INC
4808 White Plains Rd (10470-1102)
PHONE.....................718 324-5017
Fax: 718 324-5017
Barbara Deangelo, *President*
EMP: 5
SQ FT: 2,400
SALES (est): 320K **Privately Held**
SIC: 2752 Commercial printing, offset

(G-1407)
N & L FUEL CORP
2014 Blackrock Ave (10472-6104)
PHONE.....................718 863-3538
Nick Leandro, *Principal*
EMP: 8
SALES (est): 966.1K **Privately Held**
SIC: 2869 Fuels

(G-1408)
NATIONAL EQUIPMENT CORPORATION
Also Called: Union Standard & Un Conf McHy
801 E 141st St (10454-1917)
PHONE.....................718 585-0200
Eddie Greenberg, *Manager*
EMP: 30
SALES (corp-wide): 11.8MM **Privately Held**
SIC: 3556 3559 3565 5084 Food products machinery; confectionery machinery; chemical machinery & equipment; pharmaceutical machinery; packaging machinery; processing & packaging equipment
PA: National Equipment Corporation
600 Mmaroneck Ave Ste 400
Harrison NY 10528
718 585-0200

(G-1409)
NATIONAL STEEL RULE DIE INC
2407 3rd Ave (10451-6301)
PHONE.....................718 402-1396
Frank G Curatolo, *President*
Mark Sanders, *Manager*
Ray Farina, *Executive*
EMP: 14 EST: 1945
SQ FT: 5,000
SALES: 900K **Privately Held**
SIC: 3544 Dies, steel rule

(G-1410)
NEW YORK BOTTLING CO INC
Also Called: Mayim Chaim Beverages
626 Whittier St (10474-6121)
PHONE.....................718 963-3232
Zvi Hold, *President*
Joseph Hold, *Vice Pres*
Racheal Hold, *Admin Sec*
Esta Kohn, *Admin Sec*
EMP: 12 EST: 1967
SQ FT: 10,000
SALES (est): 2.4MM **Privately Held**
SIC: 2086 Soft drinks: packaged in cans, bottles, etc.

(G-1411)
NEW YORK INDUSTRIAL WORKS INC (PA)
796 E 140th St (10454-1915)
PHONE.....................718 292-0615
Gary Mahoni, *President*
Eve Polanco, *Admin Mgr*
EMP: 8 EST: 1979
SQ FT: 6,000
SALES (est): 2.4MM **Privately Held**
WEB: www.newdraulictools.com
SIC: 3546 Power-driven handtools; guns, pneumatic: chip removal

(G-1412)
NEX-GEN READY MIX CORP
530 Faile St (10474-6908)
PHONE.....................347 231-0073
Salvatore Bullaro, *Chairman*
EMP: 7
SALES (est): 752K **Privately Held**
SIC: 3273 Ready-mixed concrete

(G-1413)
NICHOLAS DFINE FURN DECORATORS
546 E 170th St 48 (10456-2302)
PHONE.....................914 245-8982
Fax: 718 538-1201
Helen Savastano, *President*
Frank Savastano, *Owner*
Vincent Savastano, *Corp Secy*
Nicholas Savastano, *Vice Pres*
EMP: 15
SQ FT: 6,600
SALES (est): 1.7MM **Privately Held**
SIC: 2511 2512 2521 7641 Wood household furniture; upholstered household furniture; wood office furniture; antique furniture repair & restoration

(G-1414)
NOROC ENTERPRISES INC
415 Concord Ave (10455-4801)
PHONE.....................718 585-3230
Fax: 718 292-2243
Elias Wexler, *CEO*
Jerry Heid, *Vice Pres*
Constantin Constantinide, *Research*
Steve Petko, *Sales Staff*
◆ EMP: 150 EST: 1928
SQ FT: 27,000
SALES (est): 20MM **Privately Held**
WEB: www.zerointernational.com
SIC: 3251 3053 Fireproofing tile, clay; gasket materials

(G-1415)
NORTH BRONX RETINAL & OPHTHLMI
3725 Henry Hudson Pkwy (10463-1527)
PHONE.....................347 535-4932
Daniel Chechik MD, *Ch of Bd*
EMP: 8
SALES (est): 849.8K **Privately Held**
SIC: 3851 Ophthalmic goods

(G-1416)
NYSCO PRODUCTS LLC
2350 Lafayette Ave (10473-1104)
P.O. Box 725 (10473-0725)
PHONE.....................718 792-9000
Barry Kramer, *Principal*
Chuck Levin, *Senior VP*
Glenn Smith, *Vice Pres*
Stephen Yeh, *Design Engr*
Patricia Albright, *Human Res Dir*
▲ EMP: 60 EST: 1935
SQ FT: 80,000
SALES (est): 11.9MM **Privately Held**
WEB: www.nysco.com
SIC: 3993 Signs & advertising specialties

(G-1417)
OMC INC
4010 Park Ave (10457-7397)
PHONE.....................718 731-5001
James O'Halpin, *President*
Mike Checci, *Corp Secy*
Robert Moteti, *Vice Pres*
Joe Checchi, *Manager*
EMP: 110
SQ FT: 25,000
SALES (est): 19.1MM **Privately Held**
WEB: www.omcdrafting.com
SIC: 3444 Sheet metalwork

(G-1418)
OPERATIVE CAKE CORP
Also Called: Lady Linda Cakes
711 Brush Ave (10465-1839)
P.O. Box 1017 (10465-0623)
PHONE.....................718 278-5600
Matthew Jacobson, *President*
Mark Jacobson, *President*
Sam Jacobson, *Vice Pres*
EMP: 50
SQ FT: 60,000
SALES (est): 6.4MM
SALES (corp-wide): 43.5MM **Privately Held**
WEB: www.groceryhaulers.com
SIC: 2051 5149 Bread, cake & related products; bakery products
PA: Grocery Haulers, Inc.
581 Main St Ste 510
Woodbridge NJ 07095
732 499-3745

(G-1419)
P H CUSTOM WOODWORKING CORP
830 Barry St Fl 2nd (10474-5707)
PHONE.....................917 801-1444
Kazimierz Sperling, *President*
Daniel Sperling, *Principal*
Anna Sperling, *Vice Pres*
EMP: 23
SQ FT: 8,000
SALES: 2.7MM **Privately Held**
SIC: 2431 Interior & ornamental woodwork & trim; exterior & ornamental woodwork & trim

(G-1420)
PACIFIC DESIGNS INTL INC
2743 Webster Ave (10458-3705)
PHONE.....................718 364-2867
Edward Nerenberg, *President*
Marisha Torres, *Assistant*
EMP: 5
SALES (est): 416.4K **Privately Held**
SIC: 3081 Floor or wall covering, unsupported plastic

(G-1421)
PARADIGM GROUP LLC
1357 Lafayette Ave Frnt 1 (10474-4847)
PHONE.....................718 860-1538
Vuac Heflaz, *Principal*
EMP: 5
SALES (est): 478.3K **Privately Held**
SIC: 3471 3479 Finishing, metals or formed products; hot dip coating of metals or formed products

(G-1422)
PARKCHESTER DPS LLC
2000 E Tremont Ave (10462-5703)
PHONE.....................718 823-4411
Richard Vargas, *Manager*
EMP: 107
SALES (est): 9.1MM **Privately Held**
SIC: 3841 Surgical & medical instruments

(G-1423)
PATIENT-WEAR LLC
3940 Merritt Ave (10466-2502)
PHONE.....................914 740-7770
Thomas A Keith, *President*
EMP: 8
SALES: 950K **Privately Held**
SIC: 2389 Apparel & accessories

(G-1424)
PELICAN PRODUCTS CO INC (PA)
1049 Lowell St (10459-2608)
PHONE.....................718 860-3220
Fax: 718 860-4415
Kenneth Silver, *President*
David Silver, *Vice Pres*
Jan Pawelec, *Treasurer*
▲ EMP: 23 EST: 1946
SQ FT: 20,000
SALES (est): 2.8MM **Privately Held**
WEB: www.pelicanproducts.com
SIC: 3951 3089 Pens & mechanical pencils; novelties, plastic

(G-1425)
PEPSI-COLA BOTTLING CO NY INC
650 Brush Ave (10465-1804)
PHONE.....................718 892-1570
Michael Moral, *Manager*
EMP: 75
SALES (corp-wide): 473.9MM **Privately Held**
SIC: 2086 Soft drinks: packaged in cans, bottles, etc.

Bronx - Bronx County (G-1426) GEOGRAPHIC SECTION

PA: Pepsi-Cola Bottling Company Of New York, Inc.
11402 15th Ave Ste 5
College Point NY 11356
718 392-1000

(G-1426)
PERRIGO COMPANY
1625 Bathgate Ave (10457-8101)
PHONE 718 960-9900
Ange François, *Project Mgr*
Duane Austin, *Human Resources*
Joseph C Papa, *Branch Mgr*
Vikrant Bandekar, *Manager*
Michael Fissehaye, *Manager*
EMP: 21 **Privately Held**
SIC: 2834 Pharmaceutical preparations; analgesics; cold remedies; vitamin preparations
HQ: Perrigo Company
515 Eastern Ave
Allegan MI 49010
269 673-8451

(G-1427)
PERRIGO NEW YORK INC
455 Claremont Pkwy (10457-8301)
PHONE 718 901-2800
Oscar Camejo, *Manager*
EMP: 15 **Privately Held**
WEB: www.agis-group.com
SIC: 2834 Pharmaceutical preparations; ointments; dermatologicals
HQ: Perrigo New York, Inc.
1700 Bathgate Ave
Bronx NY 10457
718 960-9900

(G-1428)
PERRIGO NEW YORK INC (DH)
Also Called: Suppositoria Laboratory
1700 Bathgate Ave (10457-7512)
PHONE 718 960-9900
Joseph C Papa, *Ch of Bd*
Giora Carni, *President*
Ofir Sova, *Vice Pres*
Prisco Cornejo, *Facilities Mgr*
Laura Umpleby, *Purch Agent*
▲ **EMP:** 500
SQ FT: 300,000
SALES (est): 103.6MM **Privately Held**
WEB: www.agis-group.com
SIC: 2834 Pharmaceutical preparations; ointments; dermatologicals
HQ: Perrigo Company
515 Eastern Ave
Allegan MI 49010
269 673-3451

(G-1429)
POLYSEAL PACKAGING CORP
1178 E 180th St (10460-2401)
P.O. Box 1171, New York (10035-0807)
PHONE 718 792-5530
Fax: 718 792-5582
Lewis Matthews, *President*
Carol Smith, *Vice Pres*
EMP: 20
SQ FT: 20,000
SALES (est): 1.9MM **Privately Held**
SIC: 2673 2674 Plastic bags: made from purchased materials; paper bags: made from purchased materials

(G-1430)
PONCIO SIGNS
3007 Albany Cres (10463-5960)
PHONE 718 543-4851
Poncio Salcedo *Owner*
EMP: 7 **EST:** 1962
SQ FT: 700
SALES (est): 290K **Privately Held**
SIC: 3993 Signs, not made in custom sign painting shops

(G-1431)
POORAN PALLET INC
319 Barretto St (10474-6722)
PHONE 718 938-7970
Zainool Pooran, *President*
EMP: 5
SQ FT: 5,000
SALES: 300K **Privately Held**
SIC: 2448 Pallets, wood & wood with metal

(G-1432)
PORK KING SAUSAGE INC
F22 Hunts Point Co Op Mkt (10474-7568)
PHONE 718 542-2810
Fax: 718 542-2847
Dominick Puntolillo, *President*
Frank Puntolillo, *Vice Pres*
Sean McGonigle, *Manager*
EMP: 25
SQ FT: 10,000
SALES (est): 5.1MM **Privately Held**
SIC: 2013 Sausages & other prepared meats

(G-1433)
PRECISION ORNA IR WORKS INC
Also Called: Precision Furniture
1838 Adee Ave (10469-3245)
PHONE 718 379-5200
Fax: 718 320-1270
Joseph Napolitano, *President*
Anthony Napolitano, *Vice Pres*
Philip Napolitano, *Admin Sec*
EMP: 9
SQ FT: 40,000
SALES: 700K **Privately Held**
WEB: www.precisionfurniture.com
SIC: 2514 Household furniture: upholstered on metal frames

(G-1434)
PREMIUM OCEAN LLC
1271 Ryawa Ave (10474-7114)
PHONE 917 231-1061
Marie Joseph, *Manager*
Esraim Basson,
Juliana Paparizou,
▲ **EMP:** 15
SALES (est): 4.1MM **Privately Held**
SIC: 2091 Seafood products: packaged in cans, jars, etc.

(G-1435)
PULSE PLASTICS PRODUCTS INC
1156 E 165th St (10459-2693)
P.O. Box 1228 (10459-1164)
PHONE 718 328-5224
Alan J Backelman, *President*
Mike Backelman, *General Mgr*
EMP: 25
SQ FT: 23,000
SALES: 1.5MM **Privately Held**
WEB: www.pulseplastics.com
SIC: 3089 Molding primary plastic

(G-1436)
QUALITY HM BRANDS HOLDINGS LLC (PA)
125 Rose Feiss Blvd (10454-3624)
PHONE 718 292-2024
Maurice Feiss, *Mng Member*
Thomas Bilbrough,
William J Haley,
▲ **EMP:** 833
SALES (est): 49.1MM **Privately Held**
SIC: 3645 5063 Residential lighting fixtures; lighting fixtures; lighting fixtures, residential

(G-1437)
QUALITY MILLWORK CORP
425 Devoe Ave (10460-2309)
P.O. Box 479 (10460-0241)
PHONE 718 892-2250
Anthony Guarino, *President*
▲ **EMP:** 28
SQ FT: 45,000
SALES (est): 3.6MM **Privately Held**
SIC: 2431 Doors, wood

(G-1438)
R GOLDSMITH
1974 Mayflower Ave (10461-4007)
PHONE 718 239-1396
Claudine Bryan, *Branch Mgr*
EMP: 10
SALES (est): 486.8K **Privately Held**
SIC: 3914 Silversmithing

(G-1439)
REEFER TEK LLC
885a E 149th St Fl 2 (10455-5010)
PHONE 347 590-1067

Michael Liedman, *Managing Dir*
EMP: 12 **EST:** 2010
SQ FT: 12,000
SALES (est): 1.4MM **Privately Held**
SIC: 3559 Automotive related machinery

(G-1440)
ROANWELL CORPORATION
2564 Park Ave (10451-6014)
PHONE 718 401-0288
Fax: 718 401-0663
Barbara Labarre, *CEO*
Jonathan Labarre, *President*
William Rathban, *Principal*
Marcelle Wahba, *Purch Mgr*
Lech Perdowski, *Chief Engr*
▼ **EMP:** 45
SQ FT: 28,000
SALES: 6MM **Privately Held**
WEB: www.roanwellcorp.com
SIC: 3669 Intercommunication systems, electric

(G-1441)
ROCKING THE BOAT INC
812 Edgewater Rd (10474-4902)
PHONE 718 466-5799
Amy Kantroitz, *President*
Adam Green, *Exec Dir*
Bryce Lefort, *Director*
Michael Robinson, *Admin Sec*
EMP: 10
SALES: 2.1MM **Privately Held**
WEB: www.rockingtheboat.org
SIC: 3732 Non-motorized boat, building & repairing

(G-1442)
S & S FASHIONS INC
941 Longfellow Ave (10474-4810)
PHONE 718 328-0001
Sageev Mangal, *President*
▲ **EMP:** 5
SQ FT: 18,000
SALES: 4MM **Privately Held**
SIC: 2329 Men's & boys' sportswear & athletic clothing

(G-1443)
S & S SOAP CO INC
815 E 135th St (10454-3584)
PHONE 718 585-2900
Fax: 718 585-2902
Zvi Sebrow, *President*
Joseph Sebrow, *Admin Sec*
EMP: 20 **EST:** 1930
SQ FT: 40,000
SALES (est): 4.2MM **Privately Held**
WEB: www.blutex.com
SIC: 2841 Detergents, synthetic organic or inorganic alkaline

(G-1444)
S & V RESTAURANT EQP MFRS INC
Also Called: Custom Cool
4320 Park Ave (10457-2442)
PHONE 718 220-1140
Fax: 718 364-1764
Sam Zeltser, *CEO*
Shlomo Zeltser, *President*
Vyacheslav Ulman, *Corp Secy*
Zelig Zeltser, *Vice Pres*
Michael Bardin, *Engineer*
EMP: 46
SQ FT: 35,000
SALES (est): 9.7MM **Privately Held**
WEB: www.customcool.com
SIC: 3585 Refrigeration equipment, complete

(G-1445)
SACCOMIZE INC
1554 Stillwell Ave (10461-2212)
PHONE 818 287-3000
Fax: 718 918-0081
Anthony Saccommanno, *President*
Thomas Saccommanno, *Vice Pres*
EMP: 9
SQ FT: 5,000
SALES (est): 789K **Privately Held**
WEB: www.saccomize.com
SIC: 3471 7542 Finishing, metals or formed products; washing & polishing, automotive

(G-1446)
SANJAY PALLETS INC
424 Coster St (10474-6811)
PHONE 347 590-2485
Mohamed Salem Shaheed, *CEO*
EMP: 8
SALES (est): 1.1MM **Privately Held**
SIC: 2448 Pallets, wood & wood with metal

(G-1447)
SARABETHS KITCHEN LLC
1161 E 156th St (10474-6226)
PHONE 718 589-2900
Fax: 718 589-8412
Sarabeth Levine,
EMP: 7
SALES (est): 110.5K **Privately Held**
SIC: 2033 Jams, jellies & preserves: packaged in cans, jars, etc.

(G-1448)
SBK PRESERVES INC
Also Called: Sarabeth's Bakery
1161 E 156th St (10474-6226)
PHONE 800 773-7378
William Levine, *Ch of Bd*
Suzanne B Levine, *Vice Pres*
Jason Albucker, *Marketing Staff*
Sigal Seeber, *Marketing Staff*
▲ **EMP:** 40
SQ FT: 15,000
SALES (est): 6.4MM **Privately Held**
SIC: 2033 5149 5961 Jams, including imitation: packaged in cans, jars, etc.; preserves, including imitation: in cans, jars, etc.; pickles, preserves, jellies & jams; food, mail order

(G-1449)
SCACCIANOCE INC
Also Called: Daisy Brand Confectionery
1165 Burnett Pl (10474-5716)
PHONE 718 991-4462
Fax: 718 991-0154
Donald Beck, *President*
Anthony Scaccianoce, *Vice Pres*
Allen Gross, *CPA*
▲ **EMP:** 10 **EST:** 1904
SQ FT: 10,000
SALES (est): 964.8K **Privately Held**
SIC: 2064 2068 Candy & other confectionery products; salted & roasted nuts & seeds

(G-1450)
SHARON METAL STAMPING CORP
Also Called: Aai Manufacturing Div
1457 Bassett Ave (10461-2393)
PHONE 718 828-4510
Hyman Kramer, *President*
Rhoda Kramer, *Corp Secy*
EMP: 5
SQ FT: 5,000
SALES (est): 438.4K **Privately Held**
SIC: 3469 3544 Metal stampings; special dies & tools

(G-1451)
SIDCO FOOD DISTRIBUTION CORP
2324 Webster Ave (10458-7506)
P.O. Box 379, Fort Lee NJ (07024-0379)
PHONE 718 733-3939
Fax: 718 584-1863
Jose Negron, *Ch of Bd*
Lois Rodriguez, *Vice Pres*
Maria Marte, *Accounting Mgr*
EMP: 15
SQ FT: 10,000
SALES (est): 6MM **Privately Held**
SIC: 3556 1541 Food products machinery; food products manufacturing or packing plant construction

(G-1452)
SIGMA MANUFACTURING INDS INC
1361 E Bay Ave (10474-7025)
PHONE 718 842-9180
Fax: 718 991-4094
Apostolos Siantos, *President*
Yuri Reznik, *Corp Secy*
EMP: 13
SQ FT: 12,000

SALES (est): 3MM **Privately Held**
WEB: www.sigma-mfg.com
SIC: 3599 Machine shop, jobbing & repair

(G-1453)
SIGNATURE METAL MBL MAINT LLC
791 E 132nd St (10454-3512)
PHONE.................................718 292-8280
Gary Swartz,
EMP: 100
SALES (est): 15.1MM **Privately Held**
SIC: 3449 Miscellaneous metalwork

(G-1454)
SKECHERS USA INC
Also Called: Skechers Factory Outlet 315
651 River Ave (10451-2113)
PHONE.................................718 585-3024
Fax: 718 585-3034
Daniel Lugo, *Branch Mgr*
EMP: 18
SALES (corp-wide): 3.5B **Publicly Held**
SIC: 3021 Rubber & plastics footwear
PA: Skechers U.S.A., Inc.
228 Manhattan Beach Blvd # 200
Manhattan Beach CA 90266
310 318-3100

(G-1455)
SML BROTHERS HOLDING CORP
820 E 140th St (10454-1904)
PHONE.................................718 402-2000
Michael Landau, *CEO*
Jason Landau, *Research*
Mel Weinzimer, *Sales Staff*
Trish Brosnan, *MIS Dir*
Stephen Landau, *Admin Sec*
▲ **EMP:** 85 **EST:** 1976
SALES (est): 17.7MM **Privately Held**
WEB: www.polytexink.com
SIC: 3952 2851 2865 Ink, drawing: black & colored; paints & paint additives; color pigments, organic

(G-1456)
SOFA DOCTOR INC
Also Called: Dr Sofa
220 E 134th St Frnt 1b (10451-6410)
PHONE.................................718 292-6300
Shlomie Eini, *President*
Max Bar-Nahum, *Marketing Staff*
EMP: 8 **EST:** 2004
SALES (est): 899K **Privately Held**
SIC: 2512 7641 Upholstered household furniture; furniture upholstery repair

(G-1457)
SPACE AGE PLSTC FBRCATORS INC
4519 White Plains Rd (10470-1680)
PHONE.................................718 324-4062
Fax: 212 994-0582
Arthur Barsky, *President*
Joel Barsky, *Vice Pres*
Loel Barsky, *Vice Pres*
Helena Barsky, *Human Res Mgr*
EMP: 15
SQ FT: 12,000
SALES: 2.6MM **Privately Held**
WEB: www.plastic64.com
SIC: 3089 Plastic hardware & building products

(G-1458)
SPARROW MINING CO (PA)
3743 White Plains Rd (10467-5754)
PHONE.................................718 519-6600
Randolph Silverstein, *Partner*
David Silverstein, *Partner*
EMP: 7
SALES (est): 1.3MM **Privately Held**
SIC: 1442 Sand mining

(G-1459)
SPECIALTY STEEL FABG CORP
Also Called: Specialty Steel of America.
544 Casanova St (10474-6712)
PHONE.................................718 893-6326
Fax: 718 861-5805
Gregory Burns, *President*
Warren Wilhelm, *Vice Pres*
EMP: 14
SQ FT: 12,000

SALES (est): 2.4MM **Privately Held**
WEB: www.specialtysteelinternational.com
SIC: 3441 5051 5084 Fabricated structural metal; metals service centers & offices; industrial machinery & equipment

(G-1460)
ST RAYMOND MONUMENT CO
2727 Lafayette Ave (10465-2228)
PHONE.................................718 824-3600
Raymond Carotenuto, *President*
Ethel Carotenuto, *Corp Secy*
EMP: 5
SQ FT: 1,200
SALES (est): 403.6K **Privately Held**
SIC: 3272 5999 Monuments, concrete; tombstones, precast terrazzo or concrete; monuments, finished to custom order

(G-1461)
STANDARD PAPER BOX MACHINE CO
347 Coster St Fl 2 (10474-6813)
PHONE.................................718 328-3300
Fax: 718 842-7772
Aaron Adams, *Ch of Bd*
Bruce Adams, *President*
Larry Wilson, *Vice Pres*
Vicki Adams, *Treasurer*
▲ **EMP:** 25
SQ FT: 35,000
SALES (est): 3.6MM **Privately Held**
SIC: 3554 3542 Box making machines, paper; die cutting & stamping machinery, paper converting; machine tools, metal forming type

(G-1462)
STARLITE PNT & VARNISH CO INC
Also Called: Starlight Paint Factory
724 E 140th St (10454-2405)
PHONE.................................718 292-6420
Peter J Gorynski Jr, *President*
Leo Gorynski, *Vice Pres*
EMP: 5 **EST:** 1938
SQ FT: 9,000
SALES: 2.5MM **Privately Held**
SIC: 2851 5231 Paints & paint additives; paint

(G-1463)
STEVEN JOHN OPTICIANS
5901 Riverdale Ave (10471-1602)
PHONE.................................718 543-3336
Steven John, *Owner*
EMP: 9
SALES (est): 670K **Privately Held**
SIC: 3827 Optical instruments & lenses

(G-1464)
STREAMLINE PLASTICS CO INC
2590 Park Ave (10451-6014)
PHONE.................................718 401-4000
Fax: 718 401-8540
Joseph Bartner, *President*
Stewart Bartner, *Vice Pres*
Beatrice Bartner, *Admin Sec*
EMP: 35 **EST:** 1939
SALES (est): 7.1MM **Privately Held**
SIC: 3089 Extruded finished plastic products; injection molded finished plastic products

(G-1465)
SUPERMARKET EQUIPMENT DEPO INC
1135 Bronx River Ave (10472-3101)
P.O. Box 368, Mountain Dale (12763-0368)
PHONE.................................718 665-6200
Daniel Resnick, *President*
Randy Resnick, *Sales Mgr*
EMP: 7
SALES: 2.5MM **Privately Held**
SIC: 3585 Refrigeration & heating equipment

(G-1466)
SUPREME FIRE-PROOF DOOR CO INC
391 Rider Ave (10451-5905)
PHONE.................................718 665-4224
Fax: 718 402-5807
Wazier Mahmood, *President*
Khan Fizul, *Manager*

EMP: 10 **EST:** 1942
SQ FT: 2,500
SALES (est): 1.2MM **Privately Held**
SIC: 3442 Fire doors, metal

(G-1467)
SVYZ TRADING CORP
4320 Park Ave (10457-2442)
PHONE.................................718 220-1140
Sam Zeltser, *Principal*
Zelk Zeltser, *Vice Pres*
Steve Ulman, *Admin Sec*
▲ **EMP:** 6
SQ FT: 5,000
SALES (est): 797.5K **Privately Held**
SIC: 3822 Refrigeration/air-conditioning defrost controls

(G-1468)
T J RONAN PAINT CORP
Also Called: Ronan Paints
749 E 135th St (10454-3408)
PHONE.................................718 292-1100
Fax: 718 292-0406
Dennis Doran, *Ch of Bd*
John A Doran Jr, *Corp Secy*
John Doran, *Treasurer*
John A Doran Jr, *Treasurer*
▼ **EMP:** 25 **EST:** 1984
SQ FT: 35,000
SALES (est): 5MM **Privately Held**
WEB: www.ronanpaints.com
SIC: 2851 Paints & paint additives

(G-1469)
T M INTERNATIONAL LLC
Also Called: Mazzella Blasting Mat Co
413 Faile St 15 (10474-6907)
P.O. Box 10930, Fairfield NJ (07004-6930)
PHONE.................................718 842-0949
Fax: 718 328-6021
Frank Stagnito, *President*
EMP: 7
SQ FT: 45,000
SALES (est): 1MM **Privately Held**
WEB: www.tmi2001.com
SIC: 2298 Blasting mats, rope

(G-1470)
TARA RIFIC SCREEN PRINTING INC
4197 Park Ave (10457-6033)
PHONE.................................718 583-6864
Sandy Stein, *President*
Jason Holden, *Manager*
EMP: 7
SALES (est): 170K **Privately Held**
SIC: 2759 Screen printing

(G-1471)
TOSCA BRICK OVEN PIZZA REAL
4038 E Tremont Ave (10465-3018)
PHONE.................................718 430-0026
Osa R Rref, *Owner*
EMP: 8
SALES (est): 399.4K **Privately Held**
SIC: 2045 5461 Pizza doughs, prepared: from purchased flour; bread

(G-1472)
TREMONT OFFSET INC
1500 Ericson Pl (10461-5414)
PHONE.................................718 892-7333
Robert Del Greco, *President*
Janet Del Greco, *Vice Pres*
Janet Delgreco, *Vice Pres*
EMP: 9
SQ FT: 2,000
SALES (est): 1.3MM **Privately Held**
SIC: 2752 Commercial printing, offset

(G-1473)
TRENCH & MARINE PUMP CO INC
3466 Park Ave (10456-4307)
P.O. Box 543 (10456-0525)
PHONE.................................212 423-9098
Fax: 212 423-0871
Herman Azia, *President*
Malcolm Azia, *Vice Pres*
Yvette Azia, *Treasurer*
EMP: 40 **EST:** 1918
SQ FT: 10,000

SALES (est): 1.8MM **Privately Held**
SIC: 3561 3594 Pumps, domestic: water or sump; fluid power pumps & motors

(G-1474)
TRI-STATE BIODIESEL LLC
531 Barretto St (10474-6724)
PHONE.................................718 860-6600
Brent Baker, *CEO*
Henry Dotson, *Opers Mgr*
Dehran Duckworth,
EMP: 63
SALES (est): 15MM **Privately Held**
SIC: 2911 Diesel fuels

(G-1475)
TRICEUTICAL INC
1652 Hering Ave (10461-2006)
PHONE.................................631 249-0003
Richard Zhang, *President*
EMP: 12 **EST:** 2009
SALES (est): 1.1MM **Privately Held**
SIC: 2834 Druggists' preparations (pharmaceuticals)

(G-1476)
TRICON DES LLC
2428 Tiemann Ave (10469-6206)
PHONE.................................619 227-0778
Arthur Castiglia,
Omer Ibrahim,
Brian Morris,
John Waldheim,
EMP: 7
SALES (est): 350.9K **Privately Held**
SIC: 2911 5172 Petroleum refining; jet fuels; oils, fuel; diesel fuels; petroleum products

(G-1477)
TRINE ROLLED MOULDING CORP
1421 Ferris Pl (10461-3610)
PHONE.................................718 828-5200
Fax: 718 828-4052
Frank J Rella, *CEO*
Betsy Schildwachter, *CFO*
Harry Jones, *Manager*
James Lange, *Director*
Blanca Cintron, *Administration*
EMP: 45 **EST:** 1942
SQ FT: 66,000
SALES: 6MM **Privately Held**
WEB: www.trinecorp.com
SIC: 3499 Metal ladders

(G-1478)
TROY SIGN & PRINTING
Also Called: Troy Sign Printing Center
4827 White Plains Rd (10470-1125)
PHONE.................................718 994-4482
Leslie Peterson, *Owner*
EMP: 6
SALES (est): 497.8K **Privately Held**
SIC: 2752 Commercial printing, lithographic

(G-1479)
TRUXTON CORP
Also Called: Howard Formed Steel Pdts Div
1357 Lafayette Ave (10474-4846)
P.O. Box 225, Yonkers (10704-0225)
PHONE.................................718 842-6000
Fax: 718 842-6001
Howard Schwartz, *President*
Steve Meier, *Sales Staff*
EMP: 5
SQ FT: 5,000
SALES (est): 809.3K **Privately Held**
WEB: www.mailcart.com
SIC: 3799 Pushcarts & wheelbarrows

(G-1480)
TRYLON WIRE & METAL WORKS INC
526 Tiffany St (10474-6614)
PHONE.................................718 542-4472
Fax: 718 589-0177
Mark Herrmann, *President*
EMP: 25
SQ FT: 20,000
SALES (est): 3.2MM **Privately Held**
SIC: 2542 3496 3444 Stands, merchandise display: except wood; miscellaneous fabricated wire products; sheet metalwork

Bronx - Bronx County (G-1481) — GEOGRAPHIC SECTION

(G-1481)
TWI-LAQ INDUSTRIES INC
Also Called: Stone Glo Products
1345 Seneca Ave (10474-4611)
PHONE 718 638-5860
Lorin Wels, *President*
Robert Wels, *Vice Pres*
Steven Wels, *VP Sales*
David Wels, *Director*
EMP: 30
SQ FT: 25,000
SALES (est): 6.4MM **Privately Held**
WEB: www.stoneglo.com
SIC: 2842 Sanitation preparations

(G-1482)
U S EMBROIDERY INC
Also Called: US Clothing Company
728 E 136 h St Ste 1 (10454-3431)
PHONE 718 585-9662
Fax: 718 292-6131
Muhammad Jahangir, *President*
▲ **EMP:** 11
SQ FT: 20,000
SALES: 900K **Privately Held**
SIC: 2395 Embroidery & art needlework

(G-1483)
ULMER SALES LLC
Also Called: U K Sailmakers
175 City Island Ave (10464-1537)
PHONE 718 885-1700
Fax: 718 885-1726
Charles Ulmer, *President*
Kerry Klinler, *Vice Pres*
EMP: 12
SQ FT: 6,500
SALES (est): 1.3MM **Privately Held**
SIC: 2394 Sails: made from purchased materials

(G-1484)
UNITED FARM PROCESSING CORP (PA)
4366 Park Ave (10457-2442)
PHONE 718 933-6060
Marvin Weirhaus, *President*
Stephen Leibowitz, *Vice Pres*
EMP: 150
SQ FT: 31,000
SALES: 5.2MM **Privately Held**
SIC: 2035 Pickled fruits & vegetables

(G-1485)
UNITED PICKLE PRODUCTS CORP
4366 Park Ave (10457-2442)
PHONE 718 933-6060
Fax: 718 367-8522
Marvin Weishaus, *President*
Stephen Leibowitz, *Vice Pres*
Marc Leibowitz, *Sales Mgr*
Gregg Smith, *Manager*
EMP: 49
SQ FT: 60,000
SALES: 25MM **Privately Held**
SIC: 2035 Vegetables, pickled

(G-1486)
VALENCIA BAKERY INC (PA)
801 Edgewater Rd (10474-4995)
PHONE 718 991-6400
Fax: 718 991-6403
Roy List, *President*
Mike Eberle, *Vice Pres*
EMP: 20
SQ FT: 40,000
SALES: 2MM **Privately Held**
SIC: 2051 Bread, cake & related products

(G-1487)
VANITY FAIR BATHMART INC
2971 Webster Ave (10458-2424)
PHONE 718 584-6700
John P O'Boyle, *President*
EMP: 10
SQ FT: 3,500
SALES (est): 1MM **Privately Held**
WEB: www.varityfairbathmart.com
SIC: 3431 3469 5023 5031 Bathroom fixtures, including sinks; kitchen fixtures & equipment: metal, except cast aluminum; kitchenware; lumber, plywood & millwork

(G-1488)
VELVET HEALING BY ALMA CORP
645 Melrose Ave Frnt 1 (10455-2552)
PHONE 347 271-4220
Alfonsina Pena, *Owner*
EMP: 5
SALES (est): 265.8K **Privately Held**
SIC: 3221 Medicine bottles, glass

(G-1489)
VICTORIA PLATING CO INC
650 Tiffany St (10474-6289)
P.O. Box 740486 (10474-0009)
PHONE 718 589-1550
Fax: 718 378-0739
Charles Antmann, *President*
Jeffrey S Higdon, *Vice Pres*
▲ **EMP:** 51
SQ FT: 45,000
SALES (est): 5.3MM **Privately Held**
WEB: www.victoriaplating.com
SIC: 3471 Electroplating of metals or formed products

(G-1490)
VIELE MANUFACTURING CORP
Also Called: Gary Plastic
1340 Viele Ave (10474-7134)
PHONE 718 893-2200
Gary Hellinger, *CEO*
Marilyn Hellinger, *Vice Pres*
◆ **EMP:** 500
SQ FT: 25,000
SALES (est): 54MM **Privately Held**
SIC: 3089 Plastic processing

(G-1491)
WACOAL AMERICA INC
1543 Saint Lawrence Ave (10460-3226)
PHONE 718 794-1032
EMP: 115
SALES (corp-wide): 1.7B **Privately Held**
SIC: 2342 Brassieres
HQ: Wacoal America, Inc.
1 Wacoal Plz
Lyndhurst NJ 07071
201 933-8400

(G-1492)
WALDORF BAKERS INC
Also Called: Festival Bakers
909 E 135th St (10454-3611)
PHONE 718 665-2253
Milton Bier, *Ch of Bd*
Errol M Bier, *President*
Nancy Bier, *Vice Pres*
EMP: 15
SQ FT: 13,328
SALES (est): 1MM **Privately Held**
SIC: 2051 Bread, cake & related products

(G-1493)
WALTERS & WALTERS INC
961 E 224th St (10466-4677)
PHONE 347 202-8535
EMP: 8 **EST:** 2013
SALES (est): 88.7K **Privately Held**
SIC: 7692 Welding repair

(G-1494)
WENIG CORPORATION
230 Manida St Fl 2 (10474-7199)
PHONE 718 542-3600
Fax: 718 542-3979
EMP: 30 **EST:** 1924
SQ FT: 50,000
SALES (est): 5.1MM **Privately Held**
SIC: 3444 Mfg Sheet Metalwork

(G-1495)
WEST AFRICAN MOVIES
1692 Webster Ave (10457-7307)
PHONE 718 731-2190
Francis Okyere, *Owner*
EMP: 6
SALES (est): 664.9K **Privately Held**
SIC: 3695 Audio range tape, blank

(G-1496)
YANKEE CORP
Also Called: Yankee Wiping Cloth
1180 Randall Ave (10474-6217)
PHONE 718 589-1377
Fax: 718 589-9577

Todd W Hooper, *Chairman*
Richard Kocher, *Vice Pres*
▲ **EMP:** 10
SQ FT: 16,250
SALES (est): 1.2MM **Privately Held**
SIC: 2299 5093 7218 Fabrics: linen, jute, hemp, ramie; waste rags; wiping towel supply

(G-1497)
YULA CORPORATION
330 Bryant Ave (10474-7197)
PHONE 718 991-0900
Fax: 718 842-4239
Larry Feldman, *CEO*
Fred Feldman, *President*
Charles Robinson, *QC Mgr*
Raymond Levin, *Chief Engr*
Adam Nguyen, *Engineer*
▲ **EMP:** 40 **EST:** 1926
SQ FT: 20,000
SALES (est): 10.1MM **Privately Held**
WEB: www.yulacorp.com
SIC: 3443 Heat exchangers, plate type

(G-1498)
ZARO BAKE SHOP INC (PA)
Also Called: Zaro's Bread Basket
138 Bruckner Blvd (10454-4620)
PHONE 718 993-7327
Fax: 718 292-9353
Stuart D Zaro, *Ch of Bd*
Philip Zaro, *Ch of Bd*
Stewart Zaro, *President*
Joseph Zaro, *Vice Pres*
EMP: 110
SQ FT: 40,000
SALES (est): 77.8MM **Privately Held**
WEB: www.zaro.com
SIC: 2051 2052 Bread, cake & related products; cookies & crackers

Bronxville
Westchester County

(G-1499)
ARTISANAL BRANDS INC
42 Forest Ln (10708-1936)
PHONE 914 441-3591
Fax: 914 337-0846
Daniel W Dowe, *President*
James Lillis, *CFO*
EMP: 34
SQ FT: 10,000
SALES: 3.5MM **Privately Held**
SIC: 2022 5451 Cheese, natural & processed; cheese

(G-1500)
CLARK BOTANICALS INC
9 Paradise Rd (10708-2205)
P.O. Box 988 (10708-0988)
PHONE 914 826-4319
Frangesco Clark, *President*
EMP: 10
SALES (est): 1.4MM **Privately Held**
SIC: 2844 Cosmetic preparations

(G-1501)
MNM SERVICE DISTRIBUTORS INC
1 Greystone Cir (10708-2314)
PHONE 914 337-5268
Mitchell Camarda, *President*
EMP: 6
SALES: 3MM **Privately Held**
SIC: 2086 Fruit drinks (less than 100% juice): packaged in cans, etc.

(G-1502)
NOMAD EDITIONS LLC
123 Ellison Ave (10708-2728)
PHONE 212 918-0992
Mark Edminston, *CEO*
Marjorie Martay, *Exec VP*
Samuel Spivy, *Vice Pres*
Cristine De Pedro, *CTO*
EMP: 18
SALES (est): 1MM **Privately Held**
SIC: 2759 Advertising literature: printing

(G-1503)
SOVEREIGN SERVICING SYSTEM LLC
1 Stone Pl Ste 200 (10708-3431)
PHONE 914 779-1400
Stewart Alpert, *Principal*
EMP: 18
SALES (est): 1MM **Privately Held**
SIC: 1389 Roustabout service

Brookhaven
Suffolk County

(G-1504)
AMNEAL PHARMACEUTICALS LLC
50 Horseblock Rd (11719-9509)
PHONE 908 231-1911
EMP: 50
SALES (corp-wide): 430MM **Privately Held**
SIC: 2834 Mfg Pharmaceutical Preparations
PA: Amneal Pharmaceuticals, Llc
400 Crossing Blvd Fl 3
Bridgewater NJ 08807
631 952-0214

(G-1505)
AMNEAL PHARMACEUTICALS LLC
50 Horseblock Rd (11719-9509)
PHONE 631 952-0214
EMP: 41 **Privately Held**
SIC: 2834 5122 Pharmaceutical preparations; pharmaceuticals
HQ: Amneal Pharmaceuticals Llc
50 Horseblock Rd
Brookhaven NY 11719
908 947-3120

(G-1506)
AMNEAL PHARMACEUTICALS LLC (DH)
50 Horseblock Rd (11719-9509)
PHONE 908 947-3120
Fax: 631 656-1009
Chintu Patel, *CEO*
Chirag Patel, *President*
Shankar Hariharan, *Exec VP*
Jim Luce, *Exec VP*
Johnny Mikell, *Senior VP*
▲ **EMP:** 50
SQ FT: 75,000
SALES (est): 104.5MM **Privately Held**
WEB: www.amneal.com
SIC: 2834 5122 Pharmaceutical preparations; pharmaceuticals

(G-1507)
GEOTECH ASSOCIATES LTD
20 Stiriz Rd (11719-9717)
PHONE 631 286-0251
Fax: 631 286-6313
Michael Verruto Jr, *President*
Linda Billski, *Bookkeeper*
EMP: 6
SQ FT: 1,500
SALES: 600K **Privately Held**
SIC: 3272 Concrete stuctural support & building material

(G-1508)
LONG ISLAND PRECAST INC
20 Stiriz Rd (11719-9717)
PHONE 631 286-0240
Fax: 631 286-6316
Michael Verruto, *Ch of Bd*
Dan Lambertson, *Sales Engr*
EMP: 30
SQ FT: 1,500
SALES (est): 6.1MM **Privately Held**
WEB: www.li-precast.com
SIC: 3272 Concrete products, precast

(G-1509)
SALSBURG DIMENSIONAL STONE
18 Pine St (11719-9409)
PHONE 631 653-6790
Fax: 631 653-3317
Jay Salsburg, *President*

▲ = Import ▼ = Export
◆ = Import/Export

Brooklyn
Kings County

EMP: 11
SALES (est): 1MM **Privately Held**
SIC: **3281** Marble, building: cut & shaped; granite, cut & shaped

(G-1510)
12PT PRINTING LLC
2053 E 1st St (11223-4026)
PHONE..................................718 376-2120
Joseph Sutton, *Owner*
EMP: 5 EST: 2014
SALES (est): 205.1K **Privately Held**
SIC: **2752** Commercial printing, lithographic

(G-1511)
16 TONS INC
27 Knickerbocker Ave (11237-1409)
PHONE..................................718 418-8446
Fax: 718 418-8447
David Goltl, *CEO*
EMP: 20
SQ FT: 16,000
SALES (est): 3.3MM **Privately Held**
WEB: www.16tons.net
SIC: **2541** Display fixtures, wood; store & office display cases & fixtures

(G-1512)
212KIDDISH INC
168 Spencer St (11205-3929)
PHONE..................................718 705-7227
Nachum Weberman, *President*
EMP: 5 EST: 2010
SALES (est): 344K **Privately Held**
SIC: **2099** 5149 2052 Food preparations; cookies; cookies

(G-1513)
2P AGENCY USA INC
1674 E 22nd St Apt 3a (11229-1534)
PHONE..................................212 203-5586
Robert Azaryev, *CEO*
Anton Cosenco, *Director*
EMP: 2
SQ FT: 1,000
SALES (est): 29.5MM
SALES (corp-wide): 221.1MM **Privately Held**
SIC: **3663** 5999 Mobile communication equipment; mobile telephones & equipment
PA: 2p Commercial Agency S.R.O.
U Zvonarky 291/3
Praha - Vinohrady

(G-1514)
3PHASE INDUSTRIES LLC
Also Called: Token
481 Van Buren St Unit 9a (11221-3046)
PHONE..................................347 763-2942
ABI Scholz, *Manager*
Will Kavesh,
Nicole Cornell,
EMP: 6 EST: 2007
SQ FT: 4,000
SALES: 500K **Privately Held**
SIC: **2522** 2519 Office furniture, except wood; household furniture, except wood or metal: upholstered

(G-1515)
3RD AVENUE DOUGHNUT INC
7111 3rd Ave (11209-1308)
PHONE..................................718 748-3294
Ahmesh Bratea, *President*
EMP: 10
SALES (est): 505.5K **Privately Held**
SIC: **2051** Doughnuts, except frozen

(G-1516)
3V COMPANY INC
Also Called: Three V
110 Bridge St Ste 3 (11201-1575)
PHONE..................................718 858-7333
Fax: 718 858-7371
Clara Crombo, *CEO*
Sam Gombo, *President*
Dan Gombo, *Vice Pres*
Tommy Marieno, *Production*
Harrison Gombo, *Manager*
EMP: 47
SQ FT: 22,000
SALES (est): 7.7MM **Privately Held**
WEB: www.threev.com
SIC: **2087** 2834 2099 2086 Syrups, flavoring (except drink); pharmaceutical preparations; food preparations; bottled & canned soft drinks

(G-1517)
40 STREET BAKING INC
8617 17th Ave (11214-3601)
PHONE..................................212 683-4700
Mohammed Irfan,
EMP: 8
SALES (est): 467.5K **Privately Held**
SIC: **2051** Bread, cake & related products

(G-1518)
461 NEW LOTS AVENUE LLC
461 New Lots Ave (11207-6411)
P.O. Box 20540 (11202-0540)
PHONE..................................347 303-9305
Desmond R John Sr,
EMP: 6
SALES (est): 394.5K **Privately Held**
SIC: **2759** 7991 Commercial printing; spas

(G-1519)
5TH AVENUE PHARMACY INC
4818 5th Ave Ste 1 (11220-1936)
PHONE..................................718 439-8585
Avraham Pudel, *President*
EMP: 9
SALES (est): 1.2MM **Privately Held**
SIC: **2834** Pharmaceutical preparations

(G-1520)
6727 11TH AVE CORP
Also Called: Prestige Printing Company
6727 11th Ave (11219-5904)
PHONE..................................718 837-8787
Vincent Costanza, *President*
Luke Spano, *Vice Pres*
EMP: 10 EST: 1973
SQ FT: 3,200
SALES (est): 1.6MM **Privately Held**
SIC: **2752** 2759 Commercial printing, lithographic; offset & photolithographic printing; letterpress printing

(G-1521)
786 IRON WORKS CORP
50 Morgan Ave (11237-1605)
PHONE..................................718 418-4808
Fax: 718 418-4803
Baudin Canka, *President*
EMP: 5
SQ FT: 5,000
SALES (est): 736K **Privately Held**
SIC: **3446** Fences or posts, ornamental iron or steel

(G-1522)
888 PHARMACY INC
4821 8th Ave (11220-2213)
PHONE..................................718 871-8833
Larisa Golubets, *President*
EMP: 10 EST: 2012
SALES (est): 1.4MM **Privately Held**
SIC: **2834** Pharmaceutical preparations

(G-1523)
999 BAGELS INC
1410 86th St (11228-3408)
PHONE..................................718 915-0742
Stefano Mannino, *CEO*
Jaime Guli, *Manager*
Salvatore Mannino, *Director*
EMP: 8
SALES (est): 678.7K **Privately Held**
SIC: **2051** 5461 Bagels, fresh or frozen; bagels

(G-1524)
A & B FINISHING INC
401 Park Ave (11205-1406)
PHONE..................................718 522-4702
Fax: 718 624-4916
EMP: 40
SQ FT: 20,000
SALES: 800K **Privately Held**
SIC: **2253** 5199 2339 Knit Outerwear Mill Whol Nondurable Goods Mfg Women's/Misses' Outerwear

(G-1525)
A & L ASSET MANAGEMENT LTD
143 Alabama Ave (11207-2911)
PHONE..................................718 566-1500
Meir Akerman, *CEO*
Eugene Loevinger, *Admin Sec*
EMP: 150
SQ FT: 120,000
SALES (est): 12MM **Privately Held**
SIC: **3999** Candles

(G-1526)
A & L PEN MANUFACTURING CORP
145 12th St (11215-3818)
PHONE..................................718 499-8966
Fax: 718 499-5231
Angel L Martinez Sr, *President*
Felix Terrero, *Purch Agent*
Luz Martinez, *Treasurer*
Paul Richeer, *Controller*
Jerry Birkett, *Manager*
▲ EMP: 100
SQ FT: 27,000
SALES (est): 13.7MM **Privately Held**
WEB: www.aandlpen.com
SIC: **3951** Pens & mechanical pencils

(G-1527)
A & MT REALTY GROUP LLC
1979 Pacific St Fl 1 (11233-3803)
PHONE..................................718 974-5871
Aboubacar Tounkara, *Mng Member*
EMP: 10
SALES: 1MM **Privately Held**
SIC: **1389** 8741 Construction, repair & dismantling services; management services

(G-1528)
A & S ELECTRIC
952 Flushing Ave (11206-4720)
PHONE..................................212 228-2030
EMP: 7 EST: 2011
SALES (est): 1.2MM **Privately Held**
SIC: **3699** 1731 Mfg Electrical Equipment/Supplies Electrical Contractor

(G-1529)
A 3-D SIGNS & AWNINGS INC
6404 14th Ave (11219-5314)
PHONE..................................718 252-7575
Fax: 718 998-4686
Samuel Shosham, *President*
EMP: 6
SQ FT: 2,000
SALES: 800K **Privately Held**
SIC: **3993** 5999 Signs & advertising specialties; awnings

(G-1530)
A B C ELASTIC CORP
889 Metropolitan Ave (11211-2513)
PHONE..................................718 388-2953
Morris Freund, *President*
Herman Freund, *Admin Sec*
EMP: 8 EST: 1966
SQ FT: 10,000
SALES: 2MM **Privately Held**
SIC: **2221** Elastic fabrics, manmade fiber & silk

(G-1531)
A B S BRASS PRODUCTS INC
185 Moore St (11206-3707)
PHONE..................................718 497-2115
Fax: 718 458-0860
Mark Azerrad, *President*
EMP: 11
SQ FT: 6,000
SALES (est): 970K **Privately Held**
SIC: **3432** Plumbers' brass goods: drain cocks, faucets, spigots, etc.

(G-1532)
A G M DECO INC
305 Wallabout St 307 (11206-4325)
PHONE..................................718 624-6200
Leib Rosenberg, *Manager*
EMP: 15 **Privately Held**
SIC: **3442** Sash, door or window: metal
PA: A. G. M. Deco Inc.
741 Myrtle Ave
Brooklyn NY 11205

(G-1533)
A G M DECO INC (PA)
Also Called: Steiner Doors
741 Myrtle Ave (11205-3924)
PHONE..................................718 624-6200
Gabrielle Steiner, *President*
Jole Steiner, *General Mgr*
Eli Frid, *Manager*
Judy Friend, *Manager*
▲ EMP: 10
SQ FT: 2,000
SALES: 120MM **Privately Held**
SIC: **3442** Sash, door or window: metal

(G-1534)
A HEALTH OBSESSION LLC
2184 Mcdonald Ave (11223-3926)
PHONE..................................347 850-4587
Joseph Chehebar,
EMP: 30
SALES (est): 2.1MM
SALES (corp-wide): 9MM **Privately Held**
SIC: **2086** 5149 Fruit drinks (less than 100% juice): packaged in cans, etc.; beverages, except coffee & tea
PA: Jusbyjulie.Com Llc
2184 Mcdonald Ave
Brooklyn NY 11223
917 270-6040

(G-1535)
A TO Z KOSHER MEAT PRODUCTS CO
Also Called: Empire National
123 Borinquen Pl (11211)
PHONE..................................718 384-7400
Fax: 718 384-7403
Edward Weinberg, *President*
Karen Weinberg, *Manager*
EMP: 20
SQ FT: 20,000
SALES (est): 2.6MM **Privately Held**
SIC: **2011** Meat packing plants

(G-1536)
A VAN HOEK WOODWORKING LIMITED
71 Montrose Ave (11206-2005)
PHONE..................................718 599-4388
Andre Van Hoek, *President*
EMP: 5
SALES: 300K **Privately Held**
SIC: **2499** 5712 Decorative wood & woodwork; cabinet work, custom

(G-1537)
A&B IRON WORKS INC
137 Conover St (11231-1102)
PHONE..................................347 466-3193
Ashley Beygelman, *President*
Igor Kasner, *General Mgr*
Boris Beygelman, *Vice Pres*
EMP: 9
SQ FT: 30,000
SALES: 150K **Privately Held**
SIC: **3315** Fence gates posts & fittings: steel

(G-1538)
A-1 IRON WORKS INC
2413 Atlantic Ave (11233-3416)
PHONE..................................718 927-4766
Fax: 718 345-2958
Mario Palermo, *CEO*
Alberto Palermo, *President*
EMP: 6 EST: 1997
SQ FT: 4,000
SALES (est): 1.1MM **Privately Held**
SIC: **3312** Hot-rolled iron & steel products

(G-1539)
A-1 PRODUCTS INC
165 Classon Ave (11205-2636)
PHONE..................................718 789-1818
Fax: 718 789-7522
Imre David Kaufman, *President*
EMP: 9
SQ FT: 7,000
SALES (est): 1.3MM **Privately Held**
WEB: www.a1prepaid.com
SIC: **3111** 2789 3089 Cutting of leather; paper cutting; plastic processing

Brooklyn - Kings County (G-1540)

(G-1540)
A-1 SKULL CAP CORP
Also Called: A1 Skullcaps
1212 36th St (11218-2010)
PHONE.....................718 633-9333
Fax: 718 633-8028
Henny Blau, *President*
▲ EMP: 25
SALES (est): 1.3MM **Privately Held**
WEB: www.skullcap.com
SIC: 2353 5999 Hats & caps; religious goods

(G-1541)
A-ONE LAMINATING CORP
1636 Coney Island Ave 2b (11230-5808)
PHONE.....................718 266-6002
Fax: 718 265-2047
Sol Chaimovits, *CEO*
Reizel Chaimovits, *Admin Sec*
▲ EMP: 6
SALES: 3MM **Privately Held**
SIC: 2295 2621 2672 Laminating of fabrics; asphalt paper, laminated; coated & laminated paper

(G-1542)
A-ONE MOVING & STORAGE INC
1725 Avenue M (11230-5303)
PHONE.....................718 266-6002
EMP: 25
SQ FT: 35,000
SALES (est): 3.5MM **Privately Held**
SIC: 2295 2257 Mfg Coated Fabrics Weft Knit Fabric Mill

(G-1543)
A-PLUS RESTAURANT EQUIPMENT
623 Sackett St (11217-3116)
PHONE.....................718 522-2656
Alex Picav, *Principal*
▼ EMP: 8
SALES (est): 879.2K **Privately Held**
SIC: 2599 Carts, restaurant equipment

(G-1544)
A1 ORNAMENTAL IRON WORKS INC
61 Jefferson St (11206-6108)
PHONE.....................718 265-3055
Matt Barsily, *President*
EMP: 5
SALES (est): 386.2K **Privately Held**
SIC: 3446 Architectural metalwork

(G-1545)
AB FIRE INC
1554 61st St 11219-5431)
P.O. Box 230581 (11223-0581)
PHONE.....................917 416-6444
Ave Kay, *President*
EMP: 8
SALES (est): 667.8K **Privately Held**
SIC: 3711 Fire department vehicles (motor vehicles), assembly of

(G-1546)
ABC CHECK PRINTING CORP
544 Park Ave Ste 308 (11205-1647)
PHONE.....................718 855-4702
Joe Gold, *President*
EMP: 14
SQ FT: 3,000
SALES: 300K **Privately Held**
SIC: 2752 2782 Color lithography; bank checkbooks & passbooks

(G-1547)
ABETTER PROCESSING CORP
984 E 35th St (1210-3423)
PHONE.....................718 252-2223
EMP: 15
SALES (est): 919.1K **Privately Held**
SIC: 3471 Plating/Polishing Service

(G-1548)
ABLE ANODIZING CORP
1767 Bay Ridge Ave (11204-5016)
PHONE.....................718 252-0660
Brenda Clark, *Vice Pres*
Mary Di Nicola, *Treasurer*
EMP: 13
SQ FT: 8,000
SALES: 2.3MM **Privately Held**
SIC: 3471 Anodizing (plating) of metals or formed products

(G-1549)
ABLE NATIONAL CORP
49 Wyckoff Ave (11237-8001)
PHONE.....................718 386-8801
Fax: 718 456-4583
Abraham Katz, *President*
EMP: 20
SQ FT: 150,000
SALES (est): 4MM **Privately Held**
WEB: www.ablenational.com
SIC: 2675 3469 2891 Paper die-cutting; metal stampings; adhesives & sealants

(G-1550)
ACCURATE KNITTING CORP
1478 E 26th St (11210-5233)
PHONE.....................646 552-2216
Chajim Philip Franzos, *President*
EMP: 7
SQ FT: 5,800
SALES (est): 1.2MM **Privately Held**
SIC: 2253 Sweaters & sweater coats, knit

(G-1551)
ACCURATE PRECAST
1957 Pitkin Ave (11207-3305)
PHONE.....................718 345-2910
Fax: 718 345-2950
Fred Lermer, *Principal*
EMP: 18
SALES (est): 2MM **Privately Held**
SIC: 3272 Precast terrazo or concrete products

(G-1552)
ACCURATE SIGNS & AWNINGS INC
247 Prospect Ave Ste 2 (11215-8403)
PHONE.....................718 788-0302
Fax: 718 788-0315
Jim Coppersmith, *President*
EMP: 10
SQ FT: 4,000
SALES: 2MM **Privately Held**
SIC: 3993 Signs & advertising specialties

(G-1553)
ACME ARCHITECTURAL PRODUCTS
513 Porter Ave (11222)
PHONE.....................718 360-0700
Jack Teich, *President*
Buddy Martin, *Treasurer*
Jeff Ackner, *Manager*
EMP: 500 EST: 1924
SQ FT: 15,000
SALES (est): 25.4MM **Privately Held**
WEB: www.acmesteel.com
SIC: 3469 Spinning metal for the trade; stamping metal for the trade

(G-1554)
ACME ARCHITECTURAL PDTS INC (PA)
Also Called: Acme Architectural Walls
251 Lombardy St (11222-5516)
PHONE.....................718 384-7800
Fax: 718 384-1062
Jack Teich, *President*
Joel Licari, *Vice Pres*
Michael Teich, *Vice Pres*
Mark Teich, *Treasurer*
▲ EMP: 57
SQ FT: 250,000
SALES (est): 54MM **Privately Held**
WEB: www.acmearchitecturalwalls.com
SIC: 3442 3444 3446 Metal doors; sheet metalwork; partitions & supports/studs, including accoustical systems

(G-1555)
ACME PARTS INC
901 Elton St (11208-5315)
PHONE.....................718 649-1750
Allan Rodolitz, *President*
EMP: 26
SQ FT: 20,000
SALES (est): 3.3MM **Privately Held**
WEB: www.acmeparts.com
SIC: 3432 Plumbers' brass goods: drain cocks, faucets, spigots, etc.

(G-1556)
ACME SMOKED FISH CORP (PA)
30 Gem St 56 (11222-2804)
PHONE.....................954 942-5598
Fax: 347 586-0310
Eric Caslow, *Ch of Bd*
Mark Brownstein, *Vice Pres*
David Caslow, *Vice Pres*
Robert Caslow, *Vice Pres*
Eduardo Carbajosa, *CFO*
◆ EMP: 100
SQ FT: 70,000
SALES (est): 20.9MM **Privately Held**
WEB: www.acmesmokedfish.com
SIC: 2091 Fish, smoked; fish, cured

(G-1557)
ACTION RACK DISPLAY MFG
980 Alabama Ave (11207-8327)
PHONE.....................718 257-7111
Fax: 718 257-7171
Joseph Berkovitz, *President*
EMP: 12
SQ FT: 40,000
SALES (est): 1MM **Privately Held**
WEB: www.actionrack.com
SIC: 2653 5046 Corrugated & solid fiber boxes; store fixtures

(G-1558)
ACTIVE WORLD SOLUTIONS INC
Also Called: M/Wbe
609 Fountain Ave (11208-6006)
PHONE.....................718 922-9404
Fax: 718 922-9438
Alvaro Vazquez, *President*
Maria Vazquez, *Principal*
▲ EMP: 6
SALES (est): 696.9K **Privately Held**
SIC: 2759 2395 7389 Screen printing; embroidery & art needlework; advertising, promotional & trade show services

(G-1559)
ADAR MEDICAL UNIFORM LLC
307 Richardson St (11222-5709)
PHONE.....................718 935-1197
Mayer Teitelbauml, *Owner*
▲ EMP: 10
SALES (est): 891.5K **Privately Held**
SIC: 2337 2326 Uniforms, except athletic: women's, misses' & juniors'; medical & hospital uniforms, men's

(G-1560)
ADEL ROOTSTEIN (USA) INC
145 18th St (11215-5313)
PHONE.....................718 499-5650
Fax: 718 499-5583
Patty Marino, *Manager*
EMP: 42
SQ FT: 16,572
SALES (corp-wide): 133.1MM **Privately Held**
SIC: 3999 Mannequins
HQ: Adel Rootstein (Usa) Inc
205 W 19th St
New York NY
212 645-2020

(G-1561)
ADIR PUBLISHING CO
1212 36th St (11218-2010)
PHONE.....................718 633-9437
Matt Fef, *Owner*
EMP: 10
SALES: 910K **Privately Held**
WEB: www.a1skullcap.com
SIC: 2731 Books; publishing & printing

(G-1562)
ADRIATIC WOOD PRODUCTS INC
1994 Industrial Park Rd (11207-3335)
PHONE.....................718 922-4621
Fax: 718 922-4625
Anthony Grbic, *President*
John Grbic, *Vice Pres*
Paula Radushimsky, *Controller*
John Grisie, *CIO*
Miljenka Grbic, *Admin Sec*
▲ EMP: 38
SQ FT: 80,000
SALES (est): 4.5MM **Privately Held**
WEB: www.adriaticwood.com
SIC: 2431 Moldings, wood: unfinished & prefinished

(G-1563)
ADS-N-COLOR INC
20 Jay St Ste 530 (11201-8324)
PHONE.....................718 797-0900
Fax: 212 633-2743
Anthony Masi, *President*
Nicholas Masi, *Vice Pres*
EMP: 50
SQ FT: 5,000
SALES (est): 3.5MM **Privately Held**
SIC: 2752 Commercial printing, offset

(G-1564)
ADVANCE CHEMICALS USA INC
1230 57th St (11219-4523)
PHONE.....................718 633-1030
Heldon Eross, *President*
EMP: 4
SQ FT: 2,000
SALES (est): 1MM **Privately Held**
SIC: 3087 Custom compound purchased resins

(G-1565)
ADVANCED READY MIX CORP
239 Ingraham St (11237-1512)
PHONE.....................718 497-5020
Rocco Mancione, *President*
Maria Singh, *Manager*
EMP: 17
SALES (est): 2.8MM **Privately Held**
SIC: 3273 Ready-mixed concrete

(G-1566)
ADVANTAGE WHOLESALE SUPPLY LLC
172 Empire Blvd Brooklyn (11225)
PHONE.....................718 284-5346
Sarah Ahmaz, *Bookkeeper*
David Smetana,
EMP: 55
SALES (est): 10.2MM **Privately Held**
SIC: 3429 Manufactured hardware (general)

(G-1567)
AESTHONICS INC
Also Called: Remains Lighting
21 Belvidere St Fl 3 (11206-4501)
PHONE.....................646 723-2463
David Callegaros, *President*
▲ EMP: 100
SQ FT: 50,000
SALES (est): 15.9MM **Privately Held**
SIC: 3645 3646 Residential lighting fixtures; commercial indusl & institutional electric lighting fixtures

(G-1568)
AFRO TIMES NEWSPAPER
Also Called: New American
1195 Atlantic Ave (11216-2709)
P.O. Box 160397 (11216-0397)
PHONE.....................718 636-9500
Tom Watkins, *Owner*
▲ EMP: 10
SQ FT: 7,500
SALES (est): 341.1K **Privately Held**
WEB: www.newamerican.com
SIC: 2711 Newspapers

(G-1569)
AGE MANUFACTURERS INC
10624 Avenue D (11236-1910)
PHONE.....................718 927-0048
Fax: 718 832-0696
Yosel Avtzon, *President*
▲ EMP: 65 EST: 1958
SQ FT: 43,000
SALES (est): 6.2MM **Privately Held**
SIC: 3999 3131 2339 2337 Hair & hair-based products; footwear cut stock; trimmings (leather), shoe; scarves, hoods, headbands, etc.: women's; women's & misses' suits & coats

(G-1570)
AIR FLOW PUMP CORP
Also Called: Air Flow Pump Supply
8412 Foster Ave (11236-3205)
PHONE.....................718 241-2800

Joseph Weinstock, *President*
David Weinstock, *Vice Pres*
EMP: 8
SQ FT: 6,000
SALES: 1.5MM **Privately Held**
SIC: 3561 5084 Pumps & pumping equipment; water pumps (industrial)

(G-1571)
AIR SKATE & AIR JUMP CORP (PA)
Also Called: Solo
2208 E 5th St (11223-4827)
P.O. Box 7453, New York (10116-7453)
PHONE...................212 967-1201
Morris Tawil, *CEO*
EMP: 12
SALES: 6.2MM **Privately Held**
SIC: 3143 5139 Men's footwear, except athletic; footwear, athletic

(G-1572)
AJMADISON CORP
3605 13th Ave (11218-3707)
PHONE...................718 532-1800
Michael Gross, *Ch of Bd*
Matthew Ortiz, *Editor*
Robert Zuckerman, *CFO*
Shulamis Neuburger, *Accounts Mgr*
Jacob Dahan, *Sales Staff*
▼ **EMP:** 55
SALES (est): 17.3MM **Privately Held**
SIC: 3639 7389 Major kitchen appliances, except refrigerators & stoves;

(G-1573)
ALADDIN BAKERS INC (PA)
240 25th St (11232-1338)
PHONE...................718 499-1818
Fax: 718 788-5174
Joseph Ayoub, *President*
Maria Andrzejewski, *Production*
Ed Curran, *Production*
Cosmo Locriccihio, *Purch Mgr*
Don Guzzi, *Finance Dir*
EMP: 120
SALES (est): 23.3MM **Privately Held**
WEB: www.aladdinbakers.com
SIC: 2051 Bread, all types (white, wheat, rye, etc): fresh or frozen

(G-1574)
ALBERT KEMPERLE INC
890 E 51st St (11203-6736)
PHONE...................718 629-1084
Albert Kemperle, *Owner*
EMP: 25
SALES (corp-wide): 221.9MM **Privately Held**
SIC: 3465 Body parts, automobile: stamped metal
PA: Albert Kemperle, Inc.
8400 New Horizons Blvd
Amityville NY 11701
631 841-1241

(G-1575)
ALBEST METAL STAMPING CORP
1 Kent Ave (11249-1000)
PHONE...................718 388-6000
Alexander Fischer, *President*
Nathan Hirsch, *Corp Secy*
Yakov Fischer, *Vice Pres*
Martin Nussbaum, *Engineer*
Mark Knieberg, *Controller*
▲ **EMP:** 65
SQ FT: 120,000
SALES (est): 14.9MM **Privately Held**
WEB: www.albest.com
SIC: 3469 3364 3089 3496 Stamping metal for the trade; nonferrous die-castings except aluminum; casting of plastic; miscellaneous fabricated wire products; aluminum die-castings

(G-1576)
ALBRIZIO INC
Also Called: Albrizio Couture
257 Varet St Ste Mgmt (11206-3859)
PHONE...................212 719-5290
David Cicalese, *Chairman*
Ann Albrizio, *Executive*
EMP: 6
SALES (est): 657.5K **Privately Held**
SIC: 2353 Millinery

(G-1577)
ALDO FRUSTACCI IRON WORKS INC
165 27th St (11232-1624)
PHONE...................718 768-0707
Aldo Frustaci, *President*
Connie Giglio, *Office Mgr*
EMP: 10
SQ FT: 8,000
SALES (est): 710K **Privately Held**
SIC: 3446 3444 3441 Architectural metalwork; stairs, staircases, stair treads: prefabricated metal; sheet metalwork; fabricated structural metal

(G-1578)
ALDOS IRON WORKS INC
75 Van Brunt St (11231-1428)
PHONE...................718 834-0408
Fax: 718 243-2353
Enzo Frustaci, *President*
Fausto Frustaci, *Sales Mgr*
EMP: 7 **EST:** 1974
SQ FT: 2,700
SALES (est): 950K **Privately Held**
SIC: 3446 Architectural metalwork

(G-1579)
ALETA INDUSTRIES INC
40 Ash St (11222-1102)
PHONE...................718 349-0040
Fax: 718 349-3247
Zinovy Malinov, *President*
Michael Guitonowitz, *Vice Pres*
Alex Sandler, *Treasurer*
EMP: 18
SQ FT: 15,000
SALES (est): 2.8MM **Privately Held**
WEB: www.aletastjames.com
SIC: 3444 Sheet metalwork

(G-1580)
ALEXANDRA FERGUSON LLC
67 35th St Unit 1 (11232-2200)
PHONE...................718 788-7768
Alexandra Ferguson, *Mng Member*
EMP: 8
SALES (est): 630.7K **Privately Held**
SIC: 2392 Cushions & pillows

(G-1581)
ALEXIS BITTAR LLC (PA)
45 Main St Ste 725 (11201-1076)
PHONE...................718 422-7580
Fax: 718 422-7584
Alexis Bittar, *President*
Tara Kurobe, *Principal*
Natasha Moench, *Principal*
Sandy Clarke, *COO*
Lorraine Oddo, *Vice Pres*
▲ **EMP:** 175
SQ FT: 11,000
SALES (est): 61.3MM **Privately Held**
SIC: 3961 Costume jewelry

(G-1582)
ALGEMEINER JOURNAL INC
508 Montgomery St (11225-3023)
P.O. Box 250746 (11225-0746)
PHONE...................718 771-0400
Fax: 718 771-0308
Gershon Jacobson, *President*
Dovid Efune, *Managing Dir*
Sagy Braun, *Manager*
Astra Taylor, *Director*
EMP: 5
SALES (est): 300K **Privately Held**
WEB: www.algemeiner.com
SIC: 2711 Newspapers

(G-1583)
ALL AMERICAN CONCRETE CORP
239 Ingraham St (11237-1512)
PHONE...................718 497-3301
Fax: 718 497-3197
Walter Charles, *President*
Anne Kresse, *Vice Pres*
EMP: 4
SALES (est): 1.8MM **Privately Held**
SIC: 3271 Concrete block & brick

(G-1584)
ALL AMERICAN TRANSIT MIX CORP
46 Knickerbocker Ave (11237-1410)
PHONE...................718 417-3654
Catherine Manzione, *President*
Anne Kressi, *Office Mgr*
EMP: 9
SALES (est): 800K **Privately Held**
SIC: 3273 Ready-mixed concrete

(G-1585)
ALL IN AUDIO INC
5314 16th Ave Ste 83 (11204-1425)
P.O. Box 68, Monroe (10949-0068)
PHONE...................718 506-0948
Joe Feder, *Ch of Bd*
Debbie Kastow, *General Mgr*
Steve Silver, *Info Tech Mgr*
EMP: 19
SALES (est): 6.5MM **Privately Held**
SIC: 3651 Household audio & video equipment

(G-1586)
ALL OUT DIE CUTTING INC
49 Wyckoff Ave Ste 1 (11237-2650)
PHONE...................718 346-6666
Abraham Katc, *President*
EMP: 25 **EST:** 1980
SQ FT: 20,000
SALES (est): 1.9MM **Privately Held**
SIC: 3544 3469 2891 2675 Special dies & tools; metal stampings; adhesives & sealants; die-cut paper & board

(G-1587)
ALL UNITED WINDOW CORP
Also Called: ABC Showerdoors
85 Classon Ave 97 (11205-1401)
PHONE...................718 624-0490
Fax: 718 624-3070
Tommy Eng, *President*
Sherry Ing, *President*
EMP: 21
SQ FT: 10,000
SALES (est): 3.1MM **Privately Held**
WEB: www.allunitedwindow.com
SIC: 3442 5211 Storm doors or windows, metal; windows, storm: wood or metal

(G-1588)
ALLIED FOOD PRODUCTS INC
251 Saint Marks Ave (11238-3503)
PHONE...................718 230-4227
Ernest Stern, *President*
David Weill, *Marketing Mgr*
Laya Gross, *Manager*
▲ **EMP:** 10
SQ FT: 10,000
SALES (est): 1.1MM **Privately Held**
WEB: www.alliedfoodproducts.com
SIC: 2034 2024 Dried & dehydrated soup mixes; pudding pops, frozen; gelatin pops, frozen

(G-1589)
ALLIED SAMPLE CARD CO INC
140 58th St Ste 7a (11220-2524)
PHONE...................718 238-0523
Fax: 718 238-0696
Marc Trager, *President*
Thomas Firavanti, *Vice Pres*
EMP: 30 **EST:** 1938
SQ FT: 22,000
SALES: 1MM **Privately Held**
SIC: 2675 Cards, folders & mats: die-cut

(G-1590)
ALPHA INCORPORATED
265 80th St (11209-3611)
PHONE...................718 765-1614
Michael Gerovich, *Owner*
EMP: 5 **EST:** 2010
SALES (est): 377K **Privately Held**
SIC: 3089 Identification cards, plastic

(G-1591)
ALPHA KNITTING MILLS INC
41 Varick Ave Ste Mgmt (11237-1527)
PHONE...................718 628-6300
Fax: 718 628-0743
Rose Fuchs, *President*
Bernard Fried, *Corp Secy*
Alex Fried, *Vice Pres*
William Fried, *Vice Pres*
EMP: 15
SQ FT: 15,000
SALES (est): 1.2MM **Privately Held**
SIC: 2253 Knit outerwear mills

(G-1592)
ALPINE PAPER BOX CO INC
2246 Fulton St (11233-3306)
PHONE...................718 345-4040
Fax: 718 345-7039
Anthony Caggiano, *President*
Renate Caggiano, *Controller*
EMP: 30 **EST:** 1953
SQ FT: 15,000
SALES (est): 5MM **Privately Held**
SIC: 3499 2631 Boxes for packing & shipping, metal; paperboard mills

(G-1593)
ALTRONIX CORP
140 58th St Bldg A3w (11220-2521)
PHONE...................718 567-8181
Fax: 718 567-9056
Jonathan Sohnis, *Ch of Bd*
Alan Forman, *President*
Jacqueline Joseph, *General Mgr*
Matt Doumitt, *Vice Pres*
Beverly Kowara, *Purch Mgr*
◆ **EMP:** 100
SQ FT: 52,000
SALES (est): 32.1MM **Privately Held**
SIC: 3699 3625 5063 Security control equipment & systems; control equipment, electric; burglar alarm systems

(G-1594)
AMBER BEVER INC
8604 Avenue M 1 (11236-4918)
PHONE...................212 391-4911
Beverly Brown, *CEO*
Mark Brown, *President*
▲ **EMP:** 4
SQ FT: 1,500
SALES: 2MM **Privately Held**
SIC: 2339 Women's & misses' athletic clothing & sportswear

(G-1595)
AMBY INTERNATIONAL INC
1460 E 12th St (11230-6606)
PHONE...................718 645-0964
Ben Wallerstein, *President*
▲ **EMP:** 5
SALES (est): 740K **Privately Held**
SIC: 2673 Plastic bags: made from purchased materials

(G-1596)
AMCO INTL MFG & DESIGN INC
10 Conselyea St (11211-2202)
PHONE...................718 388-8668
Adam Milewski, *President*
Amanda Bey, *Manager*
EMP: 26
SALES: 950K **Privately Held**
SIC: 3691 Storage batteries

(G-1597)
AMERICAN ALMOND PDTS CO INC (PA)
103 Walworth St (11205-2807)
P.O. Box 5247, Parsippany NJ (07054-6247)
PHONE...................718 875-8310
Fax: 718 935-1505
Victor Frumolt, *President*
Patrick Holsgrove, *Plant Engr*
Warren Bendiner, *Manager*
▲ **EMP:** 77 **EST:** 1924
SQ FT: 23,000
SALES (est): 9MM **Privately Held**
SIC: 2087 2099 2068 Pastes, flavoring; almond pastes; salted & roasted nuts & seeds

(G-1598)
AMERICAN CRAFT JEWELERS INC (PA)
3611 14th Ave Ste 522 (11218-3750)
PHONE...................718 972-0945
Fax: 718 854-5727
Stanley Grimstein, *President*
EMP: 9
SQ FT: 2,000

Brooklyn - Kings County (G-1599)

SALES: 8MM **Privately Held**
SIC: 3911 Jewelry, precious metal

(G-1599)
AMERICAN DIES INC
37 Provost St (11222-1813)
PHONE 718 387-1900
Fax: 718 387-1110
Joel Lefkowitz, *President*
EMP: 14
SALES (est): 1.5MM **Privately Held**
SIC: 3544 Dies & die holders for metal cutting, forming, die casting

(G-1600)
AMERICAN INTL TRIMMING
80 39th S (11232-2604)
PHONE 718 369-9643
Fax: 718 369-9649
Tony Wu, *President*
▲ **EMP:** 6
SQ FT: 32,000
SALES (est): 537K **Privately Held**
WEB: www.aiglifeus.com
SIC: 3089 3496 Clothes hangers, plastic; garment hangers, made from purchased wire

(G-1601)
AMERICAN LEATHER SPECIALTIES
87 34th St Unit 1 (11232-2009)
PHONE 800 556-6488
Fax: 718 439-2481
Paul Weinberg, *President*
Jeff Weinberg, *General Mgr*
Alan Weinberg, *Corp Secy*
George Schuman, *Vice Pres*
Joel Weinberg, *Vice Pres*
▲ **EMP:** 100 **EST:** 1931
SQ FT: 70,000
SALES (est): 7.9MM **Privately Held**
WEB: www.americanleatherspecialties.com
SIC: 2399 5199 Pet collars, leashes, etc.: non-leather; pet supplies

(G-1602)
AMERICAN MTAL STMPING SPINNING
1 Nassau Ave (11222-3115)
PHONE 718 384-1500
Stephanie Esenberg, *President*
EMP: 15
SALES (est): 1.5MM **Privately Held**
SIC: 3469 Stamping metal for the trade; spinning metal for the trade

(G-1603)
AMERICAN PACKAGE COMPANY INC
Also Called: Ampaco
226 Franklin St (11222-1382)
PHONE 718 389-4444
Martin C Kofman, *President*
EMP: 40 **EST:** 1921
SQ FT: 120,000
SALES (est): 7.1MM **Privately Held**
SIC: 2652 3089 Setup paperboard boxes; boxes, plastic

(G-1604)
AMERICAN PRINT SOLUTIONS INC
561 President St (11215-1018)
PHONE 718 246-7800
Fax: 718 246-7830
Steven Klein, *Branch Mgr*
EMP: 25
SALES (corp-wide): 3.9MM **Privately Held**
SIC: 2752 Commercial printing, lithographic
PA: American Print Solutions Inc.
2233 Nostrand Ave Ste 7
Brooklyn NY 11210
718 208-2309

(G-1605)
AMERICAN PRINT SOLUTIONS INC (PA)
2233 Nostrand Ave Ste 7 (11210-3029)
PHONE 718 208-2309
Erica Braun, *President*
Isaac Braun, *Vice Pres*
Malki Lipshitz, *Treasurer*
Israel Izzy Braun, *Finance Dir*
Mark Lipschitz, *Admin Sec*
EMP: 5
SQ FT: 20,000
SALES (est): 3.9MM **Privately Held**
SIC: 2754 5112 Business forms: gravure printing; business forms

(G-1606)
AMERICAN SCIENTIFIC LTG CORP
Also Called: A S L
25 12th St Ste 4 (11215-8019)
PHONE 718 369-1100
Yaakov Singer, *President*
John Deola, *Manager*
Ben Leifer, *Manager*
Chaya Singer, *Manager*
▲ **EMP:** 25 **EST:** 1979
SQ FT: 25,000
SALES (est): 6MM **Privately Held**
WEB: www.asllighting.com
SIC: 3646 Commercial indusl & institutional electric lighting fixtures

(G-1607)
AMERICAN SHIP REPAIRS COMPANY
1011 38th St 13 (11219-1012)
PHONE 718 435-5570
Fax: 718 871-9050
Peter Gianopulos, *President*
Andy Vellios, *Director*
▲ **EMP:** 10 **EST:** 1952
SQ FT: 7,000
SALES (est): 1.8MM **Privately Held**
SIC: 3561 7699 Pumps & pumping equipment; industrial pumps & parts; pumps & pumping equipment repair

(G-1608)
AMERICAN WOOD COLUMN CORP
913 Grand St (11211-2785)
PHONE 718 782-3163
Fax: 718 387-9099
Thomas Lupo, *President*
EMP: 8 **EST:** 1916
SQ FT: 12,000
SALES (est): 920.7K **Privately Held**
SIC: 2431 3299 Woodwork, interior & ornamental; ornamental & architectural plaster work

(G-1609)
AMIRAM DROR INC (PA)
Also Called: Black Hound
226 India St (11222-1804)
P.O. Box 170, Short Hills NJ (07078-0170)
PHONE 212 979-9505
Amiram Dror, *President*
EMP: 16
SQ FT: 7,500
SALES: 1.8MM **Privately Held**
WEB: www.blackhoundny.com
SIC: 2051 2064 2066 2033 Bakery: wholesale or wholesale/retail combined; chocolate candy, except solid chocolate; chocolate bars, solid; chocolate candy, solid; fruits & fruit products in cans, jars, etc.; chocolate; canned goods: fruit, vegetables, seafood, meats, etc.; candy

(G-1610)
AMJ DOT LLC
Also Called: City Fashion, The
1726 E 7th St (11223-2216)
PHONE 718 775-3288
Assaf Joseth, *CEO*
Assaf Joseph, *CEO*
Ruth Elmann, *COO*
David Yakobov, *CFO*
Sara Joseph, *Manager*
▲ **EMP:** 7
SQ FT: 1,200
SALES (est): 3MM **Privately Held**
SIC: 2335 5621 Women's, juniors' & misses' dresses; women's clothing stores

(G-1611)
ANGEL-MADE IN HEAVEN INC
Also Called: 116 26 Street
116 26th St (11232-1405)
PHONE 718 832-4778
Fax: 718 832-9768
Morris Dahan, *President*
EMP: 9
SQ FT: 29,800
SALES (corp-wide): 1.2MM **Privately Held**
WEB: www.angelmih.com
SIC: 2339 Women's & misses' outerwear
PA: Angel-Made In Heaven, Inc.
525 Fashion Ave Rm 1710
New York NY 10018
212 869-5678

(G-1612)
ANIIWE INC
774 Rockaway Ave Apt 3k (11212-5830)
PHONE 347 683-1891
Tamaris King, *President*
Tiffany King, *Principal*
EMP: 5
SALES (est): 318.9K **Privately Held**
SIC: 3961 5139 2679 Bracelets, except precious metal; shoe accessories; wallboard, decorated: made from purchased material

(G-1613)
ANNE TAINTOR INC
Also Called: ATI
137 Montague St (11201-3548)
PHONE 718 483-9312
Anne Taintor, *President*
Nathan Janoff, *Vice Pres*
▲ **EMP:** 6
SALES (est): 643K **Privately Held**
WEB: www.annetaintor.com
SIC: 2771 2752 2678 7389 Greeting cards; post cards, picture: lithographed; poster & decal printing, lithographic; notebooks: made from purchased paper;

(G-1614)
ANNOINTED BUTY MINISTRIES LLC
1697 E 54th St (11234-3921)
P.O. Box 340437 (11234-0437)
PHONE 646 867-3796
Rachel Ineus, *CEO*
EMP: 5
SALES (est): 235.7K **Privately Held**
SIC: 2721 Periodicals

(G-1615)
APEX AIRTRONICS INC (PA)
2465 Atlantic Ave (11207-2346)
PHONE 718 485-8560
William Rosenblum, *President*
▲ **EMP:** 22 **EST:** 1948
SQ FT: 14,000
SALES (est): 2.4MM **Privately Held**
SIC: 3663 Radio broadcasting & communications equipment

(G-1616)
APEX REAL HOLDINGS INC
Also Called: Pak 21
1640 40th St Ste A (11218-5541)
PHONE 877 725-2150
Mark Loewy, *President*
Goldy Loewy, *Manager*
EMP: 8
SQ FT: 2,000
SALES (est): 95.6K **Privately Held**
WEB: www.pak21.com
SIC: 2392 Bags, garment storage: except paper or plastic film

(G-1617)
APOLLO WINDOWS & DOORS INC
1003 Metropolitan Ave (11211-2605)
PHONE 718 386-3326
Fax: 718 386-6060
Hang Hsin Cheng, *President*
Wen Tsui Ping, *Admin Sec*
EMP: 10
SQ FT: 20,000
SALES (est): 1MM **Privately Held**
WEB: www.apollowindows.com
SIC: 2431 Doors & door parts & trim, wood; windows & window parts & trim, wood

(G-1618)
APPLE BANK FOR SAVINGS
Also Called: Williamsburg Branch
44 Lee Ave (11211-7216)
PHONE 718 486-7294
EMP: 5
SALES (corp-wide): 2.2MM **Privately Held**
SIC: 3571 Personal computers (microcomputers)
HQ: Apple Bank For Savings
1395 Northern Blvd
Manhasset NY 11030
516 627-1800

(G-1619)
APPLE CORE ELECTRONICS INC
991 Flushing Ave (11206-4721)
PHONE 718 628-4068
Fax: 718 628-4082
Michael Arnold, *President*
Gregory Arnold, *Vice Pres*
EMP: 11
SQ FT: 4,000
SALES (est): 1.8MM **Privately Held**
SIC: 3669 5065 Intercommunication systems, electric; intercommunication equipment, electronic

(G-1620)
APPLIED MINERALS INC (PA)
55 Washington St Ste 301 (11201-1077)
PHONE 212 226-4265
Mario Concha, *Ch of Bd*
John F Levy, *Vice Ch Bd*
Andre Zeitoun, *President*
Christopher T Carney, *CFO*
Christopher Carney, *CFO*
▲ **EMP:** 32
SALES: 4MM **Publicly Held**
WEB: www.atlasmining.com
SIC: 1459 2816 Clays, except kaolin & ball; iron oxide pigments (ochers, siennas, umbers)

(G-1621)
APPSBIDDER INC
55 Clark St 772 (11201-2415)
PHONE 917 880-4269
Oladapo Ajayi, *CEO*
EMP: 5
SALES (est): 166.2K **Privately Held**
SIC: 7372 Prepackaged software

(G-1622)
APSCO SPORTS ENTERPRISES INC
Also Called: Abercrombie & Fitch
50th & 1st Ave Bldg 57 (11232)
PHONE 718 965-9500
Philip Livoti, *President*
Philip Di Pietro, *Vice Pres*
Christine De Chirico, *Controller*
Fran Di Pietro, *Accountant*
▲ **EMP:** 60 **EST:** 1968
SQ FT: 30,000
SALES (est): 8.2MM **Privately Held**
SIC: 2396 Screen printing on fabric articles

(G-1623)
ARCHITCTRAL DSIGN ELEMENTS LLC
52 Box St (11222-1150)
PHONE 718 218-7800
Alan Paulenoff, *Mng Member*
Tess Cross, *Manager*
EMP: 7
SALES: 850K **Privately Held**
SIC: 3083 Laminated plastics plate & sheet

(G-1624)
ARCHITECTURAL COATINGS INC
538 Johnson Ave (11237-1226)
PHONE 718 418-9584
Fax: 718 418-9587
Nick Comaianni, *President*
Daniel France, *Vice Pres*
Margaret Karnick, *Admin Sec*
EMP: 18
SALES: 1.2MM **Privately Held**
SIC: 3599 Machine & other job shop work

GEOGRAPHIC SECTION
Brooklyn - Kings County (G-1654)

(G-1625)
ARCTIC GLACIER NEWBURGH INC
335 Moffat St (11237-6408)
PHONE..................................718 456-2013
Vincent Losquadro, *Branch Mgr*
EMP: 6
SALES (corp-wide): 240.7MM **Privately Held**
SIC: 2097 Manufactured ice
HQ: Arctic Glacier Newburgh Inc.
225 Lake St
Newburgh NY 12550
845 561-0549

(G-1626)
ARES BOX LLC
63 Flushing Ave Unit 224 (11205-1073)
PHONE..................................718 858-8760
Mary Filippidis,
EMP: 85
SALES (est): 4.9MM **Privately Held**
SIC: 2671 Packaging paper & plastics film, coated & laminated

(G-1627)
ARES PRINTING AND PACKG CORP
Brooklyn Navy Yard Bldg (11205)
PHONE..................................718 858-8760
Mary Filippidis, *President*
Bob Filippidis, *Vice Pres*
George Filippidis, *Vice Pres*
Jerry Filippidis, *Vice Pres*
EMP: 125
SQ FT: 150,000
SALES (est): 16.6MM **Privately Held**
WEB: www.aresny.com
SIC: 2752 2653 Commercial printing, offset; corrugated & solid fiber boxes; boxes, corrugated: made from purchased materials; display items, corrugated: made from purchased materials

(G-1628)
ARIMED ORTHOTICS PROSTHETICS P (PA)
302 Livingston St (11217-1002)
PHONE..................................718 875-8754
Steven Mirones, *President*
Gary E Korbel, *COO*
Frank Murtaugh, *Director*
EMP: 14
SQ FT: 10,000
SALES (est): 3.7MM **Privately Held**
WEB: www.arimed.com
SIC: 3842 5661 5999 7251 Surgical appliances & supplies; shoes, orthopedic; orthopedic & prosthesis applications; shoe repair shop

(G-1629)
ARISTA STEEL DESIGNS CORP
788 3rd Ave (11232-1418)
PHONE..................................718 965-7077
Steve Viglis, *President*
Maria Holmeerg, *Office Mgr*
EMP: 5
SALES: 1,000K **Privately Held**
SIC: 3449 Bars, concrete reinforcing: fabricated steel

(G-1630)
ARISTOCRAT LIGHTING INC
104 Halleck St (11231-2100)
PHONE..................................718 522-0003
Leon Gross, *President*
Michael Gross, *Vice Pres*
EMP: 12 EST: 1983
SQ FT: 18,000
SALES (est): 1.5MM **Privately Held**
SIC: 3646 Commercial indusl & institutional electric lighting fixtures

(G-1631)
ARNOLDS MEAT FOOD PRODUCTS
274 Heyward St (11206-2994)
PHONE..................................718 384-8071
Fax: 718 963-2303
Sheldon Dosik, *President*
Jason Judd, *Vice Pres*
EMP: 25
SALES (est): 3.8MM **Privately Held**
SIC: 2013 Sausages from purchased meat

(G-1632)
AROMASONG USA INC
35 Frost St (11211-1202)
PHONE..................................718 838-9669
Sam Neustein, *President*
EMP: 10
SALES (est): 495.5K **Privately Held**
SIC: 2844 2099 Bath salts; seasonings & spices

(G-1633)
ART AND COOK INC
14 C 53rd St Fl 2 (11232)
PHONE..................................718 567-7778
Ester Harosh, *VP Opers*
Allan Ben, *Exec Dir*
▲ EMP: 15
SALES: 10MM **Privately Held**
SIC: 3229 Cooking utensils, glass or glass ceramic

(G-1634)
ART BEDI-MAKKY FOUNDRY CORP
227 India St Ste 31 (11222-1803)
PHONE..................................718 383-4191
Fax: 718 349-8998
Istvan Makky, *President*
EMP: 8
SQ FT: 7,500
SALES: 400K **Privately Held**
SIC: 3366 Castings (except die): bronze

(G-1635)
ART CRAFT LEATHER GOODS INC
1970 Pitkin Ave (11207-3329)
PHONE..................................718 257-7401
Bernard Kandler, *President*
Jo Kandler, *Sales Executive*
EMP: 15
SQ FT: 15,000
SALES (est): 1.6MM **Privately Held**
SIC: 3199 Leather garments

(G-1636)
ART DIGITAL TECHNOLOGIES LLC
85 Debevoise Ave (11222-5608)
PHONE..................................646 649-4820
Fax: 646 861-6580
Meryl Adler, *Controller*
Dan Bright,
EMP: 11
SALES (est): 1.2MM **Privately Held**
WEB: www.artdigitaltech.com
SIC: 2752 7336 Commercial printing, lithographic; commercial art & graphic design

(G-1637)
ARTEMIS STUDIOS INC
Also Called: Diane Artemis Studios
34 35th St Ste 2b (11232-2212)
PHONE..................................718 788-6022
Martin Kurant, *President*
Valerie Hennessy, *Office Mgr*
EMP: 70 EST: 1964
SQ FT: 30,000
SALES (est): 5MM **Privately Held**
WEB: www.artemisstudios.com
SIC: 3999 3645 Shades, lamp or candle; residential lighting fixtures

(G-1638)
ARTHUR GLUCK SHIRTMAKERS INC
871 E 24th St (11210-2821)
PHONE..................................212 755-8165
Fax: 212 758-0627
Michael Spitzer, *President*
EMP: 10
SALES (est): 1.5MM **Privately Held**
WEB: www.shirtcreations.com
SIC: 2321 Men's & boys' dress shirts

(G-1639)
ASA MANUFACTURING INC
3611 14th Ave (11218-3773)
PHONE..................................718 853-3033
Fax: 718 435-8486
Alex Klein, *President*
Sam Hershkovich, *Vice Pres*
EMP: 20
SQ FT: 4,000
SALES (est): 3.8MM **Privately Held**
WEB: www.par4shelters.com
SIC: 3915 Jewelry parts, unassembled

(G-1640)
ASAP RACK RENTAL INC
33 35th St5 (11232-2022)
PHONE..................................718 499-4495
David Fox, *President*
EMP: 7
SQ FT: 6,000
SALES: 969.3K **Privately Held**
SIC: 2542 3537 5051 5021 Garment racks: except wood; industrial trucks & tractors; pipe & tubing, steel; racks

(G-1641)
ASHLEY RESIN CORP
1171 59th St (11219-4909)
P.O. Box 190733 (11219-0733)
PHONE..................................718 851-8111
Nathan Freedman, *President*
Misem Moskobics, *Admin Sec*
▼ EMP: 5
SALES (est): 1.3MM **Privately Held**
WEB: www.ashleypoly.com
SIC: 2821 Plastics materials & resins

(G-1642)
ASPECT PRINTING INC
904 E 51st St (11203-6736)
PHONE..................................347 789-4284
Olga Belenkaya, *Ch of Bd*
Anatoly Fusman, *Manager*
EMP: 20
SALES (est): 3MM **Privately Held**
SIC: 2711 2759 Commercial printing & newspaper publishing combined; magazines: printing

(G-1643)
ASTRO LABEL & TAG LTD
5820 Fort Hamilton Pkwy (11219)
PHONE..................................718 435-4474
Sheldon Kustin, *President*
Lew Kustin, *Vice Pres*
Ellis Amies, *Admin Sec*
EMP: 5
SQ FT: 5,000
SALES: 600K **Privately Held**
SIC: 2759 Flexographic printing; tags: printing; labels & seals: printing

(G-1644)
ATAIR AEROSPACE INC
63 Flushing Ave Unit 262 (11205-1077)
PHONE..................................718 923-1709
Fax: 718 923-1733
Paul Casner Jr, *President*
Vlad Kopman, *CTO*
EMP: 17
SALES (est): 3.2MM **Privately Held**
WEB: www.extremefly.com
SIC: 3812 Aircraft/aerospace flight instruments & guidance systems

(G-1645)
ATALLA HANDBAGS INC
117 57th St (11220-2513)
PHONE..................................718 965-5500
Sami Atalla, *President*
EMP: 4 EST: 1978
SQ FT: 1,300
SALES: 1.1MM **Privately Held**
SIC: 3171 Handbags, women's

(G-1646)
ATELIER VIOLLET CORP
505 Driggs Ave (11211-2020)
PHONE..................................718 782-1727
Jean Paul Violiet, *President*
EMP: 6
SQ FT: 7,500
SALES (est): 778.7K **Privately Held**
WEB: www.ateliervioliet.com
SIC: 2511 5712 2499 Wood household furniture; custom made furniture, except cabinets; decorative wood & woodwork

(G-1647)
ATERES PUBLISHING & BK BINDERY
Also Called: Ateres Book Binding
845 Bedford Ave (11205-2801)
PHONE..................................718 935-9355
Fax: 718 935-9335
Sam Greenfield, *President*
Simon Pollak, *Sales Executive*
Joseph Greenfield, *Admin Sec*
▲ EMP: 14 EST: 1975
SQ FT: 20,000
SALES (est): 1.6MM **Privately Held**
SIC: 2789 2731 Bookbinding & repairing: trade, edition, library, etc.; book publishing

(G-1648)
ATLANTIC ELECTRONIC TECH LLC
Also Called: Atlantic Electronic Technology
285 5th Ave Apt 2b (11215-2421)
PHONE..................................800 296-2177
Absalam Ottafa,
▲ EMP: 5
SQ FT: 1,500
SALES: 500K **Privately Held**
SIC: 3699 Security control equipment & systems

(G-1649)
ATLANTIC STAIRS CORP
Also Called: Design Interiors
284a Meserole St (11206-2242)
PHONE..................................718 417-8818
Fax: 718 381-5501
Stanley Majkut, *President*
Elizabeth Wozniak, *Admin Sec*
EMP: 6
SQ FT: 3,000
SALES (est): 797.4K **Privately Held**
WEB: www.atlanticstairs.com
SIC: 2431 Doors & door parts & trim, wood; staircases, stairs & railings

(G-1650)
ATLAS COATINGS GROUP CORP (PA)
4808 Farragut Rd (11203-6612)
PHONE..................................718 469-8787
Ben Berman, *CEO*
Jeff Berman, *President*
Lance Berman, *Vice Pres*
EMP: 75 EST: 2001
SALES (est): 4.2MM **Privately Held**
SIC: 2851 5231 Paints & paint additives; paint

(G-1651)
ATTIAS OVEN CORP
Also Called: Cannon Co
926 3rd Ave (11232-2002)
PHONE..................................718 499-0145
Simon Attias, *President*
Carrie Gorelick, *Manager*
▲ EMP: 6
SQ FT: 5,000
SALES (est): 1MM **Privately Held**
WEB: www.attiasco.com
SIC: 3589 Commercial cooking & food-warming equipment

(G-1652)
AUDIBLE DIFFERENCE INC
Also Called: ADI
110 8th St (11215-3116)
PHONE..................................212 662-4848
Erich R Bechtel, *President*
EMP: 25 **Privately Held**
SIC: 3699 Electric sound equipment
PA: Audible Difference, Inc.
110 8th St
Brooklyn NY 11215

(G-1653)
AUDIBLE DIFFERENCE INC (PA)
Also Called: Audible Difference Lnc
110 8th St (11215-3116)
PHONE..................................212 662-4848
Erich R Bechtel, *President*
Levy Vargas, *Director*
EMP: 2
SALES (est): 2.8MM **Privately Held**
WEB: www.adigroup.net
SIC: 3699 Electric sound equipment

(G-1654)
AUDIO TECHNOLOGY NEW YORK INC
Also Called: Audiology
129 31st St (11232-1824)
PHONE..................................718 369-7528

Brooklyn - Kings County (G-1655)

Alan Safdiah, *Senior VP*
Charles Safdiah, *CFO*
Jamie Safdiah, *Director*
▲ **EMP:** 10
SQ FT: 30,000
SALES (est): 1.7MM **Privately Held**
SIC: 3651 Audio electronic systems

(G-1655)
AZURRX BIOPHARMA INC
760 Parkside Ave Ste 304 (11226-1784)
PHONE 646 699-7855
Edward J Borkowski, *Ch of Bd*
Johan M Spoor, *President*
Maged Shenouda, *CFO*
Daniel Dupret, *Security Dir*
EMP: 11
SQ FT: 687
SALES (est): 1.4MM **Privately Held**
SIC: 2834 Pharmaceutical preparations

(G-1656)
B & B SWEATER MILLS INC (PA)
1160 Flushing Ave (11237-1747)
PHONE 718 456-8693
Fax: 718 821-3150
Berl Biderman, *President*
Sol Biderman, *Corp Secy*
Joseph Cohen, *Accountant*
▲ **EMP:** 10 **EST:** 1954
SQ FT: 42,000
SALES (est): 975.4K **Privately Held**
SIC: 2253 5137 Sweaters & sweater coats, knit; sweaters, women's & children's

(G-1657)
B & K DYE CUTTING INC
245 Varet St (11206-3823)
PHONE 718 497-5216
EMP: 6
SQ FT: 5,000
SALES: 300K **Privately Held**
SIC: 2261 Dyeing & Cutting Materials

(G-1658)
B CAKE NY LLC
702 Washington Ave (11238-2264)
PHONE 347 787-7199
Miriam Milord, *Principal*
EMP: 8
SALES (est): 787.5K **Privately Held**
SIC: 2051 Cakes, pies & pastries

(G-1659)
B D B TYPEWRITER SUPPLY WORKS
6215 14th Ave (11219-5338)
PHONE 718 232-4800
Albert Brauner, *Owner*
EMP: 25 **EST:** 1948
SQ FT: 3,160
SALES (est): 1.3MM **Privately Held**
SIC: 2521 2752 Wood office furniture; commercial printing, lithographic

(G-1660)
BABY CENTRAL LLC
2436 Mcdonald Ave (11223-5231)
PHONE 718 372-2229
Mike Seda, *Principal*
EMP: 6 **EST:** 2007
SALES (est): 620K **Privately Held**
SIC: 2023 Baby formulas

(G-1661)
BACKSTAGE LLC (PA)
45 Main St Ste 416 (11201-1093)
PHONE 212 493-4243
James Reynolds, *President*
Pete Keeley, *Editor*
Melinda Loewenstein, *Editor*
Rebecca Welch, *Editor*
Michael Rieck, *Senior VP*
EMP: 21
SALES (est): 9.8MM **Privately Held**
SIC: 2721 Periodicals

(G-1662)
BAGGU
109 Ingraham St (11237-1205)
PHONE 347 457-5266
Emily Sugihara, *Owner*
EMP: 5 **EST:** 2010

SALES (est): 464K **Privately Held**
SIC: 2673 Plastic bags: made from purchased materials

(G-1663)
BANNER SMOKED FISH INC
2715 W 15th St (11224-2705)
PHONE 718 449-1992
Abraham A Attias, *Ch of Bd*
Eddie Flores, *Asst Controller*
Alan Levitz, *Admin Sec*
▲ **EMP:** 54
SQ FT: 20,000
SALES (est): 6.3MM **Privately Held**
SIC: 2091 Fish, smoked

(G-1664)
BAR FIELDS INC
2614 W 13th St (11223-5815)
PHONE 347 587-7795
Rose Ranna, *Ch of Bd*
Steve Jacobs, *General Mgr*
EMP: 10 **EST:** 2011
SALES (est): 526.4K **Privately Held**
SIC: 3728 Aircraft parts & equipment

(G-1665)
BARCLAY BROWN CORP
47 Lancaster Ave (11223-5533)
PHONE 718 376-7166
Gladys Hedaya, *President*
Maurice Hedaya, *Vice Pres*
EMP: 10
SALES (est): 848.2K **Privately Held**
WEB: www.barclaybrowncorp.com
SIC: 3161 3086 Satchels; packaging & shipping materials, foamed plastic

(G-1666)
BASE CONTAINER INC
Also Called: M. C. Container
180 Classon Ave (11205-2637)
PHONE 718 636-2004
Malka Katz, *President*
EMP: 12
SALES (est): 1MM **Privately Held**
SIC: 2631 5113 Container, packaging & boxboard; boxes & containers

(G-1667)
BASS OIL & CHEMICAL LLC
136 Morgan Ave (11237-1220)
PHONE 718 628-4444
Leonard Roz, *CEO*
EMP: 17
SALES (est): 1.5MM **Privately Held**
SIC: 1389 Oil & gas field services

(G-1668)
BASS OIL COMPANY INC
136 Morgan Ave (11237-1220)
PHONE 718 628-4444
Gregory Bass, *Ch of Bd*
EMP: 30
SQ FT: 28,000
SALES (est): 6.6MM **Privately Held**
SIC: 2899 5172 Antifreeze compounds; engine fuels & oils

(G-1669)
BATAMPTE PICKLE PRODUCTS INC (PA)
77 Brooklyn Terminal Mkt (11236-1511)
PHONE 718 251-2100
Fax: 718 531-9212
Barry Silberstein, *President*
Howard Silberstein, *Corp Secy*
Scott Silberstein, *Vice Pres*
Shimon Horowitz, *Office Mgr*
Mike Field, *Manager*
EMP: 60 **EST:** 1955
SQ FT: 12,000
SALES (est): 8.7MM **Privately Held**
SIC: 2035 5149 Pickles, vinegar; pickles, preserves, jellies & jams

(G-1670)
BATOR BINTOR INC
42 Delevan St (11231-1808)
PHONE 347 546-6503
Max Connolly, *President*
EMP: 10

SALES (est): 587.7K **Privately Held**
WEB: www.batorbintor.com
SIC: 2431 2541 1521 Windows & window parts & trim, wood; cabinets, lockers & shelving; general remodeling, single-family houses

(G-1671)
BAYIT HOME AUTOMATION CORP
2299 Mcdonald Ave (11223-4737)
PHONE 973 988-2638
Eliav Scaba, *CEO*
Marco Scaba, *Principal*
▲ **EMP:** 30
SQ FT: 180,000
SALES (est): 5.4MM **Privately Held**
SIC: 3651 Household audio & video equipment; video camera-audio recorders, household use; electronic kits for home assembly: radio, TV, phonograph

(G-1672)
BDB TECHNOLOGIES LLC
Also Called: Fingertech USA
768 Bedford Ave (11205-1508)
PHONE 800 921-4270
Norana Johar, *COO*
Henry Pang, *Technical Mgr*
Fazalina Zamidon, *Sales Mgr*
Nattalina Zainal, *Marketing Staff*
Hershey Goldstein, *Manager*
▲ **EMP:** 8
SQ FT: 1,200
SALES: 1MM **Privately Held**
SIC: 3699 Security control equipment & systems; security devices

(G-1673)
BEAST VAPES NYC
182 30th St (11232-1706)
PHONE 718 714-8139
Nelson Rivera Jr, *Principal*
EMP: 7 **EST:** 2015
SALES (est): 94.4K **Privately Held**
SIC: 3999 Cigar & cigarette holders

(G-1674)
BEDESSEE IMPORTS LTD
140 Varick Ave (11237-1219)
PHONE 718 272-1300
Fax: 718 628-7790
Verman Bedessee, *Branch Mgr*
EMP: 20
SALES (corp-wide): 14.5MM **Privately Held**
SIC: 2098 Noodles (e.g. egg, plain & water), dry
PA: Bedessee Imports Ltd
2 Golden Gate Crt
Scarborough ON M1P 3
416 292-2400

(G-1675)
BEDFORD DOWNING GLASS
220 Ingraham St Ste 2 (11237-1514)
P.O. Box 220015 (11222-0015)
PHONE 718 418-6409
Ingo Williams, *Owner*
▼ **EMP:** 9
SQ FT: 25,000
SALES: 605K **Privately Held**
SIC: 3229 5999 Glassware, art or decorative; art, picture frames & decorations

(G-1676)
BEIS MOSHIACH INC
744 Eastern Pkwy (11213-3409)
PHONE 718 778-8000
Menachem Hendel, *President*
Boruch Merkur, *Editor*
Naftoli Greenfield, *Admin Sec*
Rami Antian,
EMP: 35
SALES (est): 3.3MM **Privately Held**
SIC: 2759 Publication printing

(G-1677)
BELTRAN ASSOCIATES INC
1133 E 35th St Ste 1 (11210-4243)
PHONE 718 252-2996
Fax: 718 253-9028
Michael Beltran, *Ch of Bd*
Ichael Beltran, *Ch of Bd*
Michael R Beltran, *Ch of Bd*
Debbie Zarneski, *Manager*

Atanu Bose, *Technology*
EMP: 40
SQ FT: 10,000
SALES (est): 9.1MM **Privately Held**
WEB: www.beltranassociates.com
SIC: 3564 Air purification equipment

(G-1678)
BELTRAN TECHNOLOGIES INC
1133 E 35th St (11210-4243)
PHONE 718 338-3311
Michael R Beltran, *Ch of Bd*
Debbie Zarneski, *Admin Asst*
▲ **EMP:** 25
SALES (est): 4.9MM **Privately Held**
SIC: 3564 8711 Precipitators, electrostatic; engineering services

(G-1679)
BENCHMARK FURNITURE MFG
300 Dewitt Ave (11236-1912)
PHONE 718 257-4707
Fax: 718 257-4757
Sandy Marks, *President*
Russell Marks, *Treasurer*
Hal Levenstein, *Manager*
Arthur Dichiara, *Info Tech Mgr*
▲ **EMP:** 70
SQ FT: 50,000
SALES (est): 8.1MM **Privately Held**
WEB: www.benchmarkfurnituremfg.com
SIC: 2511 Wood household furniture

(G-1680)
BENNETT MULTIMEDIA INC
1087 Utica Ave (11203-5318)
PHONE 718 629-1454
David Newman, *President*
EMP: 10
SQ FT: 4,000
SALES (est): 870K **Privately Held**
SIC: 2752 Commercial printing, lithographic

(G-1681)
BENNETT PRINTING CORPORATION
1087 Utica Ave (11203-5390)
PHONE 718 629-1454
Fax: 718 451-1799
Lawrence Newman, *President*
David Newman, *Vice Pres*
Ellen Newman, *Treasurer*
EMP: 10
SQ FT: 5,800
SALES: 950K **Privately Held**
SIC: 2752 Commercial printing, lithographic

(G-1682)
BENSON MILLS INC
140 58th St Ste 7j (11220-2538)
PHONE 718 236-6743
Fax: 718 532-1406
Keith Levy, *CEO*
Gabriel Levy, *President*
Ralph Levy, *Vice Pres*
◆ **EMP:** 22
SQ FT: 5,000
SALES (est): 3.6MM **Privately Held**
SIC: 2299 Fabrics: linen, jute, hemp, ramie

(G-1683)
BENSON SALES CO INC
6813 20th Ave (11204-4504)
PHONE 718 236-6743
Fax: 718 236-6736
Gabriel Levy, *President*
Keith Levy, *Vice Pres*
EMP: 13 **EST:** 1962
SQ FT: 10,000
SALES: 2.9MM **Privately Held**
SIC: 2392 5023 5199 Tablecloths: made from purchased materials; linens, table; general merchandise, non-durable

(G-1684)
BERKMAN BROS INC
538 Johnson Ave (11237-1226)
PHONE 718 782-1827
Gerald R Berkman, *President*
▲ **EMP:** 21
SQ FT: 20,000

GEOGRAPHIC SECTION
Brooklyn - Kings County (G-1716)

SALES (est): 1.7MM **Privately Held**
WEB: www.berkmanbrothers.com
SIC: 3471 3479 Electroplating of metals or formed products; lacquering of metal products

(G-1685)
BEST BOILERS INC
2402 Neptune Ave (11224-2316)
P.O. Box 240607 (11224-0607)
PHONE.................................718 372-4210
Aaron Ganguli, *President*
Raymond Miele, *Treasurer*
EMP: 10
SALES (est): 869.8K **Privately Held**
WEB: www.bestboilers.com
SIC: 3433 Boilers, low-pressure heating: steam or hot water

(G-1686)
BEST MEDICAL WEAR LTD
21 Hall St (11205-1315)
P.O. Box 50221 (11205-0221)
PHONE.................................718 858-5544
Fax: 718 858-5545
Herman Schwartz, *CEO*
Gittel Schwartz, *President*
Naftuli Schwartz, *Vice Pres*
Jack Schwartz, *Manager*
▲ EMP: 8 EST: 1997
SALES (est): 2.5MM **Privately Held**
WEB: www.bestmedicalwear.com
SIC: 2326 Work uniforms; medical & hospital uniforms, men's

(G-1687)
BEST TOY MANUFACTURING LTD
43 Hall St Ste B1 (11205-1395)
PHONE.................................718 855-9040
Fax: 718 875-5934
Abraham Hammer, *President*
Angie Rempersad, *Bookkeeper*
▲ EMP: 15
SQ FT: 22,500
SALES (est): 2.3MM **Privately Held**
SIC: 3942 Stuffed toys, including animals

(G-1688)
BETTER FRESH CORP
41 Varick Ave (11237-1521)
PHONE.................................718 628-3682
Hamish McCall, *Finance Dir*
EMP: 5
SQ FT: 600
SALES (est): 169.2K **Privately Held**
SIC: 2087 Beverage bases

(G-1689)
BEVERAGE WORKS INCORPORATED
70 Hamilton Ave 8 (11231-1305)
PHONE.................................718 834-0500
Fax: 914 961-0597
Pat Mezzatesta, *Office Mgr*
Steve Dimario, *Manager*
EMP: 5
SALES (est): 474.4K **Privately Held**
SIC: 2086 Carbonated beverages, nonalcoholic: bottled & canned

(G-1690)
BEVERAGE WORKS NY INC
70 Hamilton Ave 8 (11231-1305)
PHONE.................................718 812-2034
Fax: 718 834-9526
Gerald Ponfigslione, *Principal*
EMP: 20
SALES (corp-wide): 56.2MM **Privately Held**
WEB: www.beverageworks.com
SIC: 2086 Bottled & canned soft drinks
PA: The Beverage Works Nj Inc
 1800 State Route 34 # 203
 Wall Township NJ 07719
 732 938-7600

(G-1691)
BEYOND VAPE ✪
602 Pacific St (11217-2008)
PHONE.................................917 909-1413
EMP: 7 EST: 2017
SALES (est): 94.4K **Privately Held**
SIC: 3999 Cigar & cigarette holders

(G-1692)
BIEN CUIT LLC
120 Smith St (11201-6217)
PHONE.................................718 852-0200
Alex Copeland, *Office Mgr*
David Golper, *Mng Member*
EMP: 41 EST: 2011
SALES: 3MM **Privately Held**
SIC: 2051 Bakery: wholesale or wholesale/retail combined

(G-1693)
BIG APPLE WELDING SUPPLY
236 47th St (11220-1010)
PHONE.................................718 439-3959
Vincent Pampillonia, *President*
EMP: 5
SALES (est): 691.7K **Privately Held**
SIC: 7692 Automotive welding

(G-1694)
BIGROW PAPER MFG CORP
Also Called: Bigrow Paper Product
930 Bedford Ave (11205-4502)
PHONE.................................718 624-4439
David Greenwald, *President*
▲ EMP: 10
SQ FT: 13,000
SALES (est): 1.4MM **Privately Held**
SIC: 2621 Business form paper; envelope paper

(G-1695)
BILLIE-ANN PLASTICS PKG CORP
360 Troutman St (11237-2614)
PHONE.................................718 497-3409
Toll Free:.................................888 -
Fax: 718 497-6095
William Rubinstein, *President*
Joan Rubinstein, *Vice Pres*
▲ EMP: 30
SQ FT: 15,000
SALES (est): 5.6MM **Privately Held**
WEB: www.billieannplastics.com
SIC: 3089 Plastic containers, except foam

(G-1696)
BILLING CODING AND PRTG INC
455 Grant Ave (11208-3056)
PHONE.................................718 827-9409
Omirta Rickheeram, *President*
EMP: 7
SALES (est): 673.1K **Privately Held**
SIC: 2752 Commercial printing, lithographic

(G-1697)
BINAH MAGAZINES CORP
207 Foster Ave (11230-2195)
PHONE.................................718 305-5200
Chanie Berger, *Marketing Staff*
Ruth Lichtenstein, *Manager*
EMP: 5
SALES (est): 598.5K **Privately Held**
SIC: 2721 Periodicals

(G-1698)
BINDLE AND KEEP
47 Hall St Ste 109 (11205-1315)
PHONE.................................917 740-5002
Fax: 718 935-0495
Daniel Friedman, *Owner*
EMP: 8 EST: 2013
SALES (est): 680K **Privately Held**
SIC: 2311 2337 Suits, men's & boys': made from purchased materials; women's & misses' suits & skirts

(G-1699)
BLACKBIRDS BROOKLYN LLC
Also Called: Four &TWenty Blackbirds
597 Sackett St (11217-3116)
PHONE.................................917 362-4080
Kathryn Morrissette, *Administration*
Emily Elsen,
Melissa Elsen,
EMP: 25
SALES (est): 890.1K **Privately Held**
SIC: 2051 Bakery: wholesale or wholesale/retail combined

(G-1700)
BLUE MARBLE ICE CREAM
220 36th St Unit 33 (11232-2405)
PHONE.................................718 858-5551
Jennie Dundas, *Owner*
Alexis Miesen, *Co-Owner*
Sarah Green, *Manager*
EMP: 12
SALES (est): 1.1MM **Privately Held**
SIC: 2024 Ice cream, bulk

(G-1701)
BLUE OCEAN FOOD TRADING LLC
154 42nd St (11232-3317)
PHONE.................................718 689-4291
Guo Wen Lin, *Mng Member*
EMP: 6
SALES (est): 445.5K **Privately Held**
SIC: 2091 Canned & cured fish & seafoods

(G-1702)
BLUE SKY PLASTIC PRODUCTION
305 Johnson Ave (11206-2804)
PHONE.................................718 366-3966
▲ EMP: 11
SALES (est): 1.5MM **Privately Held**
SIC: 3083 Plastic finished products, laminated

(G-1703)
BLUE STAR BEVERAGES CORP
1099 Flushing Ave (11237-1830)
PHONE.................................718 381-3535
Albert Shtainer, *Principal*
▲ EMP: 9
SALES (est): 921.2K **Privately Held**
SIC: 2086 Carbonated beverages, nonalcoholic: bottled & canned

(G-1704)
BLUEBERRY KNITTING INC (PA)
138 Ross St (11211-7705)
PHONE.................................718 599-6520
Phillip Werzberger, *President*
EMP: 2
SQ FT: 1,000
SALES (est): 2.2MM **Privately Held**
SIC: 2253 Sweaters & sweater coats, knit

(G-1705)
BNC INNOVATIVE WOODWORKING
555 Liberty Ave (11207-3109)
PHONE.................................718 277-2800
Hyman Cassuto, *Owner*
EMP: 10
SQ FT: 11,202
SALES (est): 1.1MM **Privately Held**
SIC: 2431 Millwork

(G-1706)
BNEI ARAM SOBA INC
Also Called: Community Magazine
1616 Ocean Pkwy (11223-2144)
PHONE.................................718 645-4460
Fax: 347 504-4246
Jack Cohen, *President*
AVI Selvman, *Opers-Prdtn-Mfg*
Jacob Savdie, *VP Sls/Mktg*
David Sitt, *Treasurer*
Max Sharp, *Controller*
EMP: 11
SQ FT: 8,000
SALES (est): 1.1MM **Privately Held**
WEB: www.communitym.com
SIC: 2721 Periodicals

(G-1707)
BODY BUILDERS INC
Also Called: Red Line Networx Screen Prtg
5518 3rd Ave (11220-2609)
PHONE.................................718 492-7997
Richard Baez, *Ch of Bd*
EMP: 6
SALES (est): 565.7K **Privately Held**
SIC: 2759 Commercial printing

(G-1708)
BOOKLINKS PUBLISHING SVCS LLC
55 Washington St Ste 253c (11201-1073)
PHONE.................................718 852-2116
Maria Villela, *President*
Jose Schettino, *Bd of Directors*
EMP: 6
SQ FT: 5,000
SALES: 2MM **Privately Held**
SIC: 2731 Textbooks: publishing only, not printed on site

(G-1709)
BOOKLYN ARTISTS ALLIANCE
37 Greenpoint Ave Ste C4 (11222-1553)
PHONE.................................718 383-9621
Bridget Elmer, *President*
Chris Wilde, *President*
Mark Wagner, *Treasurer*
EMP: 5
SALES (est): 319.1K **Privately Held**
WEB: www.booklyn.org
SIC: 2731 Books: publishing & printing

(G-1710)
BRACCI IRONWORKS INC
1440 Utica Ave (11203-6617)
PHONE.................................718 629-2374
Fax: 718 629-9101
Cory Bracci, *President*
Charlie Smith, *General Mgr*
Jonathan Bracci, *Vice Pres*
Vanessa Vargas, *Accounts Mgr*
Michael Bracci, *Admin Sec*
EMP: 10
SQ FT: 9,000
SALES: 1.6MM **Privately Held**
SIC: 3446 7692 Stairs, staircases, stair treads: prefabricated metal; welding repair

(G-1711)
BRAGLEY MFG CO INC
Also Called: Bragley Shipp Carrying Cases
924 Bergen St (11238-3301)
PHONE.................................718 622-7469
Neil Lurie, *President*
Vincent Lorello, *Vice Pres*
Leila Lurie, *Admin Sec*
Teabicha Jenkins, *Administration*
EMP: 50 EST: 1946
SQ FT: 20,000
SALES (est): 4.8MM **Privately Held**
WEB: www.bragleycases.com
SIC: 2441 3089 3161 Cases, wood; cases, plastic; luggage

(G-1712)
BRAZEN STREET LLC
734 Pennsylvania Ave (11207-6903)
PHONE.................................516 305-7951
Dr Ade Bushansky, *CEO*
Dr Tyrone Johnson, *CFO*
EMP: 50
SALES (est): 4.1MM **Privately Held**
SIC: 2082 Beer (alcoholic beverage)

(G-1713)
BRIDES INC
4817 New Utrecht Ave (11219-3042)
PHONE.................................718 435-6092
Hindy Werzberger, *Principal*
EMP: 5
SALES (est): 415.7K **Privately Held**
SIC: 2335 Bridal & formal gowns

(G-1714)
BRIDGE ENTERPRISES INC
544 Park Ave (11205-1600)
PHONE.................................718 625-6622
Sara Lev, *President*
EMP: 5
SALES (est): 415.9K **Privately Held**
SIC: 2732 Book music: printing & binding, not published on site

(G-1715)
BRIDGE FULFILLMENT INC
493 Flushing Ave Ste 19 (11205-5122)
PHONE.................................718 625-6622
Chaim Eigner, *Ch of Bd*
EMP: 3 EST: 2007
SQ FT: 500
SALES: 2MM **Privately Held**
SIC: 2759 Commercial printing

(G-1716)
BRIGHT WAY SUPPLY INC
6302 Fort Hamilton Pkwy (11219-5122)
PHONE.................................718 833-2882

Brooklyn - Kings County (G-1717)

Phillip Lee, *Ch of Bd*
▲ **EMP:** 15
SQ FT: 10,000
SALES (est): 1.8MM Privately Held
SIC: 3677 Transformers power supply, electronic type

(G-1717)
BRODER MFG INC
566 Johnson Ave (11237-1305)
P.O. Box 370182 (11237-0182)
PHONE..................718 366-1667
Fax: 718 386-9671
Martin Broder, *President*
▲ **EMP:** 6
SQ FT: 6,000
SALES (est): 440K Privately Held
SIC: 2392 5162 Tablecloths & table settings; plastics products

(G-1718)
BROOKLYN BABY CAKES INC
411 Hancock St (11216-2414)
PHONE..................917 334-2518
EMP: 5
SALES (est): 245.6K Privately Held
SIC: 2053 Frozen bakery products, except bread

(G-1719)
BROOKLYN BANGERS LLC
111 Atlantic Ave Ste 1r (11201-6726)
PHONE..................718 875-3535
Joseph Del Prete, *Mng Member*
Saul Bolton,
Ben Daitz,
EMP: 17
SQ FT: 1,800
SALES (est): 186.3K Privately Held
SIC: 2013 5147 Sausages & other prepared meats; meats & meat products

(G-1720)
BROOKLYN BREW SHOP LLC
20 Jay St Ste 410 (11201-8311)
PHONE..................718 874-0119
Stephen Valard,
▲ **EMP:** 12
SQ FT: 2,000
SALES: 3.5MM Privately Held
SIC: 3556 5084 Beverage machinery; industrial machinery & equipment

(G-1721)
BROOKLYN CASING CO INC
412 3rd St (11215-2882)
PHONE..................718 522-0866
Morris Klasbole *President*
EMP: 6
SALES (est): 410K Privately Held
SIC: 2013 Sausage casings, natural

(G-1722)
BROOKLYN CIRCUS (PA)
150 Nevins St (11217-2986)
PHONE..................718 858-0919
Ouigi Theordore, *Owner*
Isaac Muwaswes, *Store Mgr*
Ouigi Theodore, *Creative Dir*
EMP: 10
SALES (est): 760.7K Privately Held
SIC: 2752 Letters, circular or form: lithographed

(G-1723)
BROOKLYN CSTM MET FBRCTION INC
48 Prospect Park Sw (11215-5915)
PHONE..................718 499-1573
David Stanavich, *President*
EMP: 5
SALES (est): 498.4K Privately Held
SIC: 3499 Fabricated metal products

(G-1724)
BROOKLYN DENIM CO
85 N 3rd St (11249-3944)
PHONE..................718 782-2600
Frank Pizzurro, *Principal*
Marika Krudysz, *Manager*
EMP: 10
SALES (est): 980K Privately Held
SIC: 2211 2389 5651 Denims; apparel for handicapped; jeans stores

(G-1725)
BROOKLYN INDUSTRIES LLC
328 7th Ave (11215-4105)
PHONE..................718 788-5250
Lindsey Stamps, *Manager*
EMP: 8
SALES (corp-wide): 25.1MM Privately Held
SIC: 3999 Barber & beauty shop equipment
PA: Brooklyn Industries Llc
45 Main St Ste 413
Brooklyn NY 11201
718 801-8900

(G-1726)
BROOKLYN INDUSTRIES LLC
162 Bedford Ave Ste A (11249-1369)
PHONE..................718 486-6464
Fax: 718 943-1278
Vahap Avsar, *Branch Mgr*
EMP: 13
SALES (corp-wide): 25.1MM Privately Held
SIC: 3999 Barber & beauty shop equipment
PA: Brooklyn Industries Llc
45 Main St Ste 413
Brooklyn NY 11201
718 801-8900

(G-1727)
BROOKLYN INDUSTRIES LLC
206 5th Ave Ste 1 (11217-4431)
PHONE..................718 789-2764
EMP: 10
SALES (corp-wide): 25.1MM Privately Held
SIC: 3999 Barber & beauty shop equipment
PA: Brooklyn Industries Llc
45 Main St Ste 413
Brooklyn NY 11201
718 801-8900

(G-1728)
BROOKLYN JOURNAL PUBLICATIONS
Also Called: Brooklyn Heights Press
16 Court St 30 (11241-0102)
PHONE..................718 422-7400
Fax: 718 857-3291
John Dozier Hasty, *President*
EMP: 20
SALES (est): 1MM Privately Held
WEB: www.brooklyneagle.net
SIC: 2711 Newspapers

(G-1729)
BROOKLYN RAIL INC
99 Commercial St Apt 15 (11222-1081)
PHONE..................718 349-8427
Theodore Hann, *President*
Phong Bui, *Publisher*
Sara Christoph, *Managing Dir*
Corina Larkin, *Editor*
Chloe Wyma, *Assoc Editor*
EMP: 12
SALES (est): 751K Privately Held
WEB: www.brooklynrail.org
SIC: 2711 Newspapers

(G-1730)
BROOKLYN REMEMBERS INC
9201 4th Ave (11209-7065)
PHONE..................718 491-1705
Patrick Condon, *Admin Sec*
Lisa Deljanin, *Administration*
EMP: 17
SALES (est): 842K Privately Held
SIC: 3299 Architectural sculptures: gypsum, clay, papier mache, etc.

(G-1731)
BROOKLYN ROASTING WORKS LLC
45 Washington St (11201-1029)
PHONE..................718 855-1000
EMP: 5 Privately Held
SIC: 2095 Coffee extracts
PA: Brooklyn Roasting Works Llc
50 John St
Brooklyn NY 11201

(G-1732)
BROOKLYN SIGNS LLC
Also Called: Signs New York
6404 14th Ave (11219-5314)
PHONE..................718 252-7575
Tahir Salemi, *President*
EMP: 6
SQ FT: 1,200
SALES (est): 319.2K Privately Held
SIC: 3993 Letters for signs, metal; neon signs; displays & cutouts, window & lobby; name plates: except engraved, etched, etc.: metal

(G-1733)
BROOKLYN STORE FRONT CO INC
62 Throop Ave (11206-4307)
PHONE..................718 384-4372
Samuel Greenberg, *President*
EMP: 5
SQ FT: 5,000
SALES (est): 277.6K Privately Held
SIC: 3442 1542 Metal doors, sash & trim; store front construction

(G-1734)
BROOKLYN SWEET SPOT INC
366 Myrtle Ave (11205-2441)
PHONE..................718 522-2577
EMP: 5 **EST:** 2013
SALES (est): 302.2K Privately Held
SIC: 2051 Cakes, pies & pastries

(G-1735)
BROOKLYN VAPE
53 5th Ave (11217-2687)
PHONE..................917 336-7363
EMP: 7
SALES (est): 94.4K Privately Held
SIC: 3999 Cigar & cigarette holders

(G-1736)
BROOKLYN WINERY LLC (PA)
213 N 8th St (11211-2007)
PHONE..................347 763-1506
Fax: 347 763-1507
Pam Wroblewski, *Finance Mgr*
Rachel Sackheim, *Sales Dir*
Kara Taylor, *Sales Mgr*
Emily Dolan-Leach, *Social Dir*
Jessica Wittwer, *Social Dir*
EMP: 11
SALES (est): 2MM Privately Held
SIC: 2084 Wines, brandy & brandy spirits

(G-1737)
BSD ALUMINUM FOIL LLC
260 Hewest St (11211)
PHONE..................347 689-3875
Esther Klein, *President*
EMP: 25 **EST:** 2009
SQ FT: 100,000
SALES (est): 1.8MM Privately Held
SIC: 2621 3421 3353 Towels, tissues & napkins: paper & stock; table & food cutlery, including butchers'; aluminum sheet, plate & foil

(G-1738)
BUDD WOODWORK INC
54 Franklin St (11222-2089)
PHONE..................718 389-1110
Fax: 718 389-7712
Serafin Caamano, *President*
Belen Caamano, *Shareholder*
EMP: 15 **EST:** 1952
SQ FT: 14,000
SALES (est): 2.3MM Privately Held
SIC: 2499 Decorative wood & woodwork

(G-1739)
BUNA BESTA TORTILLAS
219 Johnson Ave (11206-2713)
PHONE..................347 987-3995
Francis Forgione, *Principal*
EMP: 6
SALES (est): 493.6K Privately Held
SIC: 2099 Tortillas, fresh or refrigerated

(G-1740)
BUPERIOD PBC
5414 6th Ave 2 (11220-3119)
PHONE..................917 406-9804
Vanessa Siverls, *CEO*

EMP: 5
SALES (est): 177.6K Privately Held
SIC: 2299 7389 Pads, fiber: henequen, sisal, istle;

(G-1741)
BUSHWICK KITCHEN LLC
630 Flushing Ave Fl 5 (11206-5026)
PHONE..................917 297-1045
Casey Elsas, *Mng Member*
Ped Barbeau,
EMP: 5
SQ FT: 1,400
SALES: 500K Privately Held
SIC: 2035 Seasonings & sauces, except tomato & dry

(G-1742)
BUSINESS DIRECTORY INC
Also Called: Community Directory
137 Division Ave Ste A (11211-8270)
PHONE..................718 486-8099
Shie Krausz, *President*
EMP: 10
SALES (est): 850K Privately Held
SIC: 2741 Telephone & other directory publishing

(G-1743)
BUST INC
Also Called: Bust Magazine
253 36th St Unit 3 (11232-2415)
P.O. Box 1016, New York (10276-1016)
PHONE..................212 675-1707
Laura Henzel, *President*
Debbie Stoller, *Vice Pres*
EMP: 5
SALES (est): 601.7K Privately Held
WEB: www.bust.com
SIC: 2721 Periodicals

(G-1744)
BYFUSION INC
350 Manhattan Ave Apt 104 (11211-2446)
PHONE..................347 563-5286
Gregory Gomory, *CEO*
Gregor Gomory, *CEO*
Heidi Kujawa, *COO*
Steve Rocco, *CFO*
EMP: 5
SALES (est): 228K Privately Held
SIC: 3559 Plastics working machinery

(G-1745)
C B S FOOD PRODUCTS CORP
770 Chauncey St (11207-1120)
PHONE..................718 452-2500
Fax: 718 452-2516
Bernard Steinberg, *Ch of Bd*
Chaim Stein, *President*
Phillip Shapiro, *Vice Pres*
EMP: 15 **EST:** 1939
SQ FT: 34,000
SALES (est): 5.9MM Privately Held
SIC: 2079 Cooking oils, except corn: vegetable refined; shortening & other solid edible fats

(G-1746)
C K PRINTING
267 41st St (11232-2811)
PHONE..................718 965-0388
Bo Chen, *Owner*
EMP: 7
SALES (est): 777.2K Privately Held
SIC: 2752 Commercial printing, lithographic

(G-1747)
CAB SIGNS INC
Also Called: Cab Plastics
38 Livonia Ave (11212-4011)
PHONE..................718 479-2424
Fax: 718 385-1187
Christopher Bayer, *President*
Charles Bayer, *Vice Pres*
EMP: 26
SQ FT: 14,000
SALES (est): 3.6MM Privately Held
WEB: www.cabplastics.com
SIC: 3993 Signs & advertising specialties

(G-1748)
CABEZON DESIGN GROUP INC
197 Waverly Ave (11205-3605)
PHONE..................718 488-9868

Kurt Lebeck, *President*
EMP: 7
SALES: 220K **Privately Held**
WEB: www.cabezondesign.com
SIC: 3446 7389 Architectural metalwork; business services

(G-1749)
CABINETS BY STANLEY INC
46 Hall St (11205)
PHONE 718 222-5861
Stanley Stryszowski, *CEO*
Lukasz Stryszowski, *Exec VP*
Tom Stryszowski, *Project Mgr*
EMP: 7
SALES (est): 517.2K **Privately Held**
SIC: 2434 Wood kitchen cabinets

(G-1750)
CALIPER ARCHITECTURE PC
67 Metropolitan Ave Ste 2 (11249-4038)
PHONE 718 302-2427
Stephen Lynch, *President*
EMP: 6
SALES (est): 509.1K **Privately Held**
WEB: www.caliperstudio.com
SIC: 3446 Architectural metalwork

(G-1751)
CALIPERSTUDIO CO
75 Scott Ave (11237-1320)
PHONE 718 302-2427
Steve Lynch, *President*
Jonathan Taylor, *Vice Pres*
Stephen Dunn, *Project Mgr*
Jackson Barry, *Prdtn Mgr*
Pavel Pepeliaev, *Manager*
EMP: 6
SALES (est): 1.2MM **Privately Held**
SIC: 3446 Architectural metalwork

(G-1752)
CAM FUEL INC
50 Commerce St (11231-1643)
PHONE 718 246-4306
Robert Petrillo, *Principal*
John Zambardi, *Vice Pres*
EMP: 6
SALES (est): 887.2K **Privately Held**
SIC: 2869 Fuels

(G-1753)
CAMEO METAL PRODUCTS INC
127 12th St (11215-3891)
PHONE 718 788-1106
Fax: 718 788-3761
Vito Di Maio, *Ch of Bd*
Antonio D Maio, *President*
Frank Spodnick, *General Mgr*
Anthony Di Maio, *Vice Pres*
Adolpho Polo, *Manager*
▲ **EMP:** 40
SQ FT: 48,988
SALES (est): 8.2MM **Privately Held**
WEB: www.cameometal.com
SIC: 3559 3469 Metal finishing equipment for plating, etc.; metal stampings

(G-1754)
CANARSIE COURIER INC
1142 E 92nd St 44 (11236-3698)
PHONE 718 257-0600
Fax: 718 272-0870
Donna Marra, *Publisher*
Sandra Greco, *Principal*
Catherine Rosa, *Business Mgr*
EMP: 10
SALES (est): 470K **Privately Held**
WEB: www.canarsiecourier.com
SIC: 2711 Newspapers

(G-1755)
CANDLE IN THE WINDOW INC
Also Called: Aura Essence
43 Hall St Ste C10 (11205-1393)
P.O. Box 230123, New York (10023-0003)
PHONE 718 852-5743
Marni Bouchardy, *Ch of Bd*
Barnard Bouchardy, *Manager*
▲ **EMP:** 16
SQ FT: 8,000
SALES (est): 1.1MM **Privately Held**
SIC: 3999 5199 Candles; candles

(G-1756)
CANNIZZARO SEAL & ENGRAVING CO
435 Avenue U (11223-4007)
P.O. Box 230304 (11223-0304)
PHONE 718 513-6125
Fax: 718 645-7296
Janet Cannizzaro, *President*
▲ **EMP:** 5
SQ FT: 1,200
SALES (est): 672K **Privately Held**
WEB: www.cannizzaroseal.com
SIC: 3953 5199 Embossing seals & hand stamps; gifts & novelties

(G-1757)
CAPITOL POLY CORP
101 Spencer St (11205-2805)
P.O. Box 270, Haverstraw (10927-0270)
PHONE 718 855-6000
Fax: 718 855-6800
Benny Green, *President*
EMP: 20
SALES (est): 2.4MM **Privately Held**
WEB: www.capitalpoly.com
SIC: 2673 Bags: plastic, laminated & coated

(G-1758)
CAPUTO BAKERY INC
Also Called: Caputo's Bake Shop
329 Court St Ste 1 (11231-4390)
PHONE 718 875-6871
John Caputo, *President*
Francis Tunzi, *Vice Pres*
EMP: 5
SQ FT: 2,000
SALES (est): 300K **Privately Held**
SIC: 2051 5461 Bakery: wholesale or wholesale/retail combined; bakeries

(G-1759)
CARDINAL TANK CORP
Also Called: Cardinal Boiler and Tank
700 Hicks St (11231-1823)
PHONE 718 625-4350
Fax: 718 852-4592
William J Weidmann, *President*
Joe Snow, *Manager*
Patricia Helmer, *Admin Asst*
EMP: 50
SQ FT: 31,000
SALES (est): 9.5MM **Privately Held**
WEB: www.cardinal-detecto.centralcarolinascale.com
SIC: 3443 Fuel tanks (oil, gas, etc.): metal plate

(G-1760)
CARECONNECTOR
177 Concord St Apt 2a (11201-2091)
PHONE 919 360-2987
Sima Pendharkar, *Principal*
EMP: 5 **EST:** 2015
SALES (est): 199.7K **Privately Held**
SIC: 7372 Business oriented computer software

(G-1761)
CARRY-ALL CANVAS BAG CO INC
1983 Coney Island Ave (11223-2328)
PHONE 718 375-4230
Fax: 718 375-4230
Michel Kraut, *President*
▲ **EMP:** 7
SQ FT: 3,800
SALES: 500K **Privately Held**
WEB: www.carryalibag.com
SIC: 3161 Traveling bags

(G-1762)
CARTER ENTERPRISES LLC (PA)
Also Called: Mil-Spec. Enterprises
4610 12th Ave (11219-2556)
PHONE 718 853-5052
Chaim Wolf, *Mng Member*
Sarah Tannbm, *Executive Asst*
▲ **EMP:** 40
SALES (est): 57.1MM **Privately Held**
WEB: www.carterny.com
SIC: 2389 Men's miscellaneous accessories

(G-1763)
CARTS MOBILE FOOD EQP CORP
Also Called: Cfe
113 8th St (11215-3115)
PHONE 718 788-5540
Fax: 718 788-4962
Jeno Rosenberg, *President*
Florence Rosenberg, *Corp Secy*
Dave Nader, *Exec VP*
David Nadler, *Sales Mgr*
Michelle Burstein, *Manager*
EMP: 22
SQ FT: 15,000
SALES (est): 4.1MM **Privately Held**
WEB: www.cartsfoodeqp.com
SIC: 2599 3589 3556 Food wagons, restaurant; carts, restaurant equipment; commercial cooking & foodwarming equipment; food products machinery

(G-1764)
CASA COLLECTION INC
106 Ferris St (11231-1066)
PHONE 718 694-0272
Roberto Gil, *President*
EMP: 5
SALES (est): 480K **Privately Held**
WEB: www.casacollection.com
SIC: 2434 5712 Wood kitchen cabinets; juvenile furniture

(G-1765)
CASA INNOVATIONS INC
Also Called: Shredder Essentials
140 58th St Ste 5h-1 (11220-2525)
PHONE 718 965-6600
Aron Abramson, *CEO*
Charles Sued, *President*
▲ **EMP:** 6
SQ FT: 5,300
SALES (est): 810K **Privately Held**
SIC: 3678 Electronic connectors

(G-1766)
CATALINA PRODUCTS CORP (PA)
2455 Mcdonald Ave (11223-5232)
PHONE 718 336-8288
Fax: 718 375-9028
Victor Salama, *President*
Marie Mireille Salama, *Corp Secy*
Linda Reyzis, *Vice Pres*
Paul Yedin, *Vice Pres*
▲ **EMP:** 35 **EST:** 1968
SQ FT: 75,000
SALES (est): 2.1MM **Privately Held**
WEB: www.catalinabath.com
SIC: 2392 Shower curtains: made from purchased materials

(G-1767)
CCC PUBLICATIONS INC
12020 Flatlands Ave (11207-8203)
PHONE 718 306-1008
AR Bernard, *CEO*
Robin Hogan, *General Mgr*
Karen Bernard, *Vice Pres*
EMP: 8
SQ FT: 2,500
SALES: 600K
SALES (corp-wide): 7.5MM **Privately Held**
SIC: 2731 Book publishing
PA: Christian Cultural Center, Inc
 12020 Flatlands Ave
 Brooklyn NY 11207
 718 306-1000

(G-1768)
CELLULAR EMPIRE INC
Also Called: Pom Gear
2614 W 13th St (11223-5815)
PHONE 800 778-3513
Doris Mosseri, *President*
Steve Jacobs, *President*
EMP: 56
SQ FT: 8,500
SALES (est): 2MM **Privately Held**
SIC: 3629 Electronic generation equipment

(G-1769)
CELONIS INC
1820 Avenue M Unit 544 (11230-5347)
PHONE 941 615-9670
Alexander Rinke, *CEO*
EMP: 5
SALES (est): 196.7K **Privately Held**
SIC: 7372 Prepackaged software

(G-1770)
CERTIFIED HEALTH PRODUCTS INC
67 35th St Unit 12 (11232-2200)
PHONE 718 339-7498
Fax: 718 946-6727
Gene Kisselman, *President*
Steve Zeltser, *Vice Pres*
Denis Korablev, *QC Mgr*
EMP: 35
SQ FT: 12,000
SALES (est): 3.9MM **Privately Held**
SIC: 3069 Orthopedic sundries, molded rubber

(G-1771)
CHAIR FACTORY
1355 Atlantic Ave (11216-2810)
PHONE 718 363-2383
AB Bellsky, *Owner*
EMP: 50 **EST:** 1970
SALES (est): 4.5MM **Privately Held**
WEB: www.thechairfactory.com
SIC: 2531 5712 Chairs, table & arm; furniture stores

(G-1772)
CHAMBORD LLC
4302 Farragut Rd (11203-6520)
PHONE 718 859-1110
Daniel Faks, *President*
EMP: 20
SQ FT: 12,000
SALES (est): 1.3MM **Privately Held**
SIC: 2051 Bread, cake & related products

(G-1773)
CHAN & CHAN (USA) CORP
2 Rewe St (11211-1708)
PHONE 718 388-9633
EMP: 8
SALES (est): 569.6K **Privately Held**
SIC: 2099 3999 Food preparations; atomizers, toiletry

(G-1774)
CHAN KEE DRIED BEAN CURD INC
71 Steuben St (11205-2608)
PHONE 718 622-0820
Alex Luk, *President*
Tan Muneng Sing, *Principal*
Tran Van Track, *Principal*
EMP: 6
SQ FT: 1,000
SALES: 500K **Privately Held**
SIC: 2099 Tofu, except frozen desserts

(G-1775)
CHARLOTTE NEUVILLE DESIGN LLC
Also Called: Fashion Chef, The
882 3rd Ave (11232-1904)
PHONE 646 530-4570
Charlotte Neuville, *President*
EMP: 6
SQ FT: 2,000
SALES (est): 539.2K **Privately Held**
SIC: 2051 Cakes, bakery: except frozen

(G-1776)
CHEFS DELIGHT PACKING CO
94 N 8th St (11249-2802)
PHONE 718 388-8581
Bradford Karroll, *President*
Doug Karroll, *Vice Pres*
EMP: 13 **EST:** 1956
SQ FT: 3,000
SALES (est): 1.1MM **Privately Held**
SIC: 2011 Meat packing plants

(G-1777)
CHROMOSENSE LLC
1 Metrotech Ctr Fl 19 (11201-3949)
PHONE 347 770-5421
Filip Mlekicki, *COO*
EMP: 6
SALES (est): 79K **Privately Held**
SIC: 3826 Analytical instruments

Brooklyn - Kings County (G-1778)

(G-1778)
CIC INTERNATIONAL LTD
1118 42nd St (11219-1213)
P.O. Box 533, New York (10011)
PHONE..................212 213-0089
S G Fassoulis, *President*
David Ceja, *Exec VP*
James Chladek, *Vice Pres*
Robert Perry, *Vice Pres*
Larry Thompson, *Vice Pres*
EMP: 98
SQ FT: 14,656
SALES (est): 6.3MM **Privately Held**
SIC: 3812 3711 3482 3483 Aircraft/aerospace flight instruments & guidance systems; military motor vehicle assembly; small arms ammunition; ammunition components rocket launchers; helicopters

(G-1779)
CIDC CORP
Also Called: Ocs Industries
2015 Pitkin Ave (11207-3424)
PHONE..................718 342-5820
Henry Gutman, *President*
▲ **EMP:** 15
SALES (est): 1.8MM **Privately Held**
SIC: 2514 3433 Cabinets, radio & television: metal; heating equipment, except electric

(G-1780)
CITY COOLING ENTERPRISES INC
1624 61st St (11204-2109)
PHONE..................718 331-7400
Fax: 718 331-5524
Derick Pearlin, *President*
Joel Zuller, *CPA*
EMP: 8
SQ FT: 5,000
SALES (est): 760K **Privately Held**
SIC: 3444 1711 Sheet metalwork; heating & air conditioning contractors

(G-1781)
CITY OF NEW YORK
Also Called: HRA Poster Project
4014 1st Ave Fl 3 (11232-2700)
PHONE..................718 965-8787
David Hall, *Branch Mgr*
EMP: 30 **Privately Held**
WEB: www.nyc.gov
SIC: 2741 9199 Shopping news: publishing & printing; general government administration;
PA: City Of New York
City HI
New York NY 10007
212 788-3000

(G-1782)
CITY OF NEW YORK
Also Called: Department of Sanitation
5602 19th Ave (11204-2049)
PHONE..................718 236-2693
Jay Ryan, *Superintendent*
EMP: 117 **Privately Held**
WEB: www.nyc.gov
SIC: 2842 9511 Sanitation preparations; waste management program administration, government;
PA: City Of New York
City HI
New York NY 10007
212 788-3000

(G-1783)
CITY SIGNS INC
1940 Mcdonald Ave (11223-1829)
PHONE..................718 375-5933
Fax: 718 382-0876
Yehuda Mizrahi, *President*
Eyal Mizrahi, *Vice Pres*
Smadar Mizrahi, *Treasurer*
EMP: 5
SQ FT: 12,000
SALES (est): 655.3K **Privately Held**
WEB: www.citysignsinc.com
SIC: 3993 2399 5999 Signs & advertising specialties; neon signs; flags, fabric; awnings

(G-1784)
CITY SITES SPORTSWEAR INC (PA)
2421 Mcdonald Ave (11223-5230)
P.O. Box 230187 (11223-0187)
PHONE..................718 375-2990
Fax: 718 998-4112
Sui Tong MA, *President*
David Schwitzer, *Corp Secy*
▲ **EMP:** 24
SQ FT: 8,000
SALES (est): 2.6MM **Privately Held**
SIC: 2339 Sportswear, women's

(G-1785)
CLASSIC ALBUM
343 Lorimer St (11206-1998)
PHONE..................718 388-2818
Fax: 718 436-1650
Barry Himmel, *President*
EMP: 30
SQ FT: 12,500
SALES (est): 2.7MM **Privately Held**
SIC: 2782 7221 2789 2759 Blankbooks & looseleaf binders; photographic studios, portrait; bookbinding & related work; commercial printing

(G-1786)
CLASSIC ALBUM LLC
343 Lorimer St (11206-1998)
PHONE..................718 388-2818
Fax: 718 388-0214
Barry Himmel,
▲ **EMP:** 75 **EST:** 1952
SQ FT: 10,000
SALES (est): 9.3MM **Privately Held**
SIC: 2782 7221 Albums; photographic studios, portrait

(G-1787)
CLEANSE TEC
1000 Linwood St (11208-5320)
PHONE..................718 346-9111
Fax: 718 346-9133
Steven Feig, *President*
Bob Clark, *Senior VP*
Bruce Hittner, *Vice Pres*
Andy Feig, *Opers Staff*
Philip T Seng, *Controller*
EMP: 29
SQ FT: 14,000
SALES (est): 7.2MM **Privately Held**
WEB: www.soapman.com
SIC: 2841 2842 Detergents, synthetic organic or inorganic alkaline; specialty cleaning, polishes & sanitation goods

(G-1788)
CNV ARCHITECTURAL COATINGS INC
538 Johnson Ave (11237-1226)
PHONE..................718 418-9584
Nicola Comaianni, *President*
EMP: 6 **EST:** 2015
SQ FT: 10,000
SALES (est): 297.5K **Privately Held**
SIC: 3479 Metal coating & allied service

(G-1789)
CODA RESOURCES LTD (PA)
Also Called: Cambridge Resources
960 Alabama Ave (11207-8327)
PHONE..................718 649-1666
Hillel Tropper, *CEO*
Moshe Tropper, *Vice Pres*
Solomon Tropper, *Vice Pres*
Larry Lasher, *VP Opers*
Baruch Travitsky, *CFO*
▲ **EMP:** 86
SQ FT: 100,000
SALES (est): 34.9MM **Privately Held**
WEB: www.codaresources.com
SIC: 3469 2821 Metal stampings; molding compounds, plastics

(G-1790)
COLONIAL REDI RECORD CORP
1225 36th St (11218-2023)
PHONE..................718 972-7433
Fax: 718 972-7438
Joe Berkobits, *President*
EMP: 25
SQ FT: 12,000
SALES: 2.5MM **Privately Held**
SIC: 3993 Signs & advertising specialties

(G-1791)
COLUMBIA BUTTON NAILHEAD CORP
306 Stagg St 316 (11206-1702)
PHONE..................718 386-3414
Fax: 718 386-3881
Robert Matz, *President*
Charles J Matz Jr, *Corp Secy*
EMP: 17 **EST:** 1946
SQ FT: 20,000
SALES (est): 2.2MM **Privately Held**
SIC: 3965 Studs, shirt, except precious/semiprecious metal or stone; buttons & parts; buckles & buckle parts

(G-1792)
COMBOLAND PACKING CORP
2 Cumberland St (11205-1040)
PHONE..................718 858-4200
Marvin Eisenstadt, *President*
Ira Eisenstadt, *Vice Pres*
Tony Buccola, *Executive*
EMP: 99
SALES (est): 8.8MM **Privately Held**
SIC: 2869 Perfumes, flavorings & food additives

(G-1793)
COMFORT BEDDING INC
13 Christopher Ave (11212-8038)
PHONE..................718 485-7662
Fax: 718 485-7499
Mark Kohn, *President*
Moses Kohn, *Vice Pres*
Moses Weiner, *Sales Executive*
▲ **EMP:** 30 **EST:** 2000
SQ FT: 3,000
SALES (est): 4.9MM **Privately Held**
SIC: 2515 Mattresses & bedsprings

(G-1794)
COMMODORE MANUFACUTRING CORP
Also Called: Commodore Tool
3913 2nd Ave (11232-2707)
PHONE..................718 788-2600
Abraham Damast, *Branch Mgr*
EMP: 50
SALES (corp-wide): 22.2MM **Privately Held**
SIC: 3542 Machine tools, metal forming type
PA: Commodore Manufacutring Corporation
4312 2nd Ave
Brooklyn NY 11232
718 788-2600

(G-1795)
COMMUNITY NEWS GROUP LLC (PA)
Also Called: Bronx Times Reporter
1 Metrotech Ctr Fl 10 (11201-3949)
PHONE..................718 260-2500
Les Goodstein, *CEO*
Jennifer Goodstein, *President*
Ralph D'Onofrio, *VP Sales*
Cynthia Soto, *Office Mgr*
Eric Hercules, *Info Tech Dir*
EMP: 105
SQ FT: 14,000
SALES (est): 29.3MM **Privately Held**
SIC: 2711 Commercial printing & newspaper publishing combined

(G-1796)
CONFRTRNITY OF PRESCIOUS BLOOD
5300 Fort Hamilton Pkwy (11219)
PHONE..................718 436-1120
Fax: 718 854-6058
Susan Pergolizzi, *Principal*
Austin Bennett, *Director*
EMP: 8
SALES (est): 690K **Privately Held**
WEB: www.confraternitypb.org
SIC: 2731 Books: publishing only

(G-1797)
CONSUMER FLAVORING EXTRACT CO
921 Mcdonald Ave (11218-5611)
PHONE..................718 435-0201
Louis Fontana, *President*
Frank Biscello, *Executive*
EMP: 14 **EST:** 1962
SQ FT: 5,000
SALES (est): 1.9MM **Privately Held**
WEB: www.consumersflavoring.com
SIC: 2079 2087 Edible oil products, except corn oil; concentrates, flavoring (except drink)

(G-1798)
CONTINENTAL LATEX CORP
1489 Shore Pkwy Apt 1g (11214-6321)
PHONE..................718 783-7883
George Miller, *President*
EMP: 10 **EST:** 1953
SALES (est): 800K **Privately Held**
SIC: 3069 3089 Air-supported rubber structures; plastic processing

(G-1799)
CONTROL ELECTROPOLISHING CORP
109 Walworth St (11205-2897)
P.O. Box 50237 (11205-0237)
PHONE..................718 858-6634
Fax: 718 596-6127
Nancy Zapata, *President*
Manuel Acosta, *Safety Mgr*
Lina De-La-Cruz, *Office Mgr*
EMP: 15 **EST:** 1959
SQ FT: 7,000
SALES (est): 1.2MM **Privately Held**
SIC: 3471 Polishing, metals or formed products

(G-1800)
CONVERGENT MED MGT SVCS LLC
7513 3rd Ave (11209-3103)
PHONE..................718 921-6159
Anthony Pennacchio, *President*
EMP: 6
SALES (est): 614.7K **Privately Held**
SIC: 3674 Semiconductors & related devices

(G-1801)
COPY CAT
3177 Coney Island Ave A (11235-6443)
PHONE..................718 934-2192
Horace Bryan, *President*
Araceli Bryan, *Vice Pres*
EMP: 5 **EST:** 1977
SQ FT: 3,000
SALES (est): 415.2K **Privately Held**
SIC: 3647 Vehicular lighting equipment

(G-1802)
COPY CORNER INC
200 Division Ave (11211)
PHONE..................718 388-4545
Fax: 718 388-4949
Zalman Eizikovits, *President*
EMP: 5
SQ FT: 1,500
SALES (est): 410K **Privately Held**
SIC: 2754 2789 Commercial printing, gravure; bookbinding & related work

(G-1803)
CORNELL BEVERAGES INC
105 Harrison Pl (11237-1403)
PHONE..................718 381-3000
Helene Hoffman, *President*
Donna Hoffman, *Corp Secy*
Allen Hoffman, *Vice Pres*
EMP: 10
SALES (est): 890K **Privately Held**
WEB: www.cornellbev.com
SIC: 2086 Soft drinks: packaged in cans, bottles, etc.

(G-1804)
CORONET PARTS MFG CO INC (PA)
883 Elton St (11208-5315)
PHONE..................718 649-1750
Fax: 718 272-2956
Allan Rodolitz, *President*

GEOGRAPHIC SECTION
Brooklyn - Kings County (G-1834)

Jeffrey Rodolitz, *President*
Mark Silfen, *General Mgr*
Armand Salvati, *Sales Staff*
Joel Poretz, *Branch Mgr*
EMP: 20 **EST:** 1945
SQ FT: 15,000
SALES (est): 7.3MM **Privately Held**
WEB: www.coronetparts.com
SIC: 3432 5074 Plumbers' brass goods: drain cocks, faucets, spigots, etc.; plumbers' brass goods & fittings

(G-1805)
CORONET PARTS MFG CO INC
901 Elton St Fl 1 (11208-5315)
PHONE 718 649-1750
Joel Poretz, *Branch Mgr*
EMP: 20
SALES (corp-wide): 7.3MM **Privately Held**
WEB: www.coronetparts.com
SIC: 3432 Plumbers' brass goods: drain cocks, faucets, spigots, etc.
PA: Coronet Parts Mfg. Co. Inc.
 883 Elton St
 Brooklyn NY 11208
 718 649-1750

(G-1806)
COSMIC ENTERPRISE
147 Rockaway Ave Ste A (11233-3289)
PHONE 718 342-6257
Marjorie Thorne, *Owner*
EMP: 6
SALES (est): 320K **Privately Held**
SIC: 2833 5499 Drugs & herbs: grading, grinding & milling; health & dietetic food stores

(G-1807)
COUNTY ENERGY CORP
65 S 11th St Apt 1e (11249-7003)
PHONE 718 626-7000
David Rosner, *President*
Theresa Goihman, *Executive Asst*
EMP: 4
SALES: 20MM **Privately Held**
SIC: 1311 4911 Natural gas production; electric services

(G-1808)
COURIER PACKAGING INC
220 West St (11222-1350)
PHONE 718 349-2390
Fax: 718 349-2394
Isaac Markstein, *President*
Peter Sanabria, *Executive*
EMP: 25
SQ FT: 20,000
SALES (est): 4.9MM **Privately Held**
SIC: 2673 Plastic bags: made from purchased materials

(G-1809)
COURIER-LIFE INC
Also Called: Courier Life Publications
1 Metrotech Ctr (11201-3948)
PHONE 718 260-2500
Fax: 718 260-2592
Les Goodstein, *CEO*
Jennifer Goodstein, *President*
EMP: 218
SQ FT: 11,300
SALES (est): 11.6MM
SALES (corp-wide): 29.3MM **Privately Held**
WEB: www.courierlife.net
SIC: 2711 Newspapers: publishing only, not printed on site
PA: Community News Group Llc
 1 Metrotech Ctr Fl 10
 Brooklyn NY 11201
 718 260-2500

(G-1810)
CRAFT PACKAGING INC
1274 49th St Ste 350 (11219-3011)
PHONE 718 633-4045
Fax: 718 633-4046
Fhia Rothstein, *President*
Rothstein Shia, *Owner*
EMP: 5
SALES (est): 445K **Privately Held**
SIC: 2671 Packaging paper & plastics film, coated & laminated

(G-1811)
CREAM BEBE
694 Myrtle Ave Ste 220 (11205-3916)
PHONE 917 578-2088
Yossi Greenburg, *Owner*
EMP: 10 **EST:** 2012
SALES (est): 380K **Privately Held**
SIC: 2361 Shirts: girls', children's & infants'

(G-1812)
CREATIONS IN LUCITE INC
165 Franklin Ave Apt 5 (11205-2760)
PHONE 718 871-2000
Davin Rand, *President*
David Rand, *President*
Shaye Gross, *Vice Pres*
Brenda Gross, *Office Mgr*
EMP: 9
SALES: 150K **Privately Held**
WEB: www.creationsinlucite.com
SIC: 2821 Acrylic resins

(G-1813)
CREATIVE GOLD LLC
1425 37th St Ste 5 (11218-3771)
PHONE 718 686-2225
▲ **EMP:** 23 **EST:** 2003
SALES: 500K **Privately Held**
SIC: 3911 Manufacture Precious Metals

(G-1814)
CREATIVE SCENTS USA INC
183 Wilson St Ste 106 (11211-7578)
PHONE 718 522-5901
Adolf Kraus, *CEO*
EMP: 3
SALES: 2MM **Privately Held**
SIC: 2392 Household furnishings

(G-1815)
CREATIVE VAPE ✪
894 Wyckoff Ave (11237-6116)
PHONE 347 927-0982
EMP: 7 **EST:** 2017
SALES (est): 94.4K **Privately Held**
SIC: 3999 Cigar & cigarette holders

(G-1816)
CREPINI LLC
Also Called: Crepe Team, The
5600 1st Ave (11220-2550)
PHONE 347 422-0829
Paula Rimer, *CEO*
Charles Rabinovich, *President*
Tatyana Tom, *Marketing Mgr*
Eugene Tulman, *Officer*
Eric Shkolnik,
▲ **EMP:** 30
SQ FT: 12,000
SALES (est): 12MM **Privately Held**
WEB: www.crepini.com
SIC: 2024 5084 Ice cream & frozen desserts; dairy based frozen desserts; food product manufacturing machinery

(G-1817)
CREST LOCK CO INC
342 Herzl St (11212-4442)
PHONE 718 345-9898
Samuel Sheiman, *President*
▲ **EMP:** 15 **EST:** 1938
SQ FT: 20,000
SALES (est): 1.4MM **Privately Held**
WEB: www.crestlock.net
SIC: 3429 Luggage hardware

(G-1818)
CRITERION BELL & SPECIALTY
4312 2nd Ave (11232-3306)
PHONE 718 788-2600
Fax: 718 788-4071
Abraham Damast, *President*
Donald Damast, *Corp Secy*
Gary Damast, *Vice Pres*
EMP: 40
SQ FT: 30,000
SALES (est): 3.6MM **Privately Held**
SIC: 3499 3999 Novelties & specialties, metal; Christmas tree ornaments, except electrical & glass

(G-1819)
CROWN WOODWORKING CORP
583 Montgomery St (11225-3009)
PHONE 718 974-6415
Mendel Barber, *President*
EMP: 9
SALES (est): 350K **Privately Held**
SIC: 2431 Millwork

(G-1820)
CRUSADER CANDLE CO INC
325 Nevins St Ste 327329 (11215-1084)
PHONE 718 625-0005
Fax: 718 855-7195
Paul J Morra, *President*
◆ **EMP:** 28 **EST:** 1946
SQ FT: 14,500
SALES: 4.9MM **Privately Held**
SIC: 3999 Candles

(G-1821)
CT INDUSTRIAL SUPPLY CO INC
305 Ten Eyck St (11206-1724)
P.O. Box 60338 (11206-0338)
PHONE 718 417-3226
Charles Tolkin, *President*
Addy Gonanzalez, *Manager*
EMP: 10
SALES (est): 1MM **Privately Held**
SIC: 3089 Garbage containers, plastic

(G-1822)
CTAC HOLDINGS LLC
68 35th Street Brooklyn (11232)
PHONE 212 924-2280
Anthony Cirone, *President*
EMP: 20
SALES (est): 2.7MM **Privately Held**
SIC: 2066 Chocolate

(G-1823)
CUMBERLAND PACKING CORP (PA)
2 Cumberland St (11205-1000)
PHONE 718 858-4200
Fax: 718 260-9017
Steven Eisenstadt, *CEO*
Jeffrey Eisenstadt, *Principal*
Rob Bowen, *Exec VP*
Michael Briskey, *Exec VP*
Ira Eisenstadt, *Senior VP*
◆ **EMP:** 390
SQ FT: 13,000
SALES: 150MM **Privately Held**
WEB: www.cpack.com
SIC: 2869 Sweeteners, synthetic; flavors or flavoring materials, synthetic

(G-1824)
CURRICULUM ASSOCIATES LLC
55 Prospect St (11201-1497)
PHONE 978 313-1355
Stephanie Lawkins, *Manager*
EMP: 12
SALES (corp-wide): 61MM **Privately Held**
SIC: 2731 Book publishing
PA: Curriculum Associates, Llc
 153 Rangeway Rd
 North Billerica MA 01862
 978 667-8000

(G-1825)
CUSTOM FIXTURES INC
129 13th St (11215-4603)
PHONE 718 965-1141
Fax: 718 832-0448
Michael Lerich, *President*
Joseph Waknine, *Manager*
EMP: 9
SQ FT: 8,000
SALES (est): 960K **Privately Held**
WEB: www.customfixturesonline.com
SIC: 2542 Fixtures: display, office or store: except wood

(G-1826)
CUSTOM LAMPSHADES INC
Also Called: Creative Custom Shades
544 Park Ave Ste 503 (11205-1788)
P.O. Box 50186 (11205-0186)
PHONE 718 254-0500
Nachman Heller, *President*
EMP: 16 **EST:** 1979
SALES (est): 1.8MM **Privately Held**
SIC: 3645 5719 Lamp & light shades; lamps & lamp shades

(G-1827)
CUSTOM LUCITE CREATIONS INC
165 Franklin Ave Apt 5 (11205-2760)
PHONE 718 871-2000
David L Rand, *CEO*
EMP: 10
SALES (est): 816K **Privately Held**
SIC: 3089 Plastic processing

(G-1828)
CUSTOM WOOD INC
770 E 94th St (11236-1817)
PHONE 718 927-4700
Fax: 718 345-0341
James Campo, *President*
EMP: 8 **EST:** 1980
SQ FT: 3,200
SALES (est): 750K **Privately Held**
SIC: 2541 2431 Store fixtures, wood; woodwork, interior & ornamental

(G-1829)
D BEST SERVICE CO INC
Also Called: D Best Glass & Mirror
729 Church Ave (11218-3305)
PHONE 718 972-6133
William Omalley Jr, *President*
Grace Fradella O'Malley, *Admin Sec*
EMP: 7
SQ FT: 400
SALES (est): 947K **Privately Held**
SIC: 3429 1751 7699 Metal fasteners; window & door installation & erection; mirror repair shop

(G-1830)
D MALDARI & SONS INC
557 3rd Ave (11215-4600)
PHONE 718 499-3555
Fax: 718 499-6071
Chris Maldari, *President*
Daniel Maldari, *Vice Pres*
▲ **EMP:** 30 **EST:** 1902
SQ FT: 16,000
SALES (est): 5.3MM **Privately Held**
WEB: www.maldari.com
SIC: 3544 Extrusion dies

(G-1831)
D ORO ONOFRIO INC
1051 73rd St Apt 1 (11228-1939)
PHONE 718 491-2961
Onofrio Demattia, *President*
EMP: 5
SALES (est): 291.9K **Privately Held**
SIC: 3911 Jewelry, precious metal

(G-1832)
D V S IRON & ALUMINUM WORKS
117 14th St (11215-4607)
PHONE 718 768-7961
Fax: 718 369-6814
Louis Di Janic, *President*
Steve Janic, *Manager*
EMP: 9 **EST:** 1969
SQ FT: 1,000
SALES (est): 1.3MM **Privately Held**
SIC: 3446 Architectural metalwork; railings, prefabricated metal; fire escapes, metal; guards, made from pipe

(G-1833)
DADDARIO & COMPANY INC
Also Called: D'Addario & Company Inc
1000 Dean St Ste 410 (11238-3385)
PHONE 718 599-6660
EMP: 22
SALES (corp-wide): 210.7MM **Privately Held**
SIC: 3931 Musical instruments
PA: D'addario & Company, Inc.
 595 Smith St
 Farmingdale NY 11735
 631 439-3300

(G-1834)
DAHILL DISTRIBUTORS INC
975 Dahill Rd (11204-1738)
PHONE 347 371-9453
Hirsch Stengel, *President*
Yitty Stengel, *Office Mgr*
EMP: 8
SQ FT: 500

Brooklyn - Kings County (G-1835)

SALES: 300K **Privately Held**
WEB: www.filmart.com
SIC: 3699 5199 Electrical equipment & supplies; general merchandise, non-durable

(G-1835)
DAILY WEAR SPORTSWEAR CORP (FA)
2308 Mcconald Ave (11223-4739)
PHONE 718 972-0533
Isaac Abed, *President*
Joey Abed, *Vice Pres*
Michael Abed, *Vice Pres*
▲ EMP: 8
SQ FT: 20,000
SALES (est): 1MM **Privately Held**
SIC: 2339 Sportswear, women's

(G-1836)
DAIRY MAID RAVIOLO MFG (PA)
216 Avenue U Fl 1 (11223-3825)
PHONE 718 449-2620
Louis Ballarino, *President*
Salvatore Ballarino, *Vice Pres*
EMP: 10 EST: 1953
SQ FT: 4,000
SALES: 1.5MM **Privately Held**
WEB: www.dairymaidravioli.com
SIC: 2098 5499 Macaroni & spaghetti; macaroni products (e.g. alphabets, rings & shells), dry; spaghetti, dry; gourmet food stores

(G-1837)
DALY MEGHAN
78 5th Ave 11217-4647)
PHONE 347 699-3259
Meghan Daly, *Owner*
EMP: 10
SALES (est): 283.4K **Privately Held**
SIC: 2051 Eakery: wholesale or wholesale/retail combined

(G-1838)
DAMASCUS BAKERY INC
56 Gold St (11201-1297)
PHONE 718 855-1456
Fax: 718 403-0948
Edward Mafoud, *President*
David Mafouc, *Exec VP*
Peter Guerci, *Plant Mgr*
Rodolfo Toledo, *Safety Mgr*
Julio Llovet, *Opers Staff*
EMP: 140 EST: 1930
SQ FT: 20,000
SALES (est): 28.9MM **Privately Held**
WEB: www.damascusbakery.com
SIC: 2051 5149 Bread, cake & related products; bread, all types (white, wheat, rye, etc); fresh or frozen; bakery products

(G-1839)
DANET INC
Also Called: Russian Bazaar
8518 17th Ave Fl 2 (11214-2810)
PHONE 718 266-4444
Nathasha Shapiro, *President*
Anatoli Shapiro, *Vice Pres*
Margarita Shapiro, *Director*
EMP: 12
SALES (est): 490K **Privately Held**
WEB: www.danet.com
SIC: 2711 7319 Newspapers: publishing only, not printed on site; transit advertising services

(G-1840)
DAPPER DADS INC
45 Rochester Ave (11233-3011)
PHONE 917 903-8045
Mario Daniels, *President*
Geayse Williams, *Vice Pres*
EMP: 5
SALES (est): 227K **Privately Held**
SIC: 2741 7389 Miscellaneous publishing;

(G-1841)
DAS YIDISHE LICHT INC
66 Middleton St Apt 1 (11206-5088)
PHONE 718 387-3166
Mike Kraus, *President*
EMP: 5
SQ FT: 1,500

SALES (est): 290K **Privately Held**
SIC: 2711 Newspapers: publishing only, not printed on site

(G-1842)
DAVEL SYSTEMS INC
1314 Avenue M (11230-5206)
PHONE 718 382-6024
Fax: 718 336-4420
David Liberman, *President*
EMP: 6
SALES (est): 477.1K **Privately Held**
SIC: 7372 Prepackaged software

(G-1843)
DAWNEX INDUSTRIES INC
861 Park Ave (11206-7300)
PHONE 718 384-0199
Fax: 718 709-1331
EMP: 10
SALES (est): 600K **Privately Held**
SIC: 3089 Mfg Plastic Products

(G-1844)
DBG MEDIA
358 Classon Ave (11238-1306)
PHONE 718 599-6828
David Greaves, *Owner*
EMP: 8
SQ FT: 900
SALES (est): 230K **Privately Held**
WEB: www.ourtimepress.com
SIC: 2711 Newspapers: publishing only, not printed on site

(G-1845)
DE ANS PORK PRODUCTS INC (PA)
899 4th Ave (11232-2150)
PHONE 718 788-2464
Fax: 718 832-2817
Frank De Angelis, *President*
Anthony Gaglia, *Vice Pres*
Guy De Angelis, *Treasurer*
Guy Deangelis, *Treasurer*
Bernadette Petrella, *Office Mgr*
EMP: 20
SQ FT: 13,000
SALES (est): 4.5MM **Privately Held**
SIC: 2013 Sausages from purchased meat

(G-1846)
DEAN TRADING CORP
200 Junius St (11212-8103)
PHONE 718 485-0600
Robert Clemente, *Ch of Bd*
EMP: 18 EST: 1966
SQ FT: 20,000
SALES (est): 6.7MM **Privately Held**
SIC: 2299 Textile mill waste & remnant processing

(G-1847)
DECOR BY DENE INC
2569 Mcdonald Ave (11223-5995)
PHONE 718 376-5566
Fax: 718 375-3822
Michael Dene, *President*
Maurice Dene, *Corp Secy*
Joe Pentangello, *Manager*
EMP: 12
SQ FT: 10,000
SALES (est): 910K **Privately Held**
SIC: 3645 Residential lighting fixtures; wall lamps

(G-1848)
DECORATIVE NOVELTY CO INC
74 20th St (11232-1101)
PHONE 718 965-8600
Fax: 718 965-8600
Dr Leonard Feldman, *President*
Robert Notine, *Corp Secy*
Matt Notine, *Vice Pres*
Margret Hickey, *Manager*
▼ EMP: 10
SQ FT: 10,000
SALES (est): 760K **Privately Held**
WEB: www.decorativenovelty.com
SIC: 2391 5947 Curtains & draperies; draperies, plastic & textile: from purchased materials; party favors

(G-1849)
DELLET INDUSTRIES INC
1 43rd St Ste L8 (11232-2621)
PHONE 718 965-0101
Mike Brown, *Regional Mgr*
EMP: 16
SALES (est): 1.5MM **Privately Held**
SIC: 2599 Furniture & fixtures

(G-1850)
DELLS CHERRIES LLC
Also Called: Dell's Maraschino Cherries Co
175 Dikeman St Ste 177 (11231-1199)
PHONE 718 624-4380
Dana Bentz, *President*
Dominique Mondella, *Vice Pres*
EMP: 30
SQ FT: 30,000
SALES (est): 942.1K **Privately Held**
SIC: 2033 Maraschino cherries: packaged in cans, jars, etc.

(G-1851)
DELLS CHERRIES LLC
81 Ferris St (11231-1105)
PHONE 718 624-4380
Dana Bentz, *President*
EMP: 30
SQ FT: 17,540 **Privately Held**
WEB: www.dellscherry.com
SIC: 2033 Maraschino cherries: packaged in cans, jars, etc.

(G-1852)
DELTA METAL PRODUCTS CO INC
476 Flushing Ave (11205-1614)
P.O. Box 50239 (11205-0239)
PHONE 718 855-4200
Fax: 718 237-0979
Mark Beer, *President*
Nathan Mazurek, *Vice Pres*
EMP: 50
SALES (est): 6.3MM **Privately Held**
SIC: 3644 3643 Noncurrent-carrying wiring services; switch boxes, electric; electric switches; sockets, electric

(G-1853)
DELUXE TRAVEL STORE INC
Also Called: Deluxe Passport Express
5014 12th Ave (11219-3407)
PHONE 718 435-8111
Yitzchok Isaac Stern, *CEO*
EMP: 5
SALES (est): 282.8K **Privately Held**
SIC: 3161 3199 5099 Luggage; corners, luggage: leather; luggage

(G-1854)
DENVIN INC
6520 New Utrecht Ave (11219-5725)
PHONE 718 232-3389
Joseph Otranto, *President*
Vinny Mongelli, *Vice Pres*
Dennis Otranto, *Treasurer*
EMP: 50 EST: 1941
SQ FT: 16,000
SALES (est): 5MM **Privately Held**
WEB: www.empiresilver.com
SIC: 3914 Silversmithing

(G-1855)
DER YID INC
Also Called: DER YID PUBLICATION
84 Bay St (11231)
P.O. Box 110556 (11211-0556)
PHONE 718 797-3900
Fax: 718 797-1985
Moses Freidman, *Owner*
Aron Friedman, *Editor*
EMP: 35
SQ FT: 2,900
SALES (est): 1.7MM **Privately Held**
SIC: 2711 Newspapers

(G-1856)
DESIGNS BY ROBERT SCOTT INC
Also Called: Closet Systems Group, The
810 Humboldt St Ste 3 (11222-1913)
PHONE 718 609-2535
Fax: 718 609-2538
Robert S Feingold, *President*
Jason Kesselman, *Vice Pres*

EMP: 20
SQ FT: 16,000
SALES: 1.8MM **Privately Held**
WEB: www.robertscottinc.com
SIC: 2511 2521 2499 Wood household furniture; wood office furniture; kitchen, bathroom & household ware: wood

(G-1857)
DESKU GROUP INC
7206 7th Ave (11209-2617)
PHONE 646 436-1464
Kriste Desku, *President*
EMP: 8 EST: 2010
SQ FT: 5,000
SALES: 30MM **Privately Held**
SIC: 1241 Coal mining services

(G-1858)
DIANA KANE INCORPORATED
229 5th Ave Ste B (11215-7708)
PHONE 718 638-6520
Diana Kane, *President*
Tanya Lewellyl, *Accounts Mgr*
EMP: 5
SQ FT: 600
SALES: 500K **Privately Held**
WEB: www.dianakane.com
SIC: 3911 5094 Jewelry, precious metal; jewelry

(G-1859)
DIANE STUDIOS INC (PA)
34 35th St Ste 2b (11232-2212)
PHONE 718 788-6007
Fax: 718 499-7849
Martin Kurant, *President*
EMP: 55
SQ FT: 30,000
SALES (est): 4.9MM **Privately Held**
WEB: www.dianestudios.com
SIC: 3999 Shades, lamp or candle

(G-1860)
DIB MANAGMNT INC
Also Called: Airtech Lab
251 53rd St (11220-1716)
PHONE 718 439-8190
Rollads Dib, *President*
EMP: 10
SALES (est): 1.1MM **Privately Held**
SIC: 2869 Fuels

(G-1861)
DICK BAILEY SERVICE INC
Also Called: Dick Bailey Printers
25 Chapel St Ste 602 (11201-1916)
PHONE 718 522-4363
Fax: 718 522-4024
Richard Bailey, *President*
William Bailey, *Vice Pres*
EMP: 14
SALES (est): 2.1MM **Privately Held**
SIC: 2752 8111 Commercial printing, offset; legal services

(G-1862)
DIGIORANGE INC
Also Called: Shhhmouse
5620 1st Ave Ste 4 (11220-2519)
PHONE 718 787-1500
▲ EMP: 7
SALES (est): 222.9K **Privately Held**
SIC: 3577 Computer peripheral equipment

(G-1863)
DIGITAC INC (PA)
2076 Ocean Pkwy (11223-4045)
PHONE 732 215-4020
Jacob Elmann, *Ch of Bd*
▲ EMP: 15
SQ FT: 80,000
SALES (est): 2.5MM **Privately Held**
SIC: 3651 3089 3827 Video camera-audio recorders, household use; plastic kitchenware, tableware & houseware; spyglasses

(G-1864)
DIJIFI LLC
1166 Manhattan Ave # 100 (11222-1036)
PHONE 646 519-2447
Anthony Pinder, *Manager*
Jesse Crowder,
EMP: 11

GEOGRAPHIC SECTION
Brooklyn - Kings County (G-1893)

SALES (est): 1.1MM Privately Held
SIC: 2754 Photogravure printing

(G-1865)
DINETTE DEPOT LTD
Also Called: Dining Furniture
350 Dewitt Ave (11207-6618)
P.O. Box 696, Bay Shore (11706-0845)
PHONE..................516 515-9623
Walter Lustig, Partner
Barry Lustig, Partner
Salie Jagroop, Bookkeeper
▲ EMP: 75 EST: 1919
SQ FT: 60,000
SALES (est): 8.9MM Privately Held
SIC: 2511 Kitchen & dining room furniture

(G-1866)
DISPLAY PRESENTATIONS LTD
16 Court St Fl 14 (11241-1014)
PHONE..................631 951-4050
Fax: 631 951-4015
Stanley Zaneski, Ch of Bd
Fabian Zaneski, President
Stan Zaneski, Vice Pres
Mike Fabian, Marketing Staff
Lillian Mancuso, Manager
EMP: 52
SQ FT: 56,000
SALES (est): 6.1MM Privately Held
WEB: www.displaypresentations.net
SIC: 3993 Displays & cutouts, window & lobby

(G-1867)
DIVINE ART FURNITURE INC
43 Hall St Ste C9 (11205-1393)
PHONE..................718 834-0111
David Masarsky, President
EMP: 8
SQ FT: 6,000
SALES: 100K Privately Held
WEB: www.davineartwood.com
SIC: 2521 Wood office furniture

(G-1868)
DIXIE FOAM LTD
Also Called: Dixiefoam Beds
1205 Manhattan Ave # 311 (11222-6155)
PHONE..................212 645-8999
Fax: 212 691-3092
MD Taracido-Bram, President
Roger Wade, Sales Dir
EMP: 5 EST: 1971
SQ FT: 2,000
SALES: 600K Privately Held
WEB: www.dixiefoam.com
SIC: 2515 Mattresses, containing felt, foam rubber, urethane, etc.

(G-1869)
DLC COMPREHENSIVE MEDICAL PC
979 Fulton St (11238-2346)
P.O. Box 216, Old Westbury (11568-0216)
PHONE..................718 857-1200
Fax: 718 857-1222
Katie Cheng, Manager
EMP: 10 EST: 1997
SALES (est): 692K Privately Held
SIC: 2741 5961 Miscellaneous publishing; magazines, mail order

(G-1870)
DLX INDUSTRIES INC
Also Called: Columbia Seal N Sew
225 25th St (11232-1337)
PHONE..................718 272-9420
Fax: 718 522-6636
Martin Prince, President
Marc Stewart, Vice Pres
Mark Stuart, Manager
▲ EMP: 100 EST: 1950
SQ FT: 70,000
SALES (est): 14.5MM Privately Held
SIC: 3161 Attache cases; briefcases; cases, carrying

(G-1871)
DOLCE VITE INTERNATIONAL LLC
386 12th St (11215-5002)
PHONE..................713 962-5767
Christina Summers, Mng Member
EMP: 5 EST: 2015

SALES (est): 227.9K Privately Held
SIC: 2066 Chocolate

(G-1872)
DOMANI FASHIONS CORP
86 S 1st St (11249-4171)
PHONE..................718 797-0505
Fax: 718 875-8028
Moses Rosenberg, President
Benjamin Schlesinger, Vice Pres
▲ EMP: 9
SQ FT: 3,000
SALES (est): 840K Privately Held
SIC: 2369 2253 Girls' & children's outerwear; sweaters & sweater coats, knit

(G-1873)
DOMESTIC CASING CO
410 3rd Ave (11215-3179)
PHONE..................718 522-1902
Fax: 718 260-8291
Morris Klagsbald, Partner
Harold Klagsbald, Partner
▲ EMP: 6
SQ FT: 12,000
SALES (est): 1.9MM Privately Held
SIC: 2013 2011 Sausage casings, natural; meat packing plants

(G-1874)
DONNE DIEU
63 Flushing Ave Unit 112 (11205-1069)
PHONE..................212 226-0573
Susan Gosin, President
Lisa Switalski, Prdtn Mgr
Paul Wong, Treasurer
Kathleen Flynn, Exec Dir
Dona Warner, Director
EMP: 7
SQ FT: 5,000
SALES: 809.8K Privately Held
WEB: www.dieudonne.org
SIC: 2621 8999 7999 Art paper; artist's studio; arts & crafts instruction

(G-1875)
DOORTEC ARCHTCTURAL MET GL LLC
234 46th St (11220-1008)
PHONE..................718 567-2730
Boris Barskiy,
EMP: 27
SALES (corp-wide): 4.8MM Privately Held
SIC: 3444 Sheet metalwork
PA: Doortec Architectural Metal & Glass, L.L.C.
303 Martin St
River Vale NJ 07675
201 497-5056

(G-1876)
DOUBLE STAR USA INC
307 Kingsland Ave (11222-3708)
PHONE..................212 929-2210
Fax: 212 863-8901
Jean Chau, President
▲ EMP: 8
SQ FT: 4,500
SALES (est): 504.4K Privately Held
SIC: 1499 Gemstone & industrial diamond mining

(G-1877)
DOVELIN PRINTING COMPANY INC
43 Hall St Ste C2 (11205-1393)
PHONE..................718 302-3951
Fax: 718 599-4929
Stanley Darmachman, President
EMP: 12
SQ FT: 12,000
SALES (est): 970K Privately Held
SIC: 2752 Commercial printing, lithographic

(G-1878)
DR JACOBS NATURALS LLC
2615 Coney Island Ave 2nd (11223-5501)
PHONE..................718 265-1522
Joe Aini, Mng Member
EMP: 24
SALES (est): 263.5K Privately Held
SIC: 2841 Soap & other detergents

(G-1879)
DR PEPPER SNAPPLE GROUP INC
212 Wolcott St (11231-1130)
PHONE..................718 246-6200
Joseph Poli, CEO
M McCrodden, Financial Exec
EMP: 8 Publicly Held
SIC: 2086 Bottled & canned soft drinks
PA: Dr Pepper Snapple Group, Inc.
5301 Legacy Dr
Plano TX 75024

(G-1880)
DREAM STATUARY INC
Also Called: Original Dream Statuary
251 Cleveland St (11208-1004)
PHONE..................718 647-2024
Kumar Budhu, President
EMP: 6
SALES: 100K Privately Held
SIC: 3299 Statuary: gypsum, clay, papier mache, metal, etc.; art goods: plaster of paris, papier mache & scagliola

(G-1881)
DREAMS TO PRINT
Also Called: Hard Ten
10101 Foster Ave (11236-2107)
PHONE..................718 483-8020
Michael Azafrani, Owner
EMP: 1
SALES: 3MM Privately Held
SIC: 2731 Book clubs: publishing & printing

(G-1882)
DRESSER-ARGUS INC
36 Bridge St (11201-1170)
PHONE..................718 643-1540
Warren Frank, Ch of Bd
Bonita Wetmore, Admin Sec
▲ EMP: 5
SQ FT: 6,000
SALES (est): 817.2K Privately Held
SIC: 3728 3423 Military aircraft equipment & armament; hand & edge tools

(G-1883)
DRNS CORP
Also Called: Carousel ADS
140 58th St Ste 3f (11220-2561)
PHONE..................718 369-4530
Fax: 718 265-3722
Mark Nacson, President
Robert Barber, Manager
Joan Kalmanowitz, Admin Sec
▲ EMP: 11
SQ FT: 19,500
SALES (est): 1.3MM Privately Held
WEB: www.directpromos.com
SIC: 2759 8743 Letterpress & screen printing; screen printing; promotion service

(G-1884)
DURALL DOLLY LLC
48 Spencer St (11205-1737)
PHONE..................802 728-7122
EMP: 15 EST: 1981
SQ FT: 14,000
SALES (est): 990K Privately Held
SIC: 2599 Mfg Harwood Dollies

(G-1885)
DWECK INDUSTRIES INC (PA)
Also Called: Stephen Dweck Industries
2455 Mcdonald Ave Fl 2 (11223-5232)
PHONE..................718 615-1695
Edmond Dweck, President
Gregory Dweck, Corp Secy
Stephen Dweck, Vice Pres
EMP: 2
SQ FT: 8,000
SALES (est): 3.3MM Privately Held
WEB: www.stephendweck.com
SIC: 3911 Pearl jewelry, natural or cultured

(G-1886)
DWECK INDUSTRIES INC
2247 E 16th St Fl 2 (11229-4424)
PHONE..................718 615-1695
Fax: 718 934-3303
Edmond Dweck, Branch Mgr
EMP: 36

SALES (corp-wide): 3.3MM Privately Held
WEB: www.stephendweck.com
SIC: 3915 Lapidary work, contract or other
PA: Dweck Industries, Inc.
2455 Mcdonald Ave Fl 2
Brooklyn NY 11223
718 615-1695

(G-1887)
DYNAMIC HEALTH LABS INC
Also Called: Pet Authority
110 Bridge St Ste 2 (11201-1575)
PHONE..................718 858-0100
Bruce Burwick, President
Esther Troupe, Bookkeeper
▲ EMP: 33
SQ FT: 24,000
SALES (est): 11.7MM Privately Held
SIC: 2037 Fruit juices

(G-1888)
DYNAMIC PACKAGING INC
1567 39th St (11218-4413)
PHONE..................718 388-0800
Fax: 718 388-7733
Stanley Freund, Ch of Bd
David Brown, Manager
EMP: 10
SQ FT: 10,000
SALES (est): 1.1MM Privately Held
WEB: www.dynamicpackaging.net
SIC: 2759 5113 Bags, plastic: printing; bags, paper & disposable plastic

(G-1889)
DYNATABS LLC
Also Called: Www.dynatabs.com
1600 Ocean Pkwy Apt 1f (11230-7037)
PHONE..................718 376-6084
Harold Baum, Managing Dir
Setty Baum, CFO
EMP: 11
SQ FT: 3,900
SALES (est): 1.3MM Privately Held
WEB: www.dynatabs.com
SIC: 2023 Dietary supplements, dairy & non-dairy based

(G-1890)
E & G BEDDING CORP
1901 8th Ave (11215-6201)
P.O. Box 60978, Staten Island (10306-0978)
PHONE..................718 369-1092
Walkiria Murphy, President
Wilmina Musto, Vice Pres
EMP: 30 EST: 1980
SALES (est): 2.2MM Privately Held
SIC: 2515 7699 Mattresses & foundations; mattress renovating & repair shop

(G-1891)
E CHABOT LTD
Also Called: Chabot Jewelry
1544 E 13th St Apt 1a (11230-7196)
PHONE..................212 575-1026
Ezra Shabot, President
Bob Shabot, Treasurer
EMP: 50
SQ FT: 5,000
SALES: 5.5MM Privately Held
WEB: www.echabot.com
SIC: 3911 5094 Jewelry apparel; jewelry

(G-1892)
E G M RESTAURANT EQUIPMENT MFG
688 Flushing Ave (11206-5025)
PHONE..................718 782-9800
Scott Michaels, President
EMP: 7
SQ FT: 2,500
SALES (est): 640K Privately Held
SIC: 3444 Restaurant sheet metalwork

(G-1893)
E GRAPHICS CORPORATION
160 Havemeyer St (11211-8772)
PHONE..................718 486-9767
Esmeralda Lora, President
Daniel Beleski, Manager
EMP: 5
SALES (est): 405.6K Privately Held
SIC: 2732 Book printing

Brooklyn - Kings County (G-1894)

(G-1894)
E S P METAL CRAFTS INC
379 Harman St (11237-4701)
PHONE.................................718 381-2443
Fax: 718 381-1061
Edward Crancagnolo, *President*
▲ EMP: 9
SALES: 1MM **Privately Held**
SIC: 3446 Railings, bannisters, guards, etc.: made from metal pipe

(G-1895)
E-Z GLOBAL WHOLESALE INC
925 E 14th St (11230-3648)
PHONE.................................888 769-7888
Shakhim Mamedov, *President*
EMP: 5 EST: 2012
SALES (est): 174.3K **Privately Held**
SIC: 3999 Manufacturing industries

(G-1896)
E-Z WARE DISHES INC
1002 Quentin Rd (11223-2228)
PHONE.................................718 376-3244
Joseph Messry, *President*
▲ EMP: 3 EST: 2010
SQ FT: 2,000
SALES: 1MM **Privately Held**
SIC: 3089 Plastic kitchenware, tableware & houseware

(G-1897)
EAGLE FINISHING
Also Called: Eagle Fashions U S A
49 Wyckoff Ave (11237-8001)
PHONE.................................718 497-7875
Ariam Kurti, *Principal*
Ermir Kurti, *Manager*
EMP: 20
SALES (est): 605.5K **Privately Held**
SIC: 2396 Apparel findings & trimmings

(G-1898)
EAST WEST GLOBAL SOURCING INC
425 Neptune Ave Apt 22a (11224-4587)
PHONE.................................917 887-2286
Michael Zeicner, *CEO*
EMP: 8
SQ FT: 2,000
SALES (est): 306.6K **Privately Held**
SIC: 3199 Leather garments

(G-1899)
EASTERN FEATHER & DOWN CORP
Also Called: Yugo Landau
1027 Metropolitan Ave (11211-2710)
PHONE.................................718 387-4100
Fax: 718 387-2001
Joseph Landau, *President*
Yehoshua Weiner, *Vice Pres*
▲ EMP: 8
SQ FT: 45,000
SALES: 4MM **Privately Held**
SIC: 3999 Down (feathers)

(G-1900)
EASTERN SILVER OF BORO PARK
4901 16th Ave (11204-1115)
PHONE.................................718 854-5600
Bernard Gelbstein, *President*
EMP: 5
SQ FT: 4,500
SALES: 1MM **Privately Held**
SIC: 3479 Engraving jewelry silverware, or metal

(G-1901)
ECONOMY 24/7 INC
167 6th Ave (11217-3508)
PHONE.................................917 403-8876
Marius Meland, *President*
EMP: 20
SALES (est): 635.4K **Privately Held**
SIC: 2741 Miscellaneous publishing

(G-1902)
ECOPLAST & PACKAGING LLC
4619 Surf Ave 11224-1047)
PHONE.................................718 996-0800
Shifra Lefkowitz, *CEO*
Larry Lefkowitz, *President*
EMP: 6 EST: 2009
SALES: 2.5MM **Privately Held**
SIC: 2673 2671 3081 2754 Bags: plastic, laminated & coated; plastic film, coated or laminated for packaging; unsupported plastics film & sheet; commercial printing, gravure

(G-1903)
ECS GLOBAL
Also Called: E C S
55 Washington St Ste 302a (11201-1077)
PHONE.................................718 855-5888
Luther Garcia, *President*
Ricky Dweck, *Vice Pres*
James Crespo, *Treasurer*
Connie Harrigan, *Finance Mgr*
Dina Depalma, *Accounts Mgr*
EMP: 15
SQ FT: 2,200
SALES: 13.5MM **Privately Held**
WEB: www.enerconsupply.com
SIC: 3646 Commercial indusl & institutional electric lighting fixtures

(G-1904)
ED NEGRON FINE WOODWORKING
43 Hall St Fl 5 (11205-1315)
PHONE.................................718 246-1016
Ed Negron, *President*
EMP: 8
SALES (est): 722.4K **Privately Held**
SIC: 2431 2499 Millwork; decorative wood & woodwork

(G-1905)
EDCO SUPPLY CORPORATION
323 36th St (11232-2599)
PHONE.................................718 788-8108
Fax: 718 788-7481
Carl Freyer, *CEO*
Howard Greenberg, *General Mgr*
Joaquin Celis, *Safety Mgr*
Arlene Amuso, *Human Res Mgr*
Justin Daniels, *Marketing Staff*
EMP: 53 EST: 1955
SQ FT: 25,000
SALES (est): 9.5MM **Privately Held**
WEB: www.edcosupply.com
SIC: 3081 5113 2673 Packing materials, plastic sheet; pressure sensitive tape; bags: plastic, laminated & coated

(G-1906)
EDISON POWER & LIGHT CO INC
204 Van Dyke St Ste 207 (11231-1038)
PHONE.................................718 522-0002
Leon Gross, *President*
EMP: 14
SQ FT: 36,000
SALES (est): 1.3MM **Privately Held**
SIC: 3648 5719 Lighting equipment; lighting fixtures

(G-1907)
EDSAL MACHINE PRODUCTS INC (PA)
126 56th St (11220-2575)
PHONE.................................718 439-9163
Fax: 718 748-4984
Evangelos S Tsevdos, *Ch of Bd*
Steven Tsevdos, *President*
Dessie Tsevdos, *Admin Sec*
▲ EMP: 11
SQ FT: 20,000
SALES (est): 1.8MM **Privately Held**
SIC: 3599 Machine shop, jobbing & repair

(G-1908)
EFS DESIGNS
610 Smith St Ste 3 (11231-2113)
PHONE.................................718 852-9511
Robert Burns, *President*
EMP: 6
SQ FT: 20,000
SALES (est): 532.3K **Privately Held**
SIC: 2262 2759 Screen printing: man-made fiber & silk broadwoven fabrics; screen printing

(G-1909)
EKS MANUFACTURING INC
577 Wortman Ave (11208-5415)
P.O. Box 21325 (11202-1325)
PHONE.................................917 217-0784
William Socolov, *Owner*
Yoseph Moriah, *General Mgr*
EMP: 10
SALES (est): 1.1MM **Privately Held**
SIC: 3652 Phonograph records, prerecorded

(G-1910)
EL DIARIO LLC
1 Metrotech Ctr Fl 1801 (11201-3949)
PHONE.................................212 807-4600
Rossana Rosado, *CEO*
Pedro Frisneda, *Editor*
Oscar Hernandez, *Accounts Exec*
George Ruiz, *Accounts Exec*
Veronica Romero, *Relations*
EMP: 122
SQ FT: 28,000
SALES (est): 7.7MM **Privately Held**
WEB: www.eldiariony.com
SIC: 2711 Newspapers

(G-1911)
EL ERMAN INTERNATIONAL LTD
1205 E 29th St (11210-4630)
PHONE.................................212 444-9440
Shelley Cohen, *President*
Moshe Cohen, *Vice Pres*
David Elan, *Vice Pres*
◆ EMP: 3
SALES: 2MM **Privately Held**
SIC: 2844 5122 Face creams or lotions; hair preparations
PA: E.L. Erman Cosmetic Production Ltd
  1 Haplada
  Ashdod

(G-1912)
ELECTRIC MOTORS AND PUMPS INC
466 Carroll St (11215-1012)
PHONE.................................718 935-9118
Jorge Fraticelli, *President*
Maria Fraticelli, *Vice Pres*
EMP: 7
SQ FT: 4,500
SALES (est): 790K **Privately Held**
SIC: 3469 5999 5084 Machine parts, stamped or pressed metal; engine & motor equipment & supplies; motors, electric; plumbing & heating supplies; pumps & pumping equipment

(G-1913)
ELECTRONIC DIE CORP
19th St Fl 2 (11232)
PHONE.................................718 455-3200
Joseph Assenza, *President*
Michael Reiss, *Principal*
Alfred Torez, *Treasurer*
EMP: 10
SQ FT: 10,000
SALES (est): 650K **Privately Held**
WEB: www.electronicdiecorp.com
SIC: 3544 Special dies, tools, jigs & fixtures

(G-1914)
ELEGANT DESSERTS BY METRO INC
868 Kent Ave (11205-2702)
PHONE.................................718 388-1323
Martin Weisz, *President*
Benjamin Weisz, *Principal*
EMP: 12
SQ FT: 7,500
SALES (est): 830K **Privately Held**
SIC: 2024 Ices, flavored (frozen dessert)

(G-1915)
ELEGANT LINEN INC
200 60th St (11220-3712)
PHONE.................................718 492-0297
Benjamin Barber, *President*
EMP: 5
SALES (corp-wide): 3.1MM **Privately Held**
SIC: 2392 Household furnishings
PA: Elegant Linen Inc.
  5719 New Utrecht Ave
  Brooklyn NY 11219
  718 871-3535

(G-1916)
ELEGANT LINEN INC (PA)
5719 New Utrecht Ave (11219-4634)
PHONE.................................718 871-3535
Fax: 718 437-4160
Benjamin Barber, *President*
Richard Citron, *Vice Pres*
▲ EMP: 23
SQ FT: 4,000
SALES (est): 3.1MM **Privately Held**
WEB: www.elegantlinen.com
SIC: 2392 Sheets, fabric: made from purchased materials

(G-1917)
ELEPATH INC
110 Kent Ave 9 (11249-2812)
PHONE.................................347 417-4975
Bryan Goldberg, *CFO*
EMP: 5
SALES (est): 330.7K **Privately Held**
SIC: 7372 Application computer software

(G-1918)
ELEPHANTS CUSTOM FURNITURE INC
67 Van Dam St (11222-3806)
PHONE.................................917 509-3581
Gokhan Doguer, *President*
EMP: 51
SQ FT: 10,000
SALES (est): 8.3MM **Privately Held**
SIC: 2499 Decorative wood & woodwork

(G-1919)
ELRAMIDA HOLDINGS INC
2555 E 29th St (11235-2020)
PHONE.................................646 280-0503
Mark Harris, *CEO*
Eldar Rakhamineov, *Ch of Bd*
EMP: 22
SALES (est): 4.5MM **Privately Held**
SIC: 3537 Trucks, tractors, loaders, carriers & similar equipment

(G-1920)
EMCO CHEMICAL (USA) CORP
334 Douglass St (11217-3114)
PHONE.................................718 797-3652
Andy Uchitel, *President*
Mary Ellen Limer, *Vice Pres*
EMP: 25
SQ FT: 6,000
SALES (est): 3.1MM **Privately Held**
SIC: 2819 Industrial inorganic chemicals

(G-1921)
EMERALD HOLDINGS INC
Also Called: Emerald Knitting
63 Flushing Ave Unit 201 (11205-1072)
PHONE.................................718 797-4404
Michael Engle, *President*
Arnold Shulman, *Vice Pres*
▲ EMP: 5
SALES (est): 890K **Privately Held**
SIC: 2339 2253 Women's & misses' outerwear; knit outerwear mills

(G-1922)
EMES MOTOR INC
876 Metropolitan Ave (11211-2515)
PHONE.................................718 387-2445
Abraham Mertz, *President*
EMP: 5
SALES (est): 600K **Privately Held**
SIC: 3621 5999 Motors & generators; motors, electric

(G-1923)
EMILIA INTERIORS INC (PA)
867 E 52nd St (11203-6701)
PHONE.................................718 629-4202
Nicholas Vignapiano, *President*
Jennie Vignapiano, *Corp Secy*
EMP: 19
SQ FT: 20,000
SALES (est): 1.5MM **Privately Held**
WEB: www.girardemilia.com
SIC: 2511 Wood household furniture

Brooklyn - Kings County (G-1952)

(G-1924)
EMPIRE AIR SYSTEMS LLC
Also Called: Empire Air Hvac
2535 65th St (11204-3528)
PHONE..................718 377-1549
Ana Cohen, *Office Mgr*
Lior Binyamin,
Shmuel Cohen Zada,
EMP: 15
SALES: 1.5MM **Privately Held**
SIC: 3585 Air conditioning equipment, complete

(G-1925)
EMPIRE CITY VAPE LLC
535 Neptune Ave Apt 20e (11224-4039)
PHONE..................718 676-6166
Vladimir Kalman, *Principal*
EMP: 7
SALES (est): 94.4K **Privately Held**
SIC: 3999 Cigar & cigarette holders

(G-1926)
EMPIRE PRESS CO (PA)
550 Empire Blvd (11225-3131)
PHONE..................718 756-9500
Fax: 718 604-7633
Mordechai Chein, *Owner*
Joe Katz, *Office Mgr*
EMP: 5
SQ FT: 6,000
SALES (est): 513.8K **Privately Held**
WEB: www.empirepress.com
SIC: 2791 2752 Typesetting; commercial printing, offset

(G-1927)
EMPIRE TRANSIT MIX INC
430 Maspeth Ave (11211-1704)
PHONE..................718 384-3000
Fax: 718 384-3113
Rocco Tomassetti, *Ch of Bd*
Dina Tammaro, *Office Mgr*
EMP: 40
SALES (est): 7.9MM **Privately Held**
SIC: 3273 Ready-mixed concrete

(G-1928)
EMUNAS SALES INC
947 E 27th St (11210-3727)
PHONE..................718 621-3138
Usher Orzel, *President*
EMP: 16
SQ FT: 3,000
SALES (est): 422.2K **Privately Held**
SIC: 2323 Men's & boys' neckwear

(G-1929)
ENTERPRISE NETWORK NY INC
1407 E 101st St Ste B (11236-5507)
PHONE..................516 263-0641
Richmond Fox, *President*
Sanjay Fernandez, *Engineer*
EMP: 10 **EST:** 1997
SALES: 105.5K **Privately Held**
SIC: 7372 Operating systems computer software

(G-1930)
ENTERPRISE WOOD PRODUCTS INC
4712 18th Ave (11204-1260)
PHONE..................718 853-9243
Fax: 718 474-0776
Jan Koegel, *President*
Leonard Rosenberg, *Treasurer*
EMP: 11
SQ FT: 7,500
SALES (est): 1.3MM **Privately Held**
SIC: 2434 Wood kitchen cabinets

(G-1931)
ENTICING LINGERIE INC
166 Gravesend Neck Rd (11223-4707)
PHONE..................718 998-8625
David Gindi, *President*
Arlette Gindi, *Corp Secy*
EMP: 20
SQ FT: 8,000
SALES: 5MM **Privately Held**
WEB: www.enticinglingerie.com
SIC: 2341 2342 Women's & children's underwear; bras, girdles & allied garments

(G-1932)
ENZO MANZONI LLC
2896 W 12th St (11224-2907)
PHONE..................212 464-7000
Gene Isaac, *Director*
EMP: 5
SQ FT: 5,000
SALES (est): 368.4K **Privately Held**
SIC: 2326 5136 Work apparel, except uniforms; men's & boys' clothing; men's & boys' sportswear & work clothing

(G-1933)
EPNER TECHNOLOGY INCORPORATED (PA)
78 Kingsland Ave (11222-5603)
PHONE..................718 782-5948
David Epner, *President*
Paul J Brancato, *General Mgr*
Stephen V Candiloro, *Corp Secy*
Steven A Candiloro Sr, *Vice Pres*
Michel Coury, *Exec Sec*
▼ **EMP:** 35
SQ FT: 40,000
SALES (est): 5.2MM **Privately Held**
WEB: www.epner.com
SIC: 3471 Electroplating of metals or formed products

(G-1934)
EPNER TECHNOLOGY INCORPORATED
78 Kingsland Ave (11222-5603)
PHONE..................718 782-8722
Gerald Epner, *Engineer/R&D Mgr*
David Epner, *Marketing Staff*
Stephen V Candilaro, *Systems Mgr*
EMP: 35
SALES (corp-wide): 5.2MM **Privately Held**
WEB: www.epner.com
SIC: 3471 Plating & polishing
PA: Epner Technology Incorporated
78 Kingsland Ave
Brooklyn NY 11222
718 782-5948

(G-1935)
EPUFFER INC
2348 80th St Fl 1 (11214-2025)
PHONE..................718 374-6030
Shawn Shalmiev, *President*
EMP: 5
SQ FT: 2,000
SALES: 45MM **Privately Held**
SIC: 2111 Cigarettes

(G-1936)
EQUITYARCADE LLC
33 Nassau Ave (11222-3132)
PHONE..................678 232-1301
Aaron Kaplan, *CEO*
Ponsius Odaga, *Manager*
EMP: 5
SALES (est): 143.6K **Privately Held**
SIC: 2741

(G-1937)
ERCOLE NYC INC (PA)
142 26th St (11232)
PHONE..................212 675-2218
Fax: 718 797-4291
Ornella Pisano, *President*
Nancy Henry, *Office Mgr*
▲ **EMP:** 18
SQ FT: 15,000
SALES (est): 1.8MM **Privately Held**
WEB: www.ercolehome.com
SIC: 3253 2511 Ceramic wall & floor tile; tables, household: wood

(G-1938)
ERNEX CORPORATION INC
Also Called: Ernex Chocolate
5518 Avenue N (11234-4006)
PHONE..................718 951-2251
Fax: 718 951-2254
Ernest Grunhut, *President*
Carl Grunhut, *President*
Jack Grunhut, *Vice Pres*
Lenny Grunhut, *Opers Staff*
Alia Calderon, *Admin Sec*
▲ **EMP:** 35
SQ FT: 15,000
SALES (est): 5.3MM **Privately Held**
WEB: www.empresschocolate.com
SIC: 2066 Chocolate

(G-1939)
ESER REALTY CORP (PA)
62 Greenpoint Ave 64 (11222-2057)
PHONE..................718 383-0565
Robert Frenkel, *Ch of Bd*
Morton Frenkel, *President*
◆ **EMP:** 50
SQ FT: 30,000
SALES (est): 5.4MM **Privately Held**
SIC: 3999 Feathers, renovating

(G-1940)
ESKAYEL INC
75 S 6th St (11249-6027)
PHONE..................347 703-8084
Shannan Campanaro, *Principal*
EMP: 5
SALES (est): 411.9K **Privately Held**
SIC: 2299 2273 2679 8999 Broadwoven fabrics: linen, jute, hemp & ramie; dyeing & finishing of tufted rugs & carpets; wallpaper; artist's studio

(G-1941)
ESQUIRE MECHANICAL CORP
79 Sandford St (11205)
PHONE..................718 625-4006
Geoffrey Thaw, *President*
EMP: 7
SQ FT: 5,000
SALES: 1.2MM **Privately Held**
WEB: www.dunhill-esquire.com
SIC: 3556 Food products machinery

(G-1942)
ESS BEE INDUSTRIES INC
95 Evergreen Ave (11206-6124)
PHONE..................718 894-5202
Alex Stein, *President*
Iza Stein, *Vice Pres*
EMP: 30
SQ FT: 40,000
SALES (est): 1.8MM **Privately Held**
SIC: 2221 2392 5023 Comforters & quilts, manmade fiber & silk; household furnishings; bedspreads

(G-1943)
ESSEX WORKS LTD
446 Riverdale Ave (11207-6121)
PHONE..................718 495-4575
Fax: 718 218-8048
Douglas Schickler, *President*
EMP: 19 **EST:** 1995
SQ FT: 3,000
SALES (est): 1.8MM **Privately Held**
WEB: www.essexworks.com
SIC: 3299 Architectural sculptures: gypsum, clay, papier mache, etc.

(G-1944)
EURO WOODWORKING INC
303 Park Ave Fl 8 (11205-1307)
PHONE..................718 246-9172
Wolfgang Michelitsch, *President*
EMP: 6
SALES (est): 597.6K **Privately Held**
SIC: 3089 Prefabricated plastic buildings

(G-1945)
EVER-NU-METAL PRODUCTS INC
471 20th St (11215-6294)
PHONE..................646 423-5833
Fax: 718 788-0656
Frank Gagliardi Jr, *President*
Rocco Gagliardi, *Corp Secy*
▲ **EMP:** 12
SQ FT: 14,000
SALES (est): 1.4MM **Privately Held**
WEB: www.evernumetal.com
SIC: 3471 Finishing, metals or formed products

(G-1946)
EVERLAST SEALS AND SUPPLY LLC
41 Montrose Ave (11206-2381)
PHONE..................718 388-7373
Joshua Benjamin, *Managing Prtnr*
John Martini, *Sls & Mktg Exec*
Barry Himmel,
▲ **EMP:** 10
SQ FT: 15,000
SALES: 1MM **Privately Held**
SIC: 3053 Gaskets & sealing devices

(G-1947)
EXCALBUR BRNZE SCULPTURE FNDRY
309 Starr St (11237-2611)
PHONE..................718 366-3444
William R Gold, *President*
Rachel Gold, *Vice Pres*
Eleanor Brown, *Office Mgr*
EMP: 28
SQ FT: 13,500
SALES: 1MM **Privately Held**
WEB: www.excaliburbronze.com
SIC: 3366 8711 3645 Bronze foundry; engineering services; residential lighting fixtures

(G-1948)
EXCELLENT POLY INC
820 4th Ave (11232-1612)
PHONE..................718 768-6555
Joshua Silber, *CEO*
Isaac Stern, *President*
Harry Weingarten, *Exec VP*
EMP: 15 **EST:** 1959
SQ FT: 55,000
SALES (est): 3.7MM **Privately Held**
WEB: www.excellentpoly.com
SIC: 2673 3081 Plastic bags: made from purchased materials; unsupported plastics film & sheet

(G-1949)
EXCELLENT PRINTING INC
Also Called: Excellent Photocopies
165 Hooper St (11211-7911)
PHONE..................718 384-7272
Fax: 718 384-7366
Gubor Rubin, *President*
Joseph Weinburger, *Vice Pres*
EMP: 6
SALES (est): 540K **Privately Held**
WEB: www.yeshivanet.com
SIC: 2759 Commercial printing

(G-1950)
EXECUTIVE MACHINES INC
Also Called: Jeam Imports
882 3rd Ave Unit 8 (11232-1902)
P.O. Box 320150 (11232-0150)
PHONE..................718 965-6600
Aron Abramson, *CEO*
Charles Sued, *President*
▲ **EMP:** 30
SQ FT: 20,000
SALES: 20K **Privately Held**
WEB: www.executivemachines.com
SIC: 3678 Electronic connectors

(G-1951)
EXPERT INDUSTRIES INC
848 E 43rd St (11210-3502)
PHONE..................718 434-6060
Fax: 718 434-6174
Cynthia Rubinberg, *President*
Martin Sterling, *General Mgr*
Michael Rubinberg, *Vice Pres*
Erenst Senatore, *Sales Staff*
EMP: 25
SQ FT: 25,000
SALES (est): 4.5MM **Privately Held**
SIC: 3443 3556 3444 Fabricated plate work (boiler shop); vessels, process or storage (from boiler shops): metal plate; mixers, commercial, food; sheet metalwork

(G-1952)
EY INDUSTRIES INC
Also Called: Ruckel Manufacturing Co
63 Flushing Ave Unit 331 (11205-1083)
PHONE..................718 624-9122
Fax: 718 643-8008
Joseph Friedman, *President*
Sam Friedman, *General Mgr*
Aaron Parnes, *COO*
Keigo Shimomura, *Consultant*
EMP: 15 **EST:** 1937
SQ FT: 15,000

Brooklyn - Kings County (G-1953)

SALES (est): 980K **Privately Held**
WEB: www.yarmulka.com
SIC: 2392 Comforters & quilts: made from purchased materials; pillowcases: made from purchased materials; mattress protectors except rubber; sheets, fabric: made from purchased materials

(G-1953)
EYE GRAPHICS & PRINTING INC
499 Van Brunt St Ste 3a (11231-1051)
P.O. Box 110314 (11211-0314)
PHONE..................................718 488-0606
Faisal Iqbal, *Ch of Bd*
Mohamad Ikhmies, *Vice Pres*
EMP: 15
SALES (est): 1.9MM **Privately Held**
WEB: www.eyeprinters.com
SIC: 2759 7336 7311 Commercial printing; commercial art & graphic design; advertising consultant

(G-1954)
EZ NEWSLETTER LLC
1449 Bay Ridge Ave 2 (11219-6232)
PHONE..................................412 943-7777
Eric V Hileman, *Mng Member*
EMP: 10
SALES (est): 890K **Privately Held**
SIC: 7372 Prepackaged software

(G-1955)
EZ SYSTEMS US INC
Also Called: EZ CMS Systems US
35 Meadow St Ste 103 (11206-1759)
PHONE..................................212 634-6899
Gabriele Viebach, *CEO*
Tom Jergensen, *Ch of Bd*
Bard Farstad, *Co-Founder*
Svein Arne Gusland, *CFO*
Dylan Williams, *Manager*
EMP: 105
SALES (est): 3.9MM
SALES (corp-wide): 9.2MM **Privately Held**
SIC: 7372 Business oriented computer software
PA: Ez Systems As
Porselensvegen 18
Porsgrunn 3920
355 870-20

(G-1956)
F R A M TECHNOLOGIES INC
3048 Bedford Ave (11210-3714)
PHONE..................................718 338-6230
Mordechai Flotsker, *President*
EMP: 6
SALES (est): 50.2K **Privately Held**
WEB: www.framtech.com
SIC: 7372 Prepackaged software

(G-1957)
FACTORY EAST
Also Called: Factory Nyc
723 Kent Ave (11249-7807)
PHONE..................................718 280-1558
Paul Outlaw, *Owner*
Melissa Gollance, *Project Mgr*
EMP: 20
SALES (est): 2.4MM **Privately Held**
SIC: 3499 Fabricated metal products

(G-1958)
FAIRVIEW BELL AND INTERCOM
502 Gravesend Neck Rd B (11223-4800)
PHONE..................................718 627-8621
Grzegorz Butry, *President*
Florence Kachman, *Manager*
David Rozenbyum, *Manager*
EMP: 5
SQ FT: 600
SALES (est): 200K **Privately Held**
SIC: 3699 Security devices

(G-1959)
FAL COFFEE INC
Also Called: Novatree Coffee
240 Kent Ave Ste A8 (11249-4121)
PHONE..................................718 305-4255
John Moore, *CEO*
Sue Fawver, *Director*
EMP: 10
SQ FT: 7,500
SALES: 2MM **Privately Held**
SIC: 2095 Roasted coffee

(G-1960)
FALCONES COOKIE LAND LTD (PA)
Also Called: Falcone Food Distribution
1648 61st St (11204-2109)
PHONE..................................718 236-4200
Fax: 718 259-6133
Carmine Falcone Jr, *Ch of Bd*
Angelo Falcone, *President*
Francis Falcone, *Vice Pres*
EMP: 6
SQ FT: 24,000
SALES (est): 5.8MM **Privately Held**
SIC: 2052 Cookies

(G-1961)
FANCY WINDOWS & DOORS MFG CORP
Also Called: Fancy Window & Door
312 Ten Eyck St (11206-1723)
PHONE..................................718 366-7800
Jin Hu Ye, *Ch of Bd*
Jackson Ye, *President*
Jian Xu Chung, *Shareholder*
▲ EMP: 7
SQ FT: 4,000
SALES (est): 935.5K **Privately Held**
SIC: 2431 Doors & door parts & trim, wood; windows & window parts & trim, wood

(G-1962)
FANTASY HOME IMPROVEMENT CORP
2731 Atlantic Ave (11207-2803)
PHONE..................................718 277-4021
Fax: 718 277-4022
Dominic Trimarchi, *President*
Lucy Trimarchi, *Admin Sec*
EMP: 5 EST: 1974
SALES: 300K **Privately Held**
SIC: 2434 1521 Wood kitchen cabinets; single-family housing construction

(G-1963)
FASTENERS DEPOT LLC
5308 13th Ave (11219-3804)
PHONE..................................718 622-4222
Mandle Sandle, *Office Mgr*
▲ EMP: 12
SALES (est): 1.7MM **Privately Held**
SIC: 3965 Fasteners

(G-1964)
FAVORITE PLASTIC CORP
1465 Utica Ave (11234-1108)
PHONE..................................718 253-7000
Fax: 718 377-1918
Hershey Friedman, *President*
Mitch Kirschner, *Vice Pres*
▲ EMP: 110 EST: 1956
SQ FT: 75,000
SALES (est): 16.8MM **Privately Held**
WEB: www.favoriteplastics.com
SIC: 3081 3083 Plastic film & sheet; laminated plastics plate & sheet

(G-1965)
FAYDA MANUFACTURING CORP
Also Called: Fay Da Mott St
259 Meserole St (11206-2244)
PHONE..................................718 456-9331
Han Chieh Chou, *President*
Kelen Chow, *Manager*
EMP: 10
SALES (est): 1.1MM **Privately Held**
SIC: 2051 Bakery: wholesale or wholesale/retail combined

(G-1966)
FAYE BERNARD LOUNGEWEAR
2604 Avenue M (11210-4611)
PHONE..................................718 951-7245
Faye Zola, *Partner*
Bernard Zola, *Partner*
EMP: 8
SQ FT: 2,000
SALES (est): 600K **Privately Held**
SIC: 2341 Nightgowns & negligees: women's & children's

(G-1967)
FEDERAL PUMP CORPORATION (PA)
1144 Utica Ave (11203-5319)
PHONE..................................718 451-2000
Fax: 718 629-0367
John Marr, *President*
Jeff Mayzus, *General Mgr*
Annette Applebaum, *Purchasing*
Annette Applebaum, *Accountant*
Robert Rosen, *Manager*
▲ EMP: 45 EST: 1935
SQ FT: 53,000
SALES (est): 9.3MM **Privately Held**
SIC: 3561 Pumps & pumping equipment

(G-1968)
FELDMAN JEWELRY CREATIONS INC
4821 16th Ave (11204-1109)
PHONE..................................718 438-8895
Fax: 718 438-8895
Susan Feldman, *President*
Mordecai Feldman, *Vice Pres*
EMP: 5
SQ FT: 650
SALES (est): 490K **Privately Held**
SIC: 3911 Necklaces, precious metal; rings, finger: precious metal

(G-1969)
FELDWARE INC
250 Avenue W (11223-5288)
PHONE..................................718 372-0486
Fax: 718 372-3421
Sidney Feldman, *President*
Charles Feldman, *Vice Pres*
Sam Farrell, *Manager*
▲ EMP: 25 EST: 1959
SQ FT: 15,000
SALES (est): 4MM **Privately Held**
SIC: 3469 Stamping metal for the trade

(G-1970)
FENCE PLAZA CORP
1601 Nostrand Ave (11226-5101)
PHONE..................................718 469-2200
Fax: 718 469-3735
George Prince, *President*
EMP: 6
SQ FT: 300
SALES (est): 1.1MM **Privately Held**
WEB: www.fenceplaza.com
SIC: 3446 1799 5211 3441 Fences or posts, ornamental iron or steel; fence construction; fencing; fabricated structural metal

(G-1971)
FERRO FABRICATORS INC
1117 38th St (11218-1926)
PHONE..................................718 703-0007
Gregory Dec, *President*
EMP: 13 EST: 2003
SQ FT: 10,000
SALES (est): 2.4MM **Privately Held**
SIC: 3449 Bars, concrete reinforcing: fabricated steel

(G-1972)
FIBERWAVE CORPORATION
140 58th St Ste 37 (11220-2524)
PHONE..................................718 802-9011
Fax: 718 802-0116
John Romeo, *President*
Ed Kirchgessner, *CFO*
Sal Agnello, *Controller*
▲ EMP: 200
SALES (est): 31.8MM **Privately Held**
WEB: www.fiberwave.com
SIC: 3661 Fiber optics communications equipment

(G-1973)
FIL DOUX INC
227 5th Ave (11215-1202)
PHONE..................................212 202-1459
Leonardo Novik, *Ch of Bd*
Crystal Henry, *Director*
EMP: 10
SALES: 3MM **Privately Held**
SIC: 2299 Broadwoven fabrics: linen, jute, hemp & ramie

(G-1974)
FILTA CLEAN CO INC
Also Called: Belton Industries
107 Georgia Ave (11207-2489)
PHONE..................................718 495-3800
Tommy Weber, *President*
Ron Weber, *Vice Pres*
EMP: 35
SQ FT: 10,000
SALES (est): 8.1MM **Privately Held**
WEB: www.multidisplayandpanel.com
SIC: 3564 7349 Filters, air: furnaces, air conditioning equipment, etc.; air duct cleaning

(G-1975)
FINE AND RAW CHOCOLATE
288 Seigel St (11206-3813)
PHONE..................................718 366-3633
Daniel Sklaar, *Owner*
EMP: 5
SALES (est): 150K **Privately Held**
SIC: 2064 Candy bars, including chocolate covered bars

(G-1976)
FINELINE THERMOGRAPHERS INC
544 Park Ave Ste 308 (11205-1647)
PHONE..................................718 643-1100
Fax: 718 643-6952
Samuel Fried, *President*
Themmy Sixler, *Admin Sec*
EMP: 7
SQ FT: 7,000
SALES (est): 805.3K **Privately Held**
SIC: 2759 Thermography

(G-1977)
FINESSE CREATIONS INC
3004 Avenue J (11210-3838)
PHONE..................................718 692-2100
Fax: 718 692-3303
Esther Machlis, *President*
Daniel Machlis, *Manager*
▲ EMP: 10
SQ FT: 2,500
SALES (est): 2.4MM **Privately Held**
WEB: www.finessecreations.com
SIC: 3599 5044 3569 Custom machinery; office equipment; baling machines, for scrap metal, paper or similar material

(G-1978)
FIRE FOX SECURITY CORP
2070 72nd St Apt B1 (11204-5823)
PHONE..................................917 981-9280
John Mansi, *President*
EMP: 7
SQ FT: 800
SALES: 250K **Privately Held**
SIC: 3699 5045 Security control equipment & systems; computers, peripherals & software

(G-1979)
FISH TO DISH INC
5516 16th Ave (11204-1855)
PHONE..................................718 972-7600
Shia Langson, *Manager*
EMP: 10
SALES: 1MM **Privately Held**
SIC: 2092 Seafoods, fresh: prepared

(G-1980)
FIVE BORO HOLDING LLC
1425 37th St Ste 3 (11218-3771)
PHONE..................................718 431-9500
Monique Cohen, *Office Mgr*
Joey Cohen, *Mng Member*
EMP: 10
SQ FT: 18,000
SALES (est): 138.2K **Privately Held**
WEB: www.fiveboroughprinting.com
SIC: 2761 Computer forms, manifold or continuous

(G-1981)
FIVE BURROUGHS BREWING CO
215 47th St (11220-1009)
PHONE..................................718 355-8575
Blake W Tomnitz, *CEO*
EMP: 6

GEOGRAPHIC SECTION
Brooklyn - Kings County (G-2010)

SALES (est): 91.3K **Privately Held**
SIC: 2082 Beer (alcoholic beverage)

(G-1982)
FJS INDUSTRIES INC
Also Called: S & T Machine
970 E 92nd St (11236-1720)
PHONE......917 428-3797
Sam Accardi, *President*
EMP: 10
SALES: 1MM **Privately Held**
SIC: 3446 Gratings, tread: fabricated metal

(G-1983)
FLARE MULTICOPY CORP
Also Called: Flare Multi Copy
1840 Flatbush Ave (11210-4831)
PHONE......718 258-8860
Fax: 718 252-5568
Steven Zeller, *President*
Sam Stempler, *Treasurer*
EMP: 22
SALES (est): 3.2MM **Privately Held**
SIC: 2752 2791 2789 2732 Commercial printing, offset; typesetting; bookbinding & related work; book printing

(G-1984)
FLATCUT LLC
68 Jay St Ste 901 (11201-8364)
PHONE......212 542-5732
Tomer Ben-Gal, *Principal*
Jay Schainholz, *Principal*
Daniel Ramirez, *Research*
Deven Pravin Shah, *Marketing Staff*
EMP: 5 EST: 2010
SALES (est): 523.8K **Privately Held**
SIC: 3498 3532 3496 Fabricated pipe & fittings; mining machinery; miscellaneous fabricated wire products

(G-1985)
FLAVOR PAPER LTD
Also Called: Flavor League
216 Pacific St (11201-5888)
PHONE......718 422-0230
Emily Cangie, *COO*
Jon Sherman, *Administration*
EMP: 13
SQ FT: 3,500
SALES (est): 1.4MM **Privately Held**
WEB: www.flavorleague.com
SIC: 2679 Wallpaper

(G-1986)
FLEETWOOD CABINET CO INC (PA)
673 Livonia Ave (11207-5407)
PHONE......516 379-2139
Fax: 718 345-7164
Eric Belgraier, *President*
EMP: 8 EST: 1948
SQ FT: 12,000
SALES: 1MM **Privately Held**
SIC: 2541 Cabinets, except refrigerated: show, display, etc.: wood; counters or counter display cases, wood; table or counter tops, plastic laminated; sink tops, plastic laminated

(G-1987)
FLICKINGER GLASSWORKS INC
175 Van Dyke St Ste 321ap (11231-1079)
PHONE......718 875-1531
Fax: 718 875-4264
Charles Flickinger, *President*
EMP: 8
SQ FT: 7,000
SALES (est): 1.1MM **Privately Held**
WEB: www.flickingerglassworks.com
SIC: 3231 5231 Glass sheet, bent: made from purchased glass; glass, leaded or stained

(G-1988)
FLUSHING BOILER & WELDING CO
8720 Ditmas Ave (11236-1606)
PHONE......718 463-1266
EMP: 7
SALES (est): 470K **Privately Held**
SIC: 7692 7699 5074 1799 Welding Repair Repair Services Whol Plumbing Equip/Supp Special Trade Contractor

(G-1989)
FLUSHING PHARMACY INC
414 Flushing Ave Ste 1 (11205-1548)
PHONE......718 260-8999
Michell Wifemen, *President*
EMP: 250
SALES (est): 326.2K **Privately Held**
SIC: 2834 5813 Druggists' preparations (pharmaceuticals); night clubs

(G-1990)
FOCUS CAMERA INC (PA)
Also Called: Asavings.com
895 Mcdonald Ave (11218-5611)
PHONE......718 437-8800
Fax: 718 437-8811
Anthony Z Berkowitz, *Ch of Bd*
Ernest Berkowitz, *President*
Abe Berkowitz, *Vice Pres*
Barry Plaut, *Senior Buyer*
Jacob Harari, *Buyer*
▲ EMP: 145
SQ FT: 30,000
SALES (est): 68.3MM **Privately Held**
WEB: www.focus-camera.com
SIC: 3861 Cameras & related equipment

(G-1991)
FODERA GUITARS INC
68 34th St Unit 3 (11232-2000)
PHONE......718 832-3455
Vincent Fodera, *President*
Jason Desalvo, *Principal*
Joseph Lauricella, *Principal*
Mika Goines, *Manager*
EMP: 15
SQ FT: 6,800
SALES (est): 2.1MM **Privately Held**
WEB: www.fodera.ssl-central.com
SIC: 3931 7699 5736 Musical instruments; guitars & parts, electric & nonelectric; musical instrument repair services; musical instrument stores

(G-1992)
FOLENE PACKAGING LLC
2509 Avenue M (11210-4544)
P.O. Box 300965 (11230-0965)
PHONE......917 626-6740
Edward Weiss,
▲ EMP: 5
SALES (est): 586.6K **Privately Held**
SIC: 2671 Plastic film, coated or laminated for packaging

(G-1993)
FOLIO GRAPHICS CO INC
2759 E 66th St (11234-6806)
PHONE......718 763-2076
Stanley Drate, *President*
Rochelle Drate, *Vice Pres*
EMP: 6
SQ FT: 780
SALES (est): 420K **Privately Held**
SIC: 2731 7335 Books: publishing only; commercial photography

(G-1994)
FORD REGULATOR VALVE CORP
199 Varet St (11206-3704)
PHONE......718 497-3255
Joseph Tuzzolo, *President*
Paula Tuzollo, *Treasurer*
EMP: 5 EST: 1889
SQ FT: 5,000
SALES (est): 520K **Privately Held**
WEB: www.fordregulatorvalve.com
SIC: 3494 5085 Valves & pipe fittings; industrial supplies

(G-1995)
FORO MARBLE CO INC
166 2nd Ave (11215-4619)
PHONE......718 852-2322
Fax: 718 802-0143
Joseph P Guido, *President*
Joseph A Guido Jr, *Exec VP*
Joan Foro, *Vice Pres*
John Addario, *Controller*
EMP: 25
SQ FT: 25,000

SALES (est): 4.4MM **Privately Held**
WEB: www.foromarble.net
SIC: 3272 5032 Tile, precast terrazzo or concrete; slabs, crossing: concrete; tile, clay or other ceramic, excluding refractory

(G-1996)
FORTUNE SIGN
1334 39th St (11218-3616)
PHONE......646 383-8682
Fax: 646 383-5913
Anatoliy Kreychmar, *Principal*
EMP: 5
SALES (est): 320K **Privately Held**
SIC: 3993 Signs & advertising specialties

(G-1997)
FOSTER REEVE & ASSOCIATES INC (PA)
1155 Manhattan Ave # 1011 (11222-6161)
PHONE......718 609-0090
Foster Reeve, *CFO*
Cathy Reilly, *CFO*
Heidi Hulse, *Bookkeeper*
Nancy Roscoe, *Office Mgr*
▲ EMP: 6
SQ FT: 4,000
SALES (est): 3.4MM **Privately Held**
WEB: www.fraplaster.com
SIC: 3299 1742 Moldings, architectural: plaster of paris; plastering, plain or ornamental

(G-1998)
FOUNTAIN TILE OUTLET INC
609 Fountain Ave Ste A (11208-6007)
PHONE......718 927-4555
Frank Lapetina, *Principal*
EMP: 6
SALES (est): 297.3K **Privately Held**
SIC: 2426 Flooring, hardwood

(G-1999)
FOUR DEE INC
2247 E 16th St (11229-4424)
PHONE......718 615-1695
Edmond Dweck, *President*
EMP: 62
SQ FT: 10,000
SALES: 750K **Privately Held**
SIC: 2339 Women's & misses' accessories

(G-2000)
FOUR S SHOWCASE MANUFACTURING
1044 Linwood St (11208-5422)
PHONE......718 649-4900
Tony Razi, *President*
Isabel Razi, *Vice Pres*
EMP: 8
SQ FT: 12,000
SALES (est): 770K **Privately Held**
WEB: www.4sshowcase.com
SIC: 2542 Office & store showcases & display fixtures

(G-2001)
FOX 416 CORP
Also Called: Fox's U-Bet Syrups
416 Thatford Ave (11212-5810)
PHONE......718 385-4600
Fax: 718 345-4283
David Fox, *Ch of Bd*
Karen Fox, *Corp Secy*
EMP: 30 EST: 1900
SQ FT: 36,000
SALES (est): 6.7MM **Privately Held**
WEB: www.foxs-u-bet.com
SIC: 2087 2066 Syrups, flavoring (except drink); chocolate coatings & syrup

(G-2002)
FRANKLIN POLY FILM INC
1149 56th St (11219-4504)
PHONE......718 492-3523
Fax: 718 492-1149
Isidore Handler, *President*
Rose Frankel, *Principal*
Israel Kahan, *Corp Secy*
Angela Rice, *Plant Mgr*
Mory Eigner, *Manager*
▼ EMP: 39
SQ FT: 26,000

SALES (est): 5.4MM **Privately Held**
SIC: 2673 3082 3081 Plastic bags: made from purchased materials; unsupported plastics profile shapes; unsupported plastics film & sheet

(G-2003)
FRANZ FISCHER INC
1267 Flushing Ave (11237-2302)
P.O. Box 370715 (11237-0715)
PHONE......718 821-1300
Franz Fischer, *President*
EMP: 10
SQ FT: 14,000
SALES: 1.5MM **Privately Held**
WEB: www.franzfischer.com
SIC: 2511 Wood household furniture

(G-2004)
FRENCH & ITLN FURN CRAFTSMEN
Also Called: French Itln Furn Craftsmen Cor
999 Grand St (11211-2704)
PHONE......718 599-5000
Patrick F Molloy, *President*
EMP: 7
SQ FT: 6,000
SALES (est): 490K **Privately Held**
WEB: www.frenchanditalian.com
SIC: 2511 5712 Wood household furniture; furniture stores

(G-2005)
FRESH FANATIC INC
88 Washington Ave (11205-1202)
PHONE......516 521-6574
Andrew Goldin, *CEO*
David Goldin, *President*
EMP: 8
SALES (est): 1MM **Privately Held**
SIC: 2033 5146 5149 Fruit juices: fresh; fish, fresh; sandwiches

(G-2006)
FRESH ICE CREAM COMPANY LLC
630 Flushing Ave 4 (11206-5026)
PHONE......347 603-6021
Gerard Tucci, *Manager*
EMP: 10 **Privately Held**
SIC: 2024 5143 Ice cream & frozen desserts; ice cream & ices
PA: The Fresh Ice Cream Company Llc
278 6th St Apt 3b
Brooklyn NY 11215

(G-2007)
FRIENDLY STAR FUEL INC
889 3rd Ave (11232-1907)
PHONE......718 369-8801
Gurpal Cheema, *Principal*
EMP: 7
SALES (est): 674.4K **Privately Held**
SIC: 2869 Fuels

(G-2008)
FUTURE DIAGNOSTICS LLC
266 47th St (11220-1010)
PHONE......347 434-6700
Hindy Sobel, *Mng Member*
Charles Sobel, *Mng Member*
◆ EMP: 42
SQ FT: 20,000
SALES: 15MM **Privately Held**
SIC: 3841 Medical instruments & equipment, blood & bone work

(G-2009)
FUTURE STAR DIGATECH
713 Monroe St (11221-2813)
PHONE......718 666-0350
Kertena Seabrook, *Owner*
EMP: 10
SALES (est): 760.6K **Privately Held**
SIC: 3577 Printers, computer

(G-2010)
FWC NETWORKS INC
1615 Carroll St (11213-5409)
PHONE......718 408-1558
Boruch Lowenbein, *CEO*
Barbara Nowha, *Ch of Bd*
Shlomo Oved, *President*
Bashie Lowenbein, *CFO*
EMP: 18

Brooklyn - Kings County (G-2011)   **GEOGRAPHIC SECTION**

SQ FT: 6,000
SALES (est): 2.1MM **Privately Held**
SIC: 3699 Electrical welding equipment

(G-2011)
G S COMMUNICATIONS USA INC
Also Called: Gs Communications USA
179 Greenpoint Ave (11222-7088)
PHONE................................718 389-7371
Helen Juszczak, *President*
David Pasirstein, *Vice Pres*
Louis Makowski, *Network Mgr*
EMP: 22
SQ FT: 11,250
SALES (est): 2MM **Privately Held**
WEB: www.gscomm.com
SIC: 3571 5734 Personal computers (microcomputers); computer & software stores

(G-2012)
G Z G REST & KIT MET WORKS
120 13th St (11215-4604)
PHONE................................718 788-8621
Fax: 718 788-0482
Gregory Uchatel, *President*
Alex Blyusein, *Vice Pres*
EMP: 15
SQ FT: 5,500
SALES (est): 920K **Privately Held**
SIC: 2599 Bar, restaurant & cafeteria furniture; carts, restaurant equipment

(G-2013)
GALIVA INC
236 Broadway Ste 214 (11211-6289)
PHONE................................903 600-5755
Joel Gelb, *COO*
EMP: 4
SQ FT: 10,000
SALES: 1.4MM **Privately Held**
SIC: 2252 Socks

(G-2014)
GARCO MANUFACTURING CORP INC
4802 Farragut Rd (11203-6612)
PHONE................................718 287-3330
EMP: 7 EST 1960
SQ FT: 4,000
SALES (est): 64.5K **Privately Held**
SIC: 2851 Mfg Paints/Allied Products

(G-2015)
GARY GELBFISH MD
2502 Avenue I (11210-2830)
PHONE................................718 258-3004
Fax: 718 421-0628
Gary Gelbfish, *Owner*
Abigail Falk, *Manager*
EMP: 8
SALES (est): 690K **Privately Held**
SIC: 3845 Surgical support systems: heart-lung machine, exc. iron lung

(G-2016)
GCM METAL INDUSTRIES INC
454 Troutman St (11237-2604)
PHONE................................718 386-4059
Baldo Ciaravino, *President*
EMP: 15
SALES (est): 1.4MM **Privately Held**
SIC: 3449 1731 5051 1799 Bars, concrete reinforcing: fabricated steel; structural steel erection; structural shapes, iron or steel; ornamental metal work

(G-2017)
GCM STEEL PRODUCTS INC
454 Troutman St (11237-2604)
PHONE................................718 386-3346
Giovanna Mattarella, *President*
Josephine Dolce, *General Mgr*
EMP: 10
SALES (est): 1.1MM **Privately Held**
SIC: 3499 Metal household articles

(G-2018)
GCNS TECHNOLOGY GROUP INC (PA)
597 Rutland Rd (11203-1703)
PHONE................................347 713-8160
Onyike Adjaero, *President*
EMP: 6

SALES (est): 1.3MM **Privately Held**
SIC: 3825 Network analyzers

(G-2019)
GENERAL VY-COAT LLC
1636 Coney Island Ave 2b (11230-5808)
PHONE................................718 266-6002
Allen Gottfried, *General Mgr*
Sol Chaimovits,
▲ **EMP:** 40
SQ FT: 80,000
SALES (est): 5.2MM **Privately Held**
SIC: 2851 3086 2821 Vinyl coatings, strippable; plastics foam products; plastics materials & resins

(G-2020)
GENIUS MEDIA GROUP INC
Also Called: Rap Genius
92 3rd St (11231-4808)
PHONE................................509 670-7502
Thomas Lehman, *President*
EMP: 15
SALES (est): 880K **Privately Held**
SIC: 2741 Miscellaneous publishing

(G-2021)
GERI-GENTLE CORPORATION (PA)
3841 Ocean View Ave (11224-1343)
PHONE................................917 804-7807
Joseph Grun, *CEO*
Harold Rubin, *President*
▲ **EMP:** 2
SQ FT: 5,000
SALES: 2MM **Privately Held**
SIC: 3069 Medical & laboratory rubber sundries & related products

(G-2022)
GFL USA INC
Also Called: Gfl Amenities
81 Prospect St (11201-1473)
PHONE................................917 297-8701
Guido Bonadonna, *CEO*
Anna Childs, *Sales Mgr*
EMP: 2
SQ FT: 100
SALES (est): 1.2MM **Privately Held**
SIC: 2841 2844 Soap & other detergents; shampoos, rinses, conditioners: hair; towelettes, premoistened
PA: Gfl Sa
    Via Per Sorengo 1
    Lugano TI
    919 607-500

(G-2023)
GHANI TEXTILES INC
2459 Coyle St Fl 2 (11235-1207)
PHONE................................718 859-4561
Muhammad Aslam, *CEO*
▲ **EMP:** 1
SALES: 1MM **Privately Held**
SIC: 2299 Acoustic felts

(G-2024)
GILLIES COFFEE COMPANY
150 19th St (11232-1005)
PHONE................................718 499-7766
Fax: 718 499-7771
Donald N Schoenholt, *President*
Hy Chabbott, *Treasurer*
EMP: 25
SQ FT: 14,000
SALES: 3.3MM **Privately Held**
WEB: www.gilliescoffee.com
SIC: 2095 2099 Coffee roasting (except by wholesale grocers); tea blending

(G-2025)
GIULIETTA LLC
649 Morgan Ave Ste 3h (11222-3765)
PHONE................................212 334-1859
Sofia Sizzi, *Principal*
EMP: 5
SALES (est): 489.4K **Privately Held**
SIC: 2339 Women's & misses' accessories

(G-2026)
GIUMENTA CORP (PA)
Also Called: Utility Brass & Bronze Div
42 2nd Ave (11215-3102)
PHONE................................718 832-1200
Fax: 718 832-1390
Anthony J Giumenta, *President*

Anthony F Giumenta, *Vice Pres*
Stephen Giumenta, *Treasurer*
▲ **EMP:** 46
SQ FT: 55,000
SALES (est): 12.9MM **Privately Held**
SIC: 3446 Architectural metalwork; ornamental metalwork; grillwork, ornamental metal

(G-2027)
GLENNYS INC
1960 59th St (11204-2340)
PHONE................................516 377-1400
Mendel Fischer, *Vice Pres*
EMP: 8
SQ FT: 15,000
SALES (est): 770.5K **Privately Held**
SIC: 2064 2096 Breakfast bars; corn chips & other corn-based snacks

(G-2028)
GLENWOOD CAST STONE INC
Also Called: Glenwood Mason Supply
4106 Glenwood Rd (11210-2025)
PHONE................................718 859-6500
Constance M Cincotta, *President*
EMP: 5
SALES (est): 445.2K **Privately Held**
SIC: 3272 Concrete products, precast

(G-2029)
GLISSEN CHEMICAL CO INC (PA)
1321 58th St (11219-4594)
P.O. Box 190034 (11219-0034)
PHONE................................718 436-4200
Fax: 718 851-2938
Joseph W Lehr, *President*
Barbara Lehr, *Exec VP*
Rosita Barca, *Administration*
EMP: 27 EST: 1930
SQ FT: 25,000
SALES (est): 8.1MM **Privately Held**
SIC: 2841 Detergents, synthetic organic or inorganic alkaline

(G-2030)
GLOBEX KOSHER FOODS INC
Also Called: Interntonal Glatt Kosher Meats
5600 1st Ave Ste 19 (11220-2551)
PHONE................................718 630-5555
Fax: 718 921-1542
Abraham Chaimovitz, *Ch of Bd*
Leib Chaimovitz, *President*
◆ **EMP:** 23
SALES (est): 4.3MM **Privately Held**
SIC: 2011 Meat packing plants

(G-2031)
GLOBMARBLE LLC
2201 Neptune Ave Ste 5 (11224-2362)
PHONE................................347 717-4088
Iryna Semenenko, *Mng Member*
▲ **EMP:** 6 EST: 2010
SALES (est): 316.8K **Privately Held**
SIC: 3544 5031 Industrial molds; molding, all materials

(G-2032)
GM SHEET METAL INC
193 Newell St (11222-2421)
PHONE................................718 349-2830
Fax: 718 349-2968
Michael Flatley, *President*
EMP: 16
SALES (est): 1.5MM **Privately Held**
SIC: 3444 Metal ventilating equipment

(G-2033)
GMS HICKS STREET CORPORATION
214 Hicks St (11201-4110)
PHONE................................718 858-1010
Greg Markman, *Principal*
EMP: 40
SALES (est): 2.3MM **Privately Held**
SIC: 3088 Plastics plumbing fixtures

(G-2034)
GNI COMMERCE INC
Also Called: Yourhealth911.com
458 Neptune Ave Apt 11f (11224-4319)
PHONE................................347 275-1155
Vladimir Gouliaev, *President*
Bella Bomze, *Vice Pres*

▼ **EMP:** 7
SQ FT: 3,500
SALES: 3.1MM **Privately Held**
WEB: www.gnicommerce.com
SIC: 2023 Dietary supplements, dairy & non-dairy based

(G-2035)
GODDARD DESIGN CO
51 Nassau Ave Ste 1b (11222-3171)
PHONE................................718 599-0170
Robert Goddard, *Owner*
Rosemary Heath, *Office Mgr*
EMP: 7
SQ FT: 2,000
SALES: 500K **Privately Held**
WEB: www.goddarddesign.com
SIC: 3648 3625 3669 Lighting equipment; control equipment, electric; intercommunication systems, electric

(G-2036)
GODIVA CHOCOLATIER INC
5378 Kings Plz (11234-5216)
PHONE................................718 677-1452
Osbert James, *Branch Mgr*
EMP: 24 **Privately Held**
SIC: 2066 Chocolate
HQ: Godiva Chocolatier, Inc.
    333 W 34th St Fl 6
    New York NY 10001
    212 984-5900

(G-2037)
GOLD & DIAMONDS WHOLESALE OUTL
4417 5th Ave (11220-6834)
PHONE................................718 438-7888
Alex Gattif, *President*
EMP: 4
SALES: 2MM **Privately Held**
SIC: 3911 5094 Jewel settings & mountings, precious metal; diamonds (gems)

(G-2038)
GOLDEN LEAVES KNITWEAR INC
43 Hall St Ste B3 (11205-1395)
PHONE................................718 875-8235
Cheskel Gluck, *President*
▲ **EMP:** 40
SQ FT: 25,000
SALES: 2.3MM **Privately Held**
SIC: 2253 2339 Sweaters & sweater coats, knit; women's & misses' outerwear

(G-2039)
GOLDMARK INC
Also Called: Gold Mark Mfg Co
3611 14th Ave Ste B01 (11218-3750)
PHONE................................718 438-0295
Fax: 718 438-1274
Shimson Jalas, *President*
EMP: 20
SQ FT: 20,000
SALES (est): 3.3MM **Privately Held**
WEB: www.goldmark.com
SIC: 3915 Jewelers' findings & materials

(G-2040)
GOODMAN MAIN STOPPER MFG CO
523 Atlantic Ave (11217-1913)
PHONE................................718 875-5140
Joseph Petrone, *President*
EMP: 12 EST: 1897
SQ FT: 10,000
SALES (est): 1.2MM **Privately Held**
SIC: 3494 5999 Valves & pipe fittings; medical apparatus & supplies

(G-2041)
GORILLA COFFEE INC
472 Bergen St Ste A (11217-2438)
PHONE................................917 297-8947
EMP: 6
SALES (corp-wide): 545.2K **Privately Held**
SIC: 2095 Coffee roasting (except by wholesale grocers)
PA: Gorilla Coffee Inc.
    97 5th Ave
    Brooklyn NY 11217
    718 230-3244

GEOGRAPHIC SECTION

Brooklyn - Kings County (G-2071)

(G-2042)
GORILLA COFFEE INC (PA)
97 5th Ave (11217-3201)
PHONE...................718 230-3244
Darleen Scherer, *Ch of Bd*
EMP: 5
SALES (est): 545.2K **Privately Held**
WEB: www.gorillacoffee.com
SIC: 2095 Coffee roasting (except by wholesale grocers)

(G-2043)
GOTENNA INC
81 Willoughby St Fl 3 (11201-5232)
PHONE...................415 894-2616
Daniela Perdomo, *President*
John Levy, *Principal*
Jorge Perdomo, *Chief Engr*
Paul Vizzio, *Engineer*
EMP: 13
SALES (est): 1.1MM **Privately Held**
SIC: 3679 Headphones, radio

(G-2044)
GOURMET CRAFTS INC
152 Highlawn Ave (11223-2636)
P.O. Box 200006 (11220-0006)
PHONE...................718 372-0505
Borris Tulman, *President*
Eugene Tulman, *Vice Pres*
Eric Shkolnik, *CFO*
EMP: 16
SQ FT: 4,000
SALES (est): 925K **Privately Held**
WEB: www.thecrepeteam.com
SIC: 2099 Food preparations

(G-2045)
GOURMET TOAST CORP
345 Park Ave (11205-1389)
PHONE...................718 852-4536
Jack Feld, *President*
EMP: 8 **EST:** 1958
SQ FT: 8,000
SALES (est): 600K **Privately Held**
SIC: 2099 2051 Bread crumbs, not made in bakeries; bread, cake & related products

(G-2046)
GOVERNMENT DATA PUBLICATION
1661 Mcdonald Ave (11230-6312)
PHONE...................347 789-8719
Fax: 718 998-5960
Siegfried Lobel, *President*
Barbara Calabrese, *Director*
EMP: 35 **EST:** 1959
SQ FT: 10,000
SALES (est): 3.1MM **Privately Held**
WEB: www.govdata.com
SIC: 2731 2741 2721 2752 Books: publishing only; miscellaneous publishing; directories: publishing only, not printed on site; periodicals: publishing only; commercial printing, lithographic

(G-2047)
GRADO LABORATORIES INC
4614 7th Ave Ste 1 (11220-1499)
PHONE...................718 435-5340
Fax: 718 633-6941
John A Grado, *President*
John Chen, *Vice Pres*
Todd Green, *Manager*
▲ **EMP:** 10 **EST:** 1953
SQ FT: 10,000
SALES (est): 1.8MM **Privately Held**
SIC: 3679 Phonograph needles; headphones, radio

(G-2048)
GRANADA ELECTRONICS INC
485 Kent Ave (11249-5927)
PHONE...................718 387-1157
Fax: 718 486-6995
Nachman Brach, *President*
EMP: 6
SQ FT: 55,000
SALES (est): 540K **Privately Held**
SIC: 3651 Audio electronic systems; television receiving sets

(G-2049)
GRAND PROCESSING INC
1050 Grand St (11211-1701)
PHONE...................718 388-0600
Iggy Panadora, *President*
EMP: 30
SQ FT: 30,000
SALES (est): 1.3MM **Privately Held**
SIC: 2253 Dyeing & finishing knit outerwear, excl. hosiery & glove

(G-2050)
GRECO BROS RDYMX CON CO INC
381 Hamilton Ave (11231-3943)
PHONE...................718 855-6271
Joseph Greco, *President*
EMP: 8
SALES (corp-wide): 10.1MM **Privately Held**
SIC: 3273 Ready-mixed concrete
PA: Greco Bros. Ready Mix Concrete Co. Inc.
8713 Rockaway Blvd
Ozone Park NY 11416
718 849-5200

(G-2051)
GREEN BEAM LED INC
Also Called: Greenbeam Led
4601b 1st Ave (11232-4200)
PHONE...................718 439-6262
Elliot Gellar, *CEO*
EMP: 3 **EST:** 2014
SALES: 5MM **Privately Held**
SIC: 3646 Ceiling systems, luminous

(G-2052)
GREEN WAVE INTERNATIONAL INC
5423 1st Ave (11220-2503)
P.O. Box 90288 (11209-0288)
PHONE...................718 499-3371
Kay Dan Wong, *President*
Gerry Callaghan, *Sales Mgr*
Garret Fong, *Manager*
Ivan Hui, *Manager*
Abel Leung, *Technical Staff*
▲ **EMP:** 7
SQ FT: 12,000
SALES (est): 996.5K **Privately Held**
SIC: 3263 Commercial tableware or kitchen articles, fine earthenware

(G-2053)
GREENBUDS LLC
1434 57th St (11219-4619)
PHONE...................718 483-9212
Miriam Mandel,
EMP: 5 **EST:** 2010
SQ FT: 1,000
SALES: 500K **Privately Held**
SIC: 2221 Bedding, manmade or silk fabric

(G-2054)
GREENEBUILD LLC
390a Lafayette Ave (11238-1406)
PHONE...................917 562-0556
Winston Greene,
EMP: 12
SALES (est): 755.8K **Privately Held**
SIC: 1442 Construction sand & gravel

(G-2055)
GREENTREE PHARMACY INC
291 7th Ave (11215-7263)
PHONE...................718 768-2700
Fax: 718 768-6500
Julia Nudelman, *Owner*
EMP: 10 **EST:** 2013
SALES (est): 1.6MM **Privately Held**
SIC: 2834 5961 Pharmaceutical preparations; pharmaceuticals, mail order

(G-2056)
GUERNICA
Also Called: Guernica Magazine
63 3rd Pl Apt 4r (11231-4047)
PHONE...................914 414-7318
Fax: 917 280-1443
Joel Whitney, *Principal*
Elizabeth Onusko, *Principal*
EMP: 15
SALES: 20K **Privately Held**
SIC: 2721 Periodicals

(G-2057)
H & H LABORATORIES INC (PA)
61 4th St (11231-4809)
PHONE...................718 624-8041
Fax: 718 246-2738
George Hoffmann, *President*
Trina Moslih, *Assistant*
▲ **EMP:** 14
SQ FT: 5,000
SALES (est): 1.6MM **Privately Held**
WEB: www.hhlabs.com
SIC: 2844 2841 Toilet preparations; soap & other detergents

(G-2058)
H & H LABORATORIES INC
409 Hoyt St (11231-4858)
PHONE...................718 624-8041
George Hoffman, *Branch Mgr*
EMP: 5
SALES (corp-wide): 1.6MM **Privately Held**
SIC: 2844 2841 Toilet preparations; soap & other detergents
PA: H & H Laboratories Inc.
61 4th St
Brooklyn NY 11231
718 624-8041

(G-2059)
H T L & S LTD
Also Called: Peerless Envelopes & Prtg Co
5820 Fort Hamilton Pkwy (11219-4832)
PHONE...................718 435-4474
Fax: 718 438-1750
Sheldon Kustin, *Partner*
Lewis Kustin, *Partner*
EMP: 11 **EST:** 1933
SQ FT: 20,000
SALES: 700K **Privately Held**
SIC: 2752 2759 Commercial printing, offset; letterpress printing; flexographic printing

(G-2060)
HADDAD BROS INC
1200 Mcdonald Ave (11230-3321)
PHONE...................718 377-5505
Fax: 718 252-2426
John Isseco, *Executive*
EMP: 50
SALES (corp-wide): 7.2MM **Privately Held**
WEB: www.haddadbros.com
SIC: 2361 2369 2335 Girls' & children's dresses, blouses & shirts; girls' & children's outerwear; women's, juniors' & misses' dresses
PA: Haddad Bros. Inc.
28 W 36th St Rm 1026
New York NY 10018
212 563-2117

(G-2061)
HAGADAH PASSOVER BAKERY
814 Bergen St (11238-3702)
PHONE...................718 638-1589
Fax: 718 623-6681
P Woodsberger, *Owner*
Joe Castri, *Manager*
EMP: 8
SALES (est): 453.6K **Privately Held**
SIC: 2051 Bread, cake & related products

(G-2062)
HALMARK ARCHITECTURAL FINSHG
353 Stanley Ave (11207-7601)
PHONE...................718 272-1831
Fax: 718 272-1835
Hal Spergel, *President*
EMP: 24
SQ FT: 10,000
SALES (est): 2.9MM **Privately Held**
SIC: 3471 2843 3449 Finishing, metals or formed products; surface active agents; miscellaneous metalwork

(G-2063)
HAMODIA CORP
Also Called: Daily Newspr For Torah Jewry
207 Foster Ave (11230-2195)
PHONE...................718 853-9094
Fax: 718 853-9103
Ruth Lichtenstein, *CEO*
Andrew Relkin, *Editor*
Moshe Vatalion, *Controller*
EMP: 15 **EST:** 1998
SALES (est): 947.2K **Privately Held**
SIC: 2711 Newspapers

(G-2064)
HANA PASTRIES INC
34 35th St Unit 9 (11232-2212)
P.O. Box 320154 (11232-0154)
PHONE...................718 369-7593
Michael Schwartz, *Principal*
EMP: 6
SALES (est): 757.2K **Privately Held**
SIC: 2051 5411 Bread, cake & related products; supermarkets

(G-2065)
HANCO METAL PRODUCTS INC
25 Jay St (11201-1139)
PHONE...................212 787-5992
Fax: 718 243-2915
Mark Meyer Hantman, *President*
Myles Hantman, *General Mgr*
Debra Hantman, *Corp Secy*
EMP: 10 **EST:** 1934
SQ FT: 2,000
SALES (est): 800K **Privately Held**
SIC: 3451 3432 Screw machine products; faucets & spigots, metal & plastic

(G-2066)
HANDMADE FRAMES INC
1013 Grand St Ste 2 (11211-1720)
PHONE...................718 782-8364
Fax: 718 782-6146
Paul Baumann, *President*
Angel Lopez, *General Mgr*
Marilyn Gold, *Vice Pres*
EMP: 14
SQ FT: 9,000
SALES: 983.6K **Privately Held**
SIC: 3999 3952 Framed artwork; frames for artists' canvases

(G-2067)
HANDY TOOL & MFG CO INC
1205 Rockaway Ave (11236-2132)
P.O. Box 360524 (11236-0524)
PHONE...................718 478-9203
Fax: 718 429-5062
Rochelle Sherman, *Treasurer*
Raquel Genao, *Admin Asst*
EMP: 22 **EST:** 1948
SQ FT: 13,600
SALES (est): 5.8MM **Privately Held**
SIC: 3728 3544 Aircraft assemblies, sub-assemblies & parts; special dies, tools, jigs & fixtures

(G-2068)
HEALTHONE PHARMACY INC
119 Pennsylvania Ave (11207-2428)
PHONE...................718 495-9015
Fax: 718 495-9017
Mel Springer, *President*
EMP: 15
SALES (est): 3.5MM **Privately Held**
SIC: 2834 Pharmaceutical preparations

(G-2069)
HEALTHY WAY OF LIFE MAGAZINE
1529 Voorhies Ave (11235-3912)
PHONE...................718 616-1681
Boris Zat, *President*
EMP: 5
SALES (est): 287.8K **Privately Held**
SIC: 2721 Periodicals

(G-2070)
HECHT & SOHN GLASS CO INC
406 Willoughby Ave (11205-4509)
PHONE...................718 782-8295
Fax: 718 486-6414
Abe Sabel, *President*
▲ **EMP:** 6
SQ FT: 11,000
SALES (est): 754K **Privately Held**
WEB: www.entrances.com
SIC: 3211 Flat glass; doors, glass: made from purchased glass

(G-2071)
HELLO AND HOLA MEDIA INC
1 Metrotech Ctr Fl 18 (11201-3948)
PHONE...................212 807-4795

Brooklyn - Kings County (G-2072)

Eduardo Sanchez Perez, *CEO*
EMP: 22
SALES (est): 686.4K **Privately Held**
SIC: 2721 Magazines: publishing & printing

(G-2072)
HENRYS DEALS INC
Also Called Allstateelectronics
1002 Quentin Rd Ste 2009 (11223-2248)
PHONE................................347 821-4685
David Mats, *CEO*
Simon Sarweh, *CEO*
EMP: 20
SALES: 1MM **Privately Held**
SIC: 3861 Photographic equipment & supplies

(G-2073)
HERCULES HEAT TREATING CORP
101 Classon Ave 113 (11205-1401)
PHONE................................718 625-1266
Anthony Rizzo Jr, *President*
Joseph Rizzo, *Vice Pres*
Gabriel Giraldo, *Engineer*
EMP: 27
SQ FT: 25,000
SALES (est): 5.9MM **Privately Held**
WEB: www.herculesht.com
SIC: 3398 Metal heat treating

(G-2074)
HERMAN H STICHT COMPANY INC
Also Called: Megohmer Vibrating Reed Standco
45 Main St Ste 401 (11201-1084)
PHONE................................718 852-7602
Fax: 718 852-7915
Paul H Plotkin, *President*
Glenn A Butterfield, *Vice Pres*
Edna E Brown, *Treasurer*
EMP: 6
SQ FT: 6,000
SALES (est): 1.1MM **Privately Held**
WEB: www.stichtco.com
SIC: 3825 3823 3829 Measuring instruments & meters, electric; industrial instrmnts msrmnt display/control process variable; measuring & controlling devices

(G-2075)
HERMAN HALL COMMUNICATIONS
Also Called: Everybodys Carribbean Magazine
1630 Nostrand Ave (11226-5516)
PHONE................................718 941-1879
Fax: 718 941 1886
Herman Hall, *President*
Helen Lucas, *Treasurer*
EMP: 12
SQ FT: 5,000
SALES: 500K **Privately Held**
SIC: 2721 Magazines: publishing only, not printed on site

(G-2076)
HERRIS GOURMET INC
536 Grand St (11211-3503)
PHONE................................917 578-2308
Herman Francroz, *Vice Pres*
EMP: 5
SQ FT: 2,500
SALES (est): 297.2K **Privately Held**
SIC: 2051 5812 5499 Bread, cake & related products; contract food services; gourmet food stores

(G-2077)
HERTLING TROUSERS INC
236 Greenpoint Ave (11222-2493)
PHONE................................718 784-6100
Fax: 718 784-7015
Julius Hertling, *President*
▲ **EMP:** 40
SQ FT: 8,000
SALES (est): 4.4MM **Privately Held**
SIC: 2325 2253 Men's & boys' trousers & slacks; pants, slacks or trousers, knit

(G-2078)
HMO BEVERAGE CORP
68 33rd St Unit 4 (11232-1912)
PHONE................................917 371-6100
Georgios Papanastasatos, *Principal*
EMP: 6
SALES (est): 510.7K **Privately Held**
SIC: 2086 Carbonated beverages, nonalcoholic: bottled & canned

(G-2079)
HOLLYWOOD SIGNS INC
388 3rd Ave (11215-2705)
PHONE................................917 577-7333
Steve Kokonovich, *President*
EMP: 9
SALES (est): 690K **Privately Held**
SIC: 3993 Signs & advertising specialties

(G-2080)
HOLYOKE FITTINGS INC
850 Stanley Ave (11208-5226)
PHONE................................718 649-0710
Allan Rodolitz, *President*
Joan Tipia, *Manager*
EMP: 15
SQ FT: 18,000
SALES (est): 2.1MM **Privately Held**
WEB: www.holyokefittings.com
SIC: 3432 Plumbers' brass goods: drain cocks, faucets, spigots, etc.

(G-2081)
HOME REPORTER INC
Also Called: Home Reporter & Sunset News
8723 3rd Ave (11209-5103)
PHONE................................718 238-6600
Fax: 718 238-6610
James F Griffin Jr, *President*
Alex Kalas, *Corp Secy*
Marvile Griffin, *Vice Pres*
Sara Otey, *Advt Staff*
EMP: 50 **EST:** 1956
SQ FT: 2,000
SALES (est): 2.3MM **Privately Held**
WEB: www.homereporter.net
SIC: 2711 Newspapers, publishing & printing

(G-2082)
HOME4U INC
152 Skillman St Apt 8 (11205-3906)
PHONE................................347 262-7214
Abraham Goldstein, *CEO*
Joel Teitelbaum, *CFO*
▲ **EMP:** 7
SQ FT: 2,000
SALES (est): 413.3K **Privately Held**
SIC: 2541 Cabinets, lockers & shelving

(G-2083)
HONEYBEE ROBOTICS LTD (PA)
Also Called: Honeybee Rbtics Cft Mechanisms
Suit Bldg 128 (11205)
PHONE................................212 966-0661
Fax: 646 459-7898
Kiel Davis, *President*
Stephen Gorvan, *Chairman*
Jason Herman, *Vice Pres*
Erik Mumm, *Vice Pres*
Kris Zacny, *Vice Pres*
EMP: 44
SQ FT: 110,000
SALES (est): 9.1MM **Privately Held**
WEB: www.honeybeerobotics.com
SIC: 3569 Robots, assembly line: industrial & commercial

(G-2084)
HOSKIE CO INC
132 Harrison Pl (11237-1522)
PHONE................................718 628-8672
Fax: 718 628-5545
Glenn Ho, *CEO*
◆ **EMP:** 80
SQ FT: 38,000
SALES (est): 17.4MM **Privately Held**
WEB: www.hoskiecompanyinc.com
SIC: 2015 3999 Poultry slaughtering & processing; atomizers, toiletry

(G-2085)
HPI CO INC (PA)
1656 41st St (11218-5512)
PHONE................................718 851-2753
Moshe Kenner, *President*
Peggy Oberland, *Vice Pres*
▲ **EMP:** 5
SQ FT: 3,000
SALES: 100K **Privately Held**
WEB: www.hpico.net
SIC: 3567 Industrial furnaces & ovens

(G-2086)
HUDSON POWER TRANSMISSION CO
241 Halsey St (11216-2403)
PHONE................................718 622-3869
Fax: 718 622-9396
Lawrence Saft, *President*
EMP: 5
SQ FT: 880
SALES (est): 440K **Privately Held**
SIC: 3568 Power transmission equipment

(G-2087)
HUNTINGTON ICE & CUBE CORP (PA)
335 Moffat St (11237-6408)
PHONE................................718 456-2013
Gaspar Piccolo, *Vice Pres*
EMP: 10
SALES (est): 1.1MM **Privately Held**
SIC: 2097 Block ice

(G-2088)
HYGRADE
30 Warsoff Pl (11205-1638)
PHONE................................718 488-9000
Follman Lazar, *President*
EMP: 7
SALES (est): 139.5K **Privately Held**
SIC: 3842 7218 4959 Personal safety equipment; wiping towel supply; environmental cleanup services

(G-2089)
HYMAN PODRUSNICK CO INC
212 Foster Ave (11230-2197)
P.O. Box 300158 (11230-0158)
PHONE................................718 853-4502
David Binder, *President*
Mae Binder, *Vice Pres*
▲ **EMP:** 5
SQ FT: 5,000
SALES (est): 410K **Privately Held**
SIC: 3469 3821 Household cooking & kitchen utensils, porcelain enameled; laboratory apparatus & furniture

(G-2090)
HYPERLINE SYSTEMS INC
9322 3rd Ave Ste 406 (11209-6802)
PHONE................................613 736-8500
Gregory Shields, *Branch Mgr*
EMP: 7 **Privately Held**
SIC: 3357 5063 Coaxial cable, nonferrous; wire & cable
PA: Hyperline Systems Inc.
700 Pinnacle Ct Ste 170
Norcross GA 30071

(G-2091)
IAMMALIAMILLS LLC
Also Called: Malia Mills
32 33rd St Unit 13 (11232-1924)
PHONE................................805 845-2137
Malian Mills,
EMP: 6
SALES (est): 646.2K **Privately Held**
SIC: 2253 Bathing suits & swimwear, knit

(G-2092)
IBERIA FOODS CORP (HQ)
1900 Linden Blvd (11207-6806)
PHONE................................718 272-8900
Eric Miller, *President*
Jay Shmulewitz, *Sls & Mktg Exec*
William Schneible, *CFO*
John Pierrard, *Controller*
Ada White, *Human Res Dir*
◆ **EMP:** 80
SQ FT: 240
SALES: 28.8MM
SALES (corp-wide): 39.9MM **Privately Held**
SIC: 2032 Ethnic foods: canned, jarred, etc.
PA: Brooklyn Bottling Of Milton, New York, Inc.
643 South Rd
Milton NY 12547
845 795-2171

(G-2093)
ICESTONE LLC
63 Flushing Ave Unit 283b (11205-1079)
PHONE................................718 624-4900
Dal Lamagna, *CEO*
Jana Milcikova, *President*
Arti Bhatt, *Vice Pres*
Alison Tester, *Purch Dir*
Raymond Chen, *Research*
▲ **EMP:** 37
SQ FT: 55,000
SALES (est): 6.7MM **Privately Held**
SIC: 3281 2541 1752 3499 Building stone products; counter & sink tops; ceramic floor tile installation; furniture parts, metal

(G-2094)
IEH CORPORATION
140 58th St Ste 8e (11220-2525)
PHONE................................718 492-4440
Fax: 718 492-9898
Michael Offerman, *Ch of Bd*
Mark Iskin, *Purchasing*
Robert Knoth, *CFO*
David Offerman, *Natl Sales Mgr*
Joan Prideaux, *Marketing Staff*
EMP: 160 **EST:** 1937
SQ FT: 20,400
SALES: 20.1MM **Privately Held**
WEB: www.iehcorp.com
SIC: 3678 Electronic connectors

(G-2095)
IMPERIAL FRAMES & ALBUMS LLC
8200 21st Ave (11214-2506)
PHONE................................718 832-9793
Moshe Wigdder, *Mng Member*
▲ **EMP:** 5
SALES: 2.5MM **Privately Held**
WEB: www.imperialframes.com
SIC: 2499 Woodenware, kitchen & household

(G-2096)
IMPERIAL LAMINATORS CO INC
961 Elton St (11208-5417)
P.O. Box 7367, Hicksville (11802-7361)
PHONE................................718 272-9500
Fax: 718 649-1292
Bernard Brown, *President*
David Brown, *Treasurer*
▲ **EMP:** 10
SQ FT: 40,000
SALES (est): 756.2K **Privately Held**
SIC: 2295 2297 Laminating of fabrics; bonded-fiber fabrics, except felt

(G-2097)
IMPERIAL POLYMERS INC
534 Grand St (11211-3503)
PHONE................................718 387-4741
Joseph Freund, *President*
EMP: 6
SALES (est): 550K **Privately Held**
SIC: 2821 3089 Molding compounds, plastics; plastic processing

(G-2098)
IMPERIAL SWEATER MILLS INC
Also Called: Eagle Nesher
1365 38th St (11218-3634)
PHONE................................718 871-4414
Fax: 718 871-5463
Shalom Katz, *President*
Benjamin Katz, *Admin Sec*
EMP: 6 **EST:** 1955
SQ FT: 18,500
SALES (est): 584.6K **Privately Held**
SIC: 2253 Sweaters & sweater coats, knit

(G-2099)
IMPREMEDIA LLC (DH)
Also Called: La Raza
1 Metrotech Ctr Fl 18 (11201-3948)
PHONE................................212 807-4785
Damian Mazzotta, *General Mgr*
Patricia Prieto, *Editor*
Carmen Villavicencio, *Editor*
Olga Casabona, *Vice Pres*
John Paton, *Mng Member*
▲ **EMP:** 99

GEOGRAPHIC SECTION

Brooklyn - Kings County (G-2126)

SALES (est): 61.2MM **Privately Held**
WEB: www.impremedia.com
SIC: 2711 Newspapers: publishing only, not printed on site
HQ: Us Hispanic Media Inc
  1 Metrotech Ctr Fl 18
  Brooklyn NY 11201
  212 885-8000

(G-2100)
INDIAN LARRY LEGACY
400 Union Ave (11211-3429)
PHONE..................................718 609-9184
EMP: 5
SALES: 500K **Privately Held**
SIC: 3751 Mfg Motorcycles/Bicycles

(G-2101)
INDUSTRIAL ELECTRONIC HARDWARE
140 58th St Ste 8e (11220-2525)
PHONE..................................718 492-4440
Fax: 718 492-9897
Bob Offman, *President*
Robert Romeo, *Vice Pres*
Reggie Johnson, *Manager*
Cindy Sciascia, *Manager*
Rolando Velez, *Manager*
EMP: 70
SALES (est): 6MM **Privately Held**
SIC: 3429 Manufactured hardware (general)

(G-2102)
INDUSTRIAL FINISHING PRODUCTS
820 Remsen Ave (11236-1611)
PHONE..................................718 342-4871
Andrew Galgano, *Manager*
EMP: 12
SALES (corp-wide): 12.4MM **Privately Held**
WEB: www.industrialfinishings.com
SIC: 2851 Plastics base paints & varnishes
PA: Industrial Finishing Products Inc
  465 Logan St
  Brooklyn NY 11208
  718 277-3333

(G-2103)
INFANT FORMULA LABORATORY SVC
711 Livonia Ave (11207-5497)
PHONE..................................718 257-3000
Richard C Miller, *President*
EMP: 10 EST: 1947
SQ FT: 20,000
SALES (est): 1MM **Privately Held**
SIC: 2023 5149 Bottled baby formula; groceries & related products

(G-2104)
INK PUBLISHING CORPORATION
68 Jay St Ste 315 (11201-8360)
PHONE..................................347 294-1220
Steve Oconnor, *Sales Dir*
Phyll Castle, *Branch Mgr*
EMP: 6
SALES (corp-wide): 77.8MM **Privately Held**
SIC: 2721 Periodicals
HQ: Ink Publishing Corporation
  800 Suth Dglas Rd Ste 250
  Miami FL 33134
  786 482-2065

(G-2105)
INK WELL
1440 Coney Island Ave (11230-4120)
PHONE..................................718 253-9736
Yosef Oratz, *Owner*
EMP: 5
SQ FT: 4,000
SALES (est): 340K **Privately Held**
SIC: 2752 Commercial printing, lithographic

(G-2106)
INLAND PAPER PRODUCTS CORP
Also Called: Wew Container
444 Liberty Ave (11207)
P.O. Box 70137 (11207-0137)
PHONE..................................718 827-8150

Daniel Weicher, *President*
Joel Einbinoer, *Corp Secy*
▲ EMP: 20
SQ FT: 30,000
SALES (est): 3.6MM **Privately Held**
SIC: 3083 Laminated plastics plate & sheet

(G-2107)
INTEGRA MICROSYSTEM 1988 INC
Also Called: All-Tech
61 Greenpoint Ave Ste 412 (11222-1526)
PHONE..................................718 609-6099
Israel Haber, *Ch of Bd*
EMP: 5
SQ FT: 1,000
SALES (est): 826.8K **Privately Held**
SIC: 3575 Computer terminals, monitors & components

(G-2108)
INTERIOR METALS
Also Called: M&A Metals
255 48th St (11220-1011)
PHONE..................................718 439-7324
Fax: 718 439-8723
Michael Tommasi, *President*
Antonella Tommasi, *Corp Secy*
Eric Ulmer, *Project Mgr*
John Fina, *Manager*
Laura Lopez, *Assistant*
EMP: 27
SQ FT: 13,000
SALES (est): 4.7MM **Privately Held**
WEB: www.interiormetals.com
SIC: 3444 Radiator shields or enclosures, sheet metal

(G-2109)
INTERNATIONAL AIDS VACCINE INI
140 58th St (11220-2521)
PHONE..................................646 381-8066
EMP: 19
SALES (corp-wide): 72.3MM **Privately Held**
SIC: 2836 8731 Vaccines; commercial physical research
PA: International Aids Vaccine Initative Inc
  125 Broad St Fl 9
  New York NY 10004
  212 847-1111

(G-2110)
INTERNATIONAL STONE ACCESSRS
703 Myrtle Ave (11205-3903)
PHONE..................................718 522-5399
Fax: 718 596-6373
Abraham Levy, *President*
Sanny Levy, *Vice Pres*
▲ EMP: 6
SQ FT: 7,500
SALES (est): 907.4K **Privately Held**
WEB: www.stonecityexpo.com
SIC: 3281 Marble, building: cut & shaped

(G-2111)
INTERNTIONAL FIREPROF DOOR INC
1005 Greene Ave (11221-2910)
PHONE..................................718 783-1310
Fax: 718 783-4308
Eric Arrow, *President*
EMP: 10
SQ FT: 7,500
SALES (est): 990K **Privately Held**
WEB: www.firedoor.com
SIC: 3442 Fire doors, metal; window & door frames

(G-2112)
INTERNTNAL STRPPING DIECUTTING
Also Called: Deslauriers
200 Franklin St (11222-1633)
PHONE..................................718 383-7720
Fax: 718 349-2954
Jan Chielewski, *President*
EMP: 6 EST: 1955
SQ FT: 10,000
SALES (est): 460K **Privately Held**
SIC: 3554 7699 Paper industries machinery; box making machines, paper; printing trades machinery & equipment repair

(G-2113)
IQUIT CIG LLC
4014 13th Ave (11218-3502)
PHONE..................................718 475-1422
Zelman Pollak,
EMP: 6
SQ FT: 250
SALES (est): 335.6K **Privately Held**
SIC: 3999 Cigarette & cigar products & accessories

(G-2114)
ISH PRECISION MACHINE CORP (PA)
786 Mcdonald Ave (11218-5606)
PHONE..................................718 436-8858
Fax: 718 436-8858
Issac Sheran, *President*
Aleksandr Sherman, *Vice Pres*
EMP: 11
SALES (est): 1.5MM **Privately Held**
SIC: 3541 Machine tools, metal cutting type

(G-2115)
ISSACS YISROEL
Also Called: Benchers Unlimited
4424 18th Ave (11204-1201)
PHONE..................................718 851-7430
Yisroel Issacs, *Owner*
EMP: 5
SALES: 600K **Privately Held**
WEB: www.benchers.com
SIC: 2759 5947 Imprinting; gifts & novelties

(G-2116)
IT COMMODITY SOURCING INC
Also Called: Federal Contract MGT Svcs
1640 E 22nd St (11210-5125)
PHONE..................................718 677-1577
Aviva Tabak, *CEO*
Vevel Tabak, *President*
Peretz Charach, *Vice Pres*
EMP: 5
SALES (est): 370K **Privately Held**
SIC: 3663 Radio & TV communications equipment

(G-2117)
ITAC LABEL & TAG CORP
179 Lexington Ave (11216-1114)
PHONE..................................718 625-2148
Fax: 718 625-3806
ARI Adler, *President*
Rarzy Schwartz, *Manager*
EMP: 7
SQ FT: 17,500
SALES: 700K **Privately Held**
SIC: 2672 Labels (unprinted), gummed: made from purchased materials

(G-2118)
ITIN SCALE CO INC
4802 Glenwood Rd (11234-1106)
PHONE..................................718 336-5900
Samuel Racer, *President*
Lance Gregor, *Sales Mgr*
Philip Levinson, *Manager*
◆ EMP: 20 EST: 1970
SQ FT: 4,500
SALES (est): 5.1MM **Privately Held**
WEB: www.itinscales.com
SIC: 3829 3699 3596 3821 Measuring & controlling devices; electrical equipment & supplies; scales & balances, except laboratory; laboratory apparatus & furniture; scales, except laboratory; commercial cooking & food service equipment

(G-2119)
IVALUA INC
195 Montague St (11201-3628)
PHONE..................................650 930-9710
Daniel Olivier Amzallag, *CEO*
EMP: 10
SALES (corp-wide): 19.6MM **Privately Held**
SIC: 7372 Business oriented computer software
HQ: Ivalua, Inc.
  805 Veterans Blvd Ste 230
  Redwood City CA 94063

(G-2120)
J & J BRONZE & ALUMINUM CAST
Also Called: All Cast Foundry
249 Huron St (11222-1801)
PHONE..................................718 383-2111
Fax: 718 383-3893
Vincent Grosso, *Vice Pres*
Robert Grosso, *Vice Pres*
EMP: 34
SQ FT: 23,000
SALES (est): 4.2MM **Privately Held**
SIC: 3366 3365 3369 Castings (except die): bronze; aluminum & aluminum-based alloy castings; nonferrous foundries

(G-2121)
J H C FABRICATIONS INC (PA)
Also Called: Jhc Labresin
595 Berriman St (11208-5203)
P.O. Box 80377 (11208-0377)
PHONE..................................718 649-0065
Henry L Calamari, *President*
John Calamari, *Corp Secy*
Christopher Delgrosso, *Marketing Staff*
Michael Manachevtz, *Manager*
▲ EMP: 20 EST: 1986
SQ FT: 16,000
SALES (est): 3MM **Privately Held**
WEB: www.jhclabresin.com
SIC: 3821 3644 Laboratory furniture; insulators & insulation materials, electrical

(G-2122)
J H M ENGINEERING
4014 8th Ave (11232-3706)
PHONE..................................718 871-1810
J H Maliga, *Owner*
Bud Hammen, *Sales/Mktg Mgr*
Carmen Martinez, *Bookkeeper*
EMP: 25 EST: 1966
SQ FT: 15,000
SALES (est): 2MM **Privately Held**
SIC: 3841 3843 3845 3699 Surgical & medical instruments; dental equipment; electromedical equipment; electrical equipment & supplies

(G-2123)
J LOWY CO
Also Called: J Lowy Lea Skullcaps Mfg Co
940 E 19th St (11230-3805)
PHONE..................................718 338-7324
Jerry Lowy, *Owner*
▲ EMP: 8
SALES: 1MM **Privately Held**
WEB: www.kippott.com
SIC: 2386 5999 Hats & caps, leather; religious goods

(G-2124)
J M C BOW CO INC
1271 39th St Ste 3 (11218-1981)
PHONE..................................718 686-8110
Bernard Kalisch, *President*
EMP: 15 EST: 1952
SQ FT: 7,500
SALES (est): 1.4MM **Privately Held**
SIC: 2323 2389 Bow ties, men's & boys': made from purchased materials; cummerbunds

(G-2125)
J M L PRODUCTIONS INC
162 Spencer St (11205-3929)
PHONE..................................718 643-1674
Jay Cohen, *President*
Michael Dymburt, *Admin Sec*
EMP: 60
SQ FT: 30,000
SALES (est): 2.3MM **Privately Held**
SIC: 2396 2759 Screen printing on fabric articles; screen printing

(G-2126)
J M P DISPLAY FIXTURE CO INC
760 E 96th St (11236-1821)
PHONE..................................718 649-0333
Fax: 718 485-4125
Joseph Cangelosi, *President*
Rosalie Angelosi, *Vice Pres*
EMP: 7
SQ FT: 7,200
SALES (est): 1MM **Privately Held**
SIC: 2541 Display fixtures, wood

(PA)=Parent Co (HQ)=Headquarters (DH)=Div Headquarters
✪ = New Business established in last 2 years

Brooklyn - Kings County (G-2127)

(G-2127)
J ZELUCK INC (PA)
5300 Kings Hwy (11234-1016)
PHONE.................................718 251-8060
Roy Zeluck, *President*
Kevin Zeluck, *Vice Pres*
Tommy Morrone, *Plant Mgr*
Michael Sincaglia, *Project Mgr*
Everett Philpot, *Manager*
◆ **EMP:** 50 **EST:** 1921
SALES (est): 8.9MM **Privately Held**
WEB: www.zeluck.com
SIC: 2431 Windows, wood; doors, wood

(G-2128)
JACKS GOURMET LLC
1000 Dean St Ste 214 (11238-3382)
PHONE.................................718 954-4681
Jack Silberstein, *CEO*
EMP: 12
SALES: 15MM **Privately Held**
SIC: 2013 Sausages & other prepared meats

(G-2129)
JACMAX INDUSTRIES LLC
Also Called: Expressive Scent
473 Wortman Ave (11208-5425)
PHONE.................................718 439-3743
Max Antar, *CEO*
Jack Eida, *President*
EMP: 5
SQ FT: 150,000
SALES (est): 455.6K **Privately Held**
SIC: 2677 Envelopes

(G-2130)
JACOB INC
287 Keap St (11211-7477)
PHONE.................................646 450-3067
Solomon Breuer, *CEO*
EMP: 40
SQ FT: 8,000
SALES: 20MM **Privately Held**
SIC: 3554 Paper industries machinery

(G-2131)
JACOBS JUICE CORP
388 Avenue X Apt 2h (11223-6025)
PHONE.................................646 255-2860
Jacob Prig, *President*
EMP: 5
SALES (est): 183.4K **Privately Held**
SIC: 3999 Novelties, bric-a-brac & hobby kits

(G-2132)
JACOBY ENTERPRISES LLC
1615 54th St (11204-1438)
PHONE.................................718 435-0289
Shraga Jacobowitz, *Vice Pres*
Jose Marmolejos, *Sales Associate*
Abraham Jacobowitz,
Karen Zheng, *Assoc Prof*
▲ **EMP:** 7
SQ FT: 1,500
SALES (est): 1.2MM **Privately Held**
WEB: www.jacobygems.com
SIC: 3911 5094 Bracelets, precious metal; cigarette lighters, precious metal; precious stones & metals; jewelry

(G-2133)
JAKES SNEAKERS INC
845 Classon Ave (11238-6103)
PHONE.................................718 233-1132
Jake Zebak, *President*
Beatrellia Francis, *Manager*
EMP: 1
SALES: 1.2MM **Privately Held**
SIC: 2393 5661 Cushions, except spring & carpet: purchased materials; children's shoes

(G-2134)
JAXIS INC (PA)
Also Called: Jaxis Sportswear
1365 38th St (11218-3634)
PHONE.................................212 302-7611
Ezra Abed, *President*
Nathan Mann, *Vice Pres*
Eddy Mann, *Admin Sec*
EMP: 8
SQ FT: 1,100
SALES (est): 560K **Privately Held**
SIC: 2339 5137 Sportswear, women's; sportswear, women's & children's

(G-2135)
JAY TUROFF
Also Called: Jay-Art Nvelties/Tower Grafics
681 Coney Island Ave (11218-4306)
PHONE.................................718 856-7300
Jay Turoff, *Owner*
EMP: 11 **EST:** 1965
SQ FT: 3,500
SALES: 1.2MM **Privately Held**
SIC: 3993 7336 3961 Signs & advertising specialties; commercial art & graphic design; costume novelties

(G-2136)
JERRY TOMASELLI
Also Called: Express Tag & Label
141 32nd St (11232-1809)
PHONE.................................718 965-1400
Fax: 718 965-1648
Jerry Tomaselli, *Owner*
EMP: 10
SQ FT: 10,000
SALES: 500K **Privately Held**
SIC: 2679 Tags, paper (unprinted): made from purchased paper

(G-2137)
JEWELERS SOLDER SUPPLY INC
Also Called: Jewler's Solder Sheet & Wire
1362 54th St (11219-4219)
P.O. Box 190141 (11219-0141)
PHONE.................................718 637-1256
Michael Goldenberg, *Owner*
Connie Klinger, *Principal*
Rachel Goldenberg, *Vice Pres*
EMP: 11
SQ FT: 10,000
SALES (est): 145.2K **Privately Held**
SIC: 3356 Solder: wire, bar, acid core, & rosin core

(G-2138)
JEWISH HERITAGE FOR BLIND
1655 E 24th St (11229-2401)
PHONE.................................718 338-4999
Fax: 718 338-0653
Rabbi David Toiv, *President*
EMP: 8
SQ FT: 2,000
SALES (est): 607.1K **Privately Held**
WEB: www.jhftb.org
SIC: 2741 Miscellaneous publishing

(G-2139)
JEWISH JOURNAL
7014 13th Ave (11228-1604)
PHONE.................................718 630-9350
EMP: 5
SALES (est): 160K **Privately Held**
SIC: 2711 Newspapers-Publishing/Printing

(G-2140)
JEWISH PRESS INC
4915 16th Ave (11204-1115)
PHONE.................................718 330-1100
Fax: 718 797-2717
Sidney Klass, *President*
Shelia Abrams, *Editor*
Jerry Greenwald, *Vice Pres*
Harry Rosenthal, *Vice Pres*
Arthur Federman, *Controller*
EMP: 149 **EST:** 1949
SQ FT: 40,000
SALES (est): 9.6MM **Privately Held**
WEB: www.jewishpress.com
SIC: 2711 Newspapers: publishing only, not printed on site

(G-2141)
JILL FENICHELL INC
Also Called: Bongenre.com
169 Prospect Pl (11238-3801)
PHONE.................................718 237-2490
Jill Fenichell, *President*
▲ **EMP:** 6
SALES: 250K **Privately Held**
SIC: 3263 Tableware, household & commercial: semivitreous

(G-2142)
JO-MART CANDIES CORP
Also Called: Jo Mart Chocolates
2917 Avenue R (11229-2525)
PHONE.................................718 375-1277
Fax: 718 382-7144
Michael Rogak, *President*
EMP: 11 **EST:** 1946
SQ FT: 3,000
SALES (est): 1.4MM **Privately Held**
WEB: www.jomartchocolates.com
SIC: 2064 5441 2066 Candy & other confectionery products; candy; chocolate & cocoa products

(G-2143)
JOEL ZELCER
102 S 8th St (11249-8632)
PHONE.................................917 525-6790
Joel Zelcer, *Owner*
EMP: 10
SALES (est): 520.7K **Privately Held**
SIC: 3944 7389 Games, toys & children's vehicles;

(G-2144)
JOHN AUGULIARO PRINTING CO
Also Called: John V Augugliaro Printing
2533 Mcdonald Ave (11223-5232)
PHONE.................................718 382-5283
Fax: 718 382-5283
Justin Augugliaro, *President*
EMP: 8
SALES (est): 760K **Privately Held**
SIC: 2759 Commercial printing

(G-2145)
JOMAT NEW YORK INC
4100 1st Ave Ste 3 (11232-3303)
PHONE.................................718 369-7641
Marc Landman, *President*
EMP: 35
SQ FT: 12,000
SALES: 1MM **Privately Held**
SIC: 2339 2369 Women's & misses' outerwear; girls' & children's outerwear

(G-2146)
JORDACHE WOODWORKING CORP
276 Greenpoint Ave # 1303 (11222-2451)
PHONE.................................718 349-3373
Fax: 718 349-3372
Nicholas Jordache, *President*
EMP: 14
SALES: 500K **Privately Held**
SIC: 2434 2499 Wood kitchen cabinets; decorative wood & woodwork

(G-2147)
JOS H LOWENSTEIN AND SONS INC
420 Morgan Ave (11222-5705)
PHONE.................................718 218-8013
Fax: 718 387-3806
Stephen J Lowenstein, *Ch of Bd*
David Lowenstein, *President*
Sue Papish, *Exec VP*
Richard Cahayla-Wynne, *Vice Pres*
Thomas Sowpel, *Vice Pres*
▲ **EMP:** 85 **EST:** 1897
SQ FT: 100,000
SALES (est): 29.5MM **Privately Held**
WEB: www.jhlowenstein.com
SIC: 2869 2865 Industrial organic chemicals; dyes, synthetic organic

(G-2148)
JOSEPH PAUL
Also Called: Perfect Publications
1064 Rogers Ave Apt 3 (11226-6234)
P.O. Box 1087, New York (10163-1087)
PHONE.................................718 693-4269
Joseph Paul, *Owner*
A Bourne, *Manager*
◆ **EMP:** 6
SALES (est): 340K **Privately Held**
SIC: 2752 Commercial printing, lithographic

(G-2149)
JOSEPH SHALHOUB & SON INC
1258 Prospect Ave (11218-1304)
PHONE.................................718 871-6300
Fax: 718 871-6300
Joseph Shalhoub Jr, *President*
Ray Shalhoub, *Vice Pres*
EMP: 14
SQ FT: 15,000
SALES (est): 710K **Privately Held**
SIC: 2064 Fruits: candied, crystallized, or glazed

(G-2150)
JOSEPH ZAKON WINERY LTD
Also Called: Kesser Wine
586 Montgomery St (11225-3130)
PHONE.................................718 604-1430
Joseph Zakon, *President*
EMP: 3
SQ FT: 5,000
SALES: 1.5MM **Privately Held**
SIC: 2084 Wines

(G-2151)
JOY OF LEARNING
992 Gates Ave (11221-3602)
PHONE.................................718 443-6463
C Clay Berry, *Owner*
EMP: 7
SALES: 200K **Privately Held**
SIC: 2211 Broadwoven fabric mills, cotton

(G-2152)
JOYA LLC
Also Called: Joya Studio
19 Vanderbilt Ave (11205-1113)
PHONE.................................718 852-6979
Bernard Bouchardy, *CEO*
Mayra Miranda, *Manager*
EMP: 15
SALES (est): 1.2MM **Privately Held**
SIC: 3999 Candles

(G-2153)
JOYVA CORP (PA)
53 Varick Ave (11237-1523)
PHONE.................................718 497-0170
Fax: 718 366-8504
Milton Radutzky, *President*
Sanford Wiener, *Treasurer*
Sandy Wienner, *Manager*
Richard Radutzky, *Admin Sec*
▲ **EMP:** 60 **EST:** 1906
SQ FT: 26,370
SALES (est): 12.3MM **Privately Held**
WEB: www.joyva.com
SIC: 2064 2066 2099 Candy & other confectionery products; halvah (candy); chocolate & cocoa products; food preparations

(G-2154)
JTA USA INC
63 Flushing Ave Unit 339 (11205-1084)
PHONE.................................718 722-0902
Alex Rub, *President*
EMP: 7 **EST:** 2012
SQ FT: 2,000
SALES (est): 731.9K **Privately Held**
SIC: 3291 Wheels, abrasive

(G-2155)
JUDAICA PRESS INC
123 Ditmas Ave (11218-4930)
PHONE.................................718 972-6202
Fax: 718 972-6204
Gloria Goldman, *President*
Chaim Schneider, *Sales Mgr*
▲ **EMP:** 8 **EST:** 1963
SQ FT: 2,325
SALES (est): 1MM **Privately Held**
WEB: www.judaicapress.com
SIC: 2731 Books: publishing only

(G-2156)
JUDIS LAMPSHADES INC
1495 E 22nd St (11210-5122)
PHONE.................................917 561-3921
Fax: 718 336-0416
Judith Sadan, *President*
Judi Sadan, *President*
EMP: 5 **EST:** 1998
SQ FT: 1,000
SALES: 310K **Privately Held**
WEB: www.judislampshades.com
SIC: 3645 Lamp shades, metal

GEOGRAPHIC SECTION
Brooklyn - Kings County (G-2186)

(G-2157)
JUICES ENTERPRISES INC
1142 Nostrand Ave (11225-5414)
PHONE..................718 953-1860
Patrick Brown, *President*
Juliet McNaughton, *President*
EMP: 6
SALES (est): 437.1K **Privately Held**
SIC: 2086 Carbonated beverages, nonalcoholic: bottled & canned

(G-2158)
JULIANS RECIPE LLC
128 Norman Ave (11222-3382)
PHONE..................888 640-8880
Joe Cancilleri, *Controller*
Tim Wike, *VP Sales*
Alexander Dzieduszycki, *Mng Member*
Roza Jacquez, *Administration*
▲ **EMP:** 8
SQ FT: 1,100
SALES (est): 9.2MM **Privately Held**
SIC: 2038 Frozen specialties

(G-2159)
JULIUS COHEN JEWELERS INC
169 Richardson St (11222-5016)
PHONE..................212 371-3050
Fax: 212 593-2771
Leslie Steinweiss, *President*
Anderson King, *Manager*
Parsley Steinweiss, *Director*
EMP: 7 **EST:** 1956
SALES (est): 909.8K **Privately Held**
WEB: www.juliuscohen.com
SIC: 3911 5944 Bracelets, precious metal; rings, finger: precious metal; pins (jewelry), precious metal; jewelry stores

(G-2160)
JUNIORS CHEESECAKE INC
386 Flatbush Avenue Ext (11201-5331)
PHONE..................212 302-2000
Alan Rosen, *President*
Walter Rosen, *Chairman*
Kevin Rosen, *Vice Pres*
Allison Lazaris, *Transptn Dir*
Anna Poselenova, *Opers Staff*
EMP: 7
SQ FT: 30,000
SALES (est): 913.9K **Privately Held**
WEB: www.juniorscheesecake.com
SIC: 2051 Cakes, pies & pastries

(G-2161)
K & R ALLIED INC
Also Called: Allied K & R Broom & Brush Co
39 Pearl St Fl 2 (11201-8302)
PHONE..................718 625-6610
Fax: 718 643-3741
Karl Chang, *President*
Kam Lau, *Vice Pres*
EMP: 10
SQ FT: 18,000
SALES (est): 960K **Privately Held**
WEB: www.alliedkr.com
SIC: 3991 Brooms & brushes; brooms

(G-2162)
K & S CHILDRENS WEAR INC
Also Called: Elegant Sportswear
204 Wallabout St (11206-5418)
PHONE..................718 624-0006
Fax: 718 596-8770
Thomas Klein, *President*
Jacob Klein, *Vice Pres*
EMP: 47
SQ FT: 20,000
SALES: 7.5MM **Privately Held**
SIC: 2253 2369 Sweaters & sweater coats, knit; jackets: girls', children's & infants'

(G-2163)
K DISPLAYS
1363 47th St (11219-2612)
PHONE..................718 854-6045
Fax: 718 854-5983
Malvin Boehm, *President*
EMP: 10
SALES (est): 486.4K **Privately Held**
SIC: 3172 Cases, jewelry

(G-2164)
K M DRIVE LINE INC
966 Grand St (11211-2707)
PHONE..................718 599-0628
Salvatore Bucchio Jr, *President*
John Smith, *Accounts Mgr*
EMP: 8
SQ FT: 5,000
SALES (est): 1.2MM **Privately Held**
WEB: www.kmdriveline.com
SIC: 3714 5013 5531 Drive shafts, motor vehicle; motor vehicle supplies & new parts; automobile & truck equipment & parts

(G-2165)
K T A V PUBLISHING HOUSE INC
527 Empire Blvd (11225-3121)
PHONE..................201 963-9524
Sol Scharfstein, *President*
Bernard Scharfstein, *Corp Secy*
▲ **EMP:** 13
SQ FT: 25,000
SALES (est): 1.3MM **Privately Held**
WEB: www.ktav.com
SIC: 2731 Books: publishing only

(G-2166)
KALE FACTORY INC
790 Washington Ave (11238-7706)
PHONE..................917 363-6361
EMP: 6
SALES (est): 474.4K **Privately Held**
SIC: 2099 Food preparations

(G-2167)
KAMMETAL INC (PA)
29 Imlay St (11231-1336)
PHONE..................718 722-9991
Samuel Kusack, *President*
Alastair Kusack, *Vice Pres*
Kate Dubois, *Project Mgr*
David Weinstein, *Controller*
EMP: 18
SQ FT: 1,500
SALES (est): 4.9MM **Privately Held**
SIC: 3446 Architectural metalwork

(G-2168)
KARO SHEET METAL INC
Also Called: Karosheet Metal
229 Russell St (11222-3004)
PHONE..................718 542-8420
Fax: 718 383-6145
Kathleen Portman, *President*
EMP: 40
SQ FT: 10,000
SALES (est): 5.7MM **Privately Held**
SIC: 3444 Ducts, sheet metal; ventilators, sheet metal

(G-2169)
KENDI IRON WORKS INC (PA)
236 Johnson Ave (11206-2819)
PHONE..................718 821-2722
Fax: 718 456-8006
Zadok Zvi, *President*
Anna Zvi, *Vice Pres*
EMP: 8
SQ FT: 16,500
SALES (est): 680.6K **Privately Held**
SIC: 3446 Ornamental metalwork

(G-2170)
KINFOLK STUDIOS INC
90 Wythe Ave (11249-1923)
PHONE..................347 799-2946
Ryan Carney, *President*
Jeremiah Mandel, *Director*
EMP: 30
SQ FT: 900
SALES: 950K **Privately Held**
SIC: 2599 Bar, restaurant & cafeteria furniture

(G-2171)
KING RESEARCH INC
114 12th St Ste 1 (11215-3892)
PHONE..................718 788-0122
Fax: 718 788-0290
Bernard R King, *President*
Carol Ordyk, *Asst Sec*
◆ **EMP:** 23 **EST:** 1947
SQ FT: 23,500
SALES (est): 3.2MM **Privately Held**
SIC: 2842 2841 2844 3229 Disinfectants, household or industrial plant; detergents, synthetic organic or inorganic alkaline; toilet preparations; glassware, art or decorative

(G-2172)
KING SALES INC
284 Wallabout St (11206-4927)
PHONE..................718 301-9862
David Schwimmer, *Owner*
▲ **EMP:** 10
SALES (est): 480.7K **Privately Held**
SIC: 2329 Athletic (warmup, sweat & jogging) suits: men's & boys'

(G-2173)
KING STEEL IRON WORK CORP
2 Seneca Ave (11237)
PHONE..................718 384-7500
Fax: 718 384-8647
Eliran Galapo, *Vice Pres*
Jorge Fernandez, *Manager*
EMP: 15
SALES (est): 2.9MM **Privately Held**
SIC: 3441 Fabricated structural metal

(G-2174)
KINGS FILM & SHEET INC
Also Called: Kings Specialty Co
482 Baltic St (11217-2508)
P.O. Box 170144 (11217-0144)
PHONE..................718 624-7510
Forrest T Weisburst, *President*
Joel Leonard, *General Mgr*
Paulette Anderson, *Purchasing*
Richard Blalock, *CTO*
EMP: 24
SQ FT: 15,000
SALES (est): 3.8MM **Privately Held**
WEB: www.kingsspecialty.com
SIC: 3081 Plastic film & sheet

(G-2175)
KMS CONTRACTING INC
Also Called: Sure Iron Works
86 Georgia Ave (11207-2402)
PHONE..................718 495-6500
Fax: 718 495-6503
Steven Horn, *President*
EMP: 14
SQ FT: 11,500
SALES (est): 2.9MM **Privately Held**
WEB: www.sureiron.com
SIC: 3446 Architectural metalwork

(G-2176)
KNIGHT LIFE ENTERTAINMENT
674 Lincoln Pl Apt 9 (11216-4434)
P.O. Box 160525 (11216-0525)
PHONE..................646 733-8911
Keisha Knight, *Owner*
EMP: 6 **EST:** 2010
SALES (est): 3.8K **Privately Held**
SIC: 7372 Application computer software

(G-2177)
KO FRO FOODS INC
4418 18th Ave 4420 (11204-1201)
PHONE..................718 972-6480
Kalman Mendelsohn, *President*
Abraham Mendelsohn, *Chairman*
Heshy Mendelsohn, *Treasurer*
EMP: 20
SQ FT: 4,300
SALES (est): 2MM **Privately Held**
WEB: www.mendelsohns.com
SIC: 2053 Frozen bakery products, except bread

(G-2178)
KODIAK STUDIOS INC
3030 Emmons Ave Apt 3t (11235-2226)
PHONE..................718 769-5399
Alex Tish, *President*
EMP: 5
SALES (est): 384.4K **Privately Held**
WEB: www.kodiakstudios.com
SIC: 3299 Architectural sculptures: gypsum, clay, papier mache, etc.

(G-2179)
KON TAT GROUP CORPORATION
Also Called: Ametal International
1491 E 34th St (11234-2601)
PHONE..................718 207-5022
Kong Tat Yee, *CEO*
David Kong, *Exec VP*
▼ **EMP:** 8
SQ FT: 4,000
SALES (est): 179.7K **Privately Held**
SIC: 7692 Welding repair

(G-2180)
KURRIER INC
145 Java St (11222-1602)
PHONE..................718 389-3018
Wladyslaw Wawrzonek, *President*
EMP: 5
SALES (est): 310K **Privately Held**
WEB: www.kurrier.com
SIC: 2759 5813 Newspapers: printing; drinking places

(G-2181)
KWADAIR LLC
137 Kent St (11222-2127)
PHONE..................646 824-2511
▲ **EMP:** 5
SALES (est): 457.1K **Privately Held**
SIC: 3812 Aircraft/aerospace flight instruments & guidance systems

(G-2182)
KWESI LEGESSE LLC
Also Called: K.E.Y.S. Publishers
203 Remsen Ave (11212-1342)
PHONE..................347 581-9872
Kayode Smith, *Co-Owner*
EMP: 5
SALES (est): 163.9K **Privately Held**
SIC: 2731 Book publishing

(G-2183)
KWIK TICKET INC (PA)
Also Called: Jon Barry Company Division
4101 Glenwood Rd (11210-2024)
PHONE..................718 421-3800
Fax: 718 421-5328
Larry Spiewak, *Principal*
Brian Katz, *Sales Staff*
Malky Jacobovits, *Office Mgr*
Ike Betesh, *Manager*
Michelle Jacubovits, *Manager*
◆ **EMP:** 15
SQ FT: 30,000
SALES (est): 2MM **Privately Held**
WEB: www.kwikticket.com
SIC: 2752 Tags, lithographed; tickets, lithographed

(G-2184)
KWONG CHI METAL FABRICATION
166 41st St (11232-3320)
PHONE..................718 369-6429
Larry Lang, *President*
EMP: 8
SALES (est): 400K **Privately Held**
SIC: 3479 3499 Metal coating & allied service; fabricated metal products

(G-2185)
L & M UNISERV CORP
4416 18th Ave Pmb 133 (11204-1201)
PHONE..................718 854-3700
Morris Wizel, *President*
EMP: 6
SALES (est): 585.9K **Privately Held**
SIC: 2759 Magazines: printing; catalogs: printing

(G-2186)
L MAGAZINE LLC
45 Main St Ste 806 (11201-1076)
PHONE..................212 807-1254
Scott Stedman, *Mng Member*
Lauren Rosenkranz, *Manager*
Daniel Stedman,
EMP: 18
SQ FT: 2,500
SALES: 1.2MM **Privately Held**
WEB: www.thelmagazine.com
SIC: 2721 Magazines: publishing & printing

Brooklyn - Kings County (G-2187) GEOGRAPHIC SECTION

(G-2187)
L Y Z CREATIONS LTD INC
78 18th St (11232-1010)
PHONE.................718 768-2977
Fax: 718 768-3157
Amram Weinstock, *President*
EMP: 20
SQ FT: 10,000
SALES: 950K **Privately Held**
SIC: 3172 3993 Wallets; watch straps, except metal; leather money holders; signs & advertising specialties

(G-2188)
LACE MARBLE & GRANITE INC
1465 39th St (11218-3617)
PHONE.................347 425-1645
Anthony Lanza, *President*
▲ EMP: 5
SQ FT: 5,000
SALES (est): 448.5K **Privately Held**
WEB: www.lacemarble.com
SIC: 3281 Marble, building: cut & shaped

(G-2189)
LADYBIRD BAKERY INC
1112 8th Ave (11215-4314)
PHONE.................718 499-8108
Mary L Clemens, *Ch of Bd*
Christy Jones, *Manager*
EMP: 6
SQ FT: 750
SALES (est): 634.9K **Privately Held**
WEB: www.twolittleredhens.com
SIC: 2051 2052 Bakery: wholesale or wholesale/retail combined; cookies & crackers

(G-2190)
LAGE INDUSTRIES CORPORATION
9814 Ditmas Ave (11236-1914)
PHONE.................718 342-3400
Daniel Lage, *Owner*
EMP: 12
SALES: 2MM **Privately Held**
SIC: 3271 Blocks, concrete or cinder: standard

(G-2191)
LAGUNATIC MUSIC & FILMWORKS
Also Called: Blackheart Records
456 Johnson Ave 202 (11237-1202)
PHONE.................212 353-9600
Fax: 212 353-8300
Kenny Laguna, *President*
Meryl Laguna, *Corp Secy*
Joan Jett, *Vice Pres*
Zander Wolff, *Sls & Mktg Exec*
Alena Amante, *CFO*
EMP: 10
SALES (est): 878.9K **Privately Held**
WEB: www.blackheart.com
SIC: 2741 Music book & sheet music publishing

(G-2192)
LAKEVIEW SPORTSWEAR CORP
Also Called: All Weather Outerwear
1425 37th St Ste 607 (11218-3755)
PHONE.................800 965-6550
Jerome Lieberman, *President*
Miriam Mann, *Admin Sec*
▲ EMP: 8
SQ FT: 18,000
SALES (est): 1.2MM **Privately Held**
SIC: 2329 Men's & boys' sportswear & athletic clothing; hunting coats & vests, men's

(G-2193)
LAMM INDUSTRIES INC
Also Called: Lamm Audio Lab
2621 E 24th St Ste 1 (11235-2609)
PHONE.................718 368-0181
Vladimir Lamm, *President*
EMP: 6
SALES (est): 530K **Privately Held**
WEB: www.lammindustries.com
SIC: 3651 5731 Audio electronic systems; radio, television & electronic stores

(G-2194)
LANCASTER QUALITY PORK INC
5600 1st Ave Ste 6 (11220-2558)
PHONE.................718 439-8822
David Kaplan, *Owner*
EMP: 16
SALES (est): 2.3MM **Privately Held**
SIC: 2013 Prepared pork products from purchased pork

(G-2195)
LANOVES INC
72 Anthony St (11222-5329)
PHONE.................718 384-1880
Sebastian Antoniuk, *President*
Maria Antoniuk, *Manager*
EMP: 8
SALES (est): 710K **Privately Held**
SIC: 2511 Wood household furniture

(G-2196)
LANTERN HALL LLC
52 Harrison Pl (11237-1402)
PHONE.................718 381-2122
Luis Carlos Wong, *President*
EMP: 7 EST: 2015
SALES (est): 101.4K **Privately Held**
SIC: 2711 Newspapers

(G-2197)
LAYTON MANUFACTURING CORP (PA)
864 E 52nd St (11203-6702)
PHONE.................718 498-6000
Fax: 718 498-6003
Steve Layton, *President*
Antonia Layton, *Vice Pres*
Lola Pearson, *CFO*
Marina Marshalova, *Bookkeeper*
Walter Straughter, *Sales Mgr*
EMP: 24
SQ FT: 9,000
SALES (est): 3.1MM **Privately Held**
WEB: www.laytonmfg.com
SIC: 3585 1711 5075 Air conditioning equipment, complete; heating & air conditioning contractors; air conditioning & ventilation equipment & supplies

(G-2198)
LAZER MARBLE & GRANITE CORP
1053 Dahill Rd (11204-1741)
PHONE.................718 859-9644
Lazer Mechlovitz, *CEO*
Nachman Mechlovitz, *President*
▲ EMP: 7
SQ FT: 4,200
SALES (est): 1.1MM **Privately Held**
SIC: 3211 3253 Building glass, flat; ceramic wall & floor tile

(G-2199)
LDI LIGHTING INC (PA)
240 Broadway Ste C (11211-8409)
PHONE.................718 384-4490
Allen Mundle, *President*
EMP: 9
SQ FT: 5,000
SALES (est): 2.7MM **Privately Held**
SIC: 3646 Ornamental lighting fixtures, commercial

(G-2200)
LDI LIGHTING INC
193 Williamsburg St W A (11211-7984)
PHONE.................718 384-4490
Alex Menzlowitz, *Branch Mgr*
EMP: 5
SALES (corp-wide): 2.7MM **Privately Held**
SIC: 3646 Commercial indust & institutional electric lighting fixtures
PA: Ldi Lighting, Inc
    240 Broadway Ste C
    Brooklyn NY 11211
    718 384-4490

(G-2201)
LE HOOK ROUGE LLC
275 Conover St Ste 3q-3p (11231-1035)
PHONE.................212 947-6272
Esther Chen, *President*
▲ EMP: 1 EST: 2014
SQ FT: 10,000
SALES: 8MM **Privately Held**
SIC: 3911 Jewelry apparel

(G-2202)
LE LABO HOLDING LLC
80 39th St Fl Ground (11232-2614)
PHONE.................646 719-1740
Jean B Mondesir Jr, *Principal*
EMP: 25
SALES (corp-wide): 11.8B **Publicly Held**
SIC: 2844 Perfumes & colognes
HQ: Le Labo Holding Llc
    233 Elizabeth St
    New York NY 10012
    844 316-9319

(G-2203)
LEARNIMATION
55 Washington St Ste 454 (11201-1045)
PHONE.................917 868-7261
Sarah Manning, *Owner*
EMP: 9
SALES (est): 429.7K **Privately Held**
SIC: 3999 Education aids, devices & supplies

(G-2204)
LEARNINGATEWAY LLC
106 Saint James Pl (11238-1831)
PHONE.................212 920-7969
Catherine Gichenje, *President*
EMP: 5
SALES (est): 347.2K **Privately Held**
SIC: 7372 Educational computer software

(G-2205)
LED WAVES INC
4100 1st Ave Ste 3n (11232-3303)
PHONE.................347 416-6182
Joel Slavis, *CEO*
Nancy Ahn, *Marketing Staff*
Kori Lozinski, *Manager*
▲ EMP: 12
SALES (est): 2.4MM **Privately Held**
SIC: 3641 5063 Electric lamps; light bulbs & related supplies

(G-2206)
LEE PRINTING INC
188 Lee Ave (11211-8028)
PHONE.................718 237-1651
Fax: 718 852-1862
Leo Wollner, *President*
EMP: 5
SQ FT: 1,800
SALES: 800K **Privately Held**
SIC: 2752 Commercial printing, offset

(G-2207)
LEE SPRING COMPANY LLC (HQ)
140 58th St Ste 3c (11220-2560)
PHONE.................718 362-5183
Al Mangels Jr, *President*
Ralph Mascolo, *Vice Pres*
Paul Ng, *Vice Pres*
Jamie Collazo, *Plant Mgr*
Jorge Cortes, *Plant Mgr*
▲ EMP: 150
SQ FT: 33,000
SALES (est): 43.6MM **Privately Held**
WEB: www.leespring.com
SIC: 3495 3493 3315 5085 Mechanical springs, precision; steel springs, except wire; wire & fabricated wire products; springs
PA: Unimex Corporation
    54 E 64th St
    New York NY 10065
    212 755-8800

(G-2208)
LEE SPRING LLC (PA)
140 58th St Ste 3c (11220-2560)
PHONE.................718 236-2222
Al Amangels, *President*
Jim Papagni, *Plant Supt*
Chris Emick, *Plant Mgr*
Jenny Ceccacci, *Purch Mgr*
Elvis Jarvis, *QC Mgr*
EMP: 37 EST: 1918
SALES (est): 7.6MM **Privately Held**
SIC: 3495 Wire springs

(G-2209)
LEGION LIGHTING CO INC
221 Glenmore Ave (11207-3307)
PHONE.................718 498-1770
Sheldon Bellovin, *President*
Evan Bellovin, *Vice Pres*
Michael Bellovin, *Vice Pres*
Wayne Cowell, *Engineer*
▲ EMP: 30 EST: 1946
SQ FT: 75,000
SALES: 7.3MM **Privately Held**
WEB: www.legionlighting.com
SIC: 3646 Fluorescent lighting fixtures, commercial

(G-2210)
LEITER SUKKAHS INC
1346 39th St (11218-3616)
PHONE.................718 436-0303
Gitel Goldman, *President*
▲ EMP: 7
SQ FT: 8,000
SALES (est): 989.2K **Privately Held**
WEB: www.leiterssukkah.com
SIC: 2394 5049 5999 Tents: made from purchased materials; religious supplies; tents; religious goods

(G-2211)
LEMRAL KNITWEAR INC
70 Franklin Ave (11205-1504)
PHONE.................718 210-0175
Fax: 718 596-7601
Eva Freund, *President*
Andrew Freund, *Treasurer*
A Schon, *Admin Sec*
EMP: 60 EST: 1968
SQ FT: 30,000
SALES (est): 3.6MM **Privately Held**
SIC: 2257 2339 Weft knit fabric mills; women's & misses' outerwear

(G-2212)
LENS LAB EXPRESS
Also Called: Vision Quest
482 86th St (11209-4708)
PHONE.................718 921-5488
Sherri Smith, *Owner*
EMP: 6
SALES (est): 420K **Privately Held**
SIC: 3851 5995 5049 Ophthalmic goods; opticians; optical goods

(G-2213)
LENS LAB EXPRESS OF GRAHAM AVE
28 Graham Ave (11206-4008)
PHONE.................718 486-0117
Candido Diaz, *Principal*
EMP: 5
SQ FT: 7,600
SALES (est): 585.1K **Privately Held**
SIC: 3851 Ophthalmic goods

(G-2214)
LEO INTERNATIONAL INC
471 Sutter Ave (11207-3905)
PHONE.................718 290-8005
Gary Stern, *President*
▲ EMP: 25
SQ FT: 65,000
SALES (est): 6.4MM **Privately Held**
WEB: www.leointernational.com
SIC: 3498 Fabricated pipe & fittings

(G-2215)
LEWIS MACHINE CO INC
Also Called: Lewis, S J Machine Co
209 Congress St (11201-6415)
PHONE.................718 625-0799
Gene Wayda, *President*
EMP: 8 EST: 1933
SQ FT: 2,000
SALES: 750K **Privately Held**
SIC: 3599 Machine shop, jobbing & repair

(G-2216)
LIBERTY FABRICATION INC
226 Glenmore Ave (11207-3323)
PHONE.................718 495-5735
Jimmy Hsu, *President*
EMP: 5
SALES (est): 757.8K **Privately Held**
SIC: 3315 Wire & fabricated wire products

GEOGRAPHIC SECTION
Brooklyn - Kings County (G-2246)

(G-2217)
LIBERTY PANEL CENTER INC (PA)
Also Called: Liberty Panel & Home Center
1009 Liberty Ave (11208-2812)
PHONE..................................718 647-2763
Fax: 718 647-0450
Irwin Kandel, *President*
Cory Kandel, *Vice Pres*
Craig Kandel, *Vice Pres*
EMP: 19
SQ FT: 25,000
SALES (est): 2.6MM **Privately Held**
SIC: 2851 Paints & paint additives

(G-2218)
LIDDABIT SWEETS
330 Wythe Ave Apt 2g (11249-4153)
PHONE..................................917 912-1370
EMP: 5
SALES (est): 556.8K **Privately Held**
SIC: 2053 Buns, sweet: frozen

(G-2219)
LIDS CORPORATION
5385 Kings Plz (11234-5220)
PHONE..................................718 338-7790
Stephanie Marin, *Manager*
EMP: 37
SALES (corp-wide): 2.8B **Publicly Held**
WEB: www.hatworld.com
SIC: 2353 Hats & caps
HQ: Lids Corporation
7555 Woodland Dr
Indianapolis IN 46278

(G-2220)
LIFESTYLE-TRIMCO (PA)
Also Called: Lifestyle-Trimco Viaggo
323 Malta St (11207-8210)
PHONE..................................718 257-9101
Charles Rosenthal, *President*
Chuck Rosenthal, *Principal*
Lloyd Kielson, *Vice Pres*
Gary Jacob, *Controller*
Dianna Murphy, *CTO*
▲ EMP: 39
SQ FT: 12,000
SALES: 18MM **Privately Held**
SIC: 3999 2542 2541 5046 Mannequins; garment racks: except wood; garment racks, wood; mannequins; display equipment, except refrigerated; signs & advertising specialties

(G-2221)
LIGHT BLUE USA LLC
1421 Locust Ave (11230-5220)
PHONE..................................718 475-2515
Isaac Markowitz, *Director*
EMP: 7 EST: 2012
SALES (est): 355K **Privately Held**
SIC: 3674 3648 1731 Light emitting diodes; lighting equipment; lighting contractor

(G-2222)
LIGHT PHONE INC (PA)
49 Bogart St Apt 44 (11206-3837)
PHONE..................................415 595-0044
Joe Hollier, *Founder*
Kaiwei Tang, *Founder*
EMP: 5
SALES: 500K **Privately Held**
SIC: 3669 Communications equipment

(G-2223)
LIGHT WAVES CONCEPT INC
Also Called: Led Waves
4100 1st Ave (11232-2609)
PHONE..................................212 677-6400
Fax: 212 677-6945
Joel Slavis, *President*
▲ EMP: 13
SALES: 2MM **Privately Held**
WEB: www.lightwavesconcept.com
SIC: 3646 3544 Commercial indusl & institutional electric lighting fixtures; special dies, tools, jigs & fixtures

(G-2224)
LIGHTING COLLABORATIVE INC
275 Park Ave Apt 6k (11205-2562)
PHONE..................................212 253-7220
Fax: 212 239-7111
Lewis Herman, *Ch of Bd*
Amelia Froom, *Vice Pres*
Nicholas Fisfis, *Manager*
EMP: 6
SQ FT: 1,600
SALES (est): 974.2K **Privately Held**
WEB: www.lightingcollaborative.com
SIC: 3648 Lighting fixtures, except electric: residential

(G-2225)
LILLYS HOMESTYLE BAKESHOP INC
6210 9th Ave (11220-4726)
PHONE..................................718 491-2904
Ethan Lieberman, *Ch of Bd*
Mendel Brach, *President*
Giji Stern, *Accountant*
Diane Adams, *Manager*
EMP: 60 EST: 2003
SALES (est): 9.8MM **Privately Held**
SIC: 2051 Bakery: wholesale or wholesale/retail combined

(G-2226)
LIN JIN FENG
7718 18th Ave (11214-1110)
PHONE..................................718 232-3039
Lin Jinfeng, *Owner*
EMP: 7 EST: 2010
SALES (est): 579.2K **Privately Held**
SIC: 2674 Grocers' bags: made from purchased materials

(G-2227)
LINDA TOOL & DIE CORPORATION
163 Dwight St (11231-1539)
PHONE..................................718 522-2066
Fax: 718 522-2075
Michael Di Marino, *President*
Linda Cataffo, *Vice Pres*
Arlene Di Marino, *Vice Pres*
David Holmes, *Plant Mgr*
Shlomo Mordechai, *Engineer*
▲ EMP: 23 EST: 1952
SQ FT: 17,500
SALES (est): 4.5MM **Privately Held**
WEB: www.lindatool.com
SIC: 3599 Machine shop, jobbing & repair

(G-2228)
LINDA WINE & SPIRIT
1219 Flatbush Ave (11226-7004)
PHONE..................................718 703-5707
Pierre Raoul, *Owner*
EMP: 6
SALES (est): 578.7K **Privately Held**
SIC: 2086 Bottled & canned soft drinks

(G-2229)
LINDEN FORMS & SYSTEMS INC
40 S 6th St (11249-5938)
PHONE..................................212 219-1100
Leo Green, *President*
EMP: 25 EST: 1975
SQ FT: 8,000
SALES (est): 2MM **Privately Held**
SIC: 2761 2759 Computer forms, manifold or continuous; commercial printing

(G-2230)
LINDSEY ADELMAN
27 Prospect Park W (11215-1706)
PHONE..................................718 623-3013
Lindsey Adelman, *Owner*
EMP: 28
SALES (est): 1.3MM **Privately Held**
SIC: 3648 Decorative area lighting fixtures

(G-2231)
LION DIE-CUTTING CO INC
95 Dobbin St Ste 1 (11222-2851)
PHONE..................................718 383-8841
Fax: 718 383-7801
Leo Friedman, *President*
Moshe Lieberman, *Vice Pres*
Mendel Friedman, *Manager*
EMP: 27 EST: 1958
SQ FT: 40,000
SALES: 3MM **Privately Held**
SIC: 2675 2621 Cutouts, cardboard, die-cut: from purchased materials; card paper

(G-2232)
LION IN THE SUN PARK SLOPE LTD
232 7th Ave (11215-3041)
PHONE..................................718 369-4006
Melinda Morris, *CEO*
David Morris, *Vice Pres*
EMP: 9
SQ FT: 2,000
SALES (est): 1.2MM **Privately Held**
WEB: www.lioninthesuninvitations.com
SIC: 2759 Invitation & stationery printing & engraving; invitations: printing

(G-2233)
LITE BRITE MANUFACTURING INC
575 President St (11215)
PHONE..................................718 855-9797
David Kabasso, *President*
Shaul Kabasso, *Vice Pres*
EMP: 15
SQ FT: 20,000
SALES (est): 1.2MM **Privately Held**
SIC: 3646 3643 Fluorescent lighting fixtures, commercial; current-carrying wiring devices

(G-2234)
LIVID MAGAZINE
1055 Bedford Ave Apt 4c (11216-4730)
PHONE..................................929 340-7123
Daniel Watson, *Owner*
EMP: 11
SALES (est): 473.1K **Privately Held**
SIC: 2721 Magazines: publishing & printing

(G-2235)
LLCS PUBLISHING CORP
2071 Flatbush Ave Ste 189 (11234-4340)
PHONE..................................718 569-2703
Matt Cunningham, *Owner*
Alex Englard, *Accounts Exec*
EMP: 10 EST: 2007
SALES (est): 602.1K **Privately Held**
WEB: www.llcpublishing.com
SIC: 2741 Miscellaneous publishing

(G-2236)
LO & SONS INC
55 Prospect St (11201-1497)
PHONE..................................917 775-4025
Helen Lo, *CEO*
Jan Lo, *President*
▲ EMP: 10
SALES (est): 192.1K **Privately Held**
SIC: 3161 Traveling bags

(G-2237)
LONDON PARIS LTD
4211 13th Ave (11219-1334)
PHONE..................................718 564-4793
Elias Brach, *President*
▲ EMP: 7
SALES: 1.4MM **Privately Held**
SIC: 2329 Men's & boys' sportswear & athletic clothing

(G-2238)
LOPEZ RESTORATIONS INC (PA)
394 Mcguinness Blvd Ste 4 (11222-1201)
PHONE..................................718 383-1555
Fax: 718 383-0908
Angel Lopez, *President*
EMP: 11
SQ FT: 3,500
SALES (est): 1MM **Privately Held**
SIC: 3952 Frames for artists' canvases

(G-2239)
LOPOPOLO IRON WORKS INC
2495 Mcdonald Ave (11223-5232)
PHONE..................................718 339-0572
Fax: 718 336-3073
Joseph Lopopolo, *President*
Mike Lopopolo, *Shareholder*
EMP: 7 EST: 1965
SQ FT: 4,000
SALES (est): 1.2MM **Privately Held**
SIC: 3446 Architectural metalwork; gates, ornamental metal; fences or posts, ornamental iron or steel; stairs, staircases, stair treads: prefabricated metal

(G-2240)
LOTUS AWNINGS ENTERPRISES INC
157 11th St (11215-3815)
PHONE..................................718 965-4824
Fax: 718 965-1166
Susana Merchan, *President*
EMP: 7
SQ FT: 5,000
SALES (est): 867K **Privately Held**
SIC: 3444 5999 Awnings & canopies; awnings

(G-2241)
LOWEL-LIGHT MANUFACTURING INC
140 58th St Ste 8c (11220-2524)
PHONE..................................718 921-0600
Fax: 718 921-0303
Marvin Seligman, *President*
Toni Pearl, *Administration*
▲ EMP: 40
SQ FT: 34,000
SALES (est): 5.2MM **Privately Held**
WEB: www.lowel.com
SIC: 3861 3641 Photographic equipment & supplies; electric lamps

(G-2242)
LYN JO KITCHENS INC
1679 Mcdonald Ave (11230-6312)
PHONE..................................718 336-6060
Fax: 718 336-5238
Hal Grosshandler, *President*
EMP: 5 EST: 1964
SQ FT: 2,400
SALES: 260K **Privately Held**
SIC: 2434 Wood kitchen cabinets

(G-2243)
LYNCH KNITTING MILLS INC
538 Johnson Ave (11237-1226)
PHONE..................................718 821-3436
Fax: 718 821-3461
Joseph Rotstein, *President*
EMP: 35 EST: 1965
SQ FT: 15,000
SALES (est): 3.1MM **Privately Held**
SIC: 2253 Knit outerwear mills

(G-2244)
M & C FURNITURE
Also Called: M C Kitchen & Bath
375 Park Ave (11205-2635)
PHONE..................................718 422-2136
Moshe Chayun, *President*
Erez Chayun, *Vice Pres*
▲ EMP: 6
SQ FT: 9,000
SALES (est): 769.2K **Privately Held**
WEB: www.fintec-usa.com
SIC: 2511 5031 1751 Wood household furniture; kitchen cabinets; cabinet & finish carpentry

(G-2245)
M & D INSTALLERS INC (PA)
Also Called: M & D Fire Door
70 Flushing Ave (11205-1064)
PHONE..................................718 782-6978
Fax: 718 782-6360
Moshe Deutsch, *Ch of Bd*
David Posner, *President*
Jay Posner, *CFO*
▼ EMP: 52
SQ FT: 50,000
SALES: 30MM **Privately Held**
WEB: www.mdfiredoor.com
SIC: 3442 5211 5031 Fire doors, metal; door & window products; metal doors, sash & trim

(G-2246)
M & M FOOD PRODUCTS INC
Also Called: Flaum Appetizing
286 Scholes St (11206-1728)
PHONE..................................718 821-1970
Morris Grunhut, *Ch of Bd*
EMP: 14
SQ FT: 23,000
SALES: 940K **Privately Held**
WEB: www.flaumappetizing.com
SIC: 2099 Salads, fresh or refrigerated

Brooklyn - Kings County (G-2247)

(G-2247)
M & R WOODWORKING & FINISHING
49 Withers St (11211-6891)
PHONE 718 486-5480
Fax: 718 486-5501
Robert Wieczorkowski, *President*
Milgorzata Wieczorkowski, *Vice Pres*
EMP: 7
SQ FT: 5,625
SALES: 500K **Privately Held**
SIC: 2499 Decorative wood & woodwork

(G-2248)
M A M KNITTING MILLS CORP
Also Called: Mam Knitg
43 Hall St (11205-1315)
PHONE 800 570-0093
Fax: 718 237-1169
Michael Ergel, *President*
Pinchas Brach, *Treasurer*
▲ **EMP:** 40
SQ FT: 32,000
SALES (est): 1.6MM **Privately Held**
SIC: 2253 2329 2339 Sweaters & sweater coats, knit; sweaters & sweater jackets: men's & boys'; women's & misses' outerwear

(G-2249)
M B C METAL INC
Also Called: Milgo Industrial
68 Lombarcy St (11222-5207)
PHONE 718 384-6713
Fax: 718 963-0614
Bruce Gitlin, *President*
EMP: 10
SQ FT: 5,000
SALES (est): 750K **Privately Held**
SIC: 3446 Architectural metalwork

(G-2250)
M B M MANUFACTURING INC
331 Rutledge St Ste 203 (11211-7546)
PHONE 718 769-4148
David Goldstein, *President*
Susan Goldstein, *Vice Pres*
Eugene Goldstein, *Manager*
▲ **EMP:** 15 **EST:** 1978
SQ FT: 25,000
SALES (est): 1.2MM **Privately Held**
SIC: 2253 Sweaters & sweater coats, knit

(G-2251)
M FACTORY USA INC (HQ)
32 33rd St Unit 5 (11232-1911)
PHONE 917 410-7878
Alessandro Lenaro, *President*
Tara Montoneri, *Director*
Rebecca Gieser, *Admin Sec*
EMP: 4 **EST:** 2016
SQ FT: 6,000
SALES: 4MM
SALES (corp-wide): 25.8MM **Privately Held**
SIC: 3851 Eyeglasses, lenses & frames
PA: Tworoger Associates, Ltd.
594 Broadway Rm 801
New York NY 10012
212 965-4900

(G-2252)
MAC ARTSPRAY FINISHING CORP
Also Called: Mac-Artspray Finshg
799 Sheffield Ave (11207-7797)
PHONE 718 649-3800
Fax: 718 927-2389
Howard Moskovitz, *President*
EMP: 12
SQ FT: 10,000
SALES: 800K **Privately Held**
SIC: 3479 Painting of metal products

(G-2253)
MACEDONIA LTD
Also Called: Carlton Ice Cream Co
34 E 29th St (11226-5027)
PHONE 718 462-3596
Fax: 718 469-3277
Aristides Saketos, *President*
Zeno Gianopoulos, *Vice Pres*
Belinda Turpitt, *Office Mgr*
▲ **EMP:** 12
SQ FT: 8,500
SALES (est): 2.1MM **Privately Held**
WEB: www.macedonia.com
SIC: 2024 5143 Ice cream & frozen desserts; ice cream & ices

(G-2254)
MAD SCNTSTS BRWING PRTNERS LLC
Also Called: Sixpoint Brewery
40 Van Dyke St (11231-1529)
PHONE 347 766-2739
Shane Welch, *President*
▲ **EMP:** 23
SALES (est): 7.1MM **Privately Held**
SIC: 2082 Malt beverages

(G-2255)
MADE CLOSE LLC
141 Meserole Ave (11222-2744)
PHONE 917 837-1357
David Mehlman, *CEO*
EMP: 6
SALES (est): 185.1K **Privately Held**
SIC: 2051 Bakery: wholesale or wholesale/retail combined

(G-2256)
MAJESTIC HOME IMPRVS DISTR
5902 Fort Hamilton Pkwy (11219-4834)
PHONE 718 853-5079
Man L Wong, *President*
▲ **EMP:** 5
SALES (est): 399.3K **Privately Held**
WEB: www.majesticimprovements.com
SIC: 2514 1521 Kitchen cabinets: metal; single-family home remodeling, additions & repairs

(G-2257)
MAKERBOT INDUSTRIES LLC (DH)
1 Metrotech Ctr Fl 21 (11201-3949)
PHONE 347 334-6800
Jenny Lawton, *CEO*
Kathryn Hurley, *Counsel*
Gil Maman, *Vice Pres*
Matthew Jones, *Opers Mgr*
Steven McGriff, *Production*
▲ **EMP:** 150
SQ FT: 15,000
SALES (est): 88.7MM
SALES (corp-wide): 699.1MM **Privately Held**
SIC: 3621 3625 5084 Motors & generators; actuators, industrial; industrial machinery & equipment
HQ: Stratasys, Inc.
7665 Commerce Way
Eden Prairie MN 55344
952 937-3000

(G-2258)
MALIA MILLS INC
32 33rd St Unit 13 (11232-1924)
PHONE 212 354-4200
EMP: 11
SALES (est): 654.2K **Privately Held**
SIC: 2339 5699 Mfg Women's/Misses' Outerwear Ret Misc Apparel/Accessories

(G-2259)
MANDALAY FOOD PRODUCTS INC
640 Dean St (11238-3021)
PHONE 718 230-3370
U Han Kyu, *President*
EMP: 5
SQ FT: 300
SALES (est): 356.5K **Privately Held**
WEB: www.mandalay.org
SIC: 2099 5411 Food preparations; grocery stores, independent

(G-2260)
MANGO USA INC
5620 1st Ave Ste 1 (11220-2519)
PHONE 718 998-6050
Kheder Fatiha, *CEO*
▲ **EMP:** 20
SALES (est): 3.8MM **Privately Held**
SIC: 3144 3021 3149 2339 Dress shoes, women's; canvas shoes, rubber soled; athletic shoes, except rubber or plastic; women's & misses' athletic clothing & sportswear; women's & children's clothing

(G-2261)
MANHATTAN POLY BAG CORPORATION
1228 47th St (11219-2501)
PHONE 917 689-7549
Fax: 718 326-1887
William Kaufman, *President*
Sylvia Kaufman, *Vice Pres*
Gary Kaufman, *Controller*
EMP: 32
SQ FT: 88,500
SALES (est): 4.1MM **Privately Held**
SIC: 2673 Plastic bags: made from purchased materials

(G-2262)
MANHATTAN SPECIAL BOTTLING
342 Manhattan Ave (11211-2404)
PHONE 718 388-4144
Fax: 718 384-0244
Aurora Passaro, *President*
Louis Passaro, *Exec VP*
EMP: 10
SQ FT: 7,500
SALES (est): 930K **Privately Held**
WEB: www.manhattanspecial.com
SIC: 2086 Soft drinks: packaged in cans, bottles, etc.

(G-2263)
MANNING LEWIS DIV RUBICON INDS
848 E 43rd St (11210-3502)
PHONE 908 687-2400
Michael Rubinberg, *President*
EMP: 25
SALES (est): 1.2MM **Privately Held**
SIC: 3585 Refrigeration & heating equipment

(G-2264)
MANOR ELECTRIC SUPPLY CORP
2737 Ocean Ave (11229-4700)
PHONE 718 648-8003
Fax: 718 648-7351
Kenneth Rabinowitz, *Ch of Bd*
Lawrence Rafalovich, *President*
Christine Gandee, *Manager*
EMP: 10
SQ FT: 10,000
SALES (est): 2.4MM **Privately Held**
SIC: 3699 Electrical equipment & supplies

(G-2265)
MANZIONE READY MIX CORP
Also Called: Manzione Enterprises
46 Knickerbocker Ave (11237-1410)
PHONE 718 628-3837
Rocco Manzione, *President*
Gary Snolpava, *President*
EMP: 4 **EST:** 1999
SQ FT: 45,000
SALES (est): 3MM **Privately Held**
SIC: 3273 Ready-mixed concrete

(G-2266)
MARAMONT CORPORATION (PA)
5600 1st Ave (11220-2550)
PHONE 718 439-8900
Fax: 718 238-0974
George Chivari, *President*
David Goldfarb, *Purch Agent*
Celia Lyons, *Purchasing*
Linda Jannzzkowski, *CFO*
Warren Schmitgall, *Controller*
▲ **EMP:** 420
SQ FT: 65,000
SALES (est): 108.9MM **Privately Held**
SIC: 2099 8322 Ready-to-eat meals, salads & sandwiches; salads, fresh or refrigerated; sandwiches, assembled & packaged: for wholesale market; individual & family services

(G-2267)
MARBLE KNITS INC
Also Called: Marble Knitting Mills
544 Park Ave Ste 3 (11205-1608)
PHONE 718 237-7990
Fax: 718 237-2781
Kalman Sinay, *President*
David Bark, *Vice Pres*
EMP: 20
SQ FT: 55,000
SALES (est): 2.6MM **Privately Held**
SIC: 2253 Sweaters & sweater coats, knit

(G-2268)
MARCY BUSINESS FORMS INC
1468 40th St (11218-3510)
PHONE 718 935-9100
Samuel Roth, *Ch of Bd*
EMP: 5
SALES (est): 550K **Privately Held**
WEB: www.marcybusinessforms.com
SIC: 2761 Manifold business forms

(G-2269)
MARCY PRINTING INC
777 Kent Ave Ste A (11205-1543)
P.O. Box 110199 (11211-0199)
PHONE 718 935-9100
Fax: 718 935-9349
Charles H Laufer, *President*
Jano Roth, *Manager*
EMP: 5
SQ FT: 12,000
SALES (est): 808.9K **Privately Held**
SIC: 2752 Commercial printing, offset; letters, circular or form: lithographed

(G-2270)
MARINA HOLDING CORP
Also Called: Venice Marina
3939 Emmons Ave (11235-1001)
PHONE 718 646-9283
Fax: 718 646-5889
Albert Levi, *Managing Dir*
Chuck Rondot, *Manager*
EMP: 15
SQ FT: 6,000
SALES (est): 1.3MM
SALES (corp-wide): 1.3B **Privately Held**
WEB: www.venicemarina.com
SIC: 2339 5551 5541 Women's & misses' outerwear; boat dealers; gasoline service stations
PA: Jordache Enterprises Inc.
1400 Broadway Rm 1404b
New York NY 10018
212 643-8400

(G-2271)
MARINA ICE CREAM
888 Jamaica Ave (11208-1525)
PHONE 718 235-3000
Frank Birone, *Owner*
EMP: 5 **EST:** 2007
SALES (est): 368.8K **Privately Held**
SIC: 2024 5143 Ice cream & frozen desserts; ice cream & ices

(G-2272)
MARINE PARK APPLIANCES LLC
3412 Avenue N (11234-2607)
PHONE 718 513-1808
Issac Wizel, *President*
EMP: 1
SALES (est): 5MM **Privately Held**
SIC: 3639 Major kitchen appliances, except refrigerators & stoves

(G-2273)
MARK POSNER
1950 52nd St (11204-1731)
PHONE 718 258-6241
Mark Posner, *Owner*
EMP: 5
SALES (est): 218.2K **Privately Held**
SIC: 3432 Plastic plumbing fixture fittings, assembly

(G-2274)
MARLBOROUGH JEWELS INC
67 35th St Unit 2 (11232-2200)
P.O. Box 320673 (11232-0673)
PHONE 718 768-2000
Fax: 718 788-1653
Donald Calaman, *President*
EMP: 8
SALES (est): 1MM **Privately Held**
SIC: 3961 5094 3911 Costume jewelry, ex. precious metal & semiprecious stones; jewelry; jewelry, precious metal

Brooklyn - Kings County

(G-2275)
MARLOW PRINTING CO INC
Also Called: Nap Industries
667 Kent Ave (11249-7530)
PHONE.................718 625-4948
Jack Freund, *President*
Morris Lowy, *Vice Pres*
EMP: 30 EST: 1977
SQ FT: 35,000
SALES (est): 3.9MM **Privately Held**
WEB: www.napind.com
SIC: 2759 2752 Flexographic printing; commercial printing, lithographic

(G-2276)
MARLY HOME INDUSTRIES USA INC
181 Lombardy St (11222-5417)
PHONE.................718 388-3030
EMP: 7
SALES (est): 142.9K **Privately Held**
SIC: 2824 2221 Polyester fibers; polyester broadwoven fabrics

(G-2277)
MAROVATO INDUSTRIES INC
100 Dobbin St (11222-2806)
PHONE.................718 389-0800
Fax: 718 389-0258
Margaret Rotondi, *Ch of Bd*
Marty Pietanza, *Opers Mgr*
Gabriel Xu, *Engineer*
Rosemarie Rotondi, *Treasurer*
▲ EMP: 15
SALES (est): 4MM **Privately Held**
WEB: www.marovato.com
SIC: 3441 8711 Building components, structural steel; structural engineering; mechanical engineering

(G-2278)
MARTIN CHAFKIN
Also Called: Perfection Electricks
1155 Manhattan Ave # 431 (11222-6102)
P.O. Box 220023 (11222-0023)
PHONE.................718 383-1155
Martin Chafkin, *Owner*
Myles Ambrose, *Manager*
EMP: 7
SALES: 400K **Privately Held**
WEB: www.perfectionelectric.com
SIC: 3999 7922 3446 Stage hardware & equipment, except lighting; equipment rental, theatrical; architectural metalwork

(G-2279)
MARTIN GREENFIELD CLOTHIERS
Also Called: Greenfield Martin Clothiers
239 Varet St (11206-3823)
PHONE.................718 497-5480
Fax: 718 456-3365
Martin Greenfield, *President*
Jay Greenfield, *Exec VP*
Todd Greenfield, *Vice Pres*
Michelle Guiseppone, *Manager*
▲ EMP: 140 EST: 1978
SQ FT: 40,000
SALES (est): 15MM **Privately Held**
SIC: 2311 2325 Suits, men's & boys': made from purchased materials; jackets, tailored suit-type: men's & boys'; topcoats, men's & boys': made from purchased materials; slacks, dress: men's, youths' & boys'

(G-2280)
MARVEL EQUIPMENT CORP INC
215 Eagle St (11222-1210)
PHONE.................718 383-6597
Carl Ungenheuer, *President*
Barbara Maxwell, *Vice Pres*
Emma Ungenheuer, *Admin Sec*
EMP: 7
SALES: 200K **Privately Held**
SIC: 3612 Generator voltage regulators

(G-2281)
MASON WOODWORKS LLC
127 Chester Ave (11218-3021)
PHONE.................917 363-7052
Robert Mason, *Principal*
EMP: 5
SALES (est): 380.9K **Privately Held**
SIC: 2431 Millwork

(G-2282)
MASS APPEAL MAGAZINE
261 Vandervoort Ave (11211-1718)
PHONE.................718 858-0979
Adrian Moeller, *Partner*
Patrick Elasik, *Partner*
Owen Strock, *Vice Pres*
EMP: 7 EST: 1998
SQ FT: 1,100
SALES (est): 830.6K **Privately Held**
SIC: 2721 Magazines: publishing only, not printed on site

(G-2283)
MAST BROTHERS INC
63 Flushing Ave Unit 341 (11205-1084)
PHONE.................718 388-2625
Rick Mast, *Owner*
EMP: 29
SALES (est): 5MM **Privately Held**
SIC: 2066 Chocolate & cocoa products

(G-2284)
MASTER WINDOW & DOOR CORP
199 Starr St (11237-2607)
PHONE.................718 782-5407
Penn Ku, *President*
EMP: 13
SALES (est): 2.2MM **Privately Held**
SIC: 3442 Window & door frames

(G-2285)
MATCHABLES INC
Also Called: Bara Fashions
106 Green St Ste G1 (11222-1352)
PHONE.................718 389-9318
Raphael Blumenstock, *President*
Ruth Malach, *Vice Pres*
EMP: 10
SQ FT: 8,000
SALES (est): 750K **Privately Held**
SIC: 2253 Sweaters & sweater coats, knit

(G-2286)
MATERIAL PROCESS SYSTEMS INC
87 Richardson St Ste 2 (11211-1319)
PHONE.................718 302-3081
Fax: 718 302-9043
Steven Urbatsch, *President*
Matthew Josephs, *Vice Pres*
▲ EMP: 14
SALES (est): 1.2MM **Privately Held**
WEB: www.materialprocess.com
SIC: 2434 3446 Wood kitchen cabinets; architectural metalwork

(G-2287)
MATRIX STEEL COMPANY INC
50 Bogart St (11206-3818)
PHONE.................718 381-6800
Francesca Montagna, *President*
Anna Pedri, *Bookkeeper*
EMP: 6
SALES (est): 1.5MM **Privately Held**
SIC: 3312 3321 Structural & rail mill products; gray & ductile iron foundries

(G-2288)
MATTHEWS HATS
99 Kenilworth Pl Fl 1 (11210-2423)
PHONE.................718 859-4683
Fax: 212 704-0583
Larry S Matthews, *Partner*
Merrill Matthews, *Partner*
EMP: 7
SALES: 410K **Privately Held**
SIC: 2353 Hats, trimmed: women's, misses' & children's

(G-2289)
MAXWELL BAKERY INC
2700 Atlantic Ave (11207-2893)
PHONE.................718 498-2200
George Jograj, *Owner*
Earl Wheelin, *General Mgr*
EMP: 25
SQ FT: 10,000
SALES (est): 1.2MM **Privately Held**
WEB: www.maxwellbakery.com
SIC: 2051 Bakery: wholesale or wholesale/retail combined

(G-2290)
MAZEL SUPPLY
1439 Ocean Ave Apt B10 (11230-3913)
PHONE.................212 947-2213
EMP: 8 EST: 2010
SALES (est): 1.3MM **Privately Held**
SIC: 2653 Corrugated & solid fiber boxes

(G-2291)
MDCARE911 LLC
Also Called: Gocare247
30 Main St Apt 5c (11201-8213)
PHONE.................917 640-4869
Anthony Schweinzer,
EMP: 5
SALES (est): 128.9K **Privately Held**
SIC: 7372 Home entertainment computer software

(G-2292)
MDEK INC
9728 3rd Ave (11209-7742)
P.O. Box 90318 (11209-0318)
PHONE.................347 569-7318
Rick Manak, *President*
EMP: 1
SQ FT: 15,000
SALES: 3.5MM **Privately Held**
SIC: 3799 8711 Electrocars for transporting golfers; consulting engineer

(G-2293)
MDS HOT BAGELS DELI INC
127 Church Ave (11218-3917)
PHONE.................718 438-5650
Alex Esalias, *Manager*
EMP: 1
SQ FT: 1,000
SALES (est): 483.3K **Privately Held**
SIC: 2051 5461 5411 Bagels, fresh or frozen; bagels; delicatessens

(G-2294)
MECHANICAL DISPLAYS INC
4420 Farragut Rd (11203-6522)
PHONE.................718 258-5588
Fax: 718 258-6202
Hugo Paulucci, *President*
Lou Nasti, *Vice Pres*
Dean Townsend, *Vice Pres*
▲ EMP: 7
SQ FT: 7,500
SALES: 1MM **Privately Held**
WEB: www.mechanicaldisplays.com
SIC: 3944 7389 Trains & equipment; toy: electric & mechanical; convention & show services

(G-2295)
MEDI-TECH INTERNATIONAL CORP (PA)
Also Called: Spandage
26 Court St Ste 1301 (11242-1113)
PHONE.................800 333-0109
Fax: 718 855-1618
Jacqueline Fortunato, *CEO*
Marilyn Geiger, *Principal*
Derrick Brown, *Regional Mgr*
Carol Callahan, *Regional Mgr*
Steve Dejoe, *Regional Mgr*
▲ EMP: 40
SQ FT: 1,000
SALES (est): 5MM **Privately Held**
WEB: www.medi-techintl.com
SIC: 3842 2339 Bandages: plastic, muslin, plaster of paris, etc.; dressings, surgical; maternity clothing

(G-2296)
MEDIA SIGNS LLC
6404 14th Ave (11219-5314)
PHONE.................718 252-7575
EMP: 7
SALES (est): 300.9K **Privately Held**
SIC: 2759 Commercial printing

(G-2297)
MEEKER SALES CORP
551 Sutter Ave (11207-4001)
PHONE.................718 384-5400
Harvey Worth, *President*
Jim Kaye, *Manager*
EMP: 1
SQ FT: 150
SALES: 1.2MM **Privately Held**
SIC: 2514 Metal household furniture

(G-2298)
MEGA VISION INC
1274 Flushing Ave (11237-2303)
P.O. Box 370715 (11237-0715)
PHONE.................718 228-1065
Michael Chiriac, *President*
Joe Baboola, *Sales Executive*
Katica Chiriac, *Admin Sec*
EMP: 35
SQ FT: 22,000
SALES (est): 7.9MM **Privately Held**
WEB: www.megavision.net
SIC: 3444 2542 Sheet metalwork; office & store showcases & display fixtures; fixtures: display, office or store: except wood

(G-2299)
MEISEL-PESKIN CO INC (PA)
349 Scholes St 353 (11206-1787)
PHONE.................718 497-1840
Garry Meisel, *President*
▲ EMP: 78
SQ FT: 18,000
SALES (est): 4.9MM **Privately Held**
SIC: 3999 Furs, dressed: bleached, curried, scraped, tanned or dyed

(G-2300)
MENPIN SUPPLY CORP
1229 60th St (11219-4930)
PHONE.................718 415-4168
David Hiehs, *President*
EMP: 18 EST: 2016
SQ FT: 150
SALES: 2.8MM **Privately Held**
SIC: 3589 Water filters & softeners, household type

(G-2301)
MENUCHA PUBLISHERS INC
1221 38th St (11218-1928)
PHONE.................718 232-0856
Hirsch Traube, *President*
▲ EMP: 16
SALES (est): 1.6MM **Privately Held**
SIC: 2741 Miscellaneous publishing

(G-2302)
MEP ALASKA LLC
Also Called: Magnum Energy Partners
3619 Bedford Ave Apt 4e (11210-5206)
PHONE.................646 535-9005
Mark Steinmetz, *Owner*
Terrence Manning, *COO*
EMP: 5
SALES (est): 207.7K **Privately Held**
SIC: 1389 3569 1382 Construction, repair & dismantling services; gas producers, generators & other gas related equipment; oil & gas exploration services

(G-2303)
MERCURY PAINT CORPORATION (PA)
4808 Farragut Rd (11203-6612)
PHONE.................718 469-8787
Fax: 718 469-0858
Jeff Berman, *President*
Frank Corchia, *Controller*
Ronald Alli, *Sales Mgr*
John Van, *Manager*
▲ EMP: 75 EST: 1961
SQ FT: 100,000
SALES (est): 25.2MM **Privately Held**
WEB: www.mercurypaintcorp.com
SIC: 2851 5231 Paints & paint additives; paint

(G-2304)
MERCURY PLASTICS CORP
989 Utica Ave 995 (11203-4399)
PHONE.................718 498-5400
Fax: 718 498-1103
William Wright, *President*
George Wheigl Jr, *Corp Secy*
▲ EMP: 20 EST: 1945
SQ FT: 8,000
SALES (est): 3MM **Privately Held**
SIC: 3089 Molding primary plastic

Brooklyn - Kings County (G-2305)

(G-2305)
MERKOS LINYONEI CHINUCH INC
Also Called: Merkos Bookstore
291 Kingston Ave (11213-3402)
PHONE..............................718 778-0226
Fax: 718 778-4148
Malka Ahern, Manager
EMP: 20
SALES (corp-wide): 950K **Privately Held**
WEB: www.chabad.org
SIC: 2731 Book publishing
PA: Merkos L'inyonei Chinuch, Inc.
   770 Eastern Pkwy
   Brooklyn NY 11213
   718 774-4000

(G-2306)
MERZON LEATHER CO INC
810 Humboldt St Ste 2 (11222-1913)
PHONE..............................718 782-6260
Richard Merzon, President
▲ EMP: 130 EST: 1943
SQ FT: 50,000
SALES (est): 16.3MM **Privately Held**
SIC: 3161 3172 Cases, carrying; suitcases; camera carrying bags; personal leather goods

(G-2307)
MESORAH PUBLICATIONS LTD
4401 2nd Ave (11232-4212)
PHONE..............................718 921-9000
Fax: 718 680-1875
Martin Zlotowitz, President
Abe Biderman, Publisher
Jacob Brander, Vice Pres
Efraim Perlowitz, Marketing Staff
Bernard Kempler, MIS Dir
▲ EMP: 43
SQ FT: 20,000
SALES (est): 8MM **Privately Held**
WEB: www.artscroll.com
SIC: 2731 Books: publishing only; pamphlets: publishing only, not printed on site

(G-2308)
METAL CRAFTS INC
Also Called: Metalcraft By N Barzel
650 Berrimar St (11208-5304)
PHONE..............................718 443-3333
Norman Barzel, President
Norman Bars, President
EMP: 6
SALES (est): 590K **Privately Held**
SIC: 3441 Fabricated structural metal

(G-2309)
METPAK INC
320 Roebling St Ste 601 (11211-6262)
PHONE..............................917 309-0196
Izzy Katz, President
EMP: 4
SALES: 1MM **Privately Held**
SIC: 2673 Bags: plastic, laminated & coated

(G-2310)
METRO KITCHENS CORP
1040 E 45th St (11203-6542)
PHONE..............................718 434-1166
Fax: 718 531-1374
John Ciavattoni, President
Kevin Taflin, Vice Pres
▲ EMP: 11
SQ FT: 10,000
SALES (est): 680K **Privately Held**
WEB: www.metro-kitchens.com
SIC: 2434 5031 1751 Wood kitchen cabinets; kitchen cabinets; cabinet & finish carpentry

(G-2311)
METRO PRODUCTS & SERVICES LLC (PA)
Also Called: Gumbusters of New York
1424 74th St (11228-2208)
PHONE..............................866 846-8486
Anthony Mule, Owner
Andrea Mule, Co-Owner
▲ EMP: 14
SQ FT: 5,000
SALES (est): 1.2MM **Privately Held**
SIC: 2861 Gum & wood chemicals

(G-2312)
METROPOLITAN PACKG MFG CORP
68 Java St (11222-1519)
PHONE..............................718 383-2700
Fax: 718 383-7952
Malka Katz, President
Herman Katz, Vice Pres
▲ EMP: 35 EST: 1964
SQ FT: 20,000
SALES (est): 6.8MM **Privately Held**
WEB: www.metropack.com
SIC: 2673 Plastic bags: made from purchased materials

(G-2313)
MICHAEL BERNSTEIN DESIGN ASSOC
361 Stagg St Fl 4 (11206-1734)
PHONE..............................718 456-9277
Fax: 718 456-9284
Michael Bernstein, President
EMP: 20
SQ FT: 10,000
SALES (est): 2MM **Privately Held**
WEB: www.mbda.com
SIC: 2431 2434 Woodwork, interior & ornamental; wood kitchen cabinets

(G-2314)
MICHAEL STUART INC
199 Cook St (11206-3701)
P.O. Box 60267 (11206-0267)
PHONE..............................718 821-0704
Michael Stuart Fuchs, President
EMP: 20 EST: 1975
SQ FT: 20,000
SALES (est): 1.4MM **Privately Held**
SIC: 2369 2392 2211 2361 Girls' & children's outerwear; tablecloths: made from purchased materials; bathmats, cotton; girls' & children's dresses, blouses & shirts

(G-2315)
MICRO ESSENTIAL LABORATORY
4224 Avenue H (11210-3518)
P.O. Box 100824 (11210-0824)
PHONE..............................718 338-3618
Fax: 718 692-4491
Joel Florin, President
Mark Florin, Vice Pres
Evelyn La Nier, Office Mgr
Evelyn Lanier, Office Mgr
EMP: 30
SQ FT: 7,500
SALES (est): 7.3MM **Privately Held**
WEB: www.microessentiallab.com
SIC: 2672 Chemically treated papers: made from purchased materials

(G-2316)
MIDWOOD SIGNS & DESIGN INC
202 28th St (11232-1604)
PHONE..............................718 499-9041
Ron Guercio, President
Maryanne Bowman, Principal
EMP: 3
SALES: 1.5MM **Privately Held**
SIC: 3993 2431 Signs & advertising specialties; awnings, wood

(G-2317)
MILGO INDUSTRIAL INC (PA)
Also Called: Milgo/Bufkin
68 Lombardy St (11222-5234)
PHONE..............................718 388-6476
Fax: 718 388-3154
Bruce J Gitlin, President
Rose Gitlin, Vice Pres
Gina Jordan, Vice Pres
Barbara Kanter, CFO
Michelle O'Donnell, Controller
EMP: 70 EST: 1918
SQ FT: 30,000
SALES (est): 11.6MM **Privately Held**
WEB: www.milgo-bufkin.com
SIC: 3446 3442 3398 Architectural metalwork; metal doors, sash & trim; store fronts, prefabricated, metal; brazing (hardening) of metal

(G-2318)
MILGO INDUSTRIAL INC
514 Varick Ave (11222-5400)
PHONE..............................718 387-0406
Alex Kveton, Branch Mgr
EMP: 6
SALES (corp-wide): 11.6MM **Privately Held**
WEB: www.milgo-bufkin.com
SIC: 3446 3442 3398 Architectural metalwork; metal doors, sash & trim; brazing (hardening) of metal
PA: Milgo Industrial Inc.
   68 Lombardy St
   Brooklyn NY 11222
   718 388-6476

(G-2319)
MILLA GLOBAL INC
Also Called: Concepts New York, The
1301 Metropolitan Ave (11237-1102)
PHONE..............................516 488-3601
Glen Parproff, Director
EMP: 4
SALES: 10MM **Privately Held**
SIC: 2673 3911 Bags: plastic, laminated & coated; jewelry, precious metal

(G-2320)
MILLENNIUM STL RACK RNTALS INC (PA)
253 Bond St (11217-2919)
PHONE..............................718 965-4736
Toll Free:..............................877 -
Fax: 718 868-1128
David Fox, President
Rachael Wilson, Manager
▲ EMP: 9 EST: 1999
SALES (est): 1.2MM **Privately Held**
WEB: www.millenniumsteelservice.com
SIC: 2542 7359 Garment racks: except wood; equipment rental & leasing

(G-2321)
MINDBODYGREEN LLC
45 Main St Ste 422 (11201-1093)
PHONE..............................347 529-6952
Jason Wacob,
Stephen Anderson,
EMP: 29
SQ FT: 2,500
SALES (est): 1.9MM **Privately Held**
SIC: 2741

(G-2322)
MINI-CIRCUITS FORT WAYNE LLC
13 Neptune Ave (11235-4404)
P.O. Box 350166 (11235-0166)
PHONE..............................718 934-4500
Jennifer Fogel, Human Res Mgr
Harvey Kaylie,
EMP: 500
SALES (est): 66.2MM **Privately Held**
WEB: www.matchingpad.com
SIC: 3679 3678 3677 3674 Attenuators; electronic connectors; electronic coils, transformers & other inductors; semiconductors & related devices; radio & TV communications equipment; current-carrying wiring devices

(G-2323)
MISHPACHA MAGAZINE INC
5809 16th Ave (11204-2112)
PHONE..............................718 686-9339
Eli Peli, President
Barbara Bensoussan, Editor
Nomee Shaingarten, COO
Nina Feiner, Adv Mgr
Moti Rezmovich, Manager
EMP: 5
SALES (est): 512.5K **Privately Held**
SIC: 2721 Magazines: publishing & printing

(G-2324)
MISS SPORTSWEAR INC
117 9th St (11215-3108)
PHONE..............................212 391-2535
Moses Fallas, Ch of Bd
EMP: 11 **Privately Held**
SIC: 2339 Women's & misses' athletic clothing & sportswear
PA: M.I.S.S. Sportswear, Inc.
   117 9th St
   Brooklyn NY 11215

(G-2325)
MISS SPORTSWEAR INC (PA)
Also Called: Miss Group, The
117 9th St (11215-3108)
PHONE..............................212 391-2535
Fax: 718 391-2543
Moses Fallas, Ch of Bd
Moey Fallas, President
Alan Fallas, Vice Pres
Sammy Fallas, Manager
Irene Chang, Admin Asst
▲ EMP: 3
SQ FT: 8,000
SALES (est): 22.9MM **Privately Held**
SIC: 2339 Women's & misses' athletic clothing & sportswear

(G-2326)
MISS SPORTSWEAR INC
Also Called: Miss Group, The
117 9th St (11215-3108)
PHONE..............................718 369-6012
Sammy Fallas, Branch Mgr
EMP: 14 **Privately Held**
SIC: 2339 Women's & misses' athletic clothing & sportswear
PA: M.I.S.S. Sportswear, Inc.
   117 9th St
   Brooklyn NY 11215

(G-2327)
MISSIONTEX INC
236 Greenpoint Ave Ste 12 (11222-2495)
PHONE..............................718 532-9053
Jay McLaughlin, Principal
▲ EMP: 5
SALES (est): 320K **Privately Held**
SIC: 2281 5949 5632 5651 Yarn spinning mills; fabric stores piece goods; fur apparel; family clothing stores

(G-2328)
MJK CUTTING INC
Also Called: M J K
117 9th St (11215-3108)
PHONE..............................718 384-7613
Wing Lau, President
EMP: 10
SALES (est): 750K **Privately Held**
SIC: 3552 Jacquard card cutting machines

(G-2329)
MJK ENTERPRISES LLC
Also Called: M & J Custom Lampshade Company
34 35th St (11232-2021)
PHONE..............................917 653-9042
Martin Kuranc, Managing Prtnr
EMP: 8 EST: 2011
SALES: 50MM **Privately Held**
SIC: 3648 Lanterns: electric, gas, carbide, kerosene or gasoline

(G-2330)
MJM JEWELRY CORP
Also Called: Berry Jewelry Company
400 3rd Ave (11215-2738)
PHONE..............................718 596-1600
Percival S Mijares, Branch Mgr
EMP: 70
SALES (corp-wide): 14.6MM **Privately Held**
WEB: www.berryjewelry.com
SIC: 3911 Jewelry, precious metal
PA: Mjm Jewelry Corp.
   29 W 38th St Rm 1601
   New York NY 10018
   212 354-5014

(G-2331)
MNN HOLDING COMPANY LLC
Also Called: Mother Nature & Partners
155 Water St Ste 616 (11201-1016)
PHONE..............................404 558-5251
Michael Jacobson, CFO
EMP: 15 **Privately Held**
SIC: 7372 8748 Publishers' computer software; publishing consultant
PA: Mnn Holding Company, Llc
   191 Peachtree St Ne Ste 4
   Atlanta GA 30303

Brooklyn - Kings County (G-2361)

(G-2332)
MODERN PLASTIC BAGS MFG INC
63 Flushing Ave Unit 303 (11205-1080)
PHONE..................718 237-2985
Abrahm Stossel, *President*
EMP: 5
SQ FT: 3,000
SALES: 450K Privately Held
SIC: 2673 Plastic & pliofilm bags

(G-2333)
MOES WEAR APPAREL INC
1020 E 48th St Ste 8 (11203-6605)
PHONE..................718 940-1597
Selly Nessry, *President*
Jeff Saad, *Vice Pres*
Morris Saad, *Vice Pres*
Mellisa Clark, *Office Mgr*
▲ EMP: 13
SQ FT: 50,000
SALES (est): 2.1MM Privately Held
SIC: 2339 Women's & misses' outerwear

(G-2334)
MOLDOVA PICKLES & SALADS INC
1060 E 46th St (11203-6516)
PHONE..................718 284-2220
Naum Zozulya, *President*
Vitality Pinchev, *Vice Pres*
▲ EMP: 5
SALES (est): 420K Privately Held
SIC: 2035 Pickles, vinegar

(G-2335)
MOLLY VAPES INC
3235 Emmons Ave Apt 608 (11235-1167)
PHONE..................718 743-0120
EMP: 7
SALES (est): 110.2K Privately Held
SIC: 3999 Cigar & cigarette holders

(G-2336)
MONFEFO LLC
630 Flushing Ave 5q (11206-5026)
PHONE..................347 779-2600
Justin Monsul, *Mng Member*
EMP: 5 EST: 2016
SQ FT: 600
SALES: 300K Privately Held
SIC: 2086 Soft drinks: packaged in cans, bottles, etc.

(G-2337)
MONTROSE EQUIPMENT SALES INC
Also Called: Ace
202 N 10th St (11211-1109)
PHONE..................718 388-7446
Fax: 718 218-8422
Emil Romotzki, *President*
Jack Pivovarov, *Corp Secy*
▲ EMP: 12
SQ FT: 8,000
SALES (est): 1.1MM Privately Held
SIC: 3541 Machine tools, metal cutting type

(G-2338)
MORCO PRODUCTS CORP
556 39th St (11232-3002)
PHONE..................718 853-4005
Fax: 718 436-0692
Michael Morgan, *President*
Neil Falcone, *Vice Pres*
EMP: 15
SQ FT: 6,200
SALES (est): 1.1MM Privately Held
SIC: 3599 Machine shop, jobbing & repair

(G-2339)
MORRIS KITCHEN INC
30 Chester Ct (11225-5605)
PHONE..................646 413-5186
Kari Morris, *Owner*
EMP: 15
SALES (est): 2.2MM Privately Held
SIC: 2099 2032 2033 Food preparations; chicken soup: packaged in cans, jars, etc.; tomato products: packaged in cans, jars, etc.

(G-2340)
MOTI INC
4118 13th Ave (11219-1333)
PHONE..................718 436-4280
Mordechai Fleicher, *President*
▲ EMP: 16
SQ FT: 8,000
SALES (est): 1.2MM Privately Held
SIC: 3999 Wigs, including doll wigs, toupees or wiglets

(G-2341)
MOTOROLA SOLUTIONS INC
335 Adams St Fl 7 (11201-3754)
PHONE..................718 330-2163
Tom Driscoll, *Manager*
Christopher Sparrow, *Senior Mgr*
EMP: 153
SALES (corp-wide): 6B Publicly Held
SIC: 3663 Radio & TV communications equipment
PA: Motorola Solutions, Inc.
500 W Monroe St Ste 4400
Chicago IL 60661
847 576-5000

(G-2342)
MOZNAIM PUBLISHING CO INC
Also Called: Moznaim Co
4304 12th Ave (11219-1301)
PHONE..................718 853-0525
Fax: 718 438-1305
Menachem Wagshol, *President*
Monshe Sternlicht, *Vice Pres*
▲ EMP: 6
SALES (est): 360K Privately Held
WEB: www.moznaim.com
SIC: 2731 5192 5999 Books: publishing only; books; religious goods

(G-2343)
MPR MAGAZINE APP INC
Also Called: Soldi
2653 E 19th St Fl 2 (11235-3302)
PHONE..................718 403-0303
Gady Kohanov, *President*
Gary Porat, *Vice Pres*
EMP: 20
SQ FT: 5,000
SALES (est): 933.6K Privately Held
SIC: 7372 Application computer software

(G-2344)
MR DISPOSABLE INC
101 Richardson St Ste 2 (11211-1344)
PHONE..................718 388-8574
Raymond Cora, *CEO*
Victor Morales, *Vice Pres*
Debbie Cora, *Admin Sec*
▲ EMP: 10
SALES: 400K Privately Held
WEB: www.mrdisposable.com
SIC: 2676 Diapers, paper (disposable): made from purchased paper

(G-2345)
MR PIEROGI LLC
126 12th St (11215-3817)
PHONE..................718 499-7821
Leonard Sherman,
EMP: 11
SALES (est): 1.2MM Privately Held
SIC: 2013 Sausages & other prepared meats

(G-2346)
MR SIGN USA INC
1920 Atlantic Ave (11233-3004)
PHONE..................718 218-3321
Michael Leivowitz, *President*
Ester Atran, *Manager*
EMP: 15
SALES (est): 1.2MM Privately Held
SIC: 3993 Signs & advertising specialties

(G-2347)
MRCHOCOLATECOM LLC
Also Called: Jacques Torres Chocolate
66 Water St Ste 2 (11201-1048)
PHONE..................718 875-9772
Fax: 718 875-2167
Jacques Torres, *Partner*
Keitaro Goto, *Partner*
Kris Kruid, *Partner*
Linda Lee, *Sales Dir*
▲ EMP: 18
SALES (est): 910K Privately Held
WEB: www.jacquestorres.com
SIC: 2064 5145 5441 Candy & other confectionery products; confectionery; candy, nut & confectionery stores

(G-2348)
MS PAPER PRODUCTS CO INC
930 Bedford Ave (11205-4502)
PHONE..................718 624-0248
Fax: 718 625-4748
Solomon Schwimmer, *President*
Hirsh Krauss, *Empl Benefits*
EMP: 6 EST: 1970
SQ FT: 12,000
SALES: 500K Privately Held
SIC: 2631 Paperboard mills

(G-2349)
MUSICSKINS LLC
140 58th St Ste 197 (11220-2539)
PHONE..................646 827-4271
Robert Scarcello, *Senior VP*
Vince Bartozzi, *Mng Member*
Jed Seifert,
EMP: 11
SQ FT: 4,000
SALES: 1.5MM Privately Held
SIC: 2851 5099 Vinyl coatings, strippable; musical instruments parts & accessories

(G-2350)
MY HANKY INC
680 81st St Apt 4d (11228-2833)
PHONE..................646 321-0869
Frank Marino, *President*
EMP: 10
SQ FT: 500
SALES: 500K Privately Held
SIC: 2389 Handkerchiefs, except paper

(G-2351)
MYSTIC DISPLAY CO INC
909 Remsen Ave (11236-1624)
PHONE..................718 485-2651
David Censi, *President*
Barry Censi, *Corp Secy*
Hank Lombardi, *Vice Pres*
Anthony Valentine, *Vice Pres*
Dorothy Sylvester, *Controller*
▼ EMP: 2
SQ FT: 47,000
SALES: 8MM Privately Held
WEB: www.mysticdisplay.com
SIC: 3993 7319 Displays & cutouts, window & lobby; display advertising service

(G-2352)
N C IRON WORKS INC
1117 60th St (11219-4925)
PHONE..................718 633-4660
Fax: 718 436-0334
Nicholas Sorrentino, *President*
EMP: 5
SQ FT: 3,900
SALES (est): 976.6K Privately Held
SIC: 3312 Hot-rolled iron & steel products

(G-2353)
NAGAD CABINETS INC
1039 Mcdonald Ave (11230-1020)
PHONE..................718 382-7200
Naftali Grueberger, *President*
EMP: 5
SQ FT: 2,000
SALES (est): 704.4K Privately Held
SIC: 2434 Vanities, bathroom: wood

(G-2354)
NANOTRONICS IMAGING INC
63 Flushing Ave Unit 128 (11205-1059)
PHONE..................212 401-6209
Matthew Putman, *CEO*
EMP: 20
SALES (corp-wide): 2.4MM Privately Held
SIC: 3826 Analytical instruments
PA: Nanotronics Imaging, Inc.
2251 Front St Ste 109-111
Cuyahoga Falls OH 44221
330 926-9809

(G-2355)
NAP INDUSTRIES INC
Also Called: N A P
667 Kent Ave (11249-7500)
PHONE..................718 625-4948
Fax: 718 596-4342
Leopold Lowy, *President*
Morris Lowy, *Chairman*
Jack Freund, *Vice Pres*
Ram Sirupurapu, *Exec Dir*
▲ EMP: 90 EST: 1961
SQ FT: 55,000
SALES (est): 18.4MM Privately Held
SIC: 2673 Plastic bags: made from purchased materials

(G-2356)
NARRATIVELY INC
697 Hancock St 2 (11233-1202)
PHONE..................203 536-0332
Noah Rosenberg, *President*
EMP: 25 EST: 2012
SQ FT: 20,000
SALES (est): 1.1MM Privately Held
SIC: 2741

(G-2357)
NATIONAL DIE & BUTTON MOULD CO
Also Called: Eisen Bros
1 Kent Ave (11249-1014)
PHONE..................201 939-7800
Fax: 212 575-2153
Louis Eisenpresser, *Chairman*
George Eisenpresser, *Chairman*
EMP: 50 EST: 1911
SQ FT: 65,000
SALES (est): 5.1MM Privately Held
WEB: www.nailheads.com
SIC: 3965 3469 Buttons & parts; buckles & buckle parts; eyelets, metal: clothing, fabrics, boots or shoes; metal stampings

(G-2358)
NATIONAL PRFMCE SOLUTIONS INC
Also Called: Squeaky Clean
7106 13th Ave (11228-1606)
PHONE..................718 833-4767
Lola Bizas, *Ch of Bd*
Jacob Kahle, *Principal*
Greg Bowman, *Co-Owner*
Michell Bowman, *Co-Owner*
EMP: 100
SQ FT: 400
SALES (est): 20.1MM Privately Held
SIC: 3993 Advertising artwork

(G-2359)
NATIONWIDE DAIRY INC
792 E 93rd St (11236-1831)
PHONE..................347 689-8148
Eduard Magidov, *CEO*
◆ EMP: 5
SQ FT: 9,000
SALES (est): 423.4K Privately Held
SIC: 2023 Dry, condensed, evaporated dairy products

(G-2360)
NATURAL STONE & CABINET INC
1365 Halsey St (11237-6102)
PHONE..................718 388-2988
Sally Lee, *Owner*
▲ EMP: 5
SALES (est): 423.1K Privately Held
SIC: 2522 Cabinets, office: except wood

(G-2361)
NAUTICAL MARINE PAINT CORP
Also Called: Nautical Paint
4802 Farragut Rd (11203-6690)
PHONE..................718 462-7000
Fax: 718 462-4100
Michael Schnurr, *President*
EMP: 25
SQ FT: 4,000
SALES (corp-wide): 7.2MM Privately Held
SIC: 2851 5231 Paints & allied products; paint

Brooklyn - Kings County (G-2362)

PA: Nautical Marine Paint Corp
1993 Elizabeth St
North Brunswick NJ 08902
732 821-3200

(G-2362)
NB ELECTRCAL ENCLSURES MFRS INC
902 903 Shepherd Ave (11208)
PHONE...............................718 272-8792
Neville Bearam, *President*
Travis Maynard, *Business Mgr*
EMP: 7
SALES: 2MM **Privately Held**
SIC: 3441 Fabricated structural metal

(G-2363)
NCC NY LLC
1840 Mcdonald Ave (11223-1827)
PHONE...............................718 943-7000
Michelle Cohen, *COO*
Liane Yee, *Manager*
Sharon Miller, *Executive*
Joey Haber,
Joe Nakash,
▲ EMP: 20 EST: 1999
SQ FT: 9,000
SALES (est): 4.8MM **Privately Held**
WEB: www.ehalacha.com
SIC: 3699 Extension cords
PA: Nakash Five Points Llc
1400 Broadway Fl 15
New York NY 10018

(G-2364)
NEO CAB NETRY LLC
400 Liberty Ave (11207-3032)
PHONE...............................718 403-0456
Louis Doucet, *Owner*
EMP: 10
SALES (est): 945.9K **Privately Held**
SIC: 2434 Wood kitchen cabinets

(G-2365)
NEPTUNE MACHINE INC
521 Carroll St (11215-1011)
PHONE...............................718 852-4100
Fax: 718 797-5113
Nicholas G Karkas, *President*
John Karkas, *Vice Pres*
Camille Manzo, *Controller*
Farrah Ficco Vasquez, *Admin Asst*
EMP: 20
SQ FT: 12,500
SALES (est): 3.9MM **Privately Held**
WEB: www.neptunemachine.com
SIC: 3599 Machine & other job shop work; machine shop, jobbing & repair

(G-2366)
NEW AGE IRONWORKS INC
183 Van Siclen Ave (11207-2605)
PHONE...............................718 277-1895
Fax: 718 277-1897
Yair Tapia, *President*
EMP: 14
SALES (est): 1.7MM **Privately Held**
SIC: 7692 Welding repair

(G-2367)
NEW ART PUBLICATIONS INC
Also Called: BOMB MAGAZINE
80 Hanson Pl Ste 703 (11217-2998)
PHONE...............................718 636-9100
Fax: 718 636-9200
Betsy Sussler, *President*
Ryan Chapman, *Managing Dir*
Alexis Boehmler, *Principal*
Raluca Albu, *Editor*
Lucy Raven, *Editor*
EMP: 10
SALES: 1.4MM **Privately Held**
WEB: www.bombsite.com
SIC: 2721 Magazines: publishing only, not printed on site

(G-2368)
NEW CONCEPTS OF NEW YORK LLC
89 19th St 91 (11232-1055)
PHONE...............................212 695-4999
Anna Martinez, *Manager*
Robert Schwartz,
▲ EMP: 20
SALES (est): 2.4MM **Privately Held**
WEB: www.newconceptsllc.com
SIC: 2339 Women's & misses' accessories

(G-2369)
NEW DIMENSION AWARDS INC (PA)
Also Called: New Dimension Trophies
6505 11th Ave (11219-5602)
PHONE...............................718 236-8200
Fax: 718 236-6979
Joseph S Cardinale, *President*
Michael S Fasano, *Vice Pres*
EMP: 9 EST: 1979
SQ FT: 16,000
SALES (est): 1MM **Privately Held**
WEB: www.newdimensioninc.com
SIC: 3499 Trophies, metal, except silver; novelties & specialties, metal

(G-2370)
NEW DIMENSIONS OFFICE GROUP
Also Called: Acme Office Group
540 Morgan Ave (11222-5227)
PHONE...............................718 387-0995
Fax: 718 387-1162
Ernest Eager, *President*
Bertran Teich, *Vice Pres*
Buddy Martin, *Treasurer*
Joseph Klinsky, *Controller*
Jack Teich, *Admin Sec*
EMP: 52
SQ FT: 20,000
SALES (est): 3.5MM **Privately Held**
SIC: 2521 3446 2541 2522 Wood office furniture; panel systems & partitions (free-standing), office: wood; architectural metalwork; wood partitions & fixtures; office furniture, except wood

(G-2371)
NEW YORK CHRISTAN TIMES INC
1061 Atlantic Ave (11238-2902)
PHONE...............................718 638-6397
Fax: 718 638-1810
Dennis Dillon, *President*
Karen Granger, *Vice Pres*
EMP: 6
SALES (est): 460K **Privately Held**
SIC: 2759 Publication printing

(G-2372)
NEW YORK DAILY CHALLENGE INC (PA)
1195 Atlantic Ave Fl 2 (11216-2709)
P.O. Box 160252 (11216-0252)
PHONE...............................718 636-9500
Fax: 718 857-9115
Thomas H Watkins Jr, *President*
Tatsianna Singleton, *Office Mgr*
Duwad Philip, *Manager*
EMP: 20
SQ FT: 1,000
SALES (est): 1MM **Privately Held**
SIC: 2711 Newspapers: publishing only, not printed on site

(G-2373)
NEW YORK HOSPITAL DISPOSABLE
101 Richardson St Ste 1 (11211-1344)
PHONE...............................718 384-1620
Fax: 718 599-1183
Rosa Ramos, *President*
Victor Cora, *President*
Ricardo Cora, *Vice Pres*
Zitzor Cora, *Admin Sec*
EMP: 20
SQ FT: 12,000
SALES (est): 1.7MM **Privately Held**
SIC: 2389 2326 Hospital gowns; men's & boys' work clothing

(G-2374)
NEW YORK PASTA AUTHORITY INC
640 Parkside Ave (11226-1506)
PHONE...............................347 787-2130
Chavi Katzman, *Exec Dir*
EMP: 10
SALES (est): 629.3K **Privately Held**
SIC: 2033 Spaghetti & other pasta sauce: packaged in cans, jars, etc.

(G-2375)
NEW YORK POPLIN LLC
4611 1st Ave (11232-4200)
PHONE...............................718 768-3296
Wayne Yip,
▲ EMP: 8
SQ FT: 8,000
SALES (est): 4.5MM **Privately Held**
SIC: 2221 Apparel & outerwear fabric, manmade fiber or silk

(G-2376)
NEW YORK POPULAR INC
Also Called: Popularity Products
168 39th St Unit 3 (11232-2714)
PHONE...............................718 499-2020
Benjamin Tebele, *CEO*
Albert Tebele, *Ch of Bd*
Edward Tebele, *Admin Sec*
▲ EMP: 100
SQ FT: 50,000
SALES (est): 14.9MM **Privately Held**
WEB: www.popularityproducts.com
SIC: 2389 5136 5137 Men's miscellaneous accessories; men's & boys' clothing; women's & children's clothing

(G-2377)
NEW YORK QRTRLY FOUNDATION INC
322 76th St (11209-3106)
P.O. Box 2015, New York (10113-2015)
PHONE...............................917 843-8825
Raymond Hammond, *President*
Neil Smith, *Vice Pres*
Linda Tieber, *Treasurer*
Andrea Lockett, *Admin Sec*
EMP: 12
SALES: 52K **Privately Held**
SIC: 2731 7389 Book publishing;

(G-2378)
NEWCASTLE FABRICS CORP
Also Called: Newtown Finishing
86 Beadel St (11222-5232)
PHONE...............................718 388-6600
Daniel Aldalezo, *Manager*
EMP: 5
SALES (corp-wide): 6.2MM **Privately Held**
WEB: www.newcastlefabrics.com
SIC: 2269 7389 Finishing plants; textile & apparel services
PA: Newcastle Fabrics Corp.
140 58th St Ste 112
Brooklyn NY 11220
718 782-5560

(G-2379)
NEWS REPORT INC
Also Called: Diyzeitung
1281 49th St Ste 3 (11219-3055)
PHONE...............................718 851-6607
Albert Friedman, *Ch of Bd*
Rose Friedman, *Vice Pres*
EMP: 25
SALES (est): 1.1MM **Privately Held**
SIC: 2711 Newspapers: publishing only, not printed on site

(G-2380)
NEWYORK PEDORTHIC ASSOCIATES
Also Called: Rosenbaum Foot
2102 63rd St (11204-3058)
PHONE...............................718 236-7700
Fax: 718 234-3380
Mark Rosenbaum, *President*
EMP: 6
SALES (est): 854.9K **Privately Held**
SIC: 3069 Orthopedic sundries, molded rubber

(G-2381)
NIFT GROUP INC
14 Woodbine St (11221-4302)
PHONE...............................504 505-1144
Timothee Dumain, *Principal*
EMP: 1 EST: 2016
SALES: 3MM **Privately Held**
SIC: 7372 Business oriented computer software

(G-2382)
NITEL INC
199 Lee Ave Ste 119 (11211-8919)
PHONE...............................347 731-1558
Solomon Rubin, *President*
EMP: 5
SALES (est): 234.6K **Privately Held**
SIC: 7372 Application computer software

(G-2383)
NOBLE CHECKS INC
1682 43rd St Apt 2 (11204-1059)
PHONE...............................212 537-6241
Isaac Dresdner, *Ch of Bd*
EMP: 5
SALES (est): 564.8K **Privately Held**
WEB: www.noblechecks.com
SIC: 2759 Commercial printing

(G-2384)
NORTHERN ADHESIVES INC
97 Apollo St (11222-3802)
PHONE...............................718 388-5834
Fax: 718 388-6355
Herbert Rosen, *President*
Richard Rosen, *Vice Pres*
Elaine Rosen, *Admin Sec*
EMP: 30
SQ FT: 25,000
SALES (est): 5.3MM **Privately Held**
WEB: www.northernadhesives.com
SIC: 2891 Adhesives

(G-2385)
NORTHSIDE MEDIA GROUP LLC (HQ)
55 Washington St Ste 652 (11201-1063)
PHONE...............................917 318-6513
Jesse Smith, *Vice Pres*
Scott Stedman, *Mng Member*
Daniel Stedman,
EMP: 14
SALES (est): 2.3MM
SALES (corp-wide): 8.3MM **Privately Held**
SIC: 2721 Magazines: publishing & printing
PA: Zealot Networks, Inc.
2114 Narcissus Ct
Venice CA 90291
310 821-3737

(G-2386)
NORTHSIDE MEDIA GROUP LLC
55 Washington St Ste 652 (11201-1063)
PHONE...............................917 318-6513
Fax: 718 596-3662
Scott Stedman, *Branch Mgr*
EMP: 25
SALES (corp-wide): 8.3MM **Privately Held**
SIC: 2721 Magazines: publishing & printing
HQ: Northside Media Group Llc
55 Washington St Ste 652
Brooklyn NY 11201
917 318-6513

(G-2387)
NOSTRAND PHARMACY LLC
Also Called: Vanderveer Pharmacy
1913 Nostrand Ave (11226-7917)
PHONE...............................718 282-2956
Fax: 718 282-6556
EMP: 8 EST: 2015
SALES (est): 228.7K **Privately Held**
SIC: 2834 Pharmaceutical preparations

(G-2388)
NOVEL BOX COMPANY LTD
659 Berriman St (11208-5303)
PHONE...............................718 965-2222
Fax: 718 965-0815
Moishe Sternhill, *President*
Abe Kwadrat, *Vice Pres*
▲ EMP: 25 EST: 1942
SQ FT: 41,000
SALES (est): 4.7MM **Privately Held**
WEB: www.novelbox.com
SIC: 2657 3469 3089 Folding paperboard boxes; boxes, stamped metal; boxes, plastic

GEOGRAPHIC SECTION
Brooklyn - Kings County (G-2419)

(G-2389)
NOVOYE RSSKOYE SLOVO PUBG CORP
Also Called: Russian Daily
2614 Voorhies Ave (11235-2414)
PHONE..................646 460-4566
Fax: 646 218-6951
Yuri Ivnitsky, Ch of Bd
Lawrence Weinberg, President
Michael German, Business Mgr
Alexander Goldfarb, Controller
Victoria Gikaeva, Financial Exec
EMP: 52
SQ FT: 16,000
SALES (est): 2MM Privately Held
WEB: www.nrs.com
SIC: 2711 Newspapers: publishing only, not printed on site

(G-2390)
NUHART & CO INC
49 Dupont St (11222-1008)
P.O. Box 786, Deer Park (11729-0786)
PHONE..................718 383-8484
Fax: 718 383-7215
Alex Folkman, President
Joseph Folkman, Vice Pres
David Rauch, Vice Pres
Roopriarane Dan, Controller
EMP: 76
SQ FT: 130,000
SALES (est): 9.2MM Privately Held
SIC: 3081 Vinyl film & sheet

(G-2391)
NUVITE CHEMICAL COMPOUNDS CORP
213 Freeman St 215 (11222-1400)
PHONE..................718 383-8351
Fax: 718 383-0008
Clifford Lester, President
Robert McHugh, VP Mktg
EMP: 11 EST: 1949
SQ FT: 7,000
SALES: 1MM Privately Held
WEB: www.nuvitechemical.com
SIC: 2842 Specialty cleaning preparations

(G-2392)
NY CABINET FACTORY INC
6901 14th Ave (11228-1701)
PHONE..................718 256-6541
Vin Burratto, President
Frank Burratto, Vice Pres
EMP: 11 EST: 2015
SQ FT: 2,500
SALES: 2MM Privately Held
SIC: 2434 5211 Wood kitchen cabinets; counter tops

(G-2393)
NY ORTHOPEDIC USA INC
63 Flushing Ave Unit 333 (11205-1083)
PHONE..................718 852-5330
Fax: 718 852-4095
Michael Rozenberg, President
Michael Blatt, Vice Pres
▲ EMP: 80
SQ FT: 24,000
SALES (est): 10MM Privately Held
WEB: www.nyorthousa.com
SIC: 3842 2389 5999 Personal safety equipment; uniforms & vestments; medical apparatus & supplies

(G-2394)
NY TILEMAKERS
331 Grand St (11211-4464)
PHONE..................989 278-8453
Andru Eron, Owner
EMP: 5 EST: 2012
SALES: 80K Privately Held
SIC: 3253 Ceramic wall & floor tile

(G-2395)
NYC COMMUNITY MEDIA LLC
Also Called: Villager, The
1 Metrotech Ctr N Fl 10 (11201-3875)
PHONE..................212 229-1890
Justin Hendrix, Exec Dir
Jennifer Goodstein,
EMP: 18 EST: 2012
SQ FT: 1,200
SALES (est): 1.1MM Privately Held
SIC: 2711 Newspapers: publishing only, not printed on site

(G-2396)
NYP HOLDINGS INC
Also Called: New York Post
1 Metrotech Ctr N Fl 10 (11201-3875)
PHONE..................718 260-2500
Cliff Luster, Principal
EMP: 60
SALES (corp-wide): 8.1B Publicly Held
SIC: 2711 Newspapers
HQ: Nyp Holdings, Inc.
1211 Ave Of The Americas
New York NY 10036

(G-2397)
OBSERVER
81 Prospect St Fl 4 (11201-1473)
PHONE..................347 915-5638
EMP: 7
SALES (est): 94.4K Privately Held
SIC: 2711 Newspapers, publishing & printing

(G-2398)
OFFICE GRABS NY INC
1303 53rd St 105 (11219-3823)
PHONE..................212 444-1331
Meir Barminka, CEO
Moshe Rosenberg, President
EMP: 6
SALES (est): 695K Privately Held
SIC: 2752 Commercial printing, lithographic

(G-2399)
OGOSPORT LLC
63 Flushing Ave Unit 137 (11205-1070)
PHONE..................718 554-0777
Matthew Romano, Project Mgr
Jenie Fu,
Charlotte Kreitmann, Admin Sec
Kevin Williams,
▲ EMP: 5
SQ FT: 5,000
SALES (est): 580K Privately Held
WEB: www.ogosport.com
SIC: 3944 Games, toys & children's vehicles

(G-2400)
OLD POLAND FOODS LLC
Also Called: Pipkarnia Starodolska
149 N 8th St (11249-2001)
PHONE..................718 486-7700
Richard Podedworny,
Teresa Kramer,
▲ EMP: 16
SALES (est): 2.1MM Privately Held
SIC: 2051 Pastries, e.g. danish: except frozen

(G-2401)
OLD WILLIAMSBURGH CANDLE CORP
143 Alabama Ave (11207-2911)
P.O. Box 6, Suffern (10901-0006)
PHONE..................718 566-1500
Merav Gold, CEO
Shrage Marasow, General Mgr
Niv Zikdershtein, Principal
S H Fischer, Vice Pres
Joel Kaliroff, Vice Pres
▲ EMP: 150
SQ FT: 120,000
SALES (est): 28MM Privately Held
WEB: www.palacecandlesusa.com
SIC: 3999 Candles

(G-2402)
OLOLLO INC
43 Hall St Ste B8 (11205-1395)
PHONE..................877 701-0110
Regan Chen, President
▲ EMP: 7 EST: 2009
SQ FT: 10,000
SALES (est): 1MM Privately Held
SIC: 2519 Household furniture, except wood or metal: upholstered

(G-2403)
ONE GIRL COOKIES LTD
68 Dean St Ste A (11201-7749)
PHONE..................212 675-4996
Dawn Casale, Ch of Bd
EMP: 10
SALES (est): 1.1MM Privately Held
WEB: www.onegirlcookies.com
SIC: 2052 Cookies

(G-2404)
ONE STORY INC
232 3rd St Ste A108 (11215-2708)
PHONE..................917 816-3659
Maribeth Batcha, President
Hannah Tinti, Vice Pres
Lynn Beckenstein, Manager
EMP: 8
SALES: 355.4K Privately Held
SIC: 2741 Miscellaneous publishing

(G-2405)
ONE TECHNOLOGIES LLC
44 Court St Ste 1217 (11201-4410)
PHONE..................718 509-0704
Yevhenii Lozovyi,
Polina Lozovyi,
EMP: 6
SALES: 2.2MM Privately Held
SIC: 3571 Electronic computers

(G-2406)
ORIGINAL CONVECTOR SPECIALIST
Also Called: Ocs
2015 Pitkin Ave (11207-3424)
PHONE..................718 342-5820
Fax: 718 338-8529
Henry Gutman, President
Sol Breuer, Vice Pres
Shirley Fisher, Bookkeeper
Chaim Breuer, Admin Sec
▲ EMP: 8
SALES (est): 979.3K Privately Held
SIC: 3433 Radiators, except electric

(G-2407)
ORTEX HOME TEXTILE INC
Also Called: Ortex Home Textiles
523 E 82nd St (11236-3118)
PHONE..................718 241-7298
Merry Lati, President
David Ausi, Vice Pres
▲ EMP: 6
SQ FT: 15,000
SALES (est): 7.2MM Privately Held
SIC: 2211 Sheets, bedding & table cloths: cotton

(G-2408)
ORTHOCRAFT INC
1477 E 27th St (11210-5308)
PHONE..................718 951-1700
Herschel Sauber, President
Avrumi Friedman, COO
Nina Sauber, Manager
EMP: 6
SQ FT: 800
SALES (est): 767.7K Privately Held
SIC: 3842 5999 Prosthetic appliances; orthopedic appliances; orthopedic & prosthesis applications

(G-2409)
ORTHOPEDIC ARTS LABORATORY INC
141 Atlantic Ave Apt 1 (11201-5516)
PHONE..................718 858-2400
Fax: 718 858-9258
Stephan Manucharian, CEO
EMP: 5
SQ FT: 850
SALES: 950K Privately Held
SIC: 3842 Prosthetic appliances

(G-2410)
OSO INDUSTRIES INC
1205 Manhattan Ave (11222-6154)
PHONE..................917 709-2050
Eric Weil, Principal
EMP: 8
SALES (est): 318.5K Privately Held
SIC: 3999 Manufacturing industries

(G-2411)
OTHER HALF BREWING CO
195 Centre St (11231-3907)
PHONE..................347 987-3527
EMP: 5
SALES (est): 218.8K Privately Held
SIC: 2082 Mfg Malt Beverages

(G-2412)
OUTREACH PUBLISHING CORP
546 Montgomery St (11225-3023)
PHONE..................718 773-0525
Shlomo Lakein, President
Reuben Lakein, Vice Pres
EMP: 7
SALES (est): 660K Privately Held
WEB: www.outreach770.com
SIC: 2741 Miscellaneous publishing

(G-2413)
P M BELTS USA INC
131 32nd St (11232-1809)
PHONE..................800 762-3580
Fax: 718 369-9700
Gregory O'Neil, President
EMP: 45 EST: 1986
SQ FT: 12,500
SALES (est): 1.9MM Privately Held
WEB: www.pmbelt.com
SIC: 2387 Apparel belts

(G-2414)
P8H INC ✪
Also Called: Paddle8
81 Prospect St 7 (11201-1473)
PHONE..................212 343-1142
EMP: 40 EST: 2017
SALES: 20MM Privately Held
SIC: 7372 7389 Prepackaged Software Services Business Services

(G-2415)
PALAGONIA BAKERY CO INC
Also Called: Palagonia Italian Bread
508 Junius St (11212-7199)
PHONE..................718 272-5400
Christopher Palagonia, President
Joseph A Palagonia, General Mgr
Steve Toto, QC Dir
Dennis Pizzer, Research
▲ EMP: 100
SQ FT: 25,000
SALES (est): 14.5MM Privately Held
SIC: 2051 Bread, cake & related products

(G-2416)
PANOPLY MEDIA LLC (HQ)
15 Metrotech Ctr Fl 8 (11201-3826)
PHONE..................646 382-5423
Brendan Monaghan, CEO
Ava Lubell, General Mgr
Christopher Landry, Director
EMP: 20 EST: 2016
SQ FT: 21,000
SALES (est): 2.4MM
SALES (corp-wide): 2.4B Publicly Held
SIC: 2741
PA: Graham Holdings Company
1300 17th St N Ste 1700
Arlington VA 22209
703 345-6300

(G-2417)
PAP CHAT INC
3105 Quentin Rd (11234-4234)
PHONE..................516 350-1888
Justin Schwartz, CEO
EMP: 5
SALES (est): 171.6K Privately Held
SIC: 7372 7389 Prepackaged software;

(G-2418)
PAPER SOLUTIONS INC
342 37th St (11232-2506)
PHONE..................718 499-4226
Wing FAI Lam, CEO
Natalie Lam, Manager
▲ EMP: 12
SALES (est): 2.1MM Privately Held
SIC: 2621 Paper mills

(G-2419)
PARADISE PLASTICS LLC
116 39th St (11232-2712)
PHONE..................718 788-3733
Kathy Cooper, Sales Staff
Max Berg,
Judith Berg,
Ernest Grossberger,
Gabriella Grossberger,
EMP: 25 EST: 1952

Brooklyn - Kings County (G-2420)

SQ FT: 40,000
SALES (est): 4.7MM Privately Held
WEB: www.paradiseplastics.com
SIC: 2673 Plastic bags: made from purchased materials

(G-2420)
PARAGON PUBLISHING INC
97 Harrison Ave (11206-2918)
PHONE 718 302-2093
Mendel Sicherman, *President*
Suzanne Holtman, *Controller*
EMP: 5
SALES (est): 440K Privately Held
SIC: 2741 Miscellaneous publishing

(G-2421)
PARK AVE BLDG & ROOFG SUPS LLC
2120 Atlantic Ave (11233-3162)
PHONE 718 403-0100
Bob Groeninger, *CEO*
Raymond Rivera, *President*
Tom Huffey, *CFO*
Tom Hussey, *CFO*
Margarita Ptaszek, *Controller*
EMP: 40
SQ FT: 15,000
SALES (est): 40.2MM Privately Held
SIC: 3531 5033 Aerial work platforms: hydraulic/elec. truck/carrier mounted; roofing & siding materials

(G-2422)
PARK AVENUE SPORTSWEAR LTD (PA)
820 4th Ave (11232-1612)
PHONE 718 369-0520
Fax: 718 369-0521
Joseph Steg, *President*
Martin Perlstein, *Vice Pres*
EMP: 12 EST: 1962
SQ FT: 15,000
SALES (est): 2.2MM Privately Held
SIC: 2339 Sportswear, women's

(G-2423)
PATRICK MACKIN CUSTOM FURN
Also Called: Art Boards
612 Degraw St (11217-3112)
PHONE 718 237-2592
Patrick Mackin, *President*
▲ **EMP:** 7
SALES (est): 600K Privately Held
WEB: www.art-boards.com
SIC: 2511 Wood household furniture

(G-2424)
PECORARO DAIRY PRODUCTS INC (PA)
287 Leonard St (11211-3618)
PHONE 718 388-2379
Cesare Pecoraro, *President*
Ralph Parlato, *Vice Pres*
EMP: 6
SQ FT: 4,000
SALES (est): 959.9K Privately Held
SIC: 2022 Natural cheese

(G-2425)
PEELED INC
Also Called: Peeled Snacks
65 15th St Ste 1 (11215-4653)
PHONE 212 706-2001
Noha Waibsnaider, *President*
Cassie Abrams, *Principal*
Jessica Aquila, *Principal*
Ian Kelleher, *Principal*
Dawn Techow, *COO*
▲ **EMP:** 12
SALES (est): 6.7MM Privately Held
SIC: 2068 2034 Nuts: dried, dehydrated, salted or roasted; dried & dehydrated fruits

(G-2426)
PEKING FOOD LLC
47 Stewart Ave (11237-1517)
PHONE 718 628-8080
Lawrence Wu, *Mng Member*
Teresa Wu,
EMP: 30
SQ FT: 28,000
SALES: 4MM Privately Held
SIC: 2051 Bread, cake & related products

(G-2427)
PENN SIGNS INC
Also Called: Mr Sign
1920 Atlantic Ave (11233-3004)
PHONE 718 797-1112
Fax: 718 797-1153
Shulm Miller, *President*
Leo Lew, *Manager*
EMP: 20
SALES (est): 2MM Privately Held
SIC: 3993 Signs & advertising specialties

(G-2428)
PENN STATE METAL FABRI
810 Humboldt St Ste 9 (11222-1913)
PHONE 718 786-8814
Herbert Engler, *President*
Ron Desena, *Manager*
EMP: 4
SQ FT: 7,500
SALES: 1MM Privately Held
SIC: 3531 3463 Construction machinery; pump & compressor forgings, nonferrous

(G-2429)
PERALTA METAL WORKS INC
602 Atkins Ave (11208-5202)
PHONE 718 649-8661
Fax: 718 384-5450
Omar Peralta, *President*
Yvette Peralta, *Vice Pres*
EMP: 8
SQ FT: 3,500
SALES (est): 1.5MM Privately Held
SIC: 3441 Fabricated structural metal

(G-2430)
PERFECT PRINT INC
220 36th St Unit 2a (11232-2413)
PHONE 718 832-5280
Fax: 718 832-5272
Orly Masry, *President*
Alla Goldenburg, *Prdtn Mgr*
EMP: 20
SALES (est): 250K Privately Held
SIC: 2211 Print cloths, cotton

(G-2431)
PHILLIP TISSICHER
Also Called: Fao Printing
5107 Avenue H (11234-1630)
PHONE 718 282-3310
Phillip Tissicher, *Owner*
EMP: 12
SALES (est): 103.3K Privately Held
SIC: 2752 Commercial printing, lithographic

(G-2432)
PICTURE PERFECT FRAMING
1758 50th St (11204-1220)
PHONE 718 851-1884
Harry Gruber, *Owner*
Chaya Gruber, *Owner*
EMP: 5 EST: 1990
SALES: 30K Privately Held
SIC: 2499 3499 Picture & mirror frames, wood; picture frames, metal

(G-2433)
PILGRIM SURF & SUPPLY
68 N 3rd St (11249-3925)
PHONE 718 218-7456
Chris Gentile, *Owner*
Chelsea Burcz, *Editor*
EMP: 7
SALES (est): 580.2K Privately Held
SIC: 3949 Surfboards

(G-2434)
PILLOW PERFECTIONS LTD INC
252 Norman Ave Ste 101 (11222-6412)
PHONE 718 383-2259
Fax: 718 383-3151
Kenny Fried, *President*
▼ **EMP:** 8
SQ FT: 7,000
SALES: 700K Privately Held
SIC: 2511 5712 Wood household furniture; furniture stores

(G-2435)
PINK BOX ACCESSORIES LLC
Also Called: Blue Box
1170 72nd St (11228-1306)
PHONE 716 777-4477
Mariano Uy, *Mng Member*
Michael Uy,
▲ **EMP:** 5
SALES: 500K Privately Held
SIC: 3911 7389 Jewelry, precious metal;

(G-2436)
PIROKE TRADE INC
1430 35th St Fl 2 (11218-3706)
PHONE 646 515-1537
Keitaro Maruyama, *President*
EMP: 5
SALES (est): 280K Privately Held
SIC: 2789 Trade binding services

(G-2437)
PIVOT RECORDS LLC
600 Johnson Ave (11237-1318)
P.O. Box 70276 (11207-0276)
PHONE 718 417-1213
EMP: 11
SALES (est): 490K Privately Held
SIC: 3652 Mfg Prerecorded Records/Tapes

(G-2438)
PLATFORM EXPERTS INC
2938 Quentin Rd (11229-1825)
PHONE 646 843-7100
Joshua Newman, *President*
Zev Graber, *Manager*
EMP: 8
SQ FT: 4,000
SALES (est): 801.9K Privately Held
WEB: www.platformexperts.com
SIC: 7372 Prepackaged software

(G-2439)
PLAYGROUND NY INC
55 Hope St Apt 212 (11211-4865)
PHONE 505 920-7236
Linda Yang, *CEO*
EMP: 11
SALES (est): 239.1K Privately Held
SIC: 7372 7389 Application computer software;

(G-2440)
POLYTECH POOL MFG INC
Also Called: Wet & Wild Pools & Spas
262 48th St 262 (11220-1012)
P.O. Box 544, Cedarhurst (11516-0544)
PHONE 718 492-8991
Fax: 718 439-1254
EMP: 10 EST: 1975
SQ FT: 60,000
SALES (est): 870K Privately Held
SIC: 3949 Mfg Sporting/Athletic Goods

(G-2441)
PONTI ROSSI INC
186 Franklin St Apt C16 (11222-1690)
PHONE 347 506-9616
Alessandro Capuano, *President*
EMP: 5
SALES (est): 207K Privately Held
SIC: 2099 Food preparations

(G-2442)
POP PRINTING INCORPORATED
288 Hamilton Ave (11231-3208)
PHONE 212 808-7800
Stephen Stein, *Ch of Bd*
EMP: 14
SALES (est): 1.8MM Privately Held
SIC: 2752 Commercial printing, lithographic

(G-2443)
POTENTIAL POLY BAG INC
1253 Coney Island Ave (11230-3520)
PHONE 718 258-0800
Mark Katz, *President*
Jerry Millman, *Vice Pres*
Chaya Freilich, *Manager*
▲ **EMP:** 9
SQ FT: 10,000
SALES (est): 1.6MM Privately Held
WEB: www.potentialpolybag.com
SIC: 3081 Polyethylene film

(G-2444)
POWERHOUSE CULTURAL ENTRMT INC
Also Called: Powerhouse Books
126a Front St (11201-1116)
PHONE 212 604-9074
Daniel Power, *CEO*
Craig Cohen, *President*
Rob Davidson, *Director*
Jennifer Dunn, *Director*
▲ **EMP:** 17
SQ FT: 10,200
SALES (est): 2.8MM Privately Held
WEB: www.powerhousebooks.com
SIC: 2731 Book publishing

(G-2445)
POWERMATE CELLULAR
140 58th St Ste 1d (11220-2525)
PHONE 718 833-9400
Fax: 718 567-7020
▲ **EMP:** 7
SALES (est): 730.8K Privately Held
SIC: 3661 Mfg Telephone/Telegraph Apparatus

(G-2446)
PPR DIRECT INC
Also Called: Icommunicator
74 20th St Fl 2 (11232-1101)
PHONE 718 965-8600
Leonard Feldman, *President*
Larry Brown, *Vice Pres*
Steve Bruner, *Vice Pres*
Robert Notine, *Treasurer*
Richard Kirschner, *Controller*
▲ **EMP:** 15
SQ FT: 8,000
SALES (est): 2.2MM
SALES (corp-wide): 3.7MM Privately Held
WEB: www.pprdirect.com
SIC: 3089 Novelties, plastic
PA: Professional Product Research Co. Inc.
74 20th St
Brooklyn NY 11232
718 965-8600

(G-2447)
PPR DIRECT MARKETING LLC (PA)
74 20th St (11232-1101)
PHONE 718 965-8600
Robert Notine,
Richard Carvalho,
Margaret Hickey,
▲ **EMP:** 8 EST: 2010
SALES (est): 3.9MM Privately Held
SIC: 2389 Men's miscellaneous accessories

(G-2448)
PR & STONE & TILE INC
Also Called: Stone Crafters International
17 Beadel St (11222-5110)
PHONE 718 383-1115
Edward Rynkosky, *President*
Arakdiusz Rakowski, *Vice Pres*
EMP: 5
SALES: 900K Privately Held
SIC: 3281 Granite, cut & shaped

(G-2449)
PRECISION MTAL FABRICATORS INC
Also Called: PMF
236 39th St (11232-2820)
PHONE 718 832-9805
Fax: 718 832-9405
Dimitrios Theodoru, *President*
Frank Theodorou, *Vice Pres*
EMP: 12
SQ FT: 8,000
SALES (est): 2.1MM Privately Held
SIC: 3444 Sheet metalwork

(G-2450)
PRECISION PRODUCT INC
18 Steuben St (11205-1306)
PHONE 718 852-7127
Sonny K Chan, *President*
▲ **EMP:** 5 EST: 1997
SQ FT: 6,000
SALES (est): 650.5K Privately Held
SIC: 3531 Construction machinery

(G-2451)
PREEBRO PRINTING
5319 Fort Hamilton Pkwy (11219-4036)
PHONE.....................718 633-7300
Zur Getter, *Owner*
EMP: 5
SALES (est): 537.4K **Privately Held**
WEB: www.preebroprinting.com
SIC: 2752 Commercial printing, lithographic

(G-2452)
PREMIUM ASSURE INC ✪
1726 Mcdonald Ave Ste 201 (11230-6942)
PHONE.....................605 252-9999
Nick Hager,
EMP: 5 EST: 2017
SALES (est): 150.7K **Privately Held**
SIC: 3999 Hair & hair-based products

(G-2453)
PRESSER KOSHER BAKING CORP
1720 Avenue M (11230-5304)
PHONE.....................718 375-5088
Fax: 718 375-2050
Sam Klein, *President*
Judy Klein, *Human Res Dir*
EMP: 20
SQ FT: 2,500
SALES: 750K **Privately Held**
SIC: 2051 5461 Bakery: wholesale or wholesale/retail combined; bakeries

(G-2454)
PRESTIGE HANGERS STR FIXS CORP
1026 55th St (11219-4024)
PHONE.....................718 522-6777
Abe Minkosf, *President*
Mozes Parnes, *Principal*
EMP: 5
SQ FT: 5,000
SALES: 370K **Privately Held**
WEB: www.prestigestorefixtures.com
SIC: 3089 Clothes hangers, plastic

(G-2455)
PRIME FOOD PROCESSING CORP
300 Vandervoort Ave (11211-1715)
PHONE.....................718 963-2323
Albert Chan, *Ch of Bd*
Yee Hung Chan, *President*
Tommy Ng, *Accounting Mgr*
Raymond Leung, *Manager*
▲ EMP: 80
SQ FT: 35,000
SALES (est): 12.5MM **Privately Held**
SIC: 2013 2037 Frozen meats from purchased meat; vegetables, quick frozen & cold pack, excl. potato products

(G-2456)
PRIMO FROZEN DESSERTS INC
Also Called: Ices Queen
1633 Utica Ave (11234-1524)
PHONE.....................718 252-2312
Fax: 718 253-1202
Dan Lazzaro, *CEO*
Dominick Lazzaro, *Vice Pres*
EMP: 8
SQ FT: 4,500
SALES: 400K **Privately Held**
SIC: 2024 Ices, flavored (frozen dessert)

(G-2457)
PRIMO PLASTICS INC
162 Russell St (11222-3619)
P.O. Box 220187 (11222-0187)
PHONE.....................718 349-1000
Fax: 718 349-1036
John Primo, *President*
Pete Krutros, *Vice Pres*
Stanley Primo, *Vice Pres*
▲ EMP: 20
SQ FT: 7,800
SALES (est): 2.3MM **Privately Held**
SIC: 2673 5113 Plastic & pliofilm bags; bags, paper & disposable plastic

(G-2458)
PRINCE SEATING CORP
1355 Atlantic Ave (11216-2810)
PHONE.....................718 363-2300
Fax: 718 363-9800
Abe Belsky, *President*
Henry Bodner, *Vice Pres*
Bluma Staruss, *Controller*
▲ EMP: 25
SQ FT: 80,000
SALES (est): 3.5MM **Privately Held**
WEB: www.chairfactory.net
SIC: 2522 2521 Tables, office: except wood; chairs, office: padded or plain, except wood; stools, office: except wood; tables, office: wood; chairs, office: padded, upholstered or plain: wood; stools, office: wood

(G-2459)
PRINT HOUSE INC
Also Called: Printhouse, The
538 Johnson Ave (11237-1226)
PHONE.....................718 443-7500
Fax: 718 628-6900
Sholom Laine, *Ch of Bd*
Yousef Laine, *Manager*
Rebecca Laine, *Administration*
▲ EMP: 60
SQ FT: 71,000
SALES (est): 11.3MM **Privately Held**
SIC: 2759 Commercial printing

(G-2460)
PRINT MALL
4122 16th Ave (11204-1052)
PHONE.....................718 437-7700
Sara Olewski, *Owner*
EMP: 5 EST: 1997
SALES (est): 453K **Privately Held**
WEB: www.invitations123.com
SIC: 2759 Commercial printing

(G-2461)
PRINT SEFORIM BZUL INC
8 Lynch St Apt 6r (11206-5528)
PHONE.....................718 679-1011
EMP: 5
SALES (est): 122.8K **Privately Held**
SIC: 2752 Commercial printing, lithographic

(G-2462)
PRINTING FACTORY LLC
1940 Utica Ave (11234-3214)
PHONE.....................718 451-0500
Lisa Blitman,
EMP: 12
SALES (est): 891K **Privately Held**
SIC: 2732 Book printing

(G-2463)
PRINTING MAX NEW YORK INC
2282 Flatbush Ave (11234-4518)
PHONE.....................718 692-1400
George Blair, *Principal*
EMP: 6
SALES (est): 490K **Privately Held**
SIC: 2759 Commercial printing

(G-2464)
PRINTING SALES GROUP LIMITED
Also Called: Flair Printers
1856 Flatbush Ave (11210-4831)
PHONE.....................718 258-8860
Steven Zulier, *President*
EMP: 20
SALES (est): 2.2MM **Privately Held**
SIC: 2752 Offset & photolithographic printing

(G-2465)
PRINTOUT COPY CORP
829 Bedford Ave (11205-2801)
PHONE.....................718 855-4040
Sinai Roth, *President*
Jacob Sabel, *Vice Pres*
EMP: 21
SQ FT: 3,500
SALES (est): 3.7MM **Privately Held**
SIC: 2759 Commercial printing

(G-2466)
PRINTUTOPIA
393 Prospect Ave (11215-5608)
P.O. Box 150528 (11215-0528)
PHONE.....................718 788-1545
Hamlet Villa, *General Mgr*
EMP: 10

(G-2467)
PRODUCTAND DESIGN INC
63 Flushing Ave Unit 322 (11205-1082)
PHONE.....................718 858-2440
John Milich, *President*
▲ EMP: 10
SALES (est): 2MM **Privately Held**
SIC: 3441 8712 Fabricated structural metal; architectural services

(G-2468)
PROFOOT INC
74 20th St Fl 2 (11232-1101)
PHONE.....................718 965-8600
Leonard Feldman, *President*
Robert Notine, *Corp Secy*
Larry Brown, *Vice Pres*
Richard Carvalho, *Controller*
Eileen Fennell, *Sales Staff*
▲ EMP: 45
SQ FT: 35,000
SALES (est): 7.9MM
SALES (corp-wide): 3.7MM **Privately Held**
WEB: www.profootcare.com
SIC: 3842 Orthopedic appliances; foot appliances, orthopedic
PA: Professional Product Research Co. Inc.
74 20th St
Brooklyn NY 11232
718 965-8600

(G-2469)
PROFORMANCE FOODS INC
44 Dobbin St Fl 1 (11222-3110)
PHONE.....................703 869-3413
Ryan Wiltse, *President*
EMP: 6
SALES (est): 5MM **Privately Held**
SIC: 2096 Potato chips & similar snacks

(G-2470)
PROJECT ENERGY SAVERS LLC
Also Called: PES Group
68 Jay St Ste 516 (11201-8362)
PHONE.....................718 596-4231
Alexandra Preefer, *Project Mgr*
Joshua Wolfe, *Mng Member*
Marcy Rubenstein, *Manager*
Joshua F Wolfe, *Manager*
Mark Wolfe,
EMP: 14
SALES: 1.2MM **Privately Held**
SIC: 2731 8748 Textbooks: publishing only, not printed on site; energy conservation consultant

(G-2471)
PROMOTIONAL DEVELOPMENT INC
Also Called: P D I
909 Remsen Ave (11236-1624)
PHONE.....................718 485-8550
Henry Lombardi, *President*
Anthony Valentine, *Vice Pres*
David Censi, *CFO*
Barry Censi, *Treasurer*
Joe Tata, *Sales Staff*
▲ EMP: 80
SQ FT: 60,000
SALES (est): 14.4MM **Privately Held**
WEB: www.promotionaldevelopment.com
SIC: 3999 3993 Advertising display products; signs & advertising specialties

(G-2472)
PROTECTIVE LINING CORP
601 39th St (11232-3101)
PHONE.....................718 854-3838
Fax: 718 854-4658
Steven Howard, *President*
Morton Howard, *Vice Pres*
Mary Ann, *Finance*
▲ EMP: 65 EST: 1950
SQ FT: 28,000
SALES (est): 18.7MM **Privately Held**
WEB: www.prolining.com
SIC: 2673 Plastic bags: made from purchased materials

(G-2473)
PROVISIONAIRE & CO LLC
Also Called: Field Trip Jerky
630 Flushing Ave Fl 4 (11206-5026)
PHONE.....................646 681-8600
Thomas Donigan,
M Scott Fiesinger,
Matthew Levey,
EMP: 20
SALES (est): 1.9MM **Privately Held**
SIC: 2013 Snack sticks, including jerky: from purchased meat

(G-2474)
PURE ACOUSTICS INC
18 Fuller Pl (11215-6007)
PHONE.....................718 788-4411
Rami Ezratty, *CEO*
EMP: 7 EST: 2003
SALES: 2MM **Privately Held**
SIC: 3651 Speaker systems

(G-2475)
PURE PLANET WATERS LLC
4809 Avenue N Ste 185 (11234-3711)
PHONE.....................718 676-7900
Gary Cucuzza, *COO*
James Falce, *Manager*
Denise Piccolo,
Gary Cucuza,
EMP: 10
SQ FT: 2,000
SALES: 1MM **Privately Held**
SIC: 3589 Water filters & softeners, household type

(G-2476)
PUTNAM ROLLING LADDER CO INC
444 Jefferson St (11237-2326)
PHONE.....................718 381-8219
Fax: 718 497-1703
Henry Skiba, *Manager*
EMP: 17
SALES (corp-wide): 3.6MM **Privately Held**
WEB: www.putnamrollingladder.com
SIC: 2499 Ladders, wood
PA: Putnam Rolling Ladder Co Inc
32 Howard St
New York NY 10013
212 226-5147

(G-2477)
PYX INC
Also Called: Pyx Enterprise
143 E 29th St (11226-5505)
PHONE.....................718 469-4253
Omega Ashanti, *President*
EMP: 9
SALES: 250K **Privately Held**
SIC: 3993 Advertising artwork

(G-2478)
QUALITY CARPET ONE FLOOR & HM
214 Ditmas Ave (11218-4900)
PHONE.....................718 941-4200
Fax: 718 941-4298
Herbert Frank, *Principal*
EMP: 7
SALES (est): 159.5K **Privately Held**
SIC: 2273 1743 5023 Carpets & rugs; tile installation, ceramic; floor coverings

(G-2479)
QUALITY FOAM INC
137 Gardner Ave (11237-1107)
PHONE.....................718 381-3644
Paul Minarsky, *President*
Kyle Minarsky, *Vice Pres*
◆ EMP: 12
SALES (est): 1.5MM **Privately Held**
WEB: www.qualityfoamproducts.com
SIC: 2515 Mattresses, containing felt, foam rubber, urethane, etc.

(G-2480)
QUALITY NATURE INC
8225 5th Ave Ste 215 (11209-4508)
PHONE.....................718 484-4666
Sagie Gernshteyn, *President*
EMP: 5
SQ FT: 300

Brooklyn - Kings County (G-2481)

SALES: 733.6K **Privately Held**
SIC: 2834 Vitamin, nutrient & hematinic preparations for human use

(G-2481)
QUALITY STAINLESS STEEL NY INC (PA)
865 63rd St (11220-4727)
PHONE.................................718 748-1785
Hong Guang Huang, *Ch of Bd*
EMP: 10
SALES (est): 1.1MM **Privately Held**
SIC: 3312 Stainless steel

(G-2482)
QUALITY STRAPPING INC
55 Meadow St (11206-1700)
PHONE.................................718 418-1111
Fax: 718 418-1639
Imre Oberlander, *President*
Aharon L Grossman, *Vice Pres*
Abraham Stern, *CFO*
Lea Rose, *Bookkeeper*
Ben Friedman, *Sales Staff*
▲ EMP: 53
SQ FT: 60,000
SALES: 6.7MM **Privately Held**
WEB: www.qualitystrapping.com
SIC: 3559 Plastics working machinery

(G-2483)
QUALITY WOODWORKING CORP
260 Butler St (11217-3006)
PHONE.................................718 875-3437
Fax: 718 875-0036
Joseph Boruso Sr, *President*
Denise Jacob, *Office Mgr*
Anthony Boruso, *Admin Sec*
EMP: 17 EST: 1943
SQ FT: 16,000
SALES (est): 2.3MM **Privately Held**
SIC: 2441 Nailed wood boxes & shook; boxes, wood

(G-2484)
QUEBRACHO INC
421 Troutman St (11237-2601)
PHONE.................................718 326-3605
Miguel Bavaro, *President*
Miguel Erich, *Mayor*
EMP: 5
SQ FT: 8,000
SALES (est): 460K **Privately Held**
SIC: 2499 Picture frame molding, finished

(G-2485)
QUEEN ANN MACARONI MFG CO INC
Also Called: Queen Ann Ravioli
7205 18th Ave (11204-5634)
PHONE.................................718 256-1061
Fax: 718 256-1189
Alfred Ferrara, *President*
Anna Ferrara, *Vice Pres*
EMP: 7
SQ FT: 4,000
SALES (est): 628.1K **Privately Held**
WEB: www.queenanravioliandmacaroni.com
SIC: 2098 5499 Macaroni products (e.g. alphabets, rings & shells); dry; gourmet food stores

(G-2486)
QUIP NYC INC
45 Main St Ste 628 (11201-1085)
PHONE.................................703 615-1076
Simon Enever *President*
EMP: 5
SALES (est): 316.6K **Privately Held**
SIC: 2844 3634 Toothpastes or powders, dentifrices; toothbrushes, electric

(G-2487)
QUIST INDUSTRIES LTD
204 Van Dyke St Ste 320a (11231-1005)
P.O. Box 150083 (11215-0083)
PHONE.................................718 243-2800
Rebecca Steinman, *President*
Paul Steinman, *Controller*
EMP: 10
SQ FT: 3,500
SALES (est): 849.6K **Privately Held**
WEB: www.quistindustries.com
SIC: 2759 2395 Letterpress & screen printing; emblems, embroidered

(G-2488)
R & F BOARDS & DIVIDERS INC
1678 57th St (11204-1800)
PHONE.................................718 331-1529
Regina Frankl, *Ch of Bd*
EMP: 5
SALES (est): 480K **Privately Held**
SIC: 3081 Unsupported plastics film & sheet

(G-2489)
R & H BAKING CO INC
19 5th St (11231-4514)
PHONE.................................718 852-1768
Humayun Kabir, *Owner*
EMP: 25 EST: 2003
SQ FT: 15,000
SALES: 1.5MM **Privately Held**
WEB: www.kabirbakery.com
SIC: 2051 Bread, cake & related products

(G-2490)
R H GUEST INCORPORATED
Also Called: Guesthouse Division
1300 Church Ave (11226-2602)
PHONE.................................718 675-7600
Fax: 718 675-7660
Robert Guest, *President*
Gloria Caprio, *Treasurer*
EMP: 8
SQ FT: 1,000
SALES: 1.7MM **Privately Held**
WEB: www.rhgexhibits.com
SIC: 2542 2541 Showcases (not refrigerated): except wood; showcases, except refrigerated: wood

(G-2491)
R HOCHMAN PAPERS INCORPORATED
1000 Dean St Ste 315 (11238-3384)
PHONE.................................516 466-6414
Fax: 516 466-6535
Ronald Hochman, *President*
Erik Rimalovski, *COO*
▲ EMP: 11
SQ FT: 2,100
SALES (est): 12.1MM **Privately Held**
WEB: www.hochmanpapers.com
SIC: 2752 Commercial printing, lithographic

(G-2492)
RAGS KNITWEAR LTD
850 Metropolitan Ave (11211-2515)
P.O. Box 420, Lynbrook (11563-0420)
PHONE.................................718 782-8417
Paul Gross, *President*
EMP: 10
SQ FT: 40,000
SALES (est): 980K **Privately Held**
SIC: 2253 Sweaters & sweater coats, knit

(G-2493)
RAILINGS BY NEW STAR BRASS
Also Called: J Ironwork
26 Cobeck Ct (11223-6147)
PHONE.................................516 358-1153
Carlo Lopopolo, *President*
Al Grancagnolo, *President*
Mary Ann Harmon, *Purchasing*
EMP: 20 EST: 1917
SQ FT: 25,000
SALES (est): 3.8MM **Privately Held**
SIC: 3446 Architectural metalwork

(G-2494)
RAINBOW PLASTICS INC
371 Vandervoort Ave (11211-1712)
PHONE.................................718 218-7288
Maggie Zheng, *Vice Pres*
▲ EMP: 13
SALES (est): 2MM **Privately Held**
SIC: 3089 Garbage containers, plastic

(G-2495)
RAINBOW POLY BAG CO INC
179 Morgan Ave (11237-1015)
PHONE.................................718 386-3500
Fax: 718 386-2300
Gladys Harmanoglu, *President*
Hank Harmanoglu, *Vice Pres*
Hikmet Harmanoglu, *Vice Pres*
Sibel Harman, *Manager*
Susan Harmanoglu, *Manager*
EMP: 40
SQ FT: 50,000
SALES (est): 7.5MM **Privately Held**
WEB: www.rainbowpolybag.com
SIC: 2673 3081 Plastic bags: made from purchased materials; unsupported plastics film & sheet

(G-2496)
RALPH PAYNE
Also Called: A-R Payne Cabinet Comp
475 Van Buren St Ste 11c (11221-3009)
PHONE.................................718 222-4200
Ralph Payne, *Owner*
EMP: 7
SQ FT: 5,000
SALES: 300K **Privately Held**
WEB: www.ralphpayne.com
SIC: 2434 5087 1751 Wood kitchen cabinets; beauty parlor equipment & supplies; cabinet & finish carpentry

(G-2497)
RAPID-LITE FIXTURE CORPORATION
249 Huron St (11222-1801)
PHONE.................................347 599-2600
Fax: 718 292-6461
Joel Eskin, *Ch of Bd*
EMP: 10 EST: 1946
SQ FT: 4,500
SALES (est): 1MM **Privately Held**
WEB: www.rapidlite.com
SIC: 3645 3646 5063 5719 Residential lighting fixtures; commercial indusl & institutional electric lighting fixtures; lighting fixtures, residential; lighting fixtures, commercial & industrial; lighting fixtures

(G-2498)
RAWPOTHECARY INC
630 Flushing Ave (11206-5026)
PHONE.................................917 783-7770
Stephanie Walzack, *President*
EMP: 8
SALES (est): 722.5K **Privately Held**
SIC: 2099 5812 Ready-to-eat meals, salads & sandwiches; eating places

(G-2499)
RAY GOLD SHADE INC
16 Wellington Ct (11230-2424)
PHONE.................................718 377-8892
Martin Rosenbaum, *President*
Sonia Rosenbaum, *Vice Pres*
EMP: 10
SQ FT: 18,000
SALES (est): 560K **Privately Held**
WEB: www.goldrayshades.com
SIC: 3999 Shades, lamp or candle

(G-2500)
RBHM INCORPORATED
Also Called: Abco Printing Company
1885 E 2nd St (11223-2822)
PHONE.................................609 259-4900
Fax: 609 259-4901
Howard Matthews, *President*
Lorry McAlister, *Admin Asst*
EMP: 16
SQ FT: 20,000
SALES (est): 4.3MM **Privately Held**
SIC: 2752 2759 Commercial printing, lithographic; letterpress printing

(G-2501)
RBW STUDIO LLC
Also Called: Rich Brilliant Willing
67 34th St Unit 5 (11232-2010)
PHONE.................................212 388-1621
Theodore Richardson, *President*
Charles Brill, *Vice Pres*
Alex Williams, *Vice Pres*
Lory Avery, *Sales Staff*
Olivia Sholler, *Marketing Staff*
EMP: 25 EST: 2009
SQ FT: 2,000
SALES: 4.2MM **Privately Held**
SIC: 3699 Christmas tree lighting sets, electric

(G-2502)
REAR VIEW SAFETY INC
1797 Atlantic Ave (11233-3040)
PHONE.................................855 815-3842
Gila Newman, *CEO*
▲ EMP: 25
SQ FT: 6,000
SALES (est): 4.5MM
SALES (corp-wide): 24.3MM **Privately Held**
SIC: 3861 Cameras & related equipment
PA: Safe Fleet Investments Llc
6800 E 163rd St
Belton MO 64012
844 258-8178

(G-2503)
RECORDED ANTHLOGY OF AMRCN MUS
Also Called: New World Records
20 Jay St Ste 1001 (11201-8346)
PHONE.................................212 290-1695
Fax: 646 224-9638
Herman E Krawitz, *President*
Auther Moorhaed, *Treasurer*
Mogi Oke, *Accounts Mgr*
Paul Herzman, *Manager*
Robert McNeill, *Manager*
▲ EMP: 12
SALES: 1.2MM **Privately Held**
WEB: www.newworldrecords.org
SIC: 3652 Pre-recorded records & tapes

(G-2504)
RECYCLED BROOKLYN GROUP LLC
236 Van Brunt St (11231-1211)
PHONE.................................917 902-0662
Matthew Lostice,
Alberto Baudo,
Nilesh Dawda,
Andrea De Sanctis,
Marco Gentilucci,
EMP: 14
SQ FT: 8,000
SALES (est): 1MM **Privately Held**
SIC: 2511 5712 Wood household furniture; furniture stores

(G-2505)
REDI RECORDS PAYROLL
1225 36th St (11218-2023)
PHONE.................................718 854-6990
Joe Burke, *President*
EMP: 10
SALES (est): 594.9K **Privately Held**
SIC: 2752 Calendars, lithographed

(G-2506)
REGIONAL MGT & CONSULTING INC
79 Bridgewater St (11222-3818)
PHONE.................................718 599-3718
Fax: 718 599-4454
Henryk Jarosz, *President*
Bogdan Szczurek, *Exec VP*
EMP: 10
SQ FT: 4,200
SALES (est): 1.4MM **Privately Held**
SIC: 3292 5033 Asbestos products; insulation materials

(G-2507)
REISMAN BROS BAKERY INC
Also Called: Reismans Bros. Bakery
110 Avenue O (11204-6501)
P.O. Box 40112 (11204-0112)
PHONE.................................718 331-1975
Fax: 718 256-0833
Bernat Reisman, *Ch of Bd*
Larry Fisler, *Vice Pres*
Esther Friedman, *Admin Sec*
EMP: 15
SQ FT: 4,000
SALES (est): 4.5MM **Privately Held**
WEB: www.reismansbakery.com
SIC: 2051 5411 Bread, cake & related products; cakes, bakery: except frozen; supermarkets

(G-2508)
RELIABLE PRESS II INC
Also Called: Printing
148 39th St Unit 6 (11232-2713)
PHONE.................................718 840-5812

GEOGRAPHIC SECTION

Brooklyn - Kings County (G-2535)

Fax: 718 431-6843
Ira Cohen, *President*
Sam Kowlessar, *Manager*
▲ **EMP:** 16
SALES (est): 1.1MM **Privately Held**
SIC: 2741 Miscellaneous publishing

(G-2509)
REMEDIES SURGICAL SUPPLIES
331 Rutledge St Ste 204 (11211-7546)
PHONE..................718 599-5301
Mordchai Hirsch, *President*
EMP: 7
SQ FT: 2,000
SALES (est): 5MM **Privately Held**
SIC: 3634 3069 Humidifiers, electric: household; medical & laboratory rubber sundries & related products

(G-2510)
REMSEN GRAPHICS CORP
52 Court St 2 (11201-4901)
PHONE..................718 643-7500
Greg Vellanti, *President*
Frank Vellanti, *Vice Pres*
Piero Galluzzo, *Admin Sec*
EMP: 5
SQ FT: 1,200
SALES: 1MM **Privately Held**
SIC: 2752 7389 Offset & photolithographic printing; brokers' services

(G-2511)
RENE PORTIER INC
3611 14th Ave Ste 6 (11218-3750)
PHONE..................718 853-7896
Charlotte Fixler, *President*
Aaron Fixler, *Vice Pres*
EMP: 9
SQ FT: 6,000
SALES (est): 1MM **Privately Held**
SIC: 2339 Sportswear, women's

(G-2512)
REVIVN INC
63 Flushing Ave Unit 231 (11205-1074)
PHONE..................347 762-8193
John Fazzolari, *Principal*
EMP: 15
SALES (est): 2.1MM **Privately Held**
SIC: 3571 7372 Electronic computers; application computer software

(G-2513)
RICHARD MANUFACTURING CO INC
63 Flushing Ave Unit 327 (11205-1083)
PHONE..................718 254-0958
Fax: 718 254-0959
Solomon Mayer, *President*
Janet Mayer, *Admin Sec*
EMP: 8 **EST:** 1943
SALES: 200K **Privately Held**
SIC: 2326 2339 Aprons, work, except rubberized & plastic: men's; aprons, except rubber or plastic: women's, misses, juniors'

(G-2514)
RINI TANK & TRUCK SERVICE
327 Nassau Ave (11222-3811)
PHONE..................718 384-6606
Richard V Rini, *President*
EMP: 16
SQ FT: 10,000
SALES (est): 978.7K **Privately Held**
SIC: 7692 Welding repair

(G-2515)
RIOT NEW MEDIA GROUP INC
147 Prince St Ste 1 (11201-3011)
PHONE..................604 700-4896
Jeffrey O'Neal, *CEO*
Amanda Nelson, *Editor*
Jeff Oneal, *Editor*
Clinton Kabler, *COO*
EMP: 6
SALES (est): 516.3K **Privately Held**
SIC: 2741

(G-2516)
RIP VAN WAFELS INC
67 West St Ste 705 (11222-5393)
PHONE..................415 529-5403
Abhishek Pruisken, *CEO*
Marco De Leon, *Co-CEO*
EMP: 22
SQ FT: 1,600
SALES (est): 3.1MM **Privately Held**
SIC: 2066 5947 Chocolate; gifts & novelties

(G-2517)
RIVA JEWELRY MANUFACTURING INC
140 58th St Ste 8b (11220-2524)
PHONE..................718 361-3100
Ted Doudak, *President*
Joe Perillo, *COO*
John Badee, *Engineer*
Alfonse Grace, *Controller*
Edgar Andrade, *Manager*
▲ **EMP:** 125
SQ FT: 20,000
SALES (est): 21.3MM **Privately Held**
WEB: www.rivajewelry.com
SIC: 3911 Jewelry apparel

(G-2518)
RIVERSIDE MACHINERY COMPANY (PA)
Also Called: Sns Machinery
140 53rd St (11232-4319)
PHONE..................718 492-7400
Simon Srybnik, *President*
Louis Srybnik, *Vice Pres*
Saul Waller, *Treasurer*
Jay B Srybnik, *Admin Sec*
EMP: 5
SQ FT: 30,000
SALES (est): 4.3MM **Privately Held**
SIC: 3599 Machine shop, jobbing & repair

(G-2519)
RIVERSIDE MACHINERY COMPANY
132 54th St (11220-2506)
PHONE..................718 492-7400
Simon Srybnik, *Manager*
EMP: 20
SQ FT: 35,060
SALES (corp-wide): 4.3MM **Privately Held**
SIC: 3549 5084 Metalworking machinery; industrial machinery & equipment
PA: Riverside Machinery Company Inc
140 53rd St
Brooklyn NY 11232
718 492-7400

(G-2520)
ROB HERSCHENFELD DESIGN INC
304 Boerum St (11206-3590)
PHONE..................718 456-6801
Rob Herschenfeld, *President*
EMP: 10
SQ FT: 10,000
SALES (est): 1.2MM **Privately Held**
SIC: 2512 1522 Upholstered household furniture; remodeling, multi-family dwellings

(G-2521)
ROBERT PORTEGELLO GRAPHICS
2028 Utica Ave (11234-3216)
PHONE..................718 241-8118
Fax: 718 241-3894
Robert Portegello, *President*
Grace Portegello, *Vice Pres*
EMP: 7
SQ FT: 9,000
SALES: 350K **Privately Held**
SIC: 2752 Commercial printing, lithographic

(G-2522)
ROBIN INDUSTRIES LTD
56 N 3rd St (11249-3925)
PHONE..................718 218-9616
Fax: 718 218-8922
Monica Vega, *President*
Raul Sillau, *Manager*
EMP: 11
SQ FT: 10,000

SALES (est): 1.2MM **Privately Held**
WEB: www.robinindustries.com
SIC: 3632 1711 Household refrigerators & freezers; heating & air conditioning contractors

(G-2523)
ROGER MICHAEL PRESS INC (PA)
499 Van Brunt St Ste 6b (11231-1053)
P.O. Box 27176 (11202-7176)
PHONE..................732 752-0800
Michael Held, *President*
Deborah Held, *Vice Pres*
Walter Kovac, *Plant Mgr*
Amy Neufeld, *Marketing Staff*
▲ **EMP:** 18
SQ FT: 20,000
SALES (est): 200K **Privately Held**
WEB: www.mrogerpress.com
SIC: 2782 2789 Blankbooks & looseleaf binders; looseleaf binders & devices; bookbinding & related work

(G-2524)
ROMANTIC TIMES INC
Also Called: Romantic Times Magazine
81 Willoughby St Ste 701 (11201-5233)
PHONE..................718 237-1097
Fax: 718 624-4231
Kathryn Falk, *President*
Nancy Collaco, *Office Mgr*
EMP: 17
SQ FT: 6,000
SALES (est): 2.2MM **Privately Held**
WEB: www.romantictimes.com
SIC: 2721 5942 Magazines: publishing & printing; book stores

(G-2525)
ROODE HOEK & CO INC
55 Ferris St (11231-1194)
PHONE..................718 522-5921
Edward R Butler, *President*
EMP: 13 **EST:** 2000
SALES: 750K
SALES (corp-wide): 4.7MM **Privately Held**
WEB: www.erbutler.com
SIC: 2431 Millwork
PA: E.R. Butler & Co., Inc.
55 Prince St Frnt A
New York NY 10012
212 925-3565

(G-2526)
ROOM AT THE TOP INC
Also Called: Hat Depot
632 Hegeman Ave (11207-7111)
PHONE..................718 257-0766
Shellie McDowell, *President*
EMP: 5
SALES (est): 630.3K **Privately Held**
SIC: 2353 Hats, caps & millinery

(G-2527)
ROSE SOLOMON CO
63 Flushing Ave Unit 330 (11205-1083)
PHONE..................718 855-1788
Fax: 718 855-1800
Mendel Reichman, *President*
▲ **EMP:** 21 **EST:** 1908
SQ FT: 7,000
SALES (est): 1.1MM **Privately Held**
SIC: 2389 5049 2869 Burial garments; religious supplies; industrial organic chemicals

(G-2528)
ROTH CLOTHING CO INC (PA)
300 Penn St (11211-7405)
PHONE..................718 384-4927
Fax: 718 486-7438
Mates Roth, *President*
▲ **EMP:** 3
SQ FT: 30,000
SALES: 1.2MM **Privately Held**
SIC: 2389 2311 Clergymen's vestments; suits, men's & boys': made from purchased materials

(G-2529)
ROTH DESIGN & CONSULTING INC
Also Called: Roth's Metal Works
132 Bogart St (11206)
PHONE..................718 209-0193
Arnold Roth, *President*
Jake Roth, *Vice Pres*
Abe Jaros, *Controller*
EMP: 40
SQ FT: 40,000
SALES (est): 7MM **Privately Held**
SIC: 3441 8711 1791 Fabricated structural metal; building construction consultant; structural engineering; structural steel erection

(G-2530)
ROYAL CLOTHING CORP
1316 48th St Apt 1 (11219-3167)
PHONE..................718 436-5841
Fax: 718 436-5841
Abraham Sports, *President*
EMP: 6
SQ FT: 2,000
SALES (est): 2MM **Privately Held**
SIC: 2311 5611 Suits, men's & boys': made from purchased materials; suits, men's

(G-2531)
ROYAL INDUSTRIES INC (PA)
Also Called: Royal Line The
225 25th St (11232-1337)
PHONE..................718 369-3046
Michael Rudensky, *President*
ARI Rudensky, *Vice Pres*
Jonathan Rudensky, *Vice Pres*
Marybeth Chichetti, *Marketing Staff*
◆ **EMP:** 39 **EST:** 1985
SQ FT: 75,000
SALES (est): 13.6MM **Privately Held**
WEB: www.royalindustries.com
SIC: 3089 3161 Novelties, plastic; luggage

(G-2532)
ROYAL MOLDS INC
1634 Marine Pkwy (11234-4217)
PHONE..................718 382-7686
EMP: 15 **EST:** 1946
SQ FT: 10,000
SALES (est): 1.1MM **Privately Held**
SIC: 3544 3423 Mfg Dies/Tools/Jigs/Fixtures Mfg Hand/Edge Tools

(G-2533)
ROYAL PLASTICS CORP
2840 Atlantic Ave Ste 1 (11207-2692)
PHONE..................718 647-7500
Fax: 718 647-7503
Donald Marchese, *President*
Joann Foster, *Controller*
▲ **EMP:** 19 **EST:** 1958
SQ FT: 40,000
SALES (est): 2.4MM **Privately Held**
WEB: www.royalplastics.com
SIC: 3081 Plastic film & sheet

(G-2534)
ROYAL SWEET BAKERY INC
119 49th St (11232-4229)
PHONE..................718 567-7770
Fax: 718 567-7375
Mikhail Yusim, *President*
Joseph Dubinski, *Manager*
◆ **EMP:** 10
SALES (est): 1.1MM **Privately Held**
SIC: 2051 Bread, cake & related products

(G-2535)
RUBICON INDUSTRIES CORP (PA)
848 E 43rd St (11210-3500)
PHONE..................718 434-4700
Michael Rubinberg, *President*
Mathew Rubinberg, *General Mgr*
Matthew Rubinberg, *General Mgr*
▲ **EMP:** 24
SQ FT: 20,000
SALES (est): 4.7MM **Privately Held**
WEB: www.rubiconhx.com
SIC: 3585 Evaporative condensers, heat transfer equipment

Brooklyn - Kings County (G-2536)

(G-2536)
RUBY ENGINEERING LLC
354 Sackett St (11231-4702)
PHONE...................646 391-4600
Phillip Roach, *Vice Pres*
Dennis Roach,
EMP: 5
SQ FT: 1,000
SALES (est): 310K **Privately Held**
WEB: www.rubyengineering.com
SIC: 1442 Construction sand mining

(G-2537)
RUSSIAN MIX INC
2225 Benson Ave Apt 74 (11214-5245)
PHONE...................347 385-7198
EMP: 5
SALES (est): 339.4K **Privately Held**
SIC: 3273 Ready-mixed concrete

(G-2538)
RUSSKAYA REKLAMA INC
2699 Coney Island Ave (11235-5004)
PHONE...................718 769-3000
Fax: 718 769-4700
Paul Reklama, *President*
EMP: 20
SALES (est): 1MM **Privately Held**
SIC: 2711 Newspapers

(G-2539)
RYBA GENERAL MERCHANDISE INC
63 Flushing Ave Unit 332 (11205-1083)
PHONE...................718 522-2028
Fax: 718 522-2476
Sam Ryba, *President*
Marvin Ryba, *Vice Pres*
Chaya Knopfler, *Admin Sec*
◆ **EMP:** 7
SQ FT: 25,000
SALES (est): 710K **Privately Held**
WEB: www.rybagen.com
SIC: 2325 5136 Slacks, dress: men's, youths' & boys'; men's & boys' clothing; shirts, men's & boys'

(G-2540)
S & J SHEET METAL SUPPLY
70 Grand Ave (11205-2505)
PHONE...................718 384-0800
David Gottlieb, *Branch Mgr*
EMP: 5
SALES (corp-wide): 111.2MM **Privately Held**
SIC: 3444 5033 Sheet metalwork; roofing & siding materials
PA: S. & J. Sheet Metal Supply Inc
608 E 133rd St
Bronx NY 10454
718 993-0460

(G-2541)
S & S MACHINERY CORP (PA)
Also Called: CAM Machinery Co
140 53rd St (11232-4319)
PHONE...................718 492-7400
Fax: 718 439-3930
Simon Srybnik, *President*
Louis Srybnik, *Vice Pres*
Spiros Dendrios, *Research*
Adam Zheng, *Engineer*
▲ **EMP:** 30 **EST:** 1939
SQ FT: 100,000
SALES (est): 6.4MM **Privately Held**
WEB: www.sandsmachinery.com
SIC: 3541 3549 5084 3545 Machine tools, metal cutting type; metalworking machinery; metalworking machinery; machine tools & accessories; machine tool accessories

(G-2542)
S & S MACHINERY CORP
132 54th St (11220-2506)
PHONE...................718 492-7400
Al Testa, *Branch Mgr*
EMP: 40
SALES (corp-wide): 6.4MM **Privately Held**
WEB: www.sandsmachinery.com
SIC: 3541 3549 5084 Machine tools, metal cutting type; metalworking machinery; machine tools & accessories; metalworking machinery

PA: S. & S. Machinery Corp.
140 53rd St
Brooklyn NY 11232
718 492-7400

(G-2543)
S & S PRTG DIE-CUTTING CO INC
488 Morgan Ave Ste A (11222-5703)
PHONE...................718 388-8990
Fax: 718 388-0306
Felix Sikar, *President*
▲ **EMP:** 14
SQ FT: 21,000
SALES (est): 1.4MM **Privately Held**
WEB: www.printdiecut.com
SIC: 3469 7389 2759 2675 Stamping metal for the trade; metal cutting services; letterpress printing; die-cut paper & board; coated & laminated paper

(G-2544)
S & T MACHINE INC
970 E 92nd St Fl 1 (11236-1720)
PHONE...................718 272-2484
Saverio Accardi, *President*
Tinal Accardi, *Vice Pres*
EMP: 15
SQ FT: 5,000
SALES (est): 1.4MM **Privately Held**
SIC: 3444 Sheet metalwork

(G-2545)
S & W KNITTING MILLS INC
703 Bedford Ave Fl 3 (11206)
PHONE...................718 237-2416
Fax: 718 797-3710
Henry Weiss, *President*
Manachem Samuel, *Treasurer*
Mindy Friedlander, *Controller*
EMP: 50 **EST:** 1977
SQ FT: 35,000
SALES (est): 3.6MM **Privately Held**
SIC: 2253 2329 2339 2257 Sweaters & sweater coats, knit; sweaters & sweater jackets: men's & boys'; women's & misses' outerwear; weft knit fabric mills

(G-2546)
S & W LADIES WEAR
3611 14th Ave Ste 601 (11218-3750)
PHONE...................718 431-2800
Fax: 718 431-2899
Elias Bochner, *Owner*
EMP: 7 **EST:** 2015
SALES (est): 124.7K **Privately Held**
SIC: 3144 Boots, canvas or leather: women's

(G-2547)
S & W METAL TRADING CORP
1601 E 7th St (11230-7002)
PHONE...................212 719-5070
Fax: 212 719-5753
Abraham Slomovics, *President*
Abraham Weisz, *Vice Pres*
EMP: 8
SQ FT: 1,000
SALES (est): 960.6K **Privately Held**
SIC: 3339 3341 Primary nonferrous metals; secondary nonferrous metals

(G-2548)
S D Z METAL SPINNING STAMPING
1807 Pacific St (11233-3505)
PHONE...................718 778-3600
Fax: 718 604-8481
Kenny Mersand, *President*
EMP: 15
SQ FT: 10,000
SALES (est): 971.2K **Privately Held**
SIC: 3469 Spinning metal for the trade; stamping metal for the trade

(G-2549)
S HELLERMAN INC (PA)
242 Green St (11222-1208)
PHONE...................718 622-2995
Fax: 718 622-2916
Robert Hellerman, *President*
Joseph Hellerman, *Vice Pres*
EMP: 11
SQ FT: 20,000

SALES: 750K **Privately Held**
SIC: 2299 Textile mill waste & remnant processing

(G-2550)
S2 SPORTSWEAR INC
4100 1st Ave Ste 5n (11232-3303)
PHONE...................347 335-0713
Saul Chakkall, *CEO*
Albert Zayat, *Vice Pres*
Ronnie Chakkall, *CFO*
▲ **EMP:** 10
SQ FT: 6,000
SALES (est): 1.3MM **Privately Held**
SIC: 2339 5137 Sportswear, women's; sportswear, women's & children's

(G-2551)
SABBSONS INTERNATIONAL INC
Also Called: Simple Elegance New York
474 50th St (11220-1913)
PHONE...................718 360-1947
Isaac Sabbagh, *CEO*
Victor Sabbagh, *CFO*
◆ **EMP:** 10
SALES (est): 492.2K **Privately Held**
SIC: 2299 Linen fabrics

(G-2552)
SAFCORE LLC
23 Van Dam St (11222-4509)
PHONE...................917 627-5263
Safwat Riad,
EMP: 10
SALES (est): 322.9K **Privately Held**
SIC: 2519 Household furniture

(G-2553)
SAGA INTERNATIONAL RECYCL LLC
6623 13th Ave (11219-6122)
PHONE...................718 621-5900
Akiva Klein, *Principal*
▲ **EMP:** 6
SQ FT: 3,000
SALES (est): 1MM **Privately Held**
SIC: 2821 Plastics materials & resins

(G-2554)
SAHADI FINE FOODS INC
4215 1st Ave (11232-3300)
PHONE...................718 369-0100
Fax: 718 369-0800
Pat Whelan, *Managing Dir*
Audrey Sahadi, *Director*
Charles Sahadi, *Director*
Robert Sahadi, *Director*
Ron Sahadi, *Director*
◆ **EMP:** 22
SQ FT: 116,000
SALES (est): 4.8MM **Privately Held**
WEB: www.sahadifinefoods.com
SIC: 2068 2032 5149 5145 Nuts: dried, dehydrated, salted or roasted; seeds: dried, dehydrated, salted or roasted; beans & bean sprouts, canned, jarred, etc.; fruits, dried; nuts, salted or roasted

(G-2555)
SALTY ROAD INC
190 Bedford Ave 404 (11249-2904)
PHONE...................347 673-3925
Marisa Wu, *CEO*
EMP: 8
SALES (est): 696.3K **Privately Held**
SIC: 2064 Candy & other confectionery products

(G-2556)
SANGSTER FOODS INC
225 Parkside Ave Apt 3p (11226-1352)
PHONE...................212 993-9129
Peter Sangster, *President*
Tania Sangster, *Director*
EMP: 10 **EST:** 2015
SALES (est): 326.8K **Privately Held**
SIC: 2032 2043 2091 5149 Ethnic foods: canned, jarred, etc.; infants' foods, cereal type; canned & cured fish & seafoods; health foods; instant coffee

(G-2557)
SARES INTERNATIONAL INC
95 Evergreen Ave Ste 5 (11206-6129)
PHONE...................718 366-8412
Fax: 718 366-8415
Manuel Barretto, *President*
EMP: 45
SQ FT: 15,000
SALES (est): 4.7MM **Privately Held**
SIC: 2253 Sweaters & sweater coats, knit

(G-2558)
SARUG INC
2055 Mcdonald Ave (11223-2821)
PHONE...................718 339-2791
Henrik Zylberstein, *President*
EMP: 55
SQ FT: 3,000
SALES (est): 3.3MM **Privately Held**
SIC: 2253 Sweaters & sweater coats, knit

(G-2559)
SAS MAINTENANCE SERVICES INC
8435 Bay 16th St Ste A (11214-2844)
PHONE...................718 837-2124
Maria Locascio, *President*
Steven Locascio, *Controller*
EMP: 17
SALES (est): 2.8MM **Privately Held**
WEB: www.sasmaint.com
SIC: 3471 Cleaning, polishing & finishing

(G-2560)
SATELLITE NETWORK INC
2030 Mcdonald Ave (11223-2819)
PHONE...................718 336-2698
Boris Demchenko, *Executive*
EMP: 14
SALES (est): 954.9K **Privately Held**
SIC: 2711 Newspapers

(G-2561)
SCHLESS BOTTLES INC (PA)
4616 16th Ave (11204-1104)
PHONE...................718 236-2790
Fax: 718 236-2791
Mark Schlesinger, *Ch of Bd*
Judy Schlesinger, *President*
Lia Rose, *Manager*
▲ **EMP:** 16
SQ FT: 40,000
SALES (est): 4.2MM **Privately Held**
SIC: 3085 Plastics bottles

(G-2562)
SCHWARTZ TEXTILE CONVERTING CO
Also Called: Protege
160 7th St (11215-3107)
PHONE...................718 499-8243
Mitchell Schwartz, *Partner*
Irving Schwartz, *Partner*
Marc Schwartz, *Partner*
Kewal Sukhoo, *Business Mgr*
▲ **EMP:** 25
SQ FT: 60,000
SALES (est): 2.2MM **Privately Held**
SIC: 2329 2321 Sweaters & sweater jackets: men's & boys'; men's & boys' furnishings

(G-2563)
SCIENTIFIC COMPONENTS CORP (PA)
Also Called: Mini-Circuits
13 Neptune Ave (11235-4404)
P.O. Box 350199 (11235-0199)
PHONE...................718 934-4500
Harvey Kaylie, *President*
Gloria Kaylie, *Corp Secy*
Behnam Tabrizi, *Vice Pres*
Luis E Zambrano, *Production*
Anthony Blugh, *Purchasing*
▲ **EMP:** 475
SQ FT: 50,000
SALES (est): 109.8MM **Privately Held**
WEB: www.minicircuits.com
SIC: 3679 Electronic switches; electronic circuits

Brooklyn - Kings County (G-2593)

(G-2564)
SCIENTIFIC COMPONENTS CORP
Also Called: Mini Circuits
2450 Knapp St (11235-1006)
PHONE.................718 368-2060
EMP: 264
SALES (corp-wide): 109.8MM **Privately Held**
SIC: 3679 Electronic circuits
PA: Scientific Components Corp
13 Neptune Ave
Brooklyn NY 11235
718 934-4500

(G-2565)
SCULPTGRAPHICZ INC
67 35th St Unit B520 (11232-2018)
PHONE.................646 837-7302
Marvin Seligman, *President*
Germann Vesterman, *General Mgr*
Robert Chiari, *VP Sales*
EMP: 5 EST: 2011
SALES (est): 407.4K **Privately Held**
SIC: 7372 Prepackaged software

(G-2566)
SEALCRAFT INDUSTRIES INC
5308 13th Ave Ste 251 (11219-3804)
PHONE.................718 517-2000
Fax: 718 517-2020
Joshua Benjamin, *CEO*
EMP: 10
SALES (est): 850K **Privately Held**
SIC: 3053 Gaskets, packing & sealing devices

(G-2567)
SEASONS SOYFOOD INC
605 Degraw St (11217-3120)
PHONE.................718 797-9896
Fax: 718 722-7922
Johnny Hong, *President*
▲ EMP: 8
SALES (est): 500K **Privately Held**
SIC: 2099 Tofu, except frozen desserts

(G-2568)
SEETIN DESIGN GROUP INC
57 Grand Street Ext (11211)
PHONE.................718 486-5610
Robert Seetin, *Ch of Bd*
◆ EMP: 10
SQ FT: 2,000
SALES (est): 202.7K **Privately Held**
SIC: 3499 Furniture parts, metal

(G-2569)
SEPHARDIC YELLOW PAGES
2150 E 4th St (11223-4037)
PHONE.................718 998-0299
David Benhorren, *Owner*
EMP: 20 EST: 1998
SALES (est): 1.6MM **Privately Held**
SIC: 2759 2741 Publication printing; miscellaneous publishing

(G-2570)
SERGE DUCT DESIGNS INC
535 Dean St Apt 124 (11217-5207)
PHONE.................718 783-7799
Fax: 718 783-9499
Serge Rozenbaum, *President*
Micha Rozenbaug, *Vice Pres*
EMP: 20
SALES (est): 3.2MM **Privately Held**
SIC: 3549 Metalworking machinery

(G-2571)
SETTEPANI INC (PA)
Also Called: Settapani Bakery
602 Lorimer St (11211-2220)
PHONE.................718 349-6524
Fax: 718 349-2149
Nino Settepani, *President*
Biagio Settepani, *Vice Pres*
Antonio Settepani, *Admin Sec*
EMP: 28
SQ FT: 5,000
SALES (est): 700K **Privately Held**
WEB: www.settepani.com
SIC: 2051 5461 Bakery: wholesale or wholesale/retail combined; bakeries

(G-2572)
SFOGLINI LLC
630 Flushing Ave Fl 2 (11206-5026)
PHONE.................646 872-1035
Steven Gonzalez, *Mng Member*
Scott Ketchum, *Mng Member*
EMP: 10
SQ FT: 4,000
SALES (est): 1.2MM **Privately Held**
SIC: 2099 Pasta, uncooked: packaged with other ingredients

(G-2573)
SG BLOCKS INC (PA)
195 Montague St Fl 14 (11201-3631)
PHONE.................615 585-2639
Paul M Galvin, *CEO*
Stevan Armstrong, *President*
Tim Kennedy, *Vice Pres*
Brian Wasserman, *CFO*
Kevin King, *Controller*
▼ EMP: 7
SALES: 868.1K **Publicly Held**
WEB: www.newvalley.com
SIC: 2448 5032 8711 8741 Cargo containers, wood & metal combination; building blocks; engineering services; construction management

(G-2574)
SH LEATHER NOVELTY COMPANY
123 Clymer St Bsmt (11249-6708)
PHONE.................718 387-7742
Shiee Handler, *President*
Solmen Delowitz, *Vice Pres*
Feiga Handler, *Treasurer*
EMP: 3 EST: 1954
SQ FT: 4,000
SALES (est): 1MM **Privately Held**
SIC: 2387 Apparel belts

(G-2575)
SHAKUFF LLC
34 35th St Unit 29 (11232-2209)
PHONE.................212 675-0383
Leah Hartell, *Manager*
Joseph Sidof,
EMP: 6
SALES (est): 142.3K **Privately Held**
SIC: 3648 Lighting equipment

(G-2576)
SHALAM IMPORTS INC (PA)
Also Called: Shalamex
1552 Dahill Rd Ste B (11204-3572)
PHONE.................718 686-6271
Sasson Shalam, *President*
Abraham Shalam, *Vice Pres*
◆ EMP: 12 EST: 1955
SQ FT: 1,800
SALES (est): 1.2MM **Privately Held**
SIC: 2674 Shipping bags or sacks, including multiwall & heavy duty

(G-2577)
SHANGHAI STOVE INC
78 Gerry St 82 (11206-4326)
PHONE.................718 599-4583
Fax: 718 599-1250
James Wong, *President*
Sylvia Wong, *Admin Sec*
EMP: 15 EST: 1979
SALES (est): 1.6MM **Privately Held**
SIC: 3444 Restaurant sheet metalwork

(G-2578)
SHOWERAY CO (PA)
225 25th St (11232-1337)
P.O. Box 320141 (11232-0141)
PHONE.................718 965-3633
Fax: 718 965-3647
Abraham Grazi, *President*
Jack Grazi, *Vice Pres*
Maurice Grazi, *Admin Sec*
EMP: 99 EST: 1938
SQ FT: 60,000
SALES (est): 4.6MM **Privately Held**
SIC: 2392 2391 Shower curtains: made from purchased materials; tablecloths: made from purchased materials; mattress protectors, except rubber; curtains & draperies

(G-2579)
SIGN & SIGNS
785 Coney Island Ave (11218-5309)
PHONE.................718 941-6200
Ali Chashir, *Principal*
EMP: 6
SALES (est): 431.8K **Privately Held**
SIC: 3993 Signs & advertising specialties

(G-2580)
SIGN GROUP INC
Also Called: Boro Park Signs
5215 New Utrecht Ave (11219-3829)
PHONE.................718 438-7103
Fax: 718 871-7446
Ushe Steinmetz, *President*
Jerry Greenberger, *Accounts Mgr*
Solomon Gutter, *Admin Sec*
EMP: 25
SQ FT: 9,000
SALES (est): 3.3MM **Privately Held**
WEB: www.signgroup.com
SIC: 3993 Signs & advertising specialties

(G-2581)
SIGN WORLD INC
1194 Utica Ave (11203-5997)
PHONE.................212 619-9000
Herman Weiss, *President*
Carl Weiss, *Corp Secy*
EMP: 25 EST: 1964
SQ FT: 10,000
SALES (est): 1.9MM **Privately Held**
SIC: 3993 2752 Signs & advertising specialties; commercial printing, lithographic

(G-2582)
SIGNS & DECAL CORP
410 Morgan Ave (11211-1640)
PHONE.................718 486-6400
Abdulrasul M Khalfan, *President*
Abdulrasul Khalfan, *President*
Oana Baciu, *Sales Staff*
Babu M Khalfan, *Info Tech Dir*
Tazzim U Khalfan, *Technology*
▲ EMP: 30
SQ FT: 25,000
SALES (est): 5.7MM **Privately Held**
WEB: www.signsanddecal.com
SIC: 3993 Displays & cutouts, window & lobby; signs, not made in custom sign painting shops

(G-2583)
SILLY PHILLIE CREATIONS INC
Also Called: Swisse Cheeks
140 58th St Ste 6f (11220-2526)
PHONE.................718 492-6300
Fax: 718 492-3003
Richard S'Dao, *President*
Phyllis G S'Dao, *Vice Pres*
▲ EMP: 30
SQ FT: 30,000
SALES (est): 2.7MM **Privately Held**
WEB: www.sillyphillie.com
SIC: 2369 2392 2361 Girls' & children's outerwear; sun suits: girls', children's & infants'; bathrobes: girls', children's & infants'; household furnishings; girls' & children's dresses, blouses & shirts

(G-2584)
SILVER OAK PHARMACY INC
5105 Church Ave (11203-3511)
PHONE.................718 922-3400
Axay B Joshi, *Principal*
EMP: 6
SALES (est): 536.7K **Privately Held**
SIC: 2834 Pharmaceutical preparations

(G-2585)
SILVERMAN & GORF INC
60 Franklin Ave (11205-1594)
PHONE.................718 625-1309
Edward Gorf, *President*
Harry Moorer, *Vice Pres*
EMP: 6
SQ FT: 30,000
SALES (est): 490K **Privately Held**
SIC: 3471 Plating of metals or formed products

(G-2586)
SILVERSTONE SHTMTL FBRICATIONS
66 Huntington St (11231)
PHONE.................718 422-0380
Rustem Duka, *President*
EMP: 5
SQ FT: 10,000
SALES (est): 1MM **Privately Held**
SIC: 3441 Fabricated structural metal

(G-2587)
SIMON LIU INC
5113 2nd Ave (11232-4308)
PHONE.................718 567-2011
Fax: 718 567-2015
Simon Liu, *President*
▲ EMP: 12
SQ FT: 7,500
SALES (est): 750K **Privately Held**
WEB: www.simonliuinc.com
SIC: 3952 5999 Artists' equipment; artists' supplies & materials

(G-2588)
SIMON S DECORATING INC
1670 E 19th St (11229-1312)
PHONE.................718 339-2931
Simon Poldanl, *President*
EMP: 5
SALES (est): 433.1K **Privately Held**
SIC: 2512 Upholstered household furniture

(G-2589)
SIMPLE ELEGANCE NEW YORK INC
474 50th St (11220-1913)
PHONE.................718 360-1947
Isaac Sabbagh, *President*
Victor Sabbagh, *Vice Pres*
Abraham Sabbagh, *CFO*
▲ EMP: 15
SQ FT: 6,000
SALES (est): 1MM **Privately Held**
SIC: 2299 5131 Linen fabrics; linen piece goods, woven

(G-2590)
SINCERUS LLC
2478 Mcdonald Ave (11223-5233)
PHONE.................800 419-2804
Marc Poirier,
EMP: 5
SQ FT: 5,000
SALES (est): 229.7K **Privately Held**
SIC: 2834 Pharmaceutical preparations

(G-2591)
SING AH POULTRY
114 Sackett St (11231-1414)
PHONE.................718 625-7253
Fax: 718 260-9212
Perry Chen, *Owner*
EMP: 5
SQ FT: 2,400
SALES (est): 290.1K **Privately Held**
SIC: 2015 Poultry, slaughtered & dressed

(G-2592)
SING TAO NEWSPAPERS NY LTD
5317 8th Ave (11220-3259)
PHONE.................212 431-9030
Rick Ho, *Manager*
EMP: 10 **Privately Held**
WEB: www.nysingtao.com
SIC: 2711 Newspapers
PA: Sing Tao Newspapers New York Ltd.
188 Lafayette St
New York NY 10013

(G-2593)
SING TAO NEWSPAPERS NY LTD
905 Flushing Ave Fl 2 (11206-4602)
PHONE.................718 821-0123
Fax: 718 628-0121
Patrick Seto, *Manager*
EMP: 30
SQ FT: 20,900 **Privately Held**
WEB: www.nysingtao.com
SIC: 2711 Newspapers, publishing & printing

Brooklyn - Kings County (G-2594)

PA: Sing Tao Newspapers New York Ltd.
188 Lafayette St
New York NY 10013

(G-2594)
SITA FINISHING INC
Also Called: Sita Knitting
207 Starr St Ste 1 (11237-2639)
PHONE..................718 417-5295
Fax: 718 417-5295
Loan Sita, President
Ioan Sita, President
George Sita, Vice Pres
▲ EMP: 10
SQ FT: 8,000
SALES (est): 1MM Privately Held
WEB: www.sitafashion.com
SIC: 2211 Canvas

(G-2595)
SLAVA INDUSTRIES INCORPORATED (PA)
Also Called: Nfk International
555 16th St (11215-5914)
PHONE..................718 499-4850
Nevio Kovacevic, Principal
Ilaria Sialino, CFO
Gerard Bary, Accounting Mgr
▲ EMP: 2
SQ FT: 1,200
SALES: 38MM Privately Held
SIC: 2512 2514 Upholstered household furniture; metal household furniture

(G-2596)
SLEEPING PARTNERS INTL INC
Also Called: Sleeping Partners Home Fashion
140 58th St Ste 11 (11220-2522)
PHONE..................212 254-1515
Fax: 718 254-5553
Salvo Stoch, CEO
Salvatore Stoch, Ch of Bd
Kathy Lander, Opers Mgr
Cathy Randa, Manager
▲ EMP: 15
SQ FT: 25,000
SALES: 5MM Privately Held
SIC: 2392 Household furnishings

(G-2597)
SLEEPY HEAD INC
230 3rd St (11215-2714)
PHONE..................718 237-9655
Victor Daniels, President
Haim Zeitoune, Vice Pres
EMP: 10
SQ FT: 17,000
SALES (est): 720K Privately Held
WEB: www.sleepyheadinc.com
SIC: 2369 Pantsuits: girls', children's & infants'; shorts (outerwear): girls' & children's

(G-2598)
SLN GROUP INC
2172 E 26th St (11229-4955)
PHONE..................718 677-5969
Luiza Shamilova, Principal
EMP: 5
SALES (est): 421.2K Privately Held
SIC: 3679 Electronic components

(G-2599)
SLOANE DESIGN INC
226 52nd St (11220-1715)
PHONE..................212 539-0184
Sloane Madureira, President
Tim Chapman, Vice Pres
EMP: 5 EST: 2005
SALES (est): 250.3K Privately Held
SIC: 2752 Commercial printing, lithographic

(G-2600)
SMARTONERS INC (PA)
289 Keap St Ste A (11211-7459)
PHONE..................718 975-0197
Aidel Appel, President
EMP: 4
SQ FT: 3,000
SALES (est): 8.9MM Privately Held
SIC: 3955 Print cartridges for laser & other computer printers

(G-2601)
SMITH STREET BREAD CO LLC
17 5th St (11231-4514)
PHONE..................718 797-9712
Mark Rubin, Mng Member
Humayun Kabir, Manager
EMP: 12
SQ FT: 500
SALES: 1MM Privately Held
SIC: 2051 Bread, cake & related products

(G-2602)
SOCIAL BICYCLES INC
Also Called: Sobi
55 Prospect St Ste 304 (11201-1497)
P.O. Box F9 (11205)
PHONE..................917 746-7624
Stephen Ryan Rzepecki, CEO
Edward Rayner, CFO
▲ EMP: 25
SQ FT: 700
SALES (est): 5MM Privately Held
SIC: 3751 7372 Bicycles & related parts; prepackaged software

(G-2603)
SOCKS AND MORE OF NY INC
1605 Avenue Z Fl 1 (11235-3809)
PHONE..................718 769-1785
Irene Dubrovsky, Chairman
EMP: 9
SALES (est): 906.7K Privately Held
SIC: 2252 Socks

(G-2604)
SOHO LETTERPRESS INC
68 35th St Unit 6 (11232-2211)
PHONE..................718 788-2518
Fax: 212 334-4357
Anne Noonan, President
EMP: 12
SALES: 1MM Privately Held
WEB: www.soholetterpress.com
SIC: 2759 Commercial printing

(G-2605)
SOLA HOME EXPO INC
172 Neptune Ave (11235-5317)
PHONE..................718 646-3383
Sergiy Orlov, President
▲ EMP: 6
SALES (est): 80K Privately Held
SIC: 3431 Bathroom fixtures, including sinks

(G-2606)
SOLAR ENERGY SYSTEMS LLC (PA)
1205 Manhattan Ave # 1210 (11222-6156)
PHONE..................718 389-1545
Fax: 718 389-2820
David Buckner, President
Christopher Moustakis, Vice Pres
Nadja Bruder, Admin Asst
EMP: 12
SQ FT: 1,300
SALES (est): 4MM Privately Held
WEB: www.solaresystems.com
SIC: 3433 1711 Solar heaters & collectors; solar energy contractor

(G-2607)
SOLARWATERWAY INC
Also Called: Solarelectricway
882 3rd Ave Ste 353 (11232-1904)
PHONE..................888 998-5337
Jacqueline Sarway, President
Murray Sarway, Vice Pres
▲ EMP: 20
SQ FT: 5,000
SALES: 4MM Privately Held
SIC: 3645 3646 5063 Residential lighting fixtures; commercial indusl & institutional electric lighting fixtures; lighting fixtures

(G-2608)
SOLARZ BROS PRINTING CORP
231 Norman Ave Ste 105 (11222-1559)
PHONE..................718 383-1330
Sbigniew Solarz, Principal
EMP: 5
SALES (est): 363.4K Privately Held
SIC: 2759 Commercial printing

(G-2609)
SONAAL INDUSTRIES INC
210 Kingsland Ave (11222-4303)
PHONE..................718 383-3860
Rana P Mukhopadhyay, Principal
EMP: 7
SALES (est): 205.5K Privately Held
SIC: 3999 Manufacturing industries

(G-2610)
SOURCE TECHNOLOGIES
9728 3rd Ave (11209-7742)
PHONE..................718 708-0305
Nick Anthony, Owner
EMP: 12
SQ FT: 2,000
SALES: 1MM Privately Held
SIC: 3599 Machine & other job shop work

(G-2611)
SOUTH CENTRAL BOYZ
2568 Bedford Ave Apt 1a (11226-7071)
PHONE..................718 496-7270
Keith Bessor, President
EMP: 5
SALES (est): 280K Privately Held
SIC: 2389 7389 Costumes;

(G-2612)
SPACE 150
20 Jay St Ste 928 (11201-8354)
PHONE..................612 332-6458
EMP: 120 EST: 2003
SALES (est): 11.6MM Privately Held
SIC: 2741 Misc Publishing

(G-2613)
SPFM CORP (PA)
Also Called: Spray Market, The
162 2nd Ave (11215-4619)
PHONE..................718 788-6800
Jacob Kloc, President
Ann Marie Wolf, Administration
EMP: 5
SALES: 500K Privately Held
SIC: 3563 Spraying & dusting equipment

(G-2614)
SPRING PUBLISHING CORPORATION
Also Called: Polska Gazeta
419 Manhattan Ave (11222-4914)
PHONE..................718 782-0881
Janus Czuj, President
EMP: 6 EST: 2001
SALES (est): 501.2K Privately Held
WEB: www.polskagazeta.com
SIC: 2711 Newspapers

(G-2615)
SQUOND INC
185 Marcy Ave Ste 302 (11211-6261)
P.O. Box 110873 (11211-0873)
PHONE..................718 778-6630
Moshe Teitelbaum, Principal
EMP: 25
SQ FT: 2,100
SALES (est): 982.3K Privately Held
SIC: 7372 4812 Business oriented computer software; cellular telephone services

(G-2616)
ST JOHN
1700 Saint Johns Pl (11233-4906)
PHONE..................718 771-4541
EMP: 5 EST: 2010
SALES (est): 363.4K Privately Held
SIC: 2339 Mfg Women's/Misses' Outerwear

(G-2617)
STAG BROTHERS CAST STONE CO
909 E 51st St (11203-6735)
PHONE..................718 629-0975
Sal Stagliano, President
EMP: 8
SALES: 310K Privately Held
SIC: 3272 Concrete products

(G-2618)
STANLEY M INDIG
2173 E 38th St (11234-4929)
PHONE..................718 692-0648
Fax: 718 692-0648
Stanley M Indig, Owner
EMP: 8
SQ FT: 10,000
SALES: 1.2MM Privately Held
SIC: 2731 Textbooks: publishing only, not printed on site

(G-2619)
STAPLEX COMPANY INC
777 5th Ave (11232-1695)
PHONE..................718 768-3333
Fax: 718 965-0750
James J Cussani Jr, President
Gregory Cussani, Vice Pres
David Hill, Vice Pres
R Powers, Vice Pres
Harry Winters, Mfg Staff
▲ EMP: 20 EST: 1949
SQ FT: 20,000
SALES (est): 4.3MM Privately Held
SIC: 3579 3821 Stapling machines (hand or power); laboratory apparatus & furniture

(G-2620)
STAR POLY BAG INC (PA)
200 Liberty Ave (11207-2904)
PHONE..................718 384-3130
Fax: 718 384-2342
Rachel Posen, CEO
Joel Posen, Principal
Jay Kaufman, Manager
EMP: 17 EST: 1961
SQ FT: 22,000
SALES (est): 3.6MM Privately Held
WEB: www.starpoly.com
SIC: 2673 Plastic bags: made from purchased materials

(G-2621)
STARLINER SHIPPING & TRAVEL
5305 Church Ave Ste 1 (11203-3638)
PHONE..................718 385-1515
Fax: 718 385-2890
Rhea Murray, President
Leighton Murray, Vice Pres
Blueth Murray-Ogunnoiki, Vice Pres
Anthia Murray, Treasurer
▼ EMP: 7
SALES (est): 540K Privately Held
SIC: 2599 Ship furniture

(G-2622)
STEALTH ARCHTCTRAL WINDOWS INC
Also Called: Stealth Window
232 Varet St (11206-3822)
PHONE..................718 821-6666
Barry Borgen, President
EMP: 19
SQ FT: 52,000
SALES (est): 2.1MM Privately Held
WEB: www.avantguards.com
SIC: 2431 Windows, wood

(G-2623)
STEALTH INC
1129 E 27th St (11210-4620)
PHONE..................718 252-7900
Fax: 718 252-7935
Jack Edelstein, President
EMP: 16
SQ FT: 3,000
SALES: 1.7MM Privately Held
SIC: 2326 Industrial garments, men's & boys'

(G-2624)
STEELCRAFT MANUFACTURING CO
Also Called: Steel Craft
352 Pine St (11208-2807)
PHONE..................718 277-2404
Fax: 718 277-0507
Louis Massa, President
David Massa, Vice Pres
EMP: 11 EST: 1945
SQ FT: 9,000
SALES (est): 790K Privately Held
SIC: 2514 3444 2541 Metal household furniture; kitchen cabinets: metal; radiator shields or enclosures, sheet metal; wood partitions & fixtures

Brooklyn - Kings County

(G-2625)
STEELDECK NY INC
141 Banker St (11222-3147)
PHONE..................718 599-3700
Fax: 718 599-3800
Philip Parsons, *President*
Gail Moorcroft, *Vice Pres*
Alexandra Berch, *Production*
Allan Dias, *Production*
Joshua Marmer, *Administration*
▲ EMP: 15 EST: 2001
SQ FT: 20,000
SALES (est): 3.2MM **Privately Held**
SIC: 3999 5049 2541 2531 Stage hardware & equipment, except lighting; theatrical equipment & supplies; partitions for floor attachment, prefabricated: wood; theater furniture

(G-2626)
STEELMASTERS INC
135 Liberty Ave (11212-8008)
PHONE..................718 498-2854
Matthew Rosio, *President*
Anthony Masi, *Vice Pres*
EMP: 23 EST: 1994
SQ FT: 14,000
SALES (est): 3MM **Privately Held**
SIC: 3442 Rolling doors for industrial buildings or warehouses, metal

(G-2627)
STEINBOCK-BRAFF INC
Also Called: Kat Nap Products
3611 14th Ave (11218-3773)
PHONE..................718 972-6500
Fax: 718 435-4202
Corey Steinbock, *President*
▲ EMP: 30 EST: 1933
SQ FT: 80,000
SALES (est): 3.8MM **Privately Held**
WEB: www.sleepmattress.com
SIC: 2515 5021 Mattresses & foundations; household furniture

(G-2628)
STEINWAY PASTA & GELATI INC
37 Grand Ave Ste 1 (11205-1309)
PHONE..................718 246-5414
Fax: 718 246-5236
Vincenzo Arpaia, *President*
▲ EMP: 15
SALES (est): 2.3MM **Privately Held**
SIC: 2099 5149 Packaged combination products: pasta, rice & potato; pasta & rice

(G-2629)
STEVE & ANDYS ORGANICS INC
630 Flushing Ave (11206-5026)
PHONE..................718 499-7933
Michelle Schwartz, *President*
Arjan Khiani, *Vice Pres*
Steve Marino, *Treasurer*
Quinn Rhone, *Director*
EMP: 5
SALES (est): 339.9K **Privately Held**
SIC: 2064 Candy & other confectionery products

(G-2630)
STIEGELBAUER ASSOCIATES INC (PA)
Bldg 280 (11205)
PHONE..................718 624-0835
Michael Stiegelbauer, *President*
Dawn Stiegelbauer, *Corp Secy*
Steven Paone, *Vice Pres*
Butch Huerta, *Project Mgr*
Kimberly Amato, *Mktg Dir*
EMP: 22
SQ FT: 180,000
SALES (est): 3MM **Privately Held**
SIC: 3999 Theatrical scenery

(G-2631)
STONE AND BATH GALLERY
856 39th St (11232-3230)
PHONE..................718 438-4500
Samuel Stru, *Owner*
▲ EMP: 8
SALES (est): 246.8K **Privately Held**
SIC: 3261 3251 Bathroom accessories/fittings, vitreous china or earthenware; brick & structural clay tile

(G-2632)
STREET BEAT SPORTSWEAR INC (PA)
Also Called: Visual F-X
462 Kent Ave Fl 2 (11249-5922)
PHONE..................718 302-1500
Fax: 718 387-8012
Albert Papouchado, *President*
Allen Smith, *CFO*
Micheal Amar, *Treasurer*
▲ EMP: 11
SQ FT: 66,000
SALES (est): 3.6MM **Privately Held**
SIC: 2339 Sportswear, women's

(G-2633)
STRONG TEMPERING GL INDUST LLC
530 63rd St Ste B (11220-4608)
PHONE..................718 765-0007
Joy Huang, *Sales Staff*
Mark Chen,
EMP: 12
SALES (est): 1.1MM **Privately Held**
SIC: 3211 Tempered glass

(G-2634)
STUDIO 21 LA INC
13 42nd St Fl 5 (11232-2616)
PHONE..................718 965-6579
Leonid Tszang, *President*
▲ EMP: 20
SQ FT: 5,000
SALES (est): 1.4MM **Privately Held**
WEB: www.studio21usa.com
SIC: 2531 5399 5712 Picnic tables or benches, park; catalog showrooms; furniture stores

(G-2635)
STUDIO 40 INC
810 Humboldt St Ste 4 (11222-1913)
PHONE..................212 420-8631
Richard Temerian, *President*
EMP: 6 **Privately Held**
SIC: 3446 Architectural metalwork
PA: Studio 40 Inc
 40 Great Jones St Apt 1
 New York NY 10012

(G-2636)
STUDIO DELLARTE
74 Bayard St (11222-3905)
PHONE..................718 599-3715
Fax: 718 599-4738
Jeremy Lebensohn, *Owner*
EMP: 5
SALES (est): 320K **Privately Held**
WEB: www.studiodellarte.com
SIC: 3446 Architectural metalwork

(G-2637)
STUHRLING ORIGINAL LLC
449 20th St (11215-6247)
PHONE..................718 840-5760
Jay Schiss, *CFO*
Israel Jacobson, *Controller*
Shifra Birnhack, *Accounts Mgr*
Tali Brach, *Accounts Mgr*
Yiddy Lemmer, *Info Tech Dir*
▲ EMP: 7
SQ FT: 20,000
SALES: 10MM **Privately Held**
SIC: 3873 5094 Watches, clocks, watchcases & parts; clocks, watches & parts; watches & parts

(G-2638)
STURDY STORE DISPLAYS INC
110 Beard St (11231-1502)
PHONE..................718 389-9919
Fax: 718 389-9929
Michael Fried, *President*
Sam Grossinger, *General Mgr*
Jacob Brauner, *Vice Pres*
Moshe Nathan Neuman, *Controller*
Yoel Schlesinger, *Sales Staff*
▲ EMP: 23
SQ FT: 35,000
SALES (est): 3.2MM **Privately Held**
WEB: www.sturdystoredisplays.com
SIC: 2542 Partitions & fixtures, except wood

(G-2639)
STYLIST PLEATING CORP
109 S 5th St (11249-5869)
PHONE..................718 384-8181
Fax: 718 384-9108
Kenneth Stier, *President*
EMP: 18 EST: 1938
SQ FT: 11,000
SALES (est): 862.5K **Privately Held**
SIC: 2395 Permanent pleating & pressing, for the trade

(G-2640)
SUE & SAM CO INC (PA)
Also Called: W & G Manufacturing
720 39th St 720 (11232-3200)
PHONE..................718 436-1672
Fax: 718 436-7508
Howard Wollman, *President*
Martin Stern, *Controller*
▲ EMP: 25
SQ FT: 37,000
SALES (est): 5.2MM **Privately Held**
SIC: 2321 2361 Polo shirts, men's & boys': made from purchased materials; shirts: girls', children's & infants'

(G-2641)
SUN MING JAN INC
145 Noll St (11206-4714)
PHONE..................718 418-8221
Ben Chen, *CEO*
▲ EMP: 10 EST: 1999
SALES (est): 912.9K **Privately Held**
SIC: 2013 Sausages & other prepared meats

(G-2642)
SUNBURST STUDIOS INC
584 3rd Ave (11215-4612)
PHONE..................718 768-6360
Ihor Nykolak, *President*
Peter Friedman, *Treasurer*
EMP: 5 EST: 1976
SQ FT: 3,600
SALES (est): 400K **Privately Held**
WEB: www.sunburststudio.com
SIC: 3231 8999 Stained glass: made from purchased glass; cut & engraved glassware: made from purchased glass; art restoration

(G-2643)
SUNRISE BAKING CO LLC
4564 2nd Ave (11232-4215)
PHONE..................718 499-0800
Frank S Laferlita, *Mng Member*
Michael Laferlita,
EMP: 115
SQ FT: 32,000
SALES (est): 11.3MM **Privately Held**
SIC: 2051 Bakery: wholesale or wholesale/retail combined

(G-2644)
SUNWIRE ELECTRIC CORP
70 Wyckoff Ave Apt 4h (11237-3385)
PHONE..................718 456-7500
Chen Birbaul, *Vice Pres*
EMP: 6
SALES (est): 700K **Privately Held**
SIC: 3699 Electrical equipment & supplies

(G-2645)
SUPER NEON LIGHT CO INC
7813 16th Ave (11214-1003)
PHONE..................718 236-5667
Fax: 718 236-6101
James Coccaro Jr, *President*
EMP: 8 EST: 1939
SQ FT: 1,600
SALES (est): 550K **Privately Held**
SIC: 3993 Neon signs

(G-2646)
SUPERFLEX LTD
152 44th St (11232-3310)
PHONE..................718 768-1400
Fax: 718 768-5065
Shimon Elbaz, *Ch of Bd*
Yigal Elbaz, *President*
Adna Elbaz, *Admin Asst*
▲ EMP: 50
SQ FT: 60,000
SALES (est): 19.6MM **Privately Held**
WEB: www.superflex.com
SIC: 3644 3052 Electric conduits & fittings; plastic hose

(G-2647)
SUPERIOR BLOCK CORP
Also Called: Glenwood Masonry Products
4106 Glenwood Rd (11210-2025)
PHONE..................718 421-0900
Constance Cincotta, *President*
EMP: 10 EST: 1997
SQ FT: 75,000
SALES (est): 1.8MM **Privately Held**
SIC: 3271 Concrete block & brick

(G-2648)
SUPERIOR ELEC ENCLOSURE INC
16 Spencer St (11205-1605)
PHONE..................718 797-9090
Harris Grant, *President*
EMP: 7
SALES (est): 933K **Privately Held**
SIC: 3444 Metal housings, enclosures, casings & other containers

(G-2649)
SUPERIOR FIBER MILLS INC
181 Lombardy St (11222-5417)
P.O. Box 306, East Norwich (11732-0306)
PHONE..................718 782-7500
Helen Burney, *President*
Henry Burney, *Vice Pres*
EMP: 40
SQ FT: 125,000
SALES (est): 4.9MM **Privately Held**
WEB: www.superiorfibers.com
SIC: 2299 2221 Batts & batting: cotton mill waste & related material; broadwoven fabric mills, manmade

(G-2650)
SUPERLEAF LLC
Also Called: Detox Water
212 7th St 1 (11215-3208)
PHONE..................888 887-4318
Kenneth Park, *CEO*
Dennis Chen, *CFO*
EMP: 5
SQ FT: 1,300
SALES (est): 169.2K **Privately Held**
SIC: 2086 Water, pasteurized: packaged in cans, bottles, etc.

(G-2651)
SUPREME BOILERS INC
9221 Ditmas Ave (11236-1711)
PHONE..................718 342-2220
Aaron Ganguli, *President*
David Rakst, *Vice Pres*
EMP: 5 EST: 2007
SALES (est): 540K **Privately Held**
SIC: 3443 Boiler & boiler shop work

(G-2652)
SUPREME POLY PLASTICS INC
299 Meserole St (11206-1732)
PHONE..................718 456-9300
Fax: 718 821-8170
Abe Eilander, *President*
Abe Wertaberger, *General Mgr*
Chick Lam, *Director*
EMP: 25
SQ FT: 45,000
SALES (est): 3.9MM **Privately Held**
WEB: www.supremepoly.com
SIC: 2673 Plastic bags: made from purchased materials

(G-2653)
SURE-KOL REFRIGERATOR CO INC
490 Flushing Ave (11205-1615)
PHONE..................718 625-0601
Fax: 718 624-1719
Steven Waslin, *President*
David J Waslin, *Corp Secy*
Jack Waslin, *Vice Pres*
EMP: 10 EST: 1947
SQ FT: 13,000
SALES (est): 1.5MM **Privately Held**
SIC: 3632 Household refrigerators & freezers

Brooklyn - Kings County (G-2654)

(G-2654)
SURPRISE PLASTICS INC
124 57th St (11220-2576)
PHONE.................................718 492-6355
Fax: 718 492-0258
Joseph M Tancredi, *President*
Kenneth Tancredi, *Corp Secy*
Christopher Tancredi, *Vice Pres*
Vincent Tancredi, *Vice Pres*
Raymond Tancredi, *Treasurer*
▲ EMP: 15
SQ FT: 48,000
SALES (est): 16.8MM **Privately Held**
WEB: www.surpriseplastics.com
SIC: 3089 Injection molding of plastics

(G-2655)
SWEATER BRAND INC
Also Called: Domain
86 S 1st St (11249-4171)
PHONE.................................718 797-0505
Moshe Rosenberg, *Manager*
EMP: 6
SALES (corp-wide): 3.2MM **Privately Held**
SIC: 2253 Sweaters & sweater coats, knit
PA: Sweater Brand Inc.
22 Wallenberg Cir
Monsey NY
718 797-0505

(G-2656)
SWISS MADISON LLC
498 Liberty Ave (11207-3104)
PHONE.................................434 623-4766
Mendel Grieman, *Mng Member*
EMP: 19
SALES: 500K **Privately Held**
SIC: 2499 Seats, toilet

(G-2657)
SYNERGY DIGITAL
43 Hall St (11205-1315)
PHONE.................................718 643-2742
Fax: 718 643-9212
EMP: 15
SALES (est): 720K **Privately Held**
SIC: 3691 Mfg Storage Batteries

(G-2658)
T & L TRADING CO
17 Meserole St (11206-1901)
PHONE.................................718 782-5550
Fax: 718 599-4342
David Tang, *Owner*
▲ EMP: 5
SQ FT: 5,000
SALES (est): 636.4K **Privately Held**
SIC: 2621 Stationery, envelope & tablet papers; bond paper

(G-2659)
T M I PLASTICS INDUSTRIES INC
28 Wythe Ave (11249-1036)
PHONE.................................718 383-0363
Sam Yuen, *President*
▲ EMP: 15
SALES (est): 2.2MM **Privately Held**
SIC: 2673 Plastic bags: made from purchased materials

(G-2660)
T MIX INC
6217 5th Ave (11220-4611)
PHONE.................................646 379-6814
Lin Jian, *CEO*
EMP: 7
SALES (est): 633.7K **Privately Held**
SIC: 3273 Ready-mixed concrete

(G-2661)
T&K PRINTING INC
Also Called: T & K Printing
262 44th St (11232-2816)
PHONE.................................718 439-9454
Fax: 718 439-9455
Hien Khuu, *President*
Dianna SOO, *Administration*
EMP: 10
SALES (est): 1.5MM **Privately Held**
SIC: 3577 2759 Optical scanning devices; commercial printing

(G-2662)
TAAM TOV FOODS INC
Also Called: Ko-Sure Food Distributors
188 28th St (11232-1604)
PHONE.................................718 788-8880
Meyer Thurm, *President*
Max Thurm, *Vice Pres*
Sam Sherer, *Treasurer*
Marvin Weinstein, *Intl Dir*
▲ EMP: 7
SALES (est): 658.1K **Privately Held**
SIC: 2022 Cheese, natural & processed; cheese spreads, dips, pastes & other cheese products

(G-2663)
TABLE TOPS PAPER CORP
47 Hall St Ste C-2 (11205-1315)
P.O. Box 220443 (11222-0443)
PHONE.................................718 831-6440
Ben Ruiz, *President*
EMP: 8
SALES: 660K **Privately Held**
SIC: 2759 5111 5999 Financial note & certificate printing & engraving; printing & writing paper; alarm signal systems

(G-2664)
TABLET PUBLISHING COMPANY INC
Also Called: Tablet Newspaper, The
1712 10th Ave (11215-6215)
PHONE.................................718 965-7333
Monsignor Anthony Danna, *Publisher*
Ed Wilkinson, *Principal*
Leonard W Kaiser, *Business Mgr*
Carrie White, *Manager*
EMP: 25
SQ FT: 18,000
SALES (est): 1.4MM **Privately Held**
SIC: 2711 2741 Newspapers: publishing only, not printed on site; miscellaneous publishing

(G-2665)
TAI SENG
106 Lexington Ave (11238-1412)
PHONE.................................718 399-6311
▲ EMP: 6
SALES (est): 330K **Privately Held**
SIC: 2673 Mfg Bags-Plastic/Coated Paper

(G-2666)
TALAERA
81 Fleet Pl Apt 11a (11201-8016)
PHONE.................................206 229-0631
Anita Anthonj, *CEO*
Mel Macmahon, *Manager*
EMP: 6
SALES (est): 135.3K **Privately Held**
SIC: 7372 Business oriented computer software

(G-2667)
TANEN CAP CO
Also Called: Tanen & Co
397 Bridge St Fl 8 (11201-5238)
PHONE.................................212 254-7100
Fax: 212 581-0011
David Steinberg, *Partner*
Aaron Steinberg, *Partner*
EMP: 12 EST: 1975
SQ FT: 5,000
SALES (est): 1.1MM **Privately Held**
SIC: 2353 Uniform hats & caps

(G-2668)
TARGUM PRESS USA INC
Also Called: Horizons Magazine
1946 59th St (11204-2340)
PHONE.................................248 355-2266
Sydney Choncow, *President*
David Dombey, *Admin Sec*
EMP: 8
SALES (est): 534.3K **Privately Held**
SIC: 2731 Book publishing

(G-2669)
TAYLOR TANK COMPANY INC
848 E 43rd St (11210-3502)
PHONE.................................718 434-1300
Michael Rubinberg, *President*
Cynthia Rubinberg, *Admin Sec*
EMP: 30 EST: 1947
SQ FT: 20,000
SALES (est): 4.7MM
SALES (corp-wide): 4.7MM **Privately Held**
WEB: www.rubiconhx.com
SIC: 3443 Tanks, standard or custom fabricated: metal plate
PA: Rubicon Industries Corp.
848 E 43rd St
Brooklyn NY 11210
718 434-4700

(G-2670)
TECHNICAL LIBRARY SERVICE INC
Also Called: Talas
330 Morgan Ave (11211-2716)
PHONE.................................212 219-0770
Jacob Salik, *Ch of Bd*
Marjorie Salik, *President*
Aaron Salik, *Vice Pres*
EMP: 11 EST: 1962
SQ FT: 25,000
SALES (est): 1.3MM **Privately Held**
WEB: www.talas-nyc.com
SIC: 2653 8231 5199 Corrugated boxes, partitions, display items, sheets & pad; boxes, corrugated: made from purchased materials; libraries; law library; packaging materials

(G-2671)
TECHNIPOLY MANUFACTURING INC
Also Called: T M I of New York
20 Wythe Ave (11249-1036)
PHONE.................................718 383-0363
Fax: 718 383-2769
Kam S Yuen, *Owner*
Lip Foo Yee, *Vice Pres*
Allen Yuen, *Admin Sec*
EMP: 28
SQ FT: 16,000
SALES (est): 4.4MM **Privately Held**
SIC: 2673 2752 Plastic bags: made from purchased materials; commercial printing, lithographic

(G-2672)
TECNOLUX INCORPORATED
103 14th St (11215-4607)
PHONE.................................718 369-3900
Fax: 718 369-2845
David Ablon, *President*
Robert Tinkelman, *CTO*
▲ EMP: 7
SQ FT: 10,000
SALES (est): 710K **Privately Held**
WEB: www.tecnolux.com
SIC: 3648 Lighting equipment

(G-2673)
TEKA FINE LINE BRUSHES INC
3691 Bedford Ave (11229-1703)
PHONE.................................718 692-2928
Terry Ettkins, *President*
EMP: 7
SALES (est): 923.6K **Privately Held**
WEB: www.tekabrush.com
SIC: 3991 Hair pencils (artists' brushes)

(G-2674)
TELLER PRINTING CORP
317 Division Ave (11211-7307)
PHONE.................................718 486-3662
James Teller, *President*
EMP: 6
SALES (est): 510K **Privately Held**
SIC: 2752 Commercial printing, lithographic

(G-2675)
THATS MY GIRL INC (PA)
80 39th St Ste 501 (11232-2604)
P.O. Box 230317 (11223-0317)
PHONE.................................212 695-0020
Salomon Salem, *President*
Raymond Kassin, *Vice Pres*
Connie LI, *Bookkeeper*
Chelsea Reizner, *Accounts Exec*
Steven Salem, *Manager*
EMP: 2
SQ FT: 800
SALES (est): 1.7MM **Privately Held**
SIC: 2361 Girls' & children's dresses, blouses & shirts

(G-2676)
THE EARTH TIMES FOUNDATION
195 Adams St Apt 6j (11201-1808)
PHONE.................................718 297-0488
Pranay Gupte, *President*
Ranjit Sahni, *Treasurer*
Nandini Ansari, *Director*
Jon Quint, *Director*
EMP: 5
SALES: 984.9K **Privately Held**
SIC: 2711 Newspapers, publishing & printing

(G-2677)
THEMIS CHIMNEY INC
190 Morgan Ave (11237-1014)
PHONE.................................718 937-4716
Mark Papadimitriou, *President*
EMP: 12
SQ FT: 12,000
SALES (est): 2.3MM **Privately Held**
SIC: 3443 3444 Liners/lining; sheet metalwork

(G-2678)
THOMPSON OVERHEAD DOOR CO INC
47 16th St (11215-4613)
PHONE.................................718 788-2470
Fax: 718 788-3344
Olav M Thompson, *President*
Edward Thompson, *Corp Secy*
Lynn Murray, *Treasurer*
Bob Kligman, *Sales Mgr*
Robert Kligman, *Sales Mgr*
EMP: 15
SQ FT: 16,000
SALES (est): 2.9MM **Privately Held**
SIC: 3442 5211 Rolling doors for industrial buildings or warehouses, metal; door & window products

(G-2679)
TIE KING INC (PA)
Also Called: Jimmy Sales
243 44th St (11232-2815)
PHONE.................................718 768-8484
Fax: 718 768-0355
Jimmy Azizo, *President*
Solomon Azizo, *Treasurer*
David Azizo, *Controller*
Steven Azizo, *Manager*
Jack Azizo, *Admin Sec*
▲ EMP: 50
SQ FT: 20,000
SALES (est): 4.6MM **Privately Held**
WEB: www.thetieking.com
SIC: 2323 Men's & boys' neckties & bow ties

(G-2680)
TIE VIEW NECKWEAR CO INC
1559 58th St (11219-4748)
PHONE.................................718 853-4156
Irving Spierer, *President*
EMP: 7 EST: 1967
SQ FT: 2,000
SALES: 700K **Privately Held**
SIC: 2323 Men's & boys' neckwear

(G-2681)
TLI IMPORT INC
151 2nd Ave (11215-4615)
PHONE.................................917 578-4568
Nouri Arabi, *President*
EMP: 6 EST: 2010
SALES (est): 315.9K **Privately Held**
SIC: 2221 Textile warping, on a contract basis

(G-2682)
TONER-N-MORE INC
2220 65th St Ste 103 (11204-4035)
PHONE.................................718 232-6200
Yoni Glatzer, *President*
EMP: 5
SQ FT: 10,000
SALES (est): 591.2K **Privately Held**
WEB: www.tonernmore.com
SIC: 3861 Toners, prepared photographic (not made in chemical plants)

GEOGRAPHIC SECTION
Brooklyn - Kings County (G-2712)

(G-2683)
TOOLS & STAMPING CORP
Also Called: Balint Tool
48 Eagle St (11222-1013)
P.O. Box 220375 (11222-0375)
PHONE..................................718 392-4040
Ernest Feldman, *President*
Judah Feldman, *Vice Pres*
M Feldman, *Admin Sec*
EMP: 5 **EST:** 1960
SALES (est): 390K **Privately Held**
WEB: www.jnet.com
SIC: 3469 3544 3429 Stamping metal for the trade; special dies & tools; luggage hardware

(G-2684)
TOOTTER INC
1470 Royce St (11234-5924)
PHONE..................................212 204-7937
Sade Metellus, *Vice Pres*
EMP: 25
SQ FT: 1,200
SALES (est): 654.8K **Privately Held**
SIC: 7372 Application computer software

(G-2685)
TOPOO INDUSTRIES INCORPORATED
7815 16th Ave (11214-1003)
PHONE..................................718 331-3755
▲ **EMP:** 8
SALES (est): 826.4K **Privately Held**
SIC: 3999 Manufacturing industries

(G-2686)
TOPRINT LTD
6110 7th Ave (11220-4107)
PHONE..................................718 439-0469
Thomas Corey, *Principal*
EMP: 5
SALES (est): 340K **Privately Held**
SIC: 2759 Commercial printing

(G-2687)
TORTILLERIA CHINANTLA INC
975 Grand St (11211-2704)
PHONE..................................718 302-0101
Fax: 718 302-0608
Erasmo Ponce, *Manager*
EMP: 7
SALES (corp-wide): 2MM **Privately Held**
SIC: 2096 Tortilla chips
PA: Tortilleria Chinantla Inc
  86 Central Ave
  Brooklyn NY 11206
  718 456-2828

(G-2688)
TOTAL METAL RESOURCE
Also Called: Pmrnyc
175 Bogart St (11206-1720)
PHONE..................................718 384-7818
Scott Behr, *President*
Susan Hutter, *Sales Mgr*
EMP: 10
SALES (est): 1.5MM **Privately Held**
SIC: 3499 Fabricated metal products

(G-2689)
TOURA LLC
392 2nd St 2 (11215-2404)
PHONE..................................646 652-8668
Kathleen Schnoor, *Principal*
Aaron Radin,
EMP: 10
SALES (est): 730.4K **Privately Held**
SIC: 3663 Mobile communication equipment

(G-2690)
TOWER ISLES FROZEN FOODS LTD
Also Called: Tower Isles Patties
2025 Atlantic Ave (11233-3131)
P.O. Box 330625 (11233-0625)
PHONE..................................718 495-2626
Fax: 718 342-6437
Patrick Jolly, *President*
Johnr Lokhandwala, *General Mgr*
James Jobson, *Vice Pres*
Joel Bower, *Accounts Mgr*
EMP: 73 **EST:** 1969
SQ FT: 32,600
SALES: 20MM **Privately Held**
WEB: www.towerislespatties.com
SIC: 2013 Boneless meat, from purchased meat

(G-2691)
TOWN FOOD SERVICE EQP CO INC (PA)
72 Beadel St (11222-5232)
PHONE..................................718 388-5650
Fax: 718 388-5860
Robert Pavlovich, *President*
▲ **EMP:** 15 **EST:** 1929
SQ FT: 1,500
SALES (est): 5MM **Privately Held**
SIC: 3491 Industrial valves

(G-2692)
TRADE MARK GRAPHICS INC
4502 Avenue N (11234-3613)
PHONE..................................718 306-0001
Avery Marder, *President*
EMP: 7
SQ FT: 24,000
SALES (est): 924.2K **Privately Held**
SIC: 2752 Commercial printing, offset

(G-2693)
TRANSCNTINENTAL ULTRA FLEX INC
975 Essex St (11208-5419)
PHONE..................................718 272-9100
Fax: 718 272-5424
Eli Blatt, *CEO*
Todd Addison, *Treasurer*
Radek Danielewicz, *Info Tech Mgr*
◆ **EMP:** 270
SQ FT: 115,000
SALES (est): 54.4MM
SALES (corp-wide): 1.5B **Privately Held**
WEB: www.ultraflex.com
SIC: 2759 2671 2752 Flexographic printing; packaging paper & plastics film, coated & laminated; commercial printing, lithographic
PA: Transcontinental Inc
  1 Place Ville-Marie Bureau 3240
  Montreal QC H3B 0
  514 954-4000

(G-2694)
TRANSLAND SOURCING LLC
5 Lynch St (11249-9223)
PHONE..................................718 596-5704
Jacob Frankl, *CEO*
EMP: 4
SALES: 5MM **Privately Held**
SIC: 3571 Electronic computers

(G-2695)
TRI STATE SHEARING BENDING INC
366 Herzl St (11212-4442)
P.O. Box 120002 (11212-0002)
PHONE..................................718 485-2200
Alan Blaier, *President*
Michele Blaier, *Vice Pres*
Ronald Blaier, *Manager*
EMP: 15
SQ FT: 12,000
SALES (est): 4.1MM **Privately Held**
SIC: 3446 Stairs, staircases, stair treads: prefabricated metal

(G-2696)
TRI-STATE FOOD JOBBERS INC
5600 1st Ave Unit A5 (11220-2550)
PHONE..................................718 921-1211
Maor Ohana, *President*
EMP: 6 **EST:** 2009
SALES (est): 2.6MM **Privately Held**
SIC: 3497 Foil containers for bakery goods & frozen foods

(G-2697)
TRIANGLE LABEL TAG INC
525 Dekalb Ave (11205-4818)
PHONE..................................718 875-3030
Fax: 718 875-9830
Joseph Kahan, *President*
Herman Frankel, *Vice Pres*
EMP: 8
SQ FT: 5,000
SALES: 1.3MM **Privately Held**
SIC: 2672 2759 5131 2241 Adhesive papers, labels or tapes: from purchased material; labels & seals: printing; piece goods & notions; labels, woven

(G-2698)
TRICO MANUFACTURING CORP
196 Dupont St (11222-1241)
PHONE..................................718 349-6565
Elizabeth Fling, *President*
EMP: 6 **EST:** 2000
SQ FT: 7,000
SALES (est): 537.9K **Privately Held**
SIC: 3429 Door locks, bolts & checks; door opening & closing devices, except electrical

(G-2699)
TRIMET COAL LLC
1615 Avenue I Apt 420 (11230-3041)
PHONE..................................718 951-3654
EMP: 21
SALES (est): 1.3MM **Privately Held**
SIC: 1241 Coal Mining Services

(G-2700)
TRIPI ENGRAVING CO INC
Also Called: Royal Engraving
60 Meserole Ave (11222-2638)
PHONE..................................718 383-6500
Phil Tripi, *President*
EMP: 25
SQ FT: 10,000
SALES (est): 2.2MM **Privately Held**
SIC: 2759 5143 5943 2796 Engraving; stationery; stationery stores; platemaking services; typesetting; commercial printing, lithographic

(G-2701)
TRIPLE J BEDDING LLC
63 Flushing Ave Unit 331 (11205-1083)
PHONE..................................718 643-8005
Joseph Friedman, *CEO*
▲ **EMP:** 7
SALES (est): 26K **Privately Held**
SIC: 2511 Wood household furniture

(G-2702)
TRM LINEN INC
1546 59th St (11219-5028)
PHONE..................................718 686-6075
Chaim Cohen, *Ch of Bd*
▼ **EMP:** 5
SALES (est): 457.7K **Privately Held**
SIC: 2299 5961 Linen fabrics; mail order house

(G-2703)
TROVE INC
20 Jay St Ste 846 (11201-8306)
PHONE..................................212 268-2046
Jee Levin, *Principal*
Randall Buck, *Buyer*
EMP: 15
SALES (est): 1.6MM **Privately Held**
SIC: 3999 5199 Fire extinguishers, portable; gifts & novelties

(G-2704)
TROVVIT INC
445 7th St (11215-3614)
PHONE..................................718 908-5376
Torrance Robinson, *CEO*
EMP: 9
SALES (est): 271.8K **Privately Held**
SIC: 7372 7389 Educational computer software;

(G-2705)
TRU-TONE METAL PRODUCTS INC
1261 Willoughby Ave (11237-2904)
P.O. Box 370711 (11237-0711)
PHONE..................................718 386-5960
Fax: 718 386-1021
James P Murtha, *President*
Catherine Murtha, *Vice Pres*
Nick Murtha, *Director*
EMP: 20
SQ FT: 5,000
SALES (est): 2.5MM **Privately Held**
SIC: 3471 Anodizing (plating) of metals or formed products; coloring & finishing of aluminum or formed products

(G-2706)
TUNECORE INC (PA)
45 Main St Ste 705 (11201-1075)
P.O. Box 20256 (11202-0256)
PHONE..................................646 651-1060
Scott Ackerman, *CEO*
Troy Denkinger, *Vice Pres*
Elise Holzheimer, *Vice Pres*
Gillian Morris, *Vice Pres*
Matt Barrington, *Controller*
EMP: 32
SALES (est): 1.4MM **Privately Held**
SIC: 3651 Music distribution apparatus

(G-2707)
TUROFF TOWER GRAPHICS INC
Also Called: Tower Sales Co
681 Coney Island Ave (11218-4306)
PHONE..................................718 856-7300
Jay Turoff, *President*
Rose Turoff, *Corp Secy*
Georgina Snyder, *Vice Pres*
EMP: 14 **EST:** 1969
SQ FT: 1,000
SALES (est): 1.3MM **Privately Held**
SIC: 3993 Neon signs

(G-2708)
TUV TAAM CORP
502 Flushing Ave (11205-1616)
PHONE..................................718 855-2207
Aaron Nutovich, *President*
Rivka Nutovich, *Treasurer*
Lea Gold, *Admin Sec*
▲ **EMP:** 50
SQ FT: 10,000
SALES (est): 7.4MM **Privately Held**
SIC: 2099 2038 Food preparations; salads, fresh or refrigerated; frozen specialties

(G-2709)
TWI WATCHES LLC
Also Called: Akribos Watches
4014 1st Ave (11232-2606)
PHONE..................................718 663-3969
Ben Rosenbaum, *Sales Dir*
Chaim Sischer, *Mng Member*
▲ **EMP:** 35
SALES: 2MM **Privately Held**
SIC: 3873 Watches, clocks, watchcases & parts

(G-2710)
TWIN MARQUIS INC (HQ)
7 Bushwick Pl (11206-2815)
PHONE..................................718 386-6868
Fax: 718 386-0516
Hyung Kyun Kim, *Ch of Bd*
Jing Lin, *Engineer*
Flora Lin, *Office Mgr*
Chung Pun Tang, *Admin Sec*
▲ **EMP:** 65
SQ FT: 33,000
SALES (est): 11.8MM
SALES (corp-wide): 4.1B **Privately Held**
WEB: www.twinmarquis.com
SIC: 2098 2099 2035 Macaroni & spaghetti; noodles, fried (Chinese); pickles, sauces & salad dressings
PA: Cj Cheiljedang Corp.
  Cj Jeiljedang Center
  Seoul SEO 04560
  267 401-114

(G-2711)
TWO SISTERS KIEV BAKERY INC (PA)
2737 W 15th St (11224-2705)
PHONE..................................718 769-2626
Rita Shoikhetman, *President*
Pauline Rusanovsky, *Vice Pres*
EMP: 5
SQ FT: 5,000
SALES (est): 1.2MM **Privately Held**
SIC: 2051 Bakery: wholesale or wholesale/retail combined

(G-2712)
TWO SISTERS KIEV BAKERY INC
1627 E 18th St (11229-1203)
PHONE..................................718 627-5438
Rita Shoikhetman, *Branch Mgr*
EMP: 10

Brooklyn - Kings County (G-2713)

SALES (corp-wide): 1.2MM **Privately Held**
SIC: 2051 Bakery: wholesale or wholesale/retail combined
PA: Two Sisters Kiev Bakery Inc
2737 W 15th St
Brooklyn NY 11224
718 769-2626

(G-2713)
TWO WORLDS ARTS LTD
307 Kingsland Ave (11222-3708)
PHONE 212 929-2210
Fax: 718 349-6420
Jean Chau, *Manager*
EMP: 6
SALES (corp-wide): 631.9K **Privately Held**
SIC: 2512 Upholstered household furniture
PA: Two Worlds Arts Ltd
122 W 18th St
New York NY 10011
212 929-2210

(G-2714)
ULANO PRODUCT INC
110 3rd Ave (11217-2397)
PHONE 718 622-5200
David Eisenbeiss, *Chairman*
Gary Gayton, *Sales Mgr*
John Burgher, *Manager*
EMP: 108
SQ FT: 20,000
SALES (est): 6.5MM **Privately Held**
SIC: 3953 Screens, textile printing

(G-2715)
ULTRAPEDICS LTD (PA)
355 Ovington Ave Ste 104 (11209-1457)
P.O. Box 90384 (11209-0384)
PHONE 718 748-4806
Eric Schwelke, *President*
Tulio Rivera *Senior Mgr*
EMP: 7
SQ FT: 3,400
SALES (est): 570.3K **Privately Held**
SIC: 3842 5999 Surgical appliances & supplies; artificial limbs

(G-2716)
UNIFIED SOLUTIONS FOR CLG INC
1829 Pacific St (11233-3505)
PHONE 718 782-8800
Fax: 718 782-8801
Mendel Jacobowitz, *President*
Lipa Jacobovitz, *Vice Pres*
EMP: 15 **EST:** 2009
SALES (est): 3MM **Privately Held**
SIC: 2869 Butadiene (industrial organic chemical)

(G-2717)
UNIFORMS BY PARK COATS INC
790 3rd Ave (11232-1510)
PHONE 718 499-1182
Fax: 718 499-1646
Nick Haymandos, *President*
Despina Haymandos, *Vice Pres*
Mary Jane, *Manager*
EMP: 28 **EST:** 1973
SQ FT: 8,000
SALES (est): 2.9MM **Privately Held**
WEB: www.uniformsbypark.com
SIC: 2311 2337 Men's & boys' uniforms; uniforms, except athletic: women's, misses' & juniors'

(G-2718)
UNIMED OPTICAL (PA)
175 Marcy Ave (11211-6259)
PHONE 718 384-3600
David Cohen, *Principal*
EMP: 7 **EST:** 2014
SALES (est): 1.7MM **Privately Held**
SIC: 3827 Optical instruments & lenses

(G-2719)
UNIMEX CORPORATION
Lee Spring Company Division
1462 62nd St (11219-5413)
PHONE 718 236-2222
Albert Mangels, *President*
Carmela Papagni, *Chf Purch Ofc*
Richard Carpaino, *Sales Mgr*
John Salvaggio, *Manager*
EMP: 160
SALES (corp-wide): 43.6MM **Privately Held**
SIC: 3495 Mechanical springs, precision
PA: Unimex Corporation
54 E 64th St
New York NY 10065
212 755-8800

(G-2720)
UNITED GEMDIAM INC
Also Called: UGI
1537 52nd St (11219-3910)
PHONE 718 851-5083
Morris Friedman, *President*
Isaac Friedman, *Office Mgr*
EMP: 43
SQ FT: 5,000
SALES (est): 2.8MM **Privately Held**
WEB: www.ugi.com
SIC: 3915 5094 Diamond cutting & polishing; diamonds (gems)

(G-2721)
UNITED PLASTICS INC
640 Humboldt St Ste 1 (11222-4121)
P.O. Box 220363 (11222-0363)
PHONE 718 389-2255
Mike Reno, *Vice Pres*
Charles Smiley, *Sales Executive*
Gary Mayo, *Manager*
Kenneth Farina, *Manager*
EMP: 7
SALES (corp-wide): 1.6MM **Privately Held**
SIC: 2673 3089 Plastic bags: made from purchased materials; plastic processing
PA: United Plastics, Inc
219 Nassau Ave
Brooklyn NY
718 389-2255

(G-2722)
UNITED SHIP REPAIR INC
54 Richards St (11231-1626)
PHONE 718 237-2800
Jim Tampakis, *President*
EMP: 10 **EST:** 1975
SALES (est): 890K **Privately Held**
SIC: 3731 Shipbuilding & repairing; military ships, building & repairing

(G-2723)
UNITED TRANSIT MIX INC
318 Boerum St (11206-3505)
P.O. Box 370647 (11237-0647)
PHONE 718 416-3400
Fax: 718 416-4329
Tony Mastronardi, *President*
EMP: 14
SALES (est): 4MM **Privately Held**
SIC: 3273 Ready-mixed concrete

(G-2724)
UNITED WIND INC
20 Jay St Ste 928 (11201-8354)
PHONE 800 268-9896
Russell Tencer, *CEO*
Aaron Lubowitz, *COO*
Dan Svejnar, *COO*
Jodhi Tarr, *Vice Pres*
Joseph Yurcisin, *Vice Pres*
EMP: 19 **EST:** 2013
SALES (est): 3.9MM **Privately Held**
SIC: 3443 Wind tunnels

(G-2725)
UNIVERSAL COOLERS INC
120 13th St (11215-4604)
PHONE 718 788-8621
Gregory Uchitel, *Ch of Bd*
▲ **EMP:** 6 **EST:** 1995
SALES (est): 1.1MM **Privately Held**
SIC: 3585 Parts for heating, cooling & refrigerating equipment

(G-2726)
UNIVERSAL FIRE PROOF DOOR
1171 Myrtle Ave (11206-6007)
PHONE 718 455-8442
Abelardo Galicia, *President*
Al Bender, *Finance Other*
Mendy Deutch, *Sales Executive*
Joseph Epstein, *Executive*
EMP: 25 **EST:** 1924
SQ FT: 24,000
SALES (est): 4.9MM **Privately Held**
SIC: 3442 Fire doors, metal

(G-2727)
UNIVERSAL PARENT AND YOUTH
Also Called: Upayori
1530 Pa Ave Apt 17e (11239-2620)
PHONE 917 754-2426
Vincent Riggins, *Exec Dir*
EMP: 10
SALES (est): 537.8K **Privately Held**
SIC: 3585 Refrigeration & heating equipment

(G-2728)
UNIVERSAL SCREENING ASSOCIATES
Also Called: USA Tees.com
6509 11th Ave (11219-5602)
PHONE 718 232-2744
Fax: 718 232-3793
David Cardinale, *President*
Jodi Cardinale, *Sales Executive*
Eugene Polishchuk, *Graphic Designe*
▲ **EMP:** 12
SQ FT: 500
SALES: 500K **Privately Held**
SIC: 2759 Screen printing

(G-2729)
UNIVERSAL STEEL FABRICATORS
90 Junius St (11212-8029)
PHONE 718 342-0782
Fax: 718 342-0382
Harvinder Paul, *President*
Emilio Franza, *Treasurer*
EMP: 15
SQ FT: 3,500
SALES: 1MM **Privately Held**
SIC: 3446 5051 1799 Architectural metalwork; structural shapes, iron or steel; fence construction

(G-2730)
URBAN WOODWORKS LTD
18 Crescent St (11208-1516)
PHONE 718 827-1570
Gewan Bharatlall, *President*
Gabriela Bharatlall, *Vice Pres*
Akela Etienne-Forbes, *Admin Mgr*
EMP: 5
SALES: 1.8MM **Privately Held**
SIC: 2431 Millwork

(G-2731)
US CONCRETE INC
Also Called: Kings Material
692 Mcdonald Ave (11218-4914)
PHONE 718 438-6800
Robert Bruzzese, *Branch Mgr*
EMP: 20
SALES (corp-wide): 1.1B **Publicly Held**
SIC: 3273 Ready-mixed concrete
PA: U.S. Concrete, Inc.
331 N Main St
Euless TX 76039
817 835-4105

(G-2732)
US HISPANIC MEDIA INC (DH)
1 Metrotech Ctr Fl 18 (11201-3948)
PHONE 212 885-8000
Eduardo Lomanto, *President*
EMP: 7
SALES (est): 61.7MM **Privately Held**
SIC: 2711 Newspapers: publishing only, not printed on site

(G-2733)
VAAD LHAFOTZAS SICHOES
788 Eastern Pkwy (11213-3409)
PHONE 718 778-5436
Fax: 718 774-7494
Zalmen Chanin, *President*
Nachman Shapiro, *Treasurer*
Sholom Jacobson, *Admin Sec*
▲ **EMP:** 13
SQ FT: 10,000
SALES: 1MM **Privately Held**
SIC: 2731 Books: publishing only

(G-2734)
VALENTINE PRINTING CORP
509 E 79th St (11236-3134)
P.O. Box 940096, Rockaway Park (11694-0096)
PHONE 718 444-4400
Fax: 718 444-3722
Herb Villanueva, *President*
Raymond Villanueva, *Med Doctor*
EMP: 5
SQ FT: 2,200
SALES (est): 460K **Privately Held**
SIC: 2752 Commercial printing, offset

(G-2735)
VAN BLARCOM CLOSURES INC (PA)
156 Sanford St (11205)
PHONE 718 855-3810
Vincent Scuderi Jr, *Ch of Bd*
Ron Camuto, *Vice Pres*
Anthony Scuderi, *QC Mgr*
John Scuderi, *Treasurer*
Amir S Maximos, *Controller*
▲ **EMP:** 195 **EST:** 1947
SQ FT: 160,000
SALES: 49.3MM **Privately Held**
WEB: www.vbcpkg.com
SIC: 3089 3466 3549 Closures, plastic; caps, plastic; closures, stamped metal; bottle caps & tops, stamped metal; jar tops & crowns, stamped metal; assembly machines, including robotic

(G-2736)
VAN LEEUWEN ARTISAN ICE CREAM
56 Dobbin St (11222-3110)
PHONE 718 701-1630
Ben Van Leeuwen, *Principal*
▲ **EMP:** 7
SALES (est): 446K **Privately Held**
SIC: 2024 Ice cream & frozen desserts

(G-2737)
VANS INC
25 Franklin St (11222-2007)
PHONE 718 349-2311
EMP: 10
SALES (corp-wide): 12B **Publicly Held**
SIC: 3021 Canvas shoes, rubber soled
HQ: Vans, Inc.
6550 Katella Ave
Cypress CA 90630
714 889-6100

(G-2738)
VAPE4STYLE INC
1762 Gerritsen Ave (11229-2613)
PHONE 718 395-0406
EMP: 7
SALES (est): 94.4K **Privately Held**
SIC: 3999 Cigar & cigarette holders

(G-2739)
VENTURE RESPIRATORY INC
1413 38th St (11218-3613)
PHONE 718 437-3633
Moshe Richard, *President*
Barry Zee, *Purchasing*
ARI Pearl, *Office Mgr*
EMP: 13
SQ FT: 5,000
SALES (est): 2.8MM **Privately Held**
WEB: www.venturerespiratory.com
SIC: 3842 Respiratory protection equipment, personal

(G-2740)
VERSO INC
20 Jay St Ste 1010 (11201-8346)
PHONE 718 246-8160
Jacob Stevens, *Director*
EMP: 8
SQ FT: 2,500
SALES: 959.9K **Privately Held**
SIC: 2731 Book publishing
PA: New Left Books Limited
6 Meard Street
London
207 437-3546

GEOGRAPHIC SECTION

Brooklyn - Kings County (G-2768)

(G-2741)
VIAMEDIA CORPORATION
2610 Atlantic Ave (11207-2415)
PHONE..................718 485-7792
James Underwood, *President*
Michael Underwood, *Vice Pres*
EMP: 5
SQ FT: 3,200
SALES (est): 272.5K **Privately Held**
WEB: www.via-indy.com
SIC: 2741 Miscellaneous publishing

(G-2742)
VICTORIA FINE FOODS LLC (DH)
443 E 100th St (11236-2103)
PHONE..................718 649-1635
Tim Shanley, *CEO*
Brian Dean, *President*
Gerald Aquilina, *Senior VP*
Jerry Aquilina, *Vice Pres*
Kevin Oliva, *Maintenance Dir*
◆ **EMP:** 100 **EST:** 2011
SQ FT: 90,000
SALES (est): 43.7MM
SALES (corp-wide): 1.3B **Publicly Held**
SIC: 2035 2099 2033 5149 Pickles, sauces & salad dressings; spices, including grinding; canned fruits & specialties; pasta & rice
HQ: Victoria Fine Foods Holding Company
443 E 100th St
Brooklyn NY 11236
718 649-1635

(G-2743)
VICTORY VISION CARE INC
565 Atlantic Ave (11217-1913)
PHONE..................718 622-2020
Fax: 718 622-5404
Viktor Kolesnyk, *President*
EMP: 9
SALES (est): 960K **Privately Held**
SIC: 3827 Optical instruments & lenses

(G-2744)
VIKING MAR WLDG SHIP REPR LLC
14 Raleigh Pl (11226-4218)
PHONE..................718 758-4116
Floyd Ricketts,
EMP: 10
SALES (est): 520.5K **Privately Held**
SIC: 3731 Shipbuilding & repairing

(G-2745)
VINEGAR HILL ASSET LLC
436 E 34th St (11203-5034)
PHONE..................718 469-0342
EMP: 5 **EST:** 2015
SALES (est): 83K **Privately Held**
SIC: 2099 Vinegar

(G-2746)
VINELAND KOSHER POULTRY INC
Also Called: Poultry Dist
5600 1st Ave A7 (11220-2550)
PHONE..................718 921-1347
Fax: 718 921-8913
Armin Silberstein, *Finance Mgr*
David Lefkowitz, *Systems Mgr*
EMP: 10
SALES (corp-wide): 19.3MM **Privately Held**
WEB: www.vinelandkosherpoultry.com
SIC: 2015 5144 Poultry slaughtering & processing; poultry & poultry products
PA: Vineland Kosher Poultry Inc
1050 S Mill Rd
Vineland NJ 08360
856 692-1871

(G-2747)
VIRGINIA DARE EXTRACT CO INC (PA)
Also Called: V & E Kohnstamm & Co Div
882 3rd Ave Unit 2 (11232-1902)
PHONE..................718 788-6320
Fax: 718 768-3978
Howard Smith Jr, *President*
Stephen Balter, *Vice Pres*
Laura McCord, *Purchasing*
◆ **EMP:** 147
SQ FT: 165,000
SALES (est): 42.1MM **Privately Held**
SIC: 2087 Flavoring extracts & syrups; extracts, flavoring

(G-2748)
VIRTUALAPT CORP
45 Main St Ste 613 (11201-1099)
PHONE..................917 293-3173
Bryan Colin, *CEO*
EMP: 8
SALES (est): 363.8K **Privately Held**
SIC: 3812 Search & detection systems & instruments; distance measuring equipment

(G-2749)
VISITAINER CORP
Also Called: Plastifold Industries Division
148 Classon Ave (11205-2637)
PHONE..................718 636-0300
Fax: 718 636-0302
William Lefkovitz, *President*
William Leskowitz, *Manager*
EMP: 25 **EST:** 1962
SQ FT: 30,000
SALES (est): 2.2MM **Privately Held**
SIC: 2657 3089 Folding paperboard boxes; plastic containers, except foam

(G-2750)
VISTA PACKAGING INC
1425 37th St Ste 6 (11218-3769)
PHONE..................718 854-9200
William Schwartz, *President*
Judy Weinberg, *Accounts Mgr*
▲ **EMP:** 35 **EST:** 2000
SQ FT: 43,000
SALES (est): 5.3MM **Privately Held**
WEB: www.vistatubes.com
SIC: 3085 Plastics bottles

(G-2751)
VITAROSE CORP OF AMERICA
2615 Nostrand Ave Ste 1 (11210-4643)
PHONE..................718 951-9700
Joe Derose, *President*
EMP: 6 **EST:** 1959
SQ FT: 2,625
SALES: 1MM **Privately Held**
SIC: 2541 3231 3089 3444 Window backs, store or lunchroom, prefabricated: wood; products of purchased glass; awnings, fiberglass & plastic combination; awnings & canopies

(G-2752)
VITO & SONS BAKERY
Also Called: Mima S Bakery
1423 72nd St (11228-1711)
PHONE..................201 617-8501
Fax: 201 864-3088
Vito Bavaro, *Owner*
EMP: 10
SALES (est): 612.1K **Privately Held**
SIC: 2051 Bread, cake & related products

(G-2753)
VLINE INC
81 Prospect St (11201-1473)
PHONE..................512 222-5464
Jack Strong, *CEO*
EMP: 5
SALES (est): 295.8K **Privately Held**
SIC: 7372 Utility computer software

(G-2754)
VOLCKENING INC (PA)
6700 3rd Ave (11220-5296)
PHONE..................718 748-0294
Fax: 718 748-2811
William J Schneider, *Ch of Bd*
Frederick C Schneider, *President*
Henry Schneider, *Vice Pres*
Michael Rutigliano, *Mfg Staff*
James Pelosis, *Engineer*
EMP: 45
SQ FT: 30,000
SALES (est): 6.6MM **Privately Held**
WEB: www.volckening.com
SIC: 3565 3991 Packaging machinery; brushes, household or industrial

(G-2755)
VOODOO MANUFACTURING INC
361 Stagg St Ste 408 (11206-1743)
PHONE..................646 893-8366
Max Friefeld, *CEO*
EMP: 5
SALES (est): 100K **Privately Held**
SIC: 3555 Printing trades machinery

(G-2756)
VSG INTERNATIONAL LLC
Also Called: Kustom Collabo
196 Clinton Ave Apt A2 (11205-3411)
PHONE..................718 300-8171
Yusef Sirius-El, *Mng Member*
Nicholas Vasilopoulos,
▲ **EMP:** 5 **EST:** 2012
SQ FT: 5,000
SALES (est): 311.8K **Privately Held**
SIC: 3149 Athletic shoes, except rubber or plastic

(G-2757)
W E W CONTAINER CORPORATION
189 Wyona St (11207-3009)
PHONE..................718 827-8150
Daniel Weicher, *Branch Mgr*
EMP: 20
SALES (corp-wide): 3.5MM **Privately Held**
SIC: 2673 2671 Bags: plastic, laminated & coated; plastic film, coated or laminated for packaging
PA: W E W Container Corporation
200 Bradford St
Brooklyn NY
718 827-8150

(G-2758)
WALLY PACKAGING INC (HQ)
1168 E 21st St (11210-3618)
PHONE..................718 377-5323
Fax: 718 258-2324
Ray Wallerstein, *President*
Chumie Wallerstein, *Vice Pres*
▲ **EMP:** 5
SQ FT: 15,000
SALES: 607.1K
SALES (corp-wide): 1.1MM **Privately Held**
SIC: 2673 Bags: plastic, laminated & coated
PA: Quest Packaging Llc
525 E County Line Rd # 8
Lakewood NJ 08701
732 276-7767

(G-2759)
WALTER P SAUER LLC
Also Called: Morris Fine Furniture Workshop
276 Greenpoint Ave # 8400 (11222-2434)
PHONE..................718 937-0600
Renee Tavares, *Accounts Mgr*
Andrew Dron, *Manager*
Anthony Morris,
Shanika Hudson, *Admin Sec*
EMP: 43
SQ FT: 2,100
SALES (est): 2MM **Privately Held**
WEB: www.walterpsauer.com
SIC: 2511 Wood household furniture

(G-2760)
WARNACO INC
70 Washington St Fl 10 (11201-1442)
PHONE..................718 722-3000
Smitty Seelall, *Branch Mgr*
EMP: 10
SALES (corp-wide): 8.2B **Publicly Held**
WEB: www.warnaco.com
SIC: 2342 2341 2321 2253 Bras, girdles & allied garments; brassieres; girdles & panty girdles; panties: women's, misses', children's & infants'; women's & children's nightwear; men's & boys' dress shirts; shirts (outerwear), knit; sweaters & sweater coats, knit; athletic (warmup, sweat & jogging) suits: men's & boys'; underwear, men's & boys': made from purchased materials
HQ: Warnaco Inc.
501 Fashion Ave Fl 14
New York NY 10018
212 287-8000

(G-2761)
WATERMARK DESIGNS HOLDINGS LTD
350 Dewitt Ave (11207-6618)
PHONE..................718 257-2800
AVI Abel, *President*
Jack Abel, *Vice Pres*
▲ **EMP:** 55
SQ FT: 20,000
SALES (est): 10.5MM **Privately Held**
SIC: 3431 3432 Bathroom fixtures, including sinks; plumbing fixture fittings & trim

(G-2762)
WETLOOK DETAILING INC
1125 Banner Ave Apt 11a (11235-5267)
PHONE..................212 390-8877
Dylan Valentine, *COO*
EMP: 8 **EST:** 2016
SALES (est): 364.1K **Privately Held**
SIC: 3589 Car washing machinery

(G-2763)
WG SHEET METAL CORP
341 Amber St (11208-5104)
PHONE..................718 235-3093
Andy Tolta, *Admin Sec*
EMP: 5
SALES: 700K **Privately Held**
SIC: 3444 Sheet metalwork

(G-2764)
WHITLEY EAST LLC
Brooklyn Navy Yd Bg 2 Fl (11205)
PHONE..................718 403-0050
William McShane, *General Mgr*
EMP: 79
SALES (corp-wide): 96.7MM **Privately Held**
WEB: www.capsyscorp.com
SIC: 2452 Modular homes, prefabricated, wood
HQ: Whitley East, Llc
64 Hess Rd
Leola PA 17540
717 656-2081

(G-2765)
WIDE FLANGE INC
176 27th St (11232-1625)
PHONE..................718 492-8705
Joyce Cavagnaro, *President*
Blaze Bono, *Vice Pres*
Annette Opulente, *Manager*
EMP: 11
SQ FT: 5,500
SALES: 1.8MM **Privately Held**
SIC: 3449 Bars, concrete reinforcing: fabricated steel

(G-2766)
WIGGBY PRECISION MACHINE CORP
140 58th St Ste 56 (11220-2526)
PHONE..................718 439-6900
Ronald Wiggberg, *CEO*
Robert G Wiggberg, *Corp Secy*
EMP: 30 **EST:** 1949
SALES (est): 4.4MM **Privately Held**
SIC: 3599 Machine shop, jobbing & repair

(G-2767)
WILCO FINISHING CORP
1288 Willoughby Ave (11237-2905)
P.O. Box 370708 (11237-0708)
PHONE..................718 417-6405
Julius Medwin, *Principal*
Bob Augi, *Vice Pres*
EMP: 38
SQ FT: 20,000
SALES (est): 3.3MM **Privately Held**
WEB: www.wilcoplating.com
SIC: 3471 Plating & polishing

(G-2768)
WILLIAM BROOKS WOODWORKING
856 Saratoga Ave (11212-4350)
PHONE..................718 495-9767
William Brooks, *Owner*

Brooklyn - Kings County (G-2769)

EMP: 10
SALES: 275K Privately Held
SIC: 2434 Wood kitchen cabinets

(G-2769)
WILLIAM HARVEY STUDIO INC
214 N 8th St (11211-2008)
PHONE..................................718 599-4343
William Harvey, *President*
Reed Harvey, *Admin Sec*
EMP: 5
SQ FT: 2,500
SALES (est): 290K Privately Held
WEB: www.williamharveydesign.com
SIC: 2392 Household furnishings

(G-2770)
WILLIAM KANES MFG CORP
23 Alabama Ave (11207-2303)
PHONE..................................718 346-1515
Fax: 718 346-1537
William Kanes, *President*
EMP: 7
SQ FT: 5,000
SALES: 500K Privately Held
SIC: 3444 3599 Sheet metalwork; machine shop, jobbing & repair

(G-2771)
WILLIAMSBURG BULLETIN
136 Ross St (11211-7705)
PHONE..................................718 387-0123
EMP: 6
SALES (est): 377.9K Privately Held
SIC: 2711 Newspapers, publishing & printing

(G-2772)
WIND PRODUCTS INC
20 Jay St Ste 936 (11201-8354)
PHONE..................................212 292-3135
Russell Tencer, *President*
William Jacoby, *Vice Pres*
Jian Sun, *Consultant*
EMP: 6
SALES (est): 500K Privately Held
SIC: 3511 Turbines & turbine generator sets

(G-2773)
WINDOW-FIX INC
331 37th St Fl 1 (11232-2505)
PHONE..................................718 854-3475
Ernesto Cappello, *President*
John Cappello, *Vice Pres*
Louie Rinaldi, *Manager*
EMP: 20
SALES (est): 3.3MM Privately Held
SIC: 3211 1751 7699 Window glass, clear & colored; window & door installation & erection; window blind repair services

(G-2774)
WINDOWMAN INC (USA)
460 Kingsland Ave (11222-1906)
PHONE..................................718 246-2626
Fax: 718 246-2455
Bruce Schmuter, *President*
EMP: 6
SALES (est): 630K Privately Held
WEB: www.windowmanusa.com
SIC: 3442 3699 1796 1751 Metal doors, sash & trim; door opening & closing devices, electrical; installing building equipment; window & door installation & erection; safety & security specialization

(G-2775)
WINDOWS MEDIA PUBLISHING LLC
369 Remsen Ave (11212-1245)
PHONE..................................917 732-7892
Mark McLean, *Vice Pres*
EMP: 25
SALES (est): 759K Privately Held
SIC: 2731 Books: publishing & printing

(G-2776)
WINGHING 8 LTD
6215 6th Ave (11220-4704)
PHONE..................................718 439-0021
Jennifer Hui, *President*
Frank Wong, *Manager*
EMP: 6
SQ FT: 59,640
SALES (est): 666.2K Privately Held
SIC: 2679 Paperboard products, converted

(G-2777)
WINTER WATER FACTORY
191 33rd St (11232-2109)
PHONE..................................646 387-3247
Stefanie Lynen, *Owner*
EMP: 6
SALES (est): 250K Privately Held
SIC: 2253 Dresses, knit

(G-2778)
WONTON FOOD INC (PA)
220 Moore St 222 (11206-3708)
PHONE..................................718 628-6868
Norman Wong, *CEO*
Ching Sun Wong, *Ch of Bd*
Foo Kam Wong, *Vice Pres*
Jian Chen, *VP Opers*
Ralph Chan, *Plant Mgr*
▲ EMP: 160
SQ FT: 55,000
SALES (est): 76.5MM Privately Held
WEB: www.wontonfood.com
SIC: 2099 2052 5149 Noodles, fried (Chinese); cookies; canned goods: fruit, vegetables, seafood, meats, etc.

(G-2779)
WOODWARD/WHITE INC
45 Main St Ste 820 (11201-1076)
PHONE..................................718 509-6082
Bradley Silberberg, *Branch Mgr*
EMP: 10
SALES (corp-wide): 7.6MM Privately Held
SIC: 2731 Book publishing
PA: Woodward/White, Inc.
  237 Park Ave Sw
  Aiken SC 29801
  803 648-0300

(G-2780)
WORLD CHEESE CO INC
178 28th St (11232-1604)
PHONE..................................718 965-1700
Leo S Thurm, *President*
Meyer Thurm, *President*
Easter Swartz, *Controller*
Sruly Sherer, *VP Sales*
Jay Sherer, *Marketing Staff*
◆ EMP: 16
SQ FT: 25,000
SALES (est): 4.8MM Privately Held
SIC: 2022 Cheese, natural & processed; cheese spreads, dips, pastes & other cheese products

(G-2781)
WORLD JOURNAL LLC
6007 8th Ave (11220-4337)
PHONE..................................718 871-5000
Fax: 718 871-5024
Boby Chou, *CEO*
EMP: 12
SALES (corp-wide): 54.9MM Privately Held
WEB: www.wjnews.net
SIC: 2711 Newspapers, publishing & printing
HQ: World Journal Llc
  14107 20th Ave Fl 2
  Whitestone NY 11357
  718 746-8889

(G-2782)
WORLDS FINEST CHOCOLATE INC
73 Exeter St (11235-3703)
PHONE..................................718 332-2442
Edward Opler Jr, *CEO*
EMP: 150
SALES (corp-wide): 207.7MM Privately Held
SIC: 2064 Candy & other confectionery products
PA: World's Finest Chocolate, Inc.
  4801 S Lawndale Ave
  Chicago IL 60632
  773 847-4600

(G-2783)
WORLDWIDE RESOURCES INC
1908 Avenue O (11230-6721)
PHONE..................................718 760-5000
David Pick, *President*
EMP: 16 EST: 2012
SQ FT: 1,200
SALES (est): 994.3K Privately Held
SIC: 3324 Aerospace investment castings, ferrous

(G-2784)
XSTATIC PRO INC
Proxcases
901 Essex St (11208-5317)
PHONE..................................718 237-2299
Gabriel Menashe, *Branch Mgr*
EMP: 11
SALES (corp-wide): 686.8K Privately Held
SIC: 3161 Musical instrument cases
PA: Xstatic Pro, Inc.
  901 Essex St
  Brooklyn NY 11208
  718 237-2299

(G-2785)
Y & A TRADING INC
Also Called: Sukkah Center
1365 38th St (11218-3634)
PHONE..................................718 436-6333
Joe Biston, *President*
▲ EMP: 10
SALES (est): 771.9K Privately Held
WEB: www.sukkah.com
SIC: 2394 5999 Canvas & related products; religious goods

(G-2786)
YALOZ MOULD & DIE CO INC
Also Called: Yaloz Mold & Die
239 Java St Fl 2 (11222-1893)
PHONE..................................718 389-1131
Fax: 718 389-5997
Yehuda Leon Yaloz, *President*
EMP: 30
SQ FT: 45,000
SALES (est): 2.6MM Privately Held
SIC: 2542 3429 Fixtures, store: except wood; manufactured hardware (general)

(G-2787)
YEPES FINE FURNITURE
72 Van Dam St (11222-3807)
PHONE..................................718 383-0221
Tiberio Yepes, *Owner*
EMP: 20
SALES (est): 1.4MM Privately Held
SIC: 2512 5712 Upholstered household furniture; furniture stores

(G-2788)
YOFAH RELIGIOUS ARTICLES INC
2001 57th St Ste 1 (11204-2035)
PHONE..................................718 435-3288
Jacob Leser, *President*
▲ EMP: 13
SQ FT: 2,000
SALES: 1.4MM Privately Held
SIC: 3911 Rosaries or other small religious articles, precious metal

(G-2789)
YOLAND CORPORATION
253 36th St Unit 2 (11232-2415)
PHONE..................................718 499-4803
Ayal Adler, *President*
Roni Ginat, *General Mgr*
Tal Ganet, *Vice Pres*
ADI Ginat, *Manager*
EMP: 40
SQ FT: 8,000
SALES (est): 4.8MM Privately Held
WEB: www.yolandcorp.com
SIC: 2399 Parachutes
PA: D. Yoland Ltd.
  17 Hamasger
  Netanya

(G-2790)
YORK FUEL INCORPORATED
1760 Flatbush Ave (11210-4203)
PHONE..................................718 951-0202
Gurmeet Singh Buttar, *President*
EMP: 6
SALES (est): 598.7K Privately Held
SIC: 2869 Fuels

(G-2791)
YS MARKETING INC
Also Called: Numed Pharmaceuticals
2004 Mcdonald Ave (11223-2819)
PHONE..................................718 778-6080
Joel Silberstein, *President*
Joy Azar, *Administration*
EMP: 20
SALES: 15MM Privately Held
SIC: 2834 Pharmaceutical preparations

(G-2792)
Z-STUDIOS DSIGN FBRICATION LLC
30 Haven Pl (11233-3408)
PHONE..................................347 512-4210
Zachary Zaus,
EMP: 5
SQ FT: 2,500
SALES (est): 200K Privately Held
SIC: 3446 Architectural metalwork

(G-2793)
ZAM BARRETT DIALOGUE INC
128 32nd St 112 (11232-1920)
PHONE..................................646 649-0140
Zam Barrett, *CEO*
EMP: 9
SQ FT: 2,000
SALES: 300K Privately Held
SIC: 2389 Men's miscellaneous accessories

(G-2794)
ZAN OPTICS PRODUCTS INC
982 39th St (11219-1035)
P.O. Box 110695, Lakewood Rch FL (34211-0009)
PHONE..................................718 435-0533
Fax: 718 435-8215
Walter Mazzanti, *President*
Kathy Mazzanti, *Vice Pres*
EMP: 25 EST: 1933
SQ FT: 10,000
SALES (est): 2MM Privately Held
WEB: www.zanenterprises.com
SIC: 2759 3089 2789 2396 Engraving; plastic processing; molding primary plastic; bookbinding & related work; automotive & apparel trimmings

(G-2795)
ZIPARI INC
45 Main St Ste 406 (11201-1084)
PHONE..................................855 558-7884
Mark Nathan, *CEO*
Janelle Taylor, *Marketing Staff*
EMP: 50
SALES (est): 814K Privately Held
SIC: 7372 Application computer software

(G-2796)
ZOOMERS INC (PA)
Also Called: Liz Lange
32 33rd St (11232-1901)
PHONE..................................718 369-2656
Fax: 212 244-1372
Gary Jay Schulman, *CEO*
Deborah Schulman, *President*
Wayne Sternberg, *Vice Pres*
▲ EMP: 28
SQ FT: 20,000
SALES (est): 5.2MM Privately Held
SIC: 2339 Maternity clothing; sportswear, women's

Brownville
Jefferson County

(G-2797)
FLORELLE TISSUE CORPORATION
1 Bridge St (13615-7765)
PHONE..................................647 997-7405
Harry Minas, *President*
▲ EMP: 50
SALES (est): 1.2MM Privately Held
SIC: 2676 Towels, napkins & tissue paper products

▲ = Import ▼ = Export
◆ = Import/Export

GEOGRAPHIC SECTION

Buffalo - Erie County (G-2823)

(G-2798)
NEENAH NORTHEAST LLC
101 Bridge St (13615)
PHONE.................................315 782-5800
Joe Hurd, *Branch Mgr*
Larry Kiefer, *Manager*
EMP: 80
SALES (corp-wide): 941.5MM **Publicly Held**
SIC: 2631 2621 Pressboard; specialty papers
HQ: Neenah Northeast, Llc
  70 Front St
  West Springfield MA 01089
  413 533-0699

Buchanan
Westchester County

(G-2799)
CONTINENTAL BUCHANAN LLC
350 Broadway (10511-1000)
PHONE.................................703 480-3800
Ike Preston, *President*
Dennis Romps, *CFO*
Robbe Pearson, *Director*
▲ **EMP:** 100
SALES (est): 9.3MM **Privately Held**
SIC: 2493 3275 2891 Building board & wallboard, except gypsum; building board, gypsum; sealing compounds for pipe threads or joints

(G-2800)
LAFARGE NORTH AMERICA INC
350 Broadway (10511-1000)
PHONE.................................914 930-3027
Criss Fraley, *Opers-Prdtn-Mfg*
James Tierney, *Sales Mgr*
Christopher Conrad, *Maintence Staff*
EMP: 100
SALES (corp-wide): 26.6B **Privately Held**
SIC: 3241 3275 Cement, hydraulic; gypsum products
HQ: Lafarge North America Inc.
  8700 W Bryn Mawr Ave Li
  Chicago IL 60631
  703 480-3600

(G-2801)
SILVA CABINETRY INC
12 White St Ste C (10511-1665)
PHONE.................................914 737-7697
Fax: 914 737-7553
Antonio Dasilva, *President*
Xiomara Machado, *Admin Sec*
EMP: 25
SALES (est): 2.9MM **Privately Held**
SIC: 2434 Wood kitchen cabinets

Buffalo
Erie County

(G-2802)
260 OAK STREET INC
260 Oak St (14203-1626)
PHONE.................................877 852-4676
Glenn Snyder, *Ch of Bd*
EMP: 5
SQ FT: 6,233
SALES (est): 423.6K **Privately Held**
SIC: 2542 Cabinets: show, display or storage: except wood

(G-2803)
4695 MAIN STREET SNYDER INC
Also Called: Industrial Elec & Automtn
358 Walton Dr (14226-4846)
PHONE.................................716 833-3270
Herb Segiel, *President*
EMP: 6
SALES (corp-wide): 492.2K **Privately Held**
SIC: 3535 7699 Conveyors & conveying equipment; industrial machinery & equipment repair
PA: 4695 Main Street Snyder, Inc
  4695 Main St
  Amherst NY

(G-2804)
5TH & OCEAN CLOTHING INC
160 Delaware Ave (14202-2404)
PHONE.................................716 604-9000
Daisy Reyes, *Controller*
Robert Fonseca, *Sales Dir*
Luis Leiter Jr, *Mng Member*
Alex A Leiter, *Director*
Esther Fung-Pontiff, *Director*
◆ **EMP:** 115
SQ FT: 40,000
SALES (est): 10.9MM
SALES (corp-wide): 529.4MM **Privately Held**
WEB: www.5thocean.com
SIC: 2339 Women's & misses' outerwear; women's & misses' accessories
PA: New Era Cap Co., Inc.
  160 Delaware Ave
  Buffalo NY 14202
  716 604-9000

(G-2805)
760 NL HOLDINGS
760 Northland Ave (14211-1041)
PHONE.................................716 821-1391
Fax: 716 821-1380
Daryl Zurawski, *General Mgr*
Tim George, *Principal*
EMP: 30
SQ FT: 20,000
SALES (est): 8.4MM **Privately Held**
WEB: www.nfcf.net
SIC: 3441 Fabricated structural metal

(G-2806)
A J M ENTERPRISES
348 Cayuga Rd (14225-1927)
PHONE.................................716 626-7294
Fax: 716 626-6717
Jarek Chelpinski, *Partner*
EMP: 10
SALES (est): 546.9K **Privately Held**
SIC: 3915 Jewelers' castings

(G-2807)
A-FAB INITIATIVES INC
99 Bud Mil Dr (14206-1801)
PHONE.................................716 877-5257
Edward Raimonde, *President*
◆ **EMP:** 7
SALES (est): 886.4K **Privately Held**
SIC: 3441 3354 Fabricated structural metal; aluminum extruded products

(G-2808)
ACCENTA INCORPORATED
150 Lawrence Bell Dr # 108 (14221-8403)
PHONE.................................716 565-6262
Ulf Ernetoft, *Owner*
EMP: 5 **EST:** 2012
SALES (est): 422.5K **Privately Held**
SIC: 3999 Advertising display products

(G-2809)
ACCESS PRODUCTS INC
241 Main St Ste 100 (14203-2703)
PHONE.................................800 679-4022
Kenneth E J Szekely, *President*
Sean Morrison, *Principal*
David Murray, *Vice Pres*
George Kozman, *Controller*
EMP: 6
SALES (est): 5.3MM **Privately Held**
SIC: 3272 Building materials, except block or brick: concrete

(G-2810)
ACCUMED CORP
2564 Walden Ave Ste 101 (14225-4759)
PHONE.................................716 853-1800
EMP: 7
SALES (corp-wide): 96.8MM **Privately Held**
SIC: 3841 Medical instruments & equipment, blood & bone work
PA: Accumed Corp.
  155 Boyce Dr
  Mocksville NC 27028
  800 278-6796

(G-2811)
ACME NIPPLE MFG CO INC
1930 Elmwood Ave (14207-1902)
PHONE.................................716 873-7491
John Hurley, *President*
EMP: 8 **EST:** 1945
SQ FT: 10,000
SALES (est): 1MM **Privately Held**
SIC: 3321 Pressure pipe & fittings, cast iron

(G-2812)
ACME SCREENPRINTING LLC
247 Cayuga Rd Ste 25e (14225-1949)
PHONE.................................716 565-1052
Joe Strepason,
EMP: 7
SALES (est): 275.7K **Privately Held**
SIC: 2759 Screen printing

(G-2813)
ADCO INNVTIVE PRMTNAL PDTS INC
300 Delaware Ave Ste 202 (14202-1807)
PHONE.................................716 805-1076
Fax: 716 805-1228
Antoinette Dugas, *President*
Toni Eldury, *Sales Mgr*
EMP: 5
SALES (est): 850K **Privately Held**
SIC: 2759 Screen printing

(G-2814)
ADM MILLING CO
250 Ganson St (14203-3048)
P.O. Box 487 (14240-0487)
PHONE.................................716 849-7333
Charles Bayless, *Vice Pres*
Andreas Martin, *Vice Pres*
Brad Heald, *Plant Mgr*
Yvette Ceser, *Manager*
George Siradis, *Manager*
EMP: 75
SALES (corp-wide): 62.3B **Publicly Held**
WEB: www.admmilling.com
SIC: 2041 Flour & other grain mill products
HQ: Adm Milling Co.
  8000 W 110th St Ste 300
  Overland Park KS 66210
  913 491-9400

(G-2815)
ADPRO SPORTS LLC
55 Amherst Villa Rd (14225-1432)
PHONE.................................716 854-5116
Ron Raccuia, *President*
Thomas Naples, *Exec VP*
Jeffrey Diebel, *Senior VP*
Paul Schintzius, *Senior VP*
Jason Davis, *Sales Staff*
EMP: 76 **EST:** 2010
SALES (est): 1MM **Privately Held**
SIC: 2329 2339 3949 Men's & boys' sportswear & athletic clothing; women's & misses' athletic clothing & sportswear; team sports equipment

(G-2816)
ADSCO MANUFACTURING CORP
4979 Lake Ave (14219-1398)
PHONE.................................716 827-5450
Fax: 716 827-5460
Gustav Linda, *President*
James Treantis, *Controller*
EMP: 60
SQ FT: 32,000
SALES (est): 12.1MM **Privately Held**
WEB: www.adscomfg.com
SIC: 3441 Expansion joints (structural shapes, iron or steel

(G-2817)
ADVANCED MACHINE DESIGN CO INC
45 Roberts Ave (14206-3130)
PHONE.................................716 826-2000
Fax: 716 826-2394
Heinrich Moelbert, *Ch of Bd*
Reiner Moelbert, *President*
Ursula Moelbert, *Corp Secy*
Trisha Bard, *Admin Sec*
EMP: 30
SQ FT: 102,000

SALES (est): 5.9MM **Privately Held**
WEB: www.amd-co.com
SIC: 3541 3542 8711 3549 Machine tools, metal cutting type; machine tools, metal forming type; presses: hydraulic & pneumatic, mechanical & manual; shearing machines, power; industrial engineers; metalworking machinery; cutlery

(G-2818)
AEP ENVIRONMENTAL LLC
2495 Main St Ste 230 (14214-2156)
PHONE.................................716 446-0739
Lynn Zier, *Mng Member*
Renee Larcom, *Manager*
Anthony Zier, *Admin Sec*
Scott Meacham,
Kenneth Pronti,
EMP: 10
SALES (est): 500K **Privately Held**
SIC: 3646 2844 5122 5047 Commercial indusl & institutional electric lighting fixtures; toilet preparations; drugs, proprietaries & sundries; medical & hospital equipment; household furnishings

(G-2819)
ALLEN BOAT CO INC
370 Babcock St Rear (14206-2802)
PHONE.................................716 842-0800
Fax: 716 842-0113
Thomas Allen Jr, *President*
Michael Huffman, *Vice Pres*
Sharon Hicok, *Controller*
EMP: 6 **EST:** 1961
SQ FT: 10,000
SALES (est): 997.3K **Privately Held**
WEB: www.allenboatco.com
SIC: 3732 2394 Sailboats, building & repairing; sails: made from purchased materials

(G-2820)
ALLIED CIRCUITS LLC
22 James E Casey Dr (14206-2367)
PHONE.................................716 551-0285
Carol Schreckengost, *Vice Pres*
Terrence Hayes, *Prdtn Mgr*
Chester Szewczyk, *Purch Agent*
Jason Litto, *Project Engr*
Chris Aquiline,
EMP: 50
SQ FT: 10,400
SALES (est): 9.6MM **Privately Held**
WEB: www.alliedcircuits.com
SIC: 3613 Panelboards & distribution boards, electric

(G-2821)
ALP STEEL CORP
650 Exchange St (14210-1303)
P.O. Box 1085 (14220-8085)
PHONE.................................716 854-3030
Fax: 716 854-3070
Robert W Waver Jr, *CEO*
John T Klosko, *Project Mgr*
Mike Fetes, *Safety Mgr*
Donna G Waver, *CFO*
Bill Miller, *Manager*
EMP: 39
SQ FT: 126,000
SALES (est): 10.3MM **Privately Held**
WEB: www.alpsteel.com
SIC: 3441 5051 Fabricated structural metal; building components, structural steel; structural shapes, iron or steel

(G-2822)
AMBIND CORP
Cheektowaga (14225)
P.O. Box 886 (14231-0886)
PHONE.................................716 836-4365
David Spiezer, *President*
EMP: 5
SALES (est): 660.1K **Privately Held**
SIC: 2241 Bindings, textile

(G-2823)
AMERICAN CITY BUS JOURNALS INC
465 Main St Ste 100 (14203-1717)
PHONE.................................716 541-1654
Fax: 716 845-7960
Jack Connors, *Principal*
Bo Sunshine, *Marketing Staff*
Donna Collins, *Senior Editor*

Buffalo - Erie County (G-2824)

Sean Connors, *Graphic Designe*
EMP: 32
SALES (corp-wide): 1.5B **Privately Held**
SIC: 2711 Newspapers: publishing only, not printed on site
HQ: American City Business Journals, Inc.
  120 W Morehead St Ste 400
  Charlotte NC 28202
  704 973-1000

(G-2824)
AMERICAN DOUGLAS METALS INC
Also Called: Afab Initiative
99 Bud Mil Dr (14206-1801)
PHONE.................................716 856-3170
Edward Raimonde, *CEO*
Kevin Blake, *Branch Mgr*
EMP: 12
SQ FT: 29,700
SALES (corp-wide): 27.4MM **Privately Held**
WEB: www.americandouglasmetals.com
SIC: 1099 3353 3291 Aluminum ore mining; aluminum sheet, plate & foil; abrasive products
PA: American Douglas Metals, Inc.
  783 Thorpe Rd
  Orlando FL 32824
  407 855-6590

(G-2825)
AMERICAN IMAGES INC
25 Imson St (14210-1615)
PHONE.................................716 825-8888
Fax: 716 821-7991
Steve Wojtkowiak, *President*
EMP: 10
SALES (est): 1.4MM **Privately Held**
SIC: 2397 Schiffli machine embroideries

(G-2826)
AMETA INTERNATIONAL CO LTD
2221 Kenmore Ave Ste 108 (14207-1360)
PHONE.................................416 992-8036
EMP: 6
SALES (est): 571.4K
SALES (corp-wide): 2.2MM **Privately Held**
SIC: 3699 Security control equipment & systems
PA: Ameta International Co. Ltd
  80 Shields Crt
  Markham ON L3R 9
  905 415-1234

(G-2827)
AMHERST MEDIA INC
175 Rano St Ste 200 (14207-2176)
P.O. Box 538 (14213-0538)
PHONE.................................716 874-4450
Fax: 716 874-4508
Craig Alesse *President*
Barbara Lynch-Johnt, *Assoc Editor*
EMP: 5
SALES (est) 705K **Privately Held**
WEB: www.amherstmedia.com
SIC: 2731 7812 Books: publishing only; video production

(G-2828)
AMHERST SYSTEMS INC (DH)
1740 Wehrle Dr (14221-7032)
PHONE.................................716 631-0610
Jeffrey D Palombo, *Ch of Bd*
John Stanfill, *President*
Joshua Johnson, *General Mgr*
Glen Sharpe, *Managing Dir*
Andy Ryan, *Facilities Dir*
EMP: 169
SQ FT: 150,000
SALES (est): 31MM **Publicly Held**
WEB: www.amherst-systems.com
SIC: 3812 8731 7373 Search & navigation equipment; radar systems & equipment; commercial physical research; value-added resellers, computer systems
HQ: Northrop Grumman Systems Corporation
  2980 Fairview Park Dr
  Falls Church VA 22042
  703 280-2900

(G-2829)
AMSCO INC
925 Bailey Ave (14206-2338)
PHONE.................................716 823-4213
Norm Brodfuhrersrin, *President*
Jack Kraus, *Vice Pres*
Maria Opoka, *Purchasing*
Linda Nowak, *Treasurer*
EMP: 16
SQ FT: 18,000
SALES (est): 1.3MM **Privately Held**
SIC: 3544 3444 Jigs & fixtures; sheet metalwork

(G-2830)
ANDUJAR ASBESTOS AND LEAD
473 4th St (14201-1603)
PHONE.................................716 228-6757
Alfredo Andujar, *President*
David Jones, *Manager*
EMP: 9 **EST:** 2015
SQ FT: 24,000
SALES (est): 200K **Privately Held**
SIC: 3292 Asbestos products

(G-2831)
ANNESE & ASSOCIATES INC
500 Corporate Pkwy # 106 (14226-1263)
PHONE.................................716 972-0076
Raymond Apy, *Branch Mgr*
EMP: 7
SALES (corp-wide): 686.3MM **Privately Held**
SIC: 3577 Data conversion equipment, media-to-media: computer
HQ: Annese & Associates, Inc.
  747 Pierce Rd Ste 2
  Clifton Park NY 12065
  518 877-7058

(G-2832)
ANTIQUES & COLLECTIBLE AUTOS
35 Dole St (14210-1603)
PHONE.................................716 825-3990
Joseph Trombley, *President*
EMP: 3
SALES: 1.6MM **Privately Held**
WEB: www.acrods.com
SIC: 3711 Automobile bodies, passenger car, not including engine, etc.

(G-2833)
ANTONICELLI VITO RACE CAR
3883 Broadway St (14227-1105)
PHONE.................................716 684-2205
Vito Antonicelli, *Owner*
EMP: 5
SQ FT: 6,000
SALES (est): 75K **Privately Held**
SIC: 3711 Motor vehicles & car bodies

(G-2834)
API HEAT TRANSF THERMASYS CORP (HQ)
2777 Walden Ave (14225-4788)
PHONE.................................716 684-6700
Joseph Cordosi, *President*
◆ **EMP:** 664
SALES (est): 34K
SALES (corp-wide): 465.8MM **Privately Held**
SIC: 3443 3714 Heat exchangers: coolers (after, inter), condensers, etc.; radiators & radiator shells & cores, motor vehicle
PA: Api Heat Transfer Company
  2777 Walden Ave Ste 1
  Buffalo NY 14225
  716 684-6700

(G-2835)
API HEAT TRANSFER COMPANY (PA)
2777 Walden Ave Ste 1 (14225-4788)
PHONE.................................716 684-6700
Mike Laisure, *President*
EMP: 9 **EST:** 2005
SALES (est): 465.8MM **Privately Held**
SIC: 3443 Heat exchangers: coolers (after, inter), condensers, etc.

(G-2836)
APPLE IMPRINTS APPAREL INC
2336 Bailey Ave (14211-1738)
PHONE.................................716 893-1130
Fax: 716 893-7701
Jack Lipomi, *President*
Kevin Lipomi, *Vice Pres*
▲ **EMP:** 22 **EST:** 1981
SQ FT: 15,000
SALES (est): 2.8MM **Privately Held**
WEB: www.appleimprints.com
SIC: 2396 7319 Screen printing on fabric articles; display advertising service

(G-2837)
APPLINCE INSTALLATION SVC CORP (PA)
3190 Genesee St (14225-2607)
PHONE.................................716 884-7425
Fax: 716 884-0410
Paul Glowlacki, *CEO*
Wayne Stoutner, *President*
Kim Carney, *Warehouse Mgr*
Andrew Glowacki, *Manager*
Dave Glowacki, *Manager*
EMP: 24
SALES (est): 13.4MM **Privately Held**
SIC: 3631 5085 7699 Household cooking equipment; industrial supplies; restaurant equipment repair

(G-2838)
ARCHER-DANIELS-MIDLAND COMPANY
Also Called: ADM
250 Ganson St (14203-3048)
P.O. Box 487 (14240-0487)
PHONE.................................716 849-7333
Brad Heald, *Branch Mgr*
Andrew Van Thyne, *Manager*
David Brick, *Director*
EMP: 100
SALES (corp-wide): 62.3B **Publicly Held**
WEB: www.admworld.com
SIC: 2048 Prepared feeds
PA: Archer-Daniels-Midland Company
  77 W Wacker Dr Ste 4600
  Chicago IL 60601
  312 634-8100

(G-2839)
ARTVOICE
810 Main St (14202-1501)
P.O. Box 695 (14205-0695)
PHONE.................................716 881-6604
Fax: 716 881-6682
Jamie Moses, *Owner*
Seth Hughes, *Sales Staff*
Agathi Georgiou, *Advt Staff*
Deborah Allis, *Manager*
EMP: 15
SQ FT: 3,000
SALES (est): 653.5K **Privately Held**
WEB: www.artvoice.com
SIC: 2711 Newspapers

(G-2840)
ASSOCIATED PUBLISHING COMPANY (HQ)
61 John Muir Dr (14228-1147)
PHONE.................................325 676-4032
Fax: 325 676-4084
Robert N Allen III, *President*
Bobby Jones, *Area Mgr*
Racker Monty, *Sales Executive*
Todd McKnight, *VP Mktg*
Carrie Carver, *Manager*
EMP: 40
SALES (est): 7MM
SALES (corp-wide): 6.4B **Privately Held**
WEB: www.associatedpublishingcompany.com
SIC: 2741 Directories, telephone: publishing only, not printed on site; telephone & other directory publishing
PA: The Hearst Corporation
  300 W 57th St Fl 42
  New York NY 10019
  212 649-2000

(G-2841)
ATECH-SEH METAL FABRICATOR
330 Greene St (14206-1025)
PHONE.................................716 895-8888

EMP: 20
SALES (est): 1.8MM **Privately Held**
SIC: 3499 Fabricated metal products

(G-2842)
ATHENEX INC
1001 Main St Ste 600 (14203-1009)
PHONE.................................716 427-2950
Michael Scribner, *Branch Mgr*
EMP: 182
SALES (corp-wide): 78.9MM **Publicly Held**
SIC: 2834 Pharmaceutical preparations
PA: Athenex, Inc.
  1001 Main St Ste 600
  Buffalo NY 14203
  716 427-2950

(G-2843)
ATHENEX INC (PA)
1001 Main St Ste 600 (14203-1009)
PHONE.................................716 427-2950
Johnson Lau, *Ch of Bd*
William Zuo, *President*
Jeffrey Yordon, *COO*
Nick Riehle, *CFO*
Rudolf Kwan, *Chief Mktg Ofcr*
EMP: 67
SALES (est): 78.9MM **Publicly Held**
WEB: www.kinexpharma.com
SIC: 2834 8731 Pharmaceutical preparations; medical research, commercial

(G-2844)
AURUBIS BUFFALO INC
600 Military Rd (14207-1750)
PHONE.................................716 879-6700
Raymond Mercer, *President*
EMP: 10
SALES (corp-wide): 10.6B **Privately Held**
SIC: 3351 Copper rolling & drawing
HQ: Aurubis Buffalo, Inc.
  70 Sayre St
  Buffalo NY 14207
  716 879-6700

(G-2845)
AURUBIS BUFFALO INC (HQ)
70 Sayre St (14207-2225)
P.O. Box 981 (14240-0981)
PHONE.................................716 879-6700
Fax: 716 879-6961
Raymond Mercer, *President*
Todd Heusner, *Vice Pres*
Brian Young, *VP Opers*
Thomas Fuchs, *Plant Mgr*
Joan Murray, *Project Mgr*
▲ **EMP:** 276
SQ FT: 1,214,500
SALES (est): 216.1MM
SALES (corp-wide): 10.6B **Privately Held**
WEB: www.luvata.com
SIC: 3351 Copper rolling & drawing
PA: Aurubis Ag
  Hovestr. 50
  Hamburg 20539
  407 883-0

(G-2846)
AUSTIN AIR SYSTEMS LIMITED
500 Elk St (14210-2208)
PHONE.................................716 856-3700
Fax: 716 856-6023
Richard Taylor, *President*
Joyce Taylor, *Vice Pres*
Brian Popovich, *Prdtn Mgr*
Jason Armstrong, *Mfg Staff*
Lauren Bert, *Sales Mgr*
◆ **EMP:** 60
SQ FT: 173,000
SALES (est): 19.5MM **Privately Held**
SIC: 3564 Air purification equipment

(G-2847)
AVALON COPY CENTERS AMER INC
Also Called: Avalon Document Services
741 Main St (14203-1321)
PHONE.................................716 995-7777
Donald Gleason, *Marketing Staff*
Hilary Kleppe, *Branch Mgr*
EMP: 25

▲ = Import ▼ = Export
◆ = Import/Export

GEOGRAPHIC SECTION

Buffalo - Erie County (G-2873)

SALES (corp-wide): 19.6MM **Privately Held**
SIC: 2741 7375 7336 7334 Art copy: publishing & printing; information retrieval services; commercial art & graphic design; photocopying & duplicating services
PA: Avalon Copy Centers Of America, Inc.
901 N State St
Syracuse NY 13208
315 471-3333

(G-2848)
AVANTI ADVANCED MFG CORP
673 Ontario St (14207-1614)
PHONE.................................716 541-8945
Jim WEI, *Ch of Bd*
▲ **EMP:** 9 **EST:** 2013
SALES (est): 736.9K **Privately Held**
SIC: 3999 Atomizers, toiletry

(G-2849)
AVF INC (PA)
2775 Broadway St Ste 200 (14227-1043)
PHONE.................................951 360-7111
Jerry Jacobs, *President*
Brenda Gaines, *Sales Mgr*
▲ **EMP:** 14
SALES (est): 3.6MM **Privately Held**
WEB: www.avf.com
SIC: 2542 Partitions & fixtures, except wood

(G-2850)
B & K COMPONENTS LTD
2100 Old Union Rd (14227-2725)
PHONE.................................323 776-4277
Fax: 716 656-1241
John L Beyer III, *President*
Dr Charles A Marchetta, *Admin Sec*
▲ **EMP:** 70 **EST:** 1981
SQ FT: 18,500
SALES (est): 8.6MM **Privately Held**
WEB: www.bkcomp.com
SIC: 3651 Audio electronic systems

(G-2851)
B & P JAYS INC
Also Called: Mecca Printing
19 N Hill Dr (14224-2582)
PHONE.................................716 668-8408
Betty Mecca, *President*
Paul Mecca, *Vice Pres*
EMP: 5
SQ FT: 1,400
SALES: 200K **Privately Held**
SIC: 2752 Commercial printing, offset

(G-2852)
BAK USA TECHNOLOGIES CORP
425 Michigan Ave Ste 4 (14203-2240)
PHONE.................................716 248-2704
J P Folsgaard Bak, *Ch of Bd*
Ulla Bak, *President*
Ryan Litt, *Vice Pres*
Alan Jankowski, *Controller*
EMP: 32
SQ FT: 15,000
SALES (est): 2.5MM **Privately Held**
SIC: 2678 Stationery products

(G-2853)
BARRON GAMES INTL CO LLC
84 Aero Dr Ste 5 (14225-1435)
PHONE.................................716 630-0054
Gregory Bacorn, *President*
Anna Zykina, *Vice Pres*
Alyssa Chawgo, *Office Mgr*
◆ **EMP:** 11
SQ FT: 4,500
SALES: 2MM **Privately Held**
WEB: www.barrongames.com/
SIC: 3944 5092 Electronic games & toys; video games

(G-2854)
BATAVIA PRECISION GLASS LLC
231 Currier Ave (14212-2262)
PHONE.................................585 343-6050
Steve Barber,
EMP: 6
SQ FT: 9,000
SALES: 63K **Privately Held**
SIC: 3231 8748 Leaded glass; business consulting

(G-2855)
BATES JACKSON ENGRAVING CO INC
17 Elm St 21 (14203-2605)
PHONE.................................716 854-3000
Fax: 716 847-1965
Rozanne Flammer, *CEO*
Edward Flammer, *President*
Gregory Flammer, *Controller*
EMP: 35
SQ FT: 19,000
SALES (est): 3.7MM **Privately Held**
SIC: 2759 2752 2791 Engraving; commercial printing, offset; typesetting

(G-2856)
BATTENFELD-AMERICAN INC
1575 Clinton St (14206-3064)
P.O. Box 728, North Tonawanda (14120-0728)
PHONE.................................716 822-8410
Fax: 716 822-8410
John A Bellanti Sr, *CEO*
Barbara A Bellanti, *Ch of Bd*
Barbara Bellanti, *President*
Debbi Carpenter, *Vice Pres*
Sara Dumont, *Manager*
▼ **EMP:** 38
SQ FT: 110,000
SALES (est): 9.2MM
SALES (corp-wide): 44.4MM **Privately Held**
WEB: www.battenfeld-grease.com
SIC: 2992 Oils & greases, blending & compounding
PA: Battenfeld Management, Inc.
1174 Erie Ave
North Tonawanda NY 14120
716 695-2100

(G-2857)
BEAR METAL WORKS INC
39 Scoville Ave (14206-2932)
P.O. Box 2528 (14240-2528)
PHONE.................................716 824-4350
Barrett E Price, *Ch of Bd*
Gloria Gau, *Project Mgr*
January Delaney, *Office Mgr*
Catherine Jasinski, *Admin Sec*
EMP: 10 **EST:** 1999
SALES (est): 2.4MM **Privately Held**
SIC: 3441 Fabricated structural metal

(G-2858)
BEKA WORLD LP
258 Sonwil Dr (14225-5516)
PHONE.................................905 821-1050
EMP: 7
SALES (corp-wide): 1.5MM **Privately Held**
SIC: 2992 Lubricating oils & greases
PA: Beka World Lp
2775 N Hills Dr Ne
Atlanta GA 30305
404 841-1133

(G-2859)
BELRIX INDUSTRIES INC
3590 Jeffrey Blvd (14219-2390)
PHONE.................................716 821-5964
Gail Maurer, *President*
Ann Skummer, *Manager*
EMP: 6
SQ FT: 15,000
SALES (est): 1.1MM **Privately Held**
WEB: www.belrix.com
SIC: 3469 Machine parts, stamped or pressed metal

(G-2860)
BEMCO OF WESTERN NY INC
122 Roberts Ave (14206-3120)
PHONE.................................716 823-8400
Fax: 716 823-8441
Barry E Medwin, *President*
Paul Kunkes, *Vice Pres*
EMP: 6
SQ FT: 60,000
SALES (est): 780K **Privately Held**
SIC: 3625 Motor control accessories, including overload relays

(G-2861)
BENTON ANNOUNCEMENTS INC
3006 Bailey Ave 3010 (14215-2898)
PHONE.................................716 836-4100
Fax: 716 836-4161
Philip J Guerra, *President*
Michael J Guerra Jr, *Vice Pres*
EMP: 10 **EST:** 1935
SQ FT: 13,500
SALES (est): 920K **Privately Held**
SIC: 2754 5719 5944 Commercial printing, gravure; invitations: gravure printing; stationery: gravure printing; glassware; china; silverware

(G-2862)
BETTER WIRE PRODUCTS INC
1255 Niagara St (14213-1591)
PHONE.................................716 883-3377
Fax: 716 883-5075
William Breeser, *President*
Lynn Youngman, *Sales Associate*
Betty Breeser, *Manager*
Maria Dinezza, *Manager*
Dennis McCarthy, *Data Proc Exec*
▲ **EMP:** 35 **EST:** 1952
SQ FT: 30,000
SALES (est): 8.3MM **Privately Held**
SIC: 3496 Miscellaneous fabricated wire products

(G-2863)
BFG MANUFACTURING SERVICES INC
3949 Jeffrey Blvd (14219-2334)
P.O. Box 825, Hamburg (14075-0825)
PHONE.................................716 362-0888
Fax: 716 362-0835
Minta Marie, *Branch Mgr*
EMP: 27
SALES (corp-wide): 12.6MM **Privately Held**
WEB: www.bfgelectroplating.com
SIC: 3471 Electroplating of metals or formed products
PA: Bfg Manufacturing Services, Inc.
701 Martha St
Punxsutawney PA 15767
814 938-9164

(G-2864)
BIG HEART PET BRANDS
Del Monte Foods
243 Urban St (14211-1532)
PHONE.................................716 891-6566
Greg Pastore, *General Mgr*
Todd Verost, *Opers Mgr*
Greg Bala, *Engineer*
Les Wagner, *Engnr/R&D Mgr*
Terry Wolcott, *Controller*
EMP: 31
SALES (corp-wide): 7.3B **Publicly Held**
WEB: www.kraftfoods.com
SIC: 2066 Chocolate & cocoa products
HQ: Big Heart Pet Brands
1 Maritime Plz Fl 2
San Francisco CA 94111
415 247-3000

(G-2865)
BLACK & DECKER (US) INC
881 W Delavan Ave (14209-1297)
PHONE.................................716 884-6220
Mike Eaton, *Manager*
EMP: 5
SQ FT: 4,112
SALES (corp-wide): 11.4B **Publicly Held**
WEB: www.dewalt.com
SIC: 3546 Power-driven handtools
HQ: Black & Decker (U.S.) Inc.
1000 Stanley Dr
New Britain CT 06053
860 225-5111

(G-2866)
BMC LLC
3155 Broadway St (14227-1034)
PHONE.................................716 681-7755
Richard Neal, *President*
▲ **EMP:** 24
SQ FT: 4,500
SALES (est): 2.3MM **Privately Held**
SIC: 3084 Plastics pipe

(G-2867)
BRYANT MACHINE & DEVELOPMENT
63 Stanley St (14206-1017)
PHONE.................................716 894-8282
Michael Denz, *President*

Matthew Bryant Jr, *Corp Secy*
Cindy White, *Office Mgr*
EMP: 10
SQ FT: 8,000
SALES: 200K **Privately Held**
SIC: 3599 Machine shop, jobbing & repair

(G-2868)
BRYANT MACHINE CO INC
63 Stanley St (14206-1017)
PHONE.................................716 894-8282
Fax: 716 894-8283
Kip Laviolette, *President*
Erica Laviolette, *Office Mgr*
EMP: 10 **EST:** 1946
SQ FT: 5,000
SALES (est): 1.1MM **Privately Held**
WEB: www.bryantmachine.com
SIC: 3469 Machine parts, stamped or pressed metal

(G-2869)
BRYANT MANUFACTURING WNY INC
63 Stanley St (14206-1017)
PHONE.................................716 894-8282
Kip A Laviolette, *CEO*
EMP: 6
SALES: 950K **Privately Held**
SIC: 3312 Stainless steel

(G-2870)
BUFFALO ARMORY LLC
1050 Military Rd (14217-2528)
PHONE.................................716 935-6346
John Bastiste, *President*
Scott Sulzbach, *Mktg Dir*
Brent Nicholson, *Manager*
EMP: 5
SALES (est): 832.4K **Privately Held**
SIC: 3398 Metal heat treating

(G-2871)
BUFFALO BLENDS INC (PA)
1400 William St (14206-1813)
PHONE.................................716 825-4422
Fax: 716 825-1505
Timothy Sheehy, *President*
Kevin Prise, *Corp Secy*
Liz Hichcock, *Manager*
▲ **EMP:** 22 **EST:** 1999
SQ FT: 35,000
SALES (est): 3.2MM **Privately Held**
WEB: www.buffaloblends.com
SIC: 2087 Beverage bases, concentrates, syrups, powders & mixes

(G-2872)
BUFFALO CRUSHED STONE INC (HQ)
500 Como Park Blvd (14227-1606)
PHONE.................................716 826-7310
Fax: 716 826-1342
Steven B Detwiler, *Ch of Bd*
Gary Blum, *Vice Pres*
David Firmstone, *Vice Pres*
Jamie Hypnarowski, *Vice Pres*
Richard Mirabelli, *Vice Pres*
EMP: 40
SQ FT: 25,000
SALES (est): 36.8MM
SALES (corp-wide): 651.9MM **Privately Held**
SIC: 3272 Concrete products
PA: New Enterprise Stone & Lime Co., Inc.
3912 Brumbaugh Rd
New Enterprise PA 16664
814 224-6883

(G-2873)
BUFFALO FINISHING WORKS INC
1255 Niagara St (14213-1501)
PHONE.................................716 893-5266
John Warchocki, *President*
Ulrike Warchocki, *Vice Pres*
Duane Warchocki, *Manager*
EMP: 5
SQ FT: 7,000
SALES: 250K **Privately Held**
SIC: 3479 Painting of metal products; enameling, including porcelain, of metal products

Buffalo - Erie County (G-2874)

(G-2874)
BUFFALO GAMES INC
Also Called: Buffalo Games & Puzzles
220 James E Casey Dr (14206-2362)
PHONE.................................716 827-8393
Fax: 716 827-8163
Paul A Dedrick, *CEO*
Jennifer Mengay, *President*
Eden Scott-Dedrick, *Vice Pres*
Pete Beaty, *Systems Mgr*
▲ **EMP:** 70
SQ FT: 88,000
SALES (est): 11.3MM **Privately Held**
WEB: www.buffalogames.com
SIC: 3944 Puzzles

(G-2875)
BUFFALO LAW JOURNAL
465 Main St Ste 100 (14203-1717)
PHONE.................................716 541-1600
Fax: 716 854-3394
Kim Schaus, *General Mgr*
EMP: 6
SALES (est): 310K **Privately Held**
WEB: www.buffalolawjournal.com
SIC: 2711 Newspapers: publishing only, not printed on site

(G-2876)
BUFFALO LINING & FABRICATING
73 Gillette Ave (14214-2702)
PHONE.................................716 883-6500
Bruce F Meyers, *President*
James Meyers, *Vice Pres*
Robert Murray, *Vice Pres*
Charlotte Boorman, *Office Mgr*
EMP: 6 **EST:** 1956
SQ FT: 12,000
SALES (est): 695.3K **Privately Held**
SIC: 3069 Molded rubber products

(G-2877)
BUFFALO METAL CASTING CO INC
1875 Elmwood Ave (14207-1997)
PHONE.................................716 874-6211
Fax: 716 874-6213
John Klodzinski, *President*
Justin Klodzinski, *General Mgr*
Jennifer Patterson, *Manager*
EMP: 40
SQ FT: 80,000
SALES (est): 7.6MM **Privately Held**
WEB: www.buffalometalcasting.com
SIC: 3369 Castings, except die-castings, precision

(G-2878)
BUFFALO METAL FINISHING CO (PA)
135 Dart St (14213-1087)
P.O. Box 1012 (14213-7012)
PHONE.................................716 883-2751
Fax: 716 883-6177
Frank Bonare, *President*
EMP: 8 **EST:** 1941
SQ FT: 11,000
SALES: 500K **Privately Held**
SIC: 3471 3479 Plating of metals or formed products; polishing, metals or formed products; anodizing (plating) of metals or formed products; painting of metal products

(G-2879)
BUFFALO NEWS INC
1 News Plz (14203-2994)
P.O. Box 100 (14240-0100)
PHONE.................................716 849-4401
Fax: 716 849-4554
Stanford Lipsey, *CEO*
Karen Colville, *President*
Warren Colville, *President*
Mike Connelly, *Editor*
Edward L Cuddihy, *Editor*
▲ **EMP:** 900
SQ FT: 1,000
SALES: 186.5K
SALES (corp-wide): 223.6B **Publicly Held**
WEB: www.berkshirehathaway.com
SIC: 2711 Newspapers, publishing & printing
PA: Berkshire Hathaway Inc.
3555 Farnam St Ste 1440
Omaha NE 68131
402 346-1400

(G-2880)
BUFFALO NEWSPRESS INC
200 Broadway St (14204-1439)
P.O. Box 648 (14240-0648)
PHONE.................................716 852-1600
Fax: 716 856-2017
Warren T Colville, *President*
Mark Korzelius, *President*
Michael A Kibler, *Chairman*
Joan Holzman, *Vice Pres*
Marcus Regoord, *Vice Pres*
EMP: 120
SQ FT: 80,000
SALES (est): 22.6MM **Privately Held**
WEB: www.buffalonewspress.com
SIC: 2759 Newspapers: printing; advertising literature: printing

(G-2881)
BUFFALO SPREE PUBLISHING INC (PA)
1738 Elmwood Ave Ste 103 (14207-2465)
PHONE.................................716 783-9119
Laurence Levite, *CEO*
Wendy Swearingen, *Editor*
Lucy Cieply, *Business Mgr*
Theresa Clair, *CFO*
Louis Aguglia, *Accounts Exec*
EMP: 25
SQ FT: 10,000
SALES (est): 2.3MM **Privately Held**
WEB: www.buffalospree.com
SIC: 2721 Magazines: publishing only, not printed on site

(G-2882)
BUFFALO STANDARD PRINTING CORP
Also Called: Am-Pol Eagle
3620 Harlem Rd Ste 5 (14215-2042)
PHONE.................................716 835-9454
Fax: 716 835-9457
Irene Harzewski, *President*
EMP: 10 **EST:** 1958
SALES (est): 687.1K **Privately Held**
SIC: 2711 Commercial printing & newspaper publishing combined; job printing & newspaper publishing combined

(G-2883)
BUFLOVAK LLC (PA)
750 E Ferry St (14211-1106)
PHONE.................................716 895-2100
Todd Murray, *COO*
Mike Durusky, *Plant Mgr*
Tami McNamara, *Materials Mgr*
Maliek Likely, *Engineer*
Dave Bielecki, *Controller*
▼ **EMP:** 28
SQ FT: 225,000
SALES (est): 11.7MM **Privately Held**
WEB: www.buffalotechnologies.com
SIC: 3556 5084 3567 3443 Food products machinery; industrial machinery & equipment; industrial furnaces & ovens; fabricated plate work (boiler shop)

(G-2884)
BUSINESS FIRST OF NEW YORK (DH)
465 Main St Ste 100 (14203-1793)
PHONE.................................716 854-5822
Jack Connors, *President*
Jeff Wright, *Editor*
Shelley Rohauer, *Advt Staff*
Larry Ponzi, *Manager*
Maureen R Twist, *Manager*
EMP: 44
SQ FT: 10,000
SALES (est): 4.5MM
SALES (corp-wide): 1.5B **Privately Held**
SIC: 2711 Newspapers: publishing only, not printed on site
HQ: American City Business Journals, Inc.
120 W Morehead St Ste 400
Charlotte NC 28202
704 973-1000

(G-2885)
BUXTON MACHINE AND TOOL CO INC
2181 Elmwood Ave (14216-1002)
PHONE.................................716 876-2312
Fax: 716 876-0161
James P Hettrick, *President*
Mildred Di Luca, *Admin Sec*
EMP: 12 **EST:** 1984
SQ FT: 12,000
SALES (est): 1.8MM **Privately Held**
SIC: 3599 Machine shop, jobbing & repair

(G-2886)
CALSPAN CORPORATION (HQ)
4455 Genesee St (14225-1955)
P.O. Box 400 (14225)
PHONE.................................716 631-6955
Fax: 716 631-6969
Louis H Knotts, *President*
Derek Garner, *General Mgr*
Peter Sauer, *COO*
Thomas Pleban, *Exec VP*
John Yurtchuk, *Exec VP*
◆ **EMP:** 129
SQ FT: 170,200
SALES (est): 46MM
SALES (corp-wide): 16.3MM **Privately Held**
WEB: www.windtunnel.com
SIC: 3721 Research & development on aircraft by the manufacturer
PA: Calspan Holdings, Llc
4455 Genesee St
Buffalo NY 14225
716 631-6955

(G-2887)
CAMELLIA GENERAL PROVISION CO
Also Called: Camellia Foods
1333 Genesee St (14211-2227)
PHONE.................................716 893-5352
Fax: 716 895-7713
Peter J Cichocki, *Ch of Bd*
Edmund J Cichocki Jr, *President*
Eric Cichocki, *Vice Pres*
Patrick Cichocki, *Vice Pres*
Joell Gilley, *Manager*
EMP: 46 **EST:** 1937
SQ FT: 40,000
SALES (est): 10MM **Privately Held**
WEB: www.camelliafoods.com
SIC: 2013 5147 Sausage casings, natural; bologna from purchased meat; smoked meats from purchased meat; meats, fresh; meats, cured or smoked

(G-2888)
CARAUSTAR INDUSTRIES INC
25 Dewberry Ln (14227-2709)
PHONE.................................716 874-0393
Lynn Ramsey, *Branch Mgr*
EMP: 8
SALES (corp-wide): 1.4B **Privately Held**
SIC: 2655 Tubes, fiber or paper: made from purchased material
PA: Caraustar Industries, Inc.
5000 Astell Pwdr Sprng Rd
Austell GA 30106
770 948-3101

(G-2889)
CCL LABEL INC
685 Howard St (14206-2210)
P.O. Box 550 (14240-0550)
PHONE.................................716 852-2155
Fax: 716 852-2175
Joe Langan, *Plant Mgr*
Matt Piejda, *Buyer*
Blaine Jackson, *Engineer*
Peter Lowry, *Engineer*
Robert Wilson, *Design Engr*
EMP: 150
SQ FT: 25,883
SALES (corp-wide): 145.9K **Privately Held**
WEB: www.avery.com
SIC: 2672 2671 Coated & laminated paper; packaging paper & plastics film, coated & laminated
HQ: Ccl Label, Inc.
161 Worcester Rd Ste 504
Framingham MA 01701
508 872-4511

(G-2890)
CENO TECHNOLOGIES INC
1234 Delaware Ave (14209-1430)
PHONE.................................716 885-5050
Fax: 716 885-4040
Scott Patrick, *President*
Alan Rowdon, *Vice Pres*
EMP: 5
SALES (est): 661.9K **Privately Held**
SIC: 3531 Construction machinery

(G-2891)
CERTAINTEED CORPORATION
Pipe and Plastic Div
231 Ship Canal Pkwy (14218-1026)
PHONE.................................716 827-7560
Bob Kearful, *Branch Mgr*
Derrick Campbell, *Manager*
Tom Flaws, *Manager*
David Sence, *Manager*
Dave Senne, *Manager*
EMP: 400
SALES (corp-wide): 185.8MM **Privately Held**
WEB: www.certainteed.net
SIC: 3089 Extruded finished plastic products
HQ: Certainteed Corporation
20 Moores Rd
Malvern PA 19355
610 893-5000

(G-2892)
CHOCOLATE DELIVERY SYSTEMS INC (PA)
Also Called: Tomric Plastic
85 River Rock Dr Ste 202 (14207-2170)
PHONE.................................716 854-6050
Timothy M Thill, *CEO*
Anne Rosa, *Vice Pres*
Melissa Benzee, *Sales Mgr*
Thomas Elsinghorst, *Admin Sec*
◆ **EMP:** 55 **EST:** 1962
SQ FT: 30,000
SALES (est): 21.8MM **Privately Held**
WEB: www.tomric.com
SIC: 3089 5145 3086 Molding primary plastic; candy; packaging & shipping materials, foamed plastic

(G-2893)
CHOCOMAKER INC
85 River Rock Dr Ste 202 (14207-2170)
PHONE.................................716 877-3146
Timothy Thill, *President*
Anne Rosa, *Vice Pres*
▲ **EMP:** 6
SALES (est): 249.8K
SALES (corp-wide): 21.8MM **Privately Held**
SIC: 2064 Candy bars, including chocolate covered bars
PA: Chocolate Delivery Systems, Inc.
85 River Rock Dr Ste 202
Buffalo NY 14207
716 854-6050

(G-2894)
CILYOX INC
Also Called: New Rosen Printing
345 Broadway St (14204-1541)
PHONE.................................716 853-3809
Fax: 716 853-1075
Michael Cimato, *President*
Bryan Knox, *Vice Pres*
EMP: 10 **EST:** 1963
SQ FT: 43,000
SALES (est): 1.3MM **Privately Held**
SIC: 2752 Commercial printing, offset

(G-2895)
CLEARVIEW SOCIAL INC
77 Goodell St Ste 430 (14203-1257)
PHONE.................................801 414-7675
Adrian Dayton, *CEO*
EMP: 5 **EST:** 2013
SALES (est): 171.6K **Privately Held**
SIC: 7372 Business oriented computer software

(G-2896)
CLEVELAND BIOLABS INC
73 High St (14203-1149)
PHONE.................................716 849-6810
Fax: 716 849-6820
Yakov Kogan, *CEO*

GEOGRAPHIC SECTION
Buffalo - Erie County (G-2920)

Lea Verny, *Ch of Bd*
Langdon Miller, *Chief Mktg Ofcr*
Andrei Gudkov, *Security Dir*
EMP: 25
SQ FT: 32,000
SALES: 3.5MM **Privately Held**
WEB: www.cbiolabs.com
SIC: 2834 8731 Pharmaceutical preparations; biological research

(G-2897)
COBEY INC (PA)
1 Ship Canal Pkwy (14218-1024)
PHONE..........................716 362-9550
Fax: 716 362-9551
John J Obey, *Ch of Bd*
Robert J Castle, *Vice Pres*
Neil Ackerman, *Project Mgr*
Jonathan Gesicki, *Project Mgr*
Dean Rozler, *Purch Mgr*
▲ **EMP:** 110
SQ FT: 117,000
SALES (est): 48.1MM **Privately Held**
WEB: www.cobey.com
SIC: 3498 Fabricated pipe & fittings

(G-2898)
COGNIGEN CORPORATION
Also Called: Cognigen Acquisition
1780 Wehrle Dr Ste 110 (14221-7000)
PHONE..........................716 633-3463
Ted Grasela, *President*
Cynthia Walawander, *Exec VP*
Jill Fiedler-Kelly, *Vice Pres*
Rebecca Humphrey, *Manager*
Andrew Rokitka, *Manager*
EMP: 65
SALES (est): 8.8MM **Publicly Held**
SIC: 2834 8999 Druggists' preparations (pharmaceuticals); scientific consulting
PA: Simulations Plus, Inc.
42505 10th St W Ste 103
Lancaster CA 93534

(G-2899)
COHENS BAKERY INC
Also Called: Al Cohens Famous Rye Bread Bky
1132 Broadway St (14212-1502)
PHONE..........................716 892-8149
Fax: 716 892-8150
Mark Didomenico, *President*
John J Blando, *Vice Pres*
Gary East Abrook, *Accountant*
Mary Russo, *Admin Asst*
EMP: 45
SQ FT: 25,000
SALES (est): 5.7MM **Privately Held**
SIC: 2045 5149 2051 Doughs & batters: from purchased flour; groceries & related products; bread, cake & related products

(G-2900)
COLAD GROUP LLC (HQ)
693 Seneca St Fl 5 (14210-1324)
PHONE..........................716 961-1776
Fax: 716 961-1753
Wayne Coverley, *Controller*
F Martin Anson, *Mng Member*
Cindy Flonrino, *Data Proc Dir*
J Todd Anson,
EMP: 81
SALES (est): 11.3MM
SALES (corp-wide): 19.2MM **Privately Held**
WEB: www.colad.com
SIC: 2782 2671 2752 2759 Blankbooks & looseleaf binders; packaging paper & plastics film, coated & laminated; commercial printing, lithographic; commercial printing; signs & advertising specialties
PA: Bindagraphics, Inc.
2701 Wilmarco Ave
Baltimore MD 21223
410 362-7200

(G-2901)
COMET FLASHER INC (PA)
1 Babcock St (14210-2253)
PHONE..........................716 821-9595
James Casey, *President*
Jamie Rybij, *Admin Sec*
EMP: 9
SALES (est): 1.6MM **Privately Held**
SIC: 3669 Traffic signals, electric

(G-2902)
COMMERCIAL PRINT & IMAGING
4778 Main St (14226-4020)
PHONE..........................716 597-0100
Fax: 716 597-0232
Kevin Preston, *President*
John A Polvino, *Vice Pres*
EMP: 25
SQ FT: 6,500
SALES (est): 4MM **Privately Held**
SIC: 2752 Commercial printing, lithographic

(G-2903)
COMMITMENT 2000 INC
Also Called: Father Sam's Bakery
105 Msgr Valente Dr (14206-1815)
PHONE..........................716 439-1206
Fax: 716 853-1062
William A Sam, *Ch of Bd*
Samuel A Sam II, *Treasurer*
Glenn Povitz, *VP Sales*
Tony Said, *Regl Sales Mgr*
Kelly Bernacki, *Manager*
EMP: 40
SQ FT: 40,000
SALES (est): 8.9MM **Privately Held**
WEB: www.fathersams.com
SIC: 2051 Bread, all types (white, wheat, rye, etc): fresh or frozen

(G-2904)
COMPLEMAR PRINT LLC
Also Called: Merrill Press
3034 Genesee St (14225-2641)
PHONE..........................716 875-7238
Fax: 716 875-7189
Michael Gotthelf, *President*
Christine Gotthelf, *Vice Pres*
Joan Gotthelf, *Admin Sec*
EMP: 12
SQ FT: 7,000
SALES (est): 1.7MM
SALES (corp-wide): 29.9MM **Privately Held**
WEB: www.quickbizcards.com
SIC: 2752 Commercial printing, offset
PA: Complemar Partners, Inc.
500 Lee Rd Ste 200
Rochester NY 14606
585 647-5800

(G-2905)
CONAX TECHNOLOGIES LLC (PA)
2300 Walden Ave (14225-4765)
PHONE..........................716 684-4500
Fax: 716 684-7433
Daniel Mitchell, *Vice Pres*
Ed Wilson, *Mfg Mgr*
Dale Tanski, *Facilities Mgr*
Greg Wittmann, *Mfg Staff*
Joe Kelly, *Purch Mgr*
EMP: 126
SQ FT: 83,000
SALES (est): 18.5MM **Privately Held**
WEB: www.conaxbuffalo.com
SIC: 3823 Industrial process control instruments

(G-2906)
CONNIES LAUNDRY
1494 S Park Ave (14220-1075)
PHONE..........................716 822-2800
Fax: 716 822-2800
Froncell Clifton, *Owner*
EMP: 5
SQ FT: 1,000
SALES: 500K **Privately Held**
SIC: 2842 Laundry cleaning preparations

(G-2907)
CONSUMERS BEVERAGES INC
3025 Sheridan Dr (14226-1910)
PHONE..........................716 837-3087
Fax: 716 837-3087
James E Kavanaugh, *President*
EMP: 38
SALES (corp-wide): 21.6MM **Privately Held**
WEB: www.consumersbeverage.com
SIC: 2086 Bottled & canned soft drinks
PA: Consumers Beverages, Inc.
2230 S Park Ave
Buffalo NY
716 826-9200

(G-2908)
CONTRACT PHRMCTCALS LTD NAGARA
100 Forest Ave (14213-1032)
PHONE..........................716 887-3400
John Ross, *Branch Mgr*
Todd Burdick, *Manager*
Michele Miller, *Manager*
Dale Jacobs, *Info Tech Dir*
Rick Fairess, *Info Tech Mgr*
EMP: 200
SALES (corp-wide): 33.9MM **Privately Held**
WEB: www.cplltd.com
SIC: 2834 Pharmaceutical preparations
PA: Contract Pharmaceuticals Limited Canada
7600 East Danbro Cres
Mississauga ON L5N 6
905 821-7600

(G-2909)
COOKIEBAKER LLC
1 Robert Rich Way (14213-1701)
PHONE..........................716 878-8000
Sam Stolbun, *President*
EMP: 6
SALES (est): 498.8K **Privately Held**
SIC: 2099 Food preparations

(G-2910)
COOPER TURBOCOMPRESSOR INC (DH)
3101 Broadway St (14227-1034)
P.O. Box 209 (14225-0209)
PHONE..........................716 896-6600
Fax: 716 896-1233
Jeff Altamari, *Vice Pres*
Frank Athearn, *Vice Pres*
Ron Flecknoe, *Vice Pres*
Ray Plachta, *Vice Pres*
Ed Roper, *Vice Pres*
▲ **EMP:** 485
SQ FT: 273,000
SALES (est): 81.4MM **Privately Held**
SIC: 3511 3563 Turbines & turbine generator sets; air & gas compressors

(G-2911)
COSTANZOS BAKERY INC
30 Innsbruck Dr (14227-2736)
PHONE..........................716 656-9093
Fax: 716 656-9218
Jeffrey A Costanzo, *Ch of Bd*
Michael Costanzo, *Vice Pres*
Chris Clark, *Opers Mgr*
Mike Costanzo, *Opers Mgr*
Sarah Rouleau, *Opers Mgr*
EMP: 130 EST: 1933
SQ FT: 20,000
SALES (est): 28.2MM **Privately Held**
WEB: www.costanzosbakery.com
SIC: 2051 5461 5149 Bread, cake & related products; bakeries; bakery products

(G-2912)
CRANDALL FILLING MACHINERY INC
80 Gruner Rd (14227-1007)
PHONE..........................716 897-3486
Fax: 716 897-3488
David Reed, *President*
Heather Wood, *Corp Secy*
Charles Wood, *VP Sales*
Dian Reed, *Shareholder*
EMP: 6 EST: 1906
SQ FT: 7,000
SALES (est): 664.9K **Privately Held**
SIC: 3569 Liquid automation machinery & equipment

(G-2913)
CROSBY COMPANY
183 Pratt St (14204-1519)
PHONE..........................716 852-3522
Peter W Crosby, *CEO*
Leslie Richardson, *Vice Pres*
Jack Spencer, *Buyer*
Art Machuca, *Engineer*
Paul Marun, *Engineer*
EMP: 50
SQ FT: 300,000
SALES (est): 11.3MM **Privately Held**
WEB: www.crosbycompany.com
SIC: 3469 Metal stampings

(G-2914)
CRYSTAL ROCK LLC
100 Stradtman St Ste 1 (14206-2665)
PHONE..........................716 626-7460
Tom Gawel, *Division Mgr*
EMP: 25
SALES (corp-wide): 65.3MM **Publicly Held**
SIC: 2086 Water, pasteurized: packaged in cans, bottles, etc.
HQ: Crystal Rock Llc
1050 Buckingham St
Watertown CT 06795
877 302-4241

(G-2915)
CURTIS L MACLEAN L C (HQ)
Also Called: Maclean Curtis
50 Thielman Dr (14206-2364)
PHONE..........................716 898-7800
Duncan Mac Lean, *CEO*
Paul Hojnacki, *President*
Bob Filipski, *Facilities Mgr*
Daryle Shaw, *CFO*
Greg Blaszak, *Manager*
EMP: 300
SALES (est): 48.9MM
SALES (corp-wide): 1.5B **Privately Held**
SIC: 3714 Motor vehicle engines & parts
PA: Mac Lean-Fogg Company
1000 Allanson Rd
Mundelein IL 60060
847 566-0010

(G-2916)
CURTIS SCREW CO INC
50 Thielman Dr (14206-2364)
PHONE..........................716 898-7800
John Hoskins, *Chairman*
EMP: 36
SALES (est): 7.9MM **Privately Held**
SIC: 3451 Screw machine products

(G-2917)
CUSTOM CANVAS MANUFACTURING CO
775 Seneca St (14210-1487)
PHONE..........................716 852-6372
Fax: 716 852-2328
Anthony L Guido Jr, *President*
Phyllis Guido, *Vice Pres*
William Sal Guido, *Prdtn Mgr*
▲ **EMP:** 28 EST: 1961
SQ FT: 32,000
SALES (est): 3.4MM **Privately Held**
SIC: 2394 7699 Canvas covers & drop cloths; liners & covers, fabric: made from purchased materials; tarpaulins, fabric: made from purchased materials; tents: made from purchased materials; tent repair shop

(G-2918)
D & G WELDING INC
249 Hertel Ave (14207-2153)
PHONE..........................716 873-3088
Toll Free:.........................888 -
Fax: 716 873-3088
David M Black, *President*
EMP: 5
SQ FT: 2,300
SALES (est): 425.7K **Privately Held**
SIC: 7692 3498 Welding repair; pipe fittings, fabricated from purchased pipe

(G-2919)
D-C THEATRICKS
747 Main St (14203-1321)
PHONE..........................716 847-0180
David Dejac, *Partner*
Douglas Caskey, *Partner*
EMP: 5
SQ FT: 4,600
SALES (est): 430K **Privately Held**
WEB: www.costume.com
SIC: 2389 5699 5136 5137 Theatrical costumes; costumes, masquerade or theatrical; men's & boys' clothing; women's & children's clothing

(G-2920)
DAN TRENT COMPANY INC
Also Called: D & D Printing
1728 Clinton St (14206-3151)
PHONE..........................716 822-1422
Fax: 716 822-3876

Buffalo - Erie County (G-2921)

Daniel Trent, *President*
EMP: 5
SQ FT: 5,610
SALES (est): 1.1MM **Privately Held**
SIC: 2752 Commercial printing, lithographic

(G-2921)
DATES WEISER FURNITURE CORP
1700 Broadway St (14212-2031)
PHONE..................................716 891-1700
Fax: 716 891-0399
Allan S Weiser, *President*
Joseph Iannello, *Vice Pres*
Michelle Myers, *Project Mgr*
Joseph S Iannello, *CFO*
EMP: 60
SQ FT: 90,000
SALES (est): 11.7MM **Privately Held**
WEB: www.datesweiser.com
SIC: 2521 Wood office furniture

(G-2922)
DAVIS
283 Minnesota Ave (14215-1013)
PHONE..................................716 833-4678
Arthur L Davis, *Principal*
EMP: 9
SALES (est): 668.9K **Privately Held**
SIC: 2389 Clergymen's vestments

(G-2923)
DECK BROS INC
222 Chicago St (14204-2249)
PHONE..................................716 852-0262
Ronald P Kellner, *President*
Karl J Kellner, *Vice Pres*
Randy Sanders, *Plt & Fclts Mgr*
Russell Reczek, *Engineer*
Hazel Weaver, *Controller*
EMP: 25 **EST:** 1952
SQ FT: 45,000
SALES: 3MM **Privately Held**
SIC: 3599 7692 Machine shop, jobbing & repair; welding repair

(G-2924)
DELAWARE VALLEY FORGE INC
241 Rano St (14207-2149)
P.O. Box 220, Kenmore (14217-0220)
PHONE..................................716 447-9140
Fax: 716 447-9122
Margaret Duggan, *President*
EMP: 20
SALES (est): 1.7MM **Privately Held**
SIC: 3462 Iron & steel forgings

(G-2925)
DELTACRAFT PAPER COMPANY LLC
Also Called: Nicraft
99 Bud Mil Dr (14206-1801)
PHONE..................................716 856-5135
Fax: 716 856-1113
Frank Kohl, *Purchasing*
James Lauck, *Director*
Charles Mlakar,
William Grubich,
Chuck Mlakar Jr,
▲ **EMP:** 190
SQ FT: 85,000
SALES (est): 15.3MM **Privately Held**
WEB: www.millcraft.com
SIC: 2679 Paperboard products, converted
HQ: The Millcraft Paper Company
6800 Grant Ave
Cleveland OH 44105
216 441-5505

(G-2926)
DENNY MACHINE CO INC
20 Norris St (14207-2207)
PHONE..................................716 873-6865
Frank Deni, *President*
Joseph Deni, *Vice Pres*
Leonard Deni, *Vice Pres*
George Macholtz, *Manager*
Jennie Deni, *Admin Sec*
EMP: 65 **EST:** 1957
SQ FT: 10,000
SALES (est): 8.4MM **Privately Held**
WEB: www.deni.com
SIC: 3599 Machine shop, jobbing & repair

(G-2927)
DERONDE DOORS AND FRAMES INC
330 Greene St (14206-1025)
P.O. Box 686 (14240-0686)
PHONE..................................716 895-8888
Grace W Munschauer, *Ch of Bd*
Grace Munschauer, *President*
EMP: 15 **EST:** 2008
SALES (est): 2.7MM **Privately Held**
SIC: 3442 Window & door frames

(G-2928)
DERRICK CORPORATION (PA)
Also Called: Derrick Equipment
590 Duke Rd (14225-5102)
PHONE..................................716 683-9010
James W Derrick, *Ch of Bd*
William W Derrick, *President*
John J Bakula, *Exec VP*
John Bakula, *Exec VP*
Robert G Derrick, *Exec VP*
◆ **EMP:** 200 **EST:** 1951
SQ FT: 210,000
SALES (est): 195.8MM **Privately Held**
WEB: www.derrickcorp.com
SIC: 3533 Oil & gas field machinery

(G-2929)
DESIGNERS FOLDING BOX CORP
84 Tennessee St (14204-2797)
PHONE..................................716 853-5141
Fax: 716 853-5149
Jeffrey P Winney, *President*
Brian Webb, *Opers Mgr*
James Winney, *Treasurer*
Teri McAndrews, *Admin Sec*
EMP: 25 **EST:** 1950
SQ FT: 38,000
SALES (est): 2.5MM **Privately Held**
WEB: www.designersfoldingbox.com
SIC: 2657 Folding paperboard boxes

(G-2930)
DIA-NIELSEN USA INCORPORATED (DH)
400 Exchange St (14204-2064)
PHONE..................................856 642-9700
Rick Tillinghast, *General Mgr*
Rick Tallinghast, *General Mgr*
▲ **EMP:** 6
SQ FT: 11,200
SALES (est): 801.6K
SALES (corp-wide): 1B **Privately Held**
WEB: www.dianielsen.com
SIC: 3577 Graphic displays, except graphic terminals
HQ: Dia-Nielsen Gmbh & Co. Kg Zubehor Fur MeB- Und Labortechnik
Industriestr. 8
Duren
242 159-010

(G-2931)
DILESE INTERNATIONAL INC
Also Called: Choco-Logo
141 Broadway St (14203-1629)
PHONE..................................716 855-3500
Fax: 716 855-3501
Daniel Johnson, *President*
EMP: 10
SQ FT: 10,000
SALES (est): 942.2K **Privately Held**
WEB: www.chocologo.com
SIC: 2066 2064 Chocolate; candy & other confectionery products

(G-2932)
DKM SALES LLC
Also Called: Dkm Ad Art
1352 Genesee St (14211-2296)
PHONE..................................716 893-7777
Ken Krzeminski, *Partner*
Ryan Carpenter, *Manager*
EMP: 40
SQ FT: 65,000
SALES (est): 5.2MM **Privately Held**
WEB: www.dkm-sales.com
SIC: 2759 3993 2399 Screen printing; advertising novelties; banners, made from fabric

(G-2933)
DORIC VAULT OF WNY INC
73 Gilbert St (14206-2948)
PHONE..................................716 828-1776
Fax: 716 828-9018
Dennis Schultz, *President*
Carol Schultz, *Vice Pres*
EMP: 12
SQ FT: 27,000
SALES: 1MM **Privately Held**
SIC: 3272 Burial vaults, concrete or precast terrazzo

(G-2934)
DRESCHER PAPER BOX INC
459 Broadway St (14204-1634)
PHONE..................................716 854-0288
J Baird Langworthy, *President*
J Macleod, *Div Sub Head*
John Langworthy, *Exec VP*
EMP: 14 **EST:** 1867
SQ FT: 48,000
SALES (est): 1.2MM **Privately Held**
WEB: www.drescherpuzzle.com
SIC: 2652 3944 Setup paperboard boxes; games, toys & children's vehicles; puzzles

(G-2935)
DUALL FINISHING INC
53 Hopkins St (14220-2130)
PHONE..................................716 827-1707
Fax: 716 827-5848
Richard Duman, *President*
EMP: 8
SALES: 325K **Privately Held**
SIC: 3549 Metalworking machinery

(G-2936)
DURO-SHED INC (PA)
721 Center Rd (14224-2181)
PHONE..................................585 344-0800
Dave Delagrange, *President*
Dawn Ulm, *Finance Mgr*
EMP: 33
SQ FT: 6,000
SALES (est): 2.6MM **Privately Held**
WEB: www.duro-shed.com
SIC: 2452 Prefabricated wood buildings

(G-2937)
E B ATLAS STEEL CORP
120 Tonawanda St (14207-3117)
PHONE..................................716 876-0900
Brian Hogle, *President*
Mary Gibbons, *Manager*
EMP: 16
SQ FT: 7,000
SALES (est): 3.5MM **Privately Held**
SIC: 3441 Fabricated structural metal

(G-2938)
E I DU PONT DE NEMOURS & CO
Also Called: Dupont
3115 River Rd (14207-1059)
P.O. Box 88 (14207-0088)
PHONE..................................716 876-4420
Fax: 716 879-4692
Betty Czyz, *Area Mgr*
Rich Gentilucci, *Safety Mgr*
Robert Taylor, *Engineer*
John A Wacek, *Engineer*
John Wacek, *Engineer*
EMP: 50
SALES (corp-wide): 72.7B **Publicly Held**
WEB: www.dupont.com
SIC: 2823 2253 2821 Cellulosic man-made fibers; knit outerwear mills; plastics materials & resins
HQ: E. I. Du Pont De Nemours And Company
974 Centre Rd
Wilmington DE 19805
302 774-1000

(G-2939)
EAC HOLDINGS OF NY CORP
701 Willet Rd (14218-3756)
PHONE..................................716 822-2500
Kristine Ramming, *President*
Betty Ramming, *Chairman*
James Kintzel, *Corp Secy*
▼ **EMP:** 23
SQ FT: 70,000
SALES (est): 3MM **Privately Held**
WEB: www.electroabrasives.com
SIC: 3291 Abrasive grains

(G-2940)
EAST CAST ORTHTICS PROSTHETICS
505 Delaware Ave (14202-1309)
PHONE..................................716 856-5192
Vincent Benenati, *President*
Larry Benenati, *Vice Pres*
EMP: 12
SALES (est): 1.1MM **Privately Held**
SIC: 3842 Orthopedic appliances

(G-2941)
EAST COAST TOOL & MFG
1 Alliance Dr (14218-2529)
PHONE..................................716 826-5183
Fax: 716 827-0871
Richard R Stjohn, *President*
Robert Dewey, *Treasurer*
Bernie Pruchniewski, *Admin Sec*
Michael Bauer, *Administration*
Jeanine St John, *Administration*
EMP: 6
SQ FT: 5,000
SALES (est): 1MM **Privately Held**
SIC: 3541 Machine tools, metal cutting type; grinding machines, metalworking

(G-2942)
EASTERN NIAGRA RADIOLOGY
899 Main St (14203-1109)
PHONE..................................716 882-6544
Joseph Serghany MD, *Partner*
Phillip J Silberberg, *Bd of Directors*
Cynithia Selmensburger, *Admin Sec*
EMP: 22
SALES: 300K **Privately Held**
SIC: 3829 Medical diagnostic systems, nuclear

(G-2943)
EASTMAN MACHINE COMPANY
779 Washington St (14203-1396)
PHONE..................................716 856-2200
Robert L Stevenson, *CEO*
Marla Coniglio, *Exec VP*
Lenny Gallant, *Vice Pres*
Timothy McCarthy, *Vice Pres*
Trevor Stevenson, *Vice Pres*
◆ **EMP:** 110 **EST:** 1888
SQ FT: 130,000
SALES (est): 36.6MM **Privately Held**
WEB: www.eastmancuts.com
SIC: 3552 Textile machinery

(G-2944)
EATON CORPORATION
55 Pineview Dr Ste 600 (14228-2170)
PHONE..................................716 691-0008
Brian Noble, *Sales Staff*
Bratt Nanna, *Manager*
EMP: 7 **Privately Held**
WEB: www.eaton.com
SIC: 3625 Relays & industrial controls
HQ: Eaton Corporation
1000 Eaton Blvd
Cleveland OH 44122
216 523-5000

(G-2945)
EAZY MOVEMENTS
337 Hoyt St (14213-1246)
PHONE..................................716 837-2083
Everard Shaw, *Owner*
EMP: 7
SALES (est): 297.4K **Privately Held**
SIC: 2542 Racks, merchandise display or storage: except wood

(G-2946)
EDWIN J MCKENICA & SONS INC
Also Called: E.J. McKenica & Sons Inc
1200 Clinton St (14206-2824)
PHONE..................................716 823-4646
Fax: 716 823-6253
Richard E McKenica, *Ch of Bd*
Glenn Milbrand, *President*
Bob Brigham, *General Mgr*
Ronald K McKenica, *Vice Pres*
Kisha Johnson, *Manager*
▲ **EMP:** 15 **EST:** 1974
SQ FT: 28,000

GEOGRAPHIC SECTION

Buffalo - Erie County (G-2974)

SALES (est): 4MM **Privately Held**
SIC: 3599 Machine shop, jobbing & repair

(G-2947)
ELECTRO ABRASIVES LLC
701 Willet Rd (14218-3798)
PHONE.................................716 822-2500
Fax: 716 822-2858
Kristine L Ramming, *President*
Robert A Mesanovic, *Superintendent*
James R Kintzel, *Plant Mgr*
Charles Hubbard, *QC Mgr*
Robert G Christensen, *Engineer*
◆ EMP: 20
SALES (est): 3.3MM **Privately Held**
SIC: 3291 Abrasive products

(G-2948)
ELWOOD SPECIALTY PRODUCTS INC
2180 Elmwood Ave (14216-1003)
PHONE.................................716 877-6622
Peter McGennis Jr, *President*
Bill Easton, *Mfg Staff*
EMP: 13
SQ FT: 20,000
SALES (est): 1.5MM **Privately Held**
WEB: www.coolsac.com
SIC: 3842 Clothing, fire resistant & protective

(G-2949)
EM-KAY MOLDS INC
398 Ludington St (14206-1446)
PHONE.................................716 895-6180
Richard Boehler, *President*
C F Boehler, *Vice Pres*
EMP: 6
SQ FT: 24,000
SALES: 400K **Privately Held**
SIC: 3089 Injection molding of plastics; molding primary plastic

(G-2950)
EMCOM INDUSTRIES INC
235 Genesee St (14204-1456)
PHONE.................................716 852-3711
Daniel A Higgins, *President*
EMP: 5
SQ FT: 40,000
SALES: 290K **Privately Held**
SIC: 3322 3599 Malleable iron foundries; machine shop, jobbing & repair

(G-2951)
EMPIRE INNOVATION GROUP LLC
410 Main St Ste 5 (14202-3735)
PHONE.................................716 852-5000
Nicolas Knab,
EMP: 10
SALES (est): 1MM **Privately Held**
SIC: 7372 Application computer software

(G-2952)
ENERTECH LABS INC
714 Northland Ave (14211-1045)
P.O. Box 732, Getzville (14068-0732)
PHONE.................................716 332-9074
Michael Hall, *President*
Ronald Greene, *Principal*
EMP: 6
SQ FT: 30,000
SALES (est): 906.7K **Privately Held**
WEB: www.enertechlabs.com
SIC: 2911 Fuel additives

(G-2953)
ENGINEERED COMPOSITES INC
Also Called: Armor Tile
55 Roberts Ave (14206-3119)
PHONE.................................716 362-0295
Daniel Bolubash, *President*
Roman Bolubash, *Vice Pres*
David Holmes, *Manager*
▲ EMP: 30
SQ FT: 43,000
SALES (est): 11.7MM **Privately Held**
WEB: www.armortile.com
SIC: 3089 Floor coverings, plastic

(G-2954)
ENRG INC
155 Rano St Ste 300 (14207-2132)
PHONE.................................716 873-2939
Fax: 716 873-3196
John Olenick, *President*
Viswanathan Venkateswaran, *Manager*
EMP: 15
SQ FT: 13,000
SALES (est): 1.5MM **Privately Held**
WEB: www.enrg-inc.com
SIC: 3299 3674 Ceramic fiber; solid state electronic devices

(G-2955)
ENTERPRISE FOLDING BOX CO INC
75 Isabelle St (14207-1739)
PHONE.................................716 876-6421
Fax: 716 876-7197
Andrew Baranyi, *CEO*
Lynette Ovitt, *President*
Lynette Lodestro, *Branch Mgr*
Tom Hartman, *Manager*
EMP: 24
SQ FT: 100,000
SALES (est): 9MM **Privately Held**
WEB: www.enterprisebox.com
SIC: 2631 Folding boxboard

(G-2956)
EXTEN II LLC
50 Stradtman St (14206-1908)
P.O. Box 875, Orchard Park (14127-0875)
PHONE.................................716 895-2214
Richard Swanson, *President*
EMP: 18
SALES (est): 1.9MM **Privately Held**
SIC: 3714 Motor vehicle parts & accessories

(G-2957)
F X GRAPHIX INC
3043 Delaware Ave (14217-2059)
PHONE.................................716 871-1511
Fax: 716 871-1232
Thomas Giambra, *President*
Pamela Gittins, *Partner*
EMP: 6
SQ FT: 1,600
SALES (est): 686.4K **Privately Held**
WEB: www.fxgraphix.com
SIC: 2395 7336 Embroidery products, except schiffli machine; commercial art & graphic design

(G-2958)
FAMOUS DOUGHNUTS INC
3043 Main St (14214-1333)
PHONE.................................716 834-6356
Richard Roehm Sr, *President*
EMP: 8
SQ FT: 6,000
SALES (est): 791.7K **Privately Held**
SIC: 2051 Doughnuts, except frozen

(G-2959)
FARTHING PRESS INC
260 Oak St (14203-1676)
PHONE.................................716 852-4674
Fax: 716 852-4677
David W Snyder, *President*
Carolyn Snyder, *Vice Pres*
EMP: 9 EST: 1908
SQ FT: 6,800
SALES (est): 1.1MM **Privately Held**
SIC: 2752 2759 Commercial printing, offset; letterpress & screen printing; letterpress printing; screen printing

(G-2960)
FIBERGLASS REPLACEMENT PARTS
200 Colorado Ave (14215-4006)
PHONE.................................716 893-6471
Thomas E Hall, *President*
Roger Drew, *Mfg Staff*
EMP: 15
SQ FT: 37,500
SALES (est): 1.1MM **Privately Held**
WEB: www.speedwayone.com
SIC: 3713 3711 Truck bodies & parts; motor vehicles & car bodies

(G-2961)
FIBRON PRODUCTS INC
Also Called: Real Wood Tiles
170 Florida St (14208-1212)
PHONE.................................716 886-2378
Fax: 716 886-2394

Robert C Oshei Jr, *President*
Jack Oshei, *Purchasing*
EMP: 50 EST: 1949
SQ FT: 65,000
SALES (est): 3.5MM **Privately Held**
SIC: 2499 2426 Handles, wood; hardwood dimension & flooring mills

(G-2962)
FLASHFLO MANUFACTURING INC
88 Hopkins St (14220-2131)
PHONE.................................716 826-9500
Fax: 716 854-5585
Lawrence Speiser, *President*
EMP: 10
SALES (est): 1.7MM **Privately Held**
SIC: 3545 Machine tool accessories

(G-2963)
FLETCHER ENTERPRISES INC
Also Called: Fastsigns
4913 Genesee St (14225-2411)
PHONE.................................716 837-7446
Fax: 716 837-7449
Mary Ellen Fletcher, *President*
EMP: 5
SALES (est): 508.9K **Privately Held**
SIC: 3993 Signs & advertising specialties

(G-2964)
FLEXIBLE LIFELINE SYSTEMS INC ✪
100 Stradtman St (14206-2666)
PHONE.................................716 896-4949
Murry Mike Mumau, *President*
Austin Townsend, *General Mgr*
Megan Quinn, *Vice Pres*
EMP: 44 EST: 2017
SALES (est): 1.6MM **Privately Held**
SIC: 3842 Surgical appliances & supplies

(G-2965)
FLEXLUME SIGN CORPORATION
1464 Main St (14209-1780)
P.O. Box 804 (14209-0804)
PHONE.................................716 884-2020
Fax: 716 881-0361
Alfred P Rowell Sr, *CEO*
Alfred P Rowell Jr, *President*
Shirley J Rowell, *Corp Secy*
EMP: 9 EST: 1904
SQ FT: 22,000
SALES (est): 1.2MM **Privately Held**
WEB: www.flexlume.com
SIC: 3993 1799 Electric signs; sign installation & maintenance

(G-2966)
FLEXO TRANSPARENT LLC
28 Wasson St (14210-1544)
P.O. Box 128 (14240-0128)
PHONE.................................716 825-7710
Fax: 716 825-0139
Brian Mabry, *President*
Candace Richardson, *General Mgr*
Ronald D Mabry, *Chairman*
Sharon Mabry, *Vice Pres*
Kate Howard, *Accounts Mgr*
▲ EMP: 115 EST: 1987
SQ FT: 120,000
SALES (est): 20.2MM **Privately Held**
WEB: www.flexotransparent.com
SIC: 2759 Bags, plastic: printing

(G-2967)
FORD MOTOR COMPANY
3663 Lake Shore Rd (14219-2397)
PHONE.................................716 821-4000
Fax: 716 821-4009
Mario Ciach, *Plant Mgr*
Joey Williams, *Maint Spvr*
John Nowak, *Design Engr Mgr*
Mark McGiveron, *Sales Mgr*
David Buvo, *Manager*
EMP: 500
SQ FT: 2,446,347
SALES (corp-wide): 151.8B **Publicly Held**
WEB: www.ford.com
SIC: 3465 Body parts, automobile: stamped metal
PA: Ford Motor Company
  1 American Rd
  Dearborn MI 48126
  313 322-3000

(G-2968)
FORSYTH INDUSTRIES INC
1195 Colvin Blvd (14223-1909)
PHONE.................................716 652-1070
Fax: 585 652-0414
Joseph Takats III, *President*
Daniel Grew, *General Mgr*
Ellen A Mormul, *Finance*
EMP: 29 EST: 1890
SQ FT: 50,000
SALES (est): 4.2MM **Privately Held**
SIC: 3469 3315 Metal stampings; wire products, ferrous/iron: made in wiredrawing plants

(G-2969)
FPPF CHEMICAL CO INC (PA)
117 W Tupper St Ste 1 (14201-2171)
PHONE.................................716 856-9607
Fax: 716 856-0750
Christopher Lory, *President*
Jim Thurston, *Buyer*
Mark Jacobs, *Sales Staff*
EMP: 8
SQ FT: 4,000
SALES (est): 1.4MM **Privately Held**
WEB: www.fppf.com
SIC: 2911 2899 Fuel additives; antifreeze compounds

(G-2970)
FRANK WARDYNSKI & SONS INC
336 Peckham St (14206-1717)
P.O. Box 336 (14240-0336)
PHONE.................................716 854-6083
Fax: 716 854-4887
Raymond F Wardynski, *Ch of Bd*
Betsy Hooey, *Controller*
Edmund Wardynski, *Admin Sec*
EMP: 40
SQ FT: 24,000
SALES (est): 6.7MM **Privately Held**
WEB: www.wardynski.com
SIC: 2013 5149 2011 Sausage casings, natural; canned goods: fruit, vegetables, seafood, meats, etc.; meat packing plants

(G-2971)
FREDERICK MACHINE REPAIR INC
405 Ludington St (14206-1445)
PHONE.................................716 332-0104
Fax: 716 892-1426
Alan Frederick, *President*
EMP: 8 EST: 1945
SQ FT: 11,000
SALES (est): 1.3MM **Privately Held**
SIC: 3599 Machine shop, jobbing & repair

(G-2972)
FRONTIER HT-DIP GLVANIZING INC
1740 Elmwood Ave (14207-2410)
P.O. Box 199 (14207-0199)
PHONE.................................716 875-2091
Fax: 716 875-5435
Lewis G Pierce, *President*
James Abel, *Prdtn Mgr*
Diane Goodwin, *Office Mgr*
▲ EMP: 18 EST: 1971
SQ FT: 65,000
SALES: 3.2MM **Privately Held**
WEB: www.frontierhdgalvanizing.com
SIC: 3479 Galvanizing of iron, steel or endformed products

(G-2973)
FRONTIER HYDRAULICS CORP
1738 Elmwood Ave Ste 2 (14207-2465)
PHONE.................................716 694-2070
Fax: 716 874-0211
Steve M Jackson, *President*
EMP: 12
SQ FT: 10,000
SALES: 750K **Privately Held**
WEB: www.frontierhydraulics.com
SIC: 3511 Hydraulic turbines

(G-2974)
FRONTIER PLATING
Also Called: Frontier Plating Co
68 Dignity Cir (14211-1053)
PHONE.................................716 896-2811
Fax: 716 896-3430

Buffalo - Erie County (G-2975)

Arnold Collier Jr, *Owner*
EMP: 6 **EST:** 1942
SALES (est): 480.2K **Privately Held**
SIC: 3471 Electroplating of metals or formed products; polishing, metals or formed products

(G-2975)
FULL CIRCLE STUDIOS LLC
710 Main St (14202-1915)
PHONE.....................716 875-7740
Fax: 716 875-7162
Kevin Crosby, *General Mgr*
Terry Fisher,
Jim Phillips,
EMP: 7
SALES (est): 864.1K **Privately Held**
WEB: www.fullcirclestudios.com
SIC: 3699 Electronic training devices

(G-2976)
FUTURE MOBILITY PRODUCTS INC
1 Buffalo River Pl (14210-2153)
PHONE.....................716 783-9130
Abdul Samad Panchbhaya, *President*
Sahid Aquib, *Branch Mgr*
Mohammed Aswat, *Supervisor*
EMP: 20
SALES (est): 732.9K **Privately Held**
SIC: 3842 Wheelchairs

(G-2977)
GALLAGHER PRINTING INC
Also Called: Rocket Communications
2518 Delaware Ave (14216-1702)
PHONE.....................716 873-2434
David Gallagher, *President*
Dean Gallagher, *Corp Secy*
Daryl Gallagher, *Vice Pres*
Dennis Gallagher, *Treasurer*
EMP: 30
SQ FT: 30,000
SALES (est): 3.6MM **Privately Held**
WEB: www.gallagherprinting.com
SIC: 2752 2711 6513 Commercial printing, offset; newspapers; apartment building operators

(G-2978)
GALLE & ZINTER INC
Also Called: Galle Memorial
3405 Harlem Rd (14225-2019)
PHONE.....................716 833-4212
Paul Zinter, *President*
Rick Zinter, *Principal*
Tina Zinter, *Admin Sec*
EMP: 7
SQ FT: 2,198
SALES (est): 594.1K **Privately Held**
SIC: 3272 Monuments & grave markers, except terrazo

(G-2979)
GARLAND TECHNOLOGY LLC (PA)
199 Delaware Ave (14202-2102)
P.O. Box 711 (14205-0711)
PHONE.....................716 242-8500
Christopher Bihary, *CEO*
George Bouchard, *Engineer*
Renee Straney, *Design Engr*
Pam Makofski, *Finance*
Chris Pieri, *Sales Mgr*
EMP: 15
SALES (est): 2.9MM **Privately Held**
SIC: 3572 Computer storage devices

(G-2980)
GAS TCHNLGY ENRGY CNCEPTS LLC
Also Called: G Tech Natureal Gasses Systems
201 Dutton Ave (14211-1011)
PHONE.....................716 831-9695
Sam Ho, *Business Dir*
David Reichard,
William Hess,
EMP: 8
SQ FT: 5,000
SALES (est): 1.3MM **Privately Held**
SIC: 3563 Air & gas compressors

(G-2981)
GAY SHEET METAL DIES INC
301 Hinman Ave (14216-1093)
PHONE.....................716 877-0208
Dolores Dewey, *President*
David Jaworski, *Executive*
EMP: 8 **EST:** 1936
SQ FT: 6,500
SALES (est): 1.3MM **Privately Held**
SIC: 3469 3544 Stamping metal for the trade; die sets for metal stamping (presses)

(G-2982)
GEAR MOTIONS INCORPORATED
Also Called: Oliver Gear
1120 Niagara St (14213-1714)
PHONE.....................716 885-1080
Mike Barron, *Branch Mgr*
Jamie McAllister, *Manager*
EMP: 22
SALES (corp-wide): 18MM **Privately Held**
WEB: www.gearmotions.com
SIC: 3462 Gears, forged steel
PA: Gear Motions Incorporated
 1750 Milton Ave
 Syracuse NY 13209
 315 488-0100

(G-2983)
GEMTROL INC
1800 Broadway St Bldg 1c (14212-2001)
PHONE.....................716 894-0716
Fax: 716 894-0717
Jeffrey Dombek, *President*
EMP: 8
SQ FT: 4,400
SALES (est): 1.4MM **Privately Held**
WEB: www.gemtrol.com
SIC: 3625 Electric controls & control accessories, industrial

(G-2984)
GENERAL MILLS INC
54 S Michigan Ave (14203-3086)
PHONE.....................716 856-6060
Fax: 716 857-3799
Jon Blake, *Plant Mgr*
Bryan Clark, *Research*
Diane Phillips, *Research*
Christine Shearer, *Research*
Bill Shields, *Research*
EMP: 50
SALES (corp-wide): 15.6B **Publicly Held**
WEB: www.generalmills.com
SIC: 2041 Flour: blended, prepared or self-rising; flour mixes
PA: General Mills, Inc.
 1 General Mills Blvd
 Minneapolis MN 55426
 763 764-7600

(G-2985)
GENERAL MILLS INC
315 Ship Canal Pkwy (14218-1018)
PHONE.....................716 856-6060
EMP: 58
SALES (corp-wide): 15.6B **Publicly Held**
SIC: 2043 Wheat flakes: prepared as cereal breakfast food
PA: General Mills, Inc.
 1 General Mills Blvd
 Minneapolis MN 55426
 763 764-7600

(G-2986)
GENERAL MOTORS LLC
2995 River Rd 2 (14207-1059)
PHONE.....................716 879-5000
Fax: 716 879-5425
Joseph Felong, *Superintendent*
Kevin Hamilton, *VP Opers*
Lewis Campbell, *Prdtn Mgr*
Darla Flatt, *Mfg Mgr*
Brian Day, *Safety Mgr*
EMP: 900 **Publicly Held**
SIC: 3462 Automotive & internal combustion engine forgings
HQ: General Motors Llc
 300 Renaissance Ctr L1
 Detroit MI 48243

(G-2987)
GENERAL WELDING & FABG INC
1 Walden Galleria (14225-5408)
PHONE.....................716 681-8200
EMP: 7
SALES (corp-wide): 5.9MM **Privately Held**
SIC: 7692 Welding repair
PA: General Welding & Fabricating, Inc.
 991 Maple Rd
 Elma NY 14059
 716 652-0033

(G-2988)
GENESEE RESERVE BUFFALO LLC
300 Bailey Ave (14210-2211)
P.O. Box 20619, Rochester (14602-0619)
PHONE.....................716 824-3116
Bob Victor,
EMP: 30
SALES (est): 2.5MM **Privately Held**
SIC: 2491 Structural lumber & timber, treated wood

(G-2989)
GIBRALTAR INDUSTRIES INC (PA)
3556 Lake Shore Rd # 100 (14219-1400)
P.O. Box 2028 (14219-0228)
PHONE.....................716 826-6500
Fax: 716 826-1592
William P Montague, *Ch of Bd*
Frank G Heard, *President*
Cherri L Syvrud, *Senior VP*
Jeffrey Watorek, *Vice Pres*
Timothy F Murphy, *CFO*
◆ **EMP:** 82
SALES: 1B **Publicly Held**
WEB: www.gibraltar1.com
SIC: 3499 3316 3441 3398 Strapping, metal; cold finishing of steel shapes; strip steel, cold-rolled: from purchased hot-rolled; sheet, steel, cold-rolled: from purchased hot-rolled; bars, steel, cold finished, from purchased hot-rolled; fabricated structural metal; metal heat treating

(G-2990)
GLAXOSMITHKLINE LLC
17 Mahogany Dr (14221-2420)
PHONE.....................716 913-5679
EMP: 26
SALES (corp-wide): 34.3B **Privately Held**
SIC: 2834 Pharmaceutical preparations
HQ: Glaxosmithkline Llc
 5 Crescent Dr
 Philadelphia PA 19112
 215 751-4000

(G-2991)
GLOBAL EARTH ENERGY
534 Delaware Ave Ste 412 (14202-1340)
PHONE.....................716 332-7150
Sydney A Harland, *Owner*
EMP: 6
SALES (est): 20K **Privately Held**
SIC: 2911 Petroleum refining

(G-2992)
GLOBALQUEST SOLUTIONS INC
2813 Wehrle Dr Ste 3 (14221-7384)
PHONE.....................716 601-3524
Fax: 716 601-3527
Aaron Fox, *President*
Chris Lorenz, *Sales Executive*
Denise Sisti, *Manager*
Michael Morlock, *CTO*
Tom Orschek, *Director*
EMP: 12
SQ FT: 2,000
SALES (est): 3.4MM **Privately Held**
WEB: www.globalquestinc.com
SIC: 7372 Business oriented computer software

(G-2993)
GOERGEN-MACKWIRTH CO INC
765 Hertel Ave (14207-1992)
P.O. Box 750 (14207-0750)
PHONE.....................716 874-4800
Fax: 716 874-4715
Jeffrey Mertz, *President*
Katherine Schreckenberger, *Vice Pres*

Katherine Schreckenberge, *Human Resources*
Katherine Smith, *Manager*
Gail Strassburg, *Executive Asst*
EMP: 45
SQ FT: 24,000
SALES (est): 11.1MM **Privately Held**
WEB: www.goergenmackwirth.com
SIC: 3444 1761 Sheet metalwork; sheet metalwork

(G-2994)
GRAPHIC CNTRLS ACQISITION CORP (DH)
400 Exchange St (14204-2064)
P.O. Box 1271 (14240-1271)
PHONE.....................716 853-7500
Fax: 716 847-7565
Sam Heleba, *CEO*
Sam Haleba, *General Mgr*
Jeffrey A Blair, *COO*
Brandon Hoffman, *Vice Pres*
John Belotti, *VP Mfg*
▲ **EMP:** 275
SQ FT: 235,000
SALES (est): 140.7MM
SALES (corp-wide): 1B **Privately Held**
WEB: www.graphiccontrols.com
SIC: 2752 2679 Tag, ticket & schedule printing: lithographic; paper products, converted
HQ: Graphic Controls Holdings, Inc.
 400 Exchange St
 Buffalo NY 14204
 716 853-7500

(G-2995)
GRAPHIC CONTROLS HOLDINGS INC (HQ)
400 Exchange St (14204-2064)
PHONE.....................716 853-7500
Samuel Heleba, *CEO*
Thomas Reardon, *Corp Secy*
EMP: 13
SQ FT: 235,000
SALES (est): 140.7MM
SALES (corp-wide): 1B **Privately Held**
SIC: 2752 2679 6719 Tag, ticket & schedule printing: lithographic; paper products, converted; investment holding companies, except banks
PA: Nissha Printing Co.,Ltd.
 3, Mibuhanaicho, Nakagyo-Ku
 Kyoto KYO 604-8
 758 118-111

(G-2996)
GREAT LAKES ORTHOPEDIC LABS
219 Bryant St (14222-2006)
PHONE.....................716 878-7307
Fax: 716 878-1174
Blanche Daley, *Manager*
EMP: 5 **Privately Held**
SIC: 3842 Prosthetic appliances; orthopedic appliances; braces, orthopedic
PA: Great Lakes Orthopedic Labs Inc
 2362 Genesee St
 Cheektowaga NY 14225

(G-2997)
GREAT LAKES PLASTICS CO INC
2371 Broadway St (14212-2313)
PHONE.....................716 896-3100
Fax: 716 896-3244
Thomas Barzycki, *CEO*
Curtis Rice, *President*
Phil Coleman, *General Mgr*
Amy Nelson, *Corp Secy*
Catherine Barzycki, *Vice Pres*
EMP: 28 **EST:** 1946
SQ FT: 28,000
SALES (est): 5.1MM **Privately Held**
WEB: www.greatlakesplastic.com
SIC: 3082 3081 Rods, unsupported plastic; unsupported plastics film & sheet

(G-2998)
GREAT LAKES PRESSED STEEL CORP
1400 Niagara St (14213-1302)
PHONE.....................716 885-4037
Fax: 716 885-4038
Timothy O Nichols, *President*

Maryjane Nichols, *Vice Pres*
Linda Ajdaj, *Manager*
Mary Jane Nichols, *Admin Sec*
EMP: 20
SQ FT: 21,000
SALES (est): 4.1MM **Privately Held**
WEB: www.glpscorp.com
SIC: 3469 3544 Metal stampings; dies, steel rule

(G-2999)
GREEN APPLE COURAGE INC
Also Called: BP Magazine
374 Delaware Ave Ste 240 (14202-1623)
P.O. Box 59 (14205-0059)
PHONE 716 614-4673
Joanne Doan, *Ch of Bd*
EMP: 3 **EST:** 2004
SALES: 1.3MM **Privately Held**
SIC: 2721 Magazines: publishing & printing

(G-3000)
GREENBELT INDUSTRIES INC
45 Comet Ave (14216-1710)
PHONE 800 668-1114
Fax: 716 873-1728
Jim McFarlane, *President*
Sue King, *Plant Mgr*
Bryan Cormack, *CFO*
Mark Lewis, *Manager*
Gale Lipaka, *Manager*
▲ **EMP:** 40
SQ FT: 25,758
SALES: 12MM **Privately Held**
SIC: 3535 Belt conveyor systems, general industrial use
HQ: Ammeraal Beltech International Beheer B.V.
Comeniusstraat 8
Alkmaar
725 751-212

(G-3001)
HABASIT AMERICA INC
1400 Clinton St (14206-2919)
PHONE 716 824-8484
Frank Sabatino, *District Mgr*
Maureen Beecher, *Human Res Mgr*
Tim Eldridge, *Branch Mgr*
John Berdysiak, *Manager*
Mike Berdysiak, *Info Tech Mgr*
EMP: 75
SQ FT: 50,000
SALES (corp-wide): 663.9MM **Privately Held**
WEB: www.habasit.com
SIC: 3496 3052 Conveyor belts; rubber & plastics hose & beltings
HQ: Habasit America, Inc.
805 Satellite Blvd Nw
Suwanee GA 30024
678 288-3600

(G-3002)
HADLEY EXHIBITS INC (PA)
1700 Elmwood Ave (14207-2408)
PHONE 716 874-3666
Fax: 716 874-9994
Theodore K Johnson, *President*
Ralph Allen, *Vice Pres*
Greg Kerl, *Project Mgr*
Robert Riehle, *Project Mgr*
Lynn Olson, *CFO*
EMP: 87
SQ FT: 180,000
SALES (est): 13.1MM **Privately Held**
WEB: www.hadleyexhibits.com
SIC: 3993 Displays & cutouts, window & lobby

(G-3003)
HAGNER INDUSTRIES INC
95 Botsford Pl (14216-2601)
PHONE 716 873-5720
Fax: 716 873-4250
Peter Hagner, *President*
EMP: 8
SQ FT: 3,800
SALES: 400K **Privately Held**
SIC: 3599 1799 Machine shop, jobbing & repair; welding on site

(G-3004)
HANKIN BROTHERS CAP CO
Also Called: Han-Kraft Uniform Headwear
1910 Genesee St (14211-1818)
PHONE 716 892-8840
Fax: 716 892-8840
Benjamin Hankin, *Partner*
Richard Hankin, *Partner*
EMP: 10 **EST:** 1938
SQ FT: 2,800
SALES (est): 1MM **Privately Held**
SIC: 2353 Uniform hats & caps

(G-3005)
HARD MANUFACTURING CO INC
230 Grider St (14215-3797)
PHONE 716 893-1800
Fax: 716 896-2579
William Godin, *Ch of Bd*
◆ **EMP:** 65
SQ FT: 180,000
SALES (est): 9.9MM **Privately Held**
WEB: www.hardmfg.com
SIC: 2514 2599 2515 2511 Cribs: metal; hospital beds; mattresses & bedsprings; wood household furniture

(G-3006)
HARMAC MEDICAL PRODUCTS INC (PA)
2201 Bailey Ave (14211-1797)
PHONE 716 897-4500
Fax: 716 897-0016
John F Somers, *President*
John Czamara, *Manager*
Lou Ann Digiacomo, *Manager*
Elaine Beiter, *Supervisor*
Robert Moran, *Director*
▲ **EMP:** 187
SQ FT: 80,000
SALES (est): 72.3MM **Privately Held**
WEB: www.harmac.com
SIC: 3841 Surgical & medical instruments

(G-3007)
HAROLD WOOD CO INC
329 Hinman Ave (14216-1096)
PHONE 716 873-1535
Fax: 716 873-9974
Richard L Wood, *President*
Jane Wood, *Admin Sec*
EMP: 5 **EST:** 1927
SQ FT: 3,200
SALES (est): 607.9K **Privately Held**
WEB: www.haroldwood.com
SIC: 3479 Name plates: engraved, etched, etc.

(G-3008)
HARPER INTERNATIONAL CORP
4455 Genesee St Ste 123 (14225-1965)
PHONE 716 276-9900
Tom Kittell, *CEO*
Charles Miller, *President*
Waldron Bamford, *Chairman*
Ronald Vacek, *Project Dir*
Donald Alderson, *Purch Mgr*
◆ **EMP:** 100 **EST:** 1988
SALES: 50MM **Privately Held**
WEB: www.harperintl.com
SIC: 3567 Industrial furnaces & ovens

(G-3009)
HEALTH MATTERS AMERICA INC
2501 Broadway St Unit 2 (14227-1042)
P.O. Box 1482 (14225-8482)
PHONE 716 235-8772
▲ **EMP:** 14
SALES (est): 1.7MM **Privately Held**
SIC: 2393 Tea bags, fabric: made from purchased materials

(G-3010)
HEINTZ & WEBER CO INC
150 Reading St (14220-2156)
PHONE 716 852-7171
Fax: 716 852-7173
Steven D Desmond, *CEO*
Suzanne M Desmond, *Exec VP*
EMP: 7 **EST:** 1922
SQ FT: 12,500

SALES (est): 921.4K **Privately Held**
WEB: www.webersmustard.com
SIC: 2035 Pickles, vinegar; mustard, prepared (wet); relishes, fruit & vegetable

(G-3011)
HERITAGE CONTRACT FLOORING LLC
29 Depot St (14206-2203)
PHONE 716 853-1555
William H Russell, *CEO*
Don Faltisio, *CEO*
Bill Russell, *CEO*
Jeff Friedman, *Vice Pres*
Joseph Pantano, *Vice Pres*
EMP: 45
SALES (est): 8.5MM **Privately Held**
SIC: 3996 Hard surface floor coverings

(G-3012)
HI-TEMP FABRICATION INC
15 Lawrence Bell Dr (14221-7075)
PHONE 716 852-5655
Shelly Kent, *President*
Dave Schedlbauer, *Vice Pres*
John Lent, *Sales Mgr*
Bill Oreilly, *Manager*
EMP: 13
SQ FT: 40,000
SALES (est): 2.1MM **Privately Held**
WEB: www.hi-tempfab.com
SIC: 2493 Hardboard & fiberboard products

(G-3013)
HOHL MACHINE & CONVEYOR CO INC
Also Called: Hohlveyor
1580 Niagara St (14213-1199)
PHONE 716 882-7210
Fax: 716 882-9575
Richard Milazzo, *President*
EMP: 50 **EST:** 1945
SQ FT: 30,000
SALES (est): 14.9MM **Privately Held**
SIC: 3535 3599 Conveyors & conveying equipment; belt conveyor systems, general industrial use; robotic conveyors; machine & other job shop work

(G-3014)
HOOD INDUSTRIES INC
580 Tifft St (14220-1813)
PHONE 716 836-0301
Fax: 716 825-8229
Steven R Doraski, *President*
EMP: 10
SQ FT: 60,000
SALES (est): 1.4MM **Privately Held**
SIC: 2449 Shipping cases & drums, wood: wirebound & plywood

(G-3015)
HOSPIRA INC
2501 Walden Ave (14225-4737)
PHONE 716 684-9400
Carlos E Simon, *Opers Mgr*
Wayne Dreibelbis, *Mfg Spvr*
Paul Lesniak, *Opers Staff*
Steve Wisniewski, *Engineer*
Jane Jontz, *Human Res Dir*
EMP: 193
SALES (corp-wide): 52.8B **Publicly Held**
SIC: 2834 Pharmaceutical preparations
HQ: Hospira, Inc.
275 N Field Dr
Lake Forest IL 60045
224 212-2000

(G-3016)
HUTCHINSON INDUSTRIES INC
Rodgard
92 Msgr Valente Dr (14206-1822)
PHONE 716 852-1435
Bill Barrett, *Branch Mgr*
EMP: 30
SALES (corp-wide): 7.3B **Publicly Held**
SIC: 2821 Elastomers, nonvulcanizable (plastics)
HQ: Hutchinson Industries, Inc.
460 Southard St
Trenton NJ 08638
609 394-1010

(G-3017)
HYDRA TECHNOLOGY CORP
179 Grider St (14215-3724)
PHONE 716 896-8316
Fax: 716 896-4629
Kenneth Brown, *President*
May Fehmer, *Manager*
EMP: 5
SQ FT: 24,000
SALES: 2MM **Privately Held**
WEB: www.hydra-tek.com
SIC: 3593 Fluid power cylinders, hydraulic or pneumatic; fluid power actuators, hydraulic or pneumatic

(G-3018)
HYDRO-AIR COMPONENTS INC
Also Called: Zehnder Rittling
100 Rittling Blvd (14220-1885)
PHONE 716 827-6510
Scott Pallotta, *CEO*
Tony Scime, *COO*
Robert Daigler, *Vice Pres*
Bill Putney, *Purchasing*
Jim Blount, *Engineer*
▲ **EMP:** 130
SQ FT: 80,000
SALES: 37.2MM
SALES (corp-wide): 532.7MM **Privately Held**
SIC: 3585 1711 Refrigeration & heating equipment; plumbing, heating, air-conditioning contractors
PA: Zehnder Group Ag
Moortalstrasse 1
GrAnichen AG
628 551-500

(G-3019)
I ON YOUTH
115 Godfrey St (14215-2361)
PHONE 716 832-6509
Marilyn Nixon, *President*
EMP: 5
SALES (est): 304.6K **Privately Held**
SIC: 2721 Periodicals

(G-3020)
ICYNENE US ACQUISITION CORP (HQ)
438 Main St Ste 100 (14202-3207)
PHONE 800 758-7325
Bill Sommers, *CFO*
EMP: 3
SALES (est): 2MM
SALES (corp-wide): 11.9MM **Privately Held**
SIC: 2899 Foam charge mixtures
PA: Friedman Fleischer & Lowe, Llc
1 Maritime Plz Fl 22
San Francisco CA 94111
415 402-2100

(G-3021)
IMAGE TECH
96 Donna Lea Blvd (14221-3104)
PHONE 716 635-0167
Joan Hudack, *Owner*
EMP: 15
SALES (est): 520K **Privately Held**
SIC: 3999 Pet supplies

(G-3022)
IMMCO DIAGNOSTICS INC (HQ)
60 Pineview Dr (14228-2120)
PHONE 716 691-6911
Fax: 716 691-0466
William Maggio, *CEO*
Thomas C Shanahan, *Senior VP*
Rajmish Mittal, *CFO*
Robert Greene, *Controller*
Alfredo Aguirre, *Director*
EMP: 64 **EST:** 1971
SQ FT: 20,000
SALES (est): 19.2MM **Privately Held**
WEB: www.immco.com
SIC: 3231 8071 2835 Medical & laboratory glassware: made from purchased glass; medical laboratories; in vitro & in vivo diagnostic substances

(G-3023)
IN ROOM PLUS INC
2495 Main St Ste 217 (14214-2154)
PHONE 716 838-9433
Fax: 716 838-9437

Buffalo - Erie County (G-3024) GEOGRAPHIC SECTION

Mike Amrose, *CEO*
Wanda Jones, *President*
Madelyn George, *Purch Agent*
Kim Hamilton, *Director*
Elizabeth Jones, *Director*
▼ **EMP:** 32
SQ FT: 21,000
SALES (est): 5.3MM **Privately Held**
WEB: www.inroomplus.com
SIC: 2064 Candy & other confectionery products

(G-3024)
INDUSTRIAL SUPPORT INC
36 Depot St (14206-2204)
PHONE...............................716 662-2954
Fax: 716 827-2782
David P Sullivan, *President*
John Hess, *Manager*
▲ **EMP:** 75
SQ FT: 55,000
SALES (est): 16.9MM **Privately Held**
WEB: www.industrialsupportinc.com
SIC: 3441 5999 2541 Fabricated structural metal; electronic parts & equipment; wood partitions & fixtures

(G-3025)
INGERSOLL-RAND COMPANY
3101 Broadway St (14227-1034)
P.O. Box 209 (14217-0209)
PHONE...............................716 896-6600
Pasquale Cariello, *Project Mgr*
Brian Fleming, *Project Mgr*
Brian Flemming, *Project Mgr*
Joe Gross, *Project Mgr*
Ernie Pead, *Project Mgr*
EMP: 40 **Privately Held**
SIC: 3511 Turbines & turbine generator set units, complete
HQ: Ingersoll-Rand Company
800 Beaty St Ste B
Davidson NC 28036
704 655-4000

(G-3026)
INHANCE TECHNOLOGIES LLC
Also Called: Fluoro Seal
1951 Hamburg Tpke Ste 5 (14218-1046)
PHONE...............................716 825-9031
Fax: 716 825-9036
Jim Doush, *Manager*
EMP: 21
SALES (corp-wide): 54.3MM **Privately Held**
WEB: www.fluoroseal.com
SIC: 3089 2851 Plastic processing; paints & allied products
PA: Inhance Technologies Llc
16223 Park Row Ste 100
Houston TX 77084
800 929-1743

(G-3027)
INSTANTWHIP OF BUFFALO INC
2117 Genesee St (14211-1907)
PHONE...............................716 892-7031
Fax: 716 892-2921
John Beck, *General Mgr*
EMP: 20
SALES (corp-wide): 44.3MM **Privately Held**
SIC: 2099 2035 2026 2022 Food preparations; pickles, sauces & salad dressings; fluid milk; cheese, natural & processed; sample distribution
HQ: Instantwhip Of Buffalo, Inc
2200 Cardigan Ave
Columbus OH 43215
614 488-2536

(G-3028)
INTERIOR SOLUTIONS OF WNY LLC
472 Franklin St (14202-1302)
PHONE...............................716 332-0372
Jan Malof,
EMP: 9
SALES (est): 1MM **Privately Held**
SIC: 2521 Chairs, office: padded, upholstered or plain: wood

(G-3029)
INTERNATIONAL PAPER COMPANY
100 Bud Mil Dr (14206-1802)
PHONE...............................716 852-2144
Pam Regans, *Branch Mgr*
EMP: 15
SALES (corp-wide): 21B **Publicly Held**
WEB: www.tin.com
SIC: 2653 Corrugated & solid fiber boxes
PA: International Paper Company
6400 Poplar Ave
Memphis TN 38197
901 419-9000

(G-3030)
J D COUSINS INC
667 Tifft St (14220-1890)
PHONE...............................716 824-1098
Fax: 716 823-7745
Gregory N Pauly, *CEO*
Gary Bailey, *Opers Staff*
Jonathan Whitehead, *Project Engr*
Jim Howard, *Bookkeeper*
George Morris, *Accounts Mgr*
EMP: 24 **EST:** 1904
SQ FT: 30,000
SALES (est): 5.1MM **Privately Held**
WEB: www.jdcousins.com
SIC: 3599 Machine shop, jobbing & repair

(G-3031)
JAYS FURNITURE PRODUCTS INC
321 Ramsdell Ave (14216-1030)
PHONE...............................716 876-8854
Fax: 716 876-1279
James Gianni, *President*
Dean Gianni, *Plant Mgr*
Janie Gianni, *Admin Sec*
EMP: 30
SQ FT: 25,000
SALES (est): 5.2MM **Privately Held**
WEB: www.jaysfurnitureproducts.com
SIC: 2531 2512 2431 Benches for public buildings; upholstered household furniture; millwork

(G-3032)
JBREN CORP
Also Called: Lancaster Tanks and Steel Pdts
107 Dorothy St (14206-2939)
PHONE...............................716 332-5928
John Brennan, *CEO*
Mark Stutzman, *Sales Dir*
EMP: 16
SALES (est): 2.6MM **Privately Held**
SIC: 3443 Water tanks, metal plate

(G-3033)
JENTSCH & CO INC
107 Dorothy St (14206-2939)
PHONE...............................716 852-4111
Fax: 716 852-4270
Christopher Jentsch, *President*
Walter Peters, *Corp Secy*
EMP: 6 **EST:** 1931
SQ FT: 28,500
SALES (est): 944.3K **Privately Held**
WEB: www.jentschandcompany.com
SIC: 3441 Fabricated structural metal

(G-3034)
JERRY MILLER MOLDED SHOES INC (PA)
Also Called: Jerry Miller I.D. Shoes
36 Mason St (14213-1505)
PHONE...............................716 881-3920
Fax: 716 881-0349
Hussain Syed, *President*
Sarah Syed, *Vice Pres*
Wayne Weisedel, *Sls & Mktg Exec*
Wayne Weisdel, *Sales Mgr*
◆ **EMP:** 11
SQ FT: 26,000
SALES (est): 1.2MM **Privately Held**
WEB: www.jerrymillershoes.com
SIC: 3143 3144 Orthopedic shoes, men's; orthopedic shoes, women's

(G-3035)
JERSEY EXPRESS INC
3080 Main St (14214-1304)
PHONE...............................716 834-6151
Nancy Miranda, *President*
Scott Simard, *Principal*
Michael Miranda, *Vice Pres*
EMP: 15
SALES (est): 1.4MM **Privately Held**
WEB: www.jerseyexpress.com
SIC: 2389 Footlets

(G-3036)
JET-BLACK SEALERS INC
Also Called: Sealmaster
555 Ludwig Ave (14227-1026)
P.O. Box 7257 (14240-7257)
PHONE...............................716 891-4197
Fax: 716 891-4244
William C Smith, *Ch of Bd*
Eric Moggaffin, *Sales Mgr*
John Smith, *Manager*
Rosemary Smith, *Admin Sec*
EMP: 6
SQ FT: 6,400
SALES (est): 1.4MM **Privately Held**
WEB: www.sealmasterbuffalo.com
SIC: 2951 Asphalt paving mixtures & blocks

(G-3037)
JOHNSON CONTROLS INC
130 John Muir Dr Ste 100 (14228-1139)
PHONE...............................716 688-7340
Fax: 716 688-7453
Harold Witschi, *Branch Mgr*
EMP: 50 **Privately Held**
SIC: 3822 Auto controls regulating residntl & coml environmt & applncs
HQ: Johnson Controls, Inc.
5757 N Green Bay Ave
Milwaukee WI 53209
414 524-1200

(G-3038)
JOHNSON MANUFACTURING COMPANY
Also Called: SA Day Buffalo Flux Facility
1489 Niagara St (14213-1103)
P.O. Box 1084, Tonawanda (14151-1084)
PHONE...............................716 881-3030
Jackson Bowling, *General Mgr*
Gary Lampka, *Sales Staff*
EMP: 10 **Privately Held**
WEB: www.johnsonmfg.com
SIC: 2899 Fluxes: brazing, soldering, galvanizing & welding
PA: Johnson Manufacturing Company, Inc
114 Lost Grove Rd
Princeton IA 52768

(G-3039)
JUST LAMPS OF NEW YORK INC
334 Harris Hill Rd Apt 1 (14221-7473)
PHONE...............................716 626-2240
Dave Bethell, *CEO*
Eric Lanham, *President*
Eric Laham, *General Mgr*
Mark Murray, *CFO*
Dave Fromm, *Controller*
EMP: 12
SALES (est): 2.2MM **Privately Held**
WEB: www.justlamps.us.com
SIC: 3861 Projectors, still or motion picture, silent or sound

(G-3040)
K & E FABRICATING COMPANY INC
40 Stanley St (14206-1018)
PHONE...............................716 829-1829
Fax: 716 823-2183
Peter Fasolino, *President*
David Fasolino, *Manager*
EMP: 12
SQ FT: 10,000
SALES (est): 2.7MM **Privately Held**
SIC: 3441 Fabricated structural metal

(G-3041)
K D M DIE COMPANY INC
620 Elk St (14210-2237)
PHONE...............................716 828-9000
Fax: 716 828-9100
Gary Posluszny, *CEO*
Carl Posluszny, *Treasurer*
Linn Emser, *Finance*
EMP: 17
SQ FT: 32,000
SALES: 2.5MM **Privately Held**
SIC: 3544 3599 Special dies & tools; machine shop, jobbing & repair

(G-3042)
K-TECHNOLOGIES INC
4090 Jeffrey Blvd (14219-2338)
PHONE...............................716 828-4444
Jeffrey Kryszak, *President*
Edward Tierney, *Vice Pres*
David Ankenbauer, *Mfg Mgr*
Rob Desjardins, *Chief Engr*
Guy Allan, *Manager*
EMP: 40
SQ FT: 5,400
SALES (est): 4MM **Privately Held**
WEB: www.k-technologies.net
SIC: 3824 Electromechanical counters

(G-3043)
KALNITZ KITCHENS INC
Also Called: K Kitchen
2620 Walden Ave (14225-4736)
PHONE...............................716 684-1700
Fax: 716 684-4733
Jamie Kalnitz, *President*
▲ **EMP:** 10 **EST:** 1980
SQ FT: 6,000
SALES (est): 1.3MM **Privately Held**
WEB: www.kkitchen.com
SIC: 2434 Wood kitchen cabinets

(G-3044)
KEHR-BUFFALO WIRE FRAME CO INC
Also Called: Rogers Industrial Spring
127 Kehr St (14211-1522)
P.O. Box 806, Grand Island (14072-0806)
PHONE...............................716 897-2288
George Rogers, *President*
James Rogers III, *Vice Pres*
EMP: 30
SQ FT: 27,000
SALES (est): 5.2MM **Privately Held**
WEB: www.kbwf.net
SIC: 3496 Miscellaneous fabricated wire products

(G-3045)
KELLER BROS & MILLER INC
401 Franklin St (14202-1586)
PHONE...............................716 854-2374
Fax: 716 856-7978
Ralph Salerno, *President*
EMP: 9
SQ FT: 8,600
SALES (est): 1.5MM **Privately Held**
WEB: www.kbmprinting.com
SIC: 2752 Commercial printing, lithographic

(G-3046)
KEY TECH FINISHING
2929 Main St Ste 2 (14214-1760)
PHONE...............................716 832-1232
Fax: 716 832-1298
Jack Karet, *President*
Jennifer Masse, *General Mgr*
Joan Karet, *Corp Secy*
Melanie Sandquist, *Plant Mgr*
EMP: 30
SQ FT: 80,000
SALES (est): 3MM
SALES (corp-wide): 8.1MM **Privately Held**
WEB: www.keyfinishing.com
SIC: 3471 Electroplating of metals or formed products; electroplating & plating
PA: Keystone Corporation
2929 Main St
Buffalo NY 14214
716 832-1232

(G-3047)
KEYNOTE SYSTEMS CORPORATION
2810 Sweet Home Rd (14228-1347)
PHONE...............................716 564-1332
Leonard Gostowski, *President*
EMP: 5
SALES (est): 560.8K **Privately Held**
SIC: 7372 Prepackaged software

GEOGRAPHIC SECTION
Buffalo - Erie County (G-3071)

(G-3048)
KEYSTONE CORPORATION (PA)
2929 Main St (14214-1719)
PHONE...................716 832-1232
Fax: 716 836-8885
Jack A Karet, *President*
Joan Karet, *Corp Secy*
Michael Karet, *Vice Pres*
Sam Goorevich, *Sales Mgr*
EMP: 40 **EST:** 1923
SQ FT: 45,000
SALES (est): 8.4MM **Privately Held**
WEB: www.keyfinishing.com
SIC: 3471 Electroplating of metals or formed products; electroplating & plating; anodizing (plating) of metals or formed products

(G-3049)
KINEQUIP INC
365 Old Niagara Fls Blvd (14228-1636)
PHONE...................716 694-5000
Scott Fotheringham, *Marketing Staff*
John Mistreda, *Manager*
Eric Lee, *Consultant*
Jon Kreiss, *Executive Asst*
EMP: 13
SALES (corp-wide): 12.4MM **Privately Held**
WEB: www.buywika.com
SIC: 3563 5084 Vacuum pumps, except laboratory; industrial machinery & equipment
PA: Kinequip Inc.
   365 Old Niagara Fls Blvd
   Amherst NY 14228
   716 694-5000

(G-3050)
KITTINGER COMPANY INC
4675 Transit Rd (14221-6022)
PHONE...................716 876-1000
Raymond C Bialkowski, *CEO*
EMP: 50
SQ FT: 60,000
SALES (est): 7.8MM **Privately Held**
WEB: www.kittingerfurniture.com
SIC: 2521 2512 2511 Wood office furniture; upholstered household furniture; wood household furniture

(G-3051)
KNOLL INC
1700 Broadway St (14212-2031)
PHONE...................716 891-1700
EMP: 60
SALES (corp-wide): 1.1B **Publicly Held**
SIC: 2521 Wood office furniture
PA: Knoll, Inc.
   1235 Water St
   East Greenville PA 18041
   215 679-7991

(G-3052)
KOCH METAL SPINNING CO INC
74 Jewett Ave (14214-2421)
PHONE...................716 835-3631
Fax: 716 833-0834
Eric Koch, *President*
McManigle Robert, *Purch Mgr*
Candace Farrell, *Bookkeeper*
▼ **EMP:** 52 **EST:** 1939
SQ FT: 50,000
SALES: 4MM **Privately Held**
WEB: www.kochmetalspinning.com
SIC: 3469 Spinning metal for the trade

(G-3053)
KOEHLR-GIBSON MKG GRAPHICS INC
Also Called: Koehler-Gibson Mkg & Graphics
875 Englewood Ave (14223-2334)
PHONE...................716 838-5960
Fax: 716 835-5960
David Koehler, *President*
Roselyn Kieffer, *Purchasing*
EMP: 20 **EST:** 1958
SQ FT: 13,000
SALES (est): 2.8MM **Privately Held**
SIC: 3953 2796 Date stamps, hand: rubber or metal; postmark stamps, hand: rubber or metal; printing dies, rubber or plastic, for marking machines; photoengraving plates, linecuts or halftones

(G-3054)
KOHLER AWNING INC
2600 Walden Ave (14225-4736)
PHONE...................716 685-3333
John M Kohler III, *President*
Craig Kohler, *Corp Secy*
Jesse W Kohler, *Vice Pres*
Patricia Kusz, *Office Mgr*
EMP: 30 **EST:** 1924
SQ FT: 2,182
SALES: 4.4MM **Privately Held**
WEB: www.kohlerawning.com
SIC: 2394 7699 Awnings, fabric: made from purchased materials; awning repair shop

(G-3055)
KREPE KRAFT INC
Also Called: Krepe-Kraft
1801 Elmwood Ave (14207-2463)
P.O. Box 1907 (14219-0107)
PHONE...................716 826-7086
Fax: 716 826-7239
Daniel Keane, *President*
Leo Eckman, *President*
Kevin T Keane, *Principal*
Donna Eckman, *Vice Pres*
John M Yessa, *Treasurer*
EMP: 370
SQ FT: 47,300
SALES (est): 25.6MM
SALES (corp-wide): 59.2MM **Privately Held**
WEB: www.krepekraft.com
SIC: 2754 5947 Commercial printing, gravure; invitations: gravure printing; cards, except greeting: gravure printing; gift, novelty & souvenir shop
PA: Mod-Pac Corp.
   1801 Elmwood Ave Ste 1
   Buffalo NY 14207
   716 898-8480

(G-3056)
KYNTEC CORPORATION
2100 Old Union Rd (14227-2725)
PHONE...................716 810-6956
Patrick Lee, *Ch of Bd*
Scott Taylor, *President*
Gerald Spyche, *Vice Pres*
Rich Ryan, *Treasurer*
EMP: 6 **EST:** 2012
SALES (est): 1.3MM **Privately Held**
SIC: 3569 3484 3429 3531 Industrial shock absorbers; rifles or rifle parts, 30 mm. & below; aircraft hardware; marine related equipment

(G-3057)
L LLC
106 Soldiers Pl (14222-1261)
PHONE...................716 885-3918
Mohsen Lachaal, *Mng Member*
EMP: 20 **EST:** 2001
SALES (est): 2MM **Privately Held**
SIC: 2079 Olive oil

(G-3058)
LABATT USA LLC
50 Fountain Plz Ste 900 (14202-2214)
PHONE...................716 604-1050
Fax: 716 604-1055
Glen Walter, *President*
Thomas Cardella, *Vice Pres*
Frank Oostdyk, *Engineer*
Elyse Brown, *Human Resources*
Shari Keisow, *Manager*
▲ **EMP:** 60
SALES (est): 9.1MM **Privately Held**
SIC: 2082 Beer (alcoholic beverage)
HQ: North American Breweries, Inc.
   445 Saint Paul St
   Rochester NY 14605

(G-3059)
LACTALIS AMERICAN GROUP INC
2375 S Park Ave (14220-2653)
PHONE...................716 827-2622
Sean Paul Quiblier, *Principal*
Sharon Pusateri, *Assistant*
Laurie Siwy, *Clerk*
EMP: 100
SALES (corp-wide): 98.8K **Privately Held**
SIC: 2022 Cheese, natural & processed
HQ: Lactalis American Group, Inc.
   2376 S Park Ave
   Buffalo NY 14220
   716 823-6262

(G-3060)
LACTALIS AMERICAN GROUP INC (DH)
Also Called: Sorrento Lactalis
2376 S Park Ave (14220-2670)
PHONE...................716 823-6262
Frederick Bouisset, *CEO*
Aliza Manzella, *Business Mgr*
Pierre Lorieau, *Vice Pres*
Paul Peterson, *Vice Pres*
Elena Umanskaya, *Vice Pres*
◆ **EMP:** 500
SALES (est): 550.5MM
SALES (corp-wide): 98.8K **Privately Held**
WEB: www.lactalisamericangroup.com
SIC: 2022 Cheese, natural & processed
HQ: Parmalat Spa
   Via Delle Nazioni Unite 4
   Collecchio PR 43044
   052 180-81

(G-3061)
LAFARGE NORTH AMERICA INC
575 Ohio St (14203-3119)
PHONE...................716 854-5791
Fax: 716 854-3112
Edward Hickey, *Manager*
Robert Lloyd, *Manager*
EMP: 5
SALES (corp-wide): 26.6B **Privately Held**
WEB: www.lafargenorthamerica.com
SIC: 3241 Cement, hydraulic
HQ: Lafarge North America Inc.
   8700 W Bryn Mawr Ave Ll
   Chicago IL 60631
   703 480-3600

(G-3062)
LANDIES CANDIES CO INC
2495 Main St Ste 350 (14214-2154)
PHONE...................716 834-8212
Fax: 716 833-9113
Larry Szrama, *President*
Andrew Gaiek, *Vice Pres*
Alan Nowak, *Safety Dir*
Matthew Halizak, *Facilities Mgr*
Dennis Hussak, *Marketing Staff*
▲ **EMP:** 10
SALES (est): 1.7MM **Privately Held**
WEB: www.landiescandies.com
SIC: 2066 Chocolate candy, solid

(G-3063)
LAURUS DEVELOPMENT INC
3556 Lake Shore Rd # 121 (14219-1460)
PHONE...................716 823-1202
Vincent Coppola, *President*
John Feuerstein, *Vice Pres*
Todd Eberwine, *Software Dev*
EMP: 14
SALES (est): 1MM **Privately Held**
WEB: www.laurusdevelopment.com
SIC: 7372 7371 8748 7379 Business oriented computer software; computer software systems analysis & design, custom; computer software development & applications; systems engineering consultant, ex. computer or professional; computer related maintenance services

(G-3064)
LIME ENERGY CO
1a Elk Terminal (14204-2212)
PHONE...................704 892-4442
Adam Procell, *Branch Mgr*
EMP: 5
SALES (corp-wide): 112.6MM **Privately Held**
SIC: 3274 Lime
PA: Lime Energy Co.
   4 Gateway Ctr Fl 4
   Newark NJ 07102
   201 416-2575

(G-3065)
LINDE LLC
101 Katherine St (14210-2005)
PHONE...................716 847-0748
Jack Pederson, *Opers-Prdtn-Mfg*
EMP: 40
SALES (corp-wide): 17.9B **Privately Held**
SIC: 2813 Nitrogen; oxygen, compressed or liquefied
HQ: Linde Llc
   200 Somerset Corporate Bl
   Bridgewater NJ 08807
   908 464-8100

(G-3066)
LINE WARD CORPORATION
157 Seneca Creek Rd (14224-2347)
PHONE...................716 675-7373
Fax: 716 674-5334
Cheryl Gustavel, *President*
Roger Gustavel, *Vice Pres*
Robert J Ward, *Plant Mgr*
EMP: 7
SQ FT: 3,000
SALES (est): 800K **Privately Held**
WEB: www.lineward.com
SIC: 3531 Construction machinery

(G-3067)
LITELAB CORP (PA)
251 Elm St (14203-1603)
PHONE...................716 856-4300
Fax: 716 856-0156
Frederick A Spaulding, *CEO*
Jacob Levin, *President*
Ellen Conrad, *General Mgr*
Dawn M Casati, *Corp Secy*
Lawrence Christ, *COO*
▲ **EMP:** 135
SQ FT: 80,000
SALES (est): 25.7MM **Privately Held**
WEB: www.litelab.com
SIC: 3646 3645 Commercial indusl & institutional electric lighting fixtures; residential lighting fixtures

(G-3068)
LOCKHOUSE DISTILLERY
41 Columbia St Ste 200 (14204-2133)
PHONE...................716 768-4898
Chad Vosseller, *President*
EMP: 5
SALES (est): 266K **Privately Held**
SIC: 2084 Wines, brandy & brandy spirits

(G-3069)
LOY L PRESS INC
Also Called: Allegra Printing
3959 Union Rd (14225-4253)
PHONE...................716 634-5966
Fax: 716 634-0841
Richard Delong, *President*
Joyce S Delong, *Vice Pres*
EMP: 5
SQ FT: 1,894
SALES (est): 765.3K **Privately Held**
SIC: 2752 2791 2789 2759 Commercial printing, lithographic; typesetting; bookbinding & related work; commercial printing

(G-3070)
M A MOSLOW & BROS INC
375 Norfolk Ave (14215-3108)
PHONE...................716 896-2950
Fax: 716 896-2699
David Moslow, *President*
Joe Moslow, *Vice Pres*
Laurie Keggins, *Office Mgr*
▲ **EMP:** 40
SQ FT: 21,000
SALES (est): 4.3MM **Privately Held**
WEB: www.moslowbros.com
SIC: 2499 Trophy bases, wood

(G-3071)
M K ULRICH CONSTRUCTION INC
Also Called: Bison Iron & Step
1601 Harlem Rd (14206-1923)
PHONE...................716 893-5777
Fax: 716 893-1125
Don Ulrich, *President*
Marie Ulrich, *Vice Pres*
EMP: 12
SQ FT: 4,800
SALES: 900K **Privately Held**
SIC: 3272 1799 Concrete products; steps, prefabricated concrete; ornamental metal work

Buffalo - Erie County (G-3072)

(G-3072)
MAC INNES ENTERPRISES INC
Also Called: Associated Publishing Co
61 John Muir Dr (14228-1147)
PHONE.................................325 676-4032
Robert Allen III, *President*
Richard Rayburn, *Vice Pres*
EMP: 20
SALES (est): 733.1K **Privately Held**
SIC: 2741 Directories, telephone: publishing only, not printed on site; telephone & other directory publishing

(G-3073)
MACNEIL POLYMERS INC (PA)
3155 Broadway St (14227-1034)
PHONE.................................716 681-7755
Richard Neil, *President*
EMP: 15 **EST:** 2000
SQ FT: 35,097
SALES (est): 1MM **Privately Held**
WEB: www.macneilpolymers.com
SIC: 2821 Plastics materials & resins

(G-3074)
MAGAZINES & BROCHURES INC
Also Called: Labels X Press
2205 Kenmore Ave Ste 107 (14207-1329)
PHONE.................................716 875-9699
Fax: 716 875-9996
Craig Boggs, *President*
Scott Boggs, *Treasurer*
EMP: 5
SALES (est): 546.7K **Privately Held**
WEB: www.labelsxpress.com
SIC: 2759 2752 Commercial printing; commercial printing, lithographic

(G-3075)
MAGTROL INC
70 Gardenville Pkwy W (14224-1394)
PHONE.................................716 668-5555
Fax: 716 668-8705
William A Mulroy III, *President*
Thomas Rymarczyk, *General Mgr*
◆ **EMP:** 50 **EST:** 1953
SQ FT: 35,000
SALES (est): 13.1MM **Privately Held**
WEB: www.magtrol.com
SIC: 3829 3625 3568 3825 Measuring & controlling devices; aircraft & motor vehicle measurement equipment; brakes, electromagnetic; clutches, except vehicular; instruments to measure electricity; industrial instrmnts msrmnt display/control process variable; motor vehicle parts & accessories

(G-3076)
MAKE-WAVES INSTRUMENT CORP (PA)
4172 Vinewood Dr (14221-7518)
PHONE.................................716 681-7524
Fax: 716 681-3412
John R Patterson, *President*
Brian Cory, *Vice Pres*
Richard Rang, *Controller*
▲ **EMP:** 25
SQ FT: 36,000
SALES (est): 2.4MM **Privately Held**
WEB: www.makewavesinstrumentcorp.com
SIC: 3825 3829 3641 3545 Tachometer generators; gauges, motor vehicle: oil pressure, water temperature; electric lamps; machine tool accessories; valves & pipe fittings; gaskets, packing & sealing devices

(G-3077)
MARKIN TUBING LP
Also Called: Markin Tubing Division
400 Ingham Ave (14218-2536)
PHONE.................................585 495-6211
Fax: 716 824-3525
Ivan Zahariev, *Production*
Tom Stamper, *Manager*
EMP: 17
SALES (corp-wide): 19.9MM **Privately Held**
SIC: 3312 3317 Tubes, steel & iron; steel pipe & tubes
PA: Markin Tubing, Lp
1 Markin Ln
Wyoming NY 14591
585 495-6211

(G-3078)
MASSIMO FRIEDMAN INC
Also Called: Great Arrow Graphics
2495 Main St Ste 457 (14214-2154)
PHONE.................................716 836-0408
Fax: 716 736-0702
Alan Friedman, *President*
Donna M Massimo, *Corp Secy*
Lisa Samar, *Vice Pres*
EMP: 20
SALES (est): 2.2MM **Privately Held**
WEB: www.greatarrow.com
SIC: 2771 Greeting cards

(G-3079)
MATERION ADVANCED MATERIALS (DH)
2978 Main St (14214-1004)
PHONE.................................800 327-1355
Donald Klinkowicz, *President*
Jeff Hazlett, *General Mgr*
Matthew Willson, *Vice Pres*
Jason Maher, *Mfg Dir*
Charisse Brown, *Opers Mgr*
▲ **EMP:** 198 **EST:** 1912
SQ FT: 150,000
SALES (est): 104.4MM
SALES (corp-wide): 969.2MM **Publicly Held**
WEB: www.williams-adv.com
SIC: 3339 Primary nonferrous metals
HQ: Materion Brush Inc.
6070 Parkland Blvd Ste 1
Mayfield Heights OH 44124
216 486-4200

(G-3080)
MAXSECURE SYSTEMS INC
300 International Dr # 100 (14221-5781)
PHONE.................................800 657-4336
Ken Szekely, *President*
Ken Lawrence, *Admin Sec*
EMP: 3
SALES (est): 1.3MM **Privately Held**
WEB: www.max-secure.com
SIC: 2531 Public building & related furniture

(G-3081)
MC IVOR MANUFACTURING INC
400 Ingham Ave (14218-2536)
P.O. Box 13 (14220-0013)
PHONE.................................716 825-1808
Fax: 716 825-1809
Bruce Mc Ivor, *President*
EMP: 6
SQ FT: 13,000
SALES (est): 632.2K **Privately Held**
SIC: 3599 Machine shop, jobbing & repair

(G-3082)
MEDICAL ACOUSTICS LLC
640 Ellicott St Ste 407 (14203-1253)
P.O. Box 327, Bowmansville (14026-0327)
PHONE.................................716 218-7353
Nicolaas Smith, *Vice Pres*
Frank Codella, *Mng Member*
Joel Castlevetere,
EMP: 12
SALES (est): 1MM **Privately Held**
SIC: 3842 Respirators

(G-3083)
MERZ METAL & MACHINE CORP
237 Chelsea Pl (14211-1003)
PHONE.................................716 893-7786
Fax: 716 893-8727
Dave Nieman, *President*
Joe Huefner, *Vice Pres*
Kathy Charczuk, *Human Resources*
EMP: 22 **EST:** 1948
SQ FT: 13,000
SALES (est): 5MM **Privately Held**
WEB: www.merzmetal.com
SIC: 3444 1711 Sheet metalwork; ventilators, sheet metal; ducts, sheet metal; ventilation & duct work contractor

(G-3084)
MIBRO GROUP
Also Called: Allied
4039 Genesee St (14225-1904)
PHONE.................................716 631-5713
Fax: 716 837-9500
Leon Lapidus, *President*
Sharon McNutt, *COO*
Barry J Smith, *CFO*
Silvia Garcia, *Finance Mgr*
Elaine Cruise-Smith, *Human Res Dir*
◆ **EMP:** 75 **EST:** 1954
SQ FT: 100,000
SALES (est): 11.9MM
SALES (corp-wide): 34.4MM **Privately Held**
WEB: www.mibro.com
SIC: 3545 Drill bits, metalworking
PA: Mibro Partners
111 Sinnott Rd
Scarborough ON M1L 4
416 285-9000

(G-3085)
MIKEN COMPANIES INC
75 Boxwood Ln (14227-2707)
P.O. Box 178 (14231-0178)
PHONE.................................716 668-6311
Fax: 716 668-7630
Walter J Jaworski, *CEO*
Michael Bolas, *President*
Pauline Jaworski, *Vice Pres*
Ralph Leskiw, *Purchasing*
Rick Brzezicki, *Manager*
EMP: 100 **EST:** 1929
SQ FT: 65,000
SALES (est): 13.5MM **Privately Held**
WEB: www.mikencompanies.com
SIC: 2752 2759 2675 2672 Commercial printing, lithographic; commercial printing; die-cut paper & board; coated & laminated paper

(G-3086)
MILLCRAFT PAPER COMPANY
Also Called: Deltacraft Paper Company
99 Bud Mil Dr (14206-1801)
PHONE.................................716 856-5135
Bill Grubich, *Branch Mgr*
EMP: 50 **Privately Held**
WEB: www.millcraft.com
SIC: 2679 Paper products, converted
HQ: The Millcraft Paper Company
6800 Grant Ave
Cleveland OH 44105
216 441-5505

(G-3087)
MINEO & SAPIO MEATS INC
Also Called: Minero & Sapio Sausage
410 Connecticut St (14213-2641)
PHONE.................................716 884-2398
Fax: 716 884-2515
Michael Pierro, *President*
Nadine Pierro, *Treasurer*
EMP: 6
SALES (est): 1.4MM **Privately Held**
WEB: www.mineosapio.com
SIC: 2013 5421 Sausages & other prepared meats; meat markets, including freezer provisioniers

(G-3088)
MIRION TECH CONAX NUCLEAR INC
Also Called: Ist Conax Nuclear
402 Sonwil Dr (14225-5530)
PHONE.................................716 681-1973
Fax: 716 681-1193
Iain Wilson, *CEO*
Jukka Kahilainen, *Vice Pres*
Jack Pacheco, *CFO*
Seth B Rosen, *Admin Sec*
EMP: 23
SQ FT: 26,200
SALES (est): 4.6MM
SALES (corp-wide): 169.2MM **Privately Held**
WEB: www.mirion.com
SIC: 3829 Nuclear radiation & testing apparatus
HQ: Mirion Technologies (Ist) Corporation
315 Daniel Zenker Dr # 204
Horseheads NY 14845
607 562-4300

(G-3089)
MM OF EAST AURORA LLC
Also Called: Buffalo Hardwood Floor Center
3801 Harlem Rd (14215-1907)
PHONE.................................716 651-9663
Fax: 716 683-7446
Greg Tramont, *CFO*
Marlena Maloney, *Mng Member*
EMP: 10
SALES (est): 1.5MM **Privately Held**
SIC: 2426 Hardwood dimension & flooring mills

(G-3090)
MOBILEAPP SYSTEMS LLC
4 Grand View Trl (14217)
PHONE.................................716 667-2780
EMP: 5 **EST:** 2012
SALES (est): 310.6K **Privately Held**
SIC: 7372 Prepackaged software

(G-3091)
MOD-PAC CORP (PA)
1801 Elmwood Ave Ste 1 (14207-2496)
PHONE.................................716 898-8480
Fax: 716 873-6008
Kevin T Keane, *Ch of Bd*
Daniel G Keane, *President*
Robert J McKenna, *Principal*
Howard Zemsky, *Principal*
David B Lupp, *COO*
◆ **EMP:** 170
SQ FT: 333,000
SALES (est): 59.2MM **Privately Held**
WEB: www.modpac.com
SIC: 2657 5999 Food containers, folding: made from purchased material; alarm & safety equipment stores

(G-3092)
MOD-PAC CORP
1801 Elmwood Ave Ste 1 (14207-2496)
P.O. Box 1907, Blasdell (14219-0107)
PHONE.................................716 447-9013
Robert Heilman, *Vice Pres*
Leo Eckman, *Manager*
EMP: 100
SALES (corp-wide): 59.2MM **Privately Held**
WEB: www.modpac.com
SIC: 2754 2752 Commercial printing, gravure; commercial printing, lithographic
PA: Mod-Pac Corp.
1801 Elmwood Ave Ste 1
Buffalo NY 14207
716 898-8480

(G-3093)
MODERN HEAT TRTING FORGING INC (PA)
1112 Niagara St (14213-1714)
PHONE.................................716 884-2176
Fax: 716 884-1419
Douglas Feind Sr, *President*
Scott Feind, *Vice Pres*
Pamela Feind, *Office Mgr*
EMP: 16 **EST:** 1929
SQ FT: 17,000
SALES (est): 2.1MM **Privately Held**
WEB: www.modernheattreat.com
SIC: 3398 Metal heat treating

(G-3094)
MONO-SYSTEMS INC
180 Hopkins St (14220-1854)
PHONE.................................716 821-1344
Fax: 716 821-1345
Bill Lignos, *Purchasing*
Jim Sutton, *Manager*
EMP: 30
SALES (corp-wide): 10.4MM **Privately Held**
WEB: www.monosystems.com
SIC: 3443 3643 3549 Cable trays, metal plate; current-carrying wiring devices; metalworking machinery
PA: Mono-Systems, Inc.
4 International Dr # 280
Rye Brook NY 10573
914 934-2075

(G-3095)
MOOR ELECTRONICS INC
95 Dorothy St Ste 6 (14206-2900)
P.O. Box 765 (14240-0765)
PHONE.................................716 821-5304
Duane Simano, *President*
Henry Zagara, *Corp Secy*
▲ **EMP:** 6
SQ FT: 5,000
SALES: 274K **Privately Held**
SIC: 3812 7699 Nautical instruments; nautical & navigational instrument repair

GEOGRAPHIC SECTION
Buffalo - Erie County (G-3120)

(G-3096)
MOZZARELLA FRESCA INCORPORATED
2376 S Park Ave (14220-2670)
PHONE..................................559 752-4823
Brandy Benderson, *President*
EMP: 5 EST: 2008
SALES (est): 306.8K
SALES (corp-wide): 98.8K Privately Held
SIC: 2022 Cheese, natural & processed
HQ: Lactalis American Group, Inc.
2376 S Park Ave
Buffalo NY 14220
716 823-6262

(G-3097)
MRI NORTHTOWNS GROUP PC
Also Called: Northtown Imaging
199 Park Club Ln Ste 300 (14221-5269)
PHONE..................................716 836-4646
Fax: 716 836-4696
James Rinaldi, *Manager*
Elizabeth M Sobieraj, *Diag Radio*
EMP: 11
SALES (corp-wide): 2.7MM Privately Held
WEB: www.lockportmri.com
SIC: 3231 Medical & laboratory glassware: made from purchased glass
PA: Mri Northtown's Group Pc
1020 Youngs Rd Ste 120w
Williamsville NY 14221
716 689-4406

(G-3098)
MULLER TOOL INC
74 Anderson Rd (14225-4979)
PHONE..................................716 895-3658
Fax: 716 895-3972
Gary D Reisweber, *President*
Bruce Reisweber, *Vice Pres*
Sheryl Demarco, *Purch Mgr*
Paul Banko, *QC Mgr*
EMP: 20 EST: 1941
SQ FT: 12,000
SALES (est): 3.7MM Privately Held
WEB: www.mullertool.com
SIC: 3599 3451 Machine shop, jobbing & repair; screw machine products

(G-3099)
MULTISORB TECH INTL LLC (PA)
325 Harlem Rd (14224-1825)
PHONE..................................716 824-8900
James Renda, *President*
Laxmikant Khaitan, *Business Mgr*
Jim Balon, *Vice Pres*
Rich Burke, *Opers Staff*
Sarah Cook, *Opers Staff*
EMP: 1
SALES (est): 31.4MM Privately Held
SIC: 2819 Industrial inorganic chemicals

(G-3100)
MULTISORB TECHNOLOGIES INC
Also Called: Ecto Tech Automation
10 French Rd (14227)
PHONE..................................716 656-1402
Fax: 716 662-8281
John S Cullen, *CEO*
Andrew Zippiroli, *Engineer*
Mark Morelli, *Manager*
EMP: 30
SALES (corp-wide): 104.8MM Privately Held
SIC: 2819 Industrial inorganic chemicals
PA: Multisorb Technologies, Inc.
325 Harlem Rd
Buffalo NY 14224
716 824-8900

(G-3101)
N MAKE MOLD INC
Also Called: Chocolate Delivery Systems
85 River Rock Dr Ste 202 (14207-2170)
PHONE..................................716 877-3146
Timothy Thill, *President*
Nancy Hnowski, *Credit Mgr*
▲ EMP: 50
SALES (est): 15.6MM
SALES (corp-wide): 21.8MM Privately Held
SIC: 2064 Candy bars, including chocolate covered bars
PA: Chocolate Delivery Systems, Inc.
85 River Rock Dr Ste 202
Buffalo NY 14207
716 854-6050

(G-3102)
NAS QUICK SIGN INC
Also Called: North American Signs Buffalo
1628 Elmwood Ave (14207-3014)
PHONE..................................716 876-7599
Fax: 716 876-7729
Frank Strada, *President*
Mike Francano, *Prdtn Mgr*
Paul Strada, *Sales Mgr*
Agnes Strada, *Shareholder*
EMP: 9
SQ FT: 7,000
SALES (est): 1.3MM Privately Held
SIC: 3993 Signs, not made in custom sign painting shops; electric signs

(G-3103)
NC INDUSTRIES INC (PA)
Also Called: Niagara Cutter
200 John James Audubon (14228-1120)
P.O. Box 279, Reynoldsville PA (15851-0279)
PHONE..................................248 528-5200
Fax: 716 693-5050
Roger D Bollier, *Ch of Bd*
Sherwood L Bollier, *Vice Pres*
William C Szabo, *Treasurer*
William Rees, *Office Mgr*
Dan Wells, *Manager*
EMP: 15
SQ FT: 8,500
SALES (est): 52.8MM Privately Held
SIC: 3545 3479 5084 Cutting tools for machine tools; coating of metals & formed products; machine tools & accessories

(G-3104)
NEW AVON LLC
433 Thorncliff Rd (14223-1128)
PHONE..................................716 572-4842
Kathy Gleason, *Principal*
EMP: 12
SALES (corp-wide): 36.1B Publicly Held
SIC: 2844 Toilet preparations
HQ: New Avon Llc
1 Liberty Plz
New York NY 10006
212 282-8500

(G-3105)
NEW BUFFALO SHIRT FACTORY INC
1979 Harlem Rd (14212-2410)
PHONE..................................716 436-5839
John Weiss, *President*
David Swart, *Director*
Pamela Thayer, *Director*
EMP: 8
SQ FT: 14,000
SALES: 1MM Privately Held
SIC: 2759 Screen printing

(G-3106)
NEW ERA CAP CO INC
160 Delaware Ave (14202-2404)
PHONE..................................716 604-9000
Michael Thorton, *Manager*
EMP: 300
SALES (corp-wide): 529.4MM Privately Held
WEB: www.neweracap.com
SIC: 2353 Uniform hats & caps; baseball caps
PA: New Era Cap Co., Inc.
160 Delaware Ave
Buffalo NY 14202
716 604-9000

(G-3107)
NEW ERA CAP CO INC (PA)
160 Delaware Ave (14202-2404)
P.O. Box 208, Derby (14047-0208)
PHONE..................................716 604-9000
Fax: 716 604-9299
Christopher Koch, *Ch of Bd*
Peter M Augustine, *President*
Valerie Koch, *Corp Secy*
Jim Patterson, *COO*
Gerry Matos, *Senior VP*
◆ EMP: 200
SQ FT: 120,000
SALES (est): 529.4MM Privately Held
WEB: www.neweracap.com
SIC: 2353 Uniform hats & caps; baseball caps

(G-3108)
NIAGARA DISPENSING TECH INC
170 Northpointe Pkwy (14228-1991)
PHONE..................................716 636-9827
Fax: 716 636-5095
Glenn Kaufmann, *CEO*
Thomas Gagliano, *CEO*
Carlo Petermann, *COO*
Neil Fischer, *Sales Dir*
▲ EMP: 10 EST: 2007
SQ FT: 3,000
SALES: 2MM Privately Held
SIC: 3585 Beer dispensing equipment

(G-3109)
NIAGARA FIBERGLASS INC
88 Okell St (14220-2133)
PHONE..................................716 822-3921
Fax: 716 822-0406
Stephen Gale, *President*
Philip O'Donnell, *Vice Pres*
Gordon Dickinson, *Sales Staff*
EMP: 45
SQ FT: 23,000
SALES: 2.3MM Privately Held
SIC: 3089 3544 Molding primary plastic; special dies, tools, jigs & fixtures

(G-3110)
NIAGARA GEAR CORPORATION
941 Military Rd (14217-2590)
PHONE..................................716 874-3131
Fax: 716 874-9003
Matthew Babisz, *President*
Robert C Barden, *Vice Pres*
Marcia Iore, *Finance Mgr*
EMP: 25 EST: 1952
SQ FT: 30,000
SALES: 4.2MM Privately Held
WEB: www.niagaragear.com
SIC: 3566 Gears, power transmission, except automotive

(G-3111)
NIAGARA LASALLE CORPORATION
110 Hopkins St (14220-2195)
P.O. Box 399 (14240-0399)
PHONE..................................716 827-7010
Margo Mack, *Sales Staff*
Craig Zito, *Sales Staff*
Mike Slood, *Manager*
EMP: 75
SALES (corp-wide): 184.5MM Privately Held
SIC: 3316 Bars, steel, cold finished, from purchased hot-rolled
HQ: Niagara Lasalle Corporation
1412 150th St
Hammond IN 46327
219 853-6000

(G-3112)
NIAGARA PUNCH & DIE CORP
176 Gruner Rd (14227-1090)
PHONE..................................716 896-7619
Fax: 716 896-8958
Jay Czerniak, *President*
Jean Czerniak, *Admin Sec*
EMP: 8 EST: 1956
SQ FT: 5,000
SALES (est): 1.7MM Privately Held
WEB: www.npd123.com
SIC: 3544 Special dies & tools

(G-3113)
NIAGARA TRANSFORMER CORP
1747 Dale Rd (14225-4964)
P.O. Box 233 (14225-0233)
PHONE..................................716 896-6500
Fax: 716 896-8871
John F Darby, *President*
Robert Fishlock, *Vice Pres*
Sheldon Kennedy, *Vice Pres*
Bob Murphy, *QC Mgr*
Brian Porterfield, *Engineer*
▲ EMP: 75 EST: 1928
SQ FT: 100,000
SALES (est): 27.5MM Privately Held
WEB: www.niagaratransformer.com
SIC: 3612 Power transformers, electric

(G-3114)
NIAGARA TYING SERVICE INC
176 Dingens St (14206-2308)
PHONE..................................716 825-0066
Fax: 716 825-0542
Albert J Barrato, *President*
James Smith, *Manager*
Antoinette Barrato, *Admin Sec*
▲ EMP: 38
SALES (est): 5.9MM Privately Held
WEB: www.niagaratyingservice.com
SIC: 2013 Sausage casings, natural

(G-3115)
NICKEL CITY STUDIOS PHOTO JOUR
45 Linwood Ave (14209-2203)
PHONE..................................716 200-0956
Rich Mattingly, *Principal*
EMP: 5
SALES (est): 430.3K Privately Held
SIC: 3356 Nickel

(G-3116)
NORAZZA INC (PA)
3938 Broadway St (14227-1104)
PHONE..................................716 706-1160
Thomas J Sperazza, *CEO*
Cindy Judd, *Accounting Mgr*
Mike Moran, *Director*
▲ EMP: 4
SALES (est): 1.6MM Privately Held
WEB: www.norazza.com
SIC: 3577 3861 Computer peripheral equipment; photographic equipment & supplies

(G-3117)
NORSE ENERGY CORP USA
3556 Lake Shore Rd # 700 (14219-1445)
PHONE..................................716 568-2048
EMP: 5 EST: 1993
SALES (est): 690K Privately Held
SIC: 1382 Oil/Gas Exploration Services

(G-3118)
NORTHROP GRUMMAN INTL TRDG INC
Also Called: Land Self Prtction Systems Div
1740 Wehrle Dr (14221-7032)
PHONE..................................716 626-7233
Patrick Duffey, *General Mgr*
Michael Clark, *Senior Engr*
Brian Schmidt, *Marketing Staff*
Robert Britton, *Manager*
Kevin Ruggiero, *Manager*
EMP: 6
SALES (est): 636.5K Publicly Held
SIC: 3699 Flight simulators (training aids), electronic
HQ: Northrop Grumman Overseas Holding, Inc.
2980 Fairview Park Dr
Falls Church VA 22042
703 280-4069

(G-3119)
NORTHROP GRUMMAN SYSTEMS CORP
1740 Wehrle Dr (14221-7032)
PHONE..................................716 626-4600
Tim Green, *Principal*
Kevin Ditondo, *Engineer*
James Heimbueger, *Engineer*
Angelo Morgante, *Engineer*
Mark Perrego, *Engineer*
EMP: 99 Publicly Held
SIC: 3721 Aircraft
HQ: Northrop Grumman Systems Corporation
2980 Fairview Park Dr
Falls Church VA 22042
703 280-2900

(G-3120)
OEHLERS WLDG & FABRICATION INC
242 Elk St (14210-2102)
PHONE..................................716 821-1800
Mark Appelbaum, *President*
EMP: 15

Buffalo - Erie County (G-3121) GEOGRAPHIC SECTION

SQ FT: 45,000
SALES: 1.4MM **Privately Held**
SIC: 3441 Fabricated structural metal

(G-3121)
OERLIKON BLZERS CATING USA INC
6000 N Bailey Ave Ste 3 (14226-5102)
PHONE.................................716 564-8557
John Jesnowski, *Branch Mgr*
EMP: 30
SALES (corp-wide): 2.3B **Privately Held**
WEB: www.balzers.com
SIC: 3479 3471 Coating of metals & formed products; finishing, metals or formed products
HQ: Oerlikon Balzers Coating Usa Inc.
    1475 E Wdfield Rd Ste 201
    Schaumburg IL 60173
    847 619-5541

(G-3122)
OLIVER GEAR INC
1120 Niagara St (14213-1790)
PHONE.................................716 885-1080
Fax: 716 885-1145
Sam Haines, *President*
Mike Barron, *Vice Pres*
Dan Sweeney, *Engineer*
Barbara Stone, *CFO*
Linda Manuszewski, *Human Res Mgr*
EMP: 25
SQ FT: 21,000
SALES (est): 6.3MM
SALES (corp-wide): 18MM **Privately Held**
WEB: www.gearmotions.com
SIC: 3566 7699 Speed changers, drives & gears; industrial equipment services
PA: Gear Motions Incorporated
    1750 Milton Ave
    Syracuse NY 13209
    315 488-0100

(G-3123)
ONEIDA SALES & SERVICE INC (PA)
Also Called: Oneida Concrete Products
155 Commerce Dr (14218-1041)
PHONE.................................716 822-8205
Frederick Saia, *President*
Jeff Kramer, *Controller*
EMP: 40
SALES (est): 9.4MM **Privately Held**
WEB: www.oneidagroup.com
SIC: 3531 1799 3496 Concrete plants; fence construction; miscellaneous fabricated wire products

(G-3124)
ONY INC BAIRD RESEARCHPARK
1576 Sweet Home Rd (14228-2710)
PHONE.................................716 636-9096
Edmond Egan, *President*
EMP: 30
SALES (est): 1.7MM **Privately Held**
SIC: 2834 Druggists' preparations (pharmaceuticals)

(G-3125)
OPTA MINERALS
266 Elmwood Ave (14222-2202)
P.O. Box 818 (14222)
PHONE.................................905 689-7361
Bernie Rumbold, *CEO*
John Dietrich, *President*
▲ EMP: 14
SALES (est): 2.5MM **Privately Held**
SIC: 3295 Magnesite, crude: ground, calcined or dead-burned

(G-3126)
ORBITAL HOLDINGS INC
2775 Broadway St Ste 200 (14227-1043)
PHONE.................................951 360-7100
Jerry Jacobs, *Vice Pres*
▲ EMP: 20
SQ FT: 35,160
SALES (est): 3.6MM **Privately Held**
WEB: www.avf.com
SIC: 3449 3429 Miscellaneous metalwork; manufactured hardware (general)
PA: Avf Inc.
    2775 Broadway St Ste 200
    Buffalo NY 14227

(G-3127)
OTIS BEDDING MFG CO INC (PA)
80 James E Casey Dr (14206-2367)
PHONE.................................716 825-2599
Fax: 716 824-2073
John Roma Sr, *President*
John Roma Jr, *Vice Pres*
Carol Roma, *Treasurer*
▲ EMP: 20 EST: 1882
SQ FT: 40,000
SALES (est): 2MM **Privately Held**
WEB: www.otisbed.com
SIC: 2515 5712 Mattresses & bedsprings; mattresses

(G-3128)
P J R INDUSTRIES INC
Also Called: Southside Precast Products
1951 Hamburg Tpke Ste 17 (14218-1047)
PHONE.................................716 825-9300
Fax: 716 825-1155
Richard Workman, *President*
Larry Gold, *Engineer*
Jerrell Bihm, *Info Tech Mgr*
Ron Hayden, *Info Tech Mgr*
Jody Tucker, *Administration*
EMP: 32
SQ FT: 18,500
SALES (est): 3.5MM **Privately Held**
WEB: www.southsideprecast.com
SIC: 3272 Concrete products, precast

(G-3129)
P P I BUSINESS FORMS INC
94 Spaulding St (14220-1238)
PHONE.................................716 825-1241
Fax: 716 685-4740
EMP: 9
SQ FT: 9,500
SALES (est): 900K **Privately Held**
SIC: 2761 Manifold Busines Forms

(G-3130)
P&G METAL COMPONENTS CORP
54 Gruner Rd (14227-1007)
PHONE.................................716 896-7900
Fax: 716 896-4129
Scott Bauer, *General Mgr*
David E Ponkow, *Chairman*
Andrew Ponkow, *Exec VP*
Thomas Brush, *CFO*
▲ EMP: 100 EST: 1955
SQ FT: 75,000
SALES (est): 33.7MM **Privately Held**
WEB: www.pgsteel.com
SIC: 3469 3544 4961 Metal stampings; special dies, tools, jigs & fixtures; steam & air-conditioning supply

(G-3131)
P-HGH 2 CO INC
180 Cambridge Ave (14215-3702)
PHONE.................................954 534-6058
Matthew Taylor, *President*
EMP: 6
SALES (est): 265.8K **Privately Held**
SIC: 2099 Food preparations

(G-3132)
PACKAGE PRINT TECHNOLOGIES
1831 Niagara St (14207-3112)
PHONE.................................716 871-9905
Tracy Wettlaufer, *President*
Ward Wettlaufer, *General Mgr*
Tony Collini, *Admin Sec*
▲ EMP: 21
SQ FT: 5,000
SALES (est): 4.1MM **Privately Held**
WEB: www.packageprinttech.com
SIC: 3555 3069 Printing trades machinery; printers' rolls & blankets: rubber or rubberized fabric

(G-3133)
PACKSTAR GROUP INC
215 John Glenn Dr (14228-2227)
PHONE.................................716 853-1688
Fax: 716 853-0974
Andrew Sharp, *Ch of Bd*
Todd Mann, *Prdtn Mgr*
Paul Johnson, *CFO*
Janice Bauer, *Cust Mgr*
Robert Herman, *Sales Staff*
▲ EMP: 95 EST: 1997
SQ FT: 50,000
SALES (est): 21.2MM **Privately Held**
WEB: www.packstargroup.com
SIC: 2671 4789 Plastic film, coated or laminated for packaging; cargo loading & unloading services
PA: Brook & Whittle Limited
    260 Branford Rd
    North Branford CT 06471

(G-3134)
PANASONIC CORP NORTH AMERICA
Panasonic Eco So
1339 S Park Ave (14220-1035)
PHONE.................................888 765-2489
Peter Vicoria, *Branch Mgr*
EMP: 100
SALES (corp-wide): 64.6B **Privately Held**
SIC: 3674 Solar cells
HQ: Panasonic Corporation Of North America
    2 Riverfront Plz Ste 200
    Newark NJ 07102
    201 348-7000

(G-3135)
PAR-FOAM PRODUCTS INC
239 Van Rensselaer St (14210-1345)
PHONE.................................716 855-2066
Fax: 716 855-2119
Kaushik A Shah, *President*
Rolandd J Neuffer, *Vice Pres*
George Captain, *Engineer*
Larry Parker, *Sales Mgr*
EMP: 130
SQ FT: 64,000
SALES (est): 14.7MM **Privately Held**
SIC: 3069 3714 3086 Foam rubber; motor vehicle parts & accessories; plastics foam products

(G-3136)
PARK AVENUE IMPRINTS LLC (PA)
2955 S Park Ave (14218-2613)
PHONE.................................716 822-5737
Fax: 716 822-5700
Josh Holtzman, *Sales Dir*
James Roorda, *Mng Member*
Cindy B Anticola, *Department Mgr*
EMP: 6
SQ FT: 1,200
SALES (est): 490.4K **Privately Held**
SIC: 2396 Screen printing on fabric articles

(G-3137)
PARKSIDE CANDY CO INC (PA)
3208 Main St Ste 1 (14214-1379)
PHONE.................................716 833-7540
Fax: 716 833-7560
Phillip J Buffamonte, *President*
EMP: 17 EST: 1978
SALES (est): 1.5MM **Privately Held**
WEB: www.parksidecandy.com
SIC: 2066 5441 Chocolate bars, solid; chocolate candy, solid; candy

(G-3138)
PARRINELLO PRINTING INC
84 Aero Dr (14225-1435)
PHONE.................................716 633-7780
Colleen Parrinello, *President*
Renee Shone, *Manager*
EMP: 14
SALES (est): 2.1MM **Privately Held**
SIC: 2752 Commercial printing, lithographic

(G-3139)
PDI CONE CO INC
Also Called: Dutchtreat
69 Leddy St (14210-2134)
PHONE.................................716 825-8750
Fax: 716 827-8615
Geoge Page, *Principal*
EMP: 67 EST: 2008
SALES (est): 8.2MM **Privately Held**
SIC: 2052 Cones, ice cream

(G-3140)
PELLICANO SPECIALTY FOODS INC
195 Reading St (14220-2157)
P.O. Box 34, Lake View (14085-0034)
PHONE.................................716 822-2366
Mario Pellicano, *President*
EMP: 18 EST: 1996
SALES (est): 4MM **Privately Held**
SIC: 2099 Food preparations

(G-3141)
PENINSULA PLASTICS LTD
161 Marine Dr Apt 6e (14202-4214)
P.O. Box 1179 (14202)
PHONE.................................716 854-3050
Craig Bolton, *Owner*
EMP: 54
SALES (est): 2.1MM **Privately Held**
WEB: www.penplast.com
SIC: 3089 Injection molding of plastics

(G-3142)
PEOPLES CHOICE M R I
125 Galileo Dr (14221-2776)
PHONE.................................716 681-7377
Vafeem Iqbal, *President*
EMP: 10
SALES (est): 919K **Privately Held**
WEB: www.peoplesmri.com
SIC: 3577 Magnetic ink & optical scanning devices

(G-3143)
PERAFLEX HOSE INC
155 Great Arrow Ave Ste 4 (14207-3010)
PHONE.................................716 876-8806
Fax: 716 876-8708
Newell Kraik, *President*
James Nelson, *Manager*
Mark Montgomery, *Director*
◆ EMP: 15
SQ FT: 13,000
SALES (est): 3MM **Privately Held**
WEB: www.peraflex.com
SIC: 3052 5085 Rubber & plastics hose & beltings; industrial supplies

(G-3144)
PERKINS INTERNATIONAL INC (HQ)
672 Delaware Ave (14209-2202)
PHONE.................................309 675-1000
Michael J Baunton, *CEO*
Dan Hagan, *Analyst*
EMP: 5
SALES (est): 3.1MM
SALES (corp-wide): 38.5B **Publicly Held**
WEB: www.tuckaway.com
SIC: 3519 Internal combustion engines
PA: Caterpillar Inc.
    100 Ne Adams St
    Peoria IL 61629
    309 675-1000

(G-3145)
PERMA TECH INC
363 Hamburg St (14204-2086)
PHONE.................................716 854-0707
Fax: 716 854-0774
Richard E Lund Jr, *President*
EMP: 22
SQ FT: 45,000
SALES (est): 3MM **Privately Held**
WEB: www.permatechinc.com
SIC: 2394 3441 3089 Awnings, fabric: made from purchased materials; fabricated structural metal; doors, folding: plastic or plastic coated fabric

(G-3146)
PHILCOM LTD
1144 Military Rd (14217-2232)
PHONE.................................716 875-8005
Bruce G Phillips, *Ch of Bd*
Karen Phillips, *Vice Pres*
EMP: 1
SALES (est): 3.8MM **Privately Held**
SIC: 3089 Boxes, plastic

(G-3147)
PHILPAC CORPORATION (PA)
1144 Military Rd (14217-2232)
PHONE.................................716 875-8005
Fax: 716 875-9908

GEOGRAPHIC SECTION

Buffalo - Erie County (G-3171)

Bruce G Phillips, *President*
Karen Phillips, *Corp Secy*
Courtney Gorman, *Materials Mgr*
Randy Steele, *Draft/Design*
Stephen Dysert, *Sales Mgr*
EMP: 50
SALES (est): 15.3MM **Privately Held**
SIC: 2653 5085 3086 2655 Boxes, corrugated: made from purchased materials; packing, industrial; padding, foamed plastic; fiber cans, drums & similar products; nailed wood boxes & shook

(G-3148)
PIERCE ARROW DRAPERY MFG
Also Called: Pierce Arrow Draperies
1685 Elmwood Ave Ste 312 (14207-2435)
PHONE..................................716 876-3023
Robert Merkel, *President*
EMP: 5
SQ FT: 2,000
SALES (est): 360K **Privately Held**
SIC: 2221 Draperies & drapery fabrics, manmade fiber & silk

(G-3149)
PII HOLDINGS INC (DH)
2150 Elmwood Ave (14207-1910)
PHONE..................................716 876-9951
Mike McLelland, *CEO*
Ray Baran, *Treasurer*
EMP: 2
SALES (est): 220MM
SALES (corp-wide): 2.8B **Privately Held**
SIC: 3089 3822 6719 Molding primary plastic; temperature controls, automatic; investment holding companies, except banks
HQ: Berwind Consolidated Holdings, Inc.
  3000 Ctr Sq W 1500 Mkt St 1500 W
  Philadelphia PA 19102
  215 563-2800

(G-3150)
PINE HILL FABRICATORS
2731 Seneca St (14224-1895)
PHONE..................................716 823-2474
Fax: 716 823-2475
Joseph L Neuner, *Owner*
Liz Eichelberger, *Office Mgr*
EMP: 6
SQ FT: 4,000
SALES (est): 789.7K **Privately Held**
SIC: 2541 Counter & sink tops

(G-3151)
PLASLOK CORP
3155 Broadway St (14227-1034)
PHONE..................................716 681-7755
Fax: 716 681-9142
Richard A Neil, *President*
Donald Bauman, *Research*
Gregory Maher, *Controller*
EMP: 43
SQ FT: 75,000
SALES (est): 7MM **Privately Held**
SIC: 2821 Molding compounds, plastics

(G-3152)
PLASTIC SYS/GR BFLO INC
465 Cornwall Ave (14215-3125)
PHONE..................................716 835-7555
Daniel McNamara, *President*
Sean Lobue, *General Mgr*
EMP: 5 **EST:** 1980
SQ FT: 9,200
SALES (est): 728K **Privately Held**
WEB: www.plasticsystems.com
SIC: 3089 Plastic containers, except foam; trays, plastic; thermoformed finished plastic products; cases, plastic

(G-3153)
POINTMAN LLC
Also Called: Swremote
403 Main St Ste 200 (14203-2107)
PHONE..................................716 842-1439
Stephen Kiernan, *President*
Steven Raines, *Vice Pres*
EMP: 5
SQ FT: 18,000
SALES: 1.6MM **Privately Held**
SIC: 7372 5734 5045 Business oriented computer software; software, business & non-game; computer software

(G-3154)
POL-TEK INDUSTRIES LTD
2300 Clinton St (14227-1735)
PHONE..................................716 823-1502
Fax: 716 823-5871
Martin Ostrowski, *CEO*
Wanda Ostrowski, *Corp Secy*
Natalie Handzlik, *Office Mgr*
EMP: 15
SQ FT: 11,000
SALES (est): 2MM **Privately Held**
WEB: www.pol-tek.com
SIC: 3599 Machine shop, jobbing & repair

(G-3155)
POWER DRIVES INC (PA)
801 Exchange St (14210-1434)
PHONE..................................716 822-3600
Fax: 716 824-4817
Louis P Panzica, *President*
David Word, *President*
Sue Harvey, *Editor*
Kristin Linn, *Corp Secy*
Peter Daigler, *VP Opers*
▲ **EMP:** 60 **EST:** 1945
SQ FT: 14,000
SALES (est): 43.4MM **Privately Held**
WEB: www.powerdrives.com
SIC: 3492 Hose & tube fittings & assemblies, hydraulic/pneumatic

(G-3156)
POWER UP MANUFACTURING INC
275 N Pointe Pkwy Ste 100 (14228-1895)
PHONE..................................716 876-4890
Dean T Wright, *President*
Elizabeth Wright, *Admin Dir*
▲ **EMP:** 25
SQ FT: 15,000
SALES (est): 3.6MM **Privately Held**
WEB: www.powerupmfg.com
SIC: 3069 Battery boxes, jars or parts, hard rubber

(G-3157)
POWERFLOW INC
1714 Broadway St (14212-2090)
P.O. Box 905 (14240-0905)
PHONE..................................716 892-1014
Douglas K Ward, *Ch of Bd*
Douglas Capps, *Vice Pres*
Gary Schweigert, *Plant Mgr*
Robert Dilski, *Purchasing*
Donald R Halt, *VP Finance*
▲ **EMP:** 66 **EST:** 1978
SQ FT: 55,000
SALES (est): 17.7MM **Privately Held**
WEB: www.powerflowinc.com
SIC: 3714 Motor vehicle parts & accessories

(G-3158)
PRECISION PHOTO-FAB INC
Also Called: Switzer
4020 Jeffrey Blvd (14219-2393)
PHONE..................................716 821-9393
Fax: 716 821-9399
Bernie Switzer, *Ch of Bd*
Dennis Switzer, *President*
Patrick Haefner, *Principal*
Joseph Dunlop, *VP Sales*
Kim Heimburg, *Representative*
EMP: 55
SQ FT: 20,000
SALES (est): 12.8MM **Privately Held**
WEB: www.precisionphotofab.com
SIC: 3469 Metal stampings

(G-3159)
PRECISION SPCLTY FBRCTIONS LLC
51 N Gates Ave (14218-1029)
PHONE..................................716 824-2108
Fax: 716 827-1364
Dennis Switzer,
John Maher,
EMP: 20
SALES (est): 2.6MM **Privately Held**
SIC: 3499 Strapping, metal

(G-3160)
PREMIER MACHINING TECH INC
2100 Old Union Rd (14227-2725)
PHONE..................................716 608-1311

William G Belcher, *President*
Kimberly Belcher, *Admin Sec*
EMP: 8
SQ FT: 18,500
SALES (est): 1.2MM **Privately Held**
SIC: 3599 Machine shop, jobbing & repair

(G-3161)
PRINCE RUBBER & PLAS CO INC (PA)
137 Arthur St (14207-2098)
PHONE..................................225 272-1653
Fax: 716 877-0743
S Warren Prince Jr, *Ch of Bd*
Mary Churchman, *Controller*
Tom Hashar, *Marketing Staff*
Lary Terzian, *Manager*
John G Putnam, *Admin Sec*
▲ **EMP:** 25
SQ FT: 35,000
SALES (est): 7.5MM **Privately Held**
WEB: www.princerp.com
SIC: 3069 3089 3084 3053 Hard rubber & molded rubber products; plastic processing; plastics pipe; gaskets, packing & sealing devices

(G-3162)
PRINTED IMAGE
1906 Clinton St (14206-3206)
PHONE..................................716 821-1880
Richard Zavarella, *Owner*
EMP: 5
SQ FT: 3,000
SALES (est): 410.1K **Privately Held**
SIC: 2759 Commercial printing

(G-3163)
PRINTING PREP INC
707 Washington St (14203-1308)
PHONE..................................716 852-5071
Harold S Leader, *President*
John Wulf, *Financial Exec*
Jamie Baco, *Accounts Exec*
Don Gordon, *Accounts Exec*
Scott Polley, *Supervisor*
EMP: 32
SQ FT: 11,365
SALES (corp-wide): 2.5MM **Privately Held**
WEB: www.printleader.us
SIC: 2752 Commercial printing, lithographic
PA: Printing Prep, Inc
  12 E Tupper St
  Buffalo NY
  716 852-5011

(G-3164)
PRO-GEAR CO INC
1120 Niagara St (14213-1714)
PHONE..................................716 684-3811
Fax: 716 684-7717
Gary Rackley, *President*
Dolores Reidy, *Office Mgr*
Kevin Rackley, *Manager*
EMP: 5
SQ FT: 6,500
SALES (est): 377.2K
SALES (corp-wide): 18MM **Privately Held**
SIC: 3462 Gears, forged steel
PA: Gear Motions Incorporated
  1750 Milton Ave
  Syracuse NY 13209
  315 488-0100

(G-3165)
PROTECTIVE INDUSTRIES INC (DH)
Also Called: Caplugs
2150 Elmwood Ave (14207-1910)
PHONE..................................716 876-9951
Fax: 716 874-1680
Steven Smith, *Senior VP*
Susan McElligott, *Vice Pres*
Kennery Rob, *Vice Pres*
Thomas Valentine, *Vice Pres*
James Ray, *VP Opers*
◆ **EMP:** 250
SALES (est): 220MM
SALES (corp-wide): 2.8B **Privately Held**
WEB: www.mokon.com
SIC: 3089 3822 Molding primary plastic; temperature controls, automatic

HQ: Pii Holdings, Inc.
  2150 Elmwood Ave
  Buffalo NY 14207
  716 876-9951

(G-3166)
PROTECTIVE INDUSTRIES INC
Also Called: Caplugs
2150 Elmwood Ave (14207-1910)
PHONE..................................716 876-9855
Jeff Smith, *Branch Mgr*
EMP: 238
SALES (corp-wide): 2.8B **Privately Held**
WEB: www.mokon.com
SIC: 3089 Molding primary plastic
HQ: Protective Industries, Inc.
  2150 Elmwood Ave
  Buffalo NY 14207
  716 876-9951

(G-3167)
PROTECTIVE INDUSTRIES INC
Mokon
2510 Elmwood Ave (14217-2223)
PHONE..................................716 876-9951
Robert Kennery, *General Mgr*
EMP: 55
SALES (corp-wide): 2.8B **Privately Held**
WEB: www.mokon.com
SIC: 3822 Temperature controls, automatic
HQ: Protective Industries, Inc.
  2150 Elmwood Ave
  Buffalo NY 14207
  716 876-9951

(G-3168)
PVS CHEMICAL SOLUTIONS INC
55 Lee St (14210-2109)
PHONE..................................716 825-5762
Patrick Murphy, *Opers Mgr*
Jane Lamanna, *Engineer*
Chris Cancilla, *Manager*
EMP: 51
SALES (corp-wide): 497MM **Privately Held**
SIC: 2819 2899 Sulfur chloride; chemical preparations
HQ: Pvs Chemical Solutions, Inc.
  10900 Harper Ave
  Detroit MI 48213

(G-3169)
PVS TECHNOLOGIES INC
Also Called: PVS Chemical Solutions
55 Lee St (14210-2109)
PHONE..................................716 825-5762
William Decker, *Manager*
EMP: 48
SQ FT: 65,268
SALES (corp-wide): 497MM **Privately Held**
SIC: 2819 Metal salts & compounds, except sodium, potassium, aluminum
HQ: Pvs Technologies, Inc.
  10900 Harper Ave
  Detroit MI 48213
  313 571-1100

(G-3170)
QLS SOLUTIONS GROUP INC
701 Seneca St Ste 600 (14210-1361)
PHONE..................................716 852-2203
Fax: 716 852-2204
Gary Skalyo, *President*
Debbie Besaw, *Supervisor*
EMP: 24
SQ FT: 30,000
SALES (est): 4.3MM **Privately Held**
WEB: www.qualitylaser.com
SIC: 3955 3861 Print cartridges for laser & other computer printers; reproduction machines & equipment

(G-3171)
QTA MACHINING INC
Also Called: Quick Turn Around Machining
876 Bailey Ave (14206-2300)
PHONE..................................716 862-8108
Fax: 716 837-5002
Suzanne M Pelczynski, *President*
Roxanne Pelczynski, *Vice Pres*
John Hake, *Materials Mgr*
Tom Pelczynski, *Manager*
EMP: 12
SQ FT: 10,000

(PA)=Parent Co (HQ)=Headquarters (DH)=Div Headquarters
✪ = New Business established in last 2 years

2018 Harris
New York Manufacturers Directory

Buffalo - Erie County (G-3172)   GEOGRAPHIC SECTION

SALES (est): 1.3MM **Privately Held**
WEB: www.qtanow.com
SIC: 3599 Machine shop, jobbing & repair

(G-3172)
QUAKER BONNET INC
54 Irving Pl (14201-1521)
PHONE 716 885-7208
Fax: 716 885-7245
Elizabeth Kolken, *President*
Ben Kolken, *Vice Pres*
EMP: 5 EST: 1930
SQ FT: 4,400
SALES (est): 494.2K **Privately Held**
WEB: www.quakerbonnet.com
SIC: 2051 2052 2024 Bakery: wholesale or wholesale/retail combined; cookies; ice cream & frozen desserts

(G-3173)
QUALITY BINDERY SERVICE INC
501 Amherst St (14207-2913)
PHONE 716 883-5185
Fax: 716 883-1598
Kathleen Hartmans, *President*
Cathy Rajca, *Mktg Dir*
EMP: 34
SQ FT: 4,000
SALES (est): 4.1MM **Privately Held**
SIC: 2789 Trade binding services

(G-3174)
QUANTUM ASSET RECOVERY
482 Niagara Falls Blvd (14223-2634)
PHONE 716 393-2712
EMP: 6
SALES (est): 326.9K **Privately Held**
SIC: 3572 Computer storage devices

(G-3175)
QUEEN CITY MALTING LLC
644 N Forest Rd (14221-4965)
PHONE 716 481-1313
Joseph S Kirby Jr, *CEO*
EMP: 8
SALES (est): 278.8K **Privately Held**
SIC: 2083 Malt

(G-3176)
QUEEN CITY MANUFACTURING INC
333 Henderson Ave (14217-1538)
PHONE 716 877-1102
Fax: 716 773-7071
Robert Maranto, *President*
Joseph Mallare, *Vice Pres*
Steve Nappo, *Vice Pres*
Nancy Natto, *Manager*
▲ **EMP:** 5
SALES (est): 1.4MM **Privately Held**
WEB: www.queencitymanufacturing.com
SIC: 2821 Melamine resins, melamine-formaldehyde

(G-3177)
R & A INDUSTRIAL PRODUCTS
Also Called: R&A Prods
30 Cornelia St (14210-1202)
PHONE 716 823-4300
Fax: 716 825-2080
Tony Onello, *President*
EMP: 5
SQ FT: 2,600
SALES (est): 376.6K **Privately Held**
SIC: 3061 Mechanical rubber goods

(G-3178)
R & B MACHINERY CORP
400 Kennedy Rd Ste 3 (14227-1073)
PHONE 716 894-3332
Fax: 716 894-3335
EMP: 4
SQ FT: 28,000
SALES (est): 2.2MM **Privately Held**
SIC: 3559 Mfg Misc Industry Machinery

(G-3179)
RAPID RAYS PRINTING & COPYING
300 Broadway St (14204-1433)
P.O. Box 442 (14205-0442)
PHONE 716 852-0550
Fax: 716 852-5208
Raymond Wellence, *President*
Kathleen Wellence, *Vice Pres*

Victor Garrow, *Opers Mgr*
Jeffery Steinborn, *Manager*
EMP: 9
SQ FT: 4,100
SALES (est): 1.1MM **Privately Held**
WEB: www.rapidrays.com
SIC: 2752 Photo-offset printing

(G-3180)
RAPID SERVICE ENGRAVING CO
1593 Genesee St (14211-1634)
PHONE 716 896-4555
Fax: 716 896-4557
James F Egloff, *President*
Dolores Webb, *Manager*
John F Egloff, *Admin Sec*
EMP: 6
SQ FT: 6,000
SALES (est): 558.9K **Privately Held**
SIC: 2796 2752 Photoengraving plates, linecuts or halftones; commercial printing, lithographic

(G-3181)
REALTIMETRADERSCOM
1325 N Forest Rd Ste 240 (14221-2143)
P.O. Box 387, Getzville (14068-0387)
PHONE 716 632-6600
Andrew Marthiasan, *President*
EMP: 33 EST: 1995
SQ FT: 2,000
SALES (est): 1.4MM **Privately Held**
SIC: 2711 7375 Newspapers; information retrieval services

(G-3182)
REIMANN & GEORGER CORPORATION
1849 Harlem Rd (14212-2401)
P.O. Box 681 (14240-0681)
PHONE 716 895-1156
Fax: 716 895-1547
E Eric Von Dungen, *Principal*
Joseph Quadrone, *Opers Mgr*
Phil Ventura, *Purchasing*
John Stegner, *Marketing Staff*
Donna Cooke, *Supervisor*
▲ **EMP:** 42
SQ FT: 38,000
SALES (est): 18.9MM **Privately Held**
WEB: www.rgcproducts.com
SIC: 3536 3546 Hoists; boat lifts; power-driven handtools

(G-3183)
REUSE ACTION INCORPORATED
279 Northampton St (14208-2304)
PHONE 716 949-0900
Michael Gainer, *Principal*
EMP: 5 EST: 2011
SALES (est): 579.6K **Privately Held**
SIC: 3822 Building services monitoring controls, automatic

(G-3184)
RICH HOLDINGS INC
1 Robert Rich Way (14213-1701)
PHONE 716 878-8000
Christopher T Dunstan, *Principal*
◆ **EMP:** 75
SALES (est): 7.5MM **Privately Held**
SIC: 2053 Frozen bakery products, except bread

(G-3185)
RICH PRODUCTS CORPORATION (PA)
1 Robert Rich Way (14213-1701)
P.O. Box 245 (14240-0245)
PHONE 716 878-8000
Fax: 716 878-8008
William G Gisel, *CEO*
Melinda R Rich, *Vice Ch Bd*
Joel Bearfield, *General Mgr*
Tim Falken, *Principal*
Robert Rich Jr, *Chairman*
◆ **EMP: 1375 EST:** 1993
SQ FT: 60,000

SALES (est): 3.6B **Privately Held**
WEB: www.richs.com
SIC: 2053 2092 2023 2099 Frozen bakery products, except bread; fresh or frozen packaged fish; shrimp, frozen: prepared; shellfish, frozen: prepared; dry, condensed, evaporated dairy products; whipped topping, dry mix; cream substitutes; dessert mixes & fillings

(G-3186)
RIGIDIZED METALS CORPORATION
Also Called: Rigidized-Metal
658 Ohio St (14203-3185)
PHONE 716 849-4703
Fax: 716 849-0401
Richard S Smith Jr, *Ch of Bd*
Richard S Smith III, *President*
Douglas F Lum, *Treasurer*
Patty Hammer, *Manager*
▲ **EMP: 48 EST:** 1940
SQ FT: 58,060
SALES (est): 22MM **Privately Held**
WEB: www.rigidized.com
SIC: 3469 3444 2796 Rigidizing metal; sheet metalwork; platemaking services

(G-3187)
RLP HOLDINGS INC
Also Called: Belt Maintenance Systems
1049 Military Rd (14217-2228)
PHONE 716 852-0832
Fax: 716 852-4198
Joe Hooley, *President*
Brian RE, *VP Sales*
▲ **EMP:** 8
SQ FT: 18,000
SALES (est): 1.1MM **Privately Held**
SIC: 3535 Conveyors & conveying equipment

(G-3188)
ROBERTS-GORDON LLC (HQ)
Also Called: RG
1250 William St (14206-1819)
P.O. Box 44 (14240-0044)
PHONE 716 852-4400
Mark J Dines, *President*
Mark Murdoch, *Vice Pres*
Richard G Jasiura, *CFO*
Sarah Kosprzewa, *Personnel Exec*
Geraldine Zolonowski, *Personnel*
▲ **EMP: 100 EST:** 1998
SQ FT: 107,000
SALES (est): 78MM
SALES (corp-wide): 78.1MM **Privately Held**
WEB: www.rg-inc.com
SIC: 3675 3433 Condensers, electronic; unit heaters, domestic

(G-3189)
ROBINSON KNIFE
2615 Walden Ave (14225-4735)
PHONE 716 685-6300
Fax: 716 685-4916
Robert Skerker, *CEO*
Joseph Jalbert, *Regional Mgr*
Larry Skerker, *Vice Pres*
Mark Abraszek, *VP Finance*
Candace Larotonda, *Natl Sales Mgr*
EMP: 12
SALES (est): 1.7MM **Privately Held**
SIC: 3089 Plastic kitchenware, tableware & houseware

(G-3190)
ROCKET COMMUNICATIONS INC
Also Called: Buffalo Rocket
2507 Delaware Ave (14216-1712)
PHONE 716 873-2594
David Gallagher, *CEO*
Dennis Gallagher, *Vice Pres*
Dean Gallagher, *Treasurer*
Daryl Gallagher, *Admin Sec*
EMP: 12 EST: 1996
SQ FT: 30,000
SALES (est): 657.7K **Privately Held**
WEB: www.buffalorocket.com
SIC: 2711 Newspapers

(G-3191)
RODGARD CORPORATION
92 Msgr Valente Dr (14206-1822)
PHONE 716 852-1435

Richard E Hauck, *Ch of Bd*
EMP: 30
SALES (est): 32.4K
SALES (corp-wide): 633.1MM **Publicly Held**
WEB: www.rodgard.com
SIC: 2821 Elastomers, nonvulcanizable (plastics)
PA: Astronics Corporation
130 Commerce Way
East Aurora NY 14052
716 805-1599

(G-3192)
ROLLERS INC
2495 Main St Ste 359 (14214-2154)
PHONE 716 837-0700
Frank Reppenhagen, *Owner*
EMP: 9
SALES (est): 640K **Privately Held**
WEB: www.rollers.com
SIC: 2515 3555 5085 Mattresses, containing felt, foam rubber, urethane, etc.; printing trade parts & attachments; industrial supplies

(G-3193)
ROSINA FOOD PRODUCTS INC (HQ)
Also Called: Ceoentano
170 French Rd (14227-2777)
PHONE 716 668-0123
Russell A Corigliano, *Ch of Bd*
James Corigliano, *Ch of Bd*
John Zimmerman, *President*
Frank Corigliano, *Vice Pres*
Jon Anderson, *Facilities Mgr*
EMP: 178
SQ FT: 60,000
SALES (est): 39.8MM
SALES (corp-wide): 50.3MM **Privately Held**
SIC: 2013 5812 Sausages & other prepared meats; eating places
PA: Rosina Holding, Inc.
170 French Rd
Buffalo NY 14227
716 668-0123

(G-3194)
ROSINA HOLDING INC (PA)
170 French Rd (14227-2717)
PHONE 716 668-0123
Fax: 716 656-0548
Russell A Corigliano, *Ch of Bd*
Todd Palczewski, *Research*
Frank Corigliano, *Treasurer*
James Corigliano Jr, *VP Human Res*
Randy Bernick, *Manager*
EMP: 3
SQ FT: 40,000
SALES (est): 50.3MM **Privately Held**
SIC: 2013 Sausages & other prepared meats

(G-3195)
ROSS L SPORTS SCREENING INC
2756 Seneca St (14224-1866)
PHONE 716 824-5350
Dave Cellino, *Owner*
EMP: 15 EST: 1973
SALES (est): 443.6K **Privately Held**
SIC: 2395 Embroidery & art needlework

(G-3196)
ROUGH BROTHERS HOLDING CO (HQ)
Also Called: Sunlight US Co., Inc.
3556 Lake Shore Rd # 100 (14219-1445)
PHONE 716 826-6500
Frank Heard, *President*
Paul M Murray, *Senior VP*
Kenneth W Smith, *CFO*
Timothy F Murphy, *Treasurer*
EMP: 8
SALES (est): 113.4MM
SALES (corp-wide): 1B **Publicly Held**
SIC: 3499 3316 3441 3398 Strapping, metal; cold finishing of steel shapes; fabricated structural metal; metal heat treating
PA: Gibraltar Industries, Inc.
3556 Lake Shore Rd # 100
Buffalo NY 14219
716 826-6500

Buffalo - Erie County (G-3221)

(G-3197)
ROYAL BEDDING CO BUFFALO INC
Also Called: Restonic
201 James E Casey Dr (14206-2363)
PHONE 716 895-1414
Thomas Comer Jr, *President*
Laura Tokarz, *VP Sls/Mktg*
Judy Houlanhan, *Manager*
Jennifer Beaman, *Executive*
▲ EMP: 25
SQ FT: 110,000
SALES (est): 5MM **Privately Held**
SIC: 2515 Mattresses, innerspring or box spring; box springs, assembled

(G-3198)
RWB CONTROLS INC
471 Connecticut St (14213-2645)
PHONE 716 897-4341
Fax: 716 882-1575
EMP: 6
SQ FT: 4,000
SALES (est): 600K **Privately Held**
SIC: 3823 5063 Mfg Industrial Process Control Instruments & Displays

(G-3199)
S & H MACHINE COMPANY INC
83 Clyde Ave (14215-2237)
PHONE 716 834-1194
EMP: 5
SQ FT: 5,500
SALES: 400K **Privately Held**
SIC: 3599 Machine Shop

(G-3200)
S J B FABRICATION
430 Kennedy Rd (14227-1032)
PHONE 716 895-0281
Sean Brubckman, *Owner*
EMP: 10
SALES (est): 310.1K **Privately Held**
SIC: 7692 Welding repair

(G-3201)
S J McCULLAGH INC (PA)
Also Called: McCullagh Coffee
245 Swan St (14204-2051)
PHONE 716 856-3473
Warren E Emblidge Jr, *President*
Dan Phillips, *CFO*
Mark Crotty, *Controller*
Rose Vohwinkel, *Executive Asst*
Carol Emblidge, *Admin Sec*
▲ EMP: 50
SQ FT: 16,000
SALES (est): 12.4MM **Privately Held**
SIC: 2095 5113 5149 Roasted coffee; cups, disposable plastic & paper; groceries & related products; dried or canned foods; sugar, refined; chocolate

(G-3202)
SAFETEC OF AMERICA INC
887 Kensington Ave (14215-2720)
PHONE 716 895-1822
Fax: 716 895-2969
Scott A Weinstein, *CEO*
Peter Weinstein, *Vice Pres*
Denise Bailey, *Purch Agent*
Dee Ciminelli, *Accountant*
Joe Vizzi, *Natl Sales Mgr*
▲ EMP: 60
SQ FT: 80,000
SALES: 10.3MM **Privately Held**
WEB: www.safetec.net
SIC: 2842 2834 Specialty cleaning, polishes & sanitation goods; drugs affecting parasitic & infective diseases

(G-3203)
SAFETY-KLEEN SYSTEMS INC
60 Katherine St (14210-2006)
PHONE 716 855-2212
James Drozdowski, *Branch Mgr*
EMP: 16
SQ FT: 24,259
SALES (corp-wide): 2.7B **Publicly Held**
SIC: 2992 Re-refining lubricating oils & greases
HQ: Safety-Kleen Systems, Inc.
2600 N Central Expy # 400
Richardson TX 75080
972 265-2000

(G-3204)
SAHLEN PACKING COMPANY INC
318 Howard St (14206-2760)
P.O. Box 280 (14240-0280)
PHONE 716 852-8677
Fax: 716 852-8684
Joseph E Sahlen, *Ch of Bd*
Christopher Cauley, *Vice Pres*
Deborah Howell, *Vice Pres*
Laura McKenrick, *QC Mgr*
Ed Colburn, *Controller*
▲ EMP: 85 EST: 1869
SQ FT: 53,789
SALES (est): 16.3MM **Privately Held**
WEB: www.sahlen.com
SIC: 2011 Sausages from meat slaughtered on site; hams & picnics from meat slaughtered on site; bacon, slab & sliced from meat slaughtered on site

(G-3205)
SANTORO SIGNS INC
3180 Genesee St Ste 1 (14225-2682)
PHONE 716 895-9931
Fax: 716 895-9931
Rocco Santoro, *President*
John Santoro, *Vice Pres*
EMP: 8
SALES (est): 1.2MM **Privately Held**
SIC: 3993 7389 Signs & advertising specialties; electric signs; neon signs; sign painting & lettering shop

(G-3206)
SCHULER-SUBRA INC
Also Called: Eskay Metal Fabricating
83 Doat St (14211-2048)
PHONE 716 893-3100
Fax: 716 893-0443
Jeff Subra, *President*
Ken White, *Sales Executive*
Kathy Bristol, *Manager*
EMP: 6 EST: 1944
SQ FT: 16,500
SALES (est): 648.9K **Privately Held**
WEB: www.specialtystainless.com
SIC: 3441 Fabricated structural metal

(G-3207)
SCHUTTE-BUFFALO HAMMERMILL LLC
Also Called: Schutte-Buffalo Hammer Mill
61 Depot St (14206-2203)
PHONE 716 855-1202
Fax: 716 855-3417
Thomas E Warne, *President*
Jim Klopfer, *VP Mfg*
Matthew Moliterno, *Design Engr*
Mark Podgorny, *Design Engr*
Dick Hambridge, *Sales Staff*
▲ EMP: 25 EST: 1933
SQ FT: 22,500
SALES (est): 9.9MM **Privately Held**
WEB: www.hammermills.com
SIC: 3531 Hammer mills (rock & ore crushing machines), portable

(G-3208)
SCREW COMPRESSOR TECH INC
158 Ridge Rd (14218-1035)
PHONE 716 827-6600
John Zahner, *President*
EMP: 13
SALES (est): 2.4MM **Privately Held**
SIC: 3563 Air & gas compressors

(G-3209)
SECOND AMENDMENT FOUNDATION
Also Called: Gun Week
267 Linwood Ave Ste A (14209-1816)
PHONE 716 885-6408
Fax: 716 884-4471
Joseph Tartaro, *President*
Peggy Tartaro, *Editor*
EMP: 5
SALES (corp-wide): 858.4K **Privately Held**
WEB: www.saf.org
SIC: 2711 Newspapers, publishing & printing
PA: Second Amendment Foundation Inc
12500 Ne 10th Pl
Bellevue WA 98005
425 454-7012

(G-3210)
SECONDARY SERVICES INC
757 E Ferry St (14211-1105)
PHONE 716 896-4000
Dan O'Connor, *CEO*
EMP: 12
SALES (est): 1.9MM **Privately Held**
WEB: www.secondaryservice.com
SIC: 3599 Machine shop, jobbing & repair

(G-3211)
SERVICE CANVAS CO INC
149 Swan St Unit 155 (14203-2624)
PHONE 716 853-0558
Fax: 716 845-6071
Jerald H Eron, *President*
EMP: 12 EST: 1946
SQ FT: 80,000
SALES (est): 1.2MM **Privately Held**
WEB: www.servicecanvas.com
SIC: 2394 Canvas & related products; canopies, fabric: made from purchased materials; tarpaulins, fabric: made from purchased materials; liners & covers, fabric: made from purchased materials
PA: Synthetic Textiles Inc
398 Broadway St
Buffalo NY 14204

(G-3212)
SERVICE MFG GROUP INC (PA)
400 Scajaquada St (14211-1722)
PHONE 716 893-1482
Linda Casoni, *CEO*
Vito Casoni, *President*
George Smith, *Sales Mgr*
Rounld Rusin, *Manager*
Bridget Kashmer, *Info Tech Mgr*
EMP: 12
SQ FT: 150,000
SALES (est): 8.4MM **Privately Held**
WEB: www.t-smg.com
SIC: 3625 3444 Relays & industrial controls; sheet metal specialties, not stamped

(G-3213)
SERVICE MFG GROUP INC
Also Called: Smg Control Systems
400 Scajaquada St (14211-1722)
PHONE 716 893-1482
Fax: 716 893-1495
Linda Casoni, *Vice Pres*
James Ochal, *Plant Mgr*
Carl Sellato, *Opers Mgr*
George W Leone, *Mfg Mgr*
Bob Kulp, *Mfg Staff*
EMP: 35
SALES (corp-wide): 8.4MM **Privately Held**
WEB: www.t-smg.com
SIC: 3444 Sheet metalwork
PA: The Service Manufacturing Group Inc
400 Scajaquada St
Buffalo NY 14211
716 893-1482

(G-3214)
SIEMENS INDUSTRY INC
85 Northpointe Pkwy Ste 8 (14228-1886)
PHONE 716 568-0983
Fax: 716 568-1449
Tom Strollo, *General Mgr*
Rob Lightfoot, *Vice Pres*
Patrick Parlane, *Branch Mgr*
Jerry K Wilson, *Manager*
EMP: 50
SALES (corp-wide): 89.6B **Privately Held**
WEB: www.sibt.com
SIC: 3585 7373 1541 Heating equipment, complete; computer integrated systems design; industrial buildings & warehouses
HQ: Siemens Industry, Inc.
1000 Deerfield Pkwy
Buffalo Grove IL 60089
847 215-1000

(G-3215)
SIMREX CORPORATION
1223 William St (14206-1805)
PHONE 716 206-0174
Donna Neuperger, *President*
Michael Aquilino, *Exec VP*
Frank Neuperger, *Vice Pres*
Shari Tona, *Manager*
▼ EMP: 8
SQ FT: 3,200
SALES (est): 1.2MM **Privately Held**
SIC: 3669 3661 Intercommunication systems, electric; modems

(G-3216)
SMARTPILL CORPORATION
847 Main St (14203-1109)
PHONE 716 882-0701
David Barthel, *President*
Broadhurst Austin, *Mng Member*
Kelli Regan, *Manager*
Laura Matott, *Director*
Austin Broadhurst, *Bd of Directors*
EMP: 31
SQ FT: 7,500
SALES (est): 3.7MM **Privately Held**
WEB: www.smartpill.com
SIC: 3826 Analytical instruments

(G-3217)
SOMERSET PRODUCTION CO LLC
338 Harris Hill Rd # 102 (14221-7470)
PHONE 716 932-6480
Thomas H O'Neil Jr, *Principal*
Suzan Willhauck, *Webmaster*
William A Ziegler,
EMP: 7
SQ FT: 6,000
SALES (est): 620K **Privately Held**
SIC: 1382 Oil & gas exploration services

(G-3218)
SOMMER AND SONS PRINTING INC
2222 S Park Ave (14220-2296)
PHONE 716 822-4311
Dennis Sommer, *President*
EMP: 11
SQ FT: 10,000
SALES (est): 1.3MM **Privately Held**
SIC: 2754 Job printing, gravure

(G-3219)
SOPARK CORP (PA)
3300 S Park Ave (14218-3530)
PHONE 716 822-0434
Fax: 716 822-5062
Gerald Murak, *Ch of Bd*
Kevin M Wyckoff, *Exec VP*
John Kasperek, *Controller*
▲ EMP: 150
SQ FT: 28,000
SALES (est): 32.3MM **Privately Held**
WEB: www.sopark.com
SIC: 3672 3679 3621 3694 Printed circuit boards; electronic circuits; motors, electric; engine electrical equipment

(G-3220)
SOROC TECHNOLOGY CORP
1051 Clinton St (14206-2823)
PHONE 716 849-5913
Rudy Cheddie, *President*
EMP: 2
SALES (est): 1MM
SALES (corp-wide): 61.5MM **Privately Held**
WEB: www.soroc.com
SIC: 7372 Prepackaged software
PA: Soroc Technology Inc
607 Chrislea Rd
Woodbridge ON L4L 8
905 265-8000

(G-3221)
SORRENTO LACTALIS INC
2375 S Park Ave (14220-2653)
PHONE 716 823-6262
James Binner, *Manager*
Victoire Visseaux, *Manager*
EMP: 8
SALES (est): 576.7K
SALES (corp-wide): 98.8K **Privately Held**
SIC: 2022 Cheese, natural & processed
HQ: Lactalis American Group, Inc.
2376 S Park Ave
Buffalo NY 14220
716 823-6262

Buffalo - Erie County (G-3222)   GEOGRAPHIC SECTION

(G-3222)
SOUND VIDEO SYSTEMS WNY LLC
1720 Military Rd (14217-1148)
PHONE.................................716 684-8200
Joseph Caprino,
▲ EMP: 10
SALES (est): 1.4MM Privately Held
SIC: 3651 Household audio & video equipment

(G-3223)
SPEEDWAYS CONVEYORS INC
1210 E Ferry St (14211-1615)
PHONE.................................716 893-2222
Fax: 716 893-3067
John T Thorn, President
John Jacobowitz, Exec VP
Donald Sauer, VP Finance
Dan Buckley, Marketing Staff
Debbie Doran, Office Mgr
EMP: 47 EST: 1945
SQ FT: 100,000
SALES: 4.3MM Privately Held
SIC: 3535 5084 3537 Conveyors & conveying equipment; industrial machinery & equipment; industrial trucks & tractors

(G-3224)
STEPHEN M KIERNAN
Also Called: Big Bear
701 Seneca St Ste 300 (14210-1351)
PHONE.................................716 836-6300
Stephen M Kiernan, CEO
David M Thiemecke, COO
EMP: 40
SALES (est): 1.6MM Privately Held
SIC: 2395 Embroidery & art needlework

(G-3225)
STETRON INTERNATIONAL INC (PA)
90 Broadway St Ste 1 (14203-1687)
PHONE.................................716 854-3443
Fax: 716 854-3448
Edward R Steger, Ch of Bd
Monique Steger, President
Caroline A Steger, Exec VP
Roy T Chao, Senior VP
R Hogwood, Vice Pres
▲ EMP: 14
SQ FT: 13,000
SALES (est): 3MM Privately Held
WEB: www.stetron.com
SIC: 3679 8734 3676 3674 Electronic circuits; electronic loads & power supplies; electronic switches; testing laboratories; electronic resistors, semiconductors & related devices; printed circuit boards; relays & industrial controls

(G-3226)
STORYBOOKS FOREVER
4 Magnolia Ave (14220-2005)
P.O. Box 1234 (14220-8234)
PHONE.................................716 822-7845
Dan Devlin, Owner
EMP: 14 EST: 2001
SALES (est): 530.2K Privately Held
SIC: 2731 Book publishing

(G-3227)
SUIT-KOTE CORPORATION
505 Como Park Blvd (14227-1605)
PHONE.................................716 683-8850
Scott Harris, Opers Staff
Gary Thompson, Branch Mgr
EMP: 15
SALES (corp-wide): 226MM Privately Held
WEB: www.suit-kote.com
SIC: 2843 Surface active agents
PA: Suit-Kote Corporation
1911 Lorings Crossing Rd
Cortland NY 13045
607 753-1100

(G-3228)
SUPER PRICE CHOPPER INC
1580 Genesee St (14211-1635)
PHONE.................................716 893-3323
AK Kaid, President
EMP: 10
SALES (est): 441.6K Privately Held
SIC: 3751 Motorcycles & related parts

(G-3229)
SURMET CERAMICS CORPORATION
699 Hertel Ave Ste 290 (14207-2341)
PHONE.................................716 875-4091
Timothy Davis, CEO
Terry McInerney, Finance Mgr
Tom Mroz, Manager
Mark Smith, Manager
Ashock Gunda, MIS Dir
EMP: 17
SALES (est): 1.9MM
SALES (corp-wide): 14MM Privately Held
SIC: 3297 Graphite refractories: carbon bond or ceramic bond
PA: Surmet, Corp.
31 B St
Burlington MA 01803
781 345-5721

(G-3230)
SWEETWORKS INC (PA)
Also Called: Niagara Chocolates
3500 Genesee St (14225-5015)
PHONE.................................716 634-4545
Philip Terranova, CEO
Joel Bearfield, Plant Mgr
Pascal Bieri, Opers Mgr
Jeffrey Geiger, Prdtn Mgr
Rosaline Williams, Prdtn Mgr
◆ EMP: 153
SQ FT: 115,000
SALES (est): 131.4MM Privately Held
WEB: www.sweetworks.net
SIC: 2066 2067 2064 Chocolate; chewing gum; candy & other confectionery products; chocolate candy, except solid chocolate; lollipops & other hard candy

(G-3231)
SYNTHETIC TEXTILES INC (PA)
398 Broadway St (14204-1546)
P.O. Box 1465 (14240-1465)
PHONE.................................716 842-2598
Jerald H Eron, President
Margaret Syracuse, General Mgr
EMP: 2
SQ FT: 88,000
SALES (est): 1.2MM Privately Held
WEB: www.synthetictextile.com
SIC: 3083 Plastic finished products, laminated

(G-3232)
SYSTEMS DRS C3 INC (DH)
485 Cayuga Rd (14225-1368)
PHONE.................................716 631-6200
Alan Dietrich, President
Robert Riordan, Exec VP
Bill Collins, Vice Pres
Keith Doucet, Vice Pres
Jason Rinsky, Vice Pres
EMP: 300
SQ FT: 300,000
SALES (est): 137.6MM
SALES (corp-wide): 8.3B Privately Held
WEB: www.drs-ewns.com
SIC: 3812 8713 Radar systems & equipment;
HQ: Leonardo Drs, Inc.
2345 Crystal Dr Ste 1000
Arlington VA 22202
973 898-1500

(G-3233)
T M MACHINE INC
176 Reading St (14220-2198)
PHONE.................................716 822-0817
Fax: 716 822-2340
Theodore S Michalski, President
Dennis Michalski, Vice Pres
EMP: 9
SQ FT: 7,000
SALES: 1.5MM Privately Held
SIC: 3599 Machine shop, jobbing & repair

(G-3234)
TAILORED COATINGS INC
1800 Brdwy St Bldg 2a (14212)
PHONE.................................716 893-4869
David R Mohamed, Ch of Bd
Fred Tafelski, Principal
EMP: 24
SALES (est): 4MM Privately Held
SIC: 3479 Painting of metal products

(G-3235)
TCHNOLOGIES N MRC AMEERICA LLC
Also Called: M R C
25 Roberts Ave (14206-3130)
PHONE.................................716 822-4300
Fax: 716 822-4432
Lynn Leimkuehler, Vice Pres
James Leimkuehler,
EMP: 9 EST: 1980
SQ FT: 150,000
SALES (est): 1.3MM Privately Held
SIC: 3599 7699 Machine shop, jobbing & repair; industrial machinery & equipment repair

(G-3236)
TEACHSPIN INC
2495 Main St Ste 409 (14214-2157)
PHONE.................................716 725-6116
Fax: 716 836-1077
Jonathan Reichert, President
Barbara Wolff, Marketing Staff
EMP: 13
SQ FT: 10,000
SALES (est): 1.7MM Privately Held
WEB: www.teachspin.com
SIC: 3999 Education aids, devices & supplies

(G-3237)
TECTRAN MFG INC (HQ)
2345 Walden Ave Ste 1 (14225-4770)
PHONE.................................800 776-5549
Bruce McKie, Ch of Bd
David Levan, General Mgr
Janet Heiderman, Credit Mgr
Janet Rodgers, Accountant
▲ EMP: 86
SALES (est): 19.4MM Privately Held
WEB: www.tectran.com
SIC: 3713 Truck bodies & parts

(G-3238)
TEGNA INC
Also Called: W G R Z - T V Channel 2
259 Delaware Ave (14202-2008)
PHONE.................................716 849-7602
Fax: 716 849-7602
Jim Toellner, General Mgr
Tim Bonk, Business Mgr
Deanna Russo, Exec Dir
Peter Gambacorta, Director
EMP: 130
SALES (corp-wide): 3.3B Publicly Held
WEB: www.gannett.com
SIC: 2711 4833 Newspapers; television broadcasting stations
PA: Tegna Inc.
7950 Jones Branch Dr
Mc Lean VA 22102
703 873-6600

(G-3239)
TENT AND TABLE COM LLC
2845 Bailey Ave (14215-3242)
PHONE.................................716 570-0258
▲ EMP: 15
SALES (est): 7MM Privately Held
SIC: 3999 Mfg Misc Products

(G-3240)
TERRAPIN STATION LTD
1172 Hertel Ave (14216-2704)
PHONE.................................716 874-6677
Barry Cohen, President
Robert Colsanti, Vice Pres
EMP: 13
SALES (est): 1.1MM Privately Held
WEB: www.terrapinstationbuffalo.com
SIC: 2337 Women's & misses' suits & coats

(G-3241)
THE CHOCOLATE SHOP
871 Niagara St (14213-2114)
PHONE.................................716 882-5055
Fax: 716 835-6008
Vincent Caruana, Owner
James Vincent, Manager
EMP: 6
SQ FT: 3,500
SALES (est): 381.6K Privately Held
WEB: www.chocolateshopandmore.com
SIC: 2066 5441 Chocolate & cocoa products; candy

(G-3242)
THERMAL FOAMS/SYRACUSE INC (PA)
2101 Kenmore Ave (14207-1695)
PHONE.................................716 874-6474
William F Wopperer, Ch of Bd
John P Jeffery, President
David Wopperer, Vice Pres
Larry Brady, Treasurer
▲ EMP: 2
SQ FT: 150,000
SALES (est): 5.8MM Privately Held
SIC: 3086 Insulation or cushioning material, foamed plastic

(G-3243)
THERMOTECH CORP
3 Bradford St (14210-1601)
PHONE.................................716 823-3311
Fred Muhitch, President
Bruce Smith, Vice Pres
EMP: 9
SQ FT: 18,000
SALES (est): 1.2MM Privately Held
WEB: www.thermalprecision.com
SIC: 3443 Air coolers, metal plate

(G-3244)
TIEDEMANN WALDEMAR INC
Also Called: Roofing Consultant
1720 Military Rd Ste 2 (14217-1148)
PHONE.................................716 875-5665
Waldemar Tiedemann, President
EMP: 11 EST: 1964
SALES (est): 1.2MM Privately Held
SIC: 2431 1761 Millwork; roofing contractor

(G-3245)
TIME RELEASE SCIENCES INC
Also Called: Trs Packaging
205 Dingens St (14206-2309)
PHONE.................................716 823-4580
Fax: 716 823-4625
Jeffrey Dorn, Ch of Bd
Jim Pasvek, Controller
Dennis McGee, Supervisor
▲ EMP: 20
SALES (est): 4.8MM Privately Held
SIC: 2671 Packaging paper & plastics film, coated & laminated

(G-3246)
TMP TECHNOLOGIES INC (PA)
Also Called: Advanced Foam Products Div
1200 Northland Ave (14215-3835)
PHONE.................................716 895-6100
Fax: 716 895-6396
Jeffrey T Doran, Ch of Bd
Gary R Ashe, Vice Pres
Don Phister, Vice Pres
Bob Schultz, Safety Mgr
Wayne Fabiszewski, QA Dir
▼ EMP: 65 EST: 1993
SQ FT: 47,000
SALES (est): 19.7MM Privately Held
WEB: www.tmptech.com
SIC: 3069 3086 2834 2821 Sponge rubber & sponge rubber products; molded rubber products; foam rubber; plastics foam products; pharmaceutical preparations; plastics materials & resins

(G-3247)
TOMRIC SYSTEMS INC
85 River Rock Dr (14207-2178)
PHONE.................................716 854-6050
Timothy Thill, Ch of Bd
Anne Rosa, Vice Pres
Sean Tucci, Sales Mgr
◆ EMP: 9
SALES (est): 302.6K
SALES (corp-wide): 21.8MM Privately Held
SIC: 2064 Candy & other confectionery products
PA: Chocolate Delivery Systems, Inc.
85 River Rock Dr Ste 202
Buffalo NY 14207
716 854-6050

(G-3248)
TOOLING ENTERPRISES INC
680 New Babcock St Ste 1 (14206-2285)
PHONE.................................716 842-0445
Fax: 716 842-0305

GEOGRAPHIC SECTION

Buffalo - Erie County (G-3272)

Eugene Joseph, *President*
Art Beyer, *General Mgr*
Thomas Deangelo, *Branch Mgr*
EMP: 10
SQ FT: 21,000
SALES (est): 1.2MM **Privately Held**
SIC: 3469 3544 Metal stampings; special dies, tools, jigs & fixtures

(G-3249)
TOVIE ASARESE ROYAL PRTG CO
351 Grant St (14213-1423)
PHONE...................716 885-7692
Fax: 716 885-0533
Ottoviano Asarese, *President*
Grace Campanella, *Office Mgr*
EMP: 7 **EST:** 1952
SQ FT: 1,500
SALES (est): 915.1K **Privately Held**
SIC: 2752 2759 Commercial printing, offset; letterpress printing

(G-3250)
TRANE US INC
45 Earhart Dr Ste 103 (14221-7809)
PHONE...................716 626-1260
Fax: 716 626-9412
Ronald Gerster, *Branch Mgr*
Bruce Siebert, *Data Proc Exec*
EMP: 50 **Privately Held**
SIC: 3585 Refrigeration & heating equipment
HQ: Trane U.S. Inc.
  1 Centennial Ave Ste 101
  Piscataway NJ 08854
  732 652-7100

(G-3251)
TRINITY PACKAGING CORPORATION
Cello-Pack Spclty Flms Lmntion
55 Innsbruck Dr (14227-2703)
PHONE...................716 668-3111
Craig Miller, *Vice Pres*
EMP: 25
SALES (corp-wide): 1.2B **Privately Held**
SIC: 3081 2673 Unsupported plastics film & sheet; bags: plastic, laminated & coated
HQ: Trinity Packaging Corporation
  357 Main St
  Armonk NY 10504
  914 273-4111

(G-3252)
TRIPP PLATING WORKS INC
1491 William St (14206-1807)
PHONE...................716 894-2424
Fax: 716 893-9377
Steven E Jagielo, *President*
Cherie Jagielo, *Vice Pres*
EMP: 7 **EST:** 1922
SQ FT: 6,000
SALES (est): 752.4K **Privately Held**
SIC: 3471 Electroplating of metals or formed products; polishing, metals or formed products; buffing for the trade

(G-3253)
TRU MOLD SHOES INC
42 Breckenridge St (14213-1555)
PHONE...................716 881-4484
Fax: 716 837-6663
Ahmed Syed, *President*
Wayne Weisedel, *General Mgr*
Andrea Syed, *Vice Pres*
Cheryl Garrow, *Office Mgr*
Sharon Huber, *Director*
EMP: 35
SQ FT: 11,000
SALES (est): 3.9MM **Privately Held**
WEB: www.trumold.com
SIC: 3143 3144 Orthopedic shoes, men's; orthopedic shoes, women's

(G-3254)
TWENTY-FIRST CENTURY PRESS INC
501 Cornwall Ave (14215-3125)
PHONE...................716 837-0800
Tracy B Lach, *President*
Mary Crimmen, *Vice Pres*
▲ **EMP:** 18 **EST:** 1979
SQ FT: 40,000
SALES (est): 3.4MM **Privately Held**

(G-3255)
TYSON DELI INC (HQ)
Also Called: MGM
665 Perry St (14210-1355)
PHONE...................716 826-6400
Fax: 716 826-9186
Howard Zemsky, *Chairman*
Richard Bond, *COO*
Viren Sitwala, *Vice Pres*
Ken Murray, *Plant Mgr*
Robert Neely, *Plant Mgr*
EMP: 450
SQ FT: 85,000
SALES (est): 41.7MM
SALES (corp-wide): 36.8B **Publicly Held**
SIC: 2013 Sausages & other prepared meats
PA: Tyson Foods, Inc.
  2200 W Don Tyson Pkwy
  Springdale AR 72762
  479 290-4000

(G-3256)
U S SUGAR CO INC
692 Bailey Ave (14206-3003)
PHONE...................716 828-1170
Fax: 716 828-1509
Tom Ferlito, *CEO*
Ed Jackson, *Senior VP*
Vern Milier, *Vice Pres*
Vernessa Roberts, *Vice Pres*
Steve Ward, *Vice Pres*
▲ **EMP:** 50
SQ FT: 300,000
SALES (est): 20.6MM **Privately Held**
SIC: 2099 Sugar

(G-3257)
UC COATINGS CORPORATION
2250 Fillmore Ave (14214-2119)
P.O. Box 1066 (14215-6066)
PHONE...................716 833-9366
Fax: 716 833-0120
Norman E Murray, *CEO*
Thomas D Johel, *President*
Thuy N Murray, *Corp Secy*
Eleanor Murray, *Vice Pres*
Paulette Welker, *Cust Mgr*
▼ **EMP:** 23
SQ FT: 30,000
SALES (est): 6.1MM **Privately Held**
WEB: www.uccoatings.com
SIC: 2851 Wood fillers or sealers; lacquers, varnishes, enamels & other coatings

(G-3258)
UNICELL BODY COMPANY INC (PA)
571 Howard St (14206-2195)
PHONE...................716 853-8628
Fax: 716 854-7208
Roger J Martin, *Ch of Bd*
Scott Vader, *President*
Anthony Lista, *General Mgr*
Paul Martin, *Vice Pres*
Dale Wunsch, *Purch Mgr*
EMP: 45 **EST:** 1963
SQ FT: 67,000
SALES (est): 20MM **Privately Held**
WEB: www.unicell.com
SIC: 3713 5013 Truck bodies (motor vehicles); truck parts & accessories

(G-3259)
UNIFORM NAMEMAKERS INC
55 Amherst Villa Rd (14225-1432)
PHONE...................716 626-5474
Warren Clark, *President*
EMP: 10
SQ FT: 7,000
SALES (est): 550K **Privately Held**
WEB: www.uniformnamemakers.com
SIC: 2395 Embroidery & art needlework

(G-3260)
UNILOCK LTD
510 Smith St (14210-1288)
PHONE...................716 822-6074
David Mc Intyre, *Branch Mgr*
EMP: 20
SALES (corp-wide): 87.2MM **Privately Held**
SIC: 3271 Paving blocks, concrete
PA: Unilock Ltd
  401 The West Mall Suite 610
  Etobicoke ON M9C 5
  905 453-1438

(G-3261)
UNITED RICHTER ELECTRICAL MTRS
106 Michigan Ave (14204-2111)
PHONE...................716 855-1945
Fax: 716 852-2589
Thomas Weiner, *President*
John Cook, *Vice Pres*
Judith Weiner, *Admin Sec*
EMP: 10
SQ FT: 10,000
SALES (est): 1.7MM **Privately Held**
SIC: 7694 5063 Electric motor repair; power transmission equipment, electric

(G-3262)
UPSTATE MEDICAL SOLUTIONS INC
25 Minnetonka Rd (14220-2411)
PHONE...................716 799-3782
Brian Huck, *Director*
EMP: 5
SALES (est): 416.3K **Privately Held**
SIC: 3842 Surgical appliances & supplies

(G-3263)
UPSTATE NIAGARA COOP INC (PA)
Also Called: Bison Products
25 Anderson Rd (14225-4905)
P.O. Box 650 (14225-0650)
PHONE...................716 892-3156
Fax: 716 892-3157
Larry Webster, *CEO*
Daniel Wolf, *President*
Doug Ricketts, *General Mgr*
Penney J Arnone, *Business Mgr*
Penney McGough, *Business Mgr*
EMP: 700 **EST:** 1930
SALES (est): 228.8MM **Privately Held**
SIC: 2026 Fermented & cultured milk products

(G-3264)
UPSTATE NIAGARA COOP INC
Also Called: Upstate Milk Co-Operatives
1730 Dale Rd (14225-4921)
P.O. Box 650 (14225-0650)
PHONE...................716 892-2121
Fax: 716 892-3159
Larry Darch, *Principal*
Brenda Melligan, *Manager*
Colleen Keller, *Executive*
EMP: 200
SQ FT: 53,690
SALES (corp-wide): 228.8MM **Privately Held**
SIC: 2023 2026 Ice cream mix, unfrozen: liquid or dry; fluid milk
PA: Upstate Niagara Cooperative, Inc.
  25 Anderson Rd
  Buffalo NY 14225
  716 892-3156

(G-3265)
V LAKE INDUSTRIES INC
1555 Niagara St (14213-1101)
PHONE...................716 885-9141
Keith McCoy, *President*
David Russell, *Project Mgr*
EMP: 8
SQ FT: 24,000
SALES (est): 1.2MM **Privately Held**
SIC: 3599 Machine & other job shop work

(G-3266)
VENT-A-KILN CORPORATION
Also Called: Vent-A-Fume
51 Botsford Pl (14216-2601)
PHONE...................716 876-2023
Fax: 716 876-4383
Susan Lee, *President*
Richard Smith Jr, *Opers-Prdtn-Mfg*
EMP: 5
SQ FT: 1,200
SALES (est): 871.7K **Privately Held**
WEB: www.ventakiln.com
SIC: 3567 Kilns

(G-3267)
VERMED INC
400 Exchange St (14204-2064)
PHONE...................800 669-6905
Sam Heleba, *President*
Ayu Vitous, *Mfg Staff*
Abel Rich, *Purch Agent*
Colleen Mollica, *VP Human Res*
Mollica Colleen, *Personnel Exec*
▲ **EMP:** 85
SQ FT: 45,000
SALES (est): 9.6MM
SALES (corp-wide): 1B **Privately Held**
WEB: www.vermed.com
SIC: 3845 3825 Electromedical equipment; instruments for measuring electrical quantities
HQ: Graphic Controls Acquisition Corp.
  400 Exchange St
  Buffalo NY 14204
  716 853-7500

(G-3268)
VIDBOLT INC
4 Elam Pl (14214-1911)
PHONE...................716 560-8944
John Hutchinson, *President*
Jerod Sikorskyj, *Admin Sec*
EMP: 6
SALES (est): 241.1K **Privately Held**
SIC: 2741

(G-3269)
VINCENT MARTINO DENTAL LAB
74 Ransier Dr (14224-2244)
PHONE...................716 674-7800
Vincent Martino, *President*
Deborah Martino, *Admin Sec*
EMP: 10 **EST:** 1976
SQ FT: 800
SALES: 300K **Privately Held**
SIC: 3843 8072 Orthodontic appliances; orthodontic appliance production

(G-3270)
VISIMETRICS CORPORATION
2290 Kenmore Ave (14207-1312)
PHONE...................716 871-7070
Fax: 716 871-1308
Kenneth Luczkiewicz, *President*
William Umiker, *Vice Pres*
EMP: 8
SQ FT: 22,000
SALES (est): 1MM **Privately Held**
WEB: www.visicnc.com
SIC: 3599 Machine shop, jobbing & repair

(G-3271)
VOYAGER EMBLEMS INC
Also Called: Voyager Custom Products
701 Seneca St Ste D (14210-1351)
PHONE...................416 255-3421
Donald B Grant, *Ch of Bd*
Sally Grant, *President*
Henry Maurer, *Vice Pres*
James Klein, *Purch Mgr*
Peter Barker, *Controller*
EMP: 108
SQ FT: 38,000
SALES (est): 5.3MM
SALES (corp-wide): 364.8K **Privately Held**
WEB: www.voyager-emblems.com
SIC: 2395 Emblems, embroidered
HQ: Grant Emblems Limited
  55 Fieldway Rd Suite A
  Etobicoke ON M8Z 3
  416 255-3421

(G-3272)
VULCAN STEAM FORGING CO
247 Rano St (14207-2189)
P.O. Box 87 (14207-0087)
PHONE...................716 875-3680
Fax: 716 875-3226
Michael Duggan, *President*
Frank Attea, *Opers Mgr*
Daniel Disinger, *Engineer*
Andrew Andersen, *Sales Mgr*
Mary Joe, *Manager*
▲ **EMP:** 27

Buffalo - Erie County (G-3273) — GEOGRAPHIC SECTION

SQ FT: 30,000
SALES (est): 5.4MM **Privately Held**
WEB: www.vulcansf.com
SIC: 3462 Iron & steel forgings; flange, valve & pipe fitting forgings, ferrous

(G-3273)
WARD INDUSTRIAL EQUIPMENT INC (PA)
Also Called: Ward Iron Works Limited
1051 Clinton St (14206-2823)
PHONE..................................716 856-6966
Guy Nelson, *President*
▲ EMP: 1 EST: 1980
SQ FT: 500
SALES (est): 4.3MM **Privately Held**
WEB: www.devansco.com
SIC: 3535 5084 Bulk handling conveyor systems; industrial machinery & equipment

(G-3274)
WARNER
514 Hopkins Rd (14221-2415)
PHONE..................................716 446-0663
Alan Warner, *Principal*
EMP: 9
SALES (est): 573.7K **Privately Held**
SIC: 2389 Clergymen's vestments

(G-3275)
WEB ASSOCIATES INC
1255 Niagara St (14213-1501)
PHONE..................................716 883-3377
William E Breeser, *President*
EMP: 6
SALES (est): 480.3K **Privately Held**
WEB: www.betterwire.com
SIC: 3315 3469 Wire & fabricated wire products; metal stampings

(G-3276)
WEBB-MASON INC
300 Airborne Pkwy Ste 210 (14225-1491)
PHONE..................................716 276-8792
Jon Webber, *Manager*
EMP: 23
SALES (corp-wide): 126.1MM **Privately Held**
SIC: 2752 Business form & card printing, lithographic
PA: Webb-Mason, Inc.
    10830 Gilroy Rd
    Hunt Valley MD 21031
    410 785-1111

(G-3277)
WENDT CORPORATION
2555 Walden Ave (14225-4737)
PHONE..................................716 391-1200
Fax: 716 873-9309
Thomas A Wendt Sr, *CEO*
Mike Fialkowski, *President*
Joseph Bertozzi, *Vice Pres*
Joe Stein, *Engineer*
David Kaminski, *Regl Sales Mgr*
◆ EMP: 100
SQ FT: 66,000
SALES (est): 37.4MM **Privately Held**
SIC: 3599 Custom machinery

(G-3278)
WEST METAL WORKS INC
Also Called: W M W
68 Hayes Pl (14210-1614)
PHONE..................................716 895-4900
Fax: 716 895-4861
James Stermer, *President*
Jennifer Stermer, *Vice Pres*
David Wojtkowiak, *Marketing Staff*
Gail Perona, *Office Mgr*
Gail Strassburg, *Manager*
EMP: 20 EST: 1946
SALES (est): 3.5MM **Privately Held**
WEB: www.westmetalworks.com
SIC: 7692 3559 3443 3449 Welding repair; chemical machinery & equipment; plate work for the metalworking trade; miscellaneous metalwork

(G-3279)
WESTERN NEW YORK FAMILY MAG
3147 Delaware Ave Ste B (14217-2002)
PHONE..................................716 836-3486
Fax: 716 836-3680
Michelle J Miller, *Owner*
EMP: 5
SALES (est): 517.2K **Privately Held**
WEB: www.wnyfamilymagazine.com
SIC: 2721 Magazines: publishing only, not printed on site

(G-3280)
WILCRO INC
90 Earhart Dr Ste 19 (14221-7802)
PHONE..................................716 632-4204
Fax: 716 632-4263
Richard Crooks Sr, *President*
Richard Crooks Jr, *Vice Pres*
Robert Crooks, *Admin Sec*
EMP: 9
SALES (est): 468K **Privately Held**
WEB: www.wilcro.com
SIC: 3571 2796 Personal computers (microcomputers); engraving on copper, steel, wood or rubber: printing plates

(G-3281)
WILLARD MACHINE
73 Forest Ave (14213-1093)
PHONE..................................716 885-1630
Fax: 716 885-1632
Jeffrey Rathmann, *President*
EMP: 13
SQ FT: 10,000
SALES (est): 1.1MM **Privately Held**
WEB: www.willardmachine.com
SIC: 3599 Machine shop, jobbing & repair

(G-3282)
WILLIAM S HEIN & CO INC
Also Called: Metro Center Western New York
1575 Main St (14209-1513)
PHONE..................................716 882-2600
Kevin Marmion, *President*
EMP: 100
SALES (corp-wide): 15.2MM **Privately Held**
WEB: www.foreign-law.com
SIC: 2731 Books: publishing only
PA: William S. Hein & Co., Inc.
    2350 N Forest Rd Ste 14a
    Getzville NY 14068
    716 882-2600

(G-3283)
WINTERS INSTRUMENTS INC (HQ)
Also Called: Winters Instruments
455 Cayuga Rd Ste 650 (14225-1317)
PHONE..................................281 880-8607
Jeffrey Smith, *President*
Brian McClure, *Exec VP*
Thom Milligan, *Vice Pres*
Brad Taylor, *VP Mfg*
John Bernotas, *Regl Sales Mgr*
▲ EMP: 45
SQ FT: 10,000
SALES (est): 5.1MM
SALES (corp-wide): 4.3MM **Privately Held**
SIC: 3823 5084 Industrial instrmnts msrmnt display/control process variable; instruments & control equipment
PA: Winters Instruments Ltd
    121 Railside Rd
    North York ON M3A 1
    416 444-2345

(G-3284)
X-L ENVELOPE AND PRINTING INC
701 Seneca St Ste 100 (14210-1376)
P.O. Box 344 (14224-0344)
PHONE..................................716 852-2135
Terry Allen, *CEO*
Bob Woollacott, *Treasurer*
EMP: 11
SQ FT: 20,000
SALES (est): 2.3MM **Privately Held**
SIC: 2677 2752 Envelopes; commercial printing, lithographic

(G-3285)
XEROX CORPORATION
450 Corporate Pkwy # 100 (14226-1268)
PHONE..................................716 831-3300
Frank Bov, *Marketing Staff*
Susan Ready, *Manager*
EMP: 75
SALES (corp-wide): 10.7B **Publicly Held**
WEB: www.xerox.com
SIC: 3861 Photographic equipment & supplies
PA: Xerox Corporation
    201 Merritt 7
    Norwalk CT 06851
    203 968-3000

(G-3286)
YOUNG & SWARTZ INC
39 Cherry St (14204-1298)
PHONE..................................716 852-2171
Fax: 716 852-5652
Raphael Winzig, *President*
EMP: 10 EST: 1886
SQ FT: 15,000
SALES (est): 1.2MM **Privately Held**
SIC: 3991 5198 Brushes, household or industrial; paint brushes, rollers, sprayers

(G-3287)
YR BLANC & CO LLC
Also Called: Renovatio Med & Surgical Sups
1275 Main St Ste 120 (14209-1911)
PHONE..................................716 800-3999
Yves-Richard Blanc, *CEO*
EMP: 5
SALES (est): 839K **Privately Held**
SIC: 2899 3589 1781 5078 ; sewage & water treatment equipment; water well servicing; drinking water coolers, mechanical

(G-3288)
ZEPTOMETRIX CORPORATION (PA)
847 Main St (14203-1109)
PHONE..................................716 882-0920
Gregory Chiklis, *President*
Chris Collins, *Vice Pres*
John Paul, *Vice Pres*
Jacyln Gross, *QA Dir*
Ronald Urmson, *CFO*
▼ EMP: 80
SQ FT: 20,000
SALES (est): 21MM **Privately Held**
WEB: www.zeptometrix.com
SIC: 2836 Biological products, except diagnostic

Bullville
Orange County

(G-3289)
WOODARDS CONCRETE PRODUCTS INC
629 Lybolt Rd (10915)
P.O. Box 8 (10915-0008)
PHONE..................................845 361-3471
Fax: 845 361-1050
Robert Zwart, *President*
Gayle Cortright, *Corp Secy*
Allen Zwart, *Vice Pres*
Steve Zwart, *Vice Pres*
EMP: 25 EST: 1955
SQ FT: 14,000
SALES (est): 4.2MM **Privately Held**
WEB: www.woodardsconcrete.com
SIC: 3272 Concrete products; septic tanks, concrete; steps, prefabricated concrete

Burdett
Schuyler County

(G-3290)
ATWATER ESTATE VINEYARDS LLC
5055 State Route 414 (14818-9816)
PHONE..................................607 546-8463
Ted Marks, *Partner*
Denise Clappier, *Manager*
Katie Marks, *Manager*
George Nosisi, *Assistant*
EMP: 20 EST: 2000
SQ FT: 672
SALES (est): 2.3MM **Privately Held**
WEB: www.atwatervineyards.com
SIC: 2084 Wines

(G-3291)
FINGER LAKES DISTILLING
4676 State Route 414 (14818-9730)
PHONE..................................607 546-5510
Brian McKenzie, *President*
EMP: 15
SALES (est): 2.1MM **Privately Held**
SIC: 2085 Distilled & blended liquors

Burke
Franklin County

(G-3292)
CREST HAVEN PRECAST INC
4925 State Route 11 (12917-2410)
PHONE..................................518 483-4750
Fax: 518 483-7577
Gary Boileau, *President*
Eva Boileau, *Vice Pres*
EMP: 7
SALES: 800K **Privately Held**
SIC: 3271 Concrete block & brick

Burnt Hills
Saratoga County

(G-3293)
MAMAS
119 Lake Hill Rd (12027-9519)
PHONE..................................518 399-2828
Panayiotis J Menagias, *Principal*
EMP: 6 EST: 2007
SALES (est): 345.6K **Privately Held**
SIC: 2024 Ice cream, bulk

Burt
Niagara County

(G-3294)
AKZO NOBEL CHEMICALS LLC
2153 Lockport Olcott Rd (14028-9788)
PHONE..................................716 778-8554
Fax: 716 778-7930
Gordon Martens, *Manager*
EMP: 8
SALES (corp-wide): 15B **Privately Held**
WEB: www.akzo-nobel.com
SIC: 2869 2899 Industrial organic chemicals; chemical preparations
HQ: Akzo Nobel Chemicals Llc
    525 W Van Buren St # 1600
    Chicago IL 60607
    312 544-7000

Byron
Genesee County

(G-3295)
OXBO INTERNATIONAL CORPORATION (HQ)
7275 Batavia Byron Rd (14422-9599)
PHONE..................................585 548-2665
Gary C Stich, *CEO*
Richard Glazier, *Ch of Bd*
Paul Dow, *Vice Pres*
Andrew Talbott, *Vice Pres*
John Borrelli, *Senior Buyer*
▲ EMP: 100
SQ FT: 43,500
SALES (est): 52MM
SALES (corp-wide): 197.8MM **Privately Held**
WEB: www.oxbocorp.com
SIC: 3523 5083 Farm machinery & equipment; farm & garden machinery
PA: Ploeger Oxbo Group B.V.
    Electronweg 5
    Roosendaal
    165 319-333

Cairo
Greene County

(G-3296)
B & B FOREST PRODUCTS LTD
251 Route 145 (12413-2659)
P.O. Box 907 (12413-0907)
PHONE.................518 622-0811
William Fabian, *President*
▼ **EMP:** 13 **EST:** 1993
SALES (est): 1.3MM **Privately Held**
SIC: 2411 Logging

(G-3297)
BILBEE CONTROLS INC
628 Main St (12413-2806)
PHONE.................518 622-3033
Fax: 518 622-3163
Robert Leivnn, *President*
Barbara Powell, *Owner*
EMP: 12
SQ FT: 12,000
SALES: 1.5MM **Privately Held**
WEB: www.bilbeecontrols.com
SIC: 3822 Thermostats, except built-in

(G-3298)
HIGHLAND MUSEUM & LIGHTHOUSE
111 M Simons Rd (12413-3135)
PHONE.................508 487-1121
Dan Sanders, *President*
Gordon S Russell, *President*
Francine Webster, *Treasurer*
EMP: 15
SALES: 180.5K **Privately Held**
SIC: 3731 Lighthouse tenders, building & repairing

(G-3299)
JRS FUELS INC
8037 Route 32 (12413-2526)
PHONE.................518 622-9939
John Vandenburgh, *Principal*
EMP: 5 **EST:** 2009
SALES (est): 652.4K **Privately Held**
SIC: 2869 Fuels

(G-3300)
K & B WOODWORKING INC
133 Rolling Meadow Rd (12413-2201)
PHONE.................518 634-7253
Fax: 518 634-7863
Peter Vogel, *President*
Richard Vogel, *Corp Secy*
Melissa Hulbert, *Office Mgr*
EMP: 9
SQ FT: 10,000
SALES (est): 726K **Privately Held**
WEB: www.kbwoodworking.com
SIC: 2511 2499 Wood household furniture; decorative wood & woodwork

(G-3301)
OAK VALLEY LOGGING INC
558 Frank Hitchcock Rd (12413-2626)
P.O. Box 1260 (12413-1260)
PHONE.................518 622-8249
Glenn Defrancesco, *Chairman*
EMP: 5 **EST:** 2008
SALES (est): 346.9K **Privately Held**
SIC: 2411 Logging

Caledonia
Livingston County

(G-3302)
ADVIS INC
2218 River Rd (14423-9518)
PHONE.................585 568-0100
Mark F Bocko, *CEO*
Donna REA, *Business Mgr*
Stephen Glaser, *Sales Staff*
Scott Housel, *Director*
EMP: 9
SALES: 950K **Privately Held**
SIC: 3674 Semiconductors & related devices

(G-3303)
ALLEN-BAILEY TAG & LABEL INC (PA)
3177 Lehigh St (14423-1053)
P.O. Box 123 (14423-0123)
PHONE.................585 538-2324
Fax: 585 538-2800
Eugene S Tonucci, *Ch of Bd*
Michael Chapman, *Finance*
Patricia Kenfield, *Sales Staff*
Lilian Larrabee, *Sales Staff*
Kelly Jones, *Manager*
▲ **EMP:** 86 **EST:** 1911
SQ FT: 60,000
SALES (est): 16.6MM **Privately Held**
WEB: www.abtl.com
SIC: 2679 2672 2671 Tags, paper (unprinted): made from purchased paper; labels, paper: made from purchased material; labels (unprinted), gummed: made from purchased materials; packaging paper & plastics film, coated & laminated

(G-3304)
APPLIED ENERGY SOLUTIONS LLC
1 Technology Pl (14423-1246)
PHONE.................585 538-3270
Peter Morris, *Engineer*
Jonathan Oliva, *VP Sales*
Pat Bayers, *Sales Mgr*
Vern Fleming,
EMP: 44
SQ FT: 60,000
SALES (est): 11.7MM **Privately Held**
WEB: www.appliedenergysol.com
SIC: 3629 Battery chargers, rectifying or nonrotating

(G-3305)
COMMODITY RESOURCE CORPORATION
2773 Caledonia Leroy Rd (14423-9538)
P.O. Box 576, Lakeville (14480-0576)
PHONE.................585 538-9500
Fax: 585 538-9511
Leslie Cole, *President*
EMP: 12
SALES (est): 1.7MM **Privately Held**
WEB: www.crcconnect.com
SIC: 2875 2048 Fertilizers, mixing only; feed premixes

(G-3306)
GROWMARK FS LLC
2936 Telephone Rd (14423-9708)
PHONE.................585 538-2186
Dale Bartholomew, *Managing Dir*
Tim Howard, *Manager*
EMP: 10
SALES (corp-wide): 7B **Privately Held**
WEB: www.growmarkfs.com
SIC: 2875 Fertilizers, mixing only
HQ: Growmark Fs, Llc
  308 Ne Front St
  Milford DE 19963
  302 422-3002

(G-3307)
GULDENSCHUH LOGGING & LBR LLC
143 Wheatland Center Rd (14423-9750)
P.O. Box 191 (14423-0191)
PHONE.................585 538-4750
Fax: 585 538-6993
Don Guldenschuh, *Mng Member*
Garrett Guldenschuh,
EMP: 9
SQ FT: 50,000
SALES (est): 1.3MM **Privately Held**
SIC: 2426 2411 5099 5211 Furniture stock & parts, hardwood; logging; timber products, rough; lumber products

(G-3308)
HORNS & HALOS CFT BREWING LLC
3154 State St (14423-1222)
PHONE.................585 507-7248
Justin Caccamise,
John Kabrovski,
EMP: 20
SQ FT: 8,200
SALES (est): 671.8K **Privately Held**
SIC: 2082 Near beer

(G-3309)
RHETT M CLARK INC
Also Called: Gregson-Clark
3213 Lehigh St (14423-1073)
PHONE.................585 538-9570
Rhett M Clark, *President*
EMP: 6
SQ FT: 5,000
SALES (est): 1MM **Privately Held**
SIC: 3524 5083 Lawn & garden equipment; lawn & garden machinery & equipment

(G-3310)
SPECIALIZED PRINTED FORMS INC
Also Called: Spforms
352 Center St (14423-1202)
P.O. Box 118 (14423-0118)
PHONE.................585 538-2381
Fax: 585 538-4922
Kevin Johnston, *General Mgr*
Russell Shepard, *Plant Mgr*
Jody Bailey, *Accountant*
▲ **EMP:** 20 **EST:** 1951
SQ FT: 135,000
SALES (est): 3MM
SALES (corp-wide): 356.8MM **Publicly Held**
WEB: www.spforms.com
SIC: 2761 Continuous forms, office & business
PA: Ennis, Inc.
  2441 Presidential Pkwy
  Midlothian TX 76065
  972 775-9801

(G-3311)
TSS FOAM INDUSTRIES CORP
2770 W Main St (14423-9560)
P.O. Box 119 (14423-0119)
PHONE.................585 538-2321
Fax: 585 538-2876
Samuel L Dilberto Jr, *Ch of Bd*
EMP: 15
SQ FT: 60,000
SALES (est): 2.9MM **Privately Held**
SIC: 3086 5047 7389 Plastics foam products; medical & hospital equipment; sewing contractor

Callicoon
Sullivan County

(G-3312)
CATSKILL DELAWARE PUBLICATIONS (PA)
Also Called: Sullivan County Democrat
5 Lower Main St (12723-5000)
P.O. Box 308 (12723-0308)
PHONE.................845 887-5200
Fax: 845 887-5386
Frederick W Stabbert III, *President*
Frank Rizzo, *Editor*
Dan Hust, *Advt Staff*
Susan Owens, *Office Mgr*
Christine Nappi, *Manager*
EMP: 19 **EST:** 1900
SQ FT: 5,704
SALES: 1MM **Privately Held**
WEB: www.sc-democrat.com
SIC: 2711 2752 Commercial printing & newspaper publishing combined; commercial printing, lithographic

(G-3313)
ELECTRO-KINETICS INC
51 Creamery Rd (12723-7710)
P.O. Box 188 (12723-0188)
PHONE.................845 887-4930
Fax: 845 887-4745
Eric Andkjar, *President*
Jesse Ballew, *Sales Executive*
EMP: 13
SQ FT: 8,000
SALES (est): 2.6MM **Privately Held**
WEB: www.electro-kinetics.com
SIC: 3625 Motor controls & accessories

Calverton
Suffolk County

(G-3314)
BONSAL AMERICAN INC
931 Burman Blvd (11933-3027)
PHONE.................631 208-8073
John Cardona, *Principal*
EMP: 20
SALES (corp-wide): 28.6B **Privately Held**
WEB: www.bonsalamerican.com
SIC: 1442 Construction sand & gravel
HQ: Bonsal American, Inc.
  625 Griffith Rd Ste 100
  Charlotte NC 28217
  704 525-1621

(G-3315)
BUNCEE LLC
4603 Middle Country Rd (11933-4104)
PHONE.................631 591-1390
Claire Cucchi, *COO*
Loulou Gaget, *Corp Comm Staff*
Shafique Arnab, *Prgrmr*
Marie Arturi,
EMP: 10
SALES (est): 881.1K **Privately Held**
SIC: 7372 Prepackaged software

(G-3316)
COASTAL PIPELINE PRODUCTS CORP
55 Twomey Ave (11933-1374)
P.O. Box 575 (11933-0575)
PHONE.................631 369-4000
Fax: 631 369-4006
Alexander Koke, *President*
▲ **EMP:** 50
SQ FT: 32,000
SALES (est): 11.8MM **Privately Held**
WEB: www.coastalpipeline.com
SIC: 3272 Precast terrazo or concrete products

(G-3317)
COOKING WITH CHEF MICHELLE LLC
Also Called: Ms. Michelles
4603 Middle Country Rd (11933-4104)
PHONE.................516 662-2324
Michelle Gilette-Kelly, *President*
Michelle Marie Gilette-Kelly, *President*
Christopher Kelly, *CFO*
EMP: 6
SQ FT: 8,400
SALES: 229.6K **Privately Held**
SIC: 2052 5149 Cookies; crackers, cookies & bakery products

(G-3318)
EAST END COUNTRY KITCHENS INC
Also Called: Pezera Associates
121 Edwards Ave (11933-1602)
PHONE.................631 727-2258
Fax: 631 727-0771
Henry Pazera, *President*
EMP: 10
SALES (est): 1MM **Privately Held**
SIC: 2511 Kitchen & dining room furniture

(G-3319)
GLOBAL MARINE POWER INC
Also Called: Hustler Powerboats
221 Scott Ave (11933-3039)
PHONE.................631 208-2933
Fax: 631 208-2942
Joe Logiudice, *Owner*
Richard Logiudice, *Vice Pres*
Linda Shrine, *Manager*
EMP: 40
SQ FT: 32,000
SALES (est): 8.3MM **Privately Held**
WEB: www.hustlerpowerboats.com
SIC: 3089 3732 5551 Plastic boats & other marine equipment; boat building & repairing; boat dealers

(G-3320)
LONG ISLAND SPIRITS INC
2182 Sound Ave (11933-1280)
PHONE.................631 630-9322

Calverton - Suffolk County (G-3321)

Richard Stabile, *President*
EMP: 10
SALES (est): 516.5K **Privately Held**
SIC: 2085 Distilled & blended liquors

(G-3321)
LUMINATI AEROSPACE LLC
400 David Ct (11933-3007)
PHONE..........................631 574-2616
Daniel Preston, *CEO*
April Chapple, *Vice Pres*
EMP: 16
SALES (est): 998.5K **Privately Held**
SIC: 3721 Research & development on aircraft by the manufacturer

(G-3322)
PELLA CORPORATION
Also Called: Reilly Windows & Doors
901 Burman Blvd (11933-3027)
PHONE..........................631 208-0710
Brian Goodale, *General Mgr*
Michael P Reilly, *Chairman*
James Schaub, *CFO*
Michael Iwanyczko, *Mktg Dir*
EMP: 126
SALES (corp-wide): 1.9B **Privately Held**
SIC: 2431 5211 5031 2499 Millwork; millwork & lumber; doors & windows; decorative wood & woodwork; window & door (prefabricated) installation
PA: Pella Corporation
102 Main St
Pella IA 50219
641 621-1000

(G-3323)
PORTABLE TECH SOLUTIONS LLC
221 David Ct (11933-3053)
PHONE..........................631 727-8084
Sharon Taylor, *Accountant*
Bradley Horn,
Daniel Peluso,
EMP: 10
SALES (est): 980K **Privately Held**
WEB: www.ptshome.com
SIC: 7372 Prepackaged software

(G-3324)
RACING INDUSTRIES INC
901 Scott Ave (11933-3033)
PHONE..........................631 905-0100
Ameet Bambami, *President*
▲ **EMP:** 20
SQ FT: 20,000
SALES (est): 4.5MM **Privately Held**
WEB: www.racingindustries.com
SIC: 3465 Body parts, automobile: stamped metal

(G-3325)
ROAR BIOMEDICAL INC
4603 Middle Country Rd (11933-4104)
PHONE..........................631 591-2749
Robert Brocia, *Branch Mgr*
EMP: 5
SALES (corp-wide): 2.4MM **Privately Held**
SIC: 2836 5122 Biological products, except diagnostic; biologicals & allied products
PA: Roar Biomedical Inc
3960 Broadway
New York NY 10032
212 280-2983

(G-3326)
STONY BROOK MFG CO INC (PA)
652 Scott Ave (11933-3046)
PHONE..........................631 369-9530
Fax: 631 369-9513
Ella Scaife, *President*
Marek Hyrycz, *Vice Pres*
Graham Scaife, *Vice Pres*
Peter Day, *Project Mgr*
Peter Candela, *Engineer*
EMP: 30
SQ FT: 11,000
SALES (est): 5.1MM **Privately Held**
WEB: www.stonybrookmfg.com
SIC: 3317 Steel pipe & tubes

(G-3327)
SUFFOLK CEMENT PRECAST INC (PA)
1813 Middle Rd (11933-1450)
P.O. Box 261 (11933-0261)
PHONE..........................631 727-4432
Kenneth Lohr, *President*
Sherrill Meshel, *Bookkeeper*
EMP: 9
SQ FT: 500
SALES (est): 1.1MM **Privately Held**
SIC: 3272 Septic tanks, concrete

(G-3328)
SUFFOLK CEMENT PRODUCTS INC
1843 Middle Rd (11933-1450)
PHONE..........................631 727-2317
Fax: 631 727-6211
Mark A Lohr, *Ch of Bd*
Linda Hagen, *Vice Pres*
EMP: 29
SQ FT: 4,500
SALES (est): 14.6MM **Privately Held**
WEB: www.suffolkcement.com
SIC: 3273 3271 Ready-mixed concrete; blocks, concrete or cinder: standard

(G-3329)
TEBBENS STEEL LLC
800 Burman Blvd (11933-3024)
PHONE..........................631 208-8330
Thomas A Tebbens II, *Mng Member*
Elsie Tebbens,
EMP: 18 **EST:** 2001
SQ FT: 9,000
SALES (est): 4.8MM **Privately Held**
SIC: 3449 8711 Miscellaneous metalwork; structural engineering

(G-3330)
US HOISTS CORP
Also Called: Acme Marine
800 Burman Blvd (11933-3024)
PHONE..........................631 472-3030
Thomas A Tebbens II, *President*
Kelly Tebbens, *Vice Pres*
Michael Bonner, *Manager*
◆ **EMP:** 7
SALES (est): 1.1MM **Privately Held**
SIC: 3536 Hoists, cranes & monorails

Cambria Heights
Queens County

(G-3331)
MADISON ELECTRIC
21916 Linden Blvd (11411-1619)
PHONE..........................718 358-4121
Pete Danielsson, *Owner*
Larry Zassman, *Office Mgr*
EMP: 18
SQ FT: 2,000
SALES: 300K **Privately Held**
SIC: 3699 Electrical equipment & supplies

Cambridge
Washington County

(G-3332)
B & J LUMBER CO INC
1075 State Route 22 (12816-2501)
P.O. Box 40 (12816-0040)
PHONE..........................518 677-3845
John Merriman, *President*
Barbara Merriman, *Vice Pres*
EMP: 5 **EST:** 1955
SALES: 100K **Privately Held**
SIC: 2421 5989 0115 Sawmills & planing mills, general; wood (fuel); corn

(G-3333)
CAMBRIDGE-PACIFIC INC
Also Called: CTX Printing
891 State Rd 22 (12816)
P.O. Box 159 (12816-0159)
PHONE..........................518 677-5988
Chris Belnap, *President*
▲ **EMP:** 33 **EST:** 1986
SQ FT: 12,000
SALES (est): 6.7MM **Privately Held**
WEB: www.cpacific.com
SIC: 2677 Envelopes

(G-3334)
COMMON SENSE NATURAL SOAP
7 Pearl St (12816-1127)
PHONE..........................518 677-0224
Robert Racine, *Owner*
EMP: 30 **EST:** 2014
SALES: 5.5MM **Privately Held**
SIC: 2844 Toilet preparations

(G-3335)
EASTERN CASTINGS CO
2 Pearl St (12816-1107)
P.O. Box 129 (12816-0129)
PHONE..........................518 677-5610
Fax: 518 677-5610
Anthony McDonald, *President*
Andrew Nolan, *Treasurer*
EMP: 15
SQ FT: 25,000
SALES (est): 1.5MM **Privately Held**
SIC: 3365 Aluminum & aluminum-based alloy castings

(G-3336)
ED LEVIN INC
Also Called: Ed Levin Jewelry
52 W Main St (12816-1158)
PHONE..........................518 677-8595
Fax: 518 677-8597
Peter Tonjes, *President*
Ed Levin, *Chairman*
Marianne Dallaird, *Purchasing*
Leslie Resio, *Controller*
EMP: 25
SQ FT: 10,000
SALES: 2MM **Privately Held**
WEB: www.edlevinjewelry.com
SIC: 3911 Jewelry, precious metal

(G-3337)
MORCON INC (PA)
879 State Rd 22 (12816)
PHONE..........................518 677-8511
Fax: 518 677-5984
Joseph Raccuia, *President*
Brian Stidd, *Controller*
EMP: 180
SALES: 40MM **Privately Held**
SIC: 2621 Tissue paper

(G-3338)
ROBERT RACINE (PA)
Also Called: Common Sense Natural Soap
41 N Union St (12816-1025)
PHONE..........................518 677-0224
Robert Racine, *Owner*
▲ **EMP:** 41
SALES (est): 7MM **Privately Held**
WEB: www.commonsensefarm.com
SIC: 2841 2844 Soap & other detergents; toilet preparations

(G-3339)
WAYMOR1 INC
Hc 22 (12816)
PHONE..........................518 677-8511
Susan H Morris, *Owner*
Wayne R Morris, *Owner*
EMP: 50
SALES (corp-wide): 46.7MM **Privately Held**
SIC: 2679 2676 Paper products, converted; sanitary paper products
PA: Waymor1, Inc.
879 State Rte 22
Cambridge NY 12816

Camden
Oneida County

(G-3340)
CAMDEN NEWS INC
Also Called: Queens Central News
39 Main St (13316-1301)
P.O. Box 117 (13316-0117)
PHONE..........................315 245-1849
Fax: 315 245-1880
James Van Winkle, *President*
James Winkle, *Editor*
EMP: 5 **EST:** 1974
SQ FT: 7,000
SALES (est): 270K **Privately Held**
SIC: 2711 Newspapers

(G-3341)
CAMDEN WIRE CO INC
Also Called: International Wire Group
12 Masonic Ave (13316-1294)
PHONE..........................315 245-3800
Rodney Kent, *President*
Charles Knapp, *General Mgr*
Vince Donaldson, *Vice Pres*
Chuck Lovengoth, *Vice Pres*
Ken Suits, *Plant Mgr*
EMP: 700 **EST:** 1929
SQ FT: 400,000
SALES: 120.2MM
SALES (corp-wide): 432.1MM **Privately Held**
SIC: 3351 3357 Wire, copper & copper alloy; nonferrous wiredrawing & insulating
HQ: International Wire Group, Inc.
12 Masonic Ave
Camden NY 13316

(G-3342)
DAVIS LOGGING & LUMBER
1450 Curtiss Rd (13316-5006)
PHONE..........................315 245-1040
Leonard Davis, *Principal*
EMP: 5 **EST:** 1985
SALES (est): 438.1K **Privately Held**
SIC: 2411 Logging

(G-3343)
INTERNATIONAL WIRE GROUP (PA)
12 Masonic Ave (13316-1202)
PHONE..........................315 245-3800
Rodney Kent, *CEO*
Donald Dekay, *CFO*
EMP: 13
SALES (est): 432.1MM **Privately Held**
SIC: 3351 Wire, copper & copper alloy

(G-3344)
INTERNATIONAL WIRE GROUP INC (HQ)
Also Called: Bare Wire Division
12 Masonic Ave (13316-1202)
PHONE..........................315 245-2000
Fax: 315 245-4014
Rodney D Kent, *Ch of Bd*
William L Pennington, *Vice Chairman*
Geoff Kent, *Vice Pres*
Charles Lovenguth, *Vice Pres*
James Mills, *Vice Pres*
▲ **EMP:** 300
SALES (est): 432.1MM **Privately Held**
SIC: 3357 Nonferrous wiredrawing & insulating
PA: International Wire Group
12 Masonic Ave
Camden NY 13316
315 245-3800

(G-3345)
KEVIN REGAN LOGGING LTD
1011 Hillsboro Rd (13316-4518)
P.O. Box 439 (13316-0439)
PHONE..........................315 245-3890
Kevin Regan, *President*
Sharlene Regan, *Office Mgr*
EMP: 5
SALES (est): 585.6K **Privately Held**
SIC: 2411 1629 Logging; land clearing contractor

(G-3346)
OMEGA WIRE INC (DH)
Also Called: Bare Wire Div
12 Masonic Ave (13316-1202)
P.O. Box 131 (13316-0131)
PHONE..........................315 245-3800
Fax: 315 964-2148
Rodney D Kent, *President*
Peter Ernenwein, *Vice Pres*
Matthew Dolansky, *Controller*
Donald De Kay, *VP Finance*
Jim Stoughton, *Manager*
▲ **EMP:** 325
SQ FT: 200,000

SALES (est): 95.9MM
SALES (corp-wide): 432.1MM **Privately Held**
WEB: www.omegawire.com
SIC: 3351 Wire, copper & copper alloy

(G-3347)
OWI CORPORATION
Also Called: Bare Wire Division
12 Masonic Ave (13316-1202)
P.O. Box 131 (13316-0131)
PHONE....................................315 245-4305
Fax: 315 245-0750
Rodney Kent, *President*
Donald De Kay, *VP Finance*
▲ EMP: 6
SALES (est): 907.4K
SALES (corp-wide): 432.1MM **Privately Held**
SIC: 3351 Wire, copper & copper alloy
HQ: International Wire Group, Inc.
12 Masonic Ave
Camden NY 13316

(G-3348)
PERFORMANCE WIRE & CABLE INC
9482 State Route 13 (13316-4947)
P.O. Box 126 (13316-0126)
PHONE....................................315 245-2594
Steven Benjamin, *President*
Eddie Edwards, *VP Sales*
EMP: 13
SQ FT: 37,500
SALES (est): 2.5MM **Privately Held**
WEB: www.performancewire.com
SIC: 3351 Wire, copper & copper alloy

Camillus
Onondaga County

(G-3349)
AQUARII INC
17 Genesee St (13031-1126)
PHONE....................................315 672-8807
Ray Carrock, *President*
Hannah Carrock, *Marketing Mgr*
Charles Shatzkin, *Director*
EMP: 8
SALES (est): 1.6MM **Privately Held**
SIC: 3646 Commercial indusl & institutional electric lighting fixtures

(G-3350)
CLEARSTEP TECHNOLOGIES LLC
213 Emann Dr (13031-2009)
PHONE....................................315 952-3628
Scott Buehler,
EMP: 7 EST: 2007
SQ FT: 2,000
SALES (est): 1.8MM **Privately Held**
WEB: www.clearsteptech.com
SIC: 2741 Technical manual & paper publishing

(G-3351)
KSA MANUFACTURING LLC
5050 Smoral Rd (13031-9726)
PHONE....................................315 488-0809
Fax: 315 488-5142
Tyler Hudlick, *Prdtn Mgr*
Adam Kudlick,
Jane Kudlick,
▲ EMP: 12
SQ FT: 8,500
SALES (est): 1.4MM **Privately Held**
WEB: www.ksamanufacturing.com
SIC: 3492 Hose & tube fittings & assemblies, hydraulic/pneumatic

(G-3352)
STEVE POLI SALES
Also Called: Imprinted Sportswear
102 Farmington Dr (13031-2113)
PHONE....................................315 487-0394
Steve Poli, *Owner*
EMP: 5
SALES (est): 283.6K **Privately Held**
SIC: 2261 Screen printing of cotton broadwoven fabrics

(G-3353)
TOSCH PRODUCTS LTD
25 Main St (13031-1126)
PHONE....................................315 672-3040
Fax: 315 672-3318
Todd Oudemool, *President*
Liz Fkllon, *Office Mgr*
Dirk J Oudemool,
EMP: 6
SQ FT: 12,000
SALES: 500K **Privately Held**
WEB: www.toschltd.com
SIC: 3949 Lacrosse equipment & supplies, general

(G-3354)
UPSTATE TUBE INC
5050 Smoral Rd (13031-9726)
PHONE....................................315 488-5636
Michael Kudlick, *President*
Kristy Kudlick, *Principal*
Tyler Kudlick, *Vice Pres*
EMP: 5
SALES (est): 350.8K **Privately Held**
SIC: 3492 Fluid power valves & hose fittings

(G-3355)
WESTROCK - SOUTHERN CONT LLC
100 Southern Dr (13031-1578)
PHONE....................................315 487-6111
Fax: 315 488-4310
Sandy Lewek, *Office Mgr*
Dave Atkwell, *Manager*
EMP: 120
SALES (corp-wide): 14.1B **Publicly Held**
WEB: www.southerncontainer.com
SIC: 2653 3412 Boxes, corrugated: made from purchased materials; metal barrels, drums & pails
HQ: Westrock - Southern Container, Llc
133 River Rd
Cos Cob CT 06807
631 232-5704

(G-3356)
WESTROCK RKT COMPANY
4914 W Genesee St (13031-2374)
PHONE....................................770 448-2193
David Atwell, *Plant Mgr*
EMP: 161
SALES (corp-wide): 14.1B **Publicly Held**
WEB: www.rocktenn.com
SIC: 2653 Partitions, solid fiber: made from purchased materials
HQ: Westrock Rkt Company
504 Thrasher St
Norcross GA 30071
770 448-2193

Campbell
Steuben County

(G-3357)
FT SEISMIC SUPPORT INC
5596 Mills Rd (14821-9534)
PHONE....................................607 527-8595
Melinda A Comstock, *President*
Michael Comstock, *Opers Mgr*
EMP: 130
SALES (est): 19.3MM **Privately Held**
SIC: 1382 Oil & gas exploration services

(G-3358)
KRAFT HEINZ FOODS COMPANY
8596 Main St (14821-9636)
PHONE....................................607 527-4584
Fax: 607 527-8060
Kenneth Blake, *Principal*
Henry Mapes, *Branch Mgr*
EMP: 350
SALES (corp-wide): 26.4B **Publicly Held**
WEB: www.kraftfoods.com
SIC: 2022 2026 Cheese, natural & processed; fluid milk
HQ: Kraft Heinz Foods Company
1 Ppg Pl Ste 3200
Pittsburgh PA 15222
412 456-5700

Canaan
Columbia County

(G-3359)
HILLTOWN PORK INC (PA)
12948 State Route 22 (12029-2118)
PHONE....................................518 781-4050
Fax: 518 781-4139
Richard A Beckwith, *President*
Edwin S Beckwith, *Vice Pres*
Paula Beckwith, *Office Mgr*
Robert A Beckwith, *Admin Sec*
EMP: 22
SALES (est): 3.3MM **Privately Held**
SIC: 2011 2013 Pork products from pork slaughtered on site; sausages & other prepared meats

Canajoharie
Montgomery County

(G-3360)
GRAVYMASTER INC
Also Called: Dryden & Palmer Co
101 Erie Blvd (13317-1148)
PHONE....................................203 453-1893
Stephen A Besse, *President*
John M Mills, *Treasurer*
EMP: 44
SQ FT: 31,000
SALES (est): 4.6MM **Privately Held**
WEB: www.gravy.com
SIC: 2064 2035 2099 Candy & other confectionery products; seasonings & sauces, except tomato & dry; food preparations

(G-3361)
RICHARDSON BRANDS COMPANY (HQ)
Also Called: Richardson Foods
101 Erie Blvd (13317-1148)
PHONE....................................800 839-8938
Fax: 518 673-2451
Arnold J D'Angelo, *CEO*
Kathy Hiserodt, *Vice Pres*
Tracey Burton, *VP Opers*
John Almaviva, *Opers Mgr*
Harold Rabe, *Warehouse Mgr*
▲ EMP: 150
SQ FT: 180,000
SALES (est): 30.1MM
SALES (corp-wide): 516.9MM **Privately Held**
WEB: www.richardsonbrands.com
SIC: 2064 Candy & other confectionery products
PA: Founders Equity, Inc.
545 5th Ave Rm 401
New York NY 10017
212 829-0900

(G-3362)
W W CUSTOM CLAD INC
75 Creek St (13317-1446)
PHONE....................................518 673-3322
Fax: 518 673-3343
April Chamberlain, *Human Res Dir*
EMP: 62
SQ FT: 23,804
SALES (corp-wide): 5.2MM **Privately Held**
WEB: www.wwcustomclad.com
SIC: 3479 Coating of metals & formed products
PA: W. W. Custom Clad, Inc.
337 E Main St
Canajoharie NY

Canandaigua
Ontario County

(G-3363)
AKOUSTIS INC
5450 Campus Dr (14424-8259)
PHONE....................................585 919-3073
Mary Winters, *Opers Staff*
EMP: 30

SALES (corp-wide): 486.5K **Publicly Held**
SIC: 3674 4813 Integrated circuits, semiconductor networks, etc.; data telephone communications
HQ: Akoustis, Inc.
9805 Northcross Center Ct H
Huntersville NC 28078
704 756-2981

(G-3364)
BADGE MACHINE PRODUCTS INC
2491 Brickyard Rd (14424-7969)
PHONE....................................585 394-0330
Fax: 585 394-0446
Gail Flugel, *President*
Christian Flugel, *Vice Pres*
Cindy Baxter, *Materials Mgr*
Dan Pospula, *QA Dir*
Francis Flugel, *Treasurer*
EMP: 30
SQ FT: 24,000
SALES (est): 5.2MM **Privately Held**
WEB: www.badgemachine.com
SIC: 3599 Machine shop, jobbing & repair

(G-3365)
BRISTOL CORE INC
5310 North St (14424-7965)
P.O. Box 507 (14424-0507)
PHONE....................................585 919-0302
Morgan Curtice, *President*
EMP: 19
SALES (est): 3.6MM **Privately Held**
SIC: 2621 Bristols

(G-3366)
CANANDAIGUA MSGNR INCORPORATED (PA)
Also Called: Daily Messenger
73 Buffalo St (14424-1001)
PHONE....................................585 394-0770
Fax: 585 394-1675
George Ewing Jr, *President*
George Ewing Sr, *Chairman*
Andrew Kavulich, *Vice Pres*
Joy Daggett, *Purchasing*
Lynn Brown, *Sls & Mktg Exec*
EMP: 100 EST: 1910
SALES (est): 13.2MM **Privately Held**
SIC: 2711 2752 Newspapers; commercial printing, lithographic

(G-3367)
CARGES ENTPS OF CANANDAIGUA
Also Called: Canandaigua Quick Print
330 S Main St (14424-2117)
PHONE....................................585 394-2600
Fax: 585 394-2616
Elizabeth Carges, *President*
Kevin Carges, *Vice Pres*
Robert Carges, *Vice Pres*
Jeremy Luke, *Graphic Designe*
EMP: 6
SQ FT: 2,000
SALES (est): 1.1MM **Privately Held**
WEB: www.quickprintny.com
SIC: 2752 7334 Commercial printing, offset; photocopying & duplicating services

(G-3368)
CONSTELLATION BRANDS INC
3325 Marvin Sands Dr (14424-8405)
PHONE....................................585 393-4880
EMP: 31
SALES (corp-wide): 7.3B **Publicly Held**
WEB: www.cbrands.com
SIC: 2084 Wines, brandy & brandy spirits
PA: Constellation Brands, Inc.
207 High Point Dr # 100
Victor NY 14564
585 678-7100

(G-3369)
CONSTELLATION BRANDS US OPRS
116 Buffalo St (14424-1012)
PHONE....................................585 396-7600
Karan Long, *Purch Mgr*
Christopher Benziger, *Branch Mgr*
EMP: 773
SALES (corp-wide): 7.3B **Publicly Held**
SIC: 2084 Wines

Canandaigua - Ontario County

HQ: Constellation Brands U.S. Operations, Inc.
235 N Bloomfield Rd
Canandaigua NY 14424
585 396-7600

(G-3370)
CONSTELLATION BRANDS US OPRS (HQ)
Also Called: Centerra Wine Company
235 N Bloomfield Rd (14424-1059)
PHONE..................585 396-7600
John Wright, *CEO*
William F Hackett, *President*
Scott McCain, *District Mgr*
Jim Debonis, *COO*
Kocoloski Jim, *Senior VP*
▲ EMP: 277
SALES (est): 659.8MM
SALES (corp-wide): 7.3B **Publicly Held**
SIC: 2084 Wines
PA: Constellation Brands, Inc.
207 High Point Dr # 100
Victor NY 14564
585 678-7100

(G-3371)
DENNIES MANUFACTURING INC
2543 State Route 21 (14424-8718)
PHONE..................585 393-4646
Fax: 585 396-9693
Richard Warkentin, *President*
Norma Vanderwall, *Accountant*
Dina Bennett, *Manager*
EMP: 27
SQ FT: 10,000
SALES (est): 4.8MM **Privately Held**
SIC: 3599 3441 7692 Machine shop, jobbing & repair; fabricated structural metal; welding repair

(G-3372)
DOUGS MACHINE SHOP INC
5300 North St (14424-7965)
P.O. Box 699 (14424-0699)
PHONE..................585 905-0004
Douglas Leonard, *Ch of Bd*
EMP: 9
SALES (est): 1.2MM **Privately Held**
SIC: 3599 Machine shop, jobbing & repair

(G-3373)
EATON CORPORATION
2375 State Route 332 # 250 (14424-7517)
PHONE..................585 394-1780
EMP: 217
SIC: 3625 Motor controls & accessories
HQ: Eaton Corporation
1000 Eaton Blvd
Cleveland OH 44122
216 523-5000

(G-3374)
EXFO BURLEIGH PDTS GROUP INC
181 S Main St Ste 10 (14424-1911)
PHONE..................585 301-1530
Germain Lamonde, *Ch of Bd*
Sue Yoffee, *Principal*
Pierre Plamondon, *Vice Pres*
Jim Bluett, *Opers Mgr*
Peter Battisti, *VP Finance*
EMP: 87
SQ FT: 20,000
SALES (est): 12.8MM **Privately Held**
WEB: www.burleigh.com
SIC: 3625 3827 3699 3826 Relays & industrial controls; optical instruments & lenses; laser systems & equipment; analytical optical instruments

(G-3375)
FINGER LAKES EXTRUSION CORP
Also Called: Flex Tubing
2437 State Route 21 (14424-8716)
PHONE..................585 905-0632
Fax: 315 889-7708
William Scott, *President*
Erica Wright, *VP Finance*
▲ EMP: 21 EST: 1998
SQ FT: 56,000
SALES: 5.6MM **Privately Held**
WEB: www.flextubing.com
SIC: 3089 3082 Extruded finished plastic products; tubes, unsupported plastic

(G-3376)
GATEHOUSE MEDIA LLC
Mpnnow
73 Buffalo St (14424-1001)
PHONE..................585 394-0770
James Marotta, *Vice Pres*
Carl Helbig, *Branch Mgr*
Beth Kesel, *Manager*
EMP: 100
SALES (corp-wide): 1.2B **Publicly Held**
WEB: www.gatehousemedia.com
SIC: 2711 2752 Newspapers; commercial printing, lithographic
HQ: Gatehouse Media, Llc
175 Sullys Trl Ste 300
Pittsford NY 14534
585 598-0030

(G-3377)
JUST RIGHT CARBINES LLC
231 Saltonstall St (14424-8301)
PHONE..................585 261-5331
Richard J Cutri,
EMP: 6
SALES: 900K **Privately Held**
SIC: 3999 Manufacturing industries

(G-3378)
MOORE PRINTING COMPANY INC
9 Coy St (14424-1595)
PHONE..................585 394-1533
Donna Miller, *President*
Burton Moore, *President*
EMP: 8
SQ FT: 3,500
SALES (est): 1MM **Privately Held**
SIC: 2752 2759 Commercial printing, offset; letterpress printing

(G-3379)
NUPRO TECHNOLOGIES LLC
23 Coach St Ste 2a (14424-1529)
P.O. Box 182 (14424-0182)
PHONE..................412 422-5922
Greg Novack, *Controller*
Patty Sim, *Bookkeeper*
Sam Altman, *Mng Member*
Marro Vidal,
▲ EMP: 15
SQ FT: 2,500
SALES (est): 2.7MM **Privately Held**
SIC: 3315 Wire & fabricated wire products

(G-3380)
PACTIV LLC
2480 Sommers Dr (14424-5250)
PHONE..................585 394-1525
Richard Wambold, *Chairman*
Dave Klas, *Plant Mgr*
Bill Howard, *Engineer*
Tom Morscheimer, *Engineer*
Scott Snyder, *Engineer*
EMP: 9 **Privately Held**
WEB: www.pactiv.com
SIC: 2621 Pressed & molded pulp & fiber products
HQ: Pactiv Llc
1900 W Field Ct
Lake Forest IL 60045
847 482-2000

(G-3381)
PACTIV LLC
2651 Brickyard Rd (14424-7990)
PHONE..................585 394-5125
Ernie Calahan, *Plant Mgr*
Sally Ferguson, *Cust Mgr*
Margaret Finucane, *Branch Mgr*
Daniel Farnam, *Supervisor*
David Vadney, *Supervisor*
EMP: 238 **Privately Held**
SIC: 2673 3089 5113 Food storage & frozen food bags, plastic; food storage & trash bags (plastic); food casings, plastic; containers, paper & disposable plastic; cups, disposable plastic & paper; dishes, disposable plastic & paper

HQ: Pactiv Llc
1900 W Field Ct
Lake Forest IL 60045
847 482-2000

(G-3382)
PACTIV LLC
5310 North St (14424-7965)
PHONE..................847 482-2000
Phil Korenscra, *Manager*
David Chung, *Technology*
EMP: 8 **Privately Held**
WEB: www.pactiv.com
SIC: 3089 Plastic containers, except foam
HQ: Pactiv Llc
1900 W Field Ct
Lake Forest IL 60045
847 482-2000

(G-3383)
PACTIV LLC
5250 North St (14424-1026)
PHONE..................585 393-3229
Richard Wambold, *CEO*
David C Jones, *Facilities Mgr*
Allan Rickett, *Info Tech Dir*
EMP: 207 **Privately Held**
WEB: www.pactiv.com
SIC: 3089 Plates, plastic
HQ: Pactiv Llc
1900 W Field Ct
Lake Forest IL 60045
847 482-2000

(G-3384)
PACTIV LLC
Also Called: Canandaigua Technology Center
5250 North St (14424-1026)
PHONE..................585 393-3149
David Class, *Branch Mgr*
EMP: 800 **Privately Held**
WEB: www.pactiv.com
SIC: 3089 Tableware, plastic; composition stone, plastic; doors, folding: plastic or plastic coated fabric
HQ: Pactiv Llc
1900 W Field Ct
Lake Forest IL 60045
847 482-2000

(G-3385)
PLURES TECHNOLOGIES INC (PA)
4070 County Road 16 (14424-8314)
PHONE..................585 905-0554
Aaron Dobrinsky, *President*
EMP: 1
SALES: 5.5MM **Privately Held**
SIC: 3674 Integrated circuits, semiconductor networks, etc.

(G-3386)
QUICKPRINT
330 S Main St (14424-2117)
PHONE..................585 394-2600
Kevin Carges, *CEO*
Robert Carges, *Vice Pres*
Jim Paro, *Sales Mgr*
Dawn Miles, *Manager*
EMP: 5
SALES (est): 356K **Privately Held**
SIC: 2752 Commercial printing, offset

(G-3387)
SELECT FABRICATORS INC
5310 North St Bldg 5 (14424-7965)
P.O. Box 119 (14424-0119)
PHONE..................585 393-0650
Fax: 585 393-1378
David A Yearsley, *President*
Eleanor Yearsley, *Vice Pres*
Kristin Lupien, *Production*
Gary W Winch, *CFO*
Brian Smith, *Sales Associate*
▼ EMP: 15 EST: 2000
SQ FT: 19,728
SALES (est): 2.3MM **Privately Held**
WEB: www.selectfabricatorsinc.com
SIC: 2393 3812 2673 2394 Duffle bags, canvas; made from purchased materials; aircraft/aerospace flight instruments & guidance systems; bags: plastic, laminated & coated; tents: made from purchased materials

(G-3388)
TIMBER FRAMES INC
5557 State Route 64 (14424-9382)
PHONE..................585 374-6405
Alan R Milanette, *President*
Brenda Milanette, *Office Mgr*
EMP: 7
SQ FT: 800
SALES (est): 1.3MM **Privately Held**
WEB: www.timberframesinc.com
SIC: 2439 1751 Structural wood members; framing contractor

(G-3389)
WOLFE PUBLICATIONS INC (PA)
Also Called: Messenger Post Media
73 Buffalo St (14424-1001)
PHONE..................585 394-0770
Kathy Hammond, *President*
Rick Jensen, *Editor*
Marie Ewing, *Vice Pres*
John Bowman, *Prdtn Mgr*
Martha Hagerman, *Bookkeeper*
EMP: 110 EST: 1956
SQ FT: 17,500
SALES (est): 7.4MM **Privately Held**
WEB: www.mpnewspapers.com
SIC: 2711 Commercial printing & newspaper publishing combined

(G-3390)
YOUNG EXPLOSIVES CORP
Also Called: Display Fireworks
2165 New Michigan Rd (14424-7918)
P.O. Box 18653, Rochester (14618-0653)
PHONE..................585 394-1783
James R Young, *President*
Nancy Calvey, *Corp Comm Staff*
▲ EMP: 70
SQ FT: 400
SALES (est): 12MM **Privately Held**
WEB: www.youngexplosives.com
SIC: 2899 7999 Fireworks; fireworks display service

Canaseraga
Allegany County

(G-3391)
BEAVER CREEK INDUSTRIES INC
11530 White Rd (14822-9607)
PHONE..................607 545-6382
Fax: 607 545-6383
Gary Bajus, *President*
Gary Bajus II, *Vice Pres*
Mary Bajus, *Treasurer*
Ethan Flint, *Associate*
EMP: 9
SQ FT: 8,000
SALES: 1MM **Privately Held**
SIC: 2431 Interior & ornamental woodwork & trim

Canastota
Madison County

(G-3392)
BLADING SERVICES UNLIMITED LLC
40 Madison Blvd (13032-3500)
PHONE..................315 875-5313
Stephen Stevens,
EMP: 14
SALES (est): 2.4MM **Privately Held**
SIC: 3599 Machine shop, jobbing & repair

(G-3393)
CALLANAN INDUSTRIES INC
6375 Tuttle Rd (13032-4168)
PHONE..................315 697-9569
Fax: 315 697-7501
Tim Hauck, *Principal*
EMP: 25
SALES (corp-wide): 28.6B **Privately Held**
SIC: 3272 Concrete products, precast
HQ: Callanan Industries, Inc.
8 Southwoods Blvd Ste 4
Albany NY 12211
518 374-2222

GEOGRAPHIC SECTION

Carle Place - Nassau County (G-3419)

(G-3394)
CANASTOTA PUBLISHING CO INC
130 E Center St (13032-1307)
PHONE..................315 697-9010
Fax: 315 697-8496
Patrick Milmoe, *President*
EMP: 5
SQ FT: 3,200
SALES (est): 695.4K **Privately Held**
SIC: 2752 Commercial printing, offset

(G-3395)
DEBRUCQUE CLEVELAND TRAMRAIL S
3 Technology Blvd (13032-3517)
PHONE..................315 697-5160
Ron Debrucque, *Mng Member*
EMP: 6
SQ FT: 4,500
SALES (est): 670K **Privately Held**
SIC: 3536 Cranes & monorail systems

(G-3396)
OWL WIRE & CABLE LLC
3127 Seneca Tpke (13032-3514)
PHONE..................315 697-2011
Fax: 315 697-2123
Philip J Kemper, *President*
Robert J Ratti, *Chairman*
Josh Levesque, *Opers Mgr*
Dave Wright, *Maint Spvr*
Emily Sorbello, *Purch Agent*
▲ EMP: 180 EST: 1951
SQ FT: 400,000
SALES (est): 72.8MM
SALES (corp-wide): 223.6B **Publicly Held**
WEB: www.owlwire.com
SIC: 3315 Wire & fabricated wire products
HQ: The Marmon Group Llc
 181 W Madison St Ste 2600
 Chicago IL 60602
 312 372-9500

(G-3397)
PRIME MATERIALS RECOVERY INC
51 Madison Blvd (13032-3501)
PHONE..................315 697-5251
Francis Pratt, *Branch Mgr*
EMP: 8
SALES (corp-wide): 186.9MM **Privately Held**
SIC: 3441 Fabricated structural metal
PA: Prime Materials Recovery Inc.
 99 E River Dr
 East Hartford CT 06108
 860 622-7626

(G-3398)
SALARINOS ITALIAN FOODS INC
Also Called: Basilio's
110 James St (13032-1410)
PHONE..................315 697-9766
Fax: 315 697-2551
Vincent Salamone Jr, *President*
Debra Salamone, *Vice Pres*
EMP: 10
SQ FT: 4,050
SALES (est): 997K **Privately Held**
SIC: 2013 2038 Sausages from purchased meat; pizza, frozen

(G-3399)
SIDE HILL FARMERS COOP INC
8275 State Route 13 (13032-4470)
PHONE..................315 447-4693
Paul O'Mara, *President*
Kirsten Tolman, *Treasurer*
EMP: 6
SALES: 1MM **Privately Held**
SIC: 2011 Meat packing plants

(G-3400)
THERMOLD CORPORATION
7059 Harp Rd (13032-4583)
PHONE..................315 697-3924
Fax: 315 697-7177
Jeremy Schwimmer, *Ch of Bd*
Dan Emmons, *President*
Michael Dunn, *Vice Pres*
Ashish Mare, *Project Mgr*
Jonathan Martin, *Research*

▲ EMP: 106 EST: 1945
SQ FT: 35,000
SALES (est): 27.5MM **Privately Held**
WEB: www.thermold.com
SIC: 3089 Molding primary plastic

(G-3401)
TRICON PIPING SYSTEMS INC
2 Technology Blvd (13032-3520)
P.O. Box 361 (13032-0361)
PHONE..................315 655-4178
Hugh Roszel, *President*
Sara Jeffris, *Manager*
▼ EMP: 12 EST: 1999
SALES (est): 3.3MM **Privately Held**
WEB: www.triconpiping.com
SIC: 3317 Steel pipe & tubes

(G-3402)
VICTORY SIGNS INC
8915 Old State Route 13 (13032-5417)
PHONE..................315 762-0220
Anthony Deperno, *President*
Jennifer Deperno, *Vice Pres*
EMP: 8
SQ FT: 2,000
SALES (est): 1MM **Privately Held**
SIC: 3993 Signs & advertising specialties

Candor
Tioga County

(G-3403)
H L ROBINSON SAND & GRAVEL (PA)
535 Ithaca Rd (13743)
P.O. Box 121 (13743-0121)
PHONE..................607 659-5153
Hannah L Robinson, *President*
Shane Reeves, *Sales Mgr*
Brad Robinson, *Manager*
Raymond Dailey, *Director*
EMP: 18
SQ FT: 5,000
SALES (est): 2.6MM **Privately Held**
SIC: 1442 Sand mining; gravel mining

(G-3404)
MARCELLUS ENERGY SERVICES LLC
3 Mill St Ste 6 (13743-1400)
PHONE..................607 236-0038
Gloria Tubbs, *Mng Member*
EMP: 20
SALES (est): 1.3MM **Privately Held**
SIC: 1389 Oil field services

Canisteo
Steuben County

(G-3405)
SIVKO FURS INC
3089 County Route 119 (14823-9681)
PHONE..................607 698-4827
Fax: 607 698-4827
Ann Farkas, *President*
EMP: 9
SQ FT: 3,675
SALES (est): 1MM **Privately Held**
SIC: 2299 Grease, wool

Canton
St. Lawrence County

(G-3406)
BIMBO BAKERIES USA INC
19 Miner St Ste D (13617-1231)
PHONE..................315 379-9069
Jeff Ward, *Manager*
EMP: 18 **Privately Held**
SIC: 2051 Bread, cake & related products
HQ: Bimbo Bakeries Usa, Inc
 255 Business Center Dr # 200
 Horsham PA 19044
 215 347-5500

(G-3407)
COMMERCIAL PRESS INC
6589 Us Highway 11 (13617-3980)
PHONE..................315 274-0028
Fax: 315 386-5259
David Charleson, *President*
Tracy Charleson, *Vice Pres*
EMP: 6
SQ FT: 1,200
SALES (est): 620K **Privately Held**
SIC: 2752 2759 Commercial printing, offset; commercial printing

(G-3408)
CORNING INCORPORATED
334 County Route 16 (13617-3135)
PHONE..................315 379-3200
Fax: 315 379-3211
Joseph Neubert, *Plant Mgr*
Daniel Cassavaw, *Engineer*
David Navan, *Engineer*
Lindsay Miller, *Human Res Mgr*
Joe Neubert, *Manager*
EMP: 86
SALES (corp-wide): 9.3B **Publicly Held**
WEB: www.corning.com
SIC: 3229 3211 Pressed & blown glass; flat glass
PA: Corning Incorporated
 1 Riverfront Plz
 Corning NY 14831
 607 974-9000

(G-3409)
FRAZER COMPUTING INC
6196 Us Highway 11 (13617-3967)
P.O. Box 569 (13617-0569)
PHONE..................315 379-3500
Michael Frazer, *President*
Josh Clark, *Marketing Staff*
EMP: 26
SALES (est): 3.9MM **Privately Held**
WEB: www.frazercomputing.com
SIC: 7372 Prepackaged software

Cape Vincent
Jefferson County

(G-3410)
METALCRAFT MARINE US INC
583 E Broadway St (13618)
PHONE..................315 501-4015
Tom Wroe, *President*
Michael Allen, *General Mgr*
Paul Cooledge, *Project Mgr*
Rob Phippen, *Controller*
Bob Clark, *Admin Sec*
▼ EMP: 17
SQ FT: 4,000
SALES: 547K
SALES (corp-wide): 3.6MM **Privately Held**
SIC: 3732 3731 Boat building & repairing; shipbuilding & repairing; barges, building & repairing; combat vessels, building & repairing; fireboats, building & repairing
PA: Metal Craft Marine Incorporated
 347 Wellington St
 Kingston ON K7K 6
 613 549-7747

Carle Place
Nassau County

(G-3411)
APOLLO ORTHOTICS CORP
320 Westbury Ave (11514-1607)
PHONE..................516 333-3223
Caleb Lee, *CEO*
EMP: 5
SALES: 500K **Privately Held**
SIC: 3842 Orthopedic appliances

(G-3412)
BEE GREEN INDUSTRIES INC
322 Westbury Ave (11514-1607)
PHONE..................516 334-3525
Harold Livine, *President*
EMP: 6
SALES (est): 312.1K **Privately Held**
SIC: 3999 Manufacturing industries

(G-3413)
BIOTEMPER
Also Called: Biotemper Plus
516 Mineola Ave (11514-1716)
PHONE..................516 302-7985
Nadeem Khan, *Administration*
EMP: 5 EST: 2015
SALES (est): 229.7K **Privately Held**
SIC: 2833 Medicinal chemicals

(G-3414)
FORMED PLASTICS INC
207 Stonehinge Ln (11514-1743)
P.O. Box 347 (11514-0347)
PHONE..................516 334-2300
Fax: 516 334-2679
Patrick K Long, *President*
Steve Zamprelli, *President*
David Long, *Exec VP*
Matthew Desmond, *Vice Pres*
Ron Joannou, *VP Mfg*
EMP: 80 EST: 1946
SQ FT: 74,000
SALES (est): 20.3MM **Privately Held**
WEB: www.formedplastics.com
SIC: 3089 Plastic processing

(G-3415)
GENNARIS ITLN FRENCH BKY INC
Also Called: Cardinali Bakery
465 Westbury Ave (11514-1401)
PHONE..................516 997-8968
Giuseppe A Mauro, *President*
Joe Mauro, *Sales Executive*
Mary Lou Makelski, *Admin Sec*
EMP: 6 EST: 1935
SALES (est): 500K **Privately Held**
SIC: 2051 5461 Bread, cake & related products; bakeries

(G-3416)
GOOD TIMES MAGAZINE
346 Westbury Ave Ste Ll (11514-1654)
PHONE..................516 280-2100
Rich Braciforte, *Owner*
EMP: 8
SALES (est): 648.2K **Privately Held**
WEB: www.goodtimesmag.com
SIC: 2721 Periodicals

(G-3417)
JEFF COOPER INC
288 Westbury Ave (11514-1605)
P.O. Box 361 (11514-0361)
PHONE..................516 333-8200
Fax: 516 333-0620
Jeff Cooper, *President*
Laurie Cooper, *Vice Pres*
David Cooper, *Manager*
EMP: 12 EST: 1978
SALES (est): 1.9MM **Privately Held**
WEB: www.jcplatinum.com
SIC: 3911 Jewelry, precious metal; rings, finger; precious metal; pins (jewelry), precious metal; bracelets, precious metal

(G-3418)
JOHNSON & HOFFMAN LLC
40 Voice Rd (11514-1511)
P.O. Box 343 (11514-0343)
PHONE..................516 742-3333
Brad Ansary, *President*
Larry Zettwoch, *VP Opers*
Drew Taormina, *Plant Mgr*
Barry Trontz, *Purch Dir*
Albert Costabile, *Purch Mgr*
EMP: 90
SQ FT: 65,000
SALES (est): 19.2MM **Privately Held**
WEB: www.aecjh.com
SIC: 3469 Metal stampings
PA: Ansaco, Llc
 56 E 13th St Apt 4
 New York NY 10003
 602 323-0653

(G-3419)
LOW-COST MFG CO INC
318 Westbury Ave (11514-1607)
P.O. Box 147 (11514-0147)
PHONE..................516 627-3282
Fax: 516 997-9890
Harold Rothlin, *President*
Freddy Malamud, *General Mgr*
▲ EMP: 6

Carle Place - Nassau County (G-3420)

SQ FT: 4,000
SALES (est): 1MM **Privately Held**
WEB: www.lowcostmfg.com
SIC: **3564** 5087 Purification & dust collection equipment; laundry equipment & supplies

(G-3420)
M&M PRINTING INC
Also Called: MARsid-M&m Group, The
245 Westbury Ave (11514-1604)
PHONE.................................516 796-3020
Barry Caputo, *President*
Sidney Halpern, *Vice Pres*
Giovanni Jaramillo, *Marketing Staff*
Adham Zaid, *Art Dir*
EMP: 15
SALES (est): 1.4MM **Privately Held**
SIC: **2731** Book publishing

(G-3421)
MARKET PLACE PUBLICATIONS
Also Called: J & F Advertising
234 Silverlake Blvd Ste 2 (11514-1644)
PHONE.................................516 997-7909
Fax: 516 997-7906
Gonzalez Jose, *Principal*
EMP: 40 EST: 1987
SALES (est): 1.5MM **Privately Held**
SIC: **2711** 7313 Newspapers; newspaper advertising representative

(G-3422)
MARSID GROUP LTD
Also Called: Marsid Press
245 Westbury Ave (11514-1604)
PHONE.................................516 334-1603
Sidney Halpern, *President*
Mike Halpern, *Vice Pres*
▼ EMP: 9
SALES (est): 940K **Privately Held**
WEB: www.mmprint.com
SIC: **2752** Commercial printing, offset

(G-3423)
SCIENTIFIC SOLUTIONS GLOBL LLC
326 Westbury Ave (11514-1607)
PHONE.................................516 543-3376
Felicia Accius, *Manager*
Aurangzeb Pirzada,
EMP: 10
SQ FT: 3,600
SALES (est): 500K **Privately Held**
SIC: **2844** Cosmetic preparations

(G-3424)
STAMAPRO INC
Also Called: Pharmacena Labs
516 Mineola Ave (11514-1716)
PHONE.................................888 623-5003
Danny Capusano, *CEO*
Adil Palwala, *Principal*
EMP: 5
SQ FT: 3,300
SALES (est): 229.7K **Privately Held**
SIC: **2844** Cosmetic preparations

(G-3425)
VINCENTS FOOD CORP
179 Old Country Rd (11514-1907)
PHONE.................................516 481-3544
Anthony Marisi, *President*
Robert Marisi, *Treasurer*
EMP: 12
SALES (est): 720K **Privately Held**
SIC: **2033** Tomato sauce: packaged in cans, jars, etc.

Carmel
Putnam County

(G-3426)
BIODESIGN INC OF NEW YORK (PA)
1 Sunset Rdg (10512-1118)
P.O. Box 1050 (10512-8050)
PHONE.................................845 454-6610
Fax: 845 454-6608
Susanne Ruddnick PHD, *President*
Michael Payne PHD, *Vice Pres*
EMP: 15
SQ FT: 26,000
SALES (est): 1.2MM **Privately Held**
WEB: www.biodesignofny.com
SIC: **3821** 3829 Laboratory apparatus & furniture; measuring & controlling devices

(G-3427)
EASTERN JUNGLE GYM INC (PA)
30 Commerce Dr (10512-3026)
PHONE.................................845 878-9800
Fax: 845 878-1088
Scott Honigsberg, *President*
Rolf Zimmerman, *President*
Mark Honigsberg, *Vice Pres*
Naim Brahimi, *Store Mgr*
Ashley Tarr, *Manager*
◆ EMP: 30
SQ FT: 30,000
SALES: 6MM **Privately Held**
WEB: www.playsystem.com
SIC: **3949** 5941 Playground equipment; playground equipment

(G-3428)
J & J TL DIE MFG & STAMPG CORP
594 Horsepound Rd (10512-4703)
PHONE.................................845 228-0242
Ronald C Johnson, *President*
EMP: 5 EST: 1981
SQ FT: 4,800
SALES (est): 576.5K **Privately Held**
SIC: **3599** Machine & other job shop work

(G-3429)
JAMES A STALEY CO INC
5 Bowen Ct (10512-4535)
PHONE.................................845 878-3344
Fax: 845 878-3429
James A Staley, *President*
J David Mori, *Vice Pres*
Chris Staley, *Foreman/Supr*
Kevin Loffredo, *Engineer*
Boris Shnitser, *Engineer*
EMP: 18
SQ FT: 15,800
SALES (est): 5.2MM **Privately Held**
WEB: www.staleyco.com
SIC: **3829** 7699 Aircraft & motor vehicle measurement equipment; testers for checking hydraulic controls on aircraft; fuel system instruments, aircraft; aircraft & heavy equipment repair services; hydraulic equipment repair

(G-3430)
NORTHEAST MESA LLC (PA)
10 Commerce Dr (10512-3026)
PHONE.................................845 878-9344
Fax: 845 878-9351
Denise Persek, *Sales Staff*
Giulio Burra,
Phil Waylonis,
EMP: 6 EST: 1995
SQ FT: 8,400
SALES (est): 1.2MM **Privately Held**
WEB: www.northeastmesa.com
SIC: **3271** Blocks, concrete: landscape or retaining wall

(G-3431)
PATTERSON BLACKTOP CORP
Also Called: Peckham Materials
1181 Route 6 (10512-1645)
PHONE.................................845 628-3425
Kurt Gabrielson, *Branch Mgr*
EMP: 6
SALES (corp-wide): 200.6MM **Privately Held**
SIC: **3531** Asphalt plant, including gravel-mix type
HQ: Patterson Blacktop Corp
20 Haarlem Ave
White Plains NY 10603
914 949-2000

(G-3432)
PRECISION ARMS INC
Also Called: Time Precision
421 Route 52 (10512-6063)
PHONE.................................845 225-1130
Art Cocchia, *President*
Steven Cocchia, *Vice Pres*
Josephine Cocchia, *Admin Sec*
EMP: 6
SQ FT: 3,500
SALES (est): 524.2K **Privately Held**
WEB: www.precisionarms.com
SIC: **3599** 7699 Machine shop, jobbing & repair; gunsmith shop

(G-3433)
SILARX PHARMACEUTICALS INC (HQ)
Also Called: Lannett Company
1033 Stoneleigh Ave (10512-2414)
P.O. Box 449, Spring Valley (10977-0449)
PHONE.................................845 352-4020
Fax: 845 352-4037
Rohit Desai, *President*
Vipin Patel, *Vice Pres*
Nayan Raval, *Vice Pres*
Rashmi Gandhi, *Research*
Pramit Patel, *Research*
▲ EMP: 98
SQ FT: 30,000
SALES (est): 17.6MM
SALES (corp-wide): 633.3MM **Publicly Held**
SIC: **2834** Pharmaceutical preparations
PA: Lannett Company, Inc.
9000 State Rd
Philadelphia PA 19136
215 333-9000

(G-3434)
TPA COMPUTER CORP
531 Route 52 Apt 4 (10512-6073)
PHONE.................................877 866-6044
Steven Barnes, *President*
EMP: 10
SQ FT: 1,000
SALES (est): 1.2MM **Privately Held**
WEB: www.tpacomputer.com
SIC: **7372** 5734 Application computer software; computer & software stores

Carthage
Jefferson County

(G-3435)
A B C MC CLEARY SIGN CO INC
40230 State Route 3 (13619-9727)
PHONE.................................315 493-3550
Fax: 315 493-3573
Ronald Moore, *President*
Jo Anne Moore, *Corp Secy*
EMP: 11
SQ FT: 15,000
SALES (est): 730K **Privately Held**
SIC: **3993** Signs & advertising specialties; electric signs

(G-3436)
CARTHAGE FIBRE DRUM INC (PA)
14 Hewitt Dr (13619-1101)
P.O. Box 109 (13619-0109)
PHONE.................................315 493-2730
Fax: 315 493-6818
Timothy Wright, *President*
Cathy Wright, *Corp Secy*
Ford Wright Sr, *Vice Pres*
EMP: 15 EST: 1915
SQ FT: 1,509
SALES (est): 1.9MM **Privately Held**
SIC: **2655** Fiber cans, drums & similar products

(G-3437)
CARTHAGE SPECIALTY PPRBD INC
Also Called: Climax Paperboard
30 Champion St (13619-1156)
PHONE.................................315 493-2120
Patrick Purdy, *CEO*
EMP: 51
SALES (est): 20.9MM **Privately Held**
SIC: **2631** Paperboard mills

(G-3438)
CEM MACHINE INC (PA)
571 W End Ave (13619-1038)
PHONE.................................315 493-4258
Fax: 315 493-4236
Mark Robinson, *President*
Roxanne Robinson, *Corp Secy*
Jason Flint, *Engineer*
Timothy Nettles, *Treasurer*
Richard Mayo, *Director*
◆ EMP: 48
SQ FT: 80,000
SALES (est): 8.5MM **Privately Held**
WEB: www.cem-machine.com
SIC: **3553** Woodworking machinery

(G-3439)
CHAMPION MATERIALS INC (PA)
502 S Washington St (13619-1533)
P.O. Box 127 (13619-0127)
PHONE.................................315 493-2654
Fax: 315 493-2672
James D Uhlinger Jr, *Ch of Bd*
Turnbull Zoay, *Manager*
Corina Houppert, *Admin Asst*
Heather Walker, *Admin Asst*
Arrianne Turnbell, *Administration*
EMP: 6
SALES (est): 6.7MM **Privately Held**
WEB: www.championmaterials.com
SIC: **3273** 5211 Ready-mixed concrete; sand & gravel

(G-3440)
CHAMPION MATERIALS INC
21721 Cole Rd (13619-9559)
PHONE.................................315 493-2654
James Uhlinger, *Branch Mgr*
EMP: 44
SALES (corp-wide): 6.7MM **Privately Held**
SIC: **3273** 5211 Ready-mixed concrete; sand & gravel
PA: Champion Materials, Inc.
502 S Washington St
Carthage NY 13619
315 493-2654

(G-3441)
DAVID JOHNSON
Also Called: Poly Can
Deer River Rd (13619)
PHONE.................................315 493-4735
Fax: 315 493-4735
David Johnson, *Owner*
EMP: 12
SQ FT: 12,000
SALES (est): 2MM **Privately Held**
SIC: **3085** Plastics bottles

Cassadaga
Chautauqua County

(G-3442)
CASSADAGA DESIGNS INC
309 Maple Ave (14718-9723)
P.O. Box 289 (14718-0289)
PHONE.................................716 595-3030
Fax: 716 595-2312
Harold Hawkins, *President*
Daniel Hicks, *Vice Pres*
EMP: 6
SQ FT: 25,000
SALES: 500K **Privately Held**
SIC: **2426** 2511 Frames for upholstered furniture, wood; chairs, household, except upholstered: wood

(G-3443)
WRIGHTS HARDWOODS INC
Also Called: Livermoore Logging
6868 Route 60 (14718)
P.O. Box 1021, Sinclairville (14782-1021)
PHONE.................................716 595-2345
Fax: 716 595-2585
Michael A Livermore, *President*
L Phillip Wright, *Vice Pres*
EMP: 22
SQ FT: 2,832
SALES (est): 1.6MM **Privately Held**
SIC: **2426** Dimension, hardwood

Castile
Wyoming County

(G-3444)
DON BECK INC
5249 State Route 39 (14427-9518)
PHONE.................................585 493-3040

▲ = Import ▼ = Export
◆ = Import/Export

Fax: 585 493-2256
Richard T Beck, *President*
EMP: 7
SALES (est): 1.1MM **Privately Held**
SIC: 3523 Farm machinery & equipment

Castle Creek
Broome County

(G-3445)
A D BOWMAN & SON LUMBER CO
1737 Us Highway 11 (13744-1107)
PHONE.................................607 692-2595
Fax: 607 692-4176
Melvin Bowman, *Ch of Bd*
Joanne Bowman, *President*
Joel Bowman, *Vice Pres*
EMP: 28
SALES (est): 4.3MM **Privately Held**
SIC: 2426 2448 2421 Lumber, hardwood dimension; pallets, wood & wood with metal; sawmills & planing mills, general

Castleton On Hudson
Rensselaer County

(G-3446)
CELL-NIQUE CORPORATION
22 Hamilton Way (12033-1015)
PHONE.................................888 417-9343
Dan Ratner, *CEO*
▲ **EMP:** 1
SQ FT: 1,000,000
SALES (est): 3.9MM **Privately Held**
WEB: www.cell-nique.com
SIC: 2086 Iced tea & fruit drinks, bottled & canned

(G-3447)
IN NORTHEAST PRECISION WELDING
1177 Route 9 (12033-1910)
P.O. Box 109, East Greenbush (12061-0109)
PHONE.................................518 441-2260
Christine W Dwileski, *Principal*
EMP: 5 **EST:** 2008
SALES (est): 547K **Privately Held**
SIC: 7692 Automotive welding

(G-3448)
MOORADIAN HYDRAULICS & EQP CO (PA)
1190 Route 9 (12033-9686)
PHONE.................................518 766-3866
Fax: 518 766-3183
Richard Mooradian, *President*
Thomas Mooradian, *Vice Pres*
EMP: 12
SQ FT: 17,200
SALES (est): 2.5MM **Privately Held**
SIC: 7692 7699 5085 Welding repair; hydraulic equipment repair; hose, belting & packing

(G-3449)
SAXTON CORPORATION
1320 Route 9 (12033-9686)
PHONE.................................518 732-7716
Fax: 518 732-7716
Mike Kellog, *President*
EMP: 30
SALES (est): 2.7MM **Privately Held**
SIC: 3993 Signs & advertising specialties

Castorland
Lewis County

(G-3450)
BLACK RIVER WOODWORKING LLC
4773 State Route 410 (13620-2301)
PHONE.................................315 376-8405
Melvin Hess,
Brian Ball,
Ronald Hess,
EMP: 5 **EST:** 1993
SQ FT: 6,000
SALES (est): 500K **Privately Held**
SIC: 2511 Wood household furniture

(G-3451)
DANIEL & LOIS LYNDAKER LOGGING
10460 Monnat School Rd (13620-1270)
PHONE.................................315 346-6527
Lois Lyndaker, *Principal*
EMP: 7 **EST:** 2010
SALES (est): 732.7K **Privately Held**
SIC: 2411 Logging

(G-3452)
LYNDAKER TIMBER HARVESTING LLC
10204 State Route 812 (13620-1268)
PHONE.................................315 346-1328
David R Lyndaker,
Anita Lyndaker,
EMP: 11
SALES (est): 1.2MM **Privately Held**
SIC: 2411 Timber, cut at logging camp

Cato
Cayuga County

(G-3453)
ZAPPALA FARMS AG SYSTEMS INC
11404 Schuler Rd (13033-4276)
PHONE.................................315 626-6293
James R Zappala, *President*
Samuel Zappala, *Vice Pres*
Mark Ferlito, *Treasurer*
John R Zappala, *Admin Sec*
EMP: 30
SALES (est): 2.5MM **Privately Held**
SIC: 3523 5531 Farm machinery & equipment; automotive accessories

Catskill
Greene County

(G-3454)
CIMENT ST-LAURENT INC
Also Called: St Lawrence Cement Co
6446 Route 9w (12414-5322)
P.O. Box 31 (12414-0031)
PHONE.................................518 943-4040
Fax: 518 943-6894
Clifford Graves, *Site Mgr*
Ken Dewitt, *Purchasing*
Georges Hubin, *Branch Mgr*
EMP: 140
SALES (corp-wide): 28.6B **Privately Held**
SIC: 3241 Masonry cement
HQ: Crh Canada Group Inc
   2300 Steeles Ave W Suite 300
   Concord ON L4K 5
   905 532-3000

(G-3455)
DAILY MAIL & GREENE CNTY NEWS (HQ)
414 Main St (12414-1303)
P.O. Box 484 (12414-0484)
PHONE.................................518 943-2100
Roger Coleman, *President*
Raymond Pignone, *Principal*
Sara Tully, *Editor*
Michael Higgins, *Vice Pres*
Brenda Nickles, *Exec Dir*
EMP: 15 **EST:** 1951
SQ FT: 5,000
SALES (est): 3.7MM
SALES (corp-wide): 32MM **Privately Held**
WEB: www.thedailymail.org
SIC: 2711 Newspapers, publishing & printing
PA: Johnson Newspaper Corporation
   260 Washington St
   Watertown NY
   315 782-1000

(G-3456)
GOLUB CORPORATION
Also Called: Price Chopper Pharmacy
320 W Bridge St (12414-1730)
PHONE.................................518 943-3903
Fax: 518 943-9280
Kathleen Bryant, *Branch Mgr*
EMP: 74
SALES (corp-wide): 3.4B **Privately Held**
SIC: 3751 Motorcycles & related parts
PA: The Golub Corporation
   461 Nott St
   Schenectady NY 12308
   518 355-5000

(G-3457)
HILL CREST PRESS
Also Called: E & G Press
138 Grandview Ave (12414-1934)
PHONE.................................518 943-0671
Christine French, *Principal*
EMP: 8 **EST:** 1965
SQ FT: 1,500
SALES (est): 1.1MM **Privately Held**
SIC: 2752 2759 Commercial printing, offset; letterpress printing

(G-3458)
LEHIGH CEMENT COMPANY
120 Alpha Rd (12414-6902)
PHONE.................................518 943-5940
Jeff Fetty, *Opers Staff*
Cheryl McElroy, *Manager*
Al Austin, *Manager*
EMP: 20
SALES (corp-wide): 247.4MM **Privately Held**
WEB: www.gfcement.com
SIC: 3273 5032 Ready-mixed concrete; cement
HQ: Lehigh Cement Company
   313 Warren St
   Glens Falls NY 12801
   518 792-1137

(G-3459)
MARK T WESTINGHOUSE
Also Called: Pro Printers of Greene County
138 Grandview Ave (12414-1934)
PHONE.................................518 678-3262
Mark T Westinghouse, *Owner*
EMP: 6 **EST:** 1970
SQ FT: 2,000
SALES (est): 600K **Privately Held**
SIC: 2752 2759 Commercial printing, offset; letterpress printing

(G-3460)
MOUNTAIN T-SHIRTS INC
Also Called: Mountain T-Shirts & Sign Works
8 W Bridge St (12414-1620)
PHONE.................................518 943-4533
Fax: 518 943-4577
Craig Remaley, *President*
Daniel Webster, *Corp Secy*
Michael Marciante, *Treasurer*
EMP: 6 **EST:** 1984
SALES (est): 380K **Privately Held**
WEB: www.mountaintshirts.com
SIC: 2396 2261 5136 5199 Printing & embossing on plastics fabric articles; printing of cotton broadwoven fabrics; men's & boys' clothing; gifts & novelties

(G-3461)
PECKHAM INDUSTRIES INC
7065 Us Highway 9w (12414-5311)
P.O. Box 146, Ashland (12407-0146)
PHONE.................................518 943-0155
Gary Metcalf, *Principal*
EMP: 18
SALES (corp-wide): 200.6MM **Privately Held**
SIC: 2951 Concrete, asphaltic (not from refineries)
PA: Peckham Industries, Inc.
   20 Haarlem Ave Ste 200
   White Plains NY 10603
   914 949-2000

(G-3462)
WILLIAM MOON IRON WORKS INC
Also Called: Moon, Wm
80 Main St (12414-1805)
PHONE.................................518 943-3861
Fax: 518 943-3135
Paul Moon, *President*
Shelly Moon, *Bookkeeper*
EMP: 10
SQ FT: 6,000
SALES: 450K **Privately Held**
SIC: 3599 Machine shop, jobbing & repair

(G-3463)
WOLFGANG B GOURMET FOODS INC
117 Cauterskill Ave (12414-1748)
PHONE.................................518 719-1727
Wolfgang Brandl, *President*
Penelope Queen, *Vice Pres*
Bruce Johnson, *Executive*
Dr Fereidoon Behin, *Shareholder*
EMP: 14
SQ FT: 10,000
SALES (est): 2.3MM **Privately Held**
SIC: 2033 Spaghetti & other pasta sauce; packaged in cans, jars, etc.

Cattaraugus
Cattaraugus County

(G-3464)
ADAMS LUMBER CO INC
6052 Adams Rd (14719-9567)
PHONE.................................716 358-2815
Fax: 716 358-2220
Leona Adams, *President*
Robert Adams, *Vice Pres*
Dennis Adams, *Treasurer*
EMP: 16 **EST:** 1961
SQ FT: 10,000
SALES (est): 2MM **Privately Held**
SIC: 2421 Lumber: rough, sawed or planed

(G-3465)
CHESTER-JENSEN COMPANY
124 S Main St (14719-1240)
PHONE.................................610 876-6276
Fax: 716 257-3764
Steven Miller, *Vice Pres*
Albert Gimbrone, *Opers-Prdtn-Mfg*
Larry Barr, *Engineer*
EMP: 40
SQ FT: 52,232
SALES (corp-wide): 5.2MM **Privately Held**
WEB: www.chester-jensen.com
SIC: 3556 Food products machinery
PA: Chester-Jensen Company
   345 Tilghman St
   Chester PA 19013
   610 876-6276

(G-3466)
P & C GAS MEASUREMENTS SERVICE
Also Called: P & C Service
9505 Tannery Rd (14719-9761)
PHONE.................................716 257-3412
Fax: 716 257-5253
James Perkins, *CEO*
Marie Robbons, *Manager*
EMP: 11
SQ FT: 5,000
SALES (est): 826.6K **Privately Held**
SIC: 1389 Oil sampling service for oil companies

Cayuta
Schuyler County

(G-3467)
WAGNER HARDWOODS LLC
6307 St Route 224 (14824)
P.O. Box 68 (14824-0068)
PHONE.................................607 594-3321
Les Wagner, *Mng Member*
◆ **EMP:** 30
SALES (est): 5.4MM **Privately Held**
SIC: 2426 Hardwood dimension & flooring mills

(G-3468)
WAGNER HARDWOODS LLC
6307 St Route 224 (14824)
P.O. Box 68 (14824-0068)
PHONE.................................607 594-3321
Les Wagner, *Branch Mgr*
EMP: 200 Privately Held
WEB: www.wagner-hardwoods.com
SIC: 2426 Hardwood dimension & flooring mills
PA: Wagner Hardwoods Llc
6052 County Road 20
Friendship NY 14739

Cazenovia
Madison County

(G-3469)
BYS PUBLISHING LLC
118 Albany St (13035-1257)
PHONE.................................315 655-9431
Brent Selleck,
◆ **EMP:** 5
SALES (est): 316.5K **Privately Held**
SIC: 2741 Miscellaneous publishing

(G-3470)
CONTINENTAL CORDAGE CORP (DH)
75 Burton St (13035-1156)
P.O. Box 623 (13035-0623)
PHONE.................................315 655-9800
Fax: 315 655-9686
Rodney D Kent, *President*
Jim Murphy, *Division Mgr*
▲ **EMP:** 100
SQ FT: 60,000
SALES (est): 5.2MM
SALES (corp-wide): 432.1MM **Privately Held**
WEB: www.iwgbwd.com
SIC: 2298 3357 3496 3356 Cordage: abaca, sisal, henequen, hemp, jute or other fiber; nonferrous wiredrawing & insulating; miscellaneous fabricated wire products; nonferrous rolling & drawing; copper rolling & drawing; steel wire & related products

(G-3471)
D R CORNUE WOODWORKS
3206 Us Route 20 (13035-8408)
PHONE.................................315 655-9463
Dale R Cornue, *Owner*
EMP: 6
SQ FT: 6,000
SALES: 600K **Privately Held**
SIC: 2431 Doors, wood; woodwork, interior & ornamental; windows, wood

(G-3472)
FITZSIMMONS SYSTEMS INC
53 Nelson St (13035-1306)
PHONE.................................315 214-7010
Fax: 315 708-5424
Lowell Todd Fitzsimmons, *President*
Lucy McClaine, *Accountant*
Todd Fitzsimmons, *Associate*
▼ **EMP:** 13 **EST:** 1998
SQ FT: 1,500
SALES (est): 2.2MM **Privately Held**
WEB: www.fuelstoragetank.com
SIC: 2899 Chemical preparations

(G-3473)
KNOWLES CAZENOVIA INC (HQ)
Also Called: Dli
2777 Us Route 20 (13035-8444)
PHONE.................................315 655-8710
Fax: 315 655-0445
Michael P Busse, *Ch of Bd*
David Wightman, *President*
Howard Ingleson, *Managing Dir*
Jon Keenan, *Production*
Vicky Thurston, *QC Mgr*
▲ **EMP:** 179
SQ FT: 120,000
SALES: 34MM
SALES (corp-wide): 859.3MM **Publicly Held**
WEB: www.dilabs.com
SIC: 3675 Electronic capacitors

PA: Knowles Corporation
1151 Maplewood Dr
Itasca IL 60143
630 250-5100

(G-3474)
MADISON COUNTY DISTILLERY LLC
2420 Rte 20 (13035-8438)
PHONE.................................315 391-6070
Patrick Ruddy,
EMP: 5
SALES (est): 205K **Privately Held**
SIC: 2085 Gin (alcoholic beverage); vodka (alcoholic beverage)

(G-3475)
MARQUARDT SWITCHES INC (DH)
2711 Us Route 20 (13035-9405)
PHONE.................................315 655-8050
Fax: 607 754-7517
Harold Marquardt, *Ch of Bd*
Jochen Becker, *President*
John Jelfo, *CFO*
Christine Dillingham, *Accounts Mgr*
Peter Mitchell, *Admin Sec*
▲ **EMP:** 200 **EST:** 1975
SQ FT: 98,000
SALES: 219.7MM **Privately Held**
WEB: www.switches.com
SIC: 3625 3613 Switches, electric power; switchgear & switchboard apparatus
HQ: Marquardt Gmbh
SchloBstr. 16
Rietheim-Weilheim 78604
742 499-0

(G-3476)
PDJ INC
Also Called: Johnson Bros Lumber
2550 E Ballina Rd (13035-8475)
PHONE.................................315 655-8824
Fax: 315 655-4449
Paul Johnson, *President*
Judith Johnson, *Vice Pres*
Joel Struebing, *VP Sales*
Kara Connellan, *Office Spvr*
Heather Johnson, *Admin Sec*
EMP: 30
SQ FT: 39,400
SALES (est): 5.3MM **Privately Held**
SIC: 2421 Sawmills & planing mills, general

(G-3477)
PEAKS COFFEE COMPANY
3264 Rte 20 (13035-8408)
PHONE.................................315 565-1900
Kelsey Ball, *Co-Owner*
Samuel Bender, *Co-Owner*
EMP: 5
SQ FT: 1,100
SALES (est): 139.9K **Privately Held**
SIC: 2095 Coffee roasting (except by wholesale grocers)

(G-3478)
PRICET PRINTING
3852 Charles Rd (13035-4505)
PHONE.................................315 655-0369
Nathan Hoak, *President*
EMP: 6
SALES (est): 726.3K **Privately Held**
SIC: 2752 Commercial printing, lithographic

(G-3479)
STK ELECTRONICS INC
Also Called: Air-O-Tronics
2747 Rte 20 (13035-8444)
PHONE.................................315 655-8476
Fax: 800 634-0285
Bill Merlini, *Ch of Bd*
Peter M Kip, *Principal*
Peter Mitchell, *Principal*
William Merlini, *CFO*
Dan Koehl, *Manager*
▲ **EMP:** 40
SQ FT: 20,000
SALES (est): 9.4MM **Privately Held**
WEB: www.stkelectronics.com
SIC: 3675 5063 Electronic capacitors; electrical apparatus & equipment; circuit breakers

(G-3480)
TRONSER INC
3066 John Trush Jr Blvd (13035-9541)
PHONE.................................315 655-9528
Michael Tronser, *President*
Mike Beckett, *General Mgr*
James Dowd, *Vice Pres*
James Biando, *Mfg Mgr*
Peter Mitchell, *Admin Sec*
▲ **EMP:** 6
SQ FT: 7,000
SALES (est): 1.3MM
SALES (corp-wide): 11.6MM **Privately Held**
WEB: www.tronser.com
SIC: 3675 Electronic capacitors
PA: Alfred Tronser Gmbh
Quellenweg 14
Engelsbrand 75331
708 279-80

(G-3481)
VOLTRONICS LLC
Also Called: Trimmer Capacitor Company, The
2777 Us Route 20 (13035-8444)
PHONE.................................410 749-2424
Aaron Goldberg, *General Mgr*
Mary Finkelstein, *Manager*
EMP: 48 **EST:** 1963
SQ FT: 200,000
SALES (est): 8.2MM
SALES (corp-wide): 6.7B **Publicly Held**
WEB: www.variablecap.com
SIC: 3675 Electronic capacitors
PA: Dover Corporation
3005 Highland Pkwy # 200
Downers Grove IL 60515
630 541-1540

Cedarhurst
Nassau County

(G-3482)
ABLE KITCHEN
Also Called: Able Kitchen Supplies
540 Willow Ave Unit B (11516-2211)
PHONE.................................877 268-1264
Schulman Joseph, *Owner*
EMP: 15
SALES (est): 994.2K **Privately Held**
SIC: 2434 Wood kitchen cabinets

(G-3483)
ELMAT QUALITY PRINTING LTD
79 Columbia Ave (11516-2011)
PHONE.................................516 569-5722
Fax: 516 569-5913
Matt Friedman, *President*
Ellen Friedman, *Treasurer*
EMP: 16
SQ FT: 4,000
SALES (est): 1.5MM **Privately Held**
SIC: 2752 Commercial printing, offset

(G-3484)
M & M BAGEL CORP
Also Called: Bagelry
507 Central Ave (11516-2010)
PHONE.................................516 295-1222
Vincent Matuozzi, *President*
Robert Madorsky, *Vice Pres*
EMP: 12
SALES (est): 1MM **Privately Held**
SIC: 2051 5461 Bagels, fresh or frozen; bagels

(G-3485)
MARK F ROSENHAFT N A O
538 Central Ave (11516-2127)
PHONE.................................516 374-1010
Mark F Rosenhaft, *Owner*
EMP: 8
SALES (est): 429.8K **Privately Held**
SIC: 3851 5999 Eyes, glass & plastic; miscellaneous retail stores

(G-3486)
NANO VIBRONIX INC
601 Chestnut St (11516-2228)
PHONE.................................516 374-8330
Harold Jacobs, *President*
EMP: 17

SALES: 16K **Privately Held**
SIC: 3841 Surgical & medical instruments

(G-3487)
NJR MEDICAL DEVICES
390 Oak Ave (11516-1824)
P.O. Box 582, New York (10021-0034)
PHONE.................................440 258-8204
Nicholas Pastron, *CEO*
EMP: 20
SALES (est): 1.9MM **Privately Held**
SIC: 3841 Suction therapy apparatus

(G-3488)
STJ ENTERPRISES
540 Willow Ave (11516-2211)
PHONE.................................516 612-0110
Joseph Schulman, *CEO*
Spencer Silverstein, *CFO*
EMP: 65
SALES (est): 2.5MM **Privately Held**
SIC: 3845 3841 Ultrasonic medical equipment, except cleaning; surgical & medical instruments

Center Moriches
Suffolk County

(G-3489)
DIAMOND PRECAST PRODUCTS INC
170 Railroad Ave (11934-1906)
PHONE.................................631 874-3777
Rick Cerrone, *President*
Dominic Iannuci, *Treasurer*
Steven Cerrone, *Manager*
Jeff Lashley, *Manager*
Ronald Notaranonio, *Admin Sec*
EMP: 15 **EST:** 1999
SALES (est): 1.8MM **Privately Held**
SIC: 3272 Concrete products

(G-3490)
EASTEND ENFORCEMENT PRODUCTS
24 Chichester Ave (11934-2402)
P.O. Box 309 (11934-0309)
PHONE.................................631 878-8424
John Koenig, *Owner*
Edityh Koenig, *Manager*
EMP: 5
SALES (est): 359.4K **Privately Held**
SIC: 3559 Ammunition & explosives, loading machinery

(G-3491)
GLASS STAR AMERICA INC
15 Frowein Rd Bldg E2 (11934-1609)
P.O. Box 495, East Moriches (11940-0495)
PHONE.................................631 291-9432
Fax: 631 951-0676
Anthony Jacino, *President*
Joseph Jacino, *Vice Pres*
▲ **EMP:** 11
SQ FT: 15,000
SALES (est): 2.3MM **Privately Held**
SIC: 3559 Automotive maintenance equipment

(G-3492)
ISLAND READY MIX INC
170 Railroad Ave (11934-1906)
PHONE.................................631 874-3777
Fax: 631 874-2860
Rice Cerrone, *President*
Dominic Iannuci, *Treasurer*
Ronald Notarantonio, *Admin Sec*
EMP: 25 **EST:** 1961
SALES (est): 4.3MM **Privately Held**
WEB: www.islandreadymix.com
SIC: 3273 3272 Ready-mixed concrete; concrete products, precast

(G-3493)
RED TAIL MOULDING & MLLWK LLC
23 Frowein Rd Ste 1 (11934-1606)
PHONE.................................516 852-4613
Tom Smith,
EMP: 3
SALES: 1.2MM **Privately Held**
SIC: 2431 Doors & door parts & trim, wood

Centereach
Suffolk County

(G-3494)
A M S SIGN DESIGNS
2360 Middle Country Rd (11720-3523)
PHONE..................................631 467-7722
Mark Saccone, *Owner*
Suzanna Saccone, *Co-Owner*
EMP: 5
SALES (est): 415.3K **Privately Held**
SIC: 3993 Signs & advertising specialties

(G-3495)
CALIBRATION TECHNOLOGIES INC
30 Woodland Blvd (11720-3636)
PHONE..................................631 676-6133
Thomas J Accardi, *President*
EMP: 5
SALES (est): 526K **Privately Held**
SIC: 3629 Electrical industrial apparatus

(G-3496)
ELEGANCE LIGHTING LTD
2426 Middle Country Rd (11720-3532)
PHONE..................................631 509-0640
▲ **EMP:** 10
SALES (est): 2.2MM **Privately Held**
SIC: 3646 Commercial indusl & institutional electric lighting fixtures

(G-3497)
I FIX SCREEN
203 Centereach Mall (11720-2751)
PHONE..................................631 421-1938
Alberto Cruz, *Principal*
EMP: 6
SALES (est): 382.9K **Privately Held**
SIC: 3442 Screen & storm doors & windows

(G-3498)
QUANTA ELECTRONICS INC
48 Fran Ln (11720-4441)
PHONE..................................631 961-9953
Fax: 631 615-0044
Martin Czerniewski, *President*
Carolina Zuniga, *Info Tech Mgr*
EMP: 12
SALES (est): 1.4MM **Privately Held**
SIC: 3663 Radio & TV communications equipment

(G-3499)
WIN SET TECHNOLOGIES LLC
2364 Middle Country Rd (11720-3502)
P.O. Box 2007, Miller Place (11764-8786)
PHONE..................................631 234-7077
Fax: 631 582-5777
Philip Settepani,
Frederick Winter III,
▼ **EMP:** 10 **EST:** 2001
SQ FT: 3,000
SALES (est): 750K **Privately Held**
WEB: www.winset.net
SIC: 3542 Presses: forming, stamping, punching, sizing (machine tools)

Centerport
Suffolk County

(G-3500)
BLONDIE S BAKESHOP INC
90 Washington Dr (11721-1831)
PHONE..................................631 424-4545
Jeff Kennaugh, *President*
EMP: 8
SALES (est): 592.2K **Privately Held**
SIC: 2051 Bakery: wholesale or wholesale/retail combined

(G-3501)
FORUM PUBLISHING CO
Also Called: Marketer's Forum Magazine
383 E Main St (11721-1538)
PHONE..................................631 754-5000
Fax: 631 754-0630
Martin B Stevens, *Owner*
EMP: 9
SQ FT: 3,000
SALES: 1.4MM **Privately Held**
WEB: www.forum123.com
SIC: 2721 Trade journals: publishing & printing

(G-3502)
FUEL TANK ENVMTL SVCS CORP
674 Washington Dr (11721-1809)
PHONE..................................631 374-9083
Murad Sevinch, *President*
EMP: 1 **EST:** 2005
SALES (est): 1MM **Privately Held**
SIC: 2869 Fuels

(G-3503)
LEESA DESIGNS LTD
31 Glenn Cres (11721-1715)
P.O. Box 488 (11721-0488)
PHONE..................................631 261-3991
Helen L Dello-Iacona, *President*
Helen L Dello-Iacora, *President*
Sara Mazzola, *Treasurer*
EMP: 5 **EST:** 1997
SALES: 200K **Privately Held**
SIC: 2339 Neckwear & ties: women's, misses' & juniors'

(G-3504)
LIBERTY INSTALL INC
100 Centershore Rd (11721-1527)
PHONE..................................631 651-5655
Sheri Stevens, *President*
EMP: 11
SALES (est): 423.3K **Privately Held**
SIC: 3841 Surgical & medical instruments

(G-3505)
MSP TECHNOLOGYCOM LLC
77 Bankside Dr (11721-1738)
PHONE..................................631 424-7542
Walter Stark, *CEO*
Jeanne Connor-Stark,
EMP: 3
SQ FT: 1,200
SALES (est): 1.2MM **Privately Held**
WEB: www.msptechnology.com
SIC: 3585 5075 Humidifiers & dehumidifiers; dehumidifiers, except portable

(G-3506)
SURVIVAL INC
90 Washington Dr Ste C (11721-1831)
PHONE..................................631 385-5060
Sanjay Lakhani, *President*
Rebecca Lakhani, *Vice Pres*
▲ **EMP:** 8
SALES (est): 1.1MM **Privately Held**
WEB: www.survivalrules.com
SIC: 2339 Women's & misses' outerwear

Central Bridge
Schoharie County

(G-3507)
AMERICAN STANDARD MFG INC
Also Called: Asm
106 Industrial Park Ln (12035)
P.O. Box 164 (12035-0164)
PHONE..................................518 868-2512
Coleman Vickary, *Chairman*
Aaron Haig, *Prdtn Mgr*
David Dane, *Manager*
William Cleveland, *Director*
Connie Vickary, *Admin Sec*
EMP: 25
SQ FT: 28,000
SALES (est): 6MM **Privately Held**
WEB: www.amrstd.com
SIC: 3499 2542 Machine bases, metal; partitions & fixtures, except wood

Central Islip
Suffolk County

(G-3508)
ABK ENTERPRISES INC
Also Called: Beval Engine & Machine
403 E Suffolk Ave (11749-2352)
PHONE..................................631 348-0555
Beverly Kaiser, *Vice Pres*
EMP: 6
SQ FT: 8,500
SALES (est): 58.3K **Privately Held**
SIC: 3599 Machine shop, jobbing & repair

(G-3509)
AH ELCTRONIC TEST EQP REPR CTR
7 Olive St (11722-4017)
PHONE..................................631 234-8979
Audley Haynes, *Principal*
EMP: 12
SALES (corp-wide): 1.7MM **Privately Held**
WEB: www.ahelectronics.com
SIC: 1389 3825 7629 Testing, measuring, surveying & analysis services; standards & calibration equipment for electrical measuring; electronic equipment repair
PA: Ah Electronic Test Equipment Repair Center Inc
374 Islip Ave Ste 201
Islip NY 11751
631 277-6282

(G-3510)
AUTRONIC PLASTICS INC
Also Called: API
1150 Motor Pkwy (11722-1217)
PHONE..................................516 333-7577
Fax: 516 333-7695
Michael Lax, *President*
Tim Keuning, *President*
Phil Tjimos, *Project Mgr*
Agjah I Libohova, *Research*
Agjah Libohova, *Research*
▲ **EMP:** 70 **EST:** 1961
SQ FT: 55,000
SALES (est): 27.4MM **Privately Held**
WEB: www.apisolution.com
SIC: 3089 5162 Injection molding of plastics; plastics products

(G-3511)
AVCO INDUSTRIES INC
120 Windsor Pl (11722-3331)
P.O. Box 416, Huntington Station (11746-0338)
PHONE..................................631 851-1555
Fax: 631 232-9504
Gil Korine, *Ch of Bd*
Marcela Lazo, *Accountant*
▲ **EMP:** 15
SQ FT: 40,000
SALES (est): 9.3MM **Privately Held**
SIC: 2679 Pressed fiber & molded pulp products except food products

(G-3512)
BERKSHIRE TRANSFORMER (PA)
Also Called: Custom Power Systems
77 Windsor Pl Ste 18 (11722-3334)
PHONE..................................631 467-5328
Paul Alessandrini, *Owner*
EMP: 5
SALES (est): 916.7K **Privately Held**
SIC: 3679 3612 Electronic loads & power supplies; transformers, except electric

(G-3513)
BI NUTRACEUTICALS INC
120 Hoffman Ln (11749-5008)
PHONE..................................631 232-1105
Fax: 631 232-0369
Francisco Rivera, *Opers Mgr*
Robin Corcella, *Purchasing*
Terri Wright, *Sales Executive*
Bob Harvey, *Manager*
EMP: 52
SALES (corp-wide): 33MM **Privately Held**
WEB: www.botanicals.com
SIC: 2834 Vitamin preparations
PA: Bi Nutraceuticals, Inc.
2384 E Pacifica Pl
Rancho Dominguez CA 90220
310 669-2100

(G-3514)
CELLU TISSUE - LONG ISLAND LLC
555 N Research Pl (11722-4417)
PHONE..................................631 232-2626
Russell C Taylor,
▲ **EMP:** 210
SALES (est): 22.5MM
SALES (corp-wide): 1.7B **Publicly Held**
SIC: 2676 Sanitary paper products
HQ: Cellu Tissue Holdings, Inc.
12725 Morris Road Ext # 210
Alpharetta GA 30004

(G-3515)
CENTRAL ISLIP PHARMACY INC
1629 Islip Ave (11722-2701)
PHONE..................................631 234-6039
Ronald Goodstadt, *Principal*
EMP: 7
SALES (est): 847.4K **Privately Held**
SIC: 2834 Adrenal pharmaceutical preparations

(G-3516)
COLOR CARD LLC
Also Called: Limo-Print.com
1065 Islip Ave (11722-4203)
PHONE..................................631 232-1300
Robert Haller Sr, *President*
Marilyn Haller, *Vice Pres*
EMP: 18
SQ FT: 110,000
SALES (est): 1.4MM **Privately Held**
SIC: 2752 5961 2759 Business form & card printing, lithographic; cards, mail order; invitations: printing

(G-3517)
CREATIVE HOME FURNISHINGS (PA)
Also Called: Dakotah
250 Creative Dr (11722-4404)
PHONE..................................631 582-8000
Gunther Bartsch, *President*
▲ **EMP:** 3
SALES (est): 9MM **Privately Held**
WEB: www.dakotah.com
SIC: 2392 Household furnishings; cushions & pillows; blankets, comforters & beddings; slip covers & pads

(G-3518)
CVD EQUIPMENT CORPORATION (PA)
355 S Technology Dr (11722-4416)
PHONE..................................631 981-7081
Fax: 631 981-7095
Leonard A Rosenbaum, *CEO*
Steven Aragon, *COO*
Kevin R Collins, *Vice Pres*
William S Linss, *Vice Pres*
Karlheinz Strobl, *Vice Pres*
▲ **EMP:** 175
SQ FT: 130,000
SALES: 20.9MM **Publicly Held**
WEB: www.cvdequipment.com
SIC: 3559 Semiconductor manufacturing machinery

(G-3519)
CVD EQUIPMENT CORPORATION
Also Called: Conceptronic
355 S Technology Dr (11722-4416)
PHONE..................................631 582-4365
Leonard Rosenbaum, *President*
Jorge Bilstein, *Prdtn Mgr*
EMP: 15
SALES (corp-wide): 20.9MM **Publicly Held**
WEB: www.cvdequipment.com
SIC: 3559 3567 Semiconductor manufacturing machinery; heating units & devices, industrial: electric
PA: Cvd Equipment Corporation
355 S Technology Dr
Central Islip NY 11722
631 981-7081

Central Islip - Suffolk County (G-3520) — GEOGRAPHIC SECTION

(G-3520)
D & R SILK SCREENING LTD
201 Creative Dr (11722-4405)
PHONE............................631 234-7464
Dominick De Ricco, *President*
Rose De Ricco, *Admin Sec*
EMP: 15
SQ FT: 4,000
SALES (est): 1.2MM **Privately Held**
SIC: 2261 2396 Screen printing of cotton broadwoven fabrics; automotive & apparel trimmings

(G-3521)
EUGENE G DANNER MFG INC
Also Called: Danner, Eg Mfg
160 Oval Dr (11749-1403)
PHONE............................631 234-5261
Fax: 631 234-4778
Eugene G Danner, *President*
Bill Minnick, *General Mgr*
Josephine Danner, *Corp Secy*
Michael Danner, *Vice Pres*
▲ EMP: 38 EST: 1948
SQ FT: 31,000
SALES (est): 7.9MM **Privately Held**
WEB: www.dannermfg.com
SIC: 3089 Aquarium accessories, plastic

(G-3522)
FAR EASTERN COCONUT COMPANY
200 Corporate Plz 201a (11749-1552)
PHONE............................631 851-8800
Fax: 631 851-7950
Richard Martino, *President*
Mitchell Bauman, *Treasurer*
Anthony Armen, *Sales Staff*
▲ EMP: 10
SQ FT: 2,000
SALES (est): 640K **Privately Held**
SIC: 2099 Coconut, desiccated & shredded

(G-3523)
FREEPORT PAPER INDUSTRIES INC
120 Windsor Pl (11722-3331)
PHONE............................631 851-1555
Gil Korine, *Ch of Bd*
Debby Steiner, *Controller*
Marcela Lazo, *Accountant*
Linda Franca, *Bookkeeper*
◆ EMP: 60
SQ FT: 40,000
SALES (est): 14.1MM **Privately Held**
SIC: 2621 Paper mills

(G-3524)
GMR MANUFACTURING INC
Also Called: George Raum Manufacturing
101 Windsor Pl Unit D (11722-3329)
PHONE............................631 582-2600
Fax: 631 582-0548
George Raum, *President*
EMP: 6 EST: 1976
SQ FT: 2,300
SALES (est): 520.4K **Privately Held**
SIC: 3599 Machine shop, jobbing & repair

(G-3525)
INVAGEN PHARMACEUTICALS INC
550 S Research Pl (11722-4415)
PHONE............................631 949-6367
Fakiha Rana, *Branch Mgr*
EMP: 150
SALES (corp-wide): 23.6MM **Privately Held**
SIC: 2834 Tablets, pharmaceutical
HQ: Invagen Pharmaceuticals Inc.
7 Oser Ave Ste 4
Hauppauge NY 11788
631 231-3233

(G-3526)
ISLAND RECYCLING CORP
228 Blydenburg Rd (11749-5006)
PHONE............................631 234-6688
Fax: 631 234-4201
Mary Dimatteo, *President*
EMP: 5
SQ FT: 10,000
SALES (est): 572.3K **Privately Held**
SIC: 3341 Recovery & refining of nonferrous metals

(G-3527)
ISLANDIA MRI ASSOCIATES PC
200 Corporate Plz Ste 203 (11749-1507)
PHONE............................631 234-2828
Joel Reiter, *President*
Maggie Hernandez, *Office Mgr*
EMP: 15
SALES (est): 1.5MM **Privately Held**
SIC: 3826 Magnetic resonance imaging apparatus

(G-3528)
J&R FUEL OF LI INC
97 W Suffolk Ave (11722-2143)
PHONE............................631 234-1959
James R Reed, *Owner*
EMP: 5
SALES (est): 350.1K **Privately Held**
SIC: 2869 Fuels

(G-3529)
LENARO PAPER CO INC
31 Windsor Pl (11722-3301)
P.O. Box 9024 (11722-9024)
PHONE............................631 439-8800
Fax: 631 439-8801
Leonard Aronica, *Ch of Bd*
Anthony J Aronica, *Vice Pres*
John McClung, *Controller*
◆ EMP: 18
SQ FT: 143,000
SALES (est): 10.3MM **Privately Held**
WEB: www.lenaropaper.com
SIC: 2621 5111 Paper mills; fine paper

(G-3530)
M & M MOLDING CORP
250 Creative Dr (11722-4404)
PHONE............................631 582-1900
Mathias Meinzinger, *President*
John McLaughlin, *CFO*
Gunther Bartsch, *Treasurer*
▲ EMP: 200 EST: 1977
SQ FT: 50,000
SALES (est): 27.2MM **Privately Held**
SIC: 3089 Injection molded finished plastic products

(G-3531)
MONARCH GRAPHICS INC
1065 Islip Ave (11722-4203)
PHONE............................631 232-1300
Fax: 631 232-1392
Marilyn Haller, *President*
Robert Haller, *Vice Pres*
EMP: 18
SQ FT: 11,000
SALES (est): 2.8MM **Privately Held**
WEB: www.monarchgraphics.com
SIC: 2752 Commercial printing, lithographic

(G-3532)
NATIONWIDE EXHIBITOR SVCS INC
Also Called: Nationwide Displays
110 Windsor Pl (11722-3331)
PHONE............................631 467-2034
Steven Griffith, *President*
William Griffith, *Vice Pres*
Jim Reardon, *Project Mgr*
Ashley Zere, *Project Mgr*
Robin Matthews, *Bookkeeper*
EMP: 10
SQ FT: 20,000
SALES (est): 2MM **Privately Held**
SIC: 3993 3999 2542 Displays & cutouts, window & lobby; advertising display products; fixtures: display, office or store: except wood

(G-3533)
NETEGRITY INC (HQ)
1 Ca Plz (11749-5305)
PHONE............................631 342-6000
Barry N Bycoff, *President*
Erik Hansen, *General Mgr*
William C Bartow, *Vice Pres*
Sharyn Dodson, *Vice Pres*
Steve McLaughlin, *Vice Pres*
EMP: 160
SALES (est): 22.8MM
SALES (corp-wide): 4B **Publicly Held**
WEB: www.netegrity.com
SIC: 7372 Prepackaged software
PA: Ca, Inc.
520 Madison Ave Fl 22
New York NY 10022
800 225-5224

(G-3534)
NORTH AMERICAN ENCLOSURES INC (PA)
Also Called: Nae
85 Jetson Ln Ste B (11722-1202)
P.O. Box 913, Westbury (11590-0126)
PHONE............................631 234-9500
Fax: 631 234-9504
Richard Schwartz, *Ch of Bd*
Norman S Grafstein, *President*
Marie Neubert, *Corp Secy*
Nick Dibenedittto, *Purchasing*
Alan Streisfeld, *Credit Mgr*
▲ EMP: 40 EST: 1962
SQ FT: 55,000
SALES (est): 64.9MM **Privately Held**
WEB: www.naeframes.com
SIC: 2499 3827 Picture & mirror frames, wood; mirrors, optical

(G-3535)
QUALITY ENCLOSURES INC (PA)
101 Windsor Pl Unit H (11722-3339)
PHONE............................631 234-0115
Manny Schwartz, *Ch of Bd*
Michael Schwartz, *President*
Stephen Kady, *Opers Mgr*
John Berger, *Prdtn Mgr*
▲ EMP: 23
SQ FT: 27,000
SALES (est): 5.7MM **Privately Held**
WEB: www.qualityenclosures.com
SIC: 3088 3231 Plastics plumbing fixtures; products of purchased glass

(G-3536)
RICHARD RUFFNER
Also Called: Dynamic Printing
69 Carleton Ave (11722-3018)
PHONE............................631 234-4600
Richard Ruffner, *Owner*
Rosie Dejesus, *Exec Dir*
EMP: 15
SQ FT: 6,000
SALES (est): 1.1MM **Privately Held**
SIC: 2759 7349 5943 2789 Commercial printing; building maintenance services; office forms & supplies; bookbinding & related work; manifold business forms; commercial printing, lithographic

(G-3537)
SPECTRUM CATALYSTS INC
69 Windsor Pl (11722-3300)
P.O. Box 472, Smithtown (11787-0472)
PHONE............................631 560-3683
John Plunkett, *President*
Michael Plunkett, *Senior VP*
EMP: 5
SQ FT: 100,000
SALES: 1MM **Privately Held**
SIC: 3559 Chemical machinery & equipment

(G-3538)
SYNERGY RESOURCES INC
320 Carleton Ave Ste 6200 (11722-4538)
PHONE............................631 665-2050
Gene Caiola, *Ch of Bd*
Mark Lilly, *Principal*
Marion Sornieri, *Office Mgr*
Marianne Fornieri, *Manager*
Lou Miranda, *Manager*
EMP: 43
SQ FT: 3,500
SALES: 12MM **Privately Held**
WEB: www.synergyresources.net
SIC: 7372 Business oriented computer software

(G-3539)
SYSTEM OF AME BINDING
95 Hoffman Ln (11749-5020)
PHONE............................631 390-8560
William Stross, *Vice Pres*
EMP: 10
SALES (est): 1.7MM **Privately Held**
SIC: 3111 Bookbinders' leather

(G-3540)
UNITED BAKING CO INC
16 Bronx Ave (11722-2406)
PHONE............................631 413-5116
EMP: 17 **Privately Held**
SIC: 2052 Cookies & crackers
PA: United Baking Co., Inc.
41 Natcon Dr
Shirley NY 11967

(G-3541)
VANGUARD METALS INC
135 Brightside Ave (11722-2709)
PHONE............................631 234-6500
Fax: 631 234-5304
Joel Frank, *President*
Helene Frank, *Vice Pres*
EMP: 15
SQ FT: 6,000
SALES: 1.6MM **Privately Held**
WEB: www.vanguardmetals.com
SIC: 3451 3599 Screw machine products; machine shop, jobbing & repair

Central Square
Oswego County

(G-3542)
ALLOY METAL PRODUCTS LLC
193 Us Route 11 (13036-9760)
P.O. Box 2 (13036-0002)
PHONE............................315 676-2405
James Thayer, *Mng Member*
▲ EMP: 10
SQ FT: 14,000
SALES: 1MM **Privately Held**
WEB: www.alloymetalproducts.com
SIC: 3714 Motor vehicle parts & accessories

(G-3543)
AMERITOOL MFG INC
64 Corporate Park Dr (13036-9595)
P.O. Box 213 (13036-0213)
PHONE............................315 668-2172
Fax: 315 668-6853
Jerome E Beck, *President*
Cheryl Joyce, *Vice Pres*
▲ EMP: 20
SALES (est): 3.9MM **Privately Held**
SIC: 3593 Fluid power cylinders & actuators

(G-3544)
NASIFF ASSOCIATES INC
841 County Route 37 (13036-2133)
P.O. Box 88, Brewerton (13029-0088)
PHONE............................315 676-2346
Fax: 315 676-4711
Roger Nasiff, *President*
Anita Bourdeau, *Marketing Mgr*
Anita M Bourdeau, *Corp Comm Staff*
EMP: 6
SALES (est): 1MM **Privately Held**
WEB: www.nasiff.com
SIC: 3841 8711 Surgical & medical instruments; professional engineer

(G-3545)
TORRINGTON INDUSTRIES INC
Also Called: Mid-State Ready Mix
90 Corporate Park Dr (13036-9595)
PHONE............................315 676-4662
Fax: 315 676-5006
Theodore Zoli, *President*
EMP: 6
SALES (corp-wide): 1.9MM **Privately Held**
SIC: 3273 Ready-mixed concrete
PA: Torrington Industries Inc
112 Wall St
Torrington CT 06790
860 489-9261

(G-3546)
UPSTATE INSULATED GLASS INC
47 Weber Rd (13036-2109)
PHONE............................315 475-4960
Fax: 315 423-7189

GEOGRAPHIC SECTION

Champlain - Clinton County (G-3571)

James R Markert, *President*
EMP: 6
SQ FT: 3,100
SALES: 800K Privately Held
SIC: 3231 1793 5231 Insulating units, multiple-glazed: made from purchased glass; glass & glazing work; glass

Central Valley
Orange County

(G-3547)
AG ADRIANO GOLDSCHMIED INC
216 Red Apple Ct (10917-6605)
PHONE...................................845 928-8616
Nicole Linda, *Principal*
EMP: 8
SALES (corp-wide): 45.2MM Privately Held
SIC: 3663 Television closed circuit equipment
PA: Ag Adriano Goldschmied, Inc.
2741 Seminole Ave
South Gate CA 90280
323 357-1111

(G-3548)
CRABTREE & EVELYN LTD
928 Adirondack Way (10917-6206)
PHONE...................................845 928-4831
Tara Hammer, *Principal*
EMP: 6 Privately Held
SIC: 2869 Perfume materials, synthetic
HQ: Crabtree & Evelyn Ltd.
102 Peake Brook Rd
Woodstock CT 06281
800 272-2873

(G-3549)
CROCS INC
498 Red Apple Ct (10917-6620)
PHONE...................................845 928-3002
Debbie Heffern, *Manager*
EMP: 14
SALES (corp-wide): 1B Publicly Held
SIC: 3021 Shoes, rubber or rubber soled fabric uppers
PA: Crocs, Inc.
7477 Dry Creek Pkwy
Niwot CO 80503
303 848-7000

(G-3550)
DAVID YURMAN ENTERPRISES LLC
484 Evergreen Ct (10917-6716)
PHONE...................................845 928-8660
EMP: 9
SALES (corp-wide): 46.9MM Privately Held
SIC: 3911 Mfg Precious Metal Jewelry
PA: David Yurman Enterprises Llc
24 Vestry St
New York NY 10013
212 896-1550

(G-3551)
FRAGRANCE OUTLET INC
404 Dune Rd (10917-6201)
PHONE...................................845 928-1408
Fax: 845 928-1408
Kerry Donbrowski, *Manager*
EMP: 10
SALES (corp-wide): 48.3MM Privately Held
SIC: 2844 Perfumes & colognes
PA: The Fragrance Outlet Inc
11920 Miramar Pkwy
Miramar FL 33025
888 919-6613

(G-3552)
GUESS INC
498 Red Apple Ct (10917-6620)
PHONE...................................845 928-3930
EMP: 25
SALES (corp-wide): 2.2B Publicly Held
SIC: 2325 Men's & boys' jeans & dungarees

PA: Guess , Inc.
1444 S Alameda St
Los Angeles CA 90021
213 765-3100

(G-3553)
MAX LEON INC
825 Adirondack Way (10917-6205)
PHONE...................................845 928-8201
Fax: 845 928-2601
Kristen Osbourne, *Branch Mgr*
EMP: 11
SALES (corp-wide): 124.8MM Privately Held
SIC: 2339 Sportswear, women's
PA: Max Leon Inc
3100 New York Dr
Pasadena CA 91107
626 797-6886

(G-3554)
SARAR USA INC
Also Called: Woodbury Cmmon Premium Outlets
873 Adirondack Way (10917-6205)
PHONE...................................845 928-8874
Tufan Aksahin, *Opers Mgr*
Zafer Zere, *Branch Mgr*
Jim Riley, *Manager*
EMP: 6
SALES (corp-wide): 33MM Privately Held
WEB: www.sararusa.com
SIC: 2326 Men's & boys' work clothing
PA: Sarar Usa, Inc
1585 Us Highway 46
Little Falls NJ 07424
973 837-8600

(G-3555)
SCHILLER STORES INC
Also Called: Lecreuset of America
869 Adirondack Way (10917-6205)
PHONE...................................845 928-4316
Marcia York, *Branch Mgr*
EMP: 5 Privately Held
WEB: www.lecreusetofamerica.com
SIC: 3269 Cookware: stoneware, coarse earthenware & pottery
PA: Schiller Stores Inc
509 Tanger Mall Dr
Riverhead NY 11901

(G-3556)
VF OUTDOOR LLC
Also Called: North Face
461 Dune Rd (10917-6201)
PHONE...................................845 928-4900
Fax: 845 928-4940
Justin Dobson, *Manager*
EMP: 25
SALES (corp-wide): 12B Publicly Held
WEB: www.thenorthface.com
SIC: 2329 2339 Men's & boys' leather, wool & down-filled outerwear; women's & misses' outerwear
HQ: Vf Outdoor, Llc
2701 Harbor Bay Pkwy
Alameda CA 94502
510 618-3500

(G-3557)
WOODBURY PRINTING PLUS + INC
96 Turner Rd (10917-4001)
PHONE...................................845 928-6610
Frank Collins, *President*
EMP: 7
SQ FT: 3,800
SALES (est): 832.4K Privately Held
WEB: www.wprintingplus.com
SIC: 2752 7334 2791 3993 Commercial printing, offset; photocopying & duplicating services; typesetting; signs & advertising specialties

Chadwicks
Oneida County

(G-3558)
NEW YORK STATE TOOL CO INC
3343 Oneida St (13319)
PHONE...................................315 737-8985

Fax: 315 737-7784
David Wilsey, *President*
Matthew Wilsey, *President*
EMP: 11
SQ FT: 6,000
SALES (est): 1.6MM Privately Held
WEB: www.nystool.com
SIC: 3599 Machine shop, jobbing & repair

(G-3559)
WILLIAMS TOOL INC
9372 Elm St (13319-3515)
P.O. Box 430 (13319-0430)
PHONE...................................315 737-7226
Ray Williams, *President*
Jeffery Gerling, *Managing Dir*
Bob Prichard, *Prdtn Mgr*
Frances Gerling, *Manager*
Dan Petrie, *Manager*
EMP: 38 **EST:** 1957
SQ FT: 17,000
SALES: 3.3MM Privately Held
WEB: www.wmstool.com
SIC: 3599 Machine shop, jobbing & repair

Chaffee
Erie County

(G-3560)
DIAMOND SAW WORKS INC (PA)
12290 Olean Rd (14030-9767)
PHONE...................................716 496-7417
Fax: 585 496-6057
James Ziemer, *President*
James M Ziemer, *President*
Robert Gust, *Opers Staff*
Ed Duschen, *Engineer*
Charles Lafonte, *Engineer*
▲ **EMP:** 50
SQ FT: 55,000
SALES (est): 5MM Privately Held
WEB: www.diamondsaw.com
SIC: 3425 Saw blades & handsaws

(G-3561)
DONALD STEFAN
Also Called: Stefan & Sons Welding
3428 W Yorkshire Rd (14030-9619)
PHONE...................................716 492-1110
Donald Stefan, *Owner*
EMP: 5
SALES (est): 140.3K Privately Held
SIC: 7692 3441 Welding repair; fabricated structural metal

(G-3562)
HART TO HART INDUSTRIES INC
Also Called: Arcade Glass Works
13520 Chaffee Curriers Rd (14030-9701)
PHONE...................................716 492-2709
Bill Harter, *President*
EMP: 5
SQ FT: 3,500
SALES: 516.1K Privately Held
SIC: 3444 3089 Awnings & canopies; window frames & sash, plastic

(G-3563)
P & R TRUSS CO
Also Called: Uft New York
13989 E Schutt Rd (14030-9763)
PHONE...................................716 496-5484
Fax: 585 496-5490
Steven Slowick, *Manager*
EMP: 20
SALES (est): 1.6MM Privately Held
SIC: 2439 Trusses, wooden roof

(G-3564)
UFP NEW YORK LLC
Also Called: Universal Forest Products
13989 E Schutt Rd (14030-9763)
PHONE...................................716 496-5484
Fax: 716 496-5490
Steven Slowick, *Site Mgr*
Jim Howard, *Sales Staff*
Steve Slowik, *Branch Mgr*
EMP: 40
SQ FT: 18,720
SALES (corp-wide): 3.2B Publicly Held
WEB: www.ufpinc.com
SIC: 2439 Trusses, wooden roof

HQ: Ufp New York, Llc
11 Allen St
Auburn NY 13021
315 253-2758

Champlain
Clinton County

(G-3565)
AWAKEN LED COMPANY
477 State Route 11 # 1050 (12919-4819)
PHONE...................................802 338-5971
Douglas Schwartz, *President*
EMP: 15
SALES (est): 1.6MM Privately Held
SIC: 3646 Commercial indusl & institutional electric lighting fixtures

(G-3566)
BOW INDUSTRIAL CORPORATION
178 W Service Rd (12919-4440)
PHONE...................................518 561-0190
Fax: 800 526-5668
Samuel Bern, *President*
John Coney, *Controller*
▼ **EMP:** 96
SQ FT: 60,000
SALES (est): 1.4MM Privately Held
SIC: 3088 Plastics plumbing fixtures

(G-3567)
BURTON CORPORATION
Also Called: Burton Snowboards
21 Lawrence Paquette Dr (12919-4857)
PHONE...................................802 862-4500
EMP: 100
SALES (corp-wide): 147.9MM Privately Held
WEB: www.burton.com
SIC: 3949 Sporting & athletic goods
PA: The Burton Corporation
80 Industrial Pkwy
Burlington VT 05401
802 862-4500

(G-3568)
ELEGANCE COATING LTD
33 W Service Rd 100 (12919-4438)
PHONE...................................386 668-8379
Mario Morin, *CEO*
Emilie Morin, *Business Mgr*
Yoland Cloutier, *Finance Mgr*
Stephene Polequein, *Shareholder*
EMP: 25 **EST:** 2007
SALES (est): 2.2MM Privately Held
SIC: 3479 Painting, coating & hot dipping

(G-3569)
GREAT WESTERN MALTING CO
16 Beeman Way (12919-4965)
PHONE...................................800 496-7732
Will Jackson, *President*
▲ **EMP:** 9
SALES (est): 412.1K Privately Held
SIC: 2083 Malt

(G-3570)
HUMANWARE USA INC (PA)
1 Ups Way (12919-4569)
P.O. Box 800 (12919-0800)
PHONE...................................800 722-3393
Phillip Rance, *President*
Lou Lipschultz, *Vice Pres*
Vincent Rappa, *Vice Pres*
Greg Brown, *CFO*
Dan Brown, *Sales Staff*
EMP: 21
SQ FT: 3,800
SALES (est): 5.5MM Privately Held
SIC: 3851 Eyeglasses, lenses & frames

(G-3571)
KOREGON ENTERPRISES INC
Also Called: Nite Train R
102 W Service Rd (12919-4440)
PHONE...................................450 218-6836
H J Park, *President*
▲ **EMP:** 5
SQ FT: 3,300

Champlain - Clinton County (G-3572)

SALES (est): 655.4K **Privately Held**
WEB: www.nitetrain-r.com
SIC: 3699 5047 Electrical equipment & supplies; incontinent care products & supplies

(G-3572)
MODERN MECHANICAL FAB INC
100 Walnut St Ste 7 (12919-5337)
PHONE.................................518 298-5177
Fax: 518 298-3226
Heather Trombly, *President*
John Trombly, *Corp Secy*
▲ EMP: 9
SALES (est): 1.5MM **Privately Held**
WEB: www.modmechfab.com
SIC: 7692 Welding repair

(G-3573)
STARCYL USA CORP
348 State Route 11 (12919-4816)
PHONE.................................877 782-7295
Terry Allardin, *President*
EMP: 15
SQ FT: 10,000
SALES (est): 4MM **Privately Held**
SIC: 3593 Fluid power cylinders, hydraulic or pneumatic

(G-3574)
TESTORI INTERIORS INC
107 Lwrnce Paqtte Indstrl (12919)
PHONE.................................518 298-4400
Lindo Lapegna, *CEO*
Peter George, *Principal*
Russell Paynter, *Business Mgr*
Ajay Thakker, *CFO*
◆ EMP: 43 EST: 2000
SQ FT: 100,000
SALES (est): 8.9MM **Privately Held**
SIC: 2531 Public building & related furniture

(G-3575)
UNI SOURCE TECHNOLOGY
1320 Rt 9 (12919)
PHONE.................................514 748-8888
Lawrence Rutenberg, *Branch Mgr*
EMP: 10
SALES (corp-wide): 1.6MM **Privately Held**
SIC: 3812 Defense systems & equipment
PA: Unisource Technology Inc
  9010 Ryan Ave
  Dorval QC H9P 2
  514 748-8888

(G-3576)
UNIQUE PACKAGING CORPORATION
1320 State Route 9 # 3807 (12919-5007)
P.O. Box 219, Plattsburgh (12901-0219)
PHONE.................................514 341-5872
Fax: 518 561-2242
Fred Povitz, *President*
Earl Povitz, *Opers Staff*
EMP: 5
SALES (est): 496.8K **Privately Held**
SIC: 3053 3172 Packing materials; cases, jewelry

(G-3577)
WATER SPLASH INC
25 Locust St Ste 421 (12919-5001)
PHONE.................................800 936-3430
Gokhan Celik, *CEO*
Tara Menon, *Manager*
▲ EMP: 5
SALES (est): 364.4K **Privately Held**
SIC: 3999 Manufacturing industries

Chappaqua
Westchester County

(G-3578)
AIR ENGINEERING FILTERS INC
17 Memorial Dr (10514-3528)
P.O. Box 174 (10514-0174)
PHONE.................................914 238-5945
Pam Rubin, *President*
EMP: 9
SQ FT: 2,000

SALES (est): 1.3MM **Privately Held**
SIC: 3564 Filters, air: furnaces, air conditioning equipment, etc.

(G-3579)
DECORATIVE HARDWARE
180 Hunts Ln (10514-2602)
P.O. Box 627 (10514-0627)
PHONE.................................914 238-5251
Ronald Lawrence Prezener, *President*
Marie Anne Prezener, *Vice Pres*
▲ EMP: 10 EST: 1976
SQ FT: 2,000
SALES (est): 1.2MM **Privately Held**
WEB: www.decorative-hardware.com
SIC: 3429 Furniture builders' & other household hardware; furniture hardware

(G-3580)
INSIGHT UNLIMITED INC
660 Quaker Rd (10514-1505)
PHONE.................................914 861-2090
Shmuel Kliger, *President*
EMP: 6
SALES (est): 282K **Privately Held**
SIC: 7372 Prepackaged software

(G-3581)
NANORX INC
6 Devoe Pl (10514-3601)
PHONE.................................914 671-0224
Palayakopai Raghavan, *President*
EMP: 2
SALES: 1MM **Privately Held**
SIC: 2834 Medicines, capsuled or ampuled

(G-3582)
PROFESSIONAL ACCESS LLC
88 Old Farm Rd N (10514-3706)
PHONE.................................212 432-2844
Radhika Venkatesh,
EMP: 5
SALES (est): 342.2K **Privately Held**
SIC: 7372 Prepackaged software

Charlotteville
Schoharie County

(G-3583)
FLY-TYERS CARRY-ALL LLC
Also Called: Folstaf Company, The
112 Meade Rd (12036-1612)
PHONE.................................607 821-1460
Lee Stoliar,
EMP: 5
SQ FT: 850
SALES (est): 611.9K **Privately Held**
WEB: www.folstaf.com
SIC: 3949 5091 Fishing equipment; fishing tackle, general; fishing equipment & supplies; fishing tackle

Chateaugay
Franklin County

(G-3584)
AGRI-MARK INC
39 Mccadam Ln (12920-4306)
P.O. Box 900 (12920-0900)
PHONE.................................518 497-6644
Pat Dragon, *Warehouse Mgr*
Jerry Bessette, *Purch Mgr*
Tom Sorrell, *Engineer*
David McNiece, *Treasurer*
Jerry Besette, *Personnel*
EMP: 100
SALES (corp-wide): 288.2MM **Privately Held**
WEB: www.agrimark.net
SIC: 2022 Cheese, natural & processed
PA: Agri-Mark, Inc.
  100 Milk St Ste 5
  Methuen MA 01844
  978 689-4442

Chatham
Columbia County

(G-3585)
CRAFTECH
5 Dock St (12037)
PHONE.................................518 828-5011
Linda Geblanski, *CEO*
Erwin Gerard, *Owner*
EMP: 55
SALES (est): 2.6MM **Privately Held**
SIC: 2821 3089 Molding compounds, plastics; molding primary plastic

(G-3586)
KLING MAGNETICS INC
343 State Route 295 (12037-3713)
P.O. Box 348 (12037-0348)
PHONE.................................518 392-4000
Jody Rael, *President*
▲ EMP: 20
SQ FT: 20,000
SALES (est): 2.2MM **Privately Held**
SIC: 3993 3089 2752 3944 Advertising novelties; novelties, plastic; commercial printing, lithographic; games, toys & children's vehicles

(G-3587)
RAPID INTELLECT GROUP INC
77b Church St (12037-1319)
P.O. Box 131, Stuyvesant Falls (12174-0131)
PHONE.................................518 929-3210
Steve Grzeskow, *President*
Peter Grzeskow, *Vice Pres*
EMP: 12 EST: 1997
SALES (est): 888.4K **Privately Held**
SIC: 2731 Book publishing

(G-3588)
SONOCO-CRELLIN INTL INC (HQ)
87 Center St (12037-1032)
PHONE.................................518 392-2000
Fax: 518 392-6213
Bob Puechl, *Vice Pres*
David Marche, *Vice Pres*
Michael Tucker, *Vice Pres*
Ralph Tassone, *CFO*
▲ EMP: 500
SQ FT: 70,000
SALES (est): 159.2MM
SALES (corp-wide): 4.7B **Publicly Held**
SIC: 3089 Molding primary plastic
PA: Sonoco Products Company
  1 N 2nd St
  Hartsville SC 29550
  843 383-7000

Chazy
Clinton County

(G-3589)
JP SIGNS
9592 State Route 9 (12921-3102)
PHONE.................................518 569-3907
Jessica Macnerland, *Owner*
EMP: 5
SALES: 150K **Privately Held**
SIC: 3993 7389 5699 Signs & advertising specialties; printers' services: folding, collating; T-shirts, custom printed

Cheektowaga
Erie County

(G-3590)
ACCOLADE USA INC
Also Called: Level Wear
60 Industrial Pkwy # 397 (14227-2774)
PHONE.................................866 423-5071
Hilton Ngo, *President*
EMP: 200
SQ FT: 100,000
SALES: 1MM **Privately Held**
SIC: 2211 Apparel & outerwear fabrics, cotton

(G-3591)
BUFFALO COMPRESSED AIR INC
2727 Broadway St Ste 3a (14227-1070)
P.O. Box 468, Lancaster (14086-0468)
PHONE.................................716 783-8673
Greg Fuer, *Principal*
EMP: 6
SALES (est): 320K **Privately Held**
SIC: 3563 Air & gas compressors

(G-3592)
COMAIRCO EQUIPMENT INC (DH)
3250 Union Rd (14227-1044)
PHONE.................................716 656-0211
Roland Nadeau, *President*
Edward Murphy, *Vice Pres*
Judy Cook, *Manager*
EMP: 7
SQ FT: 6,000
SALES (est): 6.5MM
SALES (corp-wide): 5.9MM **Privately Held**
WEB: www.comairco.com
SIC: 3563 Air & gas compressors
HQ: Equipement Comairco Ltee
  5535 Rue Ernest-Cormier
  Montreal QC H7C 2
  450 665-8780

(G-3593)
CRS NUCLEAR SERVICES LLC
840 Aero Dr Ste 150 (14225-1451)
PHONE.................................716 810-0688
Kevin Connor, *Mng Member*
Daniel Guarasci, *Director*
▲ EMP: 12
SALES (est): 5.4MM **Privately Held**
SIC: 2834 Pharmaceutical preparations

(G-3594)
CULINARY ARTS SPECIALTIES INC
Also Called: Cas
2268 Union Rd (14227-2726)
PHONE.................................716 656-8943
Fax: 716 656-8945
Arthur L Keller, *President*
Andrew P Keller, *Vice Pres*
Jonathan Polly, *Purch Mgr*
Thomas Dagonese, *Controller*
Nancy Keller, *Financial Exec*
EMP: 85
SQ FT: 50,000
SALES (est): 20.5MM **Privately Held**
SIC: 2053 Cakes, bakery: frozen

(G-3595)
DERRICK CORPORATION
2540 Walden Ave (14225-4744)
PHONE.................................716 685-4892
EMP: 208
SALES (corp-wide): 195.8MM **Privately Held**
SIC: 3533 Derricks, oil or gas field
PA: Derrick Corporation
  590 Duke Rd
  Buffalo NY 14225
  716 683-9010

(G-3596)
DORM COMPANY CORPORATION
Also Called: Dorm Co.
575 Kennedy Rd Ste 2 (14227-1040)
P.O. Box 485, Clarence Center (14032-0485)
PHONE.................................502 551-6195
Jeff Gawronski, *President*
▲ EMP: 5
SQ FT: 6,000
SALES (est): 1MM **Privately Held**
SIC: 2431 Dormers, wood

(G-3597)
DUAL PRINT & MAIL LLC
340 Nagel Dr (14225-4731)
PHONE.................................716 684-3825
Thomas Salisbury, *Ch of Bd*
EMP: 73
SALES (corp-wide): 20.2MM **Privately Held**
SIC: 2752 Commercial printing, lithographic

GEOGRAPHIC SECTION — Chemung - Chemung County (G-3622)

HQ: Dual Print & Mail, Llc
3235 Grand Island Blvd
Grand Island NY 14072
716 775-8001

(G-3598)
ECOLAB INC
3719 Union Rd Ste 121 (14225-4250)
PHONE.................................716 683-6298
Fax: 716 683-0679
Dave Beckwith, *Branch Mgr*
EMP: 17
SALES (corp-wide): 13.1B **Publicly Held**
WEB: www.ecolab.com
SIC: 2841 Soap & other detergents
PA: Ecolab Inc.
1 Ecolab Pl
Saint Paul MN 55102
800 232-6522

(G-3599)
FLUID HANDLING LLC
Standard Xchange
175 Standard Pkwy (14227-1233)
PHONE.................................716 897-2800
Daniel Leschuitta, *Regl Sales Mgr*
Tony Scioli, *Regl Sales Mgr*
William Blankemeier, *Marketing Staff*
Joseph McMara, *Branch Mgr*
Nick Baker, *Systems Mgr*
EMP: 240 **Publicly Held**
WEB: www.ittind.com
SIC: 3443 Industrial vessels, tanks & containers
HQ: Fluid Handling, Llc
175 Standard Pkwy
Cheektowaga NY 14227
716 897-2800

(G-3600)
FLUID HANDLING LLC (HQ)
Also Called: Xylem
175 Standard Pkwy (14227-1233)
PHONE.................................716 897-2800
Ken Napolitano, *President*
Scott Alford,
Mike Romance, *Assistant*
▲ **EMP:** 1
SALES (est): 266.3MM **Publicly Held**
SIC: 3561 Pumps & pumping equipment

(G-3601)
GEMINI MANUFACTURES
160 Holtz Dr (14225)
PHONE.................................716 633-0306
Fax: 716 633-2564
Todd Lehmann, *Partner*
Irene Turski, *Partner*
EMP: 14
SQ FT: 4,200
SALES: 860K **Privately Held**
SIC: 3915 Jewelers' materials & lapidary work

(G-3602)
HAMMOND MANUFACTURING CO INC
475 Cayuga Rd (14225-1309)
PHONE.................................716 630-7030
Fax: 716 630-7042
Robert F Hammond, *CEO*
Marc A Dube, *Principal*
Kevin Bond, *COO*
Ray Schatzel, *Vice Pres*
Doug Hutt, *Engineer*
▲ **EMP:** 14
SQ FT: 17,000
SALES (est): 3.3MM
SALES (corp-wide): 85.5MM **Privately Held**
WEB: www.hammfg.com
SIC: 3677 5063 Transformers power supply, electronic type; electrical apparatus & equipment; transformers, electric
PA: Hammond Manufacturing Company Limited
394 Edinburgh Rd N
Guelph ON N1H 1
519 822-2960

(G-3603)
HANZLIAN SAUSAGE INCORPORATED
Also Called: Hanzlian Sausage Deli
2351 Genesee St (14225-2839)
PHONE.................................716 891-5247

David Hanzlian, *President*
George J Hanzlian Jr, *Vice Pres*
EMP: 8
SQ FT: 7,800
SALES (est): 950.7K **Privately Held**
SIC: 2013 Sausages from purchased meat

(G-3604)
HUGH F MCPHERSON INC
Also Called: Franklin's Printing
70 Innsbruck Dr (14227-2735)
PHONE.................................716 668-6107
Hugh F McPherson, *President*
Barbara L McPherson, *Vice Pres*
EMP: 7
SALES (est): 766.8K **Privately Held**
SIC: 2752 2791 Commercial printing, lithographic; typesetting

(G-3605)
HVR ADVNCED PWR COMPONENTS INC
2090 Old Union Rd (14227-2770)
PHONE.................................716 693-4700
Richard Arndt, *Principal*
Eugene Feind, *Principal*
David M Yanko, *Principal*
William Glodzik II, *Vice Pres*
Ronald Wills, *QC Mgr*
EMP: 10
SQ FT: 4,000
SALES (est): 1.9MM **Privately Held**
WEB: www.hvrapc.com
SIC: 3676 Electronic resistors

(G-3606)
LEO SCHULTZ
Also Called: Cuore Technology
1144 Maryvale Dr (14225-2312)
PHONE.................................716 969-0945
Kevin Ryan, *Branch Mgr*
EMP: 5
SALES (corp-wide): 1.5MM **Privately Held**
SIC: 3822 Auto controls regulating residntl & coml environmt & applncs
PA: Leo Rue Schultz
821 Panelli Pl
Santa Clara CA 95050
716 969-0945

(G-3607)
MP CAROLL INC
4822 Genesee St (14225-2494)
PHONE.................................716 683-8520
Fax: 716 683-8510
Michael Carrol, *President*
Brian Murphy, *Sales Staff*
Amy Huntingcon, *Office Mgr*
◆ **EMP:** 12
SALES (est): 2MM **Privately Held**
SIC: 2426 Flooring, hardwood

(G-3608)
MULTI-HEALTH SYSTEMS INC
Indus Pkwy Ste 70660 60 (14227)
PHONE.................................800 456-3003
Steven J Stein, *Branch Mgr*
Steven Stein, *Security Mgr*
Alasdair Maclean, *Information Mgr*
Brian Boutilier, *Systems Analyst*
Theresa Murray, *Software Dev*
EMP: 90
SALES (corp-wide): 13MM **Privately Held**
WEB: www.mhs.com
SIC: 3695 2741 Computer software tape & disks: blank, rigid & floppy; miscellaneous publishing
PA: Multi-Health Systems Inc
3770 Victoria Park Ave
North York ON
416 492-2627

(G-3609)
MULTISORB TECHNOLOGIES INC
20 French Rd (14227-2702)
PHONE.................................716 668-4191
John Cullen, *Branch Mgr*
EMP: 5
SALES (corp-wide): 104.8MM **Privately Held**
SIC: 2819 Industrial inorganic chemicals

PA: Multisorb Technologies, Inc.
325 Harlem Rd
Buffalo NY 14224
716 824-8900

(G-3610)
NEVILLE MFG SVC & DIST INC (PA)
2320 Clinton St (14227-1735)
PHONE.................................716 834-3038
Patrick Crowe, *President*
Russ Villa, *Director*
Erica Druzbik, *Admin Sec*
EMP: 10 **EST:** 1951
SQ FT: 4,000
SALES (est): 2.6MM **Privately Held**
SIC: 2448 Pallets, wood; skids, wood

(G-3611)
NOVATECH INC
190 Gruner Rd (14225-1022)
PHONE.................................716 892-6682
Fax: 716 892-1403
John Popovich Sr, *President*
John Popovich Jr, *Vice Pres*
Nova Popovich, *Vice Pres*
EMP: 20
SQ FT: 8,000
SALES (est): 3.4MM **Privately Held**
WEB: www.novatechmachining.com
SIC: 3545 Precision tools, machinists'

(G-3612)
ORIGINAL FOWLERS CHOCLAT INC
2563 Union Rd Ste 101 (14227-2275)
PHONE.................................716 668-2113
Fax: 716 668-1009
Sue Ortman, *Manager*
Judy Almond, *Manager*
EMP: 5 **Privately Held**
WEB: www.fowlerschocolate.com
SIC: 2024 Ice cream & frozen desserts
PA: Original Fowler's Chocolate Co., Inc.
100 River Rock Dr
Buffalo NY

(G-3613)
POLE POSITION RACEWAY
1 Walden Galleria (14225-5408)
PHONE.................................716 683-7223
EMP: 5
SALES (est): 378.1K **Privately Held**
SIC: 3644 Raceways

(G-3614)
PROSTHETICS BY NELSON INC (PA)
Also Called: Nelson Prsthtics Orthotics Lab
2959 Genesee St (14227-2653)
PHONE.................................716 894-6666
Christopher Vandusen, *President*
EMP: 13
SQ FT: 8,500
SALES (est): 1.2MM **Privately Held**
SIC: 3842 5999 Prosthetic appliances; orthopedic appliances; orthopedic & prosthesis applications

(G-3615)
QUALITY GRAPHICS WEST SENECA
2460 Union Rd (14227-2238)
PHONE.................................716 668-4528
Fax: 716 668-3502
Charles Lauck, *President*
Barbara Lauck, *Vice Pres*
EMP: 5
SQ FT: 3,500
SALES: 750K **Privately Held**
SIC: 2759 Commercial printing

(G-3616)
REDLAND FOODS CORP
40 Sonwil Dr (14225-2425)
PHONE.................................716 288-9061
Eva Mounsteven, *Director*
▲ **EMP:** 12
SALES (est): 982K **Privately Held**
SIC: 2099 Emulsifiers, food

(G-3617)
STEREO ADVANTAGE INC
Also Called: Advantage Wood Shop
45 Boxwood Ln (14227-2707)
PHONE.................................716 656-7161
Fax: 716 656-7166
Anthony Ragusa Jr, *Partner*
EMP: 10
SALES (corp-wide): 42.8MM **Privately Held**
SIC: 2541 Store & office display cases & fixtures
PA: Stereo Advantage, Inc.
1955 Wehrle Dr Ste B
Williamsville NY 14221
716 204-2346

(G-3618)
SUPERIOR PRINTING INK CO INC
2483 Walden Ave (14225-4717)
PHONE.................................716 685-6763
EMP: 7
SALES (corp-wide): 116.8MM **Privately Held**
SIC: 2893 Printing ink
PA: Superior Printing Ink Co Inc
100 North St
Teterboro NJ 07608
201 478-5600

(G-3619)
TECTRAN INC
2345 Walden Ave Ste 100 (14225-4770)
PHONE.................................800 776-5549
Bruce McKie, *President*
EMP: 9
SALES (est): 1.1MM **Privately Held**
SIC: 3699 3799 Cleaning equipment, ultrasonic, except medical & dental; carriages, horse drawn

(G-3620)
USA SEALING INC
356 Sonwil Dr (14225-5520)
PHONE.................................716 288-9952
David Cassert, *President*
EMP: 50
SALES (est): 1.6MM **Privately Held**
SIC: 3053 Gaskets & sealing devices

Chemung
Chemung County

(G-3621)
DALRYMPLE GRAV & CONTG CO INC
Chemung Flats Rd (14825)
P.O. Box 278 (14825-0278)
PHONE.................................607 529-3235
Fax: 607 529-3434
Hank Dalrymple, *President*
EMP: 30
SALES (corp-wide): 108.4MM **Privately Held**
SIC: 1442 5032 Gravel mining; stone, crushed or broken
HQ: Dalrymple Gravel And Contracting Company, Inc.
2105 S Broadway
Pine City NY 14871
607 739-0391

(G-3622)
VULCRAFT OF NEW YORK INC (HQ)
621 M St (14825)
P.O. Box 280 (14825-0280)
PHONE.................................607 529-9000
Peggy Peters, *Principal*
Ray Napolitan, *Exec VP*
John Giovenco, *Traffic Mgr*
Doreen Yackel, *Production*
Andy Deguire, *Financial Exec*
EMP: 105
SQ FT: 300,000
SALES (est): 53.2MM
SALES (corp-wide): 16.2B **Publicly Held**
WEB: www.nucor.com
SIC: 3441 Expansion joints (structural shapes), iron or steel

Chenango Bridge
Broome County

(G-3623)
ATWOOD TOOL & MACHINE INC
39 Kattelville Rd (13745)
PHONE.................................607 648-6543
Fax: 607 648-6300
H Blair Atwood, *President*
Brent Atwood, *Vice Pres*
Danny Winchester, *Purchasing*
David Atwood, *Treasurer*
Laurie Atwood, *Treasurer*
EMP: 22 EST: 1963
SQ FT: 23,000
SALES (est): 4.1MM **Privately Held**
WEB: www.atwoodknives.com
SIC: 3545 Tools & accessories for machine tools

Cherry Valley
Otsego County

(G-3624)
THISTLE HILL WEAVERS
101 Chestnut Ridge Rd (13320-2405)
PHONE.................................518 284-2729
Fax: 518 284-2729
Rabbit Goody, *Owner*
Jill Maney, *Manager*
EMP: 5
SALES (est): 422.9K **Privately Held**
WEB: www.thistlehillweavers.com
SIC: 2299 7219 Hand woven fabrics; reweaving textiles (mending service)

Chester
Orange County

(G-3625)
ADVERTISER PUBLICATIONS INC
Also Called: Marketplace, The
148 State Route 17m (10918)
PHONE.................................845 783-1111
Howard Kaplan, *President*
Seth Kaplan, *Vice Pres*
Marc M Hennion, *Personnel Exec*
Steve Herman, *Manager*
EMP: 13
SQ FT: 2,200
SALES: 1.9MM **Privately Held**
SIC: 2711 7331 7313 Newspapers; direct mail advertising services; newspaper advertising representative

(G-3626)
AMSCAN INC
Also Called: Amscan Everyday Warehouse
47 Elizabeth Dr (10918-1367)
PHONE.................................845 469-9116
Jim Harrison, *President*
EMP: 11
SALES (corp-wide): 2.2B **Publicly Held**
SIC: 2656 Plates, paper: made from purchased material
HQ: Amscan Inc.
  80 Grasslands Rd Ste 3
  Elmsford NY 10523
  914 345-2020

(G-3627)
B J S ELECTRIC
1000 Craigville Rd (10918-4116)
PHONE.................................845 774-8166
Jack Sherry, *Partner*
Elizabeth Sherry, *Partner*
EMP: 9
SALES (est): 968.4K **Privately Held**
SIC: 7694 1731 Electric motor repair; electrical work

(G-3628)
BRAKEWELL STL FABRICATORS INC
55 Leone Ln (10918-1363)
PHONE.................................845 469-9131
Fax: 845 469-7618
Dan Doyle, *President*
Dave Bendlin, *Project Mgr*
Robert McGrath, *Project Mgr*
William Valentin, *Project Mgr*
Carol Vandemark, *Project Mgr*
EMP: 45
SQ FT: 26,000
SALES: 7MM **Privately Held**
WEB: www.brakewell.com
SIC: 3411 3499 Metal cans; metal ladders

(G-3629)
BYK USA INC
48 Leone Ln (10918-1362)
PHONE.................................845 469-5800
Stephan Glander, *Branch Mgr*
EMP: 29 **Privately Held**
SIC: 2819 Industrial inorganic chemicals
HQ: Byk Usa Inc.
  524 S Cherry St
  Wallingford CT 06492
  203 265-2086

(G-3630)
COMMUNITY PRODUCTS LLC
Also Called: Community Playthings
359 Gibson Hill Rd (10918-2321)
PHONE.................................845 658-7720
Gary Frase, *Purchasing*
Andy Keiderling, *Marketing Staff*
John Rhodes, *Branch Mgr*
EMP: 24
SALES (corp-wide): 88.5MM **Privately Held**
SIC: 3842 Surgical appliances & supplies
PA: Community Products, Llc
  2032 Route 213 St
  Rifton NY 12471
  845 658-8799

(G-3631)
COMMUNITY PRODUCTS LLC
24 Elizabeth Dr (10918-1366)
PHONE.................................845 572-3433
Ben Maendel, *Branch Mgr*
EMP: 20
SALES (corp-wide): 88.5MM **Privately Held**
SIC: 3842 Orthopedic appliances
PA: Community Products, Llc
  2032 Route 213 St
  Rifton NY 12471
  845 658-8799

(G-3632)
DURASOL SYSTEMS INC (HQ)
445 Bellvale Rd (10918-3115)
PHONE.................................845 610-1100
Fax: 845 610-1100
Vince Best, *President*
Paolo Galliani, *President*
Frank Dorr, *Vice Pres*
Trace Feinstein, *Vice Pres*
Tim Robinson, *Vice Pres*
◆ EMP: 51
SQ FT: 65,000
SALES (est): 23.7MM
SALES (corp-wide): 28.2MM **Privately Held**
WEB: www.durasol.com
SIC: 2394 Awnings, fabric: made from purchased materials
PA: Bat Spa
  Via H. Ford 2
  Noventa Di Piave VE 30020
  042 165-672

(G-3633)
F A ALPINE WINDOWS MFG
1683 State Route 17m (10918-1020)
PHONE.................................845 469-5700
Larry Maddaloni, *President*
John Maddaloni, *Opers Mgr*
▲ EMP: 10
SALES (est): 1.5MM **Privately Held**
WEB: www.faalpinewindowmfg.com
SIC: 3442 Metal doors, sash & trim

(G-3634)
G SCHIRMER INC
Also Called: Music Sales
2 Old Rt 17 (10918)
P.O. Box 572 (10918-0572)
PHONE.................................845 469-4699
Ella Winfield, *Manager*
EMP: 50
SALES (corp-wide): 13.6MM **Privately Held**
WEB: www.schirmer.com
SIC: 2741 Music books: publishing only, not printed on site
HQ: G Schirmer Inc
  180 Madison Ave Ste 2400
  New York NY 10016
  212 254-2100

(G-3635)
GREEN ENERGY CONCEPTS INC
37 Elkay Dr Ste 51 (10918-3025)
P.O. Box 1023, Harriman (10926-1023)
PHONE.................................845 238-2574
Richard Mueller, *President*
▲ EMP: 6
SALES: 950K **Privately Held**
SIC: 3646 Commercial indusl & institutional electric lighting fixtures

(G-3636)
KE DURASOL AWNINGS INC
445 Bellvale Rd (10918-3115)
PHONE.................................845 610-1100
Paolo Galliani, *President*
Vince Best, *Principal*
Mary Corsini, *Controller*
EMP: 8
SALES (est): 960.1K **Privately Held**
SIC: 3444 Awnings & canopies

(G-3637)
NEXANS ENERGY USA INC
Also Called: Industrial Cables
25 Oakland Ave (10918-1011)
PHONE.................................845 469-2141
Gordon Thursfield, *President*
Steve Hall, *Principal*
Sande Aivaliotis, *Vice Pres*
Julie Land, *CFO*
Marianne Calicchio, *Human Resources*
▲ EMP: 160
SQ FT: 350,000
SALES (est): 56.3MM
SALES (corp-wide): 23.1MM **Privately Held**
SIC: 3496 Cable, uninsulated wire: made from purchased wire
HQ: Nexans Canada Inc
  140 Allstate Pky Suite 300
  Markham ON L3R 0
  905 944-4300

(G-3638)
PDJ COMPONENTS INC
35 Brookside Ave (10918-1409)
PHONE.................................845 469-9191
George W Ketchum, *CEO*
Pamela Ketchum, *Vice Pres*
David Crandall, *Buyer*
Christin Keating, *Accountant*
Tim Schultz, *Sales Staff*
EMP: 40
SQ FT: 30,000
SALES (est): 7.2MM **Privately Held**
WEB: www.pdjtruss.com
SIC: 2439 2499 Trusses, wooden roof; trusses, except roof: laminated lumber; decorative wood & woodwork

(G-3639)
REPRO MED SYSTEMS INC
Also Called: RMS Medical Products
24 Carpenter Rd Ste 1 (10918-1065)
PHONE.................................845 469-2042
Andrew I Sealfon, *Ch of Bd*
Eric Bauer, *COO*
Karen Fisher, *CFO*
Fred MA, *Chief Mktg Ofcr*
▲ EMP: 69
SALES: 12.2MM **Privately Held**
SIC: 3841 Surgical & medical instruments; suction therapy apparatus

(G-3640)
RIC-LO PRODUCTIONS LTD
Also Called: Lycian Stage Lighting
1144 Kings Hwy (10918-3100)
P.O. Box 214, Sugar Loaf (10981-0214)
PHONE.................................845 469-2285
Fax: 845 469-5355
Richard F Logothetis, *Chairman*
▲ EMP: 43
SQ FT: 17,400
SALES (est): 8.3MM **Privately Held**
SIC: 3648 3641 Stage lighting equipment; electric lamps

(G-3641)
S A BAXTER LLC (PA)
37 Elkay Dr Ste 33 (10918-3025)
PHONE.................................845 469-7995
Colin Gentle, *Manager*
Scott Baxter,
▲ EMP: 3
SALES: 2MM **Privately Held**
SIC: 3446 5072 Architectural metalwork; builders' hardware

(G-3642)
SATIN FINE FOODS INC
32 Leone Ln (10918-1362)
PHONE.................................845 469-1034
Kevin O' Reilly, *Ch of Bd*
Alan Standish, *General Mgr*
Chris Palmer, *Prdtn Mgr*
Maria D Laboy, *Export Mgr*
Susan Gillinder, *Finance*
◆ EMP: 75
SQ FT: 96,000
SALES (est): 5.5MM **Privately Held**
SIC: 2064 Candy & other confectionery products

(G-3643)
STRAUS COMMUNICATIONS
Also Called: Straus Newspaper
20 West Ave Ste 201 (10918-1053)
PHONE.................................845 782-4000
Stan Martin, *Manager*
EMP: 15
SALES (corp-wide): 2.5MM **Privately Held**
WEB: www.strausnews.com
SIC: 2711 Newspapers, publishing & printing
PA: Straus Communications
  57 W 57th St Ste 1204
  New York NY
  212 751-0400

(G-3644)
STRAUS NEWSPAPERS INC
20 West Ave (10918-1032)
PHONE.................................845 782-4000
Fax: 845 782-1711
Jeanne Straus, *President*
Seth Miller, *Publisher*
Juan Ayala, *Principal*
Daniel Fitzsimmons, *Editor*
Heidi Robertson, *Accounts Exec*
EMP: 24 EST: 1991
SALES (est): 1.7MM **Privately Held**
SIC: 2711 Newspapers

(G-3645)
SYMRISE INC
45 Leone Ln (10918-1363)
PHONE.................................845 469-7675
Fax: 845 469-7675
Wayne Millazo, *Director*
EMP: 45
SALES (corp-wide): 3B **Privately Held**
WEB: www.belmay.com
SIC: 2869 2844 5122 Perfumes, flavorings & food additives; toilet preparations; perfumes
HQ: Symrise Inc.
  300 North St
  Teterboro NJ 07608
  201 462-5559

(G-3646)
TELE-VUE OPTICS INC
32 Elkay Dr (10918-3001)
PHONE.................................845 469-4551
Albert Nagler, *CEO*
David Nagler, *President*
Sandy Nagler, *Vice Pres*
▲ EMP: 20

GEOGRAPHIC SECTION

SQ FT: 14,000
SALES (est): 4.3MM **Privately Held**
WEB: www.televue.com
SIC: 3827 Optical instruments & lenses

(G-3647)
THEODORE A RAPP ASSOCIATES
728 Craigville Rd (10918-4014)
PHONE 845 469-2100
Theodore A Rapp, *President*
EMP: 7
SALES (est): 718.8K **Privately Held**
SIC: 3651 Microphones

(G-3648)
TRISTATE CONTRACT SALES LLC
164 Dug Rd (10918-2652)
PHONE 845 782-2614
Ross Elliot, *Principal*
EMP: 5
SALES (est): 442.6K **Privately Held**
SIC: 2434 Vanities, bathroom: wood

Chestertown
Warren County

(G-3649)
CETTEL STUDIO OF NEW YORK INC
636 Atateka Dr (12817-2010)
PHONE 518 494-3622
Peter Heonis, *President*
EMP: 6
SALES: 350K **Privately Held**
SIC: 3843 Orthodontic appliances

(G-3650)
PECKHAM MATERIALS CORP
5983 State Route 9 (12817-2513)
PHONE 518 494-2313
Fax: 518 494-2065
John McClure, *Opers-Prdtn-Mfg*
EMP: 10
SQ FT: 208
SALES (corp-wide): 200.6MM **Privately Held**
SIC: 2951 5032 Asphalt paving mixtures & blocks; brick, stone & related material
HQ: Peckham Materials Corp
20 Haarlem Ave Ste 200
White Plains NY 10603
914 686-2045

Chestnut Ridge
Rockland County

(G-3651)
GENERICS BIDCO I LLC
Also Called: Par Pharmaceutical
1 Ram Ridge Rd (10977-6714)
P.O. Box 456, Devault PA (19432-0456)
PHONE 256 859-4011
Marvin Samson, *CEO*
Aaron Ayres, *Plant Mgr*
Gina Harris, *Accounts Mgr*
Lois Bright, *Manager*
Phil Cupero,
▲ **EMP:** 4
SQ FT: 5,800
SALES (est): 39.4MM **Privately Held**
WEB: www.qualitestrx.com
SIC: 2834 5122 5961 Pharmaceutical preparations; pharmaceuticals; pharmaceuticals, mail order
HQ: Generics International (Us), Inc.
130 Vintage Dr Ne
Huntsville AL 35811

(G-3652)
MEHRON INC
Also Called: Lechler Labs
100 Red Schoolhouse Rd C2 (10977-7056)
PHONE 845 426-1700
Martin Melik, *President*
Gene Flaharty, *Sales Mgr*
Mary Cavallini, *Marketing Staff*
Shelly Farber, *Manager*
Christine Samiel, *Information Mgr*
▲ **EMP:** 35
SQ FT: 15,000
SALES (est): 12MM **Privately Held**
WEB: www.mehron.com
SIC: 2844 Cosmetic preparations

(G-3653)
PAR PHARMACEUTICAL INC (DH)
1 Ram Ridge Rd (10977-6714)
PHONE 845 573-5500
Fax: 845 425-7907
Paul V Campanelli, *CEO*
Thomas J Haughey, *President*
Kenneth I Sawyer, *Principal*
Michael A Tropiano, *Exec VP*
Joseph Barbarite, *Senior VP*
▲ **EMP:** 277 **EST:** 1978
SQ FT: 92,000
SALES (est): 180.8MM **Privately Held**
SIC: 2834 Pharmaceutical preparations; druggists' preparations (pharmaceuticals); tablets, pharmaceutical; medicines, capsuled or ampuled
HQ: Par Pharmaceutical Companies, Inc.
1 Ram Ridge Rd
Chestnut Ridge NY 10977
845 573-5500

(G-3654)
PAR PHRMCEUTICAL COMPANIES INC (DH)
1 Ram Ridge Rd (10977-6714)
PHONE 845 573-5500
Paul V Campanelli, *CEO*
Tony Pera, *President*
Linda Casazza, *General Mgr*
Tony Cere, *General Mgr*
Jamie Dannhauser, *General Mgr*
EMP: 45 **EST:** 2012
SALES (est): 463.1MM **Privately Held**
SIC: 2834 Pharmaceutical preparations
HQ: Endo Health Solutions Inc.
1400 Atwater Dr
Malvern PA 19355
484 216-0000

(G-3655)
PAR STERILE PRODUCTS LLC (DH)
1 Ram Ridge Rd (10977-6714)
PHONE 845 573-5500
Paul V Campanelli, *CEO*
Eric Bruce, *Opers Staff*
Michael Tropiano, *CFO*
Melissa Williams, *Controller*
Valerie Luczak, *Sales Mgr*
EMP: 32
SALES (est): 72.9MM **Privately Held**
WEB: www.jnppharma.com
SIC: 2834 Pharmaceutical preparations
HQ: Par Pharmaceutical, Inc.
1 Ram Ridge Rd
Chestnut Ridge NY 10977
845 573-5500

(G-3656)
TELEDYNE LECROY INC (HQ)
700 Chestnut Ridge Rd (10977-6435)
PHONE 845 425-2000
Fax: 845 578-5985
Thomas H Reslewic, *Ch of Bd*
Sui LI, *General Mgr*
Martina Rogan, *General Mgr*
Scott R Bausback, *Vice Pres*
Luis B Boza, *Vice Pres*
▲ **EMP:** 204 **EST:** 1964
SQ FT: 95,000
SALES: 168.6MM
SALES (corp-wide): 2.1B **Publicly Held**
WEB: www.lecroy.com
SIC: 3825 3829 Oscillographs & oscilloscopes; measuring & controlling devices
PA: Teledyne Technologies Inc
1049 Camino Dos Rios
Thousand Oaks CA 91360
805 373-4545

(G-3657)
U S PLYCHMICAL OVERSEAS CORP
584 Chestnut Ridge Rd # 586 (10977-5646)
PHONE 845 356-5530
David Cherry, *President*
Bruce W Gebhardt, *General Mgr*
Ralph Almonte, *Controller*
Richard E Knipe Jr, *VP Sales*
Mark Paul, *Director*
EMP: 20
SQ FT: 20,000
SALES (est): 3.2MM **Privately Held**
WEB: www.uspoly.com
SIC: 2842 Cleaning or polishing preparations; sanitation preparations

Childwold
St. Lawrence County

(G-3658)
LEATHER ARTISAN
Also Called: Artisan Bags
9740 State Highway 3 (12922-2028)
PHONE 518 359-3102
Thomas Amoroso, *Partner*
EMP: 5
SQ FT: 7,000
SALES (est): 610.7K **Privately Held**
WEB: www.leatherartisan.com
SIC: 3172 5699 5199 Personal leather goods; leather garments; leather, leather goods & furs

Chittenango
Madison County

(G-3659)
A L SEALING
2280 Osborne Rd (13037-8791)
PHONE 315 699-6900
John C Thomas, *Ch of Bd*
EMP: 5
SALES (est): 312.3K **Privately Held**
SIC: 3053 Gaskets & sealing devices

(G-3660)
CONSOLDTED PRECISION PDTS CORP
901 E Genesee St (13037-1325)
PHONE 315 687-0014
Mark Gaspari, *Manager*
EMP: 350
SALES (corp-wide): 6.3B **Privately Held**
SIC: 3365 3324 Aluminum foundries; steel investment foundries
HQ: Consolidated Precision Products Corp.
1621 Euclid Ave Ste 1850
Cleveland OH 44115
909 595-2252

(G-3661)
CPP - GUAYMAS
901 E Genesee St (13037-1325)
PHONE 315 687-0014
Carl Bratt, *General Mgr*
Catherine Renfer, *Engineer*
Dale Vibbert, *Engineer*
Bill Kehoe, *Plant Engr*
John Derosia, *Controller*
EMP: 200
SQ FT: 1,000
SALES (est): 27.3MM
SALES (corp-wide): 6.3B **Privately Held**
WEB: www.escocorp.com
SIC: 3321 Cast iron pipe & fittings
HQ: Cpp-Syracuse, Inc.
901 E Genesee St
Chittenango NY 13037
315 687-0014

(G-3662)
CPP-SYRACUSE INC (DH)
901 E Genesee St (13037-1325)
PHONE 315 687-0014
James Stewart, *CEO*
Tom Cacace, *Mfg Dir*
Barry Weary, *Opers Mgr*
Joe Perechinsky, *Finance*
John Derosia, *Sales Mgr*
▲ **EMP:** 30
SQ FT: 95,000
SALES (est): 89.8MM
SALES (corp-wide): 6.3B **Privately Held**
SIC: 3324 3369 3356 Aerospace investment castings, ferrous; nonferrous foundries; nonferrous rolling & drawing
HQ: Consolidated Precision Products Corp.
1621 Euclid Ave Ste 1850
Cleveland OH 44115
909 595-2252

Churchville
Monroe County

(G-3663)
AMA PRECISION SCREENING INC
456 Sanford Rd N (14428-9503)
PHONE 585 293-0820
Fax: 585 293-0822
George Pietropaolo, *President*
Robert Hubbard, *Human Res Dir*
Kelley Copani, *Manager*
EMP: 18
SALES (est): 2.1MM **Privately Held**
WEB: www.amatech.com
SIC: 2759 Commercial printing

(G-3664)
BURNT MILL SMITHING
127 Burnt Mill Rd (14428-9405)
PHONE 585 293-2380
Fax: 585 293-1372
Dennis Schreiber, *Owner*
Dennis Schriber, *Owner*
EMP: 5
SALES (est): 295K **Privately Held**
WEB: www.burnt-mill.com
SIC: 3949 5941 Sporting & athletic goods; sporting goods & bicycle shops

(G-3665)
CUSTOM MOLDING SOLUTIONS INC
456 Sanford Rd N (14428-9503)
PHONE 585 293-1702
Dwight Campbell, *President*
EMP: 21
SALES (est): 4.4MM **Privately Held**
SIC: 3544 Industrial molds

(G-3666)
DYNAK INC
530 Savage Rd (14428-9614)
PHONE 585 271-2255
Fax: 585 271-6048
Bob Vorndran, *President*
Barbara Klink, *Vice Pres*
Michael R Petes, *Engineer*
Michael Allen, *Manager*
EMP: 13
SQ FT: 25,000
SALES (est): 2MM **Privately Held**
WEB: www.dynak.com
SIC: 3599 Custom machinery

(G-3667)
INLAND VACUUM INDUSTRIES INC (PA)
35 Howard Ave (14428-8008)
P.O. Box 373 (14428-0373)
PHONE 585 293-3330
Fax: 585 293-3093
Peter C Yu, *Ch of Bd*
Lusanne Lam, *Vice Pres*
Carol Taylor, *Manager*
Cindy Oliver, *CIO*
▲ **EMP:** 12
SQ FT: 1,000
SALES (est): 1.8MM **Privately Held**
WEB: www.inlandvacuum.com
SIC: 2992 Lubricating oils & greases

(G-3668)
INTEK PRECISION
539 Attridge Rd (14428-9712)
PHONE 585 293-0853
Susan Kurucz, *Partner*
Paul Kurucz, *Partner*
EMP: 8
SQ FT: 3,000

SALES: 200K **Privately Held**
WEB: www.intekprecision.com
SIC: 3544 Special dies, tools, jigs & fixtures

(G-3669)
QUALICOAT INC
14 Sanford Rd N (14428-9503)
PHONE.................................585 293-2650
Michael Pontarelli, *Ch of Bd*
Don Lawson, *Plant Mgr*
Ross Mazzola, *QC Dir*
Joe Pontarelli, *Engineer*
Debbie Ray, *Human Res Mgr*
▲ EMP: 80
SQ FT: 48,000
SALES (est): 9.9MM **Privately Held**
WEB: www.qualicoat.com
SIC: 3479 Coating of metals & formed products; painting of metal products

Cicero
Onondaga County

(G-3670)
ADD ASSOCIATES INC
Also Called: Image Press, The
6333 Daedalus Rd (13039-8889)
PHONE.................................315 449-3474
Toll Free:...............................888   -
Fax: 315 449-3480
Chris Arnone, *President*
Lonnie Dahl, *Vice Pres*
Christine Staniec, *Senior Buyer*
Bill Brokhoff, *Purchasing*
Stan Patte, *Manager*
EMP: 8
SQ FT: 10,000
SALES (est): 1.3MM **Privately Held**
SIC: 2741 Miscellaneous publishing

(G-3671)
AWNING MART INC
5665 State Route 31 (13039-8513)
PHONE.................................315 699-5928
Doug Loguidice, *President*
Tina Loguidice, *General Mgr*
EMP: 7
SQ FT: 4,400
SALES (est): 749.3K **Privately Held**
SIC: 2394 1799 5199 5999 Awnings, fabric: made from purchased materials; awning installation; canvas products; awnings; canvas products

(G-3672)
CLINTONS DITCH COOP CO INC
8478 Pardee Rd (13039-8531)
PHONE.................................315 699-2695
Ronald Anania, *President*
Michael Moehringer, *General Mgr*
Bill Fitzgerald, *Vice Pres*
Tim Tenney, *Vice Pres*
Thomas Millert, *Plant Mgr*
EMP: 155
SQ FT: 250,000
SALES: 62.6MM **Privately Held**
WEB: www.clintonsditch.com
SIC: 2086 Carbonated soft drinks, bottled & canned

(G-3673)
DAF OFFICE NETWORKS INC
6121 Jemola Runne (13039-8238)
PHONE.................................315 699-7070
David A Farabee, *President*
EMP: 9
SALES (est): 1.1MM **Privately Held**
SIC: 2521 5112 5044 Wood office furniture; office supplies; office equipment

(G-3674)
EJ GROUP INC
6177 S Bay Rd (13039-9303)
PHONE.................................315 699-2601
EMP: 9 **Privately Held**
SIC: 3446 Architectural metalwork
PA: Ej Group, Inc.
   301 Spring St
   East Jordan MI 49727

(G-3675)
GIBAR INC
7838 Brewerton Rd (13039-9536)
PHONE.................................315 452-5656
EMP: 244
SALES (corp-wide): 9MM **Privately Held**
SIC: 3421 Table & food cutlery, including butchers'
PA: Gibar, Inc
   1 Technology Pl
   East Syracuse NY 13057
   315 432-4546

(G-3676)
LIBERTY MACHINE & TOOL
7908 Ontario Ave (13039-9759)
PHONE.................................315 699-3242
Fax: 315 699-1314
Thomas Burgmeier, *Owner*
EMP: 1
SQ FT: 2,500
SALES: 1MM **Privately Held**
SIC: 3599 Machine shop, jobbing & repair

(G-3677)
MACHINE TOOL SPECIALTY
8125 Thompson Rd (13039-9454)
P.O. Box 2398, Syracuse (13220-2398)
PHONE.................................315 699-5287
Fax: 315 699-7604
David Carrington, *Owner*
EMP: 5
SQ FT: 1,000
SALES (est): 437.6K **Privately Held**
SIC: 3544 Special dies & tools

(G-3678)
PAUL DE LIMA COMPANY INC
8550 Pardee Rd (13039-8519)
PHONE.................................315 457-3725
Fax: 315 457-3730
Jim Sarner, *Vice Pres*
Steve Zaremba, *CFO*
Peter Sansone, *Human Res Dir*
Karen Huntley, *Mktg Dir*
W Drescher, *Branch Mgr*
EMP: 23
SALES (corp-wide): 13.7MM **Privately Held**
SIC: 2095 Roasted coffee
PA: Paul De Lima Company, Inc.
   7546 Morgan Rd Ste 1
   Liverpool NY 13090
   315 457-3725

(G-3679)
PAUL DELIMA COFFEE COMPANY
8550 Pardee Rd (13039-8519)
PHONE.................................315 457-3725
Paul De Lima, *Principal*
Steve Janeosik, *Info Tech Mgr*
▲ EMP: 9
SALES (est): 1.1MM **Privately Held**
SIC: 2095 Roasted coffee

(G-3680)
THERMAL FOAMS/SYRACUSE INC
6173 S Bay Rd (13039-9303)
P.O. Box 1981 (13039-1981)
PHONE.................................315 699-8734
Fax: 315 699-4969
John Jeffery, *Branch Mgr*
EMP: 25
SALES (corp-wide): 5.8MM **Privately Held**
SIC: 3053 Packing materials
PA: Thermal Foams/Syracuse, Inc.
   2101 Kenmore Ave
   Buffalo NY 14207
   716 874-6474

Cincinnatus
Cortland County

(G-3681)
DAVID CHRISTY
Also Called: Uniform Professionals
2810 Cincinnatus Rd (13040)
P.O. Box 180 (13040-0180)
PHONE.................................607 863-4610
David Christy, *Owner*

Janice Livermore, *Manager*
EMP: 9
SALES (est): 878.7K **Privately Held**
WEB: www.uniformpro.com
SIC: 2326 Work uniforms

Clarence
Erie County

(G-3682)
A C T ASSOCIATES
10100 Main St (14031-2049)
P.O. Box 510 (14031-0510)
PHONE.................................716 759-8348
William Thalmann, *Principal*
EMP: 12 EST: 2010
SALES (est): 1.8MM **Privately Held**
SIC: 3823 Water quality monitoring & control systems

(G-3683)
ANABEC INC
9393 Main St (14031-1912)
P.O. Box 433 (14031-0433)
PHONE.................................716 759-1674
Fax: 716 759-7829
Stephen Meyers, *President*
Nancy Ewing, *Vice Pres*
Michael Whipple, *Natl Sales Mgr*
Lisa Pawlowski, *Manager*
EMP: 5 EST: 1995
SQ FT: 3,200
SALES (est): 792.5K **Privately Held**
WEB: www.anabec.com
SIC: 2899 Chemical preparations

(G-3684)
ATHENEX PHARMA SOLUTIONS LLC
11342 Main St (14031-1718)
PHONE.................................877 463-7823
Stephen A Panaro, *CEO*
Mark Czopp, *Project Mgr*
Ryan Downey, *Director*
Leanne Kisicki, *Director*
EMP: 7 EST: 2012
SQ FT: 18,000
SALES (est): 1.9MM
SALES (corp-wide): 65.2MM **Publicly Held**
SIC: 2834 Pharmaceutical preparations
PA: Athenex, Inc.
   1001 Main St Ste 600
   Buffalo NY 14203
   716 427-2950

(G-3685)
DIMAR MANUFACTURING CORP
10123 Main St (14031-2164)
P.O. Box 597 (14031-0597)
PHONE.................................716 759-0351
Fax: 716 759-0389
Gregory A Fry, *President*
Thomas J Kowalski, *CFO*
Karen Seeberg, *Executive*
EMP: 140
SQ FT: 93,000
SALES: 15.3MM **Privately Held**
WEB: www.dimarmfg.com
SIC: 3499 3444 Furniture parts, metal; sheet metalwork

(G-3686)
DYNABRADE INC (PA)
8989 Sheridan Dr (14031-1490)
PHONE.................................716 631-0100
Fax: 716 631-2073
Walter N Welsch, *Ch of Bd*
Ned T Librock, *President*
Scott Nolt, *General Mgr*
Steven D Briggs, *Vice Pres*
Chip Case, *Vice Pres*
▲ EMP: 175
SQ FT: 95,000
SALES (est): 38.3MM **Privately Held**
WEB: www.dynabrade.com
SIC: 3546 Power-driven handtools

(G-3687)
EASTERN HILLS PRINTING (PA)
9195 Main St (14031-1931)
PHONE.................................716 741-3300
Fax: 716 741-4225

Geoffrey Mohring, *CEO*
EMP: 9
SQ FT: 400
SALES (est): 867.5K **Privately Held**
SIC: 2752 Commercial printing, offset

(G-3688)
ELECTROCHEM SOLUTIONS INC (DH)
10000 Wehrle Dr (14031-2086)
PHONE.................................716 759-5800
Joseph Flanagan, *Exec VP*
Scott McGregor, *Project Mgr*
Jo Rezendes, *Opers Staff*
Steven Towne, *Senior Buyer*
William Spooner, *Buyer*
▲ EMP: 53
SALES (est): 45.9MM
SALES (corp-wide): 1.3B **Publicly Held**
SIC: 3692 Primary batteries, dry & wet
HQ: Greatbatch Ltd.
   10000 Wehrle Dr
   Clarence NY 14031
   612 331-6750

(G-3689)
EXCEL INDUSTRIES INC
11737 Main St (14031)
P.O. Box 409 (14031-0409)
PHONE.................................716 542-5468
Fax: 716 542-5820
Francis Nicholas, *President*
Mark Steck, *General Mgr*
Donald Nicholas, *Vice Pres*
Diana Fiske, *Treasurer*
Craig Nicholas, *Office Mgr*
EMP: 40 EST: 1947
SQ FT: 35,000
SALES (est): 6.3MM **Privately Held**
WEB: www.excelindustriesinc.com
SIC: 3599 3441 Machine shop, jobbing & repair; fabricated structural metal

(G-3690)
INTEGER HOLDINGS CORPORATION
Engineered Components Division
4098 Barton Rd (14031-1814)
PHONE.................................716 759-5200
Fax: 716 634-0306
Jerry Hale, *Draft/Design*
Ralph Bendlin, *Marketing Staff*
Charles Wemhoff, *Manager*
EMP: 100
SALES (corp-wide): 1.3B **Publicly Held**
WEB: www.greatbatch.com
SIC: 3841 3842 Surgical & medical instruments; surgical appliances & supplies
PA: Integer Holdings Corporation
   2595 Dallas Pkwy Ste 310
   Frisco TX 75034
   214 618-5243

(G-3691)
MCDUFFIES OF SCOTLAND INC
Also Called: Mc Duffies Bakery
9920 Main St (14031-2043)
P.O. Box 427 (14031-0427)
PHONE.................................716 759-8510
Fax: 716 759-6082
David Thomas, *President*
Brian Thomas, *Vice Pres*
EMP: 20
SQ FT: 10,000
SALES (est): 2.7MM **Privately Held**
WEB: www.mcduffies.com
SIC: 2052 Cookies

(G-3692)
MCHUGH PAINTING CO INC
10335 Clarence Center Rd (14031-1003)
PHONE.................................716 741-8077
Michael McHugh, *President*
Michael Mc Hugh, *President*
Rosalie McHugh, *Admin Sec*
EMP: 14
SALES (est): 1.4MM **Privately Held**
SIC: 3479 Painting of metal products

(G-3693)
MEDIMA LLC
Also Called: Medima Metals
5727 Strickler Rd (14031-1372)
PHONE.................................716 741-0400
Barry Lazar, *Mng Member*
◆ EMP: 250

GEOGRAPHIC SECTION

Cleveland - Oswego County (G-3718)

SALES: 425MM Privately Held
SIC: 3339 3313 Silicon & chromium; ferroalloys

(G-3694)
OEM SOLUTIONS INC
4995 Rockhaven Dr (14031-2438)
PHONE 716 864-9324
Michael King, CEO
▲ EMP: 4
SQ FT: 3,000
SALES: 1MM Privately Held
SIC: 3469 3699 Metal stampings; electrical equipment & supplies

(G-3695)
PEAK MOTION INC
11190 Main St (14031-1702)
PHONE 716 534-4925
Douglas Webster, President
EMP: 7
SALES (est): 1.9MM Privately Held
WEB: www.peakmotion.com
SIC: 3499 3544 Aerosol valves, metal; special dies, tools, jigs & fixtures

(G-3696)
PRECIMED INC
Also Called: Greatbatch Medical
10000 Wehrle Dr (14031-2086)
PHONE 716 759-5600
Patrick White, CEO
Patrick Berdoz, President
Alan Booker, Opers Mgr
Charles Andrews, Treasurer
Barbara Lyons, Director
EMP: 46
SQ FT: 2,000
SALES (est): 4.5MM
SALES (corp-wide): 1.3B Publicly Held
WEB: www.precimed.com
SIC: 3841 5047 Surgical & medical instruments; medical & hospital equipment
HQ: Greatbatch Ltd.
  10000 Wehrle Dr
  Clarence NY 14031
  612 331-6750

(G-3697)
RLS HOLDINGS INC
11342 Main St (14031-1718)
PHONE 716 418-7274
Stephen A Panaro PHD, President
Mark Czopp, Project Mgr
Ryan Downey, QA Dir
Leanna Kisicki, Director
EMP: 5 EST: 2010
SALES (est): 747.2K Privately Held
SIC: 2834 Pharmaceutical preparations

(G-3698)
RODAC USA CORP
5605 Kraus Rd (14031-1342)
PHONE 716 741-3931
Daniel Primeau, CEO
EMP: 25
SALES (est): 2.2MM Privately Held
SIC: 3648 Lighting equipment

Clarence Center
Erie County

(G-3699)
CLARENCE RESINS AND CHEMICALS
9585 Keller Rd (14032-9230)
PHONE 716 406-9804
James G Lawrence, President
EMP: 8
SQ FT: 800
SALES (est): 1.3MM Privately Held
SIC: 2821 5169 Plastics materials and resins; synthetic resins, rubber & plastic materials

(G-3700)
EASTERN MANUFACTURING INC
9760 County Rd (14032-9651)
P.O. Box 379 (14032-0379)
PHONE 716 741-4572
Fax: 716 741-4572
Barbara Gomlar, President

EMP: 10
SQ FT: 8,000
SALES (est): 1.4MM Privately Held
SIC: 3441 Fabricated structural metal

(G-3701)
EXACTA LLC
8955 Williams Ct (14032-9414)
PHONE 716 406-2303
Peter Buchbinder, Owner
James B Schleer, Mng Member
EMP: 9
SQ FT: 1,200
SALES (est): 640K Privately Held
WEB: www.exacta.com
SIC: 3555 Copy holders, printers'

(G-3702)
ITALIAN MARBLE & GRANITE INC
8526 Roll Rd (14032-9761)
PHONE 716 741-1800
Mark K Zografos, President
Virginia Sorrentino, Office Mgr
▲ EMP: 16
SQ FT: 21,000
SALES (est): 2.3MM Privately Held
SIC: 3281 Marble, building: cut & shaped

(G-3703)
J R PRODUCTS INC
9680 County Rd (14032-9240)
PHONE 716 633-7565
Doug Rouba, President
Sally Moore, Financial Exec
Brian Roba, VP Sales
Susan Carpenter, Manager
Sharon Thriftjpg, Admin Sec
▲ EMP: 9
SALES (est): 730K Privately Held
WEB: www.jrprvinc.com
SIC: 3949 Camping equipment & supplies

(G-3704)
JW BURG MACHINE & TOOL INC
7430 Rapids Rd (14032-9501)
P.O. Box 372 (14032-0372)
PHONE 716 434-0015
Joe Burg, President
EMP: 8
SALES (est): 241.5K Privately Held
SIC: 3545 Machine tool accessories

(G-3705)
MALYN INDUSTRIAL CERAMICS INC
8640 Roll Rd (14032-9139)
P.O. Box 469 (14032-0469)
PHONE 716 741-1510
Fax: 585 542-4329
Michael Malyn, President
Pat Malyn, Vice Pres
EMP: 7
SQ FT: 7,000
SALES (est): 930K Privately Held
WEB: www.malyn.com
SIC: 3291 3432 Grinding balls, ceramic; plumbing fixture fittings & trim

(G-3706)
TECHNIFLO CORPORATION
9730 County Rd (14032-9651)
P.O. Box 307, Clarence (14031-0307)
PHONE 716 741-3500
Fax: 716 741-4100
Richard F Whitesell, CEO
EMP: 9 EST: 1975
SQ FT: 8,000
SALES (est): 1.6MM Privately Held
SIC: 3625 Relays & industrial controls; noise control equipment

(G-3707)
UNICENTER MILLWORK INC
9605 Clarence Center Rd (14032-9748)
PHONE 716 741-8201
Terrance Reilly, President
EMP: 9
SALES (est): 680K Privately Held
SIC: 2431 Millwork

(G-3708)
ZINERVA PHARMACEUTICALS LLC
6017 Corinne Ln (14032-9517)
PHONE 630 729-4184
Evan Zhao, CEO
Thomas Kwok, COO
Webster Guan, CFO
Alex Pien, CFO
EMP: 5
SALES (est): 275.6K Privately Held
SIC: 2834 7389 Insulin preparations;

Clay
Onondaga County

(G-3709)
MS SPARES LLC
8055 Evesborough Dr (13041-9140)
PHONE 607 223-3024
Michael Slater, President
EMP: 5
SALES (est): 532.4K Privately Held
SIC: 3061 3599 3444 7692 Mechanical rubber goods; machine & other job shop work; sheet metalwork; welding repair

Clayton
Jefferson County

(G-3710)
AMERICAN METALCRAFT MARINE
690 Riverside Dr (13624-1043)
P.O. Box 961, Cape Vincent (13618-0961)
PHONE 315 686-9891
Kenneth I Johnson, President
Leon Rusho Jr, Vice Pres
▼ EMP: 7 EST: 1997
SALES (est): 567.9K Privately Held
WEB: www.americanmetalcraftmarine.com
SIC: 3732 Boat building & repairing

(G-3711)
COYOTE MOON LLC (PA)
Also Called: Coyote Moon Vineyards
17371 County Route 3 (13624-2193)
P.O. Box 497 (13624-0497)
PHONE 315 686-5600
Kristina Ives, Marketing Staff
Elena Comiskey, Manager
David Countryman, Manager
Valerie Hickman, Manager
Phillip Randazzo, Manager
EMP: 12
SALES (est): 1.8MM Privately Held
SIC: 2084 5182 5921 Wines; wine; wine

Clayville
Oneida County

(G-3712)
BARRETT PAVING MATERIALS INC
363 Rasbach Rd (13322-2538)
PHONE 315 737-9471
Fax: 315 737-9471
Kevin Crabe, Facilities Mgr
Doug Henry, Facilities Mgr
Robert Bard, Branch Mgr
EMP: 13
SALES (corp-wide): 77.1MM Privately Held
WEB: www.barrettpaving.com
SIC: 2951 1429 3272 1422 Asphalt & asphaltic paving mixtures (not from refineries); igneous rock, crushed & broken-quarrying; concrete products; crushed & broken limestone
HQ: Barrett Paving Materials Inc.
  3 Becker Farm Rd Ste 307
  Roseland NJ 07068
  973 533-1001

(G-3713)
CLAYVILLE ICE CO INC
2514 Foundry Pl (13322-1600)
P.O. Box 12 (13322-0012)
PHONE 315 839-5405
Gareth A Evans, President
EMP: 8
SQ FT: 17,000
SALES: 340.1K Privately Held
SIC: 2097 Block ice; ice cubes

(G-3714)
HMI METAL POWDERS
Also Called: Pratt With ME Hmi Met Powders
2395 Main St (13322-1102)
P.O. Box 294 (13322-0294)
PHONE 315 839-5421
John Letisky, Treasurer
Keith Sterling, Info Tech Mgr
EMP: 120
SQ FT: 140,000
SALES (est): 14.7MM Privately Held
SIC: 3312 Blast furnaces & steel mills

(G-3715)
HOMOGENEOUS METALS INC
Also Called: Hmi Metal Powders
2395 Main St (13322-1102)
P.O. Box 294 (13322-0294)
PHONE 315 839-5421
Fax: 315 839-5609
Mark Hewko, Ch of Bd
Greg Treacy, Ch of Bd
Mark Huwko, General Mgr
Jim Coyle, Plant Mgr
John Lapinski, Treasurer
▲ EMP: 56 EST: 1965
SQ FT: 129,000
SALES (est): 14.3MM
SALES (corp-wide): 57.2B Publicly Held
WEB: www.hmipowder.com
SIC: 3312 Billets, steel
PA: United Technologies Corporation
  10 Farm Springs Rd
  Farmington CT 06032
  860 728-7000

(G-3716)
VALLEY CREEK SIDE INC
Also Called: Valley Signs
1960 State Route 8 (13322-1312)
P.O. Box 287 (13322-0287)
PHONE 315 839-5526
Lee Wratten, President
Daniel Zinger, General Mgr
EMP: 7
SALES: 240K Privately Held
SIC: 3993 Signs & advertising specialties

(G-3717)
WOLAK INC
2360 King Rd (13322-1214)
PHONE 315 839-5366
Fax: 315 736-3365
J Wolak, President
EMP: 7 EST: 1941
SQ FT: 20,000
SALES (est): 560K Privately Held
SIC: 2541 Counter & sink tops

Cleveland
Oswego County

(G-3718)
GOT WOOD LLC
28 North St (13042-3278)
P.O. Box 337, Central Square (13036-0337)
PHONE 315 440-8857
Michael Fullmer, Owner
EMP: 6
SALES (est): 410.3K Privately Held
SIC: 2411 3531 Timber, cut at logging camp; rakes, land clearing: mechanical

Clifton Park
Saratoga County

(G-3719)
A GARYS TREASURES
629 Plank Rd (12065-2050)
PHONE.................................518 383-1171
Fax: 518 383-1197
Lynn Massaroni, *Owner*
EMP: 10
SQ FT: 2,300
SALES (est): 455.7K **Privately Held**
WEB: www.garystreasures.com
SIC: 2395 Emblems, embroidered

(G-3720)
ADVANCED MFG TECHNIQUES
453 Kinns Rd (12065-2408)
P.O. Box 617 (12065-0617)
PHONE.................................518 877-8560
Fax: 518 877-8606
Steve Petronis, *President*
Richard Carusone, *Vice Pres*
Becky Davenport, *Office Mgr*
EMP: 7
SQ FT: 10,000
SALES (est): 1.1MM **Privately Held**
WEB: www.advmfgtech.com
SIC: 3599 3699 Machine shop, jobbing & repair; electrical equipment & supplies

(G-3721)
ANTHROPOSOPHIC PRESS INC (PA)
15 Greenridge Dr (12065-6628)
PHONE.................................518 851-2054
Gordon Edwards, *Ch of Bd*
Michael Dobson, *President*
Christopher Bamford, *Admin Sec*
▲ EMP: 2
SQ FT: 6,500
SALES: 1.1MM **Privately Held**
SIC: 2731 5192 5961 Books: publishing only; books; books, mail order (except book clubs)

(G-3722)
ATLANTIC PROJECTS COMPANY INC
5 Southside Dr Ste 11s (12065-3870)
P.O. Box 782 (12065-0782)
PHONE.................................518 878-2065
Judith Brodeur, *CFO*
Tom Lynch, *Manager*
EMP: 10
SALES (est): 1.6MM
SALES (corp-wide): 675MM **Publicly Held**
SIC: 3511 Hydraulic turbines
HQ: Atlantic Projects Company Limited
3 Marine Road
Dun Laoghaire

(G-3723)
BOBRICK WASHROOM EQUIPMENT INC
200 Commerce Dr (12065-1399)
PHONE.................................518 877-7444
Fax: 518 877-5029
Susan White, *Human Res Dir*
Rich Ross, *Manager*
Jude Snyder, *Office Admin*
EMP: 100
SALES (corp-wide): 101.9MM **Privately Held**
SIC: 2542 5074 3446 Partitions & fixtures, except wood; plumbing & hydronic heating supplies; architectural metalwork
HQ: Bobrick Washroom Equipment, Inc.
6901 Tujunga Ave
North Hollywood CA 91605
818 764-1000

(G-3724)
HECTOR PT SR REHAB SVC PLLC
1 Wall St (12065-3851)
PHONE.................................518 371-5554
Hector Jasen, *Branch Mgr*
EMP: 5 **Privately Held**
SIC: 3949 Sporting & athletic goods
PA: Hector Pt Sr Rehab Service Pllc
1 Wall St
Clifton Park NY 12065

(G-3725)
LASERTECH CRTRIDGE REBUILDERS
7 Longwood Dr (12065-7614)
PHONE.................................518 373-1246
Enn Epner, *Owner*
William Hougeich, *Vice Pres*
EMP: 9
SALES: 400K **Privately Held**
SIC: 3861 5734 Toners, prepared photographic (not made in chemical plants); computer & software stores

(G-3726)
M MANASTRIP-M CORPORATION
821 Main St (12065-1002)
PHONE.................................518 664-2089
David Scagnelli, *President*
George Scagnelli, *General Mgr*
EMP: 5
SQ FT: 3,000
SALES (est): 503.7K **Privately Held**
WEB: www.manastrip.com
SIC: 3498 3451 3494 Manifolds, pipe: fabricated from purchased pipe; screw machine products; valves & pipe fittings

(G-3727)
MACRODYNE INC
1 Fairchild Sq Ste 5 (12065-1261)
PHONE.................................518 383-3800
Fax: 518 383-0049
Richard Murphy, *President*
Roy Paige, *Officer*
▲ EMP: 12
SQ FT: 5,500
SALES: 1.2MM **Privately Held**
WEB: www.macrodyneusa.com
SIC: 3825 Signal generators & averagers

(G-3728)
MICROB PHASE SERVICES
Also Called: Brittish American Envmtl
14 Nottingham Way S (12065-1727)
PHONE.................................518 877-8948
Fax: 518 877-8348
Ron Shongar, *Owner*
EMP: 15
SALES (est): 830K **Privately Held**
SIC: 3822 Auto controls regulating residntl & coml environmt & applncs

(G-3729)
NYI BUILDING PRODUCTS INC (PA)
5 Southside Dr Ste 204 (12065-3870)
PHONE.................................518 458-7500
Jay Torani, *Principal*
Susanne Brook, *Vice Pres*
Natalie Vitelli, *Accounts Mgr*
▲ EMP: 16
SQ FT: 1,500
SALES (est): 4.1MM **Privately Held**
WEB: www.nyionline.com
SIC: 3315 5169 Nails, spikes, brads & similar items; adhesives & sealants

(G-3730)
PRINT & GRAPHICS GROUP
12 Fire Rd (12065-3110)
PHONE.................................518 371-4649
Fax: 518 371-1554
Frank Papasso, *Owner*
EMP: 6
SALES (est): 435.3K **Privately Held**
SIC: 2752 Commercial printing, lithographic

(G-3731)
ROBAT INC
1 Fairchild Sq Ste 114 (12065-1266)
PHONE.................................518 812-6244
Gregory Miczek, *Vice Pres*
EMP: 5
SALES: 400K **Privately Held**
SIC: 3823 Industrial process measurement equipment

(G-3732)
SENSIO AMERICA
800 Route 146 (12065-3903)
PHONE.................................877 501-5337
Paul Bardwell, *General Mgr*
Terry V Delong, *Principal*
EMP: 15
SALES (est): 2.3MM **Privately Held**
SIC: 3648 Lighting equipment

(G-3733)
SILICON PULSED POWER LLC
958 Main St Ste A (12065-1004)
PHONE.................................610 407-4700
Harshad Mehta,
EMP: 7
SALES (est): 478.5K **Privately Held**
SIC: 3674 Semiconductors & related devices

(G-3734)
SIMPLEXGRINNELL LP
1399 Vischer Ferry Rd (12065)
PHONE.................................518 952-6040
Dan Bullis, *Manager*
Amy Nichols, *Manager*
EMP: 30 **Privately Held**
WEB: www.simplexgrinnell.com
SIC: 3669 Emergency alarms
HQ: Simplexgrinnell Lp
4700 Exchange Ct
Boca Raton FL 33431
561 988-7200

(G-3735)
ST SILICONES CORPORATION
821 Main St (12065-1002)
PHONE.................................518 406-3208
David A Scagnelli, *President*
EMP: 15
SALES (est): 1MM **Privately Held**
SIC: 3841 Surgical & medical instruments

(G-3736)
THE GRAMECY GROUP
4 Gramecy Ct (12065-2329)
PHONE.................................518 348-1325
Fax: 518 373-1855
Bill Sommers, *Owner*
EMP: 8
SALES (est): 721.8K **Privately Held**
WEB: www.gramecy.com
SIC: 2759 3479 Commercial printing; name plates: engraved, etched, etc.

(G-3737)
WORLDWIDE GAS TURBINE PDTS INC
Also Called: Gt Parts & Services
300 Commerce Dr (12065-1317)
PHONE.................................518 877-7200
Anthony Campana, *CEO*
Stephen P Campana, *Ch of Bd*
Anita Clemente, *Manager*
Antoinette Campana, *Admin Sec*
EMP: 8
SQ FT: 1,200
SALES (est): 1.9MM **Privately Held**
SIC: 3511 Turbines & turbine generator sets

(G-3738)
YO FRESH INC
5 Southside Dr (12065-3870)
PHONE.................................518 982-0659
EMP: 23
SALES (corp-wide): 10.5MM **Privately Held**
SIC: 2026 Yogurt
PA: Yo Fresh Inc.
38 E 29th St Fl 6
New York NY 10016
212 260-4416

Clifton Springs
Ontario County

(G-3739)
MERCHANDISER INC
70 Stephens St (14432-1051)
P.O. Box 642 (14432-0642)
PHONE.................................315 462-6411
Fax: 315 462-7627
Cheryl Tears, *President*
James Tears, *Vice Pres*
Dawn Colangelo, *Sales Staff*
Megan Defrance, *Sales Staff*
EMP: 5
SQ FT: 1,792
SALES: 450K **Privately Held**
WEB: www.themerchandiser.net
SIC: 2759 2711 Publication printing; newspapers

(G-3740)
RJ WELDING & FABRICATING INC
2300 Wheat Rd (14432-9312)
PHONE.................................315 523-1288
Robert Crosby, *Principal*
EMP: 5
SALES (est): 556.2K **Privately Held**
SIC: 7692 Welding repair

(G-3741)
TOWNLINE MACHINE CO INC
3151 Manchester (14432)
PHONE.................................315 462-3413
Fax: 315 462-6149
Scott Converse, *President*
Patrick Converse, *Treasurer*
EMP: 16
SQ FT: 25,000
SALES: 3MM **Privately Held**
SIC: 3545 Precision tools, machinists'

Clinton
Oneida County

(G-3742)
CAZENOVIA EQUIPMENT CO INC
8186 Seneca Tpke (13323-1022)
PHONE.................................315 736-0898
Fax: 315 734-9305
Brad Hathorn, *Manager*
EMP: 9
SALES (corp-wide): 5.4MM **Privately Held**
WEB: www.cazenoviaequipment.com
SIC: 3524 Lawn & garden equipment
PA: Cazenovia Equipment Co., Inc.
2 Remington Park Dr
Cazenovia NY 13035
315 655-8620

(G-3743)
CLINTON CLRS & EMB SHOPPE INC
43 College St (13323-1690)
PHONE.................................315 853-8421
Fax: 315 853-3191
Stephen J Kaminski Sr, *President*
Cynthia A Kaminski, *Vice Pres*
EMP: 8
SQ FT: 1,400
SALES (est): 488K **Privately Held**
SIC: 2395 7212 Embroidery & art needlework; laundry & drycleaner agents

(G-3744)
GERMANIUM CORP AMERICA INC
34 Robinson Rd (13323-1419)
PHONE.................................315 853-4900
Gregory P Evans, *Ch of Bd*
John Rosker, *Chief Acct*
▲ EMP: 11
SALES (est): 1.6MM
SALES (corp-wide): 193.5MM **Privately Held**
WEB: www.indium.com
SIC: 3341 2819 Secondary nonferrous metals; chemicals, high purity: refined from technical grade
PA: Indium Corporation Of America
34 Robinson Rd
Clinton NY 13323
800 446-3486

GEOGRAPHIC SECTION

(G-3745)
INDIUM CORPORATION OF AMERICA (PA)
34 Robinson Rd (13323-1419)
P.O. Box 269, Utica (13503-0269)
PHONE...................................800 446-3486
Fax: 315 853-7001
William N Macartney III, *Ch of Bd*
Gregory P Evans, *President*
Paul Gassensmith, *General Mgr*
Wenglye Tang, *General Mgr*
Greg Hayes, *Regional Mgr*
▲ **EMP:** 45 **EST:** 1934
SQ FT: 12,000
SALES (est): 193.5MM **Privately Held**
WEB: www.indium.com
SIC: 3356 Solder: wire, bar, acid core, & rosin core

(G-3746)
POWER LINE CONSTRUCTORS INC
24 Robinson Rd (13323-1419)
P.O. Box 385 (13323-0385)
PHONE...................................315 853-6183
Fax: 315 853-3176
David L Critelli, *President*
En M Critelli, *Exec VP*
Steven M Critelli, *Exec VP*
Allen Kobbe, *Vice Pres*
Michael E Lopata, *Vice Pres*
EMP: 30
SQ FT: 7,500
SALES (est): 7.3MM **Privately Held**
WEB: www.powerlineconstructors.com
SIC: 3669 Traffic signals, electric

(G-3747)
TENNEY MEDIA GROUP (PA)
Also Called: Omp Printing & Graphics
28 Robinson Rd (13323-1419)
P.O. Box 325 (13323-0325)
PHONE...................................315 853-5569
Claudia Cleary, *Ch of Bd*
Robert Tenney, *Admin Sec*
EMP: 67
SQ FT: 25,000
SALES (est): 27.8MM **Privately Held**
WEB: www.psaver.com
SIC: 2741 2711 Shopping news: publishing & printing; newspapers

Clinton Corners
Dutchess County

(G-3748)
CLINTON VINEYARDS INC
450 Schultzville Rd (12514-2402)
PHONE...................................845 266-5372
Fax: 845 266-3395
Phyllis Feder, *President*
EMP: 5
SALES (est): 425.6K **Privately Held**
WEB: www.clintonvineyards.com
SIC: 2084 Wines

Clyde
Wayne County

(G-3749)
ADVANCED ATOMIZATION TECH LLC
Also Called: Aatech
124 Columbia St (14433-1049)
PHONE...................................315 923-2341
Leanne Collazzo, *General Mgr*
Christopher Harrison, *CFO*
Ruben Colon, *Program Mgr*
Michael Portela, *Manager*
James Mazzarell, *CTO*
EMP: 300 **EST:** 2012
SQ FT: 60,000
SALES (est): 136MM
SALES (corp-wide): 12B **Publicly Held**
SIC: 3724 Aircraft engines & engine parts
PA: Parker-Hannifin Corporation
     6035 Parkland Blvd
     Cleveland OH 44124
     216 896-3000

(G-3750)
ENERGY PANEL STRUCTURES INC
Also Called: Fingerlakes Construction
10269 Old Route 31 (14433-9777)
PHONE...................................315 923-7777
Kirt Burghdorf, *Vice Pres*
EMP: 7
SALES (corp-wide): 700K **Privately Held**
SIC: 3448 2452 Prefabricated metal buildings; prefabricated wood buildings
HQ: Energy Panel Structures, Inc.
     603 N Van Gordon Ave
     Graettinger IA 51342
     712 859-3219

(G-3751)
ENERGY PANEL STRUCTURES INC
Also Called: Fingerlakes Construction
10269 Old Route 31 (14433-9777)
PHONE...................................585 343-1777
Fax: 585 344-3859
Kirt Burghdorf, *Vice Pres*
Dan Hoffman, *Sales Mgr*
EMP: 8
SALES (corp-wide): 700K **Privately Held**
SIC: 3448 2452 Prefabricated metal buildings; prefabricated wood buildings
HQ: Energy Panel Structures, Inc.
     603 N Van Gordon Ave
     Graettinger IA 51342
     712 859-3219

(G-3752)
FUEL EFFICIENCY LLC
101 Davis Pkwy (14433)
PHONE...................................315 923-2511
Karl Simon, *Sales Staff*
Joseph Connelly,
Karen Connelly,
EMP: 8
SQ FT: 12,700
SALES (est): 1.4MM **Privately Held**
WEB: www.fuelefficency.com
SIC: 3443 Boilers: industrial, power, or marine; boiler shop products: boilers, smokestacks, steel tanks

(G-3753)
MEADE MACHINE CO INC
31 Ford St (14433-1306)
PHONE...................................315 923-1703
Fax: 315 923-2811
Mark Clinton Meade, *President*
Elizabeth Meade, *Vice Pres*
EMP: 6 **EST:** 1943
SQ FT: 8,000
SALES: 800K **Privately Held**
SIC: 3599 7539 Machine shop, jobbing & repair; machine shop, automotive

(G-3754)
MODERN BLOCK LLC
2440 Wyne Zandra Rose Vly (14433)
PHONE...................................315 923-7443
Andy Martin,
Glen S Martin,
EMP: 8
SALES: 600K **Privately Held**
SIC: 3271 Concrete block & brick

(G-3755)
PARKER-HANNIFIN CORPORATION
Also Called: Parker-Hannifin Aerospace
124 Columbia St (14433-1049)
PHONE...................................631 231-3737
Fax: 315 923-7759
Horace Bassaragh, *Engineer*
Brian Cario, *Engineer*
AVI Korenshtein, *Engineer*
David Wright, *Manager*
EMP: 248
SALES (corp-wide): 12B **Publicly Held**
SIC: 3728 Aircraft parts & equipment
PA: Parker-Hannifin Corporation
     6035 Parkland Blvd
     Cleveland OH 44124
     216 896-3000

(G-3756)
PRODUCTS SUPERB INC
231 Clyde Marengo Rd (14433-9528)
PHONE...................................315 923-7057
Fax: 315 923-1593
Ellen Bellizzi, *President*
EMP: 7
SQ FT: 8,000
SALES (est): 665K **Privately Held**
SIC: 3471 7389 Finishing, metals or formed products; packaging & labeling services

(G-3757)
THOMAS ELECTRONICS INC (PA)
208 Davis Pkwy (14433-9550)
PHONE...................................315 923-2051
Fax: 315 923-4401
David A Ketchum, *President*
Dennis Young, *President*
Jeff Culmo, *General Mgr*
Douglas Ketchum, *Exec VP*
Fred Cornelius, *Mfg Dir*
▲ **EMP:** 160
SQ FT: 71,180
SALES (est): 23.1MM **Privately Held**
SIC: 3671 Cathode ray tubes, including rebuilt

Clymer
Chautauqua County

(G-3758)
CUSTOM SHIPPING PRODUCTS INC
8661 Knowlton Rd (14724-9706)
P.O. Box 245 (14724-0245)
PHONE...................................716 355-4437
Fax: 716 355-4439
John Holthouse, *President*
Shelly Schenck, *Corp Secy*
Mike Schenck, *Vice Pres*
EMP: 10
SQ FT: 3,000
SALES (est): 890K **Privately Held**
SIC: 2448 Pallets, wood

Cobleskill
Schoharie County

(G-3759)
CLAPPER HOLLOW DESIGNS INC
369 N Grand St (12043-4140)
PHONE...................................518 234-9561
Michael Lambert, *President*
Brigette Belka, *Vice Pres*
Tony Lee, *Vice Pres*
EMP: 20
SQ FT: 10,000
SALES (est): 1.6MM **Privately Held**
SIC: 3952 Frames for artists' canvases

(G-3760)
COBLESKILL STONE PRODUCTS INC (PA)
112 Rock Rd (12043-5738)
P.O. Box 220 (12043-0220)
PHONE...................................518 234-0221
Emil Galasso, *Chairman*
Michael Galasso, *Vice Pres*
Daniel Kleeschulte, *Vice Pres*
Michael Moore, *Vice Pres*
Craig Watson, *Admin Sec*
EMP: 15 **EST:** 1954
SQ FT: 5,000
SALES (est): 115.2MM **Privately Held**
WEB: www.cobleskillstone.com
SIC: 1422 Crushed & broken limestone

(G-3761)
DIVISION STREET NEWS CORP
Also Called: Time Journal
108 Division St Apt 7 (12043-4606)
PHONE...................................518 234-2515
James Poole, *President*
Patsy Nicosia, *Manager*
EMP: 18
SALES (est): 1.9MM **Privately Held**
WEB: www.schohariechamber.com
SIC: 2752 5994 2711 Commercial printing, lithographic; newsstand; newspapers

(G-3762)
EFJ INC
Also Called: Mill Services
128 Macarthur Ave (12043-3603)
P.O. Box 577 (12043-0577)
PHONE...................................518 234-4799
Daniel W Holt, *President*
James Place, *Vice Pres*
James Bender, *Manager*
Vickie McDonald, *Manager*
EMP: 60 **EST:** 1993
SQ FT: 80,000
SALES: 10.6MM **Privately Held**
WEB: www.millservices.com
SIC: 2431 Millwork

(G-3763)
KELLEY FARM & GARDEN INC
Also Called: Agway
239 W Main St (12043-1713)
P.O. Box 37 (12043-0037)
PHONE...................................518 234-2332
Fax: 518 234-2017
Scott F Kelley, *President*
Kathy Kelley, *Corp Secy*
Scott Kelly, *Plant Mgr*
Barbara Robarge, *Manager*
EMP: 20
SQ FT: 3,700
SALES (est): 6.7MM **Privately Held**
SIC: 3546 5191 5261 Saws & sawing equipment; animal feeds; lawnmowers & tractors

(G-3764)
T A S SALES SERVICE LLC
105 Kenyon Rd (12043-5713)
PHONE...................................518 234-4919
Thomas Sachs, *Principal*
EMP: 9
SALES (est): 1.1MM **Privately Held**
SIC: 1389 Gas field services

Cochecton
Sullivan County

(G-3765)
COCHECTON MILLS INC (PA)
30 Depot Rd (12726-5221)
PHONE...................................845 932-8282
Fax: 570 932-8865
Dennis E Nearing, *President*
Robert Nearing Jr, *Treasurer*
Sean Nearing, *Manager*
EMP: 20
SQ FT: 8,500
SALES (est): 2.1MM **Privately Held**
SIC: 2048 2041 Poultry feeds; livestock feeds; flour & other grain mill products

(G-3766)
JML QUARRIES INC
420 Bernas Rd (12726-5423)
PHONE...................................845 932-8206
Fax: 845 888-4198
Rodney Cornelius, *President*
EMP: 25
SQ FT: 2,000
SALES (est): 3.2MM **Privately Held**
SIC: 1422 Crushed & broken limestone

(G-3767)
MASTEN ENTERPRISES LLC (PA)
420 Bernas Rd (12726-5423)
PHONE...................................845 932-8206
Fax: 845 932-8139
John Bernas, *Principal*
Mauren Cowger, *Manager*
EMP: 150
SQ FT: 2,000
SALES (est): 12.4MM **Privately Held**
SIC: 1429 Grits mining (crushed stone)

(G-3768)
MORLYN ASPHALT CORP
420 Bernas Rd (12726-5423)
PHONE...................................845 888-2695
John Bernas, *President*
Bob Burgio, *CFO*
Warrien Cowger, *Manager*
EMP: 6
SQ FT: 2,000

SALES (est): 717.5K
SALES (corp-wide): 12.4MM **Privately Held**
SIC: 2951 Asphalt paving mixtures & blocks
PA: Masten Enterprises Llc
420 Bernas Rd
Cochecton NY 12726
845 932-8206

(G-3769)
SULLIVAN CONCRETE INC
Also Called: Sullivan Structures
420 Bernas Rd (12726-5423)
PHONE.................................845 888-2235
John Bernas, *President*
Bob Burgio, *CFO*
Richard Messina, *Sales Mgr*
EMP: 12
SQ FT: 2,000
SALES (est): 2.4MM **Privately Held**
WEB: www.sullivanstructures.com
SIC: 3273 Ready-mixed concrete

Coeymans
Albany County

(G-3770)
TRACEY WELDING CO INC
29 Riverview Dr (12045-7719)
P.O. Box 799 (12045-0799)
PHONE.................................518 756-6309
Richard Tracey, *President*
Richard J Tracey, *Vice Pres*
EMP: 8
SQ FT: 15,200
SALES (est): 1.3MM **Privately Held**
WEB: www.traceywelding.com
SIC: 7692 Welding repair

Cohoes
Albany County

(G-3771)
ELECTRONIC COATING TECH INC (PA)
1 Mustang Dr Ste 4 (12047-4856)
PHONE.................................518 688-2048
Tom Charlton, *President*
Michelle Hughes, *Controller*
▲ EMP: 12
SALES (est): 1.3MM **Privately Held**
SIC: 3479 Coating of metals & formed products; coating of metals with silicon

(G-3772)
JAY MOULDING CORPORATION
7 Bridge Ave Ste 1 (12047-4799)
PHONE.................................518 237-4200
Fax: 518 237-6576
Christy Smagala, *President*
Nancy Uvin, *Office Mgr*
Richard Smagala, *Shareholder*
EMP: 10
SQ FT: 9,000
SALES: 1MM **Privately Held**
WEB: www.jaymoulding.com
SIC: 3083 Thermosetting laminates: rods, tubes, plates & sheet; thermoplastic laminates: rods, tubes, plates & sheet

(G-3773)
LINDE GAS NORTH AMERICA LLC
Also Called: Lifegas
10 Arrowhead Ln (12047-4812)
PHONE.................................518 713-2015
Fax: 518 713-2019
Casey Hilligas, *Branch Mgr*
EMP: 40
SALES (corp-wide): 17.9B **Privately Held**
SIC: 2813 Nitrogen; oxygen, compressed or liquefied
HQ: Linde Gas North America Llc
200 Somerset Corp Blvd # 7000
Bridgewater NJ 08807

(G-3774)
MATHESON TRI-GAS INC
15 Green Mountain Dr (12047-4807)
PHONE.................................518 203-5003
Scott Kallman, *Branch Mgr*
EMP: 6
SALES (corp-wide): 29.7B **Privately Held**
SIC: 2813 Industrial gases; nitrogen; oxygen, compressed or liquefied; argon
HQ: Matheson Tri-Gas, Inc.
150 Allen Rd Ste 302
Basking Ridge NJ 07920
908 991-9200

(G-3775)
MOHAWK FINE PAPERS INC (PA)
465 Saratoga St (12047-4626)
P.O. Box 497 (12047-0497)
PHONE.................................518 237-1740
Fax: 518 233-7102
Thomas D O'Connor, *Ch of Bd*
Walter Duignan, *Vice Ch Bd*
John F Haren, *President*
Kevin P Richard, *COO*
George Milner, *Senior VP*
▲ EMP: 300 EST: 1876
SQ FT: 207,000
SALES (est): 244.2MM **Privately Held**
WEB: www.mohawkpaper.com
SIC: 2672 2621 Coated & laminated paper; paper mills; uncoated paper

(G-3776)
MOHAWK FINE PAPERS INC
465 Saratoga St (12047-4626)
PHONE.................................518 237-1741
Dave Raley, *Manager*
EMP: 30
SALES (corp-wide): 244.2MM **Privately Held**
WEB: www.mohawkpaper.com
SIC: 2621 Paper mills
PA: Mohawk Fine Papers Inc.
465 Saratoga St
Cohoes NY 12047
518 237-1740

(G-3777)
NIS MANUFACTURING INC
Also Called: Northern Indus Svces Mech Div
1 Mustang Dr Ste 5 (12047-4856)
PHONE.................................518 456-2566
William Nattress, *Branch Mgr*
EMP: 9
SALES (corp-wide): 4.8MM **Privately Held**
WEB: www.northernindustrial.com
SIC: 3829 Testing equipment: abrasion, shearing strength, etc.
PA: Nis Manufacturing, Inc.
1 Mustang Dr Ste 5
Cohoes NY 12047
518 456-2566

(G-3778)
NORLITE LLC
Also Called: Norlite Corporation
628 Saratoga St (12047-4644)
P.O. Box 694 (12047-0694)
PHONE.................................518 235-0030
Fax: 518 235-0233
Michael Ferraro, *Corp Secy*
Brian Abely, *Vice Pres*
Robert O'Brien, *Mng Member*
Becky Mc-Clellam, *Manager*
Mark Hewitt, *Info Tech Dir*
EMP: 325 EST: 1973
SQ FT: 5,000
SALES (est): 38.9MM
SALES (corp-wide): 196.5K **Privately Held**
WEB: www.norliteagg.com
SIC: 3295 Shale, expanded
HQ: Tradebe Environmental Services, Llc
1433 E 83rd Ave Ste 200
Merrillville IN 46410

(G-3779)
PRECISION VALVE & AUTOMTN INC (PA)
Also Called: PVA
1 Mustang Dr Ste 3 (12047-4856)
PHONE.................................518 371-2684
Anthony J Hynes, *Ch of Bd*
Craig Tuttle, *Mfg Dir*
Jeremy Prusky, *Opers Mgr*
Marc Rogner, *Production*
Larry Hynes, *Purchasing*
▲ EMP: 185
SQ FT: 115,000
SALES (est): 36.8MM **Privately Held**
WEB: www.pva.net
SIC: 3491 Industrial valves

(G-3780)
REO WELDING INC
5 New Cortland St (12047-2628)
PHONE.................................518 238-1022
Fax: 518 238-9004
Robert J REO Jr, *President*
Michael REO, *Vice Pres*
Janet Hems, *Office Mgr*
EMP: 17
SQ FT: 6,000
SALES (est): 4.5MM **Privately Held**
WEB: www.reowelding.com
SIC: 3441 7692 Fabricated structural metal; welding repair

(G-3781)
ROBERTS NICHOLS FIRE APPARATUS
84 Island View Rd (12047-4995)
PHONE.................................518 431-1945
Harry Roberts, *CEO*
EMP: 9
SALES (est): 1.3MM **Privately Held**
SIC: 3711 Motor vehicles & car bodies

(G-3782)
SCHONWETTER ENTERPRISES INC
Also Called: Bilinski Sausage Mfg Co
41 Lark St (12047-4618)
PHONE.................................518 237-0171
Fax: 518 237-0205
Steven M Schonwetter, *Ch of Bd*
Stacie Waters, *COO*
Carrie Coddington, *Transptn Dir*
Sagar Agarwal, *QC Mgr*
Cathie Schonwetter, *Sales Executive*
EMP: 25
SQ FT: 20,000
SALES (est): 5.5MM **Privately Held**
WEB: www.bilinski.com
SIC: 2013 Sausages & related products, from purchased meat

(G-3783)
SHELTER ENTERPRISES INC
8 Saratoga St (12047-3109)
P.O. Box 618 (12047-0618)
PHONE.................................518 237-4100
Jeffory J Myers, *Principal*
Dan Bartolucci, *Plant Mgr*
Robert Lang, *Sales Staff*
Dan Oconnor, *Manager*
▲ EMP: 60
SQ FT: 110,000
SALES (est): 14.7MM **Privately Held**
WEB: www.shelter-ent.com
SIC: 3086 2452 Insulation or cushioning material, foamed plastic; prefabricated buildings, wood

(G-3784)
TROYS LANDSCAPE SUPPLY CO INC
1266 Loudon Rd (12047)
PHONE.................................518 785-1526
Troy Miller, *President*
Monica Mickman, *Vice Pres*
EMP: 11
SQ FT: 2,520
SALES (est): 904.2K **Privately Held**
SIC: 3271 Blocks, concrete: landscape or retaining wall

(G-3785)
VITAL SIGNS & GRAPHICS CO INC
251 Saratoga St (12047-3120)
PHONE.................................518 237-8372
Fax: 518 237-0607
Alexander Coloruotolo, *President*
EMP: 5
SQ FT: 1,200
SALES (est): 496.4K **Privately Held**
SIC: 3993 7336 Signs & advertising specialties; graphic arts & related design

(G-3786)
W N VANALSTINE & SONS INC (PA)
Also Called: Macaran Printed Products
18 New Cortland St (12047-2628)
P.O. Box 380 (12047-0380)
PHONE.................................518 237-1436
Fax: 518 237-0194
Nicholas V Alstine, *President*
William N Van Astine III, *Chairman*
Edward Wixted, *CFO*
Patrick Degnan, *Accounts Exec*
Joan Godzik, *Manager*
EMP: 65 EST: 1952
SQ FT: 52,000
SALES (est): 14.5MM **Privately Held**
WEB: www.printandapply.com
SIC: 2759 5199 Flexographic printing; packaging materials

Cold Spring
Putnam County

(G-3787)
DI VICO CRAFT PRODUCTS LTD
Also Called: Divico Products
3441 Route 9 (10516-3851)
PHONE.................................845 265-9390
Fax: 845 265-9390
David Di Vico Jr, *President*
EMP: 5
SQ FT: 5,500
SALES: 700K **Privately Held**
SIC: 2499 Fencing, docks & other outdoor wood structural products

(G-3788)
MID-HUDSON CONCRETE PDTS INC
3504 Route 9 (10516-3862)
PHONE.................................845 265-3141
Fax: 845 265-3741
Joe Giachinta, *President*
Katie Demarco, *Marketing Staff*
EMP: 7
SQ FT: 3,000
SALES (est): 650K **Privately Held**
WEB: www.midhudsonconcreteproducts.com
SIC: 3272 Concrete products; septic tanks, concrete

(G-3789)
PUTNAM CNTY NEWS RECORDER LLC
144 Main St Ste 1 (10516-2854)
P.O. Box 185 (10516-0185)
PHONE.................................845 265-2468
Joseph P Lindsley Jr, *Editor*
Brian Odonnell, *Network Mgr*
Elizabeth Ailes,
EMP: 12
SALES (est): 631.2K **Privately Held**
WEB: www.pcnr.com
SIC: 2711 Newspapers

(G-3790)
RIVERVIEW INDUSTRIES INC
3012 Route 9 Ste 1 (10516-3675)
PHONE.................................845 265-5284
Kevin Reichard, *President*
Paul Reichard, *Vice Pres*
EMP: 7
SALES (est): 949.4K **Privately Held**
SIC: 3548 7538 7549 Welding apparatus; general truck repair; high performance auto repair & service

(G-3791)
SCANGA WOODWORKING CORP
22 Corporate Park W (10516)
PHONE.................................845 265-9115
Laura Hammond, *Ch of Bd*
Hugo Scanga, *President*
John Scagna, *Vice Pres*
Mark Scanga, *Vice Pres*
Laura Hammont, *Controller*
▲ EMP: 38
SQ FT: 9,000

SALES (est): 6.2MM **Privately Held**
SIC: 2431 Moldings, wood: unfinished & prefinished; interior & ornamental woodwork & trim; panel work, wood

Cold Spring Harbor
Suffolk County

(G-3792)
CIRRUS HEALTHCARE PRODUCTS LLC (PA)
60 Main St (11724-1433)
P.O. Box 220 (11724-0220)
PHONE................................631 692-7600
Drew O'Connell, *General Mgr*
Joanne Calabria, *VP Opers*
Malcolm Boothman, *Director*
▲ EMP: 28
SALES (est): 6MM **Privately Held**
WEB: www.cirrushealthcare.com
SIC: 3842 Ear plugs

(G-3793)
DANI ACCESSORIES INC
204 Lawrence Hill Rd (11724-1910)
PHONE................................631 692-4505
Daniel Montefusco, *President*
EMP: 30
SQ FT: 4,000
SALES (est): 2MM **Privately Held**
SIC: 3171 Handbags, women's

(G-3794)
INFOSERVICES INTERNATIONAL
Also Called: Itelinso
1 Saint Marks Pl (11724-1825)
PHONE................................631 549-1805
Michael Dohan, *President*
Akademika Skryabina, *General Mgr*
Deirdre Bluemer, *Vice Pres*
Keith Andersen, *Manager*
EMP: 15
SALES (est): 840K **Privately Held**
WEB: www.infoservices.com
SIC: 2741 Telephone & other directory publishing

(G-3795)
PRINT CENTER INC
3 Harbor Rd Ste 21 (11724-1514)
PHONE................................718 643-9559
Robert Hershon, *President*
EMP: 6
SALES (est): 479K **Privately Held**
WEB: www.rhinography.com
SIC: 2752 Commercial printing, lithographic

(G-3796)
WATER RESOURCES GROUP LLC
Also Called: Ice Box Water
84 Main St (11724-1441)
P.O. Box 178 (11724-0178)
PHONE................................631 824-9088
Andrew Reynolds, *President*
▲ EMP: 9
SALES (est): 877.6K **Privately Held**
SIC: 2086 Pasteurized & mineral waters, bottled & canned

Colden
Erie County

(G-3797)
O & S MACHINE & TOOL CO INC
8143 State Rd (14033-9713)
P.O. Box 303 (14033-0303)
PHONE................................716 941-5542
Fax: 716 941-5553
Philip J Schueler, *President*
Connie Caruso, *Manager*
EMP: 9 EST: 1977
SQ FT: 5,000
SALES (est): 1MM **Privately Held**
SIC: 3599 Machine shop, jobbing & repair

College Point
Queens County

(G-3798)
A ANGONOA INC (PA)
11505 15th Ave (11356-1597)
P.O. Box 560089 (11356-0089)
PHONE................................718 762-4466
Fax: 718 359-1013
Peter Zampieri, *President*
Andrew Zampieri, *VP Opers*
John Armao, *Plant Mgr*
Gregg Desantis, *Natl Sales Mgr*
Christopher Desantis, *Sales Staff*
EMP: 77
SQ FT: 60,000
SALES (est): 9.2MM **Privately Held**
WEB: www.angonoa.com
SIC: 2051 Bread, cake & related products

(G-3799)
AABACS GROUP INC
1509 132nd St (11356-2441)
PHONE................................718 961-3577
Michael Shin, *Principal*
Tom Park, *Manager*
EMP: 10
SALES (est): 990.8K **Privately Held**
SIC: 3699 Security control equipment & systems

(G-3800)
ABC WINDOWS AND SIGNS CORP
12606 18th Ave (11356-2326)
PHONE................................718 353-6210
Lin Yang, *Ch of Bd*
EMP: 11
SALES (est): 1.1MM **Privately Held**
SIC: 3993 Signs & advertising specialties

(G-3801)
AEROSPACE WIRE & CABLE INC
12909 18th Ave (11356-2407)
PHONE................................718 358-2345
Fax: 718 358-2522
Richard Chen, *President*
Leo Tong, *Sales Mgr*
Devin Rosenberg, *Marketing Staff*
Al Lee, *Manager*
Justin Chui, *Director*
▲ EMP: 30
SQ FT: 3,500
SALES (est): 7.3MM **Privately Held**
WEB: www.aerospacewire.com
SIC: 3315 Wire, steel: insulated or armored; cable, steel: insulated or armored

(G-3802)
AFC INDUSTRIES INC
1316 133rd Pl Ste 1 (11356-2024)
PHONE................................718 747-0237
Fax: 718 747-0726
Avner Farkash, *General Mgr*
Anat Barnes, *Chairman*
Len Pushkantser, *Exec VP*
Patrick Bowen, *Sls & Mktg Exec*
Curt Robertson, *VP Finance*
▲ EMP: 100
SQ FT: 20,000
SALES: 11MM **Privately Held**
WEB: www.afcindustries.com
SIC: 2599 Hospital furniture, except beds

(G-3803)
AMERICAN ORTHOTIC LAB CO INC
924 118th St (11356-1557)
PHONE................................718 961-6487
Kevin John Renart, *President*
Kathleen Dodson, *Manager*
EMP: 7
SQ FT: 1,080
SALES (est): 917.5K **Privately Held**
SIC: 3544 Industrial molds

(G-3804)
BEL AIRE OFFSET CORP
Also Called: Bel Aire Printing
1853 College Point Blvd (11356-2220)
PHONE................................718 539-8233
Fax: 718 321-9800
Carmine Nicoletti, *President*
Michael Vogell, *Manager*
EMP: 5 EST: 1973
SQ FT: 5,000
SALES (est): 693.5K **Privately Held**
WEB: www.belaireprintingcorp.com
SIC: 2752 Commercial printing, offset

(G-3805)
CAPITAL KIT CAB & DOOR MFRS
Also Called: Capital Ktchens Cab Doors Mfrs
1425 128th St (11356-2335)
PHONE................................718 886-0303
Fax: 718 445-4630
Tom Catalanotto Sr, *President*
Steven Catalanotto, *Corp Secy*
Tom Catalanotto Jr, *Vice Pres*
EMP: 7
SQ FT: 10,000
SALES: 700K **Privately Held**
WEB: www.capitalkitchens.com
SIC: 2434 2431 5031 1751 Wood kitchen cabinets; doors, wood; kitchen cabinets; cabinet & finish carpentry

(G-3806)
CITY STORE GATES MFG CORP
Also Called: None
1520 129th St (11356-2400)
PHONE................................718 939-9700
Fax: 212 353-0724
Vincent Greco Jr, *Ch of Bd*
Darlene Leavens, *Manager*
Red Leavens, *Manager*
Steve Morisco, *Manager*
▲ EMP: 25
SQ FT: 35,000
SALES (est): 6MM **Privately Held**
SIC: 3446 5211 1799 3429 Gates, ornamental metal; door & window products; fence construction; manufactured hardware (general); millwork

(G-3807)
EAST COAST THERMOGRAPHERS INC
1558 127th St Ste 1 (11356-2347)
PHONE................................718 321-3211
Fax: 718 321-3222
Barry Schwartz, *President*
EMP: 30
SQ FT: 6,000
SALES: 2MM **Privately Held**
SIC: 2759 3953 2752 Thermography; marking devices; commercial printing, lithographic

(G-3808)
FILLING EQUIPMENT CO INC
1539 130th St (11356-2481)
PHONE................................718 445-2111
Fax: 718 463-6034
Robert A Hampton, *President*
George Hite, *Admin Mgr*
EMP: 11 EST: 1959
SQ FT: 6,800
SALES (est): 2.7MM **Privately Held**
WEB: www.fillingequipment.com
SIC: 3565 5084 Bottling machinery: filling, capping, labeling; industrial machinery & equipment

(G-3809)
GLOPAK USA CORP (PA)
1816 127th St Ste 2 (11356-2334)
PHONE................................347 869-9252
Kenneth Wang, *CEO*
▲ EMP: 48
SALES: 35MM **Privately Held**
SIC: 3221 Bottles for packing, bottling & canning: glass

(G-3810)
GMD INDUSTRIES INC
Also Called: Designer Glass
12920 18th Ave (11356-2408)
PHONE................................718 445-8779
Fax: 718 358-8614
Jorge Rodriguez, *President*
Maria Rodriguez, *Vice Pres*
Greg Macpherson, *Engineer*
Diego Rodriguez, *Data Proc Staff*
▲ EMP: 8
SQ FT: 1,500
SALES (est): 1.1MM **Privately Held**
WEB: www.gmdindustries.com
SIC: 3231 Decorated glassware: chipped, engraved, etched, etc.; mirrored glass

(G-3811)
HEAT USA II LLC (PA)
11902 23rd Ave (11356-2506)
P.O. Box 560240 (11356-0240)
PHONE................................212 254-4328
Mark Kohan, *General Mgr*
EMP: 11
SALES (est): 2.4MM **Privately Held**
SIC: 2911 Oils, fuel

(G-3812)
IN-HOUSE INC
1535 126th St Ste 3 (11356-2346)
PHONE................................718 445-9007
Fax: 718 445-9043
Joseph Passarella, *President*
EMP: 10
SQ FT: 5,000
SALES: 1.5MM **Privately Held**
SIC: 2752 2791 2789 2732 Commercial printing, offset; typesetting; bookbinding & related work; book printing

(G-3813)
INK-IT PRINTING INC
Also Called: Ink-It Prtg Inc/Angle Offset
1535 126th St Ste 1 (11356-2346)
PHONE................................718 229-5590
Fax: 718 631-5530
Michael Igoe, *President*
EMP: 8
SQ FT: 750
SALES (est): 701.8K **Privately Held**
SIC: 2752 Commercial printing, offset

(G-3814)
INTER-FENCE CO INC
1520 129th St (11356-2400)
PHONE................................718 939-9700
Vincent Greco Sr, *President*
Vincent Greco Jr, *Vice Pres*
Thomas A Greco, *Treasurer*
Angela Greco, *Admin Sec*
EMP: 40
SQ FT: 35,000
SALES (est): 6MM **Privately Held**
SIC: 3442 3446 Metal doors; gates, ornamental metal

(G-3815)
ISLAND CIRCUITS INTERNATIONAL
1318 130th St Fl 2 (11356-1917)
PHONE................................516 625-5555
Maurizio Lanza, *Branch Mgr*
EMP: 7
SALES (corp-wide): 1.8MM **Privately Held**
SIC: 3679 Electronic circuits
PA: Island Circuits International
100 E 2nd St Ste 201
Mineola NY 11501
516 625-5555

(G-3816)
JAD CORP OF AMERICA
2048 119th St (11356-2123)
PHONE................................718 762-8900
Fax: 718 762-7320
Joseph A Dussich Jr, *President*
David Newell, *Business Mgr*
James Jozkowski, *Purchasing*
Henry Schaeffer, *CFO*
Trina Laxa, *Controller*
EMP: 50
SQ FT: 45,000
SALES (est): 24.4MM **Privately Held**
WEB: www.jad.com
SIC: 2673 5087 5169 Trash bags (plastic film): made from purchased materials; cleaning & maintenance equipment & supplies; chemicals & allied products

(G-3817)
JPMORGAN CHASE BANK NAT ASSN
13207 14th Ave (11356-2001)
PHONE................................718 767-3592
EMP: 6

College Point - Queens County (G-3818)

SALES (corp-wide): 105.4B **Publicly Held**
SIC: 3578 Automatic teller machines (ATM)
HQ: Jpmorgan Chase Bank, National Association
1111 Polaris Pkwy
Columbus OH 43240
614 436-3055

(G-3818)
LAHOYA ENTERPRISE INC
Also Called: Kourosh
1842 College Point Blvd (11356-2221)
PHONE.................................718 886-8799
Kourosh Tehrani, *Ch of Bd*
Daphne Hwang, *Manager*
▲ **EMP:** 30
SALES (est): 2MM **Privately Held**
SIC: 2339 Women's & misses' outerwear

(G-3819)
LIBERTY CONTROLS INC
1505 132nd St Fl 2 (11356-2441)
PHONE.................................718 461-0600
Fax: 718 461-3613
Charles Papalcure, *President*
Chris Kellner, *Vice Pres*
David Derose, *Project Mgr*
EMP: 7 **EST:** 1998
SALES (est): 660K **Privately Held**
WEB: www.liberty-controls.com
SIC: 3829 Measuring & controlling devices

(G-3820)
M T M PRINTING CO INC
2321 College Point Blvd (11356-2596)
PHONE.................................718 353-3297
Fax: 718 353-4500
Steven Kolman, *President*
Tracy Kolman, *Vice Pres*
Tracy K Silverman, *Manager*
EMP: 14 **EST:** 1940
SQ FT: 5,500
SALES (est): 2.6MM **Privately Held**
WEB: www.mtmprinting.com
SIC: 2752 2759 Commercial printing, offset; letterpress printing

(G-3821)
MATIC INDUSTRIES INC
1540 127th St (11356-2332)
PHONE.................................718 886-5470
Fax: 718 886-5132
Roland Tatzel, *President*
EMP: 7
SALES (est): 580K **Privately Held**
SIC: 3599 Machine shop, jobbing & repair

(G-3822)
MINT-X PRODUCTS CORPORATION
2048 119th St (11356-2123)
PHONE.................................877 646-8224
Joseph Dussich, *President*
Bill Wertz, *VP Sales*
Rich Wilson, *Director*
EMP: 10
SALES: 10MM **Privately Held**
SIC: 2673 Food storage & trash bags (plastic)

(G-3823)
NAS CP CORP (DH)
Also Called: Interplex Nas Electronics
1434 110th St Apt 4a (11356-1445)
PHONE.................................718 961-6757
Jack Seidler, *President*
John Pease, *Exec VP*
Irving Klein, *Treasurer*
Mohamed Yar, *Maintence Staff*
▲ **EMP:** 50
SQ FT: 41,000
SALES (est): 24.6MM **Privately Held**
SIC: 3544 3471 3825 Dies & die holders for metal cutting, forming, die casting; plating of metals or formed products; test equipment for electronic & electric measurement
HQ: Interplex Industries, Inc.
231 Ferris Ave
Rumford RI 02916
718 961-6212

(G-3824)
NORDIC INTERIOR INC
11025 14th Ave (11356-1403)
PHONE.................................718 456-7000
Fax: 718 456-9340
Helge Halvorsen, *President*
Lloyd Jacobsen, *Corp Secy*
Harald Haegeland, *Vice Pres*
Gene Wong, *Manager*
▲ **EMP:** 150
SQ FT: 55,000
SALES (est): 23.1MM **Privately Held**
WEB: www.nordicinterior.com
SIC: 2431 1742 Woodwork, interior & ornamental; drywall

(G-3825)
OLIVE LED LIGHTING INC
1310 111th St (11356-1453)
PHONE.................................718 746-0830
Junho Lee, *President*
Alex Kang, *Manager*
◆ **EMP:** 7
SQ FT: 8,800
SALES (est): 888.3K **Privately Held**
SIC: 3648 5063 Lighting equipment; light bulbs & related supplies

(G-3826)
PEPSI-COLA BOTTLING CO NY INC
11202 15th Ave (11356-1496)
PHONE.................................718 649-2465
Stephen Del Priore, *General Mgr*
Stephen Delpriore, *General Mgr*
Harold Honickman, *Chairman*
Charlie Zimmerman, *Plant Mgr*
EMP: 300
SALES (corp-wide): 473.9MM **Privately Held**
SIC: 2086 Soft drinks: packaged in cans, bottles, etc.
PA: Pepsi-Cola Bottling Company Of New York, Inc.
11402 15th Ave Ste 5
College Point NY 11356
718 392-1000

(G-3827)
PRECISION GEAR INCORPORATED
11207 14th Ave (11356-1407)
PHONE.................................718 321-7200
Mathew S Forelli, *Ch of Bd*
M Briggs Forelli, *President*
Attila Mozsolits, *General Mgr*
Jack Rockstad, *Vice Pres*
Giovanni Esposito, *Prdtn Mgr*
▲ **EMP:** 147
SQ FT: 56,000
SALES (est): 43MM **Privately Held**
WEB: www.precisiongearinc.com
SIC: 3728 Aircraft power transmission equipment; beaching gear, aircraft

(G-3828)
QUALITY LIFE INC
2047 129th St (11356-2725)
PHONE.................................718 939-5787
Fax: 718 939-7393
Ping Ping Huang, *Ch of Bd*
▲ **EMP:** 15
SALES (est): 1.1MM **Privately Held**
SIC: 3634 Massage machines, electric, except for beauty/barber shops

(G-3829)
RAINBOW LEATHER INC
1415 112th St (11356-1435)
PHONE.................................718 939-8762
Fax: 718 461-7908
Richard Lipson, *President*
Nax Pierrot, *General Mgr*
Maria LI, *Production*
Danny Pilpe, *Sales Staff*
▲ **EMP:** 10 **EST:** 1981
SQ FT: 8,000
SALES (est): 1.8MM **Privately Held**
WEB: www.rainbowleather.com
SIC: 3111 Embossing of leather

(G-3830)
RKL BUILDING SPC CO INC
1530 131st St (11356-2423)
PHONE.................................718 728-7788
Joseph Kucich, *President*
Claire Kucich, *Corp Secy*
Gary Kucich, *Vice Pres*
▲ **EMP:** 5 **EST:** 1953
SQ FT: 5,000
SALES (est): 823K
SALES (corp-wide): 223.6B **Publicly Held**
HQ: Hohmann & Barnard, Inc.
30 Rasons Ct
Hauppauge NY 11788
631 234-0600
SIC: 3429 Builders' hardware

(G-3831)
SCHUSTER & RICHARD LABORTORIES
Also Called: Schuster & Richard Lab
1420 130th St (11356-2416)
PHONE.................................718 358-8607
Fax: 718 358-8764
Charles Boudiette, *President*
EMP: 6
SQ FT: 1,500
SALES (est): 540K **Privately Held**
SIC: 3842 Foot appliances, orthopedic

(G-3832)
SESCO INDUSTRIES INC
11019 15th Ave (11356-1425)
P.O. Box 560242 (11356-0242)
PHONE.................................718 939-5137
Fax: 718 461-0553
Steven Shulman, *President*
Allen Franceschi, *QC Mgr*
Colleen Valerio, *Sales Mgr*
▲ **EMP:** 11 **EST:** 1976
SQ FT: 4,000
SALES (est): 1.8MM **Privately Held**
WEB: www.sescoindustries.com
SIC: 3452 Bolts, nuts, rivets & washers

(G-3833)
SIGN CITY OF NEW YORK INC
13212 11th Ave (11356-1958)
P.O. Box 527015, Flushing (11352-7015)
PHONE.................................718 661-1118
EMP: 5
SALES (est): 74.2K **Privately Held**
SIC: 3993 Signs & advertising specialties

(G-3834)
SPACE SIGN
1525 132nd St (11356-2441)
PHONE.................................718 961-1112
Fax: 718 961-5577
Chang Kon Hahn, *President*
Joyce Hahn, *Vice Pres*
EMP: 11
SQ FT: 5,000
SALES (est): 1.3MM **Privately Held**
WEB: www.spacesign.com
SIC: 3993 3089 3444 1799 Signs & advertising specialties; awnings, fiberglass & plastic combination; awnings, sheet metal; awning installation; awnings

(G-3835)
TAG ENVELOPE CO INC
1419 128th St (11356-2335)
P.O. Box 220372, Brooklyn (11222-0372)
PHONE.................................718 389-6844
Fax: 718 383-6188
Geraldine Wald, *President*
Eric Wald, *Vice Pres*
Ian Wald, *Vice Pres*
EMP: 22 **EST:** 1919
SQ FT: 10,000
SALES: 3MM **Privately Held**
SIC: 2621 2679 Envelope paper; tags, paper (unprinted): made from purchased paper

(G-3836)
WEDCO FABRICATIONS INC
2016 130th St (11356-2732)
PHONE.................................718 852-6330
Dan Gordon, *President*
EMP: 7
SALES (est): 700K **Privately Held**
WEB: www.wedcofab.com
SIC: 3498 Fabricated pipe & fittings

(G-3837)
YOGA IN DAILY LIFE - NY INC
1438 132nd St (11356-2020)
PHONE.................................718 539-8548
Denis Licul, *Principal*
EMP: 5 **EST:** 2010
SALES (est): 287.4K **Privately Held**
SIC: 2711 Newspapers, publishing & printing

(G-3838)
ZERED INC (PA)
12717 20th Ave (11356-2317)
PHONE.................................718 353-7464
Fax: 718 353-7149
Hakjin Han, *President*
James Han, *Director*
▲ **EMP:** 10
SALES (est): 1.3MM **Privately Held**
SIC: 3211 Plate glass, polished & rough

Colliersville
Otsego County

(G-3839)
C & F FABRICATORS & ERECTORS
Rr 7 (13747)
PHONE.................................607 432-3520
Fax: 607 432-6435
Matthew Centofante, *President*
EMP: 6
SQ FT: 2,000
SALES (est): 580K **Privately Held**
SIC: 3443 Fabricated plate work (boiler shop)

Collins
Erie County

(G-3840)
COUNTRY SIDE SAND & GRAVEL (HQ)
Taylor Hollow Rd (14034)
PHONE.................................716 988-3271
Daniel Gernatt Jr, *President*
EMP: 1
SQ FT: 10,000
SALES (est): 1.2MM
SALES (corp-wide): 27.5MM **Privately Held**
SIC: 1442 Sand mining; gravel mining
PA: Gernatt Asphalt Products, Inc.
13870 Taylor Hollow Rd
Collins NY 14034
716 532-3371

(G-3841)
EAST END
1995 Lenox Rd (14034-9785)
PHONE.................................716 532-2622
Cheryl Whiteparker, *Owner*
EMP: 10
SALES (est): 1.1MM **Privately Held**
WEB: www.eastend.com
SIC: 2111 Cigarettes

(G-3842)
GERNATT ASPHALT PRODUCTS INC (PA)
Also Called: Gernatt Companies
13870 Taylor Hollow Rd (14034-9713)
P.O. Box 400 (14034-0400)
PHONE.................................716 532-3371
Daniel R Gernatt Jr, *Ch of Bd*
Randall Best, *Vice Pres*
Bill Schmitz, *Vice Pres*
John Redman, *Safety Mgr*
Randy Best, *Controller*
EMP: 20
SQ FT: 10,000
SALES (est): 27.5MM **Privately Held**
WEB: www.gernatt.com
SIC: 2951 Asphalt paving mixtures & blocks

(G-3843)
STEEL CITY SALT LLC
13870 Taylor Hollow Rd (14034-9713)
PHONE.................................716 532-0000

Bill Schmitz, *Principal*
EMP: 6
SALES: 500K **Privately Held**
SIC: 1479 Rock salt mining

(G-3844)
ZEBROWSKI INDUSTRIES INC
4345 Route 39 (14034-9765)
PHONE.................................716 532-3911
Peter Zebrowski, *Chairman*
EMP: 8
SALES (est): 805.9K **Privately Held**
SIC: 3999 Chairs, hydraulic, barber & beauty shop

Colonie
Albany County

(G-3845)
COLONIE BLOCK AND SUPPLY CO
124 Lincoln Ave (12205-4917)
PHONE.................................518 869-8411
Fax: 518 456-6209
Thomas Gentile, *President*
Donald Countermine, *Vice Pres*
Marlene Countermine, *Treasurer*
EMP: 5
SQ FT: 5,000
SALES (est): 693.3K **Privately Held**
SIC: 3271 5032 Blocks, concrete or cinder: standard; masons' materials

(G-3846)
GERALD MCGLONE
17 Zoar Ave (12205-3531)
PHONE.................................518 482-2613
Gerald McGlone, *Owner*
EMP: 5
SALES (est): 423.6K **Privately Held**
SIC: 2679 Wallpaper

(G-3847)
SNYDERS NEON DISPLAYS INC
Also Called: Snyder Neon & Plastic Signs
5 Highland Ave (12205-5458)
PHONE.................................518 857-4100
Fax: 518 437-9285
Mary Elizabeth Orminski, *President*
Mark Orminski, *Vice Pres*
EMP: 6 **EST:** 1931
SQ FT: 5,800
SALES: 230K **Privately Held**
SIC: 3993 7389 Signs & advertising specialties; crane & aerial lift service

Commack
Suffolk County

(G-3848)
AVENTURA TECHNOLOGIES INC (PA)
48 Mall Dr (11725-5704)
PHONE.................................631 300-4000
Frances Cabasso, *CEO*
Boris Katzenberg, *Vice Pres*
Lavonne Lazarus, *Vice Pres*
Kevin A Lichtman, *Vice Pres*
Kevin Lichtman, *Vice Pres*
▲ **EMP:** 40
SQ FT: 40,000
SALES (est): 15.5MM **Privately Held**
WEB: www.ati247.com
SIC: 3577 3812 1731 Computer peripheral equipment; search & navigation equipment; voice, data & video wiring contractor; closed circuit television installation

(G-3849)
AVERY BIOMEDICAL DEVICES INC
61 Mall Dr Ste 1 (11725-5725)
PHONE.................................631 864-1600
Martin Dobelle, *CEO*
Antonio Martins, *CEO*
Claire Dobelle, *President*
George Lapinski, *Prdtn Mgr*
Rommel Caguicla, *Technical Mgr*
EMP: 16

SQ FT: 4,000
SALES (est): 1.7MM **Privately Held**
WEB: www.dobelle.com
SIC: 3841 Surgical instruments & apparatus

(G-3850)
BEYER GRAPHICS INC
30 Austin Blvd Ste A (11725-5747)
PHONE.................................631 543-3900
Fax: 631 543-3916
Jose Beyer, *CEO*
William Beyer Sr, *Ch of Bd*
Daniel Byer, *CFO*
John Amabile, *Manager*
Susan Rosen, *Manager*
▲ **EMP:** 99
SQ FT: 40,000
SALES (est): 35.9MM **Privately Held**
SIC: 2752 2791 2789 7374 Commercial printing, offset; typesetting; bookbinding & related work; computer graphics service

(G-3851)
BREN-TRNICS BATTERIES INTL INC
10 Brayton Ct (11725-3104)
PHONE.................................631 499-5155
Leo A Brenna, *President*
Kathleen Menikos, *VP Finance*
EMP: 7
SALES (est): 620K **Privately Held**
SIC: 3691 Batteries, rechargeable

(G-3852)
BREN-TRNICS BATTERIES INTL LLC
10 Brayton Ct (11725-3104)
PHONE.................................631 499-5155
Leo Brenna,
EMP: 20
SQ FT: 94,000
SALES (est): 2.4MM **Privately Held**
SIC: 3691 Alkaline cell storage batteries

(G-3853)
BREN-TRONICS INC
10 Brayton Ct (11725-3104)
PHONE.................................631 499-5155
Fax: 631 499-5504
SAI W Fung, *President*
Gregor Ritchie, *President*
Sylvain Lhuissier, *Vice Pres*
Leigh Straub, *Opers Staff*
Elliot Manaker, *Buyer*
◆ **EMP:** 200
SQ FT: 80,000
SALES (est): 56.2MM **Privately Held**
WEB: www.bren-tronics.com
SIC: 3691 3692 3699 Storage batteries; primary batteries, dry & wet; electrical equipment & supplies

(G-3854)
COMFORT CARE TEXTILES INC (HQ)
368 Veterans Memorial Hwy # 5 (11725-4322)
PHONE.................................631 543-0531
Scott Janicola, *Chairman*
Cynthia Langhauser, *Finance Dir*
▲ **EMP:** 40
SQ FT: 26,000
SALES: 6.5MM
SALES (corp-wide): 20MM **Privately Held**
SIC: 2295 Coated fabrics, not rubberized
PA: Jan Lew Textile Corp
368 Veterans Memorial Hwy # 5
Commack NY 11725
631 543-0531

(G-3855)
CORAL COLOR PROCESS LTD
50 Mall Dr (11725-5704)
PHONE.................................631 543-5200
Fax: 631 543-0264
Edward Aiello, *President*
Ediedie D Npolis, *Vice Pres*
EMP: 37
SQ FT: 20,000
SALES (est): 13.3MM **Privately Held**
SIC: 2752 Commercial printing, lithographic

(G-3856)
DREAMSEATS LLC
60 Austin Blvd (11725-5702)
PHONE.................................631 656-1066
Dave Fibo, *Accountant*
Scott Suprina, *Mng Member*
Desiree Cain, *Info Tech Mgr*
▲ **EMP:** 27
SQ FT: 10,000
SALES: 3.8MM **Privately Held**
SIC: 3429 Furniture hardware

(G-3857)
FOREST LABORATORIES LLC
500 Commack Rd (11725-5020)
P.O. Box 9025 (11725)
PHONE.................................631 858-6010
Fax: 631 462-2794
Richard Overt, *Vice Pres*
Lori J Nuckols, *Project Mgr*
James Hamilton, *Opers Staff*
Bob Gilmartin, *QC Mgr*
John Dibella, *Controller*
EMP: 130 **Privately Held**
WEB: www.frx.com
SIC: 2834 Pharmaceutical preparations; antibiotics, packaged; drugs acting on the respiratory system; thyroid preparations
HQ: Forest Laboratories, Llc
909 3rd Ave Fl 23
New York NY 10022
212 421-7850

(G-3858)
GASSER & SONS INC (PA)
440 Moreland Rd (11725-5778)
PHONE.................................631 543-6600
Fax: 631 543-6649
Richard F Gasser, *Chairman*
Jack Gasser, *Vice Pres*
Christine Valenti, *Finance Mgr*
Rod Bush, *Manager*
▲ **EMP:** 125 **EST:** 1916
SQ FT: 30,000
SALES (est): 22.2MM **Privately Held**
WEB: www.gasser.com
SIC: 3469 Metal stampings

(G-3859)
GEMINI PHARMACEUTICALS INC
87 Modular Ave Ste 1 (11725-5718)
PHONE.................................631 543-3334
Andrew Finamore, *President*
Mark Gaeta, *COO*
Joni Foley, *Senior VP*
Bianca Eulloqui, *Vice Pres*
Michael Finamore, *Vice Pres*
▲ **EMP:** 150
SALES: 36.4MM **Privately Held**
WEB: www.geminipharm.com
SIC: 2833 Pharmaceutical preparations; vitamins, natural or synthetic: bulk, uncompounded

(G-3860)
HAROME DESIGNS LLC
75 Modular Ave (11725-5705)
PHONE.................................631 864-1900
Alan J Cohen, *Mng Member*
EMP: 22
SALES (est): 1.2MM **Privately Held**
SIC: 2519 Household furniture, except wood or metal: upholstered

(G-3861)
HOBART CORPORATION
71 Mall Dr Ste 1 (11725-5728)
PHONE.................................631 864-3440
Fax: 631 864-4042
Paul Todoro, *Manager*
EMP: 24
SALES (corp-wide): 13.6B **Publicly Held**
WEB: www.hobartcorp.com
SIC: 3639 5084 7629 7699 Major kitchen appliances, except refrigerators & stoves; food product manufacturing machinery; electrical repair shops; restaurant equipment repair
HQ: Hobart Corporation
701 S Ridge Ave
Troy OH 45374
937 332-3000

(G-3862)
ISLAND AUDIO ENGINEERING
7 Glenmere Ct (11725-5607)
PHONE.................................631 543-2372
George Alexandrovich, *Owner*
EMP: 5 **EST:** 1972
SALES (est): 389.8K **Privately Held**
SIC: 3677 Inductors, electronic

(G-3863)
MALOYA LASER INC
65a Mall Dr Ste 1 (11725-5726)
PHONE.................................631 543-2327
Fax: 631 543-2374
Reto Hug, *President*
Marc Anderes, *Vice Pres*
Paul H Ug, *Human Res Dir*
Roger Hug, *VP Sales*
Michael Boccio, *Sales Executive*
EMP: 27
SQ FT: 22,500
SALES (est): 6.4MM **Privately Held**
WEB: www.maloyalaser.com
SIC: 3444 Mail (post office) collection or storage boxes, sheet metal

(G-3864)
MOBILE MINI INC
1158 Jericho Tpke (11725-3020)
PHONE.................................631 543-4900
Ryan Catarelli, *Branch Mgr*
EMP: 20
SALES (corp-wide): 508.6MM **Publicly Held**
WEB: www.mobilemini.com
SIC: 3448 Buildings, portable: prefabricated metal
PA: Mobile Mini, Inc.
4646 E Van Buren St # 400
Phoenix AZ 85008
480 894-6311

(G-3865)
RCE MANUFACTURING LLC
10 Brayton Ct (11725-3104)
PHONE.................................631 856-9005
Kathleen Menikos, *VP Finance*
SAI Fung, *Mng Member*
EMP: 5
SQ FT: 5,000
SALES (est): 384.1K **Privately Held**
SIC: 3672 Printed circuit boards

(G-3866)
ROPACK USA INC
49 Mall Dr (11725-5722)
PHONE.................................631 482-7777
Yves Massicotta, *CEO*
EMP: 10 **EST:** 2015
SALES (est): 1.8MM **Privately Held**
SIC: 2834 Pharmaceutical preparations

(G-3867)
RPF ASSOCIATES INC
Also Called: Signs By Tomorrow
2155 Jericho Tpke Ste A (11725-2919)
PHONE.................................631 462-7446
Fax: 631 462-5330
Ron Facchiano, *President*
Patricia Facchiano, *Controller*
EMP: 5
SQ FT: 1,250
SALES (est): 605K **Privately Held**
SIC: 3993 Signs & advertising specialties

(G-3868)
SETTONS INTL FOODS INC (PA)
Also Called: Setton Farms
85 Austin Blvd (11725-5701)
PHONE.................................631 543-8090
Fax: 631 543-8070
Joshua Setton, *CEO*
Morris Setton, *Exec VP*
Jeff Gibbons, *Plant Mgr*
Patrick Braddock, *Opers Mgr*
Alfredo Nunez, *Maint Spvr*
◆ **EMP:** 50
SQ FT: 55,000
SALES (est): 69.6MM **Privately Held**
WEB: www.settonfarms.com
SIC: 2034 2068 2099 2066 Dried & dehydrated fruits; nuts: dried, dehydrated, salted or roasted; food preparations; chocolate & cocoa products; candy & other confectionery products

Commack - Suffolk County (G-3869)

(G-3869)
SIMPLY NATURAL FOODS LLC
Also Called: Simply Lite Foods
74 Mall Dr (11725-5711)
PHONE...................................631 543-9600
Pat Buechler, *Purch Agent*
Norman Gross, *CFO*
Solomon Gluck, *Controller*
Abe Rach,
Russ Asaro,
▲ **EMP:** 50
SQ FT: 55,000
SALES (est): 19MM **Privately Held**
WEB: www.simplylite.com
SIC: 3556 2064 2066 Food products machinery; candy & other confectionery products; chocolate & cocoa products

(G-3870)
VEHICLE TRACKING SOLUTIONS LLC
152 Veterans Memorial Hwy (11725-3634)
PHONE...................................631 586-7400
John Cunningham, *President*
Glenn Reed, *COO*
Karen Cunningham, *CFO*
Alfred Napolitano, *VP Sales*
Matthew Neuwirth, *Manager*
EMP: 50
SQ FT: 17,000
SALES (est): 15.4MM **Privately Held**
WEB: www.vehicletrackingsolutions.com
SIC: 7372 Prepackaged software

(G-3871)
VITAMIX LABORATORIES INC
69 Mall Dr (11725-5727)
PHONE...................................631 465-9245
Michael Koschitz, *President*
John Greenough, *Facilities Dir*
Angelica Rodriguez, *Human Resources*
Amelia Connelly, *Manager*
Eric Haller, *Manager*
EMP: 25
SALES (est): 1MM **Privately Held**
SIC: 2833 Vitamins, natural or synthetic: bulk, uncompounded

(G-3872)
WICKERS SPORTSWEAR INC (PA)
Also Called: Wickers Performance Wear
88 Wyandanch Blvd (11725-4310)
PHONE...................................631 543-1700
Fax: 631 543-1378
Anthony Mazzenga, *CEO*
Diane Basso, *President*
Carol Mazzenga, *Principal*
Maryann D'Erario, *Treasurer*
▲ **EMP:** 7
SQ FT: 2,000
SALES (est): 1.1MM **Privately Held**
WEB: www.wickers.com
SIC: 2322 2341 Underwear, men's & boys': made from purchased materials; women's & children's underwear

(G-3873)
WINDOW RAMA ENTERPRISES INC
6333 Jericho Tpke Ste 11 (11725-2824)
PHONE...................................631 462-9054
John Wood, *Manager*
EMP: 5
SALES (corp-wide): 40.1MM **Privately Held**
WEB: www.windowrama.com
SIC: 3442 Window & door frames
PA: Window Rama Enterprises, Inc.
71 Heartland Blvd
Edgewood NY 11717
631 667-2555

Conesus
Livingston County

(G-3874)
EAGLE CREST VINEYARD LLC
Also Called: O-Neh-Da Vineyard
7107 Vineyard Rd (14435-9521)
PHONE...................................585 346-5760
Fax: 585 346-2322
Sally Brown, *Manager*

Bob Quinn, *Manager*
Elizabeth Goldstone,
▲ **EMP:** 5
SQ FT: 20,000
SALES (est): 525.5K **Privately Held**
SIC: 2084 0172 Wines; grapes

Congers
Rockland County

(G-3875)
ANKA TOOL & DIE INC
150 Wells Ave (10920-2096)
PHONE...................................845 268-4116
Fax: 845 268-2159
Agnes Karl, *Corp Secy*
Anton Karl Jr, *Vice Pres*
Anthony Pisello, *Engineer*
Patricia McCoy, *Manager*
▲ **EMP:** 35 **EST:** 1970
SQ FT: 6,400
SALES (est): 5.8MM **Privately Held**
WEB: www.ankatool.com
SIC: 3544 3089 Special dies & tools; injection molding of plastics

(G-3876)
APTARGROUP INC
Also Called: Aptar Congers
250 N Route 303 (10920-1450)
PHONE...................................845 639-3700
Raymond Scheire, *Project Mgr*
Kevin Hoover, *Engineer*
Sylvia Gonzalez, *Human Res Mgr*
Jim Henkel, *VP Sales*
Pascaline Desmarchelier, *Sales Dir*
EMP: 150 **Publicly Held**
SIC: 3586 Measuring & dispensing pumps
PA: Aptargroup, Inc.
475 W Terra Cotta Ave E
Crystal Lake IL 60014

(G-3877)
BEAN KING INTERNATIONAL LLC
36 N Route 9w (10920-2459)
PHONE...................................845 268-3135
Faustino Larios, *Mng Member*
Jose Moreno, *Mng Member*
▲ **EMP:** 10
SALES (est): 4MM **Privately Held**
SIC: 3523 Driers (farm): grain, hay & seed

(G-3878)
BOURGHOL BROTHERS INC
73 Lake Rd (10920-2323)
P.O. Box 80 (10920-0080)
PHONE...................................845 268-9752
Fax: 845 268-4562
Charles Bourghol, *President*
Alexander Bourghol, *Treasurer*
EMP: 7
SQ FT: 1,200
SALES (est): 1.1MM **Privately Held**
WEB: www.bourgholbrosjewelers.com
SIC: 3911 5944 Jewelry, precious metal; jewelry, precious stones & precious metals

(G-3879)
CHARTWELL PHARMA NDA B2 HOLDIN
77 Brenner Dr (10920-1307)
PHONE...................................845 268-5000
Kimberly Ezdebski, *Vice Pres*
EMP: 5
SALES (est): 229.7K **Privately Held**
SIC: 2834 Tablets, pharmaceutical

(G-3880)
CHARTWELL PHARMACEUTICALS LLC
77 Brenner Dr (10920-1307)
PHONE...................................845 268-5000
David I Chipkin, *COO*
Francis Ezdebski, *Vice Pres*
EMP: 75
SALES (est): 18.2MM **Privately Held**
SIC: 2834 Pharmaceutical preparations

(G-3881)
F M GROUP INC
100 Wells Ave (10920-2037)
PHONE...................................845 589-0102
Josef Feldman, *President*
Solomon Feldman, *Marketing Staff*
EMP: 10
SALES (est): 1.7MM **Privately Held**
WEB: www.functionalmaterials.com
SIC: 2899 2865 Ink or writing fluids; dyes & pigments

(G-3882)
HUDSON VALLEY COATINGS LLC
175 N Route 9w Ste 12 (10920-1780)
PHONE...................................845 398-1778
Joseph Montana,
EMP: 5 **EST:** 2008
SALES (est): 416.7K **Privately Held**
SIC: 3479 Coating of metals with plastic or resins

(G-3883)
KERRY INC
225 N Route 303 Ste 109 (10920-3001)
PHONE...................................845 584-3081
EMP: 7 **Privately Held**
SIC: 2099 Food preparations
HQ: Kerry Inc.
3330 Millington Rd
Beloit WI 53511
608 363-1200

(G-3884)
LINDEN COOKIES INC
25 Brenner Dr (10920-1307)
PHONE...................................845 268-5050
Fax: 845 268-5055
Paul L Sturz, *President*
Patricia Neuenhoff, *Vice Pres*
C Ronald Sturz, *Vice Pres*
Ronald C Sturz, *Vice Pres*
EMP: 50 **EST:** 1960
SQ FT: 33,000
SALES (est): 10.1MM **Privately Held**
WEB: www.lindencookies.com
SIC: 2052 Cookies

(G-3885)
STAR KAY WHITE INC (PA)
151 Wells Ave (10920-1398)
PHONE...................................845 268-2600
Fax: 845 268-3572
Walter Katzenstein, *Principal*
Rick Francolino, *Business Mgr*
Benjamin Katzenstein, *Vice Pres*
Richard Sroka, *Opers Staff*
Florence Larosa, *Purch Mgr*
◆ **EMP:** 65 **EST:** 1890
SQ FT: 45,000
SALES (est): 14.3MM **Privately Held**
WEB: www.starkaywhite.com
SIC: 2087 Flavoring extracts & syrups

(G-3886)
VALOIS OF AMERICA INC
250 N Route 303 (10920-1450)
PHONE...................................845 639-3700
Fax: 845 639-3900
Alex Thoedorakis, *President*
Pamela Moran, *Sales Associate*
Jennifer Diaz, *Office Mgr*
Lidiette Celado, *Manager*
Carl Lund, *Manager*
▲ **EMP:** 150
SQ FT: 3,500
SALES (est): 21.5MM **Publicly Held**
WEB: www.aptargroup.com
SIC: 3586 Measuring & dispensing pumps
PA: Aptargroup, Inc.
475 W Terra Cotta Ave E
Crystal Lake IL 60014

(G-3887)
VITANE PHARMACEUTICALS INC
125 Wells Ave (10920-2036)
PHONE...................................845 267-6700
Mohammed Hassan, *CEO*
Ezz Hamza, *President*
Deepali Bhole, *Manager*
▲ **EMP:** 24
SQ FT: 15,000

SALES: 7.4MM **Privately Held**
SIC: 2834 Pharmaceutical preparations

(G-3888)
WYNN STARR FLAVORS INC (PA)
225 N Route 303 Ste 109 (10920-3001)
PHONE...................................845 584-3080
Steven B Zavagli, *Chairman*
Mark Laslo, *Vice Pres*
Barry Friedson, *VP Mfg*
Gary Raff, *VP Finance*
Joe Arias, *Sales Associate*
EMP: 25
SQ FT: 12,000
SALES (est): 12MM **Privately Held**
WEB: www.wynnstarr.com
SIC: 2087 Flavoring extracts & syrups; beverage bases

Conklin
Broome County

(G-3889)
ARDAGH METAL PACKAGING USA INC
379 Broome Corporate Pkwy (13748-1513)
PHONE...................................607 584-3300
EMP: 126 **Privately Held**
SIC: 3411 Metal cans
HQ: Ardagh Metal Packaging Usa Inc.
600 N Bell Ave Ste 200
Carnegie PA 15106
412 923-1080

(G-3890)
CADMUS JOURNAL SERVICES INC
Also Called: Digital Printing
136 Carlin Rd (13748-1533)
PHONE...................................607 762-5365
Gordie Gottlieb, *Branch Mgr*
Gordon Gottlieb, *Manager*
EMP: 75 **Publicly Held**
SIC: 2752 Commercial printing, lithographic
HQ: Cadmus Journal Services, Inc.
2901 Byrdhill Rd
Henrico VA 23228
804 287-5680

(G-3891)
CBA GROUP LLC
33 Broome Corporate Pkwy (13748-1510)
P.O. Box 825, Binghamton (13902-0825)
PHONE...................................607 779-7522
Jeroen Schmits, *President*
Patrick J Gillard, *President*
Koen A Gieskes, *Vice Pres*
EMP: 1000
SALES (est): 4.7MM
SALES (corp-wide): 1.8B **Privately Held**
SIC: 3559 Electronic component making machinery
HQ: Francisco Partners, L.P.
1 Letterman Dr Bldg C
San Francisco CA 94129
415 418-2900

(G-3892)
DOLMEN
216 Broome Corporate Pkwy (13748-1506)
PHONE...................................912 596-1537
Steve Hanratty, *Principal*
EMP: 10
SALES (est): 400K **Privately Held**
SIC: 3999 Manufacturing industries

(G-3893)
E-SYSTEMS GROUP LLC (HQ)
Also Called: SMC
100 Progress Pkwy (13748-1320)
PHONE...................................607 775-1100
Diana Smith, *Transportation*
Francisco Rodriguez, *Production*
John Lion, *Buyer*
Richard Bullers, *Engineer*
Ken Overby, *Design Engr*
▲ **EMP:** 26 **EST:** 1952
SQ FT: 30,000

SALES (est): 6.2MM
SALES (corp-wide): 48.4MM **Privately Held**
WEB: www.smcplus.com
SIC: **2521** 2522 5045 3571 Wood office furniture; office furniture, except wood; computers, peripherals & software; computer peripheral equipment; electronic computers; partitions & fixtures, except wood
PA: Celeritas Group, Llc
6800 W 117th Ave
Broomfield CO 80020
303 465-2800

(G-3894)
INTERNATIONAL PAPER COMPANY
1240 Conklin Rd (13748-1407)
PHONE..................................607 775-1550
Don Bonualas, *Engineer*
David Davenport, *Sls & Mktg Exec*
Edward Badyna, *Manager*
EMP: 150
SALES (corp-wide): 21B **Publicly Held**
SIC: **2621** 2653 2656 2631 Paper mills; printing paper; text paper; bristols; boxes, corrugated: made from purchased materials; food containers (liquid tight), including milk cartons; cartons, milk: made from purchased material; container, packaging & boxboard; container board; packaging board; pulp mills
PA: International Paper Company
6400 Poplar Ave
Memphis TN 38197
901 419-9000

(G-3895)
IRVING WOODLANDS LLC
53 Shaw Rd (13748-1007)
PHONE..................................607 723-4862
Michael Senneway, *General Mgr*
Graham Smith, *QC Mgr*
Paul G Sherrard, *Treasurer*
EMP: 28
SQ FT: 63,350
SALES (corp-wide): 1.3B **Privately Held**
WEB: www.jdirving.com
SIC: **3441** Fabricated structural metal
HQ: Irving Woodlands Llc
1798 St John Rd
St John Plt ME 04743
207 834-5767

(G-3896)
NEWSPAPER PUBLISHER LLC
Also Called: Independent Baptist Voice
1035 Conklin Rd (13748-1102)
P.O. Box 208 (13748-0208)
PHONE..................................607 775-0472
Fax: 607 775-8563
Don Einstein, *President*
EMP: 10
SQ FT: 15,000
SALES (est): 540.1K **Privately Held**
WEB: www.automarketpaper.com
SIC: **2711** 2791 7011 Newspapers: publishing only, not printed on site; typesetting; bed & breakfast inn

(G-3897)
OCEAN STEEL CORPORATION
53 Shaw Rd (13748-1007)
P.O. Box 421 (13748-0421)
PHONE..................................607 584-7500
Hans W Klohn, *President*
Rod Macintosh, *General Mgr*
Brian Smith, *Regional Mgr*
Mark Friebel, *Safety Dir*
Steve Adams, *Credit Mgr*
EMP: 25
SALES (est): 6.7MM
SALES (corp-wide): 75.3MM **Privately Held**
SIC: **3317** Steel pipe & tubes
HQ: Ocean Steel & Construction Ltd
400 Chesley Dr
Saint John NB E2K 5
506 632-2600

(G-3898)
PERFORATED SCREEN SURFACES
216 Broome Corporate Pkwy (13748-1506)
PHONE..................................866 866-8690

Davis Fleming, *President*
Kurt Behrenfeld, *Info Tech Dir*
EMP: 20
SALES (est): 3.2MM **Privately Held**
SIC: **3443** Perforating on heavy metal

(G-3899)
RELX INC
Also Called: Lexisnexis
136 Carlin Rd (13748-1533)
PHONE..................................607 772-2600
Les Howard, *Vice Pres*
James Davern, *Facilities Mgr*
EMP: 110
SALES (corp-wide): 8.4B **Privately Held**
SIC: **2731** Book publishing
HQ: Relx Inc.
230 Park Ave Ste 700
New York NY 10169
212 309-8100

(G-3900)
S & T KNITTING CO INC (PA)
Also Called: Derby Fashion Center
1010 Conklin Rd (13748-1004)
P.O. Box 1512, Binghamton (13902-1512)
PHONE..................................607 722-7558
Richard Horner, *President*
Bridgette Harvey, *Admin Sec*
EMP: 27 EST: 1958
SQ FT: 65,000
SALES (est): 1.9MM **Privately Held**
SIC: **2253** 5651 Sweaters & sweater coats, knit; family clothing stores

(G-3901)
SAMSCREEN INC
216 Broome Corporate Pkwy (13748-1506)
PHONE..................................607 722-3979
Fax: 607 722-7128
Fintan D Fleming, *CEO*
Bill McMahon, *Plant Mgr*
William McMahon, *Research*
Ryan McCann, *Engineer*
Roger Doane, *Information Mgr*
▼ EMP: 28
SQ FT: 30,000
SALES (est): 7.3MM **Privately Held**
WEB: www.samscreen.com
SIC: **3429** Piano hardware

(G-3902)
TOOLROOM EXPRESS INC
Also Called: Four Square Tool
1010 Conklin Rd (13748-1004)
PHONE..................................607 723-5373
Richard Haddock, *President*
Shelly Haddock, *Manager*
▲ EMP: 55
SQ FT: 20,000
SALES (est): 11.2MM **Privately Held**
WEB: www.toolroomexpress.com
SIC: **3089** 3599 Injection molding of plastics; machine shop, jobbing & repair

(G-3903)
UI ACQUISITION HOLDING CO (PA)
33 Broome Corporate Pkwy (13748-1510)
PHONE..................................607 779-7522
Jean-Luc Pelissier, *President*
Keith O'Leary, *Vice Pres*
EMP: 2
SALES (est): 138.7MM **Privately Held**
SIC: **3559** Electronic component making machinery

(G-3904)
UI HOLDING COMPANY (HQ)
33 Broome Corporate Pkwy (13748-1510)
PHONE..................................607 779-7522
Jeroen Schmits, *President*
Koen A Gieskes, *Vice Pres*
Patrick J Gillard, *CFO*
EMP: 3
SALES (est): 138.7MM **Privately Held**
SIC: **3559** Electronic component making machinery

(G-3905)
UNIVERSAL INSTRUMENTS CORP (DH)
33 Broome Corporate Pkwy (13748-1510)
PHONE..................................800 842-9732
Jean-Luc Pelissier, *CEO*
Lynn Tilton, *CEO*

Keith O'Leary, *CFO*
Lisa D'Angelo, *Treasurer*
Jay Smith, *Controller*
◆ EMP: 200
SALES (est): 123MM **Privately Held**
WEB: www3.uic.com
SIC: **3559** Electronic component making machinery
HQ: Ui Holding Company
33 Broome Corporate Pkwy
Conklin NY 13748
607 779-7522

Constantia
Oswego County

(G-3906)
BRIDGEPORT METALCRAFT INC
567 County Route 23 (13044-2737)
P.O. Box 470 (13044-0470)
PHONE..................................315 623-9597
Fax: 315 623-9145
Donald Deitz Jr, *President*
Cristy Deitz, *Vice Pres*
EMP: 5 EST: 1965
SQ FT: 5,000
SALES (est): 550K **Privately Held**
WEB: www.bridgeportmetalcraft.com
SIC: **3469** Spinning metal for the trade

(G-3907)
MICHAEL P MMARR
Also Called: Mike's Custom Cabinets
1358 State Route 49 (13044-2769)
P.O. Box 91 (13044-0091)
PHONE..................................315 623-9380
Fax: 315 623-7416
Michael Marr, *Owner*
Michael P Marr, *Owner*
EMP: 9
SALES: 325K **Privately Held**
SIC: **2434** 5211 2541 Wood kitchen cabinets; cabinets, kitchen; wood partitions & fixtures

(G-3908)
UNITED WIRE TECHNOLOGIES INC
1804 State Route 49 (13044-2604)
P.O. Box 502, Cleveland (13042-0502)
PHONE..................................315 623-7203
James E Ransom, *Ch of Bd*
Paul Coates, *President*
Mike Schatzberg, *COO*
Donald Ransom, *Vice Pres*
Michael Ransom, *CFO*
▲ EMP: 15
SQ FT: 17,000
SALES (est): 2.4MM **Privately Held**
SIC: **3357** Nonferrous wiredrawing & insulating

Cooperstown
Otsego County

(G-3909)
BREWERY OMMEGANG LTD
656 County Highway 33 (13326-4737)
PHONE..................................607 286-4144
Simon Thorpe, *President*
Sean Bolger, *Store Mgr*
Phil Leinhart, *Opers Staff*
Bobbie Boehler, *QC Mgr*
Rick Debar, *Technical Mgr*
▲ EMP: 30
SQ FT: 35,000
SALES (est): 7.1MM **Privately Held**
WEB: www.ommegang.com
SIC: **2082** Malt beverages

(G-3910)
COOPERSTOWN BAT CO INC
118 Main St (13326-1225)
PHONE..................................607 547-2415
Fax: 607 547-6156
Timothy Haney, *Owner*
Kyle Liner, *Marketing Staff*
EMP: 5

SALES (corp-wide): 1.1MM **Privately Held**
WEB: www.cooperstownbat.com
SIC: **3949** 5941 Sporting & athletic goods; sporting goods & bicycle shops
PA: Cooperstown Bat Co Inc
Rr 28
Fly Creek NY 13337
607 547-2415

(G-3911)
DUVEL MORTGAGE USA INC
656 County Highway 33 (13326-4737)
PHONE..................................607 267-6121
Fax: 607 544-1801
Tom Gardner, *Executive*
EMP: 5 EST: 2015
SALES (est): 238.4K **Privately Held**
SIC: **2082** Malt beverages

(G-3912)
VANBERG & DEWULF CO INC
52 Pioneer St Ste 4 (13326-1231)
PHONE..................................607 547-8184
Fax: 607 547-8374
Don Feinberg, *Principal*
▲ EMP: 7
SALES (est): 444.3K **Privately Held**
SIC: **2082** Beer (alcoholic beverage)

Copake
Columbia County

(G-3913)
HIGH VOLTAGE INC
31 County Route 7a (12516-1214)
PHONE..................................518 329-3275
Fax: 518 329-3271
Stephen S Peschel, *Ch of Bd*
Michael Peschel, *Chairman*
James Grayson, *Vice Pres*
EMP: 37
SQ FT: 23,760
SALES: 10MM **Privately Held**
WEB: www.hvinc.com
SIC: **3826** Analytical instruments

Copake Falls
Columbia County

(G-3914)
ALUMISEAL CORP
Also Called: C T Hogan
118 N Mountain Rd (12517-5329)
PHONE..................................518 329-2820
Fax: 518 329-2822
James J Golden, *President*
Robert Callahan, *General Mgr*
Mary C Golden, *Corp Secy*
Gregg Miller, *Admin Sec*
EMP: 23 EST: 1951
SQ FT: 2,000
SALES (est): 2.1MM **Privately Held**
SIC: **3644** 1711 5169 Insulators & insulation materials, electrical; refrigeration contractor; chemicals & allied products

Copiague
Suffolk County

(G-3915)
ACTAVIS LABORATORIES NY INC
33 Ralph Ave (11726-1532)
PHONE..................................631 693-8000
Brenton Saunders, *CEO*
▲ EMP: 80
SALES (est): 7.7MM **Privately Held**
SIC: **2834** Pharmaceutical preparations; druggists' preparations (pharmaceuticals); medicines, capsuled or ampuled
HQ: Activis Llc
400 Interpace Pkwy
Parsippany NJ 07054
862 261-7000

Copiague - Suffolk County (G-3916)

(G-3916)
ACTION MACHINED PRODUCTS INC
1355 Bangor St (11726-2911)
PHONE..................................631 842-2333
Fax: 516 842-5902
Edward G Korndoerfer, *President*
Chris Derrig, *Sales & Mktg St*
Nancy Gallagher, *Controller*
EMP: 13 EST: 1967
SQ FT: 8,750
SALES (est): 1.6MM **Privately Held**
SIC: 3469 Machine parts, stamped or pressed metal

(G-3917)
AJES PHARMACEUTICALS LLC
11a Lincoln St (11726-1530)
PHONE..................................631 608-1728
Cheatan Patel, *Controller*
Asha Patel,
Jatendra Patel,
▼ EMP: 20
SQ FT: 25,000
SALES (est): 4.6MM **Privately Held**
SIC: 2833 5499 Vitamins, natural or synthetic: bulk, uncompounded; health & dietetic food stores

(G-3918)
ARCHITECTURAL FIBERGLASS CORP
1395 Marconi Blvd (11726-2814)
P.O. Box 116 (11726-0116)
PHONE..................................631 842-4772
Fax: 516 842-4790
Charles Wittman, *President*
EMP: 22
SALES (est): 2.1MM **Privately Held**
WEB: www.afcornice.com
SIC: 2295 5999 Varnished glass & coated fiberglass fabrics; fiberglass materials, except insulation

(G-3919)
ARGENCORD MACHINE CORP INC
10 Reith St (11726-1414)
PHONE..................................631 842-8990
Emilio Benenati, *Ch of Bd*
Gustavo Sanchez, *COO*
Steven Peltier, *CFO*
EMP: 7 EST: 1967
SQ FT: 10,000
SALES (est): 300K **Privately Held**
SIC: 3599 Machine shop, jobbing & repair

(G-3920)
ART PRECISION METAL PRODUCTS
1465 S Strong Ave (11726-3253)
PHONE..................................631 842-8889
Fax: 516 842-8897
Steven Triola, *President*
Sam Levine, *Business Mgr*
EMP: 10
SQ FT: 13,500
SALES (est): 1.8MM **Privately Held**
SIC: 3599 3469 3444 3544 Machine shop, jobbing & repair; spinning metal for the trade; sheet metalwork; special dies & tools

(G-3921)
ASTRA PRODUCTS INC
6 Bethpage Rd (11726-1413)
P.O. Box 479, Baldwin (11510-0479)
PHONE..................................631 464-4747
Fax: 631 242-1260
Mark Bogin, *President*
Jeffrey Bogin, *Vice Pres*
▲ EMP: 6 EST: 1979
SQ FT: 4,000
SALES: 3MM **Privately Held**
SIC: 3081 5162 Plastic film & sheet; plastics sheets & rods

(G-3922)
BALDWIN MACHINE WORKS INC
20 Grant Ave 2040 (11726-3817)
PHONE..................................631 842-9110
Kenneth Roblin, *President*
John Comporato, *Manager*
▲ EMP: 6
SQ FT: 6,000
SALES (est): 788.3K **Privately Held**
SIC: 3541 3545 Drill presses; machine tool accessories; drills (machine tool accessories); drilling machine attachments & accessories

(G-3923)
CHIVVIS ENTERPRISES INC
10 Grant St (11726-1504)
PHONE..................................631 842-9055
Fax: 516 842-7624
Floyd G Chivvis, *President*
Douglas J Chivvis, *Treasurer*
Yolanda Cudrado, *Office Mgr*
EMP: 10
SQ FT: 10,000
SALES (est): 1.6MM **Privately Held**
WEB: www.chivvisent.com
SIC: 3469 Metal stampings

(G-3924)
D & C CLEANING INC
1095 Campagnoli Ave (11726-2309)
PHONE..................................631 842-1114
Fax: 631 842-1114
Joan Estrella, *President*
EMP: 12
SALES (est): 842.4K **Privately Held**
SIC: 3635 Household vacuum cleaners

(G-3925)
ELWOOD INTERNATIONAL INC
Also Called: Elwood, William J
89 Hudson St (11726-1505)
P.O. Box 180 (11726-0180)
PHONE..................................631 842-6600
Fax: 631 842-6603
Stuart Roll, *Ch of Bd*
Richard Roll, *President*
EMP: 18
SQ FT: 37,000
SALES (est): 4.4MM **Privately Held**
WEB: www.elwoodintl.com
SIC: 2035 Seasonings & sauces, except tomato & dry

(G-3926)
ENGINEERED METAL PRODUCTS INC
10 Reith St (11726-1414)
PHONE..................................631 842-3780
Gustavo Sanchez, *President*
Michael Dantona, *Opers Mgr*
EMP: 9
SALES (est): 511.3K **Privately Held**
SIC: 3728 Aircraft parts & equipment; aircraft assemblies, subassemblies & parts

(G-3927)
GABILA & SONS MFG INC
Also Called: Gabila's Knishes
100 Wartburg Ave (11726-2919)
PHONE..................................631 789-2220
Fax: 718 384-8621
Elliott Gabay, *President*
Sophie Levy, *Chairman*
Pauline Santiago, *Controller*
EMP: 50 EST: 1921
SQ FT: 20,000
SALES (est): 8.2MM **Privately Held**
SIC: 2051 Bread, cake & related products; knishes, except frozen

(G-3928)
GABILA FOOD PRODUCTS INC
100 Wartburg Ave (11726-2919)
PHONE..................................631 789-2220
Elliot Gabay, *President*
EMP: 50
SALES: 7MM **Privately Held**
SIC: 2043 Cereal breakfast foods

(G-3929)
GLOBE GRINDING CORP
1365 Akron St (11726-2909)
PHONE..................................631 694-1970
Fax: 631 694-1886
Jeffrey Rapisarda, *President*
Robert Rapisarda, *Vice Pres*
Janette Rapisarda, *Office Mgr*
EMP: 10
SQ FT: 10,000
SALES (est): 2MM **Privately Held**
SIC: 3599 Machine shop, jobbing & repair

(G-3930)
H & M LEASING CORP
1245 Marconi Blvd (11726-2815)
PHONE..................................631 225-5246
Fax: 631 225-5293
Mark Field, *President*
Marc B Field, *President*
EMP: 6 EST: 1997
SALES (est): 670K **Privately Held**
SIC: 3444 Bins, prefabricated sheet metal

(G-3931)
HERMANN GERDENS INC
1725 N Strongs Rd (11726-2926)
PHONE..................................631 841-3132
Joseph Gerdens, *President*
EMP: 6
SALES (est): 762.5K **Privately Held**
SIC: 3444 Sheet metalwork

(G-3932)
HOLLYWOOD ADVERTISING BANNERS
Also Called: Hollywood Banners
539 Oak St (11726-3215)
PHONE..................................631 842-3000
Timothy Cox, *President*
EMP: 24
SALES (est): 1.3MM **Privately Held**
SIC: 2396 Fabric printing & stamping

(G-3933)
HOLLYWOOD BANNERS INC
539 Oak St (11726-3261)
PHONE..................................631 842-3000
Fax: 516 842-3148
Daniel F Mahoney, *Ch of Bd*
Mike Hartman, *Sales Staff*
Carmen Laren, *Manager*
Tony Connelli, *Graphic Designe*
EMP: 30
SQ FT: 22,000
SALES (est): 3.4MM **Privately Held**
WEB: www.hollywoodbanners.com
SIC: 2399 Banners, made from fabric

(G-3934)
JAF CONVERTERS INC
60 Marconi Blvd (11726-2098)
PHONE..................................631 842-3131
Fax: 516 842-3185
John Flandina, *CEO*
Rudy Ruiss, *Engineer*
Claudia Ruiz, *Human Resources*
Emily Flandina, *Admin Sec*
▲ EMP: 45
SQ FT: 10,000
SALES (est): 6MM **Privately Held**
WEB: www.jafstamp.com
SIC: 3993 Signs & advertising specialties

(G-3935)
LONG ISLAND TOOL & DIE INC
1445 S Strong Ave (11726-3227)
PHONE..................................631 225-0600
Fax: 631 225-0608
Richard Cohen, *Principal*
EMP: 5
SALES (est): 396.8K **Privately Held**
SIC: 3544 Special dies & tools

(G-3936)
LUBOW MACHINE CORP
1700 N Strongs Rd (11726-2930)
PHONE..................................631 226-1700
Fax: 631 226-8701
Myron J Lubow, *President*
▲ EMP: 19 EST: 1952
SQ FT: 20,000
SALES (est): 3.5MM **Privately Held**
SIC: 3569 5084 3548 3542 Assembly machines, non-metalworking; industrial machinery & equipment; welding apparatus; machine tools, metal forming type; machine tools, metal cutting type; miscellaneous fabricated wire products

(G-3937)
MALISA BRANKO INC
95 Garfield Ave (11726-3222)
PHONE..................................631 225-9741
Fax: 631 225-2437
Branko Malisa, *President*
Regina Malisa, *Corp Secy*
EMP: 12

SQ FT: 5,600
SALES (est): 1.3MM **Privately Held**
SIC: 3599 Machine shop, jobbing & repair

(G-3938)
MARK - 10 CORPORATION
11 Dixon Ave (11726-1902)
PHONE..................................631 842-9200
Fax: 631 822-5301
William Fridman, *President*
James McGurk, *Production*
Vera Friedman, *Marketing Staff*
Vera Sabov, *Manager*
EMP: 20
SQ FT: 12,000
SALES (est): 5.3MM **Privately Held**
WEB: www.mark-10.com
SIC: 3823 5084 8731 Electrolytic conductivity instruments, industrial process; industrial process control instruments; industrial machinery & equipment; electronic research

(G-3939)
NELL-JOY INDUSTRIES INC (PA)
8 Reith St Ste 10 (11726-1414)
PHONE..................................631 842-8989
Fax: 631 842-8040
Emilio L Benenati, *CEO*
Steven Peltier, *President*
Regina Booker, *General Mgr*
Ro Kwan, *Engineer*
Melissa Gavin, *Controller*
EMP: 32
SQ FT: 35,000
SALES (est): 3.4MM **Privately Held**
SIC: 3724 5088 Aircraft engines & engine parts; aircraft & space vehicle supplies & parts; aeronautical equipment & supplies

(G-3940)
NORJAC BOXES INC
Also Called: PATCO PACKAGING
570 Oak St (11726-3216)
PHONE..................................631 842-1300
Robert Reilly, *President*
William Mc Elwain, *Vice Pres*
Lenore Mc Knight, *Office Mgr*
EMP: 25
SQ FT: 30,000
SALES: 188.7K **Privately Held**
SIC: 2441 Boxes, wood

(G-3941)
NORTH EAST FINISHING CO INC
Also Called: Nefco
245 Ralph Ave (11726-1514)
PHONE..................................631 789-8000
Fax: 631 789-8094
Bill Dechirico, *President*
Donna Ward, *Corp Secy*
Joseph Ricchetti, *Vice Pres*
Chris Deangelo, *Manager*
EMP: 11
SQ FT: 7,500
SALES (est): 1.1MM **Privately Held**
SIC: 3471 Plating & polishing

(G-3942)
PIPER PLASTICS CORP
102 Ralph Ave (11726-1510)
PHONE..................................631 842-6889
Fax: 631 842-6870
Andrew Weiss, *Production*
Charles Weiss, *Vice Pres*
EMP: 29
SQ FT: 16,000
SALES (est): 4.9MM **Privately Held**
WEB: www.piper-plastics.com
SIC: 3089 3479 Molding primary plastic; coating of metals with plastic or resins

(G-3943)
PRECISION ELECTRONICS INC
1 Di Tomas Ct (11726-1943)
PHONE..................................631 842-4900
Fax: 516 842-4904
Dominick Scaringella, *President*
Joseph Corrigan, *Vice Pres*
Joseph A Whalen Jr, *Treasurer*
Rita Scaringella, *Admin Sec*
EMP: 15 EST: 1955
SQ FT: 13,000

SALES: 3.5MM Privately Held
WEB: www.precisionelect.com
SIC: 3677 3625 3612 Coil windings, electronic; electronic transformers; relays, for electronic use; voltage regulators, transmission & distribution

(G-3944)
PROTOFAST HOLDING CORP
182 N Oak St (11726-1223)
PHONE..................................631 753-2549
Fax: 631 753-2553
Marco Gil, President
EMP: 6
SQ FT: 5,600
SALES (est): 700K Privately Held
SIC: 3444 Sheet metalwork

(G-3945)
QUALITY CANDLE MFG CO INC
121 Cedar St (11726-1201)
PHONE..................................631 842-8475
Joseph Arnone, President
EMP: 10 EST: 1955
SQ FT: 6,000
SALES (est): 870K Privately Held
WEB: www.qualitycandlecompany.com
SIC: 3999 Candles

(G-3946)
REESE MANUFACTURING INC
16 Reith St (11726-1414)
PHONE..................................631 842-3780
Emilio Benenati, President
Terri Martin, Vice Pres
EMP: 8
SALES (est): 367.8K Privately Held
SIC: 3728 Aircraft body assemblies & parts

(G-3947)
RMW FILTRATION PRODUCTS CO LLC
230 Lambert Ave (11726-3207)
P.O. Box 573, Lindenhurst (11757-0573)
PHONE..................................631 226-9412
EMP: 3
SQ FT: 4,000
SALES: 2MM Privately Held
SIC: 3599 Custom Machine Shop

(G-3948)
SCAN-A-CHROME COLOR INC
555 Oak St (11726-3215)
PHONE..................................631 532-6146
Brian Geiger, President
EMP: 5
SALES (est): 697.5K Privately Held
SIC: 2759 7336 7389 Commercial printing; commercial art & graphic design;

(G-3949)
SEAL REINFORCED FIBERGLASS INC (PA)
19 Bethpage Rd (11726-1421)
PHONE..................................631 842-2230
Fax: 516 842-2276
Patrick Kaler, President
Kevin Kaler, Vice Pres
Timothy Kaler, Shareholder
Helen Kaler, Admin Sec
Laura Kaler, Admin Asst
EMP: 30 EST: 1961
SQ FT: 20,000
SALES: 3MM Privately Held
WEB: www.sealfiberglass.com
SIC: 3089 Plastic processing

(G-3950)
SEAL REINFORCED FIBERGLASS INC
23 Bethpage Rd (11726-1421)
PHONE..................................631 842-2230
Thomas Kaler, Branch Mgr
EMP: 9
SQ FT: 11,000
SALES (corp-wide): 3MM Privately Held
WEB: www.sealfiberglass.com
SIC: 3089 Plastic processing
PA: Seal Reinforced Fiberglass, Inc.
19 Bethpage Rd
Copiague NY 11726
631 842-2230

(G-3951)
SIGN SHOP INC
1272 Montauk Hwy (11726-4908)
PHONE..................................631 226-4145
Fax: 631 957-9338
John Prete, President
Bill Prete, Vice Pres
EMP: 6
SQ FT: 6,500
SALES: 500K Privately Held
WEB: www.thesignshopinc.com
SIC: 2759 7389 Screen printing; lettering & sign painting services

(G-3952)
STEEL CRAFT ROLLING DOOR
5 Di Tomas Ct (11726-1943)
PHONE..................................631 608-8662
Joan Palmieri, General Mgr
EMP: 10
SALES (est): 1.3MM Privately Held
SIC: 3325 Steel foundries

(G-3953)
SUNRISE DOOR SOLUTIONS
Also Called: Sunrise Installation
1215 Sunrise Hwy (11726-1405)
PHONE..................................631 464-4139
EMP: 5
SALES (est): 466.7K Privately Held
SIC: 3442 Mfg Metal Doors/Sash/Trim

(G-3954)
SWISS TOOL CORPORATION
100 Court St (11726-1287)
PHONE..................................631 842-7766
Fax: 631 842-7743
Anton Croenlein, President
Anna Croenlein, Corp Secy
EMP: 40
SQ FT: 20,000
SALES (est): 7.5MM Privately Held
WEB: www.swisstoolcorp.com
SIC: 3354 Aluminum extruded products

(G-3955)
TATRA MFG CORPORATION
30 Railroad Ave (11726-2717)
PHONE..................................631 691-1184
Fax: 631 691-1187
Joseph Tyminski, President
Lana Tyminski, Corp Secy
EMP: 15
SQ FT: 10,000
SALES (est): 2.5MM Privately Held
SIC: 3444 Sheet metalwork

(G-3956)
TII INDUSTRIES INC
1385 Akron St (11726-2932)
PHONE..................................631 789-5000
Fax: 516 789-5063
Thomas Smith, President
T Roach, Principal
Gerald Smith, QC Dir
Maribel Rivera, Sales Associate
EMP: 12 EST: 2013
SALES (est): 893.3K Privately Held
SIC: 3999 Manufacturing industries

(G-3957)
TOBAY PRINTING CO INC
1361 Marconi Blvd (11726-2898)
PHONE..................................631 842-3300
Fax: 516 842-3305
Robert Rogers, President
Chuck Williams Jr, General Mgr
Jean Rogers, Vice Pres
Bob Rogers, Financial Exec
Anthony Martino, Supervisor
EMP: 40
SALES (est): 6.1MM Privately Held
WEB: www.tobayprinting.com
SIC: 2732 2752 2796 2791 Book printing; commercial printing, lithographic; platemaking services; typesetting; bookbinding & related work

(G-3958)
TRIL INC
320 Pioxi St (11726-2132)
PHONE..................................631 645-7989
Sushe Zhang, Principal
Xiaoling Wang, Vice Pres
EMP: 9

SALES (est): 683.6K Privately Held
SIC: 3841 Surgical & medical instruments

(G-3959)
VIBRATION ELIMINATOR CO INC (PA)
15 Dixon Ave (11726-1902)
PHONE..................................631 841-4000
Fax: 631 841-0020
Stuart Levy, President
Pat Gagliano, Vice Pres
Don Warick Jr, Vice Pres
Kevin Tur, Manager
▲ EMP: 41 EST: 1933
SQ FT: 13,000
SALES (est): 6.3MM Privately Held
WEB: www.veco-ny.com
SIC: 3625 Noise control equipment

(G-3960)
VIN MAR PRECISION METAL INC
1465 S Strong Ave (11726-3210)
PHONE..................................631 563-6608
Catherine Leo, President
Anthony Leo, Vice Pres
EMP: 15
SQ FT: 6,000
SALES (est): 2.3MM Privately Held
WEB: www.vin-mar.com
SIC: 3444 Sheet metalwork

(G-3961)
W A BAUM CO INC
620 Oak St (11726-3217)
P.O. Box 209 (11726-0209)
PHONE..................................631 226-3940
Fax: 631 226-3969
William A Baum Jr, Ch of Bd
John C Baum Sr, President
James M Baum, Vice Pres
Michael Hayes, Vice Pres
Margaret Faber, Export Mgr
▲ EMP: 80 EST: 1916
SQ FT: 31,000
SALES (est): 11.7MM Privately Held
WEB: www.wabaum.com
SIC: 3841 Blood pressure apparatus

(G-3962)
WORLDWIDE ARNTCAL CMPNENTS INC (PA)
10 Reith St (11726-1414)
PHONE..................................631 842-3780
Fax: 516 842-8040
Steven Peltier, President
Carol Peltier, Treasurer
Jacob Weingarten, Accountant
Selwin Mohan, Bookkeeper
Henry Deutsch, Sales Mgr
▼ EMP: 19 EST: 1965
SQ FT: 10,000
SALES: 4MM Privately Held
WEB: www.aeronauticalcomponents.com
SIC: 3812 5088 Search & navigation equipment; aircraft equipment & supplies

(G-3963)
WORLDWIDE ARNTCAL CMPNENTS INC
Also Called: Beryllium Manufacturing
10 Reith St (11726-1414)
P.O. Box 407, Lindenhurst (11757-0407)
PHONE..................................631 842-3780
Steve Paltier, CFO
EMP: 6
SALES (corp-wide): 4MM Privately Held
WEB: www.aeronauticalcomponents.com
SIC: 3812 5088 Search & navigation equipment; transportation equipment & supplies
PA: Worldwide Aeronautical Components Inc.
10 Reith St
Copiague NY 11726
631 842-3780

Coram
Suffolk County

(G-3964)
BAYSHORE WIRE PRODUCTS CORP
480 Mill Rd (11727-4108)
PHONE..................................631 451-8825
Socratis Stavropoulos, President
EMP: 11
SQ FT: 11,000
SALES (est): 1.1MM Privately Held
SIC: 3496 Miscellaneous fabricated wire products

(G-3965)
G L 7 SALES PLUS LTD
Also Called: Land and Sea Trailer Shop
125 Middle Country Rd F (11727-4474)
PHONE..................................631 696-8290
George Applescott, Owner
EMP: 6
SALES (est): 532.2K Privately Held
SIC: 3715 Truck trailers

(G-3966)
HAMPTON TRANSPORT INC
3655 Route 112 (11727-4123)
PHONE..................................631 716-4445
Keith Lewin, President
EMP: 12 EST: 1993
SALES: 100K Privately Held
SIC: 2399 4119 Horse harnesses & riding crops, etc.: non-leather; local passenger transportation

(G-3967)
HUNT GRAPHICS INC
43 Pineview Ln (11727-5105)
PHONE..................................631 751-5349
Jeffrey Homire, President
EMP: 6
SALES: 1.5MM Privately Held
WEB: www.huntgraphics.com
SIC: 2752 7336 Commercial printing, lithographic; business form & card printing, lithographic; commercial art & graphic design

(G-3968)
ISLAND INDUSTRIES CORP
480 Mill Rd (11727-4108)
PHONE..................................631 451-8825
Fax: 631 451-8829
Socratis Stavropoulos, President
▲ EMP: 7
SALES (est): 1.3MM Privately Held
SIC: 3315 Wire & fabricated wire products

(G-3969)
NATURES VALUE INC (PA)
468 Mill Rd (11727-4108)
PHONE..................................631 846-2500
Oscar Ramjeet, CEO
Carl Ramjeet, COO
Joe Kramer, CFO
Tara Inzinna, Manager
▲ EMP: 143
SQ FT: 224,000
SALES (est): 61.7MM Privately Held
WEB: www.naturesvalue.com
SIC: 2834 Vitamin preparations

(G-3970)
NEW YORK FAN COIL LLC
7 Chesapeake Bay Rd (11727-2004)
PHONE..................................646 580-1344
Seth Rubin,
EMP: 7
SALES (est): 784.5K Privately Held
SIC: 3677 Electronic coils, transformers & other inductors

(G-3971)
NOTO INDUSTRIAL CORP
11 Thomas St (11727-3153)
PHONE..................................631 736-7600
John Noto, President
EMP: 8
SALES (est): 1MM Privately Held
SIC: 3535 Conveyors & conveying equipment

Coram - Suffolk County (G-3972) — GEOGRAPHIC SECTION

(G-3972)
PREMIUM MULCH & MATERIALS INC
482 Mill Rd (11727-4108)
PHONE..................................631 320-3666
Nicholas Sorge, *President*
EMP: 10
SALES (est): 91K Privately Held
SIC: 2499 Mulch or sawdust products, wood

(G-3973)
SHARONANA ENTERPRISES INC
52 Sharon Dr (11727-1923)
PHONE..................................631 875-5619
Orlando Vizcaino, *Principal*
EMP: 20
SALES: 1MM Privately Held
SIC: 2541 Store & office display cases & fixtures

(G-3974)
SUFFOLK INDUS RECOVERY CORP
Also Called: Pk Metals
3542 Route 112 (11727-4101)
PHONE..................................631 732-6403
Fax: 631 732-6917
Philip L Fava, *CEO*
Richard Smith, *Vice Pres*
Louis Fava, *Human Resources*
Leslie Combs, *Admin Asst*
EMP: 65 **EST:** 1934
SALES (est): 15.8MM Privately Held
WEB: www.pkmetals.com
SIC: 2611 4212 Pulp mills, mechanical & recycling processing; garbage collection & transport, no disposal

Corfu
Genesee County

(G-3975)
CORFU MACHINE INC (PA)
1977 Genesee St (14036-9656)
PHONE..................................585 418-4083
David Johnson, *President*
Dale Choate, *General Mgr*
Elaine Johnson, *Vice Pres*
Cary Dixson, *Director*
▲ **EMP:** 22 **EST:** 1978
SQ FT: 20,000
SALES (est): 4.6MM Privately Held
WEB: www.corfumachine.com
SIC: 3511 Hydraulic turbines

(G-3976)
DELAVAL INC
Also Called: Beck, Don
850 Main Rd (14036-9753)
PHONE..................................585 599-4696
Fax: 585 599-4698
Donald M Beck, *Branch Mgr*
John Donnelly, *Branch Mgr*
EMP: 18
SQ FT: 8,100
SALES (corp-wide): 6.4B Privately Held
WEB: www.donbeckinc.com
SIC: 3556 Milk processing machinery
HQ: Delaval Inc.
11100 N Congress Ave
Kansas City MO 64153
816 891-7700

(G-3977)
IDEAL BURIAL VAULT COMPANY
1166 Vision Pkwy (14036-9794)
PHONE..................................585 599-2242
George Tilley, *President*
EMP: 8 **EST:** 1953
SQ FT: 4,500
SALES (est): 1.2MM Privately Held
SIC: 3272 Burial vaults, concrete or pre-cast terrazzo

(G-3978)
KUTTERS CHEESE FACTORY INC
857 Main Rd (14036-9709)
PHONE..................................585 599-3693
Fax: 585 599-4103
Richard Kutter, *Ch of Bd*
EMP: 30 **EST:** 1971
SALES (est): 3.2MM Privately Held
SIC: 2022 Natural cheese

Corinth
Saratoga County

(G-3979)
CURTIS/PALMER HYDROELECTRIC LP
15 Pine St (12822-1319)
PHONE..................................518 654-6297
David Liebetreu, *Plant Mgr*
EMP: 9
SALES (est): 1.3MM
SALES (corp-wide): 5.7MM Privately Held
SIC: 3629 Power conversion units, a.c. to d.c.: static-electric
PA: Atlantic Power Limited Partnership
200 University Ave Suite 1301
Toronto ON M5H 3
416 773-7400

(G-3980)
EVERGREEN BLEACHERS INC
122 Maple St (12822-1026)
PHONE..................................518 654-9084
Louis R McArthur Jr, *Principal*
EMP: 9
SALES (est): 1.3MM Privately Held
SIC: 3827 Telescopic sights

(G-3981)
MANUF APPLD RENOVA SYS
Also Called: Mars
105 Mill St (12822-1090)
PHONE..................................518 654-9084
Fax: 518 654-2232
Louis McArthur, *President*
Sharon J Komsa, *Treasurer*
Doris Lohfink, *Admin Sec*
EMP: 9
SQ FT: 8,868
SALES (est): 630K Privately Held
WEB: www.bleacherman.com
SIC: 3599 7699 Machine shop, jobbing & repair; miscellaneous building item repair services

Corning
Steuben County

(G-3982)
CORNING CABLE SYSTEMS CR UN
1 Riverfront Plz (14831-0002)
PHONE..................................607 974-9000
Clay Franklin, *Marketing Staff*
Clark S Kinlin, *Manager*
Donna Gotshall, *Programmer Anys*
Gail Baity, *Director*
EMP: 7
SALES (corp-wide): 9.3B Publicly Held
SIC: 3357 Nonferrous wiredrawing & insulating
HQ: Corning Cable Systems Credit Union
800 17th St Nw
Hickory NC 28601
828 327-5290

(G-3983)
CORNING INCORPORATED (PA)
1 Riverfront Plz (14831-0002)
PHONE..................................607 974-9000
Fax: 607 974-8830
Wendell P Weeks, *Ch of Bd*
Thomas Appelt, *President*
James P Clappin, *President*
Martin J Curran, *Exec VP*
Clark S Kinlin, *Exec VP*
◆ **EMP:** 6300 **EST:** 1851
SALES: 9.3B Publicly Held
WEB: www.corning.com
SIC: 3229 3357 3661 3674 Glass fiber products; glass tubes & tubing; TV tube blanks, glass; fiber optic cable (insulated); telephone & telegraph apparatus; semiconductors & related devices

(G-3984)
CORNING INCORPORATED
Decker Bldg (14831-0001)
PHONE..................................607 974-9000
Jamie Houghton, *Branch Mgr*
EMP: 51
SALES (corp-wide): 9.3B Publicly Held
WEB: www.corning.com
SIC: 3229 Pressed & blown glass
PA: Corning Incorporated
1 Riverfront Plz
Corning NY 14831
607 974-9000

(G-3985)
CORNING INCORPORATED
1 Riverfront Plz (14831-0002)
PHONE..................................607 974-9000
Fax: 607 974-2065
Dick Jack, *General Mgr*
EMP: 45
SALES (corp-wide): 9.3B Publicly Held
WEB: www.corning.com
SIC: 3229 Pressed & blown glass
PA: Corning Incorporated
1 Riverfront Plz
Corning NY 14831
607 974-9000

(G-3986)
CORNING INCORPORATED
Hp-Ab-01-A9b (14831-0001)
PHONE..................................607 248-1200
Kirk Gregg, *Officer*
EMP: 48
SALES (corp-wide): 9.3B Publicly Held
SIC: 3229 3661 3674 3357 Glass fiber products; glass tubes & tubing; TV tube blanks, glass; telephone & telegraph apparatus; semiconductors & related devices; fiber optic cable (insulated)
PA: Corning Incorporated
1 Riverfront Plz
Corning NY 14831
607 974-9000

(G-3987)
CORNING INCORPORATED
1 W Market St Ste 601 (14830-2673)
PHONE..................................607 974-4488
Olajuwon Ogunsanwo, *Electrical Engi*
John Holliday, *Branch Mgr*
Katherine Funk, *Exec Dir*
Sheree Vail, *Bd of Directors*
EMP: 6
SALES (corp-wide): 9.3B Publicly Held
WEB: www.corning.com
SIC: 3229 Pressed & blown glass
PA: Corning Incorporated
1 Riverfront Plz
Corning NY 14831
607 974-9000

(G-3988)
CORNING INCORPORATED
1 Museum Way (14830-2253)
PHONE..................................607 974-8496
Sean Keenan, *Engineer*
Rashid Rahman, *Engineer*
Pete Knott, *Manager*
Jon Chester, *Manager*
Ryan Ehrhart, *Project Leader*
EMP: 20
SQ FT: 7,500
SALES (corp-wide): 9.3B Publicly Held
WEB: www.corning.com
SIC: 3211 Flat glass
PA: Corning Incorporated
1 Riverfront Plz
Corning NY 14831
607 974-9000

(G-3989)
CORNING INTERNATIONAL CORP (HQ)
1 Riverfront Plz (14831-0002)
PHONE..................................607 974-9000
Wendell P Weeks, *CEO*
John W Loose, *Ch of Bd*
James W Wheat, *President*
Kirk P Gregg, *Vice Pres*
Kenneth C KAO, *Vice Pres*
▼ **EMP:** 7
SQ FT: 15,000
SALES (est): 733.6MM
SALES (corp-wide): 9.3B Publicly Held
WEB: www.corningware.com
SIC: 3229 5945 Pressed & blown glass; ceramics supplies
PA: Corning Incorporated
1 Riverfront Plz
Corning NY 14831
607 974-9000

(G-3990)
CORNING OPTCAL CMMNCATIONS LLC
22 W 3rd St (14831-3114)
P.O. Box 2306, Hickory NC (28603-2306)
PHONE..................................607 974-7543
Tony Tripeny, *Manager*
Sherry Derose, *Manager*
EMP: 12
SALES (corp-wide): 9.3B Publicly Held
WEB: www.corningcablesystems.com
SIC: 3357 Communication wire
HQ: Corning Optical Communications Llc
800 17th St Nw
Hickory NC 28601
828 901-5000

(G-3991)
CORNING SPECIALTY MTLS INC
1 Riverfront Plz (14831-0002)
PHONE..................................607 974-9000
Wendell P Weeks, *Ch of Bd*
Jim Dennison, *Credit Mgr*
EMP: 6
SALES (est): 2.3MM
SALES (corp-wide): 9.3B Publicly Held
SIC: 3357 3229 3674 Fiber optic cable (insulated); glass fiber products; glass tubes & tubing; TV tube blanks, glass; semiconductors & related devices
PA: Corning Incorporated
1 Riverfront Plz
Corning NY 14831
607 974-9000

(G-3992)
CORNING VITRO CORPORATION
Also Called: Corning Consumer Products Co
1 Riverfront Plz (14830-2556)
PHONE..................................607 974-8605
Peter Campanella, *President*
John W Loose, *President*
Hayward R Gipson, *Senior VP*
Thomas E Blumer, *Vice Pres*
Dawn M Cross, *Vice Pres*
◆ **EMP:** 7000
SALES (est): 228.8MM
SALES (corp-wide): 9.3B Publicly Held
WEB: www.corning.com
SIC: 3229 3469 Pressed & blown glass; household cooking & kitchen utensils, metal
PA: Corning Incorporated
1 Riverfront Plz
Corning NY 14831
607 974-9000

(G-3993)
GATEHOUSE MEDIA LLC
Also Called: Leader, The
34 W Pulteney St (14830-2211)
P.O. Box 1017 (14830-0817)
PHONE..................................607 936-4651
Fax: 607 936-9939
Denny Bruen, *Principal*
Jeff Kovaleski, *Editor*
Becky Jenkins, *Bookkeeper*
Bill Blake, *Manager*
Heather Falkey, *Manager*
EMP: 85
SALES (corp-wide): 1.2B Publicly Held
WEB: www.the-leader.com
SIC: 2711 Newspapers
HQ: Gatehouse Media, Llc
175 Sullys Trl Ste 300
Pittsford NY 14534
585 598-0030

(G-3994)
HERFF JONES LLC
262 W 2nd St (14830-2438)
PHONE..................................607 936-2366
Virginia Caumlake, *Manager*
EMP: 25

SALES (corp-wide): 1.1B Privately Held
WEB: www.herffjones.com
SIC: 2741 Yearbooks: publishing & printing
HQ: Herff Jones, Llc
4501 W 62nd St
Indianapolis IN 46268
800 419-5462

(G-3995)
JOSEPH H NAVAIE
Also Called: Soul Full Cup
81 W Market St (14830-2526)
PHONE.....................607 936-9030
Joseph H Navaie, Owner
EMP: 11
SALES (est): 420K Privately Held
SIC: 2095 Roasted coffee

(G-3996)
KABRICS
2737 Forest Hill Dr (14830-3690)
PHONE.....................607 962-6344
Kathy Wilson, Owner
EMP: 8
SALES (est): 300K Privately Held
SIC: 2395 Embroidery & art needlework

(G-3997)
MULTIMEDIA SERVICES INC
11136 River Rd 40 (14830-9324)
PHONE.....................607 936-3186
Fax: 607 936-3187
Richard Bartholomew, President
Daniel Flatt, Vice Pres
Rose Flatt, Vice Pres
Belinda Wilcox, VP Finance
EMP: 21
SQ FT: 13,000
SALES (est): 5.4MM Privately Held
SIC: 2752 Commercial printing, lithographic

(G-3998)
PANELOGIC INC
366 Baker Street Ext (14830-1639)
PHONE.....................607 962-6319
Fax: 607 936-0619
George Welch, CEO
Douglas Brown, President
Jim Cunnigham, Engineer
Moza Kealec, Office Mgr
Rich Pavlick, Network Mgr
EMP: 32
SQ FT: 14,500
SALES (est): 9MM Privately Held
WEB: www.panelogic.com
SIC: 3625 Relays & industrial controls; control equipment, electric; electric controls & control accessories, industrial

(G-3999)
RISING SONS 6 BREWING CO INC
Also Called: Iron Flamingo Brewery
196 Baker St (14830-2074)
P.O. Box 1064 (14830-0864)
PHONE.....................607 368-4836
Nadia Mauer, Principal
Mark Mauer, Principal
EMP: 5
SQ FT: 5,400
SALES (est): 300.8K Privately Held
SIC: 2082 Malt beverages; ale (alcoholic beverage); porter (alcoholic beverage); stout (alcoholic beverage)

(G-4000)
RYERS CREEK CORP
Also Called: Mill, The
1330 Mill Dr (14830-9020)
PHONE.....................607 523-6617
Fax: 607 523-8260
Graham Howard, Manager
EMP: 20
SQ FT: 7,500
SALES (est): 2.2MM Privately Held
WEB: www.gotothemill.com
SIC: 2499 3999 Novelties, wood fiber; tobacco pipes, pipestems & bits

(G-4001)
SECTOR4VAPES
106 Bridge St (14830-1929)
PHONE.....................607 377-2224
Ryan Tong, Principal
EMP: 1

SALES (est): 94.4K Privately Held
SIC: 3999 Cigar & cigarette holders

(G-4002)
SIEMENS INDUSTRY INC
23 W Market St Ste 3 (14830-2600)
PHONE.....................607 936-9512
Fax: 607 936-9551
EMP: 9
SALES (corp-wide): 89.6B Privately Held
SIC: 3661 Telephones & telephone apparatus
HQ: Siemens Industry, Inc.
1000 Deerfield Pkwy
Buffalo Grove IL 60089
847 215-1000

(G-4003)
STORFLEX HOLDINGS INC
Also Called: Storflex Fixture
392 Pulteney St (14830-2134)
PHONE.....................607 962-2137
Fax: 607 962-7655
Timothy Purdie, Ch of Bd
Ralph Santell, Production
Connie Santell, Treasurer
▼ EMP: 152
SQ FT: 160,000
SALES (est): 41.7MM Privately Held
WEB: www.storflex.com
SIC: 3585 Lockers, refrigerated

(G-4004)
TOBEYCO MANUFACTURING CO INC
165 Cedar St (14830-2603)
PHONE.....................607 962-2446
Stephen Tobey, President
EMP: 12
SQ FT: 16,000
SALES (est): 800K Privately Held
SIC: 3599 Machine & other job shop work; machine shop, jobbing & repair

(G-4005)
VITRIX INC
Also Called: Vitrix Hot Glass and Crafts
77 W Market St (14830-2526)
PHONE.....................607 936-8707
Fax: 607 936-2488
Thomas Kelly, President
EMP: 6
SALES (est): 661.7K Privately Held
WEB: www.vitrixhotglass.com
SIC: 3231 5719 Products of purchased glass; glassware

Cornwall
Orange County

(G-4006)
ADVANCE D TECH INC
2 Mill St Stop 19 (12518-1265)
P.O. Box 38 (12518-0038)
PHONE.....................845 534-8248
Fax: 845 534-8255
Samuel Brach, President
Matty Wolner, Office Mgr
EMP: 10
SQ FT: 6,000
SALES: 1.5MM Privately Held
SIC: 3545 Diamond cutting tools for turning, boring, burnishing, etc.

(G-4007)
ASPIRE ONE COMMUNICATIONS LLC
245 Main St Ste 8 (12518-1564)
PHONE.....................201 281-2998
Laura Soles, Creative Dir
Steven Mandel,
EMP: 12
SQ FT: 20,000
SALES: 4MM Privately Held
SIC: 2721 8999 Magazines: publishing & printing; communication services

(G-4008)
COSTUME ARMOUR INC
Also Called: Christo-Vac
2 Mill St Stop 4 (12518-1265)
P.O. Box 85 (12518-0085)
PHONE.....................845 534-9120

Fax: 845 534-8602
Nino Novellino, President
Susan Truncale, Admin Asst
Susan Truncale, Admin Asst
EMP: 16 EST: 1962
SQ FT: 20,000
SALES (est): 1.9MM Privately Held
WEB: www.costumearmour.com
SIC: 2389 3999 Theatrical costumes; theatrical scenery

(G-4009)
MOMN POPS INC
13 Orr Hatch (12518-1727)
PHONE.....................845 567-0640
EMP: 25
SALES (est): 3.6MM Privately Held
SIC: 2064 2066 Mfg Candy/Confectionery & Chocolate/Cocoa Products

(G-4010)
NEW YORK STATE FOAM ENRGY LLC
2 Commercial Dr (12518-1484)
P.O. Box 175 (12518-0175)
PHONE.....................845 534-4656
Dennis Bender, General Mgr
Bryan Bender, Financial Exec
Jeanine Nicholson, Office Mgr
EMP: 8
SALES (est): 1.2MM Privately Held
SIC: 3086 1742 Insulation or cushioning material, foamed plastic; acoustical & insulation work

(G-4011)
NEWS OF THE HIGHLANDS INC (PA)
Also Called: Cornwall Local
35 Hasbrouck Ave (12518-1603)
P.O. Box 518 (12518-0518)
PHONE.....................845 534-7771
Fax: 845 534-3855
Constantine Eristoff, President
Anne Phipps Sidamon-Eristoff, Vice Pres
Henry J Sylvestri, Treasurer
EMP: 12
SALES (est): 871.9K Privately Held
WEB: www.newsofthehighlands.com
SIC: 2711 Newspapers, publishing & printing

(G-4012)
RANDOB LABS LTD
45 Quaker Ave Ste 207 (12518-2146)
P.O. Box 440 (12518-0440)
PHONE.....................845 534-2197
Jim Creagan, President
EMP: 3
SALES (est): 1.8MM Privately Held
SIC: 2834 Pharmaceutical preparations

Cornwall On Hudson
Orange County

(G-4013)
EXECUTIVE SIGN CORP
43 Boulevard (12520-1809)
PHONE.....................212 397-4050
Isaac Goldman, Owner
EMP: 6
SALES (est): 250K Privately Held
WEB: www.executivesigncorp.com
SIC: 3993 Signs & advertising specialties

Corona
Queens County

(G-4014)
BONO SAWDUST SUPPLY CO INC
Also Called: Bono Sawdust Co
3330 127th Pl (11368-1508)
PHONE.....................718 446-1374
Fax: 718 446-6715
EMP: 6 EST: 1931
SQ FT: 12,000
SALES (est): 750K Privately Held
SIC: 2421 2842 Mfg Sawdust & Shavings

(G-4015)
CAZAR PRINTING & ADVERTISING
4215 102nd St (11368-2460)
PHONE.....................718 446-4606
Herman Cazar, Owner
▲ EMP: 5
SALES (est): 320K Privately Held
SIC: 2752 Commercial printing, lithographic

(G-4016)
CORONA PLUMBING & HTG SUP INC
10466 Roosevelt Ave (11368-2328)
PHONE.....................718 424-4133
Apolinar A Ferreira, Ch of Bd
EMP: 5
SALES (est): 118.3K Privately Held
SIC: 3432 1711 Plumbing fixture fittings & trim; hydronics heating contractor

(G-4017)
CORONA READY MIX INC
5025 97th Pl (11368-3028)
PHONE.....................718 271-5940
Fax: 718 592-2650
Paul Melis, President
John Vasilantonakis, Vice Pres
Tommy Phillips, Plant Mgr
Lisa Kuchinski, Office Mgr
EMP: 10
SQ FT: 6,500
SALES (est): 1.5MM Privately Held
SIC: 3273 Ready-mixed concrete

(G-4018)
CT PUBLICATIONS CO
Also Called: Queens Times
4808 111th St (11368-2920)
PHONE.....................718 592-2196
James Lisa, President
EMP: 7
SALES (est): 240K Privately Held
WEB: www.queenstimes.com
SIC: 2711 Newspapers

(G-4019)
DELICIOUS FOODS INC
11202 Roosevelt Ave (11368-2624)
PHONE.....................718 446-9352
Berminder Chahal, President
EMP: 11
SALES (est): 1MM Privately Held
WEB: www.deliciousasianfood.com
SIC: 2038 2032 5812 Ethnic foods, frozen; ethnic foods: canned, jarred, etc.; caterers

(G-4020)
GREEN ZONE FOOD SERVICE INC
9906 Christie Ave 3a (11368-3149)
PHONE.....................917 709-1728
Jian Lin, CEO
Ryan Su, Vice Pres
EMP: 6
SQ FT: 2,000
SALES (est): 221.3K Privately Held
SIC: 2086 Carbonated beverages, nonalcoholic: bottled & canned; soft drinks: packaged in cans, bottles, etc.

(G-4021)
IMAGE IRON WORKS INC
5050 98th St (11368-3023)
PHONE.....................718 592-8276
Fax: 718 592-8786
Sigi Fredo Gomez, President
EMP: 8
SALES (est): 720K Privately Held
SIC: 3312 Hot-rolled iron & steel products

(G-4022)
JASON & JEAN PRODUCTS INC
104 Corona Ave (11368)
PHONE.....................718 271-8300
Chin Ho Kim, President
EMP: 10
SQ FT: 6,000
SALES (est): 710K Privately Held
SIC: 3999 Hair & hair-based products

Corona - Queens County

(G-4023)
KENAN INTERNATIONAL TRADING
Also Called: Moo Goong Hwa
10713 Northern Blvd (11368-1235)
PHONE.................................718 672-4922
Fax: 718 672-1501
Young Kim, *Owner*
▲ EMP: 5
SQ FT: 6,720
SALES (est): 535.6K Privately Held
WEB: www.kenandigital.com
SIC: 3444 3993 2759 5999 Awnings, sheet metal; signs & advertising specialties; commercial printing; awnings

(G-4024)
MAGELLAN AEROSPACE BETHEL INC
9711 50th Ave (11368-2740)
PHONE.................................203 798-9373
James Butyniec, *CEO*
Sergio Lugo, *Engineer*
David Toupin, *Engineer*
Randall Stewart, *Controller*
Tami Niemer, *Chief Mktg Ofcr*
▲ EMP: 125
SQ FT: 37,250
SALES (est): 19.4MM
SALES (corp-wide): 742.4MM Privately Held
WEB: www.ambel.net
SIC: 3728 3599 3724 Aircraft assemblies, subassemblies & parts; machine & other job shop work; aircraft engines & engine parts
PA: Magellan Aerospace Corporation
3160 Derry Rd E
Mississauga ON L4T 1
905 677-1889

(G-4025)
MAGELLAN AEROSPACE NY INC (HQ)
9711 50th Ave (11368-2740)
P.O. Box 847256, Boston MA (02284-7256)
PHONE.................................718 699-4000
Fax: 718 592-0722
N Murray Edwards, *Ch of Bd*
John Marcello, *Ch of Bd*
James S Butyniec, *President*
Henry David, *General Mgr*
Jo-Ann Ball, *Vice Pres*
▲ EMP: 200 EST: 1939
SQ FT: 205,000
SALES (est): 44MM
SALES (corp-wide): 742.4MM Privately Held
WEB: www.magellan.aero
SIC: 3728 3812 3769 3489 Aircraft parts & equipment; aircraft assemblies, subassemblies & parts; wing assemblies & parts, aircraft; gears, aircraft power transmission; search & navigation equipment; guided missile & space vehicle parts & auxiliary equipment; ordnance & accessories
PA: Magellan Aerospace Corporation
3160 Derry Rd E
Mississauga ON L4T 1
905 677-1889

(G-4026)
MILAN PROVISION CO INC
10815 Roosevelt Ave (11368-2538)
PHONE.................................718 899-7678
Fax: 718 335-3354
Sal Laurita, *President*
EMP: 20
SQ FT: 3,000
SALES (est): 2.3MM Privately Held
SIC: 2013 Sausages & other prepared meats

(G-4027)
NATURAL DREAMS LLC
5312 104th St (11368-3222)
PHONE.................................718 760-4202
Fax: 718 760-3664
Kaston Etal, *President*
EMP: 5
SALES (est): 334.8K Privately Held
SIC: 2515 Mattresses & bedsprings

(G-4028)
RUTCARELE INC
3449 110th St (11368-1333)
PHONE.................................347 830-5353
Alex Rovira, *CEO*
EMP: 8
SALES: 950K Privately Held
SIC: 3999 Manufacturing industries

(G-4029)
S S PRECISION GEAR & INSTR
4512 104th St (11368-2890)
PHONE.................................718 457-7474
Salvatore Silvestri, *President*
Michael Silvestri, *General Mgr*
EMP: 7
SQ FT: 2,500
SALES: 500K Privately Held
SIC: 3545 Machine tool accessories

(G-4030)
SOLAR SCREEN CO INC
5311 105th St (11368-3297)
PHONE.................................718 592-8222
Fax: 718 271-0891
Miles Joseph, *President*
Michelle Rubin, *Manager*
Gia Spencer, *Manager*
EMP: 9 EST: 1955
SQ FT: 10,000
SALES: 2MM Privately Held
WEB: www.solar-screen.com
SIC: 2591 Window shades

(G-4031)
UNITED STEEL PRODUCTS INC
3340 127th Pl (11368-1508)
PHONE.................................718 478-5330
Fax: 516 779-3202
Fred Budetti, *President*
Alfred Franza, *Vice Pres*
▲ EMP: 80
SQ FT: 22,000
SALES: 9.1MM Privately Held
WEB: www.unitedsteelproducts.com
SIC: 3442 1542 7699 Metal doors; commercial & office building contractors; door & window repair

(G-4032)
YONG JI PRODUCTIONS INC
10219 44th Ave (11368-2430)
PHONE.................................917 559-4616
Wanchang Yin, *President*
EMP: 20
SALES (est): 1.2MM Privately Held
SIC: 2311 Men's & boys' suits & coats

Cortland
Cortland County

(G-4033)
ACTUANT CORPORATION
Also Called: Cortland
44 River St (13045-2311)
PHONE.................................607 753-8276
John Stidd, *CEO*
Gladys Dougan, *Admin Asst*
EMP: 47
SALES (corp-wide): 1.2B Publicly Held
SIC: 3593 Fluid power cylinders, hydraulic or pneumatic
PA: Actuant Corporation
N86w12500 Westbrook Xing
Menomonee Falls WI 53051
262 293-1500

(G-4034)
BESTWAY ENTERPRISES INC (PA)
3877 Luker Rd (13045-9339)
PHONE.................................607 753-8261
Fax: 607 753-9948
Karl D Ochs, *CEO*
David Hayes, *Sales Mgr*
Doug McGuire, *Sales Mgr*
Steve Everle, *Sales Associate*
Jim Fish, *Sales Associate*
EMP: 50
SQ FT: 200,000
SALES (est): 57.7MM Privately Held
SIC: 2491 5031 Structural lumber & timber, treated wood; building materials, exterior

(G-4035)
BESTWAY OF NEW YORK INC
3877 Luker Rd (13045-9385)
PHONE.................................607 753-8261
Karl D Ochs, *President*
EMP: 1
SALES (est): 6.1MM
SALES (corp-wide): 52.9MM Privately Held
SIC: 2491 Structural lumber & timber, treated wood
PA: Bestway Enterprises Inc.
3877 Luker Rd
Cortland NY 13045
607 753-8261

(G-4036)
BFMA HOLDING CORPORATION
37 Huntington St (13045-3096)
PHONE.................................607 753-6746
Barry W Florescue, *Ch of Bd*
Sue Vanbuskirk, *Executive Asst*
EMP: 9
SQ FT: 3,000
SALES (est): 1.1MM Privately Held
SIC: 2841 5122 5131 5139 Soap: granulated, liquid, cake, flaked or chip; toiletries; sewing accessories; shoe accessories; display equipment, except refrigerated; packaging & labeling services

(G-4037)
BORGWARNER MORSE TEC LLC
3690 Luker Rd (13045-9397)
PHONE.................................607 257-6700
Roger Wood, *Branch Mgr*
EMP: 90
SALES (corp-wide): 9B Publicly Held
WEB: www.borgwarnermorsetec.com
SIC: 3714 Motor vehicle parts & accessories
HQ: Borgwarner Morse Tec Llc
800 Warren Rd
Ithaca NY 14850
607 257-6700

(G-4038)
BP DIGITAL IMAGING LLC
Also Called: Carbon Copies
87 Main St (13045-2610)
P.O. Box 5396 (13045-5396)
PHONE.................................607 753-0022
Fax: 607 753-0026
Betsy Allen, *Mng Member*
Jeff Czimmer, *Technology*
Jim Coon, *Graphic Designe*
Paul Allen,
▼ EMP: 8
SQ FT: 1,800
SALES: 500K Privately Held
SIC: 2752 Photolithographic printing

(G-4039)
CORTLAND CABLE COMPANY INC
44 River St (13045-2335)
P.O. Box 330 (13045-0330)
PHONE.................................607 753-8276
John Stidd, *CEO*
Neil McAdam, *Managing Dir*
John Cobb, *Vice Pres*
Richard Nye, *Vice Pres*
Steve Davis, *Plant Mgr*
◆ EMP: 50
SALES (est): 49.7K
SALES (corp-wide): 1.1B Publicly Held
WEB: www.cortlandcable.com
SIC: 3496 3357 2823 Cable, uninsulated wire: made from purchased wire; nonferrous wiredrawing & insulating; cellulosic manmade fibers
HQ: Cortland Company, Inc.
44 River St
Cortland NY 13045

(G-4040)
CORTLAND COMPANY INC (HQ)
44 River St (13045-2311)
P.O. Box 330 (13045-0330)
PHONE.................................607 753-8276
Fax: 607 753-3183
John A Stidd, *CEO*
John Thomas, *President*
Sam Bull, *Vice Pres*
John G Greco, *Vice Pres*
Stephen A Breen, *CFO*
EMP: 88
SALES (est): 35.6MM
SALES (corp-wide): 1.1B Publicly Held
WEB: www.actuant.com
SIC: 2298 5063 Ropes & fiber cables; wire & cable; electronic wire & cable
PA: Actuant Corporation
N86w12500 Westbrook Xing
Menomonee Falls WI 53051
262 293-1500

(G-4041)
CORTLAND LINE MFG LLC
3736 Kellogg Rd (13045-8818)
PHONE.................................607 756-2851
Randy Brown, *President*
Ralph Canfield, *CFO*
EMP: 30
SALES (est): 2MM Privately Held
SIC: 3949 Fishing equipment

(G-4042)
CORTLAND MACHINE AND TOOL CO
60 Grant St (13045-2173)
P.O. Box 27 (13045-0027)
PHONE.................................607 756-5852
Fax: 607 756-5985
Stan Pierce, *President*
Debbie Hoyt, *Human Res Mgr*
Scott Rogers, *Technology*
EMP: 11 EST: 1913
SQ FT: 10,000
SALES: 900K Privately Held
SIC: 3599 Machine shop, jobbing & repair

(G-4043)
CORTLAND PLASTICS INTL LLC
211 S Main St (13045)
PHONE.................................607 662-0120
David Kievit, *General Mgr*
Harlen Desotell, *Prdtn Mgr*
Fritz Kern, *Engineer*
Kay Breed, *Controller*
Christine Leyburn, *Office Mgr*
EMP: 26
SALES (est): 5.6MM Privately Held
SIC: 3085 Plastics bottles

(G-4044)
CORTLAND READY MIX INC
6 Locust Ave Ofc Rte 13 (13045-1412)
PHONE.................................607 753-3063
Fax: 607 753-8719
Michael Saunders, *President*
Jim Giddings, *Plant Mgr*
Dick Maloney, *Controller*
EMP: 12 EST: 1944
SQ FT: 4,000
SALES: 200K
SALES (corp-wide): 8.7MM Privately Held
WEB: www.saundersconcrete.com
SIC: 3273 Ready-mixed concrete
PA: Saunders Concrete Co. Inc.
5126 S Onondaga Rd
Nedrow NY 13120
315 469-3217

(G-4045)
CORTLAND STANDARD PRINTING CO
110 Main St (13045-6607)
P.O. Box 5548 (13045-5548)
PHONE.................................607 756-5665
Fax: 607 756-5665
Kevin R Howe, *President*
Kevin Conlon, *Editor*
Scott Conroe, *Editor*
Ann G Howe, *Vice Pres*
Rachel Costanpino, *Human Res Mgr*
EMP: 65 EST: 1867
SQ FT: 15,000

SALES (est): 4.2MM **Privately Held**
WEB: www.cortlandstandard.com
SIC: **2711** 2791 Newspapers; typesetting

(G-4046)
COUTURE LOGGING INC
3060 State Route 13 (13045-9743)
PHONE..................................607 753-6445
Lisa Couture, *President*
Bruno Couture, *Vice Pres*
EMP: 9
SQ FT: 5,100
SALES (est): 721.6K **Privately Held**
SIC: **2411** Logging camps & contractors

(G-4047)
CROWN INDUSTRIAL
839 State Route 13 (13045-8997)
PHONE..................................607 745-8709
Kevin Patterson, *General Mgr*
▲ EMP: 7
SALES (est): 1MM **Privately Held**
SIC: **3462** Gear & chain forgings

(G-4048)
FORKEY CONSTRUCTION & FABG INC
3690 Luker Rd (13045-9397)
PHONE..................................607 849-4879
Fax: 607 849-4882
Charles Forkey, *President*
Borey Bliss, *Manager*
EMP: 30
SQ FT: 27,000
SALES (est): 7.9MM **Privately Held**
SIC: **3469** Machine parts, stamped or pressed metal

(G-4049)
GRAPH-TEX INC
46 Elm St (13045-2225)
P.O. Box 109 (13045-0109)
PHONE..................................607 756-7791
Brent Riley, *President*
Donna Lee, *General Mgr*
Shawn Riley, *Director*
EMP: 10
SALES (corp-wide): 3.1MM **Privately Held**
WEB: www.graph-tex.com
SIC: **2759** Screen printing
PA: Graph-Tex, Inc.
    24 Court St
    Cortland NY 13045
    607 756-1875

(G-4050)
GRAPH-TEX INC (PA)
24 Court St (13045-2685)
P.O. Box 109 (13045-0109)
PHONE..................................607 756-1875
Fax: 607 756-5479
Brent Riley, *President*
Mindy Myers, *Store Mgr*
Donna Lee, *Office Mgr*
EMP: 8
SQ FT: 3,600
SALES (est): 3.1MM **Privately Held**
WEB: www.graph-tex.com
SIC: **2759** 5941 5091 Screen printing; sporting goods & bicycle shops; sporting & recreation goods

(G-4051)
GRAPHICS PLUS PRINTING INC
215 S Main St (13045-3266)
PHONE..................................607 299-0500
Fax: 607 753-0115
Robert Eckard, *President*
Patty Batsford, *Marketing Staff*
EMP: 24
SQ FT: 47,000
SALES (est): 5.6MM **Privately Held**
SIC: **2752** 2759 7336 Commercial printing, offset; screen printing; art design services

(G-4052)
GUTCHESS LUMBER CO INC (PA)
890 Mclean Rd (13045-9293)
PHONE..................................607 753-3393
Fax: 607 753-6234
Gary H Gutchess, *Ch of Bd*
Matthew F Gutchess, *President*
Andrew Middleton, *Plant Mgr*
Jeffrey D Breed, *Treasurer*
Madalyn Kalning, *Controller*
◆ EMP: 250 EST: 1904
SQ FT: 3,500
SALES: 150MM **Privately Held**
WEB: www.gutchess.com
SIC: **2421** 2426 Building & structural materials, wood; lumber, hardwood dimension

(G-4053)
ITHACA PREGANCY CENTER
4 Church St (13045-2710)
PHONE..................................607 753-3909
EMP: 5
SALES (corp-wide): 183.1K **Privately Held**
SIC: **2835** Pregnancy test kits
PA: Ithaca Pregancy Center
    210 W Green St
    Ithaca NY 14850
    607 273-4673

(G-4054)
JACKSONS WELDING LLC
Also Called: Jacksons Welding Service & Sls
215 N Homer Ave (13045)
PHONE..................................607 756-2725
EMP: 7
SQ FT: 8,000
SALES (est): 252.2K **Privately Held**
SIC: **7692** 5084 1799 Welding Repair Whol Industrial Equipment Trade Contractor

(G-4055)
JM MURRAY CENTER INC (PA)
823 State Route 13 Ste 1 (13045-8731)
PHONE..................................607 756-9913
Floyd Moon, *President*
Jerry Gebhard, *General Mgr*
Judy O Brien, *Vice Pres*
Dale Davis, *Vice Pres*
Gerald Gebhard, *Vice Pres*
▲ EMP: 110
SQ FT: 110,000
SALES: 17.8MM **Privately Held**
WEB: www.jmmurray.com
SIC: **2673** 3843 7349 Bags: plastic, laminated & coated; dental equipment & supplies; building maintenance services

(G-4056)
JM MURRAY CENTER INC
4057 West Rd (13045-1637)
PHONE..................................607 756-0246
Judy O'Brien, *Branch Mgr*
EMP: 110
SALES (corp-wide): 17.8MM **Privately Held**
WEB: www.jmmurray.com
SIC: **2673** 3843 7349 Bags: plastic, laminated & coated; dental equipment & supplies; building maintenance services
PA: J.M. Murray Center, Inc.
    823 State Route 13 Ste 1
    Cortland NY 13045
    607 756-9913

(G-4057)
MARIETTA CORPORATION (HQ)
37 Huntington St (13045-3098)
P.O. Box 5250 (13045-5250)
PHONE..................................607 753-6746
Fax: 607 756-0648
Donald W Sturdivant, *CEO*
Eileen Anderson, *COO*
Chris Calhoun, *Senior VP*
Beth Corl, *Senior VP*
Ray Ferretti, *Senior VP*
▲ EMP: 500
SQ FT: 550,000
SALES (est): 398.5MM
SALES (corp-wide): 296.5MM **Privately Held**
SIC: **2844** 2834 2541 Cosmetic preparations; toilet preparations; druggists' preparations (pharmaceuticals); store & office display cases & fixtures
PA: Marietta Holding Corporation, Inc.
    37 Huntington St
    Cortland NY 13045
    607 753-6746

(G-4058)
MARIETTA CORPORATION
106 Central Ave (13045)
PHONE..................................607 753-0982
Greg Rudy, *Branch Mgr*
EMP: 350
SALES (corp-wide): 296.5MM **Privately Held**
SIC: **2841** 7389 Soap: granulated, liquid, cake, flaked or chip; packaging & labeling services
HQ: Marietta Corporation
    37 Huntington St
    Cortland NY 13045
    607 753-6746

(G-4059)
PALL CORPORATION
Also Called: Pall Trinity Micro
3643 State Route 281 (13045-3591)
P.O. Box 2030 (13045-0930)
PHONE..................................607 753-6041
Fax: 607 753-9653
David Berger, *President*
Steven Chisolm, *Vice Pres*
Douglas Conn, *Vice Pres*
Greg Walter, *Mfg Mgr*
Carl Boise, *Opers Staff*
EMP: 750
SALES (corp-wide): 16.8B **Publicly Held**
WEB: www.pall.com
SIC: **3842** 3841 3569 3599 Surgical appliances & supplies; surgical & medical instruments; IV transfusion apparatus; filters; filters, general line: industrial; filter elements, fluid, hydraulic line; air intake filters, internal combustion engine, except auto; gasoline filters, internal combustion engine, except auto; oil filters, internal combustion engine, except automotive; filters: oil, fuel & air, motor vehicle; perforated metal, stamped
HQ: Pall Corporation
    25 Harbor Park Dr
    Port Washington NY 11050
    516 484-5400

(G-4060)
PALL CORPORATION
3669 State Route 281 (13045-8957)
PHONE..................................607 753-6041
Eric Edlund, *Project Mgr*
Jim Bair, *Research*
Angela Griffin, *Engineer*
Ruth A Wood, *Engineer*
Brian Palermo, *Design Engr*
EMP: 750
SALES (corp-wide): 16.8B **Publicly Held**
WEB: www.pall.com
SIC: **3842** Surgical appliances & supplies
HQ: Pall Corporation
    25 Harbor Park Dr
    Port Washington NY 11050
    516 484-5400

(G-4061)
PALL CORPORATION
Also Called: Pall's Advnced Sprtons Systems
839 State Route 13 Ste 12 (13045-8998)
P.O. Box 2030 (13045-0930)
PHONE..................................607 753-6041
Carl Boise, *Principal*
Charles Casterline, *Mfg Staff*
Sandy Conway, *Buyer*
Lance Benjamin, *Engineer*
Kathy Mosier, *Engineer*
EMP: 750
SALES (corp-wide): 16.8B **Publicly Held**
SIC: **3842** Surgical appliances & supplies
HQ: Pall Corporation
    25 Harbor Park Dr
    Port Washington NY 11050
    516 484-5400

(G-4062)
PAUL BUNYAN PRODUCTS INC
890 Mclean Rd (13045-9393)
PHONE..................................315 696-6164
Fax: 315 696-6649
Judith Greene, *President*
Margaret Hudson, *Corp Secy*
William Oustad, *Vice Pres*
EMP: 20
SQ FT: 36,000
SALES (est): 3.8MM **Privately Held**
SIC: **2448** Pallets, wood

(G-4063)
PRECISION EFORMING LLC
839 State Route 13 Ste 1 (13045-8999)
PHONE..................................607 753-7730
Jodi Marie, *Export Mgr*
Scott Selbach,
Doug Ondrack,
EMP: 13
SQ FT: 7,000
SALES (est): 1.8MM **Privately Held**
WEB: www.precisioneforming.com
SIC: **3542** Electroforming machines

(G-4064)
PYROTEK INCORPORATED
641 State Route 13 (13045-8836)
PHONE..................................607 756-3050
Thomas Howard, *Manager*
Dave Quilter, *Manager*
EMP: 97
SALES (corp-wide): 582MM **Privately Held**
SIC: **3365** Aluminum foundries
PA: Pyrotek Incorporated
    705 W 1st Ave
    Spokane WA 99201
    509 926-6212

(G-4065)
QUADRA FLEX CORP
Also Called: Quadra Flex Quality Labels
1955 State Route 13 (13045-9619)
P.O. Box 286 (13045-0286)
PHONE..................................607 758-7066
Fax: 607 758-4943
David Masri, *President*
Christopher Meddaugh, *General Mgr*
Thresa Meddaugh, *Treasurer*
Ben Masri, *Director*
Elizabeth Masri, *Admin Sec*
EMP: 5
SQ FT: 2,500
SALES: 700K **Privately Held**
WEB: www.quadraflex.com
SIC: **2759** 2679 Commercial printing; labels, paper: made from purchased material

(G-4066)
REDDING-HUNTER INC
Also Called: Redding Reloading Equipment
1089 Starr Rd (13045-8806)
PHONE..................................607 753-3331
Fax: 607 756-8445
Richard W Beebe, *President*
Robin Sharpless, *VP Sales*
▼ EMP: 25
SQ FT: 15,000
SALES (est): 5MM **Privately Held**
WEB: www.redding-reloading.com
SIC: **3484** 3599 Small arms; machine shop, jobbing & repair

(G-4067)
SAUNDERS CONCRETE CO INC
Also Called: Cortland Ready Mix
6 Locust Ave (13045-1412)
PHONE..................................607 756-7905
Wilbur Hayes, *Manager*
EMP: 15
SALES (corp-wide): 8.7MM **Privately Held**
SIC: **3273** Ready-mixed concrete
PA: Saunders Concrete Co. Inc.
    5126 S Onondaga Rd
    Nedrow NY 13120
    315 469-3217

(G-4068)
SELLCO INDUSTRIES INC
58 Grant St (13045-2174)
P.O. Box 70 (13045-0070)
PHONE..................................607 756-7594
Fax: 607 756-7511
George Delorenzo Jr, *President*
Marilyn De Lorenzo, *Vice Pres*
EMP: 20
SQ FT: 19,000
SALES (est): 2.5MM **Privately Held**
WEB: www.sellcoinc.com
SIC: **3993** 2782 2399 2396 Signs & advertising specialties; looseleaf binders & devices; banners, made from fabric; automotive & apparel trimmings

Cortland - Cortland County (G-4069)

(G-4069)
SUIT-KOTE CORPORATION (PA)
1911 Lorings Crossing Rd (13045-9775)
PHONE 607 753-1100
Frank H Suits Jr, *President*
Steve Sanfilippo, *Regional Mgr*
Scott Harris, *Vice Pres*
Dan Quinlan, *Vice Pres*
Steve Rebman, *Vice Pres*
◆ EMP: 200
SQ FT: 10,000
SALES (est): 226MM **Privately Held**
WEB: www.suit-kote.com
SIC: **2951** 1611 Asphalt & asphaltic paving mixtures (not from refineries); highway & street paving contractor

(G-4070)
TECHNOLOGIES APPLICATION LLC
Also Called: Glyph Production Technologies
3736 Kellogg Rd (13045-8818)
PHONE 607 275-0345
Liran Shathi,
Eyal Shathi,
◆ EMP: 14
SQ FT: 15,000
SALES (est): 7MM **Privately Held**
WEB: www.glyphtech.com
SIC: **3572** Computer storage devices

(G-4071)
WILBEDONE INC
1133 State Route 222 (13045-9352)
PHONE 607 756-8813
Fax: 607 756-8818
Thomas L Beames, *President*
Diana Simpson, *Human Resources*
Rusty Perkins, *Office Mgr*
David Motyl, *Manager*
EMP: 33
SQ FT: 18,000
SALES (est): 4.8MM **Privately Held**
WEB: www.wilbedone.com
SIC: **2541** Counter & sink tops

Cortlandt Manor
Westchester County

(G-4072)
ABLE INDUSTRIES INC
Also Called: Able Wire Co
18 Brook Ln (10567-6502)
PHONE 914 739-5685
Warren Button, *President*
Louis Malano, *Sales Staff*
Patricia Button, *Admin Sec*
▲ EMP: 12 EST: 1980
SQ FT: 18,000
SALES (est): 1.1MM **Privately Held**
WEB: www.ablewire.com
SIC: **3315** Wire, steel: insulated or armored

(G-4073)
DURANM INC
101 Dale Ave (10567-1617)
PHONE 914 774-3367
Martin F Duran, *CEO*
EMP: 5
SALES (est): 633.3K **Privately Held**
SIC: **3272** Floor slabs & tiles, precast concrete

(G-4074)
ELMSFORD SHEET METAL WORKS INC
23 Arlo Ln (10567-2631)
PHONE 914 739-6300
Donald J Trier, *President*
Mark Dipasquale, *Vice Pres*
Joseph Jasiel, *Manager*
EMP: 75
SQ FT: 24,000
SALES: 14MM
SALES (corp-wide): 18.9B **Privately Held**
WEB: www.elmsfordsheetmetal.com
SIC: **3444** 7389 7699 Sheet metalwork; metal cutting services; metal reshaping & replating services

HQ: Engie North America Inc.
1990 Post Oak Blvd # 1900
Houston TX 77056
713 636-0000

(G-4075)
GC MOBILE SERVICES INC
Also Called: G C Mobile Svces
32 William Puckey Dr (10567-6216)
PHONE 914 736-9730
Garth Cooperman, *President*
EMP: 6
SALES (est): 250K **Privately Held**
SIC: **7692** Welding repair

(G-4076)
HIGHRANGE FUELS INC
96 Oregon Rd (10567-1246)
PHONE 914 930-8300
Sajan Augustine, *Principal*
EMP: 6
SALES (est): 416.2K **Privately Held**
SIC: **2869** Fuels

(G-4077)
LEONORE DOSKOW INC
1 Juniper Ln (10567-6551)
PHONE 914 737-1335
Fax: 914 737-5049
David Doskow, *Ch of Bd*
Lynn Doskow, *President*
Gloria Burchman, *Office Mgr*
EMP: 20 EST: 1936
SQ FT: 14,000
SALES (est): 2.4MM **Privately Held**
WEB: www.leonoredoskow.com
SIC: **3961** 5944 Costume jewelry; costume novelties; jewelry stores

(G-4078)
MINES PRESS INC
231 Croton Ave (10567-5284)
PHONE 914 788-1800
Fax: 914 788-1698
Steven Mines, *Ch of Bd*
Daniel Mines, *Ch of Bd*
Cynthia Mines, *Corp Secy*
Carl Hutt, *CFO*
Bernadetta Depinna, *Bookkeeper*
▲ EMP: 115 EST: 1933
SQ FT: 100,000
SALES (est): 34.1MM **Privately Held**
WEB: www.minespress.com
SIC: **2752** 2759 2789 2791 Commercial printing, offset; letterpress printing; gold stamping on books; typesetting

(G-4079)
PRONTO PRINTER
2085 E Main St Ste 3 (10567-2616)
PHONE 914 737-0800
Fax: 914 737-4921
John P Marvin, *Owner*
EMP: 6 EST: 1974
SQ FT: 7,000
SALES: 650K **Privately Held**
SIC: **2752** Photo-offset printing

(G-4080)
TERRACE MANAGEMENT INC
Also Called: Colonial Terrace Hotel
119 Oregon Rd (10567-1200)
P.O. Box 142, Peekskill (10566-0142)
PHONE 914 737-0400
Fax: 914 737-0467
Sheila Drogy, *President*
Alan Drogy, *Vice Pres*
EMP: 25
SALES (est): 3.2MM **Privately Held**
SIC: **2099** Food preparations

Cossayuna
Washington County

(G-4081)
FRONHOFER TOOL COMPANY INC
4197 County Rd 48 (12823)
P.O. Box 84 (12823-0084)
PHONE 518 692-2496
Fax: 518 692-2450
Paul Fronhofer II, *Ch of Bd*
Kyle Fronhofer, *Vice Pres*

Heidi Griffin, *Manager*
EMP: 30
SQ FT: 10,000
SALES: 5MM **Privately Held**
WEB: www.fronhofertool.com
SIC: **3545** Tools & accessories for machine tools

Coxsackie
Greene County

(G-4082)
DUCOMMUN AEROSTRUCTURES NY INC
171 Stacey Rd (12051-2613)
PHONE 518 731-2791
Michael D Grosso, *CEO*
Anthony J Reardon, *Ch of Bd*
Hugh J Quigley, *President*
Paul Burton, *Vice Pres*
Rose Rogers, *VP Human Res*
EMP: 270
SQ FT: 65,000
SALES (est): 54.5MM
SALES (corp-wide): 550.6MM **Publicly Held**
WEB: www.dynabil.com
SIC: **3728** Aircraft parts & equipment
HQ: Ducommun Aerostructures, Inc.
268 E Gardena Blvd
Gardena CA 90248
310 380-5390

Cranberry Lake
St. Lawrence County

(G-4083)
FORM A ROCKLAND PLASTICS INC
7152 Main St (12927)
P.O. Box 670 (12927-0670)
PHONE 315 848-3300
Donald Lashomb II, *President*
Cynthia Whitmore Lashomb, *Treasurer*
EMP: 5 EST: 1963
SQ FT: 6,000
SALES (est): 623.7K **Privately Held**
SIC: **3089** 3172 Plastic containers, except foam; key cases

Croghan
Lewis County

(G-4084)
GRAND SLAM SAFETY LLC
9793 S Bridge St (13327-2329)
P.O. Box 35 (13327-0035)
PHONE 315 766-7008
Robert K Lyndaker, *President*
Robert Chamberlain,
Mick Lehman,
David Moore,
EMP: 6
SALES: 300K **Privately Held**
SIC: **3949** Sporting & athletic goods

Cropseyville
Rensselaer County

(G-4085)
R J VALENTE GRAVEL INC
3349 Rte 2 (12052)
PHONE 518 279-1001
Tim Banks, *Branch Mgr*
EMP: 29
SALES (corp-wide): 25.9MM **Privately Held**
SIC: **1442** Construction sand & gravel
PA: R. J. Valente Gravel, Inc.
1 Madison St
Troy NY 12180
518 432-4470

Cross River
Westchester County

(G-4086)
VEPO SOLUTIONS LLC ⊙
3 Fairview Ct (10518-1127)
PHONE 914 384-2121
Alan Seiler, *President*
EMP: 5 EST: 2017
SALES: 2MM **Privately Held**
SIC: **3824** 7371 Water meters; computer software development & applications

Croton Falls
Westchester County

(G-4087)
GARY STOCK CORPORATION
597 Rte 22 (10519)
P.O. Box 609 (10519-0609)
PHONE 914 276-2700
Fax: 914 276-2941
Gary Stock, *President*
Michele Ryan, *Mktg Dir*
EMP: 7
SALES (est): 1MM **Privately Held**
WEB: www.gstockco.com
SIC: **2759** Promotional printing

Croton On Hudson
Westchester County

(G-4088)
BLUE PIG ICE CREAM FACTORY
121 Maple St (10520-2538)
PHONE 914 271-3850
Julia Horowitz, *Owner*
EMP: 5
SALES: 250K **Privately Held**
SIC: **2024** 5812 Ice cream & frozen desserts; ice cream stands or dairy bars

(G-4089)
GENERAL SPLICE CORPORATION
Hwy 129 (10520)
PHONE 914 271-5131
Fax: 914 271-2665
Ralph Milano, *President*
Nicole Milano, *Treasurer*
EMP: 6
SQ FT: 7,000
SALES (est): 878.8K **Privately Held**
SIC: **3535** Conveyors & conveying equipment

(G-4090)
HEALTHY N FIT INTL INC
435 Yorktown Rd (10520-3703)
PHONE 914 271-6040
Fax: 914 271-6042
Robert Sepe Jr, *Ch of Bd*
Irene Sepe, *Vice Pres*
EMP: 13 EST: 1976
SALES (est): 4MM **Privately Held**
SIC: **2833** 5122 Vitamins, natural or synthetic: bulk, uncompounded; vitamins & minerals

(G-4091)
NK ELECTRIC LLC
22 Scenic Dr (10520-1848)
P.O. Box 171 (10520-0171)
PHONE 914 271-0222
Fax: 914 271-0223
James Brophy, *Principal*
EMP: 7
SALES (est): 1MM **Privately Held**
SIC: **3699** Electrical equipment & supplies

(G-4092)
VERY BEST IRTJ
435 Yorktown Rd (10520-3703)
PHONE 914 271-6585
Robert Supe, *President*
EMP: 15
SALES (est): 1.3MM **Privately Held**
SIC: **2834** Vitamin preparations

Crown Point
Essex County

(G-4093)
MOUNTAIN FOREST PRODUCTS INC
3281 Nys Route 9n (12928-2405)
PHONE 518 597-3674
Kevin Mero, *President*
Vicki Mero, *Corp Secy*
EMP: 6
SQ FT: 1,152
SALES (est): 733.8K **Privately Held**
SIC: 2411 Logging

Cuba
Allegany County

(G-4094)
D F STAUFFER BISCUIT CO INC
8670 Farnsworth Rd (14727-9720)
PHONE 585 968-2700
Fax: 716 968-2722
Jim Clubine, *Senior Engr*
Maria Defaria, *Human Res Mgr*
Jeff Howard, *Manager*
Dawn Snyder, *Manager*
Larry Chandler, *Maintence Staff*
EMP: 50
SALES (corp-wide): 10.9B **Privately Held**
WEB: www.stauffers.net
SIC: 2052 Cookies
HQ: D F Stauffer Biscuit Co Inc
  360 S Belmont St
  York PA 17403
  717 815-4600

(G-4095)
EMPIRE CHEESE INC
4520 County Road 6 (14727-9598)
PHONE 585 968-1552
Fax: 585 968-2660
Gary Vanic, *CEO*
John Epprecht, *Corp Secy*
Russell Mullins, *Vice Pres*
Loren Sweet, *Transptn Dir*
Thomas Eastham, *Plant Mgr*
EMP: 175
SQ FT: 100,000
SALES (est): 83.2MM
SALES (corp-wide): 1.6B **Privately Held**
WEB: www.empirecheese.com
SIC: 2022 Cheese, natural & processed
PA: Great Lakes Cheese Co., Inc.
  17825 Great Lakes Pkwy
  Hiram OH 44234
  440 834-2500

(G-4096)
SPS MEDICAL SUPPLY CORP
Also Called: Sterilator Company
31 Water St Ste 1 (14727-1030)
PHONE 585 968-2377
Fax: 585 359-0167
Shawn Doyle, *Branch Mgr*
EMP: 10
SALES (corp-wide): 770.1MM **Publicly Held**
SIC: 3842 3821 Sterilizers, hospital & surgical; autoclaves, laboratory
HQ: Sps Medical Supply Corp.
  6789 W Henrietta Rd
  Rush NY 14543
  585 359-0130

Cutchogue
Suffolk County

(G-4097)
DI BORGHESE CASTELLO LLC
17150 County Road 48 (11935-1041)
P.O. Box 957 (11935-0957)
PHONE 631 734-5111
Marco Borghese, *Mng Member*
EMP: 10
SALES (est): 780.6K **Privately Held**
WEB: www.castellodiborghese.com
SIC: 2084 Wines, brandy & brandy spirits

(G-4098)
PELLEGRINI VINEYARDS LLC
23005 Main Rd (11935-1331)
PHONE 631 734-4111
Fax: 631 734-4159
Rita Pellegrini, *Partner*
Robert Pellegrini, *Partner*
Joyce Pellegrini, *Vice Pres*
EMP: 5
SALES (est): 559.7K **Privately Held**
WEB: www.pellegrinivineyards.com
SIC: 2084 Wines

(G-4099)
PUGLIESE VINEYARDS INC
34515 Main Rd Rr 25 (11935)
P.O. Box 467 (11935-0467)
PHONE 631 734-4057
Patricia Pugliese, *President*
EMP: 5
SALES (est): 460K **Privately Held**
WEB: www.pugliesevineyards.com
SIC: 2084 Wines

(G-4100)
VEDELL NORTH FORK LLC
Also Called: Corey Creek Vineyards
36225 Main Rd (11935-1346)
PHONE 631 323-3526
Peggy Lauber,
Jean Partridge,
EMP: 7
SALES (est): 590K **Privately Held**
SIC: 2084 Wines

Dansville
Livingston County

(G-4101)
AMERICAN MOTIVE POWER INC
9431 Foster Wheeler Rd (14437-9178)
PHONE 585 335-3132
Lawrence Mehlenbacher, *CEO*
Richard Tamborski, *President*
Fred Olinger, *General Mgr*
Richard Rizzieri, *General Mgr*
Frank Larkin, *Exec VP*
EMP: 20
SALES (est): 3.7MM **Privately Held**
WEB: www.magnetech.com
SIC: 3743 Lubrication systems, locomotive

(G-4102)
DANSVILLE LOGGING & LUMBER
10903 State Route 36 (14437-9444)
PHONE 585 335-5879
Fax: 585 335-8089
Timothy Rauber, *President*
EMP: 23
SQ FT: 900
SALES: 1.4MM **Privately Held**
SIC: 2421 Lumber: rough, sawed or planed

(G-4103)
GPM ASSOCIATES LLC
Also Called: Forbes Products
10 Forbes St (14437-9268)
PHONE 585 335-3940
Fax: 585 335-7285
Linda Donovan, *Purch Mgr*
Linda Demartinis, *Purch Agent*
Ron Van Duyne, *Engineer*
Nancy Barrett, *Human Res Mgr*
Elroy Power, *Manager*
EMP: 20
SALES (corp-wide): 15.8MM **Privately Held**
SIC: 2782 3089 2752 2393 Blankbooks & looseleaf binders; novelties, plastic; commercial printing, lithographic; textile bags
PA: Gpm Associates Llc
  45 High Tech Dr
  Rush NY 14543
  585 334-4800

(G-4104)
JUST IN TIME CNC MACHINING
88 Ossian St (14437-9101)
PHONE 585 335-2010
Kelly Alexander, *President*
EMP: 14
SQ FT: 10,000
SALES (est): 1.6MM **Privately Held**
SIC: 3599 Machine shop, jobbing & repair

Davenport
Delaware County

(G-4105)
GREENE LUMBER CO LP
16991 State Highway 23 (13750-8304)
PHONE 607 278-6101
Fax: 607 278-6919
Jeffrey Meyer,
EMP: 35
SQ FT: 13,888
SALES (est): 5.8MM
SALES (corp-wide): 300.9MM **Privately Held**
SIC: 2421 Sawmills & planing mills, general
PA: Baillie Lumber Co., L.P.
  4002 Legion Dr
  Hamburg NY 14075
  800 950-2850

De Ruyter
Madison County

(G-4106)
KELLEY BROS HARDWARE CORP
1714 Albany St (13052-6566)
PHONE 315 852-3302
EMP: 7
SALES (corp-wide): 38.4MM **Privately Held**
SIC: 3429 Builders' hardware
HQ: Kelley Bros. Hardware Corp
  317 E Brighton Ave
  Syracuse NY 13210
  315 478-2151

(G-4107)
USA BODY INC
994 Middle Lake Rd (13052-1244)
PHONE 315 852-6123
Fax: 315 852-9514
Bruce Macrae, *President*
Kristine Macrae, *Admin Sec*
EMP: 8
SALES (est): 1.7MM **Privately Held**
SIC: 3713 Truck bodies (motor vehicles)

De Witt
Onondaga County

(G-4108)
MAXI COMPANIES INC
4317 E Genesee St (13214-2114)
PHONE 315 446-1002
Charles C Giancola, *President*
▼ **EMP:** 6
SALES (est): 532.9K **Privately Held**
SIC: 3582 Dryers, laundry: commercial, including coin-operated

Deansboro
Oneida County

(G-4109)
BUELL FUEL LLC
2676 State Route 12b (13328-1128)
PHONE 315 841-3000
Michael Buell, *Principal*
EMP: 12
SALES (est): 2.5MM **Privately Held**
SIC: 2869 Fuels

Deer Park
Suffolk County

(G-4110)
ABLE WELDBUILT INDUSTRIES INC
1050 Grand Blvd (11729-5710)
PHONE 631 643-9700
Steve Laganas, *President*
EMP: 15
SALES (est): 3.4MM **Privately Held**
SIC: 3713 Truck & bus bodies

(G-4111)
ABRA-KA-DATA SYSTEMS LTD
39 W Jefryn Blvd Ste 1 (11729-5792)
PHONE 631 667-5550
Fax: 631 667-5572
Robert A Berding, *Ch of Bd*
Kenneth Berding, *President*
Dorothy Berding, *Admin Sec*
▲ **EMP:** 22
SQ FT: 15,000
SALES (est): 2.2MM **Privately Held**
SIC: 2761 Manifold business forms

(G-4112)
AD MAKERS LONG ISLAND INC
60 E Jefryn Blvd Ste 3 (11729-5798)
PHONE 631 595-9100
Fax: 631 595-1975
Arthur Lituchy, *President*
Evan Navarret, *General Mgr*
Henry Houston, *Vice Pres*
EMP: 10
SQ FT: 1,500
SALES (est): 930K **Privately Held**
WEB: www.admadvertising.com
SIC: 3993 7311 Signs & advertising specialties; advertising agencies

(G-4113)
ADVANCED STRUCTURES CORP (PA)
235 W Industry Ct (11729-4688)
PHONE 631 667-5000
Fax: 631 667-5015
James Henderson, *President*
Eloise Foot, *Corp Secy*
Thomas Findlayson, *Vice Pres*
Dennis Shipman, *Manager*
EMP: 14
SQ FT: 22,000
SALES (est): 3.7MM **Privately Held**
WEB: www.advancedstructurescorp.com
SIC: 3469 3083 Metal stampings; laminated plastic sheets

(G-4114)
AERO SPECIALTIES MANUFACTURING
20 Burt Dr (11729-5770)
PHONE 631 242-7200
Donald Carter, *President*
Elizabeth A Smith, *Vice Pres*
EMP: 12 EST: 1999
SQ FT: 1,400
SALES: 3.4MM **Privately Held**
SIC: 3599 Machine shop, jobbing & repair

(G-4115)
ALL COLOR BUSINESS SPC LTD
305 Suburban Ave (11729-6806)
PHONE 516 420-0649
Fax: 516 753-2506
William Bogue, *Ch of Bd*
EMP: 6
SALES (est): 760K **Privately Held**
SIC: 2752 Commercial printing, lithographic

(G-4116)
ALLSTATE GASKET & PACKING INC
31 Prospect Pl (11729-3713)
PHONE 631 254-4050
Fax: 516 254-4330
Angelo Romano, *President*
Jeff Mandell, *Sales Executive*
Rosanne Kelly, *Manager*
▲ **EMP:** 17
SQ FT: 2,000

Deer Park - Suffolk County (G-4117)

SALES (est): 1.7MM **Privately Held**
WEB: www.allstategasket.com
SIC: 3053 5085 3443 Gaskets, all materials; industrial supplies; fabricated plate work (boiler shop)

(G-4117)
ALLSTATE SIGN & PLAQUE CORP
70 Burt Dr (11729-5702)
P.O. Box 725 (11729-0725)
PHONE 631 242-2828
Fax: 631 242-2433
David Fick, *President*
Mark Fick, *Vice Pres*
Peter Fick, *Treasurer*
EMP: 15 EST: 1956
SQ FT: 15,000
SALES (est): 2.6MM **Privately Held**
WEB: www.allstatesign.com
SIC: 3993 2796 Signs, not made in custom sign painting shops; engraving platemaking services

(G-4118)
AMALFI INGREDIENTS LLC
94 E Jefryn Blvd Ste H (11729-5728)
PHONE 631 392-1526
Serge Jean Charles, *Principal*
Charlie Monteleone, *Vice Pres*
▲ EMP: 5
SALES (est): 618.8K **Privately Held**
SIC: 2099 Molasses, mixed or blended: from purchased ingredients

(G-4119)
AMERICAN CASINO EQUIPMENT MFG
Also Called: Acem
45 W Jefryn Blvd Ste 107 (11729-5722)
PHONE 631 242-2440
Fax: 631 242-2410
John Makowski, *CEO*
EMP: 10
SALES (est): 2.5MM **Privately Held**
WEB: www.acemcasino.com
SIC: 2499 Laundry products, wood

(G-4120)
AMERICAN RACING HEADERS INC
Also Called: Arh
880 Grand Blvd (11729-5708)
PHONE 631 608-1427
Nick Filippides, *CEO*
Jose Cruz, *Principal*
Alex M Cfe, *Controller*
EMP: 30 EST: 2011
SALES (est): 6.8MM **Privately Held**
SIC: 3542 Headers

(G-4121)
AMERICAN SEALING TECHNOLOGY
31 Prospect Pl (11729-3713)
P.O. Box 545, Levittown (11756-0545)
PHONE 631 254-0019
Angelo Romano, *President*
Dominico Bono, *Purch Mgr*
EMP: 12
SQ FT: 10,000
SALES (est): 960K **Privately Held**
SIC: 3053 Gaskets, packing & sealing devices

(G-4122)
ANAND PRINTING MACHINERY INC
188 W 16th St (11729-4909)
PHONE 631 667-3079
Amand Kumar, *President*
EMP: 1
SALES: 8MM **Privately Held**
SIC: 3555 Printing trades machinery

(G-4123)
ANTHONY MANNO & CO INC
307 Skidmore Rd Ste 2 (11729-7117)
P.O. Box 32, Freeport (11520-0032)
PHONE 631 445-1834
Anthony Manno, *President*
Russell Fragala, *Senior VP*
EMP: 7
SQ FT: 5,000

SALES (est): 644.2K **Privately Held**
SIC: 3452 Screws, metal

(G-4124)
APOGEE TRANSLITE INC
593 Acorn St Ste B (11729-3613)
PHONE 631 254-6975
Lynn Nicoali, *President*
Marty Gaon, *Exec VP*
Dominick Persichilli, *Production*
Keith Stegemann, *Engineer*
Ted Rykowski, *Senior Engr*
EMP: 25
SQ FT: 30,000
SALES (est): 7.9MM **Privately Held**
WEB: www.apogeetranslite.com
SIC: 3548 3646 Welding apparatus; commercial indusl & institutional electric lighting fixtures

(G-4125)
ARMA CONTAINER CORP
65 N Industry Ct (11729-4601)
PHONE 631 254-1200
Fax: 631 254-3600
Bruce Margolis, *CEO*
Howard Gottfried, *Vice Pres*
Jack Hausman, *Treasurer*
Kim Geraci, *Controller*
Howard Glass, *Admin Sec*
▼ EMP: 50 EST: 1946
SQ FT: 70,000
SALES (est): 12.7MM **Privately Held**
WEB: www.armacontainer.com
SIC: 2653 Boxes, corrugated: made from purchased materials

(G-4126)
ARTHUR BROWN W MFG CO
49 E Industry Ct Ste I (11729-4711)
PHONE 631 243-5594
Fax: 631 243-5596
Philip Sabatino, *President*
Anthony Sabatino, *Vice Pres*
EMP: 15
SQ FT: 8,000
SALES (est): 1.8MM **Privately Held**
WEB: www.arthurwbrown.com
SIC: 2511 Wood household furniture

(G-4127)
ARTSAICS STUDIOS INC
1006 Grand Blvd (11729-5710)
PHONE 631 254-2558
Fax: 631 254-2451
Nelson Londono, *President*
EMP: 6
SALES (est): 649.3K **Privately Held**
WEB: www.artsaics.com
SIC: 3253 Mosaic tile, glazed & unglazed: ceramic

(G-4128)
AUTO DATA SYSTEMS INC (PA)
Also Called: Auto Data Labels
2000 Deer Park Ave (11729-2730)
PHONE 631 667-2382
Scott Saal, *President*
▼ EMP: 28
SQ FT: 3,000
SALES (est): 2.2MM **Privately Held**
SIC: 2679 5131 Tags & labels, paper; labels

(G-4129)
AUTO MARKET PUBLICATIONS INC
1641 Deer Park Ave Ste 5 (11729-5209)
PHONE 631 667-0500
Corey Franklin, *President*
EMP: 8
SALES (est): 640.2K **Privately Held**
SIC: 2741 Telephone & other directory publishing

(G-4130)
BEST WAY TOOLS BY ANDERSON INC
171 Brook Ave (11729-7204)
PHONE 631 586-4702
Arleen Anderson CPA, *CEO*
Wayne Anderson, *President*
Warren Anderson, *Vice Pres*
Paul Cassutti, *Vice Pres*
EMP: 4
SQ FT: 15,000

SALES (est): 8MM **Privately Held**
WEB: www.bestwaytools.com
SIC: 3423 5072 Hand & edge tools; hardware

(G-4131)
BICON PHARMACEUTICAL INC
75 N Industry Ct (11729-4601)
PHONE 631 593-4199
Brian LI, *Director*
EMP: 10
SALES (est): 630K **Privately Held**
SIC: 2834 Pharmaceutical preparations

(G-4132)
BIMBO BAKERIES
955 Grand Blvd (11729-5707)
PHONE 631 274-4906
EMP: 8
SALES (est): 545.2K **Privately Held**
SIC: 2051 Bread, cake & related products

(G-4133)
BLI INTERNATIONAL INC
Also Called: Allegiant Health
75 N Industry Ct (11729-4601)
PHONE 631 940-9000
Brian LI, *President*
Lee Rudibaugh, *Senior VP*
Jerry Maleh, *Vice Pres*
John Zhong, *Vice Pres*
Roy Kasenchak, *Software Engr*
EMP: 130
SALES (est): 38.9MM **Privately Held**
SIC: 2834 Tablets, pharmaceutical

(G-4134)
BLUE SKIES
859 Long Island Ave (11729-3426)
PHONE 631 392-1140
Lisa Delvecchio, *Owner*
EMP: 5
SALES (est): 419.7K **Privately Held**
SIC: 3577 Printers & plotters

(G-4135)
BRENSEKE GEORGE WLDG IR WORKS
Also Called: Brenseke's
915 Long Island Ave Ste A (11729-3731)
PHONE 631 271-4870
Carol Brenseke, *President*
George Brenseke, *Vice Pres*
EMP: 6 EST: 1974
SALES: 800K **Privately Held**
SIC: 7692 Welding repair

(G-4136)
BROOKS LITHO DIGITAL GROUP INC
35 W Jefryn Blvd Ste A (11729-5784)
PHONE 631 789-4500
Fax: 631 789-4505
David Brooks, *President*
Linda Brooks, *Vice Pres*
EMP: 5
SQ FT: 500
SALES (est): 923.6K **Privately Held**
WEB: www.brookslitho.com
SIC: 2752 2791 2789 2759 Commercial printing, lithographic; typesetting; bookbinding & related work; commercial printing

(G-4137)
C F PRINT LTD INC
35 W Jefryn Blvd Ste 2 (11729-5784)
PHONE 631 567-2110
Fax: 631 567-2695
Steve Scelfo, *President*
EMP: 10
SALES (est): 1MM **Privately Held**
WEB: www.cfprintltd.com
SIC: 2759 Commercial printing

(G-4138)
CHALLENGE GRAPHICS SVCS INC (PA)
22 Connor Ln (11729-7234)
PHONE 631 586-0171
Fax: 631 586-0174
Anthony Brancato, *Ch of Bd*
Jim McLoone, *General Mgr*
William Boublik, *Sr Corp Ofcr*
Joseph Brancato, *Vice Pres*

Kurt Hochreiter, *Prdtn Mgr*
EMP: 42
SQ FT: 32,000
SALES (est): 6.6MM **Privately Held**
SIC: 2752 2791 2789 Lithographing on metal; typesetting; bookbinding & related work

(G-4139)
CHAPMAN SKATEBOARD CO INC
Also Called: New York Skateboards
87 N Industry Ct Ste A (11729-4607)
PHONE 631 321-4773
Greg Chapman, *President*
Christine Chapman, *Vice Pres*
Glenn Chapman, *Administration*
▲ EMP: 5
SQ FT: 2,000
SALES (est): 582.4K **Privately Held**
WEB: www.chapmanskateboards.com
SIC: 3949 5941 Skates & parts, roller; skateboarding equipment

(G-4140)
CHEMARK INTERNATIONAL USA INC
729 Acorn St (11729-3234)
PHONE 631 593-4566
Wayne Chao, *President*
EMP: 6
SALES (est): 707.5K **Privately Held**
SIC: 3621 Electric motor & generator parts

(G-4141)
COLUMBIA SPORTSWEAR COMPANY
152 The Arches Cir (11729-7057)
PHONE 631 274-6091
EMP: 250
SALES (corp-wide): 2.3B **Publicly Held**
SIC: 2329 Men's & boys' sportswear & athletic clothing
PA: Columbia Sportswear Company
14375 Nw Science Park Dr
Portland OR 97229
503 985-4000

(G-4142)
CONTINENTAL KNITTING MILLS
Also Called: La-Mar Fashions
156 Brook Ave (11729-7251)
PHONE 631 242-5330
Pat Marini, *President*
Jennifer Marini, *Vice Pres*
EMP: 5
SQ FT: 4,000
SALES: 300K **Privately Held**
SIC: 2329 2339 5131 Men's & boys' sportswear & athletic clothing; women's & misses' athletic clothing & sportswear; sportswear, women's; knit fabrics

(G-4143)
COUSINS FURNITURE & HM IMPRVS
Also Called: Cousin's Furniture
515 Acorn St (11729-3601)
PHONE 631 254-3752
Fax: 631 254-3752
Joaquim L Rodrigues, *President*
Ilidio Rodrigues, *Vice Pres*
Maria Mejia, *Bookkeeper*
Barton Bienenstock, *Executive*
EMP: 42
SQ FT: 10,200
SALES (est): 5.3MM **Privately Held**
SIC: 2511 2431 Wood household furniture; millwork

(G-4144)
CROSLEY MEDICAL PRODUCTS INC
Also Called: Cmp Adaptive Equipment Supply
60 S 2nd St Ste E (11729-4717)
PHONE 631 595-2547
Fax: 631 595-1732
Gary Kornberg, *President*
Anthony Potenzone, *Mfg Staff*
EMP: 10
SQ FT: 4,000
SALES: 1.5MM **Privately Held**
SIC: 3842 Wheelchairs

GEOGRAPHIC SECTION — Deer Park - Suffolk County (G-4170)

(G-4145)
CTI SOFTWARE INC
44 W Jefryn Blvd Ste P (11729-4721)
PHONE .... (631) 253-3550
Eric Meyn, *Ch of Bd*
EMP: 13
SALES (est): 1MM **Privately Held**
WEB: www.ctisoftware.com
SIC: 7372 Prepackaged software

(G-4146)
CUBBIES UNLIMITED CORPORATION
74 N Industry Ct (11729-4602)
PHONE 631 586-8572
Stefanie Stein, *President*
Joel Fromkin, *Treasurer*
Cyrus J Fromkin, *Admin Sec*
Chrysatll Tellacani, *Admin Sec*
▲ EMP: 15
SQ FT: 7,000
SALES (est): 1.2MM **Privately Held**
WEB: www.cubbiesunlimited.com
SIC: 3089 5211 Organizers for closets, drawers, etc.: plastic; stock shapes, plastic; closets, interiors & accessories

(G-4147)
D W S ASSOCIATES INC
Also Called: D W S Printing
89 N Industry Ct (11729-4601)
PHONE 631 667-6666
Thomas Staib, *President*
Andrew Staib, *Vice Pres*
Sal Addotta, *Project Mgr*
Courtney Casey, *Asst Controller*
Craig Smith, *Financial Exec*
EMP: 36
SQ FT: 20,000
SALES (est): 11.3MM **Privately Held**
WEB: www.dwsprinting.com
SIC: 2672 Labels (unprinted), gummed: made from purchased materials

(G-4148)
DAVINCI DESIGNS INC
Also Called: Davinci Dsgns Distinctive Furn
20 Lucon Dr Unit A (11729-5789)
PHONE 631 595-1095
Ralph Vinci, *CEO*
Chris Vinci, *Vice Pres*
Patricia Kennedy, *Manager*
EMP: 15
SQ FT: 3,000
SALES (est): 1.5MM **Privately Held**
WEB: www.davincidesigns.com
SIC: 2522 2521 Office furniture, except wood; wood office furniture

(G-4149)
DEER PARK DRIVESHAFT & HOSE
Also Called: Deer Park Drv Shaft & Hose Co
85 Brook Ave Ste C (11729-7202)
PHONE 631 667-4091
Fax: 631 242-6814
Nick Monastero, *President*
Richard Desena, *Vice Pres*
EMP: 4
SALES (est): 1MM **Privately Held**
SIC: 3714 3052 5013 Drive shafts, motor vehicle; axles, motor vehicle; automobile hose, plastic; automotive supplies & parts

(G-4150)
DEER PARK MACARONI CO INC (PA)
Also Called: Dpr Food Service
1882 Deer Park Ave (11729-4318)
PHONE 631 667-4600
Fax: 631 667-3565
Ernest Oliviero, *President*
Tom McDonald, *Vice Pres*
Phil Litrel, *Human Res Mgr*
Christopher Litrel, *Admin Sec*
EMP: 5 EST: 1949
SQ FT: 5,000
SALES (est): 1MM **Privately Held**
WEB: www.deerparkravioli.com
SIC: 2098 Macaroni & spaghetti

(G-4151)
DEER PARK MACARONI CO INC
Also Called: Deer Park Ravioli & Macaroni
1882 Deer Park Ave (11729-4318)
PHONE 631 667-4600
Fax: 631 667-4741
Earnest Olivero, *Manager*
EMP: 10
SALES (corp-wide): 1MM **Privately Held**
WEB: www.deerparkravioli.com
SIC: 2098 5149 Macaroni & spaghetti; pasta & rice
PA: Deer Park Macaroni Co Inc
1882 Deer Park Ave
Deer Park NY 11729
631 667-4600

(G-4152)
DESIGN DISTRIBUTORS INC
300 Marcus Blvd (11729-4500)
PHONE 631 242-2000
Fax: 631 242-7367
Stuart J Avrick, *Ch of Bd*
Adam G Avrick, *President*
Mark F Rice, *Vice Pres*
Michael Glanzman, *VP Opers*
Vincent Granberg, *Plant Mgr*
▲ EMP: 85 EST: 1962
SQ FT: 80,000
SALES (est): 19.1MM **Privately Held**
SIC: 2759 2752 7331 Envelopes: printing; commercial printing, lithographic; direct mail advertising services

(G-4153)
DOVER MARINE MFG & SUP CO INC
98 N Industry Ct (11729-4602)
PHONE 631 667-4300
Fax: 718 899-6876
Theodore Cerrito, *President*
Lisa Cerrito, *Treasurer*
EMP: 5
SQ FT: 5,000
SALES (est): 480K **Privately Held**
WEB: www.dovermfg.com
SIC: 3429 Marine hardware

(G-4154)
DP MURPHY CO INC
945 Grand Blvd (11729-5707)
PHONE 631 673-9400
Timothy M Schratwieser, *President*
Peter Q Murphy, *Project Dir*
Adriane Gray, *Opers Staff*
Mary Peters, *Sales Mgr*
EMP: 66 EST: 1873
SQ FT: 20,000
SALES (est): 9.8MM **Privately Held**
WEB: www.dpmurphy.com
SIC: 2752 7374 7331 2791 Commercial printing, offset; data processing service; mailing service; typesetting; bookbinding & related work

(G-4155)
EAST COAST EMBROIDERY LTD
74 Brook Ave Ste 1 (11729-7227)
PHONE 631 254-3878
Susan Simione, *President*
EMP: 7
SALES: 750K **Privately Held**
SIC: 2395 Embroidery products, except schiffli machine

(G-4156)
EAST COAST ORTHOIC & PROS COR (PA)
75 Burt Dr (11729-5701)
PHONE 516 248-5566
Vincent A Benenati, *CEO*
Lawrence J Benenati, *President*
John Fernandez, *Opers Mgr*
George Mitchell, *Controller*
Lola Menghi, *Human Res Mgr*
▲ EMP: 52 EST: 1997
SALES (est): 9.1MM **Privately Held**
WEB: www.ec-op.com
SIC: 3841 Medical instruments & equipment, blood & bone work

(G-4157)
EC WOOD & COMPANY INC
110 E Industry Ct (11729-4706)
PHONE 718 388-2287
Joseph Fontana, *President*
Crystal Corcez, *Office Mgr*
EMP: 15
SQ FT: 13,000
SALES (est): 1.4MM **Privately Held**
SIC: 2434 Wood kitchen cabinets

(G-4158)
ELITE CELLULAR ACCESSORIES INC
61 E Industry Ct (11729-4725)
PHONE 877 390-2502
John Nordstrom, *President*
Stephen Conlon, *Exec VP*
EMP: 30
SQ FT: 10,000
SALES (est): 2.5MM **Privately Held**
SIC: 3663 5065 5731 Mobile communication equipment; intercommunication equipment, electronic; video cameras, recorders & accessories

(G-4159)
ELSENER ORGAN WORKS INC
120 E Jefryn Blvd Ste A (11729-5723)
PHONE 631 254-2744
Fax: 631 254-8723
Josephine Elsener, *President*
EMP: 7
SQ FT: 5,000
SALES: 500K **Privately Held**
WEB: www.elsenerorganworks.com
SIC: 3931 Blowers, pipe organ

(G-4160)
EMBASSY DINETTES INC
78 E Industry Ct (11729-4704)
PHONE 631 253-2292
Michael Walman, *Vice Pres*
◆ EMP: 5
SQ FT: 15,000
SALES (est): 456.8K **Privately Held**
SIC: 2514 Dinette sets: metal

(G-4161)
EMPIRE INDUSTRIAL BURNER SVC
550 Brook Ave (11729-6802)
PHONE 631 242-4619
Edward Roufberg, *President*
Rose Marie Price, *Administration*
EMP: 10
SQ FT: 37,000
SALES (est): 1.1MM **Privately Held**
SIC: 3433 1711 Burners, furnaces, boilers & stokers; boiler maintenance contractor; heating systems repair & maintenance
PA: Empire Industrial Systems Corp.
40 Corbin Ave
Bay Shore NY 11706
631 242-4619

(G-4162)
EMPIRE SCIENTIFIC
Also Called: Empire Central
151 E Industry Ct (11729-4705)
P.O. Box 817 (11729-0981)
PHONE 630 510-8636
Jeff English, *Owner*
▲ EMP: 5
SALES (est): 376.4K **Privately Held**
WEB: www.empirescientific.com
SIC: 3692 Primary batteries, dry & wet

(G-4163)
FABRICATION SPECIALTIES CORP
2 Saxwood St Ste G (11729-4790)
PHONE 631 242-0326
Fax: 631 242-0344
David Conroy, *President*
Joseph W Schneider, *President*
Natale Marcellino, *Vice Pres*
EMP: 5 EST: 1972
SQ FT: 5,000
SALES (est): 750K **Privately Held**
SIC: 3469 Electronic enclosures, stamped or pressed metal

(G-4164)
FLOW X RAY CORPORATION
Also Called: Flow Dental
100 W Industry Ct (11729-4604)
PHONE 631 242-9729
Fax: 631 242-1001
Howard Wolf, *President*
Martin B Wolf, *Chairman*
Arlene Wolf, *Vice Pres*
Hugo Burbano, *Project Mgr*
Carolyn Price, *CFO*
▲ EMP: 96 EST: 1974
SQ FT: 70,000
SALES (est): 13.4MM **Privately Held**
SIC: 3844 X-ray apparatus & tubes

(G-4165)
FORCE DIGITAL MEDIA INC
39 W Jefryn Blvd Ste 2 (11729-5792)
PHONE 631 243-0243
John Mazzio, *President*
EMP: 5
SALES (est): 172.6K **Privately Held**
SIC: 2759 7336 Commercial printing; package design

(G-4166)
FORMATS UNLIMITED INC
Also Called: Mf Digital
19 W Jefryn Blvd Ste 2 (11729-5749)
PHONE 631 249-9200
Fax: 631 249-9273
Anthony Cosentino, *Ch of Bd*
Joyce Cosentino, *Vice Pres*
Rob Derita, *Sales Mgr*
John McGrath, *Manager*
EMP: 10
SQ FT: 2,500
SALES (est): 2.4MM **Privately Held**
WEB: www.formats-unlimited.com
SIC: 7372 5045 3572 5065 Prepackaged software; disk drives; disk drives, computer; diskettes, computer

(G-4167)
FOSSIL INDUSTRIES INC
44 W Jefryn Blvd Ste A (11729-4721)
PHONE 631 254-9200
Howard Decesare, *President*
Howard De, *General Mgr*
Mark Decesare, *Vice Pres*
Steve Melisi, *VP Opers*
Rhiannon Cesare, *Project Mgr*
▼ EMP: 25
SQ FT: 25,000
SALES (est): 3MM **Privately Held**
WEB: www.fossilinc.com
SIC: 3993 Signs & advertising specialties

(G-4168)
FUTURE SPRAY FINISHING CO
78 Brook Ave Ste A (11729-7226)
PHONE 631 242-6252
Fax: 631 242-6252
Josephine Galea, *Owner*
EMP: 5
SQ FT: 4,500
SALES (est): 364K **Privately Held**
SIC: 3479 Coating of metals & formed products

(G-4169)
GLOBAL STEEL PRODUCTS CORP (HQ)
95 Marcus Blvd (11729-4501)
PHONE 631 586-3455
Peter Rolla, *President*
Max Moore, *General Mgr*
Adrienne Rolla, *Treasurer*
Mike Ramzey, *Controller*
Dana Patient, *Manager*
◆ EMP: 150
SQ FT: 85,000
SALES (est): 19.1MM
SALES (corp-wide): 195.7MM **Privately Held**
WEB: www.globalpartitions.com
SIC: 2542 3446 3443 3442 Partitions for floor attachment, prefabricated: except wood; architectural metalwork; fabricated plate work (boiler shop); metal doors, sash & trim
PA: ltr Industries, Inc
441 Saw Mill River Rd
Yonkers NY 10701
914 964-7063

(G-4170)
HI-TEMP BRAZING INC
539 Acorn St (11729-3601)
PHONE 631 491-4917
Raymond M Gentner, *President*

Deer Park - Suffolk County (G-4171)

Raymond M Gentner III, *Opers Mgr*
EMP: 30
SQ FT: 7,500
SALES (est): 5.2MM **Privately Held**
WEB: www.hitempbrazing.com
SIC: 3398 Brazing (hardening) of metal

(G-4171)
HIGH FREQUENCY TECH CO INC
172 Brook Ave Ste D (11729-7243)
PHONE..................631 242-3020
Fax: 631 242-4823
Andrew Amabile, *President*
Mary Ann Amabile, *Shareholder*
▲ **EMP:** 12
SQ FT: 10,000
SALES (est): 2.2MM **Privately Held**
WEB: www.hftinc.com
SIC: 3559 5065 5084 Plastics working machinery; electronic parts & equipment; materials handling machinery

(G-4172)
HIGHLAND ORGANIZATION CORP
435 Unit 23 Brook Ave (11729)
PHONE..................631 991-3240
Marc Piacenti, *President*
Jennifer McGee, *Comptroller*
EMP: 35 **EST:** 1999
SQ FT: 3,200
SALES: 5MM **Privately Held**
SIC: 2431 Millwork

(G-4173)
HRD METAL PRODUCTS INC
120 E Jefryn Blvd Ste A (11729-5723)
PHONE..................631 243-6700
Fax: 631 243-2585
Hector Lasalle, *President*
Martin Michie, *Vice Pres*
EMP: 8
SQ FT: 4,000
SALES: 800K **Privately Held**
SIC: 3444 Sheet metalwork

(G-4174)
ICE CUBE INC (PA)
171 E Industry Ct Ste B (11729-4732)
PHONE..................613 254-0071
Cono Simino, *President*
EMP: 7
SALES (est): 848.3K **Privately Held**
SIC: 2097 Ice cubes

(G-4175)
ISLAND INSTRUMENT CORP
65 Burt Dr (11729-5701)
PHONE..................631 243-0550
Patrick McKeever, *President*
Dawn Bannwarth, *Office Mgr*
Candice McLellan, *Manager*
EMP: 9
SQ FT: 12,500
SALES (est): 1.3MM **Privately Held**
WEB: www.sonnart.com
SIC: 3599 Machine shop, jobbing & repair

(G-4176)
J & J SWISS PRECISION INC
160 W Industry Ct Ste F (11729-4677)
P.O. Box 408 (11729-0408)
PHONE..................631 243-5584
Fax: 631 243-5583
John Dojlidko, *President*
Tom Mak, *QC Mgr*
John Mroz, *Treasurer*
EMP: 30
SQ FT: 10,000
SALES (est): 4.7MM **Privately Held**
SIC: 3599 3451 Machine shop, jobbing & repair; screw machine products

(G-4177)
JAMAR PRECISION PRODUCTS CO
5 Lucon Dr (11729-5711)
PHONE..................631 254-0234
Fax: 631 254-0284
James Lewandoski, *President*
Joy Lewandoski, *Vice Pres*
EMP: 12
SQ FT: 10,500
SALES (est): 726K **Privately Held**
SIC: 3599 Machine shop, jobbing & repair

(G-4178)
JAMCO AEROSPACE INC
121a E Industry Ct (11729)
PHONE..................631 586-7900
Fax: 631 586-7505
Jack Lee, *CEO*
Linette Lee, *President*
Ronald Lee, *Project Engr*
Hanna LI, *Admin Sec*
EMP: 50
SQ FT: 30,000
SALES (est): 11MM **Privately Held**
WEB: www.jamco-aerospace.com
SIC: 3728 Aircraft parts & equipment

(G-4179)
JAVCON MACHINE INC
255 Skidmore Rd (11729-7102)
PHONE..................631 586-1890
Fax: 631 586-1868
Eric Clauss, *President*
Debra Fetsch, *Manager*
EMP: 9 **EST:** 1977
SALES: 1.5MM **Privately Held**
SIC: 3599 Machine shop, jobbing & repair

(G-4180)
JED LIGHTS INC (HQ)
10 Connor Ln (11729-7210)
PHONE..................516 812-5001
Frank Wess, *Bookkeeper*
Doug Flank, *Manager*
EMP: 10
SQ FT: 10,000
SALES (est): 5.5MM
SALES (corp-wide): 17.2MM **Privately Held**
SIC: 3648 5063 3053 3052 Lighting equipment; lighting fittings & accessories; gasket materials; rubber & plastics hose & beltings
PA: Green Logic Led Electrical Supply Inc.
75 Marine St
Farmingdale NY 11735
877 285-2733

(G-4181)
JOHN J MAZUR INC
94 E Jefryn Blvd Ste K (11729-5728)
PHONE..................631 242-4554
Fax: 631 242-4093
John J Mazur Jr, *President*
Peter Strouse, *QC Mgr*
Alice Mazur, *Admin Sec*
EMP: 15 **EST:** 1957
SQ FT: 15,000
SALES: 2.3MM **Privately Held**
SIC: 3599 Machine shop, jobbing & repair

(G-4182)
JUSTIN GREGORY INC
94 E Jefryn Blvd Ste E (11729-5728)
PHONE..................631 249-5187
Justin Gregory, *CEO*
Renee Levin, *President*
EMP: 6
SALES (est): 639.9K **Privately Held**
SIC: 3111 Accessory products, leather

(G-4183)
KONAR PRECISION MFG INC
62 S 2nd St Ste F (11729-4716)
PHONE..................631 242-4466
Fax: 631 242-4467
Daruisz Konarski, *President*
Slawomir Konarski, *Vice Pres*
Monika Konarska, *Accounting Mgr*
Karol Konarski, *Office Mgr*
EMP: 5
SQ FT: 2,000
SALES: 500K **Privately Held**
SIC: 3599 Machine shop, jobbing & repair

(G-4184)
KTD SCREW MACHINE INC
70 E Jefryn Blvd Ste D (11729-5754)
PHONE..................631 243-6861
Fax: 631 243-6862
Kevin Dorman, *President*
Michael Dorman, *Vice Pres*
EMP: 8
SQ FT: 3,700
SALES (est): 1.1MM **Privately Held**
SIC: 3451 Screw machine products

(G-4185)
L & K GRAPHICS INC
Also Called: Minuteman Press
1917 Deer Park Ave (11729-3302)
PHONE..................631 667-2269
Fax: 631 667-2346
Richard Crockett, *Ch of Bd*
Robert Mason, *President*
EMP: 6 **EST:** 1975
SQ FT: 2,000
SALES (est): 1MM **Privately Held**
SIC: 2752 Commercial printing, lithographic

(G-4186)
L MILLER DESIGN INC
Also Called: Bank Displays.com
100 E Jefryn Blvd Ste F (11729-5729)
PHONE..................631 242-1163
Fax: 631 242-7308
Robert L Miller, *President*
Leena Miller, *Corp Secy*
Mike Malone, *Vice Pres*
Lisa Melloni, *Office Mgr*
Michele Melloni, *Manager*
EMP: 7
SALES: 650K **Privately Held**
WEB: www.lmillerdesign.com
SIC: 3993 7319 Signs & advertising specialties; display advertising service

(G-4187)
LA STRADA DANCE FOOTWEAR INC
770 Grand Blvd Ste 1 (11729-5725)
PHONE..................631 242-1401
Daniel Cerasuolo, *President*
Linda O'Shea, *Corp Secy*
EMP: 6
SQ FT: 3,300
SALES: 350K **Privately Held**
SIC: 3149 2252 Ballet slippers; socks

(G-4188)
LEADING EDGE FABRICATION
699 Acorn St Ste B (11729-4235)
PHONE..................631 274-9797
Mitch Bard, *Owner*
EMP: 6
SALES (est): 662.2K **Privately Held**
SIC: 3441 Fabricated structural metal

(G-4189)
LESLY ENTERPRISE & ASSOCIATES
29 Columbo Dr (11729-1808)
P.O. Box 190 (11729-0190)
PHONE..................631 988-1301
Lesly Senat, *Principal*
EMP: 5
SALES: 50K **Privately Held**
SIC: 3721 Aircraft

(G-4190)
LIGHTING SCULPTURES INC
Also Called: Versapoints
66 N Industry Ct (11729-4602)
PHONE..................631 242-3387
Chet Yaswen, *President*
Laura Yaswen, *Vice Pres*
EMP: 10
SALES (est): 2.3MM **Privately Held**
SIC: 3648 Lighting equipment

(G-4191)
LONG ISLAND METALFORM INC
12 Lucon Dr (11729-5712)
PHONE..................631 242-9088
Fax: 631 586-4711
George Seitz Jr, *President*
Tom McCormack, *Vice Pres*
EMP: 14
SQ FT: 14,000
SALES (est): 2.8MM **Privately Held**
WEB: www.longislandmetalform.com
SIC: 3469 Spinning metal for the trade

(G-4192)
LUCIA GROUP INC
45 W Jefryn Blvd Ste 108 (11729-5722)
PHONE..................631 392-4900
Craig Lucia, *President*
Guly Rothwell, *Project Mgr*
▲ **EMP:** 5 **EST:** 1994
SQ FT: 1,000
SALES (est): 610K **Privately Held**
WEB: www.theluciagroup.com
SIC: 2522 2542 Office furniture, except wood; shelving, office & store: except wood

(G-4193)
M H STRYKE CO INC
181 E Industry Ct Ste A (11729-4718)
PHONE..................631 242-2660
Kenneth Winter, *President*
EMP: 10 **EST:** 1931
SQ FT: 3,000
SALES (est): 812K **Privately Held**
SIC: 3965 Fasteners, snap

(G-4194)
MARKSMEN MANUFACTURING CORP
355 Marcus Blvd (11729-4509)
PHONE..................800 305-6942
Peter Guttieri, *President*
◆ **EMP:** 48
SQ FT: 14,800
SALES (est): 11.7MM **Privately Held**
WEB: www.marksmenmfg.com
SIC: 3452 3599 Bolts, nuts, rivets & washers; machine shop, jobbing & repair

(G-4195)
MASTER CRAFT FINISHERS INC
30 W Jefryn Blvd Ste 1 (11729-4730)
PHONE..................631 586-0540
Fax: 631 586-0180
Roger J Fox, *President*
EMP: 40
SQ FT: 15,000
SALES (est): 4.5MM **Privately Held**
SIC: 3479 3471 2396 Coating of metals & formed products; finishing, metals or formed products; automotive & apparel trimmings

(G-4196)
MCG ELECTRONICS INC
Also Called: McG Surge Protection
12 Burt Dr (11729-5778)
PHONE..................631 586-5125
Fax: 631 586-5120
Michael Coyle, *President*
Suzanne Baron, *General Mgr*
Cecilia Coyle, *Vice Pres*
Kim Connors, *Purch Mgr*
Glenn Clifford, *Engng Exec*
▼ **EMP:** 50
SQ FT: 10,000
SALES (est): 7.7MM **Privately Held**
WEB: www.mcgsurge.com
SIC: 3674 Semiconductors & related devices

(G-4197)
MD INTERNATIONAL INDUSTRIES
Also Called: M D I Industries
120 E Jefryn Blvd Ste Aa (11729-5739)
PHONE..................631 254-3100
Fax: 631 254-3325
Martin Michie, *President*
Blanche Michie, *Shareholder*
EMP: 24
SQ FT: 10,000
SALES (est): 4.4MM **Privately Held**
WEB: www.mdiindustries.com
SIC: 3728 3444 Aircraft parts & equipment; sheet metalwork

(G-4198)
MINI-MAX DNTL REPR EQPMNTS INC
25 W Jefryn Blvd Ste B (11729-5740)
PHONE..................631 242-0322
Brad Vollmer, *Principal*
Michael Gavris, *Principal*
Bill Smith, *Service Mgr*
EMP: 7
SALES: 1.2MM **Privately Held**
SIC: 3843 Dental equipment & supplies

(G-4199)
MODERN PACKAGING INC
505 Acorn St (11729-3601)
PHONE..................631 595-2437
Fax: 631 595-2742
Syed Zaki Hossai, *Ch of Bd*

▲ = Import ▼ = Export
◆ = Import/Export

GEOGRAPHIC SECTION

Deer Park - Suffolk County (G-4227)

Syed Zaki Hossain, *Ch of Bd*
Towhidul Islam, *General Mgr*
Jaroslaw Dabek, *Vice Pres*
Mohammed Hossain, *Research*
▲ **EMP:** 62
SQ FT: 20,000
SALES (est): 15.6MM **Privately Held**
WEB: www.modernpackaginginc.com
SIC: 3599 3565 5084 Custom machinery; packaging machinery; packaging machinery & equipment

(G-4200)
NANZ CUSTOM HARDWARE INC
105 E Jefryn Blvd (11729-5713)
PHONE................................212 367-7000
EMP: 125
SALES (corp-wide): 26.8MM **Privately Held**
WEB: www.nanz.com
SIC: 3429 5031 Door opening & closing devices, except electrical; building materials, interior
PA: Nanz Custom Hardware, Inc.
20 Vandam St Fl 5l
New York NY 10013
212 367-7000

(G-4201)
NATIONAL COMPUTER & ELECTRONIC
Also Called: Nceec
367 Bay Shore Rd Ste D (11729-7244)
PHONE................................631 242-7222
Neal Morofsky, *Chairman*
Lynn Nicolai, *Vice Pres*
Ruth Morofsky, *Manager*
EMP: 8
SQ FT: 5,000
SALES (est): 859K **Privately Held**
WEB: www.ncee.com
SIC: 3469 Electronic enclosures, stamped or pressed metal

(G-4202)
NELCO LABORATORIES INC
154 Brook Ave (11729-7251)
P.O. Box 58 (11729-0058)
PHONE................................631 242-0082
Fax: 631 242-3290
April Catanzaro, *President*
Noelle Park, *Vice Pres*
Holly Mangieri, *Bookkeeper*
Fabio Cipolla, *Lab Dir*
EMP: 22
SQ FT: 6,800
SALES (est): 3.2MM **Privately Held**
WEB: www.nelcolabs.com
SIC: 2836 Allergens, allergenic extracts

(G-4203)
NEW WOP RECORDS
Also Called: Artists, Doo Wop
317 W 14th St (11729-6301)
PHONE................................631 617-9732
Giro Manuele, *Owner*
EMP: 5
SALES (est): 210K **Privately Held**
SIC: 3651 Household audio & video equipment

(G-4204)
NIJON TOOL CO INC
12 Evergreen Pl 12 (11729-3708)
PHONE................................631 242-3434
Franklin Trama, *President*
John Burns, *Vice Pres*
EMP: 10
SQ FT: 12,500
SALES (est): 870K **Privately Held**
SIC: 3544 Special dies & tools

(G-4205)
NIKE INC
102 The Arches Cir (11729-7057)
PHONE................................631 242-3014
EMP: 38
SALES (corp-wide): 32.3B **Publicly Held**
SIC: 3021 Rubber & plastics footwear
PA: Nike, Inc.
1 Sw Bowerman Dr
Beaverton OR 97005
503 671-6453

(G-4206)
NUTEC COMPONENTS INC
81 E Jefryn Blvd Ste A (11729-5733)
PHONE................................631 242-1224
Fax: 631 242-1310
Rene H Schnetzler, *President*
Glenn Stanley, *Vice Pres*
Ruth Ketay, *Director*
EMP: 15
SQ FT: 10,500
SALES (est): 3.6MM **Privately Held**
WEB: www.nutec1.com
SIC: 3823 Industrial instrmnts msrmnt display/control process variable

(G-4207)
NUTRA SOLUTIONS USA INC
Also Called: Nsusa
1019 Grand Blvd (11729-5709)
PHONE................................631 392-1900
Latiful Hakue, *CEO*
Kalsar Sultana, *Principal*
Sheila Andre, *Accounts Mgr*
EMP: 25
SALES (est): 9.5MM **Privately Held**
SIC: 2833 7389 Vitamins, natural or synthetic: bulk, uncompounded; packaging & labeling services

(G-4208)
NY FROYO LLC
324 W 19th St (11729-6342)
PHONE................................516 312-4588
EMP: 5
SALES (est): 254.2K **Privately Held**
SIC: 2024 Yogurt desserts, frozen

(G-4209)
OCEAN CARDIAC MONITORING
38 W 17th St (11729-3902)
PHONE................................631 777-3700
Roberto Garcia, *Owner*
EMP: 5
SALES (est): 586.2K **Privately Held**
SIC: 3845 Patient monitoring apparatus

(G-4210)
OVERNIGHT LABELS INC
151 W Industry Ct Ste 15 (11729-4600)
PHONE................................631 242-4240
Fax: 631 242-4385
Donald Earl, *President*
Maria Bordonari, *Accountant*
Maureen Earl, *Human Resources*
Diane Tennezol, *Sales Mgr*
Tony De Moraes, *Art Dir*
▲ **EMP:** 20
SQ FT: 3,400
SALES (est): 4.9MM **Privately Held**
WEB: www.overnightlabels.com
SIC: 2672 Coated & laminated paper

(G-4211)
PAULS RODS & RESTOS INC
131 Brook Ave Ste 13 (11729-7221)
PHONE................................631 665-7637
Paul R Dimauro, *Principal*
EMP: 6
SALES (est): 830.5K **Privately Held**
SIC: 3531 Automobile wrecker hoists

(G-4212)
PDF SEAL INCORPORATED
503 Acorn St (11729-3601)
PHONE................................631 595-7035
Jaroslaw Dabek, *Ch of Bd*
Syed Zaki Hossain, *Vice Pres*
Jeremy Bank, *Opers Mgr*
Adeeb Hakim, *Prdtn Mgr*
EMP: 25
SQ FT: 16,000
SALES (est): 6.5MM **Privately Held**
SIC: 2631 Container, packaging & boxboard

(G-4213)
PHOTO MEDIC EQUIPMENT INC
Also Called: Precise Optics
3 Saxwood St Ste E (11729-4700)
PHONE................................631 242-6700
Fax: 631 242-4421
Len Corso, *Ch of Bd*
R Hannington, *Purchasing*
Ann Alonzo, *Controller*
R Corso, *Marketing Staff*
Gordon Kellogg, *Systems Mgr*
EMP: 90
SQ FT: 50,000
SALES (est): 7.7MM **Privately Held**
WEB: www.preciseoptics.com
SIC: 3844 X-ray apparatus & tubes

(G-4214)
PLX INC (PA)
Also Called: P L X
25 W Jefryn Blvd Ste A (11729-5740)
PHONE................................631 586-4190
Jack Lipkins, *President*
Zvi Bleier, *Vice Pres*
Doinel Blaj, *Engineer*
Mary Youssef, *Bookkeeper*
Susan Lipkins, *Admin Sec*
EMP: 40 **EST:** 1953
SQ FT: 15,000
SALES (est): 6.7MM **Privately Held**
WEB: www.plxinc.com
SIC: 3827 Optical instruments & apparatus

(G-4215)
PNC SPORTS
1880 Deer Park Ave (11729-4318)
PHONE................................516 665-2244
Richard Knowles, *Principal*
EMP: 7
SALES (est): 688.1K **Privately Held**
SIC: 3949 Sporting & athletic goods

(G-4216)
PRECISION CNC
71 E Jefryn Blvd (11729-5713)
PHONE................................631 847-3999
Sal Napolitano, *Owner*
EMP: 6
SALES (est): 782.4K **Privately Held**
SIC: 3728 Aircraft parts & equipment

(G-4217)
PRIME ELECTRONIC COMPONENTS
Also Called: Prime Components
150 W Industry Ct (11729-4604)
PHONE................................631 254-0101
Fax: 631 242-8896
Daniel Martin, *President*
EMP: 12
SALES (est): 1.1MM **Privately Held**
WEB: www.primecomponents.com
SIC: 3679 Electronic loads & power supplies

(G-4218)
PRINT MARKET INC
66 E Jefryn Blvd Ste 1 (11729-5760)
PHONE................................631 940-8181
EMP: 8
SALES (est): 62.8K **Privately Held**
SIC: 2752 Lithographic Commercial Printing

(G-4219)
PROFESSIONAL MANUFACTURERS
475 Brook Ave (11729-7208)
P.O. Box 282 (11729-0282)
PHONE................................631 586-2440
Fax: 631 586-2443
Richard Lizio, *President*
EMP: 10
SALES (est): 960K **Privately Held**
SIC: 3843 Dental equipment & supplies

(G-4220)
PVH CORP
Also Called: Van Heusen
1358 The Arches Cir (11729-7069)
PHONE................................631 254-8200
Shannon Wright, *Branch Mgr*
EMP: 9
SALES (corp-wide): 8.2B **Publicly Held**
SIC: 2321 Men's & boys' dress shirts
PA: Pvh Corp.
200 Madison Ave Bsmt 1
New York NY 10016
212 381-3500

(G-4221)
R E F PRECISION PRODUCTS
517 Acorn St Ste A (11729-3610)
PHONE................................631 242-4471
Robert Fleece, *Partner*
Raymond Crisafulli, *Partner*
EMP: 17
SQ FT: 3,600
SALES (est): 1.5MM **Privately Held**
WEB: www.refprecisionproducts.com
SIC: 3599 Custom machinery

(G-4222)
R J S DIRECT MARKETING INC
561 Acorn St Ste E (11729-3600)
PHONE................................631 667-5768
Micheal Manfre, *President*
EMP: 15
SALES (est): 1.5MM **Privately Held**
WEB: www.rjsmarketingonline.com
SIC: 2834 Solutions, pharmaceutical

(G-4223)
RAINBOW POWDER COATING CORP
86 E Industry Ct (11729-4704)
PHONE................................631 586-4019
Fax: 631 586-4118
Ron Vincent, *President*
EMP: 5
SQ FT: 5,800
SALES (est): 496.4K **Privately Held**
SIC: 3471 Finishing, metals or formed products

(G-4224)
REFLEX OFFSET INC
305 Suburban Ave (11729-6806)
PHONE................................516 746-4142
Fax: 516 746-4750
John Banks, *President*
Richard Banks, *Vice Pres*
EMP: 8
SQ FT: 5,400
SALES (est): 1MM **Privately Held**
WEB: www.reflexoffset.com
SIC: 2752 Commercial printing, offset

(G-4225)
ROCKPORT COMPANY LLC
1288 The Arches Cir (11729-7068)
PHONE................................631 243-0418
EMP: 54
SALES (corp-wide): 327.7MM **Privately Held**
SIC: 3143 Men's footwear, except athletic
HQ: The Rockport Company Llc
1220 Washington St
Newton MA 02465
617 213-6100

(G-4226)
ROSEMONT PRESS INCORPORATED
35 W Jefryn Blvd Ste A (11729-5784)
PHONE................................212 239-4770
Czarina Anif, *Branch Mgr*
EMP: 9
SALES (corp-wide): 9.6MM **Privately Held**
WEB: www.rosemontpress.com
SIC: 2741 Miscellaneous publishing
PA: Rosemont Press Incorporated
253 Church St Apt 2
New York NY 10013
212 239-4770

(G-4227)
ROSS METAL FABRICATORS INC
225 Marcus Blvd (11729-4503)
P.O. Box 12308, Hauppauge (11788-0615)
PHONE................................631 586-7000
Fax: 631 586-7006
Richard Ross, *President*
Ron Reid, *Vice Pres*
Lawrence Perez, *Treasurer*
EMP: 40
SQ FT: 30,000
SALES (est): 6.6MM
SALES (corp-wide): 37.8MM **Privately Held**
SIC: 3443 Metal parts
PA: Charles Ross & Son Company
710 Old Willets Path
Hauppauge NY 11788
631 234-0500

Deer Park - Suffolk County (G-4228)

(G-4228)
RSM ELECTRON POWER INC (PA)
Also Called: Sensitron Semiconductor
221 W Industry Ct (11729-4605)
PHONE..............................631 586-7600
Fax: 631 242-9798
Steve Saunders, *President*
Susan Saunders, *Accounts Mgr*
Kristie White, *Manager*
Mary Saunders, *Admin Sec*
▲ EMP: 90 EST: 1969
SQ FT: 20,000
SALES (est): 21.2MM **Privately Held**
WEB: www.sensitron.com
SIC: 3674 Semiconductors & related devices

(G-4229)
SCHENCK CORPORATION (DH)
535 Acorn St (11729-3698)
PHONE..............................631 242-4010
Ulrik Flodermann, *President*
Peter Brooks, *Corp Secy*
Catherine Bohnhorst, *Project Mgr*
Ronald Jackson, *Engineer*
Michele Bornholdt, *Personnel*
◆ EMP: 70
SQ FT: 40,000
SALES (est): 63.2MM
SALES (corp-wide): 3.7B **Privately Held**
SIC: 3545 3829 Balancing machines (machine tool accessories); measuring & controlling devices
HQ: Schenck Industrie-Beteiligungen Ag
  C/O Dr. Thomas Hefti
  Glarus GL
  556 402-544

(G-4230)
SCHENCK TREBEL CORP (DH)
535 Acorn St (11729-3616)
PHONE..............................631 242-4397
Fax: 631 242-4308
Ulrik Frodermann, *President*
David Bayley, *District Mgr*
Ronald Kapps, *Facilities Mgr*
Ronald Jackson, *Engineer*
Judith Foddy, *Accountant*
◆ EMP: 60
SQ FT: 44,000
SALES (est): 18.4MM
SALES (corp-wide): 3.7B **Privately Held**
WEB: www.schenck-usa.com
SIC: 3545 3829 Balancing machines (machine tool accessories); measuring & controlling devices
HQ: Schenck Corporation
  535 Acorn St
  Deer Park NY 11729
  631 242-4010

(G-4231)
SCIENTIFIC COMPONENTS CORP
Also Called: Mini Circuits Lab
161 E Industry Ct (11729-4705)
PHONE..............................631 243-4901
Al Chasinov, *Branch Mgr*
Robert Jasinkonis, *Manager*
EMP: 40
SALES (corp-wide): 109.8MM **Privately Held**
SIC: 3825 Instruments to measure electricity
PA: Scientific Components Corp
  13 Neptune Ave
  Brooklyn NY 11235
  718 934-4500

(G-4232)
SECTOR MICROWAVE INDS INC
999 Grand Blvd (11729-5799)
PHONE..............................631 242-2245
Fax: 631 242-8158
Victor Hnelson, *President*
Thomas J Nelson, *Vice Pres*
Jim Tracy, *Info Tech Mgr*
Patricia Nelson, *Admin Sec*
▼ EMP: 60
SQ FT: 28,000
SALES: 7.7MM **Privately Held**
SIC: 3643 Electric switches

(G-4233)
SHANKER INDUSTRIES INC (PA)
301 Suburban Ave (11729-6806)
PHONE..............................631 940-9889
Fax: 516 437-8866
John Shanker, *President*
Frances Shanker, *Vice Pres*
David Shanker, *Sales Mgr*
▲ EMP: 5
SQ FT: 5,700
SALES (est): 1.3MM **Privately Held**
WEB: www.shanko.com
SIC: 3446 Ornamental metalwork

(G-4234)
SHARON MANUFACTURING CO INC
540 Brook Ave (11729-6802)
PHONE..............................631 242-8870
Robert Stamm, *President*
John Zaikowski, *Purch Agent*
EMP: 8
SQ FT: 7,500
SALES (est): 1.8MM **Privately Held**
SIC: 3565 3469 Packaging machinery; bag opening, filling & closing machines; machine parts, stamped or pressed metal

(G-4235)
SOMERS STAIN GLASS INC
108 Brook Ave Ste A (11729-7238)
PHONE..............................631 586-7772
Ronald Somers, *President*
Tricia Somers, *Office Mgr*
Tricia Franqueiro, *Manager*
EMP: 10
SQ FT: 10,000
SALES: 700K **Privately Held**
SIC: 3231 3229 Stained glass: made from purchased glass; lamp parts & shades, glass

(G-4236)
SOUNDCOAT COMPANY INC (DH)
1 Burt Dr (11729-5756)
PHONE..............................631 242-2200
Fax: 631 242-2246
Louis Nenninger, *CEO*
Jim Mills, *Regl Sales Mgr*
Dennis Shand, *Marketing Mgr*
◆ EMP: 65 EST: 1963
SQ FT: 70,000
SALES: 15.2MM
SALES (corp-wide): 313.4MM **Privately Held**
WEB: www.soundcoat.com
SIC: 3086 2299 3625 3296 Insulation or cushioning material, foamed plastic; acoustic felts; noise control equipment; mineral wool
HQ: Recticel Foam Corporation
  5600 Bow Pointe Dr
  Clarkston MI 48346
  248 241-9100

(G-4237)
SPEAQUA CORP
46 W Jefryn Blvd (11729-4736)
PHONE..............................858 334-9042
Steven Patsis, *President*
Steve Patsis, *Vice Pres*
EMP: 40
SQ FT: 20,000
SALES (est): 1.4MM **Privately Held**
SIC: 3651 Loudspeakers, electrodynamic or magnetic

(G-4238)
SUFFOLK COMMUNITY COUNCIL INC (PA)
819 Grand Blvd Ste 1 (11729-5780)
PHONE..............................631 434-9277
Tom Williams, *Exec Dir*
Judith Pannullo, *Director*
Robert E Detor Jr,
EMP: 9
SQ FT: 2,000
SALES (est): 194.3K **Privately Held**
WEB: www.suffolkcommunitycouncil.org
SIC: 2721 8322 Periodicals: publishing only; individual & family services

(G-4239)
SUPER STEELWORKS CORPORATION
12 Lucon Dr (11729-5712)
PHONE..............................718 386-4770
Carlos Mery, *Principal*
▲ EMP: 5
SALES (est): 391.2K **Privately Held**
SIC: 3317 Steel pipe & tubes

(G-4240)
TAE TRANS ATLANTIC ELEC INC (PA)
Also Called: Empire Scientific
151 E Industry Ct (11729-4705)
P.O. Box 817 (11729-0981)
PHONE..............................631 595-9206
Fax: 631 595-9384
Janet English, *President*
Jeffrey English, *Vice Pres*
Spencer Slipko, *Vice Pres*
▲ EMP: 23 EST: 1965
SQ FT: 1,500
SALES (est): 4MM **Privately Held**
WEB: www.empirebat.com
SIC: 3692 5063 Primary batteries, dry & wet; batteries

(G-4241)
TEK PRECISION CO LTD
205 W Industry Ct (11729-4613)
PHONE..............................631 242-0330
Fax: 631 242-1481
John Krause, *CEO*
Steve Longobardi, *President*
Randall Strauss, *Vice Pres*
John A Kruse, *Project Dir*
Pat Sweeney, *Production*
EMP: 24
SQ FT: 21,000
SALES: 10.8MM **Privately Held**
WEB: www.tekprecision.com
SIC: 3728 Aircraft assemblies, subassemblies & parts

(G-4242)
TRI-STATE WINDOW FACTORY CORP
360 Marcus Blvd (11729-4504)
PHONE..............................631 667-8600
John Kypreos, *President*
Nichole Oberst, *Accountant*
David McMahon, *CPA*
EMP: 75
SQ FT: 31,000
SALES (est): 13.8MM **Privately Held**
SIC: 3089 1761 1751 Windows, plastic; siding contractor; window & door (prefabricated) installation

(G-4243)
ULTRA THIN READY TO BAKE PIZZA
Also Called: Ultra Thin Pzza Shlls Fltbrads
151 E Industry Ct (11729-4705)
PHONE..............................516 679-6655
Cherise Kramer, *Vice Pres*
Douglas Bronsky, *Mng Member*
EMP: 30
SQ FT: 15,000
SALES (est): 5.6MM **Privately Held**
SIC: 2099 Pizza, refrigerated: except frozen

(G-4244)
UNIVERSAL SHIELDING CORP
20 W Jefryn Blvd (11729-5769)
PHONE..............................631 667-7900
Fax: 631 667-7912
Irwin Newman, *Ch of Bd*
Lois Newman, *Vice Pres*
Michael Newman, *Vice Pres*
Lou Solano, *CPA*
Ruth Quiles, *Manager*
EMP: 50
SQ FT: 20,000
SALES (est): 12.7MM **Privately Held**
WEB: www.universalshielding.com
SIC: 3448 3469 3444 Buildings, portable: prefabricated metal; metal stampings; sheet metalwork

(G-4245)
UNIVERSAL SIGNS AND SVC INC
435 Brook Ave Unit 2 (11729-6826)
PHONE..............................631 446-1121
Marcos Marmol, *President*
EMP: 27
SQ FT: 20,000
SALES: 3MM **Privately Held**
SIC: 3993 Signs & advertising specialties

(G-4246)
USA SIGNS OF AMERICA INC
172 E Industry Ct (11729-4706)
PHONE..............................631 254-6900
John Prahalis, *President*
Lynn Loder, *Vice Pres*
EMP: 75
SALES (est): 7.3MM **Privately Held**
WEB: www.usasignsofamerica.com
SIC: 3993 Signs & advertising specialties

(G-4247)
VEJA ELECTRONICS INC (PA)
Also Called: Stack Electronics
46 W Jefryn Blvd Ste A (11729-4736)
PHONE..............................631 321-6086
Fax: 631 321-5662
Steven Patsis, *CEO*
Steve Patsis, *President*
Richard Rogers, *Accounts Mgr*
Brenda Wright, *Info Tech Dir*
▲ EMP: 100
SQ FT: 40,000
SALES (est): 32.6MM **Privately Held**
WEB: www.stackny.com
SIC: 3644 5063 5065 Terminal boards; electrical fittings & construction materials; electronic parts

(G-4248)
VERSAPONENTS INC
Also Called: Writing Sculptures
66 N Industry Ct (11729-4602)
PHONE..............................631 242-3387
Fax: 631 242-3461
Chet Yaswen, *President*
Laura Yaswen, *Vice Pres*
EMP: 16
SQ FT: 4,500
SALES (est): 2.7MM **Privately Held**
SIC: 3646 Commercial indusl & institutional electric lighting fixtures

(G-4249)
VINYL MATERIALS INC
365 Bay Shore Rd (11729-7201)
PHONE..............................631 586-9444
Alex Folkman, *President*
Joseph Folkman, *Vice Pres*
Roop Narine Dhanrag, *Controller*
EMP: 50
SQ FT: 65,000
SALES (est): 9MM **Privately Held**
SIC: 3081 5162 3089 Vinyl film & sheet; plastics products; plastic processing

(G-4250)
VISUAL MILLWORK & FIX MFG INC
95 Marcus Blvd (11729-4501)
PHONE..............................718 267-7800
Mario Fichera Sr, *CEO*
Mario Fichera Jr, *Vice Pres*
Lydia Fichara, *CFO*
Roy White, *CFO*
EMP: 60
SQ FT: 50,000
SALES (est): 6MM **Privately Held**
WEB: www.visualdisplayinc.com
SIC: 2542 Office & store showcases & display fixtures

(G-4251)
WESTROCK RKT COMPANY
140 W Industry Ct (11729-4604)
PHONE..............................330 296-5155
Ron Byers, *General Mgr*
Kathy Telesca, *Purchasing*
Tim Anderson, *Engineer*
Bart Cully, *Cust Mgr*
EMP: 130
SQ FT: 120,000

GEOGRAPHIC SECTION

Depew - Erie County (G-4275)

SALES (corp-wide): 14.1B **Publicly Held**
WEB: www.rocktenn.com
SIC: 2653 5113 Boxes, corrugated: made from purchased materials; bags, paper & disposable plastic
HQ: Westrock Rkt Company
504 Thrasher St
Norcross GA 30071
770 448-2193

(G-4252)
WOLF X-RAY CORPORATION
100 W Industry Ct (11729-4604)
PHONE..............................631 242-9729
Martin Wolf, *President*
Carol Price, *Credit Mgr*
Howard Wolf, *Sales Mgr*
William Winters, *Director*
Melissa Ferguson, *Executive Asst*
◆ **EMP:** 60 **EST:** 1931
SQ FT: 80,000
SALES (est): 10.2MM **Privately Held**
WEB: www.wolfxray.com
SIC: 3844 X-ray apparatus & tubes

(G-4253)
WOLO MFG CORP
1 Saxwood St Ste 1 (11729-4779)
PHONE..............................631 242-0333
Fax: 631 242-0720
Stanley Solow, *President*
▲ **EMP:** 21
SQ FT: 10,000
SALES (est): 4MM **Privately Held**
SIC: 3429 3714 3647 Motor vehicle hardware; motor vehicle parts & accessories; vehicular lighting equipment

(G-4254)
WORLD LLC
Also Called: Wmw Machinery Company
513 Acorn St Ste B (11729-3611)
PHONE..............................631 940-9121
Fax: 845 358-2378
Cornel Circiumaru, *Mng Member*
Lester White, *Info Tech Mgr*
▼ **EMP:** 15
SQ FT: 8,000
SALES: 1.5MM **Privately Held**
SIC: 3541 Machine tools, metal cutting type

(G-4255)
Z BEST PRINTING INC
699 Acorn St Ste B (11729-4235)
PHONE..............................631 595-1400
Fax: 516 845-1439
Ronald S Bard, *President*
Craig Bard, *Vice Pres*
Gayle Bard, *Admin Sec*
EMP: 10
SQ FT: 5,000
SALES: 1.5MM **Privately Held**
SIC: 2252 2261 Leg warmers; screen printing of cotton broadwoven fabrics

(G-4256)
ZACMEL GRAPHICS LLC
500 Brook Ave Ste B (11729-6835)
PHONE..............................631 944-6031
David Warheit,
EMP: 7 **EST:** 2003
SALES (est): 1MM **Privately Held**
SIC: 2752 7336 Commercial printing, lithographic; commercial art & graphic design

Delanson
Schenectady County

(G-4257)
BENZSAY & HARRISON INC
Railroad Ave (12053)
PHONE..............................518 895-2311
Fax: 518 895-8475
Rudolph Benzsay, *President*
Sema Benzsay, *Admin Sec*
EMP: 6
SQ FT: 25,000
SALES: 900.1K **Privately Held**
WEB: www.bh-inc.com
SIC: 2819 Aluminum compounds

(G-4258)
ELECTRCAL INSTRUMENTATION CTRL
1253 Youngs Rd (12053-1711)
P.O. Box 24, Duanesburg (12056-0024)
PHONE..............................518 861-5789
Michael Weiss, *President*
EMP: 11
SALES: 2MM **Privately Held**
SIC: 3823 Industrial process control instruments

(G-4259)
HARVEST HOMES INC
1331 Cole Rd (12053-3109)
PHONE..............................518 895-2341
Fax: 518 895-2287
Timothy O Brien, *Ch of Bd*
Robert A Guay, *Vice Pres*
Christian Guay, *Sales Mgr*
Dan Steiner, *Office Mgr*
Gary Shufelt, *Info Tech Mgr*
EMP: 26
SQ FT: 27,000
SALES: 4.9MM **Privately Held**
SIC: 2452 2439 Panels & sections, prefabricated, wood; structural wood members

Delevan
Cattaraugus County

(G-4260)
HALEY CONCRETE INC (PA)
10413 Delevan Elton Rd (14042-9613)
PHONE..............................716 492-0849
Fax: 585 492-0884
Lawrence Haley II, *President*
Lawrence Haley III, *Admin Sec*
EMP: 15
SQ FT: 1,250
SALES (est): 2MM **Privately Held**
SIC: 3273 4212 Ready-mixed concrete; local trucking, without storage

(G-4261)
KENDOR MUSIC INC
21 Grove St (14042-9682)
P.O. Box 278 (14042-0278)
PHONE..............................716 492-1254
Fax: 716 492-5124
Craig Cornwall, *President*
Jackie Cornwall, *Controller*
EMP: 12
SQ FT: 10,000
SALES (est): 1MM **Privately Held**
WEB: www.kendormusic.com
SIC: 2741 Music, sheet: publishing & printing

Delhi
Delaware County

(G-4262)
DELAWARE COUNTY TIMES INC
56 Main St (13753-1121)
PHONE..............................607 746-2176
Fax: 607 746-3135
Donald F Bishop II, *President*
David Ketchum, *Sls & Mktg Exec*
Thomas Briggs, *Exec Dir*
EMP: 6
SALES (est): 250K **Privately Held**
SIC: 2711 2721 Newspapers; periodicals

(G-4263)
EXCELSIOR PUBLICATIONS
133 Main St (13753-1219)
PHONE..............................607 746-7600
Fax: 607 746-2750
Francis P Ruggiero, *President*
EMP: 5 **EST:** 1999
SALES (est): 479.5K **Privately Held**
SIC: 2721 Magazines: publishing & printing

(G-4264)
FRIESLNDCMPINA INGRDNTS N AMER
40196 State Hwy 10 Delhi (13753)
PHONE..............................607 746-0196
Don Combs, *Principal*
Irene Oerlemans, *Human Res Dir*
Joann Schreurs, *Office Mgr*
Tom Heijkant, *Manager*
EMP: 35
SALES (corp-wide): 11.6B **Privately Held**
SIC: 2023 Dry, condensed, evaporated dairy products
HQ: Frieslandcampina Ingredients North America, Inc
61 S Paramus Rd Ste 535
Paramus NJ 07652
201 655-7780

(G-4265)
MARTIN D WHITBECK
68 Meredith St (13753-1034)
PHONE..............................607 746-7642
Martin Whitbeck, *Owner*
Martin D Whitbeck, *Principal*
EMP: 6 **EST:** 2016
SALES (est): 179.5K **Privately Held**
SIC: 2011 Variety meats, fresh edible organs

(G-4266)
PROMATS ATHLETICS LLC (PA)
41155 State Highway 10 (13753-3213)
P.O. Box 231 (13753-0231)
PHONE..............................607 746-8911
Edward Rosa, *Vice Pres*
Dave Cloud, *Sales Mgr*
Liam Miller, *Sales Staff*
Danny Nance, *Sales Staff*
Dave Rama, *Sales Staff*
EMP: 33
SALES (est): 6MM **Privately Held**
WEB: www.promats.com
SIC: 3949 Sporting & athletic goods

(G-4267)
SAPUTO DAIRY FOODS USA LLC
Also Called: Morningstar Foods
40236 State Highway 10 (13753-3207)
P.O. Box 1 (13753-0001)
PHONE..............................607 746-2141
Elizabeth Banburen, *Manager*
EMP: 100
SALES (corp-wide): 1.9B **Privately Held**
WEB: www.morningstarfoods.com
SIC: 2026 Fluid milk
HQ: Saputo Dairy Foods Usa, Llc
2711 N Haske Ave Ste 3700
Dallas TX 75204
214 863-2300

(G-4268)
SPORTSFIELD SPECIALTIES INC
41155 State Highway 10 (13753-3213)
P.O. Box 231 (13753-0231)
PHONE..............................607 746-8911
Fax: 607 746-8481
Wayne Oliver, *President*
Ed Rosa, *Vice Pres*
Eric Hulbert, *Opers Mgr*
Phuong Mokay, *Engineer*
Lynn Pickett, *Credit Mgr*
EMP: 45
SQ FT: 46,000
SALES (est): 15.8MM **Privately Held**
WEB: www.sportsfieldspecialties.com
SIC: 3949 Sporting & athletic goods

Delmar
Albany County

(G-4269)
COMMUNITY MEDIA GROUP LLC (PA)
Also Called: Spotlight Newspaper
125 Adams St (12054-3211)
PHONE..............................518 439-4949
Fax: 518 439-5198
Bo Berezansky, *Vice Pres*
John McLntyre Jr, *Vice Pres*
Bill Decker, *Consultant*
John A McIntyre Jr,
Daniel E Alexander,
EMP: 11
SALES (est): 1.7MM **Privately Held**
SIC: 2711 Newspapers

(G-4270)
NEWSGRAPHICS OF DELMAR INC
Also Called: The Spotlight
125 Adams St (12054-3211)
P.O. Box 100 (12054-0100)
PHONE..............................518 439-5363
Richard Ahlstrom, *President*
Mary Ahlstrom, *Admin Sec*
EMP: 25
SQ FT: 2,500
SALES (est): 2.2MM **Privately Held**
SIC: 2721 2752 Magazines: publishing only, not printed on site; commercial printing, offset

(G-4271)
SANZDRANZ LLC (PA)
Also Called: Gatherer's Gourmet Granola
83 Dumbarton Dr (12054-4418)
PHONE..............................518 894-8625
Sandro Gerbini, *President*
EMP: 5 **EST:** 2010
SQ FT: 3,700
SALES (est): 210K **Privately Held**
SIC: 2043 Cereal breakfast foods

Depew
Erie County

(G-4272)
AUBURN-WATSON CORP (PA)
3295 Walden Ave (14043-2313)
PHONE..............................716 876-8000
Fax: 716 206-0799
Wayne Watson, *President*
Natalie Watson, *Vice Pres*
Laszlo Szlabonyi, *Prdtn Mgr*
James Fitzsimmons, *Manager*
EMP: 10 **EST:** 1946
SQ FT: 8,000
SALES (est): 754.5K **Privately Held**
SIC: 2434 1751 Wood kitchen cabinets; cabinet building & installation

(G-4273)
BISON STEEL INCORPORATED
2 Main St Ste 103 (14043-3323)
P.O. Box 454 (14043-0454)
PHONE..............................716 683-0900
Fax: 716 683-3529
Edwin C Bailey, *President*
Gus Schiralli, *Admin Sec*
▲ **EMP:** 5
SQ FT: 27,000
SALES (est): 714.7K **Privately Held**
SIC: 3442 Screens, window, metal

(G-4274)
BUFFALO ENVELOPE INC
Also Called: Buffalo Envelope Company
2914 Walden Ave Ste 300 (14043-2694)
PHONE..............................716 686-0100
Fax: 716 686-9005
Lorne Hill, *Managing Dir*
Dany Paradis, *Principal*
EMP: 12
SQ FT: 12,800
SALES (est): 2.7MM
SALES (corp-wide): 118.7MM **Privately Held**
SIC: 2677 5112 Envelopes; envelopes
PA: Supremex Inc
7213 Rue Cordner
Lasalle QC H8N 2
514 595-0555

(G-4275)
BUFFALO POWER ELEC CTR DE
166 Taylor Dr Ste 1 (14043-2021)
PHONE..............................716 651-1600
William Gates, *Ch of Bd*
Dennis M Cascio, *President*
Frank Stasio, *Vice Pres*
Mel Davis, *Mfg Mgr*
Jim Tokasz, *Sales Engr*
EMP: 45
SQ FT: 38,000
SALES (est): 6MM **Privately Held**
WEB: www.buffalopower.com
SIC: 3612 5065 3566 Transformers, except electric; transformers, electronic; speed changers, drives & gears

Depew - Erie County (G-4276)   **GEOGRAPHIC SECTION**

(G-4276)
BUFFALO TUNGSTEN INC
2 Main St (14043-3323)
P.O. Box 397 (14043-0397)
PHONE..................................716 759-6353
Ralph V Shopwalter, *Ch of Bd*
Roger Showlte, *Prdtn Mgr*
Jeffrey Showalter, *Engineer*
Tibed Showalte, *Accountant*
Jason Lahti, *Finance*
◆ **EMP:** 60
SQ FT: 500,000
SALES (est): 17.5MM **Privately Held**
WEB: www.buffalotungsten.com
SIC: 3399 2819 Powder, metal; tungsten carbide powder, except abrasive or metallurgical

(G-4277)
CUSTOM COUNTERTOPS INC (PA)
3192 Walden Ave (14043-2846)
PHONE..................................716 685-2871
Gloria Marino, *President*
EMP: 8
SALES: 750K **Privately Held**
WEB: www.customcountertops.com
SIC: 3131 2541 Counters; wood partitions & fixtures

(G-4278)
D R M MANAGEMENT INC (PA)
Also Called: Fresh Bake Pizza Co
3430 Transit Rd (14043-4853)
PHONE..................................716 668-0333
Ronald Digiore, *President*
Daniel J Digiore, *Vice Pres*
Colleen Tranquilli, *Manager*
Mark Digiore, *Admin Sec*
EMP: 25
SQ FT: 1,200
SALES (est): 5.3MM **Privately Held**
WEB: www.drminc.us
SIC: 2099 2038 8741 Food preparations; pizza, refrigerated: except frozen; pizza, frozen; restaurant management

(G-4279)
DESU MACHINERY CORPORATION
200 Gould Ave (14043-3134)
P.O. Box 245 (14043-0245)
PHONE..................................716 681-5798
Martin W Golden II, *CEO*
Mark L Dalquist, *President*
William Livingston, *Purchasing*
Thomas Depczynski, *Sls & Mktg Exec*
Tom Russles, *Human Res Dir*
EMP: 85
SALES (est): 8MM **Privately Held**
SIC: 3556 3565 Packing house machinery; bottling machinery: filling, capping, labeling

(G-4280)
ELMAR INDUSTRIES INC
200 Gould Ave (14043-3138)
P.O. Box 245 (14043-0245)
PHONE..................................716 681-5650
Fax: 716 681-4660
Martin W Golden II, *Ch of Bd*
Mark L Dahlquist, *Ch of Bd*
Mark Vaughn, *Engineer*
James Krypel, *Design Engr*
Linda Gregorio, *Finance*
▲ **EMP:** 62
SQ FT: 21,000
SALES (est): 17.6MM **Privately Held**
WEB: www.elmarworldwide.com
SIC: 3556 Food products machinery

(G-4281)
FIBRIX LLC
Buffalo Batt A Div of Polyeste
3307 Walden Ave (14043-2347)
PHONE..................................716 683-4100
Bob Heilman, *Manager*
Chuck Bushsmer, *Manager*
Chuck Ramen, *Administration*
EMP: 50
SQ FT: 43,000
SALES (corp-wide): 74MM **Privately Held**
WEB: www.leggett.com
SIC: 2299 2824 2221 Batting, wadding, padding & fillings; pillow fillings: curled hair, cotton waste, moss, hemp tow; organic fibers, noncellulosic; broadwoven fabric mills, manmade
HQ: Fibrix, Llc
1820 Evans St Ne
Conover NC 28613

(G-4282)
FLADO ENTERPRISES INC
Also Called: Quality Quick Signs
1380 French Rd Ste 6 (14043-4800)
PHONE..................................716 668-6400
Christopher R Flejtuch, *President*
EMP: 7
SQ FT: 7,000
SALES (est): 798.2K **Privately Held**
WEB: www.qualityquicksigns.com
SIC: 3993 Signs & advertising specialties

(G-4283)
HOWDEN NORTH AMERICA INC (DH)
Also Called: Howdens
2475 George Urban Blvd # 120 (14043-2022)
PHONE..................................803 741-2700
Matthew Ingle, *CEO*
Karl Kimmerling, *President*
Will Samuel, *Chairman*
Grahame Gurney, *Vice Pres*
David Smith, *Plant Mgr*
◆ **EMP:** 85 **EST:** 1980
SALES (est): 277.2MM
SALES (corp-wide): 3.6B **Publicly Held**
WEB: www.howdenbuffalo.com
SIC: 3564 3568 Exhaust fans: industrial or commercial; couplings, shaft: rigid, flexible, universal joint, etc.
HQ: Anderson Group Inc.
3411 Silverside Rd # 103
Wilmington DE 19810
302 478-6160

(G-4284)
HOWDEN NORTH AMERICA INC
Also Called: Howden Fan Company
2475 George Urban Blvd (14043-2022)
PHONE..................................716 817-6900
Fax: 716 817-6901
Darryl Halter, *Principal*
Joe Okoniewski, *Accountant*
Robert Pheil, *Human Res Dir*
Leona Backus, *Human Resources*
Greg Brill, *Accounts Mgr*
EMP: 100
SALES (corp-wide): 3.6B **Publicly Held**
WEB: www.howdenbuffalo.com
SIC: 3564 8711 Ventilating fans: industrial or commercial; engineering services
HQ: Howden North America Inc.
2475 George Urban Blvd # 120
Depew NY 14043
803 741-2700

(G-4285)
LEGNO VENETO USA
3283 Walden Ave (14043-2311)
PHONE..................................716 651-9169
James Carol II, *Owner*
James Caroll, *Owner*
Jerrie Janis, *Bookkeeper*
▲ **EMP:** 9
SQ FT: 26,000
SALES (est): 1MM **Privately Held**
WEB: www.lvwoodfloors.com
SIC: 2426 Flooring, hardwood

(G-4286)
LEICA MICROSYSTEMS INC
Also Called: Opd
3362 Walden Ave (14043-2475)
P.O. Box 123, Cragsmoor (12420-0123)
PHONE..................................716 686-3000
Fax: 716 686-3085
Tom Tonner, *QC Mgr*
Mark Wood, *Personnel Exec*
John Burgess, *Branch Mgr*
EMP: 8
SALES (corp-wide): 16.8B **Publicly Held**
SIC: 3827 Optical instruments & apparatus; microscopes, except electron, proton & corneal
HQ: Leica Microsystems Inc.
1700 Leider Ln
Buffalo Grove IL 60089
847 405-0123

(G-4287)
LIFEFORMS PRINTING
786 Terrace Blvd Ste 2 (14043-3729)
PHONE..................................716 685-4500
Nick Sanders, *Principal*
EMP: 6
SQ FT: 7,500
SALES (est): 624.7K **Privately Held**
SIC: 2759 Business forms: printing

(G-4288)
MOLDCRAFT INC
240 Gould Ave (14043-3130)
PHONE..................................716 684-1126
Fax: 716 684-0932
John Chase, *President*
Henry Lewandowski, *Treasurer*
Sharon Winkler, *Manager*
Jimmy Gray, *Admin Sec*
EMP: 20
SQ FT: 8,000
SALES (est): 3.8MM **Privately Held**
WEB: www.moldcraftinc.com
SIC: 3544 Forms (molds), for foundry & plastics working machinery

(G-4289)
NIAGARA REFINING LLC
5661 Transit Rd (14043-3227)
P.O. Box 398 (14043-0398)
PHONE..................................716 706-1400
▲ **EMP:** 27
SALES (est): 7.9MM **Privately Held**
SIC: 2819 Tungsten carbide powder, except abrasive or metallurgical

(G-4290)
NORTHEAST METROLOGY CORP
4490 Broadway (14043-2904)
PHONE..................................716 827-3770
Fax: 716 827-3775
Basil Korbut, *President*
Fred Miller, *Research*
Ursula Korbut, *Office Mgr*
EMP: 10
SQ FT: 6,120
SALES (est): 2MM **Privately Held**
WEB: www.vantek-nem.com
SIC: 3825 8734 Test equipment for electronic & electric measurement; testing laboratories

(G-4291)
OSMOSE HOLDINGS INC
2475 George Urban Blvd # 160 (14043-2022)
PHONE..................................716 882-5905
James R Spengler Jr, *President*
Elias Akle, *General Mgr*
John Kile, *General Mgr*
Joe Dobyns, *District Mgr*
David L Bradley, *Vice Pres*
◆ **EMP:** 1335
SALES (est): 228.8MM **Publicly Held**
WEB: www.fireretardanttreatedwood.com
SIC: 2491 Preserving (creosoting) of wood
HQ: Oaktree Capital Management, L.P.
333 S Grand Ave Ste 2800
Los Angeles CA 90071

(G-4292)
PCB GROUP INC (HQ)
Also Called: ICP
3425 Walden Ave (14043-2417)
PHONE..................................716 684-0001
Mike Lally, *CEO*
James F Lally, *Ch of Bd*
Graham Turgoose, *Managing Dir*
John Betzig, *Opers Mgr*
Larry Dick, *Opers Mgr*
EMP: 50
SQ FT: 64,000
SALES (est): 220MM
SALES (corp-wide): 650.1MM **Publicly Held**
SIC: 3679 3823 Transducers, electrical; industrial instrmnts msrmnt display/control process variable
PA: Mts Systems Corporation
14000 Technology Dr
Eden Prairie MN 55344
952 937-4000

(G-4293)
PCB PIEZOTRONICS INC
Larson Davis
3425 Walden Ave (14043-2495)
PHONE..................................716 684-0001
Fax: 716 926-8215
Jeff Williams, *Marketing Staff*
EMP: 8
SALES (corp-wide): 650.1MM **Publicly Held**
SIC: 3829 Measuring & controlling devices
HQ: Pcb Piezotronics, Inc.
3425 Walden Ave
Depew NY 14043
716 684-0001

(G-4294)
PCB PIEZOTRONICS INC
Industrl Mntrng Instrmntatn Dv
3425 Walden Ave (14043-2495)
PHONE..................................716 684-0003
John Cornaccio, *Vice Pres*
Sue Wood, *Purchasing*
Steve Boisvert, *Engineer*
Eric Vogel, *Engineer*
Susan Ruhland, *Human Res Dir*
EMP: 400
SALES (corp-wide): 650.1MM **Publicly Held**
WEB: www.pcb.com
SIC: 3679 5063 Electronic circuits; electrical apparatus & equipment
HQ: Pcb Piezotronics, Inc.
3425 Walden Ave
Depew NY 14043
716 684-0001

(G-4295)
QMC TECHNOLOGIES INC
4388 Broadway (14043-2998)
PHONE..................................716 681-0810
Fax: 716 681-0881
James A Serafin, *President*
Rachael S Serafin, *General Mgr*
Bob Serafin, *Vice Pres*
▲ **EMP:** 16
SQ FT: 5,500
SALES (est): 5.1MM **Privately Held**
WEB: www.qmctechnologies.com
SIC: 3315 Fence gates posts & fittings: steel

(G-4296)
REICHERT INC
Also Called: Reichert Technologies
3362 Walden Ave (14043-2437)
PHONE..................................716 686-4500
Bruce Wilson, *Ch of Bd*
Timothy Levindofske, *President*
Karen Garbacz, *General Mgr*
Jerry C Cirino, *Vice Pres*
Nick Dimatteo, *Engineer*
▲ **EMP:** 147
SQ FT: 48,000
SALES (est): 41.2MM
SALES (corp-wide): 3.8B **Publicly Held**
WEB: www.leicams.com
SIC: 3841 Surgical & medical instruments
PA: Ametek, Inc.
1100 Cassatt Rd
Berwyn PA 19312
610 647-2121

(G-4297)
RMF PRINT MANAGEMENT GROUP
786 Terrace Blvd Ste 3 (14043-3729)
P.O. Box 329, Lancaster (14086-0329)
PHONE..................................716 683-4351
Sharon Doherty, *Manager*
EMP: 12
SALES (est): 1.8MM **Privately Held**
SIC: 2752 Commercial printing, lithographic

▲ = Import ▼ = Export
◆ = Import/Export

GEOGRAPHIC SECTION

(G-4298)
SAFELITE GLASS CORP
2918 Walden Ave (14043-2600)
PHONE.................................716 685-1358
Fax: 716 517-7279
EMP: 5
SALES (corp-wide): 3.1B **Privately Held**
SIC: 3231 Products of purchased glass
HQ: Safelite Glass Corp.
    7400 Safelite Way
    Columbus OH 43235
    614 210-9000

Deposit
Broome County

(G-4299)
CANNONSVILLE LUMBER INC
199 Old Route 10 (13754-2100)
PHONE.................................607 467-3380
Fax: 607 467-3376
Adolf Schaffer Jr, *President*
EMP: 5 EST: 1998
SALES (est): 814.8K **Privately Held**
SIC: 3553 Sawmill machines

(G-4300)
COURIER PRINTING CORP
24 Laurel Bank Ave Ste 2 (13754-1244)
PHONE.................................607 467-2191
Hilton Evans, *President*
Brenda Degraw, *Manager*
Alice Martin, *Manager*
Sarah Evans, *Admin Sec*
EMP: 30 EST: 1848
SQ FT: 55,000
SALES: 1.7MM **Privately Held**
WEB: www.courierprintingcorp.com
SIC: 2752 Commercial printing, lithographic

(G-4301)
INTEGRATED WOOD COMPONENTS INC
Also Called: Iwci
791 Airport Rd (13754-1277)
P.O. Box 145 (13754-0145)
PHONE.................................607 467-1739
Fax: 607 467-2035
John Kamp, *President*
Tom Stobert, *Corp Secy*
Gerard Kamp, *Vice Pres*
Cork Faulkner, *Accounts Exec*
Dave Mills, *Supervisor*
EMP: 49
SQ FT: 2,800
SALES (est): 5.3MM **Privately Held**
SIC: 2541 Wood partitions & fixtures

(G-4302)
SANFORD STONE LLC
185 Latham Rd (13754-1271)
PHONE.................................607 467-1313
George W Sanford,
EMP: 21
SALES (est): 2.3MM **Privately Held**
SIC: 3281 Cut stone & stone products

(G-4303)
SCHAEFER ENTPS OF DEPOSIT
315 Old Route 10 (13754-2106)
PHONE.................................607 467-4990
Larry Schaefer, *President*
EMP: 30
SALES (est): 3.3MM **Privately Held**
SIC: 1422 Cement rock, crushed & broken-quarrying

(G-4304)
SCHAEFER LOGGING INC
315 Old Route 10 (13754-2106)
PHONE.................................607 467-4990
Larry Schaefer, *President*
EMP: 10
SALES (est): 983.9K **Privately Held**
SIC: 2411 5411 Logging; convenience stores

(G-4305)
WALTER R TUCKER ENTPS LTD
Also Called: E-Z Red Co
8 Leonard Way (13754-1240)
P.O. Box 80 (13754-0080)
PHONE.................................607 467-2866
Fax: 607 467-2323
Mark Tucker, *President*
Bob Cacciabeve, *Exec VP*
Schayne Bowen, *Foreman/Supr*
Luke Tucker, *Sales Mgr*
▲ EMP: 25 EST: 1966
SQ FT: 13,000
SALES (est): 5.9MM **Privately Held**
WEB: www.ezred.com
SIC: 3825 3824 3991 3629 Battery testers, electrical; test equipment for electronic & electric measurement; liquid meters; brushes, except paint & varnish; battery chargers, rectifying or nonrotating; motor vehicle supplies & new parts; testing equipment, electrical: automotive

Derby
Erie County

(G-4306)
GREYLINE SIGNS INC
6681 Schuyler Dr (14047-9644)
PHONE.................................716 947-4526
Linda Scritchfield, *President*
Everett Scritchfield, *Vice Pres*
EMP: 5
SALES (est): 430K **Privately Held**
SIC: 3993 Signs & advertising specialties

(G-4307)
NEW ERA CAP CO INC
8061 Erie Rd (14047-9503)
PHONE.................................716 549-0445
Fax: 716 923-9996
Eileen Beiter, *COO*
Sheila Halloran, *Auditor*
EMP: 11
SALES (corp-wide): 529.4MM **Privately Held**
SIC: 2353 Uniform hats & caps; baseball caps
PA: New Era Cap Co., Inc.
    160 Delaware Ave
    Buffalo NY 14202
    716 604-9000

Dexter
Jefferson County

(G-4308)
HANA SPORTSWEAR INC
321 Lakeview Dr (13634)
PHONE.................................315 639-6332
Fax: 315 639-6136
Robert Hartz, *President*
Beth Laster, *Treasurer*
Hartz Robert, *Manager*
▲ EMP: 20
SQ FT: 13,000
SALES (est): 2.1MM **Privately Held**
SIC: 3949 2339 2311 Sporting & athletic goods; women's & misses' outerwear; men's & boys' suits & coats

(G-4309)
I ABC CORPORATION
349 Lakeview Dr (13634)
PHONE.................................315 639-3100
Gretchen Young, *General Mgr*
▲ EMP: 30
SALES (est): 2.5MM **Privately Held**
SIC: 2339 Bathing suits: women's, misses' & juniors'

(G-4310)
VENUS MANUFACTURING CO INC (PA)
349 Lakeview Dr (13634)
P.O. Box 551 (13634-0551)
PHONE.................................315 639-3100
Fax: 315 639-3101
Roger Reifensnyder, *CEO*
Michael J Hennegan, *President*
▲ EMP: 90
SQ FT: 14,000
SALES (est): 6.2MM **Privately Held**
WEB: www.venusswimwear.com
SIC: 2339 Bathing suits: women's, misses' & juniors'

Dix Hills
Suffolk County

(G-4311)
A & D TOOL INC
30 Pashen Pl (11746-6600)
PHONE.................................631 243-4339
Dimitrios Margiellos, *President*
Tatiana Labate, *Corp Secy*
EMP: 7
SALES: 360K **Privately Held**
WEB: www.adtool.com
SIC: 3544 Forms (molds), for foundry & plastics working machinery

(G-4312)
AKA SPORT INC
16 Princeton Dr (11746-4826)
P.O. Box 1088, Commack (11725-0942)
PHONE.................................631 858-9888
Jon Bihn, *President*
Xiping Bihn, *Corp Secy*
▲ EMP: 11
SALES: 2MM **Privately Held**
SIC: 2393 3161 7389 Canvas bags; traveling bags;

(G-4313)
ALTERNATIVES FOR CHILDREN
600 S Service Rd (11746-6015)
PHONE.................................631 271-0777
Vivienne Viera, *Director*
EMP: 31
SALES (corp-wide): 14.1MM **Privately Held**
SIC: 3949 Windsurfing boards (sailboards) & equipment
PA: Alternatives For Children
    14 Research Way
    East Setauket NY 11733
    631 331-6400

(G-4314)
AUTHORITY TRANSPORTATION INC
Also Called: Authority On Transportation
167 Oakfield Ave (11746-6327)
PHONE.................................888 933-1268
Jinya Kato, *Principal*
David Lipsky, *Principal*
EMP: 12
SQ FT: 40,000
SALES (est): 1MM **Privately Held**
SIC: 3716 Motor homes

(G-4315)
KENT ELECTRO-PLATING CORP
5 Dupont Ct (11746-6258)
PHONE.................................718 358-9599
Fax: 718 358-9799
Anthony Galluccio, *President*
Anthony Galluccio Jr, *Vice Pres*
Michael Galluccio, *Vice Pres*
Vera Galluccio, *Treasurer*
EMP: 10 EST: 1954
SQ FT: 7,500
SALES: 1.5MM **Privately Held**
SIC: 3471 Electroplating of metals or formed products

(G-4316)
MAYFLOWER SPLINT CO
16 Arbor Ln (11746-5127)
P.O. Box 381, Huntington Station (11746-0309)
PHONE.................................631 549-5131
Fax: 631 424-6451
Inge Krueger, *Owner*
EMP: 25
SALES (est): 1.6MM **Privately Held**
SIC: 3842 Surgical appliances & supplies

(G-4317)
MCG GRAPHICS INC
101 Village Hill Dr (11746-8335)
PHONE.................................631 499-0730
Fax: 631 499-0731
Michael Goldsmith, *President*
EMP: 6
SQ FT: 800
SALES (est): 747.1K **Privately Held**
SIC: 2752 2754 Commercial printing, lithographic; commercial printing, gravure

(G-4318)
PREMIERE LIVING PRODUCTS LLC
22 Branwood Dr (11746-5710)
PHONE.................................631 873-4337
Sandy Cohen, *Mng Member*
◆ EMP: 10
SALES (est): 477.2K **Privately Held**
SIC: 2511 Storage chests, household: wood

(G-4319)
PRINTING X PRESS IONS
5 Dix Cir (11746-6033)
PHONE.................................631 242-1992
Fax: 631 254-8911
Christine Sigel, *Owner*
EMP: 7
SALES: 1.5MM **Privately Held**
WEB: www.printingxpresns.com
SIC: 2752 Commercial printing, lithographic

(G-4320)
SAFE CIRCUITS INC
15 Shoreham Dr W (11746-6580)
PHONE.................................631 586-3682
James Ptucha, *Principal*
EMP: 6 EST: 2008
SALES (est): 784.1K **Privately Held**
SIC: 3679 Electronic circuits

(G-4321)
SENTRY DEVICES CORP
33 Rustic Gate Ln (11746-6136)
PHONE.................................631 491-3191
Alex Feibush, *President*
EMP: 5
SALES (est): 400K **Privately Held**
SIC: 3669 1731 Burglar alarm apparatus, electric; marine horns, electric; fire detection & burglar alarm systems specialization

(G-4322)
TREBOR INSTRUMENT CORP
39 Balsam Dr (11746-7724)
PHONE.................................631 423-7026
Fax: 516 293-2065
Zygmunt Grzesiak, *President*
EMP: 8
SQ FT: 2,200
SALES (est): 855.5K **Privately Held**
WEB: www.treborinst.com
SIC: 3599 Machine shop, jobbing & repair

(G-4323)
YING KE YOUTH AGE GROUP INC
1 Campbell Dr (11746-7901)
PHONE.................................929 402-8458
Mark Bestercy, *Vice Pres*
EMP: 12
SALES (est): 241.2K **Privately Held**
SIC: 3751 5137 5065 Motor scooters & parts; women's & children's clothing; electronic parts & equipment

Dobbs Ferry
Westchester County

(G-4324)
AKZO NOBEL CHEMICALS LLC
Also Called: Akzo Nobel Central Research
7 Livingstone Ave (10522-3401)
PHONE.................................914 674-5008
Richard Fennelly, *Counsel*
Louis Morris, *Counsel*
Richard Lendecky, *Controller*
Al Williams, *Human Res Mgr*
Mark Buczek, *Marketing Staff*
EMP: 250

Dobbs Ferry - Westchester County (G-4325)

SALES (corp-wide): 15B **Privately Held**
WEB: www.akzo-nobel.com
SIC: **2819** 8731 2899 Industrial inorganic chemicals; commercial physical research; chemical preparations
HQ: Akzo Nobel Chemicals Llc
525 W Van Buren St # 1600
Chicago IL 60607
312 544-7000

(G-4325)
AKZO NOBEL INC
7 Livingstone Ave (10522-3401)
PHONE..................................914 674-5181
Traci Lee, *Accountant*
Mark Schroeder, *Marketing Staff*
EMP: 6
SALES (est): 119.8K **Privately Held**
SIC: **2869** Industrial organic chemicals

(G-4326)
REMBAR COMPANY LLC
67 Main St (10522-2152)
P.O. Box 67 (10522-0067)
PHONE..................................914 693-2620
Fax: 914 693-2247
Frank H Firor, *CEO*
Walter Pastor, *President*
Audra Haase, *Vice Pres*
▼ EMP: 23 EST: 1950
SQ FT: 8,000
SALES (est): 2.7MM **Privately Held**
WEB: www.rembar.com
SIC: **3297** 3399 Nonclay refractories; metal powders, pastes & flakes

(G-4327)
SUN SCIENTIFIC INC
145 Palisade St (10522-1617)
PHONE..................................914 479-5108
Sundram Ravikumar, *President*
Shridhar Shanmugam, *COO*
Arti Ravikumar, *Vice Pres*
EMP: 7
SQ FT: 1,500
SALES (est): 660.8K **Privately Held**
SIC: **3845** Electromedical equipment

(G-4328)
W H WHITE PUBLICATIONS INC
Also Called: Rivertowns Enterprise
95 Main St (10522-1673)
PHONE..................................914 725-2500
Deborah White, *President*
EMP: 8 EST: 1981
SALES (est): 370K **Privately Held**
SIC: **2711** Newspapers

Dolgeville
Herkimer County

(G-4329)
GEHRING TRICOT CORPORATION
68 Ransom St Ste 272 (13329-1461)
PHONE..................................315 429-8551
Robert Lumley, *Vice Pres*
Ray Moissonnier, *QC Dir*
Paul Gutowski, *Controller*
Richard Patrick, *Data Proc Dir*
EMP: 125
SALES (corp-wide): 60.9MM **Privately Held**
SIC: **2257** 2258 Dyeing & finishing circular knit fabrics; warp & flat knit products
PA: Gehring Tricot Corporation
1225 Franklin Ave Ste 300
Garden City NY 11530
315 429-8551

(G-4330)
NORTH HUDSON WOODCRAFT CORP
152 N Helmer Ave (13329-2826)
P.O. Box 192 (13329-0192)
PHONE..................................315 429-3105
Fax: 315 429-3479
Jeffrey C Slifka, *Ch of Bd*
William Slifka, *Treasurer*
Michael Jorrey, *Controller*
Doug Wein, *Manager*
EMP: 50 EST: 1871
SQ FT: 100,000
SALES (est): 7.4MM **Privately Held**
WEB: www.northhudsonwoodcraft.com
SIC: **2426** 3995 Furniture dimension stock, hardwood; burial caskets

(G-4331)
RAWLINGS SPORTING GOODS CO INC
52 Mckinley Ave (13329-1139)
PHONE..................................315 429-8511
Fax: 315 429-8507
Ronald Van Dergroef, *Principal*
Robert Johnson, *Production*
Kevin Griffin, *Purch Agent*
Allen Mosier, *Purchasing*
EMP: 52
SQ FT: 62,884
SALES (corp-wide): 13.2B **Publicly Held**
SIC: **3949** Sporting & athletic goods
HQ: Rawlings Sporting Goods Company, Inc.
510 Maryville University
Saint Louis MO 63141

(G-4332)
REAL DESIGN INC
187 S Main St (13329-1455)
PHONE..................................315 429-3071
Sam Camardello, *President*
EMP: 10
SALES (est): 400K **Privately Held**
WEB: www.realdesigninc.com
SIC: **3429** Furniture hardware

(G-4333)
TUMBLE FORMS INC (PA)
1013 Barker Rd (13329-2401)
PHONE..................................315 429-3101
Fax: 315 429-9739
Dave Faulchner, *General Mgr*
EMP: 20
SQ FT: 25,200
SALES (est): 10.6MM **Privately Held**
SIC: **3842** Surgical appliances & supplies

Douglaston
Queens County

(G-4334)
SALVADOR COLLETTI BLANK
25141 Van Zandt Ave (11362-1735)
PHONE..................................718 217-6725
Salvador Colletti, *Principal*
EMP: 5
SALES (est): 240.9K **Privately Held**
SIC: **2099** Food preparations

(G-4335)
SOLID-LOOK CORPORATION
4628 243rd St (11362-1129)
PHONE..................................917 683-1780
Raffaello Galli, *CEO*
EMP: 2
SQ FT: 2,000
SALES (est): 1MM **Privately Held**
SIC: **3841** Surgical & medical instruments

(G-4336)
SPRINGFIELD CONTROL SYSTEMS
4056 Douglaston Pkwy (11363-1507)
PHONE..................................718 631-0870
William Boetjer, *President*
EMP: 8
SALES (est): 680K **Privately Held**
SIC: **3823** Temperature measurement instruments, industrial

(G-4337)
TAMKA SPORT LLC
225 Beverly Rd (11363-1122)
PHONE..................................718 224-7820
Kathleen Derienzo, *Mng Member*
EMP: 8
SALES: 90K **Privately Held**
SIC: **2329** 2339 Men's & boys' athletic uniforms; uniforms, athletic: women's, misses' & juniors'

Dover Plains
Dutchess County

(G-4338)
CENTRAL DOVER DEVELOPMENT
247 Dover Furnace Rd (12522-5773)
PHONE..................................917 709-3266
Wayne Tanner, *President*
Elaine Tanner, *Vice Pres*
EMP: 4
SALES (est): 1MM **Privately Held**
SIC: **1442** 0191 Gravel mining; general farms, primarily crop

(G-4339)
J & J LOG & LUMBER CORP
528 Old State Route 22 (12522-5821)
P.O. Box 1139 (12522-1139)
PHONE..................................845 832-6535
Fax: 845 832-3757
Randolph L Williams, *CEO*
Julie Tuz, *VP Human Res*
Mil Oltman, *Technology*
◆ EMP: 80
SQ FT: 10,200
SALES (est): 15.6MM **Privately Held**
SIC: **2421** 2426 Sawmills & planing mills, general; hardwood dimension & flooring mills

(G-4340)
PALUMBO BLOCK CO INC
365 Dover Furnace Rd (12522-5775)
P.O. Box 810 (12522-0810)
PHONE..................................845 832-6100
Fax: 845 832-6431
Fortunato Palumbo, *President*
Anthony Palumbo, *Vice Pres*
Mary Palumbo, *Vice Pres*
Tony Palumbo, *Vice Pres*
Mary Palumbo Sprong, *Vice Pres*
EMP: 25
SQ FT: 28,000
SALES (est): 5.1MM **Privately Held**
SIC: **3271** 5082 5211 Concrete block & brick; masonry equipment & supplies; masonry materials & supplies

(G-4341)
PALUMBO SAND & GRAVEL COMPANY
Also Called: Palumbo Block
155 Sherman Hill Rd (12522-5625)
P.O. Box 810 (12522-0810)
PHONE..................................845 832-3356
Fortunato Palumbo, *President*
EMP: 45 EST: 1968
SQ FT: 20,000
SALES (est): 4.8MM **Privately Held**
SIC: **1442** Construction sand mining; gravel mining

Dresden
Yates County

(G-4342)
ABTEX CORPORATION
89 Main St (14441-9708)
P.O. Box 188 (14441-0188)
PHONE..................................315 536-7403
Fax: 315 536-0280
D Mark Fultz, *President*
Christian Donovan, *Opers Mgr*
Judy Roman, *Purch Agent*
David Burlew, *Project Engr*
Jason Saner, *VP Sales*
EMP: 21
SQ FT: 20,000
SALES (est): 4.4MM **Privately Held**
WEB: www.abtex.com
SIC: **3991** 3541 Brushes, household or industrial; machine tools, metal cutting type

(G-4343)
FAULKNER TRUSS COMPANY INC
1830 King Hill Rd (14441)
P.O. Box 407, Hammondsport (14840-0407)
PHONE..................................315 536-8894
Richard C Faulkner, *Ch of Bd*
EMP: 5
SALES (est): 573.2K **Privately Held**
SIC: **2439** Structural wood members

Dryden
Tompkins County

(G-4344)
AMISH STRUCTURE
32 North St (13053-8514)
P.O. Box 2 (13053-0002)
PHONE..................................607 257-1070
Virginia Jordan, *Partner*
Christoper Jordan, *Partner*
EMP: 9
SALES (est): 998.5K **Privately Held**
SIC: **2421** Outdoor wood structural products

(G-4345)
BAGELOVERS INC
42 Elm St (13053)
P.O. Box 62 (13053-0062)
PHONE..................................607 844-3683
Fax: 607 844-5269
Charles Tallman, *President*
Gary Westphal, *Vice Pres*
EMP: 18
SQ FT: 12,500
SALES (est): 2.4MM **Privately Held**
SIC: **2051** 5142 Bagels, fresh or frozen; packaged frozen goods

(G-4346)
INTEGRATED WATER MANAGEMENT
Also Called: I W M
289 Cortland Rd (13053-9517)
P.O. Box 523 (13053-0523)
PHONE..................................607 844-4276
David Duffett, *President*
▲ EMP: 5
SQ FT: 3,700
SALES (est): 1MM **Privately Held**
SIC: **3589** Water treatment equipment, industrial

(G-4347)
ROSCOE BROTHERS INC
15 Freeville Rd (13053-9537)
PHONE..................................607 844-3750
Chris Roscoe, *President*
Nick Roscoe, *Vice Pres*
EMP: 13 EST: 2014
SALES: 1MM **Privately Held**
SIC: **2452** 7389 Prefabricated buildings, wood;

(G-4348)
STURGES ELEC PDTS CO INC
Also Called: Sepco-Sturges Electronics
23 North St (13053)
P.O. Box 532 (13053-0532)
PHONE..................................607 844-8604
Fax: 607 844-8416
James Koch, *President*
Dick Biviano, *Manager*
EMP: 45
SQ FT: 15,000
SALES (est): 6.2MM **Privately Held**
WEB: www.sturgeselectronics.com
SIC: **3679** Harness assemblies for electronic use: wire or cable

Duanesburg
Schenectady County

(G-4349)
AMERICAN CAR SIGNS INC
1483 W Duane Lake Rd (12056-2713)
PHONE..................................518 227-1173
Eulaila Kulikoff, *CEO*

GEOGRAPHIC SECTION

Dunkirk - Chautauqua County (G-4372)

EMP: 6
SALES: 50K Privately Held
SIC: 3993 Signs & advertising specialties

(G-4350)
CUSTOM DESIGN KITCHENS INC
1700 Duanesburg Rd (12056-4310)
PHONE...............................518 355-4446
Fax: 518 355-4325
Terry Zarrillo, *President*
Dawn Zarrillo, *Corp Secy*
EMP: 10
SQ FT: 10,000
SALES (est): 920K Privately Held
SIC: 2541 5031 5211 3131 Cabinets, except refrigerated: show, display, etc.: wood; kitchen cabinets; cabinets, kitchen; counter tops, counters

Dundee
Yates County

(G-4351)
EAST BRANCH WINERY INC (PA)
Also Called: Mc Gregor Vineyard Winery
5503 Dutch St (14837-9746)
PHONE...............................607 292-3999
Fax: 607 292-6929
Robert Mc Gregor, *President*
David Payne, *Shareholder*
Marge Mc Gregor, *Admin Sec*
EMP: 8
SQ FT: 2,000
SALES: 402K Privately Held
SIC: 2084 0172 Wines, brandy & brandy spirits; wines; grapes

(G-4352)
FINGER LAKES MEDIA INC
Also Called: The Observer
45 Water St (14837-1029)
P.O. Box 127 (14837-0127)
PHONE...............................607 243-7600
Fax: 607 243-5833
George Lawson, *President*
EMP: 12
SALES (est): 558.1K Privately Held
WEB: www.fingerlakesmedia.com
SIC: 2711 Newspapers

(G-4353)
GLENORA WINE CELLARS INC
5435 State Route 14 (14837-8804)
PHONE...............................607 243-9500
Fax: 607 243-5514
Eugene Pierce, *President*
Scott Welliver, *Treasurer*
Tracey Dwyer, *Controller*
John Terry, *Controller*
Barbara Stone, *Human Res Mgr*
EMP: 34 EST: 1977
SQ FT: 18,000
SALES (est): 5.3MM Privately Held
WEB: www.glenora.com
SIC: 2084 Wines

(G-4354)
HERMANN J WIEMER VINEYARD
3962 Rte 14 (14837)
P.O. Box 38 (14837-0038)
PHONE...............................607 243-7971
Fax: 607 243-7983
Hermann J Wiemer, *President*
Osker Bynke, *Mktg Dir*
▲ EMP: 5
SALES (est): 467.9K Privately Held
WEB: www.wiemer.com
SIC: 2084 0172 Wines; grapes

(G-4355)
HICKORY ROAD LAND CO LLC
Also Called: Hickory Hollow Wind Cellars
5289 Route 14 (14837-8800)
P.O. Box 37 (14837-0037)
PHONE...............................607 243-9114
Edward Woodland, *Mng Member*
Suzanne Kendall, *Manager*
EMP: 5
SALES (est): 363.2K Privately Held
SIC: 2084 Wine cellars, bonded: engaged in blending wines

Dunkirk
Chautauqua County

(G-4356)
AMCOR RIGID PLASTICS USA LLC
1 Cliffstar Ave (14048-2800)
PHONE...............................716 366-2440
Fax: 716 366-2707
Rob Schulze, *Maint Spvr*
Jan Szymanski, *VP Mktg*
Bryan Cotton, *Branch Mgr*
EMP: 50
SALES (corp-wide): 9.4B Privately Held
WEB: www.slpcamericas.com
SIC: 3089 Plastic containers, except foam
HQ: Amcor Rigid Plastics Usa, Llc
935 Technology Dr Ste 100
Ann Arbor MI 48108

(G-4357)
BERRY PLASTICS GROUP INC
3565 Chadwick Dr (14048-9652)
PHONE...............................716 366-2112
Michael Kubera, *Supervisor*
EMP: 9
SALES (corp-wide): 6.4B Publicly Held
SIC: 3089 Air mattresses, plastic
PA: Berry Global Group, Inc.
101 Oakley St
Evansville IN 47710
812 424-2904

(G-4358)
CAPTIVE PLASTICS LLC
3565 Chadwick Dr (14048-9652)
PHONE...............................716 366-2112
Bob Humberger, *Branch Mgr*
EMP: 97
SALES (corp-wide): 6.4B Publicly Held
WEB: www.captiveplastics.com
SIC: 3089 Bottle caps, molded plastic
HQ: Captive Plastics, Inc.
101 Oakley St
Evansville IN 47710
812 424-2904

(G-4359)
CHAUTAUQUA CIRCUITS INC
855 Main St (14048-3505)
PHONE...............................716 366-5771
William E Wragge, *President*
EMP: 6
SALES: 250K Privately Held
SIC: 3672 Printed circuit boards

(G-4360)
CHAUTAUQUA WOODS CORP
134 Franklin Ave (14048-2806)
P.O. Box 130 (14048-0130)
PHONE...............................716 366-3808
Fax: 716 366-3814
Khalid Khan, *President*
Steve Dean, *Vice Pres*
Bia Khan, *Treasurer*
Donna Bolling, *Office Mgr*
Bia Kahn, *Manager*
EMP: 40
SQ FT: 50,000
SALES: 2.3MM Privately Held
WEB: www.chautauquawoods.com
SIC: 2431 Doors, wood

(G-4361)
CLIFFSTAR LLC (HQ)
Also Called: Cott Beverages
1 Cliffstar Dr (14048-2800)
PHONE...............................716 366-6100
Fax: 716 366-6161
Monica Consonery, *Exec VP*
Kevin Sanvidge, *Exec VP*
Richard Star, *Exec VP*
Kevin M Sanvidge, *VP Admin*
Mark Obrien, *Vice Pres*
◆ EMP: 700 EST: 1997
SALES (est): 380.2MM
SALES (corp-wide): 3.2B Privately Held
SIC: 2033 2086 Fruit juices: fresh; bottled & canned soft drinks; pasteurized & mineral waters, bottled & canned
PA: Cott Corporation
6525 Viscount Rd
Mississauga ON L4V 1
905 672-1900

(G-4362)
DUNKIRK CONSTRUCTION PRODUCTS
852 Main St (14048-3506)
P.O. Box 149 (14048-0149)
PHONE...............................716 366-5220
Patrick Pacos, *President*
James Pacos, *Vice Pres*
Dorothy Pacos, *Treasurer*
EMP: 5
SQ FT: 3,800
SALES (est): 643.3K Privately Held
SIC: 3273 Ready-mixed concrete

(G-4363)
DUNKIRK METAL PRODUCTS WNY LLC (PA)
3575 Chadwick Dr (14048-9652)
PHONE...............................716 366-2555
Fax: 716 366-4726
Joe Shull, *President*
▲ EMP: 22 EST: 1946
SQ FT: 50,000
SALES (est): 6.9MM Privately Held
SIC: 3469 Metal stampings

(G-4364)
DUNKIRK SPECIALTY STEEL LLC
830 Brigham Rd (14048-3473)
P.O. Box 319 (14048-0319)
PHONE...............................716 366-1000
Dennis Oates, *President*
Wendel Crosby, *General Mgr*
Connie Carlson, *COO*
William W Beible Jr, *Senior VP*
Paul A McGrath, *VP Admin*
◆ EMP: 166
SALES (est): 36.1MM Publicly Held
WEB: www.dunkirkspecialtysteel.com
SIC: 3312 Blast furnaces & steel mills
PA: Universal Stainless & Alloy Products, Inc.
600 Mayer St
Bridgeville PA 15017

(G-4365)
ECR INTERNATIONAL INC
Dunkirk Division
85 Middle Rd (14048-1311)
P.O. Box 32 (14048-0032)
PHONE...............................716 366-5500
Fax: 716 366-1209
Steve Lilly, *Plant Mgr*
Warren Welka, *Site Mgr*
Todd Eggleston, *Buyer*
Dennis Keppel, *QA Dir*
Thomas Poweski, *Manager*
EMP: 130
SQ FT: 17,087
SALES (corp-wide): 100.9MM Privately Held
WEB: www.ecrinternational.com
SIC: 3433 3443 Boilers, low-pressure heating: steam or hot water; fabricated plate work (boiler shop)
PA: Ecr International, Inc.
2201 Dwyer Ave
Utica NY 13501
315 797-1310

(G-4366)
FFC HOLDING CORP SUBSIDIARIES (PA)
1 Ice Cream Dr (14048-3300)
PHONE...............................716 366-5400
Kenneth A Johnson, *President*
Bob Bogdanowicz, *Purch Mgr*
Brenda Tabone, *Purch Mgr*
Jack Lockwood, *QC Dir*
Ron Odebralski, *Controller*
EMP: 12
SQ FT: 280,000
SALES (est): 110.9MM Privately Held
SIC: 2024 Ice cream & frozen desserts

(G-4367)
FIELDBROOK FOODS CORPORATION (HQ)
1 Ice Cream Dr (14048-3300)
P.O. Box 1318 (14048-6318)
PHONE...............................716 366-5400
Fax: 716 366-3588
Kenneth A Johnson, *CEO*
Mary Lind, *Editor*
James Masood, *Senior VP*
Robert Griewisch, *Vice Pres*
Ronald Odebralski, *Vice Pres*
▼ EMP: 228
SQ FT: 280,000
SALES (est): 110.9MM Privately Held
SIC: 2024 Ice cream & frozen desserts

(G-4368)
LAKESIDE PRECISION INC
208 Dove St (14048-1598)
PHONE...............................716 366-5030
Fax: 716 366-5041
Christopher Anson, *CEO*
Hugh Graves, *Opers Staff*
Patty Dechart, *Controller*
Mary Barbknecht, *Office Mgr*
EMP: 22 EST: 1963
SQ FT: 11,300
SALES: 1.7MM Privately Held
WEB: www.lakesideprecision.com
SIC: 3599 Machine shop, jobbing & repair; custom machinery

(G-4369)
NESTLE PURINA PETCARE COMPANY
Also Called: Nestle Purina Factory
3800 Middle Rd (14048-9750)
PHONE...............................716 366-8080
Ron Bowers, *Branch Mgr*
John Palmer, *Systems Staff*
Stacey Olsen, *Training Super*
EMP: 300
SALES (corp-wide): 88.4B Publicly Held
WEB: www.purina.com
SIC: 2047 Dog & cat food; dog food
HQ: Nestle Purina Petcare Company
901 Chouteau Ave
Saint Louis MO 63102
314 982-1000

(G-4370)
OBSERVER DAILY SUNDAY NEWSPPR
Also Called: The Observer
10 E 2nd St (14048-1602)
P.O. Box 391 (14048-0391)
PHONE...............................716 366-3000
Fax: 716 366-3005
Karl T Davis, *General Mgr*
Gib Snyder, *Editor*
James Austin, *Plant Mgr*
Jerry Reilly, *Loan Officer*
Berney Alexander, *Manager*
EMP: 100
SALES (est): 13.8MM Privately Held
WEB: www.observertoday.com
SIC: 2752 2711 Commercial printing, lithographic; newspapers

(G-4371)
PERSCH SERVICE PRINT INC (PA)
11 W 3rd St (14048-2060)
PHONE...............................716 366-2677
Fax: 716 366-3626
Robert H Persch, *President*
Margaret T Persch, *Treasurer*
Margaret P Triaga, *Admin Sec*
EMP: 9 EST: 1911
SALES (est): 1MM Privately Held
SIC: 2752 7334 Commercial printing, lithographic; photocopying & duplicating services

(G-4372)
REM-TRONICS INC
659 Brigham Rd (14048-2361)
PHONE...............................716 934-2697
Fax: 716 934-9538
Abe M Kadis, *President*
Mathew Karalunas, *General Mgr*
Patricia Karalunas, *Purchasing*
Ron Towers, *Controller*
Kathy Rock, *Admin Asst*

Dunkirk - Chautauqua County (G-4373)

EMP: 58
SQ FT: 20,000
SALES (est): 9.7MM **Privately Held**
WEB: www.rem-tronics.com
SIC: 3679 Electronic circuits

(G-4373)
REXFORD SERVICES INC
4849 W Lake Rd (14048-9613)
PHONE.................716 366-6671
William Rexford, *President*
Trisha Rexford, *Vice Pres*
EMP: 5
SALES (est): 666.8K **Privately Held**
SIC: 3713 Specialty motor vehicle bodies

(G-4374)
SHAANT INDUSTRIES INC
134 Franklin Ave (14048-2806)
P.O. Box 130 (14048-0130)
PHONE.................716 366-3654
Fax: 716 366-0041
Khalid Khan, *President*
Rebecca Berger, *Manager*
▲ EMP: 40
SQ FT: 50,000
SALES (est): 7.6MM **Privately Held**
WEB: www.ultrapak.net
SIC: 3081 2671 Polyvinyl film & sheet; packaging paper & plastics film, coated & laminated

(G-4375)
SPECIAL METALS CORPORATION
100 Willowbrook Ave (14048-3479)
P.O. Box 304 (14048-0304)
PHONE.................716 366-5663
Fax: 716 366-7436
Fred A Schweizer, *Opers Staff*
Peter Eckman, *Production*
Greg Caserta, *Technical Mgr*
Don Borowski, *Manager*
George Gaston, *Manager*
EMP: 60
SALES (corp-wide): 223.6B **Publicly Held**
SIC: 3542 3463 3462 3341 Forging machinery & hammers; extruding machines (machine tools); metal; die casting machines; nonferrous forgings; iron & steel forgings; secondary nonferrous metals
HQ: Special Metals Corporation
4832 Richmond Rd Ste 100
Warrensville Heights OH 44128
216 755-3030

(G-4376)
UNIVERSAL STAINLESS & ALLOY
830 Brigham Rd (14048-3473)
PHONE.................716 366-1000
EMP: 60 **Publicly Held**
SIC: 3312 Blast furnaces & steel mills
PA: Universal Stainless & Alloy Products, Inc.
600 Mayer St
Bridgeville PA 15017

(G-4377)
X PRESS SCREEN PRINTING
4867 W Lake Rd (14048-9613)
PHONE.................716 679-7788
Chad Rizzo, *President*
EMP: 7
SALES (est): 584.7K **Privately Held**
SIC: 2759 Commercial printing

Durham
Greene County

(G-4378)
ADVANCED YARN TECHNOLOGIES INC
Also Called: Cidega American Trim
4750 State Hwy 145 (12422-5306)
PHONE.................518 239-8600
Fax: 518 239-8153
Richard Gangi, *President*
Daniel Gangi, *Vice Pres*
Sabastian Gangi, *Vice Pres*
EMP: 50

SALES (est): 5.3MM **Privately Held**
SIC: 2281 5199 Yarn spinning mills; fabrics, yarns & knit goods

(G-4379)
AMERICAN TRIM MFG INC
4750 State Hwy 145 (12422-5306)
PHONE.................518 239-8151
Richard Gangi, *President*
Daniel Gangi, *Vice Pres*
Sabastian Gangi, *Vice Pres*
▲ EMP: 50
SQ FT: 30,000
SALES (est): 12.5MM **Privately Held**
SIC: 2241 Trimmings, textile

Eagle Bridge
Rensselaer County

(G-4380)
EAGLE BRIDGE MACHINE & TL INC
135 State Route 67 (12057-2446)
PHONE.................518 686-4541
Fax: 518 686-3125
Robert Farrara, *President*
Raymond Farrara, *Corp Secy*
Peter Gardner, *Manager*
▲ EMP: 35 EST: 1965
SQ FT: 12,000
SALES (est): 4.3MM **Privately Held**
WEB: www.eaglebridgemachine.com
SIC: 3599 3743 Machine shop, jobbing & repair; railroad equipment

(G-4381)
PROFESSIONAL PACKG SVCS INC
Also Called: Pro Pack
62 Owlkill Rd (12057-2609)
PHONE.................518 677-5100
Ronald Dooley, *President*
Lorraine Dooley, *Corp Secy*
Donald E Pacher Sr, *Sales Mgr*
EMP: 30
SQ FT: 25,000
SALES (est): 5.6MM **Privately Held**
SIC: 2653 2631 3086 Boxes, corrugated: made from purchased materials; paperboard mills; plastics foam products

(G-4382)
PROPAK INC
70 Owlkill Rd (12057)
PHONE.................518 677-5100
Fax: 518 677-5933
Jack Baratta, *Principal*
Frank Bowles, *Controller*
EMP: 6
SALES (est): 588.4K **Privately Held**
SIC: 2652 Setup paperboard boxes

(G-4383)
STRATO TRANSIT COMPONENTS LLC
155 State Route 67 (12057-2446)
PHONE.................518 686-4541
Michael Foxx,
Michael Corridon,
Steven Foxx,
▲ EMP: 9
SALES (est): 1.1MM **Privately Held**
SIC: 3743 Railroad equipment

Earlville
Chenango County

(G-4384)
DAN BEERS
807 County Road 22 (13332-3025)
PHONE.................607 316-8895
Dan Beers, *Principal*
EMP: 5 EST: 2014
SALES (est): 302.3K **Privately Held**
SIC: 2411 Logging

(G-4385)
EARLVILLE PAPER BOX CO INC
19 Clyde St (13332)
PHONE.................315 691-2131

Fax: 315 691-2050
Richard T Upton, *President*
Marilyn J Upton, *Treasurer*
Steve Upton, *Sales Staff*
EMP: 20
SQ FT: 7,200
SALES (est): 3.8MM **Privately Held**
WEB: www.earlvillepaperbox.com
SIC: 2652 Setup paperboard boxes

East Amherst
Erie County

(G-4386)
ELITE ROASTERS INC (PA)
Also Called: Elite Coffee Roasters
8600 Transit Rd Ste 1b (14051-2615)
PHONE.................716 626-0307
Gerald Dewes, *CFO*
William Klein, *Director*
EMP: 11 EST: 2015
SALES (est): 1.6MM **Privately Held**
SIC: 2095 5149 7389 Roasted coffee; coffee, green or roasted; packaging & labeling services

(G-4387)
INTEGRTED WORK ENVRONMENTS LLC
Also Called: Iwe
6346 Everwood Ct N (14051-2032)
P.O. Box 1514, Williamsville (14231-1514)
PHONE.................716 725-5088
Evan M Casey, *Mng Member*
EMP: 7
SALES (est): 974.7K **Privately Held**
SIC: 3821 5047 5049 Laboratory apparatus & furniture; medical laboratory equipment; laboratory equipment, except medical or dental

(G-4388)
SUPERIOR EXTERIORS OF BUFFALO
57 Insbrook Ct (14051-1496)
PHONE.................716 873-1000
Salvatore Dinatale, *President*
Patty Parker, *Office Mgr*
EMP: 10
SQ FT: 15,000
SALES (est): 1MM **Privately Held**
SIC: 3444 Awnings & canopies

(G-4389)
SWEET MELODYS LLC
8485 Transit Rd (14051-1059)
PHONE.................716 580-3227
Chuck Incorvia,
▲ EMP: 20
SALES (est): 2MM **Privately Held**
SIC: 2024 Dairy based frozen desserts

East Aurora
Erie County

(G-4390)
AMERICAN PRECISION INDS INC
API Delevan
270 Quaker Rd (14052-2192)
P.O. Box 449 (14052-0449)
PHONE.................716 652-3600
Fax: 716 652-4814
Daniel A Raskas, *President*
Steve Chandler, *Production*
David Benedict, *QC Mgr*
Joseph Calkins, *QC Mgr*
James Cadwallader, *Engrg Mgr*
EMP: 95
SALES (corp-wide): 16.8B **Publicly Held**
WEB: www.apischmidtbretten.com
SIC: 3677 Coil windings, electronic; inductors, electronic
HQ: American Precision Industries Inc.
45 Hazelwood Dr
Amherst NY 14228
716 691-9100

(G-4391)
ASTRONICS CORPORATION (PA)
130 Commerce Way (14052-2164)
PHONE.................716 805-1599
Fax: 716 655-0309
Kevin T Keane, *Ch of Bd*
Peter J Gundermann, *President*
James S Kramer, *Exec VP*
Mark A Peabody, *Exec VP*
David C Burney, *CFO*
▲ EMP: 189
SQ FT: 125,000
SALES (est): 633.1MM **Publicly Held**
SIC: 3728 3647 Aircraft parts & equipment; aircraft lighting fixtures

(G-4392)
AURORA TECHNICAL SERVICES LTD
11970 Parker Rd (14052-9533)
P.O. Box 103 (14052-0103)
PHONE.................716 652-1463
Karen Wright, *President*
Steven Wright, *Vice Pres*
Richard Ceier, *Manager*
EMP: 5
SQ FT: 1,100
SALES (est): 651.1K **Privately Held**
WEB: www.auroratechserv.com
SIC: 3829 3825 Ultrasonic testing equipment; meters: electric, pocket, portable, panelboard, etc.

(G-4393)
COLDEN CLOSET LLC
1375 Boies Rd (14052-9726)
PHONE.................716 713-6125
Kevin Lindberg, *Owner*
EMP: 9
SALES (est): 1MM **Privately Held**
SIC: 2673 Wardrobe bags (closet accessories): from purchased materials

(G-4394)
DIREKT FORCE LLC
455 Olean Rd Ste 3 (14052-9791)
PHONE.................716 652-3022
Kurt Knolle, *Sales Staff*
EMP: 25 EST: 2001
SQ FT: 7,000
SALES (est): 4.9MM **Privately Held**
WEB: www.direktforce.com
SIC: 3492 3593 3443 Control valves, fluid power: hydraulic & pneumatic; fluid power cylinders, hydraulic or pneumatic; fabricated plate work (boiler shop)

(G-4395)
EVERFAB INC
12928 Big Tree Rd (14052-9524)
PHONE.................716 655-1550
Fax: 716 655-4398
Alan L Everett, *Ch of Bd*
Lee Everett, *Vice Pres*
Scott Everett, *Vice Pres*
Jim Leonard, *Production*
Mike Spink, *Purch Mgr*
EMP: 55
SQ FT: 45,000
SALES (est): 12.7MM **Privately Held**
WEB: www.everfab.com
SIC: 2821 3441 3545 3544 Elastomers, nonvulcanizable (plastics); molding compounds, plastics; fabricated structural metal; machine tool accessories; special dies, tools, jigs & fixtures; machine & other job shop work

(G-4396)
GRANT HAMILTON (PA)
Also Called: East Aurora Advertiser
710 Main St (14052-2406)
P.O. Box 5 (14052-0005)
PHONE.................716 652-0320
Fax: 716 652-8383
Grant Hamilton, *Owner*
Sandra Cunningham, *Office Mgr*
Bonnie Cecala, *Manager*
EMP: 15 EST: 1872
SQ FT: 2,850
SALES (est): 1MM **Privately Held**
WEB: www.eastaurorany.com
SIC: 2741 5943 Newsletter publishing; office forms & supplies

(G-4397)
GUARDIAN SYSTEMS TECH INC
659 Oakwood Ave (14052-2511)
PHONE....................716 481-5597
Edward Seebald, *CEO*
Meighan Lloyd, *Principal*
EMP: 10
SALES (est): 686.6K **Privately Held**
SIC: 3699 Electrical equipment & supplies

(G-4398)
LUMINESCENT SYSTEMS INC (HQ)
Also Called: L S I
130 Commerce Way (14052-2191)
PHONE....................716 655-0800
Peter Gundermann, *President*
Frank Johns, *Vice Pres*
James Kramer, *Vice Pres*
Richard Miller, *Vice Pres*
Richard Glinski, *Engineer*
EMP: 300
SALES (est): 65.8MM
SALES (corp-wide): 633.1MM **Publicly Held**
SIC: 3647 3646 3648 3577 Aircraft lighting fixtures; commercial indusl & institutional electric lighting fixtures; lighting equipment; computer peripheral equipment
PA: Astronics Corporation
130 Commerce Way
East Aurora NY 14052
716 805-1599

(G-4399)
MATTEL INC
609 Girard Ave (14052)
PHONE....................716 714-8514
Chris Schaden, *Senior VP*
Robynn Rich, *Opers Staff*
Regis Oconnor, *Engng Exec*
Teresa G Ruiz, *VP Mktg*
Lisa McKnight, *Mktg Dir*
EMP: 15
SALES (corp-wide): 5.4B **Publicly Held**
WEB: www.mattel.com
SIC: 3944 3942 3949 Games, toys & children's vehicles; dolls, except stuffed toy animals; stuffed toys, including animals; sporting & athletic goods
PA: Mattel, Inc.
333 Continental Blvd
El Segundo CA 90245
310 252-2000

(G-4400)
MOOG INC
Moog Industrial Group
300 Jamison Rd (14052)
Po Box 18
PHONE....................716 687-4954
Donna Ward, *Mktg Coord*
Sylvia Wright, *Program Mgr*
EMP: 300
SALES (corp-wide): 2.4B **Publicly Held**
WEB: www.moog.com
SIC: 3492 3721 Fluid power valves & hose fittings; aircraft
PA: Moog Inc.
400 Jamison Rd Plant26
Elma NY 14059
716 652-2000

(G-4401)
MOOG INC
Moog Systems Group
7021 Sneca St At Jmson Rd (14052)
PHONE....................716 805-8100
Fax: 716 687-4467
James Riedel, *Vice Pres*
Sandra Reczek, *Buyer*
Emmanuel Jeanlouis, *Engineer*
Paul Bogucki, *Senior Engr*
Kristine Karnath, *Human Resources*
EMP: 225
SALES (corp-wide): 2.4B **Publicly Held**
WEB: www.moog.com
SIC: 3625 Relays & industrial controls
PA: Moog Inc.
400 Jamison Rd Plant26
Elma NY 14059
716 652-2000

(G-4402)
NORTHERN DESIGN INC
12990 Old Big Tree Rd (14052-9525)
PHONE....................716 652-7071
Robert Lippert, *President*
Gabor Bertalan, *Vice Pres*
EMP: 6
SQ FT: 550
SALES: 500K **Privately Held**
WEB: www.northerndesign.com
SIC: 3544 Forms (molds), for foundry & plastics working machinery; dies & die holders for metal cutting, forming, die casting

(G-4403)
SLOSSON EDCTL PUBLICATIONS INC
538 Buffalo Rd (14052-9456)
P.O. Box 280 (14052-0280)
PHONE....................716 652-0930
Fax: 585 655-3840
Steven Slosson, *President*
Janet Slosson, *Chairman*
EMP: 12
SQ FT: 2,400
SALES (est): 1MM **Privately Held**
WEB: www.slosson.com
SIC: 2741 8748 Miscellaneous publishing; business consulting

(G-4404)
WEST FALLS MACHINE CO INC
Also Called: West Falls Machine Co 1
11692 E Main Rd (14052-9597)
PHONE....................716 655-0440
Fax: 716 655-4048
Matthew Creps, *CEO*
Mary Ann George, *Vice Pres*
EMP: 15
SQ FT: 15,000
SALES (est): 2.7MM **Privately Held**
SIC: 3599 3471 Machine shop, jobbing & repair; chromium plating of metals or formed products

East Berne
Albany County

(G-4405)
RUDY STEMPEL & FAMILY SAWMILL
73 Stemple Rd (12059-2843)
PHONE....................518 872-0431
Rudolph Stempel, *President*
EMP: 6
SALES (est): 480.2K **Privately Held**
SIC: 2421 Sawmills & planing mills, general

East Bethany
Genesee County

(G-4406)
SANDVOSS FARMS LLC
Also Called: First Light Farm & Creamery
10198 East Rd (14054-9754)
PHONE....................585 297-7044
Peter R Sandvoss, *Owner*
Peter Sandvoss,
Stephen Sandvoss,
EMP: 8
SALES (est): 344.5K **Privately Held**
SIC: 2022 Natural cheese

East Concord
Erie County

(G-4407)
MCEWAN TRUCKING & GRAV PRODUC
11696 Route 240 (14055-9717)
PHONE....................716 609-1828
Mary McEwan, *Principal*
EMP: 6
SALES (est): 545.1K **Privately Held**
SIC: 1442 Construction sand & gravel

(G-4408)
WENDELS POULTRY FARM
12466 Vaughn St (14055-9747)
PHONE....................716 592-2299
Martin Wendel, *Partner*
Denise Wendel, *Partner*
David Wendel, *Partner*
EMP: 8
SQ FT: 12,000
SALES (est): 881.6K **Privately Held**
SIC: 2015 0254 Poultry, processed; poultry hatcheries

East Durham
Greene County

(G-4409)
GLAXOSMITHKLINE LLC
Also Called: Glaxosmthkline Cnsmr Heathcare
3169 Route 145 (12423-1416)
PHONE....................518 239-6901
Max Van Veem, *Vice Pres*
Mark Matlosz, *Plant Supt*
Caitlin Cunningham, *Opers Mgr*
Ron Pelak, *QC Dir*
Max Van Vessem, *Branch Mgr*
EMP: 75
SALES (corp-wide): 34.3B **Privately Held**
SIC: 2834 3843 Pharmaceutical preparations; procaine pharmaceutical preparations; dental equipment & supplies
HQ: Glaxosmithkline Llc
5 Crescent Dr
Philadelphia PA 19112
215 751-4000

East Elmhurst
Queens County

(G-4410)
ARM CONSTRUCTION COMPANY INC
10001 27th Ave (11369-1647)
PHONE....................646 235-6520
Abdul Motaleb, *President*
EMP: 5
SALES: 383K **Privately Held**
SIC: 1389 7389 Construction, repair & dismantling services;

(G-4411)
BROTHERS ROOFING SUPPLIES CO
10514 Astoria Blvd (11369-2097)
PHONE....................718 779-0280
Fax: 718 446-8069
Robert Kersch, *Ch of Bd*
Michael Kersch, *Vice Pres*
EMP: 20 **EST:** 1969
SQ FT: 16,000
SALES (est): 4.3MM **Privately Held**
WEB: www.brothersroofingsupply.com
SIC: 3444 Metal roofing & roof drainage equipment

(G-4412)
CITROS BUILDING MATERIALS CO
10514 Astoria Blvd (11369-2027)
PHONE....................718 779-0727
Bobby Kersh, *President*
EMP: 40
SQ FT: 1,600
SALES (est): 5.2MM **Privately Held**
SIC: 3444 Skylights, sheet metal

(G-4413)
DOROSE NOVELTY CO INC
Also Called: Dorose Albums
3107 103rd St (11369-2013)
PHONE....................718 451-3088
Fax: 718 451-3089
Sam Krauthamer, *President*
Alex Brodsky, *Vice Pres*
Regina Krauthamer, *Treasurer*
EMP: 14 **EST:** 1958
SALES (est): 1.1MM **Privately Held**
SIC: 2782 Albums

(G-4414)
I RAUCHS SONS INC
3220 112th St (11369-2590)
PHONE....................718 507-8844
Fax: 718 565-6018
Milton Levine, *President*
Joel Levine, *Corp Secy*
EMP: 21
SQ FT: 12,000
SALES (est): 3.5MM **Privately Held**
SIC: 3444 Sheet metalwork

(G-4415)
KESSO FOODS INC
Also Called: Mediterranean Thick Yogurt
7720 21st Ave (11370-1219)
PHONE....................718 777-5303
Fax: 718 777-5303
Fotini Kessissoglou, *President*
EMP: 5
SALES: 100K **Privately Held**
SIC: 2026 5143 Fluid milk; yogurt

(G-4416)
LIBERTY AWNINGS & SIGNS INC
Also Called: Empire Signs
7705 21st Ave (11370-1250)
PHONE....................347 203-1470
Panayiotis Panayi, *CEO*
Spiro Avlonitis, *Manager*
EMP: 2
SQ FT: 5,000
SALES (est): 2.3MM **Privately Held**
SIC: 3993 Advertising artwork

(G-4417)
MOON GATES COMPANY
3243 104th St (11369-2515)
PHONE....................718 426-0023
Stephen Vieira, *Principal*
EMP: 6
SQ FT: 2,000
SALES (est): 400K **Privately Held**
SIC: 3446 1791 Gates, ornamental metal; iron work, structural

(G-4418)
T RJ SHIRTS INC
3050 90th St (11369-1706)
PHONE....................347 642-3071
Femd Rocky, *Principal*
EMP: 6
SALES (est): 487.3K **Privately Held**
SIC: 2331 T-shirts & tops, women's: made from purchased materials

(G-4419)
WESTCHSTR CRNKSHFT GRNDNG
Also Called: Westchester Crankshaft Grinding
3263 110th St (11369-2525)
PHONE....................718 651-3900
Fax: 718 651-3035
Marco Albanese, *Vice Pres*
▲ **EMP:** 9
SALES (est): 1.1MM **Privately Held**
SIC: 3599 Crankshafts & camshafts, machining

East Greenbush
Rensselaer County

(G-4420)
AUTOMATED & MGT SOLUTIONS LLC
743 Columbia Tpke (12061-2266)
PHONE....................518 283-5352
Fax: 518 283-0370
Sharon Hemmes, *Research*
Russ Streifert, *Programmer Anys*
Francis Clifford,
EMP: 5 **EST:** 2011
SALES (est): 128.9K **Privately Held**
SIC: 7372 Application computer software; operating systems computer software

(G-4421)
CURTIS PRTG CO THE DEL PRESS
711 Columbia Tpke (12061-2212)
PHONE....................518 477-4820

East Greenbush - Rensselaer County (G-4422)

Fax: 518 689-0224
Richard Lieberman, *President*
EMP: 5
SQ FT: 4,000
SALES (est): 645.7K **Privately Held**
WEB: www.curtisprinting.com
SIC: 2759 Commercial printing; letterpress printing

(G-4422)
GARELICK FARMS LLC
504 Third Avenue Ext (12061)
PHONE..................................518 283-0820
Paul Nero, *Sales Executive*
Bill Hogan, *Branch Mgr*
Charles Smith, *Technology*
EMP: 210 **Publicly Held**
SIC: 2026 Cottage cheese
HQ: Garelick Farms, Llc
 1199 W Central St Ste 1
 Franklin MA 02038
 508 528-9000

(G-4423)
LEONARD CARLSON
Also Called: Carlson, L A Co
90 Waters Rd (12061-3422)
PHONE..................................518 477-4710
Leonard Carlson, *Owner*
▲ **EMP:** 6 **EST:** 1956
SQ FT: 6,000
SALES: 425K **Privately Held**
SIC: 3931 Organs, all types: pipe, reed, hand, electronic, etc.

(G-4424)
SABIC INNOVATIVE PLASTICS
1 Gail Ct (12061-1750)
PHONE..................................713 448-7474
Narendra Mansharamani, *Principal*
Shelia Naab, *Vice Pres*
Jason Fuller, *Project Mgr*
Steve Hurley, *Mfg Mgr*
Dominic Bruno, *Safety Mgr*
EMP: 35 **EST:** 2012
SALES (est): 5.9MM **Privately Held**
SIC: 3089 Plastics products

East Hampton
Suffolk County

(G-4425)
BISTRIAN CEMENT CORPORATION
225 Springs Fireplace Rd (11937-4823)
P.O. Box 5048 (11937-6079)
PHONE..................................631 324-1123
Barry Bistrian, *President*
Betsy Avallone, *Shareholder*
Bruce Bistrian, *Shareholder*
Pat Bistrian, *Shareholder*
Barbara Borg, *Shareholder*
EMP: 12
SQ FT: 20,000
SALES: 1.7MM **Privately Held**
SIC: 3272 3259 Septic tanks, concrete; drain tile, clay

(G-4426)
C E KING & SONS INC
10 Saint Francis Pl (11937-4330)
PHONE..................................631 324-4944
Fax: 631 329-3669
Clarence E King III, *President*
David King, *Treasurer*
Deanna Tikkanen, *Admin Sec*
EMP: 7
SQ FT: 1,650
SALES: 600K **Privately Held**
WEB: www.kingsawnings.com
SIC: 2394 5999 Awnings, fabric: made from purchased materials; fire extinguishers

(G-4427)
CHESU INC
81 Newtown Ln (11937-2323)
PHONE..................................239 564-2803
Chet Borgida, *President*
Susan Borgida, *Vice Pres*
EMP: 10 **EST:** 2012

SALES (est): 1MM **Privately Held**
SIC: 3086 5111 7389 Packaging & shipping materials, foamed plastic; printing paper; notary publics

(G-4428)
EAST HAMPTON IND NEWS INC
Also Called: East Hampton Independent The
74 Montauk Hwy Unit 19 (11937-3268)
PHONE..................................631 324-2500
Fax: 631 324-2351
James Mackim, *President*
James J Mackin, *Publisher*
Kitty Merrill, *Editor*
Jodi Della Femina, *Vice Pres*
Lee Minitree, *Treasurer*
EMP: 28
SQ FT: 1,400
SALES (est): 1.7MM **Privately Held**
WEB: www.indyeastend.com
SIC: 2711 Newspapers

(G-4429)
EAST HAMPTON STAR INC
153 Main St (11937-2716)
P.O. Box 5002 (11937-6005)
PHONE..................................631 324-0002
Fax: 631 324-7943
Helen Rattray, *President*
Angie Carpenter, *Treasurer*
Min Spear, *Advt Staff*
EMP: 40 **EST:** 1886
SQ FT: 6,400
SALES (est): 2.6MM **Privately Held**
WEB: www.easthamptonstar.com
SIC: 2711 Newspapers, publishing & printing

(G-4430)
ELIE TAHARI LTD
1 Main St (11937-2701)
PHONE..................................631 329-8883
Brenda Bolin, *Branch Mgr*
EMP: 75
SALES (corp-wide): 271.7MM **Privately Held**
SIC: 2337 Suits: women's, misses' & juniors'
PA: Elie Tahari Ltd.
 16 Bleeker St
 Millburn NJ 07041
 973 671-6300

(G-4431)
IRONY LIMITED INC (PA)
Also Called: Hedges and Gardens
53 Sag Harbor Tpke (11937-4905)
PHONE..................................631 329-4065
Robert Linker, *President*
Elizabeth Linker, *Vice Pres*
EMP: 2
SQ FT: 2,200
SALES (est): 1.2MM **Privately Held**
SIC: 3441 7641 3446 1799 Fabricated structural metal; antique furniture repair & restoration; stairs, staircases, stair treads: prefabricated metal; ornamental metal work

(G-4432)
KEENERS EAST END LITHO INC
10 Prospect Blvd (11937-5800)
PHONE..................................631 324-8565
Charles Keener, *President*
Lynn Keener, *Corp Secy*
Greg Keener, *Vice Pres*
EMP: 8
SALES (est): 783.3K **Privately Held**
SIC: 2752 Commercial printing, lithographic

(G-4433)
LURIA COMMUNICATIONS INC
Also Called: Card Pak Start Up
31 Shorewood Dr Fl 1 (11937-3402)
PHONE..................................631 329-4922
Jay Blatt, *President*
Vicki Luria, *Vice Pres*
EMP: 8
SALES: 500K **Privately Held**
SIC: 2721 7311 7331 Trade journals: publishing only, not printed on site; advertising agencies; mailing list brokers

(G-4434)
NATURPATHICA HOLISTIC HLTH INC
74 Montauk Hwy Unit 23 (11937-3268)
PHONE..................................631 329-8792
Barbara Close, *CEO*
Jonathan Keattch, *COO*
Becky Discipio, *Finance*
Andrea Hallett, *Finance*
EMP: 100
SQ FT: 750
SALES (est): 4.4MM **Privately Held**
SIC: 2844 Cosmetic preparations

(G-4435)
SABIN METAL CORPORATION (PA)
300 Pantigo Pl Ste 102 (11937-2630)
PHONE..................................631 329-1695
Fax: 631 329-1985
Andrew Sabin, *President*
Jonathan Sabin, *Exec VP*
Kevin Beirne, *Vice Pres*
Yanan Sui, *Opers Mgr*
Scott Yarnes, *Opers Staff*
▲ **EMP:** 14 **EST:** 1945
SQ FT: 4,000
SALES (est): 43.2MM **Privately Held**
WEB: www.sabinmetal.com
SIC: 3341 Secondary precious metals

(G-4436)
STAR READY MIX EAST INC
225 Springs Fireplace Rd (11937-4823)
P.O. Box 371, Medford (11763-0371)
PHONE..................................631 289-8787
Fax: 631 324-2258
Thomas Hess, *President*
Frank Otero, *Vice Pres*
EMP: 15
SALES (est): 1.1MM **Privately Held**
SIC: 3273 Ready-mixed concrete

East Islip
Suffolk County

(G-4437)
KEY CONTAINER CORP
135 Hollins Ln (11730-3006)
PHONE..................................631 582-3847
Frank Giaquinko, *President*
EMP: 6 **EST:** 2010
SALES: 800K **Privately Held**
SIC: 2653 Corrugated & solid fiber boxes

East Meadow
Nassau County

(G-4438)
ARTYS SPRNKLR SVC INSTLLATION
234 E Meadow Ave Unit B (11554-2455)
PHONE..................................516 538-4371
Arthur R Wolf, *President*
Helen Wolf, *Treasurer*
EMP: 13
SALES: 700K **Privately Held**
SIC: 3432 Lawn hose nozzles & sprinklers

(G-4439)
CHV PRINTED COMPANY
1905 Hempstead Tpke B (11554-1047)
PHONE..................................516 997-1101
Andrew Mazzone, *Principal*
Timothy Chant, *Administration*
EMP: 19
SALES (est): 1.4MM **Privately Held**
SIC: 2759 Commercial printing

(G-4440)
COMPLETE ORTHOPEDIC SVCS INC
2094 Front St (11554-1709)
PHONE..................................516 357-9113
Fax: 516 357-9186
Noreen Diaz, *Ch of Bd*
Alexandra Divito, *Marketing Staff*
Anne Feret, *Practice Mgr*
Annne Genovese, *Manager*

EMP: 20 **EST:** 1999
SALES (est): 3MM **Privately Held**
SIC: 3842 Braces, orthopedic

(G-4441)
DATASONIC INC
1413 Cleveland Ave (11554-4405)
PHONE..................................516 248-7330
Richard Mintz, *President*
EMP: 5
SALES (est): 320K **Privately Held**
SIC: 3669 Burglar alarm apparatus, electric

(G-4442)
E M T MANUFACTURING INC
Also Called: Engineering Mfg & Tech
273 Cherry Pl (11554-2936)
PHONE..................................516 333-1917
Ernest Hippner, *President*
Marion Hippner, *Corp Secy*
EMP: 12
SQ FT: 10,000
SALES (est): 1.7MM **Privately Held**
SIC: 3599 3365 Machine shop, jobbing & repair; aerospace castings, aluminum

(G-4443)
EATON CORPORATION
280 Bellmore Rd (11554-3538)
PHONE..................................516 353-3017
John Pierro, *Principal*
EMP: 222 **Privately Held**
SIC: 3625 Motor controls & accessories
HQ: Eaton Corporation
 1000 Eaton Blvd
 Cleveland OH 44122
 216 523-5000

(G-4444)
HI TECH SIGNS OF NY INC
415 E Meadow Ave (11554-3952)
PHONE..................................516 794-7880
Fax: 516 794-0410
Scott Abrecht, *President*
EMP: 5
SQ FT: 2,000
SALES (est): 430K **Privately Held**
SIC: 3993 5999 Signs & advertising specialties; banners, flags, decals & posters

(G-4445)
HIBU INC (DH)
90 Merrick Ave Ste 530 (11554-1575)
PHONE..................................516 730-1900
Mike Pocock, *CEO*
John Condron, *Ch of Bd*
Joseph Walsh, *President*
Dan Perti, *General Mgr*
Bob Wigley, *Chairman*
◆ **EMP:** 200
SQ FT: 30,000
SALES (est): 1.8B
SALES (corp-wide): 913MM **Privately Held**
SIC: 2741 Directories: publishing & printing
HQ: Yell Limited
 23 Forbury Road
 Reading BERKS RG1 3
 800 838-200

(G-4446)
JOHN PRIOR
2545 Hempstead Tpke # 402 (11554-2144)
PHONE..................................516 520-9801
John Prior, *Principal*
Barbara Gordon, *Human Resources*
Maria Lawrence, *Sales Staff*
Ronald Prior, *Sales Executive*
Jeffrey Arway, *Info Tech Mgr*
EMP: 8 **EST:** 2007
SALES (est): 746.6K **Privately Held**
SIC: 3999 Manufacturing industries

(G-4447)
PJ DECORATORS INC
257 Pontiac Pl (11554-1231)
PHONE..................................516 735-9693
David Brill, *President*
EMP: 25
SALES (est): 2MM **Privately Held**
SIC: 2591 5023 5719 Drapery hardware & blinds & shades; vertical blinds; vertical blinds

GEOGRAPHIC SECTION

(G-4448)
TRIPLE H CONSTRUCTION INC
832 Bethlynn Ct (11554-4911)
PHONE..................................516 280-8252
Hesham Hassane, *President*
Venaal Hassane, *Vice Pres*
EMP: 22
SQ FT: 1,600
SALES: 700K **Privately Held**
SIC: 3446 1751 Fences or posts, ornamental iron or steel; window & door installation & erection

East Moriches
Suffolk County

(G-4449)
KEY SIGNALS
47 Tuthill Point Rd (11940-1216)
PHONE..................................631 433-2962
Mark Gartung, *Principal*
EMP: 7
SALES (est): 605K **Privately Held**
SIC: 3629 Electrical industrial apparatus

(G-4450)
RINGHOFF FUEL INC
72 Atlantic Ave (11940-1324)
P.O. Box 510 (11940-0510)
PHONE..................................631 878-0663
William J Ringhoff, *Principal*
EMP: 5
SALES (est): 370.5K **Privately Held**
SIC: 2911 Oils, fuel

(G-4451)
TATES WHOLESALE LLC
Also Called: Tate's Bake Shop
62 Pine St (11940-1117)
PHONE..................................631 780-6511
Kathleen King, *President*
Michel Dobbs, *Opers Mgr*
Robert Panarella, *Warehouse Mgr*
Margaret Brock, *Accounting Mgr*
EMP: 130
SALES (est): 26.9MM **Privately Held**
SIC: 2051 Bakery: wholesale or wholesale/retail combined

East Northport
Suffolk County

(G-4452)
ADVANTAGE ORTHOTICS INC
337 Larkfield Rd (11731-2904)
PHONE..................................631 368-1754
Claire Ann Ketcham, *Principal*
EMP: 9
SALES (est): 1.1MM **Privately Held**
SIC: 3842 Orthopedic appliances

(G-4453)
ARCHITCTRAL MLLWK INSTALLATION
590 Elwood Rd (11731-5629)
PHONE..................................631 499-0755
Shaun Hanley, *President*
EMP: 23
SALES: 2MM **Privately Held**
SIC: 2431 2439 Millwork; structural wood members

(G-4454)
COMPUTER CONVERSIONS CORP
6 Dunton Ct (11731-1704)
PHONE..................................631 261-3300
Fax: 631 261-3308
Stephen Renard, *President*
Paul Waldman, *Vice Pres*
Les Levy, *Project Engr*
Margaret Librizzi, *Human Res Mgr*
Craig J Hughes, *Sales Mgr*
EMP: 32
SQ FT: 5,000
SALES (est): 6.9MM **Privately Held**
WEB: www.computer-conversions.com
SIC: 3571 Electronic computers

(G-4455)
EAST TO WEST ARCHITECTRAL PDTS
103 Tinton Pl Ste 1a (11731-5330)
PHONE..................................631 433-9690
Dean Nichol, *President*
EMP: 1
SALES: 3MM **Privately Held**
WEB: www.easttowestsales.com
SIC: 3996 Hard surface floor coverings

(G-4456)
FASTNET SOFTWARE INTL INC
459 Elwood Rd (11731-4006)
PHONE..................................888 740-7790
Uzma Abbas, *President*
EMP: 10
SALES (est): 813.4K **Privately Held**
SIC: 7372 Prepackaged software

(G-4457)
FORTE NETWORK
Also Called: Forte Security Group
75 Lockfield Rd (11731)
PHONE..................................631 390-9050
Richard Allen, *President*
EMP: 40
SALES (est): 4.6MM **Privately Held**
SIC: 3699 Security control equipment & systems

(G-4458)
ISLAND SILKSCREEN INC
Also Called: Connie's T Shirt Shop
328 Larkfield Rd (11731-2945)
PHONE..................................631 757-4567
Fax: 631 757-5080
Mike Sambur, *President*
EMP: 5
SALES (est): 453.4K **Privately Held**
SIC: 2759 Screen printing

(G-4459)
JORDAN PANEL SYSTEMS CORP (PA)
196 Laurel Rd Unit 2 (11731-1441)
PHONE..................................631 754-4900
Fax: 631 754-4643
John A Finamore Sr, *President*
Monique Green, *Controller*
Monique Greene, *Controller*
Kathi Benjes, *Accounts Mgr*
Dianna Gannon, *Administration*
▼ **EMP:** 25
SQ FT: 5,000
SALES (est): 10MM **Privately Held**
WEB: www.jordanpanel.com
SIC: 3499 1761 1793 5033 Aerosol valves, metal; roofing, siding & sheet metal work; glass & glazing work; roofing, asphalt & sheet metal

(G-4460)
LOUDON LTD
Also Called: Minuteman Press
281 Larkfield Rd (11731-2417)
PHONE..................................631 757-4447
Kathy Loudon, *President*
David Loudon, *General Mgr*
EMP: 5
SQ FT: 1,800
SALES (est): 740.2K **Privately Held**
SIC: 2752 2791 Commercial printing, lithographic; typesetting

(G-4461)
MONASANI SIGNS INC
Also Called: Mr Sign
22 Compton St (11731-5510)
PHONE..................................631 266-2635
Fax: 631 689-7039
William Monahan, *President*
EMP: 5
SQ FT: 1,500
SALES: 400K **Privately Held**
SIC: 3993 7532 Signs & advertising specialties; truck painting & lettering

(G-4462)
PROGRESSIVE HARDWARE CO INC
63 Brightside Ave (11731-1903)
PHONE..................................631 445-1826
Fax: 631 757-8870
William Zilz, *President*
▲ **EMP:** 9
SQ FT: 11,000
SALES: 960K **Privately Held**
WEB: www.progressive-hardware.com
SIC: 3429 Builders' hardware

(G-4463)
READY CHECK GLO INC
23 Bruce Ln Ste E (11731-2701)
PHONE..................................516 547-1849
Celestina Pugliese, *CEO*
EMP: 5 **EST:** 2010
SALES: 175K **Privately Held**
SIC: 2752 7389 Menus, lithographed;

East Norwich
Nassau County

(G-4464)
CATHAY RESOURCES INC
38 Cord Pl (11732-1155)
P.O. Box 314 (11732-0314)
PHONE..................................516 922-2839
Walter Belous, *President*
▲ **EMP:** 3
SQ FT: 3,000
SALES: 10MM **Privately Held**
SIC: 3356 Tin & tin alloy bars, pipe, sheets, etc.

(G-4465)
GOLDEN EGRET LLC
38 Cord Pl (11732-1155)
P.O. Box 314 (11732-0314)
PHONE..................................516 922-2839
Walter Belous, *Mng Member*
▲ **EMP:** 6
SALES (est): 766.7K **Privately Held**
SIC: 3313 Tungsten carbide powder

East Patchogue
Suffolk County

(G-4466)
G & M DEGE INC
250 Orchard Rd Bldg 1 (11772-5535)
PHONE..................................631 475-1450
Fax: 631 475-1238
Nick Gallipoli, *President*
Angela Gallipoli, *Vice Pres*
EMP: 14
SQ FT: 3,000
SALES (est): 3.4MM **Privately Held**
SIC: 2851 Removers & cleaners

(G-4467)
HUNTER METAL INDUSTRIES INC
Also Called: Hunter Displays
14 Hewlett Ave (11772-5499)
PHONE..................................631 475-5900
Fax: 631 475-5950
Harry Stoll, *CEO*
Sandy Stoll, *Senior VP*
Ken Kasper, *Vice Pres*
Renee Heuer, *Purch Mgr*
Susan Anastasia, *Accounting Mgr*
EMP: 100 **EST:** 1951
SQ FT: 75,000
SALES (est): 17.3MM **Privately Held**
WEB: www.hunterdisplays.com
SIC: 2542 2541 Fixtures: display, office or store: except wood; display fixtures, wood

(G-4468)
PROGRESSIVE ORTHOTICS LTD
285 Sills Rd Bldg 8c (11772-8800)
PHONE..................................631 447-3860
Bruce Goodman, *Branch Mgr*
EMP: 12
SALES (corp-wide): 905.9K **Privately Held**
WEB: www.progressiveorthotics.com
SIC: 3842 5999 Orthopedic appliances; orthopedic & prosthesis applications
PA: Progressive Orthotics Ltd
280 Middle Country Rd G
Selden NY 11784
631 732-5556

East Quogue
Suffolk County

(G-4469)
EAST COAST MINES LTD
Also Called: East Coast Mines & Material
2 Lewis Rd (11942)
PHONE..................................631 653-5445
Fax: 631 653-5743
William Tintle, *President*
EMP: 20
SQ FT: 5,000
SALES (est): 2.9MM **Privately Held**
SIC: 1442 5261 5032 Construction sand & gravel; top soil; brick, stone & related material

(G-4470)
HAMPTON SHIPYARDS INC
7 Carter Ln (11942-4334)
P.O. Box 3007 (11942-2008)
PHONE..................................631 653-6777
Fax: 631 653-6801
Fred Scopinich, *President*
Doris Scopinich, *Vice Pres*
EMP: 10 **EST:** 1956
SQ FT: 21,000
SALES (est): 1.1MM **Privately Held**
SIC: 3732 Boat building & repairing

(G-4471)
SITEWATCH TECHNOLOGY LLC
22 Sunset Ave (11942-4200)
PHONE..................................207 778-3246
Fred York, *Principal*
David B Horn,
EMP: 6
SALES (est): 590.8K **Privately Held**
SIC: 3678 Electronic connectors

East Rochester
Monroe County

(G-4472)
ART PARTS SIGNS INC
100 Lincoln Pkwy (14445-1450)
PHONE..................................585 381-2134
Patricia Ransco, *President*
EMP: 7
SQ FT: 8,000
SALES: 500K **Privately Held**
SIC: 3993 Signs, not made in custom sign painting shops

(G-4473)
CARDIAC LIFE PRODUCTS INC
349 W Coml St Ste 1400 (14445)
P.O. Box 25755, Rochester (14625-0755)
PHONE..................................585 267-7775
Mary Wynne, *President*
Robert Wynne, *Vice Pres*
Nancy Marone, *Sales Mgr*
Robin Vogt, *Mktg Dir*
Deb Hustis, *Manager*
EMP: 3
SALES: 3MM **Privately Held**
SIC: 3845 Electromedical equipment

(G-4474)
CARPENTIER INDUSTRIES LLC
Also Called: Rochester Magnet
119 Despatch Dr (14445-1447)
PHONE..................................585 385-5550
Fax: 585 385-4440
Andrew Carpentier, *President*
Jeffrey C Gilbert, *Sales Dir*
Brian Phillips, *Sales Dir*
▲ **EMP:** 15
SQ FT: 10,000
SALES (est): 2.2MM **Privately Held**
WEB: www.rochestermagnet.com
SIC: 3499 Magnets, permanent: metallic

(G-4475)
CONNOVER PACKAGING INC
119 Despatch Dr (14445-1447)
PHONE..................................585 377-2510
Fax: 585 377-2604
Andrew Carpentier, *President*
Leslie Childs, *Accounts Mgr*
Judy Stephens, *Office Mgr*

East Rochester - Monroe County (G-4476)   **GEOGRAPHIC SECTION**

Kim Koronas, *Info Tech Mgr*
EMP: 6
SQ FT: 15,000
SALES (est): 1.2MM Privately Held
WEB: www.connoverpackaging.com
SIC: 2673 Plastic bags: made from purchased materials

(G-4476)
EKOSTINGER INC
140 Despatch Dr (14445-1448)
PHONE.................................585 739-0450
Parr Wiegel, *CEO*
Steven Chatwin, *Principal*
Ania Makuch, *Business Mgr*
EMP: 11 EST: 2012
SQ FT: 13,500
SALES (est): 920.3K Privately Held
SIC: 3713 Truck bodies & parts

(G-4477)
FERRO CORPORATION
603 W Commercial St (14445-2253)
P.O. Box 389 (14445-0389)
PHONE.................................585 586-8770
Richard Veeder, *Branch Mgr*
EMP: 35
SQ FT: 30,000
SALES (corp-wide): 1.1B Publicly Held
WEB: www.ferro.com
SIC: 2819 Industrial inorganic chemicals
PA: Ferro Corporation
    6060 Parkland Blvd # 250
    Mayfield Heights OH 44124
    216 875-5600

(G-4478)
FILTROS LTD
Also Called: Filtros Plant
603 W Commercial St (14445-2253)
P.O. Box 389 (14445-0389)
PHONE.................................585 586-8770
Fax: 585 586-7154
Byron Anderson, *CEO*
Allan Schilling, *Vice Pres*
Bob Ayers, *Plant Mgr*
Linda Wendt, *Accountant*
George Goeller, *Sales Mgr*
EMP: 35 EST: 1999
SQ FT: 45,000
SALES (est): 5.6MM Privately Held
WEB: www.filtrosltd.com
SIC: 3255 3564 3297 3264 Clay refractories; blowers & fans; nonclay refractories; porcelain electrical supplies

(G-4479)
GREATER RCHSTER ADVERTISER INC
Also Called: Shopping Bag, The
201 Main St (14445-1703)
P.O. Box 760 (14445-0760)
PHONE.................................585 385-1974
Fax: 585 385-3507
Peter John Stahlbrodt, *President*
Kay C Kolb, *General Mgr*
Betty Stahlbrodt, *Vice Pres*
Brenda Pitoni, *Info Tech Mgr*
EMP: 26
SQ FT: 6,600
SALES (est): 1.5MM Privately Held
WEB: www.rochesteradvertiser.com
SIC: 2741 Shopping news: publishing only, not printed on site

(G-4480)
HOERCHER INDUSTRIES INC
A1 Country Club Rd Ste 1 (14445-2230)
PHONE.................................585 398-2982
Fax: 585 383-1608
Lawrence Hoercher, *President*
EMP: 5
SQ FT: 3,500
SALES (est): 360K Privately Held
SIC: 3599 Electrical discharge machining (EDM)

(G-4481)
IDEAL MANUFACTURING INC
80 Bluff Dr (14445-1300)
PHONE.................................585 872-7190
Ben Stroyer, *President*
Arthur Stroyer, *Vice Pres*
Bruce Stroyer, *Accountant*
Jay Stroyer, *Sales Dir*
▼ EMP: 32

SQ FT: 7,000
SALES (est): 9.1MM Privately Held
SIC: 2515 Foundations & platforms

(G-4482)
KEMCO SALES LLC
119 Despatch Dr (14445-1447)
PHONE.................................203 762-1902
Andrew Carpentier, *President*
EMP: 15
SQ FT: 15,000
SALES (est): 2.8MM Privately Held
WEB: www.securpak.com
SIC: 2673 Bags: plastic, laminated & coated

(G-4483)
KRONENBERGER MFG CORP
115 Despatch Dr (14445-1447)
P.O. Box 650 (14445-0650)
PHONE.................................585 385-2340
Gunter Kronenberger, *President*
Eric Kronenberger, *Vice Pres*
Kevin Kronenberger, *Vice Pres*
Bertha Parnusie, *Office Mgr*
John Girvin, *Manager*
EMP: 45
SQ FT: 40,000
SALES (est): 7.5MM Privately Held
SIC: 3599 Machine shop, jobbing & repair

(G-4484)
LINCDOC LLC
Also Called: Lincware
401 Main St (14445-1707)
PHONE.................................585 563-1669
Darren Mathis, *CEO*
Donna Moss, *Sales Staff*
Eileen Gaisser, *Business Anlyst*
James Avery, *Software Dev*
Adam Lenio, *Creative Dir*
EMP: 7
SALES (est): 520.7K Privately Held
SIC: 7372 Prepackaged software

(G-4485)
RICHARDS & WEST INC
Also Called: Rw Manufacturing Company
501 W Commercial St Ste 1 (14445-2258)
PHONE.................................585 461-4088
Fax: 585 461-0716
John R Keim, *Ch of Bd*
Gary Keim, *Vice Pres*
John E Miner, *Vice Pres*
Gene Rozewski, *Purchasing*
EMP: 54 EST: 1982
SQ FT: 10,000
SALES (est): 8.5MM Privately Held
WEB: www.rwmfg.com
SIC: 3911 7631 5944 Jewelry, precious metal; jewelry repair services; jewelry, precious stones & precious metals

(G-4486)
YOG N GO INC
163 W Commercial St (14445-2151)
PHONE.................................585 319-8110
Lorelei Sapienza, *Principal*
EMP: 5 EST: 2013
SALES (est): 213.6K Privately Held
SIC: 2024 Yogurt desserts, frozen

East Rockaway
Nassau County

(G-4487)
ADULTS AND CHILDREN WITH LEARN
22 Alice Ct (11518-1902)
PHONE.................................516 593-8230
EMP: 32
SALES (corp-wide): 68.3MM Privately Held
SIC: 3999 Barber & beauty shop equipment
PA: Adults And Children With Learning And Developmental Disabilities, Inc.
    807 S Oyster Bay Rd
    Bethpage NY 11714
    516 681-4500

(G-4488)
CIRCUITS & SYSTEMS INC
Also Called: Arlyn Scales
59 2nd St (11518-1236)
PHONE.................................516 593-4301
Arnold Gordon, *President*
Lynne Gordon, *Corp Secy*
Helen Berwind, *Plant Mgr*
Robert Hirsch, *Sales Staff*
▲ EMP: 22 EST: 1977
SQ FT: 6,000
SALES (est): 5.4MM Privately Held
WEB: www.chaverware.com
SIC: 3596 7373 Scales & balances, except laboratory; computer-aided design (CAD) systems service

(G-4489)
DAWN PAPER CO INC (PA)
Also Called: Dawn Printing Company
4 Leonard Dr (11518-1609)
PHONE.................................516 596-9110
Fax: 516 596-0167
Stephen Kucker, *President*
Jonathan Greenberg, *Vice Pres*
Marla Perrino, *Vice Pres*
EMP: 12
SQ FT: 5,000
SALES (est): 2.4MM Privately Held
SIC: 2752 5113 5085 Commercial printing, lithographic; bags, paper & disposable plastic; boxes, crates, etc., other than paper

(G-4490)
KEYSTONE IRON & WIRE WORKS INC
Also Called: Keystone Iron Elevator
15 Main St (11518-2058)
PHONE.................................844 258-7986
Diana Macchia, *President*
EMP: 8 EST: 1924
SQ FT: 5,000
SALES (est): 1.4MM Privately Held
WEB: www.keystoneironandwireworks.com
SIC: 3534 Elevators & equipment

(G-4491)
SEXTET FABRICS INC
21 Ryder Pl Ste 4 (11518-1200)
P.O. Box 10 (11518-0010)
PHONE.................................516 593-0608
Fax: 516 593-0430
Gordon Stern, *CEO*
Barbara Ross, *President*
Ronald Ross, *Principal*
Adam Ackerman, *Vice Pres*
Gail Koppel, *Treasurer*
EMP: 12 EST: 1971
SQ FT: 8,500
SALES (est): 1.4MM Privately Held
SIC: 2259 Convertors, knit goods

(G-4492)
STERLING PIERCE COMPANY INC
395 Atlantic Ave (11518-1423)
PHONE.................................516 593-1170
William Burke, *President*
Isabel Burke, *Vice Pres*
▼ EMP: 29
SQ FT: 5,000
SALES (est): 3.3MM Privately Held
WEB: www.sterlingpierce.com
SIC: 2789 2732 2752 Binding only: books, pamphlets, magazines, etc.; book printing; commercial printing, lithographic

(G-4493)
STYLEBUILT ACCESSORIES INC (PA)
Also Called: Stylebuilt Acesries
45 Rose Ln (11518-2126)
PHONE.................................917 439-0578
Jonathan Greenfield, *President*
Jerome Greenfield, *Vice Pres*
Jackie Greenfield, *Treasurer*
Carla Polizzi, *Comptroller*
Lois Kreiner, *Intl Dir*
▲ EMP: 12 EST: 1946
SQ FT: 65,000
SALES: 950K Privately Held
WEB: www.stylebuilt.com
SIC: 3499 Novelties & specialties, metal

East Setauket
Suffolk County

(G-4494)
ALPINE OVERHEAD DOORS INC
8 Hulse Rd Ste 1 (11733-3649)
PHONE.................................631 456-7800
Sebastian Nagro, *Owner*
EMP: 30
SALES (corp-wide): 17.1MM Privately Held
WEB: www.alpinedoors.com
SIC: 3442 Metal doors
PA: Alpine Overhead Doors, Inc.
    8 Hulse Rd Ste 1
    East Setauket NY 11733
    631 473-9300

(G-4495)
ANORAD CORPORATION
41 Research Way (11733-3454)
PHONE.................................631 380-2100
Fax: 631 344-6601
Marco H Wishart, *Ch of Bd*
Geoffrey Storms, *President*
Theodore D Crandall, *Senior VP*
John Callahan, *Vice Pres*
Thomas Derosa, *CFO*
▲ EMP: 102
SALES (est): 18.2MM Publicly Held
WEB: www.anorad.com
SIC: 3577 3827 Computer peripheral equipment; optical instruments & lenses
PA: Rockwell Automation, Inc.
    1201 S 2nd St
    Milwaukee WI 53204

(G-4496)
B & Z TECHNOLOGIES LLC
Also Called: Bnz Tech
7 Technology Dr (11733-4000)
PHONE.................................631 675-9666
Javed Siddiqui, *President*
David Hlinka, *General Mgr*
Asma Siddiqui, *CFO*
EMP: 7
SQ FT: 2,000
SALES: 2MM Privately Held
WEB: www.bnztech.com
SIC: 3812 Antennas, radar or communications; radar systems & equipment

(G-4497)
BASF CORPORATION
Also Called: BASF The Chemical Company
361 Sheep Pasture Rd (11733-3614)
PHONE.................................631 689-0200
Meredith Culver, *Branch Mgr*
Anthony Asselta, *Manager*
EMP: 157
SALES (corp-wide): 60.8B Privately Held
SIC: 2819 Industrial inorganic chemicals
HQ: Basf Corporation
    100 Park Ave
    Florham Park NJ 07932
    973 245-6000

(G-4498)
COLLABORATIVE LABORATORIES (DH)
3 Technology Dr Ste 400 (11733-4078)
PHONE.................................631 689-0200
James Hayward PHD, *President*
Joseph Ceccoli, *COO*
EMP: 60
SQ FT: 25,000
SALES: 3.2MM
SALES (corp-wide): 60.8B Privately Held
WEB: www.collabo.com
SIC: 2844 2869 2833 8731 Toilet preparations; industrial organic chemicals; medicinals & botanicals; biotechnical research, commercial
HQ: Basf Catalysts Llc
    25 Middlesex Tpke
    Iselin NJ 08830
    732 205-5000

(G-4499)
EATING EVOLVED INC
10 Technology Dr Unit 4 (11733-4063)
PHONE.................................516 510-2601
EMP: 8 EST: 2015

GEOGRAPHIC SECTION

East Syracuse - Onondaga County (G-4523)

SALES (est): 630.8K **Privately Held**
SIC: 2066 Chocolate & cocoa products

(G-4500)
FEDDERS ISLANDAIRE INC
Also Called: Fedders Islandaire Company
22 Research Way (11733-3453)
PHONE..................631 471-2900
Robert Hansen, *President*
EMP: 85
SQ FT: 32,000
SALES (est): 23.7K
SALES (corp-wide): 141.1MM **Privately Held**
SIC: 3585 3822 3433 5722 Air conditioning equipment, complete; heat pumps, electric; auto controls regulating residntl & coml environmt & applncs; heating equipment, except electric; air conditioning room units, self-contained; heating & air conditioning contractors
PA: Fedders Corporation
   13455 Noel Rd Ste 2200
   Dallas TX 75240
   604 908-8686

(G-4501)
FLAGPOLES INCORPORATED
95 Gnarled Hollow Rd (11733-1934)
P.O. Box 833 (11733-0643)
PHONE..................631 751-5500
Fax: 631 751-7955
Jack Seferian, *CEO*
Haig Seferian, *Principal*
Gregory Seferian, *Vice Pres*
▼ EMP: 90
SQ FT: 96,000
SALES (est): 19.1MM **Privately Held**
WEB: www.flagpole.net
SIC: 3446 3441 3354 Flagpoles, metal; lamp posts, metal; fabricated structural metal; aluminum extruded products

(G-4502)
GOLDBERG PROSTHETIC & ORTHOTIC
9 Technology Dr (11733-4000)
PHONE..................631 689-6606
Mark E Goldberg, *President*
Lisa Wilson, *Accountant*
EMP: 14
SALES (est): 2.3MM **Privately Held**
SIC: 3842 8021 5999 Limbs, artificial; prosthodontist; artificial limbs

(G-4503)
HYPUR PRECISION MACHINING INC
10 Technology Dr Unit 8 (11733-4063)
P.O. Box 2785 (11733-0858)
PHONE..................631 584-8498
Fax: 631 584-8445
James Benaburger Jr, *President*
EMP: 10
SQ FT: 4,000
SALES (est): 737.4K **Privately Held**
SIC: 3599 Machine shop, jobbing & repair

(G-4504)
MEDICINE RULES INC
2 Constance Ct (11733-3730)
PHONE..................631 334-5395
Joseph Agartner, *President*
EMP: 5
SALES (est): 309.6K **Privately Held**
SIC: 3695 Computer software tape & disks: blank, rigid & floppy

(G-4505)
MILLER MOHR DISPLAY INC
12 Technology Dr Unit 6 (11733-4049)
PHONE..................631 941-2769
Fax: 631 941-1147
Marilyn Mohr, *President*
Miller Mohr, *Principal*
EMP: 5
SALES: 950K **Privately Held**
SIC: 3993 Signs & advertising specialties

(G-4506)
MML SOFTWARE LTD
Also Called: Finance Manager
45 Research Way Ste 207 (11733-6401)
PHONE..................631 941-1313
Ron Bovich, *President*
Andrew Miller, *President*

Wendy Gottlieb, *Mktg Coord*
EMP: 20
SQ FT: 5,000
SALES (est): 2MM **Privately Held**
WEB: www.financemgr.com
SIC: 7372 6163 Prepackaged software; loan brokers

(G-4507)
PENETRON INTERNATIONAL LTD
45 Research Way Ste 203 (11733-6401)
PHONE..................631 941-9700
Fax: 631 941-9777
Robert G Reuera, *CEO*
Sue Yi, *Info Tech Mgr*
Jozef Van Beeck, *Director*
Ann Martucci, *Executive Asst*
▲ EMP: 14
SQ FT: 60,000
SALES (est): 5.5MM **Privately Held**
WEB: www.penetron.com
SIC: 2899 Waterproofing compounds

(G-4508)
POLE-TECH CO INC
Also Called: Poletech Flagpole Manufaturer
97 Gnarled Hollow Rd (11733-1980)
P.O. Box 715 (11733-0770)
PHONE..................631 689-5525
Fax: 631 689-5528
Karnik M Seferian, *Ch of Bd*
Ralph Barbarite, *Vice Pres*
Nigg Pappu, *Manager*
Lori Jane, *Admin Sec*
◆ EMP: 17
SQ FT: 20,000
SALES (est): 4.7MM **Privately Held**
WEB: www.poletech.com
SIC: 3446 Flagpoles, metal

(G-4509)
PRINTING SPECTRUM INC
12 Research Way Ste 1 (11733-3531)
PHONE..................631 689-1010
Fax: 631 689-7030
James Altebrando, *Ch of Bd*
John Visconti, *Sales Mgr*
EMP: 12
SQ FT: 10,000
SALES (est): 2MM **Privately Held**
WEB: www.printingspectrum.com
SIC: 2752 Commercial printing, lithographic

(G-4510)
RE HANSEN INDUSTRIES INC (PA)
Also Called: Islandaire
22 Research Way (11733-3453)
PHONE..................631 471-2900
Robert Hansen Jr, *Ch of Bd*
Robert Altner, *Prdtn Mgr*
Donna Thompson, *Controller*
Jason Alexander, *Sales Dir*
George Correa, *Sales Dir*
◆ EMP: 118
SALES (est): 25.2MM **Privately Held**
SIC: 3585 3822 3433 5722 Air conditioning equipment, complete; heat pumps, electric; auto controls regulating residntl & coml environmt & applncs; heating equipment, except electric; air conditioning room units, self-contained; plumbing, heating, air-conditioning contractors

(G-4511)
SKYLINE LLC
16 Hulse Rd Ste 1 (11733-3645)
PHONE..................631 403-4131
Erin Argyris, *Controller*
Louis Bove, *Mng Member*
Lawrence Schreiber,
EMP: 20
SALES: 3.5MM **Privately Held**
SIC: 3295 Perlite, aggregate or expanded

(G-4512)
TECHNOMAG INC
12 Technology Dr Unit 5 (11733-4049)
PHONE..................631 246-6142
Vujay Katukota, *President*
▲ EMP: 5

SALES (est): 605K **Privately Held**
SIC: 3499 3577 7319 Magnets, permanent: metallic; computer peripheral equipment; distribution of advertising material or sample services

(G-4513)
TIMES BEACON RECORD NEWSPAPERS (PA)
Also Called: Village Times, The
185 Route 25a Ste 4 (11733-2870)
P.O. Box 707 (11733-0769)
PHONE..................631 331-1154
Fax: 631 751-7744
Leah E Dunaeif, *President*
Leah Dunaief, *Owner*
Elana Glowatz, *Editor*
Beth H Mason, *Prdtn Dir*
Marie Murtagh, *Advt Staff*
EMP: 17
SALES (est): 1.8MM **Privately Held**
SIC: 2711 Newspapers: publishing only, not printed on site

(G-4514)
TUCKER JONES HOUSE INC
1 Enterprise Dr (11733-4086)
P.O. Box 231 (11733-0231)
PHONE..................631 642-9092
Donna Sucilsky, *President*
EMP: 20
SQ FT: 8,000
SALES (est): 2.3MM **Privately Held**
WEB: www.tavernpuzzle.com
SIC: 3944 Puzzles

(G-4515)
VISUAL LISTING SYSTEMS INC
19 Technology Dr (11733-4000)
P.O. Box 856, Stony Brook (11790-0856)
PHONE..................631 689-7222
Dale Robins, *President*
Paul Singer, *Vice Pres*
EMP: 5
SALES (est): 419.4K **Privately Held**
WEB: www.vlshomes.com
SIC: 7372 8742 Prepackaged software; real estate consultant

(G-4516)
ZEPPELIN ELECTRIC COMPANY INC
26 Deer Ln (11733-3407)
PHONE..................631 928-9467
William Zeppelin, *President*
EMP: 7
SQ FT: 1,250
SALES: 525.4K **Privately Held**
SIC: 3625 1731 Relays & industrial controls; electronic controls installation

---

East Syracuse
Onondaga County

(G-4517)
ALEXSCOE LLC
Also Called: Atlas Fence
6852 Manlius Center Rd (13057-9522)
PHONE..................315 463-9207
Fax: 315 433-8561
Christopher Polimino, *President*
Debbie Corley, *Vice Pres*
EMP: 40 EST: 2012
SALES: 9.7MM **Privately Held**
SIC: 3315 Fence gates posts & fittings: steel

(G-4518)
ALLEN TOOL PHOENIX INC
6821 Ellicott Dr (13057-1148)
P.O. Box 3024, Liverpool (13089-3024)
PHONE..................315 463-7533
Fax: 315 463-0303
Cheryl Maines, *President*
Jack Quartier, *Engineer*
Heath Severn, *Engineer*
Joan Cooney, *Accountant*
Ed McCarthy, *Manager*
EMP: 20
SQ FT: 18,000

SALES (est): 3.5MM **Privately Held**
WEB: www.allentoolphoenix.com
SIC: 3599 7692 Machine shop, jobbing & repair; welding repair

(G-4519)
ANAREN INC (PA)
6635 Kirkville Rd (13057-9672)
PHONE..................315 432-8909
Lawrence A Sala, *CEO*
David E Kopf, *President*
Jeff Liebl, *President*
Timothy Ross, *President*
David Whitaker, *General Mgr*
▲ EMP: 880
SQ FT: 159,000
SALES (est): 228.8MM **Privately Held**
WEB: www.anaren.com
SIC: 3679 Electronic circuits; microwave components

(G-4520)
ANAREN MICROWAVE INC
6635 Kirkville Rd (13057-9600)
PHONE..................315 432-8909
Fax: 315 432-9121
Lawrence A Sala, *CEO*
George Blanton, *Senior VP*
Brian Buyea, *Project Mgr*
Doreen R Barney, *Buyer*
Jim Budd, *Engineer*
EMP: 1
SALES (est): 75MM
SALES (corp-wide): 228.8MM **Privately Held**
SIC: 3821 Micromanipulator
PA: Anaren, Inc.
   6635 Kirkville Rd
   East Syracuse NY 13057
   315 432-8909

(G-4521)
ARMSTRONG MOLD CORPORATION (PA)
6910 Manlius Center Rd (13057-8507)
PHONE..................315 437-1517
Fax: 315 437-9198
John Alfred Armstrong, *CEO*
Peter Armstrong, *President*
Mark Garofano, *President*
John Matthews, *General Mgr*
Christopher Tiffault, *General Mgr*
▼ EMP: 50
SQ FT: 90,000
SALES (est): 19.6MM **Privately Held**
WEB: www.armstrongmold.com
SIC: 3365 3089 3543 Aluminum & aluminum-based alloy castings; injection molding of plastics; industrial patterns

(G-4522)
ARMSTRONG MOLD CORPORATION
5860 Fisher Rd (13057-2962)
PHONE..................315 437-1517
John Alfred Armstrong, *Principal*
Greg Mork, *Engineer*
EMP: 75
SQ FT: 31,060
SALES (corp-wide): 19.6MM **Privately Held**
WEB: www.armstrongmold.com
SIC: 3599 3365 3089 3543 Custom machinery; machine shop, jobbing & repair; aluminum & aluminum-based alloy castings; injection molding of plastics; industrial patterns
PA: Armstrong Mold Corporation
   6910 Manlius Center Rd
   East Syracuse NY 13057
   315 437-1517

(G-4523)
ARTISTRY IN WOOD OF SYRACUSE
6804 Manlius Center Rd # 2 (13057-1394)
PHONE..................315 431-4022
Fax: 315 431-0887
Gregory W McCartney, *President*
Kim Fanke, *Controller*
Peggy Thomas, *Finance Mgr*
EMP: 17
SALES (est): 3.6MM **Privately Held**
SIC: 2599 2531 5046 Factory furniture & fixtures; public building & related furniture; library furniture; store fixtures

East Syracuse - Onondaga County (G-4524)

(G-4524)
ASSA ABLOY ENTRANCE SYSTEMS US
Also Called: Besam Entrance Solutions
28 Corporate Cir Ste 1 (13057-1283)
PHONE...............................315 492-6600
Fax: 315 492-6767
Shane Stone, *Branch Mgr*
EMP: 22
SALES (corp-wide): 7.7B **Privately Held**
SIC: 3699 1796 3442 Door opening & closing devices, electrical; installing building equipment; metal doors
HQ: Assa Abloy Entrance Systems Us Inc.
1900 Airport Rd
Monroe NC 28110
704 290-5520

(G-4525)
AURORA STONE GROUP LLC
114 Marcy St (13057-2143)
PHONE...............................315 471-6869
Sandra Murphy,
EMP: 10
SALES (est): 900K **Privately Held**
SIC: 3281 1743 Granite, cut & shaped; marble installation, interior

(G-4526)
B P NASH CO INC
5841 Butternut Dr (13057-9514)
PHONE...............................315 445-1310
Fax: 315 449-1003
Barry Nash, *President*
EMP: 15
SQ FT: 12,000
SALES: 1.5MM **Privately Held**
SIC: 3441 Fabricated structural metal

(G-4527)
BELLOTTI PACKAGING INC
Also Called: Bell-Pac
6881 Schuyler Rd (13057-9752)
PHONE...............................315 433-0131
Fax: 315 433-8514
Louis Bellotti Jr, *President*
Kathlyn Bellotti, *Vice Pres*
Esther Shelley, *Manager*
EMP: 13
SQ FT: 26,100
SALES (est): 2.2MM **Privately Held**
WEB: www.bell-pak.com
SIC: 2653 Corrugated & solid fiber boxes

(G-4528)
BK PRINTING INC
Also Called: Speedpro Imaging
6507 Basile Rowe (13057-2928)
PHONE...............................315 565-5396
Fax: 315 565-5397
Robert Kellher, *President*
Lori Parker, *CFO*
EMP: 7 **EST:** 2010
SQ FT: 5,000
SALES: 700K **Privately Held**
SIC: 2752 Commercial printing, lithographic

(G-4529)
BRISTOL-MYERS SQUIBB COMPANY
6000 Thompson Rd (13057-5050)
P.O. Box 4755, Syracuse (13221-4755)
PHONE...............................315 432-2000
Fax: 315 432-2202
Steven Lee, *Branch Mgr*
John Sharak, *Security Mgr*
Sellie Bittner, *Manager*
Mary Bronchetti, *Manager*
Srinivasan Balaji, *Associate Dir*
EMP: 40
SALES (corp-wide): 19.4B **Publicly Held**
WEB: www.bms.com
SIC: 2834 Druggists' preparations (pharmaceuticals)
PA: Bristol-Myers Squibb Company
345 Park Ave Bsmt Lc3
New York NY 10154
212 546-4000

(G-4530)
CARRIER CORPORATION
6390 Fly Rd (13057-9349)
PHONE...............................315 463-5744
Ralph Bott, *Branch Mgr*
Leslie Franklin, *Manager*
EMP: 293
SALES (corp-wide): 57.2B **Publicly Held**
WEB: www.carrier.com
SIC: 3585 Air conditioning equipment, complete
HQ: Carrier Corporation
13995 Pasteur Blvd
Jupiter FL 33458
561 796-2000

(G-4531)
CARRIER CORPORATION
Carrier Transicold
Kinne St (13057)
P.O. Box 4805, Syracuse (13221-4805)
PHONE...............................315 432-6000
Fax: 315 432-3099
Nick Pinchuk, *Manager*
EMP: 293
SALES (corp-wide): 57.2B **Publicly Held**
WEB: www.carrier.com
SIC: 3585 Air conditioning equipment, complete
HQ: Carrier Corporation
13995 Pasteur Blvd
Jupiter FL 33458
561 796-2000

(G-4532)
CARRIER CORPORATION
Transicold
Carrier Pkwy Bldg Tr 20 (13057)
P.O. Box 4805, Syracuse (13221-4805)
PHONE...............................315 432-3844
Nick Pinchuk, *President*
Scott Lindsay, *Design Engr*
EMP: 293
SALES (corp-wide): 57.2B **Publicly Held**
WEB: www.carrier.com
SIC: 3585 Lockers, refrigerated
HQ: Carrier Corporation
13995 Pasteur Blvd
Jupiter FL 33458
561 796-2000

(G-4533)
CLEARWOOD CUSTOM CARPENTRY AND
617 W Manlius St Ste 1 (13057-2276)
PHONE...............................315 432-8422
Fax: 315 432-8469
Amy Steinbrecher, *Bookkeeper*
Kathy Stay, *Office Mgr*
Kyle Latray, *Mng Member*
Andrew McDonald,
EMP: 30
SQ FT: 33,856
SALES (est): 5.1MM **Privately Held**
WEB: www.clearwoodccm.com
SIC: 2431 2434 Millwork; wood kitchen cabinets

(G-4534)
CONSTRUCTION PARTS WHSE INC
5841 Butternut Dr (13057-9514)
PHONE...............................315 445-1310
Bruce P Nash Jr, *President*
Dale Spuches, *Vice Pres*
EMP: 6
SALES: 1MM **Privately Held**
SIC: 3444 Sheet metal specialties, not stamped

(G-4535)
DAIRY FARMERS AMERICA INC
5001 Brittonfield Pkwy (13057-9201)
P.O. Box 4844, Syracuse (13221-4844)
PHONE...............................816 801-6440
Diana Cordes, *Human Res Mgr*
David Geisler, *Manager*
Nichole Owens, *Manager*
Frank King, *Master*
EMP: 41
SALES (corp-wide): 13.5B **Privately Held**
WEB: www.dfamilk.com
SIC: 2026 Fluid milk
PA: Dairy Farmers Of America, Inc.
1405 N 98th St
Kansas City KS 66111
816 801-6455

(G-4536)
DANCKER SELLEW & DOUGLAS INC
6067 Corporate Dr (13057-1082)
PHONE...............................908 231-1600
EMP: 6
SALES (corp-wide): 141.1MM **Privately Held**
SIC: 2869 Industrial organic chemicals
PA: Dancker, Sellew & Douglas, Inc.
291 Evans Way
Branchburg NJ 08876
908 429-1200

(G-4537)
DATACOM SYSTEMS INC
9 Adler Dr (13057-1201)
PHONE...............................315 463-9541
Fax: 315 463-9557
Kevin Formby, *President*
Timothy Crofton, *President*
Sam Lanzafane, *Chairman*
Gilbert Kaufman, *Vice Pres*
Andy Mather, *Vice Pres*
EMP: 33
SQ FT: 16,000
SALES (est): 7.4MM **Privately Held**
WEB: www.datacomsystems.com
SIC: 3571 Electronic computers

(G-4538)
DEAN FOODS COMPANY
6867 Schuyler Rd (13057-9752)
PHONE...............................315 452-5001
Fax: 315 452-3238
Leah Curcio, *Principal*
EMP: 87 **Publicly Held**
SIC: 2026 Fluid milk; milk processing (pasteurizing, homogenizing, bottling)
PA: Dean Foods Company
2711 N Haskell Ave
Dallas TX 75204

(G-4539)
E F THRESH INC
6000 Galster Rd (13057-2917)
PHONE...............................315 437-7301
Eric F Thresh, *President*
Janet Thresh, *Corp Secy*
William Thresh, *Vice Pres*
EMP: 6 **EST:** 1955
SQ FT: 35,000
SALES: 728K **Privately Held**
SIC: 2541 6512 Cabinets, except refrigerated: show, display, etc.: wood; commercial & industrial building operation

(G-4540)
EASTSIDE PRINTERS
Also Called: East Side Printers
6163 E Molloy Rd (13057-1067)
PHONE...............................315 437-6515
Matthew Brennan, *Owner*
Cinthia Brennan, *Systems Mgr*
EMP: 12
SQ FT: 4,000
SALES (est): 1.7MM **Privately Held**
SIC: 2752 2789 Commercial printing, offset; bookbinding & related work

(G-4541)
EUCHNER USA INC
6723 Lyons St (13057-9332)
PHONE...............................315 701-0315
Michael Ladd, *President*
Holly Piazza, *Finance*
Ricardo Davalos, *Manager*
▲ **EMP:** 18 **EST:** 2000
SQ FT: 3,136
SALES (est): 3.2MM **Privately Held**
WEB: www.euchner-usa.com
SIC: 3699 Electrical equipment & supplies

(G-4542)
FBM GALAXY INC
6741 Old Collamer Rd (13057-1119)
PHONE...............................315 463-5144
Glen Markam, *Manager*
Danny Parella, *Senior Mgr*
EMP: 18
SALES (corp-wide): 622.4MM **Publicly Held**
WEB: www.spi-co.com
SIC: 3089 3296 3554 Plastic processing; fiberglass insulation; die cutting & stamping machinery, paper converting
HQ: Fbm Galaxy, Inc.
1650 Manheim Pike Ste 202
Lancaster PA 17601
717 569-3900

(G-4543)
FIBERONE LLC
5 Technology Pl Ste 4 (13057-9738)
PHONE...............................315 434-8877
Rich Brown, *Manager*
Craig Mead,
EMP: 15 **EST:** 2000
SALES (est): 2MM **Privately Held**
SIC: 2298 Cable, fiber

(G-4544)
FLEX-HOSE COMPANY INC
6801 Crossbow Dr (13057-1026)
PHONE...............................315 437-1903
Fax: 315 437-1903
Philip Argersinger, *President*
Joanna Carter, *Vice Pres*
Chuck Philips, *Vice Pres*
David Rauch, *Vice Pres*
Chuck Phillips, *VP Mfg*
▲ **EMP:** 28 **EST:** 1968
SQ FT: 15,000
SALES (est): 7.6MM **Privately Held**
SIC: 3599 Hose, flexible metallic

(G-4545)
FOREST MEDICAL LLC
6700 Old Collamer Rd # 114 (13057-1167)
PHONE...............................315 434-9000
Fax: 315 432-8064
Donald Greenfield, *COO*
Dick Bowman, *Technology*
Raymond Lichorobiec,
EMP: 9
SQ FT: 4,000
SALES (est): 1.1MM **Privately Held**
WEB: www.forestmedical.com
SIC: 3845 Electromedical equipment

(G-4546)
GEI INTERNATIONAL INC (PA)
Also Called: Gaebel Enterprises
100 Ball St (13057-2359)
P.O. Box 6849, Syracuse (13217-6849)
PHONE...............................315 463-9261
Fax: 315 463-9034
Peter Anderson, *President*
Maureen Anderson, *Vice Pres*
William Parker, *Sales Staff*
EMP: 18 **EST:** 1960
SALES (est): 2MM **Privately Held**
WEB: www.geionline.com
SIC: 3423 3531 5199 3829 Rules or rulers, metal; scrapers (construction machinery); art goods & supplies; measuring & controlling devices

(G-4547)
GREENWOOD WINERY LLC
6475 Collamer Rd (13057-1031)
P.O. Box 2949, Syracuse (13220-2949)
PHONE...............................315 432-8132
Tom Greenwood, *Owner*
Robyn Bombard, *Sales Mgr*
EMP: 30
SALES: 800K **Privately Held**
SIC: 2084 2066 Wines; chocolate

(G-4548)
H F W COMMUNICATIONS INC (HQ)
Also Called: Holstein World
6437 Collamer Rd Ste 1 (13057-1559)
PHONE...............................315 703-7979
Scott Smith, *CEO*
Joel Hastings, *President*
John Montandon, *President*
Eleanor Jacobs, *Editor*
Art Sweum, *Vice Pres*
EMP: 15
SALES (est): 6.5MM **Privately Held**
SIC: 2721 Trade journals: publishing & printing
PA: Multi-Ag Media L.L.C.
6437 Collamer Rd
East Syracuse NY
315 703-7979

GEOGRAPHIC SECTION
East Syracuse - Onondaga County (G-4571)

(G-4549)
HARDWARE SPECIALTY CO INC
23 Corporate Cir Ste 5 (13057-1077)
PHONE.....................315 434-9093
Fax: 315 434-9096
Susan Martin, *Sales Staff*
Kevin Wood, *Sales Associate*
John Olin, *Branch Mgr*
Patrick Sheehan, *Branch Mgr*
Ann Forceno, *Assistant*
EMP: 14
SALES (corp-wide): 114.9MM **Privately Held**
WEB: www.hardwarespeciality.com
SIC: 3965 Fasteners
PA: Hardware Specialty Co. Inc.
4875 36th St
Long Island City NY 11101
718 361-9320

(G-4550)
HENRY SCHEIN INC
6057 Corporate Dr Ste 2 (13057-1068)
PHONE.....................315 431-0340
Fax: 315 431-0971
Kristen Esler, *Branch Mgr*
EMP: 24
SALES (corp-wide): 11.5B **Publicly Held**
SIC: 3843 Dental equipment & supplies
PA: Henry Schein, Inc.
135 Duryea Rd
Melville NY 11747
631 843-5500

(G-4551)
HERCULES CANDY CO
Also Called: Hercules Gift & Gormet
209 W Heman St (13057-2258)
PHONE.....................315 463-4339
Fax: 315 463-2796
Terry L Andrianos, *Partner*
EMP: 10
SALES: 232K **Privately Held**
WEB: www.herculescandy.com
SIC: 2064 5441 Candy & other confectionery products; candy

(G-4552)
ILLUMINATION TECHNOLOGIES INC
5 Adler Dr (13057-1262)
P.O. Box 1153, Elbridge (13060-1153)
PHONE.....................315 463-4673
Fax: 315 463-1401
Michael Muehlemann, *President*
Jean Vurraro, *Manager*
EMP: 10
SQ FT: 6,000
SALES (est): 2MM **Privately Held**
WEB: www.illuminationtech.com
SIC: 3648 Lighting equipment

(G-4553)
INDUSTRIAL FABRICATING CORP (PA)
6201 E Molloy Rd (13057-1021)
PHONE.....................315 437-3353
Fax: 315 437-4075
Myron R Kocan, *President*
Jim McVicar, *Manager*
EMP: 33
SQ FT: 60,000
SALES: 13.1MM **Privately Held**
WEB: www.industrialfabricating.com
SIC: 3441 3444 Fabricated structural metal; sheet metalwork

(G-4554)
INDUSTRIAL FABRICATING CORP
4 Collamer Cir (13057)
PHONE.....................315 437-8234
Fax: 315 432-1669
Gary Cristal, *Manager*
EMP: 29
SQ FT: 32,886
SALES (corp-wide): 13.1MM **Privately Held**
WEB: www.industrialfabricating.com
SIC: 3443 Weldments
PA: Industrial Fabricating Corp
6201 E Molloy Rd
East Syracuse NY 13057
315 437-3353

(G-4555)
INFICON INC (HQ)
2 Technology Pl (13057-9714)
PHONE.....................315 434-1149
Fax: 315 437-3803
Peter Maier, *President*
Darren Lee, *General Mgr*
Hoang Cao, *Vice Pres*
Stephen Chabot, *Vice Pres*
Terry Perkins, *Vice Pres*
▲ **EMP:** 250
SQ FT: 135,000
SALES: 143.9K
SALES (corp-wide): 309.6MM **Privately Held**
WEB: www.inficon.com
SIC: 3823 3812 Industrial process control instruments; search & navigation equipment
PA: Inficon Holding Ag
Hintergasse 15b
Bad Ragaz SG 7310
813 004-980

(G-4556)
INFICON HOLDING AG
2 Technology Pl (13057-9714)
PHONE.....................315 434-1100
William Busher, *QC Mgr*
Paul Mahunik, *Engineer*
Peter G Maier, *CFO*
Peter Maeir, *CFO*
Janice Smeall, *VP Finance*
EMP: 5
SALES (est): 370.3K **Privately Held**
SIC: 3823 Industrial instrmnts msrmnt display/control process variable

(G-4557)
INFITEC INC
6500 Badgley Rd (13057-9667)
P.O. Box 2956, Syracuse (13220-2956)
PHONE.....................315 433-1150
Fax: 315 433-1521
George W Ehegartner, *Ch of Bd*
David Lawrie, *Vice Pres*
Bob Eichenlaub, *Purch Mgr*
Kathy Ehegartner, *Purchasing*
Tom Kissmer, *Engineer*
▲ **EMP:** 60
SQ FT: 22,000
SALES: 4.3MM **Privately Held**
WEB: www.infitec.com
SIC: 3625 3822 Timing devices, electronic; auto controls regulating residntl & coml environmt & applncs

(G-4558)
INTERSURGICAL INCORPORATED (PA)
6757 Kinne St (13057-1215)
PHONE.....................315 451-2900
Howard Bellm, *Managing Dir*
Kristin Purdy, *Vice Pres*
Mary Sweeney, *Vice Pres*
Susan Jaeger, *Accountant*
Rhonda Steward, *Accountant*
EMP: 11
SQ FT: 7,000
SALES (est): 2.5MM **Privately Held**
SIC: 3841 Surgical & medical instruments; anesthesia apparatus

(G-4559)
J W STEVENS CO INC
6059 Corporate Dr (13057-1040)
PHONE.....................315 472-6311
Jeff Salanger, *Vice Pres*
Gary Archer, *VP Sales*
EMP: 6
SALES (est): 711.8K **Privately Held**
SIC: 3443 Boiler shop products: boilers, smokestacks, steel tanks

(G-4560)
JE MILLER INC
747 W Manlius St (13057-2177)
PHONE.....................315 437-6811
Fax: 315 463-4597
Dennis J Hile, *President*
Barbara Hile, *Vice Pres*
Lana Woods, *Sales Staff*
Audrey More, *Manager*
EMP: 16 **EST:** 1951
SQ FT: 15,000
SALES (est): 3.6MM **Privately Held**
WEB: www.jemiller.com
SIC: 3625 3585 Relays & industrial controls; air conditioning units, complete: domestic or industrial

(G-4561)
JOY EDWARD COMPANY
Also Called: Joy Process Mechanical
6747 W Benedict Rd (13057-9391)
P.O. Box 338 (13057-0338)
PHONE.....................315 474-3360
Fax: 315 474-2416
Leonard P Markert III, *CEO*
Gerald Carhart, *Vice Pres*
Jim Condon, *Project Mgr*
Lyn Markert Hathaway, *Admin Sec*
EMP: 40 **EST:** 1875
SQ FT: 40,000
SALES (est): 17.5MM **Privately Held**
SIC: 3441 1711 Fabricated structural metal; mechanical contractor

(G-4562)
KERNER AND MERCHANT
104 Johnson St (13057-2840)
PHONE.....................315 463-8023
Benjamin R Merchant, *President*
Albert H Arnold, *Corp Secy*
Andrea Martin, *Bookkeeper*
EMP: 7
SQ FT: 3,600
SALES: 300K **Privately Held**
SIC: 3931 7699 Pipes, organ; organ tuning & repair

(G-4563)
MD4 HOLDINGS INC
6713 Collamer Rd (13057-9759)
PHONE.....................315 434-1869
Mike Rufo, *President*
Dan Simmons, *Treasurer*
EMP: 17
SQ FT: 17,000
SALES: 1.2MM **Publicly Held**
WEB: www.dpt-fast.com
SIC: 3089 Plastic processing
PA: 3d Systems Corporation
333 Three D Systems Cir
Rock Hill SC 29730

(G-4564)
MICROWAVE FILTER COMPANY INC (PA)
6743 Kinne St (13057-1269)
PHONE.....................315 438-4700
Fax: 315 463-1467
Paul W Mears, *CEO*
Carl F Fahrenkrug Jr, *Exec VP*
David Barnello, *Purch Dir*
Robert Paul, *Chief Engr*
Richard L Jones, *CFO*
EMP: 44
SQ FT: 40,000
SALES: 3.5MM **Publicly Held**
WEB: www.microwavefilter.com
SIC: 3677 3679 Filtration devices, electronic; microwave components

(G-4565)
MUTUAL LIBRARY BINDERY INC
6295 E Molloy Rd Ste 3 (13057-1104)
P.O. Box 6026, Syracuse (13217-6026)
PHONE.....................315 455-6638
Otto E Rausch, *President*
Robert Rausch, *Vice Pres*
Stephen Rausch, *Vice Pres*
EMP: 25 **EST:** 1915
SALES (est): 2.6MM **Privately Held**
SIC: 2789 Bookbinding & repairing: trade, edition, library, etc.

(G-4566)
NIAGARA SCIENTIFIC INC
Also Called: Schroeder Machine Div
6743 Kinne St (13057-1215)
P.O. Box 146 (13057-0146)
PHONE.....................315 437-0821
Fax: 315 437-0242
Carl Fahrenkrug, *President*
Milo Peterson, *Exec VP*
Bill Admo, *Opers Staff*
Dave Barnello, *Purchasing*
Robert Hamister, *VP Engrg*
EMP: 54
SQ FT: 16,000
SALES (est): 4.3MM
SALES (corp-wide): 3.5MM **Publicly Held**
WEB: www.microwavefilter.com
SIC: 3565 3826 Carton packing machines; environmental testing equipment
PA: Microwave Filter Company, Inc.
6743 Kinne St
East Syracuse NY 13057
315 438-4700

(G-4567)
NIDEC MOTOR CORPORATION
Advanced Motors & Drives
6268 E Molloy Rd (13057-1047)
PHONE.....................315 434-9303
Fax: 315 432-9290
EMP: 14
SALES (corp-wide): 10.5B **Privately Held**
SIC: 3621 Motors & generators
HQ: Nidec Motor Corporation
8050 West Florissant Ave
Saint Louis MO 63136

(G-4568)
POWER-FLO TECHNOLOGIES INC
Also Called: Auburn Armature
6500 New Venture Gear Dr (13057-1076)
PHONE.....................315 399-5801
Mike Capfilo, *Manager*
Joe Corbin, *Manager*
John Lemczak, *Manager*
EMP: 93
SALES (corp-wide): 32.2MM **Privately Held**
WEB: www.auburnarmature.com
SIC: 7694 Armature rewinding shops
PA: Power-Flo Technologies, Inc.
270 Park Ave
New Hyde Park NY 11040
516 812-6800

(G-4569)
PPC BROADBAND INC (HQ)
6176 E Molloy Rd (13057-4010)
P.O. Box 278 (13057-0278)
PHONE.....................315 431-7200
John D Mezzalingua, *CEO*
Jose Rosa, *General Mgr*
Milos Dvorak, *Area Mgr*
Scott Claver, *Vice Pres*
Brian Kelly, *Vice Pres*
◆ **EMP:** 500 **EST:** 2002
SQ FT: 21,000
SALES (est): 281.9MM
SALES (corp-wide): 2.3B **Publicly Held**
WEB: www.ppc-online.com
SIC: 3678 Electronic connectors
PA: Belden Inc.
1 N Brentwood Blvd # 1500
Saint Louis MO 63105
314 854-8000

(G-4570)
RAYMOND CORPORATION
Also Called: Raymond Leasing
6650 Kirkville Rd (13057-9355)
PHONE.....................607 656-2311
Fax: 315 463-0053
Jim Schaefer, *General Mgr*
William Kosina, *Facilities Mgr*
Beryl Baldwin, *Warehouse Mgr*
Janet Sexton, *Buyer*
John Perun, *Sls & Mktg Exec*
EMP: 137
SQ FT: 51,584
SALES (corp-wide): 19.8B **Privately Held**
WEB: www.raymondcorp.com
SIC: 3537 Forklift trucks
HQ: The Raymond Corporation
22 S Canal St
Greene NY 13778
800 235-7200

(G-4571)
RAYMOND CORPORATION
6517 Chrysler Ln (13057-1228)
PHONE.....................315 463-5000
Leon A Eccleston, *Branch Mgr*
EMP: 469
SALES (corp-wide): 19.8B **Privately Held**
SIC: 3537 Forklift trucks
HQ: The Raymond Corporation
22 S Canal St
Greene NY 13778
800 235-7200

East Syracuse - Onondaga County (G-4572)

(G-4572)
RAYMOND CORPORATION
6533 Chrysler Ln (13057-1375)
PHONE.................................315 643-5000
Jim Schaefer, *Branch Mgr*
EMP: 30
SALES (corp-wide): 19.8B *Privately Held*
SIC: 3535 3537 7359 Conveyors & conveying equipment; industrial trucks & tractors; equipment rental & leasing
HQ: The Raymond Corporation
  22 S Canal St
  Greene NY 13778
  800 235-7200

(G-4573)
REYNOLDS TECH FABRICATORS INC
6895 Kinne St (13057-1217)
PHONE.................................315 437-0532
Fax: 315 437-1390
Joan J Reynolds, *CEO*
Michael Nakoski, *Vice Pres*
Raoma Stevenson, *Manager*
EMP: 37
SQ FT: 35,000
SALES (est): 6.8MM *Privately Held*
SIC: 3559 3471 Refinery, chemical processing & similar machinery; plating of metals or formed products

(G-4574)
RICHLAR INDUSTRIES INC
Also Called: Richlar Custom Foam Div
6741 Old Collamer Rd (13057-1119)
PHONE.................................315 463-5144
Fax: 315 463-0362
Richard Bruntarger, *President*
Dawn Popenfuss, *Vice Pres*
John Hakes, *Opers Mgr*
Bob Taldage, *Purch Mgr*
EMP: 18
SQ FT: 32,000
SALES (est): 2.8MM *Privately Held*
SIC: 3089 3296 3554 Plastic processing; fiberglass insulation; die cutting & stamping machinery, paper converting

(G-4575)
SAAB DEFENSE AND SEC USA LLC
5717 Enterprise Pkwy (13057-2905)
PHONE.................................315 445-5009
Laurence Harris, *Principal*
Michael Owen, *Engineer*
Jim Sullivan, *Director*
EMP: 12
SALES (corp-wide): 3B *Privately Held*
SIC: 3812 Search & detection systems & instruments
HQ: Saab Defense And Security Usa Llc
  20700 Loudoun County Pkwy
  Ashburn VA 20147
  703 406-7200

(G-4576)
SBB INC
1 Gm Dr Ste 5 (13057)
PHONE.................................315 422-2376
Fax: 315 437-6501
Robert McKenty, *Principal*
Tony Meehl, *Project Mgr*
John Bazinet, *Sales Executive*
Brian Kearney, *Associate*
EMP: 5
SALES (est): 1.2MM *Privately Held*
SIC: 3564 Air purification equipment

(G-4577)
SHAKO INC
6191 E Molloy Rd (13057-1038)
PHONE.................................315 437-1294
Fax: 315 437-0351
Brian Mayfield, *Principal*
EMP: 8
SALES (est): 892.9K *Privately Held*
SIC: 3535 Pneumatic tube conveyor systems

(G-4578)
SIMPLEXGRINNELL LP
6731 Collamer Rd Ste 4 (13057-8704)
PHONE.................................315 437-4660
William Knodel, *Manager*
EMP: 29 *Privately Held*

WEB: www.simplexgrinnell.com
SIC: 3669 Emergency alarms
HQ: Simplexgrinnell Lp
  4700 Exchange Ct
  Boca Raton FL 33431
  561 988-7200

(G-4579)
SIMPLEXGRINNELL LP
6731 Collamer Rd Ste 4 (13057-8704)
PHONE.................................607 338-5100
Richard Burke, *Sales Staff*
Mike Delsanto, *Manager*
EMP: 10 *Privately Held*
WEB: www.simplexgrinnell.com
SIC: 3669 Emergency alarms
HQ: Simplexgrinnell Lp
  4700 Exchange Ct
  Boca Raton FL 33431
  561 988-7200

(G-4580)
SOUTHERN STATES COOP INC
6701 Manlius Center Rd # 240 (13057-2999)
PHONE.................................315 438-4500
Sall McGarraty, *Manager*
EMP: 12
SALES (corp-wide): 2.2B *Privately Held*
SIC: 2048 Prepared feeds
PA: Southern States Cooperative, Incorporated
  6606 W Broad St Ste B
  Richmond VA 23230
  804 281-1000

(G-4581)
STF SERVICES INC
26 Corporate Cir Ste 2 (13057-1105)
PHONE.................................315 463-8506
Fax: 315 437-8244
Michael Smith, *President*
John Siedlicki, *COO*
Therese Pearce, *Accounting Mgr*
Sam Froio, *Technology*
EMP: 50
SQ FT: 20,000
SALES (est): 3.7MM
SALES (corp-wide): 2.4B *Privately Held*
WEB: www.superforms.com
SIC: 2731 2741 Books: publishing only; miscellaneous publishing
HQ: The Bureau Of National Affairs Inc
  1801 S Bell St Ste Cn110
  Arlington VA 22202
  703 341-3000

(G-4582)
SYRACUSE CORRUGATED BOX CORP
302 Stoutenger St (13057-2841)
P.O. Box 126 (13057-0126)
PHONE.................................315 437-9901
Fax: 315 437-6131
David R Wilde, *President*
Charles Wilde, *Vice Pres*
John Wilde, *Admin Sec*
EMP: 14 EST: 1969
SQ FT: 24,000
SALES (est): 2.5MM *Privately Held*
SIC: 2653 Boxes, corrugated: made from purchased materials

(G-4583)
THE PRS GROUP INC (PA)
Also Called: Political Risk Services, The
5800 Hrtge Lndng Dr Ste E (13057)
PHONE.................................315 431-0511
Fax: 315 431-0200
Christopher McKee, *CEO*
Christa Mosher, *Production*
Dianna Spinner, *Treasurer*
Patricia Davis, *Admin Sec*
EMP: 10 EST: 2000
SQ FT: 2,100
SALES (est): 737.4K *Privately Held*
WEB: www.prsgroup.com
SIC: 2721 Periodicals: publishing & printing; statistical reports (periodicals): publishing & printing

(G-4584)
TPC INC
6780 Nthrn Blvd Ste 401 (13057)
P.O. Box 2581, Syracuse (13220-2581)
PHONE.................................315 438-8605

Fax: 315 438-8605
Max Bablok, *President*
EMP: 6
SALES: 24.3MM *Privately Held*
SIC: 3728 Aircraft parts & equipment

(G-4585)
TRANE US INC
15 Technology Pl (13057-9713)
PHONE.................................315 234-1500
Tyler Malm, *Sales Engr*
Mike Carey, *Branch Mgr*
EMP: 36
SQ FT: 4,500 *Privately Held*
SIC: 3585 Refrigeration & heating equipment
HQ: Trane U.S. Inc.
  1 Centennial Ave Ste 101
  Piscataway NJ 08854
  732 652-7100

(G-4586)
TYCO SIMPLEXGRINNELL
6731 Collamer Rd Ste 4 (13057-9715)
PHONE.................................315 437-9664
Kevin Hache, *Branch Mgr*
EMP: 40
SALES (corp-wide): 1.4B *Privately Held*
SIC: 3569 3491 Sprinkler systems, fire: automatic; automatic regulating & control valves
PA: Tyco Simplexgrinnell
  1501 Nw 51st St
  Boca Raton FL 33431
  561 988-3658

(G-4587)
U S TECH CORPORATION
6511 Basile Rowe (13057-2928)
P.O. Box 816, Skaneateles (13152-0816)
PHONE.................................315 437-7207
Fax: 315 432-0225
Alexander E Gelston II, *President*
Janis J Soule, *Vice Pres*
EMP: 12
SALES: 6MM *Privately Held*
SIC: 3812 Search & detection systems & instruments

(G-4588)
UNITED TECHNOLOGIES CORP
6304 Carrier Pkwy (13057-6300)
PHONE.................................315 432-7849
EMP: 9
SALES (corp-wide): 57.2B *Publicly Held*
SIC: 3724 Aircraft engines & engine parts
PA: United Technologies Corporation
  10 Farm Springs Rd
  Farmington CT 06032
  860 728-7000

(G-4589)
UNIVERSAL STEP INC
5970 Butternut Dr (13057-8526)
PHONE.................................315 437-7611
David Smith, *President*
EMP: 5 EST: 2009
SALES (est): 580K *Privately Held*
SIC: 3272 Steps, prefabricated concrete

(G-4590)
US OPTICAL LLC
6848 Ellicott Dr (13057-1046)
PHONE.................................315 463-4800
Ronald Cotran, *Vice Pres*
Hank Delfavero, *Sales Mgr*
Tim Wooster, *Sales Mgr*
Christopher Salvage, *Marketing Mgr*
Ronald Potran, *Mng Member*
EMP: 50
SALES (est): 9.1MM *Privately Held*
SIC: 3827 Optical instruments & lenses

(G-4591)
VILLAGE DECORATION LTD
20 Corporate Cir (13057-1015)
PHONE.................................315 437-2522
Michael Robinson, *President*
Shawn Robinson, *Plant Mgr*
EMP: 30
SQ FT: 13,500
SALES: 1.5MM *Privately Held*
SIC: 3599 Machine & other job shop work

(G-4592)
WERMA (USA) INC
6731 Collamer Rd Ste 1 (13057-9793)
PHONE.................................315 414-0200
Michael Oneill, *President*
▲ EMP: 4 EST: 2011
SQ FT: 4,500
SALES (est): 3MM
SALES (corp-wide): 42.2MM *Privately Held*
SIC: 3669 Signaling apparatus, electric
PA: Werma Signaltechnik Gmbh + Co. Kg
  Durbheimer Str. 15
  Rietheim-Weilheim 78604
  742 495-570

East Yaphank
Suffolk County

(G-4593)
FIREMATIC SUPPLY CO INC (PA)
10 Ramsey Rd (11967-4704)
P.O. Box 187, Yaphank (11980-0187)
PHONE.................................631 924-3181
Fax: 631 924-5202
Michael Hanratty, *Ch of Bd*
Peter Hanratty, *President*
Barbara Hanratty, *Corp Secy*
George Barbieri, *Prdtn Mgr*
Marcel Rosenfeld, *Director*
EMP: 46
SQ FT: 22,000
SALES (est): 29.2MM *Privately Held*
WEB: www.firematic.com
SIC: 3569 Firefighting apparatus

Eastchester
Westchester County

(G-4594)
EASTCHESTER PHOTO SERVICES
Also Called: Eastchester Photo Svce
132 Fisher Ave (10709-2602)
P.O. Box 86 (10709-0086)
PHONE.................................914 961-6596
Fax: 914 961-6684
George Longobardo, *President*
Lorinda Longobardo, *Corp Secy*
EMP: 5
SQ FT: 2,400
SALES (est): 599.6K *Privately Held*
WEB: www.eastchesterphoto.com
SIC: 3861 5946 Developers, photographic (not made in chemical plants); camera & photographic supply stores

(G-4595)
W D TECHNOLOGY INC
42 Water St Ste B (10709-5502)
PHONE.................................914 779-8738
Vincent Rende, *President*
Joe Beard, *Sales Staff*
EMP: 6
SQ FT: 1,000
SALES: 1.5MM *Privately Held*
SIC: 3679 3825 Liquid crystal displays (LCD); radio frequency measuring equipment

Eastport
Suffolk County

(G-4596)
MEDIA TECHNOLOGIES LTD
220 Sonata Ct (11941-1617)
PHONE.................................631 467-7900
Rainer Zopfy, *President*
EMP: 12
SQ FT: 6,800
SALES (est): 2.7MM *Privately Held*
WEB: www.mediatechmail.com
SIC: 3652 5044 Compact laser discs, prerecorded; duplicating machines

Eden
Erie County

(G-4597)
AARFID LLC (PA)
3780 Yochum Rd (14057-9519)
PHONE.................................716 992-3999
Chad Carpenter, *President*
EMP: 5
SALES (est): 920.8K **Privately Held**
SIC: 7372 3695 Business oriented computer software; magnetic & optical recording media

(G-4598)
E B TROTTNOW MACHINE SPC
8955 Woodside Dr (14057-1460)
PHONE.................................716 694-0600
Fax: 716 694-0742
Mary Pietsch, *President*
EMP: 18 **EST:** 1948
SQ FT: 55,000
SALES (est): 3MM **Privately Held**
SIC: 3599 Machine shop, jobbing & repair

(G-4599)
EDEN TOOL & DIE INC
2721 Hemlock Rd (14057-1390)
P.O. Box 296 (14057-0296)
PHONE.................................716 992-4240
Fax: 716 992-4785
James Rettig, *President*
Gary Rettig, *Vice Pres*
Raymond Rettig, *Admin Sec*
▼ **EMP:** 8
SALES (est): 1.1MM **Privately Held**
SIC: 3544 Special dies & tools

(G-4600)
JOHN F RAFTER INC
Also Called: Jf Rafter The Lexington Co
2746 W Church St (14057-1011)
P.O. Box 300 (14057-0300)
PHONE.................................716 992-3425
Fax: 716 992-3426
John Rafter Jr, *President*
EMP: 5
SQ FT: 2,500
SALES (est): 567.8K **Privately Held**
SIC: 3452 Screws, metal

(G-4601)
MUSTANG-MAJOR TOOL & DIE CO
3243 N Boston Rd (14057-9500)
PHONE.................................716 992-9200
Fax: 716 992-9257
David Kolodczak, *President*
EMP: 6 **EST:** 1965
SQ FT: 8,200
SALES: 800K **Privately Held**
WEB: www.mmtooldie.com
SIC: 3544 Special dies & tools

Edgewood
Suffolk County

(G-4602)
ABH NATURES PRODUCTS INC
131 Heartland Blvd (11717-8315)
PHONE.................................631 249-5783
Jahirul Islam, *President*
Harsh Vyas, *CFO*
Sahina Islam, *Director*
David Rabinowit, *Director*
EMP: 28
SQ FT: 40,000
SALES (est): 9.2MM **Privately Held**
WEB: www.abhnature.com
SIC: 2833 Vitamins, natural or synthetic: bulk, uncompounded

(G-4603)
ABH PHARMA INC
131 Heartland Blvd (11717-8315)
PHONE.................................631 392-4692
Frank Cantone, *CEO*
EMP: 70 **EST:** 2016
SALES (est): 7.4MM **Privately Held**
SIC: 2834 Pharmaceutical preparations

(G-4604)
ADVANCE FOOD SERVICE CO INC
200 Heartland Blvd (11717-8380)
PHONE.................................631 242-4800
Fax: 631 242-6900
Milton Schwartz, *Corp Secy*
Daniel Schwartz, *Vice Pres*
Jerry Nolan, *Purchasing*
EMP: 200 **EST:** 1955
SQ FT: 60,000
SALES (est): 27.7MM **Privately Held**
SIC: 3589 Cooking equipment, commercial

(G-4605)
ADVANCE TABCO INC (HQ)
200 Heartland Blvd (11717-8379)
PHONE.................................631 242-8270
Fax: 631 242-6900
Penny Schwartz-Hutner, *President*
Alice Schwartz, *Chairman*
Daniel Schwartz, *Vice Pres*
Chris Pacicca, *Warehouse Mgr*
Ryan Fee, *Purch Mgr*
◆ **EMP:** 85
SQ FT: 70,000
SALES (est): 23.6MM
SALES (corp-wide): 87.6MM **Privately Held**
SIC: 3589 3431 Commercial cooking & foodwarming equipment; metal sanitary ware
PA: Kinplex Corp.
  200 Heartland Blvd
  Edgewood NY 11717
  631 242-4800

(G-4606)
ALL ISLAND MEDIA INC (PA)
Also Called: Pennysaver/Town Crier
1 Rodeo Dr (11717-8318)
PHONE.................................631 698-8400
Paul E Gregory, *Principal*
Robert Sussi, *Vice Pres*
Brenda Colonna, *Prdtn Dir*
Arleen Butler, *Sales Mgr*
Gregg Robinson, *Sales Mgr*
EMP: 110
SQ FT: 20,000
SALES (est): 12.9MM **Privately Held**
WEB: www.allislandmedia.com
SIC: 2711 Newspapers, publishing & printing

(G-4607)
AZTEC TOOL CO INC
180 Rodeo Dr (11717-8340)
PHONE.................................631 243-1144
Fax: 631 243-1149
Stewart Swiss, *President*
James Evarts, *Vice Pres*
Harry Herz, *Marketing Staff*
EMP: 20
SQ FT: 24,000
SALES (est): 4.3MM **Privately Held**
WEB: www.aztectool.com
SIC: 3089 Injection molded finished plastic products; injection molding of plastics

(G-4608)
BEMIS COMPANY INC
Also Called: Bemis North America
100 Wilshire Blvd (11717-8302)
PHONE.................................631 794-2900
Thomas Sperlazzo, *Buyer*
Igor Rakhmanskiy, *Engineer*
Linda Elkin, *Human Resources*
EMP: 171
SALES (corp-wide): 4B **Publicly Held**
SIC: 2671 Packaging paper & plastics film, coated & laminated
PA: Bemis Company, Inc.
  1 Neenah Ctr Fl 4
  Neenah WI 54956
  920 527-5000

(G-4609)
BIOCHEMICAL DIAGNOSTICS INC
180 Heartland Blvd (11717-8314)
PHONE.................................631 595-9200
Fax: 631 595-9204
Allen Panetz, *President*
Amir Forooqi, *Corp Secy*
Rich Gordon, *Vice Pres*
EMP: 25
SQ FT: 30,000
SALES (est): 4.1MM **Privately Held**
WEB: www.biochemicaldiagnostics.com
SIC: 3841 2835 Diagnostic apparatus, medical; in vitro & in vivo diagnostic substances

(G-4610)
CPI AEROSTRUCTURES INC
91 Heartland Blvd (11717-8330)
PHONE.................................631 586-5200
Fax: 631 586-5840
Eric S Rosenfeld, *Ch of Bd*
Douglas McCrosson, *President*
Vincent Palazzolo, *CFO*
EMP: 259 **EST:** 1980
SQ FT: 171,000
SALES (est): 81.3MM **Privately Held**
WEB: www.cpiaero.com
SIC: 3728 Aircraft parts & equipment

(G-4611)
EMDA INC
250 Executive Dr Ste J (11717-8354)
P.O. Box 378, Plainview (11803-0378)
PHONE.................................631 243-6363
Alan Steinbok, *President*
EMP: 10
SALES: 1MM **Privately Held**
WEB: www.emdainc.com
SIC: 3861 Photographic equipment & supplies

(G-4612)
FLEXIM AMERICAS CORPORATION (HQ)
250 Executive Dr Ste V (11717-8354)
PHONE.................................631 492-2300
Jens Hilpert, *President*
John Obrien, *Vice Pres*
Sherry Stanley, *Manager*
EMP: 12
SQ FT: 7,250
SALES (est): 2.4MM
SALES (corp-wide): 23.6MM **Privately Held**
SIC: 3824 Impeller & counter driven flow meters
PA: Flexim Flexible IndustriemeBtechnik Gmbh
  Wolfener Str. 36
  Berlin 12681
  309 366-7660

(G-4613)
GLOBAL MARKET DEVELOPMENT INC
Also Called: Accusonic Voice Systems
200 Executive Dr Ste G (11717-8322)
PHONE.................................631 667-1002
Fax: 631 667-1001
Anthony Mazzeo, *President*
Phillip Glickman, *Vice Pres*
Chris Scocco, *VP Opers*
Daniel Pizarro, *QC Mgr*
Laura Reizner, *Finance*
▲ **EMP:** 30
SQ FT: 4,200
SALES (est): 5.5MM **Privately Held**
WEB: www.accusonicproducts.com
SIC: 3651 Loudspeakers, electrodynamic or magnetic

(G-4614)
IBA INDUSTRIAL INC
Also Called: Rdi
151 Heartland Blvd (11717-8315)
PHONE.................................631 254-6800
Richard A Galloway, *Ch of Bd*
Frederic Genin, *President*
Rick Galloway, *Vice Pres*
Chris McKittrick, *Mfg Staff*
Linda Frey, *Purch Mgr*
▲ **EMP:** 41 **EST:** 1958
SQ FT: 42,000
SALES (est): 13.2MM
SALES (corp-wide): 231.1MM **Privately Held**
WEB: www.e-beam-rdi.com
SIC: 3699 5065 Electron linear accelerators; electronic parts & equipment
PA: Ion Beam Application Sa
  Chemin Du Cyclotron 3
  Ottignies-Louvain-La-Neuve 1348
  104 758-11

(G-4615)
INTERNATIONAL LEISURE PDTS INC
191 Rodeo Dr (11717-8319)
PHONE.................................631 254-2155
Larry Schwimmer, *President*
▲ **EMP:** 20
SALES (est): 1.7MM
SALES (corp-wide): 18.6MM **Privately Held**
SIC: 3949 Billiard & pool equipment & supplies, general
PA: Swimline Corp.
  191 Rodeo Dr
  Edgewood NY 11717
  631 254-2155

(G-4616)
KELTA INC (PA)
141 Rodeo Dr (11717-8378)
PHONE.................................631 789-5000
Parag Mehta, *President*
Jyotindra Mehta, *Admin Sec*
▲ **EMP:** 22
SQ FT: 25,000
SALES (est): 103.5MM **Privately Held**
SIC: 3089 3643 3661 Plastic hardware & building products; current-carrying wiring devices; telephone & telegraph apparatus

(G-4617)
KINPLEX CORP (PA)
200 Heartland Blvd (11717-8380)
PHONE.................................631 242-4800
Penny Hunter, *President*
Penny S Hunter, *President*
Daniel Schwartz, *Vice Pres*
Regina Dombal, *Credit Mgr*
▲ **EMP:** 50
SQ FT: 70,000
SALES (est): 87.6MM **Privately Held**
SIC: 3589 Commercial cooking & foodwarming equipment

(G-4618)
KINPLEX CORP
Also Called: Tables Manufacturing
200 Heartland Blvd (11717-8380)
PHONE.................................631 242-4800
Maragret Ramsey, *Manager*
EMP: 50
SALES (corp-wide): 87.6MM **Privately Held**
SIC: 3589 2599 3556 Commercial cooking & foodwarming equipment; food wagons, restaurant; food products machinery
PA: Kinplex Corp.
  200 Heartland Blvd
  Edgewood NY 11717
  631 242-4800

(G-4619)
MERIT ELECTRONIC DESIGN CO INC
Also Called: Medco
190 Rodeo Dr (11717-8317)
PHONE.................................631 667-9699
Fax: 631 667-9853
Guy Intoci, *President*
Tony Petroccione, *Purchasing*
Cheryl Sickles, *CFO*
▲ **EMP:** 115
SQ FT: 20,000
SALES (est): 43.7MM **Privately Held**
WEB: www.medcomfg.com
SIC: 3679 Electronic circuits

(G-4620)
POLY-FLEX CORP (PA)
250 Executive Dr Ste S (11717-8354)
PHONE.................................631 586-9500
Barry Neustein, *President*
Roland Razon, *General Mgr*
Talbert Paola, *Principal*
▲ **EMP:** 10 **EST:** 1977
SQ FT: 8,000
SALES (est): 1.9MM **Privately Held**
WEB: www.poly-flexcorp.com
SIC: 2759 Envelopes: printing

(G-4621)
POLYGEN PHARMACEUTICALS INC
41 Mercedes Way Unit 17 (11717-8334)
PHONE.................................631 392-4044

Edgewood - Suffolk County (G-4622)

Zhoumin LI, *President*
Albert Assa, *Controller*
Andrew Fischman, *Marketing Staff*
Bipin Sharma, *Director*
EMP: 42
SQ FT: 32,000
SALES: 4.5MM **Privately Held**
SIC: 2834 5122 Pharmaceutical preparations; pharmaceuticals

(G-4622)
RSQUARED NY INC
100 Heartland Blvd (11717-8313)
P.O. Box 807, Deer Park (11729-0971)
PHONE..................631 521-8700
Fax: 631 274-0005
Altaf Hirji, *President*
Lisa Candurard, *Manager*
Shane Hirji, *Director*
▲ **EMP:** 98
SQ FT: 30,000
SALES (est): 15.2MM **Privately Held**
WEB: www.redvisuals.com
SIC: 3993 Signs & advertising specialties; advertising artwork

(G-4623)
S G NEW YORK LLC
Also Called: Penny Saver News
1 Rodeo Dr (11717-8318)
PHONE..................631 698-8400
Bob Sussy, *Manager*
EMP: 17
SALES (corp-wide): 5.9MM **Privately Held**
SIC: 2711 Newspapers, publishing & printing
PA: S G New York Llc
2950 Vtrans Mem Hwy Ste 1
Bohemia NY 11716
631 665-4000

(G-4624)
SATCO PRODUCTS INC (PA)
Also Called: Satco Lighting
110 Heartland Blvd (11717-8303)
PHONE..................631 243-2022
Fax: 631 243-2027
Herbert Gildin, *CEO*
William Gildin, *Ch of Bd*
Luis Melendez, *General Mgr*
Allen Nathan, *General Mgr*
Alan Karen, *Vice Pres*
◆ **EMP:** 90
SQ FT: 80,000
SALES (est): 42.2MM **Privately Held**
WEB: www.satco.com
SIC: 3641 3645 5063 Electric lamps; residential lighting fixtures; lighting fixtures; light bulbs & related supplies

(G-4625)
SPACE-CRAFT WORLDWIDE INC
91 Rodeo Dr (11717-8318)
PHONE..................631 603-3000
Mazher Khalfan, *President*
▲ **EMP:** 40
SALES (est): 9MM **Privately Held**
SIC: 2541 Store & office display cases & fixtures

(G-4626)
SWIMLINE CORP (PA)
191 Rodeo Dr (11717-8319)
PHONE..................631 254-2155
Fax: 631 254-2363
Herman Schwimmer, *Ch of Bd*
Larry Schwimmer, *President*
Dennis Smith, *General Mgr*
David Schwartz, *Opers Mgr*
Kieran Glackin, *Sales Mgr*
◆ **EMP:** 39
SALES (est): 18.6MM **Privately Held**
SIC: 3949 3081 Swimming pools, plastic; unsupported plastics film & sheet

(G-4627)
SWIMLINE INTERNATIONAL CORP
191 Rodeo Dr (11717-8319)
PHONE..................631 254-2155
Larry Schwimmer, *President*
Cynthia Schwimmer, *Vice Pres*
Lisa Melnick, *Manager*
◆ **EMP:** 125
SALES (est): 9.7MM
SALES (corp-wide): 18.6MM **Privately Held**
SIC: 3423 Leaf skimmers or swimming pool rakes
PA: Swimline Corp.
191 Rodeo Dr
Edgewood NY 11717
631 254-2155

(G-4628)
SYLHAN LLC (PA)
210 Rodeo Dr (11717-8317)
PHONE..................631 243-6600
Fax: 631 243-2800
Steven Pasco, *COO*
Ronald Manganiello, *VP Opers*
Maria Gruner, *Admin Asst*
Edward N Epstein,
Steven Paskoff,
▲ **EMP:** 20
SQ FT: 20,000
SALES (est): 2MM **Privately Held**
WEB: www.sylhan.com
SIC: 3599 Machine shop, jobbing & repair

(G-4629)
TII TECHNOLOGIES INC (HQ)
141 Rodeo Dr (11717-8378)
PHONE..................516 364-9300
Parag Mehta, *President*
Thomas Smith, *President*
Bruce C Barksdale, *Exec VP*
Albert Rosenthaler, *Senior VP*
Gini Hall, *VP Admin*
▲ **EMP:** 29
SQ FT: 25,000
SALES (est): 10.4MM
SALES (corp-wide): 103.5MM **Privately Held**
WEB: www.tiinettech.com
SIC: 3089 3643 3661 Plastic hardware & building products; lightning protection equipment; telephone & telegraph apparatus
PA: Kelta, Inc.
141 Rodeo Dr
Edgewood NY 11717
631 789-5000

(G-4630)
TIME BASE CORPORATION (PA)
Also Called: Time Base Consoles
170 Rodeo Dr (11717-8317)
PHONE..................631 293-4068
Jerry Hahn, *President*
Jansen Hahn, *General Mgr*
Frank Lapallo, *Vice Pres*
Rene Maradiaga, *Foreman/Supr*
Daniel Giebel, *Senior Engr*
EMP: 47
SQ FT: 20,000
SALES (est): 33.8MM **Privately Held**
SIC: 2517 5712 Wood television & radio cabinets; cabinet work, custom

(G-4631)
TOGA MANUFACTURING INC (HQ)
200 Heartland Blvd (11717-8379)
PHONE..................631 242-4800
Alice Schwartz, *President*
Penny Schwartz Hutner, *Vice Pres*
Daniel Schwartz, *Vice Pres*
▲ **EMP:** 4
SQ FT: 40,000
SALES (est): 12.4MM
SALES (corp-wide): 87.6MM **Privately Held**
SIC: 3589 Commercial cooking & food-warming equipment
PA: Kinplex Corp.
200 Heartland Blvd
Edgewood NY 11717
631 242-4800

(G-4632)
US ALLIANCE PAPER INC
101 Heartland Blvd (11717-8315)
PHONE..................631 254-3030
Fax: 631 254-8697
John Sarraf, *President*
Steve Sarrafzadeh, *Vice Pres*
Bogdan Sujka, *Site Mgr*
Steve Saraf, *VP Sales*
Franklin Dejesus, *Accounts Mgr*
▲ **EMP:** 220
SQ FT: 250,000
SALES (est): 68.6MM **Privately Held**
WEB: www.usalliancepaper.com
SIC: 2676 Towels, napkins & tissue paper products

(G-4633)
WAYNE INTEGRATED TECH CORP
160 Rodeo Dr (11717-8317)
PHONE..................631 242-0213
Helen Moks, *CEO*
Joseph V Moks Jr, *Vice Pres*
Joseph Moks, *VP Opers*
Jim Donovan, *Opers Staff*
Karen Moks, *Office Mgr*
EMP: 38
SQ FT: 15,000
SALES (est): 8.1MM **Privately Held**
WEB: www.gowayne.com
SIC: 3443 3444 3599 Containers, shipping (bombs, etc.): metal plate; metal housings, enclosures, casings & other containers; machine shop, jobbing & repair

(G-4634)
WEICO WIRE & CABLE INC
Also Called: Magnet Wire Division
161 Rodeo Dr (11717-8359)
PHONE..................631 254-2970
Fax: 631 254-2099
Theodore Weill, *President*
Ellen Moore, *Controller*
Susan Smith, *Administration*
▲ **EMP:** 28
SQ FT: 35,000
SALES: 12.5K **Privately Held**
SIC: 3496 Cable, uninsulated wire: made from purchased wire

Edmeston
Otsego County

(G-4635)
BISHOP PRINT SHOP INC
Also Called: Ecclesiastical Press
9 East St (13335-2428)
PHONE..................607 965-8155
Fax: 607 965-2007
Michael Lampron, *President*
Walter Flores, *Manager*
EMP: 9 **EST:** 1949
SALES (est): 1.3MM **Privately Held**
WEB: www.bishopprintshop.com
SIC: 2752 2893 Commercial printing, offset; letterpress or offset ink

Elbridge
Onondaga County

(G-4636)
ACCURATE MCHNING INCORPORATION
Also Called: Acrolite
251 State Route 5 (13060-9640)
P.O. Box 1010 (13060-1010)
PHONE..................315 689-1428
Fax: 315 689-1582
Ronald E Drake Sr, *President*
Karen Coleman, *Manager*
Matthew Dake, *Manager*
Matthew R Drake, *Admin Sec*
EMP: 19
SQ FT: 13,600
SALES (est): 4.8MM **Privately Held**
WEB: www.acrolite.com
SIC: 3559 Fiber optics strand coating machinery

(G-4637)
ALLRED & ASSOCIATES INC
321 Rte 5 W (13060)
PHONE..................315 252-2559
Jimmie B Allred III, *President*
Cherie R Allred, *Exec VP*
Joseph Kummer, *Sales Mgr*
Cherie R Alled, *Marketing Staff*
Andy Morabito, *Info Tech Dir*
EMP: 40
SALES (est): 7.7MM **Privately Held**
WEB: www.evi-inc.com
SIC: 3083 Laminated plastics plate & sheet; laminated plastic sheets; plastic finished products, laminated; retroflective sheeting, plastic

(G-4638)
DUCK FLATS PHARMA
245 E Main St (13060-8706)
P.O. Box 101 (13060-0101)
PHONE..................315 689-3407
Luana Pescokoplowitz, *Owner*
Karen Ralston, *Manager*
EMP: 9
SALES (est): 570K **Privately Held**
SIC: 2678 Tablets & pads, book & writing: from purchased materials

(G-4639)
TESSY PLASTICS CORP
488 State Route 5 (13060-9501)
PHONE..................315 689-3924
Roland Beck, *President*
EMP: 750
SALES (corp-wide): 274.2MM **Privately Held**
SIC: 3089 Injection molding of plastics
PA: Tessy Plastics Corp.
700 Visions Dr
Skaneateles NY 13152
315 689-3924

Elizabethtown
Essex County

(G-4640)
DENTON PUBLICATIONS INC (PA)
Also Called: Free Trader
14 Hand Ave (12932)
P.O. Box 338 (12932-0338)
PHONE..................518 873-6368
Fax: 518 873-6360
Daniel Alexander, *President*
Gayle Alexander, *Vice Pres*
Leslie Teriele, *Sales Staff*
Jeff Davey, *Manager*
Cheryl Mitchell, *Manager*
EMP: 80 **EST:** 1948
SQ FT: 11,000
SALES (est): 6MM **Privately Held**
WEB: www.denpubs.com
SIC: 2711 2752 Commercial printing & newspaper publishing combined; commercial printing, lithographic

(G-4641)
E C C CORP
7 Church St (12932)
P.O. Box 567 (12932-0567)
PHONE..................518 873-6494
Fax: 518 873-2355
Peter Belzer, *President*
▲ **EMP:** 6
SQ FT: 5,304
SALES: 1MM **Privately Held**
SIC: 3944 Banks, toy

(G-4642)
HALFWAY HOUSE LLC
7158 Us Route 9 (12932-1712)
PHONE..................518 873-2198
Tina Croff, *Partner*
Gifford Croff, *Partner*
EMP: 7
SALES (est): 680.1K **Privately Held**
SIC: 2599 Bar, restaurant & cafeteria furniture

Elka Park
Greene County

(G-4643)
CHURCH COMMUNITIES NY INC
Also Called: Community Playthings
2255 Platte Clove Rd (12427-1014)
PHONE..................518 589-5103
Martin Mathis, *Branch Mgr*
Peter Alexander, *Manager*

EMP: 40
SALES (corp-wide): 10.7MM Privately Held
WEB: www.churchcommunitiesfoundation.org
SIC: 3944 3842 Games, toys & children's vehicles; orthopedic appliances
PA: Church Communities Ny Inc.
   2032 Route 213 St
   Rifton NY 12471
   845 658-7700

(G-4644)
CHURCH COMMUNITIES NY INC
Also Called: Community Playthings
Platte Clove Rd (12427)
PHONE.............................518 589-5103
Martin Mathis, Branch Mgr
EMP: 40
SALES (corp-wide): 10.7MM Privately Held
WEB: www.churchcommunitiesfoundation.org
SIC: 3944 3842 Games, toys & children's vehicles; orthopedic appliances
PA: Church Communities Ny Inc.
   2032 Route 213 St
   Rifton NY 12471
   845 658-7700

(G-4645)
COMMUNITY PRODUCTS LLC
2255 Platte Clove Rd (12427-1014)
PHONE.............................518 589-5103
EMP: 24
SALES (corp-wide): 88.5MM Privately Held
WEB: www.communityplaythings.com
SIC: 3842 3942 Surgical appliances & supplies; dolls & stuffed toys
PA: Community Products, Llc
   2032 Route 213 St
   Rifton NY 12471
   845 658-8799

Ellenville
Ulster County

(G-4646)
BROSS QUALITY PAVING
4 Kossar Pl (12428-2414)
PHONE.............................845 532-7116
Julio Moya, Partner
EMP: 6
SALES (est): 479.2K Privately Held
SIC: 2951 Asphalt paving mixtures & blocks

(G-4647)
DEVIL DOG MANUFACTURING CO INC (PA)
23 Market St (12428-2107)
P.O. Box 588 (12428-0588)
PHONE.............................845 647-4411
Carl J Rosenstock, President
Richard Rosenstock, Vice Pres
Herbert Rosenstock, Treasurer
Karen Rosselli, Manager
Tony Shananahan, Manager
▲ EMP: 6 EST: 1952
SQ FT: 30,000
SALES (est): 22.2MM Privately Held
WEB: www.sportwear.com
SIC: 2369 Girls' & children's outerwear; jeans: girls', children's & infants'

(G-4648)
JM ORIGINALS INC
Also Called: Sbi Enterprises
70 Berme Rd (12428-5605)
P.O. Box 563 (12428-0563)
PHONE.............................845 647-3003
Fax: 845 647-1059
Martha Arginsky, President
Myrna Jargowsky, Vice Pres
Robert Rue, Purchasing
Miriam Lyons, Manager
Jenifer Weed, MIS Dir
◆ EMP: 140 EST: 1976
SQ FT: 35,000
SALES (est): 13.4MM Privately Held
WEB: www.jmoriginals.com
SIC: 2361 5137 5641 2369 Girls' & children's dresses, blouses & shirts; women's & children's clothing; children's wear; girls' & children's outerwear

(G-4649)
MASTER JUVENILE PRODUCTS INC
Also Called: Sbi Enterprises
70 Berme Rd (12428-5605)
P.O. Box 563 (12428-0563)
PHONE.............................845 647-8400
Irwin Arginsky, President
EMP: 10
SQ FT: 40,000
SALES (est): 966.6K Privately Held
WEB: www.pogosticks.com
SIC: 3944 Games, toys & children's vehicles

(G-4650)
OPTIMUM WINDOW MFG CORP
28 Canal St (12428-1226)
PHONE.............................845 647-1900
Fax: 845 647-1494
Candido Perez, Ch of Bd
Maria E Perez, Corp Secy
◆ EMP: 37
SALES (est): 10MM Privately Held
WEB: www.optimumwindow.com
SIC: 3442 Screen & storm doors & windows

(G-4651)
REED SYSTEMS LTD
17 Edwards Pl (12428-1601)
P.O. Box 209 (12428-0209)
PHONE.............................845 647-3660
Fax: 845 647-5651
James Reed, President
Joan E Reed, Vice Pres
EMP: 15
SQ FT: 1,600
SALES: 4.9MM Privately Held
WEB: www.reedsystemsltd.com
SIC: 3399 Powder, metal

(G-4652)
ROCK MOUNTAIN FARMS INC
11 Spring St (12428-1329)
PHONE.............................845 647-9084
Karen Osterhoudt, President
Howard Osterhoudt, Vice Pres
EMP: 5
SALES (est): 540K Privately Held
SIC: 1442 6519 Gravel mining; landholding office

(G-4653)
TOP SHELF JEWELRY INC
Also Called: Touch By A Memory
206 Canal St (12428-1600)
PHONE.............................845 647-4661
Fax: 845 647-3314
Barbara Hoff, President
Michael Atcheson, Manager
EMP: 14
SQ FT: 6,000
SALES: 550K Privately Held
SIC: 3961 Costume jewelry, ex. precious metal & semiprecious stones

Ellicottville
Cattaraugus County

(G-4654)
AMERICAN LCKR SEC SYSTEMS INC
12 Martha St (14731-9714)
PHONE.............................716 699-2773
Fax: 716 699-2775
EMP: 25
SQ FT: 4,800
SALES (corp-wide): 30.1MM Privately Held
SIC: 3581 Mfg Vending Machines
PA: American Locker Security Systems, Inc.
   700 Freeport Pkwy Ste 300
   Coppell TX 75019
   817 329-1600

(G-4655)
FITZPATRICK AND WELLER INC
12 Mill St (14731-9614)
P.O. Box 490 (14731-0490)
PHONE.............................716 699-2393
Gregory J Fitzpatrick, Ch of Bd
Dana G Fitzpatrick, Chairman
Daniel Fitzpatrick, Vice Pres
Dave Hellwig, Prdtn Mgr
Connie Hellwig, Sales Staff
▼ EMP: 85 EST: 1892
SQ FT: 220,000
SALES (est): 16.2MM Privately Held
WEB: www.fitzweller.com
SIC: 2426 Hardwood dimension & flooring mills; furniture dimension stock, hardwood

(G-4656)
MERITOOL LLC
5 Park Ave Ste 1 (14731-9705)
P.O. Box 148, Salamanca (14779-0148)
PHONE.............................716 699-6005
Fax: 716 699-6337
Kevin Whited, Opers Mgr
Timm Herman,
Sonya Keenen, Admin Asst
Donna R Finnegan, Administration
John Bares,
▲ EMP: 15 EST: 1939
SQ FT: 20,000
SALES (est): 3.2MM Privately Held
WEB: www.meritool.com
SIC: 3546 Power-driven handtools

(G-4657)
NORTH PK INNOVATIONS GROUP INC (PA)
6442 Route 242 E (14731-9742)
P.O. Box 900 (14731-0900)
PHONE.............................716 699-2031
William Northrup, CEO
Lori Northrup, Chairman
Geoff Kroeger, Controller
▲ EMP: 5
SQ FT: 13,000
SALES (est): 16.2MM Privately Held
SIC: 3433 Heating equipment, except electric

Ellington
Chautauqua County

(G-4658)
ELLIOT INDUSTRIES INC
Leach Rd (14732)
PHONE.............................716 287-3100
Fax: 716 287-2005
Thomas A Elliot, President
Ann Elliot, Treasurer
EMP: 8
SQ FT: 5,000
SALES: 500K Privately Held
SIC: 3296 Fiberglass insulation

Elma
Erie County

(G-4659)
CLUB PROTECTOR INC
191 Buffalo Creek Rd (14059-9021)
PHONE.............................716 652-4787
William T Held, President
Carol Held, Vice Pres
▲ EMP: 2
SQ FT: 3,500
SALES (est): 1MM Privately Held
WEB: www.clubprotectorinc.com
SIC: 3799 Golf carts, powered

(G-4660)
COMGRAPH SALES SERVICE
7491 Clinton St (14059-8807)
PHONE.............................716 601-7243
Brian Schiemant, Owner
EMP: 5
SALES (est): 448.5K Privately Held
SIC: 2759 Commercial printing

(G-4661)
FREDERICK COON INC
Also Called: Elma Press
5751 Clinton St (14059-9424)
PHONE.............................716 683-6812
Fax: 716 683-5037
Frederick H Coon Jr, President
Douglas Coon, Vice Pres
Joel Coon, Vice Pres
Betty Coon, Treasurer
EMP: 23
SQ FT: 2,708
SALES: 900K Privately Held
SIC: 2752 2759 Commercial printing, offset; letterpress printing

(G-4662)
GENERAL WELDING & FABG INC (PA)
991 Maple Rd (14059-9530)
PHONE.............................716 652-0033
Fax: 585 652-0746
Mark S Andol, President
Edwin Pierrot, Manager
Richard Andol, Info Tech Mgr
EMP: 3
SQ FT: 14,000
SALES (est): 5.9MM Privately Held
SIC: 7692 3715 5531 Welding repair; truck trailers; truck equipment & parts

(G-4663)
KENS SERVICE & SALES INC
11500 Clinton St (14059-8830)
PHONE.............................716 683-1155
Kenneth Kelchlin Jr, President
Matt Kelchlin, Vice Pres
EMP: 14 EST: 1955
SQ FT: 25,000
SALES (est): 2.6MM Privately Held
SIC: 3799 All terrain vehicles (ATV)

(G-4664)
MOOG INC (PA)
400 Jamison Rd Plant26 (14059-9497)
P.O. Box 18, East Aurora (14052-0018)
PHONE.............................716 652-2000
Fax: 716 687-4457
John R Scannell, Ch of Bd
Richard A Aubrecht, Vice Ch Bd
Maureen M Athoe, Vice Pres
Lawrence J Ball, Vice Pres
R Eric Burghardt, Vice Pres
◆ EMP: 2100 EST: 1951
SQ FT: 22,000
SALES: 2.4B Publicly Held
WEB: www.moog.com
SIC: 3812 3492 3625 3769 Aircraft control systems, electronic; fluid power valves for aircraft; relays & industrial controls; actuators, industrial; guided missile & space vehicle parts & auxiliary equipment; aircraft parts & equipment; surgical & medical instruments

(G-4665)
MOOG INC
160 Jamison Rd (14059)
PHONE.............................716 687-4778
Dave Golda, Manager
EMP: 25
SALES (corp-wide): 2.4B Publicly Held
SIC: 3812 Aircraft control systems, electronic
PA: Moog Inc.
   400 Jamison Rd Plant26
   Elma NY 14059
   716 652-2000

(G-4666)
R W PUBLICATIONS DIV OF WTRHS (PA)
Also Called: Akron-Corfu Pennysaver
6091 Seneca St Bldg C (14059-9807)
PHONE.............................716 714-5620
Fax: 716 662-0740
Robert Rozeski Sr, President
Thomas Rybczynski, Vice Pres
Cheryl Kowalski, Treasurer
EMP: 30 EST: 1961
SQ FT: 5,800
SALES (est): 12.9MM Privately Held
WEB: www.rwpennysaver.com
SIC: 2711 2741 Newspapers, publishing & printing; miscellaneous publishing

Elma - Erie County (G-4667)

(G-4667)
R W PUBLICATIONS DIV OF WTRHS
Also Called: Pennysavers Rw Publications
6091 Seneca St Bldg C (14059-9807)
PHONE.................................716 714-5620
Fax: 716 675-3044
Meg Bourdette, *General Mgr*
Tom Rybczynski, *Sales Mgr*
EMP: 20
SALES (corp-wide): 12.9MM **Privately Held**
WEB: www.rwpennysaver.com
SIC: 2711 Newspapers, publishing & printing
PA: R W Publications Div Of Waterhouse Publication Inc
6091 Seneca St Bldg C
Elma NY 14059
716 714-5620

(G-4668)
SERVOTRONICS INC (PA)
1110 Maple Rd (14059-9573)
PHONE.................................716 655-5990
Fax: 585 655-6012
Nicholas D Trbovich, *Ch of Bd*
Kenneth D Trbovich, *President*
Salvatore San Filippo, *Senior VP*
James Takacs, *Senior VP*
James C Takacs, *Vice Pres*
EMP: 142 EST: 1959
SQ FT: 83,000
SALES: 38.5MM **Publicly Held**
WEB: www.servotronics.com
SIC: 3492 3728 3769 3421 Fluid power valves & hose fittings; electrohydraulic servo valves, metal; control valves, aircraft: hydraulic & pneumatic; aircraft parts & equipment; guided missile & space vehicle parts & auxiliary equipment; cutlery

(G-4669)
STEUBEN FOODS INCORPORATED
1150 Maple Rd (14059-9597)
PHONE.................................716 655-4000
Tom Taggart, *VP Engrg*
Al Tokar, *QC Mgr*
Norman Bower, *Branch Mgr*
EMP: 200
SALES (corp-wide): 123.1MM **Privately Held**
SIC: 2026 Milk processing (pasteurizing, homogenizing, bottling)
PA: Steuben Foods, Incorporated
15504 Liberty Ave
Jamaica NY 11433
718 291-3333

(G-4670)
STONY MANUFACTURING INC
591 Pound Rd (14059-9602)
PHONE.................................716 652-6730
Fax: 585 652-9601
James A Wyzykiewicz, *President*
Michael C Wyzykiewicz, *Vice Pres*
Ronald P Wyzykiewicz, *Vice Pres*
EMP: 9
SQ FT: 12,500
SALES (est): 1.5MM **Privately Held**
SIC: 3599 Machine shop, jobbing & repair

Elmhurst
Queens County

(G-4671)
BUFFALO PROVISIONS CO INC
4009 76th St (11373-1033)
PHONE.................................718 292-4300
Rene Armendariz, *President*
Staci Armendariz, *Vice Pres*
Andres Mendez, *Manager*
EMP: 15
SQ FT: 10,000
SALES (est): 1.6MM **Privately Held**
SIC: 2013 Sausages from purchased meat

(G-4672)
COACH INC
90 Queens Blvd (11373)
PHONE.................................718 760-0624
EMP: 14
SALES (corp-wide): 4.1B **Publicly Held**
SIC: 3171 Mfg Women's Handbags/Purses
PA: Coach, Inc.
516 W 34th St Bsmt 5
New York NY 10001
212 594-1850

(G-4673)
FEDERAL SAMPLE CARD CORP
4520 83rd St (11373-3599)
PHONE.................................718 458-1344
Michael Cronin, *President*
EMP: 100
SQ FT: 40,000
SALES (est): 7.4MM **Privately Held**
SIC: 2782 3999 Sample books; advertising display products

(G-4674)
GO GO APPLE INC
4126 Benham St (11373-1750)
PHONE.................................646 264-8909
Xiu Qin Lin, *Administration*
EMP: 5
SALES (est): 176.7K **Privately Held**
SIC: 3571 Personal computers (microcomputers)

(G-4675)
GODIVA CHOCOLATIER INC
9015 Queens Blvd Ste 2045 (11373-4923)
PHONE.................................718 271-3603
Nicole Keaton, *Manager*
EMP: 24 **Privately Held**
SIC: 2066 Chocolate candy, solid
HQ: Godiva Chocolatier, Inc.
333 W 34th St Fl 6
New York NY 10001
212 984-5900

(G-4676)
GOLDEN BRIDGE GROUP INC
7416 Grand Ave (11373-4127)
PHONE.................................718 335-8882
Roger Yang, *President*
▲ EMP: 6
SALES (est): 143.4K **Privately Held**
SIC: 3161 Luggage

(G-4677)
LA CALENITA BAKERY & CAFETERIA
4008 83rd St (11373-1307)
PHONE.................................718 205-8273
Dilia Lindo, *Owner*
EMP: 8
SALES (est): 377.1K **Privately Held**
SIC: 2051 Bread, cake & related products

(G-4678)
MAJESTIC CURTAINS LLC
4410 Ketcham St Apt 2g (11373-3686)
PHONE.................................718 898-0774
Fax: 718 505-4011
Robert Connor,
Barbara Tisdale,
EMP: 7
SALES: 660K **Privately Held**
SIC: 2391 1799 Curtains & draperies; window treatment installation

(G-4679)
PENNER ELBOW COMPANY INC
4700 76th St (11373-2946)
PHONE.................................718 526-9000
Fax: 718 235-6112
Sheldon Flatow, *President*
EMP: 12
SQ FT: 10,000
SALES (est): 1.4MM **Privately Held**
SIC: 3444 3321 Elbows, for air ducts, stovepipes, etc.: sheet metal; pressure pipe & fittings, cast iron

(G-4680)
ROCKPORT COMPANY LLC
9015 Queens Blvd Ste 1025 (11373-4923)
PHONE.................................718 271-3627
Miguel Mendez, *District Mgr*
EMP: 8
SALES (corp-wide): 327.7MM **Privately Held**
SIC: 3143 Men's footwear, except athletic
HQ: The Rockport Company Llc
1220 Washington St
Newton MA 02465
617 213-6100

(G-4681)
ROKON TECH LLC
5223 74th St (11373-4108)
PHONE.................................718 429-0729
Manfred Konrad, *Mng Member*
EMP: 5
SALES (est): 657.2K **Privately Held**
SIC: 3534 Elevators & moving stairways

Elmira
Chemung County

(G-4682)
AFI CYBERNETICS CORPORATION
713 Batavia St (14904-2011)
PHONE.................................607 732-3244
Fax: 607 732-1542
Kenneth Doyle, *President*
Tim Blampied, *Opers Mgr*
Tracy Haines, *Purch Agent*
Mike Walls, *Supervisor*
Jerry Windows, *Info Tech Mgr*
EMP: 28
SQ FT: 25,000
SALES (est): 6.8MM **Privately Held**
WEB: www.aficybernetics.com
SIC: 3625 Relays & industrial controls

(G-4683)
AIR FLOW MANUFACTURING
365 Upper Oakwood Ave (14903-1127)
PHONE.................................607 733-8284
Tom Musso, *Manager*
EMP: 10
SALES (est): 2.4MM **Privately Held**
SIC: 3999 3711 Manufacturing industries; truck & tractor truck assembly

(G-4684)
AIR-FLO MFG CO INC
365 Upper Oakwood Ave (14903-1127)
PHONE.................................607 733-8284
Fax: 607 522-4412
Charles Musso Jr, *President*
Tom Musso, *Vice Pres*
Stacey Eustace, *Opers Mgr*
Kevin Foster, *Opers Mgr*
Velma Andrews, *Accountant*
EMP: 75 EST: 1950
SQ FT: 60,000
SALES (est): 33MM **Privately Held**
WEB: www.air-flo.com
SIC: 3531 Construction machinery

(G-4685)
CAMERON BRIDGE WORKS LLC
1051 S Main St (14904-2713)
PHONE.................................607 734-9456
Christopher Goll, *President*
Jim Ellis, *Business Mgr*
Tommy Radford, *Project Mgr*
Katie Fairbanks, *Info Tech Mgr*
EMP: 20
SQ FT: 85,000
SALES (est): 3.9MM
SALES (corp-wide): 33MM **Privately Held**
SIC: 3441 Fabricated structural metal for bridges
PA: Cameron Manufacturing & Design, Inc.
727 Blostein Blvd
Horseheads NY 14845
607 739-3606

(G-4686)
CARBAUGH TOOL COMPANY INC
126 Philo Rd W (14903-9755)
PHONE.................................607 739-3293
Fax: 607 739-3274
Harold Dota, *President*
Terry Catlin, *Manager*
EMP: 30 EST: 1966
SQ FT: 10,600
SALES (est): 4.6MM **Privately Held**
SIC: 3599 3544 Machine & other job shop work; special dies & tools

(G-4687)
CARBIDE-USA LLC
100 Home St (14904-1859)
P.O. Box 4005 (14904-0005)
PHONE.................................607 331-9353
EMP: 8
SALES (est): 1.1MM **Privately Held**
SIC: 2819 Carbides

(G-4688)
CHEMUNG CNTY CHPTER NYSARC INC (HQ)
Also Called: ARC of Chemung, The
711 Sullivan St (14901-2322)
PHONE.................................607 734-6151
Fax: 607 734-2943
Nikki May, *President*
Peter Honsberger, *Division Mgr*
Jim Scott, *Sr Corp Ofcr*
Joanne Conley, *Human Res Dir*
Joanne Conley-Pease, *Human Res Dir*
EMP: 150
SQ FT: 33,000
SALES: 17.3MM
SALES (corp-wide): 1.3B **Privately Held**
WEB: www.chemungarc.org
SIC: 3861 8331 8361 3577 Photographic equipment & supplies; job training & vocational rehabilitation services; home for the mentally retarded; computer peripheral equipment; wood pallets & skids
PA: Nysarc, Inc.
29 British American Blvd # 2
Latham NY 12110
518 439-8311

(G-4689)
COMMUNITY GLASS INC
139 W 17th St (14903-1215)
PHONE.................................607 737-8860
Fax: 607 737-8890
Patrick M Crouse, *President*
EMP: 6
SALES (est): 632.3K **Privately Held**
SIC: 3231 Scientific & technical glassware: from purchased glass

(G-4690)
COURSER INC
802 County Road 64 # 100 (14903-7984)
PHONE.................................607 739-3861
Daniel Herman, *Ch of Bd*
Christophe Seeley, *Engineer*
Steve Seeley, *Finance*
Bob Cleveland, *Manager*
EMP: 25
SQ FT: 50,000
SALES (est): 5MM **Privately Held**
WEB: www.courser.com
SIC: 3599 Machine & other job shop work

(G-4691)
CREATIVE ORTHOTICS & PROSTHET (DH)
1300 College Ave Ste 1 (14901-1154)
PHONE.................................607 734-7215
Fax: 607 733-5281
Vinit Asar, *Ch of Bd*
John Renz, *President*
EMP: 15
SALES (est): 42.1MM
SALES (corp-wide): 451.4MM **Publicly Held**
WEB: www.creativeoandp.com
SIC: 3842 5999 5047 Limbs, artificial; artificial limbs; hospital equipment & furniture
HQ: Hanger Prosthetics & Orthotics, Inc.
10910 Domain Dr Ste 300
Austin TX 78758
512 777-3800

(G-4692)
EASTERN METAL OF ELMIRA INC (PA)
1430 Sullivan St (14901-1698)
PHONE.................................607 734-2295
Kevin Harrison, *Ch of Bd*
John Pendleton, *Vice Pres*
Kevin Burdick, *Purch Mgr*
Tom Aber, *VP Sales*

GEOGRAPHIC SECTION
Elmira - Chemung County (G-4716)

Ron Gray, *Sales Associate*
▼ **EMP:** 80 **EST:** 1947
SALES (est): 20MM **Privately Held**
WEB: www.usa-sign.com
SIC: 3993 7336 Signs & advertising specialties; graphic arts & related design

(G-4693)
EASTSIDE OXIDE CO
211 Judson St (14901-3308)
PHONE 607 734-1253
Greg Wheeler, *Principal*
John Short, *Principal*
EMP: 40
SALES (est): 1.7MM **Privately Held**
WEB: www.eastsiderailnow.org
SIC: 3471 Finishing, metals or formed products

(G-4694)
ELMIRA COUNTRY CLUB INC
1538 W Church St (14905-1993)
PHONE 607 734-6251
Fax: 607 734-6253
Tom Newkirk, *Superintendent*
Joe Steigerwald, *Manager*
EMP: 4
SALES: 2.7MM **Privately Held**
WEB: www.elmiracountryclub.com
SIC: 3949 Shafts, golf club

(G-4695)
ELMIRA HEAT TREATING INC
407 S Kinyon St (14904-2398)
PHONE 607 734-1577
Fax: 607 734-2572
Terry Youngs, *CEO*
Richard Youngs, *President*
Mark Youngs, *Sales Mgr*
Ann Borden, *Manager*
EMP: 40 **EST:** 1962
SQ FT: 20,000
SALES (est): 9.9MM **Privately Held**
WEB: www.elmiraht.com
SIC: 3398 Tempering of metal

(G-4696)
ELMIRA METAL WORKS INC
1493 Cedar St (14904-2932)
P.O. Box 4110 (14904-0110)
PHONE 607 734-9813
Jim Biggs, *President*
EMP: 6
SALES (est): 441.1K **Privately Held**
WEB: www.snowhog.com
SIC: 3441 Fabricated structural metal

(G-4697)
F M HOWELL & COMPANY (PA)
Also Called: Howell Packaging
79 Pennsylvania Ave (14904-1455)
P.O. Box 286 (14902-0286)
PHONE 607 734-6291
Fax: 607 734-8667
Katherine H Roehlke, *CEO*
James Haley, *Division Mgr*
Trevor Ball, *Vice Pres*
Susan Hendy, *Vice Pres*
Douglas M McGinnis, *Vice Pres*
▲ **EMP:** 74 **EST:** 1883
SQ FT: 168,000
SALES: 36.1MM **Privately Held**
WEB: www.howellpkg.com
SIC: 2657 2671 7389 2652 Folding paperboard boxes; thermoplastic coated paper for packaging; packaging & labeling services; setup paperboard boxes

(G-4698)
FENNELL INDUSTRIES LLC (PA)
Also Called: United Dividers
108 Stephens Pl (14901-1539)
PHONE 607 733-6693
Fax: 607 733-0340
Tom Fennell, *Owner*
Martin Fennell, *Mng Member*
Thomas Fennell,
EMP: 30
SQ FT: 13,500
SALES (est): 4.1MM **Privately Held**
SIC: 2653 Corrugated & solid fiber boxes; partitions, corrugated: made from purchased materials

(G-4699)
GEORGE CHILSON LOGGING
54 Franklin St (14904-1738)
PHONE 607 732-1558
George Chilson, *Owner*
EMP: 1
SALES: 1.6MM **Privately Held**
SIC: 2411 Logging

(G-4700)
HANGER PRSTHETCS & ORTHO INC
1300 College Ave Ste 1 (14901-1154)
PHONE 607 795-1220
Sheryl Price, *Manager*
Vickie Preston, *Manager*
EMP: 99
SALES (corp-wide): 451.4MM **Publicly Held**
SIC: 3842 Braces, orthopedic
HQ: Hanger Prosthetics & Orthotics, Inc.
10910 Domain Dr Ste 300
Austin TX 78758
512 777-3800

(G-4701)
HARDINGE INC (PA)
1 Hardinge Dr (14902)
PHONE 607 734-2281
Fax: 607 734-8819
Christopher Disantis, *Ch of Bd*
Charles P Dougherty, *President*
James P Langa, *Senior VP*
URS Baumgartner, *Vice Pres*
Richard Savin, *Vice Pres*
▲ **EMP:** 277 **EST:** 1890
SALES: 292MM **Publicly Held**
WEB: www.hardinge.com
SIC: 3541 3545 3553 3549 Machine tools, metal cutting type; lathes; grinding, polishing, buffing, lapping & honing machines; collets (machine tool accessories); lathes, wood turning: including accessories; metalworking machinery

(G-4702)
HAUN WELDING SUPPLY INC
1100 Sullivan St (14901-1640)
PHONE 607 846-2289
Fax: 607 846-2292
Mike Cesaro, *Manager*
EMP: 10
SALES (corp-wide): 63.5MM **Privately Held**
SIC: 7692 5999 5169 Welding repair; welding supplies; industrial gases
PA: Haun Welding Supply, Inc.
5921 Court Street Rd
Syracuse NY 13206
315 463-5241

(G-4703)
HILLIARD CORPORATION (PA)
100 W 4th St (14901-2190)
P.O. Box 866 (14902-0866)
PHONE 607 733-7121
Fax: 607 737-1108
Arie J Van Den Blink, *Ch of Bd*
Gene A Ebbrecht, *President*
Laura Blew, *General Mgr*
Steven J Chesebro, *Exec VP*
Lindsey Canfield, *Vice Pres*
◆ **EMP:** 277 **EST:** 1905
SQ FT: 326,000
SALES: 106.5MM **Privately Held**
SIC: 3564 3569 3823 Purification & dust collection equipment; filters; industrial instrmnts msrmnt display/control process variable

(G-4704)
HILLIARD CORPORATION
1420 College Ave (14901-1153)
PHONE 607 733-7121
Arie J Van Den Blink, *Branch Mgr*
Doug Canfield, *Manager*
James Graham, *Manager*
Doug Henry, *Manager*
Gordon Webster, *Manager*
EMP: 10
SALES (corp-wide): 106.5MM **Privately Held**
SIC: 3564 3569 3823 Purification & dust collection equipment; filters; industrial instrmnts msrmnt display/control process variable
PA: The Hilliard Corporation
100 W 4th St
Elmira NY 14901
607 733-7121

(G-4705)
I D MACHINE INC
Also Called: I Do Machining
1580 Lake St (14901-1248)
PHONE 607 796-2549
Fax: 607 796-9024
John Meier, *Ch of Bd*
EMP: 7
SALES (est): 1.1MM **Privately Held**
WEB: www.idomachining.com
SIC: 3599 Machine shop, jobbing & repair

(G-4706)
JRSMM LLC
Also Called: Jetwrx Rotable Services
1316 College Ave (14901-1169)
PHONE 607 331-1549
Robert Salluzzo, *CFO*
Tina McGrane, *Human Resources*
EMP: 6 **EST:** 2016
SQ FT: 12,000
SALES (est): 259K **Privately Held**
SIC: 3728 Aircraft parts & equipment

(G-4707)
KITCHEN SPECIALTY CRAFTSMEN
2366 Corning Rd (14903-1045)
PHONE 607 739-0833
Fax: 607 739-5902
Douglas Wells, *President*
Kenneth Wells, *Vice Pres*
Phillis Wells, *Treasurer*
EMP: 9 **EST:** 1968
SALES (est): 1.1MM **Privately Held**
SIC: 2541 Table or counter tops, plastic laminated

(G-4708)
MCWANE INC
Also Called: Kennedy Valve Division
1021 E Water St (14901-3332)
P.O. Box 931 (14902-0931)
PHONE 607 734-2211
Fax: 607 734-1003
Arne Feyling, *General Mgr*
Doug Bond, *Plant Mgr*
Thomas Shaw, *Safety Mgr*
Tim Decker, *Purch Mgr*
Chris Burris, *Buyer*
EMP: 376
SALES (corp-wide): 1.1B **Privately Held**
WEB: www.mcwane.com
SIC: 3491 3561 3321 5085 Industrial valves; pumps & pumping equipment; gray & ductile iron foundries; valves & fittings
PA: Mcwane, Inc.
2900 Highway 280 S # 300
Birmingham AL 35223
205 414-3100

(G-4709)
MEGA TOOL & MFG CORP
1023 Caton Ave (14904-2620)
PHONE 607 734-8398
Fax: 607 734-8549
Craig Spencer, *President*
Nancy Ellison, *Controller*
Larry Lovell, *Executive*
Mary Lou Spencer, *Admin Sec*
EMP: 25
SQ FT: 18,000
SALES (est): 3.8MM **Privately Held**
WEB: www.megatool-mfg.com
SIC: 3599 3469 7692 3544 Machine shop, jobbing & repair; machine parts, stamped or pressed metal; welding repair; special dies, tools, jigs & fixtures

(G-4710)
NARDE PAVING COMPANY INC
400 E 14th St (14903-1817)
PHONE 607 737-7177
Fax: 607 733-7887
Ann Narde, *CEO*
Donald A Narde Sr, *President*
Daniel Narde, *Vice Pres*
Donal Narde Jr, *Admin Sec*
EMP: 30
SQ FT: 7,000
SALES (est): 4.4MM **Privately Held**
SIC: 2951 Asphalt paving mixtures & blocks

(G-4711)
PC SOLUTIONS & CONSULTING
407 S Walnut St (14904-1637)
PHONE 607 735-0466
Roy Brotherhood, *President*
Katherine Brotherhood, *Vice Pres*
EMP: 5
SQ FT: 1,800
SALES (est): 792K **Privately Held**
WEB: www.powerpcs.com
SIC: 3575 7371 Computer terminals, monitors & components; custom computer programming services

(G-4712)
QUICKER PRINTER INC
210 W Gray St (14901-2907)
P.O. Box 1257 (14902-1257)
PHONE 607 734-8622
Fax: 607 737-0648
Robert Lavarnway Jr, *President*
Karl Schweisinger, *Vice Pres*
Lorrie Lavarnway, *Office Mgr*
EMP: 7
SQ FT: 5,500
SALES (est): 950.1K **Privately Held**
WEB: www.quickerprinter.com
SIC: 2752 2791 Commercial printing, offset; typesetting

(G-4713)
RAINBOW LETTERING
1329 College Ave (14901-1133)
PHONE 607 732-5751
Tom Wolfe, *Owner*
EMP: 5
SALES: 150K **Privately Held**
SIC: 2396 2759 Screen printing on fabric articles; screen printing

(G-4714)
SEPAC INC
1580 Lake St (14901-1248)
PHONE 607 732-2030
Fax: 607 732-0273
John H Meier, *President*
Jeffrey Ryan, *Engineer*
Mike Vieira, *Engineer*
Martha Zoerb, *Accounting Mgr*
Luke Morse, *Manager*
▲ **EMP:** 35
SQ FT: 17,352
SALES (est): 8.5MM **Privately Held**
SIC: 3568 Power transmission equipment

(G-4715)
STAR-GAZETTE FUND INC
Also Called: Elmira Star-Gazette
310 E Church St (14901-2704)
PHONE 607 734-5151
Fax: 607 733-4408
Monte I Trammer, *President*
Rose Cooper, *Editor*
Linda Rockwell, *Manager*
Jay Keller, *Info Tech Mgr*
Jay Peak, *Director*
EMP: 150
SALES: 20MM
SALES (corp-wide): 3B **Publicly Held**
SIC: 2711 Newspapers
HQ: Gannett Satellite Information Network, Llc
7950 Jones Branch Dr
Mc Lean VA 22102
703 854-6000

(G-4716)
SURFACE FINISH TECHNOLOGY
215 Judson St (14901-3308)
PHONE 607 732-2909
Fax: 607 733-6119
John Short, *President*
Linda Short, *Corp Secy*
Jack Slocum, *Engineer*
Carrie Roadarmel, *CFO*
Laura Walters, *Human Res Mgr*
EMP: 35
SQ FT: 18,000
SALES (est): 4.3MM **Privately Held**
WEB: www.surfacefinishtech.com
SIC: 3471 Finishing, metals or formed products

Elmira - Chemung County

(G-4717)
TDS FITNESS EQUIPMENT
160 Home St (14904-1811)
P.O. Box 4189 (14904-0189)
PHONE.....................607 733-6789
Thugginni D Seethapathy, *President*
▲ EMP: 45
SQ FT: 100,000
SALES (est): 4.6MM Privately Held
WEB: www.tdsfitnessequipment.com
SIC: 3949 3842 Dumbbells & other weightlifting equipment; exercise equipment; surgical appliances & supplies

(G-4718)
WINCHESTER OPTICAL COMPANY (DH)
1935 Lake St (14901-1239)
P.O. Box 1515 (14902-1515)
PHONE.....................607 734-4251
Fax: 607 732-0901
Ben E Lynch, *President*
Karla Lynch, *General Mgr*
Michael P Lynch, *Vice Pres*
Deborah Lynch, *Treasurer*
Art Waite, *Loan Officer*
EMP: 45
SQ FT: 32,500
SALES (est): 14.2MM
SALES (corp-wide): 938.9MM Privately Held
WEB: www.winoptical.com
SIC: 3851 5048 Frames, lenses & parts, eyeglass & spectacle; ophthalmic goods
HQ: Essilor Laboratories Of America Holding Co., Inc.
13555 N Stemmons Fwy
Dallas TX 75234
214 496-4141

(G-4719)
WRIGHTCUT EDM & MACHINE INC
951 Carl St (14904-2662)
PHONE.....................607 733-5018
Fax: 607 735-0126
Byron Wright, *President*
Michelle Wright, *Vice Pres*
EMP: 9
SQ FT: 3,500
SALES (est): 1.3MM Privately Held
WEB: www.wrightcutedm.com
SIC: 3599 Machine shop, jobbing & repair

(G-4720)
X-GEN PHARMACEUTICALS INC
744 Baldwin St (14901-2226)
P.O. Box 150, Northport (11768-0150)
PHONE.....................631 261-8188
Susan Badia, *Branch Mgr*
EMP: 30
SALES (corp-wide): 4.4MM Privately Held
SIC: 2834 Pharmaceutical preparations
PA: X-Gen Pharmaceuticals, Inc.
300 Daniel Zenker Dr
Big Flats NY 14814
607 562-2700

Elmira Heights
Chemung County

(G-4721)
ANCHOR GLASS CONTAINER CORP
151 E Mccanns Blvd (14903-1955)
PHONE.....................607 737-1933
Fax: 607 737-1286
Bill Butler, *Purchasing*
Michael Sopp, *Manager*
Jim Housworth, *Manager*
EMP: 370
SALES (corp-wide): 317.9K Privately Held
WEB: www.anchorglass.com
SIC: 3221 Glass containers
HQ: Anchor Glass Container Corporation
401 E Jackson St Ste 1100
Tampa FL 33602

(G-4722)
CAF USA INC
300 E 18th St (14903-1333)
PHONE.....................607 737-3004
Teresa Machado, *General Mgr*
Hoyos V Manuel, *General Mgr*
Rebeca Mellado, *General Mgr*
Juneldy Salazar, *General Mgr*
Octavio Rosselli, *Vice Pres*
EMP: 100
SALES (corp-wide): 976.8MM Privately Held
SIC: 3743 Railroad equipment
HQ: Caf Usa, Inc.
1401 K St Nw Ste 1003
Washington DC 20005
202 898-4848

(G-4723)
GOLOS PRINTING INC
110 E 9th St (14903-1733)
PHONE.....................607 732-1896
Fax: 607 732-2356
Thomas L Golos Sr, *President*
Thomas L Corp Sr, *President*
Hank Corp, *Vice Pres*
EMP: 6 EST: 1921
SQ FT: 10,000
SALES: 300K Privately Held
SIC: 2752 2759 Commercial printing, offset; letterpress printing

(G-4724)
MOTOR COMPONENTS LLC
2243 Corning Rd (14903-1031)
PHONE.....................607 737-8011
Reeve Howland, *Facilities Mgr*
Dave Demarco, *Controller*
Anita Mawhir, *HR Admin*
Tony Bonfardeci, *Manager*
Kris Miller, *Manager*
▲ EMP: 68
SQ FT: 300,000
SALES (est): 18.8MM
SALES (corp-wide): 43.3MM Privately Held
WEB: www.motorcomponents.com
SIC: 3714 Motor vehicle wheels & parts
PA: Bam Enterprises, Inc.
2937 Alt Blvd
Grand Island NY 14072
716 773-7634

(G-4725)
SERVICE MACHINE & TOOL COMPANY
206 E Mccanns Blvd (14903-1958)
P.O. Box 2118 (14903-0118)
PHONE.....................607 732-0413
Fax: 607 734-9872
Keith Knowlden, *President*
Axieann Knowlden, *Corp Secy*
Marilyn Smith, *Manager*
Hal Fitzsimmons, *Tech/Comp Coord*
▲ EMP: 25
SALES (est): 4.8MM Privately Held
WEB: www.servicemachinetool.com
SIC: 3599 Machine shop, jobbing & repair

(G-4726)
STAMPED FITTINGS INC
217 Lenox Ave (14903-1118)
PHONE.....................607 733-9988
Shana Graham, *President*
Mike Graham, *Vice Pres*
▲ EMP: 25 EST: 1997
SQ FT: 25,000
SALES (est): 4.8MM Privately Held
WEB: www.stampedfittings.com
SIC: 3469 Metal stampings

(G-4727)
SWIFT GLASS CO INC
131 22nd St (14903-1329)
P.O. Box 879, Elmira (14902-0879)
PHONE.....................607 733-7166
Fax: 607 732-5829
Daniel J Burke, *President*
Gary Palmowski, *Plant Mgr*
Kevin Wheeler, *Opers Mgr*
Carlotta Munson, *Opers Staff*
Mary Owens, *Purch Agent*
▲ EMP: 85 EST: 1882
SQ FT: 80,000
SALES (est): 19.1MM Privately Held
WEB: www.swiftglass.com
SIC: 3231 Products of purchased glass; scientific & technical glassware: from purchased glass; tempered glass: made from purchased glass; industrial glassware: made from purchased glass

Elmont
Nassau County

(G-4728)
ANDREW SAPIENZA BAKERY INC
553 Meacham Ave (11003-3807)
PHONE.....................516 437-1715
Fax: 516 775-5719
Paul Tolomeo, *President*
Ronald Luisi, *Vice Pres*
Jack Tolomeo, *Treasurer*
EMP: 40
SQ FT: 6,000
SALES (est): 5.1MM Privately Held
SIC: 2051 Bread, cake & related products

(G-4729)
ARCHITECTURAL SIGN GROUP INC
145 Meacham Ave (11003-2633)
PHONE.....................516 326-1800
Abbas Jaffer, *President*
Rehana Jaffer, *Vice Pres*
EMP: 5
SQ FT: 4,000
SALES (est): 657.8K Privately Held
WEB: www.archsigngroup.com
SIC: 3993 Signs & advertising specialties

(G-4730)
AWT SUPPLY CORP
Also Called: American Printing Eqp & Sup
153 Meacham Ave (11003-2633)
P.O. Box 356, Franklin Square (11010-0356)
PHONE.....................516 437-9105
Fax: 718 437-9107
Greg Mandel, *President*
Josh Solomon, *Vice Pres*
Max Mandel, *Admin Sec*
▲ EMP: 8
SQ FT: 45,000
SALES (est): 1.5MM Privately Held
WEB: www.americanprintingequipment.com
SIC: 3555 5051 3546 Printing trades machinery; wire; power-driven handtools

(G-4731)
ELMONT NORTH LITTLE LEAGUE
1532 Clay St (11003-1046)
PHONE.....................516 775-8210
Ronald Levin, *Owner*
Tom Laietta, *Vice Pres*
EMP: 7
SALES (est): 462.1K Privately Held
SIC: 2721 Trade journals: publishing only, not printed on site

(G-4732)
GM INSULATION CORP
1345 Rosser Ave (11003-3244)
P.O. Box 2188, New Hyde Park (11040-8188)
PHONE.....................516 354-6000
Izabel Skugor, *President*
EMP: 13
SALES (est): 2.4MM Privately Held
SIC: 2295 Sealing or insulating tape for pipe: coated fiberglass

(G-4733)
HOLLYWOOD CABINETS CO
182 Hendrickson Ave (11003-1255)
PHONE.....................516 354-0857
Mike Howie, *Owner*
EMP: 6
SALES: 500K Privately Held
SIC: 2434 Wood kitchen cabinets

(G-4734)
MARTIN ORNA IR WORKS II INC
266 Elmont Rd (11003-1600)
PHONE.....................516 354-3923
Martin Boventre, *President*
Charles Cascio, *Principal*
EMP: 5 EST: 1962
SQ FT: 5,000
SALES (est): 635.2K Privately Held
SIC: 3446 Architectural metalwork

(G-4735)
MERIDIAN TECHNOLOGIES INC
700 Elmont Rd (11003-4027)
PHONE.....................516 285-1000
Fax: 516 285-6300
Denise Shay, *Ch of Bd*
Michael Barry, *Managing Dir*
Tim Medved, *Regl Sales Mgr*
David Rabin, *Manager*
Rachel Shifrin, *Systems Staff*
EMP: 22
SQ FT: 10,000
SALES: 2.2MM Privately Held
WEB: www.meridian-tech.com
SIC: 3679 Electronic circuits

(G-4736)
PROFESSNL SPT PBLICATIONS INC
570 Elmont Rd (11003-3535)
PHONE.....................516 327-9500
Michael Shabsels, *Ch of Bd*
EMP: 18
SALES (est): 1.8MM Privately Held
SIC: 2741 Miscellaneous publishing

(G-4737)
PROFESSNL SPT PBLICATIONS INC
Also Called: Pspi
570 Elmont Rd Ste 202 (11003-3535)
PHONE.....................516 327-9500
EMP: 100
SALES (corp-wide): 19.4MM Privately Held
WEB: www.pspsports.com
SIC: 2721 Periodicals
PA: Professional Sports Publications Inc.
519 8th Ave
New York NY 10018
212 697-1460

(G-4738)
RPC INC
Also Called: RPC Car Service
165 Emporia Ave (11003-1837)
PHONE.....................347 873-3935
Michelle Franklin, *Branch Mgr*
EMP: 39
SALES (corp-wide): 728.9MM Publicly Held
SIC: 1389 Oil field services
PA: Rpc, Inc.
2801 Buford Hwy Ne # 520
Brookhaven GA 30329
404 321-2140

(G-4739)
SAPIENZA PASTRY INC
Also Called: Sapienza Bake Shop
1376 Hempstead Tpke (11003-2539)
PHONE.....................516 352-5232
Fax: 516 352-2459
Paul Sapienza, *President*
EMP: 25
SQ FT: 3,600
SALES (est): 3.3MM Privately Held
SIC: 2051 5461 2099 2052 Bakery: wholesale or wholesale/retail combined; bakeries; food preparations; cookies & crackers

(G-4740)
TIMELY SIGNS INC
2135 Linden Blvd (11003-3901)
PHONE.....................516 285-5339
Fax: 516 285-9637
Eugene Goldsmith, *President*
EMP: 6
SQ FT: 2,000
SALES: 600K Privately Held
SIC: 3993 Displays & cutouts, window & lobby

Elmsford
Westchester County

(G-4741)
A GATTY PRODUCTS INC
Also Called: A Gatty Svce
1 Warehouse Ln (10523-1538)
P.O. Box 725 (10523-0725)
PHONE..............................914 592-3903
Andy Gattyan, *President*
Eva Gattyan, *Vice Pres*
EMP: 6
SQ FT: 5,000
SALES (est): 396K **Privately Held**
SIC: 3639 1799 Trash compactors, household; hydraulic equipment, installation & service

(G-4742)
ANCHOR TECH PRODUCTS CORP
4 Vernon Ln Ste 2 (10523-1947)
PHONE..............................914 592-0240
Dan Esposito, *President*
Phyllis Loomis, *Treasurer*
Steve Ebanks, *Manager*
▲ **EMP:** 20
SQ FT: 3,000
SALES (est): 2MM **Privately Held**
SIC: 3052 Vacuum cleaner hose, rubber; vacuum cleaner hose, plastic; v-belts, rubber

(G-4743)
ARTINA GROUP INC
250 Clearbrook Rd Ste 245 (10523-1332)
P.O. Box 681, Tarrytown (10591-0681)
PHONE..............................914 592-1850
INA Shapiro, *President*
Rick Horn, *Vice Pres*
Adrienne Karlson, *Purch Agent*
Mark Spinozza, *Controller*
Gene Tedrow, *Natl Sales Mgr*
EMP: 34 **EST:** 1971
SQ FT: 25,000
SALES (est): 6.1MM **Privately Held**
SIC: 2752 Commercial printing, lithographic; business forms, lithographed

(G-4744)
BEST PRICED PRODUCTS INC
250 Clearbrook Rd Ste 240 (10523-1332)
P.O. Box 1174, White Plains (10602-1174)
PHONE..............................914 345-3800
Linda Goldberg, *President*
EMP: 5
SQ FT: 30,000
SALES (est): 290K **Privately Held**
WEB: www.bpp2.com
SIC: 3999 Novelties, bric-a-brac & hobby kits

(G-4745)
BH COFFEE COMPANY LLC (PA)
Also Called: Barrie House Coffee & Tea
4 Warehouse Ln Ste 121 (10523-1541)
PHONE..............................914 377-2500
David Goldstein, *CEO*
Paul Goldstein, *President*
Miles Lewis, *Business Mgr*
Ronald Goldstein, *Vice Pres*
Karan Magee, *Vice Pres*
▲ **EMP:** 75 **EST:** 1934
SQ FT: 35,000
SALES (est): 20MM **Privately Held**
WEB: www.barriehouse.com
SIC: 2095 Coffee roasting (except by wholesale grocers)

(G-4746)
BLINDTEK DESIGNER SYSTEMS INC
1 Hayes St (10523-2531)
PHONE..............................914 347-7100
Lee Miller, *President*
Anthony Ash, *Vice Pres*
Steve Beamand, *Vice Pres*
Paul Berliner, *Webmaster*
▲ **EMP:** 18
SALES (est): 2.5MM **Privately Held**
SIC: 2591 Blinds vertical

(G-4747)
C & F IRON WORKS INC
14 N Payne St Ste 1 (10523-1839)
PHONE..............................914 592-2450
Fax: 914 592-2718
Fernando Pastilha, *President*
Michael Boino, *Manager*
EMP: 15
SQ FT: 1,600
SALES (est): 800K **Privately Held**
SIC: 3446 Railings, bannisters, guards, etc.: made from metal pipe

(G-4748)
C & F STEEL CORP
14 N Payne St Ste 2 (10523-1841)
PHONE..............................914 592-3928
Arthur Boino, *CEO*
EMP: 18 **EST:** 2000
SALES (est): 2.6MM **Privately Held**
SIC: 3446 Fences, gates, posts & flagpoles

(G-4749)
CHAMART EXCLUSIVES INC
68 Williams St (10523-2515)
PHONE..............................914 345-3870
Lenny Davidson, *President*
Gaines Davidson, *Vice Pres*
▲ **EMP:** 8
SALES (est): 560K **Privately Held**
SIC: 3469 Porcelain enameled products & utensils

(G-4750)
COCA-COLA BTLG CO OF NY INC
111 Fairview Pk Dr Ste 1 (10523-1536)
PHONE..............................914 592-4574
Fax: 914 592-3219
Kevin Stewart, *Safety Mgr*
Edward Bryan, *Branch Mgr*
EMP: 18
SALES (corp-wide): 41.8B **Publicly Held**
SIC: 2086 Bottled & canned soft drinks
HQ: The Coca-Cola Bottling Company Of New York Inc
2500 Windy Ridge Pkwy Se
Atlanta GA 30339
770 989-3000

(G-4751)
COCA-COLA BTLG CO OF NY INC
115 Fairview Pk Dr Ste 1 (10523-1535)
PHONE..............................914 789-1580
Margerite Lopiccollo, *Principal*
Frank Cllen, *Technical Staff*
EMP: 10
SALES (corp-wide): 41.8B **Publicly Held**
SIC: 2086 Bottled & canned soft drinks
HQ: The Coca-Cola Bottling Company Of New York Inc
2500 Windy Ridge Pkwy Se
Atlanta GA 30339
770 989-3000

(G-4752)
CORAL BLOOD SERVICE
525 Executive Blvd # 285 (10523-1240)
PHONE..............................800 483-4888
Fax: 914 872-6007
Rose Shaw, *Vice Pres*
EMP: 15
SALES (est): 1.7MM **Privately Held**
SIC: 2836 Plasmas

(G-4753)
CRAFTERS WORKSHOP INC
116 S Central Ave Ste 1 (10523-3503)
PHONE..............................914 345-2838
Fax: 914 345-0575
Jaime Echt, *President*
Rj Farr, *Marketing Mgr*
▼ **EMP:** 9
SQ FT: 3,000
SALES (est): 512.4K **Privately Held**
WEB: www.thecraftersworkshop.com
SIC: 3953 Stencils, painting & marking

(G-4754)
CRONIN ENTERPRISES INC
Also Called: Minuteman Press
70 E Main St Ste 2 (10523-3146)
PHONE..............................914 345-9600
Fax: 914 347-2563
Gary Cronin, *President*
Jacquiline Cronin, *Vice Pres*
Christina Sabbia, *Vice Pres*
Tom Hughes, *Marketing Staff*
EMP: 9
SQ FT: 4,000
SALES (est): 900K **Privately Held**
SIC: 2752 Commercial printing, lithographic

(G-4755)
CUSTOM PINS INC
150 Clearbrook Rd Ste 139 (10523-1148)
PHONE..............................914 690-9378
James Zendman, *President*
EMP: 6
SALES (est): 511.2K **Privately Held**
WEB: www.custompins.com
SIC: 3961 Pins (jewelry), except precious metal

(G-4756)
DR PEPPER SNAPPLE GROUP INC
55 Hunter Ln (10523-1334)
PHONE..............................914 846-2300
John Romano, *Warehouse Mgr*
Sam Suleiman, *Warehouse Mgr*
Bill Byron, *Manager*
Marcus Pucci, *Manager*
Tim Holz, *Director*
EMP: 100 **Publicly Held**
SIC: 2086 Bottled & canned soft drinks
PA: Dr Pepper Snapple Group, Inc.
5301 Legacy Dr
Plano TX 75024

(G-4757)
EMKAY TRADING CORP (PA)
250 Clearbrook Rd Ste 127 (10523-1332)
P.O. Box 504 (10523-0504)
PHONE..............................914 592-9000
Fax: 914 592-9000
Howard Kravitz, *President*
Ruth Kravitz, *Vice Pres*
EMP: 2
SQ FT: 2,500
SALES (est): 1.9MM **Privately Held**
WEB: www.emkaytrading.org
SIC: 2022 Cheese, natural & processed

(G-4758)
EMPIRE GYPSUM PDTS & SUP CORP
25 Haven St (10523-1831)
P.O. Box 779 (10523-0779)
PHONE..............................914 592-8141
Carl Nicolosi, *President*
John Nicolosi, *Financial Exec*
EMP: 5
SALES (est): 1.2MM **Privately Held**
SIC: 3275 Gypsum products

(G-4759)
ENGAGEMENT TECHNOLOGY LLC
33 W Main St Ste 303 (10523-2413)
PHONE..............................914 591-7600
Glen Holden, *General Mgr*
Andrea Lightman, *Vice Pres*
Bruce Bolger,
EMP: 10
SALES (est): 1.5MM **Privately Held**
SIC: 3679 Electronic loads & power supplies

(G-4760)
EXECUTIVE PRTG & DIRECT MAIL
8 Westchester Plz Ste 117 (10523-1604)
PHONE..............................914 592-3200
Fax: 914 592-3103
Gary Dieckman, *President*
Andrew Dieckman, *General Mgr*
EMP: 9
SQ FT: 5,200
SALES (est): 1MM **Privately Held**
WEB: www.exprint.com
SIC: 2752 Commercial printing, lithographic

(G-4761)
FABRICATION ENTERPRISES INC
250 Clearbrook Rd Ste 240 (10523-1332)
P.O. Box 1500, White Plains (10602-1500)
PHONE..............................914 591-9300
Fax: 914 345-9800
Elliott Goldberg, *President*
Linda Green, *VP Prdtn*
Jason Drucker, *VP Sales*
Joseph Cardone, *Sales Mgr*
Greg Guerci, *Accounts Mgr*
◆ **EMP:** 45
SQ FT: 30,000
SALES: 50MM **Privately Held**
WEB: www.fabricationenterprises.com
SIC: 3841 2297 Physiotherapy equipment, electrical; nonwoven fabrics

(G-4762)
G C D M IRONWORKS INC
Also Called: G C Ironworks
55 N Evarts Ave (10523-3215)
PHONE..............................914 347-2058
Fax: 914 347-4916
Arrel Gordon, *President*
Michael Creegan, *Vice Pres*
Blondell Hill, *Manager*
EMP: 20
SQ FT: 650
SALES (est): 3.5MM **Privately Held**
SIC: 3446 Stairs, fire escapes, balconies, railings & ladders

(G-4763)
HUDSON SOFTWARE CORPORATION
3 W Main St Ste 106 (10523-2414)
PHONE..............................914 773-0400
Glenn Polin, *President*
Mike Gulley, *COO*
James Mott, *Opers Mgr*
Ralph Santoni, *Manager*
John Rodriguez, *Technical Staff*
EMP: 35
SQ FT: 6,000
SALES (est): 2.5MM **Privately Held**
WEB: www.hudsonsoft.com
SIC: 7372 7371 7374 Prepackaged software; custom computer programming services; service bureau, computer

(G-4764)
HYPRES INC (PA)
175 Clearbrook Rd (10523-1109)
PHONE..............................914 592-1190
Fax: 914 347-2239
Richard E Hitt Jr, *Ch of Bd*
Richard Hitt, *President*
Dr Oleg Mukhanov, *Senior VP*
Dr Deepnarayan Gupta, *Vice Pres*
Michael Kamkar, *Engineer*
EMP: 37
SQ FT: 17,250
SALES: 8MM **Privately Held**
WEB: www.hypres.com
SIC: 3679 3565 Electronic circuits; packaging machinery

(G-4765)
IRON ART INC
14 N Payne St (10523-1835)
PHONE..............................914 592-7977
Fernando Pastilha, *President*
EMP: 5
SALES: 200K **Privately Held**
SIC: 3446 Ornamental metalwork

(G-4766)
JAM PRINTING PUBLISHING INC
11 Clearbrook Rd Ste 133 (10523-1126)
PHONE..............................914 345-8400
Fax: 914 345-6767
Judith Millman, *President*
Mitch Schilkraut, *General Mgr*
EMP: 7
SALES (est): 949.8K **Privately Held**
WEB: www.jamprinting.com
SIC: 2752 Commercial printing, lithographic

Elmsford - Westchester County (G-4767)

(G-4767)
JP BUS & TRUCK REPAIR LTD (PA)
Also Called: Bird Bus Sales
1 Warehouse Ln (10523-1538)
PHONE..................914 592-2872
Fax: 516 767-2703
Robert Reichenbach, *President*
Stephanie Chavez, *Principal*
James Filomena, *Principal*
Ivan Soto, *Vice Pres*
Marie Birnbaum, *Accountant*
EMP: 19 **EST:** 2004
SALES (est): 7.3MM **Privately Held**
SIC: 3711 Buses, all types, assembly of

(G-4768)
JUDSCOTT HANDPRINTS LTD (PA)
2269 Saw Mill River Rd 4d (10523-3832)
PHONE..................914 347-5515
Fax: 914 347-3192
Sally Lefkowitz, *President*
Stephen Rabin, *Opers Staff*
EMP: 12
SQ FT: 8,000
SALES (est): 2.8MM **Privately Held**
WEB: www.judscott.com
SIC: 2262 2261 2221 Screen printing: manmade fiber & silk broadwoven fabrics; screen printing of cotton broadwoven fabrics; wall covering fabrics, manmade fiber & silk

(G-4769)
KIMBER MFG INC
555 Taxter Rd Ste 235 (10523-2314)
PHONE..................406 758-2222
George Hawthorn, *Engineer*
Elliot Orenstein, *Engineer*
Brigit Salgado, *Engineer*
Daniel Sapio, *Engineer*
Jordan Walker, *Engineer*
EMP: 85
SALES (corp-wide): 92.3MM **Privately Held**
WEB: www.kimbermfg.com
SIC: 3599 Machine shop, jobbing & repair
PA: Kimber Mfg., Inc.
1 Lawton St
Yonkers NY 10705
914 964-0771

(G-4770)
LUXO CORPORATION
5 Westchester Plz Ste 110 (10523-1613)
PHONE..................914 345-0067
Fax: 914 345-0068
Sam Gumins, *President*
Michael Vuolo, *Opers Mgr*
Lynn Green, *Production*
Bob Grinnell, *CFO*
Robert Grinnell, *CFO*
▲ **EMP:** 19 **EST:** 1953
SALES: 7.5MM
SALES (corp-wide): 758.2MM **Privately Held**
WEB: www.luxous.com
SIC: 3646 Commercial indusl & institutional electric lighting fixtures
HQ: Glamox As
Birger Hatlebakks Veg 15
Molde 6415
712 460-00

(G-4771)
MAGNETIC ANALYSIS CORPORATION (PA)
Also Called: M A C
103 Fairview Pk Dr Ste 2 (10523-1544)
PHONE..................914 530-2000
JI Vitulli, *Ch of Bd*
Zhongqing You, *President*
Billy Beasley, *General Mgr*
William S Gould III, *Chairman*
Fred Fundy, *District Mgr*
▲ **EMP:** 90 **EST:** 1928
SQ FT: 26,000
SALES: 25MM **Privately Held**
WEB: www.mac-ndt.com
SIC: 3829 3825 Testing equipment: abrasion, shearing strength, etc.; instruments to measure electricity

(G-4772)
MASTER IMAGE PRINTING INC
75 N Central Ave Ste 202 (10523-2548)
PHONE..................914 347-4400
Fax: 914 347-4955
John Sabatino, *President*
Mary Jane Yollen, *Vice Pres*
EMP: 5
SQ FT: 5,000
SALES: 1MM **Privately Held**
WEB: www.masterimage.com
SIC: 2759 2752 2396 2679 Commercial printing; commercial printing, lithographic; automotive & apparel trimmings; labels, paper: made from purchased material

(G-4773)
MASTERDISK CORPORATION
134 S Central Ave Ste C (10523-3539)
PHONE..................212 541-5022
Douglas Levine, *CEO*
Graham Goldman, *Engineer*
Laksham Fernando, *Treasurer*
EMP: 15
SQ FT: 10,000
SALES: 981K **Privately Held**
WEB: www.masterdisk.com
SIC: 3652 3651 2851 Master records or tapes, preparation of; household audio & video equipment; vinyl coatings, strippable

(G-4774)
MMO MUSIC GROUP INC
Also Called: Music Minus One
50 Executive Blvd Ste 236 (10523-1341)
PHONE..................914 592-1188
Fax: 914 592-3116
Irving Kratka, *CEO*
Patricia Dichek, *Office Mgr*
EMP: 9
SQ FT: 35,000
SALES (est): 1.7MM **Privately Held**
WEB: www.musicminusone.com
SIC: 3652 Compact laser discs, prerecorded; magnetic tape (audio): prerecorded

(G-4775)
MOTTS LLP (HQ)
Also Called: Motts
55 Hunter Ln (10523-1334)
P.O. Box 869077, Plano TX (75086-9077)
PHONE..................972 673-8088
Angela Stephens, *Controller*
Jeff Morgan, *MIS Dir*
Victor Dominich, *Network Analyst*
Jim Baldwin, *General Counsel*
Larry D Young,
◆ **EMP:** 250
SQ FT: 160,000
SALES (est): 202.3MM **Publicly Held**
WEB: www.maunalai.com
SIC: 2033 5149 2087 Fruit juices: packaged in cans, jars, etc.; apple sauce: packaged in cans, jars, etc.; beverage concentrates; cocktail mixes, nonalcoholic

(G-4776)
MYPUBLISHER INC (HQ)
8 Westchester Plz Ste 145 (10523-1604)
PHONE..................914 773-4312
Jeffrey T Housenbold, *Ch of Bd*
Lisa Heck, *Accountant*
Igor Karpov, *Software Engr*
Jude Niles, *Administration*
▲ **EMP:** 17
SALES (est): 3.9MM
SALES (corp-wide): 1.1B **Publicly Held**
WEB: www.mypublisher.com
SIC: 2782 Albums
PA: Shutterfly, Inc.
2800 Bridge Pkwy Ste 100
Redwood City CA 94065
650 610-5200

(G-4777)
NANOVIBRONIX INC
525 Executive Blvd (10523-1240)
PHONE..................914 233-3004
William Stern, *CEO*
EMP: 12
SALES (est): 482.9K **Privately Held**
SIC: 3845 Ultrasonic medical equipment, except cleaning

(G-4778)
NANTUCKET ALLSERVE INC
Also Called: Nantucket Nectars
55 Hunter Ln (10523-1334)
PHONE..................914 612-4000
Mark Hellendrung, *President*
Thomas First, *Co-COB*
Thomas Scott, *Co-COB*
Tim Chan, *Treasurer*
Ellen Ludwig, *Human Resources*
EMP: 400
SALES (est): 17.9MM **Privately Held**
SIC: 2086 5499 Fruit drinks (less than 100% juice): packaged in cans, etc.; juices, fruit or vegetable

(G-4779)
NOVAMED-USA INC
4 Westchester Plz Ste 137 (10523-1612)
PHONE..................914 789-2100
Robert Gates, *General Mgr*
Carol Schuler, *Exec VP*
Maggie Wang, *Purch Mgr*
▲ **EMP:** 40
SQ FT: 30,000
SALES (est): 5.9MM **Privately Held**
SIC: 3841 3845 Catheters; patient monitoring apparatus

(G-4780)
OLYMPIA SPORTS COMPANY INC
Also Called: Olympia Company
500 Executive Blvd # 170 (10523-1239)
PHONE..................914 347-4737
Roger Heumann, *President*
Ed Brodsky, *Vice Pres*
Peter Kiernan, *Vice Pres*
▲ **EMP:** 10
SQ FT: 7,200
SALES (est): 1.3MM **Privately Held**
WEB: www.olympiagloves.com
SIC: 3949 Gloves, sport & athletic: boxing, handball, etc.

(G-4781)
PRESS EXPRESS
400 Executive Blvd # 146 (10523-1243)
PHONE..................914 592-3790
Al Tiso, *President*
EMP: 5
SALES (est): 337.7K **Privately Held**
SIC: 2741 7313 Miscellaneous publishing; printed media advertising representatives

(G-4782)
RADON TESTING CORP OF AMERICA (PA)
Also Called: R T C A
2 Hayes St (10523-2502)
PHONE..................914 345-3380
Michael Osterer, *CEO*
Nancy Bredhoff, *President*
Alan S Bande, *Vice Pres*
Alan S Bandes, *Vice Pres*
Mark A Goodman, *Vice Pres*
EMP: 12
SQ FT: 4,500
SALES (est): 1.9MM **Privately Held**
WEB: www.rtca.com
SIC: 3821 Laboratory apparatus & furniture

(G-4783)
RALPH MARTINELLI
Also Called: Suburban Marketing Assoc
100 Clearbrook Rd Ste 170 (10523-1135)
PHONE..................914 345-3055
Fax: 914 345-3515
Ralph Martinelli, *Owner*
EMP: 30
SALES (est): 1.2MM **Privately Held**
WEB: www.sub-pub.com
SIC: 2721 Periodicals

(G-4784)
RELIABLE AUTMTC SPRNKLR CO INC (PA)
103 Fairview Pk Dr Ste 1 (10523-1523)
PHONE..................800 431-1588
Fax: 914 592-3676
Frank J Fee III, *President*
Candida M Fee, *Vice Pres*
Kevin T Fee, *Vice Pres*
Michael R Fee, *Vice Pres*
Robert C Hultgren, *Vice Pres*
◆ **EMP:** 350 **EST:** 1920
SQ FT: 64,000
SALES (est): 377.3MM **Privately Held**
SIC: 3569 Sprinkler systems, fire: automatic

(G-4785)
SAVE O SEAL CORPORATION INC
90 E Main St (10523-3218)
P.O. Box 553 (10523-0553)
PHONE..................914 592-3031
Fax: 914 592-4511
Tullio Muscariello, *President*
Rose Muscariello, *Vice Pres*
EMP: 7
SQ FT: 3,000
SALES (est): 1.2MM **Privately Held**
SIC: 3565 5085 Packaging machinery; knives, industrial

(G-4786)
SCHOTT CORPORATION (DH)
555 Taxter Rd Ste 470 (10523-2363)
PHONE..................914 831-2200
Fax: 914 831-2346
Linda S Mayer, *Ch of Bd*
Greg Wolters, *Ch of Bd*
Dr Andreas F Liebenberg, *President*
Robert Galante, *General Mgr*
Nikhil Krishna, *Business Mgr*
▲ **EMP:** 70
SQ FT: 70,000
SALES (est): 827.1MM **Privately Held**
SIC: 3211 3829 3221 3229 Flat glass; measuring & controlling devices; glass containers; vials, glass; glass fiber products
HQ: Schott Ag
Hattenbergstr. 10
Mainz 55122
613 166-0

(G-4787)
SCHOTT GEMTRON CORPORATION
555 Taxter Rd Ste 470 (10523-2352)
PHONE..................423 337-3522
Linda S Mayer, *President*
Tony Springate, *Accounts Mgr*
EMP: 194 **Privately Held**
SIC: 3211 Flat glass
HQ: Schott Gemtron Corporation
615 Highway 68
Sweetwater TN 37874
423 337-3522

(G-4788)
SCHOTT GOVERNMENT SERVICES LLC
Also Called: Schott Defense
555 Taxter Rd Ste 470 (10523-2352)
PHONE..................703 418-1409
Scott Custer, *President*
Mona Roche, *Business Mgr*
EMP: 7 **EST:** 2007
SALES (est): 559.3K **Privately Held**
SIC: 3211 Flat glass
HQ: Schott North America, Inc.
555 Taxter Rd Ste 470
Elmsford NY 10523
914 831-2200

(G-4789)
SCHOTT LITHOTEC USA CORP
555 Taxter Rd Ste 470 (10523-2352)
PHONE..................845 463-5300
Patrick Markschlaeger, *President*
EMP: 80
SQ FT: 36,115
SALES (est): 6.3MM **Privately Held**
SIC: 3674 Semiconductors & related devices

(G-4790)
SCHOTT SOLAR PV INC
555 Taxter Rd Ste 470 (10523-2352)
PHONE..................888 457-6527
Mark Finocchario, *President*
Hans-Juergen Gebel, *Vice Pres*
Doug Jenks, *CFO*
Lauren Lake, *Human Resources*
Manfred Jaeckel, *Admin Sec*
▲ **EMP:** 8

▲ = Import ▼ = Export
◆ = Import/Export

SALES (est): 748.2K **Privately Held**
SIC: 3674 3211 Solar cells; flat glass
HQ: Schott Solar Ag
Hattenbergstr. 10
Mainz
613 166-0

(G-4791)
SEQUENTIAL ELECTRONICS SYSTEMS
399 Executive Blvd (10523-1205)
PHONE..................914 592-1345
Fax: 914 592-6014
Lewis S Schiller, *Ch of Bd*
Norman Wheatcroft, *Vice Pres*
Elliott Laitman, *CFO*
EMP: 22
SQ FT: 15,000
SALES (est): 1.9MM
SALES (corp-wide): 2.5MM **Privately Held**
SIC: 3577 3625 3823 3663 Encoders; computer peripheral equipment; positioning controls, electric; industrial instrmnts msrmnt display/control process variable; radio & TV communications equipment
PA: Trinity Group Acquisition Corp
249 Saw Mill River Rd
Elmsford NY

(G-4792)
SIGN WORKS INCORPORATED
150 Clearbrook Rd Ste 118 (10523-1142)
PHONE..................914 592-0700
Fax: 914 592-4971
Lynn Feiner, *President*
Allen Abramson, *Sls & Mktg Exec*
Anthony Martinelli, *Marketing Staff*
Roseanne Bocknik, *Manager*
EMP: 25
SQ FT: 11,000
SALES (est): 2.5MM **Privately Held**
SIC: 3993 1799 Signs & advertising specialties; sign installation & maintenance

(G-4793)
SML ACQUISITION LLC
33 W Main St Ste 505 (10523-2453)
PHONE..................914 592-3130
Robert B Wetzel, *President*
Laura Hutter, *Controller*
EMP: 179 EST: 2011
SQ FT: 35,000
SALES (est): 12.5MM **Privately Held**
SIC: 2844 Toilet preparations

(G-4794)
SPOTLIGHT PUBLICATIONS LLC
100 Clearbrook Rd Ste 170 (10523-1135)
PHONE..................914 345-9473
John Jordan, *Principal*
EMP: 5
SALES (est): 470K **Privately Held**
SIC: 2721 Magazines: publishing only, not printed on site

(G-4795)
TRANE US INC
3 Westchester Plz Ste 198 (10523-1623)
PHONE..................914 593-0303
Terry Connor, *Manager*
EMP: 5 **Privately Held**
SIC: 3585 Refrigeration & heating equipment
HQ: Trane U.S. Inc.
1 Centennial Ave Ste 101
Piscataway NJ 08854
732 652-7100

(G-4796)
TRI-STATE METALS LLC
Also Called: Tsm
41 N Lawn Ave (10523-2632)
PHONE..................914 347-8157
Patti Carone, *Manager*
Ray Ayerbe,
EMP: 10
SQ FT: 10,000
SALES (est): 2MM **Privately Held**
SIC: 3444 Culverts, flumes & pipes

(G-4797)
U E SYSTEMS INCORPORATED (PA)
14 Hayes St (10523-2536)
PHONE..................914 592-1220

Fax: 914 347-2181
Michael Osterer, *Ch of Bd*
Blake Canham, *Regional Mgr*
Joe Edelen, *Regional Mgr*
Mike Naro, *Regional Mgr*
Mike Pierce, *Regional Mgr*
EMP: 30
SALES (est): 5.2MM **Privately Held**
WEB: www.uesystems.com
SIC: 3829 3812 3699 Ultrasonic testing equipment; search & navigation equipment; electrical equipment & supplies

(G-4798)
VISIPLEX INSTRUMENTS CORP
250 Clearbrook Rd (10523-1305)
PHONE..................845 365-0190
David Vozick, *Ch of Bd*
Donald Rabinovitch, *President*
Elise Nissen, *CFO*
Thalia Rosales, *Controller*
EMP: 62
SALES: 20MM **Privately Held**
WEB: www.afpimaging.com
SIC: 3845 Electromedical equipment
PA: Biowave Innovations, Llc
274 Ridgefield Rd
Wilton CT 06897

(G-4799)
VITERION CORPORATION
565 Taxter Rd Ste 175 (10523-2371)
PHONE..................914 333-6033
Toru Ide, *President*
EMP: 16 EST: 2012
SALES (est): 2.5MM **Privately Held**
SIC: 3841 Surgical & medical instruments

(G-4800)
WESTINGHOUSE A BRAKE TECH CORP
Also Called: Metro Service Center
4 Warehouse Ln Ste 144 (10523-1556)
PHONE..................914 347-8650
Doug Cavallo, *Manager*
EMP: 13
SALES (corp-wide): 2.9B **Publicly Held**
WEB: www.wabco-rail.com
SIC: 3743 Rapid transit cars & equipment
PA: Westinghouse Air Brake Technologies Corporation
1001 Airbrake Ave
Wilmerding PA 15148
412 825-1000

(G-4801)
WHITE PLAINS MARBLE INC
186 E Main St (10523-3302)
PHONE..................914 347-6000
John Bargellini, *President*
Judy Birdsall, *Manager*
EMP: 7
SQ FT: 5,000
SALES (est): 700K **Privately Held**
SIC: 3281 1743 Marble, building: cut & shaped; statuary, marble; terrazzo, tile, marble, mosaic work

Endicott
Broome County

(G-4802)
311 INDUSTRIES CORP
434 Airport Rd (13760-4406)
PHONE..................607 846-4520
John Galli, *President*
▲ **EMP:** 6
SALES (est): 193.9K **Privately Held**
SIC: 3089 Boot or shoe products, plastic

(G-4803)
AMPHENOL INTRCONNECT PDTS CORP (HQ)
20 Valley St (13760-3600)
PHONE..................607 754-4444
Fax: 607 786-4234
Richard Adam Norwitt, *CEO*
Martin H Loeffler, *President*
Craig Lampo, *Vice Pres*
Sue Dodge, *Purch Agent*
Sue Thompson, *Buyer*
▲ **EMP:** 5
SQ FT: 140,000

SALES (est): 94.4MM
SALES (corp-wide): 6.2B **Publicly Held**
WEB: www.amphenol-aipc.com
SIC: 3679 Harness assemblies for electronic use: wire or cable
PA: Amphenol Corporation
358 Hall Ave
Wallingford CT 06492
203 265-8900

(G-4804)
BAE SYSTEMS CONTROLS INC (DH)
1098 Clark St (13760-2815)
PHONE..................607 770-2000
Thomas A Asrseneault, *President*
Joyce Sherwood, *Principal*
Pete Pepaj, *Opers Mgr*
Steve Butterworth, *Safety Mgr*
Joe Zeilman, *Mfg Staff*
▲ **EMP:** 1400 EST: 2000
SALES (est): 439.3MM
SALES (corp-wide): 21.9B **Privately Held**
WEB: www.baesystemscontrols.com
SIC: 3812 Aircraft/aerospace flight instruments & guidance systems
HQ: Bae Systems, Inc.
1101 Wilson Blvd Ste 2000
Arlington VA 22209
703 312-6100

(G-4805)
BROOME COUNTY
Central Foods & Nutrition Svcs
2001 E Main St (13760-5622)
P.O. Box 1766, Binghamton (13902-1766)
PHONE..................607 785-9567
Fax: 607 748-0268
Michelle Hauf, *Director*
EMP: 20
SQ FT: 11,076 **Privately Held**
WEB: www.bcstopdwi.com
SIC: 2099 Emulsifiers, food
PA: Broome County
60 Hawley St
Binghamton NY 13901
607 778-2452

(G-4806)
CHAKRA COMMUNICATIONS INC
32 Washington Ave (13760-5305)
PHONE..................607 748-7491
Jim Arnold, *Branch Mgr*
EMP: 20 **Privately Held**
WEB: www.chakracentral.com
SIC: 2752 7334 2791 2789 Commercial printing, offset; photocopying & duplicating services; typesetting; bookbinding & related work; commercial printing
HQ: Chakra Communications, Inc.
80 W Drullard Ave
Lancaster NY 14086
716 505-7300

(G-4807)
CROWLEY FABG MACHINING CO INC (PA)
403 N Nanticoke Ave (13760-4138)
PHONE..................607 484-0299
Thomas Crowley, *President*
Mike Crowley, *General Mgr*
Jim Macuch, *Manager*
Mike Newfrock, *Info Tech Mgr*
EMP: 4
SQ FT: 30,000
SALES (est): 4.5MM **Privately Held**
WEB: www.crowleyfab.com
SIC: 3541 Machine tools, metal cutting type

(G-4808)
DATUM ALLOYS INC
407 Airport Rd (13760-4405)
PHONE..................607 239-6274
Ben Scott, *President*
Kevin Graham, *General Mgr*
Duncan Watey, *Vice Pres*
Urban Torto, *Opers Mgr*
◆ **EMP:** 6
SQ FT: 800
SALES (est): 685.5K **Privately Held**
SIC: 3291 Abrasive metal & steel products

(G-4809)
ELTEE TOOL & DIE CO
404 E Franklin St (13760-4124)
PHONE..................607 748-4301
William Andrew Keeler, *Owner*
EMP: 10
SQ FT: 10,000
SALES (est): 1.2MM **Privately Held**
SIC: 3559 Automotive related machinery

(G-4810)
ENDICOTT INTERCONNECT TECH INC
Also Called: Ei
1701 North St (13760-5587)
P.O. Box 5250, Binghamton (13902-5250)
PHONE..................866 820-4820
James J Mc Namara Jr, *Ch of Bd*
Michael Cummings, *President*
Jeff Knight, *General Mgr*
David Giordani, *Production*
Frank Egitto, *Research*
▲ **EMP:** 600
SQ FT: 1,400,000
SALES (est): 90.2K **Privately Held**
WEB: www.endicottinterconnect.com
SIC: 3674 Semiconductors & related devices

(G-4811)
ENDICOTT PRECISION INC
1328-30 Campville Rd (13760-4414)
PHONE..................607 754-7076
Fax: 607 754-7150
Ronald Oliveira, *General Mgr*
Tammie Romich, *General Mgr*
Douglas Walters, *General Mgr*
Manuel Oliveira, *Chairman*
Dolores Oliveira, *Vice Pres*
EMP: 125 EST: 1959
SQ FT: 85,000
SALES: 19.1MM **Privately Held**
WEB: www.endicottprecision.com
SIC: 3444 3443 3599 3469 Sheet metalwork; fabricated plate work (boiler shop); weldments; custom machinery; metal stampings

(G-4812)
ENDICOTT RESEARCH GROUP INC
2601 Wayne St (13760-3207)
PHONE..................607 754-9187
Fax: 607 754-9255
Nathan Burd, *President*
Scott Barney, *Vice Pres*
Anna Quick, *Mfg Staff*
Scott Dittrich, *Buyer*
Kate Walsh, *Purchasing*
EMP: 64
SQ FT: 30,000
SALES (est): 13.9MM **Privately Held**
WEB: www.ergpower.com
SIC: 3629 Power conversion units, a.c. to d.c.: static-electric; inverters, nonrotating: electrical

(G-4813)
ENGINEERING MFG TECH LLC
101 Delaware Ave (13760-6106)
PHONE..................607 754-7111
Fax: 607 754-2237
Patricia Marconi, *President*
Wyoma Chambala, *Vice Pres*
Michael Nowalk, *Vice Pres*
Cary Simon, *Manager*
EMP: 90 EST: 1946
SQ FT: 80,000
SALES (est): 21MM **Privately Held**
WEB: www.endicottmachine.com
SIC: 3444 3599 3496 3469 Sheet metalwork; machine & other job shop work; miscellaneous fabricated wire products; metal stampings

(G-4814)
EVERLASTING IMAGES
504 Shady Dr (13760-5918)
PHONE..................607 785-8743
John C Kupiec, *Principal*
EMP: 7
SALES (est): 477.1K **Privately Held**
SIC: 3479 Etching & engraving

Endicott - Broome County (G-4815)

(G-4815)
FAMBUS INC
Also Called: Village Printing
2800 Watson Blvd (13760-3512)
PHONE..................607 785-3700
David Labelle, *President*
Frank Labelle, *Consultant*
EMP: 6
SQ FT: 2,100
SALES (est): 590K **Privately Held**
WEB: www.fambus.com
SIC: 2752 7334 Commercial printing, offset; photocopying & duplicating services

(G-4816)
FELIX ROMA & SONS INC
2 S Page Ave (13760-4693)
P.O. Box 5547 (13763-5547)
PHONE..................607 748-3336
Fax: 607 748-3607
Eugene F Roma, *President*
Eugene Romask, *Vice Pres*
Lucille Fetsko, *Bookkeeper*
EMP: 60
SQ FT: 43,000
SALES (est): 8.1MM **Privately Held**
WEB: www.felixroma.com
SIC: 2051 Bread, cake & related products; bread, all types (white, wheat, rye, etc): fresh or frozen; rolls, bread type: fresh or frozen

(G-4817)
G B INTERNATIONAL TRDG CO LTD
408 Airport Rd (13760-4494)
PHONE..................607 785-0938
Fax: 607 785-1109
August Garufy, *President*
◆ EMP: 250
SQ FT: 30,000
SALES (est): 40.9MM **Privately Held**
WEB: www.gbint.com
SIC: 3629 5065 5999 Power conversion units, a.c. to d.c.: static-electric; electronic parts & equipment; electronic parts & equipment

(G-4818)
GEORGE INDUSTRIES LLC
1 S Page Ave (13760-4695)
PHONE..................607 748-3371
Fax: 607 754-9883
John Ferro, *Purch Mgr*
Kellen Kafka, *Engineer*
Marilyn Cline, *Manager*
Kathy Snyder, *Information Mgr*
Shankar Kiru,
EMP: 117 EST: 1951
SQ FT: 100,000
SALES (est): 27.2MM **Privately Held**
WEB: www.georgeindustries.com
SIC: 3441 Fabricated structural metal

(G-4819)
INTERNATIONAL BUS MCHS CORP
Also Called: IBM
1701 North St (13760-5587)
PHONE..................607 754-9558
Fax: 607 755-3527
Mike Cadigan, *Vice Pres*
Ed Cervantes, *Vice Pres*
Bill Cosnett, *Project Mgr*
John Spalik, *Project Mgr*
Mario Monaco, *Production*
EMP: 2000
SALES (corp-wide): 79.9B **Publicly Held**
WEB: www.ibm.com
SIC: 3571 Electronic computers
PA: International Business Machines Corporation
1 New Orchard Rd Ste 1
Armonk NY 10504
914 499-1900

(G-4820)
JARETS STUFFED CUPCAKES
116 Oak Hill Ave (13760-2810)
PHONE..................607 658-9096
EMP: 8
SALES (est): 406.6K **Privately Held**
SIC: 2051 Bread, cake & related products

(G-4821)
JAX SIGNS AND NEON INC
108 Odell Ave (13760)
PHONE..................607 727-3420
James E Taber, *Ch of Bd*
EMP: 7
SALES (est): 860.8K **Privately Held**
SIC: 3993 Signs & advertising specialties

(G-4822)
JD TOOL INC
521 E Main St (13760-5023)
PHONE..................607 786-3129
Jeffrey Dibble, *President*
Mandy Esposito, *Office Mgr*
Mandy Hill, *Manager*
EMP: 3
SALES (est): 1.8MM **Privately Held**
WEB: www.jdtool.net
SIC: 3545 Tools & accessories for machine tools

(G-4823)
JIM ROMAS BAKERY INC
202 N Nanticoke Ave (13760-4135)
PHONE..................607 748-7425
James Roma, *President*
Carl Roma, *Vice Pres*
EMP: 30
SQ FT: 5,200
SALES: 800K **Privately Held**
SIC: 2051 5411 Bakery: wholesale or wholesale/retail combined; delicatessens

(G-4824)
MEDSIM-EAGLE SIMULATION INC
811 North St (13760-5127)
PHONE..................607 658-9354
Nimrod Goor, *President*
Christopher Paulsen, *Vice Pres*
EMP: 12
SALES (est): 692.5K **Privately Held**
WEB: www.medsim.com
SIC: 3571 3577 7373 Electronic computers; graphic displays, except graphic terminals; systems integration services
HQ: Medsim Inc
741 Curlew Rd
Delray Beach FL 33444

(G-4825)
MICROCHIP TECHNOLOGY INC
3301 Country Club Rd (13760-3401)
PHONE..................607 785-5992
Steve Sanghi, *Branch Mgr*
EMP: 166
SALES (corp-wide): 3.4B **Publicly Held**
SIC: 3674 Semiconductors & related devices
PA: Microchip Technology Inc
2355 W Chandler Blvd
Chandler AZ 85224
480 792-7200

(G-4826)
NANOMAS TECHNOLOGIES INC
1093 Clark St (13760-2815)
PHONE..................607 821-4208
John J Hannafin, *President*
Tom Xu, *Vice Pres*
Zhihao Yang, *Vice Pres*
EMP: 10
SQ FT: 300
SALES (est): 115.5K **Privately Held**
SIC: 3674 Semiconductor circuit networks

(G-4827)
NEW VISION INDUSTRIES INC
1239 Campville Rd (13760-4424)
P.O. Box 570, Apalachin (13732-0570)
PHONE..................607 687-7700
Michael R Copt, *President*
Betsy Copt, *Vice Pres*
Diane Horne, *Assistant*
EMP: 18
SQ FT: 4,100
SALES (est): 5.5MM **Privately Held**
WEB: www.newvisionindustries.com
SIC: 3569 3441 Assembly machines, non-metalworking; fabricated structural metal

(G-4828)
NORTH POINT TECHNOLOGY LLC
816 Buffalo St (13760-1780)
PHONE..................866 885-3377
Ryan Kane, *Engineer*
Robert P Lee,
EMP: 10
SALES (est): 660K **Privately Held**
WEB: www.northpointusa.com
SIC: 3625 Relays & industrial controls

(G-4829)
PALMER INDUSTRIES INC
2320 Lewis St (13760-6157)
PHONE..................607 754-8741
Jeck Palmer Jr, *Manager*
EMP: 7
SALES (corp-wide): 2.2MM **Privately Held**
WEB: www.palmerind.com
SIC: 3842 3534 Wheelchairs; elevators & moving stairways
PA: Palmer Industries Inc
509 Paden St
Endicott NY 13760
607 754-2957

(G-4830)
PALMER INDUSTRIES INC (PA)
509 Paden St (13760-4631)
P.O. Box 5707 (13763-5707)
PHONE..................607 754-2957
Fax: 607 754-1954
Jack Palmer Sr, *President*
Jack Palmer Jr, *General Mgr*
▲ EMP: 21
SALES (est): 2.2MM **Privately Held**
WEB: www.palmerind.com
SIC: 3842 Wheelchairs

(G-4831)
PALMER INDUSTRIES INC
1 Heath St (13760-6110)
P.O. Box 5707 (13763-5707)
PHONE..................607 754-1954
Jack Palmer Jr, *Manager*
EMP: 6
SALES (corp-wide): 2.2MM **Privately Held**
WEB: www.palmerind.com
SIC: 3751 3842 Motorcycles, bicycles & parts; wheelchairs
PA: Palmer Industries Inc
509 Paden St
Endicott NY 13760
607 754-2957

(G-4832)
PHOTONIX TECHNOLOGIES INC
48 Washington Ave (13760-5305)
PHONE..................607 786-4600
John Urban, *President*
Sam Cucci, *Vice Pres*
EMP: 12
SQ FT: 2,500
SALES: 1,000K **Privately Held**
WEB: www.photonixtechnologies.com
SIC: 3825 Test equipment for electronic & electric measurement

(G-4833)
SAM A LUPO & SONS INC (PA)
1219 Campville Rd (13760-4411)
P.O. Box 5721 (13763-5721)
PHONE..................800 388-5352
Sam A Lupo Jr, *President*
Stephen J Lupo, *Vice Pres*
Diane Peris, *Manager*
Jennifer Perkins, *Admin Sec*
EMP: 3
SALES (est): 9.7MM **Privately Held**
WEB: www.spiedies.com
SIC: 2011 5411 Meat by-products from meat slaughtered on site; delicatessens

(G-4834)
SMARTYS CORNER
501 W Main St (13760-4621)
PHONE..................607 239-5276
Laura Cla, *Principal*
EMP: 6 EST: 2008
SALES (est): 423.7K **Privately Held**
SIC: 2024 Ice cream, bulk

(G-4835)
TIOGA TOOL INC (PA)
160 Glendale Dr (13760-3704)
PHONE..................607 785-6005
Fax: 607 625-2155
Jeff Rudler, *President*
Jeff Koprevich, *Sales Mgr*
EMP: 12 EST: 1965
SQ FT: 5,500
SALES (est): 1.7MM **Privately Held**
WEB: www.tiogatool.com
SIC: 3599 1799 Machine & other job shop work; welding on site

(G-4836)
TNTPAVING
1077 Taft Ave (13760-7201)
PHONE..................607 372-4911
Dale Thomas, *Owner*
EMP: 5
SALES (est): 186.3K **Privately Held**
SIC: 2952 Asphalt felts & coatings

(G-4837)
TRUEBITE INC
129 Squires Ave (13760-2936)
PHONE..................607 786-3184
Ed Calafut, *President*
▲ EMP: 12
SALES (est): 825K **Privately Held**
WEB: www.fotofiles.com
SIC: 3545 Drills (machine tool accessories)

(G-4838)
VESTAL ELECTRONIC DEVICES LLC
635 Dickson St (13760-4527)
PHONE..................607 773-8461
Fax: 607 772-8184
Walter H Kintner Jr, *Mng Member*
Joel Osborne, *Manager*
▲ EMP: 17
SQ FT: 110,000
SALES (est): 3.4MM **Privately Held**
WEB: www.vestalelectronics.com
SIC: 3679 3356 Electronic circuits; tin & tin alloy bars, pipe, sheets, etc.

(G-4839)
WEDDING GOWN PRESERVATION CO
707 North St (13760-5011)
PHONE..................607 748-7999
Fax: 607 754-9863
Michael Schapiro, *Owner*
Susan Schapiro, *Vice Pres*
Mary Roberts, *CFO*
Colby Schapiro, *Manager*
Vicki Raposo, *Data Proc Staff*
EMP: 60
SALES (est): 7.3MM **Privately Held**
WEB: www.gownpreservation.com
SIC: 2842 Drycleaning preparations

Endwell
Broome County

(G-4840)
EMPIRE PLASTICS INC
2011 E Main St (13760-5622)
PHONE..................607 754-9132
Fax: 607 748-0391
John Witinski Sr, *President*
John Witinski Jr, *Vice Pres*
Shirley Westover, *Data Proc Dir*
EMP: 33 EST: 1958
SQ FT: 11,000
SALES (est): 5.4MM **Privately Held**
SIC: 3599 3699 2821 Machine shop, jobbing & repair; laser welding, drilling & cutting equipment; thermosetting materials; acrylic resins; nylon resins; polytetrafluoroethylene resins (teflon)

(G-4841)
J T SYSTEMATIC
Also Called: Just In Time Company
39 Valley St (13760-3659)
PHONE..................607 754-0929
Fax: 607 754-7509
Roger Carr, *Owner*
EMP: 5
SQ FT: 6,000

GEOGRAPHIC SECTION — Fairport - Monroe County (G-4866)

SALES: 350K Privately Held
SIC: 3544 3999 3089 3599 Industrial molds; models, general, except toy; injection molded finished plastic products; machine shop, jobbing & repair

(G-4842)
LIGHTSPIN TECHNOLOGIES INC
616 Lowell Dr (13760-2525)
PHONE...............................301 656-7600
Jared Bowling, *President*
Richard Clayton, *Chairman*
EMP: 6
SALES: 1MM Privately Held
WEB: www.polychip.com
SIC: 3674 Semiconductors & related devices

(G-4843)
PRIMARY PLASTICS INC
315 Scarborough Dr (13760-5887)
PHONE...............................607 785-4865
Joseph Flannigan, *President*
Brian Flannigan, *Vice Pres*
EMP: 12
SQ FT: 10,000
SALES (est): 1.1MM Privately Held
WEB: www.primaryplastics.com
SIC: 3296 1799 Fiberglass insulation; fiberglass work

(G-4844)
PROGRESSIVE TOOL COMPANY INC
3221 Lawndale St (13760-3593)
PHONE...............................607 748-8294
Fax: 607 748-5683
Gordon E Markoff, *CEO*
Ronald G Markoff, *President*
Sandra J Roloson, *Corp Secy*
Lorraine Markoff, *Vice Pres*
Pat Crowley, *Plant Mgr*
EMP: 35 EST: 1956
SQ FT: 15,900
SALES: 5MM Privately Held
SIC: 3599 Machine shop, jobbing & repair

(G-4845)
PTC PRECISION LLC ✪
3221 Lawndale St (13760-3523)
PHONE...............................607 748-8294
Wayne Keller, *CFO*
EMP: 21 EST: 2017
SALES: 5MM
SALES (corp-wide): 43.3MM Privately Held
SIC: 3545 Precision tools, machinists'
PA: Bam Enterprises, Inc.
2937 Alt Blvd
Grand Island NY 14072
716 773-7634

Esperance
Montgomery County

(G-4846)
US SANDER LLC
4131 Rte 20 (12066)
PHONE...............................518 875-9157
Gary Rudolph, *Mng Member*
David Rudolph,
Peggy Rudolph,
EMP: 9
SQ FT: 10,000
SALES (est): 1.9MM Privately Held
WEB: www.ussander.com
SIC: 3553 Sanding machines, except portable floor sanders: woodworking

(G-4847)
WIND SOLUTIONS LLC
251 County Road 156 (12066)
P.O. Box 57, Sanford NC (27331-0057)
PHONE...............................518 813-8029
Christopher Winslow, *Principal*
▲EMP: 5
SALES (est): 668.3K Privately Held
SIC: 3621 Windmills, electric generating

Fabius
Onondaga County

(G-4848)
VILLAGE WROUGHT IRON INC
7756 Main St (13063-9749)
PHONE...............................315 683-5589
Gary Host, *President*
Adam Host, *Vice Pres*
EMP: 12
SQ FT: 15,000
SALES (est): 1.1MM Privately Held
SIC: 3446 Architectural metalwork

Fairport
Monroe County

(G-4849)
ARCTIC GLACIER MINNESOTA INC
900 Turk Hill Rd (14450-8747)
PHONE...............................585 388-0080
EMP: 39
SALES (corp-wide): 240.7MM Privately Held
SIC: 2097 Manufactured ice
HQ: Arctic Glacier Minnesota Inc.
1601 Halbur Rd
Marshall MN 56258
507 532-5411

(G-4850)
ARCTIC GLACIER PA INC
900 Turk Hill Rd (14450-8747)
PHONE...............................610 494-8200
John Stratman, *Executive*
EMP: 50
SALES (est): 4.7MM
SALES (corp-wide): 1MM Privately Held
SIC: 2097 Manufactured ice
PA: Arctic Glacier Income Fund
625 Henry Ave
Winnipeg MB R3A 0
204 772-2473

(G-4851)
ARCTIC GLACIER TEXAS INC
900 Turk Hill Rd (14450-8747)
PHONE...............................215 283-0326
EMP: 38
SALES (corp-wide): 240.7MM Privately Held
SIC: 2097 Block ice
HQ: Arctic Glacier Texas Inc.
130 E 42nd St
Lubbock TX

(G-4852)
ARCTIC GLACIER USA
900 Turk Hill Rd (14450-8747)
PHONE...............................215 283-0326
Peter Stack, *President*
EMP: 25
SALES (est): 5MM Privately Held
SIC: 2097 Ice cubes

(G-4853)
BERNARD HALL
Also Called: Minuteman Press
10 Perinton Hills Mall (14450-3621)
PHONE...............................585 425-3340
Fax: 585 425-4924
Bernard Hall, *Owner*
EMP: 5
SALES (est): 482.4K Privately Held
SIC: 2752 2791 2789 Commercial printing, lithographic; typesetting; bookbinding & related work

(G-4854)
BREED ENTERPRISES INC
34 Water St (14450-1549)
PHONE...............................585 388-0126
Fax: 585 388-0125
Ronald Reding, *President*
Bruce Caruana, *Vice Pres*
Dave Kirsher, *Manager*
EMP: 5

SALES: 1.1MM Privately Held
WEB: www.bullittmansparts.com
SIC: 3599 Machine shop, jobbing & repair

(G-4855)
CASA LARGA VINEYARDS (PA)
27 Emerald Hill Cir (14450-9504)
P.O. Box 400 (14450-0400)
PHONE...............................585 223-4210
Ann Colaruotolo, *President*
Andrew Colaruotolo, *President*
John Colaruotolo, *Vice Pres*
Maria Digiambattista, *Financial Analy*
EMP: 3
SALES (est): 1.4MM Privately Held
WEB: www.casalarga.com
SIC: 2084 5921 7299 Wines; wine; banquet hall facilities

(G-4856)
CASA LARGA VINEYARDS
2287 Turk Hill Rd (14450-9579)
P.O. Box 400 (14450-0400)
PHONE...............................585 223-4210
Fax: 585 223-8899
John Colaruotolo, *Facilities Mgr*
Andrea Oneill, *Opers Staff*
Ann Colaruottolo, *Manager*
EMP: 7
SALES (corp-wide): 1.6MM Privately Held
WEB: www.casalarga.com
SIC: 2084 Wines
PA: Casa Larga Vineyards
27 Emerald Hill Cir
Fairport NY 14450
585 223-4210

(G-4857)
CORNING TROPEL CORPORATION
60 Oconnor Rd (14450-1328)
PHONE...............................585 377-3200
Fax: 585 377-1966
Curt Weinstein, *Ch of Bd*
John Burning, *President*
Dan Gales, *Mfg Mgr*
Kelly Scott, *Purchasing*
Lou Lombardo, *Engineer*
EMP: 195
SQ FT: 100,000
SALES (est): 28.6MM
SALES (corp-wide): 9.3B Publicly Held
WEB: www.tropel.com
SIC: 3841 3827 3229 Ophthalmic instruments & apparatus; optical instruments & lenses; pressed & blown glass
PA: Corning Incorporated
1 Riverfront Plz
Corning NY 14831
607 974-9000

(G-4858)
D BAG LADY INC
183 Perinton Pkwy (14450-9104)
PHONE...............................585 425-8095
Debra Perry, *President*
Rick Perry, *QC Mgr*
EMP: 8
SQ FT: 8,500
SALES (est): 1MM Privately Held
WEB: www.dbaglady.com
SIC: 3081 Unsupported plastics film & sheet

(G-4859)
DAVIS INTERNATIONAL INC
388 Mason Rd (14450-9561)
PHONE...............................585 421-8175
Timothy M McGraw, *President*
James R Davis, *Principal*
Ryan McGraw, *Sales Staff*
Lynn Davis, *Manager*
EMP: 7
SQ FT: 5,000
SALES (est): 770K Privately Held
WEB: www.davisinternational.net
SIC: 3555 5084 Printing trades machinery; printing trades machinery, equipment & supplies

(G-4860)
DUNDEE FOODS LLC (PA)
Also Called: Dundeespirits
815 Whitney Rd W (14450-1030)
PHONE...............................585 377-7700

Fax: 607 243-3877
Giovanni Lidestri, *CEO*
Robyn Ott, *QC Mgr*
Holly Feily, *Accounts Mgr*
Linda Vance, *Regl Sales Mgr*
Keith Silsbee, *Manager*
▲EMP: 19
SALES (est): 2.9MM Privately Held
SIC: 2099 Food preparations

(G-4861)
EAST PATTERN & MODEL CORP (PA)
75 N Main St (14450-1544)
PHONE...............................585 461-3240
Fax: 585 461-0798
Warren H Kellogg, *President*
Mark Landers, *General Mgr*
Lisa Smyder, *Opers Mgr*
Michelle E Kellogg, *Treasurer*
EMP: 26
SQ FT: 15,000
SALES: 3MM Privately Held
SIC: 3544 3089 3365 3275 Industrial molds; injection molding of plastics; aluminum foundries; gypsum products

(G-4862)
HANDONE STUDIOS INC
388 Mason Rd (14450-9561)
PHONE...............................585 421-8175
Fax: 585 421-8707
Jim Davis, *President*
Chris Stewart, *Opers Mgr*
Anatol Topolewski, *Purch Mgr*
Lynn Davis, *Office Mgr*
EMP: 9
SQ FT: 6,000
SALES: 300K Privately Held
SIC: 2759 Screen printing

(G-4863)
IRON SMOKE WHISKEY LLC
111 Parce Ave Ste 5 (14450-1467)
PHONE...............................585 388-7584
Thomas J Brunett, *President*
EMP: 6 EST: 2015
SALES (est): 566.5K Privately Held
SIC: 2085 Bourbon whiskey

(G-4864)
J & N COMPUTER SERVICES INC
1387 Fairport Rd Ste 900j (14450-2087)
PHONE...............................585 388-8780
Fax: 585 388-8783
Nancy E Jacobsen, *Ch of Bd*
Jerold Jacobsen, *General Mgr*
Jonathon Hull, *Opers Mgr*
Matt Jacobus, *Manager*
Justin Gonzales, *Consultant*
EMP: 11
SQ FT: 3,000
SALES (est): 4.1MM Privately Held
SIC: 3571 5734 Electronic computers; computer & software stores

(G-4865)
JASCO HEAT TREATING INC
75 Macedon Center Rd (14450-9763)
P.O. Box 60620, Rochester (14606-0620)
PHONE...............................585 388-0071
Eugine W Baldino, *CEO*
Diane Simons, *CFO*
Ed Bessette, *Human Resources*
Bryan Jerman, *Marketing Staff*
Rick Hook, *Supervisor*
EMP: 23
SQ FT: 50,000
SALES: 5.8MM Privately Held
WEB: www.jascotools.com
SIC: 3398 Metal heat treating

(G-4866)
LAHR RECYCLING & RESINS INC
Also Called: Lahr Plastics
164 Daley Rd (14450-9524)
PHONE...............................585 425-8608
Fax: 585 425-2849
Craig A Lahr, *President*
EMP: 15
SQ FT: 20,000

Fairport - Monroe County (G-4867)

SALES (est): 1.9MM **Privately Held**
SIC: 3087 Custom compound purchased resins

(G-4867)
LIDESTRI FOODS INC (PA)
Also Called: Lidestri Food and Drink
815 Whitney Rd W (14450-1030)
PHONE.....................585 377-7700
John Lidestri, *CEO*
Phil Viruso, *General Mgr*
Joe Ferrigno, *Principal*
Robert Schiefer, *Principal*
Edward P Salzano, *COO*
◆ **EMP:** 400
SQ FT: 260,000
SALES (est): 247.4MM **Privately Held**
WEB: www.francescorinaldi.com
SIC: 3221 2033 Bottles for packing, bottling & canning: glass; canned fruits & specialties; spaghetti & other pasta sauce: packaged in cans, jars, etc.

(G-4868)
LMG NATIONAL PUBLISHING INC (HQ)
350 Willowbrook Office Pa (14450-4222)
P.O. Box 580, Middletown (10940-0580)
PHONE.....................585 598-6874
Leslie Hinton, *Ch of Bd*
EMP: 26
SALES (est): 13.1MM
SALES (corp-wide): 1.2B **Publicly Held**
SIC: 2711 2752 Newspapers; commercial printing, lithographic
PA: New Media Investment Group Inc.
1345 Avenue Of The Americ
New York NY 10105
212 479-3160

(G-4869)
MASTERCRAFT DECORATORS INC
Also Called: Caldwell Cor
320 Macedon Center Rd (14450-9759)
PHONE.....................585 223-5150
James Yonosko, *President*
Rosemary Smith, *Vice Pres*
Christine Pollock, *Controller*
Tim Bayer, *Credit Mgr*
Ben McAllister, *CTO*
◆ **EMP:** 40
SQ FT: 6,000
SALES (est): 5.5MM
SALES (corp-wide): 3.6MM **Privately Held**
WEB: www.guildlines.com
SIC: 2759 Screen printing
PA: Zenan Custom Cresting Inc
430 Flint Rd
North York ON M3J 2
416 736-6652

(G-4870)
MOONLIGHT CREAMERY
36 West Ave (14450-2158)
PHONE.....................585 223-0880
Hiedi Grenik, *Owner*
EMP: 6
SALES (est): 572.1K **Privately Held**
SIC: 2024 Ice cream & frozen desserts

(G-4871)
MURPHY MANUFACTURING CO INC
38 West Ave (14450-2159)
P.O. Box 119 (14450-0119)
PHONE.....................585 223-0100
Fax: 585 223-0101
Gordon D Murphy Sr, *President*
Donna Faust, *Database Admin*
▲ **EMP:** 5 **EST:** 1946
SQ FT: 6,500
SALES (est): 360K **Privately Held**
WEB: www.murphymanufacturing.com
SIC: 3451 3491 Screw machine products; industrial valves

(G-4872)
OMEGA TOOL MEASURING MCHS INC (PA)
101 Perinton Pkwy (14450-9104)
PHONE.....................585 598-7800
Fax: 585 425-7542
Michael R Nuccitelli, *CEO*

Mark Higgins, *Exec VP*
Ronald S Ricotta, *Vice Pres*
Jay Nuccitelli, *VP Opers*
Bash Nanayakkara, *Project Mgr*
▲ **EMP:** 35
SQ FT: 100,000
SALES: 30MM **Privately Held**
WEB: www.parlec.com
SIC: 3541 3545 Numerically controlled metal cutting machine tools; machine tool accessories

(G-4873)
ORACLE AMERICA INC
Sun Microsystems
345 Woodcliff Dr Ste 1 (14450-4210)
PHONE.....................585 317-4648
Fax: 585 385-8754
Fritz Rupp, *Engineer*
Kevin Regan, *Manager*
Jeff Barteld, *Director*
EMP: 55
SALES (corp-wide): 37.7B **Publicly Held**
SIC: 3571 Minicomputers
HQ: Oracle America, Inc.
500 Oracle Pkwy
Redwood City CA 94065
650 506-7000

(G-4874)
PARKER-HANNIFIN CORPORATION
Also Called: Chomerics Div
83 Estates Dr W (14450-8425)
PHONE.....................585 425-7000
Patrick Malone, *CEO*
Brian Smith, *QC Mgr*
Duane Potter, *Manager*
EMP: 126
SALES (corp-wide): 12B **Publicly Held**
SIC: 3594 Fluid power pumps & motors
PA: Parker-Hannifin Corporation
6035 Parkland Blvd
Cleveland OH 44124
216 896-3000

(G-4875)
PENNSAUKEN PACKING COMPANY LLC
815 Whitney Rd W (14450-1030)
PHONE.....................585 377-7700
EMP: 5
SALES (est): 336.6K
SALES (corp-wide): 247.4MM **Privately Held**
SIC: 3221 Food containers, glass
PA: Lidestri Foods, Inc.
815 Whitney Rd W
Fairport NY 14450
585 377-7700

(G-4876)
PERFORMANCE DESIGNED BY PETERS
Also Called: Poerformance Design
7 Duxbury Hts (14450-3331)
PHONE.....................585 223-9062
Peter R Geib, *President*
Todd Geib, *Vice Pres*
EMP: 19
SALES: 5MM **Privately Held**
SIC: 3714 Motor vehicle parts & accessories

(G-4877)
PRINTER COMPONENTS INC (HQ)
100 Photikon Dr Ste 2 (14450-8430)
PHONE.....................585 924-5190
Richard Dipasquale, *Vice Pres*
Rick Dipasquale, *Vice Pres*
◆ **EMP:** 9
SQ FT: 16,000
SALES (est): 1.5MM
SALES (corp-wide): 83.7MM **Privately Held**
WEB: www.pcivictor.com
SIC: 3861 5112 3955 5999 Printing equipment, photographic; laserjet supplies; print cartridges for laser & other computer printers; photocopy machines; printers, computer

PA: Floturn, Inc.
4236 Thunderbird Ln
West Chester OH 45014
513 860-8040

(G-4878)
QIOPTIQ INC (DH)
78 Schuyler Baldwin Dr (14450-9100)
PHONE.....................585 223-2370
William Gilman, *Ch of Bd*
Herv Passot, *Exec VP*
Bernd Schnakenberg, *Exec VP*
Steve Shaw, *Exec VP*
Teow Tzing, *Exec VP*
▲ **EMP:** 45
SQ FT: 41,000
SALES (est): 4.1MM **Privately Held**
SIC: 3826 3827 Analytical optical instruments; optical instruments & lenses
HQ: Qioptic North America Inc
78 Schuyler Baldwin Dr
Fairport NY 14450
585 223-2370

(G-4879)
QUALITROL COMPANY LLC (HQ)
Also Called: Otiwti
1385 Fairport Rd (14450-1399)
PHONE.....................586 643-3717
Fax: 585 377-0220
Ronald Meyer, *President*
John Piper, *President*
Richard M Kloc, *General Mgr*
Jay Cunningham, *Vice Pres*
Brian English, *Vice Pres*
▲ **EMP:** 111
SQ FT: 50,000
SALES (est): 129.2MM
SALES (corp-wide): 6.2B **Publicly Held**
WEB: www.qualitrolcorp.com
SIC: 3825 Instruments for measuring electrical quantities
PA: Fortive Corporation
6920 Seaway Blvd
Everett WA 98203
425 446-5000

(G-4880)
QUALTECH TOOL & MACHINE INC
1000 Turk Hill Rd Ste 292 (14450-8755)
P.O. Box 356 (14450-0356)
PHONE.....................585 223-9227
Fax: 585 223-4348
Anita Palmer, *President*
Richard T Palmer III, *Vice Pres*
EMP: 10
SQ FT: 10,500
SALES (est): 1.4MM **Privately Held**
SIC: 3599 Machine shop, jobbing & repair

(G-4881)
R STEINER TECHNOLOGIES INC
180 Perinton Pkwy (14450-9107)
PHONE.....................585 425-5912
Rudolph Steiner, *CEO*
Andy Nolan, *President*
Tyler Nolan, *Marketing Staff*
EMP: 20
SQ FT: 12,000
SALES (est): 1.5MM **Privately Held**
WEB: www.steinertechnologies.com
SIC: 3541 Machine tools, metal cutting type

(G-4882)
SELBY MARKETING ASSOCIATES INC (PA)
Also Called: Direct 2 Market Solutions
1387 Fairport Rd Ste 800 (14450-2002)
PHONE.....................585 377-0750
Fax: 585 377-0763
Richard L Selby, *President*
Trina Selby, *Manager*
EMP: 15
SQ FT: 6,000
SALES: 3MM **Privately Held**
SIC: 2741 7319 Miscellaneous publishing; media buying service

(G-4883)
SENDEC CORP (DH)
Also Called: API Technologies
72 Perinton Pkwy (14450-9107)
PHONE.....................585 425-3390
Fax: 585 425-3392

Kenton W Fiske, *President*
Tom Tette, *CFO*
▲ **EMP:** 140
SQ FT: 86,000
SALES (est): 19.1MM
SALES (corp-wide): 303.2MM **Privately Held**
WEB: www.sendec.com
SIC: 3679 Electronic circuits
HQ: Api Technologies Corp.
400 Nickerson Rd
Marlborough MA 01752
855 294-3800

(G-4884)
SENDEC CORP
Sendec Corp Product Division
151 Perinton Pkwy (14450-9104)
PHONE.....................585 425-5965
David Sestito, *General Mgr*
EMP: 22
SALES (corp-wide): 303.2MM **Privately Held**
WEB: www.sendec.com
SIC: 3679 Microwave components
HQ: Sendec Corp.
72 Perinton Pkwy
Fairport NY 14450
585 425-3390

(G-4885)
SENECA TEC INC
73 Country Corner Ln (14450-3034)
PHONE.....................585 381-2645
Fax: 585 381-6308
John Kidd, *President*
James Kidd, *Vice Pres*
Art Trimble, *Vice Pres*
EMP: 9
SQ FT: 1,500
SALES (est): 765.7K **Privately Held**
WEB: www.senecatec.com
SIC: 3861 3841 Photographic processing equipment & chemicals; surgical & medical instruments

(G-4886)
SIEMENS PRODUCT LIFE MGMT SFTW
345 Woodcliff Dr (14450-4210)
PHONE.....................585 389-8699
EMP: 34
SALES (corp-wide): 89.6B **Privately Held**
SIC: 7372 Business oriented computer software
HQ: Siemens Product Lifecycle Management Software Inc.
5800 Granite Pkwy Ste 600
Plano TX 75024
972 987-3000

(G-4887)
STEINER TECHNOLOGIES INC
180 Perinton Pkwy (14450-9107)
PHONE.....................585 425-5910
Fax: 585 425-5913
Andrew Nolan, *President*
Ryan Nolan, *Opers Mgr*
EMP: 19 **EST:** 2008
SALES (est): 3.9MM **Privately Held**
SIC: 3545 Cutting tools for machine tools

(G-4888)
STREAMLINE PRECISION INC
205 Turk Hill Park (14450-8728)
PHONE.....................585 421-9050
Kelly Palladino, *President*
Robert Levitsky, *Vice Pres*
Tom Gore, *Engineer*
EMP: 8
SQ FT: 1,000
SALES (est): 926.4K **Privately Held**
SIC: 3545 Precision tools, machinists'

(G-4889)
STREAMLINE PRECISION INC
Also Called: Steamline Machine
1000 Turk Hill Rd Ste 205 (14450-8755)
PHONE.....................585 421-9050
Fax: 585 421-9198
Robert Levitsky, *President*
EMP: 6
SALES (est): 650K **Privately Held**
SIC: 3545 Machine tool accessories

GEOGRAPHIC SECTION

Falconer - Chautauqua County (G-4915)

(G-4890)
SUHOR INDUSTRIES INC (PA)
Also Called: Si Funeral Services
72 Oconnor Rd (14450-1328)
PHONE.....................585 377-5100
Joe Suhor, *President*
▲ **EMP:** 14
SQ FT: 4,250
SALES (est): 2.2MM **Privately Held**
WEB: www.wilbertservices.com
SIC: 3272 Burial vaults, concrete or precast terrazzo

(G-4891)
THALES LASER SA
78 Schuyler Baldwin Dr (14450-9100)
PHONE.....................585 223-2370
Ariane Andreani, *General Mgr*
Joe Blackie, *Senior Buyer*
EMP: 65
SALES (est): 3.4MM **Privately Held**
SIC: 3674 Semiconductors & related devices

(G-4892)
VIDEK INC
1387 Fairport Rd 1000c (14450-2004)
PHONE.....................585 377-0377
Thomas Slechta, *President*
Moreen Jorjensen, *Controller*
EMP: 25
SQ FT: 14,861
SALES (est): 5.5MM **Privately Held**
WEB: www.videk.com/
SIC: 3827 3829 Optical test & inspection equipment; measuring & controlling devices

(G-4893)
VOLT TEK INC
111 Parce Ave (14450-1467)
PHONE.....................585 377-2050
Fax: 585 377-2654
Steve Holland, *President*
Mike Buczko, *Manager*
▲ **EMP:** 15
SALES (est): 1.4MM **Privately Held**
WEB: www.volttek.com
SIC: 3644 Insulators & insulation materials, electrical

(G-4894)
WORKPLACE INTERIORS LLC
400 Packetts Lndg (14450-1576)
PHONE.....................585 425-7420
Liz Kiefer, *Opers Mgr*
Scott Maccaull, *Mng Member*
EMP: 13 EST: 2015
SQ FT: 6,000
SALES: 8.9MM **Privately Held**
SIC: 2522 5021 Office furniture, except wood; office furniture

(G-4895)
XEROX CORPORATION
1387 Fairport Rd Ste 200 (14450-2003)
PHONE.....................585 425-6100
Fax: 585 383-7517
Tim Conlin, *Principal*
Chris Snyder, *Manager*
EMP: 75
SQ FT: 1,485
SALES (corp-wide): 10.7B **Publicly Held**
WEB: www.xerox.com
SIC: 3861 Photographic equipment & supplies
PA: Xerox Corporation
201 Merritt 7
Norwalk CT 06851
203 968-3000

Falconer
Chautauqua County

(G-4896)
AJ GENCO MCH SP MCHY RDOUT SVC
Also Called: A J Gnco Mch Shp/Mchnery Rdout
235 Carter St (14733-1409)
PHONE.....................716 664-4925
Anthony J Genco, *President*
EMP: 10

SQ FT: 23,940
SALES: 610K **Privately Held**
SIC: 3599 7692 3444 Machine shop, jobbing & repair; welding repair; sheet metal-work

(G-4897)
ALLIED INSPECTION SERVICES LLC
4 Carter St (14733-1406)
PHONE.....................716 489-3199
Scott M Lynn, *Director*
EMP: 13
SALES (est): 2MM **Privately Held**
SIC: 3569 Sprinkler systems, fire: automatic

(G-4898)
ARCONIC INC
Also Called: Alcoa
2632 S Work St Ste 24 (14733-1705)
PHONE.....................716 358-6451
Dave Groetsch, *Branch Mgr*
EMP: 8
SALES (corp-wide): 12.3B **Publicly Held**
SIC: 3542 High energy rate metal forming machines
PA: Arconic Inc.
390 Park Ave
New York NY 10022
212 836-2758

(G-4899)
BARTON TOOL INC
1864 Lyndon Blvd (14733-1735)
P.O. Box 17 (14733-0017)
PHONE.....................716 665-2801
Fax: 716 665-4713
Jo Anne Barton, *President*
John Barton, *Vice Pres*
Joanne Barton, *Admin Sec*
EMP: 7
SQ FT: 20,000
SALES (est): 1.1MM **Privately Held**
WEB: www.bartontool.com
SIC: 3089 3599 Injection molding of plastics; machine shop, jobbing & repair

(G-4900)
CHAUTAUQUA SIGN CO INC
2164 Allen Street Ext (14733-1703)
PHONE.....................716 665-2222
Gregory J Winter, *President*
EMP: 8
SALES (est): 796.2K **Privately Held**
WEB: www.chautauquasportshalloffame.org
SIC: 3993 Signs & advertising specialties

(G-4901)
CPI OF FALCONER INC
1890 Lyndon Blvd (14733-1731)
PHONE.....................716 664-4444
EMP: 22
SQ FT: 20,000
SALES (est): 266.7K **Privately Held**
SIC: 3089 3965 Mfg Plastic Products Mfg Fasteners/Buttons/Pins

(G-4902)
ELLISON BRONZE INC
125 W Main St (14733-1698)
PHONE.....................716 665-6522
Fax: 716 665-5552
Peter Stark, *Ch of Bd*
Mark Graves, *President*
Billy Emerson, *Vice Pres*
Roger Overend, *Vice Pres*
Marty Ericsson, *VP Finance*
◆ **EMP:** 59 EST: 1913
SQ FT: 65,000
SALES (est): 12.1MM **Privately Held**
WEB: www.ellisonbronze.com
SIC: 3442 Metal doors, sash & trim

(G-4903)
EMC FINTECH
1984 Allen Street Ext (14733-1717)
PHONE.....................716 488-9071
Eric Corey, *Vice Pres*
EMP: 11
SALES (est): 900K **Privately Held**
SIC: 3552 3585 Dyeing, drying & finishing machinery & equipment; air conditioning equipment, complete

(G-4904)
FALCON CHAIR AND TABLE INC
121 S Work St (14733-1433)
P.O. Box 8 (14733-0008)
PHONE.....................716 664-7136
Fax: 716 664-3157
Peter Scheira, *President*
Gary Henry, *Vice Pres*
Sue Freeburg, *Bookkeeper*
Joan Erickson, *Admin Sec*
EMP: 49
SQ FT: 23,000
SALES (est): 4.7MM **Privately Held**
SIC: 2511 Dining room furniture: wood

(G-4905)
FALCONER ELECTRONICS INC (PA)
421 W Everett St (14733-1647)
PHONE.....................716 665-4176
Fax: 716 665-2017
Roger E Hall, *President*
Janine Hall, *Vice Pres*
Kurt Sturzenbecker, *Plant Mgr*
EMP: 61
SQ FT: 20,000
SALES (est): 10.8MM **Privately Held**
WEB: www.falconer-electronics.com
SIC: 3672 5065 Printed circuit boards; electronic parts

(G-4906)
FALCONER PRINTING & DESIGN INC
Also Called: Jamestown Envelope
66 E Main St (14733-1390)
P.O. Box 262 (14733-0262)
PHONE.....................716 665-2121
Fax: 716 665-6328
Stephen E Roach, *President*
James M Roach, *Vice Pres*
Karen Mazzu, *Bookkeeper*
Julie Norblund, *Product Mgr*
Misty Johnson, *Marketing Staff*
EMP: 17
SQ FT: 12,000
SALES (est): 2.1MM **Privately Held**
WEB: www.falconerprinting.com
SIC: 2752 2735 5112 2791 Commercial printing, lithographic; commercial printing, offset; photo-offset printing; photographic studio, commercial; office supplies; typesetting; commercial printing

(G-4907)
HANSON AGGREGATES EAST LLC
4419 S 9 Mile Rd (14733)
PHONE.....................716 372-1574
Mike Shumack, *Manager*
Robert Wilson, *Supervisor*
EMP: 17
SALES (corp-wide): 16B **Privately Held**
SIC: 3273 Ready-mixed concrete
HQ: Hanson Aggregates East Llc
3131 Rdu Center Dr
Morrisville NC 27560
919 380-2500

(G-4908)
HANSON SIGN SCREEN PRCESS CORP
Also Called: Hanson Sign Companies
82 Carter St (14733-1406)
PHONE.....................716 661-3900
Edward Sullivan, *CEO*
Shelly Cooper, *Business Mgr*
Patricia Reynolds, *Purch Mgr*
EMP: 34 EST: 1949
SQ FT: 25,000
SALES: 4.6MM **Privately Held**
WEB: www.hansonsign.com
SIC: 3993 Signs, not made in custom sign painting shops

(G-4909)
INSCAPE (NEW YORK) INC (HQ)
Also Called: Inscape Archtectural Interiors
221 Lister Ave 1 (14733-1459)
PHONE.....................716 665-6210
Rod Turgeon, *CEO*
Craig Dunlop, *Ch of Bd*
Nic Balderi, *Vice Pres*
Gwen Keanary, *Safety Mgr*
Stephen Holland, *Purch Mgr*

◆ **EMP:** 82
SALES (est): 20.7MM
SALES (corp-wide): 71.5MM **Privately Held**
SIC: 2542 3442 3441 3449 Partitions for floor attachment, prefabricated: except wood; metal doors; fabricated structural metal; custom roll formed products;
PA: Inscape Corporation
67 Toll Rd
Holland Landing ON L9N 1
905 836-7676

(G-4910)
INSCAPE INC
221 Lister Ave (14733-1459)
PHONE.....................716 665-6210
Aziz Hirji, *CFO*
EMP: 40
SQ FT: 130,000
SALES (est): 1.8MM **Privately Held**
SIC: 2522 2542 Office furniture, except wood; partitions & fixtures, except wood

(G-4911)
JAMES TOWN MACADAM INC
1946 New York Ave (14733-1739)
PHONE.....................716 665-4504
Fax: 716 665-6040
Jim Ells, *Principal*
Mike Wellman, *Manager*
EMP: 56
SQ FT: 2,000
SALES (est): 5.2MM **Privately Held**
SIC: 3273 Ready-mixed concrete

(G-4912)
JAMESTOWN CONTAINER CORP (PA)
14 Deming Dr (14733-1697)
P.O. Box 8, Jamestown (14702-0008)
PHONE.....................716 665-4623
Fax: 716 665-2954
Bruce Janowsky, *Ch of Bd*
Larry Hudson, *General Mgr*
Dick Weimer, *Corp Secy*
Richards Emmerick, *Vice Pres*
Joseph R Palmeri, *Vice Pres*
▼ **EMP:** 110 EST: 1956
SQ FT: 100,000
SALES (est): 136.3MM **Privately Held**
WEB: www.jamestowncontainer.com
SIC: 2653 3086 Corrugated & solid fiber boxes; packaging & shipping materials, foamed plastic

(G-4913)
JAMESTOWN IRON WORKS INC
2022 Allen Street Ext (14733-1793)
PHONE.....................716 665-2818
Fax: 716 665-2851
David W Maher, *President*
Michelle Maher, *Manager*
EMP: 16 EST: 1881
SQ FT: 3,600
SALES (est): 3.9MM **Privately Held**
SIC: 3321 3599 Ductile iron castings; machine shop, jobbing & repair

(G-4914)
LANDPRO EQUIPMENT LLC
1756 Lindquist Dr (14733-9710)
PHONE.....................716 665-3110
Tracy Buck, *President*
Ryan Payment, *Vice Pres*
Jonathon Lindstrom, *Sales Mgr*
Cynthia Fiore, *Manager*
EMP: 300
SALES (est): 40MM **Privately Held**
SIC: 3523 Farm machinery & equipment

(G-4915)
MONOFRAX LLC
1870 New York Ave (14733-1797)
PHONE.....................716 483-7200
Bill Andrews, *President*
Sarah Callen, *Controller*
Daryl Clendenen, *Marketing Mgr*
Alan Lindquist, *Manager*
Rowland Crosby, *Executive*
◆ **EMP:** 250
SQ FT: 300,000

Falconer - Chautauqua County (G-4916)

SALES (est): 54.5MM
SALES (corp-wide): 940.5K **Privately Held**
WEB: www.monofrax.com
SIC: 3297 Nonclay refractories
PA: Callista Holdings Gmbh & Co. Kg
Steinstr. 48
Munchen 81667
892 314-1600

(G-4916)
RAND MACHINE PRODUCTS INC (PA)
2072 Allen Street Ext (14733-1709)
P.O. Box 72 (14733-0072)
PHONE..................716 665-5217
Fax: 716 665-3374
Herman C Ruhlman Jr, *President*
Chad Ruhlman, *Exec VP*
Jason Ruhlman, *Vice Pres*
Tiffany Joyner, *Safety Dir*
Carl Hornstrom, *Plant Mgr*
EMP: 51 EST: 1964
SQ FT: 15,000
SALES (est): 22.7MM **Privately Held**
WEB: www.randmachine.com
SIC: 3544 3494 3743 3599 Special dies, tools, jigs & fixtures; special dies & tools; valves & pipe fittings; industrial locomotives & parts; custom machinery

(G-4917)
RAPID REMOVAL LLC
1599 Route 394 (14733-9716)
P.O. Box 498 (14733-0498)
PHONE..................716 665-4663
Brian Hasson,
EMP: 10
SALES (est): 512.5K **Privately Held**
SIC: 2851 Removers & cleaners

(G-4918)
REYNOLDS PACKAGING MCHY INC
Also Called: Csi
2632 S Work St Ste 24 (14733-1705)
PHONE..................716 358-6451
Fax: 716 358-6459
Rochard Kelson, *Exec VP*
Valeria Muka, *Purch Mgr*
Joe Schrecengost, *Purch Mgr*
Angela Hymen, *Engineer*
Pat Depas, *Design Engr*
EMP: 55 **Privately Held**
SIC: 3565 3643 3466 Canning machinery, food; current-carrying wiring devices; crowns & closures
HQ: Reynolds Packaging Machinery Inc.
2632 S Work St Ste 24
Falconer NY 14733

(G-4919)
SKF USA INC
Also Called: SKF Aeroengine North America
1 Maroco St (14733-9705)
P.O. Box 263 (14733-0263)
PHONE..................716 661-2869
Jerry Lindsey, *Mfg Staff*
Brandon Green, *Engineer*
Joseph Sienicki, *Engineer*
Wayne Wilson, *Engineer*
Heather Willie, *Accountant*
EMP: 61
SALES (corp-wide): 546.3MM **Privately Held**
WEB: www.skfusa.com
SIC: 3562 3769 Ball bearings & parts; guided missile & space vehicle parts & auxiliary equipment
HQ: Skf Usa Inc.
890 Forty Foot Rd
Lansdale PA 19446
267 436-6000

(G-4920)
SKF USA INC
Also Called: SKF Aeroengine North America
1 Maroco St (14733-9705)
PHONE..................716 661-2600
Mark Ragen, *Senior Engr*
Steve Koehler, *Branch Mgr*
Pascal Wanderoild, *Manager*
Eugene Olofson, *Associate*
EMP: 61

SALES (corp-wide): 546.3MM **Privately Held**
WEB: www.skfusa.com
SIC: 3562 3769 Ball bearings & parts; guided missile & space vehicle parts & auxiliary equipment
HQ: Skf Usa Inc.
890 Forty Foot Rd
Lansdale PA 19446
267 436-6000

(G-4921)
STUART MOLD & MANUFACTURING
560 N Work St (14733-1115)
PHONE..................716 488-9765
Fax: 716 488-9767
Randall Stuart, *President*
Charles Stuart, *Vice Pres*
Mike Malinoski, *Opers Mgr*
Tina Himes, *Office Mgr*
EMP: 12
SQ FT: 10,000
SALES (est): 1.3MM **Privately Held**
WEB: www.stumold.com
SIC: 3089 Injection molding of plastics

(G-4922)
STUART TOOL & DIE INC
600 N Work St (14733-1117)
PHONE..................716 488-1975
Fax: 716 488-1977
Ronald Rothleder, *President*
Patrick J Degnan, *Vice Pres*
Corinne Beckstrom, *Bookkeeper*
Dawn Johnson, *Office Mgr*
EMP: 40
SQ FT: 10,000
SALES: 9MM **Privately Held**
WEB: www.stu-t-d.com
SIC: 3544 Industrial molds; special dies & tools; jigs & fixtures

(G-4923)
TRUCK-LITE CO LLC
310 E Elmwood Ave (14733-1421)
PHONE..................716 665-2614
Chris Richardson, *Regional Mgr*
Greg Pond, *Materials Mgr*
Cindy Franklin, *Hum Res Coord*
Greg Certo, *Manager*
Brian Melquist, *MIS Mgr*
EMP: 20 **Privately Held**
WEB: www.truck-lite.com
SIC: 3647 3648 Vehicular lighting equipment; lighting equipment
PA: Truck-Lite Co., Llc
310 E Elmwood Ave
Falconer NY 14733

(G-4924)
TRUCK-LITE CO LLC (PA)
310 E Elmwood Ave (14733-1421)
PHONE..................716 665-6214
Fax: 716 665-4825
Brian Kupchella, *President*
Jeff Church, *COO*
Chris Ross, *Project Engr*
Robert Reed, *Manager*
Donald Alexander, *CIO*
◆ EMP: 245
SALES (est): 500MM **Privately Held**
SIC: 3647 Vehicular lighting equipment

(G-4925)
TRUCK-LITE SUB INC
310 E Elmwood Ave (14733-1421)
PHONE..................800 888-7095
Fax: 716 665-6403
EMP: 5 EST: 2015
SALES (est): 126K **Privately Held**
SIC: 3799 Transportation equipment

Far Rockaway
Queens County

(G-4926)
BUSINESS ADVISORY SERVICES
Also Called: Universal Water Technology
1104 Bay 25th St (11691-1749)
PHONE..................718 337-3740
Michael Walfish, *President*
EMP: 5

SALES: 750K **Privately Held**
SIC: 3589 Water treatment equipment, industrial

(G-4927)
EAZY LOCKS LLC
1914 Mott Ave (11691-4102)
PHONE..................718 327-7770
Carl Roberts, *CEO*
EMP: 6
SQ FT: 1,000
SALES: 304.2K **Privately Held**
SIC: 3429 Locks or lock sets

(G-4928)
EMPIRE PUBLISHING INC
Also Called: West End Journal
1525 Central Ave Ste 1 (11691-4020)
PHONE..................516 829-4000
Fax: 516 829-4776
Jerome Lippman, *President*
EMP: 15
SQ FT: 2,000
SALES (est): 870.4K **Privately Held**
SIC: 2711 Newspapers: publishing only, not printed on site

(G-4929)
FAR ROCKAWAY DRUGS INC
Also Called: Ocean Park Drugs & Surgical
1727 Seagirt Blvd (11691-4513)
PHONE..................718 471-2500
Fax: 718 471-0840
Russell Shvartsshteyn, *President*
Steven Blick, *Vice Pres*
EMP: 16
SQ FT: 4,000
SALES (est): 3.1MM **Privately Held**
WEB: www.mynucare.com
SIC: 3842 5912 Surgical appliances & supplies; drug stores & proprietary stores

(G-4930)
J P R PHARMACY INC
Also Called: Vista Pharmacy & Surgical
529 Beach 20th St (11691-3645)
PHONE..................718 327-0600
Fax: 718 327-8019
Jeffrey Rosenberg, *President*
Russell Shvartsshteyn, *Vice Pres*
EMP: 11
SQ FT: 800
SALES: 4.6MM **Privately Held**
SIC: 3842 5912 Surgical appliances & supplies; drug stores & proprietary stores

(G-4931)
ROCKAWAY STAIRS LTD
1011 Bay 24th St (11691-1801)
PHONE..................718 945-0047
Nollah Pastor, *President*
EMP: 5
SALES (est): 334.7K **Privately Held**
SIC: 2431 Stair railings, wood

Farmingdale
Nassau County

(G-4932)
A & J MACHINE & WELDING INC
6040 New Hwy (11735)
PHONE..................631 845-7586
Ahalya Narine, *Manager*
EMP: 15 **Privately Held**
SIC: 7692 Welding repair
PA: A & J Machine & Welding Inc.
8776 130th St
Jamaica NY

(G-4933)
A C ENVELOPE INC
51 Heisser Ln Ste B (11735-3321)
PHONE..................516 420-0646
Bob Kuhlmann, *President*
William Bogue, *Corp Secy*
EMP: 5
SALES: 500K **Privately Held**
SIC: 3555 5112 2759 2752 Presses, envelope, printing; envelopes; commercial printing; commercial printing, lithographic

(G-4934)
A R V PRECISION MFG INC
60 Baiting Place Rd Ste B (11735-6228)
PHONE..................631 293-9643
Fax: 631 293-9166
Fred Freyre, *President*
EMP: 5
SQ FT: 2,000
SALES (est): 899.8K **Privately Held**
SIC: 3679 3599 3089 Electronic circuits; machine shop, jobbing & repair; injection molded finished plastic products

(G-4935)
AAA CATALYTIC RECYCLING INC
345 Eastern Pkwy (11735-2713)
PHONE..................631 920-7944
Drew Vecchionem, *CEO*
▲ EMP: 10 EST: 2011
SALES: 10MM **Privately Held**
SIC: 3339 Platinum group metal refining (primary)

(G-4936)
ABBE LABORATORIES INC
1095 Broadhollow Rd Ste E (11735-4815)
PHONE..................631 756-2223
Eleanor Posner, *President*
Robert Posner, *Corp Secy*
EMP: 10
SALES (est): 1.8MM **Privately Held**
WEB: www.abbelabs.com
SIC: 2844 5122 Cosmetic preparations; cosmetics

(G-4937)
ADVANCED AEROSPACE MACHINING
154 Rome St (11735-6609)
PHONE..................631 694-7745
Bruce Hambrecht, *President*
EMP: 6
SQ FT: 4,000
SALES (est): 655.9K **Privately Held**
SIC: 3599 Custom machinery

(G-4938)
AFCO SYSTEMS INC
Also Called: Afco Modular Enclosure Systems
200 Finn Ct Ste 1 (11735-1119)
PHONE..................631 249-9441
Fax: 516 249-9450
Michael Mallia, *CEO*
Gerard Becker, *President*
Lawrence Mallia, *Exec VP*
Graham Leonard, *Vice Pres*
Joe Busini, *Plant Mgr*
EMP: 102
SQ FT: 65,000
SALES (est): 25MM
SALES (corp-wide): 16.3MM **Privately Held**
WEB: www.afcosystems.com
SIC: 2522 3469 3444 Panel systems & partitions, office: except wood; metal stampings; sheet metalwork
HQ: Legrand North America, Llc
60 Woodlawn St
West Hartford CT 06110
860 233-6251

(G-4939)
AIRFLEX CORP
965 Conklin St (11735-2412)
PHONE..................631 752-1219
Jonathan Fogelman, *President*
Lorraine Mazzella, *Manager*
EMP: 89
SQ FT: 10,000
SALES (est): 16MM **Privately Held**
SIC: 3441 Fabricated structural metal

(G-4940)
AIRFLEX INDUSTRIAL INC (PA)
965 Conklin St (11735-2412)
PHONE..................631 752-1234
Jonathan Fogelman, *Ch of Bd*
Lorraine Mazzella, *Manager*
EMP: 41
SQ FT: 10,000

GEOGRAPHIC SECTION
Farmingdale - Nassau County (G-4965)

SALES (est): 16.4MM **Privately Held**
WEB: www.airflexind.com
SIC: 3446 3822 3365 Louvers, ventilating; damper operators: pneumatic, thermostatic, electric; aluminum & aluminum-based alloy castings

(G-4941)
AIRFLEX INDUSTRIAL INC
937 Conklin St (11735-2412)
PHONE.................................631 752-1234
Jonathan Fogelman, *Branch Mgr*
EMP: 59
SALES (corp-wide): 16.4MM **Privately Held**
SIC: 3446 Louvers, ventilating
PA: Airflex Industrial, Inc.
    965 Conklin St
    Farmingdale NY 11735
    631 752-1234

(G-4942)
ALA SCIENTIFIC INSTRUMENTS INC
60 Marine St Ste 1 (11735-5660)
PHONE.................................631 393-6401
Alan Kriegstein, *President*
Andrew Pomerantz, *Vice Pres*
Christena Lopez, *Manager*
Irene Pomerantz, *Manager*
EMP: 13
SQ FT: 6,000
SALES: 2.5MM **Privately Held**
WEB: www.alascience.com
SIC: 3841 5047 Surgical & medical instruments; medical equipment & supplies

(G-4943)
ALL COLOR OFFSET PRINTERS INC
Also Called: All Color Business Specialties
51 Henry St Ste A (11735)
PHONE.................................516 420-0649
Fax: 631 753-2506
William Bogue, *President*
Tim Dorman, *Vice Pres*
Donald Romano, *Vice Pres*
Louis Divito, *Sales Executive*
Paul Currao, *Manager*
EMP: 5
SQ FT: 2,500
SALES (est): 912.2K **Privately Held**
SIC: 2752 Commercial printing, offset

(G-4944)
ALLANSON INC (HQ)
99 Adams Blvd (11735-6612)
PHONE.................................631 293-3880
Fax: 631 293-3470
Rick Woodgate, *President*
David Alt, *Office Mgr*
EMP: 2
SQ FT: 8,000
SALES (est): 1MM
SALES (corp-wide): 20.1MM **Privately Held**
WEB: www.allanson.net
SIC: 3612 Specialty transformers; ignition transformers, for use on domestic fuel burners
PA: Allanson International Inc
    33 Cranfield Rd
    Toronto ON M4B 3
    800 661-7251

(G-4945)
ALLOY METAL WORKS INC
146 Verdi St (11735-6324)
PHONE.................................631 694-8163
Fax: 631 694-1213
Phillip Rajotte Jr, *President*
EMP: 5
SQ FT: 2,500
SALES: 250K **Privately Held**
SIC: 7692 Welding repair

(G-4946)
ALPHA MANUFACTURING CORP
152 Verdi St (11735-6324)
PHONE.................................631 249-3700
Fax: 516 249-3705
George Sparacio, *President*
EMP: 10
SQ FT: 6,000
SALES: 1MM **Privately Held**
SIC: 3599 Machine shop, jobbing & repair

(G-4947)
AMANA TOOL CORP
Also Called: Age Timberline Mamba
120 Carolyn Blvd (11735-1525)
PHONE.................................631 752-1300
Fax: 631 752-1674
Eitan Spiegel, *CEO*
Aaron Einstein, *Chairman*
John P McInerney, *Vice Pres*
Zygmunt L Miewski, *Vice Pres*
Zygmunt L Milewski, *Vice Pres*
◆ EMP: 52
SQ FT: 80,000
SALES (est): 10.5MM **Privately Held**
WEB: www.amanatool.com
SIC: 3425 Saw blades & handsaws

(G-4948)
AMERICAN AEROSPACE CONTRLS INC
Also Called: A A C
570 Smith St (11735-1115)
PHONE.................................631 694-5100
Fax: 516 694-6739
Ruth Gitlin, *CEO*
Philip Koch, *Opers Mgr*
John Zatwarnicki, *Purch Mgr*
Celeste Morrissey, *QC Mgr*
Steve Lucey, *Controller*
EMP: 47 EST: 1965
SQ FT: 16,000
SALES (est): 9.6MM **Privately Held**
WEB: www.a-a-c.com
SIC: 3679 Transducers, electrical

(G-4949)
AMERICAN VISUALS INC
Also Called: American Visual Display
90 Gazza Blvd (11735-1402)
PHONE.................................631 694-6104
Morris Charnow, *President*
EMP: 7
SQ FT: 8,200
SALES (est): 825.6K **Privately Held**
WEB: www.americanvisuals.com
SIC: 3993 3089 Displays & cutouts, window & lobby; plastic processing

(G-4950)
ANDREA SYSTEMS LLC
140 Finn Ct (11735-1107)
PHONE.................................631 390-3140
Tony Macri, *QC Mgr*
Luis Rivera, *Electrical Engi*
Tal Barak, *Sales Mgr*
Robert J Carton, *Sales Mgr*
Frank Randazzo, *Mng Member*
EMP: 23
SQ FT: 15,000
SALES: 5MM **Privately Held**
WEB: www.andreasystems.com
SIC: 3669 Intercommunication systems, electric

(G-4951)
APEX PACKING & RUBBER CO INC
1855 New Hwy Ste D (11735-1557)
PHONE.................................631 420-8150
Fax: 631 756-9639
Ralph Oppenheim, *President*
EMP: 13 EST: 1940
SQ FT: 8,000
SALES (est): 2.1MM **Privately Held**
WEB: www.apexgaskets.com
SIC: 3053 Gaskets & sealing devices

(G-4952)
APSIS USA INC
1855 New Hwy Ste B (11735-1557)
PHONE.................................631 421-6800
Jersey Wu, *President*
Terry Wu, *Vice Pres*
EMP: 15
SQ FT: 5,000
SALES: 4MM **Privately Held**
WEB: www.apsisusa.com
SIC: 3714 7532 Motor vehicle parts & accessories; motor vehicle body components & frame; customizing services, non-factory basis

(G-4953)
ARBE MACHINERY INC
54 Allen Blvd (11735-5623)
PHONE.................................631 756-2477
Fax: 516 756-2485
Artin Karakaya, *President*
Burc Karakaya, *Vice Pres*
◆ EMP: 10
SQ FT: 30,000
SALES (est): 2.3MM **Privately Held**
SIC: 3559 5084 3599 Jewelers' machines; industrial machinery & equipment; machine shop, jobbing & repair

(G-4954)
ATI MODEL PRODUCTS INC (PA)
Also Called: Model Power
180 Smith St (11735-1023)
PHONE.................................631 694-7022
Fax: 516 694-7133
Michael Tager, *Ch of Bd*
Matthew Tager, *President*
Joshua Tager, *Vice Pres*
Ida Yonenson, *Treasurer*
William Larkin, *Manager*
▲ EMP: 50
SQ FT: 44,000
SALES (est): 5.6MM **Privately Held**
SIC: 3944 Trains & equipment, toy: electric & mechanical

(G-4955)
AUSCO INC
425 Smith St Ste 1 (11735-1124)
PHONE.................................516 944-9882
Fax: 516 944-8522
Kenneth Bram, *Ch of Bd*
Jackie Gregus, *General Mgr*
Marguerite Fenech, *Vice Pres*
Thai Tong, *Vice Pres*
Glenn Davis, *Mfg Mgr*
EMP: 100
SQ FT: 11,000
SALES (est): 23.6MM **Privately Held**
WEB: www.auscoinc.com
SIC: 3728 Aircraft parts & equipment

(G-4956)
AUTEL US INC (HQ)
Also Called: Autel North America
175 Central Ave Ste 200 (11735-6917)
PHONE.................................631 923-2620
Arthur Jacobsen, *CEO*
▲ EMP: 5
SQ FT: 20,000
SALES (est): 1.8MM
SALES (corp-wide): 60.8MM **Privately Held**
SIC: 3694 Automotive electrical equipment
PA: Autel Intelligent Technology Corp., Ltd.
    8th Floor, Building B1, Zhiyuan
    Xueyuan Road, Xili, Nanshan
    Shenzhen
    755 861-4777

(G-4957)
AVANTI FURNITURE CORP
497 Main St (11735-3579)
PHONE.................................516 293-8220
Fax: 631 293-9335
Joan Bagnasco, *President*
Kevin Bagnasco, *Treasurer*
▲ EMP: 12
SQ FT: 10,000
SALES (est): 1.6MM **Privately Held**
SIC: 2512 Chairs: upholstered on wood frames

(G-4958)
B & R ELECTRIC MOTOR INC
5919 Central Ave (11735)
PHONE.................................631 752-7533
Ellen M McQuade, *President*
Roy A Mack, *Vice Pres*
EMP: 5
SQ FT: 3,000
SALES (est): 602.7K **Privately Held**
SIC: 7694 7629 Electric motor repair; electrical equipment repair services

(G-4959)
BDR CREATIVE CONCEPTS INC
141 Central Ave Ste B (11735-6903)
PHONE.................................516 942-7768
Fax: 516 938-7302
Ronald Cohen, *President*
Pearl Cohen, *Vice Pres*
Judie Seaton, *Office Mgr*
Bruce Beckerman, *Shareholder*
Debra Beckerman, *Shareholder*
EMP: 14
SQ FT: 7,000
SALES (est): 1.4MM **Privately Held**
WEB: www.bdrcc.com
SIC: 2759 Poster & decal printing & engraving; posters, including billboards: printing

(G-4960)
BESCOR VIDEO ACCESSORIES LTD
244 Route 109 (11735-1503)
PHONE.................................631 420-1717
Fax: 516 420-0106
Douglas Brandwin, *President*
David Issacs, *Sales Mgr*
▲ EMP: 16
SQ FT: 8,000
SALES (est): 3.1MM **Privately Held**
SIC: 3861 5065 5043 Cameras & related equipment; video equipment, electronic; photographic cameras, projectors, equipment & supplies

(G-4961)
BEVERAGE WORKS NJ INC
16 Dubon Ct (11735-1008)
PHONE.................................631 293-3501
Fax: 631 293-3505
Jeffrey Brown, *VP Opers*
Iles Hantman, *Manager*
EMP: 20
SALES (corp-wide): 56.2MM **Privately Held**
WEB: www.beverageworks.com
SIC: 2086 Bottled & canned soft drinks
PA: The Beverage Works Nj Inc
    1800 State Route 34 # 203
    Wall Township NJ 07719
    732 938-7600

(G-4962)
BST UNITED CORP
59 Central Ave (11735-6902)
PHONE.................................631 777-2110
Shakil Shahriar, *Owner*
EMP: 12
SALES: 250K **Privately Held**
SIC: 3089 Blow molded finished plastic products

(G-4963)
C & C BINDERY CO INC
Also Called: C&C Diecuts
25 Central Ave Unit B (11735-6920)
PHONE.................................631 752-7078
Fax: 631 752-2249
Joe Spalone, *President*
Mitch Holsborg, *Vice Pres*
EMP: 30
SQ FT: 11,000
SALES: 4.3MM **Privately Held**
SIC: 2789 Bookbinding & related work

(G-4964)
C A M GRAPHICS CO INC
24 Central Dr (11735-1202)
PHONE.................................631 842-3400
Emanuel Cardinale, *President*
Jorge Reyes, *Vice Pres*
Jose Vargas, *Mfg Mgr*
Juneth Webson, *Manager*
Elizabeth Heiser, *Admin Sec*
EMP: 27
SQ FT: 20,000
SALES (est): 4.5MM **Privately Held**
WEB: www.camgraphics.com
SIC: 3672 3679 3643 3613 Printed circuit boards; electronic switches; current-carrying wiring devices; switchgear & switchboard apparatus

(G-4965)
CANDID LITHO PRINTING LTD (PA)
210 Route 109 (11735-1503)
PHONE.................................212 431-3800
Howard Weinstein, *President*
Scott Weinstein, *Corp Secy*
Lewis Rosenberg, *Vice Pres*
Jhamar Brown, *Controller*
Mary Milazzo, *Human Resources*

Farmingdale - Nassau County (G-4966)

EMP: 60 EST: 1964
SQ FT: 109,285
SALES (est): 15.9MM Privately Held
WEB: www.candidlitho.com
SIC: 2752 Commercial printing, lithographic; commercial printing, offset

(G-4966)
CANDID WORLDWIDE LLC (HQ)
210 Route 109 (11735-1503)
PHONE.....................212 799-5300
David Stadler, CEO
Howard Weinstein, President
Jhamar Brown, Controller
EMP: 6
SALES (est): 6.7MM
SALES (corp-wide): 15.9MM Privately Held
SIC: 2759 Posters, including billboards: printing
PA: Candid Litho Printing Ltd.
210 Route 109
Farmingdale NY 11735
212 431-3800

(G-4967)
CEMTREX INC (PA)
19 Engineers Ln (11735-1207)
PHONE.....................631 756-9116
Fax: 631 845-0541
Saagar Govil, Ch of Bd
Ravi Narayan, Vice Pres
Renato Dela Rama, CFO
Mayuri Shah, Human Resources
Bob Dachert, Natl Sales Mgr
EMP: 244
SQ FT: 4,000
SALES: 93.7MM Publicly Held
SIC: 3823 7389 Industrial instrmnts msrmnt display/control process variable; controllers for process variables, all types; air pollution measuring service

(G-4968)
CHIM-CAP CORP
120 Schmitt Blvd (11735-1424)
PHONE.....................800 262-9622
Fax: 631 454-7535
Fred Giumenta Jr, President
▲ EMP: 20
SQ FT: 40,000
SALES (est): 3.8MM Privately Held
WEB: www.chimcapcorp.com
SIC: 3272 Fireplace & chimney material: concrete; chimney caps, concrete

(G-4969)
CIGAR OASIS INC
79 Heisser Ct (11735-3310)
PHONE.....................516 520-5258
Albert P Foundos, President
Christine Beno, Vice Pres
Donna Oswald, Vice Pres
Philip Foundos, Treasurer
▲ EMP: 5
SQ FT: 2,000
SALES (est): 510K Privately Held
SIC: 3911 Cigar & cigarette accessories

(G-4970)
COCO ARCHITECTUREAL GRILLES
173 Allen Blvd (11735-5616)
PHONE.....................631 482-9449
Jim Coco, President
EMP: 5
SALES (est): 675K Privately Held
SIC: 3441 Fabricated structural metal

(G-4971)
COLONIAL PRECISION MACHINERY
Also Called: Colonial Electric
134 Rome St (11735-6607)
PHONE.....................631 249-0738
James Tormey, President
Scott Tormey, Vice Pres
EMP: 7
SQ FT: 15,000
SALES (est): 650K Privately Held
SIC: 3469 Machine parts, stamped or pressed metal

(G-4972)
COMMERCE SPRING CORP
143 Allen Blvd (11735-5616)
PHONE.....................631 293-4844
Fax: 516 293-4859
Bruno Rotellini, President
Janet Halleran, Office Mgr
EMP: 12
SQ FT: 10,000
SALES (est): 1.2MM Privately Held
WEB: www.commercespring.com
SIC: 3495 Wire springs

(G-4973)
COSMO ELECTRONIC MACHINE CORP
Also Called: D & L Electronic Die
113 Gazza Blvd (11735-1421)
PHONE.....................631 249-2535
Fax: 631 694-2349
Kenneth Arutt, President
Bruce Mc Kee, Vice Pres
Vladimir Lipkin, Manager
EMP: 50
SQ FT: 3,000
SALES (est): 5.2MM Privately Held
SIC: 3544 Special dies, tools, jigs & fixtures

(G-4974)
COSMOS ELECTRONIC MACHINE CORP (PA)
140 Schmitt Blvd (11735-1461)
PHONE.....................631 249-2535
Kenneth Arutt, President
Bruce McKee, Vice Pres
Wayne Nelson, Purch Mgr
Paul Abriola, Sales Mgr
Rick Cabrera, Manager
EMP: 43
SQ FT: 20,000
SALES (est): 8.6MM Privately Held
SIC: 3567 Industrial furnaces & ovens

(G-4975)
CPW DIRECT MAIL GROUP LLC
110 Schmitt Blvd (11735-1424)
P.O. Box 216, Bohemia (11716-0216)
PHONE.....................631 588-6565
Fax: 631 588-6502
John Plate, Mng Member
Loraine Chaudrhy Ekinci, Mng Member
Mark Krevitski, Mng Member
Todd Meties, Mng Member
Dave Swanson, Mng Member
EMP: 28
SQ FT: 42,000
SALES (est): 2.9MM Privately Held
SIC: 2759 2677 3577 Laser printing; envelopes: printing; envelopes; bar code (magnetic ink) printers

(G-4976)
CRISRAY PRINTING CORP
50 Executive Blvd Ste A (11735-4712)
PHONE.....................631 293-3770
Fax: 631 249-1954
Raymond J Marro, President
Angelo Berardi, General Mgr
Anthony Conti, Vice Pres
Patricia Marro, Vice Pres
Lucy Forgione, Accounts Mgr
EMP: 30 EST: 1971
SQ FT: 10,000
SALES (est): 5MM Privately Held
WEB: www.crisray.com
SIC: 2759 Labels & seals: printing

(G-4977)
CURTISS-WRIGHT CONTROLS
Also Called: Curtiss-Wrght Intgrted Sensing
175 Central Ave Ste 100 (11735-6917)
P.O. Box 7751, Philadelphia PA (19101-7751)
PHONE.....................631 756-4740
Thomas P Quinly, COO
Christopher Kelly, Engineer
Dora Pinones, Manager
EMP: 14
SALES (corp-wide): 2.1B Publicly Held
SIC: 3674 Semiconductors & related devices
HQ: Curtiss-Wright Controls Integrated Sensing, Inc.
28965 Avenue Penn
Valencia CA 91355
626 851-3100

(G-4978)
CURTISS-WRIGHT FLOW CTRL CORP (HQ)
Also Called: Target Rock
1966 Broadhollow Rd Ste E (11735-1726)
PHONE.....................631 293-3800
Fax: 516 293-6144
Martin Benante, Ch of Bd
David Linton, President
David C Adams, COO
Joseph Callaghan, Vice Pres
Greg Hempfling, Vice Pres
◆ EMP: 236 EST: 1950
SQ FT: 100,000
SALES (est): 511.9MM
SALES (corp-wide): 2.1B Publicly Held
SIC: 3491 3494 Industrial valves; valves & pipe fittings
PA: Curtiss-Wright Corporation
13925 Balntyn Corp Pl
Charlotte NC 28277
704 869-4600

(G-4979)
CURTISS-WRIGHT FLOW CTRL CORP
1966 Broadhollow Rd Ste E (11735-1726)
P.O. Box 379 (11735-0379)
PHONE.....................631 293-3800
Bill Hughes, Purch Agent
Steve Jung, Branch Mgr
Donald Leatherman, Manager
EMP: 160
SALES (corp-wide): 2.1B Publicly Held
SIC: 3491 Industrial valves
HQ: Curtiss-Wright Flow Control Corporation
1966 Broadhollow Rd Ste E
Farmingdale NY 11735
631 293-3800

(G-4980)
CUSTOM DOOR & MIRROR INC
Also Called: Flex Supply
148 Milbar Blvd (11735-1425)
PHONE.....................631 414-7725
Angelo Sciubba, Ch of Bd
Philip Sciubba, Vice Pres
Vincent Barbagallo, Project Mgr
▲ EMP: 20 EST: 1996
SQ FT: 17,000
SALES: 3MM Privately Held
WEB: www.paniflex.com
SIC: 3089 2431 Doors, folding: plastic or plastic coated fabric; millwork

(G-4981)
CUSTOM SITECOM LLC
Also Called: Buckle Down
470 Smith St (11735-1105)
PHONE.....................631 420-4238
Eric Swope, COO
Jason Dorf,
▲ EMP: 11
SALES (est): 2.1MM Privately Held
SIC: 3714 Motor vehicle parts & accessories

(G-4982)
DADDARIO & COMPANY INC (PA)
595 Smith St (11735-1120)
P.O. Box 290 (11735-0290)
PHONE.....................631 439-3300
Fax: 631 439-3336
James D'Addario, Ch of Bd
Rick Drumm, President
John D'Addario III, Exec VP
John D'Addario Jr, Vice Pres
David Via, Vice Pres
◆ EMP: 700
SQ FT: 110,000
SALES (est): 210.7MM Privately Held
WEB: www.daddario.com
SIC: 3931 String instruments & parts; strings, musical instrument

(G-4983)
DAKOTA SYSTEMS MFG CORP
Also Called: Dakota Wall
1885 New Hwy Ste 2 (11735-1518)
PHONE.....................631 249-5811
Fax: 631 249-5819
Edward Owsinski, President
Jimmy Eowinski, Bookkeeper
EMP: 6
SQ FT: 3,000
SALES (est): 1.3MM Privately Held
SIC: 2542 3312 Partitions & fixtures, except wood; stainless steel

(G-4984)
DANBURY PHARMA LLC
220 Smith St (11735-1024)
PHONE.....................631 393-6333
Lou Ferreira, Manager
Carmen Martinez, Manager
BJ Harid,
▲ EMP: 33
SQ FT: 19,000
SALES (est): 9MM Privately Held
SIC: 2834 Vitamin preparations

(G-4985)
DESKTOP PUBLISHING CONCEPTS
Also Called: Toledo Graphics Group
855 Conklin St Ste T (11735-2409)
P.O. Box 34 (11735-0034)
PHONE.....................631 752-1934
Fax: 631 752-1423
Nicholas Sachs, President
Jennifer Plattman, Graphic Designe
EMP: 12
SQ FT: 2,500
SALES (est): 1.4MM Privately Held
WEB: www.toledogroup.com
SIC: 2791 7336 Typesetting; graphic arts & related design

(G-4986)
DIGICOM INTERNATIONAL INC
145 Rome St (11735-6610)
PHONE.....................631 249-8999
Fax: 631 249-5536
Chia I Chen, CEO
Linn Grieshaber, Controller
Jammy Chen, Executive
▲ EMP: 15
SQ FT: 20,000
SALES (est): 3MM Privately Held
SIC: 3571 5045 Electronic computers; computer peripheral equipment

(G-4987)
DIGITAL MATRIX CORP
34 Sarah Dr Ste B (11735-1218)
PHONE.....................516 481-7990
Fax: 516 481-7320
Alex Greenspan, President
Freeman Peng, Managing Prtnr
Jan Berman, Vice Pres
Alexsandr Davelman, Engineer
Boris Lopantnikov, Engineer
EMP: 21
SQ FT: 20,000
SALES (est): 3.7MM Privately Held
WEB: www.galvanics.com
SIC: 3559 Electroplating machinery & equipment

(G-4988)
DUCON TECHNOLOGIES INC
19 Engineers Ln (11735-1207)
PHONE.....................631 420-4900
Bill Papa, VP Opers
Lou Paparella, Purch Mgr
Renato Delarama, Controller
Tony Maccari, Sales Dir
Robert Dachert, Sales Mgr
EMP: 45
SALES (corp-wide): 479.4MM Privately Held
SIC: 3564 3537 Blowers & fans; industrial trucks & tractors
PA: Ducon Technologies Inc.
5 Penn Plz Ste 2403
New York NY 10001
631 694-1700

▲ = Import ▼ = Export
◆ = Import/Export

Farmingdale - Nassau County (G-5013)

(G-4989)
DURO DYNE CORPORATION (HQ)
130 Broadhollow Rd (11735-4828)
P.O. Box 9117, Bay Shore (11706-9117)
PHONE...................................631 249-9000
Fax: 631 249-8346
Randall Hinden, *President*
Joe Auriemmo, *Purchasing*
Paul Thompson, *VP Sales*
▲ **EMP:** 150 **EST:** 1952
SQ FT: 130,000
SALES (est): 37.5MM
SALES (corp-wide): 126.3MM **Privately Held**
SIC: 3585 Air conditioning equipment, complete; heating equipment, complete
PA: Dyne Duro National Corp
81 Spence St
Bay Shore NY 11706
631 249-9000

(G-4990)
E B INDUSTRIES LLC (PA)
90 Carolyn Blvd (11735-1525)
PHONE...................................631 293-8565
Fax: 631 752-7866
Dominic Rocco, *Engineer*
John De Lalio, *Marketing Staff*
Steven Delalio, *Prgrmr*
Steven M Delalio,
Devorah Lisnoff, *Admin Asst*
EMP: 25 **EST:** 1965
SQ FT: 16,000
SALES (est): 3.3MM **Privately Held**
WEB: www.ebindustries.com
SIC: 3599 Machine shop, jobbing & repair

(G-4991)
E B INDUSTRIES LLC
90 Carolyn Blvd (11735-1525)
PHONE...................................631 293-8565
Steven Delalio, *Mng Member*
EMP: 25
SALES (est): 440.7K
SALES (corp-wide): 3.3MM **Privately Held**
WEB: www.ebindustries.com
SIC: 7692 Welding repair
PA: E B Industries, Llc
90 Carolyn Blvd
Farmingdale NY 11735
631 293-8565

(G-4992)
EAST COAST CYCLE LLC
80 Smith St Ste 1 (11735-1011)
PHONE...................................631 780-5360
Joshua Kohn, *Manager*
Jeffrey Bruno,
▲ **EMP:** 9
SQ FT: 2,500
SALES (est): 900K **Privately Held**
SIC: 3751 5091 Bicycles & related parts; bicycles

(G-4993)
EAST COAST ENVMTL GROUP INC
136 Allen Blvd (11735-5659)
PHONE...................................516 352-1946
Edwin Rincon, *President*
Jennifer Mosquera, *Manager*
EMP: 5
SQ FT: 15,000
SALES: 1MM **Privately Held**
SIC: 3826 Differential thermal analysis instruments

(G-4994)
EDLAW PHARMACEUTICALS INC
195 Central Ave Ste B (11735-6904)
PHONE...................................631 454-6888
Fax: 516 454-4846
Scott Giroux, *General Mgr*
Bonnie Hilton Green, *Principal*
▼ **EMP:** 20
SQ FT: 6,500
SALES (est): 3.8MM **Privately Held**
SIC: 2834 Pharmaceutical preparations

(G-4995)
EEG ENTERPRISES INC
586 Main St (11735-3546)
PHONE...................................516 293-7472
Fax: 516 293-7417
Philip McLaughlin, *President*
Bill McLaughlin, *President*
William Jorden, *Vice Pres*
Frank Zovko, *Engineer*
Eric McErlain, *Sales Dir*
EMP: 12
SQ FT: 5,000
SALES (est): 2.1MM **Privately Held**
WEB: www.eegent.com
SIC: 3663 Cable television equipment; television antennas (transmitting) & ground equipment

(G-4996)
ELLIOT GANTZ & COMPANY INC
115 Schmitt Blvd (11735-1403)
P.O. Box 756, Commack (11725-0756)
PHONE...................................631 249-0680
Elliot Gantz, *President*
Barbara Yacker, *Controller*
Elliot Guntz, *Personnel Exec*
Rachel Allgood, *CTO*
EMP: 40
SQ FT: 20,000
SALES (est): 4.3MM **Privately Held**
WEB: www.elliotgantz.com
SIC: 3299 Architectural sculptures: gypsum, clay, papier mache, etc.

(G-4997)
ENZO LIFE SCIENCES INC (HQ)
Also Called: Enzo Diagnostics
10 Executive Blvd (11735-4710)
PHONE...................................631 694-7070
Fax: 516 694-7501
Elazar Rabbani, *Ch of Bd*
Jo-Marie Chan, *Business Mgr*
Jennifer Norman, *Business Mgr*
Barry W Weiner, *Exec VP*
Herbert Bass, *Vice Pres*
EMP: 30
SQ FT: 40,000
SALES (est): 14.6MM
SALES (corp-wide): 102.7MM **Publicly Held**
SIC: 2835 2834 5049 In vitro & in vivo diagnostic substances; pharmaceutical preparations; laboratory equipment, except medical or dental
PA: Enzo Biochem, Inc.
527 Madison Ave Rm 901
New York NY 10022
212 583-0100

(G-4998)
ENZO LIFE SCIENCES INTL INC
10 Executive Blvd (11735-4710)
PHONE...................................610 941-0430
Robert Zipkin, *President*
Ira Taffer, *Vice Pres*
Debbie Dejzak, *Credit Mgr*
Debbie Lilley, *Accountant*
◆ **EMP:** 28
SQ FT: 20,000
SALES (est): 3.3MM
SALES (corp-wide): 102.7MM **Publicly Held**
WEB: www.biomol.com
SIC: 2834 Pharmaceutical preparations
HQ: Enzo Life Sciences, Inc.
10 Executive Blvd
Farmingdale NY 11735
631 694-7070

(G-4999)
EVANS MANUFACTURING LLC
595 Smith St (11735-1116)
P.O. Box 290 (11735-0290)
PHONE...................................631 439-3300
James D'Addario,
John D'Addario Jr,
Robert Dodaro,
Michael Russo,
Domenick Scarfogliero,
▲ **EMP:** 75 **EST:** 1995
SQ FT: 110,000
SALES (est): 6MM **Privately Held**
WEB: www.dadario.com
SIC: 3931 Musical instruments; heads, drum

(G-5000)
FARMINGDALE IRON WORKS INC
105 Florida St (11735-6305)
PHONE...................................631 249-5995
John Cardullo, *President*
Vita Cardullo, *Corp Secy*
EMP: 6 **EST:** 1959
SQ FT: 4,500
SALES: 642.4K **Privately Held**
SIC: 3441 Fabricated structural metal

(G-5001)
FERRARO MANUFACTURING COMPANY
150 Central Ave (11735-6900)
PHONE...................................631 752-1509
Fax: 631 752-2233
Joseph Ferraro, *President*
Sharon Allocco, *Admin Sec*
EMP: 6
SALES (est): 800.9K **Privately Held**
WEB: www.ferrarofirm.com
SIC: 3599 Machine shop, jobbing & repair

(G-5002)
FIBER FOOT APPLIANCES INC
34 Sarah Dr Ste A (11735-1218)
PHONE...................................631 465-9199
Jeffrey Fiber, *President*
Allan Fiber, *Treasurer*
Helene Fiber, *Admin Sec*
EMP: 13
SQ FT: 6,500
SALES (est): 1.3MM **Privately Held**
SIC: 3842 Foot appliances, orthopedic

(G-5003)
FRUITCROWN PRODUCTS CORP (PA)
250 Adams Blvd (11735-6615)
PHONE...................................631 694-5800
Fax: 516 694-6467
Robert E Jagenburg, *President*
Bruce Jagenburg, *Vice Pres*
Frank Poma, *VP Opers*
Nick Mendola, *Warehouse Mgr*
Peter Pace, *Purchasing*
▼ **EMP:** 45
SQ FT: 40,000
SALES (est): 21.4MM **Privately Held**
WEB: www.fruitcrown.com
SIC: 2033 Fruits: packaged in cans, jars, etc.

(G-5004)
FUN INDUSTRIES OF NY
111 Milbar Blvd (11735-1426)
PHONE...................................631 845-3805
Bryan Spodek, *Principal*
EMP: 13
SALES (est): 1.4MM **Privately Held**
SIC: 3999 Manufacturing industries

(G-5005)
GAVIN MFG CORP
25 Central Ave Unit A (11735-6920)
PHONE...................................631 467-0040
Christopher Gavin, *President*
Brian Gavin, *Vice Pres*
Michael Gavin, *Vice Pres*
Ryan Gavin, *Vice Pres*
EMP: 45 **EST:** 1953
SQ FT: 15,000
SALES (est): 7.7MM **Privately Held**
WEB: www.gavinmfgcorp.com
SIC: 2679 2653 2657 Paper products, converted; paperboard products, converted; corrugated & solid fiber boxes; folding paperboard boxes

(G-5006)
GILD-RITE INC
51 Carolyn Blvd (11735-1527)
PHONE...................................631 752-9000
Howard Schneider, *President*
Morris D Schneider, *Chairman*
Roert Schneider, *Vice Pres*
Sylvia K Zang, *Treasurer*
EMP: 5
SQ FT: 7,000
SALES: 250K
SALES (corp-wide): 15.7MM **Privately Held**
SIC: 2789 Gilding books, cards or paper
PA: Leather Craftsmen, Inc.
24 Seaview Blvd
Port Washington NY 11735
631 752-9000

(G-5007)
GLISSADE NEW YORK LLC
399 Smith St (11735-1106)
PHONE...................................631 756-4800
Jed Leadman,
▲ **EMP:** 25
SQ FT: 30,000
SALES (est): 3MM **Privately Held**
WEB: www.glissade.com
SIC: 2434 2514 Wood kitchen cabinets; vanities, bathroom: wood; medicine cabinets & vanities: metal

(G-5008)
GOLDMARK PRODUCTS INC
855 Conklin St Ste D (11735-2409)
PHONE...................................631 777-3343
Stanley Dabrowski, *President*
Matthew Paliwoda, *Treasurer*
EMP: 30
SQ FT: 5,000
SALES (est): 3.2MM **Privately Held**
SIC: 3911 3339 Jewelry, precious metal; primary nonferrous metals

(G-5009)
GREENMAKER INDUSTRIES LLC
885 Conklin St (11735-2400)
PHONE...................................866 684-7800
Bruce Respler, *Principal*
Aj Rego, *Buyer*
EMP: 11 **EST:** 2005
SALES (est): 2MM **Privately Held**
SIC: 2841 2842 Soap & other detergents; rug, upholstery, or dry cleaning detergents or spotters; sanitation preparations, disinfectants & deodorants; degreasing solvent; window cleaning preparations

(G-5010)
GUSTBUSTER LTD
Also Called: Sunbuster
855 Conklin St Ste O (11735-2409)
PHONE...................................631 391-9000
Steven Asman, *President*
Cathy Hamel, *Manager*
▲ **EMP:** 8
SQ FT: 17,000
SALES: 2MM **Privately Held**
WEB: www.gustbuster.com
SIC: 3999 Umbrellas, canes & parts

(G-5011)
HADES MANUFACTURING CORP
135 Florida St (11735-6307)
PHONE...................................631 249-4244
Fax: 631 249-1618
Eugene L Brand, *President*
Ken Norris, *Vice Pres*
EMP: 10 **EST:** 1966
SQ FT: 3,000
SALES (est): 2.1MM **Privately Held**
WEB: www.hadesmfgcorp.com
SIC: 3823 5084 Industrial instrmnts msrmnt display/control process variable; temperature instruments: industrial process type; industrial machinery & equipment

(G-5012)
HAHNS OLD FASHIONED CAKE CO
75 Allen Blvd (11735-5614)
PHONE...................................631 249-3456
Fax: 516 492-3492
Regina C Hahn, *President*
Andrew M Hahn, *Corp Secy*
EMP: 12
SQ FT: 4,550
SALES: 1MM **Privately Held**
WEB: www.crumbcake.net
SIC: 2051 5149 Cakes, bakery: except frozen; bakery products

(G-5013)
HIRSCH OPTICAL CORP
91 Carolyn Blvd (11735-1409)
PHONE...................................516 752-2211
Fax: 516 752-0104
Harold M Rothstein, *President*

Farmingdale - Nassau County (G-5014)

Kenneth Mitel, *Vice Pres*
Michael Weinstein, *Vice Pres*
Joanne Rosalia, *Comptroller*
EMP: 60 **EST:** 1978
SQ FT: 12,000
SALES (est): 6.8MM **Privately Held**
WEB: www.hirschoptical.com
SIC: 3851 Eyeglasses, lenses & frames

(G-5014)
HORNE PRODUCTS INC
144 Verdi St (11735-6324)
PHONE..................................631 293-0773
John Hind, *President*
Joanne Incalcatera, *Corp Secy*
Patricia A O'Neill, *Vice Pres*
EMP: 6
SQ FT: 2,200
SALES (est): 964.1K **Privately Held**
WEB: www.horneproducts.com
SIC: 3743 5088 Railroad equipment; railroad equipment & supplies

(G-5015)
HURON TL CUTTER GRINDING INC
2045 Wellwood Ave (11735-1212)
PHONE..................................631 420-7000
Fax: 631 420-7007
James Cosenza, *President*
Richard Cosenza, *Vice Pres*
Robert Gooch, *Manager*
Blanche Silbert, *Admin Sec*
EMP: 30 **EST:** 1955
SQ FT: 25,000
SALES: 4MM **Privately Held**
WEB: www.hurontool.com
SIC: 3545 3841 3568 3423 Tools & accessories for machine tools; knives, surgical; power transmission equipment; hand & edge tools

(G-5016)
I J WHITE CORPORATION
20 Executive Blvd (11735-4710)
PHONE..................................631 293-3788
Fax: 516 293-3788
Peter J White, *Ch of Bd*
Niv Eldor, *COO*
Andy Cohn, *Vice Pres*
Roy Berntsen, *Plant Mgr*
Joyce Bridges, *Controller*
▼ **EMP:** 70 **EST:** 1919
SQ FT: 42,500
SALES (est): 20.7MM **Privately Held**
WEB: www.ijwhite.com
SIC: 3556 3535 Food products machinery; conveyors & conveying equipment

(G-5017)
IMPRESSIVE IMPRINTS INC
195 Central Ave Ste N (11735-6904)
PHONE..................................631 293-6161
Howard Lang, *President*
EMP: 5
SQ FT: 3,000
SALES (est): 593.3K **Privately Held**
SIC: 3993 Signs & advertising specialties

(G-5018)
INNOVATIVE AUTOMATION INC
595 Smith St (11735-1116)
P.O. Box 290 (11735-0290)
PHONE..................................631 439-3300
Fax: 631 391-5410
James D'Addario, *President*
Michael Russo, *Exec VP*
John D'Addario Jr, *Vice Pres*
EMP: 12
SQ FT: 25,000
SALES (est): 1.4MM **Privately Held**
WEB: www.innovativeautomation.net
SIC: 3545 Machine tool attachments & accessories

(G-5019)
INSTANT VERTICALS INC
330 Broadhollow Rd (11735-4807)
PHONE..................................631 501-0001
Fax: 631 501-0952
Michael Moran, *President*
John Joy, *Vice Pres*
EMP: 10
SALES (est): 1.2MM **Privately Held**
WEB: www.instantverticals.com
SIC: 2591 1799 Window blinds; window treatment installation

(G-5020)
INTERNATIONAL KEY SUPPLY LLC
Also Called: Ik Supply
32 Gazza Blvd (11735-1402)
PHONE..................................631 983-6096
Sean McAuliffe, *Partner*
EMP: 10
SALES (est): 1.2MM **Privately Held**
SIC: 3429 3694 3643 Keys & key blanks; automotive electrical equipment; connectors & terminals for electrical devices

(G-5021)
J M HALEY CORP
151 Toledo St Ste 1 (11735-6640)
PHONE..................................631 845-5200
Fax: 516 334-8382
John Ackerson, *President*
Jerry Iavarone, *CFO*
Cynthia Bissoon, *HR Admin*
Julia Giangrasso, *HR Admin*
Terri Carson, *Office Mgr*
EMP: 140
SQ FT: 10,000
SALES: 16MM **Privately Held**
WEB: www.jmhaleycorp.com
SIC: 3441 Fabricated structural metal

(G-5022)
J P MACHINE PRODUCTS INC
144 Rome St (11735-6609)
P.O. Box 1243, East Northport (11731-0500)
PHONE..................................631 249-9229
Fax: 631 249-1619
Joseph Piliero, *President*
Yoland Coulaz, *Principal*
Frank Piliero, *Treasurer*
EMP: 11
SQ FT: 7,600
SALES: 500K **Privately Held**
SIC: 3469 Machine parts, stamped or pressed metal

(G-5023)
J P PRINTING INC (PA)
Also Called: Minuteman Press
331 Main St (11735-3508)
PHONE..................................516 293-6110
Fax: 516 293-7692
Jeff Miller, *President*
Susan Miller, *Vice Pres*
EMP: 5
SQ FT: 1,200
SALES: 385K **Privately Held**
SIC: 2752 5943 Commercial printing, lithographic; office forms & supplies

(G-5024)
JAMES WOERNER INC
130 Allen Blvd (11735-5617)
PHONE..................................631 454-9330
James Woerner, *President*
Barbara Woerner, *Vice Pres*
EMP: 6 **EST:** 1972
SQ FT: 7,000
SALES (est): 1MM **Privately Held**
SIC: 3498 3441 7538 Fabricated pipe & fittings; fabricated structural metal; general automotive repair shops

(G-5025)
JANED ENTERPRISES
48 Allen Blvd Unit B (11735-5642)
PHONE..................................631 694-4494
Joseph Pileri, *CEO*
Claudia Montuori, *President*
EMP: 15
SQ FT: 14,000
SALES (est): 2.5MM **Privately Held**
WEB: www.janed.net
SIC: 3449 Miscellaneous metalwork

(G-5026)
JOE P INDUSTRIES INC
Also Called: Carrmet Industries
6 Commerce Dr (11735-1206)
PHONE..................................631 293-7889
Fax: 516 293-2160
Joseph Parente, *President*
Maryann Young, *Bookkeeper*
EMP: 17
SQ FT: 3,500
SALES: 1MM **Privately Held**
SIC: 3444 Sheet metalwork; metal housings, enclosures, casings & other containers

(G-5027)
JUNK IN MY TRUNK INC
266 Route 109 (11735-1503)
PHONE..................................631 420-5865
Tomasz Myszke, *Principal*
EMP: 5
SALES (est): 611.7K **Privately Held**
SIC: 3161 Trunks

(G-5028)
K SIDRANE INC
24 Baiting Place Rd (11735-6227)
PHONE..................................631 393-6974
Fax: 516 378-3580
Michael Liff, *General Mgr*
Neil Sidrane, *Chairman*
Andrew Hersh, *Accounts Mgr*
▲ **EMP:** 45 **EST:** 1948
SQ FT: 10,000
SALES (est): 12MM **Privately Held**
SIC: 2679 2671 2672 Tags & labels, paper; packaging paper & plastics film, coated & laminated; coated & laminated paper; adhesive papers, labels or tapes; from purchased material

(G-5029)
KABAR MANUFACTURING CORP (HQ)
140 Schmitt Blvd (11735-1461)
PHONE..................................631 694-6857
Fax: 516 694-6846
Bruce Mc Kee, *President*
Ken Arutt, *Treasurer*
▲ **EMP:** 31 **EST:** 1945
SQ FT: 12,000
SALES (est): 6.8MM
SALES (corp-wide): 8.6MM **Privately Held**
WEB: www.cosmos-kabar.com
SIC: 3565 3559 Packaging machinery; plastics working machinery
PA: Cosmos Electronic Machine Corp.
140 Schmitt Blvd
Farmingdale NY 11735
631 249-2535

(G-5030)
KABAR MANUFACTURING CORP
113 Gazza Blvd (11735-1421)
PHONE..................................631 694-1036
Bruce Mc Kee, *President*
EMP: 30
SALES (corp-wide): 8.6MM **Privately Held**
WEB: www.cosmos-kabar.com
SIC: 3559 Plastics working machinery
HQ: Kabar Manufacturing Corp.
140 Schmitt Blvd
Farmingdale NY 11735
631 694-6857

(G-5031)
KAZAC INC
Also Called: Corzane Cabinets
55 Allen Blvd Ste C (11735-5643)
PHONE..................................631 249-7299
Fax: 631 249-1454
EMP: 5
SQ FT: 4,200
SALES: 450K **Privately Held**
SIC: 2511 2521 Mfg Wood Household Furniture Mfg Wood Office Furniture

(G-5032)
KEDCO INC
Also Called: Kedco Wine Storage Systems
564 Smith St (11735-1115)
PHONE..................................516 454-7800
Fax: 631 454-4876
Helene Windt, *President*
David Windt, *Corp Secy*
Ken Windt, *Vice Pres*
EMP: 12 **EST:** 1970
SQ FT: 20,000
SALES (est): 2MM **Privately Held**
SIC: 3585 2599 3556 Refrigeration & heating equipment; bar, restaurant & cafeteria furniture; beverage machinery

(G-5033)
KELLY WINDOW SYSTEMS INC
460 Smith St (11735-1105)
PHONE..................................631 420-8500
Fax: 516 420-8628
Carl J Giugliano, *President*
Frank Giugliano, *Vice Pres*
Pat Giugliano, *Vice Pres*
EMP: 32
SQ FT: 20,000
SALES (est): 4.6MM **Privately Held**
WEB: www.kellywindows.com
SIC: 2431 3442 Windows, wood; metal doors, sash & trim

(G-5034)
KEM MEDICAL PRODUCTS CORP (PA)
400 Broadhollow Rd Ste 2 (11735-4824)
PHONE..................................631 454-6565
Fax: 631 454-8083
Douglas A Kruger, *President*
Joseph Ebenstein, *Vice Pres*
EMP: 3
SQ FT: 2,500
SALES (est): 1.4MM **Privately Held**
WEB: www.kemmed.com
SIC: 3842 3829 Personal safety equipment; measuring & controlling devices

(G-5035)
KINEMOTIVE CORPORATION
222 Central Ave Ste 1 (11735-6958)
PHONE..................................631 249-6440
Fax: 516 249-6482
Arthur Szeglin, *Ch of Bd*
William Niedzwiecki, *President*
Charles Szeglin, *Principal*
Engin Oge, *Vice Pres*
Robert Skidmore, *Sales Mgr*
EMP: 48 **EST:** 1959
SQ FT: 20,000
SALES (est): 10.8MM **Privately Held**
WEB: www.kinemotive.com
SIC: 3492 3452 3599 3568 Fluid power valves & hose fittings; screws, metal; bellows, industrial: metal; couplings, shaft: rigid, flexible, universal joint, etc.; pivots, power transmission; precision springs; pressure transducers

(G-5036)
KROGER PACKAGING INC
215 Central Ave Ste M (11735-6905)
PHONE..................................631 249-6690
Fax: 631 249-8492
Alfred Knapp, *President*
Joseph Deangelo, *CFO*
Terri Brennan, *Bookkeeper*
Claudya McPhail, *Admin Asst*
EMP: 33
SQ FT: 15,000
SALES: 8MM **Privately Held**
WEB: www.krogerpackaging.com
SIC: 2759 Labels & seals: printing

(G-5037)
L AND S PACKING CO
Also Called: Paesana
101 Central Ave (11735-6915)
P.O. Box 709 (11735-0709)
PHONE..................................631 845-1717
Fax: 631 420-7309
Louis J Scaramelli III, *Ch of Bd*
Louis Scarmelli IV, *President*
Stan Staszewski, *General Mgr*
Jacqueline Massaro, *Exec VP*
Lorraine Scaramelli, *Exec VP*
▲ **EMP:** 72
SQ FT: 73,000
SALES (est): 18.2MM **Privately Held**
WEB: www.paesana.com
SIC: 2033 2035 Olives: packaged in cans, jars, etc.; vegetables: packaged in cans, jars, etc.; maraschino cherries: packaged in cans, jars, etc.; spaghetti & other pasta sauce: packaged in cans, jars, etc.; pickles, sauces & salad dressings

Farmingdale - Nassau County (G-5063)

(G-5038)
L P R PRECISION PARTS & TLS CO
108 Rome St Ste 1 (11735-6637)
PHONE..................631 293-7334
Fax: 631 293-7819
Tarquin Rattotti Jr, *President*
Tarquin Rattotti Sr, *Principal*
Lucy Rattotti, *Corp Secy*
Clarke Mizuk, *Foreman/Supr*
EMP: 10
SQ FT: 5,000
SALES (est): 1.8MM Privately Held
WEB: www.lprprecision.com
SIC: 3599 Machine shop, jobbing & repair

(G-5039)
LA MAR LIGHTING CO INC
485 Smith St (11735-1106)
P.O. Box 9013 (11735-9013)
PHONE..................631 777-7700
Fax: 631 454-0599
Jeffrey Goldstein, *CEO*
Barry Kugel, *Ch of Bd*
Bill Phillips, *Vice Pres*
Keith Briggs, *Purch Mgr*
Gregory Calise, *Technical Mgr*
▲ EMP: 65 EST: 1957
SQ FT: 40,000
SALES (est): 16.1MM Privately Held
WEB: www.lamarlighting.com
SIC: 3646 3648 3641 2542 Fluorescent lighting fixtures, commercial; lighting equipment; electric lamps; partitions & fixtures, except wood

(G-5040)
LADY BURD EXCLUSIVE COSMT INC (PA)
Also Called: Lady Burd Private Label Cosmt
44 Executive Blvd Ste 1 (11735-4706)
PHONE..................631 454-0444
Fax: 631 454-0599
Roberta Burd, *Chairman*
Allan Burd, *Vice Pres*
Christina Burd, *Vice Pres*
Lawrence Burd, *Vice Pres*
Tina Burd, *Vice Pres*
▲ EMP: 109
SQ FT: 40,000
SALES (est): 20.8MM Privately Held
WEB: www.ladyburd.com
SIC: 2844 Cosmetic preparations

(G-5041)
LEATHER CRAFTSMEN INC (PA)
6 Dubon Ct (11735-1008)
PHONE..................631 752-9000
Fax: 516 752-9220
Howard Schneider, *President*
Joseph Fiore, *Vice Pres*
David Willis, *Sales Associate*
Ira Gershoff, *Director*
Robert Schneider, *Admin Sec*
EMP: 120
SQ FT: 18,000
SALES (est): 14.6MM Privately Held
WEB: www.leathercraftsmen.com
SIC: 2782 Albums

(G-5042)
LEATHER CRAFTSMEN INC
Also Called: Leather Craftsmen West
6 Dubon Ct (11735-1008)
PHONE..................714 429-9763
Howard Schneider, *President*
Ira Gershoff, *Sales Staff*
EMP: 50
SALES (corp-wide): 14.6MM Privately Held
WEB: www.leathercraftsmen.com
SIC: 2782 Albums
PA: Leather Craftsmen, Inc.
  6 Dubon Ct
  Farmingdale NY 11735
  631 752-9000

(G-5043)
LEVON GRAPHICS CORP
210 Route 109 (11735-1503)
P.O. Box 9073 (11735-9073)
PHONE..................631 753-2022
Donna A Dickran, *Ch of Bd*
Harry L Dickran, *President*
Larry Dupkin, *Opers Staff*
Mario Devita, *Director*
Debbie Kubler, *Admin Asst*
EMP: 80
SQ FT: 42,000
SALES (est): 17.7MM Privately Held
WEB: www.levongraphics.com
SIC: 2752 2759 Commercial printing, offset; commercial printing

(G-5044)
LOGOMAX INC
242 Route 109 Ste B (11735-1500)
PHONE..................631 420-0484
Victor Rouse, *President*
Annette Regan, *Sales Staff*
EMP: 4 EST: 1998
SALES: 1.1MM Privately Held
WEB: www.logomaxusa.com
SIC: 2759 Screen printing

(G-5045)
LONG ISLAND ICED TEA CORP (PA)
12 Dubon Ct Ste 1 (11735-1025)
PHONE..................855 542-2832
Philip J Thomas, *CEO*
Julian Davidson, *Ch of Bd*
Peter Dydensborg, *COO*
Richard B Allen, *CFO*
James Meehan,
EMP: 29
SQ FT: 5,000
SALES: 4.5MM Publicly Held
SIC: 2086 Iced tea & fruit drinks, bottled & canned

(G-5046)
LOS OLIVOS LTD
105 Bi County Blvd (11735-3919)
PHONE..................631 773-6439
Ester Alvarado, *Ch of Bd*
EMP: 135
SALES (est): 3.2MM Privately Held
SIC: 3556 Smokers, food processing equipment

(G-5047)
M C PACKAGING CORPORATION (PA)
200 Adams Blvd (11735-6615)
P.O. Box 1031, Melville (11747-0031)
PHONE..................631 694-3012
Fax: 631 694-6135
Robert M Silverberg, *Ch of Bd*
Marc Silverberg, *President*
John Kurek, *Vice Pres*
Kerstein Carter, *Manager*
▲ EMP: 21
SQ FT: 9,000
SALES (est): 25.1MM Privately Held
WEB: www.mcpkg.com
SIC: 2679 Cardboard products, except die-cut

(G-5048)
MACHINIT INC
400 Smith St (11735-1105)
PHONE..................631 454-9297
Tony Kusturic, *President*
Edward Grcic, *General Mgr*
Tony Kustics, *Controller*
EMP: 4
SALES: 2MM Privately Held
SIC: 2253 Knit outerwear mills

(G-5049)
MAN PRODUCTS INC
99 Milbar Blvd Unit 1 (11735-1407)
PHONE..................631 789-6500
Fax: 631 789-1313
Attilio Mancusi, *President*
Corrain Bar, *General Mgr*
EMP: 30
SALES (est): 4.9MM Privately Held
WEB: www.manproducts.com
SIC: 3448 Prefabricated metal buildings

(G-5050)
MARKEN LLP
123 Smith St (11735-1004)
PHONE..................631 396-7454
Steve Roese, *Partner*
James Schaitel, *Manager*
EMP: 8
SQ FT: 10,000
SALES (corp-wide): 60.9B Publicly Held
SIC: 2834 4731 Tablets, pharmaceutical; freight forwarding
HQ: Marken Llp
  1009 Slater Rd Ste 120
  Durham NC 27703
  919 474-6892

(G-5051)
MAROTTA DENTAL STUDIO INC
130 Finn Ct (11735-1107)
PHONE..................631 249-7520
Fax: 631 249-2343
Leonard Marotta, *President*
Steven Pigliacelli, *Vice Pres*
Chris Marotta, *Treasurer*
Joshua Marotta, *Manager*
Chelsea Rodland, *Executive Asst*
EMP: 40
SQ FT: 15,000
SALES (est): 7.4MM Privately Held
WEB: www.marottadental.com
SIC: 3843 8021 8072 Dental materials; offices & clinics of dentists; dental laboratories

(G-5052)
MART-TEX ATHLETICS INC
180 Allen Blvd (11735-5617)
PHONE..................631 454-9583
Fax: 516 454-1604
Richard Marte, *President*
Raymond Marte Jr, *Corp Secy*
EMP: 35
SQ FT: 15,000
SALES (est): 3.9MM Privately Held
WEB: www.mart-tex.com
SIC: 2396 Screen printing on fabric articles

(G-5053)
MASTER MOLDING INC
97 Gazza Blvd (11735-1401)
PHONE..................631 694-1444
Fax: 631 694-6230
Peter Innvar, *President*
EMP: 15
SQ FT: 11,000
SALES (est): 2.3MM Privately Held
SIC: 3089 Injection molding of plastics

(G-5054)
MAXUS PHARMACEUTICALS INC
Also Called: Island Vitamin
50 Executive Blvd Ste B (11735-4712)
PHONE..................631 249-0003
Bob Kathuria, *President*
Survir Salaria, *Vice Pres*
EMP: 12
SALES: 1MM Privately Held
SIC: 2834 Pharmaceutical preparations

(G-5055)
MAZZA CLASSICS INCORPORATED
117 Gazza Blvd (11735-1415)
PHONE..................631 390-9060
Jim Rivera, *President*
Esther Rivera, *Office Mgr*
EMP: 7
SQ FT: 5,000
SALES: 500K Privately Held
SIC: 2512 Upholstered household furniture

(G-5056)
MEMORY PROTECTION DEVICES INC
200 Broadhollow Rd Ste 4 (11735-4814)
PHONE..................631 249-0001
Fax: 631 249-0002
Thomas Blaha, *President*
Charles Engelstein, *Chairman*
Daniel Lynch, *Vice Pres*
Dan Lynch, *Info Tech Mgr*
Letitia Dicicco, *Admin Asst*
EMP: 10
SQ FT: 3,000
SALES: 7MM Privately Held
WEB: www.memoryprotectiondevices.com
SIC: 3089 Battery cases, plastic or plastic combination

(G-5057)
MERB LLC
Also Called: Belgian Boys USA
140 Carolyn Blvd (11735-1525)
PHONE..................631 393-3621
Michael Berro, *President*
Ricardo Dellajiovanna, *Vice Pres*
EMP: 10 EST: 2013
SQ FT: 2,000
SALES: 10MM Privately Held
SIC: 2099 Food preparations

(G-5058)
METADURE DEFENSE & SEC LLC
165 Gazza Blvd (11735-1415)
PHONE..................631 249-2141
Gary Templeton, *President*
Nickos Chatzis, *Vice Pres*
George Strouzakis, *Vice Pres*
EMP: 12
SALES (est): 574.3K Privately Held
SIC: 3448 9711 Prefabricated metal buildings; national security

(G-5059)
METADURE PARTS & SALES INC
Also Called: Sbcontract.com
165 Gazza Blvd (11735-1415)
PHONE..................631 249-2141
Gary Templeton, *President*
Mike Foster, *QA Dir*
Nicholas Picon, *QC Mgr*
Cristine Tesimone, *Manager*
EMP: 12
SQ FT: 10,000
SALES (est): 2.2MM Privately Held
SIC: 3728 Military aircraft equipment & armament

(G-5060)
METROPLTAN DATA SLTONS MGT INC
279 Conklin St (11735-2608)
P.O. Box 11394, Newark NJ (07101-4394)
PHONE..................516 586-5520
John Dankowitz, *President*
Jonathan Friedfertig, *Accounts Mgr*
Patricia Dankowitz, *Administration*
EMP: 11
SQ FT: 1,500
SALES (est): 2MM Privately Held
SIC: 3089 Identification cards, plastic

(G-5061)
MICROWAVE CIRCUIT TECH INC
45 Central Dr (11735-1201)
PHONE..................631 845-1041
Brit Andresen, *CEO*
Edward Frankoski, *President*
Leif Andresen, *Vice Pres*
Elsie Andresen, *CFO*
Kariann Hunter, *Director*
EMP: 30
SQ FT: 5,700
SALES (est): 4.1MM Privately Held
WEB: www.mct-rf.com
SIC: 3679 Microwave components

(G-5062)
MID ISLAND DIE CUTTING CORP
77 Schmitt Blvd (11735-1403)
PHONE..................631 293-0180
Robert Geier, *President*
Matt Brenner, *Info Tech Mgr*
Ruth Geier, *Admin Sec*
EMP: 200
SQ FT: 12,000
SALES (est): 33.4MM Privately Held
SIC: 2675 Die-cut paper & board

(G-5063)
MID ISLAND GROUP
Also Called: Geier Bindery Co
77 Schmitt Blvd (11735-1403)
PHONE..................631 293-0180
Robert Geier, *President*
Bob Russo, *Vice Pres*
EMP: 25
SQ FT: 40,000
SALES (est): 4MM Privately Held
WEB: www.midislandgroup.com
SIC: 2789 Binding only: books, pamphlets, magazines, etc.

Farmingdale - Nassau County (G-5064)

(G-5064)
MID-ISLAND BINDERY INC
77 Schmitt Blvd (11735-1403)
PHONE................................631 293-0180
Robert Geier, *CEO*
EMP: 48
SQ FT: 30,000
SALES (est): 6.2MM **Privately Held**
SIC: 2789 Pamphlets, binding

(G-5065)
MILLER TECHNOLOGY INC
61 Gazza Blvd (11735-1401)
PHONE................................631 694-2224
Walter Miller Jr, *President*
Joane Miller, *Treasurer*
EMP: 5 **EST:** 1954
SQ FT: 3,000
SALES: 250K **Privately Held**
SIC: 3089 3369 3599 Casting of plastic; castings, except die-castings, precision; machine shop, jobbing & repair

(G-5066)
MIRAGE MOULDING MFG INC
Also Called: Mirage Moulding & Supply
160 Milbar Blvd (11735-1425)
PHONE................................631 843-6168
Hashim Ismailzadah, *President*
▲ **EMP:** 10
SALES (est): 1.3MM **Privately Held**
SIC: 3089 Molding primary plastic

(G-5067)
MISONIX INC (PA)
1938 New Hwy (11735-1214)
PHONE................................631 694-9555
Fax: 516 694-9412
Stavros G Vizirgianakis, *CEO*
Marc Sconzo, *Area Mgr*
Robert S Ludecker, *Senior VP*
Michael C Ryan, *Senior VP*
Joseph J Brennan, *Vice Pres*
▲ **EMP:** 85
SQ FT: 34,400
SALES: 27.2MM **Publicly Held**
WEB: www.misonix.com
SIC: 3841 3845 3677 Surgical & medical instruments; electromedical equipment; electronic coils, transformers & other inductors

(G-5068)
MKT329 INC
Also Called: Superior Packaging
565 Broadhollow Rd Ste 5 (11735-4826)
P.O. Box 667, North Bellmore (11710-0667)
PHONE................................631 249-5500
Marlene Tallon, *President*
▲ **EMP:** 17 **EST:** 2014
SQ FT: 121
SALES (est): 3.1MM **Privately Held**
SIC: 2653 Corrugated & solid fiber boxes

(G-5069)
MOREY PUBLISHING
Also Called: Long Island Press
20 Hempstead Tpke Unit B (11735-2043)
PHONE................................516 284-3300
Fax: 516 284-3310
Jed Morey, *Ch of Bd*
Beverly Fortune, *Publisher*
Timothy Bolger, *Editor*
Jon Sasala, *Editor*
Jamie Castagna, *Business Mgr*
EMP: 30
SALES (est): 4.4MM **Privately Held**
SIC: 2741 Miscellaneous publishing

(G-5070)
NAMEPLATE MFRS OF AMER
65 Toledo St (11735-6520)
PHONE................................631 752-0055
Bill Williams, *CEO*
Darren Cash, *COO*
Connie Case, *Office Mgr*
EMP: 40
SQ FT: 8,000
SALES (est): 4.9MM **Privately Held**
WEB: www.nameplateamerica.com
SIC: 3479 3993 2752 2671 Name plates: engraved, etched, etc.; signs & advertising specialties; commercial printing, lithographic; packaging paper & plastics film, coated & laminated

(G-5071)
NATIONWIDE SALES AND SERVICE
303 Smith St Ste 4 (11735-1110)
PHONE................................631 491-6625
Mark Genoa, *Ch of Bd*
Scott Genoa, *Vice Pres*
▲ **EMP:** 10
SQ FT: 10,000
SALES (est): 1.6MM **Privately Held**
WEB: www.shopnss.com
SIC: 3635 5087 5722 Household vacuum cleaners; janitors' supplies; vacuum cleaning systems; vacuum cleaners

(G-5072)
NEIGHBOR NEWSPAPERS
565 Broadhollow Rd Ste 3 (11735-4826)
PHONE................................631 226-2636
Richard A Freedman, *Principal*
EMP: 7
SALES (est): 378.6K **Privately Held**
SIC: 2711 Newspapers, publishing & printing

(G-5073)
NEILSON INTERNATIONAL INC
144 Allen Blvd Ste B (11735-5644)
P.O. Box 784, Hicksville (11802-0784)
PHONE................................631 454-0400
Kamlesh Mehta, *President*
▲ **EMP:** 3
SQ FT: 8,000
SALES: 1MM **Privately Held**
WEB: www.neilsoninc.com
SIC: 2211 Print cloths, cotton

(G-5074)
NESTLE HEALTHCARE NTRTN INC
Also Called: Haagen-Dazs
565 Broadhollow Rd (11735-4831)
PHONE................................516 249-5085
Bill Boraczek, *Principal*
EMP: 6
SALES (corp-wide): 88.4B **Publicly Held**
SIC: 2099 5812 Food preparations; ice cream, soft drink & soda fountain stands
HQ: Nestle Healthcare Nutrition, Inc.
12 Vreeland Rd Fl 2
Florham Park NJ 07932
952 848-6000

(G-5075)
NETECH CORPORATION
110 Toledo St (11735-6623)
PHONE................................631 531-0100
Fax: 631 433-7458
Mohan Das, *President*
Nicole Nipp, *Opers Staff*
Amelia Voccola, *Opers Staff*
Jessica Roush, *Engineer*
Ginger Spray, *Engineer*
EMP: 11
SQ FT: 4,500
SALES (est): 1.9MM **Privately Held**
WEB: www.gonetech.com
SIC: 3845 Electromedical equipment

(G-5076)
NOGA DAIRIES INC
Also Called: Dairy Delite
175 Price Pkwy (11735-1318)
PHONE................................516 293-5448
Eli Paz, *CEO*
Zami Leinson, *President*
▲ **EMP:** 10
SQ FT: 22,000
SALES (est): 1.3MM **Privately Held**
SIC: 2026 2022 Yogurt; spreads, cheese

(G-5077)
NORTECH LABORATORIES INC
125 Sherwood Ave (11735-1717)
PHONE................................631 501-1452
Fax: 631 501-1453
Caryn Nazarieh, *President*
David Nazarieh, *Vice Pres*
Jonathan Nazarieh, *VP Sales*
Daniel Dunleavy, *Mktg Dir*
Sandra Spencer, *Admin Sec*
EMP: 17
SQ FT: 16,200
SALES (est): 2.9MM **Privately Held**
WEB: www.nortechlabs.com
SIC: 3842 Surgical appliances & supplies

(G-5078)
NUTRASCIENCE LABS INC
70 Carolyn Blvd (11735-1525)
PHONE................................631 247-0660
Steve Rolfes, *CEO*
Vincent Tricarico, *Vice Pres*
Blayney McEneaney, *VP Sales*
EMP: 27 **EST:** 2014
SALES (est): 1MM
SALES (corp-wide): 86.3MM **Privately Held**
SIC: 2834 2833 Pharmaceutical preparations; druggists' preparations (pharmaceuticals); botanical products, medicinal; ground, graded or milled
PA: Twinlab Consolidated Holdings Inc.
4800 T Rex Ave Ste 305
Boca Raton FL 33431
561 443-4301

(G-5079)
O C P INC
Also Called: Morania Oil of Long Island
500 Bi County Blvd # 209 (11735-3931)
PHONE................................516 679-2000
Ronald I Shields, *President*
Chris Westad, *Financial Exec*
EMP: 40
SQ FT: 6,000
SALES (est): 5.6MM **Privately Held**
SIC: 3433 Heaters, swimming pool: oil or gas

(G-5080)
ORICS INDUSTRIES INC
240 Smith St (11735-1113)
PHONE................................718 461-8613
Ori Cohen, *Ch of Bd*
Suzi Oneill, *Executive Asst*
▲ **EMP:** 50
SQ FT: 15,000
SALES (est): 24.2MM **Privately Held**
WEB: www.orics.com
SIC: 3565 3841 Packaging machinery; surgical & medical instruments

(G-5081)
ORLANDI INC (PA)
Also Called: Orlandi Scented Products
131 Executive Blvd (11735-4719)
PHONE................................631 756-0110
Sven Dobler, *Ch of Bd*
Kenneth Kane, *Senior VP*
Douglas M Whitaker, *Senior VP*
Per Dobler, *Vice Pres*
Henri Liesenfelt, *Vice Pres*
▲ **EMP:** 100
SQ FT: 80,000
SALES (est): 34.2MM **Privately Held**
WEB: www.orlandi-usa.com
SIC: 3993 3999 7389 2752 Signs & advertising specialties; novelties, bric-a-brac & hobby kits; packaging & labeling services; commercial printing, lithographic

(G-5082)
ORLANDI INC
121 Executive Blvd (11735-4719)
PHONE................................631 756-0110
Sven Dobler, *President*
Kevin O'Leary, *Controller*
EMP: 50
SQ FT: 45,500
SALES (corp-wide): 34.2MM **Privately Held**
SIC: 3993 3999 7389 2752 Signs & advertising specialties; novelties, bric-a-brac & hobby kits; packaging & labeling services; commercial printing, lithographic
PA: Orlandi, Inc.
131 Executive Blvd
Farmingdale NY 11735
631 756-0110

(G-5083)
OSI PHARMACEUTICALS LLC
500 Bi County Blvd # 118 (11735-3959)
PHONE................................631 847-0175
EMP: 84
SALES (corp-wide): 10.4B **Privately Held**
SIC: 2834 Mfg Pharmaceutical Preparations
HQ: Osi Pharmaceuticals, Llc
1 Bioscience Way Dr
Farmingdale NY 11735
631 962-2000

(G-5084)
OSI PHARMACEUTICALS LLC (DH)
1 Bioscience Way Dr (11735)
PHONE................................631 962-2000
Fax: 631 845-5671
Colin Goddard PHD, *CEO*
Gabriel Leung, *President*
Anker Lundemose MD PHD, *President*
Robert L Simon, *Exec VP*
Linda E Amper PHD, *Senior VP*
▼ **EMP:** 5
SALES (est): 83.3MM
SALES (corp-wide): 11.5B **Privately Held**
WEB: www.osip.com
SIC: 2834 8731 Drugs affecting neoplasms & endocrine systems; drugs acting on the central nervous system & sense organs; commercial physical research
HQ: Astellas Us Holding, Inc.
1 Astellas Way
Northbrook IL 60062
224 205-8800

(G-5085)
PCX AEROSTRUCTURES LLC
60 Milbar Blvd (11735-1406)
PHONE................................631 467-2632
David Duryea, *Engineer*
Leisa White, *Benefits Mgr*
Mike Iannotta, *Branch Mgr*
EMP: 25
SALES (corp-wide): 100MM **Privately Held**
SIC: 3441 Fabricated structural metal
PA: Pcx Aerostructures, Llc
300 Fenn Rd
Newington CT 06111
860 666-2471

(G-5086)
PEERLESS INSTRUMENT CO INC
1966 Broadhollow Rd Ste D (11735-1726)
PHONE................................631 396-6500
Fax: 631 243-5408
Martin R Benante, *CEO*
David Linton, *President*
Frederic Borah, *General Mgr*
Klaus Steinmeyer, *Vice Pres*
Fran Vargas, *Buyer*
EMP: 109 **EST:** 1938
SQ FT: 55,000
SALES (est): 28.7MM
SALES (corp-wide): 2.1B **Publicly Held**
WEB: www.peerlessny.com
SIC: 3829 7389 3825 3625 Measuring & controlling devices; design services; instruments to measure electricity; relays & industrial controls
PA: Curtiss-Wright Corporation
13925 Balntyn Corp Pl
Charlotte NC 28277
704 869-4600

(G-5087)
PHARBEST PHARMACEUTICALS INC
14 Engineers Ln Ste 1 (11735-1219)
PHONE................................631 249-5130
Munir Islam, *President*
Intekhab Ahmed, *Manager*
Nishant Parikh, *Manager*
▲ **EMP:** 41
SQ FT: 22,000
SALES (est): 8MM **Privately Held**
WEB: www.pharbestusa.com
SIC: 2834 Druggists' preparations (pharmaceuticals)

(G-5088)
PHARMALIFE INC
130 Gazza Blvd (11735-1420)
PHONE................................631 249-4040
Larry Sayage, *President*
EMP: 5 **EST:** 1999
SQ FT: 4,300
SALES (est): 692.9K **Privately Held**
SIC: 2834 Vitamin, nutrient & hematinic preparations for human use

Farmingdale - Nassau County

(G-5089)
PHOENIX LABORATORIES INC
200 Adams Blvd (11735-6615)
PHONE..................................516 822-1230
Melvin Rich, *President*
Stephen R Stern, *Exec VP*
Al Assa, *Controller*
Steven Tuohey, *Director*
Charlotte Rich, *Admin Sec*
EMP: 180 EST: 1966
SQ FT: 40,000
SALES (est): 24.9MM **Privately Held**
WEB: www.phoenixlaboratories.com
SIC: 2834 Vitamin, nutrient & hematinic preparations for human use; vitamin preparations

(G-5090)
PIRNAT PRECISE METALS INC
Also Called: F & M Precise Metals Co
127 Marine St (11735-5609)
PHONE..................................631 293-9169
Frank Pirnat, *President*
Mark Pirnat, *Vice Pres*
EMP: 7 EST: 1967
SQ FT: 10,000
SALES (est): 1.2MM **Privately Held**
SIC: 3444 Sheet metalwork

(G-5091)
PLASCAL CORP
361 Eastern Pkwy (11735-2713)
P.O. Box 590 (11735-0590)
PHONE..................................516 249-2200
Fax: 516 249-2256
Mark Hurd, *CEO*
Fred Hurd, *President*
Sheldon Eskowitz, *Corp Secy*
Thomas Blackler, *Vice Pres*
Raymond Brown, *Vice Pres*
▲ **EMP:** 4 EST: 1975
SQ FT: 75,000
SALES: 6MM **Privately Held**
WEB: www.plascal.com
SIC: 3081 Vinyl film & sheet

(G-5092)
PLATINUM PRINTING & GRAPHICS
70 Carolyn Blvd Ste C (11735-1525)
PHONE..................................631 249-3325
Fax: 516 249-3318
Paul Currao, *President*
EMP: 5 EST: 1996
SALES (est): 474.8K **Privately Held**
SIC: 2752 Commercial printing, lithographic

(G-5093)
POLYPLASTIC FORMS INC
49 Gazza Blvd (11735-1401)
PHONE..................................631 249-5011
Fax: 516 249-8504
Thomas Garrett, *President*
Diane Garrett, *Corp Secy*
Richard Garrett, *Vice Pres*
Nancy Behrens, *Administration*
EMP: 35
SQ FT: 10,000
SALES (est): 5.2MM **Privately Held**
WEB: www.polyplasticforms.com
SIC: 3993 Displays & cutouts, window & lobby; signs, not made in custom sign painting shops

(G-5094)
POSILLICO MATERIALS LLC
1750 New Hwy (11735-1562)
PHONE..................................631 249-1872
Joseph K Posillico, *CEO*
Michael J Posillico, *President*
Mario A Posillico, *Chairman*
Joseph D Posillico, *Senior VP*
Paul F Posillico, *Senior VP*
EMP: 11 EST: 1971
SQ FT: 2,500
SALES (est): 15.2MM **Privately Held**
SIC: 2951 Asphalt & asphaltic paving mixtures (not from refineries)

(G-5095)
PRECIPART CORPORATION
120 Finn Ct Ste 2 (11735-1121)
PHONE..................................631 694-3100
Fax: 631 694-4016
John P Walter, *President*
Lloyd W Miller, *Chairman*
Georges Assimilalo, *COO*
Karl Walter, *Vice Pres*
Donald Weinzimer, *Vice Pres*
EMP: 216
SQ FT: 16,200
SALES: 43.6MM **Privately Held**
WEB: www.precipart.com
SIC: 3566 Speed changers, drives & gears
PA: Precipart Group, Inc.
100 Finn Ct
Farmingdale NY 11735

(G-5096)
PRECISION ENVELOPE CO INC
Also Called: H & R Precision
110 Schmitt Blvd 7a (11735-6961)
PHONE..................................631 694-3990
Fax: 631 694-3998
Gilbert M Colombo Jr, *President*
Jane Colombo, *Corp Secy*
EMP: 9
SQ FT: 7,000
SALES (est): 1.3MM **Privately Held**
SIC: 2759 2752 Envelopes: printing; stationery: printing; business forms, lithographed

(G-5097)
PRECISION LABEL CORPORATION
175 Marine St (11735-5609)
PHONE..................................631 270-4490
Bradley A Cohn, *CEO*
EMP: 12
SQ FT: 4,000
SALES (est): 1.7MM **Privately Held**
SIC: 2759 2679 Labels & seals: printing; labels, paper: made from purchased material

(G-5098)
PRINT PACK INC (DH)
70 Schmitt Blvd (11735-1404)
PHONE..................................404 460-7000
Barbara Drillings, *Marketing Staff*
◆ **EMP:** 150
SQ FT: 100,000
SALES (est): 21.5MM
SALES (corp-wide): 1.3B **Privately Held**
WEB: www.sealitinc.com
SIC: 2671 2759 Packaging paper & plastics film, coated & laminated; labels & seals: printing
HQ: Printpack, Inc.
2800 Overlook Pkwy Ne
Atlanta GA 30339
404 460-7000

(G-5099)
PROMPT PRINTING INC
160 Rome St (11735-6609)
PHONE..................................631 454-6524
Fax: 631 454-6370
John Probst, *President*
EMP: 6 EST: 1980
SQ FT: 2,000
SALES: 370K **Privately Held**
SIC: 2752 Commercial printing, offset

(G-5100)
PROOF INDUSTRIES INC
125 Rome St (11735-6606)
PHONE..................................631 694-7663
Vincent Cacioppo, *President*
Christie Cacioppo, *Office Mgr*
EMP: 9
SQ FT: 3,000
SALES (est): 1.3MM **Privately Held**
WEB: www.proofroof.com
SIC: 2439 5999 1751 Trusses, wooden roof; awnings; window & door (prefabricated) installation

(G-5101)
PROPER CHEMICAL LTD
280 Smith St (11735-1113)
PHONE..................................631 420-8000
Emil Backstrom, *President*
EMP: 5
SQ FT: 20,000
SALES (est): 400K **Privately Held**
SIC: 2833 Medicinal chemicals

(G-5102)
QUALIFIED MANUFACTURING CORP
134 Toledo St (11735-6625)
PHONE..................................631 249-4440
Donald Wojnar, *President*
EMP: 11 EST: 1970
SQ FT: 7,000
SALES (est): 1.5MM **Privately Held**
SIC: 3599 Machine shop, jobbing & repair

(G-5103)
QUALITY STAIR BUILDERS INC
95 Schmitt Blvd (11735-1403)
PHONE..................................631 694-0711
Fax: 516 694-0712
Esta Topal, *President*
Sherri Sugar, *Corp Secy*
EMP: 16 EST: 1955
SQ FT: 10,000
SALES (est): 2.2MM **Privately Held**
SIC: 2431 Staircases & stairs, wood

(G-5104)
QUICK SIGN F X
6 Powell St (11735-4019)
PHONE..................................516 249-6531
Steve Levine, *President*
EMP: 13
SALES (est): 825.7K **Privately Held**
SIC: 3993 Signs & advertising specialties

(G-5105)
R & J GRAPHICS INC
45 Central Ave (11735-6901)
PHONE..................................631 293-6611
Fax: 631 293-0303
John Merendino, *President*
Vinnie Farrell, *Sales Staff*
Ann Merendino, *Admin Sec*
EMP: 16
SQ FT: 15,000
SALES (est): 2.9MM **Privately Held**
SIC: 2752 Commercial printing, offset

(G-5106)
R D PRINTING ASSOCIATES INC
1865 New Hwy Ste 1 (11735-1501)
PHONE..................................631 390-5964
Fax: 516 694-8489
Ralph Demartino Jr, *President*
EMP: 14
SQ FT: 10,000
SALES (est): 1.4MM **Privately Held**
SIC: 2752 Commercial printing, offset

(G-5107)
RASON ASPHALT INC (PA)
Rr 110 (11735)
P.O. Box 530, Old Bethpage (11804-0530)
PHONE..................................631 293-6210
Fax: 631 293-6849
Anthony J Shakesby, *President*
Tony Shakesby, *Vice Pres*
Donna Bryan, *Manager*
Kim Hartley, *Manager*
John F Hendrickson, *Admin Sec*
EMP: 7 EST: 1950
SALES (est): 10.2MM **Privately Held**
WEB: www.rason1.com
SIC: 2951 Asphalt paving mixtures & blocks

(G-5108)
RENEWAL BY ANDERSEN LLC
Also Called: Renewal By Andrsen Long Island
2029 New Hwy (11735-1103)
PHONE..................................631 843-1716
EMP: 43
SALES (corp-wide): 2.7B **Privately Held**
SIC: 3442 Screens, window, metal
HQ: Renewal By Andersen Llc
9900 Jamaica Ave S
Cottage Grove MN 55016
855 871-7377

(G-5109)
RICO INTERNATIONAL
8484 San Fernando Rd (11735)
P.O. Box 290 (11735-0290)
PHONE..................................818 767-7711
Dan Fasani, *General Mgr*
EMP: 5 EST: 2009
SALES (est): 616.9K **Privately Held**
SIC: 3931 Reeds for musical instruments

(G-5110)
RIPI PRECISION CO INC (PA)
92 Toledo St (11735-6623)
PHONE..................................631 694-2453
Fax: 631 694-2458
Michael Perciballi, *President*
EMP: 12
SQ FT: 12,000
SALES (est): 2.5MM **Privately Held**
SIC: 3728 Aircraft parts & equipment

(G-5111)
ROBOCOM US LLC (HQ)
Also Called: Robocom Systems International
1111 Broadhollow Rd # 100 (11735-4819)
PHONE..................................631 861-2045
Fred Radcliffe, *President*
Richard Adamo, *Vice Pres*
Raymond Oconnor, *Vice Pres*
Steve Pharo, *Purchasing*
Elias Jubran, *Engineer*
EMP: 13
SQ FT: 4,000
SALES: 7MM
SALES (corp-wide): 219K **Privately Held**
WEB: www.avantce.com
SIC: 7372 Prepackaged software
PA: Avantc, Llc
3838 Tamiami Trl N # 416
Naples FL 34103
407 312-8445

(G-5112)
ROLI RETREADS INC
Also Called: Roli Tire and Auto Repair
212 E Carmans Rd Unit A (11735-4722)
PHONE..................................631 694-7670
Fax: 631 694-7625
Richard Bucci, *Owner*
EMP: 20
SQ FT: 6,500
SALES (est): 4.2MM **Privately Held**
WEB: www.rolitire.com
SIC: 3011 7549 Tire & inner tube materials & related products; automotive maintenance services

(G-5113)
ROTA PACK INC
34 Sarah Dr Ste B (11735-1218)
PHONE..................................631 274-1037
Adrian Spirea, *Ch of Bd*
EMP: 11
SALES: 525K **Privately Held**
WEB: www.rotaindustries.com
SIC: 3565 3535 Packaging machinery; conveyors & conveying equipment

(G-5114)
ROZAL INDUSTRIES INC
151 Marine St (11735-5609)
PHONE..................................631 420-4277
Brian Casio, *President*
Gary Grieber, *Vice Pres*
EMP: 47
SALES (est): 3.8MM **Privately Held**
SIC: 3599 Machine shop, jobbing & repair

(G-5115)
RS PRECISION INDUSTRIES INC
295 Adams Blvd (11735-6632)
PHONE..................................631 420-0424
Fax: 516 249-2624
Robert Savitzky, *President*
John Popescu, *Mfg Staff*
George Macy, *Engineer*
Thomas Shelby, *Engineer*
Eileen Levine, *Manager*
EMP: 24
SQ FT: 6,700
SALES (est): 6.6MM **Privately Held**
WEB: www.rsprecision.com
SIC: 3339 Primary nonferrous metals

(G-5116)
S & V KNITS INC
117 Marine St (11735-5607)
PHONE..................................631 752-1595
Steve Sustrean, *President*
Virginia Sustrean, *Vice Pres*
Doris Alfson, *Accountant*
EMP: 30
SQ FT: 14,000

Farmingdale - Nassau County (G-5117)

SALES (est): 2.8MM **Privately Held**
SIC: **2253** 2339 Knit outerwear mills; sweaters & sweater coats, knit; women's & misses' outerwear

(G-5117)
SABRA DIPPING COMPANY LLC
535 Smith St (11735-1116)
PHONE..................516 249-0151
Abner Hornick, *Exec Dir*
EMP: 10 **Privately Held**
SIC: **2099** 5148 Food preparations; fresh fruits & vegetables
HQ: Sabra Dipping Company, Llc
777 Westchester Ave Fl 3
White Plains NY 10604

(G-5118)
SEANAIR MACHINE CO INC
95 Verdi St (11735-6320)
PHONE..................631 694-2820
Fax: 631 694-2859
Laura Abel Nawrocki, *Ch of Bd*
Dorothy Abel, *President*
Thomas J Nawrochi, *Vice Pres*
Laura Abel, *Info Tech Mgr*
EMP: 18 EST: 1955
SQ FT: 16,000
SALES (est): 3.3MM **Privately Held**
SIC: **3599** Machine shop, jobbing & repair

(G-5119)
SIMTEC INDUSTRIES CORPORATION
65 Marine St Ste A (11735-5638)
PHONE..................631 293-0080
Jean J Simon, *President*
EMP: 6
SALES: 1MM **Privately Held**
SIC: **3552** Textile machinery

(G-5120)
SKYLINE CUSTOM CABINETRY INC
200 Verdi St Unit A (11735-6337)
PHONE..................631 393-2983
Lisa Mumalo, *Principal*
EMP: 5
SALES (est): 506.1K **Privately Held**
SIC: **2434** Wood kitchen cabinets

(G-5121)
SMITH GRAPHICS INC
40 Florida St (11735-6301)
PHONE..................631 420-4180
Rick Smith, *President*
Beryl Smith, *Vice Pres*
David Smith, *Sales Mgr*
EMP: 8
SQ FT: 2,500
SALES: 1.2MM **Privately Held**
WEB: www.smithgraphicsinc.com
SIC: **3993** Signs & advertising specialties

(G-5122)
SOURCE ENVELOPE INC
104 Allen Blvd Ste I (11735-5627)
PHONE..................866 284-0707
Fred Blustein, *President*
Alan Blustein, *Vice Pres*
David Blustein, *Treasurer*
EMP: 9
SQ FT: 2,000
SALES (est): 963.4K **Privately Held**
WEB: www.source-envelope.com
SIC: **2752** 2759 Commercial printing, lithographic; letterpress printing

(G-5123)
SPACE COAST SEMICONDUCTOR INC
1111 Broadhollow Rd Fl 3 (11735-4881)
PHONE..................631 414-7131
Anthony Tamborrino, *Director*
EMP: 10
SALES (est): 682.4K **Privately Held**
WEB: www.spacecoastsemi.com
SIC: **3679** Electronic components

(G-5124)
STANDWILL PACKAGING INC
220 Sherwood Ave (11735-1718)
PHONE..................631 752-1236
Fax: 516 752-8036
William Standwill Jr, *President*
Stacy Bardavid, *Opers Mgr*
Randy Hallam, *Prdtn Mgr*
▲ EMP: 25 EST: 1976
SQ FT: 15,000
SALES (est): 4.6MM **Privately Held**
WEB: www.standwill.com
SIC: **2752** 2759 Commercial printing, offset; commercial printing

(G-5125)
STAR DRAPERIES INC
24 Florida St (11735-6301)
PHONE..................631 756-7121
Fax: 631 756-7121
Jacqueline Stolberg, *CEO*
EMP: 10
SQ FT: 3,200
SALES (est): 1.1MM **Privately Held**
SIC: **2211** 5023 Draperies & drapery fabrics, cotton; draperies

(G-5126)
STAR MOLD CO INC
125 Florida St (11735-6307)
PHONE..................631 694-2283
Fax: 516 694-2283
Guenther Merz, *President*
EMP: 6
SQ FT: 2,400
SALES (est): 320K **Privately Held**
SIC: **3544** Industrial molds

(G-5127)
STEPHEN J LIPKINS INC
855 Conklin St Ste A (11735-2409)
PHONE..................631 249-8866
Fax: 631 420-0862
Jonathan Lipkins, *President*
EMP: 5
SQ FT: 2,800
SALES (est): 420K **Privately Held**
SIC: **3915** Jewel cutting, drilling, polishing, recutting or setting; jewelry polishing for the trade

(G-5128)
STERLING INDUSTRIES INC
410 Eastern Pkwy (11735-2431)
PHONE..................631 753-3070
Fax: 631 753-3075
Brian Lewis, *President*
EMP: 25
SALES (est): 4.4MM **Privately Held**
SIC: **3444** Sheet metalwork

(G-5129)
SUPERIOR METAL & WOODWORK INC
70 Central Ave (11735-6906)
PHONE..................631 465-9004
John Cipri, *President*
Joseph Cipri, *Vice Pres*
EMP: 25
SQ FT: 12,500
SALES (est): 6.5MM **Privately Held**
SIC: **3446** Architectural metalwork

(G-5130)
SUPERIOR MOTION CONTROLS INC
40 Smith St (11735-1005)
PHONE..................516 420-2921
Frank Grieco, *CEO*
Tony Reda, *Engineer*
EMP: 40
SQ FT: 20,000
SALES (est): 9.6MM **Privately Held**
WEB: www.superior-ny.com
SIC: **3728** 3679 3462 Aircraft assemblies, subassemblies & parts; electronic loads & power supplies; iron & steel forgings

(G-5131)
SWIMWEAR ANYWHERE INC (PA)
Also Called: Liz Claiborne Swimwear
85 Sherwood Ave (11735-1717)
PHONE..................631 420-1400
Rosemarie Dilorenzo, *Chairman*
Joseph Dilorenzo, *COO*
Mark Griem, *Facilities Mgr*
Joseph Roehrig, *CFO*
James Lamanna, *Accounting Mgr*
◆ EMP: 75 EST: 1998

SALES (est): 43.4MM **Privately Held**
SIC: **2339** Bathing suits: women's, misses' & juniors'

(G-5132)
SYNTHO PHARMACEUTICALS INC
230 Sherwood Ave (11735-1718)
PHONE..................631 755-9898
Hosneara Malik, *President*
EMP: 7
SALES (est): 2.1MM **Privately Held**
WEB: www.synthopharmaceutical.com
SIC: **2834** Pharmaceutical preparations

(G-5133)
T A TOOL & MOLDING INC
Also Called: Konrad Design
185 Marine St (11735-5609)
PHONE..................631 293-0172
Fax: 631 293-2647
Ludwig Konrad, *President*
Maryann Konrad, *Vice Pres*
EMP: 18
SALES (est): 2.2MM **Privately Held**
SIC: **3089** 3544 Injection molding of plastics; industrial molds

(G-5134)
TANGENT MACHINE & TOOL CORP
108 Gazza Blvd (11735-1489)
PHONE..................631 249-3088
Fax: 631 249-5503
Joseph A Scafidi, *President*
Charles C Piola, *CFO*
EMP: 20 EST: 1953
SQ FT: 30,000
SALES (est): 3.6MM **Privately Held**
SIC: **3599** 7692 3728 Machine shop, jobbing & repair; welding repair; aircraft parts & equipment

(G-5135)
TAPE PRINTERS INC
155 Allen Blvd Ste A (11735-5640)
PHONE..................631 249-5585
Alexander J Kruk, *President*
▲ EMP: 15
SQ FT: 10,000
SALES (est): 2.9MM **Privately Held**
WEB: www.tapeprinters.com
SIC: **2759** Bag, wrapper & seal printing & engraving; labels & seals: printing

(G-5136)
TELEPHONICS CORPORATION
Also Called: Communications Systems Div
815 Broadhollow Rd (11735-3937)
PHONE..................631 755-7659
EMP: 99
SALES (corp-wide): 1.9B **Publicly Held**
SIC: **3661** Telephone & telegraph apparatus
HQ: Telephonics Corporation
815 Broadhollow Rd
Farmingdale NY 11735
631 755-7000

(G-5137)
TELEPHONICS CORPORATION (HQ)
815 Broadhollow Rd (11735-3937)
PHONE..................631 755-7000
Fax: 631 755-7046
Joseph Battaglia, *President*
Mel French, *President*
Alan Bryan, *Principal*
Garfield Gray, *Business Mgr*
Thomas Barber, *Vice Pres*
▲ EMP: 667
SQ FT: 160,000
SALES (est): 347.2MM
SALES (corp-wide): 1.9B **Publicly Held**
SIC: **3669** 3661 3679 3812 Intercommunication systems, electric; telephone & telegraph apparatus; electronic circuits; radar systems & equipment; air traffic control systems & equipment, electronic; radio & TV communications equipment
PA: Griffon Corporation
712 5th Ave Fl 18
New York NY 10019
212 957-5000

(G-5138)
TELEPHONICS CORPORATION
Also Called: Command Systems Division
815 Broadhollow Rd (11735-3937)
PHONE..................631 755-7000
Joseph Battaglia, *CEO*
EMP: 99
SALES (corp-wide): 1.9B **Publicly Held**
SIC: **3699** Electronic training devices
HQ: Telephonics Corporation
815 Broadhollow Rd
Farmingdale NY 11735
631 755-7000

(G-5139)
THERMAL PROCESS CNSTR CO
19 Engineers Ln (11735-1207)
PHONE..................631 293-6400
Al Gupta, *President*
EMP: 22
SQ FT: 10,000
SALES (est): 1.5MM **Privately Held**
SIC: **3567** 3497 Incinerators, metal: domestic or commercial; metal foil & leaf

(G-5140)
TIGER SUPPLY INC
99 Sherwood Ave (11735-1717)
PHONE..................631 293-2700
Fax: 631 293-2707
Anthony Davanzo, *President*
Anthony Devanzo, *Human Res Dir*
EMP: 5
SALES (est): 789.4K **Privately Held**
WEB: www.tigersupplyinc.com
SIC: **3843** Dental equipment & supplies

(G-5141)
TIME-CAP LABORATORIES INC
Also Called: Custom Coatings
7 Michael Ave (11735-3921)
PHONE..................631 753-9090
Fax: 516 753-2220
Mark Saldanha, *Ch of Bd*
Irene McGregor, *Principal*
Robert Azzara, *COO*
Bob Azzara, *VP Opers*
Alex Martinez, *Production*
▲ EMP: 160
SQ FT: 45,000
SALES (est): 49.1MM **Privately Held**
SIC: **2834** Proprietary drug products
PA: Marksans Pharma Limited
Floor 11th Floor, Grandeur, Veera Desai Extension Road,
Mumbai MH 40005

(G-5142)
TIN BOX COMPANY OF AMERICA INC (PA)
216 Sherwood Ave (11735-1718)
P.O. Box 9068 (11735)
PHONE..................631 845-1600
Lloyd Roth, *President*
Andy Siegel, *Vice Pres*
Michael Siegel, *Vice Pres*
Stephen Siegel, *CFO*
Cathy Callahan-Pallone, *Manager*
▲ EMP: 25
SQ FT: 20,000
SALES (est): 2.9MM **Privately Held**
SIC: **2631** 5051 Container, packaging & boxboard; tin & tin base metals, shapes, forms, etc.

(G-5143)
TRI-FLEX LABEL CORP
48 Allen Blvd Unit A (11735-5642)
PHONE..................631 293-0411
Fax: 631 293-1496
Kevin Duckman, *President*
Kevin Duckham, *President*
Rich Arens, *Marketing Staff*
Denise Duckham, *Office Mgr*
Gene Saraniero, *Manager*
▲ EMP: 20
SQ FT: 6,000
SALES (est): 4.4MM **Privately Held**
WEB: www.triflexlabel.com
SIC: **2672** 2679 Labels (unprinted), gummed: made from purchased materials; labels, paper: made from purchased material

GEOGRAPHIC SECTION

(G-5144)
TRI-SUPREME OPTICAL LLC
Also Called: Tri Supreme Optical
91 Carolyn Blvd (11735-1527)
PHONE..................................631 249-2020
Fax: 516 249-0577
Michael Cooper, *General Mgr*
Robert Grecco, *Purchasing*
Eileen Lewis, *Personnel*
Richard Salberg, *Sales Mgr*
Larry Yellin, *Sales Mgr*
▲ EMP: 95
SQ FT: 18,000
SALES (est): 12.6MM
SALES (corp-wide): 938.9MM **Privately Held**
WEB: www.essilor.com
SIC: 3851 5049 Lenses, ophthalmic; optical goods
HQ: Essilor Of America, Inc.
13555 N Stemmons Fwy
Dallas TX 75234
214 496-4000

(G-5145)
TRONIC PLATING CO INC
37 Potter St (11735-4200)
PHONE..................................516 293-7883
Herbert Buckstone, *President*
Gerald Alletto, *President*
Stanley J Buckstone, *Vice Pres*
EMP: 11 EST: 1955
SQ FT: 6,000
SALES: 629.2K **Privately Held**
SIC: 3471 Electroplating of metals or formed products; finishing, metals or formed products

(G-5146)
ULTIMATE PRCISION MET PDTS INC
200 Finn Ct (11735-1119)
PHONE..................................631 249-9441
Fax: 631 777-1828
Michael Mallia, *CEO*
Vincent Mallia, *President*
Paul Mallia, *Principal*
Larry Mallia, *Vice Pres*
Joseph Reid, *Vice Pres*
▼ EMP: 125
SQ FT: 70,000
SALES (est): 25.3MM **Privately Held**
WEB: www.ultimateprecision.com
SIC: 3469 3544 3444 Stamping metal for the trade; special dies & tools; sheet metalwork

(G-5147)
VELOCITY PHARMA LLC
226 Sherwood Ave Unit B (11735-1732)
PHONE..................................516 312-7585
Ankur Shah, *President*
Nicholas Monte, *Director*
▲ EMP: 8
SQ FT: 20,000
SALES: 5.8MM **Privately Held**
SIC: 2834 Vitamin, nutrient & hematinic preparations for human use

(G-5148)
VITA-NAT INC
298 Adams Blvd (11735-6615)
PHONE..................................631 293-6000
Mohd M Alam, *President*
Khurshid Anwar, *Vice Pres*
Anwar Khurshid, *Vice Pres*
▲ EMP: 6
SQ FT: 7,000
SALES: 861.1K **Privately Held**
SIC: 2834 Vitamin, nutrient & hematinic preparations for human use

(G-5149)
W R P WELDING LTD
Also Called: Ramick Welding
126 Toledo St (11735-6625)
PHONE..................................631 249-8859
William R Pontecorvo, *President*
EMP: 6
SQ FT: 3,500
SALES (est): 542.1K **Privately Held**
SIC: 7692 Brazing

(G-5150)
WALNUT PACKAGING INC
450 Smith St (11735-1105)
PHONE..................................631 293-3836
Fax: 631 293-3878
Jose Alvarado, *President*
Sheila Haile, *Vice Pres*
Leslee Marin, *Controller*
Elba Radriguez, *Office Mgr*
EMP: 21
SQ FT: 14,000
SALES (est): 3.3MM **Privately Held**
WEB: www.wpiplasticbags.com
SIC: 3086 Packaging & shipping materials, foamed plastic

(G-5151)
WEL MADE ENTERPRISES INC
1630 New Hwy (11735-1510)
PHONE..................................631 752-1238
EMP: 14 EST: 1950
SQ FT: 1,800
SALES: 1.1MM **Privately Held**
SIC: 3272 Mfg Concrete Products

(G-5152)
WELLMILL LLC
Also Called: Vitamix Laboratories
141 Central Ave Ste B (11735-6903)
PHONE..................................631 465-9245
Robert Martino, *Opers Staff*
Michael Kochitz, *Mng Member*
EMP: 17
SALES: 750K **Privately Held**
SIC: 2834 Vitamin preparations

(G-5153)
XYLON INDUSTRIES INC
79 Florida St (11735-6305)
PHONE..................................631 293-4717
Fax: 631 293-4748
Joseph Jones, *President*
EMP: 5
SQ FT: 4,200
SALES: 850K **Privately Held**
SIC: 3842 2431 Radiation shielding aprons, gloves, sheeting, etc.; millwork

(G-5154)
ZINGS COMPANY LLC
250 Adams Blvd (11735-6615)
PHONE..................................631 454-0339
Fax: 631 694-2326
Robert Jagenburg,
EMP: 5
SALES (est): 385.1K **Privately Held**
WEB: www.zingsco.com
SIC: 2024 Juice pops, frozen

Farmington
Ontario County

(G-5155)
BADGER TECHNOLOGIES INC
5829 County Road 41 (14425-9103)
PHONE..................................585 869-7101
Fax: 315 531-9883
Dave Bronger, *Vice Pres*
Lauren Moran, *Personnel Exec*
Gary Gray, *Manager*
EMP: 45
SALES (corp-wide): 10.7MM **Privately Held**
WEB: www.badgertech.com
SIC: 3679 Harness assemblies for electronic use: wire or cable
PA: Badger Technologies, Inc.
5829 County Road 41
Farmington NY 14425
585 869-7101

(G-5156)
BADGER TECHNOLOGIES INC (PA)
5829 County Road 41 (14425-9103)
PHONE..................................585 869-7101
Fax: 585 869-7199
Manoj Shekar, *President*
Jim Harris, *General Mgr*
Jeff Sullivan, *CFO*
Barbara Jensen, *Accounts Mgr*
Nancy Rakiewicz, *Manager*
▲ EMP: 51

SQ FT: 15,000
SALES (est): 10.7MM **Privately Held**
WEB: www.badgertech.com
SIC: 3679 Harness assemblies for electronic use: wire or cable

(G-5157)
CROSMAN CORPORATION
1360 Rural Rte 8 (14425)
PHONE..................................585 398-3920
Steve Burley, *Branch Mgr*
EMP: 30
SALES (corp-wide): 978.3MM **Publicly Held**
SIC: 3484 3482 3563 Pellet & BB guns; pellets & BB's, pistol & air rifle ammunition; shot, steel (ammunition); air & gas compressors
HQ: Crosman Corporation
7629 State Route 5 And 20
Bloomfield NY 14469
585 657-6161

(G-5158)
EBSCO INDUSTRIES INC
Global Point Products
5815 County Road 41 (14425-9103)
PHONE..................................585 398-2000
David Testa, *Vice Pres*
EMP: 5
SALES (corp-wide): 1.8B **Privately Held**
WEB: www.ebscoind.com
SIC: 3861 Photographic equipment & supplies
PA: Ebsco Industries, Inc.
5724 Highway 280 E
Birmingham AL 35242
205 991-6600

(G-5159)
EMORY MACHINE & TOOL CO INC
6176 Hunters Dr (14425-1122)
PHONE..................................585 436-9610
James Fowler Jr, *President*
Rob Roney, *Manager*
EMP: 45
SQ FT: 30,000
SALES (est): 4.4MM **Privately Held**
WEB: www.emory-rockwood.com
SIC: 3599 3451 Machine shop, jobbing & repair; screw machine products

(G-5160)
GANNETT CO INC
Also Called: Democrat & Chronicle
6300 Collett Rd (14425-1075)
PHONE..................................585 924-3406
Karen Beach, *Manager*
EMP: 8
SALES (corp-wide): 3B **Publicly Held**
WEB: www.gannett.com
SIC: 2711 Newspapers
PA: Gannett Co., Inc.
7950 Jones Branch Dr
Mc Lean VA 22102
703 854-6000

(G-5161)
HANSEN STEEL
Also Called: Hansen Metal Fabrications
6021 County Road 41 (14425-8938)
PHONE..................................585 398-2020
Fax: 585 398-3138
Thomas Hansen, *Owner*
Mike Hansen, *Sales Executive*
EMP: 25
SQ FT: 13,500
SALES (est): 4MM **Privately Held**
SIC: 3441 7692 3444 Fabricated structural metal; welding repair; sheet metalwork

(G-5162)
INGLESIDE MACHINE CO INC
1120 Hook Rd (14425-8956)
PHONE..................................585 924-3046
Fax: 585 924-7904
Jan Marie Veomett, *Ch of Bd*
Gary Voemett, *Plant Mgr*
EMP: 80
SQ FT: 40,000
SALES (est): 11.6MM **Privately Held**
WEB: www.inglesidemachine.com
SIC: 7692 3599 Welding repair; machine shop, jobbing & repair

(G-5163)
ROCHESTER ASPHALT MATERIALS
5929 Loomis Rd (14425-9526)
PHONE..................................585 924-7360
Daniel Coe, *Branch Mgr*
EMP: 60
SALES (corp-wide): 28.6B **Privately Held**
SIC: 3273 Ready-mixed concrete
HQ: Rochester Asphalt Materials Inc
1150 Penfield Rd
Rochester NY 14625
585 381-7010

(G-5164)
ROCHESTER LUMBER COMPANY
Also Called: Trusses & Trim Division
6080 Collett Rd (14425-9531)
PHONE..................................585 924-7171
Fax: 585 924-7173
Paul Rickner, *Branch Mgr*
EMP: 30
SALES (corp-wide): 10.2MM **Privately Held**
SIC: 2439 2431 3442 Trusses, wooden roof; doors, wood; staircases & stairs, wood; metal doors, sash & trim
PA: Rochester Lumber Company
2040 East Ave
Rochester NY 14610
585 473-8080

(G-5165)
TCS ELECTRONICS INC
1124 Corporate Dr (14425-9570)
PHONE..................................585 337-4301
Jim Harris, *General Mgr*
Renee Strong, *Manager*
EMP: 27
SALES (est): 6MM **Privately Held**
SIC: 3672 3679 Circuit boards, television & radio printed; harness assemblies for electronic use: wire or cable

(G-5166)
VR FOOD EQUIPMENT INC
5801 County Road 41 (14425-9103)
P.O. Box 216, Penn Yan (14527-0216)
PHONE..................................315 531-8133
Fax: 315 531-8134
Steven A Von Rhedey, *Ch of Bd*
Isaac Von Rhedey, *Vice Pres*
Steven P Von Rhedey, *Vice Pres*
Peter Von Rhedey, *CFO*
Mary Guild, *Manager*
▲ EMP: 10
SQ FT: 15,000
SALES (est): 2.7MM **Privately Held**
WEB: www.vrfoodequipment.com
SIC: 3556 5084 Food products machinery; food industry machinery

Farmingville
Suffolk County

(G-5167)
BUD BARGER ASSOC INC
Also Called: Carduner Sales Company
3 Mount Mckinley Ave (11738-2107)
PHONE..................................631 696-6703
Bud Barger, *President*
EMP: 5
SALES (est): 609.7K **Privately Held**
SIC: 3679 Electronic components

(G-5168)
MIND DESIGNS INC (PA)
5 Gregory Ct (11738-4202)
PHONE..................................631 563-3644
Anibal Rodriguez, *President*
Joshua Rodriguez, *COO*
Dorothea Rodriguez, *CFO*
EMP: 8
SQ FT: 8,800
SALES (est): 1.5MM **Privately Held**
WEB: www.mindglow.com
SIC: 2431 5211 Planing mill, millwork; cabinets, kitchen

Farmingville - Suffolk County (G-5169)

(G-5169)
PEI/GENESIS INC
2410 N Ocean Ave Ste 401 (11738-2917)
PHONE................631 256-1747
Donald Wood, *Branch Mgr*
EMP: 7
SALES (corp-wide): 332MM **Privately Held**
SIC: 3643 Electric connectors
PA: Pei/Genesis, Inc.
  2180 Hornig Rd Ste 2
  Philadelphia PA 19116
  215 464-1410

Fayette
Seneca County

(G-5170)
SENECA STONE CORPORATION
Cty Rd 121 Hoster Cors Rd (13065)
P.O. Box 76 (13065-0076)
PHONE................315 549-8253
Tom Cleare, *Manager*
EMP: 15
SALES (corp-wide): 108.4MM **Privately Held**
SIC: 3281 5032 Cut stone & stone products; stone, crushed or broken
HQ: Seneca Stone Corporation
  2105 S Broadway
  Pine City NY 14871
  607 737-6200

Fayetteville
Onondaga County

(G-5171)
CARTERS INC
537 Towne Dr (13066-1331)
PHONE................315 637-3128
Fax: 315 637-3129
EMP: 9
SALES (corp-wide): 3.2B **Publicly Held**
SIC: 2361 Girls' & children's dresses, blouses & shirts
PA: Carter's, Inc.
  3438 Peachtree Rd Ne # 1800
  Atlanta GA 30326
  678 791-1000

(G-5172)
DATA KEY COMMUNICATION LLC
7573 Hunt Ln (13066-2560)
PHONE................315 445-2347
Fax: 315 445-9336
Carole Jesiolowski, *Editor*
Judy Flannagan, *Mng Member*
EMP: 15
SALES (est): 1.5MM **Privately Held**
WEB: www.datakeyllc.com
SIC: 2721 7375 7371 Magazines: publishing only, not printed on site; information retrieval services; custom computer programming services

(G-5173)
JENLOR LTD
523 E Genesee St (13066-1536)
PHONE................315 637-9080
Joseph Ophir, *President*
Ron Darby, *Manager*
▲ EMP: 10
SQ FT: 5,000
SALES (est): 1.3MM **Privately Held**
WEB: www.jenlor-samatic.com
SIC: 3679 Electronic circuits

(G-5174)
P B & H MOULDING CORPORATION
7121 Woodchuck Hill Rd (13066-9714)
PHONE................315 455-1756
Fax: 315 455-8748
Timothy Orcutt, *President*
Douglas Hatch, *Vice Pres*
Jo Dean Hall Orcutt, *Vice Pres*
EMP: 22
SQ FT: 33,000
SALES (est): 2.5MM **Privately Held**
WEB: www.pbhmoulding.com
SIC: 2499 Picture frame molding, finished

Felts Mills
Jefferson County

(G-5175)
CRANESVILLE BLOCK CO INC
Also Called: Drum Ready-Mix
23903 Cemetery Rd (13638-3113)
P.O. Box 210 (13638-0210)
PHONE................315 773-2296
Edward Bailey, *Regional Mgr*
Robert Vancoughnett, *Opers Mgr*
James Buckley, *Sales Executive*
EMP: 35
SALES (corp-wide): 45.4MM **Privately Held**
SIC: 3271 3273 Blocks, concrete or cinder: standard; ready-mixed concrete
PA: Cranesville Block Co., Inc.
  1250 Riverfront Ctr
  Amsterdam NY 12010
  518 684-6154

Ferndale
Sullivan County

(G-5176)
CHIPITA AMERICA INC
Also Called: Mamma Says
1243 Old Route 17 (12734-5422)
PHONE................845 292-2540
Karen McCann, *Purch Agent*
Norm Gallagher, *Plant Engr*
Ed McDermott, *Manager*
EMP: 50
SALES (corp-wide): 121.1MM **Privately Held**
SIC: 2052 Cookies
HQ: Chipita America, Inc.
  1 Westbrook Corporate Ctr
  Westchester IL 60154
  708 731-2434

(G-5177)
DC FABRICATION & WELDING INC
17 Radcliff Rd (12734-5300)
PHONE................845 295-0215
Dan Coutermash, *President*
Bill Fredrick, *Treasurer*
EMP: 6
SQ FT: 8,000
SALES: 600K **Privately Held**
SIC: 2296 Cord & fabric for reinforcing industrial belting

(G-5178)
GETEC INC
624 Harris Rd (12734-5135)
P.O. Box 583 (12734-0583)
PHONE................845 292-0800
Jean Bader, *President*
Hans Bader Jr, *Vice Pres*
▲ EMP: 15
SQ FT: 10,000
SALES: 3.1MM **Privately Held**
WEB: www.getec.com
SIC: 3621 Generators & sets, electric

(G-5179)
HUDSON VALLEY FOIE GRAS LLC
80 Brooks Rd (12734-5101)
PHONE................845 292-2500
Michael Ginor, *Principal*
EMP: 11 EST: 2008
SALES (est): 2MM **Privately Held**
SIC: 2015 Ducks, processed; ducks, processed: canned; ducks, processed: fresh; ducks, processed: frozen

Feura Bush
Albany County

(G-5180)
LINDE LLC
76 W Yard Rd (12067-9739)
PHONE................518 439-8187
Paul L Giudice, *Project Mgr*
John Cox, *Branch Mgr*
Paul Marton, *Manager*
Debbi Lacey, *Administration*
EMP: 55
SALES (corp-wide): 17.9B **Privately Held**
SIC: 2813 Nitrogen; oxygen, compressed or liquefied
HQ: Linde Llc
  200 Somerset Corporate Bl
  Bridgewater NJ 08807
  908 464-8100

(G-5181)
MATHESON TRI-GAS INC
1297 Feura Bush Rd (12067-1719)
PHONE................518 439-0362
Fax: 518 439-3871
Roger Corvasce, *Manager*
Roger Corbasce, *Manager*
Jim Vincent, *Manager*
EMP: 14
SALES (corp-wide): 29.7B **Privately Held**
WEB: www.mgindustries.com
SIC: 2813 5084 Industrial gases; nitrogen; oxygen, compressed or liquefied; argon; welding machinery & equipment; safety equipment
HQ: Matheson Tri-Gas, Inc.
  150 Allen Rd Ste 302
  Basking Ridge NJ 07920
  908 991-9200

(G-5182)
OWENS CORNING SALES LLC
1277 Feura Bush Rd (12067-1719)
P.O. Box 98, Delmar (12054-0098)
PHONE................518 475-3600
Fax: 518 439-3646
Craig Burroughs, *Branch Mgr*
Donna Baumann, *Director*
Anthony Williams, *Director*
EMP: 465
SQ FT: 1,860
SALES (corp-wide): 5.6B **Publicly Held**
WEB: www.owenscorning.com
SIC: 3229 3296 Pressed & blown glass; mineral wool
HQ: Owens Corning Sales, Llc
  1 Owens Corning Pkwy
  Toledo OH 43659
  419 248-8000

Fillmore
Allegany County

(G-5183)
CUBA SPECIALTY MFG CO INC
Also Called: Tackle Factory
81 S Genesee St (14735-8700)
P.O. Box 195 (14735-0195)
PHONE................585 567-4176
Fax: 585 567-2366
Dana R Pickup, *President*
Stephen Fentz, *President*
Edward Fox, *President*
Michelle Popovice, *Controller*
▲ EMP: 10 EST: 1931
SQ FT: 23,000
SALES (est): 1.6MM **Privately Held**
SIC: 3496 Traps, animal & fish

(G-5184)
PRIMESOUTH INC
11537 Route 19 (14735-8667)
PHONE................585 567-4191
John Kingston, *Manager*
EMP: 10 EST: 1991
SALES (est): 740K **Privately Held**
SIC: 3825 Electrical power measuring equipment

Findley Lake
Chautauqua County

(G-5185)
OUR OWN CANDLE COMPANY INC (PA)
10349 Main St (14736-9722)
P.O. Box 99 (14736-0099)
PHONE................716 769-5000
Lawrence S Gross, *President*
Kurt M Duska, *Vice Pres*
◆ EMP: 12
SALES (est): 2.1MM **Privately Held**
SIC: 3999 Shades, lamp or candle

Fishers
Ontario County

(G-5186)
GORBEL INC (PA)
600 Fishers Run (14453)
P.O. Box 593 (14453-0593)
PHONE................585 924-6262
Fax: 585 924-6273
David Reh, *CEO*
Brian D Reh, *Ch of Bd*
Gay Card, *General Mgr*
David Butwid, *Vice Pres*
David Pritchard, *VP Opers*
▲ EMP: 130 EST: 1977
SQ FT: 64,000
SALES (est): 78.2MM **Privately Held**
WEB: www.gorbel.com
SIC: 3536 Hoists, cranes & monorails; cranes, industrial plant

Fishkill
Dutchess County

(G-5187)
ACADIA STAIRS
73 Route 9 Ste 3 (12524-2944)
PHONE................845 765-8600
▲ EMP: 8
SALES (est): 1.2MM **Privately Held**
SIC: 3441 Fabricated structural metal

(G-5188)
BIONIC EYE TECHNOLOGIES INC
4 Willow Lake Dr (12524-2952)
PHONE................845 505-5254
Richard Birney, *CEO*
EMP: 7
SALES (est): 427.3K **Privately Held**
SIC: 3842 Implants, surgical

(G-5189)
CRANESVILLE BLOCK CO INC
70 Route 9 (12524-2962)
PHONE................845 896-5687
John Tesrro, *CEO*
EMP: 20
SQ FT: 3,960
SALES (corp-wide): 45.4MM **Privately Held**
SIC: 3273 Ready-mixed concrete
PA: Cranesville Block Co., Inc.
  1250 Riverfront Ctr
  Amsterdam NY 12010
  518 684-6154

(G-5190)
ENTERPRISE BAGELS INC
Also Called: Bagel Shoppe, The
986 Main St Ste 3 (12524-3508)
PHONE................845 896-3823
Joe Raffele, *CEO*
EMP: 12
SALES (est): 1.3MM **Privately Held**
SIC: 2051 Bagels, fresh or frozen

(G-5191)
FAMILY HEARING CENTER
18 Westage Dr Ste 16 (12524-2289)
PHONE................845 897-3059
Lori Biasotti, *Owner*

EMP: 5
SALES (est): 440.6K Privately Held
SIC: 3842 8049 Hearing aids; audiologist

(G-5192)
LAM RESEARCH CORPORATION
300 Westage Bus Ctr Dr # 190 (12524-4201)
PHONE..............................845 896-0606
Fax: 845 896-4151
Craig Bitzell, *Manager*
Dean Turnbaugh, *Manager*
EMP: 50
SALES (corp-wide): 8B Publicly Held
WEB: www.lamrc.com
SIC: 3559 Semiconductor manufacturing machinery
PA: Lam Research Corporation
4650 Cushing Pkwy
Fremont CA 94538
510 572-0200

(G-5193)
LOVINGLY LLC
1399 Route 52 Ste 100 (12524-3250)
PHONE..............................845 977-0775
Russ Taylor, *Regional Mgr*
Mahima Kurian, *QA Dir*
Edward Castillo, *Sales Dir*
Lindsay Santoro, *Sales Staff*
Ken Garland, *Mng Member*
EMP: 36
SQ FT: 10,000
SALES: 379.6K Privately Held
WEB: www.unitedfloristnetwork.com
SIC: 7372 Application computer software

(G-5194)
MONTFORT BROTHERS INC
44 Elm St (12524-1804)
PHONE..............................845 896-6694
Fax: 845 896-4456
Jacqueline Montfort, *President*
Melissa Oberle, *Controller*
Daniel Polanco, *Manager*
Karen Piga, *Executive Asst*
EMP: 30
SQ FT: 15,000
SALES (est): 6.4MM Privately Held
WEB: www.montfortgroup.com
SIC: 3271 Blocks, concrete or cinder: standard

(G-5195)
N SKETCH BUILD INC
982 Main St Ste 4-130 (12524-3506)
PHONE..............................800 975-0597
Jacqueline Ellison, *Ch of Bd*
◆ EMP: 8
SALES (est): 570K Privately Held
SIC: 2499 Decorative wood & woodwork

(G-5196)
SUBURBAN PUBLISHING INC (PA)
Also Called: Hudson Valley Magazine
1 Summit Ct Ste 200a (12524-1370)
PHONE..............................845 463-0542
Fax: 845 463-1544
Jack Driscoll, *Publisher*
Nancy Walbridge, *Publisher*
Angelo Martinello, *Chairman*
Robert Martinella, *Vice Pres*
Robert Martinelli, *Vice Pres*
EMP: 12
SQ FT: 3,000
SALES (est): 969.8K Privately Held
WEB: www.hudsonvalleymagazine.com
SIC: 2721 Magazines: publishing only, not printed on site

Floral Park
Nassau County

(G-5197)
A D MFG CORP
24844 Jericho Tpke (11001-4002)
PHONE..............................516 352-6161
Fax: 516 352-8502
Howard Karmitz, *President*
EMP: 15
SQ FT: 6,000
SALES (est): 2.3MM Privately Held
WEB: www.adtrophy.com
SIC: 3499 Trophies, metal, except silver

(G-5198)
ALLIANCE SERVICES CORP
23 Van Siclen Ave (11001-2012)
PHONE..............................516 775-7600
Frank De Oliveira, *President*
Peter Smith, *General Mgr*
Victor De Oliveira, *Vice Pres*
EMP: 14
SQ FT: 18,000
SALES: 1.6MM Privately Held
WEB: www.alliancewelding.com
SIC: 7692 Welding repair

(G-5199)
ALLIANCE WELDING & STEEL FABG
15 Van Siclen Ave (11001-2012)
PHONE..............................516 775-7600
Fax: 516 775-5955
Victor De Oliveira, *President*
Frank De Oliveira, *Corp Secy*
Joe King, *Sales Mgr*
EMP: 18
SQ FT: 18,000
SALES (est): 2MM Privately Held
SIC: 3444 7692 Sheet metalwork; welding repair

(G-5200)
ALLOMATIC PRODUCTS COMPANY
Also Called: Sales Department
102 Jericho Tpke Ste 104 (11001-2004)
PHONE..............................516 775-0330
Fax: 516 775-5543
Bob Clark, *Vice Pres*
Bob Tichy, *Marketing Mgr*
Israel Tabaksblat, *Marketing Staff*
John Butz, *Manager*
EMP: 5
SALES (corp-wide): 123.9MM Privately Held
WEB: www.allomatic.com
SIC: 3714 Motor vehicle parts & accessories
HQ: Allomatic Products Company Inc
609 E Chaney St
Sullivan IN 47882
812 268-0322

(G-5201)
ART DENTAL LABORATORY INC
199 Jericho Tpke Ste 402 (11001-2190)
PHONE..............................516 437-1882
Fax: 516 437-1887
James Pratap, *President*
Janice Schlin, *Exec Dir*
EMP: 8
SQ FT: 800
SALES (est): 1.2MM Privately Held
SIC: 3843 Dental equipment & supplies

(G-5202)
AUTOMATED BLDG MGT SYSTEMS INC (PA)
54 Cherry Ln (11001-1611)
PHONE..............................516 216-5603
Alkesh Amin, *President*
Aika Patel, *Manager*
EMP: 35
SQ FT: 2,000
SALES: 27.5MM Privately Held
WEB: www.abmsys.com
SIC: 3822 Temperature controls, automatic

(G-5203)
BARCLAY TAGG RACING
86 Geranium Ave (11001-3035)
PHONE..............................631 404-8269
Barclay Tagg, *Owner*
EMP: 30
SALES (est): 1.1MM Privately Held
SIC: 3721 Aircraft

(G-5204)
BUTTER COOKY BAKERY
217 Jericho Tpke (11001-2143)
PHONE..............................516 354-3831
Ben Borgognone, *President*
EMP: 8
SALES (est): 605.5K Privately Held
SIC: 2051 Cakes, bakery: except frozen

(G-5205)
C & A SERVICE INC (PA)
Also Called: Citrus and Allied Essences
65 S Tyson Ave (11001-1821)
PHONE..............................516 354-1200
Richard Pisano Jr, *President*
Marie Taormina, *Purchasing*
Nancy McDonald, *Controller*
◆ EMP: 5
SALES (est): 1MM Privately Held
SIC: 2899 2911 Chemical preparations; aromatic chemical products

(G-5206)
CB PUBLISHING LLC
Also Called: CB Products
50 Carnation Ave Bldg 2-1 (11001-1741)
P.O. Box 280, New Hyde Park (11040-0280)
PHONE..............................516 354-4888
Fax: 516 354-4889
Clifford Brechner, *President*
EMP: 7
SQ FT: 1,400
SALES (est): 577.4K Privately Held
WEB: www.cbproducts.com
SIC: 2731 Books: publishing only

(G-5207)
CITRUS AND ALLIED ESSENCES LTD (PA)
Also Called: C&A Aromatics
65 S Tyson Ave (11001-1898)
PHONE..............................516 354-1200
Fax: 516 354-1262
Stephen Pisano, *CEO*
Richard C Pisano Jr, *CEO*
Christopher Pisano, *Vice Pres*
Carl Lembo, *Plant Mgr*
Rob Haedrich, *Purch Dir*
◆ EMP: 29
SQ FT: 11,000
SALES (est): 28.6MM Privately Held
WEB: www.citrusandallied.com
SIC: 2087 2899 2911 Flavoring extracts & syrups; chemical preparations; aromatic chemical products

(G-5208)
CREATRON SERVICES INC
Also Called: Lanel
504 Cherry Ln (11001-1646)
PHONE..............................516 437-5119
Fax: 516 352-0465
Isidore Epstein, *President*
Alan Rosen, *Vice Pres*
EMP: 20
SQ FT: 10,000
SALES (est): 1.5MM Privately Held
SIC: 3861 Photographic equipment & supplies

(G-5209)
DECREE SIGNS & GRAPHICS INC
Also Called: Manhattan Signs
91 Tulip Ave Apt Kd1 (11001-1983)
PHONE..............................973 278-3603
Anthony Decrescenzo, *President*
Jeff Taborda, *Asst Controller*
EMP: 15
SALES (est): 1.3MM Privately Held
SIC: 3993 Signs & advertising specialties

(G-5210)
EASTERN UNIT EXCH RMNFACTURING
186 Beech St (11001-3318)
P.O. Box 180346, Richmond Hill (11418-0346)
PHONE..............................718 739-7113
Fax: 718 739-9005
Chester Brown, *President*
Mehendra Sarwan, *Manager*
EMP: 15
SQ FT: 15
SALES (est): 1.8MM Privately Held
SIC: 3694 Alternators, automotive; generators, automotive & aircraft; motors, starting: automotive & aircraft

(G-5211)
FULL SERVICE AUTO BODY INC
Also Called: Lakeville Service Station
25601 Jericho Tpke (11001-1707)
PHONE..............................718 831-9300
Anthony Coppolino, *President*
Steven Coppolino Jr, *Vice Pres*
EMP: 12
SQ FT: 25,000
SALES: 3MM Privately Held
SIC: 3715 Bus trailers, tractor type

(G-5212)
LANEL INC
504 Cherry Ln Ste 3 (11001-1643)
PHONE..............................516 437-5119
Fax: 516 354-2194
Isidore Epstein, *President*
ARI Rosenberg, *Manager*
▲ EMP: 12
SALES (est): 1.3MM Privately Held
SIC: 3861 5099 Photographic equipment & supplies; video & audio equipment

(G-5213)
P T E INC
36 Ontario Rd (11001-4113)
PHONE..............................516 775-3839
Fax: 631 842-5227
Gustave Loos, *President*
EMP: 19 EST: 1957
SQ FT: 10,125
SALES (est): 1.8MM Privately Held
SIC: 3599 Machine shop, jobbing & repair

(G-5214)
TWO BILLS MACHINE & TOOL CO
17 Concord St (11001-2819)
PHONE..............................516 437-2585
Wilhelm Sangen, *President*
Frederick Sangen, *Vice Pres*
EMP: 11
SQ FT: 7,000
SALES (est): 1.3MM Privately Held
SIC: 3599 Machine shop, jobbing & repair

Floral Park
Queens County

(G-5215)
INDIRA FOODS INC
25503 Hillside Ave # 255 (11004)
PHONE..............................718 343-1500
Indira Mathur, *President*
EMP: 10
SALES (est): 820K Privately Held
SIC: 2032 Italian foods: packaged in cans, jars, etc.

(G-5216)
S & J TRADING INC
8030 263rd St (11004-1517)
P.O. Box 40337, Glen Oaks (11004-0337)
PHONE..............................718 347-1323
Surinder Chawla, *President*
▲ EMP: 8
SALES: 800K Privately Held
SIC: 3299 5063 5033 Mica products; electrical apparatus & equipment; roofing, siding & insulation

Florida
Orange County

(G-5217)
BRACH KNITTING MILLS INC
12 Roosevelt Ave (10921-1808)
P.O. Box 13 (10921-0013)
PHONE..............................845 651-4450
Fax: 845 651-1068
Shea Brach, *President*
Joseph Fried, *Manager*
EMP: 15 EST: 1965
SQ FT: 32,000
SALES: 500K Privately Held
SIC: 2251 2331 Panty hose; tights, women's; shirts, women's & juniors': made from purchased materials

Florida - Orange County (G-5218)   GEOGRAPHIC SECTION

(G-5218)
CONVERGENT CNNCTIVITY TECH INC
1751 State Route 17a (10921-1061)
P.O. Box 454 (10921-0454)
PHONE..................................845 651-5250
Joseph T Moore, *Ch of Bd*
Mary L Van Sise, *Info Tech Mgr*
▲ **EMP:** 5
SALES (est) 789.9K **Privately Held**
SIC: 3357 Nonferrous wiredrawing & insulating

(G-5219)
EMPIRE VENTILATION EQP CO INC (PA)
9 Industrial Dr (10921-1000)
PHONE..................................718 728-2143
Fax: 718 267-0143
George R Taylor, *President*
Linda L Taylor, *Vice Pres*
Robert E Warnken, *Treasurer*
Brian G Taylor, *Admin Sec*
EMP: 12 **EST:** 1936
SQ FT: 15,000
SALES: 1.5MM **Privately Held**
WEB: www.empirevent.com
SIC: 3444 Ventilators, sheet metal

(G-5220)
ISLAND NAMEPLATE INC
124 S Main St (10921-1818)
P.O. Box 548 (10921-0548)
PHONE..................................845 651-4005
Fax: 845 651-0609
Joseph C Sicina III, *President*
EMP: 5
SQ FT: 1,860
SALES: 260K **Privately Held**
SIC: 3993 Name plates: except engraved, etched, etc.: metal

(G-5221)
NEW ENGLAND TOOL CO LTD
Also Called: Fine Architectural Met Smiths
44 Jayne St (10921-1109)
P.O. Box 30, Chester (10918-0030)
PHONE..................................845 651-7550
Fax: 845 651-7857
Rhoda Mack, *President*
EMP: 6
SQ FT: 4,000
SALES: 250K **Privately Held**
WEB: www.iceforge.com
SIC: 3446 Architectural metalwork

(G-5222)
STAUBER CALIFORNIA INC
Also Called: Pharmline
41 Bridge St (10921-1323)
PHONE..................................845 651-4443
EMP: 10
SALES (corp-wide): 483.5MM **Publicly Held**
SIC: 2833 Medicinals & botanicals
HQ: Stauber California, Inc.
4120 N Palm St
Fullerton CA 92835
714 441-3900

(G-5223)
ZIRCAR CERAMICS INC (PA)
100 N Main St Ste 2 (10921-1329)
P.O. Box 519 (10921-0519)
PHONE..................................845 651-6600
Phil Hamling, *President*
David Hamling, *Vice Pres*
Jay Magnelli, *Prdtn Mgr*
Jessica Tan, *Sales Engr*
Marilyn Sweeney, *Manager*
▲ **EMP:** 34
SQ FT: 30,000
SALES: 4.8MM **Privately Held**
WEB: www.zircarceramics.com
SIC: 2899 Insulating compounds

(G-5224)
ZIRCAR REFR COMPOSITES INC
14 Golden Hill Ter (10921-1116)
PHONE..................................845 651-2200
Julie Sterns, *Branch Mgr*
EMP: 12 **Privately Held**
WEB: www.zrci.com
SIC: 2493 Reconstituted wood products

PA: Zircar Refractory Composites, Inc.
46 Jayne St
Florida NY 10921

(G-5225)
ZIRCAR REFR COMPOSITES INC (PA)
46 Jayne St (10921-1109)
P.O. Box 489 (10921-0489)
PHONE..................................845 651-4481
Tom Hamling, *Ch of Bd*
Peter Hamling, *President*
Michael Cauda, *Sales Engr*
Julie Stern, *Manager*
▲ **EMP:** 8
SQ FT: 4,000
SALES (est): 3.3MM **Privately Held**
WEB: www.zrci.com
SIC: 3297 Nonclay refractories

(G-5226)
ZIRCAR ZIRCONIA INC
87 Meadow Rd (10921-1112)
P.O. Box 287 (10921-0287)
PHONE..................................845 651-3040
Craig Hamling, *President*
Clare Hamling, *Vice Pres*
John Koar, *Engineer*
David Hoskins, *Sales Mgr*
▲ **EMP:** 24
SQ FT: 20,800
SALES (est): 3.8MM **Privately Held**
WEB: www.zircarzirconia.com
SIC: 3297 Nonclay refractories

Flushing
Queens County

(G-5227)
5 STARS PRINTING CORP
13330 32nd Ave (11354-1921)
PHONE..................................718 461-4612
Fax: 718 461-4612
S K Han, *President*
EMP: 10
SALES (est) 894.5K **Privately Held**
WEB: www.bocasoccer.com
SIC: 2759 Commercial printing

(G-5228)
ACCREDO HEALTH INCORPORATED
14330 38th Ave Apt 1f (11354-5720)
PHONE..................................718 353-3012
Amber Dorr, *Sales Executive*
Nakia Jefferson, *Branch Mgr*
EMP: 5
SALES (corp-wide): 100.2B **Publicly Held**
SIC: 2833 Medicinals & botanicals
HQ: Accredo Health, Incorporated
1640 Century Center Pkwy # 110
Memphis TN 38134

(G-5229)
ACE PRINTING & PUBLISHING INC
Also Called: Ace Printing Co
14951 Roosevelt Ave (11354-4939)
PHONE..................................718 939-0040
Sung N Kang, *CEO*
EMP: 10
SQ FT: 3,000
SALES (est): 800K **Privately Held**
SIC: 2752 Offset & photolithographic printing

(G-5230)
AIR EXPORT MECHANICAL
4108 Parsons Blvd Apt 4r (11355-1940)
PHONE..................................917 709-5310
Gricelio Nosquera, *President*
EMP: 5
SALES (est): 480K **Privately Held**
SIC: 3564 Filters, air: furnaces, air conditioning equipment, etc.

(G-5231)
ALBERT SIY
Also Called: Avant Garde Screen Printing Co
13508 Booth Memorial Ave (11355-5009)
PHONE..................................718 359-0389
Albert Siy, *Owner*

EMP: 8
SALES: 1MM **Privately Held**
SIC: 2752 2759 2396 Commercial printing, lithographic; screen printing; automotive & apparel trimmings

(G-5232)
ALL ABOUT ART INC
4128 Murray St (11355-1055)
PHONE..................................718 321-0755
Gee Book Jeung, *President*
EMP: 11
SALES (est): 900K **Privately Held**
WEB: www.myallaboutart.com
SIC: 2395 2261 Embroidery products, except schiffli machine; finishing plants, cotton

(G-5233)
AMERICAN AUTO ACC INCRPORATION (PA)
3506 Leavitt St Apt Cfc (11354-2967)
PHONE..................................718 886-6600
Henry Hsu, *President*
Betty L Hsu, *Vice Pres*
Nina Sung, *Accountant*
EMP: 20
SQ FT: 50,000
SALES (est): 1.5MM **Privately Held**
WEB: www.3aracing.com
SIC: 3714 5013 Motor vehicle parts & accessories; motor vehicle supplies & new parts

(G-5234)
ARRINGEMENT INTERNATIONAL INC
16015 45th Ave (11358-3135)
PHONE..................................347 323-7974
WEI Huang, *President*
EMP: 6 **EST:** 2013
SQ FT: 1,500
SALES (est): 200K **Privately Held**
SIC: 3911 Jewelry, precious metal

(G-5235)
ATI TRADING INC
13631 41st Ave Ste 5a (11355-2446)
PHONE..................................718 888-7918
EMP: 16
SALES (est): 3.5MM **Privately Held**
SIC: 3823 Computer interface equipment for industrial process control

(G-5236)
BEST CONCRETE MIX CORP
3510 College Point Blvd (11354-2719)
PHONE..................................718 463-5500
Fax: 718 762-0804
Michael Emanuele, *President*
EMP: 35
SQ FT: 20,000
SALES (est): 6.2MM **Privately Held**
SIC: 3273 Ready-mixed concrete

(G-5237)
CENTURY TOM INC
3344 Farrington St (11354-2821)
PHONE..................................347 654-3179
Yanru Lin, *CEO*
EMP: 4 **EST:** 2012
SQ FT: 1,800
SALES: 1.7MM **Privately Held**
SIC: 2023 Dietary supplements, dairy & non-dairy based

(G-5238)
CFP PURCHASING INC
4760 197th St (11358-3937)
PHONE..................................705 806-0383
Robert Mantrop, *President*
▼ **EMP:** 2
SALES: 3MM **Privately Held**
SIC: 2499 7389 Yard sticks, wood;

(G-5239)
CHINESE MEDICAL REPORT INC
3907 Prince St Ste 5b (11354-5308)
PHONE..................................718 359-5676
Fax: 718 359-3816
Ava Lee, *President*
▲ **EMP:** 5
SALES (est): 210K **Privately Held**
WEB: www.chinesemedical.com
SIC: 2711 Newspapers

(G-5240)
CHRISTIAN PRESS INC
14317 Franklin Ave (11355-2116)
PHONE..................................718 886-4400
Fax: 718 886-0074
Young-Choon Chang, *President*
EMP: 5
SQ FT: 1,200
SALES: 250K **Privately Held**
SIC: 2711 8661 Newspapers, publishing & printing; miscellaneous denomination church

(G-5241)
COFIRE PAVING CORPORATION
12030 28th Ave (11354-1049)
PHONE..................................718 463-1403
Fax: 718 358-8522
Ross J Holland, *President*
John D Ficarelli, *Treasurer*
Linda Myer, *Office Mgr*
Robert Ficarelli, *Admin Sec*
EMP: 30 **EST:** 1946
SQ FT: 29,000
SALES (est): 4.6MM **Privately Held**
SIC: 2951 1611 Asphalt paving mixtures & blocks; surfacing & paving

(G-5242)
COURTLANDT BOOT JACK CO INC
3334 Prince St (11354-2731)
PHONE..................................718 445-6200
Fax: 718 353-1524
John K Parlante Jr, *President*
▲ **EMP:** 35 **EST:** 1940
SQ FT: 30,000
SALES (est): 3.9MM **Privately Held**
SIC: 3199 2387 Holsters, leather; apparel belts

(G-5243)
DAHUA ELECTRONICS CORPORATION
13412 59th Ave (11355-5244)
PHONE..................................718 886-2188
Gomita Junkiji, *President*
Scott Russel, *Manager*
EMP: 20
SALES: 156MM **Privately Held**
SIC: 3676 Electronic resistors

(G-5244)
DELICIAS ANDINAS FOOD CORP
5750 Maspeth Ave (11378-2212)
PHONE..................................718 416-2922
Fax: 718 416-2929
Manuel Midonda, *President*
Juanita Midonda, *Vice Pres*
Maritza Sanchez, *Manager*
EMP: 33
SALES (est): 5.6MM **Privately Held**
SIC: 2051 Bread, cake & related products

(G-5245)
DIGITAL ONE USA INC
Also Called: Akhon Samoy Weekly
7230 Roosevelt Ave (11372-6335)
PHONE..................................718 396-4890
Fax: 718 396-4810
Kazi S Hoque, *President*
EMP: 15
SALES (est): 735.5K **Privately Held**
SIC: 2711 Newspapers

(G-5246)
DRAGON VAPES NYC
13527 Roosevelt Ave (11354-5337)
PHONE..................................718 801-7855
EMP: 7
SALES (est): 94.4K **Privately Held**
SIC: 3999 Cigar & cigarette holders

(G-5247)
EXCELSIOR MLT-CLTURAL INST INC
13340 Roosevelt Ave 7g (11354-5263)
P.O. Box 14332, Augusta GA (30919-0332)
PHONE..................................706 627-4285
Rhonda Jackson, *CEO*
Ronald Nurse, *Director*
EMP: 14
SALES (est): 704.3K **Privately Held**
SIC: 3812 Cabin environment indicators

GEOGRAPHIC SECTION

Flushing - Queens County (G-5275)

(G-5248)
FERRARA BROS LLC (HQ)
12005 31st Ave (11354-2516)
PHONE.............................718 939-3030
Fax: 718 939-7286
William J Sandbrook, *President*
EMP: 20
SQ FT: 16,000
SALES (est): 14.4MM
SALES (corp-wide): 1.1B **Publicly Held**
WEB: www.ferraraconcrete.com
SIC: **3273** 5211 5033 Ready-mixed concrete; masonry materials & supplies; roofing, siding & insulation
PA: U.S. Concrete, Inc.
 331 N Main St
 Euless TX 76039
 817 835-4105

(G-5249)
FIBER USA CORP
13620 38th Ave Ste 11f (11354-4232)
PHONE.............................718 888-1512
Pengyu Zhu, *President*
EMP: 8
SQ FT: 3,000
SALES (est): 1.7MM
SALES (corp-wide): 22.6MM **Privately Held**
SIC: **2653** 5093 Corrugated & solid fiber boxes; plastics scrap
PA: Jiangyin Mighty Chemical Fiber Co., Ltd.
 Mazhen Industrial Park
 Wuxi
 510 827-1150

(G-5250)
FLUSHING IRON WELD INC
13125 Maple Ave (11355-4224)
PHONE.............................718 359-2208
Fax: 718 461-6376
Dario Toro, *President*
Hector Munoz, *Vice Pres*
Paula Munoz, *Manager*
EMP: 20
SQ FT: 5,000
SALES: 2.5MM **Privately Held**
SIC: **3446** Architectural metalwork

(G-5251)
GILDAN MEDIA CORP
6631 Wetherole St (11374-4640)
PHONE.............................718 459-6299
Fax: 718 459-6299
Gilles Dana, *President*
▲ EMP: 12
SALES (est): 1MM **Privately Held**
WEB: www.gildanmedia.com
SIC: **2731** Books: publishing only

(G-5252)
GLOBAL GRAPHICS INC
Also Called: Wen Hwa Printing
3711 Prince St Ste D (11354-4428)
PHONE.............................718 939-4967
Rong Fang, *President*
Chen Wang, *Manager*
EMP: 10
SALES: 500K **Privately Held**
SIC: **2752** Commercial printing, lithographic

(G-5253)
GROUP INTERNATIONAL LLC
14711 34th Ave (11354-3755)
PHONE.............................718 475-8805
John Liriano, *CEO*
EMP: 5 EST: 2013
SALES (est): 169.2K **Privately Held**
SIC: **2043** Infants' foods, cereal type

(G-5254)
H H B BAKERY OF LITTLE NECK
Also Called: Richer's Bakery
24914 Horace Harding Expy (11362-2050)
PHONE.............................718 631-7004
Eugene Stanko, *President*
EMP: 5
SALES (est): 230K **Privately Held**
SIC: **2051** Bakery: wholesale or wholesale/retail combined

(G-5255)
H&L COMPUTERS INC
13523 Northern Blvd (11354-4006)
PHONE.............................516 873-8088
Bothen Lin, *President*
EMP: 20
SQ FT: 5,000
SALES (est): 1.6MM **Privately Held**
SIC: **3571** Electronic computers

(G-5256)
HAIR COLOR RESEARCH GROUP INC
13320 Whitestone Expy (11354-2509)
PHONE.............................718 445-6026
Armando Petruccelli, *President*
EMP: 26
SALES: 2.5MM **Privately Held**
SIC: **3999** Hair & hair-based products

(G-5257)
HARVY SURGICAL SUPPLY CORP
Also Called: Harvy Canes
3435 Collins Pl (11354-2720)
PHONE.............................718 939-1222
Fax: 718 939-1222
Harvey Murtha, *President*
Paul Murtha, *Vice Pres*
Sara Moss, *Finance Other*
Judith Murtha, *Sales Mgr*
▲ EMP: 30 EST: 1897
SALES (est): 5.2MM **Privately Held**
SIC: **3842** Surgical appliances & supplies; canes, orthopedic

(G-5258)
HISUN OPTOELECTRONICS CO LTD
Also Called: Hisun Led
4109 College Point Blvd (11355-4226)
PHONE.............................718 886-6966
Eugene L Yu, *President*
Jane Wen, *Manager*
▲ EMP: 15
SALES (est): 1.8MM **Privately Held**
SIC: **3674** Light emitting diodes

(G-5259)
HOME IDEAL INC
4528 159th St (11358-3148)
PHONE.............................718 762-8998
Fax: 718 353-3507
Henry Chin, *President*
Cheryl Lyn, *Corp Secy*
Winston Lyn, *Vice Pres*
EMP: 7
SALES: 300K **Privately Held**
SIC: **2434** 5712 1751 2541 Wood kitchen cabinets; cabinets, except custom made: kitchen; cabinet building & installation; wood partitions & fixtures

(G-5260)
INTER PACIFIC CONSULTING CORP
Also Called: Ipcc
14055 34th Ave Apt 3n (11354-3038)
PHONE.............................718 460-2787
Fax: 718 460-9433
John Tsao, *President*
▲ EMP: 5
SALES: 1MM **Privately Held**
SIC: **3499** 5023 Picture frames, metal; frames & framing, picture & mirror

(G-5261)
INTERCULTURAL ALLIANCE ARTISTS
Also Called: Iaas , The
4510 165th St (11358-3229)
P.O. Box 4378, New York (10163-4378)
PHONE.............................917 406-1202
Gabrielle David, *President*
Stephanie Agosto, *Vice Pres*
Michelle Aragon, *Vice Pres*
Joan Edmonds Ashman, *Vice Pres*
Naydene Brickus, *Vice Pres*
EMP: 5
SALES: 11.8K **Privately Held**
SIC: **2721** Magazines: publishing & printing

(G-5262)
INTREPID CONTROL SERVICE INC
2904 Francis Lewis Blvd (11358-1536)
PHONE.............................718 886-8771
William Varrone, *President*
James Colleran, *Corp Secy*
Andrew Manesis, *Vice Pres*
Dean Pecoraro, *Vice Pres*
EMP: 5
SQ FT: 750
SALES (est): 907.2K **Privately Held**
SIC: **3822** Temperature controls, automatic

(G-5263)
J D STEWARD INC
4537 162nd St (11358-3157)
PHONE.............................718 358-0169
Dominick Savino, *President*
Jean Stephens, *Vice Pres*
Joseph Savino, *Treasurer*
EMP: 5
SALES: 900K **Privately Held**
WEB: www.jdsteward.com
SIC: **3498** Fabricated pipe & fittings

(G-5264)
JOHN A VASSILAROS & SON INC
Also Called: Vassilaros Coffee
2905 120th St (11354-2505)
PHONE.............................718 886-4140
John Vassilaros, *President*
Irene Vassilaros, *Vice Pres*
Maria Peterson, *Manager*
EMP: 42
SQ FT: 25,000
SALES: 11MM **Privately Held**
WEB: www.vassilaroscoffee.com
SIC: **2095** Coffee roasting (except by wholesale grocers)

(G-5265)
KALEL PARTNERS LLC
7012 170th St Ste 101 (11365-3332)
PHONE.............................347 561-7804
Todd Friedman, *CEO*
EMP: 15
SALES (est): 493.8K **Privately Held**
SIC: **2741** Miscellaneous publishing

(G-5266)
KEPCO INC (PA)
13138 Sanford Ave (11355-4245)
PHONE.............................718 461-7000
Fax: 718 767-1102
Martin Kupferberg, *President*
Max Kupferberg, *Chairman*
Saul Kupferberg, *Vice Pres*
Seth Kupferberg, *Vice Pres*
Mark Kupferberg, *VP Mfg*
EMP: 40 EST: 1946
SQ FT: 145,000
SALES (est): 21.8MM **Privately Held**
SIC: **3612** Power & distribution transformers

(G-5267)
KEPCO INC
13140 Maple Ave (11355-4225)
PHONE.............................718 461-7000
Martin Kupferberg, *President*
EMP: 90
SALES (corp-wide): 21.8MM **Privately Held**
SIC: **3612** Power & distribution transformers
PA: Kepco, Inc.
 13138 Sanford Ave
 Flushing NY 11355
 718 461-7000

(G-5268)
KEPCO INC
13138 Sanford Ave (11355-4245)
PHONE.............................718 461-7000
EMP: 50
SALES (corp-wide): 21.8MM **Privately Held**
SIC: **3612** Power & distribution transformers
PA: Kepco, Inc.
 13138 Sanford Ave
 Flushing NY 11355
 718 461-7000

(G-5269)
KOREA TIMES NEW YORK INC
15408 Nthrn Blvd Ste 2b (11354)
PHONE.............................718 961-7979
Jae Chang, *President*
EMP: 7
SALES (corp-wide): 83.9MM **Privately Held**
SIC: **2711** Newspapers: publishing only, not printed on site
HQ: The Korea Times New York Inc
 3710 Skillman Ave
 Long Island City NY 11101
 718 784-4526

(G-5270)
KOREAN YELLOW PAGES
14809 Northern Blvd (11354-4346)
PHONE.............................718 461-0073
Gwanseo Pak, *Owner*
▲ EMP: 10
SALES: 300K **Privately Held**
SIC: **2741** Telephone & other directory publishing

(G-5271)
LB LAUNDRY INC
4431 Kissena Blvd (11355-3055)
PHONE.............................347 399-8030
Ll Xinli, *Owner*
EMP: 3
SQ FT: 700
SALES: 2MM **Privately Held**
SIC: **2842** 3582 Laundry cleaning preparations; commercial laundry equipment

(G-5272)
LEVI STRAUSS & CO
13432 Blossom Ave (11355-4639)
PHONE.............................917 213-6263
Chip Bergh, *Branch Mgr*
EMP: 19
SALES (corp-wide): 4.5B **Privately Held**
SIC: **2325** Jeans: men's, youths' & boys'
PA: Levi Strauss & Co.
 1155 Battery St
 San Francisco CA 94111
 415 501-6000

(G-5273)
LIFE WATCH TECHNOLOGY INC
Also Called: My Life My Health
42-10 Polen St Ste 412 (11355)
PHONE.............................917 669-2428
Jiping Zhu, *CEO*
EMP: 56
SQ FT: 1,200
SALES (est): 2MM **Privately Held**
SIC: **3873** Watches & parts, except crystals & jewels

(G-5274)
LONG ISLAND PIPE SUPPLY INC
5858 56th St (11378-3106)
PHONE.............................718 456-7877
David Pargon, *Manager*
EMP: 6
SALES (corp-wide): 59.6MM **Privately Held**
WEB: www.lipipe.com
SIC: **3498** Fabricated pipe & fittings
PA: Long Island Pipe Supply Inc
 586 Commercial Ave
 Garden City NY 11530
 516 222-8008

(G-5275)
LOOSELEAF LAW PUBLICATIONS INC
4308 162nd St (11358-3131)
P.O. Box 650042, Fresh Meadows (11365-0042)
PHONE.............................718 359-5559
Fax: 718 539-0941
Warren Taylor, *President*
Michael Loughrey, *Vice Pres*
Hilliary McKeon, *President*
Hilary McKeon, *Manager*
Lynette Piper, *Admin Sec*
EMP: 10
SQ FT: 5,000
SALES: 1MM **Privately Held**
WEB: www.looseleaflaw.com
SIC: **2731** 5961 Books: publishing only; books, mail order (except book clubs)

Flushing - Queens County (G-5276)

(G-5276)
MDS USA INC
13244 Booth Memorial Ave (11355-5128)
PHONE.....................................718 358-5588
Kim Jong Hag, *President*
EMP: 20
SALES (est): 1.6MM **Privately Held**
SIC: 3993 Neon signs

(G-5277)
NATURAL LAB INC
13538 39th Ave Ste 4 (11354-4423)
PHONE.....................................718 321-8848
Michael Chang, *Manager*
▲ EMP: 6
SALES (est): 543.2K **Privately Held**
SIC: 2099 5149 Food preparations; organic & diet foods

(G-5278)
NEW STAR BAKERY
4121a Kissena Blvd (11355-3138)
PHONE.....................................718 961-8868
Huantang Liang, *Owner*
EMP: 20
SALES (est): 1.2MM **Privately Held**
SIC: 2051 Bread, cake & related products

(G-5279)
NEW YORK IL BO INC
Also Called: Korean New York Daily, The
4522 162nd St Fl 2 (11358-3280)
PHONE.....................................718 961-1538
Fax: 718 358-7243
Grace Chung, *CEO*
▲ EMP: 15
SALES (est): 120K **Privately Held**
SIC: 2711 Newspapers

(G-5280)
NEW YORK TIMES COMPANY
1 New York Times Plz (11354-1200)
PHONE.....................................718 281-7000
Fax: 718 281-7219
Thomas P Lombardo, *Plant Mgr*
Mike Joyce, *Foreman/Supr*
EMP: 12
SALES (corp-wide): 1.5B **Publicly Held**
WEB: www.nytco.com
SIC: 2711 Newspapers, publishing & printing
PA: The New York Times Company
  620 8th Ave
  New York NY 10018
  212 556-1234

(G-5281)
NORTH AMERICA PASTEL ARTISTS
13303 41st Ave Apt 1a (11355-5840)
PHONE.....................................718 463-4701
Jason Chang, *President*
EMP: 8
SALES: 3.8K **Privately Held**
SIC: 3952 Pastels, artists'

(G-5282)
NORTH SHORE NEON SIGN CO INC
4649 54th Ave (11378-1011)
PHONE.....................................718 937-4848
Fax: 718 937-0569
Nancy Byrnes, *Accountant*
Tom Brown, *Manager*
EMP: 30
SALES (corp-wide): 15MM **Privately Held**
WEB: www.northshoreneon.com
SIC: 3993 1799 Signs & advertising specialties; sign installation & maintenance
PA: North Shore Neon Sign Co. Inc.
  295 Skidmore Rd
  Deer Park NY 11729
  631 667-2500

(G-5283)
P S PIBBS INC
Also Called: Pibbs Industries
13315 32nd Ave (11354-1909)
PHONE.....................................718 445-8046
Fax: 718 461-3910
Damiano Petruccelli, *CEO*
Biagio Petruccelli, *President*
Sunny Thomas, *President*
Giulio Pertruccelli, *Vice Pres*
Antonio Petruccelli, *Vice Pres*
◆ EMP: 100
SQ FT: 30,000
SALES (est): 11.8MM **Privately Held**
WEB: www.pibbs.com
SIC: 3999 2844 Barber & beauty shop equipment; shampoos, rinses, conditioners: hair; hair preparations, including shampoos; face creams or lotions

(G-5284)
PALADINO PRTG & GRAPHICS INC
20009 32nd Ave (11361-1037)
PHONE.....................................718 279-6000
Fax: 718 352-2745
Vincent Paladino, *President*
EMP: 9
SQ FT: 1,000
SALES (est): 1.2MM **Privately Held**
SIC: 2752 Commercial printing, lithographic

(G-5285)
PALMBAY LTD
4459 Kissena Blvd Apt 6h (11355-3065)
PHONE.....................................718 424-3388
Fax: 718 396-4488
Wenchao Tao, *President*
◆ EMP: 6
SQ FT: 20,000
SALES (est): 817.3K **Privately Held**
WEB: www.disposablewear.com
SIC: 2384 2252 Robes & dressing gowns; slipper socks

(G-5286)
PARIS WEDDING CENTER CORP (PA)
42-53 42 55 Main St (11355)
PHONE.....................................347 368-4085
Yuki Lin, *President*
▲ EMP: 11
SALES (est): 1.6MM **Privately Held**
SIC: 2335 Wedding gowns & dresses

(G-5287)
PEACE TIMES WEEKLY INC
14527 33rd Ave (11354-3145)
PHONE.....................................718 762-6500
Yongil Park, *President*
Joseph Aahn, *President*
▲ EMP: 5
SALES: 408.2K **Privately Held**
SIC: 2711 Newspapers

(G-5288)
PERRY PLASTICS INC
3050 Whitestone Expy # 300 (11354-1964)
PHONE.....................................718 747-5600
Irwing Laub, *President*
Aaron Laub, *Vice Pres*
▼ EMP: 10
SALES (est): 902.3K **Privately Held**
SIC: 2295 Chemically coated & treated fabrics

(G-5289)
PLASTI-VUE CORP
4130 Murray St (11355-1055)
PHONE.....................................718 463-2300
Fax: 718 358-1903
Gary Fischer, *President*
Bill Olveari, *General Mgr*
EMP: 6
SQ FT: 12,800
SALES (est): 410K **Privately Held**
SIC: 3993 Displays & cutouts, window & lobby

(G-5290)
PORCELAIN REFINISHING CORP
19905 32nd Ave (11358-1205)
PHONE.....................................516 352-4841
Fax: 718 352-3324
Paula Weinstock, *President*
EMP: 15
SQ FT: 700
SALES (est): 2.3MM **Privately Held**
SIC: 3431 5074 Bathtubs: enameled iron, cast iron or pressed metal; sanitary ware, china or enameled iron

(G-5291)
PRIME RESEARCH SOLUTIONS LLC
7328 136th St (11367-2827)
PHONE.....................................917 836-7941
Leonid Litman, *Principal*
Jonathan Robinson, *Principal*
EMP: 5
SALES (est): 128.1K **Privately Held**
SIC: 7372 Educational computer software

(G-5292)
PURE GHEE INC (PA)
5701 225th St (11364-2042)
PHONE.....................................718 224-7399
Mahesh K Maheshwari, *President*
Sucheta Maheshwari, *Senior VP*
EMP: 6 EST: 1988
SQ FT: 9,700
SALES: 1.5MM **Privately Held**
SIC: 2021 Creamery butter

(G-5293)
PURE KEMIKA LLC
6228 136th St Apt 2 (11367-1021)
PHONE.....................................718 745-2200
Luis F Becker, *Mng Member*
EMP: 6 EST: 2013
SQ FT: 1,000
SALES: 1.5MM **Privately Held**
SIC: 2899 Chemical preparations

(G-5294)
RAJBHOG FOODS INC
4123 Murray St (11355-1048)
PHONE.....................................718 358-5105
Fax: 718 358-5123
Ajit M Mody, *CEO*
Suzy Mody, *Vice Pres*
Sachin Mody, *Treasurer*
Cherry Rajbhog, *Sales Dir*
Lalita Mody, *Sales Mgr*
▲ EMP: 30
SQ FT: 12,000
SALES (est): 4MM **Privately Held**
WEB: www.rajbhog.com
SIC: 2064 Candy & other confectionery products

(G-5295)
RIVERA
3330 109th St (11368-1216)
PHONE.....................................718 458-1488
EMP: 5
SALES (est): 214.2K **Privately Held**
SIC: 3281 Cut stone & stone products

(G-5296)
S & L AEROSPACE METALS LLC
12012 28th Ave (11354-1049)
PHONE.....................................718 326-1821
Fax: 718 894-5843
Jerry Wang, *President*
Carlos Quintana, *Vice Pres*
Ted Varvatsas, *Vice Pres*
Alan Wang, *Vice Pres*
Shao Chen, *Controller*
EMP: 100 EST: 1946
SQ FT: 50,000
SALES (est): 29.2MM **Privately Held**
WEB: www.slaerospace.com
SIC: 3728 Aircraft parts & equipment

(G-5297)
SAGE PARTS PLUS
1 Main Terminal Ste 1 (11371-1012)
PHONE.....................................718 651-1898
Ingrid Diaz, *Manager*
EMP: 5 EST: 1999
SALES (est): 377.1K **Privately Held**
SIC: 3465 Body parts, automobile: stamped metal

(G-5298)
SANFORD PRINTING INC
13335 41st Rd (11355-3667)
PHONE.....................................718 461-1202
Fax: 718 886-4258
Paul Peng, *President*
Mark Peng, *Managing Dir*
▲ EMP: 5
SALES (est): 671.9K **Privately Held**
SIC: 2752 Commercial printing, offset

(G-5299)
SNAPP TOO ENTERPRISE
3312 211th St (11361-1523)
PHONE.....................................718 224-5252
Edward Porzelt, *Owner*
EMP: 6
SALES (est): 330K **Privately Held**
SIC: 2086 Bottled & canned soft drinks

(G-5300)
SPEEDY ENTERPRISE OF USA CORP
4120 162nd St (11358-4123)
PHONE.....................................718 463-3000
Harolyn Paik, *Principal*
EMP: 8
SALES (est): 648.1K **Privately Held**
SIC: 2759 Commercial printing

(G-5301)
STAR CORRUGATED BOX CO INC
5515 Grand Ave (11378-3186)
PHONE.....................................718 386-3200
Robert Karlin, *Chairman*
Richard H Etra, *Vice Pres*
EMP: 9
SALES (est): 1.6MM **Privately Held**
SIC: 2653 Boxes, corrugated: made from purchased materials

(G-5302)
STARK AQUARIUM PRODUCTS CO INC
Also Called: Stark Fish
2914 122nd St (11354-2530)
PHONE.....................................718 445-5357
Edith Starkman, *President*
Omiros Gioroukos, *Vice Pres*
Helen Vasili, *Admin Asst*
▲ EMP: 26 EST: 1977
SQ FT: 20,000
SALES (est): 3.4MM **Privately Held**
WEB: www.starkproducts.com
SIC: 3231 Products of purchased glass; aquariums & reflectors, glass

(G-5303)
SUNRISE TILE INC
13309 35th Ave (11354-2712)
PHONE.....................................718 939-0538
Kathy Chen, *Manager*
▲ EMP: 8
SALES (est): 797.4K **Privately Held**
SIC: 2273 1752 Carpets & rugs; wood floor installation & refinishing

(G-5304)
TABI INC
488 Onderdonk Ave Apt 1l (11385-1547)
PHONE.....................................347 701-1051
Diego Tenesaca, *President*
EMP: 6
SALES (est): 199.3K **Privately Held**
SIC: 7372 Application computer software

(G-5305)
TEMPCO GLASS FABRICATION LLC
13110 Maple Ave (11355-4223)
PHONE.....................................718 461-6888
Steven Powell, *General Mgr*
▲ EMP: 9
SALES (est): 920K **Privately Held**
SIC: 3211 Building glass, flat

(G-5306)
TILCON NEW YORK INC
Also Called: Flushing Terminal
3466 College Point Blvd (11354-2717)
PHONE.....................................845 480-3249
EMP: 63
SALES (corp-wide): 28.6B **Privately Held**
SIC: 1429 Dolomitic marble, crushed & broken-quarrying
HQ: Tilcon New York Inc.
  162 Old Mill Rd
  West Nyack NY 10994
  845 358-4500

▲ = Import ▼ = Export
◆ = Import/Export

GEOGRAPHIC SECTION

Forest Hills - Queens County (G-5332)

(G-5307)
TONGLI PHARMACEUTICALS USA INC (PA)
4260 Main St Apt 6f (11355-4737)
PHONE.................................212 842-8837
Mingli Yao, *Ch of Bd*
Ailing Zhao, *Admin Sec*
EMP: 11
SALES: 11.1MM **Publicly Held**
SIC: 2834 Pharmaceutical preparations

(G-5308)
TRIBORO BAGEL CO INC
Also Called: Bagel Oasis
18312 Horace Harding Expy (11365-2123)
PHONE.................................718 359-9245
Fax: 718 539-8484
Abe Moskowitz, *President*
Mike Edelstein, *Corp Secy*
Mike Donovan, *Controller*
EMP: 20 **EST:** 1961
SQ FT: 1,200
SALES (est): 1MM **Privately Held**
WEB: www.bageloasis.com
SIC: 2051 Bakery: wholesale or wholesale/retail combined; bagels, fresh or frozen

(G-5309)
TWINKLE LIGHTING INC
13114 40th Rd (11354-5137)
PHONE.................................718 225-0939
Fuchun Lin, *President*
Cheng Zhi Lai, *Sales Mgr*
EMP: 5
SALES (est): 389.7K **Privately Held**
SIC: 3646 Commercial indusl & institutional electric lighting fixtures

(G-5310)
UNITED SATCOM INC
4555 Robinson St (11355-3444)
PHONE.................................718 359-4100
Ted Park, *President*
EMP: 7
SQ FT: 3,500
SALES: 1.5MM **Privately Held**
SIC: 3663 Microwave communication equipment

(G-5311)
UNITED STEEL PRODUCTS INC
Also Called: Ronmar
3340 127th Pl (11368-1508)
PHONE.................................914 968-7782
EMP: 60
SALES (est): 24.8K **Privately Held**
SIC: 3442 3446 Mfg Metal Doors/Sash/Trim Mfg Architectural Metalwork

(G-5312)
WARODEAN CORPORATION
Also Called: Loosesleeve Law Publications
4308 162nd St (11358-3131)
P.O. Box 650042, Fresh Meadows (11365-0042)
PHONE.................................718 359-5559
Michael Loughrey, *President*
EMP: 8
SQ FT: 1,750
SALES (est): 690K **Privately Held**
SIC: 2731 Textbooks: publishing & printing

(G-5313)
WOLSKI WOOD WORKS INC
14134 78th Rd Apt 3c (11367-3331)
PHONE.................................718 577-9816
Tadeusz Wolski, *President*
EMP: 7
SALES (est): 177.1K **Privately Held**
SIC: 2421 Outdoor wood structural products

(G-5314)
WORLD JOURNAL LLC
Also Called: World Journal Book Store
13619 39th Ave (11354)
PHONE.................................718 445-2277
Fax: 718 445-5157
Bob Chow, *Principal*
EMP: 20

SALES (corp-wide): 54.9MM **Privately Held**
WEB: www.wjnews.net
SIC: 2711 Newspapers: publishing only, not printed on site
HQ: World Journal Llc
14107 20th Ave Fl 2
Whitestone NY 11357
718 746-8889

(G-5315)
YELLOW E HOUSE INC
Also Called: Gatecomusa
18812 Northern Blvd (11358-2811)
PHONE.................................718 888-2000
Stephan Cho, *CEO*
EMP: 7 **EST:** 2013
SQ FT: 3,000
SALES (est): 499.7K **Privately Held**
SIC: 3571 5045 7629 5945 Electronic computers; computers, peripherals & software; business machine repair, electric; hobby, toy & game shops

(G-5316)
ZENITH SOLUTIONS
6922 Manse St (11375-5850)
PHONE.................................718 575-8570
P Bilello, *Principal*
Latha Vakati, *Human Resources*
EMP: 7
SALES (est): 631.8K **Privately Held**
SIC: 2834 Intravenous solutions

Fly Creek
Otsego County

(G-5317)
ADIRONDACK LEATHER PDTS INC
196 Cemetery Rd (13337-2102)
P.O. Box 180 (13337-0180)
PHONE.................................607 547-5798
Gregory M O Neil, *CEO*
Darlene O Neil, *Vice Pres*
EMP: 10
SALES (est): 1.4MM **Privately Held**
WEB: www.adirondackleatherproducts.com
SIC: 3199 7389 Holsters, leather; leggings or chaps, canvas or leather; leather belting & strapping;

(G-5318)
COOPERSTOWN BAT CO INC (PA)
Rr 28 (13337)
PHONE.................................607 547-2415
Sharon Oberriter, *President*
Don Oberriter, *Vice Pres*
EMP: 15
SQ FT: 4,000
SALES (est): 1.1MM **Privately Held**
WEB: www.cooperstownbat.com
SIC: 3949 5941 Sporting & athletic goods; sporting goods & bicycle shops

(G-5319)
FLY CREEK CDER MILL ORCHRD INC
288 Goose St (13337-2314)
PHONE.................................607 547-9692
Fax: 607 547-2826
Brenda Michaels, *President*
Howard Michaels, *Vice Pres*
Lin Molloy, *Personnel*
EMP: 5
SALES (est): 485.8K **Privately Held**
SIC: 2022 2033 2037 2084 Cheese, natural & processed; canned fruits & specialties; frozen fruits & vegetables; wines; gift shop

Fonda
Montgomery County

(G-5320)
KASSON & KELLER INC
Also Called: Kas-Kel
60 School St (12068-4809)
P.O. Box 777 (12068-0777)
PHONE.................................518 853-3421
Fax: 518 853-3929
William Keller III, *Ch of Bd*
James P Keller, *Exec VP*
Drue Wallach, *Vice Pres*
Linda Kilmartin, *Credit Mgr*
John Caruso, *Sales Mgr*
▲ **EMP:** 900 **EST:** 1946
SQ FT: 60,000
SALES (est): 169.2MM **Privately Held**
WEB: www.kas-kel.com
SIC: 3442 3089 1521 3231 Window & door frames; windows, plastic; single-family housing construction; products of purchased glass

(G-5321)
KEYMARK CORPORATION
1188 Cayadutta St (12068)
P.O. Box 626 (12068-0626)
PHONE.................................518 853-3421
Fax: 518 853-3130
William L Keller III, *Ch of Bd*
Kelly Fernet, *General Mgr*
Tony Maiolo, *COO*
James P Keller, *Exec VP*
Bob Channell, *VP Opers*
▲ **EMP:** 600 **EST:** 1964
SQ FT: 250,000
SALES (est): 228.8MM **Privately Held**
WEB: www.keymarkcorp.com
SIC: 3354 3479 3471 Aluminum extruded products; painting of metal products; anodizing (plating) of metals or formed products

(G-5322)
TEMPER CORPORATION (PA)
544 Persse Rd (12068-7700)
P.O. Box 1127 (12068-1127)
PHONE.................................518 853-3467
Fax: 518 853-4092
John Rode, *President*
Bob Francisco, *Production*
Nancy S Chmaeh, *Office Mgr*
Alice Stanawich, *Office Mgr*
Ruth Browen, *Info Tech Mgr*
EMP: 25
SQ FT: 30,000
SALES (est): 4.2MM **Privately Held**
WEB: www.tempercorp.com
SIC: 3493 3053 Steel springs, except wire; gaskets & sealing devices

(G-5323)
TEMPER CORPORATION
Temper Axle Products
544 Persse Rd (12068-7700)
PHONE.................................518 853-3467
John Rhode, *President*
EMP: 5
SALES (corp-wide): 4.2MM **Privately Held**
WEB: www.tempercorp.com
SIC: 3714 Axles, motor vehicle
PA: Temper Corporation
544 Persse Rd
Fonda NY 12068
518 853-3467

Forest Hills
Queens County

(G-5324)
2H INTERNATIONAL CORP
6766 108th St Apt D1 (11375-2904)
PHONE.................................347 623-9380
June LI, *Manager*
EMP: 5
SALES: 300K **Privately Held**
SIC: 2337 Women's & misses' suits & coats

(G-5325)
AIGNER CHOCOLATES INC (PA)
10302 Metropolitan Ave (11375-6734)
PHONE.................................718 544-1850
Peter Aigner, *Ch of Bd*
Christopher Aigner, *Vice Pres*
EMP: 6
SQ FT: 2,000
SALES (est): 879.7K **Privately Held**
WEB: www.aignerchocolates.com
SIC: 2064 2066 Chocolate candy, except solid chocolate; chocolate candy, solid

(G-5326)
ALLROUND LOGISTICS INC (PA)
Also Called: Allround Maritime Services
7240 Ingram St (11375-5927)
PHONE.................................718 544-8945
Roland Meier, *President*
Ellen Meier, *Vice Pres*
Charlie Boon, *Treasurer*
Jody Barton, *Asst Sec*
◆ **EMP:** 5
SQ FT: 3,600
SALES (est): 864.1K **Privately Held**
WEB: www.allroundlogistics.com
SIC: 3534 Escalators, passenger & freight

(G-5327)
ARIEL TIAN LLC
253 W 35th St Fl 8 (11375)
P.O. Box 296, New York (10018-0005)
PHONE.................................212 457-1266
LI Tian, *Mng Member*
EMP: 5
SALES: 100K **Privately Held**
SIC: 3111 7389 Accessory products, leather; styling of fashions, apparel, furniture, textiles, etc.

(G-5328)
COMBINE GRAPHICS CORP
10714 Queens Blvd (11375-4249)
PHONE.................................212 695-4044
Fax: 212 633-0352
Charles Caminiti, *President*
Louis Zafonte, *Vice Pres*
EMP: 5
SQ FT: 2,300
SALES (est): 590.6K **Privately Held**
SIC: 2752 Commercial printing, offset

(G-5329)
HANGER INC
Also Called: Hanger Prosthectics Orthotics
11835 Queens Blvd Ste Ll3 (11375-7205)
PHONE.................................718 575-5504
Joe Nieto, *Manager*
EMP: 8
SALES (corp-wide): 451.4MM **Publicly Held**
SIC: 3842 5999 Surgical appliances & supplies; artificial limbs
PA: Hanger, Inc.
10910 Domain Dr Ste 300
Austin TX 78758
512 777-3800

(G-5330)
HI-TECH ADVANCED SOLUTIONS INC
10525 65th Ave Apt 4h (11375-1802)
PHONE.................................718 926-3488
Nison B Isaak, *President*
EMP: 10
SALES: 100K **Privately Held**
SIC: 3571 Electronic computers

(G-5331)
LOYALTYPLANT INC (PA)
70 23 Juno St (11375)
PHONE.................................551 221-2701
Vasilii Diachenko, *President*
EMP: 10
SALES (est): 399.2K **Privately Held**
SIC: 7372 Business oriented computer software

(G-5332)
NATIVE AMERCN ENRGY GROUP INC (PA)
7211 Austin St Ste 288 (11375-5354)
PHONE.................................718 408-2323
Fax: 718 793-4034
Raj Nanvaan, *Principal*

Forest Hills - Queens County (G-5333)

EMP: 6
SALES (est): 495.9K **Privately Held**
SIC: 1382 Oil & gas exploration services

(G-5333)
NATURE ONLY INC
10420 Queens Blvd Apt 3b (11375-3602)
PHONE.....................917 922-6539
EMP: 9
SALES (est): 780K **Privately Held**
SIC: 2844 Mfg Natural Rash Creams For Kids & Facial Creams

(G-5334)
NEW YORK TYPING & PRINTING CO
10816 72nd Ave (11375-5653)
PHONE.....................718 268-7900
Jay Goldstin, *President*
EMP: 5 EST: 1981
SALES (est): 380K **Privately Held**
SIC: 2752 7338 Commercial printing, offset; secretarial & typing service

(G-5335)
PRESTON GLASS INDUSTRIES INC
Also Called: P G I
10420 Queens Blvd Apt 17a (11375-3610)
PHONE.....................718 997-8888
Ashish Karnavat, *President*
EMP: 20 EST: 1995
SALES (est): 1.3MM **Privately Held**
SIC: 3641 Electrodes, cold cathode fluorescent lamp

(G-5336)
TWIST IT TOP IT
10309 Metropolitan Ave (11375-6733)
PHONE.....................718 793-8947
EMP: 15 EST: 2012
SALES (est): 367.6K **Privately Held**
SIC: 2026 Yogurt

(G-5337)
WILSON & WILSON GROUP
Also Called: Wilson N Wilson Group & RES
6514 110th St (11375-1424)
PHONE.....................212 729-4736
Pius Wilson, *Principal*
EMP: 5
SALES: 25K **Privately Held**
SIC: 3577 Computer peripheral equipment

Forestport
Oneida County

(G-5338)
NIRVANA INC
1 Nirvana Plz (13338)
P.O. Box 200 (13338-0200)
PHONE.....................315 942-4900
Fax: 315 942-5013
Mozafar Rafizadeh, *President*
Mansur Rafizadeh, *Vice Pres*
MO Rafizadeh, *Vice Pres*
Edward Wiehl, *Vice Pres*
Heather Hughes, *Info Tech Mgr*
▲ EMP: 160
SQ FT: 250,000
SALES (est): 75.4MM **Privately Held**
WEB: www.nirvanaspring.com
SIC: 2086 Mineral water, carbonated: packaged in cans, bottles, etc.; water, pasteurized: packaged in cans, bottles, etc.

(G-5339)
TOWN OF OHIO
Also Called: Town of Ohio Highway Garage
N Lake Rd (13338)
PHONE.....................315 392-2055
Fred Reuter, *Manager*
EMP: 24
SQ FT: 2,066 **Privately Held**
SIC: 3531 Snow plow attachments
PA: Town Of Ohio
  234 Nellis Rd
  Cold Brook NY 13324
  315 826-7912

Forestville
Chautauqua County

(G-5340)
BAILEY MANUFACTURING CO LLC
10987 Bennett State Rd (14062-9714)
P.O. Box 356 (14062-0356)
PHONE.....................716 965-2731
Fax: 716 965-2764
John Hines, *President*
Dona Hines,
EMP: 50 EST: 2002
SQ FT: 40,000
SALES (est): 11MM **Privately Held**
SIC: 3469 Metal stampings

(G-5341)
MERRITT ESTATE WINERY INC
2264 King Rd (14062-9703)
PHONE.....................716 965-4800
Fax: 716 965-4800
William T Merritt, *President*
Jason Merritt, *Corp Secy*
EMP: 15
SQ FT: 20,000
SALES (est): 2.4MM **Privately Held**
WEB: www.merrittestatewinery.com
SIC: 2084 Wines

(G-5342)
P S M GROUP INC
Also Called: Pit Stop Motorsports
17 Main St (14062-9998)
P.O. Box 500 (14062-0500)
PHONE.....................716 532-6686
Jeffrey A Furash, *President*
EMP: 20 EST: 1978
SALES (est): 1.7MM **Privately Held**
WEB: www.burningasphalt.com
SIC: 2842 7948 Specialty cleaning, polishes & sanitation goods; race track operation

(G-5343)
SHYKAT PROMOTIONS
10561 Creek Rd (14062-9607)
PHONE.....................866 574-2757
Krista Miller, *Owner*
EMP: 7
SALES (est): 372.9K **Privately Held**
SIC: 2759 2395 8743 Screen printing; embroidery & art needlework; promotion service

Fort Ann
Washington County

(G-5344)
PETTEYS LUMBER
Also Called: A Petteys Lumber
10247 State Route 149 (12827-1804)
PHONE.....................518 792-5943
Alvin Petteys, *Owner*
EMP: 7
SALES: 370K **Privately Held**
SIC: 2421 2426 Lumber: rough, sawed or planed; hardwood dimension & flooring mills

Fort Drum
Jefferson County

(G-5345)
BLACK RIVER GENERATIONS LLC
Also Called: Reenergy Black River
4515 2nd St (13602)
P.O. Box 849 (13602-0849)
PHONE.....................315 773-2314
EMP: 23 EST: 2010
SALES (est): 9.8MM **Privately Held**
SIC: 3822 Mfg Environmental Controls

(G-5346)
REENERGY BLACK RIVER LLC
4515 Ephrtes River Vly Rd (13602)
PHONE.....................315 773-2314
Larry Richardson, *CEO*
Peter Lister, *Facilities Mgr*
Tom Beck, *Officer*
William Ralson, *Officer*
EMP: 33
SALES (est): 1,000K **Privately Held**
SIC: 3612 Transformers, except electric
PA: Reenergy Holdings Llc
  30 Century Hill Dr # 102
  Latham NY 12110

Fort Edward
Washington County

(G-5347)
A HYATT BALL CO LTD
School St (12828)
PHONE.....................518 747-0272
Fax: 518 747-2619
Robert Simpson, *President*
EMP: 7
SQ FT: 12,000
SALES (est): 1.2MM **Privately Held**
SIC: 3562 3949 Ball bearings & parts; billiard & pool equipment & supplies, general

(G-5348)
BURNHAM POLYMERIC INC
Also Called: Burnhams, The
1408 Route 9 (12828-2459)
P.O. Box 317, Glens Falls (12801-0317)
PHONE.....................518 792-3040
Fax: 518 792-4680
Warren Burnham Jr, *President*
William Wulfken, *President*
Eileen Jensen, *Bookkeeper*
George Pape, *Sales Staff*
EMP: 7
SQ FT: 8,400
SALES (est): 670K **Privately Held**
WEB: www.burnhams.com
SIC: 3089 Extruded finished plastic products

(G-5349)
D K MACHINE INC
48 Sullivan Pkwy (12828-1027)
PHONE.....................518 747-0626
Fax: 518 747-0889
Daniel Komarony, *President*
Jim Glacy, *Purchasing*
Theresa Komarony, *Admin Sec*
EMP: 10
SQ FT: 8,500
SALES (est): 1.7MM **Privately Held**
WEB: www.dkmachine.com
SIC: 3599 5085 Machine shop, jobbing & repair; industrial supplies

(G-5350)
IRVING CONSUMER PRODUCTS INC (HQ)
Also Called: Irving Tissue Div
1 Eddy St (12828-1711)
PHONE.....................518 747-4151
Fax: 518 747-2746
J K Irving, *Principal*
Arthur L Irving, *Vice Pres*
Bo B Lam, *Vice Pres*
Rachel Roy, *Vice Pres*
Bernice Wall, *Vice Pres*
▲ EMP: 300
SQ FT: 700,000
SALES (est): 105.8MM
SALES (corp-wide): 90.3MM **Privately Held**
SIC: 2621 Towels, tissues & napkins: paper & stock
PA: Irving Consumer Products Limited
  100 Prom Midland
  Dieppe NB E1A 6
  506 858-7777

(G-5351)
PALLETS INC
99 1/2 East St (12828-1813)
P.O. Box 326 (12828-0326)
PHONE.....................518 747-4177
Fax: 518 747-3757
Clinton Binley, *President*
Arthur Binley III, *Chairman*
Marvin Horowitz, *Admin Sec*
EMP: 45 EST: 1942
SQ FT: 100,000
SALES (est): 6.6MM **Privately Held**
WEB: www.palletsincorporated.com
SIC: 2448 2421 Pallets, wood; sawmills & planing mills, general; lumber: rough, sawed or planed

(G-5352)
PARKER MACHINE COMPANY INC
28 Sullivan Pkwy (12828-1027)
PHONE.....................518 747-0675
Fax: 518 747-2930
Tammy Aust, *President*
Patrick A Whaley, *Vice Pres*
EMP: 17
SQ FT: 17,400
SALES (est): 3.4MM **Privately Held**
WEB: www.parkermachine.com
SIC: 3599 5251 Machine shop, jobbing & repair; tools

(G-5353)
REAL BARK MULCH LLC
1380 Towpath Ln (12828-1757)
PHONE.....................518 747-3650
Jack Bullard, *General Mgr*
Patrick Gulsha,
Patrick Bulsha,
EMP: 9
SALES (est): 1.6MM **Privately Held**
SIC: 3524 Lawn & garden equipment

(G-5354)
RFB ASSOCIATES INC
Also Called: Bruno Associates
35 Sullivan Pkwy (12828-1028)
P.O. Box 14825, Albany (12212-4825)
PHONE.....................518 271-0551
Robert Bruno Sr, *President*
Sean P Bruno Sr, *Vice Pres*
EMP: 12
SQ FT: 60,000
SALES: 3MM **Privately Held**
SIC: 3559 3569 3565 3552 Automotive related machinery; assembly machines, non-metalworking; packaging machinery; textile machinery

(G-5355)
STONEGATE STABLESS
106 Reynolds Rd (12828-9244)
PHONE.....................518 746-7133
William Johnson, *Owner*
EMP: 8
SALES (est): 540.6K **Privately Held**
SIC: 2399 Horse harnesses & riding crops, etc.: non-leather

Fort Plain
Montgomery County

(G-5356)
ELITE PRECISE MANUFACTURER LLC
55 Willett St (13339-1134)
PHONE.....................518 993-3040
Ross Stevenson, *Principal*
EMP: 8
SQ FT: 10,000
SALES (est): 430.9K **Privately Held**
SIC: 3599 Machine & other job shop work

(G-5357)
PERFORMANCE PRECISION MFG LLC
55 Willett St (13339-1134)
PHONE.....................518 993-3033
Joeseph Stevenson, *Owner*
EMP: 8
SALES (est): 952.2K **Privately Held**
SIC: 3999 Manufacturing industries

Frankfort
Herkimer County

(G-5358)
ABDO SHTMTL & FABRICATION INC
4293 Acme Rd (13340-3505)
P.O. Box 4071, Utica (13504-4071)
PHONE 315 894-4664
Michael Abdo, *President*
Trish McGowan, *Manager*
Laurie Rose, *Admin Sec*
EMP: 7
SQ FT: 8,000
SALES (est): 1.7MM **Privately Held**
WEB: www.abdosheetmetal.com
SIC: 3444 1721 1799 Sheet metalwork; painting & paper hanging; welding on site

(G-5359)
C-FLEX BEARING CO INC
104 Industrial Dr (13340-1139)
PHONE 315 895-7454
D Joanne Willcox, *President*
Wayne Smith, *Vice Pres*
EMP: 10
SQ FT: 6,200
SALES: 1.4MM **Privately Held**
WEB: www.c-flex.com
SIC: 3568 3812 3556 3825 Bearings, bushings & blocks; search & navigation equipment; food products machinery; instruments to measure electricity

(G-5360)
DI SANOS CREATIVE CANVAS INC
113 W Main St (13340-1007)
PHONE 315 894-3137
Fax: 315 894-0210
John Di Sano, *President*
EMP: 5
SQ FT: 2,400
SALES (est): 425.3K **Privately Held**
WEB: www.disanoscreativecanvas.com
SIC: 2394 5999 5091 Awnings, fabric: made from purchased materials; canvas covers & drop cloths; awnings; canvas products; boat accessories & parts

(G-5361)
F E HALE MFG CO
120 Benson Pl (13340-3752)
P.O. Box 186 (13340-0186)
PHONE 315 894-5490
Fax: 315 894-5046
Jim Benson, *President*
Cindy Cole, *Credit Mgr*
Brooke Benson, *Admin Sec*
EMP: 65 EST: 1907
SQ FT: 80,000
SALES (est): 12.7MM **Privately Held**
WEB: www.halebookcases.com
SIC: 2521 Bookcases, office: wood

(G-5362)
FIBERDYNE LABS INC
127 Business Park Dr (13340-3700)
PHONE 315 895-8470
Fax: 315 895-8436
A Peter Polus III, *CEO*
Carl Fredlund, *President*
Chad A Polus, *President*
Eric Grossman, *Managing Prtnr*
Don Fariel, *Vice Pres*
▲ **EMP:** 96
SQ FT: 20,000
SALES: 10.5MM **Privately Held**
WEB: www.fiberdyne.com
SIC: 3357 4822 4899 Fiber optic cable (insulated); telegraph & other communications; communication signal enhancement network system

(G-5363)
JBF STAINLESS LLC
148 Industrial Park Dr (13340-4745)
P.O. Box 632, Cazenovia (13035-0632)
PHONE 315 569-2800
John Feldmeier, *President*
Margaret Feldmeier, *Principal*
EMP: 26
SQ FT: 4,500
SALES (est): 6.5MM **Privately Held**
SIC: 3324 Steel investment foundries

(G-5364)
MAPLEHURST BAKERIES LLC
Also Called: Grannys Kitchens
178 Industrial Park Dr (13340-4745)
PHONE 315 735-5000
EMP: 280
SALES (corp-wide): 35.5B **Privately Held**
SIC: 2051 2053 Bread, cake & related products; doughnuts, frozen
HQ: Maplehurst Bakeries, Llc
50 Maplehurst Dr
Brownsburg IN 46112
317 858-9000

(G-5365)
MOHAWK VALLEY MANUFACTURING
2237 Broad St (13340-5101)
PHONE 315 797-0851
EMP: 7
SALES (est): 630K **Privately Held**
SIC: 3556 Mfg Food Products Machinery

(G-5366)
PRECISION POLISH LLC
144 Adams St (13340-3751)
PHONE 315 894-3792
Nial Williams, *President*
Jack Dunderdale, *Vice Pres*
Michelle Williams, *Manager*
EMP: 25
SALES: 1.4MM **Privately Held**
SIC: 3441 Fabricated structural metal

(G-5367)
SOFT-NOZE USA INC
2216 Broad St (13340-5100)
PHONE 315 732-2726
Fax: 315 732-2963
Brett Truett, *President*
Krista Petrowski, *Finance Mgr*
Haris Dervisevic, *Technology*
▲ **EMP:** 5
SQ FT: 4,500
SALES (est): 510K **Privately Held**
WEB: www.softnoze.com
SIC: 3625 Electric controls & control accessories, industrial

(G-5368)
TURBO MACHINED PRODUCTS LLC
102 Industrial Dr (13340-1139)
PHONE 315 895-3010
Fax: 315 895-3011
John A Kabot Jr, *President*
Robert Cartmell, *Vice Pres*
Robert Partmell, *Vice Pres*
Brett Brewer, *QC Mgr*
Charles Gross, *Engineer*
EMP: 35
SQ FT: 20,000
SALES (est): 8.1MM **Privately Held**
WEB: www.turbomp.com
SIC: 3824 3511 Impeller & counter driven flow meters; turbines & turbine generator sets & parts

Franklin Square
Nassau County

(G-5369)
514 ADAMS CORPORATION
Also Called: Adams Press
781 Hempstead Tpke (11010-4328)
PHONE 516 352-6948
Daniel Rummo, *President*
Chris Rummo, *Vice Pres*
Theresa Rummo, *Admin Sec*
EMP: 7
SQ FT: 3,000
SALES (est): 1MM **Privately Held**
SIC: 2752 2791 2789 Commercial printing, offset; typesetting; bookbinding & related work

(G-5370)
ARTISTICS PRINTING CORP
746 Franklin Ave Ste 2 (11010-1101)
PHONE 516 561-2121
Richard Farruggia, *President*
EMP: 5
SQ FT: 1,200
SALES (est): 400K **Privately Held**
SIC: 2759 Commercial printing

(G-5371)
BONURA AND SONS IRON WORKS
957 Lorraine Dr (11010-1812)
PHONE 718 381-4100
Frank Bonura, *Principal*
Enzo Bonuro, *Principal*
EMP: 15
SALES (est): 1.2MM **Privately Held**
SIC: 3312 1799 Fence posts, iron & steel; ornamental metal work

(G-5372)
D C I TECHNICAL INC
475 Franklin Ave Fl 2 (11010-1228)
PHONE 516 355-0464
Fax: 516 355-0467
Andrea Mannheim, *President*
Harold Adler, *Vice Pres*
Merideth Hilton, *Vice Pres*
Sidney Platt, *Vice Pres*
EMP: 12
SQ FT: 2,700
SALES (est): 882.8K **Privately Held**
SIC: 2731 2741 Books: publishing & printing; miscellaneous publishing

(G-5373)
FEMTECH WOMEN POWERED SOFTWARE
1230 Hempstead Tpke (11010-1534)
PHONE 516 328-2631
Colleen Simeone, *President*
EMP: 99
SALES (est): 2.6MM **Privately Held**
WEB: www.femtech.at
SIC: 7372 Prepackaged software

(G-5374)
LESSOILCOM
672 Dogwood Ave (11010-3247)
PHONE 516 319-5052
Mike Gregoretti, *Principal*
Joseph Lamacchia, *Vice Pres*
Rae Crenshaw, *Admin Asst*
EMP: 6
SALES (est): 363K **Privately Held**
SIC: 1241 Bituminous coal mining services, contract basis

(G-5375)
MOVIN ON SOUNDS AND SEC INC
Also Called: M O S S Communications
636 Hempstead Tpke (11010-4326)
PHONE 516 489-2350
Fax: 516 489-9536
Bruce Cirillo, *President*
Paul Cirillo, *Vice Pres*
Jean Ulsheimer, *Manager*
EMP: 35
SALES (est): 6.9MM **Privately Held**
WEB: www.movinon.com
SIC: 3663 Radio & TV communications equipment

(G-5376)
NYCOM BUSINESS SOLUTIONS INC
804 Hempstead Tpke (11010-4321)
PHONE 516 345-6000
Jerry Sperduto, *President*
EMP: 3
SQ FT: 800
SALES (est): 1.2MM **Privately Held**
SIC: 3663 Cellular radio telephone

(G-5377)
STUDENT LIFELINE INC
Also Called: Student Safety Books
922 Hempstead Tpke (11010-3628)
P.O. Box 570200, Whitestone (11357-0200)
PHONE 516 327-0800
Richard Signarino, *President*
Bonnie Meehan, *Sales Mgr*
Jennifer Tores-Ebert, *Manager*
EMP: 42
SQ FT: 2,200
SALES (est): 4.1MM **Privately Held**
WEB: www.studentlifeline.com
SIC: 2741 Miscellaneous publishing

Franklinville
Cattaraugus County

(G-5378)
BUFFALO CRUSHED STONE INC
Rr 16 (14737)
P.O. Box 106 (14737-0106)
PHONE 716 566-9636
John Lentz, *Manager*
EMP: 11
SALES (corp-wide): 651.9MM **Privately Held**
SIC: 1442 5032 Gravel mining; stone, crushed or broken
HQ: Buffalo Crushed Stone, Inc.
500 Como Park Blvd
Buffalo NY 14227
716 826-7310

(G-5379)
CATTARAUGUS CONTAINERS INC
21 Elm St 23 (14737-1052)
P.O. Box 174 (14737-0174)
PHONE 716 676-2000
Fax: 716 676-3552
Jane Lemke, *President*
Paul Wagner, *Vice Pres*
Tammy Mooney, *Controller*
Tammy Webster, *Controller*
EMP: 33
SQ FT: 33,000
SALES: 3.8MM **Privately Held**
SIC: 2653 2657 5113 Boxes, corrugated: made from purchased materials; folding paperboard boxes; corrugated & solid fiber boxes

(G-5380)
ONTARIO KNIFE COMPANY
26 Empire St Ste 1 (14737-1099)
P.O. Box 145 (14737-0145)
PHONE 716 676-5527
Fax: 716 676-5535
Nicholas D Trbovich Jr, *CEO*
Kenneth Trbovich, *Ch of Bd*
Nicholas D Trbovich, *Chairman*
Robert J Breton, *Vice Pres*
John O'Brien, *Vice Pres*
▲ **EMP:** 63
SQ FT: 10,000
SALES: 6.5MM
SALES (corp-wide): 38.5MM **Publicly Held**
WEB: www.ontarioknife.com
SIC: 3421 Cutlery
PA: Servotronics, Inc.
1110 Maple Rd
Elma NY 14059
716 655-5990

Fredonia
Chautauqua County

(G-5381)
D & F PALLET INC
134 Clinton Ave (14063-1406)
PHONE 716 672-2984
Fax: 716 679-3525
Jeremy Poehler, *Ch of Bd*
Thomas J Ivory, *President*
Richard Ivory, *Vice Pres*
Vickie Ivory, *Treasurer*
Mary Ivory, *Admin Sec*
EMP: 18
SQ FT: 26,000
SALES (est): 2.8MM **Privately Held**
SIC: 2448 Pallets, wood

Fredonia - Chautauqua County (G-5382) GEOGRAPHIC SECTION

(G-5382)
FREDONIA PENNYSAVER INC (PA)
Also Called: Lakeshore Pennysaver
276 W Main St Ste 1 (14063-2099)
P.O. Box 493 (14063-0493)
PHONE.................................716 679-1509
Fax: 716 672-2626
Thomas K Webb Jr, *President*
Maureen Webb, *Vice Pres*
EMP: 5
SQ FT: 1,000
SALES (est): 805.8K **Privately Held**
WEB: www.fredoniapennysaver.com
SIC: 2741 2711 Guides: publishing only, not printed on site; newspapers, publishing & printing

(G-5383)
GREAT LAKES SPECIALITES
9491 Route 60 (14063-9729)
P.O. Box 351 (14063-0351)
PHONE.................................716 672-4622
Fax: 716 672-4620
Michael J Gloss, *Owner*
EMP: 20
SQ FT: 10,000
SALES (est): 1.8MM **Privately Held**
SIC: 2448 2449 2441 Pallets, wood; wood containers; nailed wood boxes & shook

(G-5384)
TUBE FABRICATION COMPANY INC
183 E Main St Ste 10 (14063-1435)
PHONE.................................716 673-1871
Daniel Sturniolo, *President*
Charles Sturniolo, *Purchasing*
EMP: 12
SALES (est): 2MM **Privately Held**
SIC: 3498 5051 Tube fabricating (contract bending & shaping); tubing, metal

(G-5385)
URBAN TECHNOLOGIES INC
3451 Stone Quarry Rd (14063-9722)
PHONE.................................716 672-2709
John Urbanik, *President*
EMP: 5
SALES (est): 656.5K **Privately Held**
SIC: 3677 Electronic transformers; inductors, electronic

(G-5386)
WOODBURY VINEYARDS INC
Also Called: Noble Vintages
3215 S Roberts Rd (14063-9417)
PHONE.................................716 679-9463
Joseph Carney, *Branch Mgr*
EMP: 5
SALES (corp-wide): 1.5MM **Privately Held**
WEB: www.woodburyvineyards.com
SIC: 2084 Wines
PA: Woodbury Vineyards, Inc.
2001 Crocker Rd Ste 440
Westlake OH 44145
440 835-2828

Freedom
Cattaraugus County

(G-5387)
GUTCHESS FREEDOM INC
10699 Maple Grove Rd (14065-9774)
PHONE.................................716 492-2824
Larry Lines, *Manager*
EMP: 70 EST: 2007
SALES (est): 9.3MM
SALES (corp-wide): 150MM **Privately Held**
SIC: 2421 Custom sawmill
PA: Gutchess Lumber Co., Inc.
890 Mclean Rd
Cortland NY 13045
607 753-3393

Freeport
Nassau County

(G-5388)
5TH AVENUE CHOCOLATIERE LTD (PA)
114 Church St (11520-3833)
PHONE.................................212 935-5454
Joseph E Whaley, *President*
John Whaley, *Vice Pres*
▲ EMP: 4
SQ FT: 4,500
SALES: 1.6MM **Privately Held**
SIC: 2064 2066 5441 Candy & other confectionery products; chocolate & cocoa products; candy

(G-5389)
ACCESS DISPLAY GROUP INC
Also Called: Swing Frame
151 S Main St (11520-3845)
PHONE.................................516 678-7772
Fax: 516 867-7073
Charles Abrams, *President*
Barbara Abrams, *Vice Pres*
Brian McAley, *Info Tech Mgr*
Craig R Abrams, *Exec Dir*
John Klimiuk, *Graphic Designe*
▲ EMP: 14
SQ FT: 6,000
SALES (est): 2.7MM **Privately Held**
WEB: www.swingframe.com
SIC: 3499 Picture frames, metal

(G-5390)
AIRMARINE ELECTROPLATING CORP
388 Woodcleft Ave (11520-6379)
PHONE.................................516 623-4406
Fax: 516 623-6215
Ernest Rieger III, *President*
EMP: 6
SALES (est): 724.4K **Privately Held**
WEB: www.airmarine.com
SIC: 3471 Electroplating of metals or formed products

(G-5391)
ALABASTER GROUP INC
188 N Main St (11520-2232)
PHONE.................................516 867-8223
Orna Alabaster, *President*
Zeev Alabaster, *Vice Pres*
EMP: 5
SQ FT: 7,300
SALES (est): 356.4K **Privately Held**
SIC: 2791 7336 7389 Typesetting; graphic arts & related design; printing broker

(G-5392)
ALL AMERICAN METAL CORPORATION (PA)
200 Buffalo Ave (11520-4732)
P.O. Box 108 (11520-0108)
PHONE.................................516 223-1760
Fax: 516 378-0638
Bernard Pechter, *President*
Laury Ryan, *Clerk*
▲ EMP: 8
SQ FT: 50,000
SALES (est): 5MM **Privately Held**
WEB: www.allamericanmetal.com
SIC: 2542 Partitions for floor attachment, prefabricated: except wood

(G-5393)
ALL AMERICAN METAL CORPORATION
200 Buffalo Ave (11520-4732)
P.O. Box 108 (11520-0108)
PHONE.................................516 623-0222
Bernard Pechter, *Manager*
EMP: 32
SALES (corp-wide): 5MM **Privately Held**
WEB: www.allamericanmetal.com
SIC: 2542 3446 Partitions & fixtures, except wood; architectural metalwork
PA: All American Metal Corporation
200 Buffalo Ave
Freeport NY 11520
516 223-1760

(G-5394)
ALPHA FASTENERS CORP
154 E Merrick Rd (11520-4020)
PHONE.................................516 867-6188
Fax: 516 867-6189
Koula Perdios, *President*
Archie Perdios, *Vice Pres*
Michael Perdios, *Vice Pres*
▲ EMP: 5
SQ FT: 3,000
SALES (est): 657.3K **Privately Held**
SIC: 3599 Machine shop, jobbing & repair

(G-5395)
AMADEO SERRANO
36 Frankel Ave (11520-4846)
PHONE.................................516 608-8359
Amaeeo Serrano, *Owner*
EMP: 6
SALES (est): 733K **Privately Held**
SIC: 3089 Fences, gates & accessories: plastic

(G-5396)
AMERICAN PUFF CORP
225 Buffalo Ave (11520-4794)
PHONE.................................516 379-1300
Fax: 516 378-2844
William Ostrower, *President*
EMP: 100
SQ FT: 70,000
SALES (est): 6.6MM **Privately Held**
SIC: 3172 2399 Personal leather goods; powder puffs & mitts

(G-5397)
ANNA YOUNG ASSOC LTD
Also Called: Lombardi Design & Mfg
100 Doxsee Dr (11520-4716)
PHONE.................................516 546-4400
Fax: 516 546-4413
Carl M Lombardi, *President*
Jodi Stern, *Purchasing*
Steve Ash, *CFO*
Alice Weiber, *Accountant*
▲ EMP: 150
SQ FT: 50,000
SALES (est): 52.3MM **Privately Held**
WEB: www.lombardi.cc
SIC: 3089 Injection molded finished plastic products

(G-5398)
ARROW CHEMICAL CORP
28 Rider Pl (11520-4612)
PHONE.................................516 377-7770
Sherry Bernstein, *CEO*
EMP: 17 EST: 1960
SQ FT: 8,000
SALES (est): 4.2MM **Privately Held**
WEB: www.arrowchemical.net
SIC: 2842 Cleaning or polishing preparations

(G-5399)
BELLO LLC
178 Hanse Ave (11520-4609)
PHONE.................................516 623-8800
John Alair Garcia, *Mng Member*
EMP: 144 EST: 2016
SQ FT: 65,000
SALES (est): 16.4MM **Privately Held**
SIC: 2053 Frozen bakery products, except bread

(G-5400)
BRAMSON HOUSE INC
151 Albany Ave (11520-4710)
PHONE.................................516 764-5006
Jules Abramson, *CEO*
Ellis Abramson, *President*
Betty Abramson, *Vice Pres*
Mark Hecht, *Sales Dir*
Neal Wilkinson, *Sales Mgr*
◆ EMP: 120
SQ FT: 80,000
SALES (est): 17MM **Privately Held**
WEB: www.bramsonhouse.com
SIC: 2392 2391 Bedspreads & bed sets: made from purchased materials; curtains & draperies

(G-5401)
BRUETON INDUSTRIES INC (PA)
146 Hanse Ave Ste 1 (11520-4636)
PHONE.................................516 379-3400
Ralph Somma, *President*
Daniel Dayao, *Controller*
EMP: 60 EST: 1920
SQ FT: 55,000
SALES (est): 6.9MM **Privately Held**
WEB: www.brueton.com
SIC: 2522 2514 2511 2521 Office furniture, except wood; metal household furniture; wood household furniture; wood office furniture

(G-5402)
CASTLEREAGH PRINTCRAFT INC
Also Called: Castle Reagh Print Craft
320 Buffalo Ave (11520-4711)
PHONE.................................516 623-1728
Fax: 516 379-2386
James Vollaro, *President*
Robert Quadrino, *Vice Pres*
Steven Quadrino, *Vice Pres*
Donna Vollaro, *CFO*
EMP: 70
SQ FT: 35,000
SALES (est): 10.5MM **Privately Held**
WEB: www.printcraftonline.com
SIC: 3555 2791 2789 2752 Printing trades machinery; typesetting; bookbinding & related work; commercial printing, lithographic

(G-5403)
CELLGEN INC
55 Commercial St (11520-2831)
PHONE.................................516 889-9300
Nicholas Capriotti, *CEO*
EMP: 9
SALES (est): 332K **Privately Held**
SIC: 3621 Generators & sets, electric

(G-5404)
DART AWNING INC
365 S Main St (11520-5114)
PHONE.................................718 945-4224
Thomas Hart, *President*
Richard Hart, *Admin Sec*
EMP: 12
SQ FT: 5,000
SALES (est): 1.6MM **Privately Held**
WEB: www.dartawnings.com
SIC: 3444 5999 1799 Awnings, sheet metal; awnings; fence construction

(G-5405)
DORAL REFINING CORP
533 Atlantic Ave (11520-5211)
PHONE.................................516 223-3684
Fax: 516 223-3936
Stephen Faliks, *President*
Alan Zaret, *Vice Pres*
EMP: 20
SQ FT: 10,000
SALES (est): 6MM **Privately Held**
WEB: www.doralcorp.com
SIC: 3339 Precious metals

(G-5406)
EDR INDUSTRIES INC
Also Called: Wil-Nic
100 Commercial St (11520-2832)
PHONE.................................516 868-1928
Don Capriglione, *President*
Christopher Cullinan, *Vice Pres*
EMP: 19
SQ FT: 10,000
SALES (est): 3.4MM **Privately Held**
SIC: 3599 Machine shop, jobbing & repair

(G-5407)
EXCLUSIVE DESIGNS
84 Albany Ave (11520-4011)
PHONE.................................516 378-5258
Bob Mazzella, *Owner*
EMP: 10
SALES (est): 864.6K **Privately Held**
SIC: 2542 Stands, merchandise display: except wood

(G-5408)
FARBER PLASTICS INC
162 Hanse Ave (11520-4644)
PHONE.................................516 378-4860
Fax: 516 378-4312
Lewis Farber, *President*
Janet Hunn, *Bookkeeper*
David Garfinkel, *Sales Mgr*

▲ = Import ▼ = Export
◆ = Import/Export

GEOGRAPHIC SECTION

Freeport - Nassau County (G-5435)

Kc Calderone, *Office Mgr*
Tracy Calderone, *Office Mgr*
EMP: 23
SALES (est): 4.5MM **Privately Held**
SIC: 3081 Plastic film & sheet

(G-5409)
FARBER TRUCKING CORP
162 Hanse Ave (11520-4644)
PHONE..........................516 378-4860
Lewis Farber, *President*
Kasey Calderone, *Manager*
EMP: 23
SQ FT: 35,000
SALES (est): 3MM **Privately Held**
SIC: 3081 Plastic film & sheet

(G-5410)
FORM-TEC INC
216 N Main St Ste E (11520-2200)
PHONE..........................516 867-0200
Fax: 516 867-7724
Howard Lebow, *President*
EMP: 20
SQ FT: 10,000
SALES (est): 3.6MM **Privately Held**
WEB: www.form-tec.com
SIC: 3089 Molding primary plastic

(G-5411)
FORSYTHE COSMETIC GROUP LTD
Also Called: Forsythe Licensing
10 Niagara Ave (11520-4704)
P.O. Box 431, Lawrence (11559-0431)
PHONE..........................516 239-4200
Harriet Rose, *Ch of Bd*
Michael Rose, *President*
Whitney Matza, *Vice Pres*
Cathy Cheong, *Sales Staff*
David Zhou, *Info Tech Mgr*
▲ **EMP:** 75
SQ FT: 20,000
SALES (est): 15MM **Privately Held**
WEB: www.cosmeticgroup.com
SIC: 2844 Cosmetic preparations

(G-5412)
FREEPORT SCREEN & STAMPING
31 Hanse Ave (11520-4601)
PHONE..........................516 379-0330
Stan Papot, *President*
▲ **EMP:** 20
SQ FT: 13,500
SALES (est): 2.4MM **Privately Held**
SIC: 3469 2759 2396 Metal stampings; screen printing; automotive & apparel trimmings

(G-5413)
GLENN FOODS INC (PA)
Also Called: Glenny's
371 S Main St Ste 119-405 (11520-5114)
PHONE..........................516 377-1400
Glenn Schacher, *President*
Philip Fruchter, *Vice Pres*
Steven Fruchter, *Treasurer*
Demress Stockman, *Manager*
▼ **EMP:** 10
SALES (est): 880K **Privately Held**
WEB: www.glennys.com
SIC: 2099 Food preparations

(G-5414)
GREENFIELD DIE CASTING CORP
99 Doxsee Dr (11520-4717)
PHONE..........................516 623-9230
Fax: 516 623-6275
Peter Greenfield, *President*
Michael Greenfield, *Vice Pres*
Douglas Greenfield, *Admin Sec*
EMP: 50
SQ FT: 56,000
SALES (est): 7.3MM **Privately Held**
SIC: 3364 3369 Zinc & zinc-base alloy die-castings; nonferrous foundries

(G-5415)
GREENFIELD INDUSTRIES INC
99 Doxsee Dr (11520-4717)
PHONE..........................516 623-9230
Peter Greenfield, *President*
Douglas Greenfield, *Vice Pres*

Michael Greenfield, *Vice Pres*
Barry Krompier, *Controller*
Linda Teti, *Manager*
▲ **EMP:** 75
SQ FT: 70,000
SALES (est): 12.2MM **Privately Held**
WEB: www.greenfieldny.com
SIC: 3363 Aluminum die-castings

(G-5416)
HARWITT INDUSTRIES INC
61 S Main St Unit A (11520-3864)
PHONE..........................516 623-9787
Louis Harwitt, *President*
EMP: 13 **EST:** 2002
SALES (est): 920K **Privately Held**
SIC: 3599 Machine & other job shop work

(G-5417)
INTEX COMPANY INC (PA)
Also Called: Semtex Industrial
80 Commercial St (11520-2832)
PHONE..........................516 223-0200
Henrietta Rivman, *President*
EMP: 61
SQ FT: 20,000
SALES (est): 6MM **Privately Held**
SIC: 3674 5065 Semiconductors & related devices; electronic parts

(G-5418)
KNICKERBOCKER PARTITION CORP (PA)
193 Hanse Ave (11520-4633)
P.O. Box 690 (11520-0690)
PHONE..........................516 546-0550
Fax: 516 546-0549
Stewart Markbreiter, *President*
Albert Giorgianni, *Vice Pres*
Mark Reiss, *VP Opers*
Andrew Kennedy, *Treasurer*
Ken Kuprian, *Manager*
▲ **EMP:** 90
SQ FT: 60,000
SALES (est): 17.5MM **Privately Held**
WEB: www.knickerbockerpartition.com
SIC: 2542 Partitions for floor attachment, prefabricated: except wood

(G-5419)
LAMAR PLASTICS PACKAGING LTD
216 N Main St Ste F (11520-2200)
PHONE..........................516 378-2500
Fax: 516 378-6192
Lawrence Aronson, *Ch of Bd*
Marc Aronson, *President*
Karen Persico, *Purchasing*
Barry Reimel, *VP Sales*
▲ **EMP:** 60 **EST:** 1966
SQ FT: 60,000
SALES (est): 10.9MM **Privately Held**
SIC: 3086 3993 Packaging & shipping materials, foamed plastic; displays & cutouts, window & lobby

(G-5420)
MARCON ELECTRONIC SYSTEMS LLC
152 Westend Ave (11520-5245)
PHONE..........................516 633-6396
Grace Connelly,
EMP: 6
SALES (est): 750K **Privately Held**
SIC: 3679 Electronic components

(G-5421)
MARCON SERVICES
152 Westend Ave (11520-5245)
PHONE..........................516 223-8019
Grace Connelly, *Owner*
EMP: 6
SALES (est): 66.5K **Privately Held**
WEB: www.graceconnelly.com
SIC: 3674 Semiconductors & related devices

(G-5422)
MELTO METAL PRODUCTS CO INC
37 Hanse Ave (11520-4696)
PHONE..........................516 546-8766
Fax: 516 867-4339
Bernard Liebman, *Ch of Bd*
Peter Sheridan, *Vice Pres*

Juan Costa, *Project Mgr*
Elaine Rezny, *Manager*
▲ **EMP:** 35
SQ FT: 15,000
SALES (est): 7.9MM **Privately Held**
WEB: www.meltometalproducts.com
SIC: 3446 Architectural metalwork

(G-5423)
MICA INTERNATIONAL LTD
126 Albany Ave (11520-4702)
PHONE..........................516 378-3400
Fax: 516 379-0560
EMP: 12
SQ FT: 5,500
SALES (est): 820K **Privately Held**
SIC: 2511 Mfg Wood Household Furniture

(G-5424)
MIDBURY INDUSTRIES INC
86 E Merrick Rd (11520-4034)
PHONE..........................516 868-0600
Fax: 516 868-0659
Diane Jones, *President*
Michael Natilli Jr, *Vice Pres*
EMP: 15
SQ FT: 10,000
SALES: 900K **Privately Held**
WEB: www.midbury.com
SIC: 3089 Injection molding of plastics

(G-5425)
NEW YORK VANITY AND MFG CO
10 Henry St (11520-3910)
PHONE..........................718 417-1010
Teddy Foukalas, *President*
Helen Samaklis, *Bookkeeper*
George Mantikas, *Manager*
Tony Fotou, *Shareholder*
▲ **EMP:** 25
SQ FT: 30,000
SALES (est): 3.6MM **Privately Held**
WEB: www.nyvanity.com
SIC: 2434 Vanities, bathroom: wood

(G-5426)
ON TIME PLASTICS INC
121 Henry St (11520-3821)
PHONE..........................516 442-4280
Franklin Toribio, *President*
EMP: 7
SALES: 600K **Privately Held**
SIC: 3083 Thermoplastic laminates: rods, tubes, plates & sheet

(G-5427)
ONDRIVESUS CORP
Also Called: Rino
216 N Main St Bldg B2 (11520-2200)
PHONE..........................516 771-6777
Fax: 516 867-5656
Dennis G Berg, *CEO*
D Lee Berg, *President*
Jayne Berg, *Vice Pres*
◆ **EMP:** 35
SQ FT: 11,000
SALES (est): 10.4MM **Privately Held**
WEB: www.ondrives.us
SIC: 3566 Speed changers, drives & gears

(G-5428)
ORAMAAX DENTAL PRODUCTS INC
216 N Main St Ste A (11520-2200)
PHONE..........................516 771-8514
Fax: 516 771-8518
Robert Endelson, *President*
Gary Galluzzo, *Engineer*
EMP: 15
SQ FT: 12,500
SALES (est): 1.4MM **Privately Held**
WEB: www.flosscard.com
SIC: 3843 5047 Dental equipment & supplies; dental equipment & supplies

(G-5429)
PENTHOUSE MANUFACTURING CO INC
Also Called: Penthouse Group, The
225 Buffalo Ave (11520-4709)
PHONE..........................516 379-1300
William Ostrower, *President*
Chris Gannotta, *Sales Staff*
David Ramos, *Manager*

▲ **EMP:** 350 **EST:** 1952
SALES (est): 36.4MM **Privately Held**
SIC: 3172 2399 Cosmetic bags; powder puffs & mitts

(G-5430)
PRESTI READY MIX CONCRETE INC
Also Called: Presti Stone and Mason
210 E Merrick Rd (11520-4029)
PHONE..........................516 378-6006
Joseph Prestigiacomo, *President*
EMP: 7
SQ FT: 2,500
SALES: 1.2MM **Privately Held**
SIC: 3273 3531 Ready-mixed concrete; bituminous, cement & concrete related products & equipment

(G-5431)
PRIMELITE MANUFACTURING CORP
407 S Main St (11520-5194)
PHONE..........................516 868-4411
Fax: 516 868-4609
Benjamin Heit, *President*
Emma Warren, *Office Mgr*
EMP: 9 **EST:** 1962
SQ FT: 12,000
SALES (est): 1.7MM **Privately Held**
WEB: www.primelite-mfg.com
SIC: 3646 Commercial indusl & institutional electric lighting fixtures

(G-5432)
QUALITY LINEALS USA INC
105 Bennington Ave Ste 1 (11520-3946)
PHONE..........................516 378-6577
Jill Kaiserman, *President*
EMP: 43
SQ FT: 40,000 **Privately Held**
SIC: 3544 Dies, plastics forming
PA: Quality Lineals Usa, Inc.
1 Kees Pl
Merrick NY 11566

(G-5433)
RAND & PASEKA MFG CO INC
10 Hanse Ave (11520-4602)
PHONE..........................516 867-1500
Fax: 516 867-0230
Marc Schwab, *President*
Andrea Schwab, *Senior VP*
Bogdan Chojnacki, *Manager*
EMP: 22
SQ FT: 19,000
SALES (est): 3.3MM **Privately Held**
SIC: 3911 Rosaries or other small religious articles, precious metal

(G-5434)
ROSE FENCE INC (PA)
345 W Sunrise Hwy (11520-3120)
PHONE..........................516 223-0777
Fax: 516 223-0791
Janice Rosenzeig, *Ch of Bd*
Dorrie Lobe, *Manager*
▲ **EMP:** 42
SQ FT: 2,000
SALES (est): 20.2MM **Privately Held**
WEB: www.rosefence.com
SIC: 3496 Fencing, made from purchased wire

(G-5435)
SAJ OF FREEPORT CORP
Also Called: Love & Quiches Desserts
178 Hanse Ave (11520-4609)
PHONE..........................516 623-8800
Fax: 516 623-8817
Irwin Axelrod, *CEO*
Andrew Axelrod, *President*
Susan Axelrod, *Chairman*
Andy Axelrod, *Vice Pres*
Michael J Goldstein, *Vice Pres*
▼ **EMP:** 250
SALES (est): 72.1MM **Privately Held**
WEB: www.loveandquiches.com
SIC: 2053 Frozen bakery products, except bread

Freeport - Nassau County (G-5436)

(G-5436)
SEA ISLE CUSTOM ROD BUILDERS
495 Guy Lombardo Ave (11520-6293)
PHONE...................516 868-8855
Fax: 516 546-2983
Robert Feuring, *President*
EMP: 7
SQ FT: 1,710
SALES: 900K **Privately Held**
SIC: 3949 5941 Fishing tackle, general; fishing equipment

(G-5437)
SEMITRONICS CORP (HQ)
80 Commercial St (11520-2832)
PHONE...................516 223-0200
Fax: 516 623-6954
Henrietta Rivman, *President*
Brian Jipp, *Manager*
Roz Sollinger, *Manager*
EMP: 45 **EST:** 1944
SQ FT: 10,000
SALES (est): 5.5MM
SALES (corp-wide): 6MM **Privately Held**
WEB: www.semitronics.com
SIC: 3674 5065 Semiconductors & related devices; electronic parts & equipment
PA: Intex Company Inc
80 Commercial St
Freeport NY 11520
516 223-0200

(G-5438)
SEVILLE CENTRAL MIX CORP (PA)
157 Albany Ave (11520-4710)
PHONE...................516 868-3000
Fax: 516 293-9088
Peter Scalamandre, *Ch of Bd*
Joseph L Scalamandre, *Vice Pres*
Marty McCarthy, *Controller*
Christine Demacy, *Manager*
EMP: 67
SQ FT: 8,000
SALES (est): 13.1MM **Privately Held**
WEB: www.sevillecentralmix.com
SIC: 3273 Ready-mixed concrete

(G-5439)
SIGNATURE INDUSTRIES INC
32 Saint Johns Pl (11520-4618)
PHONE...................516 679-5177
Fax: 516 771-8186
Emil Petschauer, *President*
Ante Vulin, *Vice Pres*
James Calderon, *Treasurer*
EMP: 15
SALES (est): 1.7MM **Privately Held**
WEB: www.signatureindustries.com
SIC: 3993 Signs & advertising specialties

(G-5440)
TEENA CREATIONS INC
10 Hanse Ave (11520-4628)
PHONE...................516 867-1500
Jules Rand, *President*
Michael Rand, *Treasurer*
Mark Schwab, *Admin Sec*
EMP: 5
SQ FT: 19,000
SALES (est): 520K **Privately Held**
SIC: 3911 Jewelry, precious metal

(G-5441)
TEMREX CORPORATION (PA)
300 Buffalo Ave (11520-4720)
P.O. Box 182 (11520-0182)
PHONE...................516 868-6221
Fax: 516 868-5700
Alda Levander, *CEO*
Ethan Levander, *President*
Ruth Fusci, *Admin Sec*
EMP: 37
SQ FT: 5,000
SALES (est): 4.5MM **Privately Held**
WEB: www.temrex.com
SIC: 3843 Dental equipment & supplies

(G-5442)
THREE STAR OFFSET PRINTING
188 N Main St (11520-2232)
PHONE...................516 867-8223
Fax: 516 867-8227
Zeev Alabaster, *President*
Orna Alabaster, *Corp Secy*
EMP: 10 **EST:** 1958
SQ FT: 7,300
SALES (est): 1.9MM **Privately Held**
SIC: 2752 Photo-offset printing

(G-5443)
TRIUMPH ACTUATION SYSTEMS LLC
417 S Main St (11520-5144)
PHONE...................516 378-0162
EMP: 55
SALES (corp-wide): 3.8B **Publicly Held**
SIC: 3593 3728 3724 3594 Mfg Fluid Power Cylinder Mfg Aircraft Parts/Equip Mfg Aircraft Engine/Part Mfg Fluid Power Pump/Mtr Whol Industrial Equip
HQ: Triumph Actuation Systems, Llc
4520 Hampton Rd
Clemmons NC 27012
336 766-9036

(G-5444)
UNIQUE DISPLAY MFG CORP (PA)
216 N Main St Ste D (11520-2200)
PHONE...................516 546-3800
Philip Boxer, *President*
Eleanor Boxer, *Corp Secy*
EMP: 8 **EST:** 1976
SQ FT: 50,000
SALES (est): 1MM **Privately Held**
SIC: 3993 Displays & cutouts, window & lobby

(G-5445)
WL CONCEPTS & PRODUCTION INC
1 Bennington Ave (11520-3953)
PHONE...................516 538-5300
Fax: 516 565-5115
William Levine, *President*
Walter Nikles, *VP Opers*
Marian Keilson, *Director*
▲ **EMP:** 7
SQ FT: 4,500
SALES (est): 1MM **Privately Held**
WEB: www.wlconcepts.com
SIC: 3993 Signs & advertising specialties

(G-5446)
Z VAPE STATION/ATLANTIC SMOKE
384 Atlantic Ave (11520-5286)
PHONE...................516 442-0548
EMP: 9
SALES (est): 193.2K **Privately Held**
SIC: 3999 Cigar & cigarette holders

Freeville
Tompkins County

(G-5447)
FREEVILLE PUBLISHING CO INC
Also Called: Cortland-Ithaca Subn Shopper
9 Main St (13068-9599)
P.O. Box 210 (13068-0210)
PHONE...................607 844-9119
Fax: 607 844-3381
Michael Down, *President*
EMP: 10 **EST:** 1949
SQ FT: 1,998
SALES (est): 899.7K **Privately Held**
SIC: 2741 2752 2759 Shopping news: publishing only, not printed on site; commercial printing, offset; commercial printing

(G-5448)
GENOA SAND & GRAVEL LNSG
390 Peruville Rd (13068-9732)
PHONE...................607 533-4551
Tracy Pinney, *Owner*
EMP: 4
SALES (est): 210K **Privately Held**
SIC: 1442 Construction sand & gravel

(G-5449)
INCODEMA3D LLC
330 Main St (13068-9701)
P.O. Box 429 (13068-0429)
PHONE...................607 269-4390
Terry Posecznick, *Controller*
Scott Volk, *Director*
EMP: 38
SALES: 5MM **Privately Held**
SIC: 2759 Commercial printing

(G-5450)
WEAVER WIND ENERGY LLC
7 Union St (13068-3201)
PHONE...................607 379-9463
Art Weaver, *President*
EMP: 5
SQ FT: 5,000
SALES (est): 526.4K **Privately Held**
SIC: 3511 Turbines & turbine generator sets

Fresh Meadows
Queens County

(G-5451)
AMERICAN CIGAR
6940 Fresh Meadow Ln (11365-3422)
PHONE...................718 969-0008
Allen Schuster, *President*
EMP: 6
SALES (est): 450K **Privately Held**
WEB: www.smokeyscigars.com
SIC: 2121 Cigars

(G-5452)
CDML COMPUTER SERVICES LTD
5343 198th St (11365-1719)
PHONE...................718 428-9063
Leonard Kaplan, *President*
EMP: 6
SALES: 281.3K **Privately Held**
WEB: www.cdml.com
SIC: 7372 7371 Prepackaged software; custom computer programming services

(G-5453)
DYNAMIC DECISIONS INC (PA)
18519 64th Ave (11365-2707)
PHONE...................908 755-5000
Alan Fan, *President*
Jake Shaikh, *Marketing Mgr*
▲ **EMP:** 10
SQ FT: 6,500
SALES (est): 2.7MM **Privately Held**
WEB: www.ddidynex.com
SIC: 3571 3577 Electronic computers; computer peripheral equipment

(G-5454)
FRENCH ASSOCIATES INC
Also Called: French Pdts Frnch Pickle Works
7339 172nd St (11366-1420)
PHONE...................718 387-9880
Seymour Rosen, *President*
Jerry Rosen, *Vice Pres*
EMP: 10 **EST:** 1919
SQ FT: 20,000
SALES (est): 650K **Privately Held**
WEB: www.frenchassociates.com
SIC: 2035 5199 5149 Pickles, vinegar; general merchandise, non-durable; groceries & related products

(G-5455)
HACULLA NYC INC
6805 Fresh Meadow Ln (11365-3438)
PHONE...................718 886-3163
Jonathan Koon, *Principal*
EMP: 10 **EST:** 2014
SALES (est): 530K **Privately Held**
SIC: 2329 Men's & boys' sportswear & athletic clothing

(G-5456)
KOON ENTERPRISES LLC
6805 Fresh Madow Ln Ste B (11365)
PHONE...................718 886-3163
Jonathan M Koon, *Mng Member*
Katherine Koon,
EMP: 5
SALES: 1.2MM **Privately Held**
SIC: 2389 Costumes

(G-5457)
KOONICHI INC
6805 Fresh Madow Ln Ste B (11365)
PHONE...................718 886-8338
Jonathan Koon, *President*
Katherine Koon, *Vice Pres*
Raymond Koon, *CFO*
▲ **EMP:** 7
SQ FT: 2,500
SALES (est): 590K **Privately Held**
WEB: www.koonichi.com
SIC: 3089 Automotive parts, plastic

(G-5458)
MANIFESTATION-GLOW PRESS INC
7740 164th St (11366-1227)
PHONE...................718 380-5259
Fax: 718 380-7651
IA Konopiaty, *Ch of Bd*
Abakash Konopiaty, *President*
EMP: 5
SQ FT: 1,800
SALES (est): 540K **Privately Held**
WEB: www.heart-light.com
SIC: 2752 Commercial printing, offset

(G-5459)
RYBA SOFTWARE INC
7359 186th St (11366-1719)
PHONE...................718 264-9352
Alexander J Ryba, *Principal*
EMP: 5
SALES (est): 180.4K **Privately Held**
SIC: 7372 Prepackaged software

(G-5460)
TOROTRON CORPORATION
18508 Union Tpke Ste 101 (11366-1700)
PHONE...................718 428-6992
Oscar Zanger, *President*
Donny Korblit, *Engineer*
Steve Bortnicker, *Controller*
Miriam Zanger, *Admin Sec*
EMP: 8 **EST:** 1950
SQ FT: 3,000
SALES (est): 350K **Privately Held**
SIC: 3679 Electronic circuits

(G-5461)
VR CONTAINMENT LLC
17625 Union Tpke Ste 175 (11366-1515)
PHONE...................917 972-3441
EMP: 6
SALES (est): 644K **Privately Held**
SIC: 3442 3446 Metal doors; gates, ornamental metal

Frewsburg
Chautauqua County

(G-5462)
ARTISAN MANAGEMENT GROUP INC
39 Venman St (14738-9565)
PHONE...................716 569-4094
Kevin Delong, *President*
EMP: 7
SALES: 950K **Privately Held**
SIC: 3544 3599 Special dies, tools, jigs & fixtures; machine shop, jobbing & repair

(G-5463)
COLBURNS AC RFRGN
17 White Dr (14738-9553)
P.O. Box 9430 (14738-1443)
PHONE...................716 569-3695
Fax: 716 569-6362
George M Colburn, *President*
EMP: 10
SQ FT: 3,600
SALES (est): 1.7MM **Privately Held**
SIC: 3585 7623 Heating & air conditioning combination units; refrigeration repair service

(G-5464)
FREW RUN GRAVEL PRODUCTS INC
984 Frew Run Rd (14738-9746)
PHONE...................716 569-4712
Michael Nelson, *President*

EMP: 6
SALES (est): 441.4K **Privately Held**
SIC: 1442 Construction sand & gravel

(G-5465)
MONARCH PLASTICS INC
225 Falconer St (14738-9506)
P.O. Box 648 (14738-0648)
PHONE.................................716 569-2175
Donald Olander, *President*
Charles Moffett, *Engineer*
Steve Luzzi, *Sales Mgr*
Bamry Muro, *Manager*
▲ EMP: 30 EST: 1960
SQ FT: 16,000
SALES (est): 5.7MM **Privately Held**
WEB: www.monarchplastic.com
SIC: 3089 Molding primary plastic

Friendship
Allegany County

(G-5466)
FRIENDSHIP DAIRIES LLC
6701 County Road 20 (14739-8660)
PHONE...............................585 973-3031
Fax: 585 973-2401
Ron Klein, *President*
John Albanese, *Vice Pres*
Sherry Crawford, *Buyer*
Steve Bacharach, *Purchasing*
Bobby Budinger, *Purchasing*
EMP: 250
SQ FT: 15,000
SALES (est): 39.8MM
SALES (corp-wide): 1.9B **Privately Held**
WEB: www.deanfoods.com
SIC: 2023 2022 Dry, condensed, evaporated dairy products; cheese, natural & processed
HQ: Saputo Dairy Foods Usa, Llc
2711 N Haske Ave Ste 3700
Dallas TX 75204
214 863-2300

Fulton
Oswego County

(G-5467)
C & C METAL FABRICATIONS INC
159 Hubbard St (13069-1247)
PHONE.................................315 598-7607
Fax: 315 598-7613
Judy Davis, *Manager*
John F Sharkey IV,
EMP: 19
SQ FT: 32,000
SALES (est): 3.2MM **Privately Held**
WEB: www.candcfabrication.com
SIC: 3441 Fabricated structural metal

(G-5468)
CANFIELD MACHINE & TOOL LLC
121 Howard Rd (13069-4278)
PHONE.................................315 593-8062
Fax: 315 592-5963
Chris Canfield, *CIO*
Debra Canfield, *Director*
EMP: 41
SQ FT: 24,000
SALES (est): 5.7MM **Privately Held**
SIC: 3599 Machine shop, jobbing & repair

(G-5469)
D-K MANUFACTURING CORP
Also Called: DK
551 W 3rd St S (13069-2824)
P.O. Box 600 (13069-0600)
PHONE.................................315 592-4327
Fax: 315 593-2252
Norman W Kesterke, *President*
Donald L Kesterke, *General Mgr*
Lorry Bailey, *Manager*
Sue Kesterke, *CIO*
EMP: 20
SQ FT: 30,000
SALES: 2MM **Privately Held**
WEB: www.d-kmfg.com
SIC: 3469 3599 Stamping metal for the trade; machine shop, jobbing & repair

(G-5470)
DOT PUBLISHING
Also Called: Fulton Daily News
117 Cayuga St (13069-1709)
PHONE.................................315 593-2510
Fax: 315 593-2515
Monica Mackenzie, *President*
EMP: 10
SQ FT: 2,048
SALES (est): 581.9K **Privately Held**
SIC: 2711 Newspapers, publishing & printing

(G-5471)
FULTON NEWSPAPERS INC
Also Called: Fulton Patriot
67 S 2nd St (13069-1725)
PHONE.................................315 598-6397
Vincent R Caravan, *President*
Ronald Caravan, *Vice Pres*
EMP: 20
SQ FT: 8,000
SALES (est): 928.2K **Privately Held**
SIC: 2711 2752 2791 2789 Newspapers: publishing only, not printed on site; commercial printing, offset; typesetting; bookbinding & related work

(G-5472)
FULTON TOOL CO INC
802 W Broadway Ste 1 (13069-1522)
PHONE.................................315 598-2900
Fax: 315 598-4210
Bruce Phelps, *President*
Barbara Phelps, *Corp Secy*
Peter Russell, *Vice Pres*
Jim Bowers, *QC Mgr*
Peter Russells, *Sales Mgr*
EMP: 21 EST: 1959
SQ FT: 32,000
SALES (est): 4.3MM **Privately Held**
WEB: www.fultontool.com
SIC: 3599 Machine shop, jobbing & repair

(G-5473)
GONE SOUTH CONCRETE BLOCK INC
Also Called: John Deere Authorized Dealer
2809 State Route 3 (13069-5805)
P.O. Box 787 (13069-0787)
PHONE.................................315 598-2141
Thomas S Venezia, *President*
Desire Descastalzo, *Controller*
Cory Murray, *Controller*
Melissa Gentile, *Human Res Dir*
Mark Lalomia, *Sales Mgr*
EMP: 30
SQ FT: 2,000
SALES (est): 8.3MM **Privately Held**
SIC: 3271 5211 5082 Blocks, concrete or cinder: standard; lumber & other building materials; construction & mining machinery

(G-5474)
HAUN WELDING SUPPLY INC
214 N 4th St (13069-1216)
PHONE.................................315 592-5012
Fax: 315 592-2447
Patty Sasso, *Manager*
EMP: 7
SQ FT: 1,938
SALES (corp-wide): 63.5MM **Privately Held**
SIC: 7692 5084 Welding repair; welding machinery & equipment
PA: Haun Welding Supply, Inc.
5921 Court Street Rd
Syracuse NY 13206
315 463-5241

(G-5475)
HUHTAMAKI INC
Huhtamaki Consumer Packaging
100 State St (13069-2518)
PHONE.................................315 593-5311
Fax: 315 593-5378
Dietmar Johann, *Opers Mgr*
Rick Davis, *Engineer*
George Zeiler, *Engineer*
Jim Carroll, *Manager*
Stephen Horth, *Manager*
EMP: 585
SALES (corp-wide): 3B **Privately Held**
SIC: 2621 Pressed pulp products
HQ: Huhtamaki, Inc.
9201 Packaging Dr
De Soto KS 66018
913 583-3025

(G-5476)
INTERFACE PERFORMANCE MTLS INC
2885 State Route 481 (13069-4221)
PHONE.................................315 592-8100
Richard Isbell, *QC Dir*
Dave Meritech, *Marketing Mgr*
Debra Morris, *Technology*
Michael Kerker, *Technology*
EMP: 219
WEB: www.sealinfo.com
SIC: 3053 Gaskets, packing & sealing devices
PA: Interface Performance Materials, Inc.
216 Wohlsen Way
Lancaster PA 17603

(G-5477)
IVES FARM MARKET
Also Called: Ives Slaughterhouse
2652 Rr 176 (13069)
PHONE.................................315 592-4880
Ronald Ives, *Owner*
Jean Ives, *Partner*
EMP: 5
SALES (est): 360K **Privately Held**
SIC: 2011 5411 5421 Meat packing plants; grocery stores; meat markets, including freezer provisioners

(G-5478)
JOHN CRANE INC
2314 County Route 4 (13069-3659)
PHONE.................................315 593-6237
John Crane, *Branch Mgr*
EMP: 64
SALES (corp-wide): 4.1B **Privately Held**
SIC: 3053 Gaskets & sealing devices
HQ: John Crane Inc.
227 W Monroe St Ste 1800
Chicago IL 60606
312 605-7800

(G-5479)
K&NS FOODS USA LLC
607 Phillips St (13069-1520)
PHONE.................................315 598-8080
Jimmy Koid, *Mng Member*
▲ EMP: 30 EST: 2012
SALES (est): 7.6MM **Privately Held**
SIC: 2015 Chicken, processed: frozen
PA: K&N's Foods (Private) Limited
Business Centre, Shadman Second Floor
Lahore
423 742-1710

(G-5480)
KENWELL CORPORATION
871 Hannibal St (13069-4186)
P.O. Box 207 (13069-0207)
PHONE.................................315 592-4263
Fax: 315 593-2063
Roger Horning Jr, *President*
Bruce Horning, *Vice Pres*
Douglas Horning, *Finance*
Bob Flack, *Manager*
EMP: 52
SQ FT: 13,000
SALES (est): 10.8MM **Privately Held**
WEB: www.kenwellcorp.com
SIC: 3599 Machine shop, jobbing & repair

(G-5481)
KRENGEL MANUFACTURING CO INC
Also Called: American Marking Systems
121 Fulton Ave Fl 2 (13069)
PHONE.................................212 227-1901
EMP: 18
SALES (est): 980K **Privately Held**
SIC: 3953 Mfg Marking Devices

(G-5482)
LE ROI INC
21 S 2nd St (13069-1706)
PHONE.................................315 342-3681
Fax: 315 343-0388
Terry Leroy, *President*
Julie Symons, *Office Mgr*
EMP: 12 EST: 1997
SQ FT: 3,400
SALES (est): 1.7MM **Privately Held**
WEB: www.leroi.com
SIC: 3911 Jewelry, precious metal

(G-5483)
LINDE MERCHANT PRODUCTION INC
370 Owens Rd (13069-4619)
PHONE.................................315 593-1360
Richard Olinger, *Principal*
Randy Draving, *Opers Staff*
EMP: 8
SALES (corp-wide): 17.9B **Privately Held**
SIC: 2813 Carbon dioxide
HQ: Linde Merchant Production, Inc.
575 Mountain Ave
New Providence NJ 07974

(G-5484)
NET & DIE INC
24 Foster St (13069)
P.O. Box 240 (13069-0240)
PHONE.................................315 592-4311
Fax: 315 598-1232
Richard N Shatrau, *President*
Helena Rockwood, *Corp Secy*
EMP: 38 EST: 1963
SQ FT: 30,000
SALES (est): 6.7MM **Privately Held**
SIC: 3599 Machine shop, jobbing & repair

(G-5485)
NORTH END PAPER CO INC
702 Hannibal St (13069-1020)
PHONE.................................315 593-8100
William F Shafer III, *President*
Sam Gabriele, *Manager*
EMP: 7
SQ FT: 40,000
SALES (est): 1.1MM
SALES (corp-wide): 8.7MM **Privately Held**
WEB: www.flowercitytissue.com
SIC: 2621 Tissue paper
PA: Flower City Tissue Mills Company, Inc.
700 Driving Park Ave
Rochester NY 14613
585 458-9200

(G-5486)
NORTHERN BITUMINOUS MIX INC
32 Silk Rd (13069-4862)
P.O. Box 787 (13069-0787)
PHONE.................................315 598-2141
Thomas Venezia Sr, *President*
EMP: 6
SQ FT: 2,000
SALES (est): 784K **Privately Held**
SIC: 2951 Asphalt & asphaltic paving mixtures (not from refineries)

(G-5487)
NORTHERN READY-MIX INC (PA)
32 Silk Rd (13069-4862)
P.O. Box 787 (13069-0787)
PHONE.................................315 598-2141
Fax: 315 593-8252
Thomas S Venezia, *President*
Desiree Capousis, *Controller*
Cris Yates, *Credit Mgr*
Melissa Gentile, *Human Res Mgr*
EMP: 30
SQ FT: 2,000
SALES (est): 6.4MM **Privately Held**
WEB: www.northerncompanies.com
SIC: 3273 Ready-mixed concrete

(G-5488)
PATHFINDER INDUSTRIES INC
117 N 3rd St (13069-1256)
PHONE.................................315 593-2483
Fax: 315 593-3311
Marsha Ives, *President*
Maribeth Myers, *Vice Pres*
Mike Cook, *Foreman/Supr*
Bud Hauswirth, *QC Mgr*
Wally Corzett, *Prgrmr*
EMP: 21
SQ FT: 22,000

Fulton - Oswego County (G-5489) — **GEOGRAPHIC SECTION**

SALES (est): 4.6MM **Privately Held**
WEB: www.pathfinderind.com
SIC: **3444** Sheet metalwork

(G-5489)
SYRACUSE SAND & GRAVEL LLC
1902 County Route 57 (13069-4909)
PHONE................................315 548-8207
EMP: 6
SALES (est): 580K **Privately Held**
SIC: **1442** Construction sand & gravel

(G-5490)
UNIVERSAL METAL WORKS LLC
159 Hubbard St (13069-1247)
PHONE................................315 598-7607
John F Sharkey IV,
EMP: 19
SALES: 4.5MM **Privately Held**
SIC: **3441** Fabricated structural metal

Fultonville
Montgomery County

(G-5491)
ANDERSON INSTRUMENT CO INC (HQ)
156 Auriesville Rd (12072-2031)
PHONE................................518 922-5315
Fax: 518 922-8997
Andrew Hicer, *CEO*
Deanne Brassard, *Purch Agent*
Peter Cannellos, *Buyer*
David Chatt, *VP Finance*
George Sherman, *Finance Mgr*
▲ EMP: 70
SQ FT: 40,000
SALES (est): 27.1MM
SALES (corp-wide): 6.2B **Publicly Held**
WEB: www.andinst.com
SIC: **3823 5084 3822 3625** Controllers for process variables, all types; industrial machinery & equipment; auto controls regulating residntl & coml environmt & applncs; relays & industrial controls
PA: Fortive Corporation
    6920 Seaway Blvd
    Everett WA 98203
    425 446-5000

(G-5492)
CONSOLIDATED BARRICADES INC
179 Dillenbeck Rd (12072-3311)
PHONE................................518 922-7944
Joseph Melideo, *President*
EMP: 8
SQ FT: 7,000
SALES (est): 1.2MM **Privately Held**
WEB: www.consolidatedbarricades.com
SIC: **3499** Barricades, metal

(G-5493)
FULTONVILLE MACHINE & TOOL CO
73 Union St (12072-1836)
P.O. Box 426 (12072-0426)
PHONE................................518 853-4441
Fax: 518 853-3445
Randolf C Snyder, *President*
Patricia Snyder, *Corp Secy*
EMP: 11 EST: 1945
SQ FT: 18,000
SALES: 1.2MM **Privately Held**
SIC: **3599** Machine shop, jobbing & repair

(G-5494)
MOHAWK RIVER LEATHER WORKS
32 Broad St (12072)
PHONE................................518 853-3900
Fax: 518 853-3729
Joseph H Sicilia, *President*
Robert Hojohn, *Vice Pres*
Tammy Plantt, *Bookkeeper*
EMP: 17
SQ FT: 3,534
SALES (est): 2.6MM **Privately Held**
SIC: **3111** Coloring of leather

(G-5495)
PARTLOW CORPORATION
Also Called: Partlow West
156 Auriesville Rd (12072-2031)
PHONE................................518 922-5315
Craig Purse, *President*
Donald D'Amico, *Vice Pres*
Frank Stagliano, *Vice Pres*
Dominick Caracas, *Engineer*
Carol Bennett, *Human Res Mgr*
EMP: 175
SQ FT: 60,000
SALES: 34.8MM **Privately Held**
SIC: **3823** Industrial process control instruments

(G-5496)
PERRONE LEATHER LLC (PA)
Also Called: Perrone Aerospace
182a Riverside Dr (12072)
PHONE................................518 853-4300
Bartle Avery, *CEO*
William T Perrone Jr, *President*
Janei Speal, *Manager*
Sarah Mans, *Director*
Rick McGinn,
▲ EMP: 57
SQ FT: 69,221
SALES (est): 13.7MM **Privately Held**
WEB: www.perroneleather.com
SIC: **3199 5611** Leather garments; men's & boys' clothing stores

Gainesville
Wyoming County

(G-5497)
DRASGOW INC
4150 Poplar Tree Rd (14066-9723)
PHONE................................585 786-3603
Karl Drasgow, *President*
Bryan Schabloski, *Production*
Crystal Hilton, *Info Tech Mgr*
EMP: 25
SQ FT: 17,946
SALES: 1.7MM **Privately Held**
SIC: **3569** Filters

Galway
Saratoga County

(G-5498)
WHALENS HORSERADISH PRODUCTS
1710 Route 29 (12074-2213)
PHONE................................518 587-6404
Kim Bibens, *President*
EMP: 5
SALES (est): 450.7K **Privately Held**
SIC: **2035** Horseradish, prepared

Gansevoort
Saratoga County

(G-5499)
AUREONIC
13 Whispering Pines Rd (12831-1443)
PHONE................................518 791-9331
Shawn Lescault, *CEO*
Nicholas Karker, *Co-Owner*
Patrick Roden, *Co-Owner*
Robert Schramm, *Co-Owner*
Ian Tucker, *CFO*
EMP: 5
SALES (est): 350K **Privately Held**
SIC: **3823 7389** Combustion control instruments;

(G-5500)
GRANITE & MARBLE WORKS INC
8 Commerce Park Dr (12831-2240)
PHONE................................518 584-2800
Margaret P Roohan, *President*
▲ EMP: 20
SALES (est): 3.2MM **Privately Held**
SIC: **3281** Granite, cut & shaped

(G-5501)
PALLETTE STONE CORPORATION
269 Ballard Rd (12831-1597)
PHONE................................518 584-2421
Thomas Longe, *President*
D Alan Collins, *Corp Secy*
Todd Cochran, *Project Mgr*
Rob Montague, *Project Mgr*
Dennis Cenci, *Sales Staff*
EMP: 40
SQ FT: 3,000
SALES (est): 7.5MM
SALES (corp-wide): 41.5MM **Privately Held**
SIC: **3281 2951 3241 5032** Cut stone & stone products; concrete, bituminous; portland cement; stone, crushed or broken; asphalt mixture; concrete & cinder block; paving stones; concrete & cinder block
PA: D. A. Collins Construction Co., Inc.
    269 Ballard Rd
    Gansevoort NY 12831
    518 664-9855

(G-5502)
RASP INCORPORATED
8 Dukes Way (12831-1668)
PHONE................................518 747-8020
Fax: 518 747-8729
Ronald Richards, *Vice Pres*
Jeff Bruno, *Engineer*
Michael Close, *Treasurer*
EMP: 27 EST: 1995
SQ FT: 8,000
SALES: 6.4MM **Privately Held**
WEB: www.rasp-controls.com
SIC: **3625** Industrial controls: push button, selector switches, pilot

(G-5503)
ROCK HILL BAKEHOUSE LTD
21 Saratoga Rd (12831-1554)
PHONE................................518 743-1627
Fax: 518 743-9623
Matthew Funiciello, *President*
Michael London, *Vice Pres*
Adam Witt, *Treasurer*
Wendy London, *Admin Sec*
EMP: 30
SALES (est): 2.4MM **Privately Held**
WEB: www.rockhillbakehouse.com
SIC: **2051 5461** Bread, all types (white, wheat, rye, etc): fresh or frozen; bread

(G-5504)
STONE BRIDGE IRON AND STL INC
426 Purinton Rd (12831-2193)
PHONE................................518 695-3752
Fax: 518 695-3056
Brian Carmer, *Principal*
Britt Carmer, *Exec VP*
Mark Hutchinson, *Vice Pres*
James Mulholland, *Plant Mgr*
Peter Dunham, *Project Mgr*
▲ EMP: 60
SQ FT: 45,000
SALES (est): 17.3MM **Privately Held**
WEB: www.stonebridgeiron.com
SIC: **3441** Building components, structural steel

(G-5505)
TRUARC FABRICATION
1 Commerce Park Dr (12831-2239)
PHONE................................518 691-0430
Cris Edgrely, *President*
EMP: 9
SALES (est): 956.8K **Privately Held**
SIC: **3599** Flexible metal hose, tubing & bellows

Garden City
Nassau County

(G-5506)
A G MASTER CRAFTS LTD
5 South St Ste A (11530-4926)
PHONE................................516 745-6262
Fax: 516 745-6276
Tom Gardianos, *President*
Diana Gardianos, *Vice Pres*
Cynthia Herman, *Manager*
▲ EMP: 15
SALES (est): 1.9MM **Privately Held**
WEB: www.agmastercrafts.com
SIC: **2521** Wood office furniture; cabinets, office: wood

(G-5507)
AAR ALLEN SERVICES INC
AAR Aircraft Component
747 Zeckendorf Blvd (11530-2188)
PHONE................................516 222-9000
Rob Bruinsna, *General Mgr*
Salim Khamze, *Engineer*
Christine Sebor, *Manager*
EMP: 35
SALES (corp-wide): 1.7B **Publicly Held**
SIC: **3679** Electronic circuits
HQ: Aar Allen Services, Inc.
    1100 N Wood Dale Rd
    Wood Dale IL 60191
    630 227-2410

(G-5508)
AMETEK INC
Also Called: Hughes-Treitler
300 Endo Blvd (11530-6708)
PHONE................................516 832-7710
Fax: 516 832-8054
Colleen Maloney, *Principal*
Ronald Brasser, *Vice Pres*
Anthony Salucci, *Mfg Staff*
Fabrizio Coduri, *Production*
Joe Bacino, *Engineer*
EMP: 175
SALES (corp-wide): 3.8B **Publicly Held**
SIC: **3443** Fabricated plate work (boiler shop)
PA: Ametek, Inc.
    1100 Cassatt Rd
    Berwyn PA 19312
    610 647-2121

(G-5509)
ATLAS SWITCH CO INC
969 Stewart Ave (11530-4816)
PHONE................................516 222-6280
Fax: 516 222-6287
Gina Paradise, *President*
Javier Castagnola, *Engineer*
Fred Creda, *Engineer*
Billy Falcone, *Engineer*
John Paradise, *Engineer*
EMP: 33
SQ FT: 30,000
SALES (est): 11.2MM **Privately Held**
WEB: www.atlasswitch.com
SIC: **3613 3699** Switches, electric power except snap, push button, etc.; electrical equipment & supplies

(G-5510)
BHARAT ELECTRONICS LIMITED
53 Hilton Ave (11530-2806)
PHONE................................516 248-4021
Fax: 516 741-5894
Siva Muthuswamy, *Manager*
EMP: 7
SALES (corp-wide): 1B **Privately Held**
WEB: www.bel-india.com
SIC: **3674** Solid state electronic devices
PA: Bharat Electronics Limited
    Outer Ring Road, Nagavara,
    Bengaluru KAR 56004
    802 503-9300

(G-5511)
BRISTOL-MYERS SQUIBB COMPANY
1000 Stewart Ave (11530-4814)
PHONE................................516 832-2191
Richard Serafin, *Branch Mgr*
Patrick McFarland, *Associate Dir*
Leacy Pryor, *Associate Dir*
EMP: 225
SALES (corp-wide): 19.4B **Publicly Held**
WEB: www.bms.com
SIC: **2834** Pharmaceutical preparations
PA: Bristol-Myers Squibb Company
    345 Park Ave Bsmt Lc3
    New York NY 10154
    212 546-4000

GEOGRAPHIC SECTION

Garden City - Nassau County (G-5538)

(G-5512)
CAMPUS COURSE PAKS INC
1 South Ave Fl 1 (11530-4213)
PHONE..................516 877-3967
Wayne Piskin, *President*
Stanley Rosenfeld, *Financial Exec*
Sabine Dorcean, *Manager*
EMP: 5
SQ FT: 1,500
SALES: 237.4MM **Privately Held**
WEB: www.ccpaks.com
SIC: 2731 Books: publishing only

(G-5513)
DYNA-EMPIRE INC
1075 Stewart Ave (11530-4871)
PHONE..................516 222-2700
Fax: 516 222-1896
G Patrick Mc Carthy, *President*
Richard Shaper, *Vice Pres*
Syd Crossley, *Opers Staff*
John Sallami, *Opers Staff*
Dennis Harty, *Purch Agent*
▲ **EMP:** 145 **EST:** 1941
SQ FT: 52,000
SALES (est): 29.4MM **Privately Held**
WEB: www.dyna-empire.com
SIC: 3724 3728 3829 3823 Aircraft engines & engine parts; aircraft landing assemblies & brakes; measuring & controlling devices; industrial instrmnts msrmnt display/control process variable; search & navigation equipment

(G-5514)
EDGEWOOD INDUSTRIES INC
635 Commercial Ave (11530-6409)
PHONE..................516 227-2447
Frank Suppa, *President*
EMP: 6
SALES (est): 551.9K **Privately Held**
SIC: 3271 Concrete block & brick

(G-5515)
ELEVATOR SYSTEMS INC
465 Endo Blvd Unit 1 (11530-4924)
PHONE..................516 239-4044
Fax: 516 239-5793
Ignatius Alcamo Jr, *President*
Annie-Marie Alcamo, *Corp Secy*
James Sullivan, *Sales Mgr*
Alma Ignites, *Shareholder*
▲ **EMP:** 25
SQ FT: 10,000
SALES (est): 4.9MM **Privately Held**
SIC: 3625 Relays & industrial controls

(G-5516)
EURO FINE PAPER INC
220 Nassau Blvd (11530-5500)
PHONE..................516 238-5253
Tom McShea Sr, *President*
EMP: 8
SALES (est): 640K **Privately Held**
SIC: 2621 Paper mills

(G-5517)
EUROPEAN MARBLE WORKS CO INC
Also Called: Puccio Marble and Onyx
54 Nassau Blvd (11530-4139)
PHONE..................718 387-9778
Paul Puccio, *President*
John Puccio, *Vice Pres*
▲ **EMP:** 12 **EST:** 1956
SQ FT: 70,000
SALES (est): 1.2MM **Privately Held**
SIC: 3281 Cut stone & stone products

(G-5518)
EXERGY LLC
320 Endo Blvd Unit 1 (11530-6747)
PHONE..................516 832-9300
Jordan Finkelstein, *President*
Bob Scott, *President*
Robert Scott, *Vice Pres*
EMP: 37
SQ FT: 20,000
SALES (est): 7.2MM **Privately Held**
WEB: www.exergyllc.com
SIC: 3443 8711 Heat exchangers, condensers & components; consulting engineer

(G-5519)
GAFFNEY KROESE SUPPLY CORP
Also Called: Gaffney Kroese Electrial
377 Oak St Ste 202 (11530-6542)
PHONE..................516 228-5091
Fax: 516 334-2794
John Kroese, *President*
Gregory Poli, *Opers Staff*
Robert Jouas, *Controller*
Ilene Paulvin, *Accounting Mgr*
Michel Burrel, *Sales Staff*
▼ **EMP:** 15 **EST:** 2012
SALES (est): 1.7MM **Privately Held**
SIC: 3621 Motors & generators

(G-5520)
GEHRING TRICOT CORPORATION (PA)
Also Called: Gehring Textiles
1225 Franklin Ave (11530-1659)
P.O. Box 272, Dolgeville (13329-0272)
PHONE..................315 429-8551
Fax: 516 747-8885
George G Gehring Jr, *President*
Brenda Gehring, *Principal*
Marie Bevilaqua, *Vice Pres*
Martin Callahan, *Vice Pres*
Paul Gutowski, *Vice Pres*
▲ **EMP:** 71 **EST:** 1952
SQ FT: 50,000
SALES (est): 60.9MM **Privately Held**
SIC: 2258 2262 Dyeing & finishing lace goods & warp knit fabric; tricot fabrics; finishing plants, manmade fiber & silk fabrics

(G-5521)
GEM FABRICATION OF NC
586 Commercial Ave (11530-6418)
PHONE..................704 278-6713
Greg Smith, *Branch Mgr*
EMP: 7
SALES (est): 2MM **Privately Held**
SIC: 3569 Sprinkler systems, fire: automatic

(G-5522)
H&E SERVICE CORP
Also Called: Gimbel & Associates
400 Garden Cy Plz Ste 405 (11530)
PHONE..................646 472-1936
Audrey Gimbel, *CEO*
Roger Gimbel, *President*
Keston Parsard, *Controller*
EMP: 98 **EST:** 1960
SQ FT: 30,000
SALES (est): 4.9MM **Privately Held**
SIC: 2752 Commercial printing, offset

(G-5523)
IMACOR INC
821 Franklin Ave Ste 301 (11530-4519)
PHONE..................516 393-0970
Fax: 516 393-0969
Peter Pellerito, *President*
Scott Roth, *Vice Pres*
Torrel Harris, *Marketing Staff*
EMP: 20
SALES (est): 3.6MM **Privately Held**
SIC: 3845 Ultrasonic scanning devices, medical

(G-5524)
ISSCO CORPORATION (PA)
Also Called: Industrial SEC Systems Contrls
111 Cherry Valley Ave # 410 (11530-1573)
PHONE..................212 732-8748
Fax: 516 334-7064
Arthur R Katon, *President*
Marsha Katon, *Corp Secy*
Flavie Aronowicz, *Admin Asst*
EMP: 18
SQ FT: 14,000
SALES (est): 1.4MM **Privately Held**
SIC: 3699 Security control equipment & systems

(G-5525)
L & M PUBLICATIONS INC
Also Called: Freeport Baldwin Leader
2 Endo Blvd (11530-6707)
PHONE..................516 378-3133
Linda Laursen Toscano, *President*
Paul Laursen, *Vice Pres*
John Laursen, *Shareholder*
EMP: 33
SALES (est): 1.6MM **Privately Held**
WEB: www.merricklife.com
SIC: 2711 7313 Newspapers; newspaper advertising representative

(G-5526)
LIFETIME BRANDS INC (PA)
1000 Stewart Ave (11530-4814)
PHONE..................516 683-6000
Fax: 516 555-0101
Jeffrey Siegel, *Ch of Bd*
Daniel Siegel, *President*
Ronald Shiftan, *COO*
Tony Arancio, *Senior VP*
Steven Bracco, *Vice Pres*
◆ **EMP:** 277
SQ FT: 159,000
SALES: 592.6MM **Publicly Held**
WEB: www.lifetimebrands.com
SIC: 3421 5023 5719 Cutlery; home furnishings; kitchen tools & utensils; stainless steel flatware; kitchenware; cutlery; glassware

(G-5527)
LITMOR PUBLISHING CORP (PA)
Also Called: Litmor Publications
821 Franklin Ave Ste 208 (11530-4519)
PHONE..................516 931-0012
Fax: 516 931-0027
Margaret Norris, *Publisher*
Edward Norris, *General Mgr*
EMP: 15
SQ FT: 3,000
SALES (est): 1.3MM **Privately Held**
SIC: 2711 2791 2752 Newspapers, publishing & printing; typesetting; commercial printing, lithographic

(G-5528)
LONG ISLAND PIPE SUPPLY INC (PA)
Also Called: LI Pipe Supply
586 Commercial Ave (11530-6418)
PHONE..................516 222-8008
Robert Moss, *CEO*
Larry Greenberg, *General Mgr*
Kim Smith, *Controller*
Kyle Heffner, *Sales Staff*
Anthony Kritis, *Sales Associate*
EMP: 40
SQ FT: 35,000
SALES (est): 23.5MM **Privately Held**
SIC: 3569 Sprinkler systems, fire: automatic

(G-5529)
LONG ISLAND PIPE SUPPLY INC (PA)
586 Commercial Ave (11530-6418)
PHONE..................516 222-8008
Fax: 516 222-9234
Robert Moss, *President*
Kim Smith, *Manager*
EMP: 28
SQ FT: 35,000
SALES (est): 59.6MM **Privately Held**
WEB: www.lipipe.com
SIC: 3498 5074 Fabricated pipe & fittings; plumbing fittings & supplies

(G-5530)
M AND J HAIR CENTER INC
Also Called: Natural Image Hair Concepts
1103 Stewart Ave Ste 100 (11530-4886)
PHONE..................516 872-1010
Jean Dreyfuss, *President*
EMP: 15
SQ FT: 1,600
SALES (est): 1.4MM **Privately Held**
WEB: www.mjhair.com
SIC: 3999 Wigs, including doll wigs, toupees or wiglets

(G-5531)
MCQUILLING PARTNERS INC (PA)
1035 Stewart Ave Ste 100 (11530-4825)
PHONE..................516 227-5718
John F Desantes, *Ch of Bd*
Dick Barnard, *Vice Pres*
Christopher Desantis, *Vice Pres*
Andy Berlin, *Opers Staff*
Alison Omelio, *Marketing Staff*
EMP: 26 **EST:** 1964
SALES (est): 3.5MM **Privately Held**
WEB: www.mcquilling.com
SIC: 3731 Tankers, building & repairing

(G-5532)
MEADOWBROOK DISTRIBUTING CORP
95 Jefferson St (11530-3931)
PHONE..................516 226-9000
Patrick O'Conner, *Branch Mgr*
EMP: 60
SALES (corp-wide): 2.2B **Privately Held**
SIC: 2086 Carbonated soft drinks, bottled & canned
HQ: Meadowbrook Distributing Corp
550 New Horizons Blvd
Amityville NY 11701
631 226-9000

(G-5533)
MELWOOD PARTNERS INC (PA)
100 Qentin Roosevelt Blvd (11530-4874)
PHONE..................516 307-8030
Brian Wasserman, *Ch of Bd*
EMP: 4
SALES (est): 2.2MM **Privately Held**
SIC: 2331 2335 Women's & misses' blouses & shirts; blouses, women's & juniors': made from purchased material; shirts, women's & juniors': made from purchased materials; women's, juniors' & misses' dresses

(G-5534)
META PHARMACY SYSTEMS INC
401 Franklin Ave Ste 106 (11530-5942)
PHONE..................516 488-6189
Fax: 516 488-6647
Salvatore M Barcia, *President*
EMP: 25
SALES (est): 1.8MM **Privately Held**
WEB: www.metapharmacy.com
SIC: 7372 Prepackaged software

(G-5535)
MITCO MANUFACTURING
605 Locust St (11530-6552)
PHONE..................800 338-8908
Daniel Kornfeld, *Sls & Mktg Exec*
▲ **EMP:** 6
SALES (est): 400.9K **Privately Held**
SIC: 3999 Manufacturing industries

(G-5536)
NEW YORK PACKAGING II LLC
Also Called: Redi Bag Brand
135 Fulton Ave (11530)
P.O. Box 1039, New Hyde Park (11040-7039)
PHONE..................516 746-0600
Jeffrey Rabiea, *President*
▲ **EMP:** 249
SALES (est): 32.9MM **Privately Held**
SIC: 2673 Plastic bags: made from purchased materials

(G-5537)
NORCATEC LLC (PA)
100 Garden Cy Plz Ste 530 (11530)
PHONE..................516 222-7070
Fax: 516 222-8811
Eytan Erez, *President*
Doreen Romanello, *Editor*
Danny Vinluan, *Purch Dir*
Shelley Bengyak, *Purchasing*
Theresa Hurley, *Purchasing*
▼ **EMP:** 25
SQ FT: 65,000
SALES (est): 23.5MM **Privately Held**
WEB: www.norcatec.com
SIC: 3714 Motor vehicle parts & accessories

(G-5538)
OPTIONLINE LLC
100 Hilton Ave Apt 23 (11530-1564)
PHONE..................516 218-3225
Luiz Grossmann, *President*
EMP: 25
SALES (est): 694.2K **Privately Held**
SIC: 2721 7375 Periodicals: publishing only; statistical reports (periodicals): publishing only; on-line data base information retrieval

Garden City - Nassau County (G-5539)

(G-5539)
PINCHARMING INC
215 Brixton Rd (11530-1339)
PHONE..................516 663-5115
Susan Smith, *President*
Barry Smith, *Vice Pres*
EMP: 12
SALES (est): 1MM **Privately Held**
SIC: 3961 Costume jewelry

(G-5540)
PRACTICEPRO SOFTWARE SYSTEMS
666 Old Country Rd Bsmt (11530-2079)
PHONE..................516 222-0010
Gary J Balsamo, *President*
EMP: 5
SALES: 313.6K **Privately Held**
WEB: www.practicepro.com
SIC: 7372 Prepackaged software

(G-5541)
PROGINET CORPORATION
200 Garden Cy Plz Ste 220 (11530)
PHONE..................516 535-3600
Fax: 516 248-3360
Sandison E Weil, *President*
Stephen M Flynn, *COO*
John W Gazzola, *Senior VP*
Jennifer Mundy, *Vice Pres*
Joe Christel, *CFO*
EMP: 37
SALES: 9.3MM **Privately Held**
WEB: www.proginet.com
SIC: 7372 Application computer software; business oriented computer software; operating systems computer software

(G-5542)
PUCCIO DESIGN INTERNATIONAL
Also Called: Puccio European Marble & Onyx
54 Nassau Blvd (11530-4139)
PHONE..................516 248-6426
Paul Puccio, *President*
EMP: 15 EST: 1968
SQ FT: 4,000
SALES (est): 170.8K **Privately Held**
WEB: www.puccio.info
SIC: 3281 Furniture, cut stone

(G-5543)
RICHNER COMMUNICATIONS INC (PA)
Also Called: Prime Time
2 Endo Blvd (11530-6707)
PHONE..................516 569-4000
Stuart Richner, *CEO*
Jeff Bessen, *Editor*
Scott Brinton, *Editor*
John Connell, *Editor*
Alex Costello, *Editor*
EMP: 130
SQ FT: 90,000
SALES (est): 16.3MM **Privately Held**
SIC: 2711 Commercial printing & newspaper publishing combined

(G-5544)
ROBECO/ASCOT PRODUCTS INC
100 Ring Rd W (11530-3219)
PHONE..................516 248-1521
EMP: 0
SALES (est): 1.2MM **Privately Held**
SIC: 3081 Unsupported Plastics Film And Sheet, Nsk

(G-5545)
SAVENERGY INC
645 South St Unit A (11530-4928)
PHONE..................516 239-1958
John Hyung Choi, *President*
Turab Syed, *General Mgr*
Raaed Junaid, *Project Mgr*
▲ EMP: 9 EST: 2010
SALES (est): 1.1MM **Privately Held**
SIC: 3646 Commercial indusl & institutional electric lighting fixtures

(G-5546)
SEVIROLI FOODS INC (PA)
601 Brook St (11530-6431)
PHONE..................516 222-6220
Fax: 516 222-0534
Joseph Seviroli Jr, *Ch of Bd*
Paul Vertullo, *COO*
Alan Bronstein, *VP Opers*
Ovidio Campos, *Plant Mgr*
Bert Singh, *Purch Mgr*
▲ EMP: 167
SQ FT: 80,000
SALES (est): 71.9MM **Privately Held**
WEB: www.seviroli.com
SIC: 2038 Frozen specialties

(G-5547)
STANDARD WEDDING BAND CO
951 Franklin Ave (11530-2909)
PHONE..................516 294-0954
Walter E Soderlund, *President*
Mabel T Soderlund, *Treasurer*
EMP: 6
SALES: 500K **Privately Held**
SIC: 3911 Rings, finger: precious metal

(G-5548)
THERMAL TECH DOORS INC (PA)
576 Brook St (11530-6416)
PHONE..................516 745-0100
Emanuel Karavas, *President*
Stephanos Kourtis, *Vice Pres*
George Gregory, *Comptroller*
EMP: 28
SQ FT: 25,000
SALES (est): 4.3MM **Privately Held**
SIC: 3442 Sash, door or window: metal

(G-5549)
VIRAJ - USA INC (DH)
100 Quentin Roosevelt Blv (11530-4848)
PHONE..................516 280-8380
Dhruv Kochhar, *President*
Daulat Tannan, *Vice Pres*
Imran Hassan, *Admin Asst*
◆ EMP: 6
SALES (est): 2.1MM **Privately Held**
SIC: 3312 Stainless steel

(G-5550)
WILDER MANUFACTURING CO INC
439 Oak St (11530-6453)
PHONE..................516 222-0433
Jonathan J Holtz, *President*
Richard Leads, *General Mgr*
Jeff Herbert, *Vice Pres*
John Jameson, *Vice Pres*
John Mc Laughlin, *CFO*
EMP: 55
SQ FT: 37,500
SALES (est): 3.3MM **Privately Held**
SIC: 3589 3556 Commercial cooking & foodwarming equipment; food products machinery

(G-5551)
WIN-HOLT EQUIPMENT CORP
439 Oak St Ste 1 (11530-6453)
PHONE..................516 222-0433
Fax: 516 222-0371
Ed Campbell, *Branch Mgr*
Milton Perez, *Manager*
EMP: 120
SQ FT: 45,000
SALES (corp-wide): 83.7MM **Privately Held**
WEB: www.winholt.com
SIC: 3499 3556 3537 Machine bases, metal; food products machinery; industrial trucks & tractors
PA: Win-Holt Equipment Corp.
20 Crossways Park Dr N # 205
Woodbury NY 11797
516 222-0335

(G-5552)
WON & LEE INC
Also Called: Unicorn Graphics
971 Stewart Ave (11530-4816)
PHONE..................516 222-0712
Jong Suk Lee, *President*
Jong Hoon Lee, *Vice Pres*
Won Lee, *Prdtn Mgr*
Jason Lee, *Manager*
Michael Park, *Director*
▲ EMP: 35
SQ FT: 30,000

Garden City Park
Nassau County

(G-5553)
DENTON STONEWORKS INC
94 Denton Ave (11040-4036)
PHONE..................516 746-1500
Fax: 516 746-6776
Boguslaw Kaczor, *CEO*
Monika Krasuska, *Manager*
EMP: 14
SQ FT: 15,000
SALES (est): 1.6MM **Privately Held**
SIC: 3281 Cut stone & stone products

(G-5554)
PERFECT GEAR & INSTRUMENT
125 Railroad Ave (11040-5016)
PHONE..................516 873-6122
Karen Hearne, *Principal*
EMP: 24
SALES (corp-wide): 113.2MM **Privately Held**
SIC: 3462 Gears, forged steel
HQ: Perfect Gear & Instrument Corp
55 Denton Ave S
New Hyde Park NY 11040
516 328-3330

(G-5555)
SQUARE ONE PUBLISHERS INC
115 Herricks Rd (11040-5341)
PHONE..................516 535-2010
Rudy Shur, *President*
Bob Love, *Finance*
Ariel Colletti, *Manager*
Rob Benson, *Director*
▲ EMP: 12
SQ FT: 8,000
SALES (est): 3.5MM **Privately Held**
SIC: 2731 Book publishing

(G-5556)
STRIANO ELECTRIC CO INC
246 Park Ave (11040-5318)
PHONE..................516 408-4969
Vincent T Striano, *Ch of Bd*
Stan Komorowski, *Superintendent*
Lynn Gallagher, *Opers Staff*
Patrick Hickey, *Assistant*
Dave Murphy, *Contractor*
EMP: 34
SALES (est): 9.9MM **Privately Held**
SIC: 3699 Electrical equipment & supplies

(G-5557)
WINDOWCRAFT INC
77 2nd Ave (11040-5030)
PHONE..................516 294-3580
Fax: 516 294-0444
Joseph Daniels, *President*
Ellen Caro, *Accountant*
▲ EMP: 18
SQ FT: 6,000
SALES (est): 3.1MM **Privately Held**
SIC: 2591 Window shades

(G-5558)
WINDOWTEX INC
77 2nd Ave (11040-5030)
PHONE..................877 294-3580
Dara Centonze, *Business Mgr*
David Lin, *Opers Mgr*
Fang Lin, *Design Engr*
Faith Daniels, *Accounting Mgr*
Eric Dudley, *Cust Mgr*
EMP: 10
SALES (est): 121.4K **Privately Held**
SIC: 2591 Window shade rollers & fittings

(G-5559)
YORK INDUSTRIES INC
303 Nassau Blvd (11040-5213)
PHONE..................516 746-3736
Fax: 516 746-3741
Lee E Smith, *Ch of Bd*
Paul Byers, *Vice Pres*
Janne Allen, *Purchasing*
Frank Filadelfo, *Engineer*
Maria Maqueda, *VP Sales*
EMP: 50 EST: 1942
SQ FT: 9,000
SALES (est): 11.1MM **Privately Held**
WEB: www.york-ind.com
SIC: 3829 3568 3462 3429 Measuring & controlling devices; ball joints, except aircraft & automotive; iron & steel forgings; manufactured hardware (general); hand & edge tools; tire cord & fabrics

Gardiner
Ulster County

(G-5560)
ARTHUR LAUER INC
47 Steves Ln (12525-5322)
P.O. Box 745, Dublin OH (43017-0845)
PHONE..................845 255-7871
Jeremy Smith, *President*
Joyce Salimeno, *Partner*
Kathleen Martin, *Controller*
▲ EMP: 29
SALES (est): 2.7MM **Privately Held**
WEB: www.arthurlauer.com
SIC: 2511 2512 Wood household furniture; upholstered household furniture

(G-5561)
BYCMAC CORP
Also Called: Kiss My Face
144 Main St (12525-5245)
P.O. Box 224 (12525-0224)
PHONE..................845 255-0884
Robert Macleod, *President*
Steve Byckiewicz, *Exec VP*
Betty Jordan, *Vice Pres*
Renee Smitherman, *Research*
Letitia Baviello, *CFO*
▲ EMP: 45
SQ FT: 20,000
SALES (est): 9.5MM **Privately Held**
WEB: www.kissmyface.com
SIC: 2844 Cosmetic preparations

(G-5562)
DAVID KUCERA INC
42 Steves Ln (12525-5319)
PHONE..................845 255-1044
Fax: 845 255-1597
David Kucera, *President*
Ted Fair, *Project Mgr*
Melanie Prouty, *Project Mgr*
Ann Kramer, *Purchasing*
Dan Couse, *Sales Staff*
EMP: 35
SQ FT: 15,000
SALES (est): 6.6MM **Privately Held**
WEB: www.davidkucerainc.com
SIC: 3272 Concrete products, precast

(G-5563)
S P INDUSTRIES INC
Also Called: Sp Scientific
815 Rte 208 (12525)
PHONE..................845 255-5000
David T Sutherland, *Vice Pres*
Duane Richards, *Production*
Drli Mylie, *Purchasing*
Kenneth Tenedini, *Sales Mgr*
Dan De Beau, *Branch Mgr*
EMP: 82
SQ FT: 7,200
SALES (corp-wide): 1.4B **Privately Held**
WEB: www.virtis.com
SIC: 3829 3821 Measuring & controlling devices; laboratory apparatus & furniture
HQ: S P Industries, Inc.
935 Mearns Rd
Warminster PA 18974
215 672-7800

(G-5564)
TUTHILLTOWN SPIRITS LLC
14 Gristmill Ln (12525-5528)
P.O. Box 320 (12525-0320)
PHONE..................845 255-1527
Cathy Erenzo, *Opers Mgr*
Gable Lnd, *Manager*
Brian Lee,
Ralph Erenzo,

GEOGRAPHIC SECTION

▲ EMP: 15
SALES (est): 2.8MM
SALES (corp-wide): 1.3B Privately Held
SIC: 2085 Distilled & blended liquors
HQ: William Grant & Sons Limited
Strathclyde Business Park
Bellshill
169 884-3843

(G-5565)
UTILITY CANVAS INC (PA)
2686 Route 44 55 (12525)
PHONE................................845 255-9290
Fax: 845 255-9293
Hal Grano, *President*
Jillian Kaufman, *Vice Pres*
EMP: 4
SQ FT: 4,000
SALES: 1MM Privately Held
SIC: 2394 Canvas & related products

Garnerville
Rockland County

(G-5566)
A & W METAL WORKS INC
55 W Railroad Ave 5 (10923-1261)
P.O. Box 276 (10923-0276)
PHONE................................845 352-2346
Martin Weinstock, *Admin Sec*
EMP: 10 EST: 2016
SALES (est): 363.6K Privately Held
SIC: 3999 Manufacturing industries

(G-5567)
AM ARCHITECTURAL METAL & GLASS
5 Bridge St (10923-1201)
PHONE................................845 942-8848
Paula Maunsell, *CEO*
Philip Gordon, *Sales Executive*
▲ EMP: 35
SALES: 1.5MM Privately Held
SIC: 3449 Curtain walls for buildings, steel

(G-5568)
FIRST DUE FIRE EQUIPMENT INC
130 W Ramapo Rd (10923-2134)
PHONE................................845 222-1329
David Leiser, *CEO*
Mike Humphrey, *General Mgr*
Eric Beill, *Sales Staff*
Jeffrey Belschwinder, *Sales Staff*
Kevin Dann, *Sales Staff*
EMP: 10
SALES (est): 1.9MM Privately Held
WEB: www.jeffola.com
SIC: 3569 Firefighting apparatus & related equipment; firefighting apparatus

Garrison
Putnam County

(G-5569)
ELEANORS BEST
15 Peacock Way (10524-3107)
P.O. Box 9 (10524-0009)
PHONE................................845 809-5621
Jennifer Mercurio, *Mng Member*
EMP: 10
SALES (est): 596.6K Privately Held
SIC: 2033 Jams, jellies & preserves: packaged in cans, jars, etc.

Gasport
Niagara County

(G-5570)
AG-PAK INC
8416 Telegraph Rd (14067-9246)
P.O. Box 304 (14067-0304)
PHONE................................716 772-2651
Fax: 716 772-2555
James W Currie, *CEO*
Andy Currie, *President*
◆ EMP: 15
SQ FT: 14,000
SALES (est): 3.5MM Privately Held
WEB: www.agpak.com
SIC: 3556 Food products machinery

(G-5571)
COSMICOAT OF WNY INC
Also Called: Star Seal of New York
8419 East Ave (14067-9102)
P.O. Box 376 (14067-0376)
PHONE................................716 772-2644
Fax: 716 772-2648
John Rouch, *President*
EMP: 4
SQ FT: 10,000
SALES (est): 1.7MM Privately Held
WEB: www.starsealny.com
SIC: 2951 Asphalt & asphaltic paving mixtures (not from refineries)

(G-5572)
GASPORT WELDING & FABG INC
8430 Telegraph Rd (14067-9246)
P.O. Box 410 (14067-0410)
PHONE................................716 772-7205
Fax: 716 772-7388
Edward J Wojtkowski Jr, *President*
Beverly Wojtkowski, *Corp Secy*
Edward J Wotkowski, *Marketing Staff*
Christine Pittler, *Office Mgr*
EMP: 10
SQ FT: 14,000
SALES (est): 1.6MM Privately Held
SIC: 3443 7692 3441 Tanks, standard or custom fabricated: metal plate; hoppers, metal plate; containers, shipping (bombs, etc.): metal plate; welding repair; fabricated structural metal

(G-5573)
MAKIPLASTIC
4904 Gasport Rd (14067-9506)
P.O. Box 2 (14067-0002)
PHONE................................716 772-2222
Scott Brauer, *Owner*
EMP: 5
SALES (est): 347.7K Privately Held
SIC: 3949 Bait, artificial: fishing

(G-5574)
MILNE MFG INC
8411 State St (14067-9246)
P.O. Box 159 (14067-0159)
PHONE................................716 772-2536
Janet Filipovich, *Human Res Mgr*
Ann Cain, *Branch Mgr*
Lyle Demmin, *Manager*
EMP: 11
SALES (corp-wide): 3.3MM Privately Held
WEB: www.mmplastics.com
SIC: 3089 7389 Injection molding of plastics; telephone answering service
PA: M M Plastic (Mfg) Company, Inc
1301 Blundell Rd
Mississauga ON L4Y 1
905 277-5514

(G-5575)
WOLFE LUMBER MILL INC
8416 Ridge Rd (14067-9415)
PHONE................................716 772-7750
Fax: 716 772-7750
David C Caldwell, *President*
Sandy Lawrence, *Admin Sec*
EMP: 7
SQ FT: 11,000
SALES: 800K Privately Held
SIC: 2449 2448 2431 Fruit crates, wood: wirebound; pallets, wood; millwork

Gates
Monroe County

(G-5576)
KEYES MACHINE WORKS INC
147 Park Ave (14606-3818)
PHONE................................585 426-5059
Fax: 585 426-5063
John Ritchie, *President*
Fraser Ritchie, *Vice Pres*
EMP: 5
SQ FT: 2,500
SALES (est): 490K Privately Held
SIC: 3544 3599 7699 Special dies & tools; custom machinery; industrial equipment services

(G-5577)
QSF INC
Also Called: Quality Stainless Fabrication
140 Cherry Rd (14624-2510)
PHONE................................585 247-6200
Fax: 585 247-7093
Clyde Wingate, *President*
Gail Craig, *Office Mgr*
EMP: 7
SQ FT: 10,000
SALES (est): 1MM Privately Held
WEB: www.qsfportal.com
SIC: 3312 1731 7692 Stainless steel; electronic controls installation; welding repair

(G-5578)
R D A CONTAINER CORPORATION
70 Cherry Rd (14624-2592)
PHONE................................585 247-2323
Fax: 585 247-5680
Alan P Brant, *Ch of Bd*
Steve Douglass, *Dept Chairman*
Theodre Brant, *Treasurer*
Sharon Hall, *Sales Staff*
Brian Burger, *Marketing Staff*
EMP: 42
SQ FT: 103,000
SALES (est): 9.3MM Privately Held
WEB: www.rdacontainer.com
SIC: 2653 3086 2449 Boxes, corrugated: made from purchased materials; packaging & shipping materials, foamed plastic; rectangular boxes & crates, wood

Geneseo
Livingston County

(G-5579)
CLARION PUBLICATIONS INC
38 Main St (14454-1216)
P.O. Box 236 (14454-0236)
PHONE................................585 243-3530
Fax: 585 243-3764
M Corrin Strong, *President*
Howard Appell, *Editor*
Phil Livingston, *Editor*
EMP: 12
SQ FT: 1,600
SALES (est): 603.3K Privately Held
WEB: www.clarioncall.com
SIC: 2711 2721 2754 7334 Newspapers: publishing only, not printed on site; magazines: publishing & printing; color printing, gravure; photocopying & duplicating services

(G-5580)
DEER RUN ENTERPRISES INC
Also Called: Deer Run Winery
3772 W Lake Rd (14454-9743)
PHONE................................585 346-0850
George Kuyon, *President*
Joan Kuyon, *Vice Pres*
Scott Kuyon, *Manager*
EMP: 6
SQ FT: 4,000
SALES (est): 621.9K Privately Held
WEB: www.deerrunwinery.com
SIC: 2084 Wines

(G-5581)
LIVINGSTON COUNTY NEWS
122 Main St (14454-1230)
PHONE................................585 243-1234
Tom Turanvull, *President*
Howard Aggell, *Manager*
EMP: 7
SALES (est): 442.3K
SALES (corp-wide): 32MM Privately Held
WEB: www.ogd.com
SIC: 2711 Newspapers, publishing & printing
PA: Johnson Newspaper Corporation
260 Washington St
Watertown NY
315 782-1000

Geneva
Ontario County

(G-5582)
BILLSBORO WINERY
4760 State Route 14 (14456-9746)
PHONE................................315 789-9538
Kim Aliberti, *President*
Evan Pierce, *Sales Associate*
Jessica McGuigan, *Manager*
EMP: 6 EST: 1999
SALES (est): 529.4K Privately Held
SIC: 2084 Wines

(G-5583)
CCMI INC
88 Middle St (14456-1836)
PHONE................................315 781-3270
Fax: 315 781-3271
Wells C Lewis, *President*
Anthony Lewis, *President*
James Hartman, *Treasurer*
Faye Bentley, *Sales Dir*
Rose Hammond-Hoose, *Office Mgr*
EMP: 8
SQ FT: 7,500
SALES (est): 931.7K Privately Held
WEB: www.ccmi-reedco.com
SIC: 2821 7389 Plastics materials & resins; packaging & labeling services

(G-5584)
CCN INTERNATIONAL INC
200 Lehigh St (14456-1096)
PHONE................................315 789-4400
Fax: 315 789-0376
Charles Richard Conoyer, *President*
Justin Mahoney, *General Mgr*
Anne Nenneau, *Exec VP*
Michael Hryzak, *Vice Pres*
Timothy Lesslie, *Vice Pres*
▼ EMP: 74 EST: 1970
SQ FT: 85,000
SALES (est): 9.6MM Privately Held
WEB: www.ccnintl.com
SIC: 2521 Wood office furniture; desks, office: wood; tables, office: wood; bookcases, office: wood

(G-5585)
CHERIBUNDI INC (PA)
500 Technology Farm Dr (14456-1325)
PHONE................................800 699-0460
Steve Pear, *Principal*
Ed Maguire, *Vice Pres*
Katie Hyland, *QC Mgr*
Mary Sterling, *QC Mgr*
Carol Langdon, *Controller*
EMP: 21
SQ FT: 8,300
SALES (est): 4.4MM Privately Held
SIC: 2037 2033 2086 Fruit juices; fruit juice concentrates, frozen; fruit juices: fresh; fruit drinks (less than 100% juice): packaged in cans, etc.

(G-5586)
ENVIROFORM RECYCLED PDTS INC
287 Gambee Rd (14456-1025)
P.O. Box 553 (14456-0553)
PHONE................................315 789-1810
Robert L Bates, *President*
Joe Bates, *Project Mgr*
Amanda Wright, *Office Mgr*
EMP: 9
SQ FT: 5,000
SALES: 2.5MM Privately Held
WEB: www.enviroform.com
SIC: 3069 Molded rubber products; rubber automotive products

(G-5587)
FAHY-WILLIAMS PUBLISHING INC
171 Reed St (14456-2137)
P.O. Box 1080 (14456-8080)
PHONE................................315 781-6820

Geneva - Ontario County (G-5588)

Fax: 315 789-4263
Kevin Fahy, *President*
Tim Braden, *Vice Pres*
Trisha McKenna, *Office Mgr*
EMP: 13
SQ FT: 3,200
SALES (est): 1.8MM **Privately Held**
WEB: www.fwpi.com
SIC: 2721 Periodicals: publishing only

(G-5588)
FINGER LAKES PRINTING CO INC (HQ)
218 Genesee St (14456-2323)
P.O. Box 393 (14456-0393)
PHONE 315 789-3333
Fax: 315 789-4077
William L McLean III, *President*
EMP: 50
SQ FT: 20,000
SALES (est): 8.1MM
SALES (corp-wide): 79.2MM **Privately Held**
WEB: www.fltimes.com
SIC: 2711 Newspapers
PA: Independent Publications, Inc.
945 E Haverford Rd Ste 5
Bryn Mawr PA
610 527-6330

(G-5589)
FINGER LAKES RADIOLOGY LLC
196 North St (14456-1651)
PHONE 315 787-5399
John Oates, *Information Mgr*
Leza Hassett, *Director*
Rich Laurenzo, *Director*
Andre Forcier,
Terri Haskins,
EMP: 6
SALES (est): 1.3MM **Privately Held**
SIC: 3826 Magnetic resonance imaging apparatus

(G-5590)
GENEVA GRANITE CO INC (PA)
272 Border City Rd (14456-1988)
P.O. Box 834 (14456-0834)
PHONE 315 789-8142
Fax: 315 781-2900
Ralph Fratto Jr, *President*
Joseph Fratto, *Corp Secy*
Jean Fratto, *Vice Pres*
EMP: 15
SQ FT: 1,200
SALES (est): 3MM **Privately Held**
SIC: 3281 1771 Curbing, paving & walkway stone; concrete work; curb construction

(G-5591)
GENEVA PRINTING COMPANY INC
40 Castle St (14456-2679)
PHONE 315 789-8191
Fax: 315 789-1618
Ronald Alcock, *President*
Jo Ellen Alcock, *Vice Pres*
EMP: 8
SQ FT: 7,500
SALES (est): 1.2MM **Privately Held**
WEB: www.genevaprinting.com
SIC: 2752 Commercial printing, offset

(G-5592)
GUARDIAN INDUSTRIES LLC
50 Forge Ave (14456-1281)
PHONE 315 787-7000
Fax: 315 787-7065
Christopher Housman, *General Mgr*
Dean Cambell, *Principal*
Cheryl Hess, *Human Resources*
Mark Bennett, *Manager*
Laura Neubauer, *Manager*
EMP: 332
SALES (corp-wide): 27.8B **Privately Held**
WEB: www.guardian.com
SIC: 3211 Flat glass
HQ: Guardian Industries, Llc
2300 Harmon Rd
Auburn Hills MI 48326
248 340-1800

(G-5593)
HANGER PRSTHETCS & ORTHO INC
787 State Route 5 And 20 (14456-2001)
PHONE 315 789-4810
Thomas Kirk PHD, *CEO*
Sheryl Price, *Director*
EMP: 5
SALES (corp-wide): 451.4MM **Publicly Held**
SIC: 3842 Limbs, artificial; braces, orthopedic
HQ: Hanger Prosthetics & Orthotics, Inc.
10910 Domain Dr Ste 300
Austin TX 78758
512 777-3800

(G-5594)
MCINTOSH BOX & PALLET CO INC
40 Doran Ave (14456-1224)
PHONE 315 789-8750
Fax: 315 789-8820
Robert Randall, *Facilities Mgr*
William Wester, *Opers Staff*
Joshua Stasik, *Sales Staff*
Vayeli Rivera, *Manager*
Danielle Wester, *Manager*
EMP: 18
SQ FT: 14,400
SALES (corp-wide): 26.9MM **Privately Held**
WEB: www.mcintoshbox.com
SIC: 2441 2448 Shipping cases, wood: nailed or lock corner; wood pallets & skids
PA: Mcintosh Box & Pallet Co., Inc.
5864 Pyle Dr
East Syracuse NY 13057
315 446-9350

(G-5595)
NEGYS NEW LAND VINYRD WINERY
Also Called: Three Brothers Winery
623 Lerch Rd Ste 1 (14456-9295)
PHONE 315 585-4432
Nancy Burdick, *President*
Dave Mansfield, *Owner*
Erica Ridley, *General Mgr*
Jon Mansfield, *Assistant*
EMP: 7
SALES (est): 100K **Privately Held**
SIC: 2084 5921 Wines; wine

(G-5596)
R M REYNOLDS (PA)
Also Called: Point of Sale Outfitters
504 Exchange St (14456-3407)
PHONE 315 789-7365
R M Reynolds, *Owner*
EMP: 5
SQ FT: 5,500
SALES (est): 550.4K **Privately Held**
SIC: 3911 5094 Jewelry, precious metal; jewelry

(G-5597)
SENECA FOODS CORPORATION
Also Called: Vegetable Operations
100 Gambee Rd (14456-1099)
PHONE 315 781-8733
Fax: 315 789-1586
Warren Fredericksen, *Plant Mgr*
Gary Hadyk, *Plant Mgr*
Mark Forsting, *Opers-Prdtn-Mfg*
Katie Gushlaw, *Human Res Mgr*
William Gardinier, *Director*
EMP: 150
SALES (corp-wide): 1.2B **Publicly Held**
SIC: 2033 Sauerkraut: packaged in cans, jars, etc.; vegetables: packaged in cans, jars, etc.
PA: Seneca Foods Corporation
3736 S Main St
Marion NY 14505
315 926-8100

(G-5598)
SENECA TRUCK & TRAILER INC
2200 State Route 14 (14456-9511)
PHONE 315 781-1100
Patrick O'Connor, *President*
Patrick O Connor, *President*
EMP: 6
SALES (est): 350K **Privately Held**
WEB: www.senecatruck.com
SIC: 3715 Truck trailers

(G-5599)
TRAMWELL INC
Also Called: Graphic Connections
70 State St (14456-1760)
PHONE 315 789-2762
Fax: 315 789-2910
William D Whitwell, *President*
Nancy F Whitwell, *Vice Pres*
EMP: 5
SQ FT: 4,000
SALES (est): 300K **Privately Held**
SIC: 2261 Screen printing of cotton broadwoven fabrics

(G-5600)
VANCE METAL FABRICATORS INC
251 Gambee Rd (14456-1025)
PHONE 315 789-5626
Fax: 315 789-1848
Joseph A Hennessy, *Ch of Bd*
William Dobbin Jr, *Chairman*
Len Visco, *Opers Mgr*
Brian Mott, *Safety Mgr*
John Sabin, *Foreman/Supr*
▲ **EMP:** 85 **EST:** 1880
SQ FT: 36,000
SALES (est): 43.4MM **Privately Held**
WEB: www.vancemetal.com
SIC: 3441 3444 Fabricated structural metal; sheet metalwork

(G-5601)
ZOTOS INTERNATIONAL INC
Joico Laboratories
300 Forge Ave (14456-1294)
PHONE 315 781-3207
Fax: 315 789-0744
Herb Nieporent, *Principal*
Doug Parkinson, *Vice Pres*
Komal Ladd, *Research*
John Mahon, *Research*
Jim Hannan, *Electrical Engi*
EMP: 289
SALES (corp-wide): 7.6B **Privately Held**
WEB: www.zotos.com
SIC: 2844 Hair preparations, including shampoos; cosmetic preparations
HQ: Zotos International, Inc.
100 Tokeneke Rd
Darien CT 06820
203 655-8911

Genoa
Cayuga County

(G-5602)
STONE WELL BODIES & MCH INC
625 Sill Rd (13071-4182)
PHONE 315 497-3512
Fax: 315 497-1550
Luigi Sposito, *CEO*
Todd Mix, *COO*
Robert Todd Mix, *Vice Pres*
▼ **EMP:** 37
SQ FT: 30,000
SALES (est): 4.7MM **Privately Held**
WEB: www.stonewellbodies.com
SIC: 3715 3441 8711 Truck trailers; fabricated structural metal; engineering services

Germantown
Columbia County

(G-5603)
ON THE DOUBLE INC
Also Called: John Patrick
178 Viewmont Rd (12526-5808)
PHONE 518 431-3571
Walter Fleming, *Ch of Bd*
EMP: 5
SALES (est): 446.8K **Privately Held**
SIC: 2339 2329 Women's & misses' athletic clothing & sportswear; men's & boys' sportswear & athletic clothing

Gerry
Chautauqua County

(G-5604)
COBBE INDUSTRIES INC
Also Called: Valley Industries
1397 Harris Hollow Rd (14740-9515)
PHONE 716 287-2661
Fax: 716 287-2663
Daniel W Cobbe, *President*
Tad Henderson, *Engineer*
Tina Godfrey, *Manager*
EMP: 30 **EST:** 1976
SQ FT: 22,000
SALES (est): 4.7MM **Privately Held**
WEB: www.valleyindustries.com
SIC: 3469 3441 Metal stampings; fabricated structural metal

(G-5605)
SWANSON LUMBER
5273 N Hill Rd (14740-9521)
PHONE 716 499-1726
Charles Swanson, *Owner*
EMP: 5
SQ FT: 2,688
SALES (est): 311.2K **Privately Held**
SIC: 2421 Sawmills & planing mills, general

(G-5606)
UNIVERSAL TOOLING CORPORATION
4533 Route 60 (14740-9540)
P.O. Box 364 (14740-0364)
PHONE 716 985-4691
Fax: 716 985-4430
Nichole Segrue, *CEO*
Warren Piazza, *President*
Scott Sando, *Manager*
Ray Ord, *Supervisor*
EMP: 13 **EST:** 1981
SQ FT: 10,630
SALES (est): 1.4MM **Privately Held**
WEB: www.u-t-c.com
SIC: 3544 3545 Forms (molds), for foundry & plastics working machinery; dies, plastics forming; machine tool accessories

Getzville
Erie County

(G-5607)
COLUMBUS MCKINNON CORPORATION (PA)
205 Crosspoint Pkwy (14068-1605)
PHONE 716 689-5400
Fax: 716 689-5598
Ernest R Verebelyi, *Ch of Bd*
Mark D Morelli, *President*
Alan S Korman, *Vice Pres*
Gregory P Rustowicz, *CFO*
Mark Paradowski, *VP Info Sys*
◆ **EMP:** 145 **EST:** 1875
SALES: 637.1M **Publicly Held**
WEB: www.cmworks.com
SIC: 3536 3496 3535 3537 Hoists; cranes, industrial plant; cranes, overhead traveling; chain, welded; conveyor belts; conveyors & conveying equipment; tables, lift: hydraulic

(G-5608)
COLUMBUS MCKINNON CORPORATION
Also Called: Coffing
205 Crosspoint Pkwy (14068-1605)
PHONE 716 689-5400
Fax: 716 689-5514
EMP: 134
SALES (corp-wide): 637.1MM **Publicly Held**
WEB: www.cmworks.com
SIC: 3536 3496 3535 3537 Hoists; cranes, industrial plant; cranes, overhead traveling; chain, welded; conveyor belts; conveyors & conveying equipment; tables, lift: hydraulic

PA: Columbus Mckinnon Corporation
205 Crosspoint Pkwy
Getzville NY 14068
716 689-5400

(G-5609)
COLUMBUS MCKINNON CORPORATION
Also Called: Yale
205 Crosspoint Pkwy (14068-1605)
PHONE...................716 689-5400
EMP: 134
SALES (corp-wide): 637.1MM **Publicly Held**
WEB: www.cmworks.com
SIC: 3536 3496 3535 3537 Hoists; cranes, industrial plant; cranes, overhead traveling; chain, welded; conveyor belts; conveyors & conveying equipment; tables, lift: hydraulic
PA: Columbus Mckinnon Corporation
205 Crosspoint Pkwy
Getzville NY 14068
716 689-5400

(G-5610)
COLUMBUS MCKINNON CORPORATION
Also Called: Columbus McKnnon- Lift TEC Div
205 Crosspoint Pkwy (14068-1605)
PHONE...................716 689-5400
Maureen Strimple, *Business Anlyst*
Linda Riggi, *Manager*
EMP: 100
SALES (corp-wide): 637.1MM **Publicly Held**
WEB: www.cmworks.com
SIC: 3462 Iron & steel forgings
PA: Columbus Mckinnon Corporation
205 Crosspoint Pkwy
Getzville NY 14068
716 689-5400

(G-5611)
INTEL CORPORATION
55 Dodge Rd (14068-1205)
PHONE...................408 765-8080
Victor Arabagian, *Sales Staff*
Mike Brunner, *Branch Mgr*
EMP: 60
SALES (corp-wide): 59.3B **Publicly Held**
WEB: www.intel.com
SIC: 3674 7372 Microprocessors; application computer software
PA: Intel Corporation
2200 Mission College Blvd
Santa Clara CA 95054
408 765-8080

(G-5612)
MISSION CRITICAL ENERGY INC
Also Called: Starboard Sun
1801 N French Rd (14068-1032)
PHONE...................716 276-8465
Mark Dettmer, *President*
EMP: 5 **EST:** 2012
SALES (est): 435.3K **Privately Held**
SIC: 3511 Turbines & turbine generator sets

(G-5613)
NINAS CUSTARD
2577 Millersport Hwy (14068-1445)
PHONE...................716 636-0345
Fax: 716 689-2258
Merry Scioli, *Partner*
EMP: 30
SALES (est): 3.6MM **Privately Held**
SIC: 2024 Ice cream & frozen desserts

(G-5614)
OLD DUTCHMANS WROUGH IRON INC
2800 Millersport Hwy (14068-1449)
P.O. Box 632 (14068-0632)
PHONE...................716 688-2034
Keith Deck, *Principal*
▲ **EMP:** 6
SQ FT: 2,416
SALES: 100K **Privately Held**
WEB: www.oldutchman.com
SIC: 3446 Architectural metalwork

(G-5615)
PETIT PRINTING CORP
42 Hunters Gln (14068-1264)
PHONE...................716 871-9490
Fax: 716 871-0760
Richard Petit, *President*
EMP: 8
SQ FT: 14,000
SALES: 540K **Privately Held**
WEB: www.petitprinting.com
SIC: 2752 Commercial printing, offset

(G-5616)
SPX FLOW TECH SYSTEMS INC (HQ)
Also Called: SPX Flow Tech Systems Inc
105 Crosspoint Pkwy (14068-1603)
PHONE...................716 692-3000
Christopher J Kearney, *CEO*
Marc Michael, *President*
Patrick J O'Leary, *President*
Katie Masters, *Safety Mgr*
Brian Goff, *CFO*
▲ **EMP:** 80
SALES (est): 287MM
SALES (corp-wide): 2B **Publicly Held**
SIC: 3556 8742 Food products machinery; food & beverage consultant
PA: Spx Flow, Inc.
13320 Balntyn Corp Pl
Charlotte NC 28277
704 752-4400

(G-5617)
U S ENERGY DEVELOPMENT CORP (PA)
2350 N Forest Rd (14068-1296)
PHONE...................716 636-0401
Fax: 716 636-0418
Joseph M Jayson, *Ch of Bd*
Douglas Walch, *President*
Jerry Jones, *Opers Mgr*
Mark Goc, *Accounting Mgr*
Judy Jayson, *Marketing Staff*
EMP: 53
SQ FT: 5,000
SALES (est): 50.7MM **Privately Held**
WEB: www.usenergydevcorp.com
SIC: 1382 1381 1389 Oil & gas exploration services; drilling oil & gas wells; oil field services

(G-5618)
VADER SYSTEMS LLC
385 Crsspint Pkwy Ste 104 (14068)
PHONE...................716 688-1600
Scott Vader, *CEO*
Zachary Vader, *Co-Owner*
EMP: 11
SALES (est): 7.2MM **Privately Held**
SIC: 3599 3542 3577 3549 Machine & other job shop work; metal deposit forming machines; computer peripheral equipment; metalworking machinery

(G-5619)
WILLIAM S HEIN & CO INC (PA)
Also Called: Metro Storage Center
2350 N Forest Rd Ste 14a (14068-1296)
PHONE...................716 882-2600
Fax: 716 883-8100
William S Hein Sr, *Ch of Bd*
Kevin Marmion, *President*
Richard Spinnelli, *Senior VP*
Len Grieco, *Vice Pres*
Susan H Mc Clinton, *Vice Pres*
EMP: 100
SQ FT: 140,000
SALES: 53.7K **Privately Held**
WEB: www.foreign-law.com
SIC: 2731 5942 3572 Books: publishing only; book stores; computer storage devices

Ghent
Columbia County

(G-5620)
J D HANDLING SYSTEMS INC
1346 State Route 9h (12075-3415)
PHONE...................518 828-9676
Fax: 518 828-9629
Joseph Cardinale Jr, *President*
Joseph Cardinale Sr, *Shareholder*
Diane Cardinale, *Admin Sec*
▲ **EMP:** 12
SQ FT: 53,000
SALES: 1.5MM **Privately Held**
WEB: www.jdhand.com
SIC: 3535 5599 Conveyors & conveying equipment; utility trailers

Glen Cove
Nassau County

(G-5621)
A LOSEE & SONS
68 Landing Rd (11542-1844)
PHONE...................516 676-3060
Fax: 516 676-1520
Allan Losee, *President*
Mark Losee, *Treasurer*
EMP: 7 **EST:** 1963
SQ FT: 3,000
SALES: 500K **Privately Held**
SIC: 2431 Woodwork, interior & ornamental

(G-5622)
ALLEN PICKLE WORKS INC
36 Garvies Point Rd (11542-2821)
PHONE...................516 676-0640
Fax: 516 759-5780
Ronald Horman, *President*
Nick Horman, *Vice Pres*
EMP: 19
SQ FT: 20,000
SALES (est): 9MM **Privately Held**
SIC: 2035 Pickles, vinegar

(G-5623)
AUGUST THOMSEN CORP
36 Sea Cliff Ave (11542-3635)
PHONE...................516 676-7100
Fax: 516 676-7108
Jeffrey G Schneider, *President*
Douglas J Schneider, *Vice Pres*
Douglass Schnieder, *Sales Dir*
Ingrid Schneider, *Shareholder*
◆ **EMP:** 40
SQ FT: 25,000
SALES (est): 8.1MM **Privately Held**
WEB: www.atecousa.com
SIC: 3365 Cooking/kitchen utensils, cast aluminum

(G-5624)
AVALONBAY COMMUNITIES INC
1100 Avalon Sq (11542-2877)
PHONE...................516 484-7766
Fax: 516 484-7801
Karen Griemsmann, *Vice Pres*
EMP: 33
SALES (corp-wide): 2B **Publicly Held**
SIC: 3843 Dental equipment & supplies
PA: Avalonbay Communities, Inc.
671 N Glebe Rd Ste 800
Arlington VA 22203
703 329-6300

(G-5625)
COMMUNITY CPONS FRNCHISING INC
100 Carney St Ste 2 (11542-3687)
PHONE...................516 277-1968
Fax: 516 671-6399
Matthew Rosencrans, *President*
Dennis Coupons, *Sales Mgr*
Stu Golden, *Regl Sales Mgr*
EMP: 25
SQ FT: 3,200
SALES: 3.5MM **Privately Held**
SIC: 2741 7313 Miscellaneous publishing; newspaper advertising representative

(G-5626)
COMPS INC
3 School St Ste 101b (11542-2548)
P.O. Box 255, Sea Cliff (11579-0255)
PHONE...................516 676-0400
Keith Larson, *President*
EMP: 12
SALES (est): 887.8K **Privately Held**
WEB: www.compsny.com
SIC: 2741 Miscellaneous publishing

(G-5627)
EXPO FURNITURE DESIGNS INC
Also Called: Expo Lighting Design
1 Garvies Point Rd (11542-2821)
PHONE...................516 674-1420
Fax: 516 674-6778
Brian Landau, *President*
Mary Miluso, *Sales Mgr*
Maria Landau, *Admin Sec*
▲ **EMP:** 10
SQ FT: 5,000
SALES: 900K **Privately Held**
WEB: www.expodesigninc.com
SIC: 3648 5063 5072 Lighting fixtures, except electric: residential; lighting fixtures; hardware

(G-5628)
G SICURANZA LTD
4 East Ave (11542-3917)
PHONE...................516 759-0259
Gaetano Sicuranza, *Ch of Bd*
EMP: 5
SALES (est): 510.4K **Privately Held**
SIC: 3432 Plumbing fixture fittings & trim

(G-5629)
GADDIS INDUSTRIAL EQUIPMENT
Also Called: Gaddis Engineering
140 Pratt Oval (11542-1482)
P.O. Box 915, Locust Valley (11560-0915)
PHONE...................516 759-3100
Fax: 516 759-3175
M Francis Gaddis, *President*
Marie B Gaddis, *Treasurer*
Paul Gaddis, *Asst Treas*
L C Hills, *Admin Sec*
EMP: 12
SALES (est): 1.2MM **Privately Held**
SIC: 3053 Packing materials

(G-5630)
GLEN PLAZA MARBLE & GRAN INC
75 Glen Cove Ave Ste A (11542-3261)
PHONE...................516 671-1100
Fax: 516 759-0970
Frank Caruso, *President*
Joe Caruso, *Corp Secy*
Angelo Caruso, *Vice Pres*
▲ **EMP:** 7
SQ FT: 7,500
SALES (est): 702.1K **Privately Held**
SIC: 3281 5032 5999 5211 Granite, cut & shaped; marble, building: cut & shaped; granite building stone; marble building stone; monuments & tombstones; tile, ceramic

(G-5631)
HORIZON POWER SOURCE LLC
50 Glen St (11542-4304)
PHONE...................877 240-0580
David Shaoulpour,
Derrick Shaoulpour,
EMP: 20
SALES (est): 1.4MM **Privately Held**
SIC: 2899 Battery acid

(G-5632)
KCH PUBLICATIONS INC
Also Called: Gold Coast Gazette
57 Glen St Ste 1 (11542-2785)
PHONE...................516 671-2360
Fax: 516 671-2361
Kevin Horton, *President*
EMP: 20
SALES (est): 955.9K **Privately Held**
WEB: www.goldcoastgazette.net
SIC: 2711 Newspapers, publishing & printing

(G-5633)
KORE INFRASTRUCTURE LLC (PA)
4 High Pine (11542-1422)
PHONE...................646 532-9060
Cornelius Shields, *Mng Member*
David Harding, *Officer*
EMP: 3
SQ FT: 3,000
SALES (est): 3.5MM **Privately Held**
SIC: 2869 4953 Fuels; recycling, waste materials

Glen Cove - Nassau County (G-5634)

(G-5634)
MIL-SPEC INDUSTRIES CORP
42 Herb Hill Rd (11542-2817)
PHONE..................516 625-5787
Fax: 516 625-0988
Ron Nanne, *President*
Jin Park, *Finance Dir*
Bill Morris, *Accounts Exec*
Ayse Erguner, *Manager*
▼ **EMP:** 7
SALES (est): 2.1MM **Privately Held**
WEB: www.mil-spec-industries.com
SIC: 3489 Ordnance & accessories

(G-5635)
NORESCO INDUSTRIAL GROUP INC
3 School St Ste 103 (11542-2548)
PHONE..................516 759-3355
Fax: 516 759-3497
Daan Hu, *President*
Julie Lee, *Exec VP*
▲ **EMP:** 40
SALES (est): 9.1MM **Privately Held**
WEB: www.norescoindustrial.com
SIC: 3321 5013 5084 3322 Ductile iron castings; automotive supplies & parts; industrial machinery & equipment; malleable iron foundries

(G-5636)
NOVITA FABRICS FURNISHING CORP
1 Brewster St (11542-2571)
PHONE..................516 299-4500
David Rahimi, *President*
EMP: 12 **EST:** 2014
SQ FT: 12,000
SALES: 2.5MM **Privately Held**
SIC: 2299 Linen fabrics

(G-5637)
PLEATCO LLC
28 Garvies Point Rd (11542-2821)
PHONE..................516 609-0200
Fax: 516 609-0204
Howard Smith, *President*
John Antretter, *Vice Pres*
Jeff Manno, *Vice Pres*
Richard Medina, *Vice Pres*
Mary Bethray, *VP Opers*
▲ **EMP:** 80
SQ FT: 21,000
SALES (est): 31.2MM **Privately Held**
SIC: 3589 Swimming pool filter & water conditioning systems

(G-5638)
PROFESSIONAL TAPE CORPORATION
100 Pratt Oval (11542-1482)
P.O. Box 234271, Great Neck (11023-4271)
PHONE..................516 656-5519
Fax: 516 656-5519
Morris Kamkar, *President*
Jeff Levigne, *Warehouse Mgr*
▲ **EMP:** 4
SQ FT: 10,000
SALES: 7MM **Privately Held**
WEB: www.proftapeco.com
SIC: 3695 7819 5099 Magnetic tape; video tape or disk reproduction; video & audio equipment

(G-5639)
RASON ASPHALT INC
44 Morris Ave (11542-2816)
PHONE..................516 671-1500
Fax: 516 671-0234
Gene Sullivan, *Manager*
EMP: 5
SALES (corp-wide): 10.2MM **Privately Held**
WEB: www.rason1.com
SIC: 2951 Asphalt paving mixtures & blocks
PA: Rason Asphalt Inc.
 Rr 110
 Farmingdale NY 11735
 631 293-6210

(G-5640)
SHERCO SERVICES LLC
2 Park Pl Ste A (11542-2566)
PHONE..................516 676-3028
Shawn Sheridan,
EMP: 10
SALES (est): 1.2MM **Privately Held**
SIC: 3537 Trucks, tractors, loaders, carriers & similar equipment

(G-5641)
SLANTO MANUFACTURING INC
40 Garvies Point Rd (11542-2887)
PHONE..................516 759-5721
Mel Dubin, *President*
EMP: 25
SALES (est): 1.6MM **Privately Held**
SIC: 3442 Baseboards, metal

(G-5642)
STEVENSON PRINTING CO INC
1 Brewster St Ste 2 (11542-2556)
PHONE..................516 676-1233
Fax: 516 676-1250
Anthony Messineo, *President*
Cindy Messineo Hawkhurst, *Vice Pres*
Glenn Messineo, *Vice Pres*
EMP: 6 **EST:** 1909
SQ FT: 12,800
SALES (est): 800.8K **Privately Held**
WEB: www.printingedgemarketing.com
SIC: 2752 Commercial printing, offset

(G-5643)
SUNNYSIDE DECORATIVE PRINTS CO
Also Called: Etcetera Wallpapers
67 Robinson Ave (11542-2944)
PHONE..................516 671-1935
Douglas Fletcher Jr, *President*
Melissa Wolf, *Manager*
EMP: 9
SQ FT: 12,000
SALES (est): 1.2MM **Privately Held**
SIC: 2679 Wallpaper

(G-5644)
WELLS RUGS INC
Also Called: Wells, George Ruggery
44 Sea Cliff Ave (11542-3627)
PHONE..................516 676-2056
Joseph Misiak, *President*
EMP: 6
SALES (est): 404.7K **Privately Held**
SIC: 2273 Carpets & rugs

Glen Head
Nassau County

(G-5645)
DEANGELIS LTD
262 Glen Head Rd (11545-1974)
PHONE..................212 348-8225
Fax: 212 286-3950
Kenneth Deangelis, *President*
Kayel Deangelis, *Vice Pres*
Kristine Deangelis, *MIS Dir*
EMP: 50 **EST:** 1957
SQ FT: 1,500
SALES (est): 4.8MM **Privately Held**
SIC: 2512 2391 Upholstered household furniture; draperies, plastic & textile: from purchased materials

(G-5646)
HALM INDUSTRIES CO INC (PA)
180 Glen Head Rd (11545-1995)
PHONE..................516 676-6700
Donald Lyon, *President*
Donald Schanck, *Vice Pres*
John Lampitt, *Opers Staff*
Mark Winkler, *Purch Mgr*
Joe Puma, *CFO*
◆ **EMP:** 90
SQ FT: 32,000
SALES (est): 15MM **Privately Held**
SIC: 3555 Printing trades machinery

(G-5647)
HALM INSTRUMENT CO INC
180 Glen Head Rd (11545-1924)
PHONE..................516 676-6700
Fax: 516 676-6751
Floyd A Lyon, *President*
Steven Lyon, *Vice Pres*
Donald Schanck, *Vice Pres*
EMP: 76 **EST:** 1945
SQ FT: 32,000
SALES (est): 5MM **Privately Held**
SIC: 3555 Printing trades machinery

(G-5648)
INCREDIBLE SCENTS INC
1009 Glen Cove Ave Ste 6 (11545-1592)
PHONE..................516 656-3300
Howard Rabinowitz, *President*
Richard Davi, *Exec VP*
EMP: 5
SQ FT: 1,500
SALES: 10MM **Privately Held**
WEB: www.incrediblescents.com
SIC: 3841 Surgical & medical instruments

(G-5649)
INTERNATIONAL NEWSPPR PRTG CO
Also Called: International Newspaper Prntng
18 Carlisle Dr (11545-2120)
PHONE..................516 626-6095
Fax: 718 392-4777
Richard Schwartz, *Vice Pres*
Gilda Schwartz, *Admin Sec*
EMP: 25 **EST:** 1932
SQ FT: 12,500
SALES (est): 3.1MM **Privately Held**
SIC: 2752 Commercial printing, offset

(G-5650)
LOMIN CONSTRUCTION COMPANY
Also Called: O'Neil Construction
328 Glen Cove Rd (11545-2273)
PHONE..................516 759-5734
Steven O'Neil, *Partner*
EMP: 6
SALES (est): 490K **Privately Held**
SIC: 3531 1629 1611 Pavers; tennis court construction; surfacing & paving

(G-5651)
NEW ART SIGNS CO INC
78 Plymouth Dr N (11545-1127)
PHONE..................718 443-0900
Fax: 718 455-2340
Steven Weiss, *President*
EMP: 5
SALES (est): 350K **Privately Held**
SIC: 3993 2759 Signs & advertising specialties; screen printing

(G-5652)
NIRX MEDICAL TECHNOLOGIES LLC
15 Cherry Ln (11545-2215)
PHONE..................516 676-6479
Doug Maxwell, *Branch Mgr*
EMP: 15
SALES (corp-wide): 1.4MM **Privately Held**
WEB: www.nirx.net
SIC: 3845 Position emission tomography (PET scanner)
PA: Nirx Medical Technologies, Llc
 7083 Hollywood Blvd Fl 4
 Los Angeles CA 90028
 424 264-0556

(G-5653)
NORTH SHORE MONUMENTS INC
667 Cedar Swamp Rd Ste 5 (11545-2267)
PHONE..................516 759-2156
Fax: 516 671-2885
Hugh A Tanchuck, *President*
Maggie L Tanchuck, *President*
EMP: 6
SQ FT: 3,100
SALES: 734.4K **Privately Held**
WEB: www.northshoremonuments.com
SIC: 3281 5999 1799 Cut stone & stone products; monuments & tombstones; sandblasting of building exteriors

Glen Oaks
Queens County

(G-5654)
BAYSIDE BEEPERS & CELLULAR
25607 Hillside Ave (11004-1617)
PHONE..................718 343-3888
Albert Castro, *Owner*
EMP: 5 **EST:** 2013
SALES (est): 335.2K **Privately Held**
SIC: 3663 4812 Pagers (one-way); cellular telephone services

(G-5655)
SHINE FOODS USA INC
7824 266th St (11004-1325)
PHONE..................516 784-9674
Joby Joseph, *CEO*
▲ **EMP:** 5
SALES (est): 258.5K **Privately Held**
SIC: 2092 5149 Fresh or frozen fish or seafood chowders, soups & stews; groceries & related products

(G-5656)
WYNCO PRESS ONE INC
Also Called: Minuteman Press
7839 268th St (11004-1330)
PHONE..................516 354-6145
Fax: 516 354-6145
Jeff Wheeler, *President*
EMP: 6
SQ FT: 1,000
SALES: 750K **Privately Held**
SIC: 2752 2791 2789 Commercial printing, lithographic; typesetting; bookbinding & related work

Glendale
Queens County

(G-5657)
A & S WINDOW ASSOCIATES INC
8819 76th Ave (11385-7992)
PHONE..................718 275-7900
Fax: 718 997-7683
Alan Herman, *President*
▲ **EMP:** 20 **EST:** 1952
SQ FT: 14,000
SALES (est): 3.5MM **Privately Held**
WEB: www.aswindowassociates.com
SIC: 3442 Storm doors or windows, metal

(G-5658)
ALFA CARD INC
7915 Cooper Ave (11385-7528)
PHONE..................718 326-7107
Fax: 718 326-7532
George Chase, *President*
Judy Chase, *Vice Pres*
EMP: 8
SQ FT: 1,400
SALES (est): 385K **Privately Held**
WEB: www.alfacard.com
SIC: 2754 Business form & card printing, gravure

(G-5659)
ALLEN WILLIAM & COMPANY INC
Also Called: Alvin J Bart
7119 80th St Ste 8315 (11385-7733)
PHONE..................212 675-6461
Fax: 718 821-2486
EMP: 200 **EST:** 1884
SALES (est): 24MM **Privately Held**
SIC: 2678 2752 Mfg Stationery Products Lithographic Commercial Printing

(G-5660)
ALVIN J BART & SONS INC
7119 80th St Ste 8315 (11385-7733)
PHONE..................718 417-1300
Fax: 718 366-7940
Richard Bart, *Ch of Bd*
Alvin J Bart, *President*
Ira Bart, *Vice Pres*
Denise Crafa, *Vice Pres*

GEOGRAPHIC SECTION

Glens Falls - Warren County (G-5685)

Terri Fiero, *Manager*
▲ **EMP:** 150 **EST:** 1956
SQ FT: 170,000
SALES (est): 26.4MM **Privately Held**
WEB: www.ajbartny.com
SIC: 2759 Commercial printing; bank notes: engraved

(G-5661)
BOWE INDUSTRIES INC (PA)
Also Called: Changes
8836 77th Ave (11385-7826)
PHONE.................................718 441-6464
Fax: 718 441-8624
Daniel Barasch, *CEO*
Marek Kiyashka, *Co-President*
Michael Ohlstein, *Senior VP*
Michael Olsten, *Human Res Dir*
Dawn Stober, *Accounts Exec*
◆ **EMP:** 100
SQ FT: 62,000
SALES (est): 57.4MM **Privately Held**
SIC: 2321 2331 2361 Men's & boys' furnishings; T-shirts & tops, women's: made from purchased materials; shirts, women's & juniors': made from purchased materials; t-shirts & tops: girls', children's & infants'; shirts: girls', children's & infants'

(G-5662)
BOWE INDUSTRIES INC
8836 77th Ave (11385-7826)
PHONE.................................718 441-6464
Michael Ohlsten, *Branch Mgr*
EMP: 75
SALES (corp-wide): 57.4MM **Privately Held**
SIC: 2321 Men's & boys' furnishings
PA: Bowe Industries Inc.
8836 77th Ave
Glendale NY 11385
718 441-6464

(G-5663)
C F PETERS CORP
7030 80th St Ste 2 (11385-7735)
PHONE.................................718 416-7800
Dr Don Gillespie, *Vice Pres*
Richie Anichiarico, *Warehouse Mgr*
Shili Uddin, *Finance*
Frank Billack, *Sales Dir*
Martin Gonzalez, *Sales Staff*
▲ **EMP:** 27 **EST:** 1948
SQ FT: 7,200
SALES (est): 3.3MM **Privately Held**
WEB: www.petersedition.com
SIC: 2741 Music book & sheet music publishing

(G-5664)
COSTUME CULTURE BY FRANCO LLC
7017 83rd St (11385-7716)
PHONE.................................718 821-7100
Michelle Umano, *CEO*
▲ **EMP:** 1
SALES (est): 1.2MM **Privately Held**
SIC: 2389 Costumes

(G-5665)
COTTON EMPORIUM INC (PA)
8000 Cooper Ave (11385-7739)
PHONE.................................718 894-3365
Josef Moshevili, *President*
Nana Moshevili, *Vice Pres*
Mzia Krikhely, *Bookkeeper*
▲ **EMP:** 8
SQ FT: 8,500
SALES (est): 2.6MM **Privately Held**
SIC: 2329 Sweaters & sweater jackets: men's & boys'

(G-5666)
DISPLAYS & BEYOND INC
8816 77th Ave (11385-7826)
PHONE.................................718 805-7786
Dilawar Syed, *President*
EMP: 12
SALES (est): 2MM **Privately Held**
SIC: 2653 3993 5999 Display items, corrugated: made from purchased materials; signs & advertising specialties; trophies & plaques; banners, flags, decals & posters

(G-5667)
FM BRUSH CO INC
7002 72nd Pl (11385-7307)
PHONE.................................718 821-5939
Fred J Mink Jr, *Ch of Bd*
Beatrice Mink, *Corp Secy*
Jeffrey A Mink, *Vice Pres*
Linda Mayer, *Human Res Mgr*
Veronica Towney, *Mktg Dir*
▲ **EMP:** 120 **EST:** 1929
SQ FT: 20,000
SALES (est): 16.2MM **Privately Held**
WEB: www.fmbrush.com
SIC: 3991 Brushes, household or industrial

(G-5668)
FRED M VELEPEC CO INC
7172 70th St (11385-7246)
PHONE.................................718 821-6636
Fax: 718 821-5874
Fredric A Velepec, *President*
Gerda Velepec, *Vice Pres*
Dolores Quigley, *Office Mgr*
Terry Reilly, *Manager*
EMP: 21 **EST:** 1942
SQ FT: 6,000
SALES (est): 1.8MM **Privately Held**
SIC: 3545 Tools & accessories for machine tools

(G-5669)
GLENDALE ARCHITECTURAL WD PDTS
Also Called: Glendale Products
7102 80th St (11385-7715)
PHONE.................................718 326-2700
Fax: 718 894-2528
Vincenzo Alcamo, *President*
Ben Alcamo, *Purchasing*
Ben Larocca, *CTO*
EMP: 30
SALES (est): 4.2MM **Privately Held**
WEB: www.glendalecustomfurniture.com
SIC: 2521 2511 Wood office furniture; wood household furniture

(G-5670)
GLENRIDGE FABRICATORS INC
7945 77th Ave (11385-7522)
PHONE.................................718 456-2297
Fax: 718 386-1286
Albert Putre, *Ch of Bd*
Kampta Persaud, *Vice Pres*
Marilyn White, *Manager*
EMP: 10
SQ FT: 36,000
SALES (est): 2.1MM **Privately Held**
SIC: 3441 3443 1799 Fabricated structural metal; weldments; welding on site

(G-5671)
HANSEL N GRETEL BRAND INC
7936 Cooper Ave (11385-7530)
P.O. Box 60452, Florence MA (01062-0452)
PHONE.................................718 326-0041
Fax: 718 326-2069
Milton Rattner, *President*
Ruth Rattner, *Exec VP*
Eddie Olkano, *Manager*
Robert Shapiro, *Admin Sec*
▲ **EMP:** 150
SQ FT: 30,000
SALES (est): 19.6MM **Privately Held**
SIC: 2013 2015 Prepared pork products from purchased pork; prepared beef products from purchased beef; turkey processing & slaughtering

(G-5672)
LEA APPAREL INC
6126 Cooper Ave (11385-6115)
PHONE.................................718 418-2800
Fax: 718 418-2805
Leonard Novick, *President*
Ellen Novick, *Vice Pres*
Andrew Porter, *Manager*
EMP: 5
SQ FT: 8,000
SALES: 5MM **Privately Held**
SIC: 2339 Sportswear, women's

(G-5673)
MARK I PUBLICATIONS INC
Also Called: Queens Chronicle
7119 80th St Ste 8201 (11385-7733)
P.O. Box 747769, Rego Park (11374-7769)
PHONE.................................718 205-8000
Fax: 718 205-0150
Mark Wilder, *President*
Raymond G Sito, *General Mgr*
Betty M Cooney, *Editor*
Rebecca Cooney, *Counsel*
Stanley Merzon, *Vice Pres*
EMP: 50
SQ FT: 1,800
SALES (est): 3.2MM **Privately Held**
WEB: www.qchron.com
SIC: 2711 Newspapers

(G-5674)
NEW DAY WOODWORK INC
Also Called: John Bossone
8861 76th Ave (11385-7910)
PHONE.................................718 275-1721
Fax: 718 275-3220
Jay Levtow, *President*
EMP: 30
SQ FT: 14,000
SALES (est): 2.5MM **Privately Held**
WEB: www.newdaywoodwork.com
SIC: 2511 Wood household furniture

(G-5675)
NORTH STAR KNITTING MILLS INC
7030 80th St (11385-7737)
PHONE.................................718 894-4848
Fax: 718 894-4884
Todor Stefan, *President*
Marian Stefan, *Admin Sec*
EMP: 7
SQ FT: 12,500
SALES: 900K **Privately Held**
SIC: 2253 5199 Knit outerwear mills; knit goods

(G-5676)
REGENT PAINTS INC
6944 Cooper Ave (11385-7103)
PHONE.................................917 966-6011
Huzaifa Matawala, *President*
Fatema Matawala, *Vice Pres*
EMP: 5
SALES (est): 229.7K **Privately Held**
SIC: 2851 5198 Paints & allied products; paints, varnishes & supplies

(G-5677)
ROLLING GATE SUPPLY CORP
7919 Cypress Ave (11385-6038)
PHONE.................................718 366-5258
Miguel Molinare, *President*
▲ **EMP:** 9
SALES (est): 970K **Privately Held**
SIC: 3315 Steel wire & related products

(G-5678)
SCHINDLER ELEVATOR CORPORATION
8400 72nd Dr Ste 2 (11385-7900)
PHONE.................................718 417-3131
Linda Marchese, *Manager*
EMP: 110
SALES (corp-wide): 9.5B **Privately Held**
WEB: www.us.schindler.com
SIC: 3534 Elevators & equipment
HQ: Schindler Elevator Corporation
20 Whippany Rd
Morristown NJ 07960
973 397-6500

(G-5679)
SMART USA INC
6907 69th Pl (11385-6639)
PHONE.................................718 416-4400
Jim Soleiman, *Ch of Bd*
Yosi Soleimany, *Vice Pres*
EMP: 20
SALES (est): 4MM **Privately Held**
SIC: 2671 3365 Thermoplastic coated paper for packaging; cooking/kitchen utensils, cast aluminum

(G-5680)
SUPERIOR DECORATORS INC
Also Called: Superior Plastic Slipcovers
7416 Cypress Hills St (11385-6946)
PHONE.................................718 381-4793
Fax: 718 381-2500
Peter Cassar, *Owner*
Charlie Heavens, *Manager*
EMP: 16
SQ FT: 3,500
SALES (est): 710K **Privately Held**
SIC: 2392 Slipcovers: made of fabric, plastic etc.

(G-5681)
T & R KNITTING MILLS INC (PA)
8000 Cooper Ave Ste 6 (11385-7734)
PHONE.................................718 497-4017
Rocco Marini, *President*
Christine Fumei, *Prdtn Mgr*
Carol Schultz, *CFO*
▲ **EMP:** 24
SQ FT: 100,000
SALES: 20MM **Privately Held**
SIC: 2253 Sweaters & sweater coats, knit

Glenmont
Albany County

(G-5682)
AIR PRODUCTS AND CHEMICALS INC
461 River Rd (12077-4307)
PHONE.................................518 463-4273
Micheal Joczak, *Branch Mgr*
Scott Loupe, *Manager*
EMP: 53
SQ FT: 8,624
SALES (corp-wide): 9.5B **Publicly Held**
WEB: www.airproducts.com
SIC: 2813 Oxygen, compressed or liquefied
PA: Air Products And Chemicals, Inc.
7201 Hamilton Blvd
Allentown PA 18195
610 481-4911

(G-5683)
DEMARTINI OIL EQUIPMENT SVC
214 River Rd (12077-4604)
P.O. Box 9 (12077-0009)
PHONE.................................518 463-5752
Fax: 518 426-4240
James Demartini, *President*
James De Martini, *President*
Marianne Carner, *Vice Pres*
Mathew Carner, *Treasurer*
EMP: 6 **EST:** 1945
SQ FT: 4,000
SALES (est): 1MM **Privately Held**
SIC: 3713 7699 Truck bodies (motor vehicles); industrial machinery & equipment repair

(G-5684)
INNOVATIVE MUNICIPAL PDTS US
Also Called: Innovative Surface Solutions
454 River Rd (12077-4306)
PHONE.................................800 387-5777
Greg Baun, *President*
▲ **EMP:** 30
SALES: 20MM
SALES (corp-wide): 4.1MM **Privately Held**
SIC: 2819 Industrial inorganic chemicals
HQ: Innovative Building Products Inc
78 Orchard Rd
Ajax ON L1S 6
905 427-0318

Glens Falls
Warren County

(G-5685)
AMES GOLDSMITH CORP
21 Rogers St (12801-3803)
PHONE.................................518 792-7435
Fax: 518 792-1034

Glens Falls - Warren County (G-5686)

Bill Hamelin, *President*
Mike Delsignore, *General Mgr*
Frank Barber, *Vice Pres*
Tim Russell, *Plant Mgr*
Michelle Sellick, *Purchasing*
EMP: 16
SALES (corp-wide): 35.6MM **Privately Held**
SIC: 3399 2819 3339 2869 Silver powder; flakes, metal; catalysts, chemical; primary nonferrous metals; industrial organic chemicals
PA: Ames Goldsmith Corp.
50 Harrison Ave
South Glens Falls NY 12803
518 792-5808

(G-5686)
ANDRITZ INC
Also Called: Ahlstrom Kamyr
13 Pruyns Island Dr (12801-4706)
PHONE..................518 745-2988
Michael Kingsley, *Manager*
EMP: 20
SALES (corp-wide): 6.3B **Privately Held**
SIC: 2611 Pulp manufactured from waste or recycled paper
HQ: Andritz Inc.
500 Technology Dr
Canonsburg PA 15317
724 597-7801

(G-5687)
ANGIODYNAMICS INC
10 Glens Fls Technical Pa (12801)
PHONE..................518 792-4112
Mark Frost, *President*
Myles Donnelly, *Info Tech Mgr*
EMP: 275
SALES (corp-wide): 349.6MM **Publicly Held**
SIC: 3841 Surgical & medical instruments
PA: Angiodynamics, Inc.
14 Plaza Dr
Latham NY 12110
518 795-1400

(G-5688)
BARTON MINES COMPANY LLC (PA)
Also Called: Barton International
6 Warren St (12801-4531)
PHONE..................518 798-5462
Fax: 518 798-5728
Charles Bracken Jr, *Ch of Bd*
William Flint, *President*
Rick Strain, *Plant Mgr*
John Swertner, *Sls & Mktg Exec*
Barton Mines, *CFO*
◆ **EMP:** 200 **EST:** 1996
SQ FT: 5,000
SALES (est): 57.6MM **Privately Held**
WEB: www.barton.com
SIC: 1499 3291 5085 Garnet mining; coated abrasive products; abrasives

(G-5689)
BRENNANS QUICK PRINT INC
Also Called: Bqp
6 Collins Dr (12804-1493)
P.O. Box 4221, Queensbury (12804-0221)
PHONE..................518 793-4999
Fax: 518 793-5075
Sue Brennan, *President*
EMP: 6
SALES (est): 685.1K **Privately Held**
WEB: www.bqprinting.com
SIC: 2752 Commercial printing, offset

(G-5690)
C R BARD INC
Glens Falls Manufacturing
289 Bay Rd (12804-2015)
PHONE..................518 793-2531
Ron Green, *Safety Mgr*
Tammy Monahan, *Purchasing*
Anne Linehan, *Engineer*
Mike Lockhart, *Engineer*
Marna Moore, *Human Res Dir*
EMP: 960
SALES (corp-wide): 3.7B **Publicly Held**
WEB: www.crbard.com
SIC: 3841 3845 Surgical & medical instruments; electromedical equipment
PA: C. R. Bard, Inc.
730 Central Ave
New Providence NJ 07974
908 277-8000

(G-5691)
CONVERTER DESIGN INC (PA)
25 Murdock Ave (12801-2456)
PHONE..................518 745-7138
Jim Wood, *President*
EMP: 1
SALES: 1.2MM **Privately Held**
SIC: 3599 Custom machinery

(G-5692)
COOPERS CAVE ALE CO S-CORP
2 Sagamore St (12801-3179)
PHONE..................518 792-0007
Edward Bethel, *Partner*
Patricia Bethel, *Partner*
EMP: 15 **EST:** 1999
SALES (est): 2.1MM **Privately Held**
WEB: www.cooperscaveale.com
SIC: 2082 Malt beverages

(G-5693)
DOHENY NICE AND EASY
Also Called: Doheny's Mobil
150 Broad St (12801-4253)
PHONE..................518 793-1733
EMP: 8
SALES (est): 380K **Privately Held**
SIC: 2086 Mfg Bottled/Canned Soft Drinks

(G-5694)
ERBESSD RELIABILITY LLC
Also Called: Erbessd Reliability Instrs
2c Glens Falls Tech Park (12801-3864)
PHONE..................518 874-2700
Michael Howard, *President*
EMP: 27
SALES (est): 1.3MM **Privately Held**
SIC: 3829 Measuring & controlling devices

(G-5695)
FLOMATIC CORPORATION
Also Called: Flomatic Valves
15 Pruyns Island Dr (12801-4706)
PHONE..................518 761-9797
Fax: 518 761-9798
Bo Andersson, *President*
Nick Farrrara, *Vice Pres*
Mark Girard, *Plant Mgr*
George Swenson, *Research*
Chris Bauder, *Engineer*
◆ **EMP:** 50
SQ FT: 50,000
SALES (est): 12.7MM
SALES (corp-wide): 11.5MM **Privately Held**
WEB: www.flomatic.com
SIC: 3494 3491 Valves & pipe fittings; water works valves
HQ: Boshart Industries Inc
25 Whaley Ave
Milverton ON N0K 1
519 595-4444

(G-5696)
GLENS FALLS NEWSPAPERS INC
76 Lawrence St (12801-3741)
P.O. Box 2157 (12801-2157)
PHONE..................518 792-3131
James Marshall, *Principal*
EMP: 6
SALES (est): 358K **Privately Held**
SIC: 2711 Newspapers, publishing & printing

(G-5697)
GLENS FALLS PRINTING LLC
51 Hudson Ave (12801-4347)
PHONE..................518 793-0555
Fax: 518 793-8624
George Beyerbach,
Barbara Beyerbach,
Robert Beyerbach,
EMP: 12 **EST:** 1966
SQ FT: 4,800
SALES (est): 2.6MM **Privately Held**
SIC: 2752 Commercial printing, offset

(G-5698)
GREAT PACIFIC ENTPS US INC (DH)
Also Called: Genpak
68 Warren St (12801-4530)
P.O. Box 727 (12801-0727)
PHONE..................518 761-2593
Michael Korenberg, *CEO*
James Pattison, *Ch of Bd*
James Reilly, *Chairman*
Nick Geer, *Vice Pres*
Mike Linacre, *Controller*
▲ **EMP:** 45
SQ FT: 36,000
SALES (est): 1.1B
SALES (corp-wide): 12B **Privately Held**
SIC: 3089 Plastic containers, except foam
HQ: Great Pacific Enterprises Inc
1067 Cordova St W Unit 1800
Vancouver BC V6C 1
604 688-6764

(G-5699)
JUST BEVERAGES LLC
31 Broad St (12801-4301)
P.O. Box 4392, Queensbury (12804-0392)
PHONE..................480 388-1133
Jim Jacobs, *CFO*
EMP: 10
SALES (est): 1.1MM **Privately Held**
SIC: 2086 Mineral water, carbonated: packaged in cans, bottles, etc.

(G-5700)
KADANT INC
436 Quaker Rd (12804-1535)
PHONE..................518 793-8801
Steve Fielding, *Opers Staff*
Eric Gerrebos, *Chief Engr*
Jeff Bachand, *Branch Mgr*
Thomas Kozloski, *Associate*
EMP: 12
SALES (corp-wide): 414.1MM **Publicly Held**
SIC: 3554 Paper industries machinery
PA: Kadant Inc.
1 Technology Park Dr # 210
Westford MA 01886
978 776-2000

(G-5701)
KMA CORPORATION
153 Maple St Ste 5 (12801-3796)
PHONE..................518 743-1330
Fax: 518 743-9450
Eric Ukauf, *President*
Joe Congel, *Office Mgr*
▲ **EMP:** 9
SALES (est): 1.1MM **Privately Held**
SIC: 3599 Machine & other job shop work

(G-5702)
LEE ENTERPRISES INCORPORATED
Also Called: Post Star
76 Lawrence St (12801-3741)
P.O. Box 2157 (12801-2157)
PHONE..................518 792-3131
Fax: 518 761-1255
Terry Doomes, *President*
Greg Brownell, *Editor*
Lisa Malan, *Editor*
Ken Pingley, *Editor*
Rona Rahlf, *Editor*
EMP: 160
SQ FT: 5,000
SALES (est): 10.3MM
SALES (corp-wide): 614.3MM **Publicly Held**
SIC: 2711 Newspapers: publishing only, not printed on site
HQ: Lee Publications, Inc.
201 N Harrison St Ste 600
Davenport IA 52801
563 383-2100

(G-5703)
LEHIGH CEMENT COMPANY (DH)
Also Called: Lehigh Northeast Cement
313 Warren St (12801-3820)
P.O. Box 440 (12801-0440)
PHONE..................518 792-1137
Helmut S Erhard, *Ch of Bd*
Dan Harrington, *President*
Vince Fischer, *Foreman/Supr*
Karen Toorop, *Buyer*
Mark Trybendis, *QC Mgr*
▲ **EMP:** 122
SQ FT: 20,000
SALES (est): 22.6MM
SALES (corp-wide): 247.4MM **Privately Held**
WEB: www.gfcement.com
SIC: 3241 Portland cement; masonry cement
HQ: Dyckerhoff Gmbh
Biebricher Str. 68
Wiesbaden 65203
611 676-0

(G-5704)
MEDTEK LIGHTING CORPORATION (PA)
Also Called: Phototherapeutix
206 Glen St Ste 5 (12801-3585)
PHONE..................518 745-7264
Fax: 518 745-1402
Jack Springer, *President*
Anthony Ianniello, *Vice Pres*
Emmett Haydel, *Sales Mgr*
Jerri Corlew, *Executive Asst*
EMP: 4
SQ FT: 9,000
SALES (est): 3.3MM **Privately Held**
WEB: www.uvbiotek.com
SIC: 3648 Sun tanning equipment, incl. tanning beds

(G-5705)
MILLER MECHANICAL SERVICES INC
55-57 Walnut St (12801)
P.O. Box 504 (12801-0504)
PHONE..................518 792-0430
Fax: 518 792-2956
Elizabeth Miller, *President*
Ken Lofton, *Superintendent*
Ken Pagels, *Opers Staff*
Frank Burkhardt, *Engineer*
Ted Schfelt, *Manager*
EMP: 20
SQ FT: 2,240
SALES (est): 5.6MM **Privately Held**
WEB: www.millermech.com
SIC: 3542 Machine tools, metal forming type

(G-5706)
NATIONAL VAC ENVMTL SVCS CORP
80 Park Rd (12804-7614)
PHONE..................518 743-0563
Fax: 518 743-0463
Roger Letendre, *Branch Mgr*
EMP: 20
SALES (corp-wide): 9.6MM **Privately Held**
SIC: 3589 Vacuum cleaners & sweepers, electric: industrial
PA: National Vacuum Environmental Services Corp.
408 47th St
Niagara Falls NY 14304
716 773-1167

(G-5707)
NAVILYST MEDICAL INC
10 Glens Fls Technical Pa (12801)
PHONE..................800 833-9973
Fax: 518 742-4397
▲ **EMP:** 670
SALES (est): 150.8MM
SALES (corp-wide): 349.6MM **Publicly Held**
SIC: 3841 Surgical & medical instruments
PA: Angiodynamics, Inc.
14 Plaza Dr
Latham NY 12110
518 795-1400

(G-5708)
OAK LONE PUBLISHING CO INC
Also Called: Chronicle, The
15 Ridge St (12801-3608)
P.O. Box 153 (12801-0153)
PHONE..................518 792-1126
Fax: 518 793-1587
Mark Frost, *President*
Gordon Woodworth, *Editor*
Patricia Maddock, *Vice Pres*

GEOGRAPHIC SECTION

Teresa Hackett, *Office Mgr*
EMP: 27
SQ FT: 5,280
SALES (est): 1.8MM **Privately Held**
WEB: www.loneoak.com
SIC: 2711 Newspapers: publishing only, not printed on site

(G-5709)
PACTIV CORPORATION
6 Haskell Ave (12801-3854)
P.O. Box 148 (12801-0148)
PHONE..........................518 743-3100
Christopher G Angus, *Vice Pres*
Gene Tomczak, *CTO*
Stan Lucas, *Info Tech Dir*
EMP: 207 **Privately Held**
WEB: www.pactiv.com
SIC: 3089 Thermoformed finished plastic products
HQ: Pactiv Llc
  1900 W Field Ct
  Lake Forest IL 60045
  847 482-2000

(G-5710)
PACTIV LLC
18 Peck Ave (12801-3833)
PHONE..........................518 793-2524
Gene Tomzzac, *Plant Mgr*
Mitch Brehm, *Plant Mgr*
Paul Ostwald, *Manager*
Brian Williams, *MIS Dir*
EMP: 110 **Privately Held**
WEB: www.pactiv.com
SIC: 2673 3497 3089 Food storage & trash bags (plastic); trash bags (plastic film): made from purchased materials; food storage & frozen food bags, plastic; metal foil & leaf; plastic containers, except foam; plastic kitchenware, tableware & houseware
HQ: Pactiv Llc
  1900 W Field Ct
  Lake Forest IL 60045
  847 482-2000

(G-5711)
PRECISION EXTRUSION INC
12 Glens Fls Technical Pa (12801)
PHONE..........................518 792-1199
Fax: 518 792-3805
Michael J Badera, *Ch of Bd*
Leta Beecher, *Opers Staff*
Barbara Samiley, *Human Resources*
EMP: 35
SQ FT: 15,000
SALES (est): 5.2MM
SALES (corp-wide): 1.3B **Privately Held**
WEB: www.precisionextrusion.com
SIC: 3061 Medical & surgical rubber tubing (extruded & lathe-cut)
HQ: Pexco Llc
  2500 Northwinds Pkwy # 472
  Alpharetta GA 30009
  404 564-8560

(G-5712)
PREGIS LLC
18 Peck Ave (12801-3833)
P.O. Box 148 (12801-0148)
PHONE..........................518 743-3100
Barbara Blanchette, *Opers Mgr*
Sharon Pugh, *Sales Associate*
Gene Pomczak, *Manager*
Jennifer Lawrence, *Director*
EMP: 65
SALES (corp-wide): 5.6B **Privately Held**
SIC: 2671 Plastic film, coated or laminated for packaging
HQ: Pregis Llc
  1650 Lake Cook Rd Ste 400
  Deerfield IL 60015
  847 597-9330

(G-5713)
UMICORE TECHNICAL MATERIALS
9 Pruyns Island Dr (12801-4706)
PHONE..........................518 792-7700
Marc Grynberg, *CEO*
Jens-Uwe Heitsch, *General Mgr*
Martin Boarder, *Chairman*
Stephan Csoma, *Exec VP*
Filip Platteeuw, *CFO*
▲ **EMP:** 110

SALES (est): 21.6MM
SALES (corp-wide): 2.4B **Privately Held**
SIC: 3339 Silver refining (primary)
HQ: Umicore Usa Inc.
  3600 Glenwood Ave Ste 250
  Raleigh NC 27612

(G-5714)
UMICORE USA INC
9 Pruyns Island Dr (12801-4706)
PHONE..........................919 874-7171
Allen Molvar, *Branch Mgr*
EMP: 25
SALES (corp-wide): 2.4B **Privately Held**
SIC: 3339 5051 5052 5169 Cobalt refining (primary); nonferrous metal sheets, bars, rods, etc.; metallic ores; industrial chemicals; metal scrap & waste materials
HQ: Umicore Usa Inc.
  3600 Glenwood Ave Ste 250
  Raleigh NC 27612

(G-5715)
VIBRO-LASER INSTRS CORP LLC
2c Glens Falls Tech Park (12801-3864)
PHONE..........................518 874-2700
Megh McCane Howard,
EMP: 5
SALES (est): 258.6K **Privately Held**
SIC: 3823 Analyzers, industrial process type

Glenville
Schenectady County

(G-5716)
DSM NUTRITIONAL PRODUCTS LLC
Fortitech
300 Tech Park (12302-7107)
PHONE..........................518 372-5155
Chris Nulmerrick, *Manager*
EMP: 152
SALES (corp-wide): 8.3B **Privately Held**
SIC: 2834 3295 2087 Vitamin, nutrient & hematinic preparations for human use; vitamin preparations; minerals, ground or treated; flavoring extracts & syrups
HQ: Dsm Nutritional Products, Llc
  45 Waterview Blvd
  Parsippany NJ 07054
  800 526-0189

(G-5717)
INTERNATIONAL PAPER COMPANY
803 Corporation Park (12302-1057)
PHONE..........................518 372-6461
EMP: 92
SALES (corp-wide): 21B **Publicly Held**
WEB: www.tin.com
SIC: 2653 Corrugated & solid fiber boxes
PA: International Paper Company
  6400 Poplar Ave
  Memphis TN 38197
  901 419-9000

Glenwood
Erie County

(G-5718)
LK INDUSTRIES INC
9731 Center St (14069-9611)
PHONE..........................716 941-9202
Larry Krzeminski, *President*
John Brennan, *Manager*
EMP: 5
SQ FT: 3,000
SALES: 600K **Privately Held**
SIC: 3541 Machine tools, metal cutting type

Gloversville
Fulton County

(G-5719)
ADIRONDACK STAINED GLASS WORKS
29 W Fulton St Ste 6 (12078-2937)
PHONE..........................518 725-0387
Fax: 518 725-0384
Donald Dwyer, *President*
Brenda Dwyer, *Treasurer*
Patrick Duell, *Admin Sec*
EMP: 6
SQ FT: 9,600
SALES: 275K **Privately Held**
SIC: 3231 Stained glass: made from purchased glass

(G-5720)
AMERICAN TARGET MARKETING INC
11 Cayadutta St (12078-3816)
PHONE..........................518 725-4369
Richard Denero, *President*
Al Parillo, *Treasurer*
EMP: 31
SQ FT: 18,000
SALES: 700K **Privately Held**
SIC: 3151 Leather gloves & mittens

(G-5721)
ANDROME LEATHER INC
21 Foster St (12078-1600)
P.O. Box 826 (12078-0826)
PHONE..........................518 773-7945
Fax: 518 773-7942
Frank A Garguilo, *President*
Christopher Garguilo, *Vice Pres*
Richard Mancini, *Executive*
Lisa Garguilo, *Admin Sec*
▲ **EMP:** 15
SQ FT: 10,000
SALES (est): 1.9MM **Privately Held**
SIC: 3111 2843 Finishing of leather; leather finishing agents

(G-5722)
AVANTI CONTROL SYSTEMS INC
1 Hamilton St Fl 2 (12078-2321)
P.O. Box 113 (12078-0113)
PHONE..........................518 921-4368
Timothy M Tesiero, *President*
Annette Greg, *Manager*
EMP: 6
SALES (est): 1.3MM **Privately Held**
SIC: 3613 8711 Control panels, electric; engineering services

(G-5723)
BEEBIE PRINTING & ART AGCY INC
40 E Pine St (12078-4339)
P.O. Box 1277 (12078-0011)
PHONE..........................518 725-4528
Fax: 518 773-3855
Craig J Beebie, *President*
EMP: 7
SQ FT: 10,000
SALES (est): 560K **Privately Held**
SIC: 2759 7336 Commercial printing; graphic arts & related design

(G-5724)
COLONIAL TANNING CORPORATION (PA)
8 Wilson St 810 (12078-1500)
P.O. Box 1068 (12078-0009)
PHONE..........................518 725-7171
Fax: 518 773-8195
William Studenic, *President*
Matthew Smrtic, *General Mgr*
George Bradt, *Opers Mgr*
Leslie Smrtic, *Controller*
▲ **EMP:** 7 **EST:** 1971
SQ FT: 50,000
SALES (est): 1.1MM **Privately Held**
SIC: 3111 Tanneries, leather

(G-5725)
CURTIN-HEBERT CO INC
Also Called: Curtin-Hebert Machines
11 Forest St (12078-3999)
P.O. Box 511 (12078-0005)
PHONE..........................518 725-7157
Fax: 518 773-3805
James Curtin, *Ch of Bd*
George Wells, *Office Mgr*
Bruce Anderson, *Director*
EMP: 11 **EST:** 1908
SQ FT: 11,000
SALES (est): 1.3MM **Privately Held**
WEB: www.curtinhebert.com
SIC: 3559 Rubber working machinery, including tires; leather working machinery; metal pickling equipment

(G-5726)
FOWNES BROTHERS & CO INC
204 County Highway 157 (12078-6043)
PHONE..........................518 752-4411
Rennie Sanges, *Branch Mgr*
EMP: 30
SALES (corp-wide): 67.4MM **Privately Held**
SIC: 3151 2381 5136 5137 Gloves, leather: dress or semidress; gloves, woven or knit: made from purchased materials; gloves, men's & boys'; gloves, women's & children's; gloves, sport & athletic: boxing, handball, etc.
PA: Fownes Brothers & Co Inc
  16 E 34th St Fl 5
  New York NY 10016
  212 683-0150

(G-5727)
GREENFIBER ALBANY INC
Also Called: US Greenfiber
210 County Highway 102 (12078-7023)
PHONE..........................518 842-1470
Dennis Barrineau, *Ch of Bd*
Richard Linek, *Plant Mgr*
EMP: 51 **EST:** 1986
SALES (est): 15.6MM **Privately Held**
SIC: 2679 Building, insulating & packaging paperboard
HQ: Us Greenfiber, Llc
  5500 77 Center Dr Ste 100
  Charlotte NC 28217

(G-5728)
HALO OPTICAL PRODUCTS INC
9 Phair St Ste 1 (12078-4398)
P.O. Box 1369 (12078-0011)
PHONE..........................518 773-4256
Fax: 518 773-8992
Peter Leonardi, *President*
EMP: 65 **EST:** 1964
SQ FT: 32,000
SALES (est): 8.5MM **Privately Held**
SIC: 3827 Optical instruments & apparatus

(G-5729)
HAWKINS FABRICS INC (PA)
111 Woodside Ave Ste 1 (12078-2744)
P.O. Box 351 (12078-0351)
PHONE..........................518 773-9550
James Batty, *President*
Ted Sweet, *Controller*
▲ **EMP:** 38
SQ FT: 50,000
SALES (est): 14.9MM **Privately Held**
WEB: www.safeind.com
SIC: 2259 2231 Gloves, knit, except dress & semidress gloves; mittens, knit; work gloves, knit; broadwoven fabric mills, wool

(G-5730)
HOHENFORST SPLITTING CO INC
152 W Fulton St (12078-2799)
PHONE..........................518 725-0012
Robert Hohenforst, *President*
Loretta Hohenforst, *Vice Pres*
Richard Hohenforst, *Manager*
EMP: 6 **EST:** 1965
SQ FT: 6,000
SALES (est): 780.2K **Privately Held**
SIC: 3111 Cutting of leather

Gloversville - Fulton County (G-5731)

(G-5731)
HUDSON DYING & FINISHING LLC
68 Harrison St (12078-4732)
PHONE...................518 752-4389
Mark Shore,
EMP: 30 EST: 2009
SALES (est): 2MM Privately Held
SIC: 2389 Men's miscellaneous accessories

(G-5732)
LITCHFIELD FABRICS OF NC (PA)
111 Woodside Ave (12078-2741)
PHONE...................518 773-9500
William Conroy, President
Dale Steenburgh, CFO
Morris Evans, Treasurer
EMP: 3
SQ FT: 2,000
SALES (est): 3.2MM Privately Held
SIC: 2258 Tricot fabrics

(G-5733)
MOHAWK CABINET COMPANY INC
137 E State St (12078-1200)
PHONE...................518 725-0645
James Law, President
EMP: 12
SALES (est): 2.1MM Privately Held
SIC: 3585 Cabinets, show & display, refrigerated

(G-5734)
PROTECH (LLC)
Also Called: Pro-TEC V I P
11 Cayadutta St (12078-3816)
PHONE...................518 725-7785
Fax: 518 725-7783
Al Parillo, Mng Member
Richard Denero,
EMP: 26
SALES (est): 2.3MM Privately Held
SIC: 3151 5699 Gloves, leather: work; work clothing

(G-5735)
SAMCO LLC
122 S Main St Ste 2 (12078-3842)
PHONE...................518 725-4705
Fax: 518 725-4705
Tobin Cash, Accountant
Richard Warner,
EMP: 50
SQ FT: 30,000
SALES (est): 4.6MM Privately Held
SIC: 3151 Leather gloves & mittens; gloves, leather: dress or semidress; gloves, leather: work

(G-5736)
SOMERSET DYEING & FINISHING
68 Harrison St (12078-4732)
P.O. Box 1189 (12078-0010)
PHONE...................518 773-7383
Edward Falk, Corp Secy
EMP: 42
SQ FT: 24,000
SALES: 5.5MM Privately Held
SIC: 2258 Dyeing & finishing lace goods & warp knit fabric

(G-5737)
SOMERSET INDUSTRIES INC (PA)
Also Called: CJ Indstries A Div Smrset Inds
68 Harrison St (12078-4732)
P.O. Box 1189 (12078-0010)
PHONE...................518 773-7383
Fax: 518 773-7383
Ed Falk, CEO
Bruce Dingman, Controller
▲ EMP: 32
SQ FT: 35,000
SALES (est): 12.8MM Privately Held
WEB: www.somersetindustries.com
SIC: 2258 Lace & warp knit fabric mills

(G-5738)
STEPHEN MILLER GEN CONTRS INC
Also Called: Miller's Ready Mix
301 Riceville Rd (12078-6958)
P.O. Box 291, Mayfield (12117-0291)
PHONE...................518 661-5601
Fax: 518 661-6264
Stephen Miller, CEO
Lynn Holland, Bookkeeper
Patricia Miller, Manager
Trish Miller, Officer
EMP: 25 EST: 1971
SQ FT: 640
SALES (est): 5.8MM Privately Held
SIC: 3273 1541 1761 1542 Ready-mixed concrete; industrial buildings, new construction; roofing, siding & sheet metal work; nonresidential construction

(G-5739)
TAYLOR MADE GROUP LLC (HQ)
66 Kingsboro Ave (12078-3415)
PHONE...................518 725-0681
Brian Castleman, Plant Engr
Mark Kenyon, Controller
Mike Oathout, Marketing Mgr
John Taylor, Mng Member
▲ EMP: 50
SQ FT: 5,000
SALES (est): 164.4MM
SALES (corp-wide): 230.5MM Privately Held
SIC: 3231 3429 Windshields, glass: made from purchased glass; marine hardware
PA: Taylor Made Group Holdings, Inc.
 66 Kingsboro Ave
 Gloversville NY 12078
 518 725-0681

(G-5740)
TAYLOR PRODUCTS INC (PA)
66 Kingsboro Ave (12078-3415)
P.O. Box 1190 (12078-0190)
PHONE...................518 773-9312
James W Taylor, Ch of Bd
Dennis F Flint, President
Cindy Walsh, Manager
▲ EMP: 2
SQ FT: 20,000
SALES (est): 5.4MM Privately Held
SIC: 3231 Tempered glass: made from purchased glass; safety glass: made from purchased glass

(G-5741)
TIC TAC TOES MFG CORP
1 Hamilton St (12078-2321)
P.O. Box 953 (12078-0953)
PHONE...................518 773-8187
Fax: 518 725-8116
Robert Winig, President
Ed Wager, Human Res Dir
Edward Wagar, Office Mgr
▲ EMP: 75
SQ FT: 75,000
SALES (est): 10MM Privately Held
WEB: www.tictactoes.com
SIC: 3143 3144 Men's footwear, except athletic; women's footwear, except athletic

(G-5742)
WADSWORTH LOGGING INC
3095 State Highway 30 (12078-7601)
P.O. Box 177, Northville (12134-0177)
PHONE...................518 863-6870
Stephen S Wadsworth, President
EMP: 10 EST: 1996
SALES (est): 910K Privately Held
SIC: 2411 Logging camps & contractors

(G-5743)
WASHBURNS DAIRY INC
145 N Main St (12078-3078)
P.O. Box 551 (12078-0005)
PHONE...................518 725-0629
Fax: 518 725-0098
Richard J Washburn, President
Alfred J Washburn, Corp Secy
Bill Washburn, Vice Pres
William Washburn, Vice Pres
EMP: 45
SQ FT: 6,000
SALES (est): 5.3MM Privately Held
SIC: 2024 5143 Ice cream & ice milk; ice cream & ices

(G-5744)
WILLIAM B COLLINS COMPANY (HQ)
Also Called: Leader Herald, The
8 E Fulton St (12078-3227)
PHONE...................518 773-8272
Fax: 518 725-3556
George Ogden Nutting, President
Steve Herron, Publisher
Patricia Older, Editor
Jason Subik, Editor
Paul Wager, Editor
EMP: 70 EST: 1961
SQ FT: 15,000
SALES (est): 8.9MM
SALES (corp-wide): 627.3MM Privately Held
WEB: www.lhprint.com
SIC: 2711 Newspapers, publishing & printing
PA: The Ogden Newspapers Inc
 1500 Main St
 Wheeling WV 26003
 304 233-0100

(G-5745)
WOOD & HYDE LEATHER CO INC
68 Wood St (12078-1695)
P.O. Box 786 (12078-0007)
PHONE...................518 725-7105
Fax: 518 725-5158
Randall Doerter, CEO
James Keiffer, President
Thomas Porter, CFO
Greg Patterson, Executive
◆ EMP: 30
SQ FT: 266,000
SALES (est): 3.5MM Privately Held
WEB: www.woodandhyde.com
SIC: 3111 Tanneries, leather

Goshen
Orange County

(G-5746)
BIMBO BAKERIES USA INC
Also Called: Stroehmann Bakeries 72
9 Police Dr (10924-6730)
PHONE...................845 294-5282
Fax: 845 294-0615
Phil Tobin, Manager
EMP: 19 Privately Held
SIC: 2051 5149 Breads, rolls & buns; groceries & related products
HQ: Bimbo Bakeries Usa, Inc
 255 Business Center Dr # 200
 Horsham PA 19044
 215 347-5500

(G-5747)
BLASER PRODUCTION INC
31 Hatfield Ln (10924-6712)
PHONE...................845 294-3200
Peter Blaser, Ch of Bd
Nick Blaser, Vice Pres
Doris Martini, Vice Pres
Judy Villiers, Accountant
▲ EMP: 11
SALES (est): 16.8MM Privately Held
WEB: www.blaser.com
SIC: 2992 Lubricating oils
HQ: Blaser Swisslube Holding Corp
 31 Hatfield Ln
 Goshen NY 10924

(G-5748)
BLASER SWISSLUBE HOLDING CORP (HQ)
31 Hatfield Ln (10924-6712)
PHONE...................845 294-3200
Fax: 914 428-1914
Peter Blaser, CEO
Ulrich Krahenbuhl, President
Bob Green, Area Mgr
Richard Surico, Vice Pres
Linda Aldorasi, Controller
◆ EMP: 17
SQ FT: 40,000
SALES (est): 84.3MM Privately Held
SIC: 2992 Lubricating oils & greases
PA: Koras Ag
 Winterseistrasse 22
 Hasle-RUegsau BE
 344 600-101

(G-5749)
FG GALASSI MOULDING CO INC
699 Pulaski Hwy (10924-6009)
PHONE...................845 258-2100
John Petromilli, President
Linda Petromilli, Marketing Staff
Alice Hicks, Manager
▲ EMP: 9
SQ FT: 11,000
SALES (est): 1MM Privately Held
WEB: www.fggalassi.com
SIC: 2499 Picture & mirror frames, wood

(G-5750)
JUNO CHEFS
Also Called: Milmar Food Group
1 6 1/2 Station Rd (10924-6723)
PHONE...................845 294-5400
Julius Spessot, President
Luisa Spessot, President
Roy Makinen, Exec VP
Rita Oconnor, Vice Pres
Barry Werk, Purch Dir
EMP: 65
SQ FT: 25,000
SALES (est): 12.7MM Privately Held
WEB: www.junofoundation.org
SIC: 2038 Breakfasts, frozen & packaged

(G-5751)
KONICA MNOLTA SUPS MFG USA INC
51 Hatfield Ln (10924-6712)
PHONE...................845 294-8400
Fax: 845 294-2689
Miyako Asai, President
Randy Jamerson, Production
Richard Shields, Production
Crysty Leininger, Engineer
John Oliva, Engineer
▲ EMP: 75
SQ FT: 88,039
SALES: 100MM
SALES (corp-wide): 8.4B Privately Held
WEB: www.konicabt.com
SIC: 3861 Toners, prepared photographic (not made in chemical plants)
HQ: Konica Minolta Holdings U.S.A. Inc.
 100 Williams Dr
 Ramsey NJ 07446
 201 825-4000

(G-5752)
MILMAR FOOD GROUP II LLC
1 6 1/2 Station Rd (10924-6777)
PHONE...................845 294-5400
Roy Makinen, Exec VP
Barry Luvsdiks, Purch Mgr
Judah Koolyk, MIS Dir
Martin Hoffman,
Marie Triantafillou, Executive Asst
▲ EMP: 250
SQ FT: 66,000
SALES (est): 64.8MM Privately Held
WEB: www.milmarfoodgroup.com
SIC: 2038 8748 Frozen specialties; business consulting

(G-5753)
SKIN ATELIER INC
Also Called: Skinprint
1997 Route 17m (10924-5229)
PHONE...................845 294-1202
Robert P Manzo, President
James Hannan, Vice Pres
Devon Houghtalin, Cust Mgr
▼ EMP: 10
SQ FT: 4,000
SALES (est): 1.9MM Privately Held
WEB: www.skinprint.com
SIC: 2844 Toilet preparations

(G-5754)
TILCON NEW YORK INC
Also Called: Goshen Quarry
2 Quarry Rd (10924-6045)
PHONE...................845 615-0216
Bob Portice, Manager
EMP: 63

SALES (corp-wide): 28.6B **Privately Held**
SIC: 1429 Dolomitic marble, crushed & broken-quarrying
HQ: Tilcon New York Inc.
162 Old Mill Rd
West Nyack NY 10994
845 358-4500

(G-5755)
VALUE FRAGRANCES & FLAVORS INC
7 Musket Ct (10924)
PHONE.....................845 294-5726
Fax: 845 294-7230
Alexander Vernon, *President*
Gerald Vernon, *CFO*
EMP: 18 **EST:** 2014
SQ FT: 30,000
SALES: 15MM **Privately Held**
SIC: 2869 Perfumes, flavorings & food additives

(G-5756)
VALUE FRAGRANCES INC
Also Called: Value Fragrances & Flavors
7 Musket Ct (10924)
P.O. Box 550 (10924-0550)
PHONE.....................845 294-5726
Debra Mitzner, *President*
B Mitzner, *Network Mgr*
▼ **EMP:** 9
SQ FT: 8,268
SALES (est): 1.7MM **Privately Held**
SIC: 2844 5122 Perfumes & colognes; perfumes

Gouverneur
St. Lawrence County

(G-5757)
BAKERY & COFFEE SHOP
274 W Main St (13642-1333)
PHONE.....................315 287-1829
John Yerdon, *Owner*
EMP: 5
SALES: 230K **Privately Held**
SIC: 2051 Bakery: wholesale or wholesale/retail combined

(G-5758)
CIVES CORPORATION
Also Called: Cives Steel Company Nthrn Div
8 Church St (13642-1416)
PHONE.....................315 287-2200
Fax: 315 287-4569
Richard Cowles, *Plant Supt*
Tyler Estabrooks, *Project Mgr*
Norm Newvine, *Purchasing*
Thomas M Farr, *Engineer*
Kim Pistolesi, *Accounting Dir*
EMP: 150
SALES (corp-wide): 453.1MM **Privately Held**
WEB: www.cives.com
SIC: 3441 1791 Fabricated structural metal; structural steel erection
PA: Cives Corporation
3700 Mansell Rd Ste 500
Alpharetta GA 30022
770 993-4424

(G-5759)
CLEARWATER PAPER CORPORATION
4921 State Highway 58 (13642-3207)
PHONE.....................315 287-1200
John E Keel, *Human Resources*
Jeremery Bartholomew, *Branch Mgr*
EMP: 85
SALES (corp-wide): 1.7B **Publicly Held**
SIC: 2621 Paper mills
PA: Clearwater Paper Corporation
601 W Riverside Ave # 1100
Spokane WA 99201
509 344-5900

(G-5760)
DUNN PAPER - NATURAL DAM INC
4921 St Rt 58 (13642-3207)
PHONE.....................315 287-1200
Brent Earnshaw, *President*
Greg Howe, *Vice Pres*
Jeremy Bartholomew, *Mill Mgr*
Darzy Fehnekenburger, *VP Sls/Mktg*
Al Magnan, *CFO*
EMP: 88
SALES: 48MM
SALES (corp-wide): 1.7B **Publicly Held**
SIC: 2621 Specialty papers
HQ: Dunn Paper, Inc.
218 Riverview St
Port Huron MI 48060
810 984-5521

(G-5761)
IMERYS USA INC
16a Main St Hailesboro Rd (13642-3360)
P.O. Box 479 (13642-0479)
PHONE.....................315 287-0780
Bob Snyder, *Branch Mgr*
EMP: 17
SQ FT: 30,000
SALES (corp-wide): 1.7MM **Privately Held**
SIC: 1411 Granite, dimension-quarrying; marble, dimension-quarrying
HQ: Imerys Usa, Inc.
100 Mansell Ct E Ste 300
Roswell GA 30076
770 645-3300

(G-5762)
RIVERSIDE IRON LLC
26 Water St (13642-1438)
PHONE.....................315 535-4864
Fax: 315 287-2250
Eric Tessmer, *President*
EMP: 12
SALES (est): 777.7K **Privately Held**
SIC: 3441 3446 3449 Dam gates, metal plate; architectural metalwork; miscellaneous metalwork

Gowanda
Cattaraugus County

(G-5763)
TTE FILTERS LLC (HQ)
1 Magnetic Pkwy (14070-1526)
P.O. Box 111 (14070-0111)
PHONE.....................716 532-2234
Claude Badawy, *President*
Thomas Norsen, *CFO*
EMP: 8
SALES: 1.5MM
SALES (corp-wide): 18.7MM **Privately Held**
SIC: 3677 Filtration devices, electronic
PA: Gowanda Holdings, Llc
1 Magnetic Pkwy
Gowanda NY 14070
716 532-2234

Grand Island
Erie County

(G-5764)
ABRAXIS BIOSCIENCE LLC
3159 Staley Rd (14072-2028)
PHONE.....................716 773-0800
Mark Forell, *Manager*
EMP: 7
SALES (corp-wide): 11.2B **Publicly Held**
SIC: 2834 Pharmaceutical preparations
HQ: Abraxis Bioscience, Llc
11755 Wilshire Blvd Fl 20
Los Angeles CA 90025

(G-5765)
ASI SIGN SYSTEMS INC
2957 Alt Blvd (14072-1220)
PHONE.....................716 775-0104
Fax: 716 775-3329
Robin Wright, *Controller*
Andy Bernatovicz, *Branch Mgr*
Laura Thorne, *Info Tech Mgr*
EMP: 7
SALES (corp-wide): 20.4MM **Privately Held**
SIC: 3993 Signs & advertising specialties
PA: Asi Sign Systems, Inc.
8181 Jetstar Dr Ste 110
Irving TX 75063
214 352-9140

(G-5766)
BAKED CUPCAKERY
1879 Whitehaven Rd (14072-1803)
PHONE.....................716 773-2050
EMP: 8
SALES (est): 755K **Privately Held**
SIC: 2051 Bread, cake & related products

(G-5767)
BAM ENTERPRISES INC (PA)
2937 Alt Blvd (14072-1285)
PHONE.....................716 773-7634
Gary Moose, *CEO*
Victor Alfiero, *CFO*
Linda Smth, *Administration*
EMP: 2
SQ FT: 310,000
SALES (est): 43.3MM **Privately Held**
SIC: 3714 Motor vehicle wheels & parts

(G-5768)
DUAL PRINT & MAIL LLC (HQ)
3235 Grand Island Blvd (14072-1284)
PHONE.....................716 775-8001
Michael Vitch, *CEO*
Thomas Salisbury, *Ch of Bd*
Joanne Sabio, *Vice Pres*
EMP: 76
SALES (est): 12MM
SALES (corp-wide): 20.2MM **Privately Held**
SIC: 2752 Commercial printing, lithographic
PA: Compu-Mail, Llc
3235 Grand Island Blvd
Grand Island NY 14072
716 775-8001

(G-5769)
DYLIX CORPORATION
347 Lang Blvd (14072-3123)
PHONE.....................719 773-2985
Nathaniel G Bargar, *President*
Bryan Barrett, *General Mgr*
Nicole Gwiazdowski, *Mfg Staff*
Will Bargar, *VP Sales*
Tom Glynn, *Sales Staff*
EMP: 25
SALES (est): 4.9MM **Privately Held**
WEB: www.dylixcorp.com
SIC: 3829 Pressure transducers

(G-5770)
FAST BY GAST INC
120 Industrial Dr (14072-1270)
PHONE.....................716 773-1536
Fax: 716 773-7509
Paul Gast, *President*
Dana Gast, *Vice Pres*
Kevin Gilham, *Sales Staff*
▲ **EMP:** 9
SQ FT: 4,240
SALES (est): 1.2MM **Privately Held**
WEB: www.fastbygast.com
SIC: 3714 Motor vehicle parts & accessories

(G-5771)
FRESENIUS KABI USA LLC
3159 Staley Rd (14072-2028)
PHONE.....................716 773-0053
Peter Martinez, *Vice Pres*
Bob Brockman, *Project Mgr*
David Marzec, *Engineer*
Richard J Tajak, *CFO*
Arthur Senf, *Manager*
EMP: 450
SALES (corp-wide): 31.1B **Privately Held**
WEB: www.appdrugs.com
SIC: 2834 Pharmaceutical preparations
HQ: Fresenius Kabi Usa, Inc.
3 Corporate Dr Ste 300
Lake Zurich IL 60047
847 969-2700

(G-5772)
FRESENIUS KABI USA LLC
3159 Staley Rd (14072-2028)
PHONE.....................716 773-0800
Fax: 716 773-0878
Nicholas Bateman, *Opers Staff*
Rich Rowles, *QA Dir*
Valerie Maggard, *QC Mgr*
Scott Gorenflo, *Engineer*
Frank Harmon, *Branch Mgr*
EMP: 35
SALES (corp-wide): 31.1B **Privately Held**
SIC: 2834 Pharmaceutical preparations
HQ: Fresenius Kabi Usa, Llc
3 Corporate Dr Ste 300
Lake Zurich IL 60047
847 550-2300

(G-5773)
GRAND ISLAND ANIMAL HOSPITAL
Also Called: Grand Island Research & Dev
2323 Whitehaven Rd (14072-1505)
PHONE.....................716 773-7645
Robert Harper, *President*
Lysa P Posner Dvm, *Principal*
EMP: 20
SALES (est): 1.4MM **Privately Held**
SIC: 3999 0742 Pet supplies; veterinary services, specialties

(G-5774)
ISLECHEM LLC
2801 Long Rd (14072-1244)
PHONE.....................716 773-8401
Fax: 716 773-8517
Daniel Canavan, *Vice Pres*
Dave Ernst, *Manager*
Kevin Rader, *Manager*
Vivian Hoffman, *Analyst*
Richard Morlok, *Analyst*
▲ **EMP:** 25
SALES (est): 9.6MM **Privately Held**
WEB: www.islechem.com
SIC: 2869 8731 Industrial organic chemicals; commercial physical research

(G-5775)
LIFE TECHNOLOGIES CORPORATION
3175 Staley Rd (14072-2028)
PHONE.....................716 774-6700
Fax: 716 774-6694
Lyle Turner, *Vice Pres*
Kelli A Richard, *Vice Pres*
Doug Evans, *Opers Staff*
Carl Bennett, *Mfg Staff*
Melanie Lenz, *Mfg Staff*
EMP: 100
SALES (corp-wide): 18.2B **Publicly Held**
SIC: 2836 Biological products, except diagnostic
HQ: Life Technologies Corporation
5781 Van Allen Way
Carlsbad CA 92008
760 603-7200

(G-5776)
LINDE LLC
3279 Grand Island Blvd (14072-1216)
PHONE.....................716 773-7552
Jeffrey Schutrum, *Division Mgr*
Darin Hippner, *Engineer*
Glen Murray, *VP Mktg*
Jeff Schutrum, *Manager*
David Kryszak, *Agent*
EMP: 60
SALES (corp-wide): 17.9B **Privately Held**
SIC: 3825 3625 3567 3561 Instruments to measure electricity; relays & industrial controls; industrial furnaces & ovens; pumps & pumping equipment; machine tool accessories
HQ: Linde Llc
200 Somerset Corporate Bl
Bridgewater NJ 08807
908 464-8100

(G-5777)
MINIMAX CONCRETE CORP
2735 Bedell Rd (14072-1258)
PHONE.....................716 444-8908
Julianne Thompson, *Principal*
EMP: 5
SALES (est): 328K **Privately Held**
SIC: 3531 Mixers, concrete

Grand Island - Erie County (G-5778)

(G-5778)
NIDEC INDUS AUTOMTN USA LLC
Also Called: Emerson Control Techniques
359 Lang Blvd Bldg B (14072-3123)
PHONE..................716 774-1193
Fax: 716 774-8327
Jim Hovey, *Technical Mgr*
Diane Thompson, *Branch Mgr*
John Johnson, *Manager*
Ken Siddall, *Manager*
Don Hubbard, *IT/INT Sup*
EMP: 30
SALES (corp-wide): 10.5B **Privately Held**
SIC: 3566 3823 Drives, high speed industrial, except hydrostatic; industrial process control instruments
HQ: Nidec Industrial Automation Usa, Llc
7078 Shady Oak Rd
Eden Prairie MN 55344
952 995-8000

(G-5779)
NRD LLC
2937 Alt Blvd (14072-1292)
P.O. Box 310 (14072-0310)
PHONE..................716 773-7634
Fax: 716 773-7744
Douglas J Fiegel, *President*
Chandana Desilva, *Project Mgr*
Sarah Escutia, *Engineer*
Jim Smith, *Engineer*
Charles Dunn, *Sales Dir*
▲ EMP: 50
SQ FT: 32,000
SALES (est): 10.4MM
SALES (corp-wide): 43.3MM **Privately Held**
WEB: www.nrdstaticcontrol.com
SIC: 3629 3669 3499 Static elimination equipment, industrial; smoke detectors; fire- or burglary-resistive products
PA: Bam Enterprises, Inc.
2937 Alt Blvd
Grand Island NY 14072
716 773-7634

(G-5780)
OCCIDENTAL CHEMICAL CORP
2801 Long Rd (14072-1244)
PHONE..................716 773-8100
Fax: 716 773-8110
Charles G Radar, *Branch Mgr*
EMP: 30
SALES (corp-wide): 10.4B **Publicly Held**
WEB: www.oxychem.com
SIC: 2812 Alkalies & chlorine
HQ: Occidental Chemical Corporation
5005 Lyndon B Johnson Fwy # 2200
Dallas TX 75244
972 404-3800

(G-5781)
RR DONNELLEY & SONS COMPANY
Also Called: Moore Business Forms
300 Lang Blvd (14072-3122)
PHONE..................716 773-0647
Thomas Johnson, *VP Mktg*
Jeffrey Gebhart, *Branch Mgr*
Ted Cyman, *Manager*
EMP: 56
SALES (corp-wide): 6.9B **Publicly Held**
WEB: www.moore.com
SIC: 2761 Manifold business forms
PA: R. R. Donnelley & Sons Company
35 W Wacker Dr Ste 3650
Chicago IL 60601
312 326-8000

(G-5782)
RR DONNELLEY & SONS COMPANY
Also Called: Moore Research Center
300 Lang Blvd (14072-3122)
PHONE..................716 773-0300
Fax: 716 773-1091
Anthony D Joseph, *Vice Pres*
Edward J Zurbugh Jr, *Librarian*
EMP: 65
SALES (corp-wide): 6.9B **Publicly Held**
WEB: www.moore.com
SIC: 2761 Manifold business forms

PA: R. R. Donnelley & Sons Company
35 W Wacker Dr Ste 3650
Chicago IL 60601
312 326-8000

(G-5783)
SAINT-GOBAIN ADFORS AMER INC (DH)
Also Called: Saint-Gobain-Paris France
1795 Baseline Rd (14072-2010)
PHONE..................716 775-3900
Fax: 716 775-3901
John Bedell, *CEO*
Rudy Coetzee, *General Mgr*
Marilyn Woomer, *Credit Mgr*
◆ EMP: 55
SALES (est): 153.3MM
SALES (corp-wide): 185.8MM **Privately Held**
WEB: www.sgtf.com
SIC: 2297 Nonwoven fabrics

(G-5784)
SIHI PUMPS INC (DH)
303 Industrial Dr (14072-1293)
P.O. Box 460 (14072-0460)
PHONE..................716 773-6450
Fax: 716 773-2330
David P Moran, *Ch of Bd*
Ian Reynolds, *Business Mgr*
Frank Papp, *Vice Pres*
Mike Pastore, *Vice Pres*
▲ EMP: 47
SQ FT: 37,500
SALES (est): 9.2MM **Privately Held**
WEB: www.sihi.com
SIC: 3561 Pumps & pumping equipment
HQ: S.F. Americas Inc
303 Industrial Dr
Grand Island NY
716 773-6450

(G-5785)
STARLINE USA INC
3036 Alt Blvd (14072-1274)
PHONE..................716 773-0100
Fax: 716 773-2332
Joshua Lapsker, *CEO*
Dennis Mincks, *President*
Daniel Norris, *President*
Ron Lapsker, *Chairman*
Patrick Moran, *CFO*
EMP: 120
SQ FT: 80,000
SALES (est): 15.9MM **Privately Held**
SIC: 2396 Printing & embossing on plastics fabric articles

(G-5786)
THERMO FISHER SCIENTIFIC INC
3175 Staley Rd (14072-2028)
PHONE..................716 774-6700
EMP: 5
SALES (corp-wide): 18.2B **Publicly Held**
SIC: 3826 Analytical instruments
PA: Thermo Fisher Scientific Inc.
168 3rd Ave
Waltham MA 02451
781 622-1000

(G-5787)
TULLY PRODUCTS INC
2065 Baseline Rd (14072-2060)
PHONE..................716 773-3166
Fax: 716 773-7894
Richard Ray, *President*
EMP: 5
SQ FT: 8,000
SALES: 500K **Privately Held**
SIC: 3089 Trays, plastic

(G-5788)
US PEROXIDE
1815 Love Rd Ste 1 (14072-2248)
PHONE..................716 775-5585
Paul Faulise, *Manager*
EMP: 8
SALES (est): 1.3MM **Privately Held**
SIC: 2819 Peroxides, hydrogen peroxide

Granville
Washington County

(G-5789)
CENTRAL TIMBER CO INC
Also Called: Central Timber Research/Devt
9088 State Route 22 (12832-4805)
PHONE..................518 638-6338
Fax: 518 638-6121
Ralph Jameson II, *President*
EMP: 5
SQ FT: 52,704
SALES (est): 326.6K **Privately Held**
SIC: 2411 Logging

(G-5790)
LOCKER MASTERS INC
10329 State Route 22 (12832-5024)
PHONE..................518 288-3203
Martha Lyng, *President*
William Lyng, *Treasurer*
Carmen Dodge, *Bookkeeper*
Allan Lyng, *Admin Sec*
EMP: 12
SQ FT: 12,000
SALES: 600K **Privately Held**
SIC: 2542 7699 Lockers (not refrigerated): except wood; industrial machinery & equipment repair

(G-5791)
MANCHESTER NEWSPAPER INC (PA)
Also Called: Whitehall Times
14 E Main St (12832-1334)
P.O. Box 330 (12832-0330)
PHONE..................518 642-1234
Fax: 518 642-1344
John Manchester, *President*
Darell Beebe, *Editor*
John Manchester, *Editor*
Bill Toscano, *Editor*
Lisa Manchester, *Vice Pres*
EMP: 33 EST: 1875
SQ FT: 10,000
SALES (est): 3.4MM **Privately Held**
WEB: www.manchesternewspapers.com
SIC: 2711 Newspapers: publishing only, not printed on site

(G-5792)
MANCHESTER WOOD INC
1159 County Route 24 (12832-9438)
P.O. Box 180 (12832-0180)
PHONE..................518 642-9518
Fax: 518 642-9682
Edward Eriksen, *President*
Priscilla Eriksen, *Treasurer*
Laurie Grottoli, *Accountant*
EMP: 148 EST: 1976
SQ FT: 54,000
SALES (est): 19.2MM **Privately Held**
WEB: www.manchesterwood.com
SIC: 2511 Wood household furniture; chairs, household, except upholstered: wood; tables, household: wood

(G-5793)
METTOWEE LUMBER & PLASTICS CO
82 Church St (12832-1662)
PHONE..................518 642-1100
Henry V Derminden IV, *President*
Robert Vanderminden Jr, *Vice Pres*
Paul Parker, *Purch Agent*
Rick Doyle, *Manager*
EMP: 250 EST: 1936
SQ FT: 20,000
SALES (est): 22MM
SALES (corp-wide): 62.8MM **Privately Held**
SIC: 2421 0811 3089 Sawmills & planing mills, general; timber tracts; plastic processing
PA: Telescope Casual Furniture, Inc.
82 Church St
Granville NY 12832
518 642-1100

(G-5794)
NORTH AMERICAN SLATE INC
50 Columbus St (12832-1024)
PHONE..................518 642-1702

Robert Tatko, *President*
EMP: 7 EST: 1998
SQ FT: 3,500
SALES (est): 495.1K **Privately Held**
SIC: 3281 Slate products

(G-5795)
NORTON PERFORMANCE PLAS CORP
1 Sealants Park (12832-1652)
PHONE..................518 642-2200
Fax: 518 642-1792
Robert C Ayotte, *President*
Dean Mason, *Purchasing*
Trish Tulenko, *Controller*
Edward Canning, *Manager*
Mark Godfrey, *CTO*
EMP: 6
SALES (est): 500.5K **Privately Held**
SIC: 3083 Laminated plastics plate & sheet

(G-5796)
SAINT-GOBAIN PRFMCE PLAS CORP
1 Sealants Park (12832-1652)
PHONE..................518 642-2200
Dave Williams, *General Mgr*
Robert J Lewandusky, *Purch Mgr*
Bryan W Harrison, *Engineer*
Edward K Prunier, *Engineer*
Dean Waldenberger, *Enginr/R&D Mgr*
EMP: 150
SALES (corp-wide): 185.8MM **Privately Held**
SIC: 2891 3086 2821 2671 Sealants; plastics foam products; plastics materials & resins; packaging paper & plastics film, coated & laminated
HQ: Saint-Gobain Performance Plastics Corporation
31500 Solon Rd
Solon OH 44139
440 836-6900

(G-5797)
WINN MANUFACTURING INC
12 Burtis Ave (12832)
P.O. Box 308 (12832-0308)
PHONE..................518 642-3515
Steve Winn, *President*
Sandra Winn, *Vice Pres*
EMP: 6
SQ FT: 4,500
SALES: 500K **Privately Held**
SIC: 3599 Machine shop, jobbing & repair

Great Bend
Jefferson County

(G-5798)
HANSON AGGREGATES EAST LLC
County Rt 47 (13643)
P.O. Box 130, Watertown (13601-0130)
PHONE..................315 493-3721
Fax: 315 493-3539
Dan Oconnor, *Superintendent*
EMP: 15
SQ FT: 910
SALES (corp-wide): 16B **Privately Held**
SIC: 3281 Limestone, cut & shaped
HQ: Hanson Aggregates East Llc
3131 Rdu Center Dr
Morrisville NC 27560
919 380-2500

Great Neck
Nassau County

(G-5799)
ADVANCED BARCODE TECH INC
Also Called: ABT
175 E Shore Rd Ste 228 (11023-2430)
PHONE..................516 570-8100
Fax: 516 829-2955
Charles Bibas, *President*
Stephen A Bauman, *President*
Dafna Bibas, *Vice Pres*
EMP: 16

▲ = Import ▼ = Export
◆ = Import/Export

GEOGRAPHIC SECTION
Great Neck - Nassau County (G-5828)

SQ FT: 7,500
SALES (est): 3.8MM **Privately Held**
WEB: www.abtworld.com
SIC: 3577 7371 Bar code (magnetic ink) printers; computer software development

(G-5800)
AFP MANUFACTURING CORP
9 Park Pl (11021-5034)
PHONE....................516 466-6464
Attilio F Petrocelli, *Principal*
EMP: 18
SALES (est): 3.6MM **Privately Held**
SIC: 3999 Manufacturing industries

(G-5801)
ALFRED BUTLER INC
107 Grace Ave (11021-1608)
PHONE....................516 829-7460
Jerome Butler, *President*
Diana Schavaria, *Manager*
▲ EMP: 16
SQ FT: 8,000
SALES (est): 1.8MM **Privately Held**
WEB: www.alfredbutler.com
SIC: 3911 Rings, finger: precious metal

(G-5802)
ALFRED KHALILY INC
Also Called: Alfa Chem
2 Harbor Way (11024-2117)
PHONE....................516 504-0059
Alfred Khalily, *President*
Farry Khalliy, *Vice Pres*
Freshteh Khalily, *Treasurer*
▲ EMP: 14
SQ FT: 5,000
SALES (est): 2.7MM **Privately Held**
WEB: www.alfachem1.com
SIC: 2834 Pharmaceutical preparations

(G-5803)
ALL NET LTD
15 Cuttermill Rd Ste 145 (11021-3252)
PHONE....................516 504-4559
Fax: 212 760-2710
Kishore Hemrajani, *President*
Priya Najrani, *Corp Secy*
EMP: 12
SQ FT: 1,500
SALES (est): 987.5K **Privately Held**
SIC: 2329 5136 Basketball uniforms: men's, youths' & boys'; men's & boys' clothing

(G-5804)
ALLURE FASHIONS INC
8 Barstow Rd Apt 2e (11021-3543)
PHONE....................516 829-2470
Jay Confino, *President*
Abdool S Ali, *Vice Pres*
EMP: 2
SQ FT: 800
SALES: 1.5MM **Privately Held**
SIC: 2341 Women's & children's nightwear

(G-5805)
AMERICAN APPAREL LTD
15 Cuttermill Rd Ste 145 (11021-3252)
PHONE....................516 504-4559
Kishore Hemrajani, *President*
EMP: 8
SQ FT: 1,000
SALES (est): 550.5K **Privately Held**
SIC: 2326 Men's & boys' work clothing

(G-5806)
ARCADIA CHEM PRESERVATIVE LLC
100 Great Neck Rd Apt 5b (11021-3349)
PHONE....................516 466-5258
Richard Rofe, *Mng Member*
EMP: 5
SQ FT: 3,000
SALES (est): 6.5MM **Privately Held**
SIC: 2869 5169 Industrial organic chemicals; alkalines & chlorine; drilling mud; industrial chemicals; silicon lubricants

(G-5807)
ARGON CORP (PA)
160 Great Neck Rd (11021-3304)
PHONE....................516 487-5314
Fax: 516 487-5121
Moshe Albaum, *CEO*
Mike Forde, *COO*

Steve Wilkinson, *Vice Pres*
Cynthia Panter, *QC Mgr*
Leonid Fabisevich, *Engineer*
▲ EMP: 18
SQ FT: 10,000
SALES (est): 7.6MM **Privately Held**
WEB: www.argoncorp.com
SIC: 3571 8731 Electronic computers; computer (hardware) development

(G-5808)
ASHER JEWELRY COMPANY INC
Also Called: Asher Collection
175 Great Neck Rd Ste 201 (11021-3351)
PHONE....................212 302-6233
Fax: 212 302-6279
Ben Asher, *Ch of Bd*
Fred Asher, *Vice Pres*
Tamara Asher, *Treasurer*
▲ EMP: 60
SQ FT: 6,000
SALES (est): 9.5MM **Privately Held**
WEB: www.asherjewelry.com
SIC: 3911 Jewelry apparel

(G-5809)
AUTOMOTIVE LEATHER GROUP LLC
17 Barstow Rd Ste 206 (11021-2213)
PHONE....................516 627-4000
Bob Kamali, *Mng Member*
EMP: 10
SQ FT: 5,000
SALES (est): 362.1K **Privately Held**
SIC: 3111 Accessory products, leather

(G-5810)
AVANTE
35 Hicks Ln (11024-2026)
PHONE....................516 782-4888
Arash Ouriel, *Partner*
Albert Alishahi, *Partner*
John Haskin, *Manager*
▲ EMP: 6
SALES (est): 567.4K **Privately Held**
WEB: www.avante.net
SIC: 2371 Fur goods

(G-5811)
BEAUTY AMERICA LLC
10 Bond St Ste 296 (11021-2454)
PHONE....................917 744-1430
AVI Sivan,
EMP: 30
SALES: 1.9MM **Privately Held**
SIC: 3823 4813 Viscosimeters, industrial process type;

(G-5812)
CADDY CONCEPTS INC
15 Cuttermill Rd (11021-3252)
PHONE....................516 570-6279
Kishore Hemrajani, *President*
▲ EMP: 10
SALES (est): 1.2MM **Privately Held**
SIC: 2392 Household furnishings

(G-5813)
CARDONA INDUSTRIES USA LTD (PA)
505 Northern Blvd Ste 213 (11021-5112)
P.O. Box 7778, Delray Beach FL (33482-7778)
PHONE....................516 466-5200
Ben Feinsod, *President*
Edward Streim, *Chairman*
Douglas Knapp, *Vice Pres*
Joyce Campisi, *Manager*
▲ EMP: 8
SQ FT: 2,500
SALES (est): 1.3MM **Privately Held**
SIC: 3369 5094 White metal castings (lead, tin, antimony), except die; jewelers' findings

(G-5814)
CHAMELEON GEMS INC
98 Cuttermill Rd Ste 398n (11021-3009)
PHONE....................516 829-3333
Aaron Hakimian, *CEO*
Abraham Hakimian, *President*
EMP: 12
SALES (est): 1.6MM **Privately Held**
SIC: 3911 Jewelry, precious metal

(G-5815)
CLASSIC CREATIONS INC
Also Called: Viducci
1 Linden Pl Ste 409 (11021-2640)
PHONE....................516 498-1991
Tony Nemati, *Owner*
EMP: 5
SALES (est): 412.2K **Privately Held**
SIC: 3915 Jewel cutting, drilling, polishing, recutting or setting

(G-5816)
COLONIAL TAG & LABEL CO INC
425 Northern Blvd Ste 36 (11021-4803)
PHONE....................516 482-0508
Eric Kono, *President*
Marc Kono, *Sales Associate*
Peggy Esterman, *Systems Staff*
▲ EMP: 13 EST: 1966
SQ FT: 10,000
SALES (est): 9.7MM **Privately Held**
WEB: www.cdscds.com
SIC: 2759 2241 Commercial printing; tags: printing; labels & seals: printing; business forms: printing; labels, woven

(G-5817)
CONFORMER PRODUCTS INC
60 Cuttermill Rd Ste 411 (11021-3104)
PHONE....................516 504-6300
Marvin Makofsky, *CEO*
EMP: 13
SALES (est): 2.2MM **Privately Held**
SIC: 2677 Envelopes

(G-5818)
CONNIE FRENCH CLEANERS INC
Also Called: Connie Cleaners
801 Middle Neck Rd (11024-1932)
PHONE....................516 487-1343
Michael Estivo, *President*
EMP: 9 EST: 1938
SQ FT: 2,000
SALES (est): 1.1MM **Privately Held**
SIC: 2842 7219 Drycleaning preparations; garment alteration & repair shop

(G-5819)
DALCOM USA LTD
Also Called: Dalfon
11 Middle Neck Rd Ste 301 (11021-2301)
PHONE....................516 466-7733
Fred Hakim, *President*
EMP: 11
SQ FT: 4,000
SALES (est): 2.5MM **Privately Held**
WEB: www.dalfon.com
SIC: 2326 Men's & boys' work clothing

(G-5820)
DSR INTERNATIONAL CORP
107 Northern Blvd Ste 401 (11021-4312)
PHONE....................631 427-2600
Thil NA, *President*
Harvey Drill, *Director*
▲ EMP: 6
SALES (est): 705.4K **Privately Held**
SIC: 3315 5063 Cable, steel: insulated or armored; electronic wire & cable

(G-5821)
ELITE UNIFORMS LTD
310 Northern Blvd Ste A (11021-4806)
PHONE....................516 487-5481
Fax: 516 487-5483
Corey Greenberg, *President*
EMP: 8 EST: 2009
SALES (est): 818.7K **Privately Held**
SIC: 2311 Men's & boys' uniforms

(G-5822)
EXPEDI-PRINTING INC
41 Red Brook Rd (11024-1437)
PHONE....................516 513-0919
Fax: 718 417-8096
Shiann Jong Chen, *Chairman*
▲ EMP: 145
SQ FT: 130,000
SALES (est): 15.7MM **Privately Held**
WEB: www.expedi.com
SIC: 2759 Newspapers: printing; periodicals: printing

(G-5823)
F L DEMETER INC
12 N Gate Rd (11023-1313)
PHONE....................516 487-5187
Fax: 516 487-1027
Debra Janke, *President*
Blair Crames, *Assistant VP*
Mark Crames, *Vice Pres*
▲ EMP: 25
SQ FT: 3,000
SALES (est): 5.3MM **Privately Held**
SIC: 2844 5122 Perfumes & colognes; cosmetics, perfumes & hair products

(G-5824)
FAB INDUSTRIES CORP (HQ)
98 Cuttermill Rd Ste 412 (11021-3006)
PHONE....................516 498-3200
Fax: 516 829-0783
Steven Myers, *President*
Sam Hiatt, *Vice Pres*
Beth Myers, *Vice Pres*
Jerry Deese, *CFO*
David A Miller, *CFO*
EMP: 33
SQ FT: 2,409
SALES (est): 58.4MM **Privately Held**
WEB: www.fab-industries.com
SIC: 2258 2211 Warp & flat knit products; lace & lace products; bedspreads, lace: made on lace machines; bed sets, lace; sheets, bedding & table cloths: cotton
PA: Ssjjj Manufacturing, Llc
98 Cuttermill Rd Ste 412
Great Neck NY 11021
516 498-3200

(G-5825)
FABRIC RESOURCES INTL LTD (PA)
9 Park Pl (11021-5034)
PHONE....................516 829-4550
Steven Richman, *President*
Stephen Gold, *COO*
◆ EMP: 16 EST: 1939
SQ FT: 5,500
SALES (est): 2.7MM **Privately Held**
SIC: 2221 2262 2231 2295 Broadwoven fabric mills, manmade; finishing plants, manmade fiber & silk fabrics; broadwoven fabric mills, wool; coated fabrics, not rubberized

(G-5826)
FIRST QLTY PACKG SOLUTIONS LLC (PA)
80 Cuttermill Rd Ste 500 (11021-3108)
PHONE....................516 829-3030
EMP: 14
SALES (est): 6.4MM **Privately Held**
SIC: 3086 Packaging & shipping materials, foamed plastic

(G-5827)
FIRST QUALITY HYGIENIC INC
80 Cuttermill Rd Ste 500 (11021-3108)
PHONE....................516 829-3030
Kambiz Damaghi, *President*
EMP: 5
SALES (est): 253.5K **Privately Held**
SIC: 2676 5137 Towels, napkins & tissue paper products; feminine hygiene paper products; diapers

(G-5828)
FIRST QUALITY PRODUCTS INC (HQ)
80 Cuttermill Rd Ste 500 (11021-3108)
P.O. Box 270, Mc Elhattan PA (17748-0270)
PHONE....................516 829-4949
Fax: 516 829-4949
Kambiz Damaghi, *Ch of Bd*
Nasser Damaghi, *Ch of Bd*
Noam Yarimi, *Business Mgr*
Scott Shingleton, *COO*
Kambiz Damagh, *Vice Pres*
◆ EMP: 11
SQ FT: 6,000
SALES (est): 372.6MM **Privately Held**
SIC: 2676 Sanitary paper products

Great Neck - Nassau County (G-5829)

(G-5829)
FLEXTRADE SYSTEMS INC (PA)
111 Great Neck Rd Ste 314 (11021-5403)
PHONE..................516 627-8993
Fax: 516 627-8994
Vijay Kedia, *President*
Vikas Kedia, *Managing Dir*
Bertrand Rassat, *Managing Dir*
Vishal Pandya, *COO*
Shailendra Balani, *Senior VP*
EMP: 140
SALES (est): 70.4MM **Privately Held**
WEB: www.flextrade.com
SIC: 7372 Prepackaged software

(G-5830)
FULLER SPORTSWEAR CO INC
10 Grenfell Dr (11020-1429)
PHONE..................516 773-3353
Robert Feinerman, *President*
Aaron Feinerman, *Corp Secy*
Robin Feinerman, *Vice Pres*
EMP: 6 EST: 1960
SQ FT: 50,000
SALES (est): 550K **Privately Held**
SIC: 2331 Blouses, women's & juniors': made from purchased material

(G-5831)
ILICO JEWELRY INC
98 Cuttermill Rd Ste 396 (11021-3008)
PHONE..................516 482-0201
Michael Ilian, *President*
Rodney Ilian, *Vice Pres*
Mirai Bechara, *Manager*
Rebecca Ilian, *Admin Sec*
EMP: 5
SQ FT: 1,200
SALES (est): 505.2K **Privately Held**
SIC: 3911 Jewelry, precious metal

(G-5832)
INTERNATIONAL CASEIN CORP CAL
111 Great Neck Rd Ste 218 (11021-5408)
PHONE..................516 466-4363
Marvin Match, *President*
Vance Perry, *Vice Pres*
EMP: 5
SQ FT: 1,500
SALES (est): 459.3K **Privately Held**
SIC: 2821 Plastics materials & resins

(G-5833)
IRIDIUM INDUSTRIES INC
Also Called: Artube
17 Barstow Rd Ste 302 (11021-2213)
PHONE..................516 504-9700
Fax: 516 504-9800
Jacques Sassouni, *Principal*
EMP: 50
SALES (corp-wide): 37.5MM **Privately Held**
SIC: 3089 3083 Plastic containers, except foam; laminated plastics plate & sheet
PA: Iridium Industries, Inc.
147 Forge Rd
East Stroudsburg PA 18301
570 476-8800

(G-5834)
KALATI COMPANY INC
14 Bond St Ste 152 (11021-2045)
PHONE..................516 423-9132
Rami Kalati, *Principal*
EMP: 6
SALES (est): 17.5K **Privately Held**
SIC: 2273 Carpets & rugs

(G-5835)
KAMALI AUTOMOTIVE GROUP INC
17 Barstow Rd Ste 206 (11021-2213)
PHONE..................516 627-4000
Joseph Kamali, *Vice Pres*
EMP: 10
SALES (est): 398.3K **Privately Held**
SIC: 3111 Upholstery leather

(G-5836)
KAMALI GROUP INC
17 Barstow Rd Ste 206 (11021-2213)
PHONE..................516 627-4000
Bahman Kamali, *Ch of Bd*
Bob Kamali, *Principal*
Joseph Kamali, *Vice Pres*
Ruth Kamali, *Vice Pres*
Selena Lau, *Vice Pres*
▲ EMP: 5
SQ FT: 3,000
SALES (est): 26.6K **Privately Held**
WEB: www.kamaligroup.com
SIC: 2399 3111 Automotive covers, except seat & tire covers; accessory products, leather

(G-5837)
LE VIAN CORP (PA)
Also Called: Arusha Tanzanite
235 Great Neck Rd (11021-3301)
PHONE..................516 466-7200
Moosa Levian, *President*
Joan A Foley, *Asst Director*
▲ EMP: 82
SQ FT: 7,000
SALES (est): 24.1MM **Privately Held**
WEB: www.levian.com
SIC: 3911 Jewelry, precious metal

(G-5838)
LINO INTERNATIONAL INC
Also Called: Lino Metal
111 Great Neck Rd 300a (11021-5403)
PHONE..................516 482-7100
Ling Hong LI, *President*
Aisan Kim, *Manager*
EMP: 7
SALES: 5MM **Privately Held**
SIC: 3312 Pipes, iron & steel

(G-5839)
MARCO MOORE INC
825 Northern Blvd Ste 201 (11021-5323)
PHONE..................212 575-2090
David Zar, *President*
EMP: 60
SQ FT: 11,000
SALES: 4MM
SALES (corp-wide): 5.8MM **Privately Held**
SIC: 3911 3873 Jewelry, precious metal; watches, clocks, watchcases & parts
PA: Royal Jewelry Manufacturing Inc.
825 Northern Blvd Fl 2
Great Neck NY 11021
212 302-2500

(G-5840)
NIBMOR PROJECT LLC
11 Middle Neck Rd (11021-2312)
PHONE..................718 374-5091
Jennifer Love, *CEO*
EMP: 14
SALES (est): 2.3MM **Privately Held**
SIC: 2066 Chocolate

(G-5841)
NUTEK DISPOSABLES INC
80 Cuttermill Rd Ste 500 (11021-3108)
PHONE..................516 829-3030
Jim Dodge, *CFO*
EMP: 6 **Privately Held**
SIC: 2676 Sanitary paper products
HQ: Nutek Disposables, Inc.
121 N Rd
Mc Elhattan PA 17748
570 769-6900

(G-5842)
OAKWOOD PUBLISHING CO
14 Bond St Ste 386 (11021-2045)
PHONE..................516 482-7720
Richard Weiss, *President*
Lisa Whitney, *CFO*
EMP: 7
SQ FT: 3,000
SALES: 100K **Privately Held**
SIC: 2741 Miscellaneous publishing

(G-5843)
OLD DUTCH MUSTARD CO INC (PA)
Also Called: Pilgrim Foods Co
98 Cuttermill Rd Ste 260s (11021-3033)
PHONE..................516 466-0522
Fax: 516 466-0762
Charles R Santich, *Ch of Bd*
Paul Santich, *President*
Renate Santich, *Vice Pres*
▼ EMP: 6 EST: 1915
SQ FT: 3,000
SALES (est): 14.6MM **Privately Held**
SIC: 2099 2033 2035 Vinegar; fruit juices: concentrated, hot pack; fruit juices: fresh; fruit juices: packaged in cans, jars, etc.; mustard, prepared (wet)

(G-5844)
ORO AVANTI INC (PA)
250 Kings Point Rd (11024-1022)
PHONE..................516 487-5185
Fax: 516 482-4369
Hersel Sarraf, *President*
Gidion Sarraf, *Vice Pres*
EMP: 7
SALES (est): 1.7MM **Privately Held**
SIC: 3295 Minerals, ground or treated

(G-5845)
OZ BAKING COMPANY LTD
114 Middle Neck Rd (11021-1245)
PHONE..................516 466-5114
Ofer Zur, *Ch of Bd*
EMP: 8
SALES (est): 568.7K **Privately Held**
SIC: 2051 Bread, cake & related products

(G-5846)
PAMA ENTERPRISES INC
60 Cuttermill Rd Ste 411 (11021-3104)
PHONE..................516 504-6300
Fax: 516 504-6374
Marvin A Makofsky, *President*
Wilner Merrill, *Finance Mgr*
Alison Hickerson, *Manager*
EMP: 5
SALES (est): 330K **Privately Held**
SIC: 3993 2752 Advertising novelties; commercial printing, lithographic

(G-5847)
PEARL LEATHER GROUP LLC
17 Barstow Rd Ste 206 (11021-2213)
PHONE..................516 627-4047
Selena Lau, *Sales Staff*
Bob Kamali,
John Ruggeiro,
▲ EMP: 50
SQ FT: 4,000
SALES: 10MM **Privately Held**
SIC: 3111 Leather processing

(G-5848)
PENFLI INDUSTRIES INC
11 Woodland Pl (11021-1035)
PHONE..................212 947-6080
Anton Fischman, *President*
Joe Fischman, *Vice Pres*
▲ EMP: 15
SALES (est): 1.6MM **Privately Held**
WEB: www.penfliusa.com
SIC: 2326 5136 2339 5137 Men's & boys' work clothing; men's & boys' clothing; women's & misses' athletic clothing & sportswear; women's & children's clothing

(G-5849)
PREMIER INGRIDIENTS INC
3 Johnstone Rd (11021-1507)
PHONE..................516 641-6763
Dennis Provda, *CEO*
▲ EMP: 4 EST: 2010
SALES (est): 1.3MM **Privately Held**
SIC: 2999 Waxes, petroleum: not produced in petroleum refineries

(G-5850)
PRESTIGE BOX CORPORATION (PA)
115 Cuttermill Rd (11021-3101)
P.O. Box 220428 (11022-0428)
PHONE..................516 773-3115
Fax: 516 773-3612
Sherry Warren, *Principal*
Ray Turin, *Vice Pres*
EMP: 38 EST: 1963
SQ FT: 12,000
SALES (est): 49.7MM **Privately Held**
SIC: 2657 2653 2631 2652 Folding paperboard boxes; boxes, corrugated: made from purchased materials; boxboard; setup paperboard boxes

(G-5851)
PROGRESSIVE COLOR GRAPHICS
122 Station Rd (11023-1723)
PHONE..................212 292-8787
Hugo Saltini, *President*
Stuart Linzer, *Vice Pres*
EMP: 41
SQ FT: 28,000
SALES (est): 4.2MM **Privately Held**
SIC: 2752 Offset & photolithographic printing

(G-5852)
ROSECORE DIVISION
Also Called: Corey Rugs
11 Grace Ave Ste 100 (11021-2417)
P.O. Box 855, Plainview (11803-0855)
PHONE..................516 504-4530
Fax: 516 504-4542
EMP: 10
SALES (est): 820K **Privately Held**
SIC: 2273 Mfg Carpets/Rugs

(G-5853)
ROYAL JEWELRY MFG INC (PA)
825 Northern Blvd Fl 2 (11021-5321)
PHONE..................212 302-2500
Fax: 212 768-0601
Parviz Hakimian, *President*
Ben Hakimian, *Vice Pres*
David Zar, *Vice Pres*
Sammy Hakimian, *Sales Staff*
Moses Zarnighian, *Sales Staff*
▲ EMP: 38
SQ FT: 9,000
SALES (est): 5.8MM **Privately Held**
WEB: www.royaljewelrymfg.com
SIC: 3911 5094 5944 Jewelry, precious metal; jewelry; jewelry stores

(G-5854)
S KASHI & SONS INC
175 Great Neck Rd Ste 204 (11021-3313)
PHONE..................212 869-9393
Fax: 212 869-9467
Sarah Kashi, *President*
Eley Kashi, *Vice Pres*
Ronen Kashi, *Admin Sec*
▲ EMP: 15
SQ FT: 1,300
SALES (est): 1.9MM **Privately Held**
WEB: www.skashi.com
SIC: 3911 5094 Jewelry, precious metal; precious stones & metals

(G-5855)
SAMUEL B COLLECTION INC
98 Cuttermill Rd (11021-3036)
PHONE..................516 466-1826
Neda Behnam, *President*
▲ EMP: 3
SALES: 3MM **Privately Held**
SIC: 3911 Jewelry, precious metal

(G-5856)
SCARGUARD LABS LLC
15 Barstow Rd (11021-2211)
PHONE..................516 482-8050
Joel Studin, *CEO*
Jim Dun, *President*
James Dunns, *Exec VP*
Alan Graham, *Exec VP*
Steve Levinson, *VP Opers*
EMP: 12
SQ FT: 5,000
SALES (est): 3.1MM **Privately Held**
SIC: 2834 Pharmaceutical preparations

(G-5857)
SPRINGFIELD OIL SERVICES INC
40 Cuttermill Rd Ste 201 (11021-3213)
PHONE..................516 482-5995
Bentley Blum, *Manager*
EMP: 5
SALES (corp-wide): 1.2MM **Privately Held**
SIC: 1382 Oil & gas exploration services
PA: Springfield Oil Services, Inc.
550 Mmaroneck Ave Ste 503
Harrison NY 10528
914 315-6812

GEOGRAPHIC SECTION

(G-5858)
SSJJJ MANUFACTURING LLC (PA)
98 Cuttermill Rd Ste 412 (11021-3006)
PHONE..................516 498-3200
Steven Myers,
Beth Myers,
EMP: 2
SALES (est): 58.4MM **Privately Held**
SIC: 2258 2211 Warp & flat knit products; lace & lace products; bedspreads, lace: made on lace machines; bed sets, lace; sheets, bedding & table cloths: cotton

(G-5859)
STANDARD GROUP (PA)
Also Called: Southern Standard Cartons
1010 Nthrn Blvd Ste 236 (11021)
PHONE..................718 335-5500
Louis Cortes, *President*
Steven D Levkoff, *Chairman*
Tony Pallini, *Info Tech Dir*
Ed Stichweh, *Art Dir*
▲ EMP: 41
SQ FT: 115,000
SALES (est): 72.9MM **Privately Held**
SIC: 2657 Folding paperboard boxes

(G-5860)
STANDARD GROUP LLC (HQ)
Also Called: Southern Standard Cartoons
1010 Nthrn Blvd Ste 236 (11021)
PHONE..................718 507-6430
Louis Cortes, *Vice Pres*
Tom Selmani, *Controller*
Cynthia Sapp, *Human Res Mgr*
Joseph Rebecca,
Steven Levkoff,
▲ EMP: 235 EST: 2009
SQ FT: 115,000
SALES (est): 58.2MM **Privately Held**
WEB: www.thestandardgroup.com
SIC: 2657 Folding paperboard boxes

(G-5861)
STAR SPORTS CORP
Also Called: American Turf Monthly
747 Middle Neck Rd # 103 (11024-1950)
PHONE..................516 773-4075
Allen Hakim, *President*
Diane Karron, *Publisher*
Scott Romick, *Manager*
Sara Rempelos, *Director*
EMP: 20
SQ FT: 2,500
SALES (est): 900K **Privately Held**
WEB: www.carteriley.com
SIC: 2711 Newspapers

(G-5862)
STYLECRAFT INTERIORS INC
22 Watermill Ln (11021-4235)
PHONE..................516 487-2133
Fax: 516 487-2199
Fred Reindl, *President*
Matthew Reindl, *Treasurer*
EMP: 10 EST: 1944
SQ FT: 5,000
SALES (est): 600K **Privately Held**
WEB: www.stylecraftinteriors.com
SIC: 3843 2521 Cabinets, dental; cabinets, office: wood

(G-5863)
TODD ENTERPRISES INC
747 Middle Neck Rd # 103 (11024-1955)
PHONE..................516 773-8087
Alan Sarfaty, *President*
EMP: 100
SQ FT: 16,000
SALES (est): 10.6MM **Privately Held**
WEB: www.scinetcorp.com
SIC: 3571 5045 3577 3572 Electronic computers; computers; computer peripheral equipment; computer storage devices

(G-5864)
TONI INDUSTRIES INC
Also Called: Hbs
111 Great Neck Rd Ste 305 (11021-5403)
PHONE..................212 921-0700
Ophelia Chung, *President*
Neil Blumstein, *Vice Pres*
EMP: 14 EST: 2002
SALES: 18MM **Privately Held**
SIC: 2339 Athletic clothing: women's, misses' & juniors'

(G-5865)
UNIQUE OVERSEAS INC
425 Northern Blvd Ste 22 (11021-4803)
PHONE..................516 466-9792
Raju Shewakramani, *President*
Ragu Ramani, *Principal*
◆ EMP: 8
SALES (est): 894K **Privately Held**
WEB: www.uniqueoverseas.com
SIC: 3199 Equestrian related leather articles

(G-5866)
UNIVERSAL METALS INC
98 Cuttermill Rd Ste 428 (11021-3006)
PHONE..................516 829-0896
Pushpa Kochar, *CEO*
Hira Kochar, *Vice Pres*
◆ EMP: 5
SALES (est): 1.7MM **Privately Held**
SIC: 3399 Metal fasteners

(G-5867)
VARIETY GEM CO INC (PA)
295 Northern Blvd Ste 208 (11021-4701)
PHONE..................212 921-1820
Effie Bezalel, *President*
Soraya Zabih, *Bookkeeper*
▲ EMP: 10
SQ FT: 2,000
SALES (est): 3.5MM **Privately Held**
WEB: www.varietygem.com
SIC: 3911 Jewelry, precious metal

(G-5868)
WEGO INTERNATIONAL FLOORS LLC
239 Great Neck Rd (11021-3301)
PHONE..................516 487-3510
Bert Eshaghpour, *CEO*
Barry Okun, *CFO*
EMP: 11 EST: 2015
SALES (est): 549.7K
SALES (corp-wide): 14.2MM **Privately Held**
SIC: 2491 5023 Flooring, treated wood block; wood flooring
PA: Wego Chemical Group Inc.
239 Great Neck Rd
Great Neck NY 11021
516 487-3510

Great River
Suffolk County

(G-5869)
HEARST BUSINESS MEDIA CORP
3500 Sunrise Hwy Ste 100 (11739-1001)
PHONE..................631 650-6151
Peter Olsen, *Principal*
EMP: 9
SALES (corp-wide): 6.4B **Privately Held**
SIC: 2721 Magazines: publishing only, not printed on site
HQ: Hearst Business Media Corp
2620 Barrett Rd
Gainesville GA 30507
770 532-4111

(G-5870)
HEARST BUSINESS MEDIA CORP
3500 Sunrise Hwy (11739-1001)
PHONE..................631 650-4441
Richard P Malloch, *President*
Gregory Dorn MD MPH, *Exec VP*
Steven A Hobbs, *Exec VP*
Donna Yeager, *Manager*
EMP: 12
SALES (est): 202.5K
SALES (corp-wide): 6.4B **Privately Held**
SIC: 2721 2731 2711 4832 Magazines: publishing only, not printed on site; books: publishing only; newspapers, publishing & printing; newspapers: publishing only, not printed on site; radio broadcasting stations; television broadcasting stations; news feature syndicate
PA: The Hearst Corporation
300 W 57th St Fl 42
New York NY 10019
212 649-2000

Green Island
Albany County

(G-5871)
ARCADIA MFG GROUP INC (PA)
80 Cohoes Ave (12183-1505)
PHONE..................518 434-6213
William T Sumner, *Ch of Bd*
Michael Werner, *President*
George Quigley, *Vice Pres*
Jen Canone, *Purch Mgr*
Charlie Schuffert, *Purch Mgr*
▲ EMP: 44
SQ FT: 20,000
SALES (est): 10.8MM **Privately Held**
WEB: www.arcadiasupply.com
SIC: 3498 3446 3444 3999 Fabricated pipe & fittings; ornamental metalwork; sheet metalwork; cigar lighters, except precious metal

(G-5872)
CASE GROUP LLC
Also Called: Case Window and Door
195 Cohoes Ave (12183-1501)
PHONE..................518 720-3100
Russell Brooks, *Mng Member*
Mike Wright, *Director*
Gerhard Loeffel,
◆ EMP: 36
SQ FT: 50,000
SALES (est): 5MM **Privately Held**
WEB: www.casewindow.com
SIC: 2431 Doors & door parts & trim, wood; windows & window parts & trim, wood

(G-5873)
GENERAL CONTROL SYSTEMS INC
60 Cohoes Ave Ste 101 (12183-1553)
PHONE..................518 270-8045
Fax: 518 270-8042
Clay Robinson, *President*
Gregory Pacifico, *General Mgr*
Daniel Robens, *Prdtn Mgr*
Rich Honsinger, *Opers Staff*
Randy Powell, *Opers Staff*
EMP: 50
SQ FT: 24,000
SALES (est): 11.5MM
SALES (corp-wide): 4.4B **Privately Held**
WEB: www.gcontrol.net
SIC: 3625 Industrial controls: push button, selector switches, pilot
PA: Talen Energy Corporation
835 Hamilton St Ste 150
Allentown PA 18101
888 211-6011

(G-5874)
GREEN ISLAND POWER AUTHORITY
20 Clinton St (12183-1117)
PHONE..................518 273-0661
John J Brown, *Chairman*
Robert Bourgeois, *Fire Chief*
Micheal Cocca, *Vice Chairman*
Justine Tesiero, *Psychologist*
Corey Fong, *Teacher*
EMP: 11
SQ FT: 8,400
SALES (est): 5.8MM **Privately Held**
WEB: www.villageofgreenisland.com
SIC: 3699 Electrical equipment & supplies

(G-5875)
HUERSCH MARKETING GROUP LLC
70 Cohoes Ave Ste 4 (12183-1533)
PHONE..................518 874-1045
Thomas R Huerter, *CEO*
EMP: 11
SALES (est): 704.7K **Privately Held**
SIC: 2711 Commercial printing & newspaper publishing combined

(G-5876)
LAI INTERNATIONAL INC
1 Tibbits Ave (12183-1430)
PHONE..................763 780-0060
Rici Smentek, *Credit Mgr*
Michael Bagel, *Manager*
EMP: 60 **Privately Held**
SIC: 3728 Aircraft assemblies, subassemblies & parts
PA: Lai International, Inc.
7645 Baker St Ne
Minneapolis MN 55432

(G-5877)
LYDALL PERFORMANCE MTL INC
68 George St (12183-1113)
PHONE..................518 273-6320
Donald Ackerman, *QC Mgr*
John Minnick, *Engineer*
Timothy Reilly, *VP Finance*
Terrence Dingman, *Director*
Chuck Carlstrom, *Director*
◆ EMP: 115
SQ FT: 300,000
SALES (est): 28MM
SALES (corp-wide): 566.8MM **Publicly Held**
WEB: www.lydall.com
SIC: 2211 Cotton broad woven goods
PA: Lydall, Inc.
1 Colonial Rd
Manchester CT 06042
860 646-1233

(G-5878)
LYDALL PERFORMANCE MTLS INC
68 George St (12183-1113)
PHONE..................518 273-6320
EMP: 12
SALES (corp-wide): 566.8MM **Publicly Held**
SIC: 3569 Filters
HQ: Lydall Performance Materials, Inc.
134 Chestnut Hill Rd
Rochester NH 03867
603 332-4600

(G-5879)
RELIABLE BROTHERS INC
185 Cohoes Ave (12183-1501)
PHONE..................518 273-6732
Fax: 518 273-6784
Kyle Buchakjiar, *Ch of Bd*
Vahan Buchakjian, *President*
EMP: 30
SALES (est): 5.9MM **Privately Held**
SIC: 2013 5147 Meat extracts from purchased meat; meats, fresh

Greene
Chenango County

(G-5880)
AMERICAN BLADE MFG LLC
Also Called: Greene Brass & Aluminum Fndry
47 Birdsall St (13778-1053)
PHONE..................607 656-4204
Fax: 607 656-4245
Tom Todd, *Manager*
EMP: 8
SALES (corp-wide): 1.3MM **Privately Held**
WEB: www.charleslay.com
SIC: 3366 3365 Bronze foundry; aluminum foundries
PA: American Blade Manufacturing Llc
138 Roundhouse Rd
Oneonta NY 13820
607 432-4518

(G-5881)
CROSS COUNTRY MFG INC
2355 Rte 206 (13778)
P.O. Box 565 (13778-0565)
PHONE..................607 656-4103
Frank M Hanrahan, *Branch Mgr*
EMP: 15
SALES (corp-wide): 3.4MM **Privately Held**
WEB: www.crosscountrymfg.com
SIC: 3715 Truck trailers

Greene - Chenango County (G-5882)

PA: Cross Country Manufacturing, Inc.
2355 State Highway 206
Greene NY 13778
607 656-4103

(G-5882)
CROSS COUNTRY MFG INC (PA)
2355 State Highway 206 (13778-2367)
P.O. Box 565 (13778-0565)
PHONE..........................607 656-4103
Fax: 607 656-7188
Frank M Hanrahan, *President*
Catherine Hanrahan, *Vice Pres*
Ruth Smith, *Manager*
Leslie Haddad, *Admin Asst*
EMP: 18
SQ FT: 2,544
SALES (est): 3.4MM **Privately Held**
WEB: www.crosscountrymfg.com
SIC: 3715 Truck trailers

(G-5883)
G C CONTROLS INC
1408 County Road 2 (13778-2257)
PHONE..........................607 656-4117
Fax: 607 656-7452
Mert Gilbert, *Ch of Bd*
Steven Gilbert, *Principal*
Dan Snowberger, *Vice Pres*
Peggy Clark, *Manager*
EMP: 40
SQ FT: 12,000
SALES (est): 8.6MM **Privately Held**
WEB: www.gccontrols.com
SIC: 3625 Relays & industrial controls; control equipment, electric; timing devices, electronic

(G-5884)
GREENE TECHNOLOGIES INC
Grand & Clinton St (13778)
PHONE..........................607 656-4166
Fax: 607 656-9363
Carol M Rosenkrantz, *Chairman*
Robert Lindridge, *Vice Pres*
George Howe, *Plant Mgr*
Douglas Ramsay, *Engineer*
Mark Rosenkrantz, *Director*
EMP: 100
SQ FT: 49,000
SALES (est): 16.4MM **Privately Held**
WEB: www.greenetech.biz
SIC: 3444 3479 3471 3469 Sheet metalwork; coating of metals & formed products; electroplating of metals or formed products; polishing, metals or formed products; metal stampings

(G-5885)
RAPP SIGNS INC
3979 State Route 206 (13778-2134)
PHONE..........................607 656-8167
Fax: 607 656-8677
Ronald J Rapp, *President*
David Rapp, *Principal*
Lorraine Detweiler, *Plant Mgr*
Darlene Wilkins, *Manager*
EMP: 13
SALES (est): 1.3MM **Privately Held**
SIC: 3993 1799 Signs, not made in custom sign painting shops; sign installation & maintenance

(G-5886)
RAYMOND CONSOLIDATED CORP (DH)
22 S Canal St (13778-1244)
PHONE..........................800 235-7200
Jim Malvaso, *President*
Timothy Combs, *Exec VP*
John Everts, *Vice Pres*
Ryan Delaney, *QC Mgr*
Edward J Rompala, *CFO*
◆ **EMP:** 200
SQ FT: 180,000
SALES (est): 768MM
SALES (corp-wide): 19.8B **Privately Held**
SIC: 3537 Industrial trucks & tractors
HQ: Toyota Material Handling Europe Ab
Svarvargatan 8
Mjolby 595 3
142 860-00

(G-5887)
RAYMOND CORPORATION (DH)
22 S Canal St (13778-1244)
P.O. Box 130 (13778-0130)
PHONE..........................800 235-7200
Michael G Field, *President*
Eric Hills, *General Mgr*
Louis J Callea, *Counsel*
Arthur A Goodell, *Counsel*
Timothy Combs, *Exec VP*
◆ **EMP:** 800 **EST:** 1887
SQ FT: 325,000
SALES (est): 768MM
SALES (corp-wide): 19.8B **Privately Held**
WEB: www.raymondcorp.com
SIC: 3537 3535 7359 Industrial trucks & tractors; lift trucks, industrial: fork, platform, straddle, etc.; forklift trucks; straddle carriers, mobile; conveyors & conveying equipment; belt conveyor systems, general industrial use; pneumatic tube conveyor systems; equipment rental & leasing; aircraft & industrial truck rental services
HQ: Raymond Consolidated Corporation
22 S Canal St
Greene NY 13778
800 235-7200

(G-5888)
RAYMOND SALES CORPORATION
22 S Canal St (13778-1244)
P.O. Box 130 (13778-0130)
PHONE..........................607 656-2311
James Malvaso, *Principal*
Diana Gurney, *Manager*
EMP: 3
SQ FT: 325,000
SALES (est): 20.9MM
SALES (corp-wide): 19.8B **Privately Held**
SIC: 3537 5084 Forklift trucks; materials handling machinery
HQ: The Raymond Corporation
22 S Canal St
Greene NY 13778
800 235-7200

Greenfield Center
Saratoga County

(G-5889)
PECKHAM INDUSTRIES INC
430 Coy Rd (12833-1042)
PHONE..........................518 893-2176
William H Peckham, *Branch Mgr*
EMP: 18
SALES (corp-wide): 200.6MM **Privately Held**
SIC: 2951 Concrete, asphaltic (not from refineries)
PA: Peckham Industries, Inc.
20 Haarlem Ave Ste 200
White Plains NY 10603
914 949-2000

Greenlawn
Suffolk County

(G-5890)
ALL CULTURES INC
Also Called: American Culture
12 Gates St (11740-1427)
PHONE..........................631 293-3143
Louis Guaneri, *CEO*
Louis Guarneri, *Manager*
◆ **EMP:** 35
SQ FT: 30,000
SALES (est): 6.7MM **Privately Held**
WEB: www.americanculturehair.com
SIC: 2844 Hair preparations, including shampoos; shampoos; rinses, conditioners: hair

(G-5891)
BAE SYSTEMS INFO & ELEC SYS
450 Pulaski Rd (11740-1606)
PHONE..........................631 912-1525
Anthony Boniciolli, *Engineer*
Richard F Brofka, *Engineer*
Steve Fischetti, *Engineer*
Robert Lafferty, *Project Engr*
Arin Lanis, *Senior Engr*
EMP: 8
SALES (corp-wide): 21.9B **Privately Held**
WEB: www.iesi.na.baesystems.com
SIC: 3823 Digital displays of process variables
HQ: Bae Systems Information And Electronic Systems Integration Inc.
65 Spit Brook Rd
Nashua NH 03060
603 885-4321

(G-5892)
MB PLASTICS INC (PA)
130 Stony Hollow Rd (11740-1511)
PHONE..........................718 523-1180
Fax: 718 526-4002
Milton Bassin, *President*
Sandra Benton, *Personnel*
Eddy Megerne, *Manager*
▲ **EMP:** 14 **EST:** 1964
SQ FT: 15,000
SALES (est): 1.5MM **Privately Held**
SIC: 2821 3911 Plastics materials & resins; jewelry apparel

(G-5893)
MEDICAL TECHNOLOGY PRODUCTS
33a Smith St (11740-1219)
PHONE..........................631 285-6640
Fax: 631 285-6641
Thomas J Hartnett Jr, *Ch of Bd*
David Hawkins, *Admin Sec*
EMP: 8
SQ FT: 5,000
SALES (est): 1MM **Privately Held**
SIC: 3841 Surgical & medical instruments

Greenport
Suffolk County

(G-5894)
125-127 MAIN STREET CORP
Also Called: Mills, William J & Company
125 Main St 127 (11944-1421)
P.O. Box 2126 (11944-0978)
PHONE..........................631 477-1500
Fax: 631 477-1504
William J Mills III, *President*
Robert Hills, *Vice Pres*
Maureen Mills, *Financial Exec*
EMP: 18 **EST:** 1880
SQ FT: 25,000
SALES (est): 2MM **Privately Held**
WEB: www.millscanvas.com
SIC: 2394 Awnings, fabric: made from purchased materials; sails: made from purchased materials

(G-5895)
STIDD SYSTEMS INC
220 Carpenter St (11944-1406)
P.O. Box 87 (11944-0087)
PHONE..........................631 477-2400
Fax: 631 477-1095
Walter A Gezari, *President*
Robert J Digregorio, *Vice Pres*
David J Wilberding, *Vice Pres*
Ian Strachan, *Engineer*
Abbey Boskoff, *Accountant*
▼ **EMP:** 36
SQ FT: 62,000
SALES (est): 10MM **Privately Held**
WEB: www.stidd.com
SIC: 2531 Vehicle furniture

(G-5896)
WOODEN BOATWORKS
190 Sterling St Unit 2 (11944-1454)
PHONE..........................631 477-6507
Robert Wahl, *Principal*
EMP: 6
SALES (est): 737.8K **Privately Held**
SIC: 3732 Boat building & repairing

Greenvale
Nassau County

(G-5897)
CALL FORWARDING TECHNOLOGIES
55 Northern Blvd Ste 3b (11548-1301)
PHONE..........................516 621-3600
Charles Hart, *President*
EMP: 7
SQ FT: 600
SALES (est): 810K **Privately Held**
SIC: 3661 Telephones & telephone apparatus

(G-5898)
DALMA DRESS MFG CO INC
3 Carman Rd (11548-1123)
PHONE..........................212 391-8296
Fax: 212 391-0076
Madalin Dipalma, *President*
Madalina Dipalma, *Owner*
Giovanna Darmiani, *Vice Pres*
EMP: 25
SQ FT: 5,500
SALES (est): 1.7MM **Privately Held**
SIC: 2335 2339 Women's, juniors' & misses' dresses; women's & misses' outerwear

(G-5899)
SLANT/FIN CORPORATION (PA)
100 Forest Dr (11548-1295)
P.O. Box 416 (11548-0416)
PHONE..........................516 484-2600
Fax: 516 484-2694
Melvin Dubin, *Ch of Bd*
Adam Dubin, *Chairman*
Gary Golden, *Plant Mgr*
Neil Segal, *Plant Mgr*
Robert Viets, *Buyer*
▲ **EMP:** 374 **EST:** 1949
SQ FT: 200,000
SALES (est): 75.4MM **Privately Held**
WEB: www.slantfin.com
SIC: 3433 3443 Heating equipment, except electric; fabricated plate work (boiler shop)

(G-5900)
SLANTCO MANUFACTURING INC (HQ)
100 Forest Dr (11548-1205)
PHONE..........................516 484-2600
Melvin Dubin, *President*
Selwyn Steinberg, *Senior VP*
John Sweiteck, *Vice Pres*
Donald Brown, *Treasurer*
Delcy Brooks, *Admin Sec*
EMP: 7 **EST:** 1976
SQ FT: 150,000
SALES (est): 1.2MM
SALES (corp-wide): 75.4MM **Privately Held**
SIC: 3443 Heat exchangers: coolers (after, inter), condensers, etc.
PA: Slant/Fin Corporation
100 Forest Dr
Greenvale NY 11548
516 484-2600

(G-5901)
WIN WOOD CABINETRY INC
200 Forest Dr Ste 7 (11548-1216)
PHONE..........................516 304-2216
Frank Lin, *President*
▲ **EMP:** 8
SALES (est): 413K **Privately Held**
SIC: 2434 Wood kitchen cabinets

Greenville
Greene County

(G-5902)
CLASSIC AUTO CRAFTS INC
Also Called: Town Line Auto
6501 State Route 32 (12083-2212)
P.O. Box 10 (12083-0010)
PHONE..........................518 966-8003
John Dolce, *President*

GEOGRAPHIC SECTION

Guilderland - Albany County (G-5925)

EMP: 8
SALES (est): 1.1MM **Privately Held**
WEB: www.townlineauto.com
SIC: 3599 Machine shop, jobbing & repair

(G-5903)
HAWKENCATSKILLS LLC
Also Called: Catskill Boiler Co.
18 Shultes Rd (12083-2032)
PHONE..................................518 966-8900
Bert Tobin,
Holly Tobin,
▲ **EMP:** 6 **EST:** 2006
SALES (est): 767.7K **Privately Held**
SIC: 3433 Burners, furnaces, boilers & stokers

Greenwich
Washington County

(G-5904)
BDP INDUSTRIES INC (PA)
Also Called: BELT DEWATERING PRESS
354 State Route 29 (12834-4518)
P.O. Box 118 (12834-0118)
PHONE..................................518 695-6851
Fax: 518 695-5417
Albert J Schmidt, *President*
Scott Enflinger, *Regional Mgr*
Kelly Falk, *Purchasing*
Steve Dobert, *Engineer*
Carl Fronhofer, *Treasurer*
EMP: 49 **EST:** 1978
SALES: 14.3MM **Privately Held**
WEB: www.bdpindustries.com
SIC: 3523 3545 3542 Turf & grounds equipment; machine tool accessories; machine tools, metal forming type

(G-5905)
BETTERBEE INC
Also Called: Southern Adirondack Honey Co.
8 Meader Rd (12834-2734)
PHONE..................................518 314-0575
Erica Stevens, *CEO*
Margaret A Stevens, *President*
Justin Stevens, *Exec VP*
John Rath, *Engineer*
Leah Sargood, *Sales Mgr*
◆ **EMP:** 15
SQ FT: 3,500
SALES (est): 2.6MM **Privately Held**
WEB: www.betterbee.com
SIC: 2499 3999 Beekeeping supplies, wood; candles

(G-5906)
FORT MILLER GROUP INC
688 Wilbur Ave (12834-4413)
P.O. Box 98, Schuylerville (12871-0098)
PHONE..................................518 695-5000
John T Hedbring, *Ch of Bd*
John Marcelle, *Exec VP*
Ira Adler, *QA Dir*
Richard Schumaker, *CFO*
Brian Myers, *Manager*
▲ **EMP:** 420
SQ FT: 160,000
SALES (est): 134MM
SALES (corp-wide): 156.8MM **Privately Held**
WEB: www.fortmiller.com
SIC: 3272 3441 Concrete products, precast; fabricated structural metal
PA: The Fort Miller Service Corp
688 Wilbur Ave
Greenwich NY 12834
518 695-5000

(G-5907)
FORT MILLER SERVICE CORP (PA)
688 Wilbur Ave (12834-4413)
P.O. Box 98, Schuylerville (12871-0098)
PHONE..................................518 695-5000
John T Hedbring, *Ch of Bd*
Mary Ann Spiezio, *Vice Pres*
Richard Schumaker, *CFO*
▼ **EMP:** 12
SQ FT: 10,000
SALES (est): 156.8MM **Privately Held**
SIC: 3272 3271 5211 1799 Concrete products, precast; burial vaults, concrete or precast terrazzo; concrete block & brick; concrete & cinder block; fence construction

(G-5908)
HOLLINGSWORTH & VOSE COMPANY
3235 County Rte 113 (12834)
PHONE..................................518 695-8000
Donald Wagner, *Opers-Prdtn-Mfg*
David Graham, *Engineer*
Ed Dunavin, *Human Res Mgr*
Paul Blinn, *Manager*
Laurie Moore, *Admin Asst*
EMP: 160
SQ FT: 3,594
SALES (corp-wide): 776.8MM **Privately Held**
WEB: www.hovo.com
SIC: 2621 3053 Filter paper; gasket materials
PA: Hollingsworth & Vose Company
112 Washington St
East Walpole MA 02032
508 850-2000

(G-5909)
ICE CREAM MAN INC
417 State Route 29 (12834-4233)
PHONE..................................518 692-8382
Fax: 518 692-1298
Julia Reynolds, *President*
EMP: 20
SALES: 200K **Privately Held**
WEB: www.the-ice-cream-man.com
SIC: 2024 Ice cream, bulk

(G-5910)
NORTHAST CTR FOR BEKEEPING LLC
Also Called: Betterbee
8 Meader Rd (12834-2734)
PHONE..................................800 632-3379
Christopher Cripps,
Joseph Cali,
John Rath,
EMP: 19
SALES (est): 1.5MM **Privately Held**
SIC: 2499 5191 3999 Beekeeping supplies, wood; beekeeping supplies (non-durable); beekeepers' supplies

(G-5911)
PHANTOM LABORATORY INC
Also Called: Phantom Laboratory, The
2727 State Route 29 (12834-3212)
P.O. Box 511, Salem (12865-0511)
PHONE..................................518 692-1190
Fax: 518 692-3329
Joshua Levy, *President*
Julie Simms, *Vice Pres*
Bonnie Hanlon, *VP Opers*
Megan Stalter, *Cust Mgr*
Ariel Dickson, *Manager*
EMP: 15
SQ FT: 65,000
SALES: 750K **Privately Held**
WEB: www.phantomlab.com
SIC: 3844 X-ray apparatus & tubes

(G-5912)
SCA TISSUE NORTH AMERICA LLC
72 County Route 53 (12834-2233)
PHONE..................................518 692-8434
Fax: 518 692-8451
Michael Bell, *Safety Mgr*
Cathy Crimmins, *Purch Agent*
Glenn Jones, *Branch Mgr*
Karen Brockway, *Manager*
William Dunphy, *Manager*
EMP: 50
SALES (corp-wide): 12.6B **Privately Held**
WEB: www.scatissue.com
SIC: 2621 Paper mills; napkin stock, paper; facial tissue stock; toilet tissue stock
HQ: Sca Tissue North America, Llc
984 Winchester Rd
Neenah WI 54956
920 727-3770

(G-5913)
SOUTHERN ADRNDCK FBR PRDCRS CP
2532 State Route 40 (12834-2300)
PHONE..................................518 692-2700
Mary Jeanne Packer, *President*
EMP: 5
SALES: 50K **Privately Held**
SIC: 2299 Textile goods

(G-5914)
TEFFT PUBLISHERS INC
Also Called: Journal Stationers
35 Salem St (12834-1320)
PHONE..................................518 692-9290
Sally Tefft, *President*
Culver Tefft, *Vice Pres*
EMP: 9 **EST:** 1980
SQ FT: 2,766
SALES (est): 384.6K **Privately Held**
SIC: 2711 5943 Newspapers: publishing only, not printed on site; writing supplies

(G-5915)
TYMETAL CORP (HQ)
678 Wilbur Ave (12834-4413)
P.O. Box 139, Schuylerville (12871-0139)
PHONE..................................518 692-9930
Fax: 518 692-9404
John T Hedbring, *President*
Rob Douglas, *President*
Douglas Blanchard, *Opers Mgr*
Peg Harrington, *Opers Staff*
O E S Hedbring, *Treasurer*
EMP: 30
SQ FT: 25,000
SALES: 15MM
SALES (corp-wide): 156.8MM **Privately Held**
WEB: www.tymetal.com
SIC: 3446 3441 Fences, gates, posts & flagpoles; fabricated structural metal
PA: The Fort Miller Service Corp
688 Wilbur Ave
Greenwich NY 12834
518 695-5000

Greenwood Lake
Orange County

(G-5916)
AUTOMATED ELEVATOR SYSTEMS
659 Jersey Ave (10925-2014)
PHONE..................................845 595-1063
Jacqueline Doyle, *Principal*
EMP: 20
SALES (est): 527.2K **Privately Held**
SIC: 3534 Elevators & moving stairways

(G-5917)
BARNABY PRINTS INC (PA)
673 Jersey Ave (10925-2014)
P.O. Box 98 (10925-0098)
PHONE..................................845 477-2501
Fax: 845 477-2739
Robert Brodhurst, *President*
William Neuhaus, *Treasurer*
Diane Eccher, *Office Mgr*
EMP: 15
SQ FT: 12,000
SALES (est): 1.1MM **Privately Held**
SIC: 2759 2396 Screen printing; automotive & apparel trimmings

Groton
Tompkins County

(G-5918)
BAY HORSE INNOVATIONS NYINC
130 Cayuga St (13073-1002)
PHONE..................................607 898-3337
Gene Velten, *President*
EMP: 5
SALES (est): 424.1K **Privately Held**
SIC: 3599 Industrial machinery

(G-5919)
C & D ASSEMBLY INC
107 Corona Ave (13073-1206)
PHONE..................................607 898-4275
Fax: 607 898-4685
Jeffrey Cronk, *President*
Barb Eberhardt, *Editor*
Michael Hammond, *Vice Pres*
John Wolff, *Prdtn Mgr*
Dale Harris, *Purchasing*
▲ **EMP:** 42
SQ FT: 10,600
SALES (est): 9.5MM **Privately Held**
WEB: www.cdassembly.com
SIC: 3672 8731 Printed circuit boards; electronic research

(G-5920)
CAYUGA TOOL AND DIE INC
182 Newman Rd (13073-8712)
PHONE..................................607 533-7400
Fax: 607 533-7401
Judson Bailey, *President*
Becky Bailey, *Treasurer*
EMP: 9
SQ FT: 3,680
SALES (est): 664.9K **Privately Held**
SIC: 3599 Machine shop, jobbing & repair

(G-5921)
LEWBRO READY MIX INC (PA)
502 Locke Rd (13073-9494)
PHONE..................................315 497-0498
Mitchell Metzgar, *President*
EMP: 6
SQ FT: 5,000
SALES (est): 833.3K **Privately Held**
SIC: 3273 Ready-mixed concrete

(G-5922)
MARTINEZ SPECIALTIES INC
205 Bossard Rd (13073-9779)
PHONE..................................607 898-3053
Philip Martinez, *President*
Dorothy Martinez, *Vice Pres*
Jamie Young, *Vice Pres*
EMP: 8
SALES (est): 1.1MM **Privately Held**
SIC: 3694 Ignition apparatus & distributors

(G-5923)
PYLANTIS NEW YORK LLC
102 E Cortland St (13073-1108)
PHONE..................................310 429-5911
Jeff Toolan, *CEO*
Eli Gill, *COO*
Matt Ruttenberg,
EMP: 5 **EST:** 2012
SALES (est): 348.9K **Privately Held**
SIC: 3089 Injection molding of plastics

Guilderland
Albany County

(G-5924)
CUSTOM PRTRS GUILDERLAND INC
Also Called: Guilderland Printing
2210 Western Ave (12084-9701)
PHONE..................................518 456-2811
Fax: 518 456-1093
Joyce Ragone, *President*
Thomas Ragone, *Vice Pres*
Kathleen Szesnat, *Manager*
EMP: 15
SQ FT: 4,000
SALES (est): 2.7MM **Privately Held**
SIC: 2759 Commercial printing

(G-5925)
PRICE CHOPPER OPERATING CO
2080 Western Ave Ste 160 (12084-9564)
PHONE..................................518 456-5115
Fax: 518 456-0494
Cathy Gorman, *Branch Mgr*
EMP: 5
SALES (corp-wide): 3.4B **Privately Held**
SIC: 3751 Motorcycles & related parts
HQ: Price Chopper Operating Co., Inc
501 Duanesburg Rd
Schenectady NY 12306
518 379-1600

Hadley
Saratoga County

(G-5926)
NORTHEASTERN ELECTRIC MOTORS
34 Hollow Rd (12835-2822)
PHONE..................518 793-5939
Walter R Burnham, *President*
EMP: 5
SQ FT: 6,500
SALES (est): 380K **Privately Held**
SIC: 7694 5063 Electric motor repair; rewinding services; motors, electric

Halcottsville
Delaware County

(G-5927)
ALTA INDUSTRIES LTD
Also Called: Alta Log Homes
46966 State Hwy 30 (12438)
PHONE..................845 586-3336
Fax: 845 586-2582
Frank Mann, *President*
David S Mann, *Vice Pres*
Ken Castle, *Plant Mgr*
Heather Davie, *Production*
Franscine Ladenheim, *Purch Mgr*
EMP: 16
SQ FT: 7,000
SALES (est): 2.2MM **Privately Held**
WEB: www.altaloghomes.com
SIC: 2452 Log cabins, prefabricated, wood

Halesite
Suffolk County

(G-5928)
MANUFACTURERS INDEXING PDTS
Also Called: Mip
53 Gristmill Ln (11743-2134)
PHONE..................631 271-0956
Charles Busk Jr, *President*
Janet Boone, *Bookkeeper*
EMP: 9 EST: 1964
SQ FT: 12,000
SALES (est): 787.7K **Privately Held**
SIC: 2821 2675 Vinyl resins; die-cut paper & board

(G-5929)
ROSE FENCE INC
356 Bay Ave (11743-1141)
PHONE..................516 790-2308
EMP: 88
SALES (corp-wide): 20.2MM **Privately Held**
SIC: 3496 Fencing, made from purchased wire
PA: Rose Fence, Inc.
  345 W Sunrise Hwy
  Freeport NY 11520
  516 223-0777

Halfmoon
Saratoga County

(G-5930)
ADVANCE ENERGY TECH INC
1 Solar Dr (12065-3402)
PHONE..................518 371-2140
Timothy K Carlo, *Ch of Bd*
EMP: 27 EST: 1965
SQ FT: 30,000
SALES (est): 6.4MM **Privately Held**
WEB: www.advanceet.com
SIC: 3585 Parts for heating, cooling & refrigerating equipment

(G-5931)
CAPITAL DISTRICT STAIRS INC
45 Dunsbach Rd (12065-7906)
PHONE..................518 383-2449
Fax: 518 371-9655
Alex Nikiforov, *President*
EMP: 7
SALES (est): 1MM **Privately Held**
WEB: www.capitaldistrictstairs.com
SIC: 2431 Staircases & stairs, wood; stair railings, wood

(G-5932)
EBELING ASSOCIATES INC (PA)
Also Called: Control Global Solutions
9 Corporate Dr Ste 1 (12065-8636)
PHONE..................518 688-8700
Allan Robison, *President*
James Colunio, *CIO*
Scott Ebeling, *Systems Analyst*
EMP: 18
SQ FT: 5,500
SALES (est): 1.9MM **Privately Held**
WEB: www.execontrol.com
SIC: 7372 Prepackaged software

(G-5933)
INFO LABEL INC
12 Enterprise Ave (12065-3424)
PHONE..................518 664-0791
Mark Dufort, *President*
EMP: 15
SQ FT: 7,000
SALES (est): 2MM **Privately Held**
WEB: www.infolabel.net
SIC: 2759 5084 Labels & seals: printing; printing trades machinery, equipment & supplies

(G-5934)
MOTOROLA SOLUTIONS INC
7 Deer Run Holw (12065-5664)
PHONE..................518 348-0833
Carolely Urgenson, *Principal*
Thomas Lee, *Electrical Engi*
Harvey Edelman, *Manager*
EMP: 148
SALES (corp-wide): 6B **Publicly Held**
WEB: www.motorola.com
SIC: 3663 Radio broadcasting & communications equipment
PA: Motorola Solutions, Inc.
  500 W Monroe St Ste 4400
  Chicago IL 60661
  847 576-5000

(G-5935)
MOVINADS & SIGNS LLC
1771 Route 9 (12065-2413)
PHONE..................518 378-3000
Fax: 518 937-9022
Rob Potter, *President*
EMP: 5 EST: 2007
SQ FT: 4,000
SALES (est): 300K **Privately Held**
SIC: 3993 Signs & advertising specialties

(G-5936)
REQUEST INC
Also Called: Request Multimedia
14 Corporate Dr Ste 6 (12065-8607)
PHONE..................518 899-1254
Fax: 518 899-1251
Peter M Cholnoky, *President*
Andy Lopez, *Sales Dir*
Susan Zelensky, *Accounts Mgr*
Scott Bartgis, *Director*
EMP: 30
SQ FT: 8,100
SALES (est): 5MM **Privately Held**
WEB: www.request.com
SIC: 3651 Home entertainment equipment, electronic

(G-5937)
REQUEST SERIOUS PLAY LLC
14 Corporate Dr (12065-8607)
PHONE..................518 899-1254
Barry Evans, *Principal*
EMP: 7
SALES (est): 680K **Privately Held**
SIC: 3651 Home entertainment equipment, electronic

(G-5938)
SAVE MORE BEVERAGE CORP
Also Called: Uptown
1512 Route 9 Ste 1 (12065-8664)
PHONE..................518 371-1764
Fax: 518 371-1764
Harold Rockowitz, *President*
Donald Morin, *Vice Pres*
Robert Popp, *Treasurer*
EMP: 8
SALES (est): 2.5MM **Privately Held**
SIC: 2086 5921 5149 5181 Carbonated beverages, nonalcoholic: bottled & canned; beer (packaged); soft drinks; beer & other fermented malt liquors

(G-5939)
ZAPPONE CHRYSLER JEEP DDGE INC
1780 Route 9 (12065-2402)
PHONE..................518 982-0610
James M Zappone, *Ch of Bd*
Ken Pelcher, *Owner*
EMP: 19
SALES (est): 3.5MM **Privately Held**
SIC: 3699 5511 Heat emission operating apparatus; new & used car dealers

Hall
Ontario County

(G-5940)
MILLCO WOODWORKING LLC
1710 Railroad Pl (14463-9005)
P.O. Box 38 (14463-0038)
PHONE..................585 526-6844
Fax: 585 526-5664
Charles L Millerd,
Mark M Millerd,
EMP: 11
SQ FT: 6,290
SALES (est): 1.6MM **Privately Held**
WEB: www.millcowoodworking.com
SIC: 2434 2431 Wood kitchen cabinets; millwork

Hamburg
Erie County

(G-5941)
ABASCO INC
5225 Southwestern Blvd (14075-3524)
P.O. Box 247 (14075-0247)
PHONE..................716 649-4790
Fax: 716 649-4791
Frank A Saeli Jr, *President*
Michael Saeli, *Vice Pres*
Bill Seipel, *Vice Pres*
Michael Hitt, *Purch Mgr*
William G Seipel, *Marketing Mgr*
▲ EMP: 30 EST: 1962
SALES (est): 8.4MM **Privately Held**
WEB: www.abasco.net
SIC: 3613 3449 Control panels, electric; miscellaneous metalwork

(G-5942)
CAPITAL CONCRETE INC
5690 Camp Rd (14075-3706)
PHONE..................716 648-8001
Rosanne Lettieri, *President*
EMP: 6
SALES (est): 912.9K **Privately Held**
SIC: 3273 Ready-mixed concrete

(G-5943)
CLASSIC AWNINGS INC
Also Called: Classic Awnings & Party Tents
1 Elmview Ave (14075-3761)
PHONE..................716 649-0390
David Vesneske, *President*
EMP: 12
SQ FT: 5,000
SALES (est): 750K **Privately Held**
WEB: www.classicawnings.com
SIC: 2394 7359 Awnings, fabric: made from purchased materials; tent & tarpaulin rental

(G-5944)
E-ONE INC
4760 Camp Rd (14075-2604)
PHONE..................716 646-6790
Kevin Nunn, *Regl Sales Mgr*
Jeffrey Hermann, *Branch Mgr*
William Graczyk, *Commissioner*
EMP: 70 **Publicly Held**
SIC: 3537 Industrial trucks & tractors
HQ: E-One, Inc.
  1601 Sw 37th Ave
  Ocala FL 34474
  352 237-1122

(G-5945)
EATON BROTHERS CORP
3530 Lakeview Rd (14075-6160)
P.O. Box 60 (14075-0060)
PHONE..................716 649-8250
Fax: 716 649-9466
Ralph D Allen, *President*
Gary Allen, *Exec VP*
Christopher Allen, *Shareholder*
▲ EMP: 9
SQ FT: 21,000
SALES (est): 2MM **Privately Held**
WEB: www.eatonbrothers.com
SIC: 3524 3272 Lawn & garden tractors & equipment; tombstones, precast terrazzo or concrete

(G-5946)
EL-DON BATTERY POST INC
4109 Saint Francis Dr (14075-1722)
PHONE..................716 627-3697
Fax: 716 896-0406
Gary K Logsdon, *Principal*
Cindy Logsdon, *Manager*
EMP: 5
SALES (est): 833.7K **Privately Held**
SIC: 3691 5063 Storage batteries; batteries

(G-5947)
EMCS LLC
4414 Manor Ln (14075-1117)
PHONE..................716 523-2002
Ed Monacelli, *President*
Rob Haefner, *Vice Pres*
EMP: 7
SALES (est): 839.5K **Privately Held**
SIC: 3572 Computer storage devices

(G-5948)
EVENHOUSE PRINTING
4783 Southwestern Blvd (14075-1926)
PHONE..................716 649-2666
Fax: 716 649-0266
Robin L Evenhouse, *Partner*
EMP: 7
SALES (est): 736.6K **Privately Held**
WEB: www.evenhouseprinting.com
SIC: 2759 Commercial printing

(G-5949)
GATEWAY PRTG & GRAPHICS INC
3970 Big Tree Rd (14075-1320)
PHONE..................716 823-3873
Jeffery Donner, *President*
Eugene Donner, *Corp Secy*
Brian Lattimore, *Production*
Brenda Blazevic, *Office Mgr*
Brenda Blazek, *Admin Sec*
EMP: 22
SQ FT: 20,000
SALES (est): 4.7MM **Privately Held**
WEB: www.gatewayprints.com
SIC: 2752 2791 2789 2761 Commercial printing, offset; typesetting; bookbinding & related work; manifold business forms

(G-5950)
GREAT AMERICAN TOOL CO INC
7223 Boston State Rd (14075-6932)
P.O. Box 600, Getzville (14068-0600)
PHONE..................716 646-5700
Fax: 716 877-2591
John Anthon, *President*
▲ EMP: 6
SALES (est): 1MM **Privately Held**
WEB: www.timberlineknives.com
SIC: 3546 3421 Power-driven handtools; table & food cutlery, including butchers'

GEOGRAPHIC SECTION

Hammond - St. Lawrence County (G-5974)

(G-5951)
HAWKEYE FOREST PRODUCTS LP (PA)
Also Called: Hawkeye Forest Products
4002 Legion Dr (14075-4508)
PHONE..................608 534-6156
Jeffrey Meyer, *President*
Andrew Lander, *Credit Mgr*
Karen Long, *Executive*
EMP: 14
SALES (est): 2.7MM **Privately Held**
SIC: 2421 Sawmills & planing mills, general

(G-5952)
JOBS WEEKLY INC
Also Called: Wny Jobs.com
31 Buffalo St Ste 2 (14075-5000)
PHONE..................716 648-5627
Fax: 716 648-5658
Thomas Kluckhohn, *President*
Carl Kluckhohn, *Vice Pres*
Steve Kluckhohn, *Treasurer*
Susan O'Connor, *Manager*
Joe Rindfuss, *Admin Sec*
EMP: 11
SALES: 1MM **Privately Held**
WEB: www.wnyjobs.com
SIC: 2711 Newspapers

(G-5953)
K & H INDUSTRIES INC (PA)
160 Elmview Ave (14075-3763)
PHONE..................716 312-0088
Fax: 716 312-0028
Joseph Pinker Jr, *Ch of Bd*
Karl A Baake, *President*
John Herc, *Vice Pres*
Joe Panker Jr, *Vice Pres*
Tim Cooke, *Purchasing*
▲ **EMP:** 17 **EST:** 1960
SQ FT: 100,000
SALES (est): 4.7MM **Privately Held**
WEB: www.khindustries.com
SIC: 3641 3643 3599 3089 Lamps, fluorescent, electric; plugs, electric; connectors & terminals for electrical devices; electrical discharge machining (EDM); injection molding of plastics

(G-5954)
K & H INDUSTRIES INC
160 Elmview Ave (14075-3763)
PHONE..................716 312-0088
Robert Kickbuslt, *Sales Dir*
Klaus Baake, *Branch Mgr*
EMP: 20
SALES (corp-wide): 4.7MM **Privately Held**
WEB: www.khindustries.com
SIC: 3089 3641 Injection molding of plastics; lamps, fluorescent, electric
PA: K & H Industries, Inc.
  160 Elmview Ave
  Hamburg NY 14075
  716 312-0088

(G-5955)
KRAGEL CO INC
Also Called: Custom Bags Unlimited
23 Lake St (14075-4940)
P.O. Box 71 (14075-0071)
PHONE..................716 648-1344
Fax: 716 648-6833
Jim Bednasz, *President*
EMP: 7
SQ FT: 4,980
SALES (est): 150K **Privately Held**
SIC: 2394 2221 2393 Canvas & related products; liners & covers, fabric: made from purchased materials; nylon broadwoven fabrics; textile bags

(G-5956)
KUSTOM KORNER
Also Called: West Herr Automotive Group
5140 Camp Rd (14075-2704)
PHONE..................716 646-0173
Scott Beiler, *President*
Eric Zimmerman, *General Mgr*
Mark Boland, *Manager*
EMP: 13
SALES (est): 1.2MM **Privately Held**
SIC: 3465 Body parts, automobile: stamped metal

(G-5957)
NITRO MANUFACTURING LLC
106 Evans St Ste E (14075-6169)
PHONE..................716 646-9900
Bill Frascella, *Manager*
EMP: 10
SALES (est): 246.8K **Privately Held**
SIC: 3999 Barber & beauty shop equipment

(G-5958)
NORTHEASTERN TRANSPARTS INC
5727 S Park Ave (14075-3022)
PHONE..................716 833-0792
Ronald Gutowski, *Owner*
Wendy Gutowski, *Manager*
EMP: 13
SQ FT: 13,500
SALES (est): 1.2MM **Privately Held**
WEB: www.northeasterntransparts.com
SIC: 3714 Transmission housings or parts, motor vehicle

(G-5959)
ON THE MARK DIGITAL PRINTING &
5758 S Park Ave (14075-3739)
PHONE..................716 823-3373
Mark Poydock, *President*
EMP: 5
SALES (est): 626.7K **Privately Held**
SIC: 3993 Signs & advertising specialties

(G-5960)
POTTER LUMBER CO LLC
4002 Legion Dr (14075-4508)
P.O. Box 9001 (14075-9091)
PHONE..................814 438-7888
Andrew Lander, *Credit Mgr*
Jeffrey Meyer, *Mng Member*
▼ **EMP:** 100 **EST:** 2013
SALES (est): 5.9MM **Privately Held**
SIC: 2426 Lumber, hardwood dimension

(G-5961)
PRAXAIR INC
5322 Scranton Rd (14075-2935)
PHONE..................716 649-1600
Jim Hodgson, *Manager*
EMP: 20
SALES (corp-wide): 10.5B **Publicly Held**
SIC: 2813 Industrial gases
PA: Praxair, Inc.
  10 Riverview Dr
  Danbury CT 06810
  203 837-2000

(G-5962)
QUEST MANUFACTURING INC
5600 Camp Rd (14075-3706)
PHONE..................716 312-8000
Kimberly M Leach, *Principal*
Dennis Crissy, *Sales Staff*
John Kennedy, *Sales Staff*
Matt Sharpless, *Sales Staff*
Gloria Obrien, *Manager*
EMP: 20
SALES (est): 2.8MM **Privately Held**
SIC: 3999 Manufacturing industries

(G-5963)
QUO VADIS EDITIONS INC
120 Elmview Ave (14075-3770)
PHONE..................716 648-2602
Oliver Beltrami, *CEO*
Jerome Malavoy, *Ch of Bd*
Richard T Lydo, *General Mgr*
Keith Porter, *Senior VP*
Sandra Fox, *Opers Staff*
▲ **EMP:** 34
SQ FT: 45,000
SALES (est): 3.9MM
SALES (corp-wide): 1.3MM **Privately Held**
SIC: 2782 Diaries
HQ: Editions Quo Vadis
  Zone Industrielle
  Carquefou 44470
  240 304-812

(G-5964)
RIEFLER CONCRETE PRODUCTS LLC
5690 Camp Rd (14075-3706)
PHONE..................716 649-3260
Michael Sheehan, *President*
Echarles Cotten, *Vice Pres*
David J Lichner, *VP Opers*
Thomas Noonan, *Treasurer*
William C Haas, *VP Sales*
EMP: 170
SQ FT: 6,700
SALES (est): 20.1MM **Privately Held**
SIC: 3273 5999 3271 3272 Ready-mixed concrete; concrete products, pre-cast; blocks, concrete or cinder: standard; concrete products

(G-5965)
ROLY DOOR SALES INC
5659 Herman Hill Rd (14075-6909)
PHONE..................716 877-1515
Frank Sowa, *President*
EMP: 5 **EST:** 1952
SALES (est): 328.6K **Privately Held**
SIC: 3442 Garage doors, overhead: metal

(G-5966)
SINCLAIR TECHNOLOGIES INC (DH)
5811 S Park Ave 3 (14075-3738)
PHONE..................716 874-3682
Valerie Sinclair, *Ch of Bd*
David Ralston, *President*
David Grinstead, *Vice Pres*
David Savel, *CFO*
Andrea Sinclair, *Treasurer*
EMP: 21 **EST:** 1960
SQ FT: 36,000
SALES (est): 1.6MM
SALES (corp-wide): 498.5MM **Privately Held**
WEB: www.sinctech.com
SIC: 3663 5065 3674 3643 Antennas, transmitting & communications; communication equipment; amateur radio communications equipment; semiconductors & related devices; current-carrying wiring devices; switchgear & switchboard apparatus; nonferrous wiredrawing & insulating
HQ: Sinclair Technologies Inc
  85 Mary St
  Aurora ON
  905 727-0165

(G-5967)
STAUB MACHINE COMPANY INC
Also Called: Staub Square
206 Lake St (14075-4471)
PHONE..................716 649-4211
Anthony J Staub, *Ch of Bd*
Tony Staub, *President*
Jim Staub, *Opers Mgr*
Rhonda Bachert, *Controller*
Erik Bauerlein, *Marketing Mgr*
EMP: 20
SQ FT: 1,500
SALES (est): 4.1MM **Privately Held**
WEB: www.staubmachine.com
SIC: 3599 Machine shop, jobbing & repair

(G-5968)
WILLIAM R SHOEMAKER INC
399 Pleasant Ave (14075-4719)
PHONE..................716 649-0511
Fax: 716 649-2750
William R Shoemaker, *President*
EMP: 5
SQ FT: 1,800
SALES (est): 708.8K **Privately Held**
SIC: 3569 Firefighting apparatus

(G-5969)
WORLDWIDE PROTECTIVE PDTS LLC
4255 Mckinley Pkwy (14075-1005)
PHONE..................877 678-4568
Fax: 716 332-9280
Matt Stucke, *Managing Prtnr*
Jennifer Zicardi, *Manager*
Ed Mesanovic,
▲ **EMP:** 200
SALES (est): 63.1MM **Privately Held**
WEB: www.wwprotective.com
SIC: 3151 Gloves, leather: work

Hamilton
Madison County

(G-5970)
COSSITT CONCRETE PRODUCTS INC
6543 Middleport Rd (13346-2275)
P.O. Box 379 (13346-0379)
PHONE..................315 824-2700
Fax: 315 824-2823
Lance Kenyon, *President*
Lance Cenyon, *Vice Pres*
Jeniffer Tfardakas, *Accounts Mgr*
EMP: 10 **EST:** 1947
SQ FT: 1,500
SALES (est): 2MM **Privately Held**
SIC: 3271 3272 3273 5211 Concrete block & brick; concrete stuctural support & building material; ready-mixed concrete; lumber & other building materials

(G-5971)
JAMES MORRIS
Also Called: Madison Manufacturing
6697 Airport Rd (13346-2118)
PHONE..................315 824-8519
James Morris, *Owner*
Bob Britton, *General Mgr*
EMP: 30
SQ FT: 6,000
SALES (est): 2.8MM **Privately Held**
WEB: www.jamesmorris.net
SIC: 3559 Electronic component making machinery

(G-5972)
PARRYS INCORPORATED
Also Called: Parry's Hardware
100 Utica St (13346-2009)
PHONE..................315 824-0002
Fax: 315 824-0086
Gwenn Werner, *Ch of Bd*
Bill Parry, *Partner*
Rebecca Parry, *Partner*
Evan Werner, *Principal*
EMP: 11
SQ FT: 9,000
SALES: 1.8MM **Privately Held**
WEB: www.morrisvilleny.com
SIC: 3663 7378 5731 Cellular radio telephone; computer maintenance & repair; consumer electronic equipment

Hamlin
Monroe County

(G-5973)
HF TECHNOLOGIES LLC
810 Martin Rd (14464-9743)
PHONE..................585 254-5030
David Fletcher,
Angela Fletcher,
EMP: 20 **EST:** 2001
SQ FT: 25,000
SALES (est): 2.3MM **Privately Held**
WEB: www.hftechnologies.com
SIC: 3577 3955 Printers, computer; print cartridges for laser & other computer printers

Hammond
St. Lawrence County

(G-5974)
YESTERYEARS VINTAGE DOORS LLC
66 S Main St (13646-3201)
PHONE..................315 324-5250
Fax: 315 324-5250
Erica Demick, *Natl Sales Mgr*
Howard Demick,
EMP: 9
SQ FT: 5,760

Hammondsport - Steuben County (G-5975)

Hammondsport
Steuben County

(G-5975)
ATLAS METAL INDUSTRIES INC
17 Wheeler Ave (14840-9566)
PHONE..............................607 776-2048
EMP: 1 EST: 2012
SALES (est): 3.4MM
SALES (corp-wide): 114.1MM Privately Held
SIC: 3999 Manufacturing industries
PA: Mercury Aircraft Inc.
  8126 County Route 88
  Hammondsport NY 14840
  607 569-4200

(G-5976)
CUSTOM MANUFACTURING INC
93 Lake St (14840-9563)
PHONE..............................607 569-2738
Carmen J Waters, President
Michael Waters, Vice Pres
▲ EMP: 5
SALES: 700K Privately Held
WEB: www.archivalboxes.com
SIC: 2655 Containers, liquid tight fiber: from purchased material

(G-5977)
HEARTWOOD SPECIALTIES INC
10249 Gibson Rd (14840-9431)
PHONE..............................607 654-0102
Bruce G Bozman, President
EMP: 7
SQ FT: 5,000
SALES (est): 680K Privately Held
SIC: 2521 2541 Wood office furniture; wood partitions & fixtures

(G-5978)
HERON HILL VINEYARDS INC (PA)
Also Called: Heron Hill Winery
9301 County Route 76 (14840-9685)
PHONE..............................607 868-4241
Fax: 607 868-3435
John Engle Jr, CEO
Chuck Oyler, General Mgr
Eric Frarey, COO
Paul Wilson, Opers Mgr
Christy Dann, CFO
EMP: 33
SQ FT: 8,640
SALES (est): 2.5MM Privately Held
WEB: www.heronhill.com
SIC: 2084 5812 0172 Wines; eating places; grapes

(G-5979)
KEUKA BREWING CO LLC
8572 Briglin Rd (14840-9633)
PHONE..............................607 868-4648
Richard Musso, President
EMP: 8
SALES (est): 678K Privately Held
SIC: 2082 Malt beverages

(G-5980)
KONSTANTIN D FRANK& SONS VINI
Also Called: Vinifera Wine Cellard
9749 Middle Rd (14840-9462)
PHONE..............................607 868-4884
Fax: 607 868-4888
Fred Frank, President
Meaghan Frank, General Mgr
Karen Smolos, Manager
Hilda Volz, Admin Sec
▲ EMP: 30
SALES (est): 3.9MM Privately Held
WEB: www.drfrankwines.com
SIC: 2084 0172 Wines; grapes

SALES (est): 930K Privately Held
WEB: www.vintagedoors.com
SIC: 2431 Doors, wood

Hampton
Washington County

(G-5981)
HADEKA STONE CORP (PA)
115 Staso Ln (12837-2214)
P.O. Box 108 (12837-0108)
PHONE..............................518 282-9605
Eileen Hadeka, President
Raymond Hadeka, Vice Pres
William Hadeka, Treasurer
Gerald Hadeka, Admin Sec
EMP: 8
SQ FT: 640
SALES (est): 1.5MM Privately Held
WEB: www.hadekastone.com
SIC: 1411 Slate, dimension-quarrying

Hampton Bays
Suffolk County

(G-5982)
BROCK AWNINGS LTD
211 E Montauk Hwy Ste 1 (11946-2035)
PHONE..............................631 765-5200
Fax: 631 728-0134
Earl Brock, President
EMP: 10 EST: 1975
SQ FT: 8,000
SALES: 693.1K Privately Held
WEB: www.brockawnings.com
SIC: 2394 5999 5199 5091 Canvas & related products; canvas products; canvas products; boat accessories & parts

(G-5983)
NEW YORK MARINE ELEC INC
124 Springville Rd Ste 1 (11946-3043)
P.O. Box 2131, Aquebogue (11931-2131)
PHONE..............................631 734-6050
Sean York, Ch of Bd
John Lamendola, Principal
Danette Carroll, Office Mgr
Candice York, Executive Asst
EMP: 9
SALES (est): 1MM Privately Held
SIC: 3845 Electromedical equipment

Hancock
Delaware County

(G-5984)
COBLESKILL STONE PRODUCTS INC
Also Called: Hancock Quarry/Asphalt
1565 Green Flats Rd (13783)
PHONE..............................607 637-4271
Fax: 607 637-4470
Ray Althiser, Branch Mgr
EMP: 10
SALES (corp-wide): 115.2MM Privately Held
WEB: www.cobleskillstone.com
SIC: 1422 2951 Crushed & broken limestone; asphalt & asphaltic paving mixtures (not from refineries)
PA: Cobleskill Stone Products, Inc.
  112 Rock Rd
  Cobleskill NY 12043
  518 234-0221

(G-5985)
COMPREHENSIVE DENTAL TECH
Rr 1 Box 69 (13783)
PHONE..............................607 467-4456
Marie Benjamin, President
Mike Archer, Vice Pres
EMP: 4
SQ FT: 2,700
SALES (est): 1.3MM Privately Held
SIC: 7372 8021 Prepackaged software; offices & clinics of dentists

(G-5986)
K TOOLING LLC
396 E Front St (13783-1169)
PHONE..............................607 637-3781
George Willis, Sales Associate
Perry Kuehn, Mng Member
EMP: 10
SQ FT: 10,000
SALES (est): 1.2MM Privately Held
WEB: www.ktooling.com
SIC: 3469 Machine parts, stamped or pressed metal

(G-5987)
MALLERY LUMBER LLC
158 Labarre St (13783)
Rural Route 4060 Gaskill Rd, Owego (13827)
PHONE..............................607 637-2236
Fax: 607 637-2283
Les Wagner, President
Lori Moore, Controller
EMP: 7
SQ FT: 2,000
SALES (est): 62.9K Privately Held
SIC: 2421 Kiln drying of lumber

(G-5988)
PETERS LLC
5259 Peas Eddy Rd (13783-4237)
PHONE..............................607 637-5470
Van Peters,
Beverly Peters,
EMP: 5
SALES (est): 360K Privately Held
SIC: 2411 Logging

(G-5989)
RUSSELL BASS
Also Called: Russell Bass & Son Lumber
59 Saw Mill Rd (13783)
P.O. Box 718 (13783-0718)
PHONE..............................607 637-5253
Russell Bass, Partner
EMP: 15
SALES (est): 1.3MM Privately Held
SIC: 2421 2411 Sawmills & planing mills, general; logging

(G-5990)
VAN CPETERS LOGGING INC
4480 Peas Eddy Rd (13783-4232)
PHONE..............................607 637-3574
Van Peters, Principal
EMP: 6
SALES (est): 515.7K Privately Held
SIC: 2411 Logging

Hannacroix
Greene County

(G-5991)
MODERN METAL FABRICATORS INC
799 Cr 111 (12087)
PHONE..............................518 966-4142
Brian Kinn, President
EMP: 7
SALES (est): 228.5K Privately Held
SIC: 2522 Office furniture, except wood

Hannibal
Oswego County

(G-5992)
ACRO-FAB LTD
55 Rochester St (13074-3139)
P.O. Box 184 (13074-0184)
PHONE..............................315 564-6688
Fax: 315 564-5599
Mike Combes, Ch of Bd
Martin Victory, Corp Secy
Darrell Baker, Vice Pres
EMP: 23
SQ FT: 12,000
SALES (est): 3.1MM Privately Held
WEB: www.acro-fab.com
SIC: 7692 3444 3599 Welding repair; sheet metalwork; machine shop, jobbing & repair

Harriman
Orange County

(G-5993)
AMSCAN INC
Kookaburra
2 Commerce Dr S (10926-3101)
PHONE..............................845 782-0490
Fax: 845 782-7442
Walter Thompson, Manager
EMP: 60
SALES (corp-wide): 2.2B Publicly Held
SIC: 2656 Plates, paper: made from purchased material
HQ: Amscan Inc.
  80 Grasslands Rd Ste 3
  Elmsford NY 10523
  914 345-2020

(G-5994)
HOME MAIDE INC
1 Short St (10926-3311)
PHONE..............................845 837-1700
Edward Fennessy, President
EMP: 14
SALES (est): 2.8MM Privately Held
SIC: 3556 Ovens, bakery

(G-5995)
PREMIER INK SYSTEMS INC
2 Commerce Dr S (10926-3101)
PHONE..............................845 782-5802
Fax: 845 782-5041
Tyring Marcus, Owner
EMP: 48
SALES (corp-wide): 14.3MM Privately Held
SIC: 2759 Commercial printing
PA: Premier Ink Systems, Inc.
  10420 N State St
  Harrison OH 45030
  513 367-4700

(G-5996)
SIMPLEXGRINNELL LP
4 Commerce Dr S Ste 3 (10926-3101)
PHONE..............................845 774-4120
Fax: 845 566-8608
Erica Wardrop, Financial Exec
Kevin Gibbons, Sales Staff
Lynette Gray, Sales Staff
Steve Walsh, Manager
Melissa Degiglio, Manager
EMP: 5 Privately Held
WEB: www.simplexgrinnell.com
SIC: 3669 5087 1731 1711 Emergency alarms; firefighting equipment; fire detection & burglar alarm systems specialization; fire sprinkler system installation
HQ: Simplexgrinnell Lp
  4700 Exchange Ct
  Boca Raton FL 33431
  561 988-7200

Harris
Sullivan County

(G-5997)
JUS-SAR FUEL INC
Also Called: Black Bear Fuels Oil
884 Old Route 17 (12742-5016)
P.O. Box 289 (12742-0289)
PHONE..............................845 791-8900
Fax: 845 791-8042
Darren Mapes, President
Tina Mapes, Admin Sec
EMP: 5
SALES (est): 793.8K Privately Held
SIC: 3433 Heaters, swimming pool: oil or gas

Harrison
Westchester County

(G-5998)
CASTLE FUELS CORPORATION
440 Mamaroneck Ave (10528-2418)
PHONE..............................914 381-6600

▲ = Import ▼=Export
◆ =Import/Export

GEOGRAPHIC SECTION

Michael Romita, *CEO*
EMP: 39
SALES (est): 4.6MM **Privately Held**
SIC: 2869 Fuels

(G-5999)
CEMAC FOODS CORP
8 Cayuga Trl (10528-1820)
PHONE 914 835-0526
Thomas May, *President*
Helen Nash May, *Corp Secy*
Mel Persily, *Vice Pres*
Mildred Nash, *CFO*
EMP: 16
SQ FT: 3,000
SALES (est): 1.6MM **Privately Held**
WEB: www.cemacfoods.com
SIC: 2022 Natural cheese; imitation cheese

(G-6000)
CHEMLUBE INTERNATIONAL LLC (PA)
500 Mmaroneck Ave Ste 306 (10528)
PHONE 914 381-5800
Fax: 914 381-8988
Robert Nobel, *CEO*
Robert Cowen, *Senior VP*
Rob Kress, *Vice Pres*
Fernando Walters, *Manager*
◆ **EMP: 13 EST:** 2012
SQ FT: 5,300
SALES (est): 5.2MM **Privately Held**
SIC: 2992 5172 5169 Lubricating oils & greases; lubricating oils & greases; chemicals & allied products

(G-6001)
CHEMLUBE MARKETING INC
500 Mamaroneck Ave (10528-1633)
PHONE 914 381-5800
Robert Nobel, *Ch of Bd*
Beverly Walter, *Finance Mgr*
◆ **EMP:** 13
SQ FT: 5,300
SALES (est): 4.9MM **Privately Held**
WEB: www.sopetra.com
SIC: 2992 5172 5169 Lubricating oils & greases; lubricating oils & greases; chemicals & allied products

(G-6002)
COUNTY WASTE MANAGEMENT INC
565 Harrison Ave (10528-1431)
PHONE 914 592-5007
Ralph Mancini, *President*
EMP: 5
SQ FT: 2,500
SALES (est): 1MM **Privately Held**
SIC: 2842 Sanitation preparations

(G-6003)
DAL-TILE CORPORATION
31 Oakland Ave (10528-3709)
PHONE 914 835-1801
Brian Scocio, *Manager*
EMP: 7
SALES (corp-wide): 8.9B **Publicly Held**
WEB: www.mohawk.com
SIC: 3253 5032 Ceramic wall & floor tile; ceramic wall & floor tile
HQ: Dal-Tile Corporation
7834 C F Hawn Fwy
Dallas TX 75217
214 398-1411

(G-6004)
GGP PUBLISHING INC
105 Calvert St Ste 201 (10528-3138)
PHONE 914 834-8896
Generosa Gina Protano, *Partner*
EMP: 10
SALES: 1MM **Privately Held**
WEB: www.ggppublishing.com
SIC: 2731 Book publishing

(G-6005)
GRACE ASSOCIATES INC
470 West St (10528-2510)
PHONE 718 767-9000
Anthony Grace, *President*
Richard Grace, *Vice Pres*
Steven Marano, *Plant Mgr*
William Urig, *Manager*
Sweeney Aleli, *Director*
EMP: 5
SQ FT: 1,500
SALES (est): 639.3K **Privately Held**
SIC: 3271 3272 2951 Concrete block & brick; concrete products; asphalt paving mixtures & blocks

(G-6006)
NATIONAL EQUIPMENT CORPORATION (PA)
Also Called: Union Standard Eqp Co Div
600 Mmaroneck Ave Ste 400 (10528)
PHONE 718 585-0200
Fax: 718 993-2650
Arthur A Greenberg, *Ch of Bd*
Andrew Greenberg, *President*
John Greenberg, *President*
Charles Greenberg, *Exec VP*
Robert Sahol, *Sales Engr*
◆ **EMP:** 18
SQ FT: 260,000
SALES (est): 11.8MM **Privately Held**
SIC: 3556 3559 5084 Food products machinery; confectionery machinery; chemical machinery & equipment; processing & packaging equipment

(G-6007)
PACE POLYETHYLENE MFG CO INC (PA)
46 Calvert St (10528-3238)
P.O. Box 385 (10528-0385)
PHONE 914 381-3000
Fax: 914 381-3062
Stan Nathanson, *President*
Marc Lawrence, *Vice Pres*
EMP: 20
SQ FT: 1,500
SALES (est): 5.9MM **Privately Held**
SIC: 3081 Unsupported plastics film & sheet; polyethylene film

(G-6008)
PROFESSIONAL MEDICAL DEVICES
10 Century Trl (10528-1702)
PHONE 914 835-0614
EMP: 10
SALES: 500K **Privately Held**
SIC: 3841 Mfg Surgical/Medical Instruments

(G-6009)
SPRINGFIELD OIL SERVICES INC (PA)
550 Mmaroneck Ave Ste 503 (10528)
PHONE 914 315-6812
Bentley Blum, *President*
Mary Irwin, *Vice Pres*
▲ **EMP:** 18
SQ FT: 1,000
SALES (est): 1.2MM **Privately Held**
SIC: 1382 Oil & gas exploration services

(G-6010)
SS&C FINANCIAL SERVICES LLC (DH)
1 South Rd (10528-3309)
PHONE 914 670-3600
Fax: 914 670-3601
William Stone, *CEO*
David Jonassen, *Managing Dir*
Hans Hufschmid, *Principal*
Vernon Barback, *COO*
John Lomurno, *Facilities Dir*
EMP: 106
SQ FT: 24,000
SALES (est): 73.3MM
SALES (corp-wide): 1.4B **Publicly Held**
WEB: www.globeop.com
SIC: 7372 Prepackaged software
HQ: Ss&C Technologies, Inc.
80 Lamberton Rd
Windsor CT 06095
860 298-4500

(G-6011)
TREO BRANDS LLC
106 Calvert St (10528-3131)
PHONE 914 341-1850
Robert Golten, *CEO*
Brian O'Byrne, *President*
EMP: 8
SQ FT: 3,800
SALES (est): 258.8K **Privately Held**
SIC: 2086 Carbonated beverages, nonalcoholic: bottled & canned

(G-6012)
UNIVERSAL REMOTE CONTROL INC (PA)
500 Mmaroneck Ave Ste 502 (10528)
PHONE 914 630-4343
Chang Park, *Chairman*
Douglas Cole, *Senior VP*
Lars Granoe, *VP Sales*
Debra Sharker, *Sales Dir*
Scott Srolis, *Sales Mgr*
▲ **EMP:** 57
SQ FT: 11,000
SALES (est): 12.8MM **Privately Held**
WEB: www.universalremote.com
SIC: 3678 Electronic connectors

(G-6013)
VALUE SPRING TECHNOLOGY INC
521 Harrison Ave (10528-1431)
PHONE 917 705-4658
EMP: 15
SALES (est): 305.2K **Privately Held**
SIC: 7372 Prepackaged Software Services

Harrisville
Lewis County

(G-6014)
CIVES CORPORATION
Also Called: Viking-Cives
14331 Mill St (13648-3331)
PHONE 315 543-2321
Fax: 315 543-2366
Larry Jeroscko, *General Mgr*
Steve Rider, *General Mgr*
Steve Chartrand, *Prdtn Mgr*
Aj Macdonald, *Prdtn Mgr*
Terri Luther, *Purchasing*
EMP: 75
SQ FT: 46,000
SALES (corp-wide): 453.1MM **Privately Held**
WEB: www.cives.com
SIC: 3531 Snow plow attachments
PA: Cives Corporation
3700 Mansell Rd Ste 500
Alpharetta GA 30022
770 993-4424

Hartford
Washington County

(G-6015)
RICHARD STEWART
4495 State Rte 149 (12838)
P.O. Box 18 (12838-0018)
PHONE 518 632-5363
Richard Stewart, *Owner*
Mary Stewart, *Owner*
EMP: 5
SALES (est): 480K **Privately Held**
SIC: 3523 Dairy equipment (farm)

Hartsdale
Westchester County

(G-6016)
APOGEE POWER USA INC
7 Verne Pl (10530-1026)
PHONE 202 746-2890
Michael Harper, *CEO*
John Hollins, *President*
Dr Kc Tsai, *Mfg Mgr*
EMP: 10
SALES (est): 14.6K **Privately Held**
SIC: 3825 3621 Electrical energy measuring equipment; storage battery chargers; motor & engine generator type

(G-6017)
FRISCH PLASTICS CORP
7 Joyce Rd (10530-2929)
PHONE 973 685-5936
Ruth Lefkowitz, *President*
Irwin Lefkowitz, *Vice Pres*
Eve Lefkowitz, *Manager*
EMP: 20
SALES: 500K **Privately Held**
WEB: www.frischplastics.com
SIC: 3089 Novelties, plastic

(G-6018)
RICHARD EDELSON
Also Called: Pinewood Marketing
80 Pinewood Rd (10530-1672)
PHONE 914 428-7573
Richard Edelson, *Owner*
EMP: 1
SALES: 2MM **Privately Held**
SIC: 2252 Hosiery

(G-6019)
SIGN HERE ENTERPRISES LLC
Also Called: Sign-A-Rama
28 N Central Ave Rear (10530-2430)
PHONE 914 328-3111
Fax: 914 682-8610
David Reichenberg,
EMP: 5
SALES (est): 350K **Privately Held**
SIC: 3993 Signs & advertising specialties

(G-6020)
TAPEMAKER SUPPLY COMPANY LLC
22 Sherbrooke Rd (10530-2938)
PHONE 914 693-3407
Ronald Huppert, *Mng Member*
EMP: 7
SALES (est): 453.1K **Privately Held**
WEB: www.tapemakersupply.com
SIC: 2759 Commercial printing

(G-6021)
TLC VISION (USA) CORPORATION
Also Called: Blinds To Go
150 Central Park Ave (10530)
PHONE 914 395-3949
Fax: 914 468-2119
Steven Shiller, *Owner*
EMP: 5
SALES (corp-wide): 950.8MM **Privately Held**
SIC: 2591 Window blinds
HQ: Tlc Vision (Usa) Corporation
16305 Swingley Ridge Rd # 300
Chesterfield MO 63017
636 534-2300

Hastings On Hudson
Westchester County

(G-6022)
ALTERNATIVE TECHNOLOGY CORP
Also Called: Marketfax Information Services
1 North St Ste 1 (10706-1542)
P.O. Box 357 (10706-0357)
PHONE 914 478-5900
Fax: 914 478-5908
Tom Kadala, *CEO*
EMP: 5
SQ FT: 3,000
SALES: 1.2MM **Privately Held**
WEB: www.marketfax.com
SIC: 3661 5065 4822 7375 Facsimile equipment; facsimile equipment; facsimile transmission services; information retrieval services

(G-6023)
FLOGIC INC
Also Called: F Logic
25 Chestnut Dr (10706-1901)
PHONE 914 478-1352
Julius Funaro, *President*
Michael Piscatelli, *Vice Pres*
Elle Lang, *Sales Staff*
Angela Vargas, *Office Mgr*
Ron Olive, *Manager*
EMP: 13
SALES (est): 1.2MM **Privately Held**
WEB: www.flinc.com
SIC: 7372 Prepackaged software

Hastings On Hudson - Westchester County (G-6024)

(G-6024)
JAMES RICHARD SPECIALTY CHEM
24 Ridge St (10706-2702)
PHONE..................914 478-7500
Katrine Barth, *President*
EMP: 6
SQ FT: 1,300
SALES: 3MM **Privately Held**
WEB: www.rjsconline.com
SIC: 2842 Specialty cleaning, polishes & sanitation goods

(G-6025)
LORENA CANALS USA INC
104 Burnside Dr (10706-3013)
PHONE..................844 567-3622
Delia Elbaum, *General Mgr*
▲ EMP: 3
SQ FT: 3,000
SALES: 1MM
SALES (corp-wide): 2.7MM **Privately Held**
SIC: 2273 5023 Carpets & rugs; rugs
PA: Lorena Canals Sl.
    Calle Alexandre Goicoechea, 6 - Loc 8
    Sant Just Desvern 08960

Hauppauge
Suffolk County

(G-6026)
A & Z PHARMACEUTICAL INC
350 Wireless Blvd Ste 200 (11788-3947)
PHONE..................631 952-3802
Frank Berstler, *Vice Pres*
EMP: 90 **Privately Held**
SIC: 2834 8734 Pills, pharmaceutical; testing laboratories
PA: A & Z Pharmaceutical Inc.
    180 Oser Ave
    Hauppauge NY 11788

(G-6027)
A & Z PHARMACEUTICAL INC (PA)
180 Oser Ave (11788-3736)
PHONE..................631 952-3800
Fax: 631 952-3900
Emma LI, *CEO*
Xu Xiaoxian, *Ch of Bd*
Frank Berstler, *Senior VP*
Xian Chen, *Vice Pres*
Clyde Granger, *QA Dir*
◆ EMP: 102
SQ FT: 73,000
SALES (est): 60MM **Privately Held**
SIC: 2834 Pharmaceutical preparations

(G-6028)
AD NOTAM LLC
135 Ricefield Ln (11788-2046)
PHONE..................631 951-2020
Hector Cadeaux, *Opers Staff*
Nurdan Citamak, *Treasurer*
Isaac Fattal, *Mng Member*
▲ EMP: 15
SALES (est): 1.8MM **Privately Held**
SIC: 3231 5023 Mirrored glass; mirrors & pictures, framed & unframed

(G-6029)
ADVANCED BACK TECHNOLOGIES
89 Ste F Cabot Ct (11788)
PHONE..................631 231-0076
David F Cuccia, *President*
Mohamed Mostafa, *Marketing Staff*
EMP: 5 EST: 1997
SALES (est): 788.9K **Privately Held**
SIC: 3069 Orthopedic sundries, molded rubber

(G-6030)
AEROFLEX PLAINVIEW INC
Integrted Electronic Solutions
350 Kennedy Dr (11788-4014)
PHONE..................631 231-9100
Fax: 631 231-8375
Jim Smith, *Division Mgr*
Richard Casper, *Vice Pres*
Boz Sharif, *Chief Engr*
Harsad Shah, *Engineer*
William Billbrown, *Branch Mgr*
EMP: 120
SALES (corp-wide): 2.3B **Privately Held**
SIC: 3679 3621 3674 3577 Electronic circuits; motors & generators; semiconductors & related devices; computer peripheral equipment
HQ: Aeroflex Plainview, Inc.
    35 S Service Rd
    Plainview NY 11803
    516 694-6700

(G-6031)
AIPING PHARMACEUTICAL INC
350w Wireless Blvd (11788)
PHONE..................631 952-3802
Jing Zou, *Principal*
Frank Berstler, *Vice Pres*
EMP: 5
SALES (est): 371.4K **Privately Held**
SIC: 2834 2899 Tablets, pharmaceutical; gelatin: edible, technical, photographic or pharmaceutical

(G-6032)
AIR INDUSTRIES GROUP (PA)
3609 Motor Pkwy Ste 100 (11788)
PHONE..................631 881-4920
Fax: 631 968-5377
Michael N Taglich, *Ch of Bd*
Luciano Melluzzo, *President*
Peter D Rettaliata, *President*
Michael E Recca, *CFO*
Mike Worhle, *Administration*
EMP: 75
SALES: 66.9MM **Publicly Held**
SIC: 3728 Aircraft body assemblies & parts; aircraft landing assemblies & brakes; aircraft assemblies, subassemblies & parts

(G-6033)
ALADDIN PACKAGING LLC
115 Engineers Rd Ste 100 (11788-4005)
PHONE..................631 273-4747
Moshe Wortzberger, *Sales Associate*
Abraham Mandell, *Mng Member*
Joel Endzweig,
▲ EMP: 60
SQ FT: 40,000
SALES (est): 16.2MM **Privately Held**
SIC: 2673 Cellophane bags, unprinted: made from purchased materials

(G-6034)
ALLCRAFT FABRICATORS INC
150 Wireless Blvd (11788-3955)
PHONE..................631 951-4100
Fax: 631 951-4040
Douglas Donaldson, *President*
Darren J Winter, *Exec VP*
Mike Donovan, *Facilities Mgr*
Nessie Cojuangco, *Controller*
Margaret Manzo, *HR Admin*
EMP: 75 EST: 1964
SALES (est): 12.1MM **Privately Held**
SIC: 2522 Office furniture, except wood

(G-6035)
ALLEN MACHINE PRODUCTS INC
120 Ricefield Ln Ste 100 (11788-2033)
PHONE..................631 630-8800
Fax: 631 630-8801
Peter Allen, *Ch of Bd*
Richard Pettenato, *Vice Pres*
Robert Renz, *Vice Pres*
Una Scheriff, *Vice Pres*
Chris Bonadonna, *Mfg Dir*
▲ EMP: 50
SQ FT: 30,000
SALES (est): 5.9MM **Privately Held**
WEB: www.allenmachine.com
SIC: 3469 3444 Machine parts, stamped or pressed metal; sheet metalwork

(G-6036)
ALPHAMED BOTTLES INC
360 Oser Ave (11788-3608)
PHONE..................631 275-5042
Subhakar Viyala, *President*
Pavan Vemula, *Opers Mgr*
▲ EMP: 17
SQ FT: 26,000
SALES: 4MM **Privately Held**
SIC: 3085 Plastics bottles

(G-6037)
ALUFOIL PRODUCTS CO INC
135 Oser Ave Ste 3 (11788-3722)
PHONE..................631 231-4141
Fax: 631 231-1435
Howard Lent, *Ch of Bd*
Elliot Lent, *Vice Pres*
Cornelius Nagel, *Vice Pres*
Duke Simms, *Vice Pres*
Estelle Lent, *Shareholder*
◆ EMP: 18 EST: 1945
SQ FT: 45,000
SALES: 3.7MM **Privately Held**
WEB: www.alufoil.com
SIC: 3497 3353 Foil, laminated to paper or other materials; foil, aluminum

(G-6038)
AMERICAN ACCESS CARE LLC
32 Central Ave (11788-4734)
PHONE..................631 582-9729
Thea Hemback, *Manager*
Phea Hemback, *Manager*
EMP: 11
SALES (corp-wide): 17.5B **Privately Held**
WEB: www.americanaccesscare.com
SIC: 3844 X-ray apparatus & tubes
HQ: American Access Care, Llc
    40 Valley Stream Pkwy
    Malvern PA 19355
    717 235-0181

(G-6039)
AMERICAN CHIMNEY SUPPLIES INC
129 Oser Ave Ste B (11788-3813)
PHONE..................631 434-2020
Fax: 631 434-2010
Chris Arbucci, *President*
Debbie Cullum, *Opers Mgr*
▲ EMP: 6 EST: 1993
SQ FT: 21,000
SALES (est): 1MM **Privately Held**
SIC: 3312 3272 3259 Stainless steel; chimney caps, concrete; clay chimney products

(G-6040)
AMERICAN DIAGNOSTIC CORP
Also Called: A D C
55 Commerce Dr (11788-3931)
PHONE..................631 273-6155
Fax: 631 273-9659
Marc Blitstein, *President*
Neal Weingart, *Vice Pres*
◆ EMP: 77
SALES (est): 15.8MM **Privately Held**
WEB: www.adctoday.com
SIC: 3841 Blood pressure apparatus; stethoscopes & stethographs

(G-6041)
AMERICAN INTRMDAL CONT MFG LLC
Also Called: Aicm
150 Motor Pkwy Ste 401 (11788-5108)
PHONE..................631 774-6790
Pat Marron, *President*
EMP: 8
SQ FT: 200
SALES (est): 888.5K **Privately Held**
SIC: 2655 Fiber shipping & mailing containers

(G-6042)
ARC SYSTEMS INC
2090 Joshuas Path (11788-4764)
PHONE..................631 582-8020
Fax: 631 582-8038
Robert Miller, *President*
Clifford Miller, *Treasurer*
John Grant, *Manager*
▲ EMP: 33 EST: 1967
SQ FT: 12,000
SALES (est): 6.5MM **Privately Held**
WEB: www.arcsystemsinc.com
SIC: 3621 3694 3724 Motors & generators; electric motor & generator parts; battery charging alternators & generators; aircraft engines & engine parts

(G-6043)
ARKAY PACKAGING CORPORATION (PA)
100 Marcus Blvd Ste 2 (11788-3749)
PHONE..................631 273-2000
Fax: 631 273-2478
Mitchell Kaneff, *Chairman*
Walter Shiels, *COO*
Craig Bradley, *Plant Mgr*
Brian Hopkins, *Plant Mgr*
Richard Legler, *Plant Mgr*
▲ EMP: 40
SQ FT: 5,000
SALES (est): 43.3MM **Privately Held**
WEB: www.arkay.com
SIC: 2657 Folding paperboard boxes

(G-6044)
ARTEMIS INC
36 Central Ave (11788-4734)
PHONE..................631 232-2424
Yuly Margulis, *CEO*
Jeffrey Dunn, *COO*
Alex Margulis, *Vice Pres*
Mike Schorr, *Engineer*
William Roe, *Design Engr*
▲ EMP: 7
SQ FT: 9,000
SALES (est): 1.4MM **Privately Held**
WEB: www.artemis.com
SIC: 3674 3812 Integrated circuits, semiconductor networks, etc.; radar systems & equipment

(G-6045)
ARTISTIC PRODUCTS LLC
125 Commerce Dr (11788-3932)
PHONE..................631 435-0200
Richard Leifer, *CEO*
Bradley Brighton, *President*
Norma Friedman, *Accountant*
▲ EMP: 45
SQ FT: 50,000
SALES (est): 5.2MM **Privately Held**
WEB: www.artistic-products.com
SIC: 2521 5044 Wood office furniture; office equipment

(G-6046)
ATLANTIC ESSENTIAL PDTS INC
7 Oser Ave Ste 1 (11788-3811)
PHONE..................631 434-8333
Fax: 631 434-8222
Maxim G Uvarov, *Ch of Bd*
Pailla Rebby, *Vice Pres*
Selven Sam, *Vice Pres*
EMP: 57
SQ FT: 22,000
SALES (est): 11MM **Privately Held**
WEB: www.atlanticep.com
SIC: 2834 7389 Pharmaceutical preparations; packaging & labeling services

(G-6047)
ATLANTIC ULTRAVIOLET CORP
375 Marcus Blvd (11788-2026)
PHONE..................631 234-3275
Fax: 631 273-0771
Hilary Boehme, *President*
Thomas Dituro, *Vice Pres*
Celeste Kopp, *Treasurer*
Ronald Henderson, *Director*
Anne Wysocki, *Admin Sec*
◆ EMP: 30 EST: 1963
SALES (est): 7MM **Privately Held**
WEB: www.ultraviolet.com
SIC: 3589 3641 Water purification equipment, household type; ultraviolet lamps

(G-6048)
AUTOMATIC CONNECTOR INC
375 Oser Ave (11788-3607)
PHONE..................631 543-5000
David Lax, *President*
EMP: 19
SALES (est): 3.1MM **Privately Held**
WEB: www.automaticconnector.com
SIC: 3678 3643 Electronic connectors; electric connectors

(G-6049)
AVM PRINTING INC
Also Called: Printers 3
43 Corporate Dr (11788-2048)
PHONE..................631 351-1331
Anthony Viscuso, *President*

EMP: 13
SQ FT: 6,000
SALES: 2MM Privately Held
SIC: 2752 Commercial printing, lithographic

(G-6050)
AVON REPRODUCTIONS INC
Also Called: Avon Press
175 Engineers Rd (11788-4020)
PHONE.................................631 273-2400
Fax: 631 420-0930
Brad Peters, *President*
James Gibb, *Vice Pres*
▲ **EMP:** 35 **EST:** 1958
SQ FT: 10,000
SALES (est): 3.7MM Privately Held
WEB: www.avonpress.com
SIC: 2752 Lithographing on metal

(G-6051)
BARRONS EDUCATIONAL SERIES INC (PA)
Also Called: Barrons Educational
250 Wireless Blvd (11788-3924)
PHONE.................................631 434-3311
Fax: 631 434-3725
Manuel H Barron, *Chairman*
Ellen Sibley, *Exec VP*
Mary E Owens, *Production*
Debbie Bacek, *Purchasing*
Jackie Raab, *Sales Staff*
◆ **EMP:** 81
SQ FT: 75,000
SALES (est): 23.4MM Privately Held
WEB: www.barronseduc.com
SIC: 2731 5942 Book publishing; book stores

(G-6052)
BEHLMAN ELECTRONICS INC (HQ)
80 Cabot Ct (11788-3729)
PHONE.................................631 435-0410
Fax: 631 951-4341
Mitchell Binder, *CEO*
Mitchell Buder, *Ch of Bd*
Mark Tublisky, *President*
Barry Nolan, *Mfg Mgr*
Fred Wolff, *QA Dir*
▲ **EMP:** 47
SQ FT: 25,000
SALES (est): 9.2MM
SALES (corp-wide): 20.7MM Publicly Held
WEB: www.behlman.com
SIC: 3679 Power supplies, all types: static
PA: Orbit International Corp.
    80 Cabot Ct
    Hauppauge NY 11788
    631 435-8300

(G-6053)
BIO-BOTANICA INC (PA)
75 Commerce Dr (11788-3943)
PHONE.................................631 231-0987
Fax: 631 231-7332
Frank D'Amelio Sr, *CEO*
Josephine Perricone, *President*
Marisol Bello, *Business Mgr*
Frank D'Amelio Jr, *Vice Pres*
Tony Perricone, *Opers Staff*
◆ **EMP:** 100
SQ FT: 100,000
SALES (est): 19.6MM Privately Held
SIC: 2833 2834 2844 Alkaloids & other botanical based products; drugs & herbs: grading, grinding & milling; botanical products, medicinal: ground, graded or milled; extracts of botanicals: powdered, pilular, solid or fluid; toilet preparations

(G-6054)
BLACK & DECKER (US) INC
180 Oser Ave Ste 100 (11788-3709)
PHONE.................................631 952-2008
Joe Rufino, *Branch Mgr*
EMP: 7
SALES (corp-wide): 11.4B Publicly Held
WEB: www.dewalt.com
SIC: 3546 Power-driven handtools
HQ: Black & Decker (U.S.) Inc.
    1000 Stanley Dr
    New Britain CT 06053
    860 225-5111

(G-6055)
BLUE STAR PRODUCTS INC
355 Marcus Blvd Ste 2 (11788-2027)
PHONE.................................631 952-3204
Gerald Jacino Sr, *President*
Tom Jacino, *Chief Mktg Ofcr*
Marie Dydland, *Manager*
EMP: 12
SQ FT: 15,000
SALES (est): 1.3MM Privately Held
WEB: www.bluestar-products.com
SIC: 3559 Automotive maintenance equipment

(G-6056)
BRICKIT
17 Central Ave (11788-4733)
PHONE.................................631 727-8977
Fax: 631 348-0400
Oscar Hernandez, *Marketing Staff*
Robert Dolinsk,
Robert Dolinsky,
EMP: 20
SALES (est): 3.5MM Privately Held
SIC: 3271 Brick, concrete

(G-6057)
BRONSON NUTRITIONALS LLC (PA)
Also Called: Bronson Labrotaries
70 Commerce Dr (11788-3962)
PHONE.................................631 750-0000
Steven Kane, *Warehouse Mgr*
Michelle Coscia, *Controller*
Cindy Warsaw, *Financial Exec*
Sheri Taubes, *Mktg Dir*
Bharat Patel, *Manager*
EMP: 20
SALES (est): 6MM Privately Held
SIC: 2834 Vitamin preparations

(G-6058)
BYSTRONIC INC
185 Commerce Dr (11788-3916)
PHONE.................................631 231-3677
Ulrich Troesch, *Principal*
EMP: 8
SALES (corp-wide): 1.2B Privately Held
SIC: 3541 Machine tools, metal cutting type
HQ: Bystronic Inc.
    200 Airport Rd
    Elgin IL 60123
    847 214-0300

(G-6059)
C & C CUSTOM METAL FABRICATORS
2 N Hoffman Ln (11788-2735)
PHONE.................................631 235-9646
Chris Drago, *President*
EMP: 6
SQ FT: 1,500
SALES (est): 483.7K Privately Held
SIC: 3441 Fabricated structural metal

(G-6060)
CASTELLA IMPORTS INC
60 Davids Dr (11788-2041)
PHONE.................................631 231-5500
Vasilios Valsamos, *Ch of Bd*
Chris Valsamos, *Vice Pres*
John Roumbos, *CFO*
Gabrielle Coriaty, *Sales Executive*
◆ **EMP:** 185
SQ FT: 110,000
SALES (est): 64.8MM Privately Held
WEB: www.castellaimports.com
SIC: 2099 5149 Food preparations; specialty food items

(G-6061)
CENTRAL SEMICONDUCTOR CORP
145 Adams Ave (11788-3603)
PHONE.................................631 435-1110
Fax: 631 435-1824
W S Radgowski, *CEO*
Susan M Ryan, *President*
T Radgowski, *General Mgr*
Tom Hambel, *Vice Pres*
Steven Radgowski, *Vice Pres*
▲ **EMP:** 80
SQ FT: 30,000
SALES (est): 22.6MM Privately Held
WEB: www.centralsemi.com
SIC: 3674 Semiconductors & related devices

(G-6062)
CHAMPION ALUMINUM CORP
Also Called: Champion Window and Door
250 Kennedy Dr (11788-4002)
PHONE.................................631 656-3424
Anthony Muraco, *CEO*
Mike Piltoff, *President*
James Trupiano, *Treasurer*
Stephanie Bellotto, *Controller*
Anthony Arcati, *Shareholder*
▲ **EMP:** 140 **EST:** 1952
SQ FT: 80,000
SALES (est): 23.4MM Privately Held
WEB: www.championwindows.com
SIC: 3442 Metal doors, sash & trim

(G-6063)
CHARL INDUSTRIES INC
225 Engineers Rd (11788-4020)
PHONE.................................631 234-0100
Fax: 631 234-5544
Richard Coronato Sr, *President*
Linda Stence, *Controller*
Kitt Tyson, *Manager*
Charlotte Coronato, *Admin Sec*
EMP: 40
SQ FT: 44,000
SALES (est): 8.1MM Privately Held
WEB: www.charlco.com
SIC: 3599 Machine shop, jobbing & repair

(G-6064)
CHARLES ROSS & SON COMPANY (PA)
Also Called: Ross Metal Fabricators Div
710 Old Willets Path (11788-4193)
P.O. Box 12308 (11788-0615)
PHONE.................................631 234-0500
Fax: 631 234-0691
Richard Ross, *President*
Joseph Martorana, *Vice Pres*
Heinz Feibert, *Mfg Dir*
Dave Almeida, *Purch Mgr*
Tom Dee-G-Norio, *Engineer*
▲ **EMP:** 60 **EST:** 1840
SQ FT: 50,000
SALES (est): 37.8MM Privately Held
WEB: www.cosmeticmixers.com
SIC: 3443 3586 3559 5084 Fabricated plate work (boiler shop); measuring & dispensing pumps; chemical machinery & equipment; pharmaceutical machinery; industrial machinery & equipment

(G-6065)
CIRCOR AEROSPACE INC
Aerodyne Controls
425 Rabro Dr Ste 1 (11788-4245)
PHONE.................................631 737-1900
Daniel R Godin, *Division Mgr*
Peter Chouinard, *QC Mgr*
Dave Hohf, *Engineer*
Cory Jordan, *Project Engr*
Jeff Horning, *Design Engr*
EMP: 70
SALES (corp-wide): 590.2MM Publicly Held
SIC: 3483 3829 3728 Ammunition, except for small arms; measuring & controlling devices; aircraft parts & equipment
HQ: Circor Aerospace, Inc.
    2301 Wardlow Cir
    Corona CA 92880
    951 270-6200

(G-6066)
CLEAN GAS SYSTEMS INC
380 Townline Rd Ste 120 (11788-2842)
PHONE.................................631 467-1600
Anil M Shah, *President*
EMP: 20
SQ FT: 4,000
SALES (est): 4.8MM Privately Held
WEB: www.cgscgs.com
SIC: 3564 8711 7389 Air purification equipment; pollution control engineering; air pollution measuring service

(G-6067)
CLICK IT INC
85 Corporate Dr (11788-2021)
PHONE.................................631 686-2900
James J Carey, *CEO*
Diane Jutting, *Cust Mgr*
Michael Simco, *Manager*
Vincent Pastore, *Technical Staff*
EMP: 60
SALES (est): 10.8MM Privately Held
WEB: www.clickitinc.com
SIC: 3663 Television closed circuit equipment

(G-6068)
COCA-COLA BTLG CO OF NY INC
375 Wireless Blvd (11788-3940)
PHONE.................................631 434-3535
Mike Chidester, *Manager*
Mike Taroli, *Manager*
Joanne Harms, *Executive*
EMP: 50
SALES (corp-wide): 41.8B Publicly Held
SIC: 2086 Bottled & canned soft drinks
HQ: The Coca-Cola Bottling Company Of New York Inc
    2500 Windy Ridge Pkwy Se
    Atlanta GA 30339
    770 989-3000

(G-6069)
COLONIAL WIRE & CABLE CO INC (PA)
40 Engineers Rd (11788-4079)
PHONE.................................631 234-8500
Fax: 631 234-8544
Thomas J Walsh III, *President*
Thomas J Walsh Jr, *Chairman*
George Stubbs, *Corp Secy*
Tony Affrunti, *Plant Mgr*
Michael Rossi, *Accountant*
EMP: 55 **EST:** 1944
SQ FT: 100,000
SALES (est): 11.3MM Privately Held
WEB: www.colonialwire.com
SIC: 3357 Nonferrous wiredrawing & insulating

(G-6070)
COMME-CI COMME-CA AP GROUP
Also Called: Male Power Apparel
380 Rabo Dr (11788)
PHONE.................................631 300-1035
Fax: 631 300-1039
Sam Baker, *President*
Marybeth Healy, *Vice Pres*
▲ **EMP:** 21
SQ FT: 12,000
SALES (est): 3.5MM Privately Held
WEB: www.malepower.com
SIC: 2322 2329 2339 2341 Underwear, men's & boys': made from purchased materials; bathing suits & swimwear: men's & boys'; bathing suits: women's, misses' & juniors'; panties: women's, misses', children's & infants'

(G-6071)
COMMUNICATION POWER CORP
80 Davids Dr Ste 3 (11788-2002)
PHONE.................................631 434-7306
Daniel P Myer, *President*
Richard Myer, *General Mgr*
John Foglio, *Engineer*
Tuna Djemil, *Manager*
Lai Lee, *Manager*
▲ **EMP:** 36
SQ FT: 11,000
SALES (est): 8.6MM Privately Held
WEB: www.cpcamps.com
SIC: 3663 3651 5065 Amplifiers, RF power & IF; household audio & video equipment; communication equipment

(G-6072)
COMPAC DEVELOPMENT CORPORATION
Also Called: Miller Stuart
110 Plant Ave Ste 1 (11788-3830)
PHONE.................................631 881-4903
Scott Cullen, *General Mgr*
Kristie Petersen, *Vice Pres*

Hauppauge - Suffolk County (G-6073)

EMP: 85 EST: 1976
SQ FT: 84,000
SALES (est): 15.5MM
SALES (corp-wide): 66.9MM Publicly Held
WEB: www.compac-rf.com
SIC: 3469 Electronic enclosures, stamped or pressed metal
PA: Air Industries Group
3609 Motor Pkwy Ste 100
Hauppauge NY 11788
631 881-4920

(G-6073)
CONTRACT PHARMACAL CORP
110 Plant Ave (11788-3830)
PHONE 631 231-4610
Mark Wolf, Manager
EMP: 20
SQ FT: 48,000
SALES (corp-wide): 310.4MM Privately Held
SIC: 2834 Pharmaceutical preparations
PA: Contract Pharmacal Corp.
135 Adams Ave
Hauppauge NY 11788
631 231-4610

(G-6074)
CONTRACT PHARMACAL CORP
1324 Motor Pkwy (11749-5262)
PHONE 631 231-4610
Mark Wolf, Manager
EMP: 125
SALES (corp-wide): 310.4MM Privately Held
SIC: 2834 Pharmaceutical preparations
PA: Contract Pharmacal Corp.
135 Adams Ave
Hauppauge NY 11788
631 231-4610

(G-6075)
CONTRACT PHARMACAL CORP
250 Kennedy Dr (11788-4002)
PHONE 631 231-4610
Matt Wolf, CEO
EMP: 50
SALES (corp-wide): 310.4MM Privately Held
SIC: 2834 Pharmaceutical preparations
PA: Contract Pharmacal Corp.
135 Adams Ave
Hauppauge NY 11788
631 231-4610

(G-6076)
CONTRACT PHARMACAL CORP
145 Oser Ave (11788-3725)
PHONE 631 231-4610
Mark Wolf, President
EMP: 79
SALES (corp-wide): 310.4MM Privately Held
SIC: 2834 Pharmaceutical preparations
PA: Contract Pharmacal Corp.
135 Adams Ave
Hauppauge NY 11788
631 231-4610

(G-6077)
CONTRACT PHARMACAL CORP
160 Commerce Dr (11788-3944)
PHONE 631 231-4610
Fax: 631 231-4156
Glenn Simonin, Maintenance Dir
Mark Wolf, Manager
EMP: 181
SALES (corp-wide): 310.4MM Privately Held
SIC: 2834 Pharmaceutical preparations
PA: Contract Pharmacal Corp.
135 Adams Ave
Hauppauge NY 11788
631 231-4610

(G-6078)
CONTRACT PHARMACAL CORP
150 Commerce Dr (11788-3930)
PHONE 631 231-4610
Mark Wolf, Manager
EMP: 19
SALES (corp-wide): 310.4MM Privately Held
SIC: 2834 Pharmaceutical preparations

PA: Contract Pharmacal Corp.
135 Adams Ave
Hauppauge NY 11788
631 231-4610

(G-6079)
CROSSTEX INTERNATIONAL INC (HQ)
10 Ranick Rd (11788-4209)
PHONE 631 582-6777
Gary Steinberg, CEO
Mitchell Steinberg, Exec VP
Ken Plunkett, Senior VP
Sheldon Fisher, Vice Pres
Dan Pitkowsky, Vice Pres
◆ EMP: 75
SQ FT: 63,000
SALES (est): 63.9MM
SALES (corp-wide): 770.1MM Publicly Held
WEB: www.crosstex.com
SIC: 3843 2621 5047 2842 Dental equipment & supplies; toweling tissue, paper; dentists' professional supplies; specialty cleaning, polishes & sanitation goods; soap & other detergents; sanitary paper products
PA: Cantel Medical Corp.
150 Clove Rd Ste 36
Little Falls NJ 07424
973 890-7220

(G-6080)
CROSSTEX INTERNATIONAL INC
2095 Express Dr N (11788-5308)
PHONE 631 582-6777
Jessica Lauper, Manager
EMP: 10
SALES (corp-wide): 770.1MM Publicly Held
SIC: 3843 Dental equipment & supplies
HQ: Crosstex International, Inc.
10 Ranick Rd
Hauppauge NY 11788
631 582-6777

(G-6081)
CURRAN MANUFACTURING CORP (PA)
Also Called: Royal Products
200 Oser Ave (11788-3724)
PHONE 631 273-1010
Fax: 631 273-1066
F Allan Curran, Ch of Bd
Christopher Jakubowsky, VP Opers
Linda Michaels, Purch Mgr
Lynn Telis, Director
▲ EMP: 49 EST: 1946
SALES (corp-wide): 10.2MM Privately Held
WEB: www.airchucks.com
SIC: 3545 5084 Machine tool attachments & accessories; machine tools & accessories

(G-6082)
CURRAN MANUFACTURING CORP
Also Called: Royal Products
210 Oser Ave (11788-3724)
PHONE 631 273-1010
Allan Curran, President
EMP: 50
SALES (corp-wide): 10.2MM Privately Held
WEB: www.airchucks.com
SIC: 3545 Machine tool attachments & accessories
PA: Curran Manufacturing Corp
200 Oser Ave
Hauppauge NY 11788
631 273-1010

(G-6083)
DEPCO INC
20 Newton Pl (11788-4752)
PHONE 631 582-1995
Fax: 631 582-2015
Greg Minuto, CEO
David W Bean, President
Linda Ifko, Office Mgr
▲ EMP: 10
SQ FT: 20,000
SALES (est): 1.9MM Privately Held
SIC: 2822 Silicone rubbers

(G-6084)
DEUTSCH RELAYS
55 Engineers Rd (11788-4007)
PHONE 631 342-1700
Fax: 631 342-9455
Thomas M Sadusky, President
Serge Belot, Vice Pres
Varin Parker, Vice Pres
Rich Stadalik, Opers Mgr
Claudio Lanza, Production
EMP: 14
SALES (est): 1.8MM Privately Held
SIC: 3625 Relays & industrial controls

(G-6085)
DISC GRAPHICS INC
30 Gilpin Ave (11788-4724)
PHONE 631 300-1129
Margaret Krumholz, President
EMP: 150
SALES (corp-wide): 64.8MM Privately Held
SIC: 2657 Folding paperboard boxes
PA: Disc Graphics, Inc.
10 Gilpin Ave
Hauppauge NY 11788
631 234-1400

(G-6086)
DISC GRAPHICS INC (PA)
10 Gilpin Ave (11788-4770)
PHONE 631 234-1400
Fax: 631 234-1460
Donald Sinkin, Ch of Bd
Margaret Krumholz, President
Stephen Frey, Senior VP
John A Rebecchi, Senior VP
Frank Bress, Vice Pres
▲ EMP: 215
SALES (est): 64.8MM Privately Held
WEB: www.discgraphics.com
SIC: 2657 Folding paperboard boxes

(G-6087)
DISPLAY LOGIC USA INC
40 Oser Ave Ste 4 (11788-3807)
PHONE 631 406-1922
Keith Morton, CEO
Stanley Schiller, General Mgr
EMP: 9 EST: 2012
SALES (est): 1.4MM Privately Held
SIC: 3823 Digital displays of process variables

(G-6088)
DOCTOR PRINT INC (PA)
Also Called: Dr Print
18 Commerce Dr Ste 1 (11788-3975)
PHONE 631 873-4560
Mitch Cohen, CEO
Anthony Bulla, Vice Pres
EMP: 20
SQ FT: 4,000
SALES (est): 3MM Privately Held
SIC: 2759 Laser printing

(G-6089)
DRI RELAYS INC (HQ)
60 Commerce Dr (11788-3929)
PHONE 631 342-1700
Michel Nespoulous, President
Diane Goerz, Vice Pres
Steve Byun, Project Mgr
Tracy Gu, Production
Murthy Kiran, Purch Mgr
▲ EMP: 100
SALES (est): 21.6MM Privately Held
SIC: 3625 Relays, for electronic use
PA: Financiere De Societes Techniques
17 Rue Vicq D Azir
Paris
142 039-420

(G-6090)
DRIVE SHAFT SHOP INC
210 Blydenburg Rd Unit A (11749-5022)
PHONE 631 348-1818
Frank J Rehak III, President
Mike Smith, Manager
EMP: 10
SQ FT: 1,600

SALES (est): 840K Privately Held
WEB: www.driveshaftshop.com
SIC: 3714 Drive shafts, motor vehicle; axle housings & shafts, motor vehicle; axles, motor vehicle; hydraulic fluid power pumps for auto steering mechanism

(G-6091)
EBC TECHNOLOGIES LLC
Also Called: Theautopartsshop.com
200 Motor Pkwy Ste D26 (11788-5116)
PHONE 631 729-8182
Jay Talluri, CEO
EMP: 55
SALES (est): 5MM Privately Held
SIC: 3571 Electronic computers

(G-6092)
EHRLICH ENTERPRISES INC
Also Called: Floymar Manufacturing
91 Marcus Blvd (11788-3712)
PHONE 631 956-0690
Don Ehrlich, President
Al Schneider, General Mgr
EMP: 16
SQ FT: 18,000
SALES (est): 1.3MM Privately Held
SIC: 3599 Machine shop, jobbing & repair

(G-6093)
ELECTRONIC MACHINE PARTS LLC
Also Called: Emp
400 Oser Ave Ste 2000 (11788-3658)
PHONE 631 434-3700
Fax: 631 434-3718
Tim McAdam, Vice Pres
Maureen McAdam, Mng Member
Tetal Scantlebury, Manager
Maureen Ramert,
EMP: 13
SQ FT: 2,100
SALES (est): 3.1MM Privately Held
WEB: www.empregister.com
SIC: 3625 3823 3714 Control equipment, electric; industrial instrmnts msrmnt display/control process variable; motor vehicle parts & accessories

(G-6094)
ELECTRONIC PRINTING INC
1200 Prime Pl (11788-4761)
P.O. Box 1439, New York (10276-1439)
PHONE 631 218-2200
John Kwiecinski, President
Eileen Abrams, Office Mgr
Paul Kwiecinski, Shareholder
EMP: 7
SQ FT: 9,000
SALES (est): 1.1MM Privately Held
WEB: www.epi-printing.com
SIC: 2732 Book printing

(G-6095)
EMBASSY INDUSTRIES INC
Also Called: Franklin Manufacturing Div
315 Oser Ave Ste 1 (11788-3680)
PHONE 631 435-0209
Fax: 631 694-1832
Robert Ramistella, President
Richard Horowitz, Chairman
Richard Cisek, COO
Joe Krowl, Sls & Mktg Exec
Sidney Horowitz, Bd of Directors
▲ EMP: 170 EST: 1950
SQ FT: 75,000
SALES (est): 84.6MM
SALES (corp-wide): 57.2MM Publicly Held
WEB: www.embassyind.com
SIC: 3433 1711 3567 Heating equipment, except electric; plumbing, heating, air-conditioning contractors; industrial furnaces & ovens
PA: P & F Industries, Inc.
445 Broadhollow Rd # 100
Melville NY 11747
631 694-9800

(G-6096)
ET OAKES CORPORATION
686 Old Willets Path (11788-4102)
PHONE 631 232-0002
Fax: 631 232-0170
W Peter Oakes, Ch of Bd
Noel Oakes, Corp Secy

Robert Peck, *Vice Pres*
EMP: 20
SQ FT: 25,000
SALES (est): 5.3MM **Privately Held**
WEB: www.oakes.com
SIC: **3556** 3531 5084 3599 Cutting, chopping, grinding, mixing & similar machinery; construction machinery; food product manufacturing machinery; machine shop, jobbing & repair

(G-6097)
F & T GRAPHICS INC
690 Old Willets Path (11788-4102)
PHONE.................................631 643-1000
Fax: 631 643-1098
John M Leone, *President*
Debbie Lioni, *Manager*
EMP: 17
SQ FT: 15,000
SALES (est): 4.3MM **Privately Held**
SIC: **2752** Commercial printing, offset

(G-6098)
FB LABORATORIES INC
Also Called: Futurebiotics
70 Commerce Dr (11788-3962)
PHONE.................................631 750-0000
Saiful Kibria, *President*
Kerilee Crennan, *Purch Mgr*
Elizabeth Brynes, *Admin Asst*
▲ EMP: 50 EST: 2010
SALES (est): 9.1MM **Privately Held**
SIC: **2834** Vitamin preparations

(G-6099)
FINISH LINE TECHNOLOGIES INC (PA)
50 Wireless Blvd (11788-3954)
PHONE.................................631 666-7300
Fax: 631 666-7391
Henry J Krause, *President*
◆ EMP: 28
SQ FT: 60,000
SALES (est): 11.6MM **Privately Held**
SIC: **2992** Lubricating oils & greases

(G-6100)
FIXTURES 2000 INC
Also Called: Premier Store Fixtures
400 Oser Ave Ste 350 (11788-3632)
P.O. Box 14177 (11788-0401)
PHONE.................................631 236-4100
Jose Tellez, *President*
Oswaldo Zurita, *Senior VP*
Nelson Goodman, *Vice Pres*
Josephine Rapp, *Accounts Mgr*
Sigal Bonilla, *Manager*
◆ EMP: 280
SQ FT: 230,978
SALES (est): 74.6MM **Privately Held**
WEB: www.premierfixtures.com
SIC: **2542** Fixtures, store: except wood

(G-6101)
FLUID MECHANISMS HAUPPAUGE INC
225 Engineers Rd (11788-4020)
PHONE.................................631 234-0100
Richard Coronato, *President*
Charlotte Coronato, *Corp Secy*
EMP: 35 EST: 1962
SQ FT: 44,000
SALES (est): 9.8MM **Privately Held**
SIC: **3728** Aircraft parts & equipment

(G-6102)
FORECAST CONSOLES INC
681 Old Willets Path (11788-4109)
PHONE.................................631 253-9000
William Haberman, *President*
Ryan Haberman, *General Mgr*
Brian Knox, *COO*
V Decesare, *Prdtn Mgr*
Steven Cirone, *Engineer*
▲ EMP: 24
SQ FT: 21,000
SALES (est): 3.6MM **Privately Held**
WEB: www.forecast-consoles.com
SIC: **2511** 2521 2521 2541 Console tables: wood; public building & related furniture; wood office furniture; shelving, office & store, wood; office furniture, except wood

(G-6103)
FOREST LABORATORIES LLC
45 Adams Ave (11788-3605)
PHONE.................................212 421-7850
Christine Stone, *Office Mgr*
Elaine Hochberg, *Branch Mgr*
EMP: 54 **Privately Held**
WEB: www.frx.com
SIC: **2834** Pharmaceutical preparations
HQ: Forest Laboratories, Llc
  909 3rd Ave Fl 23
  New York NY 10022
  212 421-7850

(G-6104)
FUNGILAB INC
89 Cabot Ct Ste K (11788-3719)
PHONE.................................631 750-6361
Ernest Buira, *CEO*
Joan Buira, *President*
Giovanni Capella, *Sales Mgr*
Diana Hernandez, *Marketing Staff*
◆ EMP: 5
SQ FT: 10,000
SALES: 1MM
SALES (corp-wide): 2.2MM **Privately Held**
SIC: **3821** Laboratory apparatus & furniture
PA: Fungi Lab Sa
  Calle Constitucio (Pg Ind Les Grases), 64 - Nave 15
  Sant Feliu De Llobregat 08980
  936 853-500

(G-6105)
FUTUREBIOTICS LLC
70 Commerce Dr (11788-3936)
PHONE.................................631 273-6300
Fax: 631 273-1165
Steve Welling, *COO*
Jay Patel, *Prdtn Mgr*
Michellle Cofcia, *Controller*
Dina Confredo, *Regl Sales Mgr*
Louise Macintosh, *Cust Mgr*
▲ EMP: 25
SALES (est): 5.8MM **Privately Held**
WEB: www.futurebiotics.com
SIC: **2834** Medicines, capsuled or ampuled

(G-6106)
GENERAL SEMICONDUCTOR INC
150 Motor Pkwy Ste 101 (11788-5167)
PHONE.................................631 300-3818
Linda Perry, *Executive*
EMP: 6
SALES (est): 313.3K **Privately Held**
SIC: **3674** Semiconductors & related devices

(G-6107)
GEOSYNC MICROWAVE INC
320 Oser Ave (11788-3608)
PHONE.................................631 760-5567
Arthur Faverio, *President*
Stephen Philips, *Vice Pres*
Timothy Jahn, *Engineer*
M Zahidi, *Engineer*
Israel Moskovitch, *Marketing Staff*
EMP: 5
SQ FT: 4,000
SALES (est): 950K **Privately Held**
WEB: www.geosyncmicrowave.com
SIC: **3663** Satellites, communications

(G-6108)
GLARO INC
735 Calebs Path Ste 1 (11788-4201)
PHONE.................................631 234-1717
Fax: 631 234-9510
Neal Glass, *President*
Robert Glass, *Division Mgr*
Kane Kessler, *Counsel*
Sherman Lawrence, *Counsel*
Robert Betensky, *Exec VP*
▲ EMP: 60 EST: 1945
SQ FT: 50,000
SALES (est): 9.6MM **Privately Held**
WEB: www.glaro.com
SIC: **2542** Office & store showcases & display fixtures

(G-6109)
GLOBECOMM SYSTEMS INC (DH)
45 Oser Ave (11788-3808)
PHONE.................................631 231-9800
Fax: 631 231-1557
Jason Juranek, *CEO*
Nick Governale, *Dean*
Julia Hanft, *Exec VP*
Dwight R Hunsicker, *Exec VP*
Michael Plourde, *Exec VP*
◆ EMP: 250
SQ FT: 122,000
SALES: 319.6MM
SALES (corp-wide): 533MM **Privately Held**
WEB: www.globecommsystems.com
SIC: **3663** 4813 Satellites, communications; telephone communication, except radio
HQ: Wasserstein Cosmos Co-Invest, L.P.
  1185 Avenue Of The Americ
  New York NY 10036
  212 702-5600

(G-6110)
GSE COMPOSITES INC
110 Oser Ave (11788-3820)
P.O. Box 13248 (11788-0593)
PHONE.................................631 389-1300
EMP: 14
SALES (est): 1.9MM **Privately Held**
SIC: **3089** Mfg Plastic Products

(G-6111)
HAIG PRESS INC
Also Called: Haig Graphic Communications
690 Old Willets Path (11788-4102)
PHONE.................................631 582-5800
Fax: 631 582-2806
James Kalousdian, *Ch of Bd*
Steve Kalousdian, *Vice Pres*
EMP: 44
SQ FT: 30,000
SALES: 7.5MM **Privately Held**
WEB: www.haigraphic.com
SIC: **2752** 2789 2759 Commercial printing, lithographic; bookbinding & related work; commercial printing

(G-6112)
HARMONIC DRIVE LLC
89 Cabot Ct Ste A (11788-3719)
PHONE.................................631 231-6630
Douglas Olson, *President*
Brian Stdenis, *Sls & Mktg Exec*
EMP: 5
SALES (corp-wide): 264.5MM **Privately Held**
WEB: www.harmonic-drive.com
SIC: **3566** Speed changers, drives & gears
HQ: Harmonic Drive L.L.C.
  247 Lynnfield St
  Peabody MA 01960
  978 532-1800

(G-6113)
HAUPPAUGE COMPUTER WORKS INC (HQ)
Also Called: Hauppuge Cmpt Dgtal Erope Sarl
909 Motor Pkwy (11788-5250)
PHONE.................................631 434-1600
Fax: 631 434-3198
Kenneth Plotkin, *Ch of Bd*
Sheila Easop, *Prdtn Mgr*
Gerald Tucciarone, *CFO*
Marlina Sheridan, *Manager*
Steve Sullivan, *Manager*
▲ EMP: 25
SQ FT: 85,000
SALES: 9MM **Publicly Held**
WEB: www.happage.com
SIC: **3577** 7371 Computer peripheral equipment; custom computer programming services

(G-6114)
HAUPPAUGE DIGITAL INC (PA)
909 Motor Pkwy (11788-5250)
PHONE.................................631 434-1600
Kenneth Plotkin, *Ch of Bd*
John Casey, *President*
Jerome Lallier, *Business Mgr*
Ron Petralia, *Vice Pres*
Steve Sullivan, *Opers Mgr*
▲ EMP: 26
SALES: 34MM **Publicly Held**
WEB: www.hauppauge.com
SIC: **3577** Computer peripheral equipment

(G-6115)
HAWK-I SECURITY INC
355 Oser Ave (11788-3607)
P.O. Box 13297 (11788-0723)
PHONE.................................631 656-1056
Joseph Smith, *CEO*
Eric Foreman, *Vice Pres*
Doug Miller, *CFO*
Anthony Matyszczyk, *Consultant*
◆ EMP: 5
SQ FT: 1,000
SALES (est): 498.7K **Privately Held**
WEB: www.hawkisecurity.com
SIC: **3699** Security devices

(G-6116)
HI-TRON SEMICONDUCTOR CORP
85 Engineers Rd (11788-4003)
PHONE.................................631 231-1500
Mel Lax, *President*
Barry Grossman, *Sales Staff*
Mindy Lax, *Admin Sec*
EMP: 20
SQ FT: 42,000
SALES (est): 1.4MM **Privately Held**
SIC: **3674** Semiconductors & related devices

(G-6117)
HILORD CHEMICAL CORPORATION
70 Engineers Rd (11788-4076)
PHONE.................................631 234-7373
Donald Balbinder, *President*
Cody Sickle, *Vice Pres*
Shawnee Sicke, *Treasurer*
Rommel Gloria, *Manager*
Michael Lani, *Information Mgr*
▲ EMP: 26 EST: 1970
SQ FT: 37,000
SALES (est): 6.3MM **Privately Held**
WEB: www.hilord.com
SIC: **3861** 2822 3479 Toners, prepared photographic (not made in chemical plants); ethylene-propylene rubbers, EPDM polymers; coating electrodes

(G-6118)
HOHMANN & BARNARD INC (DH)
Also Called: HB
30 Rasons Ct (11788-4206)
P.O. Box 5270 (11788-0270)
PHONE.................................631 234-0600
Fax: 631 234-0683
Ronald P Hohmann, *Principal*
Winfred Freeman, *Plant Mgr*
Christopher Hohmann, *Treasurer*
Saverio Minucci, *VP Sales*
Kathleen Hohmann, *Sales Staff*
▲ EMP: 25
SQ FT: 55,000
SALES (est): 43.4MM
SALES (corp-wide): 223.6B **Publicly Held**
WEB: www.foamfiller.com
SIC: **3496** 3462 3315 Clips & fasteners, made from purchased wire; iron & steel forgings; steel wire & related products
HQ: Mitek Industries, Inc.
  16023 Swinly Rdg
  Chesterfield MO 63017
  314 434-1200

(G-6119)
HUCKLEBERRY INC
Also Called: Minuteman Press
655 Old Willets Path (11788-4105)
PHONE.................................631 630-5450
Robin Eschenberg, *President*
Hayley Eschenberg, *Managing Prtnr*
EMP: 6
SALES (est): 1MM **Privately Held**
SIC: **2752** Commercial printing, lithographic

Hauppauge - Suffolk County (G-6120)

(G-6120)
ICONIX INC
40 Oser Ave Ste 4 (11788-3807)
PHONE 516 513-1420
Fax: 516 513-1421
Jacob Kohn, *Ch of Bd*
Stan Schiller, *General Mgr*
Nir Levy, *Business Mgr*
Charlie Forbes, *Buyer*
Steve Molstad, *QC Mgr*
EMP: 18
SQ FT: 6,200
SALES: 9.1MM **Privately Held**
SIC: 3699 5065 Electrical equipment & supplies; electronic parts & equipment

(G-6121)
INNOVATIVE LABS LLC
85 Commerce Dr (11788-3902)
PHONE 631 231-5522
Frank Amelio Sr, *CEO*
Frank D Amelio Jr, *President*
Dean Lafemina, *Vice Pres*
Ahsanul Aziz, *Purch Mgr*
EMP: 60
SQ FT: 25,000
SALES: 10MM **Privately Held**
WEB: www.innovativelabsny.com
SIC: 2834 Tablets, pharmaceutical; medicines, capsuled or ampuled

(G-6122)
INNOVATIVE VIDEO TECH INC
Also Called: Invid Tech
355 Oser Ave (11788-3607)
PHONE 631 388-5700
Joe Troiano, *President*
Lou Giannizzero, *Accounts Mgr*
EMP: 13
SQ FT: 10,000
SALES: 1.3MM **Privately Held**
SIC: 3699 Security control equipment & systems

(G-6123)
INVAGEN PHARMACEUTICALS INC (HQ)
7 Oser Ave Ste 4 (11788-3811)
PHONE 631 231-3233
Sudhakar Vidiyala, *President*
Madhava U Reddy, *COO*
Praveen Ale, *Mfg Staff*
Taralynn Manja, *Purchasing*
RAO Prahallada, *Purchasing*
▲ **EMP:** 330
SQ FT: 150,000
SALES: 129MM
SALES (corp-wide): 23.6MM **Privately Held**
SIC: 2834 5122 Pharmaceutical preparations; pharmaceuticals

(G-6124)
J & M PACKAGING INC
Also Called: Baron Packaging
21 Newton Rd (11788-1646)
P.O. Box 5783 (11788-0164)
PHONE 631 608-3069
Melissa Vincente, *CEO*
John Vincente, *Vice Pres*
EMP: 10
SQ FT: 7,500
SALES (est): 162.8K **Privately Held**
SIC: 2653 2449 3086 Boxes, corrugated: made from purchased materials; rectangular boxes & crates, wood; plastics foam products

(G-6125)
JACK MERKEL INC
1720 Express Dr S (11788-5302)
PHONE 631 234-2600
Jack Merkel, *President*
EMP: 5
SQ FT: 6,000
SALES: 800K **Privately Held**
SIC: 3599 7538 Machine shop, jobbing & repair; engine repair; engine rebuilding: automotive

(G-6126)
JACKNOB INTERNATIONAL LTD
Also Called: Omega Die Casting Co
290 Oser Ave (11788-3610)
P.O. Box 18032 (11788-8832)
PHONE 631 546-6560
Jerry M Loveless, *President*
Brendan Omalley, *Vice Pres*
Carole Termini, *Vice Pres*
Cristin Nilson, *Human Res Mgr*
Susan Marsh, *Info Tech Mgr*
▲ **EMP:** 90 **EST:** 1931
SQ FT: 20,000
SALES (est): 11.2MM **Privately Held**
WEB: www.jacknob.com
SIC: 3432 Plumbers' brass goods: drain cocks, faucets, spigots, etc.

(G-6127)
JOSH PACKAGING INC
245 Marcus Blvd Ste 1 (11788-2000)
PHONE 631 822-1660
Abraham Golshirazian, *Ch of Bd*
Abe Gulsh, *President*
Nejat Rahmani, *Vice Pres*
▲ **EMP:** 20
SQ FT: 30,000
SALES (est): 5MM **Privately Held**
SIC: 2673 5113 5162 Plastic bags: made from purchased materials; industrial & personal service paper; plastics materials

(G-6128)
KEEBLER COMPANY
55 Gilpin Ave (11788-4723)
PHONE 631 234-3700
Fax: 631 582-3570
Jean Meigl, *Manager*
EMP: 40
SALES (corp-wide): 13B **Publicly Held**
WEB: www.keebler.com
SIC: 2052 Cookies
HQ: Keebler Company
1 Kellogg Sq
Battle Creek MI 49017
269 961-2000

(G-6129)
KILTRONX ENVIRO SYSTEMS LLC
330 Motor Pkwy Ste 201 (11788-5118)
PHONE 917 971-7177
Gabriel Kaszovitz,
Arlen Cabale,
EMP: 30
SQ FT: 1,500
SALES (est): 10MM **Privately Held**
SIC: 2295 Chemically coated & treated fabrics

(G-6130)
KINGS PARK ASPHALT CORPORATION
201 Moreland Rd Ste 2 (11788-3922)
PHONE 631 269-9774
Michael Farino, *President*
James Farino, *Corp Secy*
Paul Farino, *Vice Pres*
EMP: 5
SQ FT: 1,000
SALES (est): 850K **Privately Held**
SIC: 2951 Asphalt paving mixtures & blocks; asphalt paving blocks (not from refineries); paving mixtures; asphalt & asphaltic paving mixtures (not from refineries)

(G-6131)
KLD LABS INC
55 Cabot Ct (11788-3717)
PHONE 631 549-4222
Steven Magnus, *President*
Daniel L Magnus, *Vice Pres*
Yury Malyarov, *Design Engr*
Ryan Danziger, *Electrical Engi*
Patricia Anwander, *Controller*
EMP: 40
SQ FT: 20,000
SALES (est): 10MM **Privately Held**
WEB: www.kldlabs.com
SIC: 3829 7373 Measuring & controlling devices; computer integrated systems design

(G-6132)
L3 TECHNOLOGIES INC
Narda Microwave East
435 Moreland Rd (11788-3926)
PHONE 631 231-1700
Joe Merenda, *President*
John Mega, *Division Pres*
Tim Fowler, *Vice Pres*
Robert Koelzer, *Vice Pres*
Michael J Sanator, *Vice Pres*
EMP: 300
SALES (corp-wide): 10.5B **Publicly Held**
SIC: 3663 Telemetering equipment, electronic
PA: L3 Technologies, Inc.
600 3rd Ave Fl 34
New York NY 10016
212 697-1111

(G-6133)
L3 TECHNOLOGIES INC
Also Called: L-3 Narda-Miteq
100 Davids Dr (11788-2043)
PHONE 631 436-7400
Steven Skpock, *President*
Wendy U Ringhiser, *Executive*
EMP: 700
SALES (corp-wide): 10.5B **Publicly Held**
SIC: 3663 3769 3661 3651 Radio & TV communications equipment; guided missile & space vehicle parts & auxiliary equipment; telephone & telegraph apparatus; household audio & video equipment; current-carrying wiring devices
PA: L3 Technologies, Inc.
600 3rd Ave Fl 34
New York NY 10016
212 697-1111

(G-6134)
L3 TECHNOLOGIES INC
Also Called: Narda Satellite Networks
435 Moreland Rd (11788-3926)
PHONE 631 231-1700
Fax: 631 231-1485
Jeff Czworniak, *Opers Mgr*
Frank Sepulveda, *Facilities Mgr*
Charles Okon, *Engineer*
Mike Callegari, *Controller*
Sherry Dowe, *Human Res Dir*
SQ FT: 60,000
SALES (corp-wide): 10.5B **Publicly Held**
SIC: 3663 8748 5731 Telemetering equipment, electronic; communications consulting; antennas, satellite dish
PA: L3 Technologies, Inc.
600 3rd Ave Fl 34
New York NY 10016
212 697-1111

(G-6135)
L3 TECHNOLOGIES INC
Also Called: L-3 Narda-Miteq
330 Oser Ave (11788-3630)
PHONE 631 436-7400
Dan Sundberg, *Dept Chairman*
Aksel Kiiss, *Manager*
EMP: 100
SALES (corp-wide): 10.5B **Publicly Held**
SIC: 3663 Radio broadcasting & communications equipment
PA: L3 Technologies, Inc.
600 3rd Ave Fl 34
New York NY 10016
212 697-1111

(G-6136)
LA FLOR PRODUCTS COMPANY INC (PA)
Also Called: La Flor Spices
25 Hoffman Ave (11788-4717)
PHONE 631 851-9601
Ruben La Torre Sr, *President*
Dan La Torre, *Exec VP*
Ruben La Torre Jr, *Vice Pres*
Chris Pappas, *Vice Pres*
▲ **EMP:** 44
SQ FT: 90,000
SALES: 9MM **Privately Held**
WEB: www.laflor.com
SIC: 2099 Seasonings & spices; seasonings: dry mixes

(G-6137)
LISTEC VIDEO CORP (PA)
90 Oser Ave (11788-3800)
PHONE 631 273-3029
William J Littler, *Ch of Bd*
Joanne Camarda, *President*
Raymond Blumenthal, *Vice Pres*
EMP: 5
SQ FT: 3,000
SALES (est): 995.9K **Privately Held**
WEB: www.listecny.com
SIC: 3663 5099 Radio & TV communications equipment; video & audio equipment

(G-6138)
LIVING WELL INNOVATIONS INC
115 Engineers Rd (11788-4005)
PHONE 646 517-3200
Arthur Danziger, *President*
EMP: 6
SQ FT: 4,000
SALES (est): 5MM **Privately Held**
SIC: 2731 5192 Book publishing; books

(G-6139)
LNK INTERNATIONAL INC
22 Arkay Dr (11788-3708)
PHONE 631 435-3500
EMP: 100
SALES (corp-wide): 53.5MM **Privately Held**
SIC: 2834 Pharmaceutical preparations
PA: L.N.K. International Inc.
60 Arkay Dr
Hauppauge NY 11788
631 435-3500

(G-6140)
LNK INTERNATIONAL INC
100 Ricefield Ln (11788-2008)
PHONE 631 435-3500
Fax: 631 435-3542
Chudgar Pk, *Manager*
EMP: 100
SALES (corp-wide): 53.5MM **Privately Held**
SIC: 2834 Pharmaceutical preparations
PA: L.N.K. International Inc.
60 Arkay Dr
Hauppauge NY 11788
631 435-3500

(G-6141)
LNK INTERNATIONAL INC
325 Kennedy Dr (11788-4006)
PHONE 631 435-3500
Joseph J Mollica, *President*
EMP: 100
SALES (corp-wide): 53.5MM **Privately Held**
SIC: 2834 Pharmaceutical preparations
PA: L.N.K. International Inc.
60 Arkay Dr
Hauppauge NY 11788
631 435-3500

(G-6142)
LNK INTERNATIONAL INC
145 Ricefield Ln (11788-2007)
PHONE 631 543-3787
Fax: 631 543-2040
Pk Chudgar, *Manager*
EMP: 100
SALES (corp-wide): 53.5MM **Privately Held**
SIC: 2834 Pharmaceutical preparations
PA: L.N.K. International Inc.
60 Arkay Dr
Hauppauge NY 11788
631 435-3500

(G-6143)
LNK INTERNATIONAL INC
40 Arkay Dr (11788-3708)
PHONE 631 435-3500
Shaji Kumar Varghese, *Branch Mgr*
EMP: 100
SALES (corp-wide): 53.5MM **Privately Held**
SIC: 2834 Pharmaceutical preparations
PA: L.N.K. International Inc.
60 Arkay Dr
Hauppauge NY 11788
631 435-3500

(G-6144)
LNK INTERNATIONAL INC
2095 Expressway Dr N (11788-5308)
PHONE 631 231-3415
Joseph J Mollica, *President*
EMP: 100
SALES (corp-wide): 53.5MM **Privately Held**
SIC: 2834 Pharmaceutical preparations

GEOGRAPHIC SECTION

Hauppauge - Suffolk County (G-6168)

PA: L.N.K. International Inc.
60 Arkay Dr
Hauppauge NY 11788
631 435-3500

(G-6145)
LNK INTERNATIONAL INC
55 Arkay Dr (11788-3707)
PHONE...............................631 231-4020
Joseph J Mollica Sr, *Branch Mgr*
EMP: 100
SALES (corp-wide): 53.5MM **Privately Held**
SIC: 2834 Pharmaceutical preparations
PA: L.N.K. International Inc.
60 Arkay Dr
Hauppauge NY 11788
631 435-3500

(G-6146)
LOURDES INDUSTRIES INC (PA)
65 Hoffman Ave (11788-4798)
PHONE...............................631 234-6600
Fax: 631 234-7595
William J Jakobsen, *Ch of Bd*
Bruce Jacobson, *Vice Pres*
Peter McKenna, *Vice Pres*
Paul Vaughan, *Opers Mgr*
Dave Hertling, *Engineer*
EMP: 90 EST: 1954
SQ FT: 26,000
SALES (est): 20.5MM **Privately Held**
SIC: 3795 3492 3643 3724 Tanks & tank components; fluid power valves & hose fittings; current-carrying wiring devices; aircraft engines & engine parts; engineering services

(G-6147)
LOURDES SYSTEMS INC
21 Newton Pl (11788-4815)
PHONE...............................631 234-7077
George Powell, *Ch of Bd*
Peter Maguire, *President*
George Meyerle, *Vice Pres*
Peter McKenna, *Treasurer*
Jeff Jordan, *MIS Dir*
EMP: 12
SQ FT: 5,000
SALES (est): 1.3MM **Privately Held**
SIC: 3542 Machine tools, metal forming type

(G-6148)
M&C ASSOCIATES LLC
700 Vets Memrl Hwy 335 (11788)
PHONE...............................631 467-8760
Fax: 631 467-8767
Lou Marianacci, *President*
Kelly Palacios, *President*
Leanora Gordon, *Principal*
Dave Depietro, *Vice Pres*
Russell Asceri, *Manager*
EMP: 40
SALES (est): 6.9MM **Privately Held**
SIC: 3571 Electronic computers

(G-6149)
MACHINERY MOUNTINGS INC
41 Sarah Dr (11788)
PHONE...............................631 851-0480
Bernard H Kass, *President*
Steven Kass, *Vice Pres*
Wayne Kass, *Vice Pres*
EMP: 14
SALES (est): 1.6MM **Privately Held**
SIC: 3499 Machine bases, metal

(G-6150)
MAGGIO DATA FORMS PRINTING LTD
1735 Express Dr N (11788-5312)
PHONE...............................631 348-0343
Fax: 631 348-4422
Robert Maggio, *President*
James Maggio, *Vice Pres*
Charlie Johnson, *Sales Staff*
Charles Maggio, *Admin Sec*
EMP: 110
SQ FT: 30,000
SALES (est): 13.2MM **Privately Held**
WEB: www.maggio.com
SIC: 2761 Manifold business forms

(G-6151)
MAKERS NUTRITION LLC (PA)
315 Oser Ave Ste 3 (11788-3680)
PHONE...............................631 456-5397
Stephen Finnegan, *General Mgr*
Rosa Ciaccio, *Manager*
EMP: 25 EST: 2014
SALES: 12MM **Privately Held**
SIC: 2023 Dietary supplements, dairy & non-dairy based

(G-6152)
MASON INDUSTRIES INC (PA)
Also Called: M I
350 Rabro Dr (11788-4237)
P.O. Box 410, Smithtown (11787-0410)
PHONE...............................631 348-0282
Fax: 631 348-0279
Norm Mason, *Ch of Bd*
Patrick Lama, *Vice Pres*
Armando Gamble, *Safety Mgr*
Yuewei Chang, *Purchasing*
Valerie J Angel, *Engineer*
◆ EMP: 350 EST: 1958
SQ FT: 60,000
SALES (est): 64.7MM **Privately Held**
WEB: www.mercer-rubber.com
SIC: 3625 3829 3052 3069 Noise control equipment; measuring & controlling devices; rubber hose; hard rubber & molded rubber products; fabricated structural metal; electronic connectors

(G-6153)
MASON INDUSTRIES INC
33 Ranick Rd Ste 1 (11788-4250)
PHONE...............................631 348-0282
Patricia Gowicki, *Manager*
EMP: 7
SALES (corp-wide): 64.7MM **Privately Held**
SIC: 3625 Noise control equipment
PA: Mason Industries, Inc.
350 Rabro Dr
Hauppauge NY 11788
631 348-0282

(G-6154)
MCKEE FOODS CORPORATION
111 Serene Pl (11788-3534)
PHONE...............................631 979-9364
John Meyer, *Branch Mgr*
EMP: 609
SALES (corp-wide): 1.8B **Privately Held**
WEB: www.mckeefoods.com
SIC: 2051 Cakes, bakery: except frozen
PA: Mckee Foods Corporation
10260 Mckee Rd
Collegedale TN 37315
423 238-7111

(G-6155)
MEDICAL ACTION INDUSTRIES INC
150 Motor Pkwy Ste 205 (11788-5180)
PHONE...............................631 231-4600
Fax: 631 231-3075
Paul Meringola, *Manager*
EMP: 215 **Publicly Held**
WEB: www.medical-action.com
SIC: 3842 4226 5999 5047 Sponges, surgical; sterilizers, hospital & surgical; surgical appliances & supplies; special warehousing & storage; medical apparatus & supplies; hospital equipment & furniture
HQ: Medical Action Industries Inc.
25 Heywood Rd
Arden NC 28704
631 231-4600

(G-6156)
MELLAND GEAR INSTR OF HUPPAUGE
225 Engineers Rd (11788-4020)
PHONE...............................631 234-0100
Richard C Coronato, *CEO*
Richard Coronato Sr, *President*
Oscar Duarte, *Purchasing*
Charlotte Coronato, *Admin Sec*
EMP: 35 EST: 1959
SQ FT: 44,000
SALES (est): 4.9MM **Privately Held**
SIC: 3824 3545 Mechanical counters; precision tools, machinists'

(G-6157)
MEOPTA USA INC
Also Called: Tyrolit Company
50 Davids Dr (11788-2040)
PHONE...............................631 436-5900
Fax: 631 436-5920
Gerald J Rausnitz, *President*
Alois Bell, *General Mgr*
David Rausnitz, *COO*
Marcel Kappeler, *Vice Pres*
Carlos Arango, *Purch Mgr*
▲ EMP: 140 EST: 1957
SQ FT: 41,500
SALES: 42.1MM
SALES (corp-wide): 97.7MM **Privately Held**
WEB: www.meopta.com
SIC: 3827 Lenses, optical: all types except ophthalmic
PA: Meopta - Optika, S.R.O.
Kabelikova 2682/1
Prerov - Prerov I-Mesto 75002
581 242-153

(G-6158)
MERCER RUBBER CO
350 Rabro Dr (11788-4257)
PHONE...............................631 348-0282
Norman J Mason, *President*
Mary P Ryan, *Corp Secy*
Pat Lama, *Vice Pres*
▲ EMP: 150 EST: 1866
SQ FT: 60,000
SALES (est): 20.6MM
SALES (corp-wide): 64.7MM **Privately Held**
WEB: www.mercer-rubber.com
SIC: 3069 3052 Expansion joints, rubber; rubber hose
PA: Mason Industries, Inc.
350 Rabro Dr
Hauppauge NY 11788
631 348-0282

(G-6159)
MERGENCE STUDIOS LTD
135 Ricefield Ln (11788-2046)
PHONE...............................212 288-5616
Douglas Schulman, *CEO*
▲ EMP: 11
SALES (est): 1.3MM **Privately Held**
SIC: 2241 Glass narrow fabrics

(G-6160)
METAL DYNAMICS INTL CORP
Also Called: Mdi
25 Corporate Dr (11788-2021)
P.O. Box 13248 (11788-0593)
PHONE...............................631 231-1153
Daniel Shybunko, *President*
Anne D Shybunko-Moore, *President*
Tim Austin, *Vice Pres*
Amy Pitarra, *Purchasing*
Ann Curran, *Controller*
◆ EMP: 5
SQ FT: 28,600
SALES (est): 892.7K **Privately Held**
WEB: www.metaldynamicsintl.com
SIC: 3728 Aircraft parts & equipment

(G-6161)
MICROCAD TRNING CONSULTING INC
77 Arkay Dr Ste C2 (11788-3742)
PHONE...............................631 291-9484
Michael F Frey, *Branch Mgr*
EMP: 7 **Privately Held**
SIC: 7372 Prepackaged software
PA: Microcad Training & Consulting, Inc.
440 Arsenal St Ste 3
Watertown MA

(G-6162)
MICROCHIP TECHNOLOGY INC
80 Arkay Dr Ste 100 (11788-3705)
PHONE...............................631 233-3280
Fax: 631 249-8178
Kenneth Smalley, *Engineer*
Daniel Thornton, *Engineer*
Dan Levesser, *Manager*
Dennis Cho, *Manager*
Andrew Odlivak, *Manager*
EMP: 6

SALES (corp-wide): 3.4B **Publicly Held**
WEB: www.microchip.com
SIC: 3674 Microcircuits, integrated (semiconductor)
PA: Microchip Technology Inc
2355 W Chandler Blvd
Chandler AZ 85224
480 792-7200

(G-6163)
MICROSOFT CORPORATION
2929 Expressway Dr N # 300 (11749-5302)
PHONE...............................516 380-1531
Fax: 631 630-8521
Wilhelm Gerbert, *General Mgr*
Charles Baker, *Project Mgr*
John Reumann, *Human Res Mgr*
Tom Marsh, *Sales Mgr*
Matt Destefano, *Accounts Mgr*
EMP: 100
SALES (corp-wide): 89.9B **Publicly Held**
WEB: www.microsoft.com
SIC: 7372 Prepackaged software
PA: Microsoft Corporation
1 Microsoft Way
Redmond WA 98052
425 882-8080

(G-6164)
MILSO INDUSTRIES INC
25 Engineers Rd (11788-4019)
PHONE...............................631 234-1133
Al Orsi, *Branch Mgr*
EMP: 12
SQ FT: 10,000
SALES (corp-wide): 1.4B **Publicly Held**
SIC: 3995 5087 Burial caskets; caskets
HQ: Milso Industries Inc.
534 Union St
Brooklyn NY 11215
718 624-4593

(G-6165)
MINI GRAPHICS INC
Also Called: Mgi
140 Commerce Dr (11788-3948)
PHONE...............................516 223-6464
James Delise, *CEO*
Chris La Pak, *Managing Dir*
Charles J Delise, *Principal*
Steven Delise, *Principal*
Mark Dlhopolsky, *Project Mgr*
EMP: 100
SALES (est): 23.3MM **Privately Held**
WEB: www.minigraphics.net
SIC: 2759 Commercial printing

(G-6166)
MMC ENTERPRISES CORP
175 Commerce Dr Ste E (11788-3920)
PHONE...............................800 435-1088
Jin Sun, *President*
▲ EMP: 8
SALES (est): 972.6K **Privately Held**
SIC: 3826 Instruments measuring magnetic & electrical properties

(G-6167)
MMC MAGNETICS CORP
175 Commerce Dr Ste E (11788-3920)
PHONE...............................631 435-9888
Huai Sheu Zhou, *Ch of Bd*
EMP: 17
SALES (est): 1.4MM **Privately Held**
SIC: 3674 3499 Photoelectric magnetic devices; magnets, permanent: metallic

(G-6168)
MOBILE FLEET INC (PA)
10 Commerce Dr (11788-3968)
P.O. Box 1240, Farmingdale (11735-0855)
PHONE...............................631 206-2920
Robert E Squicciarini Sr, *CEO*
Jeff Beutel, *General Mgr*
Jennifer Clark, *Principal*
Kevin Walker, *Vice Pres*
Matt Tannenbaum, *CFO*
▼ EMP: 8
SQ FT: 16,500
SALES: 15MM **Privately Held**
SIC: 3647 Automotive lighting fixtures

Hauppauge - Suffolk County (G-6169)

(G-6169)
MONITOR ELEVATOR PRODUCTS LLC
Also Called: Monitor Controls
125 Ricefield Ln (11788-2007)
PHONE..................631 543-4334
Fax: 631 543-4372
Paul Horney, *President*
Kathryn Byszewski, *Vice Pres*
Kevin White, *Production*
Louise Russo, *Purchasing*
Bill Higbee, *Regl Sales Mgr*
▲ EMP: 65 EST: 2011
SQ FT: 30,000
SALES (est): 16.6MM
SALES (corp-wide): 22.6MM **Privately Held**
WEB: www.mcontrols.com
SIC: 3534 Elevators & equipment
PA: Innovation Industries, Inc.
3500 E Main St
Russellville AR 72802
800 843-1004

(G-6170)
MULTIFOLD DIE CTNG FINSHG CORP
120 Ricefield Ln Ste B (11788-2033)
PHONE..................631 232-1235
William Collins, *Ch of Bd*
Christine Collins, *President*
EMP: 5
SALES (est): 561.8K **Privately Held**
SIC: 3544 Special dies & tools

(G-6171)
NATUS MEDICAL INCORPORATED
Also Called: Neometrics
150 Motor Pkwy Ste 106 (11788-5167)
PHONE..................631 457-4430
Fax: 631 457-4444
Joe Amato, *Principal*
EMP: 8
SALES (corp-wide): 381.8MM **Publicly Held**
SIC: 3845 Electromedical equipment
PA: Natus Medical Incorporated
6701 Koll Center Pkwy # 150
Pleasanton CA 94566
925 223-6700

(G-6172)
NEOPOST USA INC
415 Oser Ave Ste K (11788-3637)
PHONE..................631 435-9100
Joanne Lafrance, *Principal*
EMP: 50
SALES (corp-wide): 47.4MM **Privately Held**
SIC: 3579 7359 7629 Postage meters; business machine & electronic equipment rental services; business machine repair, electric
HQ: Neopost Usa Inc.
478 Wheelers Farms Rd
Milford CT 06461
203 301-3400

(G-6173)
NEW HORIZON GRAPHICS INC
1200 Prime Pl (11788-4761)
PHONE..................631 231-8055
Fax: 516 249-2127
Anthony Guida, *Chairman*
Annette Guida, *Corp Secy*
Rachel Guida, *Office Mgr*
Steve Guida, *Manager*
EMP: 45
SQ FT: 25,000
SALES (est): 10.8MM **Privately Held**
WEB: www.newhorizongraphic.com
SIC: 2752 2675 Commercial printing, offset; cards, folders & mats: die-cut

(G-6174)
NIKISH SOFTWARE CORP
801 Motor Pkwy (11788-5256)
PHONE..................631 754-1618
Kishin Bharwani, *President*
Nitsha Bharwani, *Vice Pres*
Catherine Kraemer, *Administration*
EMP: 6

SALES (est): 700K **Privately Held**
WEB: www.nikish.com
SIC: 7372 Prepackaged software

(G-6175)
NOVA SCIENCE PUBLISHERS INC
400 Oser Ave Ste 1600 (11788-3667)
PHONE..................631 231-7269
Frank Columbus, *President*
Richard Schortemeyer, *Editor*
Nadezhda Columbus, *Vice Pres*
Maria Pontillo, *Prdtn Mgr*
Nese Kaya, *Marketing Staff*
EMP: 12
SQ FT: 1,500
SALES (est): 1.6MM **Privately Held**
SIC: 2721 2731 Periodicals; book publishing

(G-6176)
NUBIAN HERITAGE
367 Old Willets Path (11788-1217)
PHONE..................631 265-3551
Edwin McCray, *Owner*
EMP: 5
SALES (est): 249.3K **Privately Held**
SIC: 3999 5199 Fire extinguishers, portable; gifts & novelties

(G-6177)
OLAN LABORATORIES INC
Also Called: Prolocksusa
20 Newton Pl (11788-4752)
PHONE..................631 582-2082
Maurice Gregory Minuto, *President*
Lisa Minuto, *Vice Pres*
EMP: 9
SQ FT: 20,000
SALES (est): 1.7MM **Privately Held**
SIC: 2844 Cosmetic preparations; hair preparations, including shampoos

(G-6178)
OLDCASTLE BUILDINGENVELOPE INC
895 Motor Pkwy (11788-5232)
P.O. Box 18039 (11788-8839)
PHONE..................631 234-2200
Kathy Blays, *General Mgr*
Jeff Duty, *General Mgr*
Greg Grothoff, *General Mgr*
Robert Wheeler, *General Mgr*
Lauren McMillon, *Project Mgr*
EMP: 125
SALES (corp-wide): 28.6B **Privately Held**
WEB: www.crh.ie
SIC: 3231 5231 Tempered glass: made from purchased glass; insulating glass: made from purchased glass; glass
HQ: Oldcastle Buildingenvelope, Inc.
5005 Lndn B Jnsn Fwy 10 Ste 1050
Dallas TX 75244
214 273-3400

(G-6179)
OLYMPIC MANUFACTURING INC
195 Marcus Blvd (11788-3702)
PHONE..................631 231-8900
Donald Molloy Jr, *President*
EMP: 20
SQ FT: 6,000
SALES (est): 2.2MM **Privately Held**
SIC: 3444 Sheet metalwork

(G-6180)
ORBIT INTERNATIONAL CORP (PA)
80 Cabot Ct (11788-3771)
PHONE..................631 435-8300
Mitchell Binder, *President*
Donna Holzeis, *Human Res Mgr*
John Goodfellow, *Director*
David Goldman, *Officer*
Mark Tublisky, *Admin Sec*
EMP: 122 EST: 1957
SQ FT: 60,000
SALES: 20.7MM **Publicly Held**
WEB: www.orbitintl.com
SIC: 3679 3674 3643 3577 Power supplies, all types: static; solid state electronic devices; current-carrying wiring devices; computer peripheral equipment; computer terminals

(G-6181)
ORBIT INTERNATIONAL CORP
Tulip Development Laboratory
80 Cabot Ct (11788-3771)
PHONE..................631 435-8300
Mitchell Binder, *Branch Mgr*
EMP: 53
SALES (corp-wide): 19.1MM **Publicly Held**
SIC: 3679 Static power supply converters for electronic applications
PA: Orbit International Corp.
80 Cabot Ct
Hauppauge NY 11788
631 435-8300

(G-6182)
ORGANIC FROG INC
Also Called: Frog International
85 Commerce Dr (11788-3902)
PHONE..................516 897-0369
Ellen Piernick, *President*
EMP: 8
SQ FT: 2,200
SALES: 1.5MM **Privately Held**
SIC: 2834 5122 Vitamin, nutrient & hematinic preparations for human use; drugs, proprietaries & sundries

(G-6183)
PARKER-HANNIFIN CORPORATION
Also Called: Electronics Systems Division
300 Marcus Blvd (11788-2044)
PHONE..................631 231-3737
Fax: 631 273-2817
Donald Washkewicz, *President*
Lee Banks, *Vice Pres*
Jon Marten, *Vice Pres*
Thomas A Piraino Jr, *Vice Pres*
Daniel Serbin, *Vice Pres*
EMP: 335
SQ FT: 150,000
SALES (corp-wide): 12B **Publicly Held**
WEB: www.parker.com
SIC: 3829 Instrument board gauges, automotive: computerized
PA: Parker-Hannifin Corporation
6035 Parkland Blvd
Cleveland OH 44124
216 896-3000

(G-6184)
PDK LABS INC
145 Ricefield Ln (11788-2007)
PHONE..................631 273-2630
Fax: 631 434-9145
Reginald Spinello, *President*
Carmella Staugaitis, *Purch Mgr*
Richerd Rodriguez, *Controller*
Stephanie Dalio, *Cust Mgr*
Donna Ellis, *Info Tech Mgr*
EMP: 80
SQ FT: 44,000
SALES (est): 1.4MM **Privately Held**
SIC: 2834 2844 Pharmaceutical preparations; vitamin, nutrient & hematinic preparations for human use; cold remedies; analgesics; toilet preparations; oral preparations; cosmetic preparations

(G-6185)
PEELLE COMPANY (PA)
373 Smithtown Byp 311 (11788-2516)
PHONE..................631 231-6000
R B Peelle Jr, *Ch of Bd*
Henry E Peelle III, *President*
Michael J Ryan, *Vice Pres*
Dan Nieves, *Engineer*
Brad Hunt, *Sales Mgr*
▲ EMP: 7
SQ FT: 6,000
SALES (est): 10.9MM **Privately Held**
SIC: 3499 Aerosol valves, metal

(G-6186)
PEER SOFTWARE INCORPORATED (PA)
1363 Veterans Hwy Ste 44 (11788-3046)
PHONE..................631 979-1770
Paul J Marsala, *Principal*
EMP: 7
SALES (est): 2.6MM **Privately Held**
SIC: 7372 Prepackaged software

(G-6187)
PETER KWASNY INC
400 Oser Ave Ste 1650 (11788-3669)
PHONE..................727 641-1462
Hans Peter Kwasny, *President*
▲ EMP: 6
SALES (est): 730K
SALES (corp-wide): 61.3MM **Privately Held**
SIC: 2851 Paints & allied products
PA: Peter Kwasny Gmbh
Heilbronner Str. 96
Gundelsheim 74831
626 995-0

(G-6188)
PETS N PEOPLE INC
2100 Pacific St (11788-4737)
PHONE..................631 232-1200
Fax: 631 232-1206
Mindy D Weiss Lasman, *President*
Marcia Weiss, *Corp Secy*
Mark Stern, *Personnel Exec*
▲ EMP: 8
SALES (est): 520K **Privately Held**
SIC: 3999 Pet supplies

(G-6189)
PHOENIX MCH PDTS OF HAUPPAUGE
225 Engineers Rd (11788-4020)
PHONE..................631 234-0100
Richard F Coronato Sr, *President*
EMP: 5
SQ FT: 15,000
SALES (est): 357.8K **Privately Held**
SIC: 3599 Machine shop, jobbing & repair

(G-6190)
PINDER INTERNATIONAL INC (PA)
1140 Motor Pkwy Ste A (11788-5255)
PHONE..................631 273-0324
Jatinder Dhall, *Ch of Bd*
▲ EMP: 5 EST: 2011
SQ FT: 15,000
SALES (est): 769.4K **Privately Held**
SIC: 2231 Apparel & outerwear broadwoven fabrics

(G-6191)
PIROD INC
Also Called: Valmont Site Pro 1
15 Oser Ave (11788-3808)
PHONE..................631 231-7660
Joe Catapano, *General Mgr*
Joseph Cadapano, *Branch Mgr*
EMP: 33
SALES (corp-wide): 2.5B **Publicly Held**
SIC: 3441 Fabricated structural metal
HQ: Pirod Inc.
1545 Pidco Dr
Plymouth IN 46563
574 936-7221

(G-6192)
PNEUMERCATOR COMPANY INC
1785 Express Dr N (11788-5303)
PHONE..................631 293-8450
Fax: 631 293-8533
Jonathan Levy, *President*
Agnes Amundsen, *Manager*
▲ EMP: 35 EST: 1914
SQ FT: 11,500
SALES (est): 7.9MM **Privately Held**
WEB: www.pneumercator.com
SIC: 3823 Gas flow computers, industrial process type; pressure gauges, dial & digital

(G-6193)
POLY CRAFT INDUSTRIES CORP
40 Ranick Rd (11788-4209)
PHONE..................631 630-6731
Fax: 718 392-4044
Samuel Brach, *President*
Sylvia Brach, *Admin Sec*
▲ EMP: 25
SQ FT: 13,000
SALES (est): 5.9MM **Privately Held**
SIC: 2673 5113 Plastic bags: made from purchased materials; bags, paper & disposable plastic

GEOGRAPHIC SECTION

Hauppauge - Suffolk County (G-6218)

(G-6194)
PRECARE CORP
Also Called: Premier Care Industries
400 Wireless Blvd (11788-3938)
PHONE..................631 524-5171
Fax: 631 952-7478
Abraham Micheal, *Branch Mgr*
EMP: 5 Privately Held
SIC: 2676 Sanitary paper products
PA: Precare Corp.
 100 Oser Ave
 Hauppauge NY 11788

(G-6195)
PRECARE CORP (PA)
100 Oser Ave (11788-3809)
PHONE..................631 667-1055
Matthew Neman, *COO*
Ouri Neman, *Vice Pres*
Bill Lutz, *VP Sales*
▲ **EMP:** 5
SQ FT: 35,000
SALES: 16.4MM Privately Held
SIC: 2621 2676 Tissue paper; napkins, sanitary: made from purchased paper; diapers, paper (disposable): made from purchased paper; tampons, sanitary: made from purchased paper

(G-6196)
PRELOAD CONCRETE STRUCTURES
60 Commerce Dr (11788-3929)
PHONE..................631 231-8100
Andrew E Tripp Jr, *President*
Nancy Coll, *Corp Secy*
Jack Hornstein, *Vice Pres*
Stephen G Kravitz, *Network Mgr*
EMP: 42
SQ FT: 29,000
SALES (est): 6.9MM Privately Held
WEB: www.preload.com
SIC: 3272 Tanks, concrete

(G-6197)
PREMIER WOODWORKING INC
400 Oser Ave (11788-3619)
P.O. Box 14177 (11788-0401)
PHONE..................631 236-4100
Jose Tellez, *President*
Carlos Zurita, *Vice Pres*
Jasmin Gonzalez, *Administration*
▲ **EMP:** 35
SQ FT: 230,000
SALES: 2.5MM Privately Held
SIC: 2541 Wood partitions & fixtures

(G-6198)
PRINTERS 3 INC
43 Corporate Dr Ste 2 (11788-2048)
PHONE..................631 351-1331
Fax: 631 351-1384
Sal Viscuso, *Ch of Bd*
Anthony Viscuso, *President*
Christal Viscuso, *Corp Secy*
EMP: 10
SQ FT: 4,200
SALES (est): 1.1MM Privately Held
SIC: 2752 Commercial printing, lithographic

(G-6199)
PROFESSIONAL BUTY HOLDINGS INC
150 Motor Pkwy Ste 401 (11788-5108)
PHONE..................631 787-8576
Bruce Kowalsky, *Managing Prtnr*
Gari Dawn Tingler, *Treasurer*
EMP: 10
SQ FT: 100,000
SALES: 10MM Privately Held
SIC: 2844 Toilet preparations

(G-6200)
PROFESSIONAL SOLUTIONS PRINT
125 Wireless Blvd Ste E (11788-3937)
PHONE..................631 231-9300
Karl Snyder, *President*
EMP: 6
SALES: 750K Privately Held
SIC: 2752 Commercial printing, lithographic

(G-6201)
PROFILE PRINTING & GRAPHICS (PA)
275 Marcus Blvd (11788-2022)
PHONE..................631 273-2727
Michael Munda, *President*
EMP: 7
SQ FT: 3,000
SALES (est): 508.8K Privately Held
WEB: www.profileprinting.com
SIC: 2752 Commercial printing, lithographic

(G-6202)
QUOIZEL INC
590 Old Willets Path # 1 (11788-4119)
PHONE..................631 436-4402
Sandy Stone, *Accounting Mgr*
Carolyn Fredrickson, *Cust Mgr*
Patrick Slater, *Marketing Staff*
Toni Phillips, *Branch Mgr*
Alex Jen, *Director*
EMP: 27
SALES (corp-wide): 77.6MM Privately Held
WEB: www.quoizel.com
SIC: 3645 5063 8741 Residential lighting fixtures; lighting fixtures; management services
PA: Quoizel, Inc.
 6 Corporate Pkwy
 Goose Creek SC 29445
 843 553-6700

(G-6203)
RENTSCHLER BIOTECHNOLOGIE GMBH
400 Oser Ave Ste 1650 (11788-3669)
PHONE..................631 656-7137
Nikolaus F Rentschler, *CEO*
Daniela Ceixeira, *Accountant*
EMP: 5
SALES (est): 426.6K Privately Held
SIC: 2836 Biological products, except diagnostic

(G-6204)
ROBERT BUSSE & CO INC
Also Called: Busse Hospital Disposables
75 Arkay Dr (11788-3707)
PHONE..................631 435-4711
Fax: 631 435-4721
Jane Cardinale, *President*
Raymond O'Hara, *Vice Pres*
Dean Cardinale, *Plant Mgr*
Ruth Ripley, *Traffic Mgr*
Mary Sherman, *Purch Agent*
◆ **EMP:** 280 **EST:** 1964
SQ FT: 78,000
SALES (est): 61.1MM Privately Held
WEB: www.busseinc.com
SIC: 3842 Surgical appliances & supplies

(G-6205)
RODALE WIRELESS INC
Also Called: Rodale Electronics
20 Oser Ave Ste 2 (11788-3815)
PHONE..................631 231-0044
John B Clement, *President*
Terry Colford, *General Mgr*
Vince Maida, *Vice Pres*
Mary Licciardi, *Purch Dir*
Robert Ponzio, *Buyer*
EMP: 25
SQ FT: 10,000
SALES (est): 4.7MM Privately Held
SIC: 3699 3825 3812 3663 Electrical equipment & supplies; countermeasure simulators, electric; instruments to measure electricity; search & navigation equipment; radio & TV communications equipment; current-carrying wiring devices; computer peripheral equipment

(G-6206)
ROTRONIC INSTRUMENT CORP (DH)
135 Engineers Rd Ste 150 (11788-4018)
P.O. Box 11241 (11788-0703)
PHONE..................631 348-6844
David Love, *Managing Dir*
Patrick J Lafarie, *Senior VP*
David P Love, *Vice Pres*
Anthony Cordero, *Sales Mgr*
Rose Mannarino, *Sales Mgr*
▲ **EMP:** 18
SALES (est): 2.1MM Privately Held
WEB: www.rotronic-usa.com
SIC: 3823 Temperature measurement instruments, industrial; temperature instruments: industrial process type; humidity instruments, industrial process type
HQ: Rotronic Ag
 Grindelstrasse 6
 Bassersdorf ZH 8303
 448 381-111

(G-6207)
RSM ELECTRON POWER INC
Also Called: Sensitron Semiconductor
100 Engineers Rd Ste 100 (11788-4023)
PHONE..................631 586-7600
Bryan Rogers, *Vice Pres*
Susan Panagopoulos, *Opers Staff*
Steve Saunders, *Branch Mgr*
EMP: 90
SALES (corp-wide): 21.2MM Privately Held
SIC: 3674 Semiconductors & related devices
PA: Rsm Electron Power, Inc.
 221 W Industry Ct
 Deer Park NY 11729
 631 586-7600

(G-6208)
SANTA FE MANUFACTURING CORP
225 Engineers Rd (11788-4020)
PHONE..................631 234-0100
Richard Coronato Sr, *President*
Charlotte Coronato, *Vice Pres*
EMP: 5
SQ FT: 44,000
SALES (est): 605.2K Privately Held
SIC: 3728 3827 Aircraft parts & equipment; optical instruments & lenses

(G-6209)
SAPTALIS PHARMACEUTICALS LLC
45 Davids Dr (11788-2038)
PHONE..................631 231-2751
Polireddy Dondeti, *President*
Tatiana Akimova, *Exec VP*
Venkataramana Mudium, *Director*
EMP: 17
SQ FT: 10,000
SALES (est): 1MM Privately Held
SIC: 2834 Pharmaceutical preparations

(G-6210)
SCALAMANDRE WALLPAPER INC
Also Called: Scalamandre Silks
350 Wireless Blvd (11788-3947)
PHONE..................631 467-8800
▲ **EMP:** 401
SQ FT: 30,000
SALES (est): 40.2MM Privately Held
SIC: 2621 5198 2231 2221 Paper Mill Whol Paints/Varnishes Wool Brdwv Fabric Mill Manmad Brdwv Fabric Mill Cotton Brdwv Fabric Mill

(G-6211)
SCIEGEN PHARMACEUTICALS INC (PA)
330 Oser Ave (11788-3630)
PHONE..................631 434-2723
Pailla Malla Reddy, *CEO*
Siva Reddy, *Vice Pres*
Venkata Reddy, *Vice Pres*
Krishna Chilakamarphy, *Opers Mgr*
Renee Reynolds, *CFO*
▲ **EMP:** 70
SQ FT: 89,000
SALES: 15MM Privately Held
SIC: 2834 Pharmaceutical preparations

(G-6212)
SCOTTS COMPANY LLC
65 Engineers Rd (11788-4003)
PHONE..................631 478-6843
Peter Pirro, *Principal*
EMP: 8
SALES (corp-wide): 2.8B Publicly Held
SIC: 2873 Fertilizers: natural (organic), except compost
HQ: The Scotts Company Llc
 14111 Scottslawn Rd
 Marysville OH 43040
 937 644-3729

(G-6213)
SIEMENS INDUSTRY INC
Process Instrmntation Bus Unit
155 Plant Ave (11788-3801)
PHONE..................631 231-3600
Joseph Chilleme, *Engineer*
Frank Fromm, *Engineer*
Orban Fedak, *Financial Exec*
Jonas Norinder, *Sales Staff*
Allan Cottrell, *Manager*
EMP: 120
SALES (corp-wide): 89.6B Privately Held
WEB: www.sea.siemens.com
SIC: 3824 Totalizing meters, consumption registering
HQ: Siemens Industry, Inc.
 1000 Deerfield Pkwy
 Buffalo Grove IL 60089
 847 215-1000

(G-6214)
SIGN A RAMA INC
Also Called: Sign-A-Rama
663 Old Willets Path C (11788-4117)
PHONE..................631 952-3324
Fax: 631 952-3259
Jim Reardon, *Manager*
EMP: 5
SALES (corp-wide): 98.9MM Privately Held
WEB: www.franchisemart.com
SIC: 3993 Signs & advertising specialties
HQ: Sign A Rama Inc.
 2121 Vista Pkwy
 West Palm Beach FL 33411
 561 640-5570

(G-6215)
SIMA TECHNOLOGIES LLC
125 Commerce Dr (11788-3983)
PHONE..................412 828-9130
George Simolin, *CFO*
Storm Orion, *Director*
Richard Leifer,
Bob Pennington, *Products*
Robert S Leifer,
▲ **EMP:** 7
SQ FT: 27,000
SALES (est): 1MM Privately Held
WEB: www.simacorp.com
SIC: 3651 3861 5999 3577 Household audio & video equipment; photographic processing equipment & chemicals; mobile telephones & equipment; computer peripheral equipment; electrical equipment & supplies; motors & generators

(G-6216)
SIR INDUSTRIES INC
208 Blydenburg Rd Unit C (11749-5023)
PHONE..................631 234-2444
Fax: 631 234-5063
Stanley Rabinowitz, *President*
▲ **EMP:** 6
SQ FT: 7,000
SALES: 30.4K Privately Held
SIC: 3648 5063 5719 Stage lighting equipment; light bulbs & related supplies; lighting fixtures

(G-6217)
SLV LABS LLC
320 Oser Ave (11788-3608)
PHONE..................631 901-1170
Mohamed Bilal Doria, *Mng Member*
Vinod Vera Reddy, *Manager*
EMP: 5
SALES (est): 229.7K Privately Held
SIC: 2834 Ointments

(G-6218)
SPECTRON GLASS & ELECTRONICS
595 Old Willets Path A (11788-4112)
P.O. Box 13368 (11788-0744)
PHONE..................631 582-5600
Fax: 631 582-5671
Robert S Marshall, *Ch of Bd*
Pastall Lemarie, *Vice Pres*
Norman Goldsobel, *VP Mfg*
Jennifer Marshall, *Human Res Mgr*

Hauppauge - Suffolk County (G-6219)

Danny Dalfonso, *Human Resources*
▲ **EMP:** 16
SQ FT: 16,000
SALES (est): 2.9MM
SALES (corp-wide): 3.2MM **Privately Held**
WEB: www.spectronsensors.com
SIC: 3679 3674 Electronic switches; semi-conductors & related devices
PA: Spectron Systems Technology Inc
595 Old Willets Path A
Hauppauge NY 11788
631 582-5600

(G-6219)
SPECTRON SYSTEMS TECHNOLOGY (PA)
595 Old Willets Path A (11788-4113)
P.O. Box 13368 (11788-0744)
PHONE 631 582-5600
Robert Marshall, *President*
Pascal Lemarie, *Exec VP*
Nancy Chereb, *Treasurer*
Bruce Smart, *Natl Sales Mgr*
EMP: 14
SQ FT: 14,000
SALES (est): 3.2MM **Privately Held**
WEB: www.tiltsensors.com
SIC: 3679 Electronic switches

(G-6220)
SPECTRUM BRANDS INC
Also Called: United Pet Group
2100 Pacific St (11788-4737)
PHONE 631 232-1200
Mark Stern, *Branch Mgr*
EMP: 275
SALES (corp-wide): 5.2B **Publicly Held**
SIC: 3999 Pet supplies
HQ: Spectrum Brands, Inc.
3001 Deming Way
Middleton WI 53562
608 275-3340

(G-6221)
SPECTRUM THIN FILMS INC
135 Marcus Blvd (11788-3702)
PHONE 631 901-1010
Anthony Pirera, *President*
Carlos Penalbert, *Opers Staff*
Donna Mulz, *Administration*
EMP: 35
SQ FT: 3,400
SALES (est): 12.6MM **Privately Held**
WEB: www.spectrumthinfilms.com
SIC: 3827 5049 Lenses, optical: all types except ophthalmic; optical goods

(G-6222)
SPELLMAN HIGH VLTAGE ELEC CORP (PA)
475 Wireless Blvd (11788-3951)
PHONE 631 630-3000
Loren Skeist, *President*
Dennis Bay, *Managing Dir*
Mitch Alexander, *Vice Pres*
Robert Barone, *Vice Pres*
Ira Elias, *Vice Pres*
▲ **EMP:** 500
SQ FT: 100,000
SALES (est): 283.8MM **Privately Held**
SIC: 3612 Transformers, except electric

(G-6223)
STANDARD MICROSYSTEMS CORP (HQ)
Also Called: Smsc
80 Arkay Dr Ste 100 (11788-3774)
PHONE 631 435-6000
Fax: 631 435-6110
Christine King, *President*
Ian Harris, *President*
David Coller, *Senior VP*
Aaron L Fisher, *Senior VP*
Gene Sheridan, *Senior VP*
▲ **EMP:** 84
SQ FT: 200,000
SALES (est): 134.2MM
SALES (corp-wide): 3.4B **Publicly Held**
SIC: 3674 Integrated circuits, semiconductor networks, etc.
PA: Microchip Technology Inc
2355 W Chandler Blvd
Chandler AZ 85224
480 792-7200

(G-6224)
STAR QUALITY PRINTING INC
Also Called: Star Communications
270 Oser Ave (11788-3610)
PHONE 631 273-1900
Alka Parikh, *Ch of Bd*
Kalpesh Parikh, *President*
James Gibb, *Vice Pres*
Adhish Parikh, *Vice Pres*
Fernando Basurto, *Production*
▲ **EMP:** 12
SQ FT: 7,500
SALES (est): 2.8MM **Privately Held**
WEB: www.sqprinting.com
SIC: 2752 Commercial printing, offset

(G-6225)
STERLING NORTH AMERICA INC
270 Oser Ave (11788-3610)
PHONE 631 243-6933
Ed McAllister, *Ch of Bd*
EMP: 28
SQ FT: 40,000
SALES (est): 7.2MM **Privately Held**
SIC: 2752 Commercial printing, lithographic

(G-6226)
SUMMIT APPAREL INC (PA)
91 Cabot Ct (11788-3717)
PHONE 631 213-8299
Morad Mayeri, *Ch of Bd*
Abraham Mayeri, *Vice Pres*
▲ **EMP:** 48
SQ FT: 25,000
SALES (est): 10.6MM **Privately Held**
WEB: www.summitapparel.com
SIC: 2253 Dresses, knit

(G-6227)
SUPERIOR WASHER & GASKET CORP (PA)
170 Adams Ave (11788-3612)
P.O. Box 5407 (11788-0407)
PHONE 631 273-8282
Fax: 631 273-8088
Allan Lippolis, *Principal*
Robert Lippolis, *Purchasing*
Jason Garrick, *QC Mgr*
Marie Panfilio, *VP Sales*
Luann Racca, *Sales Mgr*
EMP: 65
SQ FT: 42,000
SALES (est): 16.5MM **Privately Held**
WEB: www.superiorwasher.com
SIC: 3452 Washers, metal; washers

(G-6228)
SUPERITE GEAR INSTR OF HPPAUGE (PA)
225 Engineers Rd (11788-4020)
PHONE 631 234-0100
Richard Coronato Sr, *President*
Barbara Knox, *Human Res Mgr*
Charlotte Coronato, *Admin Sec*
EMP: 8 EST: 1955
SQ FT: 44,000
SALES (est): 2.4MM **Privately Held**
SIC: 3462 Gears, forged steel

(G-6229)
SYMWAVE INC (DH)
80 Arkay Dr (11788-3705)
PHONE 949 542-4400
Yossi Cohen, *President*
Jun Ye, *Vice Pres*
Adam Spice, *CFO*
Wanda Knight, *Manager*
Christopher Thomas, *CTO*
EMP: 6
SALES (est): 733K
SALES (corp-wide): 3.4B **Publicly Held**
WEB: www.symwave.com
SIC: 3674 Semiconductors & related devices
HQ: Standard Microsystems Corporation
80 Arkay Dr Ste 100
Hauppauge NY 11788
631 435-6000

(G-6230)
TARSIA TECHNICAL INDUSTRIES
Also Called: TTI
93 Marcus Blvd (11788-3712)
PHONE 631 231-8322
Joe Tarsia, *President*
EMP: 7
SALES (est): 664.2K **Privately Held**
WEB: www.ttiind.com
SIC: 3599 Machine shop, jobbing & repair

(G-6231)
TDK-LAMBDA AMERICAS INC
145 Marcus Blvd Ste 3 (11788-3760)
PHONE 631 967-3000
Fax: 631 967-3022
Hiroshi Osawa, *President*
Greg Laufman, *Design Engr*
EMP: 15
SALES (corp-wide): 10.3B **Privately Held**
WEB: www.lambdapower.com
SIC: 3677 Transformers power supply, electronic type
HQ: Tdk-Lambda Americas Inc.
405 Essex Rd
Tinton Falls NJ 07753
732 922-9300

(G-6232)
TDL MANUFACTURING INC
Also Called: Tulip Development Labs
80 Cabot Ct (11788-3729)
PHONE 215 538-8820
Dennis Sunshine, *Chairman*
Bruce Reissman, *Exec VP*
Mitch Binder, *CFO*
Edward Rusin, *Accounts Mgr*
EMP: 19
SQ FT: 9,000
SALES (est): 1.8MM
SALES (corp-wide): 19.1MM **Publicly Held**
WEB: www.orbitintl.com
SIC: 3728 Aircraft parts & equipment
PA: Orbit International Corp.
80 Cabot Ct
Hauppauge NY 11788
631 435-8300

(G-6233)
TECHNAPULSE LLC
400 Oser Ave Ste 1950 (11788-3639)
PHONE 631 234-8700
Bernard Rachowitz, *President*
Joseph Schneider, *Plant Mgr*
▲ **EMP:** 17 EST: 1999
SALES (est): 376.5K **Privately Held**
SIC: 7692 Welding repair

(G-6234)
TECHNIMETAL PRECISION INDS
195 Marcus Blvd (11788-3796)
PHONE 631 231-8900
Fax: 631 231-8928
Donald T Molloy, *President*
Stephen J Miller, *Exec VP*
EMP: 50 EST: 1967
SQ FT: 27,000
SALES (est): 9MM **Privately Held**
WEB: www.tpimetals.com
SIC: 3444 Sheet metalwork

(G-6235)
TEK WELD
45 Rabro Dr Unit 1 (11788-4260)
PHONE 631 694-5503
Maryanne Coopersmith, *Principal*
Randy Seltzer, *VP Sls/Mktg*
Stacy Reiter, *Accounting Mgr*
Patrick Hale, *Credit Mgr*
Val Johnson, *Sales Staff*
▲ **EMP:** 16
SALES (est): 1.7MM **Privately Held**
SIC: 7692 Welding repair

(G-6236)
TELEBYTE INC (PA)
355 Marcus Blvd Ste 2 (11788-2027)
PHONE 631 423-3232
Dr Kenneth S Schneider, *CEO*
Michael Breneisen, *President*
Kenneth Schneicer, *Vice Pres*
Victoria Twomey, *Sales Dir*
Abraham Weber, *Manager*
EMP: 25
SQ FT: 3,500
SALES (est): 4MM **Privately Held**
WEB: www.telebyteusa.com
SIC: 3669 Intercommunication systems, electric

(G-6237)
TELESITE USA INC
89 Arkay Dr (11788-3727)
PHONE 631 952-2288
Larry Greenwald, *President*
EMP: 11
SQ FT: 7,000
SALES (est): 779.3K
SALES (corp-wide): 35.7MM **Publicly Held**
WEB: www.viconindustries.com
SIC: 3669 Intercommunication systems, electric
PA: Vicon Industries, Inc.
135 Fell Ct
Hauppauge NY 11788
631 952-2288

(G-6238)
THREAD CHECK INC
390 Oser Ave Ste 2 (11788-3682)
PHONE 631 231-1515
Hyman Jack Kipnes, *President*
Irving Kipnes, *Vice Pres*
Mark Koszyk, *Sales Dir*
EMP: 99
SQ FT: 74,000
SALES (est): 11.5MM **Privately Held**
WEB: www.threadcheck.com
SIC: 3552 5084 3823 Thread making machines, spinning machinery; industrial machinery & equipment; industrial instrmnts msrmnt display/control process variable

(G-6239)
TIFFEN COMPANY LLC
Also Called: Tiffen Co, The
80 Oser Ave (11788-3809)
PHONE 631 273-2500
EMP: 9
SALES (corp-wide): 24.1MM **Privately Held**
SIC: 3861 Photographic equipment & supplies
PA: The Tiffen Company Llc
90 Oser Ave
Hauppauge NY 11788
631 273-2500

(G-6240)
TIFFEN COMPANY LLC (PA)
90 Oser Ave (11788-3809)
PHONE 631 273-2500
Michael Cannata, *COO*
Bill Funicello, *Opers Staff*
Eric Jackson, *Engineer*
Stacy Gonzalez, *Controller*
Edward Ranieri, *Credit Mgr*
▲ **EMP:** 60
SALES (est): 24.1MM **Privately Held**
WEB: www.tiffen.com
SIC: 3861 Photographic equipment & supplies

(G-6241)
TRUE ERP NEW YORK
2150 Joshuas Path Ste 11f (11788-4767)
PHONE 631 582-7210
EMP: 30
SALES (est): 767.2K **Privately Held**
SIC: 7372 Application computer software

(G-6242)
TUNAVERSE MEDIA INC
750 Veterans Hwy Ste 200 (11788-2943)
PHONE 631 778-8350
Ross Pirtle, *President*
Hal Denton, *Vice Pres*
Tom Diemidil, *Vice Pres*
Barbara Pirtle, *Bookkeeper*
EMP: 8
SALES: 500K **Privately Held**
SIC: 7372 Prepackaged software

(G-6243)
TWINCO MFG CO INC
30 Commerce Dr (11788-3904)
PHONE 631 231-0022
Fax: 631 231-0314
John A Schatz, *President*

GEOGRAPHIC SECTION

Ellen Wilcken, *Vice Pres*
Walter Weiss, *Chief Engr*
Veronica Broome, *Manager*
▲ **EMP:** 44 **EST:** 1965
SQ FT: 50,000
SALES: 9.3MM **Privately Held**
WEB: www.twincomfg.com
SIC: 3669 3469 3599 3743 Railroad signaling devices, electric; machine parts, stamped or pressed metal; machine & other job shop work; railroad equipment

(G-6244)
UNITED-GUARDIAN INC (PA)
230 Marcus Blvd (11788-3731)
P.O. Box 18050 (11788-8850)
PHONE 631 273-0900
Kenneth H Globus, *Ch of Bd*
Peter A Hiltunen, *Vice Pres*
Joseph J Vernice, *Vice Pres*
Robert S Rubinger, *CFO*
EMP: 34
SQ FT: 50,000
SALES: 10.7MM **Publicly Held**
WEB: www.u-g.com
SIC: 2844 2834 Toilet preparations; cosmetic preparations; pharmaceutical preparations

(G-6245)
UNIVERSAL PACKG SYSTEMS INC (PA)
Also Called: Paklab
380 Townline Rd Ste 130 (11788-2800)
PHONE 631 543-2277
Andrew Young III, *Ch of Bd*
Alan Kristel, *COO*
Peter Belinsky, *Exec VP*
Nancy Weinmaster, *Vice Pres*
Rita Arellano, *Project Mgr*
▲ **EMP:** 750
SQ FT: 115,000
SALES (est): 423.8MM **Privately Held**
SIC: 2844 7389 3565 2671 Cosmetic preparations; packaging & labeling services; bottling machinery: filling, capping, labeling; plastic film, coated or laminated for packaging

(G-6246)
UNLIMITED INK INC
595 Old Willets Path B (11788-4114)
PHONE 631 582-0696
Josh Disamone, *President*
EMP: 20
SALES (est): 934.8K **Privately Held**
SIC: 2759 5699 Screen printing; sports apparel

(G-6247)
VEHICLE MANUFACTURERS INC
Also Called: Skyguard
400 Oser Ave Ste 100 (11788-3600)
PHONE 631 851-1700
George J Wafer, *CEO*
Scott Wafer, *President*
Thomas Tomlinson, *Business Mgr*
Angelo Addesso, *COO*
Brent Depeppe, *Vice Pres*
EMP: 22
SQ FT: 3,000
SALES: 10MM **Privately Held**
SIC: 3069 Rubber automotive products

(G-6248)
VENUS PHARMACEUTICALS INTL INC
55a Kennedy Dr (11788-4038)
PHONE 631 249-4140
Bharat Kakumanu, *CEO*
Survir Singh Salaria, *President*
▼ **EMP:** 15
SQ FT: 25,000
SALES (est): 3.5MM **Privately Held**
WEB: www.venuspharmaceuticals.com
SIC: 2834 Pharmaceutical preparations

(G-6249)
VETRA SYSTEMS CORPORATION
275 Marcus Blvd Unit J (11788-2022)
PHONE 631 434-3185
Fax: 631 434-3516
Jonas Ulenas, *President*

Paul Sabatino, *Vice Pres*
George Zahn, *QC Dir*
Paul Wieties, *CIO*
Valdas Douba, *Shareholder*
EMP: 8
SALES (est): 1.1MM **Privately Held**
WEB: www.vetra.com
SIC: 3823 5084 Computer interface equipment for industrial process control; controllers for process variables, all types; conveyor systems

(G-6250)
VICON INDUSTRIES INC (PA)
135 Fell Ct (11788-4351)
PHONE 631 952-2288
Fax: 631 951-2288
Eric S Fullerton, *CEO*
Julian A Tiedemann, *Ch of Bd*
Bret M McGowan, *Senior VP*
Peter A Horn, *Vice Pres*
Rochak Sharma, *Engineer*
▲ **EMP:** 148
SQ FT: 30,000
SALES: 35.7MM **Publicly Held**
WEB: www.viconindustries.com
SIC: 3663 3669 Television closed circuit equipment; visual communication systems; transportation signaling devices

(G-6251)
VIRTUE PAINTBALL LLC (PA)
40 Oser Ave Ste 14 (11788-3807)
PHONE 631 617-5560
Tom Conde, *Opers Mgr*
Michael Newman,
▲ **EMP:** 8
SQ FT: 4,000
SALES (est): 740.3K **Privately Held**
SIC: 3675 3676 3678 Electronic capacitors; electronic resistors; electronic connectors

(G-6252)
VISIONTRON CORP
720 Old Willets Path (11788-4102)
PHONE 631 582-8600
Lisa Torsiello, *President*
Donna Goroshko, *General Mgr*
Kevin McDonald, *Business Mgr*
Joseph Torsiello, *Vice Pres*
Laurence Torsiello, *Vice Pres*
◆ **EMP:** 25
SQ FT: 20,000
SALES (est): 6.1MM **Privately Held**
WEB: www.visiontron.com
SIC: 3669 Intercommunication systems, electric

(G-6253)
VITAMIN POWER INCORORATED
75 Commerce Dr (11788-3902)
PHONE 631 676-5790
David Friedlander, *President*
Edward Friedlander, *Chairman*
Robert Edwards, *Marketing Staff*
EMP: 7
SQ FT: 20,000
SALES: 1.2MM **Privately Held**
WEB: www.vitaminpower.com
SIC: 2023 Dietary supplements, dairy & non-dairy based

(G-6254)
W & H STAMPINGS INC
45 Engineers Rd (11788-4019)
PHONE 631 234-6161
Fax: 631 582-1540
Ernest E Hoffmann, *President*
Ron Marcisak, *General Mgr*
Al Toepfer, *Purchasing*
Maria Alfieri, *Bookkeeper*
Nerissa Hoffman, *Financial Exec*
EMP: 28 **EST:** 1956
SQ FT: 33,000
SALES: 1MM **Privately Held**
WEB: www.whstamp.com
SIC: 3469 Metal stampings

(G-6255)
WATSON PRODUCTIONS LLC
Also Called: Skyline New York
740 Old Willets Path # 400 (11788-4121)
PHONE 516 334-9766
Larry Centola, *General Mgr*
Judy Fairbanks, *Vice Pres*

Liz Kasavana, *Manager*
Robert Watson,
Robert T Watson,
▼ **EMP:** 12
SALES (est): 1.6MM **Privately Held**
WEB: www.watsonproductions.com
SIC: 3577 Graphic displays, except graphic terminals

(G-6256)
WELDING METALLURGY INC (HQ)
110 Plant Ave Ste 1 (11788-3830)
PHONE 631 253-0500
Fax: 631 231-4970
Gary Settoducato, *Ch of Bd*
John Canova, *General Mgr*
Kristie Petersen, *Vice Pres*
Steve Chouinard, *Engineer*
Scott Glassman, *CFO*
EMP: 48
SQ FT: 35,000
SALES (est): 9.1MM
SALES (corp-wide): 66.9MM **Publicly Held**
WEB: www.weldingmet.com
SIC: 3441 Fabricated structural metal
PA: Air Industries Group
3609 Motor Pkwy Ste 100
Hauppauge NY 11788
631 881-4920

(G-6257)
WIDEX USA INC (DH)
Also Called: Widex International
185 Commerce Dr (11788-3916)
P.O. Box 6077, Long Island City (11106-0077)
PHONE 718 360-1000
Jake Haycock, *President*
Peter Schaade, *Managing Dir*
Sren Westermann, *Exec VP*
Brian Weiss, *Manager*
▲ **EMP:** 87
SALES (est): 22.9MM
SALES (corp-wide): 631.8MM **Privately Held**
SIC: 3842 Hearing aids
HQ: Widex A/S
Nymollevej 6
Lynge 3540
443 556-00

(G-6258)
WILBAR INTERNATIONAL INC
50 Cabot Ct (11788-3716)
PHONE 631 951-9800
Steven Cohen, *President*
Richard Sobel, *Vice Pres*
Peter Rizzo, *Plant Mgr*
Bill Bezanson, *Controller*
Brian Kelley, *CIO*
▲ **EMP:** 100
SQ FT: 20,000
SALES (est): 25.1MM **Privately Held**
SIC: 3949 Swimming pools, plastic; swimming pools, except plastic

(G-6259)
WOODBINE PRODUCTS INC
110 Plant Ave (11788-3830)
PHONE 631 586-3770
Fax: 631 586-3777
Vincent J Conforti, *President*
Johanna Conforti, *Admin Sec*
EMP: 20
SQ FT: 20,000
SALES (est): 2.4MM
SALES (corp-wide): 66.9MM **Publicly Held**
WEB: www.woodbineproducts.com
SIC: 3812 Acceleration indicators & systems components, aerospace
HQ: Welding Metallurgy, Inc.
110 Plant Ave Ste 1
Hauppauge NY 11788
631 253-0500

(G-6260)
WORLD TRADING CENTER INC
115 Engineers Rd Fl 2 (11788-4005)
PHONE 631 273-3330
Arthur W Danziger Jr, *President*
Dave Love, *Project Mgr*
Robert Treyfuss, *Controller*
Anita Inklis, *Technology*

Jane Avaril, *IT/INT Sup*
◆ **EMP:** 8
SQ FT: 4,000
SALES (est): 1.6MM **Privately Held**
WEB: www.wtcco.com
SIC: 2511 3699 3634 Wood household furniture; household electrical equipment; housewares, excluding cooking appliances & utensils

---

Haverstraw
Rockland County

(G-6261)
JAGUAR INDUSTRIES INC
89 Broadway (10927-1144)
P.O. Box 385 (10927-0385)
PHONE 845 947-1800
Marvin Kigler, *President*
EMP: 15
SQ FT: 15,000
SALES (est): 2.7MM **Privately Held**
SIC: 3679 5065 3643 3357 Electronic circuits; electronic parts & equipment; current-carrying wiring devices; nonferrous wiredrawing & insulating; laminated plastics plate & sheet

(G-6262)
LEXSTAR INC (PA)
Also Called: Lites On West Soho
25 Lincoln St (10927-1106)
PHONE 845 947-1415
Fax: 845 818-9627
Uri Redlich, *President*
Kyle Anderson, *General Mgr*
David Regezv, *Vice Pres*
▲ **EMP:** 30
SQ FT: 15,000
SALES (est): 3.1MM **Privately Held**
WEB: www.lexstar.com
SIC: 3645 Residential lighting fixtures

(G-6263)
ROCKLAND INSULATED WIRE CABLE
87 Broadway (10927-1144)
P.O. Box 111 (10927-0111)
PHONE 845 429-3103
Fax: 845 947-1712
Lawrence Kigler, *President*
EMP: 7 **EST:** 1956
SQ FT: 10,000
SALES (est): 1.2MM **Privately Held**
SIC: 3357 Nonferrous wiredrawing & insulating

(G-6264)
ROSS ELECTRONICS LTD
12 Maple Ave (10927-1824)
PHONE 718 569-6643
Reuven Lakein, *President*
▲ **EMP:** 20 **EST:** 2010
SALES: 12MM **Privately Held**
SIC: 3699 5999 Electrical equipment & supplies; electronic parts & equipment

---

Hawthorne
Westchester County

(G-6265)
ADL DATA SYSTEMS INC
9 Skyline Dr Ste 4 (10532-2146)
PHONE 914 591-1800
Fax: 914 591-1818
David Pollack, *President*
Aaron Weg, *Vice Pres*
Terry Hamilton, *Sales Staff*
Fila Kolodny, *Prgrmr*
Leslie Siegel, *Exec Dir*
EMP: 40
SQ FT: 13,000
SALES (est): 4.7MM **Privately Held**
WEB: www.adldata.com
SIC: 7372 Prepackaged software

Hawthorne - Westchester County

(G-6266)
ASTRA TOOL & INSTR MFG CORP
369 Bradhurst Ave (10532-1141)
PHONE..................914 747-3863
Fax: 914 747-3925
Greg Unmann, *President*
Greg Unman, *President*
Anthony Posco, *Controller*
EMP: 22 EST: 1950
SQ FT: 10,000
SALES: 2.9MM **Privately Held**
WEB: www.astratool.net
SIC: 3841 3599 Surgical & medical instruments; machine shop, jobbing & repair

(G-6267)
BIOMED PHARMACEUTICALS INC
Also Called: Soleo Health
4 Skyline Dr Ste 5 (10532-2192)
PHONE..................914 592-0525
Drew Walk, *CEO*
John Ginzler, *CFO*
EMP: 8
SALES (est): 1.1MM
SALES (corp-wide): 28.1MM **Privately Held**
SIC: 2834 5912 Druggists' preparations (pharmaceuticals); drug stores & proprietary stores
PA: Soleo Health Holdings, Inc.
950 Calcon Hook Rd Ste 15
Sharon Hill PA 19079
888 244-2340

(G-6268)
COCA-COLA REFRESHMENTS USA INC
3 Skyline Dr (10532-2174)
PHONE..................914 592-0806
Fax: 914 789-1153
William Highberger, *Project Mgr*
John Krause, *Project Mgr*
Jeff Lumberg, *Human Res Mgr*
Brian Winn, *Branch Mgr*
EMP: 8
SALES (corp-wide): 41.8B **Publicly Held**
SIC: 2086 Bottled & canned soft drinks
HQ: Coca-Cola Refreshments Usa, Inc.
2500 Windy Ridge Pkwy Se
Atlanta GA 30339
770 989-3000

(G-6269)
FOUR BROTHERS ITALIAN BAKERY
Also Called: Sinapi's Italian Ice
332 Elwood Ave (10532-1217)
PHONE..................914 741-5434
Pat Sinapi, *President*
Angelo Sinapi, *Vice Pres*
Anthony Sinapi, *Treasurer*
Luigi Sinapi, *Admin Sec*
EMP: 5
SALES (est): 469.6K **Privately Held**
SIC: 2024 5143 Ices, flavored (frozen dessert); ice cream & ices

(G-6270)
GAS TURBINE CONTROLS CORP
6 Skyline Dr Ste 150 (10532-8102)
P.O. Box 104, Ardsley (10502-0104)
PHONE..................914 693-0830
Peter Zinman, *Ch of Bd*
Robyn Howal, *Manager*
▲ EMP: 25
SALES (est): 2.5MM **Privately Held**
SIC: 3511 Turbines & turbine generator sets

(G-6271)
JOHNSON CONTROLS INC
8 Skyline Dr Ste 115 (10532-2151)
PHONE..................914 593-5200
Rick Salon, *Manager*
EMP: 20 **Privately Held**
SIC: 3822 Energy cutoff controls, residential or commercial types
HQ: Johnson Controls, Inc.
5757 N Green Bay Ave
Milwaukee WI 53209
414 524-1200

(G-6272)
KRYTEN IRON WORKS INC
3 Browns Ln Ste 201 (10532-1546)
PHONE..................914 345-0990
Peter Lavelli, *President*
Joseph Lavelli, *Sls & Mktg Exec*
Stephen Winiarski, *Accountant*
EMP: 8
SALES (est): 1.4MM **Privately Held**
SIC: 3441 3446 Fabricated structural metal; ornamental metalwork

(G-6273)
LITHO DYNAMICS INC
17 Saw Mill River Rd (10532-1503)
PHONE..................914 769-1759
Fax: 914 347-4920
Kenneth Giustino, *President*
Ed Martin, *Vice Pres*
Joseph Giustino, *Shareholder*
EMP: 6
SQ FT: 10,000
SALES: 400K **Privately Held**
SIC: 2752 Commercial printing, offset

(G-6274)
LUDL ELECTRONIC PRODUCTS LTD
Also Called: Lep
171 Brady Ave (10532-2216)
PHONE..................914 769-6111
Fax: 914 769-4759
Helmut Ludl, *Ch of Bd*
Dirk Ludl, *President*
Mark Ludl, *President*
Petra H Ludl, *Corp Secy*
Nicholas Kucharik, *Mfg Staff*
▼ EMP: 25
SQ FT: 23,000
SALES: 2K **Privately Held**
WEB: www.ludl.com
SIC: 3825 Instruments to measure electricity

(G-6275)
MWSI INC (PA)
12 Skyline Dr Ste 230 (10532-2138)
PHONE..................914 347-4200
Mark Wasserman, *President*
David Saily, *Vice Pres*
EMP: 70
SQ FT: 12,160
SALES (est): 3.9MM **Privately Held**
SIC: 3961 5094 3911 Costume jewelry, ex. precious metal & semiprecious stones; jewelry; jewelry, precious metal

(G-6276)
PEPSICO
3 Skyline Dr (10532-2174)
PHONE..................419 252-0247
EMP: 17
SALES (est): 2.8MM **Privately Held**
SIC: 2086 Carbonated soft drinks, bottled & canned

(G-6277)
PRINCETEL INC
Also Called: Wendon Engineering
200 Saw Mill River Rd (10532-1523)
PHONE..................914 579-2410
Boying Zhang, *Branch Mgr*
EMP: 14
SALES (corp-wide): 6MM **Privately Held**
SIC: 3678 3621 Electronic connectors; sliprings, for motors or generators
PA: Princetel Inc.
2560 E State Street Ext
Hamilton NJ 08619
609 588-8801

(G-6278)
RAW INDULGENCE LTD
Also Called: Raw Revolution
200 Saw Mill River Rd (10532-1523)
P.O. Box 359 (10532-0359)
PHONE..................866 498-4671
David Friedman, *CEO*
Alice Benedetto, *President*
Belgica Tuba, *Admin Sec*
▲ EMP: 14
SQ FT: 3,000
SALES (est): 3MM **Privately Held**
SIC: 2099 Food preparations

(G-6279)
SCHMERSAL INC
15 Skyline Dr Ste 230 (10532-2152)
PHONE..................914 347-4775
Philip Schmersal, *General Mgr*
Gary Ferguson, *Managing Dir*
Joe Bussie, *Regional Mgr*
Holger Fehn, *Regional Mgr*
David Upton, *Business Mgr*
◆ EMP: 26
SQ FT: 10,000
SALES (est): 5.2MM
SALES (corp-wide): 228.3MM **Privately Held**
WEB: www.schmersal.com
SIC: 3625 Motor control accessories, including overload relays
HQ: K. A. Schmersal Gmbh & Co. Kg
Moddinghofe 30
Wuppertal 42279
202 647-40

(G-6280)
U X WORLD INC
245 Saw Mill River Rd # 106 (10532-1547)
PHONE..................914 375-6167
Vinod Pulkayath, *President*
EMP: 5
SQ FT: 300
SALES: 140K **Privately Held**
SIC: 7372 Prepackaged software

(G-6281)
WILLEMIN MACODEL INCORPORATED
10 Skyline Dr Ste 132 (10532-2160)
PHONE..................914 345-3504
Melissa Dorsey, *Principal*
▲ EMP: 16 EST: 2011
SALES (est): 2.3MM **Privately Held**
SIC: 3545 Machine tool attachments & accessories

Hector
Schuyler County

(G-6282)
HAZLITTS 1852 VINEYARDS INC
Also Called: Hazlitt 1852 Vineyards
5712 State Route 414 (14841-9714)
P.O. Box 53 (14841-0053)
PHONE..................607 546-9463
Fax: 607 546-5712
Doug Hazlitt, *CEO*
Elaine Hazlitt, *President*
Jerome Hazlitt, *President*
Fred Wickham, *Vice Pres*
Leigh Triner, *Treasurer*
EMP: 48
SQ FT: 4,500
SALES (est): 7.9MM **Privately Held**
WEB: www.hazlitt1852.com
SIC: 2084 0172 Wines, brandy & brandy spirits; grapes

(G-6283)
LAFAYETTE CHATEAU
Also Called: Chateau La Fayette Reneau
Rr 414 (14841)
PHONE..................607 546-2062
Fax: 607 546-2069
Richard Reno, *Owner*
Heather Lodge, *General Mgr*
EMP: 25
SQ FT: 5,000
SALES (est): 2MM **Privately Held**
WEB: www.clrwine.com
SIC: 2084 Wines

(G-6284)
RED NEWT CELLARS INC
3675 Tichenor Rd (14841-9675)
PHONE..................607 546-4100
Fax: 607 546-4101
David Whiting, *President*
Gregory Tumbarello, *General Mgr*
Terri Myers, *Business Mgr*
Katie Goodwin, *Manager*
Meagan Goodwin, *Manager*
EMP: 10
SQ FT: 13,000
SALES (est): 2.8MM **Privately Held**
WEB: www.rednewt.com
SIC: 2084 Wines

(G-6285)
STANDING STONE VINEYARDS
9934 State Route 414 (14841-9727)
PHONE..................607 582-6051
Martha Macinski, *Owner*
Tom Macinski, *Co-Owner*
EMP: 6
SALES (est): 416.1K **Privately Held**
WEB: www.standingstonewines.com
SIC: 2084 5921 Wines; wine

(G-6286)
TICKLE HILL WINERY
3831 Ball Diamond Rd (14841-9629)
PHONE..................607 546-7740
Valerie Rosbaugh, *Owner*
EMP: 5
SALES (est): 283.8K **Privately Held**
SIC: 2084 Wine cellars, bonded: engaged in blending wines

Hemlock
Livingston County

(G-6287)
ITT CORPORATION
4847 Main St (14466-9714)
PHONE..................585 269-7109
Rosario Pitta, *Branch Mgr*
EMP: 46
SALES (corp-wide): 2.4B **Publicly Held**
WEB: www.ittind.com
SIC: 3625 Control equipment, electric
HQ: Itt Llc
1133 Westchester Ave N-100
White Plains NY 10604
914 641-2000

Hempstead
Nassau County

(G-6288)
ANHUI SKYWORTH LLC
44 Kensington Ct (11550-2126)
PHONE..................917 940-6903
Fuzhen Ang, *Mng Member*
Fuzhen Wang, *Mng Member*
▲ EMP: 65
SALES (est): 1.8MM **Privately Held**
SIC: 2392 5023 Cushions & pillows; pillowcases

(G-6289)
ARNELL INC
73 High St (11550-3817)
PHONE..................516 486-7098
Fax: 516 292-0697
Doug Riebl, *President*
Ron Riebl, *Vice Pres*
EMP: 6 EST: 1956
SQ FT: 4,300
SALES (est): 910.3K **Privately Held**
SIC: 3469 3544 Metal stampings; special dies, tools, jigs & fixtures

(G-6290)
BP BEYOND PRINTING INC
117 Fulton Ave (11550-3706)
PHONE..................516 328-2700
Christine Persaud, *Ch of Bd*
Bryan Prasad, *Asst Mgr*
EMP: 6
SALES (est): 790.3K **Privately Held**
SIC: 2752 2759 Commercial printing, lithographic; commercial printing

(G-6291)
CENTURY-TECH INC
32 Intersection St (11550-1306)
PHONE..................718 326-9400
Peter Terranova, *Branch Mgr*
EMP: 13 **Privately Held**
SIC: 3561 Industrial pumps & parts
PA: Century-Tech Inc.
5825 63rd St
Hempstead NY 11550

▲ = Import ▼ = Export ◆ = Import/Export

GEOGRAPHIC SECTION

(G-6292)
CENTURY-TECH INC (PA)
5825 63rd St (11550)
PHONE..................516 493-9800
Peter Terranova, *President*
Jack Terranova, *Corp Secy*
Ronald Wiggberg, *Corp Secy*
Louis Mastrangelo, *Vice Pres*
◆ **EMP:** 5
SQ FT: 4,500
SALES: 5MM **Privately Held**
WEB: www.century-techinc.com
SIC: 3559 Plastics working machinery

(G-6293)
GAMMA INSTRUMENT CO INC
52 Chasner St (11550-4820)
PHONE..................516 486-5526
Fax: 516 486-4905
John Schurr, *President*
William Hansen, *Vice Pres*
EMP: 7 **EST:** 1976
SQ FT: 4,400
SALES: 500K **Privately Held**
SIC: 3599 Machine shop, jobbing & repair

(G-6294)
GENERAL REFINING & SMELTING
Also Called: Grc
106 Taft Ave (11550-4887)
PHONE..................516 538-4747
Fax: 516 538-4767
Richard Spera, *President*
Andrea Poveromo, *Bookkeeper*
Carol Spera, *Office Mgr*
EMP: 7
SQ FT: 10,000
SALES (est): 984.6K **Privately Held**
SIC: 3339 3341 Gold refining (primary); silver refining (primary); platinum group metal refining (primary); secondary non-ferrous metals

(G-6295)
GENERAL REFINING CORPORATION
59 Madison Ave (11550-4813)
PHONE..................516 538-4747
Peter Spera, *Principal*
EMP: 8
SALES (est): 850K **Privately Held**
SIC: 3339 Gold refining (primary)

(G-6296)
GOLD PURE FOOD PRODUCTS CO INC
1 Brooklyn Rd (11550-6619)
PHONE..................516 483-5600
Fax: 516 483-5798
Steven Gold, *Ch of Bd*
Howard Gold, *Vice Pres*
Marc Gold, *Vice Pres*
Neil Gold, *CFO*
Paul Altamore, *Natl Sales Mgr*
▲ **EMP:** 75 **EST:** 1932
SQ FT: 75,000
SALES (est): 15.2MM **Privately Held**
WEB: www.goldshorseradish.com
SIC: 2035 2099 Seasonings & sauces, except tomato & dry; horseradish, prepared; Worcestershire sauce; mustard, prepared (wet); food preparations

(G-6297)
HEMPSTEAD SENTINEL INC
Also Called: Sentinel Printing
55 Chasner St (11550-4807)
P.O. Box 305 (11551-0305)
PHONE..................516 486-5000
Fax: 516 486-1966
Glenn Boehmer, *President*
Joan Boehmer, *Admin Sec*
EMP: 13
SQ FT: 7,000
SALES (est): 2.8MM **Privately Held**
SIC: 2752 Commercial printing, lithographic

(G-6298)
ICELL INC
133 Fulton Ave (11550-3710)
PHONE..................516 590-0007
Arpreet Sanhi, *President*
EMP: 127
SQ FT: 4,000
SALES: 10MM **Privately Held**
SIC: 3663 Mobile communication equipment

(G-6299)
JEM SIGN CORP (PA)
Also Called: Tee Pee Signs
470 S Franklin St (11550-7419)
PHONE..................516 867-4466
Jeraldine Eid, *President*
Teddy Eid, *Vice Pres*
EMP: 5
SQ FT: 3,700
SALES (est): 560.1K **Privately Held**
WEB: www.teepeesigns.com
SIC: 3993 7532 5999 1799 Signs & advertising specialties; truck painting & lettering; trophies & plaques; sign installation & maintenance

(G-6300)
JONICE INDUSTIRES
95 Angevine Ave (11550-5618)
PHONE..................516 640-4283
EMP: 5
SALES (est): 232.3K **Privately Held**
SIC: 2299 Broadwoven fabrics: linen, jute, hemp & ramie

(G-6301)
KING CRACKER CORP
Also Called: Cristina
307 Peninsula Blvd (11550-4912)
PHONE..................516 539-9251
Leonard Morales, *President*
EMP: 15
SALES (est): 450K **Privately Held**
SIC: 2051 5149 Bread, cake & related products; bakery products

(G-6302)
MAGER & GOUGELMAN INC
230 Hilton Ave Ste 112 (11550-8116)
PHONE..................212 661-3939
Henry P Gougleman, *President*
EMP: 8
SALES (corp-wide): 855.4K **Privately Held**
WEB: www.artificial-eyes.com
SIC: 3851 Eyes, glass & plastic
PA: Mager & Gougelman Inc
345 E 37th St Rm 316
New York NY 10016
212 661-3939

(G-6303)
MAGER & GOUGELMAN INC
230 Hilton Ave Ste 112 (11550-8116)
PHONE..................516 489-0202
Denise Gougelmann, *Manager*
EMP: 9
SALES (corp-wide): 855.4K **Privately Held**
WEB: www.artificial-eyes.com
SIC: 3851 Eyes, glass & plastic
PA: Mager & Gougelman Inc
345 E 37th St Rm 316
New York NY 10016
212 661-3939

(G-6304)
MILLENNIUM SIGNS & DISPLAY INC
90 W Graham Ave (11550-6102)
PHONE..................516 292-8000
Sajjad Khalfan, *President*
Richard Seider, *Sales Staff*
▲ **EMP:** 25
SQ FT: 35,000
SALES (est): 4MM **Privately Held**
WEB: www.msdny.com
SIC: 3993 Signs & advertising specialties

(G-6305)
NASSAU AUTO REMANUFACTURER
Also Called: Nassau Auto Remanufacturers
25 Chasner St (11550-4807)
PHONE..................516 485-4500
Fax: 516 485-1124
Dorothy Pontrelli, *President*
EMP: 8
SQ FT: 9,000
SALES: 500K **Privately Held**
SIC: 3714 Motor vehicle electrical equipment

(G-6306)
NASSAU COUNTY PUBLICATIONS
Also Called: Beacon Newspapers
5 Centre St (11550-2422)
PHONE..................516 481-5400
Peter Hoegl, *President*
EMP: 5
SALES (est): 367.9K **Privately Held**
SIC: 2711 Newspapers

(G-6307)
PLANT-TECH2O INC
30 Chasner St (11550-4808)
P.O. Box 520 (11551-0520)
PHONE..................516 483-7845
William Lyon, *President*
EMP: 5
SQ FT: 5,000
SALES: 500K **Privately Held**
SIC: 3523 7359 7389 1791 Farm machinery & equipment; live plant rental; plant care service; exterior wall system installation

(G-6308)
ROYAL PRESTIGE LASTING CO
198 Jerusalem Ave (11550-6332)
PHONE..................516 280-5148
Kevin Ramos, *General Mgr*
EMP: 15
SALES (est): 871.2K **Privately Held**
SIC: 3589 Water filters & softeners, household type

(G-6309)
SHANE TEX INC
Also Called: Henry Segal Co
50 Polk Ave (11550-5416)
PHONE..................516 486-7522
Fax: 516 486-7534
Martin Segal, *Ch of Bd*
Robert Segal, *President*
Bob Silverman, *Vice Pres*
▲ **EMP:** 18 **EST:** 1926
SQ FT: 30,000
SALES: 4MM **Privately Held**
WEB: www.henrysegal.com
SIC: 2311 2337 2335 Tailored suits & formal jackets; men's & boys' uniforms; uniforms, except athletic: women's, misses' & juniors'; women's & misses' suits & skirts; bridal & formal gowns

(G-6310)
T-REX SUPPLY CORPORATION
1 Fulton Ave Ste 120 (11550-3646)
PHONE..................516 308-0505
Brunilda Medina, *President*
EMP: 6
SALES (est): 925.5K **Privately Held**
SIC: 3559 Automotive maintenance equipment

(G-6311)
ULTIMATE SIGNS & DESIGNS INC
86 Sewell St (11550-5432)
PHONE..................516 481-0800
Fax: 516 481-7480
Michael Peras, *President*
Chris Hays, *General Mgr*
Shanna Peras, *Vice Pres*
Arlene Meli, *Project Mgr*
Marguerite Martinek, *Accounting Mgr*
EMP: 26
SQ FT: 10,000
SALES (est): 3.8MM **Privately Held**
WEB: www.ultimatesigns.com
SIC: 3993 Signs & advertising specialties

(G-6312)
WOODMOTIF INC
Also Called: Woodmotif Cabinetry
42 Chasner St (11550-4820)
PHONE..................516 564-8325
George Dimitriadis, *President*
Lisa Louberel, *Manager*
EMP: 10
SALES (est): 1.3MM **Privately Held**
SIC: 2521 2511 2499 Wood office furniture; wood household furniture; decorative wood & woodwork

Henderson
Jefferson County

(G-6313)
VISHAY AMERICAS INC
14992 Snowshoe Rd (13650-2234)
PHONE..................315 938-7575
Rich Mangan, *Branch Mgr*
EMP: 127
SALES (corp-wide): 2.3B **Publicly Held**
SIC: 3676 Electronic resistors
HQ: Vishay Americas, Inc.
1 Greenwich Pl
Shelton CT 06484
203 452-5648

Henrietta
Monroe County

(G-6314)
AGRINETIX CMPT SYSTEMS LLC
Also Called: Agrinetix, LLC
370 Summit Point Dr 1a (14467-9629)
PHONE..................877 978-5477
Richard Wildman, *CEO*
Christine Wildman, *Mng Member*
EMP: 12
SALES (est): 1.5MM **Privately Held**
SIC: 7372 Business oriented computer software

(G-6315)
ANGIOTECH BIOCOATINGS CORP
336 Summit Point Dr (14467-9607)
PHONE..................585 321-1130
Richard Whitbourne, *Ch of Bd*
Richard Richmond, *President*
John F Lanzafame, *President*
Carolyn Eastman, *Vice Pres*
Gerard Whitbourne, *Vice Pres*
▲ **EMP:** 45
SQ FT: 13,000
SALES (est): 4MM
SALES (corp-wide): 73.8MM **Privately Held**
WEB: www.angiotech.com
SIC: 3479 2891 2851 Painting, coating & hot dipping; adhesives & sealants; paints & allied products
PA: Angiotech Pharmaceuticals, Inc
355 Burrard St Suite 1100
Vancouver BC V6C 2
604 221-7676

(G-6316)
ARGON MEDICAL DEVICES INC
336 Summit Point Dr (14467-9607)
PHONE..................585 321-1130
EMP: 8
SALES (corp-wide): 327.6MM **Privately Held**
SIC: 3842 3841 3845 Surgical appliances & supplies; surgical & medical instruments; electromedical equipment
HQ: Argon Medical Devices, Inc.
5151 Hdqtr Dr Ste 210
Plano TX 75024
903 675-9321

(G-6317)
HYDROACOUSTICS INC
999 Lehigh Station Rd # 100 (14467-9389)
PHONE..................585 359-1000
John V Bouyoucos, *Ch of Bd*
Michael Smith, *President*
Michael J Czora, *Vice Pres*
James Rall, *Mfg Staff*
Ken Wittlief, *Engineer*
EMP: 16
SQ FT: 45,000
SALES (est): 4.2MM
SALES (corp-wide): 3.6MM **Privately Held**
WEB: www.hydroacoustics.com
SIC: 3594 Fluid power pumps & motors

Henrietta - Monroe County (G-6318)　　　　　　　　　　　　　　　　　　　　　　　　　　　　　　　　　　**GEOGRAPHIC SECTION**

PA: Hai Technologies Inc.
11611 Tanner Rd Ste A
Houston TX 77041
281 598-3940

(G-6318)
KONECRANES INC
1020 Lehigh Station Rd # 4 (14467-9369)
PHONE..................585 359-4450
Christina Moss, *Manager*
Aaron Boutwelo, *Manager*
EMP: 12
SALES (corp-wide): 2.2B **Privately Held**
WEB: www.kciusa.com
SIC: 3536 7699 Cranes, industrial plant; industrial machinery & equipment repair
HQ: Konecranes, Inc.
4401 Gateway Blvd
Springfield OH 45502

(G-6319)
LAKE IMAGE SYSTEMS INC
205 Summit Point Dr Ste 2 (14467-9631)
PHONE..................585 321-3630
Fax: 585 321-3788
Scott Stevens, *President*
Martin Keats, *President*
Paul Stinson, *Exec VP*
Paul Smith, *Senior VP*
Alain Almeras, *Opers Mgr*
EMP: 17
SQ FT: 7,500
SALES: 5.5MM **Privately Held**
WEB: www.lakeimage.com
SIC: 3861 3554 7371 Cameras & related equipment; paper industries machinery; computer software development
PA: Lake Image Systems Limited
1 The Forum Icknield Way Industrial Estate
Tring HERTS
144 289-2700

(G-6320)
MAGPUMP LLC
235 Middle Rd Ste 600 (14467-9302)
PHONE..................585 444-9812
David Reitano,
EMP: 6
SALES (est): 237.7K **Privately Held**
SIC: 3484 Guns (firearms) or gun parts, 30 mm. & below

(G-6321)
ORAFOL AMERICAS INC
Also Called: Reflexite Precision Tech Ctr
200 Park Centre Dr (14467)
PHONE..................585 272-0309
Stephen Meissner, *Engineer*
Steven Scott, *Branch Mgr*
EMP: 25
SALES (corp-wide): 533.7MM **Privately Held**
WEB: www.reflexite.com
SIC: 3081 Vinyl film & sheet
HQ: Orafol Americas Inc.
1100 Oracal Pkwy
Black Creek GA 31308
912 851-5000

(G-6322)
TUCKER PRINTERS INC
270 Middle Rd (14467-9312)
PHONE..................585 359-3030
Fax: 585 359-3053
Joe R Davis, *CEO*
Daniel A Tucker, *President*
Peter Ashe, *Vice Pres*
Glenn Marino, *Vice Pres*
Mary Fornataro, *Purchasing*
EMP: 82 EST: 1997
SQ FT: 60,000
SALES (est): 18.7MM
SALES (corp-wide): 6.9B **Publicly Held**
WEB: www.tuckerprinters.com
SIC: 2752 Commercial printing, offset
HQ: Consolidated Graphics, Inc.
5858 Westheimer Rd # 200
Houston TX 77057
713 787-0977

(G-6323)
TURNER UNDGRD INSTLLATIONS INC
1233 Lehigh Station Rd (14467-9228)
PHONE..................585 739-0238

Robert Turner, *President*
Rhett Turner, *Vice Pres*
Abraham Brouk, *Project Mgr*
EMP: 12
SQ FT: 11,000
SALES: 3.4MM **Privately Held**
SIC: 1381 Directional drilling oil & gas wells

Herkimer
Herkimer County

(G-6324)
ELG UTICA ALLOYS INC (DH)
378 Gros Blvd Ste 3 (13350-1446)
PHONE..................315 733-0475
Fax: 315 733-2228
Dimitaij Orlov, *Ch of Bd*
Anthony Moreno, *President*
Holger Ropling, *Managing Dir*
Joseph Jiampietro, *Vice Pres*
Fred Schweizer, *Vice Pres*
▲ EMP: 50
SQ FT: 40,000
SALES (est): 35.1MM
SALES (corp-wide): 3.8B **Privately Held**
WEB: www.uticaalloys.com
SIC: 3599 Machine shop, jobbing & repair
HQ: Elg Utica Alloys International Gmbh
Kremerskamp 16
Duisburg
203 450-10

(G-6325)
GATEHOUSE MEDIA LLC
Also Called: Evening Telegram
111 Green St (13350-1914)
P.O. Box 551 (13350-0551)
PHONE..................315 866-2220
Fax: 315 866-5913
Beth Brewer, *Manager*
EMP: 10
SALES (corp-wide): 1.2B **Publicly Held**
WEB: www.gatehousemedia.com
SIC: 2711 Newspapers, publishing & printing
HQ: Gatehouse Media, Llc
175 Sullys Trl Ste 300
Pittsford NY 14534
585 598-0030

(G-6326)
HEIDELBERG GROUP INC
3056 State Hwy Rte 28 N (13350)
PHONE..................315 866-0999
Boyd Bissell, *President*
Cheryl Phillips, *Opers Staff*
▲ EMP: 40
SQ FT: 8,000
SALES (est): 6.3MM **Privately Held**
WEB: www.heidelbergbakingco.com
SIC: 2051 Bread, cake & related products

(G-6327)
HERKIMER DIAMOND MINES INC
800 Mohawk St (13350-2261)
PHONE..................315 891-7355
Renee Scialdo Schevat, *Ch of Bd*
EMP: 25
SALES (est): 3.2MM **Privately Held**
WEB: www.herkimerdiamond.com
SIC: 1499 5094 Gemstone & industrial diamond mining; diamonds (gems)

(G-6328)
HERKIMER TOOL & MACHINING CORP
Also Called: Herkimer Tool & Equipment Co
125 Marginal Rd (13350-2305)
PHONE..................315 866-2110
Fax: 315 866-7129
F Ellis Green Jr, *President*
Francis E Green III, *Vice Pres*
Nancy J Green, *Admin Sec*
EMP: 10
SQ FT: 14,000
SALES (est): 1.3MM **Privately Held**
SIC: 3599 Machine shop, jobbing & repair

(G-6329)
LENNONS LITHO INC
Also Called: Mohawk Valley Printing Co
234 Kast Hill Rd (13350-4402)
PHONE..................315 866-3156
Robert J Lennon, *Ch of Bd*
Elfrieda Lennon, *Treasurer*
EMP: 10
SQ FT: 6,400
SALES (est): 730K **Privately Held**
WEB: www.mohawkvalleyprinting.com
SIC: 2752 2759 Commercial printing, offset; commercial printing; letterpress printing

Hewlett
Nassau County

(G-6330)
ABS METAL CORP
58 Holly Rd (11557-1411)
PHONE..................646 302-9018
Alan Minchenberg, *Principal*
EMP: 5 EST: 2012
SALES (est): 465.7K **Privately Held**
SIC: 3471 Finishing, metals or formed products

(G-6331)
ALGAFUEL AMERICA
289 Meadowview Ave (11557-2106)
PHONE..................516 295-2257
Allan Roffe, *Principal*
EMP: 7
SALES (est): 464.7K **Privately Held**
SIC: 2911 Diesel fuels

(G-6332)
LADY BRASS CO INC
1717 Broadway Unit 2 (11557-1682)
PHONE..................516 887-8040
Fax: 516 887-8025
Lauren Brasco, *President*
EMP: 6
SALES (est): 1MM **Privately Held**
SIC: 2337 2326 Uniforms, except athletic: women's, misses' & juniors'; work uniforms

(G-6333)
LIFEWATCH INC
Also Called: Lifewatch Personal Mergency
1344 Broadway Ste 106 (11557-1356)
PHONE..................800 716-1433
Fax: 516 837-3852
Evan Sirlin, *President*
Art Sirlin, *Vice Pres*
Sarai Baker, *Opers Staff*
Art Mitchell, *Treasurer*
Mitchell Evan, *Manager*
EMP: 10
SALES: 700K **Privately Held**
WEB: www.lifewatch.net
SIC: 3669 5063 5999 Emergency alarms; alarm systems; alarm signal systems

(G-6334)
NEW PRIMECARE
1184 Broadway (11557-2322)
PHONE..................516 822-4031
Fred Tylutki, *CFO*
EMP: 5 EST: 2007
SALES (est): 366.5K **Privately Held**
SIC: 3845 Laser systems & equipment, medical

(G-6335)
PETLAND DISCOUNTS INC
1340 Peninsula Blvd (11557-1226)
PHONE..................516 821-3194
EMP: 6
SALES (corp-wide): 151.8MM **Privately Held**
SIC: 3999 Pet supplies
PA: Petland Discounts, Inc.
355 Crooked Hill Rd
Brentwood NY 11717
631 273-6363

(G-6336)
S & M RING CORP
1080 Channel Dr (11557-2638)
PHONE..................212 382-0900

Fax: 212 398-1963
Wally Schafran, *President*
▲ EMP: 12
SALES (est): 622K **Privately Held**
SIC: 3911 Jewelry, precious metal; rings, finger; precious metal

(G-6337)
TORSAF PRINTERS INC
Also Called: Minuteman Press
1315 Broadway Unit B (11557-2104)
PHONE..................516 569-5577
Fax: 516 569-4740
David Toron, *President*
Michael Toron, *Corp Secy*
EMP: 6
SQ FT: 4,800
SALES (est): 876.7K **Privately Held**
SIC: 2752 2791 Commercial printing, lithographic; typesetting

(G-6338)
UNITED PIPE NIPPLE CO INC
1602 Lakeview Dr (11557-1818)
PHONE..................516 295-2468
Fax: 718 756-3016
Roger Desimone, *CEO*
Selma Dolgov, *President*
▲ EMP: 15
SQ FT: 25,000
SALES: 5MM **Privately Held**
WEB: www.unitedpipenipple.com
SIC: 3494 Pipe fittings

(G-6339)
VENUS PRINTING COMPANY
1420 Kew Ave (11557-1413)
PHONE..................212 967-8900
Fax: 516 967-8992
Erwin Goodman, *President*
Carol Goodman, *Treasurer*
Tom Shields, *Manager*
EMP: 15
SALES (est): 1MM **Privately Held**
SIC: 2759 Commercial printing

(G-6340)
WASHINGTON FOUNDRIES INC
1434 Vian Ave (11557-1423)
PHONE..................516 374-8447
Jyotsna Kejriwal, *CEO*
Ramesh Kejriwal, *President*
EMP: 4
SQ FT: 2,100
SALES (est): 1.1MM **Privately Held**
SIC: 3674 Semiconductors & related devices

(G-6341)
YES WERE NUTS LTD
Also Called: I'M Nuts
1215 Broadway (11557-2001)
PHONE..................516 374-1940
Fax: 516 374-2643
Catherine Davi, *President*
EMP: 6
SQ FT: 2,500
SALES (est): 484.6K **Privately Held**
SIC: 2066 Chocolate

Hicksville
Nassau County

(G-6342)
AJAX WIRE SPECIALTY CO INC
119 Bloomingdale Rd (11801-6508)
PHONE..................516 935-2333
Fax: 516 935-2334
Patricia Ellner, *CEO*
David Ellner, *President*
EMP: 15
SQ FT: 5,000
SALES: 1MM **Privately Held**
SIC: 3495 Wire springs

(G-6343)
ALL ISLAND MEDIA INC
Also Called: Carrier News
325 Duffy Ave Unit 2 (11801-3644)
PHONE..................516 942-8400
Fax: 516 942-3730
Robert Sussi, *Branch Mgr*
EMP: 26

GEOGRAPHIC SECTION

Hicksville - Nassau County (G-6367)

SALES (corp-wide): 12.9MM **Privately Held**
WEB: www.allislandmedia.com
SIC: 2711 Newspapers, publishing & printing
PA: All Island Media, Inc.
1 Rodeo Dr
Edgewood NY 11717
631 698-8400

(G-6344)
ALL THE RAGE INC
147 W Cherry St Unit 1 (11801-3885)
PHONE 516 605-2001
Michael J Demarco, *President*
Sridat Rambarren, *Manager*
EMP: 7
SQ FT: 3,000
SALES (est): 5MM **Privately Held**
SIC: 3911 Jewelry apparel

(G-6345)
ALLIES GF GOODIES LLC
1b W Village Grn (11801-3911)
PHONE 516 216-1719
Donna Miller,
EMP: 10
SALES (est): 805.3K **Privately Held**
SIC: 2051 Bakery: wholesale or wholesale/retail combined

(G-6346)
APPLIED POWER SYSTEMS INC
Also Called: A P S
124 Charlotte Ave (11801-2620)
PHONE 516 935-2230
Fax: 516 935-2603
James Murphy, *CEO*
Les Doti, *Vice Pres*
Andres Romay, *Vice Pres*
Paul Kowal, *Engineer*
Tom Murray, *Engineer*
▲ **EMP:** 25
SALES (est): 4.8MM **Privately Held**
WEB: www.appliedps.com
SIC: 3679 3677 3629 3823 Power supplies, all types: static; transformers power supply, electronic type; inverters, nonrotating: electrical; controllers for process variables, all types; frequency converters (electric generators)

(G-6347)
APX TECHNOLOGIES INC
264 Duffy Ave (11801-3605)
PHONE 516 433-1313
Yuval Ofek, *President*
Tony Nicotra, *Engineer*
Roberto Paniccia, *Engineer*
Jeanette Kahn, *Office Mgr*
▲ **EMP:** 20
SQ FT: 3,500
SALES (est): 3MM **Privately Held**
SIC: 3679 Harness assemblies for electronic use: wire or cable; electronic loads & power supplies

(G-6348)
ARSTAN PRODUCTS INTERNATIONAL
Also Called: Apx Arstan Products
264 Duffy Ave (11801-3605)
PHONE 516 433-1313
Fax: 516 433-1457
Yuval Ofek, *President*
EMP: 15
SQ FT: 3,500
SALES (est): 1.2MM **Privately Held**
WEB: www.apxonline.com
SIC: 3679 3612 Power supplies, all types: static; transformers, except electric

(G-6349)
AUTO-MAT COMPANY INC
69 Hazel St (11801-5340)
PHONE 516 938-7373
Fax: 516 931-8438
Timothy S Browner, *President*
Marilyn Browner, *Corp Secy*
Roger Browner, *Vice Pres*
EMP: 21 **EST:** 1956
SQ FT: 12,000

SALES (est): 1.5MM **Privately Held**
SIC: 2273 5013 7532 Automobile floor coverings, except rubber or plastic; automotive supplies & parts; interior repair services

(G-6350)
BALANCE ENTERPRISES INC
12 W Cherry St (11801-3802)
PHONE 516 822-3183
Robert Philips, *President*
EMP: 8
SALES (est): 446.3K **Privately Held**
SIC: 3999 Education aids, devices & supplies

(G-6351)
BATTSCO LLC
190 Lauman Ln Unit A (11801-6570)
PHONE 516 586-6544
Fred Hentschel, *Managing Prtnr*
John R Garnett, *Mng Member*
▲ **EMP:** 5
SQ FT: 2,500
SALES (est): 2MM **Privately Held**
SIC: 3691 Storage batteries

(G-6352)
C Q COMMUNICATIONS INC
Also Called: Cq Magazine
17 W John St Unit 1 (11801-1004)
PHONE 516 681-2922
Richard Ross, *President*
Joe Lynch, *Editor*
Wayne Yoshida, *Editor*
Dorothy Kehrwieder, *Prdtn Dir*
S Del Grosso, *Accounting Dir*
EMP: 22
SQ FT: 10,000
SALES (est): 3.3MM **Privately Held**
WEB: www.cq-vhf.com
SIC: 2721 Magazines: publishing only, not printed on site

(G-6353)
CAMBRIDGE KITCHENS MFG INC
280 Duffy Ave Unit 1 (11801-3656)
PHONE 516 935-5100
Neoklis Vasiliades, *President*
Barbara Narene, *Admin Sec*
EMP: 15
SQ FT: 32,000
SALES (est): 2.6MM **Privately Held**
WEB: www.cambridgekitchens.com
SIC: 2434 Wood kitchen cabinets

(G-6354)
CLASSIC COLOR GRAPHICS INC (PA)
268 N Broadway Unit 8 (11801-2923)
P.O. Box 599, Jericho (11753-0599)
PHONE 516 822-9090
Daniel Fischer, *President*
Meryl Fischer, *Treasurer*
EMP: 7
SALES (est): 508.8K **Privately Held**
SIC: 2752 Commercial printing, lithographic

(G-6355)
CLASSIC COLOR GRAPHICS INC
87 Broadway (11801-4272)
PHONE 516 822-9090
Dan Fisher, *President*
Barry Moscowitz, *Accountant*
EMP: 5
SALES (corp-wide): 508.8K **Privately Held**
SIC: 2752 Commercial printing, lithographic
PA: Classic Color Graphics, Inc
268 N Broadway Unit 8
Hicksville NY 11801
516 822-9090

(G-6356)
CLASSIC CONCRETE CORP
29a Midland Ave (11801-1509)
PHONE 516 822-1800
Saverio Potente Jr, *President*
EMP: 10
SQ FT: 700
SALES (est): 1.1MM **Privately Held**
SIC: 3273 5032 Ready-mixed concrete; paving materials

(G-6357)
CLEARY CUSTOM CABINETS INC
794 S Broadway (11801-5017)
PHONE 516 939-2475
Tom Cleary, *President*
Lora Cleary, *Vice Pres*
EMP: 15
SALES (est): 1.3MM **Privately Held**
WEB: www.clearycustomcabinets.com
SIC: 2517 Home entertainment unit cabinets, wood

(G-6358)
COOPER LIGHTING LLC
Also Called: Neo Ray Lighting Products
100 Andrews Rd Ste 1 (11801-1725)
PHONE 516 470-1000
Aida Rivera, *General Mgr*
Harry Mangru, *Buyer*
Dennis Detore, *Controller*
Lisa Goodman,
▲ **EMP:** 110 **EST:** 2007
SALES (est): 18.5MM **Privately Held**
WEB: www.neoray-lighting.com
SIC: 3646 3645 Commercial indusl & institutional electric lighting fixtures; residential lighting fixtures
HQ: Cooper Industries Unlimited Company
41 A B Drury Street
Dublin

(G-6359)
CORAL GRAPHIC SERVICES INC (DH)
Also Called: Coral Graphic Svce
840 S Broadway (11801-5066)
PHONE 516 576-2100
David Liess, *Ch of Bd*
Frank Cappo, *President*
Robert Vitale, *Exec VP*
Walter Keane, *VP Opers*
Manny Paiva, *Plant Mgr*
▲ **EMP:** 171
SQ FT: 56,000
SALES (est): 72MM
SALES (corp-wide): 17.9B **Privately Held**
SIC: 2752 Commercial printing, offset
HQ: Dynamic Graphic Finishing, Inc.
945 Horsham Rd
Horsham PA 19044
215 441-8880

(G-6360)
CORAL GRAPHIC SERVICES INC
840 S Broadway (11801-5066)
PHONE 516 576-2100
Dave Lieff, *President*
EMP: 102
SALES (corp-wide): 17.9B **Privately Held**
SIC: 2752 Commercial printing, lithographic
HQ: Coral Graphic Services, Inc.
840 S Broadway
Hicksville NY 11801
516 576-2100

(G-6361)
CRAIG ENVELOPE CORP
220 Miller Pl (11801-1826)
PHONE 718 786-4277
Fax: 718 937-8178
Lawrence Aaronson, *President*
Susan Aaronson, *Corp Secy*
Robert Aaronson, *VP Opers*
Manny Ramos, *Prdtn Mgr*
John Lundgren, *Human Res Mgr*
EMP: 39
SQ FT: 20,000
SALES (est): 6MM **Privately Held**
SIC: 2752 2759 Commercial printing, offset; letterpress printing

(G-6362)
CREATIVE MODELS & PROTOTYPES
160 Lauman Ln Unit A (11801-6557)
PHONE 516 433-6828
Deborah Dinoia, *President*
Brian Allbin, *Prdtn Mgr*
William Dinoia, *Manager*
EMP: 8
SALES: 40K **Privately Held**
SIC: 3999 Models, except toy

(G-6363)
CROWN EQUIPMENT CORPORATION
Also Called: Crown Lift Trucks
5 Charlotte Ave Ste 1 (11801-3607)
PHONE 516 822-5100
Fax: 516 822-0205
Jim Casey, *Manager*
EMP: 68
SALES (corp-wide): 5.5B **Privately Held**
SIC: 3537 Lift trucks, industrial: fork, platform, straddle, etc.
PA: Crown Equipment Corporation
44 S Washington St
New Bremen OH 45869
419 629-2311

(G-6364)
CULICOVER & SHAPIRO INC
270 Duffy Ave Ste K (11801-3600)
PHONE 516 597-4888
Fax: 631 918-4561
Richard Shapiro, *President*
David Shapiro, *Treasurer*
▲ **EMP:** 4 **EST:** 1929
SALES (est): 1.2MM **Privately Held**
SIC: 3991 Brushes, household or industrial

(G-6365)
CYNOSURE INC
Also Called: Ellman International
400 Karin Ln (11801-5352)
PHONE 516 594-3333
Tom Oliveri, *VP Opers*
EMP: 7
SALES (corp-wide): 2.8B **Publicly Held**
SIC: 3841 3843 Surgical & medical instruments; dental equipment & supplies
HQ: Cynosure, Inc.
5 Carlisle Rd
Westford MA 01886
978 256-4200

(G-6366)
DESIGNATRONICS INCORPORATED (PA)
Also Called: Sdp/Si
250 Duffy Ave Unit A (11801-3654)
P.O. Box 5416, New Hyde Park (11042-5416)
PHONE 516 328-3300
Fax: 516 326-2784
Michael Walsh, *Ch of Bd*
Richard Kufner, *President*
Sue Anderson, *Exec VP*
Robert Lindemann, *Vice Pres*
Daniel Raleigh, *Vice Pres*
▲ **EMP:** 2
SQ FT: 40,000
SALES (est): 113.2MM **Privately Held**
WEB: www.designatronics.com
SIC: 3824 3559 3545 3625 Mechanical & electromechanical counters & devices; electronic component making machinery; cams (machine tool accessories); relays & industrial controls; iron & steel forgings

(G-6367)
DESIGNATRONICS INCORPORATED
Also Called: Stock Drive Products Div
250 Duffy Ave Unit A (11801-3654)
PHONE 516 328-3300
Anthony Pagliughi, *Principal*
Robert Lindemann, *Vice Pres*
Billal Hossian, *Engineer*
Herb Arum, *Marketing Mgr*
Shawn Silver, *Data Proc Staff*
EMP: 296
SALES (corp-wide): 113.2MM **Privately Held**
WEB: www.designatronics.com
SIC: 3625 3621 3568 3566 Motor controls & accessories; motors & generators; power transmission equipment; speed changers, drives & gears; manufactured hardware (general); tire cord & fabrics
PA: Designatronics Incorporated
250 Duffy Ave Unit A
Hicksville NY 11801
516 328-3300

Hicksville - Nassau County (G-6368)

(G-6368)
DESIGNATRONICS INCORPORATED
250 Duffy Ave Unit A (11801-3654)
PHONE..................................516 328-3970
Chris Garwig, *Product Mgr*
George Klein, *Branch Mgr*
Richard Mittasch, *Info Tech Mgr*
EMP: 50
SALES (corp-wide): 113.2MM **Privately Held**
WEB: www.designatronics.com
SIC: 3824 Mechanical & electromechanical counters & devices
PA: Designatronics Incorporated
250 Duffy Ave Unit A
Hicksville NY 11801
516 328-3300

(G-6369)
DESIGNATRONICS INCORPORATED
Also Called: Sterling Instruments Div
250 Duffy Ave Unit A (11801-3654)
PHONE..................................516 328-3300
Dan Raleigh, *Vice Pres*
James Mastrorilli, *Sales Executive*
Susan Anderson, *Manager*
Linda Shuett, *Manager*
Daniel Raleigh, *Info Tech Dir*
EMP: 10
SALES (corp-wide): 113.2MM **Privately Held**
SIC: 3568 Power transmission equipment
PA: Designatronics Incorporated
250 Duffy Ave Unit A
Hicksville NY 11801
516 328-3300

(G-6370)
E-BEAM SERVICES INC (PA)
270 Duffy Ave Ste H (11801-3600)
PHONE..................................516 622-1422
Fax: 516 622-1425
Paul R Minbiole, *President*
Mary C Daly, *Vice Pres*
Greg Shavzian, *Info Tech Mgr*
Mary Daly, *Admin Sec*
▲ EMP: 4
SQ FT: 2,000
SALES: 5MM **Privately Held**
WEB: www.e-beamservices.com
SIC: 3671 Electron beam (beta ray) generator tubes

(G-6371)
EDGIAN PRESS INC
10 Bethpage Rd (11801-1512)
PHONE..................................516 931-2114
Fax: 516 931-7989
Edward E Giannelli, *President*
Ian R Fuller, *Principal*
Edward C Giannelli, *Principal*
EMP: 8
SQ FT: 6,000
SALES (est): 1.1MM **Privately Held**
SIC: 2752 2759 Commercial printing, offset; letterpress printing

(G-6372)
EISEMAN-LUDMAR CO INC
56 Bethpage Dr (11801-1502)
PHONE..................................516 932-6990
Andrew Ludmar, *President*
Carol Ludmar, *Vice Pres*
David Ludmar, *Vice Pres*
Delores Becker, *Bookkeeper*
EMP: 10
SQ FT: 4,200
SALES (est): 891.8K **Privately Held**
WEB: www.elcaccessories.com
SIC: 2395 2241 Embroidery & art needlework; lace & decorative trim, narrow fabric

(G-6373)
FLEXFIT LLC
350 Karin Ln Unit A (11801-5360)
PHONE..................................516 932-8800
Leslie Umphrey, *General Mgr*
Mike Son, *Design Engr*
John Micheal, *Credit Mgr*
Austin OH, *Sales Dir*
Allison Jeon, *Sales Staff*
▲ EMP: 60

SALES (est): 97MM **Privately Held**
SIC: 2353 Hats, caps & millinery

(G-6374)
FOOT LOCKER RETAIL INC
Also Called: Champs Sports
358 Broadway Mall (11801-2709)
PHONE..................................516 827-5306
Jamie Blas, *Manager*
EMP: 10
SALES (corp-wide): 7.7B **Publicly Held**
WEB: www.venatorgroup.com
SIC: 2389 5611 Men's miscellaneous accessories; clothing, sportswear, men's & boys'
HQ: Foot Locker Retail, Inc.
330 W 34th St
New York NY 10001

(G-6375)
FOUGERA PHARMACEUTICALS INC
55 Cantiague Rock Rd (11801-1126)
P.O. Box 2006, Melville (11747-0103)
PHONE..................................631 454-7677
Robert Faivre, *Managing Dir*
James Cherry, *VP Mfg*
Richard Sanchez, *Manager*
EMP: 158
SALES (corp-wide): 48.5B **Privately Held**
SIC: 2834 Druggists' preparations (pharmaceuticals)
HQ: Fougera Pharmaceuticals Inc.
60 Baylis Rd
Melville NY 11747
631 454-7677

(G-6376)
GE POLYMERSHAPES
120 Andrews Rd (11801-1704)
PHONE..................................516 433-4092
Mike Grimm, *Manager*
◆ EMP: 10
SALES (est): 878.8K **Privately Held**
SIC: 2295 Resin or plastic coated fabrics

(G-6377)
GIM ELECTRONICS CORP
270 Duffy Ave Ste H (11801-3600)
PHONE..................................516 942-3382
Fax: 516 942-3389
Mark Douenias, *President*
William Cardenas, *Vice Pres*
Mac E Fetner, *Plant Mgr*
Mike Morand, *Rsch/Dvlpt Dir*
EMP: 15
SQ FT: 7,800
SALES: 10MM **Privately Held**
WEB: www.gimelectronics.com
SIC: 3572 5961 Computer storage devices; computer equipment & electronics, mail order

(G-6378)
GLOBAL GLASS CORP
134 Woodbury Rd (11801-3025)
PHONE..................................516 681-2309
Fax: 516 937-0389
Jack Flax, *President*
▲ EMP: 6
SQ FT: 2,000
SALES (est): 662.4K **Privately Held**
SIC: 3211 3231 5231 5719 Flat glass; products of purchased glass; glass; mirrors; glass & glazing work

(G-6379)
GLOPAK USA CORP
35 Engel St Ste B (11801-2648)
PHONE..................................516 433-3214
EMP: 58
SALES (corp-wide): 35MM **Privately Held**
SIC: 3221 Bottles for packing, bottling & canning: glass
PA: Glopak Usa Corp
1816 127th St Ste 2
College Point NY 11356
347 869-9252

(G-6380)
GOLFING MAGAZINE
Also Called: Long Island Golfer Magazine
22 W Nicholai St Ste 200 (11801-3881)
PHONE..................................516 822-5446
Fax: 516 822-5446

John Glozek Jr, *President*
▲ EMP: 8
SALES (est): 411K **Privately Held**
WEB: www.ligolfer.com
SIC: 2721 5736 Magazines: publishing only, not printed on site; sheet music

(G-6381)
GREENWOOD GRAPHICS INC
960 S Broadway Ste 106 (11801-5028)
PHONE..................................516 822-4856
Michael Boker, *President*
EMP: 12
SALES (est): 1MM **Privately Held**
WEB: www.greenwoodgraphics.com
SIC: 2752 7336 7319 Commercial printing, offset; graphic arts & related design; display advertising service

(G-6382)
HANAN PRODUCTS COMPANY INC
196 Miller Pl (11801-1826)
PHONE..................................516 938-1000
Fax: 516 938-1925
Stuart M Hanan, *President*
Francis Hanan, *Vice Pres*
Bruce Meyeroff, *Director*
Doris Hanan, *Admin Sec*
▼ EMP: 20 EST: 1950
SQ FT: 23,000
SALES (est): 3.9MM **Privately Held**
WEB: www.hananproducts.com
SIC: 2026 Whipped topping, except frozen or dry mix

(G-6383)
HICKSVILLE MACHINE WORKS CORP
761 S Broadway (11801-5098)
PHONE..................................516 931-1524
Fax: 516 931-2308
Gioachino Jack Spiezio, *Ch of Bd*
John Spiezio, *General Mgr*
Holly Pasquarella, *Purchasing*
Debby Snyder, *Manager*
Betty Spiezio, *Admin Sec*
EMP: 18
SQ FT: 35,000
SALES (est): 4MM **Privately Held**
WEB: www.hicksvillemachine.com
SIC: 3728 Aircraft parts & equipment

(G-6384)
JAY-AIMEE DESIGNS INC
99 Railroad Station Plz # 200 (11801-2850)
PHONE..................................718 609-0333
Isaac Matalon, *CEO*
Shlomi Matalon, *President*
Diana Maldimado, *Bookkeeper*
EMP: 175
SQ FT: 4,000
SALES (est): 21.8MM **Privately Held**
WEB: www.jayaimee.com
SIC: 3911 Jewelry, precious metal; earrings, precious metal; bracelets, precious metal

(G-6385)
JOHN E POTENTE & SONS INC
114 Woodbury Rd Unit 1 (11801-3047)
PHONE..................................516 935-8585
Fax: 516 935-8546
Eugene Potente, *CEO*
Ralph J Potente, *President*
Saverio Potente, *Vice Pres*
EMP: 6 EST: 1925
SQ FT: 5,000
SALES (est): 929.9K **Privately Held**
SIC: 3272 Concrete products

(G-6386)
KINGFORM CAP COMPANY INC
121 New South Rd (11801-5230)
PHONE..................................516 822-2501
Fax: 516 822-2536
Leonard Ochs, *President*
▲ EMP: 60 EST: 1955
SQ FT: 33,000
SALES (est): 6.7MM **Privately Held**
WEB: www.kingformcap.com
SIC: 2353 Uniform hats & caps

(G-6387)
KOZY SHACK ENTERPRISES LLC (HQ)
83 Ludy St (11801-5114)
PHONE..................................516 870-3000
Robert Striano, *Principal*
Nancy Roberts, *Manager*
Joanne Caridi, *Admin Sec*
◆ EMP: 250 EST: 1967
SQ FT: 70,000
SALES (est): 90.2MM
SALES (corp-wide): 14.9B **Privately Held**
WEB: www.kozyshack.com
SIC: 2099 5149 Desserts, ready-to-mix; gelatin dessert preparations; groceries & related products
PA: Land O'lakes, Inc.
4001 Lexington Ave N
Arden Hills MN 55126
651 375-2222

(G-6388)
KOZY SHACK ENTERPRISES LLC
Also Called: Freshway Distributors
50 Ludy St (11801-5115)
PHONE..................................516 870-3000
Frank Gilmartin, *Mfg Spvr*
Brian Duffy, *QC Mgr*
Roy Kasenchak, *Engineer*
Joe Anderson, *VP Sales*
Stephen Harrigan, *Sales Dir*
EMP: 200
SALES (corp-wide): 14.9B **Privately Held**
WEB: www.kozyshack.com
SIC: 2099 5149 2024 Desserts, ready-to-mix; gelatin dessert preparations; groceries & related products; ice cream & frozen desserts
HQ: Kozy Shack Enterprises, Llc
83 Ludy St
Hicksville NY 11801
516 870-3000

(G-6389)
KUNO STEEL PRODUCTS CORP
132 Duffy Ave (11801-3640)
PHONE..................................516 938-8500
Fax: 516 938-8516
Kuno Weckenmann, *President*
Irmgard Weckenmann, *Corp Secy*
W Weckenmann, *Vice Pres*
EMP: 10
SQ FT: 1,500
SALES: 1.2MM **Privately Held**
WEB: www.kunosteel.com
SIC: 3441 Building components, structural steel

(G-6390)
LAND OLAKES INC
50 Ludy St (11801-5115)
PHONE..................................516 681-2980
EMP: 9
SALES (corp-wide): 14.9B **Privately Held**
SIC: 2099 Food preparations
PA: Land O'lakes, Inc.
4001 Lexington Ave N
Arden Hills MN 55126
651 375-2222

(G-6391)
LEATHER INDEXES CORP
174a Miller Pl (11801-1826)
P.O. Box 1350, Port Washington (11050-7350)
PHONE..................................516 827-1900
Fax: 516 827-1920
Paul Ellenberg, *President*
Kay Ellenberg, *Vice Pres*
EMP: 60
SQ FT: 15,000
SALES: 1.5MM **Privately Held**
SIC: 2678 2782 2675 Stationery products; blankbooks & looseleaf binders; die-cut paper & board

(G-6392)
M F MANUFACTURING ENTERPRISES
2 Ballad Ln (11801-4529)
PHONE..................................516 822-5135
Michael Funk, *CEO*
Fern Funk, *Vice Pres*
EMP: 5

GEOGRAPHIC SECTION

Hicksville - Nassau County (G-6420)

SALES (est): 325K **Privately Held**
SIC: 3469 Machine parts, stamped or pressed metal

(G-6393)
MARCAL PRINTING INC
Also Called: PIP Printing
85 N Broadway (11801-2948)
PHONE..................516 942-9500
Fax: 516 942-9502
Marc Saltzman, *President*
Alan Smith, *Vice Pres*
EMP: 6
SQ FT: 3,000
SALES (est): 720K **Privately Held**
SIC: 2752 Commercial printing, offset

(G-6394)
MARIAH METAL PRODUCTS INC
89 Tec St (11801-3618)
PHONE..................516 938-9783
Fax: 516 938-9784
Raymond O Leary, *President*
EMP: 5
SQ FT: 2,000
SALES (est): 676.2K **Privately Held**
SIC: 3444 Sheet metalwork

(G-6395)
MARIGOLD SIGNS INC
Also Called: Sign-A-Rama
485 S Broadway Ste 34 (11801-5071)
PHONE..................516 433-7446
Fax: 516 433-8023
Vincent Marino, *President*
Robert Goldaber, *Vice Pres*
Benjamin Lichtiger, *Consultant*
Mark Lifshitz, *Director*
Michael Eaton,
EMP: 10
SALES (est): 790K **Privately Held**
SIC: 3993 Signs & advertising specialties

(G-6396)
MARKWIK CORP
309 W John St (11801-1024)
PHONE..................516 470-1990
Jane A Groene, *President*
Taylor Groene, *General Mgr*
EMP: 18 EST: 1949
SQ FT: 9,000
SALES (est): 2.3MM **Privately Held**
WEB: www.markwik.com
SIC: 3089 Plastic hardware & building products

(G-6397)
MICRO CONTACTS INC (PA)
1 Enterprise Pl Unit E (11801-2694)
PHONE..................516 433-4830
Fax: 516 433-6379
Gerald F Tucci, *Ch of Bd*
Michael F Tucci, *President*
Robert Stinson, *General Mgr*
Steven Klekman, *Vice Pres*
Philip Uruburu, *Vice Pres*
▲ EMP: 50 EST: 1963
SQ FT: 40,000
SALES (est): 5.7MM **Privately Held**
WEB: www.microcontacts.com
SIC: 3643 Contacts, electrical

(G-6398)
MISON CONCEPTS INC
485 S Broadway Ste 33 (11801-5071)
PHONE..................516 933-8000
Fax: 516 933-8001
Joseph Jaroff, *President*
Bhavani Morganstern, *Vice Pres*
JP Proskauer, *Project Mgr*
Sandra Fiore, *Administration*
▲ EMP: 8
SQ FT: 2,000
SALES (est): 690K **Privately Held**
WEB: www.mison.com
SIC: 3446 Architectural metalwork

(G-6399)
MOD-A-CAN INC (PA)
178 Miller Pl (11801-1890)
PHONE..................516 931-8545
Fax: 516 931-8545
Stan Buoninfante, *President*
Stan L Buoninfante, *President*
Bill Sammon, *General Mgr*
Roberta Wolfe, *General Mgr*

Michael Iannotta, *VP Opers*
EMP: 20 EST: 1966
SQ FT: 19,400
SALES (est): 7.6MM **Privately Held**
WEB: www.modacan.com
SIC: 3812 Aircraft flight instruments

(G-6400)
MULTI PACKAGING SOLUTIONS INC
325 Duffy Ave Unit 1 (11801-3644)
PHONE..................516 488-2000
Michael Greenberg, *Branch Mgr*
EMP: 113
SALES (corp-wide): 14.1B **Publicly Held**
SIC: 2671 Packaging paper & plastics film, coated & laminated
HQ: Multi Packaging Solutions, Inc.
  150 E 52nd St Ste 2800
  New York NY 10022
  646 885-0005

(G-6401)
NOASPENCE INC
Also Called: Edible Arrangement Store 1373
1040 S Broadway Unit 6 (11801-5027)
PHONE..................516 433-7848
Hillary B Friedland, *President*
EMP: 6
SALES (est): 499K **Privately Held**
SIC: 2099 5441 Dessert mixes & fillings; confectionery

(G-6402)
NU - COMMUNITEK LLC
108 New South Rd Ste A (11801-5262)
PHONE..................516 433-3553
Allison Waserman, *Controller*
Gary Calmenson,
Jarret Calmenson,
EMP: 10
SQ FT: 1,500
SALES (est): 2.4MM **Privately Held**
WEB: www.loyaltykiosk.com
SIC: 3575 Computer terminals

(G-6403)
NY EMBROIDERY INC
Also Called: New York Embroidery & Monogram
25 Midland Ave (11801-1509)
PHONE..................516 822-6456
Fax: 516 822-6461
John La Rocca, *President*
Annette Snow, *Vice Pres*
▲ EMP: 20
SALES (est): 1.5MM **Privately Held**
WEB: www.nyembroidery.com
SIC: 2395 Embroidery products, except schiffli machine

(G-6404)
OLMSTEAD PRODUCTS CORP
1 Jefry Ln (11801-5394)
PHONE..................516 681-3700
Fax: 516 681-3702
Jack Tepper, *President*
Nicholas Lucarello, *Vice Pres*
▲ EMP: 12 EST: 1954
SQ FT: 7,000
SALES (est): 1.9MM **Privately Held**
SIC: 3556 Food products machinery

(G-6405)
OXYGEN INC (PA)
Also Called: Rodan
6 Midland Ave (11801-1510)
PHONE..................516 433-1144
Fax: 516 433-8450
Daniel Joory, *President*
Ronnie Zubli, *CFO*
Kenny Miller, *Manager*
◆ EMP: 8
SQ FT: 2,000
SALES (est): 955.8K **Privately Held**
SIC: 2369 Bathing suits & swimwear: girls', children's & infants'; leggings: girls', children's & infants'

(G-6406)
OYSTER BAY PUMP WORKS INC
78 Midland Ave Unit 1 (11801-1537)
P.O. Box 725 (11802-0725)
PHONE..................516 933-4500
Fax: 516 933-4501
Patrick Gaillard, *CEO*

Andrew Mancura, *Purch Mgr*
▲ EMP: 18
SALES (est): 5.2MM **Privately Held**
WEB: www.obpw.com
SIC: 3561 3829 3589 Pumps & pumping equipment; medical diagnostic systems, nuclear; liquor dispensing equipment & systems

(G-6407)
P & F BAKERS INC
640 S Broadway (11801-5016)
PHONE..................516 931-6821
P Zamparelli, *CEO*
EMP: 8
SALES (est): 449.4K **Privately Held**
SIC: 2026 Bakers' cheese

(G-6408)
PAL ALUMINUM INC (PA)
Also Called: Pal Industries
230 Duffy Ave Unit B (11801-3641)
PHONE..................516 937-1990
Pana Giotis Mar Neris, *President*
Laurel Marneris, *Vice Pres*
EMP: 3
SQ FT: 70,000
SALES (est): 4.7MM **Privately Held**
SIC: 3444 5033 5031 Metal roofing & roof drainage equipment; gutters, sheet metal; roof deck, sheet metal; siding, except wood; doors

(G-6409)
PAL MANUFACTURING CORP
230 Duffy Ave Unit B (11801-3641)
PHONE..................516 937-1990
Laurel Marneris, *President*
Panagiotis Marneris, *Vice Pres*
Paul Baricelli, *Controller*
EMP: 28
SQ FT: 70,000
SALES (est): 4.4MM **Privately Held**
WEB: www.palwindows.com
SIC: 3442 3231 Screen & storm doors & windows; products of purchased glass

(G-6410)
PB08 INC
40 Bloomingdale Rd (11801-6507)
PHONE..................347 866-7353
Jajtar Kular, *Owner*
Neeraj Sherma, *Principal*
EMP: 2
SALES (est): 3MM **Privately Held**
SIC: 3537 Trucks: freight, baggage, etc.: industrial, except mining

(G-6411)
PEDRE CORP (PA)
Also Called: Pedre Watch
270 Duffy Ave Ste G (11801-3600)
PHONE..................212 868-2935
Fax: 212 868-3646
R Peter Gunshor, *President*
Jill Kiviat, *Vice Pres*
Cornelia Bourne, *Credit Mgr*
◆ EMP: 20
SQ FT: 10,000
SALES (est): 2.8MM **Privately Held**
WEB: www.pedrewatch.com
SIC: 3873 Watches, clocks, watchcases & parts

(G-6412)
PETRO INC
477 W John St (11801-1029)
PHONE..................516 686-1900
Rodney Roberts, *Branch Mgr*
EMP: 8 **Publicly Held**
SIC: 1389 Oil field services
HQ: Petro, Inc.
  9 W Broad St Ste 3
  Stamford CT 06902
  203 325-5400

(G-6413)
PHOENIX METAL DESIGNS INC
175 Lauman Ln (11801-6548)
PHONE..................516 597-4100
Voula Nikitopoulos, *Chairman*
EMP: 5 EST: 2016
SALES (est): 635.5K **Privately Held**
SIC: 3446 Architectural metalwork

(G-6414)
PIONEER WINDOW HOLDINGS INC (PA)
Also Called: Pioneer Windows Manufacturing
15 Frederick Pl (11801-4205)
PHONE..................516 822-7000
Fax: 516 933-3607
Vincent Amato, *Ch of Bd*
Anthony J Ross, *President*
EMP: 12
SALES (est): 15.1MM **Privately Held**
WEB: www.pwindows.com
SIC: 3442 Storm doors or windows, metal

(G-6415)
PORTA DECOR
290 Duffy Ave Unit 3 (11801-3638)
PHONE..................516 826-6900
Andrew Zaino, *Owner*
Christopher Michaels, *Vice Pres*
▼ EMP: 7
SALES (est): 710.3K **Privately Held**
SIC: 2599 Furniture & fixtures

(G-6416)
REPAPERS CORPORATION (PA)
268 N Broadway Unit 9 (11801-2923)
PHONE..................305 691-1635
Andres Patino, *Principal*
Deisy Bonilla, *Purchasing*
Gregory Frazier, *Manager*
◆ EMP: 14
SALES (est): 5MM **Privately Held**
SIC: 2611 Pulp manufactured from waste or recycled paper

(G-6417)
RUI XING INTERNATIONAL TRDG CO
89 Jerusalem Ave (11801-4950)
PHONE..................516 298-2667
Ke Yi Sun, *Ch of Bd*
Katie Huang, *Manager*
▲ EMP: 5
SALES: 500K **Privately Held**
SIC: 3089 Boxes, plastic

(G-6418)
SAMSON TECHNOLOGIES CORP (HQ)
278 Duffy Ave Unit B (11801-3642)
PHONE..................631 784-2200
Fax: 516 784-2201
Richard Ash, *Ch of Bd*
Scott Goodman, *President*
David Hakim, *General Mgr*
David Ash, *COO*
Douglas Bryant, *Vice Pres*
◆ EMP: 70
SALES (est): 14.4MM
SALES (corp-wide): 274.6MM **Privately Held**
WEB: www.samsontech.com
SIC: 3651 3931 5099 5065 Sound reproducing equipment; musical instruments; musical instruments; sound equipment, electronic
PA: Sam Ash Music Corporation
  278 Duffy Ave Unit A
  Hicksville NY 11801
  516 932-6400

(G-6419)
SCHINDLER ELEVATOR CORPORATION
7 Midland Ave (11801-1509)
PHONE..................516 860-1321
Fax: 516 860-1350
Jim Mistretta, *Project Mgr*
Bob Delaney, *Branch Mgr*
EMP: 58
SALES (corp-wide): 9.5B **Privately Held**
WEB: www.us.schindler.com
SIC: 3534 Elevators & equipment
HQ: Schindler Elevator Corporation
  20 Whippany Rd
  Morristown NJ 07960
  973 397-6500

(G-6420)
SCIARRA LABORATORIES INC
48509 S Broadway (11801)
PHONE..................516 933-7853
Fax: 516 933-7807
John J Sciarra, *President*

Hicksville - Nassau County (G-6421)

Christopher J Sciarra, *Vice Pres*
Neil Brown, *Plant Mgr*
Caroline Laregina, *Office Mgr*
EMP: 6
SALES (est): 1.2MM **Privately Held**
WEB: www.sciarralabs.com
SIC: 2834 Pharmaceutical preparations

(G-6421)
SI PARTNERS INC
15 E Carl St Unit 1 (11801-4290)
PHONE..........................516 433-1415
Amit Singhvi, *President*
Aj Shaah, *Manager*
▲ **EMP:** 8
SALES (est): 930.9K **Privately Held**
SIC: 3355 Aluminum wire & cable

(G-6422)
STS REFILL AMERICA LLC
399 W John St Unit A (11801-1043)
PHONE..........................516 934-8008
Shahar Turgeman,
Mark Freedman,
Uri Hason,
Scott Robert,
▲ **EMP:** 6
SQ FT: 2,500
SALES (est): 501.1K **Privately Held**
WEB: www.stsrefill.com
SIC: 3951 Cartridges, refill: ball point pens

(G-6423)
SUMMIT INSTRUMENT CORP
99 Engineers Dr (11801-6594)
PHONE..........................516 433-0140
Fax: 516 433-0281
Arthur Petschauer, *CEO*
Tom Petschauer, *President*
Stefanie Petschauer, *Corp Secy*
EMP: 8
SQ FT: 7,500
SALES: 750K **Privately Held**
SIC: 3599 Machine shop, jobbing & repair

(G-6424)
SUNQUEST PHARMACEUTICALS INC
385 W John St Ste 1 (11801-1033)
PHONE..........................855 478-6779
Atul Sharma, *President*
EMP: 15
SALES (est): 3.8MM **Privately Held**
SIC: 2834 Pharmaceutical preparations

(G-6425)
TAMPERPROOF SCREW COMPANY INC
30 Laurel St (11801-2641)
PHONE..........................516 931-1616
Fax: 516 931-1654
Lewis Friedman, *President*
George Friedman, *Corp Secy*
Alaina Picitelli, *Vice Pres*
▲ **EMP:** 12
SQ FT: 5,000
SALES: 2.3MM **Privately Held**
WEB: www.tamperproof.com
SIC: 3452 Screws, metal

High Falls
Ulster County

(G-6426)
ALE-TECHNIQUES INC
2452b Lucas Tpke (12440-5920)
PHONE..........................845 687-7200
Daniel Ale, *CEO*
Richard Kodnia, *Vice Pres*
EMP: 15
SQ FT: 35,000
SALES (est): 1.3MM **Privately Held**
SIC: 3545 Machine tool accessories

(G-6427)
DELTA PRESS INC
2426 Lucas Tpke (12440-5920)
PHONE..........................212 989-3445
Fax: 212 989-3668
Joel Sachs, *President*
EMP: 30
SALES (est): 2.5MM **Privately Held**
WEB: www.deltapress.com
SIC: 2752 Commercial printing, offset

(G-6428)
FIELD WARES LLC
Also Called: Field Company
244 Rock Hill Rd (12440-5442)
PHONE..........................508 380-6545
Stephen Muscarella, *Mng Member*
Chris Muscarella,
EMP: 6
SQ FT: 1,000
SALES: 2MM **Privately Held**
SIC: 3321 Cooking utensils, cast iron

(G-6429)
ULSTER COUNTY PRESS OFFICE
Also Called: Blue Stone Press
1209 State Route 213 (12440-5714)
P.O. Box 149, Stone Ridge (12484-0149)
PHONE..........................845 687-4480
Fax: 845 691-1424
Lori Childerss, *President*
Gregory Childress, *Principal*
Rochelle Riservato, *Associate*
EMP: 5
SALES (est): 572.2K **Privately Held**
WEB: www.ulstercountypress.com
SIC: 2711 Newspapers, publishing & printing

Highland
Ulster County

(G-6430)
BORABORA FRUIT JUICES INC
255 Milton (12528-2256)
P.O. Box 383, Pound Ridge (10576-0383)
PHONE..........................845 795-1027
Fax: 914 470-5940
EMP: 8
SQ FT: 10,000
SALES: 1MM **Privately Held**
SIC: 2086 Mfg Bottled/Canned Soft Drinks

(G-6431)
GORDON FIRE EQUIPMENT LLC
3199 Us Highway 9w (12528-2633)
PHONE..........................845 691-5700
Fax: 845 691-8700
Mary Anne Hein, *Mng Member*
EMP: 5
SALES (est): 450K **Privately Held**
SIC: 2899 Fire retardant chemicals

(G-6432)
M M TOOL AND MANUFACTURING
175 Chapel Hill Rd (12528-2105)
PHONE..........................845 691-4140
Fax: 845 691-4911
Matt Mc Cluskey, *President*
Kenneth P Castelo, *Director*
EMP: 8
SQ FT: 10,000
SALES: 1.2MM **Privately Held**
SIC: 3585 Air conditioning equipment, complete; air conditioning units, complete: domestic or industrial

(G-6433)
PHOENIX CABLES CORPORATION
131 Tillson Avenue Ext (12528-1828)
PHONE..........................845 691-6253
Fax: 845 691-7989
Frank Roberto, *President*
Jonathan Heptinstall, *Vice Pres*
Cathy Cassells, *Purch Mgr*
Dorothy Roberto, *Treasurer*
Maritza Crespo, *Accounts Mgr*
EMP: 135
SQ FT: 26,000
SALES (est): 12.6MM **Privately Held**
SIC: 3679 Harness assemblies for electronic use: wire or cable

(G-6434)
PRISM SOLAR TECHNOLOGIES INC (PA)
180 South St (12528-2439)
PHONE..........................845 883-4200
Fax: 845 883-4394
Kevin R Stewart, *CEO*
David Waserstein, *Ch of Bd*
Carolyn Lewandowski, *Corp Secy*
Jeff Rosenberg, *Opers Mgr*
John Neidhardt, *Facilities Mgr*
▲ **EMP:** 38
SQ FT: 93,000
SALES (est): 4.1MM **Privately Held**
SIC: 3433 Solar heaters & collectors

(G-6435)
SELUX CORPORATION
5 Lumen Ln (12528-1903)
P.O. Box 1060 (12528-8060)
PHONE..........................845 691-7723
Fax: 845 691-6749
Felix Groenwaldt, *Ch of Bd*
Peter Stanway, *President*
Thomas Mindt, *Managing Dir*
Mike Seckler, *VP Mfg*
Randy Adams, *Plant Mgr*
▲ **EMP:** 164
SQ FT: 85,000
SALES: 42.5MM
SALES (corp-wide): 1.9MM **Privately Held**
WEB: www.selux.com
SIC: 3646 Commercial indusl & institutional electric lighting fixtures
PA: Selux Benelux Nv
  Grotesteenweg 50
  Kontich 2550

(G-6436)
ZUMTOBEL LIGHTING INC (DH)
3300 Route 9w (12528-2630)
PHONE..........................845 691-6262
Kevin Maddy, *CEO*
Debbie Cohen-Lampitok, *Controller*
Michael J Baudo, *Regl Sales Mgr*
Ed Tessier, *Technology*
▲ **EMP:** 130
SQ FT: 80,000
SALES: 44MM
SALES (corp-wide): 1.4B **Privately Held**
WEB: www.zumtobel.com
SIC: 3646 Commercial indusl & institutional electric lighting fixtures
HQ: Zumtobel Lighting Gmbh
  SchweizerstraBe 30
  Dornbirn 6850
  557 239-00

Highland Falls
Orange County

(G-6437)
SKD TACTICAL INC
291 Main St (10928-1803)
PHONE..........................845 897-2889
Dani Seuk, *CEO*
Joe Seuk, *Vice Pres*
▲ **EMP:** 6 EST: 1999
SALES: 1.5MM **Privately Held**
SIC: 2399 Military insignia, textile

Highland Mills
Orange County

(G-6438)
ALL MERCHANDISE DISPLAY CORP
Also Called: AM Display
4 Pheasant Run (10930-2140)
PHONE..........................718 257-2221
Eddie Minkoff, *President*
Abraham J Minkoff, *Vice Pres*
EMP: 7
SALES (est): 627.8K **Privately Held**
SIC: 2541 Display fixtures, wood

(G-6439)
M &L INDUSTRY OF NY INC
583 State Route 32 Ste 1u (10930-5229)
PHONE..........................845 827-6255
Melech Krauf, *CEO*
Tiffany Vesley, *Office Mgr*
EMP: 9
SALES (est): 770K **Privately Held**
SIC: 2441 Boxes, wood

(G-6440)
SPEYSIDE HOLDINGS LLC
911 State Route 32 (10930-2309)
P.O. Box 1007 (10930-1007)
PHONE..........................845 928-2221
Anthony Williams, *Chairman*
EMP: 25
SALES (est): 855.3K **Privately Held**
SIC: 1442 Construction sand & gravel

Hillburn
Rockland County

(G-6441)
HILLBURN GRANITE COMPANY INC
166 Sixth St (10931-1100)
P.O. Box 832, Tuxedo Park (10987-0832)
PHONE..........................845 357-8900
Leeann Matthews, *Info Tech Mgr*
EMP: 5
SQ FT: 1,000
SALES (est): 259.4K **Privately Held**
SIC: 1411 Dimension stone; granite dimension stone

(G-6442)
MERCO HACKENSACK INC
Also Called: Merco Tape
201 Route 59 Ste D2 (10931-1189)
P.O. Box 875 (10931-0875)
PHONE..........................845 357-3699
David Rose, *President*
Susan Hofmann, *General Mgr*
Adam Riskin, *Vice Pres*
Eleanor Rose, *Sales Staff*
Joshua Rose, *Sales Staff*
◆ **EMP:** 6 EST: 1972
SQ FT: 18,000
SALES: 4.7MM **Privately Held**
WEB: www.maskingtape.com
SIC: 2672 Tape, pressure sensitive: made from purchased materials

Hilton
Monroe County

(G-6443)
CUDDEBACK MACHINING INC
18 Draffin Rd (14468-9708)
PHONE..........................585 392-5889
Fax: 585 392-5888
Lawrence Cuddeback, *President*
Michael Ahl, *Managing Dir*
Sandra Cuddeback, *Admin Sec*
EMP: 7
SQ FT: 4,200
SALES (est): 1.1MM **Privately Held**
WEB: www.cuddebackmachining.com
SIC: 3496 3544 Miscellaneous fabricated wire products; special dies & tools

(G-6444)
MONROE FLUID TECHNOLOGY INC
36 Draffin Rd (14468-9717)
PHONE..........................585 392-3434
Alan Christodaro, *President*
Jeff Cliff, *VP Mfg*
Paul Silloway, *Prdtn Mgr*
Tim Kelley, *Sales Mgr*
Alan Eckard, *Director*
▲ **EMP:** 25
SALES: 10MM **Privately Held**
SIC: 2992 2899 2841 Lubricating oils; cutting oils, blending: made from purchased materials; chemical preparations; soap & other detergents

GEOGRAPHIC SECTION

Holbrook - Suffolk County (G-6471)

(G-6445)
OMEGA CONSOLIDATED CORPORATION
101 Heinz St (14468-1226)
PHONE..................................585 392-9262
Fax: 585 392-4868
Martin Hunte, *President*
Robert Hunte, *Vice Pres*
Thomas Hunte, *Vice Pres*
Linda Kokorotsis, *Manager*
▼ EMP: 20 EST: 1981
SQ FT: 30,000
SALES (est): 3.1MM **Privately Held**
WEB: www.omegacon.com
SIC: 3541 Machine tools, metal cutting type

(G-6446)
RC IMAGING INC
50 Old Hojack Ln (14468-1147)
PHONE..................................585 392-4336
Eric Bostley, *President*
Harry Bostley, *Vice Pres*
Michelle Rose, *Office Mgr*
Kim Manuel, *Manager*
▼ EMP: 9
SQ FT: 7,900
SALES (est): 1.7MM **Privately Held**
WEB: www.rochestercassette.com
SIC: 3844 7699 X-ray apparatus & tubes; X-ray equipment repair

(G-6447)
WILLIAM J RYAN
Also Called: Ryan Printing
1365 Hamlin Parma Townlne (14468-9749)
PHONE..................................585 392-6200
Fax: 585 392-5229
William Ryan, *Owner*
EMP: 5
SQ FT: 3,000
SALES: 200K **Privately Held**
WEB: www.ryanprinting.com
SIC: 2752 7334 2759 Commercial printing, lithographic; photocopying & duplicating services; commercial printing

Himrod
Yates County

(G-6448)
LAPP MANAGEMENT CORP
Also Called: Wood-Tex Products
3700 Route 14 (14842-9802)
PHONE..................................607 243-5141
Barbara Lapp, *President*
EMP: 7
SQ FT: 12,000
SALES (est): 1.2MM **Privately Held**
WEB: www.woodtexproducts.com
SIC: 2452 Prefabricated buildings, wood

(G-6449)
WOOD TEX PRODUCTS LLC
3700 Route 14 (14842-9802)
PHONE..................................607 243-5141
Fax: 607 243-5767
Kent Lapp, *General Mgr*
Travis Beachy, *Exec VP*
Ben Lapp, *Exec VP*
Myron Glick, *Vice Pres*
Amy Coon, *Sales Staff*
EMP: 54
SALES: 7.2MM **Privately Held**
SIC: 2452 Prefabricated wood buildings

Hinsdale
Cattaraugus County

(G-6450)
SIMPLICITY BANDSAW INC
3674 Main St (14743-9817)
PHONE..................................716 557-8805
Norbert J Witzigman, *Principal*
EMP: 8
SALES (est): 796.9K **Privately Held**
SIC: 2421 Sawmills & planing mills, general

Hobart
Delaware County

(G-6451)
HATHERLEIGH COMPANY LTD
62545 State Highway 10 (13788-3019)
PHONE..................................607 538-1092
Frederic Flach, *Ch of Bd*
EMP: 9
SALES: 8.7K **Privately Held**
WEB: www.bodysculptingbible.com
SIC: 2721 7812 Trade journals: publishing only, not printed on site; audio-visual program production

(G-6452)
MALLINCKRODT LLC
Also Called: Mallinckrodt Pharmaceuticals
172 Railroad Ave (13788)
P.O. Box P (13788-0416)
PHONE..................................607 538-9124
Fax: 607 538-2501
Seth Merwin, *Opers Mgr*
Rick West, *Opers Mgr*
Tammi Tully, *Purch Agent*
Paul Dibble, *Engineer*
Carolyn Ehrhart, *Engineer*
EMP: 630 **Privately Held**
WEB: www.mallinckrodt.com
SIC: 2834 Pharmaceutical preparations
HQ: Mallinckrodt Llc
675 Jmes S Mcdonnell Blvd
Hazelwood MO 63042
314 654-2000

Hogansburg
Franklin County

(G-6453)
JACOBS TOBACCO COMPANY
Also Called: Jacobs Manufacturing
344 Frogtown Rd (13655-3137)
PHONE..................................518 358-4948
Roseley Jacobs, *Owner*
Stiifny Codroy, *Accountant*
EMP: 24
SALES (est): 4.4MM **Privately Held**
SIC: 2111 Cigarettes

(G-6454)
OHSERASE MANUFACTURING LLC
393 Frogtown Rd (13655-3138)
PHONE..................................518 358-9309
Justin Tarbell, *Vice Pres*
▲ EMP: 6
SALES (est): 77.3K **Privately Held**
SIC: 3999 Manufacturing industries

Holbrook
Suffolk County

(G-6455)
ACCENT SPEAKER TECHNOLOGY LTD
Also Called: Nola Speaker
1511 Lincoln Ave (11741-2216)
PHONE..................................631 738-2540
Carl Marchisotto, *CEO*
▲ EMP: 7
SALES (est): 1MM **Privately Held**
SIC: 3651 Household audio & video equipment

(G-6456)
ACCURATE INDUSTRIAL MACHINING
1711 Church St (11741-5921)
PHONE..................................631 242-0566
Fax: 631 242-6469
Jerome Bricker, *President*
Marguerite Bricker, *Corp Secy*
▲ EMP: 20
SQ FT: 30,000
SALES (est): 2.7MM **Privately Held**
SIC: 3599 5084 Machine shop, jobbing & repair; industrial machinery & equipment

(G-6457)
ADVANCED DOOR SOLUTIONS INC
Also Called: Advanced Doors
1363 Lincoln Ave Ste 7 (11741-2274)
PHONE..................................631 773-6100
James McGonigle, *President*
EMP: 7
SQ FT: 2,300
SALES: 1MM **Privately Held**
SIC: 3442 7699 1796 1793 Metal doors, sash & trim; lock & key services; lock parts made to individual order; installing building equipment; glass & glazing work; window & door installation & erection

(G-6458)
ADVANCED PLACEMENT LLC
60 Lorraine Ct (11741-1540)
PHONE..................................949 281-9086
Dr Mark Resasco,
EMP: 49 EST: 2016
SQ FT: 2,850
SALES: 6.2MM **Privately Held**
SIC: 3841 Surgical & medical instruments

(G-6459)
ALWAYS BAKED FRESH
331 Dante Ct Ste F (11741-3800)
PHONE..................................631 648-0811
Victoria Kim, *Principal*
EMP: 8 EST: 2009
SALES (est): 432.7K **Privately Held**
SIC: 2051 Cakes, bakery: except frozen

(G-6460)
BNM PRODUCT SERVICE
1561 Lincoln Ave (11741-2217)
PHONE..................................631 750-1586
Sergio Lorenzo, *President*
EMP: 5
SALES (est): 642.3K **Privately Held**
SIC: 3545 Machine tool accessories

(G-6461)
BRYIT GROUP LLC
Also Called: Jentronics
1724 Church St (11741-5918)
PHONE..................................631 563-6603
Fax: 631 563-6509
Larry Boas, *Vice Pres*
Laura Erwig, *Bookkeeper*
Barbara Weiss, *Mng Member*
EMP: 16
SQ FT: 4,000
SALES (est): 1.6MM **Privately Held**
WEB: www.jentronics.com
SIC: 3672 3679 Printed circuit boards; harness assemblies for electronic use: wire or cable

(G-6462)
BRZOZKA INDUSTRIES INC
Also Called: Felber Metal Fabricators
790 Broadway Ave (11741-4906)
PHONE..................................631 588-8164
Waldmar Brazozka, *CEO*
Hans Felber, *President*
EMP: 10
SQ FT: 3,600
SALES (est): 1.5MM **Privately Held**
SIC: 3499 Machine bases, metal

(G-6463)
CALMETRICS INC
1340 Lincoln Ave Ste 6 (11741-2255)
PHONE..................................631 580-2522
Frank Ferrandino, *President*
David Cernese, *Vice Pres*
Justina Kortus, *Manager*
Justina Corpus, *Admin Sec*
EMP: 6
SQ FT: 1,650
SALES (est): 585.6K **Privately Held**
SIC: 3825 Standards & calibrating equipment, laboratory

(G-6464)
CAREFREE KITCHENS INC
925 Lincoln Ave Ste 1 (11741-2200)
PHONE..................................631 567-2120
Leonard Daino, *President*
Carolina Daino, *Vice Pres*
Mike Nikel, *Manager*
EMP: 5
SALES (est): 440K **Privately Held**
SIC: 2434 5031 5211 Wood kitchen cabinets; kitchen cabinets; cabinets, kitchen

(G-6465)
CJN MACHINERY CORP
917 Lincoln Ave Ste 13 (11741-2250)
PHONE..................................631 244-8030
Fax: 631 563-9850
Josephine Chillemi, *President*
Josephine Chllemi, *President*
Vivian Chillemi, *General Mgr*
EMP: 7
SQ FT: 4,000
SALES (est): 2MM **Privately Held**
SIC: 3599 Machine shop, jobbing & repair

(G-6466)
CLEAN ROOM DEPOT INC
1730 Church St (11741-5918)
PHONE..................................631 589-3033
Ken Lorello, *President*
Alexis Lorello, *Vice Pres*
Frank Vandeplanck, *Engineer*
EMP: 10
SQ FT: 3,600
SALES (est): 1MM **Privately Held**
WEB: www.cleanroomdepot.com
SIC: 3822 Auto controls regulating residntl & coml environmt & applncs

(G-6467)
COIL STAMPING INC
1340 Lincoln Ave Ste 1 (11741-2255)
PHONE..................................631 588-3040
Fax: 631 588-8912
Edward Kiss, *President*
EMP: 15
SALES (est): 1.5MM **Privately Held**
WEB: www.coilstamping.com
SIC: 3544 Special dies & tools

(G-6468)
COLORSPEC COATINGS INTL INC
1716 Church St (11741-5918)
P.O. Box 493, Bohemia (11716-0493)
PHONE..................................631 472-8251
Lisa Bancalari, *President*
Robert Pein, *Vice Pres*
Tim Strohsnitter, *Office Mgr*
Bincent Rotondi, *Manager*
▲ EMP: 10
SQ FT: 5,200
SALES (est): 1.4MM **Privately Held**
WEB: www.colorspeccoatings.com
SIC: 2491 Preserving (creosoting) of wood

(G-6469)
CRYSTALIZATIONS SYSTEMS INC
1401 Lincoln Ave (11741-2215)
PHONE..................................631 467-0090
Patricia Ellenwood, *President*
Kim Torregrosa, *Bookkeeper*
Nelson Young, *Admin Sec*
EMP: 15
SQ FT: 12,000
SALES (est): 2.3MM **Privately Held**
SIC: 3499 Fire- or burglary-resistive products

(G-6470)
CTB ENTERPRISE LLC
1170 Lincoln Ave Unit 7 (11741-2286)
PHONE..................................631 563-0088
Tom Passaro, *Mng Member*
Thomas Passaro Jr, *Mng Member*
EMP: 10
SALES (est): 774.2K **Privately Held**
WEB: www.ctbenterprise.com
SIC: 3826 Instruments measuring magnetic & electrical properties

(G-6471)
DATA DISPLAY USA INC
1330 Lincoln Ave Ste 2 (11741-2268)
P.O. Box 5135, Brookings SD (57006-5135)
PHONE..................................631 218-2130
Fax: 631 218-2140
Marie Neville, *CEO*
Kevin Neville, *President*
Staci Shannon, *Sls & Mktg Exec*
Robert Giglio, *Accounts Mgr*
Kathy Lawson, *Manager*

Holbrook - Suffolk County (G-6472)

▲ EMP: 120
SQ FT: 5,000
SALES (est): 14.8MM
SALES (corp-wide): 586.5MM Publicly Held
WEB: www.data-display.com
SIC: 3674 Light emitting diodes
HQ: Daktronics Ireland Co. Limited
Co Clare
Ballymote

(G-6472)
DYNOCOAT INC
1738 Church St (11741-5918)
PHONE....................631 244-9344
Fax: 631 244-9436
Patrick Dimaio, President
Donald Cowdell, Vice Pres
Terry Dimaio, Bookkeeper
Matt Dienna, Director
EMP: 10
SQ FT: 6,500
SALES: 850K Privately Held
WEB: www.dynocoat.com
SIC: 3479 Coating of metals & formed products

(G-6473)
ELECTRONIC SYSTEMS INC
Also Called: Esi
1742 Church St (11741-5918)
PHONE....................631 589-4389
Gregory Quirk, President
EMP: 4 EST: 1997
SALES: 1.2MM Privately Held
SIC: 3571 Electronic computers

(G-6474)
ENCORE REFINING AND RECYCLEING
1120 Lincoln Ave (11741-2260)
PHONE....................631 319-1910
Joseph Crisera, Partner
Robert Gaslindo, Partner
EMP: 9
SALES: 432.3K Privately Held
SIC: 3341 Secondary precious metals

(G-6475)
ENERAC INC
1320 Lincoln Ave Ste 1 (11741-2267)
PHONE....................516 997-1554
Bill Dascal Sr, President
Kurt Makoske, Vice Pres
Russell Drago, Plant Mgr
Fred Dascal, Purch Mgr
Mary Kearney, Financial Exec
EMP: 14
SALES (est): 1.4MM Privately Held
WEB: www.enerac.com
SIC: 3823 3829 Analyzers, industrial process type; measuring & controlling devices

(G-6476)
FLANAGAN ELECTRIC CORP
630 Broadway Ave Ste 7 (11741-4900)
PHONE....................631 567-2976
EMP: 5
SALES (est): 261.7K Privately Held
SIC: 3699 Electrical equipment & supplies

(G-6477)
GEOMETRIC CIRCUITS INC
920 Lincoln Ave Unit 1 (11741-2257)
PHONE....................631 249-0230
Fax: 631 249-0286
John Pollina, President
Kurt J Meyer, Corp Secy
Kathy Whittaker, Manager
EMP: 60
SQ FT: 36,000
SALES (est): 8.4MM Privately Held
WEB: www.geometriccircuits.com
SIC: 3672 Printed circuit boards

(G-6478)
GRAND PRIX LITHO INC
101 Colin Dr Unit 5 (11741-4332)
PHONE....................631 242-4182
Craig Lennon, President
EMP: 25 EST: 1968
SQ FT: 6,000
SALES: 4MM Privately Held
WEB: www.grandprixlitho.com
SIC: 2752 Commercial printing, lithographic

(G-6479)
IMAGE TYPOGRAPHY INC
Also Called: Starfire Printing
751 Coates Ave Ste 31 (11741-6039)
P.O. Box 5250, Miller Place (11764-7901)
PHONE....................631 218-6932
Fax: 631 218-6935
James Bryant, President
EMP: 5 EST: 2001
SALES (est): 450.7K Privately Held
WEB: www.starfireprinting.com
SIC: 2759 Commercial printing

(G-6480)
INGHAM INDUSTRIES INC
Also Called: Authentic Parts
1363 Lincoln Ave Ste 1 (11741-2274)
PHONE....................631 242-2493
Fax: 631 563-5853
Donna Miller, President
EMP: 3
SQ FT: 2,500
SALES: 1MM Privately Held
WEB: www.authelectric.com
SIC: 3699 5065 5251 3429 Chimes, electric; intercommunication equipment, electronic; builders' hardware; manufactured hardware (general)

(G-6481)
INNOVATIVE POWER PRODUCTS INC
1170 Lincoln Ave Unit 7 (11741-2286)
PHONE....................631 563-0088
Thomas Passaro Jr, President
Thomas Dowling, Vice Pres
EMP: 22
SQ FT: 5,200
SALES (est): 3.1MM Privately Held
SIC: 3679 Passive repeaters

(G-6482)
ISLAND COMPONENTS GROUP INC
101 Colin Dr Unit 4 (11741-4332)
PHONE....................631 563-4224
Fax: 631 563-4363
Demetris Agrotis, CEO
Ali Ghanbarian, Vice Pres
Edith Powers, Manager
Fran Close, Admin Asst
EMP: 17
SQ FT: 5,000
SALES: 2MM Privately Held
WEB: www.islandcomponents.com
SIC: 3621 Motors & generators; electric motor & generator parts; electric motor & generator auxillary parts

(G-6483)
JAGS MANUFACTURING NETWORK INC
13403 Lincoln Ave (11741)
PHONE....................631 750-6367
Ubalco Filippetti, CEO
Pat Filippetti, General Mgr
EMP: 6 EST: 2010
SQ FT: 3,200
SALES (est): 618.2K Privately Held
SIC: 3999 Barber & beauty shop equipment

(G-6484)
LATIUM USA TRADING LLC (PA)
Also Called: Four Seasons Buildings Pdts
5005 Veterans Mem Hwy (11741-4506)
PHONE....................631 563-4000
Shaun Kennedy, President
EMP: 70
SALES (est): 43.2MM Privately Held
SIC: 3448 Sunrooms, prefabricated metal

(G-6485)
LAWN ELEMENTS INC
1150 Lincoln Ave Ste 4 (11741-2251)
PHONE....................631 656-9711
Veronica Concilio, Principal
EMP: 10
SALES (est): 1.4MM Privately Held
SIC: 2819 Industrial inorganic chemicals

(G-6486)
LIBERTY LABEL MFG INC
21 Peachtree Ct (11741-4615)
PHONE....................631 737-2365
Fax: 631 737-2366
Mike Fernandez, President
Lawrence Fernandez, Vice Pres
Sandra Iannuzzi, Office Mgr
EMP: 15
SALES (est): 1.8MM Privately Held
WEB: www.libertylabel.com
SIC: 2754 2752 2672 Labels: gravure printing; commercial printing, lithographic; coated & laminated paper

(G-6487)
LONG ISLAND ANALYTICAL LABS
110 Colin Dr (11741-4306)
PHONE....................631 472-3400
Fax: 631 472-8505
Mike Veraldi, President
Domenik Veraldi Jr, Vice Pres
Nancy Fava, Analyst
Micheal Matulock, Assistant
EMP: 18 EST: 1998
SQ FT: 6,000
SALES (est): 3.7MM Privately Held
WEB: www.lialinc.com
SIC: 3822 Auto controls regulating residntl & coml environmt & applncs

(G-6488)
M C PRODUCTS
Also Called: Division of Emergency Services
1330 Lincoln Ave Ste 2 (11741-2268)
P.O. Box 821 (11741-0821)
PHONE....................631 471-4070
Fax: 631 471-4254
William Barnes, President
Joyce Doolin, Sls & Mktg Exec
Jennifer Riccobono, Office Mgr
James Krogh, Info Tech Mgr
Steve Walter, Director
EMP: 25
SALES (est): 4.5MM Privately Held
WEB: www.mcproducts.com
SIC: 3674 Semiconductors & related devices

(G-6489)
MACHINE TOOL REPAIR & SALES
1537 Lincoln Ave (11741-2263)
PHONE....................631 580-2550
Michael Cohen, President
EMP: 5
SALES: 1MM Privately Held
WEB: www.machineryselection.com
SIC: 3569 Assembly machines, non-metalworking

(G-6490)
MARKETPLACE SLUTIONS GROUP LLC
48 Nimbus Rd Ste 303 (11741-4417)
PHONE....................631 868-0111
Paul Pensabene, Mng Member
EMP: 25
SQ FT: 30,000
SALES: 4MM Privately Held
SIC: 2032 8742 8748 Italian foods: packaged in cans, jars, etc.; management consulting services; business consulting

(G-6491)
METALS BUILDING PRODUCTS
5005 Veterans Mem Hwy (11741-4506)
PHONE....................844 638-2527
Shaun Kennedy, President
EMP: 44
SALES (est): 7.3MM
SALES (corp-wide): 43.2MM Privately Held
SIC: 3448 Prefabricated metal buildings
PA: Latium Usa Trading Llc
5005 Veterans Mem Hwy
Holbrook NY 11741
631 563-4000

(G-6492)
METALSMITH INC
1340 Lincoln Ave Ste 13 (11741-2255)
PHONE....................631 467-1500
Fax: 631 467-1504
Jeff Smith, President
EMP: 5
SQ FT: 3,500
SALES (est): 420K Privately Held
SIC: 3444 Sheet metalwork

(G-6493)
NATURES BOUNTY CO
4320 Veterans Mem Hwy (11741-4501)
PHONE....................631 588-3492
Albert Anastafi, Manager
EMP: 19 Publicly Held
SIC: 2833 Vitamins, natural or synthetic: bulk, uncompounded
HQ: The Nature's Bounty Co
2100 Smithtown Ave
Ronkonkoma NY 11779
631 200-2000

(G-6494)
OMICRON TECHNOLOGIES INC
1736 Church St (11741-5918)
PHONE....................631 434-7697
Fax: 631 434-7699
Bob Levine, President
John Kennedy, Vice Pres
EMP: 20
SALES (est): 901.2K Privately Held
SIC: 3999 Manufacturing industries

(G-6495)
PERCEPTION IMAGING INC
90 Colin Dr Unit 11 (11741-4333)
PHONE....................631 676-5262
Jeanine A Segall, President
Douglas Segall, Exec VP
EMP: 10
SQ FT: 5,000
SALES: 2MM Privately Held
SIC: 2752 7311 7331 Commercial printing, offset; advertising agencies; direct mail advertising services

(G-6496)
READ MANUFACTURING COMPANY INC
330 Dante Ct (11741-3845)
PHONE....................631 567-4487
Fax: 631 580-4830
Ronald H Read Sr, CEO
Heather Read-Connor, President
Joanne Gacho, Controller
EMP: 21
SQ FT: 10,000
SALES: 2.6MM Privately Held
WEB: www.readmfg.com
SIC: 3444 3479 Sheet metalwork; painting, coating & hot dipping

(G-6497)
ROADIE PRODUCTS INC
Also Called: Hybrid Cases
1121 Lincoln Ave Unit 20 (11741-2264)
P.O. Box 98, Oakdale (11769-0098)
PHONE....................631 567-8588
Frank Maiella, President
Jennifer Moran, Manager
▲ EMP: 25
SQ FT: 15,000
SALES (est): 4.7MM Privately Held
WEB: www.islandcases.com
SIC: 3161 3171 Musical instrument cases; handbags, women's

(G-6498)
RV PRINTING
39 Portside Dr (11741-5814)
PHONE....................631 567-8658
Robert Viola, Owner
EMP: 7
SALES: 1.4MM Privately Held
SIC: 2752 Commercial printing, lithographic

(G-6499)
SELECT-A-FORM INC
4717 Veterans Mem Hwy (11741-4515)
PHONE....................631 981-3076
Fax: 631 981-3073
Dave Walters, President
John Candia, Vice Pres
Gwen Little, Office Mgr
EMP: 52
SQ FT: 17,000

SALES (est): 4.2MM Privately Held
SIC: 2759 2761 2752 Business forms: printing; manifold business forms; color lithography

(G-6500)
SOLAR METROLOGY LLC
1340 Lincoln Ave Ste 6 (11741-2255)
PHONE..................................845 247-4701
Francis Reilly,
EMP: 9
SALES (est): 640.8K Privately Held
SIC: 3823 Industrial instrmnts msrmnt display/control process variable

(G-6501)
SPEEDCARD INC
Also Called: B C T
133 Glenmere Way (11741-5013)
PHONE..................................631 472-1904
Jeffery Lewis, President
Sharon Lewis, Manager
EMP: 8
SQ FT: 3,000
SALES: 320K Privately Held
WEB: www.speedcard.com
SIC: 2752 Commercial printing, lithographic

(G-6502)
SUMMIT TECHNOLOGIES LLC
Also Called: Summit Laser Products
723 Broadway Ave (11741-4955)
PHONE..................................631 590-1040
Steven Hecht, Mng Member
Mike Kosiah,
▲ EMP: 38
SQ FT: 25,300
SALES (est): 3.7MM Privately Held
WEB: www.uninetimaging.com
SIC: 3955 Print cartridges for laser & other computer printers
PA: Uninet Imaging, Inc.
   3232 W El Segundo Blvd
   Hawthorne CA 90250

(G-6503)
SUPERIOR WELDING
331 Dante Ct Ste G (11741-3800)
PHONE..................................631 676-2751
Steve Takats, Executive
EMP: 7
SALES (est): 802.6K Privately Held
SIC: 3599 Machine shop, jobbing & repair

(G-6504)
SYMBOL TECHNOLOGIES LLC
25 Andrea Rd (11741-4310)
PHONE..................................631 218-3907
James Rawson, Manager
EMP: 16
SALES (corp-wide): 3.5B Publicly Held
WEB: www.symbol.com
SIC: 3577 Magnetic ink & optical scanning devices
HQ: Symbol Technologies, Llc
   1 Zebra Plz
   Holtsville NY 11742
   631 737-6851

(G-6505)
TENS MACHINE COMPANY INC
800 Grundy Ave (11741-2606)
PHONE..................................631 981-3321
Fax: 631 981-3372
Toni Coffaro, President
Fabio Berlingieri, Vice Pres
Mike Berlingieri, Vice Pres
Salvatore Berlingieri, Vice Pres
Diane Terrell, Purchasing
EMP: 28
SQ FT: 9,620
SALES: 5.5MM Privately Held
WEB: www.tensmachine.com
SIC: 3728 Aircraft parts & equipment

(G-6506)
UNISOURCE FOOD EQP SYSTEMS INC
1505 Lincoln Ave (11741-2216)
PHONE..................................516 681-0537
Ronald Mondello, President
Rita Tenaglia, Manager
▲ EMP: 9

SALES (est): 896.7K Privately Held
SIC: 3556 2499 Bakery machinery; bakers' equipment, wood

Holland
Erie County

(G-6507)
BUFFALO POLYMER PROCESSORS INC
42 Edgewood Dr (14080-9784)
PHONE..................................716 537-3153
Miro O Staroba, Ch of Bd
Barbara Staroba, Manager
EMP: 40
SQ FT: 180,000
SALES (est): 7.8MM Privately Held
SIC: 3089 Plastic processing

(G-6508)
INEX INC
9229 Olean Rd (14080-9773)
PHONE..................................716 537-2270
Fax: 716 537-3218
Michael Kasprzyk, President
Curt Colopy, Vice Pres
EMP: 9
SALES (est): 1.6MM Privately Held
WEB: www.schunk-inex.com
SIC: 3443 Heat exchangers, plate type

(G-6509)
MULLICAN FLOORING LP
209 Vermont St (14080-9735)
P.O. Box 342 (14080-0342)
PHONE..................................716 537-2642
Rick Tyburski, Manager
EMP: 45
SALES (corp-wide): 300.9MM Privately Held
WEB: www.mullicanlumberco.com
SIC: 2426 Flooring, hardwood
HQ: Mullican Flooring, L.P.
   655 Woodlyn Rd
   Johnson City TN 37601
   423 262-8440

(G-6510)
PRO-TECK COATING INC
7785 Olean Rd (14080-9709)
P.O. Box 372 (14080-0372)
PHONE..................................716 537-2619
Fax: 716 537-2083
Wayne Rutkowski Sr, President
Jeff Weber, Vice Pres
EMP: 13
SQ FT: 22,000
SALES (est): 1MM Privately Held
WEB: www.proteckcoating.com
SIC: 3479 Coating of metals with plastic or resins

(G-6511)
STAROBA PLASTICS INC
42 Edgewood Dr (14080-9784)
PHONE..................................716 537-3153
Fax: 716 537-9536
Miro Staroba, CEO
Barbara Staroba, Vice Pres
Ed Staroba, Manager
EMP: 125
SALES (est): 17.9MM Privately Held
SIC: 3089 Injection molding of plastics

(G-6512)
UHMAC INC
136 N Main St (14080-9704)
PHONE..................................716 537-2343
Fax: 716 537-2955
James McBride, President
Rhonda B Juhasz, Corp Secy
EMP: 10
SQ FT: 9,973
SALES (est): 1.6MM Privately Held
WEB: www.uhmac.com
SIC: 3542 Rebuilt machine tools, metal forming types

Holland Patent
Oneida County

(G-6513)
CUSTOM KLEAN CORP
Also Called: Pressure Washer Sales
8890 Boak Rd E (13354-3608)
PHONE..................................315 865-8101
Fax: 315 865-8101
Paul Sears, President
EMP: 15
SQ FT: 30,000
SALES (est): 1.8MM Privately Held
WEB: www.pressurewashersales.com
SIC: 3589 7363 High pressure cleaning equipment; domestic help service

(G-6514)
STEFFEN PUBLISHING INC
Also Called: Adirondack Home News
9584 Main St (13354-3819)
P.O. Box 403 (13354-0403)
PHONE..................................315 865-4100
Fax: 315 865-4000
Sally M Steffen, President
Preston P Steffen Jr, Publisher
G Mann, Division Mgr
Jack Behrens, Manager
Pam Kulig, Manager
EMP: 100
SQ FT: 20,000
SALES (est): 4.4MM Privately Held
SIC: 2711 2752 2732 2731 Newspapers: publishing only, not printed on site; commercial printing, lithographic; book printing; book publishing; periodicals

Holley
Orleans County

(G-6515)
AMY PAK PUBLISHING INC
3997 Roosevelt Hwy (14470-9201)
PHONE..................................585 964-8188
Amy Pak, Principal
EMP: 9
SALES (est): 784.5K Privately Held
SIC: 2741 Miscellaneous publishing

(G-6516)
ORLEANS CUSTOM PACKING INC
101 Cadbury Way (14470-1079)
PHONE..................................585 314-8227
Donald Ward, Ch of Bd
EMP: 6
SALES (est): 622.4K Privately Held
SIC: 2011 Meat packing plants

(G-6517)
PRECISION PACKAGING PDTS INC
88 Nesbitt Dr (14470-1078)
PHONE..................................585 638-8200
Fax: 585 638-4600
Michael Evans, CEO
Mike Bankes, Plant Mgr
Kerry Kyle, Plant Mgr
Kenneth Knopick, Warehouse Mgr
Greg Piedmonte, Purch Mgr
▲ EMP: 110
SQ FT: 68,000
SALES (est): 9.5MM
SALES (corp-wide): 13.2B Publicly Held
WEB: www.prepackpro.com
SIC: 3081 Packing materials, plastic sheet
PA: Newell Brands Inc.
   221 River St
   Hoboken NJ 07030
   201 610-6600

(G-6518)
SEAWARD CANDIES
3588 N Main Street Rd (14470-9305)
PHONE..................................585 638-6761
Donna Seaward,
EMP: 6
SALES: 75K Privately Held
SIC: 2064 5441 Candy & other confectionery products; candy

(G-6519)
WADDINGTON NORTH AMERICA INC
Also Called: Wna Holley
88 Nesbitt Dr (14470-1078)
PHONE..................................585 638-8200
EMP: 11
SALES (corp-wide): 13.2B Publicly Held
SIC: 3089 Plastic kitchenware, tableware & houseware; plastic processing
HQ: Waddington North America, Inc
   50 E Rivercenter Blvd # 650
   Covington KY 41011
   859 292-8028

Hollis
Queens County

(G-6520)
BORDEN & RILEY PAPER CO INC
18410 Jamaica Ave Ste W3 (11423-2434)
PHONE..................................718 454-9494
Fax: 718 454-0791
Zoila P Woodward, President
Juan Guerra, Vice Pres
▲ EMP: 25
SQ FT: 31,500
SALES (est): 5.3MM Privately Held
WEB: www.bordenandriley.com
SIC: 2675 Die-cut paper & board

(G-6521)
CHINA RUITAI INTL HOLDINGS LTD
8710 Clover Pl (11423-1252)
PHONE..................................718 740-2278
James Herbst, Principal
EMP: 3
SALES: 43.1MM Privately Held
SIC: 2869 Industrial organic chemicals

(G-6522)
CRUMBRUBBER TECHNOLOGY INC
18740 Hollis Ave (11423-2808)
PHONE..................................718 468-3988
Angelo Reali, President
Michael Reali, Vice Pres
EMP: 10
SQ FT: 60,000
SALES: 5MM Privately Held
SIC: 3559 4953 Recycling machinery; recycling, waste materials

(G-6523)
G & J RDYMX & MASNRY SUP INC
18330 Jamaica Ave (11423-2302)
PHONE..................................718 454-0800
John Cervoni, President
John Cerzoni, President
Mark Blankson, Office Mgr
EMP: 12
SQ FT: 80,000
SALES (est): 1.2MM Privately Held
SIC: 3273 Ready-mixed concrete

(G-6524)
NEW ATLANTIC READY MIX CORP
18330 Jamaica Ave (11423-2302)
PHONE..................................718 812-0739
John Cervoni, President
EMP: 7
SALES (est): 1MM Privately Held
SIC: 3273 Ready-mixed concrete

Holtsville
Suffolk County

(G-6525)
ADVANCE PHARMACEUTICAL INC (PA)
895 Waverly Ave (11742-1109)
PHONE..................................631 981-4600
Fax: 631 981-4112
Tasrin Hossain, President
Liaquat Hossain, Exec VP

Holtsville - Suffolk County (G-6526)

EMP: 30
SQ FT: 80,000
SALES: 9MM **Privately Held**
SIC: 2834 Pharmaceutical preparations

(G-6526)
BROOKHAVEN INSTRUMENTS CORP
750 Blue Point Rd (11742-1896)
PHONE.................................631 758-3200
Fax: 631 758-3255
Walther Tscharnuter, *CEO*
Joe Pozzolano, *Ch of Bd*
Bruce Weiner, *President*
Eric Farrell, *General Mgr*
Scott Lee, *Sales Engr*
EMP: 24
SQ FT: 15,000
SALES (est): 5MM **Privately Held**
WEB: www.bic.com
SIC: 3826 Analytical instruments

(G-6527)
C & H PRECISION TOOLS INC
194 Morris Ave Ste 20 (11742-1451)
PHONE.................................631 758-3806
Fax: 631 758-3539
Donald Schwabe, *President*
EMP: 20
SALES (est): 1.9MM **Privately Held**
SIC: 3469 Metal stampings

(G-6528)
CUTTING EDGE METAL WORKS
12 Long Island Ave (11742-1803)
PHONE.................................631 981-8333
Tom Richards, *Owner*
Lou Tancredi, *Vice Pres*
EMP: 24
SALES: 3.1MM **Privately Held**
SIC: 3444 Sheet metalwork

(G-6529)
KOEHLER INSTRUMENT COMPANY INC
85 Corporate Dr (11742-2007)
PHONE.................................631 589-3800
Fax: 631 589-3815
Roy Westerhaus, *Ch of Bd*
Rene Nack, *Purch Mgr*
Chris Koenig, *Engineer*
Peter Brey, *Treasurer*
Donna Tabano, *Human Res Dir*
▲ EMP: 55
SQ FT: 28,500
SALES (est): 18.3MM **Privately Held**
WEB: www.koehlerinstrument.com
SIC: 3823 Industrial instrmnts msrmnt display/control process variable

(G-6530)
METAVAC LLC
4000 Point St (11742-2008)
PHONE.................................631 207-2344
Fax: 631 447-7715
Samuel E Fox, *Controller*
Richard Vinkiewicz, *Manager*
Michael J Kessler,
Robert Longo,
EMP: 46
SQ FT: 33,000
SALES (est): 7.2MM
SALES (corp-wide): 18.2B **Publicly Held**
WEB: www.medavac.com
SIC: 3827 Optical elements & assemblies, except ophthalmic
HQ: Fisher Scientific International Llc
81 Wyman St
Waltham MA 02451
781 622-1000

(G-6531)
OASIS COSMETIC LABS INC
182 Long Island Ave (11742-1815)
PHONE.................................631 758-0038
Thomas Murray, *CEO*
EMP: 12
SALES (est): 1.2MM **Privately Held**
SIC: 2844 Cosmetic preparations

(G-6532)
PAVCO ASPHALT INC
615 Furrows Rd (11742-2001)
PHONE.................................631 289-3223
Ronald Marone, *President*
Ronald Fehr, *Treasurer*
Sally Marone, *Admin Sec*
EMP: 20
SQ FT: 2,000
SALES (est): 2.3MM **Privately Held**
SIC: 2951 1611 Asphalt paving mixtures & blocks; highway & street paving contractor

(G-6533)
PRIMA ASPHALT AND CONCRETE
615 Furrows Rd (11742-2099)
PHONE.................................631 289-3223
Fax: 631 758-3958
William Fehr, *Vice Pres*
Ronald Fehr, *Treasurer*
Kathy Stanley, *Controller*
Sally Marone, *Admin Sec*
EMP: 11
SQ FT: 2,000
SALES (est): 3.3MM **Privately Held**
SIC: 2951 Asphalt paving mixtures & blocks

(G-6534)
SCREEN THE WORLD INC
Also Called: Crazy Hatter
658 Blue Point Rd (11742-1848)
PHONE.................................631 475-0023
Jeff Liebowitz, *President*
Jeffery Leibowitz, *Sr Corp Ofcr*
EMP: 12
SQ FT: 5,000
SALES (est): 1.5MM **Privately Held**
WEB: www.crazyhatter.com
SIC: 2759 2395 Screen printing; art needlework: made from purchased materials

(G-6535)
STARFIRE PRINTING INC
28 Washington Ave (11742-1027)
PHONE.................................631 736-1495
EMP: 5
SALES (est): 230K **Privately Held**
SIC: 2759 Commercial Printing

(G-6536)
SYMBOL TECHNOLOGIES LLC (HQ)
Also Called: Symbol Technologies Delaware
1 Zebra Plz (11742-1300)
PHONE.................................631 737-6851
Fax: 631 738-3824
Edward Fitzpatrick, *CEO*
Paul Kiernen, *Principal*
James M Conboy, *Vice Pres*
Timothy T Yates, *CFO*
Cary Schmiedel, *Treasurer*
▲ EMP: 1800 EST: 1987
SQ FT: 299,000
SALES (est): 1.8B
SALES (corp-wide): 3.5B **Publicly Held**
WEB: www.symbol.com
SIC: 3577 Optical scanning devices
PA: Zebra Technologies Corporation
3 Overlook Pt
Lincolnshire IL 60069
847 634-6700

(G-6537)
SYMBOL TECHNOLOGIES LLC
1 Zebra Plz (11742-1300)
PHONE.................................631 738-3346
EMP: 5
SALES (corp-wide): 3.5B **Publicly Held**
SIC: 3577 Magnetic ink & optical scanning devices
HQ: Symbol Technologies, Llc
1 Zebra Plz
Holtsville NY 11742
631 737-6851

(G-6538)
TANGRAM COMPANY LLC
125 Corporate Dr (11742-2007)
PHONE.................................631 758-0460
Sheila Mandl, *Manager*
Philip Gillette,
John Takakjian,
▼ EMP: 25
SQ FT: 32,000
SALES: 6.4MM **Privately Held**
WEB: www.tangramco.com
SIC: 2819 2899 Industrial inorganic chemicals; chemical preparations

(G-6539)
TELXON CORPORATION (DH)
1 Zebra Plz (11742-1300)
PHONE.................................631 738-2400
John W Paxton, *Ch of Bd*
Kenneth A Cassady, *President*
David H Briggs, *Vice Pres*
Laurel Meissner, *Vice Pres*
Woody M McGee, *CFO*
▲ EMP: 35
SALES (est): 76.2MM
SALES (corp-wide): 3.5B **Publicly Held**
WEB: www.telxon.com
SIC: 3571 7373 3663 Personal computers (microcomputers); systems integration services; radio & TV communications equipment
HQ: Symbol Technologies, Llc
1 Zebra Plz
Holtsville NY 11742
631 737-6851

(G-6540)
TOPAZ INDUSTRIES INC
130 Corporate Dr (11742-2005)
PHONE.................................631 207-0700
Fax: 631 207-0705
Craig Stowell, *President*
▲ EMP: 10
SQ FT: 3,000
SALES (est): 2MM **Privately Held**
SIC: 2899 Salt

(G-6541)
WEISS INSTRUMENTS INC
905 Waverly Ave (11742-1109)
PHONE.................................631 207-1200
Fax: 631 207-0900
William Weiss, *CEO*
John Weiss, *President*
Andrea Rocco, *Editor*
Phillip J Weiss, *Chairman*
John A Carnival, *Vice Pres*
▲ EMP: 100 EST: 1882
SQ FT: 50,000
SALES (est): 25.6MM **Privately Held**
WEB: www.weissinstruments.com
SIC: 3823 3829 Temperature instruments: industrial process type; pressure gauges, dial & digital; measuring & controlling devices

(G-6542)
ZEBRA TECHNOLOGIES ENTP CORP
1 Zebra Plz (11742-1325)
PHONE.................................800 722-6234
Anders Gustafsson, *CEO*
Alan Berni, *Engineer*
Kenneth Rivalsi, *Engineer*
Ming Sun, *Senior Engr*
Michael Smiley, *CFO*
EMP: 39
SALES (est): 23MM
SALES (corp-wide): 3.5B **Publicly Held**
SIC: 3577 1541 5088 Computer peripheral equipment; prefabricated building erection, industrial; transportation equipment & supplies
PA: Zebra Technologies Corporation
3 Overlook Pt
Lincolnshire IL 60069
847 634-6700

Homer
Cortland County

(G-6543)
ALBANY INTERNATIONAL CORP
156 S Main St (13077-1600)
PHONE.................................607 749-7226
Fax: 607 749-7216
Tim Stevens, *Safety Mgr*
Gary R Seales, *Manager*
Jay Jandris, *Associate*
EMP: 115
SALES (corp-wide): 779.8MM **Publicly Held**
WEB: www.albint.com
SIC: 2298 3089 2284 Cordage & twine; extruded finished plastic products; thread mills
PA: Albany International Corp.
216 Airport Dr
Rochester NH 03867
603 330-5850

(G-6544)
DEWEY MACHINE & TOOL INC
49 James St (13077-1221)
PHONE.................................607 749-3930
Chris Dewey, *President*
Sandra Dewey, *Vice Pres*
EMP: 6
SQ FT: 2,000
SALES (est): 864.4K **Privately Held**
SIC: 3599 Machine shop, jobbing & repair

(G-6545)
F M L INDUSTRIES INC
10 Hudson St (13077-1043)
P.O. Box 398 (13077-0398)
PHONE.................................607 749-7273
Fax: 607 749-7520
Paul Dries, *President*
Paul Drief, *Manager*
EMP: 9
SQ FT: 12,000
SALES (est): 1.2MM **Privately Held**
SIC: 7692 3444 3599 Welding repair; sheet metalwork; machine shop, jobbing & repair

(G-6546)
HASKELL MACHINE & TOOL INC
5 S Fulton St (13077-1232)
PHONE.................................607 749-2421
Fax: 607 749-7386
James E Harris, *President*
Roberta J Harris, *Vice Pres*
EMP: 10 EST: 1947
SQ FT: 7,000
SALES (est): 1.2MM **Privately Held**
WEB: www.haskellmachine.com
SIC: 3599 7692 Machine shop, jobbing & repair; welding repair

(G-6547)
HOMER IRON WORKS LLC
5130 Us Route 11 (13077-9528)
PHONE.................................607 749-3963
Dan Gustasson, *General Mgr*
Mike Park,
EMP: 7
SQ FT: 2,100
SALES: 700K **Privately Held**
SIC: 3441 7692 7538 Fabricated structural metal; welding repair; general automotive repair shops

(G-6548)
HOMER LOGGING CONTRACTOR
6176 Sunnyside Dr (13077-9321)
PHONE.................................607 753-8553
Steve Hubbard, *Principal*
EMP: 5
SALES (est): 339.5K **Privately Held**
SIC: 2411 Logging camps & contractors

(G-6549)
PHOTON VISION SYSTEMS INC (PA)
1 Technology Pl (13077-1526)
PHONE.................................607 749-2689
Thomas L Vogelsong, *President*
Jeffrey J Zarnowski, *COO*
EMP: 15 EST: 1997
SALES (est): 1.6MM **Privately Held**
SIC: 3571 Electronic computers

(G-6550)
SOLIDUS INDUSTRIES INC
Also Called: Pb Industries
6849 N Glen Haven Rd (13077-9522)
PHONE.................................607 749-4540
Frank Girardi, *President*
Steve Tak, *Opers Mgr*
Chris Figures, *Controller*
EMP: 96
SQ FT: 28,000
SALES (est): 13MM **Privately Held**
WEB: www.pb-industries.com
SIC: 3444 3469 3479 2396 Sheet metalwork; machine parts, stamped or pressed metal; coating of metals & formed products; automotive & apparel trimmings

▲ = Import ▼ = Export
◆ = Import/Export

Honeoye
Ontario County

(G-6551)
CY PLASTICS WORKS INC
8601 Main St (14471-9603)
P.O. Box 560 (14471-0560)
PHONE.................585 229-2555
Fax: 585 229-5520
Andy Molodetz, *President*
Edgar White, *Prdtn Mgr*
Eric Kunisch, *QC Mgr*
Julie Molodetz, *Controller*
Stephen Craine, *Sales Mgr*
▲ EMP: 40
SQ FT: 35,000
SALES (est): 9.9MM **Privately Held**
SIC: 3089 3544 3842 3949 Injection molding of plastics; special dies, tools, jigs & fixtures; industrial molds; surgical appliances & supplies; sporting & athletic goods

(G-6552)
ROOME TECHNOLOGIES INC
4796 Honeoye Business Par (14471-8808)
P.O. Box 742 (14471-0742)
PHONE.................585 229-4437
David Roome, *President*
EMP: 7
SQ FT: 8,500
SALES: 2MM **Privately Held**
WEB: www.roometechnologies.com
SIC: 3564 Filters, air: furnaces, air conditioning equipment, etc.

Honeoye Falls
Monroe County

(G-6553)
BRANSON ULTRASONICS CORP
475 Quaker Meeting Hse Rd (14472-9754)
PHONE.................585 624-8000
Fax: 585 359-1189
Nancy Parmeter, *Opers Staff*
Ken Nelson, *Project Engr*
Craig Birrittella, *Manager*
Scott Latona, *Manager*
Paul Rooney, *Manager*
EMP: 20
SQ FT: 78,580
SALES (corp-wide): 14.5B **Publicly Held**
WEB: www.bransonic.com
SIC: 3699 Welding machines & equipment, ultrasonic
HQ: Branson Ultrasonics Corporation
41 Eagle Rd Ste 1
Danbury CT 06810
203 796-0400

(G-6554)
CUSTOM BREWCRAFTERS INC
300 Village Square Blvd (14472-1180)
PHONE.................585 624-4386
Fax: 585 624-5756
Walter Alcorn, *President*
EMP: 12 EST: 1997
SQ FT: 4,800
SALES (est): 1.7MM **Privately Held**
WEB: www.custombrewcrafters.com
SIC: 2082 Malt beverages

(G-6555)
EQUICENTER INC
3247 Rush Mendon Rd (14472-9333)
PHONE.................585 742-2522
Jonathan Friedlander, *President*
EMP: 30
SALES: 622.2K **Privately Held**
SIC: 3199 Equestrian related leather articles

(G-6556)
GRAVER TECHNOLOGIES LLC
300 W Main St (14472-1197)
PHONE.................585 624-1330
Herbert J Ego, *General Mgr*
Bob Simpson, *Plant Mgr*
Jack Schultz, *Mfg Staff*
Virginia Marble, *Production*
Gary Clements, *Purch Mgr*
EMP: 40
SQ FT: 34,000
SALES (est): 9.4MM
SALES (corp-wide): 223.6B **Publicly Held**
SIC: 3569 Filters, general line: industrial
HQ: Graver Technologies Llc
200 Lake Dr
Newark DE 19702

(G-6557)
HANSON AGGREGATES PA LLC
2049 County Rd 6 (14472)
PHONE.................585 624-3800
Bob Lange, *Sales Staff*
Douglas Fuess, *Manager*
Larry Clark, *Manager*
EMP: 35
SALES (corp-wide): 16B **Privately Held**
SIC: 2951 1442 5032 Asphalt & asphaltic paving mixtures (not from refineries); gravel mining; brick, stone & related material
HQ: Hanson Aggregates Pennsylvania, Llc
7660 Imperial Way
Allentown PA 18195
610 366-4626

(G-6558)
HANSON AGGREGATES PA LLC
2049 Honeoye Falls 6 Rd (14472-8913)
P.O. Box 151 (14472-0151)
PHONE.................585 624-1220
Mike Clark, *Branch Mgr*
Larry Clark, *Manager*
EMP: 30
SALES (corp-wide): 16B **Privately Held**
SIC: 1442 5999 1422 5032 Gravel mining; stones, crystalline: rough; crushed & broken limestone; asphalt mixture
HQ: Hanson Aggregates Pennsylvania, Llc
7660 Imperial Way
Allentown PA 18195
610 366-4626

(G-6559)
HONEOYE FALLS DISTILLERY LLC (PA)
168 W Main St (14472-1135)
PHONE.................201 780-4618
Scott M Stanton, *Mng Member*
John D Marshall,
Robert Teal Schlegel,
EMP: 10 EST: 2014
SQ FT: 7,000
SALES: 200K **Privately Held**
SIC: 2085 Applejack (alcoholic beverage)

(G-6560)
K & H PRECISION PRODUCTS INC
45 Norton St (14472-1032)
PHONE.................585 624-4894
Fax: 585 624-1553
Steven Hogarth, *President*
Alex Ferguson, *Vice Pres*
George Reeners, *CFO*
Colin Hogarth, *Manager*
Rachel Roblee, *Manager*
EMP: 40
SQ FT: 20,000
SALES (est): 8.1MM **Privately Held**
WEB: www.kandhprecision.com
SIC: 3543 3089 3599 3544 Industrial patterns; injection molded finished plastic products; machine shop, jobbing & repair; special dies, tools, jigs & fixtures; nonferrous foundries

(G-6561)
KADDIS MANUFACTURING CORP
Enerco Plant
1175 Bragg St (14472-8602)
P.O. Box 92985, Rochester (14692-9085)
PHONE.................585 624-3070
Bruce Whitmore, *Manager*
Robert Dardenne, *Supervisor*
EMP: 8
SALES (corp-wide): 11.2MM **Privately Held**
WEB: www.kaddis.com
SIC: 3451 3621 3568 Screw machine products; motors & generators; power transmission equipment
PA: Kaddis Manufacturing Corp.
293 Patriot Way
Rochester NY 14624
585 464-9000

(G-6562)
MICROPEN TECHNOLOGIES CORP
Also Called: MICROPEN DIVISION
93 Papermill St (14472-1252)
PHONE.................585 624-2610
Fax: 585 624-2692
Edwin P Petrazzolo, *CEO*
William Grande, *Vice Pres*
Eric Van Wormer, *Vice Pres*
Eric Wormer, *Vice Pres*
Leigh Barry, *Purchasing*
▼ EMP: 75
SQ FT: 38,000
SALES: 11.4MM **Privately Held**
WEB: www.ohmcraft.com
SIC: 3625 3676 Resistors & resistor units; electronic resistors

(G-6563)
RUSH GRAVEL CORP
130 Kavanaugh Rd (14472-9599)
PHONE.................585 533-1740
Marie Schillinger, *Treasurer*
David Schillinger Jr, *Shareholder*
Timothy Schillinger, *Shareholder*
EMP: 8
SALES (est): 770K **Privately Held**
WEB: www.rushgravel.com
SIC: 1442 Sand mining; gravel mining

(G-6564)
SOUTHCO INC
Honeoye Falls Div
250 East St (14472-1298)
PHONE.................585 624-2545
Fax: 585 624-4635
Eric Cook, *Engineer*
Matt Frame, *Engineer*
Terry Graham, *Engineer*
David Milne, *Engineer*
Joseph Werner, *Engineer*
EMP: 400
SQ FT: 40,000
SALES (corp-wide): 745.4MM **Privately Held**
WEB: www.southco.com
SIC: 3429 3452 Metal fasteners; bolts, nuts, rivets & washers
HQ: Southco, Inc.
210 N Brinton Lake Rd
Concordville PA 19331
610 459-4000

(G-6565)
STEVER-LOCKE INDUSTRIES INC
Also Called: Metal Stampings
179 N Main St (14472-1056)
PHONE.................585 624-3450
Fax: 585 624-3146
Elaine R Davin, *President*
Bruce Rose, *Design Engr*
▲ EMP: 9
SQ FT: 33,000
SALES (est): 6.9MM **Privately Held**
WEB: www.steverlocke.com
SIC: 3469 3672 3643 Metal stampings; wiring boards; current-carrying wiring devices

Hoosick Falls
Rensselaer County

(G-6566)
GRAPHITEK INC
4883 State Route 67 (12090-4829)
PHONE.................518 686-5966
Al Randle, *President*
Thierry Guerlain, *Vice Pres*
EMP: 18
SQ FT: 8,500
SALES: 3.5MM **Privately Held**
WEB: www.graphitek.com
SIC: 3993 Signs & advertising specialties

(G-6567)
INTERFACE PERFORMANCE MTLS INC
12 Davis St (12090-1006)
PHONE.................518 686-3400
John Messersmith, *General Mgr*
Daniel Collett, *Treasurer*
Ann Fort, *Personnel*
James Lynch, *Branch Mgr*
EMP: 60 **Privately Held**
WEB: www.sealinfo.com
SIC: 2631 3053 Paperboard mills; gaskets, packing & sealing devices
PA: Interface Performance Materials, Inc.
216 Wohlsen Way
Lancaster PA 17603

(G-6568)
LOVEJOY CHAPLET CORPORATION
12 River St (12090-1815)
P.O. Box 66 (12090-0066)
PHONE.................518 686-5232
Fax: 518 686-4919
Peter McGuire, *President*
Lisa McGuire, *Vice Pres*
James Smith, *Controller*
Mallory McGuire, *Sales Mgr*
Margaret Sargood, *Admin Asst*
EMP: 28 EST: 1911
SQ FT: 20,000
SALES (est): 5.6MM **Privately Held**
WEB: www.lovejoychaplet.com
SIC: 3545 Precision tools, machinists'

(G-6569)
OAK-MITSUI INC
1 Mechanic St Bldg 2 (12090-1011)
PHONE.................518 686-8060
EMP: 54
SALES (corp-wide): 3.8B **Privately Held**
SIC: 3497 Copper foil
HQ: Oak Mitsui, Inc.
29 Battleship Road Ext
Camden SC 29020
518 686-4961

(G-6570)
OAK-MITSUI TECHNOLOGIES LLC
80 1st St (12090-1631)
P.O. Box 501 (12090-0501)
PHONE.................518 686-4961
Fax: 518 686-8080
Fujio Kuwako,
▲ EMP: 30
SALES (est): 4.6MM
SALES (corp-wide): 3.8B **Privately Held**
WEB: www.oakmitsui.com
SIC: 3497 Copper foil
HQ: Oak Mitsui, Inc.
29 Battleship Road Ext
Camden SC 29020
518 686-4961

(G-6571)
SAINT-GOBAIN PRFMCE PLAS CORP
14 Mccaffrey St (12090-1819)
PHONE.................518 686-7301
Amanda Rawson, *Purchasing*
Scott Nelson, *Controller*
Chris Lower, *Manager*
EMP: 177
SALES (corp-wide): 185.8MM **Privately Held**
SIC: 3229 Pressed & blown glass
HQ: Saint-Gobain Performance Plastics Corporation
31500 Solon Rd
Solon OH 44139
440 836-6900

(G-6572)
SAINT-GOBAIN PRFMCE PLAS CORP
1 Liberty St (12090-1019)
P.O. Box 320 (12090)
PHONE.................518 686-7301
Chris Lower, *Prdtn Mgr*
Pat Traynor, *Branch Mgr*
Ed Yankas, *MIS Mgr*
EMP: 190

Hoosick Falls - Rensselaer County (G-6573)

SALES (corp-wide): 185.8MM **Privately Held**
SIC: 2821 Polytetrafluoroethylene resins (teflon)
HQ: Saint-Gobain Performance Plastics Corporation
31500 Solon Rd
Solon OH 44139
440 836-6900

(G-6573)
TROJAN STEEL
48 Factory Hill Rd (12090-4405)
P.O. Box 59, North Hoosick (12133-0059)
PHONE.................................518 686-7426
Ray Revenoic, Owner
EMP: 5
SQ FT: 2,000
SALES (est): 622.6K **Privately Held**
SIC: 3462 Armor plate, forged iron or steel

Hopewell Junction
Dutchess County

(G-6574)
BEECH GROVE TECHNOLOGY INC
11 Sandy Pines Blvd (12533-8211)
P.O. Box 406, Stormville (12582-0406)
PHONE.................................845 223-6844
Carol Petvai, President
Steve Petvai, Vice Pres
EMP: 5
SQ FT: 1,500
SALES (est): 480K **Privately Held**
SIC: 3674 Semiconductors & related devices

(G-6575)
EMAGIN CORPORATION (PA)
2070 Route 52 (12533-3507)
PHONE.................................845 838-7900
Fax: 845 838-7901
Jill J Wittels, Ch of Bd
Andrew G Sculley, President
Amalkumar Ghosh, Senior VP
Olivier Prache, Senior VP
Jeffrey P Lucas, CFO
EMP: 90
SQ FT: 37,000
SALES (est): 21.4MM **Publicly Held**
WEB: www.emagin.com
SIC: 3674 Light emitting diodes

(G-6576)
FRITTERS & BUNS INC
236 Blue Hill Rd (12533-6659)
PHONE.................................845 227-6609
EMP: 8 EST: 1985
SALES (est): 400K **Privately Held**
SIC: 2051 Mfg Bread/Related Products

(G-6577)
GLOBALFOUNDRIES US 2 LLC (DH)
2070 Route 52 (12533-3507)
PHONE.................................512 457-3900
Sanjay Jha, CEO
EMP: 118
SALES (est): 972.9K
SALES (corp-wide): 8.5B **Privately Held**
SIC: 3674 Semiconductors & related devices

(G-6578)
GLOBALFOUNDRIES US INC
2070 Route 52 (12533-3507)
PHONE.................................512 457-3900
Kripa N Chauhan, Engineer
David Brown, Manager
James Doyle, Manager
Chandra Reddy, Manager
Thomas Schulze, Technical Staff
EMP: 19
SALES (corp-wide): 8.5B **Privately Held**
SIC: 3559 3674 Semiconductor manufacturing machinery; semiconductors & related devices
HQ: Globalfoundries U.S. Inc.
2600 Great America Way
Santa Clara CA 95054

(G-6579)
HOPEWELL PRECISION INC
19 Ryan Rd (12533-8322)
P.O. Box 551 (12533-0551)
PHONE.................................845 221-2737
Fax: 845 226-7285
Richard Skeen, President
Sangeeta Dev, Accounts Mgr
Donna Cznarty, Admin Sec
EMP: 22
SQ FT: 25,000
SALES (est): 4.1MM **Privately Held**
WEB: www.hopewell-precision.com
SIC: 3663 Studio equipment, radio & television broadcasting

(G-6580)
INTERNATIONAL BUS MCHS CORP
Also Called: IBM
10 North Dr (12533)
PHONE.................................800 426-4968
Michel Mayer, General Mgr
Jonathan Morris, Vice Pres
Anand RAO, Opers Staff
Rich Burda, Engineer
Rich Conti, Engineer
EMP: 170
SALES (corp-wide): 79.9B **Publicly Held**
WEB: www.ibm.com
SIC: 3674 Semiconductors & related devices
PA: International Business Machines Corporation
1 New Orchard Rd Ste 1
Armonk NY 10504
914 499-1900

(G-6581)
KENT OPTRONICS INC
40 Corporate Park Rd (12533-6557)
PHONE.................................845 897-0138
Le LI, CEO
Deng Ke Yang, President
Jiangbin Zhao, Engineer
Jack Lippert, Manager
EMP: 10
SALES (est): 1.2MM **Privately Held**
WEB: www.kentoptronics.com
SIC: 3661 Fiber optics communications equipment

(G-6582)
LIFE MEDICAL TECHNOLOGIES LLC
2070 Rte 52 21a Bldg 320a (12533)
PHONE.................................845 894-2121
EMP: 10
SALES (est): 660K **Privately Held**
SIC: 3069 Mfg Fabricated Rubber Products

(G-6583)
PHILLIP J ORTIZ MANUFACTURING
44 Railroad Ave (12533-7318)
P.O. Box 116 (12533-0116)
PHONE.................................845 226-7030
Fax: 845 226-8775
Barry Ortiz, President
EMP: 6 EST: 1946
SQ FT: 10,000
SALES (est): 440K **Privately Held**
SIC: 7692 3714 Welding repair; motor vehicle parts & accessories

(G-6584)
PURESPICE LLC
173 Shagbark Ln (12533-5281)
PHONE.................................617 549-8400
Robert Wilder, Mng Member
Brian Benko,
EMP: 5
SQ FT: 2,000
SALES: 1MM **Privately Held**
SIC: 2099 Seasonings & spices

(G-6585)
SPECTRAL SYSTEMS LLC (PA)
35 Corporate Park Rd (12533-6558)
PHONE.................................845 896-2200
Fax: 845 896-2203
Scott Little, President
Carlos Guajardo, Sales Executive
Bruce Capuano,

Frank Wesley,
EMP: 47
SALES: 11MM **Privately Held**
SIC: 3827 Optical instruments & lenses

Hornell
Steuben County

(G-6586)
BOMBARDIER TRANSPORTATION
1 William K Jackson Ln (14843-1457)
PHONE.................................607 324-0216
Dave Sharma, Branch Mgr
EMP: 60
SALES (corp-wide): 16.3B **Privately Held**
SIC: 3441 3743 Fabricated structural metal; railroad equipment, except locomotives
HQ: Bombardier Transportation (Holdings) Usa Inc.
1501 Lebanon Church Rd
Pittsburgh PA 15236
412 655-5700

(G-6587)
DOLOMITE PRODUCTS COMPANY INC
Also Called: A.L. Blades
7610 County Road 65 (14843-9626)
P.O. Box 590 (14843-0590)
PHONE.................................607 324-3636
Robert Blades, Branch Mgr
EMP: 16
SALES (corp-wide): 28.6B **Privately Held**
SIC: 2951 Paving mixtures
HQ: Dolomite Products Company Inc.
1150 Penfield Rd
Rochester NY 14625
315 524-1998

(G-6588)
DYCO ELECTRONICS INC
7775 Industrial Park Rd (14843-9673)
PHONE.................................607 324-2030
Fax: 607 324-2036
Gregory D Georgek, President
Roque Santiago, General Mgr
Allan Klus, Engineer
Jeffrey Wilkins, Program Mgr
Karla Dungan, Manager
EMP: 80
SQ FT: 30,000
SALES (est): 14.7MM **Privately Held**
WEB: www.dycoelectronics.com
SIC: 3612 Specialty transformers

(G-6589)
FORTITUDE INDUSTRIES
Also Called: A T M
7200 County Route 70a (14843-9303)
PHONE.................................607 324-1500
Fax: 607 698-4851
Margaret E Walsh, President
Randy Harkenrider, President
Barry Walsh, Vice Pres
Eric Teator, Purchasing
Dan Barnett, Engineer
▲ EMP: 65
SQ FT: 13,500
SALES: 11MM **Privately Held**
SIC: 3625 Electromagnetic clutches or brakes

(G-6590)
GATEHOUSE MEDIA LLC
Also Called: Evening Tribune
32 Broadway Mall (14843-1920)
PHONE.................................607 324-1425
Dave Broderick, Sales Staff
Bonnie Willey, Sales Staff
Kelly Luvinson, Manager
EMP: 101
SALES (corp-wide): 1.2B **Publicly Held**
WEB: www.gatehousemedia.com
SIC: 2711 Newspapers
HQ: Gatehouse Media, Llc
175 Sullys Trl Ste 300
Pittsford NY 14534
585 598-0030

(G-6591)
GRAY MANUFACTURING INDS LLC
Also Called: G M I
6258 Ice House Rd (14843-9739)
P.O. Box 126 (14843-0126)
PHONE.................................607 281-1325
Fax: 607 281-1327
David Gray, CEO
Marie Stewart, Administration
Richard Head,
Dennis Mullikin,
▲ EMP: 17
SQ FT: 15,000
SALES (est): 6.3MM **Privately Held**
SIC: 3743 Railroad equipment

(G-6592)
LOGO PRINT COMPANY
135 Seneca St (14843-1329)
PHONE.................................607 324-5403
EMP: 6
SALES (est): 21.4K **Privately Held**
SIC: 2752 Commercial printing, lithographic

(G-6593)
SENECA MEDIA INC (PA)
Also Called: Genesee County Express
32 Broadway Mall (14843-1920)
PHONE.................................607 324-1425
Fax: 607 324-1462
George Sample, President
Micheal Wnek, President
Cindy Giglio, Clerk
EMP: 75
SALES (est): 6.2MM **Privately Held**
WEB: www.eveningtribune.com
SIC: 2711 8661 Newspapers; religious organizations

(G-6594)
STERN & STERN INDUSTRIES INC
188 Thacher St (14843-1293)
P.O. Box 556 (14843-0556)
PHONE.................................607 324-4485
Fax: 607 324-6274
Peter B Thornton, Ch of Bd
Stanley Cone, Vice Pres
Lee Kessler, Vice Pres
Joanne Prouty, Vice Pres
Terry Bartel, Credit Mgr
EMP: 100
SALES (est): 28.3MM **Privately Held**
WEB: www.sternandstern.com
SIC: 2221 Manmade & synthetic broadwoven fabrics

(G-6595)
TRANSIT AIR INC
Also Called: Transitair Systems
1 William K Jackson Ln (14843-1693)
PHONE.................................607 324-0216
Fax: 607 324-2930
Dave Sharma, President
Thomas J Martin, Vice Pres
Allen Wright, Vice Pres
Robert Smith, Purchasing
Karen Nisbet, Personnel
▲ EMP: 25 EST: 1991
SQ FT: 50,000
SALES (est): 9.2MM **Privately Held**
SIC: 3585 3822 3613 Air conditioning equipment, complete; auto controls regulating residntl & coml environmt & applncs; control panels, electric

Horseheads
Chemung County

(G-6596)
BEECHER EMSSN SLTN TCHNLGS LLC (PA)
Also Called: Ward Diesel Filter Systems
1250 Schweizer Rd (14845-9017)
PHONE.................................607 796-0149
Fax: 607 739-7092
Scott Beecher, President
Tricia Ketter, Manager
Sally Spring, Manager
Katie Fincz, Admin Sec
Sally Spreng, Admin Asst

GEOGRAPHIC SECTION
Horseheads - Chemung County (G-6620)

EMP: 17
SQ FT: 12,000
SALES (est): 2.4MM **Privately Held**
WEB: www.warddiesel.com
SIC: 3564 Air purification equipment

(G-6597)
BELDEN INC
Also Called: Lrc Electronics
224 N Main St Ste 4 (14845-1766)
PHONE..................607 796-5600
Greg Hamilton, *Engineer*
Larry Zuber, *Branch Mgr*
Paul Corter, *Manager*
Stanley Cullen, *Manager*
EMP: 400
SALES (corp-wide): 2.3B **Publicly Held**
WEB: www.tnb.com
SIC: 3663 3678 3643 Cable television equipment; electronic connectors; current-carrying wiring devices
PA: Belden Inc.
   1 N Brentwood Blvd # 1500
   Saint Louis MO 63105
   314 854-8000

(G-6598)
BENNETT DIE & TOOL INC
130 Wygant Rd (14845-1564)
PHONE..................607 739-5629
Fax: 607 739-3471
Jim Mc Millen, *President*
Brian Bennett, *Vice Pres*
Jim Pittman, *Plant Mgr*
Jim McMillen, *Mktg Dir*
Jane Mc Millen, *Manager*
EMP: 40
SQ FT: 25,000
SALES (est): 6.6MM **Privately Held**
WEB: www.bdandt.com
SIC: 3544 Special dies & tools; jigs & fixtures

(G-6599)
CAMERON MFG & DESIGN INC (PA)
727 Blostein Blvd (14845-2739)
P.O. Box 478 (14845-0478)
PHONE..................607 739-3606
Fax: 607 739-3786
Christopher Goll, *President*
Ronald Johnson, *President*
Guy Loomis, *Plant Mgr*
Joshua Roloson, *Plant Mgr*
Michael Chevalier, *Project Mgr*
▲ EMP: 205
SQ FT: 106,000
SALES (est): 33MM **Privately Held**
WEB: www.camfab.com
SIC: 3441 Fabricated structural metal

(G-6600)
CROWN TANK COMPANY LLC
60 Electric Pkwy (14845-1424)
PHONE..................855 276-9682
Shawn Dawson, *Regl Sales Mgr*
EMP: 8
SALES (est): 1MM **Privately Held**
SIC: 3443 Fuel tanks (oil, gas, etc.): metal plate

(G-6601)
DAVID HELSING
Also Called: Horseheads Printing
2077 Grand Central Ave (14845-2893)
PHONE..................607 796-2681
Fax: 607 796-4127
David Helsing, *Owner*
EMP: 5
SQ FT: 3,200
SALES (est): 320K **Privately Held**
SIC: 2752 7336 2789 Lithographing on metal; commercial art & graphic design; bookbinding & related work

(G-6602)
DEMETS CANDY COMPANY LLC
1 Turtle Cir (14845-1000)
PHONE..................607 562-8600
EMP: 6 **Privately Held**
SIC: 2064 Candy & other confectionery products
HQ: Demet's Candy Company, Llc
   30 Buxton Farm Rd Ste 320
   Stamford CT 06905
   203 329-4545

(G-6603)
DEPUY SYNTHES INC
Also Called: Synthes USA
35 Airport Rd (14845-1067)
PHONE..................607 271-2500
Russ Heft, *Purch Mgr*
Kyle Amberg, *Buyer*
Sandra Graham, *Buyer*
Eric Nelson, *Buyer*
Joel Buice, *QC Mgr*
EMP: 150
SALES (corp-wide): 71.8B **Publicly Held**
SIC: 3842 Surgical appliances & supplies
HQ: Depuy Synthes, Inc.
   700 Orthopaedic Dr
   Warsaw IN 46582
   574 267-8143

(G-6604)
EM PFAFF & SON INC
204 E Franklin St (14845-2425)
PHONE..................607 739-3691
Fax: 607 739-2844
Susan Alexander, *President*
John Alexander, *Vice Pres*
Tracey Stermer, *Office Mgr*
EMP: 19 EST: 1944
SQ FT: 21,000
SALES (est): 2.7MM **Privately Held**
SIC: 2431 2434 Millwork; wood kitchen cabinets

(G-6605)
EMHART GLASS MANUFACTURING INC
74 Kahler Rd (14845-1022)
PHONE..................607 734-3671
C Mobayad, *Div Sub Head*
William Gruninger, *Vice Pres*
Scott Briggs, *Engineer*
M Claypool, *Engineer*
David Passmore, *Engineer*
EMP: 150
SALES (corp-wide): 2.3B **Privately Held**
WEB: www.emhartglass.com
SIC: 3559 Glass making machinery: blowing, molding, forming, etc.
HQ: Emhart Glass Manufacturing Inc.
   123 Great Pond Dr
   Windsor CT 06095
   860 298-7340

(G-6606)
FENNELL SPRING COMPANY LLC
295 Hemlock St (14845-2721)
PHONE..................607 739-3541
Thomas Fennell, *Mng Member*
Suzanne Sandore, *Manager*
Martin Fennell,
EMP: 60
SQ FT: 75,000
SALES (est): 10MM **Privately Held**
SIC: 3495 Precision springs

(G-6607)
FUEL ENERGY SERVICES USA LTD
250 Ltta Brook Indus Pkwy (14845)
PHONE..................607 846-2650
Mitchell Liivam, *CEO*
EMP: 22
SALES (est): 6.5MM **Privately Held**
SIC: 2869 1389 2911 7699 Fuels; oil field services; oils, fuel; pumps & pumping equipment repair; industrial equipment cleaning

(G-6608)
GAS FIELD SPECIALISTS INC
224 N Main St (14845-1766)
PHONE..................716 378-6422
John Hargrave, *Superintendent*
Brad West, *Branch Mgr*
Lisa Springstead, *Manager*
EMP: 51
SALES (corp-wide): 33.3MM **Privately Held**
SIC: 1389 Oil field services; gas field services
PA: Gas Field Specialists, Inc.
   2107 State Route 44 S
   Shinglehouse PA 16748
   814 698-2122

(G-6609)
HEADS & TAILS LURE CO
283 Hibbard Rd (14845-7930)
PHONE..................607 739-7900
Clint Kellar, *Owner*
EMP: 5 EST: 2007
SQ FT: 4,000
SALES (est): 238.3K **Privately Held**
SIC: 3949 Lures, fishing: artificial

(G-6610)
MICATU INC
315 Daniel Zenker Dr # 202 (14845-1008)
PHONE..................888 705-8836
Michael Oshetski, *CEO*
EMP: 5
SALES (est): 1.3MM **Privately Held**
SIC: 3827 Optical instruments & lenses

(G-6611)
MIRION TECH IMAGING LLC
Also Called: Mirion Tech Imging Systems Div
315 Daniel Zenker Dr (14845-1008)
PHONE..................607 562-4300
David Stewart, *President*
Seth Rosen, *Admin Sec*
Emmanuelle Lee, *Asst Sec*
EMP: 23 EST: 2015
SQ FT: 15,000
SALES (est): 3.6MM
SALES (corp-wide): 169.2MM **Privately Held**
SIC: 3663 Radio & TV communications equipment
PA: Mirion Technologies, Inc.
   3000 Executive Pkwy # 518
   San Ramon CA 94583
   925 543-0800

(G-6612)
MIRION TECHNOLOGIES IST CORP (HQ)
Also Called: Imaging and Sensing Technology
315 Daniel Zenker Dr # 204 (14845-1008)
PHONE..................607 562-4300
Fax: 607 796-4482
Thomas Logan, *CEO*
David Stewart, *President*
Tim Pelot, *Vice Pres*
Hilton Harrell, *Project Dir*
Karen Harper, *Buyer*
EMP: 70
SQ FT: 105,000
SALES (est): 32.1MM
SALES (corp-wide): 169.2MM **Privately Held**
WEB: www.mirion.com
SIC: 3679 3861 3829 3812 Electronic circuits; photographic equipment & supplies; nuclear radiation & testing apparatus; search & navigation equipment; computer peripheral equipment
PA: Mirion Technologies, Inc.
   3000 Executive Pkwy # 518
   San Ramon CA 94583
   925 543-0800

(G-6613)
MRC GLOBAL (US) INC
224 N Main St Bldg 13-1 (14845-1766)
PHONE..................607 739-8575
James Griffith, *Branch Mgr*
EMP: 11 **Publicly Held**
SIC: 1311 Crude petroleum & natural gas
HQ: Mrc Global (Us) Inc.
   1301 Mckinney St Ste 2300
   Houston TX 77010
   877 294-7574

(G-6614)
ORTHSTAR ENTERPRISES INC
119 Sing Sing Rd (14845-1073)
P.O. Box 459, Big Flats (14814-0459)
PHONE..................607 562-2100
Fax: 607 562-2110
James E Orsillo, *Ch of Bd*
Joseph E Strykowski, *President*
EMP: 65
SALES (est): 3.7MM **Privately Held**
WEB: www.orthstar.com
SIC: 7372 7379 3812 3823 Business oriented computer software; ; search & navigation equipment; industrial instrmnts msrmnt display/control process variable

(G-6615)
PEPSI-COLA METRO BTLG CO INC
Also Called: Pepsico
140 Wygant Rd (14845-9126)
PHONE..................607 795-1399
Chuck Dunn, *General Mgr*
Drew White, *Facilities Mgr*
Brian Morgan, *Manager*
EMP: 85
SALES (corp-wide): 62.8B **Publicly Held**
WEB: www.pbg.com
SIC: 2086 Carbonated soft drinks, bottled & canned
HQ: Pepsi-Cola Metropolitan Bottling Company, Inc.
   1111 Westchester Ave
   White Plains NY 10604
   914 767-6000

(G-6616)
PHOTONIC CONTROLS LLC
500 1st Ctr Ste 2 (14845)
PHONE..................607 562-4585
Fax: 607 562-4704
Ronald S Karfelt, *President*
EMP: 14
SQ FT: 6,250
SALES: 1.8MM **Privately Held**
WEB: www.photoniccontrols.com
SIC: 3229 Fiber optics strands

(G-6617)
PRINT SHOP
3153 Lake Rd (14845-3117)
PHONE..................607 734-4937
Deb Dupey, *Superintendent*
Kathy Grave, *Superintendent*
Tony Micha, *Superintendent*
EMP: 7
SALES (est): 606.7K **Privately Held**
SIC: 2752 Commercial printing, lithographic

(G-6618)
REPSOL OIL & GAS USA LLC
337 Daniel Zenker Dr (14845-1008)
PHONE..................607 562-4000
Todd Normane, *Vice Pres*
Woody Pace, *Vice Pres*
Pat Minor, *Plant Mgr*
David Wozniak, *Opers Mgr*
Seanna Starner, *Production*
EMP: 5
SALES (corp-wide): 3.2B **Privately Held**
SIC: 1311 Natural gas production
HQ: Repsol Oil & Gas Usa, Llc
   2455 Tech Forest Blvd
   Spring TX 77381
   832 442-1000

(G-6619)
RIMCO PLASTICS CORP
316 Colonial Dr (14845-9034)
PHONE..................607 739-3864
Fax: 607 739-3577
Robert Reimsnyder, *President*
Nancy Kosalek, *Corp Secy*
Lester W Reimsnyder III, *Vice Pres*
EMP: 25 EST: 1966
SQ FT: 36,000
SALES (est): 4.7MM **Privately Held**
WEB: www.rimcoplastics.com
SIC: 3089 3086 Plastic processing; plastics foam products

(G-6620)
ROCHESTER COCA COLA BOTTLING
Also Called: Coca-Cola
210 Industrial Park Rd (14845-9024)
PHONE..................607 739-5678
John Kelley, *Branch Mgr*
George Keim, *Manager*
EMP: 35
SQ FT: 23,000
SALES (corp-wide): 41.8B **Publicly Held**
SIC: 2086 Bottled & canned soft drinks
HQ: Rochester Coca Cola Bottling Corp
   300 Oak St
   Pittston PA 18640
   570 655-2874

Horseheads - Chemung County (G-6621)

(G-6621)
SCHLUMBERGER TECHNOLOGY CORP
224 N Main St Bldg S (14845-1766)
PHONE...................607 378-0105
EMP: 200 Privately Held
SIC: 1382 1389 3825 3824 Geophysical exploration, oil & gas field; geological exploration, oil & gas field; well logging; cementing oil & gas well casings; pumping of oil & gas wells; oil field services; measuring instruments & meters, electric; meters: electric, pocket, portable, panelboard, etc.; controls, revolution & timing instruments; counters, revolution; oil & gas field machinery; measuring & dispensing pumps
HQ: Schlumberger Technology Corp
    100 Gillingham Ln
    Sugar Land TX 77478
    281 285-8500

(G-6622)
SILICON CARBIDE PRODUCTS INC
361 Daniel Zenker Dr (14845-1008)
PHONE...................607 562-8599
Fax: 607 562-7585
Martin Metzger, President
Joshua Dahlman, General Mgr
Mark Whitmer, Vice Pres
Rick Cleveland, Sales Mgr
Margaret Johnson, Office Mgr
▲ EMP: 30
SALES (est): 4.8MM Privately Held
WEB: www.siliconcarbideproducts.com
SIC: 3297 Nonclay refractories; cement: high temperature, refractory (nonclay); castable refractories, nonclay

(G-6623)
VAPE FLAVORIUM
940c Chemung St (14845-2260)
PHONE...................607 346-7276
Angela Franceschelli, Owner
EMP: 9
SALES (est): 114.3K Privately Held
SIC: 3999 Cigar & cigarette holders

(G-6624)
X-GEN PHARMACEUTICALS INC
300 Daniel Zenker Dr (14845-1014)
P.O. Box 445, Big Flats (14814-0445)
PHONE...................607 562-2700
Robin Liles, Vice Pres
Jared Aiello, Project Mgr
Jennifer Muto, Project Mgr
Jocelyn Polito, Project Mgr
RC Park, QC Dir
EMP: 30
SALES (corp-wide): 4.4MM Privately Held
SIC: 2834 Pharmaceutical preparations
PA: X-Gen Pharmaceuticals, Inc.
    300 Daniel Zenker Dr
    Big Flats NY 14814
    607 562-2700

Howard Beach
Queens County

(G-6625)
GRILLMASTER INC
15314 83rd St (11414-1826)
PHONE...................718 272-9191
Fax: 718 272-2268
Anne Cohen, CEO
Sherman Moss, President
Evelyn Kelly, Manager
Luis Marin, Manager
EMP: 50
SQ FT: 20,000
SALES (est): 7.8MM Privately Held
SIC: 3585 3822 3446 Parts for heating, cooling & refrigerating equipment; auto controls regulating residntl & coml environmt & applncs; architectural metalwork

(G-6626)
RAK FINISHING CORP
15934 83rd St (11414-2933)
PHONE...................718 416-4242
Fax: 718 386-6166

John Muncan, CEO
Jon Muncan, CEO
Julianna Muncan, President
EMP: 48
SQ FT: 7,000
SALES (est): 3MM Privately Held
SIC: 2339 7389 Service apparel, washable: women's; textile & apparel services

(G-6627)
VIP PRINTING
16040 95th St (11414-3801)
PHONE...................718 641-9361
Victor Ingrassia, Owner
EMP: 5
SALES: 150K Privately Held
SIC: 2752 Commercial printing, lithographic

(G-6628)
VPJ PUBLICATION INC
Also Called: Forum South, The
15519 Lahn St (11414-2858)
PHONE...................718 845-3221
Patricia Adams, President
EMP: 25
SQ FT: 1,000
SALES (est): 1.3MM Privately Held
SIC: 2711 Newspapers, publishing & printing

Howes Cave
Schoharie County

(G-6629)
W KINTZ PLASTICS INC (PA)
Also Called: K P I Plastics
165 Caverns Rd (12092-1907)
PHONE...................518 296-8513
Fax: 518 296-8309
Edwin Kintz, Ch of Bd
Laurie Dent, Plant Mgr
Roger Cusano, Engineer
Lawrence Kath, CFO
Elly Hill, Human Res Dir
◆ EMP: 122 EST: 1976
SQ FT: 60,000
SALES (est): 22.4MM Privately Held
WEB: www.kintz.com
SIC: 3089 Plastic processing

Hudson
Columbia County

(G-6630)
A & S WOODWORKING INC
9 Partition St (12534-3111)
PHONE...................518 821-0832
Arthur Cincotti, CEO
EMP: 7
SQ FT: 900
SALES: 5MM Privately Held
SIC: 2511 Wood household furniture

(G-6631)
A COLARUSSO AND SON INC (PA)
Also Called: Colarusso Blacktop Co
91 Newman Rd (12534-4040)
P.O. Box 302 (12534-0302)
PHONE...................518 828-3218
Fax: 518 828-0546
Peter G Colarusso Jr, President
Robert Colarusso, Corp Secy
Larry Gregory, Safety Dir
Robert Butler, Project Mgr
Jason Arrick, Controller
EMP: 20 EST: 1912
SQ FT: 10,000
SALES (est): 22MM Privately Held
WEB: www.acolarusso.com
SIC: 2951 5032 1611 1771 Asphalt & asphaltic paving mixtures (not from refineries); asphalt mixture; stone, crushed or broken; highway & street construction; concrete work; construction sand & gravel

(G-6632)
ACME KITCHENETTES CORP
4269 Us Route 9 (12534-4031)
PHONE...................518 828-4191

Nick Peros, President
Mike Pavlovich, Vice Pres
EMP: 20
SALES (est): 3.4MM Privately Held
WEB: www.acme3in1.com
SIC: 3469 3632 2434 5064 Kitchen fixtures & equipment: metal, except cast aluminum; household refrigerators & freezers; wood kitchen cabinets; refrigerators & freezers

(G-6633)
AMERICAN SPACER TECHNOLOGIES
35 Industrial Tract Anx (12534-1505)
PHONE...................518 828-1339
Paul Donofrio, President
EMP: 7 EST: 2008
SALES (est): 1.1MM Privately Held
SIC: 3089 Injection molding of plastics

(G-6634)
ARCHER-DANIELS-MIDLAND COMPANY
201 State Route 23b (12534-4009)
P.O. Box 398 (12534-0398)
PHONE...................518 828-4691
Fax: 518 828-7736
Andy Spirek, Branch Mgr
EMP: 50
SALES (corp-wide): 62.3B Publicly Held
SIC: 2041 Bread & bread-type roll mixes
PA: Archer-Daniels-Midland Company
    77 W Wacker Dr Ste 4600
    Chicago IL 60601
    312 634-8100

(G-6635)
ARCHER-DANIELS-MIDLAND COMPANY
Also Called: ADM
Ste B Rr 23 (12534)
P.O. Box 398 (12534-0398)
PHONE...................518 828-4691
Mark Eisler, Manager
EMP: 52
SALES (corp-wide): 62.3B Publicly Held
WEB: www.admworld.com
SIC: 2041 5149 Flour: blended, prepared or self-rising; flour
PA: Archer-Daniels-Midland Company
    77 W Wacker Dr Ste 4600
    Chicago IL 60601
    312 634-8100

(G-6636)
ATLANTIC ENGINEER PRODUCTS LLC
239 State Route 23b (12534-4009)
P.O. Box 639, Kinderhook (12106-0639)
PHONE...................518 822-1800
Robert Peloke,
Thomas Smith Sr,
Tucker Smith,
EMP: 25
SALES (est): 2.7MM Privately Held
SIC: 3537 Loading docks: portable, adjustable & hydraulic

(G-6637)
ATMOST REFRIGERATION CO INC (PA)
Also Called: R T F Manufacturing
793 Route 66 (12534-3410)
PHONE...................518 828-2180
Fax: 518 828-2257
Thomas Finck, Principal
Bob Walsh, Sls & Mktg Exec
Ashley Finck, Sales Mgr
▲ EMP: 5
SQ FT: 25,000
SALES (est): 3.6MM Privately Held
WEB: www.rtfmanufacturing.com
SIC: 3585 Refrigeration equipment, complete

(G-6638)
BENNERS GARDENS LLC
1 Hudson City Ctr (12534-2354)
PHONE...................518 828-1055
John Tonelli, Partner
EMP: 9
SALES (est): 1.1MM Privately Held
SIC: 3089 Fences, gates & accessories: plastic

(G-6639)
BERKSHIRE BUSINESS FORMS INC
829 Route 66 (12534-3406)
P.O. Box 118, Troy (12181-0118)
PHONE...................518 828-2600
Fax: 518 828-3582
Nancy Linton, President
Jeffrey C Linton, Vice Pres
John S Linton, VP Mfg
EMP: 12 EST: 1960
SQ FT: 15,000
SALES: 1.2MM Privately Held
SIC: 2759 Commercial printing

(G-6640)
CRAFTECH INDUSTRIES INC
8 Dock St (12534-2003)
P.O. Box 636 (12534-0636)
PHONE...................518 828-5001
Fax: 518 828-9468
Barbara Gerard, President
Ronald Prior, General Mgr
Tara Sterritt, General Mgr
Irving Gerard, Vice Pres
Linda Jabanski, Human Res Mgr
EMP: 55 EST: 1966
SQ FT: 18,500
SALES (est): 13.1MM Privately Held
WEB: www.craftechind.com
SIC: 3451 3089 3452 Screw machine products; injection molding of plastics; bolts, nuts, rivets & washers

(G-6641)
DIGITAL FABRICATION WKSHP INC
99 S 3rd St Ste 2 (12534-2171)
PHONE...................518 249-6500
Chris Stapleson, General Mgr
EMP: 6
SALES (est): 424.1K Privately Held
SIC: 2499 Decorative wood & woodwork

(G-6642)
DINOSAW INC (PA)
340 Power Ave (12534-2442)
PHONE...................518 828-9942
Fax: 518 828-6610
Henry J Warchol Jr, CEO
Gregg S Warchol, President
Franklin Winkler, Plant Mgr
Scott Myers, Sales Mgr
Colleen Fitzgibbon, Office Mgr
EMP: 25
SQ FT: 14,000
SALES (est): 3.9MM Privately Held
WEB: www.dinosaw.com
SIC: 3425 3545 5085 3541 Saw blades & handsaws; machine tool accessories; industrial tools; machine tools, metal cutting type

(G-6643)
EMSIG MANUFACTURING CORP
160 Fairview Ave Ste 916 (12534-8404)
PHONE...................518 828-7301
Fax: 518 828-0026
James Feane, Manager
EMP: 11
SALES (corp-wide): 26.7MM Privately Held
SIC: 3965 5131 Buttons & parts; buttons
PA: Emsig Manufacturing Corp.
    263 W 38th St Fl 5
    New York NY 10018
    718 784-7717

(G-6644)
FOSTER REFRIGERATORS ENTP
300 Fairview Ave (12534-1214)
PHONE...................518 671-6036
James Dinardi, President
Mir Pyson, Accounting Mgr
Robert E Walsh, Sales Staff
EMP: 10
SALES (est): 1.8MM Privately Held
SIC: 3585 7623 Refrigeration equipment, complete; refrigeration service & repair

(G-6645)
GOLUB CORPORATION
Also Called: Price Chopper Pharmacy
351 Fairview Ave Ste 3 (12534-1259)
PHONE...................518 822-0076

GEOGRAPHIC SECTION

Hudson Falls - Washington County (G-6669)

Stacey McGovern, *Branch Mgr*
EMP: 99
SALES (corp-wide): 3.4B **Privately Held**
SIC: 3751 Motorcycles & related parts
PA: The Golub Corporation
461 Nott St
Schenectady NY 12304
518 355-5000

(G-6646)
H & H HULLS INC
35 Industrial Tract Anx (12534-1505)
PHONE.................................518 828-1339
Fax: 518 828-5208
Thomas Halpin, *President*
EMP: 5
SQ FT: 2,604
SALES (est): 290K **Privately Held**
SIC: 3089 Injection molded finished plastic products

(G-6647)
HUDSON FABRICS LLC
128 2nd Street Ext (12534-1626)
PHONE.................................518 671-6100
Mark Schur,
EMP: 15
SALES (est): 1.6MM **Privately Held**
SIC: 2258 Tricot fabrics

(G-6648)
HUDSON VALLEY CREAMERY LLC
2986 Us Route 9 (12534-4407)
PHONE.................................518 851-2570
Veronica Madey,
▲ **EMP:** 10 **EST:** 2010
SALES (est): 1.2MM **Privately Held**
SIC: 2022 Cheese, natural & processed

(G-6649)
J V PRECISION INC
3031 Us Route 9 (12534-4320)
PHONE.................................518 851-3200
Dorothy Jahns, *President*
Scott Valentine, *Vice Pres*
Lisa Valentine, *Treasurer*
EMP: 6
SQ FT: 5,400
SALES (est): 999.2K **Privately Held**
WEB: www.jvprecision.com
SIC: 3624 Electrodes, thermal & electrolytic uses: carbon, graphite

(G-6650)
JEM WDWKG & CABINETS INC
250 Falls Rd (12534-3323)
PHONE.................................518 828-5361
Neil Schnelwar, *Chairman*
EMP: 14 **EST:** 2007
SALES (est): 1.9MM **Privately Held**
SIC: 2431 Millwork

(G-6651)
JOHNNYS IDEAL PRINTING CO
Also Called: Johnny's Ideal Prntng Co
352 Warren St (12534-2419)
PHONE.................................518 828-6666
Fax: 518 828-6970
John Brodowski, *President*
Virginia Brodowski, *Treasurer*
EMP: 5
SQ FT: 5,000
SALES (est): 460K **Privately Held**
SIC: 2752 2759 2791 2789 Commercial printing, offset; letterpress printing; typesetting; bookbinding & related work

(G-6652)
JOHNSON ACQUISITION CORP (HQ)
Also Called: Chatham Courier, The
364 Warren St (12534-2419)
PHONE.................................518 828-1616
Roger Coleman, *President*
Karrie Allen, *Editor*
Mike Labuff, *Editor*
William Lundquest, *Div Sub Head*
Pamela Geski, *Sales Staff*
EMP: 16 **EST:** 1895
SQ FT: 35,000
SALES: 401.9K
SALES (corp-wide): 32MM **Privately Held**
WEB: www.registerstar.com
SIC: 2711 Newspapers, publishing & printing
PA: Johnson Newspaper Corporation
260 Washington St
Watertown NY
315 782-1000

(G-6653)
JONAS LOUIS PAUL STUDIOS INC
304 Miller Rd (12534-4522)
PHONE.................................518 851-2211
David Merritt, *President*
Pam Merritt, *Admin Sec*
EMP: 6 **EST:** 1942
SQ FT: 10,000
SALES (est): 454.9K **Privately Held**
WEB: www.jonasstudios.com
SIC: 3299 Statuary: gypsum, clay, papier mache, metal, etc.

(G-6654)
LB FURNITURE INDUSTRIES LLC
99 S 3rd St (12534-2172)
PHONE.................................518 828-1501
Fax: 518 828-3219
Amy Mecabe, *Sr Corp Ofcr*
Craig Banta, *Vice Pres*
Wayne Amburgh, *Purch Agent*
Jenny Decker, *Cust Svc Dir*
Mark Zelinger, *Sales Mgr*
▲ **EMP:** 150
SQ FT: 300,000
SALES (est): 13.2MM **Privately Held**
WEB: www.lbempire.com
SIC: 2599 3469 Restaurant furniture, wood or metal; household cooking & kitchen utensils, metal

(G-6655)
MCCARROLL UPHL DESIGNS LLC
Also Called: Upholstery Unlimited
743 Columbia St (12534-2509)
PHONE.................................518 828-0500
Debbie Whelan, *Owner*
EMP: 8
SQ FT: 2,300
SALES (est): 250K **Privately Held**
SIC: 2591 5023 2512 2392 Drapery hardware & blinds & shades; window shades; window covering parts & accessories; window shades; decorative home furnishings & supplies; upholstered household furniture; household furnishings; curtains & draperies; slip covers

(G-6656)
MELTZ LUMBER CO OF MELLENVILLE
483 Route 217 (12534-3640)
PHONE.................................518 672-7021
Fax: 518 672-4492
Emil Meltz Jr, *President*
Jeffory Meltz, *Vice Pres*
Mary Stard, *Finance Mgr*
Betty Lou Meltz, *Admin Sec*
EMP: 20
SALES (est): 2.7MM **Privately Held**
SIC: 2421 5211 Sawmills & planing mills, general; millwork & lumber

(G-6657)
MICOSTA ENTERPRISES INC
Also Called: Easy H2b
3007 County Route 20 (12534-3384)
PHONE.................................518 822-9708
Steven A McKay, *President*
EMP: 8
SQ FT: 350
SALES (est): 811.4K **Privately Held**
WEB: www.micostaent.com
SIC: 2053 2066 Pies, bakery: frozen; chocolate bars, solid

(G-6658)
MODERN FARMER MEDIA INC
403 Warren St (12534-2414)
PHONE.................................518 828-7447
Ann M Gardner, *CEO*
EMP: 10
SALES (est): 1.1MM **Privately Held**
SIC: 2721 7371 Periodicals: publishing only; custom computer programming services

(G-6659)
OVERHEAD DOOR CORPORATION
W McGuire Co
1 Hudson Ave (12534-2807)
PHONE.................................518 828-7652
Fax: 518 828-1262
Brad Knable, *Vice Pres*
Kevin Hoyt, *Mfg Staff*
Charlie Klotz, *Human Res Mgr*
Jennifer Noblin, *Sales Staff*
Rich Moore, *Manager*
EMP: 100
SALES (corp-wide): 3.1B **Privately Held**
WEB: www.overheaddoor.com
SIC: 3442 2431 5084 3842 Garage doors, overhead: metal; doors, wood; materials handling machinery; surgical appliances & supplies; packaging machinery; prefabricated metal buildings
HQ: Overhead Door Corporation
2501 S State Hwy 121 Ste
Lewisville TX 75067
469 549-7100

(G-6660)
PERIODICAL SERVICES CO INC
351 Fairview Ave Ste 300 (12534-1259)
PHONE.................................518 822-9300
Marcia Scneider, *President*
Rob Koskey, *Vice Pres*
EMP: 15 **EST:** 2013
SALES: 3MM **Privately Held**
SIC: 2721 Periodicals

(G-6661)
PHOENIX SERVICES GROUP LLC
1 Hudson City Ctr (12534-2354)
PHONE.................................518 828-6611
John Tonelli,
Dimitri Rakopoulos,
Peter Stavropoulos,
EMP: 25
SQ FT: 70,000
SALES (est): 2.5MM **Privately Held**
SIC: 3089 Extruded finished plastic products

(G-6662)
PRINCTON ARCHTCTURAL PRESS LLC (HQ)
202 Warren St (12534-2118)
PHONE.................................518 671-6100
Fax: 212 995-9454
Joe Watson, *Manager*
Kevin Lippert,
▲ **EMP:** 16
SALES: 5.2MM
SALES (corp-wide): 28.8MM **Privately Held**
SIC: 2731 2678 Book publishing; stationery products
PA: The Mcevoy Group Llc
680 2nd St
San Francisco CA 94107
415 537-4200

(G-6663)
SATURN INDUSTRIES INC (PA)
157 Union Tpke (12534-1524)
P.O. Box 367 (12534-0367)
PHONE.................................518 828-9956
Fax: 518 828-9868
Maryanne Lee, *President*
John Lee, *Vice Pres*
Seth Neefus, *Sales Staff*
EMP: 40 **EST:** 1959
SQ FT: 25,000
SALES: 3.5MM **Privately Held**
SIC: 3624 3599 3544 3769 Electrodes, thermal & electrolytic uses: carbon, graphite; machine & other job shop work; special dies, tools, jigs & fixtures; guided missile & space vehicle parts & auxiliary equipment; current-carrying wiring devices

(G-6664)
SAUSBIERS AWNING SHOP INC
43 8th St (12534-2901)
PHONE.................................518 828-3748
Fax: 518 751-1033
William M Harp, *President*
Robert Stalker, *Business Mgr*
EMP: 8 **EST:** 1902
SQ FT: 4,000
SALES: 700K **Privately Held**
SIC: 2394 5999 7532 Awnings, fabric: made from purchased materials; fire extinguishers; upholstery & trim shop, automotive; tops (canvas or plastic), installation or repair: automotive

(G-6665)
SERVOTEC USA LLC
1 Industrial Tract Anx # 3 (12534-1514)
PHONE.................................518 671-6120
Thomas Tanguay,
EMP: 6
SALES (est): 900.9K **Privately Held**
WEB: www.servotecusa.com
SIC: 3542 Presses: hydraulic & pneumatic, mechanical & manual

(G-6666)
SMITH CONTROL SYSTEMS INC
1839 Route 9h (12534-3374)
PHONE.................................518 828-7646
Fax: 518 828-2845
Thomas H Smith Sr, *President*
Marjorie Gallagher, *General Mgr*
Jim Dodd, *Business Mgr*
Kirt Coonradt, *Vice Pres*
Michael Keating, *Vice Pres*
EMP: 17
SQ FT: 10,000
SALES (est): 4.5MM **Privately Held**
WEB: www.smithcontrol.com
SIC: 3613 Control panels, electric

(G-6667)
TWIN COUNTIES PRO PRINTERS INC
59 Fairview Ave (12534-2334)
PHONE.................................518 828-3278
Fax: 518 828-4375
David Scott, *President*
Linda D Scott, *CFO*
Ryan Scott, *Sales Mgr*
EMP: 10
SQ FT: 3,500
SALES (est): 1.1MM **Privately Held**
WEB: www.pro-printers.com
SIC: 2752 7334 Commercial printing, offset; photocopying & duplicating services

(G-6668)
UFP NEW YORK LLC
Also Called: Universal Forest Products
11 Falls Industrial Pk Rd (12534-3377)
PHONE.................................518 828-2888
Rich Flinn, *General Mgr*
EMP: 35
SALES (corp-wide): 3.2B **Publicly Held**
WEB: www.ufpinc.com
SIC: 2439 Trusses, wooden roof
HQ: Ufp New York, Llc
11 Allen St
Auburn NY 13021
315 253-2758

Hudson Falls
Washington County

(G-6669)
ADIRONDACK MACHINE CORPORATION
84 Boulevard St (12839-1026)
PHONE.................................518 792-2258
Fax: 518 792-2274
Tom Ferari, *President*
EMP: 5 **EST:** 1963
SQ FT: 6,000
SALES: 750K **Privately Held**
WEB: www.adirondackmachine.com
SIC: 3821 Laboratory apparatus & furniture

Hudson Falls - Washington County (G-6670)

(G-6670)
COLOR-AID CORPORATION
38 La Fayette St Ste 2 (12839-1247)
PHONE..................................212 673-5500
Fax: 518 475-0315
Richard O'Brien, *President*
Raymond O'Brien, *Vice Pres*
EMP: 8
SQ FT: 8,500
SALES (est): 1.3MM **Privately Held**
WEB: www.coloraid.com
SIC: 2752 Commercial printing, lithographic

(G-6671)
DIMENSIONAL MILLS INC
337 Main St (12839-1513)
PHONE..................................518 746-1047
David Lafountain, *President*
EMP: 5 EST: 1992
SALES: 600K **Privately Held**
SIC: 2448 Wood pallets & skids

(G-6672)
DWA PALLET INC
Also Called: Dimensional Mills
337 Main St (12839-1513)
PHONE..................................518 746-1047
Daniel Ellsworth, *President*
EMP: 9
SALES (est): 720K **Privately Held**
SIC: 2448 Pallets, wood & wood with metal

(G-6673)
GENERAL ELECTRIC COMPANY
446 Lock 8 Way 8th (12839)
PHONE..................................518 746-5750
Fax: 518 746-5447
Benjamin Heineman, *Senior VP*
Timothy Kilpeck, *Safety Mgr*
Matt Levin, *Purch Mgr*
Rich Young, *Engineer*
Wendy Dangelo, *Controller*
EMP: 425
SALES (corp-wide): 123.6B **Publicly Held**
SIC: 3629 Capacitors, fixed or variable
PA: General Electric Company
41 Farnsworth St
Boston MA 02210
617 443-3000

(G-6674)
GL&V USA INC
27 Allen St (12839-1901)
PHONE..................................518 747-2444
Eve Lacroix, *General Mgr*
Valere Morissette, *General Mgr*
Jim Wilson, *Manager*
Brian Stringham, *Info Tech Mgr*
EMP: 83
SALES (corp-wide): 71.5K **Privately Held**
WEB: www.glv.com
SIC: 3554 Paper industries machinery
HQ: Gl&V Usa Inc.
1 Cellu Dr Ste 200
Nashua NH 03063
603 882-2711

(G-6675)
GL&V USA INC (DH)
27 Allen St (12839-1901)
PHONE..................................518 747-2444
Fax: 518 747-1334
Laurent Verreault, *CEO*
Richard Verrault, *President*
Marc Foulger, *Business Mgr*
Bob Burns, *Purchasing*
Stefanie South, *HR Admin*
▲ EMP: 47
SQ FT: 215,000
SALES (est): 15.6MM
SALES (corp-wide): 2.5B **Privately Held**
SIC: 3554 Paper industries machinery
HQ: 9189-6175 Quebec Inc
174 West St S
Orillia ON
705 325-6181

(G-6676)
GRANVILLE GLASS & GRANITE
131 Revere Rd (12839)
PHONE..................................518 812-0492
Kyle Suchan, *President*
Scott Suchan, *Vice Pres*
EMP: 5

SALES (est): 514.4K **Privately Held**
SIC: 3231 Products of purchased glass

(G-6677)
HAANEN PACKARD MACHINERY INC (PA)
16 Allen St (12839-1941)
PHONE..................................518 747-2330
Fax: 518 747-2315
Michael Haanen, *President*
Grace Packard, *Corp Secy*
Tony Rouleau, *Prgrmr*
EMP: 2
SQ FT: 3,500
SALES (est): 1.1MM **Privately Held**
SIC: 3554 3559 Paper industries machinery; plastics working machinery

(G-6678)
HALL CONSTRUCTION PDTS & SVCS
31 Allen St (12839-1974)
P.O. Box 1392, South Glens Falls (12803-1392)
PHONE..................................518 747-7047
David Hall, *President*
Ariel Corona, *Manager*
EMP: 5
SQ FT: 7,000
SALES (est): 522.6K **Privately Held**
WEB: www.duraslot.com
SIC: 3089 Plastic hardware & building products

(G-6679)
NORTH-EAST MACHINE INC
4160 State Route 4 (12839-3716)
PHONE..................................518 746-1837
Tracy Stevenson, *President*
EMP: 7
SQ FT: 4,000
SALES: 450K **Privately Held**
SIC: 3599 Machine shop, jobbing & repair

(G-6680)
PECKHAM MATERIALS CORP
438 Vaughn Rd (12839-9644)
PHONE..................................518 747-3353
Fax: 518 747-4006
John R Peckham, *President*
EMP: 30
SALES (corp-wide): 200.6MM **Privately Held**
SIC: 1429 3531 2952 2951 Igneous rock, crushed & broken-quarrying; asphalt plant, including gravel-mix type; asphalt felts & coatings; asphalt paving mixtures & blocks; highway & street construction
HQ: Peckham Materials Corp
20 Haarlem Ave Ste 200
White Plains NY 10603
914 686-2045

(G-6681)
THE KINGSBURY PRINTING CO INC
110 Franklin St (12839-1256)
PHONE..................................518 747-6606
Fax: 518 747-8852
Robert Bombard Jr, *Ch of Bd*
Robert L Bombard Jr, *Ch of Bd*
Janette Bombard, *Vice Pres*
EMP: 8
SQ FT: 2,070
SALES (est): 1.1MM **Privately Held**
SIC: 2752 Commercial printing, lithographic

Huguenot
Orange County

(G-6682)
SOMERVILLE ACQUISITIONS CO INC
Also Called: Summit Research Laboratories
15 Big Pond Rd (12746-5003)
P.O. Box F (12746-0626)
PHONE..................................845 856-5261
Fran Baxter, *Branch Mgr*
EMP: 10

SALES (corp-wide): 27.3MM **Privately Held**
SIC: 2819 Aluminum compounds
PA: Somerville Acquisitions Co., Inc.
45 River Rd Ste 300
Flemington NJ 08822
908 782-9500

(G-6683)
SOMERVILLE TECH GROUP INC
15 Big Pond Rd (12746-5003)
P.O. Box F (12746-0626)
PHONE..................................908 782-9500
Piyush J Patel, *CEO*
EMP: 100
SALES (est): 5.9MM **Privately Held**
SIC: 2819 Aluminum compounds

(G-6684)
SUMMIT RESEARCH LABS INC (PA)
Also Called: Summitreheis
15 Big Pond Rd (12746-5003)
P.O. Box 626 (12746-0626)
PHONE..................................845 856-5261
Fax: 845 856-6516
Piyush J Patel, *Ch of Bd*
Suresh Patel, *President*
Tony Buzzelli, *Plant Mgr*
Joe Gallo, *Warehouse Mgr*
Kathleen Innella, *Purch Agent*
◆ EMP: 110
SQ FT: 106,000
SALES (est): 24.3MM **Privately Held**
SIC: 2819 Industrial inorganic chemicals

Huntington
Suffolk County

(G-6685)
ADL DESIGN INC
4 W Mall Dr (11743-6440)
PHONE..................................516 949-6658
David Pollack, *CEO*
EMP: 2
SALES: 2MM **Privately Held**
SIC: 3144 Dress shoes, women's

(G-6686)
APS ENTERPRISE SOFTWARE INC
775 Park Ave (11743-3976)
PHONE..................................631 784-7720
Peter Thiermann, *President*
Michael Sullivan, *Principal*
Steffen Heinke, *Treasurer*
EMP: 22
SALES (est): 1.2MM **Privately Held**
SIC: 7372 Prepackaged software

(G-6687)
AXLE TEKNOLOGY LLC (PA)
113 Woodbury Rd (11743-4135)
PHONE..................................631 423-3044
▲ EMP: 9
SALES (est): 1.3MM **Privately Held**
SIC: 3714 5013 Axles, motor vehicle; automotive supplies & parts

(G-6688)
BERJEN METAL INDUSTRIES LTD
645 New York Ave Unit 1 (11743-4266)
PHONE..................................631 673-7979
Robert Sentura, *President*
Barbara Santoro, *Vice Pres*
Robert J Santoro, *Admin Sec*
EMP: 6
SALES (est): 935.8K **Privately Held**
WEB: www.berjen.com
SIC: 3444 1761 Sheet metalwork; sheet metalwork

(G-6689)
BLUE CAST DENIM CO INC
10 Blue Grass Ct (11743-2512)
PHONE..................................212 719-1182
Fax: 212 719-1521
Steve Brandis, *Ch of Bd*
Joseph Rosenheck, *President*
Sal Romo, *Vice Pres*
EMP: 34
SQ FT: 3,000

SALES (est): 3.2MM **Privately Held**
WEB: www.bluecastdenim.com
SIC: 2339 Slacks: women's, misses' & juniors'; jeans: women's, misses' & juniors'

(G-6690)
BOA SECURITY TECHNOLOGIES CORP
Also Called: Boa Handcuff
586 New York Ave Unit 3 (11743-4269)
PHONE..................................516 576-0295
Alan Lurie, *President*
Alvin MA, *Vice Pres*
EMP: 6
SQ FT: 4,000
SALES (est): 941K **Privately Held**
WEB: www.cuffmaxx.com
SIC: 3429 Handcuffs & leg irons

(G-6691)
CAL BLEN ELECTRONIC INDUSTRIES
6 Kenneth Ave (11743-4925)
PHONE..................................631 242-6243
Fax: 631 242-1937
Rod Staehlin, *President*
EMP: 12 EST: 1961
SQ FT: 7,500
SALES (est): 2.4MM **Privately Held**
SIC: 3577 3823 Optical scanning devices; computer interface equipment for industrial process control

(G-6692)
COOCOO SMS INC
356 New York Ave Ste 1 (11743-3304)
PHONE..................................646 459-4260
John J Tunney III, *Mng Member*
Larry Prager,
Ryan Thompson,
EMP: 11
SALES: 500K **Privately Held**
SIC: 7372 Prepackaged software

(G-6693)
DEJANA TRCK UTILITY EQP CO LLC
Also Called: Dejana Truck & Utility Eqp Co
743 Park Ave (11743-3912)
PHONE..................................631 549-0944
Fax: 631 549-0945
Richard Nieves, *Sales Staff*
Andrew Dejana, *Manager*
EMP: 25 **Publicly Held**
WEB: www.dejana.com
SIC: 3711 Trucks, pickup, assembly of
HQ: Dejana Truck & Utility Equipment Company, Llc
490 Pulaski Rd
Kings Park NY 11754
631 544-9000

(G-6694)
FAD INC
Also Called: Fad Treasures
630 New York Ave Ste B (11743-4289)
PHONE..................................631 385-2460
Fax: 631 385-4540
Allan Axelowitz, *President*
Donna Axelowitz, *Admin Sec*
▲ EMP: 27
SQ FT: 6,000
SALES (est): 3.3MM **Privately Held**
WEB: www.fad-treasures.com
SIC: 2339 5137 5632 Women's & misses' accessories; women's & children's accessories; women's accessory & specialty stores

(G-6695)
HARBORSIDE PRESS
94 N Woodhull Rd (11743-2829)
PHONE..................................631 470-4967
Claudine Kiffer, *Editor*
Anthony Cutrone, *Exec VP*
Leslie Dubin, *Vice Pres*
Kelley Moore, *Vice Pres*
Jessica Tamasi, *Senior Mgr*
EMP: 6
SALES (est): 83.9K **Privately Held**
SIC: 2741 Miscellaneous publishing

▲ = Import ▼=Export
◆ =Import/Export

GEOGRAPHIC SECTION — Huntington - Suffolk County

(G-6696)
INTEGRATED CONTROL CORP
748 Park Ave (11743-3900)
PHONE.................................631 673-5100
Fax: 631 673-6756
Roberta Vaccaro Salerno, *President*
Roberta Salerno, *President*
Nat Cauldwell, *Engineer*
Jason Amian, *Project Engr*
Phil Caputo, *Financial Exec*
▲ EMP: 34
SQ FT: 5,000
SALES (est): 8.4MM **Privately Held**
WEB: www.integratedcontrol.com
SIC: 3823 Industrial instrmnts msrmnt display/control process variable

(G-6697)
INTELLIGENT CTRL SYSTEMS LLC
6 Inlet Pl (11743-1812)
P.O. Box 495, Plainview (11803-0495)
PHONE.................................516 340-1011
Jack Hammer, *Chief Engr*
Michael Ruff,
Celso Monge,
EMP: 5
SALES (est): 261.4K **Privately Held**
SIC: 3699 7389 Electrical equipment & supplies;

(G-6698)
INTERNATIONAL LIFE SCIENCE
23 Gloria Ln (11743-2229)
PHONE.................................631 549-0471
Roy Chavarcode, *President*
EMP: 3
SALES: 1.5MM **Privately Held**
SIC: 2834 Pharmaceutical preparations

(G-6699)
J A T PRINTING INC
Also Called: Minuteman Press
46 Gerard St Unit 2 (11743-6944)
PHONE.................................631 427-1155
Fax: 631 427-1183
John Titus, *President*
Gina Titus, *Vice Pres*
EMP: 6
SALES (est): 630K **Privately Held**
SIC: 2752 Commercial printing, lithographic

(G-6700)
JURIS PUBLISHING INC
71 New St Ste 1 (11743-3397)
PHONE.................................631 351-5430
Charles Kitzen, *President*
Michael Kitzen, *Vice Pres*
Benetta Pearson, *Prdtn Mgr*
James Martucci, *Manager*
Richard Bodt, *Info Tech Mgr*
▲ EMP: 12 EST: 1994
SALES (est): 1.8MM **Privately Held**
WEB: www.jurispub.com
SIC: 2731 Book publishing

(G-6701)
KREFAB CORPORATION
125 Chichester Rd (11743-6526)
PHONE.................................631 842-5151
Fax: 631 842-5156
Robert S Krenn, *President*
James Krenn, *Vice Pres*
Thomas Krenn, *Vice Pres*
EMP: 16
SQ FT: 12,500
SALES: 1.5MM **Privately Held**
SIC: 2431 2521 Millwork; wood office furniture

(G-6702)
LADY-N-TH-WNDOW CHOCOLATES INC
Also Called: Bon Bons Chocolatier
319 Main St (11743-6914)
PHONE.................................631 549-1059
Mary Alice Meinersman, *President*
Susanna Fasolino, *Vice Pres*
EMP: 10
SQ FT: 4,200
SALES (est): 1.3MM **Privately Held**
WEB: www.bonbonschocolatier.com
SIC: 2066 2064 5441 5947 Chocolate; candy & other confectionery products; candy; gift, novelty & souvenir shop

(G-6703)
LONG ISLAND CMNTY NWSPPERS INC
Also Called: Long Islndr Nrth/Sth Pblctns
322 Main St (11743-6923)
PHONE.................................631 427-7000
Fax: 631 427-5820
Sloggatt Peter, *Editor*
Peter Sloggatt, *Manager*
EMP: 12
SALES (corp-wide): 11.8MM **Privately Held**
WEB: www.antonnews.com
SIC: 2711 Newspapers, publishing & printing
PA: Long Island Community Newspapers Inc.
132 E 2nd St
Mineola NY 11501
516 482-4490

(G-6704)
LONG ISLANDER NEWSPAPERS LLC
14 Wall St Ste A (11743-7622)
PHONE.................................631 427-7000
Luann Dallojacono, *Editor*
Linda Gilbert, *Advt Staff*
Peter Sloggatt, *Manager*
Michael Schenkler,
EMP: 7
SALES (est): 366.1K **Privately Held**
SIC: 2711 Newspapers

(G-6705)
NORTHEASTERN PAPER CORP
2 Lilac Ct (11743-6050)
PHONE.................................631 659-3634
Jeff Singer, *President*
Scott Zelen, *Vice Pres*
EMP: 8
SQ FT: 30,000
SALES (est): 1MM **Privately Held**
SIC: 2679 Paper products, converted

(G-6706)
NORTHROP GRUMMAN SYSTEMS CORP
70 Dewey St (11743-7126)
PHONE.................................631 423-1014
Ray Schubnel, *Manager*
Mary Westerling, *Administration*
EMP: 7 **Publicly Held**
WEB: www.sperry.ngc.com
SIC: 3721 Aircraft
HQ: Northrop Grumman Systems Corporation
2980 Fairview Park Dr
Falls Church VA 22042
703 280-2900

(G-6707)
OUTDOOR LIGHTING PERSPECTIVES
1 Warner Ct (11743-5829)
PHONE.................................631 266-6200
Dennis Dowling, *President*
Amy Dowling, *Principal*
EMP: 6
SALES (est): 869.2K **Privately Held**
SIC: 3648 Outdoor lighting equipment

(G-6708)
PASSIVE-PLUS INC
48 Elm St (11743-3402)
PHONE.................................631 425-0938
Lisa Beyel, *President*
Steve Beyel, *Vice Pres*
Mark Johnson, *Sales Mgr*
Erin Hannigan, *Sales Staff*
Joan Bender, *Sales Associate*
▲ EMP: 18
SALES (est): 1.7MM **Privately Held**
SIC: 3679 3675 3676 3674 Microwave components; electronic capacitors; electronic resistors; magnetohydrodynamic (MHD) devices

(G-6709)
PHOTO AGENTS LTD
Also Called: Country Printer, The
716 New York Ave (11743-4413)
PHONE.................................631 421-0258
Fax: 631 421-0308
Gary Lerman, *President*
EMP: 5
SALES (est): 488K **Privately Held**
WEB: www.thecountryprinter.com
SIC: 2759 2752 Commercial printing; commercial printing, lithographic

(G-6710)
PUPA TEK INC
Also Called: Test Cloud
6 Queens St (11743-3725)
PHONE.................................631 664-7817
Ryan Katz, *CEO*
Arnold Katz, *Principal*
EMP: 5 EST: 2011
SALES (est): 198.2K **Privately Held**
SIC: 7372 Prepackaged software

(G-6711)
QUANTUM MECHANICS NY LLC
40 Hennessey Dr (11743-3828)
PHONE.................................917 519-7077
EMP: 6
SALES (est): 315.8K **Privately Held**
SIC: 3572 Computer storage devices

(G-6712)
RED ONYX INDUSTRIAL PDTS LLC
23 Green St Ste 310 (11743-3363)
PHONE.................................516 459-6035
▲ EMP: 5 EST: 2009
SALES (est): 326.8K **Privately Held**
SIC: 3493 Leaf springs: automobile, locomotive, etc.

(G-6713)
RESOURCE CAPITAL FUNDS LP
224 Wall St Ste 202 (11743-2186)
PHONE.................................631 692-9111
Sherri Croasdale, *Branch Mgr*
EMP: 5
SALES (corp-wide): 678.4K **Privately Held**
SIC: 1481 Mine development, nonmetallic minerals
PA: Resource Capital Funds Lp
1400 16th St Ste 200
Denver CO 80202
720 946-1444

(G-6714)
RINGLEAD INC
205 E Main St Ste 2-3a (11743-7944)
PHONE.................................310 906-0545
Jaime Muirhead, *Senior VP*
John Kosturos, *Sales Dir*
Gregg Thaler, *Officer*
EMP: 10 EST: 2016
SALES (est): 324.8K **Privately Held**
SIC: 7372 Business oriented computer software

(G-6715)
ROAR BEVERAGES LLC (PA)
125 W Shore Rd (11743-2042)
PHONE.................................631 683-5565
Roland Neffey, *CEO*
Vincent Nesi, *COO*
Andrew Zambratto, *Vice Pres*
▼ EMP: 21
SALES: 7MM **Privately Held**
SIC: 2087 Concentrates, drink

(G-6716)
ROBOT FRUIT INC
40 Radcliff Dr (11743-2649)
PHONE.................................631 423-7250
Thomas Vieweg, *CEO*
EMP: 12 EST: 2012
SALES (est): 665.6K **Privately Held**
SIC: 7372 Application computer software

(G-6717)
ROLLSON INC
10 Smugglers Cv (11743-1616)
PHONE.................................631 423-9578
Rudolph Creteur, *President*
Tom Perry, *Vice Pres*
EMP: 25 EST: 1938
SQ FT: 15,000
SALES (est): 2.7MM **Privately Held**
WEB: www.rollson.com
SIC: 3429 3444 3446 Marine hardware; sheet metalwork; architectural metalwork

(G-6718)
SC TEXTILES INC
Also Called: Affiliated Services Group
434 New York Ave (11743-3438)
PHONE.................................631 944-6262
Stephen S Cohen, *President*
EMP: 2
SQ FT: 3,500
SALES: 4MM **Privately Held**
SIC: 3679 Electronic loads & power supplies

(G-6719)
SECURITY OFFSET SERVICES INC
11 Grandview St (11743-3534)
PHONE.................................631 944-6031
Fax: 631 944-6034
George Hirsch, *President*
EMP: 9
SQ FT: 10,000
SALES (est): 939.4K **Privately Held**
SIC: 2752 Commercial printing, offset

(G-6720)
SELECT PRODUCTS HOLDINGS LLC
1 Arnold Dr Unit 3 (11743-3981)
P.O. Box 707 (11743-0707)
PHONE.................................855 777-3532
Simon Roozrokh, *CEO*
David Darouvar, *CFO*
▲ EMP: 49
SQ FT: 80,000
SALES: 30MM **Privately Held**
SIC: 2676 Towels, napkins & tissue paper products

(G-6721)
STEVEN KRAUS ASSOCIATES INC
9 Private Rd (11743-2243)
PHONE.................................631 923-2033
Steven Kraus, *President*
EMP: 5
SQ FT: 2,500
SALES: 475K **Privately Held**
SIC: 2542 Office & store showcases & display fixtures

(G-6722)
TELEPHONICS CORPORATION
Tlsi Division
770 Park Ave (11743-3974)
PHONE.................................631 549-6000
Fax: 631 549-6322
Mark Supko, *President*
Peter A Wolfe, *Senior VP*
Barry Eckstein, *Vice Pres*
Siedlewicz Russell, *Facilities Dir*
Jerry Golden, *Purch Agent*
EMP: 30
SALES (corp-wide): 1.9B **Publicly Held**
SIC: 3679 3674 Electronic circuits; semiconductors & related devices
HQ: Telephonics Corporation
815 Broadhollow Rd
Farmingdale NY 11735
631 755-7000

(G-6723)
TELEPHONICS CORPORATION
770 Park Ave (11743-3974)
PHONE.................................631 755-7000
Fax: 631 549-6100
Dominic Nocera, *Controller*
Donald Pastor, *VP Finance*
Ken Hoffman, *Manager*
EMP: 16
SALES (corp-wide): 2B **Publicly Held**
SIC: 3669 Emergency alarms
HQ: Telephonics Corporation
815 Broadhollow Rd
Farmingdale NY 11735
631 755-7000

Huntington - Suffolk County (G-6724)

(G-6724)
TELEPHONICS CORPORATION
780 Park Ave (11743-4516)
PHONE..................631 470-8800
Stephen Maroney, *Director*
EMP: 99
SALES (corp-wide): 2B **Publicly Held**
SIC: 3699 Electronic training devices
HQ: Telephonics Corporation
   815 Broadhollow Rd
   Farmingdale NY 11735
   631 755-7000

(G-6725)
TELEPHONICS TLSI CORP
780 Park Ave (11743-4516)
PHONE..................631 470-8854
Fax: 631 549-6114
Zhigang MA, *President*
Marshall Lacoff, *Senior VP*
Dan McGovern, *Engineer*
Rudy Rupe, *Engineer*
Janet Perinelli, *VP Human Res*
EMP: 200
SQ FT: 20,000
SALES (est): 5.1MM
SALES (corp-wide): 1.9B **Publicly Held**
SIC: 3674 Microcircuits, integrated (semi-conductor)
HQ: Telephonics Corporation
   815 Broadhollow Rd
   Farmingdale NY 11735
   631 755-7000

(G-6726)
TLSI INCORPORATED
780 Park Ave (11743-4516)
PHONE..................631 470-8880
Kevin McSweeney, *COO*
Russ Nenninger, *Opers Mgr*
Kerry Ebbecke, *Purchasing*
Nicolas Salamina, *Engineer*
Pawel Janczykowski, *Design Engr*
EMP: 65
SALES (est): 8.2MM
SALES (corp-wide): 1.9B **Publicly Held**
SIC: 3674 3679 Semiconductors & related devices; electronic circuits
HQ: Telephonics Corporation
   815 Broadhollow Rd
   Farmingdale NY 11735
   631 755-7000

(G-6727)
VALLEY INDUSTRIAL PRODUCTS INC
152 New York Ave (11743-2185)
PHONE..................631 385-9300
Fax: 631 385-9340
Laurel B Phelan, *CEO*
Laurel Phelan, *Ch of Bd*
Alberta Barth Dwyer, *Treasurer*
EMP: 35 EST: 1965
SQ FT: 14,000
SALES (est): 12.5MM **Privately Held**
WEB: www.valleyindustrialtape.com
SIC: 2672 2671 2241 Tape, pressure sensitive: made from purchased materials; packaging paper & plastics film, coated & laminated; narrow fabric mills

(G-6728)
VDC ELECTRONICS INC
155 W Carver St Ste 2 (11743-3376)
PHONE..................631 683-5850
Sheryl Ross, *Ch of Bd*
▲ EMP: 13
SALES (est): 1.9MM **Privately Held**
SIC: 3621 Storage battery chargers, motor & engine generator type

(G-6729)
VENCO SALES INC
755 Park Ave Ste 300 (11743-3979)
PHONE..................631 754-0782
Fax: 631 754-4659
John Venini, *President*
Gary Bosma, *Sales Staff*
Frank Brecher, *Sales Staff*
Rob Morrision, *Sales Staff*
Jake Greenwood, *Manager*
EMP: 20
SALES (est): 2.5MM **Privately Held**
SIC: 3494 Plumbing & heating valves

Huntington Station
Suffolk County

(G-6730)
AEROBIC WEAR INC
16 Depot Rd (11746-1737)
PHONE..................631 673-1830
Fax: 631 673-1834
Bradley Rosen, *President*
EMP: 5
SQ FT: 6,200
SALES: 527.8K **Privately Held**
WEB: www.aerobicwear.com
SIC: 2339 2369 Athletic clothing: women's, misses' & juniors'; girls' & children's outerwear

(G-6731)
AMERICAN CULTURE HAIR INC
159 E 2nd St (11746-1430)
PHONE..................631 242-3142
Louis Guarneri, *President*
Becky Oswald, *Opers Mgr*
Alicyn McDermott, *Advisor*
▲ EMP: 22
SALES (est): 2.1MM **Privately Held**
SIC: 3999 Hair & hair-based products

(G-6732)
AMERICAN TCHNCAL CERAMICS CORP (DH)
Also Called: Atc
1 Norden Ln (11746-2140)
PHONE..................631 622-4700
John Lawing, *CEO*
John S Gilbertson, *Principal*
Richard Monsorno, *Senior VP*
David B Ott, *Senior VP*
Bill Johnson, *Vice Pres*
◆ EMP: 440 EST: 1966
SQ FT: 18,000
SALES (est): 184.5MM
SALES (corp-wide): 12.5B **Publicly Held**
WEB: www.atceramics.com
SIC: 3672 3675 Printed circuit boards; electronic capacitors
HQ: Avx Corporation
   1 Avx Blvd
   Fountain Inn SC 29644
   864 967-2150

(G-6733)
AMERICAN TECHICAL CERAMICS
11 Stepar Pl (11746-2103)
PHONE..................631 622-4758
Eduardo Sayers, *Manager*
▲ EMP: 5
SALES (est): 391.8K **Privately Held**
SIC: 3675 Electronic capacitors

(G-6734)
AMERICAN TECHNICAL CERAMICS
17 Stepar Pl (11746-2141)
PHONE..................631 622-4700
Fax: 631 622-4748
Michael Giacalone, *Vice Pres*
Frank Bennett, *Prdtn Mgr*
Skip Wiese, *Facilities Mgr*
James Navas, *Foreman/Supr*
Ned Patel, *Production*
EMP: 400
SALES (corp-wide): 12.5B **Publicly Held**
WEB: www.atceramics.com
SIC: 3675 Electronic capacitors
HQ: American Technical Ceramics Corp.
   1 Norden Ln
   Huntington Station NY 11746
   631 622-4700

(G-6735)
AUTO SPORT DESIGNS INC
203 W Hills Rd (11746-3147)
PHONE..................631 425-1555
Fax: 631 425-6185
Tom Papadopoulos, *President*
Tomas Papadopoulos, *President*
Beveroy Higgins, *Manager*
▲ EMP: 11
SQ FT: 30,000
SALES (est): 2.1MM **Privately Held**
WEB: www.autosportdesigns.com
SIC: 3711 5511 5531 Automobile assembly, including specialty automobiles; new & used car dealers; speed shops, including race car supplies

(G-6736)
CALIFORNIA FRAGRANCE COMPANY
Also Called: Aromafloria
171 E 2nd St (11746-1430)
PHONE..................631 424-4023
Fax: 516 424-0219
Sharon Christie, *President*
Rosemary Gaynor, *Cust Mgr*
▲ EMP: 30
SQ FT: 30,000
SALES (est): 7.4MM **Privately Held**
SIC: 2844 Toilet preparations

(G-6737)
CARTERS INC
350 Walt Whitman Rd (11746-8704)
PHONE..................631 549-6781
EMP: 9
SALES (corp-wide): 3.2B **Publicly Held**
SIC: 2361 Girls' & children's dresses, blouses & shirts
PA: Carter's, Inc.
   3438 Peachtree Rd Ne # 1800
   Atlanta GA 30326
   678 791-1000

(G-6738)
COMCO PLASTICS INC
11 Stepar Pl (11746-2103)
PHONE..................718 849-9000
Fax: 775 414-5578
Michael French, *President*
Steven Johnson, *Plant Mgr*
Jason Romano, *Sales Executive*
▲ EMP: 37 EST: 1956
SQ FT: 20,000
SALES: 4.3MM **Privately Held**
WEB: www.comcoplastics.com
SIC: 3082 3081 Rods, unsupported plastic; unsupported plastics film & sheet

(G-6739)
COMPLETE SEC & CONTRLS INC
100 Hillwood Dr (11746-1345)
PHONE..................631 421-7200
Steve Krishnayah, *President*
EMP: 18
SQ FT: 7,000
SALES (est): 175.3K **Privately Held**
WEB: www.completesecuritycorp.com
SIC: 3644 Noncurrent-carrying wiring services

(G-6740)
DC CONTRACTING & BUILDING CORP
136 Railroad St (11746-1540)
PHONE..................631 385-1117
Fax: 631 385-4430
Dean Confessore, *President*
Frank Carollo, *Accountant*
Kristy Shoclin, *Manager*
EMP: 13
SQ FT: 5,000
SALES (est): 1.7MM **Privately Held**
SIC: 2431 Woodwork, interior & ornamental

(G-6741)
DILLNER PRECAST INC
200 W 9th St (11746-1667)
PHONE..................631 421-9130
John Dillner, *President*
EMP: 5
SQ FT: 4,000
SALES (corp-wide): 1MM **Privately Held**
SIC: 3272 Concrete products, precast
PA: Dillner Precast Inc
   14 Meadow Ln
   Lloyd Harbor NY 11743
   631 421-9130

(G-6742)
FERACO INDUSTRIES
3 Plumb Ct (11746-1128)
PHONE..................631 547-8120
Ray Albini, *Owner*
EMP: 8
SALES (est): 734.4K **Privately Held**
SIC: 3999 Manufacturing industries

(G-6743)
FORMAC WELDING INC
42 W Hills Rd (11746-2304)
PHONE..................631 421-5525
Fax: 631 421-2023
Joel Mc Elearney, *President*
Maureen Mc Elearney, *Admin Sec*
EMP: 7
SQ FT: 3,800
SALES (est): 852.7K **Privately Held**
SIC: 7692 Welding repair

(G-6744)
FOUR-WAY PALLET CORP
191 E 2nd St (11746-1430)
PHONE..................631 351-3401
Fax: 631 673-7345
Leonard Koppelman, *President*
Jay Koppelman, *Manager*
EMP: 28
SALES (est): 3.3MM **Privately Held**
SIC: 2448 7699 5084 Wood pallets & skids; pallet repair; materials handling machinery

(G-6745)
HART SPORTS INC
4 Roxanne Ct (11746-1122)
PHONE..................631 385-1805
James Hart, *President*
EMP: 6
SALES (est): 411.7K **Privately Held**
SIC: 3949 Hockey equipment & supplies, general

(G-6746)
HERCULES INTERNATIONAL INC
95 W Hills Rd (11746-3119)
PHONE..................631 423-6900
Michael Flaxman, *President*
EMP: 20
SALES (est): 2.2MM **Privately Held**
WEB: www.herculesintlcorp.com
SIC: 3589 Car washing machinery

(G-6747)
HUNTINGTON WELDING & IRON
139 W Pulaski Rd (11746-1693)
PHONE..................631 423-3331
Fax: 631 423-3318
Andrew Blondrage, *Owner*
EMP: 5
SALES (est): 301.5K **Privately Held**
SIC: 7692 Welding repair

(G-6748)
I A S NATIONAL INC
Also Called: Hercules
95 W Hills Rd (11746-3197)
PHONE..................631 423-6900
Fax: 631 385-3222
Michael Flaxman, *President*
Lynn Kramer, *Manager*
▼ EMP: 20
SALES (est): 2.8MM **Privately Held**
WEB: www.hercules.com
SIC: 3589 2899 Car washing machinery; chemical preparations

(G-6749)
ISLAND AUTOMATED GATE CO LLC
125 W Hills Rd (11746-3144)
PHONE..................631 425-0196
Stan Osowski,
EMP: 3
SALES: 1MM **Privately Held**
SIC: 3569 Bridge or gate machinery, hydraulic

(G-6750)
JOHN LAROCCA & SON INC
Also Called: E C Sumereau & Sons
290 Broadway (11746-1403)
PHONE..................631 423-5256
Fax: 631 423-5271
John Larocca, *President*
EMP: 6 EST: 1856
SQ FT: 10,000

GEOGRAPHIC SECTION

Ilion - Herkimer County (G-6778)

SALES (est): 741.9K Privately Held
WEB: www.ecsumereau.com
SIC: 3471 Electroplating of metals or formed products

(G-6751)
KELMAR SYSTEMS INC
284 Broadway (11746-1497)
PHONE..................631 421-1230
Fax: 631 421-1274
Andrew Marglin, *President*
Laurie Franz, *Vice Pres*
Raymond Matthews, *Engineer*
Joan Marglin, *Admin Sec*
EMP: 16
SQ FT: 4,500
SALES: 1.4MM Privately Held
WEB: www.kelmarsystems.com
SIC: 3861 Sound recording & reproducing equipment, motion picture

(G-6752)
LUCKY BRAND DUNGAREES LLC
100 Walt Whitman Rd 1090b (11746-4100)
PHONE..................631 350-7358
EMP: 36
SALES (corp-wide): 392.4MM Privately Held
SIC: 2325 Men's & boys' trousers & slacks
PA: Lucky Brand Dungarees, Llc
540 S Santa Fe Ave
Los Angeles CA 90013
213 443-5700

(G-6753)
MELBOURNE C FISHER YACHT SAILS
Also Called: Doyle Sails
1345 New York Ave Ste 2 (11746-1751)
PHONE..................631 673-5055
Fax: 631 673-6736
Mark Washeim, *President*
Diana Malkin'washeim, *Vice Pres*
▼ EMP: 6
SALES (est): 657K Privately Held
SIC: 2394 Sails: made from purchased materials

(G-6754)
MICROSOFT CORPORATION
160 Walt Whitman Rd 1006b (11746-4160)
PHONE..................631 760-2340
EMP: 5
SALES (corp-wide): 89.9B Publicly Held
SIC: 7372 Prepackaged software
PA: Microsoft Corporation
1 Microsoft Way
Redmond WA 98052
425 882-8080

(G-6755)
NEW YORK DIGITAL CORPORATION
33 Walt Whitman Rd # 117 (11746-3678)
PHONE..................631 630-9798
Salil Bandy, *President*
John Tully, *Sales Mgr*
EMP: 11
SQ FT: 30,000
SALES (est): 830K Privately Held
SIC: 3679 Electronic loads & power supplies

(G-6756)
NORTH SHORE PALLET INC
191 E 2nd St (11746-1430)
PHONE..................631 673-4700
EMP: 8
SALES (est): 1.2MM Privately Held
SIC: 2448 Pallets, wood & wood with metal

(G-6757)
ROTTKAMP TENNIS INC
100 Broadway (11746-1448)
PHONE..................631 421-0040
Richard Rottkamp, *President*
EMP: 25
SALES (est): 1.7MM Privately Held
SIC: 3949 Tennis equipment & supplies

(G-6758)
RUBBER STAMP X PRESS
7 Bradford Pl (11747-1043)
PHONE..................631 423-1322
Ilene Schleichkorn, *Chairman*
EMP: 5
SALES (est): 380.4K Privately Held
SIC: 3953 Embossing seals & hand stamps

(G-6759)
SCENT-A-VISION INC
171 E 2nd St (11746-1430)
PHONE..................631 424-4905
Fax: 631 424-0219
Sharon Christie, *President*
Mark Christie, *Admin Director*
EMP: 23
SQ FT: 5,000
SALES (est): 3.3MM Privately Held
WEB: www.aromafloria.com
SIC: 2844 5122 Toilet preparations; perfumes

(G-6760)
SELECTRODE INDUSTRIES INC (PA)
230 Broadway (11746-1403)
PHONE..................631 547-5470
Fax: 631 547-5475
Joe Paternoster, *Ch of Bd*
Paul Paternoster, *President*
Rich Oliveri, *Manager*
Randy Bruckner, *Technology*
Steve Lehecka, *Director*
▲ EMP: 6
SQ FT: 26,000
SALES (est): 13.2MM Privately Held
WEB: www.selectrode.com
SIC: 3356 3496 Nonferrous rolling & drawing; miscellaneous fabricated wire products

(G-6761)
SUPER SWEEP INC (PA)
Also Called: SMS
20 Railroad St Unit 1 (11746-1296)
PHONE..................631 223-8205
Michael P Margolin, *President*
Jarred Saperton, *COO*
EMP: 12
SALES (est): 700.8K Privately Held
SIC: 3354 Aluminum extruded products

(G-6762)
SWISSWAY INC
123 W Hills Rd (11746-3155)
PHONE..................631 351-5350
Fax: 631 351-5005
Gerard Cavalier Jr, *President*
Jody Cavalier, *Controller*
EMP: 25 EST: 1963
SQ FT: 10,000
SALES (est): 3.7MM Privately Held
WEB: www.swisswayinc.com
SIC: 3599 Machine shop, jobbing & repair

(G-6763)
TECHNOPAVING NEW YORK INC
270 Broadway (11746-1561)
PHONE..................631 351-6472
Christine Brown, *President*
EMP: 7
SALES (est): 719.9K Privately Held
SIC: 3531 Pavers

(G-6764)
TEQUIPMENT INC
Also Called: T E Q
7 Norden Ln (11746-2102)
PHONE..................516 922-3508
Fax: 631 293-4951
Robert Sugarman, *President*
Christine Sugarman, *Corp Secy*
Frank Falconeri, *Warehouse Mgr*
Alyssa Armenio, *Human Res Mgr*
Philip Iserino, *VP Sales*
EMP: 100
SQ FT: 40,000
SALES (est): 22.9MM Privately Held
WEB: www.tequipment.com
SIC: 7372 Educational computer software

(G-6765)
VAIRE LLC
200 E 2nd St Ste 34 (11746-1464)
PHONE..................631 271-4933
Fax: 631 424-1128
Robert Pearl,

EMP: 7
SQ FT: 23,000
SALES (est): 1.2MM Privately Held
SIC: 3652 5211 Compact laser discs, prerecorded; bathroom fixtures, equipment & supplies

(G-6766)
WALSH & HUGHES INC (PA)
Also Called: Velvetop Products
1455 New York Ave (11746-1706)
PHONE..................631 427-5904
Fax: 631 673-3301
John B Walsh, *President*
Linda J Walsh, *Treasurer*
EMP: 8
SQ FT: 3,800
SALES (est): 1.7MM Privately Held
WEB: www.velvetop.com
SIC: 2891 5941 5032 5091 Sealants; tennis goods & equipment; clay construction materials, except refractory; sporting & recreation goods

(G-6767)
WTBI INC
Also Called: Whats The Big Idea
200 E 2nd St Ste 12 (11746-1462)
PHONE..................631 547-1993
Jeff Vogel, *President*
▼ EMP: 7
SQ FT: 6,000
SALES (est): 710K Privately Held
WEB: www.wtbi.com
SIC: 3499 Magnets, permanent: metallic

(G-6768)
Z-CAR-D CORP
Also Called: Sign-A-Rama
403 Oakwood Rd (11746-7207)
PHONE..................631 424-2077
Fax: 631 424-2078
Dawn M Tiritter-Bent, *Ch of Bd*
Michael Ziccardi, *Vice Pres*
Krystal Eichler, *Assistant*
EMP: 28
SQ FT: 15,000
SALES (est): 3.1MM Privately Held
WEB: www.ssar.com
SIC: 3993 Signs & advertising specialties

Hurleyville
Sullivan County

(G-6769)
MONGIELLO SALES INC
250 Hilldale Rd (12747-5301)
P.O. Box 320 (12747-0320)
PHONE..................845 436-4200
Anthony Mongiello, *President*
Gary Kudrowitz, *Manager*
▼ EMP: 40
SALES (est): 4.1MM Privately Held
SIC: 2022 Natural cheese

(G-6770)
MONGIELLOS ITLN CHEESE SPC LLC
Also Called: Formaggio Italian Cheese
250 Hilldale Rd (12747-5301)
P.O. Box 320 (12747-0320)
PHONE..................845 436-4200
Fax: 845 436-7076
Anthony Mongiello, *CEO*
John Jmongiello, *COO*
Stuart Parsons, *Controller*
Gary Kudrowitz, *Manager*
Anna Rose Mongiello, *Manager*
EMP: 150
SQ FT: 65,000
SALES: 25.6MM Privately Held
SIC: 2022 Natural cheese

Hyde Park
Dutchess County

(G-6771)
ABE POOL SERVICE
793 Violet Ave (12538-1952)
PHONE..................845 473-7730
Fax: 845 229-2378

Abraham Stewart, *President*
EMP: 5
SALES (est): 618.4K Privately Held
SIC: 3589 Swimming pool filter & water conditioning systems

(G-6772)
CASTINO CORPORATION
1300 Route 9g (12538-2076)
PHONE..................845 229-0341
Eric Castaldo, *Principal*
EMP: 5 EST: 2011
SALES (est): 537.2K Privately Held
SIC: 3089 Plastics products

(G-6773)
HYDE PARK BREWING CO INC
4076 Albany Post Rd (12538-1934)
PHONE..................845 229-8277
Fax: 845 229-6146
Carmelo Decicco, *President*
EMP: 20
SQ FT: 4,000
SALES (est): 2.2MM Privately Held
WEB: www.hydeparkbrewing.com
SIC: 2082 5812 Malt beverages; eating places

(G-6774)
NEW CITY PRESS INC
202 Comforter Blvd (12538-2977)
PHONE..................845 229-0335
Fax: 845 229-0351
Patrick Markey, *General Mgr*
Gary Brandal, *Manager*
Robert Cummings, *Administration*
EMP: 5
SALES (est): 441.2K Privately Held
WEB: www.newcitypress.com
SIC: 2731 Books: publishing only

(G-6775)
RICHARD R CAIN INC
50 Scenic Dr (12538-1313)
PHONE..................845 229-7410
Fax: 845 229-6538
Richard R Cain, *President*
EMP: 11
SQ FT: 1,200
SALES (est): 1.1MM Privately Held
SIC: 3589 1629 Sewage treatment equipment; waste water & sewage treatment plant construction

(G-6776)
RIVERWOOD SIGNS BY DANDEV DESI
7 Maple Ln (12538-1223)
PHONE..................845 229-0282
Kathleen Hinz-Shaffer, *President*
EMP: 5
SALES: 100K Privately Held
SIC: 3993 7336 7389 Signs & advertising specialties; commercial art & graphic design; design, commercial & industrial

(G-6777)
VICTORIA PRECISION INC
78 Travis Rd (12538-2753)
PHONE..................845 473-9309
Vincent Slaninka, *President*
Ray Forman, *Sales Staff*
EMP: 5
SQ FT: 3,000
SALES: 270K Privately Held
WEB: www.victoriaprecisioninc.com
SIC: 3599 Machine shop, jobbing & repair

Ilion
Herkimer County

(G-6778)
ACORN PRODUCTS CORP
27 Pleasant Ave (13357-1115)
PHONE..................315 894-4868
John Thayer, *President*
EMP: 15
SALES (est): 1.5MM Privately Held
SIC: 2396 Printing & embossing on plastics fabric articles

Ilion - Herkimer County (G-6779)

(G-6779)
FERMER PRECISION INC
114 Johnson Rd (13357-3899)
PHONE..................315 822-6371
Fax: 315 822-6300
Stewart Bunce, *President*
John Tofani, *Vice Pres*
Chad Bernier, *Production*
Tina Lafountain, *Purchasing*
Steve Scheibel, *Sales Staff*
EMP: 72
SQ FT: 60,000
SALES: 8MM **Privately Held**
WEB: www.fermerprecision.com
SIC: 3599 Electrical discharge machining (EDM)

(G-6780)
ILION PLASTICS INC
27 Pleasant Ave (13357-1115)
PHONE..................315 894-4868
Fax: 315 894-4890
Steve Quinn, *President*
Kathy Quinn, *President*
EMP: 16
SQ FT: 10,000
SALES: 800K **Privately Held**
SIC: 3089 Injection molding of plastics

(G-6781)
JAMES WIRE DIE CO
138 West St (13357-2250)
PHONE..................315 894-3233
R B Roux, *President*
Alex Roux, *Vice Pres*
EMP: 5
SALES: 100K **Privately Held**
SIC: 3544 Special dies & tools

(G-6782)
ORIGINAL HRKMER CNTY CHESE INC
Also Called: Herkimer Cheese
2745 State Route 51 (13357-4299)
P.O. Box 310, Herkimer (13350-0310)
PHONE..................315 895-7428
Sheldon Basloe, *President*
Norma Basloe, *Corp Secy*
Robert Basloe, *Vice Pres*
Nora Ray, *Safety Mgr*
Jacob Basloe, *Purch Mgr*
EMP: 60 **EST:** 1949
SQ FT: 22,913
SALES (est): 8.6MM **Privately Held**
WEB: www.herkimerfoods.com
SIC: 2022 2099 Cheese, natural & processed; gelatin dessert preparations; dessert mixes & fillings

(G-6783)
REMINGTON ARMS COMPANY LLC
14 Hoefler Ave (13357-1888)
PHONE..................315 895-3482
Fax: 315 895-3237
Laird G Williams, *Principal*
Steven Taylor, *Safety Dir*
Joseph Nolan, *Opers Staff*
Robert Skinner, *Purch Mgr*
Roseann Barone, *Buyer*
EMP: 850
SALES (corp-wide): 36.1B **Publicly Held**
WEB: www.remington.com
SIC: 3484 8711 Small arms; engineering services
HQ: Remington Arms Company, Llc
870 Remington Dr
Madison NC 27025
336 548-8700

(G-6784)
REVIVAL INDUSTRIES INC
126 Old Forge Rd (13357-4200)
PHONE..................315 868-1085
Richard Jackson, *President*
Edward R Jackson, *Vice Pres*
EMP: 17
SQ FT: 16,000
SALES (est): 1MM **Privately Held**
WEB: www.revivalindustries.com
SIC: 2426 2499 Gun stocks, wood; handles, poles, dowels & stakes: wood; novelties, wood fiber

Interlaken
Seneca County

(G-6785)
AMERICANA VINEYARDS & WINERY
4367 E Covert Rd (14847-9720)
PHONE..................607 387-6801
Fax: 607 387-3852
Joseph Gober, *President*
EMP: 15
SALES: 750K **Privately Held**
SIC: 2084 Wines

(G-6786)
HIPSHOT PRODUCTS INC
Also Called: Melissa
8248 State Route 96 (14847-9655)
PHONE..................607 532-9404
Fax: 607 532-9530
David Borisoff, *President*
Zack Singer, *Engineer*
▲ **EMP:** 15
SALES (est): 2.1MM **Privately Held**
WEB: www.hipshotproducts.com
SIC: 3931 5736 Guitars & parts, electric & nonelectric; musical instrument stores

(G-6787)
LUCAS VINEYARDS & WINERY
3862 County Road 150 (14847-9805)
PHONE..................607 532-4825
Fax: 607 532-8580
Ruth Lucas, *President*
EMP: 12
SALES (est): 2MM **Privately Held**
WEB: www.lucasvineyards.com
SIC: 2084 0172 5921 Wines; grapes; liquor stores

(G-6788)
PINE TREE FARMS INC
3714 Cayuga St (14847-9607)
P.O. Box 254 (14847-0254)
PHONE..................607 532-4312
Fax: 607 532-4311
Mark Stillions, *President*
Joelle Stillions, *Corp Secy*
Neal Stillions, *Vice Pres*
Michelle Griego-Stillions, *Sales Mgr*
EMP: 30
SQ FT: 14,000
SALES (est): 4.7MM **Privately Held**
WEB: www.pinetreefarmsinc.com
SIC: 2048 Bird food, prepared

Inwood
Nassau County

(G-6789)
APEX ARIDYNE CORP
168 Doughty Blvd (11096-2010)
P.O. Box 960670 (11096-0670)
PHONE..................516 239-4400
Edward Schlussel, *President*
EMP: 5
SALES (corp-wide): 8.6MM **Privately Held**
SIC: 2258 2257 Lace & warp knit fabric mills; weft knit fabric mills
PA: Apex Aridyne Corp.
2350 Long Dairy Rd
Graham NC
516 239-4400

(G-6790)
ARLEE LIGHTING CORP
125 Doughty Blvd (11096-2003)
PHONE..................516 595-8558
Pinchaf Gralla, *President*
▲ **EMP:** 4
SQ FT: 10,000
SALES: 3MM **Privately Held**
SIC: 3646 Commercial indusl & institutional electric lighting fixtures

(G-6791)
AUDIOSAVINGS INC
Also Called: Rockville Pro
600 Bayview Ave Ste 200 (11096-1625)
PHONE..................888 445-1555
▼ **EMP:** 14
SALES (est): 2.5MM **Privately Held**
SIC: 3651 Mfg Home Audio/Video Equipment

(G-6792)
BEL TRANSFORMER INC (HQ)
Also Called: Signal Transformer
500 Bayview Ave (11096-1702)
P.O. Box 36129, Newark NJ (07188-6106)
PHONE..................516 239-5777
Fax: 516 239-7208
Daniel Bernstein, *President*
Sandy Axelrad, *General Mgr*
Colin Dunn, *Vice Pres*
Mohammad Siddiqui, *Accountant*
▲ **EMP:** 60
SQ FT: 40,000
SALES: 17MM
SALES (corp-wide): 500.1MM **Publicly Held**
WEB: www.signaltransformer.com
SIC: 3677 Electronic coils, transformers & other inductors
PA: Bel Fuse Inc.
206 Van Vorst St
Jersey City NJ 07302
201 432-0463

(G-6793)
CUSTOM CANDY CONCEPTS INC
50 Inip Dr (11096-1011)
PHONE..................516 824-3228
Barry J Bass, *President*
Leonid Kaufman, *Treasurer*
EMP: 7
SALES (est): 530K **Privately Held**
WEB: www.customcandyconcepts.com
SIC: 2064 Candy & other confectionery products

(G-6794)
EXCEL PAINT APPLICATORS INC
555 Doughty Blvd (11096-1031)
PHONE..................347 221-1968
Fax: 718 927-3662
P C Sekar, *President*
Georgio Lee, *Manager*
▲ **EMP:** 45
SQ FT: 48,000
SALES (est): 6MM **Privately Held**
SIC: 2851 Paints & allied products

(G-6795)
EXCELLENT ART MFG CORP
Also Called: Neva Slip
531 Bayview Ave (11096-1703)
PHONE..................718 388-7075
Fax: 718 388-9404
Marshall Korn, *President*
David Korn, *Vice Pres*
▲ **EMP:** 16 **EST:** 1929
SQ FT: 25,000
SALES (est): 1.3MM **Privately Held**
SIC: 2392 3949 2273 Household furnishings; mattress pads; sporting & athletic goods; carpets & rugs

(G-6796)
FIBERALL CORP
449 Sheridan Blvd (11096-1203)
PHONE..................516 371-5200
Fax: 516 371-2509
Isaac Zilber, *President*
Sophie Zilber, *Vice Pres*
▲ **EMP:** 25
SQ FT: 8,000
SALES (est): 5.6MM **Privately Held**
WEB: www.fiberall.com
SIC: 3661 Multiplex equipment, telephone & telegraph

(G-6797)
GENERAL DIARIES CORPORATION
56 John St (11096-1353)
PHONE..................516 371-2244
Fax: 516 239-0851
Mark Lebo, *President*
▲ **EMP:** 15 **EST:** 1953
SALES (est): 1.9MM **Privately Held**
WEB: www.dallasnews.com
SIC: 2782 2678 Memorandum books, printed; diaries; desk pads, paper: made from purchased materials

(G-6798)
HASTINGS HIDE INC
Also Called: A J Hollander Enterprises
372 Doughty Blvd (11096-1337)
PHONE..................516 295-2400
Howard Ganz, *President*
EMP: 6
SALES (corp-wide): 1.7MM **Privately Held**
SIC: 3111 5159 4731 Leather tanning & finishing; hides; agents, shipping
PA: Hastings Hide, Inc.
231 Road 3168
Hastings NE 68901
402 463-5308

(G-6799)
INWOOD MATERIAL
1 Sheridan Blvd (11096-1807)
PHONE..................516 371-1842
Fax: 516 671-5273
Frank Sciarrino, *President*
EMP: 11
SALES (est): 1.7MM **Privately Held**
SIC: 3273 5082 Ready-mixed concrete; masonry equipment & supplies

(G-6800)
LES CHATEAUX DE FRANCE INC
1 Craft Ave (11096-1609)
PHONE..................516 239-6795
Fax: 516 239-6215
Gerald Shapiro, *President*
Marie Cuscianna, *Vice Pres*
EMP: 28 **EST:** 1950
SQ FT: 7,000
SALES (est): 3.5MM **Privately Held**
SIC: 2038 Snacks, including onion rings, cheese sticks, etc.

(G-6801)
MGR EQUIPMENT CORP
22 Gates Ave (11096-1612)
PHONE..................516 239-3030
Fax: 516 239-3602
Gerald Ross, *President*
Robert Ross, *Corp Secy*
George Mauder, *Vice Pres*
▼ **EMP:** 25
SQ FT: 40,000
SALES (est): 4.3MM **Privately Held**
WEB: www.mgrequip.com
SIC: 3585 Refrigeration & heating equipment; ice making machinery

(G-6802)
N3A CORPORATION
345 Doughty Blvd (11096-1348)
PHONE..................516 284-6799
Niall Alli, *CEO*
Adrienne Alli, *CFO*
▲ **EMP:** 100 **EST:** 2007
SQ FT: 100,000
SALES (est): 9.3MM **Privately Held**
SIC: 2676 2599 Towels, napkins & tissue paper products; hotel furniture

(G-6803)
NEA MANUFACTURING CORP
345 Doughty Blvd (11096-1348)
PHONE..................516 371-4200
Fax: 516 239-0239
Sheik Alli, *President*
Niall Alli, *Senior VP*
Justin Alli, *CFO*
▲ **EMP:** 37
SQ FT: 4,000
SALES (est): 5MM **Privately Held**
SIC: 3672 3679 3677 3678 Printed circuit boards; electronic switches; electronic transformers; electronic connectors; household audio & video equipment; current-carrying wiring devices

(G-6804)
NOEL ASSOC
114 Henry St Ste A (11096-2350)
PHONE..................516 371-5420
EMP: 5

▲ = Import ▼=Export
◆ =Import/Export

GEOGRAPHIC SECTION

SALES (est): 300K **Privately Held**
SIC: 3993 Mfg Signs/Advertising Specialties

(G-6805)
PLUSLUX LLC
Also Called: Wascomat of America
461 Doughty Blvd (11096-1344)
PHONE..................................516 371-4400
Neal Milch,
EMP: 5 **EST:** 2015
SALES (est): 278.9K **Privately Held**
SIC: 3633 Household laundry equipment; household laundry machines, including coin-operated; drycleaning machines, household: including coin-operated; laundry dryers, household or coin-operated

(G-6806)
SCY MANUFACTURING INC
600 Bayview Ave Ste 200 (11096-1625)
PHONE..................................516 986-3083
Shmuel Freund, *President*
Chagai Freund, *Vice Pres*
Isaac Freund, *Vice Pres*
Sarah Herzberg, *Accounting Mgr*
◆ **EMP:** 3 **EST:** 2013
SQ FT: 900
SALES: 8MM **Privately Held**
SIC: 3651 Household audio & video equipment

Irving
Chautauqua County

(G-6807)
SENECA NATION ENTERPRISE
Also Called: This Business Is Tribally Owned
11482 Route 20 (14081-9539)
PHONE..................................716 934-7430
Fax: 716 934-3255
Seneca Nation, *Owner*
Julie Carry, *Exec Dir*
EMP: 12
SALES (est): 1.3MM **Privately Held**
SIC: 2111 5172 Cigarettes; gasoline

Irvington
Westchester County

(G-6808)
ABYRX INC
1 Bridge St Ste 121 (10533-1553)
PHONE..................................914 357-2600
John Pacifico, *President*
David Hart, *Vice Pres*
Jenny Enrico, *Opers Mgr*
Richard Kronenthal, *Officer*
EMP: 11 **EST:** 2013
SALES (est): 1.4MM **Privately Held**
SIC: 3841 Surgical instruments & apparatus

(G-6809)
CITY GEAR INC
213 Taxter Rd (10533-1111)
PHONE..................................914 450-4746
John Clark, *President*
Ingred Roberg, *Vice Pres*
Vanessa Pyatt, *Controller*
▼ **EMP:** 6
SQ FT: 3,000
SALES (est): 510K **Privately Held**
SIC: 3599 Machine shop, jobbing & repair

(G-6810)
EILEEN FISHER INC (PA)
Also Called: Eileen Fisher Womens Apparel
2 Bridge St Ste 230 (10533-3500)
PHONE..................................914 591-5700
Fax: 914 591-8824
Eileen Fisher, *Ch of Bd*
Christine Beisigel, *General Mgr*
Hillary Old, *Vice Pres*
Mariclare Vanbergen, *Vice Pres*
Loretta Torcicollo, *Prdtn Dir*
▲ **EMP:** 125
SQ FT: 20,000
SALES: 350MM **Privately Held**
WEB: www.eileenfisher.com
SIC: 2339 Sportswear, women's

(G-6811)
FEINKIND INC
Also Called: REFINEDKIND PET PRODUCTS
17 Algonquin Dr (10533-1007)
PHONE..................................800 289-6136
Josh Feinkind, *CEO*
▲ **EMP:** 1
SQ FT: 65,000
SALES: 1MM **Privately Held**
SIC: 2511 Novelty furniture: wood

(G-6812)
GUTTZ CORPORATION OF AMERICA
Also Called: Gutts Corporation of America
50 S Buckhout St Ste 104 (10533-2217)
PHONE..................................914 591-9600
Robert H Cohen, *President*
Ronald Roemer, *Vice Pres*
Jane Berger, *Manager*
EMP: 13
SQ FT: 7,000
SALES (est): 1.5MM **Privately Held**
WEB: www.marketvis.com
SIC: 3955 Print cartridges for laser & other computer printers

(G-6813)
HAIR VENTURES LLC
Also Called: Hairstory
94 Fargo Ln (10533-1202)
PHONE..................................718 664-7689
Eli Halliwell, *CEO*
EMP: 13
SALES (est): 715.5K **Privately Held**
SIC: 2844 7389 Hair preparations, including shampoos;

(G-6814)
ISP OPTICS CORPORATION (HQ)
50 S Buckhout St (10533-2203)
PHONE..................................914 591-3070
Mark Lifshotz, *CEO*
Joseph Menaker, *President*
Rasvana Popescu, *VP Opers*
Dale Allen, *Facilities Mgr*
Iryna Kutsiaba, *Accountant*
▲ **EMP:** 57
SQ FT: 22,000
SALES (est): 8.7MM
SALES (corp-wide): 28.3MM **Publicly Held**
WEB: www.ispoptics.com
SIC: 3827 Optical instruments & lenses
PA: Lightpath Technologies, Inc.
2603 Challenger Tech Ct # 100
Orlando FL 32826
407 382-4003

(G-6815)
ORTHOCON INC
1 Bridge St Ste 121 (10533-1553)
PHONE..................................914 357-2600
John J Pacifico, *President*
David J Hart, *Vice Pres*
Christine Moley, *Vice Pres*
Stephen Hall, *CFO*
EMP: 23 **EST:** 2006
SALES (est): 2.8MM **Privately Held**
SIC: 3841 Surgical & medical instruments

(G-6816)
PECO PALLET INC (HQ)
2 Bridge St Ste 210 (10533-1594)
PHONE..................................914 376-5444
Fax: 914 376-7376
Joseph Dagnese, *CEO*
David Lee, *President*
Jeff Euritt, *Vice Pres*
Adrian Potgieter, *Vice Pres*
Roberto Sobrino, *Vice Pres*
EMP: 24
SQ FT: 5,000
SALES (est): 32.2MM **Privately Held**
WEB: www.pecopallet.com
SIC: 2448 7359 Pallets, wood; pallet rental services

Island Park
Nassau County

(G-6817)
A-1 MANHATTAN CUSTOM FURN INC
Also Called: Manhattan Cabinets
4315 Austin Blvd (11558-1627)
PHONE..................................212 750-9800
Eric Heim, *Manager*
EMP: 7
SALES (corp-wide): 10.2MM **Privately Held**
WEB: www.manhattancabinetry.com
SIC: 2511 Wood household furniture
PA: A-1 Manhattan Custom Furniture Inc.
4315 Austin Blvd
Island Park NY 11558
718 937-4780

(G-6818)
BHI ELEVATOR CABS INC
74 Alabama Ave (11558-1116)
PHONE..................................516 431-5665
Rick Hart, *President*
Brian Holodar, *Principal*
EMP: 15
SALES (est): 3.2MM **Privately Held**
SIC: 3534 Elevators & equipment

(G-6819)
F & B PHOTO OFFSET CO INC (PA)
4 California Pl N (11558-2215)
P.O. Box 366 (11558-0366)
PHONE..................................516 431-5433
Frank Naudus, *President*
EMP: 5
SQ FT: 6,000
SALES: 1MM **Privately Held**
SIC: 2752 2759 Commercial printing, offset; letterpress printing

(G-6820)
H D M LABS INC
153 Kingston Blvd (11558-1926)
PHONE..................................516 431-8357
Hardat Singh, *President*
Natashia Singh, *COO*
EMP: 5 **EST:** 1993
SQ FT: 1,600
SALES (est): 799.9K **Privately Held**
WEB: www.hdmlabsinc.com
SIC: 3829 Medical diagnostic systems, nuclear

(G-6821)
NATHAN BERRIE & SONS INC
Also Called: Naomi Manufacturing
3956 Long Beach Rd (11558-1146)
P.O. Box 240 (11558-0240)
PHONE..................................516 432-8500
Fax: 516 432-8544
Stanley Berrie, *President*
Suzanne Berrie, *Admin Sec*
EMP: 9 **EST:** 1944
SQ FT: 4,000
SALES (est): 1.1MM **Privately Held**
SIC: 3915 Jewelers' findings & materials

(G-6822)
NORTHFELD PRECISION INSTR CORP
Also Called: NORTH FIELD
4400 Austin Blvd (11558-1621)
P.O. Box 550 (11558-0550)
PHONE..................................516 431-1112
Fax: 516 431-1928
Donald Freedman, *Ch of Bd*
Paul Defeo, *COO*
Linda Vassallo, *Accounting Mgr*
Ken Sprenger, *VP Sales*
Charles Florio, *Sales Staff*
EMP: 32
SQ FT: 15,000
SALES: 6MM **Privately Held**
WEB: www.northfield.com
SIC: 3545 Chucks: drill, lathe or magnetic (machine tool accessories)

(G-6823)
WOOD DESIGNS DELUXE CORP
4090 Austin Blvd (11558-1241)
PHONE..................................917 414-4640
EMP: 5
SALES (est): 487.2K **Privately Held**
SIC: 2782 Checkbooks

Islandia
Suffolk County

(G-6824)
A & L MACHINE COMPANY INC
200 Blydenburg Rd Ste 9 (11749-5011)
PHONE..................................631 463-3111
Fax: 631 778-8071
Horst Ehinger, *President*
George Ramos, *Principal*
EMP: 7 **EST:** 1963
SQ FT: 4,000
SALES (est): 966.7K **Privately Held**
WEB: www.anlmachine.com
SIC: 3599 Machine shop, jobbing & repair

(G-6825)
ARK SCIENCES INC
1601 Veterans Hwy Ste 315 (11749-1543)
PHONE..................................646 943-1520
Joseph Tosini, *President*
EMP: 6
SALES (est): 690.3K **Privately Held**
SIC: 2834 Veterinary pharmaceutical preparations

(G-6826)
BIG APPLE SIGN CORP
Also Called: Big Apple Visual Group
3 Oval Dr (11749-1402)
PHONE..................................631 342-0303
Amir Khalfan, *Branch Mgr*
Ahmedali Ahalsan, *Manager*
EMP: 35
SALES (corp-wide): 12.7MM **Privately Held**
WEB: www.bigapplegroup.com
SIC: 3993 2399 3552 Signs, not made in custom sign painting shops; displays & cutouts, window & lobby; banners, made from fabric; silk screens for textile industry
PA: Big Apple Sign Corp.
247 W 35th St Frnt 1
New York NY 10001
212 629-3650

(G-6827)
CENTURY DIRECT LLC
15 Enter Ln (11749-4811)
PHONE..................................212 763-0600
Michael Kellogg, *Principal*
Eric Seid, *COO*
Martin Rego, *Vice Pres*
Chris Calahan, *Plant Mgr*
Thomas McNeill, *CFO*
▲ **EMP:** 200
SQ FT: 80,000
SALES (est): 41MM **Privately Held**
WEB: www.centltr.com
SIC: 2759 7331 7379 Commercial printing; direct mail advertising services; computer related maintenance services

(G-6828)
CES INDUSTRIES INC
95 Hoffman Ln Ste S (11749-5020)
PHONE..................................631 782-7088
Fax: 516 293-8556
Mitchell B Nesenoff, *CEO*
Edward J Ermler, *Vice Pres*
Frank Ellis, *Manager*
EMP: 40
SQ FT: 20,000
SALES (est): 6.7MM **Privately Held**
WEB: www.cesindustries.com
SIC: 3699 Electronic training devices

(G-6829)
DISPLAY MARKETING GROUP INC
170 Oval Dr Ste B (11749-1419)
PHONE..................................631 348-4450
Steven Larit, *President*
EMP: 35
SQ FT: 24,000

Islandia - Suffolk County (G-6830)

SALES (est): 5.3MM **Privately Held**
SIC: 3993 Displays & cutouts, window & lobby

(G-6830)
DUETTO INTEGRATED SYSTEMS INC
Also Called: Dis
85 Hoffman Ln Ste Q (11749-5019)
PHONE..................631 851-0102
Carmela Faraci, Office Mgr
Gary Sortino, Manager
Michael Faraci, Technician
EMP: 10
SQ FT: 2,000
SALES (est): 1.5MM **Privately Held**
SIC: 3599 Custom machinery

(G-6831)
FLEXBAR MACHINE CORPORATION
Also Called: Mediflex
250 Gibbs Rd (11749-2697)
PHONE..................631 582-8440
Jon Adler, President
Juanita Adler, Corp Secy
Robert Adler, Vice Pres
Lance Larkin, Vice Pres
Steven Culver, Engineer
▲ EMP: 27
SQ FT: 10,500
SALES (est): 6.3MM **Privately Held**
WEB: www.flexbar.com
SIC: 3545 3841 Machine tool attachments & accessories; surgical & medical instruments

(G-6832)
I E D CORP
88 Bridge Rd (11749)
PHONE..................631 348-0424
Fax: 631 348-0425
Martin Ramage, President
Robert Jaffe, Engineer
EMP: 10
SQ FT: 5,000
SALES (est): 1.5MM **Privately Held**
SIC: 3674 3625 Microprocessors; relays & industrial controls

(G-6833)
ICD PUBLICATIONS INC (PA)
Also Called: Hotel Business
1377 Motor Pkwy Ste 410 (11749-5258)
PHONE..................631 246-9300
Fax: 516 246-9496
Ian Gittlitz, President
James Schultz, Publisher
Emily Cappiello, Editor
Corris Little, Editor
Christina Trauthwein, Editor
EMP: 25
SQ FT: 10,000
SALES (est): 3.5MM **Privately Held**
WEB: www.icdnet.com
SIC: 2721 7313 Magazines: publishing only, not printed on site; magazine advertising representative

(G-6834)
INNOVANT INC (PA)
Also Called: Innovant Group
135 Oval Dr (11749-1402)
PHONE..................631 348-1900
Charles Braham, President
Garrett Pluck, Vice Pres
Mary Hudson, Controller
Joan Gullans, Admin Sec
▲ EMP: 172
SALES (est): 31.3MM **Privately Held**
WEB: www.innovant.com
SIC: 2521 Wood office furniture

(G-6835)
JET COMPONENTS INC
62 Bridge Rd (11749-1411)
PHONE..................631 436-7300
Fax: 631 436-7342
Gina Pedroli, President
Charles Scarborough, General Mgr
Ken Pedroli, Vice Pres
▲ EMP: 6
SQ FT: 6,000
SALES (est): 1.3MM **Privately Held**
WEB: www.jet-components.com
SIC: 3679 Electronic circuits

(G-6836)
JOMART ASSOCIATES INC
170 Oval Dr Ste A (11749-1419)
PHONE..................212 627-2153
Walter Waltman, President
Peter Batterson, Vice Pres
Steve Perry, Manager
Walter Woltmann, Exec Dir
Evelyn Giman, Admin Sec
EMP: 30
SQ FT: 1,200
SALES (est): 2.8MM **Privately Held**
WEB: www.jomartassociates.com
SIC: 2759 Commercial printing

(G-6837)
LIF DISTRIBUTING INC
155 Oval Dr (11749-1402)
PHONE..................631 630-6900
Steven Frielander, President
Gerard Mach, Vice Pres
EMP: 13
SQ FT: 8,000
SALES (est): 1.9MM **Privately Held**
SIC: 2541 Table or counter tops, plastic laminated

(G-6838)
M & M CANVAS & AWNINGS INC
Also Called: M & M Signs & Awnings
180 Oval Dr (11749-1403)
PHONE..................631 424-5370
Fax: 631 424-5375
Mike Mere, President
EMP: 7
SALES (est): 660K **Privately Held**
WEB: www.mmawning.com
SIC: 2394 Canvas & related products

(G-6839)
METRO DOOR INC (DH)
Also Called: Apton Door
2929 Express Dr N 300b (11749-5306)
PHONE..................800 669-3667
Scott McDermott, President
Jeff Chevalier, General Mgr
Jim Karcher, Co-Founder
Brian Wilmhoff, Project Mgr
Ellen Kraus, Opers Mgr
▼ EMP: 80
SQ FT: 17,200
SALES (est): 24MM
SALES (corp-wide): 5.3B **Publicly Held**
WEB: www.metrodoor.com
SIC: 3446 1799 Fences, gates, posts & flagpoles; fence construction

(G-6840)
PRINTEX PACKAGING CORPORATION
555 Raymond Dr (11749-4844)
PHONE..................631 234-4300
Fax: 631 234-4840
David Heller, President
Joel Heller, President
Carol Heller, Vice Pres
Tom Vollmuth, Vice Pres
Barbara Colangelo, Accounting Mgr
▲ EMP: 70
SQ FT: 40,000
SALES (est): 24.5MM **Privately Held**
WEB: www.printexpackaging.com
SIC: 3089 3086 2671 Boxes, plastic; packaging & shipping materials, foamed plastic; packaging paper & plastics film, coated & laminated

(G-6841)
SOCKET PRODUCTS MFG CORP
175 Bridge Rd (11749-5202)
PHONE..................631 232-9870
Fax: 631 232-3215
Sol Kellner, President
EMP: 5
SQ FT: 5,000
SALES (est): 759.1K **Privately Held**
SIC: 3452 3545 Screws, metal; nuts, metal; bolts, metal; sockets (machine tool accessories)

(G-6842)
SONOTEC US INC
190 Blydenburg Rd (11749-5015)
PHONE..................631 415-4758
Christopher Portelli, President
Cristy Georgiades, Executive Asst
EMP: 120 EST: 2013
SALES: 1MM
SALES (corp-wide): 20MM **Privately Held**
SIC: 3674 Solid state electronic devices
PA: Sonotec Ultraschallsensorik Halle Gmbh
  Nauendorfer Str. 2
  Halle (Saale) 06112
  345 133-170

(G-6843)
WHITSONS FOOD SVC BRONX CORP
1800 Motor Pkwy (11749-5216)
PHONE..................631 424-2700
Robert Whitcomb, President
Beth Bunster, Corp Secy
Douglas Whitcomb, Vice Pres
John Whitcomb, Vice Pres
Andrew Whitcomb, Shareholder
EMP: 350
SQ FT: 65,000
SALES (est): 47.7MM **Privately Held**
SIC: 2068 2099 Salted & roasted nuts & seeds; food preparations; peanut butter

(G-6844)
ZAHK SALES INC
Also Called: Project Visual
75 Hoffman Ln Ste A (11749-5027)
PHONE..................631 348-9300
Husein Kermalli, President
Nick Kermalli, Manager
▲ EMP: 7
SALES (est): 566.3K **Privately Held**
WEB: www.zahk.com
SIC: 3444 1752 Sheet metalwork; wood floor installation & refinishing

Islip
Suffolk County

(G-6845)
AINES MANUFACTURING CORP
96 E Bayberry Rd (11751-4903)
PHONE..................631 471-3900
▼ EMP: 30
SQ FT: 10,000
SALES (est): 4.3MM **Privately Held**
SIC: 3661 Mfg Telephone/Telegraph Apparatus

(G-6846)
COOKIES UNITED LLC
141 Freeman Ave (11751-1428)
PHONE..................631 581-4000
Michael Strauss, Mktg Dir
Louis Avignone, Mng Member
▲ EMP: 120
SQ FT: 80,000
SALES (est): 6.4MM **Privately Held**
SIC: 2052 Cookies & crackers
PA: United Baking Co., Inc.
  41 Natcon Dr
  Shirley NY 11967

(G-6847)
EUGENIA SELECTIVE LIVING INC
122 Freeman Ave (11751-1417)
PHONE..................631 277-1461
Fax: 631 277-1536
Edward Smith, President
Mary Schlichting, Office Mgr
Eugenia Smith, Admin Sec
EMP: 10
SQ FT: 5,000
SALES (est): 1.2MM **Privately Held**
WEB: www.selectiveliving.com
SIC: 2511 2519 2521 2522 Wood household furniture; furniture, household; glass, fiberglass & plastic; wood office furniture; office furniture, except wood; laboratory equipment, except medical or dental; cabinet & finish carpentry

(G-6848)
JIMCO LAMP & MANUFACTURING CO
Also Called: Jimco Lamp Company
181 Freeman Ave (11751-1400)
PHONE..................631 218-2152
Fax: 631 218-6806
Marlo Lorenz, Branch Mgr
EMP: 5 **Privately Held**
SIC: 3645 3999 Residential lighting fixtures; table lamps; floor lamps; wall lamps; shades, lamp or candle
HQ: Jimco Lamp & Manufacturing Co
  11759 Highway 63 N Ste B
  Bono AR 72416
  870 935-6820

(G-6849)
MEADES WELDING AND FABRICATING
331 Islip Ave (11751-2800)
PHONE..................631 581-1555
Michelle Mede, President
EMP: 5
SALES (est): 195.3K **Privately Held**
SIC: 7692 5046 Welding repair; commercial cooking & food service equipment

(G-6850)
MJB PRINTING CORP
Also Called: Mod Printing
280 Islip Ave (11751-2818)
PHONE..................631 581-0177
Fax: 631 581-0137
Jeanine Bazata, President
Michael Bazata, Treasurer
EMP: 5
SQ FT: 2,800
SALES (est): 717.9K **Privately Held**
SIC: 2752 Commercial printing, offset

(G-6851)
RIKE ENTERPRISES INC
Also Called: Corpkit Legal Supplies
46 Taft Ave (11751-2112)
PHONE..................631 277-8338
Fax: 631 277-8448
Richard Jansen, President
Dan O'Dwyer, Sales Mgr
Amanda Jansen, Manager
▲ EMP: 15
SALES (est): 1.7MM **Privately Held**
WEB: www.corpkit.com
SIC: 2759 5112 Commercial printing; office supplies

(G-6852)
T J SIGNS UNLIMITED LLC (PA)
Also Called: American Signcrafters
171 Freeman Ave (11751-1430)
PHONE..................631 273-4800
Jeff Petersen, President
Thomas Garatina, Business Mgr
Jonathan Bell, Vice Pres
Anthony Lipari, Vice Pres
Christi Baird, Project Mgr
EMP: 50
SQ FT: 20,000
SALES: 25MM **Privately Held**
WEB: www.americansigncrafters.com
SIC: 3993 1799 7389 Electric signs; neon signs; sign installation & maintenance; personal service agents, brokers & bureaus

(G-6853)
TJ SIGNS UNLIMITED LLC
Also Called: American Signcrafters
171 Freeman Ave (11751-1430)
PHONE..................631 273-4800
Jeffrey Petersen, CEO
Jonathan Bell, President
Lisa Johnson, President
EMP: 130
SALES (est): 251.4K **Privately Held**
SIC: 3993 Signs & advertising specialties

Islip Terrace
Suffolk County

(G-6854)
BARRASSO & SONS TRUCKING INC
160 Floral Park St (11752-1399)
PHONE..................631 581-0360
Fax: 631 581-0902
Michael Barrasso, President
Joseph Longo, Corp Secy
Andres Ocampo, Sales Staff

GEOGRAPHIC SECTION
Ithaca - Tompkins County (G-6878)

Anthony Barrasso, *Director*
EMP: 30 **EST:** 1996
SQ FT: 2,500
SALES (est): 8.1MM **Privately Held**
SIC: 3271 5211 5032 Concrete block & brick; brick; brick, stone & related material

(G-6855)
NIKE INC
2675 Sunrise Hwy (11752-2119)
PHONE.................................631 960-0184
John Grasselino, *Branch Mgr*
EMP: 38
SALES (corp-wide): 32.3B **Publicly Held**
SIC: 3021 Rubber & plastics footwear
PA: Nike, Inc.
1 Sw Bowerman Dr
Beaverton OR 97005
503 671-6453

Ithaca
Tompkins County

(G-6856)
ADVANCED DIGITAL INFO CORP
10 Brown Rd (14850-1287)
PHONE.................................607 266-4000
James H Watson Jr, *Principal*
EMP: 50
SALES (corp-wide): 505.3MM **Publicly Held**
SIC: 3672 Printed circuit boards
HQ: Advanced Digital Information Corporation
11431 Willows Rd Ne
Redmond WA 98052
425 881-8004

(G-6857)
ADVION INC (PA)
10 Brown Rd Ste 101 (14850-1287)
PHONE.................................607 266-9162
David Patterson, *President*
Thomas R Kurz, *President*
Jamey Jones, *Vice Pres*
Mark Allen PH, *Vice Pres*
Gary Williams, *Vice Pres*
EMP: 20
SQ FT: 16,500
SALES (est): 11.3MM **Privately Held**
SIC: 3826 Analytical instruments; mass spectrometers; spectrometers

(G-6858)
ALPINE MACHINE INC
1616 Trumansburg Rd (14850-9213)
PHONE.................................607 272-1344
Fax: 607 272-0935
Richard Hoffman, *President*
David Osburn, *Corp Secy*
William Osburn, *Vice Pres*
Russell Timblin, *Vice Pres*
EMP: 15 **EST:** 1981
SQ FT: 6,000
SALES (est): 2MM **Privately Held**
WEB: www.alpinemachine.com
SIC: 3599 7692 3541 3444 Machine shop, jobbing & repair; welding repair; machine tools, metal cutting type; sheet metalwork

(G-6859)
ARNOLD PRINTING CORP
604 W Green St (14850-5250)
PHONE.................................607 272-7800
Fax: 607 272-2607
Robert Becker Jr, *President*
Christian J Becker, *Vice Pres*
EMP: 18 **EST:** 1963
SQ FT: 8,000
SALES (est): 2.6MM **Privately Held**
SIC: 2752 Commercial printing, offset

(G-6860)
BENNETT DIE & TOOL INC
113 Brewery Ln (14850-8814)
PHONE.................................607 273-2836
James McMillen, *President*
Brian Bennett, *Vice Pres*
EMP: 16
SALES (est): 1.2MM **Privately Held**
SIC: 3544 Special dies & tools

(G-6861)
BIGWOOD SYSTEMS INC
35 Thornwood Dr Ste 400 (14850-1284)
PHONE.................................607 257-0915
Hsiao-Dong Chiang, *President*
Pat Causgrove, *General Mgr*
Bin Wang, *Engineer*
Gilbert Chiang, *Director*
EMP: 7
SALES (est): 590K **Privately Held**
WEB: www.bigwood-systems.com
SIC: 7372 Prepackaged software

(G-6862)
BINOPTICS LLC (DH)
9 Brown Rd (14850-1247)
PHONE.................................607 257-3200
Fax: 607 257-9753
Alex Behfar, *CEO*
William Fritz, *COO*
Norman Kwong, *Exec VP*
Christopher Smith, *CFO*
Prascilla Walter, *Manager*
▼ **EMP:** 43
SQ FT: 28,600
SALES (est): 20.5MM **Publicly Held**
WEB: www.binoptics.com
SIC: 3827 Optical instruments & lenses

(G-6863)
BORGWARNER INC
780 Warren Rd (14850-1242)
PHONE.................................607 257-1800
Roger Wood, *President*
Steven Leung, *Buyer*
Rohit Meshram, *QC Mgr*
Dustin Bordonaro, *Engineer*
Ken Degraff, *Engineer*
EMP: 30
SALES (corp-wide): 9B **Publicly Held**
SIC: 3714 Motor vehicle parts & accessories
PA: Borgwarner Inc.
3850 Hamlin Rd
Auburn Hills MI 48326
248 754-9200

(G-6864)
BORGWARNER ITHACA LLC
Also Called: Morse Systems
800 Warren Rd (14850-1266)
PHONE.................................607 257-6700
James R Verrier, *President*
Steven G Carlson, *Vice Pres*
John J Gasparovic, *Vice Pres*
Alexandra Harvey, *Vice Pres*
Tom Daly, *Senior Buyer*
EMP: 300
SQ FT: 100,000
SALES (est): 31.9MM **Privately Held**
SIC: 3462 Iron & steel forgings

(G-6865)
BORGWARNER MORSE TEC INC
780 Warren Rd (14850-1242)
PHONE.................................607 266-5111
Timothy M Manganello, *CEO*
Donald Freyburger, *Chief Engr*
EMP: 90
SALES (corp-wide): 9B **Publicly Held**
WEB: www.borgwarnermorsetec.com
SIC: 3714 Motor vehicle parts & accessories
HQ: Borgwarner Morse Tec Llc
800 Warren Rd
Ithaca NY 14850
607 257-6700

(G-6866)
BORGWARNER MORSE TEC LLC (HQ)
800 Warren Rd (14850-1266)
PHONE.................................607 257-6700
Fax: 607 257-3337
James R Verrier, *President*
Ronald M Ruzic, *President*
Timothy M Manganello, *Chairman*
Steve G Carlson, *Vice Pres*
Tony Hensel, *Vice Pres*
▲ **EMP:** 184
SALES (est): 133.6MM
SALES (corp-wide): 9B **Publicly Held**
WEB: www.borgwarnermorsetec.com
SIC: 3714 3462 3568 Motor vehicle parts & accessories; iron & steel forgings; power transmission equipment

PA: Borgwarner Inc.
3850 Hamlin Rd
Auburn Hills MI 48326
248 754-9200

(G-6867)
BSU INC
445 E State St (14850-4409)
PHONE.................................607 272-8100
Christine Houseworth, *Chairman*
Denver Jones, *Vice Pres*
Richard Stillwaggon, *Purch Agent*
Dottie Highfield, *Accounts Mgr*
EMP: 42
SQ FT: 17,000
SALES (est): 7.5MM **Privately Held**
WEB: www.bsuinc.com
SIC: 3672 8711 Printed circuit boards; engineering services

(G-6868)
CAYUGA WOODEN BOATWORKS INC
381 Enfield Main Rd (14850-9346)
P.O. Box 301, Cayuga (13034-0301)
PHONE.................................315 253-7447
Fax: 607 272-1601
Phil Walker, *General Mgr*
Ken Anderson, *Principal*
EMP: 21
SQ FT: 10,000
SALES (est): 1.5MM **Privately Held**
WEB: www.cwbw.com
SIC: 3732 7699 Boat building & repairing; boat repair

(G-6869)
CBORD GROUP INC (HQ)
950 Danby Rd Ste 100c (14850-5795)
PHONE.................................607 257-2410
Fax: 607 257-1902
Max Steinhardt, *President*
Tim Tighe, *President*
Rich Imlay, *General Mgr*
Gregory Hubbell, *Business Mgr*
Bruce Lane, *Exec VP*
EMP: 250
SQ FT: 40,000
SALES (est): 134.4MM
SALES (corp-wide): 3.7B **Publicly Held**
WEB: www.cbord.com
SIC: 7372 5045 Application computer software; computer peripheral equipment; computers
PA: Roper Technologies, Inc.
6901 Prof Pkwy E Ste 200
Sarasota FL 34240
941 556-2601

(G-6870)
CHARLES A HONES INC
222 S Albany St Ste 3 (14850-5480)
PHONE.................................607 273-5720
EMP: 6 **EST:** 2013
SALES (est): 331K **Privately Held**
SIC: 3291 Hones

(G-6871)
CORNELL UNIVERSITY
Also Called: Cornell University Press
512 E State St (14850-4412)
PHONE.................................607 277-2338
Fax: 607 277-2374
Susan Specter, *Editor*
Roger Hubbs, *Controller*
A Edwards, *Ch Invest Ofcr*
Irene Hendricks, *VP Human Res*
Bonnie Bailey, *HR Admin*
EMP: 51
SALES (corp-wide): 3.8B **Privately Held**
SIC: 2731 8221 Textbooks; publishing only, not printed on site; university
PA: Cornell University
308 Duffield Hall
Ithaca NY 14853
607 254-4636

(G-6872)
CORNELL UNIVERSITY
Also Called: Cornell Laboratory Ornithology
159 Sapsucker Woods Rd (14850-1923)
PHONE.................................607 254-2473
Fax: 607 254-2415
Richard Adie, *General Mgr*
Brooke Keeney, *Editor*
Todd Pfeiffer, *Facilities Dir*

Jeffrey Payne, *Facilities Mgr*
Hannah Walker, *Production*
EMP: 20
SALES (est): 3.8MM **Privately Held**
SIC: 2721 8221 Periodicals; university
PA: Cornell University
308 Duffield Hall
Ithaca NY 14853
607 254-4636

(G-6873)
DAILY CORNELL SUN
Also Called: Dail Cornell Sun, The
139 W State St (14850-5427)
PHONE.................................607 273-0746
Fax: 607 273-0746
John Marcham, *President*
Caroline Flax, *Editor*
Nicole Hamilton, *Editor*
Maegan Nevins, *Editor*
Amanda Soule, *Business Mgr*
EMP: 25
SQ FT: 7,020
SALES (est): 1.6MM **Privately Held**
WEB: www.cornellsun.com
SIC: 2711 Newspapers: publishing only, not printed on site

(G-6874)
DUKE COMPANY
7 Hall Rd (14850-8732)
PHONE.................................607 347-4455
EMP: 7
SALES (est): 161.8K **Privately Held**
SIC: 3272 7353 Building materials, except block or brick: concrete; earth moving equipment, rental or leasing

(G-6875)
F M ABDULKY INC (PA)
527 W Seneca St (14850-4033)
PHONE.................................607 272-7373
Fax: 607 277-7106
Fareed M Abdulky, *President*
Fareed Abdulky, *President*
Lamia Abdulky, *Vice Pres*
EMP: 13
SQ FT: 4,000
SALES (est): 1.2MM **Privately Held**
WEB: www.abdulky.com
SIC: 3911 Jewelry, precious metal

(G-6876)
F M ABDULKY INC
Also Called: Buffalo Finishing Company
527 W Seneca St (14850-4033)
PHONE.................................607 272-7373
Don Covert, *Manager*
EMP: 6
SQ FT: 2,616
SALES (corp-wide): 1.2MM **Privately Held**
WEB: www.abdulky.com
SIC: 3911 Jewelry, precious metal
PA: F M Abdulky Inc
527 W Seneca St
Ithaca NY 14850
607 272-7373

(G-6877)
FINGER LAKES MASSAGE GROUP (PA)
Also Called: Finger Lakes School of Massage
215 E State St Ste 2 (14850-5547)
PHONE.................................607 272-9024
Fax: 607 272-4271
John Robinson, *Ch of Bd*
David Merwin, *President*
Linda Van Almelo, *Director*
Beth Tetreault, *Administration*
Heidi Eckerson, *Instructor*
EMP: 15
SQ FT: 8,000
SALES (est): 189K **Privately Held**
WEB: www.flsm.com
SIC: 2741 Music books: publishing & printing

(G-6878)
FINGER LAKES STONE CO INC
33 Quarry Rd (14850)
PHONE.................................607 273-4646
Fax: 607 273-4692
James Hobart, *President*
Ann Hobart, *Vice Pres*
EMP: 16

Ithaca - Tompkins County (G-6879) — GEOGRAPHIC SECTION

SQ FT: 1,000
SALES (est): 1.8MM **Privately Held**
WEB: www.fingerlakesstone.net
SIC: 1411 Dimension stone

(G-6879)
GLOBA PHONI COMPU TECHN SOLUT (PA)
21 Dutch Mill Rd (14850-9785)
P.O. Box 3959 (14852-3959)
PHONE..................607 257-7279
Fax: 607 257-3450
Danqing Kong, *Ch of Bd*
Jon Littlefield, *Accounts Exec*
Kelly Pietsch, *Office Mgr*
Kevin Kong, *Info Tech Mgr*
◆ **EMP:** 20 **EST:** 2001
SALES (est): 6.2MM **Privately Held**
SIC: 3651 Home entertainment equipment, electronic

(G-6880)
GLYCOBIA INC
33 Thornwood Dr Ste 104 (14850-1275)
PHONE..................607 339-0051
Matthew Delisa, *President*
EMP: 5
SALES (est): 299K **Privately Held**
SIC: 2834 Pharmaceutical preparations

(G-6881)
GRATITUDE & COMPANY INC
215 N Cayuga St Ste 71 (14850-4323)
PHONE..................607 277-3188
Julie Umbach, *President*
Kimberly Griffghs, *Admin Sec*
EMP: 6
SALES (est): 895K **Privately Held**
WEB: www.giftsofgratitude.com
SIC: 2621 Specialty papers

(G-6882)
HANGER PRSTHETCS & ORTHO INC
Also Called: Creative Orthotics Prosthetics
310 Taughannock Blvd 1a (14850-3251)
PHONE..................607 277-6620
Fax: 607 257-1802
Thomas Kirk PHD, *CEO*
Robert Frank, *Manager*
Christopher Lange, *Manager*
EMP: 10
SALES (corp-wide): 451.4MM **Publicly Held**
SIC: 3842 Surgical appliances & supplies
HQ: Hanger Prosthetics & Orthotics, Inc.
10910 Domain Dr Ste 300
Austin TX 78758
512 777-3800

(G-6883)
HENRY NEWMAN LLC
Also Called: Ithaca Ice Company, The
312 4th St (14850-3481)
PHONE..................607 273-8512
Henry Newman, *Owner*
Charles Everhart, *Principal*
EMP: 10
SQ FT: 8,000
SALES (est): 284.7K **Privately Held**
SIC: 2097 5999 Ice cubes; ice

(G-6884)
INCODEMA INC
407 Cliff St (14850-2009)
PHONE..................607 277-7070
Sean Whittaker, *CEO*
James Hockey, *Business Mgr*
Mike Wargo, *Opers Mgr*
Jeremy Woodman, *QC Mgr*
Chris Hern, *Engineer*
▼ **EMP:** 47
SQ FT: 30,000
SALES (est): 11.4MM **Privately Held**
SIC: 3444 Sheet metalwork

(G-6885)
INDUSTRIAL MACHINE REPAIR
1144 Taughannock Blvd (14850-9573)
PHONE..................607 272-0717
Martin J Sullivan, *Owner*
EMP: 6
SALES (est): 199.6K **Privately Held**
SIC: 3823 Computer interface equipment for industrial process control

(G-6886)
INTERNATIONAL CENTER FOR POSTG
Also Called: Icpme-Ithaca Center
179 Graham Rd Ste E (14850-1141)
PHONE..................607 257-5860
Fax: 607 257-5891
John Leyendecker, *Director*
Kenneth Zeserson,
EMP: 9
SALES (est): 858.6K
SALES (corp-wide): 97.2MM **Privately Held**
WEB: www.radinfonet.com
SIC: 2721 8741 Periodicals: publishing only; management services
PA: Jobson Medical Information Llc
440 9th Ave Fl 14
New York NY 10001
212 274-7000

(G-6887)
INTERNATIONAL CLIMBING MCHS
630 Elmira Rd (14850-8745)
PHONE..................607 288-4001
Samuel J Maggio, *President*
Carolina Osorio Gil, *Manager*
EMP: 5
SALES (est): 644.5K **Privately Held**
SIC: 3599 Custom machinery

(G-6888)
ITHACA BEER COMPANY INC
122 Ithaca Beer Dr (14850-8813)
PHONE..................607 272-1305
Fax: 607 273-0766
Dan Mitchell, *President*
Pete Browning, *Vice Pres*
Scotie Jacobs, *Facilities Mgr*
Amanda McGonigal, *Office Mgr*
Paul Wagner, *Admin Sec*
EMP: 30
SQ FT: 6,100
SALES (est): 5.8MM **Privately Held**
WEB: www.ithacabeer.com
SIC: 2082 Beer (alcoholic beverage)

(G-6889)
ITHACA JOURNAL NEWS CO INC
123 W State St Ste 1 (14850-5479)
PHONE..................607 272-2321
Fax: 607 272-4335
Sherman Bodner, *President*
John Semo, *Production*
Tad Kilgore, *Manager*
Stephen Miller, *Manager*
Steve Miller, *Manager*
EMP: 50 **EST:** 1815
SQ FT: 6,000
SALES (est): 6.5MM
SALES (corp-wide): 3B **Publicly Held**
WEB: www.ithaca.gannett.com
SIC: 2711 Commercial printing & newspaper publishing combined
PA: Gannett Co., Inc.
7950 Jones Branch Dr
Mc Lean VA 22102
703 854-6000

(G-6890)
JOE MORO
Also Called: Moro Design
214 Fayette St (14850-5263)
PHONE..................607 272-0591
Fax: 607 272-0591
Joe Moro, *Owner*
EMP: 5
SALES (est): 170K **Privately Held**
SIC: 3949 Bowling equipment & supplies

(G-6891)
KIONIX INC
36 Thornwood Dr (14850-1263)
PHONE..................607 257-1080
Fax: 607 257-1146
Nader Sadrzadeh, *President*
Paul Bryan, *Exec VP*
Timothy J Davis, *Exec VP*
Kenneth N Salky, *Exec VP*
Kenneth Hager, *Vice Pres*
▲ **EMP:** 185
SQ FT: 60,000
SALES (est): 58.3MM
SALES (corp-wide): 3.1B **Privately Held**
WEB: www.kionix.com
SIC: 3676 Electronic resistors
PA: Rohm Company Limited
21, Mizosakicho, Saiin, Ukyo-Ku
Kyoto KYO 615-0
753 112-121

(G-6892)
M2 RACE SYSTEMS INC
53 Enfield Main Rd (14850-9367)
PHONE..................607 882-9078
Ron Mielbrecht, *President*
Beth Mielbrecht, *Vice Pres*
EMP: 6
SQ FT: 7,500
SALES (est): 734.7K **Privately Held**
WEB: www.m2race.com
SIC: 3714 Cylinder heads, motor vehicle

(G-6893)
MADISON PRINTING CORP
Also Called: Instant Printing Service
704 W Buffalo St (14850-3300)
PHONE..................607 273-3535
Angelo Digiacomo, *President*
Molly Digiacomo, *Vice Pres*
EMP: 5 **EST:** 1972
SQ FT: 1,600
SALES (est): 592.3K **Privately Held**
SIC: 2752 Commercial printing, offset

(G-6894)
MAG INC
Also Called: Momentummedia Sports Pubg
20 Eastlake Rd (14850-9786)
PHONE..................607 257-6970
Mark Goldberg, *President*
Mike Gruppe, *General Mgr*
Kristin Maki, *Editor*
Eleanor Frankel, *Chief*
Penny Small, *Financial Exec*
EMP: 25
SQ FT: 3,600
SALES (est): 3.6MM **Privately Held**
WEB: www.momentummedia.com
SIC: 2721 Magazines: publishing only, not printed on site

(G-6895)
MCBOOKS PRESS INC
520 N Meadow St 2 (14850-3229)
PHONE..................607 272-2114
Fax: 607 273-6068
Alexander G Skutt, *President*
Chris Carey, *Vice Pres*
▲ **EMP:** 5
SQ FT: 750
SALES (est): 1.2MM **Privately Held**
WEB: www.mcbooks.com
SIC: 2731 Book publishing

(G-6896)
METTLER-TOLEDO INC
5 Barr Rd (14850-9117)
PHONE..................607 257-6000
Olivier Filliol, *CEO*
William P Donnelly, *Ch of Bd*
Gerald Liswoski, *General Mgr*
Tom Dorward, *Production*
Carlos Karam, *Research*
EMP: 135 **EST:** 1987
SQ FT: 45,000
SALES (est): 34.6MM
SALES (corp-wide): 2.5B **Publicly Held**
WEB: www.hispeedcheckweigher.com
SIC: 3596 3537 Weighing machines & apparatus; industrial trucks & tractors
HQ: Mettler-Toledo, Llc
1900 Polaris Pkwy Fl 6
Columbus OH 43240
614 438-4511

(G-6897)
MEZMERIZ INC
33 Thornwood Dr Ste 100 (14850-1275)
PHONE..................607 216-8140
Bradley N Treat, *President*
Cliff Lardin, *Director*
EMP: 5
SALES (est): 935K **Privately Held**
SIC: 3679 Electronic components

(G-6898)
MITEGEN LLC
95 Brown Rd Ste 1034 (14850-1277)
P.O. Box 3867 (14852-3867)
PHONE..................607 266-8877
Robert Newman, *General Mgr*
Benjamin Apker, *Opers Staff*
Stephen Hollabaugh, *Research*
Ben Apker, *Engineer*
Shane Cavanaugh, *Sales Staff*
EMP: 5
SALES: 200K **Privately Held**
WEB: www.mitegen.com
SIC: 3844 X-ray apparatus & tubes

(G-6899)
MPL INC
41 Dutch Mill Rd (14850-9785)
PHONE..................607 266-0480
Fax: 607 266-0482
Shane French, *CEO*
Michelle French, *Ch of Bd*
Bill Lanigan, *Engineer*
Betty Ford, *Manager*
Joanne Underhill, *Admin Sec*
EMP: 39
SQ FT: 7,500
SALES (est): 12.4MM **Privately Held**
WEB: www.mplinc.com
SIC: 3672 Printed circuit boards

(G-6900)
MULTIWIRE LABORATORIES LTD
95 Brown Rd 1018266a (14850-1294)
PHONE..................607 257-3378
Fax: 607 257-3201
Donald Bilderback, *President*
Bill Hawley, *Business Mgr*
Becky Bilderback, *Vice Pres*
▼ **EMP:** 6
SQ FT: 2,668
SALES (est): 855.4K **Privately Held**
WEB: www.multiwire.com
SIC: 3844 3826 X-ray apparatus & tubes; analytical instruments

(G-6901)
NCR CORPORATION
950 Danby Rd (14850-5778)
PHONE..................607 273-5310
Donald J Moses, *Opers Staff*
Paul Gardner, *Human Res Dir*
Malcom Unsworth, *Branch Mgr*
EMP: 247
SALES (corp-wide): 6.5B **Publicly Held**
WEB: www.ncr.com
SIC: 2752 3577 Commercial printing, lithographic; computer peripheral equipment
PA: Ncr Corporation
3097 Satellite Blvd # 100
Duluth GA 30096
937 445-5000

(G-6902)
NEW SKI INC
Also Called: Ithaca Times
109 N Cayuga St Ste A (14850-4340)
P.O. Box 27 (14851-0027)
PHONE..................607 277-7000
Fax: 607 277-1012
James Belinski, *President*
Andre Hafner, *Prdtn Mgr*
EMP: 30
SQ FT: 2,000
SALES (est): 1.3MM **Privately Held**
WEB: www.ithacatimes.com
SIC: 2711 Newspapers: publishing only, not printed on site

(G-6903)
ONGWEOWEH CORP (PA)
767 Warren Rd (14850-1255)
P.O. Box 3300 (14852-3300)
PHONE..................607 266-7070
Fax: 607 266-7085
Frank C Bonamie, *Ch of Bd*
Justin M Bennett, *President*
Troy Williams, *General Mgr*
Karl Lindhorst, *CFO*
Kristi Pierce, *Treasurer*
EMP: 56
SQ FT: 20,000
SALES: 180MM **Privately Held**
WEB: www.ongweoweh.com
SIC: 2448 Wood pallets & skids

▲ = Import ▼ = Export
◆ = Import/Export

GEOGRAPHIC SECTION

Jamaica - Queens County (G-6930)

(G-6904)
PERFORMANCE SYSTEMS CONTG INC
124 Brindley St (14850-5002)
PHONE..................607 277-6240
Greg Thomas, *President*
Jody Schwan, *Finance*
EMP: 50
SQ FT: 20,000
SALES (est): 4.5MM **Privately Held**
WEB: www.pscontracting.com
SIC: 3825 Energy measuring equipment, electrical

(G-6905)
PETRUNIA LLC
Also Called: Petrune
126 E State St (14850-5542)
PHONE..................607 277-1930
Dominica Brookman, *Mng Member*
EMP: 5
SALES (est): 571.4K **Privately Held**
SIC: 2339 Women's & misses' outerwear; women's & misses' accessories; service apparel, washable: women's

(G-6906)
POROUS MATERIALS INC (PA)
Also Called: Advance Pressure Products
20 Dutch Mill Rd (14850-9199)
PHONE..................607 257-5544
Krishna M Gupta, *President*
Mike Yahle, *Human Res Mgr*
Evan Sorel, *Lab Dir*
Sudha Gupta, *Admin Sec*
EMP: 25
SQ FT: 10,000
SALES: 2MM **Privately Held**
WEB: www.pmiapp.com
SIC: 3826 Laser scientific & engineering instruments

(G-6907)
PRECISION FILTERS INC (PA)
240 Cherry St (14850-5099)
PHONE..................607 277-3550
Fax: 607 277-4466
Douglas Firth, *Ch of Bd*
Donald Chandler, *President*
John Morris, *General Mgr*
Paul Costantini, *Vice Pres*
Mike Potter, *Opers Staff*
EMP: 35
SQ FT: 15,500
SALES (est): 6.6MM **Privately Held**
WEB: www.pfinc.com
SIC: 3825 Test equipment for electronic & electric measurement

(G-6908)
PURITY ICE CREAM CO INC (PA)
700 Cascadilla St Ste A (14850-3255)
PHONE..................607 272-1545
Fax: 607 272-1546
Bruce Lane, *President*
Heather Lane, *Vice Pres*
EMP: 16 **EST:** 1936
SQ FT: 10,000
SALES (est): 1.2MM **Privately Held**
WEB: www.purityicecream.com
SIC: 2024 5143 5812 2026 Ice cream & ice milk; ice cream & ices; ice cream stands or dairy bars; fluid milk

(G-6909)
RHEONIX INC (PA)
10 Brown Rd Ste 103 (14850-1287)
PHONE..................607 257-1242
Gregory J Galvin PHD, *Ch of Bd*
Richard A Montagna PHD, *Senior VP*
Peng Zhou PHD, *Senior VP*
John Brenner Ms, *Vice Pres*
Doug Olsen, *Vice Pres*
EMP: 60
SALES (est): 13.3MM **Privately Held**
WEB: www.rheonix.com
SIC: 3826 Analytical instruments

(G-6910)
RPS HOLDINGS INC
2415 N Triphammer Rd # 2 (14850-1093)
PHONE..................607 257-7778
David Johnson, *President*
EMP: 22

SALES (est): 2.6MM **Privately Held**
WEB: www.rpsolutions.com
SIC: 7372 Business oriented computer software

(G-6911)
STORK H & E TURBO BLADING INC
334 Comfort Rd (14850-8626)
P.O. Box 177 (14851-0177)
PHONE..................607 277-4968
Fax: 607 277-1193
John Slocum, *Ch of Bd*
Jeff Saunders, *General Mgr*
Joseph Walker, *General Mgr*
Tony Cain, *Purch Mgr*
Derek Bareham, *Engineer*
▲ **EMP:** 170 **EST:** 1976
SQ FT: 49,046
SALES (est): 42.4MM
SALES (corp-wide): 19B **Publicly Held**
WEB: www.he-machinery.com
SIC: 3511 Turbines & turbine generator sets
HQ: Stork Turbo Blading B.V.
Kamerlingh Onnesstraat 21
Sneek
880 891-290

(G-6912)
THERM INCORPORATED
1000 Hudson Street Ext (14850-5999)
PHONE..................607 272-8500
Fax: 607 277-5799
Robert R Sprole III, *Ch of Bd*
Valerie Daugherty, *General Mgr*
Valerie Talcott, *Manager*
Richard Grossman, *Admin Sec*
▲ **EMP:** 200
SQ FT: 130,000
SALES (est): 52.3MM **Privately Held**
WEB: www.therm.com
SIC: 3724 Aircraft engines & engine parts

(G-6913)
TOMPKINS WEEKLY INC
36 Besemer Rd (14850-9638)
P.O. Box 6404 (14851-6404)
PHONE..................607 539-7100
James Graney, *Principal*
EMP: 6
SALES (est): 296.5K **Privately Held**
SIC: 2711 Newspapers

(G-6914)
TRANSACT TECHNOLOGIES INC
Also Called: Ithaca Peripherals
20 Bomax Dr (14850-1200)
PHONE..................607 257-8901
Fax: 607 257-8922
Donald Brooks, *Vice Pres*
Dick Cole, *Vice Pres*
John Hays, *Vice Pres*
Michael Kachala, *Vice Pres*
Dave Ritchie, *Vice Pres*
EMP: 94
SQ FT: 70,000 **Publicly Held**
WEB: www.transact-tech.com
SIC: 3577 Printers, computer
PA: Transact Technologies Incorporated
2319 Whitney Ave Ste 3b
Hamden CT 06518

(G-6915)
TRANSACTION PRINTER GROUP
108 Woodcrest Ter (14850-6224)
PHONE..................607 274-2500
Dana Wardlaw, *Principal*
Barry Shaw, *Info Tech Dir*
EMP: 5 **EST:** 2009
SALES (est): 522.2K **Privately Held**
SIC: 2752 Commercial printing, lithographic

(G-6916)
VANGUARD GRAPHICS LLC
Also Called: Vanguard Printing
17 Hallwoods Rd (14850-8787)
PHONE..................607 272-1212
Fax: 607 273-0846
Steve Rossi, *President*
William Post, *Vice Pres*
Bill Post, *Plant Mgr*
Lynn Hickey, *Purch Agent*
Steven Smith, *CFO*

EMP: 140
SALES (est): 3.7MM
SALES (corp-wide): 7.1MM **Privately Held**
SIC: 2752 Commercial printing, lithographic
PA: Kappa Media, Llc
40 Skippack Pike
Fort Washington PA 19034
215 643-5800

(G-6917)
VECTOR MAGNETICS LLC
236 Cherry St (14850-5023)
PHONE..................607 273-8351
Arthur Kuckes, *CEO*
Rahn Pitzer, *President*
David Mohlet, *VP Opers*
Diana Griffin, *Manager*
EMP: 25
SQ FT: 12,000
SALES (est): 4.4MM **Privately Held**
SIC: 3829 Magnetometers

(G-6918)
VYBION INC
33 Thornwood Dr Ste 104 (14850-1275)
P.O. Box 4030 (14852-4030)
PHONE..................607 266-0860
Lee A Henderson, *Ch of Bd*
Rick Hendrick, *Manager*
EMP: 16
SQ FT: 2,500
SALES (est): 2.6MM **Privately Held**
WEB: www.vybion.com
SIC: 2824 Protein fibers

(G-6919)
WIDETRONIX INC
950 Danby Rd Ste 139 (14850-5714)
PHONE..................607 330-4752
Fax: 607 330-2804
Jonathan Greene, *President*
Samuel Portnoff, *Associate*
EMP: 5
SQ FT: 300
SALES (est): 762.8K **Privately Held**
SIC: 3674 Semiconductors & related devices

(G-6920)
ZYMTRNIX CATALYTIC SYSTEMS INC
405 Will Hall Crnell Univ (14853)
PHONE..................918 694-8206
Juan Alonso Succar, *President*
Stephane Corgie, *COO*
EMP: 6 **EST:** 2013
SALES (est): 663K **Privately Held**
SIC: 2869 Enzymes

Jackson Heights
Queens County

(G-6921)
BORNOMALA USA INC
Also Called: Weekly Bornomal
3766 72nd St Fl 3 (11372-6143)
PHONE..................347 753-2355
Mahfuzur Rahman, *President*
EMP: 5 **EST:** 2015
SALES (est): 92.2K **Privately Held**
SIC: 2711 Newspapers, publishing & printing; newspapers: publishing only, not printed on site

(G-6922)
JIN PIN MARKET INC
Also Called: Sin Yang Yang Company
8220 Roosevelt Ave (11372-7035)
PHONE..................718 898-0788
EMP: 5
SALES (est): 306.6K **Privately Held**
SIC: 3452 Pins

(G-6923)
KARISHMA FASHIONS INC
Also Called: Lavanya
3708 74th St (11372-6338)
PHONE..................718 565-5404
Shiv Dass, *President*
EMP: 5
SQ FT: 1,500

SALES (est): 300K **Privately Held**
SIC: 2395 Embroidery & art needlework

(G-6924)
TIME2VAPE LLC
9219 Roosevelt Ave (11372-7941)
PHONE..................718 335-0401
EMP: 7
SALES (est): 94.4K **Privately Held**
SIC: 3999 Cigar & cigarette holders

(G-6925)
WEEKLY AJKAL
3707 74th St Ste 8 (11372-6308)
PHONE..................718 565-2100
Jakaria Masud, *Owner*
EMP: 10
SALES (est): 375.8K **Privately Held**
SIC: 2711 Newspapers

Jamaica
Queens County

(G-6926)
ABBOTT INDUSTRIES INC (PA)
Also Called: Woodmaster Industries
9525 149th St (11435-4511)
PHONE..................718 291-0800
Fax: 718 739-0937
Leonard Grossman, *Ch of Bd*
Jeffrey Grossman, *Vice Pres*
Robert Candea, *Engineer*
Cindy Ackerman, *Controller*
Pat Iaonne, *Manager*
▲ **EMP:** 26 **EST:** 1958
SQ FT: 225,000
SALES (est): 30MM **Privately Held**
SIC: 2499 2541 3089 2542 Woodenware, kitchen & household; store fixtures, wood; plastic hardware & building products; office & store showcases & display fixtures, fryers, electric: household; heating units, for electric appliances; can openers, electric; food mixers, electric: household; miscellaneous fabricated wire products

(G-6927)
ACCORD PIPE FABRICATORS INC
9226 180th St (11433-1427)
PHONE..................718 657-3900
Fax: 718 657-3549
Harry Schwarz, *President*
Thomas S Bloom, *Vice Pres*
EMP: 35
SQ FT: 40,000
SALES (est): 5.5MM **Privately Held**
SIC: 3498 5051 Fabricated pipe & fittings; pipe & tubing, steel

(G-6928)
AMERICAN STEEL GATE CORP
10510 150th St (11435-5018)
PHONE..................718 291-4050
Tony Lohay, *President*
Anthony Lohay, *President*
EMP: 6
SQ FT: 3,000
SALES (est): 663K **Privately Held**
WEB: www.americansteelgate.com
SIC: 3442 Rolling doors for industrial buildings or warehouses, metal

(G-6929)
AMERICAN TORQUE INC
10522 150th St (11435-5018)
PHONE..................718 526-2433
Marsha McCarthy, *President*
EMP: 10
SQ FT: 4,000
SALES (est): 1MM **Privately Held**
SIC: 3566 Torque converters, except automotive

(G-6930)
ATLANTIC PORK & PROVISIONS INC
14707 94th Ave (11435-4513)
PHONE..................718 272-9550
Jack Antinori, *President*
Ronald Romeo, *Vice Pres*
Susan Antinori, *Treasurer*

Jamaica - Queens County (G-6931)

Acevedo Genis, *Manager*
EMP: 40 **EST:** 1948
SQ FT: 30,000
SALES (est): 4.3MM **Privately Held**
SIC: 2013 Bologna from purchased meat; ham, boiled: from purchased meat; ham, roasted: from purchased meat; ham, smoked: from purchased meat

(G-6931)
ATLAS CONCRETE BATCHING CORP
9511 147th Pl (11435-4507)
PHONE..................................718 523-3000
Thomas Polsinelli, *Principal*
EMP: 100
SQ FT: 12,000
SALES (est): 9MM **Privately Held**
SIC: 3273 Ready-mixed concrete

(G-6932)
ATLAS TRANSIT MIX CORP
9511 147th Pl (11435-4507)
PHONE..................................718 523-3000
Fax: 718 658-2293
Mary Polsinelli, *President*
Vincent Polsinelli, *Corp Secy*
Tom Polsinelli, *Vice Pres*
EMP: 150
SQ FT: 12,000
SALES: 900K **Privately Held**
SIC: 3273 Ready-mixed concrete

(G-6933)
B & R SHEET
10652 157th St (11433-2050)
PHONE..................................718 558-5544
Rohan Rampersaud, *Principal*
EMP: 5 **EST:** 2014
SALES (est): 502.1K **Privately Held**
SIC: 3444 1761 Sheet metalwork; sheet metalwork

(G-6934)
BAUERSCHMIDT & SONS INC
11920 Merrick Blvd (11434-2296)
PHONE..................................718 528-3500
Fax: 718 276-9021
Fred Bauerschmidt, *Ch of Bd*
Robert Bauerschmidt, *Treasurer*
Patricia Bauerschmidt, *Manager*
Douglas Wefer, *Admin Asst*
▲ **EMP:** 70 **EST:** 1948
SQ FT: 28,000
SALES (est): 11.4MM **Privately Held**
WEB: www.bauerschmidtandsons.com
SIC: 2541 2431 2521 2434 Office fixtures, wood; cabinets, except refrigerated: show, display, etc.: wood; woodwork, interior & ornamental; wood office furniture; wood kitchen cabinets

(G-6935)
C T M INDUSTRIES LTD (HQ)
22005 97th Ave (11429-1398)
PHONE..................................718 479-3300
Fax: 718 217-4451
Perry Ciarletta, *President*
Martin Silver, *Vice Pres*
Howard Cherry, *Admin Director*
EMP: 30
SQ FT: 1,000
SALES (est): 8MM
SALES (corp-wide): 13.6MM **Privately Held**
SIC: 2836 5122 Plasmas; blood plasma
PA: Life Resources Llc
71 S Bedford Rd
Mount Kisco NY
914 241-1646

(G-6936)
CAPITOL AWNING CO INC
Also Called: Capitol Awning & Shade Co
10515 180th St (11433-1818)
PHONE..................................212 505-1717
Michael Catalano, *President*
Steven Rubino, *General Mgr*
Phil Catalano, *Vice Pres*
Ryan Catalano, *Treasurer*
Mike Grosso, *Accounts Exec*
EMP: 18 **EST:** 1967
SQ FT: 8,000
SALES (est): 2MM **Privately Held**
WEB: www.capitolawning.com
SIC: 2394 Awnings, fabric: made from purchased materials

(G-6937)
CHEMCLEAN CORPORATION
13045 180th St (11434-4107)
PHONE..................................718 525-4500
Fax: 718 481-6470
Bernard Esquenet, *President*
Brian Alexander, *Sales Executive*
Miriam Ramos, *Manager*
Crispin Paul, *Supervisor*
▲ **EMP:** 28 **EST:** 1943
SQ FT: 30,000
SALES (est): 5.9MM **Privately Held**
WEB: www.chemclean.com
SIC: 2842 Specialty cleaning preparations

(G-6938)
CIRCLE 5 DELI CORP
13440 Guy R Brewer Blvd (11434-3728)
PHONE..................................718 525-5687
Yahya Alsaidi, *Principal*
EMP: 8
SALES (est): 455.7K **Privately Held**
SIC: 2051 Bakery, for home service delivery

(G-6939)
CITY MASON CORP
Also Called: Three Star Supply
10417 148th St (11435-4921)
PHONE..................................718 658-3796
Fax: 718 658-6878
Anthony Scaccia, *Ch of Bd*
Frank Landen Jr, *President*
EMP: 15
SQ FT: 20,000
SALES (est): 1.1MM **Privately Held**
SIC: 3272 Concrete products

(G-6940)
CITY POST EXPRESS INC
17518 147th Ave (11434-5402)
P.O. Box 405, Fairfield CT (06824-0405)
PHONE..................................718 995-8690
Robert Swords, *Principal*
▲ **EMP:** 9
SALES (est): 866.5K **Privately Held**
SIC: 2741 Miscellaneous publishing

(G-6941)
CLASSIC COOKING LLC
16535 145th Dr (11434-5108)
PHONE..................................718 439-0200
Andy Reichgut, *President*
Anthony Minuto, *QA Dir*
Eli Weinstock, *VP Sls/Mktg*
Julie Gould, *Marketing Staff*
Karen Velazquez, *Office Mgr*
▲ **EMP:** 100
SQ FT: 40,000
SALES: 15.8MM **Privately Held**
SIC: 2035 2037 2038 Pickles, sauces & salad dressings; vegetables, quick frozen & cold pack, excl. potato products; soups, frozen

(G-6942)
CONCORD EXPRESS CARGO INC
17214 119th Ave (11434-2260)
PHONE..................................718 276-7200
Chris Okafor, *CEO*
Maggie Burnes, *Manager*
Margaret Jones, *Admin Sec*
▼ **EMP:** 5
SALES (est): 642.5K **Privately Held**
SIC: 2448 Cargo containers, wood & wood with metal

(G-6943)
CORKHILL MANUFACTURING CO INC
Also Called: Corkhill Grp
13121 Merrick Blvd (11434-4133)
PHONE..................................718 528-7413
Dennis Wugalter, *President*
EMP: 8 **EST:** 1947
SQ FT: 7,000
SALES (est): 1.3MM **Privately Held**
SIC: 3442 Storm doors or windows, metal

(G-6944)
CRS REMANUFACTURING CO INC
9440 158th St (11433-1017)
PHONE..................................718 739-1720
Pratab Angira, *President*
Balkrishna Angira, *Vice Pres*
▲ **EMP:** 10
SALES (est): 920K **Privately Held**
SIC: 3714 Power steering equipment, motor vehicle

(G-6945)
D AND D SHEET METAL CORP
9510 218th St Ste 4 (11429-1216)
PHONE..................................718 465-7585
EMP: 12
SALES (est): 960K **Privately Held**
SIC: 3444 Mfg Sheet Metalwork

(G-6946)
ELMHURST DAIRY INC
15602 Liberty Ave Ste 2 (11433-1009)
PHONE..................................718 526-3442
Fax: 718 291-0919
Henry Schwartz, *President*
Joe Kranz, *Vice Pres*
Jay Valentine, *Vice Pres*
Sam Chadwick, *Opers Staff*
Bob Giurco, *QC Dir*
EMP: 208
SALES (est): 48.9MM **Privately Held**
WEB: www.elmhurstdairy.net
SIC: 2026 5143 Milk processing (pasteurizing, homogenizing, bottling); milk & cream, fluid

(G-6947)
EXPRESSIONS PUNCHING & DIGITIZ
Also Called: Expression Embroidery
9315 179th Pl (11433-1425)
PHONE..................................718 291-1177
George Hanakis, *President*
Evelyn Hanakis, *Vice Pres*
Alicia Clarke, *Office Mgr*
EMP: 9
SQ FT: 7,000
SALES: 980K **Privately Held**
SIC: 2395 Embroidery & art needlework

(G-6948)
FORTUNE POLY PRODUCTS INC
17910 93rd Ave (11433-1406)
PHONE..................................718 361-0767
Fax: 718 361-1756
Roger Truong, *President*
▲ **EMP:** 14
SQ FT: 25,000
SALES (est): 2.8MM **Privately Held**
SIC: 2673 Plastic bags: made from purchased materials

(G-6949)
FRANCHET METAL CRAFT INC
17832 93rd Ave (11433-1489)
PHONE..................................718 658-6400
Fax: 718 658-5627
Frank Grodio, *President*
EMP: 6
SQ FT: 4,000
SALES: 700K **Privately Held**
SIC: 3444 Sheet metal specialties, not stamped

(G-6950)
FRANKLIN ELECTRIC CO INC
17501 Rockaway Blvd # 309 (11434-5502)
PHONE..................................718 244-7744
EMP: 563
SALES (corp-wide): 949.8MM **Publicly Held**
SIC: 3621 Motors, electric
PA: Franklin Electric Co., Inc.
9255 Coverdale Rd
Fort Wayne IN 46809
260 824-2900

(G-6951)
GLEANER COMPANY LTD
Also Called: Jamaican Weekly Gleaner
9205 172nd St Fl 2 (11433-1218)
PHONE..................................718 657-0788
Fax: 718 657-0857
Lolita Long, *Manager*
Sheila Alexander, *Director*
EMP: 5
SALES (est): 629.9K **Privately Held**
WEB: www.gleaner-classifieds.com
SIC: 2711 Newspapers
HQ: Gleaner Company (Canada) Inc, The
1390 Eglinton Ave W Suite 2
Toronto ON M6C 2
416 784-3002

(G-6952)
GOURMET BOUTIQUE LLC (PA)
14402 158th St (11434-4214)
PHONE..................................718 977-1200
Fax: 718 977-0200
Jan Sussman, *President*
David Andersen, *General Mgr*
Jason Sussman, *General Mgr*
Robert Liberto, *COO*
Hugh Anderson, *Maint Spvr*
▲ **EMP:** 217
SQ FT: 60,000
SALES: 64MM **Privately Held**
WEB: www.gourmetboutique.com
SIC: 2099 Food preparations

(G-6953)
H & H FURNITURE CO
11420 101st Ave (11419-1139)
PHONE..................................718 850-5252
John Hassan, *Manager*
EMP: 5
SALES (est): 330K **Privately Held**
SIC: 2512 Upholstered household furniture

(G-6954)
H G MAYBECK CO INC
17930 93rd Ave Ste 2 (11433-1405)
PHONE..................................718 297-4410
Fax: 718 297-4213
John Arapis, *President*
Chris Arapis, *Vice Pres*
▲ **EMP:** 30
SQ FT: 26,000
SALES (est): 4.2MM **Privately Held**
SIC: 2393 2673 Canvas bags; bags: plastic, laminated & coated

(G-6955)
HILLSIDE PRINTING INC
Also Called: Printing Express
16013 Hillside Ave (11432-3982)
PHONE..................................718 658-6719
Fax: 718 658-4892
Joseph Randazzo, *President*
EMP: 10
SQ FT: 2,000
SALES: 1MM **Privately Held**
WEB: www.hillsideprinting.com
SIC: 2752 Commercial printing, offset

(G-6956)
HUDA KAWSHAI LLC
8514 168th St Ste 3 (11432-2624)
PHONE..................................929 255-7009
Nusrat Zafreen, *CEO*
EMP: 5 **EST:** 2016
SALES (est): 146.6K **Privately Held**
SIC: 2011 Meat by-products from meat slaughtered on site

(G-6957)
IMPLADENT LTD (PA)
19845 Foothill Ave (11423-1611)
PHONE..................................718 465-1810
Fax: 718 464-9620
Maurice Valen, *President*
Virginia Valen, *Vice Pres*
Stephanie Georgi, *Executive*
Gisele Sasson, *Admin Sec*
EMP: 8
SALES: 2MM **Privately Held**
WEB: www.impladentltd.com
SIC: 3843 3069 5047 Dental equipment & supplies; medical & laboratory rubber sundries & related products; dental equipment & supplies

(G-6958)
J SUSSMAN INC
10910 180th St (11433-2622)
PHONE..................................718 297-0228
Fax: 718 297-3090
David Sussman, *President*
Steve Sussman, *Vice Pres*
Robin Sussman, *Manager*

GEOGRAPHIC SECTION
Jamaica - Queens County (G-6987)

▼ EMP: 45 EST: 1906
SQ FT: 55,000
SALES (est): 11.4MM **Privately Held**
WEB: www.jsussmaninc.com
SIC: **3442** 3354 Window & door frames; aluminum extruded products

(G-6959)
JAMAICA IRON WORKS INC
10847 Merrick Blvd (11433-2992)
PHONE..................................718 657-4849
Fax: 718 526-3450
Robert Pape, *President*
EMP: 10 EST: 1927
SQ FT: 2,000
SALES (est): 830K **Privately Held**
SIC: **3446** Fences or posts, ornamental iron or steel

(G-6960)
JONATHAN METAL & GLASS LTD
17818 107th Ave (11433-1802)
PHONE..................................718 846-8000
Fax: 718 847-9397
Wilfred Smith, *President*
▲ EMP: 70
SQ FT: 6,000
SALES: 47.3MM **Privately Held**
SIC: **3446** Bank fixtures, ornamental metal; brasswork, ornamental: structural; grill-work, ornamental metal

(G-6961)
LITE-MAKERS INC
10715 180th St (11433-2617)
PHONE..................................718 739-9300
John Iorio, *President*
Priya Bery, *Research*
Gary Iorio, *Treasurer*
Paul Davis, *Director*
▲ EMP: 30 EST: 1974
SQ FT: 12,000
SALES (est): 4.9MM **Privately Held**
WEB: www.litemakers.com
SIC: **3646** Commercial indusl & institutional electric lighting fixtures; chandeliers, commercial

(G-6962)
MACHINA DEUS LEX INC
15921 Grand Central Pkwy (11432-1128)
PHONE..................................917 577-0972
Glen Kieser, *President*
EMP: 6
SALES: 150K **Privately Held**
SIC: **2421** Silo stock, wood: sawed

(G-6963)
MAIA SYSTEMS LLC
8344 Parsons Blvd Ste 101 (11432-1642)
PHONE..................................718 206-0100
Jack Najyb, *President*
EMP: 6
SALES (est): 846.4K **Privately Held**
SIC: **3661** 3577 5734 Telephone sets, all types except cellular radio; computer peripheral equipment; computer & software stores

(G-6964)
MARTIN BRASS WORKS INC
17544 Liberty Ave (11433-1391)
PHONE..................................718 523-3146
Fax: 718 523-6631
Aloysia Carl, *President*
Joseph Carl III, *Engineer*
EMP: 7
SQ FT: 2,500
SALES (est): 700K **Privately Held**
WEB: www.martinbrassworks.com
SIC: **3494** 3432 Pipe fittings; plumbing fixture fittings & trim

(G-6965)
MAUCERI SIGN INC
Also Called: Mauceri Sign & Awning Co
16725 Rockaway Blvd (11434-5222)
PHONE..................................718 656-7700
James V Mauceri, *President*
Carol Caruso, *General Mgr*
EMP: 18
SQ FT: 14,000
SALES (est): 2.6MM **Privately Held**
SIC: **3993** 2394 5999 Signs, not made in custom sign painting shops; awnings, fabric: made from purchased materials; awnings

(G-6966)
METAL WORKS OF NY INC
11603 Merrick Blvd (11434-1825)
PHONE..................................718 525-9440
Fax: 718 525-9462
Vincent Sabatino, *President*
Danny Sabatino, *Treasurer*
EMP: 5
SALES (est): 520K **Privately Held**
SIC: **3441** Fabricated structural metal

(G-6967)
METEOR EXPRESS INC
16801 Rockaway Blvd # 202 (11434-5287)
PHONE..................................718 551-9177
Ning Fang, *CEO*
EMP: 15
SALES (est): 1.1MM **Privately Held**
SIC: **3537** Trucks: freight, baggage, etc.: industrial, except mining

(G-6968)
MINUTEMAN PRESS INTL INC
24814 Union Tpke (11426-1837)
PHONE..................................718 343-5440
Rob Schiffman, *Manager*
EMP: 5
SALES (corp-wide): 23.4MM **Privately Held**
SIC: **2752** Commercial printing, lithographic
PA: Minuteman Press International, Inc.
61 Executive Blvd
Farmingdale NY 11735
631 249-1370

(G-6969)
MMS H& F INC
8745 144th St (11435-3122)
PHONE..................................718 785-6663
Hamida Begun, *Principal*
Mohhammed Rahaman, *Vice Pres*
EMP: 6 EST: 2012
SQ FT: 1,200
SALES: 350K **Privately Held**
SIC: **2392** Household furnishings

(G-6970)
MONTANA GLOBAL LLC
9048 160th St (11432-6124)
PHONE..................................212 213-1572
Mathieu Goldenberg, *President*
▲ EMP: 5
SALES: 1.4MM **Privately Held**
SIC: **3172** Cases, glasses
PA: Duval, Llc
15929 Jamaica Ave 2
Jamaica NY 11432

(G-6971)
MOUNTAIN SIDE FARMS INC
15504 Liberty Ave (11433-1038)
PHONE..................................718 526-3442
Henry Schwartz, *President*
Lonnie Stewart, *Controller*
Bruce Kinlin, *Acting Cntr*
EMP: 30 EST: 1981
SQ FT: 500
SALES (est): 29.8K **Privately Held**
SIC: **2026** Milk processing (pasteurizing, homogenizing, bottling)

(G-6972)
NEW CLASSIC TRADE INC
17211 93rd Ave (11433-1210)
PHONE..................................347 822-9052
Mustafo Masik, *CEO*
EMP: 6
SQ FT: 1,200
SALES: 1MM **Privately Held**
SIC: **2241** Trimmings, textile

(G-6973)
NEW YORK STEEL SERVICES CO
18009 Liberty Ave (11433-1434)
PHONE..................................718 291-7770
Fax: 718 291-8609
George Cromwell, *Owner*
EMP: 5
SALES (est): 390K **Privately Held**
SIC: **3449** Bars, concrete reinforcing: fabricated steel

(G-6974)
OLYMPIC ICE CREAM CO INC
Also Called: Marion's Italian Ices
12910 91st Ave (11418-3317)
PHONE..................................718 849-6200
Michael Barone, *President*
EMP: 50
SALES (corp-wide): 12.9MM **Privately Held**
WEB: www.marinositalianices.com
SIC: **2024** Ices, flavored (frozen dessert)
PA: Olympic Ice Cream Co., Inc.
12910 91st Ave
Richmond Hill NY 11418
718 849-6200

(G-6975)
PAL ALUMINUM INC
Also Called: Pal Industries
10620 180th St (11433-1828)
PHONE..................................718 262-0091
Pana Giotis Mar Neris, *Branch Mgr*
EMP: 22
SALES (corp-wide): 4.7MM **Privately Held**
SIC: **3444** Metal roofing & roof drainage equipment
PA: Pal Aluminum, Inc.
230 Duffy Ave Unit B
Hicksville NY 11801
516 937-1990

(G-6976)
PATI INC
Also Called: Airport Press, The
Jfk Intl Airprt Hngar 16 (11430)
PHONE..................................718 244-6788
Fax: 718 995-3432
EMP: 10
SQ FT: 1,000
SALES (est): 790K **Privately Held**
SIC: **2721** Periodicals-Publishing/Printing

(G-6977)
PRECISION READY MIX INC
14707 Liberty Ave (11435-4727)
PHONE..................................718 658-5600
Frank Scaccia, *President*
EMP: 6
SQ FT: 700
SALES (est): 500K **Privately Held**
SIC: **3273** Ready-mixed concrete

(G-6978)
PREMIUM SWEETS USA INC
16803 Hillside Ave (11432-4340)
PHONE..................................718 739-6000
Babu Khan, *CEO*
EMP: 8
SALES (est): 602.4K **Privately Held**
SIC: **2064** 5145 Candy & other confectionery products; candy

(G-6979)
QUEENS READY MIX INC
14901 95th Ave (11435-4521)
PHONE..................................718 526-4919
Tony Mastronardi, *President*
Jerry Mastronardi, *Vice Pres*
EMP: 7
SALES (est): 1MM **Privately Held**
SIC: **3273** Ready-mixed concrete

(G-6980)
R & M THERMOFOIL DOORS INC
14830 94th Ave (11435-4516)
PHONE..................................718 206-4991
Robby Moyal, *Ch of Bd*
Robbert Moy, *Manager*
Alison Pucorte, *Admin Asst*
EMP: 5
SALES (est): 643.2K **Privately Held**
SIC: **2434** Wood kitchen cabinets

(G-6981)
RAYCO MANUFACTURING CO INC
Also Called: Rayco Manufacturing Div
10715 180th St (11433-2617)
PHONE..................................516 431-2006
Fax: 718 626-1163
Sidney L Friedman, *President*

John Iannuzzo, *Treasurer*
EMP: 12
SQ FT: 15,000
SALES (est): 970K **Privately Held**
SIC: **3444** 3469 Sheet metalwork; machine parts, stamped or pressed metal

(G-6982)
RAYS RESTAURANT & BAKERY INC
12325 Jamaica Ave (11418-2640)
PHONE..................................718 441-7707
Ray Manharalall, *CEO*
▲ EMP: 6
SQ FT: 3,100
SALES (est): 320K **Privately Held**
SIC: **2051** Bakery: wholesale or wholesale/retail combined

(G-6983)
REHABILITATION INTERNATIONAL
15350 89th Ave Apt 1101 (11432-3977)
PHONE..................................212 420-1500
Fax: 212 505-0871
Tomas Lagerwall, *President*
Leonor Coello, *Office Mgr*
EMP: 5
SQ FT: 4,000
SALES: 182.2K **Privately Held**
SIC: **3663**

(G-6984)
RENT-A-CENTER INC
11211 Liberty Ave (11419-1813)
PHONE..................................718 322-2400
Fax: 718 322-2404
Derrick Williams, *Manager*
EMP: 6
SALES (corp-wide): 2.9B **Publicly Held**
WEB: www.rentacenter.com
SIC: **2519** Furniture, household: glass, fiberglass & plastic
PA: Rent-A-Center, Inc.
5501 Headquarters Dr
Plano TX 75024
972 801-1100

(G-6985)
ROSCO INC (PA)
9021 144th Pl (11435-4227)
PHONE..................................718 526-2601
Sol Englander, *Chairman*
Gertrude Englander, *Corp Secy*
Ben Englander, *Vice Pres*
Danny Englander, *Vice Pres*
Joe Ippolito, *Opers Staff*
◆ EMP: 170
SQ FT: 85,000
SALES (est): 37.5MM **Privately Held**
WEB: www.roscomirrors.com
SIC: **3231** 3714 3429 Mirrors, truck & automobile: made from purchased glass; motor vehicle parts & accessories; manufactured hardware (general)

(G-6986)
SKY LAUNDROMAT INC
8615 Ava Pl Apt 4e (11432-2954)
PHONE..................................718 639-7070
David Mendoza, *President*
Jay Wright, *Vice Pres*
Herman Mendoza, *Chief Mktg Ofcr*
EMP: 33
SQ FT: 5,000
SALES: 660K **Privately Held**
SIC: **2211** 7215 Laundry nets; laundry, coin-operated

(G-6987)
SSRJA LLC
Also Called: Five Star Printing
10729 180th St (11433-2617)
PHONE..................................718 725-7020
Savithri Somwaru,
Anand Jagessar,
Seelochini S Liriano,
Javier Rojas,
Sandy Shivnarayan, *Assistant*
EMP: 11
SQ FT: 10,000
SALES: 3MM **Privately Held**
SIC: **2711** Newspapers, publishing & printing

Jamaica - Queens County (G-6988)

(G-6988)
STAR MOUNTAIN JFK INC
Also Called: Star Mountain Coffee
Federal Cir Bldg 141 (11430)
PHONE..................................718 553-6787
Carmen Ham, *President*
EMP: 5
SALES: 350K **Privately Held**
SIC: 2095 Roasted coffee

(G-6989)
STEUBEN FOODS INCORPORATED (PA)
15504 Liberty Ave (11433-1000)
PHONE..................................718 291-3333
Kenneth Schlossberg, *President*
Jeffrey Sokal, *Principal*
Bruce Budinoff, *Vice Pres*
David Cantor, *Vice Pres*
Darius Schwartz, *Vice Pres*
EMP: 17
SQ FT: 10,000
SALES (est): 123.1MM **Privately Held**
SIC: 2032 2026 Puddings, except meat: packaged in cans, jars, etc.; yogurt; milk drinks, flavored

(G-6990)
SUGARBEAR CUPCAKES
14552 159th St (11434-4220)
PHONE..................................917 698-9005
Louise Torbert, *Principal*
EMP: 8
SALES (est): 315K **Privately Held**
SIC: 2051 Bread, cake & related products

(G-6991)
SUNBILT SOLAR PDTS BY SUSSMAN
10910 180th St (11433-2622)
PHONE..................................718 297-0228
Steven Sussman, *President*
David Sussman, *Vice Pres*
EMP: 55
SQ FT: 80,000
SALES (est): 5.7MM **Privately Held**
SIC: 3448 Sunrooms, prefabricated metal

(G-6992)
TECHNICAL SERVICE INDUSTRIES
Also Called: ABC Casting
17506 Devonshire Rd 5n (11432-2949)
PHONE..................................212 719-9800
Mitch Altman, *President*
Michael Hooks, *Vice Pres*
EMP: 27
SQ FT: 3,500
SALES (est): 3MM **Privately Held**
SIC: 3911 Jewelry, precious metal

(G-6993)
TEE PEE FENCE AND RAILING
Also Called: Tee Pee Fence & Rail
9312 179th Pl (11433-1426)
PHONE..................................718 658-8323
Fax: 718 297-1174
Tom Pendergast, *President*
Jim Pendergast, *Office Mgr*
EMP: 15
SQ FT: 15,000
SALES: 1.3MM **Privately Held**
SIC: 3446 Fences or posts, ornamental iron or steel; railings, prefabricated metal

(G-6994)
THE SANDHAR CORP
16427 Highland Ave (11432-3555)
PHONE..................................718 523-0819
Hardev Sandhu, *President*
Shawinder Sandhu, *Vice Pres*
Shyamal N Bastola DDS, *Fmly & Gen Dent*
EMP: 7 **EST:** 1990
SALES (est): 413.8K **Privately Held**
SIC: 2711 Newspapers

(G-6995)
TRU-ART SIGN CO INC
Also Called: Signs By Sunrise
10515 180th St (11433-1818)
PHONE..................................718 658-5068
Lawrence Amatulli, *President*
EMP: 12

SALES (corp-wide): 1.3MM **Privately Held**
SIC: 3993 Signs & advertising specialties
PA: Tru-Art Sign Co. Inc.
  187 N Main St
  Freeport NY
  516 378-0066

(G-6996)
TURBO EXPRESS INC
16019 Rockaway Blvd Ste D (11434-5100)
PHONE..................................718 723-3686
Fax: 718 723-5270
Gilberto Rosario, *Principal*
EMP: 5
SALES (est): 239.2K **Privately Held**
SIC: 2741 Miscellaneous publishing

(G-6997)
URDU TIMES
16920 Hillside Ave (11432-4435)
PHONE..................................718 297-8700
Fax: 718 658-1177
Khalil Ur Rehman, *President*
EMP: 6
SALES (est): 198.5K **Privately Held**
SIC: 2711 Newspapers

(G-6998)
VISUAL EFFECTS INC
15929 Jamaica Ave 2 (11432-6002)
PHONE..................................718 324-0011
Thomas Murphy, *President*
Henry Kwitel, *Vice Pres*
Evelyn Viera, *Office Mgr*
▲ **EMP:** 10 **EST:** 1968
SALES (est): 1.5MM **Privately Held**
SIC: 3648 5063 3993 Lighting equipment; lighting fixtures; electric signs; displays & cutouts, window & lobby

(G-6999)
WAYNE DECORATORS INC
14409 Rockaway Blvd Apt 1 (11436-1602)
PHONE..................................718 529-4200
Louis Sapodin, *President*
Alex Greenberg, *Vice Pres*
EMP: 8
SQ FT: 2,000
SALES (est): 617.1K **Privately Held**
SIC: 2391 2392 2393 Draperies, plastic & textile: from purchased materials; bedspreads & bed sets: made from purchased materials; pillows, bed: made from purchased materials; cushions, except spring & carpet: purchased materials

(G-7000)
WHITNEY FOODS INC
Also Called: Kissle
15504 Liberty Ave (11433-1038)
PHONE..................................718 291-3333
Fax: 718 291-0560
Henry Schwartz, *Ch of Bd*
Kenneth Schlossberg, *Vice Ch Bd*
D Bruce Budinoff, *Vice Pres*
Robert E Braks, *Treasurer*
EMP: 16
SALES (est): 1.3MM
SALES (corp-wide): 123.1MM **Privately Held**
SIC: 2026 Yogurt
PA: Steuben Foods, Incorporated
  15504 Liberty Ave
  Jamaica NY 11433
  718 291-3333

(G-7001)
X-TREME READY MIX INC
17801 Liberty Ave (11433-1432)
PHONE..................................718 739-3384
Michael Falco, *Ch of Bd*
EMP: 9
SALES (est): 1.2MM **Privately Held**
SIC: 3531 Mixers, concrete

Jamesport
Suffolk County

(G-7002)
NORTH HOUSE VINEYARDS INC
Also Called: Jamesport Vineyards
1216 Main Rd Rte 25a (11947)
P.O. Box 842 (11947-0842)
PHONE..................................631 779-2817
Fax: 631 722-5256
Ronald B Goerler, *President*
Ann Marie Goerler, *Treasurer*
▲ **EMP:** 5
SALES (est): 431.7K **Privately Held**
WEB: www.jamesportvineyards.com
SIC: 2084 Wines

Jamestown
Chautauqua County

(G-7003)
ACCESS ELEVATOR & LIFT INC (PA)
1209 E 2nd St (14701-1952)
PHONE..................................716 483-3696
Sean Fenton, *President*
Michelle Butman, *General Mgr*
Debra Fagerstrom, *Office Mgr*
Norm Klein, *Manager*
EMP: 1
SALES: 1.8MM **Privately Held**
SIC: 3534 Elevators & moving stairways

(G-7004)
ACU RITE COMPANIES INC
1 Precision Way (14701-9630)
PHONE..................................716 661-1700
Fax: 716 661-1888
Thomas Wright, *CEO*
John Parker, *Opers Staff*
Jerry Reynolds, *Controller*
Craig Greiner, *Manager*
Kenneth Cramer, *Software Engr*
◆ **EMP:** 5
SALES (est): 285.6K **Privately Held**
SIC: 1389 Testing, measuring, surveying & analysis services
HQ: Heidenhain Corporation
  333 E State Pkwy
  Schaumburg IL 60173
  847 490-1191

(G-7005)
ALL METAL SPECIALTIES INC
300 Livingston Ave (14701-2665)
PHONE..................................716 664-6009
Fax: 716 483-0575
Raymond Anderson, *President*
Kathy Gourley, *Admin Sec*
EMP: 21 **EST:** 1953
SQ FT: 18,500
SALES: 3MM **Privately Held**
WEB: www.allmetalspecialties.com
SIC: 3446 Architectural metalwork

(G-7006)
ALLIED INDUSTRIAL PRODUCTS CO
Also Called: Allied Industries
880 E 2nd St (14701-3824)
PHONE..................................716 664-3893
Greg Bender, *Manager*
EMP: 6
SALES (corp-wide): 90K **Privately Held**
SIC: 3599 Machine & other job shop work
PA: Allied Industrial Products Co
  180 W Olive St
  Long Beach NY

(G-7007)
ANDERSON PRECISION INC
20 Livingston Ave (14701-2844)
PHONE..................................716 484-1148
Steven Godfrey, *President*
Jason Carlson, *Prdtn Mgr*
John McCool, *Engineer*
Elise Covey, *Accountant*
David Archer, *VP Sales*
▲ **EMP:** 83
SQ FT: 80,000

SALES (est): 22MM **Privately Held**
WEB: www.andersonprecision.com
SIC: 3451 3494 Screw machine products; valves & pipe fittings

(G-7008)
ARTONE LLC
Also Called: Artone Furniture By Design
1089 Allen St (14701-2327)
PHONE..................................716 664-2232
Fax: 716 664-1511
Michael Calimeri, *President*
Vicrorian Doucette, *Senior VP*
Sebastion Calimeri, *Vice Pres*
Sally Donisi, *Controller*
Lori Crowell, *Admin Asst*
▲ **EMP:** 85
SQ FT: 240,000
SALES: 12.3MM **Privately Held**
WEB: www.artonemfg.com
SIC: 2521 2522 2531 2541 Wood office furniture; office furniture, except wood; public building & related furniture; wood partitions & fixtures; wood kitchen cabinets; upholstered household furniture

(G-7009)
BELLA INTERNATIONAL INC
111 W 2nd St Ste 4000 (14701-5207)
PHONE..................................716 484-0102
Stephen Pownell, *Principal*
EMP: 5
SALES (est): 508.3K **Privately Held**
WEB: www.bellayre.com
SIC: 2835 In vitro & in vivo diagnostic substances

(G-7010)
BIOPOOL US INC
Also Called: Trinity Biotech Distribution
2823 Girts Rd (14701-9666)
P.O. Box 1059 (14702-1059)
PHONE..................................716 483-3851
Ian Woodwards, *CEO*
Sharon Bell, *Production*
Bonnie D Joy, *QA Dir*
Brendan Fitzpatrick, *Auditor*
Teresa Pirog, *Marketing Staff*
▲ **EMP:** 48
SALES (est): 7MM **Privately Held**
SIC: 2835 In vitro & in vivo diagnostic substances
HQ: Trinity Biotech, Inc.
  2823 Girts Rd
  Jamestown NY 14701
  800 325-3424

(G-7011)
BLACKSTONE ADVANCED TECH LLC
86 Blackstone Ave (14701-2202)
PHONE..................................716 665-5410
Richard Turner, *CEO*
EMP: 101
SALES: 26.8MM **Privately Held**
SIC: 3444 3441 3443 Sheet metalwork; fabricated structural metal; fabricated plate work (boiler shop)

(G-7012)
BNO INTL TRDG CO INC
505 Chautauqua Ave (14701-7615)
P.O. Box 97 (14702-0097)
PHONE..................................716 487-1900
Benjamin N Okwumabua, *President*
Benjamin Okwumabua, *President*
Constance Okwumabua, *Vice Pres*
EMP: 4 **EST:** 1997
SQ FT: 100,000
SALES: 2.5MM **Privately Held**
WEB: www.bnointl.com
SIC: 3669 5063 Highway signals, electric; signaling equipment, electrical

(G-7013)
BUSH INDUSTRIES INC (PA)
1 Mason Dr (14701-9200)
P.O. Box 460 (14702-0460)
PHONE..................................716 665-2000
Fax: 716 665-2510
Jim Garde, *CEO*
Stephen Pettia, *President*
Mike Evans, *Exec VP*
Jerry Green, *Exec VP*
Steve Phelan, *Exec VP*
▲ **EMP:** 234 **EST:** 1959

GEOGRAPHIC SECTION — Jamestown - Chautauqua County (G-7036)

SQ FT: 440,000
SALES (est): 110.9MM **Privately Held**
WEB: www.bushindustries.com
SIC: 2511 2521 Wood household furniture; desks, office: wood; cabinets, office: wood; bookcases, office: wood; panel systems & partitions (free-standing), office: wood

(G-7014)
CLARK LABORATORIES INC (DH)
Also Called: Trinity Biotech USA
2823 Girts Rd (14701-9666)
P.O. Box 1059 (14702-1059)
PHONE..................................716 483-3851
Fax: 716 488-1990
Ian M Woodwards, *CEO*
▲ EMP: 11
SQ FT: 25,000
SALES (est): 13MM **Privately Held**
SIC: 2835 In vitro & in vivo diagnostic substances
HQ: Trinity Biotech, Inc.
2823 Girts Rd
Jamestown NY 14701
800 325-3424

(G-7015)
CLARKE-BOXIT CORPORATION
45 Norwood Ave (14701-6564)
PHONE..................................716 487-1950
Donald Zaas, *Ch of Bd*
Joel Zaas, *President*
Mark Cassese, *COO*
John Asimakopoulos, *CFO*
EMP: 6
SALES (est): 223.5K
SALES (corp-wide): 58.5MM **Privately Held**
WEB: www.boxit.com
SIC: 2652 Setup paperboard boxes
PA: The Apex Paper Box Company
5555 Walworth Ave
Cleveland OH 44102
216 631-4000

(G-7016)
CLEANING TECH GROUP LLC
Blackstone-Ney Ultrasonics
9 N Main St (14701-5213)
P.O. Box 220 (14702-0220)
PHONE..................................716 665-2340
Timothy Piazza, *President*
Alan Atcheson, *General Mgr*
Jeff Gordon, *Opers Staff*
Tony Chapman, *Purch Agent*
William Puskas, *Research*
EMP: 50
SALES (corp-wide): 13.4MM **Privately Held**
SIC: 3569 3559 Blast cleaning equipment, dustless; degreasing machines, automotive & industrial
HQ: Cleaning Technologies Group, Llc
4933 Provident Dr
West Chester OH 45246
513 870-0100

(G-7017)
CNTRY CROSS COMMUNICATIONS LLC
Also Called: W K Z A 106.9 K I S S-F M
106 W 3rd St Ste 106 (14701-5105)
PHONE..................................386 758-9696
Fax: 716 488-2169
John Newman, *Mng Member*
EMP: 10
SALES (est): 1.1MM **Privately Held**
WEB: www.1069kissfm.com
SIC: 3663 Radio receiver networks

(G-7018)
CONTAINER TSTG SOLUTIONS LLC
17 Tiffany Ave (14701-1953)
PHONE..................................716 487-3300
Brian Johnson, *Branch Mgr*
EMP: 12 **Privately Held**
SIC: 2834 Solutions, pharmaceutical
PA: Container Testing Solutions Llc
17 Lester St
Sinclairville NY 14782

(G-7019)
COPPER RIDGE OIL INC
111 W 2nd St Ste 404 (14701-5229)
P.O. Box 626, Olean (14760-0626)
PHONE..................................716 372-4021
Greg Thropp, *President*
EMP: 8
SALES (est): 950K **Privately Held**
SIC: 1381 Drilling oil & gas wells

(G-7020)
CRAWFORD FURNITURE MFG CORP
347 Broadhead Ave (14701-8163)
P.O. Box 668 (14702-0668)
PHONE..................................716 483-2102
Fax: 716 483-2634
Michael Cappa, *Ch of Bd*
Peter Cardinale, *Manager*
Catherine Cappa, *Director*
Edward Wright, *Admin Sec*
EMP: 250 EST: 1883
SQ FT: 130,000
SALES (est): 24.1MM **Privately Held**
WEB: www.crawfordfurniture.com
SIC: 2511 2421 2448 Wood household furniture; wood bedroom furniture; chairs, household, except upholstered: wood; dining room furniture: wood; sawmills & planing mills, general; pallets, wood

(G-7021)
CUMMINS INC
101-133 Jackson Ave (14701)
PHONE..................................812 377-5000
EMP: 319
SALES (corp-wide): 17.5B **Publicly Held**
SIC: 3519 3714 3694 3621 Internal combustion engines; engines, diesel & semi-diesel or dual-fuel; diesel engine rebuilding; motor vehicle parts & accessories; motor vehicle engines & parts; crankshaft assemblies, motor vehicle; filters: oil, fuel & air, motor vehicle; engine electrical equipment; generator sets: gasoline, diesel or dual-fuel
PA: Cummins Inc.
500 Jackson St
Columbus IN 47201
812 377-5000

(G-7022)
DAWSON METAL COMPANY INC
Also Called: Dawson Doors
825 Allen St (14701-3998)
P.O. Box 278 (14702-0278)
PHONE..................................716 664-3811
Fax: 716 664-3485
David G Dawson, *Principal*
Roxie Barnes, *COO*
Rick Carlson, *Senior VP*
Dennis Ewing, *Mfg Staff*
Tom Greene, *Mfg Staff*
EMP: 110 EST: 1945
SQ FT: 100,000
SALES (est): 13.1MM **Privately Held**
WEB: www.dawsondoors.com
SIC: 3444 3442 Sheet metalwork; metal doors, sash & trim; sash, door or window: metal; moldings & trim, except automobile: metal

(G-7023)
DOMINION VOTING SYSTEMS INC
221 Hopkins Ave (14701-2252)
PHONE..................................404 955-9799
John Poulos, *President*
Goran Obradovic, *Managing Dir*
Robert H Cook, *Vice Pres*
Ian Macvicar, *CFO*
Howard Cramer, *VP Sales*
EMP: 18
SALES (est): 1.2MM **Privately Held**
SIC: 3579 Voting machines

(G-7024)
ECKO FIN & TOOLING INC
221 Hopkins Ave Ste 2 (14701-2252)
PHONE..................................716 487-0200
Steve Rauschenberger, *CEO*
Lance Rauschenberger, *Vice Pres*
Walter Dunmore, *Manager*
Brenda Nelson, *Admin Sec*
▼ EMP: 11
SALES (est): 1.3MM **Privately Held**
SIC: 3542 Machine tools, metal forming type

(G-7025)
EL GRECO WOODWORKING INC (PA)
106 E 1st St Ste 1 (14701-5499)
PHONE..................................716 483-0315
Fax: 716 661-3131
George Theofilactidis, *President*
Constantina Kathleen Theofilac, *Corp Secy*
Dimitri Theofilactidis, *Vice Pres*
EMP: 20
SQ FT: 100,000
SALES (est): 1.6MM **Privately Held**
WEB: www.elgrecofurniture.com
SIC: 2511 Wood household furniture; chairs, household, except upholstered: wood; tables, household: wood; dressers, household: wood

(G-7026)
ELECTRIC MOTOR SPECIALTY INC
Also Called: Electric Motor Specialties
490 Crescent St (14701-3828)
PHONE..................................716 487-1458
Fax: 716 483-2895
William L Allen, *President*
EMP: 6
SALES (est): 638.7K **Privately Held**
SIC: 7694 5063 Electric motor repair; motors, electric

(G-7027)
EMCO FINISHING PRODUCTS INC
470 Crescent St (14701-3897)
PHONE..................................716 483-1176
Fax: 716 664-6680
Daniel S Alexander, *President*
Barbara L Sheldon, *Admin Sec*
▲ EMP: 9 EST: 1999
SQ FT: 14,000
SALES (est): 2.3MM **Privately Held**
SIC: 2851 Lacquer: bases, dopes, thinner

(G-7028)
GENCO JOHN
Also Called: S & S Enterprises
71 River St (14701-3806)
PHONE..................................716 483-5446
Fax: 716 664-6269
John Genco, *Owner*
Jon Scherzinger, *Sales Mgr*
EMP: 6
SQ FT: 21,000
SALES (est): 588.9K **Privately Held**
SIC: 3599 1541 7692 3541 Machine shop, jobbing & repair; dry cleaning plant construction; welding repair; machine tools, metal cutting type

(G-7029)
GRACE WHEELER
Also Called: Superior Bat Company
118 E 1st St (14701-5430)
P.O. Box 3331 (14702-3331)
PHONE..................................716 664-6501
Grace Wheeler, *Owner*
EMP: 6
SQ FT: 26,000
SALES (est): 565K **Privately Held**
SIC: 3949 Baseball equipment & supplies, general; softball equipment & supplies

(G-7030)
GREEN PROSTHETICS & ORTHOTICS
1290 E 2nd St (14701-1915)
PHONE..................................716 484-1088
Michelle Lohrke, *Opers-Prdtn-Mfg*
EMP: 7
SALES (corp-wide): 1.9MM **Privately Held**
SIC: 3842 5999 Limbs, artificial; artificial limbs
PA: Green Prosthetics & Orthotics, Inc
2241 Peninsula Dr
Erie PA 16506
814 833-2311

(G-7031)
H & H METAL SPECIALTY INC
153 Hopkins Ave (14701-2289)
PHONE..................................716 665-2110
Fax: 716 665-3481
Paul W Harris Jr, *President*
Bruce W Harris, *Vice Pres*
Donna Bakewell, *Manager*
Thomas Harris, *Executive*
EMP: 21 EST: 1953
SQ FT: 15,000
SALES (est): 2.4MM **Privately Held**
WEB: www.hhmetalspecialty.com
SIC: 3498 Fabricated pipe & fittings

(G-7032)
HANSON AGGREGATES NEW YORK LLC
2237 Allen Street Ext (14701-9632)
PHONE..................................716 665-4620
Scott Wheaton, *Manager*
EMP: 15
SALES (corp-wide): 16B **Privately Held**
SIC: 3273 Ready-mixed concrete
HQ: Hanson Aggregates New York Llc
8505 Freport Pkwy Ste 500
Irving TX 75063

(G-7033)
HEIDENHAIN INTERNATIONAL INC (DH)
1 Precision Way (14701-9630)
PHONE..................................716 661-1700
Michael D Metzger, *CEO*
Gerhard Hagenau, *Vice Pres*
Charles Yeskey, *Purch Mgr*
Chris Bartkowiak, *Engineer*
Ramon Rivas, *Engineer*
▲ EMP: 130
SQ FT: 118,000
SALES (est): 9.4MM **Privately Held**
SIC: 3545 3953 3823 3272 Machine tool accessories; marking devices; industrial instrmnts msrmnt display/control process variable; solid containing units, concrete
HQ: Heidenhain Holding Inc
333 E State Pkwy
Schaumburg IL 60173
716 661-1700

(G-7034)
HOPES WINDOWS INC
84 Hopkins Ave (14701-2223)
P.O. Box 580 (14702-0580)
PHONE..................................716 665-5124
Frank A Farrell Jr, *Ch of Bd*
Brian Whalen, *General Mgr*
John Brown, *Vice Pres*
Mary C Lausterer, *Vice Pres*
Randall P Manitta, *Vice Pres*
▲ EMP: 250
SQ FT: 228,000
SALES (est): 54.5MM **Privately Held**
SIC: 3442 Sash, door or window: metal

(G-7035)
HYTECH TOOL & DIE INC
2202 Washington St (14701-2028)
PHONE..................................716 488-2796
Fax: 716 488-2797
William Swanson, *President*
David Reiser, *General Mgr*
▲ EMP: 8
SQ FT: 6,625
SALES (est): 1.3MM
SALES (corp-wide): 4.8MM **Privately Held**
WEB: www.hytechmold.com
SIC: 3544 Special dies & tools; industrial molds
PA: Hytech Tool & Design Co
12076 Edinboro Rd
Edinboro PA 16412
814 734-6000

(G-7036)
INTERNATIONAL ORD TECH INC
101 Harrison St (14701-6614)
PHONE..................................716 664-1100
Fax: 716 664-1115
Tammy H Snyder, *President*
Fred Callahan, *Vice Pres*
John Hedman, *Vice Pres*
Sandy Alexander, *Cust Mgr*
EMP: 90

Jamestown - Chautauqua County (G-7037)

SALES (est): 14.1MM **Privately Held**
WEB: www.iotusa.net
SIC: 3469 3398 2874 Metal stampings; metal heat treating; phosphates

(G-7037)
JAMESTOWN ADVANCED PDTS CORP
2855 Girts Rd (14701-9666)
PHONE 716 483-3406
Fax: 716 483-5398
Wendi Lodestro, *Ch of Bd*
Wendi A Lodestro, *Ch of Bd*
Beth Woodward, *General Mgr*
Lee Lodestro, *Vice Pres*
Jon Wehrenberg, *Manager*
EMP: 46
SALES (est): 16.9MM **Privately Held**
WEB: www.jamestownadvanced.com
SIC: 3444 Sheet metalwork

(G-7038)
JAMESTOWN AWNING INC
313 Steele St (14701-6287)
PHONE 716 483-1435
Fax: 716 483-3995
Mark Saxton, *President*
EMP: 9 EST: 1964
SQ FT: 5,000
SALES (est): 896.4K **Privately Held**
SIC: 2394 Awnings, fabric: made from purchased materials

(G-7039)
JAMESTOWN BRONZE WORKS INC
174 Hopkins Ave (14701-2290)
PHONE 716 665-2302
Fax: 716 665-2980
Robert R Knobloch, *President*
Wolfgang Michael Dunker, *Vice Pres*
Rexford Knapp, *Foreman/Supr*
▼ EMP: 9
SQ FT: 10,000
SALES: 500K **Privately Held**
WEB: www.jamestownbronze.com
SIC: 3369 3363 3479 Nonferrous foundries; aluminum die-castings; etching on metals

(G-7040)
JAMESTOWN FAB STL & SUP INC
1034 Allen St (14701-2302)
PHONE 716 665-2227
Fax: 716 665-5361
Mel Duggan, *President*
Malachai Ives, *Vice Pres*
Sue Livermore, *HR Admin*
Dee Higley, *Manager*
EMP: 6
SQ FT: 20,000
SALES: 1.2MM **Privately Held**
SIC: 3446 Fire escapes, metal; railings, bannisters, guards, etc.: made from metal pipe; stairs, staircases, stair treads: prefabricated metal; fences or posts, ornamental iron or steel

(G-7041)
JAMESTOWN KITCHEN & BATH INC
1085 E 2nd St (14701-2243)
PHONE 716 665-2299
Fax: 716 665-1178
Donald Proctor, *President*
Andy Proctor, *Vice Pres*
Lora Proctor, *Admin Sec*
EMP: 7
SQ FT: 15,000
SALES (est): 1.2MM **Privately Held**
SIC: 3281 5712 Bathroom fixtures, cut stone; cabinet work, custom

(G-7042)
JAMESTOWN MACADAM INC (PA)
Also Called: Corbett Hill Gravel Products
74 Walden Ave (14701-2751)
P.O. Box 518, Celoron (14720-0518)
PHONE 716 664-5108
Fax: 716 484-0100
Michael Wellman, *Ch of Bd*
Roger R Olson, *President*
Tim Sickles, *Managing Dir*
Thomas Olson, *Vice Pres*
Steve Russo, *Mktg Dir*
EMP: 15
SQ FT: 3,000
SALES (est): 9MM **Privately Held**
WEB: www.jamestownmacadam.com
SIC: 2951 5032 Asphalt paving mixtures & blocks; gravel

(G-7043)
JAMESTOWN MATTRESS CO
150 Blackstone Ave (14701-2204)
PHONE 716 665-2247
James L Pullan Sr, *President*
EMP: 35
SALES: 950K **Privately Held**
SIC: 2515 Mattresses & bedsprings

(G-7044)
JAMESTOWN METAL PRODUCTS LLC
178 Blackstone Ave (14701-2297)
PHONE 716 665-5313
Fax: 716 665-6598
Richard McLeod, *President*
Mike Cook, *Opers Mgr*
David Gniwecki, *Engineer*
Paul Jagoda, *Engineer*
Lori Dumaine, *Controller*
▲ EMP: 105
SQ FT: 165,000
SALES (est): 29.2MM
SALES (corp-wide): 55.1MM **Privately Held**
SIC: 3821 Laboratory apparatus & furniture; laboratory equipment: fume hoods, distillation racks, etc.; laboratory furniture
PA: Institutional Casework, Incorporated
1865 Hwy 641 North Paris
Paris TN 38242
731 642-4251

(G-7045)
JAMESTOWN SCIENTIFIC INDS LLC
1300 E 2nd St (14701-1915)
PHONE 716 665-3224
Bob Trusler, *Safety Mgr*
Shannon Miller, *Facilities Mgr*
Richard O'Neill, *Sales Mgr*
Duane Smith, *Prgrmr*
John Pflaumer,
EMP: 13
SALES (est): 2.1MM **Privately Held**
WEB: www.jamestownscientific.com
SIC: 3069 Medical & laboratory rubber sundries & related products

(G-7046)
JEFFREY D MENOFF
785 Fairmount Ave (14701-2608)
PHONE 716 665-1468
Jeffrey D Menoff, *Owner*
EMP: 7
SALES (est): 619.4K **Privately Held**
SIC: 3843 Enamels, dentists'

(G-7047)
JOHNSON MCH & FIBR PDTS CO INC
142 Hopkins Ave (14701-2208)
PHONE 716 665-2003
Fax: 716 665-6516
Michael Marshall, *President*
Richard Thorpe, *General Mgr*
Dale L Marshall, *Principal*
Brian Maloy, *Manager*
Joyce Workens, *Manager*
EMP: 15
SQ FT: 11,000
SALES (est): 2.8MM **Privately Held**
SIC: 3599 3541 Machine shop, jobbing & repair; screw machines, automatic

(G-7048)
LAKESIDE CAPITAL CORPORATION
Also Called: Dahlstrom Roll Form
402 Chandler St Ste 2 (14701-3890)
P.O. Box 446 (14702-0446)
PHONE 716 664-2555
Fax: 716 661-3992
Robert G White, *Ch of Bd*
Thomas Heppeler, *VP Opers*
Peggy Ambrose, *Manager*
▲ EMP: 21
SQ FT: 73,800
SALES (est): 6.5MM **Privately Held**
WEB: www.dahlstromrollform.com
SIC: 3449 Custom roll formed products

(G-7049)
LARSON METAL MANUFACTURING CO
Also Called: Design Craft Division
1831 Mason Dr (14701-9290)
P.O. Box 1182 (14702-1182)
PHONE 716 665-6807
Fax: 716 665-6007
Melda W Larson, *President*
William E Larson, *Vice Pres*
EMP: 6
SQ FT: 31,000
SALES: 1MM **Privately Held**
SIC: 2522 Office furniture, except wood

(G-7050)
MASON CARVINGS INC
2871 Ivystone Dr (14701-9783)
PHONE 716 484-7884
Fax: 716 664-9403
Sam Mason, *President*
Thomas Mason, *Vice Pres*
Robert Parasiliti, *Manager*
Mary Jo Mason, *Admin Sec*
EMP: 8
SQ FT: 18,000
SALES: 350K **Privately Held**
SIC: 2426 Carvings, furniture: wood

(G-7051)
MASTER MACHINE INCORPORATED
155 Blackstone Ave (14701-2203)
PHONE 716 487-2555
Fax: 716 488-2668
Steven Carolus, *President*
▲ EMP: 14
SQ FT: 15,000
SALES (est): 1.4MM **Privately Held**
SIC: 3599 Machine shop, jobbing & repair

(G-7052)
MD ELECTRONICS CORPORATION
Also Called: MD Electronics of Illinois
33 Precision Way (14701-9630)
PHONE 716 488-0300
Bruce Dudgeon, *President*
Debbie Kennelley, *Manager*
▲ EMP: 77
SALES (est): 15.4MM **Privately Held**
SIC: 3643 Current-carrying wiring devices
HQ: Md Elektronik Gmbh
Neutraublinger Str. 4
Waldkraiburg 84478
863 860-40

(G-7053)
MILES MACHINE INC
85 Jones And Gifford Ave (14701-2826)
PHONE 716 484-6026
Richard Page, *President*
Michael Page, *Vice Pres*
Diane Start, *Office Mgr*
EMP: 6
SQ FT: 5,000
SALES: 588.5K **Privately Held**
SIC: 3599 Machine shop, jobbing & repair

(G-7054)
NATIONAL WIRE & METAL TECH INC
22 Carolina St (14701-2311)
PHONE 716 661-9180
Fax: 716 661-9189
Bump Hedman, *President*
John Hedman, *Vice Pres*
Tammy Snyder, *Vice Pres*
Lucy Hedman, *Treasurer*
Brenda Goodwill, *Manager*
▲ EMP: 25
SQ FT: 80,000
SALES (est): 4.4MM **Privately Held**
SIC: 3469 2392 Perforated metal, stamped; mops, floor & dust

(G-7055)
OGDEN NEWSPAPERS INC
Also Called: Post-Journal, The
15 W 2nd St (14701-5215)
P.O. Box 190 (14702-0190)
PHONE 716 487-1111
Fax: 716 664-3119
Michael Bird, *President*
Chris Murphy, *Editor*
Jim Funcell, *Prdtn Mgr*
Michael Warren, *Mfg Staff*
Debbie Brunner, *Marketing Staff*
EMP: 200
SALES (corp-wide): 617.1MM **Privately Held**
SIC: 2711 Commercial printing & newspaper publishing combined
PA: The Ogden Newspapers Inc
1500 Main St
Wheeling WV 26003
304 233-0100

(G-7056)
POST JOURNAL
412 Murray Ave (14701-4742)
PHONE 716 487-1111
Debra Brunner, *Principal*
Mike Rukavina, *Editor*
Pete Ellison, *Info Tech Mgr*
EMP: 17
SALES (est): 1.4MM **Privately Held**
SIC: 2711 Newspapers, publishing & printing

(G-7057)
PRODUCTO CORPORATION
Also Called: Ring Division Producto Machine
2980 Turner Rd (14701-9024)
P.O. Box 490 (14702-0490)
PHONE 716 484-7131
Newman Marsilius, *President*
Jack Kelly, *COO*
Gregory Timko, *Plant Mgr*
John O'Neil, *Purchasing*
Ronald Jorgenson, *Engineer*
EMP: 113
SQ FT: 40,800
SALES (corp-wide): 65.8MM **Privately Held**
WEB: www.ringprecision.com
SIC: 3541 3542 3544 Machine tools, metal cutting type; machine tools, metal forming type; special dies, tools, jigs & fixtures
HQ: The Producto Corporation
800 Union Ave
Bridgeport CT 06607
203 366-3224

(G-7058)
ROLLFORM OF JAMESTOWN INC
Also Called: Precision Locker
181 Blackstone Ave (14701-2203)
PHONE 716 665-4479
Fax: 716 665-5310
Edward F Ruttenberg, *President*
Pat Traniello, *Opers Mgr*
Al Perone, *Foreman/Supr*
Debby Walsh, *Accountant*
▲ EMP: 17
SQ FT: 43,000
SALES (est): 4.9MM **Privately Held**
WEB: www.rollform.com
SIC: 3449 Miscellaneous metalwork; custom roll formed products

(G-7059)
SHRED CENTER
20 Carroll St (14701-4755)
PHONE 716 664-3052
Ronald Mazonie, *Owner*
Monica Mazany, *Vice Pres*
EMP: 6 EST: 2008
SALES (est): 557K **Privately Held**
SIC: 3559 Tire shredding machinery

(G-7060)
SKF USA INC
Also Called: MRC Bearings
402 Chandler St (14701-3890)
P.O. Box 263, Falconer (14733-0263)
PHONE 716 661-2600
Rolf Jacobson, *Branch Mgr*
Ned Baudo, *Training Spec*
EMP: 61

SALES (corp-wide): 546.3MM **Privately Held**
WEB: www.skfusa.com
SIC: **3562** 3053 3829 Ball & roller bearings; ball bearings & parts; roller bearings & parts; gaskets & sealing devices; oil seals, rubber; vibration meters, analyzers & calibrators
HQ: Skf Usa Inc.
  890 Forty Foot Rd
  Lansdale PA 19446
  267 436-6000

(G-7061)
SPARTAN PUBLISHING INC
Also Called: Southern Tier Pennysaver
2 Harding Ave (14701-4778)
PHONE..........................716 664-7373
Fax: 716 664-7377
Robert V Stanley, *President*
Sandra Stanley, *Treasurer*
EMP: 12
SQ FT: 4,000
SALES (est): 530K **Privately Held**
SIC: **2711** Newspapers, publishing & printing

(G-7062)
SPRAY-TECH FINISHING INC
443 Buffalo St (14701-2262)
P.O. Box 278 (14702-0278)
PHONE..........................716 664-6317
Fax: 716 664-6318
David Dawson, *President*
George Fuller, *Vice Pres*
Guy Lombardo, *Treasurer*
Harold Andersen, *Admin Sec*
EMP: 11
SQ FT: 80,000
SALES: 1.1MM **Privately Held**
WEB: www.spraytechfinishing.com
SIC: **2952** Coating compounds, tar

(G-7063)
STAR TUBING CORP
53 River St (14701-3806)
P.O. Box 904 (14702-0904)
PHONE..........................716 483-1703
Fax: 716 484-8894
Gary F Johnson, *President*
Gary Johnson, *President*
Sandra Johnson, *Vice Pres*
Charles A Lawson, *Shareholder*
EMP: 6
SQ FT: 46,000
SALES: 1.3MM **Privately Held**
WEB: www.startubing.com
SIC: **3498** Tube fabricating (contract bending & shaping)

(G-7064)
SUHOR INDUSTRIES INC
Also Called: GM Pre Cast Products
584 Buffalo St (14701-2307)
PHONE..........................716 483-6818
Fax: 716 483-5063
Joel Suhor, *President*
EMP: 5
SALES (corp-wide): 2.2MM **Privately Held**
WEB: www.wilbertservices.com
SIC: **3272** Concrete products
PA: Suhor Industries, Inc.
  72 Oconnor Rd
  Fairport NY 14450
  585 377-5100

(G-7065)
SUIT-KOTE CORPORATION
57 Lister St (14701-2701)
PHONE..........................716 664-3750
Fax: 716 664-3752
George Ginter, *Branch Mgr*
EMP: 35
SALES (corp-wide): 226MM **Privately Held**
WEB: www.suit-kote.com
SIC: **2951** 1611 Asphalt & asphaltic paving mixtures (not from refineries); highway & street paving contractor
PA: Suit-Kote Corporation
  1911 Lorings Crossing Rd
  Cortland NY 13045
  607 753-1100

(G-7066)
SUNSET RIDGE HOLDINGS INC
Also Called: Electric Motor Specialty
490-496 Crescent St (14701)
PHONE..........................716 487-1458
Rebecca Ames, *President*
EMP: 5
SALES: 230K **Privately Held**
SIC: **7694** 7699 Armature rewinding shops; pumps & pumping equipment repair

(G-7067)
SUPERIOR ENERGY SERVICES INC
1720 Foote Avenue Ext (14701-9385)
PHONE..........................716 483-0100
EMP: 7 **Publicly Held**
SIC: **1389** Servicing oil & gas wells
PA: Superior Energy Services, Inc.
  1001 La St Ste 2900
  Houston TX 77002

(G-7068)
SUPERIOR STL DOOR TRIM CO INC
154 Fairmount Ave (14701-2866)
PHONE..........................716 665-3256
Fax: 716 665-3230
Ellen Connell, *President*
Bevan Connell, *Vice Pres*
Tammy Ryder, *Manager*
EMP: 15
SALES: 5MM **Privately Held**
SIC: **3442** Metal doors, sash & trim

(G-7069)
SUPERIOR WOOD TURNINGS
118 E 1st St (14701-5430)
P.O. Box 3341 (14702-3341)
PHONE..........................716 483-1254
Fax: 716 483-1264
Shane Goodwill, *Partner*
Doug Wheeler, *Partner*
EMP: 16
SQ FT: 30,000
SALES (est): 1.9MM **Privately Held**
WEB: www.superiorwoodturnings.com
SIC: **2499** Carved & turned wood

(G-7070)
TILAROS BAKERY INC
32 Willard St Ste 34 (14701-6937)
PHONE..........................716 488-3209
Robert Tilaro, *President*
Donald Sholl, *Treasurer*
EMP: 7
SQ FT: 1,250
SALES (est): 709K **Privately Held**
SIC: **2051** Bakery: wholesale or wholesale/retail combined

(G-7071)
TITANX ENGINE COOLING INC
2258 Allen Street Ext (14701-2330)
PHONE..........................716 665-7129
Stefan Nordstrm, *CEO*
Matthew Moore, *President*
Ulf Hellgesson, *Vice Pres*
Mats Hman, *Vice Pres*
Bruno Jouannet, *Vice Pres*
▲ EMP: 320
SALES (est): 155.9MM
SALES (corp-wide): 687.3K **Privately Held**
SIC: **3714** Air conditioner parts, motor vehicle
HQ: Titanx Engine Cooling Ab
  Klockskogsvagen 9
  Solvesborg 294 7
  456 550-00

(G-7072)
TYCO SIMPLEXGRINNELL
527 Foote Ave (14701-8206)
PHONE..........................716 483-0079
Michael Vito, *Principal*
EMP: 40
SALES (corp-wide): 1.4B **Privately Held**
SIC: **3569** Sprinkler systems, fire: automatic
PA: Tyco Simplexgrinnell
  1501 Nw 51st St
  Boca Raton FL 33431
  561 988-3658

(G-7073)
UPSTATE NIAGARA COOP INC
223 Fluvanna Ave (14701-2050)
PHONE..........................716 484-7178
Fax: 716 484-7142
Michael Conklin, *Manager*
EMP: 20
SALES (corp-wide): 228.8MM **Privately Held**
SIC: **2026** 0241 5143 Milk processing (pasteurizing, homogenizing, bottling); milk production; dairy products, except dried or canned
PA: Upstate Niagara Cooperative, Inc.
  25 Anderson Rd
  Buffalo NY 14225
  716 892-3156

(G-7074)
VAC AIR SERVICE INC
Also Called: Ameri Serv South
1295 E 2nd St (14701-1914)
P.O. Box 940 (14702-0940)
PHONE..........................716 665-2206
EMP: 11
SQ FT: 4,000
SALES (est): 1.4MM **Privately Held**
SIC: **3563** Mfg Air/Gas Compressors

(G-7075)
WEBER-KNAPP COMPANY (PA)
441 Chandler St (14701-3895)
PHONE..........................716 484-9135
Fax: 716 484-9142
Rex Mc Cray, *Ch of Bd*
Donald Pangborn, *Senior VP*
Rhonda Johnson, *Opers Mgr*
Kim Greyber, *Engineer*
Kory Slye, *Engineer*
▲ EMP: 102 EST: 2002
SQ FT: 146,000
SALES (est): 20.4MM **Privately Held**
WEB: www.weberknapp.com
SIC: **3429** Furniture hardware

(G-7076)
WILSTON ENTERPRISES INC
Also Called: Industrial Welding & Fabg Co
121 Jackson Ave (14701-2441)
PHONE..........................716 483-1411
Fax: 716 664-2501
Susan L Wilston, *President*
Eugene Wilston, *Vice Pres*
EMP: 18 EST: 2007
SALES (est): 1.6MM **Privately Held**
SIC: **3441** Building components, structural steel

Jamesville
Onondaga County

(G-7077)
B & B LUMBER COMPANY INC (PA)
4800 Solvay Rd (13078-9530)
P.O. Box 420 (13078-0420)
PHONE..........................866 282-0582
Fax: 315 469-4946
Jeffrey H Booher, *Ch of Bd*
Brent Booher, *Principal*
Brigham Booher, *Principal*
Pat Buff, *Principal*
Gary R Booher, *Vice Pres*
EMP: 78
SQ FT: 300,000
SALES (est): 20.3MM **Privately Held**
SIC: **2448** 2421 2426 Pallets, wood; lumber: rough, sawed or planed; hardwood dimension & flooring mills

(G-7078)
B&B ALBANY PALLET COMPANY LLC
4800 Solvay Rd (13078-9530)
P.O. Box 420 (13078-0420)
PHONE..........................315 492-1786
Ruth Manasse, *Vice Pres*
Michael Parvis, *Mfg Staff*
Jane Diehl, *Accountant*
Eric Smith,
EMP: 30 EST: 1966
SQ FT: 9,500
SALES (est): 3.5MM
SALES (corp-wide): 20.3MM **Privately Held**
SIC: **2448** Pallets, wood
PA: B & B Lumber Company Inc.
  4800 Solvay Rd
  Jamesville NY 13078
  866 282-0582

(G-7079)
CHRISTIANA MILLWORK INC (PA)
4755 Jamesville Rd (13078)
PHONE..........................315 492-9099
Fax: 315 492-6863
Lawrence J Christiana, *President*
Ross Tuzzo Lino, *President*
EMP: 26
SQ FT: 26,000
SALES (est): 2.5MM **Privately Held**
SIC: **2431** Millwork

(G-7080)
FULLER FABRICATIONS
3915 State Route 91 (13078-9613)
PHONE..........................315 469-7415
EMP: 7 EST: 2016
SALES (est): 94.4K **Privately Held**
SIC: **7692** Welding repair

(G-7081)
HANSON AGGREGATES NEW YORK LLC
2237 Allen St (13078)
PHONE..........................716 665-4620
Scott Wheaton, *Manager*
EMP: 10
SALES (corp-wide): 16B **Privately Held**
SIC: **3241** Natural cement
HQ: Hanson Aggregates New York Llc
  8505 Freport Pkwy Ste 500
  Irving TX 75063

(G-7082)
HANSON AGGREGATES NEW YORK LLC
4800 Jamesville Rd (13078)
PHONE..........................315 469-5501
Dan Meehan, *Vice Pres*
Daniel Meeham, *Vice Pres*
EMP: 120
SALES (corp-wide): 16B **Privately Held**
SIC: **3273** Ready-mixed concrete
HQ: Hanson Aggregates New York Llc
  8505 Freport Pkwy Ste 500
  Irving TX 75063

(G-7083)
HANSON AGGREGATES PA LLC
4800 Jamesville Rd (13078)
PHONE..........................315 469-5501
Dan Meehan, *Vice Pres*
Mike Cornell, *Purch Agent*
Liz Simmons, *Office Mgr*
Gary Eno, *Branch Mgr*
Roger Hutchinson, *Manager*
EMP: 20
SALES (corp-wide): 16B **Privately Held**
SIC: **1442** 1422 Common sand mining; crushed & broken limestone
HQ: Hanson Aggregates Pennsylvania, Llc
  7660 Imperial Way
  Allentown PA 18195
  610 366-4626

(G-7084)
PREMIER HARDWOOD PRODUCTS INC
4800 Solvay Rd (13078-9530)
P.O. Box 434 (13078-0434)
PHONE..........................315 492-1786
Fax: 315 492-9799
Brigham Booher, *Ch of Bd*
Lawrence G English, *President*
Jeffrey Booher, *Vice Pres*
Russ Shamblen, *Purch Agent*
Gary Booher, *Treasurer*
EMP: 50
SQ FT: 80,000
SALES (est): 9.5MM **Privately Held**
WEB: www.premierhardwood.com
SIC: **2426** Hardwood dimension & flooring mills

Jamesville — Onondaga County

(G-7085)
ROBINSON CONCRETE INC
3537 Apulia Rd (13078-9663)
PHONE..................................315 492-6200
Micheal Vitale, *President*
EMP: 12
SALES (corp-wide): 24MM **Privately Held**
SIC: 3273 Ready-mixed concrete
PA: Robinson Concrete, Inc.
 3486 Franklin Street Rd
 Auburn NY 13021
 315 253-6666

(G-7086)
U-CUT ENTERPRISES INC
4800 Solvay Rd (13078-9530)
P.O. Box 420 (13078-0420)
PHONE..................................315 492-9316
Fax: 315 492-1586
John R Storrier Jr, *President*
Nanette Hildreth, *Admin Sec*
EMP: 22
SQ FT: 8,000
SALES: 2.5MM **Privately Held**
WEB: www.u-cut.com
SIC: 3599 Machine shop, jobbing & repair

Java Village — Wyoming County

(G-7087)
FARRANT SCREW MACHINE PRODUCTS
Gulf Rd (14083)
PHONE..................................585 457-3213
Fax: 585 457-3297
Thomas Farrant, *President*
EMP: 7
SQ FT: 13,000
SALES: 1MM **Privately Held**
SIC: 3599 Machine shop, jobbing & repair

Jay — Essex County

(G-7088)
ADIRONDACK LIFE INC (PA)
Also Called: Adirondack Life Magazine
Rr 9 Box North (12941)
P.O. Box 410 (12941-0410)
PHONE..................................518 946-2191
Fax: 518 946-7461
Barry Silverstein, *President*
Tom Hughes, *Publisher*
Janine Sorrell, *Business Mgr*
Tim S Pierre, *Info Tech Dir*
Kelly Hofschneider, *Art Dir*
EMP: 17
SALES (est): 1MM **Privately Held**
WEB: www.adirondacklife.com
SIC: 2721 Magazines: publishing only, not printed on site

(G-7089)
WILLIAM WARD LOGGING
Valley Rd (12941)
P.O. Box 300 (12941-0300)
PHONE..................................518 946-7826
William L Ward Sr, *Owner*
Kathy Ward, *Finance Other*
EMP: 17
SALES (est): 1.2MM **Privately Held**
SIC: 2411 Logging

Jefferson Valley — Westchester County

(G-7090)
GEORGE PONTE INC
Also Called: Gpi Equipment Company
500 E Main St (10535-1100)
PHONE..................................914 243-4202
Fax: 914 243-2380
George Ponte, *President*
EMP: 5
SQ FT: 4,000
SALES (est): 630K **Privately Held**
WEB: www.gpiusa.com
SIC: 3559 5084 Pharmaceutical machinery; materials handling machinery

(G-7091)
LONGSTEM ORGANIZERS INC
380 E Main St (10535-1200)
P.O. Box 22 (10535-0022)
PHONE..................................914 777-2174
Alison Albanese, *President*
Gregery Alabnese, *Vice Pres*
▲ **EMP:** 6
SQ FT: 4,500
SALES (est): 600K **Privately Held**
SIC: 3449 Miscellaneous metalwork

Jeffersonville — Sullivan County

(G-7092)
A S A PRECISION CO INC
295 Jffersonville N Br Rd (12748-5825)
PHONE..................................845 482-4870
Fax: 845 482-4721
Steve Schmidt, *President*
Rich Schmidt, *Vice Pres*
EMP: 6 **EST:** 1961
SQ FT: 6,400
SALES (est): 780K **Privately Held**
SIC: 3826 Analytical instruments

(G-7093)
JEFFERSONVILLE VOLUNTEER
49 Callicoon Center Rd (12748)
P.O. Box 396 (12748-0396)
PHONE..................................845 482-3110
Dawnrenee Hauschild, *Chairman*
EMP: 50
SALES: 507.1K **Privately Held**
SIC: 3713 Ambulance bodies

Jericho — Nassau County

(G-7094)
BAMBERGER POLYMERS INTL CORP
2 Jericho Plz Ste 109 (11753-1681)
PHONE..................................516 622-3600
Steven Goldberg, *President*
Dennis Don, *Exec VP*
Alfonso Garcia, *Vice Pres*
Christine Levy, *Vice Pres*
Paul Coco, *CFO*
◆ **EMP:** 10
SQ FT: 11,000
SALES (est): 1MM **Privately Held**
WEB: www.bambergerpolymers.com
SIC: 2821 Plasticizer/additive based plastic materials
PA: Bamberger Polymers Corp.
 2 Jericho Plz Ste 109
 Jericho NY 11753

(G-7095)
CFFCO USA INC
55 Jericho Tpke Ste 302 (11753-1013)
PHONE..................................718 747-1118
Fax: 718 747-1119
James Yan, *CEO*
David Xu, *Vice Pres*
▲ **EMP:** 7
SQ FT: 1,800
SALES: 15.8MM **Privately Held**
WEB: www.cffco.com
SIC: 2499 Fencing, docks & other outdoor wood structural products

(G-7096)
CLOPAY AMES TRUE TMPER HLDNG (HQ)
100 Jericho Quadrangle # 224 (11753-2708)
PHONE..................................516 938-5544
Ronald J Kramer, *CEO*
EMP: 11
SALES (est): 389.6MM
SALES (corp-wide): 1.9B **Publicly Held**
SIC: 3423 3799 3524 Garden & farm tools, including shovels; shovels, spades (hand tools); wheelbarrows; lawn & garden equipment
PA: Griffon Corporation
 712 5th Ave Fl 18
 New York NY 10019
 212 957-5000

(G-7097)
CONTINENTAL KRAFT CORP
100 Jericho Quadrangle # 219 (11753-2708)
PHONE..................................516 681-9090
Peter J Bogan, *Ch of Bd*
David Landau, *President*
Steve Roth, *Treasurer*
Darlene Moseen, *Manager*
▼ **EMP:** 6
SQ FT: 2,264
SALES (est): 998.3K **Privately Held**
WEB: www.continentalkraft.com
SIC: 2631 Kraft linerboard

(G-7098)
D SQUARED TECHNOLOGIES INC
71 Birchwood Park Dr (11753-2238)
PHONE..................................516 932-7319
David Delman, *President*
EMP: 5
SALES (est): 246.2K **Privately Held**
WEB: www.d2tech.net
SIC: 3949 Exercise equipment

(G-7099)
DARBY DENTAL SUPPLY
105 Executive Ct (11753)
PHONE..................................516 688-6421
Gary Rosenberg, *Principal*
Anthony Ricigilano, *Vice Pres*
Liz Meyers, *VP Mktg*
EMP: 9
SALES (est): 1.7MM **Privately Held**
SIC: 3843 Dental equipment & supplies

(G-7100)
ELARA FDSRVICE DISPOSABLES LLC
420 Jericho Tpke Ste 320 (11753-1319)
Rural Route R 28089 Netw, Chicago IL (60673-0001)
PHONE..................................877 893-3244
Daniel Girnderg, *President*
Ernesto Grinberg, *Chairman*
Donna Cherulnik, *Vice Pres*
Fran Laudicina, *Vice Pres*
Darci Rodriguez, *Vice Pres*
▲ **EMP:** 7
SALES (est): 10MM **Privately Held**
SIC: 3089 5113 Work gloves, plastic; bags, paper & disposable plastic

(G-7101)
EXCHANGE MY MAIL INC
30 Jericho Executive Plz 100c (11753-1025)
PHONE..................................516 605-1835
Sal Dipiazza, *CEO*
Steven Daneshgar, *Exec VP*
EMP: 15
SQ FT: 2,500
SALES (est): 1.6MM **Privately Held**
WEB: www.exchangemymail.com
SIC: 7372 Application computer software

(G-7102)
FIRETRONICS INC (PA)
50 Jericho Tpke (11753-1014)
PHONE..................................516 997-5151
Gail Miller, *President*
John Moreno, *Accountant*
EMP: 6
SALES (est): 1.9MM **Privately Held**
SIC: 3669 Fire detection systems, electric

(G-7103)
HEALTH CARE COMPLIANCE (HQ)
30 Jericho Executive Plz 400c (11753-1098)
PHONE..................................516 478-4100
Fax: 516 478-6773
Mitchell Diamond, *CEO*
Benjamin Diamond, *President*
Lise Rauzi Chc, *Vice Pres*
Jackie Tesser, *Vice Pres*
Anthony Buttcavoli, *Manager*
EMP: 19
SQ FT: 5,350
SALES (est): 3.7MM
SALES (corp-wide): 225.9MM **Publicly Held**
WEB: www.hccsonline.com
SIC: 7372 Educational computer software
PA: Healthstream, Inc.
 209 10th Ave S Ste 450
 Nashville TN 37203
 615 301-3100

(G-7104)
INTELLICHECK MOBILISA INC (PA)
100 Jericho Quadrangle # 202 (11753-2702)
PHONE..................................516 992-1900
Bill White, *CEO*
Michael D Malone, *Ch of Bd*
Russell T Embry, *Senior VP*
Cynthia Walden, *Controller*
Bill Kotsifas, *Director*
EMP: 22
SQ FT: 9,233
SALES (est): 3.8MM **Publicly Held**
WEB: www.intellicheck.com
SIC: 3699 Security devices

(G-7105)
INTERNATIONAL TIME PRODUCTS
410 Jericho Tpke Ste 110 (11753-1318)
PHONE..................................516 931-0005
Raymond T D'Alessio, *Owner*
EMP: 6
SALES (est): 240K **Privately Held**
SIC: 3172 Watch straps, except metal

(G-7106)
JPM FINE WOODWORKING LLC
103 Estate Dr (11753-2829)
PHONE..................................516 236-7605
Mitchell Kahn,
EMP: 6
SALES (est): 241.2K **Privately Held**
SIC: 3999 Novelties, bric-a-brac & hobby kits

(G-7107)
LIGHTRON CORPORATION
Also Called: Western Synthetic Felt
100 Jericho Quadrangle (11753-2708)
PHONE..................................516 938-5544
Robert Balemian, *President*
Allen R Kaden, *Vice Pres*
Edward Kramer, *Admin Sec*
EMP: 3 **EST:** 1969
SQ FT: 2,500
SALES: 40.2MM
SALES (corp-wide): 1.9B **Publicly Held**
SIC: 3429 3585 Manufactured hardware (general); cold drink dispensing equipment (not coin-operated)
PA: Griffon Corporation
 712 5th Ave Fl 18
 New York NY 10019
 212 957-5000

(G-7108)
LUMIA ENERGY SOLUTIONS LLC
48 Jericho Tpke (11753-1004)
PHONE..................................516 478-5795
John Lee, *CEO*
Turab Syed, *COO*
Syed Turab, *COO*
EMP: 7
SQ FT: 14,000
SALES (est): 463.6K **Privately Held**
SIC: 3641 Electric lamps; electric light bulbs, complete; tubes, electric light

(G-7109)
NAK INTERNATIONAL CORP (PA)
131 Jericho Tpke Ste 204 (11753-1017)
PHONE..................................516 997-4212
Fax: 516 997-4599
Allan Seligson, *President*

GEOGRAPHIC SECTION

Johnson City - Broome County (G-7134)

Dean Musi, *Vice Pres*
▲ **EMP:** 58
SALES (est): 15.4MM **Privately Held**
SIC: 3463 Nonferrous forgings

(G-7110)
NCR CORPORATION
30 Jericho Executive Plz (11753-1057)
PHONE.................................516 876-7200
Paul Buscemi, *Manager*
EMP: 200
SALES (corp-wide): 6.5B **Publicly Held**
WEB: www.ncr.com
SIC: 3571 7622 Electronic computers; radio & television repair
PA: Ncr Corporation
    3097 Satellite Blvd # 100
    Duluth GA 30096
    937 445-5000

(G-7111)
NORTH AMERICAN PIPE CORP
Also Called: Jekerda Sales
420 Jericho Tpke Ste 222 (11753-1319)
PHONE.................................516 338-2863
Jamie Hebert, *Manager*
EMP: 10
SALES (corp-wide): 5B **Publicly Held**
SIC: 3354 3084 Pipe, extruded, aluminum; plastics pipe
HQ: North American Pipe Corporation
    2801 Post Oak Blvd # 600
    Houston TX 77056
    855 624-7473

(G-7112)
PARKSIDE PRINTING CO INC
4 Tompkins Ave (11753-1920)
PHONE.................................516 933-5423
William Goldstein, *President*
Ellen Goldstein, *Corp Secy*
EMP: 10
SQ FT: 10,000
SALES (est): 1MM **Privately Held**
SIC: 2752 Commercial printing, lithographic

(G-7113)
PITNEY BOWES INC
200 Robbins Ln Unit B2 (11753-2341)
PHONE.................................516 822-0900
Jim Sartory, *General Mgr*
Dan Hindman, *Branch Mgr*
EMP: 35
SALES (corp-wide): 3.4B **Publicly Held**
SIC: 3579 7359 Postage meters; business machine & electronic equipment rental services
PA: Pitney Bowes Inc.
    3001 Summer St Ste 3
    Stamford CT 06905
    203 356-5000

(G-7114)
PRODUCT STATION INC
366 N Broadway Ste 410 (11753-2000)
PHONE.................................516 942-4220
Scott Roberts, *President*
Peter Oliveto, *Vice Pres*
EMP: 11
SALES (est): 1.1MM **Privately Held**
SIC: 3613 Distribution cutouts

(G-7115)
ROYCE ASSOCIATES A LTD PARTNR
366 N Broadway Ste 400 (11753-2000)
PHONE.................................516 367-6298
Greg Gipson, *Plant Mgr*
Joanna Moskowitz, *Manager*
EMP: 5
SALES (corp-wide): 17.8MM **Privately Held**
SIC: 2869 3089 2842 2851 Industrial organic chemicals; plastic processing; polishing preparations & related products; varnishes; chemical preparations
PA: Royce Associates, A Limited Partnership
    35 Carlton Ave
    East Rutherford NJ 07073
    201 438-5200

(G-7116)
SATNAM DISTRIBUTORS LLC
Also Called: Lion & Bear Distributors
200 Robbins Ln Unit B (11753-2341)
PHONE.................................516 802-0600
Bila Singh, *Office Mgr*
Ann Goerler, *Exec Dir*
Rachna Sachdev,
EMP: 3
SQ FT: 6,000
SALES: 4.5MM **Privately Held**
SIC: 2834 Tablets, pharmaceutical

(G-7117)
SC MEDICAL OVERSEAS INC
Also Called: Orfit Industries America
350 Jericho Tpke Ste 302 (11753-1317)
PHONE.................................516 935-8500
Steven A Cuypres, *President*
Martin Ratner, *President*
Libby Camin, *Administration*
▲ **EMP:** 9
SQ FT: 3,000
SALES: 780K **Privately Held**
WEB: www.orfit.com
SIC: 2821 Plastics materials & resins

(G-7118)
SD EAGLE GLOBAL INC
2 Kay St (11753-2648)
PHONE.................................516 822-1778
Shaojun Liu, *President*
EMP: 7
SALES (est): 409.9K **Privately Held**
SIC: 2211 Denims

(G-7119)
SJ ASSOCIATES INC (PA)
500 N Broadway Ste 159 (11753-2111)
PHONE.................................516 942-3232
Fax: 516 216-4943
Bruce Joseph, *President*
Owen Drugan, *Controller*
Mark Wachtel, *Manager*
EMP: 25
SQ FT: 3,000
SALES (est): 6.3MM **Privately Held**
SIC: 3559 5065 Electronic component making machinery; electronic parts

(G-7120)
SKD DISTRIBUTION CORP
28 Westchester Ave (11753-1442)
PHONE.................................718 525-6000
Richard Marks, *President*
Bill Stephan, *General Mgr*
Harold Marks, *Vice Pres*
Stanley AST, *Controller*
Richard Mark, *Manager*
▲ **EMP:** 30
SQ FT: 45,000
SALES (est): 4.9MM **Privately Held**
SIC: 3089 3086 Novelties, plastic; plastics foam products

(G-7121)
WAGNERS LLC (PA)
366 N Broadway Ste 402 (11753-2027)
P.O. Box 54 (11753-0054)
PHONE.................................516 933-6580
Harry Tyre, *President*
Donald P Corr, *Senior VP*
Danielle Traietta, *Engineer*
Margaret Keller, *VP Finance*
EMP: 6
SQ FT: 1,500
SALES: 50MM **Privately Held**
WEB: www.wagnerproducts.com
SIC: 2048 Bird food, prepared

Johnson City
Broome County

(G-7122)
DONALD R HUSBAND INC
Also Called: Maine Coil & Transformer Co
1140 E Maine Rd (13790-4002)
PHONE.................................607 770-1990
Don Husband, *President*
Donald Husband, *President*
Edward E Paden, *Principal*
EMP: 8 **EST:** 1982
SQ FT: 10,000
SALES (est): 770K **Privately Held**
WEB: www.mainecoil.com
SIC: 3629 Electronic generation equipment

(G-7123)
GAGNE ASSOCIATES INC
41 Commercial Dr (13790-4111)
P.O. Box 487 (13790-0487)
PHONE.................................800 800-5954
Fax: 607 729-7644
Mary Ann Holland, *Ch of Bd*
Jeff Sampson, *President*
William Coak, *Vice Pres*
Kim Prentice, *Vice Pres*
Michelle Clark, *VP Mfg*
▲ **EMP:** 25 **EST:** 1961
SQ FT: 37,250
SALES (est): 5.3MM **Privately Held**
WEB: www.gagneinc.com
SIC: 3089 5063 Plastic hardware & building products; lighting fittings & accessories

(G-7124)
GANNETT CO INC
Also Called: Gannett NY Production Facility
10 Gannett Dr (13790-2260)
PHONE.................................607 352-2702
Kevin Crane, *Manager*
EMP: 100
SALES (corp-wide): 3B **Publicly Held**
WEB: www.gannett.com
SIC: 2741 Miscellaneous publishing
PA: Gannett Co., Inc.
    7950 Jones Branch Dr
    Mc Lean VA 22102
    703 854-6000

(G-7125)
HI-TECH INDUSTRIES NY INC
23 Ozalid Rd (13790)
PHONE.................................607 217-7361
Douglas Gardner, *Ch of Bd*
Douglas P Sterns, *President*
Rob George, *Human Res Dir*
EMP: 28 **EST:** 1999
SQ FT: 8,900
SALES (est): 3.7MM **Privately Held**
SIC: 3444 3599 Sheet metalwork; machine shop, jobbing & repair

(G-7126)
INNOVATION ASSOCIATES INC
530 Columbia Dr Ste 101 (13790-1096)
PHONE.................................607 798-9376
Fax: 607 729-5008
Mary Reno, *CEO*
Joseph Harry Boyer, *Chairman*
Thomas Boyer, *COO*
Doyle Jensen, *Exec VP*
Joe Galati, *Vice Pres*
▲ **EMP:** 150
SQ FT: 18,700
SALES (est): 62.7MM **Privately Held**
WEB: www.innovat.com
SIC: 3559 8711 Pharmaceutical machinery; consulting engineer

(G-7127)
J H ROBOTICS INC
109 Main St (13790-2482)
PHONE.................................607 729-3758
Fax: 607 797-6941
John F Hartman, *Ch of Bd*
Jason Colsten, *Engineer*
Dave Nolan, *Engineer*
Clifford Solowiej, *Engineer*
Cindy Warner, *Manager*
EMP: 35
SQ FT: 41,000
SALES (est): 9.7MM **Privately Held**
WEB: www.jhrobotics.com
SIC: 3494 3569 3545 Valves & pipe fittings; robots, assembly line: industrial & commercial; machine tool accessories

(G-7128)
KLEMMT ORTHOTICS & PROSTHETICS
Also Called: Klemmt Orthopaedic Services
130 Oakdale Rd (13790-1758)
PHONE.................................607 770-4400
Marcus Klemmt, *President*
Julie Klemmt, *Principal*
EMP: 8 **EST:** 1965
SQ FT: 3,000
SALES (est): 680K **Privately Held**
SIC: 3842 5999 Orthopedic appliances; prosthetic appliances; orthopedic & prosthesis applications

(G-7129)
KNUCKLEHEAD EMBROIDERY INC
800 Valley Plz Ste 4 (13790-1046)
PHONE.................................607 797-2725
Fax: 607 766-9554
Dave Cobb, *President*
Diane Cobb, *Vice Pres*
Matt Heier, *Treasurer*
Bridget Heier, *Admin Sec*
EMP: 5
SQ FT: 1,500
SALES: 500K **Privately Held**
WEB: www.knuckleheadinc.com
SIC: 2262 5699 2759 2395 Embossing: manmade fiber & silk broadwoven fabrics; customized clothing & apparel; screen printing; art needlework: made from purchased materials

(G-7130)
NORTH POINT TECHNOLOGIES
520 Columbia Dr Ste 105 (13790-3305)
PHONE.................................607 238-1114
Robert Lee, *Owner*
Lisa Lee, *Co-Owner*
Richard Wrobleski, *Administration*
EMP: 26
SALES (est): 3.9MM **Privately Held**
SIC: 3625 Industrial controls: push button, selector switches, pilot

(G-7131)
PELLA CORPORATION
Also Called: Pella Window Door
800 Valley Plz Ste 5 (13790-1046)
PHONE.................................607 223-2023
Chris Ward, *Branch Mgr*
EMP: 316
SALES (corp-wide): 1.9B **Privately Held**
SIC: 2431 Windows, wood
PA: Pella Corporation
    102 Main St
    Pella IA 50219
    641 621-1000

(G-7132)
PELLA CORPORATION
Also Called: Pella Window Door
800 Valley Plz Ste 5 (13790-1046)
PHONE.................................607 231-8550
Fax: 607 231-8584
Chris Ward, *Branch Mgr*
EMP: 316
SALES (corp-wide): 1.9B **Privately Held**
SIC: 2431 Windows, wood
PA: Pella Corporation
    102 Main St
    Pella IA 50219
    641 621-1000

(G-7133)
PELLA CORPORATION
Also Called: Pella Window Door
800 Valley Plz Ste 5 (13790-1046)
PHONE.................................607 238-2812
Chris Ward, *Branch Mgr*
EMP: 316
SALES (corp-wide): 1.9B **Privately Held**
SIC: 2431 Windows, wood
PA: Pella Corporation
    102 Main St
    Pella IA 50219
    641 621-1000

(G-7134)
PELLA CORPORATION
Also Called: Pella Window Door
800 Valley Plz Ste 5 (13790-1046)
PHONE.................................607 238-2812
Chris Ward, *Branch Mgr*
EMP: 316
SALES (corp-wide): 1.9B **Privately Held**
SIC: 2431 Windows, wood
PA: Pella Corporation
    102 Main St
    Pella IA 50219
    641 621-1000

(PA)=Parent Co (HQ)=Headquarters (DH)=Div Headquarters
◎ = New Business established in last 2 years

Johnson City - Broome County (G-7135)

(G-7135)
PELLA CORPORATION
Also Called: Pella Window Door
800 Valley Plz Ste 5 (13790-1046)
PHONE..................607 231-8550
Chris Ward, *Branch Mgr*
EMP: 316
SALES (corp-wide): 1.9B **Privately Held**
SIC: 2431 Windows, wood
PA: Pella Corporation
  102 Main St
  Pella IA 50219
  641 621-1000

(G-7136)
ROB SALAMIDA COMPANY INC
71 Pratt Ave Ste 1 (13790-2255)
PHONE..................607 729-4868
Robert A Salamida, *President*
▲ **EMP:** 19 **EST:** 1975
SQ FT: 9,136
SALES (est): 4.3MM **Privately Held**
WEB: www.spiedie.com
SIC: 2035 2099 Seasonings & sauces, except tomato & dry; food preparations

(G-7137)
UPSTATE OFFICE LIQUIDATORS INC
Also Called: Upstate Office Furniture
718 Azon Rd (13790-1725)
PHONE..................607 722-9234
Fax: 607 722-3148
Sylvia J Kerber, *President*
Wayne Kerber Jr, *Vice Pres*
Judy Sarr, *Manager*
▲ **EMP:** 11
SQ FT: 45,000
SALES (est): 1.9MM **Privately Held**
WEB: www.upstateofficefurniture.com
SIC: 2521 Wood office furniture

Johnstown
Fulton County

(G-7138)
ARROW LEATHER FINISHING INC
12 W State St (12095-2104)
P.O. Box 542 (12095-0542)
PHONE..................518 762-3121
Fax: 518 762-2203
Joseph De Cristofaro, *President*
▲ **EMP:** 50
SQ FT: 18,000
SALES (est): 6.2MM **Privately Held**
SIC: 3111 Finishing of leather

(G-7139)
BENJAMIN MOORE & CO
Union Ave Ext (12095)
P.O. Box 220 (12095-0220)
PHONE..................518 736-1723
Fax: 518 736-1722
Bob Nowicki, *Plant Mgr*
Robert Nowicki, *Manager*
Perry Cimo, *Mng Officer*
EMP: 40
SQ FT: 2,403
SALES (corp-wide): 223.6B **Publicly Held**
WEB: www.benjaminmoore.com
SIC: 2851 5198 Paints & allied products; paints
HQ: Benjamin Moore & Co.
  101 Paragon Dr
  Montvale NJ 07645
  201 573-9600

(G-7140)
ELECTRO-METRICS CORPORATION
231 Enterprise Rd (12095-3340)
PHONE..................518 762-2600
Fax: 518 762-2812
Leslie Apple, *CEO*
▼ **EMP:** 34
SQ FT: 42,500
SALES (est): 7.6MM **Privately Held**
WEB: www.emihq.com
SIC: 3663 Radio & TV communications equipment

(G-7141)
EMPIRE ARCHTCTURAL SYSTEMS INC
125 Belzano Rd (12095-9755)
PHONE..................518 773-5109
Paul Lusenhop, *President*
Mike Richards, *General Mgr*
EMP: 35
SQ FT: 40,000
SALES (est): 4.1MM **Privately Held**
SIC: 2541 3442 Store fronts, prefabricated: wood; store fronts, prefabricated, metal

(G-7142)
EUPHRATES INC
230 Enterprise Rd (12095-3338)
P.O. Box 977 (12095-0977)
PHONE..................518 762-3488
Hamdi Ulukaya, *President*
Besnik Fetoski, *Controller*
Peter Averell, *Maintence Staff*
▲ **EMP:** 87
SQ FT: 44,000
SALES: 34MM **Privately Held**
WEB: www.euphrates.com
SIC: 2022 Cheese, natural & processed

(G-7143)
FAGE USA DAIRY INDUSTRY INC
Also Called: Fage USA Yogurt Mfg Plant
1 Opportunity Dr (12095-3349)
PHONE..................518 762-5912
Athanasios Filippou, *CEO*
Tim Gibeau, *Business Mgr*
Robert Shea, *Corp Secy*
Spyridon Giantatas, *Vice Pres*
Ioannis Ravanis, *Vice Pres*
▲ **EMP:** 265
SALES (est): 97.6MM
SALES (corp-wide): 168.3MM **Privately Held**
WEB: www.fageusa.com
SIC: 2026 Yogurt
HQ: Fage Usa Holdings
  1 Opportunity Dr
  Johnstown NY 12095
  518 762-5912

(G-7144)
FAGE USA HOLDINGS (HQ)
1 Opportunity Dr (12095-3349)
PHONE..................518 762-5912
Anthanasios Filippou, *CEO*
Ioannis Ravanis, *Exec VP*
Tim McClarren, *Purch Mgr*
Christos Koloventzos, *Treasurer*
Charlotte Gross, *Accounts Mgr*
◆ **EMP:** 5 **EST:** 2000
SALES (est): 97.6MM
SALES (corp-wide): 168.3MM **Privately Held**
SIC: 2026 5143 Yogurt; yogurt
PA: Fage Dairy Industry S.A.
  35 Ermou
  Metamorfosi 14452
  210 289-2555

(G-7145)
FALK INDUSTRIES INC
179 Corporate Dr (12095-4062)
P.O. Box 946 (12095-0946)
PHONE..................518 725-2777
Fax: 518 725-6849
Paul Levine, *Principal*
Kathy Lobel, *Sr Corp Ofcr*
Kathy Loebel, *Director*
▼ **EMP:** 12
SQ FT: 6,000
SALES (est): 1.4MM **Privately Held**
SIC: 3999 Manufacturing industries

(G-7146)
HUDSON INDUSTRIES CORPORATION
Also Called: Milligan & Higgins Div
100 Maple Ave (12095-1041)
P.O. Box 506 (12095-0506)
PHONE..................518 762-4638
Fax: 518 762-7039
Ron Kormanek, *Branch Mgr*
EMP: 40
SQ FT: 36,025 **Privately Held**
WEB: www.milligan1868.com

SIC: 2891 Glue
HQ: Hudson Industries Corporation
  271 Us Highway 46 F207
  Fairfield NJ 07004
  973 402-0100

(G-7147)
JAG MANUFACTURING INC
26 Grecco Dr (12095-1067)
P.O. Box 957 (12095-0957)
PHONE..................518 762-9558
Fax: 518 762-2807
Joseph A Galea, *President*
Kelly L Galea, *Vice Pres*
▲ **EMP:** 45
SQ FT: 10,000
SALES (est): 5.2MM **Privately Held**
SIC: 3949 3732 2394 2393 Sporting & athletic goods; boat building & repairing; canvas & related products; textile bags; broadwoven fabric mills, manmade

(G-7148)
KAMALI LEATHER CORP
204 Harrison St (12095-4072)
PHONE..................518 762-2522
Fax: 518 762-2526
Mark Towne, *Manager*
EMP: 9
SALES (corp-wide): 4.7MM **Privately Held**
SIC: 3199 Boxes, leather
PA: Kamali Leather Llc
  44 Hillside Ave
  Manhasset NY 11030
  516 627-6505

(G-7149)
LEE DYEING COMPANY NC INC
Also Called: Merrimac Leasing
328 N Perry St (12095-1210)
P.O. Box 100 (12095-0100)
PHONE..................518 736-5232
Morris Evans, *President*
John Henley, *Manager*
EMP: 10
SQ FT: 76,063
SALES (est): 1.3MM **Privately Held**
WEB: www.leedyeing.com
SIC: 2261 Embossing cotton broadwoven fabrics

(G-7150)
PEACEFUL VALLEY MAPLE FARM (PA)
116 Lagrange Rd (12095-4031)
PHONE..................518 762-0491
Stephen M Savage, *Owner*
Barbara Kirk, *Manager*
EMP: 5
SALES: 100K **Privately Held**
SIC: 2099 Maple syrup

(G-7151)
PEARL LEATHER FINISHERS INC
11 Industrial Pkwy 21 (12095-1046)
PHONE..................518 762-4543
Fax: 518 762-2898
Carmen F Ruggiero, *CEO*
Chuck Frascatore, *Plant Mgr*
Harry Downing, *Associate*
▲ **EMP:** 95
SQ FT: 20,000
SALES (est): 11.1MM **Privately Held**
WEB: www.pearlleather.com
SIC: 3111 Leather tanning & finishing

(G-7152)
PIONEER WINDOW HOLDINGS INC
200 Union Ave (12095-3336)
P.O. Box 70 (12095-0070)
PHONE..................518 762-5526
Fax: 518 762-5527
Vincent Amato, *President*
Barbara Amato, *Vice Pres*
Robert Bridge, *Purchasing*
Joseph Boltzer, *Manager*
Ian Chan, *Manager*
EMP: 50 **Privately Held**
WEB: www.pwindows.com
SIC: 3442 3354 Storm doors or windows, metal; aluminum extruded products

PA: Pioneer Window Holdings, Inc.
  15 Frederick Pl
  Hicksville NY 11801

(G-7153)
R H CROWN CO INC
100 N Market St (12095-2126)
PHONE..................518 762-4589
Fax: 518 762-4478
Michael Gray, *President*
Kevin Capobianco, *General Mgr*
Richard Reynolds, *Exec VP*
EMP: 30 **EST:** 1965
SQ FT: 58,000
SALES (est): 9.6MM **Privately Held**
SIC: 2911 7349 Oils, lubricating; janitorial service, contract basis

(G-7154)
READYJET TECHNICAL SVCS INC
1 Warren St (12095-2009)
PHONE..................518 705-4019
Mark Farrington, *CEO*
EMP: 15
SQ FT: 13,000
SALES (est): 266.2K **Privately Held**
SIC: 2531 Seats, aircraft

(G-7155)
SILK SCREEN ART INC
1 School St (12095-2198)
PHONE..................518 762-8423
Fax: 518 736-1110
David P Sponenberg, *President*
Guy B Sponenberg, *Vice Pres*
EMP: 12
SQ FT: 20,000
SALES (est): 870K **Privately Held**
SIC: 2759 Screen printing

(G-7156)
SIMCO LEATHER CORPORATION
99 Pleasant Ave (12095-1720)
P.O. Box 509 (12095-0509)
PHONE..................518 762-7100
Fax: 518 736-1514
Gerald Simek, *President*
▲ **EMP:** 20
SQ FT: 45,000
SALES (est): 3MM **Privately Held**
SIC: 3111 Tanneries, leather

(G-7157)
SPRAY NINE CORPORATION
309 W Montgomery St (12095-2435)
PHONE..................800 477-7299
Greg Mostooler, *General Mgr*
Mary Shippee, *Asst Controller*
Amy Yackbucci, *Accounting Mgr*
Stanley Banovic, *Manager*
Jack Case, *MIS Mgr*
EMP: 80
SQ FT: 82,000
SALES (est): 12.6MM **Privately Held**
WEB: www.spraynine.com
SIC: 2842 Specialty cleaning preparations

Jordan
Onondaga County

(G-7158)
OMEGA WIRE INC
Also Called: Bare Wire Div
24 N Beaver St (13080-9531)
PHONE..................315 689-7115
Fax: 315 689-1080
C Knapp, *Manager*
EMP: 90
SALES (corp-wide): 432.1MM **Privately Held**
WEB: www.omegawire.com
SIC: 3351 3366 3315 Wire, copper & copper alloy; copper foundries; steel wire & related products
HQ: Omega Wire, Inc.
  12 Masonic Ave
  Camden NY 13316
  315 245-3800

▲ = Import ▼=Export
◆ =Import/Export

(G-7159)
WECARE ORGANICS LLC
9293 Bonta Bridge Rd (13080-9430)
PHONE..........................315 689-1937
Jeffrey Leblanc, *President*
EMP: 30
SALES (est): 11.4MM **Privately Held**
SIC: 2869 Plasticizers, organic: cyclic & acyclic

Jordanville
Herkimer County

(G-7160)
HANSON AGGREGATES PA INC
237 Kingdom Rd (13361-2603)
PHONE..........................315 858-1100
Kevin Smith, *Superintendent*
William Scherer, *Plant Mgr*
EMP: 30
SQ FT: 2,944
SALES (corp-wide): 16B **Privately Held**
SIC: 1442 1422 Common sand mining; crushed & broken limestone
HQ: Hanson Aggregates Pennsylvania, Llc
7660 Imperial Way
Allentown PA 18195
610 366-4626

Katonah
Westchester County

(G-7161)
NOVA PACKAGING LTD INC
7 Sunrise Ave (10536-2301)
P.O. Box 785, Goldens Bridge (10526-0785)
PHONE..........................914 232-8406
Fax: 914 232-8968
Greg Scott, *President*
EMP: 37
SALES (est): 5.3MM **Privately Held**
SIC: 2671 3081 2673 Packaging paper & plastics film, coated & laminated; unsupported plastics film & sheet; bags: plastic, laminated & coated

(G-7162)
RECORD REVIEW LLC
Also Called: Bedford Pund Rdge Rcord Review
16 The Pkwy Fl 3 (10536-1550)
P.O. Box 455, Bedford Hills (10507-0455)
PHONE..........................914 244-0533
Fax: 914 244-0537
Felix Carroll, *Advt Staff*
Deborah White, *Mng Member*
Rob Astorino, *Executive*
EMP: 10
SALES (est): 426.1K **Privately Held**
SIC: 2711 Newspapers, publishing & printing

(G-7163)
US AUTHENTIC LLC
11 Mt Holly Rd E (10536-2400)
PHONE..........................914 767-0295
Shaul Dover, *Mng Member*
▲ **EMP:** 6 **EST:** 2000
SQ FT: 4,000
SALES (est): 600.5K **Privately Held**
WEB: www.flightjacket.com
SIC: 2386 Garments, sheep-lined

(G-7164)
WORDWISE INC
1 Brady Ln (10536-2503)
PHONE..........................914 232-5366
Karen Gotimer, *CEO*
EMP: 3
SALES (est): 1.8MM **Privately Held**
WEB: www.wordwiseinc.com
SIC: 2731 Textbooks: publishing only, not printed on site

Kauneonga Lake
Sullivan County

(G-7165)
B H M METAL PRODUCTS CO
Horseshoe Lake Rd (12749)
PHONE..........................845 292-5297
Robert Gordon, *Owner*
EMP: 6 **EST:** 1947
SQ FT: 15,000
SALES: 100K **Privately Held**
SIC: 3469 3441 3312 3679 Metal stampings; fabricated structural metal; tool & die steel & alloys; electronic circuits

Keeseville
Clinton County

(G-7166)
ESSEX BOX & PALLET CO INC
49 Industrial Park Rd (12944-2936)
PHONE..........................518 834-7279
Fax: 518 834-9156
Michael Lemza, *President*
EMP: 22
SQ FT: 19,000
SALES (est): 2.8MM **Privately Held**
WEB: www.essexboxandpallet.com
SIC: 2449 2448 2499 Wood containers; pallets, wood; handles, poles, dowels & stakes: wood

(G-7167)
INTERNATIONAL MTLS & SUPS INC
56 Industrial Park Rd (12944-2937)
PHONE..........................518 834-9899
David Kruse, *President*
John Burns, *Vice Pres*
Martin Caouette, *Vice Pres*
Jeffrey Kinblom, *Vice Pres*
David Rumble, *Vice Pres*
▼ **EMP:** 5 **EST:** 2001
SALES (est): 490.6K
SALES (corp-wide): 1.3B **Privately Held**
SIC: 2869 Industrial organic chemicals
HQ: Virginia Materials Inc.
3306 Peterson St
Norfolk VA 23509
757 855-0155

(G-7168)
LOREMANSS EMBROIDERY ENGRAV
Also Called: Loreman's
1599 Front St (12944-3510)
P.O. Box 546 (12944-0546)
PHONE..........................518 834-9205
Fax: 518 834-9001
Jim Reisdorf, *Sales Staff*
Thomas H Loreman, *Mng Member*
Donald Loreman Sr,
EMP: 12
SQ FT: 7,000
SALES (est): 1.7MM **Privately Held**
WEB: www.loremans.com
SIC: 2261 2759 7389 2395 Screen printing of cotton broadwoven fabrics; screen printing; engraving service; embroidery & art needlework; automotive & apparel trimmings

(G-7169)
MURRAY LOGGING LLC
1535 Route 9 (12944-2848)
PHONE..........................518 834-7372
Fax: 518 834-7768
Robert Murray,
James Murray,
EMP: 5
SALES (est): 403.3K **Privately Held**
SIC: 2411 Logging

(G-7170)
UPSTATE RECORDS MANAGEMENT LLC
1729 Front St (12944-3620)
PHONE..........................518 834-1144
Barbara Davidson,
EMP: 5
SALES: 125K **Privately Held**
SIC: 7372 Prepackaged software

Kendall
Orleans County

(G-7171)
DMD MACHINING TECHNOLOGY INC
17231 Roosevelt Hwy (14476-9762)
PHONE..........................585 659-8180
David Hofer, *President*
EMP: 5
SALES (est): 250K **Privately Held**
SIC: 3599 Machine & other job shop work

(G-7172)
NORTHEAST WATER SYSTEMS LLC
2338 W Kendall Rd (14476-9786)
PHONE..........................585 943-9225
Daniel Halling, *Owner*
EMP: 6
SALES (est): 729.1K **Privately Held**
WEB: www.northeastwatersystems.com
SIC: 3589 Sewage & water treatment equipment

Kenmore
Erie County

(G-7173)
ARMENTO INCORPORATED
Also Called: Armento Architectural Arts
1011 Military Rd (14217-2225)
P.O. Box 39, Buffalo (14217-0039)
PHONE..........................716 875-2423
Fax: 716 875-8010
Robert W Pierce, *President*
Douglas Knox, *Exec Dir*
EMP: 6 **EST:** 1946
SQ FT: 5,000
SALES (est): 1MM **Privately Held**
SIC: 3446 Architectural metalwork; ornamental metalwork

(G-7174)
DENNYS DRIVE SHAFT SERVICE
1189 Military Rd (14217-1845)
PHONE..........................716 875-6640
Dennis Bringhurst, *President*
Mary Bringhurst, *Vice Pres*
EMP: 8
SALES (est): 1MM **Privately Held**
WEB: www.dennysdriveshaft.com
SIC: 3714 7538 Drive shafts, motor vehicle; general automotive repair shops

(G-7175)
HARGRAVE DEVELOPMENT
Also Called: Hargraves Bus MGT Consulting
84 Shepard Ave (14217-1914)
PHONE..........................716 877-7880
Lawrence Tanner, *Owner*
Lloyd Tanner, *Principal*
EMP: 15
SALES (est): 597.2K **Privately Held**
SIC: 1499 8742 Miscellaneous nonmetallic minerals; business consultant

(G-7176)
HERRMANN GROUP LLC
Also Called: Identity Ink & Custom Tee
2320 Elmwood Ave (14217-2645)
PHONE..........................716 876-9798
Fax: 716 876-9684
William Herrmann,
EMP: 5
SALES (est): 430.6K **Privately Held**
SIC: 2759 3552 3949 5136 Screen printing; embroidery machines; sporting & athletic goods; men's & boys' clothing; clothing, sportswear, men's & boys'

(G-7177)
HORACE J METZ
Also Called: Insty Trints
2385 Elmwood Ave (14217-2648)
PHONE..........................716 873-9103
Horace J Metz, *Owner*
Jim Metz, *Manager*
EMP: 7 **EST:** 1976
SALES (est): 280.2K **Privately Held**
SIC: 2759 Commercial printing

(G-7178)
HULLEY HOLDING COMPANY INC (PA)
Also Called: Hulley Woodworking Company
2500 Elmwood Ave (14217-2223)
PHONE..........................716 332-3982
Fax: 716 332-3983
John Hulley, *President*
EMP: 13
SQ FT: 6,400
SALES: 1MM **Privately Held**
WEB: www.hulleywoodworking.com
SIC: 2431 Millwork

(G-7179)
KEN-TON OPEN MRI PC
2882 Elmwood Ave (14217-1325)
PHONE..........................716 876-7000
Fax: 716 876-7447
Joseph Serghany, *Ch of Bd*
Dr H Chen Park, *Principal*
EMP: 7
SALES (est): 670K **Privately Held**
SIC: 3841 8071 2835 Diagnostic apparatus, medical; testing laboratories; in vivo diagnostics

(G-7180)
W H JONES & SON INC
1208 Military Rd (14217-1833)
PHONE..........................716 875-8233
Elizabeth Jones, *Ch of Bd*
W Todd Jones, *President*
Kevin B Jones, *Vice Pres*
Peter W Jones, *Vice Pres*
EMP: 10 **EST:** 1941
SQ FT: 6,800
SALES: 737.7K **Privately Held**
SIC: 3599 Custom machinery

(G-7181)
ZENGER PARTNERS LLC
1881 Kenmore Ave (14217-2523)
PHONE..........................716 876-2284
George Zenger, *Vice Pres*
Donna Benzel, *Manager*
Joseph Zenger,
EMP: 37 **EST:** 1947
SQ FT: 12,000
SALES: 3.1MM **Privately Held**
SIC: 2752 2791 2789 Commercial printing, offset; typesetting; bookbinding & related work

Kennedy
Chautauqua County

(G-7182)
CARGILL INCORPORATED
1029 Poland Center Rd (14747-9708)
PHONE..........................716 665-6570
Tim Decker, *Branch Mgr*
EMP: 7
SALES (corp-wide): 109.7B **Privately Held**
WEB: www.growmarkfs.com
SIC: 2041 Grain cereals, cracked
PA: Cargill, Incorporated
15407 Mcginty Rd W
Wayzata MN 55391
952 742-7575

Kerhonkson
Ulster County

(G-7183)
BARRA & TRUMBORE INC
40 Old Mine Rd (12446-2641)
PHONE..........................845 626-5442
Fax: 845 626-5476
David Barra, *President*
Martin Trumbore, *Vice Pres*
▲ **EMP:** 8
SALES (est): 805.8K **Privately Held**
WEB: www.barratrumbore.com
SIC: 3281 Cut stone & stone products

(G-7184)
DAVES PRECISION MACHINE SHOP
56 Webster Ave (12446-2672)
PHONE..................................845 626-7263
Fax: 845 626-7263
David Seymour, Owner
EMP: 12
SQ FT: 1,500
SALES (est): 540K Privately Held
SIC: 3599 Machine shop, jobbing & repair

(G-7185)
MORGAN FUEL & HEATING CO INC
5 Webster Ave (12446-2669)
PHONE..................................845 626-7766
EMP: 26
SALES (corp-wide): 48MM Privately Held
SIC: 2869 Fuels
PA: Morgan Fuel & Heating Co., Inc.
  2785 W Main St
  Wappingers Falls NY 12590
  845 297-5580

Kew Gardens
Queens County

(G-7186)
A & B COLOR CORP (DEL) (PA)
Also Called: Soho Guilds
8204 Lefferts Blvd # 356 (11415-1731)
PHONE..................................718 441-5482
William Rabinowitz, President
EMP: 6
SQ FT: 2,500
SALES (est): 180K Privately Held
SIC: 2851 5198 Paints & allied products; paints

(G-7187)
ADVANTAGE PRINTING INC
12034 Queens Blvd Ste 310 (11415-1231)
PHONE..................................718 820-0688
Francene Biderman, President
Angelica Rozon, Prdtn Mgr
Ruth Sommer, Production
Derrek Lyons, Manager
EMP: 11
SALES (est): 2.3MM Privately Held
WEB: www.advantages.net
SIC: 2752 5199 7336 Commercial printing, offset; advertising specialties; graphic arts & related design

(G-7188)
CUMMINS - ALLISON CORP
8002 Kew Gardens Rd # 402 (11415-3613)
PHONE..................................718 263-2482
EMP: 64
SALES (corp-wide): 377.1MM Privately Held
SIC: 3579 3519 Perforators (office machines); internal combustion engines
PA: Cummins - Allison Corp.
  852 Feehanville Dr
  Mount Prospect IL 60056
  847 759-6403

(G-7189)
CUZINS DUZIN CORP
8420 Austin St Apt 3a (11415-2213)
P.O. Box 313073, Jamaica (11431-3073)
PHONE..................................347 724-6200
Todd Jones, Manager
EMP: 8
SALES: 76K Privately Held
SIC: 2051 Doughnuts, except frozen

(G-7190)
I D E PROCESSES CORPORATION (PA)
106 81st Ave (11415-1108)
PHONE..................................718 544-1177
Fax: 718 575-8050
▲ EMP: 17
SQ FT: 500
SALES: 2.1MM Privately Held
SIC: 3625 Mfg Silencers & Industrial Noise Control Equipment

(G-7191)
ISRAELI YELLOW PAGES
12510 Queens Blvd Ste 14 (11415-1522)
PHONE..................................718 520-1000
Assaf Ran, CEO
EMP: 20
SALES (est): 756.9K Privately Held
SIC: 2741 Telephone & other directory publishing

(G-7192)
JACK L POPKIN & CO INC
12510 84th Rd (11415-2202)
PHONE..................................718 361-6700
Leonard F Popkin, President
Debra Z Popkin, Admin Sec
EMP: 8 EST: 1947
SQ FT: 6,000
SALES: 1.6MM Privately Held
SIC: 3861 7699 Printing equipment, photographic; printing trades machinery & equipment repair

(G-7193)
JG INNOVATIVE INDUSTRIES INC
8002 Kew Gardens Rd # 5002 (11415-3600)
PHONE..................................718 784-7300
Joseph Gottlieb, Ch of Bd
Anat Geula, COO
EMP: 8
SALES (est): 964.5K Privately Held
SIC: 3999 Advertising display products

(G-7194)
MANHOLE BRRIER SEC SYSTEMS INC
Also Called: Mbss
8002 Kew Gardens Rd # 901 (11415-3600)
PHONE..................................516 741-1032
Michael Manoussos, CEO
John Messer, President
EMP: 22 EST: 2001
SQ FT: 5,000
SALES (est): 3.6MM Privately Held
SIC: 3699 Security devices

Kill Buck
Cattaraugus County

(G-7195)
DONVER INCORPORATED
4185 Killbuck Rd (14748)
P.O. Box 181 (14748-0181)
PHONE..................................716 945-1910
Fax: 716 945-4047
Donald A Vershay, President
Patricia B Vershay, Vice Pres
Merry Lankow, Office Mgr
Donald A Vershy, Manager
EMP: 18
SQ FT: 900
SALES: 4.3MM Privately Held
SIC: 2421 3713 2491 2426 Sawmills & planing mills, general; truck & bus bodies; wood preserving; hardwood dimension & flooring mills

Kinderhook
Columbia County

(G-7196)
AMERICAN BIO MEDICA CORP (PA)
122 Smith Rd (12106-2819)
PHONE..................................518 758-8158
Fax: 518 758-8171
Melissa A Waterhouse, CEO
Richard P Koskey, Ch of Bd
Edmund M Jaskiewicz, President
Martin Gould, Exec VP
Douglas Casterlin, Vice Pres
EMP: 65
SQ FT: 30,000
SALES: 5.6MM Publicly Held
WEB: www.americanbiomedica.com
SIC: 2834 3841 Pharmaceutical preparations; diagnostic apparatus, medical

(G-7197)
MAPLE HILL CREAMERY LLC
5 Hudson St (12106)
PHONE..................................518 758-7777
Peter T Joseph, Mng Member
EMP: 6
SALES (corp-wide): 8MM Privately Held
SIC: 2026 Yogurt
PA: Maple Hill Creamery Llc
  285 Allendale Rd W
  Stuyvesant NY 12173
  518 758-7777

King Ferry
Cayuga County

(G-7198)
LAKE VIEW MANUFACTURING LLC
Also Called: Aurora Shoe Company
1690 State Route 90 N (13081-9713)
P.O. Box 430, Aurora (13026-0430)
PHONE..................................315 364-7892
David Binns, President
EMP: 10
SQ FT: 5,000
SALES (est): 1.3MM Privately Held
SIC: 3143 3144 Men's footwear, except athletic; women's footwear, except athletic

Kings Park
Suffolk County

(G-7199)
AMFAR ASPHALT CORP
Also Called: Farino & Sons Asphalt
137 Old Northport Rd (11754-4200)
PHONE..................................631 269-9660
Anthony Farino, President
EMP: 5 EST: 1955
SQ FT: 7,500
SALES (est): 474K Privately Held
SIC: 2951 Asphalt & asphaltic paving mixtures (not from refineries)

(G-7200)
DEJANA TRCK UTILITY EQP CO LLC (HQ)
490 Pulaski Rd (11754-1317)
PHONE..................................631 544-9000
Fax: 631 544-0942
Peter Dejana, President
Andrew Dejana, Vice Pres
Michael Canaan, Prdtn Mgr
Daniel Edelmann, Purch Agent
Jerry Dresel, CFO
EMP: 150
SQ FT: 25,000
SALES (est): 36.1MM Publicly Held
SIC: 3711 5531 Truck & tractor truck assembly; truck equipment & parts

(G-7201)
HANSA PLASTICS INC
8 Meadow Glen Rd (11754-1312)
PHONE..................................631 269-9050
Fax: 631 269-9143
Harold Schmidt, President
Nellie Schmidt, Corp Secy
Peter Schmidt Jr, Vice Pres
▲ EMP: 10 EST: 1961
SQ FT: 5,000
SALES (est): 1.6MM Privately Held
WEB: www.hansasystemsusa.com
SIC: 3089 Injection molding of plastics

(G-7202)
KINGS PARK READY MIX CORP
140 Old Northport Rd E (11754-4211)
PHONE..................................631 269-4330
Fax: 631 269-4639
Claudio Valente, President
Jason Berchoff, General Mgr
EMP: 15
SALES: 2MM Privately Held
SIC: 3273 Ready-mixed concrete

(G-7203)
PELKOWSKI PRECAST CORP
294a Old Northport Rd (11754-4200)
PHONE..................................631 269-5727
Fax: 631 269-2100
Tom Pelkowski, President
Bob Pelkowski, Vice Pres
Bryan Pelkowski, Treasurer
Bill Pelkowski, Admin Sec
EMP: 17
SQ FT: 400
SALES (est): 2.7MM Privately Held
SIC: 3272 Concrete products, precast; septic tanks, concrete; manhole covers or frames, concrete; covers, catch basin: concrete

(G-7204)
R SCHLEIDER CONTRACTING CORP
135 Old Northport Rd (11754-4200)
PHONE..................................631 269-4249
Fax: 631 269-1534
Ray Schleider, President
Loretta Schleider, Vice Pres
EMP: 5
SQ FT: 2,500
SALES (est): 853.6K Privately Held
SIC: 2951 5169 Road materials, bituminous (not from refineries); industrial salts & polishes

(G-7205)
SOFTPACK INTERNATIONAL INC
279 Kohr Rd (11754-1214)
PHONE..................................631 544-7014
Fax: 631 544-9561
Marianna Kay, President
EMP: 7
SALES: 250K Privately Held
SIC: 3565 Packaging machinery

Kingston
Ulster County

(G-7206)
ALCOA FASTENING SYSTEMS
1 Corporate Dr (12401-5536)
PHONE..................................845 334-7203
Klaus Kleinfeld, Principal
▲ EMP: 130
SQ FT: 40,000
SALES (est): 23.9MM Privately Held
SIC: 3728 Mfg Aircraft Parts/Equipment

(G-7207)
ARMOR DYNAMICS INC
138 Maple Hill Rd (12401-8616)
PHONE..................................845 658-9200
Bernard C Schaeffer, President
EMP: 15
SALES: 1.5MM Privately Held
SIC: 3711 Cars, armored, assembly of

(G-7208)
BESICORP LTD (PA)
1151 Flatbush Rd (12401-7011)
PHONE..................................845 336-7700
Fax: 845 336-7172
William Seils, President
Frederic M Zinn Sr, President
Michael F Zinn, Chairman
Jim Waleur, Plant Mgr
EMP: 14 EST: 1998
SQ FT: 8,000
SALES (est): 5.7MM Privately Held
SIC: 3674 4911 3585 Photovoltaic devices, solid state; electric services; refrigeration & heating equipment

(G-7209)
C & G OF KINGSTON INC
25 Cornell St (12401-3625)
P.O. Box 1458 (12402-1458)
PHONE..................................845 331-0148
Fax: 845 331-6218
Clyde E Wonderly, CEO
Patricia Schweikart, Controller
Drew Wonderly, Manager
Gloria M Wonderly, Admin Sec
EMP: 60
SQ FT: 20,000

GEOGRAPHIC SECTION

Kingston - Ulster County (G-7235)

SALES (est): 5.7MM **Privately Held**
WEB: www.wonderlys.com
SIC: **2391** 2392 Curtains & draperies; bedspreads & bed sets: made from purchased materials

(G-7210)
C S I G INC
721 Broadway 270 (12401-3449)
PHONE..................................845 383-3800
Jonathan Peck, *CEO*
Tim Peck, *Vice Pres*
Andrew Peck, *CFO*
Andy Peck, *Human Res Mgr*
Wendi Piper, *Associate*
EMP: 9
SQ FT: 1,450
SALES: 650K **Privately Held**
WEB: www.csiginc.com
SIC: **7372** Application computer software

(G-7211)
CALLANAN INDUSTRIES INC
Salem St (12401)
P.O. Box 1220 (12402-1220)
PHONE..................................845 331-6868
Fax: 845 331-1740
Randy Anson, *Manager*
Lew A Anthony, *Manager*
EMP: 25
SALES (corp-wide): 28.6B **Privately Held**
WEB: www.callanan.com
SIC: **3272** 3281 2951 1442 Concrete products, precast; stone, quarrying & processing of own stone products; asphalt paving mixtures & blocks; construction sand & gravel
HQ: Callanan Industries, Inc.
    8 Southwoods Blvd Ste 4
    Albany NY 12211
    518 374-2222

(G-7212)
CHARLTON PRECISION PDTS INC
461 Sawkill Rd (12401-1229)
P.O. Box 500, Mount Marion (12456-0500)
PHONE..................................845 338-2351
Fax: 845 338-9202
Robert Charlton, *President*
Bonnie Charlton, *Vice Pres*
Nancy Charlton, *Shareholder*
Katherine Charlton, *Admin Sec*
EMP: 9 EST: 1962
SQ FT: 4,000
SALES: 1.2MM **Privately Held**
WEB: www.charltonprecision.com
SIC: **3643** Current-carrying wiring devices

(G-7213)
CITY OF KINGSTON
Also Called: Kingston Wste Wtr Trment Plant
91 E Strand St (12401-6001)
PHONE..................................845 331-2490
Fax: 845 331-4648
Allen Winchell, *Director*
Dan Heitzmam, *Director*
EMP: 11 **Privately Held**
WEB: www.kingstonez.com
SIC: **3589** 9511 Sewage & water treatment equipment;
PA: City Of Kingston
    420 Broadway
    Kingston NY 12401
    845 334-3935

(G-7214)
CRANESVILLE BLOCK CO INC
637 E Chester St (12401-1738)
PHONE..................................845 331-1775
Will Longto, *Principal*
EMP: 25
SQ FT: 4,262
SALES (corp-wide): 45.4MM **Privately Held**
SIC: **3273** Ready-mixed concrete
PA: Cranesville Block Co., Inc.
    1250 Riverfront Ctr
    Amsterdam NY 12010
    518 684-6154

(G-7215)
DAILY FREEMAN
79 Hurley Ave (12401-2898)
PHONE..................................845 331-5000
Fax: 845 331-3557
Jan Dewey, *Principal*
Sam Daleo, *Principal*
Darryl Gangloff, *Editor*
Sarah Gantz, *Correspondent*
Robert R Mitchell, *Correspondent*
EMP: 11
SALES (est): 486K **Privately Held**
SIC: **2711** Newspapers

(G-7216)
DIRT T SHIRTS INC
444 Old Neighborhood Rd (12401-1508)
PHONE..................................845 336-4230
Fax: 845 336-6127
John Stote, *President*
Scott Winter, *Vice Pres*
William Stote, *Treasurer*
Daryl Morrrell, *Credit Mgr*
John Stote III, *Admin Sec*
EMP: 40
SQ FT: 25,000
SALES (est): 3.5MM **Privately Held**
SIC: **2396** 2395 Screen printing on fabric articles; art goods for embroidering, stamped: purchased materials

(G-7217)
EAST COAST CULTURES LLC
906 State Route 28 (12401-7264)
P.O. Box 220147, Brooklyn (11222-0147)
PHONE..................................917 261-3010
EMP: 10
SALES (est): 932K **Privately Held**
SIC: **2086** Mfg Bottled/Canned Soft Drinks

(G-7218)
FALA TECHNOLOGIES INC
430 Old Neighborhood Rd (12401-1508)
PHONE..................................845 336-4000
Fax: 845 336-4030
Frank Falatyn, *Ch of Bd*
Henry Dimarco, *President*
Robert Schmidt, *President*
Steve Barthel, *General Mgr*
Gerry Dimarco, *General Mgr*
EMP: 38 EST: 1946
SQ FT: 48,000
SALES: 7MM **Privately Held**
WEB: www.falatech.com
SIC: **3449** Miscellaneous metalwork

(G-7219)
HEALTHALLIANCE HOSPITAL
Also Called: Benedictine Hospital
105 Marys Ave (12401-5848)
PHONE..................................845 338-2500
Jeffrey Murphy, *Manager*
EMP: 7 **Privately Held**
SIC: **3821** Laboratory apparatus & furniture
HQ: Healthalliance Hospital Mary's Avenue Campus
    105 Marys Ave
    Kingston NY 12401
    845 338-2500

(G-7220)
HUCK INTERNATIONAL INC
Also Called: Arconic Fstening Systems Rings
1 Corporate Dr (12401-5536)
PHONE..................................845 331-7300
Fax: 845 334-7214
Steven Boderck, *Branch Mgr*
Kim Ball, *Info Tech Mgr*
Tim Barkman, *Maintence Staff*
EMP: 203
SALES (corp-wide): 12.3B **Publicly Held**
WEB: www.huck.com
SIC: **3452** 3594 3546 Bolts, nuts, rivets & washers; fluid power pumps & motors; power-driven handtools
HQ: Huck International, Inc.
    3724 E Columbia St
    Tucson AZ 85714
    520 519-7400

(G-7221)
KEEGAN ALES LLC
20 Saint James St (12401-4534)
PHONE..................................845 331-2739
Tommy Keegan, *Mng Member*
Lisa Hantes, *Manager*
EMP: 13
SALES (est): 1.1MM **Privately Held**
WEB: www.keeganales.com
SIC: **2082** Beer (alcoholic beverage)

(G-7222)
KINGSTON HOOPS SUMMER
68 Glen St (12401-6406)
P.O. Box 2606 (12402-2606)
PHONE..................................845 401-6830
Charlene Laday Hill, *Owner*
EMP: 8
SALES: 24K **Privately Held**
SIC: **3494** Valves & pipe fittings

(G-7223)
KNIGHTLY ENDEAVORS
319 Wall St Ste 2 (12401-3884)
PHONE..................................845 340-0949
John Reeder, *Owner*
EMP: 11 EST: 1996
SALES (est): 789.1K **Privately Held**
WEB: www.knightly.com
SIC: **2211** Apparel & outerwear fabrics, cotton

(G-7224)
LABELLA PASTA INC
906 State Route 28 (12401-7264)
PHONE..................................845 331-9130
Nancy Covello, *President*
Dennis Covello, *President*
EMP: 7
SQ FT: 4,800
SALES (est): 709.5K **Privately Held**
WEB: www.labellapasta.com
SIC: **2099** Pasta, uncooked: packaged with other ingredients

(G-7225)
LHV PRECAST INC
540 Ulster Landing Rd (12401-6963)
PHONE..................................845 336-8880
Fax: 845 336-8962
Henry Killian, *CEO*
Robert Willis, *President*
James Willis, *Vice Pres*
Mike Venett, *Plant Engr*
Tonya Valk, *Manager*
EMP: 50
SQ FT: 30,000
SALES (est): 8.9MM **Privately Held**
WEB: www.lhvprecast.com
SIC: **3272** Concrete products, precast

(G-7226)
LOCAL MEDIA GROUP INC
Also Called: Times Herald-Record
34 John St (12401-3822)
PHONE..................................845 340-4910
EMP: 12
SALES (corp-wide): 1.2B **Publicly Held**
SIC: **2711** Newspapers-Publishing/Printing
HQ: Local Media Group, Inc.
    40 Mulberry St
    Middletown NY 10940
    845 341-1100

(G-7227)
LUDWIG HOLDINGS CORP
Also Called: Wolf-TEC
20 Kieffer Ln (12401-2209)
PHONE..................................845 340-9727
Fax: 845 340-9732
Ralf Ludwig, *CEO*
Peter Ludwig, *Owner*
Don Tegeler, *CFO*
Melinda Beuf, *Human Res Dir*
Rolf Hammann, *Sales Mgr*
◆ EMP: 85
SQ FT: 47,500
SALES (est): 18.7MM **Privately Held**
WEB: www.wolf-tec.com
SIC: **3556** 8742 Food products machinery; meat, poultry & seafood processing machinery; industry specialist consultants; food & beverage consultant

(G-7228)
LUMINARY PUBLISHING INC
314 Wall St (12401-3820)
PHONE..................................845 334-8600
Jason Stern, *President*
Amara Projansky, *Vice Pres*
Robert Pina, *Accounts Exec*
Mathew Watzka, *Manager*
EMP: 15
SQ FT: 1,000
SALES (est): 1.8MM **Privately Held**
WEB: www.chronogram.com
SIC: **2721** 2741 Magazines: publishing & printing; art copy & poster publishing

(G-7229)
M & E MFG CO INC
19 Progress St (12401-3611)
P.O. Box 1548 (12402-1548)
PHONE..................................845 331-7890
Fax: 845 331-7898
Jeffrey Weinberger, *CEO*
Don Hall, *President*
Pam Bailey, *Purch Agent*
Mary Blauvelt, *Cust Mgr*
Jim Akin, *Info Tech Mgr*
EMP: 55
SQ FT: 54,000
SALES: 6.1MM **Privately Held**
WEB: www.zframerack.com
SIC: **3556** Food products machinery

(G-7230)
MILLROCK TECHNOLOGY INC
39 Kieffer Ln Ste 2 (12401-2210)
PHONE..................................845 339-5700
Taylor Thompson, *Chairman*
Mary Anne Whitnas, *Accounts Mgr*
◆ EMP: 20
SQ FT: 12,000
SALES (est): 4.4MM **Privately Held**
WEB: www.millrocktech.com
SIC: **3585** Refrigeration equipment, complete

(G-7231)
MONKEY JOE ROASTING COMPANY
478 Broadway Ste A (12401-4623)
PHONE..................................845 331-4598
Gabriel Cicale, *CEO*
EMP: 8
SALES (est): 733.5K **Privately Held**
SIC: **2095** Coffee roasting (except by wholesale grocers)

(G-7232)
NORTHAST COML WIN TRTMENTS INC
Also Called: Wonderly Company, The
25 Cornell St (12401-3625)
PHONE..................................845 331-0148
Al Parsons, *CEO*
Pat Schweikart, *CFO*
EMP: 65
SALES: 6MM **Privately Held**
SIC: **2391** Cottage sets (curtains): made from purchased materials

(G-7233)
NORTHEAST DATA
619 State Route 28 (12401-7466)
P.O. Box 316, West Hurley (12491-0316)
PHONE..................................845 331-5554
Mark Wachtel, *Principal*
EMP: 7
SALES (est): 1MM **Privately Held**
SIC: **3559** Tire shredding machinery
PA: National Waste Management Holdings, Inc.
    5920 N Florida Ave
    Hernando FL 34442
    352 489-6912

(G-7234)
NORTHEAST PANEL & TRUSS LLC
2 Kieffer Ln (12401-2206)
PHONE..................................845 339-3656
Fax: 845 339-5096
Ed Collins,
Bruce Hutchins,
EMP: 40
SQ FT: 50,000
SALES (est): 2.9MM **Privately Held**
WEB: www.northeastpanel.com
SIC: **2439** 2435 Trusses, wooden roof; trusses, except roof: laminated lumber; panels, hardwood plywood

(G-7235)
PEARSON EDUCATION INC
317 Wall St (12401-3819)
PHONE..................................845 340-8700
Fax: 845 339-0316

Kingston - Ulster County (G-7236)

Dan Cooper, Manager
EMP: 27
SALES (corp-wide): 5.6B Privately Held
WEB: www.phgenit.com
SIC: 2731 Book publishing
HQ: Pearson Education, Inc.
221 River St
Hoboken NJ 07030
201 236-7000

(G-7236)
R & F HANDMADE PAINTS INC
84 Ten Broeck Ave (12401-3921)
PHONE.................................845 331-3112
Richard Frumess, President
Darin Seim, Opers Staff
Jim Haskin, Treasurer
▲ EMP: 12
SQ FT: 5,000
SALES (est): 875.1K Privately Held
SIC: 3952 5199 Lead pencils & art goods; artists' materials

(G-7237)
ROBERT TABATZNIK ASSOC INC (PA)
Also Called: American Printing and Off Sups
867 Flatbush Rd (12401-7315)
PHONE.................................845 336-4555
Fax: 845 336-7717
Patricia Tabatznik, Ch of Bd
EMP: 10
SQ FT: 7,300
SALES (est): 1.7MM Privately Held
WEB: www.rtachicago.com
SIC: 2752 5112 Commercial printing, lithographic; office supplies

(G-7238)
SOLVENTS COMPANY INC
9 Cornell St (12401-3623)
P.O. Box 231015, Great Neck (11023-0015)
PHONE.................................631 595-9300
Batia Shellef, President
EMP: 10 EST: 2013
SALES (est): 1.9MM Privately Held
SIC: 2911 2869 2899 2842 Solvents; non-aromatic chemical products; industrial organic chemicals; chlorinated solvents; orange oil; degreasing solvent

(G-7239)
SPIEGEL WOODWORKS INC
Also Called: S A W
418 Old Neighborhood Rd (12401-1508)
PHONE.................................845 336-8090
Fax: 845 336-8087
Gary Spiegel, President
EMP: 10
SQ FT: 12,000
SALES: 1.6MM Privately Held
WEB: www.sawmoulding.com
SIC: 2431 2421 Moldings, wood: unfinished & prefinished; doors, wood; sawmills & planing mills, general

(G-7240)
STATEBOOK LLC
185 Fair St Ste 2 (12401-0503)
P.O. Box 3659 (12402-3659)
PHONE.................................845 383-1991
Calandra Cruickshank, Principal
Ira Schuman, Manager
EMP: 5
SALES (est): 296.1K Privately Held
SIC: 2741

(G-7241)
STAVO INDUSTRIES INC (PA)
Also Called: Ertel Alsop
132 Flatbush Ave (12401-2202)
PHONE.................................845 331-4552
George T Quigley, Vice Pres
Bianca Quigley, Vice Pres
David Thompson, Research
Jean Winter, Human Res Mgr
Bill Kearney, VP Sales
▲ EMP: 17 EST: 1966
SQ FT: 15,000
SALES (est): 9.8MM Privately Held
WEB:
SIC: 3569 3561 3443 Filters, general line: industrial; industrial pumps & parts; tanks, standard or custom fabricated: metal plate

(G-7242)
STAVO INDUSTRIES INC
Also Called: Ertel Engineering Co
132 Flatbush Ave (12401-2202)
PHONE.................................845 331-5389
Fax: 845 339-1063
George Quigley, Vice Pres
EMP: 45
SALES (corp-wide): 9.8MM Privately Held
WEB: www.ertelalsop.com
SIC: 3569 Filters
PA: Stavo Industries, Inc.
132 Flatbush Ave
Kingston NY 12401
845 331-4552

(G-7243)
TIMELY SIGNS OF KINGSTON INC
154 Clinton Ave Fl 1 (12401-4922)
PHONE.................................845 331-8710
Gerard Beichert, President
Jeff Zduniak, Principal
Joe Beichert, Vice Pres
EMP: 12
SQ FT: 15,000
SALES (est): 1.6MM Privately Held
WEB: www.timelysigns.com
SIC: 3993 Signs & advertising specialties

(G-7244)
TONNER DOLL COMPANY INC (PA)
1094 Morton Blvd (12401-8110)
P.O. Box 4410 (12402-4410)
PHONE.................................845 339-9537
Fax: 845 339-1259
Robert Tonner, CEO
Jack Kralik, Vice Pres
Lorri Booth, Manager
Noreen Morris, Manager
▲ EMP: 24
SQ FT: 8,500
SALES (est): 2.2MM Privately Held
WEB: www.tonnerdoll.com
SIC: 3942 Miniature dolls, collectors'

(G-7245)
TORTILLA HEAVEN INC
Also Called: Armadillo Bar & Grill
97 Abeel St (12401-6009)
PHONE.................................845 339-1550
Fax: 845 657-2261
Merle Borenstein, President
EMP: 20
SQ FT: 3,200
SALES (est): 2.2MM Privately Held
SIC: 2099 5812 Tortillas, fresh or refrigerated; Mexican restaurant

(G-7246)
ULSTER PRECISION INC
57 Teller St (12401-2600)
P.O. Box 1668 (12402-1668)
PHONE.................................845 338-0995
Fax: 845 338-3045
Selma Boris, President
Harold Hill, Exec VP
Lenore Eckhardt, Vice Pres
Christopher Eckhardt, Foreman/Supr
Dan Smith, Sales Staff
EMP: 20
SQ FT: 16,000
SALES (est): 4.2MM Privately Held
SIC: 3444 3441 3645 Sheet metalwork; fabricated structural metal; residential lighting fixtures

(G-7247)
ULSTER PUBLISHING CO INC (PA)
Also Called: Woodstock Times
322 Wall St Fl 1 (12401-3820)
P.O. Box 3329 (12402-3329)
PHONE.................................845 334-8205
Fax: 845 334-8809
Geddy Sveikauskas, President
Debbie Alexsa, Editor
Genia Wickwire, Director
EMP: 20 EST: 1972
SQ FT: 2,500
SALES (est): 3.6MM Privately Held
WEB: www.ulsterpublishing.com
SIC: 2711 2721 Newspapers: publishing only, not printed on site; magazines: publishing only, not printed on site

(G-7248)
UNIVERSAL METAL FABRICATORS
Also Called: Reliance Gayco
27 Emerick St (12401-3009)
PHONE.................................845 331-8248
James Hassett, President
EMP: 10
SQ FT: 50,000
SALES (est): 2MM Privately Held
WEB: www.urminc.com
SIC: 3555 3599 3569 3532 Printing trades machinery; machine shop, jobbing & repair; separators for steam, gas, vapor or air (machinery); mining machinery

(G-7249)
US HEALTH EQUIPMENT COMPANY
138 Maple Hill Rd (12401-8616)
PHONE.................................845 658-7576
Bernard Schaeffer, President
Wayne Schaeffer, President
EMP: 20 EST: 1961
SALES (est): 2.2MM Privately Held
WEB: www.saunex.com
SIC: 3634 Sauna heaters, electric

(G-7250)
USHECO INC
138 Maple Hill Rd (12401-8616)
PHONE.................................845 658-9200
Fax: 845 658-7224
Bernarr C Schaeffer, CEO
Wayne M Schaeffer, President
Lorene Schaeffer, Vice Pres
Cynthia Marketti, Bookkeeper
EMP: 16
SQ FT: 40,000
SALES: 1.3MM Privately Held
WEB: www.usheco.com
SIC: 3089 Plastic processing

(G-7251)
VINCENT CONIGLIARO
Also Called: Salvin Company
308 State Route 28 (12401-7445)
PHONE.................................845 340-0489
Fax: 845 334-9618
Vincent Conigliaro, Owner
EMP: 15
SQ FT: 12,000
SALES (est): 860K Privately Held
SIC: 3648 5719 1731 5731 Lighting equipment; lighting, lamps & accessories; lighting contractor; radio, television & electronic stores; audio electronic systems

(G-7252)
WORKSHOP ART FABRICATION
117 Tremper Ave (12401-3619)
P.O. Box 1009 (12402-1009)
PHONE.................................845 331-0385
Vincent Didonato, President
Andrew Tharmer, President
EMP: 12
SALES: 1MM Privately Held
SIC: 3562 Casters

(G-7253)
YUM YUM NOODLE BAR
275 Fair St Ste 17 (12401-3882)
PHONE.................................845 679-7992
Dorothy Lee, Owner
EMP: 8
SALES (est): 637.6K Privately Held
SIC: 2098 Noodles (e.g. egg, plain & water), dry

Kirkville
Onondaga County

(G-7254)
MANTH-BROWNELL INC
1120 Fyler Rd (13082-9445)
PHONE.................................315 687-7263
Fax: 315 687-6856
Wesley R Skinner Jr, Ch of Bd
Rob Pike, Vice Pres
James Wilsey, Opers Mgr
Pat Hachey, Purchasing
Glenn Spaarling, CFO
EMP: 180 EST: 1951
SQ FT: 140,000
SALES (est): 45.2MM Privately Held
WEB: www.manth.com
SIC: 3451 Screw machine products

(G-7255)
STANLEY INDUSTRIAL EQP LLC
8094 Saintsville Rd (13082-9325)
PHONE.................................315 656-8733
Thomas Stanley, Mng Member
EMP: 6
SQ FT: 5,200
SALES (est): 1.2MM Privately Held
SIC: 3537 Forklift trucks

(G-7256)
TITAN STEEL CORP
6333 N Kirkville Rd (13082-3300)
P.O. Box 10 (13082-0010)
PHONE.................................315 656-7046
Gretchen K Conway, President
Jeff Kealin, Vice Pres
Dave Carbone, Project Mgr
Micheal Conway, Controller
Julie Stiles, Info Tech Mgr
EMP: 12
SALES (est): 2.4MM Privately Held
SIC: 3441 Fabricated structural metal

Kirkwood
Broome County

(G-7257)
ACTIVE MANUFACTURING INC
32 Laughlin Rd (13795)
P.O. Box 332 (13795-0332)
PHONE.................................607 775-3162
Fax: 607 775-5086
Frank Sweetay, President
EMP: 12
SQ FT: 2,000
SALES (est): 1.4MM Privately Held
SIC: 3599 3999 Machine shop, jobbing & repair; models, general, except toy

(G-7258)
AKRATURN MFG INC
1743 Us Route 11 (13795-1637)
PHONE.................................607 775-2802
Fax: 607 775-2227
Douglas Gardner, President
Douglas Sterns, Corp Secy
David Gardner, Vice Pres
Kimberly Reger, Manager
EMP: 51
SQ FT: 60,000
SALES (est): 5.2MM Privately Held
WEB: www.akraturn.com
SIC: 3599 Machine shop, jobbing & repair

(G-7259)
BELDEN MANUFACTURING INC
Also Called: Dan Ann Associates
1813 Us Route 11 (13795-1608)
PHONE.................................607 238-0998
Fax: 607 238-0996
Jerry Wilson, President
Kate Molesky, Office Mgr
EMP: 20
SQ FT: 6,000
SALES: 3MM Privately Held
SIC: 3599 Machine shop, jobbing & repair

(G-7260)
FUSE ELECTRONICS INC
1223 Us Route 11 (13795-1641)
PHONE.................................607 352-3222
Susane Lewis, CEO
Patricia Mancinelli, Ch of Bd
EMP: 7
SALES (est): 1MM Privately Held
SIC: 3677 Electronic coils, transformers & other inductors

(G-7261)
L3 TECHNOLOGIES INC
265 Industrial Park Dr (13795)
PHONE..................................607 721-5465
Fax: 607 721-5458
Donald Ulmer, *Purch Agent*
Bob Hansen, *Manager*
Todd Cundey, *Info Tech Mgr*
EMP: 100
SALES (corp-wide): 10.5B **Publicly Held**
SIC: 3663 7371 3699 Telemetering equipment, electronic; custom computer programming services; electrical equipment & supplies
PA: L3 Technologies, Inc.
  600 3rd Ave Fl 34
  New York NY 10016
  212 697-1111

La Fargeville
Jefferson County

(G-7262)
HP HOOD LLC
20700 State Route 411 (13656-3228)
PHONE..................................315 658-2132
EMP: 300
SALES (corp-wide): 1.7B **Privately Held**
SIC: 2026 Fluid milk
PA: Hp Hood Llc
  6 Kimball Ln Ste 400
  Lynnfield MA 01940
  617 887-8441

(G-7263)
JOHNSON S SAND GRAVEL INC
23284 County Route 3 (13656-3111)
PHONE..................................315 771-1450
Rusty Johnson, *Principal*
EMP: 6
SALES (est): 542.4K **Privately Held**
SIC: 1442 Construction sand & gravel

(G-7264)
THOUSAND ISLAND READY MIX CON
38760 State Route 180 (13656-3108)
PHONE..................................315 686-3203
Fax: 315 686-1107
Thomas Dillenbeck, *President*
Steven Dillenbeck, *Vice Pres*
EMP: 8 **EST:** 1964
SQ FT: 2,988
SALES (est): 1.2MM **Privately Held**
WEB: www.thousandislandsconcrete.com
SIC: 3273 Ready-mixed concrete

La Fayette
Onondaga County

(G-7265)
BEAK & SKIFF CIDER MILL INC
4472 Us Route 20 (13084-9729)
PHONE..................................315 677-5105
David Pittard, *President*
Stephen F Morse, *Treasurer*
Timothy Beak, *Shareholder*
Mark Fleckenstein, *Shareholder*
Marshall Skiff, *Shareholder*
EMP: 9
SQ FT: 9,800
SALES: 1.1MM **Privately Held**
SIC: 2099 Cider, nonalcoholic

(G-7266)
BOULAY FABRICATION INC
Rr 20 Box West (13084)
P.O. Box 508 (13084-0508)
PHONE..................................315 677-5247
Fax: 315 677-5325
Timothy Foody, *President*
Daniel Foody, *Vice Pres*
Connie Foody, *Admin Sec*
EMP: 12
SQ FT: 14,000
SALES (est): 3MM **Privately Held**
WEB: www.boulayfab.com
SIC: 3613 Control panels, electric

(G-7267)
BYRNE DAIRY INC (PA)
2394 Us Route 11 (13084-9583)
P.O. Box 176 (13084-0176)
PHONE..................................315 475-2121
Fax: 315 471-0930
Carl Byrne, *Ch of Bd*
Kingsley Irobunda, *General Mgr*
James Obrist, *General Mgr*
Scott Smith, *General Mgr*
William M Byrne Jr, *Principal*
EMP: 300 **EST:** 1932
SQ FT: 32,000
SALES (est): 278.8MM **Privately Held**
WEB: www.byrnedairy.com
SIC: 2026 2024 Milk processing (pasteurizing, homogenizing, bottling); ice cream, packaged; molded, on sticks, etc.; ice cream, bulk

Lackawanna
Erie County

(G-7268)
ALLIANCE INNOVATIVE MFG INC
1 Alliance Dr (14218-2529)
PHONE..................................716 822-1626
Richard St John, *President*
Jeanine Zaleski, *Controller*
Jeanine Stjohn, *Manager*
EMP: 34 **EST:** 2007
SQ FT: 35,000
SALES: 7MM **Privately Held**
SIC: 3443 Metal parts

(G-7269)
CERTAINTEED CORPORATION
231 Ship Canal Pkwy (14218-1026)
PHONE..................................716 823-3684
EMP: 226
SALES (corp-wide): 185.8MM **Privately Held**
SIC: 3221 Glass containers
HQ: Certainteed Corporation
  20 Moores Rd
  Malvern PA 19355
  610 893-5000

(G-7270)
LINITA DESIGN & MFG CORP
1951 Hamburg Tpke Ste 24 (14218-1047)
P.O. Box 1101, Buffalo (14201-6101)
PHONE..................................716 566-7753
Carlos Vera, *President*
Sean Greenhouse, *General Mgr*
Chris Macrides, *Manager*
Andrea Vera, *Manager*
Eva Vera, *Shareholder*
EMP: 50
SQ FT: 80,000
SALES: 10.6MM **Privately Held**
SIC: 3441 7389 7692 8711 Dam gates, metal plate; design services; welding repair; engineering services

(G-7271)
ONEIDA SALES & SERVICE INC
Also Called: Oneida Concrete Products
155 Commerce Dr (14218-1041)
PHONE..................................716 270-0433
Fax: 716 822-1740
Frederick Saia, *President*
EMP: 15
SALES (corp-wide): 9.4MM **Privately Held**
WEB: www.oneidagroup.com
SIC: 3531 3272 3273 Concrete plants; building materials, except block or brick; concrete; ready-mixed concrete
PA: Oneida Sales & Service, Inc.
  155 Commerce Dr
  Buffalo NY 14218
  716 822-8205

(G-7272)
PAGE FRONT GROUP INC
2703 S Park Ave (14218-1511)
PHONE..................................716 823-8222
Fax: 716 821-0550
William Delmont, *President*
Beverly Mazur, *Corp Secy*
EMP: 6

SQ FT: 1,500
SALES (est): 386.7K **Privately Held**
SIC: 2711 Newspapers: publishing only, not printed on site

(G-7273)
QUIKRETE COMPANIES INC
Also Called: Quikrete-Buffalo
11 N Steelawanna Ave (14218-1114)
PHONE..................................716 213-2027
Fax: 716 824-3902
Chuck Morell, *Regional Mgr*
Tom Kostelny, *Sales Mgr*
Chuck Olgin, *Manager*
EMP: 30
SQ FT: 26,293 **Privately Held**
WEB: www.quikrete.com
SIC: 3272 Concrete products
HQ: The Quikrete Companies Llc
  5 Concourse Pkwy Ste 1900
  Atlanta GA 30328
  404 634-9100

(G-7274)
RJS MACHINE WORKS INC
1611 Electric Ave (14218-3021)
PHONE..................................716 826-1778
Ronald J Szewczyk, *President*
Lori Szewczyk, *Vice Pres*
EMP: 6
SQ FT: 9,000
SALES: 470K **Privately Held**
SIC: 3599 Machine shop, jobbing & repair

(G-7275)
SAMPLA BELTING NORTH AMER LLC
61 N Gates Ave (14218-1029)
PHONE..................................716 667-7450
Fax: 716 667-7428
Gary Dombrowski, *Accountant*
Steven Beecher, *Sales Staff*
Lucio Depaoli, *Mng Member*
Stefan Cristian Balint,
David Gordon,
▲ **EMP:** 20
SQ FT: 40,000
SALES (est): 4.3MM **Privately Held**
SIC: 3199 3052 Transmission belting, leather; transmission belting, rubber

(G-7276)
WELDED TUBE USA INC
2537 Hamburg Tpke (14218-2557)
PHONE..................................716 828-1111
Robert Mandel, *CEO*
▲ **EMP:** 60 **EST:** 2013
SALES (est): 19MM
SALES (corp-wide): 467.6MM **Privately Held**
SIC: 3317 Steel pipe & tubes
PA: Welded Tube Of Canada Corp
  111 Rayette Rd
  Concord ON L4K 2
  905 669-1111

Lacona
Oswego County

(G-7277)
VANHOUTEN MOTORSPORTS
27 Center Rd (13083-4127)
PHONE..................................315 387-6312
Henry N Van Houten, *Principal*
EMP: 6
SALES (est): 626.3K **Privately Held**
SIC: 3531 Automobile wrecker hoists

Lagrangeville
Dutchess County

(G-7278)
GRAPHICS SLUTION PROVIDERS INC (PA)
Also Called: Brewster Coachworks
115 Barmore Rd (12540-6601)
P.O. Box 159 (12540-0159)
PHONE..................................845 677-5088
Theresa Brewster, *President*
Alexander S Brewster, *Vice Pres*

Jack Brewster, *Vice Pres*
EMP: 8 **EST:** 1977
SQ FT: 2,500
SALES: 2.5MM **Privately Held**
WEB: www.graphics-solutions.com
SIC: 2499 7373 Novelties, wood fiber; value-added resellers, computer systems

(G-7279)
INTENTIONS JEWELRY LLC
83 Miller Hill Dr (12540-5641)
PHONE..................................845 226-4650
Bob Baff,
Shareane Baff,
EMP: 5
SALES (est): 406.6K **Privately Held**
SIC: 3911 Jewelry, precious metal

(G-7280)
MACRO TOOL & MACHINE COMPANY
1397 Route 55 (12540-5118)
PHONE..................................845 223-3824
Fax: 845 223-7306
Daniel Siegel, *President*
Gisela Siegel, *Corp Secy*
Roland Siegel, *Vice Pres*
Linda Petandrea, *Manager*
EMP: 8
SQ FT: 30,000
SALES: 500K **Privately Held**
WEB: www.macrotool.com
SIC: 3599 Amusement park equipment

(G-7281)
MICROCAD TRNING CONSULTING INC
1110 Route 55 Ste 209 (12540-5048)
PHONE..................................617 923-0500
Agustin Fernandez, *Principal*
John McCoy, *Accounts Exec*
EMP: 7 **Privately Held**
SIC: 7372 8243 Prepackaged software; software training, computer
PA: Microcad Training & Consulting, Inc.
  440 Arsenal St Ste 3
  Watertown MA

(G-7282)
PARAGON AQUATICS
Also Called: KDI Paragon
1351 Route 55 Unit 1 (12540-5128)
PHONE..................................845 452-5500
Thomas A Saldarelli, *Principal*
Devin Hare, *Safety Mgr*
▲ **EMP:** 50 **EST:** 1969
SQ FT: 38,000
SALES (est): 7.7MM
SALES (corp-wide): 14.5B **Publicly Held**
WEB: www.paragonaquatics.com
SIC: 3449 3446 Miscellaneous metalwork; railings, prefabricated metal
HQ: Pentair Water Pool And Spa, Inc.
  1620 Hawkins Ave
  Sanford NC 27330
  919 774-4151

(G-7283)
PENTAIR WATER POOL AND SPA INC
Paragon Aquatics
341 Route 55 (12540)
PHONE..................................845 452-5500
Fax: 845 452-5426
Thomas Saldarelli, *President*
EMP: 45
SALES (corp-wide): 14.5B **Publicly Held**
WEB: www.pentairpool.com
SIC: 3589 3561 Swimming pool filter & water conditioning systems; pumps, domestic; water or sump
HQ: Pentair Water Pool And Spa, Inc.
  1620 Hawkins Ave
  Sanford NC 27330
  919 774-4151

(G-7284)
STYLES AVIATION INC (PA)
Also Called: Sky Geek
30 Airway Dr Ste 2 (12540-5254)
PHONE..................................845 677-8185
Fax: 845 677-6252
Steven T Styles, *CEO*
Virginia R Styles, *Vice Pres*
Sherri Palm, *Treasurer*

Jeffery Cross, *Manager*
Robert Rose, *Web Dvlpr*
▲ **EMP:** 5
SQ FT: 5,000
SALES (est): 5.4MM **Privately Held**
SIC: 3728 5088 Aircraft parts & equipment; aircraft equipment & supplies

(G-7285)
TYMOR PARK
249 Duncan Rd (12540-5845)
PHONE.................................845 724-5691
Fax: 845 724-5692
Robert Mattes, *Director*
EMP: 5
SALES: 6.3K **Privately Held**
WEB: www.unionvaleny.us
SIC: 2531 Picnic tables or benches, park

Lake George
Warren County

(G-7286)
JOCKEY INTERNATIONAL INC
1439 State Route 9 Ste 10 (12845-3447)
P.O. Box 5 (12845-0005)
PHONE.................................518 761-0965
Beverly Schult, *Manager*
EMP: 20
SALES (corp-wide): 253.9MM **Privately Held**
SIC: 2254 Underwear, knit
PA: Jockey International, Inc.
   2300 60th St
   Kenosha WI 53140
   262 658-8111

(G-7287)
LEATHER OUTLET
1656 State Route 9 (12845-3440)
PHONE.................................518 668-0328
Fax: 518 381-3827
Kevin Clint, *Owner*
EMP: 8
SALES (est): 788.8K **Privately Held**
SIC: 3199 Leather garments

(G-7288)
PERFORMANCE CUSTOM TRAILER
230 Lockhart Mountain Rd (12845-4904)
P.O. Box 106, Hadley (12835-0106)
PHONE.................................518 504-4021
William Bunting, *President*
Diane Bunting, *Treasurer*
EMP: 7
SQ FT: 3,000
SALES (est): 1.1MM **Privately Held**
SIC: 3799 Boat trailers

(G-7289)
UNDER ARMOUR INC
1444 State Route 9 (12845-3480)
PHONE.................................518 761-6787
EMP: 29
SALES (corp-wide): 4.8B **Publicly Held**
SIC: 2329 Men's & boys' sportswear & athletic clothing
PA: Under Armour, Inc.
   1020 Hull St Ste 300
   Baltimore MD 21230
   410 454-6428

Lake Grove
Suffolk County

(G-7290)
S&B ALTERNATIVE FUELS INC
1232 Stony Brook Rd (11755-1624)
PHONE.................................631 585-6637
Scott Kunz, *Principal*
EMP: 5 **EST:** 2009
SALES (est): 464.7K **Privately Held**
SIC: 2869 Fuels

(G-7291)
SPEEDWAY LLC
2825 Middle Country Rd (11755-2105)
PHONE.................................631 738-2536
Jaswante Kor, *Branch Mgr*
EMP: 15 **Publicly Held**
SIC: 1311 Crude petroleum production
HQ: Speedway Llc
   500 Speedway Dr
   Enon OH 45323
   937 864-3000

(G-7292)
SUNDOWN SKI & SPORT SHOP INC (PA)
3060 Middle Country Rd (11755-2106)
PHONE.................................631 737-8600
Fax: 631 737-5985
Winfred Breuer, *President*
Michael Rahatigan, *Vice Pres*
▲ **EMP:** 20
SQ FT: 13,000
SALES (est): 10.9MM **Privately Held**
SIC: 2511 5091 Wood lawn & garden furniture; skiing equipment

(G-7293)
VANS INC
313 Smith Haven Mall (11755-1201)
PHONE.................................631 724-1011
EMP: 10
SALES (corp-wide): 12B **Publicly Held**
SIC: 3021 5699 Canvas shoes, rubber soled; uniforms & work clothing
HQ: Vans, Inc.
   6550 Katella Ave
   Cypress CA 90630
   714 889-6100

Lake Katrine
Ulster County

(G-7294)
COBRA MANUFACTURING CORP
68 Leggs Mills Rd (12449-5145)
P.O. Box 209, Bloomington (12411-0209)
PHONE.................................845 514-2505
Michael V Pavlov, *President*
Hillarie Pavlov, *Treasurer*
▲ **EMP:** 9 **EST:** 2000
SALES (est): 1.2MM **Privately Held**
SIC: 3315 Barbed & twisted wire

(G-7295)
WCD WINDOW COVERINGS INC
1711 Ulster Ave (12449-5426)
P.O. Box 723 (12449-0723)
PHONE.................................845 336-4511
Fax: 845 336-2071
Drew Wonderly, *President*
Vicky Delavan, *Accounting Mgr*
EMP: 50
SQ FT: 14,000
SALES (est): 1.3MM **Privately Held**
WEB: www.wcd-drapery.com
SIC: 2391 5021 2591 Draperies, plastic & textile: from purchased materials; beds & bedding; drapery hardware & blinds & shades

Lake Luzerne
Warren County

(G-7296)
KETCHUM MANUFACTURING CO INC
11 Town Shed Rd (12846)
P.O. Box 10 (12846-0010)
PHONE.................................518 696-3331
Fax: 518 696-4048
Gary Powers, *President*
Lisa Podwirny, *Vice Pres*
Helen A Powers, *Admin Sec*
EMP: 13 **EST:** 1964
SQ FT: 8,000
SALES: 1.2MM **Privately Held**
WEB: www.ketchummfg.com
SIC: 3999 2652 Identification tags, except paper; setup paperboard boxes

Lake Placid
Essex County

(G-7297)
COMSEC VENTURES INTERNATIONAL
17 Tamarack Ave (12946-1607)
PHONE.................................518 523-1600
Fax: 518 523-1971
William H Borland, *President*
Tina Preston, *Manager*
EMP: 6
SQ FT: 1,700
SALES (est): 458.2K **Privately Held**
SIC: 3699 4822 4215 7929 Security control equipment & systems; telegraph & other communications; couriers services, except by air; entertainers & entertainment groups

(G-7298)
EVERGREEN HIGH VOLTAGE LLC
140 Peninsula Way (12946)
PHONE.................................281 814-9973
Carlos Delgado,
William Larzeler,
▲ **EMP:** 5 **EST:** 2013
SALES: 2MM **Privately Held**
SIC: 3699 3825 7629 Particle accelerators, high voltage; test equipment for electronic & electric measurement; electrical equipment repair, high voltage

(G-7299)
LAKE PLACID ADVERTISERS WKSHP
Also Called: Sir Speedy
Cold Brook Plz (12946)
PHONE.................................518 523-3359
Fax: 518 523-2577
Tom Connors, *President*
Adele Pierce, *Vice Pres*
EMP: 20
SQ FT: 2,000
SALES: 4.5MM **Privately Held**
SIC: 2752 2759 2791 Commercial printing, lithographic; commercial printing; typesetting

(G-7300)
SUGAR SHACK DESERT COMPANY INC
2567 Main St (12946-3305)
PHONE.................................518 523-7540
Gina D Cimaglia, *CEO*
EMP: 6
SALES (est): 290K **Privately Held**
SIC: 2099 Sugar

Lake Pleasant
Hamilton County

(G-7301)
WILT INDUSTRIES INC
2452 State Route 8 (12108-4416)
PHONE.................................518 548-4961
Fax: 518 548-5504
Daniel Wilt, *President*
Richard Wilt, *Vice Pres*
Donna Mandon, *Bookkeeper*
EMP: 6 **EST:** 1949
SQ FT: 10,000
SALES (est): 1MM **Privately Held**
WEB: www.wiltindustries.com
SIC: 3559 Glass making machinery: blowing, molding, forming, etc.

Lake Ronkonkoma
Suffolk County

(G-7302)
J F B & SONS LITHOGRAPHERS
1700 Ocean Ave (11779-6570)
PHONE.................................631 467-1444
Fax: 631 467-2174
Joseph Brown, *President*
Randall Brown, *Corp Secy*
Gary Brown, *Vice Pres*
Dennis Ganzak, *CFO*
EMP: 75
SQ FT: 43,000
SALES (est): 3.9MM
SALES (corp-wide): 189.9MM **Privately Held**
SIC: 2752 Commercial printing, lithographic
HQ: Earth Color New York, Inc.
   249 Pomeroy Rd
   Parsippany NJ 07054
   973 884-1300

Lake View
Erie County

(G-7303)
DEEDEE DESSERTS LLC
6969 Southwestern Blvd (14085-9644)
P.O. Box 353 (14085-0353)
PHONE.................................716 627-2330
Dawn Davis,
EMP: 7
SALES (est): 330K **Privately Held**
SIC: 2099 Dessert mixes & fillings

(G-7304)
LAKESHORE CARBIDE INC
5696 Minerva Dr (14085-9633)
PHONE.................................716 462-4349
Carl Ciesla, *Chairman*
EMP: 5 **EST:** 2009
SALES (est): 763K **Privately Held**
SIC: 2819 Carbides

Lakeville
Livingston County

(G-7305)
ARCHER-DANIELS-MIDLAND COMPANY
Also Called: ADM
3401 Rochester Rd (14480-9762)
PHONE.................................585 346-2311
Lee Robinson, *Branch Mgr*
Tim Calway, *Manager*
EMP: 7
SALES (corp-wide): 62.3B **Publicly Held**
WEB: www.admworld.com
SIC: 2046 Corn sugars & syrups
PA: Archer-Daniels-Midland Company
   77 W Wacker Dr Ste 4600
   Chicago IL 60601
   312 634-8100

(G-7306)
CONESUS LAKE ASSOCIATION INC
5828 Big Tree Rd (14480)
P.O. Box 637 (14480-0637)
PHONE.................................585 346-6864
Greg Foust, *Ch of Bd*
George Coolbaugh, *President*
Burt Lyon, *Treasurer*
EMP: 30
SALES: 47.4K **Privately Held**
SIC: 3599 2511 Machine & other job shop work; wood household furniture

(G-7307)
GANNETT CO INC
Also Called: Democrat & Chronicle
3155 Rochester Rd Bldg E (14480-9713)
PHONE.................................585 346-4150
Fax: 585 346-4146
Perry Van Dunk, *Manager*
Tom Callahan, *Manager*
EMP: 6
SALES (corp-wide): 3B **Publicly Held**
WEB: www.gannett.com
SIC: 2711 Newspapers
PA: Gannett Co., Inc.
   7950 Jones Branch Dr
   Mc Lean VA 22102
   703 854-6000

GEOGRAPHIC SECTION

Lancaster - Erie County (G-7332)

(G-7308)
S & R TOOL INC
6066 Stone Hill Rd (14480-9712)
PHONE.....................585 346-2029
Fax: 585 346-5865
Samuel Dandrea, *President*
Richard Panipinto, *Vice Pres*
EMP: 6
SQ FT: 10,428
SALES (est): 936.1K **Privately Held**
SIC: 3545 Precision tools, machinists'

(G-7309)
SWEETENERS PLUS INC
5768 Sweeteners Blvd (14480-9741)
P.O. Box 520 (14480-0520)
PHONE.....................585 728-3770
Carlton Myers, *President*
Mark Rudolph, *QC Mgr*
Kyle Whitford, *Marketing Staff*
Ann Coffey, *Admin Sec*
▲ EMP: 70
SQ FT: 30,000
SALES (est): 41.4MM **Privately Held**
WEB: www.sweetenersplus.com
SIC: 2062 Cane sugar refining

Lakewood
Chautauqua County

(G-7310)
ARRO MANUFACTURING LLC
4687 Gleason Rd (14750)
P.O. Box 19 (14750-0019)
PHONE.....................716 763-6203
Scott Bauer, *President*
EMP: 18
SALES (est): 632.3K **Privately Held**
SIC: 3544 3469 Punches, forming & stamping; metal stampings

(G-7311)
ARRO TOOL & DIE INC
4687 Gleason Rd (14750)
P.O. Box 7 (14750-0007)
PHONE.....................716 763-6203
Fax: 716 763-8511
James R Lindell, *President*
Eric Corey, *Vice Pres*
Jeff A Lindell, *Vice Pres*
Richard Morris, *Vice Pres*
Timothy Raynor, *Engineer*
▼ EMP: 19 EST: 1952
SQ FT: 23,000
SALES (est): 3.2MM **Privately Held**
WEB: www.arrotool.com
SIC: 3544 3469 Special dies & tools; metal stampings

(G-7312)
CLASSIC BRASS INC
2051 Stoneman Cir (14750-9779)
P.O. Box 3563, Jamestown (14702-3563)
PHONE.....................716 763-1400
Fax: 716 664-3281
J Christopher Creighton, *President*
▲ EMP: 56
SQ FT: 30,050
SALES (est): 9.2MM **Privately Held**
SIC: 3429 Furniture builders' & other household hardware

(G-7313)
CUMMINS INC
Also Called: Jamestown Engine Plant
4720 Baker St (14750-9772)
PHONE.....................716 456-2676
Karine Ramsey, *Principal*
Howard Bryan, *Engineer*
John Findlay, *Engineer*
William Herrick, *Engineer*
Scott Lord, *Engineer*
◆ EMP: 62
SALES (est): 14.1MM **Privately Held**
SIC: 3519 Internal combustion engines

(G-7314)
CUMMINS INC
Also Called: Cummins Eng Company/James Town
4720 Baker St (14750-9772)
PHONE.....................716 456-2111
Fax: 716 456-2451
Ian Ramsay, *Managing Dir*
Maria Jones, *Opers Mgr*
Dennis C Roberg, *Foreman/Supr*
Dan Nelson, *Purchasing*
Howard M Bryan, *Engineer*
EMP: 800
SQ FT: 1,733
SALES (corp-wide): 17.5B **Publicly Held**
WEB: www.cummins.com
SIC: 3519 3714 Internal combustion engines; motor vehicle parts & accessories
PA: Cummins Inc.
500 Jackson St
Columbus IN 47201
812 377-5000

(G-7315)
DLH ENERGY SERVICE LLC
4422 W Fairmount Ave (14750-9705)
P.O. Box 40, Ashville (14710-0040)
PHONE.....................716 410-0028
Kim Helffrich, *Manager*
Charles Dubose,
EMP: 3
SQ FT: 1,000
SALES: 5MM **Privately Held**
SIC: 1311 Crude petroleum & natural gas

(G-7316)
QUALITY MANUFACTURING SYS LLC
1995 Stoneman Cir (14750-9776)
PHONE.....................716 763-0988
Patsy Jo Kosinski, *Partner*
EMP: 6
SQ FT: 12,000
SALES (est): 1.1MM **Privately Held**
SIC: 3569 Assembly machines, non-metalworking

(G-7317)
R R DONNELLEY & SONS COMPANY
Also Called: Moore Business Forms
112 Winchester Rd (14750-1739)
P.O. Box 137 (14750-0137)
PHONE.....................716 763-2613
Fax: 716 763-5948
Kevin Diluca, *Manager*
Dan Caruso, *Manager*
EMP: 12
SALES (corp-wide): 6.9B **Publicly Held**
WEB: www.moore.com
SIC: 2759 Commercial printing
PA: R. R. Donnelley & Sons Company
35 W Wacker Dr Ste 3650
Chicago IL 60601
312 326-8000

(G-7318)
R-CO PRODUCTS CORPORATION
1855 Big Tree Rd (14750-9759)
PHONE.....................800 854-7657
Fax: 716 763-0080
Edward Roemer Jr, *President*
Erika Roemer, *Treasurer*
Katy Lord, *Admin Sec*
EMP: 13 EST: 1975
SQ FT: 30,000
SALES (est): 2.1MM **Privately Held**
SIC: 2891 Sealants

(G-7319)
ULRICH PLANFILING EQP CORP
2120 4th Ave (14750-9727)
P.O. Box 135 (14750-0135)
PHONE.....................716 763-1815
Fax: 716 763-1818
Daniel Berry, *President*
Jamie Carlson, *Vice Pres*
Reid Van Every, *Plant Mgr*
Barbara Sauer, *Purch Mgr*
Joni Drocy, *Engineer*
▼ EMP: 40
SQ FT: 42,400
SALES (est): 7.7MM **Privately Held**
WEB: www.ulrichcorp.com
SIC: 2522 Office cabinets & filing drawers: except wood

(G-7320)
WATER STREET BRASS CORPORATION
4515 Gleason Rd (14750-9748)
P.O. Box 463 (14750-0463)
PHONE.....................716 763-0059
Mathew Churchill, *President*
▲ EMP: 22
SALES (est): 2.7MM **Privately Held**
SIC: 3429 Furniture hardware

Lancaster
Erie County

(G-7321)
A & T TOOLING LLC
91 Beach Ave (14086-1658)
PHONE.....................716 601-7299
Maureen Hassenbohler,
EMP: 5
SALES: 250K **Privately Held**
SIC: 3543 Industrial patterns

(G-7322)
ADVANCED THERMAL SYSTEMS INC
15 Enterprise Dr (14086-9773)
PHONE.....................716 681-1800
Fax: 716 681-0228
Edward W Patnode, *Ch of Bd*
Eugene Miliczky, *President*
Edward Patnode, *General Mgr*
EMP: 40
SQ FT: 31,000
SALES (est): 8.5MM **Privately Held**
WEB: www.advancedthermal.net
SIC: 3494 3568 3498 3441 Expansion joints pipe; ball joints, except aircraft & automotive; fabricated pipe & fittings; fabricated structural metal

(G-7323)
AFTER 50 INC
5 W Main St Rear (14086-2109)
PHONE.....................716 832-9300
Bonnie Degweck, *President*
Phyllis Goasiti, *Vice Pres*
EMP: 5
SALES (est): 500K **Privately Held**
SIC: 2711 Newspapers

(G-7324)
AIR SYSTEM PRODUCTS INC
Also Called: AFP Industries
51 Beach Ave (14086-1658)
PHONE.....................716 683-0435
Fax: 716 683-7128
Patrick Scanlon, *President*
Henry Bourg, *President*
Mike Zacharko, *Accounts Mgr*
▲ EMP: 12
SQ FT: 17,000
SALES (est): 1.7MM **Privately Held**
WEB: www.airsyspro.com
SIC: 3491 Industrial valves

(G-7325)
ALCO PLASTICS INC
35 Ward Rd (14086-9779)
PHONE.....................716 683-3020
Fax: 716 683-3739
Raymond Mazurczyk, *President*
EMP: 20 EST: 1971
SQ FT: 25,000
SALES (est): 3.1MM **Privately Held**
SIC: 2673 Plastic bags: made from purchased materials

(G-7326)
ALDEN OPTICAL LABORATORY INC
6 Lancaster Pkwy (14086-9713)
PHONE.....................716 937-9181
Fax: 716 937-3303
Charles H Creighton, *President*
Helen Creighton, *Treasurer*
EMP: 16
SQ FT: 8,000
SALES (est): 2.4MM **Privately Held**
WEB: www.aldenoptical.com
SIC: 3851 Contact lenses

(G-7327)
APPLE RUBBER PRODUCTS INC (PA)
Also Called: Express Seal Div
310 Erie St (14086-9504)
PHONE.....................716 684-6560
Fax: 716 684-1678
Steven L Apple, *President*
Carol Malaney, *Vice Pres*
Erica Patterson, *Materials Mgr*
Dale Cielinski, *Project Engr*
Andrew Rich, *Project Engr*
▲ EMP: 25
SQ FT: 11,000
SALES (est): 24.1MM **Privately Held**
WEB: www.applerubber.com
SIC: 3069 Hard rubber & molded rubber products; molded rubber products

(G-7328)
APPLE RUBBER PRODUCTS INC
Also Called: Expresseal
204 Cemetery Rd (14086-9798)
PHONE.....................716 684-7649
Fax: 716 683-7053
Steven Apple, *President*
Flo Dorman, *Purch Agent*
Joe Divissich, *Engineer*
Mark Trzepacz, *Manager*
EMP: 110
SQ FT: 49,668
SALES (corp-wide): 24.1MM **Privately Held**
WEB: www.applerubber.com
SIC: 3069 3061 3053 Hard rubber & molded rubber products; molded rubber products; mechanical rubber goods; gaskets, packing & sealing devices
PA: Apple Rubber Products, Inc.
310 Erie St
Lancaster NY 14086
716 684-6560

(G-7329)
BABULA CONSTRUCTION INC
5136 William St (14086-9447)
PHONE.....................716 681-0886
Stanley Babula, *President*
Janet Babula, *Vice Pres*
EMP: 7
SALES: 300K **Privately Held**
SIC: 1389 Construction, repair & dismantling services

(G-7330)
BIMBO BAKERIES USA INC
2900 Commerce Pkwy (14086-1741)
PHONE.....................716 706-0450
George Weston, *Owner*
EMP: 18 **Privately Held**
WEB: www.gwbakeries.com
SIC: 2051 Bread, cake & related products
HQ: Bimbo Bakeries Usa, Inc.
255 Business Center Dr # 200
Horsham PA 19044
215 347-5500

(G-7331)
BUFFALO FILTER LLC
5900 Genesee St (14086-9024)
PHONE.....................716 835-7000
Samantha Bonano, *CEO*
Samantha Palmerton, *Vice Pres*
Greg Pepe, *Vice Pres*
David McKay, *Opers Staff*
Cathy Carson, *Purch Mgr*
▲ EMP: 85
SQ FT: 15,000
SALES (est): 17.8MM **Privately Held**
WEB: www.buffalofilter.com
SIC: 3841 3845 3699 3564 Surgical & medical instruments; laser systems & equipment, medical; electrical equipment & supplies; blowers & fans

(G-7332)
CASEY MACHINE CO INC
74 Ward Rd (14086-9779)
PHONE.....................716 651-0150
Fax: 716 651-4614
Thomas Radziwon, *Ch of Bd*
Ronald C Radziwon, *President*
Peter Szulc, *Vice Pres*
Dawn Delzer, *Purch Agent*

Bill Gillan, *Purch Agent*
EMP: 95 **EST**: 1976
SQ FT: 15,000
SALES (est): 18.4MM **Privately Held**
WEB: www.caseymachine.com
SIC: 3599 Machine shop, jobbing & repair

(G-7333)
CHAKRA COMMUNICATIONS INC
80 W Drullard Ave (14086-1649)
PHONE..................716 505-7300
Joe Griffin, *Prdtn Mgr*
Sharique Ansari, *Branch Mgr*
EMP: 50 **Privately Held**
WEB: www.chakracentral.com
SIC: 2796 2791 7812 7375 Lithographic plates, positives or negatives; typesetting; motion picture & video production; information retrieval services; color lithography
HQ: Chakra Communications, Inc.
80 W Drullard Ave
Lancaster NY 14086
716 505-7300

(G-7334)
CLASSIC & PERFORMANCE SPC
Also Called: Classic Tube
80 Rotech Dr (14086-9755)
PHONE..................716 759-1800
Fax: 716 759-1014
Paul Fix, *President*
Lauren J Fix, *Vice Pres*
Jane Fix, *Manager*
Pam Ladue, *Exec Dir*
EMP: 24
SQ FT: 20,000
SALES (est): 4.5MM **Privately Held**
WEB: www.classictube.com
SIC: 3714 Motor vehicle parts & accessories

(G-7335)
DELFT PRINTING INC
1000 Commerce Pkwy (14086-1707)
PHONE..................716 683-1100
Fax: 716 683-1101
Kamal C Jowdy, *President*
EMP: 7
SQ FT: 2,200
SALES: 800K **Privately Held**
WEB: www.delftprinting.com
SIC: 2759 Commercial printing

(G-7336)
DIVERSIFIED MANUFACTURING INC
4401 Walden Ave (14086-9013)
PHONE..................716 681-7670
Walt Kempa, *Branch Mgr*
EMP: 15
SALES (corp-wide): 20.5MM **Privately Held**
WEB: www.dmimfg.com
SIC: 3441 Fabricated structural metal
PA: Diversified Manufacturing Inc.
410 Ohio St
Lockport NY 14094
716 434-5585

(G-7337)
EASTERN AIR PRODUCTS LLC
Also Called: Engineered Air Products
41 Ward Rd (14086-9779)
PHONE..................716 391-1866
Jeffrey Browne, *President*
Peter Baran, *Vice Pres*
Michael Arno, *CFO*
▲ **EMP**: 18
SQ FT: 12,500
SALES: 3.2MM **Privately Held**
SIC: 3563 Air & gas compressors including vacuum pumps

(G-7338)
ERIE ENGINEERED PRODUCTS INC
3949 Walden Ave (14086-1472)
PHONE..................716 206-0204
Barry Newman, *Ch of Bd*
Thomas Kilpatrick, *General Mgr*
Ron Korczynski, *Vice Pres*
David Vystup, *Vice Pres*
Lorne Weil, *Shareholder*
EMP: 45
SQ FT: 88,000
SALES (est): 12.2MM **Privately Held**
WEB: www.containers-cases.com
SIC: 3443 3441 3412 3411 Containers, shipping (bombs, etc.): metal plate; fabricated structural metal; metal barrels, drums & pails; metal cans

(G-7339)
FBC CHEMICAL CORPORATION
4111 Walden Ave (14086-1599)
PHONE..................716 681-1581
Fax: 716 681-1512
Joe Villafranca, *Manager*
EMP: 5
SQ FT: 4,000
SALES (corp-wide): 60MM **Privately Held**
WEB: www.fbcchem.com
SIC: 2842 5169 Cleaning or polishing preparations; chemicals & allied products
PA: Fbc Chemical Corporation
634 Route 228
Mars PA 16046
724 625-3116

(G-7340)
FLOWNET LLC
580 Lake Ave (14086-9627)
PHONE..................716 685-4036
EMP: 6 **EST**: 2012
SALES (est): 288K **Privately Held**
SIC: 1311 Natural gas production

(G-7341)
GOOD EARTH INC
5960 Broadway St (14086-9531)
PHONE..................716 684-8111
Gunter Burkhardt, *President*
Cornelia Orffeo, *Vice Pres*
EMP: 6 **EST**: 1999
SALES (est): 844.9K **Privately Held**
WEB: www.goodearth.net
SIC: 2833 Organic medicinal chemicals: bulk, uncompounded

(G-7342)
GOOD EARTH ORGANICS CORP (PA)
5960 Broadway St (14086-9531)
PHONE..................716 684-8111
Fax: 716 684-3722
Guenter H Burkhardt, *Ch of Bd*
Andreas G Burkhardt, *President*
Bernhard G Burkhardt, *Vice Pres*
Eva Burkhardt, *Vice Pres*
Cornelia Orffeo, *Purchasing*
EMP: 20
SQ FT: 180,000
SALES (est): 17MM **Privately Held**
WEB: www.goodearth.org
SIC: 3523 Planting machines, agricultural

(G-7343)
HC BRILL CO INC
3765 Walden Ave (14086-1405)
PHONE..................716 685-4000
Bob Craiglow, *Vice Pres*
Melissa Price, *Telecom Exec*
EMP: 8
SALES (est): 1.2MM **Privately Held**
SIC: 2033 Canned fruits & specialties

(G-7344)
ILLINOIS TOOL WORKS INC
United Silicone Div
4471 Walden Ave (14086-9754)
PHONE..................716 681-8222
Joseph Wukovits, *Branch Mgr*
Patrick Smith, *Manager*
EMP: 155
SALES (corp-wide): 13.6B **Publicly Held**
SIC: 3559 Plastics working machinery
PA: Illinois Tool Works Inc.
155 Harlem Ave
Glenview IL 60025
847 724-7500

(G-7345)
KZ PRECISION INC
Also Called: K Z Precision
1 Mason Pl (14086-1615)
PHONE..................716 683-3202
Kenneth Zwara, *President*
Jerome Zwara, *Manager*
EMP: 15
SQ FT: 7,500
SALES (est): 931.7K **Privately Held**
WEB: www.kzprecision.com
SIC: 3599 Machine shop, jobbing & repair

(G-7346)
LAFARGE NORTH AMERICA INC
6125 Genesee St (14086-9722)
PHONE..................716 651-9235
Fax: 716 651-9580
Ken King, *Regl Sales Mgr*
Ron Morgan, *Manager*
EMP: 25
SALES (corp-wide): 26.6B **Privately Held**
WEB: www.lafargenorthamerica.com
SIC: 3241 1442 Cement, hydraulic; construction sand & gravel
HQ: Lafarge North America Inc.
8700 W Bryn Mawr Ave LI
Chicago IL 60631
703 480-3600

(G-7347)
LANCASTER KNIVES INC (PA)
165 Court St (14086-2399)
PHONE..................716 683-5050
Fax: 716 683-5068
Scott C Cant, *President*
Allen A Turton, *Engineer*
Franes M Cant, *Accounting Mgr*
Harold Landahl, *Mktg Dir*
Brian Turton, *Manager*
▲ **EMP**: 45 **EST**: 1896
SQ FT: 46,000
SALES (est): 5.5MM **Privately Held**
WEB: www.lancasterknives.com
SIC: 3423 3545 3469 3541 Knives, agricultural or industrial; shear knives; machine parts, stamped or pressed metal; machine tools, metal cutting type

(G-7348)
LANCE VALVES
15 Enterprise Dr (14086-9749)
PHONE..................716 681-5825
Eugene Miliczky, *Vice Pres*
Geoffrey Schrott, *Manager*
EMP: 8 **EST**: 1974
SQ FT: 6,000
SALES (est): 966.3K **Privately Held**
WEB: www.lancevalves.com
SIC: 3494 Valves & pipe fittings

(G-7349)
MANHASSET TOOL & DIE CO INC
4270 Walden Ave (14086-9770)
PHONE..................716 684-6066
Fax: 716 684-6067
Mark Fenimore, *President*
EMP: 10 **EST**: 1955
SALES (est): 1MM **Privately Held**
WEB: www.manhassettool.com
SIC: 3544 3542 Jigs & fixtures; jigs: inspection, gauging & checking; die sets for metal stamping (presses); dies & die holders for metal cutting, forming, die casting; punching & shearing machines; bending machines

(G-7350)
MARKAR ARCHITECTURAL PRODUCTS
Also Called: Adams Ridge
68 Ward Rd (14086-9779)
PHONE..................716 685-4104
Fax: 716 685-3919
EMP: 8 **Privately Held**
SIC: 3442 Mfg Metal Doors/Sash/Trim

(G-7351)
MOLDTECH INC
1900 Commerce Pkwy (14086-1735)
PHONE..................716 685-3344
H Wayne Gerhart, *Ch of Bd*
Rob Paladichuk, *Vice Pres*
Eric Bittner, *Opers Staff*
James H Wittman, *CFO*
James Wittman, *CFO*
▲ **EMP**: 45
SQ FT: 35,000
SALES (est): 15.7MM **Privately Held**
SIC: 3069 3061 Molded rubber products; mechanical rubber goods

(G-7352)
ORFFEO PRINTING & IMAGING INC
99 Cambria St (14086-1952)
P.O. Box 426 (14086-0426)
PHONE..................716 681-5757
Fax: 716 684-0444
Gregory Orffeo, *Ch of Bd*
Darci Abel, *Graphic Designe*
EMP: 5
SQ FT: 27,000
SALES (est): 2.7MM **Privately Held**
SIC: 2752 7331 Commercial printing, offset; direct mail advertising services

(G-7353)
PALMA TOOL & DIE COMPANY INC
40 Ward Rd (14086-9779)
PHONE..................716 681-4685
Fax: 716 681-4785
William D Tate Sr, *President*
Jeff Parks, *General Mgr*
Thomas Owczarak, *Vice Pres*
Tom Potter, *Sales Staff*
William Cocklin, *Manager*
EMP: 42 **EST**: 1962
SQ FT: 23,000
SALES (est): 8MM **Privately Held**
WEB: www.palmatool.com
SIC: 3544 Special dies & tools

(G-7354)
PARKER-HANNIFIN CORPORATION
4087 Walden Ave (14086-1512)
PHONE..................716 686-6400
Craig Dillworth, *Manager*
William Allhusen, *Sr Software Eng*
EMP: 126
SALES (corp-wide): 12B **Publicly Held**
SIC: 3594 Fluid power pumps
PA: Parker-Hannifin Corporation
6035 Parkland Blvd
Cleveland OH 44124
216 896-3000

(G-7355)
PARKER-HANNIFIN CORPORATION
Finite Airtek Filtration
4087 Walden Ave (14086-1512)
PHONE..................248 628-6017
John Carpenter, *Facilities Mgr*
Judy Ryan, *Mfg Staff*
Dan Ryan, *Research*
Gary Stack, *Chief Engr*
Thomas Comstock, *Product Mgr*
EMP: 82
SALES (corp-wide): 12B **Publicly Held**
WEB: www.parker.com
SIC: 3569 3714 3564 Filters; motor vehicle parts & accessories; blowers & fans
PA: Parker-Hannifin Corporation
6035 Parkland Blvd
Cleveland OH 44124
216 896-3000

(G-7356)
PARKER-HANNIFIN CORPORATION
Purification, Dehydration
4087 Walden Ave (14086-1512)
PHONE..................716 685-4040
Adam Hoot, *Purch Agent*
Johanne Ipperciel, *Human Res Mgr*
David Peters, *VP Sales*
Jon Hilberg, *Branch Mgr*
Jack Mahoney, *Manager*
EMP: 85
SALES (corp-wide): 12B **Publicly Held**
WEB: www.parker.com
SIC: 3585 3567 Refrigeration & heating equipment; industrial furnaces & ovens
PA: Parker-Hannifin Corporation
6035 Parkland Blvd
Cleveland OH 44124
216 896-3000

(G-7357)
PERFORMANCE ADVANTAGE CO INC
6 W Main St Lowr Rear (14086-2110)
PHONE..................716 683-7413

Richard Young, *President*
James Everett, *General Mgr*
Barb Kozurkiewicz, *Accounting Mgr*
Mickey McGuire, *Manager*
EMP: 15
SQ FT: 13,000
SALES (est): 2.2MM **Privately Held**
WEB: www.pactoolmounts.com
SIC: 3089 Plastic hardware & building products

(G-7358)
PFANNENBERG INC
68 Ward Rd (14086-9779)
PHONE.................................716 685-6866
Fax: 716 681-1521
Andreas Pfannenberg, *President*
Meyer ISA-Bianka, *Senior VP*
William Baron, *Vice Pres*
Laura Chasalow, *Vice Pres*
George McNamara, *Vice Pres*
◆ **EMP:** 52
SQ FT: 65,000
SALES (est): 15.5MM
SALES (corp-wide): 1.6MM **Privately Held**
WEB: www.pfannenbergusa.com
SIC: 3585 Air conditioning units, complete: domestic or industrial
PA: Pfannenberg Group Holding Gmbh
Werner-Witt-Str. 1
Hamburg 21035
407 341-20

(G-7359)
PFANNENBERG MANUFACTURING LLC
68 Ward Rd (14086-9779)
PHONE.................................716 685-6866
William Baron, *President*
Laura Chasalow, *Vice Pres*
Jennifer Bialasik, *Vice Pres*
Earl Rogalski, *Vice Pres*
EMP: 60
SQ FT: 57,000
SALES (est): 1.9MM **Privately Held**
SIC: 3585 Refrigeration & heating equipment

(G-7360)
PRZ TECHNOLOGIES INC
5490 Broadway St (14086-2220)
P.O. Box 369 (14086-0369)
PHONE.................................716 683-1300
Walt Przybyl, *President*
Danielle McGraw, *Opers Mgr*
Karan Andrea, *Accountant*
Michael Giddens, *Marketing Staff*
EMP: 15
SALES (est): 3.2MM **Privately Held**
SIC: 3599 Machine & other job shop work

(G-7361)
QUICK CUT GASKET & RUBBER
192 Erie St (14086-9532)
P.O. Box 330 (14086-0330)
PHONE.................................716 684-8628
Fax: 716 684-0169
Norman J Steinbruckner, *Ch of Bd*
Scott Steinbruckner, *Vice Pres*
EMP: 13
SQ FT: 10,000
SALES (est): 2.1MM **Privately Held**
WEB: www.quickcutgasket.com
SIC: 3053 Gaskets, all materials

(G-7362)
RAM PRECISION TOOL INC
139 Gunnville Rd (14086-9017)
PHONE.................................716 759-8722
Fax: 716 759-8747
Joseph Walter, *President*
Barbara M Walter, *Vice Pres*
EMP: 6
SQ FT: 6,000
SALES (est): 760K **Privately Held**
WEB: www.ramprecisiontool.com
SIC: 3544 Special dies & tools

(G-7363)
RICHARDS MACHINE TOOL CO INC
3753 Walden Ave (14086-1496)
PHONE.................................716 683-3380
Fax: 716 683-3408
Dennis Richards, *President*
Betsy Richards, *Vice Pres*
Peter Valenti, *QC Mgr*
Jeanne Walkowski, *Manager*
EMP: 23
SQ FT: 18,000
SALES (est): 2.4MM **Privately Held**
SIC: 3599 Machine shop, jobbing & repair

(G-7364)
RMF PRINTING TECHNOLOGIES INC
Also Called: Ogilvie Press
50 Pearl St (14086-1922)
PHONE.................................716 683-7500
Fax: 716 684-9012
Monica Castano, *Ch of Bd*
Keith Makey, *Maint Spvr*
Juan Carlos Yanez, *CFO*
▲ **EMP:** 50
SQ FT: 140,000
SALES (est): 17.3MM **Privately Held**
WEB: www.rmfprinttechnology.com
SIC: 2761 Manifold business forms

(G-7365)
ROLITE MFG INC
10 Wendling Ct (14086-9766)
PHONE.................................716 683-0259
Fax: 716 683-5406
Ron Roberts, *President*
Ronald Roberts, *President*
Thomas Debbins, *Vice Pres*
Frank Gurgol, *Director*
William Yeager, *Director*
▲ **EMP:** 25
SQ FT: 65,000
SALES (est): 7MM **Privately Held**
WEB: www.rolitemfg.com
SIC: 3469 3449 Stamping metal for the trade; custom roll formed products

(G-7366)
S3J ELECTRONICS LLC
2000 Commerce Pkwy (14086-1733)
PHONE.................................716 206-1309
EMP: 20
SALES (est): 4.2MM **Privately Held**
SIC: 3674 Mfg Semiconductors/Related Devices

(G-7367)
SEIBEL MODERN MFG & WLDG CORP
38 Palmer Pl (14086-2144)
PHONE.................................716 683-1536
Fax: 716 683-2552
Leon A Seibel, *Ch of Bd*
Mark Seibel, *Vice Pres*
Jeff Heath, *Engineer*
Lynne M Sobkowiak, *Manager*
▲ **EMP:** 85 EST: 1945
SQ FT: 70,000
SALES (est): 20.9MM **Privately Held**
WEB: www.seibelmodern.com
SIC: 3441 3443 Fabricated structural metal; fabricated plate work (boiler shop)

(G-7368)
SILICONE PRODUCTS & TECHNOLOGY
4471 Walden Ave (14086-9754)
PHONE.................................716 684-1155
Fax: 716 684-0310
Kim Jackson, *President*
Bill Boquard, *Vice Pres*
Michael Robinson, *Treasurer*
Jeannine Smolarek, *VP Finance*
Paul Schneeberger, *Sales Dir*
EMP: 150
SALES (est): 11.4MM
SALES (corp-wide): 13.6B **Publicly Held**
SIC: 2822 3544 Silicone rubbers; special dies, tools, jigs & fixtures
PA: Illinois Tool Works Inc.
155 Harlem Ave
Glenview IL 60025
847 724-7500

(G-7369)
STUTZMAN MANAGEMENT CORP
11 Saint Joseph St (14086-1800)
PHONE.................................800 735-2013
Gerard Sheldon, *President*
EMP: 15
SQ FT: 32,000
SALES (est): 2.3MM **Privately Held**
SIC: 3443 Fuel tanks (oil, gas, etc.): metal plate

(G-7370)
UNITED SILICONE INC
4471 Walden Ave (14086-9778)
PHONE.................................716 681-8222
Fax: 716 681-8789
Donato Curcio, *President*
Karla Dearstyne, *Business Mgr*
Robert Le Posa, *Vice Pres*
Kevin Vincent, *Accounting Mgr*
▲ **EMP:** 81
SQ FT: 80,000
SALES (est): 14.3MM
SALES (corp-wide): 13.6B **Publicly Held**
SIC: 3953 Pads, inking & stamping
PA: Illinois Tool Works Inc.
155 Harlem Ave
Glenview IL 60025
847 724-7500

(G-7371)
W N R PATTERN & TOOL INC
21 Pavement Rd (14086-9595)
PHONE.................................716 681-9334
Fax: 716 681-3520
Gary Machniak, *President*
Jeffrey Tucker, *Vice Pres*
EMP: 6
SQ FT: 6,000
SALES (est): 360K **Privately Held**
SIC: 3544 3543 Industrial molds; forms (molds), for foundry & plastics working machinery; industrial patterns

(G-7372)
WEB-TECH PACKAGING INC
500 Commerce Pkwy (14086-1793)
PHONE.................................716 684-4520
Fax: 716 684-6433
David C Rost, *President*
Kevin Kelly, *Shareholder*
William Rost, *Shareholder*
Kathleen Visciano, *Shareholder*
EMP: 16
SQ FT: 10,000
SALES (est): 3MM **Privately Held**
SIC: 2679 Tags & labels, paper

Lansing
Tompkins County

(G-7373)
CAYUGA CRUSHED STONE INC
87 Portland Point Rd (14882-9013)
P.O. Box 41 (14882-0041)
PHONE.................................607 533-4273
Fax: 607 533-7581
Thomas Besemer, *President*
Matthew Besemer, *Vice Pres*
Ruth Teeter, *Bd of Directors*
EMP: 20
SQ FT: 1,200
SALES (est): 4.1MM **Privately Held**
SIC: 1429 Igneous rock, crushed & broken-quarrying

(G-7374)
METAL IMPROVEMENT COMPANY LLC
Also Called: IMR Test Labs
131 Woodsedge Dr (14882-8940)
PHONE.................................607 533-7000
Don Shuman, *Branch Mgr*
EMP: 69
SALES (corp-wide): 2.1B **Publicly Held**
SIC: 3398 Shot peening (treating steel to reduce fatigue)
HQ: Metal Improvement Company, Llc
80 E State Rt 4 Ste 310
Paramus NJ 07652
201 843-7800

Larchmont
Westchester County

(G-7375)
INTERNATIONAL ROBOTICS INC
2001 Palmer Ave Ste LI1 (10538-2420)
P.O. Box 11474, Naples FL (34101-1474)
PHONE.................................914 630-1060
Robert Doornic, *CEO*
Jason Doornick, *Vice Pres*
EMP: 10
SALES (est): 1.1MM **Privately Held**
SIC: 3535 Robotic conveyors

(G-7376)
SOGGY DOGGY PRODUCTIONS LLC
50 Chestnut Ave (10538-3534)
PHONE.................................877 504-4811
Joanna Rein, *Mng Member*
▲ **EMP:** 4
SALES (est): 2MM **Privately Held**
SIC: 3999 Pet supplies

Latham
Albany County

(G-7377)
AB ENGINE
4a Northway Ln (12110-4809)
PHONE.................................518 557-3510
Alexander Bakharev, *Principal*
EMP: 8
SALES (est): 370K **Privately Held**
SIC: 3519 Internal combustion engines

(G-7378)
ACCUMETRICS INC
6 British American Blvd # 100 (12110-1476)
PHONE.................................716 684-0002
John Lally, *President*
EMP: 12
SALES (est): 1.6MM
SALES (corp-wide): 650.1MM **Publicly Held**
SIC: 3674 Semiconductors & related devices
HQ: Pcb Piezotronics, Inc.
3425 Walden Ave
Depew NY 14043
716 684-0001

(G-7379)
ACCUMETRICS ASSOCIATES INC
6 British American Blvd # 100 (12110-1476)
PHONE.................................518 393-2200
Fax: 518 393-3622
John M Reschovsky, *President*
Sandra Reschovsky, *Director*
EMP: 17
SQ FT: 5,000
SALES (est): 3MM **Privately Held**
WEB: www.accumetrix.com
SIC: 3674 Semiconductors & related devices

(G-7380)
ANGIODYNAMICS INC (PA)
14 Plaza Dr (12110-2166)
PHONE.................................518 795-1400
Howard W Donnelly, *Ch of Bd*
James C Clemmer, *President*
Gary Barrett, *Senior VP*
George Bourne, *Senior VP*
Chad Campbell, *Senior VP*
EMP: 277
SQ FT: 55,000
SALES: 353.8MM **Publicly Held**
WEB: www.angiodynamics.com
SIC: 3841 Surgical & medical instruments

(G-7381)
BAJAN GROUP INC
950 New Loudon Rd Ste 280 (12110-2111)
PHONE.................................518 464-2884
Anthony Lombordo, *President*

Latham - Albany County (G-7382)   **GEOGRAPHIC SECTION**

EMP: 8
SALES (corp-wide): 5MM **Privately Held**
WEB: www.bajangroup.com
SIC: 2752 Commercial printing, offset
PA: The Bajan Group Inc
    950 New Loudon Rd Ste 280
    Latham NY 12110
    518 464-2884

(G-7382)
BRITISH AMERICAN PUBLISHING
19 British American Blvd (12110-6405)
PHONE 518 786-6000
Fax: 518 786-6001
Bernard F Conners, *Chairman*
Francis Coughlin, *Treasurer*
John T De Graff, *Admin Sec*
EMP: 60
SALES: 17MM **Privately Held**
WEB: www.bapublish.com
SIC: 2731 Books: publishing only

(G-7383)
BULLOCK BOYS LLC
400 Old Loudon Rd (12110-2908)
PHONE 518 783-6161
James Morrell, *CEO*
EMP: 15
SQ FT: 25,500
SALES (est): 780.3K **Privately Held**
SIC: 2599 Bar, restaurant & cafeteria furniture

(G-7384)
BUSINESS FIRST OF NEW YORK
Also Called: Business Review
40 British American Blvd (12110-1421)
PHONE 518 640-6800
Caroline Jones, *General Mgr*
Mike Hendricks, *Editor*
Todd Kehoe, *Engineer*
Brian Crouth, *Accounts Exec*
Melissa Mangini, *Creative Dir*
EMP: 23
SALES (corp-wide): 1.5B **Privately Held**
SIC: 2711 Newspapers: publishing only, not printed on site
HQ: Business First Of New York Inc
    465 Main St Ste 100
    Buffalo NY 14203
    716 854-5822

(G-7385)
CALLANAN INDUSTRIES INC
Also Called: Clemente Latham Concrete
9 Fonda Rd (12110)
PHONE 518 785-5666
Fax: 518 785-3846
Mark Clemente, *Manager*
EMP: 8
SALES (corp-wide): 28.6B **Privately Held**
WEB: www.callanan.com
SIC: 3272 Concrete products, precast
HQ: Callanan Industries, Inc.
    8 Southwoods Blvd Ste 4
    Albany NY 12211
    518 374-2222

(G-7386)
CARR MANUFACTURING JEWELERS
Also Called: Carr Jewelers
22 West Ln (12110-5320)
PHONE 518 783-6093
Fax: 518 783-3376
W James Dix, *President*
James E Dix, *Vice Pres*
Gloria Dix, *Treasurer*
EMP: 5
SALES (est): 351.2K **Privately Held**
SIC: 3911 7631 5944 Jewelry, precious metal; jewelry repair services; jewelry stores

(G-7387)
D & W DIESEL INC
51 Sicker Rd Ste 3 (12110-1505)
PHONE 518 437-1300
Jeffrey Hartgraves, *Manager*
EMP: 12
SALES (corp-wide): 105.2MM **Privately Held**
WEB: www.dwdiesel.com
SIC: 3519 Diesel engine rebuilding

PA: D & W Diesel, Inc.
    1503 Clark Street Rd
    Auburn NY 13021
    315 253-5300

(G-7388)
EAZYLIFT ALBANY LLC
836 Troy Schenectady Rd (12110-2424)
P.O. Box 340 (12110-0340)
PHONE 518 452-6929
Theresa Farrigan,
▲ EMP: 5
SALES: 950K **Privately Held**
SIC: 3534 Elevators & moving stairways

(G-7389)
EMERGENT POWER INC (HQ)
968 Albany Shaker Rd (12110-1401)
PHONE 201 441-3590
Andrew Marsh, *President*
EMP: 5
SALES (est): 19.7MM
SALES (corp-wide): 85.9MM **Publicly Held**
SIC: 2679 Fuel cell forms, cardboard: made from purchased material
PA: Plug Power Inc.
    968 Albany Shaker Rd
    Latham NY 12110
    518 782-7700

(G-7390)
G AND G SERVICE
21 Nelson Ave (12110-1805)
PHONE 518 785-9247
Greg Gilbert,
EMP: 5
SALES (est): 336.9K **Privately Held**
SIC: 3089 8999 Plastics products; services

(G-7391)
HOWMEDICA OSTEONICS CORP
2 Northway Ln (12110-4820)
PHONE 518 783-1880
Steve Bulger, *Branch Mgr*
EMP: 9
SALES (corp-wide): 11.3B **Publicly Held**
SIC: 3842 Surgical appliances & supplies
HQ: Howmedica Osteonics Corp.
    325 Corporate Dr
    Mahwah NJ 07430
    201 831-5000

(G-7392)
IMPERIAL POOLS INC (PA)
33 Wade Rd (12110-2613)
PHONE 518 786-1200
Fax: 518 786-0954
William Churchman, *CEO*
John V Maiuccoro, *President*
Katie Maiuccoro, *Principal*
Robert Burke, *Vice Pres*
Gary Maiuccoro, *Vice Pres*
◆ EMP: 123 EST: 1966
SQ FT: 100,000
SALES (est): 70MM **Privately Held**
WEB: www.imperialpools.com
SIC: 3949 5091 Swimming pools, except plastic; swimming pools, equipment & supplies

(G-7393)
JUNIOR ACHEVEMENT OF EASTRN NY
8 Stanley Cir Ste 8 (12110-2606)
PHONE 518 783-4336
Fax: 518 783-4346
Ed Murray, *President*
Tovah Lisky, *Marketing Staff*
EMP: 5
SALES (est): 580.1K **Privately Held**
SIC: 3613 Distribution cutouts

(G-7394)
KAFKO (US) CORP
787 Watervliet Shaker Rd (12110-2211)
PHONE 877 721-7665
Mark Laven, *President*
EMP: 5
SALES (est): 447.8K
SALES (corp-wide): 218.9MM **Privately Held**
SIC: 3999 Manufacturing industries

PA: Latham International, Inc.
    787 Watervliet Shaker Rd
    Latham NY 12110
    518 783-7776

(G-7395)
KJCKD INC (PA)
Also Called: Camelot Print & Copy Centers
630 Columbia St Ext Ste 2 (12110-3063)
PHONE 518 435-9696
John Derboghossian, *CEO*
Cristene Derboghossian, *COO*
EMP: 3 EST: 2014
SQ FT: 20,000
SALES (est): 1MM **Privately Held**
SIC: 2752 2741 7334 7336 Photo-offset printing; posters: publishing & printing; photocopying & duplicating services; commercial art & graphic design; optical scanning data service

(G-7396)
LATHAM INTERNATIONAL INC (PA)
787 Watervliet Shaker Rd (12110-2211)
PHONE 518 783-7776
Mark Laven, *President*
Ron Crowley, *VP Opers*
Gary Whitcher, *VP Opers*
Tom Correll, *Plant Mgr*
Lynn Hyatt, *Safety Mgr*
◆ EMP: 1 EST: 2004
SQ FT: 90,000
SALES (est): 218.9MM **Privately Held**
WEB: www.pacificpools.com
SIC: 3086 3081 Plastics foam products; vinyl film & sheet

(G-7397)
LATHAM POOL PRODUCTS INC (PA)
787 Watervliet Shaker Rd (12110-2211)
P.O. Box 550, Jane Lew WV (26378-0550)
PHONE 518 951-1000
Fax: 518 785-0004
Mark Laven, *President*
Ray Ludwig, *Controller*
Jennifer Lyons, *HR Admin*
Richard Piontkowski, *VP Sales*
Kieth Dodge, *Sales Mgr*
◆ EMP: 172
SQ FT: 25,000
SALES (est): 159.6MM **Privately Held**
SIC: 3949 Swimming pools, except plastic

(G-7398)
LATHAM POOL PRODUCTS INC
Also Called: Latham Manufacturing
787 Watervliet Shaker Rd (12110-2211)
PHONE 260 432-8731
Phil Grogan, *Finance Mgr*
Matt Geyman, *Branch Mgr*
Kyle Smart, *Manager*
EMP: 44 **Privately Held**
SIC: 3086 Plastics foam products
PA: Latham Pool Products, Inc.
    787 Watervliet Shaker Rd
    Latham NY 12110

(G-7399)
LATHAM SOFTWARE SCIENCES INC
678 Troy Schenectady Rd # 104 (12110-2502)
PHONE 518 785-1100
Michael Dellavilla, *President*
John D Miller, *Vice Pres*
EMP: 12
SALES (est): 840K **Privately Held**
SIC: 7372 Prepackaged software

(G-7400)
LATORRE ORTHOPEDIC LABORATORY
960 Troy Schenectady Rd (12110-1609)
PHONE 518 786-8655
Timothy Lacy, *President*
EMP: 15
SALES (est): 930K **Privately Held**
SIC: 3842 Orthopedic appliances; prosthetic appliances

(G-7401)
MARKTECH INTERNATIONAL CORP (PA)
Also Called: Marktech Optoelectronics
3 Northway Ln N (12110-2232)
PHONE 518 956-2980
Mark G Campito, *Ch of Bd*
Clive A Sofe, *President*
Joseph Andrascik, *Vice Pres*
Han CHI, *Engineer*
Vincent Forte, *Engineer*
▲ EMP: 25
SALES (est): 3.6MM **Privately Held**
WEB: www.marktechopto.com
SIC: 3674 Semiconductors & related devices

(G-7402)
PEPSI BEVERAGES CO
Also Called: Pepsico
421 Old Niskayuna Rd (12110-1566)
PHONE 518 782-2150
EMP: 6
SALES (est): 539.8K **Privately Held**
SIC: 2086 Carbonated soft drinks, bottled & canned

(G-7403)
PHILIPS MEDICAL SYSTEMS MR (DH)
Also Called: Philips Healthcare
450 Old Niskayuna Rd (12110-1569)
PHONE 518 782-1122
Stephen H Rusckowski, *CEO*
Leo Blecher, *President*
Richard Stevens, *President*
Thomas J O'Brien, *Exec VP*
Thomas J Obrien, *Exec VP*
◆ EMP: 400
SQ FT: 146,000
SALES (est): 203.1MM
SALES (corp-wide): 25.9B **Privately Held**
SIC: 3845 3674 3679 Electromedical equipment; magnetic resonance imaging device, nuclear; integrated circuits, semiconductor networks, etc.; cryogenic cooling devices for infrared detectors, masers; cores, magnetic

(G-7404)
PLUG POWER INC (PA)
968 Albany Shaker Rd (12110-1428)
PHONE 518 782-7700
Fax: 518 782-9060
George C McNamee, *Ch of Bd*
Andrew Marsh, *President*
Keith C Schmid, *COO*
Gerard L Conway Jr, *Senior VP*
John Cococcia, *Vice Pres*
▲ EMP: 277 EST: 1997
SQ FT: 140,000
SALES: 85.9MM **Publicly Held**
WEB: www.plugpower.com
SIC: 2679 Fuel cell forms, cardboard: made from purchased material

(G-7405)
RESPONSELINK INC
Also Called: Responselink of Albany
31 Dussault Dr (12110-2303)
PHONE 518 424-7776
Jason Kutey, *President*
EMP: 6
SALES (est): 365.1K **Privately Held**
SIC: 3841 Surgical & medical instruments

(G-7406)
TIRE CONVERSION TECH INC
874 Albany Shaker Rd (12110-1416)
PHONE 518 372-1600
Fax: 518 372-5505
Garen Szablewski, *CEO*
Jeff Henry, *Vice Pres*
Jack Hout, *Accounts Mgr*
▲ EMP: 25
SQ FT: 10,000
SALES (est): 4.2MM **Privately Held**
WEB: www.tire-conversion.com
SIC: 3069 Custom compounding of rubber materials

(G-7407)
TRANE US INC
301 Old Niskayuna Rd # 1 (12110-2276)
PHONE 518 785-1315

Fax: 518 785-4359
William Seward, *Branch Mgr*
EMP: 35 Privately Held
SIC: 3585 Refrigeration & heating equipment
HQ: Trane U.S. Inc.
1 Centennial Ave Ste 101
Piscataway NJ 08854
732 652-7100

(G-7408)
TRANSTECH SYSTEMS INC (PA)
900 Albany Shaker Rd (12110-1416)
PHONE..................518 370-5558
Fax: 518 370-5538
David Apkarian, *CEO*
Mike Debrino, *Vice Pres*
David Dussault, *Director*
Kevin Lynch, *Director*
Chet Opalka, *Director*
▼ **EMP: 21**
SQ FT: 14,000
SALES: 3.9MM Privately Held
WEB: www.transtechsys.com
SIC: 3823 8731 Industrial instrmnts msrmnt display/control process variable; commercial physical research

(G-7409)
UL INFORMATION & INSIGHTS INC (DH)
23 British American Blvd # 2 (12110-1429)
PHONE..................518 640-9200
Lou Desorbo, *President*
Tom Carter, *Vice Pres*
Dave Spore, *Project Mgr*
Kim Desorbo, *Controller*
Gabriel Valentin-Ramos, *Sr Project Mgr*
EMP: 39
SALES (est): 9.1MM
SALES (corp-wide): 22.6MM Privately Held
WEB: www.thewercs.com
SIC: 7372 8748 Business oriented computer software; business consulting
HQ: UI Llc
333 Pfingsten Rd
Northbrook IL 60062
847 272-8800

(G-7410)
VINYL WORKS INC
33 Wade Rd (12110-2613)
PHONE..................518 786-1200
John Maiuccoro, *President*
EMP: 50 EST: 1971
SALES (est): 3.7MM Privately Held
WEB: www.thevinylworks.com
SIC: 2394 Liners & covers, fabric: made from purchased materials

(G-7411)
WILLIAM BOYD PRINTING CO INC
Also Called: Boyd Printing Company
4 Weed Rd Ste 1 (12110-2939)
PHONE..................518 339-5832
Henry R Bosselman, *Ch of Bd*
Jane Q Carey, *President*
Stacey Dunning, *Principal*
James Blaauboer, *Vice Pres*
Carl R Johnson, *Vice Pres*
EMP: 120 EST: 1889
SQ FT: 81,000
SALES (est): 4.9MM Privately Held
SIC: 2711 2752 Commercial printing & newspaper publishing combined; commercial printing, lithographic

Laurelton
Queens County

(G-7412)
CLINTON CREAMERY INC
13221 220th St (11413-1547)
PHONE..................917 324-9699
Robyn Clinton, *President*
Cedrizk Clinton, *Vice Pres*
EMP: 14
SALES (est): 690K Privately Held
SIC: 2024 5451 Ice cream & frozen desserts; ice cream (packaged)

(G-7413)
EPIC PHARMA LLC
22715 N Conduit Ave (11413-3134)
PHONE..................718 276-8600
Manish Potti, *General Mgr*
Jai Narine, *Exec VP*
Christopher Aupperlee, *Vice Pres*
Marcus Taylor, *Research*
Paul Cook, *Engineer*
▲ **EMP: 160**
SQ FT: 110,000
SALES (est): 67.1MM Privately Held
SIC: 2834 Pharmaceutical preparations

(G-7414)
NOVARTIS CORPORATION
22715 N Conduit Ave (11413-3134)
PHONE..................718 276-8600
Kumar Rathnam, *Vice Pres*
EMP: 56
SALES (corp-wide): 48.5B Privately Held
WEB: www.novartis.com
SIC: 2834 Pharmaceutical preparations
HQ: Novartis Corporation
1 S Ridgedle Ave 122
East Hanover NJ 07936
212 307-1122

(G-7415)
NOVARTIS PHARMACEUTICALS CORP
22715 N Conduit Ave (11413-3134)
PHONE..................718 276-8600
EMP: 8
SALES (est): 2.2MM
SALES (corp-wide): 49.4B Privately Held
SIC: 2834 Pharmaceutical Preparations
PA: Novartis Ag
Lichtstrasse 35
Basel BS 4056
613 241-111

Lawrence
Nassau County

(G-7416)
ATLAZ INTERNATIONAL LTD
298 Lawrence Ave Unit 1 (11559-1268)
PHONE..................516 239-1854
Fax: 516 239-1939
Loretta Zalta, *President*
Adam Zalta, *Vice Pres*
Andre Zalta, *Vice Pres*
EMP: 11
SQ FT: 3,000
SALES (est): 2.5MM Privately Held
WEB: www.atlaz.com
SIC: 3577 5045 5112 Computer peripheral equipment; computer peripheral equipment; stationery & office supplies

(G-7417)
JOHN J RICHARDSON
Also Called: Gad Systems
12 Bernard St (11559-1245)
PHONE..................516 538-6339
John J Richardson, *Owner*
EMP: 15
SQ FT: 4,000
SALES: 900K Privately Held
SIC: 3695 Computer software tape & disks: blank, rigid & floppy

(G-7418)
LAST STRAW INC
Also Called: Zenith Promotions
22 Lawrence Ln Unit 1 (11559-1137)
P.O. Box 960177, Inwood (11096-0177)
PHONE..................516 371-2727
Fax: 516 371-2442
Sharon Hecht, *President*
Maria Lafichi, *Shareholder*
▲ **EMP: 40 EST: 1995**
SQ FT: 9,000
SALES (est): 7.3MM Privately Held
WEB: www.zenithpromotions.com
SIC: 2656 5092 Straws, drinking: made from purchased material; toys & games

(G-7419)
M W MICROWAVE CORP
45 Auerbach Ln (11559-2529)
PHONE..................516 295-1814
Fax: 631 420-0621
Mariam Wiesenfeld, *President*
EMP: 12 EST: 1970
SQ FT: 10,000
SALES (est): 1MM Privately Held
SIC: 3679 Waveguides & fittings; microwave components

(G-7420)
MEDITUB INCORPORATED
11 Wedgewood Ln (11559-1427)
P.O. Box 668 (11559-0668)
PHONE..................866 633-4882
Joseph Swartz, *President*
Mark Barnathan, *Sales Staff*
EMP: 19
SALES (est): 621.6K
SALES (corp-wide): 16.7MM Privately Held
SIC: 3272 Bathtubs, concrete
PA: Spa World Corporation
1 Oakwood Blvd Ste 200
Hollywood FL 33020
866 588-8008

(G-7421)
NEW YORK RHBILITATIVE SVCS LLC
135 Rockaway Tpke Ste 107 (11559-1023)
PHONE..................516 239-0990
Michael Nadata, *Owner*
EMP: 14
SALES (est): 1.6MM Privately Held
SIC: 3842 Prosthetic appliances

(G-7422)
PREMIER SKIRTING PRODUCTS INC
Also Called: Premier Skrting Tblecloths Too
241 Mill St (11559-1209)
PHONE..................516 239-6581
Fax: 516 239-6810
Ross Yudin, *CEO*
Beth Yudin, *President*
Linda Ehrlich, *Corp Secy*
Jessica Yudin, *Marketing Mgr*
EMP: 16
SQ FT: 8,500
SALES (est): 1.5MM Privately Held
WEB: www.premierskirting.com
SIC: 2392 Tablecloths: made from purchased materials; napkins, fabric & non-woven: made from purchased materials

(G-7423)
RASON ASPHALT INC
4 Johnson Rd (11559-1036)
PHONE..................516 239-7880
Fax: 516 239-7621
Fred Wallenquest, *Manager*
EMP: 6
SALES (corp-wide): 10.2MM Privately Held
WEB: www.rason1.com
SIC: 2951 Asphalt & asphaltic paving mixtures (not from refineries)
PA: Rason Asphalt Inc.
Rr 110
Farmingdale NY 11735
631 293-6210

(G-7424)
RICHNER COMMUNICATIONS INC
Also Called: Oceanside-Island Park Herald
379 Central Ave (11559-1607)
PHONE..................516 569-4000
Rhonda Glickman, *Vice Pres*
Karen Mengel, *Prdtn Mgr*
Ellen Frisch, *Accounts Exec*
Vicki Kaplan, *Accounts Exec*
Cliff Richner, *Branch Mgr*
EMP: 5
SALES (corp-wide): 16.3MM Privately Held
SIC: 2711 Newspapers: publishing only, not printed on site
PA: Richner Communications, Inc.
2 Endo Blvd
Garden City NY 11530
516 569-4000

(G-7425)
SEVILLE CENTRAL MIX CORP
101 Johnson Rd (11559)
PHONE..................516 239-8333
Fax: 516 239-7496
Peter Buck, *Manager*
EMP: 30
SALES (corp-wide): 13.1MM Privately Held
WEB: www.sevillecentralmix.com
SIC: 3273 Ready-mixed concrete
PA: Seville Central Mix Corp.
157 Albany Ave
Freeport NY 11520
516 868-3000

(G-7426)
TG PEPPE INC
Also Called: Doery Awning Co
299 Rockaway Tpke Unit B (11559-1269)
PHONE..................516 239-7852
Fax: 516 239-0696
Thomas Peppe, *President*
Gregory Peppe, *Vice Pres*
Sabrina Peppe, *Office Mgr*
EMP: 8
SQ FT: 6,000
SALES (est): 967.6K Privately Held
SIC: 2394 7699 Awnings, fabric: made from purchased materials; awning repair shop

Le Roy
Genesee County

(G-7427)
ALUMINUM INJECTION MOLD CO LLC
8741 Lake Street Rd Ste 4 (14482-9381)
PHONE..................585 502-6087
Gerald Ayers, *Vice Pres*
Russ Bailey, *Admin Asst*
Tom Bergman,
EMP: 8
SQ FT: 12,000
SALES (est): 1.4MM Privately Held
WEB: www.aluminuminjectionmold.com
SIC: 3089 Injection molded finished plastic products

(G-7428)
BATAVIA LEGAL PRINTING INC
7 Bank St (14482-1413)
P.O. Box 57, Stafford (14143-0057)
PHONE..................585 768-2100
Susan Duyssen, *President*
Pat Maher, *Manager*
EMP: 5
SQ FT: 4,000
SALES: 350K Privately Held
WEB: www.batavialegal.com
SIC: 2759 Laser printing

(G-7429)
CK COATINGS
57 North St Ste 150 (14482-1143)
P.O. Box 203 (14482-0203)
PHONE..................585 502-0425
Linda Wright, *Owner*
EMP: 5
SALES (est): 487.6K Privately Held
SIC: 3827 Optical instruments & lenses

(G-7430)
DOLOMITE PRODUCTS COMPANY INC
8250 Golf Rd (14482)
PHONE..................585 768-7295
Fax: 585 768-7246
Matt McCormick, *Manager*
Matt M Cormick, *Manager*
EMP: 12
SQ FT: 9,122
SALES (corp-wide): 28.6B Privately Held
WEB: www.dolomitegroup.com
SIC: 2951 Paving mixtures
HQ: Dolomite Products Company Inc.
1150 Penfield Rd
Rochester NY 14625
315 524-1998

Le Roy - Genesee County (G-7431)

(G-7431)
DRAY ENTERPRISES INC
Also Called: Le Roy Pennysaver
1 Church St (14482-1017)
P.O. Box 190 (14482-0190)
PHONE.....................................585 768-2201
Fax: 585 768-2201
David J Grayson Jr, *President*
Danette L Grayson, *Admin Sec*
EMP: 14
SQ FT: 16,000
SALES (est): 1.1MM **Privately Held**
WEB: www.leroyny.com
SIC: 2711 7389 Newspapers; embroidering of advertising on shirts, etc.

(G-7432)
DUZMOR PAINTING INC
Also Called: Finishing Line, The
7959 E Main Rd (14482-9726)
P.O. Box 135 (14482-0135)
PHONE.....................................585 768-4760
Fax: 585 768-2296
Peter Mc Quillen, *President*
Judy Mc Quillen, *Vice Pres*
EMP: 6
SQ FT: 10,000
SALES (est): 757.8K **Privately Held**
WEB: www.thefinishinglineco.com
SIC: 3479 Painting of metal products

(G-7433)
HELIOJET CLEANING TECH INC
57 North St Ste 120 (14482-1143)
PHONE.....................................585 768-8710
Russell Knisel Jr, *President*
Scott Meurer, *Vice Pres*
Katie Murrock, *Financial Exec*
Lee Nicodemus, *Marketing Mgr*
EMP: 12 **EST:** 1980
SQ FT: 11,640
SALES (est): 1.1MM **Privately Held**
WEB: www.heliojet.com
SIC: 3589 High pressure cleaning equipment

(G-7434)
ICON DESIGN LLC
9 Lent Ave (14482-1009)
PHONE.....................................585 768-6040
Fax: 585 768-7558
Wendell Castle,
EMP: 25
SALES (est): 3MM **Privately Held**
WEB: www.icondesign.com
SIC: 2511 Wood household furniture

(G-7435)
J & L PRECISION CO INC
9222 Summit Street Rd (14482-8950)
PHONE.....................................585 768-6388
James Lytle, *President*
Laurita Lytle, *Corp Secy*
EMP: 8
SQ FT: 6,500
SALES (est): 720K **Privately Held**
SIC: 3599 Machine shop, jobbing & repair; electrical discharge machining (EDM)

(G-7436)
LAPP INSULATORS LLC
130 Gilbert St (14482-1392)
PHONE.....................................585 768-6221
Fax: 585 768-5768
Bernhard Kahl, *CEO*
Rob Johnson, *President*
Wayne Subject, *Plant Mgr*
Joe Burns, *Engineer*
Andreas Stockhausen, *Engineer*
▲ **EMP:** 125
SQ FT: 651,000
SALES (est): 28.1MM **Privately Held**
WEB: www.lappinsulator.com
SIC: 3264 3644 Insulators, electrical: porcelain; noncurrent-carrying wiring services; insulators & insulation materials, electrical

(G-7437)
LEROY PLASTICS INC
20 Lent Ave (14482-1010)
PHONE.....................................585 768-8158
Fax: 585 768-4283
Ernest Truax, *President*
George Jinks, *QC Mgr*
Kay Miggins, *Office Mgr*
C Freeman, *Technical Staff*
◆ **EMP:** 61
SQ FT: 62,305
SALES: 6.9MM **Privately Held**
WEB: www.leroyplastics.com
SIC: 3498 Fabricated pipe & fittings

(G-7438)
MARMACH MACHINE INC
11 Lent Ave (14482)
PHONE.....................................585 768-8800
Fax: 585 768-4809
John M Lynch, *President*
J P Lynch, *Business Mgr*
EMP: 6
SALES (est): 873.7K **Privately Held**
SIC: 3451 Screw machine products

(G-7439)
MOFFITT FAN CORPORATION
54 Church St (14482-1037)
PHONE.....................................585 768-7010
John Moffitt, *Ch of Bd*
Terence R Wirth II, *President*
Michael Andorka, *Plant Mgr*
Barbara Snell, *Office Mgr*
EMP: 40
SQ FT: 50,000
SALES (est): 10.1MM **Privately Held**
SIC: 3564 Blowers & fans; blowers & fans

(G-7440)
PCORE ELECTRIC COMPANY INC
135 Gilbert St (14482-1353)
PHONE.....................................585 768-1200
Fax: 585 768-1235
Timothy Powers, *President*
Andrew McNulty, *Engineer*
Eric Weatherbee, *Senior Engr*
Peter G Schulpz, *Director*
▲ **EMP:** 64
SQ FT: 100,000
SALES (est): 14.6MM
SALES (corp-wide): 3.5B **Publicly Held**
WEB: www.pcoreelectric.com
SIC: 3325 Bushings, cast steel: except investment
PA: Hubbell Incorporated
40 Waterview Dr
Shelton CT 06484
475 882-4000

(G-7441)
T S P CORP
Also Called: Thom McGinnes Excavating Plbg
78 One Half Lake St (14482)
PHONE.....................................585 768-6769
Thomas W McGinnis, *President*
EMP: 10
SQ FT: 1,000
SALES: 550K **Privately Held**
SIC: 3531 Plows: construction, excavating & grading

Leicester
Livingston County

(G-7442)
CPAC INC (DH)
Also Called: Stanley Home Products
2364 State Route 20a (14481-9734)
P.O. Box 175 (14481-0175)
PHONE.....................................585 382-3223
Fax: 585 382-3031
Thomas N Hendrickson, *Principal*
David P Biehn, *Senior VP*
Thomas N Hedrickso, *Project Mgr*
Sue Doerflinger, *Opers Mgr*
Tish Johnson, *Purchasing*
▼ **EMP:** 50
SQ FT: 31,262
SALES (est): 55.4MM
SALES (corp-wide): 75.9MM **Privately Held**
SIC: 2842 3991 2392 2841 Specialty cleaning, polishes & sanitation goods; specialty cleaning preparations; sanitation preparations, disinfectants & deodorants; brooms & brushes; mops, floor & dust; soap & other detergents; shampoos, rinses, conditioners: hair; cosmetic preparations; photographic equipment & supplies; sensitized film, cloth & paper; photographic processing chemicals
HQ: Buckingham Cpac Inc
2364 State Route 20a
Leicester NY 14481
585 382-3223

(G-7443)
CPAC EQUIPMENT INC
2364 State Route 20a (14481-9734)
P.O. Box 175 (14481-0175)
PHONE.....................................585 382-3223
Thomas Weldgen, *CEO*
Natalie Gayton, *Controller*
EMP: 16
SQ FT: 15,000
SALES (est): 2.3MM **Privately Held**
WEB: www.cpacequipment.com
SIC: 3843 Sterilizers, dental; dental equipment; glue, dental
PA: Integrated Medical Technologies, Inc.
2422 E Washington St # 103
Bloomington IL 61704
309 662-3614

(G-7444)
SENECA FOODS CORPORATION
Also Called: Comstock Food
5705 Rte 36 (14481)
P.O. Box 278 (14481-0278)
PHONE.....................................585 658-2211
Fax: 585 658-3848
Cameron Ellis, *Warehouse Mgr*
Flo Mullen, *QC Mgr*
Mike Hanchette, *Manager*
EMP: 40
SALES (corp-wide): 1.2B **Publicly Held**
SIC: 2033 Vegetables: packaged in cans, jars, etc.
PA: Seneca Foods Corporation
3736 S Main St
Marion NY 14505
315 926-8100

Levittown
Nassau County

(G-7445)
APOGEE RETAIL NY
3041 Hempstead Tpke (11756-1332)
PHONE.....................................516 731-1727
EMP: 5 **EST:** 2010
SALES (est): 379.5K **Privately Held**
SIC: 2329 Men's & boys' clothing

(G-7446)
AVALONICS INC
94 Gardiners Ave Ste 164 (11756-3705)
PHONE.....................................516 238-7074
Sharjeel Ansari, *CEO*
Raheel Ansari, *President*
Chris Papas, *Manager*
EMP: 7
SALES: 1.3MM **Privately Held**
WEB: www.security-cameras-cctv.com
SIC: 3699 Security devices

(G-7447)
BEYOND BEAUTY BASICS LLC
3359 Hempstead Tpke (11756-1310)
PHONE.....................................516 731-7100
Claudie Oslian,
EMP: 17
SALES (est): 1.7MM **Privately Held**
SIC: 2899 Core wash or wax

(G-7448)
CCZ READY MIX CONCRETE CORP
2 Loring Rd (11756-1516)
PHONE.....................................516 579-7352
Michael Zampini, *President*
EMP: 5
SALES (est): 531.3K **Privately Held**
SIC: 3273 Ready-mixed concrete

(G-7449)
DEUNALL CORPORATION
147 Blacksmith Rd E (11756-3127)
PHONE.....................................516 667-8875
Kevin Park, *President*
Steve Yoon, *Vice Pres*
Myeoan Kim, *Shareholder*
Russell Lin, *Shareholder*
Hugh Thung, *Shareholder*
EMP: 205
SQ FT: 2,800
SALES (est): 4MM **Privately Held**
SIC: 2342 Foundation garments, women's

(G-7450)
GLITNIR TICKETING INC
Also Called: Glitner Ticketing
3 Snapdragon Ln (11756-3315)
PHONE.....................................516 390-5168
Gordon Krstacic, *CEO*
EMP: 5
SALES (est): 488.9K **Privately Held**
WEB: www.glitnir.com
SIC: 7372 Prepackaged software

(G-7451)
KB MILLWORK INC
36 Grey Ln (11756-4411)
P.O. Box 395 (11756-0395)
PHONE.....................................516 280-2183
Kenneth Wright, *President*
EMP: 5
SQ FT: 1,200
SALES: 1.5MM **Privately Held**
SIC: 2431 Millwork

Lewis
Essex County

(G-7452)
UPSTONE MATERIALS INC
Also Called: Lewis Sand & Gravel
Rr 9 (12950)
PHONE.....................................518 873-2275
Ron Haugh, *Manager*
EMP: 9
SALES (corp-wide): 77.1MM **Privately Held**
WEB: www.graymont-ab.com
SIC: 2951 3273 3272 3241 Asphalt paving mixtures & blocks; ready-mixed concrete; concrete products; cement, hydraulic
HQ: Upstone Materials Inc.
111 Quarry Rd
Plattsburgh NY 12901
518 561-5321

Lewiston
Niagara County

(G-7453)
450 RIDGE ST INC
Also Called: Mellen Pressroom & Bindery
450 Ridge St (14092-1206)
P.O. Box 450 (14092-0450)
PHONE.....................................716 754-2789
Ruth Koheil, *President*
Dick Cessna, *Controller*
EMP: 7
SQ FT: 1,488
SALES (est): 900K **Privately Held**
SIC: 2731 2752 2732 Books: publishing & printing; commercial printing, lithographic; book printing

(G-7454)
EASTON PHARMACEUTICALS INC
736 Center St Ste 5 (14092-1706)
PHONE.....................................347 284-0192
Joseph Slechta, *President*
Peter Rothbart, *Treasurer*
Elena Milantoni, *Administration*
EMP: 6 **EST:** 1998

SALES (est): 173.3K **Privately Held**
SIC: 2834 8731 Ointments; commercial physical research; commercial research laboratory; medical research, commercial

(G-7455)
EDWIN MELLEN PRESS INC
442 Center St (14092-1604)
PHONE..................................716 754-2796
Herbert Richardson, *President*
EMP: 38
SALES (est): 1.5MM **Privately Held**
SIC: 2731 Book publishing

(G-7456)
PROTOCASE INCORPORATED
210 S 8th St (14092-1702)
PHONE..................................866 849-3911
Steve Lilley, *President*
Doug Milburn, *Vice Pres*
Patricia McCann, *Controller*
Shirley Evely, *Sales Staff*
Shane Maclean, *Manager*
EMP: 138
SALES (est): 8.6MM **Privately Held**
WEB: www.protocase.com
SIC: 3499 3466 Furniture parts, metal; crowns & closures

(G-7457)
PSR PRESS LTD
Also Called: Mellen Press, The
415 Ridge St (14092-1205)
P.O. Box 450 (14092-0450)
PHONE..................................716 754-2266
Fax: 716 754-4056
Herbert Richardson, *CEO*
Dick Cessna, *Finance Mgr*
John Rupnow, *Director*
EMP: 12
SQ FT: 2,000
SALES (est): 1MM **Privately Held**
WEB: www.mellenpress.com
SIC: 2731 Book publishing

Liberty
Sullivan County

(G-7458)
CRANESVILLE BLOCK CO INC
Also Called: Cranesville Concrete Co
1794 State Route 52 (12754-8304)
PHONE..................................845 292-1585
Fax: 845 292-2083
Stephen Miller, *Manager*
EMP: 10
SALES (corp-wide): 45.4MM **Privately Held**
SIC: 3273 Ready-mixed concrete
PA: Cranesville Block Co., Inc.
  1250 Riverfront Ctr
  Amsterdam NY 12010
  518 684-6154

(G-7459)
IDEAL SNACKS CORPORATION
89 Mill St (12754-2038)
PHONE..................................845 292-7000
Fax: 845 292-7000
Zeke Alenick, *President*
Miriam Ehrenberg, *Vice Pres*
Steven Van Poucke, *Vice Pres*
Steven Vanpoucke, *Engineer*
Jim Pietro, *Sls & Mktg Exec*
◆ **EMP:** 200
SQ FT: 70,000
SALES (est): 50.5MM **Privately Held**
WEB: www.idealsnacks.com
SIC: 2096 Potato chips & similar snacks

(G-7460)
MAJOR-IPC INC
53 Webster Ave (12754-2005)
P.O. Box 350 (12754-0350)
PHONE..................................845 292-2200
David Feldman, *President*
Elizabeth McCalister, *Office Mgr*
▲ **EMP:** 5 **EST:** 1976
SQ FT: 9,800
SALES (est): 825.3K **Privately Held**
SIC: 3089 3441 Plastic processing; fabricated structural metal

Lido Beach
Nassau County

(G-7461)
AIRLINE CONTAINER SERVICES
Also Called: Airline Container Svces
354 Harbor Dr (11561-4907)
PHONE..................................516 371-4125
R Dino Persaud, *President*
Gomattie Persaud, *Vice Pres*
Isherwin Glabman, *Manager*
▲ **EMP:** 7
SALES (est): 1.1MM **Privately Held**
SIC: 2448 Cargo containers, wood & wood with metal

(G-7462)
JFB PRINT SOLUTIONS INC
21 Park Dr (11561-4920)
PHONE..................................631 694-8300
Randy Brown, *President*
Gary Brown, *Vice Pres*
EMP: 2
SQ FT: 2,000
SALES (est): 1.6MM **Privately Held**
SIC: 2752 Commercial printing, lithographic

(G-7463)
MARVEL DAIRY WHIP INC
258 Lido Blvd (11561-5024)
PHONE..................................516 889-4232
Pauline Seremetis, *President*
EMP: 5
SALES (est): 312.6K **Privately Held**
SIC: 2024 5451 Ice cream, bulk; ice cream (packaged)

Lima
Livingston County

(G-7464)
BEARS MANAGEMENT GROUP INC
Also Called: Bears Playgrounds
7577 E Main St (14485-9735)
PHONE..................................585 624-5694
Fax: 585 624-5694
C Daniel Bears, *President*
Marcie Bears, *Vice Pres*
EMP: 9
SQ FT: 2,000
SALES (est): 1.4MM **Privately Held**
WEB: www.bearsplaygrounds.com
SIC: 3949 Playground equipment

(G-7465)
CORNEAL DESIGN CORPORATION
3288 Plank Rd (14485-9408)
PHONE..................................301 670-7076
Daniel L Bell, *President*
Linda Adkins, *Manager*
EMP: 10
SQ FT: 4,000
SALES (est): 1.3MM **Privately Held**
SIC: 3851 Contact lenses

(G-7466)
EAST MAIN ASSOCIATES
Also Called: Lakelands Concrete
7520 E Main St (14485-9731)
PHONE..................................585 624-1990
Todd Clarke, *President*
EMP: 60
SQ FT: 28,720
SALES (est): 270K **Privately Held**
SIC: 3272 Concrete products

(G-7467)
LAKELANDS CONCRETE PDTS INC
7520 E Main St (14485-9731)
PHONE..................................585 624-1990
Fax: 585 624-2102
Todd Clarke, *President*
Gina Lathan, *Sales Mgr*
EMP: 49 **EST:** 1951
SQ FT: 40,000
SALES (est): 9.3MM **Privately Held**
WEB: www.lakelandsconcrete.com
SIC: 3272 Concrete products, precast

(G-7468)
NORTHEAST CONVEYORS INC
7620 Evergreen St (14485-9727)
P.O. Box 55, Le Roy (14482-0055)
PHONE..................................585 768-8912
Fax: 585 624-8015
Paul Hastings, *Ch of Bd*
Guy Bianchi, *Vice Pres*
Eric Ingraham, *Vice Pres*
Michael Schaffer, *Vice Pres*
Beth Bartz, *Treasurer*
EMP: 17
SQ FT: 8,024
SALES (est): 4.9MM **Privately Held**
WEB: www.neind.com
SIC: 3535 Conveyors & conveying equipment
PA: Northeast Industrial Technologies, Inc.
  7115 W Main Rd Ste 2
  Le Roy NY 14482

(G-7469)
P & H THERMOTECH INC
1883 Heath Markham Rd (14485-9529)
PHONE..................................585 624-1310
Dave Howes, *CEO*
Ray Platt, *President*
EMP: 5
SALES (est): 463.7K **Privately Held**
SIC: 2796 Platemaking services

(G-7470)
SMIDGENS INC
7336 Community Dr (14485-9772)
PHONE..................................585 624-1486
Rita Villa, *President*
Gary Villa, *Vice Pres*
EMP: 8
SQ FT: 3,000
SALES (est): 1.1MM **Privately Held**
WEB: www.smidgens.com
SIC: 3599 Machine shop, jobbing & repair

(G-7471)
SUPERIOR WALLS UPSTATE NY INC
7574 E Main St (14485-9731)
PHONE..................................585 624-9390
Fax: 585 624-9572
Gary T Hess, *President*
Liza Gfeller, *Manager*
EMP: 90
SQ FT: 200,000
SALES (est): 19.4MM **Privately Held**
SIC: 3272 Precast terrazo or concrete products

Limestone
Cattaraugus County

(G-7472)
CASE BROTHERS INC
370 Quinn Rd (14753-9713)
P.O. Box 181 (14753-0181)
PHONE..................................716 925-7172
Thomas A Case, *President*
EMP: 9
SALES (est): 949.7K **Privately Held**
SIC: 1389 Oil & gas field services

(G-7473)
JAY LITTLE OIL WELL SERVI
5460 Nichols Run (14753-9774)
PHONE..................................716 925-8905
Jay Little, *Principal*
EMP: 5
SALES (est): 333.2K **Privately Held**
SIC: 1389 Well logging

Lindenhurst
Suffolk County

(G-7474)
ALRAJS INC (PA)
Also Called: Yohay Baking Company
146 Albany Ave (11757-3628)
PHONE..................................631 225-0300
Fax: 631 225-4277
Mike Solomon, *President*
Lew Solomon, *Chairman*
Mitch Margolis, *Vice Pres*
▲ **EMP:** 27 **EST:** 1948
SQ FT: 15,000
SALES (est): 6.4MM **Privately Held**
WEB: www.yohay.com
SIC: 2051 2052 2064 Pastries, e.g. danish: except frozen; cones, ice cream; fudge (candy)

(G-7475)
ALRO MACHINE TOOL & DIE CO INC
585 W Hoffman Ave (11757-4032)
PHONE..................................631 226-5020
Fax: 631 226-5026
Ronald Young, *President*
Elizabeth Young, *Corp Secy*
Steven Young, *Vice Pres*
Maya Young, *Administration*
EMP: 15 **EST:** 1960
SQ FT: 22,000
SALES (est): 3.1MM **Privately Held**
SIC: 3728 Aircraft assemblies, subassemblies & parts

(G-7476)
ANTHONY MANUFACTURING INC
34 Gear Ave (11757-1005)
PHONE..................................631 957-9424
Jon Hatz, *President*
Benjamin Hatz, *Shareholder*
Melanie Hatz, *Shareholder*
Sandy Hatz, *Shareholder*
Kevin Jampolis, *Shareholder*
EMP: 9
SQ FT: 12,000
SALES (est): 1.2MM **Privately Held**
WEB: www.keithmachinery.com
SIC: 3547 5084 Rolling mill machinery; industrial machinery & equipment

(G-7477)
AUTO BODY SERVICES LLC
400 W Hoffman Ave (11757-4038)
PHONE..................................631 431-4640
Michael Moretti, *Officer*
EMP: 12
SALES (est): 5MM **Privately Held**
SIC: 3563 3444 5013 Spraying outfits: metals, paints & chemicals (compressor); booths, spray: prefabricated sheet metal; body repair or paint shop supplies, automotive

(G-7478)
AUTODYNE MANUFACTURING CO INC
200 N Strong Ave (11757-3629)
PHONE..................................631 957-5858
Lindsay Howe, *Ch of Bd*
Shari Kramberg, *Treasurer*
Linsy Marino, *Manager*
EMP: 10
SALES (est): 2MM **Privately Held**
WEB: www.autodyne.com
SIC: 3674 Solid state electronic devices

(G-7479)
BUXTON MEDICAL EQUIPMENT CORP
1178 Route 109 (11757-1004)
PHONE..................................631 957-4500
Fax: 631 957-3884
Carl Newman, *President*
Phillip McCann, *Vice Pres*
▲ **EMP:** 30
SALES (est): 5.3MM **Privately Held**
WEB: www.buxtonmed.com
SIC: 3841 Surgical & medical instruments

Lindenhurst - Suffolk County (G-7480)

(G-7480)
CANFIELD ELECTRONICS INC (PA)
6 Burton Pl (11757-1812)
PHONE................631 585-4100
Fax: 631 585-4200
Lynn Zaun, *President*
Laura Holme, *Manager*
▲ **EMP:** 18
SQ FT: 15,000
SALES (est): 3.1MM **Privately Held**
WEB: www.canfieldelectronics.com
SIC: 3679 5065 Electronic circuits; electronic parts & equipment

(G-7481)
CAROB INDUSTRIES INC
215 W Hoffman Ave (11757-4096)
PHONE................631 225-0900
Robert A Levey, *President*
EMP: 10
SQ FT: 8,000
SALES (est): 1.2MM **Privately Held**
SIC: 2431 Millwork

(G-7482)
CRYSTAL FUSION TECH INC
185 W Montauk Hwy (11757-5654)
PHONE................631 253-9800
Ray Doran, *President*
Gary Locicero, *Manager*
EMP: 19
SALES (est): 3.2MM **Privately Held**
SIC: 2899 Water treating compounds

(G-7483)
DELANEY MACHINE PRODUCTS LTD
150 S Alleghany Ave Ste A (11757-5062)
PHONE................631 225-1032
Fax: 516 225-5723
Bob Delaney, *President*
Sharon Delaney, *Vice Pres*
EMP: 6
SQ FT: 10,000
SALES: 850K **Privately Held**
SIC: 3599 Machine shop, jobbing & repair

(G-7484)
DERMATECH LABS INC
165 S 10th St (11757-4505)
PHONE................631 225-1700
Dan Bryle, *President*
Ava Abbati, *Manager*
▲ **EMP:** 10
SQ FT: 11,000
SALES (est): 940K **Privately Held**
SIC: 2844 5122 Cosmetic preparations; cosmetics

(G-7485)
DINE RITE SEATING PRODUCTS INC
165 E Hoffman Ave Unit 3 (11757-5036)
PHONE................631 226-8899
Fax: 631 225-2399
Phil Driesen, *President*
EMP: 20
SALES (est): 3.7MM **Privately Held**
SIC: 2599 7641 Restaurant furniture, wood or metal; upholstery work

(G-7486)
ELITE SEMI CONDUCTOR PRODUCTS
860 N Richmond Ave (11757-3007)
PHONE................631 884-8400
Fax: 631 884-8427
Robert Kravitz, *President*
Edward Kravitz, *Vice Pres*
Joan Kravitz, *Vice Pres*
EMP: 8
SQ FT: 5,000
SALES (est): 790K **Privately Held**
WEB: www.elitesemi.com
SIC: 3674 Semiconductors & related devices

(G-7487)
GABRIELA SYSTEMS LTD
135 Bangor St (11757-3632)
PHONE................631 225-7952
John Russo, *Owner*
EMP: 5 **EST:** 1999
SALES (est): 374.9K **Privately Held**
WEB: www.blendexindustrial.com
SIC: 2851 Polyurethane coatings

(G-7488)
JOHNNY MICA INC
116 E Hoffman Ave (11757-5029)
PHONE................631 225-5213
John Desimini, *President*
Karla Desimini, *Corp Secy*
EMP: 5
SALES (est): 590K **Privately Held**
WEB: www.johnnymica.com
SIC: 2541 5031 1799 1751 Cabinets, except refrigerated: show, display, etc.: wood; kitchen cabinets; counter top installation; cabinet & finish carpentry

(G-7489)
LINDENHURST FABRICATORS INC
117 S 13th St (11757-4546)
PHONE................631 226-3737
Fax: 631 226-3867
Charles Rogers, *President*
EMP: 8
SQ FT: 17,500
SALES (est): 1.6MM **Privately Held**
SIC: 3441 Fabricated structural metal

(G-7490)
LINEAR SIGNS INC
Also Called: Vista Visual Group
275 W Hoffman Ave Ste 1 (11757-4081)
PHONE................631 532-5330
Fax: 631 532-5331
Mike Shroff, *President*
Sohel Vakil, *Vice Pres*
Judy Minaya, *Consultant*
EMP: 15
SQ FT: 7,000
SALES (est): 2.5MM **Privately Held**
SIC: 3993 Signs & advertising specialties

(G-7491)
LONGO COMMERCIAL CABINETS INC
Also Called: Longo Cabinets
829 N Richmond Ave (11757-3008)
PHONE................631 225-4290
Robert Longo, *President*
Sandy Giuffrida, *Purch Mgr*
Clarke Ganshaw, *Legal Staff*
EMP: 50
SQ FT: 22,000
SALES (est): 6.1MM **Privately Held**
SIC: 2541 2521 2434 Store fixtures, wood; wood office furniture; wood kitchen cabinets

(G-7492)
MAR-A-THON FILTERS INC
369 41st St (11757-2713)
PHONE................631 957-4774
Fax: 631 957-1181
John Reinbold, *President*
Thomas Cornell, *Corp Secy*
EMP: 6
SQ FT: 7,000
SALES (est): 846.7K **Privately Held**
SIC: 3364 3599 5046 Nonferrous die-castings except aluminum; machine & other job shop work; commercial cooking & food service equipment

(G-7493)
MARIA DIONISIO WELDING INC
71 W Montauk Hwy (11757-5751)
PHONE................631 956-0815
EMP: 6
SALES (est): 107.3K **Privately Held**
SIC: 7692 Welding repair

(G-7494)
MATTHEW-LEE CORPORATION
149 Pennsylvania Ave (11757-5052)
PHONE................631 226-0100
Fax: 631 226-0226
John Ferrigno, *President*
Matthew Ferrigno, *Corp Secy*
EMP: 10
SQ FT: 13,000
SALES (est): 830K **Privately Held**
WEB: www.mattlee.com
SIC: 2759 Screen printing

(G-7495)
MIDDLEBY CORPORATION
Also Called: Marsal & Sons
175 E Hoffman Ave (11757-5013)
PHONE................631 226-6688
Fax: 631 226-6890
Rosemarie Ferrara, *Bookkeeper*
Santo Bruno, *VP Sales*
Joseph Ferrera, *Branch Mgr*
EMP: 33
SALES (corp-wide): 2.2B **Publicly Held**
SIC: 3444 Sheet metalwork; restaurant sheet metalwork
PA: The Middleby Corporation
1400 Toastmaster Dr
Elgin IL 60120
847 741-3300

(G-7496)
MODERN CRAFT BAR REST EQUIP
Also Called: Modern Craft Bar Rest Equip
165 E Hoffman Ave Unit 3 (11757-5036)
PHONE................631 226-5647
John Venticinque, *President*
Heidee Venticinque, *Admin Sec*
EMP: 7
SALES (est): 959.7K **Privately Held**
WEB: www.moderncraft.com
SIC: 2599 5046 2542 Bar, restaurant & cafeteria furniture; commercial cooking & food service equipment; bar fixtures, except wood

(G-7497)
NAS-TRA AUTOMOTIVE INDS INC
Also Called: Nastra Automotive
3 Sidney Ct (11757-1011)
PHONE................631 225-1225
James Lambert, *Ch of Bd*
Americo De Rocchis, *President*
Antonio Abbatiello, *Corp Secy*
Tim Nolan, *VP Opers*
Ramesh Lakshmanan, *Prdtn Mgr*
▲ **EMP:** 150 **EST:** 1978
SQ FT: 60,000
SALES (est): 24.1MM **Privately Held**
WEB: www.nastra.com
SIC: 3714 3694 3625 Motor vehicle parts & accessories; engine electrical equipment; relays & industrial controls

(G-7498)
NEW FINE CHEMICALS INC ◆
35 W Hoffman Ave (11757-4012)
PHONE................631 321-8151
Jim Haseez, *Director*
EMP: 7 **EST:** 2017
SALES (est): 304.1K **Privately Held**
SIC: 2899 Chemical preparations

(G-7499)
NEXGEN ENVIRO SYSTEMS INC
190 E Hoffman Ave Ste D (11757-5017)
PHONE................631 226-2930
Michael Robbins, *President*
Jason Robbins, *Vice Pres*
▲ **EMP:** 3
SALES: 1.1MM **Privately Held**
WEB: www.nexgenenviro.com
SIC: 3826 Environmental testing equipment

(G-7500)
NICOLIA CONCRETE PRODUCTS INC
Also Called: Nicolia of Long Island
640 Muncy St (11757-4318)
P.O. Box 1120, West Babylon (11704-0120)
PHONE................631 669-0700
R Glenn Schroeder, *Principal*
Robert Nicolia, *Chairman*
Antonio Nicolia, *Vice Pres*
Gian Nicolia, *Vice Pres*
Franco Nicolia, *Treasurer*
▲ **EMP:** 53
SQ FT: 22,000
SALES (est): 5.7MM **Privately Held**
SIC: 3271 3272 2951 5211 Paving blocks, concrete; concrete products; asphalt paving mixtures & blocks; masonry materials & supplies

(G-7501)
NICOLIA READY MIX INC
615 Cord Ave (11757-4314)
PHONE................631 669-7000
Antonio L Nicolia, *President*
EMP: 30
SALES (corp-wide): 17.8MM **Privately Held**
WEB: www.nicoliareadymix.com
SIC: 3273 Ready-mixed concrete
PA: Nicolia Ready Mix, Inc.
615 Cord Ave
Lindenhurst NY 11757
631 669-7000

(G-7502)
PACE UP PHARMACEUTICALS LLC
200 Bangor St (11757-3644)
PHONE................631 450-4495
Ming Yang,
EMP: 10
SALES (est): 1.5MM **Privately Held**
SIC: 2834 Druggists' preparations (pharmaceuticals)

(G-7503)
PRIDE LINES LTD
651 W Hoffman Ave (11757-4034)
PHONE................631 225-0033
Fax: 631 225-0099
EMP: 8
SQ FT: 8,000
SALES (est): 720K **Privately Held**
SIC: 3944 Manufactures Toy Trains

(G-7504)
RUSSELL PLASTICS TECH CO INC
521 W Hoffman Ave (11757-4052)
PHONE................631 963-8602
Fax: 631 226-3707
Alexander Bozza, *Ch of Bd*
EMP: 110
SQ FT: 58,000
SALES (est): 20.9MM
SALES (corp-wide): 1.7B **Privately Held**
WEB: www.russellplastics.com
SIC: 3089 Plastic processing
HQ: Vaupell Holdings, Inc.
1144 Nw 53rd St
Seattle WA 98107

(G-7505)
SIMS STEEL CORPORATION
650 Muncy St (11757-4396)
PHONE................631 587-8670
Fax: 631 587-2077
William Sims, *President*
David Geremenko, *Vice Pres*
EMP: 25
SQ FT: 4,000
SALES (est): 6.3MM **Privately Held**
WEB: www.simssteel.com
SIC: 3449 Miscellaneous metalwork

(G-7506)
STEELFLEX ELECTRO CORP
145 S 13th St (11757-4546)
P.O. Box 515 (11757-0515)
PHONE................516 226-4466
Fax: 631 226-4321
Philip Rine, *President*
Anthony Rine, *Vice Pres*
EMP: 60
SQ FT: 25,000
SALES (est): 7.6MM **Privately Held**
SIC: 3357 Nonferrous wiredrawing & insulating

(G-7507)
STJ ORTHOTIC SERVICES INC (PA)
Also Called: S T J Orthotic Svces
920 Wellwood Ave Ste B (11757-1246)
PHONE................631 956-0181
James De Francisco, *President*
Steve Goldring, *General Mgr*
Steven Levitz, *Vice Pres*
EMP: 12
SQ FT: 14,000
SALES: 3.5MM **Privately Held**
WEB: www.stjorthotic.com
SIC: 3842 Orthopedic appliances

GEOGRAPHIC SECTION

Little Neck - Queens County (G-7533)

(G-7508)
STRUX CORP
Also Called: Art Foam
100 Montauk Hwy (11757-5835)
PHONE..................516 768-3969
Fax: 631 957-7203
Robert Kjeldsen, *President*
EMP: 25 EST: 1970
SQ FT: 30,000
SALES (est): 2.1MM **Privately Held**
WEB: www.strux.com
SIC: 3083 3675 3086 Laminated plastics plate & sheet; electronic capacitors; plastics foam products

(G-7509)
SUFFOLK GRANITE MANUFACTURING
Also Called: Suffolk Monument Mfg
25 Gear Ave (11757-1006)
PHONE..................631 226-4774
Martin Solomon, *President*
Pat Leavy, *Bookkeeper*
EMP: 20
SQ FT: 17,500
SALES (est): 2.1MM **Privately Held**
WEB: www.uk-engineering.net
SIC: 3281 1423 1411 Monuments, cut stone (not finishing or lettering only); crushed & broken granite; dimension stone

(G-7510)
SUPERBOATS INC
694 Roosevelt Ave (11757-5820)
PHONE..................631 226-1761
John H Coen, *President*
EMP: 6
SQ FT: 10,000
SALES: 600K **Privately Held**
SIC: 3732 5551 7699 Boats, fiberglass: building & repairing; boat dealers; boat repair

(G-7511)
SUPERIOR AGGRAGATES SUPPLY LLC
612 Muncy St (11757-4318)
PHONE..................516 333-2923
Robert Nicolia,
Antonio L Nicolia,
Franco A Nicolia,
Gian P Nicolia,
Sandy H Nicolia,
EMP: 30
SALES: 2.9MM **Privately Held**
SIC: 3272 Precast terrazo or concrete products

(G-7512)
SUPREME STEEL INC
690 N Jefferson Ave (11757-2902)
PHONE..................631 884-1320
Fax: 718 346-3711
Jay Shikora, *President*
Vincent Caravana, *Vice Pres*
EMP: 12
SQ FT: 10,000
SALES (est): 1.1MM **Privately Held**
WEB: www.supremesteelinc.com
SIC: 3441 5051 Fabricated structural metal; structural shapes, iron or steel

(G-7513)
TENTINA WINDOW FASHIONS INC
1186 Route 109 (11757-1088)
P.O. Box 617 (11757-0617)
PHONE..................631 957-9585
Fax: 631 957-9588
Frank J Miritello, *CEO*
Andrea Miritello, *President*
Jeffery Miritello, *Vice Pres*
Neil Miritello, *Treasurer*
Barbara Guill, *Office Mgr*
EMP: 105
SQ FT: 40,000
SALES (est): 11.4MM **Privately Held**
WEB: www.tentina.com
SIC: 2591 Window blinds; window shades

(G-7514)
VELIS ASSOCIATES INC (PA)
151 S 14th St (11757-4432)
PHONE..................631 225-4220
Fax: 631 777-3127
Glenn Mastroberti, *General Mgr*
Suriya Khan, *Chairman*
Rafael Croissiert, *Vice Pres*
Brian Mastoberti, *Vice Pres*
Debbie Jelley, *Administration*
EMP: 3
SALES (est): 6.7MM **Privately Held**
SIC: 3534 Elevators & moving stairways

(G-7515)
VIKING ATHLETICS LTD
80 Montauk Hwy Ste 1 (11757-5800)
PHONE..................631 957-8000
David C Kjeldsen, *CEO*
Jerry Ehrlich, *CIO*
EMP: 40 EST: 1995
SQ FT: 28,000
SALES (est): 3.7MM **Privately Held**
WEB: www.vikingathletics.com
SIC: 3949 5949 2759 Sporting & athletic goods; needlework goods & supplies; screen printing

(G-7516)
VIKING TECHNOLOGIES LTD
80 E Montauk Hwy (11757)
PHONE..................631 957-8000
David Kjeldsen, *President*
Hugh Foster, *Finance*
EMP: 45
SQ FT: 35,000
SALES: 10MM **Privately Held**
WEB: www.cardwellcondenser.com
SIC: 3629 3674 3675 Condensers, fixed or variable; semiconductors & related devices; electronic capacitors

(G-7517)
VILLAGE LANTERN BAKING CORP
155 N Wellwood Ave (11757-4085)
PHONE..................631 225-1690
EMP: 8
SALES (est): 602.8K **Privately Held**
SIC: 2051 Bread, cake & related products

(G-7518)
VISUAL CITI INC (PA)
305 Henry St (11757-4315)
PHONE..................631 482-3030
Abbas Devji, *President*
Fazle Abbas Deyjiyani, *Chairman*
Samina Devji, *Vice Pres*
Brian Hughes, *Project Mgr*
Zahirabbas Merchant, *Project Mgr*
▲ EMP: 125
SQ FT: 28,000
SALES (est): 38.5MM **Privately Held**
WEB: www.visualciti.com
SIC: 3993 Displays & cutouts, window & lobby

Lindley
Steuben County

(G-7519)
LINDLEY WOOD WORKS INC
9625 Morgan Creek Rd (14858-9780)
P.O. Box 5 (14858-0005)
PHONE..................607 523-7786
Fax: 607 523-6697
Peter McIntosh, *President*
Peter Mc Intosh, *President*
Keith Mc Intosh, *Vice Pres*
Mary Mc Intosh, *Admin Sec*
EMP: 15
SQ FT: 10,000
SALES (est): 2.3MM **Privately Held**
SIC: 2448 Pallets, wood

Little Falls
Herkimer County

(G-7520)
BURROWS PAPER CORPORATION
Also Called: Burrows Paper Mill
730 E Mill St (13365)
PHONE..................315 823-2300
Fax: 315 823-0614
Fred Scarano, *Manager*
EMP: 70
SALES (corp-wide): 228.8MM **Privately Held**
WEB: www.burrowspaper.com
SIC: 2621 Paper mills
PA: Burrows Paper Corporation
501 W Main St Ste 1
Little Falls NY 13365
315 823-2300

(G-7521)
BURROWS PAPER CORPORATION
Also Called: Mohawk Valley Mill
489 W Main St (13365-1815)
PHONE..................315 823-2300
Fax: 315 823-1032
Duane Judd, *Manager*
EMP: 66
SALES (corp-wide): 228.8MM **Privately Held**
WEB: www.burrowspaper.com
SIC: 2621 Tissue paper; specialty papers
PA: Burrows Paper Corporation
501 W Main St Ste 1
Little Falls NY 13365
315 823-2300

(G-7522)
IDEAL WOOD PRODUCTS INC
Also Called: Ideal Stair Parts
225 W Main St (13365-1800)
PHONE..................315 823-1124
Fax: 315 823-1127
Bruce Mang, *President*
Doug Plourde, *Controller*
▲ EMP: 40
SQ FT: 14,000
SALES (est): 6.3MM **Privately Held**
WEB: www.idealstairparts.com
SIC: 2431 Staircases, stairs & railings

(G-7523)
PEMS TOOL & MACHINE INC
125 Southern Ave (13365-1906)
PHONE..................315 823-3595
Fax: 315 823-4116
Isabella Stone, *Ch of Bd*
John Brown, *QC Mgr*
Larry Laporta, *Manager*
EMP: 31
SQ FT: 17,500
SALES (est): 7.5MM **Privately Held**
WEB: www.pemstoolandmachine.com
SIC: 3599 3549 Machine shop, jobbing & repair; metalworking machinery

(G-7524)
R D S MOUNTAIN VIEW TRUCKING
Also Called: R D Drive and Shop
1600 State Route 5s (13365-5405)
P.O. Box 924 (13365-0924)
PHONE..................315 823-4265
Randall Dawley, *Owner*
EMP: 7
SALES (est): 745.9K **Privately Held**
SIC: 2611 Soda pulp

(G-7525)
REDCO FOODS INC
1 Hansen Is (13365-1997)
PHONE..................315 823-1300
Fax: 315 823-2069
Gordon Boggis, *CEO*
Doug Farrell, *General Mgr*
Debo Mukherjee, *COO*
Sandy Gokey, *Accountant*
Barbara Kuyrkendall, *HR Admin*
EMP: 75
SALES (corp-wide): 279.9MM **Privately Held**
SIC: 2393 Textile bags
HQ: Redco Foods, Inc.
1 Hansen Is
Bethlehem PA 18017
800 556-6674

(G-7526)
SUNBELT INDUSTRIES INC (PA)
540 E Mill St (13365-2027)
P.O. Box 584 (13365-0584)
PHONE..................315 823-2947
Fax: 315 823-4458
Earl Mannion, *President*
EMP: 10
SQ FT: 36,000
SALES (est): 1MM **Privately Held**
SIC: 3291 5085 Abrasive grains; abrasives

(G-7527)
TWIN RIVERS PAPER COMPANY LLC
501 W Main St (13365-1829)
PHONE..................315 823-2300
EMP: 138 **Privately Held**
SIC: 2621 Paper mills
PA: Twin Rivers Paper Company Llc
82 Bridge Ave
Madawaska ME 04756

(G-7528)
VINCENT MANUFACTURING CO INC
560 E Mill St (13365-2027)
P.O. Box 306 (13365-0306)
PHONE..................315 823-0280
Fax: 315 823-0928
Todd R Vincent, *President*
Alan N Vincent, *President*
Todd Vincent, *President*
Linda B Vincent, *Vice Pres*
EMP: 11 EST: 1892
SQ FT: 50,000
SALES: 800K **Privately Held**
SIC: 2299 5169 Batts & batting: cotton mill waste & related material; polyurethane products

Little Neck
Queens County

(G-7529)
ANGEL TIPS NAIL SALON
25473 Horace Harding Expy (11362-1816)
PHONE..................718 225-8300
Sun Kim, *Owner*
EMP: 6
SALES (est): 542.8K **Privately Held**
SIC: 2844 7231 Manicure preparations; manicurist, pedicurist

(G-7530)
BRAVE CHEFS INCORPORATED
4130 249th St Ste 2 (11363-1655)
PHONE..................347 956-5905
Michael Kim, *President*
EMP: 5 EST: 2013
SALES (est): 289.6K **Privately Held**
SIC: 2086 Carbonated beverages, nonalcoholic: bottled & canned

(G-7531)
E GLUCK CORPORATION (PA)
Also Called: Armitron Watch Div
6015 Little Neck Pkwy (11362-2500)
PHONE..................718 784-0700
Fax: 718 482-2700
Eugen Gluck, *President*
Mark Odenheimer, *Senior VP*
Jerry Dikowitz, *President*
Michael Feagan, *Vice Pres*
Michael Feagan, *Vice Pres*
▲ EMP: 151 EST: 1957
SQ FT: 200,000
SALES (est): 85.1MM **Privately Held**
WEB: www.egluck.com
SIC: 3873 5094 Watches & parts, except crystals & jewels; clocks, assembly of; watches & parts; clocks

(G-7532)
RECON CONSTRUCTION CORP
1108 Shore Rd (11363-1054)
PHONE..................718 939-1305
Fax: 718 463-6263
Gloria Kemper, *President*
EMP: 30
SQ FT: 5,000
SALES: 3.5MM **Privately Held**
SIC: 3312 Stainless steel

(G-7533)
RENEWABLE ENERGY INC
6 Cornell Ln (11363-1939)
PHONE..................718 690-2691

Little Valley - Cattaraugus County (G-7534) **GEOGRAPHIC SECTION**

EMP: 6
SALES (est): 518.5K **Privately Held**
SIC: 3674 Mfg Semiconductors/Related Devices

Little Valley
Cattaraugus County

(G-7534)
LITTLE VALLEY SAND & GRAVEL
8984 New Albion Rd (14755-9771)
P.O. Box 164 (14755-0164)
PHONE..................716 938-6676
John R Charlesworth, *President*
Jay Charlesworth, *Treasurer*
Mary Charlesworth, *Admin Sec*
EMP: 7
SQ FT: 5,000
SALES (est): 622.3K **Privately Held**
SIC: 1442 4212 Construction sand mining; gravel mining; local trucking, without storage

Liverpool
Onondaga County

(G-7535)
BRANNOCK DEVICE CO INC
116 Luther Ave (13088-6726)
PHONE..................315 475-9862
Fax: 315 475-2723
Salvatore A Leonardi Jr, *President*
Tim Follett, *Vice Pres*
Garrison Davis, *Treasurer*
James Hanley, *Director*
EMP: 20 EST: 1929
SQ FT: 10,000
SALES (est): 2.5MM **Privately Held**
WEB: www.brannock.com
SIC: 3842 Foot appliances, orthopedic

(G-7536)
C & G VIDEO SYSTEMS INC (PA)
7778 Tirrell Hill Cir (13090-2508)
P.O. Box 2476, Syracuse (13220-2476)
PHONE..................315 452-1490
Fax: 315 343-1623
Charles F Bisesi, *President*
Gail Bisesi, *Vice Pres*
EMP: 5
SQ FT: 3,600
SALES: 1MM **Privately Held**
SIC: 3699 1731 Security control equipment & systems; electrical welding equipment; electrical work

(G-7537)
C SPEED LLC
316 Commerce Blvd (13088-4511)
PHONE..................315 453-1043
David Lysack, *President*
Michael Lesmerises, *Project Mgr*
Matt Ryan, *QC Mgr*
Brian D Sherry -, *Engineer*
Kevin Francis -, *Engineer*
EMP: 32
SQ FT: 5,000
SALES (est): 6.9MM **Privately Held**
WEB: www.cspeed.com
SIC: 3812 8711 3825 Search & navigation equipment; electrical or electronic engineering; instruments to measure electricity

(G-7538)
CARGILL INCORPORATED
7700 Maltage Dr (13090-2513)
PHONE..................315 622-3533
Fax: 315 652-1043
Hugh Fordyce, *Sales/Mktg Mgr*
Brians Parham, *Manager*
Luke Reynolds, *Manager*
EMP: 25
SQ FT: 27,466
SALES (corp-wide): 109.7B **Privately Held**
WEB: www.cargill.com
SIC: 2048 Prepared feeds
PA: Cargill, Incorporated
    15407 Mcginty Rd W
    Wayzata MN 55391
    952 742-7575

(G-7539)
CASCADE HELMETS HOLDINGS INC
4697 Crssrads Pk Dr Ste 1 (13088)
PHONE..................315 453-3073
Bill Brine, *CEO*
Steve Moore, *COO*
EMP: 7
SALES (est): 3MM **Privately Held**
SIC: 3949 Helmets, athletic
PA: Old Psg Wind-Down Ltd.
    100 Domain Dr
    Exeter NH 03833

(G-7540)
CAYUGA PRESS CORTLAND INC
4707 Dey Rd (13088-3510)
PHONE..................888 229-8421
Thomas Quartier, *President*
Barney Schug, *Vice Pres*
Joe Shelton, *Accounts Exec*
Mark Binkowski, *Info Tech Mgr*
EMP: 32 EST: 2011
SALES (est): 342K **Privately Held**
SIC: 2752 2741 Commercial printing, offset; miscellaneous publishing

(G-7541)
COMPLEX BIOSYSTEMS INC
8266 Warbler Way Apt C6 (13090-1053)
PHONE..................315 464-8007
Jacques Beaumont, *Owner*
EMP: 7
SQ FT: 600
SALES (est): 366.2K **Privately Held**
SIC: 3845 7371 7373 8711 Electrotherapeutic apparatus; computer software systems analysis & design, custom; computer-aided engineering (CAE) systems service; consulting engineer

(G-7542)
CREATIVE COSTUME CO
3804 Rivers Pointe Way (13090-4917)
PHONE..................212 564-5552
Susan Handler, *Partner*
Linda Carcaci, *Partner*
EMP: 7
SALES (est): 877.3K **Privately Held**
WEB: www.creativecostume.com
SIC: 2389 Costumes

(G-7543)
EAGLE COMTRONICS INC
7665 Henry Clay Blvd (13088-3507)
P.O. Box 2457, Syracuse (13220-2457)
PHONE..................315 451-3313
Fax: 315 451-4362
William Devendorf, *CEO*
Timothy Devendorf, *President*
Ron Barry, *Purch Mgr*
Ted Jewett, *Purch Mgr*
Rob Sgarlata, *Design Engr*
▲ EMP: 200 EST: 1975
SQ FT: 100,000
SALES (est): 38.8MM **Privately Held**
WEB: www.eaglecomtronics.com
SIC: 3663 Cable television equipment

(G-7544)
FAYETTE STREET COATINGS INC
1 Burr Dr (13088)
PHONE..................315 488-5401
Bill Udovich, *Branch Mgr*
EMP: 11
SALES (corp-wide): 23.4MM **Publicly Held**
SIC: 2851 Paints & allied products
HQ: Fayette Street Coatings, Inc.
    1970 W Fayette St
    Syracuse NY 13204
    315 488-5401

(G-7545)
HEARTH CABINETS AND MORE LTD
4483 Buckley Rd (13088-2506)
P.O. Box 2700 (13089-2700)
PHONE..................315 641-1197
Richard D Hovey, *President*
Lisa Hinman, *Office Mgr*
Kim Hovey, *Manager*
Chris Yager, *Consultant*
EMP: 2
SALES (est): 2.3MM **Privately Held**
SIC: 2434 Wood kitchen cabinets

(G-7546)
HSM PACKAGING CORPORATION
4529 Crown Rd (13090-3541)
PHONE..................315 476-7996
Fax: 315 476-7998
Sheila M Martin, *Controller*
Homer S Martin III, *COO*
Jessica T Pletka, *CFO*
Joan Brady, *Admin Sec*
▲ EMP: 58
SQ FT: 30,000
SALES (est): 14.1MM **Privately Held**
WEB: www.hsmpackaging.com
SIC: 2657 Folding paperboard boxes

(G-7547)
INFIMED INC (PA)
Also Called: Varian Medical Systems
121 Metropolitan Park Dr (13088-5335)
PHONE..................315 453-4545
Fax: 315 453-4550
Robert Kluge, *CEO*
Norman Shoenfeld, *Ch of Bd*
Amy L Ryan, *President*
Bruce Perry, *Engineer*
Carrie Murphy, *Controller*
▲ EMP: 64
SQ FT: 26,000
SALES (est): 8.3MM **Privately Held**
WEB: www.digitalxrayimages.com
SIC: 3845 Electromedical equipment

(G-7548)
INFO QUICK SOLUTIONS
7460 Morgan Rd (13090-3979)
PHONE..................315 463-1400
Bernie Owens, *President*
Christine Lohr, *Opers Staff*
Dennis Owens, *Sales Staff*
Mike Prosser, *Technology*
Tony Tabone, *Database Admin*
EMP: 50
SALES (est): 4.9MM **Privately Held**
SIC: 7372 Prepackaged software

(G-7549)
INTEGRATED MEDICAL DEVICES
549 Electronics Pkwy # 200 (13088-4391)
PHONE..................315 457-4200
Stephen L Esposito, *President*
EMP: 7
SQ FT: 4,400
SALES (est): 650K **Privately Held**
WEB: www.qrstech.com
SIC: 3845 Electrocardiographs

(G-7550)
IRONSHORE HOLDINGS INC
Also Called: Lipe Automation
290 Elwood Davis Rd (13088-2100)
PHONE..................315 457-1052
Fax: 315 457-1678
Robert Offley, *CEO*
Jay Lacey, *President*
Bill Wagner, *Engineer*
Jeff Purdy, *Controller*
Ann Buerkle, *Manager*
EMP: 16
SQ FT: 27,000
SALES (est): 1.3MM **Privately Held**
SIC: 3599 Machine shop, jobbing & repair

(G-7551)
JOHN MEZZALINGUA ASSOC LLC (PA)
Also Called: Jma Wireless
7645 Henry Clay Blvd # 678 (13088-3512)
P.O. Box 678 (13088-0678)
PHONE..................315 431-7100
Christian Barb, *Vice Pres*
Gail Cawley, *Vice Pres*
Terry Kennedy, *QC Mgr*
Barbara Fowler, *HR Admin*
John Mezzalingua, *Mng Member*
▲ EMP: 150
SALES (est): 8.6MM **Privately Held**
SIC: 3663 Antennas, transmitting & communications; airborne radio communications equipment

(G-7552)
JT SYSTEMS INC
8132 Oswego Rd (13090-1500)
P.O. Box 2575 (13089-2575)
PHONE..................315 622-1980
Jit Turakhia, *Ch of Bd*
Manda Turakhia, *Admin Sec*
EMP: 10
SQ FT: 1,700
SALES (est): 2.5MM **Privately Held**
WEB: www.jtsystemsinc.com
SIC: 3564 Air purification equipment; ventilating fans: industrial or commercial

(G-7553)
LOCKHEED MARTIN CORPORATION
497 Electronics Pkwy (13088-5394)
PHONE..................315 456-1548
Steven Montagne, *General Mgr*
Peter Morin, *Principal*
Christopher Gregoire, *Vice Pres*
Anthony Stagnitta, *Project Mgr*
Linda Raymond, *Purch Agent*
EMP: 25 **Publicly Held**
SIC: 3721 Aircraft
PA: Lockheed Martin Corporation
    6801 Rockledge Dr
    Bethesda MD 20817

(G-7554)
LOCKHEED MARTIN CORPORATION
497 Electronics Pkwy # 5 (13088-5394)
P.O. Box 4840, Syracuse (13221-4840)
PHONE..................315 456-0123
T S Kires, *Principal*
Marc Heller, *Business Mgr*
Carl Bannar, *Vice Pres*
Robert Tucker, *Vice Pres*
Robert Fiorentini, *Mfg Dir*
EMP: 2200 **Publicly Held**
WEB: www.lockheedmartin.com
SIC: 3761 3812 Rockets, space & military, complete; navigational systems & instruments
PA: Lockheed Martin Corporation
    6801 Rockledge Dr
    Bethesda MD 20817

(G-7555)
LOCKHEED MARTIN GLOBAL INC (HQ)
Also Called: Lmgi
497 Electronics Pkwy # 5 (13088-5394)
PHONE..................315 456-2982
Dale M Johnson, *President*
Zachary Parmely, *General Mgr*
Christopher Gregoire, *Vice Pres*
Kenneth Possenriede, *Vice Pres*
Karen Barrett, *Admin Sec*
EMP: 48
SALES (est): 364.4MM **Publicly Held**
SIC: 3812 Search & navigation equipment

(G-7556)
LOCKHEED MARTIN OVERSEAS
497 Electronics Pkwy # 7 (13088-5394)
P.O. Box 4840, Syracuse (13221-4840)
PHONE..................315 456-0123
Fax: 315 456-3881
Kwame Otieku, *Principal*
Ralph Heath, *Exec VP*
Andrew Yeman, *Engineer*
Linda Raymond, *Branch Mgr*
Karen Barrett, *Asst Sec*
EMP: 14 **Publicly Held**
SIC: 3812 Sonar systems & equipment; radar systems & equipment
HQ: Lockheed Martin Overseas Services Corporation
    6801 Rockledge Dr
    Bethesda MD 20817
    301 897-6000

▲ = Import ▼=Export
◆ =Import/Export

Liverpool - Onondaga County (G-7580)

(G-7557)
LOCKHEED MARTIN OVERSEAS LLC
497 Electronics Pkwy Ep5 (13088-5394)
PHONE..............................301 897-6923
Scott Soyster, *Contract Mgr*
Kittrell Daniels, *Asst Sec*
EMP: 99
SALES (est): 2.8MM **Privately Held**
SIC: 3761 Space vehicles, complete

(G-7558)
MCAULIFFE PAPER INC
100 Commerce Blvd (13088-4500)
PHONE..............................315 453-2222
Fax: 315 453-2225
Charles Thiaville, *President*
Mary Y Maltbie, *Vice Pres*
Amy Caldeira, *VP Sales*
EMP: 35 **EST:** 1920
SQ FT: 40,000
SALES (est): 3.5MM **Privately Held**
WEB: www.mcauliffepad.com
SIC: 2759 Business forms: printing

(G-7559)
MERCER MILLING CO
4698 Crossroads Park Dr (13088-3598)
PHONE..............................315 701-1334
Fax: 315 701-4987
Bill Colten, *President*
Rene Lavoie II, *General Mgr*
Scott Lyndaker, *Opers Staff*
Angelo Depasquale, *QA Dir*
▲ **EMP:** 36 **EST:** 1829
SQ FT: 60,000
SALES (est): 15.8MM **Privately Held**
SIC: 2834 2833 Intravenous solutions; botanical products, medicinal: ground, graded or milled

(G-7560)
MIDSTATE PRINTING CORP
4707 Dey Rd (13088-3510)
PHONE..............................315 475-4101
Fax: 315 475-5129
John Williams III, *President*
Bob Williams, *Vice Pres*
Robert Williams, *Vice Pres*
Lee Boyce, *Project Mgr*
Thomas Keehfus, *CFO*
EMP: 49
SQ FT: 28,000
SALES (est): 1.3MM
SALES (corp-wide): 52.9K **Privately Held**
WEB: www.midstateprinting.com
SIC: 2752 Commercial printing, offset
PA: Qpc-Mpc Consolidation, Inc.
  4707 Dey Rd
  Liverpool NY 13088
  315 475-4101

(G-7561)
MODERN DECAL CO
8146 Soule Rd (13090-1536)
PHONE..............................315 622-2778
Fax: 315 622-9703
William J Hitchcock, *Owner*
Kathleen Hitchcock, *Co-Owner*
EMP: 6
SALES: 220K **Privately Held**
SIC: 2759 3993 Decals: printing; name plates: except engraved, etched, etc.: metal

(G-7562)
NANOPV CORPORATION
7526 Morgan Rd (13090-3502)
PHONE..............................609 851-3666
Anna Selvan John, *President*
EMP: 187
SALES (corp-wide): 10.4MM **Privately Held**
SIC: 3433 Solar heaters & collectors
PA: Nanopv Corporation
  122 Mountainview Rd
  Ewing NJ 08560
  609 851-3666

(G-7563)
O BRIEN GERE MFG INC
7600 Morgan Rd Ste 1 (13090-4128)
PHONE..............................315 437-6100
Terry Brown, *Owner*
EMP: 8
SALES (est): 862.9K **Privately Held**
SIC: 3999 Manufacturing industries

(G-7564)
PACKAGING CORPORATION AMERICA
Also Called: Pca/Syracuse, 384
4471 Steelway Blvd S (13090-3508)
P.O. Box 584 (13088-0584)
PHONE..............................315 457-6780
Fax: 315 457-0630
Mike Hodges, *General Mgr*
Sharon Wilbur, *Safety Mgr*
Julie Clark, *Controller*
Teresa Bashore, *Branch Mgr*
Joseph Armentrout, *Manager*
EMP: 130
SQ FT: 144,672
SALES (corp-wide): 5.7B **Publicly Held**
WEB: www.packagingcorp.com
SIC: 2653 Corrugated & solid fiber boxes
PA: Packaging Corporation Of America
  1955 W Field Ct
  Lake Forest IL 60045
  847 482-3000

(G-7565)
PACTIV LLC
4471 Steelway Blvd S (13090-3517)
P.O. Box 584 (13088-0584)
PHONE..............................315 457-6780
Teresa J Bashore, *Manager*
EMP: 130 **Privately Held**
WEB: www.pactiv.com
SIC: 2653 Boxes, corrugated: made from purchased materials; boxes, solid fiber: made from purchased materials
HQ: Pactiv Llc
  1900 W Field Ct
  Lake Forest IL 60045
  847 482-2000

(G-7566)
PAUL DE LIMA COMPANY INC (PA)
Also Called: Paul De Lima Coffee Company
7546 Morgan Rd Ste 1 (13090-3532)
PHONE..............................315 457-3725
Paul W Delima Jr, *CEO*
William J Drescher Jr, *Ch of Bd*
Michael Drescher, *Vice Pres*
Peter Miller, *Vice Pres*
Bill Kukula, *Manager*
▲ **EMP:** 55
SQ FT: 15,000
SALES (est): 13.7MM **Privately Held**
WEB: www.delimacoffee.com
SIC: 2095 5149 Roasted coffee; coffee, green or roasted

(G-7567)
PERFORMANCE LACROSSE GROUP INC (DH)
4697 Crossroads Park Dr (13088-3515)
PHONE..............................315 453-3073
Stephen Moore, *President*
▲ **EMP:** 8
SALES (est): 1.1MM **Privately Held**
WEB: www.sporthelmets.com
SIC: 3949 Helmets, athletic
HQ: Bauer Hockey, Inc.
  100 Domain Dr Ste 1
  Exeter NH 03833
  603 430-2111

(G-7568)
POINTWISE INFORMATION SERVICE
223 1st St (13088-5140)
P.O. Box 11457, Syracuse (13218-1457)
PHONE..............................315 457-4111
Richard C Jaquin, *Owner*
EMP: 10
SQ FT: 1,000
SALES (est): 837.2K **Privately Held**
SIC: 2721 Periodicals: publishing only

(G-7569)
PRAXAIR DISTRIBUTION INC
4560 Morgan Pl (13090-3522)
PHONE..............................315 457-5821
Todd Saumier, *Principal*
Donna Kline, *Office Mgr*
EMP: 7
SALES (corp-wide): 10.5B **Publicly Held**
SIC: 2813 5984 5169 Oxygen, compressed or liquefied; nitrogen; liquefied petroleum gas dealers; oxygen; industrial gases; acetylene
HQ: Praxair Distribution, Inc.
  10 Riverview Dr
  Danbury CT 06810
  203 837-2000

(G-7570)
PRECISION SYSTEMS MFG INC
4855 Executive Dr (13088-5378)
PHONE..............................315 451-3480
Theodore Jeske, *President*
Gary S Price, *Controller*
EMP: 48
SQ FT: 40,000
SALES (est): 10.8MM **Privately Held**
WEB: www.psmi.org
SIC: 3599 3444 7389 3549 Machine & other job shop work; sheet metalwork; design, commercial & industrial; metalworking machinery; special dies, tools, jigs & fixtures

(G-7571)
PRINT SOLUTIONS PLUS INC
7325 Oswego Rd (13090-3717)
PHONE..............................315 234-3801
Darren Petragnani, *President*
EMP: 6
SALES (est): 741.1K **Privately Held**
SIC: 2752 Commercial printing, lithographic

(G-7572)
ROBERTS OFFICE FURN CNCPTS INC
7327 Henry Clay Blvd (13088-3529)
PHONE..............................315 451-9185
Fax: 315 451-9325
Robert L Barcza, *CEO*
R Scott Barcza, *President*
Dave Straub, *Accounting Mgr*
Kevin Oconnor, *Sales Associate*
EMP: 25
SQ FT: 76,000
SALES (est): 5.1MM **Privately Held**
WEB: www.robertsofc.com
SIC: 2522 7641 Office furniture, except wood; office furniture repair & maintenance

(G-7573)
SCAPA NORTH AMERICA
Also Called: Great Lakes Technologies
1111 Vine St (13088-5301)
PHONE..............................315 413-1111
Fax: 315 413-1112
Duane Gordan, *Plant Mgr*
Edward Liscio, *Treasurer*
Kevin Toomey, *Human Res Dir*
Stuart Ganslaw,
Angelo Labbadia,
▲ **EMP:** 20
SQ FT: 70,000
SALES (est): 12.9MM
SALES (corp-wide): 348.6MM **Privately Held**
WEB: www.greatlakestechnologies.com
SIC: 3081 Unsupported plastics film & sheet
HQ: Scapa Tapes North America Llc
  111 Great Pond Dr
  Windsor CT 06095
  860 688-8000

(G-7574)
SEABOARD GRAPHIC SERVICES LLC
Also Called: Minuteman Press
7570 Oswego Rd (13090-2928)
PHONE..............................315 652-4200
Fax: 315 652-2546
Lawrence Kuhn, *Mng Member*
EMP: 25
SALES: 4.2MM **Privately Held**
WEB: www.seaboardgraphics.com
SIC: 2752 Commercial printing, lithographic

(G-7575)
SOLENIS LLC
Also Called: Ashland Hercules Water Tech
911 Old Liverpool Rd (13088-1504)
PHONE..............................315 461-4730
EMP: 9
SALES (corp-wide): 783.6MM **Privately Held**
SIC: 2891 Adhesives
PA: Solenis Llc
  3 Beaver Valley Rd # 500
  Wilmington DE 19803
  866 337-1533

(G-7576)
STALLION TECHNOLOGIES INC
4324 Loveland Dr (13090-6862)
PHONE..............................315 622-1176
Marshall MA, *President*
EMP: 8
SALES (est): 520K **Privately Held**
WEB: www.stalliontech.com
SIC: 3861 Photographic equipment & supplies

(G-7577)
STAMPCRETE INTERNATIONAL LTD
Also Called: Stampcrete Decorative Concrete
325 Commerce Blvd (13088-4595)
PHONE..............................315 451-2837
Fax: 315 451-2290
Karen Reith, *President*
Bob Williams, *Vice Pres*
Michael Stevens, *Plant Mgr*
Amy Michales, *Accountant*
▼ **EMP:** 20
SQ FT: 10,000
SALES (est): 7MM **Privately Held**
SIC: 3469 Metal stampings

(G-7578)
SYRACUSE PLASTICS LLC
7400 Morgan Rd (13090-3902)
PHONE..............................315 637-9881
Fax: 315 637-9260
Rick Gigon, *Manager*
David Nason, *Manager*
Thomas Falcone,
Joseph R Falcone Sr,
Joseph R Falcone Jr,
▲ **EMP:** 150 **EST:** 1953
SQ FT: 55,000
SALES (est): 34.7MM **Privately Held**
SIC: 3089 Injection molding of plastics

(G-7579)
TACTAIR FLUID CONTROLS INC
4806 W Taft Rd (13088-4810)
PHONE..............................315 451-3928
Fax: 315 451-8919
Dudley D Johnson, *Ch of Bd*
Peter Kaido, *President*
Michael Yates, *President*
Bob Powell, *Superintendent*
Matt Devendorf, *Business Mgr*
EMP: 240
SQ FT: 70,000
SALES (est): 50.9MM
SALES (corp-wide): 3.1B **Publicly Held**
WEB: www.tactair.com
SIC: 3492 3593 Fluid power valves for aircraft; fluid power actuators, hydraulic or pneumatic
HQ: Young & Franklin, Inc.
  942 Old Liverpool Rd
  Liverpool NY 13088
  315 457-3110

(G-7580)
THERMO CIDTEC INC
Also Called: Cid Technologies
101 Commerce Blvd (13088-4507)
PHONE..............................315 451-9410
Fax: 315 451-9421
Seth H Hoogasian, *Ch of Bd*
Mike Pilon, *General Mgr*
Jon Miles, *Mfg Mgr*
Mark Ptaszek, *Purchasing*
Robert Gorczynski, *Engineer*
EMP: 30
SQ FT: 14,000
SALES (est): 10MM
SALES (corp-wide): 18.2B **Publicly Held**
SIC: 3861 3674 Photographic equipment & supplies; solid state electronic devices

Liverpool - Onondaga County (G-7581)

HQ: Thermo Vision Corp
8 Forge Pkwy Ste 4
Franklin MA 02038

(G-7581)
VANSANTIS DEVELOPMENT INC
4595 Morgan Pl (13090-3521)
PHONE..............................315 461-0113
Fax: 315 461-0346
Bill Vanauken, *President*
EMP: 40
SQ FT: 16,356
SALES (est): 5.6MM **Privately Held**
SIC: 2448 Pallets, wood

(G-7582)
WARD STEEL COMPANY INC
4591 Morgan Pl (13090-3511)
P.O. Box 628 (13088-0628)
PHONE..............................315 451-4566
John E Ward, *President*
Terrance Ward, *Vice Pres*
Al Parisi, *Plant Mgr*
EMP: 25
SQ FT: 28,000
SALES (est): 7.1MM **Privately Held**
SIC: 3441 Fabricated structural metal

(G-7583)
WARNER ENERGY LLC (PA)
7526 Morgan Rd (13090-3502)
PHONE..............................315 457-3828
Steven Toomey, *Administration*
EMP: 8
SALES (est): 3.8MM **Privately Held**
SIC: 3674 Solar cells

(G-7584)
WHITACRE ENGINEERING COMPANY
4522 Wetzel Rd (13090-2548)
PHONE..............................315 622-1075
Fax: 315 622-1076
Yan Bukowy, *Financial Exec*
Samuel Conley, *Branch Mgr*
Jeff Andrews, *Manager*
Sam Poon, *Comp Tech*
EMP: 7
SQ FT: 48,359
SALES (corp-wide): 8.3MM **Privately Held**
SIC: 3441 Fabricated structural metal
PA: Whitacre Engineering Company
4645 Rebar Ave Ne
Canton OH 44705
330 455-8505

(G-7585)
XTO INCORPORATED (PA)
110 Wrentham Dr (13088-4503)
PHONE..............................315 451-7807
Fax: 315 451-2687
Donald G Kreiger, *CEO*
Ric Sill, *President*
D Keith Krieger, *Vice Pres*
Keith Hughes, *VP Sales*
Keith Krieger, *VP Sales*
▲ **EMP:** 65
SQ FT: 38,000
SALES (est): 14.9MM **Privately Held**
WEB: www.xtoinc.com
SIC: 3053 5085 3549 Gaskets & sealing devices; adhesives, tape & plasters; seals, industrial; metalworking machinery

(G-7586)
YOUNG & FRANKLIN INC (HQ)
942 Old Liverpool Rd (13088-5596)
PHONE..............................315 457-3110
W Nicholas Howley, *President*
Chuck Roberts, *Purch Mgr*
Greg Butler, *Buyer*
Andrew Stiteler, *Engineer*
Jim Weaver, *Engineer*
EMP: 100 **EST:** 1918
SQ FT: 70,000
SALES: 73MM
SALES (corp-wide): 3.1B **Publicly Held**
SIC: 3492 3625 3728 3593 Control valves, aircraft: hydraulic & pneumatic; control valves, fluid power: hydraulic & pneumatic; actuators, industrial; aircraft parts & equipment; fluid power cylinders & actuators

PA: Transdigm Group Incorporated
1301 E 9th St Ste 3000
Cleveland OH 44114
216 706-2960

Livingston
Columbia County

(G-7587)
F H STICKLES & SON INC
2590 Rr 9 (12541)
PHONE..............................518 851-9048
Bernard F Stickles Jr, *President*
EMP: 15 **EST:** 1928
SQ FT: 1,000
SALES (est): 2MM **Privately Held**
SIC: 3273 5032 Ready-mixed concrete; sand, construction; gravel

Livingston Manor
Sullivan County

(G-7588)
FLOUR POWER BAKERY CAFE
87 Debruce Rd (12758-2001)
PHONE..............................917 747-6895
Rowley, *President*
Denise Rowley, *Admin Sec*
EMP: 5
SALES (est): 275K **Privately Held**
SIC: 2051 Bakery: wholesale or wholesale/retail combined

(G-7589)
GLOBAL NATURAL FOODS INC
672 Old Route 17 Rear Ofc (12758-5031)
P.O. Box 276 (12758-0276)
PHONE..............................845 439-3292
Randy Lewis, *President*
Melissa Holden, *Vice Pres*
Lori Endriss, *Mfg Mgr*
Trish Rampe, *Accounting Mgr*
◆ **EMP:** 32
SQ FT: 2,500
SALES (est): 7.8MM **Privately Held**
WEB: www.globalnaturalfoods.com
SIC: 2037 2033 Fruit juices; fruit juice concentrates, frozen; fruit purees: packaged in cans, jars, etc.

Livonia
Livingston County

(G-7590)
AG BIOTECH INC
3578 Shoreline Dr (14487-9645)
P.O. Box 636, Lakeville (14480-0636)
PHONE..............................585 346-0020
Fax: 585 346-0048
Robert Hudack, *President*
Patti Hudack, *Vice Pres*
◆ **EMP:** 8
SALES (est): 2MM **Privately Held**
SIC: 2836 Biological products, except diagnostic

(G-7591)
FINGER LAKES TIMBER CO INC
6274 Decker Rd (14487-9528)
PHONE..............................585 346-2990
Ronald Munson, *President*
Aaron Munson, *Vice Pres*
EMP: 6
SQ FT: 1,000
SALES (est): 873.9K **Privately Held**
SIC: 2411 Logging

(G-7592)
TWISTERS
13 Commercial St (14487-9113)
P.O. Box 604 (14487-0604)
PHONE..............................585 346-3730
Jeffery Helwig, *Owner*
EMP: 6
SALES (est): 498.5K **Privately Held**
SIC: 2024 Ice cream & frozen desserts

Lloyd Harbor
Suffolk County

(G-7593)
DILLNER PRECAST INC (PA)
14 Meadow Ln (11743-9721)
PHONE..............................631 421-9130
John Dillner, *President*
Maureen Dillner, *Corp Secy*
EMP: 5
SALES (est): 1MM **Privately Held**
SIC: 3272 Concrete products, precast

(G-7594)
KANNALIFE SCIENCES INC
4 Knoll Ct (11743-9731)
PHONE..............................516 669-3219
EMP: 5
SALES (est): 514.4K **Privately Held**
SIC: 2834 2833 2835 Mfg Pharmaceutical Preparations Mfg Medicinal/Botanical Products Mfg Diagnostic Substances

Locke
Cayuga County

(G-7595)
COTE HARDWOOD PRODUCTS INC (PA)
Also Called: Cote Wood Products
4725 Cat Path Rd (13092-4135)
PHONE..............................607 898-5737
Fax: 315 497-3108
Pierre Cote, *President*
Carl Cote, *Vice Pres*
Paulette Cote, *Treasurer*
EMP: 11
SALES: 950K **Privately Held**
SIC: 2421 Sawmills & planing mills, general

Lockport
Niagara County

(G-7596)
240 MICHIGAN STREET INC
Also Called: Garb-El Products Co
240 Michigan St (14094-1708)
PHONE..............................716 434-6010
Fax: 716 434-9148
James Carbone, *President*
EMP: 10
SQ FT: 19,000
SALES (est): 1.9MM **Privately Held**
WEB: www.garb-el.com
SIC: 3589 Garbage disposers & compactors, commercial

(G-7597)
ALLVAC
695 Ohio St (14094-4221)
PHONE..............................716 433-4411
Reginald C Buri, *Principal*
Joe Gardner, *Director*
Mike Wilson, *Executive*
▲ **EMP:** 12
SALES (est): 2.6MM **Privately Held**
SIC: 3312 Blast furnaces & steel mills; stainless steel; rods, iron & steel: made in steel mills

(G-7598)
ARROWHEAD SPRING VINEYARDS LLC
4746 Townline Rd (14094-9604)
PHONE..............................716 434-8030
Duncan Ross,
EMP: 5
SALES (est): 441K **Privately Held**
WEB: www.duncanrossphoto.com
SIC: 2084 Wines

(G-7599)
BARRY STEEL FABRICATION INC (PA)
30 Simonds St (14094-4111)
P.O. Box 579 (14095-0579)
PHONE..............................716 433-2144
Fax: 716 433-7742
Steven R Barry, *President*
Jody Barry, *Vice Pres*
Randy Allen, *Project Mgr*
Kathryn Barry, *Marketing Mgr*
EMP: 34
SQ FT: 8,400
SALES (est): 11.3MM **Privately Held**
WEB: www.barrysteel.com
SIC: 3441 1791 Fabricated structural metal; structural steel erection

(G-7600)
BISON BAG CO INC
5404 Crown Dr (14094-1850)
PHONE..............................716 434-4380
Fax: 716 434-4546
James Streacher, *Ch of Bd*
Scott J Zgoda, *Ch of Bd*
Bruce Zgoda, *President*
Jim Streicher, *President*
James Streacher Jr, *Vice Pres*
▲ **EMP:** 55
SQ FT: 50,000
SALES (est): 14MM **Privately Held**
WEB: www.bisonbag.com
SIC: 2673 Plastic bags: made from purchased materials

(G-7601)
BUFFALO BIOBLOWER TECH LLC
6100 Donner Rd (14094-9227)
PHONE..............................716 625-8618
Dr John A Lordi, *CEO*
EMP: 8
SALES (est): 1.1MM **Privately Held**
SIC: 3564 Purification & dust collection equipment

(G-7602)
BUFFALO MACHINE TLS OF NIAGARA
4935 Lockport Rd (14094-9630)
PHONE..............................716 201-1310
Fax: 716 625-9850
Theresa Silva, *President*
Joseph Silva, *Vice Pres*
Karen Nuggent, *Manager*
Dara Clark, *Administration*
EMP: 11
SQ FT: 25,000
SALES (est): 500K **Privately Held**
WEB: www.bmt-usa.com
SIC: 3542 Machine tools, metal forming type

(G-7603)
CANDLELIGHT CABINETRY INC
Also Called: Renaissance Import
24 Michigan St (14094-2628)
PHONE..............................716 434-2114
Fax: 716 434-6748
Robert Sanderson, *Ch of Bd*
John Yakich, *President*
EMP: 210
SQ FT: 40,000
SALES (est): 26.6MM **Privately Held**
WEB: www.candlelightcab.com
SIC: 2434 Wood kitchen cabinets

(G-7604)
CHAMELEON COLOR CARDS LTD
6530 S Transit Rd (14094-6334)
PHONE..............................716 625-9452
Fax: 716 625-8580
Phyllis Duha, *President*
Emeric J Duha, *Corp Secy*
Ginny Dillman, *Safety Dir*
Cathy Lattanzio, *Opers Mgr*
Bill Salverberger, *Finance*
▲ **EMP:** 55
SQ FT: 16,000
SALES (est): 9.4MM
SALES (corp-wide): 26.4MM **Privately Held**
WEB: www.duhagroup.com
SIC: 3993 Displays, paint process

GEOGRAPHIC SECTION

Lockport - Niagara County (G-7630)

PA: Duha Color Services Limited
750 Bradford St
Winnipeg MB R3H 0
204 786-8961

(G-7605)
COMMUNITY NEWSPPR HOLDINGS INC
Also Called: Union Sun & Journal
135 Main St Ste 1 (14094-3728)
PHONE.................................716 439-9222
Fax: 716 439-9239
Denise Young, *Branch Mgr*
Scott Moreland, *Manager*
EMP: 33 **Privately Held**
SIC: 2711 Newspapers: publishing only, not printed on site
PA: Community Newspaper Holdings, Inc.
445 Dexter Ave Ste 7000
Montgomery AL 36104

(G-7606)
CUSTOM LASER INC
6747 Akron Rd (14094-5316)
P.O. Box 962 (14095-0962)
PHONE.................................716 434-8600
Fax: 716 439-4805
Gary Brockman, *President*
Ken Hammond, *Opers Mgr*
Jason Walling, *Opers Staff*
Carol Cambell, *Human Res Dir*
Scott Brockman, *Sales Executive*
EMP: 30
SQ FT: 9,000
SALES (est): 5.9MM **Privately Held**
WEB: www.customlaserinc.com
SIC: 3479 7692 Etching & engraving; welding repair

(G-7607)
DELPHI THERMAL SYSTEMS
350 Upper Mountain Rd (14094-1861)
PHONE.................................716 439-2454
Andrew Minarcin, *Principal*
EMP: 11 EST: 2014
SALES (est): 1.6MM **Privately Held**
SIC: 3714 Motor vehicle parts & accessories

(G-7608)
DERN MOORE MACHINE COMPANY INC
151 S Niagara St (14094-1907)
PHONE.................................716 433-6243
Fax: 716 433-7018
Ken Moore, *President*
Sally J Moore, *Vice Pres*
EMP: 9
SQ FT: 10,000
SALES (est): 840K **Privately Held**
WEB: www.moorewashsystems.com
SIC: 3599 Machine shop, jobbing & repair

(G-7609)
DOBRIN INDUSTRIES INC (PA)
210 Walnut St Ste 22 (14094-3713)
PHONE.................................800 353-2229
Fax: 716 438-5000
Paul Dobrin, *President*
EMP: 5
SQ FT: 5,000
SALES (est): 483.5K **Privately Held**
WEB: www.time-frames.com
SIC: 3499 Picture frames, metal

(G-7610)
E & R MACHINE INC
211 Grand St (14094-2198)
P.O. Box 499 (14095-0499)
PHONE.................................716 434-6639
Fax: 716 434-9857
Garry E Sauls, *Ch of Bd*
Robert Swierczynski, *Plant Mgr*
Linda Penwright, *Office Mgr*
Doug Betts, *Manager*
James Gaylord, *Manager*
EMP: 30 EST: 1961
SALES (est): 5.5MM **Privately Held**
WEB: www.er-machine.com
SIC: 3599 Machine shop, jobbing & repair

(G-7611)
E Z ENTRY DOORS INC
5299 Enterprise Dr (14094-1853)
PHONE.................................716 434-3440
Fax: 716 434-0197
Roger W Grear, *President*
Patricia R Grear, *Vice Pres*
EMP: 12
SQ FT: 5,000
SALES (est): 2.2MM **Privately Held**
WEB: www.ezentrydoors.com
SIC: 3534 Elevators & equipment

(G-7612)
EMPRO NIAGARA INC
5027 Ridge Rd (14094-8948)
PHONE.................................716 433-2769
Fax: 716 433-3353
Willa L Hand, *President*
Willa Hand, *President*
Will Hand, *Principal*
Melissa Hand, *Vice Pres*
EMP: 6
SALES: 500K **Privately Held**
WEB: www.emproniagara.com
SIC: 3599 Machine shop, jobbing & repair

(G-7613)
ENTERTRON INDUSTRIES INC
99 Robinson Pl (14094-4617)
PHONE.................................716 772-7216
Stephen Luft, *President*
Dave Polakiewicz, *Manager*
EMP: 24 EST: 1979
SQ FT: 6,000
SALES (est): 220.5K **Privately Held**
WEB: www.entertron.com
SIC: 3625 3672 Electric controls & control accessories, industrial; printed circuit boards

(G-7614)
F W ROBERTS MFG CO INC
73 Lock St (14094-2891)
P.O. Box 408, Mountville PA (17554-0408)
PHONE.................................716 434-3555
Fax: 716 439-4603
Sherri Sczepczenski, *Admin Sec*
▲ **EMP:** 13
SQ FT: 13,363
SALES (est): 2.2MM **Privately Held**
SIC: 3554 3545 Paper mill machinery: plating, slitting, waxing, etc.; machine tool accessories

(G-7615)
FISHING VALLEY LLC
7217 N Canal Rd (14094-9411)
PHONE.................................716 523-6158
Anna Zhalyalotdinova,
EMP: 5
SALES (est): 175.6K **Privately Held**
SIC: 3949 Bait, artificial; fishing

(G-7616)
FREEDOM RUN WINERY INC
5138 Lower Mountain Rd (14094-9767)
PHONE.................................716 433-4136
Larry Manning, *Manager*
EMP: 7
SALES (est): 715.8K **Privately Held**
SIC: 2084 Wines

(G-7617)
GLOBAL ABRASIVE PRODUCTS INC (PA)
62 Mill St (14094-2460)
PHONE.................................716 438-0047
John T Sidebottom, *President*
Laurie J Sidebottom, *Vice Pres*
EMP: 40
SALES (est): 4.9MM **Privately Held**
WEB: www.preson.com
SIC: 3291 Coated abrasive products; sandpaper

(G-7618)
GM COMPONENTS HOLDINGS LLC
Also Called: Gmch Lockport Ptc
200 Upper Mountain Rd (14094-1819)
PHONE.................................716 439-2237
Jerry Griffin, *Purchasing*
Pat Murtha, *Branch Mgr*
Rich Thunhorst, *Manager*
EMP: 209 **Publicly Held**
SIC: 3714 Air conditioner parts, motor vehicle; defrosters, motor vehicle; heaters, motor vehicle; radiators & radiator shells & cores, motor vehicle
HQ: Gm Components Holdings, Llc
300 Renaissance Ctr
Detroit MI 48243

(G-7619)
GM COMPONENTS HOLDINGS LLC
Also Called: Gmch Lockport
200 Upper Mountain Rd (14094-1819)
PHONE.................................716 439-2463
Jeremy Cummins, *Engineer*
Ronald Pirtle, *Branch Mgr*
EMP: 350 **Publicly Held**
SIC: 3629 3714 3585 3563 Condensers, for motors or generators; motor vehicle parts & accessories; refrigeration & heating equipment; air & gas compressors
HQ: Gm Components Holdings, Llc
300 Renaissance Ctr
Detroit MI 48243

(G-7620)
GM COMPONENTS HOLDINGS LLC
Also Called: General Mtr Cmponents Holdings
200 Upper Mountain Rd # 7 (14094-1819)
PHONE.................................716 439-2011
Ron Prabucki, *Engineer*
Tom Rush, *Engineer*
Anita Mullen, *Branch Mgr*
EMP: 300 **Publicly Held**
SIC: 3629 3714 3585 3563 Condensers, for motors or generators; motor vehicle parts & accessories; refrigeration & heating equipment; air & gas compressors
HQ: Gm Components Holdings, Llc
300 Renaissance Ctr
Detroit MI 48243

(G-7621)
GM COMPONENTS HOLDINGS LLC
Also Called: Integrated Indus Resources
200 Upper Mountain Rd # 10 (14094-1819)
PHONE.................................716 439-2402
Steven Kendall, *Engineer*
R Westby, *Engineer*
Mark Inchiosa, *Branch Mgr*
EMP: 75 **Publicly Held**
WEB: www.delphiauto.com
SIC: 3053 Gaskets & sealing devices
HQ: Gm Components Holdings, Llc
300 Renaissance Ctr
Detroit MI 48243

(G-7622)
GOODING CO INC
Also Called: Insert Outsert Experts, The
5568 Davison Rd (14094-9090)
PHONE.................................716 434-5501
Fax: 716 434-9778
Gerald J Hace, *President*
David Carver, *Manager*
April Corrao, *Director*
▼ **EMP:** 34
SQ FT: 26,500
SALES: 6.4MM **Privately Held**
WEB: www.goodingcoinc.com
SIC: 2679 2752 2621 Tags & labels, paper; commercial printing, offset; wrapping & packaging papers; packaging paper

(G-7623)
HTI RECYCLING LLC
Also Called: Manufacturing
490 Ohio St (14094-4220)
PHONE.................................716 433-9294
Derek Martin,
EMP: 50
SALES (est): 8.6MM **Privately Held**
SIC: 3069 Reclaimed rubber (reworked by manufacturing processes)

(G-7624)
J M CANTY INC
6100 Donner Rd (14094-9227)
PHONE.................................716 625-4227
Thomas Canty, *Ch of Bd*
Jean Canty, *Vice Pres*
Jack Doescher, *MIS Staff*
EMP: 30
SQ FT: 38,000
SALES (est): 8MM **Privately Held**
WEB: www.jmcanty.com
SIC: 3443 3648 2891 Vessels, process or storage (from boiler shops): metal plate; lighting equipment; sealants

(G-7625)
JACK J FLORIO JR
Also Called: Micro Graphics
36b Main St (14094-3607)
PHONE.................................716 434-9123
Fax: 716 434-9152
Jack J Florio Jr, *Owner*
Rebecca Kelley, *Vice Pres*
EMP: 5
SALES (est): 370K **Privately Held**
SIC: 2752 2754 2759 2791 Commercial printing, lithographic; commercial printing, gravure; commercial printing; typesetting; bookbinding & related work; automotive & apparel trimmings

(G-7626)
LAFARGE NORTH AMERICA INC
400 Hinman Rd (14094-9276)
PHONE.................................716 772-2621
Courtland Hess, *Plant Mgr*
Len Studley, *Safety Mgr*
Harry McCormick, *Manager*
Rebecca Hartford, *Manager*
Todd Watson, *Manager*
EMP: 30
SQ FT: 47,480
SALES (corp-wide): 26.6B **Privately Held**
WEB: www.lafargenorthamerica.com
SIC: 3241 Cement, hydraulic
HQ: Lafarge North America Inc.
8700 W Bryn Mawr Ave Ll
Chicago IL 60631
703 480-3600

(G-7627)
MAHLE BEHR USA INC
Also Called: Delphi Thrmal Lckport Model Sp
350 Upper Mountain Rd (14094-1861)
PHONE.................................716 439-2011
Daniel L Martin, *Engineer*
Dave Patterson, *Branch Mgr*
Celia Paulin, *Info Tech Mgr*
EMP: 450 **Privately Held**
SIC: 3714 Motor vehicle parts & accessories
HQ: Mahle Behr Usa Inc.
2700 Daley Dr
Troy MI 48083
248 743-3700

(G-7628)
MERRITT MACHINERY LLC
10 Simonds St (14094-4111)
PHONE.................................716 434-5558
Micheal Smith, *Purchasing*
Anna McCann,
◆ **EMP:** 20 EST: 1977
SQ FT: 30,000
SALES (est): 4.5MM **Privately Held**
WEB: www.merrittpmi.com
SIC: 3553 Woodworking machinery

(G-7629)
METAL CLADDING INC
230 S Niagara St (14094-1927)
PHONE.................................716 434-5513
Fax: 716 439-4010
Alexander F Robb, *CEO*
Raymond S Adornetto, *CFO*
Deborah Reimer, *Admin Sec*
▲ **EMP:** 87 EST: 1945
SQ FT: 70,000
SALES (est): 14.5MM **Privately Held**
WEB: www.metalcladding.com
SIC: 3479 3089 Coating of metals with plastic or resins; coating, rust preventive; plastic hardware & building products; plastic & fiberglass tanks

(G-7630)
METRO GROUP INC
Also Called: Retailer
8 South St (14094-4412)
PHONE.................................716 434-4055
Fax: 716 434-6022
Bernard Bradpiece, *President*
David Smith, *Supervisor*
EMP: 5 EST: 1948
SQ FT: 1,500

Lockport - Niagara County (G-7631) — GEOGRAPHIC SECTION

SALES (est): 246K **Privately Held**
SIC: 2741 Guides: publishing only, not printed on site; shopping news: publishing only, not printed on site

(G-7631)
MILWARD ALLOYS INC
500 Mill St (14094-1712)
PHONE 716 434-5536
Fax: 716 434-3257
Johanna Van De Mark, *President*
Allen Van De Mark, *Vice Pres*
Johanna V Mark, *Plant Mgr*
Dave Summerlee, *Plant Mgr*
Kevin Kristy, *Maint Spvr*
◆ **EMP:** 37 **EST:** 1948
SQ FT: 60,000
SALES: 5MM **Privately Held**
WEB: www.milward.com
SIC: 3351 3365 Bands, copper & copper alloy; aluminum & aluminum-based alloy castings

(G-7632)
MODERN-TEC MANUFACTURING INC
4935 Lockport Rd (14094-9630)
PHONE 716 625-8700
Christopher Matyas, *President*
EMP: 5
SQ FT: 11,000
SALES (est): 594.5K **Privately Held**
SIC: 3599 Air intake filters, internal combustion engine, except auto

(G-7633)
MOLEY MAGNETICS INC
5202 Commerce Dr (14094-1862)
PHONE 716 434-4023
John S Moley, *CEO*
Ronald Slaby, *Vice Pres*
Nicholas Moley, *Opers Staff*
Susan Davis, *Purch Agent*
Barbara Sullivan, *Sales Mgr*
▲ **EMP:** 4
SALES (est): 1.1MM **Privately Held**
SIC: 3621 Electric motor & generator parts

(G-7634)
NIAGARA COOLER INC
6605 Slyton Settlement Rd (14094-1144)
PHONE 716 434-1235
Fax: 716 434-1739
Joseph Loiacano, *President*
EMP: 7
SQ FT: 5,000
SALES: 1MM **Privately Held**
WEB: www.niagaracooler.com
SIC: 3743 Industrial locomotives & parts

(G-7635)
NIAGARA FIBERBOARD INC
140 Van Buren St (14094-2437)
P.O. Box 520 (14095-0520)
PHONE 716 434-8881
Fax: 716 434-8884
Stephen W Halas, *Ch of Bd*
Kevin Cain, *Vice Pres*
EMP: 23
SQ FT: 60,000
SALES (est): 3.9MM **Privately Held**
WEB: www.niagarafiberboard.com
SIC: 2493 2631 Fiberboard, other vegetable pulp; paperboard mills

(G-7636)
NIAGARA PRECISION INC
233 Market St (14094-2917)
PHONE 716 439-0956
Fax: 716 439-0117
Roger Hood, *President*
Dennis Hood, *Vice Pres*
Barbara Hood, *Admin Sec*
EMP: 24
SQ FT: 12,000
SALES (est): 4MM **Privately Held**
WEB: www.niagaraprecision.net
SIC: 3599 Machine shop, jobbing & repair

(G-7637)
NIAGARA TRUSS & PALLET LLC
5626 Old Saunders Settle (14094-4100)
PHONE 716 433-5400
Fax: 716 433-8400
Gary Clark, *Marketing Staff*
EMP: 18
SQ FT: 12,000
SALES (est): 2.3MM **Privately Held**
SIC: 2439 Trusses, except roof: laminated lumber

(G-7638)
NORTON PULPSTONES INCORPORATED
53 Caledonia St (14094-2829)
P.O. Box 408, Mountville PA (17554-0408)
PHONE 716 433-9400
Glen Smith, *Branch Mgr*
EMP: 8
SALES (corp-wide): 1.1MM **Privately Held**
SIC: 2611 Mechanical pulp, including groundwood & thermomechanical
PA: Norton Pulpstones Incorporated
604 Lindsay Cir
Villanova PA 19085
610 964-0544

(G-7639)
ONTARIO LABEL GRAPHICS INC
6444 Ridge Rd (14094-1015)
PHONE 716 434-8505
Fax: 716 434-8515
Richard E Verheyn, *President*
Rose M Verheyn, *Vice Pres*
EMP: 12
SQ FT: 9,000
SALES (est): 1.1MM **Privately Held**
SIC: 2759 Commercial printing; labels & seals: printing

(G-7640)
PIVOT PUNCH CORPORATION
6550 Campbell Blvd (14094-9228)
PHONE 716 625-8000
Fax: 716 625-6995
Robert H King Jr, *CEO*
Christopher C King, *President*
Robert H King, *Chairman*
Richard Chapman, *Vice Pres*
Christopher King, *Vice Pres*
EMP: 87 **EST:** 1945
SQ FT: 32,500
SALES: 7.2MM **Privately Held**
WEB: www.pivotpunch.com
SIC: 3544 Punches, forming & stamping

(G-7641)
PRECISE PUNCH CORPORATION
6550 Campbell Blvd (14094-9210)
PHONE 716 625-8000
Robert H King Jr, *President*
Christopher King, *Vice Pres*
Joseph La Monto, *Accounting Mgr*
EMP: 11
SQ FT: 3,000
SALES (est): 1.1MM **Privately Held**
SIC: 3544 Punches, forming & stamping

(G-7642)
ROSS JC INC
6722 Lincoln Ave (14094-6220)
PHONE 716 439-1161
John Ross, *President*
Natalie Ross, *Vice Pres*
EMP: 5
SQ FT: 5,452
SALES: 400K **Privately Held**
SIC: 3545 Machine tool accessories

(G-7643)
ROYALTON MILLWORK & DESIGN
7526 Tonawanda Creek Rd (14094-9350)
PHONE 716 439-4092
Thomas Herberger, *President*
Cathy Fimbel, *Office Mgr*
EMP: 5
SQ FT: 10,000
SALES (est): 743.3K **Privately Held**
SIC: 2431 Doors & door parts & trim, wood; windows & window parts & trim, wood; moldings & baseboards, ornamental & trim; staircases, stairs & railings

(G-7644)
RUBBERFORM RECYCLED PDTS LLC
75 Michigan St (14094-2629)
PHONE 716 478-0404
Bill Robbins, *CEO*
Roberta Callaghan, *Accounts Mgr*
Susie Robbins, *Accounts Mgr*
Kim Bunce, *Manager*
Susie Robbins, *Manager*
▼ **EMP:** 14
SQ FT: 30,000
SALES (est): 3.4MM **Privately Held**
WEB: www.rubberform.com
SIC: 3069 Reclaimed rubber (reworked by manufacturing processes)

(G-7645)
SENTRY METAL BLAST INC
Also Called: Sentry Metal Services
553 West Ave (14094-4116)
P.O. Box 160 (14095-0160)
PHONE 716 285-5241
Fax: 716 692-6245
Gary D Verost, *President*
James Verost, *Vice Pres*
Mark Verost, *Vice Pres*
Karen Schiro, *Manager*
EMP: 30
SQ FT: 47,000
SALES (est): 7.1MM **Privately Held**
WEB: www.sentrymetal.com
SIC: 3441 3479 Fabricated structural metal; coating of metals & formed products

(G-7646)
SUMMIT MSP LLC
6042 Old Beattie Rd (14094-7943)
PHONE 716 433-1014
Fax: 716 433-1054
John Butcher, *Mng Member*
Rose Butcher, *Mng Member*
EMP: 8
SQ FT: 1,500
SALES: 767K **Privately Held**
SIC: 2752 Commercial printing, offset

(G-7647)
SUMMIT PRINT & MAIL LLC
6042 Old Beattie Rd (14094-7943)
PHONE 716 433-1014
J Butcher, *Mng Member*
John Butcher, *Mng Member*
Cookie Butcher,
EMP: 7
SALES (est): 841.1K **Privately Held**
WEB: www.summitprintmail.com
SIC: 2752 Commercial printing, lithographic

(G-7648)
TDY INDUSTRIES LLC
Also Called: ATI Specialty Materials
695 Ohio St (14094-4221)
PHONE 716 433-4411
H Dalton, *Branch Mgr*
Gordie Martin, *Sr Sys Analyst*
Sara Newton, *Systems Staff*
EMP: 35
SQ FT: 438 **Publicly Held**
WEB: www.alleghenyludlum.com
SIC: 3312 3339 Stainless steel; primary nonferrous metals
HQ: Tdy Industries, Llc
1000 Six Ppg Pl
Pittsburgh PA 15222
412 394-2896

(G-7649)
TED WESTBROOK
Also Called: Westbrook Machinery
4736 Mapleton Rd (14094-9621)
PHONE 716 625-4443
Ted Westbrook, *Owner*
EMP: 1 **EST:** 1995
SALES: 1MM **Privately Held**
SIC: 3599 Machine shop, jobbing & repair

(G-7650)
TITANIUM DEM REMEDIATION GROUP
4907 I D A Park Dr (14094-1833)
P.O. Box 471 (14095-0471)
PHONE 716 433-4100
Angela M Bodami, *Principal*
EMP: 12
SALES (est): 4.6MM **Privately Held**
SIC: 3356 Titanium

(G-7651)
TORRENT EMS LLC
190 Walnut St (14094-3710)
PHONE 716 312-4099
Michael Dehn, *CEO*
Louise Cadwalader, *Treasurer*
EMP: 16
SALES (est): 4.3MM
SALES (corp-wide): 13.8MM **Privately Held**
SIC: 3577 Computer peripheral equipment
PA: Trek, Inc.
190 Walnut St
Lockport NY 14094
716 438-7555

(G-7652)
TREK INC (PA)
190 Walnut St (14094-3710)
PHONE 716 438-7555
Toshio Uehara, *CEO*
Mike Dehn, *President*
Louise Cadwalader, *VP Finance*
Chris Lemke, *Sales Engr*
David Abdy, *Marketing Staff*
EMP: 16
SQ FT: 30,330
SALES: 13.8MM **Privately Held**
SIC: 3825 Instruments to measure electricity

(G-7653)
TWIN LAKE CHEMICAL INC
520 Mill St (14094-1794)
P.O. Box 411 (14095-0411)
PHONE 716 433-3824
Fax: 716 433-7271
James J Hodan, *President*
William Caswell, *Engineer*
▲ **EMP:** 18
SQ FT: 10,000
SALES (est): 3.9MM **Privately Held**
WEB: www.twinlakechemical.com
SIC: 2869 Industrial organic chemicals

(G-7654)
ULRICH SIGN CO INC
177 Oakhurst St (14094-1920)
PHONE 716 434-0167
Fax: 716 434-0226
C McCaffrey, *President*
Christopher McCaffrey, *President*
Joe Reinhart, *General Mgr*
Val Cox, *Office Mgr*
EMP: 21 **EST:** 1939
SQ FT: 6,000
SALES (est): 2MM **Privately Held**
WEB: www.ulrichsigns.com
SIC: 3993 Neon signs; signs, not made in custom sign painting shops

(G-7655)
VAN DE MARK CHEMICAL CO INC (PA)
1 N Transit Rd (14094-2323)
PHONE 716 433-6764
Fax: 716 433-2850
Michael Kucharski, *CEO*
Paul Ameis, *COO*
Paul Ameb, *Exec VP*
Brian Law, *Senior VP*
William Krencik, *QC Mgr*
▲ **EMP:** 85 **EST:** 1951
SQ FT: 13,770
SALES: 27.8MM **Privately Held**
WEB: www.vdmchemical.com
SIC: 2819 Industrial inorganic chemicals

(G-7656)
VANCHLOR COMPANY INC (PA)
45 Main St (14094-2838)
PHONE 716 434-2624
Richard G Shotell, *Ch of Bd*
Dirk A Van De Mark, *Vice Pres*
Dustin Corallo, *Manager*
Judy Samuel, *Manager*
Richard White, *Manager*
◆ **EMP:** 12 **EST:** 1960
SALES (est): 2.7MM **Privately Held**
WEB: www.vanchlor.com
SIC: 2819 Aluminum chloride

(G-7657)
VANCHLOR COMPANY INC
555 W Jackson St (14094)
PHONE 716 434-2624

▲ = Import ▼ = Export
◆ = Import/Export

Richard Shotell, *Branch Mgr*
EMP: 16
SQ FT: 30,839
SALES (corp-wide): 2.7MM **Privately Held**
WEB: www.vanchlor.com
SIC: 2819 Aluminum chloride
PA: Vanchlor Company, Inc.
 45 Main St
 Lockport NY 14094
 716 434-2624

Lockwood
Tioga County

(G-7658)
H F CARY & SONS
70 Reniff Rd (14859-9753)
 PHONE..................607 598-2563
 Lewis A Cary, *Owner*
 EMP: 5
 SALES: 250K **Privately Held**
 SIC: 3272 Septic tanks, concrete

Locust Valley
Nassau County

(G-7659)
ALPHA 6 DISTRIBUTIONS LLC
Also Called: Arctix
11 Oyster Bay Rd (11560-2322)
 PHONE..................516 801-8290
 Judy Ward, *CFO*
 Brendan Schechter, *Natl Sales Mgr*
 Matthew Bruderman, *Mng Member*
 Courtney Adel, *Manager*
 Adam Smith, *Executive Asst*
 ▲ **EMP:** 12
 SQ FT: 3,000
 SALES: 25MM **Privately Held**
 SIC: 2329 5137 2339 Athletic (warmup, sweat & jogging) suits: men's & boys'; women's & children's clothing; women's & misses' athletic clothing & sportswear

(G-7660)
FILESTREAM INC
257 Buckram Rd (11560-1906)
P.O. Box 93, Glen Head (11545-0093)
 PHONE..................516 759-4100
 Fax: 516 759-3011
 Yao Chu, *President*
 Marcus Hill, *Manager*
 Tan-NA Lee, *CTO*
 EMP: 10
 SQ FT: 1,200
 SALES: 2MM **Privately Held**
 WEB: www.filestream.com
 SIC: 7372 Prepackaged software; business oriented computer software; educational computer software

(G-7661)
FOREST IRON WORKS INC
3 Elm St Ste A (11560-2149)
 PHONE..................516 671-4229
 Fax: 516 671-8613
 Mario Gallo, *President*
 EMP: 8
 SQ FT: 13,000
 SALES (est): 1.2MM **Privately Held**
 SIC: 3446 Architectural metalwork

(G-7662)
HENRY DESIGN STUDIOS INC
129 Birch Hill Rd Ste 2 (11560-1841)
 PHONE..................516 801-2760
 Fax: 212 730-2340
 Henry Perlstein, *President*
 Henri Rayski, *Vice Pres*
 Elka Perlstein, *Treasurer*
 EMP: 7
 SQ FT: 1,400
 SALES: 1MM **Privately Held**
 SIC: 3911 Jewelry, precious metal

(G-7663)
JK MANUFACTURING INC
115 Forest Ave Unit 22 (11560-4001)
 PHONE..................212 683-3535
 Joe Rubens, *Owner*

 EMP: 9
 SALES (est): 809K **Privately Held**
 SIC: 3911 Jewelry, precious metal

(G-7664)
T G S INC
6 Wildwood Ct (11560-1108)
 PHONE..................516 629-6905
 Rajesh Raichoudhury, *CEO*
 EMP: 5
 SALES (est): 370K **Privately Held**
 WEB: www.tgs.com
 SIC: 2731 Books: publishing & printing

Lodi
Seneca County

(G-7665)
LAMOREAUX LANDING WI
Also Called: Wagner Farms
9224 State Route 414 (14860-9641)
 PHONE..................607 582-6162
 Fax: 607 582-6010
 Linsey Wig, *Sales Dir*
 Michele Harris, *Marketing Staff*
 Brenda Clawson, *Office Mgr*
 Mark Wagner,
 EMP: 70
 SQ FT: 4,070
 SALES (est): 5.2MM **Privately Held**
 WEB: www.lamoreauxwine.com
 SIC: 2084 Wines

(G-7666)
WAGNER VINEYARDS & BREWING CO
Also Called: Ginny Lee Cafe
9322 State Route 414 (14860-9641)
 PHONE..................607 582-6574
 Stanley Wagner, *Owner*
 Kim Greenier, *Bookkeeper*
 John Wagner, *Manager*
 Brent Wojnowski, *Manager*
 EMP: 30
 SQ FT: 1,200
 SALES (est): 2.6MM **Privately Held**
 WEB: www.wagnervineyards.com
 SIC: 2084 0172 2082 Wines; grapes; malt beverages

Long Beach
Nassau County

(G-7667)
AIR TITE MANUFACTURING INC
Also Called: Focus Point Windows & Doors
724 Park Pl Ste B (11561-2158)
P.O. Box 149 (11561-0149)
 PHONE..................516 897-0295
 Fax: 516 897-0299
 EMP: 120
 SQ FT: 40,000
 SALES (est): 1.6MM **Privately Held**
 SIC: 3442 Mfg Storm Doors & Windows Metal

(G-7668)
BARRIER BREWING COMPANY LLC
612 W Walnut St (11561-2919)
 PHONE..................516 316-4429
 Evan Klein, *Administration*
 EMP: 5 **EST:** 2012
 SALES (est): 318K **Privately Held**
 SIC: 2082 Malt beverages

(G-7669)
DESIGNERS TOUCH INC (PA)
Also Called: Diamond Venetian Blind Shade
750 Shore Rd Apt 6b (11561-4734)
 PHONE..................718 641-3718
 Marvin Kotin, *President*
 Elaine Kotin, *Vice Pres*
 EMP: 7 **EST:** 1952
 SQ FT: 5,000
 SALES (est): 654K **Privately Held**
 SIC: 2591 5719 Blinds vertical; vertical blinds

(G-7670)
ECHO APPELLATE PRESS INC
30 W Park Ave Ste 200 (11561-2018)
 PHONE..................516 432-3601
 Stuart Davis, *President*
 Joyce Davis, *Corp Secy*
 EMP: 7
 SQ FT: 4,500
 SALES: 763K **Privately Held**
 WEB: www.echoappellate.com
 SIC: 2752 Commercial printing, lithographic

(G-7671)
FIVE STAR FIELD SERVICES
Also Called: Five Star Measurement
535 W Penn St (11561-3017)
 PHONE..................347 446-6816
 Douglas Asch, *Mng Member*
 William Cook,
 Keith Stone,
 EMP: 7
 SQ FT: 1,000
 SALES (est): 601.7K **Privately Held**
 SIC: 1389 Measurement of well flow rates, oil & gas

(G-7672)
INNOVATION IN MOTION INC
Also Called: Iim Global
780 Long Beach Blvd (11561-2238)
 PHONE..................407 878-7561
 David Jones, *CEO*
 Thomas Szoke, *COO*
 Todd Libey, *Prdtn Mgr*
 Sue Bannister, *Manager*
 Daniel Fovzati, *Director*
 ▼ **EMP:** 6
 SQ FT: 10,000
 SALES (est): 446.7K
 SALES (corp-wide): 1.9MM **Publicly Held**
 SIC: 3663 7371 3559 Mobile communication equipment; computer software development & applications; screening equipment, electric
 PA: Ipsidy Inc.
 780 Long Beach Blvd
 Long Beach NY 11561
 407 951-8640

(G-7673)
IPSIDY INC (PA)
780 Long Beach Blvd (11561-2238)
 PHONE..................407 951-8640
 Philip D Beck, *Ch of Bd*
 Stuart Stoller, *CFO*
 Thomas Szoke, *CTO*
 Douglas Solomon, *Exec Dir*
 EMP: 72
 SALES: 1.9MM **Publicly Held**
 SIC: 7372 7371 Prepackaged software; computer software development & applications

Long Eddy
Sullivan County

(G-7674)
DEDECO INTERNATIONAL SALES INC (PA)
11617 State Route 97 (12760-5603)
 PHONE..................845 887-4840
 Fax: 914 887-5281
 Steven M Antler, *President*
 Joseph Lancellotti, *Mktg Dir*
 ▲ **EMP:** 35
 SALES (est): 7.5MM **Privately Held**
 WEB: www.dedeco.com
 SIC: 3291 3843 Abrasive products; dental equipment & supplies

Long Island City
Queens County

(G-7675)
21ST CENTURY OPTICS INC (DH)
Also Called: S&G Optical
4700 33rd St Ste 1r (11101-2401)
 PHONE..................347 527-1079
 Fax: 718 685-0404

 Ralph Woythaler, *President*
 Bernard Woythaler, *Vice Pres*
 Michael Woythaler, *Vice Pres*
 Anthony Fulco, *VP Sales*
 Nicholas Cacace, *Sales Mgr*
 EMP: 26
 SQ FT: 22,000
 SALES (est): 6.6MM
 SALES (corp-wide): 938.9MM **Privately Held**
 WEB: www.21stcenturyoptics.com
 SIC: 3827 3851 5048 Optical instruments & lenses; lenses, optical: all types except ophthalmic; ophthalmic goods; lenses, ophthalmic
 HQ: Essilor Laboratories Of America Holding Co., Inc.
 13555 N Stemmons Fwy
 Dallas TX 75234
 214 496-4141

(G-7676)
A W R GROUP INC
3715 Hunters Point Ave (11101-1913)
 PHONE..................718 729-0412
 Mark Schinderman, *President*
 Mia Coppala, *Accountant*
 EMP: 10
 SALES (est): 1.1MM **Privately Held**
 SIC: 2385 7699 Waterproof outerwear; antique repair & restoration, except furniture, automobiles

(G-7677)
AAAA YORK INC
Also Called: York Ladders
3720 12th St (11101-6009)
 PHONE..................718 784-6666
 Kenneth Buettner, *President*
 ▲ **EMP:** 10
 SQ FT: 5,000
 SALES (est): 1.3MM **Privately Held**
 SIC: 3531 Construction machinery

(G-7678)
ABBOT & ABBOT BOX CORP
Also Called: Abbot & Abbot Packing Service
3711 10th St (11101-6043)
 PHONE..................888 930-5972
 Fax: 718 392-8439
 Stuart Gleiber, *President*
 Douglas Gleiber, *Vice Pres*
 Lee Schogel, *Sales Mgr*
 Carol Maiorella, *Manager*
 EMP: 17
 SQ FT: 40,000
 SALES (est): 3.3MM **Privately Held**
 WEB: www.abbotbox.com
 SIC: 2441 2448 3412 Boxes, wood; pallets, wood; skids, wood; wood containers; metal barrels, drums & pails; folding paperboard boxes

(G-7679)
ABLE STEEL EQUIPMENT CO INC
5002 23rd St (11101-4595)
 PHONE..................718 361-9240
 Fax: 718 937-5742
 Bonnie S Tarkenton, *President*
 William Tarkenton, *Mfg Staff*
 Ed Morgan, *Treasurer*
 Harris Singer, *Director*
 EMP: 15 **EST:** 1935
 SQ FT: 30,000
 SALES (est): 1.5MM **Privately Held**
 WEB: www.ablesteelequipment.com
 SIC: 2542 1799 2531 2522 Cabinets: show, display or storage: except wood; partitions for floor attachment, prefabricated: except wood; shelving, office & store: except wood; demountable partition installation; public building & related furniture; office furniture, except wood

(G-7680)
ACTION TECHNOLOGIES INC
Also Called: Active Business Systems
3809 33rd St Apt 1 (11101-2230)
 PHONE..................718 278-1000
 Francine Amendola, *President*
 EMP: 5
 SALES (est): 232.9K **Privately Held**
 SIC: 3579 Canceling machinery, post office

Long Island City - Queens County (G-7681)

(G-7681)
AIR LOUVER & DAMPER INC (PA)
2121 44th Rd (11101-5010)
PHONE.................718 392-3232
Joseph Chalpin, *President*
Harold Blake, *Div Sub Head*
EMP: 12
SQ FT: 20,000
SALES (est): 2.7MM **Privately Held**
SIC: 3822 3444 Damper operators: pneumatic, thermostatic, electric; metal ventilating equipment

(G-7682)
AKZO NOBEL COATINGS INC
4602 21st St (11101-7848)
P.O. Box 1931 (11101-0931)
PHONE.................610 603-7589
Volkan Goren, *Ch of Bd*
EMP: 34
SALES (est): 15.7MM
SALES (corp-wide): 15B **Privately Held**
SIC: 2851 Paints & allied products
PA: Akzo Nobel N.V.
    Christian Neefestraat 2
    Amsterdam
    889 697-555

(G-7683)
ALFRED MAINZER INC (PA)
2708 40th Ave (11101-3725)
PHONE.................718 392-4200
Fax: 718 392-2681
Ronald Mainzer, *President*
Barry Mainzer, *Vice Pres*
Brad Packer, *Treasurer*
Sari Mainzer, *Admin Sec*
▼ EMP: 25 EST: 1938
SQ FT: 40,000
SALES (est): 3.7MM **Privately Held**
WEB: www.alfredmainzer.com
SIC: 2741 Miscellaneous publishing

(G-7684)
ALL CITY SWITCHBOARD CORP
3541 11th St (11106-5013)
PHONE.................718 956-7244
Peter Tsimoyianis, *President*
Mark Silletti, *Sr Corp Ofcr*
Efstratios Kountouris, *Treasurer*
Joan Wittlinder, *Controller*
EMP: 26
SALES (est): 8.9MM **Privately Held**
WEB: www.allcityswbd.com
SIC: 3613 Switchgear & switchboard apparatus

(G-7685)
ALLSTATEBANNERSCOM CORPORATION
Also Called: Allstate Banners
3511 9th St (11106-5103)
PHONE.................718 300-1256
Panagiotis Panagi, *President*
Alexander Phioukas, *Vice Pres*
EMP: 9
SQ FT: 2,000
SALES (est): 1.5MM **Privately Held**
SIC: 2752 Commercial printing, offset

(G-7686)
ALP STONE INC
2520 50th Ave Fl 2 (11101-4421)
PHONE.................718 706-6166
Yunus Bickici, *President*
Hakton Bor, *Vice Pres*
Ghiridhar Khurana, *Accountant*
▲ EMP: 15
SALES: 4MM **Privately Held**
WEB: www.alpstone.com
SIC: 3272 1743 Stone, cast concrete; tile installation, ceramic

(G-7687)
ALPHA PACKAGING INDUSTRIES INC
2004 33rd St (11105-2010)
PHONE.................718 267-4115
Fax: 718 932-9549
David Zaret, *President*
Steven Zaret, *Corp Secy*
Michael Zaret, *Vice Pres*
EMP: 35
SQ FT: 25,000
SALES (est): 12MM **Privately Held**
SIC: 2657 Folding paperboard boxes

(G-7688)
AMBRAS FINE JEWELRY INC
Also Called: Ambras Fjc
3100 47th Ave Unit 3 (11101-3010)
PHONE.................718 784-5252
Fax: 212 268-1546
Morris Dweck, *Ch of Bd*
EMP: 50
SQ FT: 9,000
SALES (est): 5.7MM **Privately Held**
SIC: 3911 Jewelry, precious metal

(G-7689)
AMCI LTD
3302 48th Ave (11101-2418)
PHONE.................718 937-5858
Fax: 718 937-5867
Justo Lorenzotti, *President*
Luis Lorenzotti, *Vice Pres*
Mike Gover, *Accounts Mgr*
Kelli Schmidt, *Marketing Staff*
Nicole Bouverie, *Program Mgr*
▲ EMP: 60
SQ FT: 25,000
SALES (est): 7MM **Privately Held**
SIC: 2499 Picture & mirror frames, wood

(G-7690)
AMERICAN VINTAGE WINE BISCUIT
4003 27th St (11101-3814)
PHONE.................718 361-1003
Fax: 718 361-0204
Mary-Lynn Mondich, *President*
EMP: 7
SQ FT: 2,500
SALES (est): 464.5K **Privately Held**
WEB: www.americanvintage.com
SIC: 2051 Bread, cake & related products

(G-7691)
AMERICAN WAX COMPANY INC
Also Called: American Cleaning Solutions
3930 Review Ave (11101-2020)
P.O. Box 1943 (11101-0943)
PHONE.................718 392-8080
Fax: 718 482-9366
Alan Winik, *CEO*
Ronald Ingber, *President*
Michelle Devito, *Opers Staff*
EMP: 50
SQ FT: 65,000
SALES (est): 10.8MM **Privately Held**
WEB: www.cleaning-solutions.com
SIC: 2842 Specialty cleaning, polishes & sanitation goods

(G-7692)
AMERICAN WOODS & VENEERS WORKS
4735 27th St (11101-4410)
PHONE.................718 937-2195
Chingyu Peng, *President*
Dianna Serro, *Manager*
EMP: 30
SQ FT: 11,000
SALES (est): 4.7MM **Privately Held**
SIC: 2499 Furniture inlays (veneers); veneer work, inlaid

(G-7693)
ANIMA MUNDI HERBALS LLC
Also Called: Rainforest Apothecary
2323 Borden Ave (11101-4508)
PHONE.................415 279-5727
Adriana Ayales, *CEO*
EMP: 6
SQ FT: 1,000
SALES (est): 556K **Privately Held**
SIC: 2834 Vitamin, nutrient & hematinic preparations for human use

(G-7694)
ANTHONY LAWRENCE OF NEW YORK
Also Called: Belfair Draperies
3233 47th Ave (11101-2426)
PHONE.................212 206-8820
Joseph Calagna, *Ch of Bd*
Anthony Lawrence, *Owner*
Michael Giambattista, *Vice Pres*
EMP: 20
SALES (est): 3.1MM **Privately Held**
WEB: www.anthonylawrence.com
SIC: 2391 7641 2511 Draperies, plastic & textile: from purchased materials; re-upholstery; wood household furniture

(G-7695)
APPLE ENTERPRISES INC
Also Called: Apple Digital Printing
1308 43rd Ave (11101-6833)
PHONE.................718 361-2200
Howard N Sturm, *CEO*
Howard Sturm, *CEO*
Adam Sturm, *President*
Alexandra Rosner, *Accounts Mgr*
Jillian Rowen, *Manager*
EMP: 30 EST: 1995
SALES (est): 5.7MM **Privately Held**
WEB: www.applevisualgraphics.com
SIC: 2759 7389 Commercial printing; advertising, promotional & trade show services

(G-7696)
APPLE HEALING & RELAXATION
3114 Broadway (11106-2585)
PHONE.................718 278-1089
EMP: 5
SALES (est): 425.9K **Privately Held**
SIC: 3571 Personal computers (microcomputers)

(G-7697)
APPLIED SAFETY LLC
4349 10th St Ste 311 (11101-6941)
PHONE.................718 608-6292
Jose Hernandez,
EMP: 8
SALES: 200K **Privately Held**
SIC: 3564 Blowers & fans

(G-7698)
ARC REMANUFACTURING INC
1940 42nd St (11105-1113)
PHONE.................718 728-0701
Fax: 718 274-4348
William P Hayes, *President*
John Hayes, *Site Mgr*
▲ EMP: 60
SQ FT: 150,000
SALES (est): 9.4MM **Privately Held**
WEB: www.arcparts.com
SIC: 3714 Motor vehicle engines & parts; power steering equipment, motor vehicle; windshield wiper systems, motor vehicle; motor vehicle brake systems & parts

(G-7699)
ARCHAELOGY MAGAZINE
3636 33rd St Ste 301 (11106-2329)
PHONE.................718 472-3050
Fax: 718 472-3751
Phyliss Katz, *President*
Zachary Zorich, *General Mgr*
EMP: 20
SALES (est): 1.4MM **Privately Held**
WEB: www.archaeology.org
SIC: 2721 Periodicals

(G-7700)
ARGO ENVELOPE CORP
4310 21st St (11101-5002)
PHONE.................718 729-2700
Fax: 718 361-8950
Lawrence Chait, *President*
Eric Chait, *Vice Pres*
EMP: 60 EST: 1946
SQ FT: 50,000
SALES (est): 6.3MM **Privately Held**
SIC: 2759 2752 Envelopes: printing; commercial printing, lithographic

(G-7701)
ARGO GENERAL MACHINE WORK INC
3816 11th St (11101-6114)
PHONE.................718 392-4605
Fax: 718 204-1985
Frank Scaduto, *President*
Ignazio Scaduto, *Vice Pres*
EMP: 7
SQ FT: 2,400
SALES (est): 863.4K **Privately Held**
SIC: 3599 Machine shop, jobbing & repair

(G-7702)
ARGO LITHOGRAPHERS INC
4310 21st St (11101-5002)
PHONE.................718 729-2700
Lawrence Chait, *President*
Eric Chait, *Vice Pres*
EMP: 25
SQ FT: 5,000
SALES: 4MM **Privately Held**
WEB: www.argoenvelope.com
SIC: 2752 5112 5111 2789 Commercial printing, lithographic; stationery & office supplies; printing & writing paper; bookbinding & related work; commercial printing

(G-7703)
ASCO CASTINGS INC (PA)
3100 47th Ave Ste G (11101-3013)
PHONE.................212 719-9800
Barry Smith, *General Mgr*
EMP: 6
SQ FT: 4,000
SALES (est): 1MM **Privately Held**
WEB: www.ascocasting.com
SIC: 3915 Jewelers' castings

(G-7704)
ASIAN GLOBAL TRADING CORP
3613 36th Ave Ste 2 (11106-1306)
PHONE.................718 786-0998
Fax: 718 786-0971
Chau Pei Hsu, *President*
▲ EMP: 10
SALES (est): 1MM **Privately Held**
SIC: 2253 Knit outerwear mills

(G-7705)
ASTRON CANDLE MANUFACTURING CO
1125 30th Ave (11102-4098)
PHONE.................718 728-3330
Fax: 718 956-9583
Menelaos G Tzelios, *President*
◆ EMP: 7
SQ FT: 7,000
SALES (est): 733.7K **Privately Held**
SIC: 3999 Candles

(G-7706)
ASTUCCI US LTD
4369 9th St (11101-6907)
PHONE.................718 752-9700
Dan Benmoshe, *Branch Mgr*
EMP: 18 **Privately Held**
SIC: 3172 Personal leather goods
PA: Astucci, U.S., Ltd.
    385 5th Ave Rm 1100
    New York NY 10016

(G-7707)
ASUR JEWELRY INC
4709 30th St Ste 403 (11101-3400)
PHONE.................718 472-1687
Aydin Barka, *President*
EMP: 6
SQ FT: 2,500
SALES: 700K **Privately Held**
SIC: 3915 Jewelers' castings

(G-7708)
ATLANTIC PRECIOUS METAL CAST
4132 27th St (11101-3825)
PHONE.................718 937-7100
Fax: 718 937-6544
Ricky Barbieri, *Principal*
EMP: 9
SALES (est): 630K **Privately Held**
SIC: 3911 Jewelry, precious metal

(G-7709)
AUGUST STUDIOS
Also Called: Augusta Studios
4008 22nd St Fl 3 (11101-4826)
PHONE.................718 706-6487
August Helbling, *Owner*
EMP: 8
SALES (est): 390K **Privately Held**
SIC: 2512 7641 Upholstered household furniture; upholstery work

GEOGRAPHIC SECTION
Long Island City - Queens County (G-7736)

(G-7710)
B & B SHEET METAL INC
2540 50th Ave (11101-4421)
PHONE.....................718 433-2501
Fax: 718 433-2709
Robert Baschnagel, *President*
Robert Baschnagel III, *President*
Peter Barry, *Research*
Christopher Andreone, *Sales Mgr*
Janice Sausto, *Accounts Mgr*
◆ **EMP:** 50
SALES (est): 11.2MM **Privately Held**
SIC: 3444 Sheet metalwork

(G-7711)
BAGEL LITES LLC
Also Called: Big City Bagel Lites
240 51st Ave Apt 1f (11101-5865)
PHONE.....................855 813-7888
Raquel Salas,
EMP: 2 **EST:** 2015
SQ FT: 2,000
SALES (est): 1MM **Privately Held**
SIC: 2051 5461 Bagels, fresh or frozen; bagels

(G-7712)
BANGLA PATRIKA INC
3806 31st St 2 (11101-2719)
PHONE.....................718 482-9923
Mahabubur Rahman, *President*
EMP: 9
SQ FT: 1,250
SALES (est): 32K **Privately Held**
SIC: 2711 Newspapers

(G-7713)
BARGOLD STORAGE SYSTEMS LLC
4141 38th St (11101-1708)
PHONE.....................718 247-7000
Fax: 212 247-7007
Gerald Goldman, *Mng Member*
Alan Goldman, *Mng Member*
Jordan Goldman, *Mng Member*
Joshua Goldman, *Mng Member*
EMP: 40
SQ FT: 3,000
SALES (est): 9.1MM **Privately Held**
WEB: www.bargoldstorage.com
SIC: 3444 1796 Sheet metalwork; installing building equipment

(G-7714)
BENLEE ENTERPRISES LLC
Also Called: Luvente
3100 47th Ave Unit 2 (11101-3068)
PHONE.....................212 730-7330
Daniel Dabakarov,
EMP: 10
SALES (est): 1.1MM **Privately Held**
SIC: 3911 Jewelry, precious metal

(G-7715)
BESTEC CONCEPT INC
Also Called: Maxivision
4310 23rd St Lbby 4 (11101-5020)
PHONE.....................718 937-5848
Fax: 718 937-5825
Helen M Han, *President*
EMP: 6
SALES (est): 792.7K **Privately Held**
SIC: 2326 2311 2337 2339 Work uniforms; men's & boys' uniforms; military uniforms, men's & youths': purchased materials; policemen's uniforms: made from purchased materials; uniforms, except athletic: women's, misses' & juniors'; service apparel, washable: women's

(G-7716)
BIMBO BAKERIES USA INC
4011 34th Ave (11101-1105)
PHONE.....................718 545-0291
Al Larocca, *Branch Mgr*
EMP: 5 **Privately Held**
SIC: 2051 Cakes, pies & pastries
HQ: Bimbo Bakeries Usa, Inc
  255 Business Center Dr # 200
  Horsham PA 19044
  215 347-5500

(G-7717)
BIRCH GUYS LLC
Also Called: Birch Coffee
4035 23rd St (11101)
P.O. Box 287507, New York (10128-0026)
PHONE.....................917 763-0751
Paul Schlader,
EMP: 8
SALES (est): 396K **Privately Held**
SIC: 2095 Roasted coffee

(G-7718)
BLACK BEAR COMPANY INC
2710 49th Ave (11101-4408)
PHONE.....................718 784-7330
Barret T Schleicher, *President*
Jennifer Trubia, *Corp Secy*
Derek Chou, *Controller*
▲ **EMP:** 20
SQ FT: 25,000
SALES (est): 4.2MM **Privately Held**
WEB: www.blackbearoil.com
SIC: 2992 Lubricating oils & greases

(G-7719)
BLATT SEARLE & COMPANY LTD (PA)
4121 28th St (11101-3718)
PHONE.....................212 730-7717
Fax: 212 764-4524
Searle Blatt, *President*
Alice Blatt, *Exec VP*
▲ **EMP:** 20
SALES (est): 4.3MM **Privately Held**
WEB: www.momao.com
SIC: 2337 Suits: women's, misses' & juniors'; skirts, separate: women's, misses' & juniors'; women's & misses' capes & jackets

(G-7720)
BLEECKER PASTRY TARTUFO INC
3722 13th St (11101-6025)
PHONE.....................718 937-9830
Fax: 718 392-5965
Lucy Di Saverio, *President*
Donato Di Saverio, *Principal*
EMP: 7
SQ FT: 7,500
SALES (est): 400K **Privately Held**
WEB: www.bleeckerpastrytartufo.com
SIC: 2024 5451 Ice cream, bulk; ice cream (packaged)

(G-7721)
BRIDGE PRINTING INC
4710 32nd Pl Fl 2 (11101-2415)
PHONE.....................212 243-5390
Fax: 718 361-9123
EMP: 5
SQ FT: 8,000
SALES (est): 1MM **Privately Held**
SIC: 2752 Lithographic Commercial Printing

(G-7722)
CABINET SHAPES CORP
3721 12th St (11101-6008)
PHONE.....................718 784-6255
Fax: 718 392-4282
John Seretis, *President*
Max Tomchin, *Manager*
EMP: 15
SALES: 1.2MM **Privately Held**
WEB: www.info-s.com
SIC: 2434 2499 1751 Wood kitchen cabinets; decorative wood & woodwork; cabinet & finish carpentry

(G-7723)
CAMA GRAPHICS INC
Also Called: Altum Press
3200 Skillman Ave Ste B (11101-2308)
PHONE.....................718 707-9747
Fax: 718 707-9751
Anthony Cappuccio, *President*
EMP: 12
SQ FT: 4,800
SALES (est): 830K **Privately Held**
WEB: www.camagraphics.com
SIC: 2759 Commercial printing

(G-7724)
CASSINELLI FOOD PRODUCTS INC
3112 23rd Ave (11105-2407)
PHONE.....................718 274-4881
Anthony Bonfigli, *President*
Nella Costella, *Treasurer*
EMP: 6 **EST:** 1973
SQ FT: 3,000
SALES: 700K **Privately Held**
SIC: 2098 5411 Macaroni & spaghetti; delicatessens

(G-7725)
CENTRAL TIME CLOCK INC
Also Called: Discountclocks.com
523 50th Ave (11101-5711)
PHONE.....................718 784-4900
Fax: 718 472-9491
Sheldon Reinhardt, *President*
JP Altenau, *Managing Dir*
Hal Reinhardt, *Vice Pres*
Mathew Reinhardt, *Vice Pres*
Andrew Papadeas, *Sales Associate*
EMP: 10
SQ FT: 4,000
SALES: 1.4MM **Privately Held**
WEB: www.centraltimeclock.com
SIC: 3579 Time clocks & time recording devices

(G-7726)
CITY BAKING LLC
1041 45th Ave (11101-7017)
PHONE.....................718 392-8514
Fax: 718 392-1818
Barry Blaine, *Mng Member*
Fernando Lopez,
EMP: 7
SQ FT: 2,500
SALES: 765K **Privately Held**
SIC: 2052 Bakery products, dry

(G-7727)
CIVIL SVC RTRED EMPLOYEES ASSN
Also Called: Csrea
3427 Steinway St Ste 1 (11101-8602)
PHONE.....................718 937-0290
Kjell Kjellberg, *Editor*
EMP: 12
SALES: 560K **Privately Held**
SIC: 2721 Magazines: publishing & printing

(G-7728)
CLADDAGH ELECTRONICS LTD
1032 47th Rd (11101-5514)
PHONE.....................718 784-0571
Fax: 718 482-9471
William J Casey, *President*
Angelo Mottola, *Vice Pres*
Arthur Zagari, *Accounts Mgr*
Joanne Guidici, *Manager*
EMP: 20
SQ FT: 3,000
SALES: 3.6MM **Privately Held**
WEB: www.claddaghelectronics.com
SIC: 3613 5065 Panelboards & distribution boards, electric; electronic parts & equipment

(G-7729)
CNC MANUFACTURING CORP
Also Called: Gt Machine & Tool
3214 49th St (11103-1403)
PHONE.....................718 728-6800
Fax: 718 726-3002
Dean Theotos, *President*
EMP: 25
SALES (est): 140.5K **Privately Held**
SIC: 3469 Machine parts, stamped or pressed metal

(G-7730)
COE DISPLAYS INC
4301 22nd St Ste 603 (11101-5031)
P.O. Box 3203, Fort Lee NJ (07024-9203)
PHONE.....................718 937-5658
Fax: 212 707-3207
Joel Sgroe, *CEO*
Masimo Russo, *Co-Owner*
EMP: 5 **EST:** 1960
SQ FT: 10,000
SALES (est): 696.7K **Privately Held**
SIC: 2752 3993 2396 Commercial printing, lithographic; signs & advertising specialties; automotive & apparel trimmings

(G-7731)
COLOR INDUSTRIES LLC
3002 48th Ave Ste H (11101-3401)
PHONE.....................718 392-8301
Edward Tikkanen, *Mng Member*
Meida Costanzo, *Manager*
EMP: 8
SALES (est): 1MM **Privately Held**
SIC: 2754 Commercial printing, gravure

(G-7732)
COLUMBIA DENTOFORM CORPORATION (PA)
3110 37th Ave Ste 307 (11101-2112)
PHONE.....................718 482-1569
Jeffrey E Perelman, *CEO*
Carl Bredco, *President*
Sharon McQuirns, *COO*
Penelope Bichardo, *Vice Pres*
Phil Librach, *Purchasing*
EMP: 31
SQ FT: 25,000
SALES (est): 4.8MM **Privately Held**
WEB: www.columbiadentoform.com
SIC: 3843 3842 3999 3544 Dental equipment & supplies; models, anatomical; mannequins; special dies, tools, jigs & fixtures

(G-7733)
COOPERFRIEDMAN ELC SUP CO INC
2219 41st Ave (11101-4835)
PHONE.....................718 269-4906
EMP: 7
SALES (corp-wide): 10MM **Privately Held**
SIC: 3699 1731 Electrical equipment & supplies; electrical work
HQ: Cooperfriedman Electric Supply Co., Inc.
  1 Matrix Dr
  Monroe Township NJ 08831
  732 747-2233

(G-7734)
COSMOS COMMUNICATIONS INC
1105 44th Dr (11101-7027)
PHONE.....................718 482-1800
Jack Weiss, *Ch of Bd*
Arnold Weiss, *President*
Gerald Weiss, *Corp Secy*
Frank Ferraro, *Production*
Judy Stonehill, *CFO*
EMP: 105 **EST:** 1933
SQ FT: 54,000
SALES (est): 25.9MM **Privately Held**
WEB: www.cosmosinc.net
SIC: 2752 2791 2789 Commercial printing, lithographic; typesetting; bookbinding & related work

(G-7735)
CRISADA INC
3913 23rd St (11101-4816)
PHONE.....................718 729-9730
Fax: 718 729-9740
Chris Kole, *President*
EMP: 5
SALES: 1.2MM **Privately Held**
WEB: www.crisada.com
SIC: 2335 2311 Gowns, formal; tailored suits & formal jackets

(G-7736)
CUSTOM CAS INC
2631 1st St (11102-4124)
PHONE.....................718 726-3575
Fax: 718 721-8814
Yiota Yerolemuo, *President*
Tasos Yerolemuo, *Vice Pres*
EMP: 20
SQ FT: 10,000
SALES (est): 2.4MM **Privately Held**
WEB: www.customcas.com
SIC: 2434 Wood kitchen cabinets

Long Island City - Queens County (G-7737)

(G-7737)
CW METALS INC
3421 Greenpoint Ave (11101-2013)
PHONE............917 416-7906
Caesar Witek, *President*
EMP: 20
SALES: 1MM **Privately Held**
SIC: 3444 Sheet metalwork

(G-7738)
D3 REPRO GROUP
3401 38th Ave (11101-2223)
PHONE............347 507-1075
EMP: 7 EST: 2011
SALES (est): 30.4K **Privately Held**
SIC: 2759 Commercial printing

(G-7739)
DAVID FLATT FURNITURE LTD
3842 Review Ave Ste 2 (11101-2045)
PHONE............718 937-7944
David Flatt, *President*
▲ EMP: 10
SQ FT: 11,000
SALES (est): 943.2K **Privately Held**
SIC: 2541 Display fixtures, wood

(G-7740)
DELTA SHEET METAL CORP
3935 Skillman Ave (11104-3706)
PHONE............718 429-5805
Peter J Pappas, *President*
Eva Georgopoulos, *Vice Pres*
EMP: 202
SQ FT: 25,000
SALES (est): 31.6MM **Privately Held**
SIC: 3444 Ducts, sheet metal

(G-7741)
DEPENDABLE LITHOGRAPHERS INC
3200 Skillman Ave (11101-2309)
PHONE............718 472-4200
Fax: 718 472-5260
David Hananel, *President*
EMP: 15
SQ FT: 15,000
SALES (est): 1.5MM **Privately Held**
SIC: 2752 2789 Commercial printing, lithographic; bookbinding & related work

(G-7742)
DEPP GLASS INC
4140 38th St (11101-1709)
PHONE............718 784-8500
Fax: 718 784-9018
Wesley R Depp, *President*
Judy Depp, *Admin Sec*
▲ EMP: 12 EST: 1923
SQ FT: 14,000
SALES (est): 1.9MM **Privately Held**
WEB: www.deppglass.com
SIC: 3229 3231 Lamp parts & shades, glass; mirrored glass

(G-7743)
DEWES GUMBS DIE CO INC
3833 24th St (11101-3689)
PHONE............718 784-9755
Fax: 718 784-9755
Robert Salerni, *President*
EMP: 7 EST: 1906
SQ FT: 5,000
SALES (est): 490K **Privately Held**
SIC: 3544 Dies & die holders for metal cutting, forming, die casting

(G-7744)
DI FIORE AND SONS CUSTOM WDWKG
4202 Astoria Blvd (11103-2504)
PHONE............718 278-1663
Fax: 718 274-6848
Santino Di Fiore, *President*
Maria T Di Fiore, *Vice Pres*
Joe Mazzola, *Manager*
Joseph Mazzola, *Manager*
EMP: 5
SQ FT: 8,000

SALES (est): 596.4K **Privately Held**
SIC: 2434 5712 5031 2499 Wood kitchen cabinets; cabinet work, custom; kitchen cabinets; decorative wood & woodwork; kitchen & bathroom remodeling; single-family home remodeling, additions & repairs

(G-7745)
DIMENSION DEVELOPMENT CORP
3630 37th St Fl 1 (11101-1606)
PHONE............718 361-8825
Wiston A Williams, *President*
Sarah Lopez, *Cust Mgr*
Jeanette M Pineda, *Administration*
EMP: 9
SALES: 256K **Privately Held**
SIC: 1389 Testing, measuring, surveying & analysis services

(G-7746)
DRILLCO EQUIPMENT CO INC
3452 11th St (11106-5012)
PHONE............718 777-5986
Gus Neos, *Treasurer*
Angelo Neos, *Treasurer*
▲ EMP: 25
SALES (est): 4.6MM **Privately Held**
SIC: 3532 Drills, bits & similar equipment

(G-7747)
DRILLCO NATIONAL GROUP INC (PA)
2432 44th St (11103-2002)
P.O. Box 2182 (11102-0182)
PHONE............718 726-9801
Patrick Lacey, *President*
Jim Wieder, *Corp Secy*
Nicholas Lacey, *Vice Pres*
EMP: 36
SALES (est): 6.1MM **Privately Held**
SIC: 3531 Drags, road (construction & road maintenance equipment)

(G-7748)
DURA ENGRAVING CORPORATION
Also Called: Dura Architectural Signage
4815 32nd Pl (11101-2538)
PHONE............718 706-6400
Fax: 718 786-2863
Eva Forst, *CEO*
Ark Forst, *President*
Dan Forst, *Accountant*
Myra Hyman, *Assistant*
EMP: 25 EST: 1941
SQ FT: 20,000
SALES: 2MM **Privately Held**
WEB: www.duracorp.com
SIC: 3993 Signs, not made in custom sign painting shops; name plates: except engraved, etched, etc.: metal

(G-7749)
DURAL DOOR COMPANY INC
3128 Greenpoint Ave (11101-2006)
PHONE............718 729-1333
Fax: 718 729-1761
Peter Macari, *President*
Louis Vella, *Vice Pres*
EMP: 13 EST: 1945
SQ FT: 2,500
SALES: 1.2MM **Privately Held**
SIC: 3534 3442 Elevators & equipment; metal doors, sash & trim

(G-7750)
DWM INTERNATIONAL INC
Also Called: Society Awards
37-18 Nthrn Blvd Ste 516 (11101)
PHONE............646 290-7448
David Moritz, *President*
Jason Garcia, *Accounts Mgr*
▲ EMP: 15
SQ FT: 3,000
SALES (est): 1.2MM **Privately Held**
SIC: 3914 7336 Trophies; art design services

(G-7751)
E & T PLASTIC MFG CO INC (PA)
Also Called: E&T Plastics
4545 37th St (11101-1801)
PHONE............718 729-6226

Fax: 718 392-6277
Gary Thal, *President*
Mark Elowsky, *Vice Pres*
Shahid Bacchus, *Controller*
Samuel Allen, *Sales Associate*
Robert Nachimson, *Marketing Staff*
◆ EMP: 40 EST: 1946
SQ FT: 60,000
SALES (est): 26.8MM **Privately Held**
SIC: 3089 Extruded finished plastic products

(G-7752)
EDISON PRICE LIGHTING INC (PA)
Also Called: Epl
4150 22nd St (11101-4815)
PHONE............718 685-0700
Fax: 718 392-6648
Emma Price, *President*
Gregory Mortman, *Vice Pres*
Mary Romano, *Vice Pres*
Richard Shaver, *Vice Pres*
Joel R Siegel, *Vice Pres*
▲ EMP: 119 EST: 1952
SQ FT: 40,000
SALES (est): 18.9MM **Privately Held**
SIC: 3646 Commercial indusl & institutional electric lighting fixtures

(G-7753)
EDISON PRICE LIGHTING INC
4105 21st St (11101)
PHONE............718 685-0700
Fulgencio Bengochea, *Branch Mgr*
EMP: 80
SALES (corp-wide): 18.9MM **Privately Held**
SIC: 3646 5063 Commercial indusl & institutional electric lighting fixtures; electrical apparatus & equipment
PA: Edison Price Lighting, Inc.
4150 22nd St
Long Island City NY 11101
718 685-0700

(G-7754)
EFAM ENTERPRISES LLC
Also Called: Finestar
3731 29th St (11101-2611)
PHONE............718 204-1760
Toll Free:............888 -
Jeff Aronowitz, *Accounting Mgr*
Shai Bivas, *Mng Member*
EMP: 20
SQ FT: 12,000
SALES (est): 3MM **Privately Held**
SIC: 3861 5045 7699 Toners, prepared photographic (not made in chemical plants); computers, peripherals & software; printing trades machinery & equipment repair

(G-7755)
EFFANJAY PENS INC
2109 Borden Ave Fl 2 (11101-4531)
PHONE............212 316-9565
Carlos Evering, *President*
EMP: 40 EST: 1953
SQ FT: 26,000
SALES (est): 3.4MM **Privately Held**
SIC: 3951 3953 3952 Ball point pens & parts; pencils & pencil parts, mechanical; markers, soft tip (felt, fabric, plastic, etc.); marking devices; lead pencils & art goods

(G-7756)
EFFICIENT AUTOMATED MCH CORP
Also Called: Efficient Mach Shop
3913 23rd St Fl 1 (11101-4887)
PHONE............718 937-9393
Fax: 718 786-6849
Vasilious Vasiadis, *President*
Edward Calleja, *Vice Pres*
Robert Calleja, *Vice Pres*
EMP: 10 EST: 1938
SQ FT: 7,500
SALES (est): 1.6MM **Privately Held**
SIC: 3599 Machine shop, jobbing & repair

(G-7757)
EFRON DESIGNS LTD
2121 41st Ave Ste 5b (11101-4828)
PHONE............718 482-8440
Daniel Efron, *President*

Jill Efron, *Vice Pres*
EMP: 8
SALES (est): 1MM **Privately Held**
SIC: 3911 Jewelry apparel

(G-7758)
ELENIS NYC INC (PA)
Also Called: Eleni's Cookies
4725 34th St Ste 305 (11101-2442)
PHONE............718 361-8136
Fax: 212 361-8272
Eleni Gianopulos, *CEO*
Randall Gianopulos, *President*
Ron Levine, *Opers Staff*
Matthew Gilson, *Controller*
▲ EMP: 32
SQ FT: 4,000
SALES (est): 4MM **Privately Held**
SIC: 2052 Cookies

(G-7759)
EMPIRE BIAS BINDING CO INC
Also Called: Karter Bias Binding
3439 31st St (11106-2301)
P.O. Box 6058 (11106-0058)
PHONE............718 545-0300
Fax: 718 545-6387
Darryl S Goldberg, *President*
Seymour Goldberg, *Shareholder*
▲ EMP: 15 EST: 1923
SQ FT: 8,000
SALES: 914K **Privately Held**
WEB: www.empiregrouponline.com
SIC: 2396 5131 Bindings, bias: made from purchased materials; lace fabrics

(G-7760)
ENDEAVOR PRINTING LLC
3704 29th St (11101-2612)
PHONE............718 570-2720
Brian Baltes,
EMP: 5
SQ FT: 2,000
SALES: 650K **Privately Held**
SIC: 2759 Business forms: printing

(G-7761)
EUROCRAFT CUSTOM FURNITURE
3425 11th St (11106-5011)
PHONE............718 956-0600
Tsambikos Mahramas, *President*
EMP: 5
SQ FT: 6,200
SALES (est): 330K **Privately Held**
SIC: 2511 5031 Wood household furniture; kitchen cabinets

(G-7762)
EUROPADISK LLC
2402 Queens Plz S (11101-4602)
PHONE............718 407-7300
Fax: 718 361-7961
James P Shelton, *President*
Ron Texley, *Vice Pres*
Jeremy Guttenberg, *Mfg Staff*
Vince Sbarra, *CFO*
Kirk Oetting, *Training Super*
EMP: 50
SQ FT: 75,000
SALES: 6MM **Privately Held**
SIC: 3652 Phonograph record blanks; magnetic tape (audio): prerecorded; compact laser discs, prerecorded

(G-7763)
EXHIBIT CORPORATION AMERICA
Also Called: Exhibit Portables
4623 Crane St Ste 3 (11101-4303)
PHONE............718 937-2600
Gregory Abbate, *President*
Ronald A Abbate Jr, *Chairman*
Lorraine Pasieka, *Treasurer*
Giannina Abbate, *Admin Sec*
EMP: 30 EST: 1965
SQ FT: 50,000
SALES: 100K **Privately Held**
SIC: 3993 7389 2522 2521 Signs & advertising specialties; interior designer; office furniture, except wood; wood office furniture

GEOGRAPHIC SECTION

Long Island City - Queens County (G-7792)

(G-7764)
EXPERT MACHINE SERVICES INC
3944a 28th St (11101-3729)
PHONE..................718 786-1200
Stuart Fischer, *President*
EMP: 5
SALES (est): 500.6K **Privately Held**
SIC: 3599 Machine shop, jobbing & repair

(G-7765)
EXPERT METAL SLITTERS CORP
3740 12th St (11101-6009)
PHONE..................718 361-2735
Fax: 718 361-1808
Kent Derossi, *President*
Henry Rossi, *Vice Pres*
▲ EMP: 6
SQ FT: 22,000
SALES (est): 1.3MM **Privately Held**
SIC: 3549 Cutting & slitting machinery

(G-7766)
FALCON PERSPECTIVES INC
28 Vernon Blvd Ste 45 (11101)
PHONE..................718 706-9168
Fax: 718 433-0993
Elizabeth Toma, *President*
EMP: 8
SQ FT: 14,000
SALES (est): 1MM **Privately Held**
SIC: 3498 Coils, pipe: fabricated from purchased pipe

(G-7767)
FASHION RIBBON CO INC (PA)
Also Called: Pascale Madonna
3401 38th Ave (11101-2223)
PHONE..................718 482-0100
Fax: 718 482-0177
William Rosenzweig, *Ch of Bd*
Jeffrey Rosenzweig, *President*
Donald Rubin, *President*
▲ EMP: 35 EST: 1949
SQ FT: 28,000
SALES (est): 1.6MM **Privately Held**
WEB: www.fashionribbon.com
SIC: 2241 Ribbons

(G-7768)
FELDMAN MANUFACTURING CORP
3010 41st Ave Ste 3fl (11101-2814)
PHONE..................718 433-1700
Richard Feldman, *President*
Brenda Johnson, *Vice Pres*
Kent Chong, *Manager*
▲ EMP: 93
SALES (est): 5.4MM **Privately Held**
WEB: www.ebathingsuit.com
SIC: 2339 Bathing suits: women's, misses' & juniors'

(G-7769)
FINE ARTS FURNITURE INC
3872 13th St (11101-6120)
PHONE..................212 744-9139
Fax: 718 754-2186
Robert Longo Sr, *President*
Michelle Longo, *Corp Secy*
Robert Longo Jr, *Vice Pres*
EMP: 7
SQ FT: 12,500
SALES (est): 747.5K **Privately Held**
SIC: 2511 Wood household furniture

(G-7770)
FIREFIGHTERS JOURNAL
2420 Jackson Ave (11101-4323)
PHONE..................718 391-0283
Tony Coretto, *Officer*
EMP: 25
SALES (est): 513.7K **Privately Held**
SIC: 2711 Newspapers, publishing & printing

(G-7771)
FIRST DISPLAYS INC
2415 43rd Ave Fl 2 (11101-4623)
PHONE..................347 642-5972
Philip Wong, *Owner*
EMP: 10
SALES (est): 981.5K **Privately Held**
SIC: 2752 Advertising posters, lithographed

(G-7772)
FISONIC CORP
4402 23rd St (11101-5000)
PHONE..................212 732-3777
Robert Kremer, *CEO*
EMP: 8
SQ FT: 4,000 **Privately Held**
SIC: 3561 3433 Industrial pumps & parts; heating equipment, except electric
PA: Fisonic Corp
31-00 47th Ave Ste 106
New York NY 10023

(G-7773)
FOO YUAN FOOD PRODUCTS CO INC
2301 Borden Ave (11101-4517)
PHONE..................212 925-2840
George Chuang, *President*
▲ EMP: 9 EST: 1979
SQ FT: 1,200
SALES (est): 665.5K **Privately Held**
SIC: 2092 Fresh or frozen packaged fish; fish, fresh: prepared; fish, frozen: prepared

(G-7774)
FREEDA VITAMINS INC (PA)
4725 34th St Ste 303 (11101-2436)
PHONE..................718 433-4337
Philip W Zimmerman, *President*
Sylvia Zimmerman, *Vice Pres*
M Kaganoff, *Treasurer*
Eli Zimmerman, *Treasurer*
Samuel Zimmerman, *Treasurer*
EMP: 25
SQ FT: 3,600
SALES (est): 2.2MM **Privately Held**
SIC: 2834 Vitamin, nutrient & hematinic preparations for human use

(G-7775)
FREIRICH JULIAN CO INC (PA)
815 Kerr St (11101)
PHONE..................718 361-9111
Fax: 718 392-0396
Paul Dardiens, *President*
Jeff Freirich, *President*
Jerry Freirich, *Chairman*
Digna Freirich, *Admin Sec*
EMP: 30 EST: 1923
SQ FT: 25,000
SALES (est): 5.1MM **Privately Held**
WEB: www.freirich.com
SIC: 2013 Prepared beef products from purchased meat; corned beef from purchased meat; pastrami from purchased meat; roast beef from purchased meat

(G-7776)
GALAS FRAMING SERVICES
4224 Orchard St Fl 4 (11101-2936)
PHONE..................718 706-0007
Fax: 718 706-0731
Nilda Brothers, *President*
Elizabeth Madho, *Manager*
EMP: 15
SQ FT: 10,000
SALES: 750K **Privately Held**
WEB: www.galaframe.com
SIC: 2499 5023 7699 Picture & mirror frames, wood; frames & framing, picture & mirror; picture framing, custom

(G-7777)
GALMER LTD
Also Called: Galmer Silversmiths
4301 21st St Ste 130b (11101-5082)
PHONE..................718 392-4609
Fax: 718 472-9390
Michael Izrael, *Ch of Bd*
EMP: 9
SQ FT: 10,000
SALES (est): 770K **Privately Held**
SIC: 3499 3471 Novelties & giftware, including trophies; plating of metals or formed products

(G-7778)
GEM METAL SPINNING & STAMPING
517 47th Rd (11101-5592)
PHONE..................718 729-7014
Fax: 718 729-7014
Stephen Sloop, *President*
EMP: 5
SQ FT: 12,500
SALES: 175K **Privately Held**
SIC: 3469 Spinning metal for the trade; stamping metal for the trade

(G-7779)
GN PRINTING
4216 34th Ave (11101-1110)
PHONE..................718 784-1713
Tony Barsamin, *President*
EMP: 20
SALES (est): 1.4MM **Privately Held**
SIC: 2752 Commercial printing, lithographic

(G-7780)
GNOSIS CHOCOLATE INC
4003 27th St (11101-3814)
PHONE..................646 688-5549
Vanessa Barg, *CEO*
EMP: 8
SALES (est): 657.5K **Privately Held**
SIC: 2066 Chocolate & cocoa products

(G-7781)
GRAND MERIDIAN PRINTING INC
Also Called: GM Printing
3116 Hunters Point Ave (11101-3131)
PHONE..................718 937-3888
K Y Chow, *President*
Carol Chiu, *Vice Pres*
EMP: 20
SQ FT: 1,500
SALES (est): 3.4MM **Privately Held**
SIC: 2752 2759 Commercial printing, offset; commercial printing

(G-7782)
GRAPHICS 247 CORP
4402 23rd St Ste 113 (11101-5027)
PHONE..................718 729-2470
Fax: 718 729-2465
George Ibanez, *President*
EMP: 7
SALES (est): 410K **Privately Held**
WEB: www.graphics247.com
SIC: 2759 Publication printing

(G-7783)
GREAT WALL CORP
4727 36th St (11101-1823)
PHONE..................212 704-4372
Ping Nen Lin, *Ch of Bd*
George Lin, *President*
▲ EMP: 120
SQ FT: 86,000
SALES (est): 9.6MM **Privately Held**
SIC: 2339 Athletic clothing: women's, misses' & juniors'

(G-7784)
GUARANTEED PRINTING SVC CO INC
4710 33rd St (11101-2408)
PHONE..................212 929-2410
Fax: 212 627-0179
Bob Cohen, *President*
Gloria Vargas, *Bookkeeper*
EMP: 20 EST: 1931
SQ FT: 3,000
SALES: 3MM **Privately Held**
SIC: 2752 Commercial printing, lithographic

(G-7785)
HANNA ALTINIS CO INC
3601 48th Ave (11101-1815)
PHONE..................718 706-1134
Fax: 718 706-7824
Kenny Altinis, *President*
John Acello, *Accountant*
EMP: 50
SQ FT: 10,000
SALES (est): 4.9MM **Privately Held**
WEB: www.altunis.com
SIC: 3911 Jewelry, precious metal

(G-7786)
HEALTHY BRAND OIL CORP (PA)
5215 11th St Ste 3 (11101-5830)
PHONE..................718 937-0806
Bradly Green, *Chairman*
Jason Thomas, *Vice Pres*
Kim Goockner, *Office Mgr*
Kim Glockner, *Administration*
▲ EMP: 20
SQ FT: 1,000
SALES (est): 86.1MM **Privately Held**
SIC: 2079 Cooking oils, except corn: vegetable refined

(G-7787)
HERALD PRESS INC
3710 30th St (11101-2614)
PHONE..................718 784-5255
Anthony Diamataris, *President*
EMP: 6
SQ FT: 4,500
SALES (est): 360K **Privately Held**
SIC: 2711 Newspapers, publishing & printing

(G-7788)
HERBERT JAFFE INC
4011 Skillman Ave (11104-3203)
P.O. Box 4189 (11104-0189)
PHONE..................718 392-1956
Fax: 718 392-2748
Herbert Jaffe, *President*
Henny Jaffe, *Treasurer*
EMP: 5
SQ FT: 5,000
SALES: 350K **Privately Held**
SIC: 3559 Sewing machines & attachments, industrial

(G-7789)
HERSCO-ORTHOTIC LABS CORP
Also Called: Hersco-Arch Products
3928 Crescent St (11101-3802)
PHONE..................718 391-0416
Fax: 718 391-0406
James Kennedy, *President*
Cathal Kennedy, *Vice Pres*
EMP: 20 EST: 1939
SQ FT: 3,000
SALES (est): 1.5MM **Privately Held**
WEB: www.hersco.com
SIC: 3842 Surgical appliances & supplies; foot appliances, orthopedic

(G-7790)
HOLA PUBLISHING CO
Also Called: Spanish Tele Dirctry Hola 912
2932 Northern Blvd (11101-4013)
PHONE..................718 424-3129
Hernando Solano, *President*
EMP: 5
SALES (est): 190K **Privately Held**
SIC: 2741 Directories, telephone: publishing only, not printed on site

(G-7791)
I 2 PRINT INC
3819 24th St (11101-3619)
PHONE..................718 937-8800
Fax: 718 937-8869
Shulan Leong, *President*
EMP: 10
SALES (est): 1.7MM **Privately Held**
WEB: www.i2print.com
SIC: 2752 Commercial printing, lithographic

(G-7792)
IMPORT-EXPORT CORPORATION
Also Called: Wilda
3814 30th St (11101-2792)
PHONE..................718 707-0880
Fax: 718 707-9335
William Wu, *President*
Joe Zoo, *Officer*
▲ EMP: 15
SQ FT: 2,500
SALES: 7.5MM **Privately Held**
SIC: 3199 Equestrian related leather articles

Long Island City - Queens County (G-7793) — GEOGRAPHIC SECTION

(G-7793)
IN TOON AMKOR FASHIONS INC
Also Called: Galaxy Knitting Mills
4809 34th St (11101-2515)
PHONE..................718 937-4546
Fax: 718 729-5289
Albert Plant, *President*
EMP: 30 EST: 1985
SQ FT: 50,000
SALES (est): 1.9MM Privately Held
SIC: 2254 Knit underwear mills

(G-7794)
INNOVATIVE INDUSTRIES LLC
4322 22nd St Ste 205 (11101)
P.O. Box 92, Westernville (13486-0092)
PHONE..................718 784-7300
EMP: 8
SALES (est): 893.8K Privately Held
SIC: 3999 Barber & beauty shop equipment

(G-7795)
INTERIORS-PFT INC
Also Called: Props For Today
3200 Skillman Ave Fl 3 (11101-2308)
PHONE..................212 244-9600
Fax: 212 244-1053
Dyann Klein, *President*
EMP: 48
SALES (est): 4.8MM Privately Held
SIC: 2599 Factory furniture & fixtures

(G-7796)
J J CREATIONS INC
4742 37th St (11101-1804)
PHONE..................718 392-2828
John Thor, *President*
EMP: 50
SALES: 22MM Privately Held
WEB: www.jjcreations.com
SIC: 3911 3961 Jewelry, precious metal; earrings, precious metal; costume jewelry

(G-7797)
JACKSON DAKOTA INC
3010 41st Ave Ste 3 (11101-2817)
PHONE..................718 786-8600
Ross Conn, *Manager*
EMP: 15
SALES (corp-wide): 6.1MM Privately Held
WEB: www.dakotajackson.com
SIC: 2512 Wood upholstered chairs & couches
PA: Jackson Dakota Inc
979 3rd Ave Ste 503
New York NY 10022
212 838-9444

(G-7798)
JADO SEWING MACHINES INC
4008 22nd St (11101-4826)
PHONE..................718 784-2314
Fax: 718 784-2314
Onik Balian, *President*
Alexander Saks, *Vice Pres*
Anneke Stern, *Vice Pres*
EMP: 20
SQ FT: 14,000
SALES: 2.5MM Privately Held
WEB: www.jadosewingmachine.com
SIC: 3639 Sewing machines & attachments, domestic

(G-7799)
JOHN GAILER INC
3718 Northern Blvd Ste 3 (11101-1631)
PHONE..................212 243-5662
Steven Dourgarian, *President*
Dennis Dourgarian, *Vice Pres*
EMP: 30
SALES (est): 2.2MM Privately Held
WEB: www.gailer.com
SIC: 3999 3111 Gold stamping, except books; die-cutting of leather

(G-7800)
JOHN R ROBINSON INC
3805 30th St (11101-2716)
PHONE..................718 786-6088
Fax: 718 786-6090
Frank V Cunningham, *President*
Albert Jackson, *General Mgr*
Sharon Racette, *Vice Pres*
EMP: 20
SQ FT: 5,000
SALES (est): 4MM Privately Held
SIC: 3443 Heat exchangers, condensers & components

(G-7801)
JURIST COMPANY INC
1105 44th Dr (11101-5107)
PHONE..................212 243-8008
Joseph Jurist, *President*
David Shushansky, *Exec VP*
Jaclyn Belczyk, *Director*
EMP: 7
SQ FT: 13,000
SALES (est): 1.4MM Privately Held
WEB: www.juristprinting.com
SIC: 2752 Commercial printing, lithographic

(G-7802)
JUSTA COMPANY
3464 9th St (11106-5102)
PHONE..................718 932-6139
Fax: 718 932-8232
Janechai Sayananon, *Owner*
EMP: 8
SQ FT: 4,000
SALES: 900K Privately Held
WEB: www.justacompany.com
SIC: 3873 5199 Watches, clocks, watchcases & parts; gifts & novelties

(G-7803)
JUSTIN ASHLEY DESIGNS INC
4301 21st St Ste 212a (11101-5049)
PHONE..................718 707-0200
Scott Barcvi, *President*
▲ EMP: 6
SALES (est): 540K Privately Held
SIC: 3911 Jewelry, precious metal

(G-7804)
KADER LITHOGRAPH COMPANY INC
3002 48th Ave Ste C (11101-3401)
PHONE..................917 664-4380
Fax: 212 265-1663
Roland Katz, *President*
Jack Erlich, *Vice Pres*
EMP: 101
SQ FT: 250,000
SALES (est): 13.1MM Privately Held
SIC: 2752 7336 2789 Commercial printing, lithographic; commercial printing, offset; commercial art & graphic design; bookbinding & related work

(G-7805)
KAITERY FURS LTD
2529 49th St (11103-1120)
PHONE..................718 204-1396
Fax: 718 204-0721
Jimmy Kaitery, *President*
◆ EMP: 6
SQ FT: 7,500
SALES (est): 930.4K Privately Held
SIC: 2371 Hats, fur; apparel, fur

(G-7806)
KARR GRAPHICS CORP
2219 41st Ave Ste 2a (11101-4807)
PHONE..................212 645-6000
Larry Karr, *President*
Myron Karr, *Vice Pres*
EMP: 20
SQ FT: 25,000
SALES (est): 3.2MM Privately Held
SIC: 2754 2752 2759 2796 Commercial printing, gravure; stationery: gravure printing; commercial printing, lithographic; thermography; platemaking services

(G-7807)
KERNS MANUFACTURING CORP (PA)
3714 29th St (11101-2690)
PHONE..................718 784-4044
Fax: 718 786-0534
Simon Srybnik, *Ch of Bd*
Louis Srybnik, *President*
Robert Arrighi, *General Mgr*
Naldo Pena, *QC Dir*
Garrett Jarvis, *QC Mgr*
▲ EMP: 125
SQ FT: 60,000
SALES (est): 21.1MM Privately Held
WEB: www.kernsmfg.com
SIC: 3469 3724 3812 3714 Electronic enclosures, stamped or pressed metal; aircraft engines & engine parts; search & navigation equipment; motor vehicle parts & accessories

(G-7808)
KOENIG IRON WORKS INC
814 37th Ave (11101-6011)
PHONE..................718 433-0900
Fax: 718 433-1090
Barry Leistner, *President*
Jane Ross, *President*
Nick Morisset, *Exec VP*
Norman Rosenbaum, *Vice Pres*
Richard Velting, *Vice Pres*
EMP: 50
SQ FT: 35,000
SALES (est): 12.9MM Privately Held
WEB: www.koenigironworks.com
SIC: 3441 3446 Fabricated structural metal; ornamental metalwork

(G-7809)
KONG KEE FOOD CORP
4831 Van Dam St (11101-3101)
PHONE..................718 937-2746
Ip Kong, *President*
Alan Pierroz, *Controller*
▲ EMP: 45
SQ FT: 18,000
SALES (est): 5.8MM Privately Held
SIC: 2026 5141 Fermented & cultured milk products; groceries, general line

(G-7810)
KOREA CENTRAL DAILY NEWS INC (HQ)
4327 36th St (11101-1703)
PHONE..................718 361-7700
Fax: 718 361-8891
Byoungsoo Sohn, *CEO*
Wanseob Kong, *Publisher*
Seok J Kim, *General Mgr*
Sangmook Lee, *CFO*
Yondong Kim, *Finance Dir*
▲ EMP: 58
SQ FT: 10,000
SALES (est): 9.1MM
SALES (corp-wide): 299.2MM Privately Held
SIC: 2711 Newspapers, publishing & printing
PA: Joongang Ilbo
100 Seosomun-Ro, Jung-Gu
Seoul SEO 04513
275 191-14

(G-7811)
KOREA TIMES NEW YORK INC (HQ)
3710 Skillman Ave (11101-1731)
PHONE..................718 784-4526
Fax: 718 784-9219
Jae Min Chang, *CEO*
Hak Shin, *President*
Justin Kim, *Accounts Mgr*
▲ EMP: 80 EST: 1967
SQ FT: 16,000
SALES (est): 14.8MM
SALES (corp-wide): 83.9MM Privately Held
SIC: 2711 Newspapers: publishing only, not printed on site
PA: The Korea Times Los Angeles Inc
3731 Wilshire Blvd
Los Angeles CA 90010
323 692-2000

(G-7812)
KOREA TIMES NEW YORK INC
3710 Skillman Ave (11101-1731)
PHONE..................718 729-5555
Jae Min Chang, *Branch Mgr*
EMP: 7
SALES (corp-wide): 83.9MM Privately Held
SIC: 2711 Newspapers
HQ: The Korea Times New York Inc
3710 Skillman Ave
Long Island City NY 11101
718 784-4526

(G-7813)
L & L OVERHEAD GARAGE DOORS (PA)
3125 45th St (11103-1620)
PHONE..................718 721-2518
Louis Lauri Jr, *President*
EMP: 9
SQ FT: 5,000
SALES (est): 783.8K Privately Held
SIC: 3442 5211 Garage doors, overhead: metal; garage doors, sale & installation

(G-7814)
LARKIN ANYA LTD
4310 23rd St Ste 2b (11101-5020)
PHONE..................718 361-1827
Fax: 212 532-2854
Anya Larkin, *President*
EMP: 9
SQ FT: 4,000
SALES (est): 830K Privately Held
WEB: www.anyalarkin.com
SIC: 2679 Wallpaper

(G-7815)
LARTE DEL GELATO GRUPPO INC
3100 47th Ave (11101-3013)
PHONE..................718 383-6600
Francesco Realmuto, *Principal*
Marco Cattaneo, *Manager*
▲ EMP: 10
SALES (est): 1MM Privately Held
SIC: 2024 2053 Ice cream & frozen desserts; cakes, bakery: frozen

(G-7816)
LIFFEY SHEET METAL CORP
4555 36th St (11101-1821)
PHONE..................347 381-1134
Michael Freeman, *President*
Francisco Piscitelly, *Principal*
Priscilla Freeman, *Shareholder*
Bridgette Piscitelli, *Shareholder*
EMP: 14 EST: 2006
SALES (est): 2.7MM Privately Held
SIC: 3444 1711 Ducts, sheet metal; ventilation & duct work contractor

(G-7817)
LINCO PRINTING INC
5022 23rd St (11101-4502)
PHONE..................718 937-5141
Fax: 718 937-5142
Yu-Ou Lin, *President*
Sandy Lin, *Vice Pres*
Kelly Shu, *Accounts Mgr*
Tammy Lee, *Manager*
Sherry Mao, *Manager*
EMP: 40 EST: 1975
SQ FT: 34,000
SALES: 4.6MM Privately Held
WEB: www.lincoprinting.com
SIC: 2759 Letterpress printing

(G-7818)
LINEAR LIGHTING CORPORATION
3130 Hunters Point Ave (11101-3132)
PHONE..................718 361-7552
Stanley Deutsch, *President*
Larry Deutsch, *Principal*
Fred Jona, *Purch Dir*
Richard Coffin, *Engineer*
Phil Zayes, *Engineer*
▲ EMP: 150
SQ FT: 85,000
SALES (est): 27.1MM Privately Held
WEB: www.linearlighting.com
SIC: 3646 5063 Commercial indusl & institutional electric lighting fixtures; electrical apparatus & equipment

(G-7819)
LIQUID KNITS INC
3200 Skillman Ave Fl 2 (11101-2308)
PHONE..................718 706-6600
Jeffrey Schechter, *President*
▲ EMP: 18
SQ FT: 35,000
SALES (est): 2.7MM Privately Held
WEB: www.liquidknits.com
SIC: 2339 Women's & misses' athletic clothing & sportswear

GEOGRAPHIC SECTION
Long Island City - Queens County (G-7846)

(G-7820)
LITELAB CORP
540 54th Ave (11101-5925)
PHONE.....................718 361-6829
Rafael Ramirez, *Manager*
EMP: 6
SALES (corp-wide): 25.7MM **Privately Held**
WEB: www.litelab.com
SIC: **3646** Commercial indusl & institutional electric lighting fixtures
PA: Litelab Corp.
  251 Elm St
  Buffalo NY 14203
  716 856-4300

(G-7821)
LOCKWOOD TRADE JOURNAL CO INC
Also Called: Tea & Coffee Trade Journal
3743 Crescent St Fl 2 (11101-3516)
PHONE.....................212 391-2060
George E Lockwood Jr, *President*
Frederick Lockwood, *Publisher*
Vanessa L Facenda, *Editor*
Robert Lockwood Sr, *Vice Pres*
Edward Hoyt III, *Sales Staff*
▲ EMP: 20 EST: 1872
SQ FT: 4,000
SALES (est): 1.9MM **Privately Held**
WEB: www.lockwoodpublications.com
SIC: **2721** Trade journals: publishing & printing

(G-7822)
LONG ISLAND BRAND BEVS LLC
3788 Review Ave (11101-2052)
PHONE.....................855 542-2832
Philip Thomas, *CEO*
EMP: 100
SQ FT: 25,000
SALES (est): 3.5MM
SALES (corp-wide): 4.5MM **Publicly Held**
SIC: **2086** Iced tea & fruit drinks, bottled & canned
PA: Long Island Iced Tea Corp.
  12 Dubon Ct Ste 1
  Farmingdale NY 11735
  855 542-2832

(G-7823)
LUCINAS GOURMET FOOD INC
3646 37th St (11101-1606)
PHONE.....................646 835-9784
Desmond Morais, *President*
Pauline Morais, *Vice Pres*
EMP: 6
SQ FT: 500
SALES: 18.5K **Privately Held**
SIC: **2035** Pickles, sauces & salad dressings

(G-7824)
LUKAS LIGHTING INC
4020 22nd St Ste 11 (11101-4814)
PHONE.....................800 841-4011
Craig Corona, *CEO*
Brian K Jre, *Opers Mgr*
Max Gardiner, *Engineer*
Angela Rendon, *Sales Mgr*
Marilyn Watkins, *Office Mgr*
▲ EMP: 30
SALES (est): 7.1MM **Privately Held**
SIC: **3646** Commercial indusl & institutional electric lighting fixtures

(G-7825)
LUXERDAME CO INC
4315 Queens St Ste A (11101-2923)
PHONE.....................718 752-9800
Fax: 718 752-9888
Leonard Finkel, *President*
EMP: 20 EST: 1933
SALES (est): 1.4MM **Privately Held**
SIC: **2341 2342** Women's & children's underwear; bras, girdles & allied garments

(G-7826)
M A R A METALS LTD
2520 40th Ave (11101-3810)
PHONE.....................718 786-7868
Andreas Fiorentino, *President*
Andreas Vassiliou, *Vice Pres*
EMP: 6
SQ FT: 600
SALES (est): 500K **Privately Held**
SIC: **3911** Jewelry, precious metal

(G-7827)
MAC CRETE CORPORATION
Also Called: Mac Donuts of New York
3412 10th St (11106-5108)
PHONE.....................718 932-1803
Georga Papadopoulos, *President*
Greg Papadopoulos, *Manager*
EMP: 10
SALES (est): 1.6MM **Privately Held**
SIC: **2051 5149** Cakes, pies & pastries; bakery products

(G-7828)
MANA PRODUCTS INC (PA)
Also Called: Your Name Professional Brand
3202 Queens Blvd Fl 6 (11101-2341)
PHONE.....................718 361-2550
Fax: 718 472-1028
Nikos Mouyiaris, *Chairman*
N Masturzo, *Exec VP*
Deonarain Bisram, *Vice Pres*
Edward Ewankov, *Vice Pres*
Edward M Ewankov, *Vice Pres*
◆ EMP: 277
SALES (est): 283.7MM **Privately Held**
WEB: www.manaproducts.com
SIC: **2844 5122** Cosmetic preparations; cosmetics

(G-7829)
MANA PRODUCTS INC
Esthetic Research Group
3202 Queens Blvd Fl 6 (11101-2341)
PHONE.....................718 361-5204
Necos Mouyiaris, *Branch Mgr*
EMP: 500
SALES (corp-wide): 283.7MM **Privately Held**
SIC: **2844** Toilet preparations
PA: Mana Products, Inc.
  3202 Queens Blvd Fl 6
  Long Island City NY 11101
  718 361-2550

(G-7830)
MANE ENTERPRISES INC
3100 47th Ave Ste 5100 (11101-3010)
PHONE.....................718 472-4955
Bill Mountain, *CEO*
Nicholas Sackett, *President*
John Mountain, *Vice Pres*
Evelyn Kessler, *Manager*
▲ EMP: 55
SQ FT: 12,000
SALES (est): 4.6MM **Privately Held**
SIC: **2323** Men's & boys' neckwear

(G-7831)
MANHATTAN COOLING TOWERS INC
1142 46th Rd (11101-5322)
PHONE.....................212 279-1045
Richard Silver, *President*
EMP: 15
SQ FT: 10,400
SALES (est): 1.8MM **Privately Held**
SIC: **3443** Cooling towers, metal plate

(G-7832)
MANHATTAN DISPLAY INC
1215 Jackson Ave Ste B (11101-5551)
PHONE.....................718 392-1365
Fax: 718 392-1646
John Petursson, *President*
EMP: 6
SQ FT: 1,500
SALES (est): 520K **Privately Held**
WEB: www.manhattandisplay.com
SIC: **2542 5046** Office & store showcases & display fixtures; store fixtures & display equipment

(G-7833)
MARITIME BROADBAND INC
1143 47th Ave (11101-5465)
PHONE.....................347 404-6041
Mary Ellen Kramer, *President*
Zebi Kramer, *Admin Sec*
▲ EMP: 27
SALES (est): 5.9MM **Privately Held**
SIC: **3663** Marine radio communications equipment

(G-7834)
MASPETH STEEL FABRICATORS INC
5215 11th St Ste 21 (11101-5832)
PHONE.....................718 361-9192
Dominick Lofaso, *Ch of Bd*
EMP: 7
SALES (est): 1.1MM **Privately Held**
SIC: **3441** Fabricated structural metal

(G-7835)
MASTERCRAFT MANUFACTURING CO
3715 11th St (11101-6006)
PHONE.....................718 729-5620
Peter Borsits, *President*
EMP: 5
SALES (est): 310K **Privately Held**
SIC: **3993** Advertising novelties

(G-7836)
MATOV INDUSTRIES INC
Also Called: Roxter Lighting
1011 40th Ave (11101-6105)
PHONE.....................718 392-5060
Fax: 718 392-9811
Alan Hochster, *President*
Roberta Ackerman, *Human Res Dir*
EMP: 20
SQ FT: 15,000
SALES (est): 3.4MM **Privately Held**
SIC: **3645 3469 3646 5063** Residential lighting fixtures; metal stampings; commercial indusl & institutional electric lighting fixtures; lighting fixtures

(G-7837)
MECHO SYSTEMS
3708 34th St (11101-2213)
PHONE.....................718 729-8373
Fax: 718 729-8378
Anthony Gryak, *Manager*
EMP: 15
SALES (corp-wide): 15.8MM **Privately Held**
WEB: www.stretchwall.com
SIC: **3296** Acoustical board & tile, mineral wool
HQ: Mecho Systems
  4203 35th St
  Long Island City NY 11101
  718 729-8376

(G-7838)
MECHOSHADE SYSTEMS INC (DH)
4203 35th St (11101-2301)
PHONE.....................718 729-2020
Jan Berman, *President*
John Baucom, *Regional Mgr*
Robert Knoll, *Business Mgr*
Steve Hebeisen, *Engineer*
Norman Rathfelder, *CFO*
◆ EMP: 200
SQ FT: 45,000
SALES (est): 117.4MM **Privately Held**
WEB: www.soleilshades.com
SIC: **2591** Window shades
HQ: Springs Window Fashions, Llc
  7549 Graber Rd
  Middleton WI 53562
  608 836-1011

(G-7839)
MEDITERREAN DYRO COMPANY
1102 38th Ave (11101-6041)
PHONE.....................718 786-4888
Jimmy Austin, *President*
Amalia Malamis, *Principal*
▲ EMP: 40
SALES (est): 2.1MM **Privately Held**
SIC: **2099** Food preparations

(G-7840)
METRO DUCT SYSTEMS INC
1219 Astoria Blvd Apt 2 (11102-4478)
PHONE.....................718 278-4294
Orson Arroyo, *President*
EMP: 11
SALES (est): 1.2MM **Privately Held**
SIC: **3444 1711** Sheet metalwork; mechanical contractor

(G-7841)
METRO GROUP INC (PA)
Also Called: Metro Grouping
5023 23rd St (11101-4501)
PHONE.....................718 392-3616
Bernard Bradpiece, *CEO*
Robert H Seidman, *President*
Reynaldo Benitez, *Engineer*
Richard Blake, *Engineer*
Gary Ho, *Engineer*
EMP: 74 EST: 1925
SQ FT: 15,000
SALES (est): 21.4MM **Privately Held**
WEB: www.metrogroupinc.com
SIC: **3589 1389** Water treatment equipment, industrial; chemically treating wells

(G-7842)
MICHAEL FELDMAN INC
3010 41st Ave Ste 3 (11101-2817)
PHONE.....................718 433-1700
Richard Feldman, *President*
Grace Feldman, *Treasurer*
EMP: 95 EST: 1964
SQ FT: 20,000
SALES (est): 6.6MM **Privately Held**
WEB: www.permanentfoliage.com
SIC: **2339** Bathing suits: women's, misses' & juniors'

(G-7843)
MING PAO (NEW YORK) INC
Also Called: Ming Pao Daily News, New York
4331 33rd St Fl 2 (11101-2316)
PHONE.....................718 786-2888
Fax: 718 433-4480
Stephanie Liu, *CEO*
EMP: 20
SALES (corp-wide): 349.1MM **Privately Held**
SIC: **2711** Newspapers
HQ: Ming Pao (New York), Inc
  4331 33rd St
  Long Island City NY 11101

(G-7844)
MING PAO (NEW YORK) INC (HQ)
Also Called: Ming Pay N Y
4331 33rd St (11101-2316)
PHONE.....................718 786-2888
Ryan Low, *President*
Francis Tiong, *President*
Ka Lui, *Publisher*
Michael Liu, *Controller*
David Kwan, *Accounting Mgr*
EMP: 70
SQ FT: 21,000
SALES (est): 4.6MM
SALES (corp-wide): 349.1MM **Privately Held**
WEB: www.mingpaousa.com
SIC: **2711** Newspapers, publishing & printing
PA: Media Chinese International Limited
  15/F Ming Pao Indl Ctr Blk A
  Chai Wan HK
  259 531-11

(G-7845)
MISSION CRANE SERVICE INC (PA)
4700 33rd St (11101-2419)
PHONE.....................718 937-3333
David Chazen, *President*
EMP: 60
SQ FT: 30,000
SALES (est): 4.5MM **Privately Held**
SIC: **3999 7993** Coin-operated amusement machines; game machines

(G-7846)
MODUTANK INC
4104 35th Ave (11101-1410)
PHONE.....................718 392-1112
Fax: 718 786-1008
John Reed Margulis, *President*
Thomas G Carren, *Vice Pres*
Saul Stadtmauer, *Manager*
Hunter Carren, *CIO*
EMP: 10
SQ FT: 15,000
SALES (est): 2.6MM **Privately Held**
WEB: www.modutank.com
SIC: **3443** Tanks, lined: metal plate

Long Island City - Queens County (G-7847)   GEOGRAPHIC SECTION

(G-7847)
MONGRU NECKWEAR INC
1010 44th Ave Fl 2 (11101-7032)
PHONE.................................718 706-0406
Ramdihal Mongru, *President*
EMP: 40
SQ FT: 10,580
SALES (est): 4.8MM **Privately Held**
SIC: 2253 2323 5136 Neckties, knit; men's & boys' neckwear; neckwear, men's & boys'

(G-7848)
MUTUAL SALES CORP
Also Called: Mutual Harware
545 49th Ave (11101-5610)
PHONE.................................718 361-8373
Fax: 718 729-8296
Mary Piotrowski, *President*
Maria Stewart, *Corp Secy*
Vincent Marmallardi, *Vice Pres*
Carol Grassi, *Controller*
Maret Asaro, *Shareholder*
▲ EMP: 23
SQ FT: 10,000
SALES: 8.4MM **Privately Held**
SIC: 2391 7922 5131 Curtains & draperies; equipment rental, theatrical; textiles, woven

(G-7849)
MZB ACCESSORIES LLC
2976 Northern Blvd Fl 4 (11101-2829)
PHONE.................................718 472-7500
Paul Gengler, *Controller*
Galina Dodis, *Accountant*
AMI Alterin, *Mng Member*
▲ EMP: 100
SALES (est): 19.4MM
SALES (corp-wide): 76MM **Privately Held**
SIC: 2844 Toilet preparations; cosmetic preparations; deodorants, personal; lotions, shaving
PA: M.Z. Berger & Co. Inc.
    2976 Northern Blvd Fl 4
    Long Island City NY 11101
    718 472-7500

(G-7850)
N A ALUMIL CORPORATION
4401 21st St Ste 203 (11101-5009)
PHONE.................................718 355-9393
Kyprianos Bazehika, *Ch of Bd*
John Lombardi, *Sr Project Mgr*
▲ EMP: 8
SALES (est): 3.3MM
SALES (corp-wide): 128.7MM **Privately Held**
SIC: 3355 Aluminum rolling & drawing
PA: Alumil Aluminium Industry S.A.
    Industrial Area, Stavrochori, P.O. Box 37
    Kilkis   61100
    234 107-9300

(G-7851)
NATIONAL HERALD INC
Also Called: Greek Nat Hrald Dily Nwsppr In
3710 30th St (11101-2614)
PHONE.................................718 784-5255
Anthony H Diamataris, *President*
Andy Dabilis, *Editor*
Vasilis Magalios, *Editor*
Aris Papadopoulos, *Editor*
Victoria Diamataris, *Corp Secy*
▲ EMP: 35 EST: 1915
SQ FT: 4,200
SALES (est): 2.6MM **Privately Held**
WEB: www.nationalherald.com
SIC: 2711 Newspapers: publishing only, not printed on site

(G-7852)
NAZIM IZZAK INC
Also Called: N I Boutique
4402 23rd St Ste 517 (11101-5072)
PHONE.................................212 920-5546
Nazim I Guity, *President*
EMP: 6
SQ FT: 2,800
SALES (est): 494.4K **Privately Held**
SIC: 2231 5632 Apparel & outerwear broadwoven fabrics; apparel accessories

(G-7853)
NBC UNIVERSAL LLC
210 54th Ave (11101-5923)
PHONE.................................718 482-8310
Stacy Brady, *General Mgr*
Bruce Kallner, *Senior VP*
Marc Siry, *Senior VP*
Hilary Smith, *Senior VP*
Kelli Callanan, *Vice Pres*
EMP: 50
SALES (corp-wide): 80.4B **Publicly Held**
WEB: www.nbc.com
SIC: 3663 Radio & TV communications equipment
HQ: Nbcuniversal, Llc
    1221 Ave Of The Amer
    New York NY 10020
    212 664-4444

(G-7854)
NECESSARY OBJECTS LTD (PA)
3030 47th Ave Fl 6 (11101-3433)
PHONE.................................212 334-9888
Fax: 212 941-0114
Ady Gluck Frankel, *Ch of Bd*
Bill Kauffman, *CFO*
▲ EMP: 50
SALES (est): 12.6MM **Privately Held**
WEB: www.necessaryobjects.com
SIC: 2335 2339 2331 Women's, juniors' & misses' dresses; slacks: women's, misses' & juniors'; blouses, women's & juniors': made from purchased material

(G-7855)
NEW CLASSIC INC
4143 37th St (11101-1723)
PHONE.................................718 609-1100
Fax: 718 609-2509
Simon Yiu, *President*
Rachel Yiu, *Vice Pres*
Alex Quinones, *Sales Mgr*
▲ EMP: 14
SQ FT: 20,000
SALES (est): 1.5MM **Privately Held**
WEB: www.newclassic.net
SIC: 2387 5136 5137 Apparel belts; apparel belts, men's & boys'; apparel belts, women's & children's

(G-7856)
NEW SENSOR CORPORATION (PA)
Also Called: Electro-Harmonix
5501 2nd St (11101-5908)
PHONE.................................718 937-8300
Fax: 212 937-9111
Michael Matthews, *President*
Laura Ho, *Purch Agent*
Matthias Raabe, *Controller*
Marc Lesser, *Marketing Staff*
Ralph Trimarchi, *Marketing Staff*
▲ EMP: 51
SQ FT: 89,886
SALES (est): 14.1MM **Privately Held**
WEB: www.newsensor.com
SIC: 3931 3671 5065 Musical instruments, electric & electronic; vacuum tubes; electronic parts & equipment

(G-7857)
NEW YORK BINDING CO INC
2121 41st Ave Ste A (11101-4833)
PHONE.................................718 729-2454
Fax: 718 392-7070
Roger Levin, *President*
Linda Dine, *Manager*
Linda Van Dine, *Manager*
EMP: 40
SQ FT: 15,000
SALES (est): 4.5MM **Privately Held**
WEB: www.newyorkbindingco.com
SIC: 2241 2396 Bindings, textile; trimmings, textile; automotive & apparel trimmings

(G-7858)
NOVELTY CRYSTAL CORP (PA)
3015 48th Ave (11101-3419)
PHONE.................................718 458-6700
Rivka Michaeli, *President*
Ed Coslett, *COO*
Asher Michaeli, *Exec VP*
Daniel Weatherly, *Plant Mgr*
▲ EMP: 20 EST: 1961
SQ FT: 50,000
SALES (est): 10.3MM **Privately Held**
WEB: www.noveltycrystal.com
SIC: 3089 3421 Plastic kitchenware, tableware & houseware; kitchenware, plastic; cutlery

(G-7859)
NY IRON INC
3131 48th Ave Ste 2 (11101-3022)
PHONE.................................718 302-9000
Fax: 718 486-8382
Todd Devito, *Ch of Bd*
EMP: 15
SALES (est): 954.8K **Privately Held**
SIC: 7692 Welding repair

(G-7860)
ODEGARD INC
3030 47th Ave Ste 700 (11101-3492)
PHONE.................................212 545-0069
John Nihoul, *Manager*
EMP: 12
SALES (corp-wide): 5.6MM **Privately Held**
WEB: www.odegardinc.com
SIC: 2273 Carpets & rugs
PA: Odegard, Inc.
    200 Lexington Ave Rm 1206
    New York NY 10016
    212 545-0205

(G-7861)
OLD UE LLC
4511 33rd St (11101-2405)
PHONE.................................718 707-0700
Steve Franz, *Principal*
Stuart Grover, *Principal*
Willie Hollingswo, *Principal*
Raymond Maragh, *Principal*
John Sorrentino, *Principal*
EMP: 400
SALES (est): 21.8MM **Privately Held**
SIC: 2752 2677 Commercial printing, lithographic; envelopes

(G-7862)
P C RFRS RADIOLOGY
Also Called: Radiology Film Reading Svcs
3630 37th St Frnt (11101-1606)
PHONE.................................212 586-5700
Fax: 212 586-5726
Joseph Gottesman, *President*
EMP: 8
SQ FT: 1,000
SALES (est): 874.1K **Privately Held**
WEB: www.radiologyreadings.com
SIC: 3577 Film reader devices

(G-7863)
P RYTON CORP
504 50th Ave (11101-5712)
PHONE.................................718 937-7052
Fax: 718 729-1795
Joseph Palumbo Jr, *President*
Sergio Palumbo, *Vice Pres*
Joseph Palumbo Sr, *Shareholder*
Linda Palumbo, *Admin Sec*
▲ EMP: 11
SQ FT: 6,000
SALES (est): 1.8MM **Privately Held**
WEB: www.p-ryton.com
SIC: 3841 5122 Surgical & medical instruments; cosmetics, perfumes & hair products

(G-7864)
PACIFIC POLY PRODUCT CORP
3934 Crescent St (11101-3802)
PHONE.................................718 786-7129
Fax: 718 706-7855
Henry Ly, *President*
▲ EMP: 10
SQ FT: 10,000
SALES: 1MM **Privately Held**
SIC: 2673 Plastic bags: made from purchased materials; garment bags (plastic film): made from purchased materials

(G-7865)
PADDY LEE FASHIONS INC
4709 36th St Fl 2nd (11101-1823)
PHONE.................................718 786-6020
Fax: 718 786-6876
Ralph Covelli Jr, *CEO*

John Covelli, *Vice Pres*
EMP: 15 EST: 1955
SQ FT: 46,000
SALES (est): 3MM **Privately Held**
WEB: www.paddylee.com
SIC: 2339 2331 Slacks: women's, misses' & juniors'; blouses, women's & juniors': made from purchased material

(G-7866)
PARSONS-MEARES LTD
2107 41st Ave Ste 1I (11101-4802)
PHONE.................................212 242-3378
Fax: 212 741-1869
James Mears, *President*
Sally Ann Parsons, *Vice Pres*
EMP: 60
SQ FT: 12,000
SALES (est): 4.8MM **Privately Held**
WEB: www.parsons-meares.com
SIC: 2389 Theatrical costumes

(G-7867)
PASS EM-ENTRIES INC (PA)
3914 Crescent St (11101-3802)
PHONE.................................718 392-0100
Fax: 718 392-0639
Joseph Stegmayer, *President*
John La Salle, *Vice Pres*
EMP: 18
SALES (est): 1.1MM **Privately Held**
SIC: 2395 Pleating & stitching

(G-7868)
PEACHTREE ENTERPRISES INC
2219 41st Ave Ste 4a (11101-4807)
PHONE.................................212 989-3445
Robert Sussman, *President*
Jeffrey Alpert, *Vice Pres*
Bart Sussman, *Treasurer*
Vernice Henderson, *Manager*
EMP: 38 EST: 1976
SALES (est): 6.4MM **Privately Held**
WEB: www.peachtree-printingnyc.com
SIC: 2752 Commercial printing, offset

(G-7869)
PELICAN BAY LTD
Also Called: Ravioli Store, The
3901 22nd St (11101-4809)
PHONE.................................718 729-9300
Donna Nasoff, *Principal*
Michael Nasoff, *Principal*
EMP: 12
SALES (est): 990K **Privately Held**
SIC: 2099 Food preparations

(G-7870)
PENN & FLETCHER INC
2107 41st Ave Fl 5 (11101-4802)
PHONE.................................212 239-6868
Fax: 718 239-6914
Ernie Smith, *President*
Alma Quimomes, *Director*
EMP: 15
SQ FT: 4,500
SALES (est): 1.1MM **Privately Held**
SIC: 2395 5131 Embroidery products, except schiffli machine; lace fabrics; trimmings, apparel

(G-7871)
PETCAP PRESS CORPORATION
3200 Skillman Ave Ste F (11101-2308)
PHONE.................................718 609-0910
Joan Caputo, *President*
Peter Caputo, *Vice Pres*
EMP: 10
SALES (est): 1.1MM **Privately Held**
SIC: 2752 Commercial printing, offset

(G-7872)
PHEONIX CUSTOM FURNITURE LTD
2107 41st Ave Fl 2 (11101-4802)
PHONE.................................212 727-2648
Fax: 212 727-2332
John J Clarke, *Principal*
Pauline R De Cosimo, *Business Mgr*
Vito D'Alessandro, *Vice Pres*
Lou Monti, *Controller*
EMP: 20
SQ FT: 10,000
SALES: 2MM **Privately Held**
SIC: 2512 2521 Upholstered household furniture; wood office furniture

GEOGRAPHIC SECTION
Long Island City - Queens County (G-7900)

(G-7873)
PILOT PRODUCTS INC
2413 46th St (11103-1007)
P.O. Box 3221 (11103-0221)
PHONE 718 728-2141
Fax: 718 728-5190
Carolyn J Hebel, *President*
Herbert Hebel, *President*
Elizabeth Hammell, *Vice Pres*
EMP: 13
SQ FT: 17,000
SALES (est) 1.5MM **Privately Held**
SIC: 3061 Mechanical rubber goods

(G-7874)
PLATINUM SALES PROMOTION INC
Also Called: The Spirited Shipper
3514a Crescent St (11106-3920)
PHONE 718 361-0200
Fax: 718 784-1910
Bruce Cappels, *President*
▲ EMP: 7
SQ FT: 12,000
SALES: 1.4MM **Privately Held**
WEB: www.spiritedshipper.com
SIC: 3993 4225 8743 4213 Displays & cutouts, window & lobby; general warehousing; sales promotion; trucking, except local

(G-7875)
PRESTONE PRESS LLC
Also Called: Prestone Printing Company
4750 30th St (11101-3404)
PHONE 347 468-7900
Danielle Smith, *Opers Mgr*
Margaret Horn, *Accounts Mgr*
Ken Sassano, *Sales Executive*
Carlos Ortiz, *Manager*
Robert Adler,
EMP: 113
SALES: 24MM **Privately Held**
SIC: 2752 Commercial printing, lithographic

(G-7876)
PRIME ELECTRIC MOTORS INC
4850 33rd St (11101-2514)
P.O. Box 1374 (11101-0374)
PHONE 718 784-1124
Gul Zaman, *President*
EMP: 9
SALES (est): 820K **Privately Held**
SIC: 7694 Electric motor repair

(G-7877)
PRIMO COAT CORP
Also Called: Ciccarelli Custom Taylor
4315 Queens St Fl 3 (11101-2947)
PHONE 718 349-2070
Fax: 718 349-7150
Rocco Ciccarelli, *President*
EMP: 35 EST: 1963
SQ FT: 13,500
SALES (est): 1MM **Privately Held**
SIC: 2311 2337 2339 2325 Suits, men's & boys': made from purchased materials; suits: women's, misses & juniors'; women's & misses' outerwear; men's & boys' trousers & slacks

(G-7878)
PROMETHEUS INTERNATIONAL INC
4502 11th St (11101-5206)
PHONE 718 472-0700
Sayedd Rabb, *President*
Monjur Hossain, *Manager*
EMP: 16 EST: 1989
SALES (est): 630.3K **Privately Held**
SIC: 2711 Commercial printing & newspaper publishing combined

(G-7879)
PULSAR TECHNOLOGY SYSTEMS INC
2720 42nd Rd (11101-4112)
PHONE 718 361-9292
Fax: 718 433-4658
Rudolph Robinson, *President*
Joann Pitcher, *Manager*
EMP: 9
SQ FT: 3,750

SALES: 1.3MM **Privately Held**
WEB: www.taxi-meters.com
SIC: 3825 Test equipment for electronic & electrical circuits; meters: electric, pocket, portable, panelboard, etc.

(G-7880)
PURA FRUTA LLC
2323 Borden Ave (11101-4508)
PHONE 415 279-5727
Adriana Ayales,
EMP: 12
SALES (est): 1.3MM **Privately Held**
SIC: 2037 Fruit juices

(G-7881)
QUAD/GRAPHICS INC
4402 11th St Fl 1 (11101-5174)
PHONE 718 706-7600
James Altadonna, *Branch Mgr*
EMP: 32
SALES (corp-wide): 4.3B **Publicly Held**
SIC: 2752 Commercial printing, lithographic
PA: Quad/Graphics Inc.
   N61w23044 Harrys Way
   Sussex WI 53089
   414 566-6000

(G-7882)
QUADLOGIC CONTROLS CORPORATION
Also Called: Qlc
3300 Northern Blvd Fl 2 (11101-2215)
PHONE 212 930-9300
Fax: 212 930-9394
Sayre Swarztrauber, *Ch of Bd*
Doron Shafrir, *President*
Phil Fram, *Vice Pres*
Newman Fruitwala, *Production*
Jordon Herzog, *Technical Mgr*
▲ EMP: 75
SQ FT: 36,000
SALES (est): 17MM **Privately Held**
SIC: 3825 7389 Electrical energy measuring equipment; meters: electric, pocket, portable, panelboard, etc.; meter readers, remote

(G-7883)
QUALITY CASTINGS INC
3100 47th Ave Ste 2120b (11101-3023)
PHONE 732 409-3203
Carl Morfino, *President*
Frank Bono, *General Mgr*
EMP: 50
SQ FT: 3,200
SALES (est): 7.2MM **Privately Held**
WEB: www.qualitycasting.com
SIC: 3369 3324 Castings, except die-castings, precision; steel investment foundries

(G-7884)
QUALITY OFFSET LLC
4750 30th St (11101-3404)
PHONE 347 342-4660
Steve Wong,
EMP: 7
SQ FT: 2,000
SALES (est): 752.8K **Privately Held**
SIC: 2759 Commercial printing

(G-7885)
QUATTRO FRAMEWORKS INC
4310 23rd St Ste 307 (11101-4604)
PHONE 718 361-2620
Sebastian Ramundo, *President*
EMP: 11
SALES (est): 567K **Privately Held**
SIC: 2499 Picture frame molding, finished

(G-7886)
RAGOZIN DATA
Also Called: Sheets, The
4402 11th St Ste 613 (11101-5184)
PHONE 212 674-3123
Len Ragozin, *Owner*
Alex Wolf, *Manager*
EMP: 20
SQ FT: 2,000
SALES (est): 1.4MM **Privately Held**
WEB: www.thesheets.com
SIC: 2721 Magazines: publishing & printing

(G-7887)
RAPID FAN & BLOWER INC
2314 39th Ave (11101-3612)
PHONE 718 786-2060
Fax: 718 706-0951
George J Rogner Jr, *President*
EMP: 10 EST: 1956
SQ FT: 15,000
SALES (est): 1.8MM **Privately Held**
WEB: www.rapidfan.com
SIC: 3564 5084 Blowing fans: industrial or commercial; turbo-blowers, industrial; industrial machinery & equipment

(G-7888)
RAVIOLI STORE INC
4344 21st St (11101-5002)
PHONE 718 729-9300
Fax: 212 925-4807
Michael Nasoss, *Manager*
EMP: 5
SALES (est): 500K **Privately Held**
WEB: www.raviolistore.com
SIC: 2098 5411 Macaroni & spaghetti; grocery stores

(G-7889)
RAYANA DESIGNS INC
2520 40th Ave (11101-3810)
PHONE 718 786-2040
Andreas Vassiliou, *President*
Andreas Fiorentino, *Corp Secy*
Mihran Panossian, *Vice Pres*
Dennis Fiorentino, *Admin Sec*
EMP: 20 EST: 1979
SQ FT: 5,000
SALES (est): 2.5MM **Privately Held**
WEB: www.rayanadesigns.com
SIC: 3479 Engraving jewelry silverware, or metal

(G-7890)
RELIANCE MACHINING INC
4335 Vernon Blvd (11101-6911)
PHONE 718 784-0314
Fax: 718 729-1724
Lloyd Larsen, *President*
EMP: 30
SQ FT: 15,000
SALES (est): 3MM **Privately Held**
SIC: 3599 Machine shop, jobbing & repair

(G-7891)
RENCO MANUFACTURING INC
1040 45th Ave Fl 2 (11101-7094)
PHONE 718 392-8877
AVI Shaul, *President*
EMP: 32
SQ FT: 15,000
SALES: 660K **Privately Held**
SIC: 3915 Jewelers' findings & materials

(G-7892)
ROBERT MILLER ASSOCIATES LLC
4310 23rd St (11101-4604)
PHONE 718 392-1640
Fax: 718 392-1601
Robert Miller, *Mng Member*
EMP: 15
SALES: 1MM **Privately Held**
SIC: 2389 Men's miscellaneous accessories

(G-7893)
ROLLHAUS SEATING PRODUCTS INC
4310 21st St (11101-5002)
PHONE 718 729-9111
Fax: 718 729-9117
Michael Rollhaus, *President*
Stuart Goldstein, *General Mgr*
Jack Lebewohl, *Counsel*
EMP: 13 EST: 1945
SQ FT: 28,000
SALES (est): 1.9MM **Privately Held**
WEB: www.seatingproducts.com
SIC: 2599 Restaurant furniture, wood or metal; bar furniture

(G-7894)
RONBAR LABORATORIES INC
5202 Van Dam St (11101-3221)
PHONE 718 937-6755
Fax: 718 786-1109

Sheldon Borgen, *President*
Barry Borgen, *Vice Pres*
Helen White, *Bookkeeper*
EMP: 11
SQ FT: 12,000
SALES: 2MM **Privately Held**
SIC: 2841 7699 Detergents, synthetic organic or inorganic alkaline; restaurant equipment repair

(G-7895)
RONER INC (PA)
3553 24th St (11106-4416)
P.O. Box 6077 (11106-0077)
PHONE 718 392-6020
Ron Meltsner, *President*
Eric Spar, *Vice Pres*
Henry Meltsner, *Treasurer*
Ray Rancourt, *MIS Dir*
Harold Spar, *Admin Sec*
▲ EMP: 5 EST: 1959
SQ FT: 20,000
SALES (est): 14.7MM **Privately Held**
SIC: 3842 5047 Hearing aids; medical & hospital equipment

(G-7896)
RONER INC
1433 31st Ave (11106-4536)
PHONE 718 392-6020
Fax: 718 267-7191
Marge Weber, *Branch Mgr*
Angel Cabrera, *Supervisor*
EMP: 150
SALES (corp-wide): 14.7MM **Privately Held**
SIC: 3842 Hearing aids
PA: Roner, Inc.
   3553 24th St
   Long Island City NY 11106
   718 392-6020

(G-7897)
RUBINSTEIN JEWELRY MFG CO
3100 47th Ave (11101-3013)
PHONE 718 784-8650
Fax: 718 784-8893
EMP: 12 EST: 1956
SQ FT: 5,000
SALES (est): 74.5K **Privately Held**
SIC: 3911 Mfg Gold Jewelry

(G-7898)
S & B FASHION INC
4315 Queens St Ste B (11101-2923)
PHONE 718 482-1386
Tony Song, *President*
▲ EMP: 5 EST: 2000
SALES (est): 279.4K **Privately Held**
SIC: 2389 Apparel & accessories

(G-7899)
S BROOME AND CO INC
Also Called: Samuel Broome Uniform ACC
3300 47th Ave Fl 1 (11101-2428)
PHONE 718 663-6800
Michael Broome, *President*
Daniel Broome, *Vice Pres*
David Schaffer, *Treasurer*
ARI Wilker, *MIS Dir*
Kathy Broome, *Info Tech Mgr*
▲ EMP: 80 EST: 1917
SQ FT: 27,000
SALES (est): 7.8MM **Privately Held**
WEB: www.sbroome.com
SIC: 2339 2323 Neckwear & ties: women's, misses' & juniors'; men's & boys' neckwear

(G-7900)
SADOWSKY GUITARS LTD
2107 41st Ave Fl 4 (11101-4802)
PHONE 718 433-1990
Fax: 718 422-1125
Roger Sadowsky, *President*
Sam Sadowsky, *Marketing Staff*
Robin Phillips, *Shareholder*
▲ EMP: 10
SQ FT: 4,100
SALES: 1.3MM **Privately Held**
WEB: www.sadowsky.com
SIC: 3931 7699 String instruments & parts; musical instrument repair services

Long Island City - Queens County (G-7901) — GEOGRAPHIC SECTION

(G-7901)
SCOTTI GRAPHICS INC
3200 Skillman Ave Fl 1 (11101-2308)
PHONE 212 367-9602
Fax: 212 691-9013
Richard J Scotti, *President*
Carmen Rai, *Bookkeeper*
EMP: 50
SQ FT: 8,000
SALES (est): 7.7MM **Privately Held**
WEB: www.scottigraphics.com
SIC: **2759** 2752 2791 Commercial printing; letterpress printing; commercial printing, offset; typesetting

(G-7902)
SCREEN TEAM INC
3402c Review Ave (11101-3242)
PHONE 718 786-2424
Fax: 718 786-0399
Richard Grubman, *President*
EMP: 10
SQ FT: 10,000
SALES: 1.5MM **Privately Held**
WEB: www.screenteam.com
SIC: **3552** Silk screens for textile industry

(G-7903)
SELECT JEWELRY INC
4728 37th St Fl 3 (11101-1809)
PHONE 718 784-3626
Nissim Seliktar, *Ch of Bd*
Ronny Seliktar, *President*
▲ EMP: 60
SQ FT: 40,000
SALES (est): 16.2MM **Privately Held**
SIC: **3911** 5094 Jewelry, precious metal; jewelry

(G-7904)
SERVICE ADVERTISING GROUP INC
Also Called: Western Queens Gazette
4216 34th Ave (11101-1110)
PHONE 718 361-6161
Tony Barsamian, *President*
Tony Barsamiam, *Sales Mgr*
EMP: 15
SQ FT: 2,118
SALES (est): 820K **Privately Held**
WEB: www.qgazette.com
SIC: **2711** 2741 7311 7313 Newspapers, publishing & printing; shopping news: publishing only, not printed on site; advertising agencies; newspaper advertising representative

(G-7905)
SIGN DESIGN GROUP NEW YORK INC
3326 Northern Blvd (11101-2224)
PHONE 718 392-0779
Mazher Khalfan, *Ch of Bd*
Shokat Khalfan, *Vice Pres*
Mohan Shivram, *Manager*
Sid Walli, *Manager*
Gavinder Dhillon, *Art Dir*
▲ EMP: 18
SALES (est): 2.6MM **Privately Held**
WEB: www.sdgny.com
SIC: **3993** Signs & advertising specialties

(G-7906)
SIMS GROUP USA HOLDINGS CORP
Sims Metal
3027 Greenpoint Ave (11101-2009)
PHONE 718 786-6031
Thomas Ferretti, *Opers-Prdtn-Mfg*
EMP: 66
SALES (corp-wide): 3.8B **Privately Held**
SIC: **3312** 3341 Stainless steel; secondary nonferrous metals
HQ: Sims Group Usa Holdings Corp
16 W 22nd St Fl 10
New York NY 10010
212 604-0710

(G-7907)
SIZZAL LLC
Also Called: Influence Graphics
1105 44th Rd Fl 2 (11101)
PHONE 212 354-6123
Bill Reeve, *Vice Pres*
Paul Gonzalez, *Prdtn Mgr*

Al Weiss, *Mng Member*
Ron Sizemore,
EMP: 28
SALES (est): 2.1MM **Privately Held**
SIC: **2752** Commercial printing, lithographic; commercial printing, offset

(G-7908)
SLYDE INC
474 48th Ave Apt 18a (11109-5711)
PHONE 917 331-2114
Jason Peltz, *CEO*
Edward Ludvigsen, *Principal*
Kai Blache, *CFO*
EMP: 15
SALES (est): 587.4K **Privately Held**
SIC: **7372** 7389 Prepackaged software;

(G-7909)
SPANJER CORP
Also Called: Spanjer Signs
3856 11th St (11101-6114)
PHONE 347 448-8033
Fax: 347 448-8032
Steve Silverberg, *President*
Alissa Silverberg, *Vice Pres*
Rose Silverberg, *Admin Sec*
EMP: 6 EST: 1908
SQ FT: 5,000
SALES: 446K **Privately Held**
SIC: **3993** Signs & advertising specialties

(G-7910)
STALLION INC (PA)
3620 34th St (11106-1902)
PHONE 718 706-0111
Fax: 212 695-4569
John Georgiades, *Ch of Bd*
Ioannis Georgiades, *President*
James Charles, *CFO*
Achilleas Georgiades, *Admin Sec*
▲ EMP: 26
SQ FT: 30,000
SALES (est): 46.3MM **Privately Held**
SIC: **2371** 5621 Coats, fur; ready-to-wear apparel, women's

(G-7911)
STAMP RITE TOOL & DIE INC
4311 35th St (11101-2303)
PHONE 718 752-0334
EMP: 5
SQ FT: 1,000
SALES: 200K **Privately Held**
SIC: **3544** Manufacturer Of Tools

(G-7912)
STANDARD MOTOR PRODUCTS INC (PA)
3718 Northern Blvd # 600 (11101-1637)
PHONE 718 392-0200
Fax: 718 729-5493
Lawrence I Sills, *Ch of Bd*
Eric P Sills, *President*
Carmine J Broccole, *Senior VP*
Ray Nicholas, *Vice Pres*
Chad Bright, *Engineer*
◆ EMP: 500 EST: 1919
SQ FT: 74,800
SALES: 1B **Publicly Held**
WEB: www.smpcorp.com
SIC: **3714** 3694 3585 3564 Motor vehicle engines & parts; fuel systems & parts, motor vehicle; air conditioner parts, motor vehicle; motor vehicle electrical equipment; ignition systems, high frequency; harness wiring sets, internal combustion engines; battery cable wiring sets for internal combustion engines; compressors for refrigeration & air conditioning equipment; parts for heating, cooling & refrigerating equipment; air conditioning equipment, complete; blowers & fans; rubber & plastics hose & beltings

(G-7913)
STANLEY CREATIONS INC
Also Called: Sgg
3100 47th Ave Ste 4105 (11101-3068)
PHONE 718 361-6100
David Lowy, *Branch Mgr*
Harun Ahmed, *Executive*
EMP: 111
SALES (corp-wide): 12.7MM **Privately Held**
SIC: **3911** Jewelry, precious metal

PA: Stanley Creations, Inc.
1414 Willow Ave
Elkins Park PA 19027
215 635-6200

(G-7914)
STANLEY PLEATING STITCHING CO
2219 41st Ave Fl 3 (11101-4807)
PHONE 718 392-2417
Fax: 212 868-2939
Stuart Meyer, *President*
EMP: 50
SQ FT: 7,800
SALES (est): 3MM **Privately Held**
SIC: **2395** Permanent pleating & pressing, for the trade; decorative & novelty stitching, for the trade; embroidery products, except schiffli machine

(G-7915)
STARCRAFT PRESS INC
4402 11th St Ste 311 (11101-5150)
PHONE 718 383-6700
Robert Glickman, *President*
Jeff Glickman, *Vice Pres*
EMP: 8
SALES (est): 1.2MM **Privately Held**
SIC: **2759** Commercial printing

(G-7916)
STEINWAY INC (DH)
Also Called: Steinway Hall
1 Steinway Pl (11105-1033)
PHONE 718 721-2600
Ronald Losby, *CEO*
Logan Thomson, *Business Mgr*
Kyle R Kirkland, *Exec VP*
▲ EMP: 575
SQ FT: 449,000
SALES (est): 117.8MM
SALES (corp-wide): 41.1MM **Privately Held**
WEB: www.steinway.com
SIC: **3931** 5736 Pianos, all types: vertical, grand, spinet, player, etc.; pianos

(G-7917)
STEINWAY AND SONS (DH)
1 Steinway Pl (11105-1033)
PHONE 718 721-2600
Michael Sweeney, *Ch of Bd*
Kyle R Kirkland, *President*
Ronald Losby, *Vice Pres*
Darren Marshall, *Exec VP*
Dana D Messina, *Exec VP*
◆ EMP: 102
SQ FT: 450,000
SALES: 107.7MM
SALES (corp-wide): 41.1MM **Privately Held**
WEB: www.steinwaypiano.net
SIC: **3931** 5736 Pianos, all types: vertical, grand, spinet, player, etc.; pianos

(G-7918)
STELLAR PRINTING INC
3838 9th St (11101-6110)
PHONE 718 361-1600
Fax: 718 786-3200
Dirk Anthonis, *President*
Fred Newton, *President*
Ken Akulin, *General Mgr*
Bill Ednie, *General Mgr*
Kevin Roletter, *Warehouse Mgr*
EMP: 100
SQ FT: 35,000
SALES (est): 15.7MM
SALES (corp-wide): 488.1MM **Privately Held**
WEB: www.americasnewspaper.com
SIC: **2759** Newspapers: printing
HQ: News World Communications, Inc.
3600 New York Ave Ne
Washington DC 20002
202 636-3000

(G-7919)
STEVEN MADDEN LTD (PA)
Also Called: Steve Madden
5216 Barnett Ave (11104-1018)
PHONE 718 446-1800
Edward R Rosenfeld, *Ch of Bd*
Amelia Newton Varela, *President*
Awadhesh Sinha, *COO*
Michele Bergerac, *Exec VP*

Richard Zech, *Exec VP*
◆ EMP: 265
SQ FT: 90,000
SALES: 1.4B **Publicly Held**
WEB: www.mypinecastle.com
SIC: **3143** 3144 3149 5632 Men's footwear, except athletic; women's footwear, except athletic; children's footwear, except athletic; handbags; apparel accessories

(G-7920)
STONE & TERRAZZO WORLD INC
5132 35th St (11101-3257)
PHONE 718 361-6899
Konstadinos Hagias, *President*
Mary Hagias, *Admin Sec*
EMP: 5
SQ FT: 3,500
SALES (est): 540.8K **Privately Held**
SIC: **3281** 5032 Curbing, granite or stone; marble building stone

(G-7921)
STUART-DEAN CO INC
4350 10th St (11101-6910)
PHONE 718 472-1326
Fax: 718 472-1327
Kristen Rice, *Branch Mgr*
EMP: 13
SALES (corp-wide): 61.3MM **Privately Held**
SIC: **3479** 1741 1752 Etching & engraving; stone masonry; wood floor installation & refinishing
PA: Stuart-Dean Co. Inc.
450 Fashion Ave Ste 3800
New York NY 10123
212 273-6900

(G-7922)
SUMMIT AEROSPACE INC
4301 21st St Ste 203 (11101-5039)
PHONE 718 433-1326
Fax: 718 433-3964
Moon K Lee, *President*
EMP: 7
SQ FT: 4,000
SALES: 1.2MM **Privately Held**
SIC: **3369** Aerospace castings, nonferrous: except aluminum

(G-7923)
SUPERIOR METALS & PROCESSING
Also Called: Super Stud Building Products
801 26th Ave (11102)
PHONE 718 545-7500
Raymond Frobosilo, *President*
Brian Kimmins, *Sales Staff*
John Conneely, *Info Tech Mgr*
▲ EMP: 6
SQ FT: 20,500
SALES (est): 340K **Privately Held**
SIC: **3479** Sherardizing of metals or metal products

(G-7924)
SUPREME POULTRY INC
3788 Review Ave (11101-2052)
PHONE 718 472-0300
Nasrullah Kamran, *President*
▲ EMP: 5 EST: 2015
SALES (est): 1.5MM **Privately Held**
SIC: **3089** Tableware, plastic

(G-7925)
SUSSMAN-AUTOMATIC CORPORATION (PA)
Also Called: Mr Steam
4320 34th St (11101-2321)
PHONE 347 609-7652
Fax: 718 937-4676
Jay Wilsker, *Ch of Bd*
Richard Sussman, *Ch of Bd*
Martha Orellana, *President*
Mike Pinkus, *President*
Dan Reinert, *President*
▲ EMP: 73 EST: 1944
SQ FT: 60,000
SALES: 30MM **Privately Held**
WEB: www.sussmanelectricboilers.com
SIC: **3569** Generators: steam, liquid oxygen or nitrogen

GEOGRAPHIC SECTION

Long Island City - Queens County (G-7954)

(G-7926)
TEMPTU INC
522 46th Ave Ste B (11101-5204)
PHONE.................................718 937-9503
Fax: 718 937-9502
Steven Gary, *Manager*
EMP: 5
SALES (corp-wide): 4.8MM **Privately Held**
WEB: www.temptu.com
SIC: 2844 Cosmetic preparations
PA: Temptu Inc.
   26 W 17th St Rm 302
   New York NY 10011
   212 675-4000

(G-7927)
THEODOSIOU INC
Also Called: G T Machine & Tool
3214 49th St (11103-1403)
PHONE.................................718 728-6800
Dean Theodos, *President*
Harry Theodos, *President*
Vj Sukhu, *Manager*
EMP: 8
SQ FT: 7,500
SALES (est): 1.6MM **Privately Held**
WEB: www.gtmachine.com
SIC: 3599 Machine shop, jobbing & repair

(G-7928)
THOMAS C WILSON LLC
Also Called: Thomas C Wilson
2111 44th Ave (11101-5007)
PHONE.................................718 729-3360
Stephen Hanley, *Ch of Bd*
David Hanley, *Opers Mgr*
Sugelis Gonzalez, *Accounting Mgr*
John Heekin, *Administration*
▼ EMP: 42 EST: 2009
SQ FT: 45,600
SALES (est): 12.6MM **Privately Held**
WEB: www.tcwilson.com
SIC: 3546 Power-driven handtools

(G-7929)
THOMSON PRESS (INDIA) LIMITED
Also Called: Living Media
4 Court Sq Fl 3rm2 (11101-4327)
PHONE.................................646 318-0369
Fax: 718 729-8143
Anup Uniyal, *Branch Mgr*
EMP: 5
SALES (corp-wide): 52.2MM **Privately Held**
SIC: 2759 Commercial printing
PA: Thomson Press India Limited
   18/35, Thomson Press Building,
   Faridabad HAR 12100
   129 228-5520

(G-7930)
TOTAL SOLUTION GRAPHICS INC
2511 49th Ave (11101-4429)
PHONE.................................718 706-1540
Ricki Noto, *President*
Jeaneppe Zeh, *Manager*
EMP: 3
SALES: 3MM **Privately Held**
SIC: 2759 Imprinting

(G-7931)
TOWERIQ INC
Also Called: NAMSNET
37-18 Nthrn Blvd Ste 421 (11101)
PHONE.................................844 626-7638
Connor Crowley, *CEO*
Douglas Baena, *Vice Pres*
EMP: 18
SQ FT: 11,000
SALES: 1.5MM **Privately Held**
SIC: 3669 Fire alarm apparatus, electric

(G-7932)
TOWNE HOUSE RESTORATIONS INC
4309 Vernon Blvd (11101-6831)
PHONE.................................718 497-9200
Ivan Cerina, *Principal*
EMP: 5 EST: 2011
SALES (est): 681.9K **Privately Held**
SIC: 3272 Concrete products

(G-7933)
TRANE US INC
4518 Court Sq Ste 100 (11101-4341)
PHONE.................................718 721-8844
Fax: 718 269-3601
Lisa Hawkins, *Sales Engr*
Richard Halley, *Branch Mgr*
EMP: 70 **Privately Held**
SIC: 3585 Refrigeration & heating equipment
HQ: Trane U.S. Inc.
   3950 Business Park Dr
   1 Centennial Ave Ste 101
   Piscataway NJ 08854
   732 652-7100

(G-7934)
TRIBORO IRON WORKS INC
3830 31st St (11101-2719)
PHONE.................................718 361-9600
Fax: 718 361-5422
Salvatore Gulino, *President*
EMP: 9
SQ FT: 2,500
SALES (est): 1.7MM **Privately Held**
SIC: 3441 1799 1791 Fabricated structural metal; fire escape installation; iron work, structural

(G-7935)
UNIQUE MBL GRAN ORGNZTION CORP
3831 9th St (11101-6109)
PHONE.................................718 482-0440
John Manassakis, *President*
Hanna Manassakis, *Manager*
▲ EMP: 5
SALES (est): 436.5K **Privately Held**
SIC: 3281 Marble, building: cut & shaped; granite, cut & shaped

(G-7936)
UNITED PRINT GROUP INC
Also Called: United Business Forms
3636 33rd St Ste 303 (11106-2329)
P.O. Box 1430 (11101-0430)
PHONE.................................718 392-4242
Fax: 718 392-4650
Robert Sanchez, *Ch of Bd*
Bill Linet, *Vice Pres*
Henry Morales, *Vice Pres*
Norma Sanchez, *Treasurer*
EMP: 16
SQ FT: 6,200
SALES (est): 2.4MM **Privately Held**
WEB: www.unitedpg.com
SIC: 2759 3993 Business forms: printing; advertising artwork

(G-7937)
UNITED SHEET METAL CORP
4602 28th St (11101-3402)
PHONE.................................718 482-1197
Fax: 718 482-1197
Joseph Grgas, *President*
Siraj Bora, *Vice Pres*
EMP: 50
SQ FT: 4,000
SALES (est): 4.7MM **Privately Held**
SIC: 3444 Ducts, sheet metal

(G-7938)
UNIVERSAL DESIGNS INC
3517 31st St (11106-2320)
PHONE.................................718 721-1111
Panos Adamopoulos, *President*
Silvia Adamopoulos, *Vice Pres*
EMP: 6
SQ FT: 8,000
SALES: 700K **Privately Held**
SIC: 2511 2521 2541 5712 Wood household furniture; wood office furniture; wood partitions & fixtures; unfinished furniture

(G-7939)
USA HALAL FOODS INC
4700 Northern Blvd (11101-1028)
PHONE.................................718 291-9111
Kashif Saeed, *President*
EMP: 7
SALES (est): 724.7K **Privately Held**
SIC: 2011 Meat by-products from meat slaughtered on site

(G-7940)
VECTRA INC
Also Called: Vectra Visual
3200 Skillman Ave Fl 3 (11101-2308)
PHONE.................................718 361-1000
EMP: 6
SALES (corp-wide): 4.3B **Privately Held**
SIC: 2752 Commercial printing, lithographic
HQ: Vectra, Inc.
   3950 Business Park Dr
   Columbus OH 43204
   614 351-6868

(G-7941)
VENGO INC
4550 30th St Ste 41 (11101-3413)
PHONE.................................866 526-7054
Brian Shimmerlik, *CEO*
Adam Gargenderg, *Vice Pres*
EMP: 6
SALES (est): 1.1MM **Privately Held**
SIC: 3581 Automatic vending machines

(G-7942)
VENUE GRAPHICS SUPPLY INC
1120 46th Rd (11101-5322)
PHONE.................................718 361-1690
EMP: 13
SQ FT: 10,000
SALES (est): 1.2MM **Privately Held**
SIC: 2899 Mfr Industrial Chemical Solutions

(G-7943)
VERNON WINE & LIQUOR INC
5006 Vernon Blvd (11101-5702)
PHONE.................................718 784-5096
Fax: 718 784-5096
Adrian Bettencourt, *Manager*
EMP: 5
SALES (est): 275.4K **Privately Held**
SIC: 2082 Malt liquors

(G-7944)
VERSAILLES DRAPERY UPHOLSTERY
4709 30th St Ste 200 (11101-3400)
PHONE.................................212 533-2059
Fax: 212 995-1681
Jorge Loayza, *President*
Ricardo Loayza, *Treasurer*
EMP: 11
SQ FT: 20,000
SALES: 1MM **Privately Held**
SIC: 2512 5714 2211 Upholstered household furniture; draperies; draperies & drapery fabrics, cotton

(G-7945)
VITOBOB FURNITURE INC
3879 13th St (11101-6119)
PHONE.................................516 676-1696
Robert Longo, *President*
Michele Longo, *Admin Sec*
EMP: 5
SQ FT: 5,000
SALES (est): 490K **Privately Held**
SIC: 2426 Frames for upholstered furniture, wood

(G-7946)
VONN LLC
Also Called: Vonn Lighting
3245 Hunters Point Ave # 2 (11101-2524)
PHONE.................................888 604-8666
Sergio Magarik, *CEO*
Lenny Valdberg, *President*
EMP: 18
SQ FT: 7,000
SALES: 10MM **Privately Held**
SIC: 3645 3646 Residential lighting fixtures; commercial indusl & institutional electric lighting fixtures

(G-7947)
WALNUT PRINTING INC
2812 41st Ave (11101-3706)
PHONE.................................718 707-0100
Fax: 718 433-0510
Gerald Paul Pont, *President*
EMP: 5
SQ FT: 3,500
SALES (est): 592.6K **Privately Held**
WEB: www.walnutprinting.com
SIC: 2752 Commercial printing, lithographic

(G-7948)
WARREN PRINTING INC
3718 Northern Blvd # 418 (11101-1636)
PHONE.................................212 627-5000
Fax: 212 691-0857
Warren Pugach, *President*
Priscilla Pugach, *Corp Secy*
Seymour Pugach, *Vice Pres*
Diane Niefin, *Accountant*
EMP: 10
SQ FT: 7,500
SALES (est): 1.8MM **Privately Held**
SIC: 2752 Commercial printing, offset

(G-7949)
WATCHCRAFT INC
2214 40th Ave Ste 4 (11101-4830)
PHONE.................................347 531-0382
Eduardo Milieris, *President*
▲ EMP: 5
SALES (est): 742.5K **Privately Held**
SIC: 3873 5094 Watches, clocks, watchcases & parts; clocks, watches & parts

(G-7950)
WESTMORE LITHO CORP
Also Called: Westmore Litho Printing Co
4017 22nd St (11101-4834)
PHONE.................................718 361-9403
Fax: 718 361-9469
Spike Kalashian, *President*
EMP: 8 EST: 1959
SQ FT: 10,000
SALES (est): 590K **Privately Held**
SIC: 2752 Commercial printing, lithographic

(G-7951)
WILLIAM E WILLIAMS VALVE CORP
3850 Review Ave (11101-2019)
P.O. Box 1190 (11101-0190)
PHONE.................................718 392-1660
Fax: 718 729-5106
Richard Sherman, *President*
Nicholas Sherman, *Vice Pres*
Roy Psoncak, *Manager*
◆ EMP: 23 EST: 1918
SQ FT: 60,000
SALES (est): 6.1MM **Privately Held**
SIC: 3494 3491 Valves & pipe fittings; industrial valves

(G-7952)
WILLIAM H JACKSON COMPANY
3629 23rd St (11106-4405)
PHONE.................................718 784-4482
Eric Nelson, *Manager*
EMP: 7
SQ FT: 4,800
SALES (corp-wide): 1.5MM **Privately Held**
WEB: www.bumrails.com
SIC: 3429 Fireplace equipment, hardware: andirons, grates, screens
PA: William H Jackson Company
   18 E 17th St Frnt 1
   New York NY 10003
   212 753-9400

(G-7953)
WINNER PRESS INC
4331 33rd St 1 (11101-2316)
PHONE.................................718 937-7715
Hermi Fu, *President*
Ya Tang Fu, *Principal*
Marissa Santiago, *Admin Sec*
EMP: 25
SQ FT: 20,000
SALES (est): 3.6MM **Privately Held**
WEB: www.winnerpress.com
SIC: 2752 Commercial printing, lithographic

(G-7954)
WINSON SURNAMER INC
4402 11th St Ste 601 (11101-5149)
PHONE.................................718 729-8787
Gary Levinson, *President*
Lawrence Levinson, *Treasurer*
Robert Levinson, *Admin Sec*

Long Island City - Queens County (G-7955)

EMP: 5
SQ FT: 40,000
SALES (est): 702.1K **Privately Held**
SIC: 2752 Commercial printing, offset

(G-7955)
WONTON FOOD INC
5210 37th St (11101-2001)
PHONE.................718 784-8178
Foo Kam Wong, *Manager*
EMP: 20
SQ FT: 5,320
SALES (corp-wide): 76.5MM **Privately Held**
WEB: www.wontonfood.com
SIC: 2099 2052 Noodles, fried (Chinese); cracker meal & crumbs
PA: Wonton Food Inc.
220 Moore St 222
Brooklyn NY 11206
718 628-6868

(G-7956)
X BRAND EDITIONS
4020 22nd St Ste 1 (11101-4814)
PHONE.................718 482-7646
Robert Blanton, *President*
EMP: 8 **EST:** 2010
SALES (est): 1MM **Privately Held**
SIC: 3577 Printers & plotters

(G-7957)
XANIA LABS INC
3202 Queens Blvd Fl 6 (11101-2332)
PHONE.................718 361-2550
Nikos Mouyiaris, *President*
Brenda Gallagher, *Sales Dir*
EMP: 5
SALES (est): 435.3K
SALES (corp-wide): 283.7MM **Privately Held**
SIC: 2844 5122 Cosmetic preparations; cosmetics
PA: Mana Products, Inc.
3202 Queens Blvd Fl 6
Long Island City NY 11101
718 361-2550

(G-7958)
YORK INTERNATIONAL CORPORATION
1130 45th Rd (11101-5213)
PHONE.................718 389-4152
Ben Cohen, *Branch Mgr*
EMP: 94 **Privately Held**
SIC: 3585 Refrigeration & heating equipment
HQ: York International Corporation
631 S Richland Ave
York PA 17403
717 771-7890

(G-7959)
YORK LADDER INC
3720 12th St (11101-6098)
PHONE.................718 784-6666
Kenneth J Buettner, *President*
Daniel Buettner, *General Mgr*
John Ottulich, *Sales Staff*
David Caro, *Manager*
Tammy Wood, *Admin Asst*
▲ **EMP:** 9
SALES (est): 810K **Privately Held**
SIC: 2499 Ladders & stepladders, wood

(G-7960)
ZELMAN & FRIEDMAN JWLY MFG CO
4722 37th St (11101-1804)
P.O. Box 547, Woodbury (11797-0547)
PHONE.................718 349-3400
Fax: 718 349-8159
Irwin Friedman, *President*
Morris Zelman, *Treasurer*
Gary Zelman, *Asst Treas*
Alan Zelman, *Shareholder*
EMP: 25 **EST:** 1951
SQ FT: 5,000
SALES (est): 2.3MM **Privately Held**
SIC: 3911 Jewelry, precious metal

(G-7961)
ZENITH COLOR COMM GROUP INC (PA)
4710 33rd St (11101-2408)
PHONE.................212 989-4400
Peter D Savitt, *President*
Josh Mittleman, *Marketing Staff*
EMP: 20
SALES (est): 4MM **Privately Held**
SIC: 2711 Commercial printing & newspaper publishing combined

(G-7962)
ZIC SPORTSWEAR INC (PA)
Also Called: Zoe
2107 41st Ave Fl 3 (11101-4802)
PHONE.................718 361-9022
Fax: 718 392-2813
Susan Mandel, *President*
Alan Gold, *Manager*
EMP: 39
SQ FT: 12,000
SALES (est): 4.9MM **Privately Held**
WEB: www.zoeltd.com
SIC: 2361 2369 Dresses: girls', children's & infants'; girls' & children's outerwear

Lowville
Lewis County

(G-7963)
CLIMAX PACKAGING INC
7840 State Route 26 (13367-2926)
PHONE.................315 376-8000
Fax: 315 376-6534
Patrick Purdy, *President*
Mary Wuest, *CFO*
Patty Remick, *Controller*
Peter Dawes, *VP Sales*
EMP: 105
SQ FT: 110,000
SALES (est): 14.1MM **Privately Held**
WEB: www.stjpkg.com
SIC: 3993 2657 Signs & advertising specialties; folding paperboard boxes

(G-7964)
FARNEY LUMBER CORPORATION
7194 Brewery Rd (13367-2524)
PHONE.................315 346-6013
Fax: 315 346-1859
Duane Farney, *President*
Terry Farney, *Vice Pres*
Todd Farney, *Vice Pres*
Karen Farney, *Admin Sec*
EMP: 17
SQ FT: 20,000
SALES: 2MM **Privately Held**
SIC: 2421 Sawmills & planing mills, general

(G-7965)
KRAFT HEINZ FOODS COMPANY
7388 Utica Blvd (13367-9503)
PHONE.................315 376-6575
Fax: 315 376-2944
Tim Reagan, *Plant Mgr*
Chris Pomerville, *Warehouse Mgr*
Laura McCallops, *Production*
Wendell Kuhl, *Engineer*
Suzanne Eastham, *Human Res Mgr*
EMP: 335
SQ FT: 460
SALES (corp-wide): 26.4B **Publicly Held**
WEB: www.kraftfoods.com
SIC: 2022 Cheese, natural & processed
HQ: Kraft Heinz Foods Company
1 Ppg Pl Ste 3200
Pittsburgh PA 15222
412 456-5700

(G-7966)
LOWVILLE FARMERS COOP INC
5500 Shady Ave (13367-1698)
PHONE.................315 376-6587
Fax: 315 376-8233
John Williams, *President*
Brian Tabolt, *General Mgr*
Mark Karelus, *Vice Pres*
Tim Smithling, *CFO*
Stanley Szalch, *Treasurer*
EMP: 37
SQ FT: 20,000
SALES: 10MM **Privately Held**
SIC: 2048 5999 5251 5211 Prepared feeds; feed & farm supply; hardware; lumber products

(G-7967)
LOWVILLE NEWSPAPER CORPORATION
Also Called: Journal and Republican
7567 S State St (13367-1512)
PHONE.................315 376-3525
Fax: 315 376-4136
Cindy Aucter, *Business Mgr*
Bonnie Franklin, *Advt Staff*
Jeremiah Papineau, *Manager*
Adam Atkinson, *Manager*
EMP: 7 **EST:** 1830
SQ FT: 2,000
SALES (est): 360.5K
SALES (corp-wide): 32MM **Privately Held**
WEB: www.ogd.com
SIC: 2711 Newspapers, publishing & printing
PA: Johnson Newspaper Corporation
260 Washington St
Watertown NY
315 782-1000

(G-7968)
NEENAH NORTHEAST LLC
5492 Bostwick St (13367)
PHONE.................315 376-3571
Fax: 315 376-4916
Porter Cathy, *Personnel Exec*
Larry Kieffer, *Branch Mgr*
Roger Perkins, *Info Tech Mgr*
EMP: 179
SALES (corp-wide): 941.5MM **Publicly Held**
WEB: www.fibermark.com
SIC: 2672 Coated & laminated paper
HQ: Neenah Northeast, Llc
70 Front St
West Springfield MA 01089
413 533-0699

(G-7969)
QUBICAAMF WORLDWIDE LLC
Also Called: Pins and Lanes
7412 Utica Blvd (13367-9572)
PHONE.................315 376-6541
Wayne White, *General Mgr*
Rebecca Purvines, *Human Res Mgr*
William McDonnell, *Manager*
EMP: 150
SALES (corp-wide): 18.4MM **Privately Held**
SIC: 3949 Bowling pins
HQ: Qubicaamf Worldwide, Llc
8100 Amf Dr
Mechanicsville VA 23111
804 569-1000

(G-7970)
ROYAL CUSTOM CABINETS
6149 Patty St (13367-4206)
PHONE.................315 376-6042
David Lapp, *Owner*
EMP: 8
SALES (est): 815.8K **Privately Held**
SIC: 2434 Wood kitchen cabinets

Lynbrook
Nassau County

(G-7971)
ADF ACCESSORIES INC
Also Called: Todaysgentleman.com
381 Sunrise Hwy Unit 5r (11563-3040)
PHONE.................516 450-5755
Jack Fischman, *President*
Chanie Manheimer, *Vice Pres*
▲ **EMP:** 5
SALES (est): 689.4K **Privately Held**
WEB: www.todaysgentleman.com
SIC: 2389 Men's miscellaneous accessories

(G-7972)
ADVANCE BIOFACTURES CORP
35 Wilbur St (11563-2358)
PHONE.................516 593-7000
Fax: 516 593-7039
Edwin Wegman, *President*
Thomas Wegman, *Senior VP*
Larry Dobross, *Admin Sec*
EMP: 20 **EST:** 1957
SQ FT: 15,000
SALES (est): 1.3MM
SALES (corp-wide): 26.2MM **Publicly Held**
WEB: www.biospecifics.com
SIC: 2836 8731 Biological products, except diagnostic; biological research
PA: Biospecifics Technologies Corp.
35 Wilbur St
Lynbrook NY 11563
516 593-7000

(G-7973)
ALL METRO EMRGNCY RESPONSE SYS
50 Broadway (11563-2519)
PHONE.................516 750-9100
Irving Edwards, *President*
EMP: 6
SALES (est): 460K **Privately Held**
WEB: www.amerslifeline.com
SIC: 3669 Emergency alarms

(G-7974)
ALLOY MACHINE & TOOL CO INC
169 Vincent Ave (11563-2607)
P.O. Box 708 (11563-0708)
PHONE.................516 593-3445
Fax: 516 593-9031
Paul R Will, *President*
Gary Will, *Vice Pres*
EMP: 8 **EST:** 1967
SQ FT: 8,000
SALES: 900K **Privately Held**
SIC: 3679 Electronic circuits

(G-7975)
BIMBO BAKERIES USA INC
669 Sunrise Hwy Spc 4 (11563-3246)
PHONE.................516 887-1024
George Weston, *Branch Mgr*
EMP: 18 **Privately Held**
SIC: 2051 Bread, cake & related products
HQ: Bimbo Bakeries Usa, Inc
255 Business Center Dr # 200
Horsham PA 19044
215 347-5500

(G-7976)
BIOSPECIFICS TECHNOLOGIES CORP (PA)
35 Wilbur St (11563-2358)
PHONE.................516 593-7000
Thomas L Wegman, *CEO*
▲ **EMP:** 5
SALES: 26.2MM **Publicly Held**
WEB: www.biospecifics.com
SIC: 2834 Pharmaceutical preparations

(G-7977)
CASCADE TECHNICAL SERVICES LLC (DH)
30 N Prospect Ave (11563-1313)
PHONE.................516 596-6300
Tim Smith, *CEO*
Katarzyna Kosarska, *Business Mgr*
Gary Crueger, *Vice Pres*
Tyler Kopet, *CFO*
EMP: 17
SQ FT: 6,400
SALES: 5.3MM
SALES (corp-wide): 399.2MM **Privately Held**
SIC: 3822 Auto controls regulating residntl & coml environmt & applncs

(G-7978)
ECOLOGICAL LABORATORIES INC (PA)
13 Hendrickson Ave (11563-1201)
P.O. Box 184, Malverne (11565-0184)
PHONE.................516 823-3441
Barry Richter, *President*
Doug Dent, *Vice Pres*

Mark Krupka, *Vice Pres*
Matthew Richter, *Vice Pres*
Domenic Simone, *Vice Pres*
▲ **EMP:** 55
SQ FT: 5,500
SALES (est): 14.6MM **Privately Held**
WEB: www.propump.com
SIC: 2899 2836 5169 Water treating compounds; biological products, except diagnostic; chemicals & allied products

(G-7979)
IDC PRINTING & STY CO INC
(PA)
536 Merrick Rd (11563-2328)
PHONE 516 599-0400
Fax: 516 599-8422
Anthony Trani, *President*
Isober Trani, *Admin Sec*
EMP: 4
SQ FT: 2,400
SALES (est): 1.1MM **Privately Held**
SIC: 2759 2761 5943 Commercial printing; letterpress printing; envelopes: printing; computer forms, manifold or continuous; office forms & supplies

(G-7980)
LABGRAFIX PRINTING INC
43 Rocklyn Ave Unit B (11563-2752)
PHONE 516 280-8300
Lev Galkin, *President*
EMP: 6 **EST:** 2010
SALES: 1MM **Privately Held**
SIC: 3861 7384 Photographic equipment & supplies; photographic services

(G-7981)
MASTER CRAFT JEWELRY CO INC
Also Called: L'Etoile Jewelers
150 Vincent Ave (11563-2608)
PHONE 516 599-1012
Fax: 516 599-2817
Robert Sharaby, *President*
Marie Coakley, *Bookkeeper*
EMP: 55 **EST:** 1945
SQ FT: 10,000
SALES (est): 5.7MM **Privately Held**
WEB: www.mastercraftjewelry.net
SIC: 3911 Jewelry, precious metal; bracelets, precious metal; earrings, precious metal; rings, finger: precious metal

(G-7982)
ND LABS INC
Also Called: Nutritional Designs
202 Merrick Rd (11563-2622)
PHONE 516 612-4900
Beth Beller, *Ch of Bd*
Diane Altos, *President*
Leticia Hanysz-Narvaez, *Facilities Mgr*
Elisa Gross, *Office Mgr*
EMP: 10
SQ FT: 10,000
SALES (est): 1.7MM **Privately Held**
WEB: www.ndlabs.com
SIC: 2834 Vitamin, nutrient & hematinic preparations for human use

(G-7983)
PRO PRINTING
Also Called: PIP Printing
359 Merrick Rd (11563-2517)
PHONE 516 561-9700
Raymond Kenney Sr, *Partner*
Raymond Kenney Jr, *Partner*
EMP: 7
SQ FT: 1,000
SALES (est): 370K **Privately Held**
SIC: 2752 2791 2789 Commercial printing, offset; typesetting; bookbinding & related work

(G-7984)
RAYDON PRECISION BEARING CO
75 Merrick Rd (11563-2713)
P.O. Box 679 (11563-0679)
PHONE 516 887-2582
Fax: 516 887-2880
Dominick Pinto, *President*
Barbara Pinto, *Treasurer*
EMP: 6 **EST:** 1965
SQ FT: 1,000
SALES (est): 972.4K **Privately Held**
SIC: 3562 5085 Ball & roller bearings; bearings

(G-7985)
REGENCE PICTURE FRAMES INC
12 Cherry Ln (11563-4120)
PHONE 718 779-0888
Cecilia Litzak, *President*
Bob O'Donald, *Vice Pres*
Mary Grosse, *Bookkeeper*
EMP: 25
SQ FT: 7,500
SALES: 1MM **Privately Held**
WEB: www.regencepictureframes.com
SIC: 2499 Picture & mirror frames, wood

(G-7986)
RUSSELL INDUSTRIES INC
Also Called: E V G Division
40 Horton Ave (11563-2333)
P.O. Box 807 (11563-0807)
PHONE 516 536-5000
Adam Russell, *President*
Stacey Russell, *Manager*
▲ **EMP:** 10 **EST:** 1965
SQ FT: 20,000
SALES (est): 1.5MM **Privately Held**
SIC: 3679 3643 5065 Antennas, receiving; current-carrying wiring devices; video equipment, electronic

(G-7987)
SIGNS OF SUCCESS LTD
247 Merrick Rd Ste 101 (11563-2641)
PHONE 516 295-6000
Fax: 516 823-1023
Steven Cohen, *President*
Diane Mastorides, *Manager*
EMP: 17
SQ FT: 4,500
SALES: 700K **Privately Held**
WEB: www.signs-of-success.com
SIC: 3993 Signs & advertising specialties

(G-7988)
SKINZ INC
Also Called: Skinz Mfg
156 Union Ave (11563-3345)
PHONE 516 593-3139
Fax: 516 593-0813
Loretta Wax, *President*
Fran Babus, *Admin Sec*
EMP: 20
SQ FT: 2,500
SALES (est): 1.5MM **Privately Held**
SIC: 2335 Women's, juniors' & misses' dresses

(G-7989)
STAND UP MRI OF LYNBROOK PC
229 Broadway (11563-3295)
PHONE 516 256-1558
Fax: 516 256-0758
Theresa Gabriel, *Regional Mgr*
Laurie Leimisidi, *Manager*
EMP: 9
SALES (est): 901.7K **Privately Held**
SIC: 3845 Electromedical equipment

(G-7990)
SWIFT FULFILLMENT SERVICES
290 Broadway (11563-3293)
PHONE 516 593-1198
Barbara Fiegas, *President*
Preston D Theiber, *Vice Pres*
Swist Fulimint, *Manager*
EMP: 7
SQ FT: 5,000
SALES: 999K **Privately Held**
SIC: 2721 5192 Periodicals: publishing only; books

(G-7991)
TOP FORTUNE USA LTD
100 Atlantic Ave Ste 2 (11563-3471)
PHONE 516 608-2694
Elan Oved, *CEO*
▲ **EMP:** 5
SALES: 1,000K **Privately Held**
SIC: 2385 Waterproof outerwear

(G-7992)
VALLEY STREAM SPORTING GDS INC
Also Called: Arrowear Athletic Apparel
325 Hendrickson Ave (11563-1055)
PHONE 516 593-7800
Robert J Heller, *Ch of Bd*
Joel Napchan, *Manager*
EMP: 25
SQ FT: 16,000
SALES (est): 3.3MM **Privately Held**
WEB: www.arrowear.com
SIC: 2329 2262 Athletic (warmup, sweat & jogging) suits: men's & boys'; screen printing: manmade fiber & silk broadwoven fabrics

(G-7993)
ZEBRA ENVIRONMENTAL CORP (PA)
30 N Prospect Ave (11563-1398)
PHONE 516 596-6300
Fax: 516 596-4422
EMP: 17
SQ FT: 6,400
SALES (est): 5.2MM **Privately Held**
SIC: 3822 Mfg Environmental Controls

Lyndonville
Orleans County

(G-7994)
ANDROS BOWMAN PRODUCTS LLC
151 West Ave (14098-9744)
PHONE 540 217-4100
Fax: 585 765-2761
Jon Corscer, *Branch Mgr*
EMP: 5
SALES (corp-wide): 10.8MM **Privately Held**
SIC: 2033 2099 Fruits: packaged in cans, jars, etc.; food preparations
HQ: Bowman Andros Products, Llc
10119 Old Valley Pike
Mount Jackson VA 22842
540 217-4100

(G-7995)
MIZKAN AMERICA INC
Also Called: Nakano Foods
247 West Ave (14098-9744)
PHONE 585 765-9171
Steven Gardepe, *Principal*
Steve Fortunato, *Purchasing*
EMP: 70
SQ FT: 82,000 **Privately Held**
SIC: 2033 2099 2035 Fruit juices: packaged in cans, jars, etc.; food preparations; pickles, sauces & salad dressings
HQ: Mizkan America, Inc.
1661 Feehanville Dr # 200
Mount Prospect IL 60056
847 590-0059

(G-7996)
SHORELINE FRUIT LLC
Also Called: Atwater Foods
10190 Route 18 (14098-9785)
PHONE 585 765-2639
Fax: 585 765-9443
EMP: 70
SALES (corp-wide): 43.3MM **Privately Held**
SIC: 2034 Processor Of Fruit Products
PA: Shoreline Fruit, Llc
10850 E Traverse Hwy # 4001
Traverse City MI 49684
231 941-4336

Lyons
Wayne County

(G-7997)
CASWELL INC
7696 State Route 31 (14489-9116)
PHONE 315 946-1213
Fax: 315 946-4456
Lance Caswell, *President*
Carol Caswell, *Vice Pres*
Craige Brooks, *Sales Staff*
Mike Caswell, *Shareholder*
Kelly Campbell, *Administration*
◆ **EMP:** 10
SQ FT: 8,000
SALES (est): 2MM **Privately Held**
WEB: www.caswellplating.net
SIC: 3559 5169 Electroplating machinery & equipment; chemicals & allied products

(G-7998)
CONNEX GRINDING & MACHINING
65 Clyde Rd (14489-9364)
PHONE 315 946-4340
Carlton J Collins Jr, *President*
Barbara A Collins, *Treasurer*
EMP: 5
SQ FT: 2,400
SALES (est): 503.8K **Privately Held**
SIC: 3541 Grinding machines, metalworking

(G-7999)
DELOKA LLC
150 Dunn Rd (14489-9772)
PHONE 315 946-6910
Scott Lord,
Dercy Gordner, *Admin Asst*
Mike Kunes,
Roger Westerman,
EMP: 5
SQ FT: 21,000
SALES (est): 730.3K **Privately Held**
WEB: www.deloka.com
SIC: 3479 Coating of metals & formed products

(G-8000)
LAGASSE WORKS INC
5 Old State Route 31 (14489-9214)
PHONE 315 946-9202
Daniel Lagasse, *President*
Kate McCormick, *Controller*
Kate Vosvurgh, *Manager*
▲ **EMP:** 6
SQ FT: 10,000
SALES (est): 1.1MM **Privately Held**
WEB: www.lagasseworks.com
SIC: 7692 3599 Welding repair; machine shop, jobbing & repair

(G-8001)
PENN CAN EQUIPMENT CORPORATION
Also Called: Penn Can Asphalt Materials
300 Cole Rd (14489-9602)
PHONE 315 378-0337
EMP: 7
SALES (corp-wide): 1.1MM **Privately Held**
SIC: 3531 Mfg Construction Machinery
PA: Penn Can Equipment Corporation
555 State Fair Blvd
Syracuse NY
315 637-3168

(G-8002)
SILGAN CONTAINERS MFG CORP
8673 Lyons Marengo Rd (14489-9726)
PHONE 315 946-4826
John Anderson, *Vice Pres*
Tom Kaczynski, *Manager*
Richard Bailey, *Manager*
EMP: 150
SALES (corp-wide): 3.6B **Publicly Held**
WEB: www.silgancontainers.com
SIC: 3411 Metal cans; food containers, metal
HQ: Silgan Containers Manufacturing Corporation
21600 Oxnard St Ste 1600
Woodland Hills CA 91367

(G-8003)
TIM CRETIN LOGGING & SAWMILL
3607 Wayne Center Rd (14489-9321)
PHONE 315 946-4476
Tim Cretin, *President*
EMP: 11
SQ FT: 1,961
SALES: 2MM **Privately Held**
SIC: 2411 Logging

Lyons Falls - Lewis County (G-8004) GEOGRAPHIC SECTION

Lyons Falls
Lewis County

(G-8004)
OTIS PRODUCTS INC (PA)
Also Called: Otis Technology
6987 Laura St (13368-1802)
P.O. Box 582 (13368-0582)
PHONE................315 348-4300
Doreen Garrett, *CEO*
John McDonald, *Opers Mgr*
Mike Tuttle, *Opers Mgr*
Daniel Szalach, *Buyer*
Bob Ryan, *QC Mgr*
▲ **EMP:** 122
SQ FT: 12,000
SALES (est): 16.9MM **Privately Held**
WEB: www.otisgun.com
SIC: 3949 Shooting equipment & supplies, general

(G-8005)
TWIN RIVERS PAPER COMPANY LLC
Lyonsdale Rd (13368)
PHONE................315 348-8491
Fax: 315 348-6808
Dennis Gigliotti, *Branch Mgr*
John Dailey, *Maintence Staff*
EMP: 37
SQ FT: 67,484 **Privately Held**
WEB: www.burrowspaper.com
SIC: 2621 Tissue paper
PA: Twin Rivers Paper Company Llc
  82 Bridge Ave
  Madawaska ME 04756

Macedon
Wayne County

(G-8006)
A&M MODEL MAKERS LLC
1675 Wayneport Rd Ste 1 (14502-8770)
PHONE................626 813-9661
Derek Backus,
EMP: 6
SALES: 350K **Privately Held**
SIC: 3999 Manufacturing industries

(G-8007)
ANKOM DEVELOPMENT LLC
2052 Oneil Rd (14502-8953)
PHONE................315 986-1937
Andrew Komarek,
EMP: 5 **EST:** 2006
SALES (est): 642.7K **Privately Held**
SIC: 3534 Elevators & moving stairways

(G-8008)
ANKOM TECHNOLOGY CORP
2052 Oneil Rd (14502-8953)
PHONE................315 986-8090
Fax: 315 986-8091
Andrew Komarek, *President*
Christopher Kelley, *Vice Pres*
Ron Komarek, *Vice Pres*
Ronald Komarek, *Vice Pres*
Shawn Ritchie, *Vice Pres*
EMP: 30
SQ FT: 50,000
SALES (est): 6.7MM **Privately Held**
WEB: www.ankom.com
SIC: 3821 5049 Laboratory equipment: fume hoods, distillation racks, etc.; laboratory equipment, except medical or dental

(G-8009)
AUBURN BEARING & MFG INC
4 State Route 350 (14502-9177)
PHONE................315 986-7600
Peter Schroth, *CEO*
Barbara McMillan, *Manager*
EMP: 8
SQ FT: 1,280
SALES (est): 888.5K **Privately Held**
SIC: 3714 3599 Motor vehicle transmissions, drive assemblies & parts; custom machinery

(G-8010)
BALDWIN RICHARDSON FOODS CO
3268 Blue Heron Dr (14502-9337)
PHONE................315 986-2727
Fax: 315 986-5880
Matt Igler, *Production*
Matt Mahoney, *Technology*
EMP: 221
SALES (corp-wide): 88.5MM **Privately Held**
SIC: 2087 2035 2099 Flavoring extracts & syrups; extracts, flavoring; syrups, flavoring (except drink); fruit juices: concentrated for fountain use; pickles, sauces & salad dressings; mustard, prepared (wet); food preparations
PA: Baldwin Richardson Foods Company
  1 Tower Ln
  Oakbrook Terrace IL 60181
  815 464-9994

(G-8011)
BERRY GLOBAL INC
112 Main St (14502-8996)
PHONE................315 986-2161
Judy Gell, *Personnel*
Richard Leone, *Branch Mgr*
EMP: 200
SALES (corp-wide): 6.4B **Publicly Held**
WEB: www.6sens.com
SIC: 3089 3081 2673 Bottle caps, molded plastic; unsupported plastics film & sheet; bags: plastic, laminated & coated
HQ: Berry Global, Inc.
  101 Oakley St
  Evansville IN 47710
  812 424-2904

(G-8012)
BERRY GLOBAL GROUP INC
200 Main St (14502-8977)
PHONE................315 986-6270
Dan Blackburn, *Engineer*
Mike Waite, *Engineer*
Marty Carpie, *Branch Mgr*
Lin Jackson, *Manager*
Shawn Keddy, *Master*
EMP: 17
SALES (corp-wide): 6.4B **Publicly Held**
SIC: 3089 Plastic containers, except foam
PA: Berry Global Group, Inc.
  101 Oakley St
  Evansville IN 47710
  812 424-2904

(G-8013)
BERRY PLASTICS CORPORATION
200 Main St (14502-8977)
PHONE................315 986-6270
EMP: 400
SALES (corp-wide): 4.8B **Publicly Held**
SIC: 3081 3086 2671 Mfg Unsupported Plastic Film/Sheet Mfg Plastic Foam Products Mfg Packaging Paper/Film
HQ: Berry Plastics Corporation
  101 Oakley St
  Evansville IN 47710
  812 424-2904

(G-8014)
CLAD INDUSTRIES LLC
1704 Wayneport Rd Ste 1 (14502-9181)
PHONE................585 413-4359
Alan Brown,
EMP: 7
SQ FT: 1,200
SALES (est): 1.5MM **Privately Held**
SIC: 3499 Fire- or burglary-resistive products

(G-8015)
DAU THRMAL SLUTIONS N AMER INC
1657 E Park Dr (14502-8892)
PHONE................585 678-9025
Christopher Cutaia, *President*
David Fast, *Vice Pres*
Shelley Hilfiker, *Controller*
Michael Kulzer, *Sales Dir*
Lance Dumigan, *Sales Mgr*
◆ **EMP:** 30
SALES (est): 10.5MM
SALES (corp-wide): 719.8K **Privately Held**
SIC: 3823 Thermal conductivity instruments, industrial process type
HQ: Miba Aktiengesellschaft
  Dr. Mitterbauer-StraBe 3
  Laakirchen 4663
  761 325-410

(G-8016)
EXXONMOBIL CHEMICAL COMPANY
Also Called: Stratford Oriented
729 State Route 31 (14502-9179)
PHONE................315 966-1000
Fax: 315 966-5033
Barry Rice, *Facilities Mgr*
Todd Brooks, *Marketing Mgr*
Diane Dobriandobris, *Manager*
EMP: 200
SALES (corp-wide): 226B **Publicly Held**
SIC: 2821 Polypropylene resins
HQ: Exxonmobil Chemical Company
  22777 Sprngwoods Vlg Pkwy
  Spring TX 77389
  800 243-9966

(G-8017)
FB SALE LLC
1688 Wayneport Rd (14502-8765)
PHONE................315 986-9999
Aaron Fleischer, *Director*
Marc Fleischer,
EMP: 8 **EST:** 1974
SQ FT: 42,000
SALES (est): 1MM **Privately Held**
WEB: www.fleischersbagels.com
SIC: 2051 Bagels, fresh or frozen

(G-8018)
LAWSON M WHITING INC
15 State Route 350 (14502-9177)
PHONE................315 986-3064
Fax: 315 986-5912
Jay D Whiting, *President*
Barbara Aruck, *Controller*
Van Price, *Controller*
Lawson M Whiting, *Shareholder*
EMP: 8 **EST:** 1973
SQ FT: 14,000
SALES (est): 1.7MM **Privately Held**
WEB: www.rockcrusher.com
SIC: 3532 Mining machinery; crushing, pulverizing & screening equipment

(G-8019)
PENTA-TECH COATED PRODUCTS LLC
1610 Commons Pkwy (14502-9190)
PHONE................315 986-4098
Fax: 315 986-4669
Robert Debruin, *Branch Mgr*
EMP: 12
SALES (corp-wide): 6.6MM **Privately Held**
WEB: www.ptcp.net
SIC: 2671 Packaging paper & plastics film, coated & laminated
PA: Penta-Tech Coated Products Llc
  58 Main Rd N
  Hampden ME 04444
  207 862-3105

(G-8020)
PLIANT LLC
200 Main St (14502-8977)
PHONE................315 986-6286
Kim Kirby, *Manager*
EMP: 400
SALES (est): 48.5MM
SALES (corp-wide): 6.4B **Publicly Held**
SIC: 3081 3086 2671 Unsupported plastics film & sheet; plastics foam products; packaging paper & plastics film, coated & laminated
HQ: Berry Global, Inc.
  101 Oakley St
  Evansville IN 47710
  812 424-2904

(G-8021)
SHORT JJ ASSOCIATES INC (PA)
1645 Wayneport Rd (14502-9110)
P.O. Box 183, Fairport (14450-0183)
PHONE................315 986-3511
Fax: 315 986-2827
John Short Jr, *President*
John J Short Jr, *President*
Peter J Short, *CFO*
EMP: 11
SQ FT: 12,500
SALES: 750K **Privately Held**
WEB: www.jjshort.com
SIC: 3069 Molded rubber products

(G-8022)
WATER TECHNOLOGIES INC (PA)
Also Called: Columbia
1635 Commons Pkwy (14502-9191)
PHONE................315 986-0000
Joe Cupido, *President*
Bruce Dan, *Vice Pres*
▲ **EMP:** 5
SALES (est): 6.5MM **Privately Held**
SIC: 3589 Water filters & softeners, household type

Machias
Cattaraugus County

(G-8023)
MACHIAS FURNITURE FACTORY INC (PA)
3638 Route 242 (14101-9727)
PHONE................716 353-8687
Charles I Horning, *President*
Cindy Horning, *Vice Pres*
EMP: 9
SQ FT: 25,000
SALES (est): 473.1K **Privately Held**
SIC: 2511 Wood desks, bookcases & magazine racks

Madrid
St. Lawrence County

(G-8024)
MADRID FIRE DISTRICT
26 10 Church St (13660)
PHONE................315 322-4346
Theodore Schulz, *Chief*
Marsha Watson, *Admin Sec*
EMP: 6 **EST:** 1984
SALES (est): 377K **Privately Held**
SIC: 3711 Fire department vehicles (motor vehicles), assembly of

Mahopac
Putnam County

(G-8025)
EMD MILLIPORE CORPORATION
118 Eleanor Dr (10541-3977)
PHONE................845 621-6560
EMP: 5
SALES (corp-wide): 15.8B **Privately Held**
SIC: 3826 Analytical instruments
HQ: Emd Millipore Corporation
  400 Summit Dr
  Burlington MA 01803
  781 533-6000

(G-8026)
GATEWAY NEWSPAPERS INC
Also Called: Putnam Press
928 S Lake Blvd Apt 1e (10541-3242)
PHONE................845 628-8400
Fax: 914 628-8400
Donald Hall, *President*
EMP: 7
SQ FT: 1,000
SALES (est): 427.4K **Privately Held**
SIC: 2711 Newspapers: publishing only, not printed on site

GEOGRAPHIC SECTION

(G-8027)
MICHAEL BENALT INC
100 Buckshollow Rd (10541-3756)
PHONE 845 628-1008
Fax: 845 628-1143
Michael Benalt, *President*
Kevin Briger, *VP Sales*
Kevin Grieger, *Sales Executive*
EMP: 25 **EST:** 1975
SQ FT: 37,000
SALES (est) 665.5K **Privately Held**
WEB: www.michaelbenaltinc.com
SIC: 3559 Pharmaceutical machinery

(G-8028)
MORTECH INDUSTRIES INC
961 Route 6 (10541-1796)
P.O. Box 962 (10541-0962)
PHONE 845 628-6138
Fax: 845 628-1479
Anthony Morando, *President*
EMP: 8 **EST:** 1945
SQ FT: 12,000
SALES: 1.5MM **Privately Held**
SIC: 3541 5999 Grinding, polishing, buffing, lapping & honing machines; buffing & polishing machines; cleaning equipment & supplies

(G-8029)
NORTHEAST DOULAS
23 Hilltop Dr (10541-2815)
PHONE 845 621-0654
Debbie Aglietti, *Principal*
EMP: 5
SALES (est): 667K **Privately Held**
SIC: 2835 Pregnancy test kits

(G-8030)
RICHS STTCHES EMB SCREENPRINT
407 Route 6 (10541-3783)
PHONE 845 621-2175
Rich Schnetzinger, *Owner*
EMP: 5
SALES: 210K **Privately Held**
SIC: 2759 Screen printing

(G-8031)
RMD HOLDING INC
Also Called: X-Press Printing & Office Sup
593 Route 6 (10541-1682)
PHONE 845 628-0030
Richard De Cola, *President*
Marie De Cola, *Vice Pres*
EMP: 8
SQ FT: 2,500
SALES (est): 1MM **Privately Held**
SIC: 2752 5943 2791 2789 Commercial printing, offset; office forms & supplies; typesetting; bookbinding & related work

(G-8032)
STEERING COLUMNS GALORE INC
8 Vine Rd (10541-5429)
PHONE 845 278-5762
William Lanza, *President*
Rick Lanza, *Vice Pres*
EMP: 5
SALES: 414K **Privately Held**
WEB: www.columnsgalore.com
SIC: 3714 Steering mechanisms, motor vehicle

(G-8033)
T JN ELECTRIC
116 Cortlandt Rd (10541-3620)
PHONE 917 560-0981
Tina Giustino, *Owner*
EMP: 12
SALES (est): 1.5MM **Privately Held**
SIC: 3699 Electrical equipment & supplies

(G-8034)
T JN ELECTRIC INC
901 Route 6 (10541-1717)
PHONE 845 628-6970
Tina Giustino, *President*
EMP: 5
SALES (est): 398.7K **Privately Held**
SIC: 3699 Electrical equipment & supplies

(G-8035)
WALSH & SONS MACHINE INC
15 Secor Rd Ste 5 (10541-2078)
PHONE 845 526-0301
Fax: 845 526-8367
Frank Walsh, *President*
EMP: 6
SALES (est) 652.7K **Privately Held**
SIC: 3599 Machine shop, jobbing & repair

Malone
Franklin County

(G-8036)
ADIRONDACK ICE & AIR INC
Also Called: Adirondex
26 Railroad St (12953-1014)
PHONE 518 483-4340
Fax: 518 481-2468
James McKee, *Ch of Bd*
Tim Boyea, *Vice Pres*
Melanie Andrews, *Project Mgr*
Katie Smith, *Office Mgr*
Molly Mc Kee, *Admin Sec*
EMP: 14 **EST:** 1968
SQ FT: 4,800
SALES (est): 1.6MM **Privately Held**
SIC: 2097 4222 5499 7389 Manufactured ice; storage, frozen or refrigerated goods; water: distilled mineral or spring; coffee service

(G-8037)
ADIRONDACK POWER SPORTS
5378 State Route 37 (12953-4114)
P.O. Box 390 (12953-0390)
PHONE 518 481-6269
John Waters, *General Mgr*
EMP: 8
SQ FT: 5,000
SALES (est): 905.7K **Privately Held**
SIC: 3799 5012 Recreational vehicles; recreation vehicles, all-terrain

(G-8038)
ASEPT PAK INC
64 West St (12953-1118)
PHONE 518 651-2026
Gary L Hanley, *Ch of Bd*
EMP: 23 **EST:** 2004
SALES (est): 5.4MM **Privately Held**
SIC: 2833 Organic medicinal chemicals: bulk, uncompounded

(G-8039)
COCA-COLA BOTTLING COMPANY
15 Ida Pkwy (12953)
PHONE 518 483-0422
Ron Lavalley, *Branch Mgr*
EMP: 28
SALES (corp-wide): 18.7B **Privately Held**
SIC: 2086 Bottled & canned soft drinks
HQ: The Coca-Cola Bottling Company Of Northern New England Inc
1 Executive Park Dr # 330
Bedford NH 03110
603 627-7871

(G-8040)
FASPRINT
20 Finney Blvd (12953-1039)
P.O. Box 832 (12953-0832)
PHONE 518 483-4631
Fax: 518 483-0504
Tammi M Dupont, *Owner*
Royal Forgues, *Opers-Prdtn-Mfg*
EMP: 6
SQ FT: 2,000
SALES (est): 683.4K **Privately Held**
SIC: 2752 Commercial printing, lithographic

(G-8041)
GARLAND LOGGING LLC
587 County Route 26 (12953-5843)
PHONE 518 483-1700
EMP: 6
SALES (est): 319.8K **Privately Held**
SIC: 2411 Logging

(G-8042)
JOHNSON NEWSPAPER CORPORATION
Also Called: Malone News
469 E Main St Ste 2 (12953-2128)
PHONE 518 483-4700
Chuck Kelly, *Manager*
EMP: 20
SALES (corp-wide): 32MM **Privately Held**
WEB: www.ogd.com
SIC: 2711 Newspapers: publishing only, not printed on site
PA: Johnson Newspaper Corporation
260 Washington St
Watertown NY
315 782-1000

(G-8043)
LOMIR INC
Also Called: Lomir Biomedical Inc
213 W Main St (12953-9577)
P.O. Box 778 (12953-0778)
PHONE 518 483-7697
Fax: 518 483-8195
Teresa Price, *CEO*
Teresa Woodger, *President*
Karen Coles, *General Mgr*
Mr Tom Long, *Chairman*
EMP: 16
SQ FT: 10,000
SALES (est): 1.5MM
SALES (corp-wide): 4MM **Privately Held**
WEB: www.lomir.com
SIC: 3821 Laboratory equipment: fume hoods, distillation racks, etc.
PA: Lomir Biomedical Inc
95 Rue Huot
Notre-Dame-De-L'Ile-Perrot QC J7V 7
514 425-3604

(G-8044)
MALONE INDUSTRIAL PRESS INC
10 Stevens St (12953-1634)
P.O. Box 267 (12953-0267)
PHONE 518 483-5880
Fax: 518 483-4942
Bernard Desnoyers, *President*
EMP: 6 **EST:** 1939
SQ FT: 3,000
SALES: 725K **Privately Held**
SIC: 2752 5111 2759 Commercial printing, offset; printing paper; letterpress printing

(G-8045)
MALONE NEWSPAPERS CORP
Also Called: Malone Telegram
469 E Main St Ste 2 (12953-2128)
PHONE 518 483-2000
Fax: 518 483-8579
John B Johnson Jr, *CEO*
Connie Jenkins, *Principal*
Russell Webster, *Principal*
Elizabeth Cordes, *Editor*
Betsy McGivney, *Auditor*
EMP: 30
SQ FT: 2,000
SALES (est): 1.9MM
SALES (corp-wide): 32MM **Privately Held**
WEB: www.malonetelegram.com
SIC: 2711 Newspapers
PA: Johnson Newspaper Corporation
260 Washington St
Watertown NY
315 782-1000

(G-8046)
SCOTTS FEED INC
Also Called: Collins Pet & Garden Center
245 Elm St (12953-1541)
PHONE 518 483-3110
Fax: 518 483-3147
Scott Collins, *President*
Tom Schildkamp, *Manager*
EMP: 23
SQ FT: 6,000
SALES (est): 4.9MM **Privately Held**
SIC: 2048 5191 Prepared feeds; animal feeds

(G-8047)
SEAWAY MATS INC
Also Called: Sea Mats
252 Park St (12953-1234)
P.O. Box 407 (12953-0407)
PHONE 518 483-2560
Roy Hamilton, *CEO*
Diane Hamilton, *Vice Pres*
EMP: 7
SALES (est): 900.4K
SALES (corp-wide): 1.8MM **Privately Held**
SIC: 3069 3949 3089 2391 Mats or matting, rubber; nets: badminton, volleyball, tennis, etc.; composition stone, plastic; doors, folding: plastic or plastic coated fabric; curtains & draperies
PA: Seaway Plastics Ltd
270 Boul Saint-Joseph
Lachine QC H8S 2
514 637-2323

(G-8048)
SIGNS INC
2 Boyer Ave (12953-1628)
P.O. Box 185 (12953-0185)
PHONE 518 483-4759
Judy Sousie, *President*
Shannon Niles, *Treasurer*
EMP: 5
SALES (est): 400K **Privately Held**
SIC: 3993 Signs & advertising specialties

(G-8049)
TITUS MOUNTAIN SAND & GRAV LLC
17 Junction Rd (12953-4217)
P.O. Box 390 (12953-0390)
PHONE 518 483-3740
Dean Savage, *Sls & Mktg Exec*
William Hewitt, *Mng Member*
EMP: 6
SALES (est): 920.8K **Privately Held**
SIC: 1442 Construction sand & gravel

(G-8050)
UPSTONE MATERIALS INC
Also Called: Malone Concrete Products Div
359 Elm St (12953)
P.O. Box 457, North Bangor (12966-0457)
PHONE 518 483-2671
Fax: 518 483-7833
Jim Odis, *Manager*
EMP: 6
SALES (corp-wide): 77.1MM **Privately Held**
WEB: www.graymont-ab.com
SIC: 3272 Concrete products
HQ: Upstone Materials Inc.
111 Quarry Rd
Plattsburgh NY 12901
518 561-5321

Malta
Saratoga County

(G-8051)
GLOBALFOUNDRIES US INC
400 Stone Break Rd Ext (12020)
PHONE 518 305-9013
Bill Barrett, *Vice Pres*
Daniel Korff, *Facilities Mgr*
Deborah Leupold, *Site Mgr*
Brad Bateman, *Engineer*
Charles Baugham, *Engineer*
EMP: 105
SALES (corp-wide): 8.5B **Privately Held**
SIC: 3369 3572 Nonferrous foundries; computer disk & drum drives & components
HQ: Globalfoundries U.S. Inc.
2600 Great America Way
Santa Clara CA 95054

(G-8052)
GOLUB CORPORATION
Also Called: Price Chopper Pharmacy 184
3 Hemphill Pl Ste 116 (12020-4419)
PHONE 518 899-6063
Rob Russell, *Branch Mgr*
EMP: 99
SALES (corp-wide): 3.4B **Privately Held**
SIC: 3751 Motorcycles & related parts

Malta - Saratoga County (G-8053)

PA: The Golub Corporation
461 Nott St
Schenectady NY 12308
518 355-5000

(G-8053)
TOKYO ELECTRON AMERICA INC
2 Bayberry Dr (12020-6352)
PHONE.................518 289-3100
Fax: 518 289-3101
Tetsuo Tsuneishi, *Branch Mgr*
EMP: 6
SALES (corp-wide): 7B **Privately Held**
SIC: 3559 Semiconductor manufacturing machinery
HQ: Tokyo Electron America, Inc.
2400 Grove Blvd
Austin TX 78741
512 424-1000

(G-8054)
WIRED COFFEE AND BAGEL INC
Rr 9 (12020)
PHONE.................518 506-3194
Matthew J Michele, *President*
EMP: 12
SALES (est): 1MM **Privately Held**
SIC: 3556 5812 Roasting machinery: coffee, peanut, etc.; lunchrooms & cafeterias

Mamaroneck
Westchester County

(G-8055)
AUTOMATED BUILDING CONTROLS
629 N Barry Ave (10543-1608)
PHONE.................914 381-2860
Barry Novick, *President*
Mary Ellen Keefer, *Office Mgr*
Maryellen Kiefas, *Manager*
EMP: 8
SQ FT: 400
SALES: 800K **Privately Held**
SIC: 3822 Auto controls regulating residntl & coml environmt & applncs; temperature controls, automatic

(G-8056)
BASSIN TECHNICAL SALES CO
Also Called: Press Air
1009 W Boston Post Rd # 2 (10543-3329)
PHONE.................914 698-9358
Fax: 914 698-9456
Gilbert Bassin, *Owner*
Christopher West, *CFO*
EMP: 40
SQ FT: 450
SALES (est): 2.4MM **Privately Held**
WEB: www.pressair.com
SIC: 3643 Electric switches

(G-8057)
BRANDS WITHIN REACH LLC
Also Called: AMI Brands
141 Halstead Ave Ste 201 (10543-2652)
PHONE.................847 720-9090
Nicolas Merlen, *District Mgr*
Ryan Sowards, *Regl Sales Mgr*
Matthew Stephens, *Regl Sales Mgr*
Julie Beurier, *Marketing Mgr*
Elsa Trignac, *Marketing Staff*
▲ EMP: 24
SQ FT: 2,500
SALES (est): 5MM **Privately Held**
SIC: 2086 Bottled & canned soft drinks

(G-8058)
CARPET FABRICATIONS INTL
628 Waverly Ave Ste 1 (10543-2259)
PHONE.................914 381-6060
Fax: 914 381-6090
Thomas L Budetti, *President*
Edward Soto, *Vice Pres*
▲ EMP: 23
SQ FT: 15,000
SALES (est): 2.3MM **Privately Held**
SIC: 2273 5023 Carpets & rugs; floor coverings

(G-8059)
CATHOLIC NEWS PUBLISHING CO
Also Called: School Guide Publications
606 Halstead Ave (10543-2718)
PHONE.................914 632-7771
Fax: 914 632-3412
Myles A Ridder, *President*
Joseph Ridder, *Treasurer*
EMP: 15 EST: 1886
SQ FT: 5,500
SALES: 3MM **Privately Held**
WEB: www.schoolguides.com
SIC: 2741 7372 Directories: publishing only, not printed on site; publishers' computer software

(G-8060)
CHOCOLATIONS LLC
607 E Boston Post Rd (10543-3742)
PHONE.................914 777-3600
Maria Valente,
EMP: 5
SALES: 200K **Privately Held**
SIC: 2064 Candy & other confectionery products

(G-8061)
COLDSTREAM GROUP INC (PA)
Also Called: Nessen Lighting, The
420 Railroad Way (10543-2257)
P.O. Box 187 (10543-0187)
PHONE.................914 698-5959
Fax: 914 698-5577
Bob Henderson, *President*
Ralph Izzi, *Controller*
Jim Hayworth, *Manager*
▲ EMP: 19
SALES (est): 8.7MM **Privately Held**
SIC: 3648 Lighting equipment

(G-8062)
CORIUM CORPORATION (PA)
Also Called: Cromwell Group
147 Palmer Ave (10543-3632)
PHONE.................914 381-0100
Thomas Fleisch, *President*
Margaret Zulkowsky, *Vice Pres*
Richard Gilbert, *Plant Mgr*
Rick Derr, *Treasurer*
Nanci Maida, *Admin Asst*
▲ EMP: 18
SALES (est): 5.2MM **Privately Held**
WEB: www.coriumcorp.com
SIC: 3111 Leather tanning & finishing

(G-8063)
CULIN/COLELLA INC
632 Center Ave (10543-2206)
PHONE.................914 698-7727
Fax: 914 698-6457
Raynsford Culin, *President*
Janice Colella Culin, *Corp Secy*
EMP: 9 EST: 1975
SQ FT: 10,000
SALES (est): 1.1MM **Privately Held**
WEB: www.culincolella.com
SIC: 2521 2519 Wood office furniture; cabinets, office: wood; household furniture, except wood or metal: upholstered

(G-8064)
DAC LIGHTING INC
420 Railroad Way (10543-2257)
P.O. Box 262 (10543-0262)
PHONE.................914 698-5959
Larry K Powers, *President*
Robert Haidinger Jr, *Vice Pres*
Ralph Izzi, *Treasurer*
▲ EMP: 45
SQ FT: 32,000
SALES (est): 2.8MM
SALES (corp-wide): 8.7MM **Privately Held**
WEB: www.daclighting.com
SIC: 3646 Commercial indusl & institutional electric lighting fixtures
PA: Coldstream Group Inc
420 Railroad Way
Mamaroneck NY 10543
914 698-5959

(G-8065)
DIVISION DEN-BAR ENTERPRISES
Also Called: Arborn Printing & Graphics
745 W Boston Post Rd (10543-3320)
PHONE.................914 381-2220
Fax: 914 381-6404
Barry Arborn, *President*
Denise Arborn, *Vice Pres*
Bruce Sherling, *Vice Pres*
Michael Arborn, *Manager*
Billie Karner, *Manager*
EMP: 5
SQ FT: 1,000
SALES: 650K **Privately Held**
SIC: 2759 2789 Commercial printing; bookbinding & related work

(G-8066)
ENCORE RETAIL SYSTEMS INC (PA)
180 E Prospect Ave (10543-3709)
PHONE.................718 385-3443
Fax: 718 385-3161
Louis Fusaro, *President*
Stephen Cain, *Vice Pres*
EMP: 10
SQ FT: 10,000
SALES (est): 1.9MM **Privately Held**
SIC: 2499 2541 Display forms, boot & shoes; wood partitions & fixtures

(G-8067)
FAMILY PUBLISHING GROUP INC
Also Called: New York Familypublications
141 Halstead Ave (10543-2607)
PHONE.................914 381-7474
Fax: 914 381-7672
EMP: 20
SQ FT: 1,200
SALES (est): 1.8MM **Privately Held**
SIC: 2721 2731 Periodicals-Publishing/Printing Books-Publishing/Printing

(G-8068)
GANNETT STLLITE INFO NTWRK INC
Also Called: Gannett Suburban Newspapers
700 Waverly Ave (10543-2262)
PHONE.................914 381-3400
Larry James, *Manager*
EMP: 16
SQ FT: 6,000
SALES (corp-wide): 3B **Publicly Held**
WEB: www.usatoday.com
SIC: 2711 Newspapers
HQ: Gannett Satellite Information Network, Llc
7950 Jones Branch Dr
Mc Lean VA 22102
703 854-6000

(G-8069)
INFLATION SYSTEMS INC
500 Ogden Ave (10543-2227)
PHONE.................914 381-8070
Sandra Goldman, *President*
Robert Goldman, *Vice Pres*
Sandra Machic, *Vice Pres*
EMP: 20
SQ FT: 7,500
SALES (est): 3.4MM **Privately Held**
SIC: 3069 Valves, hard rubber; hard rubber & molded rubber products

(G-8070)
MARINE & INDUS HYDRAULICS INC
329 Center Ave (10543-2304)
PHONE.................914 698-2036
John J Wright, *President*
Howard Fessel, *Prdtn Mgr*
Brooks Wright, *VP Finance*
John Cermanski, *Manager*
Louis Pesapane, *Manager*
▲ EMP: 10
SQ FT: 10,000
SALES (est): 2.1MM **Privately Held**
SIC: 3625 Actuators, industrial

(G-8071)
MARVAL INDUSTRIES INC
Also Called: M I I
315 Hoyt Ave (10543-1899)
PHONE.................914 381-2400
Fax: 914 381-2259
Alan Zimmerman, *CEO*
Thomas Zimmerman, *Ch of Bd*
Emil Kocur, *Vice Pres*
Logan Osberg, *Opers Mgr*
Ed Greene, *Marketing Mgr*
▲ EMP: 70 EST: 1956
SQ FT: 54,000
SALES (est): 39.6MM **Privately Held**
WEB: www.marvalindustries.com
SIC: 2869 5162 3089 3087 Industrial organic chemicals; plastics materials; thermoformed finished plastic products; custom compound purchased resins

(G-8072)
MDJ SALES ASSOCIATES INC
27 Doris Rd (10543-1009)
PHONE.................914 420-5897
Michael Aaronson, *CEO*
EMP: 5
SALES: 750K **Privately Held**
SIC: 2253 Knit outerwear mills

(G-8073)
ON THE JOB EMBROIDERY & AP
154 E Boston Post Rd # 1 (10543-3755)
PHONE.................914 381-3556
Michael Federici, *President*
Joseph Bilotto, *Vice Pres*
EMP: 5
SALES (est): 320K **Privately Held**
SIC: 2395 Embroidery products, except schiffli machine

(G-8074)
PALETERIA FERNANDEZ INC
350 Mamaroneck Ave (10543-2608)
PHONE.................914 315-1598
Ignacio Fernandez, *CEO*
EMP: 28
SALES (corp-wide): 477.7K **Privately Held**
SIC: 2024 Ice cream, bulk
PA: Paleteria Fernandez Inc.
33 N Main St
Port Chester NY 10573
914 939-3694

(G-8075)
PICONE MEAT SPECIALTIES LTD
Also Called: Picone's Sausage
180 Jefferson Ave (10543-1912)
PHONE.................914 381-3002
Fax: 914 381-1139
Frank Picone, *President*
Anthony Picone, *Vice Pres*
EMP: 8
SQ FT: 6,600
SALES (est): 2.4MM **Privately Held**
SIC: 2013 Sausages & other prepared meats

(G-8076)
POLKADOT USA INC
33 Country Rd (10543-1108)
PHONE.................914 835-3697
Debra Schoenau, *President*
Howard Friedman, *Vice Pres*
EMP: 2
SQ FT: 6,000
SALES: 2MM **Privately Held**
WEB: www.polkadotusa.com
SIC: 2396 Apparel & other linings, except millinery

(G-8077)
RICHARD ENGDAL BAKING CORP
Also Called: Hudson Valley Baking Co
421 Waverly Ave (10543-2233)
PHONE.................914 777-9600
Fax: 914 937-9450
Richard Cuozzo, *President*
EMP: 10
SQ FT: 4,000
SALES (est): 1.1MM **Privately Held**
SIC: 2051 Bakery: wholesale or wholesale/retail combined

GEOGRAPHIC SECTION

Manlius - Onondaga County (G-8103)

(G-8078)
ROBERT E DERECKTOR INC
Also Called: Derecktor Shipyards
311 E Boston Post Rd (10543-3738)
PHONE....................914 698-0962
Fax: 914 698-6596
Eric P Derecktor, *Ch of Bd*
E Paul Derecktor, *Ch of Bd*
Mark S Donahue, *Vice Pres*
Mark Donahue, *Vice Pres*
Steve Drago, *Project Mgr*
▲ EMP: 80 EST: 1947
SQ FT: 64,000
SALES (est): 16MM **Privately Held**
SIC: **3732** 3731 4493 7699 Boat building & repairing; fishing boats: lobster, crab, oyster, etc.: small; yachts, building & repairing; ferryboats, building & repairing; boat yards, storage & incidental repair; boat repair; sheet metalwork; fabricated structural metal

(G-8079)
SECOR MARKETING GROUP INC
Also Called: Nisonger Instrument Sls & Svc
225 Hoyt Ave (10543-1835)
PHONE....................914 381-3600
Fax: 914 381-1786
Peter Bayer, *President*
Robert Castagnetta, *Vice Pres*
Neal Dorf, *Treasurer*
EMP: 6
SQ FT: 3,200
SALES (est): 656.1K **Privately Held**
SIC: **3714** 5521 Motor vehicle parts & accessories; fuel systems & parts, motor vehicle; automobiles, used cars only

(G-8080)
SHORE LINE MONOGRAMMING INC
Also Called: Shore Line Momogramming & EMB
115 Hoyt Ave (10543-1891)
PHONE....................914 698-8000
John Moller, *President*
Andrew Moller, *President*
David Griffith, *General Mgr*
Ann Saccomanno, *Bookkeeper*
EMP: 12
SQ FT: 18,000
SALES (est): 1.3MM **Privately Held**
SIC: **2759** 5941 Screen printing; sporting goods & bicycle shops

(G-8081)
TOM & JERRY PRINTCRAFT FORMS (PA)
960 Mamaroneck Ave (10543-1631)
P.O. Box 743 (10543-0743)
PHONE....................914 777-7468
Fax: 914 698-1085
Thomas La Guidice, *President*
Phil Caragine, *Treasurer*
Mattie Saporito, *Bookkeeper*
EMP: 22
SQ FT: 5,000
SALES (est): 2.6MM **Privately Held**
WEB: www.printcraftny.com
SIC: **2752** 2791 2789 Commercial printing, lithographic; typesetting; bookbinding & related work

(G-8082)
TRIDENT VALVE ACTUATOR CO
329 Center Ave (10543-2304)
PHONE....................914 698-2650
Fax: 914 698-5629
John Cermanski, *General Mgr*
John Samanski, *General Mgr*
John Wright, *Principal*
Lucille Rende, *Plant Mgr*
Howard Fessel, *Opers Staff*
EMP: 12
SQ FT: 10,000
SALES (est): 1.1MM **Privately Held**
SIC: **3625** 5085 Actuators, industrial; valves & fittings

(G-8083)
WHITE PLAINS DRAPERY UPHL INC
Also Called: Commercial Draperies Unlimited
801 E Boston Post Rd (10543-4143)
PHONE....................914 381-0908
Fax: 914 381-0705
James Lanera, *President*
Sally Lanera, *Vice Pres*
Philip Apap, *Project Mgr*
Rose Marie Lanera, *Treasurer*
Silvana Tucci, *Marketing Staff*
EMP: 24
SQ FT: 5,000
SALES (est): 3.3MM **Privately Held**
WEB: www.commercialdrape.com
SIC: **2221** 5714 5719 5023 Upholstery, tapestry & wall covering fabrics; draperies; curtains; upholstery materials; window furnishings; draperies; window furnishings; reupholstery & furniture repair; curtains & draperies

---

Manchester
Ontario County

(G-8084)
ELITE MACHINE INC
3 Merrick Cir (14504-9740)
P.O. Box 8 (14504-0008)
PHONE....................585 289-4733
Steve Hawkins, *President*
EMP: 5
SQ FT: 5,304
SALES (est): 451K **Privately Held**
SIC: **3599** Machine shop, jobbing & repair

(G-8085)
ROCHESTER INSULATED GLASS INC
73 Merrick Cir (14504-9740)
P.O. Box 168 (14504-0168)
PHONE....................585 289-3611
Fax: 585 289-3610
Richard S Wolk, *President*
Gretchen Wolk, *Corp Secy*
Tyler Wolk, *Vice Pres*
Linda Ralston, *Controller*
Andrew Onofrey, *Accounts Mgr*
◆ EMP: 55
SALES (est): 13.6MM **Privately Held**
WEB: www.rochesterinsulatedglass.com
SIC: **3231** Insulating glass: made from purchased glass; safety glass: made from purchased glass

(G-8086)
SIDCO FILTER CORPORATION
58 North Ave (14504-9769)
PHONE....................585 289-3100
Fax: 585 924-0777
Sidney T Cutt, *Ch of Bd*
Andrea Fitzgerald, *President*
Bill Florance, *Sales Dir*
Kathy Shattuck, *Cust Svc Mgr*
Ebba Donner, *Office Mgr*
EMP: 27
SQ FT: 20,000
SALES (est): 5.2MM **Privately Held**
WEB: www.sidcofilter.com
SIC: **3569** Filters

Manhasset
Nassau County

(G-8087)
ADVANCED PROSTHETICS ORTHOTICS
Also Called: Joyce Center
50 Maple Pl (11030-1927)
PHONE....................516 365-7225
Fax: 516 365-7112
Michael A Joyce, *President*
Cheryl Caruso, *Manager*
EMP: 10
SALES (est): 1.4MM **Privately Held**
SIC: **3842** Prosthetic appliances; orthopedic appliances

(G-8088)
CABINETRY BY TBR INC
1492 Northern Blvd (11030-3006)
PHONE....................516 365-8500
Basiliki Ypsilantis, *Principal*
EMP: 8
SALES (est): 747K **Privately Held**
SIC: **2434** Wood kitchen cabinets

(G-8089)
CALIBRATED INSTRUMENTS INC
306 Aerie Ct (11030-4053)
PHONE....................914 741-5700
John B Shroyer, *President*
Angela Perry, *Bookkeeper*
▲ EMP: 10 EST: 1954
SALES (est): 1.6MM **Privately Held**
SIC: **3823** On-stream gas/liquid analysis instruments, industrial

(G-8090)
DAVID YURMAN ENTERPRISES LLC
2046 Northern Blvd (11030-3540)
PHONE....................516 627-1700
Julie Freeman, *Store Mgr*
Caryn Amandola, *Manager*
EMP: 6
SALES (corp-wide): 276.9MM **Privately Held**
SIC: **3911** Jewelry, precious metal
PA: David Yurman Enterprises Llc
24 Vestry St
New York NY 10013
212 691-1550

(G-8091)
DEEP DYEING INC
120 Bayview Ave (11030-1849)
PHONE....................718 418-7187
Fax: 718 418-7188
Edvart Mouradian, *President*
Alis Mouradian, *Vice Pres*
Arsen Mouradian, *Vice Pres*
EMP: 13
SQ FT: 10,000
SALES (est): 1.8MM **Privately Held**
SIC: **2865** Dyes & pigments

(G-8092)
DOHNSCO INC
19 Gracewood Dr (11030-3931)
PHONE....................516 773-4800
EMP: 5
SQ FT: 2,100
SALES (est): 310K **Privately Held**
SIC: **2741** 7379 Misc Publishing Computer Related Services

(G-8093)
FRAME SHOPPE & ART GALLERY
Also Called: Frame Shoppe & Gallery
447 Plandome Rd (11030-1942)
PHONE....................516 365-6014
Demitri Kazianis, *Partner*
Thomas Walsh, *Partner*
EMP: 6
SALES (est): 429.6K **Privately Held**
SIC: **2499** 3499 7699 5999 Picture frame molding, finished; picture frames, metal; picture framing, custom; art dealers; gift shop

(G-8094)
GOLF DIRECTORIES USA INC
39 Orchard St Ste 7 (11030-1969)
PHONE....................516 365-5351
Ray Cyrgalis, *President*
EMP: 5
SQ FT: 1,000
SALES (est): 274.8K **Privately Held**
SIC: **2741** Telephone & other directory publishing

(G-8095)
MDR PRINTING CORP
Also Called: Minuteman Press
125 Plandome Rd (11030-2331)
PHONE....................516 627-3221
Fax: 516 365-8271
Les Forrai, *President*
EMP: 5
SQ FT: 1,200
SALES (est): 842.8K **Privately Held**
WEB: www.manhassetminuteman.com
SIC: **2752** Commercial printing, lithographic

(G-8096)
MITCHELL GOLD CO
1900 Northern Blvd Ste F (11030-3542)
PHONE....................516 627-3525
EMP: 96
SALES (corp-wide): 277.3MM **Privately Held**
SIC: **2512** Upholstered household furniture
PA: The Mitchell Gold Co
135 One Comfortable Pl
Taylorsville NC 28681
828 632-9200

(G-8097)
NATIONAL SECURITY SYSTEMS INC
511 Manhasset Woods Rd (11030-1663)
PHONE....................516 627-2222
Jay Baron, *President*
John W Walter, *Chairman*
William T Walter, *Vice Pres*
Joan Walter, *Admin Sec*
EMP: 26
SQ FT: 3,200
SALES (est): 34.6MM **Privately Held**
WEB: www.plazaconstruction.com
SIC: **3699** Security control equipment & systems

(G-8098)
PRISCILLA QUART CO FIRTS
160 Plandome Rd Fl 2 (11030-2326)
PHONE....................516 365-2755
EMP: 6
SALES (est): 278.8K **Privately Held**
SIC: **3131** Quarters

(G-8099)
SUPERIOR FURS INC
1697 Northern Blvd (11030-3026)
PHONE....................516 365-4123
Tom Djoganopoulos, *President*
EMP: 13
SQ FT: 1,000
SALES (est): 1.1MM **Privately Held**
SIC: **2371** 5632 Apparel, fur; furriers

(G-8100)
TEA LIFE LLC
73 Plandome Rd (11030-2330)
PHONE....................516 365-7711
Linda Villano,
EMP: 8
SQ FT: 3,000
SALES (est): 258.8K **Privately Held**
SIC: **2099** Tea blending

Manlius
Onondaga County

(G-8101)
BASILEUS COMPANY LLC
8104 Cazenovia Rd (13104-6700)
PHONE....................315 963-3516
Maribeth Homa, *Bookkeeper*
Jacqueline B Wilson, *Sales Mgr*
Gerald E Wilson, *Mng Member*
◆ EMP: 10
SQ FT: 2,215
SALES (est): 940K **Privately Held**
SIC: **2211** Apparel & outerwear fabrics, cotton

(G-8102)
CARPENTER MANUFACTURING CO
110 Fairgrounds Dr (13104-2481)
P.O. Box 188 (13104-0188)
PHONE....................315 682-9176
Fax: 315 682-9160
Thomas Carpenter, *President*
Susan C Sorensen, *Vice Pres*
Andrew Miller, *Engineer*
Alan Sorensen, *Sales Dir*
Kenneth Carpenter, *Shareholder*
EMP: 20 EST: 1955
SQ FT: 14,500
SALES (est): 4.5MM **Privately Held**
WEB: www.carpentermfg.com
SIC: **3549** Wiredrawing & fabricating machinery & equipment, ex. die; cutting & slitting machinery

(G-8103)
CREATIVE YARD DESIGNS INC
8329 Us Route 20 (13104-9536)
PHONE....................315 706-6143

Manlius - Onondaga County (G-8104)

Ron King, *Manager*
EMP: 5
SALES (est): 377.6K **Privately Held**
SIC: 3271 Blocks, concrete: landscape or retaining wall

(G-8104)
FILTER TECH INC (PA)
113 Fairgrounds Dr (13104-2497)
P.O. Box 527 (13104-0527)
PHONE.................................315 682-8815
Fax: 315 682-8825
Joseph F Scalise, *President*
Ahmad El-Hindi, *Principal*
Joseph El-Hindi, *Vice Pres*
Elizabeth Elhindi, *Vice Pres*
Ahmad E Hindi, *Treasurer*
▲ **EMP:** 59
SQ FT: 10,000
SALES (est): 12.2MM **Privately Held**
WEB: www.filtertech.com
SIC: 3569 Filters, general line: industrial; lubricating systems, centralized

(G-8105)
GLOBAL INSTRUMENTATION LLC
8104 Cazenovia Rd Ste 2/3 (13104-6700)
PHONE.................................315 682-0272
James Demaso, *Mng Member*
Scott Meyers,
Craig Sellers,
EMP: 10
SALES (est): 1.9MM **Privately Held**
WEB: www.globalinstrumentation.com
SIC: 3845 Ultrasonic scanning devices, medical

(G-8106)
L& JG STICKLEY INCORPORATED (PA)
1 Stickley Dr (13104-2485)
P.O. Box 480 (13104-0480)
PHONE.................................315 682-5500
Fax: 315 682-6306
Aminy I Audi, *Ch of Bd*
Edward Audi, *President*
John Brogan, *CFO*
Ed McCord, *Finance*
Beverly Manning, *Human Res Mgr*
▲ **EMP:** 900 **EST:** 1895
SQ FT: 400,000
SALES (est): 254.3MM **Privately Held**
WEB: www.stickley.com
SIC: 2511 2519 Wood household furniture; household furniture, except wood or metal: upholstered

(G-8107)
MAYBERRY SHOE COMPANY INC
Also Called: Kangaroo Crossing
131 W Seneca St Ste B (13104-2444)
PHONE.................................315 692-4086
Bruce Mayberry, *President*
EMP: 5
SQ FT: 500
SALES (est): 776K **Privately Held**
SIC: 3149 2329 2339 Athletic shoes, except rubber or plastic; men's & boys' athletic uniforms; uniforms, athletic: women's, misses' & juniors'

(G-8108)
MILLER ENTERPRISES CNY INC
Also Called: UPS
131 W Seneca St Ste B (13104-2444)
PHONE.................................315 682-4999
Christopher Akin, *President*
EMP: 5
SALES (est): 497.4K **Privately Held**
SIC: 2752 7334 4783 4513 Commercial printing, lithographic; offset & photolithographic printing; photocopying & duplicating services; packing goods for shipping; package delivery, private air

(G-8109)
VOSS SIGNS LLC
112 Fairgrounds Dr Ste 2 (13104-2437)
P.O. Box 553 (13104-0553)
PHONE.................................315 682-6418
Fax: 315 682-7335
Debbie Menter, *Human Resources*
Mary Walser, *Sales Mgr*

Thomas Tenerovicz, *Mktg Dir*
Diane Voss, *Office Mgr*
James Menter, *Executive*
EMP: 25
SQ FT: 31,000
SALES (est): 3.6MM **Privately Held**
WEB: www.vosssigns.com
SIC: 2759 3993 2791 Screen printing; signs & advertising specialties; typesetting

Manorville
Suffolk County

(G-8110)
B & K PRECISION CORPORATION
31 Oakwood Dr (11949-1211)
PHONE.................................631 369-2665
Ray Kreiger, *Branch Mgr*
EMP: 5 **Privately Held**
WEB: www.bkprecision.com
SIC: 3559 Automotive related machinery
PA: B&K Precision Corporation
 22820 Savi Ranch Pkwy
 Yorba Linda CA 92887

(G-8111)
CPI INDUSTRIES INC
275 Dayton Ave (11949-2029)
PHONE.................................631 909-3434
Ciro Intini, *President*
Denise Intini, *Opers Mgr*
EMP: 55
SALES: 4MM **Privately Held**
SIC: 3444 Sheet metalwork

(G-8112)
S A S INDUSTRIES INC
939 Wding River Manor Rd (11949)
P.O. Box 245 (11949-0245)
PHONE.................................631 727-1441
Fax: 631 727-1387
Steve Steckis, *President*
A Steckis, *Manager*
Mitchell Steckis, *Info Tech Mgr*
▲ **EMP:** 15 **EST:** 1973
SQ FT: 10,000
SALES (est): 3.3MM **Privately Held**
WEB: www.sasindustries.com
SIC: 3053 5085 Gaskets, all materials; industrial supplies

(G-8113)
SPLICE TECHNOLOGIES INC
625 North St (11949-2055)
P.O. Box 644 (11949-0644)
PHONE.................................631 924-8108
Robert P Auteri, *President*
Nannette M Auteri, *Admin Sec*
▼ **EMP:** 8
SQ FT: 2,000
SALES (est): 1.2MM **Privately Held**
WEB: www.splicetechnologies.com
SIC: 3661 Fiber optics communications equipment

(G-8114)
VULCAN IRON WORKS INC
190 Weeks Ave (11949-2034)
PHONE.................................631 395-6846
Carl Forster, *President*
Barbara Forster, *Office Mgr*
EMP: 4 **EST:** 1926
SQ FT: 1,800
SALES (est): 2MM **Privately Held**
WEB: www.vulcanironworks.com
SIC: 3441 Fabricated structural metal

Marathon
Cortland County

(G-8115)
KURTZ TRUCK EQUIPMENT INC
1085 Mcgraw Marathon Rd (13803-2806)
PHONE.................................607 849-3468
Mellisa Slack, *President*
Roger Smith, *President*
EMP: 18 **EST:** 1960
SQ FT: 4,000

SALES (est): 3.8MM **Privately Held**
SIC: 3713 3599 3714 Specialty motor vehicle bodies; machine shop, jobbing & repair; propane conversion equipment, motor vehicle

(G-8116)
MARATHON BOAT GROUP INC
1 Grumman Way (13803-3030)
P.O. Box 549 (13803-0549)
PHONE.................................607 849-3211
Fax: 607 849-3077
Doug Potter, *President*
Greg Harvey, *Corp Secy*
▼ **EMP:** 15
SQ FT: 24,050
SALES (est): 1.3MM **Privately Held**
WEB: www.marathonboat.com
SIC: 3732 5551 Motorized boat, building & repairing; canoes, building & repairing; boat dealers

Marcellus
Onondaga County

(G-8117)
ARMSTRONG TRANSMITTER CORP
4835 N Street Rd (13108-9715)
PHONE.................................315 673-1269
Fax: 315 673-9972
Sinan Mimaroglu, *President*
Jim Giatz, *General Mgr*
Ernie Belanger, *Mktg Dir*
Kevin Smith, *Marketing Staff*
Bill Darron, *Manager*
▲ **EMP:** 10
SQ FT: 40,000
SALES (est): 1.2MM **Privately Held**
WEB: www.armstrongtx.com
SIC: 3663 Transmitting apparatus, radio or television

(G-8118)
CHOCOLATE PIZZA COMPANY INC
3774 Lee Mulroy Rd (13108-9814)
PHONE.................................315 673-4098
Ryan Novak, *Ch of Bd*
EMP: 18
SQ FT: 7,000
SALES (est): 3.3MM **Privately Held**
WEB: www.chocolatepizza.com
SIC: 2066 2064 5149 Chocolate candy, solid; chocolate candy, except solid chocolate; chocolate

(G-8119)
QUIKRETE COMPANIES INC
4993 Limeledge Rd Ste 560 (13108-9798)
PHONE.................................315 673-2020
Joe Boucher, *Sales Executive*
Greg Breen, *Branch Mgr*
EMP: 20 **Privately Held**
SIC: 3273 Ready-mixed concrete
HQ: The Quikrete Companies Llc
 5 Concourse Pkwy Ste 1900
 Atlanta GA 30328
 404 634-9100

(G-8120)
SMITH SAND & GRAVEL INC
4782 Shepard Rd (13108-9745)
P.O. Box 166 (13108-0166)
PHONE.................................315 673-4124
David J Smith, *Ch of Bd*
Stacy Feocco, *Admin Sec*
EMP: 9 **EST:** 2005
SALES (est): 1.6MM **Privately Held**
SIC: 1442 Construction sand & gravel

Marcy
Oneida County

(G-8121)
DEANS PAVING INC
6002 Cavanaugh Rd (13403-2411)
PHONE.................................315 736-7601
James J Dean, *Principal*
EMP: 6

SALES: 700K **Privately Held**
WEB: www.deanspaving.com
SIC: 2951 4959 7521 0782 Asphalt paving mixtures & blocks; sweeping service: road, airport, parking lot, etc.; snowplowing; parking lots; lawn services

(G-8122)
PRAXAIR DISTRIBUTION INC
9432 State Route 49 (13403-2342)
PHONE.................................315 735-6153
Ron Marson, *Manager*
EMP: 11
SALES (corp-wide): 10.5B **Publicly Held**
SIC: 2813 Oxygen, compressed or liquefied; nitrogen; acetylene
HQ: Praxair Distribution, Inc.
 10 Riverview Dr
 Danbury CT 06810
 203 837-2000

Margaretville
Delaware County

(G-8123)
ROBERT GREENBURG (PA)
Cross Rd (12455)
PHONE.................................845 586-2226
Robert Greenburg, *President*
Robert Kane, *Vice Pres*
Al Bates, *Manager*
EMP: 5
SQ FT: 2,000
SALES (est): 898.5K **Privately Held**
SIC: 2851 Epoxy coatings; polyurethane coatings

Marion
Wayne County

(G-8124)
GREEN VALLEY FOODS LLC
3736 S Main St (14505-9751)
PHONE.................................315 926-4280
Kraig H Kayser,
Timothy Benjamin,
Paul Palmby,
Jeffrey Van Riper,
EMP: 7
SQ FT: 348,000
SALES (est): 285.2K
SALES (corp-wide): 1.2B **Publicly Held**
SIC: 2033 Vegetables: packaged in cans, jars, etc.; fruits: packaged in cans, jars, etc.
PA: Seneca Foods Corporation
 3736 S Main St
 Marion NY 14505
 315 926-8100

(G-8125)
HADLEYS FAB-WELD INC
4202 Sunset Dr (14505-9538)
PHONE.................................315 926-5101
Fax: 315 926-0224
Alan Hadley, *President*
Adriana Hadley, *Vice Pres*
Christopher Wahl, *Supervisor*
EMP: 9
SQ FT: 5,800
SALES (est): 1.1MM **Privately Held**
WEB: www.hadleyfabweld.com
SIC: 7692 Welding repair

(G-8126)
J & G MACHINE & TOOL CO INC
4510 Smith Rd (14505-9509)
PHONE.................................315 310-7130
Gary Prutsman, *President*
EMP: 14
SQ FT: 15,000
SALES: 1.5MM **Privately Held**
SIC: 3599 Machine shop, jobbing & repair

(G-8127)
PARKER-HANNIFIN CORPORATION
Also Called: Engineered Polymer Systems Div
3967 Buffalo St (14505-9616)
P.O. Box 6 (14505-0006)
PHONE..................................315 926-4211
Terry Gardner, *Mfg Mgr*
Sue Remmel, *Personnel*
Eric Nary, *Manager*
EMP: 30
SALES (corp-wide): 12B **Publicly Held**
WEB: www.parker.com
SIC: **2821** Plastics materials & resins
PA: Parker-Hannifin Corporation
6035 Parkland Blvd
Cleveland OH 44124
216 896-3000

(G-8128)
PETER C HERMAN INC
5395 Skinner Rd (14505-9406)
PHONE..................................315 926-4100
Fax: 315 331-0046
Matthew Herman, *President*
Joseph Herman, *Vice Pres*
Diana Harder, *Manager*
EMP: 6
SQ FT: 2,000
SALES (est): 8.1MM **Privately Held**
SIC: **2448** Pallets, wood

(G-8129)
SENECA FOODS CORPORATION (PA)
3736 S Main St (14505-9751)
PHONE..................................315 926-8100
Fax: 315 926-7008
Arthur S Wolcott, *Ch of Bd*
Kraig H Kayser, *President*
Paul L Palmby, *COO*
Jeffrey L Van Riper, *Vice Pres*
Timothy J Benjamin, *CFO*
◆ EMP: 50
SQ FT: 348,000
SALES: 1.2B **Publicly Held**
SIC: **2033** **2037** Vegetables: packaged in cans, jars, etc.; fruits: packaged in cans, jars, etc.; vegetables, quick frozen & cold pack, excl. potato products; fruits, quick frozen & cold pack (frozen); fruit juices, frozen

(G-8130)
SENECA FOODS CORPORATION
3709 Mill St (14505-9602)
PHONE..................................315 926-0531
Fax: 315 926-4296
Patricia East, *Accounting Dir*
Mike Hanchette, *Manager*
EMP: 66
SQ FT: 544
SALES (corp-wide): 1.2B **Publicly Held**
SIC: **3411** Metal cans
PA: Seneca Foods Corporation
3736 S Main St
Marion NY 14505
315 926-8100

(G-8131)
SENECA FOODS CORPORATION
Also Called: Vegetable Operations
3732 S Main St (14505-9751)
P.O. Box 996 (14505-0996)
PHONE..................................315 926-4277
Fax: 315 926-5332
Jim Haukom, *Engineer*
Dan Janke, *Manager*
Jeff Hall, *Manager*
Dennis Magtee, *Manager*
Ben Scherwitz, *Admin Sec*
EMP: 18
SALES (corp-wide): 1.2B **Publicly Held**
SIC: **2033** Vegetables: packaged in cans, jars, etc.
PA: Seneca Foods Corporation
3736 S Main St
Marion NY 14505
315 926-8100

(G-8132)
TEC GLASS & INST LLC
Also Called: Thomas R Schul TEC GL & Inst
4211 Sunset Dr (14505-9556)
PHONE..................................315 926-7639
Fax: 315 926-5731
Thomas Schul, *Mng Member*
Hope Schul,
EMP: 7
SQ FT: 3,000
SALES: 150K **Privately Held**
WEB: www.tecglass.biz
SIC: **3231** **5049** Laboratory glassware; laboratory equipment, except medical or dental

(G-8133)
VERNS MACHINE CO INC
4929 Steel Point Rd (14505-9552)
PHONE..................................315 926-4223
Fax: 315 926-1005
Al Visingard, *President*
EMP: 28 EST: 1975
SQ FT: 8,000
SALES (est): 3.6MM **Privately Held**
SIC: **3541** **3599** **3451** Machine tools, metal cutting type; machine & other job shop work; screw machine products

(G-8134)
WESSIE MACHINE INC
5229 Steel Point Rd (14505-9534)
PHONE..................................315 926-4060
Alan Wessie, *President*
EMP: 7
SALES (est): 1.1MM **Privately Held**
SIC: **3469** Machine parts, stamped or pressed metal

Marlboro
Ulster County

(G-8135)
CIGAR BOX STUDIOS INC
24 Riverview Dr (12542-5310)
PHONE..................................845 236-9283
Fax: 845 863-1016
Gary Rausenberger, *President*
Michael Girman, *General Mgr*
Scott Rausenberger, *Project Mgr*
Mike Rutski, *Project Mgr*
Rob Macdonald, *Purch Mgr*
▲ EMP: 14
SQ FT: 20,000
SALES (est): 3.6MM **Privately Held**
WEB: www.cigarboxstudios.com
SIC: **3443** Fabricated plate work (boiler shop)

(G-8136)
ROYAL WINE CORPORATION
Also Called: Royal Kedem Wine
1519 Route 9w (12542-5420)
PHONE..................................845 236-4000
Solomon Schwartz, *Purchasing*
Michael Herzog, *Branch Mgr*
EMP: 15
SALES (corp-wide): 47.4MM **Privately Held**
SIC: **2084** **5182** Wines; wine; liquor
PA: Royal Wine Corporation
63 Lefante Dr
Bayonne NJ 07002
718 384-2400

Masonville
Delaware County

(G-8137)
AXTELL BRADTKE LUMBER CO
113 Beals Pond Rd (13804-2031)
PHONE..................................607 265-3850
Stuart Axtell, *Partner*
EMP: 6
SALES (est): 554.1K **Privately Held**
SIC: **2421** **5211** Sawmills & planing mills, general; lumber products

(G-8138)
MASONVILLE STONE INCORPORATED
12999 State Highway 8 (13804-2119)
PHONE..................................607 265-3597
David Barnes, *President*
Douglas Barnes, *Vice Pres*
EMP: 8
SQ FT: 7,800
SALES (est): 937.4K **Privately Held**
SIC: **3281** Cut stone & stone products

Maspeth
Queens County

(G-8139)
A & A LINE & WIRE CORP
Also Called: Crown Brand Twine
5118 Grand Ave Ste 10 (11378-3031)
PHONE..................................718 456-2657
Fax: 718 366-8284
Walter Lach, *President*
Fayga Lach, *Treasurer*
Jacob Lach, *Admin Sec*
▲ EMP: 15 EST: 1963
SQ FT: 16,000
SALES (est): 2.6MM **Privately Held**
SIC: **2298** Twine, cord & cordage; ropes & fiber cables

(G-8140)
AGL INDUSTRIES INC
5912 57th St (11378-3112)
PHONE..................................718 326-7597
Frank Lofaso, *President*
Farooq Khan, *Controller*
EMP: 50 EST: 2012
SQ FT: 4,500
SALES (est): 10.3MM **Privately Held**
SIC: **3449** Bars, concrete reinforcing: fabricated steel

(G-8141)
AIR LOUVER & DAMPER INC
5670 58th Pl (11378-2348)
PHONE..................................718 392-3232
Fax: 718 786-5344
James Pascale, *Manager*
EMP: 24
SALES (corp-wide): 2.7MM **Privately Held**
SIC: **3822** **3444** Damper operators: pneumatic, thermostatic, electric; metal ventilating equipment
PA: Air Louver & Damper, Inc
2121 44th Rd
Long Island City NY 11101
718 392-3232

(G-8142)
ALL-CITY METAL INC
5435 46th St (11378-1035)
PHONE..................................718 937-3975
Frank J Buccola, *Ch of Bd*
Roni Lifshitz, *Vice Pres*
John Majowka, *Controller*
Mark Pukhovich, *Manager*
Alicia Barreto, *Admin Asst*
EMP: 40
SQ FT: 2,000
SALES (est): 11MM **Privately Held**
SIC: **3441** **1711** Fabricated structural metal; mechanical contractor

(G-8143)
ALLE PROCESSING CORP
Also Called: Amazing Meals
5620 59th St (11378-2314)
PHONE..................................718 894-2000
Sam Hollander, *Ch of Bd*
Albert Weinstock, *President*
Shlomi Pilo, *General Mgr*
Zevi Wienstock, *Purch Mgr*
Pinchus Gelbman, *Engineer*
▲ EMP: 250 EST: 1954
SQ FT: 75,000
SALES (est): 54.1MM **Privately Held**
WEB: www.alleprocessing.com
SIC: **2013** **2015** **2038** Sausages & other prepared meats; prepared beef products from purchased beef; poultry slaughtering & processing; dinners, frozen & packaged

(G-8144)
AMAX PRINTING INC
6417 Grand Ave (11378-2421)
PHONE..................................718 384-8600
Fax: 718 384-5628
Anton Chan, *President*
Fanny Fang, *Vice Pres*
EMP: 15
SQ FT: 8,000
SALES (est): 2.1MM **Privately Held**
WEB: www.amaxprinting.com
SIC: **2759** **2752** Commercial printing; commercial printing, lithographic

(G-8145)
AMERICA NY RI WANG FD GROUP CO
5885 58th Ave (11378-2721)
PHONE..................................718 628-8999
Lian You Ye, *President*
Alex Chang, *Administration*
▲ EMP: 50 EST: 2009
SQ FT: 40,000
SALES: 5MM **Privately Held**
SIC: **2038** Ethnic foods, frozen

(G-8146)
ANDIKE MILLWORK INC (PA)
Also Called: A & M Home Improvement
5818 64th St Fl 2 (11378-2817)
PHONE..................................718 894-1796
Fax: 718 894-0662
Andrew La Russa, *President*
Mike Machalski, *Vice Pres*
EMP: 2
SQ FT: 6,500
SALES (est): 1MM **Privately Held**
WEB: www.amhomeimprovement.com
SIC: **2434** **5211** **2499** **1521** Wood kitchen cabinets; millwork & lumber; decorative wood & woodwork; single-family home remodeling, additions & repairs

(G-8147)
APEXX OMNI-GRAPHICS INC
5829 64th St (11378-2836)
PHONE..................................718 326-3330
Fax: 718 326-7317
Larry A Peters, *Ch of Bd*
Diran Avedissian, *Sales Staff*
Luis Arroyo, *Info Tech Mgr*
EMP: 55 EST: 1963
SQ FT: 40,000
SALES (est): 10.3MM **Privately Held**
WEB: www.apexxog.com
SIC: **3555** **2656** **3861** **3089** Plates, offset; plates, paper: made from purchased material; plates, photographic (sensitized); plates, plastic; labels, paper: made from purchased material; packaging paper & plastics film, coated & laminated

(G-8148)
ARISTA COFFEE INC
5901 55th St (11378-3103)
PHONE..................................347 531-0813
Stephen Vouvoudakis, *Ch of Bd*
EMP: 5
SALES (est): 605.2K **Privately Held**
SIC: **3589** Coffee brewing equipment

(G-8149)
ASN INC
Also Called: Tri Star
6020 59th Pl Ste 2 (11378-3349)
PHONE..................................718 894-0800
Fax: 718 894-4040
Albert Nawroth, *Ch of Bd*
Rudy Bove, *Vice Pres*
Rosa Frankly, *Receptionist*
EMP: 40
SALES (est): 1.5MM **Privately Held**
SIC: **2759** **2752** Commercial printing; commercial printing, lithographic

(G-8150)
BG BINDERY INC
5877 57th St (11378-3125)
PHONE..................................631 767-4242
Barbara Michael, *CEO*
EMP: 5 EST: 2011
SALES (est): 539.6K **Privately Held**
SIC: **2789** Bookbinding & related work

Maspeth - Queens County (G-8151) — GEOGRAPHIC SECTION

(G-8151)
BIMBO BAKERIES USA INC
Also Called: Stroehmann Bakeries 33
5754 Page Pl (11378-2236)
PHONE..................718 463-6300
Fax: 718 463-1614
Steven Hartley, *Branch Mgr*
EMP: 117 **Privately Held**
SIC: 2051 5149 Bread, all types (white, wheat, rye, etc); fresh or frozen; groceries & related products
HQ: Bimbo Bakeries Usa, Inc
   255 Business Center Dr # 200
   Horsham PA 19044
   215 347-5500

(G-8152)
CASCADES NEW YORK INC
5515 Grand Ave (11378-3113)
PHONE..................718 340-2100
Robert Sattelberg, *Manager*
EMP: 100
SALES (corp-wide): 2.9B **Privately Held**
SIC: 2652 Setup paperboard boxes
HQ: Cascades New York Inc.
   1845 Emerson St
   Rochester NY 14606
   585 527-8110

(G-8153)
COCA-COLA BTLG CO OF NY INC
5902 Borden Ave (11378-1189)
PHONE..................718 326-3334
Fax: 718 326-3491
Anthony Blanchfield, *Opers Mgr*
Mike Linbugh, *Opers Mgr*
Mike Limbaugh, *Mfg Staff*
David Prespitino, *Manager*
Eric Place, *Manager*
EMP: 116
SALES (corp-wide): 41.8B **Publicly Held**
SIC: 2086 Bottled & canned soft drinks
HQ: The Coca-Cola Bottling Company Of New York Inc
   2500 Windy Ridge Pkwy Se
   Atlanta GA 30339
   770 989-3000

(G-8154)
COCA-COLA BTLG CO OF NY INC
5840 Borden Ave (11378-1106)
PHONE..................718 416-7575
Debra Carpianoco, *Finance Mgr*
Sharon Smith, *Manager*
Debra Capobianco, *Executive*
Mike Limbaugh, *Executive*
EMP: 20
SALES (corp-wide): 41.8B **Publicly Held**
SIC: 2086 Bottled & canned soft drinks
HQ: The Coca-Cola Bottling Company Of New York Inc
   2500 Windy Ridge Pkwy Se
   Atlanta GA 30339
   770 989-3000

(G-8155)
CRAFT CUSTOM WOODWORK CO INC
5949 56th Ave (11378-2324)
PHONE..................718 821-2162
Fax: 718 894-6858
Yakov Roitman, *President*
▼ EMP: 10
SQ FT: 3,500
SALES: 600K **Privately Held**
SIC: 2434 2521 Wood kitchen cabinets; cabinets, office: wood

(G-8156)
CRAFTSMEN WOODWORKERS LTD
5865 Maspeth Ave (11378-2728)
PHONE..................718 326-3350
Fax: 718 326-0269
Joseph Finocchiaro, *Principal*
Maddy Finocchiaro, *Manager*
EMP: 25
SQ FT: 13,000
SALES (est): 3.8MM **Privately Held**
WEB: www.craftsmenwoodworkers.com
SIC: 2431 Millwork

(G-8157)
CREATIVE IMAGES & APPLIQUE
Also Called: Cyber Swag Merchandise of NY
5208 Grand Ave Ste 2 (11378-3032)
PHONE..................718 821-8700
Bob Andreoli, *President*
Roger Clark, *Vice Pres*
EMP: 63
SQ FT: 14,500
SALES (est): 6.5MM **Privately Held**
SIC: 2396 Screen printing on fabric articles

(G-8158)
D & G SHEET METAL CO INC
5400 Grand Ave (11378-3006)
PHONE..................718 326-9111
Fax: 718 326-0990
Frank Doka, *President*
EMP: 12
SQ FT: 12,400
SALES (est): 1.3MM **Privately Held**
SIC: 3444 Sheet metalwork

(G-8159)
DAL-TILE CORPORATION
5840 55th Dr (11378-1152)
PHONE..................718 894-9574
Gary Guarascio, *Manager*
EMP: 6
SALES (corp-wide): 8.9B **Publicly Held**
WEB: www.mohawk.com
SIC: 2824 5032 Organic fibers, noncellulosic; ceramic wall & floor tile
HQ: Dal-Tile Corporation
   7834 C F Hawn Fwy
   Dallas TX 75217
   214 398-1411

(G-8160)
DAYLIGHT TECHNOLOGY USA INC
5971 59th St (11378-3229)
PHONE..................973 255-8100
Reawei Lee, *President*
▲ EMP: 5 EST: 2013
SQ FT: 2,000
SALES (est): 2MM **Privately Held**
SIC: 3229 Bulbs for electric lights

(G-8161)
DIAMOND CORING & CUTTING INC
5919 55th St (11378-3103)
PHONE..................718 381-4545
David Obbink, *President*
EMP: 5
SALES: 80K **Privately Held**
SIC: 3531 Construction machinery

(G-8162)
DSI GROUP INC
Also Called: Ovation Instore
5713 49th St (11378-2020)
PHONE..................800 553-2202
Benjamin S Weshler, *Ch of Bd*
Mindy Kaufman, *COO*
Emily Pelton, *Vice Pres*
Jose Mosquea, *Plant Mgr*
Barbara Gnyp, *Purch Dir*
▲ EMP: 200
SQ FT: 130,000
SALES (est): 47.1MM **Privately Held**
SIC: 3993 Displays & cutouts, window & lobby

(G-8163)
DURA FOAM INC
6302 59th Ave (11378-2808)
PHONE..................718 894-2488
Fax: 718 894-2493
Antony Fontana, *President*
Donna Broselofsky, *Manager*
Gary Hall, *Manager*
EMP: 35 EST: 1977
SQ FT: 50,000
SALES (est): 4.7MM **Privately Held**
SIC: 3086 Plastics foam products

(G-8164)
DYNASTY STAINLESS STEEL & META
5985 Maurice Ave (11378-1236)
PHONE..................718 205-6623
Peter Liou, *President*
Alicia Lee, *Manager*
Mingkunn Lee, *Manager*
EMP: 30
SQ FT: 120,000
SALES (est): 6.3MM **Privately Held**
SIC: 3444 1542 Sheet metalwork; nonresidential construction

(G-8165)
EAST CAST ENVLOPE GRAPHICS LLC
5615 55th Dr (11378-1108)
PHONE..................718 326-2424
Fax: 718 894-1570
Leslie Stern, *President*
Alfred Wilkowski, *COO*
Patrick Nunziante, *CFO*
EMP: 41
SQ FT: 78,000
SALES: 8MM **Privately Held**
WEB: www.interstate-envelope.com
SIC: 2677 Envelopes

(G-8166)
EAST COAST INTL TIRE INC
5746 Flushing Ave Bldg C (11378)
PHONE..................718 386-9088
EMP: 10
SALES (est): 1.4MM **Privately Held**
SIC: 3011 Tires & inner tubes
PA: Qingdao Taining Industry Co., Ltd.
   No.247, 308 National Highway, Hai'er Industrial Zone, Laoshan Di
   Qingdao
   532 886-0033

(G-8167)
ELDORADO COFFEE ROASTERS LTD
Also Called: Eldorado Coffee Distributors
5675 49th St (11378-2012)
PHONE..................718 418-4100
Segundo Martin, *President*
Amparo Martin, *Vice Pres*
Andres Martin, *Vice Pres*
Juan Martin, *Vice Pres*
Robert Magan, *Sales Dir*
▲ EMP: 80 EST: 1980
SQ FT: 54,000
SALES (est): 18.3MM **Privately Held**
WEB: www.eldoradocoffee.com
SIC: 2095 Coffee extracts; coffee roasting (except by wholesale grocers)

(G-8168)
EXTREME SPICES INC (PA)
Also Called: Sanaa Spices
5634 56th St Ste 36 (11378-1132)
PHONE..................917 496-4081
Marc Salih, *President*
Taha Salih, *General Mgr*
▲ EMP: 2
SQ FT: 8,000
SALES (est): 1.3MM **Privately Held**
SIC: 2099 Spices, including grinding

(G-8169)
FALLON INC
5930 56th Rd (11378-2330)
PHONE..................718 326-7226
Steven Rosenblatt, *President*
EMP: 20
SQ FT: 27,000
SALES (est): 1.4MM **Privately Held**
WEB: www.structuralprocessing.com
SIC: 3471 Anodizing (plating) of metals or formed products

(G-8170)
FERGUSON
5722 49th St (11378-2099)
PHONE..................718 937-9500
Mark Bembia, *Sales Executive*
EMP: 7
SALES (est): 130.1K **Privately Held**
SIC: 3432 Plumbing fixture fittings & trim

(G-8171)
FINAL DIMENSION INC
57-401 59th St Fl 1 (11378)
PHONE..................718 786-0100
Labros Magoutas, *President*
EMP: 5
SQ FT: 3,000
SALES: 500K **Privately Held**
SIC: 2511 Wood household furniture

(G-8172)
FRANKS CUSHIONS INC
6302 59th Ave (11378-2808)
PHONE..................718 848-1216
Anthony Fontana, *President*
Maryann Fontana, *Bookkeeper*
Donna Broseo, *Manager*
EMP: 15 EST: 1930
SQ FT: 10,000
SALES (est): 1.3MM **Privately Held**
WEB: www.frankscushions.com
SIC: 2392 Cushions & pillows

(G-8173)
GREAT AMERICAN DESSERT CO LLC
5842 Maurice Ave (11378-2333)
PHONE..................718 894-3494
Mike Goodman,
EMP: 55 EST: 1998
SALES (est): 7.6MM **Privately Held**
SIC: 2051 Cakes, bakery: except frozen

(G-8174)
GYM STORE INC
Also Called: Gym Store.com
5889 57th St (11378-3125)
PHONE..................718 366-7804
Christopher Kelly, *President*
▼ EMP: 5
SQ FT: 10,000
SALES: 1.4MM **Privately Held**
SIC: 3949 Exercise equipment; dumbbells & other weightlifting equipment; treadmills; gymnasium equipment

(G-8175)
HERGO ERGONOMIC SUPPORT (PA)
5601 55th Ave (11378-1104)
PHONE..................718 894-0639
Fax: 718 894-4724
Eli E Hertz, *CEO*
Barry J Goldsammler, *Senior VP*
Albert Hirschson, *Senior VP*
I Marilyn Hertz, *Vice Pres*
Kristen Speranza-Diamond, *Vice Pres*
◆ EMP: 40
SQ FT: 42,000
SALES (est): 5.8MM **Privately Held**
WEB: www.hergo.com
SIC: 3577 3699 3443 2542 Computer peripheral equipment; electrical equipment & supplies; sheet metalwork; partitions & fixtures, except wood; office furniture, except wood

(G-8176)
HI-TECH METALS INC
5920 56th Ave (11378-2325)
PHONE..................718 894-1212
Fax: 718 894-5021
Manny Tzilzelis, *President*
Menelaos Tzilvelis, *President*
Chris Christodoulou, *Vice Pres*
Victor Vargas, *Engineer*
Jay Valentino, *Manager*
EMP: 50
SQ FT: 10,000
SALES (est): 13.8MM **Privately Held**
WEB: www.hi-techmetals.com
SIC: 3446 Architectural metalwork

(G-8177)
J & R UNIQUE GIFTWARE
5863 56th St (11378-3105)
PHONE..................718 821-0398
John Daidone, *Owner*
EMP: 20 EST: 2008
SALES (est): 930K **Privately Held**
SIC: 3999 Manufacturing industries

(G-8178)
JACK LUCKNER STEEL SHELVING CO
Also Called: Kart
5454 43rd St (11378-1028)
PHONE..................718 363-0500
Fax: 718 784-9169
Burton J Gold, *President*
Scott Mair, *Purchasing*
Alan Sheldon, *Controller*
Gardenia McCray, *Credit Mgr*
Gold Adam, *Manager*
EMP: 75 EST: 1947

▲ = Import ▼ = Export ◆ = Import/Export

GEOGRAPHIC SECTION — Maspeth - Queens County (G-8204)

SQ FT: 12,000
SALES (est): 7.4MM
SALES (corp-wide): 21.9MM Privately Held
WEB: www.karpinc.com
SIC: 2542 Shelving, office & store: except wood
PA: Karp Associates Inc.
260 Spagnoli Rd
Melville NY 11747
631 768-8300

(G-8179)
KARP OVERSEAS CORPORATION
5454 43rd St (11378-1028)
PHONE................718 784-2105
Burton J Gold, President
EMP: 40
SQ FT: 30,000
SALES: 500K
SALES (corp-wide): 21.9MM Privately Held
WEB: www.karpinc.com
SIC: 3965 8742 Straight pins: steel or brass; sales (including sales management) consultant
PA: Karp Associates Inc.
260 Spagnoli Rd
Melville NY 11747
631 768-8300

(G-8180)
MASPETH PRESS INC
6620 Grand Ave (11378-2531)
PHONE................718 429-2363
Frederick F Strobel, President
Frederick J Strobel, President
Linda Strobel, Vice Pres
EMP: 5
SQ FT: 2,000
SALES (est): 690.9K Privately Held
SIC: 2759 Letterpress printing

(G-8181)
MASPETH WELDING INC
5930 54th St (11378-3004)
PHONE................718 497-5430
Fax: 718 386-9238
Jeffrey Anschlowar, Ch of Bd
Evelyn Agnoli, VP Finance
Lou Javier, Sr Project Mgr
Val Chua, Manager
Fred Peterson, Manager
EMP: 40 EST: 1977
SQ FT: 48,000
SALES (est): 11.9MM Privately Held
WEB: www.maspethwelding.com
SIC: 3441 7692 Fabricated structural metal; welding repair

(G-8182)
MAXSUN CORPORATION (PA)
Also Called: Maxsun Furnishings
5711 49th St (11378-2020)
PHONE................718 418-6800
Johnny Song Lin, Ch of Bd
▲ EMP: 17
SALES (est): 867.1K Privately Held
SIC: 2599 5719 Restaurant furniture, wood or metal; bar furniture; bar, restaurant & cafeteria furniture; lighting fixtures

(G-8183)
N Y CONTRACT SEATING INC
5560 60th St (11378-2338)
PHONE................718 417-9298
John Glantzis, President
EMP: 7
SQ FT: 2,100
SALES (est): 738.1K Privately Held
SIC: 2211 Upholstery fabrics, cotton

(G-8184)
N Y ELLI DESIGN CORP
5105 Flushing Ave 2 (11378-3019)
PHONE................718 228-0014
Fax: 718 418-4629
Dimitra Ligas, CEO
Lisa Opera, Manager
▲ EMP: 15
SQ FT: 30,000
SALES: 5.1MM Privately Held
WEB: www.ellicorp.com
SIC: 2434 2521 2531 Wood kitchen cabinets; cabinets, office: wood; public building & related furniture; library furniture

(G-8185)
NE & WS INC
6085 60th St (11378-3550)
PHONE................718 326-4699
Fax: 718 417-7427
Edward Nowakowski, President
Margaret Nowakowski, Admin Sec
EMP: 9
SQ FT: 4,900
SALES: 950K Privately Held
SIC: 2431 Staircases, stairs & railings

(G-8186)
NELSON AIR DEVICE CORPORATION
Also Called: C W Sheet Metal
4628 54th Ave (11378-1012)
PHONE................718 729-3801
Fax: 718 729-7181
Nelson Blitz Jr, President
Thomas Howard, COO
Michael Doff, Vice Pres
Peter Unrath, Vice Pres
Mike Fry, Opers Mgr
EMP: 200 EST: 1938
SQ FT: 20,000
SALES (est): 83.2MM Privately Held
WEB: www.nadcw.com
SIC: 3444 1711 Ducts, sheet metal; heating & air conditioning contractors

(G-8187)
NEW YORK MARBLE AND STONE CORP
4411 55th Ave (11378-1023)
PHONE................718 729-7272
Fax: 718 724-7273
Luigi Crecco, President
Cathy Crecco, Vice Pres
▲ EMP: 10
SALES: 1MM Privately Held
SIC: 3281 Stone, quarrying & processing of own stone products

(G-8188)
NEW YORK SAND & STONE LLC
5700 47th St (11378-2105)
PHONE................718 596-2897
Tom Dooley,
Randy Waterman,
▲ EMP: 9
SQ FT: 400,000
SALES (est): 1MM
SALES (corp-wide): 1.1B Publicly Held
SIC: 1442 Construction sand & gravel
HQ: Eastern Concrete Materials, Inc.
250 Pehle Ave Ste 503
Saddle Brook NJ 07663
201 843-5103

(G-8189)
NORAMPAC NEW YORK CITY INC
5515 Grand Ave (11378-3113)
PHONE................718 340-2100
Fax: 718 386-7370
Marc Andre Depin, Ch of Bd
Nilanjan Sen, Controller
Mary Norton, Human Res Dir
Richard Etra, Manager
Stephen Valjato, Supervisor
EMP: 160 EST: 1906
SQ FT: 340,000
SALES (est): 35.3MM
SALES (corp-wide): 2.9B Privately Held
SIC: 2653 3993 2675 Boxes, corrugated: made from purchased materials; display items, corrugated: made from purchased materials; signs & advertising specialties; die-cut paper & board
HQ: Norampac Inc
1061 Rue Parent
Saint-Bruno QC J3V 6
450 461-8600

(G-8190)
NY TEMPERING LLC
6021 Flushing Ave (11378-3220)
PHONE................718 326-8989
Tim LI, Manager
▲ EMP: 5 EST: 2012
SALES (est): 838.7K Privately Held
SIC: 3272 Concrete products

(G-8191)
NYC FIREPLACES & KITCHENS
5830 Maspeth Ave (11378-2214)
PHONE................718 326-4328
Frank Alesci, Principal
EMP: 5
SALES (est): 588.4K Privately Held
SIC: 3496 Grilles & grillework, woven wire

(G-8192)
OWAYNE ENTERPRISES INC
4901 Maspeth Ave (11378-2219)
PHONE................718 326-2200
Owen M Mester, President
Wayne Wattenberg, Vice Pres
EMP: 38
SQ FT: 30,000
SALES (est): 7.1MM Privately Held
SIC: 2051 Cakes, pies & pastries; cakes, bakery: except frozen

(G-8193)
P & F INDUSTRIES OF NY CORP
Also Called: P and F Machine Industries
6006 55th Dr (11378-2351)
PHONE................718 894-3501
Fax: 718 894-7820
Frank Passantino, President
▲ EMP: 6
SQ FT: 7,000
SALES (est): 440K Privately Held
SIC: 3599 Machine shop, jobbing & repair

(G-8194)
PATCO TAPES INC
Also Called: Patco Group
5927 56th St (11378-3395)
PHONE................718 497-1527
Fax: 718 366-6845
Michael Rosenberg, Corp Secy
Joel Rosenberg, Vice Pres
EMP: 8 EST: 1973
SQ FT: 30,000
SALES: 2.5MM Privately Held
WEB: www.patcogroup.com
SIC: 2672 2671 5199 Gummed tape, cloth or paper base: from purchased materials; paper coated or laminated for packaging; packaging materials

(G-8195)
PEPSI-COLA BOTTLING CO NY INC
5035 56th Rd (11378-1109)
PHONE................718 786-8550
EMP: 5
SALES (corp-wide): 473.9MM Privately Held
SIC: 2086 Soft drinks: packaged in cans, bottles, etc.
PA: Pepsi-Cola Bottling Company Of New York, Inc.
11402 15th Ave Ste 5
College Point NY 11356
718 392-1000

(G-8196)
PURVI ENTERPRISES INCORPORATED
Also Called: Sinnara
5556 44th Ave (11378-2024)
PHONE................347 808-9448
Harshi Patel, President
▲ EMP: 7
SALES (est): 616.1K Privately Held
SIC: 3556 Dehydrating equipment, food processing

(G-8197)
RISA MANAGEMENT CORP
Also Called: Risa's
5501 43rd St Fl 3 (11378-2023)
PHONE................718 361-2606
Fax: 516 338-4900
D Savi Prashad, CEO
Rishi Prashad, COO
Shafqat Tanweer, CFO
Karen Henriquez, Manager
▲ EMP: 45
SQ FT: 6,500
SALES (est): 9MM Privately Held
WEB: www.risacorp.com
SIC: 3449 3441 Miscellaneous metalwork; fabricated structural metal

(G-8198)
RM BAKERY LLC
Also Called: Rollo Mio Artisan Bakery
4425 54th Dr (11378-1017)
Rural Route 220 E 42nd St, New York (10017)
PHONE................718 472-3036
Christian Mattheus, Managing Prtnr
EMP: 22
SALES (est): 4.6MM Privately Held
SIC: 2051 Bread, cake & related products

(G-8199)
ROCKMILLS STEEL PRODUCTS CORP
5912 54th St (11378-3004)
P.O. Box 234838, Great Neck (11023-4838)
PHONE................718 366-8300
Fax: 718 894-2196
Ann O'Brien, President
Daniel Obrien, Shareholder
Mary Obrien, Shareholder
EMP: 15
SQ FT: 25,200
SALES (est): 4MM Privately Held
WEB: www.rockmillsboilers.com
SIC: 3433 Boilers, low-pressure heating: steam or hot water

(G-8200)
S R S INC
5920 56th Ave (11378-2325)
P.O. Box 4277, Metuchen NJ (08840-4277)
PHONE................732 548-6630
M Dan Bellware, President
Marilyn Russo, Vice Pres
Alex Mackenzie, Director
EMP: 20
SALES (est): 3.5MM Privately Held
WEB: www.srs-metals.com
SIC: 3446 Railings, bannisters, guards, etc.: made from metal pipe

(G-8201)
STAIN RAIL SYSTEMS INC
Also Called: SRS
5920 56th Ave (11378-2325)
P.O. Box 4277, Metuchen NJ (08840-4277)
PHONE................732 548-6630
Fax: 732 548-6885
M Daniel Bellware, President
EMP: 10 EST: 1968
SALES (est): 1.5MM Privately Held
SIC: 3446 Railings, bannisters, guards, etc.: made from metal pipe

(G-8202)
T&B BAKERY CORP
5870 56th St (11378-3106)
PHONE................646 642-4300
Tomasz Eider, President
EMP: 6
SQ FT: 6,000
SALES: 2.8MM Privately Held
SIC: 2051 Bakery products, partially cooked (except frozen)

(G-8203)
TRI-STAR OFFSET CORP
6020 59th Pl Ste 3 (11378-3349)
PHONE................718 894-5555
Brian Nawroth, CEO
Al Nawroth, President
Mark Serwetz, Vice Pres
Michael Louie, Sales Staff
EMP: 25 EST: 1977
SALES (est): 5.5MM Privately Held
SIC: 2752 Commercial printing, lithographic

(G-8204)
US ALLEGRO INC
5430 44th St (11378-1034)
PHONE................347 408-6601
Yuriy Bogutskiy, President
Marty McMahon, Vice Pres
EMP: 30
SQ FT: 10,000
SALES: 4MM Privately Held
SIC: 1442 Construction sand & gravel

Maspeth - Queens County (G-8205)

(G-8205)
VALENTINE PACKAGING CORP
6020 59th Pl Ste 7 (11378-3349)
PHONE 718 418-6000
Fax: 718 545-0618
Daniel Suchow, *Vice Pres*
Richard Suchow, *Vice Pres*
Steven Suchow, *Vice Pres*
EMP: 18 EST: 1953
SQ FT: 25,000
SALES (est): 4.9MM **Privately Held**
SIC: 2653 7389 Sheets, corrugated: made from purchased materials; packaging & labeling services

Massapequa
Nassau County

(G-8206)
A & M APPEL DISTRIBUTING INC
500 N Atlanta Ave (11758-2000)
PHONE 516 735-1172
Michael Appel, *Principal*
EMP: 5
SALES (est): 320.4K **Privately Held**
SIC: 2051 5149 Bread, cake & related products; bakery products

(G-8207)
ADAMS INTERIOR FABRICATIONS
8 Iroquois Pl (11758-7622)
PHONE 631 249-8282
Fax: 516 249-8284
Anthony E Adams, *President*
EMP: 11
SALES (est): 1.4MM **Privately Held**
SIC: 2431 2499 Millwork; decorative wood & woodwork

(G-8208)
CANOPY BOOKS LLC (PA)
28 N Wisconsin Ave 2-1 (11758-1705)
PHONE 516 354-4888
Clifford Brechner, *CEO*
Sarah Panik, *Product Mgr*
EMP: 4
SALES (est): 1.7MM **Privately Held**
SIC: 2731 Book publishing

(G-8209)
HUNTINGTON SERVICES INC
Also Called: Vox Systems
727 N Broadway Ste A4 (11758-2348)
PHONE 516 795-8500
Richard Vience, *President*
Chris Vience, *Network Enginr*
Angel Larocca, *Executive*
EMP: 6
SQ FT: 1,200
SALES (est): 850K **Privately Held**
WEB: www.hsi4service.com
SIC: 7372 Prepackaged software

(G-8210)
LIGHT DENTAL LABS INC
250 N Syracuse Ave (11758-2026)
PHONE 516 785-7730
Fax: 516 785-7731
Frank Tomasino, *President*
EMP: 5
SALES: 750K **Privately Held**
SIC: 3843 Dental equipment & supplies

(G-8211)
LITTLE BIRD CHOCOLATES INC
Also Called: Little Curios Confections
25 Fairchild Ave Ste 200 (11758)
PHONE 646 620-6395
Sara Meyer, *President*
EMP: 7 EST: 2013
SALES (est): 575.6K **Privately Held**
SIC: 2064 Candy & other confectionery products

(G-8212)
PLURA BROADCAST INC (PA)
67 Grand Ave (11758-4947)
PHONE 516 997-5675
Ray Kalo, *Owner*
Emad Hassan, *General Mgr*
Ibrahim Karim, *Opers Staff*
Azucena Soto, *Sales Mgr*
Leslie Brock, *Manager*
EMP: 7
SALES (est): 3MM **Privately Held**
SIC: 3679 Liquid crystal displays (LCD)

(G-8213)
PRINT IT HERE
185 Jerusalem Ave (11758-3308)
PHONE 516 308-7785
Shari Levine, *CEO*
EMP: 5
SALES (est): 342K **Privately Held**
SIC: 2752 Commercial printing, lithographic

(G-8214)
R KLEIN JEWELRY CO INC
Also Called: Klein & Company
39 Brockmeyer Dr (11758-7804)
PHONE 516 482-3260
Richard Klein, *President*
Fred Schrager, *Credit Mgr*
EMP: 55
SQ FT: 30,000
SALES (est): 4.7MM **Privately Held**
WEB: www.kleinjewelry.com
SIC: 3911 Jewelry, precious metal

(G-8215)
S SCHARF INC
278 N Richmond Ave (11758-3231)
PHONE 516 541-9552
Irwin Scharf, *President*
Jesse Scharf, *Treasurer*
EMP: 13 EST: 1935
SQ FT: 5,000
SALES (est): 1.2MM **Privately Held**
SIC: 3911 Jewelry, precious metal

(G-8216)
SUNRISE JEWELERS OF NY INC
1220 Sunrise Hwy (11758)
PHONE 516 541-1302
EMP: 8
SALES (est): 930K **Privately Held**
SIC: 3911 Mfg Precious Metal Jewelry

(G-8217)
WOODS KNIFE CORPORATION
19 Brooklyn Ave (11758-4855)
PHONE 516 798-4972
Fax: 516 798-5864
James S Woods, *President*
Ann Woods, *Vice Pres*
EMP: 24 EST: 1916
SQ FT: 2,600
SALES (est): 2.4MM **Privately Held**
SIC: 3423 3421 Knives, agricultural or industrial; cutlery

Massapequa Park
Nassau County

(G-8218)
CUSTOM MIX INC
31 Clark Blvd (11762-2609)
PHONE 516 797-7090
Matthew Lott, *Principal*
EMP: 9
SALES (est): 933.8K **Privately Held**
SIC: 3273 Ready-mixed concrete

(G-8219)
IMAGE SALES & MARKETING INC
106 Thornwood Rd (11762-4023)
PHONE 516 238-7023
Francine Walk, *President*
Steven Walk, *Vice Pres*
EMP: 2
SQ FT: 3,000
SALES: 4MM **Privately Held**
WEB: www.imagesalesny.com
SIC: 2754 Commercial printing, gravure

(G-8220)
INNOVATIVE SYSTEMS OF NEW YORK
201 Rose St (11762-1022)
PHONE 516 541-7410
Joseph Esposito, *President*
EMP: 5
SALES (est): 353.8K **Privately Held**
SIC: 3577 7373 7378 Computer peripheral equipment; computer integrated systems design; computer maintenance & repair

(G-8221)
MASSAPEQUA POST
Also Called: Acj Communications
1045b Park Blvd (11762-2764)
PHONE 516 798-5100
Fax: 516 798-5296
Alfred James, *President*
Carolyn James, *Vice Pres*
Karen Pennachio, *Branch Mgr*
Mary A Hayden, *Admin Sec*
Teka McCabe, *Teacher*
EMP: 21
SALES (est): 504.2K **Privately Held**
WEB: www.massapequapost.com
SIC: 2711 Newspapers

(G-8222)
PRINT COTTAGE LLC
1138 Lakeshore Dr (11762-2054)
PHONE 516 369-1749
James Altadonna, *Mng Member*
EMP: 10
SQ FT: 1,000
SALES: 4MM **Privately Held**
SIC: 2752 Commercial printing, lithographic

(G-8223)
TVI IMPORTS LLC
178 Abbey St (11762-3430)
PHONE 631 793-3077
Anthony Tisi, *Mng Member*
▲ EMP: 6
SQ FT: 2,500
SALES: 19MM **Privately Held**
SIC: 3089 Flower pots, plastic

(G-8224)
WORLD BUSINESS MEDIA LLC
Also Called: Gsn Government Security News
4770 Sunrise Hwy Ste 105 (11762-2911)
PHONE 212 344-0759
EMP: 12
SQ FT: 2,000
SALES: 2MM **Privately Held**
SIC: 2721 7313 7382 Periodicals-Publishing/Printing Advertising Representative Security Systems Services

Massena
St. Lawrence County

(G-8225)
CURRAN RENEWABLE ENERGY LLC
20 Commerce Dr (13662-2576)
PHONE 315 769-2000
Ken Ashley, *Controller*
Kelli Curran, *Marketing Mgr*
Patrick Curran, *Mng Member*
Tricia Terry, *Manager*
▲ EMP: 30
SALES: 19.1MM **Privately Held**
SIC: 2421 Sawmills & planing mills, general

(G-8226)
GENERAL MOTORS LLC
56 Chevrolet Rd (13662-1878)
PHONE 315 764-2000
Rey Hart, *Prdtn Mgr*
Jim Toth, *Prdtn Mgr*
Daniel J Carroll, *Purchasing*
Larry French, *Engineer*
Ross Johnson, *Engineer*
EMP: 500 **Publicly Held**
SIC: 3369 3714 Castings, except die-castings, precision; motor vehicle parts & accessories
HQ: General Motors Llc
  300 Renaissance Ctr L1
  Detroit MI 48243

(G-8227)
HANYAN & HIGGINS COMPANY INC
9772 State Highway 56 (13662-3416)
PHONE 315 769-8838
Fax: 315 769-8838
Donald Walters, *CEO*
EMP: 5 EST: 1999
SALES (est): 254.7K **Privately Held**
SIC: 3297 Castable refractories, nonclay

(G-8228)
KINGSTON PHARMA LLC
Also Called: Kingston Pharmaceuticals
5 County Route 42 (13662-1569)
PHONE 315 705-4019
Venkat Kakani, *CEO*
Srikanth Lingen, *Opers Mgr*
Sridhar Thyagarajan, *Controller*
EMP: 8
SQ FT: 32,778
SALES (est): 518.9K **Privately Held**
SIC: 2834 Druggists' preparations (pharmaceuticals)

(G-8229)
MASSENA METALS INC
86 S Racquette River Rd (13662-4318)
P.O. Box 5282 (13662-5282)
PHONE 315 769-3846
Fax: 315 769-0134
J Goldstein, *President*
Lawrence Leibo, *Corp Secy*
Gary Master, *Vice Pres*
EMP: 15
SQ FT: 10,000
SALES (est): 1.7MM **Privately Held**
SIC: 3365 5093 5051 Aluminum foundries; ferrous metal scrap & waste; steel

(G-8230)
PURINEPHARMA LLC
5 County Route 42 (13662-1569)
PHONE 732 485-1400
Venkat Kakani, *Manager*
EMP: 5
SALES (est): 597.4K **Privately Held**
SIC: 2834 Pharmaceutical preparations

(G-8231)
SEAWAY TIMBER HARVESTING INC (PA)
15121 State Highway 37 (13662-6194)
PHONE 315 769-5970
Patrick Curran, *President*
Tim Curran, *Vice Pres*
Tricia Terry, *Manager*
Lee Curran, *Admin Sec*
EMP: 60
SQ FT: 15,000
SALES (est): 11.1MM **Privately Held**
SIC: 2411 4789 Logging; log loading & unloading

(G-8232)
STUBBS PRINTING INC
271 E Orvis St Ste B (13662-2352)
P.O. Box 110 (13662-0110)
PHONE 315 769-8641
Fax: 315 764-9285
Karen Stubbs, *President*
Robert T Stubbs, *Vice Pres*
EMP: 5
SQ FT: 2,000
SALES (est): 390K **Privately Held**
SIC: 2752 Commercial printing, offset

(G-8233)
UPSTONE MATERIALS INC
Also Called: Massena Ready Mix
539 S Main St (13662-2537)
P.O. Box 825, Plattsburgh (12901)
PHONE 315 764-0251
James Otis, *District Mgr*
Scott Love, *Manager*
EMP: 5
SQ FT: 9,608
SALES (corp-wide): 77.1MM **Privately Held**
WEB: www.graymont-ab.com
SIC: 3273 Ready-mixed concrete

HQ: Upstone Materials Inc.
111 Quarry Rd
Plattsburgh NY 12901
518 561-5321

Mastic
Suffolk County

(G-8234)
EAST END SIGN DESIGN INC
1161 Montauk Hwy (11950-2918)
PHONE..............................631 399-2574
Joseph Colucci, President
John Dugan, Manager
Mike Powell, Manager
EMP: 5
SALES (est): 528.4K **Privately Held**
SIC: 3993 Signs & advertising specialties

(G-8235)
FUNDA-MANTELS LLC
659 Mastic Rd (11950-5012)
P.O. Box 318, Ridge (11961-0318)
PHONE..............................631 924-1404
Frank Turrigiano, Mng Member
EMP: 6
SQ FT: 3,000
SALES: 1MM **Privately Held**
WEB: www.funda-mantels.com
SIC: 2431 Mantels, wood

Mastic Beach
Suffolk County

(G-8236)
AFFLUENT DESIGN INC
48 Biltmore Dr (11951-1310)
PHONE..............................631 655-2556
Daniel Louis Levine, Principal
EMP: 10
SALES (est): 428.1K **Privately Held**
SIC: 2741 7374 Miscellaneous publishing; computer graphics service

(G-8237)
VINCENT GENOVESE
Also Called: Long Island Radiant Heat
19 Woodmere Dr (11951-2016)
PHONE..............................631 281-8170
Vincent Genovese, Owner
EMP: 6
SALES (est): 674.5K **Privately Held**
SIC: 3634 5074 8711 1711 Heating units, electric (radiant heat): baseboard or wall; heating equipment & panels, solar; heating & ventilation engineering; heating & air conditioning contractors; industrial furnaces & ovens; heating equipment, except electric

Mattituck
Suffolk County

(G-8238)
AMEREON LTD
800 Wickham Ave (11952)
P.O. Box 1200 (11952-0921)
PHONE..............................631 298-5100
Joanna Paulsen, President
John Clauss, Vice Pres
EMP: 5
SQ FT: 30,000
SALES (est): 594.3K **Privately Held**
WEB: www.amereon.com
SIC: 2731 Books: publishing only

(G-8239)
LIEB CELLARS LLC
Also Called: Lieb Cellars Tasting Room
35 Cox Neck Rd (11952-1458)
P.O. Box 907, Cutchogue (11935-0907)
PHONE..............................631 298-1942
Gary Madden, General Mgr
EMP: 20 **Privately Held**
WEB: www.liebcellars.com
SIC: 2084 Wines

PA: Lieb Cellars Llc
13050 Oregon Rd
Cutchogue NY 11935

(G-8240)
NORTH FORK WOOD WORKS INC
5175 Route 48 (11952-3260)
P.O. Box 1407, Southold (11971-0938)
PHONE..............................631 255-4028
Scott Edgett, CEO
EMP: 9
SALES (est): 1.1MM **Privately Held**
SIC: 2431 Millwork

(G-8241)
PREMIUM WINE GROUP LLC
35 Cox Neck Rd (11952-1458)
PHONE..............................631 298-1900
Russell Hearn, Principal
John Leo, Principal
Andrew Rockwell, Lab Dir
▲ **EMP:** 22
SALES (est): 3.5MM **Privately Held**
WEB: www.premiumwinegroup.com
SIC: 2084 Wines

(G-8242)
SHINN WINERY LLC
Also Called: Shinn Vineyard
2000 Oregon Rd (11952-1762)
PHONE..............................631 804-0367
Barbara Shinn,
▲ **EMP:** 7
SALES (est): 600K **Privately Held**
SIC: 2084 Wines, brandy & brandy spirits

(G-8243)
TIMES REVIEW NEWSPAPER CORP
Also Called: News Review, The
7780 Main Rd (11952-1539)
PHONE..............................631 354-8031
Fax: 631 298-3287
Troy Gustavson, President
Jean Burgond, VP Mktg
Karen Cullen, Manager
Tim Kelly, Manager
Sarah Olsen, Manager
EMP: 33
SQ FT: 6,000
SALES (est): 3.1MM **Privately Held**
WEB: www.timesreview.com
SIC: 2711 2791 Newspapers: publishing only, not printed on site; typesetting

Mayfield
Fulton County

(G-8244)
KADCO USA INC
17 W Main St (12117-3996)
P.O. Box 584, Amsterdam (12010-0584)
PHONE..............................518 661-6068
Fax: 518 661-5808
Thomas Petherick, President
Frank Mc Cleneghen, Vice Pres
◆ **EMP:** 7
SQ FT: 5,000
SALES (est): 1.1MM **Privately Held**
WEB: www.kadcousa.com
SIC: 3524 Carts or wagons for lawn & garden; lawn & garden mowers & accessories

(G-8245)
SMITH & SONS FUELS INC
36 2nd Ave (12117-3960)
P.O. Box 191 (12117-0191)
PHONE..............................518 661-6112
Jeffrey J Smith, Ch of Bd
EMP: 8
SALES (est): 1MM **Privately Held**
SIC: 2869 Fuels

Mayville
Chautauqua County

(G-8246)
EMPIRE DEVLEOPMENT
5889 Magnolia Stedman Rd (14757-9420)
PHONE..............................716 789-2097
Micah Meredith, Principal
EMP: 8 **EST:** 2007
SALES (est): 1MM **Privately Held**
SIC: 3423 Jewelers' hand tools

(G-8247)
KLEINFELDER JOHN
Also Called: Chautauqua Iron Works
5239 W Lake Rd (14757-9507)
PHONE..............................716 753-3163
Fax: 716 753-7018
John Kleinfelder, Owner
EMP: 5
SQ FT: 990
SALES (est): 467.8K **Privately Held**
SIC: 3441 3446 5947 4491 Fabricated structural metal; ornamental metalwork; artcraft & carvings; docks, incl. buildings & facilities: operation & maintenance; boat lifts; welding on site

(G-8248)
LYN JO ENTERPRISES LTD
Also Called: Standard Portable
Rr 394 Box 147 (14757)
PHONE..............................716 753-2776
Fax: 716 487-1024
Julie Baraniewicz, President
Bernie Newhouse, Purch Mgr
Gregory Goerke, Sales Mgr
EMP: 7
SQ FT: 288
SALES: 750K **Privately Held**
WEB: www.standardportable.com
SIC: 3496 3699 Lamp frames, wire; trouble lights

(G-8249)
RANGE RSURCES - APPALACHIA LLC
Also Called: Lomak Petroleum
100 E Chautauqua St (14757-1040)
P.O. Box 187 (14757-0187)
PHONE..............................716 753-3385
Fax: 716 753-3394
Doug Stebbins, Manager
EMP: 30
SALES (corp-wide): 1.1B **Publicly Held**
WEB: www.gl-energy.com
SIC: 1382 Oil & gas exploration services
HQ: Range Resources - Appalachia, Llc.
3000 Town Center Blvd
Canonsburg PA 15317
724 743-6700

(G-8250)
STEDMAN ENERGY INC
4411 Canterbury Dr (14757-9610)
P.O. Box 1006, Chautauqua (14722-1006)
PHONE..............................716 789-3018
Kevin E McChesney, President
EMP: 7
SALES: 100K **Privately Held**
SIC: 1311 Crude petroleum production; natural gas production

Mc Connellsville
Oneida County

(G-8251)
HARDEN FURNITURE LLC (PA)
8550 Mill Pond Way (13401-1844)
PHONE..............................315 675-3600
Fax: 315 245-2884
Gregory Harden, CEO
Mike Allen, Superintendent
Andy Clark, COO
Andrew Clark, Vice Pres
Pete Raynford, Vice Pres
▲ **EMP:** 170 **EST:** 1844
SQ FT: 400,000

SALES: 19.7MM **Privately Held**
WEB: www.cnywinter.com
SIC: 2511 2512 2521 5021 Wood household furniture; dining room furniture: wood; bed frames, except water bed frames: wood; dressers, household: wood; upholstered household furniture; living room furniture: upholstered on wood frames; wood office furniture; desks, office: wood; bookcases, office: wood; furniture

Mc Graw
Cortland County

(G-8252)
COUTURE TIMBER HARVESTING
2760 Phelps Rd (13101-9561)
P.O. Box 66, Cortland (13045-0066)
PHONE..............................607 836-4719
Bruno Couture, President
Bruno Coutrue, Vice Pres
EMP: 7 **EST:** 1971
SALES (est): 653.5K **Privately Held**
SIC: 2411 Logging camps & contractors

(G-8253)
HIGGINS SUPPLY COMPANY INC
Also Called: Higgins Supl Co
18-23 South St (13101-9475)
PHONE..............................607 836-6474
Fax: 607 836-6913
Terri Maxson, Ch of Bd
Cathy Gregg, President
Glenn Doran, Vice Pres
Terri L Gutchess, Vice Pres
Kristen Miller, Office Mgr
EMP: 65 **EST:** 1921
SQ FT: 30,000
SALES (est): 10.5MM **Privately Held**
SIC: 3842 2342 Orthopedic appliances; corset accessories: clasps, stays, etc.

(G-8254)
MCGRAW WOOD PRODUCTS LLC (PA)
1 Charles St (13101-9190)
P.O. Box 652 (13101-0652)
PHONE..............................607 836-6465
Fax: 607 836-6413
Christopher Ousby, Purchasing
Jenifer Crisp, Office Mgr
Harold J Ousby III, Mng Member
EMP: 30 **EST:** 2006
SQ FT: 100,000
SALES (est): 5.7MM **Privately Held**
WEB: www.mcgrawwoodproducts.com
SIC: 2511 2499 2441 2434 Silverware chests: wood; decorative wood & woodwork; nailed wood boxes & shook; wood kitchen cabinets

Mechanicville
Saratoga County

(G-8255)
ALABU INC
Also Called: Alabu Skin Care
30 Graves Rd (12118-3218)
PHONE..............................518 665-0411
Mary Claire, President
Dean Mayes, President
EMP: 7
SALES (est): 1MM **Privately Held**
WEB: www.alabu.com
SIC: 2841 Soap: granulated, liquid, cake, flaked or chip

(G-8256)
ALONZO FIRE WORKS DISPLAY INC (PA)
12 County Route 75 (12118-3357)
PHONE..............................518 664-9994
Jeff Alonzo, President
▲ **EMP:** 8

Mechanicville - Saratoga County (G-8257)

SALES (est): 654K **Privately Held**
WEB: www.alonzofireworks.com
SIC: 2899 7999 Fireworks; fireworks display service

(G-8257)
DECRESCENTE DISTRIBUTING CO
Also Called: D D C
211 N Main St (12118-1242)
P.O. Box 231 (12118-0231)
PHONE..................................518 664-9866
Don Miller, *President*
Russ Teplitzky, *General Mgr*
Carmine D Crescente Jr, *Principal*
Tom Turcotte, *VP Opers*
Andy Laing, *Facilities Mgr*
EMP: 67 EST: 2010
SALES (est): 28.4MM **Privately Held**
SIC: 2082 Beer (alcoholic beverage)

(G-8258)
EMPIRE EXHIBITS & DISPLAYS INC
Also Called: Empire Exhibits and Displays
131 Round Lake Ave (12118-1026)
PHONE..................................518 266-9362
Craig L Koehler, *CEO*
Don Wiesenforth, *President*
Sarah Taormina, *Corp Comm Staff*
Linda Jarvis, *Office Mgr*
EMP: 10
SQ FT: 1,500
SALES (est): 700K **Privately Held**
WEB: www.empireexhibits.com
SIC: 2426 Frames for upholstered furniture, wood

(G-8259)
GLAXOSMITHKLINE LLC
108 Woodfield Blvd (12118-3038)
PHONE..................................518 852-9637
EMP: 27
SALES (corp-wide): 34.3B **Privately Held**
SIC: 2834 Pharmaceutical preparations
HQ: Glaxosmithkline Llc
5 Crescent Dr
Philadelphia PA 19112
215 751-4000

(G-8260)
POLYSET COMPANY INC
65 Hudson Ave (12118-4517)
P.O. Box 111 (12118-0111)
PHONE..................................518 664-6000
Fax: 518 664-6001
Bart McGonnigal, *President*
Niladri Ghoshal, *Exec VP*
Charlie Simon, *CFO*
Rajat Ghoshal, *Treasurer*
Earl Ramlow, *Manager*
▲ EMP: 36
SQ FT: 40,000
SALES (est): 14.4MM **Privately Held**
WEB: www.polyset.com
SIC: 2819 3087 2952 2891 Industrial inorganic chemicals; custom compound purchased resins; coating compounds, tar; adhesives & sealants

(G-8261)
RALOID TOOL CO INC
Hc 146 (12118)
P.O. Box 551 (12118-0551)
PHONE..................................518 664-4261
Fax: 518 664-4087
Ronald Brownell, *President*
David Brownell, *Vice Pres*
Stephen Shafts, *Project Mgr*
Molly Montanye, *Info Tech Mgr*
EMP: 19 EST: 1945
SQ FT: 23,200
SALES (est): 3.5MM **Privately Held**
WEB: www.raloidtool.com
SIC: 3544 3542 Special dies & tools; die casting & extruding machines

(G-8262)
ST SILICONES INC
95 N Central Ave (12118-1543)
PHONE..................................518 664-0745
Fax: 518 664-4179
David A Scagnelli, *President*
EMP: 5
SQ FT: 3,500

SALES: 500K **Privately Held**
WEB: www.st-silicones.com
SIC: 1446 Silica mining

(G-8263)
VOICES FOR ALL LLC
29 Moreland Dr (12118-3630)
PHONE..................................518 261-1664
Paul Benedetti,
Stan Denis,
EMP: 8
SALES (est): 858.1K **Privately Held**
SIC: 3679 Voice controls

Medford
Suffolk County

(G-8264)
A & L LIGHTING LTD
15 Commercial Blvd (11763-1522)
PHONE..................................718 821-1188
Glen Altman, *President*
Barbara Ehrhardt, *Manager*
EMP: 10
SQ FT: 11,000
SALES (est): 960K **Privately Held**
WEB: www.allighting.com
SIC: 3646 Fluorescent lighting fixtures, commercial

(G-8265)
ACCUVEIN INC (PA)
3243 Route 112 Ste 2 (11763-1438)
P.O. Box 1303, Huntington (11743-0657)
PHONE..................................816 997-9400
Ron Goldman, *Ch of Bd*
Wayne Shepherd, *President*
Daniel Delaney, *COO*
Jeff Schou, *Vice Pres*
Fred Wood, *Engineer*
EMP: 53
SQ FT: 5,000
SALES (est): 11.1MM **Privately Held**
SIC: 3829 Thermometers, including digital: clinical

(G-8266)
AMERICAN AVIONIC TECH CORP
Also Called: Aatc
25 Industrial Blvd (11763-2243)
PHONE..................................631 924-8200
Amin J Khoury, *Ch of Bd*
Werner Lieberherr, *Ch of Bd*
Salvatore F Scilingo, *President*
Rick Lapp, *Vice Pres*
David Eckland, *CFO*
EMP: 60
SQ FT: 12,000
SALES (est): 17.6MM **Publicly Held**
WEB: www.aatcorp.com
SIC: 3699 8711 Electrical equipment & supplies; engineering services
HQ: Tsi Group, Inc.
94 Tide Mill Rd
Hampton NH 03842
603 964-0296

(G-8267)
B & R INDUSTRIES INC
Also Called: Manifold Center, The
12 Commercial Blvd (11763-1523)
PHONE..................................631 736-2275
Fax: 631 736-2725
Christian P Burian, *President*
EMP: 12
SQ FT: 64,000
SALES (est): 2MM **Privately Held**
WEB: www.bnrindustries.com
SIC: 3599 Machine & other job shop work

(G-8268)
BLAIR INDUSTRIES INC (PA)
3671 Horseblock Rd (11763-2240)
PHONE..................................631 924-6600
William R Lehmann Jr, *Ch of Bd*
Elena Feldman, *Manager*
Gabrielle Piazza, *Manager*
▲ EMP: 25
SQ FT: 8,000

SALES (est): 6.5MM **Privately Held**
WEB: www.blair-hsm.com
SIC: 3728 Aircraft parts & equipment; aircraft landing assemblies & brakes

(G-8269)
CHEMBIO DIAGNOSTIC SYSTEMS INC
3661 Horseblock Rd Ste A (11763-2244)
PHONE..................................631 924-1135
Fax: 631 924-6033
Javan Esfandiari, *Exec VP*
Tom Ippolito, *Vice Pres*
Paul Lambotte, *Vice Pres*
Michael Steele, *Vice Pres*
Bill Schneider, *Facilities Mgr*
▲ EMP: 105
SQ FT: 14,000
SALES (est): 12.1MM
SALES (corp-wide): 17.8MM **Publicly Held**
WEB: www.chembio.com
SIC: 2835 In vitro & in vivo diagnostic substances
PA: Chembio Diagnostics, Inc.
3661 Horseblock Rd Ste C
Medford NY 11763
631 924-1135

(G-8270)
CHEMBIO DIAGNOSTICS INC (PA)
3661 Horseblock Rd Ste C (11763-2225)
PHONE..................................631 924-1135
Sharon Klugewicz, *CEO*
Katherine L Davis, *Ch of Bd*
Robert Passas, *President*
John J Sperzel III, *President*
Javan Esfandiari, *Exec VP*
▲ EMP: 131
SQ FT: 39,660
SALES: 17.8MM **Publicly Held**
WEB: www.chembio.com
SIC: 2835 In vitro & in vivo diagnostic substances

(G-8271)
CHROMA COMMUNICATIONS INC
2030 Route 112 (11763-3644)
P.O. Box 340, Bohemia (11716-0340)
PHONE..................................631 289-8871
Fax: 631 289-8872
Peter Gulyas, *President*
EMP: 5
SALES (est): 310K **Privately Held**
SIC: 2759 Commercial printing

(G-8272)
CLARKE HESS COMMUNICATION RES
3243 Route 112 Ste 1 (11763-1438)
PHONE..................................631 698-3350
Fax: 631 784-2438
Kenneth Salz, *President*
Doante Alessi, *Vice Pres*
Dan Salz, *Info Tech Mgr*
EMP: 8
SQ FT: 4,500
SALES (est): 1.6MM **Privately Held**
WEB: www.clarke-hess.com
SIC: 3825 Test equipment for electronic & electrical circuits

(G-8273)
DATA FLOW INC
6 Balsam Dr (11763-4304)
PHONE..................................631 436-9200
Timothy Stead, *President*
Joseph Crook, *Vice Pres*
EMP: 8
SQ FT: 8,500
SALES (est): 1.7MM **Privately Held**
WEB: www.printtomail.com
SIC: 2759 Commercial printing

(G-8274)
ENECON CORPORATION (PA)
Also Called: High Prfmce Plymr Cmposits Div
6 Platinum Ct (11763-2251)
PHONE..................................516 349-0022
Andrew A Janczik, *Ch of Bd*
Andrew A Janczak, *President*
Michael Tedesco, *Exec VP*
Matt Goldberg, *Vice Pres*

Robert L Kneuer, *Vice Pres*
◆ EMP: 56
SQ FT: 30,000
SALES (est): 10.3MM **Privately Held**
WEB: www.enecon.com
SIC: 2851 Coating, air curing

(G-8275)
ENEFLUX ARMTEK MAGNETICS INC (HQ)
6 Platinum Ct (11763-2251)
PHONE..................................516 576-3434
Tony Mantella, *President*
Dave Gerstacker, *Plant Mgr*
Edward Krensel, *Treasurer*
Deann Dambrosio, *Accounts Mgr*
EMP: 4 EST: 1997
SQ FT: 20,000
SALES (est): 2.8MM
SALES (corp-wide): 10.3MM **Privately Held**
WEB: www.eamagnetics.com
SIC: 3264 Magnets, permanent: ceramic or ferrite
PA: Enecon Corporation
6 Platinum Ct
Medford NY 11763
516 349-0022

(G-8276)
GLOBAL TISSUE GROUP INC (PA)
870 Expressway Dr S (11763-2027)
PHONE..................................631 924-3019
Meir Elnekaveh, *CEO*
Freydoun Elhekaveh, *Ch of Bd*
David Shaoul, *President*
Daniel David, *Exec VP*
Phil Higgins, *Purch Mgr*
◆ EMP: 50
SQ FT: 90,000
SALES (est): 13.2MM **Privately Held**
WEB: www.gtgtissue.com
SIC: 2679 Paper products, converted

(G-8277)
H B MILLWORK INC (PA)
500 Long Island Ave (11763-2510)
PHONE..................................631 289-8086
Fax: 631 289-8057
Timothy Hollowell, *President*
Michael Hollowell, *Vice Pres*
EMP: 15
SQ FT: 6,000
SALES (est): 1.9MM **Privately Held**
WEB: www.hbmillwork.com
SIC: 2431 2436 2426 Millwork; softwood veneer & plywood; hardwood dimension & flooring mills

(G-8278)
HAMPTON ART LLC
19 Scouting Blvd (11763-2220)
PHONE..................................631 924-1335
Robert M Gallagher, *Mktg Dir*
Kevin Gallagher, *Marketing Mgr*
Ronald T Gallagher,
Kevin T Gallagher,
Steven G Gallagher,
▲ EMP: 44
SQ FT: 13,500
SALES (est): 5.6MM **Privately Held**
WEB: www.hamptonart.com
SIC: 3069 3953 Stationers' rubber sundries; marking devices

(G-8279)
HAMPTON TECHNOLOGIES LLC
19 Scouting Blvd (11763-2220)
PHONE..................................631 924-1335
Kevin Gallagher, *Director*
Ron Gallagher,
Ronald Gallagher, *Administration*
Steven Gallagher,
▲ EMP: 30
SQ FT: 13,500
SALES (est): 5.3MM **Privately Held**
WEB: www.hamptonsecurity.com
SIC: 3699 Security devices

(G-8280)
HEALTHY BASEMENT SYSTEMS LLC
79 Cedarhurst Ave (11763-1503)
PHONE..................................516 650-9046

William Simone,
EMP: 14
SALES (est): 1.4MM **Privately Held**
WEB: www.healthybasementsystems.com
SIC: 3272 Areaways, basement window: concrete

(G-8281)
HSM MACHINE WORKS INC (PA)
Also Called: Blair-Hsm
3671 Horseblock Rd (11763-2295)
PHONE..................................631 924-6600
Fax: 631 924-6786
William R Lehmann Jr, *Ch of Bd*
Kevin Dembinski, *President*
Bill Lehmann, *President*
Scott Wigley, *General Mgr*
Clark Early, *Plant Mgr*
▲ **EMP:** 40
SQ FT: 30,000
SALES (est): 8MM **Privately Held**
SIC: 3599 3728 Machine shop, jobbing & repair; aircraft parts & equipment

(G-8282)
ISLAND CUSTOM STAIRS INC
23 Scouting Blvd Unit C (11763-2245)
PHONE..................................631 205-5335
Christopher L Brett, *President*
Carol Hodosky, *Treasurer*
Delores Rufrano, *Director*
EMP: 7
SQ FT: 5,800
SALES: 900K **Privately Held**
SIC: 3534 Elevators & moving stairways

(G-8283)
JACOBI TOOL & DIE MFG INC
Also Called: Jacobi Industries
131 Middle Island Rd (11763-1517)
P.O. Box 50 (11763-0050)
PHONE..................................631 736-5394
Fax: 631 732-4643
Roger Jacobi, *Principal*
Dennis Oconnor, *Executive*
EMP: 6
SQ FT: 10,000
SALES (est): 1.1MM **Privately Held**
WEB: www.jacobiindustries.com
SIC: 3599 Machine shop, jobbing & repair

(G-8284)
L VII RESILIENT LLC
108 Cherry Ln (11763-4022)
PHONE..................................631 987-5819
John Scelsi, *Mng Member*
EMP: 12 **EST:** 2012
SALES (est): 1MM **Privately Held**
SIC: 2676 7389 Tampons, sanitary: made from purchased paper;

(G-8285)
LIVING DOORS INC
22 Scouting Blvd Ste 3 (11763-2260)
P.O. Box 95, Yaphank (11980-0095)
PHONE..................................631 924-5393
Fax: 631 924-5590
Don Plante, *President*
Elizabeth Plante, *Manager*
EMP: 10
SQ FT: 4,000
SALES: 700K **Privately Held**
WEB: www.livingdoors.com
SIC: 2431 Doors, wood

(G-8286)
M AND M INDUSTRIAL WELDING
2890 Route 112 (11763-1426)
PHONE..................................631 451-6044
Michael Bellasatto, *Owner*
EMP: 5
SALES (est): 232.2K **Privately Held**
SIC: 7692 Welding repair

(G-8287)
MACHOONJDGROUP ✪
18 Victorian Ln (11763-2574)
PHONE..................................856 345-4689
Alphajour Ahmed Bah III, *Principal*
Chierno Bah, *Administration*
EMP: 5 **EST:** 2017
SALES (est): 145K **Privately Held**
SIC: 2046 Starch

(G-8288)
MACROLINK INC
25 Scouting Blvd Ste 1 (11763-2243)
PHONE..................................631 924-8200
Mark Cordivari, *CEO*
Thomas Riggleman, *Supervisor*
EMP: 50 **EST:** 1975
SQ FT: 30,000
SALES (est): 17.1MM **Publicly Held**
WEB: www.macrolink.com
SIC: 3823 3577 Computer interface equipment for industrial process control; computer peripheral equipment
HQ: B/E Aerospace, Inc.
1400 Corporate Center Way
Wellington FL 33414
561 791-5000

(G-8289)
MICRO CONTRACT MANUFACTURING
27 Scouting Blvd Unit E (11763-2286)
PHONE..................................631 738-7874
Fax: 631 738-7879
Michael L Matula, *President*
Thomas Degasperi, *President*
Josephine Matula, *Corp Secy*
EMP: 90
SQ FT: 12,000
SALES (est): 16MM **Privately Held**
WEB: www.microcontractmfg.com
SIC: 3674 Semiconductors & related devices

(G-8290)
MTK ELECTRONICS INC
1 National Blvd (11763-2252)
PHONE..................................631 924-7666
David Radford, *President*
Erik F Meade, *Purch Mgr*
Joseph Alaimo, *Sales Staff*
Tony Digiacomo, *Manager*
▲ **EMP:** 35
SQ FT: 15,000
SALES (est): 8.1MM **Privately Held**
WEB: www.mtkelec.com
SIC: 3677 3675 Filtration devices, electronic; electronic capacitors

(G-8291)
PHYMETRIX INC
28 Scouting Blvd Ste C (11763-2250)
PHONE..................................631 627-3950
Bedros Bedrossian, *President*
Deborah Bedrossian, *Vice Pres*
Ani Omer, *Vice Pres*
EMP: 9
SQ FT: 10,000
SALES: 3MM **Privately Held**
SIC: 3826 8734 Moisture analyzers; calibration & certification

(G-8292)
POSIMECH INC
15 Scouting Blvd Unit 3 (11763-2254)
PHONE..................................631 924-5959
Fax: 631 924-3850
Steven R Fazio, *President*
Dan George, *VP Mfg*
Stephanie Giglio, *Bookkeeper*
▼ **EMP:** 22
SQ FT: 12,236
SALES (est): 4MM **Privately Held**
WEB: www.posimech.com
SIC: 3599 3728 Machine shop, jobbing & repair; aircraft assemblies, subassemblies & parts

(G-8293)
SAYEDA MANUFACTURING CORP
20 Scouting Blvd (11763-2221)
PHONE..................................631 345-2525
Fax: 631 345-2342
Ali Khan, *President*
EMP: 10
SQ FT: 5,000
SALES (est): 810K **Privately Held**
WEB: www.sayeda.com
SIC: 3679 Harness assemblies for electronic use: wire or cable

(G-8294)
STAR READY MIX INC
172 Peconic Ave (11763-3244)
P.O. Box 371 (11763-0371)
PHONE..................................631 289-8787
Fax: 631 289-1323
Joseph A Di Silva, *President*
Tom Heff, *Vice Pres*
Frank Otero, *Vice Pres*
Frank Oters, *Project Mgr*
Thomas Hess, *Treasurer*
EMP: 13
SQ FT: 1,000
SALES (est): 1.6MM **Privately Held**
SIC: 3273 Ready-mixed concrete

(G-8295)
TINT WORLD
3165 Route 112 (11763-1407)
PHONE..................................631 458-1999
Timothy Kjaer, *Principal*
EMP: 5
SALES (est): 484.7K **Privately Held**
SIC: 3089 5013 Automotive parts, plastic; automotive supplies & parts

(G-8296)
WAVERLY IRON CORP
25 Commercial Blvd (11763-1531)
PHONE..................................631 732-2800
Fax: 631 732-9085
Anthony Pizzichemi, *President*
CAM Jambor, *Bookkeeper*
EMP: 21
SQ FT: 7,000
SALES (est): 5.9MM **Privately Held**
WEB: www.waverlyiron.com
SIC: 3446 Architectural metalwork

(G-8297)
WOOD INNOVATIONS OF SUFFOLK
266 Middle Island Rd # 8 (11763-1525)
PHONE..................................631 698-2345
Fax: 631 698-2396
Gino Genna, *President*
Mary Weiss, *Treasurer*
EMP: 6
SQ FT: 3,000
SALES (est): 856.3K **Privately Held**
WEB: www.woodin.com
SIC: 2431 2499 5712 1799 Interior & ornamental woodwork & trim; exterior & ornamental woodwork & trim; decorative wood & woodwork; outdoor & garden furniture; fence construction

Medina
Orleans County

(G-8298)
BARNES METAL FINISHING INC
3932 Salt Works Rd (14103-9546)
P.O. Box 517 (14103-0517)
PHONE..................................585 798-4817
Fax: 585 798-4359
Wilfred Barnes, *President*
Darrel Barnes, *Vice Pres*
EMP: 15
SQ FT: 6,000
SALES: 800K **Privately Held**
SIC: 3471 Polishing, metals or formed products

(G-8299)
BAXTER HEALTHCARE CORPORATION
711 Park Ave (14103-1078)
PHONE..................................800 356-3454
Mike Smith, *Senior VP*
Dan Wellington, *QC Dir*
Rohan Thadani, *Engineer*
Nelson Tatterson, *Branch Mgr*
EMP: 380
SALES (corp-wide): 10.1B **Publicly Held**
SIC: 3841 Surgical & medical instruments
HQ: Baxter Healthcare Corporation
1 Baxter Pkwy
Deerfield IL 60015
224 948-2000

(G-8300)
BMP AMERICA INC (HQ)
Also Called: B M P
11625 Maple Ridge Rd (14103-9710)
PHONE..................................585 798-0950
Fax: 585 798-4272
Edward D Andrew, *CEO*
Peter Milicia, *President*
Robert Dunning, *Vice Pres*
Jason Gillard, *Vice Pres*
Alan Lebold, *Vice Pres*
▲ **EMP:** 112
SQ FT: 40,000
SALES (est): 29.5MM
SALES (corp-wide): 100.2MM **Privately Held**
SIC: 3555 Sticks, printers'
PA: Andrew Industries Limited
Walton House, Altham Business Park
Accrington LANCS BB5 5
128 277-8022

(G-8301)
BRUNNER INTERNATIONAL INC
3959 Bates Rd (14103-9705)
P.O. Box 111 (14103-0111)
PHONE..................................585 798-6000
Fax: 585 798-4963
Peter Brunner, *Ch of Bd*
Laurel Harrington, *QC Mgr*
Matt Gersley, *Engineer*
Roy Wagner, *Senior Engr*
Jim Carlson, *Controller*
▲ **EMP:** 122
SALES (est): 35.7MM **Privately Held**
SIC: 3713 Truck bodies & parts

(G-8302)
COMMUNITY NEWSPPR HOLDINGS INC
Also Called: Medina Journal Register
541-543 Main St (14103)
PHONE..................................585 798-1400
Mark Francis, *Publisher*
Michael Wertman, *Vice Pres*
EMP: 38
SQ FT: 14,301 **Privately Held**
WEB: www.clintonnc.com
SIC: 2711 Newspapers, publishing & printing
PA: Community Newspaper Holdings, Inc.
445 Dexter Ave Ste 7000
Montgomery AL 36104

(G-8303)
D & W ENTERPRISES LLC
10775 W Shelby Rd (14103-9584)
PHONE..................................585 590-6727
Darrel Barnes,
EMP: 17
SALES (est): 960K **Privately Held**
SIC: 3471 Finishing, metals or formed products

(G-8304)
F & H METAL FINISHING CO INC
Also Called: Fearby Enterprises
700 Genesee St (14103-1504)
P.O. Box 486 (14103-0486)
PHONE..................................585 798-2151
Fax: 585 798-2151
Timothy Fearby, *President*
Patricia Caleb, *Corp Secy*
Kim Stevens, *Vice Pres*
EMP: 18
SQ FT: 10,000
SALES: 800K **Privately Held**
SIC: 3479 3471 Enameling, including porcelain, of metal products; lacquering of metal products; varnishing of metal products; painting of metal products; cleaning, polishing & finishing; buffing for the trade; finishing, metals or formed products; polishing, metals or formed products

(G-8305)
GANNETT STLLITE INFO NTWRK INC
Also Called: Greater Niagara Newspaper
413 Main St (14103-1416)
PHONE..................................585 798-1400
Joyce Miles, *Manager*
Dan Caswell, *Director*
EMP: 88

Medina - Orleans County (G-8306)

SALES (corp-wide): 3B **Publicly Held**
WEB: www.usatoday.com
SIC: 2711 Newspapers, publishing & printing
HQ: Gannett Satellite Information Network, Llc
7950 Jones Branch Dr
Mc Lean VA 22102
703 854-6000

(G-8306)
GEOPUMP INC
213 State St (14103-1337)
PHONE 585 798-6666
James Mirand, *President*
Paul Fox, *Vice Pres*
EMP: 5
SQ FT: 1,500
SALES (est): 650.2K **Privately Held**
WEB: www.geopump.com
SIC: 3561 Pumps, domestic: water or sump

(G-8307)
HANSON AGGREGATES EAST LLC
Glenwood Ave (14103)
PHONE 585 798-0762
EMP: 15
SALES (corp-wide): 18.7B **Privately Held**
SIC: 3273 Mfg Ready-Mixed Concrete
HQ: Hanson Aggregates East Llc
2300 Gateway Centre Blvd
Morrisville NC 27560
919 380-2500

(G-8308)
HINSPERGERS POLY INDUSTRIES
430 W Oak Orchard St (14103-1551)
PHONE 585 798-6625
Fax: 585 798-6627
Greg Budd, *Manager*
EMP: 27
SALES (corp-wide): 13.1MM **Privately Held**
WEB: www.hinspergers.com
SIC: 3949 Swimming pools, plastic
PA: Hinspergers Poly Industries Ltd
645 Needham Lane
Mississauga ON L5A 1
905 272-0144

(G-8309)
MEDINA MILLWORKS LLC
10694 Ridge Rd (14103-9406)
PHONE 585 798-2969
Matt Graber,
Jerome Graber,
Philip Graber,
Steven Graber,
EMP: 8
SQ FT: 960
SALES (est): 1MM **Privately Held**
WEB: www.medinamillworks.com
SIC: 2431 Millwork

(G-8310)
MILLERS BULK FOOD AND BAKERY
10858 Ridge Rd (14103-9432)
PHONE 585 798-9700
Steven Miller, *Principal*
EMP: 8
SALES (est): 744.2K **Privately Held**
SIC: 2051 Bakery: wholesale or wholesale/retail combined

(G-8311)
MIZKAN AMERICA INC
Also Called: Nakano Foods
711 Park Ave (14103-1078)
PHONE 585 798-5720
Craig Smith, *President*
EMP: 18 **Privately Held**
SIC: 2099 2035 Vinegar; dressings, salad: raw & cooked (except dry mixes)
HQ: Mizkan America, Inc.
1661 Feehanville Dr # 200
Mount Prospect IL 60056
847 590-0059

(G-8312)
QUORUM GROUP LLC
Also Called: Takeform Archtectural Graphics
11601 Maple Ridge Rd (14103-9710)
PHONE 585 798-8888
Fax: 585 798-8889
William Hungerford, *President*
Dee Ann Courcy, *CFO*
Jim Brown, *Manager*
Carmine Giso, *Manager*
EMP: 52
SQ FT: 35,000
SALES: 6.3MM **Privately Held**
WEB: www.takeform.net
SIC: 3993 Signs, not made in custom sign painting shops

(G-8313)
S B WHISTLER & SONS INC
11023 W Center Street Ext (14103-9557)
P.O. Box 270 (14103-0270)
PHONE 585 798-3000
Brendan Whistler, *Owner*
Larry Massey, *CFO*
EMP: 46
SQ FT: 25,000
SALES (est): 14.4MM **Privately Held**
WEB: www.phinneytool.com
SIC: 3544 Special dies & tools

(G-8314)
SHELBY CRUSHED STONE INC
10830 Blair Rd (14103-9590)
PHONE 585 798-4501
Thomas S Biamonte, *CEO*
EMP: 17
SALES (est): 3.1MM **Privately Held**
SIC: 1429 1442 1422 Sandstone, crushed & broken-quarrying; gravel mining; crushed & broken limestone

(G-8315)
SIGMA INTL GEN MED APPRTUS LLC
711 Park Ave (14103-1078)
PHONE 585 798-3901
Nelson Tatterson, *President*
Mike Southworth, *Vice Pres*
Todd Underwood, *Opers Mgr*
George Kiefer, *Purch Mgr*
Katie Budine, *Engineer*
▼ **EMP:** 500
SQ FT: 40,000
SALES (est): 219.5MM
SALES (corp-wide): 10.1B **Publicly Held**
WEB: www.sigmapumps.com
SIC: 3841 IV transfusion apparatus
PA: Baxter International Inc.
1 Baxter Pkwy
Deerfield IL 60015
224 948-2000

(G-8316)
VIVUS TECHNOLOGIES LLC
591 Mahar St (14103-1612)
Rural Route 591 Mahar (14103)
PHONE 585 798-6658
David Cooper,
EMP: 7
SQ FT: 20,000
SALES (est): 184.7K **Privately Held**
SIC: 3821 Autoclaves, laboratory

(G-8317)
WESTERN NEW YORK ENERGY LLC
4141 Bates Rd (14103-9706)
P.O. Box 191 (14103-0191)
PHONE 585 798-9693
Tim Winters, *Controller*
Sara Flansburg, *Accountant*
Michelle Kingdollar, *Accountant*
Andrew L Buck, *Marketing Mgr*
Mike Langdon, *Lab Dir*
EMP: 40
SALES (est): 17.6MM **Privately Held**
WEB: www.wnyenergy.com
SIC: 2869 Ethanolamines

Medusa
Albany County

(G-8318)
DEGENNARO FUEL SERVICE LLC
242 County Route 357 (12120-2005)
PHONE 518 239-6350
EMP: 8 **EST:** 2012
SALES (est): 535.4K **Privately Held**
SIC: 2869 Fuels

Melville
Suffolk County

(G-8319)
110 SAND COMPANY (PA)
136 Spagnoli Rd (11747-3502)
PHONE 631 694-2822
Chester Broman, *Partner*
Doug Piccozi, *Controller*
EMP: 50
SQ FT: 20,000
SALES (est): 6.2MM **Privately Held**
SIC: 1442 Construction sand & gravel

(G-8320)
18 ROCKS LLC
102 Marcus Dr (11747-4212)
PHONE 631 465-9990
Richard Cotler, *Production*
Michael Schatten, *Mng Member*
EMP: 21
SQ FT: 3,000
SALES (est): 1.6MM
SALES (corp-wide): 2.2MM **Privately Held**
SIC: 2331 2335 Women's & misses' blouses & shirts; blouses, women's & juniors': made from purchased material; shirts, women's & juniors': made from purchased materials; women's, juniors' & misses' dresses
PA: Melwood Partners, Inc.
100 Qentin Roosevelt Blvd
Garden City NY 11530
516 307-8030

(G-8321)
ADVANTAGE PLUS DIAGNOSTICS INC
200 Broadhollow Rd (11747-4846)
PHONE 631 393-5044
Jason Damianio, *President*
Anthony Rollo, *Admin Sec*
EMP: 5
SALES (est): 324.5K **Privately Held**
SIC: 3841 Diagnostic apparatus, medical

(G-8322)
AERO-VISION TECHNOLOGIES INC (PA)
7 Round Tree Dr (11747-3314)
PHONE 631 643-8349
Fax: 631 952-3517
Donald P Burkhardt, *President*
EMP: 8
SQ FT: 6,200
SALES (est): 2MM **Privately Held**
WEB: www.aero-vision.com
SIC: 3577 Computer peripheral equipment

(G-8323)
AIP PUBLISHING LLC
1305 Walt Whitman Rd # 300 (11747-4300)
PHONE 516 576-2200
John Haynes, *CEO*
John Light, *Editor*
Roy Levenson, *CFO*
Madeline Babtiste, *Human Res Dir*
EMP: 125 **EST:** 2013
SALES: 48.9MM
SALES (corp-wide): 15.3MM **Privately Held**
SIC: 2731 Books: publishing only
PA: American Institute Of Physics Incorporated
1 Physics Ellipse
College Park MD 20740
301 209-3100

(G-8324)
AIR TECHNIQUES INC (HQ)
1295 Walt Whitman Rd (11747-3062)
PHONE 516 433-7676
Christoph Roeer, *CEO*
John Puswald, *General Mgr*
Lou Guellnitz, *Vice Pres*
Robert Nordquist, *Vice Pres*
Kent Searl, *Vice Pres*
▲ **EMP:** 326
SQ FT: 92,000
SALES (est): 59.1MM
SALES (corp-wide): 256.2MM **Privately Held**
WEB: www.airtechniques.com
SIC: 3861 3563 3821 3844 Photographic processing equipment & chemicals; air & gas compressors including vacuum pumps; laboratory equipment: fume hoods, distillation racks, etc.; X-ray apparatus & tubes; dental equipment & supplies; pumps & pumping equipment
PA: Durr Dental Ag
Hopfigheimer Str. 17
Bietigheim-Bissingen 74321
714 270-50

(G-8325)
ALL-PRO IMAGING CORP
1295 Walt Whitman Rd (11747-3070)
PHONE 516 433-7676
Louis E Brooks, *Ch of Bd*
Frank Bader, *President*
Mark S Brooks, *Vice Pres*
Fredrick Fischer, *Vice Pres*
Kenny Keith, *Regl Sales Mgr*
▲ **EMP:** 20
SQ FT: 10,000
SALES (est): 2.2MM **Privately Held**
WEB: www.allproimaging.com
SIC: 3861 Processing equipment, photographic

(G-8326)
AMERICAN INSTITUTE PHYSICS INC
Hntngton Qad Ste 1n1-2 (11747)
PHONE 516 576-2410
Catherine Oriordan, *Vice Pres*
Zita Murano, *Opers Staff*
Richard Baccante, *Treasurer*
Doris Lewis, *Branch Mgr*
Debra Dillon, *Manager*
EMP: 250
SALES (corp-wide): 15.3MM **Privately Held**
SIC: 2721 2731 8733 Trade journals: publishing only, not printed on site; books: publishing only; noncommercial research organizations
PA: American Institute Of Physics Incorporated
1 Physics Ellipse
College Park MD 20740
301 209-3100

(G-8327)
AMOROSO WOOD PRODUCTS CO INC
462 Old Country Rd (11747-1825)
PHONE 631 249-4998
Fax: 631 249-4576
Rocco Amoroso, *President*
EMP: 7
SQ FT: 18,000
SALES (est): 993.9K **Privately Held**
SIC: 2434 Wood kitchen cabinets

(G-8328)
AN GROUP INC
17 Scott Dr (11747-1013)
P.O. Box 895 (11747-0895)
PHONE 631 549-4090
Steve Hopfenmuller, *President*
Steven Hopfenmuller, *President*
Jill Hopfenmuller, *Vice Pres*
EMP: 5

Melville - Suffolk County (G-8352)

SALES (est): 283.2K **Privately Held**
WEB: www.smbiz.com
SIC: **2741** Business service newsletters: publishing & printing

(G-8329)
BLUE RHINO GLOBAL SOURCING INC
Also Called: Mr.-Bar-B-q-
10 Hub Dr Ste 101 (11747-3522)
PHONE.....................516 752-0670
Fax: 516 752-0683
Silvia Piccininni, *Controller*
Lauren McWhirter, *Sales Staff*
Marc Zemel, *Branch Mgr*
Wendy Sender, *Director*
EMP: 23 **Publicly Held**
SIC: **1321** 5984 Casing-head butane & propane production; propane gas, bottled
HQ: Blue Rhino Global Sourcing, Inc.
5650 University Pkwy # 400
Winston Salem NC 27105
800 258-7466

(G-8330)
BZ MEDIA LLC
Also Called: SD Times
225 Broadhollow Rd 211e (11747-4807)
PHONE.....................631 421-4158
Fax: 631 922-5258
Ted Bahr, *President*
H Ted Bahr, *President*
Christina Mulligan, *Editor*
Alan L Zeichick, *Exec VP*
Joe Fernandes, *Vice Pres*
EMP: 18 **EST:** 1999
SQ FT: 4,000
SALES: 5.5MM **Privately Held**
WEB: www.bzmedia.com
SIC: **2721** Magazines: publishing & printing

(G-8331)
CAPY MACHINE SHOP INC (PA)
114 Spagnoli Rd (11747-3502)
PHONE.....................631 694-6916
Salvatore Capacchione, *CEO*
John Vlachos, *General Mgr*
Alice Calamusa, *Technology*
Rosemary Capacchione, *Shareholder*
▲ **EMP:** 40
SQ FT: 7,500
SALES (est): 7.6MM **Privately Held**
SIC: **3599** Machine shop, jobbing & repair

(G-8332)
CHROMAGRAPHICS PRESS INC
3 Martha Dr (11747-1906)
PHONE.....................631 367-6160
Frank Cuoco, *President*
Irene Cuoco, *Vice Pres*
Thomas Cuoco, *Vice Pres*
Ed Eng Nancy Lee, *IT/INT Sup*
EMP: 5
SALES (est): 480K **Privately Held**
WEB: www.chromagraphicspress.com
SIC: **2752** 8748 Commercial printing, lithographic; business consulting

(G-8333)
CHYRONHEGO CORPORATION (HQ)
5 Hub Dr (11747-3523)
PHONE.....................631 845-2000
Fax: 631 845-2090
Johan Apel, *President*
Richard Hajdu, *General Mgr*
Katie Panza, *General Mgr*
Neil Foster, *COO*
Rickard Ohrn, *COO*
EMP: 90
SQ FT: 47,000
SALES (est): 46.5MM **Privately Held**
WEB: www.chyron.com
SIC: **3663** Radio & TV communications equipment

(G-8334)
COMAX AROMATICS CORPORATION
130 Baylis Rd (11747-3808)
PHONE.....................631 249-0505
Peter J Calabretta, *President*
Norman Katz, *Vice Pres*
Francis J Keppel, *Admin Sec*
EMP: 50

SQ FT: 40,000
SALES (est): 4.1MM **Privately Held**
SIC: **2869** Flavors or flavoring materials, synthetic

(G-8335)
COMAX MANUFACTURING CORP
Also Called: Comax Flavors
130 Baylis Rd (11747-3808)
PHONE.....................631 249-0505
Fax: 631 249-9255
Peter J Calabretta Jr, *Ch of Bd*
Catherine Armstrong, *Vice Pres*
Paul Calabretta, *Vice Pres*
◆ **EMP:** 55
SQ FT: 40,000
SALES (est): 29.9MM **Privately Held**
SIC: **2869** Flavors or flavoring materials, synthetic

(G-8336)
COMTECH PST CORP (HQ)
105 Baylis Rd (11747-3833)
PHONE.....................631 777-8900
Fax: 631 777-8877
Dr Stan Sloane, *CEO*
Michael Hrybenko, *President*
Jim Heick, *Managing Dir*
Walter Koprowski, *Vice Pres*
Anthony Scuderi, *Vice Pres*
▲ **EMP:** 120
SQ FT: 46,000
SALES (est): 76.1MM
SALES (corp-wide): 550.3MM **Publicly Held**
WEB: www.comtechpst.com
SIC: **3663** 3825 Microwave communication equipment; amplifiers, RF power & IF; test equipment for electronic & electric measurement
PA: Comtech Telecommunications Corp.
68 S Service Rd Ste 230
Melville NY 11747
631 962-7000

(G-8337)
COMTECH TELECOM CORP (PA)
68 S Service Rd Ste 230 (11747-2350)
PHONE.....................631 962-7000
Fax: 631 962-7001
Fred Kornberg, *Ch of Bd*
John Branscum Jr, *Senior VP*
Richard L Burt, *Senior VP*
Michael D Porcelain, *CFO*
◆ **EMP:** 129
SQ FT: 9,600
SALES: 550.3MM **Publicly Held**
WEB: www.comtechtel.com
SIC: **3663** Microwave communication equipment; amplifiers, RF power & IF; mobile communication equipment

(G-8338)
CROWN NOVELTY WORKS INC
42 Elkland Rd (11747-3302)
PHONE.....................631 253-0949
EMP: 7 **EST:** 1909
SQ FT: 10,000
SALES: 1.2MM **Privately Held**
SIC: **3364** Mfg Lead Curtain Weights

(G-8339)
DADDARIO & COMPANY INC
99 Marcus Dr (11747-4209)
PHONE.....................631 439-3300
EMP: 67
SALES (corp-wide): 210.7MM **Privately Held**
SIC: **3931** String instruments & parts
PA: D'addario & Company, Inc.
595 Smith St
Farmingdale NY 11735
631 439-3300

(G-8340)
DESIGNER EPOXY FINISHES INC
445 Broadhollow Rd Ste 25 (11747-3645)
PHONE.....................646 943-6044
Justin Palladino, *President*
EMP: 6 **EST:** 2007
SALES (est): 885.2K **Privately Held**
SIC: **2851** 1752 Epoxy coatings; floor laying & floor work

(G-8341)
DISTINCTION MAGAZINE INC
Also Called: Island Publications
235 Pinelawn Rd (11747-4226)
PHONE.....................631 843-3522
Fax: 631 843-4186
Madelyn Roberts, *CEO*
Patrice Golde, *President*
EMP: 25
SALES (est): 2.4MM **Privately Held**
SIC: **2721** Magazines: publishing & printing

(G-8342)
DORIS PANOS DESIGNS LTD
130 Old East Neck Rd (11747-3209)
PHONE.....................631 245-0580
Doris Panos, *President*
EMP: 6
SQ FT: 250
SALES (est): 710K **Privately Held**
SIC: **3911** Jewelry, precious metal

(G-8343)
E-Z-EM INC (DH)
155 Pinelawn Rd Ste 230n (11747-3249)
PHONE.....................609 524-2864
Vittorio Puppo, *CEO*
Adrianne Setton, *Manager*
◆ **EMP:** 32
SALES (est): 11MM **Privately Held**
WEB: www.ezem.com
SIC: **2835** 3841 In vitro & in vivo diagnostic substances; diagnostic apparatus, medical

(G-8344)
EQUAL OPPRTNITY PBLCATIONS INC
Also Called: Careers and The Disabled
445 Broadhollow Rd # 425 (11747-3669)
PHONE.....................631 421-9421
John R Miller III, *Ch of Bd*
Debra Kahn, *Business Mgr*
Tamara Flaun, *Exec VP*
Kay Miller, *Exec VP*
Christine Desmond, *Vice Pres*
EMP: 12 **EST:** 1969
SQ FT: 3,000
SALES (est): 2.1MM **Privately Held**
WEB: www.eop.com
SIC: **2721** 7361 Magazines: publishing & printing; employment agencies

(G-8345)
ESTEE LAUDER INC
125 Pinelawn Rd (11747-3135)
PHONE.....................631 531-1000
Fax: 631 531-1604
Ken Marenus, *Senior VP*
Daniel Kelly, *Vice Pres*
Louis Schapiro, *Vice Pres*
David P Yacko, *Vice Pres*
Lorraine Courter, *Purch Agent*
EMP: 100
SALES (corp-wide): 11.8B **Publicly Held**
WEB: www.esteelauder.com
SIC: **2844** 5999 5122 Perfumes & colognes; toiletries, cosmetics & perfumes; cosmetics; perfumes & colognes; drugs, proprietaries & sundries
HQ: Estee Lauder Inc.
767 5th Ave Fl 37
New York NY 10153
212 572-4200

(G-8346)
ESTEE LAUDER INC
350 S Service Rd (11747-3230)
PHONE.....................631 454-7000
Fax: 631 847-8370
Shahan Nazar, *Senior VP*
Larry Krieb, *Vice Pres*
Frank O'Neil, *Vice Pres*
Jack Deng, *Project Mgr*
Rafael Mercedes, *Mfg Staff*
EMP: 108
SALES (corp-wide): 11.8B **Publicly Held**
WEB: www.esteelauder.com
SIC: **2844** Cosmetic preparations
HQ: Estee Lauder Inc.
767 5th Ave Fl 37
New York NY 10153
212 572-4200

(G-8347)
FALCONSTOR SOFTWARE INC (PA)
2 Huntington Quadrangle 2s (11747-4501)
PHONE.....................631 777-5188
Fax: 631 501-7633
Todd Brooks, *CEO*
Eli Oxenhorn, *Ch of Bd*
Gary Quinn, *President*
John Yang, *General Mgr*
Alan Komet, *Exec VP*
EMP: 226
SQ FT: 55,000
SALES: 30.2MM **Publicly Held**
WEB: www.falconstor.com
SIC: **7372** 7371 Prepackaged software; application computer software; computer software development; computer software systems analysis & design, custom

(G-8348)
FILMPAK EXTRUSION LLC
125 Spagnoli Rd (11747-3518)
PHONE.....................631 293-6767
Peter Levy, *President*
EMP: 60
SQ FT: 100,000
SALES: 20MM **Privately Held**
SIC: **2673** Bags: plastic, laminated & coated

(G-8349)
FONAR CORPORATION (PA)
110 Marcus Dr (11747-4292)
PHONE.....................631 694-2929
Fax: 516 249-3734
Raymond V Damadian, *Ch of Bd*
Timothy R Damadian, *President*
Luciano B Bonanni, *COO*
John Greenhalgh, *Director*
Claudette J V Chan, *Admin Sec*
EMP: 127
SQ FT: 78,000
SALES: 78MM **Publicly Held**
WEB: www.fonar.com
SIC: **3845** 8741 Electromedical equipment; management services

(G-8350)
FOUGERA PHARMACEUTICALS INC (DH)
Also Called: Pharmaderm
60 Baylis Rd (11747-3838)
P.O. Box 2006 (11747-0103)
PHONE.....................631 454-7677
Fax: 631 420-1572
Brian A Markison, *CEO*
Donald Degolyer, *Ch of Bd*
Darryl Jackson, *Publisher*
Jeff Bailey, *COO*
Chris Klein, *Senior VP*
▲ **EMP:** 250 **EST:** 1963
SQ FT: 190,000
SALES (est): 348.1MM
SALES (corp-wide): 48.5B **Privately Held**
WEB: www.altanapharma-us.com
SIC: **2834** 2851 2821 3479 Pharmaceutical preparations; ointments; paints & paint additives; plasticizer/additive based plastic materials; painting, coating & hot dipping; measuring & controlling devices
HQ: Sandoz Inc.
100 College Rd W
Princeton NJ 08540
609 627-8500

(G-8351)
GPC INTERNATIONAL INC (PA)
510 Broadhollow Rd # 205 (11747-3606)
PHONE.....................631 752-9600
Steven Roth, *President*
Don Fleisheiar, *CFO*
Joan Middleton, *Manager*
EMP: 8
SQ FT: 2,500
SALES (est): 20.4MM **Privately Held**
SIC: **3861** Graphic arts plates, sensitized

(G-8352)
GRAPHIC IMAGE ASSOCIATES LLC
305 Spagnoli Rd (11747-3506)
PHONE.....................631 249-9600
EMP: 100
SQ FT: 8,500

Melville - Suffolk County (G-8353)

SALES (est): 8.5MM **Privately Held**
SIC: 3111 Leather Tanning/Finishing

(G-8353) GRAPHIC IMAGE INCORPORATED
Also Called: Gigi New York
305 Spagnoli Rd (11747-3506)
PHONE 631 249-9600
Thomas J Glazer, *President*
Carol O'Connell, *Vice Pres*
Ashley Sullivan, *Design Engr*
Edward Mesloh, *Controller*
Midari Papa, *Hum Res Coord*
◆ **EMP:** 150 **EST:** 1969
SQ FT: 50,000
SALES (est): 14.2MM **Privately Held**
WEB: www.graphicimagenewyork.com
SIC: 2782 3111 5137 5632 Blankbooks & looseleaf binders; albums; diaries; handbag leather; handbags; handbags

(G-8354) GUIDANCE GROUP INC
Also Called: Child's Work-Child's Play
1 Huntington Quad 1n03 (11747-4466)
PHONE 631 756-4618
Jon D Werz, *CEO*
Edward Werz, *Publisher*
Carmine Russo, *CFO*
Michael Surrey, *Analyst*
EMP: 12
SALES (est): 946.8K **Privately Held**
SIC: 2711 Newspapers, publishing & printing

(G-8355) HADCO METAL TRADING CO LLC
120 Spagnoli Rd Ste 1 (11747-3513)
PHONE 631 270-9724
Gilad Fishman, *CEO*
Nancy Barcus, *Sales Mgr*
EMP: 6
SALES (est): 724K **Privately Held**
SIC: 3353 Aluminum sheet, plate & foil

(G-8356) HENRY SCHEIN FINCL SVCS LLC (HQ)
Also Called: Henry Schein International Inc
135 Duryea Rd (11747-3834)
PHONE 631 843-5500
Stanley Bergman, *CEO*
Joseph Iacovino, *Engineer*
Steven Paladino, *CFO*
EMP: 9
SALES (est): 966.7K
SALES (corp-wide): 11.5B **Publicly Held**
SIC: 3843 Dental equipment & supplies
PA: Henry Schein, Inc.
135 Duryea Rd
Melville NY 11747
631 843-5500

(G-8357) HONEYWELL INTERNATIONAL INC
263 Old Country Rd (11747-2712)
P.O. Box 22324, Brooklyn (11202-2324)
PHONE 212 964-5111
EMP: 657
SALES (corp-wide): 38.5B **Publicly Held**
SIC: 3724 Aircraft Engines And Engine Parts
PA: Honeywell International Inc.
115 Tabor Rd
Morris Plains NJ 07950
973 455-2000

(G-8358) HONEYWELL INTERNATIONAL INC
2 Corporate Center Dr # 100 (11747-3269)
PHONE 516 577-2000
Ron Rothman, *President*
Mike Zimolka, *Sr Project Mgr*
Rafael Pimentel, *Manager*
Ashbel Roy, *Info Tech Mgr*
Michael Landi, *Software Engr*
EMP: 400
SALES (corp-wide): 39.3B **Publicly Held**
WEB: www.honeywell.com
SIC: 3728 Accumulators, aircraft propeller
PA: Honeywell International Inc.
115 Tabor Rd
Morris Plains NJ 07950
973 455-2000

(G-8359) I W INDUSTRIES INC (PA)
Also Called: Concinnity Division
35 Melville Park Rd (11747-3104)
PHONE 631 293-9494
Fax: 516 293-9499
Jerome Warshawsky, *President*
Murray Cohen, *Vice Pres*
ARI Warshawsky, *Vice Pres*
Glenn M Davis, *Engineer*
Terry Klein, *Credit Mgr*
▲ **EMP:** 230 **EST:** 1931
SQ FT: 110,000
SALES (est): 11.4MM **Privately Held**
WEB: www.iwindustries.com
SIC: 3451 3471 3432 Screw machine products; finishing, metals or formed products; faucets & spigots, metal & plastic

(G-8360) INTERDGITAL COMMUNICATIONS LLC
2 Huntington Quad Ste 4s (11747-4508)
PHONE 631 622-4000
Fax: 631 622-0100
Daniel Cohen, *Engineer*
Bill Hackett, *Engineer*
Gary Lomp, *Manager*
Richard Cho, *Manager*
Cynthia Hanscom, *Manager*
EMP: 125 **Publicly Held**
WEB: www.interdigital.com
SIC: 3661 8731 Telephone & telegraph apparatus; commercial physical research
HQ: Interdigital Communications, Inc.
200 Bellevue Pkwy Ste 300
Wilmington DE 19809
610 878-7800

(G-8361) INTERNATIONAL METALS TRDG LLC
25 Melville Park Rd # 114 (11747-3175)
PHONE 866 923-0182
Ian Parker, *CEO*
Joseph Kalinowski, *Principal*
Bret Bedges, *COO*
EMP: 5 **EST:** 2013
SALES: 20MM **Privately Held**
SIC: 3441 Building components, structural steel

(G-8362) KARP ASSOCIATES INC (PA)
Also Called: Adjustable Shelving
260 Spagnoli Rd (11747-3505)
PHONE 631 768-8300
Fax: 631 768-8350
Adam Gold, *Chairman*
Augustine Lopez, *Safety Mgr*
Ronnit Kessler, *Engineer*
Ronnie Peterson, *Controller*
Lawrence Mass, *VP Sales*
▲ **EMP:** 95 **EST:** 1956
SALES (est): 21.9MM **Privately Held**
WEB: www.karpinc.com
SIC: 3442 2541 Metal doors; shelving, office & store, wood

(G-8363) LEVITON MANUFACTURING CO INC (PA)
201 N Service Rd (11747-3138)
P.O. Box 10600 (11747-0056)
PHONE 631 812-6000
Stephen Sokolow, *Vice Ch Bd*
Donald J Hendler, *President*
Bruno Filio, *President*
Daryoush Larizadeh, *President*
Shady Youssef, *Regional Mgr*
◆ **EMP:** 450 **EST:** 1990
SALES (est): 1.6B **Privately Held**
WEB: www.leviton.com
SIC: 3643 3613 3357 3674 Current-carrying wiring devices; caps & plugs, electric: attachment; connectors, electric cord; sockets, electric; fuses, electric; nonferrous wiredrawing & insulating; building wire & cable, nonferrous; diodes, solid state (germanium, silicon, etc.); transistors; engine electrical equipment; electronic connectors

(G-8364) LSI COMPUTER SYSTEMS
1235 Walt Whitman Rd (11747-3086)
PHONE 631 271-0400
Fax: 631 271-0405
Alfred Musto, *CEO*
Attila Tetik, *President*
Alvin Kaplan, *Corp Secy*
Burt Cohen, *Vice Pres*
Sherri Smith, *Vice Pres*
EMP: 35
SQ FT: 13,500
SALES (est): 5.1MM **Privately Held**
WEB: www.lsicsi.com
SIC: 3674 Integrated circuits, semiconductor networks, etc.; metal oxide silicon (MOS) devices

(G-8365) MDAMERICA WELLNESS INC
225 Broadhollow Rd 110e (11747-4822)
PHONE 631 396-0991
Jason Polete, *CEO*
EMP: 10
SALES (est): 221.8K **Privately Held**
SIC: 7372 Application computer software

(G-8366) MEYCO PRODUCTS INC (PA)
1225 Walt Whitman Rd (11747-3093)
PHONE 631 421-9800
David W Weissner, *CEO*
John Ciniglio, *President*
Donnie Griffin, *Vice Pres*
John Hughes, *Prdtn Mgr*
Patricia K Weissner, *Admin Sec*
▼ **EMP:** 30 **EST:** 1898
SQ FT: 70,000
SALES (est): 21.5MM **Privately Held**
WEB: www.meycoproducts.com
SIC: 2394 Liners & covers, fabric: made from purchased materials

(G-8367) MITSUBISHI ELC PWR PDTS INC
55 Marcus Dr (11747-4209)
PHONE 516 962-2813
EMP: 7
SALES (corp-wide): 37.3B **Privately Held**
SIC: 3699 1731 Electrical equipment & supplies; electrical work
HQ: Mitsubishi Electric Power Products, Inc.
530 Keystone Dr
Warrendale PA 15086
724 772-2555

(G-8368) NATURAL ORGANICS INC (PA)
Also Called: Nature's Plus
548 Broadhollow Rd (11747-3708)
PHONE 631 293-0030
Fax: 631 249-2022
Gerald Kessler, *Ch of Bd*
James Gibbons, *President*
Ed Canavan, *Publisher*
Vic Deventer, *Publisher*
Gary Schultz, *Mfg Dir*
▲ **EMP:** 250
SQ FT: 100,000
SALES: 0 **Privately Held**
SIC: 2833 Vitamins, natural or synthetic: bulk, uncompounded

(G-8369) NEW DIMENSIONS RESEARCH CORP
260 Spagnoli Rd (11747-3593)
PHONE 631 694-1356
Fax: 631 694-6097
Timothy L Mason, *Ch of Bd*
Jeffrey Mason, *President*
Kenneth Dasrath, *Vice Pres*
Ranga Kanadam, *Opers Mgr*
Dany Espinal, *Warehouse Mgr*
▲ **EMP:** 125 **EST:** 1957
SQ FT: 155,000
SALES (est): 30.7MM **Privately Held**
WEB: www.ndrc.com
SIC: 3993 7389 Signs & advertising specialties; design, commercial & industrial

(G-8370) NEWSDAY LLC (DH)
Also Called: Newsday Media Group
235 Pinelawn Rd (11747-4250)
PHONE 631 843-4050
Fax: 516 843-2953
Patrick Dolan, *President*
William H Attwood, *Publisher*
Alicia P Riding, *Publisher*
David Blasband, *Editor*
Bobby Cassidy, *Editor*
EMP: 400 **EST:** 1940
SALES (est): 302MM
SALES (corp-wide): 21.9B **Publicly Held**
SIC: 2711 Newspapers, publishing & printing
HQ: Csc Holdings, Llc
1111 Stewart Ave
Bethpage NY 11714
516 803-2300

(G-8371) NEWSDAY LLC
25 Deshon Dr (11747-4221)
PHONE 631 843-3135
Raymond Jansen, *Branch Mgr*
EMP: 150
SALES (corp-wide): 21.9B **Publicly Held**
SIC: 2711 Newspapers, publishing & printing
HQ: Newsday Llc
235 Pinelawn Rd
Melville NY 11747
631 843-4050

(G-8372) NIKON INSTRUMENTS INC (DH)
1300 Walt Whitman Rd Fl 2 (11747-3064)
PHONE 631 547-4200
Yoshinobu Ishikawa, *Ch of Bd*
Toshiaki Nagano, *President*
James Hamlin, *Vice Pres*
Scott Monroe, *Purch Mgr*
Laura Sysko, *Engineer*
◆ **EMP:** 71
SALES (est): 40.4MM
SALES (corp-wide): 6.5B **Privately Held**
WEB: www.nikonusa.com
SIC: 3827 Optical instruments & lenses

(G-8373) OLYMPIC SOFTWARE & CONSULTING
290 Broadhollow Rd 130e (11747-4852)
PHONE 631 351-0655
Chris McLean, *Owner*
EMP: 7 **EST:** 2001
SALES (est): 596.9K **Privately Held**
SIC: 7372 Prepackaged software

(G-8374) OPUS TECHNOLOGY CORPORATION
10 Gwynne Rd (11747-1414)
PHONE 631 271-1883
James Startin, *President*
EMP: 10
SALES (est): 890K **Privately Held**
SIC: 3679 Electronic circuits

(G-8375) P & F INDUSTRIES INC (PA)
Also Called: P&F
445 Broadhollow Rd # 100 (11747-3615)
PHONE 631 694-9800
Fax: 631 694-9804
Richard A Horowitz, *Ch of Bd*
Joseph A Molino Jr, *COO*
◆ **EMP:** 43 **EST:** 1963
SQ FT: 5,000
SALES: 57.2MM **Publicly Held**
WEB: www.pfina.com
SIC: 3546 3429 3714 Power-driven handtools; grinders, portable: electric or pneumatic; manufactured hardware (general); filters: oil, fuel & air, motor vehicle

▲ = Import ▼ = Export
◆ = Import/Export

GEOGRAPHIC SECTION

Menands - Albany County (G-8401)

(G-8376)
PARK ELECTROCHEMICAL CORP (PA)
48 S Service Rd Ste 300 (11747-2335)
PHONE...................................631 465-3600
Fax: 631 465-3100
Brian E Shore, *Ch of Bd*
Christopher T Mastrogiacomo, *President*
Stephen E Gilhuley, *Exec VP*
Mark A Esquivel, *Vice Pres*
Constantine Petropoulos, *Vice Pres*
▲ EMP: 113
SQ FT: 8,000
SALES: 114.6MM **Publicly Held**
WEB: www.parkelectro.com
SIC: 3672 3674 Printed circuit boards; microcircuits, integrated (semiconductor)

(G-8377)
POLY-PAK INDUSTRIES INC (PA)
Also Called: Colorpak
125 Spagnoli Rd (11747-3518)
PHONE...................................631 293-6767
Fax: 516 454-6366
Peter Levy, *Ch of Bd*
Leonard Levy, *Chairman*
Rose Matty, *Senior VP*
Mitchell Cohen, *Vice Pres*
Doug Kiesel, *Vice Pres*
◆ EMP: 280
SQ FT: 150,000
SALES (est): 81.9MM **Privately Held**
WEB: www.poly-pak.com
SIC: 2673 2677 Plastic bags: made from purchased materials; envelopes

(G-8378)
PRECISION PHARMA SERVICES INC
155 Duryea Rd (11747-3894)
PHONE...................................631 752-7314
Jim Moose, *President*
Kathleen Beach, *Vice Pres*
Tom Lynch, *Vice Pres*
June Heck, *CFO*
Michele Barcia, *Manager*
EMP: 125
SQ FT: 100,000
SALES (est): 24.5MM **Privately Held**
WEB: www.precisionpharma.com
SIC: 2834 Pharmaceutical preparations

(G-8379)
PUBLISHERS CLEARING HOUSE LLC
265 Spagnoli Rd Ste 1 (11747-3508)
PHONE...................................516 249-4063
EMP: 31
SALES (corp-wide): 156MM **Privately Held**
SIC: 2741 Miscellaneous publishing
PA: Publishers Clearing House Llc
   300 Jericho Quadrangle De
   Jericho NY 11753
   516 883-5432

(G-8380)
QUADRANGLE QUICKPRINTS LTD
Also Called: Quadrangle Quick Print
1 Huntington Quad LI04 (11747-4401)
P.O. Box 2753, North Babylon (11703-0753)
PHONE...................................631 694-4464
Fax: 516 694-4469
Henry Schaja, *Owner*
EMP: 6
SQ FT: 1,000
SALES (est): 780.6K **Privately Held**
WEB: www.cardsandstationery.com
SIC: 2752 Commercial printing, offset

(G-8381)
ROSS COMMUNICATIONS ASSOCIATES
200 Broadhollow Rd # 207 (11747-4846)
PHONE...................................631 393-5089
Robert Ross, *President*
Jodie Ross, *Vice Pres*
EMP: 10
SALES (est): 4.8MM **Privately Held**
SIC: 2721 Magazines: publishing & printing

(G-8382)
RUBIES COSTUME COMPANY INC
1770 Walt Whitman Rd (11747-3068)
PHONE...................................516 326-1500
Howard Biege, *Vice Pres*
Richard Tinari, *Sales Staff*
Lauren Rabinowitz, *Director*
EMP: 40
SALES (corp-wide): 429.9MM **Privately Held**
SIC: 2389 5199 7299 Costumes; fabrics, yarns & knit goods; costume rental
PA: Rubie's Costume Company, Inc.
   12008 Jamaica Ave
   Richmond Hill NY 11418
   718 846-1008

(G-8383)
SIMPLY AMAZING ENTERPRISES INC
68 S Service Rd Ste 1 (11747-2354)
PHONE...................................631 503-6452
EMP: 7 EST: 2014
SALES: 390K **Privately Held**
SIC: 2842 Mfg Polish/Sanitation Goods

(G-8384)
STAR COMMUNITY PUBLISHING
Also Called: Star Community Pubg Group LLC
235 Pinelawn Rd (11747-4226)
PHONE...................................631 843-4050
Lee Aiello, *Credit Mgr*
Michael Gates, *VP Sales*
Barbara Fisher, *Manager*
EMP: 194
SALES: 45MM
SALES (corp-wide): 21.9B **Publicly Held**
WEB: www.tribune.com
SIC: 2711 Newspapers, publishing & printing
HQ: Newsday Llc
   235 Pinelawn Rd
   Melville NY 11747
   631 843-4050

(G-8385)
STERIS CORPORATION
Also Called: Vts Medical Systems
40 Melville Park Rd (11747-3173)
PHONE...................................877 887-1788
EMP: 6
SALES (corp-wide): 2.6B **Privately Held**
SIC: 3842 Surgical appliances & supplies
HQ: Steris Corporation
   5960 Heisley Rd
   Mentor OH 44060
   440 354-2600

(G-8386)
SUTTON PLACE SOFTWARE INC
13 Tappen Dr (11747-1019)
PHONE...................................631 421-1737
Steve J Sutton, *President*
EMP: 5
SALES (est): 290.2K **Privately Held**
SIC: 7372 Prepackaged software

(G-8387)
SYSTEMS TRADING INC
48 S Svc Rd Ste LI90 (11747)
PHONE...................................718 261-8900
Harold Schwartz, *Ch of Bd*
EMP: 7
SQ FT: 1,650
SALES: 8MM **Privately Held**
WEB: www.btn.net
SIC: 7372 7377 Prepackaged software; computer rental & leasing

(G-8388)
TAYLOR COMMUNICATIONS INC
155 Pinelawn Rd Ste 120s (11747-3252)
PHONE...................................937 221-1303
Bob Paradise, *Branch Mgr*
EMP: 10
SALES (corp-wide): 4.3B **Privately Held**
WEB: www.stdreg.com
SIC: 2761 Manifold business forms
HQ: Taylor Communications, Inc.
   4205 S 96th St
   Omaha NE 68127
   402 898-6200

(G-8389)
TECH SOFTWARE LLC
Also Called: BEC Acquisition Co
270 Spagnoli Rd Ste 102 (11747-3515)
PHONE...................................516 986-3050
Walden Leverich,
EMP: 6
SALES (est): 342K **Privately Held**
SIC: 7372 Prepackaged software

(G-8390)
TEL TECH INTERNATIONAL
200 Broadhollow Rd # 207 (11747-4846)
PHONE...................................516 393-5174
Donald Wuerfl, *Manager*
EMP: 40
SALES (est): 1.1MM **Privately Held**
SIC: 7372 Prepackaged software

(G-8391)
TOPTEC PRODUCTS LLC
1225 Walt Whitman Rd (11747-3010)
PHONE...................................631 421-9800
John Ciniglio, *President*
EMP: 15
SALES (est): 1.4MM **Privately Held**
SIC: 2394 Tents: made from purchased materials

(G-8392)
VINDAGRA USA INCORPORATED
1121 Walt Whitman Rd (11747-3083)
PHONE...................................516 605-1960
Karen McMahon, *President*
Steve Kunz, *Sales Mgr*
▲ EMP: 5 EST: 2010
SALES: 1MM **Privately Held**
SIC: 2084 Wines, brandy & brandy spirits
PA: Vindagra Usa Inc.
   433 Plaza Real Ste 275
   Boca Raton FL 33432

(G-8393)
XEROX CORPORATION
155 Pinelawn Rd Ste 200n (11747-3248)
PHONE...................................516 677-1500
Donna Dunlap, *Manager*
EMP: 78
SALES (corp-wide): 10.7B **Publicly Held**
SIC: 3577 Computer peripheral equipment
PA: Xerox Corporation
   201 Merritt 7
   Norwalk CT 06851
   203 968-3000

Memphis
Onondaga County

(G-8394)
MATTESSICH IRON LLC
1484 New State Route 31 (13112-8719)
PHONE...................................315 409-8496
Michael Mattessich,
EMP: 5 EST: 2010
SQ FT: 4,000
SALES: 500K **Privately Held**
SIC: 3462 Iron & steel forgings

Menands
Albany County

(G-8395)
A M & J DIGITAL
800 N Pearl St Ste 5 (12204-1893)
PHONE...................................518 434-2579
Alan Brand, *Accounts Mgr*
Lori Squadere,
Beth Cipperly, *Graphic Designe*
Laura Golon, *Graphic Designe*
EMP: 8
SALES (est): 1MM **Privately Held**
SIC: 2759 Advertising literature: printing

(G-8396)
ACKROYD METAL FABRICATORS INC
966 Broadway Ste 2 (12204-2521)
PHONE...................................518 434-1281
Fax: 518 434-8232
Paul Zabinski, *President*
Bill White, *Controller*
EMP: 12
SQ FT: 40,000
SALES: 1.5MM **Privately Held**
SIC: 3441 Fabricated structural metal

(G-8397)
ALBANY INTERNATIONAL CORP
Appleton Wire Division
1373 Broadway (12204-2697)
PHONE...................................518 445-2230
Fax: 518 445-2265
Heather Drislane, *Vice Pres*
Tom Rice, *Vice Pres*
Charles J Silva Jr, *Vice Pres*
Chris Spraggins, *Vice Pres*
Norman Fugate, *Opers Mgr*
EMP: 150
SALES (corp-wide): 779.8MM **Publicly Held**
WEB: www.albint.com
SIC: 2621 2296 Paper mills; tire cord & fabrics
PA: Albany International Corp.
   216 Airport Dr
   Rochester NH 03867
   603 330-5850

(G-8398)
ALBANY INTERNATIONAL CORP
Dryer Fabrics Division
1373 Broadway (12204-2697)
P.O. Box 1907, Albany (12201-1907)
PHONE...................................518 447-6400
Al Drinkwater, *Manager*
Alan Perfect, *Administration*
EMP: 100
SALES (corp-wide): 779.8MM **Publicly Held**
WEB: www.albint.com
SIC: 2672 Cloth lined paper: made from purchased paper
PA: Albany International Corp.
   216 Airport Dr
   Rochester NH 03867
   603 330-5850

(G-8399)
ARCADIA MFG GROUP INC
1032 Broadway (12204-2506)
PHONE...................................518 434-6213
Fax: 518 434-2527
William T Sumner, *Ch of Bd*
EMP: 6
SALES (corp-wide): 10.8MM **Privately Held**
SIC: 3498 3446 3444 3999 Fabricated pipe & fittings; ornamental metalwork; sheet metalwork; cigar lighters, except precious metal
PA: Arcadia Manufacturing Group, Inc.
   80 Cohoes Ave
   Green Island NY 12183
   518 434-6213

(G-8400)
ATLANTIC STATES DISTRIBUTING
Also Called: Atlantic States Kitchens Baths
1325 Broadway (12204-2652)
PHONE...................................518 427-6364
Fax: 518 426-8753
Philip Crane, *President*
James Flood, *Vice Pres*
Joey Flood, *VP Finance*
Jamie Flood, *Sales Mgr*
EMP: 8 EST: 1959
SALES (est): 1.6MM **Privately Held**
WEB: www.atlanticstateskitchens.com
SIC: 2434 Wood kitchen cabinets

(G-8401)
BLASCH PRECISION CERAMICS INC (PA)
580 Broadway Ste 1 (12204-2896)
PHONE...................................518 436-1263
Fax: 518 436-0098
Robert A Baker, *Ch of Bd*
David W Bobrek, *Ch of Bd*
Werner Steinheimer, *Principal*
John Parrish, *Exec VP*
William Johnson, *Vice Pres*
▲ EMP: 100

Menands - Albany County (G-8402)

SALES (est): 14.4MM Privately Held
WEB: www.powermaterials.com
SIC: 3297 Graphite refractories: carbon bond or ceramic bond

(G-8402)
DYNASTY CHEMICAL CORP
444 N Pearl St (12204-1511)
PHONE 518 463-1146
Fax: 518 463-3684
Jane Waldman, *President*
Mel R Waldman, *Vice Pres*
Birdus Waldman, *Sales Mgr*
Tabor Waldman, *Mktg Dir*
Chris Babie, *Manager*
▲ EMP: 48
SQ FT: 109,000
SALES (est): 14.8MM Privately Held
SIC: 2819 5169 Industrial inorganic chemicals; industrial chemicals

(G-8403)
FRAMES PLUS INC
991 Broadway Ste 208 (12204-2539)
PHONE 518 462-1842
Fax: 518 426-0858
Todd Richless, *President*
Brian Richless, *Vice Pres*
EMP: 18
SQ FT: 15,000
SALES (est): 1.7MM Privately Held
WEB: www.framesplusinc.com
SIC: 3952 Frames for artists' canvases

(G-8404)
GEROME TECHNOLOGIES INC
85 Broadway Ste 1 (12204-2791)
PHONE 518 463-1324
Fax: 518 689-2337
Mark Smisloff, *President*
Julie Ferraro, *Manager*
Katie Whalen, *Manager*
▲ EMP: 54
SQ FT: 54,000
SALES (est): 17.7MM Privately Held
SIC: 3644 3699 7539 Insulators & insulation materials, electrical; electrical equipment & supplies; electrical services

(G-8405)
LEXIS PUBLISHING
Also Called: Lexis Nexis Mathew Bender
1275 Broadway (12204-2638)
PHONE 518 487-3000
Fax: 518 487-3083
Lou Androzzi, *President*
Robert Wood, *Vice Pres*
Mark E Howe, *Human Res Dir*
Daniel Green, *Manager*
Nick Longinow, *Manager*
EMP: 113
SALES (est): 8.9MM Privately Held
SIC: 2731 Book publishing

(G-8406)
MCALLISTERS PRECISION WLDG INC
Also Called: Precision Co.
47 Broadway (12204-2701)
PHONE 518 221-3455
April McCallister, *President*
Jason McCallister, *Vice Pres*
EMP: 15
SQ FT: 12,000
SALES (est): 1.2MM Privately Held
SIC: 3446 3548 Fences or posts, ornamental iron or steel; welding & cutting apparatus & accessories

(G-8407)
MCCARTHY TIRE SVC CO NY INC
Also Called: McCarthy Tire and Auto Ctr
980 Broadway (12204-2504)
PHONE 518 449-5185
Fax: 518 434-2354
Rick Beckman, *Principal*
EMP: 15
SQ FT: 7,140
SALES (corp-wide): 232MM Privately Held
SIC: 3011 Automobile tires, pneumatic
HQ: Mccarthy Tire Service Company Of New York, Inc.
340 Kidder St
Wilkes Barre PA 18702

(G-8408)
MIDLAND FARMS INC (PA)
375 Broadway (12204-2708)
PHONE 518 436-7038
Demetrios E Haseotes, *CEO*
Bob Walton, *Manager*
EMP: 51
SALES (est): 14.5MM Privately Held
WEB: www.midlandfarms.com
SIC: 2026 Milk processing (pasteurizing, homogenizing, bottling)

(G-8409)
NEW YORK LEGAL PUBLISHING
120 Broadway Ste 1a (12204-2722)
PHONE 518 459-1100
Ernest Barvoets, *President*
Edward M Neiles Jr, *Vice Pres*
Suzanne Barvoets, *Sales Staff*
EMP: 7
SALES (est): 1.2MM Privately Held
WEB: www.nylp.com
SIC: 2741 2759 2731 Miscellaneous publishing; commercial printing; book publishing

(G-8410)
SIMMONS MACHINE TOOL CORP (PA)
Also Called: Nsh
1700 Broadway (12204-2701)
PHONE 518 462-5431
Fax: 518 462-0371
John O Naumann, *CEO*
Hans J Naumann, *Ch of Bd*
David William Davis, *President*
Roger Collen, *Vice Pres*
Daniel T Menoncin, *Project Mgr*
▲ EMP: 104
SQ FT: 145,000
SALES (est): 19.3MM Privately Held
WEB: www.smtgroup.com
SIC: 3541 5084 Machine tools, metal cutting type; industrial machinery & equipment

(G-8411)
T LEMME MECHANICAL INC
Selby & Smith
1074 Broadway (12204-2507)
PHONE 518 436-4136
Bill Mattfeld, *Opers Mgr*
EMP: 40 Privately Held
SIC: 3444 Sheet metalwork
PA: T. Lemme Mechanical, Inc.
67 Erie Blvd
Menands NY 12204

Mendon
Monroe County

(G-8412)
BARS PRECISION INC
5 Charleston Dr (14506-9759)
PHONE 585 742-6380
Robert Born, *President*
Marc Ramsperger, *Manager*
Jana Born, *Admin Sec*
EMP: 11
SALES (est): 1.5MM Privately Held
WEB: www.toolingonline.com
SIC: 3542 Presses: forming, stamping, punching, sizing (machine tools)

(G-8413)
N Y B P INC
Also Called: New York Blood Pressure
1355 Pittsford Mendon Rd (14506-9733)
P.O. Box 471 (14506-0471)
PHONE 585 624-2541
Gregory J Sarkis, *President*
EMP: 3
SALES: 1MM Privately Held
SIC: 3841 Blood pressure apparatus

(G-8414)
SAXBY IMPLEMENT CORP (PA)
Also Called: Kubota Authorized Dealer
180 Mendon Victor Rd (14506)
P.O. Box 333 (14506-0333)
PHONE 585 624-2938
Marvin E Hogan, *President*
Teri H Maxwell, *Vice Pres*
Randall Hogan, *Treasurer*
Joanne Hogan, *Admin Sec*
EMP: 10
SQ FT: 9,400
SALES (est): 1.2MM Privately Held
SIC: 3524 5083 Lawn & garden tractors & equipment; farm & garden machinery

Merrick
Nassau County

(G-8415)
CREATIVE MAGAZINE INC
31 Merrick Ave Ste 60 (11566-3499)
PHONE 516 378-0800
David Flasterstein, *President*
Lisa Flasterstein, *Assoc Editor*
EMP: 5 EST: 2008
SALES (est): 76K Privately Held
SIC: 2721 Periodicals: publishing only

(G-8416)
D G M GRAPHICS INC
Also Called: Printing Emporium
55 Merrick Ave (11566-3415)
P.O. Box 121 (11566-0121)
PHONE 516 223-2220
Fax: 516 223-1200
Douglas G Mills, *President*
EMP: 11
SQ FT: 3,300
SALES (est): 1.1MM Privately Held
WEB: www.printingemporium.com
SIC: 2752 2791 2789 2759 Photo-offset printing; typesetting; bookbinding & related work; commercial printing

(G-8417)
E J MANUFACTURING INC
2935 Charlotte Dr (11566-5301)
PHONE 516 313-9380
Elliot S Negrin, *President*
Jeff Negrin, *Vice Pres*
▲ EMP: 2
SQ FT: 8,000
SALES: 3MM Privately Held
SIC: 2326 Men's & boys' work clothing

(G-8418)
FIORENTINA LLC
1519 Hendrickson Ave (11566-2120)
PHONE 516 208-5448
Fax: 631 423-3514
Brett Carter, *Mng Member*
Anna Carter,
▲ EMP: 6
SQ FT: 800
SALES (est): 678.7K Privately Held
SIC: 3199 Equestrian related leather articles

(G-8419)
FUEL SOUL
188 Merrick Rd (11566-4532)
PHONE 516 379-0810
Gregory Fine, *CEO*
EMP: 5
SALES (est): 392.7K Privately Held
SIC: 2869 Fuels

(G-8420)
JON LYN INK INC
Also Called: Minuteman Press
255 Sunrise Hwy Ste 1 (11566-3700)
PHONE 516 546-2312
Fax: 516 623-0870
John Jutt, *President*
EMP: 6
SQ FT: 1,200
SALES (est): 710.3K Privately Held
SIC: 2752 7334 2759 2791 Commercial printing, lithographic; photocopying & duplicating services; invitation & stationery printing & engraving; typesetting; bookbinding & related work

(G-8421)
L I C SCREEN PRINTING INC
2949 Joyce Ln (11566-5209)
PHONE 516 546-7289
Edward Rosenblum, *President*
EMP: 25
SQ FT: 15,000
SALES (est): 1.9MM Privately Held
WEB: www.licscreenprinting.com
SIC: 2759 3089 3993 2396 Letterpress & screen printing; screen printing; plastic processing; signs & advertising specialties; automotive & apparel trimmings

(G-8422)
LEADER PRINTING INC
Also Called: Print-O-Rama Copy Center
2272 Babylon Tpke (11566-3829)
PHONE 516 546-1544
Steve Leads, *President*
EMP: 10
SALES (est): 735K Privately Held
SIC: 2752 7334 Photo-offset printing; photocopying & duplicating services

(G-8423)
LEGAL STRATEGIES INC
1795 Harvard Ave (11566-4413)
PHONE 516 377-3940
Steven Mitchell Sack, *President*
EMP: 7
SALES (est): 519.4K Privately Held
SIC: 2731 Book publishing

(G-8424)
MEGA SOURCING INC (PA)
Also Called: Mega Apparel International
1929 Edward Ln (11566-4922)
PHONE 646 682-0304
Mandy Sciortino, *President*
▲ EMP: 3 EST: 2006
SALES: 1MM Privately Held
SIC: 2331 2321 5621 5611 Women's & misses' blouses & shirts; men's & boys' furnishings; women's clothing stores; ready-to-wear apparel, women's; men's & boys' clothing stores

(G-8425)
NORTHEAST WINDOWS USA INC
1 Kees Pl (11566-3642)
P.O. Box 159 (11566-0159)
PHONE 516 378-6577
Jill Kaiserman, *President*
Jeffrey Kaiserman, *Vice Pres*
Steven Kaiserman, *Sales Dir*
Phil Reid, *Sales Executive*
▲ EMP: 48
SQ FT: 35,000
SALES (est): 6.6MM Privately Held
SIC: 3089 Window frames & sash, plastic

(G-8426)
PRESTIGE ENVELOPE & LITHOGRAPH
Also Called: Prestige Litho & Graphics
1745 Merrick Ave Ste 2 (11566-2700)
PHONE 631 521-7043
Fax: 631 434-3319
Gary Gingo, *CEO*
Angel Irimia, *President*
Gregory Catanese, *Office Mgr*
Joe Nieves, *Admin Sec*
EMP: 12
SQ FT: 30,000
SALES (est): 1.9MM Privately Held
WEB: www.prestigelg.com
SIC: 2752 2791 2789 7389 Commercial printing, lithographic; typesetting; bookbinding & related work; printing broker; envelopes

(G-8427)
QUALITY LINEALS USA INC (PA)
Also Called: Quality Fence
1 Kees Pl (11566-3642)
P.O. Box 159 (11566-0159)
PHONE 516 378-6577
Fax: 516 546-0205
Jill Kaiserman, *President*
Jeffrey Kaiserman, *Vice Pres*
EMP: 2
SALES (est): 7.5MM Privately Held
SIC: 3089 Billfold inserts, plastic

(G-8428)
SOURCE ONE PROMOTIONAL PRODUCT
2024 Brian Dr (11566-1731)
PHONE 516 208-6996
Ken Greenfield, *President*

GEOGRAPHIC SECTION

Middleport - Niagara County (G-8454)

EMP: 1
SALES: 1.5MM Privately Held
SIC: 2752 Promotional printing, lithographic

(G-8429)
WORLDWIDE TICKET CRAFT
1390 Jerusalem Ave (11566-1364)
PHONE...................516 538-6200
Fax: 516 538-4860
Eric Colts, President
EMP: 60
SALES (est): 4.4MM Privately Held
WEB: www.ticketcraft.com
SIC: 2752 2791 2759 Tickets, lithographed; typesetting; commercial printing

Mexico
Oswego County

(G-8430)
GRANDMA BROWNS BEANS INC
5837 Scenic Ave (13114-3481)
P.O. Box 230 (13114-0230)
PHONE...................315 963-7221
Fax: 315 963-4072
Sandra L Brown, President
EMP: 15 EST: 1938
SQ FT: 35,000
SALES: 19.7K Privately Held
SIC: 2032 Canned specialties

Middle Granville
Washington County

(G-8431)
EVERGREEN SLATE COMPANY INC
2027 County Route 23 (12849-4901)
P.O. Box 248, Granville (12832-0248)
PHONE...................518 642-2530
Fax: 518 642-9313
Fred Whitridge, President
Shannon Humphrey, General Mgr
Ray Loomis, Vice Pres
Jody Oakman, Credit Mgr
Jan Edwards, Sales Staff
◆ EMP: 70 EST: 1916
SQ FT: 1,000
SALES (est): 10.7MM Privately Held
WEB: www.evergreenslate.com
SIC: 3281 Slate products

(G-8432)
HILLTOP SLATE INC
Rr 22 Box A (12849)
PHONE...................518 642-1453
Fax: 518 642-1220
David Thomas, President
Adrian Curtis, Div Sub Head
John J Conlon, Sales Staff
David Lundy, Manager
▲ EMP: 30 EST: 1948
SQ FT: 50,000
SALES (est): 5.5MM Privately Held
WEB: www.hilltopslate.com
SIC: 1411 Slate, dimension-quarrying

(G-8433)
K-D STONE INC
Rr 22 (12849)
PHONE...................518 642-2082
Nelson Dunster, President
Kimberly Dunster, Vice Pres
EMP: 12
SALES (est): 1.8MM Privately Held
SIC: 2952 Roof cement: asphalt, fibrous or plastic

(G-8434)
SHELDON SLATE PRODUCTS CO INC
Fox Rd (12849)
PHONE...................518 642-1280
Fax: 518 642-9085
John Tatko Jr, President
Beverly Tatko, Manager
EMP: 50 EST: 1924
SQ FT: 1,200

SALES (est): 5.3MM Privately Held
SIC: 3281 2952 2951 Slate products; asphalt felts & coatings; asphalt paving mixtures & blocks

(G-8435)
VERMONT MULTICOLOR SLATE
146 State Route 22a (12849-5431)
P.O. Box 202 (12849-0202)
PHONE...................518 642-2400
William Enny, President
Renold Tang, CFO
EMP: 9
SQ FT: 10,000
SALES (est): 406.5K Privately Held
SIC: 1411 Slate, dimension-quarrying

(G-8436)
VERMONT NATURAL STONEWORKS
Also Called: Ritchie Brothers Slate Co
146 State Route 22a (12849)
PHONE...................518 642-2460
Fax: 518 642-9327
Bonnie Pratt, President
EMP: 30
SALES (est): 2.2MM Privately Held
SIC: 3281 Slate products

Middle Grove
Saratoga County

(G-8437)
CUCCIO-ZANETTI INC
Also Called: Zanetti Millwork
455 Middle Grove Rd (12850-1107)
PHONE...................518 587-1363
John Zanetti, President
EMP: 8
SQ FT: 9,000
SALES (est): 1MM Privately Held
SIC: 2431 Millwork

Middle Island
Suffolk County

(G-8438)
AFCO PRECAST SALES CORP
Also Called: Old Castle Precast
114 Rocky Point Rd (11953-1216)
PHONE...................631 924-7114
Fax: 631 924-2243
Richard Affenita, Ch of Bd
Peter Kaplin, President
Robert Affenita, Treasurer
Jackie Densing, Accountant
Marion Classi, Director
▲ EMP: 75
SQ FT: 1,560
SALES (est): 10.7MM Privately Held
SIC: 3272 5211 Concrete products, precast; masonry materials & supplies

(G-8439)
ALLEY CAT SIGNS INC
506 Middle Country Rd (11953-2521)
PHONE...................631 924-7446
Fax: 631 924-9772
Albert Borsella, President
EMP: 12
SALES (est): 980K Privately Held
SIC: 3993 1799 5999 Signs & advertising specialties; sign installation & maintenance; awnings

(G-8440)
MID ENTERPRISE INC
809 Middle Country Rd (11953-2511)
PHONE...................631 924-3933
Shahid Ali Khan, Principal
EMP: 5
SALES (est): 541.5K Privately Held
SIC: 3578 Automatic teller machines (ATM)

(G-8441)
SIMON DEFENSE INC
1533 Rocky Point Rd (11953-1259)
PHONE...................516 217-6000
CJ Calleson, Director
EMP: 7 EST: 2014

SQ FT: 2,000
SALES (est): 338.2K Privately Held
SIC: 3452 Bolts, metal

Middle Village
Queens County

(G-8442)
ACCURATE SPECIALTY METAL FABRI
6420 Admiral Ave (11379-1614)
PHONE...................718 418-6895
Fax: 718 456-4567
Ronald Palmerick, Ch of Bd
Sebastian Loaysa, General Mgr
Richard Veltri, Exec VP
Sebastian Loayas, Office Mgr
Gene Griffin, Manager
EMP: 35
SQ FT: 30,000
SALES (est): 7.2MM
SALES (corp-wide): 51.2MM Privately Held
WEB: www.asm-mech.com
SIC: 3444 Ducts, sheet metal
PA: Aabco Sheet Metal Co., Inc.
47 40 Metropolitan Ave
Ridgewood NY 11385
718 821-1166

(G-8443)
AGLIKA TRADE LLC
5905 74th St (11379-5216)
PHONE...................727 424-1944
Maya Petkova,
EMP: 10
SALES (est): 599.5K Privately Held
SIC: 3552 Textile machinery

(G-8444)
GOLDMONT ENTERPRISES INC
Also Called: Superior Model Form Co
7603 Caldwell Ave (11379-5233)
PHONE...................212 947-3633
Vito Montalto, President
EMP: 15 EST: 1940
SQ FT: 7,000
SALES: 1MM Privately Held
WEB: www.superiormodel.com
SIC: 3999 Forms: display, dress & show

(G-8445)
J M R PLASTICS CORPORATION
5847 78th St (11379-5305)
PHONE...................718 898-9825
Fax: 718 898-7967
John Daidone, President
Selina Daidone, Corp Secy
EMP: 8
SQ FT: 10,000
SALES: 2MM Privately Held
SIC: 3089 Plastic kitchenware, tableware & houseware

(G-8446)
JONATHAN DAVID PUBLISHERS INC
6822 Eliot Ave (11379-1131)
PHONE...................718 456-8611
Fax: 718 894-2818
Alfred J Kolatch, President
Thelma Kolatch, Corp Secy
Marvin Sekler, Vice Pres
Carol Zelezny, Accounting Mgr
▲ EMP: 10 EST: 1949
SQ FT: 2,400
SALES (est): 860K Privately Held
WEB: www.jdbooks.com
SIC: 2731 Books: publishing only

(G-8447)
JUNIPER ELBOW CO INC (PA)
Also Called: Juniper Industries
7215 Metropolitan Ave (11379-2198)
P.O. Box 148 (11379-0148)
PHONE...................718 326-2546
Fax: 718 326-3786
Jesse L Wiener, CEO
Marvin Jacobs, General Mgr
Celia Wiener, Vice Pres
Elliot Wiener, Vice Pres
▲ EMP: 185 EST: 1929
SQ FT: 100,000

SALES (est): 25.5MM Privately Held
WEB: www.juniperind.com
SIC: 3444 3498 3433 3312 Elbows, for air ducts, stovepipes, etc.: sheet metal; ventilators, sheet metal; metal ventilating equipment; fabricated pipe & fittings; heating equipment, except electric; blast furnaces & steel mills

(G-8448)
JUNIPER INDUSTRIES FLORIDA INC
7215 Metropolitan Ave (11379-2107)
PHONE...................718 326-2546
▲ EMP: 5
SALES (est): 384.6K Privately Held
SIC: 3498 Mfg Fabricated Pipe/Fittings

(G-8449)
METRO KNITTING CORP
6325 70th St (11379-1729)
PHONE...................718 894-0765
Fax: 718 597-7594
Illija Jaksic, President
EMP: 10
SQ FT: 14,000
SALES (est): 1.3MM Privately Held
SIC: 2253 Knit outerwear mills

(G-8450)
PATDAN FUEL CORPORATION
7803 68th Rd (11379-2836)
PHONE...................718 326-3668
EMP: 6
SALES (est): 743.4K Privately Held
SIC: 2869 Fuels

(G-8451)
WETHERALL CONTRACTING NY INC
8312 Penelope Ave Ste 101 (11379-2321)
PHONE...................718 894-7011
Bryan Wetherall, President
EMP: 5
SALES (est): 695.2K Privately Held
SIC: 2323 Men's & boys' neckwear

Middleburgh
Schoharie County

(G-8452)
DR REDDYS LABORATORIES NY INC
1974 State Route 145 (12122-5315)
PHONE...................518 827-7702
Alok Sonig, President
Swaninathan Chandrasekaran, Corp Secy
Sunil Kumar Chebrolu, Finance
Gv Prasad, Director
Satish Reddy, Director
EMP: 30
SALES (est): 3MM Privately Held
SIC: 2834 Pharmaceutical preparations
HQ: Dr. Reddy's Laboratories, Inc.
107 College Rd E Ste 100
Princeton NJ 08540

(G-8453)
URREY LUMBER
663 Clauverwie Rd (12122-3411)
PHONE...................518 827-4851
Fax: 518 827-4859
Allan Urrey, Partner
Jeff Urrey, Partner
Toni Urrey, Partner
EMP: 9
SALES: 2.1MM Privately Held
SIC: 2421 Sawmills & planing mills, general

Middleport
Niagara County

(G-8454)
BIRCH MACHINE & TOOL INC
80 Telegraph Rd (14105-9638)
PHONE...................716 735-9802
Fax: 716 438-0131
Jerry Stadelman, President
Mary Stadelman, Vice Pres

EMP: 7
SQ FT: 1,500
SALES (est): 500K Privately Held
SIC: 3599 Machine & other job shop work; machine shop, jobbing & repair

(G-8455)
FMC CORPORATION
Also Called: F M C Aricultural Chem Group
100 Niagara St (14105-1398)
PHONE.................................716 735-3761
Fax: 585 735-7804
Stewart Throop, *Plant Mgr*
John Velletta, *Engineer*
A M Hahn, *Finance*
Roger L Krough, *Branch Mgr*
Harry E Bacon Jr, *Manager*
EMP: 50
SALES (corp-wide): 3.2B Publicly Held
WEB: www.fmc.com
SIC: 2879 2819 Agricultural chemicals; industrial inorganic chemicals
PA: Fmc Corporation
2929 Walnut St
Philadelphia PA 19104
215 299-6668

(G-8456)
PERFORMANCE MFG INC
80 Telegraph Rd (14105-9638)
PHONE.................................716 735-3500
Jody P Herriven, *President*
Tim Worth, *Vice Pres*
EMP: 15
SALES (est): 2.2MM Privately Held
WEB: www.pmikartparts.com
SIC: 3599 Machine shop, jobbing & repair

(G-8457)
SIGMAMOTOR INC
3 N Main St (14105-1005)
P.O. Box 298 (14105-0298)
PHONE.................................716 735-3115
Fax: 716 735-3166
Donald Heschke Jr, *President*
Shari Heschke, *Corp Secy*
EMP: 22 EST: 1951
SQ FT: 6,500
SALES: 6MM Privately Held
SIC: 3599 3494 Machine shop, jobbing & repair; valves & pipe fittings

Middletown
Orange County

(G-8458)
209 DISCOUNT OIL
10 Sands Station Rd (10940-4415)
PHONE.................................845 386-2090
Steve Cortese, *Principal*
EMP: 20
SALES (est): 1.6MM Privately Held
SIC: 2911 Oils, fuel

(G-8459)
ADVANCED ENTERPRISES INC
Also Called: Wonder Products
366 Highland Ave Ext (10940-4454)
PHONE.................................845 342-1009
Eugene Polanish, *President*
Christian Al, *Principal*
Colin Dixon, *Vice Pres*
▲ EMP: 10
SQ FT: 100
SALES (est): 1.5MM Privately Held
SIC: 3842 Cotton & cotton applicators

(G-8460)
ARCHITECTURAL ENHANCEMENTS INC
135 Crotty Rd (10941-4070)
P.O. Box 4680 (10941-8680)
PHONE.................................845 343-9663
Fax: 845 343-0225
Philip Cohen, *President*
Chaim Cohen, *Exec VP*
EMP: 10 EST: 1962
SQ FT: 31,000
SALES (est): 1.6MM Privately Held
SIC: 2499 Decorative wood & woodwork

(G-8461)
BALL METAL BEVERAGE CONT CORP
Also Called: Ball Metal Beverage Cont Div
95 Ballard Rd (10941-3013)
PHONE.................................845 692-3800
Fax: 845 692-3881
Terree Angerame, *Principal*
Robert Chapin, *Principal*
Noreen Dellay, *Principal*
Rob Lauterbach, *Vice Pres*
Rich Bailey, *Safety Mgr*
EMP: 175
SALES (corp-wide): 9B Publicly Held
SIC: 3411 Aluminum cans
HQ: Ball Metal Beverage Container Corp.
9300 W 108th Cir
Westminster CO 80021

(G-8462)
BRAGA WOODWORKS
19 Montgomery St (10940-5115)
PHONE.................................845 342-4636
Leo Braga, *Owner*
EMP: 5
SALES (est): 410.6K Privately Held
SIC: 2431 Millwork

(G-8463)
BRAIDED OAK SPIRITS LLC
12 Roberts St (10940-5007)
P.O. Box 2124 (10940-0949)
PHONE.................................845 381-1525
Peter J Matos,
Peter Matos,
EMP: 17
SALES: 5.2MM Privately Held
SIC: 2085 Distilled & blended liquors

(G-8464)
CHROMALLOY GAS TURBINE LLC
Also Called: Chromalloy Middletown
105 Tower Dr (10941-2034)
PHONE.................................845 692-8912
Fax: 845 692-8992
Mark Levine, *Purch Mgr*
Dean Hoffman, *Engineer*
Scott Irwin, *Engineer*
Judith Quinn, *Engineer*
Matt Wilson, *Branch Mgr*
EMP: 28
SALES (corp-wide): 2.2B Publicly Held
WEB: www.chromalloysatx.com
SIC: 3479 3724 Painting, coating & hot dipping; aircraft engines & engine parts
HQ: Chromalloy Gas Turbine Llc
3999 Rca Blvd
Palm Beach Gardens FL 33410
561 935-3571

(G-8465)
CLASSIC HOSIERY INC
33 Mulberry St Ste 4 (10940-6359)
PHONE.................................845 342-6661
Fax: 845 342-2023
Tuvia Brach, *President*
▲ EMP: 35 EST: 1980
SQ FT: 18,000
SALES (est): 4.5MM Privately Held
SIC: 2251 Women's hosiery, except socks; panty hose; tights, women's

(G-8466)
COMMERCIAL COMMUNICATIONS LLC
Also Called: Msdivisions
14 Montgomery St (10940-5116)
PHONE.................................845 343-9078
Fax: 845 344-2175
Dee Pirtz, *Office Mgr*
Steven Rosenblatt,
EMP: 6
SALES (est): 881.8K Privately Held
WEB: www.msdspring.com
SIC: 3495 Wire springs

(G-8467)
COUNTY DRAPERIES INC
64 Genung St (10940-5317)
PHONE.................................845 342-9009
Fax: 845 342-1530
Sara Markowitz, *CEO*
Carl Markowitz, *President*
David C Markowitz, *Vice Pres*
Devi Heyer, *Project Mgr*
Jeffrey Remin, *Project Mgr*
◆ EMP: 45
SQ FT: 50,000
SALES (est): 9.3MM Privately Held
WEB: www.drape.com
SIC: 2391 2392 Draperies, plastic & textile: from purchased materials; curtains, window: made from purchased materials; bedspreads & bed sets: made from purchased materials

(G-8468)
D & W DESIGN INC (PA)
62 Industrial Pl (10940-3609)
PHONE.................................845 343-3366
Fax: 845 534-7568
Mariam Weiss, *President*
David Weiss, *Vice Pres*
Simon Kraus, *Manager*
Mike Toplamos, *Admin Sec*
▲ EMP: 26
SQ FT: 50,000
SALES: 3MM Privately Held
WEB: www.dustinwdesign.com
SIC: 2511 2514 5712 Wood household furniture; metal household furniture; furniture stores

(G-8469)
DELFORD INDUSTRIES INC
82 Washington St 84 (10940-4268)
P.O. Box 863 (10940-0863)
PHONE.................................845 342-3901
Fax: 845 342-3168
Robert L Reach Jr, *President*
Eric McCaffrey, *Opers Staff*
Richard Reynolds, *Human Resources*
Allison Reach, *Sales Staff*
EMP: 80 EST: 1983
SQ FT: 55,000
SALES: 2MM Privately Held
WEB: www.delford-industries.com
SIC: 3061 Mechanical rubber goods

(G-8470)
E TETZ & SONS INC (PA)
130 Crotty Rd (10941-4059)
PHONE.................................845 692-4486
Edward Tetz Jr, *Ch of Bd*
Corinne Tetz, *Bookkeeper*
Liz Raffa, *Manager*
Bob Weber, *Info Tech Mgr*
Denise Tetz, *Admin Sec*
EMP: 55
SQ FT: 3,000
SALES (est): 22.8MM Privately Held
WEB: www.etetz-sons.com
SIC: 3273 1442 Ready-mixed concrete; construction sand & gravel

(G-8471)
EAD CASES
43 Smith St (10940-3710)
P.O. Box 957 (10940-0957)
PHONE.................................845 343-2111
Julio Diaz, *President*
EMP: 10
SALES (est): 975.1K Privately Held
SIC: 3161 Cases, carrying

(G-8472)
ECO-BAT AMERICA LLC
Also Called: RSR
65 Ballard Rd (10941-3013)
PHONE.................................845 692-4414
Dan Demercurio, *Branch Mgr*
Steve Brooks, *Maintence Staff*
EMP: 183
SQ FT: 20,000
SALES (corp-wide): 6.3MM Privately Held
SIC: 3356 3339 3341 Nonferrous rolling & drawing; precious metals; lead smelting & refining (secondary)
HQ: Eco-Bat America Llc
2777 N Stemmons Fwy
Dallas TX 75207
214 688-4000

(G-8473)
EQUILIBRIUM BREWERY LLC
22 Henry St (10940-5709)
PHONE.................................201 245-0292
Ricardo Petroni, *CEO*
Peter Oates, *COO*
EMP: 5
SQ FT: 6,800
SALES: 700K Privately Held
SIC: 2082 Malt beverages

(G-8474)
FAIRBANKS MFG LLC
79 Industrial Pl (10940-3608)
PHONE.................................845 341-0002
Fax: 845 341-1606
Jared Swift, *General Mgr*
Michael Ruppel, *CFO*
Joyce Pitt, *Financial Exec*
Zeke Alenick, *Mng Member*
▲ EMP: 145 EST: 2011
SQ FT: 100,000
SALES: 34.5MM Privately Held
SIC: 2064 Candy & other confectionery products

(G-8475)
FUEL DATA SYSTEMS INC
772 Greenville Tpke (10940-7125)
PHONE.................................800 447-7870
Steve Michalek, *President*
EMP: 6 EST: 1989
SALES (est): 457.1K Privately Held
WEB: www.fueldatasystems.com
SIC: 7372 7371 Prepackaged software; custom computer programming services

(G-8476)
GENPAK LLC
Republic Plz (10940)
PHONE.................................845 343-7971
Fax: 845 343-0450
Betty Hager, *Opers-Prdtn-Mfg*
Ed Rider, *Engr R&D*
Jeff Cole, *Marketing Mgr*
Bill Gentes, *Facilities*
EMP: 200
SQ FT: 150,000
SALES (corp-wide): 12B Privately Held
WEB: www.genpak.com
SIC: 3089 5046 Plastic processing; commercial cooking & food service equipment
HQ: Genpak Llc
68 Warren St
Glens Falls NY 12801
518 798-9511

(G-8477)
GOLUB CORPORATION
Also Called: Price Chopper Pharmacy
511 Schutt Road Ext (10940-2569)
PHONE.................................845 344-0327
Fax: 845 344-0319
Jacky Gessner, *Co-Mgr*
EMP: 99
SALES (corp-wide): 3.4B Privately Held
SIC: 3751 Motorcycles & related parts
PA: The Golub Corporation
461 Nott St
Schenectady NY 12308
518 355-5000

(G-8478)
HISTORCAL SOC OF MDDLTOWN WALK
25 East Ave (10940-5818)
P.O. Box 34 (10940-0034)
PHONE.................................845 342-0941
Marvin H Cohen, *President*
Nicholas Cscili, *Vice Pres*
Joanne Norbury, *Treasurer*
Ann Vail, *Director*
Francis Cleary, *Admin Sec*
EMP: 6
SQ FT: 1,974
SALES: 12.6K Privately Held
SIC: 2452 8412 Prefabricated wood buildings; museum

(G-8479)
HONEYWELL INTERNATIONAL INC
13 Bedford Ave (10940-6401)
PHONE.................................845 342-4400
EMP: 673
SALES (corp-wide): 39.3B Publicly Held
SIC: 3724 Aircraft engines & engine parts
PA: Honeywell International Inc.
115 Tabor Rd
Morris Plains NJ 07950
973 455-2000

(G-8480)
LOCAL MEDIA GROUP INC
Orange County Publications
40 Mulberry St (10940-6302)
P.O. Box 2046 (10940-0558)
PHONE..................845 341-1100
Fax: 845 343-0163
Jim Moss, *Publisher*
Barry Lewis, *General Mgr*
Dick Bayne, *Editor*
Marc Davis, *Editor*
Michael Levensohn, *Editor*
EMP: 290
SALES (corp-wide): 1.2B **Publicly Held**
WEB: www.ottaway.com
SIC: 2711 Newspapers, publishing & printing
HQ: Local Media Group, Inc.
40 Mulberry St
Middletown NY 10940
845 341-1100

(G-8481)
LOCAL MEDIA GROUP INC (HQ)
40 Mulberry St (10940-6302)
P.O. Box 580 (10940-0580)
PHONE..................845 341-1100
John Wilcox, *President*
Patrick Purcell, *Chairman*
William T Kennedy, *COO*
Kurt Lozier, *Senior VP*
Patricia Gatto, *Vice Pres*
EMP: 50 **EST:** 1936
SQ FT: 10,000
SALES (est): 358.8MM
SALES (corp-wide): 1.2B **Publicly Held**
WEB: www.ottaway.com
SIC: 2711 7313 Newspapers: publishing only, not printed on site; newspaper advertising representative
PA: New Media Investment Group Inc.
1345 Avenue Of The Americ
New York NY 10105
212 479-3160

(G-8482)
LOCAL MEDIA GROUP INC
Also Called: Times Herald-Record
60 Brookline Ave (10940)
PHONE..................845 341-1100
Andy Mark, *Branch Mgr*
EMP: 68
SALES (corp-wide): 1.2B **Publicly Held**
WEB: www.ottaway.com
SIC: 2711 Commercial printing & newspaper publishing combined
HQ: Local Media Group, Inc.
40 Mulberry St
Middletown NY 10940
845 341-1100

(G-8483)
MANDARIN SOY SAUCE INC
Also Called: Wan Ja Shan
4 Sands Station Rd (10940-4415)
PHONE..................845 343-1505
Fax: 845 343-0731
Michael Wu, *Ch of Bd*
Mike Shapiro, *Vice Pres*
▲ **EMP:** 25 **EST:** 1974
SQ FT: 85,000
SALES (est): 4MM **Privately Held**
WEB: www.wanjashan.com
SIC: 2035 5149 Seasonings & sauces, except tomato & dry; soy sauce; groceries & related products
PA: Wan Ja Shan Brewery Co., Ltd.
5f-6, 9, Dehui St.,
Taipei City TAP
266 180-101

(G-8484)
MEDLINE INDUSTRIES INC
3301 Route 6 (10940-6992)
PHONE..................845 344-3301
George Vargulish, *Surgery Dir*
EMP: 276
SALES (corp-wide): 8B **Privately Held**
SIC: 3842 3841 2326 2392 Surgical appliances & supplies; surgical & medical instruments; men's & boys' work clothing; household furnishings; surgical fabrics, cotton; scrub cloths; surgical equipment & supplies; hospital equipment & supplies; hospital furniture
PA: Medline Industries, Inc.
3 Lakes Dr
Northfield IL 60093
847 949-5500

(G-8485)
MIDDLETOWN PRESS (PA)
20 W Main St 26 (10940-5716)
PHONE..................845 343-1895
Fax: 845 343-1897
Jo Cover, *Owner*
EMP: 5
SQ FT: 2,800
SALES (est): 401.6K **Privately Held**
WEB: www.mtprintandpromote.com
SIC: 2752 7311 7336 5199 Commercial printing, lithographic; advertising agencies; graphic arts & related design; advertising specialties; commercial printing

(G-8486)
MIX N MAC LLC
280 Route 211 E (10940-3109)
PHONE..................845 381-5536
EMP: 5 **EST:** 2011
SALES (est): 413.6K **Privately Held**
SIC: 3273 Ready-mixed concrete

(G-8487)
MONROE CABLE COMPANY INC
14 Commercial Ave (10941-1444)
PHONE..................845 692-2800
Fax: 845 692-8041
Isaac Wieder, *President*
Joseph Ungar, *Controller*
Abraham Wieder, *Consultant*
▲ **EMP:** 104 **EST:** 1978
SQ FT: 95,000
SALES (est): 39.3MM **Privately Held**
SIC: 3357 Shipboard cable, nonferrous; coaxial cable, nonferrous

(G-8488)
NEW DYNAMICS CORPORATION
15 Fortune Rd W (10941-1625)
PHONE..................845 692-0022
Fax: 845 692-2590
James Destefano, *President*
Walter Pawlowski, *Vice Pres*
EMP: 20
SQ FT: 35,000
SALES: 5MM **Privately Held**
WEB: www.newdynamics.net
SIC: 3842 5963 7349 Ear plugs; food services, direct sales; janitorial service, contract basis

(G-8489)
NEW YORK CUTTING & GUMMING CO
265 Ballard Rd (10941-3034)
PHONE..................212 563-4146
Jack Siegel, *President*
Richard Deteresa, *Principal*
Robert Siegel, *Vice Pres*
EMP: 45 **EST:** 1914
SQ FT: 44,000
SALES (est): 4.2MM **Privately Held**
SIC: 3089 2295 2675 2672 Laminating of plastic; laminating of fabrics; die-cut paper & board; coated & laminated paper

(G-8490)
OTTAWAY NEWSPAPERS INC
40 Mulberry St (10940-6302)
PHONE..................845 343-2181
Joe Vanderhoof, *Principal*
Robin Robinson, *Accounting Dir*
Zeke Fleet, *VP Sales*
EMP: 11 **EST:** 2010
SALES (est): 737.7K **Privately Held**
SIC: 2711 Newspapers

(G-8491)
PILLER POWER SYSTEMS INC (DH)
45 Wes Warren Dr (10941-1772)
PHONE..................845 695-6658
Fax: 845 692-0295
Dean Richards, *President*
Jonathan Davis, *Managing Dir*
Mark Nuelle, *Vice Pres*
Charles Daling, *Project Mgr*
John Brotherton, *Safety Mgr*
▲ **EMP:** 40
SQ FT: 20,000
SALES: 65MM
SALES (corp-wide): 949.8MM **Privately Held**
WEB: www.piller.com
SIC: 3699 3612 Electrical equipment & supplies; transformers, except electric
HQ: Piller Group Gmbh
Abgunst 24
Osterode Am Harz 37520
552 231-10

(G-8492)
PRESIDENT CONT GROUP II LLC
Also Called: Manufacturing Facility
290 Ballard Rd (10941-3035)
PHONE..................845 516-1600
Sabrina Washington, *Manager*
EMP: 440
SALES (corp-wide): 10.7MM **Privately Held**
SIC: 2653 Corrugated boxes, partitions, display items, sheets & pad; sheets, corrugated: made from purchased materials; display items, corrugated: made from purchased materials
PA: President Container Group Ii, Llc
200 W Commercial Ave
Moonachie NJ 07074
201 933-7500

(G-8493)
PRINCETON UPHOLSTERY CO INC (PA)
Also Called: Bright Chair Co
51 Railroad Ave (10940-5117)
P.O. Box 269 (10940-0269)
PHONE..................845 343-2196
Fax: 845 343-4958
Stan Gottlieb, *Ch of Bd*
Ross Spasato, *Vice Pres*
Roxanne Beacon, *Human Res Mgr*
Leigh Spence, *Sales Staff*
Jody Gottlieb, *Admin Sec*
◆ **EMP:** 100
SQ FT: 100,000
SALES (est): 12.6MM **Privately Held**
WEB: www.brightchair.com
SIC: 2521 2512 Wood office furniture; upholstered household furniture

(G-8494)
RIJ PHARMACEUTICAL CORPORATION
40 Commercial Ave (10941-1444)
PHONE..................845 692-5799
Fax: 845 692-3023
Hassan Zaidi, *CEO*
Brij Gupta, *President*
Nitin Gupta, *VP Opers*
Jason Nadin, *VP Opers*
Brenda Caputi, *Admin Sec*
EMP: 20
SQ FT: 52,000
SALES (est): 5.3MM **Privately Held**
WEB: www.rijpharm.com
SIC: 2834 Pharmaceutical preparations

(G-8495)
RIMS LIKE NEW INC
507 Union School Rd (10941-5018)
PHONE..................845 537-0396
Manuel P Heredia Jr, *Owner*
EMP: 10
SALES (est): 630K **Privately Held**
SIC: 3479 Painting of metal products

(G-8496)
S R & R INDUSTRIES INC
45 Enterprise Pl (10941-2043)
PHONE..................845 692-8329
Fax: 845 692-8330
Paul Rosanelli, *President*
EMP: 6
SQ FT: 10,000
SALES: 450K **Privately Held**
SIC: 3531 3462 3599 Rollers, sheepsfoot & vibratory; gears, forged steel; machine shop, jobbing & repair

(G-8497)
STAFFORD LABS ORTHOTICS/PROSTH
189 Monhagen Ave (10940-6020)
P.O. Box 1004, Goshen (10924-8004)
PHONE..................845 692-5227
Fax: 845 692-5244
Kimberly Thompson, *President*
Ellen Amodio, *Manager*
EMP: 15
SALES (est): 960K **Privately Held**
WEB: www.staffordlabsandp.com
SIC: 3842 Prosthetic appliances

(G-8498)
STERLING MOLDED PRODUCTS INC
9-17 Oliver Ave (10940-6095)
PHONE..................845 344-4546
Fax: 845 344-4548
Stephen Crescimanno, *Ch of Bd*
Janice Fumarola, *Manager*
Caitlin Gulling, *Admin Asst*
▲ **EMP:** 40
SALES (est): 7.2MM **Privately Held**
SIC: 3089 Injection molded finished plastic products; injection molding of plastics

(G-8499)
SURVING STUDIOS
17 Millsburg Rd (10940-8497)
PHONE..................845 355-1430
Fax: 845 355-1517
Natalie Surving, *Owner*
EMP: 10
SALES (est): 1.2MM **Privately Held**
SIC: 3469 8999 Tile, floor or wall: stamped metal; sculptor's studio

(G-8500)
TPI INDUSTRIES LLC (HQ)
265 Ballard Rd (10941-3034)
PHONE..................845 692-2820
Fax: 845 692-2946
John Bowe, *President*
Carl Landsman, *Controller*
▲ **EMP:** 42 **EST:** 1978
SQ FT: 50,000
SALES (est): 74.7MM
SALES (corp-wide): 202.9MM **Privately Held**
WEB: www.darlexx.com
SIC: 2295 Laminating of fabrics
PA: Shawmut Corporation
208 Manley St
West Bridgewater MA 02379
508 588-3300

(G-8501)
TRIAD PRINTING INC
Also Called: Chester Printing Service
7 Prospect St (10940-4809)
PHONE..................845 343-2722
Fax: 845 341-1319
Joseph Stewart, *President*
Ralph Carr, *Corp Secy*
EMP: 5
SALES (est): 791.1K **Privately Held**
SIC: 2752 Commercial printing, lithographic

(G-8502)
TURBINE ARFOIL CATING REPR LLC
Also Called: Tacr
105 Tower Dr (10941-2034)
PHONE..................845 692-8912
Mathew Wilson, *General Mgr*
Michael Beckert, *CFO*
Marc Lafontaine, *CFO*
Gerard Milidantri,
▲ **EMP:** 250
SQ FT: 65,000
SALES (est): 20.6MM **Privately Held**
SIC: 3479 Painting, coating & hot dipping

(G-8503)
UNIQUE QUALITY FABRICS INC
115 Wisner Ave (10940-3635)
PHONE..................845 343-3070
Henry Klein, *President*
Norman Klein, *Manager*
◆ **EMP:** 7 **EST:** 1980
SQ FT: 13,000
SALES (est): 934.7K **Privately Held**
WEB: www.uniquequalityfabrics.com
SIC: 2221 Draperies & drapery fabrics, manmade fiber & silk

(G-8504)
VAPE PARADISE INC
47 Bennett St (10940-6410)
P.O. Box 732 (10940-0732)
PHONE..................................845 467-4517
EMP: 8
SALES (est): 665.8K **Privately Held**
SIC: 3999 Cigar & cigarette holders

(G-8505)
WANJASHAN INTERNATIONAL LLC
4 Sands Station Rd (10940-4415)
PHONE..................................845 343-1505
Michael Wu, *President*
◆ EMP: 17
SALES (est): 2.9MM **Privately Held**
SIC: 2035 Soy sauce

(G-8506)
WATEC AMERICA CORPORATION
720 Route 17m Ste 4 (10940-4350)
PHONE..................................702 434-6111
Chia L Liu, *President*
EMP: 50
SALES (est): 4.3MM **Privately Held**
SIC: 3861 Cameras & related equipment

(G-8507)
ZENITH AUTOPARTS CORP
20 Industrial Pl (10940-3609)
PHONE..................................845 344-1382
Fax: 845 344-1462
Moses Goldstein, *President*
Joel Goldstein, *Vice Pres*
▲ EMP: 25
SQ FT: 38,000
SALES: 5MM **Privately Held**
SIC: 3694 Ignition systems, high frequency

Middleville
Herkimer County

(G-8508)
E J WILLIS COMPANY INC
37 N Main St (13406)
PHONE..................................315 891-7602
Fax: 315 891-3477
Evelyn Reile, *President*
Rita Huyck, *Bookkeeper*
EMP: 15
SQ FT: 75,000
SALES: 1MM **Privately Held**
SIC: 3599 Machine shop, jobbing & repair

Milford
Otsego County

(G-8509)
PRESSURE WASHING SERVICES INC
26 Maple St (13807)
P.O. Box 417 (13807-0417)
PHONE..................................607 286-7458
Mathew Johnson, *President*
EMP: 6
SALES (est): 480K **Privately Held**
SIC: 3582 Washing machines, laundry: commercial, incl. coin-operated

Millbrook
Dutchess County

(G-8510)
ALICIA ADAMS ALPACA INC
3262 Franklin Ave (12545-5918)
P.O. Box 1455 (12545-1455)
PHONE..................................845 868-3366
Alicaia Adams, *Ch of Bd*
Daniel Adams, *Principal*
▲ EMP: 8
SALES (est): 636.5K **Privately Held**
SIC: 2337 2231 Women's & misses' suits & coats; women's & misses' capes & jackets; alpacas, mohair: woven

(G-8511)
GORDON S ANDERSON MFG CO
215 N Mabbettsville Rd (12545-5358)
P.O. Box 1459 (12545-1459)
PHONE..................................845 677-3304
Fax: 845 677-5047
Stewart Anderson, *President*
Christine Horihan, *Vice Pres*
EMP: 7 EST: 1946
SQ FT: 7,000
SALES (est): 459.6K **Privately Held**
SIC: 3648 3559 Lighting equipment; pharmaceutical machinery

(G-8512)
MICRO SYSTEMS SPECIALISTS INC
Also Called: Mssi
3280 Franklin Ave Fl 2 (12545-5975)
P.O. Box 347 (12545-0347)
PHONE..................................845 677-6150
Fax: 845 677-6620
Catherine Culkin, *President*
Dawn Roeller, *Vice Pres*
Eileen Sunderland, *Treasurer*
Judy Bruning, *Admin Sec*
EMP: 5
SQ FT: 2,000
SALES (est): 431K **Privately Held**
SIC: 7372 Business oriented computer software

(G-8513)
MILLBROOK WINERY INC
Also Called: Millbrook Vineyard
26 Wing Rd (12545-5017)
PHONE..................................845 677-8383
Fax: 845 677-6186
John Dyson, *President*
John Graziano, *Vice Pres*
Stacy Hudson, *Marketing Staff*
Lynn Murphy, *Office Mgr*
Stacey Nich, *Manager*
▲ EMP: 12
SQ FT: 960
SALES (est): 1.2MM **Privately Held**
WEB: www.millbrookwine.com
SIC: 2084 Wines

Millerton
Dutchess County

(G-8514)
ILLINOIS TOOL WORKS INC
5979 N Elm Ave (12546-4525)
PHONE..................................860 435-2574
EMP: 89
SALES (corp-wide): 13.6B **Publicly Held**
SIC: 3089 Injection molding of plastics
PA: Illinois Tool Works Inc.
    155 Harlem Ave
    Glenview IL 60025
    847 724-7500

Millport
Chemung County

(G-8515)
BLUE MANUFACTURING CO INC
3852 Watkins Rd (14864-9782)
PHONE..................................607 796-2463
Fax: 607 796-4291
Teresa K Liston, *President*
Marlene Liston, *Vice Pres*
EMP: 6
SQ FT: 4,800
SALES (est): 733K **Privately Held**
WEB: www.bluemoonmanufacturing.com
SIC: 3599 Grease cups, metal

Milton
Ulster County

(G-8516)
BROOKLYN BTLG MILTON NY INC (PA)
Also Called: Hudson Valley Apple Products
643 South Rd (12547-5119)
P.O. Box 808 (12547-0808)
PHONE..................................845 795-2171
Fax: 845 795-2589
Eric Miller, *President*
Steve Kneeter, *VP Opers*
Neil Richardson, *Prdtn Mgr*
Korese Donaldson, *QC Mgr*
Dennis Morgan, *Controller*
◆ EMP: 140
SQ FT: 140,000
SALES (est): 39.9MM **Privately Held**
WEB: www.brooklynbottling.com
SIC: 2086 5149 2033 Bottled & canned soft drinks; iced tea & fruit drinks, bottled & canned; carbonated soft drinks, bottled & canned; juices; soft drinks; canned fruits & specialties

(G-8517)
PRAGMATICS TECHNOLOGY INC
14 Old Indian Trl (12547-5114)
PHONE..................................845 795-5071
Chris Mack, *President*
Carissa Dangero, *Office Mgr*
Gaberiela Hughes, *Administration*
EMP: 8 EST: 2000
SQ FT: 700
SALES (est): 1.4MM **Privately Held**
WEB: www.pragmaticstech.com
SIC: 3825 Semiconductor test equipment

(G-8518)
SONO-TEK CORPORATION (PA)
2012 Route 9w Stop 3 (12547-5034)
PHONE..................................845 795-2020
Fax: 845 795-2720
Christopher L Coccio, *Ch of Bd*
R Stephen Harshbarger, *President*
Robb W Engle, *Vice Pres*
Stephen J Bagley, *CFO*
◆ EMP: 58 EST: 1975
SQ FT: 50,000
SALES: 9.7MM **Publicly Held**
WEB: www.sprayfluxing.com
SIC: 3499 Nozzles, spray: aerosol, paint or insecticide

(G-8519)
SUNDANCE INDUSTRIES INC
36 Greentree Ln (12547-5437)
PHONE..................................845 795-5809
Alden Link, *President*
Carol Link, *Treasurer*
EMP: 5
SQ FT: 10,000
SALES: 1.5MM **Privately Held**
WEB: www.sundanceind.com
SIC: 3634 Juice extractors, electric

Mineola
Nassau County

(G-8520)
A & D OFFSET PRINTERS LTD
146 2nd St Apt 3 (11501-4079)
PHONE..................................516 746-2476
Fax: 516 746-2859
Mark A Eliassof, *President*
Adam S Eliaof, *Vice Pres*
Adam S Eliassof, *Vice Pres*
Tara A Eliassof, *Vice Pres*
Tara A Elissof, *Vice Pres*
EMP: 8
SQ FT: 2,000
SALES (est): 590K **Privately Held**
SIC: 2752 7334 7389 5943 Commercial printing, offset; photocopying & duplicating services; laminating service; office forms & supplies

(G-8521)
A & M STEEL STAMPS INC
55 Windsor Ave (11501-1923)
PHONE..................................516 741-6223
Fax: 516 248-4202
Paul Argendorf, *President*
EMP: 5
SQ FT: 2,000
SALES: 500K **Privately Held**
SIC: 3953 Embossing seals & hand stamps

(G-8522)
A K ALLEN CO INC
Also Called: Allen Air
255 E 2nd St (11501-3520)
P.O. Box 350 (11501-0350)
PHONE..................................516 747-5450
Ronald Buttner, *President*
Tim Byrnes, *General Mgr*
Jim Lyons, *Vice Pres*
Steve Werlinitsch, *Plant Mgr*
Wayne Butner, *Research*
▲ EMP: 120 EST: 1945
SQ FT: 150,000
SALES (est): 17.3MM **Privately Held**
SIC: 3679 3443 3822 3593 Electronic circuits; cylinders, pressure: metal plate; pneumatic relays, air-conditioning type; fluid power cylinders & actuators; valves & pipe fittings; fluid power valves & hose fittings

(G-8523)
AERO TRADES MFG CORP
65 Jericho Tpke (11501-2991)
PHONE..................................516 746-3360
Fax: 516 746-3417
Jeffrey E Love, *President*
John Niebuhr, *Vice Pres*
Amy Bernstein, *Manager*
Walter Trimborn, *Manager*
EMP: 33 EST: 1931
SQ FT: 60,000
SALES (est): 6.2MM **Privately Held**
WEB: www.aerotrades.com
SIC: 3728 3444 Aircraft assemblies, sub-assemblies & parts; sheet metalwork

(G-8524)
AERODUCT INC
134 Herricks Rd (11501-2205)
PHONE..................................516 248-9550
Alvin Soffler, *President*
Blanche Soffler, *Corp Secy*
Glen Soffler, *Vice Pres*
Marc Soffler, *Vice Pres*
Roberta Yobs, *Controller*
EMP: 20 EST: 1967
SQ FT: 3,500
SALES (est): 2.6MM **Privately Held**
WEB: www.aeroduct.com
SIC: 3444 1711 Sheet metalwork; ventilation & duct work contractor

(G-8525)
AGRECOLOR INC (PA)
400 Sagamore Ave (11501-1987)
PHONE..................................516 741-8700
Fax: 516 741-0698
Anthony Greco, *President*
Doreen Greco, *Corp Secy*
Anette Brady, *Bookkeeper*
Frank Ortega, *CPA*
EMP: 18 EST: 1957
SQ FT: 15,000
SALES (est): 2.7MM **Privately Held**
WEB: www.agrecolor.com
SIC: 2752 2791 2789 Commercial printing, offset; typesetting; bookbinding & related work

(G-8526)
ALLEN AVIONICS INC
255 E 2nd St (11501-3524)
P.O. Box 350 (11501-0350)
PHONE..................................516 248-8080
Fax: 516 747-6724
Alton K Allen, *President*
Jim Lyons, *General Mgr*
Richard Mintz, *General Mgr*
Sylvia G Allen, *Vice Pres*
Claudia Colon, *Admin Asst*
▲ EMP: 50
SQ FT: 80,000

Mineola - Nassau County (G-8553)

SALES (est): 7.4MM **Privately Held**
WEB: www.allenavionics.com
SIC: **3677** 3679 Filtration devices, electronic; delay lines

(G-8527)
ALLENAIR CORPORATION
255 E 2nd St (11501-3524)
P.O. Box 350 (11501-0350)
PHONE.................516 747-5450
Fax: 516 747-5450
Ronald Butner, *President*
Tim Byrnes, *General Mgr*
Daniel Paradino, *QC Dir*
Wayne Butner, *Research*
Sylvia G Allen, *Treasurer*
EMP: 100
SQ FT: 150,000
SALES (est): 13.2MM **Privately Held**
WEB: www.allenair.com
SIC: **3593** Fluid power cylinders, hydraulic or pneumatic

(G-8528)
AQUIFER DRILLING & TESTING INC (PA)
Also Called: A D T
75 E 2nd St (11501-3503)
PHONE.................516 616-6026
Fax: 516 616-6194
H Leonard Rexrode Jr, *Ch of Bd*
Richard Gregory, *Project Mgr*
Bryan Clark, *Manager*
Steffany McInery, *Assistant*
Patrick Desmond, *Assistant*
▲ **EMP:** 105
SQ FT: 22,000
SALES (est): 24MM **Privately Held**
SIC: **1382** 7375 1711 Geological exploration, oil & gas field; information retrieval services; plumbing contractors

(G-8529)
ARISTA INNOVATIONS INC
Also Called: Arista Printing
131 Liberty Ave (11501-3510)
PHONE.................516 746-2262
Edward Sikorski, *President*
Eleanor Sikorski, *Corp Secy*
Leonard Sikorski, *Vice Pres*
Raymond Sikorski, *Vice Pres*
Greg Turwilliger, *Senior Mgr*
EMP: 30
SQ FT: 25,000
SALES (est): 3.8MM **Privately Held**
WEB: www.aristaprinters.com
SIC: **2752** 2791 2789 2759 Commercial printing, offset; typesetting; bookbinding & related work; commercial printing

(G-8530)
BEARDSLEE REALTY
290 E Jericho Tpke (11501-2197)
PHONE.................516 747-5557
Kan McDowbll, *Manager*
EMP: 6
SALES (corp-wide): 688.4K **Privately Held**
SIC: **2326** 6519 Industrial garments, men's & boys'; real property lessors
PA: Beardslee Realty
27 To 22 Jackson Ave
Long Island City NY 11101
718 784-4100

(G-8531)
BIMBO BAKERIES USA INC
12 E Jericho Tpke (11501-3141)
PHONE.................516 877-2850
EMP: 25
SALES (corp-wide): 13.7B **Privately Held**
SIC: **2051** Mfg Bread/Related Products
HQ: Bimbo Bakeries Usa, Inc
255 Business Center Dr # 200
Horsham PA 19044
215 347-5500

(G-8532)
BLC TEXTILES INC
330 Old Country Rd # 201 (11501-4187)
P.O. Box 5485, New Hyde Park (11042-5485)
PHONE.................844 500-7900
Mark Lichter, *CEO*
EMP: 26

SALES (est): 2.5MM **Privately Held**
SIC: **2299** Towels & towelings, linen & linen-and-cotton mixtures

(G-8533)
CANVAS PRODUCTS COMPANY INC
234 Herricks Rd (11501-2208)
PHONE.................516 742-1058
Edwin E Youngstrom, *President*
EMP: 10
SQ FT: 1,500
SALES (est): 1MM **Privately Held**
SIC: **2394** Awnings, fabric: made from purchased materials

(G-8534)
CAROL PERETZ
Also Called: Carol Peretz Workshop
49 Windsor Ave Ste 103 (11501-1933)
PHONE.................516 248-6300
Carol Peretz, *Owner*
EMP: 18
SQ FT: 4,000
SALES (est): 1.1MM **Privately Held**
WEB: www.carolperetz.com
SIC: **2335** Dresses, paper: cut & sewn

(G-8535)
CAST-ALL CORPORATION (PA)
229 Liberty Ave (11501-3575)
P.O. Box 271 (11501-0271)
PHONE.................516 741-4025
Jack Mandell, *President*
Rose Mandell, *Corp Secy*
Chaim Mandell, *Vice Pres*
Theodore Mandell, *Vice Pres*
EMP: 35 **EST:** 1962
SALES (est): 2.6MM **Privately Held**
WEB: www.cast-all.com
SIC: **3089** 3364 3429 3369 Injection molding of plastics; zinc & zinc-base alloy die-castings; manufactured hardware (general); nonferrous foundries

(G-8536)
CAST-ALL CORPORATION
229 Liberty Ave (11501-3575)
P.O. Box 271 (11501-0271)
PHONE.................516 741-4025
Jack Mandell, *President*
EMP: 25
SALES (corp-wide): 2.6MM **Privately Held**
WEB: www.cast-all.com
SIC: **3364** 3089 Zinc & zinc-base alloy die-castings; injection molding of plastics
PA: Cast-All Corporation
229 Liberty Ave
Mineola NY 11501
516 741-4025

(G-8537)
COMPETICION MOWER REPAIR
75 Windsor Ave (11501-1983)
PHONE.................516 280-6584
Christopher Sideris, *Owner*
Lisa B Sideris, *Admin Sec*
EMP: 5
SALES (est): 495.7K **Privately Held**
SIC: **7692** Welding repair

(G-8538)
DCL FURNITURE MANUFACTURING
96 Windsor Ave (11501-1922)
PHONE.................516 248-2683
Fax: 516 248-0417
Domingos Lopes, *President*
Carlos Lopes, *Manager*
EMP: 20
SQ FT: 2,000
SALES (est): 2.2MM **Privately Held**
WEB: www.dclfurniture.com
SIC: **2511** 2522 2521 Wood household furniture; office furniture, except wood; wood office furniture

(G-8539)
DONMAR PRINTING CO
90 2nd St Ste 2 (11501-3060)
PHONE.................516 280-2239
Sanford Scharf, *President*
EMP: 10

SALES: 251.8K **Privately Held**
SIC: **2752** Commercial printing, lithographic

(G-8540)
ELIAS ARTMETAL INC
70 E 2nd St (11501-3505)
P.O. Box 1872 (11501-0909)
PHONE.................516 873-7501
Fax: 516 873-7505
Constantine Elias, *President*
Ruth Elias, *Vice Pres*
EMP: 19 **EST:** 1976
SQ FT: 9,000
SALES (est): 1MM **Privately Held**
WEB: www.eliasartmetal.com
SIC: **3499** Picture frames, metal; novelties & specialties, metal

(G-8541)
ENVIRONMENTAL TEMP SYSTEMS LLC
Also Called: Ets
111 Roosevelt Ave Ste C (11501-3056)
P.O. Box 701 (11501-0701)
PHONE.................516 640-5818
Wayman Lee,
Kwon Chan,
Joseph D'Alessio,
EMP: 5
SALES (est): 1.2MM **Privately Held**
SIC: **3585** Refrigeration & heating equipment

(G-8542)
EPS IRON WORKS INC
38 Windsor Ave Ste 101 (11501-1932)
PHONE.................516 294-5840
Edward Strocchia, *President*
Philip Strocchia, *Vice Pres*
EMP: 8
SQ FT: 2,000
SALES (est): 1.7MM **Privately Held**
SIC: **3441** Fabricated structural metal

(G-8543)
ERICEIRA INC
Also Called: Bakers All Nations
54 E Jericho Tpke (11501-3141)
PHONE.................516 294-4034
Fax: 516 877-2472
Paula Rego, *President*
Joao Malheiro, *Treasurer*
EMP: 7
SALES (est): 540K **Privately Held**
WEB: www.ericeira.com
SIC: **2051** Bakery: wholesale or wholesale/retail combined

(G-8544)
F J REMEY CO INC
121 Willis Ave (11501-2612)
P.O. Box 589 (11501-0589)
PHONE.................516 741-5112
Fax: 516 741-0523
Richard A Haas, *President*
Margarent Haas, *Manager*
Charlie Morano, *Info Tech Mgr*
EMP: 40
SQ FT: 20,000
SALES (est): 6.2MM **Privately Held**
WEB: www.fjremey.com
SIC: **2752** 5112 Commercial printing, offset; stationery

(G-8545)
GENERAL LED CORP
206 E Jericho Tpke (11501-2034)
PHONE.................516 280-2854
George Geffen, *President*
EMP: 6
SALES (est): 251.5K **Privately Held**
SIC: **3648** Lighting equipment

(G-8546)
GEOTECHNICAL DRILLING INC
Also Called: Environmental Closures
75 E 2nd St (11501-3503)
PHONE.................516 616-6055
H L Rexrode Jr, *Ch of Bd*
William Poupis, *Vice Pres*
EMP: 85
SQ FT: 1,250
SALES (est): 3.2MM **Privately Held**
SIC: **1381** Drilling oil & gas wells

(G-8547)
HYGRADE FUEL INC
260 Columbus Pkwy (11501-3137)
PHONE.................516 741-0723
R Grieco, *Principal*
EMP: 5
SALES (est): 490.2K **Privately Held**
SIC: **2911** Oils, fuel

(G-8548)
INTERCALL SYSTEMS INC
Also Called: Intercall of New York
150 Herricks Rd (11501-2205)
PHONE.................516 294-4524
Fax: 516 294-4526
Ellis Gurman, *President*
Esther Gurman, *Vice Pres*
Jaco Jacob, *Manager*
▲ **EMP:** 25
SQ FT: 10,000
SALES (est): 4.4MM **Privately Held**
WEB: www.intercallsystems.com
SIC: **3669** Intercommunication systems, electric

(G-8549)
ISLAND MARKETING CORP
95 Searing Ave Ste 2 (11501-3046)
PHONE.................516 739-0500
Fax: 516 747-4668
Frank Scarangella, *President*
EMP: 5
SALES (est): 400K **Privately Held**
SIC: **2879** 8742 Insecticides, agricultural or household; sales (including sales management) consultant

(G-8550)
ISLAND ORDNANCE SYSTEMS LLC
267 E Jericho Tpke Ste 2 (11501-2100)
PHONE.................516 746-2100
Fax: 516 746-2405
Amnon Parizat, *President*
Anne Parizat, *Treasurer*
◆ **EMP:** 13
SQ FT: 3,000
SALES (est): 2.8MM **Privately Held**
WEB: www.islandgroup.com
SIC: **3489** 5099 5169 Ordnance & accessories; firearms & ammunition, except sporting; explosives

(G-8551)
ISLAND PYROCHEMICAL INDS CORP (PA)
267 E Jericho Tpke Ste 2 (11501-2100)
PHONE.................516 746-2100
Amnon Parizat, *President*
Frank Anselmo, *Business Mgr*
Robert Massey, *Business Mgr*
Claudia Orjuela, *Vice Pres*
Anne Parizat, *Vice Pres*
◆ **EMP:** 15 **EST:** 1982
SQ FT: 6,000
SALES (est): 29.6MM **Privately Held**
WEB: www.worldvoi.com
SIC: **3081** 2899 5169 Film base, cellulose acetate or nitrocellulose plastic; pyrotechnic ammunition: flares, signals, rockets, etc.; chemicals & allied products

(G-8552)
KHK USA INC
259 Elm Pl Ste 2 (11501-2960)
PHONE.................516 248-3850
Toshiharu Kohara, *President*
Naoji Kohara, *Corp Secy*
EMP: 5 **EST:** 2015
SQ FT: 5,000
SALES: 1MM **Privately Held**
SIC: **3566** 5084 5085 Gears, power transmission, except automotive; industrial machinery & equipment; gears

(G-8553)
LI COMMUNITY NEWSPAPERS INC
132 E 2nd St (11501-3533)
PHONE.................516 747-8282
Angela Anton, *Publisher*
Billey Daelventhal, *Manager*
EMP: 5

Mineola - Nassau County (G-8554) — GEOGRAPHIC SECTION

SALES (est): 294.2K **Privately Held**
SIC: 2711 Newspapers, publishing & printing

(G-8554)
LIBERTY PIPE INCORPORATED
128 Liberty Ave (11501-3509)
PHONE..................516 747-2472
John Kritis, *President*
EMP: 5
SALES (est): 516.5K **Privately Held**
SIC: 3317 Steel pipe & tubes

(G-8555)
LONG ISLAND CMNTY NWSPPERS INC (PA)
Also Called: Anton Community Newspapers
132 E 2nd St (11501-3522)
PHONE..................516 482-4490
Fax: 516 742-5867
Angela Anton, *President*
Vicki Caruso, *Editor*
Rich Forestano, *Editor*
Steve Mosco, *Editor*
Denise Nash, *Editor*
EMP: 85
SALES (est): 11.8MM **Privately Held**
WEB: www.antonnews.com
SIC: 2711 7313 Newspapers, publishing & printing; newspaper advertising representative

(G-8556)
MAXIM HYGIENE PRODUCTS INC (PA)
Also Called: Organic Peak
121 E Jericho Tpke (11501-2031)
PHONE..................516 621-3323
Kenneth Alvandi, *Ch of Bd*
▲ EMP: 15
SALES (est): 1.9MM **Privately Held**
SIC: 2676 Feminine hygiene paper products

(G-8557)
MEDIPOINT INC
Also Called: Medipoint International,
72 E 2nd St (11501-3591)
PHONE..................516 294-8822
Fax: 516 746-6693
Peter Gollobin, *President*
EMP: 12
SQ FT: 7,200
SALES (est): 1.7MM **Privately Held**
SIC: 3841 Surgical & medical instruments; medical instruments & equipment, blood & bone work

(G-8558)
MICHAEL BRITT INC
Also Called: MBI Firearms
89 Mineola Blvd Fl 1 (11501-4063)
PHONE..................516 248-2010
Fax: 516 248-2010
Michael Britt Sr, *President*
Tatiana Britt, *Corp Secy*
EMP: 3 EST: 1949
SQ FT: 4,500
SALES: 1MM **Privately Held**
SIC: 3949 7699 7997 Sporting & athletic goods; baskets (creels), fish & bait; gunsmith shop; gun club, membership

(G-8559)
NASSAU CHROMIUM PLATING CO INC
122 2nd St (11501-3054)
PHONE..................516 746-6666
Fax: 516 747-3791
George Waring, *President*
Shirley Waring, *Corp Secy*
EMP: 45 EST: 1929
SQ FT: 10,000
SALES (est): 4.9MM **Privately Held**
WEB: www.nassaufdrant.com
SIC: 3471 Plating of metals or formed products

(G-8560)
NORTH SHORE FARMS TWO LTD
330 E Jericho Tpke (11501-2111)
PHONE..................516 280-6880
Jose Juan, *Store Mgr*
EMP: 7

SALES (est): 295.5K **Privately Held**
SIC: 2099 Food preparations

(G-8561)
NORTHEAST HARDWARE SPECIALTIES
393 Jericho Tpke Ste 103 (11501-1213)
PHONE..................516 487-6868
Wayne A Reed Jr, *Owner*
EMP: 10
SALES (est): 174.6K **Privately Held**
SIC: 3599 Industrial machinery

(G-8562)
NORWOOD SCREW MACHINE PARTS
200 E 2nd St Ste 2 (11501-3519)
PHONE..................516 481-6644
Gary Prchal, *President*
EMP: 10
SQ FT: 10,000
SALES: 1.5MM **Privately Held**
WEB: www.norwoodscrewmachine.com
SIC: 3451 Screw machine products

(G-8563)
ORIGIN PRESS INC
131 Liberty Ave (11501-3510)
PHONE..................516 746-2262
Ray Sikorski, *President*
EMP: 5
SQ FT: 3,000
SALES (est): 378.4K **Privately Held**
WEB: www.originpress.com
SIC: 2759 Commercial printing

(G-8564)
PRECISION DISC GRINDING CORP
255 E 2nd St (11501-3524)
P.O. Box 350 (11501-0350)
PHONE..................516 747-5450
Ron Buttner, *President*
Tim Byrnes, *President*
Richard Mintz, *Vice Pres*
Sylvia C Allen, *Treasurer*
Virginia Amato, *Personnel*
EMP: 15 EST: 1951
SQ FT: 150,000
SALES (est): 1MM **Privately Held**
WEB: www.precisiondiscgrinding.com
SIC: 3599 8741 Grinding castings for the trade; management services

(G-8565)
RA NEWHOUSE INC (PA)
110 Liberty Ave (11501-3509)
P.O. Box 791 (11501-0791)
PHONE..................516 248-6670
Fax: 516 747-9209
Richard A Newhouse Jr, *President*
Nancy Appey, *Accounts Mgr*
EMP: 60 EST: 1955
SQ FT: 20,000
SALES (est): 7.5MM **Privately Held**
SIC: 2389 Uniforms & vestments; academic vestments (caps & gowns)

(G-8566)
RAYTECH CORP ASBESTOS PERSONAL (PA)
190 Willis Ave (11501-2672)
PHONE..................516 747-0300
Elena Karabatos, *Vice Pres*
Ron Poepple, *Vice Pres*
Richard A Lippe, *Mng Trustee*
EMP: 8
SALES (est): 123.9MM **Privately Held**
SIC: 3499 Friction material, made from powdered metal

(G-8567)
REIS D FURNITURE MFG
327 Sagamore Ave Ste 2 (11501-1944)
PHONE..................516 248-5676
Fax: 516 746-5223
Domingos Reis, *President*
Candida C Reis, *Corp Secy*
▼ EMP: 45
SQ FT: 15,000
SALES (est): 6.3MM **Privately Held**
WEB: www.mineolachamber.com
SIC: 2511 Wood household furniture

(G-8568)
RUBBER STAMPS INC
174 Herricks Rd (11501-2206)
PHONE..................212 675-1180
Fax: 212 675-3849
Robert A Kowalsky, *President*
Elsie Cintron, *Vice Pres*
Abel Kowalsky, *Vice Pres*
Peter Leinroth, *Vice Pres*
Patricia Reber, *Vice Pres*
EMP: 25
SALES (est): 2.9MM **Privately Held**
WEB: www.rubberstampsinc.com
SIC: 3953 3555 2791 3069 Postmark stamps, hand: rubber or metal; printing plates; typographic composition, for the printing trade; stationers' rubber sundries

(G-8569)
S & V CUSTOM FURNITURE MFG
75 Windsor Ave Unit E (11501-1935)
PHONE..................516 746-8299
Carlos Silva, *President*
Norman Kurtz, *Vice Pres*
George Valente, *Treasurer*
EMP: 10
SQ FT: 2,800
SALES (est): 1.1MM **Privately Held**
SIC: 2434 Wood kitchen cabinets

(G-8570)
SCHAEFER MACHINE CO INC
100 Hudson St (11501-3581)
PHONE..................516 248-6880
Fax: 516 747-2227
Peter G Walter, *President*
Paul Rubilotta, *Vice Pres*
Paul Walter, *Vice Pres*
EMP: 22
SQ FT: 15,000
SALES (est): 3MM **Privately Held**
WEB: www.schaeferco.com
SIC: 3542 3452 Machine tools, metal forming type; bolts, nuts, rivets & washers

(G-8571)
VISUAL ID SOURCE INC
65 E 2nd St (11501-3503)
PHONE..................516 307-9759
Fayaz Khalfan, *Ch of Bd*
EMP: 15
SQ FT: 20,000
SALES: 1.5MM **Privately Held**
SIC: 3993 Signs & advertising specialties

(G-8572)
WESTBURY TIMES
Also Called: Three Village Times
132 E 2nd St (11501-3522)
PHONE..................516 747-8282
Angela Anton, *Owner*
William Delventhal Jr, *General Mgr*
EMP: 75
SALES (est): 5MM **Privately Held**
WEB: www.westburytimes.com
SIC: 2711 Newspapers

Mineville
Essex County

(G-8573)
ESSEX INDUSTRIES
17 Pilfershire Rd (12956-1092)
P.O. Box 374 (12956-0374)
PHONE..................518 942-6671
Fax: 518 942-3024
John Anello, *Manager*
EMP: 8
SALES (est): 772.2K **Privately Held**
SIC: 3999 Manufacturing industries

(G-8574)
PRE-TECH PLASTICS INC
3085 Plank Rd (12956-1050)
P.O. Box 370 (12956-0370)
PHONE..................518 942-5950
Fax: 518 942-5931
Mike Cave, *Branch Mgr*
EMP: 30
SALES (corp-wide): 11.3MM **Privately Held**
WEB: www.pretechplastics.com
SIC: 3599 Machine shop, jobbing & repair

PA: Pre-Tech Plastics, Inc.
209 Blair Park Rd
Williston VT 05495
802 879-9441

Mohawk
Herkimer County

(G-8575)
MARY F MORSE
Also Called: Kwik Kut Manufacturing Co
125 Columbia St Ste 1 (13407-1527)
P.O. Box 116 (13407-0116)
PHONE..................315 866-2741
Fax: 315 866-2654
Mary Morse, *Owner*
EMP: 8 EST: 1954
SQ FT: 3,600
SALES (est): 888.1K **Privately Held**
WEB: www.kwik-kut.com
SIC: 3556 Choppers, commercial, food

(G-8576)
R D R INDUSTRIES INC
146 W Main St (13407-1085)
PHONE..................315 866-5020
Fax: 315 866-3325
Mark Rushton, *President*
EMP: 17
SQ FT: 22,000
SALES (est): 2.9MM **Privately Held**
SIC: 3444 Sheet metalwork; metal housings, enclosures, casings & other containers; machine guards, sheet metal; forming machine work, sheet metal

Mohegan Lake
Westchester County

(G-8577)
BARONE OFFSET PRINTING CORP
89 Lake Ridge Cv (10547-1222)
PHONE..................212 989-5500
Sandra Barone, *President*
Claudio Olnos, *Manager*
EMP: 5
SALES (est): 541.3K **Privately Held**
WEB: www.baronepress.com
SIC: 2752 Commercial printing, offset

(G-8578)
ICON ENTERPRISES INTL INC
Also Called: Icon-TV
2653 Stoney St (10547-2009)
PHONE..................718 752-9764
Fax: 718 752-9768
Claudio Laraia, *President*
Moe Belin, *Vice Pres*
▲ EMP: 23
SQ FT: 7,000
SALES (est): 4.6MM **Privately Held**
WEB: www.icon-tv.org
SIC: 3663 Radio & TV communications equipment; television monitors; radio broadcasting & communications equipment; television broadcasting & communications equipment

(G-8579)
SHOPPING CENTER WINE & LIQUOR
Also Called: Kimbri Liquor
3008 E Main St (10547)
PHONE..................914 528-1600
Cathereen Lebleu, *Owner*
EMP: 5
SALES (est): 175.4K **Privately Held**
SIC: 2086 Bottled & canned soft drinks

(G-8580)
SOHO EDITIONS INC
2641 Deer St (10547-2019)
PHONE..................914 591-5100
Elliot Burns, *CEO*
Nicole Mone, *Vice Pres*
EMP: 25
SALES (est): 2.1MM **Privately Held**
WEB: www.sohoeditions.com
SIC: 2741 Art copy: publishing & printing

GEOGRAPHIC SECTION

Monsey - Rockland County (G-8610)

Moira
Franklin County

(G-8581)
MOIRA NEW HOPE FOOD PANTRY
2341 County Route 5 (12957)
PHONE..................................518 529-6524
Joanne Deno, *Director*
EMP: 20
SALES (est): 1MM **Privately Held**
SIC: 2099 Food preparations

Monroe
Orange County

(G-8582)
6TH AVE GOURMET INC
51 Forest Rd Unit 116 (10950-2948)
PHONE..................................845 782-9067
Clara Perl, *President*
EMP: 8
SQ FT: 4,000
SALES (est): 617K **Privately Held**
SIC: 2092 Fresh or frozen packaged fish

(G-8583)
ASSOCIATED DRAPERY & EQUIPMENT
Also Called: Novelty Scenic Studios Inc
3 Kosnitz Dr Unit 111 (10950-1163)
PHONE..................................516 671-5245
Fax: 516 674-2213
Feivel Weiss, *Principal*
Howard Kessler, *Corp Secy*
Leslie Kessler, *Vice Pres*
EMP: 10 **EST:** 1968
SQ FT: 19,000
SALES (est): 838.6K
SALES (corp-wide): 1.1MM **Privately Held**
SIC: 2391 Curtains & draperies
PA: Novelty Scenic Studios Inc
    3 Kosnitz Dr Unit 111
    Monroe NY
    516 671-5940

(G-8584)
B & H ELECTRONICS CORP
308 Museum Village Rd (10950-1638)
PHONE..................................845 782-5000
Fax: 845 782-0470
Harvey Horowitz, *President*
Bernard Horowitz, *Vice Pres*
EMP: 25
SQ FT: 7,300
SALES (est): 2.7MM **Privately Held**
WEB: www.bhelectronicscorp.com
SIC: 3663 8734 3651 3699 Amplifiers, RF power & IF; testing laboratories; household audio & video equipment; electrical equipment & supplies

(G-8585)
BLOOMING GROVE STAIR CO (PA)
1 Stair Way (10950-1642)
PHONE..................................845 783-4245
Fax: 845 782-2361
Glen Durant, *President*
Serena Aglaff, *Co-Owner*
EMP: 11
SALES (est): 1.1MM **Privately Held**
SIC: 2431 Stair railings, wood

(G-8586)
C T A DIGITAL INC
Also Called: SOL MARKOWITZ
326 State Route 208 (10950-2874)
PHONE..................................845 513-0433
Fax: 718 384-3509
Joseph Markowitz, *Ch of Bd*
Leo Markowitz, *President*
Eli Treitel, *Bookkeeper*
Steve Stern, *Sales Mgr*
▲ **EMP:** 25
SALES (est): 12.7K **Privately Held**
WEB: www.ctadigital.com
SIC: 3944 Video game machines, except coin-operated

(G-8587)
CHECK-O-MATIC INC
13 D A Weider Blvd # 101 (10950-6124)
P.O. Box 2141 (10949-7141)
PHONE..................................845 781-7675
Chaim Ellenbogen, *President*
Pearl Gruber, *Admin Sec*
EMP: 7
SQ FT: 2,500
SALES (est): 1.3MM **Privately Held**
WEB: www.checkomatic.com
SIC: 2759 Publication printing

(G-8588)
DER BLATT INC
6 Taitch Ct Unit 112 (10950-2195)
PHONE..................................845 783-1148
Aron Muller, *Principal*
EMP: 11
SALES (est): 1.6MM **Privately Held**
SIC: 2711 Newspapers, publishing & printing

(G-8589)
FIVE STAR CREATIONS INC
4 Preshburg Blvd Unit 302 (10950-2968)
PHONE..................................845 783-1187
Baruch Weiss, *President*
Chaya Weiss, *Admin Sec*
EMP: 20
SQ FT: 1,500
SALES (est): 1.7MM **Privately Held**
SIC: 3961 3999 3911 Costume jewelry; bric-a-brac; jewelry, precious metal

(G-8590)
G & M CLEARVIEW INC
Also Called: Clearview Glass & Mirror
112 Spring St (10950-3679)
PHONE..................................845 781-4877
Chaim Weisberg, *President*
EMP: 6
SALES (est): 436.7K **Privately Held**
SIC: 3231 Mirrored glass

(G-8591)
H&F PRODUCTS INC
51 Forest Rd Ste 360 (10950-2938)
PHONE..................................845 651-6100
Rivkah Brach, *Ch of Bd*
EMP: 6
SALES (est): 522K **Privately Held**
SIC: 2037 Frozen fruits & vegetables

(G-8592)
HOUSE OF STONE INC
1015 State Route 17m (10950-1626)
PHONE..................................845 782-7271
Raymond Krok Sr, *President*
Eva Crok, *Manager*
EMP: 6
SALES (est): 674.6K **Privately Held**
SIC: 3281 Granite, cut & shaped

(G-8593)
JOEL KIRYAS MEAT MARKET CORP
Also Called: Kirays & Joel Meat Market
51 Forest Rd Ste 345 (10950-2939)
PHONE..................................845 782-9194
Fax: 845 783-1544
Harry Polatchek, *President*
Moses Mewman, *Vice Pres*
Cheskel Landau, *Manager*
EMP: 14
SQ FT: 3,000
SALES (est): 1.8MM **Privately Held**
SIC: 2011 Meat by-products from meat slaughtered on site

(G-8594)
JW CONSULTING INC
Also Called: KJ MEAT DIRECT
20 Chevron Rd Unit 201 (10950-7432)
PHONE..................................845 325-7070
Joel Weiss, *President*
EMP: 2 **EST:** 1987
SQ FT: 1,000
SALES: 4MM **Privately Held**
SIC: 2015 Poultry slaughtering & processing

(G-8595)
LASER PRINTER CHECKS CORP
7 Vayoel Moshe Ct # 101 (10950-6389)
PHONE..................................845 782-5837
Solomon Klagsbrun, *President*
EMP: 6
SALES (est): 696.5K **Privately Held**
SIC: 2752 Commercial printing, lithographic

(G-8596)
MARKOWITZ JEWELRY CO INC
53 Forest Rd Ste 104 (10950-2903)
PHONE..................................845 774-1175
Fax: 212 774-1168
Isaac Markowitz, *President*
Baruch Markowitz, *Vice Pres*
Sam Brisk, *Personnel*
EMP: 30
SQ FT: 10,000
SALES (est): 4.4MM **Privately Held**
WEB: www.markowitzjewelry.com
SIC: 3911 Jewelry, precious metal

(G-8597)
MEDEK LABORATORIES INC
63 First Ave (10950-2063)
PHONE..................................845 943-4988
Isaac Schwartz, *COO*
EMP: 27
SALES (est): 1.2MM **Privately Held**
SIC: 2834 Solutions, pharmaceutical

(G-8598)
MONROE STAIR PRODUCTS INC (PA)
1 Stair Way (10950-1642)
PHONE..................................845 783-4245
Glen T Durant, *President*
Jesse J Kehoe, *Vice Pres*
Paul Graham, *Treasurer*
Serina Durant, *Manager*
EMP: 24
SQ FT: 21,500
SALES (est): 2.8MM **Privately Held**
WEB: www.bloominggrovestair.com
SIC: 2431 Staircases & stairs, wood

(G-8599)
STOP ENTERTAINMENT INC
408 Rye Hill Rd (10950-4509)
PHONE..................................212 242-7867
EMP: 15
SQ FT: 1,500
SALES (est): 1.1MM **Privately Held**
SIC: 2732 7311 Book Printing Advertising Agency

(G-8600)
TRI COUNTY CUSTOM VACUUM
653 State Route 17m (10950-3309)
PHONE..................................845 774-7595
Mike Zahra, *Partner*
EMP: 5
SALES (est): 200K **Privately Held**
SIC: 3635 Household vacuum cleaners

Monsey
Rockland County

(G-8601)
A&B CONSERVATION LLC
12 Maple Leaf Rd (10952-3030)
PHONE..................................845 282-7272
Baruch Tabak, *General Mgr*
Dovber Tabak, *Manager*
Judah Rominek,
EMP: 7
SQ FT: 1,000
SALES (est): 499.6K **Privately Held**
SIC: 3295 Pumice, ground or otherwise treated

(G-8602)
AMERTAC HOLDINGS INC (PA)
25 Robert Pitt Dr (10952-3365)
PHONE..................................610 336-1330
Charles Peifer, *Ch of Bd*
John Cooper, *President*
Peter Hermann, *Vice Pres*
EMP: 6

SALES (est): 29.7MM **Privately Held**
SIC: 3699 3429 5063 5072 Electrical equipment & supplies; manufactured hardware (general); metal fasteners; electrical apparatus & equipment; hardware; tacks

(G-8603)
ARONOWITZ METAL WORKS
5 Edwin Ln (10952-3102)
PHONE..................................845 356-1660
Avigdor Aronowitz, *Owner*
Sal Hurst CPA, *Accountant*
EMP: 5
SQ FT: 2,900
SALES (est): 362.7K **Privately Held**
SIC: 2522 Office furniture, except wood

(G-8604)
ATLANTIC SPECIALTY CO INC
20 Jeffrey Pl (10952-2703)
PHONE..................................845 356-2502
Mark Srulowitz, *President*
Seung Lee, *Treasurer*
EMP: 20 **EST:** 1908
SQ FT: 5,000
SALES (est): 1.4MM **Privately Held**
SIC: 3172 3161 Personal leather goods; key cases; coin purses; luggage

(G-8605)
CROWN MILL WORK CORP
12 Melnick Dr (10952-3328)
PHONE..................................845 371-2200
Benzion Lebovits, *Ch of Bd*
EMP: 5
SQ FT: 15,500
SALES (est): 1.2MM **Privately Held**
SIC: 2431 Millwork

(G-8606)
DJS NYC INC
Also Called: Deejays
15 S Remsen St (10952-2807)
PHONE..................................845 445-8618
Chaim Einhorn, *President*
Sarah Koenig, *Admin Sec*
EMP: 8
SALES (est): 1.6MM **Privately Held**
SIC: 3674 Solid state electronic devices

(G-8607)
DVASH FOODS INC
2 Brewer Rd (10952-4001)
PHONE..................................845 578-1959
Mel Gertner, *President*
▲ **EMP:** 10 **EST:** 2008
SALES (est): 2.7MM **Privately Held**
SIC: 2038 Frozen specialties

(G-8608)
LE CHOCOLAT LLC
41 Main St (10952-3005)
PHONE..................................845 352-8301
Bruce Serkez, *President*
▲ **EMP:** 5 **EST:** 1998
SQ FT: 1,500
SALES (est): 460K **Privately Held**
WEB: www.finestchocolate.com
SIC: 2066 Chocolate & cocoa products

(G-8609)
MAGCREST PACKAGING INC
Also Called: Wally Packaging
5 Highview Rd (10952-2943)
PHONE..................................845 425-0451
Fax: 845 352-8374
Aaron Rubinson, *President*
Gitty Rubinson, *Vice Pres*
Judy Gluck, *Admin Sec*
◆ **EMP:** 6
SALES (est): 1.2MM **Privately Held**
WEB: www.magcrest.com
SIC: 2673 7389 Bags: plastic, laminated & coated;

(G-8610)
MAVIANO CORP
21 Robert Pitt Dr Ste 207 (10952-5305)
PHONE..................................845 494-2598
Brenda Falk, *President*
EMP: 7
SALES (est): 549.3K **Privately Held**
SIC: 2821 Plastics materials & resins

Monsey - Rockland County (G-8611)

(G-8611)
NAVY PLUM LLC
47 Plum Rd (10952-1525)
PHONE 845 641-7441
Jonathan Joseph,
▲ EMP: 3
SQ FT: 2,500
SALES: 40MM Privately Held
SIC: 2299 5199 Fabrics: linen, jute, hemp, ramie; yarn: flax, jute, hemp & ramie; fabrics, yarns & knit goods

(G-8612)
PLASTICWARE LLC (PA)
13 Wilsher Dr (10952-2328)
PHONE 845 267-0790
Patricia Belt, Sales/Mktg Mgr
David Koegel, CFO
Rachel Meltzer, Office Mgr
Sam Meth, Mng Member
EMP: 16
SQ FT: 10,000
SALES (est): 6.3MM Privately Held
SIC: 3089 Plastic containers, except foam

(G-8613)
PRINT IT INC
59 Route 59 Ste 141 (10952-3543)
PHONE 845 371-2227
EMP: 7
SALES (est): 163.5K Privately Held
SIC: 2752 Commercial printing, lithographic

(G-8614)
S B MANUFACTURING LLC
161 Route 59 (10952-7819)
PHONE 845 352-3700
Michael Bloch, President
Ralph Heidings, CFO
EMP: 14
SALES (est): 1.9MM Privately Held
SIC: 3999 Barber & beauty shop equipment

(G-8615)
SAFE-DENT ENTERPRISES LLC
4 Orchard Hill Dr (10952-1503)
PHONE 845 362-0141
Hedy Worch, Mng Member
EMP: 5
SQ FT: 20,000
SALES (est): 442K Privately Held
SIC: 3843 Dental materials

(G-8616)
SB MOLDS LLC
161 Route 59 Ste 203a (10952-7817)
PHONE 845 352-3700
Michael Bloch, Mng Member
EMP: 80
SALES (est): 3MM Privately Held
SIC: 3544 Industrial molds

(G-8617)
SENNETH LLC
26 Ronald Dr Ste 500 (10952-2607)
PHONE 347 232-3170
Aaron Mandel,
EMP: 9 EST: 2015
SALES (est): 846.7K Privately Held
SIC: 2339 Women's & misses' athletic clothing & sportswear

(G-8618)
SZ - DESIGN & PRINT INC
Also Called: S Z Design & Prints
33 Rita Ave (10952-2699)
PHONE 845 352-0395
Shlomo Zeibe, President
EMP: 13
SALES (est): 2.3MM Privately Held
SIC: 2752 Commercial printing, lithographic

(G-8619)
TAMI GREAT FOOD CORP
22 Briarcliff Dr (10952-2503)
PHONE 845 352-7901
David Rosenberg, President
Martin Rosenberg, President
Renee Rosenberg, Vice Pres
EMP: 8
SQ FT: 6,000
SALES (est): 585.6K Privately Held
SIC: 2037 2038 Vegetables, quick frozen & cold pack, excl. potato products; frozen specialties

(G-8620)
TELE-PAK INC
Also Called: Card Printing.us
421 Route 59 (10952-2835)
P.O. Box 430 (10952-0430)
PHONE 845 426-2300
Jack Steinmetz, Ch of Bd
Shoshana Stefansky, President
Laura Brown, Production
Avram Joseph, Treasurer
Isaac Adler, Sales Dir
▲ EMP: 43
SQ FT: 7,000
SALES (est): 8.6MM Privately Held
WEB: www.tele-pak.com
SIC: 2754 2759 2752 7929 Commercial printing, gravure; commercial printing; cards, lithographed; entertainers & entertainment groups

(G-8621)
YATED NEEMAN INC
53 Olympia Ln (10952-2829)
PHONE 845 369-1600
Fax: 845 369-6397
Pinchos Lipschutz, President
AVI Yishai, Editor
▲ EMP: 12
SALES (est): 600K Privately Held
WEB: www.yated.com
SIC: 2711 Newspapers

(G-8622)
ZYLON CORPORATION
Also Called: Zylon Polymers
23 Mountain Ave (10952-2949)
PHONE 845 425-9469
Fax: 845 352-6508
Alan Zamore, President
EMP: 10
SQ FT: 2,500
SALES (est): 580K Privately Held
WEB: www.zylon.net
SIC: 3069 Reclaimed rubber & specialty rubber compounds

Montauk
Suffolk County

(G-8623)
JESSE JOECKEL
Also Called: Whalebone Creative
65 Tuthill Rd (11954-5460)
PHONE 631 668-2772
Jesse Joeckel, Owner
Bronson Lamb, Manager
EMP: 5 EST: 2010
SQ FT: 600
SALES (est): 374.2K Privately Held
SIC: 2339 Women's & misses' outerwear

(G-8624)
MONTAUK BREWING COMPANY INC
62 S Erie Ave (11954-5370)
P.O. Box 1079 (11954-0802)
PHONE 631 668-8471
Vaughan Cutillo, Vice Pres
EMP: 10
SALES (est): 25.9K Privately Held
SIC: 2082 Beer (alcoholic beverage)

(G-8625)
MONTAUK INLET SEAFOOD INC
E Lake Dr Ste 540-541 (11954)
P.O. Box 2148 (11954-0905)
PHONE 631 668-3419
Charles S Weimar, President
David Aripocth, Owner
Kevin Maguire, Owner
William Grimm, Vice Pres
Richard Jones, Treasurer
EMP: 3
SQ FT: 5,000
SALES (est): 1.1MM Privately Held
SIC: 2092 5146 5983 Fish, fresh: prepared; fish, fresh; fuel oil dealers

(G-8626)
NYEMAC INC
Also Called: On Montauk
Paradise Ln (11954)
P.O. Box 2087 (11954-0903)
PHONE 631 668-1303
Joseph Nye, President
Carol Macdonald-Nye, President
EMP: 8 EST: 1990
SQ FT: 1,200
SALES (est): 690K Privately Held
SIC: 2721 4813 Magazines: publishing only, not printed on site;

Montgomery
Orange County

(G-8627)
BAXTER INTERNATIONAL INC
500 Neelytown Rd (12549-2828)
PHONE 845 457-9370
EMP: 5
SALES (corp-wide): 10.1B Publicly Held
SIC: 2834 Pharmaceutical preparations
PA: Baxter International Inc.
  1 Baxter Pkwy
  Deerfield IL 60015
  224 948-2000

(G-8628)
CALLANAN INDUSTRIES INC
215 Montgomery Rd (12549-2814)
P.O. Box 505, Maybrook (12543-0505)
PHONE 845 457-3158
Charlie Tady, Opers Mgr
Kevin Schuler, Manager
EMP: 25
SALES (corp-wide): 28.6B Privately Held
WEB: www.callanan.com
SIC: 2951 5032 2952 Asphalt & asphaltic paving mixtures (not from refineries); stone, crushed or broken; asphalt felts & coatings
HQ: Callanan Industries, Inc.
  8 Southwoods Blvd Ste 4
  Albany NY 12211
  518 374-2222

(G-8629)
CARLISLE CONSTRUCTION MTLS LLC
9 Hudson Crossing Dr (12549-2854)
PHONE 386 753-0786
Fax: 845 336-4719
Illya Spiecker, Plant Mgr
Ron Robichaud, Prdtn Mgr
Kellie McGowan, HR Admin
Scott Pearson, Manager
Joe Lightfoot, Manager
EMP: 65
SALES (corp-wide): 3.6B Publicly Held
WEB: www.hpanels.com
SIC: 3086 Insulation or cushioning material, foamed plastic
HQ: Carlisle Construction Materials, Llc
  1285 Ritner Hwy
  Carlisle PA 17013

(G-8630)
GLAXOSMITHKLINE LLC
3 Tyler St (12549-1609)
PHONE 845 341-7590
EMP: 26
SALES (corp-wide): 34.3B Privately Held
SIC: 2834 Pharmaceutical preparations
HQ: Glaxosmithkline Llc
  5 Crescent Dr
  Philadelphia PA 19112
  215 751-4000

(G-8631)
GROSSO MATERIALS INC
90 Collabar Rd (12549-1805)
PHONE 845 361-5211
Fax: 845 361-3576
Allan Grosso, President
EMP: 10
SQ FT: 300
SALES (est): 1.5MM Privately Held
SIC: 1459 5261 5032 Shale (common) quarrying; top soil; stone, crushed or broken

(G-8632)
JOHN WILEY & SONS INC
46 Wavey Willow Ln (12549-1501)
PHONE 845 457-6250
EMP: 65
SALES (corp-wide): 1.7B Publicly Held
SIC: 2731 Textbooks: publishing only, not printed on site
PA: John Wiley & Sons, Inc.
  111 River St Ste 2000
  Hoboken NJ 07030
  201 748-6000

(G-8633)
KAL PAC CORP
10 Factory St (12549-1202)
PHONE 845 457-7013
Mike Nozawa, CEO
▲ EMP: 19
SALES (est): 4.2MM Privately Held
SIC: 2671 Plastic film, coated or laminated for packaging

(G-8634)
NORTHEAST CNSTR INDS INC
Also Called: Nci Panel Systems
657 Rte 17 K S St Ste 2 (12549)
PHONE 845 565-1000
Robert Schroeder, President
Harry Gittlitz, Vice Pres
EMP: 10 EST: 1999
SQ FT: 12,000
SALES: 630K Privately Held
SIC: 3316 Cold finishing of steel shapes

(G-8635)
ON POINT REPS INC
Also Called: Off State Water Group
20a Wellroad Ave (12549)
PHONE 518 258-2268
Antonio Goncalves, President
EMP: 5
SALES: 400K Privately Held
SIC: 3088 Plastics plumbing fixtures

(G-8636)
ORANGE COUNTY IRONWORKS LLC
36 Maybrook Rd (12549-2815)
PHONE 845 769-3000
Steve Michael, Prdtn Mgr
Daniel Teutul, Mng Member
Jenny Stafford, Manager
Marie Zeigler, Manager
EMP: 44
SQ FT: 65,000
SALES: 61.3MM Privately Held
SIC: 3449 3441 1541 Miscellaneous metalwork; fabricated structural metal; industrial buildings, new construction

(G-8637)
QUICK ROLL LEAF MFG CO INC (PA)
118 Bracken Rd (12549-2600)
P.O. Box 53, Middletown (10940-0053)
PHONE 845 457-1500
Charles E Quick, Ch of Bd
Edward Quick Jr, President
William Crowley, Vice Pres
EMP: 48
SQ FT: 80,000
SALES: 43.3MM Privately Held
SIC: 3497 Metal foil & leaf

(G-8638)
REUTER PALLET PKG SYS INC
272 Neelytown Rd (12549-2840)
PHONE 845 457-9937
Joseph A Carfizzi Sr, President
George Reuter Jr, Vice Pres
EMP: 9
SQ FT: 10,000
SALES (est): 920.4K Privately Held
SIC: 2448 2441 Wood pallets & skids; nailed wood boxes & shook

(G-8639)
TILCON NEW YORK INC
Also Called: Maybrook Asphalt
215 Montgomery Rd (12549-2814)
PHONE 845 457-3158
Ciaran Brennan, Principal
EMP: 63

SALES (corp-wide): 28.6B **Privately Held**
SIC: 1429 Dolomitic marble, crushed & broken-quarrying
HQ: Tilcon New York Inc.
162 Old Mill Rd
West Nyack NY 10994
845 358-4500

(G-8640)
VALAD ELECTRIC HEATING CORP
65 Leonards Dr (12549-2643)
Rural Route 65 Leonard (12549)
PHONE.................................888 509-4927
Fax: 845 634-4395
Arthur Cecchini, *Ch of Bd*
Lauren Cecchini, *Corp Secy*
Arthur Cecchini Jr, *Vice Pres*
Tim James, *Production*
Lauren Cecchini Janes, *Treasurer*
EMP: 12 **EST:** 1941
SQ FT: 35,000
SALES (est): 3.2MM **Privately Held**
WEB: www.valadelectric.com
SIC: 3634 Heaters, space electric; electric household cooking appliances

(G-8641)
VALID ELECTRIC CORP
65 Leonards Dr (12549-2643)
PHONE.................................914 631-9436
Arthur L Cecchini, *President*
Arthur Cechini, *President*
EMP: 25 **EST:** 1981
SALES (est): 2.6MM **Privately Held**
SIC: 3634 Heaters, space electric; electric household cooking appliances

Monticello
Sullivan County

(G-8642)
BLOOMING GROVE STAIR CO
309 E Broadway (12701-8839)
PHONE.................................845 791-4016
Glen Durant, *Principal*
EMP: 7 **Privately Held**
SIC: 2431 Stair railings, wood
PA: Blooming Grove Stair Co
1 Stair Way
Monroe NY 10950

(G-8643)
LOCAL MEDIA GROUP INC
Also Called: Times Herald-Record
479 Broadway (12701-1756)
PHONE.................................845 794-3712
EMP: 10
SALES (corp-wide): 610.2MM **Publicly Held**
SIC: 2711 Newspapers-Publishing/Printing
HQ: Local Media Group, Inc.
40 Mulberry St
Middletown NY 10940
845 294-8181

(G-8644)
MONROE STAIR PRODUCTS INC
309 E Broadway (12701-8839)
PHONE.................................845 791-4016
Glen Durant, *Manager*
EMP: 5
SALES (corp-wide): 2.8MM **Privately Held**
WEB: www.bloominggrovestair.com
SIC: 2431 Staircases & stairs, wood
PA: Monroe Stair Products Inc.
1 Stair Way
Monroe NY 10950
845 783-4245

(G-8645)
MR VAPE GURU
73 Pleasant St (12701-1419)
PHONE.................................845 796-2274
EMP: 6 **EST:** 2015
SALES (est): 92.3K **Privately Held**
SIC: 3999 Cigar & cigarette holders

(G-8646)
PATRICK ROHAN
Also Called: Wadadda.com
9 Green St (12701-1307)
PHONE.................................718 781-2573
Rohan Patrick, *Owner*
EMP: 5
SALES (est): 195.2K **Privately Held**
SIC: 2396 2759 7336 7389 Printing & embossing on plastics fabric articles; woodcuts for use in printing illustrations, posters, etc.; commercial art & graphic design; commercial art & illustration;

(G-8647)
WYDE LUMBER
419 State Route 17b (12701-3525)
PHONE.................................845 513-5571
Fax: 845 794-6420
Wallace Madnick, *Owner*
EMP: 12
SALES (est): 760K **Privately Held**
SIC: 2421 Lumber: rough, sawed or planed

Montour Falls
Schuyler County

(G-8648)
CHICONE BUILDERS LLC
Chicone Cabinetmakers
302 W South St (14865-9743)
PHONE.................................607 535-6540
Jennifer Chicone, *Office Mgr*
David H Chicone,
EMP: 5 **Privately Held**
SIC: 2521 2434 Cabinets, office: wood; wood kitchen cabinets
PA: Chicone Builders, Llc
302 W South St
Montour Falls NY 14865

(G-8649)
MALINA MANAGEMENT COMPANY INC
Also Called: Castel Grisch Winery
3620 County Road 16 (14865-9708)
PHONE.................................607 535-9614
Fax: 607 535-2994
Thomas Malina, *President*
Barbara A Malina, *Treasurer*
Scott Wachter, *Admin Sec*
EMP: 22
SQ FT: 1,250
SALES (est): 1.5MM **Privately Held**
SIC: 2084 5812 7011 Wines, brandy & brandy spirits; eating places; bed & breakfast inn

(G-8650)
ROBERT M BROWN
Also Called: Malone Welding
150 Mill St (14865-9734)
PHONE.................................607 426-6250
Robert M Brown, *Owner*
EMP: 11
SALES (est): 368.3K **Privately Held**
WEB: www.empiregp.com
SIC: 7692 Welding repair

(G-8651)
TAYLOR PRECISION MACHINING
3921 Dug Rd (14865-9722)
PHONE.................................607 535-3101
Mickey Taylor, *Owner*
EMP: 7
SQ FT: 1,056
SALES (est): 1MM **Privately Held**
SIC: 3599 Machine shop, jobbing & repair

Montrose
Westchester County

(G-8652)
CORTLANDT SMOKE AND VAPE
2153 Albany Post Rd (10548-1044)
PHONE.................................914 930-7592
Chelsea Al Marji, *Principal*
EMP: 5
SALES (est): 85.2K **Privately Held**
SIC: 3999 Cigar & cigarette holders

(G-8653)
QUALITY CIRCLE PRODUCTS INC
2108 Albany Post Rd (10548-1431)
P.O. Box 36 (10548-0036)
PHONE.................................914 736-6600
Gary Flaum, *President*
Anthony Cenname, *Vice Pres*
▲ **EMP:** 70
SQ FT: 32,500
SALES (est): 14.3MM **Privately Held**
WEB: www.qualitycircle.com
SIC: 2679 2671 Labels, paper: made from purchased material; tags, paper (unprinted): made from purchased paper; packaging paper & plastics film, coated & laminated

Mooers
Clinton County

(G-8654)
ACME ENGINEERING PRODUCTS INC
2330 State Route 11 (12958-3725)
PHONE.................................518 236-5659
Fax: 518 236-6941
G S Presser, *President*
Robert Presser, *Vice Pres*
Mohand Amroun, *Engineer*
Martin Costa, *Engineer*
Julie Hawa, *Finance*
EMP: 25
SALES (est): 4.2MM **Privately Held**
WEB: www.acmeprod.com
SIC: 3564 8711 Air cleaning systems; engineering services

Mooers Forks
Clinton County

(G-8655)
NORTHERN TIER CNC INC (PA)
733 Woods Falls Rd (12959-2111)
PHONE.................................518 236-4702
Jerry Meseck, *President*
Jamie Meseck, *Treasurer*
EMP: 9
SQ FT: 4,000
SALES: 1.2MM **Privately Held**
SIC: 3599 Custom machinery

Moravia
Cayuga County

(G-8656)
BROOKSIDE LUMBER INC
4191 Duryea St (13118-2500)
PHONE.................................315 497-0937
Fax: 315 497-0018
William Millier, *President*
Jennifer Bradshaw, *Manager*
Katherine Millier, *Shareholder*
EMP: 17
SQ FT: 10,000
SALES (est): 2.5MM **Privately Held**
SIC: 2421 Sawmills & planing mills, general

(G-8657)
CROSS FILTRATION LTD LBLTY CO
87 W Cayuga St (13118-3000)
P.O. Box 1082 (13118-1082)
PHONE.................................315 412-1539
Denise Dans, *Sales Mgr*
Joanne Cross, *Mng Member*
John Ramirez, *Manager*
◆ **EMP:** 7
SALES (est): 297.9K **Privately Held**
SIC: 3569 Filters, general line: industrial

(G-8658)
REPUBLICAN REGISTRAR INC
Also Called: Community Newspapers
6 Central St (13118-3609)
P.O. Box 591 (13118-0591)
PHONE.................................315 497-1551
Bernard McGuerty III, *President*
Cathy Robinson, *Finance Other*
Janet Mulvaney, *Sales Staff*
EMP: 8
SALES (est): 615.2K **Privately Held**
SIC: 2759 Newspapers: printing

Moriches
Suffolk County

(G-8659)
RE FUEL
210 Montauk Hwy (11955-1415)
PHONE.................................631 909-3316
Ernest Ruberto, *Principal*
EMP: 5 **EST:** 2010
SALES (est): 395.1K **Privately Held**
SIC: 2869 Fuels

Morris
Otsego County

(G-8660)
H W NAYLOR CO INC
121 Main St (13808-6920)
P.O. Box 190 (13808-0190)
PHONE.................................607 263-5145
Fax: 607 263-2416
David Lucas, *President*
Jerome Payton, *Human Res Mgr*
▲ **EMP:** 12 **EST:** 1926
SQ FT: 10,000
SALES (est): 1.3MM **Privately Held**
WEB: www.drnaylor.com
SIC: 2834 Veterinary pharmaceutical preparations

Morrisville
Madison County

(G-8661)
CDC PUBLISHING LLC
19 North St (13408-1721)
PHONE.................................215 579-1695
Ken Borah, *Branch Mgr*
EMP: 30
SALES (corp-wide): 21.3MM **Privately Held**
WEB: www.cdcpublishing.com
SIC: 2721 2711 Periodicals: publishing only; newspapers
PA: Cdc Publishing, Llc
2001 9th Ave Ste 207
Vero Beach FL 32960
772 770-6003

(G-8662)
COPESETIC INC
62 E Main St (13408)
P.O. Box 1119 (13408-1119)
PHONE.................................315 684-7780
Fax: 315 684-7790
Eric Beyer, *President*
Anthony Lee, *Vice Pres*
David Lee, *VP Opers*
Shannon Cook, *Office Mgr*
Janice Sebringe, *Office Mgr*
EMP: 15
SQ FT: 10,000
SALES: 1.7MM **Privately Held**
WEB: www.copeseticinc.com
SIC: 3999 Models, except toy

Mount Kisco
Westchester County

(G-8663)
ACCEL PRINTING & GRAPHICS
128 Radio Circle Dr Ste 2 (10549-2640)
PHONE.................914 241-3369
Bill Harden, *Owner*
Anna Harden, *Vice Pres*
Donna Corti, *Marketing Staff*
EMP: 9
SQ FT: 2,200
SALES: 625K **Privately Held**
WEB: www.accelprinting.com
SIC: 2759 Commercial printing

(G-8664)
BROOKS WOODWORKING INC
15 Kensico Dr (10549-1003)
PHONE.................914 666-2029
Fax: 914 666-2029
Richard Brooks, *President*
Kevin Wright, *Vice Pres*
▲ **EMP:** 14
SQ FT: 5,000
SALES: 1.1MM **Privately Held**
SIC: 2499 Decorative wood & woodwork

(G-8665)
COLUMBIA CABINETS LLC (PA)
332 E Main St (10549-3005)
PHONE.................212 972-7550
EMP: 4
SALES (est): 1.1MM **Privately Held**
SIC: 2434 Wood kitchen cabinets

(G-8666)
CURTIS INSTRUMENTS INC (PA)
Also Called: Curtis PMC Division
200 Kisco Ave (10549-1400)
PHONE.................914 666-2971
Fax: 914 666-2188
Stuart Marwell, *Ch of Bd*
Eugene Finger, *President*
Wang Jinghui, *General Mgr*
Randy Miller, *Business Mgr*
Mark Ankers, *Vice Pres*
▲ **EMP:** 150 **EST:** 1960
SQ FT: 35,000
SALES (est): 291.6MM **Privately Held**
SIC: 3825 3824 3629 Elapsed time meters, electronic; speed indicators & recorders, vehicle; electronic generation equipment

(G-8667)
D C I PLASMA CENTER INC (PA)
71 S Bedford Rd (10549-3407)
PHONE.................914 241-1646
Martin Silver, *President*
Perry Ciarrletta, *Treasurer*
EMP: 3
SQ FT: 700
SALES (est): 2.1MM **Privately Held**
SIC: 2836 Plasmas

(G-8668)
DATALINK COMPUTER PRODUCTS
165 E Main St 175 (10549-2923)
PHONE.................914 666-2358
Vickram Bedi, *President*
Chhaya Bedi, *Vice Pres*
Richard Niziak, *Engineer*
EMP: 10
SALES: 2.4MM **Privately Held**
SIC: 3572 7374 Computer storage devices; service bureau, computer

(G-8669)
ENTERMARKET
280 N Bedford Rd Ste 305 (10549-1148)
PHONE.................914 437-7268
Jeff Tong, *Owner*
Louis Veccaarelli, *Prdtn Mgr*
Mark Matich, *Director*
EMP: 5
SALES (est): 552.9K **Privately Held**
WEB: www.entermarket.com
SIC: 2752 Commercial printing, lithographic

(G-8670)
IAT INTERACTIVE LLC
Also Called: It's About Time
333 N Bedford Rd Ste 110 (10549-1161)
PHONE.................914 273-2233
Thomas Laster, *Shareholder*
Laurie Kreindler, *Shareholder*
EMP: 37
SQ FT: 574,600
SALES (est): 2.8MM **Privately Held**
SIC: 2731 Textbooks: publishing & printing

(G-8671)
IMMUDYNE INC
50 Spring Meadow Rd (10549-3846)
PHONE.................914 244-1777
Anthony G Bruzzese, *Ch of Bd*
Mark McLaughlin, *President*
Joseph Ditrolio, *Chief Mktg Ofcr*
EMP: 11 **EST:** 1987
SALES: 5.2MM **Privately Held**
SIC: 2833 Medicinals & botanicals

(G-8672)
INTERDYNAMICS
100 S Bedford Rd Ste 300 (10549-3444)
PHONE.................914 241-1423
Ken Motush, *Principal*
▲ **EMP:** 15
SALES (est): 2.6MM **Privately Held**
SIC: 2992 Lubricating oils & greases

(G-8673)
JEROME LEVY FORECASTING CENTER
Also Called: Industry Forecast
69 S Moger Ave Ste 202 (10549-2222)
PHONE.................914 244-8617
David Levy, *Principal*
EMP: 5
SALES (est): 384.4K **Privately Held**
SIC: 2721 Periodicals

(G-8674)
JT ROSELLE LIGHTING & SUP INC
333 N Bedford Rd Ste 120 (10549-1158)
PHONE.................914 666-3700
EMP: 14
SALES (est): 3.1MM **Privately Held**
SIC: 3648 Lighting equipment

(G-8675)
KIDZ TOYZ INC
280 N Bedford Rd Ste 203 (10549-1147)
PHONE.................914 261-4453
Scott Spiegel, *President*
EMP: 2
SALES: 2MM **Privately Held**
SIC: 3944 Games, toys & children's vehicles; electronic games & toys

(G-8676)
KOHLBERG SPORTS GROUP INC (HQ)
111 Radio Circle Dr (10549-2609)
PHONE.................914 241-7430
Walter W Farley,
EMP: 5
SALES (est): 1.1MM
SALES (corp-wide): 7.6B **Privately Held**
SIC: 3949 Hockey equipment & supplies, general
PA: Kohlberg & Co., L.L.C.
111 Radio Circle Dr
Mount Kisco NY 10549
914 241-7430

(G-8677)
LAURTOM INC
Also Called: It's About Time Publishing
333 N Bedford Rd Ste 100 (10549-1160)
PHONE.................914 273-2233
Laurie Kreindler, *CEO*
Cheryl Deese, *Vice Pres*
Sal Marottoli, *Vice Pres*
Barbara Zahm, *Vice Pres*
Tom Liao, *Controller*
EMP: 35
SQ FT: 4,000
SALES: 3.8MM
SALES (corp-wide): 1.1B **Privately Held**
WEB: www.its-about-time.com
SIC: 2721 Periodicals

HQ: Herff Jones, Llc
4501 W 62nd St
Indianapolis IN 46268
800 419-5462

(G-8678)
MOUNT KISCO TRANSFER STN INC
10 Lincoln Pl (10549-2614)
PHONE.................914 666-6350
Anthony Orlando, *CEO*
EMP: 7
SALES (est): 576.9K
SALES (corp-wide): 1.7B **Publicly Held**
SIC: 3443 4953 5722 Dumpsters, garbage; garbage: collecting, destroying & processing; garbage disposals
HQ: Covanta Energy, Llc
445 South St
Morristown NJ 07960
862 345-5000

(G-8679)
NATIONWIDE COILS INC (PA)
24 Foxwood Cir (10549-1127)
PHONE.................914 277-7396
Ross Stephens, *President*
Andre Ostacoli, *General Mgr*
Stephen Barzelatto, *Vice Pres*
Jay Feldman, *Natl Sales Mgr*
Justin Campanello, *Sales Associate*
▼ **EMP:** 4
SQ FT: 1,000
SALES (est): 1.3MM **Privately Held**
WEB: www.nationwidecoils.com
SIC: 3585 Refrigeration & heating equipment

(G-8680)
NORCORP INC
Also Called: NORTHERN WESTCHESTER HOSPITAL
400 E Main St (10549-3417)
PHONE.................914 666-1310
Joel Seligman, *President*
John Partenza, *Treasurer*
Micheal Mascia, *Manager*
EMP: 27
SALES: 186.1K
SALES (corp-wide): 266.6MM **Privately Held**
SIC: 2326 8062 Medical & hospital uniforms, men's; general medical & surgical hospitals
PA: Northern Westchester Hospital Association
400 E Main St
Mount Kisco NY 10549
914 666-1200

(G-8681)
ORBIT INDUSTRIES LLC
116 Radio Circle Dr # 302 (10549-2631)
PHONE.................914 244-1500
Marc Shur,
John Katz,
EMP: 14
SALES (est): 2.4MM **Privately Held**
SIC: 2258 Lace & lace products

(G-8682)
PECKER IRON WORKS LLC
137 Ruxton Rd (10549-4025)
PHONE.................914 665-0100
Elliott Pecker, *Mng Member*
EMP: 4
SQ FT: 1,000
SALES (est): 1.4MM **Privately Held**
SIC: 3312 Structural shapes & pilings, steel

(G-8683)
PLASTIC & RECONSTRUCTIVE SVCS
Also Called: Spa Sciara
333 N Bedford Rd (10549-1158)
PHONE.................914 584-5605
Sharon Dechiara, *President*
EMP: 5 **EST:** 2010
SQ FT: 1,800
SALES (est): 1.2MM **Privately Held**
SIC: 2844 Cosmetic preparations

(G-8684)
R L C ELECTRONICS INC
83 Radio Circle Dr (10549-2622)
PHONE.................914 241-1334
Fax: 914 241-1753
Charles Alan Borck, *CEO*
Doug Borck, *President*
Chris Medina, *Controller*
Peter Jeffery, *Sales Dir*
Linda A Agosta, *Sales Staff*
EMP: 65 **EST:** 1959
SQ FT: 20,000
SALES (est): 12.8MM **Privately Held**
WEB: www.rlcelectronics.com
SIC: 3679 Electronic circuits; microwave components

(G-8685)
RADIO CIRCLE REALTY INC
136 Radio Circle Dr (10549-2642)
PHONE.................914 241-8742
Arturo Defeo, *President*
Lucia Defeo, *Corp Secy*
Anthony D Feo, *Vice Pres*
Anthony De Feo, *Marketing Staff*
▲ **EMP:** 40
SQ FT: 11,000
SALES (est): 2.4MM **Privately Held**
SIC: 2399 6799 Glove mending on factory basis; real estate investors, except property operators

(G-8686)
RDI INC (PA)
Also Called: RDI ELECTRONICS
333 N Bedford Rd Ste 135 (10549-1160)
PHONE.................914 773-1000
Fax: 914 241-3825
James Diamond, *Ch of Bd*
Barry Miller, *President*
Greg Mozingo, *Regional Mgr*
John Horl, *CFO*
David Del Monte, *Controller*
▲ **EMP:** 18
SQ FT: 10,000
SALES: 38.9MM **Privately Held**
WEB: www.rdiusa.com
SIC: 3679 3678 3677 3577 Electronic circuits; electronic connectors; electronic coils, transformers & other inductors; computer peripheral equipment; nonferrous wiredrawing & insulating

(G-8687)
RPB DISTRIBUTORS LLC
Also Called: Protec Friction Supply
45 Kensico Dr (10549-1025)
PHONE.................914 244-3600
Fax: 914 244-3615
Roy Landesberg, *President*
Parker Silzer, *Vice Pres*
Jer Thompson, *Engineer*
Daniel Martabano, *Manager*
▲ **EMP:** 8
SALES (est): 1.2MM **Privately Held**
WEB: www.protecfriction.com
SIC: 3714 5084 5013 Motor vehicle brake systems & parts; industrial machine parts; clutches

(G-8688)
WESTCHESTER SIGNS INC
Also Called: Sign-A-Rama
145 Kisco Ave (10549-1418)
PHONE.................914 666-7446
Karl Theile, *President*
EMP: 5
SALES (est): 335.2K **Privately Held**
SIC: 3993 Signs & advertising specialties

(G-8689)
XELEUM LIGHTING LLC
333 N Bedford Rd Ste 135 (10549-1160)
PHONE.................954 617-8170
Jon Cooper, *Branch Mgr*
EMP: 11
SALES (corp-wide): 6.1MM **Privately Held**
SIC: 3646 Commercial indusl & institutional electric lighting fixtures
PA: Xeleum Lighting, Llc
3430 Quantum Blvd
Boynton Beach FL 33426
914 773-6250

GEOGRAPHIC SECTION

(G-8690)
ZIERICK MANUFACTURING CORP (PA)
131 Radio Circle Dr (10549-2623)
PHONE..................800 882-8020
Fax: 914 666-0216
Gretchen Zierick, *President*
Russell Zierick, *President*
Frank Lynster, *Plant Mgr*
Eric King, *Engineer*
Bill Searles, *Engineer*
▲ **EMP:** 80 **EST:** 1919
SQ FT: 47,500
SALES (est): 13.8MM **Privately Held**
WEB: www.zierick.com
SIC: 3643 3452 3644 3694 Connectors & terminals for electrical devices; solderless connectors (electric wiring devices); nuts, metal; noncurrent-carrying wiring services; terminal boards; ignition apparatus, internal combustion engines; machinery castings, nonferrous: ex. alum., copper, die, etc.

(G-8691)
ZUMBACH ELECTRONICS CORP
Also Called: Elvo
140 Kisco Ave (10549-1412)
PHONE..................914 241-7080
Fax: 914 241-7096
Bruno Zumbach, *Ch of Bd*
Rainer Zumbach, *President*
Jorge Lage, *Area Mgr*
Daleo James, *COO*
Sven Naegeli, *Vice Pres*
▲ **EMP:** 55
SQ FT: 15,000
SALES (est): 10.9MM **Privately Held**
SIC: 3825 Instruments to measure electricity

Mount Marion
Ulster County

(G-8692)
LAIRD TELEMEDIA
2000 Sterling Rd (12456)
PHONE..................845 339-9555
Mark Braunstein, *CEO*
Vincent Bruno, *Vice Pres*
EMP: 110
SALES (est): 8.5MM **Privately Held**
WEB: www.lairdtelemedia.com
SIC: 3651 7812 Household audio & video equipment; motion picture & video production

(G-8693)
METHODS TOOLING & MFG INC
635 Glasco Tpke (12456)
P.O. Box 400 (12456-0400)
PHONE..................845 246-7100
Fax: 845 246-0328
Keith Michaels, *President*
Michael Allen, *Vice Pres*
EMP: 31
SQ FT: 30,000
SALES (est): 5.2MM **Privately Held**
WEB: www.methodstooling.com
SIC: 3545 3444 3648 2514 Tools & accessories for machine tools; sheet metalwork; stage lighting equipment; kitchen cabinets: metal; fabricated plate work (boiler shop); wood kitchen cabinets

(G-8694)
NORTHEAST SOLITE CORPORATION
962 Kings Hwy (12456)
PHONE..................845 246-2177
Fax: 845 246-2619
Gary Green, *Branch Mgr*
Ian Leaning, *Manager*
EMP: 40
SALES (corp-wide): 16.2MM **Privately Held**
WEB: www.nesolite.com
SIC: 3295 1442 3281 Minerals, ground or treated; construction sand & gravel; slate products

PA: Northeast Solite Corporation
1135 Kings Hwy
Saugerties NY 12477
845 246-2646

Mount Morris
Livingston County

(G-8695)
MT MORRIS SHOPPER INC
85 N Main St (14510-1023)
PHONE..................585 658-3520
Fax: 585 658-2962
Jerry W Rolison, *President*
Evelyn C Rolison, *Corp Secy*
EMP: 6
SQ FT: 1,800
SALES (est): 606.5K **Privately Held**
WEB: www.mtmorrisshopper.com
SIC: 2741 Guides: publishing only, not printed on site; shopping news: publishing only, not printed on site

Mount Sinai
Suffolk County

(G-8696)
CHEM-PUTER FRIENDLY INC
1 Sevilla Walk (11766-2825)
P.O. Box 650 (11766-0650)
PHONE..................631 331-2259
Linda Ruben, *President*
Bart Ruben, *General Mgr*
EMP: 31
SALES: 3.7MM **Privately Held**
SIC: 2621 2842 3577 5112 Business form paper; specialty cleaning preparations; computer peripheral equipment; business forms; computer peripheral equipment; computer maintenance & repair

(G-8697)
KENDALL CIRCUITS INC
5507-10 Nesconset Hwy 105 (11766)
PHONE..................631 473-3636
Danielle Seaford, *President*
EMP: 37
SALES (est): 4.6MM **Privately Held**
WEB: www.wordcircuits.com
SIC: 3672 Circuit boards, television & radio printed

(G-8698)
OSPREY BOAT
96 Mount Sinai Ave (11766-2311)
P.O. Box 331, Port Jefferson (11777-0331)
PHONE..................631 331-4153
Amanda Cash, *Owner*
EMP: 5 **EST:** 2010
SALES (est): 441.1K **Privately Held**
SIC: 2399 Fishing nets

(G-8699)
TRANSPORTGISTICS INC
28 N Country Rd Ste 103 (11766-1518)
PHONE..................631 567-4100
Fax: 631 563-4698
Alan Miller, *President*
Stewart Miller, *Senior VP*
Kerry Loudenback, *Vice Pres*
Robert Munro, *Vice Pres*
EMP: 12 **EST:** 2001
SQ FT: 3,000
SALES (est): 2.1MM **Privately Held**
WEB: www.transportgistics.com
SIC: 7372 Business oriented computer software

Mount Upton
Chenango County

(G-8700)
LILAC QUARRIES LLC
1702 State Highway 8 (13809-4163)
PHONE..................607 867-4016
Russell Heath,
EMP: 6

SALES (est): 245.9K **Privately Held**
SIC: 1422 Crushed & broken limestone

Mount Vernon
Westchester County

(G-8701)
AARON GROUP LLC
Also Called: Diamond Dimensions
115 S Macquesten Pkwy (10550-1724)
PHONE..................718 392-5454
Robert Kempler, *President*
Richard Katz, *COO*
Sue MO, *Senior VP*
Shelendra Agrawal, *Controller*
Harry Schnitzer, *Sales Staff*
EMP: 100
SALES (est): 9MM
SALES (corp-wide): 223.6B **Publicly Held**
WEB: www.saaron.com
SIC: 3911 5094 5944 Jewelry, precious metal; jewelry; jewelry, precious stones & precious metals
HQ: Richline Group, Inc.
1385 Broadway Fl 12
New York NY 10018

(G-8702)
ABALON PRECISION MFG CORP (PA)
717 S 3rd Ave (10550-4905)
PHONE..................914 665-7700
Fax: 718 589-0300
Norman Orenstein, *President*
EMP: 15 **EST:** 1945
SQ FT: 9,000
SALES (est): 2.9MM **Privately Held**
SIC: 3441 Fabricated structural metal

(G-8703)
ABALON PRECISION MFG CORP
717 S 3rd Ave (10550-4905)
PHONE..................718 589-5682
Norman Orent, *Manager*
EMP: 15
SALES (corp-wide): 2.9MM **Privately Held**
SIC: 3441 Fabricated structural metal
PA: Abalon Precision Mfg Corp
717 S 3rd Ave
Mount Vernon NY 10550
914 665-7700

(G-8704)
ACCURATE METAL WEATHER STRIP
725 S Fulton Ave (10550-5086)
PHONE..................914 668-6042
Fax: 914 668-6062
Fred O Kammerer, *President*
Ronald R Kammerer, *Corp Secy*
EMP: 7 **EST:** 1898
SQ FT: 15,000
SALES: 17.5MM **Privately Held**
SIC: 3442 3449 Weather strip, metal; miscellaneous metalwork

(G-8705)
ACHILLES CONSTRUCTION CO INC
373 Hayward Ave (10552-1028)
PHONE..................718 389-4717
Fax: 718 389-4719
David Braunstein, *CEO*
EMP: 8 **EST:** 1933
SQ FT: 2,200
SALES: 1MM **Privately Held**
SIC: 3441 Fabricated structural metal

(G-8706)
ALBERT AUGUSTINE LTD
161 S Macquesten Pkwy (10550-1724)
PHONE..................718 913-9635
Fax: 917 661-0223
Stephen Griesgraber, *President*
EMP: 55 **EST:** 1945
SQ FT: 10,500
SALES (est): 648.1K **Privately Held**
WEB: www.albertaugustine.com
SIC: 3931 5736 Strings, musical instrument; musical instrument stores

(G-8707)
APPLE MED URGENT CARE PC
504 Gramatan Ave (10552-3009)
PHONE..................914 523-5965
Jeannine Raciti, *Owner*
EMP: 5
SALES (est): 215.5K **Privately Held**
SIC: 3571 Personal computers (microcomputers)

(G-8708)
ARIESUN INC
160 W 3rd St (10550-3750)
PHONE..................866 274-3049
Donny McPaggart, *President*
Dennis Everton, *General Mgr*
EMP: 50
SQ FT: 10,000
SALES (est): 300K **Privately Held**
SIC: 2086 Pasteurized & mineral waters, bottled & canned; mineral water, carbonated: packaged in cans, bottles, etc.

(G-8709)
BALL CHAIN MFG CO INC (PA)
Also Called: BCM
741 S Fulton Ave (10550-5085)
PHONE..................914 664-7500
Fax: 914 664-7460
Valentine Taubner Jr, *President*
Valentine J Taubner III, *Vice Pres*
James Taubner, *Treasurer*
Teresa Dejesus, *Asst Controller*
Susan Glaser, *Asst Controller*
▲ **EMP:** 90 **EST:** 1938
SQ FT: 35,000
SALES (est): 13.9MM **Privately Held**
WEB: www.ballchain.com
SIC: 3462 Gear & chain forgings

(G-8710)
BARRETT BRONZE INC
115 Miller Pl (10550-4728)
PHONE..................914 699-6060
Fax: 914 699-6061
Eli Ross, *President*
Jamie Ross, *Principal*
Jeff Hirshon, *Prdtn Mgr*
▲ **EMP:** 20
SALES (est): 2.1MM **Privately Held**
WEB: www.barrettbronze.com
SIC: 3299 2821 Statuary: gypsum, clay, papier mache, metal, etc.; plastics materials & resins

(G-8711)
BEACON ADHESIVES INC
Also Called: Beacon Chemical
125 S Macquesten Pkwy (10550-1724)
PHONE..................914 699-3400
Fax: 914 699-2783
Milton Meshirer, *CEO*
David Meshirer, *President*
Barbara Meshirer, *Corp Secy*
Jose Espinosa, *Vice Pres*
Debbie Meshirer-Wojcik, *Vice Pres*
◆ **EMP:** 30
SQ FT: 20,000
SALES (est): 7MM **Privately Held**
WEB: www.beacon1.com
SIC: 2891 Adhesives

(G-8712)
BRIDGE METAL INDUSTRIES LLC
717 S 3rd Ave (10550-4905)
PHONE..................914 663-9200
Alan Cowen, *Mng Member*
Frank Giordano, *Manager*
Darryl Veluez, *Manager*
▲ **EMP:** 130
SQ FT: 8,000
SALES (est): 16.4MM **Privately Held**
SIC: 2542 Partitions & fixtures, except wood

(G-8713)
BRONX WSTCHESTER TEMPERING INC
160 S Macquesten Pkwy (10550-1705)
PHONE..................914 663-9400
Miles Kiho, *President*
▲ **EMP:** 26

Mount Vernon - Westchester County (G-8714)

SALES (est): 4.4MM **Privately Held**
SIC: 3229 Art, decorative & novelty glassware

(G-8714)
CANAL ASPHALT INC
800 Canal St (10550-4708)
PHONE..............................914 667-8500
Fax: 914 667-3879
August M Nigro, *President*
Maria Dioguardi, *Vice Pres*
Sakir Thanawana, *Manager*
EMP: 10
SALES (est): 2.7MM **Privately Held**
SIC: 2951 Asphalt paving mixtures & blocks

(G-8715)
CASTOLEUM CORPORATION
240 E 7th St (10550-4615)
P.O. Box 41, Yonkers (10710-0041)
PHONE..............................914 664-5877
Fax: 914 664-9383
S V Goldrich, *President*
Leslie Schwebel, *Corp Secy*
Steve Neil, *Vice Pres*
Mark House, *Government*
EMP: 15
SQ FT: 25,000
SALES (est): 2.8MM **Privately Held**
WEB: www.sterifab.com
SIC: 2992 2842 5169 Lubricating oils & greases; disinfectants, household or industrial plant; coal tar products, primary & intermediate; gum & wood chemicals

(G-8716)
CHESTER WEST COUNTY PRESS
29 W 4th St (10550-4108)
P.O. Box 152, White Plains (10602-0152)
PHONE..............................914 684-0006
EMP: 6 EST: 1959
SALES (est): 280.2K **Privately Held**
SIC: 2711 Newspapers-Publishing/Printing

(G-8717)
CLASSIC MEDALLICS INC
520 S Fulton Ave (10550-5010)
PHONE..............................718 392-5410
Fax: 914 530-6258
Gerald Singer, *President*
Lucy Walsh, *General Mgr*
Mario Singer, *Vice Pres*
Salma Tasin, *Bookkeeper*
Mobola Sapara, *Comptroller*
▲ EMP: 50 EST: 1941
SALES (est): 9.7MM **Privately Held**
SIC: 3499 5094 Trophies, metal, except silver; jewelry

(G-8718)
COLD MIX MANUFACTURING CORP
65 Edison Ave (10550-5003)
PHONE..............................718 463-1444
Dario Amicucci, *President*
Mark Pugliese, *Plant Mgr*
EMP: 17
SQ FT: 2,000
SALES (est): 4.5MM **Privately Held**
SIC: 2951 Asphalt paving mixtures & blocks

(G-8719)
COVENTRY MANUFACTURING CO INC (PA)
115 E 3rd St (10550-3606)
PHONE..............................914 668-2212
Myron S Gorel, *President*
Edward R Gorel, *Vice Pres*
Phyllis Gorel, *Admin Sec*
EMP: 31 EST: 1953
SQ FT: 26,000
SALES (est): 2.9MM **Privately Held**
WEB: www.trulytubular.com
SIC: 3498 3317 3312 Tube fabricating (contract bending & shaping); steel pipe & tubes; blast furnaces & steel mills

(G-8720)
CROWN DIE CASTING CORP
268 W Lincoln Ave (10550-2509)
PHONE..............................914 667-5400
Fax: 914 667-4284
Sam Strober, *President*
Bill Gutwein, *Vice Pres*
Lynn Strober, *Office Mgr*
EMP: 28
SQ FT: 17,000
SALES (est): 6MM **Privately Held**
WEB: www.crowndiecasting.com
SIC: 3364 3643 3444 3369 Nonferrous die-castings except aluminum; connectors, electric cord; sheet metalwork; nonferrous foundries; aluminum foundries; aluminum die-castings

(G-8721)
CROWN SIGN SYSTEMS INC
2 South St (10550-1708)
PHONE..............................914 375-2118
Michelle Strum, *President*
Tamara Crewa, *Project Mgr*
Carolyn Cohen, *Manager*
▲ EMP: 11
SALES (est): 1.7MM **Privately Held**
SIC: 3993 Signs & advertising specialties

(G-8722)
DAB-O-MATIC CORP (PA)
896 S Columbus Ave (10550-5074)
P.O. Box 3839 (10553-3839)
PHONE..............................914 699-7070
Fax: 914 699-7052
Gerard Magaletti, *Ch of Bd*
James P Bell, *President*
Scott Bell, *Purchasing*
Daphne Maurrasse, *Manager*
EMP: 67
SQ FT: 29,000
SALES (est): 11.9MM **Privately Held**
WEB: www.dabomatic.com
SIC: 3953 Pads, inking & stamping

(G-8723)
DRG NEW YORK HOLDINGS CORP (PA)
700 S Fulton Ave (10550-5014)
PHONE..............................914 668-9000
Fax: 914 668-6900
Montague Wolfson, *Ch of Bd*
Stephen Bardfield, *Corp Secy*
Salvatore Ferrera, *Controller*
◆ EMP: 100
SQ FT: 40,000
SALES (est): 19MM **Privately Held**
WEB: www.wolfsoncasing.com
SIC: 2011 5149 Meat packing plants; sausage casings

(G-8724)
DUNCAN & SON CARPENTRY INC
1 W Prospect Ave (10550-2008)
PHONE..............................914 664-4311
EMP: 21
SQ FT: 10,000
SALES (est): 2.2MM **Privately Held**
SIC: 2431 Carpentry Contractor

(G-8725)
DUNLEA WHL GL & MIRROR INC
Also Called: J&T Macquesten Realty
147 S Macquesten Pkwy (10550-1724)
PHONE..............................914 664-5277
Fax: 914 664-4427
Timothy Dunlea, *President*
John Arminio, *Vice Pres*
Alex Puranbuda, *Vice Pres*
EMP: 6
SQ FT: 7,000
SALES (est): 837.3K **Privately Held**
SIC: 3231 Insulating glass: made from purchased glass

(G-8726)
FINA CABINET CORP
20 N Macquesten Pkwy (10550-1841)
PHONE..............................718 409-2900
Fax: 718 409-2956
Annette Alberti, *President*
John Albertti, *Vice Pres*
EMP: 5
SALES (est): 764.8K **Privately Held**
SIC: 2521 2434 2541 Cabinets, office: wood; wood kitchen cabinets; wood partitions & fixtures

(G-8727)
GERITREX LLC
144 E Kingsbridge Rd (10550-4909)
PHONE..............................914 668-4003
Fax: 914 668-4047
Boyd Relac, *President*
Tim Sawyer, *Chairman*
John Francis, *Exec VP*
Tonyalisa Thomas, *Purchasing*
David Gershen, *CFO*
▲ EMP: 40
SQ FT: 47,500
SALES (est): 8.3MM **Privately Held**
WEB: www.geritrex.com
SIC: 2834 Pharmaceutical preparations

(G-8728)
GERITREX HOLDINGS INC (PA)
144 E Kingsbridge Rd (10550-4909)
PHONE..............................914 668-4003
Mitch Blashinsky, *CEO*
EMP: 4
SALES (est): 1.5MM **Privately Held**
SIC: 2834 6719 Pharmaceutical preparations; investment holding companies, except banks

(G-8729)
GIAGNI ENTERPRISES LLC
Also Called: Qmi
550 S Columbus Ave (10550-4712)
PHONE..............................914 699-6500
Vincent Giagni, *Mng Member*
EMP: 5
SALES (est): 582.9K **Privately Held**
SIC: 3432 Faucets & spigots, metal & plastic

(G-8730)
GIAGNI INTERNATIONAL CORP
548 S Columbus Ave (10550-4712)
PHONE..............................914 699-6500
Vincent Giagni, *President*
Dan Gaulin, *Prdtn Mgr*
EMP: 5
SALES (est): 400K **Privately Held**
SIC: 3432 Faucets & spigots, metal & plastic

(G-8731)
GRACE RYAN & MAGNUS MLLWK LLC
17 N Bleeker St (10550-1801)
PHONE..............................914 665-0902
Joseph Grace, *Mng Member*
Enrique Lopez, *Manager*
Thor Magnus,
Eamonn Ryan,
EMP: 70
SQ FT: 10,000
SALES (est): 7.4MM **Privately Held**
SIC: 2431 Millwork

(G-8732)
GRANITE TOPS INC
716 S Columbus Ave (10550-4717)
PHONE..............................914 699-2909
Fax: 914 699-2425
Christopher Sanzaro, *President*
EMP: 40
SQ FT: 11,000
SALES (est): 3.4MM **Privately Held**
SIC: 3281 Cut stone & stone products

(G-8733)
H & S EDIBLE PRODUCTS CORP
119 Fulton Ln (10550-4607)
PHONE..............................914 413-3489
Fax: 914 664-8304
Mari P Sweeney, *President*
Peter J Rowan, *Vice Pres*
Chasity Misserio, *Office Mgr*
EMP: 30
SQ FT: 13,000
SALES (est): 3.2MM **Privately Held**
SIC: 2099 2051 Bread crumbs, not made in bakeries; bread, cake & related products

(G-8734)
HAMLET PRODUCTS INC
221 N Macquesten Pkwy (10550-1005)
PHONE..............................914 665-0307
Fax: 914 665-0248
Russ Hamlet, *President*
Marlo Barreto, *Vice Pres*
Randy Hamlet, *Vice Pres*
▲ EMP: 12
SQ FT: 12,000
SALES (est): 1.9MM **Privately Held**
WEB: www.hamletproducts.com
SIC: 2542 3089 5046 2541 Fixtures, store: except wood; cases, plastic; commercial equipment; wood partitions & fixtures

(G-8735)
HI SPEED ENVELOPE CO INC
560 S 3rd Ave Ste 1 (10550-4568)
PHONE..............................718 617-1600
Charles Romeo, *President*
Mary Romeo-Springman, *Corp Secy*
Anthony Romeo, *Director*
Fortunato C Romeo, *Director*
Jim Romeo, *Director*
EMP: 16 EST: 1939
SQ FT: 26,000
SALES (est): 1.9MM **Privately Held**
WEB: www.hispeedprinting.com
SIC: 2752 2759 Commercial printing, offset; letterpress printing

(G-8736)
HI-TECH CNC MACHINING CORP
13 Elm Ave (10550-2305)
PHONE..............................914 668-5090
Karl Hormann, *President*
Karl Hormann Jr, *Vice Pres*
EMP: 5 EST: 1970
SQ FT: 7,000
SALES (est): 1.2MM **Privately Held**
SIC: 3599 Machine shop, jobbing & repair

(G-8737)
ICE AIR LLC
80 Hartford Ave (10553-1327)
PHONE..............................914 668-4700
Fredric Nadel,
Moshe Siegel,
▲ EMP: 20
SQ FT: 26,000
SALES (est): 7.5MM **Privately Held**
SIC: 3585 Air conditioning units, complete: domestic or industrial

(G-8738)
INTERNATIONAL MDSE SVCS INC
336 S Fulton Ave Fl 1 (10553-1748)
PHONE..............................914 699-4000
Johnny Peralta, *President*
EMP: 5
SALES (est): 639.4K **Privately Held**
SIC: 3578 Automatic teller machines (ATM)

(G-8739)
ISO PLASTICS CORP
160 E 1st St (10550-3435)
PHONE..............................914 663-8300
Raul Silva, *President*
Jim Coughlin, *Vice Pres*
Fred Squitire, *Treasurer*
▲ EMP: 65
SQ FT: 43,000
SALES (est): 11.1MM **Privately Held**
WEB: www.isoplastics.com
SIC: 3089 3599 Molding primary plastic; machine & other job shop work

(G-8740)
J-K PROSTHETICS & ORTHOTICS
699 N Macquesten Pkwy (10552-2121)
PHONE..............................914 699-2077
Fax: 914 699-0676
Jack Caputo, *President*
Kathleen Caputo, *Corp Secy*
EMP: 22
SALES (est): 2.7MM **Privately Held**
WEB: www.trishare.com
SIC: 3842 Prosthetic appliances

(G-8741)
K & B STAMPING CO INC
Also Called: K & B Signs
29 Mount Vernon Ave (10550-2492)
PHONE..............................914 664-8555
Fax: 914 664-6667
Albert Aghabekian, *President*
Elaine Dechiara, *Manager*
EMP: 7

SQ FT: 4,500
SALES (est): 1MM Privately Held
WEB: www.kbsign.com
SIC: 2759 3993 Plateless engraving; screen printing; neon signs; displays & cutouts, window & lobby

(G-8742)
KEY DIGITAL SYSTEMS INC
521 E 3rd St (10553-1606)
PHONE..................914 667-9700
Fax: 914 668-8666
Mikhail Tsingberg, *President*
Shakil Khan, *Accounting Mgr*
Farisa Pepic, *Accountant*
Michael Lakhter, *VP Sales*
Dan O'Donnell, *Regl Sales Mgr*
▲ EMP: 20
SQ FT: 24,000
SALES (est): 4.7MM Privately Held
WEB: www.keydigital.com
SIC: 3651 Household audio & video equipment

(G-8743)
KING LITHOGRAPHERS INC (PA)
245 S 4th Ave (10550-3804)
PHONE..................914 667-4200
Fax: 914 667-5281
Martin Rego, *President*
Joseph A Rego, *Treasurer*
EMP: 35
SQ FT: 55,000
SALES (est): 4.4MM Privately Held
WEB: www.kinglitho.com
SIC: 2752 2789 Commercial printing, lithographic; bookbinding & related work

(G-8744)
KINGSTON BUILDING PRODUCTS LLC
Also Called: Century Awning Concepts
11 Brookdale Pl Ste 101 (10550-3505)
PHONE..................914 665-0707
John Kingston, *President*
EMP: 9
SALES (est): 367K Privately Held
SIC: 2394 Canvas awnings & canopies; shades, canvas: made from purchased materials

(G-8745)
LAMPARTS CO INC
160 E 3rd St Ste 2 (10550-3694)
PHONE..................914 723-8986
Fax: 914 668-5941
Anthony Sorbaro Jr, *President*
EMP: 10 EST: 1948
SQ FT: 30,000
SALES (est): 1.5MM Privately Held
SIC: 3648 3469 Lighting equipment; metal stampings

(G-8746)
LEONARDO PRINTING CORP
Also Called: Leonardo Prntng
529 E 3rd St (10553-1606)
PHONE..................914 664-7890
Fax: 914 664-6767
Frank Leonardo Jr, *President*
Mark Leonardo, *Vice Pres*
Steven Leonardo, *Admin Sec*
EMP: 5 EST: 1947
SALES (est): 691K Privately Held
SIC: 2754 Job printing, gravure

(G-8747)
LGN MATERIALS & SOLUTIONS
149 Esplanade (10553-1116)
PHONE..................888 414-0005
Maria Nonni, *President*
EMP: 12
SALES (est): 376.5K Privately Held
SIC: 2796 Steel line engraving for the printing trade

(G-8748)
LUMINATTA INC
Also Called: Apollo Lighting and Hasco Ltg
717 S 3rd Ave (10550-4905)
PHONE..................914 664-6091
Fax: 914 665-5941
Joseph Sagona, *President*
Paul Verkleij, *Vice Pres*
EMP: 8 EST: 1947
SQ FT: 14,000
SALES (est): 1.5MM Privately Held
WEB: www.apollolighting.com
SIC: 3646 Commercial indusl & institutional electric lighting fixtures

(G-8749)
M&F STRINGING LLC
2 Cortlandt St (10550-2706)
PHONE..................914 664-1600
Fax: 914 664-1455
Kenneth Jacobs, *Mng Member*
EMP: 20 EST: 1953
SQ FT: 8,000
SALES (est): 2MM Privately Held
WEB: www.mfstringing.com
SIC: 2631 Cardboard, tagboard & strawboard

(G-8750)
METAL MAN RESTORATION
254 E 3rd St Fl 1 (10553-5115)
PHONE..................914 662-4218
Fax: 914 665-4219
Anthony Bugliomo, *Principal*
EMP: 10
SALES (est): 700K Privately Held
SIC: 3471 Electroplating & plating

(G-8751)
MICHAEL ANTHONY JEWELERS LLC (DH)
115 S Macquesten Pkwy (10550-1724)
P.O. Box 31283, West Palm Beach FL (33420-1283)
PHONE..................914 699-0000
Fax: 914 664-4884
Anthony Paolercio Jr, *Vice Pres*
Linda Levin, *Purch Dir*
Betty Sou, *CFO*
Roseanne Bosco, *Human Res Mgr*
Terri Faber, *Sales Executive*
EMP: 150
SQ FT: 150,000
SALES (est): 32MM
SALES (corp-wide): 223.6B Publicly Held
SIC: 3911 5944 5094 Jewelry, precious metal; earrings, precious metal; rings, finger: precious metal; bracelets, precious metal; jewelry stores; jewelry & precious stones

(G-8752)
MICK RADIO NUCLEAR INSTRUMENT
521 Homestead Ave (10550-4619)
PHONE..................718 597-3999
Fax: 914 665-8834
Felix Mick, *President*
Verena Mick, *Corp Secy*
Maria Saltares, *Admin Asst*
EMP: 19
SQ FT: 25,000
SALES (est): 3.6MM
SALES (corp-wide): 145.8MM Privately Held
SIC: 3841 Surgical & medical instruments
HQ: Eckert & Ziegler Bebig Sa
    Zone Industrielle C
    Seneffe 7180
    645 208-01

(G-8753)
MITCHELL ELECTRONICS CORP
85 W Grand St (10552-2108)
PHONE..................914 699-3800
Fax: 914 699-1022
Nancy Lerner, *President*
Jonathan Lerner, *Corp Secy*
EMP: 25 EST: 1956
SQ FT: 5,000
SALES (est): 2.5MM Privately Held
WEB: www.mitchellxfmr.com
SIC: 3677 3612 Electronic coils, transformers & other inductors; specialty transformers

(G-8754)
MOUNT VERNON IRON WORKS INC
130 Miller Pl (10550-4706)
P.O. Box 3009 (10553-3009)
PHONE..................914 668-7064
Fax: 914 668-7122
Joeseph Lividini, *President*
Peter M Lividini, *Vice Pres*
Grace Lividini, *Treasurer*
EMP: 7 EST: 1945
SQ FT: 2,000
SALES (est): 1.4MM Privately Held
SIC: 3441 Expansion joints (structural shapes), iron or steel

(G-8755)
MUNN WORKS LLC
150 N Macquesten Pkwy (10550-1836)
PHONE..................914 665-6100
Beverly O'Keesse, *Accounting Mgr*
Max Munn, *Mng Member*
◆ EMP: 23
SALES (est): 4.7MM Privately Held
SIC: 3231 3211 Framed mirrors; antique glass

(G-8756)
NOBLE PINE PRODUCTS CO INC
240 E 7th St (10550-4615)
P.O. Box 41, Yonkers (10710-0041)
PHONE..................914 664-5877
Sylvia Goldrich, *President*
Leslie Schwebel, *Corp Secy*
Steven Goldrich, *Vice Pres*
Steve Neil, *Vice Pres*
EMP: 12
SQ FT: 12,000
SALES (est): 2.2MM Privately Held
SIC: 2842 2879 Disinfectants, household or industrial plant; insecticides, agricultural or household

(G-8757)
NSI INDUSTRIES LLC
Tork Division
50 S Macquesten Pkwy (10550-1741)
PHONE..................800 841-2505
R Sam Shankar, *Division Pres*
Leonard Caponigro, *Vice Pres*
Jerry Kerensky, *Agent*
Gil Ledoux, *Agent*
EMP: 200 Privately Held
WEB: www.nsipolaris.com
SIC: 3625 3674 Relays & industrial controls; switches, electric power; light sensitive devices
PA: Nsi Industries, Llc
    9730 Northcross Center Ct
    Huntersville NC 28078

(G-8758)
OWN INSTRUMENT INC
250 E 7th St (10550-4615)
PHONE..................914 668-6546
Fax: 914 668-8434
Gerald Chapins, *President*
Patricia Chapins, *Treasurer*
EMP: 13 EST: 1957
SQ FT: 5,000
SALES (est): 2.1MM Privately Held
WEB: www.owninstrument.com
SIC: 3492 Fluid power valves & hose fittings

(G-8759)
PCI INDUSTRIES CORP
550 Franklin Ave (10550-4516)
PHONE..................914 662-2700
Richard Persico, *President*
EMP: 22
SALES (est): 3.5MM Privately Held
SIC: 3999 Barber & beauty shop equipment

(G-8760)
PEPSI-COLA BOTTLING CO NY INC
601 S Fulton Ave (10550-5094)
PHONE..................914 699-2600
Fax: 914 699-2638
Mike Freeman, *Sales Executive*
Jim Perry, *Technology*
EMP: 376
SALES (corp-wide): 473.9MM Privately Held
SIC: 2086 Soft drinks: packaged in cans, bottles, etc.
PA: Pepsi-Cola Bottling Company Of New York, Inc.
    11402 15th Ave Ste 5
    College Point NY 11356
    718 392-1000

(G-8761)
PERFECT SHOULDER COMPANY INC
2 Cortlandt St (10550-2706)
PHONE..................914 699-8100
Harold Greenberg, *President*
Julio Figueroa, *Division Mgr*
Ketty Manno, *Sales Staff*
Julius Greenberg, *Administration*
▲ EMP: 25 EST: 1938
SQ FT: 35,000
SALES (est): 2.7MM Privately Held
SIC: 2396 Pads, shoulder: for coats, suits, etc.

(G-8762)
PRECISION COSMETICS MFG CO
519 S 5th Ave Ste 6 (10550-4476)
PHONE..................914 667-1200
Aubrey Fenton Sr, *President*
Aubrey Fenton Jr, *Treasurer*
EMP: 5
SQ FT: 5,000
SALES (est): 50K Privately Held
SIC: 2844 Lipsticks

(G-8763)
PREMIER BRANDS OF AMERICA INC (PA)
31 South St Ste 2s (10550-1748)
PHONE..................914 667-6200
Steven D Corsun, *Ch of Bd*
Glenn Livi, *VP Opers*
Osvaldo Cruz, *Prdtn Mgr*
Alex Corsun, *Purch Agent*
Pierre Mathelier, *Engineer*
▲ EMP: 120
SQ FT: 75,000
SALES (est): 35.7MM Privately Held
WEB: www.premier-brands.com
SIC: 3842 3131 2842 Surgical appliances & supplies; orthopedic appliances; footwear cut stock; shoe polish or cleaner

(G-8764)
PREMIER BRANDS OF AMERICA INC
120 Pearl St (10550-1725)
PHONE..................718 325-3000
Vinnie Gioffre, *VP Sales*
EMP: 25
SALES (corp-wide): 35.7MM Privately Held
SIC: 2842 2865 Shoe polish or cleaner; polishing preparations & related products; cyclic crudes & intermediates
PA: Premier Brands Of America Inc
    31 South St Ste 2s
    Mount Vernon NY 10550
    914 667-6200

(G-8765)
PRO-LINE SOLUTIONS INC
Also Called: Pry Care Products
18 Sargent Pl (10550-4727)
P.O. Box 651, Bronx (10465-0617)
PHONE..................914 664-0002
Alex Lodato, *President*
EMP: 7
SQ FT: 10,000
SALES (est): 894.3K Privately Held
SIC: 2841 Soap & other detergents

(G-8766)
PROACTIVE MEDICAL PRODUCTS LLC
270 Washington St (10553-1017)
PHONE..................845 205-6004
Mordecai Light, *President*
Brian Goldstein, *VP Sales*
▲ EMP: 8 EST: 2012
SQ FT: 20,000
SALES: 7MM Privately Held
SIC: 3841 Diagnostic apparatus, medical

(G-8767)
PROMPTUS ELECTRONIC HDWR INC
Also Called: Giagni Enterprises
520 Homestead Ave (10550-4620)
PHONE..................914 699-4700
Vincent Giagni Jr, *President*
Steve Giagni, *Sales Executive*

Mount Vernon - Westchester County (G-8768)

Paul Vamvaketis, *Director*
▲ **EMP:** 28
SQ FT: 15,000
SALES (est): 4.7MM **Privately Held**
WEB: www.promptusinc.com
SIC: 3699 Electrical equipment & supplies

(G-8768)
PURINE PHARMA LLC
144 E Kingsbridge Rd (10550-4909)
PHONE 315 705-4030
Mount Vernon,
EMP: 25
SQ FT: 32,778
SALES (est): 147.8K
SALES (corp-wide): 1.4MM **Privately Held**
SIC: 2834 Cough medicines; analgesics; vitamin preparations
PA: Geritrex Holdings, Inc.
144 E Kingsbridge Rd
Mount Vernon NY 10550
914 668-4003

(G-8769)
R I R COMMUNICATIONS SYSTEMS (PA)
20 Nuvern Ave (10550-4819)
P.O. Box 3660 (10553-3660)
PHONE 718 706-9957
Fax: 914 664-0329
Ralph Robinson, *President*
Inez Robinson, *Manager*
EMP: 8
SALES (est): 1.7MM **Privately Held**
SIC: 3661 Telephones & telephone apparatus

(G-8770)
R I R COMMUNICATIONS SYSTEMS
20 Nuvern Ave (10550-4819)
PHONE 718 706-9957
Ralph Robinson, *Manager*
EMP: 20
SALES (corp-wide): 1.7MM **Privately Held**
SIC: 3661 Telephones & telephone apparatus
PA: R I R Communications Systems Inc
20 Nuvern Ave
Mount Vernon NY 10550
718 706-9957

(G-8771)
R V H ESTATES INC
138 Mount Vernon Ave (10550-1719)
PHONE 914 664-9888
Robert Belluzzi, *President*
Vincent Belluzzi, *Vice Pres*
EMP: 6 **EST:** 1981
SALES: 390K **Privately Held**
SIC: 2599 Bar, restaurant & cafeteria furniture

(G-8772)
RELIABLE ELEC MT VERNON INC
519 S 5th Ave (10550-4498)
PHONE 914 668-4440
Fax: 914 668-4972
Jay Friedman, *President*
Irv Seiger, *Vice Pres*
EMP: 23
SQ FT: 8,000
SALES: 75K **Privately Held**
WEB: www.reliableelectronics.net
SIC: 3577 Computer peripheral equipment

(G-8773)
ROHLFS STINED LEADED GL STUDIO
783 S 3rd Ave (10550-4946)
PHONE 914 699-4848
Fax: 914 699-7091
Peter A Rohlf, *CEO*
Gregory Rohlf, *Vice Pres*
EMP: 25
SQ FT: 10,000
SALES (est): 3.1MM **Privately Held**
WEB: www.rohlfstudio.com
SIC: 3231 3442 Stained glass: made from purchased glass; leaded glass; casements, aluminum

(G-8774)
ROYAL CARIBBEAN JAMAICAN BKY (PA)
Also Called: Royal Caribbean Bakery
620 S Fulton Ave (10550-5012)
PHONE 914 668-6868
Jeanette Hosang, *President*
Vincent Hosang, *Vice Pres*
EMP: 50
SQ FT: 20,000
SALES (est): 8.2MM **Privately Held**
SIC: 2051 5149 Bread, cake & related products; bakery: wholesale or wholesale/retail combined; bakery products

(G-8775)
S & S GRAPHICS INC
521 E 3rd St (10553-1606)
PHONE 914 668-4230
Fax: 914 668-3674
Stuart Standard, *President*
Jason Standard, *Vice Pres*
EMP: 11
SQ FT: 21,000
SALES: 2.3MM **Privately Held**
SIC: 2759 Commercial printing

(G-8776)
SANDFORD BLVD DONUTS INC
440 E Sandford Blvd (10550-4729)
PHONE 914 663-7708
Fax: 914 663-7709
Nick Rassias, *President*
EMP: 6
SALES (est): 448.4K **Privately Held**
SIC: 2051 Doughnuts, except frozen

(G-8777)
SECS INC (PA)
550 S Columbus Ave (10550-4712)
PHONE 914 667-5600
Fax: 914 699-0377
Vincent Giagni, *Ch of Bd*
Leonora Giagni, *Ch of Bd*
Stephen Giagni, *President*
Kevin McBrien, *VP Mktg*
▲ **EMP:** 20
SQ FT: 15,000
SALES (est): 6.4MM **Privately Held**
WEB: www.prosecs.com
SIC: 3462 Gears, forged steel

(G-8778)
SECS INC
550 S Columbus Ave (10550-4712)
PHONE 914 667-5600
Nichoas Bianculli, *Principal*
EMP: 30
SALES (corp-wide): 6.4MM **Privately Held**
WEB: www.prosecs.com
SIC: 3679 3462 Electronic switches; gears, forged steel
PA: Secs, Inc.
550 S Columbus Ave
Mount Vernon NY 10550
914 667-5600

(G-8779)
SENTAGE CORPORATION
Also Called: D P Mount Vernon
161 S Macquesten Pkwy 2 (10550-1724)
PHONE 914 664-2200
Fax: 914 664-2538
Barry Rothenberg, *Vice Pres*
Michael Petschulat, *Traffic Mgr*
Herman Braverman, *Manager*
Rick West, *Executive*
EMP: 42
SALES (corp-wide): 100MM **Privately Held**
WEB: www.dentalservices.net
SIC: 3843 Dental laboratory equipment
PA: Sentage Corporation
801 12th Ave N
Minneapolis MN 55411
412 431-3353

(G-8780)
SIGMUND COHN CORP
121 S Columbus Ave (10553-1324)
PHONE 914 664-5300
Thomas Cohn, *President*
Sue Keneally, *Purchasing*
Michael Myers, *QC Mgr*
George Pilke, *CFO*
▲ **EMP:** 55 **EST:** 1901
SQ FT: 72,000
SALES (est): 13.2MM **Privately Held**
SIC: 3356 3496 3339 3315 Nonferrous rolling & drawing; precious metals; miscellaneous fabricated wire products; primary nonferrous metals; steel wire & related products

(G-8781)
TALYARPS CORPORATION
716 S Columbus Ave (10550-4717)
PHONE 914 699-3030
Fax: 914 699-3035
Jack Orentlikher, *Principal*
Tom Klapach, *Controller*
EMP: 30
SALES (corp-wide): 33.6MM **Privately Held**
WEB: www.spraylat.com
SIC: 2851 Paints & paint additives
PA: Talyarps Corporation
143 Sparks Ave
Pelham NY 10803
914 699-3030

(G-8782)
TAPE SYSTEMS INC
630 S Columbus Ave (10550-4734)
P.O. Box 8612, Pelham (10803-8612)
PHONE 914 668-3700
Fax: 914 668-3987
Aniello Scotti, *President*
Ana Tongco, *Executive*
▲ **EMP:** 10
SQ FT: 30,000
SALES (est): 2.2MM **Privately Held**
SIC: 3842 Adhesive tape & plasters, medicated or non-medicated

(G-8783)
TENNYSON MACHINE CO INC
535 S 5th Ave (10550-4483)
PHONE 914 668-5468
Fax: 914 668-5002
Lawrence A Castiglia, *President*
EMP: 16 **EST:** 1961
SQ FT: 10,000
SALES: 1.2MM **Privately Held**
SIC: 3599 Machine shop, jobbing & repair

(G-8784)
TORK INC (PA)
50 S Macquesten Pkwy (10550-1741)
PHONE 914 664-3542
Fax: 914 664-5052
Victoria White, *Ch of Bd*
R Sam Shankar, *President*
Leonard Caponigro, *Vice Pres*
Nicholas Murlo, *Vice Pres*
Janice Bastin, *Safety Mgr*
▲ **EMP:** 100 **EST:** 1934
SQ FT: 40,000
SALES (est): 12.8MM **Privately Held**
WEB: www.tork.com
SIC: 3625 3674 Relays & industrial controls; switches, electric power; light sensitive devices

(G-8785)
TRAC REGULATORS INC
160 S Terrace Ave (10550-2408)
PHONE 914 699-9352
Fax: 914 699-9367
Adelmo Costantini, *President*
Cynthia La Sorsa, *Corp Secy*
Tom Notaro, *Vice Pres*
George Witzel, *Shareholder*
EMP: 20
SQ FT: 10,000
SALES (est): 3.4MM **Privately Held**
SIC: 3613 3491 Regulators, power; industrial valves

(G-8786)
TRI STAR LABEL INC
630 S Columbus Ave (10550-4734)
PHONE 914 237-4800
Dan Mesisco, *President*
Neil Scotti, *Vice Pres*
Laura Annunziata, *Admin Sec*
▲ **EMP:** 7
SQ FT: 8,000
SALES: 900K **Privately Held**
SIC: 2672 Tape, pressure sensitive: made from purchased materials

(G-8787)
TRI-TECHNOLOGIES INC
40 Hartford Ave (10553-5119)
PHONE 914 699-2001
Fax: 914 699-2002
David Hirsch, *CEO*
Dennis Di Donato, *President*
Lisa Bertuzzi, *Admin Asst*
▲ **EMP:** 48
SQ FT: 25,000
SALES (est): 11MM **Privately Held**
SIC: 3484 3451 3444 3469 Small arms; screw machine products; sheet metalwork; metal stampings

(G-8788)
TRULY TUBULAR FITTING CORP
115 E 3rd St (10550-3606)
P.O. Box 1160 (10551-1160)
PHONE 914 664-8686
Fax: 914 668-2617
Myron S Gorel, *President*
Edward Gorel, *Vice Pres*
Phyllis Gorel, *Admin Sec*
EMP: 19
SQ FT: 26,000
SALES: 800K
SALES (corp-wide): 2.9MM **Privately Held**
WEB: www.trulytubular.com
SIC: 3498 Fabricated pipe & fittings
PA: Coventry Manufacturing Company, Inc.
115 E 3rd St
Mount Vernon NY 10550
914 668-2212

(G-8789)
TURBOFIL PACKAGING MCHS LLC
30 Beach St (10550-1702)
PHONE 914 239-3878
Deborah Smook, *VP Mktg*
Eli Uriel, *Branch Mgr*
Elaine Epps, *Director*
▲ **EMP:** 10
SQ FT: 7,000
SALES (est): 2MM **Privately Held**
WEB: www.turbofil.com
SIC: 3565 Packing & wrapping machinery

(G-8790)
UFS INDUSTRIES INC
Also Called: Sally Sherman Foods
300 N Macquesten Pkwy (10550-1008)
PHONE 718 822-1100
Fax: 914 664-2846
Thomas Recine, *President*
Felix Endico, *COO*
Michael Lodolce, *VP Opers*
Ann Colantuono, *Controller*
Debra Gentile, *Accounts Mgr*
EMP: 100 **EST:** 1930
SQ FT: 50,000
SALES (est): 23.3MM **Privately Held**
SIC: 2099 Food preparations; cole slaw, in bulk; salads, fresh or refrigerated

(G-8791)
UNITED IRON INC
6 Roslyn Pl (10550-4540)
PHONE 914 667-5700
Fax: 914 667-5925
Randall Rifelli, *President*
Teodor Valev, *Research*
Pat Zacchi, *Human Res Mgr*
EMP: 30 **EST:** 1922
SQ FT: 27,000
SALES (est): 7.3MM **Privately Held**
SIC: 3449 3441 3446 Miscellaneous metalwork; fabricated structural metal; architectural metalwork

(G-8792)
YOUR WAY CUSTOM CABINETS INC
20 N Macquesten Pkwy (10550-1841)
PHONE 914 371-1870
Annette Alberti, *President*
EMP: 7
SALES (est): 915.7K **Privately Held**
SIC: 2434 Wood kitchen cabinets

Mountainville
Orange County

(G-8793)
GLUTEN FREE BAKE SHOP INC
Also Called: Katz Gluten Free
19 Industry Dr (10953)
P.O. Box 58, Monroe (10949-0058)
PHONE..................845 782-5307
Rachel Jacobowitz, *President*
Mordche Jacobowitz, *Vice Pres*
▼ EMP: 50
SQ FT: 13,000
SALES (est): 9.3MM **Privately Held**
SIC: 2051 Bakery: wholesale or wholesale/retail combined

(G-8794)
JP FILLING INC
20 Industry Dr (10953)
PHONE..................845 534-4793
Joel Polatsek, *President*
▲ EMP: 65
SQ FT: 3,000
SALES (est): 3.2MM **Privately Held**
SIC: 2844 Perfumes & colognes

Munnsville
Madison County

(G-8795)
BRIGGS & STRATTON CORPORATION
5375 N Main St (13409-4003)
PHONE..................315 495-0100
Fax: 315 495-0109
Timothy Wild, *VP Opers*
Kevin Kiehn, *Plant Mgr*
Asmus Shannon, *Safety Mgr*
Kurt Shea, *Safety Mgr*
John Peters, *Purchasing*
EMP: 175
SALES (corp-wide): 1.7B **Publicly Held**
WEB: www.briggsandstratton.com
SIC: 3519 3524 Internal combustion engines; lawn & garden equipment
PA: Briggs & Stratton Corporation
    12301 W Wirth St
    Wauwatosa WI 53222
    414 259-5333

(G-8796)
CUSTOM WOODCRAFT LLC
2525 Perry Schumaker Rd (13409-3620)
PHONE..................315 843-4234
Fax: 315 843-7269
Daniel Stoltzfus,
EMP: 12
SQ FT: 11,000
SALES (est): 1.3MM **Privately Held**
SIC: 2434 5712 2511 Wood kitchen cabinets; cabinet work, custom; wood household furniture

Nanuet
Rockland County

(G-8797)
AZAR INTERNATIONAL INC (PA)
Also Called: Azar Displays
31 W Prospect St (10954-2620)
P.O. Box 250 (10954-0250)
PHONE..................845 624-8808
Fax: 845 624-7156
Elazar Cohen, *CEO*
Loree Cohen, *Controller*
▲ EMP: 45
SQ FT: 40,000
SALES (est): 8.1MM **Privately Held**
WEB: www.azardisplays.com
SIC: 3993 Displays & cutouts, window & lobby

(G-8798)
BRIGADOON SOFTWARE INC (PA)
119 Rockland Ctr 250 (10954-2956)
PHONE..................845 624-0909
Fax: 845 624-0990
Terrance Kawles, *President*
Martin Moran, *Vice Pres*
Frank Jones, *Sls & Mktg Exec*
Tim Albright, *VP Sales*
Cevin Moran, *Manager*
EMP: 2
SALES (est): 1.4MM **Privately Held**
WEB: www.brigadoonsoftware.com
SIC: 7372 Prepackaged software

(G-8799)
BRUNO & CANIO LTD
130 Blauvelt Rd (10954-3602)
PHONE..................845 624-3060
EMP: 37
SQ FT: 6,500
SALES: 1MM **Privately Held**
SIC: 2325 2337 Contract Manufacturer Men's Separate Trousers & Women's Skirts

(G-8800)
CITIZEN PUBLISHING CORP
Also Called: Rockland County Times
119 Main St Ste 2 (10954-2883)
PHONE..................845 627-1414
Armand Miele, *Manager*
EMP: 10
SALES (est): 452K **Privately Held**
WEB: www.rocklandcountytimes.com
SIC: 2711 Newspapers

(G-8801)
DENMAR ELECTRIC
202 Main St (10954-3324)
PHONE..................845 624-4430
Dennis Maher, *Owner*
EMP: 17
SALES (est): 3.7MM **Privately Held**
SIC: 3699 Electrical equipment & supplies

(G-8802)
EAGLE INTERNATIONAL LLC
228 E Route 59 Ste 50 (10954-2905)
PHONE..................917 282-2536
Harry Adler, *Mng Member*
EMP: 5 EST: 2013
SQ FT: 400
SALES: 600K **Privately Held**
SIC: 2835 In vitro & in vivo diagnostic substances

(G-8803)
HNST MOLD INSPECTIONS LLC (PA)
6 Kevin Ct (10954-3828)
PHONE..................845 215-9258
John Skelly, *Mng Member*
EMP: 4
SALES (est): 1.7MM **Privately Held**
SIC: 3544 Industrial molds

(G-8804)
JAR METALS INC
50 2nd Ave (10954-4405)
PHONE..................845 425-8901
Andrew Gallina, *President*
John Shepitka, *Vice Pres*
EMP: 15
SQ FT: 10,000
SALES (est): 292.8K **Privately Held**
SIC: 3444 5085 Sheet metalwork; industrial supplies

(G-8805)
MINUTEMAN PRESS INC
121 W Nyack Rd Ste 3 (10954-2962)
PHONE..................845 623-2277
Brian H Gunn, *President*
EMP: 5
SQ FT: 2,000
SALES (est): 556.3K **Privately Held**
SIC: 2752 Commercial printing, lithographic

(G-8806)
PHILIPP FELDHEIM INC (PA)
Also Called: Feldheim Publishers
208 Airport Executive Par (10954-5262)
PHONE..................845 356-2282
Fax: 845 425-1908
Yitzchak Feldheim, *President*
Mirian Mendlowitz, *Treasurer*
Suzanne Brandt, *Sales Mgr*
Judy Gruenebaum, *Office Mgr*
Eli Hollander, *Intl Dir*
▲ EMP: 9 EST: 1939
SALES (est): 607.3K **Privately Held**
WEB: www.feldheim.com
SIC: 2731 Book publishing

(G-8807)
ROCKLAND BAKERY INC (PA)
94 Demarest Mill Rd W (10954-2989)
PHONE..................845 623-5800
Fax: 845 623-6921
Ignazio Battaglia, *CEO*
Philip Battaglia, *Vice Pres*
Robert Santore, *Opers Staff*
Riccardo Anselmo, *Engineer*
Mario Battaglia, *Treasurer*
EMP: 100
SQ FT: 22,000
SALES (est): 138.9MM **Privately Held**
WEB: www.rocklandbakery.com
SIC: 2051 Bread, cake & related products

(G-8808)
WENDYS AUTO EXPRESS INC
121 Main St (10954-2800)
PHONE..................845 624-6100
Fax: 845 624-2675
Wendy Winnick, *President*
Cindy Cherny, *Manager*
EMP: 6
SALES (est): 523.1K **Privately Held**
SIC: 3711 Chassis, motor vehicle

(G-8809)
WR SMITH & SONS INC
121 W Nyack Rd (10954-2939)
P.O. Box 225, West Nyack (10994-0225)
PHONE..................845 620-9400
William Smith, *Principal*
EMP: 7
SQ FT: 1,500
SALES (est): 914.6K **Privately Held**
SIC: 2821 3469 Plastics materials & resins; metal stampings

Naples
Ontario County

(G-8810)
BAKER LOGGING & FIREWOOD
8781 Gringhuse Atlanta Rd (14512-9247)
PHONE..................585 374-5733
Richard Baker, *Owner*
EMP: 9
SALES (est): 529.5K **Privately Held**
SIC: 2411 Logging camps & contractors

(G-8811)
L & D ACQUISITION LLC
1 Lake Niagara Ln (14512-9770)
PHONE..................585 531-9000
Doug Hazlitt, *Principal*
EMP: 16
SALES (est): 950K **Privately Held**
SIC: 2084 Wines, brandy & brandy spirits

(G-8812)
LAKE COUNTRY WOODWORKERS LTD
12 Clark St (14512-9535)
P.O. Box 400 (14512-0400)
PHONE..................585 374-6353
Fax: 585 374-2505
Donna Fargo, *President*
Karen Wood, *President*
Wayne Haines, *Vice Pres*
Chris Cooney, *Project Mgr*
Ben Heibach, *Engineer*
▲ EMP: 40 EST: 1976
SQ FT: 30,000
SALES (est): 7.1MM **Privately Held**
WEB: www.lcww.com
SIC: 2521 Wood office furniture

(G-8813)
NAPLES VLY MRGERS ACQSTONS LLC
Also Called: Angelic Gourmet
154 N Main St (14512-9156)
P.O. Box 39 (14512-0039)
PHONE..................585 490-1339
Donna Nichols, *Mng Member*
▼ EMP: 9 EST: 2011
SQ FT: 6,000
SALES: 500K **Privately Held**
SIC: 2064 Cake ornaments, confectionery

Narrowsburg
Sullivan County

(G-8814)
NARROWSBURG FEED & GRAIN CO
Also Called: Honor Brand Feeds
Fifth And Main St (12764)
PHONE..................845 252-3936
Fax: 845 252-3211
Patrick C Brown, *President*
Raymond Villeneuve, *President*
Roy G Morris, *General Mgr*
EMP: 16 EST: 1970
SQ FT: 20,000
SALES (est): 2.2MM **Privately Held**
WEB: www.narrowsburg.org
SIC: 2048 Prepared feeds; poultry feeds

(G-8815)
STUART COMMUNICATIONS INC
Also Called: The River Reporter
93 Erie Ave (12764-6423)
P.O. Box 150 (12764-0150)
PHONE..................845 252-7414
Fax: 845 252-3298
Laura Stuart, *President*
EMP: 13
SALES (est): 888.1K **Privately Held**
WEB: www.riverreporter.com
SIC: 2711 Newspapers: publishing only, not printed on site

Nassau
Rensselaer County

(G-8816)
CAPITAL SAWMILL SERVICE
4119 Us Highway 20 (12123-1904)
PHONE..................518 479-0729
Fax: 518 479-0729
Steven Daniels,
Teresa Eddy,
EMP: 9
SALES (est): 907.8K **Privately Held**
WEB: www.capitalsawmill.com
SIC: 2421 Sawmills & planing mills, general

(G-8817)
COPELAND COATING COMPANY INC
3600 Us Highway 20 (12123-1934)
P.O. Box 595 (12123-0595)
PHONE..................518 766-2932
Fax: 518 766-3603
John R Copeland, *Ch of Bd*
Steven W Hinding, *Vice Pres*
Rick Kment, *Purch Agent*
Matthew Mitchell, *CFO*
Albert Giamei, *Sr Project Mgr*
▲ EMP: 15 EST: 1945
SQ FT: 10,000
SALES (est): 4.3MM **Privately Held**
WEB: www.copelandcoating.com
SIC: 3272 Paving materials, prefabricated concrete

Nedrow
Onondaga County

(G-8818)
BOWEN PRODUCTS CORPORATION
5084 S Onondaga Rd (13120-9702)
PHONE....................315 498-4481
Charles D Smith, *President*
Louise M Smith, *Vice Pres*
EMP: 9 **EST:** 1896
SQ FT: 18,000
SALES (est): 1.1MM **Privately Held**
SIC: 3469 3569 Metal stampings; lubricating equipment

(G-8819)
W F SAUNDERS & SONS INC (PA)
5126 S Onondaga Rd (13120-9789)
P.O. Box A (13120-0129)
PHONE....................315 469-3217
Fax: 315 469-3940
Sherman V Saunders Jr, *President*
Michael Saunders, *Treasurer*
EMP: 15 **EST:** 1891
SQ FT: 5,000
SALES (est): 7.7MM **Privately Held**
SIC: 3273 3281 Ready-mixed concrete; cut stone & stone products

Nelliston
Montgomery County

(G-8820)
FUCCILLO FORD NELLISTON INC
6500 State Hwy 5 (13410)
PHONE....................518 993-5555
William B Fuccillo, *CEO*
Shawn Sponable, *Sales Mgr*
EMP: 7
SALES (est): 208.1K **Privately Held**
SIC: 3429 5511 Motor vehicle hardware; new & used car dealers

Nesconset
Suffolk County

(G-8821)
C D A INC
66 Southern Blvd Ste A (11767-1092)
PHONE....................631 473-1595
Robert Tuniewicz, *President*
Gilbert D Talamo, *Vice Pres*
▲ **EMP:** 9 **EST:** 1996
SQ FT: 2,000
SALES (est): 1.1MM **Privately Held**
SIC: 3625 Industrial electrical relays & switches

(G-8822)
HUM LIMITED LIABILITY CORP
70 Deer Valley Dr (11767-1568)
PHONE....................631 525-2174
Richard Blumenfeld, *Principal*
EMP: 6
SALES (est): 185.1K **Privately Held**
SIC: 2051 7389 Bakery: wholesale or wholesale/retail combined;

(G-8823)
KEY HIGH VACUUM PRODUCTS INC
36 Southern Blvd (11767-1097)
PHONE....................631 584-5959
Fax: 631 360-3973
Anthony Kozyrski, *President*
Elizabeth Kozyrski, *Corp Secy*
Betty Janosick, *Manager*
▲ **EMP:** 30
SQ FT: 15,000
SALES (est): 5.5MM **Privately Held**
WEB: www.keyhigh.com
SIC: 3589 3494 3492 3429 Vacuum cleaners & sweepers, electric: industrial; valves & valves; fluid power valves & hose fittings; manufactured hardware (general)

(G-8824)
MOBILE DATA SYSTEMS INC
110 Lake Ave S Ste 35 (11767-1071)
PHONE....................631 360-3400
Joseph Spiteri, *President*
Clayton Decosterd, *President*
EMP: 5
SALES (est): 406.3K **Privately Held**
WEB: www.mobiledatasys.com
SIC: 7372 Prepackaged software

(G-8825)
PERFECT POLY INC
1 Gina Ct (11767-2058)
PHONE....................631 265-0539
Malke Gelbstein, *President*
Elissa Artiles, *Manager*
EMP: 20
SALES (est): 3.5MM **Privately Held**
SIC: 2821 Polyesters

New Berlin
Chenango County

(G-8826)
CHOBANI LLC
669 County Road 25 (13411-4403)
PHONE....................607 847-6181
Grace Simmons, *Senior VP*
John Wanat, *Senior VP*
Keith Williams, *Vice Pres*
Cory Grey, *Buyer*
Warren Gordon, *Research*
EMP: 8
SALES (corp-wide): 203.8MM **Privately Held**
SIC: 2026 Yogurt
HQ: Chobani, Llc
147 State Highway 320
Norwich NY 13815
607 337-1246

(G-8827)
GOLDEN ARTIST COLORS INC
188 Bell Rd (13411-3616)
PHONE....................607 847-6154
Fax: 607 847-6767
Mark Golden, *Ch of Bd*
Barbara J Schindler, *President*
Greg Sheldon, *Opers Mgr*
Ralph Gagnon, *Facilities Mgr*
Scott Turner, *Opers Staff*
◆ **EMP:** 125
SQ FT: 60,000
SALES (est): 30.6MM **Privately Held**
WEB: www.goldenpaint.com
SIC: 3952 Paints, except gold & bronze: artists'; paints, gold or bronze: artists'

New City
Rockland County

(G-8828)
A TRADITION OF EXCELLENCE INC
85b Maple Ave (10956)
PHONE....................845 638-4595
Tom Sullivan, *President*
John Cusick, *Vice Pres*
EMP: 5
SALES (est): 499.1K **Privately Held**
SIC: 2759 Screen printing

(G-8829)
DARK STAR LITHOGRAPH CORP
9 Perth Ln (10956-5808)
P.O. Box 9074, Bardonia (10954-9074)
PHONE....................845 634-3780
Fax: 845 634-2509
Richard Suben, *President*
EMP: 5
SALES (est): 510K **Privately Held**
SIC: 2752 Commercial printing, lithographic

(G-8830)
DOCTOROW COMMUNICATIONS INC
Also Called: Home Lighting & Accessories
180 Phillips Hill Rd 1b (10956-4132)
P.O. Box 293 (10956-0293)
PHONE....................845 708-5166
Jeffrey Doctorow, *President*
Jonathon Doctorow, *Manager*
EMP: 12
SALES (est): 1.2MM **Privately Held**
WEB: www.contractlighting.net
SIC: 2721 Magazines: publishing only, not printed on site

(G-8831)
E L SMITH PRINTING CO INC
3 Lisa Ct (10956-2605)
P.O. Box 6567, Carlstadt NJ (07072-0567)
PHONE....................201 373-0111
Hilton I Kaufman, *President*
Beverly Kaufman, *Admin Sec*
EMP: 20 **EST:** 1929
SALES (est): 2MM **Privately Held**
SIC: 2752 2789 Commercial printing, lithographic; bookbinding & related work

(G-8832)
EASTERN INDUSTRIAL STEEL CORP (PA)
4 Fringe Ct (10956-6802)
P.O. Box 132, Blauvelt (10913-0132)
PHONE....................845 639-9749
Peter Lacombe, *President*
EMP: 4
SALES: 1MM **Privately Held**
WEB: www.easternindustrialsteel.com
SIC: 3325 3089 Steel foundries; extruded finished plastic products

(G-8833)
JMK ENTERPRISES LLC
301 N Main St Ste 1 (10956-4021)
PHONE....................845 634-8100
John Knutsen, *Partner*
EMP: 7
SALES (est): 484.9K **Privately Held**
SIC: 2389 Apparel & accessories

(G-8834)
MSI INC
329 Strawtown Rd (10956-6634)
PHONE....................845 639-6683
Murray Steinfink, *President*
Carl Roth, *Accountant*
EMP: 10
SALES (est): 880K **Privately Held**
SIC: 3081 Unsupported plastics film & sheet

(G-8835)
MY INDUSTRIES INC ✪
368 New Hempstead Rd (10956-1900)
PHONE....................845 638-2257
EMP: 7 **EST:** 2017
SALES (est): 94.4K **Privately Held**
SIC: 3999 Manufacturing industries

(G-8836)
PRO HITTER CORP
170 S Main St (10956-3323)
P.O. Box 883 (10956-0883)
PHONE....................845 358-8670
Fax: 845 634-1191
Philip Lomedico, *President*
Robert Ingenito, *Treasurer*
EMP: 15
SALES (est): 1.4MM **Privately Held**
WEB: www.prohitter.com
SIC: 3949 Baseball equipment & supplies, general

(G-8837)
REAL GOODS SOLAR INC
22 Third St (10956-4922)
PHONE....................845 708-0800
James Albert, *Branch Mgr*
EMP: 125 **Publicly Held**
SIC: 3433 Heating equipment, except electric

PA: Real Goods Solar, Inc.
110 16th St Ste 300
Denver CO 80202

(G-8838)
SHINING CREATIONS INC
Also Called: Strawtown Jewerly
40 S Main St Ste 1 (10956-3533)
PHONE....................845 358-4911
Ellen Arkin, *President*
Glenn Arkin, *Vice Pres*
EMP: 5
SALES: 200K **Privately Held**
SIC: 3911 5944 Jewelry mountings & trimmings; jewelry, precious stones & precious metals

(G-8839)
SUPER SOFTWARE
151 S Main St Ste 303 (10956-3544)
PHONE....................845 735-0000
Fax: 845 623-3333
James Flattery, *Owner*
EMP: 6
SALES (est): 310K **Privately Held**
WEB: www.supersoftware.org
SIC: 7372 Prepackaged software

(G-8840)
YELLOW PAGES INC (PA)
222 N Main St (10956-5302)
PHONE....................845 639-6060
Robert Gazzetta, *Ch of Bd*
EMP: 4
SALES (est): 6.6MM **Privately Held**
WEB: www.ypinc.net
SIC: 2741 Telephone & other directory publishing

(G-8841)
YO FRESH INC
170 S Main St (10956-3323)
PHONE....................845 634-1616
EMP: 28
SALES (corp-wide): 10.5MM **Privately Held**
SIC: 2026 Yogurt
PA: Yo Fresh Inc.
38 E 29th St Fl 6
New York NY 10016
212 260-4416

New Hampton
Orange County

(G-8842)
BALCHEM CORPORATION (PA)
52 Sunrise Park Rd (10958-4703)
P.O. Box 600 (10958-0600)
PHONE....................845 326-5600
Fax: 845 326-5702
Theodore L Harris, *Ch of Bd*
Frank J Fitzpatrick, *Vice Pres*
David F Ludwig, *Vice Pres*
William A Backus, *CFO*
Francis J Fitzpatrick, *Treasurer*
◆ **EMP:** 277
SQ FT: 20,000
SALES: 553.2MM **Publicly Held**
WEB: www.balchem.com
SIC: 2869 2899 Industrial organic chemicals; methyl alcohol, synthetic methanol; propylene, butylene; chemical preparations

(G-8843)
BCP INGREDIENTS INC (HQ)
52 Sunrise Park Rd (10958-4703)
PHONE....................845 326-5600
Dino A Rossi, *Ch of Bd*
Richard Bendure, *COO*
John E Kuehner, *Vice Pres*
David F Ludwig, *Vice Pres*
Dana Putnam, *Vice Pres*
▼ **EMP:** 54
SALES (est): 18.2MM
SALES (corp-wide): 553.2MM **Publicly Held**
SIC: 2899 Chemical preparations
PA: Balchem Corporation
52 Sunrise Park Rd
New Hampton NY 10958
845 326-5600

GEOGRAPHIC SECTION

(G-8844)
DICKS CONCRETE CO INC (PA)
1053 County Route 37 (10958-4811)
PHONE.................845 374-5966
Fax: 845 374-7262
Richard Penaluna Jr, *President*
Barbara Penaluna, *Vice Pres*
Jan Dodd, *CFO*
Mary Smith, *Manager*
Nettie Smith, *Manager*
EMP: 40
SQ FT: 5,000
SALES (est): 11.5MM **Privately Held**
WEB: www.dicksconcrete.com
SIC: **1442** 5032 3273 3271 Sand mining; gravel mining; cement; ready-mixed concrete; concrete block & brick

(G-8845)
EAST COAST SPRING MIX INC
211 Lynch Ave (10958-4504)
PHONE.................845 355-1215
Richard Minkus Jr, *President*
EMP: 7
SALES (est): 885.2K **Privately Held**
SIC: **3273** Ready-mixed concrete

New Hartford
Oneida County

(G-8846)
B & D ENTERPRISES OF UTICA (PA)
Also Called: Hemstrought's Bakeries
2 Campion Rd Ste 7 (13413-1647)
PHONE.................315 735-3311
Fax: 315 735-5213
Thomas R Batters, *President*
Michael J Denz, *Vice Pres*
Mary Denz, *Treasurer*
Paul Remizowski, *Shareholder*
EMP: 75
SQ FT: 20,000
SALES (est): 8.6MM **Privately Held**
SIC: **2051** 5461 5149 Bread, cake & related products; bakeries; bakery products

(G-8847)
DARTCOM INCORPORATED
Also Called: Dart Communications
2 Oxford Xing Ste 1 (13413-3246)
PHONE.................315 790-5456
Michael Baldwin, *President*
Jamie Jones, *Business Mgr*
Nick Baldwin, *Administration*
EMP: 4
SQ FT: 7,500
SALES (est): 1.3MM **Privately Held**
WEB: www.dart.com
SIC: **7372** Business oriented computer software

(G-8848)
ELM GRAPHICS INC
9694 Mallory Rd (13413-3618)
PHONE.................315 737-5984
Fax: 315 737-0904
Stanley Lebiednik, *President*
Gerald Eischen, *Vice Pres*
EMP: 5
SQ FT: 1,200
SALES (est): 532.6K **Privately Held**
SIC: **2759** Commercial printing

(G-8849)
FASTER-FORM CORP
Also Called: Lifesake Division
1 Faster Form Cir Ste 1 (13413-9564)
P.O. Box 825 (13413-0825)
PHONE.................800 327-3676
Fax: 315 792-9543
J C Waszkiewicz III, *President*
Lawrence P Ulrich, *Vice Pres*
J C Waszkiewicz II, *Treasurer*
Carolyn Kearney, *Accountant*
Jeff Thorpe, *Sales Staff*
▲ EMP: 85 EST: 1959
SQ FT: 200,000
SALES (est): 9.5MM **Privately Held**
WEB: www.vincenzaflowers.com
SIC: **3999** 3993 Flowers, artificial & preserved; bric-a-brac; displays, paint process

(G-8850)
GAN KAVOD INC
2050 Tilden Ave (13413-3613)
P.O. Box 1000 (13413-0709)
PHONE.................315 797-3114
Fax: 315 797-6955
Patricia A Hays, *Principal*
EMP: 2
SALES: 5MM **Privately Held**
SIC: **3843** Enamels, dentists'

(G-8851)
HARTFORD HWY DEPT
Also Called: Chadwicks Town Park
48 Genesee St (13413-2337)
PHONE.................315 724-0654
Mike Jeffery, *Director*
EMP: 7 **Privately Held**
SIC: **9111** Picnic tables or benches, park; mayors' offices
PA: Hartford Hwy. Dept
 165 Cr 23
 Hartford NY 12838
 518 632-5255

(G-8852)
LOCKHEED MARTIN CORPORATION
8373 Seneca Tpke (13413-4957)
PHONE.................315 793-5800
Cassaundra Wilkerson, *Business Anlyst*
Richard Kahler, *Manager*
Robert E McAuliffe, *Manager*
William Bryant, *Director*
EMP: 80 **Publicly Held**
WEB: www.lockheedmartin.com
SIC: **3721** 7371 Aircraft; custom computer programming services
PA: Lockheed Martin Corporation
 6801 Rockledge Dr
 Bethesda MD 20817

(G-8853)
PAR TECHNOLOGY CORPORATION (PA)
8383 Seneca Tpke Ste 2 (13413-4991)
PHONE.................315 738-0600
Fax: 315 738-0411
Donald H Foley, *President*
Bryan A Menar, *CFO*
EMP: 99
SQ FT: 216,800
SALES: 229.6MM **Publicly Held**
WEB: www.partech.com
SIC: **7372** 7382 Prepackaged software; confinement surveillance systems maintenance & monitoring

(G-8854)
RIVERHAWK COMPANY LP
Also Called: Indikon Company
215 Clinton Rd (13413-5306)
PHONE.................315 624-7171
Allen Williams, *Manager*
EMP: 32
SALES (corp-wide): 19.1MM **Privately Held**
WEB: www.indikon.com
SIC: **3823** 3829 3674 Industrial process measurement equipment; measuring & controlling devices; semiconductors & related devices
PA: Riverhawk Company L.P.
 215 Clinton Rd
 New Hartford NY 13413
 315 768-4855

(G-8855)
SAES SMART MATERIALS INC
Also Called: Saes Memry
4355 Middle Settlement Rd (13413-5317)
PHONE.................315 266-2026
Richard Lafond, *CEO*
Giorgio Vergani, *Ch of Bd*
John Schosser, *CFO*
Steve Dayton, *Treasurer*
Ronald Rossi, *Controller*
▲ EMP: 27
SALES (est): 7MM
SALES (corp-wide): 47MM **Privately Held**
SIC: **3339** Titanium metal, sponge & granules
PA: Saes Getters Spa
 Viale Italia 77
 Lainate MI 20020
 029 317-81

(G-8856)
SPECIAL METALS CORPORATION
4317 Middle Settlement Rd (13413-5392)
PHONE.................315 798-2900
Fax: 315 798-2001
Joseph I Snowden, *CEO*
Jason Catalino, *General Mgr*
Don Stockton, *General Mgr*
Paul Jelinek, *Production*
Arlene Qualls, *Human Res Dir*
▲ EMP: 76 EST: 1964
SALES (est): 20.8MM
SALES (corp-wide): 223.6B **Publicly Held**
SIC: **3356** Nickel & nickel alloy: rolling, drawing or extruding
HQ: Precision Castparts Corp.
 4650 Sw Mcdam Ave Ste 300
 Portland OR 97239
 503 946-4800

(G-8857)
TALLMANS EXPRESS LUBE
8421 Seneca Tpke (13413-4959)
PHONE.................315 266-1033
Tim Tallman, *President*
EMP: 5
SALES (est): 517.7K **Privately Held**
SIC: **2992** Lubricating oils

(G-8858)
WESTROCK CP LLC
45 Campion Rd (13413-1601)
PHONE.................770 448-2193
Debbie Millspaugh, *Purch Agent*
Mark Thomson, *Controller*
Nancy Rudnitski, *Human Resources*
William Ross, *Manager*
Dan Fowlkes, *Manager*
EMP: 147
SALES (corp-wide): 14.1B **Publicly Held**
SIC: **2653** Corrugated boxes, partitions, display items, sheets & pad
HQ: Westrock Cp, Llc
 504 Thrasher St
 Norcross GA 30071

New Hyde Park
Nassau County

(G-8859)
ALNIK SERVICE CORPORATION
20 Tulip Pl (11040-5315)
PHONE.................516 873-7300
Robert Fuchs, *President*
Sabita Singh, *Office Mgr*
EMP: 8
SALES (est): 1.2MM **Privately Held**
SIC: **3444** Sheet metalwork

(G-8860)
AMERICAN CHALLENGE ENTERPRISES
1804 Plaza Ave Ste 6 (11040-4937)
PHONE.................631 595-7171
Fax: 516 616-0598
Robert Laker Sr, *Ch of Bd*
Robert J Laker Jr, *President*
Bruce Laker, *Vice Pres*
▲ EMP: 6
SALES (est): 400K **Privately Held**
SIC: **2329** 2339 Men's & boys' athletic uniforms; uniforms, athletic: women's, misses' & juniors'

(G-8861)
APPLE COMMUTER INC
54 Lake Dr (11040-1125)
PHONE.................917 299-0066
Shah Biren, *Principal*
EMP: 6 EST: 2001
SALES (est): 689.5K **Privately Held**
SIC: **3571** Personal computers (microcomputers)

(G-8862)
ARNOUSE DIGITAL DEVICES CORP
Also Called: Biodigitalpc
1983 Marcus Ave Ste 104 (11042-2002)
PHONE.................516 673-4444
Fax: 516 626-6001
Michael Arnouse, *President*
Daniel Dellick, *COO*
Dan Gallic, *COO*
Sid M Rezvani, *Project Mgr*
Roland Feibert, *Electrical Engi*
EMP: 62
SQ FT: 4,963
SALES (est): 5.6MM **Privately Held**
SIC: **3571** Electronic computers

(G-8863)
BARC USA INC
5 Delaware Dr Ste 2 (11042-1100)
PHONE.................516 719-1052
Joseph Jonckheere, *CEO*
Kay Philips, *Accountant*
▲ EMP: 34
SQ FT: 17,500
SALES (est): 10.2MM
SALES (corp-wide): 598.9MM **Privately Held**
WEB: www.barclab.com
SIC: **2834** Pharmaceutical preparations
HQ: Bio Analytical Research Corporation Nv
 Industriepark-Zwijnaarde 3
 Gent 9052
 932 923-26

(G-8864)
BILLANTI CASTING CO INC
Also Called: Billanti Jewelry Casting
299 S 11th St (11040-5558)
P.O. Box 1117 (11040-7117)
PHONE.................516 775-4800
Rosemarie Billanti, *Exec Officer*
Allora Doolittle, *Treasurer*
EMP: 30 EST: 1955
SALES (est): 4.3MM **Privately Held**
WEB: www.billanticasting.com
SIC: **3911** 3339 Jewelry, precious metal; primary nonferrous metals

(G-8865)
CAMBRIDGE MANUFACTURING LLC
1700 Jericho Tpke (11040-4742)
PHONE.................516 326-1350
Linda Hofmann, *Controller*
Peter Negri,
EMP: 8
SALES (est): 1.1MM **Privately Held**
SIC: **3826** Laser scientific & engineering instruments

(G-8866)
CHEMICOLLOID LABORATORIES INC
55 Herricks Rd (11040-5340)
P.O. Box 251 (11040-0251)
PHONE.................516 747-2666
Fax: 516 747-4888
Geo Ryder, *President*
John Senft, *Senior Engr*
▲ EMP: 19 EST: 1920
SQ FT: 10,000
SALES (est): 3.2MM **Privately Held**
SIC: **3556** 2099 Dairy & milk machinery; emulsifiers, food

(G-8867)
COLORS IN OPTICS LTD
Also Called: Ic Optics
120 Broadway G (11040-5301)
PHONE.................718 845-0300
Gabe Tusk, *Branch Mgr*
EMP: 100
SQ FT: 10,000
SALES (corp-wide): 9.2MM **Privately Held**
SIC: **3851** Eyeglasses, lenses & frames
PA: Colors In Optics, Ltd.
 366 5th Ave Rm 804
 New York NY
 212 465-1200

New Hyde Park - Nassau County (G-8868)

(G-8868)
COMPUCOLOR ASSOCIATES INC
2200 Marcus Ave Ste C (11042-1043)
PHONE.................................516 358-0000
Thomas Weitzmann, *President*
Sharon Nadel, *General Mgr*
Mark Rosner, *Corp Secy*
William Vitale, *Vice Pres*
Cindy Weitzman, *Accounting Mgr*
EMP: 45
SQ FT: 22,000
SALES (est): 6.1MM **Privately Held**
WEB: www.compucolor.com
SIC: 2752 Commercial printing, lithographic

(G-8869)
CONTINENTAL QUILTING CO INC
3000 Marcus Ave Ste 3e6 (11042-1006)
PHONE.................................718 499-9100
Alfred G Sayegh, *President*
Stephen Sayegh, *Vice Pres*
Peter Jabara, *Controller*
▲ **EMP:** 50 **EST:** 1919
SQ FT: 40,000
SALES (est): 4.4MM **Privately Held**
SIC: 2392 Mattress pads; mattress protectors, except rubber; comforters & quilts: made from purchased materials

(G-8870)
CORA MATERIALS CORP
Also Called: Cora Matrls
30 Nassau Terminal Rd (11040-4928)
PHONE.................................516 488-6300
Robert Raths, *President*
Elissa Raths, *Admin Sec*
EMP: 10
SQ FT: 10,000
SALES (est): 1.5MM **Privately Held**
WEB: www.corarefining.com
SIC: 3341 Secondary nonferrous metals

(G-8871)
DISPLAY TECHNOLOGIES LLC (DH)
1111 Marcus Ave Ste M68 (11042-2041)
PHONE.................................718 321-3100
Fax: 718 939-4034
Marshall Goldberg, *President*
Jon Noce, *President*
Todd Dyment, *Vice Pres*
Bruce Gommermann, *Vice Pres*
Diogo Pereira, *Vice Pres*
▲ **EMP:** 53 **EST:** 1960
SQ FT: 30,000
SALES: 76.1MM
SALES (corp-wide): 223.6B **Publicly Held**
WEB: www.display-technologies.com
SIC: 2542 Fixtures: display, office or store: except wood
HQ: The Marmon Group Llc
181 W Madison St Ste 2600
Chicago IL 60602
312 372-9500

(G-8872)
DOREEN INTERIORS LTD
76 Nottingham Rd (11040-2214)
PHONE.................................212 255-9008
Fax: 212 255-8946
Shalom Sharoni, *President*
Boaz Sharoni, *Vice Pres*
Yoav Sharoni, *Vice Pres*
Yona Sharoni, *Treasurer*
EMP: 24
SQ FT: 40,000
SALES (est): 1.9MM **Privately Held**
WEB: www.doreeninteriors.com
SIC: 2512 Upholstered household furniture

(G-8873)
DYNASTY BELTS INC
161 Railroad Ave (11040-5016)
PHONE.................................516 625-6280
Harbans Lal Chandihok, *President*
Rajinder K Chandihok, *Vice Pres*
EMP: 35
SQ FT: 8,000
SALES (est): 1.4MM **Privately Held**
SIC: 2387 5136 Apparel belts; apparel belts, men's & boys'

(G-8874)
EASTERN FINDING CORP
116 County Courthouse Rd (11040-5342)
PHONE.................................516 747-6640
Fax: 516 629-4018
Paul Posner, *President*
Anthony Millaci, *Partner*
Sylvia Posner, *Treasurer*
▲ **EMP:** 10 **EST:** 1938
SQ FT: 5,000
SALES (est): 1.3MM **Privately Held**
WEB: www.easternfindings.com
SIC: 3366 Brass foundry

(G-8875)
ELECTRIC SWTCHBARD SLTIONS LLC
270 Park Ave (11040-5318)
PHONE.................................718 643-1105
Fax: 516 855-7017
Timothy Walsh, *Purch Agent*
George Katramados, *Controller*
Steve Levine, *Sales Staff*
Jerry Dicunzolo,
EMP: 8 **EST:** 2006
SQ FT: 25,000
SALES (est): 1.7MM **Privately Held**
SIC: 3613 Switchboards & parts, power

(G-8876)
ELI LILLY AND COMPANY
Also Called: Elanco Animal Health
1979 Marcus Ave (11042-1076)
PHONE.................................516 622-2244
Derek Asay, *Financial Exec*
James Sweeny, *Manager*
EMP: 14
SALES (corp-wide): 21.2B **Publicly Held**
WEB: www.lilly.com
SIC: 2834 Pharmaceutical preparations
PA: Eli Lilly And Company
Lilly Corporate Center
Indianapolis IN 46285
317 276-2000

(G-8877)
EON LABS INC (DH)
1999 Marcus Ave Ste 300 (11042-1020)
PHONE.................................516 478-9700
Thomas Strungmann, *Ch of Bd*
Bernhard Hampl, *President*
Jefferey S Bauer, *Vice Pres*
Pranab Bhattacharyya, *Vice Pres*
Sadie Ciganek, *Vice Pres*
EMP: 19
SQ FT: 25,000
SALES (est): 29.9MM
SALES (corp-wide): 48.5B **Privately Held**
WEB: www.sandoz.com
SIC: 2834 Pharmaceutical preparations
HQ: Sandoz Inc.
100 College Rd W
Princeton NJ 08540
609 627-8500

(G-8878)
FAR EAST INDUSTRIES INC (PA)
118 Stephan Marc Ln (11040-1811)
PHONE.................................718 687-2482
Yong Xiang Cui, *Ch of Bd*
Raman Than, *General Mgr*
EMP: 4
SQ FT: 1,200
SALES (est): 6.5MM **Privately Held**
SIC: 2326 Men's & boys' work clothing

(G-8879)
FERGUSON ENTERPRISES INC
Also Called: Pollardwater
200 Atlantic Ave (11040-5057)
PHONE.................................800 437-1146
Thomas Towler, *Principal*
Steven Hancey, *Manager*
EMP: 30
SALES (est): 1.2MM **Privately Held**
SIC: 3589 Sewage & water treatment equipment

(G-8880)
GENERAL FIBRE PRODUCTS CORP
170 Nassau Terminal Rd (11040-4940)
PHONE.................................516 358-7500
Fax: 516 358-7503
Stuart Shrode, *CEO*

James Miller, *President*
Michael Petti, *Vice Pres*
Frank Anthony, *Plant Mgr*
Ruth Cartegena, *QC Mgr*
◆ **EMP:** 70
SQ FT: 52,000
SALES (est): 19.9MM **Privately Held**
WEB: www.generalfibre.com
SIC: 2653 2671 2675 2679 Corrugated boxes, partitions, display items, sheets & pad; packaging paper & plastics film, coated & laminated; die-cut paper & board; corrugated paper: made from purchased material

(G-8881)
HAIN BLUEPRINT INC
1111 Marcus Ave Ste 100 (11042-2033)
PHONE.................................212 414-5741
EMP: 21
SALES (est): 6.3MM **Publicly Held**
SIC: 2037 Fruit juices
PA: The Hain Celestial Group Inc
1111 Marcus Ave Ste 100
New Hyde Park NY 11042

(G-8882)
HAIN CELESTIAL GROUP INC (PA)
1111 Marcus Ave Ste 100 (11042-2033)
PHONE.................................516 587-5000
Fax: 631 730-2550
John Carroll, *CEO*
Irwin D Simon, *Ch of Bd*
Julie Bowerman, *Senior VP*
Michael B McGuinness, *Senior VP*
James Langrock, *Vice Pres*
◆ **EMP:** 130
SQ FT: 86,000
SALES: 2.8B **Publicly Held**
WEB: www.hain-celestial.com
SIC: 2023 2034 2096 2086 Dried & powdered milk & milk products; dried milk preparations; dietary supplements, dairy & non-dairy based; vegetable flour, meal & powder; potato chips & similar snacks; iced tea & fruit drinks, bottled & canned; toilet preparations

(G-8883)
HAL-HEN COMPANY INC
180 Atlantic Ave (11040-5028)
P.O. Box 6077, Astoria (11106-0077)
PHONE.................................516 294-3200
Fax: 516 739-5248
Ronald Meltsner, *President*
Eric Spar, *Vice Pres*
Harold Spar, *Treasurer*
Joseph A Vespe, *Director*
Henry Meltsner, *Admin Sec*
▲ **EMP:** 50 **EST:** 1946
SQ FT: 20,000
SALES (est): 7.5MM **Privately Held**
WEB: www.halhen.com
SIC: 3842 Hearing aids

(G-8884)
HARBORS MAINE LOBSTER LLC
969 Lakeville Rd (11040-3008)
PHONE.................................516 775-2400
Christian Limbereg,
Peter Cardone,
William Kienke,
EMP: 48 **EST:** 2015
SALES: 250K **Privately Held**
SIC: 2091 Seafood products: packaged in cans, jars, etc.

(G-8885)
HASCO COMPONETS
906 Jericho Tpke (11040-4604)
PHONE.................................516 328-9292
Tom Marcus, *President*
Wayne Hauser, *Exec VP*
Mike Greenbaum, *Sales Staff*
Warren Pritzker, *Sales Executive*
Larry Ruben, *Sales Executive*
▲ **EMP:** 20
SALES: 11MM **Privately Held**
SIC: 3625 Relays, for electronic use

(G-8886)
HOPP COMPANIES INC
815 2nd Ave (11040-4869)
PHONE.................................516 358-4170

Fax: 516 358-4178
Robert Hopp, *President*
Rose Fontana, *Manager*
EMP: 12
SQ FT: 5,000
SALES: 2MM **Privately Held**
WEB: www.hoppcompanies.com
SIC: 3578 3086 Point-of-sale devices; plastics foam products

(G-8887)
INTERNTNAL BUS CMMNCATIONS INC (PA)
Also Called: IBC/ Worldwide
1981 Marcus Ave Ste C105 (11042-2028)
PHONE.................................516 352-4505
Fax: 516 352-3084
Norman Kay, *President*
Philip Schoonmaker, *Exec VP*
Maggie Maher-Healion, *CFO*
Rachel Samaroo, *Director*
Diane Banks, *Admin Asst*
▲ **EMP:** 25
SQ FT: 53,000
SALES (est): 23.4MM **Privately Held**
WEB: www.ibcshell.com
SIC: 3086 2679 Packaging & shipping materials, foamed plastic; pressed fiber & molded pulp products except food products

(G-8888)
IVER PRINTING INC
124 N 12th St (11040-4265)
PHONE.................................718 275-2070
Fax: 718 275-9149
William Iverson, *President*
Ann Iverson, *Vice Pres*
Martin Iverson, *Treasurer*
John Iverson, *Admin Sec*
EMP: 5 **EST:** 1979
SQ FT: 900
SALES: 400K **Privately Held**
WEB: www.iverprinting.com
SIC: 2752 Commercial printing, offset

(G-8889)
JOSEPH STRUHL CO INC
Also Called: Super Moderna/Magic Master
195 Atlantic Ave (11040-5027)
PHONE.................................516 741-3660
Fax: 516 742-3617
Clifford Struhl, *President*
Harriet Struhl, *Corp Secy*
Joseph Struhl, *Vice Pres*
EMP: 14
SQ FT: 13,000
SALES (est): 1.7MM **Privately Held**
WEB: www.magicmaster.com
SIC: 3993 Displays & cutouts, window & lobby

(G-8890)
JSM VINYL PRODUCTS INC
44 Orchid Ln (11040-1918)
PHONE.................................516 775-4520
Fax: 516 239-2879
EMP: 15
SQ FT: 26,000
SALES: 4MM **Privately Held**
SIC: 3089 Mfg Plastic Products

(G-8891)
LAFAYETTE MIRROR & GLASS CO
2300 Marcus Ave (11042-1058)
PHONE.................................718 768-0660
Fax: 718 768-3047
Micheal Chuisano, *President*
Barbara Umbria, *Bookkeeper*
▲ **EMP:** 7 **EST:** 1910
SQ FT: 7,000
SALES (est): 881.2K **Privately Held**
SIC: 3211 3231 1793 Plate glass, polished & rough; mirrored glass; glass & glazing work

(G-8892)
LIQUID MANAGEMENT PARTNERS LLC
1983 Marcus Ave Ste E138 (11042-2000)
PHONE.................................516 775-5050
Nick Smith, *Marketing Mgr*
Michael H Lam,
▲ **EMP:** 11

SQ FT: 3,000
SALES (est): 1.1MM **Privately Held**
SIC: **2086** 5182 Carbonated beverages, nonalcoholic; bottled & canned; wine & distilled beverages

(G-8893)
MARLOU GARMENTS INC
2115 Jericho Tpke (11040-4703)
P.O. Box 407, West Hempstead (11552-0407)
PHONE..................516 739-7100
Fax: 516 739-1991
Louis De Angelo, *Ch of Bd*
Rose De Angelo, *Admin Sec*
▲ EMP: 15 EST: 1952
SQ FT: 19,200
SALES (est): 1.4MM **Privately Held**
WEB: www.marlou.com
SIC: **2337** Uniforms, except athletic: women's, misses' & juniors'

(G-8894)
MASON CONTRACT PRODUCTS LLC
85 Denton Ave (11040-4002)
P.O. Box 609, Port Washington (11050-0609)
PHONE..................516 328-6900
Robert Kaye, *Controller*
Janet Vukan, *Manager*
Kevin Connors, *CTO*
Leonard Horowitz,
Lisa Horowitz,
▼ EMP: 80
SQ FT: 100,000
SALES (est): 5.9MM **Privately Held**
SIC: **2391** 2211 Curtains & draperies; bedspreads, cotton

(G-8895)
NATURAL E CREATIVE LLC
Also Called: Be The Media
1110 Jericho Tpke (11040-4606)
PHONE..................516 488-1143
David Mathison,
Eric Mathison,
Peter Mathison,
EMP: 11
SALES (est): 75K **Privately Held**
WEB: www.bethemedia.com
SIC: **2731** Books: publishing & printing

(G-8896)
NEW YORK PACKAGING CORP
Also Called: Redi-Bag USA
135 Fulton Ave (11040-5305)
P.O. Box 1039 (11040-7039)
PHONE..................516 746-0600
Fax: 516 746-0661
Jeffrey Rabiea, *President*
▲ EMP: 90
SQ FT: 50,000
SALES (est): 25MM **Privately Held**
WEB: www.newyorkpackaging.com
SIC: **2673** Plastic bags: made from purchased materials

(G-8897)
NEW YORK RAVIOLI PASTA CO INC
12 Denton Ave S (11040-4904)
PHONE..................516 270-2852
David Creo, *President*
Paul Moncada, *Corp Secy*
Jeanne Gherity, *Sales Mgr*
Tricia Nacewicz, *Office Mgr*
EMP: 20
SQ FT: 20,000
SALES (est): 3.6MM **Privately Held**
WEB: www.nyravioli.com
SIC: **2099** 5499 5149 Packaged combination products: pasta, rice & potato; gourmet food stores; pasta & rice

(G-8898)
NY 1 ART GALLERY INC
32 3rd St (11040-4438)
PHONE..................917 698-0626
Faisal Sheikh, *President*
EMP: 4
SALES: 1MM **Privately Held**
SIC: **2389** Men's miscellaneous accessories

(G-8899)
OCALA GROUP LLC
1981 Marcus Ave Ste 227 (11042-1055)
PHONE..................516 233-2750
◆ EMP: 17
SALES (est): 2.6MM **Privately Held**
SIC: **3841** 3089 Surgical & medical instruments; plastic kitchenware, tableware & houseware

(G-8900)
OVERNIGHT MOUNTINGS INC
1400 Plaza Ave (11040-4921)
PHONE..................516 865-3000
Morris Adwar, *CEO*
Jeffery Adwar, *President*
Matthew Roth, *Vice Pres*
EMP: 55
SQ FT: 550,000
SALES (est): 7.7MM **Privately Held**
WEB: www.overnightmountings.com
SIC: **3911** Jewelry, precious metal

(G-8901)
P J D PUBLICATIONS LTD
1315 Jericho Tpke (11040-4613)
P.O. Box 966, Westbury (11590-0966)
PHONE..................516 626-0650
Fax: 516 626-5546
Siva Sankar, *CEO*
Douglas Sankar, *Vice Pres*
Jason Sankar, *Vice Pres*
Barbara Kelly, *Director*
Priscilla Wong,
EMP: 5
SALES (est): 330K **Privately Held**
WEB: www.pjdonline.com
SIC: **2731** 5045 Books: publishing only; computers, peripherals & software

(G-8902)
PERFECT GEAR & INSTRUMENT (HQ)
55 Denton Ave S (11040-4901)
PHONE..................516 328-3330
Morton Hoffman, *President*
Joseph Rubenfeld, *Vice Pres*
EMP: 10
SALES (est): 2.2MM
SALES (corp-wide): 113.2MM **Privately Held**
SIC: **3462** Gears, forged steel
PA: Designatronics Incorporated
    250 Duffy Ave Unit A
    Hicksville NY 11801
    516 328-3300

(G-8903)
QUALITY READY MIX INC
1824 Gilford Ave (11040-4031)
PHONE..................516 437-0100
Eugene Messina, *President*
Mario Messina, *Manager*
EMP: 15
SALES (est): 2.1MM **Privately Held**
SIC: **3273** Ready-mixed concrete

(G-8904)
QUANTUM LOGIC CORP
91 5th Ave (11040-5005)
PHONE..................516 746-1380
John Carbone, *Ch of Bd*
EMP: 9 EST: 2002
SALES (est): 1.1MM **Privately Held**
SIC: **3572** Computer storage devices

(G-8905)
SATCO CASTINGS SERVICE INC
Also Called: Plaza Bracelette Mounting
1400 Plaza Ave (11040-4921)
P.O. Box 1068 (11040-1068)
PHONE..................516 354-1500
Steven Feld, *President*
EMP: 45
SQ FT: 18,000
SALES (est): 7MM **Privately Held**
WEB: www.satcocasting.com
SIC: **3915** 3911 Jewelers' castings; jewelry, precious metal

(G-8906)
SHELL CONTAINERS INC (NY)
1981 Marcus Ave Ste C105 (11042-2028)
PHONE..................516 352-4505
Norman Kay, *President*
Philip Schoonmaker, *Vice Pres*
▲ EMP: 20
SQ FT: 19,000
SALES (est): 3.3MM
SALES (corp-wide): 23.4MM **Privately Held**
WEB: www.shellcontainers.com
SIC: **3086** 2679 Packaging & shipping materials, foamed plastic; building, insulating & packaging paperboard
PA: International Business Communications, Inc.
    1981 Marcus Ave Ste C105
    New Hyde Park NY 11042
    516 352-4505

(G-8907)
SNOW CRAFT CO INC
200 Fulton Ave (11040-5306)
P.O. Box 829 (11040-0829)
PHONE..................516 739-1399
Fax: 516 739-1637
Kirk Guyton, *President*
Robert Farina, *Vice Pres*
William Hess, *Admin Sec*
EMP: 28 EST: 1954
SQ FT: 22,500
SALES (est): 4MM **Privately Held**
SIC: **3086** Packaging & shipping materials, foamed plastic

(G-8908)
SONOMED INC
Also Called: Sonomed Escalon
1979 Marcus Ave Ste C105 (11042-1002)
PHONE..................516 354-0900
Fax: 516 354-5902
Barry Durante, *President*
Ronald Hueneke, *COO*
John Rich, *Vice Pres*
Frances Shanker, *Vice Pres*
Judi Herman, *Purch Agent*
EMP: 30
SQ FT: 11,000
SALES (est): 5.1MM
SALES (corp-wide): 11.2MM **Privately Held**
WEB: www.sonomedinc.com
SIC: **3845** 3841 Electromedical equipment; ophthalmic instruments & apparatus
PA: Escalon Medical Corp.
    435 Devon Park Dr Ste 100
    Wayne PA 19087
    610 688-6830

(G-8909)
SPECIAL CIRCLE INC
123 Shelter Rock Rd (11040-1328)
PHONE..................516 595-9988
Lawrence Lin, *Principal*
Kathleen Loftus, *Co-Owner*
Phoebe Lin, *COO*
Selena Zhang, *COO*
Darren Yang, *Chief Engr*
EMP: 12
SALES (est): 281.6K **Privately Held**
SIC: **7372** 7389 Educational computer software;

(G-8910)
TEXAS HOME SECURITY INC (PA)
Also Called: Medallion Security Door & Win
50 Rose Pl (11040-5312)
PHONE..................516 747-2100
Fax: 516 739-9862
Gregory E Falgoust, *President*
Brian S Falgoust, *Vice Pres*
Brian Flagoust, *Financial Exec*
EMP: 50
SALES (est): 6.5MM **Privately Held**
WEB: www.medalliondoors.com
SIC: **3442** 1521 Storm doors or windows, metal; general remodeling, single-family houses

(G-8911)
THREE GEMS INC
Also Called: Sign-A-Rama
2201 Hillside Ave (11040-2714)
PHONE..................516 248-0388
Fax: 516 248-3978
Sal Italiano, *President*
Jane Italiano, *Vice Pres*
EMP: 5

SQ FT: 1,200
SALES (est): 692.5K **Privately Held**
WEB: www.threegems.com
SIC: **3993** Signs & advertising specialties

(G-8912)
UBM LLC (HQ)
Also Called: Ubm Tech
1983 Marcus Ave Ste 250 (11042-2000)
PHONE..................516 562-7800
Scott D Schulman, *CEO*
Atif Malik, *President*
Amy Birnbach, *Publisher*
Will Wise, *Publisher*
Jennifer Jessup, *General Mgr*
EMP: 60
SQ FT: 230,000
SALES (est): 435.8MM
SALES (corp-wide): 1B **Privately Held**
WEB: www.cmp.com
SIC: **2721** 2711 7319 7389 Periodicals: publishing only; newspapers; media buying service; decoration service for special events
PA: Ubm Plc
    240 Blackfriars Road
    London SE1 8
    207 921-5000

(G-8913)
UNITED METAL INDUSTRIES INC
1008 3rd Ave (11040-5529)
PHONE..................516 354-6800
Fax: 516 354-6715
Richard M Meyers, *President*
Robert S Meyers, *Vice Pres*
▲ EMP: 8 EST: 1912
SQ FT: 8,000
SALES (est): 1.1MM **Privately Held**
WEB: www.unitedmetal.net
SIC: **3429** Clamps & couplings, hose

(G-8914)
UNITED STTES BRNZE SIGN OF FLA
811 2nd Ave (11040-4869)
PHONE..................516 352-5155
Fax: 516 352-1761
George Barbeosch, *President*
Alan Kasten, *Vice Pres*
Martha Lamberta, *Office Mgr*
EMP: 25 EST: 1927
SQ FT: 10,000
SALES (est): 2.7MM **Privately Held**
WEB: www.usbronze.com
SIC: **3993** 3953 Signs & advertising specialties; marking devices

(G-8915)
UNIVERSAL READY MIX INC
197 Atlantic Ave (11040-5048)
PHONE..................516 746-4535
Fax: 516 746-4537
Guilio Viti, *President*
Anthony Logiudice, *Vice Pres*
Rocco Viti, *Admin Sec*
EMP: 5 EST: 1997
SALES (est): 877.9K **Privately Held**
WEB: www.universalreadymix.com
SIC: **2951** Asphalt paving mixtures & blocks

(G-8916)
USE ACQUISITION LLC
Also Called: US Energy Group
270 Park Ave (11040-5318)
PHONE..................516 812-6800
Gerald Dicunzolo,
EMP: 10
SALES (est): 1.3MM **Privately Held**
SIC: **3822** Temperature controls, automatic

(G-8917)
WINE MARKET
2337 New Hyde Park Rd (11042-1212)
PHONE..................516 328-8800
Bina Gubda, *Owner*
EMP: 6
SALES (est): 390.8K **Privately Held**
SIC: **2084** Wines

New Paltz - Ulster County (G-8918)   **GEOGRAPHIC SECTION**

New Paltz
Ulster County

(G-8918)
BRUYNSWICK SALES INC
14 Bruynswick Rd (12561-4106)
PHONE.................................845 789-2049
Wayne Elliot, *President*
EMP: 12
SALES (est): 591.2K Privately Held
SIC: 3949 Lures, fishing: artificial

(G-8919)
GILDED OTTER BREWING CO
3 Main St (12561-1742)
P.O. Box 57 (12561-0057)
PHONE.................................845 256-1700
Fax: 845 256-0955
Rick Rauch, *President*
EMP: 70 EST: 1996
SQ FT: 10,000
SALES (est): 6.8MM Privately Held
WEB: www.gildedotter.com
SIC: 2082 5812 Beer (alcoholic beverage); eating places

(G-8920)
KEVCO INDUSTRIES
Also Called: Engineering Educational Eqp Co
6 Millbrook Rd (12561-1315)
PHONE.................................845 255-7407
Peter C Bowers, *Owner*
Pete Bower, *Manager*
EMP: 7
SALES (est): 480K Privately Held
WEB: www.eeeco.com
SIC: 3999 Education aids, devices & supplies

(G-8921)
LYOPHILIZATION SYSTEMS INC
14 Hickory Hill Rd (12561-3104)
PHONE.................................845 338-0456
Marc Thompson, *President*
Roger W Grange, *Opers Mgr*
EMP: 5
SQ FT: 6,000
SALES (est): 540K Privately Held
WEB: www.lyogroup.com
SIC: 3556 Food products machinery

(G-8922)
PDQ SHIPPING SERVICES
Also Called: PDQ Printing
8 New Paltz Plz 299 (12561-1616)
PHONE.................................845 255-5500
Fax: 845 255-3202
Craig Shinkles, *Owner*
Cory Bowers, *Graphic Designe*
EMP: 8
SALES (est): 340K Privately Held
SIC: 2759 7331 Promotional printing; mailing service

(G-8923)
SMALL PACKAGES INC
119 Hasbrouck Rd (12561-3531)
PHONE.................................845 255-7710
Greg Corvell, *Principal*
Greg Correll, *Creative Dir*
EMP: 5 EST: 1998
SALES (est): 366.3K Privately Held
SIC: 2631 Container, packaging & boxboard

(G-8924)
TOTAL WEBCASTING INC
8 Bruce St (12561-2101)
P.O. Box 665 (12561-0665)
PHONE.................................845 883-0909
Robert Feldman, *President*
EMP: 6
SQ FT: 3,000
SALES: 700K Privately Held
SIC: 2741

(G-8925)
ULSTER COUNTY IRON WORKS LLC
64 N Putt Corners Rd (12561-3405)
PHONE.................................845 255-0003
Steven Vasalka, *President*
EMP: 8

SQ FT: 5,000
SALES: 750K Privately Held
SIC: 3499 Metal household articles

(G-8926)
ULSTER PUBLISHING CO INC
Also Called: New Paltz Times
29 S Chestnut St Ste 101 (12561-1949)
PHONE.................................845 255-7005
Debbie Alexsa, *Principal*
Nan Wilson, *Manager*
EMP: 10
SALES (corp-wide): 3.6MM Privately Held
WEB: www.ulsterpublishing.com
SIC: 2711 Newspapers: publishing only, not printed on site
PA: Ulster Publishing Co Inc
    322 Wall St Fl 1
    Kingston NY 12401
    845 334-8205

(G-8927)
VIKING INDUSTRIES INC
89 S Ohioville Rd (12561-4012)
P.O. Box 249 (12561-0249)
PHONE.................................845 883-6325
Fax: 845 883-6228
Richard Croce, *President*
Michael Cozzolino, *Prdtn Mgr*
Mark Nowak, *Controller*
Cindy Brooks, *Finance*
Dottie Turcotte, *Cust Mgr*
EMP: 55
SQ FT: 50,000
SALES (est): 12.3MM Privately Held
WEB: www.vikingindustries.net
SIC: 2657 Folding paperboard boxes

New Rochelle
Westchester County

(G-8928)
A & T IRON WORKS INC
25 Cliff St (10801-6803)
PHONE.................................914 632-8992
Fax: 914 632-2645
Gessie Tassone, *President*
Lila Tang, *Bookkeeper*
▲ EMP: 28
SQ FT: 20,000
SALES (est): 5.5MM Privately Held
WEB: www.atironworks.com
SIC: 3446 5211 3441 Architectural metalwork; fencing; fabricated structural metal

(G-8929)
ABSOLUTE COATINGS INC
38 Portman Rd (10801-2103)
PHONE.................................914 636-0700
Fax: 914 636-0822
Brian A Demkowicz, *Principal*
Michael Lazar, *Info Tech Dir*
EMP: 35
SQ FT: 40,000
SALES (est): 1.4MM
SALES (corp-wide): 48.3MM Privately Held
SIC: 2851 Polyurethane coatings
PA: Valentus Specialty Chemicals, Inc.
    1999 Elizabeth St
    North Brunswick NJ 08902
    732 821-3200

(G-8930)
ALICIAS BAKERY INC
498 Main St Ste A (10801-6326)
PHONE.................................914 235-4689
Alicia Zapien, *President*
EMP: 5
SALES (est): 416.5K Privately Held
SIC: 2051 Doughnuts, except frozen

(G-8931)
ALLIED CONVERTERS INC
64 Drake Ave (10805-1598)
P.O. Box 548 (10802-0548)
PHONE.................................914 235-1585
Fax: 914 235-7123
Richard E Ellenbogen, *President*
Wilma J Ellenbogen, *Corp Secy*
▲ EMP: 30 EST: 1954
SQ FT: 50,000

SALES (est): 6.7MM Privately Held
WEB: www.garb-o-liner.com
SIC: 2673 2671 2679 Plastic bags: made from purchased materials; plastic film, coated or laminated for packaging; paperboard products, converted

(G-8932)
BAKERS PRIDE OVEN CO INC
145 Huguenot St Ste Mz1 (10801-6997)
PHONE.................................914 576-0200
Hylton Jones, *CEO*
Howard Kraines, *Vice Pres*
Brian Rosenbloom, *Vice Pres*
Don Wall, *CFO*
Lawrence Rosenbloom, *Admin Sec*
EMP: 150 EST: 1995
SQ FT: 120,000
SALES (est): 22MM
SALES (corp-wide): 755.2MM Publicly Held
WEB: www.associatedamericanindustries.com
SIC: 3589 3631 3556 Commercial cooking & foodwarming equipment; cooking equipment, commercial; household cooking equipment; food products machinery
HQ: Associated American Industries, Inc.
    1307 N Watters Rd
    Allen TX 75013

(G-8933)
BENCHMARK EDUCATION CO LLC (PA)
145 Huguenot St Fl 8 (10801-5233)
PHONE.................................914 637-7200
Fax: 914 738-5063
Wainright Samuel, *President*
Susan Rivers, *Senior VP*
Carrie Smith, *Vice Pres*
Barbara Andrews, *Finance*
Deloris Fox, *Human Res Mgr*
▲ EMP: 75
SALES (est): 19MM Privately Held
WEB: www.benchmarkeducation.com
SIC: 2731 Book publishing

(G-8934)
BREAD FACTORY LLC
30 Grove Ave (10801-6207)
PHONE.................................914 637-8150
Fax: 914 637-9516
Jean Yves Lebris, *Partner*
Anthony Orza, *Partner*
EMP: 24 EST: 2000
SQ FT: 10,000
SALES (est): 1.4MM Privately Held
SIC: 2051 Bread, cake & related products

(G-8935)
BRIDGE RECORDS INC
200 Clinton Ave (10801-1525)
PHONE.................................914 654-9270
Fax: 516 773-3397
David Starobin, *President*
Rob Robles, *Editor*
Doron Schachter, *Editor*
Becky Starobin, *Vice Pres*
Charlie Post, *Prdtn Mgr*
EMP: 5
SQ FT: 2,000
SALES (est): 729.4K Privately Held
SIC: 3652 Master records or tapes, preparation of

(G-8936)
CASTEK INC (HQ)
20 Jones St (10801-6000)
PHONE.................................914 636-1000
Arthur M Dinitz, *President*
Mike Stento, *Vice Pres*
Robert Welsh, *CFO*
Robert J Welsh, *Treasurer*
▲ EMP: 3
SQ FT: 42,000
SALES (est): 2.8MM
SALES (corp-wide): 7.7MM Privately Held
WEB: www.castek.net
SIC: 3272 Concrete products, precast
PA: Transpo Industries, Inc.
    20 Jones St Ste 3
    New Rochelle NY 10801
    914 636-1000

(G-8937)
CERAMICA VARM (PA)
Also Called: Ceramica V. A. R. M.
479 5th Ave (10801-2212)
PHONE.................................914 381-6215
Fax: 914 381-3785
EMP: 9
SQ FT: 4,000
SALES: 7.5MM Privately Held
SIC: 3263 Mfg Of Ceramic Earthenware-Italy

(G-8938)
CUFFS PLANNING & MODELS LTD
317 Beechmont Dr (10804-4601)
PHONE.................................914 632-1883
David K Combs, *President*
David Combs, *President*
Sandra Kirkendall, *Vice Pres*
EMP: 8
SALES (est): 508.3K Privately Held
WEB: www.cuffs88.com
SIC: 7372 Prepackaged software

(G-8939)
DERAFFELE MFG CO INC
2525 Palmer Ave Ste 4 (10801-4476)
PHONE.................................914 636-6850
Philip De Raffele Jr, *President*
Philip Deraffele, *Vice Pres*
Stephen De Raffele, *Treasurer*
Joseph De Raffele, *Admin Sec*
EMP: 25 EST: 1933
SQ FT: 30,000
SALES (est): 5.7MM Privately Held
SIC: 3448 Prefabricated metal buildings

(G-8940)
DISPLAY PRODUCERS INC
40 Winding Brook Rd (10804-2008)
PHONE.................................718 904-1200
Fax: 718 904-9843
Joseph A Laurite, *President*
Arthur E Landi, *President*
Richard Tevere, *Corp Secy*
Claudia Giron, *Personnel*
Michael Marsigliano, *Administration*
▲ EMP: 250
SQ FT: 150,000
SALES (est): 27.8MM Privately Held
WEB: www.displayproducersinc.com
SIC: 3993 Signs & advertising specialties

(G-8941)
EMERGENCY BEACON CORP
15 River St (10801-4354)
PHONE.................................914 576-2700
Joan Goodman, *President*
Mary Leonetti, *Vice Pres*
George Ramos, *Vice Pres*
Patricia Wyllie, *Vice Pres*
Judith Weber, *VP Mfg*
EMP: 15
SQ FT: 12,000
SALES: 1MM Privately Held
WEB: www.emergencybeaconcorp.com
SIC: 3812 Search & navigation equipment

(G-8942)
ENTERPRISE TECH GROUP INC
15 Irving Pl (10801-1511)
PHONE.................................914 588-0327
Liza Zaneri, *President*
EMP: 12
SALES: 950K Privately Held
SIC: 7372 Prepackaged software

(G-8943)
ERIC S TURNER & COMPANY INC
Also Called: Turner Plating
3335 Centre Ave (10801)
PHONE.................................914 235-7114
Fax: 914 235-7196
Kenneth Turner, *President*
William Vernon Turner, *Vice Pres*
Angelique Murphy, *Bookkeeper*
EMP: 12 EST: 1931
SQ FT: 10,000

SALES: 900K **Privately Held**
WEB: www.turnerplating.com
SIC: 3471 2851 Electroplating of metals or formed products; finishing, metals or formed products; polishing, metals or formed products; paints & allied products

(G-8944)
FLYNN BURNER CORPORATION
425 Fifth Ave (10801-2203)
P.O. Box 431 (10802-0431)
PHONE..................914 636-1320
Fax: 914 636-3751
Julian Modzeleski, *CEO*
Edward Flynn, *Ch of Bd*
Dom Medina, *President*
Joe Digiacomo, *Vice Pres*
Simon Walker, *Vice Pres*
◆ **EMP:** 50 **EST:** 1946
SQ FT: 25,000
SALES (est): 9.1MM **Privately Held**
WEB: www.flynnburner.com
SIC: 3433 Gas burners, industrial; oil burners, domestic or industrial

(G-8945)
FORMCRAFT DISPLAY PRODUCTS
42 Beverly Rd (10804-1703)
PHONE..................914 632-1410
George Bartoli, *President*
Joanne Bartoli, *Vice Pres*
EMP: 5
SQ FT: 5,000
SALES (est): 330K **Privately Held**
SIC: 3229 Christmas tree ornaments, from glass produced on-site

(G-8946)
FORREST ENGRAVING CO INC
Also Called: Forrest Engravg
92 1st St (10801-6121)
P.O. Box 1240, Carmel (10512-8240)
PHONE..................845 228-0200
Fax: 914 632-7416
Tom Giordano, *President*
EMP: 11
SQ FT: 3,000
SALES (est): 800K **Privately Held**
SIC: 3993 Signs & advertising specialties

(G-8947)
FRADAN MANUFACTURING CORP
499 5th Ave (10801-2212)
PHONE..................914 632-3653
Frank De Bartolo, *President*
Karen Molia, *Office Mgr*
EMP: 15
SQ FT: 12,000
SALES (est): 2.2MM **Privately Held**
SIC: 3524 Lawn & garden equipment

(G-8948)
GANNETT CO INC
Also Called: Bronxville Review
92 North Ave (10801-7413)
PHONE..................914 278-9315
Jerry McKinstry, *Principal*
EMP: 20
SALES (corp-wide): 3B **Publicly Held**
WEB: www.gannett.com
SIC: 2711 Newspapers
PA: Gannett Co., Inc.
7950 Jones Branch Dr
Mc Lean VA 22102
703 854-6000

(G-8949)
GARB-O-LINER INC
64 Drake Ave (10805-1598)
P.O. Box 548 (10802-0548)
PHONE..................914 235-1585
Richard Ellenbogen, *President*
Richard E Ellenbogen, *President*
Wilma Ellenbogen, *Treasurer*
EMP: 7 **EST:** 1986
SALES (est): 1MM **Privately Held**
SIC: 2673 5113 Trash bags (plastic film); made from purchased materials; bags, paper & disposable plastic

(G-8950)
GEN PUBLISHING INC
Also Called: Genetic Engineering News
140 Huguenot St Fl 3 (10801-5215)
PHONE..................914 834-3880
Fax: 914 740-2201
Mary Ann Liebert, *President*
Alex Philippidis, *Editor*
Sharon Spitz, *Sales Mgr*
Luc Selig, *Sales Staff*
Kwafo Anoff, *Manager*
EMP: 99
SALES: 950K **Privately Held**
WEB: www.genengnews.com
SIC: 2741 Miscellaneous publishing

(G-8951)
HAGEDORN COMMUNICATIONS INC (PA)
Also Called: Co-Op City News
662 Main St Ste 1 (10801-7145)
P.O. Box 680 (10802-0680)
PHONE..................914 636-7400
Fax: 914 636-2957
Christopher Hagedorn, *President*
Richard Kondub, *General Mgr*
Al Zezula, *Advt Staff*
▲ **EMP:** 70 **EST:** 1948
SQ FT: 20,000
SALES (est): 10.9MM **Privately Held**
WEB: www.rew-online.com
SIC: 2711 Newspapers

(G-8952)
HAITIAN TIMES INC
80 Lakeside Dr (10801-3130)
PHONE..................718 230-8700
Garry P Pierre, *President*
Muriel Fenton, *Manager*
Darlie Gervais, *Manager*
EMP: 5
SQ FT: 1,200
SALES (est): 300K **Privately Held**
WEB: www.haitiantimes.com
SIC: 2711 Newspapers

(G-8953)
HALPERN TOOL CORP (PA)
Also Called: Vernon Devices
111 Plain Ave (10801-2206)
PHONE..................914 633-0038
Fax: 914 633-0059
David Newmark, *President*
Marlene Werner, *Vice Pres*
EMP: 5
SQ FT: 12,500
SALES (est): 500K **Privately Held**
SIC: 3541 5084 Machine tools, metal cutting type; industrial machinery & equipment

(G-8954)
HARBOR ELC FABRICATION TLS INC
Also Called: Hefti
29 Portman Rd (10801-2104)
PHONE..................914 636-4400
Jerry Schiff, *President*
Bill Froehlich, *General Mgr*
Anna Campone, *Manager*
EMP: 25
SALES (est): 5.2MM **Privately Held**
SIC: 3444 Metal housings, enclosures, casings & other containers

(G-8955)
HB ATHLETIC INC (PA)
Also Called: Globe-Tex
56 Harrison St Fl 4 (10801-6517)
PHONE..................914 560-8422
Robert Hurvitz, *Ch of Bd*
Stuart Hurvitz, *President*
▲ **EMP:** 13
SQ FT: 4,500
SALES (est): 1.8MM **Privately Held**
SIC: 2339 2389 Athletic clothing: women's, misses' & juniors'; uniforms, athletic women's, misses' & juniors'; women's & misses' athletic clothing & sportswear; disposable garments & accessories

(G-8956)
HIGHLANDER REALTY INC
Also Called: Seaboard Electronics
70 Church St (10805-3204)
PHONE..................914 235-8073
Fax: 914 235-8369
Jerrold Hacker, *President*
Subhas Grandhi, *Vice Pres*
Dorothy Hacker, *Treasurer*
Amy Gibson, *Bookkeeper*
EMP: 35
SQ FT: 15,000
SALES (est): 3.9MM **Privately Held**
WEB: www.highlanderrealty.com
SIC: 3699 Security devices

(G-8957)
HOMEGROWN FOR GOOD LLC
29 Beechwood Ave (10801-6818)
PHONE..................857 540-6361
Timothy Gibb, *CEO*
Thomas Gibb,
EMP: 10
SALES (est): 1.5MM **Privately Held**
SIC: 3021 Rubber & plastics footwear

(G-8958)
IVY CLASSIC INDUSTRIES INC
40 Plain Ave (10801-2205)
PHONE..................914 632-8200
Anthony Schwartz, *President*
Greg Schwartz, *Vice Pres*
Justin Schwartz, *Vice Pres*
Stanley Schwartz, *Treasurer*
◆ **EMP:** 30
SQ FT: 30,000
SALES (est): 4.7MM **Privately Held**
SIC: 3423 3546 3547 Hand & edge tools; power-driven handtools; rolling mill machinery

(G-8959)
J P INSTALLATIONS WAREHOUSE
29 Portman Rd (10801-2104)
PHONE..................914 576-3188
Fax: 914 576-3183
John Pompi, *President*
EMP: 10
SALES (est): 1.1MM **Privately Held**
SIC: 2599 Factory furniture & fixtures

(G-8960)
JOHNS RAVIOLI COMPANY INC
15 Drake Ave (10805-1506)
PHONE..................914 576-7030
Robert Guarnero, *President*
Lee Key, *Bookkeeper*
▲ **EMP:** 15
SQ FT: 8,800
SALES (est): 2.4MM **Privately Held**
SIC: 2099 5499 Pasta, uncooked: packaged with other ingredients; gourmet food stores

(G-8961)
KORING BROS INC
30 Pine St (10801-6906)
PHONE..................888 233-1292
EMP: 4
SQ FT: 5,000
SALES: 2MM **Privately Held**
SIC: 2399 Mfg Fabricated Textile Products

(G-8962)
MARY ANN LIEBERT INC
140 Huguenot St Fl 3 (10801-5215)
PHONE..................914 740-2100
Mary Ann Liebert, *President*
Gerry Williams, *Partner*
Philip Barie, *Editor*
Durland Fish PH, *Editor*
John Sterling, *Chief*
EMP: 70
SQ FT: 4,500
SALES (est): 11.7MM **Privately Held**
WEB: www.mmsionline.com
SIC: 2721 2731 2741 Trade journals: publishing only, not printed on site; books: publishing only; miscellaneous publishing

(G-8963)
ORTHO RITE INC
65 Plain Ave (10801-2206)
PHONE..................914 235-9100
Fax: 914 235-9697
Gregory Sands, *President*
EMP: 28
SQ FT: 4,000
SALES: 3.2MM **Privately Held**
WEB: www.ortho-rite.com
SIC: 3842 Suspensories

(G-8964)
PAINT OVER RUST PRODUCTS INC
Also Called: Last N Last
38 Portman Rd (10801-2103)
PHONE..................914 636-0700
David Sherman, *CEO*
Jeff Kay, *Controller*
◆ **EMP:** 35 **EST:** 1923
SQ FT: 40,000
SALES (est): 14.5MM **Privately Held**
WEB: www.absolutecoatings.com
SIC: 2851 Polyurethane coatings; varnishes

(G-8965)
PLASTIC WORKS
26 Garden St (10801-4204)
P.O. Box 51, Crompond (10517-0051)
PHONE..................914 576-2050
Fax: 914 576-2628
David J Jeskie, *Owner*
EMP: 8 **EST:** 1978
SALES (est): 800K **Privately Held**
SIC: 3089 Plastic processing

(G-8966)
PREMCO INC
11 Beechwood Ave (10801-6818)
P.O. Box 266 (10802-0266)
PHONE..................914 636-7095
Harold Jacobs, *Ch of Bd*
EMP: 18
SQ FT: 22,000
SALES (est): 3.9MM **Privately Held**
SIC: 3621 7694 Motors & generators; motor repair services

(G-8967)
RAM TRANSFORMER TECHNOLOGIES
11 Beechwood Ave (10801-6818)
P.O. Box 266 (10802-0266)
PHONE..................914 632-3988
Fax: 914 632-3931
Harold Jacobs, *President*
Lisa Ren, *Manager*
EMP: 10
SQ FT: 7,600
SALES (est): 990K **Privately Held**
SIC: 3612 Transformers, except electric

(G-8968)
REINO MANUFACTURING CO INC
34 Circuit Rd (10805-1930)
PHONE..................914 636-8990
Fax: 914 636-0572
Florence Reino, *President*
Linda Reino, *Corp Secy*
EMP: 10 **EST:** 1945
SALES (est): 615.9K **Privately Held**
SIC: 3961 Costume jewelry

(G-8969)
REPUBLIC CONSTRUCTION CO INC
305 North Ave (10801-4169)
PHONE..................914 235-3654
Joeseph Pogostin, *President*
EMP: 6 **EST:** 1985
SALES (est): 513.2K **Privately Held**
SIC: 1442 Construction sand & gravel

(G-8970)
SCEPTER PUBLISHERS INC
56 Harrison St Ste 401 (10801-6560)
P.O. Box 360694, Strongsville OH (44136-0012)
PHONE..................212 354-0670
Fax: 212 354-0736
Robert Singerline, *President*
John Powers, *Sales Mgr*
Angel Camardese, *Manager*
Violet Sukdeo, *Manager*
◆ **EMP:** 5

SALES (est): 840.1K Privately Held
SIC: 2741 Miscellaneous publishing

(G-8971)
TOWSE PUBLISHING CO
Also Called: Furniture World
1333a North Ave (10804-2120)
PHONE...................................914 235-3095
Fax: 914 235-3278
Russell Bienenstock, President
Gary Siegel, Sales Dir
Mark Testa, Sales Mgr
Gifford Dorival, Manager
Barbara Bienenstock, Director
EMP: 11
SALES: 1MM Privately Held
WEB: www.furnitureworldmagazine.com
SIC: 2721 Magazines: publishing & printing

(G-8972)
TRANSPO INDUSTRIES INC (PA)
20 Jones St Ste 3 (10801-6098)
PHONE...................................914 636-1000
Fax: 914 636-1282
Arthur M Dinitz, Ch of Bd
Michael S Stenko, President
Joan Cornell, Vice Pres
Robert Welsh, Vice Pres
Karen Liu, CFO
▲ EMP: 38
SQ FT: 33,000
SALES (est): 7.7MM Privately Held
WEB: www.transpo.com
SIC: 3089 3272 2821 Plastic hardware & building products; hardware, plastic; concrete products, precast; plastics materials & resins

(G-8973)
VIC-GINA PRINTING COMPANY INC
Also Called: Adrean Printing
1299 North Ave (10804-2642)
PHONE...................................914 636-0200
Victor Diede, President
Louise Diede, Admin Sec
EMP: 5
SQ FT: 2,500
SALES (est): 619K Privately Held
SIC: 2752 Commercial printing, lithographic

New Windsor
Orange County

(G-8974)
24 SEVEN ENTERPRISES INC
1073 State Route 94 Ste 9 (12553-6822)
PHONE...................................845 563-9033
EMP: 9
SALES (est): 1.4MM Privately Held
SIC: 3086 Packaging & shipping materials, foamed plastic

(G-8975)
A & R CONCRETE PRODUCTS LLC
7 Ruscitti Rd (12553-6205)
PHONE...................................845 562-0640
Fax: 845 562-1518
Jay Nannini, President
Phil Segali, Sales Staff
EMP: 25 EST: 2013
SALES (est): 1.8MM Privately Held
SIC: 3272 Concrete products

(G-8976)
AIGNER LABEL HOLDER CORP
Also Called: Aigner Index,
218 Mac Arthur Ave (12553-7011)
PHONE...................................845 562-4510
Mark Aigner, President
Lisa Arestin, Accounts Mgr
Lisa Cirig, Sales Staff
▲ EMP: 11 EST: 1930
SALES (est): 2.5MM Privately Held
WEB: www.aignerindex.com
SIC: 2679 Paper products, converted

(G-8977)
AMERICAN FELT & FILTER CO INC
Also Called: Affco
361 Walsh Ave (12553-6727)
PHONE...................................845 561-3560
Fax: 845 561-0967
Wilson H Pryne, Ch of Bd
Scott H Pryne, Vice Pres
▲ EMP: 60
SQ FT: 230,000
SALES (est): 25.1MM Privately Held
WEB: www.affco.com
SIC: 3569 Filters, general line: industrial

(G-8978)
BELSITO COMMUNICATIONS INC
Also Called: 1st Responder Newspaper
1 Ardmore St (12553-8303)
PHONE...................................845 534-9700
Fax: 845 561-5059
Joseph P Belsito, President
Jim Stankiewicz, General Mgr
Wanda Rogers, Sales Staff
Kathy Ronsini, Advt Staff
Michelle Belsito, Office Mgr
EMP: 12 EST: 1997
SQ FT: 2,000
SALES (est): 1MM Privately Held
SIC: 2711 7374 Newspapers: publishing only, not printed on site; computer graphics service

(G-8979)
BLEND SMOOTHIE BAR
25 Creamery Dr (12553-8011)
PHONE...................................845 568-7366
EMP: 5
SALES (est): 337.8K Privately Held
SIC: 2037 Frozen fruits & vegetables

(G-8980)
CENTER LINE STUDIOS INC (PA)
112 Forge Hill Rd (12553-8061)
PHONE...................................845 534-7143
Fax: 845 534-4560
Roger Gray, President
Prokosch Poni, Human Resources
Alexis Gray, Sales Mgr
Jennifer Migdal, Mktg Dir
Shelley Gray, Manager
▲ EMP: 15
SQ FT: 30,000
SALES: 1.6MM Privately Held
WEB: www.centerlinestudios.com
SIC: 3999 Theatrical scenery

(G-8981)
CLASSIC TOOL DESIGN INC
31 Walnut St (12553-7021)
PHONE...................................845 562-8700
Fax: 845 562-8596
Ralph Edwards, President
Marge Edwards, Vice Pres
EMP: 20
SQ FT: 22,000
SALES (est): 1.2MM Privately Held
WEB: www.ctd4ac.com
SIC: 3423 Mechanics' hand tools

(G-8982)
COCA-COLA BTLG CO OF NY INC
10 Heampstead Rd (12553-5501)
PHONE...................................845 562-3037
Fax: 845 568-6335
John Lacey, Manager
Lennie Erlanger, Manager
James Romano, Manager
EMP: 15
SQ FT: 15,000
SALES (corp-wide): 41.8B Publicly Held
SIC: 2086 Bottled & canned soft drinks
HQ: The Coca-Cola Bottling Company Of New York Inc
2500 Windy Ridge Pkwy Se
Atlanta GA 30339
770 989-3000

(G-8983)
E W SMITH PUBLISHING CO
Also Called: Sentinel, The
36 Meriline Ave (12553-6520)
P.O. Box 406, Vails Gate (12584-0406)
PHONE...................................845 562-1218
Everett W Smith, President
Michael Smith, Vice Pres
Steven Smith, Vice Pres
EMP: 11
SALES (est): 804.8K Privately Held
WEB: www.ewsmithpublishing.com
SIC: 2711 2752 Commercial printing & newspaper publishing combined; commercial printing, lithographic

(G-8984)
GAMMA PRODUCTS INC
Also Called: A & J Washroom Accessories
509 Temple Hill Rd (12553-5532)
P.O. Box 4569 (12553-0569)
PHONE...................................845 562-3332
Anthony Granuzzo, President
Richard Rebusmen, President
Donna G Frenz, Sr Corp Ofcr
Jayne F Granuzzo, Exec VP
Horacio Sosa, Safety Mgr
▲ EMP: 70
SQ FT: 50,000
SALES (est): 10.5MM Privately Held
WEB: www.ajwashroom.com
SIC: 3261 Bathroom accessories/fittings, vitreous china or earthenware

(G-8985)
HI-TECH PACKG WORLD-WIDE LLC
110 Corporate Dr (12553-6952)
P.O. Box 4232 (12553-0232)
PHONE...................................845 947-1912
Robert Trimble, Owner
EMP: 2
SQ FT: 10,000
SALES (est): 1.1MM Privately Held
SIC: 2759 Commercial printing

(G-8986)
JUST WOOD PALLETS INC
78 Vails Gate Heights Dr (12553-8514)
PHONE...................................718 644-7013
Carlos Garcia, Principal
EMP: 8
SALES (est): 1MM Privately Held
SIC: 2448 Pallets, wood & wood with metal

(G-8987)
LARCENT ENTERPRISES INC
Also Called: Angie Washroom
509 Temple Hill Rd (12553-5532)
P.O. Box 4569 (12553-0569)
PHONE...................................845 562-3332
Anthony J Granuzzo, Ch of Bd
▲ EMP: 50
SALES (est): 6.4MM Privately Held
SIC: 3261 Bathroom accessories/fittings, vitreous china or earthenware

(G-8988)
LSI LIGHTRON INC
500 Hudson Valley Ave (12553-4744)
P.O. Box 4270 (12553-0270)
PHONE...................................845 562-5500
Fax: 845 562-3082
Gene Littman, CEO
Barry White, President
Joe Piascik, Asst Controller
▲ EMP: 1000
SQ FT: 170,000
SALES (est): 184.5MM
SALES (corp-wide): 331.3MM Publicly Held
WEB: www.lsilightron.com
SIC: 3646 5063 Commercial indusl & institutional electric lighting fixtures; electrical apparatus & equipment
PA: Lsi Industries Inc.
10000 Alliance Rd
Blue Ash OH 45242
513 793-3200

(G-8989)
METAL CONTAINER CORPORATION
1000 Breunig Rd (12553-8438)
PHONE...................................845 567-1500
Fax: 845 567-1522
Russell Lindberg, Plant Mgr
Gregg Giaquinto, QC Dir
John Voda, Engineer
George Ignarra, Human Res Mgr
Mark Stafford, Branch Mgr
EMP: 200 Privately Held
SIC: 3411 Metal cans
HQ: Metal Container Corporation
3636 S Geyer Rd Ste 100
Saint Louis MO 63127
314 577-2000

(G-8990)
NEW WINDSOR WASTE WATER PLANT
145 Caesars Ln (12553-7742)
P.O. Box 4653 (12553-0653)
PHONE...................................845 561-2550
Fax: 845 565-0626
John Egitto, Manager
EMP: 10
SALES (est): 778.8K Privately Held
SIC: 3589 Water treatment equipment, industrial

(G-8991)
NEWBURGH DISTRIBUTION CORP (PA)
463 Temple Hill Rd (12553-5527)
PHONE...................................845 561-6330
Fax: 845 561-8308
Donald Harkness, President
Sharon Harkness, Vice Pres
Mary Kratchwil, Personnel Exec
▲ EMP: 3
SALES (est): 47.6MM Privately Held
WEB: www.baricosmetics.com
SIC: 2844 Cosmetic preparations

(G-8992)
NEWLINE PRODUCTS INC
509 Temple Hill Rd (12553-5532)
PHONE...................................972 881-3318
Kevin Wang, CEO
Chris Bradford, President
William Bowers, CFO
▲ EMP: 195
SQ FT: 30,000
SALES (est): 15MM Privately Held
WEB: www.newlineproduct.com
SIC: 3993 Displays & cutouts, window & lobby

(G-8993)
PATTERSON MATERIALS CORP
322 Walsh Ave (12553-6748)
P.O. Box 800, Wingdale (12594-0800)
PHONE...................................845 832-6000
Fax: 845 832-6724
John Peckham, Manager
EMP: 20
SQ FT: 6,171
SALES (corp-wide): 200.6MM Privately Held
SIC: 1422 Crushed & broken limestone
HQ: Patterson Materials Corp
20 Haarlem Ave
White Plains NY 10603
914 949-2000

(G-8994)
PRODUCTION RESOURCE GROUP LLC
539 Temple Hill Rd (12553-5533)
PHONE...................................845 567-5700
Jerry Harris, President
Brian Edwards, General Mgr
David James, General Mgr
Kevin McKnight, General Mgr
Arthur Smith, General Mgr
EMP: 50 Privately Held
SIC: 3999 7922 Theatrical scenery; equipment rental, theatrical
PA: Production Resource Group Llc
200 Business Park Dr # 109
Armonk NY 10504

(G-8995)
PVH CORP
Also Called: Van Heusen
1073 State Route 94 (12553-6821)
PHONE...................................845 561-0233
Lenore Dunn, Branch Mgr
EMP: 9

SALES (corp-wide): 8.2B **Publicly Held**
SIC: 2321 Men's & boys' dress shirts
PA: Pvh Corp.
200 Madison Ave Bsmt 1
New York NY 10016
212 381-3500

(G-8996)
REGE INC
110 Corporate Dr (12553-6952)
P.O. Box 4417 (12553-0417)
PHONE..................845 565-7772
Fax: 845 565-9452
Cheskel Smilowitz, *CEO*
Ramon Echevarria, *President*
▲ **EMP:** 18
SQ FT: 30,000
SALES (est): 5.6MM **Privately Held**
WEB: www.polyworksinc.com
SIC: 2673 Plastic bags: made from purchased materials

(G-8997)
S M FRANK & COMPANY INC
Also Called: Medico
1073 State Route 94 Ste 7 (12553-6822)
PHONE..................914 739-3100
Fax: 914 739-3105
William F Feuerbach Jr, *President*
Lois Kessler, *Manager*
▲ **EMP:** 8 **EST:** 1924
SQ FT: 15,000
SALES (est): 1MM **Privately Held**
WEB: www.smfrankcoinc.com
SIC: 3999 Tobacco pipes, pipestems & bits; cigarette filters; cigar & cigarette holders

(G-8998)
SALKO KITCHENS INC
256 Walsh Ave (12553-5752)
PHONE..................845 565-4420
Fax: 845 565-4742
Aron Sandel, *President*
▲ **EMP:** 19
SALES: 1.5MM **Privately Held**
WEB: www.salkokitchens.com
SIC: 2434 Wood kitchen cabinets

(G-8999)
SCREEN GEMS INC
41 Windsor Hwy (12553-6225)
PHONE..................845 561-0036
Carl Friedwall, *President*
EMP: 5
SQ FT: 3,600
SALES (est): 752.7K **Privately Held**
WEB: www.screengemsny.com
SIC: 2262 2395 Screen printing: manmade fiber & silk broadwoven fabrics; embroidery & art needlework

(G-9000)
SENTINEL PRINTING SERVICES INC
Also Called: Smith, E W Publishing
36 Meriline Ave (12553-6520)
P.O. Box 406, Vails Gate (12584-0406)
PHONE..................845 562-1218
Fax: 845 562-0488
Everett Smith, *President*
Michael Smith, *Vice Pres*
Steve Smith, *Vice Pres*
EMP: 55
SQ FT: 4,000
SALES (est): 4.2MM **Privately Held**
SIC: 2741 Catalogs: publishing & printing

(G-9001)
SIMCHA CANDLE CO INC
244 Mac Arthur Ave (12553-7011)
P.O. Box 309, Monroe (10949-0309)
PHONE..................845 783-0406
Fax: 845 534-1254
Samuel Marcus, *President*
▲ **EMP:** 6
SQ FT: 15,000
SALES (est): 626.5K **Privately Held**
WEB: www.simchacandle.com
SIC: 3999 Candles

(G-9002)
USA ILLUMINATION INC
Also Called: Usai
1126 River Rd (12553-6728)
PHONE..................845 565-8500
Fax: 845 561-1130
Bonnie Littman, *Principal*
Ron Vonwerder, *Design Engr*
Janice Rosario, *Director*
▲ **EMP:** 35
SQ FT: 40,000
SALES (est): 16.5MM **Privately Held**
WEB: www.usaillumination.com
SIC: 3648 Public lighting fixtures

(G-9003)
VERLA INTERNATIONAL LTD
463 Temple Hill Rd (12553-5527)
PHONE..................845 561-2440
Fax: 845 561-0374
Mario F Maffei, *President*
Robert R Roth, *Vice Pres*
Melissa Gallardo, *Project Mgr*
Matt Haspel, *Manager*
Mike Tiedman, *Maintence Staff*
▲ **EMP:** 400
SQ FT: 60,000
SALES (est): 93.8MM **Privately Held**
SIC: 2844 Toilet preparations

New York
New York County

(G-9004)
1 ATELIER LLC
347 W 36th St (10018-6406)
PHONE..................917 916-2968
Stephanie Sarka, *CEO*
EMP: 8 **EST:** 2014
SALES (est): 275.5K **Privately Held**
SIC: 2339 5632 7389 Women's & misses' accessories; women's accessory & specialty stores; design services

(G-9005)
141 INDUSTRIES LLC
300 E 5th St Apt 11 (10003-8816)
PHONE..................978 273-8831
Nicolas Lirette,
Erin Young,
EMP: 12
SALES (est): 770K **Privately Held**
SIC: 3999 Manufacturing industries

(G-9006)
1510 ASSOCIATES LLC
1500 Lexington Ave (10029-7349)
PHONE..................212 828-8720
EMP: 6
SALES (est): 498.4K **Privately Held**
SIC: 2211 Cotton Broadwoven Fabric Mill

(G-9007)
180S LLC (HQ)
1 Liberty Plz Rm 3500 (10006-1421)
PHONE..................410 534-6320
Helen Rockey, *CEO*
Lester C Lee, *CEO*
Brian Le Gette, *President*
Shelley Foland, *Vice Pres*
Flor Andres, *CFO*
▲ **EMP:** 35
SQ FT: 45,000
SALES (est): 5.5MM **Privately Held**
SIC: 2253 Scarves & mufflers, knit
PA: 180s, Inc.
700 S Caroline St
New York NY 10006
410 534-6320

(G-9008)
2 1 2 POSTCARDS INC
121 Varick St Frnt B (10013-1408)
PHONE..................212 767-8227
Fax: 212 741-1332
Jiff Wed Work, *Manager*
EMP: 25
SALES (est): 2.9MM **Privately Held**
SIC: 2759 2752 Commercial printing; commercial printing, lithographic

(G-9009)
2 X 4 INC
180 Varick St Rm 1610 (10014-5861)
PHONE..................212 647-1170
Fax: 212 647-0454
Georgie Stout, *President*
Michael Rock, *Partner*
Douglas Freedman, *Managing Dir*
Jane Friesen, *Managing Dir*
Gala Delmont-Benatar, *Project Mgr*
EMP: 22
SQ FT: 2,000
SALES (est): 3.7MM **Privately Held**
WEB: www.2x4.org
SIC: 2752 Commercial printing, lithographic

(G-9010)
212 BIZ LLC (PA)
525 Fashion Ave Rm 2301 (10018-4923)
PHONE..................212 391-4444
Asheesh Mathur, *VP Sales*
Ira Levinas,
▲ **EMP:** 9 **EST:** 2007
SQ FT: 2,000
SALES: 12MM **Privately Held**
SIC: 3161 Clothing & apparel carrying cases

(G-9011)
212 DB CORP
Also Called: Gig-It
30 W 22nd St Fl 6 (10010-5892)
PHONE..................212 652-5600
John Acunto, *CEO*
EMP: 40 **EST:** 2013
SALES (est): 2.8MM **Privately Held**
SIC: 3944 Electronic games & toys

(G-9012)
212 MEDIA LLC
460 Park Ave S Fl 4 (10016-7561)
PHONE..................212 710-3092
Rishi Malhotra, *Managing Prtnr*
Neal Shenoy, *Mng Member*
Clint Balcom, *Creative Dir*
Brian Litvack, *Business Dir*
▲ **EMP:** 40
SALES (est): 2.9MM **Privately Held**
WEB: www.212media.com
SIC: 2741 Miscellaneous publishing

(G-9013)
21ST CENTURY FOX AMERICA INC (HQ)
1211 Ave Of The Americas (10036-8701)
PHONE..................212 852-7000
Fax: 212 575-5845
James Murdoch, *CEO*
Angie Vargo, *Vice Pres*
John Nallen, *CFO*
Ryan Schaumburg, *Account Dir*
Tina Melluse, *Analyst*
EMP: 60
SQ FT: 40,000
SALES (est): 1.9B
SALES (corp-wide): 28.5B **Publicly Held**
SIC: 2752 4833 7812 2721 Promotional printing, lithographic; television broadcasting stations; motion picture production & distribution; magazines: publishing only, not printed on site
PA: Twenty-First Century Fox, Inc.
1211 Ave Of The Americas
New York NY 10036
212 852-7000

(G-9014)
21ST CENTURY FOX AMERICA INC
Mirabella Magazine
200 Madison Ave Fl 8 (10016-3908)
PHONE..................212 447-4600
Grace Mirabella, *Director*
EMP: 85
SALES (corp-wide): 27.3B **Publicly Held**
SIC: 2721 Periodicals
HQ: 21st Century Fox America, Inc.
1211 Ave Of The Americas
New York NY 10036
212 852-7000

(G-9015)
2K INC
622 Broadway Fl 6 (10012-2600)
PHONE..................646 536-3007
Strauss Zelnick, *CEO*
Lainie Goldstein, *CFO*
EMP: 6 **EST:** 2013
SALES (est): 324.5K **Publicly Held**
SIC: 7372 Prepackaged software
PA: Take-Two Interactive Software, Inc.
622 Broadway Fl 6
New York NY 10012

(G-9016)
30DC INC (PA)
80 Broad St Fl 5 (10004-2257)
PHONE..................212 962-4400
Henry Pinskier, *Ch of Bd*
Theodore A Greenberg, *CFO*
EMP: 5
SALES: 738.1K **Publicly Held**
SIC: 7372 Prepackaged software

(G-9017)
30DC INC
80 Broad St Fl 5 (10004-2257)
PHONE..................212 962-4400
Fax: 212 962-4422
Teodore A Greenbird, *CFO*
Greg Laborde, *Director*
EMP: 12
SQ FT: 3,000
SALES: 1MM **Privately Held**
SIC: 7372 Prepackaged software; application computer software

(G-9018)
31 PHILLIP LIM LLC (PA)
304 Hudson St Fl 8 (10013-1015)
PHONE..................212 354-6540
Shirley Cheng, *Bookkeeper*
Priscilla Camacho, *Sales Dir*
Han LI, *Manager*
Bo Zhou, *Manager*
Maria Vu, *Director*
▲ **EMP:** 40
SQ FT: 2,000
SALES (est): 9.8MM **Privately Held**
WEB: www.31philliplim.com
SIC: 2339 Sportswear, women's

(G-9019)
3835 LEBRON REST EQP & SUP INC
Also Called: Lebron Equipment Supply
3835 9th Ave (10034-3740)
PHONE..................212 942-8258
Catalina Lebron, *Ch of Bd*
Manuel Lebron, *President*
Frepesvinda Perez, *Accountant*
Edward Perez, *Director*
EMP: 20
SQ FT: 400
SALES (est): 3.6MM **Privately Held**
SIC: 3679 Power supplies, all types: static

(G-9020)
3LAB INC
525 7th Ave Rm 2300 (10018-5395)
PHONE..................201 567-9100
David C Chung, *President*
Simon Hong, *Controller*
Krissy Kim, *Accounts Mgr*
Christina Oresajo, *Marketing Staff*
▲ **EMP:** 10
SQ FT: 14,000
SALES (est): 1.5MM **Privately Held**
WEB: www.3lab.com
SIC: 2844 Face creams or lotions

(G-9021)
4BUMPERS LLC
285 New Wstmnster End Ave (10023)
PHONE..................212 721-9600
Jeffrey Levine,
Alan Levine,
EMP: 10
SALES (est): 596.8K **Privately Held**
SIC: 3714 Bumpers & bumperettes, motor vehicle

(G-9022)
5 STAR APPAREL LLC
Also Called: Enyce
31 W 34th St Fl 3 (10001-3009)
PHONE..................212 563-1233
Albert Pardo, *Division Mgr*
EMP: 6
SALES (corp-wide): 63.3MM **Privately Held**
SIC: 2326 Men's & boys' work clothing
HQ: 5 Star Apparel L.L.C.
31 W 34th St Rm 401
New York NY 10001
212 563-1233

New York - New York County (G-9023)

(G-9023)
525 AMERICA LLC (PA)
525 7th Ave Rm 1000 (10018-4910)
PHONE..................212 921-5688
Fax: 212 921-5069
EMP: 7
SALES (est): 9.3MM **Privately Held**
SIC: 2339 Women's & misses' outerwear

(G-9024)
6TH AVENUE SHOWCASE INC
Also Called: Tempo Paris
241 W 37th St Frnt 2 (10018-6797)
PHONE..................212 382-0400
Fax: 212 382-0623
Shawn Assil, *President*
▲ EMP: 6
SQ FT: 5,300
SALES (est): 998.2K **Privately Held**
SIC: 2339 Women's & misses' outerwear

(G-9025)
79 METRO LTD (PA)
265 W 37th St Rm 205 (10018-5031)
PHONE..................212 944-4030
Nancy Bossio Hutnick, *President*
Reggy Puma, *Controller*
EMP: 1
SQ FT: 8,500
SALES (est): 1.1MM **Privately Held**
SIC: 2337 2253 2331 Women's & misses' suits & coats; sweaters & sweater coats, knit; blouses, women's & juniors': made from purchased material

(G-9026)
99CENT WORLD AND VARIETY CORP
4242 Broadway (10033-3708)
PHONE..................212 740-0010
Gamal Alsaidi, *CEO*
EMP: 5
SALES (est): 294.3K **Privately Held**
SIC: 3643 Outlets, electric: convenience

(G-9027)
A & M LLC
Also Called: H and B Digital
29 W 46th St (10036-4104)
PHONE..................212 354-1341
Tony Aama, *Mng Member*
EMP: 6
SQ FT: 3,000
SALES (est): 7MM **Privately Held**
SIC: 3634 Electric housewares & fans

(G-9028)
A & M ROSENTHAL ENTPS INC
Also Called: Dessy Creations
8 W 38th St Fl 4 (10018-0154)
PHONE..................646 638-9600
Alan Dessy, *President*
Ronnie Dey, *Purchasing*
Vivian G Diamond, *Treasurer*
Renee Wyatt, *Manager*
Nancy Vargas, *Supervisor*
◆ EMP: 45 EST: 1963
SQ FT: 18,400
SALES (est): 7MM **Privately Held**
SIC: 2335 Women's, juniors' & misses' dresses; wedding gowns & dresses; gowns, formal; ensemble dresses: women's, misses' & juniors'

(G-9029)
A & V CASTINGS INC
257 W 39th St Fl 16w (10018-3106)
PHONE..................212 997-0042
Fax: 212 768-3582
Alex Kvitko, *President*
EMP: 8
SALES: 1MM **Privately Held**
SIC: 3325 3911 Alloy steel castings, except investment; jewelry, precious metal

(G-9030)
A AND J APPAREL CORP
Also Called: Forwear
209 W 38th St Rm 1207 (10018-4498)
PHONE..................212 398-8899
Fax: 212 398-1302
Mahin Azizian, *President*
EMP: 9

SALES (est): 1.1MM **Privately Held**
SIC: 2211 Apparel & outerwear fabrics, cotton

(G-9031)
A ESTEBAN & COMPANY INC (PA)
132 W 36th St Rm 1000 (10018-8819)
PHONE..................212 989-7000
Fax: 212 989-6087
Alphonso C Esteban, *Ch of Bd*
Carl Bednarz, *General Mgr*
Harvey Klipper, *Sales Mgr*
Michelle Mwikoff, *Sales Mgr*
Diane Moralez, *Office Mgr*
▲ EMP: 25
SALES (est): 5.9MM **Privately Held**
WEB: www.esteban.com
SIC: 2752 7334 Commercial printing, lithographic; blueprinting service

(G-9032)
A ESTEBAN & COMPANY INC
132 W 36th St Rm 1000 (10018-8819)
PHONE..................212 714-2227
Esteban Daniel, *Vice Pres*
Tim Gibbaid, *Manager*
EMP: 25
SALES (corp-wide): 5.9MM **Privately Held**
WEB: www.esteban.com
SIC: 2752 Commercial printing, lithographic
PA: A. Esteban & Company, Inc.
132 W 36th St Rm 1000
New York NY 10018
212 989-7000

(G-9033)
A FLEISIG PAPER BOX CORP
1751 2nd Ave Apt 10a (10128-5377)
PHONE..................212 226-7490
Fax: 212 941-7840
Robert Fleisig, *President*
EMP: 10 EST: 1999
SALES: 1MM **Privately Held**
WEB: www.afleisig.com
SIC: 2652 Setup paperboard boxes

(G-9034)
A GRAPHIC PRINTING INC
49 Market St Frnt 2 (10002-7229)
PHONE..................212 233-9696
Fax: 212 233-9699
M Siam, *President*
▲ EMP: 7
SALES (est): 596.6K **Privately Held**
SIC: 2759 Commercial printing

(G-9035)
A GUIDEPOSTS CHURCH CORP
16 E 34th St Fl 21 (10016-4328)
PHONE..................212 251-8100
Fax: 212 684-0689
Rick Hamlin, *Editor*
Colleen Hughes, *Editor*
Stephanie Samoy, *Editor*
Edward Grinnan, *Sls & Mktg Exec*
Donna Kerr, *Marketing Staff*
EMP: 180
SALES (corp-wide): 22.2MM **Privately Held**
SIC: 2721 Periodicals
PA: A Guideposts Church Corp
39 Old Ridgebury Rd # 27
Danbury CT 06810
203 749-0203

(G-9036)
A H SCHREIBER CO INC (PA)
460 W 34th St Fl 10 (10001-2320)
PHONE..................212 594-7234
Fax: 212 594-7234
Joel M Schreiber, *President*
Elliott N Schreiber, *Corp Secy*
Avram Schreiber, *Vice Pres*
David Schreiber, *Vice Pres*
Seth Schreiber, *Vice Pres*
◆ EMP: 70 EST: 1923
SQ FT: 30,000
SALES (est): 40MM **Privately Held**
SIC: 2339 5621 Bathing suits: women's, misses' & juniors'; athletic clothing: women's, misses' & juniors'; women's sportswear

(G-9037)
A J C JEWELRY CONTRACTING INC
247 W 30th St Fl 3 (10001-2824)
PHONE..................212 594-3703
Fax: 212 594-3706
Dion Smith, *Owner*
EMP: 6 EST: 1993
SALES (est): 525.2K **Privately Held**
SIC: 3915 Jewel preparing: instruments, tools, watches & jewelry

(G-9038)
A JAFFE INC
Also Called: Sandberg & Sikorski Corp
592 5th Ave Fl 3 (10036-4707)
PHONE..................212 843-7464
Fax: 212 593-1989
Mihir Bhansali, *CEO*
Stanley Sikorski, *President*
Samuel Sandberg, *Chairman*
Ken Karlin, *Prdtn Mgr*
Aj Gandhi, *CFO*
EMP: 175
SQ FT: 30,000
SALES (est): 29.6MM **Privately Held**
WEB: www.ajaffe.com
SIC: 3911 Jewelry, precious metal

(G-9039)
A THOUSAND CRANES INC
Also Called: Knitty City
208 W 79th St Apt 2 (10024-6269)
PHONE..................212 724-9596
Pearl Chin, *President*
Arvin Chin, *Vice Pres*
EMP: 10
SALES (est): 1.1MM **Privately Held**
WEB: www.knittycity.com
SIC: 2299 Yarns, specialty & novelty

(G-9040)
A TO Z MEDIA INC (PA)
243 W 30th St Fl 6 (10001-2812)
PHONE..................212 260-0237
Fax: 212 260-0631
Sarah Robertson, *CEO*
Scott Pollack, *President*
Joe Vent, *General Mgr*
Bret Trach, *Vice Pres*
Stacy Karp, *VP Prdtn*
▲ EMP: 12
SALES (est): 11.3MM **Privately Held**
WEB: www.atozmedia.com
SIC: 3652 7389 Compact laser discs, prerecorded; magnetic tape (audio): prerecorded; design services

(G-9041)
A-IMPLANT DENTAL LAB CORP
10 Park Ave (10016-4338)
PHONE..................212 582-4720
Gina Martin, *Info Tech Mgr*
Bryan Glynson, *Director*
EMP: 7 EST: 2012
SALES (est): 725.3K **Privately Held**
SIC: 3843 Teeth, artificial (not made in dental laboratories)

(G-9042)
A2IA CORP
24 W 40th St Fl 3 (10018-1856)
PHONE..................917 237-0390
Fax: 917 237-0391
Jean-Louis Fages, *President*
Olivier Baret, *Senior VP*
Jorge Tavares, *Sales/Mktg Mgr*
ATI Azemoun, *Sales Mgr*
Bob Degliuomini, *Accounts Mgr*
EMP: 8
SALES: 1.3MM
SALES (corp-wide): 8.7MM **Privately Held**
SIC: 7372 Prepackaged software
PA: Analyse Image Intelli Artific
37 Au 39
Paris 75008
144 420-080

(G-9043)
A3 APPAREL LLC
1407 Broadway Rm 716a (10018-5293)
PHONE..................888 403-9669
Peter Regondo, *CEO*
EMP: 7 EST: 2014
SQ FT: 1,200

SALES: 8MM **Privately Held**
SIC: 2211 Apparel & outerwear fabrics, cotton

(G-9044)
AAA AMERCN FLAG DCTG CO INC
36 W 37th St Rm 409 (10018-7452)
PHONE..................212 279-3524
Fax: 212 695-8392
Ian Flamm, *President*
Marian Watson, *Vice Pres*
EMP: 4 EST: 1946
SQ FT: 2,500
SALES: 1MM **Privately Held**
SIC: 2399 Flags, fabric; banners, made from fabric

(G-9045)
AAA NOODLE PRODUCTS MFG
102 Bowery (10013-4727)
PHONE..................212 431-4090
David Ho, *Vice Pres*
K Phan, *Manager*
EMP: 5
SQ FT: 10,800
SALES: 1MM **Privately Held**
SIC: 2098 2052 Noodles (e.g. egg, plain & water), dry; cookies

(G-9046)
ABALENE DECORATING SERVICES
315 W 39th St Rm 611 (10018-4035)
PHONE..................718 782-2000
Mosheha Goldman, *President*
Kalmen Weiss, *President*
Miriam Weiss, *Vice Pres*
EMP: 21
SQ FT: 18,000
SALES (est): 1.8MM **Privately Held**
SIC: 2591 2391 7216 Drapery hardware & blinds & shades; curtains & draperies; curtain cleaning & repair

(G-9047)
ABBEVILLE PRESS INC
Also Called: Abbeville Publishing Group
116 W 23rd St Fl 5 (10011-2599)
PHONE..................212 366-5585
Fax: 646 375-2040
Robert E Abrams, *Ch of Bd*
Louise Kurtz, *Prdtn Dir*
Nadine Winns, *Marketing Mgr*
Misha Beletsky, *Art Dir*
Dorothy Gutterman, *Admin Sec*
▲ EMP: 33
SALES (est): 3.6MM **Privately Held**
WEB: www.abbeville.com
SIC: 2731 Books: publishing only

(G-9048)
ABC PEANUT BUTTER LLC
295 Madison Ave Ste 1618 (10017-6434)
PHONE..................212 661-6886
H J Warden, *Mng Member*
EMP: 355
SALES (est): 23.4MM **Privately Held**
SIC: 2099 Peanut butter

(G-9049)
ABEL NOSER SOLUTIONS LLC
1 Battery Park Plz # 601 (10004-1446)
PHONE..................646 432-4000
Stanley Abel, *Ch of Bd*
James Noser, *President*
Ted Morgan, *COO*
Vijay Chakka, *Manager*
Allison Keane, *Manager*
EMP: 20
SALES: 4MM **Privately Held**
SIC: 7372 Business oriented computer software

(G-9050)
ABKCO MUSIC & RECORDS INC (PA)
85 5th Ave Fl 11 (10003-3019)
PHONE..................212 399-0300
Allen Klein, *President*
Alan E Horowitz, *Vice Pres*
Peter J Howard, *Vice Pres*
Iris W Keitel, *Vice Pres*
Jody H Klein, *Vice Pres*
EMP: 67 EST: 1961

GEOGRAPHIC SECTION

New York - New York County (G-9077)

SQ FT: 11,000
SALES (est): 9.9MM **Privately Held**
SIC: **3652** 6794 2741 7922 Phonograph records, prerecorded; magnetic tape (audio): prerecorded; compact laser discs, prerecorded; copyright buying & licensing; music, sheet: publishing only, not printed on site; legitimate live theater producers; motion picture production

(G-9051)
ABP INTERNATIONAL INC
Also Called: Electronic Tech Briefs
1466 Broadway Ste 910 (10036-7309)
PHONE.....................................212 490-3999
Fax: 212 986-7864
Bill Schnirring, *Ch of Bd*
Joseph Pramberger, *President*
Cathleen Lambertson, *Editor*
Ted Selinsky, *Editor*
Domenic Mucchetti, *COO*
EMP: 40 **EST:** 1975
SQ FT: 11,000
SALES (est): 4.7MM **Privately Held**
WEB: www.emhartcontest.com
SIC: **2721** Magazines: publishing only, not printed on site

(G-9052)
ABRAHAM JWLY DESIGNERS & MFRS
37 W 47th St Ste 202 (10036-2862)
PHONE.....................................212 944-1149
Can Akdemir, *Partner*
Ibrahim Akdemir, *Partner*
Iskender Akdemir, *Partner*
EMP: 16
SALES (est): 1.5MM **Privately Held**
SIC: **3911** Jewelry, precious metal

(G-9053)
ABRIMIAN BROS CORP
48 W 48th St Ste 805 (10036-1713)
PHONE.....................................212 382-1106
Fax: 212 221-0939
Marty Abrimian, *President*
EMP: 10
SALES (est): 860.2K **Privately Held**
SIC: **3911** Jewelry, precious metal

(G-9054)
ABSOLUTE COLOR CORPORATION
109 W 27th St Frnt 2 (10001-6208)
PHONE.....................................212 868-0404
Daniel Shil, *President*
Peter Gordon, *Vice Pres*
EMP: 8
SQ FT: 2,500
SALES (est): 1MM **Privately Held**
WEB: www.absolutcolor.com
SIC: **2796** 2741 Color separations for printing; miscellaneous publishing

(G-9055)
ACADEMY OF POLITICAL SCIENCE
Also Called: POLITICAL SCIENCE QUARTERLY
475 Riverside Dr Ste 1274 (10115-1298)
PHONE.....................................212 870-2500
Fax: 212 870-2202
Demetrios Caraley, *President*
Virgil Conway, *Principal*
Abigail Moses, *Editor*
Diana Murray, *Vice Pres*
Grace Wainer, *Bookkeeper*
EMP: 6
SQ FT: 2,309
SALES: 732.7K **Privately Held**
WEB: www.psqonline.org
SIC: **2721** Periodicals: publishing only

(G-9056)
ACCELIFY SOLUTIONS LLC
16 W 36th St Rm 902 (10018-9748)
PHONE.....................................888 922-2354
Alex Brecher, *CEO*
Joe Jacobs, *President*
David Thomas, *Vice Pres*
Natalie Roth, *Marketing Staff*
EMP: 25
SQ FT: 3,000
SALES (est): 2.7MM **Privately Held**
SIC: **7372** Educational computer software

(G-9057)
ACCESS INTELLIGENCE LLC
Also Called: Pbi Media Inc.
249 W 17th St (10011-5390)
PHONE.....................................212 204-4269
John French, *President*
Andrea Persily, *COO*
Don Socteart, *Vice Pres*
Allison Witcher, *Controller*
EMP: 950
SALES (est): 35.7MM
SALES (corp-wide): 90.2MM **Privately Held**
SIC: **2721** Trade journals: publishing only, not printed on site
PA: Access Intelligence Llc
   9211 Corp Blvd Fl 4
   Rockville MD 20850
   301 354-2000

(G-9058)
ACCESSORY PLAYS LLC
29 W 36th St (10018-7907)
PHONE.....................................212 564-7301
Richard Dauplaise, *President*
EMP: 50
SQ FT: 5,000
SALES (est): 1.4MM **Privately Held**
SIC: **3961** Costume jewelry, ex. precious metal & semiprecious stones

(G-9059)
ACCESSORY STREET LLC
1370 Broadway (10018-7302)
PHONE.....................................212 686-8990
Andrew Pizzo,
Mitchell Grossman,
▲ **EMP:** 12
SALES (est): 685.8K **Privately Held**
SIC: **2339** Women's & misses' outerwear

(G-9060)
ACCESSRIES DIRECT INTL USA INC
1450 Broadway Fl 22 (10018-2222)
PHONE.....................................646 448-8200
Alberto Rosenthal, *CEO*
Rody Moreira, *President*
▲ **EMP:** 19
SALES: 11.1MM **Privately Held**
SIC: **2389** 2331 2339 Men's miscellaneous accessories; women's & misses' blouses & shirts; women's & misses' accessories

(G-9061)
ACCUTRAK INC
432 Washington St Ste 113 (10013-1721)
PHONE.....................................212 925-5330
Eli Camhi, *President*
Stanford Silverman, *Vice Pres*
EMP: 15
SALES (est): 1MM **Privately Held**
SIC: **3812** Electronic detection systems (aeronautical)

(G-9062)
ACE BANNER & FLAG COMPANY
Also Called: Ace Banner Flag & Graphics
107 W 27th St (10001-6213)
PHONE.....................................212 620-9111
Fax: 212 463-9128
Carl Calo, *President*
Elizabeth Calo, *Treasurer*
Leah Segarra, *Manager*
EMP: 12 **EST:** 1916
SQ FT: 10,000
SALES: 1MM **Privately Held**
WEB: www.acebanner.com
SIC: **2399** Banners, made from fabric; flags, fabric

(G-9063)
ACE DIAMOND CORP
30 W 47th St Ste 808r (10036-8665)
PHONE.....................................212 730-8231
Fax: 212 730-8232
Herman Witriol, *President*
Efraim Witriol, *Vice Pres*
Margaret Witriol, *Treasurer*
EMP: 3 **EST:** 1975

SALES: 1MM **Privately Held**
SIC: **3915** 5094 Diamond cutting & polishing; jewelry & precious stones; diamonds (gems)

(G-9064)
ACF INDUSTRIES HOLDING LLC (DH)
767 5th Ave (10153-0023)
PHONE.....................................212 702-4363
Keith Cozza, *CEO*
Carl C Icahn, *President*
Richard T Buonato, *Vice Pres*
EMP: 2
SALES (est): 244MM
SALES (corp-wide): 1B **Privately Held**
SIC: **3743** 4741 4789 6799 Freight cars & equipment; tank freight cars & car equipment; railroad equipment, except locomotives; rental of railroad cars; railroad car repair; security speculators for own account
HQ: Highcrest Investors Llc
   445 Hamilton Ave Ste 1210
   New York NY 10153
   212 702-4323

(G-9065)
ACKER & LI MILLS CORPORATION
44 W 62nd St Apt 3b (10023-7009)
PHONE.....................................212 307-7247
Daniel Feder, *President*
▲ **EMP:** 5
SALES: 2MM **Privately Held**
SIC: **2231** Broadwoven fabric mills, wool

(G-9066)
ACOLYTE TECHNOLOGIES CORP
44 E 32nd St Rm 901 (10016-5508)
PHONE.....................................212 629-3239
Marvin Figenbaum, *CEO*
Salvatore Guerrieri, *President*
David Hurwitz, *Controller*
Abel Gonzalez, *Sales Staff*
▲ **EMP:** 14
SALES (est): 2.1MM **Privately Held**
SIC: **3674** Light emitting diodes

(G-9067)
ACTINIUM PHARMACEUTICALS INC
275 Madison Ave Ste 702 (10016-1154)
PHONE.....................................646 677-3870
Sandesh Seth, *Ch of Bd*
Nitya Ray, *Exec VP*
Mark S Berger, *Chief Mktg Ofcr*
EMP: 23 **EST:** 1997
SALES (est): 4.1MM **Privately Held**
SIC: **2834** 8069 Pharmaceutical preparations; cancer hospital

(G-9068)
ACTV INC (DEL CORP) (DH)
233 Park Ave S Fl 10 (10003-1606)
PHONE.....................................212 995-9500
Fax: 212 995-9836
David Reese, *President*
Joel Hassell, *COO*
Bruce Crowley, *Exec VP*
Ben Bennett, *Vice Pres*
Frank Deo, *Vice Pres*
EMP: 100
SQ FT: 12,000
SALES (est): 6.3MM
SALES (corp-wide): 1B **Privately Held**
WEB: www.actv.com
SIC: **3663** 7371 Radio & TV communications equipment; custom computer programming services

(G-9069)
AD VANTAGE PRESS
481 Washington St Fl 7 (10013-1325)
PHONE.....................................212 941-8355
Fax: 212 226-6579
Edward J Kachik, *President*
Josephine Rogoff, *Treasurer*
EMP: 5
SQ FT: 2,000
SALES (est): 400K **Privately Held**
WEB: www.advantagepress.com
SIC: **2752** Commercial printing, offset

(G-9070)
ADA GEMS CORP
Also Called: Mordechai Collection
10 W 47th St Ste 707 (10036-3301)
PHONE.....................................212 719-0100
Daniel Mor, *Treasurer*
▲ **EMP:** 5
SALES (est): 457.3K **Privately Held**
SIC: **3172** Cases, jewelry

(G-9071)
ADAM SCOTT DESIGNS INC
118 E 25th St Fl 11 (10010-2966)
PHONE.....................................212 420-8866
Fax: 212 529-0309
Steven Dubler, *President*
Rosanna Rigano, *Mfg Staff*
Anthony Bello, *Controller*
▲ **EMP:** 20
SQ FT: 8,000
SALES (est): 3.3MM **Privately Held**
WEB: www.scottadamdesigns.com
SIC: **3111** 3161 3069 5199 Accessory products, leather; upholstery leather; luggage; bags, rubber or rubberized fabric; bags, textile; polyvinyl chloride resins (PVC); umbrellas, men's & boys'; hats, men's & boys'; robes, men's & boys'; men's & boys' outerwear

(G-9072)
ADAMOR INC
Also Called: Izi Creations
17 E 48th St Rm 901 (10017-1010)
PHONE.....................................212 688-8885
Izidor Kamhi, *President*
EMP: 7
SALES (est): 1.1MM **Privately Held**
WEB: www.adamor.com
SIC: **3911** Jewelry, precious metal

(G-9073)
ADC DOLLS INC
112 W 34th St Ste 1207 (10120-1207)
PHONE.....................................212 244-4500
Fax: 212 283-4263
Herbert E Brown, *Ch of Bd*
Gale Jarvis, *President*
Stu Schwartz, *Vice Pres*
Yuliya Akopova, *Production*
Rob Porell, *CFO*
◆ **EMP:** 163
SQ FT: 90,000
SALES (est): 10.5MM **Privately Held**
WEB: www.alexdoll.com
SIC: **3942** Dolls, except stuffed toy animals

(G-9074)
ADESSO INC (PA)
360 W 31st St Rm 909 (10001-2837)
PHONE.....................................212 736-4440
Lee Schaak, *President*
Marvin Traub, *Chairman*
Barney Wenograd, *Vice Pres*
Paul Berk, *VP Sales*
Lia Barbery, *Sales Staff*
◆ **EMP:** 28
SQ FT: 10,000
SALES (est): 5MM **Privately Held**
SIC: **3645** Floor lamps; table lamps

(G-9075)
ADGORITHMICS LLC (PA)
260 Madison Ave Fl 8 (10016-2418)
PHONE.....................................646 277-8728
Michael Kim, *CEO*
EMP: 3
SALES (est): 1.7MM **Privately Held**
SIC: **7372** Business oriented computer software

(G-9076)
ADITIANY INC
37 W 39th St Rm 1100 (10018-0579)
PHONE.....................................212 997-8440
Nita K Shah, *President*
EMP: 2
SALES: 1.5MM **Privately Held**
SIC: **2395** Embroidery & art needlework

(G-9077)
ADOBE SYSTEMS INC
1540 Broadway Fl 17 (10036-4039)
PHONE.....................................212 471-0904
Fax: 212 471-0990
EMP: 20

New York - New York County (G-9078) — **GEOGRAPHIC SECTION**

(G-9078)
ADOBE SYSTEMS INCORPORATED
Also Called: Behance
100 5th Ave Fl 5 (10011-6903)
PHONE.................................212 592-1400
Brittany Ancell, *Opers Mgr*
Scott Belsky, *Branch Mgr*
Malcolm Jones, *Web Dvlpr*
Gokhun Guneyhan,
Trevor Cleveland,
EMP: 250
SALES (corp-wide): 5.8B **Publicly Held**
SIC: 7372 Prepackaged software
PA: Adobe Systems Incorporated
   345 Park Ave
   San Jose CA 95110
   408 536-6000

(G-9079)
ADOBE SYSTEMS INCORPORATED
8 W 40th St Fl 8 (10018-2275)
PHONE.................................212 471-0904
Fax: 212 471-0990
Naomi Starr, *Sales Mgr*
Bruce Chizen, *Manager*
Bruno Joncour, *Manager*
Sam Telfer, *Manager*
Beatrice Noble, *Senior Mgr*
EMP: 32
SALES (corp-wide): 5.8B **Publicly Held**
WEB: www.adobe.com
SIC: 7372 Prepackaged software
PA: Adobe Systems Incorporated
   345 Park Ave
   San Jose CA 95110
   408 536-6000

(G-9080)
ADRIENNE LANDAU DESIGNS INC
519 8th Ave Fl 21 (10018-4573)
PHONE.................................212 695-8362
Fax: 212 563-2014
Adrienne Landau, *CEO*
Patti Greco, *Controller*
EMP: 15
SQ FT: 12,000
SALES (est): 1.7MM **Privately Held**
WEB: www.adriennelandau.com
SIC: 2337 Capes, except fur or rubber: women's, misses' & juniors'

(G-9081)
ADSTREAM AMERICA LLC (DH)
345 7th Ave Fl 6 (10001-5053)
PHONE.................................212 804-8498
Michael Palmer, *Mng Member*
EMP: 20
SALES (est): 4.4MM **Privately Held**
SIC: 3993 Advertising artwork
HQ: Adstream (Uk) Limited
   7th Floor, Berkshire House
   London WC1V
   207 539-8400

(G-9082)
ADTECH US INC
770 Broadway Fl 4 (10003-9558)
PHONE.................................212 402-4840
Will Schmahl, *Vice Pres*
Peter Meyer, *Vice Pres*
Owen Walsh, *Project Mgr*
Alex Aybar, *Production*
EMP: 125
SALES (est): 5.2MM
SALES (corp-wide): 125.9B **Publicly Held**
SIC: 7372 Prepackaged software
HQ: Adtech Gmbh
   Robert-Bosch-Str. 32
   Dreieich 63303
   610 357-150

(G-9083)
ADVANCE APPAREL INTL INC
265 W 37th St Rm 906 (10018-5728)
PHONE.................................212 944-0984
Charles Hu, *President*
Eugene Hu, *Vice Pres*
▲ **EMP:** 5
SALES (est): 550K **Privately Held**
SIC: 2311 Men's & boys' suits & coats

(G-9084)
ADVANCE FINANCE GROUP LLC
101 Park Ave Frnt (10178-0399)
PHONE.................................212 630-5900
Tom Summer, *CFO*
EMP: 100
SALES (est): 698.5K **Privately Held**
SIC: 2759 8721 Publication printing; auditing services

(G-9085)
ADVANCE MAGAZINE PUBLS INC (HQ)
Also Called: Conde Nast Publications
1 World Trade Ctr Fl 43 (10007-0090)
PHONE.................................212 286-2860
Fax: 212 286-6763
S I Newhouse Jr, *Ch of Bd*
Richard Beckman, *President*
Jay Felts, *President*
Daniel Lagani, *President*
Robert A Sauerberg Jr, *President*
▲ **EMP:** 2200
SALES (est): 1.1B
SALES (corp-wide): 6.2B **Privately Held**
WEB: www.condenast.com
SIC: 2721 Magazines: publishing & printing
PA: Advance Publications, Inc.
   950 W Fingerboard Rd
   Staten Island NY 10305
   718 981-1234

(G-9086)
ADVANCE MAGAZINE PUBLS INC
Also Called: Conde Nast Publications Div
1166 Ave Of The Amrcs 14 (10036-2715)
PHONE.................................212 790-4422
Siobhan Adcock, *Editor*
David Orlin, *Senior VP*
Kevin Hurley, *Prdtn Dir*
Kevin Donovan, *Finance*
Karyn Gallant-Zitomer, *Human Res Dir*
EMP: 64
SALES (corp-wide): 6.2B **Privately Held**
WEB: www.condenast.com
SIC: 2721 Magazines: publishing & printing
HQ: Advance Magazine Publishers Inc.
   1 World Trade Ctr Fl 43
   New York NY 10007
   212 286-2860

(G-9087)
ADVANCE MAGAZINE PUBLS INC
Also Called: ADVANCE MAGAZINE PUBLISHERS, INC.
1166 Ave Of The Amrcs 1 (10036-2708)
PHONE.................................212 286-2860
Alexandra Walsh, *Branch Mgr*
EMP: 64
SALES (corp-wide): 6.2B **Privately Held**
WEB: www.condenast.com
SIC: 2721 Periodicals
HQ: Advance Magazine Publishers Inc.
   1 World Trade Ctr Fl 43
   New York NY 10007
   212 286-2860

(G-9088)
ADVANCE MAGAZINE PUBLS INC
Parade Publications
711 3rd Ave Rm 700 (10017-9210)
PHONE.................................212 450-7000
John J Beni, *Vice Chairman*
John Garvey, *Senior VP*
Lee Kravitz, *Senior VP*
Marcel Schloss, *Vice Pres*
Carol Unger, *Vice Pres*
EMP: 195
SALES (corp-wide): 6.2B **Privately Held**
SIC: 2721 2711 Magazines: publishing only, not printed on site; newspapers
HQ: Advance Magazine Publishers Inc.
   1 World Trade Ctr Fl 43
   New York NY 10007
   212 286-2860

(G-9089)
ADVANCE MAGAZINE PUBLS INC
Also Called: Vogue China
750 3rd Ave Frnt G (10017-2728)
PHONE.................................212 697-0126
Chris Mitchell, *Publisher*
Bridget Foley, *Editor*
Jim Gomez, *Editor*
Molly Prior, *Editor*
Suzanne Reinhardt, *VP Finance*
EMP: 64
SALES (corp-wide): 6.2B **Privately Held**
SIC: 2721 Magazines: publishing & printing
HQ: Advance Magazine Publishers Inc.
   1 World Trade Ctr Fl 43
   New York NY 10007
   212 286-2860

(G-9090)
ADVANCED BUSINESS GROUP INC
266 W 37th St Fl 15 (10018-6615)
PHONE.................................212 398-1010
Fax: 212 398-1315
Michael J Mulligan, *President*
Kevin Kern, *Vice Pres*
Jim Mattiello, *Manager*
EMP: 15
SQ FT: 7,000
SALES (est): 3.1MM **Privately Held**
SIC: 2752 Commercial printing, lithographic

(G-9091)
ADVANCED DIGITAL PRINTING LLC
65 W 36th St Fl 11 (10018-7936)
PHONE.................................718 649-1500
Aaron Menche, *Mng Member*
Steve Toplan, *Manager*
EMP: 35 EST: 2005
SQ FT: 85,000
SALES (est): 3.7MM **Privately Held**
SIC: 2752 Commercial printing, lithographic

(G-9092)
ADVANCED FASHIONS TECHNOLOGY
110 W 40th St Rm 1100 (10018-8529)
PHONE.................................212 221-0606
EMP: 8
SALES (est): 580K **Privately Held**
SIC: 2211 Cotton Broadwoven Fabric Mill

(G-9093)
ADVANCED PRINTING NEW YORK INC
263 W 38th St (10018-4483)
PHONE.................................212 840-8108
Carlos Cruz, *President*
EMP: 8
SALES (est): 1MM **Privately Held**
WEB: www.apnyc.com
SIC: 2754 Commercial printing, gravure

(G-9094)
ADVANCED RESPONSE CORPORATION
345 W 58th St Apt 11a (10019-1140)
P.O. Box 2213 (10019)
PHONE.................................212 459-0887
Inge Rothenberg, *President*
P G Woog, *Owner*
Lionel Woog, *Director*
▲ **EMP:** 5
SALES (est): 572.7K **Privately Held**
WEB: www.broxo.com
SIC: 3634 Massage machines, electric, except for beauty/barber shops

(G-9095)
ADVANTAGE QUICK PRINT INC
Also Called: Hampshire Lithographers
30 E 33rd St Frnt B (10016-5337)
PHONE.................................212 989-5644
Stuart Menkes, *President*
▲ **EMP:** 6
SQ FT: 6,000
SALES: 350K **Privately Held**
SIC: 2752 Commercial printing, offset

(G-9096)
ADVD HEART PHYS & SURGS
130 E 77th St Fl 4 (10075-1851)
PHONE.................................212 434-3000
Fax: 212 434-2610
Michael Gorman, *Principal*
Konstadinos A Plestis, *Cardiovascular*
EMP: 10
SALES (est): 613.4K **Privately Held**
SIC: 3845 Surgical support systems: heart-lung machine, exc. iron lung

(G-9097)
ADVENTURE PUBLISHING GROUP
307 7th Ave Rm 1601 (10001-6042)
PHONE.................................212 575-4510
Fax: 212 575-4521
Laurie Schacht, *President*
Bill Reese, *Prdtn Mgr*
Lori Rubin, *Controller*
EMP: 20
SALES (est): 2.6MM **Privately Held**
WEB: www.adventurepub.com
SIC: 2721 Magazines: publishing only, not printed on site

(G-9098)
ADVERTISING LITHOGRAPHERS
121 Varick St Fl 9 (10013-1408)
PHONE.................................212 966-7771
Randolph Hafter, *President*
Robert Hafter, *Vice Pres*
EMP: 10
SQ FT: 11,250
SALES (est): 1.2MM **Privately Held**
SIC: 2752 Commercial printing, lithographic

(G-9099)
AEGIS OIL LIMITED VENTURES LLC
14 Wall St Fl 20 (10005-2123)
PHONE.................................646 233-4900
James Freiman, *Manager*
EMP: 11
SALES (corp-wide): 931K **Privately Held**
SIC: 1382 Oil & gas exploration services
PA: Aegis Oil Limited Ventures Llc
   100 Crescent Ct Ste 700
   Dallas TX 75201
   214 431-5201

(G-9100)
AEON AMERICA INC
80 5th Ave Ste 1805 (10011-8002)
PHONE.................................914 584-0275
Paul Hains, *President*
Kellen Quinn, *Director*
EMP: 8
SALES (est): 253.2K **Privately Held**
SIC: 2721 Magazines: publishing only, not printed on site

(G-9101)
AES ELECTRONICS INC
135 E 54th St Apt 10j (10022-4511)
PHONE.................................212 371-8120
Fax: 212 688-0891
Abraham E Schenfeld, *President*
Ruth Schenfeld, *Treasurer*
EMP: 7
SQ FT: 1,200
SALES (est): 430K **Privately Held**
SIC: 3633 5065 Household laundry equipment; communication equipment

(G-9102)
AF DESIGN INC
1239 Broadway Ste 310 (10001-4438)
PHONE.................................347 548-5273
Ali Ahmad, *CEO*
Behroz Ahmad, *Shareholder*
EMP: 2
SQ FT: 3,000
SALES: 3.5MM **Privately Held**
SIC: 3911 5094 Jewel settings & mountings, precious metal; jewelry

(G-9103)
AFFORDABLE LUXURY GROUP INC
Also Called: Aimee Kestenberg
10 W 33rd St Rm 615 (10001-3348)
PHONE.................................631 523-9266

GEOGRAPHIC SECTION

New York - New York County (G-9131)

Adam Protass, *COO*
▲ **EMP:** 9
SALES (est): 237.9K **Privately Held**
SIC: 3171 Women's handbags & purses

(G-9104)
AFFYMAX INC
630 5th Ave Ste 2260 (10111-2291)
PHONE................................650 812-8700
Jonathan M Couchman, *President*
John A Orwin, *Principal*
Christine Conroy, *Senior VP*
Mark G Thompson, *CFO*
▲ **EMP:** 6
SQ FT: 1,500
SALES (est): 1.4MM **Privately Held**
WEB: www.affymax.com
SIC: 2834 Pharmaceutical preparations

(G-9105)
AFH INDUSTRIES INCORPORATED ✪
110 W 34th St Fl 7 (10001-2129)
PHONE................................646 351-1700
Isaac Saideh, *CEO*
◆ **EMP:** 15 EST: 2017
SQ FT: 7,000
SALES (est): 587.6K **Privately Held**
SIC: 3661 Telephone sets, all types except cellular radio

(G-9106)
AG NEOVO PROFESSIONAL INC
Also Called: Agn Professional
156 5th Ave Ste 434 (10010-7002)
PHONE................................212 647-9080
Minson Chen, *President*
EMP: 10
SQ FT: 1,900
SALES (est): 1.3MM **Privately Held**
WEB: www.agnpro.com
SIC: 3575 Computer terminals

(G-9107)
AGI BROOKS PRODUCTION CO INC (PA)
7 E 14th St Apt 615 (10003-3130)
PHONE................................212 268-1533
Agi Brooks, *President*
Don Mc Lean, *Vice Pres*
EMP: 11
SQ FT: 5,000
SALES (est): 1.6MM **Privately Held**
WEB: www.agibrooks.com
SIC: 2337 2331 2335 Suits: women's, misses' & juniors'; blouses, women's & juniors': made from purchased material; women's, juniors' & misses' dresses

(G-9108)
AGILENT TECHNOLOGIES INC
399 Park Ave (10022-4614)
PHONE................................877 424-4536
EMP: 2498
SALES (corp-wide): 4.2B **Publicly Held**
SIC: 3825 Instruments to measure electricity
PA: Agilent Technologies, Inc.
5301 Stevens Creek Blvd
Santa Clara CA 95051
408 345-8886

(G-9109)
AGNOVOS HEALTHCARE LLC
140 Broadway Fl 46 (10005-1155)
PHONE................................646 502-5860
David Mackey, *CFO*
EMP: 8
SALES (est): 1.1MM
SALES (corp-wide): 9.3MM **Privately Held**
SIC: 3842 Implants, surgical
PA: Agnovos Healthcare Usa, Llc
7301 Calhoun Pl Ste 100
Rockville MD 20855
240 753-6500

(G-9110)
AGUILAR AMPLIFICATION LLC
599 Broadway Fl 7 (10012-3371)
PHONE................................212 431-9109
Dave Avenius, *CEO*
David Boonshoft, *CEO*
Alexander Aguilar, *President*
Goran Stankovic, *CTO*
▲ **EMP:** 10

SQ FT: 10,000
SALES (est): 1.9MM **Privately Held**
WEB: www.aguilaramp.com
SIC: 3651 Amplifiers: radio, public address or musical instrument

(G-9111)
AHHMIGO LLC
120 Cent Park S Rm 7c (10019)
PHONE................................212 315-1818
Yaacob Dabah, *Manager*
EMP: 12
SALES (est): 820K **Privately Held**
SIC: 2099 Food preparations

(G-9112)
AHQ LLC
Also Called: Accesory Headquarters
10 W 33rd St Rm 306 (10001-3340)
PHONE................................212 328-1560
Isaac Mochon, *Controller*
Abe Chehebar, *Mng Member*
▲ **EMP:** 40 EST: 2012
SALES (est): 20MM **Privately Held**
SIC: 3171 Women's handbags & purses

(G-9113)
AI ENTERTAINMENT HOLDINGS LLC (HQ)
730 5th Ave Fl 20 (10019-4105)
PHONE................................212 247-6400
Lincoln Benet, *President*
EMP: 14
SALES (est): 3.2B **Privately Held**
SIC: 2731 Book music: publishing & printing

(G-9114)
AI MEDIA GROUP INC
1359 Broadway Fl 5 (10018-7747)
PHONE................................212 660-2400
Andy Fenster, *CEO*
John Bernbach, *Ch of Bd*
Kathleen Odonnell, *Business Mgr*
Sergio Alvarez, *COO*
Amanda Peters, *Marketing Mgr*
EMP: 16
SQ FT: 2,500
SALES (est): 9.6MM **Privately Held**
SIC: 2741

(G-9115)
AIP MC HOLDINGS LLC
330 Madison Ave Fl 28 (10017-5018)
PHONE................................212 627-2360
Kim Marvin, *Partner*
Michael Aingorn, *Partner*
Jorge Amador, *Partner*
Paul Bamatter, *Partner*
Eric Baroyan, *Partner*
EMP: 1780
SALES (est): 1.1B **Privately Held**
SIC: 3541 7389 Grinding machines, metalworking; grinding, precision: commercial or industrial

(G-9116)
AIR SKATE & AIR JUMP CORP
1385 Broadway (10018-6001)
PHONE................................212 967-1201
Patrick Denihan, *Branch Mgr*
EMP: 5
SALES (corp-wide): 6.2MM **Privately Held**
SIC: 3143 5139 Men's footwear, except athletic; footwear, athletic
PA: Air Skate & Air Jump Corp.
2208 E 5th St
Brooklyn NY 11223
212 967-1201

(G-9117)
AKARI THERAPEUTICS PLC
24 W 40th St Fl 8 (10018-1028)
PHONE................................646 350-0702
Gur Aroshwalb, *CEO*
EMP: 8 EST: 2015
SALES (est): 145K **Privately Held**
SIC: 2834 Druggists' preparations (pharmaceuticals)

(G-9118)
AKH GROUP LLC
Also Called: Marchesa Accesories
601 W 26th St Rm M228 (10001-1122)
PHONE................................646 320-8720

Anneli Hofstrom, *CEO*
Ashley Kennedy, *Founder*
Debra Torres, *CFO*
Lou Wood Kennedy, *Mng Member*
EMP: 6 EST: 2015
SQ FT: 1,272
SALES: 800K **Privately Held**
SIC: 3144 3171 Women's footwear, except athletic; women's handbags & purses

(G-9119)
AKOS GROUP LTD
Also Called: Milan Accessories
315 5th Ave Fl 11 (10016-6586)
PHONE................................212 683-4747
Mark Seruya, *Ch of Bd*
Janine Ramsundar, *Director*
EMP: 35
SALES (est): 1.8MM **Privately Held**
SIC: 2326 2339 Men's & boys' work clothing; athletic clothing: women's, misses' & juniors'

(G-9120)
AL ENERGY SOLUTIONS LED LLC
1140 Ave Of The Americas (10036-5803)
PHONE................................646 380-6670
Luis Alvarez, *CEO*
Jose Alvarez, *President*
Mark Levy, *COO*
Juan Alvarez, *Vice Pres*
EMP: 21
SQ FT: 5,000
SALES (est): 2MM **Privately Held**
SIC: 3646 3648 Commercial indusl & institutional electric lighting fixtures; outdoor lighting equipment; street lighting fixtures; spotlights

(G-9121)
ALADDIN MANUFACTURING CORP
295 5th Ave Ste 1412 (10016-7124)
PHONE................................212 561-8715
Dennis Fein, *Manager*
EMP: 187
SALES (corp-wide): 8.9B **Publicly Held**
SIC: 2273 Carpets & rugs
HQ: Aladdin Manufacturing Corporation
160 S Industrial Blvd
Calhoun GA 30701
706 629-7721

(G-9122)
ALART INC
578 5th Ave Unit 33 (10036-4836)
PHONE................................212 840-1508
Alan Becer, *President*
Arthur Becer, *Vice Pres*
Vivian Becer, *Treasurer*
EMP: 3
SALES (est): 2MM **Privately Held**
SIC: 3911 3281 Jewelry, precious metal; cut stone & stone products

(G-9123)
ALBALUZ FILMS LLC
954 Lexington Ave (10021-5055)
PHONE................................347 613-2321
Carols Plasencia, *CEO*
EMP: 1
SALES (est): 1MM **Privately Held**
SIC: 3312 Blast furnaces & steel mills

(G-9124)
ALBEA COSMETICS AMERICA INC (DH)
595 Madison Ave Fl 10 (10022-1955)
PHONE................................212 371-5100
Jean P Imbert, *President*
Tina Sukapdjo, *Controller*
Nancy Gullo, *Manager*
Robert Pelliciari, *Director*
◆ **EMP:** 25
SALES (est): 252.9MM **Privately Held**
SIC: 3089 3911 5162 5051 Plastic containers, except foam; precious metal cases; plastics products; metals service centers & offices

(G-9125)
ALBION COSMETICS INC
110 E 42nd St Rm 1506 (10017-8533)
PHONE................................212 869-1052
Yusuke Kobayaski, *President*
Tetsuo Konoishi, *Manager*
▲ **EMP:** 7
SALES (est): 1MM
SALES (corp-wide): 2.3B **Privately Held**
SIC: 2844 Cosmetic preparations
HQ: Albion Co., Ltd.
1-7-10, Ginza
Chuo-Ku TKY 104-0
355 241-711

(G-9126)
ALCHEMY SIMYA INC
Also Called: Birthstone Enterprises
161 Avnue Of The Americas (10013-1205)
PHONE................................646 230-1122
Fax: 646 230-1112
Feonia Tilly, *President*
EMP: 30 EST: 2004
SALES (est): 2.3MM **Privately Held**
SIC: 3911 Jewelry, precious metal

(G-9127)
ALCOA USA CORP (HQ)
390 Park Ave (10022-4608)
PHONE................................212 518-5400
Roy C Harvey, *CEO*
EMP: 13 EST: 2016
SALES (est): 36.7MM
SALES (corp-wide): 9.3B **Publicly Held**
SIC: 3334 3353 1099 Primary aluminum; aluminum sheet & strip; bauxite mining
PA: Alcoa Corporation
201 Isabella St Ste 500
Pittsburgh PA 15212
412 992-5450

(G-9128)
ALCOHOLICS ANONYMOUS GRAPEVINE (PA)
475 Riverside Dr Ste 1264 (10115-0052)
PHONE................................212 870-3400
Fax: 212 870-3003
Robin Bromley, *CEO*
Arnold Bros, *Ch of Bd*
John Skillton, *Treasurer*
Eugene O' Brien, *Controller*
Valerie Thomas, *Finance*
▲ **EMP:** 15
SQ FT: 4,000
SALES: 3.1MM **Privately Held**
SIC: 2721 Periodicals: publishing only

(G-9129)
ALDINE INC (NY)
150 Varick St Fl 5 (10013-1218)
PHONE................................212 226-2870
Fax: 212 941-6042
Alan Zuniss, *President*
Greg Zuniss, *Vice Pres*
EMP: 62
SQ FT: 23,000
SALES (est): 12.1MM **Privately Held**
WEB: www.aldine.com
SIC: 2752 2796 2759 Commercial printing, lithographic; embossing plates for printing; engraving

(G-9130)
ALEN SANDS YORK ASSOCIATES LTD
Also Called: Stellar Alliance
236 W 26th St Rm 801 (10001-6882)
PHONE................................212 563-6305
Alen S York, *President*
Joshua Rosen, *Vice Pres*
▲ **EMP:** 10
SALES (est): 790K **Privately Held**
SIC: 2392 Comforters & quilts: made from purchased materials

(G-9131)
ALEX SEPKUS INC
42 W 48th St Ste 501 (10036-1701)
PHONE................................212 391-8466
Fax: 212 819-0709
Alex Sepkus, *President*
Candace Edelman, *COO*
Jeffrey D Feero, *Vice Pres*
EMP: 11

New York - New York County (G-9132)

(G-9132)
ALEXANDER PRIMAK JEWELRY INC
Also Called: Platina
529 5th Ave Fl 15 (10017-4674)
PHONE..................212 398-0287
Fax: 212 398-1102
Alexander Primak, *President*
Igor Shersher, *General Mgr*
EMP: 59
SQ FT: 8,000
SALES: 11.3MM **Privately Held**
WEB: www.platinacasting.com
SIC: 3911 Jewelry, precious metal

(G-9133)
ALEXANDER WANG INCORPORATED (PA)
386 Broadway Fl 3 (10013-6021)
PHONE..................212 532-3103
Aimie Wang, *CEO*
Rodrigo Bazan, *President*
Jessica Kipp, *Vice Pres*
Hana Lee, *Opers Staff*
Thiago Pereira, *Opers Staff*
▲ **EMP:** 61
SALES (est): 48.1MM **Privately Held**
SIC: 2331 2329 Blouses, women's & juniors': made from purchased material; shirt & slack suits: men's, youths' & boys'

(G-9134)
ALFRED DUNNER INC (PA)
1333 Broadway Fl 12 (10018-1064)
PHONE..................212 478-4300
Fax: 646 719-9684
Peter Aresty, *President*
Joseph Aresty, *Chairman*
Jerome Aresty, *Vice Pres*
Ray Barrick, *CFO*
Brian Buccieri, *Human Res Dir*
▲ **EMP:** 75 **EST:** 1946
SQ FT: 10,000
SALES (est): 97.9MM **Privately Held**
WEB: www.alfreddunner.com
SIC: 2337 2331 2339 Skirts, separate: women's, misses' & juniors'; jackets & vests, except fur & leather: women's; T-shirts & tops, women's: made from purchased materials; slacks: women's, misses' & juniors'; shorts (outerwear): women's, misses' & juniors'

(G-9135)
ALL RACKS INDUSTRIES INC
361 W 36th St Frnt A (10018-6408)
PHONE..................212 244-1069
Joseph Desimone, *President*
Charles Desimone, *Vice Pres*
Joseph Mensch, *Director*
EMP: 5
SQ FT: 7,000
SALES: 500K **Privately Held**
SIC: 2542 Garment racks: except wood

(G-9136)
ALLAN JOHN COMPANY
611 5th Ave Fl 7 (10022-6813)
PHONE..................212 940-2210
Fax: 212 308-5296
John Allan Meing, *CEO*
Clare Ludvigsen, *CFO*
Richard Macary, *Treasurer*
▲ **EMP:** 10
SALES (est): 649.8K
SALES (corp-wide): 2MM **Privately Held**
WEB: www.johnallans.com
SIC: 2844 Toilet preparations
PA: The John Allan Company Llc
46 E 46th St
New York NY

(G-9137)
ALLEY MUSIC CORP
126 E 38th St (10016-2602)
PHONE..................212 779-7977
Caroline Bienstock, *President*
EMP: 25
SALES (est): 1.2MM **Privately Held**
SIC: 2741 Music books: publishing & printing

(G-9138)
ALLIANCE EXPORTS LLC
22 E 127th St Apt 1 (10035-1205)
PHONE..................347 208-3547
Dicyesh Sheth, *Mng Member*
EMP: 3 **EST:** 2015
SQ FT: 700
SALES: 2MM **Privately Held**
SIC: 2211 Apparel & outerwear fabrics, cotton

(G-9139)
ALLIED BRONZE CORP (DEL CORP)
32 Avenue Of The Americas (10013-2473)
PHONE..................646 421-6400
Herbert Koenig, *President*
Sandra Browne, *Manager*
Susan Mc Cormick, *Manager*
▲ **EMP:** 40
SQ FT: 55,000
SALES (est): 4.1MM **Privately Held**
WEB: www.alliedbronze.com
SIC: 3446 Architectural metalwork; ornamental metalwork

(G-9140)
ALLIED REPRODUCTIONS INC
121 Varick St Fl 9 (10013-1408)
PHONE..................212 255-2472
Peter Bird, *President*
EMP: 20
SALES (est): 1.9MM **Privately Held**
SIC: 2752 Photo-offset printing

(G-9141)
ALLISON CHE FASHION INC (PA)
1400 Broadway Lbby 5 (10018-5362)
PHONE..................212 391-1433
Fax: 212 391-1508
Barbara Weiner, *President*
Edith Fisher, *Treasurer*
EMP: 12
SALES (est): 957.8K **Privately Held**
SIC: 2335 Women's, juniors' & misses' dresses

(G-9142)
ALLSTAR CASTING CORPORATION
240 W 37th St Frnt 7 (10018-5091)
PHONE..................212 563-0909
Robert Winters, *President*
Phyllis Vulcano, *Vice Pres*
Denise Winters, *Vice Pres*
EMP: 40
SQ FT: 2,200
SALES: 2.5MM **Privately Held**
SIC: 3915 3369 Jewelers' castings; non-ferrous foundries

(G-9143)
ALLURE JEWELRY AND ACC LLC (PA)
15 W 36th St Fl 12 (10018-7113)
P.O. Box 41305, Plymouth MN (55441-0305)
PHONE..................646 226-8057
Amy Bohaty,
Arlene Tourville,
◆ **EMP:** 36
SQ FT: 5,000
SALES (est): 3.5MM **Privately Held**
SIC: 3961 Costume jewelry

(G-9144)
ALLWORTH COMMUNICATIONS INC
Also Called: Allworth Press
10 E 23rd St Ste 510 (10010-4459)
PHONE..................212 777-8395
Tad Crawford, *President*
Marrissa Jones, *Business Mgr*
Cynthia Rivelli, *Mktg Dir*
Gebrina Roberts, *Office Mgr*
▲ **EMP:** 12
SALES (est): 930K **Privately Held**
WEB: www.allworth.com
SIC: 2731 Textbooks: publishing only, not printed on site

(G-9145)
ALLY NYC CORP ◆
230 W 39th St Rm 525 (10018-4933)
PHONE..................212 447-7277

Jenny Chen, *President*
EMP: 7 **EST:** 2017
SQ FT: 25,000
SALES: 15MM **Privately Held**
SIC: 2339 Women's & misses' outerwear

(G-9146)
ALM MEDIA LLC (HQ)
Also Called: New York Law Journal
120 Broadway Fl 5 (10271-1100)
PHONE..................212 457-9400
Fax: 646 417-7705
Bill Carter, *CEO*
Tom Larranaga, *Publisher*
Tashawna Rodwell, *Publisher*
Vanessa Blum, *Editor*
Paul Bubny, *Editor*
EMP: 350
SQ FT: 31,000
SALES (est): 235.2MM
SALES (corp-wide): 235.3MM **Privately Held**
WEB: www.alm.com
SIC: 2721 2711 2741 2731 Magazines: publishing only, not printed on site; newspapers: publishing only, not printed on site; newsletter publishing; book publishing; trade show arrangement
PA: Alm Media Holdings, Inc.
120 Broadway Fl 5
New York NY 10271
212 457-9400

(G-9147)
ALM MEDIA HOLDINGS INC (PA)
120 Broadway Fl 5 (10271-1100)
PHONE..................212 457-9400
William L Pollak, *President*
Andrew Neblett, *President*
Jack Berkowitz, *Senior VP*
Jeffrey S Litvack, *Senior VP*
Anup Bagaria, *Vice Pres*
EMP: 400
SQ FT: 31,000
SALES: 235.3MM **Privately Held**
SIC: 2721 2711 2741 2731 Magazines: publishing only, not printed on site; newspapers: publishing only, not printed on site; newsletter publishing; book publishing; trade show arrangement

(G-9148)
ALOK INC
7 W 34th St Ste 79105 (10001-8100)
PHONE..................212 643-4360
Arun Agarwaal, *CEO*
EMP: 5 **EST:** 2007
SALES (est): 371K
SALES (corp-wide): 1.7B **Privately Held**
SIC: 2299 5023 Textile goods; sheets, textile
PA: Alok Industries Limited
2nd & 3rd Floor, Tower B,
Mumbai MH 40001
226 178-7000

(G-9149)
ALPARGATAS USA INC
Also Called: Havaianas
33 E 33rd St Rm 501 (10016-5335)
PHONE..................646 277-7171
Marcio Moura, *CEO*
Afonso Fugiyama, *President*
Rona Samaniego, *Accountant*
◆ **EMP:** 30
SQ FT: 7,500
SALES (est): 7.3MM **Privately Held**
SIC: 3144 Women's footwear, except athletic
HQ: Alpargatas S/A
Av. Doutor Cardoso De Melo 1.336
Sao Paulo SP 04548

(G-9150)
ALPHA MEDIA GROUP INC (PA)
415 Madison Ave Fl 4 (10017-7945)
PHONE..................212 302-2626
Kent Brownridge, *CEO*
Felix Dennis, *Ch of Bd*
Stephen Duggan, *COO*
Karen Reed, *Controller*
Cristine Johnston, *Accountant*
▲ **EMP:** 300
SALES (est): 41.9MM **Privately Held**
WEB: www.stuffmagazine.com
SIC: 2721 Magazines: publishing & printing

(G-9151)
ALPINA COLOR GRAPHICS INC
27 Cliff St Rm 502 (10038-2850)
PHONE..................212 285-2700
Fax: 212 285-2704
Harish Sawhney, *President*
EMP: 7
SALES: 800K **Privately Held**
WEB: www.alpinaonline.com
SIC: 2752 Commercial printing, offset

(G-9152)
ALPINA COPYWORLD INC (PA)
Also Called: Alpina Digital
134 E 28th St (10016-8299)
PHONE..................212 683-3511
Harish Sawhney, *President*
Naveen Sawhney, *President*
Ian Goodwin, *Engineer*
Roy Shawney, *Accounts Mgr*
Ram Pokharel, *Sales Executive*
EMP: 15
SQ FT: 7,000
SALES: 6MM **Privately Held**
WEB: www.alpina.net
SIC: 2759 2752 Commercial printing; commercial printing, lithographic

(G-9153)
ALPINE BUSINESS GROUP INC (PA)
Also Called: Alpine Creative Group
30 E 33rd St Frnt B (10016-5337)
PHONE..................212 989-4198
Fax: 212 989-4182
Steve Paster, *President*
Angie Bhow, *Accountant*
Samantha Goldman, *Accounts Mgr*
Molly Bea, *Comms Mgr*
Rebecca Baker, *Graphic Designe*
EMP: 8
SALES (est): 1.2MM **Privately Held**
WEB: www.alpinecreativegroup.com
SIC: 2759 2752 Invitations: printing; commercial printing, lithographic

(G-9154)
ALPINE CREATIONS LTD
Also Called: TS Manufacturing
17 E 48th St Fl 6 (10017-1010)
PHONE..................212 308-9353
Fax: 212 308-9736
Samy Sanar, *President*
Zack Sanar, *Vice Pres*
▲ **EMP:** 6
SQ FT: 2,000
SALES (est): 731.9K **Privately Held**
WEB: www.alpineweddingbands.com
SIC: 3911 Jewelry, precious metal

(G-9155)
ALSTOM TRANSPORTATION INC (HQ)
641 Lexington Ave Fl 28 (10022-4503)
PHONE..................212 692-5353
Jerome Wallut, *President*
Barbara Schroeder, *Principal*
Sudha Sankaran, *CFO*
EMP: 25
SALES (est): 7.2MM
SALES (corp-wide): 54.7MM **Privately Held**
SIC: 3743 8711 7629 Railroad equipment; engineering services; electrical repair shops
PA: Alstom
48 Rue Albert Dhalenne
Saint Ouen 93400
140 101-283

(G-9156)
ALVINA VLENTA COUTURE COLLECTN
525 Fashion Ave Rm 1703 (10018-4935)
PHONE..................212 921-7058
Joe Murphy, *President*
Jim Hjelm, *Principal*
Joe O'Grady, *Admin Sec*
EMP: 10
SALES (est): 807.8K
SALES (corp-wide): 16.7MM **Publicly Held**
WEB: www.jimhelmcouture.com
SIC: 2335 Wedding gowns & dresses

GEOGRAPHIC SECTION

New York - New York County (G-9179)

PA: Jlm Couture, Inc.
525 Fashion Ave Rm 1703
New York NY 10018
212 921-7058

(G-9157)
ALVINA VLENTA COUTURE COLLECTN
225 W 37th St (10018-5703)
PHONE.................................212 921-7058
Joe Murphy, *President*
Daniel McMillan, *President*
Victoria McMillan, *President*
EMP: 8
SALES: 3MM **Privately Held**
SIC: 2335 5131 Wedding gowns & dresses; bridal supplies

(G-9158)
ALYK INC
Also Called: Lola
440 Park Ave S Fl 14 (10016-8012)
PHONE.................................917 968-2552
Jordana Kier, *CEO*
Alexandra Friedman, *President*
Jeff Martin, *Consultant*
EMP: 13
SALES (est): 2.8MM **Privately Held**
SIC: 2676 Tampons, sanitary: made from purchased paper

(G-9159)
AMCOM SOFTWARE INC
256 W 38th St Fl 8 (10018-9123)
PHONE.................................212 951-7600
Vincent D Kelly, *Branch Mgr*
Elmer Calonzo, *Software Engr*
EMP: 10
SALES (corp-wide): 179.5MM **Publicly Held**
WEB: www.amcomsoft.com
SIC: 7372 7371 Application computer software; computer software development & applications
HQ: Amcom Software, Inc.
10400 Yellow Circle Dr # 100
Eden Prairie MN 55343
952 230-5200

(G-9160)
AMEREX CORPORATION
512 7th Ave Fl 9 (10018-0861)
PHONE.................................212 221-3151
Fax: 212 391-8702
Dan Raskin, *COO*
Renee McGovern, *Manager*
EMP: 7
SALES (corp-wide): 1.1B **Privately Held**
WEB: www.amerex-fire.com
SIC: 2331 Blouses, women's & juniors': made from purchased material
HQ: Amerex Corporation
7595 Gadsden Hwy
Trussville AL 35173
205 655-3271

(G-9161)
AMERICA CAPITAL ENERGY CORP
Also Called: Acec
405 Lexington Ave Fl 65 (10174-6301)
PHONE.................................212 983-8316
Min Zhaing, *Ch of Bd*
Zhilin Feng, *President*
Kate Reulbach, *Admin Sec*
EMP: 5
SQ FT: 7,299
SALES (est): 430K **Privately Held**
SIC: 1382 Oil & gas exploration services

(G-9162)
AMERICA PRESS INC (PA)
Also Called: National Catholic Wkly Review
106 W 56th St (10019-3893)
PHONE.................................212 581-4640
Fax: 212 399-3596
Thomas Reese, *President*
Pete Catino, *Prdtn Mgr*
James Santora, *Controller*
EMP: 32 **EST:** 1909
SQ FT: 36,674
SALES (est): 4.7MM **Privately Held**
SIC: 2721 Magazines: publishing only, not printed on site

(G-9163)
AMERICAN APPAREL TRADING CORP (PA)
Also Called: Vertical Apparel
209 W 38th St Rm 1004 (10018-0391)
PHONE.................................212 764-5990
Peter Marsella, *President*
Ellen Barry, *Vice Pres*
Danny Miser, *Manager*
EMP: 3 **EST:** 2003
SALES (est): 1.4MM **Privately Held**
SIC: 2339 Sportswear, women's

(G-9164)
AMERICAN BPTST CHRCHES MTRO NY
Flemister Housing Services
527 W 22nd St (10011-1179)
PHONE.................................212 870-3195
James D Stallings, *Principal*
EMP: 8
SALES (corp-wide): 762.2K **Privately Held**
WEB: www.abcmny.org
SIC: 2531 Church furniture
PA: American Baptist Churches Of Metropolitan New York
475 Riverside Dr Ste 432
New York NY 10115
212 870-3195

(G-9165)
AMERICAN COMFORT DIRECT LLC
708 3rd Ave Fl 6 (10017-4119)
PHONE.................................201 364-8309
Benzvi Cohen, *CEO*
Timothy Enarson, *Vice Pres*
EMP: 25
SALES (est): 1.4MM **Privately Held**
SIC: 3433 3634 3635 3589 Space heaters, except electric; electric household fans, heaters & humidifiers; household vacuum cleaners; carpet sweepers, except household electric vacuum sweepers; automotive air conditioners;

(G-9166)
AMERICAN DSPLAY DIE CTTERS INC
121 Varick St Rm 301 (10013-1408)
PHONE.................................212 645-1274
Fax: 212 645-1589
Juan Leon, *President*
Christa Leon, *Treasurer*
EMP: 30
SQ FT: 20,000
SALES (est): 269.4K **Privately Held**
SIC: 2675 3544 Die-cut paper & board; dies & die holders for metal cutting, forming, die casting

(G-9167)
AMERICAN GRAPHIC DESIGN AWARDS
Also Called: Graphic Design U S A
89 5th Ave Ste 901 (10003-3046)
PHONE.................................212 696-4380
Gordon Kaye, *CEO*
Milton Kaye, *Publisher*
Eric Bauer, *Director*
Chris Grenier, *Director*
EMP: 5
SALES (est): 430K **Privately Held**
WEB: www.graphicdesignusa.com
SIC: 2721 Magazines: publishing & printing

(G-9168)
AMERICAN HEALTHCARE SUPPLY INC
304 Park Ave S (10010-4301)
PHONE.................................212 674-3636
Fax: 212 202-5173
P H Lee, *President*
Edward Letko, *Managing Dir*
▲ **EMP:** 12
SQ FT: 4,000
SALES (est): 1MM **Privately Held**
SIC: 3841 5047 Surgical & medical instruments; medical equipment & supplies

(G-9169)
AMERICAN HOME MFG LLC (HQ)
302 5th Ave (10001-3604)
PHONE.................................212 643-0680
Nathan Accad, *President*
Isaac Ades, *COO*
Benjamin Akkad, *Vice Pres*
EMP: 2 **EST:** 2012
SALES (est): 3.4MM
SALES (corp-wide): 116MM **Privately Held**
SIC: 2299 Pillow fillings: curled hair, cotton waste, moss, hemp tow
PA: Idea Nuova Inc.
302 5th Ave Fl 5
New York NY 10001
212 643-0680

(G-9170)
AMERICAN INST CHEM ENGINEERS (PA)
Also Called: AICHE
120 Wall St Fl 23 (10005-5991)
PHONE.................................646 495-1355
Fax: 212 591-8890
Shami Nayak, *Business Mgr*
Rich Sarnie, *Project Dir*
Jing Chen, *Project Mgr*
Nasim Hassan, *Research*
Kristine Togneri, *Research*
▲ **EMP:** 75
SQ FT: 18,400
SALES (est): 27.7MM **Privately Held**
WEB: www.naache.net
SIC: 2721 8621 2731 Magazines: publishing only, not printed on site; engineering association; book publishing

(G-9171)
AMERICAN JEWISH COMMITTEE
Also Called: Commentary Magazine
561 Fashion Ave Fl 16 (10018-1816)
PHONE.................................212 891-1400
David Kelsey, *Sales Staff*
Davi Birnstein, *Manager*
EMP: 7
SALES (corp-wide): 55.7MM **Privately Held**
WEB: www.projectinterchange.org
SIC: 2721 Periodicals
PA: American Jewish Committee
165 E 56th St
New York NY 10022
212 751-4000

(G-9172)
AMERICAN JEWISH CONGRESS INC (PA)
Also Called: A J Congress
825 3rd Ave Fl 181800 (10022-7519)
PHONE.................................212 879-4500
Fax: 212 758-1633
David Haberman, *Vice Chairman*
Mark Stern, *Counsel*
Simeon Saturn, *Finance Dir*
Neil Goldstein, *Director*
Belle Faber, *Director*
EMP: 20 **EST:** 1918
SQ FT: 9,000
SALES (est): 2.7MM **Privately Held**
SIC: 2721 8661 Magazines: publishing & printing; religious organizations

(G-9173)
AMERICAN JUICE COMPANY LLC
224 W 35th St Fl 11 (10001-2533)
PHONE.................................347 620-0252
Chris Wirth,
EMP: 7 **EST:** 2013
SQ FT: 400
SALES (est): 851.3K **Privately Held**
SIC: 2087 Cocktail mixes, nonalcoholic

(G-9174)
AMERICAN MEDIA INC
Also Called: AMI
4 New York Plz Fl 2 (10004-2466)
PHONE.................................212 545-4800
David Pecker, *CEO*
Dara Markus, *Adv Dir*
Ehster Maydee, *Manager*
Das Rios, *Manager*
David Bonnett, *CIO*
EMP: 74

SALES (corp-wide): 223MM **Privately Held**
SIC: 2711 2741 Newspapers; newspapers: publishing only, not printed on site; miscellaneous publishing
PA: American Media, Inc.
4 New York Plz Fl 2
New York NY 10004
212 545-4800

(G-9175)
AMERICAN MEDIA INC (PA)
4 New York Plz Fl 2 (10004-2466)
PHONE.................................212 545-4800
Fax: 561 272-8411
David Pecker, *Ch of Bd*
John Swider, *President*
Summer Federer, *Editor*
Theresa Honig, *Editor*
Ray Villwock, *Editor*
EMP: 200
SQ FT: 53,000
SALES: 223MM **Privately Held**
WEB: www.americanmediainc.com
SIC: 2711 2741 Newspapers; newspapers: publishing only, not printed on site; miscellaneous publishing

(G-9176)
AMERICAN MINERALS INC (DH)
Also Called: Prince Minerals
21 W 46th St Fl 14 (10036-4119)
PHONE.................................646 747-4222
Willson Ropp, *President*
Roderik Alewijnse, *CFO*
Kevin St Germaine, *CFO*
Anthony Weiss, *Admin Sec*
◆ **EMP:** 14 **EST:** 1963
SQ FT: 3,000
SALES (est): 33.3MM
SALES (corp-wide): 1.8B **Privately Held**
WEB: www.princeminerals.com
SIC: 1446 Silica mining; silica sand mining
HQ: Prince Minerals Llc
15311 Vantage Pkwy W
Houston TX 77032
646 747-4222

(G-9177)
AMERICAN ORIGINALS CORPORATION
Also Called: Gotham Diamonds
1156 Avenue Of The Americ (10036-2784)
PHONE.................................212 836-4155
Saumil Parikh, *President*
Nagini RAO, *Manager*
EMP: 9
SALES (est): 1.3MM **Privately Held**
SIC: 3911 5094 Jewelry, precious metal; jewelry

(G-9178)
AMERICAN REFRIGERATION INC (HQ)
142 W 57th St Fl 17 (10019-3300)
PHONE.................................212 699-4000
Stephen Presser, *President*
EMP: 4
SALES (est): 38.1MM
SALES (corp-wide): 856.8MM **Privately Held**
SIC: 3585 Refrigeration equipment, complete
PA: Monomoy Capital Partners, L.P.
600 3rd Ave Fl 27
New York NY 10016
212 699-4000

(G-9179)
AMERICAN SPRAY-ON CORP
22 W 21st St Fl 2 (10010-6949)
PHONE.................................212 929-2100
Steven Alessio, *President*
Steve Alessio, *President*
Marvin Sweet, *Chairman*
Micheal Boone, *Treasurer*
EMP: 30
SALES (est): 4.3MM **Privately Held**
SIC: 2396 2262 Automotive & apparel trimmings; fire resistance finishing: manmade & silk broadwoven

---

(PA)=Parent Co (HQ)=Headquarters (DH)=Div Headquarters
✪ = New Business established in last 2 years

New York - New York County (G-9180)   **GEOGRAPHIC SECTION**

(G-9180)
AMERICAN T SHIRTS INC
Also Called: Premium Shirts Lerma Mexico
225 W 39th St Fl 6 (10018-3103)
PHONE.................................212 563-7125
Nasser Mokhtar, *President*
American T-Shirt Group, *Shareholder*
EMP: 5
SALES: 5MM **Privately Held**
WEB: www.americantshirts.com
SIC: 2253 T-shirts & tops, knit

(G-9181)
AMERICO GROUP INC
498 7th Ave Fl 8 (10018-6944)
PHONE.................................212 563-2700
EMP: 29 **Privately Held**
SIC: 2321 Men's & boys' dress shirts
PA: Americo Group Inc.
    1411 Broadway Fl 2
    New York NY 10018

(G-9182)
AMERICO GROUP INC (PA)
Also Called: Joseph's Cloak
1411 Broadway Fl 2 (10018-3420)
PHONE.................................212 563-2700
Eli Harari, *Ch of Bd*
Paul Arking, *Vice Pres*
Marc Lieber, *Vice Pres*
Joel Weisinger, *CFO*
Kelly Moul, *Controller*
▲ **EMP:** 46
SQ FT: 30,000
SALES (est): 11.8MM **Privately Held**
WEB: www.josephscloak.com
SIC: 2321 Men's & boys' dress shirts

(G-9183)
AMERIKOM GROUP INC
247 W 30th St Rm 6w (10001-2808)
PHONE.................................212 675-1329
Yaron Ben-Horin, *COO*
Nitsan Ben-Horin, *Vice Pres*
EMP: 80
SQ FT: 50,000
SALES (est): 10MM **Privately Held**
WEB: www.amerikom.com
SIC: 2759 Commercial printing

(G-9184)
AMERIMADE COAT INC
463 Fashion Ave Rm 802 (10018-8705)
PHONE.................................212 216-0925
Gaspar Ferrara, *President*
Corey Bagget, *Opers Staff*
◆ **EMP:** 9
SQ FT: 20,000
SALES (est): 988.7K **Privately Held**
SIC: 2369 2337 2311 Girls' & children's outerwear; jackets & vests, except fur & leather; women's; men's & boys' suits & coats

(G-9185)
AMG GLOBAL LLC (HQ)
Also Called: AMG Global NY & Enchante ACC
15 W 34th St Fl 8 (10001-3015)
PHONE.................................212 602-1818
Aharon Franco, *Vice Pres*
Duvia Leigh, *Manager*
▼ **EMP:** 8
SQ FT: 5,000
SALES (est): 1.1MM
SALES (corp-wide): 50.6MM **Privately Held**
SIC: 3261 Bathroom accessories/fittings, vitreous china or earthenware
PA: Enchante Accessories Inc.
    16 E 34th St Fl 16
    New York NY 10016
    212 689-6008

(G-9186)
AMINCOR INC
1350 Ave Of Amrcas Fl 24 (10019)
PHONE.................................347 821-3452
John R Rice III, *President*
Joseph Ingrassia, *Vice Pres*
Joseph F Ingrassia, *CFO*
EMP: 166
SQ FT: 24,806
SALES: 28.6MM **Privately Held**
SIC: 2051 8734 8711 Bread, cake & related products; bakery: wholesale or wholesale/retail combined; pollution testing; petroleum engineering

(G-9187)
AMNEWS CORPORATION
2340 Frdrick Duglass Blvd (10027)
PHONE.................................212 932-7400
Elinor Tatum, *CEO*
Kristin Molroy, *Manager*
EMP: 27 **EST:** 2003
SALES: 25.3K **Privately Held**
WEB: www.amsterdamnews.com
SIC: 2711 Newspapers

(G-9188)
AMNEWYORK
330 W 34th St Fl 17 (10001-2406)
PHONE.................................212 239-5555
Fax: 212 239-2828
Paul Turcotte, *General Mgr*
Ralph Laughin, *Business Mgr*
Donna Chibbaro, *Finance*
EMP: 66
SALES (est): 362.5K
SALES (corp-wide): 21.9B **Publicly Held**
SIC: 2711 Commercial printing & newspaper publishing combined
HQ: Newsday Llc
    235 Pinelawn Rd
    Melville NY 11747
    631 843-4050

(G-9189)
AMOSEASTERN APPAREL INC (PA)
49 W 38th St Fl 7 (10018-1936)
PHONE.................................212 921-1859
Yanling Zhang, *Administration*
▲ **EMP:** 15
SALES (est): 2MM **Privately Held**
SIC: 2396 Apparel & other linings, except millinery

(G-9190)
AMPEX CASTING CORPORATION
23 W 47th St Unit 3 (10036-2826)
PHONE.................................212 719-1318
Fax: 212 719-3493
Joseph Ipek, *President*
EMP: 19
SQ FT: 3,000
SALES (est): 1.3MM **Privately Held**
SIC: 3915 Jewelers' castings

(G-9191)
AMSALE ABERRA LLC
318 W 39th St Fl 12 (10018-1484)
PHONE.................................212 695-5936
Fax: 212 971-6288
Amsale Aberra, *President*
Clarence O'Neil Brown, *Vice Pres*
EMP: 23
SALES (est): 3.3MM **Privately Held**
SIC: 2335 Gowns, formal; wedding gowns & dresses

(G-9192)
AMSCO SCHOOL PUBLICATIONS INC
315 Hudson St Fl 5 (10013-1009)
PHONE.................................212 886-6500
Fax: 212 675-7010
Henry Brun, *President*
Irene Rubin, *Vice Pres*
Laurence Beller, *Treasurer*
Inna Kushnir, *Supervisor*
Iris L Beller, *Admin Sec*
▼ **EMP:** 80 **EST:** 1935
SQ FT: 20,000
SALES (est): 6.9MM **Privately Held**
WEB: www.amscopub.com
SIC: 2731 Textbooks: publishing only, not printed on site

(G-9193)
AMY SCHERBER INC (PA)
Also Called: Amy's Bread
75 9th Ave (10011-7006)
PHONE.................................212 462-4338
Fax: 212 462-4323
Amy Scherber, *President*
Jessica Blank, *Business Mgr*
Ann Burgunder, *Human Res Dir*
Toy Dupree, *Manager*
Robin Keehner, *Manager*
▲ **EMP:** 18
SQ FT: 7,600
SALES (est): 8MM **Privately Held**
WEB: www.amysbread.com
SIC: 2051 Bread, cake & related products

(G-9194)
ANACOR PHARMACEUTICALS INC
235 E 42nd St (10017-5703)
PHONE.................................212 733-2323
Douglas E Giordano, *President*
Ryan T Sullivan, *Exec VP*
Margaret M Madden, *Vice Pres*
EMP: 110
SALES: 82.3MM
SALES (corp-wide): 52.8B **Publicly Held**
WEB: www.anacor.com
SIC: 2834 Pharmaceutical preparations
PA: Pfizer Inc.
    235 E 42nd St
    New York NY 10017
    212 733-2323

(G-9195)
ANAGE INC
530 Fashion Ave Frnt 5 (10018-4878)
PHONE.................................212 944-6533
Fax: 212 904-1787
Kenneth Berkowitz, *President*
Fred Heiser, *Vice Pres*
▲ **EMP:** 15
SALES (est): 1.1MM **Privately Held**
SIC: 2371 Jackets, fur

(G-9196)
ANALYSTS IN MEDIA (AIM) INC
55 Broad St Fl 9 (10004-2501)
PHONE.................................212 488-1777
Alexa Calvarese, *Prdtn Dir*
Garry M Chocky, *Controller*
Jan Iverson, *Manager*
Will Hamilton-Hill, *Director*
EMP: 50
SALES (est): 5.1MM **Privately Held**
SIC: 2721 Magazines: publishing only, not printed on site

(G-9197)
ANANDAMALI INC
35 N Moore St (10013-5711)
PHONE.................................212 343-8964
Cheryl Hazan, *President*
EMP: 10
SQ FT: 2,900
SALES (est): 800K **Privately Held**
SIC: 2519 Garden furniture, except wood, metal, stone or concrete

(G-9198)
ANASTASIA FURS INTERNATIONAL (PA)
Also Called: Alexandros
224 W 30th St Rm 204 (10001-4938)
PHONE.................................212 868-9241
Anastasia Dimitriades, *President*
Tommy Dimitriades, *Vice Pres*
Alex Dimitriades, *Admin Sec*
EMP: 5
SQ FT: 7,000
SALES (est): 1MM **Privately Held**
SIC: 2371 5632 7219 Fur goods; furriers; fur garment cleaning, repairing & storage

(G-9199)
ANCIENT MODERN ART LLC
Also Called: Hill, Lois Accessories
14 E 17th St Ph 1 (10003-1912)
PHONE.................................212 302-0080
Elyssa Frank, *Manager*
Lois Hill,
EMP: 10 **EST:** 1998
SQ FT: 84,000
SALES (est): 1.1MM **Privately Held**
WEB: www.loishill.com
SIC: 3911 Jewelry, precious metal

(G-9200)
ANDES GOLD CORPORATION
405 Lexington Ave (10174-0002)
PHONE.................................212 541-2495
Alejandro Diaz, *CEO*
EMP: 95
SALES (est): 2.1MM
SALES (corp-wide): 9MM **Privately Held**
SIC: 1041 Gold ores mining
PA: New World Gold Corporation
    350 Camino Gardens Blvd
    Boca Raton FL 33432
    561 962-4139

(G-9201)
ANDIGO NEW MEDIA INC
150 W 25th St Rm 900 (10001-7458)
PHONE.................................212 727-8445
Andrew Schulkind, *President*
EMP: 5
SALES (est): 509.4K **Privately Held**
WEB: www.andigo.com
SIC: 7372 Prepackaged software

(G-9202)
ANDREA STRONGWATER
Also Called: A Strongwater Designs
465 W End Ave (10024-4926)
PHONE.................................212 873-0905
Andrea Strongwater, *Owner*
EMP: 5
SALES (est): 218K **Privately Held**
SIC: 2253 Knit outerwear mills

(G-9203)
ANDREW M SCHWARTZ LLC
Also Called: Sam NY
71 Gansevoort St Ste 2a (10014-1411)
PHONE.................................212 391-7070
Mark Boloten, *Sales Staff*
Andrew M Schwartz, *Mng Member*
Suzanne Schwartz,
Jessica Avery, *Assistant*
▲ **EMP:** 9
SALES (est): 1MM **Privately Held**
SIC: 2386 Coats & jackets, leather & sheep-lined

(G-9204)
ANDY & EVAN INDUSTRIES INC
Also Called: Andy & Evan Shirt Co., The
261 W 35th St Ste 702 (10001-0127)
PHONE.................................212 967-7908
Evan Hakalir, *President*
A Jonathan Perl, *Vice Pres*
Ariella Veitlin, *Bookkeeper*
▲ **EMP:** 9
SALES: 4MM **Privately Held**
SIC: 2361 2321 Girls' & children's dresses, blouses & shirts; men's & boys' furnishings

(G-9205)
ANGEL TEXTILES INC
519 8th Ave Fl 21 (10018-4573)
P.O. Box 1169, New Paltz (12561-7169)
PHONE.................................212 532-0900
Michael Nist, *CEO*
Helen Prior, *Principal*
EMP: 8
SQ FT: 1,000
SALES (est): 1.2MM **Privately Held**
WEB: www.angelnyc.com
SIC: 3552 2396 Silk screens for textile industry; automotive & apparel trimmings

(G-9206)
ANGEL-MADE IN HEAVEN INC (PA)
525 Fashion Ave Rm 1710 (10018-0440)
PHONE.................................212 869-5678
Fax: 212 944-9698
Morris Dahan, *President*
▲ **EMP:** 3
SQ FT: 1,000
SALES (est): 1.2MM **Privately Held**
WEB: www.angelmih.com
SIC: 2339 Sportswear, women's

(G-9207)
ANGIOGENEX INC (PA)
Also Called: (A DEVELOPMENT STAGE COMPANY)
425 Madison Ave Ste 902 (10017-1110)
PHONE.................................347 468-6799
Fax: 212 874-5027
William A Garland PHD, *CEO*
Richard A Salvador PHD, *President*
Robert Benezra PHD, *Chief*
Michael M Strage, *Vice Pres*
EMP: 5

▲ = Import ▼ = Export
◆ = Import/Export

GEOGRAPHIC SECTION

New York - New York County (G-9234)

SQ FT: 700
SALES (est): 427.8K **Publicly Held**
SIC: 2834 Pharmaceutical preparations

(G-9208)
ANGLO II LTD
Also Called: Anglo Apparel Service
224 W 35th St Fl 8 (10001-2507)
PHONE..................212 563-4980
Matthew Bendix, *Manager*
EMP: 8
SALES (corp-wide): 1.1MM **Privately Held**
SIC: 2741 Patterns, paper: publishing & printing
PA: Anglo Ii Ltd.
   519 8th Ave Fl 20
   New York NY

(G-9209)
ANHEUSER-BUSCH LLC
250 Park Ave Fl 2 (10177-0299)
PHONE..................212 573-8800
Carlos Brito, *Branch Mgr*
Fabio Mazza, *Director*
EMP: 162 **Privately Held**
SIC: 2082 Beer (alcoholic beverage)
HQ: Anheuser-Busch, Llc
   1 Busch Pl
   Saint Louis MO 63118
   314 632-6777

(G-9210)
ANHEUSER-BUSCH INBEV FIN INC
250 Park Ave (10177-0001)
PHONE..................212 573-8800
Carlos Brito, *CEO*
Marianne Amssoms, *Vice Pres*
John Blood, *Vice Pres*
Ricardo Dias, *Vice Pres*
Washington Dutra, *Vice Pres*
EMP: 10
SALES (est): 1.1MM **Privately Held**
SIC: 2082 Beer (alcoholic beverage)

(G-9211)
ANIMA GROUP LLC
Also Called: 1884 Collection
435 E 79th St Ph H (10075-1079)
PHONE..................917 913-2053
Alberto Petochi,
▲ EMP: 7
SALES (est): 790K **Privately Held**
SIC: 3911 Jewelry, precious metal

(G-9212)
ANIMAL FAIR MEDIA INC
545 8th Ave Rm 401 (10018-4341)
PHONE..................212 629-0392
Wendy Diamond, *President*
Mike Wang, *Sales Dir*
EMP: 12
SQ FT: 1,200
SALES: 1.2MM **Privately Held**
WEB: www.animalfair.com
SIC: 2721 Magazines: publishing only, not printed on site

(G-9213)
ANN GISH INC (PA)
4 W 20th St (10011-4203)
PHONE..................212 969-9200
Ann P Gish Phillips, *CEO*
David Phillips, *CFO*
Richard Collymore, *Manager*
▲ EMP: 1
SQ FT: 2,000
SALES (est): 2.8MM **Privately Held**
WEB: www.anngish.com
SIC: 2211 2341 2392 2262 Broadwoven fabric mills, cotton; nightgowns & negligees: women's & children's; household furnishings; blankets, comforters & beddings; finishing plants, manmade fiber & silk fabrics; interior design services

(G-9214)
ANNA SUI CORP (PA)
250 W 39th St Fl 15 (10018-4439)
PHONE..................212 768-1951
Fax: 212 768-8825
Anna Sui, *Ch of Bd*
Bob Sui, *President*
Lauren Grover, *Design Engr*
Gladys Goldsmith, *Controller*

Amy Dougherty, *Sales Dir*
▲ EMP: 39
SQ FT: 3,000
SALES (est): 6.5MM **Privately Held**
WEB: www.annasui.com
SIC: 2331 2339 2335 2337 Blouses, women's & juniors': made from purchased material; women's & misses' athletic clothing & sportswear; slacks: women's, misses' & juniors'; women's, juniors' & misses' dresses; skirts, separate: women's, misses' & juniors'; jackets & vests, except fur & leather: women's

(G-9215)
ANNUALS PUBLISHING CO INC
Also Called: Madison Square Press
10 E 23rd St Ste 510 (10010-4459)
PHONE..................212 505-0950
Fax: 212 979-2207
EMP: 3
SQ FT: 1,000
SALES: 1.5MM **Privately Held**
SIC: 2731 Books-Publishing/Printing

(G-9216)
ANSWER PRINTING INC
505 8th Ave Rm 1101 (10018-4540)
P.O. Box 3442 (10163-3442)
PHONE..................212 922-2922
Fax: 212 681-9290
Larry Dunne, *President*
Joanne Cohen, *Sales Staff*
Billy Rodriguez, *Sales Staff*
EMP: 17
SQ FT: 3,800
SALES (est): 1.8MM **Privately Held**
WEB: www.answerprinting.com
SIC: 2741 2752 Business service newsletters: publishing & printing; commercial printing, lithographic

(G-9217)
ANTERIOS INC
60 E 42nd St Ste 1160 (10165-6206)
PHONE..................212 303-1683
Jon Edelson MD, *President*
Fabian Tenenbaum, *CFO*
Klaus Theobald MD, *Osteopathy*
EMP: 6
SALES (est): 870.6K **Privately Held**
SIC: 2834 Pharmaceutical preparations
PA: Allergan Public Limited Company
   Euro House
   Cork

(G-9218)
ANTHONY L & S LLC (PA)
Also Called: Anthony L&S Footwear Group
500 Fashion Ave Fl 16b (10018-0810)
PHONE..................212 386-7245
Ashley Ambersinos, *Sales Staff*
Joy Crook, *Manager*
Joy Krooks, *Manager*
Jenny Rosado, *Manager*
Anthony Loconte,
▲ EMP: 6
SQ FT: 6,000
SALES (est): 3.4MM **Privately Held**
WEB: www.anthonyls.com
SIC: 3021 5139 Rubber & plastics footwear; shoes

(G-9219)
ANTIMONY NEW YORK LLC ✪
120 E 34th St Apt 7g (10016-4625)
PHONE..................917 232-1836
Jason Shelowitz, *Mng Member*
Rachel Shelowitz,
EMP: 2 EST: 2017
SALES: 5MM **Privately Held**
SIC: 2844 Toilet preparations

(G-9220)
ANTWERP DIAMOND DISTRIBUTORS
581 5th Ave Fl 5 (10017-8824)
PHONE..................212 319-3300
Fax: 212 207-8168
Phyllis Lisker, *President*
Larry Lisker, *Manager*
EMP: 15 EST: 1955
SQ FT: 4,000

SALES (est): 1.5MM **Privately Held**
WEB: www.antwerpdistributors.com
SIC: 3915 5094 Diamond cutting & polishing; diamonds (gems)

(G-9221)
ANTWERP SALES INTL INC
Also Called: A.S.I. Fancies Ltd
576 5th Ave (10036-4807)
PHONE..................212 354-6515
Fax: 212 768-1209
Norbert May, *President*
Danny Klugman, *Vice Pres*
Yossel Slomovits, *CFO*
Danny Kougman, *Human Res Mgr*
EMP: 18
SQ FT: 3,500
SALES (est): 2.9MM **Privately Held**
SIC: 3915 Diamond cutting & polishing

(G-9222)
APEC PAPER INDUSTRIES LTD
Also Called: American Printing & Envelope
255 W 88th St Apt 4b (10024-1717)
PHONE..................212 730-0088
Fax: 212 730-0053
Justin Koplin, *President*
Maureen Best, *Admin Dir*
EMP: 5 EST: 1935
SQ FT: 6,000
SALES: 2.4MM **Privately Held**
SIC: 2677 5112 Envelopes; envelopes

(G-9223)
APEX TEXICON INC (PA)
295 Madison Ave (10017-6434)
P.O. Box 960670, Inwood (11096-0670)
PHONE..................516 239-4400
Edward Schlussel, *President*
John Kurz, *Vice Pres*
David Kurz, *Treasurer*
EMP: 24 EST: 1943
SQ FT: 9,000
SALES: 1.7MM **Privately Held**
SIC: 2221 2258 2257 Broadwoven fabric mills, manmade; net & netting products; tricot fabrics; weft knit fabric mills

(G-9224)
APICELLA JEWELERS INC
40 W 39th St Fl 4 (10018-2142)
PHONE..................212 840-2024
Fax: 212 575-4937
John Apicella, *President*
Anthony Apicella, *Vice Pres*
Kevin Khan, *Manager*
EMP: 30 EST: 1946
SQ FT: 2,500
SALES (est): 3.1MM **Privately Held**
SIC: 3911 Jewelry, precious metal

(G-9225)
APOGY LLC
65 N Moore St Fl 2 (10013-2363)
PHONE..................866 766-1723
Peder Regan, *CEO*
Vik Shah, *COO*
Alexander Ryzhanskiy, *Engineer*
Jeff Pfohl, *Business Dir*
EMP: 20
SQ FT: 2,000
SALES (est): 3MM **Privately Held**
SIC: 7372 Application computer software

(G-9226)
APOLLO APPAREL GROUP LLC
Also Called: Apollo Jeans
1407 Brdway Ste 2000-200 (10018)
PHONE..................212 398-6585
Salim Mann, *Mng Member*
Victor Hasbani, *Manager*
▲ EMP: 10
SALES (est): 2.2MM **Privately Held**
SIC: 2211 2389 Jean fabrics; men's miscellaneous accessories

(G-9227)
APOLLO INVESTMENT FUND VII LP
9 W 57th St Fl 43 (10019-2700)
PHONE..................212 515-3200
Martin Kelly, *CFO*
Chris Weidler, *Officer*
Leon Black,
Laurence Berg,
EMP: 7

SALES (est): 741.7K **Privately Held**
SIC: 2731 Books: publishing & printing

(G-9228)
APPARATUS LLC
Also Called: Apparatus Studio
122 W 30th St Fl 4 (10001-4009)
PHONE..................646 527-9732
Ronald Nelson, *Finance*
Jeremy Anderson, *Mng Member*
Gabriel Hendifar,
EMP: 42
SQ FT: 12,000
SALES (est): 3.9MM **Privately Held**
SIC: 3646 Commercial indusl & institutional electric lighting fixtures

(G-9229)
APPAREL GROUP LTD
Thyme
469 7th Ave Fl 8 (10018-7605)
PHONE..................212 328-1200
Thomas Bietrich, *President*
Pam Wyke, *Sales Executive*
EMP: 40 **Privately Held**
SIC: 2331 Women's & misses' blouses & shirts
HQ: The Apparel Group Ltd
   883 Trinity Dr
   Lewisville TX 75056
   214 469-3300

(G-9230)
APPAREL PARTNERSHIP GROUP LLC
250 W 39th St Rm 701 (10018-4719)
PHONE..................212 302-7722
Matthew Healy, *Mng Member*
▲ EMP: 5
SALES (est): 451.8K **Privately Held**
SIC: 2322 2341 5136 5137 Men's & boys' underwear & nightwear; women's & children's undergarments; underwear, men's & boys'; women's & children's lingerie & undergarments

(G-9231)
APPAREL PRODUCTION INC
270 W 39th St Rm 1701 (10018-0330)
PHONE..................212 278-8362
Fax: 212 278-8357
Theodore Sadaka, *President*
▲ EMP: 50
SALES (est): 518.5K **Privately Held**
SIC: 3949 Sporting & athletic goods

(G-9232)
APPFIGURES INC
133 Chrystie St Fl 3 (10002-2810)
PHONE..................212 343-7900
Eliahu Michaeli, *President*
EMP: 14
SALES (est): 1MM **Privately Held**
SIC: 7372 Business oriented computer software

(G-9233)
APPLICATION SECURITY INC (DH)
55 Broad St Rm 10a (10004-2509)
PHONE..................212 912-4100
Fax: 212 947-8788
Jack Hembrough, *President*
Madhuri Kulkarni, *QA Dir*
Gene Trog, *Research*
Peter Schwartz, *CFO*
Steve Fox, *Sales Engr*
EMP: 75
SALES: 1.6MM **Privately Held**
WEB: www.appsecinc.com
SIC: 7372 Prepackaged software
HQ: Trustwave Holdings, Inc.
   70 W Madison St Ste 600
   Chicago IL 60602
   312 750-0950

(G-9234)
APPLIEDEA INC
20 Park Ave (10016-3840)
PHONE..................212 920-6822
Yehoshua Segal, *President*
Yoram Lavi, *Vice Pres*
EMP: 5
SALES (est): 117.2K **Privately Held**
SIC: 7372 7389 Application computer software;

(PA)=Parent Co (HQ)=Headquarters (DH)=Div Headquarters
✪ = New Business established in last 2 years

New York - New York County (G-9235) — GEOGRAPHIC SECTION

(G-9235)
APRIL PRINTING CO INC
1201 Broadway Ste 403 (10001-5658)
PHONE..................212 685-7455
Brad April, *President*
Muriel April, *Vice Pres*
Muriel Horowitz, *Vice Pres*
EMP: 12 EST: 1914
SQ FT: 2,500
SALES (est): 1.6MM Privately Held
WEB: www.aprilprinting.com
SIC: 2759 Commercial printing

(G-9236)
APS AMERICAN POLYMERS SVCS INC ◇
104 W 40th St Rm 500 (10018-3770)
PHONE..................212 362-7711
Gustavo Sampaio De Souza, *CEO*
◆ EMP: 2 EST: 2017
SQ FT: 120
SALES (est): 10MM Privately Held
SIC: 2821 Polyethylene resins; polypropylene resins; polystyrene resins

(G-9237)
AR & AR JEWELRY INC
31 W 47th St Fl 15 (10036-2808)
PHONE..................212 764-7916
Fax: 212 764-7921
Aras Tirtirian, *President*
Aras Tirtir, *Vice Pres*
▲ EMP: 40 EST: 1996
SALES (est): 4.9MM Privately Held
SIC: 3911 Jewelry, precious metal

(G-9238)
AR MEDIA INC
601 W 26th St Rm 810 (10001-1153)
PHONE..................212 352-0731
Fax: 212 352-0738
Raul Martinez, *CEO*
Diane Defroches, *CEO*
Alex Gonzalez, *Founder*
Terry Waters, *COO*
Cindy Khan, *Accountant*
EMP: 50
SQ FT: 17,000
SALES (est): 5.6MM Privately Held
WEB: www.arnewyork.com
SIC: 2741 7311 Catalogs: publishing only, not printed on site; advertising agencies

(G-9239)
AR PUBLISHING COMPANY INC
55 Broad St Rm 20b (10004-2589)
PHONE..................212 482-0303
Helen Brusilovsky, *President*
EMP: 10
SALES (est): 479.6K Privately Held
WEB: www.vnsnews.com
SIC: 2711 Newspapers, publishing & printing

(G-9240)
ARABELLA TEXTILES LLC
Also Called: Deborah Connolly & Associates
303 5th Ave Rm 1402 (10016-6601)
PHONE..................212 679-0611
Fax: 212 679-0211
Deborah Connolly, *Mng Member*
▲ EMP: 5
SALES (est): 422.1K Privately Held
WEB: www.deborahconnolly.com
SIC: 2299 Batting, wadding, padding & fillings

(G-9241)
ARBEIT BROS INC
345 7th Ave Fl 20 (10001-5034)
PHONE..................212 736-9761
Sam Arbeit, *President*
EMP: 5 EST: 1948
SQ FT: 2,000
SALES (est): 390K Privately Held
SIC: 2371 Apparel, fur

(G-9242)
ARBOR BOOKS INC
244 Madison Ave (10016-2817)
PHONE..................201 236-9990
Joel Hochman, *President*
Larry Leichman, *Vice Pres*
EMP: 20
SALES: 2.5MM Privately Held
WEB: www.arborbooks.com
SIC: 2731 Book publishing

(G-9243)
ARCADE INC
1740 Broadway Fl 14 (10019-4646)
PHONE..................212 541-2600
Richard Kaleta, *Ch of Bd*
Steve Greenland, *Senior VP*
Louis Ziafonte, *Senior VP*
Jamie Ross, *Vice Pres*
Briget Tyler, *Purchasing*
EMP: 1836
SALES (est): 228.8MM
SALES (corp-wide): 13.2B Publicly Held
SIC: 2752 Commercial printing, lithographic
HQ: Visant Holding Corp.
3601 Minnesota Dr Ste 400
Minneapolis MN 55435
914 595-8200

(G-9244)
ARCANGEL INC
Also Called: Catherine Deane
209 W 38th St Rm 1001 (10018-4465)
PHONE..................347 771-0789
Catherine Deane, *CEO*
Susan Miller, *Manager*
Kathryn Hayman, *Director*
EMP: 2
SQ FT: 2,000
SALES: 1MM
SALES (corp-wide): 729.8K Privately Held
SIC: 2335 Wedding gowns & dresses
HQ: Atelier Arcangel Limited
1st Floor
London

(G-9245)
ARCHITECTS NEWSPAPER LLC
Also Called: Bd Projects
21 Murray St Fl 5 (10007-2244)
PHONE..................212 966-0630
Becca Blasdel, *Editor*
Olivia Martin, *Editor*
Molly Sullivan, *Comms Dir*
Susan Kramer, *Director*
Diana Darling,
EMP: 12
SALES (est): 840K Privately Held
WEB: www.archpaper.com
SIC: 2711 Newspapers: publishing only, not printed on site

(G-9246)
ARCHITECTURAL TEXTILES USA INC
Also Called: Architex International
36 E 23rd St Ste F (10010-4409)
PHONE..................212 213-6972
Fax: 212 213-8033
Keith Gordon, *Controller*
Victor Liss, *Manager*
Kim Matanis, *Executive*
EMP: 35
SALES (corp-wide): 59.9MM Privately Held
WEB: www.architex-ljh.com
SIC: 2299 5087 Broadwoven fabrics: linen, jute, hemp & ramie; service establishment equipment
PA: Architectural Textiles U.S.A., Inc.
3333 Commercial Ave
Northbrook IL 60062
847 205-1333

(G-9247)
ARCHIVE360 INC
165 Broadway Fl 23 (10006-1404)
P.O. Box 291, Rutherford NJ (07070-0291)
PHONE..................212 731-2438
Robert Desteno, *CEO*
Tiberiu Popp, *Founder*
EMP: 37
SQ FT: 1,000
SALES (est): 10MM Privately Held
SIC: 7372 Prepackaged software

(G-9248)
ARCONIC INC (PA)
390 Park Ave (10022-4608)
PHONE..................212 836-2758
David P Hess, *CEO*
Kay H Meggers, *President*
Timothy D Myers, *President*
Eric Roegner, *President*
Karl Tragl, *President*
◆ EMP: 100 EST: 1888
SALES: 12.3B Publicly Held
SIC: 3355 3353 3354 3463 Aluminum rolling & drawing; aluminum sheet & strip; coils, sheet aluminum; foil, aluminum; plates, aluminum; aluminum extruded products; aluminum forgings

(G-9249)
AREA INC
Also Called: Area Warehouse
58 E 11th St Fl 2 (10003-6019)
PHONE..................212 924-7084
Anki Spets, *President*
Yuko Watatami, *Executive Asst*
▲ EMP: 9
SQ FT: 6,000
SALES (est): 1MM Privately Held
WEB: www.lundstrom-id.com
SIC: 2392 Household furnishings

(G-9250)
ARGEE AMERICA INC
Also Called: Argee Sportswear
1400 Broadway Ste 2307 (10018-5300)
PHONE..................212 768-9840
Roshan L Gera, *President*
Shyama Gera, *Vice Pres*
▲ EMP: 8
SQ FT: 3,000
SALES (est): 1.2MM Privately Held
SIC: 2339 5137 Sportswear, women's; sportswear, women's & children's

(G-9251)
ARGOSY COMPOSITE ADVANCED MATE
225 W 34th St Ste 1106 (10122-1106)
PHONE..................212 268-0003
Richard Rocco, *Mng Member*
Crissy Tecerini, *Administration*
EMP: 12
SALES (est): 767.4K Privately Held
SIC: 3299 Ceramic fiber

(G-9252)
ARIELA AND ASSOCIATES INTL LLC (PA)
1359 Broadway Fl 21 (10018-7824)
PHONE..................212 683-4131
Fax: 212 683-4038
Ariela Balk, *President*
Mendel Balk, *COO*
Melissa Dietiker, *Vice Pres*
Ed Mendoza, *Vice Pres*
Toni Spinelli, *Vice Pres*
▲ EMP: 110
SQ FT: 27,741
SALES (est): 37MM Privately Held
WEB: www.ariela-alpha.com
SIC: 2341 Women's & children's undergarments

(G-9253)
ARLEE HOME FASHIONS INC (PA)
Also Called: Arlee Group
261 5th Ave Fl Mezz (10016-7600)
PHONE..................212 689-0020
Fax: 212 532-6428
David Frankel, *CEO*
Marsha Cutler, *President*
Marsha Caparelli, *Vice Pres*
Julie Polich, *Vice Pres*
Alan Mandell, *CFO*
▲ EMP: 60 EST: 1976
SQ FT: 20,000
SALES (est): 139.1MM Privately Held
SIC: 2392 Pillows, bed: made from purchased materials; chair covers & pads: made from purchased materials

(G-9254)
ARMACEL ARMOR CORPORATION
745 5th Ave Fl 7 (10151-0802)
PHONE..................805 384-1144
Asia Fernandez, *President*
David Fernandez, *Vice Pres*
EMP: 35
SALES (est): 4.6MM Privately Held
WEB: www.armacelarmorcorp.com
SIC: 3728 Military aircraft equipment & armament; aircraft assemblies, subassemblies & parts

(G-9255)
ARPA USA
62 Greene St Frnt 1 (10012-4346)
PHONE..................212 965-4099
Thomas Weissbach, *Principal*
▲ EMP: 6
SALES (est): 934.8K Privately Held
SIC: 3589 High pressure cleaning equipment

(G-9256)
ARPER USA INC
476 Broadway Ste 2f (10013-2641)
P.O. Box 1683 (10013-0870)
PHONE..................212 647-8900
Emaunele Corvo, *President*
Carmela Puleo, *Cust Mgr*
Andrew Floyd, *Manager*
▲ EMP: 6
SALES (est): 1.2MM Privately Held
SIC: 2599 Factory furniture & fixtures
HQ: Arper Spa
Via Lombardia 16
Monastier Di Treviso TV 31050
042 279-18

(G-9257)
ARRAY MARKETING GROUP INC (HQ)
200 Madison Ave Ste 2121 (10016-4000)
PHONE..................212 750-3367
Tom Hendren, *CEO*
Mike Caron, *Vice Pres*
Mark Lattimore, *Design Engr*
Kevin Pattrick, *CFO*
Alex Hagiage, *Sales Executive*
▲ EMP: 21
SALES (est): 5.4MM
SALES (corp-wide): 48.6MM Privately Held
WEB: www.arraymarketing.com
SIC: 2541 Store & office display cases & fixtures
PA: Array Canada Inc
45 Progress Ave
Scarborough ON M1P 2
416 299-4865

(G-9258)
ART ASIAPACIFIC PUBLISHING LLC
410 W 24th St Apt 14a (10011-1356)
PHONE..................212 255-6003
Elaine Ng,
EMP: 8
SALES: 800K Privately Held
SIC: 2741 Miscellaneous publishing

(G-9259)
ART FLAG COMPANY INC
8 Jay St Frnt 1 (10013-2891)
PHONE..................212 334-1890
Fax: 212 941-9631
George Weiner, *President*
Carmen Weiner, *Vice Pres*
Daniel Bright, *Manager*
Nancy Maminsky, *Art Dir*
EMP: 18 EST: 1971
SQ FT: 5,000
SALES: 1MM Privately Held
SIC: 2399 2396 Flags, fabric; banners, made from fabric; screen printing on fabric articles

(G-9260)
ART INDUSTRIES OF NEW YORK
601 W 26th St Rm 1425 (10001-1160)
PHONE..................212 633-9200
Steve Kaitz, *President*
Neal H Klein, *Vice Pres*
EMP: 50
SQ FT: 80,000
SALES: 6.4MM Privately Held
WEB: www.salinesolutions.com
SIC: 2675 Die-cut paper & board

(G-9261)
ART OF SHAVING - FL LLC
10 Columbus Cir Ste 209 (10019-1227)
PHONE..................212 823-9410

GEOGRAPHIC SECTION
New York - New York County (G-9288)

Michael Marra, *Manager*
EMP: 6
SALES (corp-wide): 65B **Publicly Held**
SIC: 3421 Scissors, shears, clippers, snips & similar tools
HQ: The Art Of Shaving - Fl Llc
6100 Blue Lagoon Dr # 150
Miami FL 33126

(G-9262)
ART OF SHAVING - FL LLC
2151 Broadway Frnt 2 (10023-8243)
PHONE.................................212 362-1493
EMP: 5
SALES (corp-wide): 65B **Publicly Held**
SIC: 2844 Toilet preparations
HQ: The Art Of Shaving - Fl Llc
6100 Blue Lagoon Dr # 150
Miami FL 33126

(G-9263)
ART PEOPLE INC
594 Broadway Rm 1102 (10012-3289)
PHONE.................................212 431-4865
Fax: 212 219-2465
Gary Golkin, *President*
Carrie Golkin, *Treasurer*
EMP: 8
SQ FT: 10,000
SALES (est): 777.9K **Privately Held**
SIC: 2221 Wall covering fabrics, manmade fiber & silk; upholstery fabrics, manmade fiber & silk

(G-9264)
ART RESOURCES TRANSFER INC
526 W 26th St Rm 614 (10001-5522)
PHONE.................................212 255-2919
Yael Meridan Schori, *President*
Bill Bartman, *Exec Dir*
Jennifer Seass, *Director*
▲ **EMP:** 5
SQ FT: 4,000
SALES: 999K **Privately Held**
WEB: www.artretran.com
SIC: 2791 Typesetting

(G-9265)
ART SCROLL PRINTING CORP
230 W 41st St Bsmt 1 (10036-7207)
PHONE.................................212 929-2413
Elliot Schwartz, *President*
EMP: 13
SALES (est): 1.8MM **Privately Held**
SIC: 2752 Commercial printing, lithographic

(G-9266)
ART-TEC JEWELRY DESIGNS LTD (PA)
48 W 48th St Ste 401 (10036-1727)
PHONE.................................212 719-2941
Fax: 212 719-9456
Edward Zylka, *President*
EMP: 20
SQ FT: 5,000
SALES (est): 4.1MM **Privately Held**
SIC: 3911 Jewelry, precious metal

(G-9267)
ARTEAST LLC
Also Called: Zadig and Voltaire
102 Franklin St Fl 4 (10013-3015)
PHONE.................................212 965-8787
Pascaline Audren, *Mng Member*
Ascher Saddah,
▲ **EMP:** 8
SALES (est): 421.5K **Privately Held**
SIC: 2335 5137 7389 Women's, juniors' & misses' dresses; women's & children's clothing; apparel designers, commercial
HQ: Zv France
11 Avenue D Iena
Paris 75116
142 218-888

(G-9268)
ARTICULATE GLOBAL INC
244 5th Ave Ste 2960 (10001-7604)
PHONE.................................800 861-4880
Adam Schwartz, *CEO*
Frazier Miller, *COO*
Tom Kuhlmann, *Vice Pres*
Lucy Suros, *Vice Pres*
Patrick Eakin, *QA Dir*

EMP: 130
SQ FT: 20,000
SALES (est): 19.3MM **Privately Held**
WEB: www.articulate.com
SIC: 7372 Prepackaged software

(G-9269)
ARTIFEX PRESS LLC
109 W 27th St (10001-6208)
PHONE.................................212 414-1482
David Groz, *President*
EMP: 15
SALES (est): 504K **Privately Held**
SIC: 2721 Periodicals: publishing & printing

(G-9270)
ARTISTIC FRAME CORP (PA)
979 3rd Ave Ste 1705 (10022-3804)
PHONE.................................212 289-2100
Fax: 212 289-2101
David Stevens, *President*
Joe Weldon, *Manager*
▲ **EMP:** 110
SQ FT: 400,000
SALES (est): 95.2MM **Privately Held**
SIC: 2426 5021 Frames for upholstered furniture, wood; office furniture

(G-9271)
ARTISTIC RIBBON NOVELTY CO INC
22 W 21st St Fl 3 (10010-6948)
P.O. Box 126, Hillsdale NJ (07642-0126)
PHONE.................................212 255-4224
Fax: 212 645-6589
Kenneth Hanz, *President*
Kenneth Handz, *President*
Steve Eigner, *Corp Secy*
▲ **EMP:** 20 **EST:** 1928
SQ FT: 15,000
SALES (est): 2.7MM **Privately Held**
WEB: www.artisticribbon.com
SIC: 2396 5131 Ribbons & bows, cut & sewed; sewing supplies & notions; ribbons

(G-9272)
ARTISTIC TYPOGRAPHY CORP (PA)
Also Called: Artistic Group, The
151 W 30th St Fl 8 (10001-4026)
PHONE.................................212 463-8880
Fax: 212 736-6668
Paul J Weinstein, *President*
▲ **EMP:** 6 **EST:** 1959
SQ FT: 7,500
SALES (est): 2.2MM **Privately Held**
WEB: www.tagimage.com
SIC: 2759 2791 Commercial printing; typographic composition, for the printing trade

(G-9273)
ARTKRAFT STRAUSS LLC
Also Called: Artkraft Sign
1776 Broadway Ste 1810 (10019-2017)
PHONE.................................212 265-5155
Fax: 212 265-5262
Tama Starr, *President*
James Manfredi, *Mfg Spvr*
Neil Vonknoblauch, *CFO*
Kim Ramos, *Office Mgr*
Amy Hu, *Manager*
EMP: 30 **EST:** 1935
SQ FT: 1,500
SALES (est): 3.7MM **Privately Held**
WEB: www.artkraft.com
SIC: 3993 7312 Electric signs; outdoor advertising services

(G-9274)
ARTNEWS LTD (PA)
Also Called: Artnewsletter
110 Greene St Ph 2 (10012-3824)
PHONE.................................212 398-1690
Fax: 212 768-4002
Peter M Brant, *Principal*
Sammy Dalati, *Editor*
Joanne Sonntecchio, *Bookkeeper*
Nicole Anderson, *Senior Editor*
Nicole De George, *Assistant*
▲ **EMP:** 18 **EST:** 1902
SQ FT: 12,000

SALES (est): 2.9MM **Privately Held**
WEB: www.artnews.com
SIC: 2721 Magazines: publishing & printing

(G-9275)
ARTSCROLL PRINTING CORP (PA)
53 W 23rd St Fl 4 (10010-4239)
PHONE.................................212 929-2413
Fax: 212 633-1264
Elliot Schwartz, *President*
David Schwartz, *Corp Secy*
Morris Pilicer, *Controller*
Maria Rojas, *Hum Res Coord*
Skip Vesell, *Branch Mgr*
EMP: 24
SALES (est): 4.4MM **Privately Held**
SIC: 2759 2791 2752 7336 Commercial printing; thermography; typesetting; commercial printing, lithographic; commercial art & graphic design; signs & advertising specialties

(G-9276)
ARUBA NETWORKS INC
556 W 22nd St (10011-1108)
PHONE.................................732 343-1305
Greg Rocha, *Director*
EMP: 5
SALES (corp-wide): 50.1B **Publicly Held**
SIC: 3577 Computer peripheral equipment
HQ: Aruba Networks, Inc.
3333 Scott Blvd
Santa Clara CA 95054
408 227-4500

(G-9277)
ARUVIL INTERNATIONAL INC (PA)
185 Madison Ave Rm 1701 (10016-7711)
PHONE.................................212 447-5020
Fax: 212 447-9812
Vilas Kulkarni, *President*
Russell Jenkins, *Vice Pres*
▲ **EMP:** 30
SQ FT: 2,800
SALES (est): 8.7MM **Privately Held**
WEB: www.aruvil.com
SIC: 3315 Fence gates posts & fittings: steel

(G-9278)
ASAHI SHIMBUN AMERICA INC
620 8th Ave (10018-1618)
PHONE.................................212 398-0257
Fax: 212 221-1734
Erika Toh, *Principal*
EMP: 15
SALES (est): 1.1MM **Privately Held**
SIC: 2711 Newspapers, publishing & printing

(G-9279)
ASCENT AEROSPACE HOLDINGS LLC (PA)
Also Called: Aip Aerospace
330 Madison Ave Fl 28 (10017-5018)
PHONE.................................212 916-8142
Michael Mahfet, *CEO*
Jonathon Levine, *CFO*
Linda Diep, *Executive Asst*
Dino Cusomano,
▲ **EMP:** 4 **EST:** 2012
SALES (est): 200MM **Privately Held**
SIC: 3721 6799 Aircraft; investors

(G-9280)
ASENCE INC
65 Broadway Fl 7 (10006-2536)
PHONE.................................347 335-2606
Fax: 212 430-6501
EMP: 21
SALES: 3MM **Privately Held**
SIC: 2834 Pharmaceutical Preparations

(G-9281)
ASHBURNS INC
Also Called: Ashburns Engravers
90 John St Rm 409 (10038-3242)
PHONE.................................212 227-5692
Fax: 212 385-1112
Daniel De Prima, *President*
Leonard Zinanti, *Vice Pres*
Jack Natter, *Manager*
EMP: 5

SQ FT: 2,000
SALES (est): 400K **Privately Held**
WEB: www.ashburns.com
SIC: 3479 Engraving jewelry silverware, or metal

(G-9282)
ASHI DIAMONDS LLC
18 E 48th St Fl 14 (10017-1014)
PHONE.................................212 319-8291
Fax: 212 319-4341
Sanjay Pandya, *Trustee*
Nilesh Shah, *Controller*
Karma Noble, *Marketing Mgr*
Sandra Morrow, *Marketing Staff*
Mahendra Pandya, *Mng Member*
▲ **EMP:** 40
SQ FT: 6,500
SALES (est): 6MM **Privately Held**
WEB: www.lazairediamond.com
SIC: 3911 Pearl jewelry, natural or cultured

(G-9283)
ASHKO GROUP LLC
10 W 33rd St Rm 1019 (10001-3306)
PHONE.................................212 594-6050
Jack Ashkenazi, *President*
Charles Ashkenazi, *COO*
David Braha, *CFO*
Antonia Collado, *Sales Dir*
▲ **EMP:** 18
SQ FT: 1,500
SALES (est): 3.6MM **Privately Held**
SIC: 2252 5139 Socks; footwear

(G-9284)
ASI SIGN SYSTEMS INC
192 Lexington Ave Rm 1002 (10016-6823)
PHONE.................................646 742-1320
EMP: 7
SALES (corp-wide): 20.4MM **Privately Held**
SIC: 3993 Signs & advertising specialties
PA: Asi Sign Systems, Inc.
8181 Jetstar Dr Ste 110
Irving TX 75063
214 352-9140

(G-9285)
ASIA CONNECTION LLC
200 E 90th St Apt 4h (10128-3559)
PHONE.................................212 369-4644
Lee Souyun,
▲ **EMP:** 12
SALES (est): 2.2MM **Privately Held**
SIC: 3949 5091 Swimming pools, except plastic; swimming pools, equipment & supplies

(G-9286)
ASITE LLC
245 W 29th St Rm 1601 (10001-5216)
PHONE.................................203 545-3089
Gordon Ashworth, *Principal*
EMP: 60
SALES (est): 1.8MM **Privately Held**
SIC: 7372 Prepackaged software

(G-9287)
ASM USA INC
73 Spring St Rm 309 (10012-5801)
PHONE.................................212 925-2906
EMP: 11
SALES (est): 953.9K
SALES (corp-wide): 188.1K **Privately Held**
SIC: 3444 5051 Sheet metal specialties, not stamped; steel
HQ: Approche Sur Mesure (A.S.M.)
63 Rue Edouard Vaillant
Levallois Perret 92300
147 481-020

(G-9288)
ASPEN PUBLISHERS INC (DH)
Also Called: Aspen Law & Business
76 9th Ave Ste 724 (10011-5222)
PHONE.................................212 771-0600
Fax: 212 771-0885
Mark Dorman, *CEO*
Anita Rosepka, *Editor*
Claudia Levine, *Chief*
Susan Yules, *Exec VP*
Gustavo Dobles, *Vice Pres*
EMP: 603

New York - New York County (G-9289)   **GEOGRAPHIC SECTION**

SALES (est): 1.2MM
SALES (corp-wide): 4.5B Privately Held
SIC: 2721 2731 2741 Trade journals: publishing only, not printed on site; book publishing; newsletter publishing
HQ: Wolters Kluwer United States Inc.
2700 Lake Cook Rd
Riverwoods IL 60015
847 580-5000

(G-9289)
ASPEN RESEARCH GROUP LTD
17 State St Fl 15 (10004-1532)
PHONE..................212 425-9588
Fax: 212 425-9349
Tony Rivera, Sales Staff
Mike Neff, Manager
EMP: 7
SALES (corp-wide): 4.1MM Privately Held
SIC: 7372 Business oriented computer software
PA: Aspen Research Group Ltd
802 Grand Ave Ste 120
Glenwood Springs CO 81601
970 945-2921

(G-9290)
ASPEX INCORPORATED
161 Hudson St Apt 1a (10013-2145)
PHONE..................212 966-0410
Fax: 212 645-8343
Gerald Henrici, President
Kenneth Lee, President
James M Herriman, Principal
John Strohbeen, Principal
Jesus Chico, Engineer
EMP: 20
SALES (est): 3.9MM Privately Held
SIC: 3823 3829 Computer interface equipment for industrial process control; measuring & controlling devices

(G-9291)
ASSOCIATED BRANDS INC
111 8th Ave (10011-5201)
P.O. Box 788, Medina (14103-0788)
PHONE..................585 798-3475
Scott Greenwood, President
Jurgen Pahl, VP Opers
Jim Dimatteo, Plant Mgr
Derek Briffett, CFO
Shahid Baloch, Controller
◆ EMP: 266
SQ FT: 340,000
SALES (est): 54.1MM
SALES (corp-wide): 6.1B Publicly Held
WEB: www.associatedbrands.com
SIC: 2034 2043 2066 2099 Fruits, dried or dehydrated, except freeze-dried; vegetables, dried or dehydrated (except freeze-dried); cereal breakfast foods; chocolate & cocoa products; food preparations
HQ: Associated Brands Inc
944 Highway 8
Stoney Creek ON L8E 5
905 643-1211

(G-9292)
ASSOCIATION FOR CMPT MCHY INC (PA)
Also Called: Acm
2 Penn Plz Rm 701 (10121-0799)
P.O. Box 30777 (10087-0777)
PHONE..................212 869-7440
Fax: 212 944-1318
John R White, CEO
Vinton Cerf, President
Wendy Hall, President
Matthew Smyth, General Mgr
John Stanik, Editor
EMP: 72
SQ FT: 30,000
SALES: 70.2MM Privately Held
SIC: 2721 8621 Periodicals: publishing only; scientific membership association

(G-9293)
ASSOULINE PUBLISHING INC (PA)
3 Park Ave Fl 27 (10016-5902)
PHONE..................212 989-6769
Fax: 212 989-6853
Prosper Assouline, President
Yaffa Assouline, Vice Pres
Eduard De Lange, Vice Pres
Stephanie Labeille, Vice Pres
Ines Gierke, Store Mgr
▲ EMP: 12
SQ FT: 3,000
SALES (est): 2.6MM Privately Held
WEB: www.assouline.com
SIC: 2731 Book publishing

(G-9294)
ASTON LEATHER INC
153 W 27th St Ste 406 (10001-6258)
PHONE..................212 481-2760
Metin Adam, Ch of Bd
▲ EMP: 6
SALES (est): 600K Privately Held
SIC: 3111 Leather tanning & finishing

(G-9295)
ASTUCCI US LTD (PA)
385 5th Ave Rm 1100 (10016-3340)
PHONE..................212 725-3171
Fax: 212 725-3236
Dan Benmoshe, President
Hanna Levy, Vice Pres
▲ EMP: 8
SQ FT: 3,000
SALES: 15MM Privately Held
SIC: 3172 Cases, jewelry; cases, glasses

(G-9296)
AT&T CORP
Also Called: Sherwin Commerce
767 5th Ave Fl 12a (10153-0023)
PHONE..................212 317-7048
Debra Surrette, Manager
EMP: 15
SALES (corp-wide): 163.7B Publicly Held
WEB: www.swbell.com
SIC: 7372 Prepackaged software
HQ: At&T Corp.
1 At&T Way
Bedminster NJ 07921
800 403-3302

(G-9297)
ATC PLASTICS LLC
Also Called: Heller Performance Polymers
555 Madison Ave Fl 5 (10022-3410)
PHONE..................212 375-2515
Herbert Heller, President
Gordon Smith, Division Mgr
EMP: 39
SALES (corp-wide): 7.9MM Privately Held
SIC: 3087 3643 2851 2821 Custom compound purchased resins; current-carrying wiring devices; paints & allied products; plastics materials & resins
PA: Atc Plastics, Llc
8425 Woodfield Crossing B
Indianapolis IN 46240
317 469-7552

(G-9298)
ATERET LLC
22 W 48th St (10036-1803)
PHONE..................212 819-0777
Khodahbaksh Levy,
Samuel Levy,
EMP: 5
SALES (est): 410K Privately Held
WEB: www.ateret.com
SIC: 3911 Jewelry, precious metal

(G-9299)
ATERIAN INVESTMENT PARTNERS LP (PA)
11 E 44th St Rm 1803 (10017-3670)
PHONE..................212 547-2806
Michael Fieldstone, Partner
Eric Dieckman, Partner
Daniel Phan, Vice Pres
Nadine Michel, Office Mgr
Isaac Chalal, Associate
EMP: 22
SALES (est): 137.5MM Privately Held
SIC: 3398 Metal heat treating

(G-9300)
ATERRA EXPLORATION LLC
230 W 56th St Apt 53d (10019-0077)
PHONE..................212 315-0030
David G Sepiashvili, President
▲ EMP: 20
SALES (est): 671K Privately Held
SIC: 1382 Oil & gas exploration services

(G-9301)
ATHALON SPORTGEAR INC
10 W 33rd St Rm 1012 (10001-3317)
PHONE..................212 268-8070
Andrew Nitkin, Ch of Bd
Robert Goldener, President
Marisol Orellana, Opers Staff
Justin Maged, Marketing Staff
Brian E Sullen, Manager
▲ EMP: 7
SALES (est): 600K Privately Held
WEB: www.athalonskyvalet.com
SIC: 3949 Bags, golf

(G-9302)
ATHLON SPT COMMUNICATIONS INC
60 E 42nd St Ste 820 (10165-0820)
PHONE..................212 478-1910
EMP: 28
SALES (corp-wide): 32.5MM Privately Held
SIC: 2721 Periodicals: publishing only
PA: Athlon Sports Communications, Inc.
2451 Atrium Way Ste 320
Nashville TN 37214
615 327-0747

(G-9303)
ATLANTIC MONTHLY GROUP INC
Also Called: Atlantic, The
60 Madison Ave (10010-1600)
PHONE..................202 266-7000
Katie Storrs, Principal
Lee Mayer, Facilities Dir
Hadley Haut, Associate Dir
Michael Proffitt, Associate Dir
Colin Manning, Admin Asst
EMP: 25
SALES (corp-wide): 11.6MM Privately Held
WEB: www.theatlantic.com
SIC: 2721 Magazines: publishing only, not printed on site
PA: The Atlantic Monthly Group Inc
600 New Hampshire Ave Nw # 4
Washington DC 20037
202 266-7000

(G-9304)
ATLANTIC RECORDING CORP (DH)
Also Called: Atlantic Records
1633 Broadway Lower 2c1 (10019-6708)
PHONE..................212 707-2000
Fax: 212 956-7232
Craig Kauman, Ch of Bd
Ahmet M Ertegun, Ch of Bd
Julie Geenwald, President
Greg Kallman, President
David Saslow, General Mgr
EMP: 325 EST: 1967
SQ FT: 133,000
SALES (est): 97.6MM Privately Held
WEB: www.ledzep.com
SIC: 3652 Compact laser discs, prerecorded; master records or tapes, preparation of; phonograph record blanks
HQ: Warner Music Group Corp.
1633 Broadway
New York NY 10019
212 275-2000

(G-9305)
ATLANTIC TROPHY CO INC
866 Avenue Of The America (10001-4168)
PHONE..................212 684-6020
Fax: 212 689-2665
Arthur Schneider, President
EMP: 6
SQ FT: 1,000
SALES (est): 758.9K Privately Held
SIC: 3914 Trophies, silver; trophies, nickel silver; trophies, pewter; trophies, plated (all metals)

(G-9306)
ATLAS & COMPANY LLC
355 Lexington Ave Fl 6 (10017-6603)
PHONE..................212 234-3100
Fax: 212 888-3650
James Atlas, President
David Barker, Manager
Peter Desrochers, Manager
Ulla Schnell, Director
EMP: 6
SALES (est): 500K Privately Held
SIC: 2731 Book publishing

(G-9307)
ATLAS MUSIC PUBLISHING LLC (PA)
6 E 39th St Ste 1104 (10016-0116)
PHONE..................646 502-5170
Richard Stumpf, CEO
Jennifer Blakeman, Creative Dir
Jennifer Blakenan, Post Master
EMP: 7
SQ FT: 3,000
SALES (est): 860.2K Privately Held
SIC: 2741 Music books: publishing & printing; music, sheet: publishing only, not printed on site

(G-9308)
ATLAS PRINT SOLUTIONS INC
589 8th Ave Fl 4 (10018-3092)
PHONE..................212 949-8775
Kathleen Tan, Finance
Fran Lupo, Accounts Exec
Gregg Morgan, Accounts Exec
Allison Philips, CTO
Ken Rosenberg, Creative Dir
EMP: 23
SALES (est): 3.6MM Privately Held
SIC: 2752 Commercial printing, lithographic

(G-9309)
ATLAS RECYCLING LLC
Also Called: Pep Realty
25 Howard St Fl 2 (10013-3164)
PHONE..................212 925-3280
John Pasquale, CEO
J Pasqual, General Mgr
EMP: 5
SALES (est): 495.9K Privately Held
SIC: 2621 Paper mills

(G-9310)
ATR JEWELRY INC
71 W 47th St Ste 402 (10036-2819)
PHONE..................212 819-0075
Fax: 212 819-0045
Aron Aranbaev, President
EMP: 10
SALES (est): 1.1MM Privately Held
WEB: www.atrjewelry.com
SIC: 3911 5944 Jewelry, precious metal; jewelry, precious stones & precious metals

(G-9311)
ATTENDS HEALTHCARE INC
200 Park Ave (10166-0005)
PHONE..................212 338-5100
Michael Fagan, CEO
Sara Weintraub, Assistant
EMP: 651
SALES (est): 29.7MM
SALES (corp-wide): 5.1B Privately Held
SIC: 2676 Sanitary paper products
PA: Domtar Corporation
395 Boul De Maisonneuve O Bureau 200
Montreal QC H3A 1
514 848-5555

(G-9312)
ATTITUDES FOOTWEAR INC
1040 1st Ave Ste 232 (10022-2991)
PHONE..................212 754-9113
Paul Mayer, President
Jeff Levy, Vice Pres
EMP: 3
SALES (est): 2MM Privately Held
SIC: 3144 Dress shoes, women's

(G-9313)
ATYPON SYSTEMS INC
330 7th Ave Fl 5 (10001-5443)
PHONE..................212 524-7060
Audrey Melkin, Branch Mgr
Dan Villa, Program Mgr
Haig Melkin, Manager
Dem Pilafian, Manager
Firas Haddad, Sr Software Eng

▲ = Import ▼=Export
◆ =Import/Export

EMP: 16 Privately Held
SIC: 2741 Miscellaneous publishing
PA: Atypon Systems, Llc
   5201 Great America Pkwy # 510
   Santa Clara CA 95054

(G-9314)
AUGURY INC
110 5th Ave Fl 5 (10011-5647)
PHONE..................................347 699-5011
Saar Yoskovitz, *CEO*
Gal Shaul, *CTO*
EMP: 11
SALES (est): 423.6K Privately Held
SIC: 7372 Business oriented computer software

(G-9315)
AUGUST SILK INC (PA)
499 7th Ave Fl 5s (10018-6868)
PHONE..................................212 643-2400
Benedict Chen, *Ch of Bd*
Fritz Penwell, *President*
May Lau, *Engineer*
Lauren Korolowicz, *Design Engr*
Ron Petraglia, *Credit Staff*
▲ EMP: 23
SQ FT: 83,000
SALES: 30MM Privately Held
SIC: 2321 2331 2335 2392 Men's & boys' furnishings; women's & misses' blouses & shirts; women's, juniors' & misses' dresses; household furnishings

(G-9316)
AUGUST SILK INC
H F G Design
499 7th Ave Fl 5s (10018-6868)
PHONE..................................212 643-2400
Fritz Penwell, *President*
EMP: 7
SALES (corp-wide): 30MM Privately Held
SIC: 2321 2331 2335 2392 Men's & boys' furnishings; women's & misses' blouses & shirts; women's, juniors' & misses' dresses; household furnishings
PA: August Silk Inc.
   499 7th Ave Fl 5s
   New York NY 10018
   212 643-2400

(G-9317)
AURA INTERNATIONAL MFG INC
512 Fashion Ave Fl 26 (10018-0804)
PHONE..................................212 719-1418
Seth Baum, *President*
Anthony Wong, *Managing Dir*
Bob Diamond, *Vice Pres*
Frances Israel, *Admin Sec*
EMP: 5
SALES (est): 770K Privately Held
SIC: 2339 Women's & misses' outerwear

(G-9318)
AURATIC INC
41 Madison Ave Ste 1402 (10010-2245)
PHONE..................................914 413-8154
Lewis Wong, *President*
▲ EMP: 6
SALES (est): 380.7K Privately Held
SIC: 2541 Counter & sink tops

(G-9319)
AUSTIN NICHOLS & CO INC (DH)
Also Called: Wild Turkey
250 Park Ave (10177-0001)
PHONE..................................519 561-5225
Paul Duffy, *CEO*
EMP: 19
SALES (est): 5.1MM Privately Held
SIC: 2086 2085 5182 2084 Soft drinks: packaged in cans, bottles, etc.; distilled & blended liquors; liquor; wines, brandy & brandy spirits
HQ: Campari America Llc
   1255 Battery St Ste 500
   San Francisco CA 94111
   415 315-8000

(G-9320)
AUTOMOTIVE ACCESSORIES GROUP
505 8th Ave Rm 12a05 (10018-6581)
PHONE..................................212 736-8100
Allan J Marrus, *President*

Stephen Delman, *Admin Sec*
EMP: 300
SALES (est): 17.9MM Privately Held
SIC: 3714 Motor vehicle parts & accessories; steering mechanisms, motor vehicle

(G-9321)
AUVEN THERAPEUTICS MGT LP
1325 Ave Of The Amrcas (10019-6026)
PHONE..................................212 616-4000
Peter B Corr, *General Ptnr*
Stephen Evans-Freke, *General Ptnr*
Tara Roulhac, *Assistant*
EMP: 10
SALES (est): 1.6MM Privately Held
SIC: 2834 Pharmaceutical preparations

(G-9322)
AV DENIM INC
230 W 38th St Fl 8r (10018-9056)
PHONE..................................212 764-6668
David Kubresi, *Ch of Bd*
▲ EMP: 30
SALES (est): 3.9MM Privately Held
SIC: 2211 Denims

(G-9323)
AV THERAPEUTICS INC
Also Called: A V T
20 E 68th St Ste 204 (10065-5836)
PHONE..................................917 497-5523
Robert Pollock, *President*
EMP: 25 EST: 2007
SALES (est): 2MM Privately Held
SIC: 2836 Vaccines

(G-9324)
AVALANCHE STUDIOS NEW YORK INC
536 Broadway (10012-3915)
PHONE..................................212 993-6447
David Grijns, *Ch of Bd*
EMP: 60
SALES (est): 4.8MM
SALES (corp-wide): 32.6MM Privately Held
SIC: 7372 Home entertainment computer software
HQ: Fatalist Holdings Ab

   Stockholm 100 6
   844 276-70

(G-9325)
AVALIN LLC
221 W 37th St Fl 3 (10018-5782)
PHONE..................................212 842-2286
Fax: 212 997-0022
Zoheir Aghravi, *President*
Matt Cohen, *Vice Pres*
Dawn Smith, *Sales Mgr*
▲ EMP: 14
SQ FT: 10,000
SALES (est): 1.6MM Privately Held
WEB: www.avalinknits.com
SIC: 2339 Women's & misses' athletic clothing & sportswear

(G-9326)
AVANTI PRESS INC
6 W 18th St Ste 6l (10011-4630)
PHONE..................................212 414-1025
Frederic Ruffner III, *Branch Mgr*
Jaisi Surowiec, *Manager*
EMP: 25
SALES (corp-wide): 14.2MM Privately Held
SIC: 2771 Greeting cards
PA: Avanti Press, Inc.
   155 W Congress St Ste 200
   Detroit MI 48226
   800 228-5684

(G-9327)
AVAYA SERVICES INC
2 Penn Plz Rm 702 (10121-1000)
PHONE..................................866 462-8292
EMP: 6
SALES (est): 426.3K
SALES (corp-wide): 4B Privately Held
SIC: 3661 Telephones & telephone apparatus

PA: Avaya Inc.
   4655 Great America Pkwy
   Santa Clara CA 95054
   908 953-6000

(G-9328)
AVENUE THERAPEUTICS INC
2 Gansevoort St Fl 9 (10014-1667)
PHONE..................................781 652-4500
Lindsay A Rosenwald, *Ch of Bd*
Lucy Lu, *President*
Joseph Vazzano, *Vice Pres*
David Horin, *CFO*
Scott A Reines, *Chief Mktg Ofcr*
EMP: 4
SALES (est): 3.6MM Publicly Held
SIC: 2834 Pharmaceutical preparations
PA: Fortress Biotech, Inc.
   3 Columbus Cir Fl 15
   New York NY 10019

(G-9329)
AVERY DENNISON CORPORATION
218 W 40th St Fl 8 (10018-1758)
PHONE..................................626 304-2000
Peter Gunshon, *Manager*
EMP: 115
SALES (corp-wide): 6B Publicly Held
SIC: 2672 Adhesive backed films, foams & foils
PA: Avery Dennison Corporation
   207 N Goode Ave Fl 6
   Glendale CA 91203
   626 304-2000

(G-9330)
AVI-SPL EMPLOYEE
8 W 38th St Rm 1101 (10018-6244)
PHONE..................................212 840-4801
EMP: 350
SALES (corp-wide): 596.9MM Privately Held
SIC: 3669 3861 3663 3651 Mfg Communications Equip Mfg Photo Equip/Supplies Mfg Radio/Tv Comm Equip Mfg Home Audio/Video Eqp Whol Photo Equip/Supply
HQ: Avi-Spl Employee Emergency Relief Fund, Inc.
   6301 Benjamin Rd Ste 101
   Tampa FL 33634
   813 884-7168

(G-9331)
AVID TECHNOLOGY INC
90 Park Ave (10016-1301)
PHONE..................................212 983-2424
Fax: 212 983-9770
Kevin Johnstone, *Sales Dir*
Adam Taylor, *Branch Mgr*
EMP: 22
SALES (corp-wide): 511.9MM Publicly Held
WEB: www.avid.com
SIC: 3861 Editing equipment, motion picture: viewers, splicers, etc.
PA: Avid Technology, Inc.
   75 Network Dr
   Burlington MA 01803
   978 640-6789

(G-9332)
AVITTO LEATHER GOODS INC
424 W Broadway Frnt A (10012-3796)
PHONE..................................212 219-7501
AVI Sharifi, *President*
EMP: 7
SALES (est): 560K Privately Held
SIC: 2211 Shoe fabrics

(G-9333)
AVOCODE INC
55 E 73rd St Apt Gf (10021-3555)
PHONE..................................646 934-8410
Tomas Hadl, *President*
EMP: 2
SALES: 500K Privately Held
SIC: 7372 Publishers' computer software

(G-9334)
AVS GEM STONE CORP
48 W 48th St Ste 1010 (10036-1713)
PHONE..................................212 944-6380
Antonio Santos, *President*
EMP: 5

SALES (est): 305.5K Privately Held
SIC: 1499 Gemstone & industrial diamond mining

(G-9335)
AWARD PUBLISHING LIMITED
40 W 55th St Apt 9b (10019-5376)
PHONE..................................212 246-0405
Iris Dodge, *Principal*
EMP: 9
SALES (est): 615.2K Privately Held
SIC: 2741 Miscellaneous publishing

(G-9336)
AXIM BIOTECHNOLOGIES INC
5 Rockefeller Plz Fl 20 (10111)
PHONE..................................212 751-0001
George E Anastassov, *Ch of Bd*
Robert Malasek, *CFO*
Philip A Van Damme, *Chief Mktg Ofcr*
Lekhram Changoer, *CTO*
EMP: 10 EST: 2010
SALES: 47K Privately Held
SIC: 2834 Pharmaceutical preparations

(G-9337)
AXIS NA LLC (PA)
Also Called: Axis Denim
70 W 40th St Fl 11 (10018-2619)
PHONE..................................212 840-4005
Shirley Zheng, *Accountant*
Ling Kwok,
Leigh Martin,
▲ EMP: 10
SALES (est): 1.2MM Privately Held
SIC: 2211 Denims

(G-9338)
AZ YASHIR BAPAZ INC
Also Called: A Yashir Bapa
134 W 37th St (10018-6911)
PHONE..................................212 947-7357
Rasael Yaghoubian, *President*
EMP: 5
SALES (est): 630K Privately Held
SIC: 2339 Sportswear, women's

(G-9339)
AZIBI LTD
Also Called: Luna Luz
270 W 39th St Rm 1501 (10018-4415)
PHONE..................................212 869-6550
Michael Samuels, *President*
Dennis Tilden, *Vice Pres*
Twana Green, *Manager*
EMP: 10
SQ FT: 8,000
SALES (est): 1MM Privately Held
WEB: www.azibi.com
SIC: 3949 Sporting & athletic goods

(G-9340)
B & F ARCHITECTURAL SUPPORT GR
Also Called: Advance Construction Group
450 7th Ave Ste 307 (10123-0307)
PHONE..................................212 279-6488
Stewart Ratzker, *President*
EMP: 30
SALES (est): 2MM Privately Held
SIC: 2851 8712 Paints & allied products; architectural services

(G-9341)
B & R PROMOTIONAL PRODUCTS
Also Called: Beal Blocks
34 W 120th St Apt 1 (10027-6478)
PHONE..................................212 563-0040
Fax: 212 465-1253
Gary Bimblick, *President*
Miriam Del Valle, *Admin Sec*
EMP: 6 EST: 1963
SQ FT: 5,000
SALES (est): 743.4K Privately Held
SIC: 3299 3999 Plaques: clay, plaster or papier mache; plaques, picture, laminated; badges, metal: policemen, firemen, etc.

(G-9342)
B K JEWELRY CONTRACTOR INC
71 W 47th St Fl 11 (10036-2819)
PHONE..................................212 398-9093

New York - New York County (G-9343)   **GEOGRAPHIC SECTION**

Fax: 212 768-1834
Jacob Solomon, *President*
Rachel Solomon, *Admin Sec*
EMP: 20
SQ FT: 5,000
SALES: 1MM **Privately Held**
SIC: 3911 Jewelry, precious metal

(G-9343)
B LIVE LLC
347 W 36th St Rm 402 (10018-7252)
PHONE.................................212 489-0721
Bill Marpet, *Managing Prtnr*
Todd Galloway, *Partner*
Russell Quy, *Partner*
Matthew Walsh, *Partner*
EMP: 9
SALES: 1.9MM **Privately Held**
SIC: 3823 Digital displays of process variables

(G-9344)
B S J LIMITED
1400 Broadway Ste 1702 (10018-5300)
PHONE.................................212 764-4600
Fax: 212 764-9340
Shari Levine, *Owner*
EMP: 24
SQ FT: 10,000 **Privately Held**
SIC: 2335 Bridal & formal gowns
PA: B S J Limited
    1375 Broadway Rm 507
    New York NY 10018

(G-9345)
B S J LIMITED (PA)
1375 Broadway Rm 507 (10018-7197)
PHONE.................................212 221-8403
Fax: 212 354-9454
Shari Levine, *Ch of Bd*
Mike Mann, *President*
Rhea Batterman, *Controller*
▲ EMP: 6
SALES (est): 5.1MM **Privately Held**
SIC: 2335 Bridal & formal gowns

(G-9346)
B SMITH FURS INC
224 W 30th St Rm 402 (10001-0406)
PHONE.................................212 967-5290
Fax: 212 736-2426
Gary Smith, *President*
Michael Hennessey, *Vice Pres*
Hennessey International, *Shareholder*
EMP: 10
SQ FT: 4,000
SALES (est): 980K **Privately Held**
SIC: 2371 Fur goods

(G-9347)
B TWEEN LLC
Also Called: Btween US
1411 Broadway Rm 2520 (10018-3468)
PHONE.................................212 819-9040
Robert Terzi, *President*
Jack Terzi, *Vice Pres*
Rochelle Terzi, *Vice Pres*
▲ EMP: 12
SQ FT: 3,000
SALES (est): 1.2MM **Privately Held**
SIC: 2339 Women's & misses' athletic clothing & sportswear

(G-9348)
B-REEL FILMS INC
401 Broadway Fl 24 (10013-3007)
PHONE.................................917 388-3836
Anders Wahlquist, *President*
Andy Williams, *General Mgr*
Cecilia Bernard, *Managing Dir*
Alistair Campbell, *Managing Dir*
Margo Mars, *Managing Dir*
EMP: 24
SALES (est): 5.2MM **Privately Held**
SIC: 3571 Computers, digital, analog or hybrid

(G-9349)
B-SQUARED INC
104 W 29th St Fl 7 (10001-5310)
PHONE.................................212 777-2044
Fax: 212 777-4655
Tim Boucher, *President*
Steve Milillo, *Vice Pres*
Micheal Scully, *Controller*
Kaitlin Gallucci, *Mktg Dir*

Megam Smith-Baltez, *Director*
EMP: 29
SQ FT: 10,000
SALES (est): 5MM **Privately Held**
SIC: 2732 Book printing

(G-9350)
B601 V2 INC
315 5th Ave Rm 903 (10016-6588)
PHONE.................................646 391-6431
Steven Cohn, *CEO*
EMP: 5
SALES (est): 117.2K **Privately Held**
SIC: 7372 Business oriented computer software

(G-9351)
BABY SIGNATURE INC (PA)
Also Called: Dainty Home
251 5th Ave Fl 2l (10016-6515)
PHONE.................................212 686-1700
Hassib Baghdadi, *President*
Merlin Quantam, *Opers Staff*
◆ EMP: 1
SQ FT: 5,000
SALES (est): 5MM **Privately Held**
SIC: 2391 2392 5023 Curtains & draperies; placemats, plastic or textile; shower curtains: made from purchased materials; curtains

(G-9352)
BABYFAIR INC
Also Called: Diversify Apparel
34 W 33rd St Rm 818 (10001-3304)
PHONE.................................212 736-7989
Fax: 212 438-0127
Maurice Shamah, *Ch of Bd*
Ralph Shamah, *Vice Pres*
Jeff Tammam, *Sales Staff*
Edward Riggio, *Manager*
▲ EMP: 35 EST: 1944
SQ FT: 8,000
SALES (est): 4.6MM **Privately Held**
WEB: www.babyfair.com
SIC: 2369 Play suits: girls', children's & infants'; rompers: infants'

(G-9353)
BACKTECH INC
2 Peter Cooper Rd Apt Mf (10010-6733)
PHONE.................................973 279-0838
Eier Rystedt, *President*
EMP: 2
SALES: 1MM **Privately Held**
SIC: 3842 Surgical appliances & supplies

(G-9354)
BADGLEY MISCHKA LICENSING LLC
Also Called: Jsc Design
550 7th Ave Fl 22 (10018-3223)
PHONE.................................212 921-1585
Fax: 212 921-4171
Kim Siu, *Exec VP*
Gail Pashka, *Office Mgr*
Neil Cole, *Mng Member*
Sonjia Winley, *Manager*
James Mischka,
EMP: 29
SQ FT: 3,000
SALES (est): 2.1MM **Privately Held**
WEB: www.badgleymischka.com
SIC: 2326 Men's & boys' work clothing

(G-9355)
BAG ARTS LTD
20 W 36th St Rm 5r (10018-9790)
PHONE.................................212 684-7020
Steve Zagha, *President*
Isaac Cohen, *Vice Pres*
▲ EMP: 7
SQ FT: 7,000
SALES (est): 896.6K **Privately Held**
WEB: www.bagarts.com
SIC: 3053 Packing materials

(G-9356)
BAG ARTS THE ART PACKAGING LLC
20 W 36th St Fl 5 (10018-8005)
PHONE.................................212 684-7020
Steve Zagha, *President*
▲ EMP: 6
SQ FT: 7,000

SALES (est): 548.4K **Privately Held**
SIC: 2673 2674 Food storage & trash bags (plastic); grocers' bags: made from purchased materials

(G-9357)
BAG BAZAAR LTD
Metro Accessories
1 E 33rd St Fl 6 (10016-5099)
PHONE.................................212 689-3508
Joey Shames, *Branch Mgr*
EMP: 25
SALES (corp-wide): 47.9MM **Privately Held**
WEB: www.aeny.com
SIC: 2339 Women's & misses' accessories
PA: Bag Bazaar Ltd.
    1 E 33rd St Fl 6
    New York NY 10016
    212 689-3508

(G-9358)
BAGZNYC CORP
Also Called: Kids
19 W 34th St Rm 318 (10001-0055)
PHONE.................................212 643-8202
Jeff Goldstein, *President*
Larry Zakarin, *Vice Pres*
▲ EMP: 18
SQ FT: 5,300
SALES (est): 1.4MM **Privately Held**
SIC: 2339 3171 Women's & misses' outerwear; women's handbags & purses

(G-9359)
BAIKAL INC (PA)
341 W 38th St Fl 3 (10018-9694)
PHONE.................................212 239-4650
Fax: 212 239-4679
Josef Itskovich, *President*
▲ EMP: 70
SQ FT: 5,000
SALES (est): 5MM **Privately Held**
WEB: www.baikal.com
SIC: 3171 Handbags, women's

(G-9360)
BAINBRIDGE & KNIGHT LLC
801 2nd Ave Fl 19 (10017-8618)
PHONE.................................212 986-5100
Carl Ruderman, *President*
Dan Gibson, *Opers Staff*
Mark Horowitz, *VP Sales*
Alla Kaplan, *Sales Mgr*
David Bernstein, *Accounts Mgr*
EMP: 50
SQ FT: 12,000
SALES (est): 5.2MM **Privately Held**
SIC: 2099 Food preparations

(G-9361)
BALAJEE ENTERPRISES INC
Also Called: Digitech Printers
150 W 30th St Frnt 2 (10001-4161)
PHONE.................................212 629-6150
Fax: 212 629-6160
Shul Khalfan, *President*
EMP: 8
SQ FT: 2,500
SALES (est): 1MM **Privately Held**
WEB: www.digitechprinters.com
SIC: 2759 Commercial printing

(G-9362)
BALANCED TECH CORP
Also Called: New Balance Underwear
37 W 37th St Fl 10 (10018-6354)
PHONE.................................212 768-8330
Ezra Jack Cattan, *Ch of Bd*
Judah Cattan, *President*
▲ EMP: 20
SALES (est): 1.2MM **Privately Held**
WEB: www.newbalanceunderwear.com
SIC: 2254 Underwear, knit

(G-9363)
BALTICARE INC (PA)
501 Fashion Ave Rm 414 (10018-8608)
PHONE.................................646 380-9470
Monika Chodkiewicz, *Sales Engr*
Al Rivera, *Sales Engr*
Edward Villela, *Manager*
EMP: 10 EST: 2007
SALES (est): 2.4MM **Privately Held**
SIC: 3585 Air conditioning units, complete: domestic or industrial

(G-9364)
BAM SALES LLC (PA)
1407 Broadway Rm 2018 (10018-2863)
PHONE.................................212 781-3000
Marc Moyal,
Alan Cohen,
Scott Danziger,
Nicole Hausman,
Robert Klein,
EMP: 3
SALES (est): 1.2MM **Privately Held**
SIC: 2339 Women's & misses' athletic clothing & sportswear

(G-9365)
BAMBOO GLOBAL INDUSTRIES
339 E 58th St Apt 7e (10022-2268)
PHONE.................................973 943-1878
Matthew Renov, *Principal*
EMP: 5
SALES (est): 347.7K **Privately Held**
SIC: 2869 Industrial organic chemicals

(G-9366)
BANDIER CORP
960 Park Ave Apt 11b (10028-0325)
PHONE.................................212 242-5400
Jeff Peterson, *President*
EMP: 8 EST: 2013
SALES (est): 1.5MM **Privately Held**
SIC: 2211 5661 2339 Apparel & outerwear fabrics, cotton; shoes, custom; women's & misses' athletic clothing & sportswear

(G-9367)
BARBARA MATERA LTD
890 Broadway Fl 5 (10003-1211)
PHONE.................................212 475-5006
Fax: 212 254-4550
Jared Aswegan, *President*
Larry Feinman, *CFO*
EMP: 100 EST: 1967
SQ FT: 8,500
SALES (est): 5.5MM **Privately Held**
SIC: 2389 Theatrical costumes

(G-9368)
BARBER BROTHERS JEWELRY MFG
Also Called: B & B Jewelry Mfg Co
580 5th Ave Ste 725 (10036-4724)
PHONE.................................212 819-0666
Fax: 212 768-8735
Abraham Barber, *President*
Simon Barber, *Vice Pres*
Ebba Bai, *Manager*
EMP: 15 EST: 1963
SQ FT: 2,200
SALES (est): 1.5MM **Privately Held**
SIC: 3911 Jewelry, precious metal

(G-9369)
BARDWIL INDUSTRIES INC (PA)
Also Called: Bardwil Linens
1071 Ave Of The Americas (10018-3777)
PHONE.................................212 944-1870
Fax: 212 869-3599
George Bardwil, *Ch of Bd*
Robert Paglieri, *Controller*
▲ EMP: 30 EST: 1906
SQ FT: 12,000
SALES (est): 27.8MM **Privately Held**
WEB: www.beyondmarketing.com
SIC: 2392 2241 Napkins, fabric & nonwoven: made from purchased materials; placemats, plastic or textile; tablecloths: made from purchased materials; chair covers & pads: made from purchased materials; trimmings, textile

(G-9370)
BARE BEAUTY LASER HAIR REMOVAL
5 E 57th St Fl 6 (10022-2553)
PHONE.................................718 278-2273
Debbie Patadopoulas, *Owner*
EMP: 6
SALES (est): 71.5K **Privately Held**
SIC: 3699 Laser systems & equipment

▲ = Import ▼ = Export
◆ = Import/Export

GEOGRAPHIC SECTION

New York - New York County (G-9396)

(G-9371)
BARE ESCENTUALS INC
Also Called: Bare Minerals
1140 3rd Ave (10065-6116)
PHONE..................646 537-0070
Fax: 646 537-0072
Lavette Tursi, *Sales Staff*
Melissa Colom, *Manager*
EMP: 7
SALES (corp-wide): 7.6B **Privately Held**
SIC: 2844 5122 Toilet preparations; toilet preparations
HQ: Bare Escentuals, Inc.
71 Stevenson St Fl 22
San Francisco CA 94105
415 489-5000

(G-9372)
BARI ENGINEERING CORP
240 Bowery (10012-3501)
PHONE..................212 966-2080
Frank Bari, *President*
EMP: 24
SQ FT: 51,000
SALES (est): 2.9MM **Privately Held**
WEB: www.bariequipment.com
SIC: 3556 5046 Food products machinery; restaurant equipment & supplies

(G-9373)
BARI-JAY FASHIONS INC (PA)
225 W 37th St Fl 7 (10018-5729)
PHONE..................212 921-1551
Fax: 212 391-0165
Bruce Cohen, *President*
EMP: 20
SQ FT: 20,000
SALES (est): 5.6MM **Privately Held**
WEB: www.barijay.com
SIC: 2335 Gowns, formal; wedding gowns & dresses

(G-9374)
BAROKA CREATIONS INC
36 W 47th St Ste 1402 (10036-8601)
P.O. Box 290744, Brooklyn (11229-0744)
PHONE..................212 768-0527
Rami Bareket, *President*
Nftali Rockah, *Vice Pres*
Sheri Baroka, *Admin Sec*
EMP: 7
SQ FT: 11,000
SALES (est): 4MM **Privately Held**
WEB: www.baroka.com
SIC: 3911 3915 Jewelry, precious metal; diamond cutting & polishing

(G-9375)
BARRAGE
401 W 47th St Frnt A (10036-2306)
PHONE..................212 586-9390
Tom Johnson, *Owner*
EMP: 20
SALES (est): 2MM **Privately Held**
WEB: www.barrage.com
SIC: 3639 Major kitchen appliances, except refrigerators & stoves

(G-9376)
BARRERA JOSE & MARIA CO LTD
29 W 36th St Fl 8 (10018-7668)
PHONE..................212 239-1994
Fax: 212 302-8480
Jose Barrera, *Owner*
Maria Barrera, *Co-Owner*
EMP: 28
SQ FT: 3,000
SALES (est): 1.7MM **Privately Held**
SIC: 2387 3961 Apparel belts; costume jewelry, ex. precious metal & semi-precious stones

(G-9377)
BARRY INDUSTRIES INC
Also Called: Barry Supply Co Div
36 W 17th St Frnt 1 (10011-5731)
PHONE..................212 242-5200
Barry Weinberger, *President*
William Wein, *Manager*
EMP: 15
SQ FT: 4,000
SALES (est): 1.1MM **Privately Held**
SIC: 3429 5072 Manufactured hardware (general); hardware

(G-9378)
BARTHOLOMEW MAZZA LTD INC
22 W 48th St Ste 805 (10036-1803)
P.O. Box 231444 (10023-0025)
PHONE..................212 935-4530
Fax: 212 355-7801
Hugo Mazza, *President*
Diane Mazza, *Treasurer*
EMP: 50
SQ FT: 4,000
SALES (est): 5.5MM **Privately Held**
WEB: www.mazzabartholomew.com
SIC: 3911 Jewelry, precious metal

(G-9379)
BASF CORPORATION
545 5th Ave Fl 11 (10017-3609)
PHONE..................212 450-8280
Julianna Wilkins, *Branch Mgr*
EMP: 368
SALES (corp-wide): 60.8B **Privately Held**
WEB: www.basf.com
SIC: 2819 Industrial inorganic chemicals
HQ: Basf Corporation
100 Park Ave
Florham Park NJ 07932
973 245-6000

(G-9380)
BASIL S KADHIM
Also Called: Eton International
280 Madison Ave Rm 912 (10016-0801)
PHONE..................888 520-5192
Basil S Kadhim, *Owner*
Stephanie Kadhim, *Manager*
Julie A Seward, *Manager*
EMP: 8
SQ FT: 1,000
SALES (est): 1.1MM **Privately Held**
WEB: www.etoninternational.com
SIC: 3663 5045 7382 5047 Television broadcasting & communications equipment; computers, peripherals & software; protective devices, security; medical equipment & supplies

(G-9381)
BASILOFF LLC
179 Bennett Ave Apt 7f (10040-4059)
PHONE..................646 671-0353
Dmitri Vassiliev, *President*
EMP: 6 EST: 2014
SALES (est): 330K **Privately Held**
SIC: 2261 Sponging cotton broadwoven cloth for the trade

(G-9382)
BASIN HOLDINGS US LLC (PA)
200 Park Ave Fl 58 (10166-5899)
PHONE..................212 695-7376
John Fitzgibbons, *CEO*
EMP: 21 EST: 2011
SALES (est): 144.5MM **Privately Held**
SIC: 3533 Oil & gas field machinery

(G-9383)
BAUBLE BAR INC
1115 Broadway Fl 5 (10010-3457)
PHONE..................646 664-4803
Nina A Hurst, *Vice Pres*
Amy McDowell, *Vice Pres*
Kristen Cruz, *Production*
Aditi Sabharwal, *Purch Mgr*
James Chu, *Manager*
▲ EMP: 55
SALES (est): 14.8MM **Privately Held**
SIC: 3172 Cases, jewelry

(G-9384)
BAUSCH & LOMB HOLDINGS INC (DH)
450 Lexington Ave (10017-3904)
PHONE..................585 338-6000
Brent L Saunders, *CEO*
Gerald M Ostrov, *Ch of Bd*
EMP: 8
SALES (est): 2.5B
SALES (corp-wide): 9.6B **Privately Held**
SIC: 3851 2834 Ophthalmic goods; pharmaceutical preparations
HQ: Valeant Pharmaceuticals International Corporation
400 Somerset Corp Blvd
Bridgewater NJ 08807
908 927-1400

(G-9385)
BAZAAR
300 W 57th St Fl 25 (10019-3741)
PHONE..................212 903-5497
Linda Crowley, *Principal*
Lyle Gulley Jr, *Vice Chairman*
John Copeland, *Bd of Directors*
Diana Kaufman, *Bd of Directors*
Ronald J Sulewski, *Admin Sec*
▲ EMP: 5
SALES (est): 250.6K **Privately Held**
SIC: 2721 Magazines: publishing & printing

(G-9386)
BDG MEDIA INC (PA)
Also Called: Bustle Digital Group
158 W 27th St Fl 11 (10001-6216)
PHONE..................917 951-9768
Bryan Goldberg, *CEO*
Tricia Dellipizzi, *Vice Pres*
EMP: 22
SQ FT: 19,200
SALES (est): 39.4MM **Privately Held**
SIC: 2741

(G-9387)
BEACHBUTTONS LLC
6 Greene St Apt 4b (10013-5817)
PHONE..................917 306-9369
Stavros Tsibiridis, *Mng Member*
EMP: 5
SALES: 100K **Privately Held**
SIC: 2253 Beachwear, knit

(G-9388)
BEAR PORT PUBLISHING COMPANY
45 W 21st St 3b (10010-6865)
PHONE..................877 337-8577
Ken Goin, *President*
Katherine Camisa, *Manager*
Adam Siegel, *Director*
Joyce Tavolacci, *Senior Editor*
EMP: 11
SQ FT: 3,000
SALES: 3MM
SALES (corp-wide): 149.6MM **Privately Held**
WEB: www.bearportpublishing.com
SIC: 2731 Book publishing
PA: Woongjin Co., Ltd.
Jongro Place Bldg.
Seoul SEO 03130
220 764-701

(G-9389)
BEAUTY FASHION INC
Also Called: Astor-Honor Division
8 W 38th St Frnt 2 (10018-0133)
PHONE..................212 840-8800
Fax: 212 840-7246
John G Ledes, *Ch of Bd*
George M Ledes, *President*
Hosu Shah, *Controller*
Tyler Stafford, *Creative Dir*
Veronica Kelly, *Admin Asst*
EMP: 20
SALES (est): 1.8MM **Privately Held**
WEB: www.astorhonor.com
SIC: 2731 2721 Book publishing; magazines: publishing only, not printed on site

(G-9390)
BECCA INC
Also Called: Becca Cosmetics
142 W 36th St Fl 15 (10018-8785)
PHONE..................646 568-6250
Robert Debaker, *CEO*
Raphaelle Curien, *Director*
Katelyn Delaney, *Director*
▲ EMP: 14 EST: 2001
SALES (est): 3.4MM
SALES (corp-wide): 11.8B **Publicly Held**
SIC: 2844 Cosmetic preparations
PA: The Estee Lauder Companies Inc
767 5th Ave Fl 37
New York NY 10153
212 572-4200

(G-9391)
BEDFORD FREEMAN & WORTH (DH)
Also Called: Scientific American Library
1 New York Plz Ste 4500 (10004-1562)
PHONE..................212 576-9400
Jessica Fiorillo, *Publisher*
Elizabeth A Widdicombe, *Senior VP*
John Britch, *Sls & Mktg Exec*
Lawrence Jankovic, *CFO*
Michael Ross, *Treasurer*
EMP: 192
SQ FT: 36,000
SALES (est): 86.4MM
SALES (corp-wide): 1.5B **Privately Held**
WEB: www.bfwpub.com
SIC: 2731 2759 2732 2721 Book publishing; textbooks: publishing only, not printed on site; commercial printing; book printing; periodicals

(G-9392)
BEDFORD FREEMAN & WORTH
Also Called: Saint Martins Press
1 New York Plz Ste 4500 (10004-1562)
PHONE..................212 375-7000
Fax: 212 614-1885
Joan Feinberg, *President*
Tom Kane, *Editor*
Cathy Shin, *Project Mgr*
Raymond Maldonado, *Info Tech Dir*
Spencer Malmad, *Webmaster*
EMP: 70
SALES (corp-wide): 1.5B **Privately Held**
WEB: www.bfwpub.com
SIC: 2731 Textbooks: publishing only, not printed on site
HQ: Bedford, Freeman & Worth Publishing Group, Llc
1 New York Plz Ste 4500
New York NY 10004
212 576-9400

(G-9393)
BEDFORD COMMUNICATIONS INC
1410 Broadway Frnt 2 (10018-9302)
PHONE..................212 807-8220
Fax: 212 807-1098
Edward D Brown, *President*
Thomas J Fink, *Editor*
Jonathan Pratt, *Editor*
Lisa Brisdane, *Finance*
Kelly Immoor, *Natl Sales Mgr*
EMP: 30
SALES (est): 3.9MM **Privately Held**
WEB: www.bedfordcommunications.com
SIC: 2721 Magazines: publishing only, not printed on site

(G-9394)
BEDROCK COMMUNICATIONS
Also Called: Facilities
152 Madison Ave Rm 802 (10016-5476)
PHONE..................212 532-4150
Fax: 212 213-6382
Susan Wexner, *President*
Michael Casffin, *Vice Pres*
EMP: 5
SQ FT: 3,500
SALES (est): 479.4K **Privately Held**
WEB: www.facilitiesonline.com
SIC: 2731 Book publishing

(G-9395)
BEILA GROUP INC
Also Called: City Hats
285 Mott St (10012-3430)
PHONE..................212 260-1948
Alexandra Tiouleneva, *CEO*
EMP: 12
SALES (est): 1MM **Privately Held**
SIC: 3942 Hats, doll

(G-9396)
BEL AMERICAS INC
122 E 42nd St Rm 2715 (10168-2700)
PHONE..................646 454-8220
Eric Deponcis, *President*
Ingrid Gonzalez, *Manager*
EMP: 5
SALES (est): 196.8K
SALES (corp-wide): 8MM **Privately Held**
SIC: 2099 Tea blending

New York - New York County (G-9397)

HQ: Bel Brands Usa, Inc.
30 S Wacker Dr Ste 3000
Chicago IL 60606
312 462-1500

(G-9397)
BELLARNO INTERNATIONAL LTD
1140 Ave Of The Americas (10036-5803)
PHONE..................212 302-4107
Fax: 212 302-5896
Donald Fishoff, *President*
EMP: 8
SALES (est): 494.5K
SALES (corp-wide): 20.2MM **Privately Held**
SIC: 2844 Toilet preparations
PA: Inter-Ocean Industries Llc
1208 Avenue M
Brooklyn NY 11280
718 375-2532

(G-9398)
BELLATAIRE DIAMONDS INC
19 W 44th St Fl 15 (10036-6101)
PHONE..................212 687-8881
Fax: 212 687-8448
Bill Moryto, *CFO*
Charles A Meyer, *Exec Dir*
EMP: 10
SALES (est): 840K **Privately Held**
WEB: www.bellatairediamonds.com
SIC: 3911 Jewelry, precious metal

(G-9399)
BELLEROPHON PUBLICATIONS INC
Also Called: Metropolis Magazine
205 Lexington Ave Fl 17 (10016-6022)
PHONE..................212 627-9977
Horace Havemeyer III, *President*
Tamara Stout, *General Mgr*
Mikki Brammer, *Editor*
Soohang Lee, *Editor*
Paul Makovsky, *Vice Pres*
EMP: 35
SQ FT: 4,000
SALES (est): 5.1MM **Privately Held**
WEB: www.metropolismag.com
SIC: 2721 Magazines: publishing only, not printed on site

(G-9400)
BELUGA INC (PA)
Also Called: Adjmi Apparel Group
463 7th Ave Fl 4 (10018-8725)
PHONE..................212 594-5511
Eric Adjmi, *Ch of Bd*
Mark Adjmi, *Vice Pres*
Gerard Agoglia, *CFO*
Gerry Agoglia, *Controller*
Jessica Fuller, *Human Resources*
▲ EMP: 40
SQ FT: 15,000
SALES (est): 7.4MM **Privately Held**
WEB: www.beluga.com
SIC: 2329 Men's & boys' sportswear & athletic clothing

(G-9401)
BEN WACHTER ASSOCIATES INC (PA)
Also Called: B W A
36 W 44th St Ste 700 (10036-8105)
PHONE..................212 736-4064
Fax: 212 764-5535
Andrew Lerner, *CEO*
Hilda McDuff, *President*
Nuno Lacerda, *Managing Dir*
Mauricio Caballero, *VP Mfg*
Carlos Mojich, *Controller*
▲ EMP: 8
SALES (est): 2.3MM **Privately Held**
SIC: 2331 5199 2321 Women's & misses' blouses & shirts; fabrics, yarns & knit goods; cotton yarns; men's & boys' furnishings

(G-9402)
BEN-AMUN CO INC (PA)
246 W 38th St Fl 12a (10018-5845)
PHONE..................212 944-6480
Fax: 212 944-9625
Isaac Manevitz, *President*
Regina Manevitz, *Vice Pres*
Marina Bolotovsky, *Sales Executive*
Alissa Kirk, *Sales Executive*
Lauren Lustica, *Sales Executive*
▼ EMP: 22 EST: 1977
SQ FT: 10,000
SALES (est): 3.5MM **Privately Held**
WEB: www.ben-amun.com
SIC: 3961 Costume jewelry, ex. precious metal & semiprecious stones

(G-9403)
BEN-SAK TEXTILE INC
Also Called: Bensak
307 W 38th St Frnt 9 (10018-9501)
PHONE..................212 279-5122
Benhour Ahdout, *CEO*
David Ahdout, *Vice Pres*
Ned Saki, *CFO*
Alka Cricahi, *Manager*
EMP: 7
SQ FT: 550
SALES (est): 960K **Privately Held**
WEB: www.getinkjet.com
SIC: 2269 Finishing plants

(G-9404)
BENARTEX INC
132 W 36th St Rm 401 (10018-8837)
PHONE..................212 840-3250
Fax: 212 921-8204
David Lochner, *President*
Jeremy Jeffries, *Sales Executive*
Susan Neill, *VP Mktg*
Janica Cantor, *Manager*
Susan Kemler, *Manager*
▲ EMP: 35
SQ FT: 7,000
SALES (est): 4.4MM **Privately Held**
WEB: www.benartex.com
SIC: 2211 Apparel & outerwear fabrics, cotton

(G-9405)
BENCHMARK GRAPHICS LTD
9 E 37th St Fl 5 (10016-2894)
PHONE..................212 683-1711
Fax: 212 889-1927
EMP: 15
SQ FT: 5,000
SALES (est): 1.8MM **Privately Held**
SIC: 2752 Lithographic Commercial Printing

(G-9406)
BENETTON TRADING USA INC (PA)
601 5th Ave Fl 4 (10017-8258)
P.O. Box 6020, Somerset NJ (08875-6020)
PHONE..................212 593-0290
ARI Hoffman, *Principal*
Diane Mravcak, *VP Finance*
◆ EMP: 7
SALES (est): 985.6K **Privately Held**
SIC: 2329 Men's & boys' sportswear & athletic clothing

(G-9407)
BENSON INDUSTRIES INC
192 Lexington Ave Rm 502 (10016-6912)
PHONE..................212 779-3230
Robyn Ryan, *Project Mgr*
John Frank, *Manager*
Julissa Maldonado, *Admin Asst*
EMP: 10
SALES (corp-wide): 223.6B **Publicly Held**
SIC: 3231 1793 5031 Products of purchased glass; glass & glazing work; lumber, plywood & millwork
HQ: Benson Industries, Inc.
1650 Nw Naito Pkwy # 250
Portland OR 97209
503 226-7611

(G-9408)
BENTLEY MANUFACTURING INC (PA)
10 W 33rd St Rm 220 (10001-3306)
PHONE..................212 714-1800
Victor Braha, *President*
Ralph Braha, *CFO*
Annett Metir, *Manager*
Eli Braha, *Admin Sec*
◆ EMP: 7
SQ FT: 5,200

SALES (est): 2MM **Privately Held**
SIC: 2676 Diapers, paper (disposable): made from purchased paper; napkins, sanitary: made from purchased paper

(G-9409)
BEOWAWE BINARY LLC
1095 Avenue Of The Ave (10036)
PHONE..................646 829-3900
James Pagano,
EMP: 30
SALES: 500K **Privately Held**
SIC: 3511 Turbines & turbine generator sets

(G-9410)
BERGER & WILD LLC
Also Called: Last Magazine, The
401 Broadway Ste 302 (10013-3005)
PHONE..................646 415-8459
Tenzen Wild, *Partner*
Migus Berger, *Partner*
Tenzen Wilt, *Partner*
Sarah Louise, *General Mgr*
▲ EMP: 5
SALES (est): 436.2K **Privately Held**
SIC: 2721 Periodicals

(G-9411)
BERNARD CHAUS INC (PA)
530 Fashion Ave Fl 18 (10018-4855)
PHONE..................212 354-1280
Fax: 646 562-4848
Josephine Chaus, *Ch of Bd*
Jaymie Brenner, *General Mgr*
Judith Leech, *Vice Pres*
William P Runge, *CFO*
Katie Burke, *Accounts Exec*
▲ EMP: 76
SQ FT: 33,000
SALES (est): 73.5MM **Privately Held**
SIC: 2339 2331 2335 Sportswear, women's; slacks: women's, misses' & juniors'; shorts (outerwear): women's, misses' & juniors'; women's & misses' blouses & shirts; wedding gowns & dresses

(G-9412)
BERNARD CHAUS INC
Also Called: Cynthia Steffe
515 7th Ave Ste 18 (10018-5902)
PHONE..................646 562-4700
Tina Cardell, *Branch Mgr*
EMP: 200
SALES (corp-wide): 73.5MM **Privately Held**
SIC: 2339 2331 Sportswear, women's; slacks: women's, misses' & juniors'; shorts (outerwear): women's, misses' & juniors'; women's & misses' blouses & shirts
PA: Bernard Chaus, Inc.
530 Fashion Ave Fl 18
New York NY 10018
212 354-1280

(G-9413)
BERNETTE APPAREL LLC
42 W 39th St Fl 2 (10018-3895)
PHONE..................212 279-5526
Adam Siskind,
Jeff Siskind,
EMP: 16
SQ FT: 7,000
SALES (est): 1.1MM **Privately Held**
WEB: www.btexusa.com
SIC: 2329 Sweaters & sweater jackets: men's & boys'

(G-9414)
BERNHARD ARNOLD & COMPANY INC (PA)
485 Lexington Ave Fl 9 (10017-2653)
PHONE..................212 907-1500
Howard Brecher, *Vice Pres*
David Henigson, *Vice Pres*
Harold Bernard, *Director*
Stephen Anastasio, *Officer*
EMP: 3 EST: 1931
SQ FT: 70,000
SALES: 36MM **Publicly Held**
WEB: www.valueline.com
SIC: 2721 6282 Periodicals: publishing only; investment advice

(G-9415)
BERRYWILD
200 E 30th St Bsmt (10016-8440)
PHONE..................212 686-5848
Samuel Mirelli, *Partner*
Harold Rosen, *Partner*
EMP: 6
SALES (est): 464K **Privately Held**
SIC: 2024 Yogurt desserts, frozen

(G-9416)
BERT WASSERERMAN
370 Lexington Ave (10017-6503)
PHONE..................212 759-5210
Fax: 212 759-5304
Bert Wasserman, *Principal*
EMP: 5
SALES (est): 513.5K **Privately Held**
SIC: 2329 Knickers, dress (separate): men's & boys'

(G-9417)
BERTELSMANN INC (HQ)
1745 Broadway Fl 20 (10019-4640)
PHONE..................212 782-1000
Fax: 212 782-1010
Jaroslaw Gabor, *CEO*
Thomas Rabe, *Ch of Bd*
Joshua Kraus, *President*
Gerd Schulte-Hillen, *Vice Chairman*
Peter Blobel, *COO*
▲ EMP: 30
SALES (est): 1.7B
SALES (corp-wide): 17.9B **Privately Held**
WEB: www.bertelsmann.com
SIC: 2731 2721 7819 3652 Books: publishing & printing; magazines: publishing & printing; trade journals: publishing & printing; video tape or disk reproduction; compact laser discs, prerecorded; commercial & industrial building operation
PA: Bertelsmann Se & Co. Kgaa
Carl-Bertelsmann-Str. 270
Gutersloh 33335
524 180-0

(G-9418)
BERTELSMANN PUBG GROUP INC (DH)
1540 Broadway Fl 24 (10036-4039)
PHONE..................212 782-1000
Thomas Middelhoff, *CEO*
Robert J Sorrentino, *CEO*
Hans-Martin Sorge, *Ch of Bd*
Peter Olson, *President*
Bernhard U Derlath, *Treasurer*
EMP: 1000
SQ FT: 710,000
SALES (est): 89.8MM
SALES (corp-wide): 17.9B **Privately Held**
SIC: 2731 2721 Books: publishing only; magazines: publishing only, not printed on site
HQ: Bertelsmann, Inc.
1745 Broadway Fl 20
New York NY 10019
212 782-1000

(G-9419)
BESPOKE APPAREL INC
214 W 39th St Rm 200b (10018-8321)
PHONE..................212 382-0330
Rong Su, *President*
Chia Hung Yu, *Vice Pres*
▲ EMP: 6
SQ FT: 1,500
SALES (est): 390K **Privately Held**
SIC: 2326 Service apparel (baker, barber, lab, etc.), washable: men's

(G-9420)
BEST BRANDS CONSUMER PDTS INC (PA)
20 W 33rd St Fl 5 (10001-3305)
PHONE..................212 684-7456
Peter Felberbaum, *President*
Meyer Kassin, *Vice Pres*
Albert Kassin, *Treasurer*
Isaac Kassin, *Admin Sec*
▲ EMP: 8
SQ FT: 26,000
SALES (est): 1.7MM **Privately Held**
SIC: 2369 2371 Headwear: girls', children's & infants'; hats, fur

▲ = Import ▼ =Export
◆ =Import/Export

(G-9421)
BESTYPE DIGITAL IMAGING LLC
285 W Broadway Frnt A (10013-2246)
PHONE..................212 966-6886
Fax: 212 966-6034
John W Lam, *Mng Member*
John Lam, *Manager*
Chick Lam,
EMP: 10
SQ FT: 3,000
SALES: 1MM **Privately Held**
SIC: 2759 Commercial printing

(G-9422)
BET NETWORKS INCORPORATED
1540 Broadway Fl 26 (10036-4039)
PHONE..................212 846-8111
Stephen Hill, *President*
Robert L Johnson, *Principal*
Pete Danielsen, *Exec VP*
MAI K Flournoy, *Senior VP*
Eddie Hill, *Senior VP*
EMP: 20 **EST:** 2008
SALES (est): 3.6MM **Privately Held**
SIC: 3663 Studio equipment, radio & television broadcasting

(G-9423)
BETH KOBLINER COMPANY LLC
1995 Broadway Ste 1800 (10023-5857)
Rural Route 120 W 45th (10036)
PHONE..................212 501-8407
Fax: 212 890-8876
Beth Kobliner,
EMP: 5
SALES (est): 305.1K **Privately Held**
SIC: 2711 Newspapers, publishing & printing

(G-9424)
BETH WARD STUDIOS LLC
133 W 25th St Rm 8e (10001-7281)
PHONE..................646 922-7575
Beth Ward, *Mng Member*
EMP: 10
SALES: 3.4MM **Privately Held**
SIC: 3961 Costume jewelry

(G-9425)
BETSY & ADAM LTD (PA)
1400 Broadway Rm 602 (10018-0779)
PHONE..................212 302-3750
Fax: 212 398-0454
Martin Sklar, *Owner*
Frank Lamourt, *Controller*
Tammy Sklar, *Sales Mgr*
▲ **EMP:** 50
SQ FT: 12,000
SALES (est): 16.1MM **Privately Held**
WEB: www.betsyandadam.com
SIC: 2253 Dresses & skirts

(G-9426)
BETTERTEX INC
Also Called: Bettertex Interiojrs
450 Broadway (10013-5822)
PHONE..................212 431-3373
Raymond Nakash, *President*
EMP: 15 **EST:** 2008
SALES (est): 1.5MM **Privately Held**
SIC: 2391 7641 Curtains & draperies; upholstery work

(G-9427)
BEVERAGE MEDIA GROUP INC (PA)
152 Madison Ave Rm 600 (10016-5471)
PHONE..................212 571-3232
Mike Roth, *President*
Kristen Wolfe, *Editor*
Jody Slone, *VP Opers*
Lauren Howery, *Marketing Staff*
Lee Stringham, *Director*
▲ **EMP:** 10
SQ FT: 13,300
SALES (est): 1.8MM **Privately Held**
WEB: www.bevmedia.com
SIC: 2721 Magazines: publishing only, not printed on site

(G-9428)
BEVERLY CREATIONS INC
Also Called: Natalie Creations
40 E 34th St Rm 1403 (10016-4501)
PHONE..................800 439-6855
Jerry Joseph, *President*
Judith Rothman, *Manager*
Dan Strauss, *Manager*
EMP: 12 **EST:** 1968
SALES (est): 770K **Privately Held**
WEB: www.beverlycreations.com
SIC: 2341 Women's & children's undergarments

(G-9429)
BEYOND LOOM INC (PA)
Also Called: Franetta
262 W 38th St Rm 203 (10018-5881)
P.O. Box 105 (10150-0105)
PHONE..................212 575-3100
Joanne Satin, *President*
Edward Storch, *Vice Pres*
Norden Hahn, *Administration*
▲ **EMP:** 6 **EST:** 1991
SQ FT: 4,000
SALES (est): 607.3K **Privately Held**
WEB: www.beyondtheloom.com
SIC: 2211 2221 2231 Cotton broad woven goods; silk broadwoven fabrics; fabric finishing: wool, mohair or similar fibers

(G-9430)
BEYONDLY INC
Also Called: Everplans
20 W 20th St Ste 1004 (10011-9252)
PHONE..................646 658-3665
Abby Schneiderman, *President*
Adam Seifer, *President*
Stan Lau, *Finance*
Peter Bogart, *Manager*
Warren Habib, *CTO*
EMP: 13 **EST:** 2012
SQ FT: 1,700
SALES (est): 1.1MM **Privately Held**
SIC: 7372 Business oriented computer software

(G-9431)
BEYONDSPRING INC
28 Liberty St Fl 39 (10005-1451)
PHONE..................646 305-6387
Lan Huang, *Ch of Bd*
Richard A Brand, *CFO*
EMP: 24
SALES (est): 1.3MM **Privately Held**
SIC: 2834 Pharmaceutical preparations

(G-9432)
BEYONDSPRING PHRMCEUTICALS INC
28 Liberty St Fl 39 (10005-1451)
PHONE..................646 305-6387
Lan Huang, *CEO*
G Kenneth Lloyd, *COO*
Steven D Reich, *Vice Pres*
Robert Dickey IV, *CFO*
Gloria Lee, *Chief Mktg Ofcr*
EMP: 11
SALES (est): 1.1MM **Privately Held**
SIC: 2834 Pharmaceutical preparations

(G-9433)
BH BRAND INC
Also Called: Bh Brands
10 W 33rd St Rm 218 (10001-3306)
PHONE..................212 239-1635
Morris Harari, *President*
Kenny Harari, *Vice Pres*
▲ **EMP:** 25
SQ FT: 4,500
SALES: 17MM **Privately Held**
SIC: 2389 2339 Men's miscellaneous accessories; women's & misses' accessories

(G-9434)
BH MULTI COM CORP (PA)
15 W 46th St Fl 6 (10036-4196)
PHONE..................212 944-0020
Fax: 212 921-7796
Fatolah Hematian, *Ch of Bd*
Effy Hematian, *President*
David Bassalalli, *Corp Secy*
Hertsel Akhavan, *Vice Pres*
Hertsal Athavan, *Controller*
▲ **EMP:** 48 **EST:** 1979
SQ FT: 6,000
SALES (est): 8.2MM **Privately Held**
WEB: www.bhmulti.com
SIC: 3911 Jewelry, precious metal

(G-9435)
BIANCA GROUP LTD
244 W 39th St Fl 4 (10018-4413)
PHONE..................212 768-3011
Ricardo Garcia, *President*
EMP: 5
SQ FT: 2,200
SALES: 200K **Privately Held**
SIC: 3953 3543 Marking devices; industrial patterns

(G-9436)
BIBO INTERNATIONAL LLC
130 Water St Apt 4g (10005-1614)
P.O. Box 492, Newport RI (02840-0492)
PHONE..................617 304-2242
Mark Lester, *Mng Member*
EMP: 18 **EST:** 2011
SALES: 1.6MM **Privately Held**
SIC: 2084 Wines, brandy & brandy spirits

(G-9437)
BICKER INC
Also Called: Holiday House Publishing
425 Madison Ave Fl 12 (10017-1135)
PHONE..................212 688-0085
Fax: 212 421-6134
John H Briggs Jr, *President*
Grace Maccarone, *Editor*
Kate Briggs, *Vice Pres*
Lisa Lee, *Opers Staff*
Regina Griffin, *VP Sales*
▲ **EMP:** 15 **EST:** 1935
SQ FT: 2,000
SALES (est): 2.1MM **Privately Held**
WEB: www.holidayhouse.com
SIC: 2731 Book publishing

(G-9438)
BIDPRESS LLC
659 Washington St Apt 5r (10014-2874)
P.O. Box 351, Asheville NC (28802-0351)
PHONE..................267 973-8876
Anthony Wavering, *CEO*
EMP: 5 **EST:** 2013
SQ FT: 1,000
SALES (est): 189.8K **Privately Held**
SIC: 2759 Screen printing

(G-9439)
BIELKA INC
136 E 57th St Ste 907 (10022-2966)
PHONE..................212 980-6841
Fax: 212 980-6852
Robert Bruce Bielka, *President*
Regina Suzanne Eros, *Vice Pres*
EMP: 5
SQ FT: 1,200
SALES (est): 562.2K **Privately Held**
WEB: www.bielkajewelry.com
SIC: 3911 Jewelry, precious metal

(G-9440)
BIG APPLE ELEVTR SRV & CONSULT
247 W 30th St (10001-2824)
PHONE..................212 279-0700
Jaclyn Hanning, *CEO*
Joseph Hanning, *President*
EMP: 8
SALES (est): 413K **Privately Held**
SIC: 3534 Elevators & moving stairways; elevators & equipment; dumbwaiters

(G-9441)
BIG APPLE SIGN CORP (PA)
Also Called: Big Apple Visual Group
247 W 35th St Frnt 1 (10001-1908)
PHONE..................212 629-3650
Fax: 212 629-4954
Amir Khalfan, *Ch of Bd*
Richi Shah, *CFO*
Habib Shahzad, *Manager*
Maria B Varga, *Consultant*
Mehul Dharia, *Administration*
▲ **EMP:** 35
SQ FT: 40,000
SALES: 12.7MM **Privately Held**
WEB: www.bigapplegroup.com
SIC: 2399 2759 3993 Banners, made from fabric; commercial printing; signs, not made in custom sign painting shops; displays & cutouts, window & lobby

(G-9442)
BIG BANG CLOTHING INC
Also Called: Big Bang Clothing Co
214 W 39th St Rm 1008 (10018-4454)
PHONE..................212 221-0379
Sam Seungwoo Lee, *Branch Mgr*
EMP: 5 **Privately Held**
SIC: 2339 Women's & misses' outerwear
PA: Big Bang Clothing, Inc
4507 Staunton Ave
Vernon CA 90058

(G-9443)
BIG FISH ENTERTAINMENT LLC
1411 Broadway Fl 16 (10018-3410)
PHONE..................646 797-4955
Daniel Cesareo, *Mng Member*
EMP: 200
SALES: 25.7MM **Privately Held**
SIC: 3663 Studio equipment, radio & television broadcasting

(G-9444)
BIG IDEA BRANDS LLC
Also Called: Flow Society
1410 Broadway Frnt 4 (10018-9343)
PHONE..................212 938-0270
Mark Elenowitz, *CEO*
Anthony Ottimo, *President*
Carlos Vazquez, *COO*
Larry Fihma, *Senior VP*
Brian Frank,
▲ **EMP:** 10
SQ FT: 4,000
SALES (est): 947.3K **Privately Held**
SIC: 2329 Athletic (warmup, sweat & jogging) suits: men's & boys'

(G-9445)
BIG WHITE WALL HOLDING INC
41 E 11th St Fl 11 (10003-4602)
PHONE..................917 281-2649
Tina Trenkler, *CEO*
EMP: 5 **EST:** 2013
SQ FT: 1,200
SALES: 250K **Privately Held**
SIC: 7372 Application computer software
HQ: Bigwhitewall Limited
Evergreen House Grafton Place
London

(G-9446)
BIGNAY INC
315 E 86th St Apt 21ge (10028-4783)
PHONE..................786 346-1673
Lucas Toledo, *CEO*
Eric Sevillia, *CFO*
EMP: 8 **EST:** 2014
SALES (est): 924K **Privately Held**
SIC: 3751 5571 5941 Bicycles & related parts; bicycles, motorized; bicycle & bicycle parts

(G-9447)
BILCO INDUSTRIES INC
214 W 39th St Rm 301 (10018-8311)
PHONE..................917 783-5008
Billy Chen, *President*
Jerry Lau, *Vice Pres*
EMP: 16 **EST:** 2013
SALES: 30MM **Privately Held**
SIC: 2329 2339 5136 5137 Men's & boys' sportswear & athletic clothing; women's & misses' athletic clothing & sportswear; men's & boys' sportswear & work clothing; work clothing, men's & boys'; women's & children's clothing

(G-9448)
BILL BLASS GROUP LLC
236 5th Ave Fl 8 (10001-7989)
PHONE..................212 689-8957
Stuart M Goldblatt, *President*
James Chang, *General Mgr*
Cin Kim, *Mng Member*
Kenny Oak, *Director*
EMP: 10

New York - New York County (G-9449)   **GEOGRAPHIC SECTION**

SALES (est): 710K **Privately Held**
SIC: **2211** Apparel & outerwear fabrics, cotton

(G-9449)
BILLION TOWER INTL LLC
Also Called: Machine Clothing Company
989 6th Ave Fl 8 (10018-0871)
PHONE.................................212 220-0608
Fax: 212 563-6879
Joeson Ko, *Manager*
Joeson Ko Cho Shun,
▲ EMP: 15
SQ FT: 3,000
SALES: 122MM **Privately Held**
SIC: **2326** 5136 Men's & boys' work clothing; men's & boys' clothing

(G-9450)
BILLION TOWER USA LLC
989 Avenue Of The America (10018-0871)
PHONE.................................212 220-0608
Joeson Cho Shun Ko,
Ceci Tan, *Executive Asst*
EMP: 5
SALES: 5MM **Privately Held**
SIC: **2329** Men's & boys' sportswear & athletic clothing

(G-9451)
BILLY BEEZ USA LLC (PA)
3 W 35th St Fl 3 (10001-2237)
PHONE.................................646 606-2249
Ron Palerico, *General Mgr*
David Agnew, *Project Mgr*
Mark Bain, *Sales Staff*
EMP: 14
SALES (est): 14.2MM **Privately Held**
SIC: **3949** 5137 7999 Playground equipment; women's & children's dresses, suits, skirts & blouses; amusement ride

(G-9452)
BIOCONTINUUM GROUP INC
116 Chambers St (10007-1336)
PHONE.................................212 406-1060
Fax: 212 406-6544
John M Dimor, *President*
EMP: 5
SQ FT: 1,200
SALES (est): 290K **Privately Held**
WEB: www.bioc.net
SIC: **3999** Education aids, devices & supplies

(G-9453)
BIOFEEDBACK INSTRUMENT CORP
Also Called: Allied Products
255 W 98th St Apt 3d (10025-5596)
PHONE.................................212 222-2665
Philip Brotman, *President*
▲ EMP: 8
SQ FT: 1,000
SALES: 800K **Privately Held**
WEB: www.biof.com
SIC: **3845** 5045 5734 Electromedical apparatus; computers, peripherals & software; computer peripheral equipment; computer & software stores

(G-9454)
BIOLITEC INC
110 E 42nd St Rm 1800 (10017-5648)
PHONE.................................413 525-0600
Wolfgang Neuberger, *CEO*
Arthur Henneberger, *Controller*
Gary Stone, *Manager*
EMP: 50
SQ FT: 16,000
SALES (est): 5.1MM
SALES (corp-wide): 601.8K **Privately Held**
WEB: www.biolitec-us.com
SIC: **3229** Fiber optics strands
HQ: Biolitec Biomedical Technology Gmbh
    Otto-Schott-Str. 15
    Jena   07745
    364 151-9530

(G-9455)
BIRNBAUM & BULLOCK LTD
151 W 25th St Rm 2a (10001-7262)
PHONE.................................212 242-2914
Fax: 212 242-0771
Robert Bullock, *CEO*

Steven Birnbaum, *President*
EMP: 8
SQ FT: 1,500
SALES (est): 1.1MM **Privately Held**
SIC: **2335** Wedding gowns & dresses

(G-9456)
BISTATE OIL MANAGEMENT CORP
10 E 40th St Rm 2705 (10016-0450)
PHONE.................................212 935-4110
Fax: 212 593-1287
Richard D Siegal, *President*
Maria Scibelli, *Principal*
Brian Grossa, *Vice Pres*
Paul H Howard, *Vice Pres*
EMP: 10
SQ FT: 4,500
SALES (est): 2.5MM **Privately Held**
SIC: **1382** Oil & gas exploration services

(G-9457)
BIZBASH MEDIA INC (PA)
Also Called: Bizbash Masterplanner
115 W 27th St Fl 8 (10001-6217)
PHONE.................................646 638-3600
Fax: 646 638-3601
David Adler, *CEO*
Richard Aaron, *President*
Michele Laufik, *Editor*
Ann Keusch, *COO*
Lee Schrager, *Vice Pres*
EMP: 45
SQ FT: 5,000
SALES (est): 11MM **Privately Held**
WEB: www.bizbash.com
SIC: **2759** Advertising literature: printing

(G-9458)
BJ MAGAZINES INC
200 Varick St (10014-4810)
PHONE.................................212 367-9705
Renu Hooda, *President*
EMP: 5
SALES (est): 530K **Privately Held**
SIC: **2721** Periodicals

(G-9459)
BJG SERVICES LLC
237 W 35th St Ste 505 (10001-1905)
PHONE.................................516 592-5692
Isaac Newmann, *CEO*
Ben Neuberg, *President*
EMP: 25
SQ FT: 1,600
SALES (est): 7MM **Privately Held**
SIC: **3911** Jewelry, precious metal

(G-9460)
BLACK BOOK PHOTOGRAPHY INC
Also Called: Black Book, The
740 Broadway Ste 202 (10003-9518)
PHONE.................................212 979-6700
Ted Rubin, *President*
▲ EMP: 19
SALES (est): 1.4MM
SALES (corp-wide): 3.3MM **Privately Held**
WEB: www.modernholdings.com
SIC: **2741** Directories: publishing only, not printed on site
PA: Modern Holding Company
    601 Lexington Ave Rm 5900
    New York NY

(G-9461)
BLACKBOOK MEDIA CORP
32 Union Sq E Ste 4l (10003-3209)
PHONE.................................212 334-1800
Robert Hoff, *CEO*
Joseph Landry, *President*
David Cohn, *Exec VP*
Haylli Weintraub, *Office Mgr*
Candice Naboicheck, *Manager*
EMP: 21
SQ FT: 1,500
SALES (est): 2.4MM **Privately Held**
SIC: **2721** Magazines: publishing & printing

(G-9462)
BLADES
659 Broadway (10012-2302)
PHONE.................................212 477-1059
George Pohntes, *Manager*
▼ EMP: 10

SALES (est): 783.8K **Privately Held**
SIC: **3949** Skateboards

(G-9463)
BLANCHE P FIELD LLC
155 E 56th St Ph (10022-2718)
PHONE.................................212 355-6616
Blanche Field, *President*
Lisa Simkin, *Manager*
EMP: 25 EST: 1942
SQ FT: 3,000
SALES (est): 1.5MM **Privately Held**
SIC: **3999** 5932 Shades, lamp or candle; antiques

(G-9464)
BLANDI PRODUCTS LLC
Also Called: Oscar Blandi
875 3rd Ave Fl 7 (10022-7226)
PHONE.................................908 377-2885
Brian Robinson,
Stuart Litman,
▲ EMP: 15
SALES (est): 1.6MM **Privately Held**
SIC: **3999** Hair & hair-based products

(G-9465)
BLISS FOODS INC
Also Called: Yorganic
275 Greenwich St Frnt 2 (10007-3824)
PHONE.................................212 732-8888
Sung Kim, *President*
Shawn Reilly, *Vice Pres*
EMP: 5
SALES (est): 466.3K **Privately Held**
SIC: **2026** Yogurt

(G-9466)
BLISS FOODS INC
Also Called: Yorganic
275 Greenwich St Frnt 2 (10007-3824)
PHONE.................................212 732-8888
EMP: 11 **Privately Held**
SIC: **2026** Mfg Fluid Milk

(G-9467)
BLISS-POSTON THE SECOND WIND
928 Broadway Ste 403 (10010-8151)
PHONE.................................212 481-1055
Fax: 212 481-7374
Marcia Poston, *Vice Pres*
John Bliss, *Exec Dir*
EMP: 6
SALES (est): 522.9K **Privately Held**
SIC: **2011** Lard from carcasses slaughtered on site

(G-9468)
BLOOMSBURG CARPET INDS INC
Also Called: Silver Creek Carpet
49 W 23rd St Fl 4 (10010-4228)
PHONE.................................212 688-7447
Fax: 212 688-9218
Thomas J Habib, *Branch Mgr*
EMP: 6
SALES (corp-wide): 50MM **Privately Held**
SIC: **2273** Carpets & rugs
PA: Bloomsburg Carpet Industries, Inc.
    4999 Columbia Blvd
    Bloomsburg PA 17815
    800 233-8773

(G-9469)
BLOOMSBURY PUBLISHING INC
Also Called: Bloomsbury USA
1385 Brdwy Fl 5 (10018)
PHONE.................................212 419-5300
Fax: 646 727-0984
Nigel Newton, *President*
George Gibson, *Publisher*
Doug White, *Principal*
Caroline Abbey, *Editor*
Richard Charkin, *Exec VP*
▲ EMP: 100
SALES (est): 20.4MM
SALES (corp-wide): 178.4MM **Privately Held**
WEB: www.bloomsburyusa.com
SIC: **2731** Book publishing
PA: Bloomsbury Publishing Plc
    50 Bedford Square
    London WC1B
    207 631-5600

(G-9470)
BLU SAND LLC
589 8th Ave Fl 9 (10018-3083)
PHONE.................................212 564-1147
Eddie Shomer, *Vice Pres*
Eddie Cheung, *Office Mgr*
Morris Sitt,
EMP: 9
SQ FT: 2,000
SALES (est): 850K **Privately Held**
WEB: www.blusand.com
SIC: **2211** Towels & toweling, cotton

(G-9471)
BLUE AND WHITE PUBLISHING INC
Also Called: Bwog
425 Riverside Dr Apt 3c (10025-7724)
PHONE.................................215 431-3339
Jake Hershman, *CEO*
James Fast, *Publisher*
Nikolas Huth, *Publisher*
EMP: 10 EST: 2013
SALES (est): 505.8K **Privately Held**
SIC: **2711** Newspapers: publishing only, not printed on site

(G-9472)
BLUE HORIZON MEDIA INC (PA)
11 Park Pl Rm 1508 (10007-2816)
PHONE.................................212 661-7878
Geoffrey D Lurie, *COO*
David Bernstein, *CFO*
EMP: 16
SQ FT: 16,000
SALES (est): 3MM **Privately Held**
WEB: www.bluehrzn.com
SIC: **2721** Magazines: publishing only, not printed on site

(G-9473)
BLUE TEE CORP (PA)
387 Park Ave S Fl 15 (10016-1495)
PHONE.................................212 598-0880
Fax: 212 598-0896
David P Alldian, *Ch of Bd*
William M Kelly, *President*
Annette Marino D'Arienzo, *Exec Dir*
Brian Hamlin, *Director*
Michelle Derosa,
◆ EMP: 900
SQ FT: 2,500
SALES (est): 219.9MM **Privately Held**
SIC: **3533** 3589 5093 3715 Water well drilling equipment; garbage disposers & compactors, commercial; ferrous metal scrap & waste; semitrailers for truck tractors; water quality monitoring & control systems; structural shapes, iron or steel

(G-9474)
BLUE WOLF GROUP LLC (HQ)
11 E 26th St Fl 21 (10010-1413)
PHONE.................................866 455-9653
Tim Anderson, *Principal*
Tom Morselli, *Vice Pres*
Eric Berridge, *Mng Member*
Tom Rahl, *Administration*
Michael Kirven,
EMP: 100
SQ FT: 5,000
SALES (est): 87.7MM
SALES (corp-wide): 79.9B **Publicly Held**
WEB: www.bluewolfgroup.com
SIC: **7372** Prepackaged software; business oriented computer software
PA: International Business Machines Corporation
    1 New Orchard Rd Ste 1
    Armonk NY 10504
    914 499-1900

(G-9475)
BLUEDUCK TRADING LTD
463 7th Ave Rm 806 (10018-8712)
PHONE.................................212 268-3122
Barry Novick, *President*
▲ EMP: 8
SQ FT: 4,500
SALES (est): 1.3MM **Privately Held**
WEB: www.blueduckshearling.com
SIC: **2339** 2311 Women's & misses' jackets & coats, except sportswear; coats, tailored, men's & boys': from purchased materials

GEOGRAPHIC SECTION — New York - New York County (G-9500)

(G-9476)
BLUESOHO (PA)
160 Varick St Fl 2 (10013-1251)
PHONE..................646 805-2583
Jennifer Bergin, *Managing Prtnr*
Janine Crowley, *Opers Mgr*
Kimberly Hansen, *Director*
Jennifer Franco, *Graphic Designe*
EMP: 10
SALES (est): 2.7MM Privately Held
SIC: 2752 Commercial printing, lithographic

(G-9477)
BLUM & FINK INC
158 W 29th St Fl 12 (10001-5300)
PHONE..................212 695-2606
Fax: 212 967-8123
Stanley Blum, *President*
▲ EMP: 12 EST: 1961
SQ FT: 10,000
SALES (est): 1.5MM Privately Held
SIC: 2371 5137 Fur coats & other fur apparel; fur clothing, women's & children's

(G-9478)
BM AMERICA LLC (DH)
Also Called: Bruno Magli
4 W 58th St Fl 10 (10019-2515)
PHONE..................201 438-7733
Jay Patel, *Accountant*
Michele Donno,
▲ EMP: 29
SQ FT: 30,000
SALES (est): 2.5MM
SALES (corp-wide): 3MM Privately Held
WEB: www.brunomagli.com
SIC: 3143 Men's footwear, except athletic
HQ: Bm Usa Incorporated
    75 Triangle Blvd
    Carlstadt NJ 07072
    800 624-5499

(G-9479)
BMC SOFTWARE INC
1114 Ave Of The Americas (10036-7703)
PHONE..................212 402-1500
Fax: 212 402-1599
Jeff Parks, *Manager*
Mark Settle, *CIO*
Ralph Crosby, *CTO*
EMP: 32
SALES (corp-wide): 1.9B Privately Held
WEB: www.bmc.com
SIC: 7372 7371 Utility computer software; custom computer programming services
HQ: Bmc Software, Inc.
    2103 Citywest Blvd # 2100
    Houston TX 77042
    713 918-8800

(G-9480)
BMG RIGHTS MANAGEMENT (US) LLC (HQ)
Also Called: Bmg Chrysalis
1745 Broadway Fl 19 (10019-4640)
PHONE..................212 561-3000
Hartwig Masuch, *CEO*
Jon Cohen, *Exec VP*
Dominique Kulling, *Vice Pres*
Pamela Lillig, *Vice Pres*
Tim Reid, *Vice Pres*
EMP: 20
SALES (est): 3.1MM
SALES (corp-wide): 17.9B Privately Held
SIC: 2731 Book publishing
PA: Bertelsmann Se & Co. Kgaa
    Carl-Bertelsmann-Str. 270
    Gutersloh 33335
    524 180-0

(G-9481)
BNNS CO INC
71 W 47th St Ste 600-601 (10036-2866)
PHONE..................212 302-1844
Fax: 212 302-1844
Nick Barhnakov, *President*
Simon Nikhamin, *Vice Pres*
EMP: 8
SALES (est): 510K Privately Held
WEB: www.bnnsco.com
SIC: 3961 Costume jewelry

(G-9482)
BOARDMAN SIMONS PUBLISHING (PA)
Also Called: Davidson Publishing
55 Broad St Fl 26 (10004-2580)
PHONE..................212 620-7200
Arthur J McGinnis Jr, *President*
Carol Franklin, *Manager*
EMP: 40
SQ FT: 12,000
SALES (est): 8.8MM Privately Held
WEB: www.sbpub.com
SIC: 2721 2731 8249 Periodicals: publishing only; books: publishing only; correspondence school

(G-9483)
BOBBI BROWN PROF COSMT INC
575 Broadway Fl 4 (10012-3237)
PHONE..................646 613-6500
Bobbi Brown, *CEO*
Leonard A Lauder, *Ch of Bd*
Donald Robertson, *Senior VP*
Veronika Ullmer, *Vice Pres*
Alicia Valencia, *Vice Pres*
▲ EMP: 33
SALES (est): 8.1MM
SALES (corp-wide): 11.8B Publicly Held
WEB: www.bobbibrown.com
SIC: 2844 Toilet preparations
PA: The Estee Lauder Companies Inc
    767 5th Ave Fl 37
    New York NY 10153
    212 572-4200

(G-9484)
BOEING COMPANY
304 Park Ave S (10010-4301)
PHONE..................201 259-9400
Donald Boeing, *Branch Mgr*
EMP: 897
SALES (corp-wide): 94.5B Publicly Held
SIC: 3721 Airplanes, fixed or rotary wing
PA: The Boeing Company
    100 N Riverside Plz
    Chicago IL 60606
    312 544-2000

(G-9485)
BONDI DIGITAL PUBLISHING LLC
88 10th Ave Frnt 6 (10011-4745)
PHONE..................212 405-1655
Murat Aktar, *Mng Member*
David Anthony, *Mng Member*
Carey Taylor, *Mng Member*
EMP: 5
SALES (est): 460.4K Privately Held
SIC: 2721 Magazines: publishing & printing

(G-9486)
BONELLI FOODS LLC
139 Fulton St Rm 314 (10038-2537)
PHONE..................212 346-0942
Tommaso Asaro, *Mng Member*
▲ EMP: 1
SQ FT: 1,000
SALES: 1.4MM Privately Held
SIC: 2079 Olive oil

(G-9487)
BONNIER PUBLISHING USA INC
251 Park Ave S Fl 12 (10010-7302)
PHONE..................212 321-0237
Shimul Tolia, *President*
Thomas Morgan, *Finance Dir*
▲ EMP: 40
SQ FT: 4,000
SALES (est): 1MM
SALES (corp-wide): 2.8B Privately Held
SIC: 2731 Books: publishing only
HQ: Bonnier Publishing Limited
    The Plaza
    London SW10

(G-9488)
BONPOINT INC (PA)
396 W Broadway Apt 3 (10012-4681)
PHONE..................212 246-3291
Fax: 212 246-3293
Bernard Kolhen, *President*
Aude Allain, *Opers Mgr*
Karine Kalocsai, *Controller*
▲ EMP: 23 EST: 1970
SALES (est): 1.7MM Privately Held
WEB: www.bonpoint.com
SIC: 2361 Dresses: girls', children's & infants'

(G-9489)
BOOM LLC
Also Called: Boom Creative Development
800 3rd Ave Fl 2 (10022-7683)
PHONE..................646 218-0752
Fax: 212 317-9062
Art Degaetano, *President*
Glenn Marks, *COO*
Karen Higgins, *Manager*
▲ EMP: 35
SQ FT: 12,000
SALES (est): 5.8MM Privately Held
WEB: www.boomllc.com
SIC: 3999 2844 Atomizers, toiletry; cosmetics, perfumes & hair products

(G-9490)
BOOSEY & HAWKES INC (DH)
Also Called: Music Library
229 W 28th St Fl 11 (10001-5915)
PHONE..................212 358-5300
Fax: 212 358-5301
Jennifer Bilfield, *General Mgr*
Bert Fink, *Senior VP*
Steven Storch, *CFO*
Alicia Fitzgerald, *Comptroller*
Linda Golding, *Personnel Exec*
▲ EMP: 20
SALES (est): 3MM
SALES (corp-wide): 337.8K Privately Held
WEB: www.christopherrouse.com
SIC: 2741 7389 Music book & sheet music publishing; music copying service; music distribution systems

(G-9491)
BORGHESE INC (PA)
Also Called: Princess Marcella Borghese
3 E 54th St Fl 20 (10022-3130)
PHONE..................212 659-5318
Fax: 212 659-5301
Georgette Mosbacher, *President*
Christopher Stephen West, *President*
Neil Petrocelli, *Vice Pres*
Gerrianne Cannon, *QC Mgr*
Frank Palladino, *CFO*
▲ EMP: 25
SQ FT: 10,000
SALES (est): 7.7MM Privately Held
WEB: www.chateauxdemeures.com
SIC: 2844 5122 5961 5999 Toilet preparations; cosmetics; cosmetics & perfumes, mail order; cosmetics

(G-9492)
BOTIFY CORPORATION
119 W 24th St (10011-1913)
PHONE..................617 576-2005
Adrien Menard, *President*
EMP: 8 EST: 2015
SALES (est): 204.7K
SALES (corp-wide): 247.3K Privately Held
SIC: 7372 Business oriented computer software
PA: Botify
    22 Rue Royale
    Paris 75002
    183 629-078

(G-9493)
BOTKIER NY LLC
19 W 34th St Fl 7 (10001-0055)
PHONE..................212 343-2782
David Seamon,
EMP: 8
SALES (est): 604.8K Privately Held
SIC: 2339 Women's & misses' accessories
PA: Trebbianno, Llc
    19 W 34th St Fl 7
    New York NY 10001

(G-9494)
BOUCHERON JOAILLERIE USA INC
Also Called: Parfums Boucheron Jewelry
460 Park Ave Fl 12 (10022-1906)
PHONE..................212 715-7330
Thomas Indermuhle, *Ch of Bd*
EMP: 7
SALES (est): 519.7K
SALES (corp-wide): 102.5MM Privately Held
SIC: 3915 3423 Jewelers' materials & lapidary work; jewelers' findings & materials; jewelers' hand tools
HQ: Boucheron Holding
    26 Place Vendome
    Paris 75001
    142 444-244

(G-9495)
BOUNDLESS SPATIAL INC
222 Broadway Fl 19 (10038-2550)
PHONE..................646 831-5531
Andy Dearing, *CEO*
Brody Stout, *COO*
Tom Ingold, *Vice Pres*
Jim Reiss, *Vice Pres*
Zach Rouse, *Vice Pres*
EMP: 35 EST: 2012
SALES (est): 4.4MM Privately Held
SIC: 7372 Business oriented computer software

(G-9496)
BOURNE MUSIC PUBLISHERS
Also Called: Bourne Co
5 W 37th St Fl 6 (10018-6275)
PHONE..................212 391-4300
Fax: 212 391-4306
Mary Elizabeth Bourne, *Owner*
EMP: 19
SQ FT: 6,500
SALES (est): 1MM Privately Held
WEB: www.bournemusic.com
SIC: 2741 Music book & sheet music publishing

(G-9497)
BOXBEE INC
134 W 26th St Rm 404 (10001-6865)
PHONE..................646 612-7839
Kristoph Matthews, *President*
EMP: 7
SQ FT: 10,000
SALES (est): 733.7K Privately Held
SIC: 7372 Business oriented computer software

(G-9498)
BOY SCOUTS OF AMERICA
271 Madison Ave Ste 401 (10016-1041)
PHONE..................212 532-0985
Fax: 212 889-4513
Leigh Novog, *Marketing Staff*
Barry Brown, *Manager*
EMP: 7
SALES (corp-wide): 335.9MM Privately Held
WEB: www.scouting.org
SIC: 2721 Magazines: publishing & printing
PA: Boy Scouts Of America
    1325 W Walnut Hill Ln
    Irving TX 75038
    972 580-2000

(G-9499)
BOYLAN BOTTLING CO INC
6 E 43rd St Fl 18 (10017-4657)
PHONE..................800 289-7978
Ronald C Fiorina, *President*
Steven Hood, *COO*
Mark Fiorina, *Vice Pres*
Nack Modujno, *Office Mgr*
▲ EMP: 30 EST: 1891
SQ FT: 25,000
SALES (est): 6.3MM Privately Held
WEB: www.boylanbottling.com
SIC: 2086 2087 Soft drinks: packaged in cans, bottles, etc.; beverage bases, concentrates, syrups, powders & mixes

(G-9500)
BPE STUDIO INC
270 W 38th St Rm 702 (10018-1520)
PHONE..................212 868-9896
Fax: 212 302-3270
Dan Ping Zhang, *President*
EMP: 5
SALES (est): 410K Privately Held
SIC: 2396 Linings, apparel: made from purchased materials

New York - New York County (G-9501)

(G-9501)
BRADLEY MARKETING GROUP INC
1431 Broadway Fl 12 (10018-1912)
PHONE...................212 967-6100
James Lemmo, *Principal*
Edward Brucia, *Vice Pres*
Kathy Reccardi, *Vice Pres*
Adam Perry, *VP Sales*
Jackie Sneyers, *Executive Asst*
EMP: 6
SALES (corp-wide): 20.1MM **Privately Held**
WEB: www.bradleymg.com
SIC: 2759 Commercial printing
PA: Bradley Marketing Group, Inc.
170 Wilbur Pl Ste 700
Bohemia NY 11716
631 231-9200

(G-9502)
BRAINPOP LLC
Also Called: Brainpop Group
71 W 23rd St Fl 17 (10010-4183)
PHONE...................212 574-6017
Raffi Kahana, *Senior VP*
Mike Watanabe, *Senior VP*
Daniel Donohue, *Vice Pres*
Demian Johnson, *Vice Pres*
Avraham Kadar, *Mng Member*
EMP: 50
SALES (est): 6MM **Privately Held**
SIC: 7372 Educational computer software

(G-9503)
BRAL NADER FINE JEWELRY INC
576 5th Ave (10036-4807)
PHONE...................800 493-1222
Nader Bral, *President*
EMP: 5
SALES: 3MM **Privately Held**
SIC: 3911 Jewelry, precious metal

(G-9504)
BRANNKEY INC (PA)
Also Called: Honora
1385 Broadway Fl 14 (10018-6001)
PHONE...................212 371-1515
Fax: 212 371-0003
Joel Schechter, *Ch of Bd*
Roberta Schechter, *Vice Pres*
Hema Ramdayal, *Opers Mgr*
Jack Jolly, *Opers Staff*
Jeannie Chan, *Human Res Mgr*
▲ EMP: 52 EST: 1969
SQ FT: 6,500
SALES (est): 10.6MM **Privately Held**
WEB: www.honora.com
SIC: 3911 Jewelry, precious metal

(G-9505)
BRANT ART PUBLICATIONS INC
Also Called: Art In America
110 Greene St Ph 2 (10012-3824)
PHONE...................212 941-2800
Sandra J Brant, *President*
Peter Brant, *Vice Pres*
Deborah Blasucci, *CFO*
Jeremy Gaspar, *Manager*
Brian Mc Keon, *Manager*
EMP: 27
SQ FT: 20,000
SALES (est): 1.5MM
SALES (corp-wide): 4.6MM **Privately Held**
WEB: www.artinamerica.com
SIC: 2721 Magazines: publishing only, not printed on site
PA: Brant Publications, Inc.
110 Greene St Ph 2
New York NY 10012
212 941-2800

(G-9506)
BRANT PUBLICATIONS INC (PA)
Also Called: Magazine Antiques, The
110 Greene St Ph 2 (10012-3824)
PHONE...................212 941-2800
Fax: 212 941-2897
Sandra J Brant, *President*
Jennifer Norton, *Publisher*
Lorrenda Sherrer, *Publisher*
Cynthia Zabel, *Publisher*
Christopher Bollen, *Editor*
▲ EMP: 28
SQ FT: 20,000
SALES (est): 4.6MM **Privately Held**
WEB: www.themagazineantiques.com
SIC: 2721 Magazines: publishing only, not printed on site

(G-9507)
BRASILANS PRESS PBLCATIONS INC
60 W 46th St Rm 302 (10036)
P.O. Box 985 (10185-0985)
PHONE...................212 764-6161
EMP: 40
SALES (est): 2.1MM **Privately Held**
SIC: 2711 Newspapers-Publishing/Printing

(G-9508)
BRAZE
263 W 38th St Fl 16 (10018-0483)
PHONE...................504 327-7269
Mark Ghermezian, *CEO*
Doug Pepper, *Principal*
Daniel Head, *Senior VP*
Matthew McRoberts, *Vice Pres*
Oliver Bell, *VP Opers*
EMP: 21 EST: 2013
SALES (est): 2.1MM **Privately Held**
SIC: 7372 Application computer software

(G-9509)
BREAD MARKET CAFE
16 W 45th St Fl 5 (10036-4204)
PHONE...................212 768-9292
Dan Millman, *President*
EMP: 5 EST: 1997
SALES (est): 324.7K **Privately Held**
WEB: www.mycafebeyond.com
SIC: 2051 Bread, cake & related products

(G-9510)
BREWER-CANTELMO CO INC
Also Called: Script-Master Div
55 W 39th St Rm 205 (10018-0573)
PHONE...................212 244-4600
Fax: 212 244-1640
Stephen Kirschenbaum, *President*
David Kirschenbaum, *Vice Pres*
Elissa Christian, *Sales Staff*
EMP: 23 EST: 1928
SQ FT: 9,000
SALES (est): 2.7MM **Privately Held**
WEB: www.brewer-cantelmo.com
SIC: 2782 Looseleaf binders & devices

(G-9511)
BRIGANTINE INC (HQ)
225 W 37th St (10018-5703)
PHONE...................212 354-8550
Isidore Friedman, *Ch of Bd*
Mark Friedman, *President*
Paul Friedman, *President*
William Fuchs, *Treasurer*
EMP: 5
SQ FT: 10,000
SALES (est): 578.6K
SALES (corp-wide): 7.3MM **Privately Held**
WEB: www.brigantine.com
SIC: 2329 2339 Men's & boys' leather, wool & down-filled outerwear; women's & misses' jackets & coats, except sportswear
PA: S. Rothschild & Co., Inc.
1407 Broadway Fl 10
New York NY 10018
212 354-8550

(G-9512)
BRIGHT KIDS NYC INC
225 Broadway Ste 1504 (10007-3704)
PHONE...................917 539-4575
Bige Doruk, *CEO*
Beth Feinkind, *Controller*
Brian Chester, *Manager*
▲ EMP: 40 EST: 2009
SALES (est): 3.6MM **Privately Held**
SIC: 2731 8299 8748 Textbooks: publishing & printing; tutoring school; testing service, educational or personnel

(G-9513)
BRIGHTLINE VENTURES I LLC
1120 Avenue Of The Americ (10036-6700)
PHONE...................212 626-6829
EMP: 26
SALES (est): 1.5MM **Privately Held**
SIC: 2099 Food preparations

(G-9514)
BRILLIANT JEWELERS/MJJ INC
Also Called: Mjj Brilliant
902 Broadway Fl 18 (10010-6038)
PHONE...................212 353-2326
Fax: 212 353-0696
Nicolay Yakubovich, *Ch of Bd*
Robert Schwartz, *COO*
Albert Kvint, *Production*
Abdul Kampani, *CFO*
Gary Astrow, *Accountant*
EMP: 120
SALES (est): 21.9MM **Privately Held**
WEB: www.mjjbrilliant.com
SIC: 3911 Jewelry, precious metal

(G-9515)
BRISTOL SEAMLESS RING CORP
209 W 86th St Apt 817 (10024-3337)
PHONE...................212 874-2645
Irving Skydell, *President*
EMP: 16 EST: 1910
SALES (est): 157.4K **Privately Held**
SIC: 3911 Jewelry, precious metal

(G-9516)
BRISTOL-MYERS SQUIBB COMPANY (PA)
345 Park Ave Bsmt Lc3 (10154-0028)
P.O. Box 4000, Princeton NJ (08543-4000)
PHONE...................212 546-4000
Fax: 212 605-9628
Giovanni Caforio, *Ch of Bd*
Louis S Schmukler, *President*
Francis Cuss, *Exec VP*
Sandra Leung, *Exec VP*
Joseph C Caldarella, *Senior VP*
EMP: 1200 EST: 1887
SALES: 19.4B **Publicly Held**
WEB: www.bms.com
SIC: 2834 Pharmaceutical preparations; drugs acting on the cardiovascular system, except diagnostic; antibiotics, packaged; drugs acting on the central nervous system & sense organs

(G-9517)
BROADCAST MANAGER INC
Also Called: Promosuite
65 Broadway Ste 602 (10006-2519)
PHONE...................212 509-1200
Fax: 212 509-6115
Rocco Macri, *CEO*
Christopher Bungo, *President*
Craig Zimmerman, *President*
CJ Knowles, *Business Mgr*
Matthew Jacobson, *Opers Mgr*
EMP: 8
SALES (est): 890K **Privately Held**
WEB: www.broadcastmanager.org
SIC: 3651 Amplifiers: radio, public address or musical instrument

(G-9518)
BROADWAY TECHNOLOGY LLC (PA)
28 Liberty St 8 (10005-1400)
PHONE...................646 912-6450
Fax: 646 437-3237
Jonathan Fieldman, *COO*
Margaret McManus, *Opers Staff*
Marek Sukk, *CFO*
Preston Mesick, *Accounts Mgr*
Lindsay Young, *Office Mgr*
EMP: 20
SALES (est): 1MM **Privately Held**
WEB: www.broadwaytechnology.com
SIC: 7372 Business oriented computer software

(G-9519)
BROKEN THREADS INC
147 W 35th St Ste 501 (10001-0070)
PHONE...................212 730-4351
Rohan Shah, *Ch of Bd*
▲ EMP: 2 EST: 2007
SQ FT: 500
SALES (est): 6.3MM **Privately Held**
SIC: 2329 Men's & boys' sportswear & athletic clothing

(G-9520)
BROOKE LEIGH LTD (PA)
Also Called: Ali & Kris
520 8th Ave Fl 20 (10018-6507)
PHONE...................212 736-9098
Fax: 212 736-9123
Mary Canter, *President*
Francis Fidel, *Bookkeeper*
EMP: 11
SALES (est): 782.3K **Privately Held**
SIC: 2331 2337 2339 Blouses, women's & juniors': made from purchased material; skirts, separate: women's, misses' & juniors'; slacks: women's, misses' & juniors'

(G-9521)
BROOKE MAYA INC
124 W 36th St Fl 7 (10018-8845)
PHONE...................212 279-2340
Allen Hakimian, *President*
▲ EMP: 35
SQ FT: 11,000
SALES (est): 2.4MM **Privately Held**
SIC: 2361 Dresses: girls', children's & infants'

(G-9522)
BROWN PRINTING COMPANY
1500 Broadway Ste 505 (10036-4055)
PHONE...................212 782-7800
Fax: 212 782-7878
Volker Peterson, *President*
Del Miller, *Materials Mgr*
Guy Christman, *Department Mgr*
EMP: 25 EST: 2010
SALES (est): 2.9MM **Privately Held**
SIC: 2752 Commercial printing, lithographic

(G-9523)
BROWN PUBLISHING NETWORK INC
122 E 42nd St Rm 2810 (10168-2893)
PHONE...................212 682-3330
Marie Brown, *Branch Mgr*
Bill Guthrie, *Branch Mgr*
EMP: 5
SALES (corp-wide): 7.2MM **Privately Held**
WEB: www.brownpubnet.com
SIC: 2731 Textbooks: publishing only, not printed on site
PA: Brown Publishing Network, Inc.
10 City Sq Ste 3
Charlestown MA 02129
781 547-7600

(G-9524)
BROWNSTONE CAPITL PARTNERS LLC
251 5th Ave Fl 3 (10016-6515)
PHONE...................212 889-0069
Lily Calle, *Manager*
Martin Alter,
EMP: 7
SQ FT: 2,500
SALES (est): 713.7K **Privately Held**
SIC: 2752 Commercial printing, offset

(G-9525)
BROWNSTONE PUBLISHERS INC
149 5th Ave Fl 10 (10010-6832)
PHONE...................212 473-8200
Fax: 212 473-8786
John Striker, *President*
George Chafeffer, *Publisher*
George Schaeffer, *Publisher*
Marion Walsh, *Editor*
Jayne Czik, *Div Sub Head*
EMP: 46
SQ FT: 10,000
SALES (est): 3.4MM **Privately Held**
SIC: 2721 2741 Periodicals: publishing only; miscellaneous publishing

(G-9526)
BSO ENERGY CORP
125 Park Ave Ste 2507 (10017-5529)
PHONE...................212 520-1827
Sergio S Correa, *President*
Rosemarie Ojeda, *Manager*
Roberto A Santos, *Director*
EMP: 10

SALES (est): 1.1MM **Privately Held**
SIC: **2821** Thermoplastic materials

(G-9527)
BUCKSENSE INC
140 West St Fl 2 (10007-2141)
PHONE...........................877 710-2825
Claudio Carnevale, *President*
Javier Barragan, *General Mgr*
Geetha Chandra, *Treasurer*
Soleidy Mendez, *Accountant*
Margherita Argenziano, *Director*
EMP: 30 EST: 2011
SALES: 25.3MM
SALES (corp-wide): 4.2MM **Privately Held**
SIC: **2741** Miscellaneous publishing
PA: Acotel Group Spa
Via Della Valle Dei Fontanili 29/37
Roma RM 00168
066 114-1000

(G-9528)
BULKLEY DUNTON (DH)
1 Penn Plz Ste 2814 (10119-2814)
PHONE...........................212 863-1800
Fax: 212 352-0929
Doehner George, *President*
EMP: 37
SALES (est): 49.7MM
SALES (corp-wide): 8.3B **Publicly Held**
SIC: **2741** Miscellaneous publishing
HQ: Veritiv Operating Company
1000 Abernathy Rd
Atlanta GA 30328
770 391-8200

(G-9529)
BULL STREET LLC
Also Called: Supdates
19 W 69th St Apt 201 (10023-4750)
PHONE...........................212 495-9855
Jared Gettinger,
EMP: 5
SALES (est): 265.4K **Privately Held**
SIC: **7372** Application computer software

(G-9530)
BULLETT MEDIA LLC
419 Lafayette St Fl 6 (10003-7013)
PHONE...........................212 242-2123
Jack Becht,
EMP: 14
SALES (est): 125.2K **Privately Held**
SIC: **2721** Magazines: publishing & printing

(G-9531)
BUREAU OF NATIONAL AFFAIRS INC
25 W 43rd St Ste 1007 (10036-7427)
PHONE...........................212 687-4530
Fax: 212 967-1727
John Herzfeld, *Manager*
EMP: 23
SALES (corp-wide): 2.4B **Privately Held**
SIC: **2711** Newspapers
HQ: The Bureau Of National Affairs Inc
1801 S Bell St Ste Cn110
Arlington VA 22202
703 341-3000

(G-9532)
BURLEN CORP
6 E 32nd St Fl 10 (10016-5415)
PHONE...........................212 684-0052
Steve Klein, *President*
EMP: 12
SALES (corp-wide): 1.1B **Privately Held**
SIC: **2342** Girdles & panty girdles
HQ: Burlen Corp.
1904 Mccormick Dr
Tifton GA 31793
229 382-4100

(G-9533)
BURNS ARCHIVE PHOTOGRAPHIC DIS
140 E 38th St Frnt 1 (10016-2686)
PHONE...........................212 889-1938
Stanley Burns MD, *Owner*
Liz Burns, *Director*
▼ EMP: 4
SQ FT: 4,000

SALES: 1MM **Privately Held**
WEB: www.burnsarchive.com
SIC: **2731** 8099 Book publishing; medical photography & art

(G-9534)
BUSINESS INTEGRITY INC (DH)
79 Madison Ave Fl 2 (10016-7805)
PHONE...........................718 238-2008
Tim Allen, *President*
Thomas Mule, *COO*
Brian Long, *Sales Staff*
EMP: 6
SQ FT: 3,000
SALES (est): 895K **Privately Held**
WEB: www.business-integrity.com
SIC: **7372** Business oriented computer software

(G-9535)
BUSINESS JOURNALS
1166 Ave Of The America (10036-2708)
PHONE...........................212 790-5100
Keith Edwards, *Manager*
EMP: 11
SALES (corp-wide): 1.5B **Privately Held**
SIC: **2711** Newspapers
HQ: The Business Journals
120 W Morehead St Ste 420
Charlotte NC 28202
704 371-3248

(G-9536)
BUTTERFLY BEAUTY LLC
150 E 52nd St Fl 14a (10022-6059)
PHONE...........................646 604-4289
Ginny Wright, *General Mgr*
Brian Royle, *Finance Mgr*
Caitlin Bohr, *Manager*
EMP: 8 EST: 2015
SALES (est): 76K
SALES (corp-wide): 12.9MM **Privately Held**
SIC: **2844** 5122 Toilet preparations; cosmetics, perfumes & hair products
PA: Batallure Beauty, Llc
104 Carnegie Ctr Ste 202
Princeton NJ 08540
609 716-1200

(G-9537)
BUTTONS & TRIMCOM INC
519 8th Ave Rm 26 (10018-5275)
PHONE...........................212 868-1971
Peter Frankel, *President*
Susan Frankel, *Vice Pres*
EMP: 13
SQ FT: 2,200
SALES (est): 1.5MM **Privately Held**
SIC: **3965** 3089 3499 Buttons & parts; buckles & buckle parts; novelties, plastic; novelties & specialties, metal

(G-9538)
BY ROBERT JAMES
74 Orchard St (10002-4515)
PHONE...........................212 253-2121
Robert Loomis, *Principal*
EMP: 5
SALES (est): 658.9K **Privately Held**
SIC: **2329** 5611 Men's & boys' clothing; men's & boys' clothing stores

(G-9539)
BYELOCORP SCIENTIFIC INC (PA)
76 Perry St (10014-3238)
PHONE...........................212 785-2580
Lowell A Mintz, *Ch of Bd*
William Begell, *President*
Kathleen Kent, *Vice Pres*
EMP: 27
SALES (est): 1.6MM **Privately Held**
SIC: **3491** 3443 Industrial valves; industrial vessels, tanks & containers

(G-9540)
BYER CALIFORNIA
1407 Broadway Rm 807 (10018-5149)
PHONE...........................212 944-8769
Fax: 212 719-4290
Amy Madus, *Sales Staff*
Martin Bernstein, *Manager*
EMP: 7

SALES (corp-wide): 378.2MM **Privately Held**
WEB: www.byer.com
SIC: **3842** Surgical appliances & supplies
PA: Byer California
66 Potrero Ave
San Francisco CA 94103
415 626-7844

(G-9541)
BYLINER INC
27 W 24th St Ste 202 (10010-3299)
PHONE...........................415 680-3608
John Tayman, *CEO*
Deanna Brown, *President*
Theodore Barnett, *COO*
EMP: 20 EST: 2010
SALES (est): 1.4MM **Privately Held**
SIC: **2731** 2741 Book publishing;

(G-9542)
BYTE CONSULTING INC
295 Madison Ave Fl 35 (10017-6414)
PHONE...........................646 500-8606
Rak Chugh, *President*
Lokesh Chugh, *Sales Staff*
Arun Murugavel, *Technology*
Dan Costin, *Director*
Thomas Loop, *Director*
EMP: 8
SALES (est): 943.6K **Privately Held**
WEB: www.byteconsulting.com
SIC: **7372** Prepackaged software

(G-9543)
CA INC (PA)
520 Madison Ave Fl 22 (10022-4327)
PHONE...........................800 225-5224
Fax: 212 827-2640
Michael P Gregoire, *CEO*
Arthur F Weinbach, *Ch of Bd*
Michael C Bisignano, *Exec VP*
David Bressler, *Vice Pres*
Brian Burba, *Vice Pres*
EMP: 1500 EST: 1976
SALES: 4B **Publicly Held**
WEB: www.cai.com
SIC: **7372** 8742 Business oriented computer software; application computer software; management consulting services

(G-9544)
CABLES AND CHIPS INC (PA)
121 Fulton St Fl 4 (10038-2795)
PHONE...........................212 619-3132
Fax: 212 619-3982
Howard Feinstein, *CEO*
Susan Feinstein, *President*
Andrew Zadorozny, *Manager*
Rick Scherer, *Shareholder*
EMP: 27
SQ FT: 5,500
SALES (est): 3MM **Privately Held**
WEB: www.cablesandchipsinc.com
SIC: **2298** 3644 5734 5063 Cable, fiber; switch boxes, electric; computer peripheral equipment; electronic wire & cable; connectors, electronic; local area network (LAN) systems integrator

(G-9545)
CABRIOLE DESIGNS INC
315 E 91st St Ste 3 (10128-5938)
PHONE...........................212 593-4528
Fax: 212 427-6913
Louis Tonna, *President*
EMP: 6
SALES (est): 476.2K **Privately Held**
WEB: www.cabrioledesign.com
SIC: **2391** Curtains & draperies

(G-9546)
CACHET INDUSTRIES INC
463 Fashion Ave Rm 601 (10018-8720)
PHONE...........................212 944-2188
Fax: 212 944-9493
David Darouvar, *President*
Mark Naim, *Admin Sec*
▲ EMP: 30
SQ FT: 12,000
SALES (est): 4.4MM **Privately Held**
SIC: **2335** Women's, juniors' & misses' dresses

(G-9547)
CAI INC (PA)
Also Called: Copen International Limited
430 E 56th St (10022-4171)
PHONE...........................212 819-0008
Fax: 212 819-0870
Carin Trundle, *CEO*
Barry Emmanuel, *President*
Tsie Persaud, *Accounts Mgr*
◆ EMP: 35
SQ FT: 2,300
SALES (est): 5MM **Privately Held**
WEB: www.midsouthmfg.com
SIC: **2211** 2396 Pocketing twill, cotton; waistbands, trouser

(G-9548)
CAI DESIGN INC
240 W 37th St Ste 303 (10018-6604)
PHONE...........................212 401-9973
Yiming Cai, *Partner*
Yisei Cai, *Partner*
▲ EMP: 14
SALES (est): 554.9K **Privately Held**
SIC: **2339** Sportswear, women's

(G-9549)
CAITHNESS EQUITIES CORPORATION (PA)
Also Called: Shepherds Flat
565 5th Ave Fl 29 (10017-2478)
PHONE...........................212 599-2112
James D Bishop Jr, *Ch of Bd*
James C Sullivan, *Senior VP*
Christopher T Mc Callion, *Vice Pres*
Gail Conboy, *Admin Sec*
EMP: 23
SALES (est): 36.1MM **Privately Held**
WEB: www.caithnessenergy.com
SIC: **3491** 4911 4961 6162 Compressed gas cylinder valves; generation, electric power; steam supply systems, including geothermal; mortgage bankers

(G-9550)
CALDEIRA USA INC
230 5th Ave Ste 300 (10001-7902)
PHONE...........................212 532-2292
Tony Caldeira, *President*
Lindsey Orrick, *General Mgr*
Jeff Shaffer, *Sales Mgr*
Fahim Khan, *Manager*
Carolyn Winderbaum, *Manager*
▲ EMP: 3 EST: 2006
SQ FT: 2,000
SALES: 2MM **Privately Held**
SIC: **2399** Emblems, badges & insignia
HQ: Caldeira Limited
Knowsley Point
Liverpool
151 290-9090

(G-9551)
CALIFORNIA PETRO TRNSPT CORP
114 W 47th St (10036-1510)
PHONE...........................212 302-5151
Frank Bilotta, *President*
EMP: 2
SALES: 1.9MM **Privately Held**
SIC: **2911** Petroleum refining

(G-9552)
CALIFORNIA US HOLDINGS INC
417 5th Ave Lbby 7th (10016-3380)
PHONE...........................212 726-6500
Bruno Bonnell, *President*
Mark Kaiman, *CFO*
Michael Pagnetti, *Controller*
Sherly Roden, *Financial Exec*
Emily Anadu, *Manager*
EMP: 564
SQ FT: 90,000
SALES: 28.4MM
SALES (corp-wide): 2.1MM **Privately Held**
SIC: **7372** 5045 Prepackaged software; computers, peripherals & software
PA: Atari Sa
Atari
Paris 75009
800 814-850

New York - New York County (G-9553)

(G-9553)
CALLAWAY ARTS & ENTRMT INC
41 Union Sq W Ste 1101 (10003-3253)
PHONE.................................646 465-4667
John Lee, CEO
Nicholas Callaway, President
Jennifer Caffrey, Administration
EMP: 11
SALES (est): 618.1K Privately Held
SIC: 2731 Books: publishing & printing

(G-9554)
CALLAWAY DIGITAL ARTS INC
41 Union Sq W Ste 1101 (10003-3253)
PHONE.................................212 675-3050
Rex Ishibashi, CEO
John Lee, President
Lisa Holton, Vice Pres
Nicholas Callaway, Officer
EMP: 30
SALES (est): 3.2MM Privately Held
SIC: 7372 Application computer software

(G-9555)
CALLIDUS SOFTWARE INC
152 W 57th St Fl 8 (10019-3386)
PHONE.................................212 554-7300
Fax: 212 554-7252
Leslie Stretch, CEO
Robert H Youngjohns, Ch of Bd
Bryan Burkhart, Vice Pres
Giles House, Vice Pres
Megan Banguis, Accountant
EMP: 15
SALES (est): 1.2MM Privately Held
SIC: 7372 Prepackaged software

(G-9556)
CALVIN KLEIN INC
654 Madison Ave (10065-8445)
PHONE.................................212 292-9000
Fax: 212 292-9001
EMP: 50
SALES (corp-wide): 8.2B Publicly Held
SIC: 3161 Mfg Luggage
HQ: Calvin Klein, Inc.
   205 W 39th St Lbby 2
   New York NY 10018
   212 719-2600

(G-9557)
CAMBRIDGE INFO GROUP INC (PA)
Also Called: C I G
888 7th Ave Ste 1701 (10106-1799)
PHONE.................................301 961-6700
Fax: 212 897-6640
Andrew M Snyder, CEO
Robert Snyder, Chairman
Michael K Chung, COO
Barbara Inkellis, Senior VP
Larisa Avner Trainor, Senior VP
EMP: 12
SQ FT: 24,000
SALES (est): 437.3MM Privately Held
WEB: www.csa.com
SIC: 2741 Technical manual & paper publishing

(G-9558)
CAMBRIDGE UNIVERSITY PRESS
165 Broadway Fl 20 (10006-1435)
PHONE.................................212 337-5000
Fax: 914 937-4712
Michael Peluse, Managing Dir
Jeffrey Brown, Editor
Sara Marcus, Editor
Chris Newton, Editor
Quin Paseka, Project Mgr
EMP: 80
SALES (corp-wide): 380.7MM Privately Held
SIC: 2731 2721 4226 Books: publishing only; periodicals; special warehousing & storage
PA: Cambridge University Press
   University Printing House
   Cambridge CAMBS CB2 8
   122 335-8331

(G-9559)
CAMINUS CORPORATION (DH)
340 Madison Ave Fl 8 (10173-0899)
PHONE.................................212 515-3600
John A Andrus, President
EMP: 65 EST: 1999
SALES (est): 11.7MM
SALES (corp-wide): 9.2B Publicly Held
SIC: 7372 7379 Business oriented computer software; computer related consulting services
HQ: Fis Data Systems Inc.
   200 Campus Dr
   Collegeville PA 19426
   484 582-2000

(G-9560)
CAMPBELL ALLIANCE GROUP INC
335 Madison Ave Fl 17 (10017-4677)
PHONE.................................212 377-2740
Patrick Manhard, CEO
Alisa Jernigan, Controller
Jennifer Krcmery, Consultant
Mengran Wang, Consultant
EMP: 24 EST: 1997
SQ FT: 50
SALES (est): 3MM Privately Held
SIC: 2834 Pharmaceutical preparations

(G-9561)
CANADA GOOSE INC
601 W 26th St Rm 1745 (10001-1141)
PHONE.................................888 276-6297
EMP: 7
SALES (corp-wide): 379.4K Privately Held
SIC: 2339 Women's & misses' outerwear
PA: Canada Goose Inc
   250 Bowie Ave
   Toronto ON M6E 4
   416 780-9850

(G-9562)
CANALI USA INC (DH)
415 W 13th St Fl 2 (10014-1114)
PHONE.................................212 767-0205
Fax: 212 586-9775
Paolo Canali, CEO
Georgio Canali, Vice Pres
Lisa Emanuel, Manager
Paul Demaio, Director
▲ EMP: 34
SALES (est): 1.8MM Privately Held
SIC: 2311 Suits, men's & boys': made from purchased materials
HQ: Canali Spa
   Via Lombardia 17
   Sovico 20845
   039 201-4226

(G-9563)
CANARY CONNECT INC
606 W 28th St Fl 7 (10001-1108)
PHONE.................................212 390-8576
Adam Sager, CEO
Jon Troutman, Ch Credit Ofcr
Chris Rill, CTO
EMP: 120 EST: 2013
SALES (est): 1.3MM Privately Held
SIC: 3699 Security devices

(G-9564)
CANCER TARGETING SYSTEMS
100 Wall St (10005-3701)
PHONE.................................212 965-4534
Raymond Tesi, CEO
EMP: 5
SALES (est): 300.5K Privately Held
SIC: 2834 Pharmaceutical preparations

(G-9565)
CANDEX SOLUTIONS INC
410 Park Ave (10022-4407)
PHONE.................................215 650-3214
Jeremy Lappin, CEO
Mark Steinke, President
Marianna Suckova, Vice Pres
Shani Vaza, Vice Pres
Melissa Deegan, Office Mgr
EMP: 5
SALES (est): 990.1K Privately Held
SIC: 7372 Prepackaged software; business oriented computer software

(G-9566)
CANDLESTICKS INC
112 W 34th St Fl 18 (10120-0911)
PHONE.................................212 947-8900
Fax: 212 643-9653
Leonard Bernstein, President
Jay Bernstein, Vice Pres
Laura Bernstein, Vice Pres
Lawrence Bernstein, Vice Pres
Marvin Cohen, Controller
▲ EMP: 10
SQ FT: 5,500
SALES (est): 1.2MM Privately Held
WEB: www.candlesticks.com
SIC: 2341 2369 2339 2322 Women's & children's nightwear; bathing suits & swimwear: girls', children's & infants'; women's & misses' outerwear; men's & boys' underwear & nightwear

(G-9567)
CANE SUGAR LLC
Also Called: Cane Simple
950 3rd Ave Ste 2200 (10022-2773)
PHONE.................................212 329-2695
Reid Chase, Mng Member
EMP: 6
SALES (est): 230K Privately Held
SIC: 2062 Cane syrup from purchased raw sugar

(G-9568)
CANOPY CANOPY CANOPY INC
Also Called: Triple Canopy
264 Canal St Ste 3w (10013-3592)
PHONE.................................347 529-5182
Peter Russo, Principal
Seth Erickson, Editor
Alexander Provan, Editor
Colby Chamberlain, Senior Editor
Franklin Bruno, Author
EMP: 1
SALES (est): 1.3MM Privately Held
SIC: 2721 Periodicals

(G-9569)
CANT LIVE WITHOUT IT LLC
Also Called: Swell Bottle
28 W 23rd St Fl 5 (10010-5259)
PHONE.................................844 517-9355
Sarah Kauss, CEO
Katie Garbis, Mktg Dir
▲ EMP: 100
SQ FT: 25,000
SALES (est): 45.4MM Privately Held
SIC: 3429 Vacuum bottles or jugs

(G-9570)
CANTON NOODLE CORPORATION
101 Mott St (10013-5093)
PHONE.................................212 226-3276
Fax: 212 226-8037
James Eng, Principal
Michelle Eng, Manager
EMP: 8 EST: 1951
SQ FT: 4,000
SALES (est): 600K Privately Held
SIC: 2098 Noodles (e.g. egg, plain & water), dry

(G-9571)
CANYON PUBLISHING INC
55 John St Ste 6 (10038-3752)
PHONE.................................212 334-0227
Sandra Vasceannie, President
EMP: 10
SALES (est): 880K Privately Held
SIC: 2752 Publication printing, lithographic

(G-9572)
CAP USA JERSEYMAN HARLEM INC (PA)
112 W 125th St (10027-4403)
PHONE.................................212 222-7942
Fax: 212 222-7946
Sung R Park, Ch of Bd
EMP: 7
SALES (est): 401.6K Privately Held
SIC: 2257 Jersey cloth

(G-9573)
CAPCO WAI SHING LLC
132 W 36th St Rm 509 (10018-8843)
PHONE.................................212 268-1976
Jim Capuano, Mng Member
EMP: 8
SALES (est): 921.9K Privately Held
SIC: 3089 Clothes hangers, plastic

(G-9574)
CAPITAL E FINANCIAL GROUP
Also Called: Victoire Latam Asset MGT LLC
598 Madison Ave Fl 9 (10022-1668)
PHONE.................................212 319-6550
Nadim Razzouck, Chairman
EMP: 10
SALES (est): 1.2MM Privately Held
SIC: 3524 6799 Hedge trimmers, electric; venture capital companies
PA: Sindicatum Holdings Limited
   Suite 225 10 Greycoat Place
   London

(G-9575)
CAPITAL GOLD CORPORATION (PA)
601 Lexington Ave Fl 36 (10022-4611)
PHONE.................................212 668-0842
▲ EMP: 8
SALES (est): 15.1MM Privately Held
SIC: 1041 1499 Gold And Mineral Exploration

(G-9576)
CAPITAL PROGRAMS INC
Also Called: CPI
420 Lexington Ave Lbby 6 (10170-0024)
PHONE.................................212 842-4640
Fax: 212 838-3176
Sabi Kanaan, CEO
Aniq Bishop, Office Mgr
EMP: 7
SQ FT: 1,000
SALES (est): 590K Privately Held
SIC: 7372 Application computer software

(G-9577)
CARANDA EMPORIUM LLC
Also Called: Serengeti Teas and Spices
2292 Frdrick Douglas Blvd (10027)
PHONE.................................212 866-7100
Oseovbie Imoukhuede,
EMP: 15
SALES (est): 703.5K Privately Held
SIC: 2095 Roasted coffee

(G-9578)
CARAVAN INTERNATIONAL CORP
641 Lexington Ave Fl 13 (10022-4503)
PHONE.................................212 223-7190
Ursula Cernuschi, President
Dennis Friedman, Vice Pres
Paulo Sanchez, Director
EMP: 6 EST: 1963
SQ FT: 32,000
SALES (est): 2.5MM Privately Held
WEB: www.caravan-ny.com
SIC: 3728 5065 Aircraft parts & equipment; communication equipment

(G-9579)
CARBERT MUSIC INC
126 E 38th St (10016-2692)
PHONE.................................212 725-9277
Freddy Bienstock, President
Frank Dimarco, Controller
Bob Golden, Mktg Dir
EMP: 30
SQ FT: 8,000
SALES (est): 1.3MM Privately Held
SIC: 2741 Music book & sheet music publishing

(G-9580)
CARL FISCHER LLC (PA)
48 Wall St 28 (10005-2903)
PHONE.................................212 777-0900
Fax: 212 477-6996
Hayden Connor, CEO
Jessica Bogwicz, Production
Casey Yu, Controller
Michael Kerr, Finance Other
Nicole Davenport, Human Resources
EMP: 20 EST: 1872

GEOGRAPHIC SECTION

New York - New York County (G-9607)

SALES (est): 2.9MM **Privately Held**
WEB: www.carlfischer.com
SIC: **2741** 5736 5099 5199 Music, sheet: publishing & printing; musical instrument stores; sheet music; musical instruments parts & accessories; sheet music

(G-9581)
CARLO MONTE DESIGNS INC
17 E 48th St Fl 8 (10017-1010)
PHONE..............................212 935-5611
Karnik Garipian, *President*
Haci Garipian, *President*
EMP: 6
SQ FT: 2,400
SALES (est): 2.5MM **Privately Held**
WEB: www.montecarlodesigns.com
SIC: **3911** Jewelry, precious metal

(G-9582)
CARNIVAL INC
284 Mott St Apt 4d (10012-3493)
PHONE..............................415 781-9815
Guy Horrocks, *CEO*
EMP: 6
SALES (est): 426.4K **Privately Held**
SIC: **7372** Prepackaged software; application computer software

(G-9583)
CARODA INC
254 W 35th St (10001-2504)
PHONE..............................212 630-9986
Ida Leigh M Law, *CEO*
EMP: 30 EST: 2009
SALES (est): 1.3MM **Privately Held**
SIC: **2329** Athletic (warmup, sweat & jogging) suits: men's & boys'

(G-9584)
CAROL DAUPLAISE LTD
134 W 37th St Fl 3 (10018-6974)
PHONE..............................212 997-5290
Jeffrey Dauplaise, *Branch Mgr*
EMP: 20
SALES (corp-wide): 5.8MM **Privately Held**
WEB: www.dauplaisejewelry.com
SIC: **3911** 5094 Jewelry, precious metal; jewelry & precious stones
PA: Carol Dauplaise Ltd
29 W 36th St Fl 12
New York NY 10018
212 564-7301

(G-9585)
CAROL FOR EVA GRAHAM INC
366 5th Ave Rm 815 (10001-2211)
PHONE..............................212 889-8686
Fax: 212 481-3299
Carol Graham, *President*
Eva C Graham, *Vice Pres*
EMP: 12
SQ FT: 10,000
SALES (est): 2.2MM **Privately Held**
SIC: **3961** Costume jewelry, ex. precious metal & semiprecious stones

(G-9586)
CAROL GROUP LTD
Also Called: Habitat Magazine
150 W 30th St Rm 902 (10001-4125)
PHONE..............................212 505-2030
Fax: 212 254-6795
Carol Ott, *President*
Paul Ukena, *Partner*
Frank Lovece, *Editor*
Frank Socci Jr, *Director*
Alvin Wasserman, *Director*
EMP: 7
SQ FT: 1,000
SALES: 891K **Privately Held**
WEB: www.habitatmag.com
SIC: **2721** Magazines: publishing only, not printed on site

(G-9587)
CAROLINA AMATO INC
270 W 38th St Rm 902 (10018-1759)
PHONE..............................212 768-9095
Carolina Amato, *President*
Elina Sidler, *Bookkeeper*
▲ EMP: 6 EST: 1977
SALES (est): 1.5MM **Privately Held**
WEB: www.carolinaamato.com
SIC: **2339** Women's & misses' accessories

(G-9588)
CAROLINA HERRERA LTD (HQ)
501 Fashion Ave Fl 17 (10018-5911)
PHONE..............................212 944-5757
Fax: 212 944-7996
Claudia Thomas, *President*
Melinda Rathke, *General Mgr*
Charles Gallardo, *Opers Mgr*
Nate Rosenberg, *CFO*
Corey Wigfall, *Sales Associate*
▼ EMP: 45
SALES (est): 17.5MM
SALES (corp-wide): 186.9K **Privately Held**
WEB: www.carolinaherrera.com
SIC: **2337** 2339 Skirts, separate: women's, misses' & juniors'; women's & misses' outerwear
PA: Equipamientos Puig Sl
Calle Lardero, 3 - Bj
Logrono
941 202-026

(G-9589)
CARRERA CASTING CORP
64 W 48th St Fl 2 (10036-1708)
PHONE..............................212 382-3296
Fax: 212 768-9124
Eric Schwartz, *Ch of Bd*
Owen Schwartz, *President*
Dean Schwartz, *Dean*
Joel Weiss, *Vice Pres*
Joseph Sorrentino, *Draft/Design*
EMP: 160
SQ FT: 8,000
SALES (est): 41.9MM **Privately Held**
WEB: www.carreracasting.com
SIC: **3915** 3369 Jewelers' castings; non-ferrous foundries

(G-9590)
CARRY HOT INC
545 W 45th St Rm 501 (10036-3409)
PHONE..............................212 279-7535
Fax: 212 279-0734
Sanford Plotkin, *President*
Ron Demaray, *Mktg Dir*
Elizabeth Werner, *Info Tech Dir*
EMP: 10
SALES (est): 1.1MM **Privately Held**
WEB: www.carryhot.com
SIC: **2393** Bags & containers, except sleeping bags: textile

(G-9591)
CARVART GLASS INC (PA)
1441 Broadway Fl 28 (10018-1905)
PHONE..............................212 675-0030
Fax: 212 675-8175
Antoly Geyman, *President*
Edward Geyman, *Vice Pres*
Bob Wessel, *Vice Pres*
Susan Kosor, *Project Mgr*
Amalia Villafranca, *Asst Controller*
▲ EMP: 10
SQ FT: 17,000
SALES (est): 5.5MM **Privately Held**
WEB: www.carvart.com
SIC: **3231** Art glass: made from purchased glass

(G-9592)
CARVIN FRENCH JEWELERS INC
515 Madison Ave Rm 1605 (10022-5445)
PHONE..............................212 755-6474
Andre Chervin, *President*
Grafinka Chunov, *Controller*
EMP: 20 EST: 1954
SQ FT: 4,000
SALES (est): 1.7MM **Privately Held**
SIC: **3911** 3961 Jewelry, precious metal; costume jewelry

(G-9593)
CASABLANCA FOODS LLC
135 E 57th St Unit 96 (10022-2168)
PHONE..............................212 317-1111
Mina Kallamni, *Managing Prtnr*
Fouad Kallamni, *Managing Prtnr*
▲ EMP: 6
SALES: 1MM **Privately Held**
SIC: **2099** Syrups

(G-9594)
CASPER SCIENCE LLC
230 Park Ave S Fl 13 (10003-1547)
PHONE..............................212 633-4309
EMP: 5 EST: 2016
SALES (est): 542.1K **Privately Held**
SIC: **2515** Mattresses, containing felt, foam rubber, urethane, etc.

(G-9595)
CASSINI PARFUMS LTD
3 W 57th St Fl 8 (10019-3407)
PHONE..............................212 753-7540
EMP: 8
SQ FT: 8,000
SALES (est): 797.6K **Privately Held**
SIC: **2844** Mfg Fragrances

(G-9596)
CASTLE BRANDS INC (PA)
122 E 42nd St Rm 5000 (10168-4700)
PHONE..............................646 356-0200
Mark E Andrews III, *Ch of Bd*
Richard J Lampen, *President*
Jason Barlow, *Editor*
John S Glover, *COO*
Alejandra Pe A, *Senior VP*
▲ EMP: 51
SQ FT: 5,000
SALES: 77.2MM **Publicly Held**
WEB: www.castlebrandsinc.com
SIC: **2082** 2085 Malt beverages; malt liquors; rum (alcoholic beverage); scotch whiskey; vodka (alcoholic beverage)

(G-9597)
CASTLE CONNOLLY MEDICAL LTD
42 W 24th St Fl 2 (10010-3201)
PHONE..............................212 367-8400
Fax: 212 367-0964
John K Castle, *Ch of Bd*
Dr John J Connolly, *President*
Mark McGinty, *President*
William Liss-Levinson, *COO*
Nicki Hughes, *Comms Mgr*
EMP: 25
SQ FT: 500
SALES (est): 3.1MM **Privately Held**
WEB: www.eldercareliving.com
SIC: **2731** 2741 Books: publishing only; miscellaneous publishing

(G-9598)
CASUALS ETC INC
Also Called: E T C
16 E 52nd St Fl 4 (10022-5306)
PHONE..............................212 838-1319
William Rondina, *President*
Steven Steinberg, *CFO*
Mark Schoenfeld, *Controller*
EMP: 100
SALES (est): 5MM **Privately Held**
SIC: **2339** 5137 Women's & misses' athletic clothing & sportswear; sportswear, women's & children's

(G-9599)
CATALYST GROUP INC
Also Called: Catalyst Group Design
345 7th Ave Rm 1100 (10001-5165)
PHONE..............................212 243-7777
Nicholas Gould, *CEO*
Jon Mysel, *President*
Tim Piatek, *Manager*
Rene Zain, *Web Dvlpr*
Peter Hughes, *Admin Sec*
EMP: 6
SQ FT: 2,000
SALES (est): 860.7K **Privately Held**
WEB: www.catalystgroupdesign.com
SIC: **7372** Application computer software

(G-9600)
CATAPULT
1140 Broadway Rm 704 (10001-7504)
PHONE..............................323 839-6204
Russell Hunter, *Principal*
EMP: 5
SALES (est): 135.2K **Privately Held**
SIC: **3599** Catapults

(G-9601)
CATCH VENTURES INC
30 W 63rd St Apt 14o (10023-7173)
PHONE..............................347 620-4351
Scott Graulich, *President*
EMP: 10
SALES (est): 229.5K **Privately Held**
SIC: **7372** 7389 Application computer software;

(G-9602)
CATHAY HOME INC (PA)
230 5th Ave Ste 215 (10001-7914)
PHONE..............................212 213-0988
Zhiming Qian, *Ch of Bd*
Liwei Fang, *COO*
Leslie Wang, *Human Res Mgr*
▲ EMP: 20
SQ FT: 10,000
SALES (est): 40MM **Privately Held**
SIC: **2392** Blankets, comforters & beddings

(G-9603)
CATHERINE STEIN DESIGNS INC
411 5th Ave Rm 600 (10016-2270)
PHONE..............................212 840-1188
Fax: 212 764-4135
Catherine Stein, *President*
EMP: 30
SQ FT: 10,000
SALES (est): 2MM **Privately Held**
WEB: www.csteindesigns.com
SIC: **3961** Costume jewelry, ex. precious metal & semiprecious stones

(G-9604)
CATHY DANIELS LTD (PA)
Also Called: Ecco Bay Sportswear
501 Fashion Ave Rm 400 (10018-8602)
PHONE..............................212 354-8000
Fax: 212 354-1076
Herb Chestler, *Ch of Bd*
Steven Chestler, *President*
Elizabeth Go, *Controller*
Jerry Passaretti, *Sales Executive*
Roseanne Barranca, *Associate*
◆ EMP: 50
SQ FT: 20,000
SALES (est): 5.9MM **Privately Held**
WEB: www.cathydaniels.com
SIC: **2339** Sportswear, women's

(G-9605)
CAVA SPILIADIS USA
200 W 57th St Ste 908 (10019-3211)
PHONE..............................212 247-8214
Martha Tsapanos, *Principal*
▲ EMP: 20 EST: 2007
SALES (est): 186.7K **Privately Held**
SIC: **2084** Wines

(G-9606)
CCT INC
Also Called: Committee For Color & Trends
60 Madison Ave Ste 1209 (10010-1635)
P.O. Box 1621 (10159-1621)
PHONE..............................212 532-3355
Ellen Campuzano, *President*
EMP: 6
SQ FT: 1,500
SALES (est): 478.4K **Privately Held**
SIC: **2732** Books: printing only

(G-9607)
CEGID CORPORATION
274 Madison Ave Rm 1400 (10016-0701)
PHONE..............................212 757-9038
Fax: 212 757-9051
Dan Friedman, *COO*
Mary Andren, *Accounts Mgr*
Lyndsey McIntosh, *Marketing Mgr*
Arnaud Coste, *Manager*
Nils Nugteren, *Manager*
EMP: 16
SALES (est): 2MM
SALES (corp-wide): 6MM **Privately Held**
SIC: **7372** Word processing computer software
PA: Cegid Group
52 Quai Paul Sedallian
Lyon 69009

(PA)=Parent Co (HQ)=Headquarters (DH)=Div Headquarters
✪ = New Business established in last 2 years

New York - New York County (G-9608)

(G-9608)
CELLVATION INC
2 Gansevoort St Fl 9 (10014-1667)
PHONE.....................212 554-4520
Frank Taffy, *CEO*
Brijesh Gill, *Consultant*
EMP: 8
SALES (est): 340K Privately Held
SIC: 2834 Pharmaceutical preparations

(G-9609)
CEMENTEX LATEX CORP
121 Varick St Frnt 2 (10013-1408)
PHONE.....................212 741-1770
Arthur Gononsky, *President*
Susan Gononsky, *Corp Secy*
Jeffrey Gononsky, *Vice Pres*
Jeff Gononsky, *Vice Pres*
▼ EMP: 10 EST: 1936
SQ FT: 12,000
SALES (est): 850K Privately Held
WEB: www.cementex.com
SIC: 3089 3069 5084 Plastic hardware & building products; reclaimed rubber & specialty rubber compounds; machine tools & accessories

(G-9610)
CEMEX CEMENT INC
590 Madison Ave Fl 41 (10022-2524)
PHONE.....................212 317-6000
Javier Garcia, *President*
EMP: 78 Privately Held
SIC: 3273 Ready-mixed concrete
HQ: Cemex Cement, Inc.
  10100 Katy Fwy Ste 300
  Houston TX 77043
  713 650-6200

(G-9611)
CEMOI INC (PA)
5 Penn Plz Ste 2325 (10001-1810)
PHONE.....................212 583-4920
Thierry Beaujeon, *CEO*
▲ EMP: 2
SALES (est): 4.3MM Privately Held
SIC: 2066 Chocolate bars, solid

(G-9612)
CENIBRA INC
335 Madison Ave Fl 23 (10017-4634)
PHONE.....................212 818-8242
James Monroe, *Manager*
Yoshida Kazuhiro, *Director*
▲ EMP: 6
SALES: 1B Privately Held
SIC: 2611 5159 Pulp mills; bristles

(G-9613)
CENTENNIAL MEDIA LLC ✪
10th Floor 40 Worth St Flr 10 (10013)
PHONE.....................646 527-7320
Sebastian Raatz, *Partner*
Benjamin Harris, *Partner*
▼ EMP: 15 EST: 2017
SALES: 12MM Privately Held
SIC: 2721 Magazines: publishing only, not printed on site

(G-9614)
CENTRAL APPAREL GROUP LTD
Also Called: Central Park Active Wear
16 W 36th St Rm 1202 (10018-9751)
PHONE.....................212 868-6505
Shalom Asher, *CEO*
Steve Goldfarb, *President*
◆ EMP: 18
SQ FT: 900
SALES (est): 10MM Privately Held
SIC: 2339 5621 Sportswear, women's; women's sportswear

(G-9615)
CENTRAL CNFRNCE OF AMRCN RBBIS
355 Lexington Ave Fl 18 (10017-6603)
PHONE.....................212 972-3636
Fax: 212 692-0819
Jonathan A Stein, *President*
Hara Person, *Publisher*
Deborah Smilow, *Editor*
Paul Menitoff, *Exec VP*
Walter Jacob, *Vice Pres*
▲ EMP: 16

SALES (est): 2.5MM Privately Held
WEB: www.ccarnet.org
SIC: 2731 Books: publishing only; pamphlets: publishing only, not printed on site

(G-9616)
CENTRAL GARDEN & PET COMPANY
2475 Broadway (10025-7450)
PHONE.....................212 877-1270
Richard Metzler, *Branch Mgr*
EMP: 9
SALES (corp-wide): 1.8B Publicly Held
WEB: www.centralgardenandpet.com
SIC: 2048 Prepared feeds
PA: Central Garden & Pet Company
  1340 Treat Blvd Ste 600
  Walnut Creek CA 94597
  925 948-4000

(G-9617)
CENTRAL MILLS INC
Also Called: Freeze Clothing
1400 Broadway Rm 1605 (10018-5200)
PHONE.....................212 221-0748
Fax: 212 944-1181
Cedric Howe, *Sales Staff*
Maurice Shalam, *Branch Mgr*
EMP: 110
SALES (corp-wide): 80.5MM Privately Held
SIC: 2329 2339 2253 Men's & boys' sportswear & athletic clothing; women's & misses' outerwear; T-shirts & tops, knit
PA: Central Mills, Inc.
  473 Ridge Rd
  Dayton NJ 08810
  732 329-2009

(G-9618)
CENTRAL TEXTILES INC
Also Called: Cotswolt Industries
10 E 40th St Rm 3410 (10016-0301)
PHONE.....................212 213-8740
Steve Rosenberg, *Sales Staff*
James McKinnon, *Manager*
EMP: 15
SALES (corp-wide): 54.1MM Privately Held
WEB: www.ctextiles.com
SIC: 2261 2262 Finishing plants, cotton; finishing plants, manmade fiber & silk fabrics
PA: Central Textiles, Inc.
  237 Mill Ave
  Central SC 29630
  864 639-2491

(G-9619)
CENTRO INC
841 Broadway Fl 6 (10003-4704)
P.O. Box 13464, Chicago IL (60613-0464)
PHONE.....................212 791-9450
Fax: 773 868-6902
Tannis McKenna, *Accounts Mgr*
Kelly Wenzel, *Chief Mktg Ofcr*
EMP: 300
SALES (corp-wide): 23.6MM Privately Held
SIC: 3089 Plastic processing
PA: Centro, Inc.
  11 E Madison St Ste 300
  Chicago IL 60602
  312 642-7348

(G-9620)
CENTURY GRAND INC
Also Called: Century Pharmacy Three
302 Grand St (10002-4465)
PHONE.....................212 925-3838
Steven T Ho, *Principal*
EMP: 10
SALES (est): 1.3MM Privately Held
SIC: 2834 Druggists' preparations (pharmaceuticals)

(G-9621)
CEO CAST INC
211 E 43rd St Rm 400 (10017-8620)
PHONE.....................212 732-4300
Kenneth Sgro, *President*
Jim Fallon, *Managing Prtnr*
EMP: 18
SQ FT: 25,000

SALES (est): 1.3MM Privately Held
WEB: www.ceocast.com
SIC: 2741 Business service newsletters: publishing & printing

(G-9622)
CEROS INC (PA)
151 W 25th St Rm 200 (10001-7262)
Drawer (10010)
PHONE.....................347 744-9250
Simon Burg, *CEO*
Aaron Wood, *QA Dir*
Kaity Ng, *Controller*
Matt Gelb, *VP Finance*
Elina Strizhak, *Human Resources*
EMP: 24
SALES (est): 1.7MM Privately Held
SIC: 7372 Publishers' computer software

(G-9623)
CFO PUBLISHING LLC (PA)
50 Broad St Frnt (10004-2354)
PHONE.....................212 459-3004
Fax: 212 258-2185
Alan Glass, *President*
Richard Rivera, *President*
Sean Allocca, *Editor*
Lissa Short, *Senior VP*
Andreas Droste, *Sales Staff*
EMP: 120
SQ FT: 7,500
SALES (est): 11.6MM Privately Held
SIC: 2721 Magazines: publishing only, not printed on site

(G-9624)
CGI TECHNOLOGIES SOLUTIONS INC
655 3rd Ave Ste 700 (10017-9124)
PHONE.....................212 682-7411
Fax: 212 682-0715
Don O'Brien, *Principal*
Edward Asip, *VP Sales*
Jeremy Douglass, *Manager*
Robert Hicks, *CTO*
Mark Chamberlin, *Info Tech Dir*
EMP: 15
SALES (corp-wide): 137.9MM Privately Held
SIC: 7372 5045 7379 Prepackaged software; computer software; computer related consulting services
HQ: Cgi Technologies And Solutions Inc.
  11325 Random Hills Rd
  Fairfax VA 22030
  703 267-8000

(G-9625)
CHAIN STORE AGE MAGAZINE
425 Park Ave (10022-3506)
PHONE.....................212 756-5000
EMP: 5
SQ FT: 30,000
SALES (est): 402.6K
SALES (corp-wide): 122.5MM Privately Held
SIC: 2731 Book Publisher
PA: Lebhar-Friedman, Inc.
  150 W 30th St Fl 19
  New York NY 10001
  212 756-5000

(G-9626)
CHAINDOM ENTERPRISES INC
48 W 48th St Ste 200 (10036-1779)
PHONE.....................212 719-4778
Fax: 212 398-1318
Fikri Akdemir, *President*
Steve Pinkin, *Treasurer*
EMP: 6
SQ FT: 2,500
SALES (est): 533.5K Privately Held
SIC: 3911 Jewelry, precious metal

(G-9627)
CHAMPION ZIPPER CORP
Also Called: Sew True
447 W 36th St Fl 2 (10018-6300)
PHONE.....................212 239-0414
Fax: 212 947-9281
Steven Silberberg, *President*
Chris Roldan, *Principal*
Eugene Silberberg, *Controller*
EMP: 6
SQ FT: 5,000

SALES: 1.3MM Privately Held
WEB: www.sewtrue.com
SIC: 3965 2241 Zipper; trimmings, textile

(G-9628)
CHAN LUU LLC
1441 Broadway (10018-1905)
PHONE.....................212 398-3163
Terence Farley, *VP Sales*
Madison Davis, *Accounts Mgr*
Natasha Hodges, *Accounts Mgr*
Chan Luu, *Branch Mgr*
EMP: 26
SALES (corp-wide): 23.7MM Privately Held
SIC: 2752 Fashion plates, lithographed
PA: Chan Luu, Llc
  818 S Broadway Ste 600
  Los Angeles CA 90014
  213 892-0245

(G-9629)
CHANSE PETROLEUM CORPORATION (PA)
828 5th Ave Apt 1f (10065-7272)
PHONE.....................212 682-3789
Fax: 212 687-5360
Kai Chang, *President*
EMP: 3 EST: 1972
SQ FT: 1,000
SALES (est): 1.5MM Privately Held
SIC: 1311 Crude petroleum production; natural gas production

(G-9630)
CHARING CROSS MUSIC INC
3 Columbus Cir Ste 1720 (10019-8708)
PHONE.....................212 541-7571
Paul Simon, *President*
EMP: 6
SQ FT: 1,000
SALES (est): 410K Privately Held
SIC: 2741 Music, sheet: publishing only, not printed on site

(G-9631)
CHARIS & MAE INC
31 W 34th St Fl 8 (10001-3030)
PHONE.....................212 641-0816
Yi Shan Su, *President*
Joseph Acevedo, *Director*
EMP: 5
SALES (est): 217.7K Privately Held
SIC: 3911 Jewelry, precious metal

(G-9632)
CHARLES HENRICKS INC
Also Called: Starkey & Henricks
121 Varick St Fl 9 (10013-1408)
PHONE.....................212 243-5800
Fax: 212 966-5913
Peter Bird, *President*
Douglas Bird, *Vice Pres*
EMP: 15
SALES (est): 1.6MM Privately Held
SIC: 2796 Gravure printing plates or cylinders, preparation of

(G-9633)
CHARLES P ROGERS BRASS BEDS (PA)
Also Called: Charles P Rogers Brass Ir Bed
26 W 17th St (10011-5710)
PHONE.....................212 675-4400
Fax: 212 675-6495
Linda Klein, *President*
David Klein, *Vice Pres*
Donnie Ray, *Vice Pres*
William Mardorf, *Marketing Staff*
Jeannine Tuttle, *Manager*
◆ EMP: 15 EST: 1979
SQ FT: 9,000
SALES (est): 4MM Privately Held
SIC: 2514 5712 5961 Beds, including folding & cabinet, household: metal; beds & accessories; furniture & furnishings, mail order

(G-9634)
CHARLES VAILLANT INC
37 W 57th St Ste 803 (10019-3411)
PHONE.....................212 752-4832
Fax: 212 486-4849
Thomas Renna, *President*
Kenneth Danielsson, *Admin Sec*
▲ EMP: 7

GEOGRAPHIC SECTION

New York - New York County (G-9662)

SALES (est): 705.3K **Privately Held**
SIC: 3911 Jewelry, precious metal

(G-9635)
CHARMING FASHION INC
247 W 38th St Rm 1400 (10018-0230)
PHONE.....................212 730-2872
Fax: 212 730-2872
Charles Kim, *President*
EMP: 5
SALES (est): 261K **Privately Held**
SIC: 2211 Apparel & outerwear fabrics, cotton

(G-9636)
CHARTER VENTURES LLC
135 W 36th St Rm 1800 (10018-6951)
PHONE.....................212 868-0222
Jennifer Lai,
Howard Cohen,
▲ EMP: 10 EST: 2000
SQ FT: 4,838
SALES (est): 1.5MM
SALES (corp-wide): 100MM **Privately Held**
SIC: 2253 Sweaters & sweater coats, knit
PA: Charter Ventures Limited
Rm A 6/F Chiap Luen Indl Bldg
Kwai Chung NT
221 106-07

(G-9637)
CHECK GROUP LLC
1385 Broadway Fl 16 (10018-6041)
PHONE.....................212 221-4700
Fax: 212 221-1561
Lawrence Jemal,
Richard Tan, *Admin Sec*
▲ EMP: 100
SALES (est): 6.8MM **Privately Held**
WEB: www.checkgroup.com
SIC: 2311 2321 2322 2325 Men's & boys' suits & coats; men's & boys' furnishings; underwear, men's & boys': made from purchased materials; men's & boys' trousers & slacks

(G-9638)
CHECKM8 INC (PA)
307 W 36th St Fl 13 (10018-6434)
PHONE.....................212 268-0048
Dana Ghavami, *CEO*
David Kedem, *General Mgr*
EMP: 16
SALES (est): 5.8MM **Privately Held**
WEB: www.checkm8.com
SIC: 7372 Business oriented computer software

(G-9639)
CHELSEA PLASTICS INC
200 Lexington Ave Rm 914 (10016-6255)
PHONE.....................212 924-4530
George Frechter, *President*
Edit Hornyak, *Financial Exec*
EMP: 12
SQ FT: 7,000
SALES (est): 1.5MM **Privately Held**
WEB: www.chelseaplastics.com
SIC: 3082 Unsupported plastics profile shapes

(G-9640)
CHERI MON BABY LLC
1412 Broadway Rm 1608 (10018-9270)
PHONE.....................212 354-5511
Ralph Kassin, *President*
▲ EMP: 6
SQ FT: 1,500
SALES (est): 605.9K **Privately Held**
SIC: 2361 Girls' & children's blouses & shirts

(G-9641)
CHERRY LANE MAGAZINE LLC
1745 Broadway 19 (10019-4640)
PHONE.....................212 561-3000
Fax: 212 683-2040
Peter Primont, *Mng Member*
EMP: 80
SQ FT: 30,000
SALES (est): 4.9MM **Privately Held**
SIC: 2741 Miscellaneous publishing

(G-9642)
CHESKY RECORDS INC
1650 Broadway Ste 900 (10019-6965)
PHONE.....................212 586-7799
Norman Chesky, *President*
David Chesky, *Vice Pres*
Lisa Hershfired, *Accounts Mgr*
EMP: 12
SQ FT: 6,000
SALES (est): 1.2MM **Privately Held**
SIC: 3652 Phonograph record blanks; compact laser discs, prerecorded

(G-9643)
CHIA USA LLC
Also Called: Chia Company
379 W Broadway (10012-5121)
PHONE.....................212 226-7512
John Foss, *CEO*
April Helliwell, *COO*
EMP: 13 EST: 2014
SQ FT: 3,000
SALES (est): 18MM
SALES (corp-wide): 26MM **Privately Held**
SIC: 2043 5153 Cereal breakfast foods; grains; barley
PA: Chia Inc.
379 W Broadway
New York NY 10012
212 226-7512

(G-9644)
CHILD NUTRITION PROG DEPT ED
1011 1st Ave Fl 6 (10022-4112)
PHONE.....................212 371-1000
Thomas Smith, *President*
Christine Plantamura, *Admin Asst*
EMP: 99
SALES (est): 3.6MM **Privately Held**
SIC: 2099 Food preparations

(G-9645)
CHILDRENS PROGRESS INC
108 W 39th St Rm 1305 (10018-8258)
PHONE.....................212 730-0905
Kevin Greaney, *President*
Pat Santo, *Business Mgr*
Sophie Gill, *Sales Associate*
Andrew Morrison, *Info Tech Dir*
EMP: 20
SQ FT: 1,700
SALES (est): 1.4MM **Privately Held**
WEB: www.childrensprogress.com
SIC: 7372 Educational computer software

(G-9646)
CHINA DAILY DISTRIBUTION CORP (HQ)
1500 Broadway Ste 2800 (10036-4097)
PHONE.....................212 537-8888
Larry Lee, *CEO*
Lili Zhou, *Admin Asst*
EMP: 20
SALES (est): 1.2MM **Privately Held**
SIC: 2711 Newspapers
PA: China Daily
No.15, Huixin East Street, Chaoyang District
Beijing
106 499-5969

(G-9647)
CHINA HUAREN ORGANIC PDTS INC
100 Wall St Fl 15 (10005-3701)
PHONE.....................212 232-0120
Cao Yushu, *CEO*
Pam Cambell, *Opers Dir*
Yushu Cao, *CFO*
▲ EMP: 3
SALES: 7.4MM **Privately Held**
WEB: www.ultradatasystems.com
SIC: 2099 2844 Food preparations; toilet preparations; cosmetic preparations

(G-9648)
CHINA INDUSTRIAL STEEL INC
110 Wall St Fl 11 (10005-3834)
PHONE.....................646 328-1502
Shenghong Liu, *Principal*
EMP: 2
SALES: 649.3MM **Privately Held**
SIC: 3312 Blast furnaces & steel mills

(G-9649)
CHINA LITHIUM TECHNOLOGIES (PA)
15 W 39th St Fl 14 (10018-0626)
PHONE.....................212 391-2688
Kun Liu, *Ch of Bd*
Jijun Zhang, *Vice Pres*
Chunping Fang, *CFO*
Fang Ai, *CTO*
EMP: 9
SQ FT: 215
SALES: 15.7MM **Privately Held**
SIC: 3691 3629 Storage batteries; batteries, rechargeable; battery chargers, rectifying or nonrotating

(G-9650)
CHINA N E PETRO HOLDINGS LTD
445 Park Ave (10022-2606)
PHONE.....................212 307-3568
Fax: 718 685-2650
Jingfu LI, *CEO*
Shaohui Chen, *CFO*
EMP: 715
SALES: 99.5MM **Privately Held**
WEB: www.cnepetroleum.com
SIC: 1311 Crude petroleum production

(G-9651)
CHINA NEWSWEEK CORPORATION
15 E 40th St Fl 11 (10016-0463)
PHONE.....................212 481-2510
WEI Xiang Peng, *Ch of Bd*
Fred Teng, *Exec Dir*
EMP: 10
SALES (est): 440K **Privately Held**
SIC: 2711 Newspapers

(G-9652)
CHINA PRESS
15 E 40th St Fl 6 (10016-0407)
PHONE.....................212 683-8282
Fax: 212 274-0688
EMP: 5 EST: 2015
SALES (est): 78K **Privately Held**
SIC: 2741 Miscellaneous publishing

(G-9653)
CHINA TING FASHION GROUP (USA)
525 7th Ave Rm 1606 (10018-0401)
PHONE.....................212 716-1600
Fax: 212 716-1605
Ren Shen, *President*
Bruce Bergquist, *Controller*
▲ EMP: 7
SALES: 8.5MM
SALES (corp-wide): 12.4MM **Privately Held**
SIC: 2269 2335 2339 Linen fabrics: dyeing, finishing & printing; dresses, paper: cut & sewn; ensemble dresses: women's, misses' & juniors'; women's & misses' outerwear
PA: Zhejiang China Ting Group Co., Ltd.
No.56, Beisha East Road, Yuhang District
Hangzhou 31110
571 862-5918

(G-9654)
CHINA XD PLASTICS COMPANY LTD
500 5th Ave Ste 960 (10110-1899)
PHONE.....................212 747-1118
Taylor Zhang, *CEO*
EMP: 6 **Privately Held**
SIC: 3086 Plastics foam products
PA: China Xd Plastics Company Limited
11 Broadway Ste 1004
New York NY

(G-9655)
CHLOE INTERNATIONAL INC
525 Fashion Ave Rm 1601 (10018-0545)
PHONE.....................212 730-6661
Leon Hedvat, *CEO*
Faramarz Hedvat, *Ch of Bd*
Behrooz Hedvat, *President*
Alex Uskach, *Controller*
Frankie Hedvat, *Director*
▲ EMP: 15

SALES (est): 2.4MM **Privately Held**
SIC: 2339 Service apparel, washable: women's

(G-9656)
CHOCNYC LLC
4996 Broadway (10034-1635)
PHONE.....................917 804-4848
Brad Jon Doles, *Principal*
Dewayne Jemal Edwards, *Principal*
Jemal Edwards, *Principal*
EMP: 6
SALES (est): 223.9K **Privately Held**
SIC: 2051 Cakes, bakery: except frozen

(G-9657)
CHOCOLAT MODERNE LLC
27 W 20th St Ste 904 (10011-3725)
PHONE.....................212 229-4797
Joan Coukos, *Mng Member*
▲ EMP: 5
SQ FT: 950
SALES (est): 250K **Privately Held**
WEB: www.chocolatmoderne.com
SIC: 2064 5145 5961 Candy & other confectionery products; candy; mail order house

(G-9658)
CHOPT CREATIVE SALAD CO LLC (PA)
853 Broadway Ste 606 (10003-4723)
PHONE.....................646 233-2923
Fax: 646 336-5513
Drew Alden, *General Mgr*
Donielle Shannon, *General Mgr*
Michael Caine, *District Mgr*
Laura Parada, *District Mgr*
Tom Kelleher, *Senior VP*
EMP: 10
SALES (est): 25.7MM **Privately Held**
SIC: 2099 Ready-to-eat meals, salads & sandwiches

(G-9659)
CHRISTIAN BOOK PUBLISHING
213 Bennett Ave (10040-2675)
PHONE.....................646 559-2533
Grace Dola Balogun, *Owner*
EMP: 33 EST: 2011
SALES (est): 1.2MM **Privately Held**
SIC: 2731 Book clubs: publishing & printing

(G-9660)
CHRISTIAN CASEY LLC (PA)
Also Called: Sean John
1440 Broadway Frnt 3 (10018-2301)
PHONE.....................212 500-2200
Frank J Dellaquila, *Vice Pres*
Vincent Panzanella, *Vice Pres*
Dawn Robertson,
Sean John,
▲ EMP: 40
SQ FT: 5,000
SALES (est): 25MM **Privately Held**
SIC: 2325 2322 2321 2311 Men's & boys' trousers & slacks; men's & boys' underwear & nightwear; men's & boys' furnishings; men's & boys' suits & coats

(G-9661)
CHRISTIAN CASEY LLC
Also Called: Sean John Clothing
1440 Broadway Frnt 3 (10018-2301)
PHONE.....................212 500-2200
Juanita Reyes, *Credit Staff*
Kevin Lowney, *Branch Mgr*
EMP: 42
SALES (corp-wide): 25MM **Privately Held**
SIC: 2325 2322 2321 2311 Men's & boys' trousers & slacks; men's & boys' underwear & nightwear; men's & boys' furnishings; men's & boys' suits & coats
PA: Christian Casey Llc
1440 Broadway Frnt 3
New York NY 10018
212 500-2200

(G-9662)
CHRISTIAN DIOR PERFUMES LLC (DH)
19 E 57th St (10022-2506)
PHONE.....................212 931-2200
Fax: 212 751-7473

New York - New York County (G-9663)   **GEOGRAPHIC SECTION**

Pamela Baxter, *CEO*
Scott Johnson, *COO*
Joanna Grillo, *Vice Pres*
Diana Miles, *Vice Pres*
Pertrand Tesra, *Vice Pres*
◆ **EMP:** 135
SALES: 34.2MM
SALES (corp-wide): 268.1MM **Privately Held**
WEB: www.saniflo.com
SIC: 2844 3999 Perfumes, natural or synthetic; cosmetic preparations; atomizers, toiletry
HQ: Parfums Christian Dior
    33 Avenue Hoche
    Paris 75008
    149 538-500

(G-9663)
CHRISTIAN SIRIANO HOLDINGS LLC
260 W 35th St Ste 403 (10001-2525)
PHONE.................................212 695-5494
Christian Siriano, *Managing Dir*
EMP: 9
SQ FT: 3,000
SALES (est): 1.3MM **Privately Held**
SIC: 2335 Women's, juniors' & misses' dresses

(G-9664)
CHRISTINA SALES INC
1441 Broadway (10018-1905)
PHONE.................................212 391-0710
Joey Schwebel, *President*
Sharon Fedele, *Credit Mgr*
Rita Mulloy, *Sales Staff*
Brittny Carbel, *Manager*
▲ **EMP:** 10
SQ FT: 5,000
SALES (est): 1.2MM **Privately Held**
SIC: 2339 5137 Bathing suits: women's, misses' & juniors'; swimsuits: women's, children's & infants'

(G-9665)
CHRISTOPHER DESIGNS INC
50 W 47th St Fl 1507 (10036-8687)
PHONE.................................212 382-1013
Fax: 212 768-8978
Christopher Slowinski, *President*
Ewa Slowinski, *Vice Pres*
Barbara Oleksiak, *Production*
Christina Grochowski, *Controller*
Izabela Rutkowski, *Accounts Exec*
▲ **EMP:** 27
SQ FT: 3,800
SALES (est): 4MM **Privately Held**
WEB: www.christopherdesigns.com
SIC: 3915 3911 Jewelers' materials & lapidary work; jewelry, precious metal

(G-9666)
CHRISTOS INC
318 W 39th St Fl 12 (10018-1484)
PHONE.................................212 921-0025
Fax: 212 921-0127
Christos Yiannakou, *President*
Michael Decuollo, *Vice Pres*
Bobbi Wager, *Bookkeeper*
▲ **EMP:** 37
SQ FT: 7,500
SALES (est): 2.4MM **Privately Held**
WEB: www.christosbridal.com
SIC: 2335 Wedding gowns & dresses

(G-9667)
CHURCH PUBLISHING INCORPORATED (HQ)
Also Called: Morehouse Publishing
445 5th Ave Frnt 1 (10016-0133)
PHONE.................................212 592-1800
Fax: 212 779-3363
Alan F Blanchard, *President*
Paul Morejon, *Vice Pres*
▼ **EMP:** 8
SALES (est): 1MM
SALES (corp-wide): 323MM **Privately Held**
WEB: www.preparingforsunday.com
SIC: 2731 Books: publishing only
PA: Church Pension Group Services Corporation
    19 E 34th St Fl 3
    New York NY 10016
    212 592-1800

(G-9668)
CINCH TECHNOLOGIES INC ✪
7 World Trade Ctr (10007-2140)
PHONE.................................212 266-0022
Maya Komerov, *CEO*
EMP: 6 **EST:** 2017
SALES: 100K **Privately Held**
SIC: 7372 Prepackaged software

(G-9669)
CINDERELLA PRESS LTD
327 Canal St 3 (10013-2513)
PHONE.................................212 431-3130
Robert Cenedella, *President*
EMP: 6
SALES (est): 548.5K **Privately Held**
SIC: 2731 Books: publishing only

(G-9670)
CINE DESIGN GROUP LLC
Also Called: Cinedeck
15 Park Row Lbby L (10038-2321)
PHONE.................................646 747-0734
Charles Dautremont,
EMP: 8
SQ FT: 5,000
SALES (est): 670.1K **Privately Held**
SIC: 3575 Cathode ray tube (CRT), computer terminal

(G-9671)
CINEDIGM SOFTWARE
45 W 36th St Fl 7 (10018-7634)
PHONE.................................212 206-9001
Dan Sherlock, *President*
Jill Calcaterra, *Principal*
Diane Anselmo, *Vice Pres*
Tom Hassell, *Vice Pres*
EMP: 5
SALES (est): 303.4K **Privately Held**
SIC: 7372 Prepackaged software

(G-9672)
CINER MANUFACTURING CO INC
20 W 37th St Fl 10 (10018-7484)
PHONE.................................212 947-3770
Fax: 212 643-0357
David Hill, *President*
Patricia Ciner Hill, *Vice Pres*
Jackie Rogers, *Sales Staff*
EMP: 28
SQ FT: 6,000
SALES (est): 3.7MM **Privately Held**
SIC: 3961 Costume jewelry, ex. precious metal & semiprecious stones

(G-9673)
CIRCLE PEAK CAPITAL MGT LLC (PA)
1325 Ave Of The Americas (10019-6026)
PHONE.................................646 230-8812
Fax: 646 349-2743
R Adam Smith, *CEO*
James H Clippard, *Principal*
Holbrook M Forusz, *Principal*
Joseph S Rhodes, *Bd of Directors*
John R Jonge Poerink,
▲ **EMP:** 30
SALES (est): 735.3MM **Privately Held**
SIC: 2053 6799 Pies, bakery: frozen; venture capital companies

(G-9674)
CIRCLE PRESS INC (PA)
Also Called: Press Room New York Division
121 Varick St Fl 7 (10013-1408)
PHONE.................................212 924-4277
Fax: 212 675-1163
Richard T Springer, *President*
Lawrence Lembo, *Vice Pres*
Benjamin Caringal, *Treasurer*
Jessie Richardson, *Accounts Exec*
Gary Lacinski, *Business Dir*
EMP: 51
SQ FT: 30,000
SALES (est): 5MM **Privately Held**
SIC: 2752 2796 Commercial printing, lithographic; platemaking services

(G-9675)
CISCO SYSTEMS INC
1 Penn Plz Ste 3306 (10119-3306)
PHONE.................................212 714-4000
Fax: 212 714-4005

Christopher Augenstein, *Regional Mgr*
Adam Pasieka, *Regional Mgr*
Jonathan Carmel, *Business Mgr*
Nick Adomo, *Vice Pres*
Hans Hwang, *Vice Pres*
EMP: 250
SALES (corp-wide): 48B **Publicly Held**
WEB: www.cisco.com
SIC: 3577 7373 Data conversion equipment, media-to-media: computer; computer integrated systems design
PA: Cisco Systems, Inc.
    170 W Tasman Dr
    San Jose CA 95134
    408 526-4000

(G-9676)
CITIFORMS INC
134 W 29th St Rm 704 (10001-5304)
PHONE.................................212 334-9671
Fax: 212 334-9887
Steven J Slutsky, *President*
EMP: 6
SQ FT: 2,900
SALES (est): 947.1K **Privately Held**
WEB: www.citiformsinc.com
SIC: 2759 Commercial printing

(G-9677)
CITIGROUP INC
388 Greenwich St (10013-2375)
PHONE.................................212 816-6000
Michael Carpenter, *CEO*
ARI Glazer, *President*
Tapodyuti Bose, *Managing Dir*
Peter Charles, *Managing Dir*
Ranjit Chatterji, *Managing Dir*
EMP: 97
SALES (corp-wide): 69.8B **Publicly Held**
SIC: 2621 Parchment, securites & bank note papers
PA: Citigroup Inc.
    388 Greenwich St
    New York NY 10013
    212 559-1000

(G-9678)
CITISOURCE INDUSTRIES INC
244 5th Ave Ste 229 (10001-7604)
PHONE.................................212 683-1033
Dino Sebastiani, *Ch of Bd*
Mario Lacava, *President*
◆ **EMP:** 30
SALES (est): 3.9MM **Privately Held**
SIC: 2231 5131 Broadwoven fabric mills, wool; woolen & worsted piece goods, woven

(G-9679)
CITIXSYS TECHNOLOGIES INC
1 Rockefeller Plz Fl 11 (10020-2073)
PHONE.................................212 745-1365
Kamal Karmakar, *CEO*
Pankaj Mathur, *COO*
Paula Da Silva, *Senior VP*
Mick Adamson, *Vice Pres*
Ajay Mamgain, *Vice Pres*
EMP: 8
SALES (est): 1MM **Privately Held**
SIC: 7372 Prepackaged software

(G-9680)
CITY AND STATE NY LLC
Also Called: Think Tank
61 Broadway Rm 1315 (10006-2721)
PHONE.................................212 268-0442
Tom Allon, *CEO*
Kelly Murphy, *Publisher*
Jeff Coltin, *Editor*
Jasmin Freeman, *Business Mgr*
Jim Katocin, *Vice Pres*
EMP: 27 **EST:** 2012
SALES (est): 1.3MM **Privately Held**
SIC: 2721 Magazines: publishing & printing

(G-9681)
CITY BAKERY INC (PA)
Also Called: Maury's Cookie Dough
3 W 18th St Frnt 1 (10011-4610)
PHONE.................................212 366-1414
Fax: 212 645-0810
Maury Rubin, *President*
Allison Dees, *General Mgr*
Cheryl Winnicki, *Admin Asst*
EMP: 30
SQ FT: 2,000

SALES (est): 3.3MM **Privately Held**
SIC: 2051 Bakery: wholesale or wholesale/retail combined

(G-9682)
CITY CASTING CORP
151 W 46th St Fl 5 (10036-8512)
PHONE.................................212 938-0511
Luis Ontiveros, *CEO*
Lily Londona, *Administration*
EMP: 7
SALES (est): 946.3K **Privately Held**
SIC: 3369 White metal castings (lead, tin, antimony), except die

(G-9683)
CITY SPORTS INC
64 W 48th St Frnt B (10036-1708)
PHONE.................................212 730-2009
EMP: 6
SALES (corp-wide): 135.8MM **Privately Held**
SIC: 3949 Mfg Sporting/Athletic Goods
PA: City Sports, Inc.
    77 N Washington St # 500
    Boston MA 02114
    617 391-9100

(G-9684)
CITY SPORTS IMAGING INC
20 E 46th St Rm 200 (10017-9287)
PHONE.................................212 481-3600
Lawrence Silverberg, *President*
EMP: 20
SALES (est): 1.1MM **Privately Held**
SIC: 3845 Magnetic resonance imaging device, nuclear

(G-9685)
CITY WINERY NAPA LLC
155 Varick St (10013-1106)
PHONE.................................212 633-4399
Michael Dorf, *Mng Member*
EMP: 10
SALES (est): 565.6K **Privately Held**
SIC: 2084 5921 Wines, brandy & brandy spirits; liquor stores

(G-9686)
CITYSCAPE OB/GYN PLLC
38 E 32nd St Fl 4 (10016-5567)
PHONE.................................212 683-3595
Heidi S Rosenberg, *Principal*
Carmit Archibald, *Obstetrician*
EMP: 19
SALES (est): 2.7MM **Privately Held**
SIC: 3842 Gynecological supplies & appliances

(G-9687)
CJ JEWELRY INC
2 W 47th St Ste 1106 (10036-3333)
PHONE.................................212 719-2464
Chaim Fischman, *President*
▲ **EMP:** 12
SALES (est): 1.3MM **Privately Held**
WEB: www.cjjewelry.com
SIC: 3911 Jewelry apparel

(G-9688)
CLARITYAD INC
833 Broadway Apt 2 (10003-4700)
PHONE.................................646 397-4198
Louis-David Mangin, *CEO*
EMP: 6
SALES (est): 190K **Privately Held**
SIC: 7372 Business oriented computer software

(G-9689)
CLARKSON N POTTER INC
1745 Broadway (10019-4640)
PHONE.................................212 782-9000
Lauren Shakely, *Director*
▲ **EMP:** 17
SALES (est): 667.4K
SALES (corp-wide): 17.9B **Privately Held**
WEB: www.anchorbooks.com
SIC: 2731 Books: publishing only
HQ: Penguin Random House Llc
    1745 Broadway
    New York NY 10019
    212 782-9000

GEOGRAPHIC SECTION

New York - New York County (G-9715)

(G-9690)
CLASSIC DESIGNER WORKSHOP INC
265 W 37th St Rm 703 (10018-5929)
PHONE 212 730-8480
Keith Lin, *General Mgr*
EMP: 8
SALES (est): 628.4K **Privately Held**
SIC: 2326 2341 Industrial garments, men's & boys'; women's & children's undergarments

(G-9691)
CLASSIC FLAVORS FRAGRANCES INC
878 W End Ave Apt 12b (10025-4957)
PHONE 212 777-0004
Fax: 212 353-0404
George Ivolin, *CEO*
EMP: 6
SQ FT: 750
SALES (est): 560K **Privately Held**
SIC: 2869 2899 5122 5169 Flavors or flavoring materials, synthetic; perfumes, flavorings & food additives; chemical preparations; essential oils; cosmetics, perfumes & hair products; aromatic chemicals; chemical additives; essential oils

(G-9692)
CLASSIC SOFA LTD
130 E 63rd St Ph B (10065-7340)
PHONE 212 620-0485
Fax: 212 924-0953
Jeffrey Stone, *President*
Randal Rogg, *CPA*
Maurice Stone, *Shareholder*
▲ EMP: 55
SQ FT: 15,000
SALES (est): 6.2MM **Privately Held**
SIC: 2512 5712 Couches, sofas & davenports: upholstered on wood frames; furniture stores

(G-9693)
CLASSPASS INC (PA)
275 7th Ave Fl 11 (10001-6708)
PHONE 888 493-5953
Payal Kadakia, *Principal*
Matt Park, *Opers Staff*
Karen Teng, *Engineer*
Chelsey Cowan, *Accounting Mgr*
Kristina Buzzo, *Human Resources*
EMP: 39
SALES (est): 4.3MM **Privately Held**
SIC: 2741

(G-9694)
CLASSROOM INC
245 5th Ave Fl 20 (10016-8728)
PHONE 212 545-8400
Fax: 212 481-7178
Lisa Holton, *President*
Mary Schearer, *Engineer*
Ja Jones, *Persnl Dir*
Jasmin Greene, *Marketing Staff*
Sharon Waddler, *Office Mgr*
EMP: 25
SALES: 4.3MM **Privately Held**
SIC: 7372 7379 Educational computer software; computer related consulting services

(G-9695)
CLAYTON DUBILIER & RICE FUN (PA)
375 Park Ave Fl 18 (10152-0144)
PHONE 212 407-5200
Joseph L Rice III, *Ch of Bd*
Donald J Gogel, *President*
Joanne Alves, *Vice Pres*
Eileen Smith, *Administration*
▲ EMP: 50 EST: 1985
SALES: 3.1MM **Privately Held**
SIC: 3825 3661 3812 3577 Test equipment for electronic & electric measurement; digital test equipment, electronic & electrical circuits; telephone & telegraph apparatus; switching equipment, telephone; headsets, telephone; search & navigation equipment; computer peripheral equipment; computer terminals; prepackaged software

(G-9696)
CLEAR CHANNEL OUTDOOR INC
Also Called: Eller
99 Park Ave Fl 2 (10016-1602)
PHONE 212 812-0000
Craig Gangi, *Exec VP*
Willie Bennett, *Chief Engr*
Zeb Huffmaster, *Chief Engr*
Cameron Stewart, *Accounts Exec*
Jeremiah Morris, *Marketing Staff*
EMP: 19 **Publicly Held**
WEB: www.clearchanneloutdoor.com
SIC: 2759 Posters, including billboards: printing
HQ: Clear Channel Outdoor, Inc
   2325 E Camelback Rd # 400
   Phoenix AZ 85016

(G-9697)
CLEVER GOATS MEDIA LLC
40 Exchange Pl Ste 1602 (10005-2727)
PHONE 917 512-0340
Lionel Crear,
EMP: 5
SALES (est): 312.6K **Privately Held**
SIC: 7372 Home entertainment computer software

(G-9698)
CLINIQUE LABORATORIES LLC (DH)
Also Called: Clinique Laboratories, Inc.
767 5th Ave Fl 41 (10153-0023)
PHONE 212 572-4200
Fax: 212 572-3857
Daniel J Brestle, *CEO*
William P Lauder, *Ch of Bd*
Selda Agic, *Business Mgr*
Argentina Aguilar, *Business Mgr*
Suzi Atchley, *Business Mgr*
▲ EMP: 2
SQ FT: 20,000
SALES: 2.8MM
SALES (corp-wide): 11.8B **Publicly Held**
WEB: www.clinique.com
SIC: 2844 5122 Cosmetic preparations; cosmetics
HQ: Estee Lauder Inc.
   767 5th Ave Fl 37
   New York NY 10153
   212 572-4200

(G-9699)
CLINIQUE SERVICES INC (DH)
767 5th Ave (10153-0023)
PHONE 212 572-4200
Fax: 212 319-9305
Lynne Greene, *Ch of Bd*
William P Lauder, *President*
Natalie Glassman, *Regional Mgr*
Ukachi Anonyuo, *Exec VP*
Melissa Knapp, *Senior VP*
EMP: 9
SALES (est): 2.8MM
SALES (corp-wide): 11.8B **Publicly Held**
SIC: 2844 Toilet preparations
HQ: Clinique Laboratories, Llc
   767 5th Ave Fl 41
   New York NY 10153
   212 572-4200

(G-9700)
CLO-SHURE INTL INC (PA)
224 W 35th St Ste 1000 (10001-2533)
PHONE 212 268-5029
Cory Liner, *Principal*
▲ EMP: 8
SALES (est): 821.8K **Privately Held**
SIC: 3965 Fasteners, buttons, needles & pins

(G-9701)
CLOUD PRINTING
66 W Broadway Frnt E (10007-2113)
PHONE 212 775-0888
EMP: 6
SALES (est): 135.1K **Privately Held**
SIC: 2752 Commercial printing, lithographic

(G-9702)
CLOUDPARC INC
122 W 27th St Fl 10 (10001-6227)
PHONE 954 665-5962

Dana Klein, *Vice Pres*
Steven Neyaroff, *Vice Pres*
EMP: 5
SALES (est): 117.2K **Privately Held**
SIC: 7372 Prepackaged software; application computer software

(G-9703)
CLOUDSENSE INC
1325 Avenue Of The Flr 28 (10019)
PHONE 917 880-6195
Jonathan Douglas, *Exec VP*
EMP: 6
SALES (est): 662.8K
SALES (corp-wide): 27MM **Privately Held**
SIC: 7372 Prepackaged software
PA: Cloudsense Ltd
   Moray House 23-31
   London W1W 7
   207 580-6685

(G-9704)
CLP PB LLC (PA)
Also Called: Perseus Books Group
1290 Ave Of The Amrcas (10104-0101)
PHONE 212 340-8100
Fax: 212 340-8105
Fred Francis, *Editor*
Melissa Veronesi, *Editor*
Joe Mangan, *COO*
Dave Diroma, *Vice Pres*
Kristin Kiser, *Vice Pres*
▲ EMP: 40
SQ FT: 16,800
SALES (est): 173.4MM **Privately Held**
WEB: www.perseusbooks.com
SIC: 2721 Comic books: publishing only, not printed on site

(G-9705)
CLYDE DUNEIER INC (PA)
415 Madison Ave Fl 6 (10017-7929)
PHONE 212 398-1122
Dana Duneier, *CEO*
Mark Duneier, *President*
Clyde Duneier, *Corp Secy*
Eddie Garcia, *IT/INT Sup*
▲ EMP: 100
SQ FT: 12,000
SALES (est): 13.5MM **Privately Held**
SIC: 3911 5094 Pearl jewelry, natural or cultured; rings, finger: precious metal; jewelry & precious stones

(G-9706)
CMX MEDIA LLC
Also Called: Complex Magazine
1271 Av Of The Americas (10020-1300)
PHONE 917 793-5831
Fax: 917 868-5168
Rich Antoniello, *CEO*
Bradley Carbone, *General Mgr*
Andrew Simon, *Editor*
Scott Cherkin, *Exec VP*
Moksha Fitzgibbons, *Exec VP*
▲ EMP: 20
SALES (est): 4.7MM **Privately Held**
WEB: www.complex.com
SIC: 2721 Magazines: publishing & printing

(G-9707)
CO2 TEXTILES LLC (PA)
88 Greenwich St Apt 1507 (10006-2238)
PHONE 212 269-2222
Melody Levy,
EMP: 3
SALES (est): 1.6MM **Privately Held**
SIC: 2295 Laminating of fabrics

(G-9708)
COACH INC
515 W 33rd St (10001-1302)
PHONE 212 615-2082
EMP: 9
SALES (corp-wide): 4.4B **Publicly Held**
SIC: 3171 Handbags, women's
PA: Coach, Inc.
   10 Hudson Yards
   New York NY 10001
   212 594-1850

(G-9709)
COACH INC
10 Columbus Cir Ste 101a (10019-1183)
PHONE 212 581-4115

Sunshine Sarff, *Manager*
EMP: 15
SALES (corp-wide): 4.4B **Publicly Held**
WEB: www.coach.com
SIC: 3171 Handbags, women's
PA: Coach, Inc.
   10 Hudson Yards
   New York NY 10001
   212 594-1850

(G-9710)
COACH INC
620 5th Ave Frnt 3 (10020-2404)
PHONE 212 245-4148
Jack Railing, *Branch Mgr*
EMP: 15
SALES (corp-wide): 4.4B **Publicly Held**
WEB: www.coach.com
SIC: 3171 Handbags, women's
PA: Coach, Inc.
   10 Hudson Yards
   New York NY 10001
   212 594-1850

(G-9711)
COACH INC
143 Prince St Frnt A (10012-3113)
PHONE 212 473-6925
Fax: 212 473-6927
Tim Zawrotney, *Branch Mgr*
Christina Colone, *Manager*
Amie Kramer, *Athletic Dir*
EMP: 20
SALES (corp-wide): 4.4B **Publicly Held**
WEB: www.coach.com
SIC: 3171 Handbags, women's
PA: Coach, Inc.
   10 Hudson Yards
   New York NY 10001
   212 594-1850

(G-9712)
COACH INC
595 Madison Ave Frnt 1 (10022-1907)
PHONE 212 754-0041
Quinn Barker, *Vice Pres*
Joe Tate, *Vice Pres*
Courtney Henry, *Branch Mgr*
Michelle Lemay, *Manager*
Alex Romaero, *Manager*
EMP: 15
SALES (corp-wide): 4.4B **Publicly Held**
WEB: www.coach.com
SIC: 3171 Handbags, women's
PA: Coach, Inc.
   10 Hudson Yards
   New York NY 10001
   212 594-1850

(G-9713)
COACH INC
79 5th Ave Frnt 3 (10003-3034)
PHONE 212 675-6403
Eliot Ko, *Site Mgr*
Jenn Wagner, *Manager*
EMP: 15
SALES (corp-wide): 4.4B **Publicly Held**
WEB: www.coach.com
SIC: 3171 Handbags, women's
PA: Coach, Inc.
   10 Hudson Yards
   New York NY 10001
   212 594-1850

(G-9714)
COACH INC (PA)
10 Hudson Yards (10001-2157)
PHONE 212 594-1850
Victor Luis, *CEO*
Jide Zeitlin, *Ch of Bd*
Kevin Wills, *CFO*
Sarah Dunn, *Officer*
Todd Kahn, *Officer*
◆ EMP: 277
SALES: 4.4B **Publicly Held**
WEB: www.coach.com
SIC: 3171 3172 2387 3143 Women's handbags & purses; handbags, women's; purses, women's; personal leather goods; apparel belts; men's footwear, except athletic; women's footwear, except athletic

(G-9715)
COACH LEATHERWARE INTL
516 W 34th St Bsmt 5 (10001-1394)
PHONE 212 594-1850

Fax: 212 594-1682
EMP: 4
SALES (est): 1MM
SALES (corp-wide): 4.4B **Publicly Held**
SIC: 3171 Mfg Women's Handbags/Purses
PA: Coach, Inc.
 10 Hudson Yards
 New York NY 10001
 212 594-1850

(G-9716)
COACH SERVICES INC
10 Hudson Yards (10001-2157)
PHONE.................................212 594-1850
Victor Luis, *Ch of Bd*
▲ EMP: 7
SALES (est): 941.5K
SALES (corp-wide): 4.4B **Publicly Held**
WEB: www.coach.com
SIC: 3171 Handbags, women's
PA: Coach, Inc.
 10 Hudson Yards
 New York NY 10001
 212 594-1850

(G-9717)
COACH STORES INC
Also Called: Coach Leatherware Company
516 W 34th St Bsmt 5 (10001-1394)
PHONE.................................212 643-9727
Fax: 212 594-8790
Lewis Frankfort, *CEO*
▲ EMP: 3000
SALES (est): 202.1MM **Privately Held**
SIC: 3171 3161 3172 2387 Handbags, women's; briefcases; personal leather goods; apparel belts; handbags; apparel belts, women's & children's; cases, carrying

(G-9718)
COALITION ON POSITIVE HEALTH
1751 Park Ave Fl 4 (10035-2809)
PHONE.................................212 633-2500
Gloria Searson, *Director*
EMP: 14
SALES: 591K **Privately Held**
SIC: 7372 Educational computer software

(G-9719)
COCKPIT USA INC
15 W 39th St Fl 12 (10018-0628)
PHONE.................................212 575-1616
Jane Chal, *CFO*
Jacky Clyman, *Branch Mgr*
EMP: 12
SALES (corp-wide): 4.4MM **Privately Held**
WEB: www.avirex.com
SIC: 2386 5136 5611 5961 Coats & jackets, leather & sheep-lined; sportswear, men's & boys'; clothing, sportswear, men's & boys'; clothing, mail order (except women's)
PA: Cockpit Usa, Inc.
 15 W 39th St Fl 12
 New York NY 10018
 212 575-1616

(G-9720)
COCKPIT USA INC (PA)
Also Called: Cockpit, The
15 W 39th St Fl 12 (10018-0628)
PHONE.................................212 575-1616
Jeffrey Clyman, *President*
Jacky Clyman, *President*
Tammy Butler, *Production*
Stewart Schuman, *Engineer*
Jeff Block, *VP Sales*
▲ EMP: 15
SQ FT: 5,000
SALES (est): 4.4MM **Privately Held**
WEB: www.avirex.com
SIC: 2386 5136 5611 5961 Sportswear, men's & boys'; coats & jackets, leather & sheep-lined; clothing, sportswear, men's & boys'; clothing, mail order (except women's)

(G-9721)
COCKPIT USA INC
15 W 39th St Fl 12 (10018-0628)
PHONE.................................908 558-9704
Andrew Baljeet, *Manager*
EMP: 10

SALES (corp-wide): 4.4MM **Privately Held**
WEB: www.avirex.com
SIC: 2386 Leather & sheep-lined clothing
PA: Cockpit Usa, Inc.
 15 W 39th St Fl 12
 New York NY 10018
 212 575-1616

(G-9722)
CODA MEDIA INC
Also Called: Coda Story
108 W 39th St Rm 1000 (10018-8267)
PHONE.................................917 478-2565
Greenberg Ilan, *Principal*
EMP: 5 EST: 2016
SALES (est): 171.1K **Privately Held**
SIC: 2721 Magazines: publishing only, not printed on site

(G-9723)
CODESTERS INC
900 Broadway Ste 903 (10003-1223)
PHONE.................................646 232-1025
Manesh Patel, *Treasurer*
Gordon Smith, *Admin Sec*
EMP: 7
SQ FT: 4,500
SALES (est): 262.6K **Privately Held**
SIC: 2731 Textbooks: publishing & printing

(G-9724)
COGNOTION INC
1407 Broadway Fl 24 (10018-5101)
PHONE.................................347 692-0640
Joanna Schneier, *CEO*
Jonathan Dariyanani, *President*
Michael Goldberg, *CFO*
Gerry Carey, *Manager*
EMP: 4
SQ FT: 1,000
SALES: 8MM **Privately Held**
SIC: 7372 Educational computer software

(G-9725)
COLGAT-PLMOLIVE CENTL AMER INC (HQ)
300 Park Ave (10022-7402)
PHONE.................................212 310-2000
Ian Cook, *Ch of Bd*
EMP: 9
SALES (est): 8MM
SALES (corp-wide): 15.2B **Publicly Held**
SIC: 2844 Toothpastes or powders, dentifrices
PA: Colgate-Palmolive Company
 300 Park Ave Fl 5
 New York NY 10022
 212 310-2000

(G-9726)
COLGATE-PALMOLIVE COMPANY (PA)
300 Park Ave Fl 5 (10022-7499)
PHONE.................................212 310-2000
Fax: 212 310-2923
Ian Cook, *Ch of Bd*
Mari Bishop, *President*
Scott Campbell, *General Mgr*
Frank Kettler, *Exec VP*
Todd Atwood, *Vice Pres*
◆ EMP: 3000
SALES: 15.2B **Publicly Held**
WEB: www.colgate.com
SIC: 2844 3991 2841 2842 Toothpastes or powders, dentifrices; mouthwashes; deodorants, personal; shaving preparations; toothbrushes, except electric; soap & other detergents; detergents, synthetic organic or inorganic alkaline; dishwashing compounds; soap: granulated, liquid, cake, flaked or chip; specialty cleaning, polishes & sanitation goods; fabric softeners; bleaches, household: dry or liquid; dog & cat food

(G-9727)
COLGATE-PALMOLIVE GLOBL TRDG
300 Park Ave Fl 8 (10022-7499)
PHONE.................................212 310-2000
Bill Shanahan, *President*
Jacklyn Pierre, *QC Mgr*
EMP: 5

SALES (est): 483.9K
SALES (corp-wide): 15.2B **Publicly Held**
WEB: www.colgate.com
SIC: 2844 Toothpastes or powders, dentifrices
PA: Colgate-Palmolive Company
 300 Park Ave Fl 5
 New York NY 10022
 212 310-2000

(G-9728)
COLGATE-PALMOLIVE NJ INC
300 Park Ave Fl 8 (10022-7499)
PHONE.................................212 310-2000
Fax: 212 310-3301
Bill Shanahan, *President*
EMP: 20
SALES (est): 3.1MM
SALES (corp-wide): 15.2B **Publicly Held**
WEB: www.colgate.com
SIC: 2841 Soap & other detergents
PA: Colgate-Palmolive Company
 300 Park Ave Fl 5
 New York NY 10022
 212 310-2000

(G-9729)
COLLECTION XIIX LTD (PA)
1370 Broadway Fl 17 (10018-7764)
PHONE.................................212 686-8990
Fax: 212 683-4789
Andrew Pizzo, *President*
Sean Rimler, *Exec VP*
Ron D'Angelo, *Senior VP*
Ron Dangelo, *Senior VP*
Amy Hersh, *Design Engr*
▲ EMP: 150
SQ FT: 14,000
SALES (est): 28.8MM **Privately Held**
WEB: www.collection18.com
SIC: 2339 Women's & misses' accessories

(G-9730)
COLONY HOLDINGS INTL LLC
131 W 35th St Fl 6 (10001-2111)
PHONE.................................212 868-2800
Douglas Chan, *CEO*
EMP: 10
SALES: 950K **Privately Held**
SIC: 2321 Men's & boys' furnishings

(G-9731)
COLOR UNLIMITED INC
244 5th Ave Frnt (10001-7604)
PHONE.................................212 802-7547
Henri Boll, *Principal*
EMP: 5
SQ FT: 1,200
SALES: 100K **Privately Held**
WEB: www.go2museum.com
SIC: 2741 Art copy: publishing & printing

(G-9732)
COLORFAST
121 Varick St Fl 9 (10013-1408)
PHONE.................................212 929-2440
Fax: 212 929-0146
John R Arbucci, *President*
Ira Schwidel, *Vice Pres*
Winnie Xil, *Bookkeeper*
EMP: 15
SALES (est): 1MM **Privately Held**
WEB: www.vividcolorinternational.com
SIC: 2752 Commercial printing, offset

(G-9733)
COLORS FASHION INC
Also Called: Cliquer's
901 Avenue Of The Ste 153 (10001)
PHONE.................................212 629-0401
Fax: 212 629-6367
John Kim, *President*
EMP: 10
SQ FT: 10,000
SALES: 2.5MM **Privately Held**
SIC: 2711 Newspapers, publishing & printing

(G-9734)
COLORTEX INC
1202 Lexington Ave 115 (10028-1439)
P.O. Box 115 (10028-0015)
PHONE.................................212 564-2000
Steven Usdan, *President*
▲ EMP: 5
SQ FT: 10,000

SALES (est): 412.8K **Privately Held**
SIC: 2281 5199 Yarn spinning mills; yarns

(G-9735)
COLUMBIA DAILY SPECTATOR
2875 Broadway Ste 303 (10025-7846)
PHONE.................................212 854-9550
Fax: 212 854-9553
Tiffany Fang, *Editor*
Maxwell Hu, *Editor*
Hannah Josi, *Editor*
Mikhail Klimentov, *Editor*
Evan Morris, *Editor*
EMP: 20
SALES: 321.7K **Privately Held**
WEB: www.columbiaspectator.com
SIC: 2711 Newspapers

(G-9736)
COLUMBIA RECORDS INC
25 Madison Ave Fl 19 (10010-8601)
PHONE.................................212 833-8000
Steven E Kober, *CEO*
Bob Semanovich, *VP Mktg*
Audra Kahn, *Marketing Staff*
Garrett Schaefer, *Marketing Staff*
James Grosso, *Manager*
EMP: 15
SALES (est): 2.1MM
SALES (corp-wide): 66.9B **Privately Held**
SIC: 3652 Pre-recorded records & tapes
HQ: Sony Music Entertainment
 25 Madison Ave Fl 19
 New York NY 10010
 212 833-8500

(G-9737)
COLUMBIA TELECOM GROUP
200 5th Ave Ste 651 (10010-4264)
PHONE.................................631 501-5000
David Giladi, *President*
Olga Bodik, *Controller*
▲ EMP: 7
SQ FT: 17,000
SALES (est): 954.3K **Privately Held**
SIC: 3661 3571 3663 3861 Telephones & telephone apparatus; electronic computers; transmitter-receivers, radio; cameras & related equipment; telephone equipment

(G-9738)
COLUMBIA UNIVERSITY PRESS (HQ)
61 W 62nd St Fl 3 (10023-7015)
PHONE.................................212 459-0600
Barbara Budrich, *Managing Dir*
Todd Lazarus, *Marketing Mgr*
Corinna Hipp, *Marketing Staff*
Kevin Kurtz, *Marketing Staff*
Anne McCoy, *Manager*
▲ EMP: 23
SQ FT: 31,500
SALES: 9.4MM
SALES (corp-wide): 3.8B **Privately Held**
SIC: 2731 Books: publishing only; pamphlets: publishing only, not printed on site
PA: The Trustees Of Columbia University In The City Of New York
 116th And Bdwy Way
 New York NY 10027
 212 854-9970

(G-9739)
COLUMBIA UNIVERSITY PRESS
61 W 62nd St Fl 3 (10023-7015)
PHONE.................................212 459-0600
EMP: 37
SALES (corp-wide): 3.8B **Privately Held**
SIC: 2731 Books: publishing only
HQ: Columbia University Press
 61 W 62nd St Fl 3
 New York NY 10023
 212 459-0600

(G-9740)
COLUMBIA UNIVERSITY PRESS
61 W 62nd St Fl 3 (10023-7015)
PHONE.................................212 459-0600
Angela Ajayi, *Branch Mgr*
EMP: 50
SALES (corp-wide): 3.8B **Privately Held**
SIC: 2731 5192 Books: publishing only; pamphlets: publishing only, not printed on site; books

HQ: Columbia University Press
61 W 62nd St Fl 3
New York NY 10023
212 459-0600

(G-9741)
COLUMBUS TRADING CORP
Also Called: Columbus Accessories
120 W 31st St Rm 600 (10001-3407)
PHONE.................................212 564-1780
Fax: 212 564-1787
Chin C S Kim, *President*
Sue Chung, *Office Mgr*
▲ EMP: 15
SALES (est): 1.4MM Privately Held
SIC: 3961 Costume jewelry

(G-9742)
COMELY INTERNATIONAL TRDG INC
303 5th Ave Rm 1903 (10016-6658)
PHONE.................................212 683-1240
Fax: 212 683-4049
Qinghe Liu, *President*
Xu Sue Wang, *Vice Pres*
▲ EMP: 5
SQ FT: 1,800
SALES (est): 2.4MM Privately Held
WEB: www.comelyinternational.com
SIC: 2519 Furniture, household: glass, fiberglass & plastic

(G-9743)
COMINT APPAREL GROUP LLC (PA)
Also Called: Sebby Clothing
463 7th Ave Fl 4 (10018-8725)
P.O. Box 630, Englewood NJ (07631-0630)
PHONE.................................212 947-7474
Graciala Donzin, *Controller*
Carlos Donzin, *Mng Member*
Graciela Donzin,
▲ EMP: 35
SQ FT: 4,000
SALES (est): 4.6MM Privately Held
WEB: www.comintapparel.com
SIC: 2339 Women's & misses' outerwear

(G-9744)
COMMENTARY INC
165 E 56th St Fl 16 (10022-2709)
PHONE.................................212 891-1400
Fax: 212 751-1174
Davi Birnstein, *Publisher*
Neal Kozodoy, *Editor*
EMP: 10
SALES: 3MM Privately Held
SIC: 2721 Magazines: publishing & printing

(G-9745)
COMMERCIAL GASKETS NEW YORK
247 W 38th St Rm 409 (10018-1047)
PHONE.................................212 244-8130
Stewart Shabman, *Principal*
EMP: 11
SALES (est): 1.3MM Privately Held
SIC: 3053 Packing, metallic

(G-9746)
COMMIFY TECHNOLOGY
228 Park Ave S (10003-1502)
PHONE.................................917 603-1822
Michael Osborn, *CEO*
EMP: 10 EST: 2016
SALES (est): 237.2K Privately Held
SIC: 7372 Prepackaged software

(G-9747)
COMMONWEAL FOUNDATION INC
Also Called: COMMONWEAL MAGAZINE
475 Riverside Dr Rm 405 (10115-0433)
PHONE.................................212 662-4200
Fax: 212 662-4183
Thomas Baker, *President*
Steven Aubrey, *Manager*
Matthew Boudway, *Assoc Editor*
Tiina Aleman, *Art Dir*
EMP: 10 EST: 1924
SALES: 2MM Privately Held
WEB: www.catholicsinpublicsquare.org
SIC: 2721 Magazines: publishing only, not printed on site

(G-9748)
COMMONWEALTH TOY NOVELTY INC (PA)
980 Ave Of The Amer # 3 (10018-7804)
PHONE.................................212 242-4070
Fax: 212 645-4279
Steven Greenfield, *Ch of Bd*
Lee Schneider, *President*
Matt Giordano, *Controller*
◆ EMP: 45 EST: 1934
SQ FT: 16,000
SALES (est): 6.7MM Privately Held
SIC: 3942 Stuffed toys, including animals

(G-9749)
COMMUNITY MEDIA LLC
Also Called: Downtown Express Newspaper
515 Canal St Fl 1 (10013-1330)
PHONE.................................212 229-1890
Fax: 212 229-2790
Zera Mussa, *Business Mgr*
Laura Rubin, *Accounts Exec*
John Sutter,
EMP: 20
SALES (est): 1MM Privately Held
WEB: www.communitymediallc.com
SIC: 2711 2752 Newspapers; commercial printing, lithographic

(G-9750)
COMPAR MANUFACTURING CORP
308 Dyckman St (10034-5351)
PHONE.................................212 304-2777
Alex Neuburger, *President*
Steven Neuburger, *Vice Pres*
EMP: 50 EST: 1965
SALES (est): 3.2MM
SALES (corp-wide): 10MM Privately Held
SIC: 3496 3469 Miscellaneous fabricated wire products; metal stampings
PA: Magic Novelty Co., Inc.
308 Dyckman St
New York NY 10034
212 304-2777

(G-9751)
COMPLETE PUBLISHING SOLUTIONS
Also Called: CPS Creative
350 W 51st St Apt 13b (10019-6445)
PHONE.................................212 242-7321
James Hohl, *Mng Member*
EMP: 5
SQ FT: 900
SALES (est): 337.6K Privately Held
WEB: www.cpspress.com
SIC: 2741 Miscellaneous publishing

(G-9752)
COMPLEX MEDIA INC (PA)
1271 6th Ave Fl 35 (10020-1309)
PHONE.................................917 793-5831
Richard Antoniello, *President*
Amy Grabisch, *Director*
Brian Kelley, *Admin Sec*
EMP: 45
SALES (est): 9.3MM Privately Held
SIC: 2721 Periodicals

(G-9753)
CONAGRA BRANDS INC
405 Lexington Ave (10174-0002)
PHONE.................................212 461-2410
EMP: 15
SALES (corp-wide): 11.6B Publicly Held
WEB: www.conagra.com
SIC: 2099 Food preparations
PA: Conagra Brands, Inc.
222 Merchandise Mart Plz
Chicago IL 60654
312 549-5000

(G-9754)
CONCEPTS NYC INC
20 W 33rd St Fl 9 (10001-3305)
PHONE.................................212 244-1033
Joseph Bibi, *President*
Reuben J Bibi, *Principal*
Elliott J Bibi, *Vice Pres*
▲ EMP: 25
SALES (est): 3.1MM Privately Held
SIC: 2221 Apparel & outerwear fabric, manmade fiber or silk

(G-9755)
CONCORD JEWELRY MFG CO LLC
Also Called: Concord Jwlry Mfrs
64 W 48th St Ste 1004 (10036-1708)
PHONE.................................212 719-4030
Fax: 212 869-4268
Ann Seregi, *President*
EMP: 25 EST: 1951
SALES (est): 1.8MM Privately Held
SIC: 3911 Jewelry, precious metal

(G-9756)
CONCORDE APPAREL COMPANY LLC (PA)
55 W 39th St Fl 11 (10018-3803)
PHONE.................................212 307-7848
Roberta Kromko, *Controller*
Lee Wattenburg,
Paul Wattenburg,
▲ EMP: 5
SALES: 20.7MM Privately Held
SIC: 2311 Men's & boys' suits & coats

(G-9757)
CONDE NAST (PA)
750 3rd Ave Fl 8 (10017-2703)
PHONE.................................212 630-3642
Charles H Townsend, *CEO*
Robert A Sauerberg Jr, *President*
John Bellando, *COO*
EMP: 32
SALES (est): 8.7MM Privately Held
SIC: 2721 2731 Periodicals: publishing only; magazines: publishing & printing; book publishing; books: publishing & printing

(G-9758)
CONDE NAST INTERNATIONAL INC (PA)
Also Called: Cond Nast's
1 World Trade Ctr (10007-0089)
PHONE.................................212 286-2860
Charles H Townsend, *CEO*
Robert A Sauerberg Jr, *CEO*
Edward Menicheschi, *President*
Gina Sanders, *President*
Matt Starker, *General Mgr*
EMP: 63
SALES (est): 271.8MM Privately Held
SIC: 2721 Magazines: publishing & printing

(G-9759)
CONDECO SOFTWARE INC (DH)
1350 Broadway Rm 1712 (10018-0900)
PHONE.................................917 677-7600
Martin Brooker, *COO*
Jeff Teddleton, *VP Opers*
Bill Mortimer, *Technical Staff*
John T Anderson, *Officer*
EMP: 31
SALES (est): 7.5MM
SALES (corp-wide): 27.4MM Privately Held
SIC: 7372 Prepackaged software
HQ: Condeco Limited
Exchange Tower
London E14 9
207 001-2020

(G-9760)
CONFERENCE BOARD INC (PA)
845 3rd Ave Fl 2 (10022-6600)
PHONE.................................212 759-0900
Fax: 212 980-7014
Jonathan Spector, *President*
Matteo Tonello, *Managing Dir*
Al Vogl, *Editor*
Jason Cross, *Pastor*
Samuel A Dipiazza, *Trustee*
EMP: 180
SQ FT: 49,750
SALES: 25.4MM Privately Held
WEB: www.conference-board.org
SIC: 2721 8299 Periodicals: publishing only; educational service, nondegree granting: continuing educ.

(G-9761)
CONGRESS FOR JEWISH CULTURE
Also Called: Di Zukunft
1133 Broadway Ste 1019 (10010-7996)
P.O. Box 1590 (10159-1590)
PHONE.................................212 505-8040
Barnett Zumoff, *President*
Shane Baker, *Exec Dir*
EMP: 5
SQ FT: 800
SALES: 94.2K Privately Held
SIC: 2731 2721 7922 Book music: publishing only, not printed on site; periodicals: publishing only; theatrical producers & services; theatrical producers

(G-9762)
CONKUR PRINTING CO INC
121 Varick St Rm 400 (10013-1451)
PHONE.................................212 541-5980
Fax: 212 541-5376
Walter Pflumm, *President*
Patricia Pflumm, *Vice Pres*
EMP: 22
SQ FT: 20,000
SALES (est): 3.1MM Privately Held
WEB: www.proprintsolutions.com
SIC: 2752 Commercial printing, offset

(G-9763)
CONNECTIVA SYSTEMS INC (PA)
19 W 44th St Ste 611 (10036-5900)
PHONE.................................646 722-8741
AVI Basu, *President*
Andrew Doyle, *Vice Pres*
Kaustav Ghosh, *Vice Pres*
Adam Maghrouri, *Vice Pres*
Shankar Mazumder, *Accounts Mgr*
EMP: 18
SALES (est): 23.8MM Privately Held
WEB: www.connectivasystems.com
SIC: 3695 Computer software tape & disks: blank, rigid & floppy

(G-9764)
CONSOLIDATED CHILDRENS AP INC (HQ)
Also Called: Bonjour For Kids
100 W 33rd St Ste 1105 (10001-2990)
PHONE.................................212 239-8615
Mark Adjmi, *President*
Jack Adjmi, *Chairman*
Joy Mahana, *Treasurer*
▲ EMP: 3
SALES (est): 7.8MM
SALES (corp-wide): 32.7MM Privately Held
SIC: 2361 Girls' & children's dresses, blouses & shirts; dresses: girls', children's & infants'; blouses: girls', children's & infants'; shirts: girls', children's & infants'
PA: Adjmi Apparel Group Llc
463 7th Ave
New York NY 10018
212 594-5511

(G-9765)
CONSOLIDATED COLOR PRESS INC
307 7th Ave Rm 607 (10001-6082)
PHONE.................................212 929-8197
Fax: 212 627-7530
William D Sommers Jr, *President*
Richard Somers, *Vice Pres*
Richard M Sommers, *Vice Pres*
Paul Cole, *Treasurer*
EMP: 12
SQ FT: 10,000
SALES (est): 1.5MM Privately Held
SIC: 2752 2791 Commercial printing, offset; typesetting

(G-9766)
CONSOLIDATED FASHION CORP
225 W 39th St Fl 12 (10018-3129)
PHONE.................................212 719-3000
Steven Sall, *President*
Angela Sall, *Corp Secy*
EMP: 6
SALES (est): 710K Privately Held
SIC: 2339 Women's & misses' outerwear

New York - New York County (G-9767)

(G-9767)
CONSOLIDATED LOOSE LEAF INC (PA)
989 Avnue Of The Americas (10018-5410)
PHONE 212 924-5800
Fax: 212 633-2461
Sol Kleinman, *President*
Martin Schneider, *Corp Secy*
EMP: 45 EST: 1943
SQ FT: 32,000
SALES (est): 3MM **Privately Held**
SIC: 2782 Looseleaf binders & devices; library binders, looseleaf

(G-9768)
CONSTELLATION BRANDS SMO LLC
111 8th Ave (10011-5201)
PHONE 585 396-7161
EMP: 5
SALES (est): 250.5K
SALES (corp-wide): 7.3B **Publicly Held**
SIC: 2084 Wines, brandy & brandy spirits
PA: Constellation Brands, Inc.
207 High Point Dr # 100
Victor NY 14564
585 678-7100

(G-9769)
CONSTELLIUM
830 3rd Ave Rm 901 (10022-6504)
PHONE 212 675-5087
Richard B Evans, *Chairman*
Rina Tran, *COO*
Didier Fontaine, *CFO*
Richelle Murray, *Manager*
Pierre Vareille, *Director*
EMP: 50 EST: 2015
SALES (est): 19.6MM
SALES (corp-wide): 5B **Privately Held**
SIC: 3354 Aluminum extruded products
HQ: Constellium France Holdco
40 44
Paris 75008

(G-9770)
CONTACTIVE INC
137 Varick St Ste 605 (10013-1105)
PHONE 646 476-9059
Inaki Berenguer, *CEO*
Julio Viera, *President*
EMP: 50
SALES (est): 2.2MM
SALES (corp-wide): 117.6MM **Privately Held**
SIC: 7372 Application computer software
PA: Fuze, Inc.
2 Copley Pl Ste 700
Boston MA 02116
617 453-2052

(G-9771)
CONTINUITY PUBLISHING INC
15 W 39th St Fl 9 (10018-0631)
PHONE 212 869-4170
Neil Adams, *President*
Kristine Adams, *Vice Pres*
Marilyn Adams, *Vice Pres*
EMP: 12
SQ FT: 4,000
SALES (est): 750K **Privately Held**
SIC: 2721 Comic books: publishing only, not printed on site

(G-9772)
CONTINUITY SOFTWARE INC
5 Penn Plz Fl 23 (10001-1810)
PHONE 646 216-8628
Gil Hecht, *CEO*
Steven B Santos, *Vice Pres*
Liav Even-Chen, *CFO*
Giza Venture Fund, *Shareholder*
EMP: 31
SALES (est): 2.5MM **Privately Held**
SIC: 3695 Computer software tape & disks: blank, rigid & floppy

(G-9773)
CONTINUUM INTL PUBG GROUP INC
15 W 26th St Fl 8 (10010-1065)
PHONE 646 649-4215
Fax: 212 953-5944
EMP: 12

SALES (corp-wide): 173.2MM **Privately Held**
SIC: 2731 Book Publishers
HQ: The Continuum International Publishing Group Inc
175 5th Ave Lbby 5
New York NY

(G-9774)
CONVENIENCE STORE NEWS
770 Broadway Fl 5 (10003-9554)
PHONE 214 217-7800
Maureen Arzato, *Principal*
EMP: 5
SALES (est): 341.5K **Privately Held**
WEB: www.csnews.com
SIC: 2721 Magazines: publishing & printing

(G-9775)
CONVERSANT LLC
150 E 62nd St (10065-8124)
PHONE 212 471-9570
Brian Belhumeur, *Branch Mgr*
EMP: 5
SALES (corp-wide): 7.1B **Publicly Held**
WEB: www.valueclick.com
SIC: 7372 Business oriented computer software
HQ: Conversant, Llc
30699 Russell Ranch Rd # 250
Westlake Village CA 91362
818 575-4500

(G-9776)
COOKIES INC
Also Called: Carnival
1 E 33rd St Fl 6 (10016-5011)
PHONE 646 452-5552
Charles Dweck, *President*
Mitch Melamed, *Director*
Carol Harris, *Legal Staff*
▲ EMP: 575
SALES (est): 31MM **Privately Held**
SIC: 2353 5947 Hats, trimmed: women's, misses' & children's; gift, novelty & souvenir shop

(G-9777)
COOKS INTL LTD LBLTY CO
7 World Trade Ctr Fl 46 (10007-2337)
PHONE 212 741-4407
Henry Mandil,
▼ EMP: 5
SQ FT: 1,500
SALES (est): 270K **Privately Held**
SIC: 2999 3567 Fuel briquettes or boulets: made with petroleum binder; metal melting furnaces, industrial: electric

(G-9778)
COPEN UNITED LLC
37 W 39th St Fl 6 (10018-3886)
PHONE 212 819-0008
◆ EMP: 8 EST: 2012
SALES (est): 844.1K
SALES (corp-wide): 30MM **Privately Held**
SIC: 2299 Ramie yarn, thread, roving & textiles
PA: Selecta International Limited
Rm 11-13 16/F One Midtown
Tsuen Wan NT
279 992-80

(G-9779)
COPIA INTERACTIVE LLC
105 Madison Ave (10016-7418)
PHONE 212 481-0520
Farimah Schuerman, *Senior VP*
Seth Kaufman, *Vice Pres*
Joann Spyker, *Vice Pres*
EMP: 15
SALES (est): 1.3MM **Privately Held**
SIC: 2711 Newspapers, publishing & printing

(G-9780)
COPRA
215 E Broadway Apt 2r (10002-5518)
PHONE 917 224-1727
Benjamin Minges, *President*
EMP: 5
SQ FT: 1,900
SALES (est): 139.9K **Privately Held**
SIC: 2037 Frozen fruits & vegetables

(G-9781)
COPY ROOM INC
885 3rd Ave Lowr 2ll (10022-4804)
PHONE 212 371-8600
Fax: 212 980-3852
George Dispigno, *President*
Chris Dispigno, *General Mgr*
EMP: 12
SQ FT: 4,000
SALES (est): 2.5MM **Privately Held**
WEB: www.nydmv.com
SIC: 2759 2789 7389 Commercial printing; magazines, binding; laminating service

(G-9782)
COPY4LES INC
146 W 29th St Rm 9w (10001-8207)
PHONE 212 487-9778
Davesham Walter Panagoda, *CEO*
Ingrid Singh, *Manager*
EMP: 11
SALES (est): 2MM **Privately Held**
SIC: 3555 Copy holders, printers'

(G-9783)
CORBERTEX LLC
1412 Broadway Rm 1100 (10018-3320)
PHONE 212 971-0008
Howard Corber, *Prgrmr*
EMP: 5
SALES (est): 310K **Privately Held**
SIC: 3552 Textile machinery

(G-9784)
COREMET TRADING INC
160 Brdwy Ste 1107 (10038)
PHONE 212 964-3600
Fax: 212 385-8591
Leo Horowitz, *Ch of Bd*
M Elliott Czermak, *Vice Pres*
Warren Katzman, *Treasurer*
Dorothy Leibowitz, *Office Mgr*
◆ EMP: 5
SQ FT: 800
SALES (est): 1.1MM **Privately Held**
SIC: 1081 Metal mining exploration & development services

(G-9785)
CORINNE MCCORMACK INC
7 W 36th St Fl 9 (10018-7158)
PHONE 212 868-7919
Corinne McCormack, *President*
Joe Mennella, *Manager*
▲ EMP: 10
SALES (est): 1.1MM
SALES (corp-wide): 938.9MM **Privately Held**
WEB: www.corinnemccormack.com
SIC: 3851 Eyeglasses, lenses & frames
HQ: Fgx International Inc.
500 George Washington Hwy
Smithfield RI 02917
401 231-3800

(G-9786)
CORNING INCORPORATED
767 5th Ave Ste 2301 (10153-0012)
PHONE 646 521-9600
Karen Nelson, *Branch Mgr*
EMP: 5
SALES (corp-wide): 9.3B **Publicly Held**
WEB: www.corning.com
SIC: 3357 Nonferrous wiredrawing & insulating
PA: Corning Incorporated
1 Riverfront Plz
Corning NY 14831
607 974-9000

(G-9787)
CORTICE BIOSCIENCES INC
1345 Avenue Of The Americ (10105-3101)
PHONE 646 747-9090
Fax: 646 607-9677
George Farmer, *CEO*
EMP: 13
SALES (est): 1.8MM **Privately Held**
SIC: 2834 Pharmaceutical preparations

(G-9788)
CORTLAND INDUSTRIES INC
1400 Broadway (10018-5300)
PHONE 212 575-2710
David White, *President*

▲ EMP: 15 EST: 2011
SALES (est): 1.1MM **Privately Held**
SIC: 2389 Disposable garments & accessories

(G-9789)
COTY INC
1 Park Ave Fl 4 (10016-5818)
PHONE 212 389-7000
Fax: 212 389-7390
Dr Peter Harf, *Ch of Bd*
Mary Brady, *President*
Rich Garzon, *Principal*
Lori Rosario, *Counsel*
Jurgen Scharfenstein, *Senior VP*
EMP: 125
SALES (est): 60.9MM **Privately Held**
SIC: 2844 Toilet preparations

(G-9790)
COTY INC (DH)
350 5th Ave Ste 2700 (10118-2700)
PHONE 212 389-7300
Camillo Pane, *CEO*
Lambertus J H Becht, *Ch of Bd*
Kert Layton, *Adv Board Mem*
Patrice Detalhout, *Exec VP*
Francoise Mariez, *Senior VP*
◆ EMP: 60
SALES: 7.6B **Publicly Held**
WEB: www.cotyshop.com
SIC: 2844 Toilet preparations; perfumes & colognes; cosmetic preparations
HQ: Jab Cosmetics B.V.
Oosterdoksstraat 80
Amsterdam
204 061-000

(G-9791)
COTY US LLC (DH)
Also Called: Private Portfolio
350 5th Ave (10118-0110)
PHONE 212 389-7000
Bart Becht, *CEO*
Patrice De Talhout, *Exec VP*
Patrice Detalhout, *Exec VP*
Camillo Pane, *Exec VP*
Mario Reis, *Exec VP*
◆ EMP: 130
SALES (est): 436.4MM **Publicly Held**
WEB: www.cotyinc.com
SIC: 2844 Perfumes & colognes; cosmetic preparations

(G-9792)
COUGAR SPORT INC
55 W 39th St Rm 305 (10018-3830)
PHONE 212 947-3054
Raymond Dayan, *Ch of Bd*
Joseph Soffer, *CFO*
Giselle Dayan, *Treasurer*
Herb Neumann, *Finance Other*
Albert Safdieh, *Admin Sec*
▲ EMP: 26
SALES (est): 1.2MM **Privately Held**
SIC: 2329 Men's & boys' sportswear & athletic clothing

(G-9793)
COUNTER EVOLUTION
37 W 17th St (10011-5503)
PHONE 212 647-7505
Jim Malone, *Owner*
EMP: 6
SALES (est): 808.5K **Privately Held**
SIC: 3131 Counters

(G-9794)
COUNTESS CORPORATION
Also Called: Terani Couture
225 W 37th St Fl 12 (10018-5726)
PHONE 212 869-7070
Fax: 212 869-7044
Daryoush Peter Tehrant, *President*
Victor Hakim, *CPA*
Joyce Hatoum, *Accounts Exec*
▲ EMP: 8
SQ FT: 10,000
SALES (est): 1.5MM **Privately Held**
SIC: 2337 Women's & misses' suits & coats

(G-9795)
COUNTESS MARA INC
120 W 45th St Fl 37 (10036-4195)
PHONE 212 768-7300

▲ = Import ▼ = Export
◆ = Import/Export

GEOGRAPHIC SECTION

Ross Gershkowitz, *President*
Ronald Griffin, *CTO*
EMP: 6
SQ FT: 3,000
SALES (est): 373.5K
SALES (corp-wide): 126.8MM **Privately Held**
WEB: www.randacorp.com
SIC: 2323 Neckties, men's & boys': made from purchased materials
HQ: Randa Corporation
417 5th Ave Fl 11
New York NY 10016
212 768-8800

(G-9796)
COURAGE CLOTHING CO INC
1407 Broadway Rm 3604 (10018-2365)
PHONE..................212 354-5690
Noreen Avallon, *CEO*
Ramya Jala, *Administration*
Harssen Mejicanos, *Administration*
▲ **EMP:** 11
SQ FT: 1,000
SALES (est): 1.4MM **Privately Held**
SIC: 2331 2326 T-shirts & tops, women's: made from purchased materials; men's & boys' work clothing

(G-9797)
COURTAULDS TEXTILES LTD
Also Called: Sara Lee Courtaulds USA
358 5th Ave Fl 6 (10001-2209)
PHONE..................212 946-8000
Jacques Moric, *Senior VP*
Shannon McKeen, *Branch Mgr*
EMP: 14
SALES (corp-wide): 5.5B **Privately Held**
SIC: 2299 Batting, wadding, padding & fillings; felts & felt products; yarns & thread, made from non-fabric materials
HQ: Courtaulds Textiles Limited
225 Bath Road
Slough BERKS
115 924-6100

(G-9798)
COUTURE INC
16 W 37th St Frnt 1 (10018-7404)
PHONE..................212 921-1166
Catherine Ansel, *Principal*
▲ **EMP:** 5 EST: 2007
SALES (est): 470K **Privately Held**
SIC: 2335 Wedding gowns & dresses

(G-9799)
COUTURE PRESS
200 Park Ave (10166-0005)
PHONE..................310 734-4831
Dorita Porter, *President*
Ashley Hammock, *Manager*
Amber Rodriguez, *Exec Dir*
EMP: 15
SALES (est): 588.2K **Privately Held**
SIC: 2741 Miscellaneous publishing

(G-9800)
COVE POINT HOLDINGS LLC (PA)
60 E 42nd St Rm 3210 (10165-0056)
PHONE..................212 599-3388
Lee Gene, *Managing Dir*
William C Morris, *Chairman*
EMP: 13
SALES: 23.5K **Privately Held**
SIC: 2671 2672 Paper coated or laminated for packaging; adhesive papers, labels or tapes: from purchased material

(G-9801)
CPT USA LLC (PA)
15 W 39th St Fl 12 (10018-0628)
PHONE..................212 575-1616
Jeffrey Clyman,
▲ **EMP:** 20
SQ FT: 4,200
SALES (est): 18.5MM **Privately Held**
SIC: 2371 Apparel, fur

(G-9802)
CRABTREE PUBLISHING INC
350 5th Ave Ste 3304 (10118-3304)
PHONE..................212 496-5040
Fax: 800 355-7166
Steve Zito, *Chief Mktg Ofcr*
Laureen Bowman, *Marketing Staff*
Mary J Hull, *Marketing Staff*
Marsha Lederfeind, *Marketing Staff*
Kathy Middleton, *Marketing Staff*
EMP: 27
SALES (corp-wide): 1.6MM **Privately Held**
WEB: www.crabtreebooks.com
SIC: 2731 Books: publishing & printing
PA: Crabtree Publishing Company Limited
616 Welland Ave
St Catharines ON L2M 5
905 682-5221

(G-9803)
CRAFT CLERICAL CLOTHES INC (PA)
Also Called: Craft Robe Co.
247 W 37th St Rm 1700 (10018-5051)
PHONE..................212 764-6122
Fax: 212 997-7318
Marvin Goldman, *President*
EMP: 8
SQ FT: 3,000
SALES: 1MM **Privately Held**
SIC: 2389 5699 Uniforms & vestments; academic vestments (caps & gowns); clergymen's vestments; uniforms; caps & gowns (academic vestments); clergy vestments

(G-9804)
CRAFTATLANTIC LLC
Also Called: Craft Atlantic
115 Greenwich Ave (10014-1915)
PHONE..................646 726-4205
Pierre Mordacq, *Mng Member*
Yvonne Cornick, *Traffic Dir*
EMP: 13
SALES (est): 1.2MM **Privately Held**
SIC: 2329 Knickers, dress (separate): men's & boys'

(G-9805)
CRAIN COMMUNICATIONS INC
Business Insurance
685 3rd Ave (10017-4024)
PHONE..................212 210-0100
Fax: 212 210-0237
Martin Ross, *Principal*
Fallon Atta-Mensah, *Editor*
Katherine Downing, *Editor*
Coleman Glenn, *Editor*
Erik Ipsen, *Editor*
EMP: 200
SALES (corp-wide): 225MM **Privately Held**
WEB: www.crainsnewyork.com
SIC: 2721 7812 Magazines: publishing only, not printed on site; motion picture & video production
PA: Crain Communications, Inc.
1155 Gratiot Ave
Detroit MI 48207
313 446-6000

(G-9806)
CRAINS NEW YORK BUSINESS
711 3rd Ave (10017-4014)
PHONE..................212 210-0250
Jill Kaplan, *Owner*
EMP: 30 EST: 2012
SALES (est): 2.5MM **Privately Held**
SIC: 2721 Periodicals

(G-9807)
CREATIVE FORMS INC
80 Varick St Apt 10a (10013-1945)
P.O. Box 1485 (10013-0878)
PHONE..................212 431-7540
Donald Macpherson, *President*
EMP: 5
SALES (est): 450K **Privately Held**
SIC: 2752 Commercial printing, offset

(G-9808)
CREATIVE PRINTING CORP
Also Called: Creative Prntng
121 Varick St Fl 9 (10013-1408)
PHONE..................212 226-3870
Mark Jackson, *President*
Candice Jackson, *Corp Secy*
Dave Bird, *Vice Pres*
Doug Bird, *Vice Pres*
EMP: 7
SQ FT: 6,000
SALES (est): 622.2K **Privately Held**
WEB: www.starkey-henricks.com
SIC: 2752 Commercial printing, offset

(G-9809)
CREATIVE RELATIONS LLC
Also Called: Three Tarts
425 W 23rd St Rm 1f (10011-1436)
PHONE..................212 462-4392
Marla Durso, *Mng Member*
Marina Brolin, *Mng Member*
EMP: 5
SALES (est): 491.6K **Privately Held**
WEB: www.creativerelations.net
SIC: 2051 Bakery: wholesale or wholesale/retail combined

(G-9810)
CREATIVE TOOLS & SUPPLY INC
Also Called: All Craft Jewelry Supply
135 W 29th St Rm 205 (10001-5191)
PHONE..................212 279-7077
Fax: 212 279-6886
Tevel Herbstman, *President*
▲ **EMP:** 9
SQ FT: 2,000
SALES (est): 1.3MM **Privately Held**
SIC: 3915 Jewelers' materials & lapidary work

(G-9811)
CREDIT UNION JOURNAL INC (PA)
Also Called: Source Media
1 State St Fl 26 (10004-1483)
PHONE..................212 803-8200
Lisa Freeman, *Editor*
Phil Albinus, *Editor*
Allison Bisbey, *Editor*
Carrie Burns, *Editor*
Allison Colter, *Editor*
EMP: 5
SALES (est): 401.6K **Privately Held**
WEB: www.cujournal.com
SIC: 2721 Magazines: publishing & printing

(G-9812)
CREDITIQ INC
270 Lafayette St Ste 608 (10012-3327)
PHONE..................888 988-4223
William Liatsis, *CEO*
Andrew Henry, *CFO*
EMP: 12
SQ FT: 800
SALES (est): 427.4K **Privately Held**
SIC: 7372 Business oriented computer software

(G-9813)
CRESCENT WEDDING RINGS INC
36 W 47th St Ste 306 (10036-8637)
PHONE..................212 869-8296
Fax: 212 869-2644
Mark Gebhardt, *President*
EMP: 7
SALES (est): 800K **Privately Held**
WEB: www.crescentweddingrings.com
SIC: 3911 Jewelry, precious metal

(G-9814)
CROSSWINDS SOURCING LLC
260 W 39th St Fl 10 (10018-4410)
PHONE..................646 438-6904
Omprakash Batheja, *Mng Member*
▲ **EMP:** 3
SQ FT: 2,500
SALES (est): 3.9MM
SALES (corp-wide): 6.7MM **Privately Held**
SIC: 2389 Apparel for handicapped
PA: Catalyst Management Holdings Llc
260 W 39th St Fl 10
New York NY 10018
212 398-9300

(G-9815)
CROWLEY TAR PRODUCTS CO INC (PA)
305 Madison Ave Ste 1035 (10165-1036)
PHONE..................212 682-1200
William A Callaman, *CEO*
Christofer Mortensen, *General Mgr*
William Jennings, *Principal*
▲ **EMP:** 7
SQ FT: 10,000
SALES (est): 3.2MM **Privately Held**
WEB: www.crowleychemical.com
SIC: 2865 Cyclic crudes, coal tar; tar

(G-9816)
CROWN JEWELERS INTL INC
168 7th Ave S (10014-2727)
PHONE..................212 420-7800
Neryo Shimunov, *Ch of Bd*
EMP: 5
SALES (est): 494.9K **Privately Held**
SIC: 3911 5094 Jewelry, precious metal; jewelry

(G-9817)
CRUNCHED INC
41 E 11th St (10003-4602)
PHONE..................415 484-9909
Sean Black, *CEO*
Roger Billerey-Mosier, *Engineer*
Kevin Farzad, *Manager*
EMP: 5
SALES (est): 420.2K
SALES (corp-wide): 25.8MM **Privately Held**
SIC: 7372 Business oriented computer software
PA: Clearslide, Inc.
45 Fremont St Ste 3200
San Francisco CA 94105
877 360-3366

(G-9818)
CRUZIN MANAGEMENT INC (DH)
401 Park Ave S Fl 7 (10016-8808)
PHONE..................212 641-8700
Jay S Maltby, *President*
Thomas A Valdes, *Exec VP*
D Chris Mitchell, *Senior VP*
Ousik Yu, *Senior VP*
Ezra Shashoua, *CFO*
▼ **EMP:** 50
SQ FT: 250,000
SALES (est): 25.8MM
SALES (corp-wide): 156.6MM **Privately Held**
WEB: www.cruzanrum.com
SIC: 2085 2084 5182 Rum (alcoholic beverage); brandy; wines; liquor; wine; brandy & brandy spirits
HQ: The Absolut Spirits Company Inc
250 Park Ave 17
New York NY 10177
914 848-4800

(G-9819)
CSCO LLC (PA)
525 7th Ave Rm 1006 (10018-0458)
PHONE..................212 221-5100
Fax: 212 221-6551
David Apperman, *CEO*
Salomon Murciano, *Vice Pres*
Penelope Savinon, *Admin Sec*
▲ **EMP:** 22 EST: 2014
SALES (est): 3.6MM **Privately Held**
SIC: 2335 Women's, juniors' & misses' dresses

(G-9820)
CTS LLC
Also Called: Costello Tagliapietra
211 E 18th St Apt 4d (10003-3624)
PHONE..................212 278-0058
Aby Saltiel,
Jeffrey Costello,
Regino Nieves,
Robert Tagliapietra,
EMP: 5
SQ FT: 5,000
SALES (est): 472.1K **Privately Held**
SIC: 2335 Women's, juniors' & misses' dresses

(G-9821)
CUBIC TRNSP SYSTEMS INC
245 W 17th St Fl 8 (10011-5373)
PHONE..................212 255-1810
Michael Ordre, *Division Mgr*
Richard Trenery, *Branch Mgr*
EMP: 15

New York - New York County (G-9822) — GEOGRAPHIC SECTION

SALES (corp-wide): 1.4B **Publicly Held**
SIC: **3829** 3714 3581 Fare registers for street cars, buses, etc.; motor vehicle parts & accessories; automatic vending machines
HQ: Cubic Transportation Systems, Inc.
5650 Kearny Mesa Rd
San Diego CA 92111
858 268-3100

(G-9822)
CULT RECORDS LLC
263 Bowery Apt 3 (10002-5656)
PHONE..................................718 395-2077
Julian Casablancas, *Co-Owner*
EMP: 5
SALES (est): 237.6K **Privately Held**
SIC: **3652** Pre-recorded records & tapes

(G-9823)
CULTUREIQ INC (PA)
7 Penn Plz Ste 1112 (10001-3390)
PHONE..................................212 755-8633
Gregory Besner, *CEO*
Erin Anderson, *Accounts Mgr*
Jeremy Hamel, *Marketing Staff*
Jamie Nichol, *Marketing Staff*
EMP: 8
SQ FT: 4,500
SALES (est): 4MM **Privately Held**
SIC: **7372** Prepackaged software

(G-9824)
CUPID FOUNDATIONS INC (PA)
Also Called: Cupid Intimates
475 Park Ave S Manhattan (10022)
PHONE..................................212 686-6224
Fax: 212 481-9357
David Welsch, *President*
Marilyn Welsch, *Corp Secy*
Ken Langston, *VP Opers*
Tom Richardson, *Sls & Mktg Exec*
Steve Canter, *CFO*
▲ EMP: 60 EST: 1943
SQ FT: 5,000
SALES: 61.7MM **Privately Held**
WEB: www.cshape.com
SIC: **2342** Brassieres; girdles & panty girdles

(G-9825)
CUREATR INC
222 Broadway Fl 201919 (10038-2510)
PHONE..................................212 203-3927
William Winkenwerder, *CEO*
Mary Stuyvesant, *President*
Oleksiy Khomenko, *COO*
Vik Shah, *Exec VP*
Julia Pulzone, *CFO*
EMP: 25 EST: 2011
SQ FT: 300
SALES (est): 1.2MM **Privately Held**
SIC: **7372** Business oriented computer software

(G-9826)
CUREMDCOM INC
120 Broadway Fl 35 (10271-3599)
PHONE..................................212 509-6200
Fax: 212 509-6206
Bilal Hashmat, *CEO*
Kamal Hashmat, *Ch of Bd*
John Fletcher, *President*
Adeel Malik, *Assistant VP*
Iman Hashmat, *Vice Pres*
EMP: 700
SQ FT: 12,100
SALES: 13.3MM **Privately Held**
WEB: www.curemd.com
SIC: **7372** 8082 8621 Prepackaged software; home health care services; health association

(G-9827)
CUSTOM PUBLISHING GROUP LTD
8 W 38th St 204 (10018-6229)
PHONE..................................212 840-8800
John G Ledges, *President*
EMP: 4
SQ FT: 2,000
SALES: 2.5MM **Privately Held**
SIC: **2741** Miscellaneous publishing

(G-9828)
CUSTOM SPORTS LAB INC
Also Called: U S Orthotic Center
515 Madison Ave Rm 1204 (10022-5484)
PHONE..................................212 832-1648
Jeff Rich, *President*
EMP: 5
SALES: 500K **Privately Held**
SIC: **3149** 3842 8734 Athletic shoes, except rubber or plastic; orthopedic appliances; product testing laboratory, safety or performance

(G-9829)
CUSTOMIZE ELITE SOCKS LLC
156 2nd Ave Apt 2c (10003-5759)
PHONE..................................212 533-8551
Roger Cheng, *Principal*
EMP: 5
SALES (est): 463.6K **Privately Held**
SIC: **2252** Socks

(G-9830)
CUSTOMSHOW INC
216 E 45th St Fl 17 (10017-3304)
PHONE..................................800 255-5303
Paul Shapiro, *CEO*
George Chevalier, *Ch of Bd*
Greg Gordon, *CTO*
EMP: 8
SQ FT: 3,000
SALES (est): 321.7K **Privately Held**
SIC: **7372** Application computer software

(G-9831)
CW FASTENERS & ZIPPERS CORP
142 W 36th St Fl 5 (10018-8796)
PHONE..................................212 594-3203
Suk Chun Wong, *Principal*
EMP: 13
SALES (est): 1.5MM **Privately Held**
SIC: **3965** Fasteners; zipper

(G-9832)
CY FASHION CORP
525 7th Ave Rm 811 (10018-0988)
PHONE..................................212 730-8600
Irene Cho, *CEO*
Barkin Eren, *President*
EMP: 3
SQ FT: 1,100
SALES: 2MM **Privately Held**
SIC: **2211** Apparel & outerwear fabrics, cotton

(G-9833)
CYBERLIMIT INC
257 W 38th St Fl 6 (10018-4457)
PHONE..................................212 840-9597
David MEI, *President*
EMP: 10
SQ FT: 2,000
SALES: 210K **Privately Held**
SIC: **2331** 2321 Women's & misses' blouses & shirts; men's & boys' furnishings

(G-9834)
CYGNET STUDIO INC
251 W 39th St Fl 17 (10018-3117)
PHONE..................................646 450-4550
Daniel Ehrenard, *Mng Member*
EMP: 12
SALES (est): 981.2K **Privately Held**
SIC: **2389** Costumes

(G-9835)
CYNTHIA ROWLEY INC (PA)
376 Bleecker St (10014-3210)
PHONE..................................212 242-3803
Cynthia Rowley, *Ch of Bd*
Peter Arnold, *President*
Irving Erin, *Prdtn Dir*
Julia Covintree, *Production*
Robert Shaw, *CFO*
▲ EMP: 12
SQ FT: 7,000
SALES (est): 2.1MM **Privately Held**
SIC: **2331** 2335 2339 Women's & misses' blouses & shirts; women's, juniors' & misses' dresses; women's & misses' outerwear; women's & misses' accessories; women's & misses' athletic clothing & sportswear

(G-9836)
CYPRESS BIOSCIENCE INC
110 E 59th St Fl 33 (10022-1315)
PHONE..................................858 452-2323
Jay D Kranzler PHD, *Ch of Bd*
Sabrina Martucci Johnson, *COO*
Sabrina Martucci, *COO*
Larry Kessel, *Marketing Staff*
Manda Hall, *Office Mgr*
EMP: 16
SQ FT: 5,700
SALES (est): 3.3MM **Privately Held**
WEB: www.cypressbio.com
SIC: **2836** Biological products, except diagnostic

(G-9837)
D & A OFFSET SERVICES INC
185 Varick St Ste 3 (10014-4607)
PHONE..................................212 924-0612
Fax: 212 924-0866
Carmine D'Elia, *President*
Al D'Elia, *President*
Henny D'Elia, *Corp Secy*
Vincent D'Elia, *Vice Pres*
EMP: 14
SQ FT: 11,000
SALES (est): 1.4MM **Privately Held**
SIC: **2796** Engraving platemaking services

(G-9838)
D & D WINDOW TECH INC (PA)
979 3rd Ave Lbby 132 (10022-1298)
PHONE..................................212 308-2822
Amos Regev, *President*
EMP: 5
SQ FT: 250
SALES (est): 401.6K **Privately Held**
SIC: **2591** 5023 Window blinds; window shades; venetian blinds; vertical blinds; window shades

(G-9839)
D J NIGHT LTD
225 W 37th St Fl 6 (10018-6741)
PHONE..................................212 302-9050
Roholah Simhaee, *President*
EMP: 30
SALES (est): 2.4MM **Privately Held**
SIC: **2335** Gowns, formal

(G-9840)
D M J CASTING INC
62 W 47th St Ste 508 (10036-3270)
PHONE..................................212 719-1951
Fax: 212 719-1956
David Green, *President*
EMP: 5
SALES: 310K **Privately Held**
SIC: **3915** Jewelers' castings

(G-9841)
D R S WATCH MATERIALS
56 W 47th St Fl 2 (10036-8625)
PHONE..................................212 819-0470
Fax: 212 354-2270
Joseph Borella, *Vice Pres*
EMP: 40 EST: 1980
SALES (est): 1.9MM **Privately Held**
SIC: **3915** Jewel preparing: instruments, tools, watches & jewelry

(G-9842)
DABBY-REID LTD
347 W 36th St Rm 701 (10018-7225)
PHONE..................................212 356-0040
Fax: 212 356-0049
Ida Reid, *President*
EMP: 15
SALES: 165.6K **Privately Held**
SIC: **3961** 5094 Costume jewelry, ex. precious metal & semiprecious stones; jewelry & precious stones

(G-9843)
DAHESHIST PUBLISHING CO LTD
1775 Broadway 501 (10019-1903)
PHONE..................................212 581-8360
Fax: 212 832-7413
Mervat Zahid, *President*
EMP: 10
SQ FT: 2,500
SALES (est): 867.9K **Privately Held**
WEB: www.daheshheritage.org
SIC: **2731** Books: publishing only

(G-9844)
DAILY BEAST COMPANY LLC (HQ)
7 Hanover Sq (10004-2616)
PHONE..................................212 445-4600
Ben Collins, *Editor*
Noah Shachtman, *Editor*
Goldie Taylor, *Editor*
William Messmer, *Vice Pres*
Paul Munsch, *Sales Mgr*
▲ EMP: 28 EST: 1936
SQ FT: 203,000
SALES: 68.3MM
SALES (corp-wide): 3.1B **Publicly Held**
WEB: www.newsweek.com
SIC: **2721** Magazines: publishing only, not printed on site
PA: Iac/Interactivecorp
555 W 18th St
New York NY 10011
212 314-7300

(G-9845)
DAILY NEWS LP (DH)
Also Called: New York Daily News
4 New York Plz Fl 6 (10004-2828)
PHONE..................................212 210-2100
Fax: 212 643-7831
William D Holiber, *President*
Linda Lindus, *Publisher*
Peggy Ackermann, *Editor*
Omar Aquije, *Editor*
Maria Bailey, *Editor*
▲ EMP: 600
SQ FT: 150,000
SALES (est): 374.9MM
SALES (corp-wide): 1.6B **Publicly Held**
WEB: www.nydailynews.com
SIC: **2711** Commercial printing & newspaper publishing combined
HQ: Trx Pubco, Llc
435 N Michigan Ave
Chicago IL 60611
312 222-9100

(G-9846)
DAILY RACING FORM INC (HQ)
708 3rd Ave Fl 12 (10017-4129)
PHONE..................................212 366-7600
Steven Crist, *President*
Irwin Cohen, *Vice Pres*
Charles Hayward, *Vice Pres*
Michael Kravchenko, *Vice Pres*
Richard Rosenbush, *Vice Pres*
▼ EMP: 140 EST: 1894
SQ FT: 34,000
SALES (est): 33.9MM
SALES (corp-wide): 215.2MM **Privately Held**
WEB: www.drf.com
SIC: **2741** Racing forms & programs: publishing only, not printing
PA: Arlington Capital Partners, L.P.
5425 Wisconsin Ave # 200
Chevy Chase MD 20815
202 337-7500

(G-9847)
DAILY RACING FORM LLC
75 Broad St (10004-2415)
PHONE..................................212 514-2180
Fax: 212 366-7773
John J Hartig, *Manager*
EMP: 11
SALES (corp-wide): 215.2MM **Privately Held**
SIC: **2711** Newspapers, publishing & printing
HQ: Daily Racing Form Llc
708 3rd Ave Fl 12
New York NY 10017
212 366-7600

(G-9848)
DAILY WORLD PRESS INC
Also Called: Daily Sun New York
228 E 45th St Rm 700 (10017-3336)
PHONE..................................212 922-9201
Fax: 212 922-9202
Yoshida Gin, *President*
Yoshiaki Takahashi, *Publisher*
EMP: 10

▲ = Import ▼ = Export ◆ = Import/Export

GEOGRAPHIC SECTION

New York - New York County (G-9878)

SALES (est): 460K **Privately Held**
SIC: 2711 Newspapers, publishing & printing

(G-9849)
DAILYCANDY INC
584 Broadway Rm 510 (10012-5244)
PHONE.................646 230-8719
Fax: 646 230-8729
Danielle Levy, *Ch of Bd*
Leonora Epstein, *Editor*
Catherine Levene, *COO*
Peter A Sheinbaum, *COO*
Alexa Wilson, *Vice Pres*
EMP: 23
SQ FT: 6,100
SALES (est): 3MM **Privately Held**
WEB: www.dailycandy.com
SIC: 2741 Miscellaneous publishing

(G-9850)
DAKOTT LLC
244 Madison Ave Ste 211 (10016-2817)
PHONE.................888 805-6795
Michael Etedgi, *CEO*
Joshua Martin, *Exec VP*
Vera A Etedgi, *CFO*
▲ EMP: 5
SQ FT: 2,500
SALES: 1MM **Privately Held**
SIC: 3944 Scooters, children's

(G-9851)
DAMPITS INTERNATIONAL INC
425 W 57th St (10019-1764)
P.O. Box 493 (10019)
PHONE.................212 581-3047
David Hollander, *President*
Tair Hollander, *Vice Pres*
EMP: 5 EST: 1966
SALES (est): 480K **Privately Held**
SIC: 3634 Humidifiers, electric: household

(G-9852)
DAN KANE PLATING CO INC
357 W 36th St (10018-6455)
PHONE.................212 675-4947
Fax: 212 929-4276
Jack Zwas, *Owner*
EMP: 16
SQ FT: 5,000
SALES (est): 1.4MM **Privately Held**
SIC: 3471 Electroplating of metals or formed products

(G-9853)
DANA MICHELE LLC
3 E 84th St (10028-0447)
PHONE.................917 757-7777
Dana Schiavo, *President*
EMP: 1
SQ FT: 5,000
SALES: 2MM **Privately Held**
SIC: 3942 3944 2339 Dolls & stuffed toys; games, toys & children's vehicles; women's & misses' outerwear

(G-9854)
DANAHER CORPORATION
445 E 14th St Apt 3f (10009-2805)
PHONE.................516 443-9432
Alison Ng, *Engineer*
EMP: 186
SALES (corp-wide): 16.8B **Publicly Held**
SIC: 3823 Water quality monitoring & control systems
PA: Danaher Corporation
2200 Penn Ave Nw Ste 800w
Washington DC 20037
202 828-0850

(G-9855)
DANGELICO GUITARS OF AMERICA
141 W 28th St Fl 4 (10001-6115)
PHONE.................732 380-0995
John M Ferolito, *CEO*
▲ EMP: 5
SALES (est): 330K **Privately Held**
WEB: www.dangelicodirect.biz
SIC: 3931 Guitars & parts, electric & non-electric

(G-9856)
DANHIER CO LLC
Also Called: Christophe Danhier
380 Rector Pl Apt 3d (10280-1442)
PHONE.................212 563-7683
Christophe Danhier,
EMP: 14
SQ FT: 1,200
SALES (est): 1.5MM **Privately Held**
WEB: www.danhier.com
SIC: 3915 Jewelers' materials & lapidary work

(G-9857)
DANI II INC (PA)
231 W 39th St Rm 1002 (10018-3167)
PHONE.................212 869-5999
Kirat Singh, *CEO*
▲ EMP: 14
SALES (est): 1.3MM **Privately Held**
SIC: 2339 Women's & misses' outerwear

(G-9858)
DANICE STORES INC
305 W 125th St (10027-3620)
PHONE.................212 665-0389
Barry Group, *Manager*
EMP: 14
SALES (corp-wide): 45MM **Privately Held**
SIC: 2339 5137 Sportswear, women's; sportswear, women's & children's
PA: Danice Stores, Inc.
525 Fashion Ave Rm 507
New York NY 10018
212 776-1001

(G-9859)
DANIEL M FRIEDMAN & ASSOC INC
19 W 34th St Fl 4 (10001-3006)
PHONE.................212 695-5545
Fax: 212 643-8464
Jamieson A Karson, *Ch of Bd*
Daniel M Friedman, *President*
Steve Lloyd, *CFO*
▲ EMP: 30
SQ FT: 5,000
SALES (est): 3.7MM
SALES (corp-wide): 1.4B **Publicly Held**
WEB: www.dmfassociates.com
SIC: 2387 Apparel belts
PA: Steven Madden, Ltd.
5216 Barnett Ave
Long Island City NY 11104
718 446-1800

(G-9860)
DANNY MACAROONS INC
2191 3rd Ave Ste 3 (10035-3520)
PHONE.................260 622-8463
Daniel Cohen, *President*
EMP: 6
SALES (est): 524K **Privately Held**
SIC: 2052 Cookies & crackers

(G-9861)
DANNY R COUTURE CORP (PA)
Also Called: Danny Couture
261 W 35th St Ground Fl (10001)
PHONE.................212 594-1095
Daniel Rochas, *President*
EMP: 3 EST: 2014
SQ FT: 5,000
SALES (est): 1MM **Privately Held**
SIC: 2389 Apparel for handicapped

(G-9862)
DANRAY TEXTILES CORP (PA)
Also Called: Dantex Trimming & Textile Co
270 W 39th St Fl 5 (10018-4409)
PHONE.................212 354-5213
Fax: 212 869-9125
Daniel Bergstein, *President*
▲ EMP: 13
SQ FT: 2,000
SALES (est): 915.3K **Privately Held**
SIC: 2241 Trimmings, textile

(G-9863)
DARCY PRINTING AND LITHOG
121 Varick St Fl 9 (10013-1408)
PHONE.................212 924-1554
James Tsiropinas, *President*
EMP: 8

SALES (est): 590K **Privately Held**
SIC: 2759 Commercial printing

(G-9864)
DARMIYAN LLC
450 E 63rd St Apt 5a (10065-7951)
PHONE.................917 689-0389
Padideh Kamali-Zare, *CEO*
Thomas Liebmann, *COO*
Kaveh Vejdani, *Development*
EMP: 5
SALES (est): 229.7K **Privately Held**
SIC: 2835 7389 In vivo diagnostics;

(G-9865)
DASAN INC
54 W 39th St Fl 8 (10018-2068)
PHONE.................212 244-5410
David Chabbott, *Ch of Bd*
EMP: 36
SALES (est): 5.4MM **Privately Held**
WEB: www.dasan.com
SIC: 3911 5094 Jewelry, precious metal; jewelry

(G-9866)
DASH PRINTING INC
153 W 27th St (10001-6203)
PHONE.................212 643-8534
David Ashendorf, *President*
Rachel Feiner, *Exec VP*
EMP: 5
SQ FT: 1,100
SALES (est): 457.1K **Privately Held**
WEB: www.dashprinting.com
SIC: 2759 Commercial printing

(G-9867)
DASHLANE INC
156 5th Ave (10010-7002)
PHONE.................212 596-7510
Emmanuel Schalit, *CEO*
Chuck Kimble, *Vice Pres*
Nishant Mani, *Vice Pres*
David Lapter, *CFO*
Jorgen Bocklage, *VP Finance*
EMP: 45
SALES (est): 2.6MM **Privately Held**
SIC: 7372 Prepackaged software

(G-9868)
DATA IMPLEMENTATION INC
5 E 22nd St Apt 14t (10010-5325)
PHONE.................212 979-2015
Gerald A Goldstein, *President*
William F Hahn, *Vice Pres*
Diana Goldstein, *Treasurer*
Debra Hahn, *Admin Sec*
EMP: 5
SALES (est): 410K **Privately Held**
SIC: 7372 Prepackaged software

(G-9869)
DATADOG INC (PA)
620 8th Ave Fl 45 (10018-1741)
PHONE.................866 329-4466
Olivier Promel, *CEO*
Alexis Le-Quoc, *President*
John Gray, *Senior VP*
Gregory Shutack, *Human Resources*
Miika Groden, *Sales Mgr*
EMP: 43
SQ FT: 7,000
SALES (est): 9.9MM **Privately Held**
SIC: 7372 Publishers' computer software

(G-9870)
DATAMAX INTERNATIONAL INC
Also Called: Data Max
132 Nassau St Rm 511 (10038-2433)
PHONE.................212 693-0933
Fax: 212 693-1706
Saul Wasser, *CEO*
Max Wasser, *Treasurer*
▲ EMP: 45
SQ FT: 15,000
SALES (est): 4.2MM **Privately Held**
WEB: www.datamaxplanners.com
SIC: 2782 3172 Blankbooks & looseleaf binders; diaries; personal leather goods

(G-9871)
DAVE & JOHNNY LTD
225 W 37th St Fl 6 (10018-6741)
PHONE.................212 302-9050
Fax: 212 764-3827

Roholah Simhaee, *President*
▲ EMP: 25
SQ FT: 9,000
SALES (est): 2MM **Privately Held**
WEB: www.daveandjohnny.com
SIC: 2335 Women's, juniors' & misses' dresses

(G-9872)
DAVES ELECTRIC MOTORS & PUMPS
282 E 7th St Apt 1 (10009-6027)
PHONE.................212 982-2930
Yefim Vinokur, *President*
EMP: 5
SQ FT: 5,600
SALES (est): 769.9K **Privately Held**
SIC: 7694 7699 Electric motor repair; pumps & pumping equipment repair

(G-9873)
DAVID & YOUNG CO INC
366 5th Ave Rm 707 (10001-2211)
PHONE.................212 594-6034
Fax: 212 594-6034
John Yoo, *President*
Jesus Arriola, *Vice Pres*
Peter Shin, *Opers Staff*
EMP: 6 EST: 2005
SALES (est): 494.7K **Privately Held**
SIC: 2389 Apparel & accessories

(G-9874)
DAVID FRIEDMAN CHAIN CO INC
Also Called: David Friedman and Sons
10 E 38th St Fl 6 (10016-0014)
PHONE.................212 684-1760
Fax: 212 532-3891
Peter Banyasz, *President*
Matthew Friedman, *Vice Pres*
EMP: 15 EST: 1913
SQ FT: 5,000
SALES (est): 1.4MM **Privately Held**
SIC: 3911 Jewelry, precious metal

(G-9875)
DAVID ISSEKS & SONS INC
298 Broome St (10002-3704)
PHONE.................212 966-8694
David Hackhauser, *President*
Joyce Hockhauser, *Exec VP*
EMP: 22
SQ FT: 5,000
SALES (est): 1.6MM **Privately Held**
SIC: 3443 7699 2449 Water tanks, metal plate; tank repair; wood containers

(G-9876)
DAVID KING LINEN INC
295 5th Ave Ste 1202 (10016-7110)
PHONE.................718 241-7298
Abraham Aosi, *Ch of Bd*
◆ EMP: 15
SQ FT: 8,000
SALES (est): 1.6MM **Privately Held**
SIC: 2299 5023 Linen fabrics; linens & towels

(G-9877)
DAVID PEYSER SPORTSWEAR INC
Also Called: 30 Degrees Weatherproof
4 Bryant Park Fl 12 (10018)
PHONE.................212 695-7716
Tony Galvao, *Exec VP*
Ken Brodsky, *CFO*
Jill Quinn, *Accounts Exec*
Eliot Peyser, *Branch Mgr*
Joyce Silverman, *Manager*
EMP: 40
SALES (corp-wide): 59.9MM **Privately Held**
WEB: www.mvsport.com
SIC: 2329 5651 Men's & boys' sportswear & athletic clothing; unisex clothing stores
PA: David Peyser Sportswear, Inc.
88 Spence St
Bay Shore NY 11706
631 231-7788

(G-9878)
DAVID S DIAMONDS INC
546 5th Ave Fl 7 (10036-5000)
PHONE.................212 921-8029
David So, *Chairman*
Joan So, *Vice Pres*

New York - New York County (G-9879) GEOGRAPHIC SECTION

▲ EMP: 15
SQ FT: 350
SALES (est): 2.3MM Privately Held
WEB: www.davidsdiamonds.com
SIC: 3911 5944 Jewelry, precious metal; jewelry, precious stones & precious metals

(G-9879)
DAVID SUTHERLAND SHOWROOMS - N (PA)
D&D Building 979 3rd (10022)
PHONE.....................212 871-9717
Thomas William, *Principal*
EMP: 5
SALES (est): 366.1K Privately Held
SIC: 2511 Wood household furniture

(G-9880)
DAVID WEEKS STUDIO
38 Walker St Frnt 1 (10013-3589)
PHONE.....................212 966-3433
David Weeks, *President*
▲ EMP: 18
SALES (est): 2.5MM Privately Held
SIC: 3645 5719 Residential lighting fixtures; lighting fixtures

(G-9881)
DAVID WEISZ & SONS INC
20 W 47th St Ste 601 (10036-3768)
PHONE.....................212 840-4747
Fax: 212 840-4852
David Weisz, *President*
EMP: 8
SALES (est): 890K Privately Held
SIC: 3911 5094 Jewelry, precious metal; diamonds (gems)

(G-9882)
DAVID YURMAN ENTERPRISES LLC (PA)
24 Vestry St (10013-1903)
PHONE.....................212 896-1550
Fax: 212 896-1592
Gabriella Forte, *CEO*
Melissa Anastasia, *General Mgr*
Carol Pennelli, *Exec VP*
Cece Coffin, *Senior VP*
Kate Harrison, *Vice Pres*
◆ EMP: 300
SQ FT: 75,000
SALES (est): 276.9MM Privately Held
SIC: 3911 Jewelry, precious metal

(G-9883)
DAVID YURMAN RETAIL LLC
712 Madison Ave (10065-7207)
PHONE.....................877 226-1400
EMP: 7
SALES (est): 881.6K
SALES (corp-wide): 275MM Privately Held
SIC: 3911 Mfg Precious Metal Jewelry
PA: David Yurman Enterprises Llc
  24 Vestry St
  New York NY 10013
  212 896-1550

(G-9884)
DAVIDOFF GNEVA MADISON AVE INC
Also Called: Davidoff of Geneva Ny. , Inc
515 Madison Ave (10022-5403)
PHONE.....................212 751-9060
Fax: 212 715-0422
James P Young, *President*
Luis Torres, *General Mgr*
Robert Seise, *Store Mgr*
Ashraf Eltoumi, *Sales Mgr*
EMP: 7
SALES (est): 940.5K Privately Held
WEB: www.davidoffmadison.com
SIC: 2121 Cigars
HQ: Davidoff Of Geneva Usa Retail, Inc.
  3001 Gateway Ctr Pkwy N
  Pinellas Park FL 33782
  727 828-5400

(G-9885)
DAVIS ZIFF PUBLISHING INC (DH)
Also Called: Ziff-Davis Publishing
28 E 28th St Fl 10 (10016-7939)
PHONE.....................212 503-3500
Fax: 212 503-5698
James Whitehead, *General Mgr*
Geoff Inns, *Managing Dir*
Sourabh Kalantri, *Editor*
Tom McGrade, *Exec VP*
Michael J Miller, *Exec VP*
▲ EMP: 100
SQ FT: 310,000
SALES (est): 70.8MM
SALES (corp-wide): 874.2MM Publicly Held
WEB: www.zdnet.com
SIC: 2721 2731 7371 Periodicals; book publishing; custom computer programming services

(G-9886)
DAVLER MEDIA GROUP LLC (PA)
498 Fashion Ave Fl 10 (10018-6957)
PHONE.....................212 315-0800
Fax: 212 271-2239
Lisa Ben-Isvry, *Publisher*
Tom Hanlon, *General Mgr*
Samantha Beranbom, *Editor*
Griffin Miller, *Editor*
Linda Sheridan, *Editor*
EMP: 30
SALES (est): 5MM Privately Held
WEB: www.davlermedia.com
SIC: 2721 Magazines: publishing & printing

(G-9887)
DAVOS BRANDS LLC
381 Park Ave S Rm 1015 (10016-8827)
PHONE.....................212 779-1911
Andrew Chrisomaois, *CEO*
Blake Bond, *COO*
◆ EMP: 10
SALES (est): 311.7K Privately Held
SIC: 2084 Neutral spirits, fruit

(G-9888)
DAXOR CORPORATION (PA)
350 5th Ave Ste 4740 (10118-0002)
PHONE.....................212 244-0555
Fax: 212 244-0806
Michael Feldschuh, *CEO*
Romeo Mendoza, *COO*
Gary Fischman, *Vice Pres*
John Blalock, *Prdtn Mgr*
Sandra Gilbert, *Research*
EMP: 37 EST: 1971
SALES: 1.6MM Publicly Held
WEB: www.daxor.com
SIC: 3841 8099 Surgical & medical instruments; sperm bank; blood bank

(G-9889)
DE MEO BROTHERS INC (PA)
Also Called: De Meo Brothers Hair
129 W 29th St Fl 5 (10001-5105)
PHONE.....................212 268-1400
Fax: 212 268-3269
Gabriel Klugmann, *President*
▲ EMP: 7
SQ FT: 6,000
SALES (est): 928.8K Privately Held
SIC: 3999 6221 Hair & hair-based products; commodity traders, contracts

(G-9890)
DEBMAR-MERCURY
75 Rockefeller Plz # 1600 (10019-6908)
PHONE.....................212 669-5025
Ira Bernstein, *President*
Liz Koman, *Exec VP*
Karen Bonck, *Senior VP*
Alexandra Jewett, *Senior VP*
Jim Kramer, *Senior VP*
EMP: 9
SALES (est): 721.7K Privately Held
SIC: 2836 Culture media

(G-9891)
DEFINITION PRESS INC
141 Greene St (10012-3201)
PHONE.....................212 777-4490
Arnold Perey, *Info Tech Mgr*
Margot Carpenter, *Exec Dir*
Anne Fielding, *Exec Dir*
Ellen Reiss, *Director*
EMP: 10 EST: 1954
SQ FT: 2,210
SALES (est): 780K Privately Held
WEB: www.definitionpress.com
SIC: 2731 Books: publishing only

(G-9892)
DEFRAN SYSTEMS INC
1 Penn Plz Ste 1700 (10119-1700)
PHONE.....................212 727-8342
Fax: 212 727-8639
Fran L Turso, *President*
Ron Aceto, *Vice Pres*
Deborah Huyer, *Vice Pres*
Greg Travis, *Vice Pres*
Chris Shaw, *Controller*
EMP: 35
SALES (est): 2.3MM Privately Held
WEB: www.defran.com
SIC: 7372 7371 Prepackaged software; custom computer programming services
PA: Netsmart Technologies, Inc.
  4950 College Blvd
  Overland Park KS 66211

(G-9893)
DELCATH SYSTEMS INC (PA)
1633 Broadway Fl 22c (10019-6708)
PHONE.....................212 489-2100
Fax: 212 489-2102
Roger G Stoll, *Ch of Bd*
Jennifer Simpson, *President*
Jennifer K Simpson, *President*
John Purpura, *Exec VP*
Barbra C Keck, *CFO*
EMP: 35
SALES (est): 1.9MM Privately Held
WEB: www.delcath.com
SIC: 3841 2834 Surgical & medical instruments; catheters; pharmaceutical preparations

(G-9894)
DELIVERY SYSTEMS INC
19 W 44th St (10036-5902)
PHONE.....................212 221-7007
Sel Silver, *President*
EMP: 15
SALES (est): 1.2MM Privately Held
SIC: 7372 Prepackaged software

(G-9895)
DELL COMMUNICATIONS INC
Also Called: Dell Graphics
109 W 27th St Frnt 2 (10001-6208)
PHONE.....................212 989-3434
Steve Dell, *President*
EMP: 5
SQ FT: 5,000
SALES (est): 713.4K Privately Held
WEB: www.dellgraphics.com
SIC: 2752 Commercial printing, offset

(G-9896)
DELTA UPHOLSTERERS INC
619 W 54th St Fl 6 (10019-3545)
PHONE.....................212 489-3308
James Congmea, *President*
EMP: 20 EST: 1952
SQ FT: 21,000
SALES (est): 1.4MM Privately Held
SIC: 2512 2391 Upholstered household furniture; draperies, plastic & textile: from purchased materials

(G-9897)
DEMOS MEDICAL PUBLISHING LLC
11 W 42nd St Ste 15c (10036-8002)
PHONE.....................516 889-1791
Fax: 212 683-0118
Phyllis Gold, *President*
Aaron Janoer, *Controller*
Reina Santana, *Sales Dir*
Ramon Simmons, *Marketing Mgr*
EMP: 10
SQ FT: 1,600
SALES (est): 970K Privately Held
WEB: www.demosmedpub.com
SIC: 2731 2721 Books: publishing only; trade journals: publishing only, not printed on site

(G-9898)
DENIZ INFORMATION SYSTEMS
Also Called: Dis
208 E 51st St Ste 129 (10022-6557)
P.O. Box 841 (10150-0841)
PHONE.....................212 750-5199
Haluk Deniz, *Ch of Bd*
Nihat Ozkaya, *VP Opers*
Karen Emer, *VP Mktg*
EMP: 9
SQ FT: 600
SALES (est): 527.2K Privately Held
SIC: 7372 5045 Prepackaged software; computers, peripherals & software

(G-9899)
DENNIS BASSO COUTURE INC
Also Called: Dennis Basso Furs
825 Madison Ave (10065-5042)
PHONE.....................212 794-4500
Dennis Basso, *President*
▲ EMP: 12
SALES (est): 1.2MM Privately Held
SIC: 2371 Fur goods

(G-9900)
DENNIS PUBLISHING INC
Also Called: Week Publications, The
55 W 39th St Fl 5 (10018-3850)
P.O. Box 111 (10018-0002)
PHONE.....................646 717-9500
Fax: 212 302-9213
Steven Kotok, *CEO*
Collingwood Harris, *Editor*
Sean Fenlon, *Mfg Dir*
Chris Mitchell, *Opers Mgr*
Karina Shu, *Opers Mgr*
EMP: 100
SALES (est): 22MM
SALES (corp-wide): 134.1MM Privately Held
SIC: 2721 Magazines: publishing only, not printed on site
HQ: Dennis Publishing Limited
  31-32 Alfred Place
  London WC1E
  203 890-3890

(G-9901)
DENTAL TRIBUNE AMERICA LLC
116 W 23rd St Ste 500 (10011-2599)
PHONE.....................212 244-7181
Sierra Rendon, *Editor*
Rob Selleck, *Editor*
Travis Gittens, *Project Mgr*
Chadette Maragh, *Marketing Staff*
Lorrie Young, *Marketing Staff*
EMP: 14
SQ FT: 4,000
SALES (est): 3MM Privately Held
SIC: 2759 Publication printing

(G-9902)
DEPARTURES MAGAZINE
Also Called: Travel & Leisure
1120 Ave Of The Amrcs 9 (10036-6700)
PHONE.....................212 382-5600
Fax: 212 768-1568
Richard Story, *Chief*
Mark Brooks, *Info Tech Dir*
Eyal Danon, *Info Tech Dir*
Patty Edwards, *Info Tech Dir*
Cynthia Garippa, *Info Tech Dir*
▲ EMP: 20
SALES (est): 1.2MM Privately Held
WEB: www.amexpub.com
SIC: 2721 Periodicals

(G-9903)
DESI TALK LLC
Also Called: Parikh Worldwide Media, LLC
115 W 30th St Rm 1206 (10001-4043)
PHONE.....................212 675-7515
Sudhir Parikh,
Shomik Chaudhuri,
EMP: 11
SALES: 300K Privately Held
SIC: 2741 Miscellaneous publishing

(G-9904)
DESIGN ARCHIVES INC
1460 Broadway (10036-7329)
PHONE.....................212 768-0617
Veena Advani, *President*
EMP: 5

▲ = Import ▼=Export
◆ =Import/Export

New York - New York County (G-9933)

SQ FT: 2,000
SALES (est): 415.5K **Privately Held**
SIC: 2395 5137 Embroidery & art needlework; women's & children's clothing

(G-9905)
DESIGN FOR ALL LLC
240 W 37th St Rm 601 (10018-5760)
PHONE....................212 523-0021
Alan Madoff, *President*
Jeffrey Zwiebel, *Vice Pres*
Ann Borton, *Manager*
▲ EMP: 22
SALES (est): 3.3MM **Privately Held**
SIC: 2339 Women's & misses' outerwear

(G-9906)
DESIGN LITHOGRAPHERS INC
519 8th Ave Ste 3 (10018-6506)
PHONE....................212 645-8900
Fax: 212 645-9459
Daniel Green, *President*
EMP: 12
SALES (est): 1.1MM **Privately Held**
WEB: www.designlitho.com
SIC: 2752 Commercial printing, offset

(G-9907)
DESIGN RESEARCH LTD
Also Called: Tom Dixon
243 Centre St (10013-3224)
PHONE....................212 228-7675
Alex Wisnioski, *Mng Member*
▲ EMP: 150
SQ FT: 2,000
SALES (est): 4.1MM **Privately Held**
SIC: 3299 Non-metallic mineral statuary & other decorative products

(G-9908)
DESIGN SOURCE BY LG INC
115 Bowery Frnt 1 (10002-4933)
PHONE....................212 274-0022
Fax: 212 334-3439
Leo Greisman, *CEO*
Florence Levi, *Manager*
Daniel Olejnik, *Manager*
▲ EMP: 23 EST: 1968
SQ FT: 1,000
SALES (est): 3.2MM **Privately Held**
SIC: 3423 Plumbers' hand tools

(G-9909)
DESIGNLOGOCOM INC
Also Called: Impressions Prtg & Graphics
200 W 37th St (10018-6603)
PHONE....................212 564-0200
Arif Jacksi, *Chairman*
Balkrishna Mehta, *Controller*
EMP: 6
SALES (est): 630K **Privately Held**
WEB: www.designlogo.com
SIC: 2752 Commercial printing, lithographic

(G-9910)
DESIGNS ON FIFTH LTD
20 W 47th St Ste 701 (10036-3451)
PHONE....................212 921-4162
David Ambalo, *Owner*
Min Tun, *Accountant*
EMP: 7
SQ FT: 8,000
SALES (est): 630K **Privately Held**
SIC: 3961 Costume jewelry

(G-9911)
DESIGNWAY LTD
27 E 21st St Fl 7 (10010-6249)
PHONE....................212 254-2220
Joan Morgan, *President*
EMP: 6
SALES (est): 1MM **Privately Held**
SIC: 2211 5712 Draperies & drapery fabrics, cotton; custom made furniture, except cabinets

(G-9912)
DESSIN/FOURNIR INC
Also Called: Rose Cumming
232 E 59th St Fl 2 (10022-1464)
PHONE....................212 758-0844
Fax: 212 888-2837
Dennis O'Hara, *Natl Sales Mgr*
Jay Shemwell, *Sales Mgr*
Stephanie Goetz, *Manager*
Ashley Dopita, *General Counsel*
EMP: 18
SALES (corp-wide): 7.7MM **Privately Held**
WEB: www.dessinfournir.com
SIC: 2511 Wood household furniture
HQ: Dessin/Fournir, Inc.
308 W Mill St
Plainville KS 67663

(G-9913)
DETNY FOOTWEAR INC
Also Called: Shane & Shawn
1 River Pl Apt 1224 (10036-4369)
PHONE....................212 423-1040
Shane Ward, *CEO*
Shawn J Ward, *President*
Adam Holmgren, *Opers Mgr*
▲ EMP: 8
SQ FT: 1,800
SALES: 1MM **Privately Held**
WEB: www.detny.com
SIC: 3143 3144 3021 Men's footwear, except athletic; women's footwear, except athletic; rubber & plastics footwear

(G-9914)
DETOUR APPAREL INC (PA)
Also Called: Chula Girls
530 7th Ave Rm 608 (10018-4888)
PHONE....................212 221-3265
Lisa Medina, *President*
EMP: 5 EST: 2003
SQ FT: 3,000
SALES (est): 10MM **Privately Held**
SIC: 2369 Jackets: girls', children's & infants'

(G-9915)
DEUX LUX INC
37 W 20th St Ste 1204 (10011-3712)
PHONE....................212 620-0801
Sarah Jones, *General Mgr*
EMP: 5
SALES (corp-wide): 2.3MM **Privately Held**
SIC: 3171 Handbags, women's
PA: Deux Lux Inc.
4535 W Valerio St
Burbank CA 91505
213 746-7040

(G-9916)
DEVA CONCEPTS LLC
Also Called: Devacurl
75 Spring St Fl 8 (10012-4071)
PHONE....................212 343-0344
Zack Zavalydriga, *VP Sales*
EMP: 50
SALES (est): 6.1MM **Privately Held**
SIC: 3999 Atomizers, toiletry

(G-9917)
DEW GRAPHICS INC
Also Called: Dew Graphics
519 8th Ave Fl 18 (10018-4577)
PHONE....................212 727-8820
Elaine Weisbrot, *President*
Don Weisbrot, *Vice Pres*
Brian Demars, *Manager*
EMP: 35
SQ FT: 17,000
SALES (est): 3.2MM **Privately Held**
SIC: 2759 Commercial printing

(G-9918)
DEZAWY LLC
Also Called: Thewritedeal
55 W 116th St Ste 327 (10026-2508)
PHONE....................917 436-8820
Yves Sorokobi, *Mng Member*
EMP: 6
SALES (est): 70K **Privately Held**
SIC: 2741 7389 Miscellaneous publishing;

(G-9919)
DFA NEW YORK LLC
318 W 39th St Fl 10 (10018-1486)
PHONE....................212 523-0021
Alan Madoff, *Mng Member*
Jeff Zwiebel, *Mng Member*
▲ EMP: 21
SALES (est): 2.1MM **Privately Held**
SIC: 2339 Women's & misses' accessories

(G-9920)
DIA
535 W 22nd St Fl 4 (10011-1119)
PHONE....................212 675-4097
Nathalie De Gunzburg, *Principal*
EMP: 1
SALES: 13.3MM **Privately Held**
SIC: 2675 Die-cut paper & board

(G-9921)
DIALASE INC
36 W 47th St Ste 709 (10036-8601)
PHONE....................212 575-8833
Isace Landerer, *President*
EMP: 5
SQ FT: 1,200
SALES (est): 330K **Privately Held**
SIC: 3915 Diamond cutting & polishing

(G-9922)
DIAMEX INC
580 5th Ave Ste 625 (10036-4725)
PHONE....................212 575-8145
Fax: 212 575-8187
David Steinmetz, *President*
Ronald Vanderlinden, *Vice Pres*
Jeffrey Greenwald, *Manager*
EMP: 4
SQ FT: 1,200
SALES (est): 554.9K **Privately Held**
SIC: 3915 5094 Diamond cutting & polishing; diamonds (gems)

(G-9923)
DIAMOND BRIDAL COLLECTION LTD
260 W 39th St Fl 17 (10018-4410)
PHONE....................212 302-0210
Fax: 212 302-8653
Paul Diamond, *President*
EMP: 25
SALES (est): 1.2MM **Privately Held**
SIC: 2335 Wedding gowns & dresses

(G-9924)
DIAMOND CONSTELLATION CORP
37 W 47th St Ste 506 (10036-2809)
P.O. Box 650466, Fresh Meadows (11365-0466)
PHONE....................212 819-0324
Fax: 212 944-9245
EMP: 6 EST: 1959
SQ FT: 2,500
SALES (est): 470K **Privately Held**
SIC: 3915 5094 Diamond Cutting & Whol Of Precious Diamonds

(G-9925)
DIAMOND DISTRIBUTORS INC (PA)
608 5th Ave Fl 10 (10020-2303)
PHONE....................212 921-9188
EMP: 8
SALES (est): 1.8MM **Privately Held**
SIC: 3911 Jewelry, precious metal

(G-9926)
DIAMOND INSCRIPTION TECH
36 W 47th St Ste 1008 (10036-8601)
PHONE....................646 366-7944
Jacob Dresdner, *Owner*
EMP: 10
SALES (est): 913.2K **Privately Held**
WEB: www.dresdiam.com
SIC: 2759 7389 Laser printing; business services

(G-9927)
DIANOS KATHRYN DESIGNS
376 Broadway Apt 13b (10013-3943)
PHONE....................212 267-1584
Kathryn Dianos, *Owner*
EMP: 5
SALES (est): 520K **Privately Held**
SIC: 2339 7389 Women's & misses' athletic clothing & sportswear; apparel designers, commercial

(G-9928)
DIGITAL COLOR CONCEPTS INC (PA)
Also Called: D C C
30 W 21st St Fl 5 (10010-6961)
PHONE....................212 989-4888
Fax: 212 989-5588
Stephen Pandolfi, *CEO*
Christine Grant, *President*
Kevin Finn, *Exec VP*
Donald Terwilliger, *Exec VP*
Theresa Bianchi, *Production*
EMP: 24
SQ FT: 15,000
SALES (est): 17.2MM **Privately Held**
WEB: www.dccnyc.com
SIC: 2752 2791 Commercial printing, lithographic; photocomposition, for the printing trade

(G-9929)
DIGITAL EVOLUTION INC (PA)
123 William St Fl 26 (10038-3832)
PHONE....................212 732-2722
Fax: 212 732-8594
Eric Pulier, *CEO*
Dominic Giordano, *President*
Nicholas Giordano, *Vice Pres*
Frankie Giordano, *Manager*
EMP: 23 EST: 2000
SQ FT: 5,000
SALES (est): 3.8MM **Privately Held**
WEB: www.digitalevolution.com
SIC: 2759 7336 7384 Commercial printing; graphic arts & related design; photograph developing & retouching

(G-9930)
DILIGENT BOARD MEMBER SVCS LLC
310 5th Ave Fl 7 (10001-3605)
PHONE....................212 741-8181
Warren Allen, *Counsel*
Bryan Zwahlen, *Vice Pres*
Caroline Emery, *QA Dir*
Linsey Manor, *Accountant*
Mayuri Rana, *Financial Analy*
EMP: 20
SQ FT: 8,000
SALES (est): 1.6MM **Privately Held**
SIC: 7372 Prepackaged software

(G-9931)
DILIGENT CORPORATION (PA)
1385 Brdwy Fl 19 (10018)
PHONE....................212 741-8181
Brian Stafford, *President*
Warren Allen, *Counsel*
Thomas N Tartaro, *Exec VP*
Johnson Garrett, *Senior VP*
Dennis Comma, *Vice Pres*
EMP: 264
SALES (est): 61.7MM **Privately Held**
SIC: 7372 Prepackaged software

(G-9932)
DIMODA DESIGNS INC
48 W 48th St Ste 403 (10036-1713)
PHONE....................212 355-8166
Fax: 212 355-3963
Karabet Koroglu, *CEO*
Hayk Ogulluk, *President*
Garo Koroglu, *Vice Pres*
EMP: 25
SALES (est): 2.1MM **Privately Held**
WEB: www.dimoda.com
SIC: 3911 Jewelry, precious metal

(G-9933)
DIRECT MKTG EDCTL FNDATION INC
Also Called: Dmef/Edge
1333 Broadway Rm 301 (10018-1170)
PHONE....................212 790-1512
Fax: 212 790-1561
Terri L Bartlett, *President*
John Taborosi, *COO*
Linda High, *Exec VP*
Gina Scala, *Vice Pres*
Anissa Lamouchi, *Project Mgr*
EMP: 8
SALES: 2MM **Privately Held**
WEB: www.the-dmef.com
SIC: 2721 Trade journals: publishing only, not printed on site

New York - New York County (G-9934) — GEOGRAPHIC SECTION

(G-9934)
DIRECT PRINT INC (PA)
77 E 125th St (10035-1622)
PHONE..................212 987-6003
Kevin Williams, *President*
EMP: 10
SALES (est): 1.7MM **Privately Held**
SIC: 2759 Commercial printing

(G-9935)
DIRTY LEMON BEVERAGES LLC
95 Grand St Apt 5 (10013-5902)
PHONE..................877 897-7784
Zak Normantin, *CEO*
EMP: 9 EST: 2015
SALES (est): 1.1MM **Privately Held**
SIC: 2086 Lemonade: packaged in cans, bottles, etc.

(G-9936)
DISCOVER CASTING INC
17 W 45th St Ste 701 (10036-4907)
PHONE..................212 302-5060
Yanneth Perlaza, *President*
Louis Perlaza, *Vice Pres*
EMP: 10
SQ FT: 1,900
SALES: 3.4MM **Privately Held**
SIC: 3366 3089 Castings (except die): brass; casting of plastic

(G-9937)
DISCOVER MEDIA LLC
Also Called: Discover Magazine
90 5th Ave Ste 1100 (10011-2051)
PHONE..................212 624-4800
Fax: 212 624-4813
Henry Donahue, *CEO*
Bob Guccione, *Ch of Bd*
Sandra Neddoff, *General Mgr*
Jane Bosveld, *Editor*
Jared Diamond, *Editor*
EMP: 35
SQ FT: 11,500
SALES (est): 3.5MM **Privately Held**
WEB: www.discovermedia.net
SIC: 2721 Magazines: publishing only, not printed on site

(G-9938)
DISPATCH GRAPHICS INC
Also Called: Dispatch Letter Service
344 W 38th St Fl 4r (10018-8432)
PHONE..................212 307-5943
Paul A Grech, *President*
Stephen Grech, *Exec VP*
EMP: 10
SQ FT: 8,000
SALES (est): 1.2MM **Privately Held**
SIC: 2752 7331 2791 2789 Commercial printing, offset; mailing service; typesetting; bookbinding & related work

(G-9939)
DISSENT MAGAZINE
120 Wall St Fl 31 (10005-4007)
PHONE..................212 316-3120
Michael Walder, *President*
EMP: 10
SALES (est): 670K **Privately Held**
SIC: 2721 Periodicals

(G-9940)
DISTINCTIVE PRINTING INC
225 W 37th St Fl 16 (10018-6637)
PHONE..................212 727-3000
Fax: 212 727-3004
Meredith Shantz, *President*
Michael Shantz, *Vice Pres*
Steve Cohen, *Manager*
EMP: 6
SQ FT: 5,000
SALES (est): 500K **Privately Held**
WEB: www.distinctiveprinting.com
SIC: 2752 Offset & photolithographic printing

(G-9941)
DISTRIBIO USA LLC
Also Called: Biologique Recherche
261 5th Ave Rm 1612 (10016-7706)
PHONE..................212 989-6077
Erica Marsh, *Manager*
Philippe Allouche,
EMP: 5
SQ FT: 18,000
SALES (est): 973.9K **Privately Held**
WEB: www.biologiquerecherche.com
SIC: 2844 Face creams or lotions

(G-9942)
DK PUBLISHING
345 Hudson St (10014-4502)
PHONE..................212 366-2000
Gary June, *CEO*
Rachel Barry, *Vice Pres*
Tom Korman, *Vice Pres*
Thomas Leddy, *Prdtn Mgr*
Jessica Lee, *Design Engr*
▲ EMP: 18 EST: 2009
SALES (est): 1.8MM **Privately Held**
SIC: 2741 Miscellaneous publishing

(G-9943)
DM2 MEDIA LLC
Also Called: Digiday
26 Mercer St Apt 4 (10013-4183)
PHONE..................646 419-4357
Newton J Friese, *CEO*
Brian Morrissey, *President*
Nancy Picker, *Exec VP*
Elaine Mershon, *Vice Pres*
Andrea Sontz, *Vice Pres*
EMP: 40
SALES (est): 644.1K **Privately Held**
SIC: 3695 Magnetic & optical recording media

(G-9944)
DNP ELECTRONICS AMERICA LLC
Also Called: Deal
335 Madison Ave Fl 3 (10017-4616)
PHONE..................212 503-1060
Masaru Suzuki, *President*
Kaoru Kando, *CFO*
Kaoru Kondo, *Treasurer*
▲ EMP: 60
SALES (est): 6.4MM
SALES (corp-wide): 12.4B **Privately Held**
SIC: 3861 Screens, projection
HQ: Dnp Corporation Usa
335 Madison Ave Fl 3
New York NY 10017
212 503-1060

(G-9945)
DO IT DIFFERENT INC
59 W 71st St (10023-4111)
PHONE..................917 842-0230
Gregory Samus, *President*
EMP: 5
SALES (est): 117.2K **Privately Held**
SIC: 7372 7389 Application computer software;

(G-9946)
DOCUMENT JOURNAL INC
264 Canal St (10013-3529)
PHONE..................646 586-3099
▲ EMP: 8
SALES (est): 399.5K **Privately Held**
SIC: 2711 Newspapers, publishing & printing

(G-9947)
DOG GOOD PRODUCTS LLC
Also Called: Victoria Stilwell Positevely
1407 Broadway Fl 41 (10018-2348)
PHONE..................212 789-7000
Steven Hanan, *Manager*
David Cayre,
Sandy Menichelli,
EMP: 6
SQ FT: 20,000
SALES (est): 563.5K **Privately Held**
SIC: 3199 2047 Dog furnishings: collars, leashes, muzzles, etc.: leather; dog food

(G-9948)
DOLBY LABORATORIES INC
1350 6th Ave Fl 28 (10019-4702)
PHONE..................212 767-1700
Fax: 212 767-1705
Richard L Hockenbrock, *Vice Pres*
Bill Allen, *Manager*
EMP: 15
SALES (corp-wide): 970.6MM **Publicly Held**
WEB: www.dolby.com
SIC: 3861 Motion picture film
PA: Dolby Laboratories, Inc.
1275 Market St
San Francisco CA 94103
415 558-0200

(G-9949)
DONALD BRUHNKE
Also Called: Chicago Watermark Company
455 W 37th St Apt 1018 (10018-4785)
PHONE..................212 600-1260
Donald Bruhnke, *Owner*
EMP: 10
SQ FT: 1,200
SALES: 1MM **Privately Held**
SIC: 2759 Commercial printing

(G-9950)
DONNA DISTEFANO LTD (PA)
37 W 20th St Ste 1106 (10011-3713)
PHONE..................212 594-3757
Donna Distefano, *President*
Kimberly Vagner, *Opers Mgr*
EMP: 9
SALES (est): 820.8K **Privately Held**
SIC: 3911 Jewelry, precious metal

(G-9951)
DONNA KARAN COMPANY LLC
Also Called: Dkny Jeans
240 W 40th St Bsmt 2 (10018-1533)
PHONE..................212 372-6500
Richard Callari, *VP Prdtn*
Mark Webber, *Branch Mgr*
Cindy Payero, *Manager*
EMP: 12
SALES (corp-wide): 2.3B **Publicly Held**
WEB: www.donnakaran.com
SIC: 2337 Women's & misses' suits & coats
HQ: The Donna Karan Company Llc
240 W 40th St
New York NY 10018
212 789-1500

(G-9952)
DONNA KARAN COMPANY LLC
240 W 40th St Bsmt (10018-1533)
PHONE..................212 789-1500
Carol Knouse, *Senior VP*
EMP: 157
SALES (corp-wide): 2.3B **Publicly Held**
WEB: www.dkny.com
SIC: 2335 2337 2331 2339 Women's, juniors' & misses' dresses; suits: women's, misses' & juniors'; skirts, separate: women's, misses' & juniors'; pantsuits: women's, misses' & juniors'; blouses, women's & juniors': made from purchased material; women's & misses' jackets & coats, except sportswear; suits, men's & boys': made from purchased materials; coats, tailored, men's & boys': from purchased materials; slacks, dress: men's, youths' & boys'
HQ: The Donna Karan Company Llc
240 W 40th St
New York NY 10018
212 789-1500

(G-9953)
DONNA KARAN COMPANY LLC (DH)
Also Called: Dkny
240 W 40th St (10018-1533)
PHONE..................212 789-1500
Fax: 212 768-4441
Donna Karan, *CEO*
Carolyn Mariani, *President*
Alexandra Deegan, *General Mgr*
Robert Wolf, *Area Mgr*
Andrew Lee, *Senior VP*
▲ EMP: 300
SQ FT: 67,000
SALES (est): 413.8MM
SALES (corp-wide): 2.3B **Publicly Held**
WEB: www.dkny.com
SIC: 2335 2337 2331 2339 Women's, juniors' & misses' dresses; suits: women's, misses' & juniors'; skirts, separate: women's, misses' & juniors'; pantsuits: women's, misses' & juniors'; blouses, women's & juniors': made from purchased material; women's & misses' jackets & coats, except sportswear; suits, men's & boys': made from purchased materials; coats, tailored, men's & boys': from purchased materials; slacks, dress: men's, youths' & boys'
HQ: Donna Karan International Inc.
240 W 40th St
New York NY 10018
212 789-1500

(G-9954)
DONNA KARAN INTERNATIONAL INC (HQ)
240 W 40th St (10018-1533)
PHONE..................212 789-1500
Fax: 212 768-6099
Patti Cohen, *Exec VP*
Louis Praino, *Senior VP*
Martha Porteus, *Vice Pres*
Barbara Rentas, *Facilities Mgr*
Patricia F Kalberer, *CFO*
◆ EMP: 10 EST: 1996
SQ FT: 80,000
SALES: 413.8MM
SALES (corp-wide): 2.3B **Publicly Held**
WEB: www.donnakaran.com
SIC: 2335 2337 2331 2339 Women's, juniors' & misses' dresses; jackets & vests, except fur & leather: women's; skirts, separate: women's, misses' & juniors'; suits: women's, misses' & juniors'; blouses, women's & juniors': made from purchased material; shirts, women's & juniors': made from purchased materials; women's & misses' outerwear; slacks: women's, misses' & juniors'; jeans: women's, misses' & juniors'; athletic clothing: women's, misses' & juniors'; men's & boys' furnishings; slacks, dress: men's, youths' & boys'; jeans: men's, youths' & boys'
PA: G-Iii Apparel Group, Ltd.
512 7th Ave Fl 35
New York NY 10018
212 403-0500

(G-9955)
DONNA KARAN INTERNATIONAL INC
240 W 40th St Bsmt (10018-1533)
PHONE..................212 768-5800
Fax: 212 768-5868
Fred Wilson, *Manager*
EMP: 8
SALES (corp-wide): 2.3B **Publicly Held**
WEB: www.donnakaran.com
SIC: 2335 2337 2331 2339 Women's, juniors' & misses' dresses; jackets & vests, except fur & leather: women's; blouses, women's & juniors': made from purchased material; women's & misses' outerwear; men's & boys' furnishings; slacks, dress: men's, youths' & boys'
HQ: Donna Karan International Inc.
240 W 40th St
New York NY 10018
212 789-1500

(G-9956)
DONNA MORGAN LLC
Also Called: Ali Ro
132 W 36th St Rm 801 (10018-8824)
PHONE..................212 575-2550
Fax: 212 575-4775
Haley Moss, *Production*
Brian Fellner, *Credit Mgr*
Kathleen Mc Feeters,
Donna Annunziata,
Milton Cahn,
EMP: 25
SALES (est): 4.1MM **Privately Held**
WEB: www.donnamorgan.com
SIC: 3161 Clothing & apparel carrying cases

▲ = Import ▼ = Export
◆ = Import/Export

New York - New York County (G-9980)

(G-9957)
DONNELLEY FINANCIAL LLC (HQ)
Also Called: RR Donnelley Financial, Inc.
55 Water St Lowr L1 (10041-0005)
PHONE 212 425-0298
Fax: 212 658-5871
Thomas J Quinlan III, *CEO*
William P Penders, *President*
Sandy McGee, *Senior VP*
Jim Palmiter, *Senior VP*
Scott L Spitzer, *Senior VP*
▲ **EMP:** 420
SQ FT: 143,000
SALES (est): 1.2B
SALES (corp-wide): 6.9B **Publicly Held**
WEB: www.bowne.com
SIC: 2752 Commercial printing, lithographic; business forms, lithographed
PA: R. R. Donnelley & Sons Company
35 W Wacker Dr Ste 3650
Chicago IL 60601
312 326-8000

(G-9958)
DONORWALL INC
125 Maiden Ln Rm 205 (10038-5099)
P.O. Box 1005 (10272-1005)
PHONE 212 766-9670
Fax: 212 766-9670
Barry Silverberg, *President*
EMP: 16
SALES (est): 1.3MM **Privately Held**
WEB: www.donorwall.com
SIC: 3999 Plaques, picture, laminated

(G-9959)
DORAL APPAREL GROUP INC
498 Fashion Ave Fl 10 (10018-6957)
PHONE 917 208-5652
Martin Ehrlich, *President*
Andrea Webster, *Manager*
EMP: 9 **EST:** 1999
SQ FT: 5,000
SALES (est): 1.1MM **Privately Held**
SIC: 2339 2326 Women's & misses' athletic clothing & sportswear; men's & boys' work clothing

(G-9960)
DOREMUS FP LLC
228 E 45th St Fl 10 (10017-3331)
PHONE 212 366-3800
Fax: 212 366-3640
Dave Wade, *President*
Greg Cunnion, *Senior VP*
Edmond Sorg, *CFO*
Jeanne Colavito, *Accounts Exec*
Charles Aranda, *Director*
EMP: 47
SQ FT: 13,800
SALES (est): 6.9MM **Privately Held**
WEB: www.doremusfp.com
SIC: 2759 Financial note & certificate printing & engraving

(G-9961)
DORLING KINDERSLEY PUBLISHING (DH)
375 Hudson St (10014-3658)
PHONE 212 213-4800
Fax: 212 689-4828
Peter Kindersley, *Ch of Bd*
Rosan Tregido, *Finance*
Nakul Bhatnagar, *Sales Mgr*
Ebony Lazare, *Sales Staff*
Todd Fries, *Mktg Dir*
▲ **EMP:** 60
SQ FT: 5,000
SALES (est): 6MM
SALES (corp-wide): 17.9B **Privately Held**
SIC: 2731 3652 Book publishing; prerecorded records & tapes
HQ: Dorling Kindersley Limited
80 Strand
London WC2R
207 010-3000

(G-9962)
DOUBLE TAKE FASHIONS INC
1407 Broadway Rm 712 (10018-5293)
PHONE 718 832-9000
Fax: 718 832-6988
Michael Mizrahi, *President*
Jeanette Mizrahi, *Vice Pres*
Daniel Marchese, *Production*
Ralfh Mizrahi, *Manager*
EMP: 8
SQ FT: 5,000
SALES (est): 1.4MM **Privately Held**
WEB: www.doubletakefashions.com
SIC: 2339 Sportswear, women's

(G-9963)
DOVER CORPORATION
500 5th Ave Ste 1828 (10110-1807)
PHONE 212 922-1640
Fax: 212 922-1656
Bob Livingston, *General Mgr*
Raymond McKay, *Vice Pres*
Robert Tyre, *Vice Pres*
Sarah Buchanan, *Director*
EMP: 5
SALES (corp-wide): 6.7B **Publicly Held**
SIC: 3632 Household refrigerators & freezers
PA: Dover Corporation
3005 Highland Pkwy # 200
Downers Grove IL 60515
630 541-1540

(G-9964)
DOVER GLOBAL HOLDINGS INC (HQ)
280 Park Ave (10017-1274)
PHONE 212 922-1640
Fax: 212 953-4326
Robert A Livingston, *President*
Kenneth Rado, *Managing Dir*
Andy Fincher, *Sr Corp Ofcr*
Lance Fleming, *Sr Corp Ofcr*
Dennis Bester, *Vice Pres*
◆ **EMP:** 18
SALES (est): 3.6MM
SALES (corp-wide): 6.7B **Publicly Held**
SIC: 3531 3542 3565 3534 Construction machinery; machine tools, metal forming type; packaging machinery; elevators & moving stairways
PA: Dover Corporation
3005 Highland Pkwy # 200
Downers Grove IL 60515
630 541-1540

(G-9965)
DOW JONES & COMPANY INC (HQ)
1211 Avenue Of The Americ (10036-8711)
P.O. Box 300, Princeton NJ (08543-0300)
PHONE 609 627-2999
Fax: 212 597-5688
William Lewis, *CEO*
Edwin Finn Jr, *President*
Gail Griffin, *General Mgr*
Greg Bartalos, *Editor*
John Bussey, *Editor*
▲ **EMP:** 500 **EST:** 1882
SALES (est): 2.3B
SALES (corp-wide): 8.1B **Publicly Held**
SIC: 2711 2721 Newspapers; magazines: publishing & printing
PA: News Corporation
1211 Ave Of The Americas
New York NY 10036
212 416-3400

(G-9966)
DOW JONES & COMPANY INC
1211 Avenue Of The Americ (10036-8711)
PHONE 212 597-5983
Edwin Finn, *Branch Mgr*
EMP: 46
SALES (corp-wide): 8.1B **Publicly Held**
SIC: 2711 2721 6289 7383 Newspapers, publishing & printing; magazines: publishing only, not printed on site; statistical reports (periodicals): publishing & printing; financial reporting; stock quotation service; news reporting services for newspapers & periodicals; business oriented computer software
HQ: Dow Jones & Company, Inc.
1211 Avenue Of The Americ
New York NY 10036
609 627-2999

(G-9967)
DOW JONES AER COMPANY INC
1211 Av Of The Am Lwr C3r (10036)
PHONE 212 416-2000
Mark Jackson, *General Mgr*
Sharon Terlep, *General Mgr*
Yun-Hee Kim, *Editor*
Patrick Purcell, *Exec VP*
Paul Meller, *Senior VP*
EMP: 701
SALES (est): 125.7MM
SALES (corp-wide): 8.1B **Publicly Held**
WEB: www.opinionjournal.com
SIC: 2721 Periodicals
HQ: Dow Jones & Company, Inc.
1211 Avenue Of The Americ
New York NY 10036
609 627-2999

(G-9968)
DOWA INTERNATIONAL CORP
370 Lexington Ave Rm 1002 (10017-6586)
PHONE 212 697-3217
Fax: 212 697-3902
Junichi Nagao, *President*
Wataru Okuda, *Marketing Mgr*
Akihisa Yamaguchi, *Marketing Mgr*
EMP: 13
SALES (corp-wide): 3.6B **Privately Held**
WEB: www.dicny.com
SIC: 1241 8732 Coal mining services; research services, except laboratory
PA: Dowa Holdings Co.,Ltd.
4-14-1, Sotokanda
Chiyoda-Ku TKY 101-0
368 471-106

(G-9969)
DOWNTOWN INTERIORS INC
250 Hudson St Lbby 1 (10013-1413)
PHONE 212 337-0230
Fax: 212 337-0231
Hertzel Abraham, *President*
Helen Conlin, *Bookkeeper*
EMP: 12
SQ FT: 3,600
SALES (est): 1MM **Privately Held**
SIC: 3553 Furniture makers' machinery, woodworking

(G-9970)
DOWNTOWN MEDIA GROUP LLC
Also Called: Tokion Magazine
12 W 27th St Ste 1000 (10001-6903)
PHONE 646 723-4510
Fax: 212 675-3276
Maxwell Williams, *Opers Staff*
Kathy Bowden, *Controller*
Larry Rosenblum,
Isam Walji,
EMP: 15 **EST:** 2005
SALES (est): 1.4MM **Privately Held**
SIC: 2721 Periodicals

(G-9971)
DOWNTOWN MUSIC LLC
485 Broadway Fl 3 (10013-3071)
PHONE 212 625-2980
Andrew Bergman, *COO*
Terence Lam,
Sean McGraw, *Administration*
EMP: 9 **EST:** 2008
SALES (est): 1MM **Privately Held**
SIC: 2741 Music book & sheet music publishing

(G-9972)
DOYLE & ROTH MFG CO INC (PA)
39 Broad St Ste 710 (10004-2513)
PHONE 212 269-7840
Fax: 212 248-4780
Mary Ann Avella, *President*
Rohit Patel, *Vice Pres*
Kathy Troise, *Buyer*
George Hahn, *Treasurer*
Fred Diestmann, *Director*
EMP: 14 **EST:** 1932
SQ FT: 3,200
SALES (est): 11.3MM **Privately Held**
WEB: www.doyleroth.com
SIC: 3443 3491 Heat exchangers, condensers & components; pressure valves & regulators, industrial

(G-9973)
DR JAYSCOM
853 Broadway Ste 1900 (10003-4703)
PHONE 888 437-5297
▼ **EMP:** 9
SALES (est): 1.1MM **Privately Held**
SIC: 2339 Women's & misses' athletic clothing & sportswear

(G-9974)
DRAGON TRADING INC
Also Called: DRAGON STEEL PRODUCTS
211 E 70th St Apt 20d (10021-5209)
PHONE 212 717-1496
James Steindecker, *President*
▲ **EMP:** 6
SQ FT: 800
SALES: 12.8MM **Privately Held**
SIC: 3462 3321 3731 3315 Iron & steel forgings; chains, forged steel; cast iron pipe & fittings; marine rigging; cable, steel: insulated or armored

(G-9975)
DRAPER ASSOCIATES INCORPORATED
121 Varick St Rm 203 (10013-1455)
PHONE 212 255-2727
Fax: 212 255-9410
Joseph Disomma, *President*
Michael Paulmasano, *Vice Pres*
EMP: 15
SQ FT: 1,200
SALES (est): 179K **Privately Held**
WEB: www.draperassociates.com
SIC: 2741 2791 Miscellaneous publishing; typesetting

(G-9976)
DREAMWAVE LLC
34 W 33rd St Fl 2 (10001-3304)
PHONE 212 594-4250
Joseph Benun, *Vice Pres*
Fred Goldstein, *Controller*
George Saade, *Controller*
Daniel Benun, *Sales Mgr*
David Grazi, *Mng Member*
▲ **EMP:** 26
SQ FT: 13,000
SALES (est): 2.5MM **Privately Held**
SIC: 2389 Men's miscellaneous accessories

(G-9977)
DRESDIAM INC
Also Called: Jacob Dresdner Co
36 W 47th St Ste 1008 (10036-8601)
PHONE 212 819-2217
Jacob Dresdner, *President*
EMP: 40
SQ FT: 3,000
SALES (est): 3.8MM **Privately Held**
SIC: 3915 Diamond cutting & polishing

(G-9978)
DRESSY TESSY INC (PA)
Also Called: Dt Industry
1410 Broadway Rm 502 (10018-9373)
PHONE 212 869-0750
Kitty Koo, *President*
Kathy Ray, *Director*
▲ **EMP:** 9
SQ FT: 5,000
SALES (est): 702.6K **Privately Held**
SIC: 2253 Knit outerwear mills

(G-9979)
DREW PHILIPS CORP (PA)
Also Called: Supply & Demand
231 W 39th St (10018-1070)
PHONE 212 354-0095
Andrew Cohen, *President*
Kasia Franuszkiewicz, *Manager*
▲ **EMP:** 7
SALES (est): 3.9MM **Privately Held**
WEB: www.supplydemand.com
SIC: 2339 Sportswear, women's

(G-9980)
DREYFUS ASHBY INC (HQ)
630 3rd Ave Rm 1501 (10017-6745)
PHONE 212 818-0770
Fax: 212 953-2366
Chris Ryan, *President*
Micheal Katz, *President*
Daniel Schmalen, *Vice Pres*
Patrick Sere, *Vice Pres*
Gary S Squires, *Vice Pres*
▲ **EMP:** 34
SQ FT: 3,000

New York - New York County (G-9981)

SALES (est): 4.9MM
SALES (corp-wide): 37.3MM Privately Held
WEB: www.dreyfusashby.com
SIC: 3645 3646 2084 Residential lighting fixtures; lamp & light shades; commercial indusl & institutional electric lighting fixtures; wines, brandy & brandy spirits
PA: Sa Maison Joseph Drouhin
7 Rue D Enfer
Beaune 21200
380 246-888

(G-9981)
DRONE USA INC (PA)
1 World Trade Ctr 285f (10007-0089)
PHONE 212 220-8795
Michael Bannon, CEO
Dennis Antonelos, CFO
Rodrigo Kuntz Rangel, CTO
Paulo Ferro, Officer
EMP: 29 EST: 1972
SALES (est): 3.9MM Privately Held
SIC: 3721 Motorized aircraft

(G-9982)
DROPCAR INC (PA)
1412 Broadway Ste 2100 (10018-9228)
PHONE 646 342-1595
Michael Richardson, CEO
EMP: 7
SALES (est): 736.8K Privately Held
SIC: 7372 Business oriented computer software

(G-9983)
DRUMMOND FRAMING INC
38 W 21st St Fl 10 (10010-6969)
PHONE 212 647-1701
Fax: 212 254-0242
Donald Delli Paoli, Owner
EMP: 14
SQ FT: 2,300
SALES (est): 1.1MM Privately Held
WEB: www.drummondframing.com
SIC: 2499 Picture & mirror frames, wood

(G-9984)
DU MONDE TRADING INC
Also Called: Up Country
1407 Brrdwy Rm 1905 (10018)
PHONE 212 944-1306
Donald Eatz, President
Dale Trienekens, COO
▲ EMP: 50
SQ FT: 4,500
SALES: 6.5MM Privately Held
SIC: 2339 2326 Women's & misses' jackets & coats, except sportswear; men's & boys' work clothing

(G-9985)
DUANE PARK PATISSERIE INC
179 Duane St Frnt 1 (10013-3397)
PHONE 212 274-8447
Madeleine Lanciani, Owner
EMP: 12
SALES (est): 1.3MM Privately Held
WEB: www.madelines.net
SIC: 2051 Bakery: wholesale or wholesale/retail combined

(G-9986)
DUCDUC LLC (PA)
Also Called: Ducduc Nyc
200 Lexington Ave Rm 715 (10016-6101)
PHONE 212 226-1868
Tracy Deland, Finance
Lelia Byrne, Mktg Dir
Philip Eidles, Mng Member
EMP: 15
SALES (est): 2.7MM Privately Held
SIC: 2511 Children's wood furniture

(G-9987)
DUCK RIVER TEXTILES INC (PA)
295 5th Ave (10016-7103)
PHONE 212 679-2980
Eili Alhakim, President
Raymond Cohen, COO
Oury Alhakim, Vice Pres
Raymond Alhakim, Controller
Joel Bren, VP Mktg
▲ EMP: 6 EST: 1997
SQ FT: 50,000
SALES (est): 2MM Privately Held
WEB: www.duckrivertextile.com
SIC: 2269 Linen fabrics: dyeing, finishing & printing

(G-9988)
DUCON TECHNOLOGIES INC (PA)
5 Penn Plz Ste 2403 (10001-1848)
PHONE 631 694-1700
Aron Govil, Chairman
William Papa, Chairman
Renato Delarama, Vice Pres
Bob Gupta, Vice Pres
◆ EMP: 15
SQ FT: 35,000
SALES (est): 479.4MM Privately Held
WEB: www.ducon.com
SIC: 3537 3564 Industrial trucks & tractors; blowers & fans

(G-9989)
DUNE INC
200 Lexington Ave Rm 200 (10016-6103)
PHONE 212 925-6171
Richard Shemtov, President
Aaron Shemtov, Vice Pres
Alicia Thibou, Production
Kristen Stocks, Sales Associate
▲ EMP: 5
SQ FT: 12,000
SALES (est): 794.6K Privately Held
WEB: www.dune-ny.com
SIC: 2511 Wood household furniture

(G-9990)
DURAN JEWELRY INC
36 W 47th St Ste 1205 (10036-8637)
PHONE 212 431-1959
Erol Civi, President
Arlet Tknezi, Manager
▲ EMP: 6
SQ FT: 1,000
SALES (est): 460K Privately Held
SIC: 3911 Jewelry, precious metal

(G-9991)
DURATA THERAPEUTICS INC
7 Times Sq Ste 3502 (10036-6540)
PHONE 646 871-6400
Paul R Edick, CEO
Richard U De Schutter, Ch of Bd
Corey N Fishman, COO
Benjamin Pe, Opers Staff
Michael Dunne, Officer
EMP: 5
SQ FT: 9,000
SALES (est): 386.3K Privately Held
SIC: 2834 8731 Antibiotics, packaged; commercial physical research

(G-9992)
DUXIANA DUX BED
235 E 58th St (10022-1201)
PHONE 212 755-2600
Fax: 212 752-4989
Bo Gustafsson, Principal
EMP: 6
SALES (est): 529K Privately Held
SIC: 2515 5712 5719 Mattresses & bedsprings; beds & accessories; beddings & linens

(G-9993)
DVF STUDIO LLC (PA)
Also Called: Diane Von Furstenberg The Shop
440 W 14th St (10014-1004)
PHONE 212 741-6607
Fax: 212 929-4051
Robert McCormick, COO
Elisa Palomino, Vice Pres
Paul Aberasturi, CFO
Amy Bobrow, Controller
April Uchitel, Sales Dir
▲ EMP: 75
SALES (est): 29.4MM Privately Held
WEB: www.dvf.com
SIC: 3199 2389 5621 Leather garments; disposable garments & accessories; women's specialty clothing stores

(G-9994)
DVF STUDIO LLC (PA)
252 W 37th St Fl 14 (10018-6636)
PHONE 646 576-8009
EMP: 6
SALES (est): 2.5MM Privately Held
SIC: 3199 2389 5621 Leather garments; disposable garments & accessories; women's specialty clothing stores

(G-9995)
DWELL LIFE INC
Also Called: Dwell Store The
60 Broad St Fl 24 (10004-2342)
PHONE 212 382-2010
Regina Flynn, Office Mgr
EMP: 25
SALES (corp-wide): 20MM Privately Held
SIC: 2741 Miscellaneous publishing
PA: Dwell Life, Inc.
901 Battery St 401
San Francisco CA 94111
415 373-5100

(G-9996)
DWNLD INC
601394 Broadway Fl 6 (10013)
PHONE 484 483-6572
Aj Framk, CEO
Alexandra Keating, CEO
EMP: 28
SALES (est): 603.5K Privately Held
SIC: 7372 Application computer software

(G-9997)
DYENAMIX INC
359 Broadway Frnt 2 (10013-3932)
PHONE 212 941-6642
Fax: 212 941-7407
Raylene Marasco, President
EMP: 7
SALES: 250K Privately Held
SIC: 2261 2262 2752 Dyeing cotton broadwoven fabrics; screen printing of cotton broadwoven fabrics; screen printing: manmade fiber & silk broadwoven fabrics; commercial printing, lithographic

(G-9998)
DYLANS CANDY BAR INC
315 E 62nd St Fl 6 (10065-7767)
PHONE 646 735-0078
EMP: 18
SALES (est): 2.9MM Privately Held
SIC: 2064 Candy & other confectionery products

(G-9999)
DYNAMIC DESIGN GROUP INC
15 W 47th St Ste 801 (10036-3765)
PHONE 212 840-9400
Amit Sanghavi, President
Harish Patel, Accountant
Steven Das, Sales Mgr
Alisha Mudaliar, Manager
Vincent Violetta, Director
▲ EMP: 6
SQ FT: 500
SALES: 3MM Privately Held
SIC: 1499 Diamond mining, industrial

(G-10000)
DYNAMICA INC
930 5th Ave Apt 3f (10021-2680)
PHONE 212 818-1900
Daniel Schwartz, President
▲ EMP: 9
SALES (est): 1MM Privately Held
SIC: 3821 Laboratory apparatus & furniture

(G-10001)
DYNAMO DEVELOPMENT INC
860 Broadway Fl 5 (10003-1228)
PHONE 212 385-1552
Dmitry I Grinberg, President
Yuri Nakonechny, Software Dev
EMP: 6
SALES (est): 2.2MM Privately Held
WEB: www.dynamodevelopment.com
SIC: 7372 Prepackaged software

(G-10002)
E M G CREATIONS INC
8 W 37th St (10018-7401)
PHONE 212 643-0960
Fax: 212 643-0963
Chasky Samet, President
Emil Weiss, Vice Pres
◆ EMP: 15
SQ FT: 2,000
SALES (est): 1.3MM Privately Held
WEB: www.emgcreations.com
SIC: 3911 Jewelry, precious metal

(G-10003)
E P SEWING PLEATING INC
327 W 36th St Frnt 2 (10018-6405)
PHONE 212 967-2575
EMP: 20 EST: 1998
SALES (est): 820K Privately Held
SIC: 2342 Mfg Bras/Girdles

(G-10004)
E SCHREIBER INC
580 5th Ave Fl 32a (10036-4716)
PHONE 212 382-0280
Norbert Steinmetz, President
Ben Moller, Vice Pres
▲ EMP: 22
SQ FT: 5,000
SALES (est): 2MM Privately Held
WEB: www.eschreiber.com
SIC: 3915 5094 Diamond cutting & polishing; diamonds (gems)

(G-10005)
E W WILLIAMS PUBLICATIONS
Also Called: LDB Interior Textiles
370 Lexington Ave Rm 1409 (10017-6583)
PHONE 212 661-1516
Fax: 212 661-1713
Aleksandra Ilnicki, Editor
Wanda Jankowski, Editor
Mark Edgar, Prdtn Mgr
Philippa Hochschild, Manager
Janys Kuznier, Director
EMP: 9
SALES (corp-wide): 42.3MM Privately Held
WEB: www.williamspublications.com
SIC: 2721 2731 Magazines: publishing only, not printed on site; textbooks: publishing only, not printed on site
HQ: E W Williams Publications
2125 Center Ave Ste 305
Fort Lee NJ 07024

(G-10006)
E&I PRINTING
545 8th Ave Rm 5e (10018-2441)
PHONE 212 206-0506
Fax: 212 268-0226
Eric Eisenberg, President
EMP: 15
SALES (est): 5MM Privately Held
WEB: www.eiprints.com
SIC: 2759 Commercial printing

(G-10007)
E-PLAY BRANDS LLC
25 W 39th St Fl 5 (10018-4075)
PHONE 212 563-2646
Joseph Esses,
EMP: 6
SQ FT: 1,000
SALES (est): 262.2K Privately Held
SIC: 2369 2361 Coat & legging sets: girls' & children's; shirts: girls', children's & infants'; dresses: girls', children's & infants'

(G-10008)
E-WON INDUSTRIAL CO INC
Also Called: New York Trading Co
625 Main St Apt 1532 (10044-0036)
PHONE 212 750-9610
Shin Han, President
Sun Yu, Vice Pres
▲ EMP: 37
SQ FT: 1,000
SALES (est): 4MM Privately Held
SIC: 3965 Buttons & parts

(G-10009)
EAGLE ART PUBLISHING INC
475 Park Ave S Rm 2800 (10016-6901)
PHONE 212 685-7411
Samuel J Lurie, President
EMP: 5
SALES (est): 330K Privately Held
SIC: 2731 Book publishing

(G-10010)
EAGLE LACE DYEING CORP
335 W 35th St Fl 2 (10001-1726)
PHONE 212 947-2712

Fax: 212 338-0848
Leonard Shally, President
EMP: 10
SALES (est): 620K **Privately Held**
SIC: 2258 2396 Dyeing & finishing lace goods & warp knit fabric; automotive & apparel trimmings

(G-10011)
EAGLES NEST HOLDINGS LLC (PA)
Also Called: Sabin Robbins
455 E 86th St (10028-6400)
PHONE 513 874-5270
Jack Turcotte, Purchasing
Wayne Penrod,
Joseph Hardiman,
EMP: 32
SQ FT: 6,000
SALES (est): 13.3MM **Privately Held**
SIC: 2679 Paper products, converted

(G-10012)
EARL G GRAVES PUBG CO INC (HQ)
Also Called: Black Enterprise
260 Madison Ave Ste 11 (10016-2413)
PHONE 212 242-8000
Earl G Graves Sr, CEO
Earl Butch Graves Jr, CEO
Jacques Jiha, Principal
Dirk J Caldwell, Senior VP
Angela Mitchell, Vice Pres
EMP: 83
SQ FT: 22,000
SALES (est): 9.7MM
SALES (corp-wide): 18.7MM **Privately Held**
SIC: 2721 Magazines: publishing only, not printed on site
PA: Earl G. Graves, Ltd.
   260 Madison Ave Ste 11
   New York NY 10016
   212 242-8000

(G-10013)
EARRING KING JEWELRY MFG INC
62 W 47th St Ste 1202 (10036-3230)
PHONE 718 544-7947
Fax: 212 471-0011
Kowk Mok, President
Jane Mok, Vice Pres
EMP: 7
SALES (est): 630K **Privately Held**
SIC: 3911 Jewelry, precious metal

(G-10014)
EAST COAST ORTHOIC & PROS COR
3927 Broadway (10032-1538)
PHONE 212 923-2161
Lawrence Benenati, Branch Mgr
EMP: 14
SALES (corp-wide): 9.1MM **Privately Held**
SIC: 3842 Orthopedic appliances
PA: East Coast Orthotic & Prosthetic Corp.
   75 Burt Dr
   Deer Park NY 11729
   516 248-5566

(G-10015)
EAST MEET EAST INC
32 W 39th St Fl 4 (10018-2166)
PHONE 646 481-0033
Mariko Tokioka, Ch of Bd
Kentaro Ejima, Admin Sec
EMP: 7 **EST:** 2014
SALES (est): 297.6K **Privately Held**
SIC: 2741

(G-10016)
EASTERN JEWELRY MFG CO INC
48 W 48th St Ste 707 (10036-1714)
PHONE 212 840-0001
Soloman Witriol, President
EMP: 50
SQ FT: 16,000
SALES (est): 3.4MM **Privately Held**
SIC: 3911 Jewelry apparel; bracelets, precious metal; earrings, precious metal; rosaries or other small religious articles, precious metal

(G-10017)
EASTERN SILK MILLS INC
148 W 37th St Fl 3 (10018-6987)
PHONE 212 730-1300
Fax: 212 302-1665
Andy Ryu, Controller
Sheena Suon, Manager
EMP: 9
SALES (corp-wide): 4.4MM **Privately Held**
SIC: 2262 2221 Dyeing: manmade fiber & silk broadwoven fabrics; broadwoven fabric mills, manmade
PA: Eastern Silk Mills Inc.
   212 Catherine St
   Elizabeth NJ

(G-10018)
EASTERN STRATEGIC MATERIALS
45 Rockefeller Plz # 2000 (10111-0100)
PHONE 212 332-1619
Kai Wong, President
Matthew Harris, Vice Pres
EMP: 41
SALES (est): 4MM **Privately Held**
SIC: 3365 3812 3822 Aerospace castings, aluminum; defense systems & equipment; space vehicle guidance systems & equipment; energy cutoff controls, residential or commercial types

(G-10019)
EASTNETS AMERICAS CORP
450 Fashion Ave Ste 1509 (10123-1509)
PHONE 212 631-0666
Hazem Mulhim, President
Mohamed E Bakkali, CFO
Chadi A Taki, Finance Mgr
Olivier Denis, Manager
Hazem Kharbat, Manager
EMP: 10
SALES (est): 1MM **Privately Held**
SIC: 7372 Prepackaged software

(G-10020)
EASTPORT OPERATING PARTNERS LP (PA)
Also Called: Eastport Management
204 E 20th St Fl 3 (10003-1802)
PHONE 212 387-8791
Fax: 212 674-6821
Edward J Kata, Partner
J Andrew McWethy, General Ptnr
Connie Ciavarella, Cust Mgr
F Patrick Smith, Manager
◆ **EMP:** 3
SALES (est): 37.4MM **Privately Held**
WEB: www.eastportlp.com
SIC: 3593 3492 Fluid power cylinders, hydraulic or pneumatic; fluid power valves & hose fittings

(G-10021)
EATON CORPORATION
830 3rd Ave Fl 7 (10022-6565)
PHONE 212 319-2100
Fax: 212 833-0250
John Mari, Sales Engr
Al Vincenzi, Manager
EMP: 218 **Privately Held**
SIC: 3625 Motor controls & accessories
HQ: Eaton Corporation
   1000 Eaton Blvd
   Cleveland OH 44122
   216 523-5000

(G-10022)
EB ACQUISITIONS LLC
444 Madison Ave Ste 501 (10022-6974)
PHONE 212 355-3310
Nachum Stein,
EMP: 100
SALES (est): 5.7MM **Privately Held**
SIC: 3643 3315 Connectors, electric cord; wire & fabricated wire products

(G-10023)
EB COUTURE LTD
Also Called: Elie Balleh Couture
110 W 34th St Rm 1002 (10001-2128)
PHONE 212 912-0190
Mari Mineh, President
▲ **EMP:** 20

SALES (est): 179.8K **Privately Held**
SIC: 2389 2329 5137 Apparel for handicapped; knickers, dress (separate): men's & boys'; women's & children's clothing

(G-10024)
EBM CARE INC
317 Madison Ave (10017-5201)
PHONE 212 500-5000
Jack Fitzgibbons, President
EMP: 7
SALES (est): 327.8K **Privately Held**
SIC: 7372 Business oriented computer software

(G-10025)
EBNER PUBLISHING INTERNATIONAL
Also Called: Watchtime Magazine
37 W 26th St Rm 412 (10010-1077)
PHONE 646 742-0740
Wolfgang Blum, President
Matthew Morse, Chief
Joe Thompson, Chief
Sara Orlando, Sls & Mktg Exec
Mark Bernardo, Manager
EMP: 5
SALES (est): 45.7K **Privately Held**
WEB: www.watchtime.com
SIC: 2721 Magazines: publishing & printing

(G-10026)
ECCELLA CORPORATION
545 8th Ave Rm 850 (10018-2431)
PHONE 855 879-3223
Meitav Harpaz, CEO
Gil Rosen, President
EMP: 8
SQ FT: 2,960
SALES (est): 420.7K
SALES (corp-wide): 30.8K **Privately Held**
SIC: 7372 7389 Business oriented computer software;
PA: Ngdata Nv
   Sluisweg 2, Internal Postal Box 10
   Gent
   933 882-20

(G-10027)
ECCLESIASTICAL COMMUNICATIONS
Also Called: Catholic New York
1011 1st Ave Fl 6 (10022-4112)
PHONE 212 688-2399
Fax: 212 688-2642
Bishop Robert A Brucato, President
Arthur L McKenna, General Mgr
Mary Gregory, Accountant
John Woods, Manager
EMP: 13
SALES (est): 750K **Privately Held**
SIC: 2711 Newspapers: publishing only, not printed on site

(G-10028)
ECHO GROUP INC
62 W 39th St Ste 1005 (10018-3818)
PHONE 917 608-7440
Fax: 212 382-2490
EMP: 15
SALES (est): 980K **Privately Held**
SIC: 3911 Mfg Precious Metal Jewelry

(G-10029)
ECLECTIC CNTRACT FURN INDS INC
450 Fashion Ave Ste 2710 (10123-2710)
PHONE 212 967-5504
Alex Marc, President
▲ **EMP:** 14
SQ FT: 1,000
SALES (est): 2MM **Privately Held**
WEB: www.eclecticcontract.com
SIC: 2511 Wood household furniture

(G-10030)
ECLIPSE COLLECTION JEWELERS
7 W 45th St Ste 1401 (10036-4905)
PHONE 212 764-6883
Fax: 212 719-2348
Vatcag Aghjayan, President
EMP: 10
SALES (est): 780K **Privately Held**
SIC: 3911 Jewelry, precious metal

(G-10031)
ECONOMIST INTELLIGENCE UNIT NA
750 3rd Ave Fl 5 (10017-2723)
PHONE 212 554-0600
Fax: 212 586-1181
Chris Stibbs, Ch of Bd
Maureen Lanigan, Business Mgr
David Cox, Senior VP
Paul Rossi, Senior VP
Peter Ceretti, Financial Analy
EMP: 68
SQ FT: 18,000
SALES (est): 11.8MM
SALES (corp-wide): 440.4MM **Privately Held**
WEB: www.eiu.com
SIC: 2721 8732 Periodicals: publishing only; business analysis
HQ: The Economist Newspaper Group Incorporated
   750 3rd Ave Fl 5
   New York NY 10017
   212 541-0500

(G-10032)
ECONOMIST NEWSPAPER GROUP INC (HQ)
Also Called: Economist Group, The
750 3rd Ave Fl 5 (10017-2723)
PHONE 212 541-0500
Chris Stibbs, CEO
James Myers, Managing Dir
Tony Tran, Vice Pres
Mary Baksh, Controller
Andre George, Credit Mgr
▲ **EMP:** 220
SALES (est): 134.2MM
SALES (corp-wide): 440.4MM **Privately Held**
SIC: 2721 7313 5963 Periodicals: publishing & printing; magazines: publishing & printing; printed media advertising representatives; magazine advertising representative; newspaper advertising representative; encyclopedias & publications, direct sales; magazine subscription sales, excl. mail order, house sales
PA: Economist Newspaper Limited(The)
   25 St James's Street
   London SW1A
   207 830-7000

(G-10033)
ECONOMIST NEWSPAPER NA INC (DH)
Also Called: Economist Magazine, The
750 3rd Ave Fl 5 (10017-2723)
PHONE 212 554-0676
Chris Stibbs, CEO
Paul Rossi, Exec VP
David Cox, CFO
Richard Hargreaves, Sales Dir
Daniel Morris, Sales Dir
EMP: 20
SQ FT: 28,900
SALES (est): 18MM
SALES (corp-wide): 440.4MM **Privately Held**
SIC: 2711 5192 Newspapers; magazines
HQ: The Economist Newspaper Group Incorporated
   750 3rd Ave Fl 5
   New York NY 10017
   212 541-0500

(G-10034)
EDITH LANCES CORP
247 W 35th St Fl 2 (10001-1927)
PHONE 212 683-1990
Jay S Gingold, President
Marsha Gingold, Vice Pres
EMP: 20
SQ FT: 3,000
SALES: 748K **Privately Held**
SIC: 2342 Brassieres

(G-10035)
EDITIONS DE PRFUMS MADISON LLC (HQ)
654 Madison Ave Rm 1609 (10065-8430)
PHONE 646 666-0527
Frederic Malle, General Mgr
EMP: 18

New York - New York County (G-10036)   **GEOGRAPHIC SECTION**

SALES (est): 1.4MM
SALES (corp-wide): 11.8B **Publicly Held**
SIC: 2844 Perfumes & colognes
PA: The Estee Lauder Companies Inc
    767 5th Ave Fl 37
    New York NY 10153
    212 572-4200

(G-10036)
EDRINGTON GROUP USA LLC (PA)
150 5th Ave Fl 11 (10011-4347)
PHONE..................................212 352-6000
Chris Spalding, *President*
Michael Schutzbank, *Opers Staff*
Jessica Tamilio, *Manager*
April Finkelstein, *Director*
EMP: 28
SALES (est): 11.2MM **Privately Held**
SIC: 2084 Wines, brandy & brandy spirits

(G-10037)
EDSIM LEATHER CO INC (PA)
131 W 35th St Fl 14 (10001-2111)
PHONE..................................212 695-8500
Simone Kamali, *President*
Edmond Kamali, *Vice Pres*
Daniel Kamali, *Sales Mgr*
Joel Kamali, *Sales Mgr*
Lauren Kamali, *Sales Staff*
▲ EMP: 20 EST: 1981
SQ FT: 7,000
SALES: 37MM **Privately Held**
WEB: www.hinet.net
SIC: 3111 Leather tanning & finishing

(G-10038)
EDWARD FIELDS INCORPORATED (PA)
Also Called: Paiping Carpets
150 E 58th St Ste 1101 (10155-1101)
PHONE..................................212 310-0400
Jim Chaplain, *Ch of Bd*
Ed Goldberg, *Vice Pres*
Jeffry Brody, *Manager*
Bethany Hopf, *Manager*
Adrian Angelini, *Contract Law*
EMP: 12 EST: 1933
SQ FT: 6,500
SALES (est): 14.5MM **Privately Held**
WEB: www.edwardfieldsinc.com
SIC: 2273 Carpets & rugs; rugs, tufted

(G-10039)
EFRONT FINANCIAL SOLUTIONS INC
Also Called: E-Front
11 E 44th St Fl 15 (10017-3608)
PHONE..................................212 220-0660
Eric Bernstein, *COO*
Daniel Martin, *COO*
Clinton McKenley, *Accountant*
Diane L Tristani, *Director*
EMP: 25
SALES (corp-wide): 1.8B **Privately Held**
SIC: 7372 Business oriented computer software
HQ: E-Front
    2 4
    Paris 75116
    149 964-060

(G-10040)
EFT ANALYTICS INC
350 5th Ave Ste 4810 (10118-4810)
PHONE..................................212 290-2300
Brent Youngers, *President*
Craig Ennis, *CTO*
EMP: 8
SALES (est): 1.1MM
SALES (corp-wide): 27.8B **Privately Held**
SIC: 7372 Application computer software
PA: Koch Industries, Inc.
    4111 E 37th St N
    Wichita KS 67220
    316 828-5500

(G-10041)
EGMONT US INC
443 Park Ave S Rm 806 (10016-7322)
PHONE..................................212 685-0102
▲ EMP: 8
SALES (est): 615K
SALES (corp-wide): 1.6B **Privately Held**
SIC: 2731 Books-Publishing/Printing
HQ: Egmont Uk Limited
    The Yellow Building
    London W11 4
    203 220-0400

(G-10042)
EIDOSMEDIA INC
14 Wall St Ste 6c (10005-2170)
PHONE..................................646 795-2100
Steven Ball, *CEO*
EMP: 20
SALES (est): 2.6MM
SALES (corp-wide): 212.8K **Privately Held**
SIC: 2721 Periodicals: publishing & printing
HQ: Eidosmedia Spa
    Corso Vercelli 40
    Milano MI 20145
    023 673-2000

(G-10043)
EIGHTEEN LIANA TRADING INC
Also Called: Liana Uniforms
110 W 40th St Rm 606 (10018-8554)
PHONE..................................718 369-4247
Fax: 718 369-4247
Arie Dervich, *President*
Helen Dervich, *Vice Pres*
▲ EMP: 22
SQ FT: 10,000
SALES (est): 2MM **Privately Held**
SIC: 2326 Medical & hospital uniforms, men's

(G-10044)
EILEENS SPECIAL CHEESECAKE
17 Cleveland Pl Frnt A (10012-4052)
PHONE..................................212 966-5585
Fax: 212 219-9558
Eileen Avezzano, *President*
EMP: 6
SQ FT: 600
SALES (est): 310K **Privately Held**
WEB: www.eileenscheesecake.com
SIC: 2051 Bakery: wholesale or wholesale/retail combined; cakes, bakery: except frozen

(G-10045)
EL AGUILA
137 E 116th St Frnt 1 (10029-1385)
PHONE..................................212 410-2450
EMP: 8
SALES (est): 433.3K **Privately Held**
SIC: 2711 Newspapers, publishing & printing

(G-10046)
EL-LA DESIGN INC
Also Called: My Apparel
209 W 38th St Rm 901 (10018-4558)
PHONE..................................212 382-1080
Fax: 212 382-1125
Elaine Lai, *President*
EMP: 5
SALES (est): 590K **Privately Held**
SIC: 2339 Sportswear, women's

(G-10047)
ELANA LADEROS LTD
Also Called: Joanna Mastroianni
230 W 38th St Fl 15 (10018-9026)
PHONE..................................212 764-0840
Fax: 212 398-6185
Joanna Mastroianni, *President*
EMP: 10
SQ FT: 3,500
SALES (est): 1.4MM **Privately Held**
WEB: www.joannamastroianni.com
SIC: 2335 Women's, juniors' & misses' dresses

(G-10048)
ELEANOR ETTINGER INC
24 W 57th St Ste 609 (10019-3918)
PHONE..................................212 925-7474
Eleanor Ettinger, *President*
Barbara Stevens, *Vice Pres*
EMP: 20
SALES (est): 1.7MM **Privately Held**
WEB: www.eleanorettinger.com
SIC: 2731 2752 Books: publishing only; commercial printing, offset

(G-10049)
ELECTRIC LIGHTING AGENCIES (PA)
Also Called: Ela
36 W 25th St Fl 6 (10010-2757)
PHONE..................................212 645-4580
EMP: 22
SALES (est): 3.8MM **Privately Held**
SIC: 3646 Mfg Commercial Lighting Fixtures

(G-10050)
ELECTRONIC ARTS INC
1515 Broadway Rm 3601 (10036-8901)
PHONE..................................212 672-0722
Barbara Gallacher, *Vice Pres*
EMP: 7
SALES (corp-wide): 4.8B **Publicly Held**
WEB: www.ea.com
SIC: 7372 Prepackaged software
PA: Electronic Arts Inc.
    209 Redwood Shores Pkwy
    Redwood City CA 94065
    650 628-1500

(G-10051)
ELEGANT HEADWEAR CO INC
Also Called: ABG Accessories
10 W 33rd St Rm 1122 (10001-3306)
PHONE..................................212 695-8520
Chris Moccia, *VP Sales*
Michael Brett, *Branch Mgr*
EMP: 8
SALES (corp-wide): 39.6MM **Privately Held**
WEB: www.elegantheadwear.com
SIC: 2253 Knit outerwear mills
PA: Elegant Headwear Co. Inc.
    1000 Jefferson Ave
    Elizabeth NJ 07201
    908 558-1200

(G-10052)
ELEGANT JEWELERS MFG CO INC
31 W 47th St Ste 301 (10036-2888)
PHONE..................................212 869-4951
Sandy Petropoulos, *President*
Nick Seretis, *Vice Pres*
EMP: 12
SQ FT: 1,500
SALES (est): 1.1MM **Privately Held**
WEB: www.elegantsilverjewellery.net
SIC: 3911 Jewelry, precious metal

(G-10053)
ELEVONDATA LABS INC
1350 Ave Of The Amrcs 2nd (10019-4702)
PHONE..................................470 222-5438
Rohit Tandon, *CEO*
EMP: 50
SALES (est): 4MM **Privately Held**
SIC: 7372 Prepackaged software

(G-10054)
ELIE TAHARI LTD
501 5th Ave Fl 2 (10017-7825)
PHONE..................................212 398-2622
Elie Tahari, *Principal*
EMP: 8
SALES (corp-wide): 271.7MM **Privately Held**
SIC: 2331 2339 2337 5621 Blouses, women's & juniors': made from purchased material; slacks: women's, misses' & juniors'; suits: women's, misses' & juniors'; jackets & vests, except fur & leather: women's; women's clothing stores; men's & boys' clothing stores
PA: Elie Tahari Ltd.
    16 Bleeker St
    Millburn NJ 07041
    973 671-6300

(G-10055)
ELIE TAHARI LTD
510 5th Ave Fl 3 (10036-7507)
PHONE..................................212 398-2622
Fax: 212 221-6776
David Elron, *Branch Mgr*
Rishi Sharma, *Software Dev*
EMP: 75

SALES (corp-wide): 271.7MM **Privately Held**
SIC: 2337 8741 2339 Suits: women's, misses' & juniors'; management services; women's & misses' outerwear
PA: Elie Tahari Ltd.
    16 Bleeker St
    Millburn NJ 07041
    973 671-6300

(G-10056)
ELIE TAHARI LTD
1114 Ave Of The Americas (10036-7703)
PHONE..................................212 763-2000
Fax: 212 763-2298
Robert Goldsmith, *Senior VP*
Julie S Deloca, *Vice Pres*
Meenakashi Lala, *VP Prdtn*
Jill Safinski, *Mktg Dir*
Arthur S Levine, *Branch Mgr*
EMP: 60
SALES (corp-wide): 271.7MM **Privately Held**
SIC: 2331 2337 Blouses, women's & juniors': made from purchased material; uniforms, except athletic: women's, misses' & juniors'
PA: Elie Tahari Ltd.
    16 Bleeker St
    Millburn NJ 07041
    973 671-6300

(G-10057)
ELIE TAHARI LTD
11 W 42nd St Fl 14 (10036-8002)
PHONE..................................973 671-6300
Lisanne Kolligs, *President*
Taylor Fleshman, *Buyer*
Danielle Kuperberg, *Sales Dir*
Dina Koutroumanis, *Marketing Mgr*
Susan Kellogg, *Manager*
EMP: 75
SALES (corp-wide): 271.7MM **Privately Held**
SIC: 2337 Suits: women's, misses' & juniors'
PA: Elie Tahari Ltd.
    16 Bleeker St
    Millburn NJ 07041
    973 671-6300

(G-10058)
ELIS BREAD (ELI ZABAR) INC (PA)
1064 Madison Ave Apt 5 (10028-0252)
PHONE..................................212 772-2011
Eli Zabar, *President*
Robert Shaloff, *VP Opers*
Ruben Flores, *Opers Staff*
Natalie Stettner, *Manager*
EMP: 10
SALES (est): 16.7MM **Privately Held**
WEB: www.elisbread.com
SIC: 2045 Bread & bread type roll mixes: from purchased flour

(G-10059)
ELITE DAILY INC
53 W 23rd St Fl 12 (10010-4313)
PHONE..................................212 402-9097
Martin Clarke, *President*
Tyler Gildin, *Director*
EMP: 301
SALES (est): 17.8MM
SALES (corp-wide): 39.4MM **Privately Held**
SIC: 2741
PA: Bdg Media, Inc.
    158 W 27th St Fl 11
    New York NY 10001
    917 951-9768

(G-10060)
ELITE PARFUMS LTD (HQ)
551 5th Ave Rm 1500 (10176-1599)
PHONE..................................212 983-2640
Jean Madar, *President*
Philippe Benacin, *President*
Bruce Elbelia, *Exec VP*
Wayne C Hamerling, *Exec VP*
Russell Greenberg, *CFO*
▲ EMP: 57
SQ FT: 12,000

GEOGRAPHIC SECTION

New York - New York County (G-10086)

SALES (est): 4MM
SALES (corp-wide): 521MM **Publicly Held**
SIC: 2844 5122 Toilet preparations; perfumes; toiletries
PA: Inter Parfums, Inc.
551 5th Ave
New York NY 10176
212 983-2640

(G-10061)
ELITE TRAVELER LLC
441 Lexington Ave Fl 3 (10017-3950)
PHONE...................................646 430-7900
Kristen Shirley, *Editor*
Lorraine Cousland, *Senior VP*
Cheryl Ricossa, *Director*
Randy Silverman, *Director*
Greg Licciardi, *Officer*
EMP: 11
SALES (est): 790.2K **Privately Held**
SIC: 2721 Magazines: publishing & printing

(G-10062)
ELIZABETH EAKINS INC (PA)
654 Madison Ave Rm 1409 (10065-8432)
PHONE...................................212 628-1950
Elizabeth Eakins, *President*
Scott Lethbridge, *Vice Pres*
Jamie Alencastro, *Manager*
▲ EMP: 10
SQ FT: 4,000
SALES (est): 2.5MM **Privately Held**
WEB: www.elizabetheakins.com
SIC: 2273 5713 5023 Carpets, hand & machine made; carpets; carpets

(G-10063)
ELIZABETH FILLMORE LLC
27 W 20th St Ste 705 (10011-3727)
PHONE...................................212 647-0863
Fax: 212 647-1562
Thomas Allen, *Vice Pres*
Elizabeth Fillmore,
EMP: 7
SQ FT: 1,900
SALES (est): 770.6K **Privately Held**
WEB: www.elizabethfillmorebridal.com
SIC: 2335 Gowns, formal

(G-10064)
ELIZABETH GILLETT LTD
Also Called: Elizabeth Gillett Designs
260 W 36th St Rm 802 (10018-8992)
PHONE...................................212 629-7993
Fax: 212 629-7993
Elizabeth Gillett, *President*
Tarafawn Marek, *Vice Pres*
Stephanie Corren, *Sales Mgr*
◆ EMP: 6
SQ FT: 1,500
SALES (est): 2.5MM **Privately Held**
WEB: www.egillett.com
SIC: 2339 Scarves, hoods, headbands, etc.: women's

(G-10065)
ELMGANG ENTERPRISES I INC
Also Called: Espostos Fnest Qlty Ssage Pdts
354 W 38th St Frnt (10018-2954)
PHONE...................................212 868-4142
Fax: 212 868-0065
David Samuels, *President*
Kimbal Musk, *General Mgr*
EMP: 10
SQ FT: 5,000
SALES (est): 1.6MM **Privately Held**
WEB: www.espositosausage.com
SIC: 2013 5147 Sausages & related products, from purchased meat; meats & meat products

(G-10066)
ELODINA INC
222 Broadway Fl 19 (10038-2550)
PHONE...................................646 402-5202
Paul Reinitz, *President*
EMP: 5
SALES (est): 128.9K **Privately Held**
SIC: 7372 Business oriented computer software

(G-10067)
ELSEVIER INC (DH)
230 Park Ave Fl 8 (10169-0123)
PHONE...................................212 633-3773
Fax: 212 633-3880
Ron Mobed, *CEO*
Hajo Oltmanns, *President*
Mj Janse, *Editor*
Barbara Makinster, *Editor*
Alan Meier, *Editor*
◆ EMP: 277 EST: 1962
SQ FT: 65,000
SALES (est): 140.8MM
SALES (corp-wide): 8.4B **Privately Held**
WEB: www.elsevierfoundation.org
SIC: 2741 Technical manuals: publishing only, not printed on site
HQ: Elsevier B.V.
Radarweg 29
Amsterdam
204 853-911

(G-10068)
ELUMINOCITY US INC
80 Pine St Fl 24 (10005-1732)
PHONE...................................651 528-1165
Sebastian Jagsch, *CEO*
Mike Rockwood Sr, *General Mgr*
EMP: 2 EST: 2015
SQ FT: 200
SALES: 1.8MM **Privately Held**
SIC: 3648 3694 3629 Street lighting fixtures; battery charging generators, automobile & aircraft; battery chargers, rectifying or nonrotating

(G-10069)
ELY BEACH SOLAR LLC
5030 Broadway Ste 819 (10034-1670)
PHONE...................................718 796-9400
Alison Karmel, *Vice Pres*
EMP: 7
SALES (est): 642.4K **Privately Held**
SIC: 3674 Solar cells

(G-10070)
EMA JEWELRY INC
246 W 38th St Fl 6 (10018-5854)
PHONE...................................212 575-8989
Fax: 212 575-9267
Michael Weiss, *CEO*
Edward Weiss, *Vice Pres*
Alex Weiss, *Treasurer*
▼ EMP: 65 EST: 1977
SQ FT: 7,500
SALES (est): 8.9MM **Privately Held**
WEB: www.emajewelry.com
SIC: 3911 3961 Jewelry, precious metal; costume jewelry

(G-10071)
EMBASSY APPAREL INC
37 W 37th St Fl 10 (10018-6354)
PHONE...................................212 768-8330
Ezra Cattan, *President*
Jack Cattan, *Vice Pres*
Judah Cattan, *Vice Pres*
Nadia Ramnauth, *Manager*
EMP: 18
SQ FT: 10,000
SALES (est): 950.8K **Privately Held**
SIC: 2331 5136 5137 Women's & misses' blouses & shirts; men's & boys' furnishings; women's & children's accessories

(G-10072)
EMBLAZE SYSTEMS INC (HQ)
Also Called: Geo Publishing
424 Madison Ave Fl 16 (10017-1137)
PHONE...................................212 371-1100
Bruce Edwards, *President*
Joe Budenholzer, *President*
Brad Grob, *Vice Pres*
Michael Weiss, *Vice Pres*
Lydia Edward, *Treasurer*
EMP: 120
SQ FT: 7,000
SALES (est): 7.6MM
SALES (corp-wide): 59.8MM **Privately Held**
SIC: 7372 Prepackaged software
PA: B.S.D Crown Ltd
7 Begin Menachem Rd
Ramat Gan 52681
976 997-55

(G-10073)
EMCO ELECTRIC SERVICES LLC
526 W 26th St Rm 1012 (10001-5541)
PHONE...................................212 420-9766
Meziar Ghavidel, *Mng Member*
Mehr Mansuri, *Mng Member*
EMP: 5 EST: 2013
SALES: 170K **Privately Held**
SIC: 3699 1731 Electrical equipment & supplies; electronic controls installation

(G-10074)
EMERSON ELECTRIC CO
1250 Broadway Ste 2300 (10001-3726)
PHONE...................................212 244-2490
Jennifer Nichols, *Principal*
EMP: 23
SALES (corp-wide): 14.5B **Publicly Held**
WEB: www.gotoemerson.com
SIC: 3823 Industrial instrmnts msrmnt display/control process variable
PA: Emerson Electric Co.
8000 West Florissant Ave
Saint Louis MO 63136
314 553-2000

(G-10075)
EMPOWRX LLC
249 E 53rd St Apt 2a (10022-4836)
PHONE...................................212 755-3577
Heather Raymond,
EMP: 5
SALES (est): 217.9K **Privately Held**
SIC: 7372 Prepackaged software

(G-10076)
EMSARU USA CORP
Also Called: Hampshire Jewels
608 5th Ave Ste 500 (10020-2303)
PHONE...................................212 459-9355
Fax: 212 459-9354
Harry Molhan, *President*
Atul Dangayach, *Managing Dir*
EMP: 5
SALES (est): 430K **Privately Held**
SIC: 3911 Jewelry, precious metal

(G-10077)
EMSIG MANUFACTURING CORP (PA)
263 W 38th St Fl 5 (10018-0291)
PHONE...................................718 784-7717
Lawrence Jacobs, *President*
John Lerner, *Vice Pres*
Nancy McCaffery, *Manager*
Arthur Klein, *Admin Sec*
◆ EMP: 15 EST: 1965
SQ FT: 19,000
SALES (est): 26.7MM **Privately Held**
SIC: 3965 Buttons & parts

(G-10078)
EMSIG MANUFACTURING CORP
263 W 38th St Fl 5 (10018-0291)
PHONE...................................718 784-7717
Fax: 212 971-0413
Lawrence Jacobs, *President*
EMP: 20
SALES (corp-wide): 26.7MM **Privately Held**
SIC: 3965 Buttons & parts
PA: Emsig Manufacturing Corp.
263 W 38th St Fl 5
New York NY 10018
718 784-7717

(G-10079)
EMUSICCOM INC (PA)
215 Lexington Ave Fl 18 (10016-6023)
PHONE...................................212 201-9240
Peter Chapman, *CEO*
Daniel Stein, *Ch of Bd*
David Packman, *President*
Madeline Milne, *General Mgr*
Emusic News, *Vice Pres*
EMP: 49
SALES (est): 10.3MM **Privately Held**
WEB: www.emusic.com
SIC: 3652 Pre-recorded records & tapes

(G-10080)
ENCHANTE ACCESSORIES INC (PA)
16 E 34th St Fl 16 (10016-4359)
PHONE...................................212 689-6008
Fax: 212 684-3622
Ezra Erani, *Ch of Bd*
Gabe Kehzrie, *Vice Pres*
Sara Rakowsky, *Project Mgr*
Tanya Kuznetsov, *Controller*
Joey Safdieh, *Cust Mgr*
◆ EMP: 170
SALES (est): 50.6MM **Privately Held**
WEB: www.emch.com
SIC: 2499 5023 Kitchen, bathroom & household ware: wood; decorative home furnishings & supplies

(G-10081)
ENCHANTE LITES LLC (HQ)
Also Called: AMG Global
15 W 34th St Fl 8 (10001-3015)
PHONE...................................212 602-1818
Ezra Erani, *President*
Abraham Weinberger, *CFO*
▲ EMP: 9
SALES (est): 2.7MM
SALES (corp-wide): 50.6MM **Privately Held**
SIC: 3648 Decorative area lighting fixtures
PA: Enchante Accessories Inc.
16 E 34th St Fl 16
New York NY 10016
212 689-6008

(G-10082)
ENCYSIVE PHARMACEUTICALS INC (HQ)
235 E 42nd St (10017-5703)
PHONE...................................212 733-2323
John M Pietruski, *Ch of Bd*
Bruce D Given, *President*
Richard A F Dixon, *Senior VP*
Paul S Manierre, *Vice Pres*
Manierre Paul, *Vice Pres*
▲ EMP: 35
SQ FT: 40,730
SALES (est): 13.9MM
SALES (corp-wide): 52.8B **Publicly Held**
SIC: 2834 8733 Pharmaceutical preparations; medical research
PA: Pfizer Inc.
235 E 42nd St
New York NY 10017
212 733-2323

(G-10083)
ENDAVA INC (HQ)
441 Lexington Ave Rm 702 (10017-3922)
PHONE...................................212 920-7240
Dan Sullivan, *President*
Dave Vioreanu, *Info Tech Mgr*
EMP: 3
SQ FT: 2,000
SALES (est): 1.5MM
SALES (corp-wide): 167.3MM **Privately Held**
SIC: 7372 7371 7375 Business oriented computer software; custom computer programming services; on-line data base information retrieval
PA: Endava Limited
125 Old Broad Street
London EC2N
207 367-1000

(G-10084)
ENDOVOR INC
1330 1st Ave Apt 1119 (10021-4792)
PHONE...................................214 679-7385
Derek Carroll, *CEO*
EMP: 5
SALES (est): 198.4K **Privately Held**
SIC: 3841 Surgical & medical instruments

(G-10085)
ENDOVOR LLC
525 E 68th St A1027 (10065-4870)
PHONE...................................214 679-7385
Derek Carroll, *Opers Staff*
EMP: 8
SALES (est): 293.5K **Privately Held**
SIC: 3841 Surgical & medical instruments

(G-10086)
ENDURANCE LLC
530 7th Ave Rm 902 (10018-4874)
PHONE...................................212 719-2500
Fax: 212 719-2507
Jason Messler, *Vice Pres*
Athanasios Nastos,
Renjie Luo,
Daidai Ni,
Qiwen Zhao,
▲ EMP: 20

New York - New York County (G-10087)   **GEOGRAPHIC SECTION**

SALES (est): 2MM Privately Held
SIC: 2329 Men's & boys' sportswear & athletic clothing

(G-10087)
ENDURART INC
Also Called: Quality Embedments Mfg Co
132 Nassau St Rm 1100 (10038-2430)
PHONE 212 473-7000
Stuart Levine, *President*
Henry Richmond, *Financial Exec*
EMP: 30
SQ FT: 18,000
SALES (est): 2.4MM Privately Held
SIC: 3914 2821 Trophies; plastics materials & resins

(G-10088)
ENER-G COGEN LLC
1261 Broadway (10001-3506)
PHONE 718 551-7170
Vishnu Barran, *Sales Staff*
Chis Hayten, *Mng Member*
EMP: 5 EST: 2011
SALES (est): 292.6K Privately Held
SIC: 3621 Power generators

(G-10089)
ENERGY BRANDS INC (HQ)
Also Called: Glaceau
260 Madison Ave Fl 10 (10016-2417)
PHONE 212 545-6000
Fax: 718 747-5900
J Darius Bikoff, *CEO*
Michael Repole, *President*
Carol Dollard, *COO*
William D Hawkins, *Vice Pres*
Glenn Ricks, *Vice Pres*
▼ EMP: 54
SQ FT: 15,000
SALES (est): 31.2MM
SALES (corp-wide): 41.8B Publicly Held
WEB: www.energybrands.com
SIC: 2086 Soft drinks: packaged in cans, bottles, etc.
PA: The Coca-Cola Company
    1 Coca Cola Plz Nw
    Atlanta GA 30313
    404 676-2121

(G-10090)
ENERGY INTELLIGENCE GROUP INC (PA)
270 Madison Ave Fl 19 (10016-0601)
PHONE 212 532-1112
Fax: 212 532-4479
Elias Saber, *President*
David Kirsch, *Managing Dir*
Megan Elmore, *Editor*
Jason Fargo, *Editor*
Tom Haywood, *Editor*
EMP: 30
SQ FT: 7,000
SALES (est): 11.5MM Privately Held
SIC: 2741 Newsletter publishing

(G-10091)
ENERTIV INC
555 W 23rd St Ph M (10011-1033)
PHONE 646 350-3525
Connell McGill, *President*
Pavel Khodorkovskiy, *Treasurer*
Felix Lipov, *Software Dev*
EMP: 6
SALES (est): 1MM Privately Held
SIC: 3825 Instruments to measure electricity

(G-10092)
ENGELACK GEM CORPORATION
36 W 47th St Ste 601 (10036-8636)
PHONE 212 719-3094
Imre England, *President*
Herman Ackerman, *Vice Pres*
EMP: 2
SALES (est): 1MM Privately Held
SIC: 3915 Lapidary work & diamond cutting & polishing

(G-10093)
ENHANCE A COLOUR CORP
211 E 43rd St Rm 700 (10017-4821)
PHONE 212 490-3620
Kevin O'Connor, *President*
EMP: 43

SALES (corp-wide): 9MM Privately Held
SIC: 2741 Posters: publishing & printing
PA: Enhance A Colour Corp.
    43 Beaver Brook Rd Ste 3
    Danbury CT 06810
    203 748-5111

(G-10094)
ENLIGHTEN AIR INC
23 E 81st St Apt 10 (10028-0225)
P.O. Box 3111, Sag Harbor (11963-0405)
PHONE 917 656-1248
William O'Boyle, *CEO*
EMP: 5
SALES: 392MM Privately Held
SIC: 3728 Target drones

(G-10095)
ENPLAS AMERICA INC
299 Park Ave Fl 41 (10171-3808)
PHONE 646 892-7811
EMP: 8
SALES (est): 992K
SALES (corp-wide): 290.2MM Privately Held
SIC: 3714 5065 3827 Gears, motor vehicle; semiconductor devices; lenses, optical: all types except ophthalmic
PA: Enplas Corporation
    2-30-1, Namiki
    Kawaguchi STM 332-0
    482 533-131

(G-10096)
ENTERPRISE PRESS INC
627 Greenwich St (10014-3327)
PHONE 212 741-2111
Fax: 212 627-7937
Robert Hort, *Ch of Bd*
Benjamin Hort, *President*
Michael Hort, *Principal*
Milton Palenbaum, *Purchasing*
Andrew Hort, *Treasurer*
EMP: 145 EST: 1915
SQ FT: 85,000
SALES (est): 12.5MM Privately Held
SIC: 2759 2752 Commercial printing; commercial printing, lithographic

(G-10097)
ENTERTAINMENT WEEKLY INC (HQ)
135 W 50th St Frnt 3 (10020-1201)
PHONE 212 522-5600
Fax: 212 522-0074
Andy Sareyan, *President*
Paul Caine, *Publisher*
Mike Bruno, *Editor*
Steve Edwards, *Vice Pres*
George Vollmuth, *Production*
▲ EMP: 135
SQ FT: 50,000
SALES (est): 15.4MM
SALES (corp-wide): 3B Publicly Held
SIC: 2731 7812 Book publishing; motion picture & video production; television film production; motion picture production
PA: Time Inc.
    225 Liberty St Ste C2
    New York NY 10281
    212 522-1212

(G-10098)
ENTRAINANT INC
Also Called: Stylesprit
1 World Trade Ctr Fl 85 (10007-0103)
PHONE 212 946-4724
Ihsan Ugurlu, *President*
EMP: 6 EST: 2015
SALES (est): 256.7K Privately Held
SIC: 2741

(G-10099)
ENUMERAL BIOMEDICAL CORP (PA)
1370 Broadway Fl 5 (10018-7350)
PHONE 347 227-4787
Arthur H Tinkelenberg, *CEO*
Gary Creason, *Vice Pres*
Kevin Sarney, *Vice Pres*
EMP: 6
SALES (est): 1MM Privately Held
SIC: 2834 Pharmaceutical preparations

(G-10100)
ENVY PUBLISHING GROUP INC
Also Called: N V Magazine
118 E 25th St Bsmt Ll (10010-2915)
PHONE 212 253-9874
Fax: 212 253-9874
Kyle Donovan, *CEO*
Maria Gordian, *President*
Kenneth Williams, *Mktg Dir*
EMP: 6
SQ FT: 3,000
SALES: 500K Privately Held
WEB: www.nvmagazine.com
SIC: 2721 6282 Periodicals; investment advice

(G-10101)
EON COLLECTIONS
247 W 35th St Rm 401 (10001-1962)
PHONE 212 695-1263
Alex Andropoulos, *Owner*
EMP: 20
SALES (est): 769K Privately Held
SIC: 2329 Men's & boys' clothing

(G-10102)
EPOCH TIMES INTERNATIONAL INC
229 W 28th St Fl 5 (10001-5905)
PHONE 212 239-2808
Fax: 646 213-1219
Peter WEI, *Vice Pres*
Amir Talai, *Sales Mgr*
Roman Balmakov, *Accounts Exec*
Echo Liu, *VP Mktg*
Dana Cheng, *Manager*
EMP: 4
SALES (est): 3.1MM Privately Held
SIC: 2711 Newspapers, publishing & printing

(G-10103)
EPOST INTERNATIONAL INC
483 10th Ave (10018-1118)
PHONE 212 352-9390
Justine Brown, *President*
EMP: 5
SALES (est): 1MM Privately Held
SIC: 2741

(G-10104)
EQUILEND HOLDINGS LLC (PA)
225 Liberty St Fl 10 (10281-1049)
PHONE 212 901-2200
Fax: 212 653-0222
Brian Lamb, *CEO*
Brent Bessire, *COO*
Chris Benedict, *Vice Pres*
Sally Chu, *Vice Pres*
Vikas Gupta, *Vice Pres*
EMP: 30
SQ FT: 5,500
SALES (est): 8MM Privately Held
WEB: www.equilend.com
SIC: 7372 Business oriented computer software

(G-10105)
EQUIPMENT APPAREL LLC
19 W 34th St Fl 8 (10001-3006)
PHONE 212 502-1890
Lisa Armstrong, *Credit Mgr*
Gila Dweck,
▲ EMP: 100
SALES (est): 7.7MM Privately Held
SIC: 2211 Apparel & outerwear fabrics, cotton

(G-10106)
EQUIVITAL INC
19 W 34th St Rm 1018 (10001-3006)
PHONE 646 513-4169
Anmol Sood, *CEO*
Anand Vasudev, *Vice Pres*
EMP: 22
SALES (est): 1.7MM Privately Held
SIC: 3845 Patient monitoring apparatus

(G-10107)
ER BUTLER & CO INC (PA)
55 Prince St (10012-3432)
P.O. Box 272 (10012-0005)
PHONE 212 925-3565
Fax: 212 925-3305
Edward R Butler, *CEO*

Christopher Albanese, *Broker*
Catherine Anello, *Office Mgr*
▲ EMP: 25
SQ FT: 11,000
SALES (est): 4.7MM Privately Held
WEB: www.erbutler.com
SIC: 3429 5072 8742 7699 Manufactured hardware (general); builders' hardware; industry specialist consultants; miscellaneous building item repair services; plumbing fixture fittings & trim; residential lighting fixtures

(G-10108)
ERIC WINTERLING INC
Also Called: Winterling, Eric Costumes
20 W 20th St Fl 5 (10011-9257)
PHONE 212 629-7686
Fax: 212 629-7543
Eric Winterling, *President*
K Larry, *Human Res Mgr*
EMP: 50
SALES (est): 4MM Privately Held
SIC: 2389 Costumes

(G-10109)
ERICKSON BEAMON LTD
498 Fashion Ave Rm 2406 (10018-6798)
PHONE 212 643-4810
Karen Foster Erickson, *President*
Eric Erickson, *Vice Pres*
Jean-Marc Flack, *Manager*
EMP: 15
SQ FT: 7,500
SALES (est): 2MM Privately Held
WEB: www.ericksonbeamon.com
SIC: 3961 Costume jewelry, ex. precious metal & semiprecious stones

(G-10110)
ERIKA T SCHWARTZ MD PC
724 5th Ave Fl 10 (10019-4106)
PHONE 212 873-3420
Erika T Schwartz, *President*
Joshua Trutt, *Vice Pres*
EMP: 6
SALES (est): 1.5MM Privately Held
SIC: 2834 8011 Hormone preparations; specialized medical practitioners, except internal

(G-10111)
ESCHEN PROSTHETIC & ORTHOTIC L
510 E 73rd St Ste 201 (10021-4010)
PHONE 212 606-1262
Fax: 212 249-6103
Andrew Meyers, *President*
Mary Eschen, *Admin Asst*
EMP: 20
SQ FT: 6,000
SALES (est): 2.7MM Privately Held
SIC: 3842 Braces, orthopedic; prosthetic appliances

(G-10112)
ESHEL JEWELRY MFG CO INC
17 E 48th St Fl 9 (10017-1010)
PHONE 212 588-8800
Fax: 212 588-1308
Manachem Noeh, *President*
Liba Noeh, *Vice Pres*
Sarah Klepner, *Controller*
EMP: 12
SQ FT: 2,000
SALES (est): 1MM Privately Held
SIC: 3911 Jewelry, precious metal

(G-10113)
ESI CASES & ACCESSORIES INC
44 E 32nd St Rm 601 (10016-5557)
PHONE 212 883-8838
Fax: 212 567-3616
Elliot Azoulay, *Ch of Bd*
Karen Kuchta, *Vice Pres*
Scott Heffes, *CFO*
Stephen Bong, *Finance*
▲ EMP: 38 EST: 1993
SQ FT: 10,000
SALES (est): 9.9MM Privately Held
WEB: www.esicellular.com
SIC: 3661 Telephone & telegraph apparatus

GEOGRAPHIC SECTION

New York - New York County (G-10138)

(G-10114)
ESSAR AMERICAS
277 Park Ave 47th (10172-0003)
PHONE..................212 292-2600
EMP: 5
SALES (est): 348.8K Privately Held
SIC: 1389 Oil & gas field services

(G-10115)
ESSAR STEEL MINNESOTA LLC (PA)
277 Park Ave Fl 35l (10172-2904)
PHONE..................212 292-2600
Carola Almonte, Administration
EMP: 7
SALES (est): 1.9MM Privately Held
SIC: 1011 Iron ore mining

(G-10116)
ESSENCE COMMUNICATIONS INC (HQ)
Also Called: Essence Magazine
225 Liberty St Fl 9 (10281-1088)
PHONE..................212 522-1212
Fax: 212 467-5017
Ed Lewis, CEO
Christian Juhl, CEO
Barbara Britton, President
Clarence O Smith, President
Donald Fries, Publisher
▲ EMP: 119
SQ FT: 30,000
SALES (est): 21.3MM
SALES (corp-wide): 3B Publicly Held
SIC: 2721 Magazines: publishing only, not printed on site
PA: Time Inc.
225 Liberty St Ste C2
New York NY 10281
212 522-1212

(G-10117)
ESSENTIAL PUBLICATIONS US LLC
Also Called: Essential Homme Magazine
14 E 4th St Rm 604 (10012-1141)
PHONE..................646 707-0898
Roger Antin, Publisher
Algis Puidokas, Principal
Terry Lu, Editor
Joshua Glass, Associate
EMP: 5 EST: 2009
SALES (est): 255.6K Privately Held
SIC: 2721 Magazines: publishing & printing

(G-10118)
ESSENTIAL RIBBONS INC
53 W 36th St Rm 405 (10018-7623)
PHONE..................212 967-4173
Jie Lin, Ch of Bd
▲ EMP: 7
SALES (est): 620.2K Privately Held
SIC: 2241 Ribbons

(G-10119)
ESSEX MANUFACTURING INC
350 5th Ave Ste 2400 (10118-0128)
P.O. Box 190, Washington GA (30673-0190)
PHONE..................212 239-0080
William Baum, CEO
Charles J Baum, Ch of Bd
Myron Baum, Ch of Bd
Peter Baum, COO
Thomas Albea, Plant Mgr
▲ EMP: 75 EST: 1961
SQ FT: 85,300
SALES (est): 8.7MM Privately Held
SIC: 2385 3171 3999 Waterproof outerwear; raincoats, except vulcanized rubber: purchased materials; women's handbags & purses; umbrellas, canes & parts

(G-10120)
ESSIE COSMETICS LTD
575 5th Ave (10017-2422)
PHONE..................212 818-1500
Fax: 718 726-7680
Esther Weingarten, President
Gerry Hill, VP Opers
Catherine Forst, Opers Mgr
Blanche Weingarten, Treasurer
Harvey Perlowitz, VP Sales
◆ EMP: 75
SQ FT: 25,000
SALES (est): 16.8MM
SALES (corp-wide): 3.2B Privately Held
WEB: www.essie.com
SIC: 2844 5122 Manicure preparations; toilet preparations; cosmetics
HQ: L'oreal Usa, Inc.
10 Hudson Yards Fl 30
New York NY 10001
212 818-1500

(G-10121)
ESTEE LAUDER COMPANIES INC
9 W 22nd St (10010-5101)
PHONE..................917 606-3240
Salima Popatia, Vice Pres
EMP: 504
SALES (corp-wide): 11.8B Publicly Held
SIC: 2844 Toilet preparations
PA: The Estee Lauder Companies Inc
767 5th Ave Fl 37
New York NY 10153
212 572-4200

(G-10122)
ESTEE LAUDER COMPANIES INC
655 Madison Ave Fl 15 (10065-8043)
PHONE..................212 756-4800
EMP: 6
SALES (corp-wide): 11.8B Publicly Held
SIC: 2844 Toilet preparations; cosmetic preparations; perfumes & colognes
PA: The Estee Lauder Companies Inc
767 5th Ave Fl 37
New York NY 10153
212 572-4200

(G-10123)
ESTEE LAUDER COMPANIES INC
767 5th Ave Fl 37 (10153-0003)
PHONE..................212 572-4200
Caroline Geerlings, Branch Mgr
EMP: 504
SALES (corp-wide): 11.8B Publicly Held
SIC: 2844 5999 Toilet preparations; cosmetic preparations; perfumes & colognes; toiletries, cosmetics & perfumes; cosmetics; perfumes & colognes
PA: The Estee Lauder Companies Inc
767 5th Ave Fl 37
New York NY 10153
212 572-4200

(G-10124)
ESTEE LAUDER COMPANIES INC (PA)
767 5th Ave Fl 37 (10153-0003)
PHONE..................212 572-4200
Fax: 212 572-6745
William P Lauder, Ch of Bd
Fabrizio Freda, President
John Demsey, President
Cedric Prouve, President
Carl Haney, Exec VP
◆ EMP: 1000
SQ FT: 741,000
SALES: 11.8B Publicly Held
WEB: www.elcompanies.com
SIC: 2844 Toilet preparations; cosmetic preparations; perfumes & colognes

(G-10125)
ESTEE LAUDER COMPANIES INC
65 Bleecker St Frnt 1 (10012-2420)
PHONE..................646 602-7590
EMP: 504
SALES (corp-wide): 11.8B Publicly Held
SIC: 2844 Toilet preparations
PA: The Estee Lauder Companies Inc
767 5th Ave Fl 37
New York NY 10153
212 572-4200

(G-10126)
ESTEE LAUDER INC (HQ)
767 5th Ave Fl 37 (10153-0003)
PHONE..................212 572-4200
Freda Fabrizio, CEO
Leonard A Lauder, Ch of Bd
John Demsey, President
Ed Straw, President
William P Lauder, Chairman
▲ EMP: 700
SQ FT: 232,000
SALES: 10.7B
SALES (corp-wide): 11.8B Publicly Held
WEB: www.esteelauder.com
SIC: 2844 5999 Toilet preparations; cosmetic preparations; perfumes & colognes; toiletries, cosmetics & perfumes; cosmetics; perfumes & colognes
PA: The Estee Lauder Companies Inc
767 5th Ave Fl 37
New York NY 10153
212 572-4200

(G-10127)
ESTEE LAUDER INC
655 Madison Ave Fl 10 (10065-8043)
PHONE..................212 756-4800
Mercedes H Alvarez, Principal
EMP: 55
SALES (corp-wide): 11.8B Publicly Held
WEB: www.esteelauder.com
SIC: 2844 Cosmetic preparations
HQ: Estee Lauder Inc.
767 5th Ave Fl 37
New York NY 10153
212 572-4200

(G-10128)
ESTEE LAUDER INTERNATIONAL INC (DH)
767 5th Ave Bsmt 1 (10153-0003)
PHONE..................212 572-4200
Fax: 212 572-3989
Patrick Bousquet-Chavanne, President
Joel Bramble, President
Larry Berger, Exec VP
Nancy Castro, Exec VP
Amy Digeso, Exec VP
▲ EMP: 7
SALES (est): 341.5MM
SALES (corp-wide): 11.8B Publicly Held
SIC: 2844 Toilet preparations; face creams or lotions; lipsticks; perfumes & lotions
HQ: Estee Lauder Inc.
767 5th Ave Fl 37
New York NY 10153
212 572-4200

(G-10129)
ET PUBLISHING INTL LLC
Also Called: Editorial America S A
150 E 58th St Ste 2200 (10155-2200)
PHONE..................212 838-7220
Cesar Ruiz, Manager
EMP: 14
SALES (corp-wide): 24.4MM Privately Held
WEB: www.buyeditorialtelevisa.com
SIC: 2721 Magazines: publishing only, not printed on site
PA: Et Publishing International
6355 Nw 36th St
Virginia Gardens FL 33166
305 871-6400

(G-10130)
ETC HOSIERY & UNDERWEAR LTD
Also Called: Every Toe Covered
350 5th Ave Ste 2525 (10118-0110)
PHONE..................212 947-5151
Richard Fink, CEO
Robert Sussaman, President
EMP: 8
SALES (est): 758.1K Privately Held
SIC: 2252 Hosiery

(G-10131)
ETERNAL FORTUNE FASHION LLC
Also Called: Profile
135 W 36th St Fl 5 (10018-6900)
PHONE..................212 965-5322
Bill Ingoglia, Sales Mgr
Roy Zou, Mng Member
Candice Wong,
◆ EMP: 12
SQ FT: 5,600
SALES (est): 2MM Privately Held
SIC: 2329 Men's & boys' sportswear & athletic clothing

(G-10132)
ETNA PRODUCTS CO INC (PA)
99 Madison Ave Fl 11 (10016-7419)
PHONE..................212 989-7591
Fax: 212 627-4860
Raymond Trinh, Ch of Bd
Jeffrey Snyder, Ch of Bd
Paula Snyder, Admin Sec
▲ EMP: 19 EST: 1957
SQ FT: 15,000
SALES (est): 3.4MM Privately Held
WEB: www.etna.com
SIC: 3089 5021 Plastic kitchenware, tableware & houseware; furniture

(G-10133)
ETNA TOOL & DIE CORPORATION
42 Bond St Frnt A (10012-2476)
PHONE..................212 475-4350
Fax: 212 533-4896
Keranus Galuppo, President
Flavia Galuppo, Manager
James Galuppo, Admin Sec
EMP: 12 EST: 1946
SQ FT: 14,000
SALES (est): 1.3MM Privately Held
WEB: www.etnatoolanddie.com
SIC: 3599 3544 7692 Machine shop, jobbing & repair; special dies & tools; welding repair

(G-10134)
ETON INSTITUTE
1 Rockefeller Plz Fl 11 (10020-2073)
PHONE..................855 334-3688
EMP: 10
SALES (est): 710K Privately Held
SIC: 3999 Mfg Misc Products

(G-10135)
EU DESIGN LLC
73 Spring St Rm 506 (10012-5802)
PHONE..................212 420-7788
Roberto Berardi, President
Maryann Russo, Sales Mgr
Leonardo Caraffini, Accounts Mgr
Kristen Maher, Accounts Mgr
Yelena Vilman, Accounts Mgr
▲ EMP: 7 EST: 1999
SALES (est): 967.9K
SALES (corp-wide): 7.7MM Privately Held
WEB: www.eu-design.com
SIC: 3965 3961 5131 Buttons & parts; costume jewelry; piece goods & other fabrics; ribbons
PA: Eu Design, Hk Limited
Rm 301-302 3/F Tins Enterprises Ctr
Cheung Sha Wan KLN
342 115-54

(G-10136)
EUPHORBIA PRODUCTIONS LTD
632 Broadway Fl 9 (10012-2614)
PHONE..................212 533-1700
Philip Glass, President
Kurt Munkaisi, Officer
EMP: 6
SALES (est): 457.7K Privately Held
WEB: www.euphorbia.com
SIC: 2741 7389 Music books: publishing only, not printed on site; music recording producer

(G-10137)
EURO BANDS INC
247 W 37th St Rm 700 (10018-5706)
PHONE..................212 719-9777
Zbigniew Jarosh, President
EMP: 16
SALES: 500K Privately Held
WEB: www.e-bands.net
SIC: 3911 Jewelry, precious metal

(G-10138)
EURO PACIFIC PRECIOUS METALS
152 Madison Ave Rm 1003 (10016-5414)
PHONE..................212 481-0310
Peter Schiff, Principal
EMP: 6 EST: 2010
SALES (est): 697.5K Privately Held
SIC: 3339 Precious metals

New York - New York County (G-10139)

(G-10139)
EUROCO COSTUMES INC
254 W 35th St Fl 15 (10001-2504)
PHONE 212 629-9665
Janet Bloor, *President*
▼ EMP: 9
SQ FT: 3,000
SALES (est): 1MM Privately Held
SIC: 2389 Theatrical costumes

(G-10140)
EUROPROJECTS INTL INC
Also Called: Adotta America
152 W 25th St Fl 8b (10001-7402)
PHONE 917 262-0795
Luigi Zannier, *President*
Mona Rubin, *Manager*
▲ EMP: 4
SALES: 8.8MM Privately Held
SIC: 3211 1751 3089 Structural glass; window & door (prefabricated) installation; fiberglass doors

(G-10141)
EV-BOX NORTH AMERICA INC
335 Madison Ave 335 (10017-4611)
PHONE 646 930-6305
Nicholas Lalli, *Director*
EMP: 5
SQ FT: 12,000
SALES (est): 216K Privately Held
SIC: 3694 Automotive electrical equipment

(G-10142)
EVADO FILIP
159 Bleecker St (10012-1457)
PHONE 917 774-8666
Craig Gainsboro, *CFO*
EMP: 12 EST: 2013
SQ FT: 2,000
SALES (est): 1MM Privately Held
SIC: 3663

(G-10143)
EVERBLOCK SYSTEMS LLC
790 Madison Ave Rm 200 (10065-6124)
PHONE 844 422-5625
Arnon Rosan, *President*
EMP: 3 EST: 2015
SALES: 1.5MM Privately Held
SIC: 3271 3251 3299 3089 Blocks, concrete: landscape or retaining wall; structural brick & blocks; blocks & brick, sand lime; injection molded finished plastic products

(G-10144)
EVERCORE PARTNERS SVCS E LLC
55 E 52nd St (10055-0002)
PHONE 212 857-3100
Stacy Dick, *Vice Pres*
Edward Merrell, *Vice Pres*
Shinji Sugiyama, *Vice Pres*
Marta Guzman, *Manager*
Takajiro Ishikawa, *Manager*
EMP: 2460
SALES (est): 128.3MM Privately Held
SIC: 2711 Newspapers, publishing & printing

(G-10145)
EVEREST BBN INC
42 Broadway Ste 1736 (10004-3853)
PHONE 212 268-7979
Ruth Shelling, *Principal*
Adrian Carel, *Network Enginr*
EMP: 11 EST: 2011
SALES (est): 1.7MM Privately Held
SIC: 3825 Network analyzers

(G-10146)
EVERLAST SPORTS MFG CORP (DH)
42 W 39th St (10018-3809)
PHONE 212 239-0990
Neil Morton, *CEO*
Frank Lekram, *Purchasing*
Richard Bonura, *Controller*
Rita C Kriss, *Finance*
Ronni Kornblul, *Manager*
▲ EMP: 41 EST: 1945
SQ FT: 300,000
SALES (est): 14.4MM
SALES (corp-wide): 4B Privately Held
SIC: 3949 5091 Sporting & athletic goods; sporting & recreation goods
HQ: Everlast Worldwide Inc.
42 W 39th St Fl 3
New York NY 10018
212 239-0990

(G-10147)
EVERLAST WORLDWIDE INC (DH)
42 W 39th St Fl 3 (10018-3832)
Rural Route 40 E 34th St (10016)
PHONE 212 239-0990
Neil Morton, *President*
Mark Hunter, *Exec VP*
Thomas K Higgerson, *Senior VP*
Jay Senzatimore, *Vice Pres*
Theresa Sutphin, *Safety Dir*
▲ EMP: 41
SQ FT: 12,087
SALES (est): 18.5MM
SALES (corp-wide): 4B Privately Held
SIC: 3949 8049 3144 3149 Boxing equipment & supplies, general; gloves, sport & athletic: boxing, handball, etc.; nutritionist; women's footwear, except athletic; children's footwear, except athletic

(G-10148)
EVIDON INC (HQ)
Also Called: Digital Governance Division
10 E 39th St Fl 8 (10016-0111)
PHONE 917 262-2530
Scott Meyer, *CEO*
Mark Rudolph, *COO*
Damian Scragg, *Senior VP*
Justin Donohoo, *Vice Pres*
Todd Ruback, *Vice Pres*
EMP: 55
SALES (est): 11.7MM Privately Held
SIC: 7372 Application computer software
PA: Crownpeak Technology, Inc.
707 17th St Ste 3800
Denver CO 80202
310 841-5920

(G-10149)
EVOLUTION SPIRITS INC
Also Called: Monkey Rum
401 Park Ave S (10016-8808)
PHONE 917 543-7880
Ian Crystal, *President*
EMP: 7
SALES (est): 589.8K Privately Held
SIC: 2085 Rum (alcoholic beverage)

(G-10150)
EWATCHFACTORY CORP (PA)
Also Called: Pacific Concepts
390 5th Ave Rm 910 (10018-8111)
PHONE 212 564-8318
Remi Chabrat, *CEO*
Andy Yeung, *Parts Mgr*
Vanessa Ramirez, *Manager*
Barbara A Rizzo, *Manager*
▲ EMP: 5
SQ FT: 1,200
SALES (est): 531.9K Privately Held
WEB: www.watchfactory.com
SIC: 3873 Watches, clocks, watchcases & parts

(G-10151)
EWT HOLDINGS III CORP (HQ)
666 5th Ave Fl 36 (10103-3102)
PHONE 212 644-5900
EMP: 10
SALES (est): 1.3B Publicly Held
SIC: 3589 3823 3826 4941 Sewage & water treatment equipment; water treatment equipment, industrial; sewage treatment equipment; water purification equipment, household type; water quality monitoring & control systems; water testing apparatus; water supply; iron & steel (ferrous) products; cast iron pipe; piling, iron & steel
PA: Ewt Holdings I Corp.
666 5th Ave Fl 36
New York NY 10103
212 644-5900

(G-10152)
EX EL ENTERPRISES LTD
630 Fort Washington Ave (10040-3900)
PHONE 212 489-4500
Henry Lehman, *President*
EMP: 11
SQ FT: 1,900
SALES (est): 960K Privately Held
WEB: www.ex-el.com
SIC: 7372 7373 Prepackaged software; systems software development services

(G-10153)
EX-IT MEDICAL DEVICES INC
1330 Ave Of The Americas (10019-5400)
PHONE 212 653-0637
Shlomo Shopen, *CEO*
EMP: 3
SALES: 10MM Privately Held
SIC: 2844 Cosmetic preparations
PA: Ex-It Medical Devices Limited
3/F Jonsim Place
Wan Chai HK

(G-10154)
EXACT SOLUTIONS INC
139 Fulton St Rm 511 (10038-2535)
PHONE 212 707-8627
Fax: 212 707-8632
Hardev Deindsa, *President*
Niraj Dube, *Senior VP*
Ned Hudson, *Sales Dir*
Narvinder Matharu, *Sales Engr*
EMP: 11
SALES (est): 1MM Privately Held
WEB: www.exact-solutions.com
SIC: 7372 Prepackaged software

(G-10155)
EXCEL GRAPHICS SERVICES INC
519 8th Ave Fl 18 (10018-4577)
PHONE 212 929-2183
Fax: 212 929-4135
Joseph Risola, *President*
Anthony Fazio III, *Vice Pres*
EMP: 12 EST: 1997
SQ FT: 16,500
SALES (est): 1.7MM Privately Held
SIC: 2752 Commercial printing, offset

(G-10156)
EXCEL TECHNOLOGY INC
780 3rd Ave (10017-2024)
PHONE 212 355-3400
Fax: 212 355-8125
Donald Hill, *CEO*
EMP: 15
SALES (corp-wide): 384.7MM Publicly Held
WEB: www.exceltechinc.com
SIC: 3845 Electromedical equipment
HQ: Excel Technology, Inc.
125 Middlesex Tpke
Bedford MA 01730
781 266-5700

(G-10157)
EXCELLED SHEEPSKIN & LEA COAT (PA)
Also Called: RG Apparel Group
1400 Broadway Fl 31 (10018-5331)
P.O. Box 659, Carteret NJ (07008-0659)
PHONE 212 594-5843
Fax: 212 967-5695
William Goldman, *President*
Myron Goldman, *Chairman*
Michael Holzberg, *Vice Pres*
Ken Walton, *CFO*
Kim Steinbach, *Manager*
▲ EMP: 12 EST: 1927
SQ FT: 50,000
SALES (est): 79.6MM Privately Held
WEB: www.leathercoatsetc.com
SIC: 2386 3172 2337 2311 Coats & jackets, leather & sheep-lined; personal leather goods; women's & misses' suits & coats; men's & boys' suits & coats

(G-10158)
EXCELSIOR GRAPHICS INC
485 Madison Ave Fl 13 (10022-5803)
PHONE 212 730-6200
Harold Siegel, *President*
Jackie Starin, *Director*
EMP: 5
SQ FT: 8,000
SALES (est): 450K Privately Held
SIC: 2752 Commercial printing, offset

(G-10159)
EXECUTIVE SIGN CORPORATION
347 W 36th St Rm 902 (10018-6491)
PHONE 212 397-4050
Fax: 212 239-9684
Isaac Goldman, *President*
Kelle Hankins, *Vice Pres*
EMP: 6
SQ FT: 1,800
SALES: 600K Privately Held
SIC: 3993 Signs, not made in custom sign painting shops

(G-10160)
EXOTIC PRINT AND PAPER INC
Also Called: Arthur Invitation
15 E 13th St (10003-4405)
PHONE 212 807-0465
Fax: 212 807-6259
Arfa Rejaei, *Ch of Bd*
Arthur Rajaei, *President*
EMP: 11
SQ FT: 1,800
SALES (est): 1.1MM Privately Held
SIC: 2759 5947 Commercial printing; gift shop

(G-10161)
EXPERIMENT LLC
260 5th Ave Fl 3 (10001-6408)
PHONE 212 889-1659
Matthew Lore, *Principal*
Peter Burn, *Principal*
▲ EMP: 5 EST: 2008
SALES (est): 450K Privately Held
SIC: 2732 Book printing

(G-10162)
EXPERIMENT PUBLISHING LLC
220 E 23rd St Ste 301 (10010-4674)
PHONE 212 889-1273
Russell Gabay, *Vice Pres*
Matthew Lore, *Mng Member*
▲ EMP: 9
SALES (est): 770K Privately Held
SIC: 2741 Miscellaneous publishing

(G-10163)
EXPRESS CHECKOUT LLC
110 E 1st St Apt 20 (10009-7977)
PHONE 646 512-2068
William Hogben, *President*
EMP: 6
SQ FT: 300
SALES (est): 313.4K Privately Held
SIC: 7372 Application computer software

(G-10164)
EXTREME GROUP HOLDINGS LLC (DH)
550 Madison Ave Fl 6 (10022-3211)
PHONE 212 833-8000
▲ EMP: 12
SALES (est): 1.8MM
SALES (corp-wide): 66.9B Privately Held
SIC: 3652 Pre-recorded records & tapes
HQ: Sony/Atv Music Publishing Llc
25 Madison Ave Fl 24
New York NY 10010
212 833-7730

(G-10165)
EYELOCK CORPORATION
355 Lexington Ave (10017-6603)
PHONE 855 393-5625
Steve Gerber, *Senior VP*
Darlene Crumbaugh, *Vice Pres*
Michael Fiorito, *Vice Pres*
Amy Romeo, *CFO*
Chris Ream, *Security Dir*
EMP: 19
SALES: 3.8MM
SALES (corp-wide): 681MM Publicly Held
SIC: 3699 Security control equipment & systems
HQ: Eyelock Llc
355 Lexington Ave Fl 12
New York NY 10017
855 393-5625

GEOGRAPHIC SECTION

New York - New York County (G-10192)

(G-10166)
EYELOCK LLC (HQ)
355 Lexington Ave Fl 12 (10017-6603)
PHONE..................................855 393-5625
Sarvesh Makthal, *President*
Jim Demitrieus,
Anthony Antolino,
Samuel Carter,
Marc Levin,
EMP: 7 EST: 2015
SALES (est): 14MM
SALES (corp-wide): 681MM **Publicly Held**
SIC: 3699 Security control equipment & systems
PA: Voxx International Corporation
2351 J Lawson Blvd
Orlando FL 32824
800 645-7750

(G-10167)
F & J DESIGNS INC
Also Called: Thalian
526 Fashion Ave Fl 8 (10018-4822)
PHONE..................................212 302-8755
Franklin Bergman, *President*
Michael Portnoy, *Accountant*
Joan Mendlinger, *Admin Sec*
▲ EMP: 9
SQ FT: 5,000
SALES (est): 1.3MM **Privately Held**
WEB: www.fjdesigns.com
SIC: 2339 5137 Sportswear, women's; sportswear, women's & children's

(G-10168)
F A PRINTING
690 10th Ave Frnt 1 (10019-7106)
PHONE..................................212 974-5982
Fax: 212 974-8769
Fazal Ali, *President*
Thomas Black, *Owner*
EMP: 5
SQ FT: 900
SALES (est): 464K **Privately Held**
SIC: 2759 Commercial printing

(G-10169)
F P H COMMUNICATIONS
225 Broadway Ste 2008 (10007-3737)
PHONE..................................212 528-1728
Steve Young, *President*
EMP: 2
SQ FT: 2,100
SALES (est): 3.5MM **Privately Held**
SIC: 2731 Book publishing

(G-10170)
F&M ORNAMENTAL DESIGNS LLC
Also Called: Desiron
200 Lexington Ave Rm 702 (10016-6123)
PHONE..................................212 353-2600
Frank J Carfaro, *Owner*
Jenna Palin, *Sales Mgr*
EMP: 6 **Privately Held**
SIC: 2514 Metal household furniture
PA: F&M Ornamental Designs L.L.C.
200 Lexington Ave Rm 702
New York NY 10016

(G-10171)
F&M ORNAMENTAL DESIGNS LLC (PA)
Also Called: Desiron
200 Lexington Ave Rm 702 (10016-6123)
PHONE..................................908 241-7776
Frank J Carfaro, *Mng Member*
Linda Rox, *Manager*
▲ EMP: 17
SQ FT: 20,000
SALES (est): 5.4MM **Privately Held**
SIC: 2514 Metal household furniture

(G-10172)
F+W MEDIA INC
1140 Broadway Fl 14 (10001-7504)
PHONE..................................212 447-1400
Jessica Canterbury, *Editor*
Jill Case, *Editor*
Megan Fitzpatrick, *Editor*
Anne Hevener, *Editor*
Rachel Randall, *Editor*
EMP: 8 **Privately Held**
SIC: 2741 Miscellaneous publishing

HQ: F+W Media, Inc.
10151 Carver Rd Ste 200
Blue Ash OH 45242
513 531-2690

(G-10173)
F-O-R SOFTWARE LLC
Also Called: Two-Four Software
757 3rd Ave Fl 20 (10017-2046)
PHONE..................................212 231-9506
Steve Davis, *Branch Mgr*
EMP: 15
SALES (corp-wide): 3MM **Privately Held**
SIC: 7372 Prepackaged software
PA: F-O-R Software Llc
10 Bank St Ste 880
White Plains NY 10606
914 220-8800

(G-10174)
F-O-R SOFTWARE LLC
100 Park Ave Rm 1600 (10017-5538)
PHONE..................................212 724-3920
Chris Davis, *Manager*
EMP: 9
SALES (corp-wide): 3MM **Privately Held**
SIC: 7372 Prepackaged software
PA: F-O-R Software Llc
10 Bank St Ste 880
White Plains NY 10606
914 220-8800

(G-10175)
F5 NETWORKS INC
600 Lexington Ave Fl 5 (10022-7634)
PHONE..................................888 882-7535
James Reardon, *Principal*
Tamin Sun, *Sales Staff*
Holly Willey, *Manager*
Jon Bartlett, *Technology*
Maxim Zavodchik, *IT/INT Sup*
EMP: 6 **Publicly Held**
SIC: 2752 Commercial printing, lithographic
PA: F5 Networks, Inc.
401 Elliott Ave W Ste 500
Seattle WA 98119

(G-10176)
FABBIAN USA CORP
307 W 38th St Rm 1103 (10018-2946)
PHONE..................................973 882-3824
Vincenzo Tersigni, *Vice Pres*
Lorie Constantinides, *Manager*
Emanuele Fraccari, *Manager*
▲ EMP: 6
SQ FT: 33,000
SALES (est): 866.8K **Privately Held**
SIC: 3648 Lighting equipment

(G-10177)
FABRITEX INC
215 W 40th St Fl 9 (10018-1575)
PHONE..................................706 376-6584
Larry Golf, *President*
▲ EMP: 5
SALES (est): 425.9K **Privately Held**
SIC: 3499 Aerosol valves, metal

(G-10178)
FACSIMILE CMMNCATIONS INDS INC (PA)
Also Called: Atlantic Business Products
134 W 26th St Fl 3 (10001-6803)
PHONE..................................212 741-6400
Fax: 212 674-2861
Larry Weiss, *Ch of Bd*
Jonathan Elson, *Project Mgr*
Russell Klin, *CFO*
Karen Flemmig, *HR Admin*
Lewis Paffile, *Sales Mgr*
EMP: 75
SQ FT: 12,000
SALES (est): 46.4MM **Privately Held**
WEB: www.tomorrowsoffice.com
SIC: 3861 3571 Photocopy machines; computers, digital, analog or hybrid

(G-10179)
FACTS ON FILE INC (HQ)
Also Called: Learn360
132 W 31st St Rm 1600 (10001-3467)
PHONE..................................212 967-8800
Fax: 212 678-3633
Mark D McDonnell, *President*
Kathy White, *General Mgr*

Jonathan Leith, *Editor*
Jared McGinley, *Regional Mgr*
Wendy Collins, *Vice Pres*
▲ EMP: 70 EST: 1940
SALES (est): 17.4MM
SALES (corp-wide): 12.7MM **Privately Held**
WEB: www.factsonfile.com
SIC: 2731 7372 Books: publishing only; prepackaged software
PA: Infobase Publishing Company
132 W 31st St Fl 17
New York NY 10001
212 967-8800

(G-10180)
FAHRENHEIT NY INC
315 W 39th St Rm 803 (10018-1492)
PHONE..................................212 354-6554
Fax: 212 354-0151
Connie Bates, *President*
Christine Bates, *Admin Sec*
EMP: 7
SQ FT: 2,200
SALES (est): 908.9K **Privately Held**
SIC: 3199 3172 Leather belting & strapping; personal leather goods

(G-10181)
FAIRCHILD PUBLICATIONS INC (DH)
Also Called: Womens Wear Daily
475 5th Ave (10017-6220)
PHONE..................................212 630-4000
Fax: 212 630-3563
Charles H Townsend, *President*
Richard Baylef, *President*
Michael Coady, *President*
Doug Fierro, *Publisher*
Pamela Firestone, *Publisher*
▲ EMP: 600
SQ FT: 150,000
SALES (est): 124.1MM
SALES (corp-wide): 6.2B **Privately Held**
WEB: www.fairchildbooks.com
SIC: 2721 2711 2731 Periodicals; newspapers; book publishing
HQ: Advance Magazine Publishers Inc.
1 World Trade Ctr Fl 43
New York NY 10007
212 286-2860

(G-10182)
FAIRCHILD PUBLISHING LLC
4 Times Sq Fl 17 (10036-6518)
PHONE..................................212 286-3897
EMP: 8
SALES (est): 803K **Privately Held**
SIC: 2721 Periodicals

(G-10183)
FAIRMOUNT PRESS
121 Varick St Fl 9 (10013-1408)
PHONE..................................212 255-2300
Fax: 212 215-2035
Peter Bird, *President*
EMP: 6
SALES (est): 518K **Privately Held**
SIC: 2759 7334 Letterpress printing; photocopying & duplicating services

(G-10184)
FAIT USA INC
350 5th Ave Fl 41 (10118-4100)
PHONE..................................215 674-5310
Massimo Bassi, *President*
Alessandro Bronzini, *Vice Pres*
▲ EMP: 4
SQ FT: 8,000
SALES: 1MM
SALES (corp-wide): 26.8MM **Privately Held**
SIC: 3568 Power transmission equipment; shafts, flexible
PA: Fait Group Spa
Via Raffaello Scarpettini 367/369
Montemurlo PO 59013
057 468-121

(G-10185)
FAM CREATIONS
7 W 45th St Ste 1404 (10036-4905)
PHONE..................................212 869-4833
Fax: 212 869-4858
Mario Scimaca, *President*
EMP: 20 EST: 1999

SALES (est): 1.6MM **Privately Held**
SIC: 3911 Jewelry apparel

(G-10186)
FAMILY PUBLICATIONS LTD
325 W 38th St Rm 804 (10018-9623)
PHONE..................................212 947-2177
Gail Granet-Velez, *President*
EMP: 12
SALES (est): 1.2MM **Privately Held**
WEB: www.familypublications.com
SIC: 2741 7999 Guides: publishing only, not printed on site; exposition operation

(G-10187)
FANCY FLAMINGO LLC
450 W 17th St Apt 528 (10011-5846)
PHONE..................................516 209-7306
Sanchali Sundaram, *CEO*
Senthil Sundaram, *COO*
EMP: 6 EST: 2011
SALES (est): 407.5K **Privately Held**
SIC: 2086 Bottled & canned soft drinks

(G-10188)
FANSHAWE FOODS LLC
5 Columbus Cir (10019-1412)
PHONE..................................212 757-3130
Lee Zalben, *President*
EMP: 10
SALES (est): 564.3K **Privately Held**
SIC: 2099 5149 Food preparations; specialty food items

(G-10189)
FANTASIA JEWELRY INC
42 W 39th St Fl 14 (10018-2082)
PHONE..................................212 921-9590
Fax: 212 398-6559
Sebastian De Serio, *President*
Joseph De Serio, *Vice Pres*
Edward Deserio, *Treasurer*
Jennifer Deserio, *Marketing Mgr*
EMP: 42
SQ FT: 7,000
SALES (est): 3.2MM **Privately Held**
WEB: www.fantasiajewelry.com
SIC: 3961 3911 Costume jewelry, ex. precious metal & semiprecious stones; jewelry, precious metal

(G-10190)
FANTASY SPORTS MEDIA GROUP INC
Also Called: Fantasy Sports Network
27 W 20th St Ste 900 (10011-3725)
PHONE..................................416 917-6002
Leonard Asper, *President*
EMP: 20
SALES (est): 2.5MM **Privately Held**
SIC: 2741 Miscellaneous publishing

(G-10191)
FANVISION ENTERTAINMENT LLC (PA)
33 W 17th St Ste 901 (10011-5520)
PHONE..................................917 297-7428
Andrew Daines, *CEO*
Sara Swager, *Accounts Mgr*
EMP: 3
SALES (est): 21MM **Privately Held**
SIC: 3861 Cameras & related equipment

(G-10192)
FARRAR STRAUS AND GIROUX LLC (DH)
Also Called: North Point Press
18 W 18th St Fl 7 (10011-4675)
PHONE..................................212 741-6900
Fax: 212 633-9385
Melanie Kroupa, *Publisher*
Debra Helfand, *Editor*
Sean McDonald, *Editor*
Tom Cansiglio, *Vice Pres*
Frances Foster, *Vice Pres*
▲ EMP: 23 EST: 1945
SQ FT: 22,500
SALES (est): 11.6MM
SALES (corp-wide): 1.5B **Privately Held**
WEB: www.petersistibet.com
SIC: 2731 Books: publishing only

New York - New York County (G-10193)

GEOGRAPHIC SECTION

(G-10193)
FARROW AND BALL INC (DH)
979 3rd Ave Ste 1519 (10022-3806)
PHONE 212 752-5544
Antonio Moreira, *Principal*
EMP: 16
SALES (est): 3.3MM
SALES (corp-wide): 105.5MM **Privately Held**
SIC: 2851 Paints & paint additives
HQ: Farrow & Ball Holdings Limited
33 Uddens Trading Estate
Wimborne BH21
120 287-6141

(G-10194)
FASHION ACCENTS LLC
366 5th Ave Rm 802 (10001-2231)
PHONE 401 331-6626
EMP: 14
SALES (corp-wide): 3.4MM **Privately Held**
SIC: 3961 Earrings, except precious metal
PA: Fashion Accents, Llc
100 Nashua St
Providence RI 02904
401 331-6626

(G-10195)
FASHION AVE SWEATER KNITS LLC
525 7th Ave Fl 4 (10018-4940)
PHONE 212 302-8282
Melvyn Weiss, *President*
Austin Mallis, *Vice Pres*
Ron Hollandsworth, *Controller*
EMP: 100
SQ FT: 18,000
SALES (est): 7.1MM **Privately Held**
SIC: 2339 Service apparel, washable: women's

(G-10196)
FASHION AVENUE KNITS INC
Also Called: Its Our Time
1400 Broadway Rm 2401 (10018-5300)
PHONE 718 456-9000
Fax: 212 221-7017
Mel Weiss, *Manager*
EMP: 10
SALES (corp-wide): 125MM **Privately Held**
WEB: www.fashionaveknits.com
SIC: 2253 Knit outerwear mills
PA: Fashion Avenue Knits Inc.
525 Fashion Ave Fl 4
New York NY 10018
718 456-9000

(G-10197)
FASHION CALENDAR INTERNATIONAL
153 E 87th St Apt 6a (10128-2705)
PHONE 212 289-0420
Fax: 212 289-5917
Ruth Finley, *Owner*
EMP: 7 **EST:** 1939
SALES (est): 665.9K **Privately Held**
WEB: www.fashioncalendar.net
SIC: 2721 Periodicals

(G-10198)
FASHIONDEX INC
153 W 27th St Ste 701 (10001-6255)
PHONE 914 271-6121
Fax: 212 691-5873
Andrea Kennedy, *President*
Max Andrews, *Vice Pres*
▲ **EMP:** 6
SALES: 150K **Privately Held**
WEB: www.fashiondex.com
SIC: 2741 5192 Telephone & other directory publishing; books, periodicals & newspapers

(G-10199)
FAST-TRAC ENTERTAINMENT LTD
7 E 74th St Apt 5 (10021-2624)
PHONE 888 758-8886
Phyllis Keitlen, *Ch of Bd*
EMP: 1
SALES: 1.5MM **Privately Held**
SIC: 2253 7922 Knit outerwear mills; agent or manager for entertainers

(G-10200)
FAVIANA INTERNATIONAL INC (PA)
320 W 37th St Fl 10 (10018-4675)
PHONE 212 594-4422
Parviz Pourmoradi, *President*
Omid Pourmoradi, *Vice Pres*
Shala Pourmoradi, *Treasurer*
Bernard Weiss, *Manager*
▲ **EMP:** 31
SQ FT: 32,000
SALES: 7.8MM **Privately Held**
WEB: www.faviana.com
SIC: 2335 Women's, juniors' & misses' dresses

(G-10201)
FEDERAL ENVELOPE INC
22 W 32nd St (10001-3807)
PHONE 212 243-8380
Fax: 212 691-8076
EMP: 10 **EST:** 1953
SQ FT: 10,000
SALES (est): 730K **Privately Held**
SIC: 2759 2752 Printer Of Printing Envelopes Letterpress & An Offset Printing Service

(G-10202)
FEDERATED MEDIA PUBLISHING LLC
31 W 27th St Fl 8 (10001-6914)
PHONE 917 677-7976
Angela Shelby, *Manager*
EMP: 7
SALES (corp-wide): 1.1B **Publicly Held**
SIC: 2741 Miscellaneous publishing
HQ: Federated Media Publishing, Llc
350 Sansome St Ste 925
San Francisco CA 94104
415 332-6955

(G-10203)
FELDMAN COMPANY INC
Also Called: Ango Home
241 W 37th St Rm 1001 (10018-7072)
PHONE 212 966-1303
Alfred Feldman, *President*
Hershel Feldman, *Vice Pres*
Eli Jeidel, *Vice Pres*
▲ **EMP:** 13
SQ FT: 6,000
SALES (est): 2.3MM **Privately Held**
WEB: www.feldmanco.com
SIC: 2299 5023 Fabrics: linen, jute, hemp, ramie; home furnishings

(G-10204)
FELLUSS RECORDING
36 E 23rd St Rm 9l (10010-4417)
PHONE 212 727-8055
Andrew Fellus, *Owner*
EMP: 6
SALES (est): 320K **Privately Held**
SIC: 3679 Recording heads, speech & musical equipment

(G-10205)
FEMINIST PRESS INC
365 5th Ave Ste 5406 (10016-4309)
PHONE 212 817-7915
Fax: 212 817-1593
Les Gribben, *Ch Admin Ofcr*
Yamberlie Tavarez, *Development*
Sebastian Persico, *CFO*
Laura Jack, *Mktg Dir*
Eric Pellerin, *Librarian*
EMP: 9
SQ FT: 2,000
SALES: 878.4K **Privately Held**
SIC: 2731 Book publishing

(G-10206)
FERRARA BAKERY & CAFE INC (PA)
195 Grand St (10013-3717)
PHONE 212 226-6150
Fax: 212 226-0667
Ernest Lepore, *Ch of Bd*
Peter Lepore, *President*
John Capirchio, *Plant Mgr*
Dennis Canciello, *Treasurer*
Adeline Sessa, *Human Res Mgr*
▲ **EMP:** 95 **EST:** 1892
SALES (est): 10.8MM **Privately Held**
WEB: www.ferraracafe.com
SIC: 2051 5461 Cakes, bakery: except frozen; pastries, e.g. danish: except frozen; bakeries; cakes; pastries

(G-10207)
FERRIS USA LLC
18 W 108th St (10025-8915)
PHONE 617 895-8102
Taylor Conlin, *CEO*
EMP: 8
SALES (est): 275.5K **Privately Held**
SIC: 2326 2321 2329 Work apparel, except uniforms; men's & boys' dress shirts; men's & boys' sportswear & athletic clothing; field jackets, military

(G-10208)
FETHERSTON DESIGN GROUP LLC
Also Called: Erin Fetherston
225 W Broadway (10013-2909)
PHONE 212 643-7537
Jane Huston, *Production*
Raschna Shah, *Finance*
Stefini Zien, *Finance*
Barbara F Fetherston, *Mng Member*
Erin F Fetherston, *Mng Member*
◆ **EMP:** 22
SALES (est): 3MM **Privately Held**
SIC: 2331 Women's & misses' blouses & shirts

(G-10209)
FIBER-SEAL OF NEW YORK INC (PA)
979 3rd Ave Ste 903 (10022-3802)
PHONE 212 888-5580
Steven Mittman, *President*
Roberta Mittman, *Corp Secy*
▲ **EMP:** 5 **EST:** 1954
SALES (est): 7MM **Privately Held**
WEB: www.lewismittman.com
SIC: 2512 2511 Upholstered household furniture; wood bedroom furniture

(G-10210)
FIBRE CASE & NOVELTY CO INC (PA)
270 Lafayette St Ste 1510 (10012-3377)
PHONE 212 254-6060
Fax: 212 460-8794
Elliot Kozer, *President*
Richard Rubin, *Treasurer*
EMP: 4 **EST:** 1956
SALES (est): 2.4MM **Privately Held**
SIC: 3161 Sample cases; trunks

(G-10211)
FIDELUS TECHNOLOGIES LLC
240 W 35th St Fl 6 (10001-2506)
PHONE 212 616-7800
Ron Rosansky, *President*
David Buckenheimer, *Exec VP*
Don Harloff, *Vice Pres*
Jerry Love, *Vice Pres*
Nancee Pronsati, *Vice Pres*
EMP: 51
SQ FT: 25,000
SALES (est): 15MM **Privately Held**
WEB: www.fidelus.com
SIC: 7372 Prepackaged software

(G-10212)
FIDESA US CORPORATION
17 State St Unit 122 (10004-1501)
PHONE 212 269-9000
Robert Thompson, *Principal*
EMP: 400
SALES (est): 20.5MM
SALES (corp-wide): 408.6MM **Privately Held**
WEB: www.royalbluefinancial.com
SIC: 7372 7371 Prepackaged software; custom computer programming services
PA: Fidessa Group Plc
2nd Floor Concourse 2
Belfast BT3 9
289 046-3000

(G-10213)
FIERCE FUN TOYS LLC
100 Riverside Dr Ste 2 (10024-4822)
P.O. Box 905 (10024-0546)
PHONE 646 322-7172
Angela Larson, *Mng Member*
EMP: 7
SALES (est): 447.2K **Privately Held**
SIC: 3942 5092 Stuffed toys, including animals; toys & hobby goods & supplies

(G-10214)
FINDMINE INC
137 Varick St Fl 2 (10013-1110)
PHONE 925 787-6181
Michelle Bacharach, *CEO*
Devon Safran, *Vice Pres*
EMP: 15 **EST:** 2014
SALES (est): 305.2K **Privately Held**
SIC: 7372 Business oriented computer software

(G-10215)
FINE CUT DIAMONDS CORPORATION
580 5th Ave Ste 901 (10036-0044)
PHONE 212 575-8780
Fax: 212 921-2676
Michael Deutsch, *President*
EMP: 5 **EST:** 1967
SQ FT: 1,100
SALES (est): 410K **Privately Held**
SIC: 3915 5094 Diamond cutting & polishing; diamonds (gems)

(G-10216)
FINE SHEER INDUSTRIES INC (PA)
350 5th Ave Ste 4710 (10118-4710)
PHONE 212 594-4224
Fax: 212 967-9039
Grace Franco, *President*
Isaac Franco, *President*
Jake Franco, *Manager*
▲ **EMP:** 18
SQ FT: 6,000
SALES (est): 275.1K **Privately Held**
SIC: 2252 2251 2369 Socks; panty hose; leggings; girls', children's & infants'

(G-10217)
FINE SOUNDS GROUP INC (PA)
Also Called: World of McIntosh
214 Lafayette St (10012-4079)
PHONE 212 364-0219
Charles Randall, *CEO*
Mauro Grange, *Ch of Bd*
Giovanni Palacardo, *CFO*
EMP: 12
SALES (est): 26.6MM **Privately Held**
SIC: 3679 Recording heads, speech & musical equipment; recording & playback heads, magnetic; recording & playback apparatus, including phonograph

(G-10218)
FIRST CHOICE NEWS INC
639 1/2 Broadway (10012-2602)
PHONE 212 477-2044
Raffie Hadibhai, *Ch of Bd*
EMP: 5
SALES (est): 208.1K **Privately Held**
SIC: 2711 5311 Newspapers, publishing & printing; department stores, discount

(G-10219)
FIRST GAMES PUBLR NETWRK INC
Also Called: 1gpn
420 Lexington Ave Rm 412 (10170-0499)
PHONE 212 983-0501
EMP: 100
SALES: 1,000K **Privately Held**
SIC: 2741 Developer & Publisher Mmog

(G-10220)
FIRST IMAGE DESIGN CORP
98 Cuttrmill Rd Ste 231 (10036)
PHONE 212 221-8282
Fax: 212 221-8484
David Hematian, *Ch of Bd*
Kathy Kamali, *Principal*
Jane Wu, *Financial Analy*
EMP: 20
SQ FT: 3,000

GEOGRAPHIC SECTION

New York - New York County (G-10246)

SALES (est): 2.4MM Privately Held
WEB: www.firstimage.net
SIC: 3911 Jewelry apparel

(G-10221)
FIRST LOVE FASHIONS LLC
1407 Broadway Rm 2010 (10018-2718)
PHONE.....................212 256-1089
Joseph Hamadani, *President*
EMP: 10
SALES (est): 1.2MM Privately Held
SIC: 2339 Women's & misses' athletic clothing & sportswear

(G-10222)
FIRST2PRINT INC
494 8th Ave Fl 12 (10001-2578)
PHONE.....................212 868-6886
Neil Brasleau, *CEO*
EMP: 7
SALES (est): 869.5K Privately Held
WEB: www.first2print.com
SIC: 2759 Commercial printing

(G-10223)
FISCHER DIAMONDS INC
1212 Avenue Of The Americ (10036-1622)
PHONE.....................212 869-1990
Fax: 212 354-9775
Jeffrey H Fisher, *President*
Neil Fischer, *Exec VP*
Marcelle Fischler, *Vice Pres*
EMP: 10
SQ FT: 5,000
SALES (est): 1.1MM Privately Held
WEB: www.fischerdiamonds.com
SIC: 3915 Lapidary work & diamond cutting & polishing

(G-10224)
FISCHLER DIAMONDS INC
580 5th Ave Ste 3100 (10036-4701)
PHONE.....................212 921-8196
Serge Fischler, *Ch of Bd*
Marcella Fischler, *Vice Pres*
▲ EMP: 5
SALES (est): 495.7K Privately Held
WEB: www.fischlerdiamonds.com
SIC: 3915 5094 Diamond cutting & polishing; diamonds (gems)

(G-10225)
FISCHLER HOCKEY SERVICE
200 W 109th St Apt C5 (10025-2252)
PHONE.....................212 749-4152
Stan Fischler, *Owner*
EMP: 10
SALES (est): 438.9K Privately Held
SIC: 2741 Newsletter publishing

(G-10226)
FISH & CROWN LTD (PA)
42 W 39th St (10018-3809)
PHONE.....................212 707-9603
Fax: 212 489-4829
Bergljot Wathne, *President*
Thorunn Wathne, *Corp Secy*
Soffia Wathne, *Vice Pres*
Thomas Faivre, *CFO*
Linda Sanducci, *Accountant*
◆ EMP: 100
SQ FT: 14,350
SALES (est): 9.3MM Privately Held
WEB: www.wathne.com
SIC: 3161 3999 Luggage; novelties, bric-a-brac & hobby kits

(G-10227)
FISONIC CORP (PA)
Also Called: Fisonic Technology
31-00 47th Ave Ste 106 (10023)
PHONE.....................716 763-0295
Fax: 917 595-5370
Robert Kremer, *CEO*
Professor Vladimir Fisenko, *Ch of Bd*
Joe Hoose, *President*
▲ EMP: 10
SQ FT: 1,000
SALES (est): 1.8MM Privately Held
WEB: www.fisonic.com
SIC: 3561 3433 Pumps & pumping equipment; heating equipment, except electric

(G-10228)
FITCH GRAPHICS LTD
229 W 28th St Fl 9 (10001-5915)
PHONE.....................212 619-3800
George Pavlides, *CEO*
John K Fitch III, *President*
Micky Padelo, *Manager*
John Fitzsimmons, *Director*
EMP: 32
SQ FT: 25,000
SALES (est): 3.2MM Privately Held
WEB: www.fitchdata.com
SIC: 2752 Commercial printing, offset

(G-10229)
FIVE STAR PRTG & MAILING SVCS
225 W 37th St Fl 16 (10018-6637)
PHONE.....................212 929-0300
Judith Magnus, *President*
Irwin Magnus, *General Mgr*
Steven Magnus, *Vice Pres*
▲ EMP: 13
SQ FT: 4,800
SALES (est): 2MM Privately Held
SIC: 2752 7331 Commercial printing, offset; mailing service

(G-10230)
FLASH VENTURES INC
Also Called: Tribeca
853 Broadway Ste 400 (10003-4725)
PHONE.....................212 255-7070
Albert OH, *CEO*
Katerina Conti, *Manager*
Dan Grabon, *Director*
▲ EMP: 12
SQ FT: 2,744
SALES (est): 2.5MM Privately Held
SIC: 3571 Electronic computers

(G-10231)
FLAVORS HOLDINGS INC (DH)
Also Called: (INDIRECT SUBSIDIARY OF MACANDREWS & FORBES INC., NEW YORK, NY)
35 E 62nd St (10065-8014)
PHONE.....................212 572-8677
Albert Mazone, *CEO*
Ken Martin, *Director*
EMP: 9 EST: 2015
SALES (est): 195.9MM Privately Held
SIC: 2869 6712 Sweeteners, synthetic; bank holding companies
HQ: Macandrews & Forbes Inc.
38 E 63rd St
New York NY 10065
212 688-9000

(G-10232)
FLIK INTERNATIONAL/COMPASS
450 Lexington Ave (10017-3904)
PHONE.....................212 450-4750
Chris Sarell, *Director*
EMP: 50
SALES (est): 3.3MM Privately Held
SIC: 2099 Food preparations

(G-10233)
FLYCELL INC
80 Pine St Fl 29 (10005-1714)
PHONE.....................212 400-1212
Cristian Carnevale, *CEO*
Guillermo Cengotita, *Senior VP*
Geetha Chandra, *Controller*
Lidiya Voloshko, *Accountant*
Michele Berardi, *Network Mgr*
EMP: 57
SQ FT: 2,000
SALES (est): 6MM
SALES (corp-wide): 4.2MM Privately Held
WEB: www.flycell.com
SIC: 3663 Mobile communication equipment
PA: Acotel Group Spa
Via Della Valle Dei Fontanili 29/37
Roma RM 00168
066 114-1000

(G-10234)
FLYNNS INC (PA)
Also Called: Flynn's Xerox
115 W 30th St (10001-4010)
PHONE.....................212 339-8700
Fax: 212 355-3738

Martin Lerner, *Ch of Bd*
Arthur Cantor, *President*
Brian Cantor, *Vice Pres*
Tony Tutura, *Manager*
▲ EMP: 27
SQ FT: 4,200
SALES (est): 3.2MM Privately Held
WEB: www.lorraineflynn.com
SIC: 2752 5943 Commercial printing, lithographic; stationery stores

(G-10235)
FOG CREEK SOFTWARE INC
1 Exchange Plz Fl 25 (10006-3745)
PHONE.....................866 364-2733
Joel Spolsky, *CEO*
Michael Pryor, *CFO*
Will Everett, *Accounts Exec*
Will L'Hommedieu, *Accounts Exec*
Anna Lewis, *Manager*
EMP: 5
SALES (est): 920.5K Privately Held
WEB: www.fogcreek.com
SIC: 7372 7371 Prepackaged software; custom computer programming services

(G-10236)
FOGEL NECKWEAR CORP
44 W 28th St Fl 15 (10001-4212)
P.O. Box 620820, Little Neck (11362-0820)
PHONE.....................212 686-7673
Fax: 212 447-9241
Sam Fogel, *President*
Freida Fogel, *Vice Pres*
Howard Fogel, *Treasurer*
EMP: 65
SQ FT: 10,000
SALES (est): 3.4MM Privately Held
SIC: 2323 Men's & boys' neckwear

(G-10237)
FOREST LABORATORIES LLC (HQ)
909 3rd Ave Fl 23 (10022-4748)
PHONE.....................212 421-7850
Fax: 212 350-5665
R Todd Joyce, *President*
Nancy Tellího, *Publisher*
Jessica McNulty, *Division Mgr*
Benjamin Gober, *Principal*
Robert Stewart, *COO*
▲ EMP: 227
SQ FT: 169,000
SALES (est): 1.5B Privately Held
WEB: www.frx.com
SIC: 2834 5122 Pharmaceutical preparations; pharmaceuticals

(G-10238)
FORMART CORP
Also Called: Bellini Collections
312 5th Ave Fl 6 (10001-3603)
PHONE.....................212 819-1819
Fax: 212 921-1992
Sheung MEI Liu, *President*
EMP: 12
SQ FT: 2,100
SALES (est): 1.5MM Privately Held
WEB: www.cancerpins.com
SIC: 3171 5094 5137 3961 Purses, women's; jewelry; watches & parts; purses; costume jewelry

(G-10239)
FORTRESS BIOTECH INC (PA)
3 Columbus Cir Fl 15 (10019-8716)
PHONE.....................781 652-4500
Lindsay A Rosenwald, *Ch of Bd*
Eric K Rowinsky, *Ch of Bd*
George Avgerinos, *Senior VP*
Robyn Hunter, *CFO*
Michael S Weiss, *Manager*
EMP: 18
SQ FT: 3,200
SALES: 16.4MM Publicly Held
SIC: 2834 Pharmaceutical preparations

(G-10240)
FOSCARINI INC
Also Called: Foscarini Showroom
20 Greene St (10013-2503)
PHONE.....................212 257-4412
Glenn Ludwig, *CEO*
▲ EMP: 8

SALES (est): 1MM
SALES (corp-wide): 45.1MM Privately Held
SIC: 3641 5719 Electric lamps; lamps, fluorescent, electric; lamps, incandescent filament, electric; lighting, lamps & accessories; lamps & lamp shades
PA: Foscarini Spa
Via Delle Industrie 27
Marcon VE 30020
041 595-3811

(G-10241)
FOUNDATION CENTER INC (PA)
1 Financial Sq Fl 24 (10005-3076)
PHONE.....................212 620-4230
Fax: 212 691-1828
Bradford K Smith, *President*
Regina Faighes, *Editor*
Christopher Hurt, *Editor*
Emily Robbins, *Editor*
Loretta Ferrari, *Vice Pres*
▲ EMP: 125
SQ FT: 150,000
SALES: 23.5MM Privately Held
WEB: www.fdncenter.net
SIC: 2741 8231 Directories: publishing only, not printed on site; libraries

(G-10242)
FOUR SEASONS FASHION MFG INC
270 W 39th St Fl 12 (10018-0338)
PHONE.....................212 947-6820
Fax: 212 354-1096
Mohan Singh, *President*
Sandra Gonsalzes, *Administration*
EMP: 45
SALES (est): 3.3MM Privately Held
SIC: 2335 2339 2337 Women's, juniors' & misses' dresses; women's & misses' outerwear; women's & misses' suits & coats

(G-10243)
FOURTYS NY INC
231 W 39th St Rm 806 (10018-0734)
PHONE.....................212 382-0301
Fax: 212 768-7690
Dawn Mayo, *President*
EMP: 10
SQ FT: 4,000
SALES: 900K Privately Held
SIC: 2331 Women's & misses' blouses & shirts

(G-10244)
FOWNES BROTHERS & CO INC (PA)
16 E 34th St Fl 5 (10016-4370)
PHONE.....................212 683-0150
Fax: 212 683-2832
Thomas Gluckman, *Ch of Bd*
Chris Giattino, *Exec VP*
Helmuth Dosch, *Vice Pres*
Bruna Maney, *Vice Pres*
Howard Samuels, *Vice Pres*
◆ EMP: 50 EST: 1887
SQ FT: 18,000
SALES (est): 67.4MM Privately Held
SIC: 3151 2381 5136 5137 Gloves, leather: dress or semidress; gloves, woven or knit: made from purchased materials; gloves, men's & boys'; gloves, women's & children's; gloves, sport & athletic: boxing, handball, etc.

(G-10245)
FOX UNLIMITED INC
345 7th Ave Rm 2b (10001-5058)
PHONE.....................212 736-3071
Marvin Levenson, *President*
EMP: 5
SQ FT: 4,000
SALES (est): 694.1K Privately Held
WEB: www.foxunlimited.com
SIC: 2371 Apparel, fur

(G-10246)
FOXHILL PRESS INC
37 E 7th St Ste 2 (10003-8027)
PHONE.....................212 995-9620
▲ EMP: 20
SQ FT: 1,600

New York - New York County (G-10247)

SALES (est): 1.1MM
SALES (corp-wide): 35.2MM **Privately Held**
SIC: 2731 Books-Publishing/Printing
PA: Mcevoy Properties Llc
85 2nd St Fl 6
San Francisco CA 94107

(G-10247) FRANCEPRESS LLC (PA)
115 E 57th St Fl 11 (10022-2120)
PHONE 646 202-9828
Louis Kyle, *Mng Member*
Lauren Weaver, *Manager*
▲ EMP: 4
SQ FT: 1,800
SALES (est): 1.2MM **Privately Held**
SIC: 2711 Newspapers, publishing & printing

(G-10248) FRANCIS EMORY FITCH INC (PA)
Also Called: Fitch Group
229 W 28th St Fl 9 (10001-5915)
PHONE 212 619-3800
Fax: 212 619-3619
George Pavlides, *CEO*
John K Fitch III, *President*
Joseph Barrett, *Exec VP*
Carl Corsi, *Prdtn Mgr*
Frank Riina, *Supervisor*
EMP: 23 EST: 1886
SQ FT: 25,000
SALES (est): 6.6MM **Privately Held**
WEB: www.fitchgroup.com
SIC: 2721 2752 Periodicals: publishing only; commercial printing, offset

(G-10249) FRANCO APPAREL GROUP INC
Also Called: Franco Apparel Group Team
1407 Broadway (10018-5100)
PHONE 212 967-7272
Fax: 212 967-7395
Ike Franco, *Ch of Bd*
Albert Shammah, *Vice Pres*
Reuben Eghbali, *Controller*
Allen Franco, *Sales Mgr*
▲ EMP: 100
SQ FT: 15,000
SALES (est): 8.9MM **Privately Held**
WEB: www.francoapparel.com
SIC: 2369 Girls' & children's outerwear

(G-10250) FRANK BILLANTI CASTING CO INC
42 W 38th St Rm 204 (10018-6220)
PHONE 212 221-0440
Frank L Billanti, *President*
Kristin N Billanti, *Principal*
Katherine O Billanti, *Vice Pres*
Frank J Billanti, *Administration*
EMP: 16
SALES: 1MM **Privately Held**
SIC: 3915 Jewelers' castings

(G-10251) FRANK BLANCATO INC
64 W 48th St Fl 16 (10036-1708)
PHONE 212 768-1495
Fax: 212 768-7204
Frank Blancato, *President*
EMP: 10
SALES: 4MM **Privately Held**
WEB: www.fblancato.com
SIC: 3911 Jewelry, precious metal

(G-10252) FRANK WINES INC
Also Called: HI Wines
345 E 80th St Apt 8b (10075-0688)
PHONE 646 765-6637
Olivier Pasquini, *Ch of Bd*
EMP: 5
SALES (est): 330K **Privately Held**
SIC: 2084 Wines

(G-10253) FRANKLIN REPORT LLC
201 E 69th St Apt 14j (10021-5470)
PHONE 212 639-9100
Fax: 212 744-3546
Elizabeth Franklin, *Owner*
Josh Maio, *Editor*
EMP: 8

SALES (est): 600K **Privately Held**
WEB: www.franklinreport.com
SIC: 2731 Book publishing

(G-10254) FRED WEIDNER & SON PRINTERS
15 Maiden Ln Ste 1505 (10038-5148)
PHONE 212 964-8676
Fred Weidner, *President*
EMP: 8
SALES (est): 830K **Privately Held**
SIC: 2759 7336 Commercial printing; commercial art & graphic design

(G-10255) FREEDOM RAINS INC
Also Called: Northern Goose Polar Project
230 W 39th St Fl 7 (10018-4977)
PHONE 646 710-4512
Bobby Reiger, *CEO*
Steven Zellman, *President*
Nick Grazione, *COO*
▲ EMP: 8
SQ FT: 3,500
SALES (est): 12MM **Privately Held**
SIC: 2253 Jackets, knit; sweaters & sweater coats, knit

(G-10256) FRENCH ACCNT RUGS & TAPESTRIES
36 E 31st St Frnt B (10016-6821)
PHONE 212 686-6097
Fax: 212 937-3928
Kevin Rahmanan, *President*
▲ EMP: 6
SQ FT: 10,000
SALES (est): 823.9K **Privately Held**
WEB: www.farugs.com
SIC: 2211 Upholstery, tapestry & wall coverings: cotton; casement cloth, cotton; tapestry fabrics, cotton

(G-10257) FRENCH ATMOSPHERE INC (PA)
Also Called: Urban Rose
421 7th Ave 525 (10001-2002)
PHONE 516 371-9100
Lawrence Kessler, *President*
Benjamin Kessler, *Vice Pres*
▲ EMP: 15
SQ FT: 1,350
SALES (est): 1MM **Privately Held**
SIC: 2339 Sportswear, women's

(G-10258) FRENCH MORNING LLC
27 W 20th St Ste 800 (10011-3726)
PHONE 646 290-7463
Emmanuel Saint-Martin, *President*
EMP: 6
SQ FT: 1,200
SALES (est): 258.9K **Privately Held**
SIC: 2711 Newspapers: publishing only, not printed on site

(G-10259) FRESH PRINTS LLC
134 E 70th St (10021-5035)
PHONE 917 826-2752
Jacob Goodman,
Josh Arbit,
EMP: 40
SALES (est): 2MM **Privately Held**
SIC: 2759 7389 Screen printing;

(G-10260) FRIDGE MAGAZINE INC
108 W 39th St Fl 4 (10018-3614)
PHONE 212 997-7673
Jonathon Levine, *President*
EMP: 5
SALES (est): 410K **Privately Held**
WEB: www.fridgemagazine.com
SIC: 2721 Magazines: publishing only, not printed on site

(G-10261) FROEBE GROUP LLC
154 W 27th St Rm 4 (10001-6215)
PHONE 646 649-2150
Thomas Daughhetee, *Opers Staff*
Troy Froebe, *Mng Member*
EMP: 8

SALES: 800K **Privately Held**
SIC: 2741 Business service newsletters: publishing & printing

(G-10262) FROZEN FOOD DIGEST INC
Also Called: Quick Frzen Foods Annual Prcss
271 Madison Ave Ste 805 (10016-1005)
PHONE 212 557-8600
Fax: 212 986-9868
Saul Beck, *President*
Audrey Beck, *Publisher*
Anna Beck, *Vice Pres*
▲ EMP: 6
SALES (est): 510K **Privately Held**
SIC: 2721 Magazines: publishing only, not printed on site

(G-10263) FRP APPAREL GROUP LLC
110 W 40th St Fl 26 (10018-3626)
PHONE 212 695-8000
Paul Burghardt, *Business Mgr*
Tsuneaki Yanagida, *Marketing Mgr*
Maggie Felm, *Manager*
Johann Cooke,
Edwin Herman,
▲ EMP: 9
SALES (est): 620K **Privately Held**
SIC: 2221 Upholstery, tapestry & wall covering fabrics

(G-10264) FRUIT ST HLTH PUB BENEFT CORP
85 Broad St Fl 18 (10004-2783)
PHONE 347 960-6400
Laurence Girard, *CEO*
Christopher Meatto, *CFO*
EMP: 5
SALES (est): 401.3K **Privately Held**
SIC: 7372 Prepackaged software

(G-10265) FSR BEAUTY LTD
411 5th Ave Rm 804 (10016-2264)
PHONE 212 447-0036
Jerrold Rauchwerger, *President*
Maxine Rauchwerger, *Vice Pres*
Falen Rauchwerger, *Marketing Staff*
▲ EMP: 6
SQ FT: 1,300
SALES (est): 752.4K **Privately Held**
SIC: 2844 Face creams or lotions; lipsticks

(G-10266) FT PUBLICATIONS INC (HQ)
Also Called: Financial Times
330 Hudson St (10013-1046)
PHONE 212 641-6500
Fax: 212 641-6556
Loredana Beg, *Ch of Bd*
David Bell, *President*
Chris Davies, *Counsel*
Richard Varey, *Vice Pres*
Jo Cunningham, *QC Mgr*
▲ EMP: 80
SQ FT: 40,000
SALES (est): 18.8MM
SALES (corp-wide): 3.2B **Privately Held**
SIC: 2711 Newspapers: publishing only, not printed on site
PA: Nikkei Inc.
1-3-7, Otemachi
Chiyoda-Ku TKY 100-0
332 700-251

(G-10267) FT PUBLICATIONS INC
Also Called: Financial Times Newspaper
330 Hudson St (10013-1046)
PHONE 212 641-2420
EMP: 46
SALES (corp-wide): 3.2B **Privately Held**
SIC: 2711 Newspapers: publishing only, not printed on site
HQ: F.T. Publications Inc.
330 Hudson St
New York NY 10013
212 641-6500

(G-10268) FUDA GROUP (USA) CORPORATION
48 Wall St Fl 11 (10005-2887)
PHONE 646 751-7488

Benjamin Wu, *CEO*
Robert Rash,
EMP: 7
SALES (est): 275.3K **Privately Held**
SIC: 1041 Gold recovery from tailings

(G-10269) FULCRUM PROMOTIONS & PRTG LLC
Also Called: Fulcrum Promos
1460 Broadway (10036-7329)
PHONE 203 909-6362
Gia-Marie Vacca, *Partner*
Vincent Miceli,
Anthony Monaco,
EMP: 4
SQ FT: 700
SALES (est): 1MM **Privately Held**
SIC: 2759 7389 Promotional printing; advertising, promotional & trade show services

(G-10270) FULL CIRCLE HOME LLC
146 W 29th St Rm 9w (10001-8207)
PHONE 212 432-0001
Tal Chitayat, *CEO*
David Chitayat, *Managing Dir*
Heather Kauffman, *COO*
Heather Tomasetti, *Manager*
▲ EMP: 9
SQ FT: 2,500
SALES: 1.5MM **Privately Held**
SIC: 3991 5199 Brooms & brushes; gifts & novelties

(G-10271) FUN MEDIA INC
1001 Ave Of The Americas (10018-5460)
PHONE 646 472-0135
Joseph Giarraputo, *President*
A Basodan, *Principal*
P Panerai, *Chairman*
Francesco Librio, *Admin Sec*
EMP: 25
SQ FT: 7,500
SALES (est): 2.5MM **Privately Held**
WEB: www.classeditori.com
SIC: 2721 7319 Magazines: publishing only, not printed on site; transit advertising services
HQ: Class Editori Spa
Via Marco Burigozzo 5
Milano MI 20122
025 821-91

(G-10272) FUNG WONG BAKERY INC
Also Called: Fung Wong Bakery Shop
30 Mott St Frnt (10013-5037)
PHONE 212 267-4037
Sherwin Choy, *President*
Eberline P Choy, *Corp Secy*
EMP: 20
SQ FT: 600
SALES (est): 1.7MM **Privately Held**
SIC: 2051 Bakery: wholesale or wholesale/retail combined

(G-10273) FUSION BRANDS AMERICA INC
444 Madison Ave Ste 700 (10022-6970)
PHONE 212 269-1387
Gregory Black, *President*
Denise Stein, *Controller*
Samuel Aracena, *Finance*
Shaliza Mithani, *Supervisor*
EMP: 25
SQ FT: 8,500
SALES: 20MM
SALES (corp-wide): 3.9MM **Privately Held**
WEB: www.fusionbrandscorp.com
SIC: 2844 5122 Cosmetic preparations; cosmetics
PA: Fusion Brands Inc
40 St Clair Ave W Suite 200
Toronto ON
800 261-9110

(G-10274) FUSION PRO PERFORMANCE LTD
Also Called: Ki Pro Performance
16 W 36th St Rm 1205 (10018-9754)
PHONE 917 833-0761

GEOGRAPHIC SECTION

New York - New York County (G-10298)

Steven Goldfarb, *President*
EMP: 16 **EST:** 2014
SQ FT: 2,000
SALES (est): 14.5MM **Privately Held**
SIC: 2339 Athletic clothing: women's, misses' & juniors'

(G-10275)
FUSION TELECOM INTL INC (PA)
420 Lexington Ave Rm 1718 (10170-1707)
PHONE..................212 201-2400
Fax: 212 972-7884
Matthew D Rosen, *CEO*
Marvin S Rosen, *Ch of Bd*
Gordon Hutchins Jr, *President*
Russell P Markman, *President*
Philip D Turits, *Corp Secy*
EMP: 114
SQ FT: 9,956
SALES: 122MM **Publicly Held**
WEB: www.fusiontel.com
SIC: 7372 4813 Business oriented computer software; telephone communication, except radio;

(G-10276)
FUTURE US INC
79 Madison Ave Fl 2 (10016-7805)
PHONE..................844 779-2822
Fax: 212 944-9279
Charlie Speight, *President*
EMP: 60
SALES (corp-wide): 76.4MM **Privately Held**
WEB: www.futureus-inc.com
SIC: 2731 Book publishing
HQ: Future Us, Inc.
1 Lombard St Ste 200
San Francisco CA 94102
650 238-2400

(G-10277)
FX INC
Also Called: Facilities Exchange
1 Penn Plz Ste 6238 (10119-0002)
PHONE..................212 244-2240
Fax: 718 235-3156
Martin Friedman, *President*
Charles Valva, *Corp Secy*
EMP: 18
SQ FT: 15,000
SALES (est): 1.7MM **Privately Held**
SIC: 2522 7641 1799 5712 Office furniture, except wood; furniture refinishing; counter top installation; office furniture

(G-10278)
G & P PRINTING INC
142 Baxter St (10013-3605)
PHONE..................212 274-8092
Fax: 212 274-1944
Stanley Chen, *President*
EMP: 5 **EST:** 1998
SALES (est): 501.1K **Privately Held**
WEB: www.gpprinting.com
SIC: 2752 Offset & photolithographic printing

(G-10279)
G I CERTIFIED INC
623 W 51st St (10019-5008)
PHONE..................212 397-1945
Michael Borrico, *Ch of Bd*
C Russonello, *Director*
Charlie Rucinelli, *Director*
EMP: 6
SALES: 500K **Privately Held**
WEB: www.certifiedny.com
SIC: 3993 Signs & advertising specialties

(G-10280)
G SCHIRMER INC (HQ)
Also Called: Music Sales
180 Madison Ave Ste 2400 (10016-5241)
PHONE..................212 254-2100
Barrie Edwards, *President*
Susan Feder, *Vice Pres*
Laurel Fay, *Opers Staff*
John Castaldo, *Controller*
Steven Wilson, *Sales Mgr*
▲ **EMP:** 4

SALES (est): 5.4MM
SALES (corp-wide): 13.6MM **Privately Held**
WEB: www.schirmer.com
SIC: 2741 7929 Music books: publishing only, not printed on site; entertainers & entertainment groups
PA: Music Sales Corporation
180 Madison Ave Ste 2400
New York NY 10016
212 254-2100

(G-10281)
G X ELECTRIC CORPORATION
8 W 38th St (10018-6229)
PHONE..................212 921-0400
Johnny Hernandez, *President*
EMP: 50 **EST:** 2013
SALES (est): 2.3MM **Privately Held**
SIC: 3699 Electrical equipment & supplies

(G-10282)
G-III APPAREL GROUP LTD (PA)
512 7th Ave Fl 35 (10018-0832)
PHONE..................212 403-0500
Morris Goldfarb, *Ch of Bd*
Sammy Aaron, *President*
Wayne S Miller, *COO*
Jeffrey Goldfarb, *Exec VP*
Neal S Nackman, *CFO*
▲ **EMP:** 277
SQ FT: 220,000
SALES: 2.3B **Publicly Held**
WEB: www.g-iii.com
SIC: 2337 2339 2311 2329 Women's & misses' suits & coats; women's & misses' outerwear; men's & boys' suits & coats; coats, overcoats & vests; jackets (suede, leatherette, etc.), sport: men's & boys'; garments, leather; coats & jackets, leather & sheep-lined; pants, leather; men's & boys' clothing

(G-10283)
G-III APPAREL GROUP LTD
Jessica Howard
512 Fashion Ave Fl 35 (10018-0832)
PHONE..................212 403-0500
Karol Gass, *Branch Mgr*
EMP: 50
SALES (corp-wide): 2.3B **Publicly Held**
SIC: 2335 Women's, juniors' & misses' dresses
PA: G-Iii Apparel Group, Ltd.
512 7th Ave Fl 35
New York NY 10018
212 403-0500

(G-10284)
G-III LEATHER FASHIONS INC
Also Called: G-III Apparel Group
512 7th Ave Fl 35 (10018-0832)
PHONE..................212 403-0500
Fax: 212 944-4081
Morris Goldfarb, *Branch Mgr*
Joe Wong, *Info Tech Mgr*
Isaure Renaud, *Director*
EMP: 20
SALES (corp-wide): 2.3B **Publicly Held**
SIC: 2386 2337 2339 Leather & sheep-lined clothing; women's & misses' suits & coats; women's & misses' outerwear
HQ: G-Iii Leather Fashions, Inc.
512 Fashion Ave Fl 35
New York NY 10018
212 403-0500

(G-10285)
G18 CORPORATION
215 W 40th St Fl 9 (10018-1575)
PHONE..................212 869-0010
Laurence Goldfarb, *President*
EMP: 2
SQ FT: 2,500
SALES: 7MM **Privately Held**
SIC: 2337 Women's & misses' suits & coats

(G-10286)
GABRIELLA IMPORTERS INC
305 W 87th St (10024-2602)
PHONE..................212 579-3945
Jacques Azoulay, *President*
EMP: 11
SALES (corp-wide): 2MM **Privately Held**
SIC: 2084 Wines

PA: Gabriella Importers, Inc.
481 Johnson Ave Ste D
Bohemia NY 11716
212 579-3945

(G-10287)
GABRIELLE ANDRA
305 W 21st St (10011-3073)
PHONE..................212 366-9624
Andra Gabrielle, *Owner*
EMP: 5
SALES (est): 220K **Privately Held**
SIC: 2331 Blouses, women's & juniors': made from purchased material

(G-10288)
GALISON PUBLISHING LLC
Also Called: Galison/Mudpuppy
70 W 36th St Fl 11 (10018-1249)
PHONE..................212 354-8840
Clairissa McLaurin, *Production*
Sam Minnitti, *CFO*
Jennifer Schroder, *VP Sales*
Steven Scott, *Mktg Dir*
Liza Rollins, *Marketing Staff*
▲ **EMP:** 20
SQ FT: 7,500
SALES (est): 3.3MM
SALES (corp-wide): 28.8MM **Privately Held**
SIC: 2621 Stationery, envelope & tablet papers
PA: The Mcevoy Group Llc
680 2nd St
San Francisco CA 94107
415 537-4200

(G-10289)
GALLERY 57 DENTAL
24 W 57th St Ste 701 (10019-3949)
PHONE..................212 246-8700
Andrew Koenigsberg DDS, *Principal*
Sandy Chemas, *Pub Rel Dir*
EMP: 20
SALES (est): 2.2MM **Privately Held**
SIC: 3843 Enamels, dentists'

(G-10290)
GALT INDUSTRIES INC
121 E 71st St (10021-4275)
PHONE..................212 758-0770
Fax: 212 758-1336
George T Votis, *Ch of Bd*
▲ **EMP:** 9
SQ FT: 2,000
SALES (est): 1.2MM **Privately Held**
SIC: 3089 Injection molding of plastics

(G-10291)
GAME TIME LLC
1407 Broadway Rm 400 (10018-3843)
PHONE..................914 557-9662
Adam Pennington, *Mng Member*
Belinda Colesanti, *Manager*
Stephanie Raw, *Manager*
Patrick McGeough, *Manager*
▲ **EMP:** 17 **EST:** 1999
SQ FT: 30,000
SALES (est): 3.5MM **Privately Held**
SIC: 3873 Watches, clocks, watchcases & parts

(G-10292)
GAMES FOR CHANGE INC
205 E 42nd St Fl 20 (10017-5706)
PHONE..................212 242-4922
Susanna Pollack, *President*
Emily Treat, *VP Prdtn*
Sara Cornish, *Project Dir*
Ling Lu, *Controller*
Meghan Ventura, *Mktg Dir*
EMP: 1 **EST:** 2004
SALES: 1.7MM **Privately Held**
SIC: 7372 Prepackaged software

(G-10293)
GAMETIME MEDIA INC
120 E 87th St Apt R8e (10128-1198)
PHONE..................212 860-2090
Robert Yan, *CEO*
Liz Yan, *President*
EMP: 6
SALES: 2MM **Privately Held**
WEB: www.gametimemedia.com
SIC: 2741 Guides: publishing & printing

(G-10294)
GARAN INCORPORATED (HQ)
200 Madison Ave Fl 4 (10016-3905)
PHONE..................212 563-1292
Fax: 212 564-7994
Seymour Lichtenstein, *CEO*
Jerald Kamiel, *President*
Wayne C Cooper, *Vice Pres*
Kathie Fiore, *Vice Pres*
Marvin S Robinson, *Vice Pres*
◆ **EMP:** 120 **EST:** 1941
SQ FT: 38,500
SALES (est): 620.5MM
SALES (corp-wide): 223.6B **Publicly Held**
WEB: www.garanimals.com
SIC: 2361 2369 2331 2339 T-shirts & tops: girls', children's & infants'; slacks: girls' & children's; T-shirts & tops, women's: made from purchased materials; shirts, women's & juniors': made from purchased materials; jeans: women's, misses' & juniors'; men's & boys' furnishings; sport shirts, men's & boys': from purchased materials
PA: Berkshire Hathaway Inc.
3555 Farnam St Ste 1440
Omaha NE 68131
402 346-1400

(G-10295)
GARAN MANUFACTURING CORP (DH)
200 Madison Ave Fl 4 (10016-3905)
PHONE..................212 563-2000
Seymour Lichtenstein, *CEO*
Jerald Kamiel, *President*
David M Fligel, *Vice Pres*
Martha Castro, *Executive*
Maria Bothos, *Executive Asst*
▼ **EMP:** 1
SALES (est): 21.2MM
SALES (corp-wide): 223.6B **Publicly Held**
SIC: 2361 2369 2331 2339 T-shirts & tops: girls', children's & infants'; slacks: girls' & children's; T-shirts & tops, women's: made from purchased materials; shirts, women's & juniors': made from purchased materials; jeans: women's, misses' & juniors'; men's & boys' furnishings; sport shirts, men's & boys': from purchased materials
HQ: Garan, Incorporated
200 Madison Ave Fl 4
New York NY 10016
212 563-1292

(G-10296)
GARYS LOFT
28 W 36th St (10018-1284)
PHONE..................212 244-0970
EMP: 6
SALES (est): 764K **Privately Held**
SIC: 3861 Photographic equipment & supplies

(G-10297)
GB GROUP INC
Umpire State Bldg 1808 (10021)
PHONE..................212 594-3748
Howard Zhanz, *President*
EMP: 8
SALES (est): 548.4K **Privately Held**
WEB: www.crystalsland.com
SIC: 3699 Laser systems & equipment

(G-10298)
GBG DENIM USA LLC (DH)
Also Called: Buffalo
350 5th Ave Lbby 9 (10118-0109)
PHONE..................646 839-7000
EMP: 13
SALES (est): 6.2MM **Privately Held**
SIC: 2325 2339 5651 Jeans: men's, youths' & boys'; jeans: women's, misses' & juniors'; jeans stores
HQ: Gbg Usa Inc.
350 5th Ave Lbby 9
New York NY 10118
646 839-7000

(G-10299)
GBG NATIONAL BRANDS GROUP LLC
350 5th Ave Lbby 9 (10118-0109)
PHONE..................................646 839-7000
Bruce Philip Rockowitz, *CEO*
Dow Peter Famulak, *President*
Ronald Ventricelli, *CFO*
Jason Andrew Rabin, *Chief Mktg Ofcr*
EMP: 5
SALES (est): 388.3K **Privately Held**
SIC: 2321 Men's & boys' furnishings
HQ: Fung Holdings (1937) Limited
G/F
Lai Chi Kok KLN
230 023-00

(G-10300)
GBG SOCKS LLC
350 5th Ave Lbby 9 (10118-0109)
PHONE..................................646 839-7000
Dow Famulak, *Mng Member*
EMP: 25
SALES (est): 1.1MM **Privately Held**
SIC: 2252 Socks

(G-10301)
GBG USA INC
350 5th Ave Fl 7 (10118-0701)
PHONE..................................646 839-7083
EMP: 93 **Privately Held**
SIC: 2387 Apparel belts
HQ: Gbg Usa Inc.
350 5th Ave Lbby 9
New York NY 10118
646 839-7000

(G-10302)
GBG USA INC
Lf USA Accessories
261 W 35th St Fl 15 (10001-1902)
PHONE..................................212 615-3400
Steven Kahn, *Branch Mgr*
EMP: 50 **Privately Held**
SIC: 2387 Apparel belts
HQ: Gbg Usa Inc.
350 5th Ave Lbby 9
New York NY 10118
646 839-7000

(G-10303)
GBG WEST LLC (DH)
Also Called: Joes Jeans
350 5th Ave Lbby 11 (10118-0108)
PHONE..................................646 839-7000
Suzy Biszantz, *CEO*
Elena Pickett, *Senior VP*
Joda Han, *Director*
EMP: 110
SQ FT: 150,000
SALES (est): 64.1MM **Privately Held**
SIC: 2339 Jeans: women's, misses' & juniors'
HQ: Gbg Usa Inc.
350 5th Ave Lbby 9
New York NY 10118
646 839-7000

(G-10304)
GCE INTERNATIONAL INC (PA)
Also Called: Great China Empire
1385 Broadway Fl 21 (10018-6022)
PHONE..................................212 704-4800
Donald Oberfield, *President*
Peter Markson, *Chairman*
Martin J Kelly, *Treasurer*
Abe Anteby, *Info Tech Mgr*
AVI Sivan, *Info Tech Mgr*
▲ **EMP:** 100 **EST:** 1920
SQ FT: 40,000
SALES: 162.9MM **Privately Held**
WEB: www.parisaccessories.com
SIC: 2253 2389 2331 5137 Hats & headwear, knit; scarves & mufflers, knit; handkerchiefs, except paper; T-shirts & tops, women's: made from purchased materials; blouses, women's & juniors': made from purchased material; scarves, women's & children's; gloves, women's & children's; scarves, men's & boys'; gloves, men's & boys'

(G-10305)
GCE INTERNATIONAL INC
Also Called: Baar & Beards
350 5th Ave Ste 616 (10118-0110)
PHONE..................................212 868-0500
Fax: 212 564-2915
Martin Kelly, *Manager*
EMP: 12
SALES (corp-wide): 162.9MM **Privately Held**
WEB: www.parisaccessories.com
SIC: 2353 2361 2381 Hats, caps & millinery; girls' & children's dresses, blouses & shirts; fabric dress & work gloves
PA: Gce International, Inc.
1385 Broadway Fl 21
New York NY 10018
212 704-4800

(G-10306)
GCE INTERNATIONAL INC
Also Called: Capital Mercury Shirtmakers Co
1359 Broadway Rm 2000 (10018-7841)
PHONE..................................773 263-1210
Peter Markson, *CEO*
Donald Mattson, *General Mgr*
Agnes Kolbig, *Credit Mgr*
EMP: 60
SALES (corp-wide): 162.9MM **Privately Held**
WEB: www.parisaccessories.com
SIC: 2321 Men's & boys' dress shirts
PA: Gce International, Inc.
1385 Broadway Fl 21
New York NY 10018
212 704-4800

(G-10307)
GDS PUBLISHING INC
40 Wall St Fl 5 (10005-1472)
PHONE..................................212 796-2000
Dave Cullinane, *Principal*
EMP: 14
SALES (est): 1.4MM
SALES (corp-wide): 32.2MM **Privately Held**
SIC: 2741 Miscellaneous publishing
HQ: Gds Publishing Limited
Queen Square House
Bristol BS1 4
117 921-4000

(G-10308)
GE HEALTHCARE FINCL SVCS INC
299 Park Ave Fl 3 (10171-0022)
PHONE..................................212 713-2000
Jay Cunningham, *Vice Pres*
Batcrio Buyo, *Branch Mgr*
EMP: 5 **Publicly Held**
SIC: 2759 Commercial printing
HQ: Ge Healthcare Financial Services, Inc.
500 W Monroe St Fl 19
Chicago IL 60661
312 697-3999

(G-10309)
GELIKO LLC
1751 2nd Ave Rm 102 (10128-5363)
PHONE..................................212 876-5620
Zach Rubin, *Mng Member*
▲ **EMP:** 20
SALES (est): 2.8MM **Privately Held**
SIC: 2899 Gelatin

(G-10310)
GEM-BAR SETTING INC
15 W 46th St (10036-4117)
PHONE..................................212 869-9238
Fred Barilla, *President*
Tina Barilla, *Admin Sec*
EMP: 8
SALES (est): 520K **Privately Held**
SIC: 3911 Jewelry, precious metal

(G-10311)
GEMFIELDS USA INCORPORATED
589 5th Ave Rm 909 (10017-8715)
PHONE..................................212 398-5400
Gabriel Jharvy, *President*
EMP: 5
SALES (est): 392.1K
SALES (corp-wide): 193.1MM **Privately Held**
SIC: 1499 Gem stones (natural) mining
PA: Gemfields Plc
4th Floor 1 New Burlington Place
London W1S 2
207 518-3400

(G-10312)
GEMORO INC
48 W 48th St Ste 1102 (10036-1703)
PHONE..................................212 768-8844
Dennis Hakim, *President*
EMP: 5
SALES (est): 530K **Privately Held**
WEB: www.gemoro.com
SIC: 3911 5094 Jewelry, precious metal; jewelry & precious stones

(G-10313)
GEMPRINT CORPORATION
580 5th Ave Bsmt LI05 (10036-4726)
PHONE..................................212 997-0007
Angelo Palmieri, *President*
EMP: 20
SQ FT: 5,500
SALES (est): 2.1MM **Privately Held**
SIC: 3826 Laser scientific & engineering instruments

(G-10314)
GEMVETO JEWELRY COMPANY INC
18 E 48th St Rm 501 (10017-1014)
PHONE..................................212 755-2522
Fax: 212 755-2027
Jean Vitau, *President*
Irene Vitau, *Corp Secy*
EMP: 20 **EST:** 1967
SQ FT: 3,500
SALES (est): 2.4MM **Privately Held**
WEB: www.gems-online.org
SIC: 3911 Jewelry, precious metal

(G-10315)
GENERAL ART COMPANY INC
Also Called: General Art Framing
14 E 38th St Fl 6 (10016-0636)
PHONE..................................212 255-1298
Jen Chan, *President*
EMP: 10
SQ FT: 4,000
SALES (est): 1MM **Privately Held**
SIC: 2499 5023 Picture frame molding, finished; frames & framing, picture & mirror

(G-10316)
GENERAL MEDIA STRATEGIES INC
Also Called: African American Observer
483 10th Ave Rm 325 (10018-1177)
PHONE..................................212 586-4141
Steve Mallory, *President*
EMP: 8 **EST:** 2001
SALES: 250K **Privately Held**
SIC: 2711 Newspapers

(G-10317)
GENERAL SPORTWEAR COMPANY INC (PA)
230 W 38th St Fl 4 (10018-9085)
P.O. Box 588, Ellenville (12428-0588)
PHONE..................................212 764-5820
Fax: 845 647-4934
Herbert Rosenstock, *Ch of Bd*
Jeffrey Rosenstock, *President*
David Rosensock, *Corp Secy*
Michael Brickner, *Plant Mgr*
Tony Shannahan, *Human Res Mgr*
◆ **EMP:** 5 **EST:** 1927
SQ FT: 20,000
SALES (est): 31.3MM **Privately Held**
WEB: www.generalsportwear.com
SIC: 2361 2369 2329 T-shirts & tops: girls', children's & infants'; jeans: girls', children's & infants'; men's & boys' sportswear & athletic clothing

(G-10318)
GENESIS MANNEQUINS USA II INC
151 W 25th St Fl 4 (10001-7204)
PHONE..................................212 505-6600
Joseph Klinow, *President*
▲ **EMP:** 8
SQ FT: 3,500
SALES (est): 3.1MM **Privately Held**
SIC: 3999 Mannequins

(G-10319)
GENEVA HOME FASHION LLC
230 5th Ave Ste 612 (10001-7704)
PHONE..................................212 213-8323
Celeste Wong, *Bookkeeper*
Jack Setton,
Toby Souleiman,
▲ **EMP:** 10 **EST:** 2014
SQ FT: 8,000
SALES (est): 1.2MM **Privately Held**
SIC: 2392 5719 Household furnishings; blankets, comforters & beddings; comforters & quilts: made from purchased materials; beddings & linens

(G-10320)
GENEVA WATCH COMPANY INC (DH)
1407 Broadway Rm 400 (10018-3843)
PHONE..................................212 221-1177
▲ **EMP:** 20
SQ FT: 15,000
SALES (est): 6.1MM
SALES (corp-wide): 98.7K **Privately Held**
SIC: 3873 Mfg Watches/Clocks/Parts
HQ: Awc Liquidating Co.
1407 Broadway Rm 400
New York NY 10018
212 221-1177

(G-10321)
GENIE INSTANT PRINTING CO INC
Also Called: Genie Instant Printing Center
37 W 43rd St (10036-7403)
PHONE..................................212 575-8258
Fax: 212 382-3408
Sal Cohen, *President*
Ronnie Cohen, *Vice Pres*
EMP: 10
SALES (est): 1MM **Privately Held**
SIC: 2759 2752 Commercial printing; photo-offset printing

(G-10322)
GENOMEWEB LLC
Also Called: Bioinformatics Publishing
40 Fulton St Rm 1002 (10038-5057)
P.O. Box 998 (10272-0998)
PHONE..................................212 651-5636
Fax: 212 269-3686
Judy Block, *Publisher*
Molika Ashford, *Editor*
Ben Butkus, *Editor*
Monica Heger, *Editor*
Doug Macron, *Editor*
EMP: 17
SQ FT: 3,600
SALES (est): 2.1MM **Privately Held**
SIC: 2721 Periodicals

(G-10323)
GEOFFREY BEENE INC
37 W 57th St Frnt 2 (10019-3410)
PHONE..................................212 371-5570
Fax: 212 980-6579
Geoffrey Beene, *President*
G Thompson Hutton, *President*
Russell Nardoza, *COO*
Russell Nardozza, *COO*
EMP: 20
SALES: 1.9MM **Privately Held**
WEB: www.geoffreybeene.com
SIC: 2335 2337 2331 2339 Women's, juniors' & misses' dresses; skirts, separate: women's, misses' & juniors'; jackets & vests, except fur & leather: women's; blouses, women's & juniors': made from purchased material; slacks: women's, misses' & juniors'

(G-10324)
GEONEX INTERNATIONAL CORP
200 Park Ave S Ste 920 (10003-1509)
PHONE..................................212 473-4555
George Nikiforov, *President*
EMP: 6
SQ FT: 1,000
SALES (est): 720K **Privately Held**
SIC: 2435 Hardwood plywood, prefinished

▲ = Import ▼=Export
◆ =Import/Export

GEOGRAPHIC SECTION

New York - New York County (G-10350)

(G-10325)
GEORGE G SHARP INC (PA)
160 Broadway (10038-4201)
PHONE.....................212 732-2800
Fax: 212 732-2809
I Hilary Rolih, *Ch of Bd*
Allen Chin, *President*
Warren Jenik, *COO*
CHI C Yang, *Vice Pres*
Robert Reehl, *QC Mgr*
EMP: 27
SQ FT: 8,000
SALES (est): 93.8MM **Privately Held**
WEB: www.ggsharp.com
SIC: 3731 4225 8712 Shipbuilding & repairing; commercial cargo ships, building & repairing; military ships, building & repairing; general warehousing; architectural services

(G-10326)
GEORGE KNITTING MILLS CORP
116 W 23rd St Fl 4 (10011-2599)
PHONE.....................212 242-3300
Lawrence Aibel, *President*
Richard Aibel, *Vice Pres*
George Paez, *Office Mgr*
EMP: 5 **EST:** 1958
SQ FT: 10,000
SALES (est): 738.7K **Privately Held**
SIC: 2258 Pile fabrics, warp or flat knit

(G-10327)
GEORGE LEDERMAN INC
515 Madison Ave Rm 1218 (10022-5452)
PHONE.....................212 753-4556
Fax: 212 888-3372
Serge Lederman, *President*
Adrienne Lederman, *Vice Pres*
Janine Lederman, *Admin Sec*
EMP: 5 **EST:** 1937
SQ FT: 800
SALES (est): 567.7K **Privately Held**
WEB: www.glederman.com
SIC: 3911 Jewelry, precious metal

(G-10328)
GEORGY CREATIVE FASHIONS INC
Also Called: Georgie Kaye
249 W 29th St (10001-5211)
PHONE.....................212 279-4885
George Kambouris, *President*
EMP: 6
SQ FT: 3,000
SALES (est): 513.8K **Privately Held**
SIC: 2371 5136 5137 2386 Fur goods; fur clothing, men's & boys'; fur clothing, women's & children's; garments, leather

(G-10329)
GERLI & CO INC (PA)
Also Called: American Silk Mills
41 Madison Ave Ste 4101 (10010-2203)
PHONE.....................212 213-1919
Fax: 212 967-5284
Robin L Slough, *President*
Cynthia Douthit, *Vice Pres*
John M Sullivan Jr, *Vice Pres*
Russell Sokolas, *Plant Mgr*
James Harowicz, *CFO*
◆ **EMP:** 35 **EST:** 1883
SQ FT: 7,500
SALES (est): 27.8MM **Privately Held**
SIC: 2211 2221 Cotton broad woven goods; broadwoven fabric mills, man-made; rayon broadwoven fabrics; silk broadwoven fabrics

(G-10330)
GERSON & GERSON INC (PA)
100 W 33rd St Ste 911 (10001-2913)
PHONE.....................212 244-6775
Fax: 212 244-6794
Matthew Gerson, *Ch of Bd*
Shelley Striar, *Prdtn Mgr*
Tania Camacho, *Purch Dir*
Barbara Zeins, *Sls & Mktg Exec*
Phyills Falsone, *Controller*
◆ **EMP:** 70 **EST:** 1933
SQ FT: 13,000
SALES (est): 21.7MM **Privately Held**
WEB: www.gersonandgerson.com
SIC: 2369 2361 Girls' & children's outerwear; dresses: girls', children's & infants'

(G-10331)
GFB FASHIONS LTD
Also Called: Jonathan Michael Coats
463 Fashion Ave Rm 1502 (10018-7596)
PHONE.....................212 239-9230
Paul Cohen, *President*
Steve Schubak, *Controller*
▲ **EMP:** 12
SALES (est): 1.1MM **Privately Held**
SIC: 2339 Women's & misses' jackets & coats, except sportswear

(G-10332)
GG DESIGN AND PRINTING
93 Henry St Frnt 1 (10002-7035)
PHONE.....................718 321-3220
Allan Yin, *President*
▲ **EMP:** 9
SQ FT: 3,500
SALES: 1MM **Privately Held**
SIC: 2791 7336 Typesetting; graphic arts & related design

(G-10333)
GH BASS & CO (DH)
512 7th Ave Fl 28 (10018-0845)
PHONE.....................646 768-4600
John Gietl, *President*
Chad Newcomer, *General Mgr*
Howard Renner, *Senior VP*
Pauline Chien, *Buyer*
Christina Merianos, *Buyer*
▲ **EMP:** 50 **EST:** 1987
SALES (est): 81.1MM
SALES (corp-wide): 2.3B **Publicly Held**
WEB: www.ghbass.com
SIC: 3144 3143 3149 5661 Women's footwear, except athletic; men's footwear, except athletic; children's footwear, except athletic; shoe stores

(G-10334)
GIFFORD GROUP INC
Also Called: Just Plastics
250 Dyckman St (10034-5354)
PHONE.....................212 569-8500
Fax: 212 569-6970
Robert C Vermann, *President*
Tammy Espaillat, *Vice Pres*
Lois Vermann, *Vice Pres*
EMP: 15
SQ FT: 25,000
SALES: 1.5MM **Privately Held**
WEB: www.justplastics.com
SIC: 3089 Plastic processing

(G-10335)
GIFTS SOFTWARE INC
360 Lexington Ave Rm 601 (10017-6562)
PHONE.....................904 438-6000
Fax: 646 838-9494
Jawaid M Khan, *CEO*
Paul Campanaro, *Vice Pres*
Nasir Farooqui, *Vice Pres*
Sydney Stone, *Vice Pres*
Paul Gdanski, *VP Sales*
EMP: 35
SQ FT: 10,000
SALES (est): 2.3MM
SALES (corp-wide): 9.2B **Publicly Held**
WEB: www.giftsoft.com
SIC: 7372 Business oriented computer software
PA: Fidelity National Information Services, Inc.
601 Riverside Ave
Jacksonville FL 32204
904 438-6000

(G-10336)
GILDAN APPAREL USA INC (DH)
Also Called: Anvil Knitwear, Inc.
48 W 38th St Fl 8 (10018-0043)
PHONE.....................212 476-0341
Fax: 212 476-0323
Anthony Corsano, *Ch of Bd*
Jacob Hollander, *Exec VP*
Heather Stefani, *Exec VP*
Chris Binnicker, *Vice Pres*
J Goldberg, *Vice Pres*
▲ **EMP:** 65
SALES (est): 534.1MM
SALES (corp-wide): 2.9B **Privately Held**
WEB: www.anvilknitwear.com
SIC: 2253 2331 Knit outerwear mills; women's & misses' blouses & shirts

(G-10337)
GILIBERTO DESIGNS INC
142 W 36th St Fl 8 (10018-8792)
PHONE.....................212 695-0216
Fax: 212 563-0524
Rosario Giliberto Jr, *President*
Anthony Giliberto, *Vice Pres*
Ken Kriegle, *CPA*
EMP: 23
SQ FT: 6,500
SALES (est): 2.1MM **Privately Held**
WEB: www.gilibertodesigns.com
SIC: 2311 5611 Men's & boys' suits & coats; clothing accessories: men's & boys'

(G-10338)
GILMORES SOUND ADVICE INC
599 11th Ave Fl 5 (10036-2110)
PHONE.....................212 265-4445
Edward Gilmore, *President*
Jennifer Pedraza, *Programmer Anys*
EMP: 12
SALES (est): 1.6MM **Privately Held**
SIC: 3651 Audio electronic systems

(G-10339)
GINA GROUP LLC
Also Called: Gina Hosiery
10 W 33rd St Ph 3 (10001-3317)
PHONE.....................212 947-2445
Paul Kubie, *President*
Jack Barasch, *Controller*
Allen Gutner, *Controller*
Morris Sakkal, *Asst Controller*
Cher Landman, *Accounts Exec*
◆ **EMP:** 35
SQ FT: 10,500
SALES (est): 6.7MM **Privately Held**
WEB: www.ginagroup.com
SIC: 2252 2251 Hosiery; socks; tights & leg warmers; women's hosiery, except socks

(G-10340)
GIOVANE LTD
Also Called: Giovane Piranesi
592 5th Ave Ste L (10036-4707)
PHONE.....................212 332-7373
Sami Hajibay, *President*
Mishel H H Piranesi, *Vice Pres*
Lavina Punwaney, *Manager*
Mishel H Handreo, *Admin Sec*
EMP: 22
SQ FT: 8,500
SALES (est): 3.2MM **Privately Held**
SIC: 3911 Jewelry, precious metal

(G-10341)
GIOVANNI BAKERY CORP
Also Called: Trio French Bakery
476 9th Ave (10018-5603)
P.O. Box 50057, Staten Island (10305-0057)
PHONE.....................212 695-4296
Mario De Giovanni, *President*
Romona De Giovanni, *Corp Secy*
John De Giovanni, *Vice Pres*
EMP: 13 **EST:** 1953
SALES (est): 40.3K **Privately Held**
SIC: 2051 5461 Bread, all types (white, wheat, rye, etc): fresh or frozen; rolls, bread type: fresh or frozen; bread

(G-10342)
GIVAUDAN FRAGRANCES CORP
40 W 57th St Fl 11 (10019-4001)
PHONE.....................212 649-8800
Fax: 212 649-8899
Laura Bowser, *QC Mgr*
Gwen Gonzalez, *Research*
Karen Flinn, *VP Sales*
Karen Elliott, *Sales Mgr*
Lauren Bitet, *Accounts Exec*
EMP: 130
SALES (corp-wide): 1.1B **Privately Held**
SIC: 2869 Perfume materials, synthetic; flavors or flavoring materials, synthetic
HQ: Givaudan Fragrances Corporation
1199 Edison Dr Ste 1-2
Cincinnati OH 45216
513 948-3428

(G-10343)
GIVI INC
16 W 56th St Fl 4 (10019-3872)
PHONE.....................212 586-5029
Mario Fabris, *President*
EMP: 10
SALES (est): 977K
SALES (corp-wide): 141.2K **Privately Held**
SIC: 3111 5661 3999 Bag leather; shoe stores; atomizers, toiletry
PA: Givi Holding Spa
Via Alessandro Manzoni 38
Milano MI
027 609-31

(G-10344)
GLACEE SKINCARE LLC
611 W 136th St Apt 4 (10031-8137)
PHONE.....................212 690-7632
Jose De La Cruz,
EMP: 6 **EST:** 2015
SALES (est): 293.2K **Privately Held**
SIC: 2844 Lotions, shaving; cosmetic preparations

(G-10345)
GLAMOUR MAGAZINE
4 Times Sq Fl 16 (10036-6625)
PHONE.....................212 286-2860
Fax: 212 286-8336
Denise Gordon, *Editor*
Wendy Naugle, *Editor*
Bill Wackermann, *Vice Pres*
Charles Townsend, *Vice Pres*
Tom Table, *Asst Controller*
EMP: 5
SALES (est): 240K **Privately Held**
SIC: 2721 Periodicals

(G-10346)
GLAMOURPUSS NYC LLC
1305 Madison Ave (10128-1327)
PHONE.....................212 722-1370
Gigi Mortimer, *Principal*
Courtney Moss, *Principal*
EMP: 9
SALES (est): 874K **Privately Held**
SIC: 2331 Women's & misses' blouses & shirts

(G-10347)
GLASS APPS LLC (PA)
11 Times Sq Ste 15 (10036-6606)
PHONE.....................310 987-1536
Thomas Lee,
Sheila Speller, *Executive Asst*
EMP: 10
SQ FT: 1,200
SALES (est): 3.7MM **Privately Held**
SIC: 3211 Laminated glass

(G-10348)
GLASSBOX US INC
234 5th Ave Ste 207 (10001-7607)
PHONE.....................917 378-2933
Yaron Morgenstern, *CEO*
Steve Dieugenio, *Human Res Mgr*
Yifat Golan, *Director*
EMP: 61
SALES (est): 922.4K **Privately Held**
SIC: 7372 Prepackaged software

(G-10349)
GLASSES USA LLC
Also Called: Glassesusa.com
954 Lexington Ave Ste 537 (10021-5055)
PHONE.....................212 784-6094
Daniel Rothman, *CEO*
Jay Engelmayer, *President*
Hili Shani, *Manager*
Roy Yamner, *CTO*
Brett Rudolph, *Director*
EMP: 14
SALES (est): 2.3MM **Privately Held**
SIC: 3851 Ophthalmic goods; glasses, sun or glare; spectacles

(G-10350)
GLASSVIEW LLC (PA)
25 E 67th St Ph A (10065-5871)
PHONE.....................646 844-4922
Kellie Christensen, *Finance Mgr*
James Brooks, *Mng Member*
EMP: 40

New York - New York County (G-10351)   **GEOGRAPHIC SECTION**

SALES: 51MM **Privately Held**
SIC: 2741 Miscellaneous publishing

(G-10351)
GLOBAL ALLIANCE FOR TB
40 Wall St Fl 24 (10005-1338)
PHONE..................212 227-7540
Fax: 212 227-7541
Melvin K Spigelman, *President*
Maarten Van Cleeff, *President*
Willo Brock, *Senior VP*
Robert C Lorette, *Senior VP*
Carl Mendel, *Senior VP*
EMP: 27
SQ FT: 8,500
SALES (est): 7.3MM **Privately Held**
WEB: www.tballiance.org
SIC: 2834 Druggists' preparations (pharmaceuticals)

(G-10352)
GLOBAL ALUMINA CORPORATION (PA)
277 Park Ave Fl 40 (10172-2902)
PHONE..................212 351-0000
Bruce J Wrobel, *CEO*
Graham Morrey, *President*
Tony McCabe, *Senior VP*
Michael J Cella, *CFO*
EMP: 9
SALES (est): 26MM **Privately Held**
SIC: 3297 Alumina fused refractories

(G-10353)
GLOBAL ALUMINA SERVICES CO
277 Park Ave Fl 40 (10172-2902)
PHONE..................212 309-8060
Bruce Wrobel, *Ch of Bd*
Bernie Cousineau, *President*
Thomas Deleo, *Counsel*
Dirk Straussfeld, *Exec VP*
Jim McGowan, *Senior VP*
EMP: 500
SQ FT: 15,400
SALES (est): 25.8MM
SALES (corp-wide): 26MM **Privately Held**
WEB: www.globalalumina.com
SIC: 3297 Alumina fused refractories
PA: Global Alumina Corporation
    277 Park Ave Fl 40
    New York NY 10172
    212 351-0000

(G-10354)
GLOBAL APPLCTIONS SOLUTION LLC
125 Park Ave Fl 25 (10017-5550)
PHONE..................212 741-9595
Russell Luke, *Managing Dir*
Vishal Khurana,
EMP: 8
SALES: 125.1K **Privately Held**
SIC: 7372 7379 Prepackaged software; computer related maintenance services

(G-10355)
GLOBAL FINANCE MAGAZINE
Also Called: Global Finance Magazine.
7 E 20th St (10003-1106)
PHONE..................212 524-3223
Josepy Giarraputo, *Principal*
Denise Bedell, *Editor*
Andrea Fiano, *Editor*
Peter McManus, *Vice Pres*
Michael Ambrosio, *Mktg Dir*
EMP: 5
SALES (est): 705.1K **Privately Held**
WEB: www.gfmag.com
SIC: 2721 Periodicals

(G-10356)
GLOBAL FINANCE MEDIA INC
Also Called: Global Finance Magazine.
7 E 20th St Fl 2 (10003-1106)
PHONE..................212 447-7900
Andrew Spindler, *CEO*
James Macdonald, *Vice Pres*
EMP: 12
SALES (est): 1.3MM **Privately Held**
SIC: 2721 5192 Periodicals; magazines

(G-10357)
GLOBAL FIRE CORPORATION
244 5th Ave Ste 2238 (10001-7604)
PHONE..................888 320-1799
Daniel Olszanski, *President*
◆ EMP: 21
SALES: 4.8MM **Privately Held**
WEB: www.globalfirecorp.com
SIC: 3711 Fire department vehicles (motor vehicles), assembly of

(G-10358)
GLOBAL GEM CORPORATION
Also Called: Global Creations
425 Madison Ave Rm 400 (10017-1141)
PHONE..................212 350-9936
Moosa Ebrahimian, *President*
Robert Ebrahimian, *Vice Pres*
Steve Ebrahimian, *Manager*
EMP: 5
SQ FT: 1,100
SALES (est): 400K **Privately Held**
WEB: www.globalcreations.com
SIC: 3911 5094 Jewelry, precious metal; diamonds (gems)

(G-10359)
GLOBAL GOLD INC
1410 Broadway Fl 8 (10018-9362)
PHONE..................212 239-4657
John Bang, *CEO*
Bruce Fisher, *President*
Jeff Fisher, *Vice Pres*
Richard Fleet, *Vice Pres*
Scott Alsberry, *CFO*
▲ EMP: 38
SALES (est): 3.7MM **Privately Held**
SIC: 2337 Women's & misses' suits & coats

(G-10360)
GLOBAL GRIND DIGITAL
512 Fashion Ave Fl 42 (10018-4603)
PHONE..................212 840-9399
Osman Eralt, *CEO*
Tricia Clarke-Stone, *Principal*
Ian Corbin, *Vice Pres*
Kat Sanchez, *Manager*
EMP: 30
SALES (est): 2MM **Privately Held**
SIC: 2741 Miscellaneous publishing

(G-10361)
GLOBAL PLASTICS LP
21 Downing St Frnt 1 (10014-0836)
PHONE..................800 417-4605
EMP: 11 **Privately Held**
SIC: 2821 Plastics materials & resins
PA: Global Plastics, Lp
    99 Middle St Ste 1
    Manchester NH 03101

(G-10362)
GLOBAL RESOURCES SG INC
Also Called: Milli Home
267 5th Ave Rm 506 (10016-7503)
PHONE..................212 686-1411
Anil Nayar, *President*
Pavan Uttam, *Exec VP*
Kush Malhotra, *Manager*
Marsha Cutler, *Director*
▲ EMP: 12
SQ FT: 800
SALES (est): 1.5MM **Privately Held**
SIC: 2299 3635 Upholstery filling, textile; household vacuum cleaners

(G-10363)
GLOBAL SECURITY TECH LLC
1407 Broadway Fl 30 (10018-2480)
PHONE..................917 838-4507
Yoram Curiel, *CEO*
Victor Franco, *President*
Samuel Franco, *VP Sales*
Victor Dabah,
EMP: 10
SALES (est): 66.5K **Privately Held**
SIC: 3089 Identification cards, plastic

(G-10364)
GLORIA APPAREL INC
256 W 38th St Rm 700 (10018-9124)
PHONE..................212 947-0869
Young H Lee, *President*
Sowon Yoon, *Accountant*
Kj Kim, *Director*

▼ EMP: 10
SALES: 59MM **Privately Held**
WEB: www.gloria-texteis.com
SIC: 2386 Coats & jackets, leather & sheep-lined

(G-10365)
GLUCK ORGELBAU INC
170 Park Row Apt 20a (10038-1156)
PHONE..................212 233-2684
Sebastian M Gluck, *President*
Albert Jensenmoulton, *General Mgr*
EMP: 5 EST: 1985
SALES: 370K **Privately Held**
SIC: 3931 Organs, all types: pipe, reed, hand, electronic, etc.

(G-10366)
GMC MERCANTILE CORP
231 W 39th St Rm 612 (10018-3109)
PHONE..................212 498-9488
Garrick Chan, *President*
Sherman Chan, *Vice Pres*
Agean Chen, *CFO*
▲ EMP: 18
SALES (est): 1.9MM **Privately Held**
SIC: 2339 Service apparel, washable: women's

(G-10367)
GNCC CAPITAL INC (PA)
244 5th Ave Ste 2525 (10001-7604)
PHONE..................702 951-9793
Peter Voss, *CEO*
Ronald Lowenthal, *Ch of Bd*
EMP: 4
SALES (est): 1.2MM **Privately Held**
SIC: 1041 Gold ores

(G-10368)
GODIVA CHOCOLATIER INC (DH)
333 W 34th St Fl 6 (10001-2566)
PHONE..................212 984-5900
Fax: 212 984-5901
Jim Goldman, *President*
Verna Armstrong, *General Mgr*
Steven Ashworth, *General Mgr*
Stephen Cady, *General Mgr*
Michelle Clark, *General Mgr*
▲ EMP: 35
SQ FT: 15,000
SALES (est): 828MM **Privately Held**
WEB: www.godiva.com
SIC: 2066 5149 5441 2064 Chocolate candy, solid; chocolate; candy; candy & other confectionery products
HQ: Yildiz Holding Anonim Sirketi
    No:6/2 Kisikli Mahallesi
    Istanbul (Anatolia) 34692
    216 524-2900

(G-10369)
GODIVA CHOCOLATIER INC
33 Maiden Ln Frnt 1 (10038-4518)
PHONE..................212 809-8990
Fax: 212 809-8890
Michelle Chin, *Vice Pres*
Erica Perretta, *Manager*
EMP: 6 **Privately Held**
WEB: www.godiva.com
SIC: 2066 Chocolate
HQ: Godiva Chocolatier, Inc.
    333 W 34th St Fl 6
    New York NY 10001
    212 984-5900

(G-10370)
GOLDARAMA COMPANY INC
Also Called: Silvertique Fine Jewelry
56 W 45th St Ste 1504 (10036-4206)
PHONE..................212 730-7299
Fax: 212 730-0288
Ernie Golan, *President*
Hagay Golan, *Vice Pres*
EMP: 7
SALES (est): 660K **Privately Held**
SIC: 3911 Jewelry, precious metal

(G-10371)
GOLDBERGER COMPANY LLC (PA)
Also Called: Goldberger International
36 W 25th St Fl 14 (10010-2749)
PHONE..................212 924-1194

Steven Strauss, *Vice Pres*
Jeffrey Holtzman, *Mng Member*
Susan Price, *Executive Asst*
Lawrence Doppelt,
Michael Pietrafesa,
▲ EMP: 16 EST: 1916
SQ FT: 10,000
SALES: 2MM **Privately Held**
WEB: www.goldbergerdoll.com
SIC: 3942 Dolls & doll clothing; stuffed toys, including animals

(G-10372)
GOLDEN EAGLE MARKETING LLC
244 5th Ave (10001-7604)
PHONE..................212 726-1242
Monika Sylvester,
EMP: 5 EST: 2009
SALES (est): 217.8K **Privately Held**
SIC: 2741

(G-10373)
GOLDEN HORSE ENTERPRISE NY INC
70 W 36th St Rm 12e (10018-1746)
PHONE..................212 594-3339
Kenny Fung, *President*
▲ EMP: 5
SALES (est): 540K **Privately Held**
SIC: 2331 T-shirts & tops, women's: made from purchased materials

(G-10374)
GOLDEN INTEGRITY INC
Also Called: B K Integrity
37 W 47th St Ste 1601 (10036-3069)
PHONE..................212 764-6753
Darek Schwartz, *President*
Khris Kornezi, *Vice Pres*
EMP: 20
SALES: 150K **Privately Held**
WEB: www.goldenintegrity.com
SIC: 3911 5944 Jewel settings & mountings, precious metal; jewelry stores

(G-10375)
GOLDEN PACIFIC LXJ INC
156 W 56th St Ste 2002 (10019-3877)
PHONE..................267 975-6537
Steve Reynolds, *President*
Joanna Ricciardi, *Sales Executive*
▲ EMP: 2 EST: 2011
SALES: 1MM **Privately Held**
SIC: 3131 Footwear cut stock

(G-10376)
GOLDSTAR LIGHTING LLC
1407 Broadway Fl 30 (10018-2480)
PHONE..................646 543-6811
EMP: 18
SQ FT: 18,000
SALES (est): 1.3MM **Privately Held**
SIC: 3641 Mfg Electric Lamps

(G-10377)
GOOD HOME CO INC
132 W 24th St (10011-1981)
PHONE..................212 352-1509
Christine Dimmick, *President*
Arni Halling, *Exec VP*
EMP: 6
SQ FT: 1,800
SALES (est): 1.1MM **Privately Held**
WEB: www.thegoodhomecompany.com
SIC: 2844 Toilet preparations; oral preparations; perfumes & colognes; cosmetic preparations

(G-10378)
GOOD SHOW SPORTWEAR INC
Also Called: Good Show Sportswear
132 Mulberry St 3 (10013-5551)
PHONE..................212 334-8751
Danny Tsui, *Owner*
EMP: 11
SALES (est): 350K **Privately Held**
SIC: 3949 Sporting & athletic goods

(G-10379)
GORGA FEHREN FINE JEWELRY LLC
Also Called: Eva Fehren
153 E 88th St (10128-2270)
PHONE..................646 861-3595

▲ = Import ▼ = Export
◆ = Import/Export

Ann Gorga, *CEO*
EMP: 6
SALES: 0 Privately Held
SIC: 3911 7389 Jewelry, precious metal;

(G-10380)
GOTHAM ENERGY 360 LLC
48 Wall St Fl 5 (10005-2911)
PHONE......................917 338-1023
Jennifer Kearney,
EMP: 10 EST: 2008
SALES (est): 451.6K Privately Held
SIC: 1389 8748 Oil consultants; energy conservation consultant

(G-10381)
GOTHAM VETERINARY CENTER PC
700 Columbus Ave Frnt 5 (10025-6662)
PHONE......................212 222-1900
Bonnie Brown, *President*
Patricia Dominguez,
Kimberly Kahn,
EMP: 20
SALES (est): 4MM Privately Held
SIC: 2835 Veterinary diagnostic substances

(G-10382)
GOTTLIEB & SONS INC
Also Called: Gottlieb Jewelery Mfg
21 W 47th St Fl 4 (10036-2825)
PHONE......................212 575-1907
Fax: 212 398-9630
Allen Gottlieb, *Owner*
EMP: 25
SALES (corp-wide): 7.9MM Privately Held
WEB: www.gottlieb-sons.com
SIC: 3911 Jewelry, precious metal
PA: Gottlieb & Sons, Inc.
    1100 Superior Ave E # 2050
    Cleveland OH 44114
    216 771-4785

(G-10383)
GOYARD INC (HQ)
Also Called: Goyard US
20 E 63rd St (10065-7210)
PHONE......................212 813-0005
Deborah Ruiz, *Manager*
Patricia Pinheiro, *Manager*
EMP: 6
SALES (est): 2.1MM
SALES (corp-wide): 55.2MM Privately Held
SIC: 3161 5137 Wardrobe bags (luggage); handbags
PA: Goyard St Honore
    16 Place Vendome
    Paris 75001
    142 601-881

(G-10384)
GOYARD MIAMI LLC (DH)
Also Called: Maison Goyard
20 E 63rd St (10065-7210)
PHONE......................212 813-0005
Deborah Ruiz,
EMP: 6 EST: 2015
SALES (est): 1MM
SALES (corp-wide): 55.2MM Privately Held
SIC: 3161 5137 Wardrobe bags (luggage); handbags
HQ: Goyard, Inc.
    20 E 63rd St
    New York NY 10065
    212 813-0005

(G-10385)
GQ MAGAZINE
4 Times Sq Fl 9 (10036-6518)
PHONE......................212 286-2860
Charles Townsend, *CEO*
Brian Coats, *Editor*
Damien Nunes, *Editor*
Daniel Riley, *Editor*
Giulio Capua, *Vice Pres*
EMP: 8
SALES (est): 570K Privately Held
SIC: 2731 Book publishing

(G-10386)
GRADIAN HEALTH SYSTEMS INC
915 Broadway Ste 1001 (10010-8268)
PHONE......................212 537-0340
Stephen M Rudy, *CEO*
Stephen Rudy, *CEO*
Erica Frenkel, *Vice Pres*
Lina Sayed, *Director*
Nicole Lund, *Administration*
EMP: 7
SQ FT: 3,400
SALES (est): 786.5K Privately Held
SIC: 3841 Anesthesia apparatus

(G-10387)
GRAMERCY JEWELRY MFG CORP
35 W 45th St Fl 5 (10036-4903)
PHONE......................212 268-0461
Fax: 212 768-2619
Danny Lai, *President*
Peter Law, *Vice Pres*
▲ EMP: 50
SQ FT: 13,000
SALES (est): 7.5MM Privately Held
WEB: www.gramercyjewelry.com
SIC: 3911 Jewelry, precious metal

(G-10388)
GRAND CENTRAL PUBLISHING (DH)
1290 Ave Of The Americas (10104-0101)
PHONE......................212 364-1200
David Young, *Ch of Bd*
Beth Ford, *Principal*
Lawrence Kirshbaum, *Principal*
Mitchell Kinzer, *Business Mgr*
Thomas Maciag, *CFO*
EMP: 240 EST: 1960
SQ FT: 140,000
SALES (est): 33.4MM
SALES (corp-wide): 62.3MM Privately Held
WEB: www.biggamesmallworld.com
SIC: 2731 Books: publishing only
HQ: Hachette Book Group, Inc.
    1290 Ave Of The Americas
    New York NY 10104
    800 759-0190

(G-10389)
GRAND SLAM HOLDINGS LLC (DH)
Also Called: Blackstone Group
345 Park Ave Bsmt Lb4 (10154-0004)
PHONE......................212 583-5000
Stephen A Schwarzman, *CEO*
EMP: 24
SALES (est): 1.4B
SALES (corp-wide): 5.1B Publicly Held
WEB: www.backstone-gro.com
SIC: 3842 Surgical appliances & supplies; implants, surgical

(G-10390)
GRANDEUR CREATIONS INC
146 W 29th St Rm 9e (10001-8207)
PHONE......................212 643-1277
Jal Billimoria, *President*
Meherukh Billimoria, *Treasurer*
EMP: 6
SQ FT: 2,450
SALES (est): 531.2K Privately Held
WEB: www.grandeurcreations.com
SIC: 3911 Rings, finger: precious metal; bracelets, precious metal

(G-10391)
GRANDMA MAES CNTRY NTURALS LLC
340 E 93rd St Apt 30h (10128-5556)
PHONE......................212 348-8171
Barry Berman, *President*
EMP: 5
SALES (est): 740K Privately Held
SIC: 2048 Canned pet food (except dog & cat); dry pet food (except dog & cat); frozen pet food (except dog & cat)

(G-10392)
GRANTOO LLC
60 Broad St Ste 3502 (10004-2356)
PHONE......................646 356-0460
Tamer Ossama Hassanein, *Vice Pres*
EMP: 5
SALES (est): 205.7K Privately Held
SIC: 7372 Application computer software

(G-10393)
GRANTS FINANCIAL PUBLISHING
Also Called: Grant's Interest Rate Observer
2 Wall St Ste 603 (10005-2000)
PHONE......................212 809-7994
Fax: 212 809-8492
James Grant, *President*
Sue Egan, *Manager*
John McCarthy, *Art Dir*
Alexander Hess, *Analyst*
Evan Lorenz, *Analyst*
EMP: 10
SALES (est): 1.6MM Privately Held
WEB: www.grantspub.com
SIC: 2721 Periodicals: publishing only

(G-10394)
GRAPHIC LAB INC
228 E 45th St Fl 4 (10017-3303)
PHONE......................212 682-1815
Fax: 212 682-5067
Richard Campisi, *President*
Carmine Campisi Jr, *Vice Pres*
Robert Campisi, *Treasurer*
Jeannette Duran, *Controller*
Albert Mahoney, *Accounts Exec*
EMP: 34
SQ FT: 7,600
SALES (est): 5.8MM Privately Held
WEB: www.gocdp.com
SIC: 2759 Commercial printing

(G-10395)
GRAPHICS FOR INDUSTRY INC
Also Called: Graphic For Industry
307 W 36th St Fl 10 (10018-6474)
PHONE......................212 889-6202
Fax: 212 545-1276
Mark Palmer, *President*
EMP: 10 EST: 1973
SQ FT: 5,000
SALES (est): 1MM Privately Held
SIC: 2759 Screen printing

(G-10396)
GRAPHIS INC
389 5th Ave Rm 1105 (10016-3350)
PHONE......................212 532-9387
Fax: 212 213-3229
B Martin Pedersen, *President*
Rachel Pedersen, *Editor*
Arna Pedersen, *Bookkeeper*
Tiffany F Washington, *Sales Mgr*
Bon Kong, *Chief Mktg Ofcr*
▲ EMP: 10
SQ FT: 5,000
SALES (est): 1.5MM Privately Held
WEB: www.graphis.com
SIC: 2721 2731 Magazines: publishing only, not printed on site; books: publishing only

(G-10397)
GRAVITY EAST VILLAGE INC
515 E 5th St (10009-6703)
PHONE......................212 388-9788
Michael J Perrine, *Chairman*
EMP: 7
SALES (est): 746.1K Privately Held
SIC: 3845 Colonoscopes, electromedical

(G-10398)
GREAT JONES LUMBER CORP
45 Great Jones St (10012-1627)
PHONE......................212 254-5560
Joseph Lauto, *President*
Anthony Lauto, *Vice Pres*
EMP: 15
SALES (est): 1.3MM Privately Held
SIC: 2421 Lumber: rough, sawed or planed; fuelwood, from mill waste

(G-10399)
GREAT NORTH ROAD MEDIA INC
Also Called: Sparkspread
3115 Broadway Apt 61 (10027-4647)
PHONE......................646 619-1355
Victor Kremer, *Ch of Bd*
Will Ainger, *Director*
EMP: 10
SALES (est): 537.5K Privately Held
SIC: 2711 Newspapers

(G-10400)
GREAT UNIVERSAL CORP
1441 Broadway Fl 5 (10018-1905)
PHONE......................917 302-0065
Grace Lu, *President*
◆ EMP: 10
SQ FT: 1,000
SALES: 10MM Privately Held
SIC: 2361 2321 Girls' & children's dresses, blouses & shirts; men's & boys' dress shirts

(G-10401)
GREEN GIRL PRTG & MSGNR INC
44 W 39th St (10018-3802)
PHONE......................212 575-0357
Alice Harford, *President*
Mark Frelow, *Manager*
EMP: 6
SALES (est): 400K Privately Held
SIC: 2752 Commercial printing, lithographic

(G-10402)
GREENBEADS LLC
Also Called: Emily and Ashley
220 E 72nd St Apt 17d (10021-4531)
PHONE......................212 327-2765
Emily Green, *Partner*
Ashley Green, *Partner*
EMP: 5
SALES (est): 350K Privately Held
WEB: www.greenbeads.com
SIC: 3961 Costume jewelry

(G-10403)
GREY STATE APPAREL LLC
305 7th Ave Ste 13a (10001-6008)
PHONE......................212 255-4216
Saima Chowdhury, *CEO*
Tara Curnen, *Manager*
EMP: 23 EST: 2015
SALES (est): 571.4K Privately Held
SIC: 2331 Women's & misses' blouses & shirts

(G-10404)
GRID TYPOGRAPHIC SERVICES INC
Also Called: Grid Typographic Svces
27 W 24th St Ste 9c (10010-3290)
PHONE......................212 627-0303
Fax: 212 627-1105
Donald Davidson, *President*
John Duffy, *Treasurer*
Robert Kerwick, *Manager*
Sy Schwartz, *Admin Sec*
EMP: 10
SQ FT: 3,300
SALES (est): 1.6MM Privately Held
WEB: www.gridtypography.com
SIC: 2791 Typesetting

(G-10405)
GRIFFON CORPORATION (PA)
712 5th Ave Fl 18 (10019-4108)
PHONE......................212 957-5000
Fax: 516 938-3779
Ronald J Kramer, *CEO*
Harvey R Blau, *Ch of Bd*
Robert F Mehmel, *President*
Seth L Kaplan, *Senior VP*
Brian G Harris, *CFO*
◆ EMP: 20
SQ FT: 10,000
SALES: 1.9B Publicly Held
WEB: www.griffoncorp.com
SIC: 3442 2431 1751 1799 Garage doors, overhead: metal; garage doors, overhead: wood; garage door, installation or erection; home/office interiors finishing, furnishing & remodeling; prefabricated fireplace installation; laminated plastics plate & sheet; laminated plastic sheets; radio & TV communications equipment

(G-10406)
GRILLBOT LLC
1562 1st Ave Ste 251 (10028-4004)
PHONE......................646 258-5639
Ethan Woods, *President*

New York - New York County (G-10407)   **GEOGRAPHIC SECTION**

EMP: 5
SALES (est): 807.2K **Privately Held**
SIC: 2842 Cleaning or polishing preparations

(G-10407)
GRIND
419 Park Ave S Fl 2 (10016-8410)
PHONE 646 558-3250
Christina Boland, *Opers Staff*
Bettina Warshaw, *Manager*
Melissa Williams, *Assistant*
EMP: 7
SALES (est): 821.2K **Privately Held**
SIC: 3599 Grinding castings for the trade

(G-10408)
GRINNELL DESIGNS LTD
260 W 39th St Rm 302 (10018-4434)
PHONE 212 391-5277
Fax: 212 391-5835
Francis De Ocampo, *President*
Larry Holliday, *Vice Pres*
Patricia Hudson, *Vice Pres*
EMP: 20
SQ FT: 4,000
SALES (est): 2MM **Privately Held**
WEB: www.grinnelldesigns.com
SIC: 3961 Costume jewelry

(G-10409)
GRIT ENERGY SERVICES INC ◆
100 Wall St Fl 11 (10005-3763)
PHONE 212 701-4500
Jennifer Wilson, *CFO*
EMP: 5 EST: 2017
SALES (est): 131.6K **Privately Held**
SIC: 1389 Oil field services

(G-10410)
GROHE AMERICA INC
160 5th Ave Fl 4 (10010-7065)
PHONE 212 206-8820
Maureen Ducret, *Human Resources*
Ivana Molzen MBA, *Manager*
Steven Rivas, *Manager*
EMP: 6 **Privately Held**
SIC: 2499 Laundry products, wood
HQ: Grohe America, Inc.
    200 N Gary Ave Ste G
    Roselle IL 60172
    630 582-7711

(G-10411)
GROLIER INTERNATIONAL INC (HQ)
557 Broadway (10012-3962)
PHONE 212 343-6100
Lisa Tarsi, *Principal*
EMP: 4
SALES (est): 2.3MM
SALES (corp-wide): 1.7B **Publicly Held**
SIC: 2731 Book publishing
PA: Scholastic Corporation
    557 Broadway Lbby 1
    New York NY 10012
    212 343-6100

(G-10412)
GROM COLUMBUS LLC
1796 Broadway (10019-1400)
PHONE 212 974-3444
Eran Keren, *Principal*
▲ EMP: 6 EST: 2010
SALES (est): 456.9K
SALES (corp-wide): 55.5B **Privately Held**
SIC: 2024 Ice cream, bulk
PA: Unilever Plc
    Unilever House
    London EC4Y
    207 822-5252

(G-10413)
GROUP COMMERCE INC (PA)
902 Broadway Fl 6 (10010-6039)
PHONE 646 346-0598
Jonty Kelt, *CEO*
David Lebow, *President*
Vibhav Prasad, *Senior VP*
Jared Augustine, *Vice Pres*
Andrea Gellert, *Vice Pres*
EMP: 13
SALES (est): 2.9MM **Privately Held**
SIC: 7372 Prepackaged software

(G-10414)
GROUP ENTERAINMENT LLC
115 W 29th St Rm 1102 (10001-5106)
PHONE 212 868-5233
Gill Holland,
EMP: 6
SALES (est): 552.6K **Privately Held**
SIC: 3571 Computers, digital, analog or hybrid

(G-10415)
GROUPE 16SUR20 LLC (PA)
Also Called: Seize Sur Vingt
198 Bowery (10012-4203)
P.O. Box 2280, Lenox MA (01240-5280)
PHONE 212 625-1620
James Jurney Jr, *Mng Member*
Karim Fresno, *Manager*
Eve Geller, *Administration*
EMP: 14
SQ FT: 2,000
SALES (est): 1.6MM **Privately Held**
SIC: 2329 2321 2325 Men's & boys' sportswear & athletic clothing; men's & boys' furnishings; men's & boys' trousers & slacks

(G-10416)
GROWNBEANS INC
110 Bank St Apt 2j (10014-2164)
PHONE 212 989-3486
Fax: 212 633-1181
Karen Groner, *President*
EMP: 5
SQ FT: 2,400
SALES (est): 458.1K **Privately Held**
SIC: 3172 Personal leather goods

(G-10417)
GRUNER & JAHR USA
375 Lexington Ave (10017-5644)
PHONE 212 782-7870
Fax: 212 499-2199
Gerd Schulte-Hillen, *President*
EMP: 13
SALES (est): 1MM **Privately Held**
SIC: 2741 Miscellaneous publishing

(G-10418)
GRUNER + JAHR PRTG & PUBG CO
Also Called: New York Times Co Mag Group
110 5th Ave Fl 7 (10011-5632)
PHONE 212 463-1000
Kari Johnston, *Sales Executive*
John Heins, *Manager*
EMP: 160
SALES (corp-wide): 522.4MM **Privately Held**
WEB: www.gjusa.com
SIC: 2721 7311 Magazines: publishing only, not printed on site; advertising agencies
PA: Gruner + Jahr Usa Group, Inc.
    1745 Broadway Fl 16
    New York NY 10019
    866 323-9336

(G-10419)
GRUNER + JAHR USA GROUP INC (PA)
Also Called: Gruner Jahr USA Publishing Div
1745 Broadway Fl 16 (10019-4640)
PHONE 866 323-9336
Mike Amundson, *President*
Gregg Black, *Exec VP*
Larry Hawkey, *Exec VP*
Dan Nitz, *Exec VP*
Yvette Miller, *Vice Pres*
◆ EMP: 500
SQ FT: 173,000
SALES (est): 522.4MM **Privately Held**
WEB: www.gjusa.com
SIC: 2721 2754 Periodicals: publishing & printing; magazines: publishing & printing; commercial printing, gravure

(G-10420)
GS DIRECT LLC
85 Broad St (10004-2434)
PHONE 212 902-1000
EMP: 4
SALES (est): 2.5MM
SALES (corp-wide): 28B **Publicly Held**
SIC: 3674 Semiconductors & related devices
PA: The Goldman Sachs Group Inc
    200 West St Bldg 200
    New York NY 10282
    212 902-1000

(G-10421)
GSCP EMAX ACQUISITION LLC
85 Broad St (10004-2434)
PHONE 212 902-1000
Henry M Paulson Jr, *CEO*
Michael Marsh, *Vice Pres*
Myo Zarny, *Vice Pres*
Nicole Gartzke, *Human Res Mgr*
EMP: 5
SALES (est): 454.4K **Privately Held**
SIC: 3442 Metal doors, sash & trim

(G-10422)
GUESS INC
575 5th Ave Lbby 1 (10017-2438)
PHONE 212 286-9856
EMP: 25
SALES (corp-wide): 2.2B **Publicly Held**
SIC: 2325 Men's & boys' jeans & dungarees
PA: Guess , Inc.
    1444 S Alameda St
    Los Angeles CA 90021
    213 765-3100

(G-10423)
GUEST INFORMAT LLC
Also Called: Quick Guide
110 E 42nd St Rm 1714 (10017-5611)
PHONE 212 557-3010
Fax: 212 557-3822
Lisa Nusynowitz, *Principal*
EMP: 13 **Privately Held**
SIC: 2741 Miscellaneous publishing
HQ: Guest Informat, L.L.C.
    21200 Erwin St
    Woodland Hills CA
    818 716-7484

(G-10424)
GUILD DIAMOND PRODUCTS INC (PA)
1212 Avenue Of The Americ (10036-1600)
PHONE 212 871-0007
Fax: 212 354-8455
Jacques H Elion, *President*
Douglas Panker, *Corp Secy*
▲ EMP: 13
SQ FT: 7,000
SALES (est): 1.4MM **Privately Held**
SIC: 3911 3915 Jewelry, precious metal; diamond cutting & polishing

(G-10425)
GUILFORD PUBLICATIONS INC
Also Called: Guilford Press
7 Penn Plz Ste 1200 (10001-1020)
PHONE 212 431-9800
Robert Matloff, *President*
Kevin Cox, *Publisher*
Judith Grauman, *Editor*
Jane Keislar, *Editor*
Anna Nelson, *Editor*
EMP: 75 EST: 1973
SQ FT: 10,000
SALES (est): 8.6MM **Privately Held**
WEB: www.guilford.com
SIC: 2741 2731 2721 7812 Miscellaneous publishing; books: publishing only; trade journals: publishing & printing; audio-visual program production

(G-10426)
GUILFORD PUBLICATIONS INC
Also Called: Guilford Press
370 7th Ave Ste 1200 (10001-1020)
PHONE 800 365-7006
Robert Matloff, *President*
Laura Patchkofsky, *Editor*
Mitch Goldblatt, *Human Res Dir*
Axel Davieau, *Marketing Staff*
Bambi Held, *Manager*
EMP: 6
SALES (est): 60.5K **Privately Held**
SIC: 2741 2731 Miscellaneous publishing; book publishing

(G-10427)
GUMUCHIAN FILS LTD
16 E 52nd St Ste 701 (10022-5307)
PHONE 212 593-3118
Fax: 212 593-9111
Irma Gumuchdjian, *President*
Patricia Jones, *Vice Pres*
Myriam Schreiber, *Vice Pres*
Andre Gumuchdjian, *Treasurer*
Chris Matty, *Accounts Mgr*
EMP: 15 EST: 1979
SQ FT: 1,700
SALES (est): 2.4MM **Privately Held**
WEB: www.gumuchianfils.com
SIC: 3911 5094 Jewelry, precious metal; precious stones (gems)

(G-10428)
GUNTHER PARTNERS LLC (HQ)
655 Madison Ave Fl 11 (10065-8043)
PHONE 212 521-2930
Fax: 212 688-0057
Barry Bloom, *Principal*
Thomas Tisch, *Mng Member*
Robert Spiegel,
Thomas M Steinberg,
EMP: 3
SALES (est): 13MM **Publicly Held**
SIC: 3577 Input/output equipment, computer
PA: Four Partners, Llc
    666 5th Ave Lowr L2
    New York NY
    212 841-1547

(G-10429)
GURWITCH PRODUCTS LLC (DH)
135 E 57th St Unit 106 (10022-2178)
PHONE 281 275-7000
Fax: 281 275-7070
Claudia Poccia, *CEO*
Joanne Chase, *Vice Pres*
Robert E Hurtte, *Vice Pres*
Renee McBride, *Vice Pres*
John Tedeschi, *Vice Pres*
▲ EMP: 56
SQ FT: 40,000
SALES (est): 52.8MM
SALES (corp-wide): 8.7B **Privately Held**
WEB: www.gurwitch.com
SIC: 2844 Cosmetic preparations
HQ: Alticor Inc.
    7575 Fulton St E
    Ada MI 49355
    616 787-1000

(G-10430)
GW ACQUISITION LLC
Also Called: G&W Industries
1370 Broadway Rm 1100 (10018-7774)
PHONE 212 736-4848
Fax: 212 736-4512
William Kawalick, *Controller*
Michael Marinoff, *Mng Member*
▲ EMP: 34
SALES (est): 4MM **Privately Held**
SIC: 2211 2361 2369 Apparel & outerwear fabrics, cotton; girls' & children's blouses & shirts; girls' & children's outerwear

(G-10431)
H & T GOLDMAN CORPORATION
2 W 46th St Ste 607 (10036-4566)
PHONE 800 822-0272
Fax: 212 869-0625
Nathan Goldman, *President*
EMP: 5
SQ FT: 1,200
SALES (est): 430K **Privately Held**
SIC: 3911 Jewelry, precious metal

(G-10432)
H BEST LTD
Moret Time
1411 Broadway Fl 8 (10018-3565)
PHONE 212 354-2400
Morris Chabott, *Director*
EMP: 10 **Privately Held**
SIC: 3873 Watches, clocks, watchcases & parts
PA: H. Best, Ltd.
    1411 Broadway Fl 8
    New York NY 10018

GEOGRAPHIC SECTION

New York - New York County (G-10458)

(G-10433)
H C KIONKA & CO INC
Also Called: Kimberley Diamond
15 Maiden Ln Ste 908 (10038-5118)
PHONE..................212 227-3155
Fax: 212 791-7731
Mark Levy, *President*
Mark Baum, *Vice Pres*
EMP: 13 EST: 1900
SQ FT: 2,500
SALES: 8MM Privately Held
WEB: www.kimberleydiamond.com
SIC: 3911 Jewelry apparel

(G-10434)
H GROUP INC
462 7th Ave Fl 9 (10018-7436)
PHONE..................212 719-5500
Joe Dahan, *President*
EMP: 15 EST: 1997
SALES (est): 157.9K Privately Held
SIC: 2241 Apparel webbing

(G-10435)
H K TECHNOLOGIES INC
303 5th Ave Rm 1707 (10016-6641)
PHONE..................212 779-0100
Fax: 212 779-4570
Rie Fechita, *Ch of Bd*
Nobutake Fujimura, *Manager*
Atsu Karino, *Manager*
Hiroto Kinoshita, *Administration*
EMP: 4
SQ FT: 800
SALES (est): 1.1MM Privately Held
WEB: www.hktechnologies.com
SIC: 3674 Semiconductors & related devices

(G-10436)
HACHETTE BOOK GROUP INC (DH)
1290 Ave Of The Americas (10104-0101)
PHONE..................800 759-0190
Fax: 212 364-0926
David Young, *Ch of Bd*
Zachary Gordon, *General Mgr*
EMI Battaglia, *Editor*
Tracy Behar, *Editor*
Deb Futter, *Editor*
◆ EMP: 350
SALES (est): 341.1MM
SALES (corp-wide): 62.3MM Privately Held
SIC: 2731 5192 Books: publishing only; books, periodicals & newspapers
HQ: Hachette Livre
   Istra Gecri Hachette Jeunesse
   Vanves 92170
   143 923-000

(G-10437)
HADDAD BROS INC (PA)
Also Called: Madonna
28 W 36th St Rm 1026 (10018-1290)
PHONE..................212 563-2117
Fax: 212 594-7325
Alan Haddad, *President*
Mac Haddad, *Chairman*
▲ EMP: 12
SQ FT: 3,500
SALES: 7.2MM Privately Held
WEB: www.haddadbros.com
SIC: 2321 2361 Men's & boys' furnishings; girls' & children's dresses, blouses & shirts

(G-10438)
HADDAD HOSIERY LLC
34 W 33rd St Rm 401 (10001-3342)
PHONE..................212 251-0022
Jack Haddad, *President*
▲ EMP: 5 EST: 2000
SALES (est): 437.6K Privately Held
SIC: 2252 Hosiery

(G-10439)
HAIGHTS CROSS CMMNICATIONS INC (PA)
136 Madison Ave Fl 8 (10016-6792)
PHONE..................212 209-0500
Fax: 212 209-0501
Rick Noble, *CEO*
Kevin R Brueggeman, *President*
Rich Freese, *President*
Julie Latzer, *Senior VP*
Diane Q Curtin, *Vice Pres*
▲ EMP: 32
SQ FT: 35,000
SALES (est): 99.1MM Privately Held
WEB: www.haightscross.com
SIC: 2731 Book publishing

(G-10440)
HAILO NETWORK USA INC
568 Broadway Fl 11 (10012-3374)
PHONE..................646 561-8552
EMP: 5 EST: 2012
SALES (est): 470K Privately Held
SIC: 7372 Prepackaged Software Services

(G-10441)
HALEYS COMET SEAFOOD CORP
605 3rd Ave Fl 34 (10158-3499)
PHONE..................212 571-1828
Robert Leone, *President*
EMP: 45
SALES: 1.5MM Privately Held
SIC: 2211 Long cloth, cotton

(G-10442)
HALMODE APPAREL INC
Also Called: Halmode Petite Div
1400 Brdwy 11th & Fl 16 (10018)
PHONE..................212 819-9114
Fax: 212 398-6462
Jay Diamond, *CEO*
Bea Myerson, *Exec VP*
Michael M Saunders, *Vice Pres*
John Winston, *CFO*
Meiling Loheng, *Manager*
▲ EMP: 600
SQ FT: 240,000
SALES (est): 31.8MM
SALES (corp-wide): 596MM Privately Held
SIC: 2339 2335 5137 Sportswear, women's; uniforms, athletic: women's, misses' & juniors'; maternity clothing; women's, juniors' & misses' dresses; women's & children's clothing
PA: Kellwood Company, Llc
   600 Kellwood Pkwy Ste 200
   Chesterfield MO 63017
   314 576-3100

(G-10443)
HALO ASSOCIATES
289 Bleecker St Fl 5 (10014-4106)
PHONE..................212 691-9549
EMP: 6
SQ FT: 7,000
SALES: 500K Privately Held
SIC: 3299 8999 Art Related Services

(G-10444)
HAMIL AMERICA INC
42 W 39th St Fl 15 (10018-2081)
PHONE..................212 244-2645
Jerry Miller, *President*
▲ EMP: 16
SALES (est): 1.4MM
SALES (corp-wide): 16.8MM Privately Held
WEB: www.algo.com
SIC: 2253 Knit outerwear mills
PA: Groupe Algo Inc
   5555 Rue Cypihot
   Saint-Laurent QC H4S 1
   514 388-8888

(G-10445)
HAMMERMAN BROS INC
Also Called: H2 At Hammerman
50 W 57th St Fl 12 (10019-3914)
PHONE..................212 956-2800
Fax: 212 956-2769
Brett Hammerman, *President*
Philip Begenstein, *General Mgr*
Darcy Hammerman, *Vice Pres*
Rose Dennis, *Controller*
EMP: 9
SQ FT: 10,000
SALES (est): 1.7MM Privately Held
WEB: www.hammermanbrothers.com
SIC: 3911 3873 Bracelets, precious metal; earrings, precious metal; necklaces, precious metal; rings, finger: precious metal; watches, clocks, watchcases & parts

(G-10446)
HAMPSHIRE SUB II INC (HQ)
114 W 41st St Fl 5 (10036-7308)
PHONE..................631 321-0923
Fax: 212 764-5747
Martin Axman, *President*
Christine Hadjigeorge, *Project Mgr*
Richard Isaacson, *CFO*
Robin Jackie, *Finance Mgr*
Mark Abramson, *VP Sales*
◆ EMP: 70
SQ FT: 7,000
SALES (est): 8.4MM
SALES (corp-wide): 91.4MM Publicly Held
WEB: www.item-eyes.com
SIC: 2337 2339 5137 Skirts, separate: women's, misses' & juniors'; jackets & vests, except fur & leather: women's; slacks: women's, misses' & juniors'; women's & children's clothing
PA: Hampshire Group, Limited
   1924 Pearman Dairy Rd A
   Anderson SC 29625
   212 540-5666

(G-10447)
HAMPTON PRESS INCORPORATED
307 7th Ave Rm 506 (10001-6079)
PHONE..................646 638-3800
Barbara Bernstein, *Owner*
EMP: 9
SALES (est): 730.5K Privately Held
SIC: 2741 Miscellaneous publishing

(G-10448)
HANDCRAFT MANUFACTURING CORP (PA)
34 W 33rd St Rm 401 (10001-3342)
PHONE..................212 251-0022
Fax: 212 251-0076
Isaac Mizrahi, *President*
Joseph I Mizrahi, *Corp Secy*
Marshall Mizrahi, *Treasurer*
Katie Voytko, *Sales Staff*
Asha Shah, *Manager*
▲ EMP: 30
SQ FT: 11,000
SALES (est): 15.2MM Privately Held
WEB: www.handcraftmfg.com
SIC: 2341 Women's & children's undergarments

(G-10449)
HANDSOME DANS LLC (PA)
186 1st Ave (10009-4002)
PHONE..................917 965-2499
EMP: 4 EST: 2012
SALES (est): 1.6MM Privately Held
SIC: 2064 Candy & other confectionery products

(G-10450)
HANDY & HARMAN LTD (DH)
Also Called: Hnh
590 Madison Ave Rm 3202 (10022-8536)
PHONE..................212 520-2300
Fax: 914 696-8684
Jack L Howard, *CEO*
Warren G Lichtenstein, *Ch of Bd*
William T Fejes Jr, *Senior VP*
James F McCabe Jr, *Senior VP*
Douglas B Woodworth, *CFO*
▼ EMP: 799
SALES: 828.3MM
SALES (corp-wide): 1.1B Publicly Held
WEB: www.whxcorp.com
SIC: 3339 3011 3312 Precious metals; tire & inner tube materials & related products; wire products, steel or iron
HQ: Sph Group Holdings Llc
   590 Madison Ave Fl 32
   New York NY 10022
   212 520-2300

(G-10451)
HANESBRANDS INC
16 E 34th St (10016-4328)
PHONE..................646 472-4117
Daphne McHone, *Sls & Mktg Exec*
Al Shealy, *Sales Executive*
Natalie Brant, *Branch Mgr*
Alison Carroll, *Manager*
William Curtiss, *Manager*
EMP: 10
SALES (corp-wide): 6B Publicly Held
SIC: 2253 T-shirts & tops, knit
PA: Hanesbrands Inc.
   1000 E Hanes Mill Rd
   Winston Salem NC 27105
   336 519-8080

(G-10452)
HANESBRANDS INC
260 Madison Ave Fl 6 (10016-2406)
PHONE..................212 576-9300
Kimberly Sorrano, *Office Mgr*
Marla Boggs, *Manager*
Bruce Blackwell, *Director*
EMP: 9
SALES (corp-wide): 6B Publicly Held
WEB: www.hanesbrands.com
SIC: 2211 5699 Apparel & outerwear fabrics, cotton; sports apparel
PA: Hanesbrands Inc.
   1000 E Hanes Mill Rd
   Winston Salem NC 27105
   336 519-8080

(G-10453)
HANIA BY ANYA COLE LLC
16 W 56th St Fl 4 (10019-3872)
PHONE..................212 302-3550
Fax: 212 302-3230
Anya Cole, *Mng Member*
Dhurata Kajtazaj, *Manager*
Sandre Verbeck, *Manager*
EMP: 8
SALES (est): 1MM Privately Held
SIC: 2253 Knit outerwear mills

(G-10454)
HANSA USA LLC
18 E 48th St Fl 3 (10017-1014)
PHONE..................646 412-6407
Abhi Gupta, *Controller*
Beth Wesel, *Accounts Mgr*
Andrew Fox, *Software Dev*
Eric Hu, *Director*
▲ EMP: 20
SALES (est): 3.4MM Privately Held
SIC: 3911 Jewelry, precious metal

(G-10455)
HANSAE CO LTD
501 Fashion Ave Rm 208 (10018-8611)
PHONE..................212 354-6690
Aesun Kim, *Mng Member*
EMP: 8
SALES (est): 855.1K
SALES (corp-wide): 1.2B Privately Held
SIC: 2331 2329 Women's & misses' blouses & shirts; T-shirts & tops, women's: made from purchased materials; men's & boys' sportswear & athletic clothing
PA: Hansae Co., Ltd.
   5/F Jungu Bldg.
   Seoul SEO 07238
   237 790-779

(G-10456)
HANSTEEL (USA) INC
230 Grand St Ste 602 (10013-4241)
PHONE..................212 226-0105
Lin Jie, *President*
EMP: 6
SALES: 4MM Privately Held
SIC: 3531 Construction machinery attachments

(G-10457)
HARD TEN CLOTHING INC
231 W 39th St Rm 606 (10018-0745)
PHONE..................212 302-1321
Jesse Battino, *Principal*
EMP: 5
SALES: 5MM Privately Held
SIC: 2361 5136 Shirts: girls', children's & infants'; shirts, men's & boys'

(G-10458)
HARLEY ROBERT D COMPANY LTD
240 W 35th St Ste 1005 (10001-2514)
PHONE..................212 947-1872
David Shapiro, *President*
▲ EMP: 6

(PA)=Parent Co (HQ)=Headquarters (DH)=Div Headquarters
◯ = New Business established in last 2 years

New York - New York County (G-10459)   GEOGRAPHIC SECTION

SALES: 5MM Privately Held
SIC: 2211 Apparel & outerwear fabrics, cotton

(G-10459)
HARPERCOLLINS
195 Broadway Fl 2 (10007-3132)
PHONE.................................212 207-7000
Erin Stadnik, Associate Dir
EMP: 9 EST: 2012
SALES (est): 153.5K Privately Held
SIC: 2741 Miscellaneous publishing

(G-10460)
HARPERCOLLINS PUBLISHERS LLC (HQ)
Also Called: William Morrow Publishing
195 Broadway Fl 2 (10007-3132)
PHONE.................................212 207-7000
Fax: 212 207-7222
Brian Murray, CEO
David Steinberger, President
Carrie Bachman, Publisher
Venetia Butterfield, Publisher
Miriam Parker, Publisher
▲ EMP: 600 EST: 1817
SQ FT: 260,000
SALES (est): 754.3MM
SALES (corp-wide): 8.1B Publicly Held
WEB: www.harpercollins.com
SIC: 2731 Books: publishing only
PA: News Corporation
1211 Ave Of The Americas
New York NY 10036
212 416-3400

(G-10461)
HARPERCOLLINS PUBLISHERS LLC
Harlequin & Silhouette Books
233 Broadway Rm 1001 (10279-1099)
PHONE.................................212 553-4200
Fax: 212 227-8969
David Galloway, Chairman
Eisbell Swift, Branch Mgr
Margaret Marbury, Manager
Leslie Wainger, Manager
Joan M Golan, Senior Editor
EMP: 43
SALES (corp-wide): 8.2B Publicly Held
SIC: 2731 Book publishing
HQ: Harpercollins Publishers L.L.C.
195 Broadway Fl 2
New York NY 10007
212 207-7000

(G-10462)
HARPERS MAGAZINE FOUNDATION
666 Broadway Fl 11 (10012-2394)
PHONE.................................212 420-5720
John Macarthur, President
John R Mc Arthur, President
Giulia Melucci, President
James Marcus, Editor
Lewis Lapham, Div Sub Head
EMP: 28
SQ FT: 7,800
SALES: 7.2MM Privately Held
SIC: 2721 Magazines: publishing only, not printed on site

(G-10463)
HARRISON SPORTSWEAR INC
Also Called: Eric Signature
260 W 39th St Fl 7 (10018-4410)
PHONE.................................212 391-1051
Eric Makofsky, President
Lemuel Shiuh, Vice Pres
Xie Ai Yi, Vice Pres
Malou Fernandez, Accountant
▲ EMP: 12
SQ FT: 3,000
SALES (est): 1.4MM Privately Held
WEB: www.randykemper.com
SIC: 2337 Pantsuits: women's, misses' & juniors'; skirts, separate: women's, misses' & juniors'; jackets & vests, except fur & leather: women's

(G-10464)
HARRY N ABRAMS INCORPORATED
Also Called: Stewart Tobori & Chang Div
195 Broadway Fl 9 (10007-3122)
PHONE.................................212 206-7715
Herve De La Martiniere, Ch of Bd
Michael Jacobs, Ch of Bd
Shawna Mullen, Publisher
Ashley Albert, Editor
Erin Barnett, Editor
▲ EMP: 94 EST: 1949
SQ FT: 30,000
SALES (est): 30.7MM
SALES (corp-wide): 408.6K Privately Held
WEB: www.hnabooks.com
SIC: 2731 Books: publishing only
PA: La Martiniere Groupe
25 Boulevard Romain Rolland
Paris
141 488-000

(G-10465)
HARRY WINSTON INC (DH)
718 5th Ave (10019-4195)
PHONE.................................212 399-1000
Fax: 212 489-6715
Nayla Hayek, CEO
Nancy Murray, Vice Pres
Robert Scott, CFO
Joseph Braun, Asst Controller
Laura Chan, Finance Mgr
▲ EMP: 110 EST: 1932
SQ FT: 18,000
SALES (est): 60.7MM
SALES (corp-wide): 7.4B Privately Held
SIC: 3911 5944 Jewelry, precious metal; jewelry, precious stones & precious metals; watches
HQ: Hw Holdings, Inc.
718 5th Ave
New York NY 10019
212 399-1000

(G-10466)
HARRYS INC (PA)
Also Called: Harry's Razor Company
161 Ave Of The (10013)
PHONE.................................888 212-6855
Fax: 212 366-1778
Andy Katz-Mayfield, CEO
Jeffrey Raider, Corp Secy
Ryan Dougherty, Prdtn Mgr
James J Borland, Branch Mgr
Rahil Esmail, Senior Mgr
▲ EMP: 59
SALES (est): 17MM Privately Held
SIC: 3634 Razors, electric

(G-10467)
HART ENERGY PUBLISHING LLLP
110 William St Fl 18 (10038-3901)
PHONE.................................212 621-4621
Kevin Higgins, Branch Mgr
EMP: 5
SALES (corp-wide): 43.3MM Privately Held
WEB: www.hartenergynetwork.com
SIC: 2721 2741 Magazines: publishing only, not printed on site; newsletter publishing
PA: Hart Energy Publishing Lllp
1616 S Voss Rd Ste 1000
Houston TX 77057
713 993-9320

(G-10468)
HART REPRODUCTION SERVICES
Also Called: Nyc Thermography
242 W 36th St Rm 801 (10018-8960)
PHONE.................................212 704-0556
Brett Greer, President
Patty Franks, Manager
EMP: 5
SQ FT: 7,400
SALES: 800K Privately Held
WEB: www.hartrepro.com
SIC: 2759 7331 Stationery: printing; mailing service

(G-10469)
HARVARD MAINTENANCE INC
245 Park Ave (10167-0002)
PHONE.................................212 682-2617
Cristina M Johns, Human Resources
EMP: 941
SALES (corp-wide): 98.4MM Privately Held
SIC: 3471 Cleaning, polishing & finishing
PA: Harvard Maintenance, Inc.
2 S Biscayne Blvd # 3650
Miami FL 33131
305 351-7300

(G-10470)
HARVARD UNIVERSITY PRESS
150 5th Ave Ste 632 (10011-4311)
PHONE.................................212 337-0280
Fax: 212 337-0259
Joyce Seltzer, Director
Kathleen McDermott, Executive
EMP: 100
SALES (est): 6.4MM Privately Held
SIC: 2731 Book publishing

(G-10471)
HASKELL JEWELS LTD (PA)
390 5th Ave Fl 2 (10018-8162)
PHONE.................................212 764-3332
Fax: 212 764-6026
Linda Fialkoss, Principal
Johanna Ortiz, Manager
▲ EMP: 50
SALES (est): 3.4MM Privately Held
SIC: 3911 Jewelry, precious metal

(G-10472)
HAUTE BY BLAIR STANLEY LLC
330 E 38th St Apt 23e (10016-2780)
PHONE.................................212 557-7868
EMP: 5
SQ FT: 1,000
SALES: 375K Privately Held
SIC: 2335 Mfg Women's/Misses' Dresses

(G-10473)
HAYMAN-CHAFFEY DESIGNS INC
137 E 25th St (10010-2314)
PHONE.................................212 889-7771
Charles R Hayman Chaffey, President
EMP: 10
SQ FT: 10,000
SALES (est): 700K Privately Held
SIC: 2511 Wood household furniture

(G-10474)
HAYMARKET GROUP LTD
Also Called: Chocolatier Magazine
12 W 37th St 9 (10018-7480)
PHONE.................................212 239-0855
Fax: 212 967-4184
EMP: 12
SQ FT: 3,000
SALES (est): 950K Privately Held
SIC: 2721 Magazine Publishers

(G-10475)
HAYMARKET MEDIA INC (DH)
Also Called: Prweek/Prescribing Reference
275 7th Ave Fl 10 (10001-6756)
PHONE.................................646 638-6000
Fax: 646 638-6150
Kevin Costello, CEO
Amey Bordikar, President
Dominic Barone, Publisher
Karmen Maurer, Publisher
Serena McMahon, Publisher
▲ EMP: 130
SQ FT: 27,000
SALES (est): 76.6MM
SALES (corp-wide): 270.3MM Privately Held
SIC: 2721 Magazines: publishing only, not printed on site

(G-10476)
HAYNES ROBERTS INC
601 W 26th St Rm 1655 (10001-1151)
PHONE.................................212 989-1901
Timothy Haynes, Owner
Vanessa Lacson, Project Mgr
Melanie Matoba, Project Mgr
Esteban Arboleda, Manager
Agustin Reynoso, Technology

▲ EMP: 15
SALES (est): 1.9MM Privately Held
SIC: 3679 Electronic components

(G-10477)
HC CONTRACTING INC
Also Called: Ferrara Manufacturing Company
318 W 39th St Fl 4 (10018-1493)
PHONE.................................212 643-9292
Fax: 212 971-5442
Carolyn Ferrara, President
Joseph Ferrara, Vice Pres
Alba Lema, Manager
◆ EMP: 60 EST: 1987
SQ FT: 25,000
SALES: 5MM Privately Held
WEB: www.ferraramfg.com
SIC: 2339 2326 Service apparel, washable: women's; service apparel (baker, barber, lab, etc.), washable: men's

(G-10478)
HEARST BUS COMMUNICATIONS INC (PA)
300 W 57th St (10019-3741)
PHONE.................................212 649-2000
Richard P Malloch, President
Barry J Green, Vice Pres
Peter Rowlinson, Vice Pres
Robert D Wilbanks, Treasurer
David L Kors, Asst Treas
EMP: 7 EST: 1980
SALES (est): 4.2MM Privately Held
SIC: 2721 Magazines: publishing only, not printed on site

(G-10479)
HEARST BUSINESS PUBLISHING INC
Also Called: Diversion Magazine
888 7th Ave Fl 2 (10106-0001)
PHONE.................................212 969-7500
Fax: 212 969-7563
Cathy Cavender, Principal
Mike Chan, MIS Dir
EMP: 16
SALES (corp-wide): 6.4B Privately Held
SIC: 2721 Periodicals
HQ: Hearst Business Publishing, Inc.
214 N Tryon St Fl 33
Charlotte NC 28202
704 348-8614

(G-10480)
HEARST COMMUNICATIONS INC (PA)
Also Called: San Francisco Chronicle
300 W 57th St (10019-3741)
PHONE.................................415 777-7825
William Hearst III, Ch of Bd
Steven Swarz, President
Oscar Villalon, Publisher
Connie Ballard, Editor
Karola Saekel Craib, Editor
▲ EMP: 1100
SQ FT: 100,000
SALES (est): 345MM Privately Held
WEB: www.telegram.com
SIC: 2711 Newspapers, publishing & printing

(G-10481)
HEARST COMMUNICATIONS INC (DH)
Also Called: Hearst Interactive Media
300 W 57th St (10019-3741)
PHONE.................................212 649-2000
Fax: 212 649-2166
Steven R Swartz, CEO
Mark E Aldam, President
Roberta Kowalishin, President
Joanna Coles, Editor
Stacy Morrison, Editor
EMP: 167
SALES (est): 25.9MM
SALES (corp-wide): 6.4B Privately Held
SIC: 2741 Miscellaneous publishing
HQ: Hearst Holdings Inc
300 W 57th St
New York NY 10019
212 649-2000

▲ = Import ▼ = Export
◆ = Import/Export

GEOGRAPHIC SECTION

New York - New York County (G-10505)

(G-10482)
HEARST CORPORATION (PA)
Also Called: Hearst Magazines
300 W 57th St Fl 42 (10019-3790)
PHONE...................................212 649-2000
Fax: 212 265-0169
Steven R Swartz, *President*
Mark E Aldam, *President*
John McKeon, *President*
David A Schirmer, *President*
Jayne Jamison, *Publisher*
▲ EMP: 2500
SQ FT: 166,612
SALES (est): 6.4B Privately Held
WEB: www.hearstcorp.com
SIC: **2721** 2731 2711 4832 Magazines: publishing only, not printed on site; books: publishing only; newspapers, publishing & printing; newspapers: publishing only, not printed on site; radio broadcasting stations; television broadcasting stations; news feature syndicate

(G-10483)
HEARST CORPORATION
Seventeen Magazine
300 W 57th St Fl 29 (10019-3741)
PHONE...................................212 649-3100
Joanna Saltz, *Editor*
EMP: 50
SALES (corp-wide): 6.4B Privately Held
SIC: **2721** Periodicals: publishing only
PA: The Hearst Corporation
   300 W 57th St Fl 42
   New York NY 10019
   212 649-2000

(G-10484)
HEARST CORPORATION
Also Called: Oprah Magazine
224 W 57th St Frnt 1 (10019-3212)
PHONE...................................212 903-5366
Fax: 212 977-4153
Jill Seelig, *Publisher*
Margaret Healy, *General Mgr*
Amy Gross, *Principal*
Naomi Barr, *Editor*
Alicia Bridgewater, *Editor*
EMP: 35
SALES (corp-wide): 6.4B Privately Held
WEB: www.hearstcorp.com
SIC: **2721** Magazines: publishing & printing
PA: The Hearst Corporation
   300 W 57th St Fl 42
   New York NY 10019
   212 649-2000

(G-10485)
HEARST CORPORATION
Also Called: Elle Magazine
1633 Broadway Fl 44 (10019-6708)
PHONE...................................212 767-5800
Laurie Abraham, *Principal*
Antoine D De Noyer, *Senior VP*
Peter Herbst, *Senior VP*
Donohue Tom, *Senior VP*
Scott Constantine, *Vice Pres*
EMP: 300
SALES (corp-wide): 6.4B Privately Held
WEB: www.popphoto.com
SIC: **2759** Magazines: printing
PA: The Hearst Corporation
   300 W 57th St Fl 42
   New York NY 10019
   212 649-2000

(G-10486)
HEARST CORPORATION
Also Called: Popular Mechanics
810 7th Ave (10019-5818)
PHONE...................................516 382-4580
Jay McGill, *Publisher*
Bob Carlquist, *General Mgr*
Greg O'Brien, *General Mgr*
Frank Bennack, *Vice Chairman*
Jeff Cohen, *Exec VP*
EMP: 60
SALES (corp-wide): 6.4B Privately Held
WEB: www.hearstcorp.com
SIC: **2721** Magazines: publishing only, not printed on site
PA: The Hearst Corporation
   300 W 57th St Fl 42
   New York NY 10019
   212 649-2000

(G-10487)
HEARST CORPORATION
Also Called: Marie Claire
1790 Broadway (10019-1412)
PHONE...................................212 830-2980
Fax: 212 541-4295
Lesley Jane Seymour, *Editor*
Liza Aelion, *Director*
EMP: 50
SALES (corp-wide): 6.4B Privately Held
WEB: www.hearstcorp.com
SIC: **2741** Miscellaneous publishing
PA: The Hearst Corporation
   300 W 57th St Fl 42
   New York NY 10019
   212 649-2000

(G-10488)
HEARST CORPORATION
Also Called: Esquire Magazine
300 W 57th St Fl 21 (10019-3741)
PHONE...................................212 649-4271
Fax: 212 649-4303
Jack Essig, *Vice Pres*
Natasha Zarinsky, *Manager*
EMP: 70
SALES (corp-wide): 6.4B Privately Held
SIC: **2721** Periodicals
PA: The Hearst Corporation
   300 W 57th St Fl 42
   New York NY 10019
   212 649-2000

(G-10489)
HEARST CORPORATION
Also Called: Seventeen Magazine
1440 Broadway Fl 13 (10018-2301)
PHONE...................................212 204-4300
Sabrina Weill, *Editor*
Kathy Riess, *Finance Mgr*
Howard Grier, *Associate*
EMP: 100
SALES (corp-wide): 6.4B Privately Held
WEB: www.hearstcorp.com
SIC: **2721** Periodicals
PA: The Hearst Corporation
   300 W 57th St Fl 42
   New York NY 10019
   212 649-2000

(G-10490)
HEARST CORPORATION
Also Called: Harper's Bazaar
300 W 57th St Fl 42 (10019-3790)
PHONE...................................212 903-5000
Fax: 212 262-7101
Jennifer Bruno, *Publisher*
Linda Nardi, *General Mgr*
Christopher Tosti, *General Mgr*
Pamela Fiori, *Editor*
Victoria Pedersen, *Editor*
EMP: 65
SALES (corp-wide): 6.4B Privately Held
WEB: www.hearstcorp.com
SIC: **2721** Magazines: publishing & printing
PA: The Hearst Corporation
   300 W 57th St Fl 42
   New York NY 10019
   212 649-2000

(G-10491)
HEARST CORPORATION
Hearst Magazines International
300 W 57th St Fl 42 (10019-3790)
PHONE...................................212 649-2275
Jane Fort, *Editor*
Charles Swift, *Vice Pres*
Ronald Doerfler, *CFO*
John Rohan Jr, *Treasurer*
Vicki Wellington, *Branch Mgr*
EMP: 50
SALES (corp-wide): 6.4B Privately Held
SIC: **2721** 2731 2711 Magazines: publishing only, not printed on site; books: publishing only; newspapers, publishing & printing; newspapers: publishing only, not printed on site
PA: The Hearst Corporation
   300 W 57th St Fl 42
   New York NY 10019
   212 649-2000

(G-10492)
HEARST DIGITAL STUDIOS INC
300 W 57th St (10019-3741)
PHONE...................................212 969-7552
Neeraj Khemlani, *Ch of Bd*
Mike Bachmann, *CFO*
EMP: 25
SQ FT: 2,500
SALES (est): 1.1MM Privately Held
SIC: **2741** 7371 ; computer software development & applications

(G-10493)
HEARST HOLDINGS INC (HQ)
300 W 57th St (10019-3741)
PHONE...................................212 649-2000
George R Hearst Jr, *Ch of Bd*
Tom Chiarella, *Editor*
Larry Doyle, *Editor*
Ken Kurson, *Editor*
John Richardson, *Editor*
▲ EMP: 10
SALES (est): 516.2MM
SALES (corp-wide): 6.4B Privately Held
SIC: **2721** 4841 Magazines: publishing only, not printed on site; cable television services
PA: The Hearst Corporation
   300 W 57th St Fl 42
   New York NY 10019
   212 649-2000

(G-10494)
HEART OF TEA
419 Lafayette St Fl 2f (10003-7033)
PHONE...................................917 725-3164
Gerami Masoud, *CEO*
EMP: 10 EST: 2014
SALES (est): 1.1MM Privately Held
SIC: **2086** Iced tea & fruit drinks, bottled & canned

(G-10495)
HEARTS OF PALM LLC
Also Called: Ruby Road
1411 Broadway Fl 23 (10018-3471)
PHONE...................................212 944-6660
Peter Aresty,
EMP: 45 Privately Held
SIC: **2339** Women's & misses' athletic clothing & sportswear
PA: Hearts Of Palm, Llc
   1411 Broadway Fl 25
   New York NY 10018

(G-10496)
HEARTS OF PALM LLC (PA)
Also Called: Ruby Road
1411 Broadway Fl 25 (10018-3496)
PHONE...................................212 944-6660
Raymond Barrick, *CFO*
Charlene Caminiti, *Credit Mgr*
Peter Aresty,
EMP: 55
SQ FT: 25,000
SALES (est): 9.2MM Privately Held
SIC: **2339** Women's & misses' athletic clothing & sportswear

(G-10497)
HEAT USA II LLC
35 E 21st St (10010-6212)
PHONE...................................212 564-4328
Mark Kohan, *Director*
EMP: 28
SALES (corp-wide): 2.4MM Privately Held
SIC: **2911** Oils, fuel
PA: Heat Usa Ii Llc
   11902 23rd Ave
   College Point NY 11356
   212 254-4328

(G-10498)
HELIUM MEDIA INC
Also Called: Heleo.com
165 Duane St Apt 7b (10013-3348)
PHONE...................................917 596-4081
Rufus Griscom, *CEO*
EMP: 5 EST: 2015
SALES (est): 157.9K Privately Held
SIC: **2741** Miscellaneous publishing

(G-10499)
HELVETICA PRESS INCORPORATED
Also Called: Vendome Press
244 5th Ave (10001-7604)
PHONE...................................212 737-1857
Fax: 212 737-5340
Mark Magowan, *President*
Alexis Gregory, *Chairman*
Steffanie Rouher, *Controller*
▲ EMP: 5
SQ FT: 3,000
SALES: 31.4K Privately Held
WEB: www.vendomepress.com
SIC: **2731** Books: publishing only

(G-10500)
HENRY B URBAN INC
Also Called: Delta Upholsterers
619 W 54th St Ste 6l (10019-3545)
PHONE...................................212 489-3308
James Congema, *CEO*
EMP: 30
SQ FT: 20,000
SALES: 3MM Privately Held
SIC: **2512** 2391 2511 7641 Upholstered household furniture; draperies, plastic & textile: from purchased materials; wood household furniture; reupholstery & furniture repair; household furnishings

(G-10501)
HENRY DUNAY DESIGNS INC
10 W 46th St Ste 1200 (10036-9312)
PHONE...................................212 768-9700
Henry Dunay, *President*
EMP: 30
SQ FT: 6,000
SALES (est): 3.8MM Privately Held
WEB: www.henrydunay.com
SIC: **3911** 5944 Jewelry, precious metal; jewelry stores

(G-10502)
HENRY HOLT AND COMPANY LLC
Also Called: Owl Books Div
175 5th Ave Ste 400 (10010-7726)
PHONE...................................646 307-5095
Sara Bershtel, *Publisher*
Gillian Blake, *Editor*
Barbara Jones, *Editor*
Jason Reigal, *Prdtn Mgr*
John Sterling, *Mng Member*
▲ EMP: 80
SQ FT: 30,000
SALES (est): 16.2MM
SALES (corp-wide): 1.5B Privately Held
WEB: www.henryholt.com
SIC: **2731** Books: publishing only
HQ: Macmillan Holdings, Llc
   175 5th Ave
   New York NY 10010

(G-10503)
HERALD PUBLISHING COMPANY LLC
4 Times Sq Fl 23 (10036-6518)
PHONE...................................315 470-2022
EMP: 6 EST: 2013
SALES (est): 273.9K Privately Held
SIC: **2711** Newspapers, publishing & printing

(G-10504)
HERBERT WOLF CORP
95 Vandam St Apt C (10013-1019)
PHONE...................................212 242-0300
Fax: 212 242-1133
Eric Wolf, *President*
EMP: 5 EST: 1947
SQ FT: 3,200
SALES: 552K Privately Held
SIC: **3534** 3599 Elevators & equipment; grinding castings for the trade

(G-10505)
HERMAN KAY COMPANY LTD
Also Called: Michael Kors
463 7th Ave Fl 12 (10018-7499)
PHONE...................................212 239-2025
Richard Kringstein, *Ch of Bd*
Barry Kringstein, *President*
▼ EMP: 250 EST: 2009
SALES (est): 13.9MM
SALES (corp-wide): 48.2MM Privately Held
SIC: **2337** 2339 2329 Women's & misses' suits & coats; women's & misses' outerwear; men's & boys' leather, wool & down-filled outerwear

New York - New York County (G-10506)

PA: Mystic Inc.
463 7th Ave Fl 12
New York NY 10018
212 239-2025

(G-10506)
HERSHEL HOROWITZ CORP
580 5th Ave Ste 901 (10036-0044)
PHONE.................................212 719-1710
Fax: 212 719-1713
Leibish Horowitz, *President*
Rachel Horowitz, *Treasurer*
Chaya Dachner, *Admin Sec*
EMP: 7
SQ FT: 1,300
SALES (est): 2.5MM **Privately Held**
SIC: 3915 Diamond cutting & polishing

(G-10507)
HESS CORPORATION (PA)
1185 Ave Of The Amer (10036-2601)
PHONE.................................212 997-8500
Fax: 212 536-8390
John B Hess, *CEO*
James H Quigley, *Ch of Bd*
Gregory P Hill, *COO*
Barclay Collins, *Exec VP*
Brian Bohling, *Senior VP*
▲ **EMP:** 254 **EST:** 1920
SALES: 4.8B **Publicly Held**
WEB: www.hess.com
SIC: 1311 2911 5171 5541 Crude petroleum production; natural gas production; petroleum refining; petroleum bulk stations; petroleum terminals; filling stations, gasoline; transmission, electric power

(G-10508)
HESS ENERGY EXPLORATION LTD (HQ)
1185 Ave Of The Americas (10036-2601)
PHONE.................................732 750-6500
Kevin B Wilcox, *Vice Pres*
Timothy B Goodell, *Vice Pres*
John P Reilly, *Vice Pres*
EMP: 3
SALES (est): 2MM
SALES (corp-wide): 4.8B **Publicly Held**
SIC: 1382 1311 Oil & gas exploration services; crude petroleum & natural gas production
PA: Hess Corporation
1185 Ave Of The Amer
New York NY 10036
212 997-8500

(G-10509)
HESS EXPLRTION PROD HLDNGS LTD (DH)
1185 Ave Of The Americas (10036-2601)
PHONE.................................732 750-6000
John P Rielly, *Vice Pres*
Kevin B Wilcox, *Vice Pres*
EMP: 3
SALES (est): 1.2MM
SALES (corp-wide): 4.8B **Publicly Held**
SIC: 1382 1311 Oil & gas exploration services; crude petroleum & natural gas production
HQ: Hess Energy Exploration Limited
1185 Ave Of The Americas
New York NY 10036
732 750-6500

(G-10510)
HESS OIL VIRGIN ISLAND CORP
1185 Ave Of The Amer 39 (10036-2603)
PHONE.................................212 997-8500
John Hess, *Ch of Bd*
Mary Quirk, *General Mgr*
Justin Mayer, *Top Exec*
Eloise Castillo, *Exec VP*
Doris Moore, *Exec VP*
EMP: 3000
SALES (est): 228.8MM
SALES (corp-wide): 4.8B **Publicly Held**
WEB: www.hess.com
SIC: 2911 Petroleum refining
PA: Hess Corporation
1185 Ave Of The Amer
New York NY 10036
212 997-8500

(G-10511)
HESS PIPELINE CORPORATION
1185 Ave Of The Amer 39 (10036-2603)
PHONE.................................212 997-8500
Fax: 212 536-8245
John Hess, *CEO*
Timothy B Goodell, *Principal*
EMP: 219
SALES (est): 25MM
SALES (corp-wide): 4.8B **Publicly Held**
WEB: www.hess.com
SIC: 1311 2911 Crude petroleum production; natural gas production; petroleum refining
PA: Hess Corporation
1185 Ave Of The Amer
New York NY 10036
212 997-8500

(G-10512)
HESS TIOGA GAS PLANT LLC
1185 Ave Of The Americas (10036-2601)
PHONE.................................212 997-8500
Jonathan C Stein, *Principal*
Theresa Hayden, *Credit Mgr*
John Hess,
EMP: 226 **EST:** 2012
SALES (est): 739.6K
SALES (corp-wide): 12.1MM **Privately Held**
SIC: 1311 Crude petroleum production; natural gas production
PA: Hess Tgp Holdings Llc
1501 Mckinney St
Houston TX

(G-10513)
HF MFG CORP (PA)
Also Called: Happy Fella
1460 Broadway (10036-7329)
P.O. Box 318, Hewlett (11557-0318)
PHONE.................................212 594-9142
Fax: 212 967-7148
Bruce Tucker, *President*
Michael Tucker, *Vice Pres*
Irene Weitz, *Controller*
Rob Juno, *Sales Associate*
◆ **EMP:** 8 **EST:** 1963
SQ FT: 2,000
SALES (est): 7.5MM **Privately Held**
WEB: www.hfmfgcorp.com
SIC: 2329 Men's & boys' sportswear & athletic clothing

(G-10514)
HFC PRESTIGE INTL US LLC
350 5th Ave (10118-0110)
PHONE.................................212 389-7800
Arelis Rodriguez, *Finance*
Patrice De Talhouet,
Kevin Monaco,
Michelle Garcia, *Asst Sec*
EMP: 3000 **EST:** 2015
SALES: 30MM
SALES (corp-wide): 65B **Publicly Held**
SIC: 2844 2676 3421 2842 Toilet preparations; towels, napkins & tissue paper products; razor blades & razors; specialty cleaning preparations; soap: granulated, liquid, cake, flaked or chip
PA: The Procter & Gamble Company
1 Procter And Gamble Plz
Cincinnati OH 45202
513 983-1100

(G-10515)
HH LIQUIDATING CORP
Also Called: Zinc Corporation America Div
110 E 59th St Fl 34 (10022-1308)
PHONE.................................646 282-2500
William E Flaherty, *Ch of Bd*
Robert D Scherich, *Vice Pres*
EMP: 843
SALES (est): 86MM **Privately Held**
SIC: 3624 2999 3356 3339 Carbon & graphite products; electrodes, thermal & electrolytic uses: carbon, graphite; carbon specialties for electrical use; coke, calcined petroleum: made from purchased materials; coke (not from refineries), petroleum; lead & zinc; zinc refining (primary), including slabs & dust

(G-10516)
HHS PHARMACEUTICALS INC
107 Hamilton Pl (10031-6821)
PHONE.................................347 674-1670
Richard Moreno, *CEO*
Wendy Chin, *COO*
EMP: 10
SALES (est): 409.5K **Privately Held**
SIC: 2899 2834 7389 Gelatin: edible, technical, photographic or pharmaceutical; lozenges, pharmaceutical; tinctures, pharmaceutical;

(G-10517)
HIGH POINT DESIGN LLC
1411 Broadway Fl 8 (10018-3565)
PHONE.................................212 354-2400
Mark Lopiparo, *CFO*
Jana Dittmer, *Executive Asst*
▲ **EMP:** 15
SQ FT: 20,000
SALES (est): 1.9MM **Privately Held**
SIC: 2252 Hosiery

(G-10518)
HIGH QUALITY VIDEO INC (PA)
12 W 27th St Fl 7 (10001-6903)
PHONE.................................212 686-9534
Fax: 212 686-9158
Hirofumy Imoto, *President*
Yuri Fukuda, *Info Tech Dir*
Fukuda Yuri, *Web Proj Mgr*
EMP: 10
SALES (est): 1.1MM **Privately Held**
SIC: 3652 Pre-recorded records & tapes

(G-10519)
HIGHCREST INVESTORS LLC (HQ)
445 Hamilton Ave Ste 1210 (10153)
PHONE.................................212 702-4323
Carl C Icahn, *Ch of Bd*
Keef Cozzi, *Manager*
EMP: 80
SQ FT: 25,000
SALES (est): 244MM
SALES (corp-wide): 1B **Privately Held**
SIC: 3743 4741 4789 4813 Freight cars & equipment; rental of railroad cars; railroad car repair; local telephone communications; long distance telephone communications;
PA: Starfire Holding Corporation
445 Hamilton Ave Ste 1210
White Plains NY 10601
914 614-7000

(G-10520)
HIGHLINE MEDIA LLC
375 Park Ave (10152-0002)
PHONE.................................859 692-2100
Andrew Goodenough, *President*
Thomas Flynn, *CFO*
EMP: 250
SALES (est): 8.2MM
SALES (corp-wide): 46.1MM **Privately Held**
WEB: www.highlinemedia.com
SIC: 2731 2711 2721 2741 Books: publishing only; pamphlets: publishing only, not printed on site; newspapers: publishing only, not printed on site; periodicals: publishing only; directories: publishing only, not printed on site
PA: Summit Business Media Holding Company
4157 Olympic Blvd Ste 225
Erlanger KY 41018
859 692-2100

(G-10521)
HILLARY MERCHANT INC
2 Wall St Ste 807 (10005-2001)
PHONE.................................646 575-9242
Zhaoxiong Zhang, *President*
EMP: 8 **EST:** 2012
SQ FT: 500
SALES: 1MM **Privately Held**
SIC: 2326 5621 Men's & boys' work clothing; ready-to-wear apparel, women's

(G-10522)
HILLS PET PRODUCTS INC (DH)
300 Park Ave (10022-7402)
PHONE.................................212 310-2000
N Thompson, *Principal*
EMP: 5
SALES (est): 4.8MM
SALES (corp-wide): 15.2B **Publicly Held**
SIC: 2047 Dog & cat food
HQ: Hill's Pet Nutrition, Inc.
400 Sw 8th Ave Ste 101
Topeka KS 66603
785 354-8523

(G-10523)
HIMATSINGKA AMERICA INC (DH)
261 5th Ave Rm 1400 (10016-7707)
PHONE.................................212 545-8929
Steve Zaffos, *President*
Dilip J Thakkar, *Chairman*
Ashutosh Halbe, *CFO*
▲ **EMP:** 24 **EST:** 2000
SQ FT: 10,600
SALES (est): 39.9MM
SALES (corp-wide): 196.3MM **Privately Held**
WEB: www.dwholdings.com
SIC: 2392 Bedspreads & bed sets: made from purchased materials

(G-10524)
HIMATSINGKA AMERICA INC
Also Called: Global Textile
261 5th Ave Rm 501 (10016-0036)
PHONE.................................212 252-0802
EMP: 24
SALES (corp-wide): 196.3MM **Privately Held**
WEB: www.divatex.com
SIC: 2221 Silk broadwoven fabrics
HQ: Himatsingka America Inc.
261 5th Ave Rm 1400
New York NY 10016
212 545-8929

(G-10525)
HIMATSINGKA HOLDINGS NA INC (HQ)
261 5th Ave Rm 1400 (10016-7707)
PHONE.................................212 545-8929
Amitabh Himatsingka, *Ch of Bd*
Shrikant Himatsingka, *President*
Ajoy Kumar Himatsingka, *Principal*
Dinesh Kumar Himatsingka, *Principal*
Rajiv Khaitan, *Chairman*
▲ **EMP:** 1
SALES (est): 43.3MM
SALES (corp-wide): 196.3MM **Privately Held**
SIC: 2221 Silk broadwoven fabrics
PA: Himatsingka Seide Limited
10/24, Kumarakrupa Road,
Bengaluru KAR 56000
802 237-8000

(G-10526)
HINGE INC
137 5th Ave Fl 5 (10010-7145)
PHONE.................................502 445-3111
Justin McLeod, *President*
Jean-Marie McGrath, *Administration*
EMP: 14
SALES (est): 960K **Privately Held**
SIC: 7372 Prepackaged software

(G-10527)
HIPPOCRENE BOOKS INC (PA)
171 Madison Ave Rm 1605 (10016-5113)
PHONE.................................212 685-4371
Fax: 212 779-9338
George Blagowidow, *President*
Jayne Salomon, *Manager*
▲ **EMP:** 6
SQ FT: 1,200
SALES (est): 825.9K **Privately Held**
WEB: www.hippocrenebooks.com
SIC: 2731 Books: publishing only

(G-10528)
HIS PRODUCTIONS USA INC
Also Called: Kingstreet Sounds
139 Fulton St Rm 317 (10038-2537)
PHONE.................................212 594-3737
Fax: 212 594-3636
Hisanao Ishioka, *President*
Robert Wunderman, *Manager*
EMP: 7

▲ = Import ▼ = Export
◆ = Import/Export

GEOGRAPHIC SECTION

New York - New York County (G-10554)

SALES (est): 1MM **Privately Held**
WEB: www.kingstreetsounds.com
SIC: 3652 5084 Pre-recorded records & tapes; recording instruments & accessories

(G-10529)
HISPANICA INTL DLGHTS AMER INC
Also Called: Hispanica Intl Delights Amer
575 Lexington Ave Fl 4 (10022-6146)
PHONE......................866 928-5070
Fernando Oswaldo Leonzo, *Ch of Bd*
John Romagosa, *President*
Robert Gunther, *COO*
Randy Berholtz, *Exec VP*
EMP: 11 **EST:** 2013
SALES: 2.4MM **Privately Held**
SIC: 2087 Beverage bases

(G-10530)
HISTORIC TW INC (HQ)
75 Rockefeller Plz (10019-6908)
PHONE......................212 484-8000
RE Turner, *Vice Ch Bd*
Richard D Parsons, *President*
Christopher P Bogart, *Exec VP*
Carl F Dill Jr, *Vice Pres*
Joseph Ripp, *CFO*
▲ **EMP:** 46
SQ FT: 451,000
SALES (est): 2.7B
SALES (corp-wide): 29.3B **Publicly Held**
SIC: 3652 6794 2741 7812 Compact laser discs, prerecorded; magnetic tape (audio): prerecorded; music licensing to radio stations; performance rights, publishing & licensing; music royalties, sheet & record; music, sheet: publishing only, not printed on site; music books: publishing only, not printed on site; motion picture production & distribution; television film production; motion picture production & distribution, television; video tape production; cable television services; magazines: publishing only, not printed on site
PA: Time Warner Inc.
1 Time Warner Ctr Bsmt B
New York NY 10019
212 484-8000

(G-10531)
HJN INC (PA)
Also Called: Bentones Enterprises
16 W 46th St Ste 900 (10036-4503)
PHONE......................212 398-9564
Fax: 212 575-1020
Joel Namdar, *Ch of Bd*
I Raj, *President*
H J Namdar, *Vice Pres*
▲ **EMP:** 15
SALES (est): 2.1MM **Privately Held**
SIC: 3911 Rings, finger: precious metal

(G-10532)
HK METAL TRADING LTD
450 Fashion Ave Ste 2300 (10123-2300)
PHONE......................212 868-3333
Kenny Chen, *Partner*
▼ **EMP:** 6
SQ FT: 350
SALES: 3MM **Privately Held**
SIC: 3399 Metal powders, pastes & flakes

(G-10533)
HKS PRINTING COMPANY INC
Also Called: Official Press, The
115 E 27th St (10016-8945)
PHONE......................212 675-2529
Fax: 212 691-6294
Inhyung You, *President*
Sue You, *Corp Secy*
EMP: 10
SALES (est): 940K **Privately Held**
SIC: 2752 2791 Lithographing on metal; typesetting

(G-10534)
HLP KLEARFOLD PACKAGING PDTS
Also Called: Hlp Klearfold Visualize
75 Maiden Ln Rm 808 (10038-4658)
PHONE......................718 554-3271
Steve Rothschild, *President*
Ada Lam, *Opers Mgr*
Glenn Levine, *Sales Mgr*

Pat McGee, *Mktg Dir*
Karen Werther, *Manager*
EMP: 10
SALES (est): 956.4K **Privately Held**
SIC: 3089 Closures, plastic

(G-10535)
HMS PRODUCTIONS INC (PA)
Also Called: Spencer Jeremy
250 W 39th St Fl 12 (10018-8215)
PHONE......................212 719-9190
Fax: 212 730-3581
Alex Goldberg, *President*
Spenser Alpern, *Chairman*
John Mow, *Exec Officer*
August Alpern, *Vice Pres*
Andrea Nimberger, *Vice Pres*
▲ **EMP:** 69
SQ FT: 14,000
SALES (est): 28.7MM **Privately Held**
WEB: www.nubby.com
SIC: 2399 Hand woven & crocheted products

(G-10536)
HNI CORPORATION
200 Lexington Ave Rm 1112 (10016-6219)
PHONE......................212 683-2232
Tom Talon, *President*
EMP: 226
SALES (corp-wide): 2.2B **Publicly Held**
WEB: www.honi.com
SIC: 2521 Wood office furniture
PA: Hni Corporation
600 E 2nd St
Muscatine IA 52761
563 272-7400

(G-10537)
HOGAN FLAVORS & FRAGRANCES
Also Called: Hogan Fragrances International
130 E 18th St Frnt (10003-2416)
PHONE......................212 598-4310
Fax: 212 477-4711
Ray Hogan, *Ch of Bd*
Kathy Ryan, *General Mgr*
Cory Warner, *Vice Pres*
Sean Hogan, *VP Sales*
EMP: 35
SQ FT: 3,000
SALES (est): 4.3MM **Privately Held**
WEB: www.hoganff.com
SIC: 2844 Perfumes & colognes

(G-10538)
HOLBROOKE INC
Also Called: Holbrooke By Sberry
444 E 20th St Apt 1b (10009-8142)
PHONE......................646 397-4674
EMP: 5
SALES (est): 322K **Privately Held**
SIC: 3961 Costume jewelry

(G-10539)
HOLDENS SCREEN SUPPLY CORP
121 Varick St (10013-1408)
PHONE......................212 627-2727
Arthur I Gononsky, *President*
EMP: 7
SALES (est): 319.8K **Privately Held**
SIC: 2711 Commercial printing & newspaper publishing combined

(G-10540)
HOLLAND & SHERRY INC (PA)
Also Called: Holland & Sherry Intr Design
330 E 59th St Ph (10022-1537)
PHONE......................212 542-8410
Sergio Casalena, *Ch of Bd*
Bryan Dicker, *President*
Tashaena Johnson, *Sales Staff*
Anna Watkins, *Manager*
▲ **EMP:** 29
SQ FT: 4,500
SALES (est): 18.9MM **Privately Held**
WEB: www.hollandandsherry.com
SIC: 2395 7389 2519 5021 Embroidery & art needlework; design services; garden furniture, except wood, metal, stone or concrete; furniture

(G-10541)
HOLLANDER HM FSHONS HLDNGS LLC
440 Park Ave S Fl 10 (10016-8012)
PHONE......................212 575-0400
Jeff Hollander, *President*
EMP: 10
SALES (corp-wide): 163MM **Privately Held**
WEB: www.hollander.com
SIC: 2392 Pillows, bed: made from purchased materials
PA: Hollander Home Fashions Holdings, Llc
6501 Congress Ave Ste 300
Boca Raton FL 33487
561 997-6900

(G-10542)
HOLLANDER SLEEP PRODUCTS LLC
440 Park Ave S (10016-8012)
PHONE......................212 575-0400
Donald Kelly, *Branch Mgr*
EMP: 79
SALES (corp-wide): 163MM **Privately Held**
SIC: 2392 Cushions & pillows
HQ: Hollander Sleep Products, Llc
6501 Congress Ave Ste 300
Boca Raton FL 33487
561 997-6900

(G-10543)
HOLMES GROUP THE INC
Also Called: Saber Awards
271 W 47th St Apt 23a (10036-1447)
PHONE......................212 333-2300
Fax: 212 333-2624
Paul Holmes, *President*
Greg Druey, *President*
Ben Edwards, *Vice Pres*
James Colman, *Corp Comm Staff*
EMP: 5
SALES (est): 540K **Privately Held**
WEB: www.holmesreport.com
SIC: 2721 Periodicals

(G-10544)
HOME FASHIONS INTL LLC (PA)
295 5th Ave Ste 1520 (10016-7126)
PHONE......................212 689-3579
Fax: 212 779-1946
Thomas Goldstein, *Controller*
David LI, *Mng Member*
EMP: 39
SQ FT: 3,600
SALES: 19MM **Privately Held**
SIC: 2392 Pillows, bed: made from purchased materials

(G-10545)
HOME FASHIONS INTL LLC
Also Called: Hfi
295 5th Ave Ste 1520 (10016-7126)
PHONE......................212 684-0091
Tom Goldstein, *Controller*
EMP: 15
SALES (corp-wide): 19MM **Privately Held**
SIC: 2392 Pillows, bed: made from purchased materials
PA: Home Fashions International, Llc
295 5th Ave Ste 1520
New York NY 10016
212 689-3579

(G-10546)
HONG HOP CO INC
Also Called: Hong Hop Noodle Company
10 Bowery (10013-5101)
P.O. Box 130364 (10013-0995)
PHONE......................212 962-1735
Fax: 212 732-0626
Dai Leong Hee, *President*
Sing Leong, *Corp Secy*
Chor Hee, *Manager*
EMP: 30 **EST:** 1931
SQ FT: 5,793
SALES (est): 3.8MM **Privately Held**
SIC: 2098 2099 2038 Noodles (e.g. egg, plain & water); dry; pasta, uncooked: packaged with other ingredients; snacks, including onion rings, cheese sticks, etc.

(G-10547)
HOOEK PRODUKTION INC
147 W 26th St Fl 6 (10001-6817)
PHONE......................212 367-9111
Joseph Primiano, *President*
▲ **EMP:** 7
SQ FT: 2,000
SALES (est): 974.3K **Privately Held**
SIC: 2752 Commercial printing, lithographic

(G-10548)
HOPE INTERNATIONAL PRODUCTIONS
315 W 57th St Apt 6h (10019-3145)
P.O. Box 237078 (10023-0029)
PHONE......................212 247-3188
David King, *Ch of Bd*
Hope King, *President*
EMP: 18
SQ FT: 1,800
SALES (est): 1.3MM **Privately Held**
SIC: 3652 3651 5099 1531 Phonograph records, prerecorded; magnetic tape (audio): prerecorded; video cassette recorders/players & accessories; phonograph records; tapes & cassettes, prerecorded; video cassettes, accessories & supplies; operative builders

(G-10549)
HORIZON FLOORS I LLC
11 Broadway Lbby 5 (10004-1330)
PHONE......................212 509-9686
Alex Shaoulpour, *President*
EMP: 1
SALES (est): 4MM **Privately Held**
SIC: 2426 Hardwood dimension & flooring mills

(G-10550)
HORLY NOVELTY CO INC
17 Ludlow St Frnt 2 (10002-6318)
PHONE......................212 226-4800
Fax: 212 226-4802
Joe Yip, *President*
Richard Joe, *Vice Pres*
Jack Lee, *Treasurer*
▲ **EMP:** 7
SALES (est): 440K **Privately Held**
SIC: 3961 Costume jewelry, ex. precious metal & semiprecious stones

(G-10551)
HORO CREATIONS LLC
Also Called: Designs By Hc
71 W 47th St Ste 404 (10036-2865)
PHONE......................212 719-4818
Suresh Krishnani, *President*
Vinay Krishnani,
EMP: 6
SALES (est): 618.8K **Privately Held**
SIC: 3911 Jewelry, precious metal

(G-10552)
HOSEL & ACKERSON INC (PA)
570 Fashion Ave Rm 805 (10018-1603)
PHONE......................212 575-1490
Monte Braverman, *President*
EMP: 5 **EST:** 1944
SALES (est): 559K **Privately Held**
SIC: 2258 2395 2269 Lace, knit; embroidery products, except schiffli machine; finishing plants

(G-10553)
HOSPITALITY GRAPHICS INC
545 8th Ave Rm 401 (10018-4341)
PHONE......................212 643-6700
Fax: 212 643-6784
Louis Melito, *President*
Marshall Silverman, *Treasurer*
Pat McNally, *Office Mgr*
EMP: 9
SQ FT: 3,500
SALES (est): 1.5MM **Privately Held**
WEB: www.hginyc.com
SIC: 2752 Commercial printing, offset

(G-10554)
HOSPITALITY INC
247 W 35th St 4 (10001-1908)
PHONE......................212 268-1930
Howard Pitler, *President*
EMP: 22

New York - New York County (G-10555) GEOGRAPHIC SECTION

SALES (est): 1.1MM **Privately Held**
SIC: 2759 6513 Commercial printing; apartment building operators

(G-10555)
HOT KISS INC
1407 Brdwy Ste 2000 (10018)
PHONE...................212 730-0404
Fax: 212 704-9687
Moshe Tsabag, *President*
EMP: 6
SALES (est): 551.8K **Privately Held**
SIC: 2325 Jeans: men's, youths' & boys'

(G-10556)
HOT SHOT HK LLC
1407 Broadway Rm 2018 (10018-2863)
PHONE...................212 921-1111
Marko Elenron, *Mng Member*
▲ EMP: 31
SALES (est): 7.1MM **Privately Held**
SIC: 2339 Women's & misses' athletic clothing & sportswear

(G-10557)
HOT SOX COMPANY INCORPORATED (PA)
Also Called: Polo Ralph Lauren Hosiery Div
95 Madison Ave Fl 15 (10016-7801)
PHONE...................212 957-2000
Fax: 212 957-1050
Gary Wolkowitz, *President*
Mark Gordon, *Senior VP*
Sarah Wolkowitz, *Treasurer*
Josephine Cordero, *Controller*
Eugene Merkushen, *Info Tech Dir*
▼ EMP: 40
SQ FT: 18,000
SALES (est): 6.4MM **Privately Held**
SIC: 2252 2251 Men's, boys' & girls' hosiery; women's hosiery, except socks

(G-10558)
HOUGHTON MIFFLIN HARCOURT PUBG
Also Called: Houghton Mifflin Clarion Books
3 Park Ave Fl 18 (10016-5902)
PHONE...................212 420-5800
Fax: 212 420-5855
Dorothy Briley, *Vice Pres*
Lori Glazer, *Vice Pres*
Dana Baylor, *Sales Mgr*
Ann Healy, *Manager*
Ruth Homberg, *Senior Mgr*
EMP: 40
SALES (corp-wide): 1.3B **Publicly Held**
WEB: www.hmco.com
SIC: 2731 Books: publishing only
HQ: Houghton Mifflin Harcourt Publishing Company
  125 High St Ste 900
  Boston MA 02110
  617 351-5000

(G-10559)
HOULES USA INC
979 3rd Ave Ste 1200 (10022-1234)
PHONE...................212 935-3900
Fax: 212 935-3923
Philippe Dasilva, *Manager*
EMP: 5
SALES (corp-wide): 1.3MM **Privately Held**
WEB: www.houlesusa.com
SIC: 3911 Trimmings for canes, umbrellas, etc.: precious metal
HQ: Houles Usa Inc
  8687 Melrose Ave Ste B617
  West Hollywood CA 90069
  310 652-6171

(G-10560)
HOUND & GATOS PET FOODS CORP
14 Wall St Fl 20 (10005-2123)
P.O. Box 11750, Atlanta GA (30355-1750)
PHONE...................212 618-1917
Will Post, *President*
EMP: 8
SQ FT: 25,000
SALES: 1.4MM **Privately Held**
WEB: www.houndgatos.com
SIC: 2047 Dog & cat food

(G-10561)
HOUSE OF HEYDENRYK JR INC
Also Called: House of Heydenryk The
601 W 26th St Rm 305 (10001-1159)
PHONE...................212 206-9611
Fax: 212 206-9615
Charles Schreiber, *President*
David Mandel, *Chairman*
Rigmor Heydenryk, *Admin Sec*
EMP: 18
SQ FT: 5,000
SALES (est): 1.4MM **Privately Held**
WEB: www.heydenryk.com
SIC: 2499 Picture & mirror frames, wood

(G-10562)
HOUSE OF PORTFOLIOS CO INC (PA)
37 W 26th St Rm 305 (10010-1047)
PHONE...................212 206-7323
Thomas Lombardo, *President*
Celia Sandiego, *Director*
EMP: 5
SQ FT: 900
SALES (est): 1.3MM **Privately Held**
WEB: www.houseofportfolios.com
SIC: 3172 5948 Personal leather goods; leather goods, except luggage & shoes

(G-10563)
HOUSE OF PORTFOLIOS CO INC
48 W 21st St (10010-6907)
PHONE...................212 206-7323
Thomas Lombardo, *Branch Mgr*
EMP: 17
SALES (corp-wide): 1.5MM **Privately Held**
WEB: www.houseofportfolios.com
SIC: 3172 Personal leather goods
PA: The House Of Portfolios Co Inc
  133 W 25th St Rm 7w
  New York NY 10010
  212 206-7323

(G-10564)
HOUSE PEARL FASHIONS (US) LTD
1410 Broadway Rm 1501 (10018-9834)
PHONE...................212 840-3183
Mehesh Seth, *President*
EMP: 10
SQ FT: 4,000
SALES (corp-wide): 106.6MM **Privately Held**
SIC: 2329 2339 Coats (oiled fabric, leatherette, etc.): men's & boys'; women's & misses' outerwear; women's & misses' accessories
HQ: House Of Pearl Fashions (Us) Ltd.
  300-2 D&E Rr 17
  Lodi NJ 07644
  973 778-7551

(G-10565)
HOVEE INC
722 Saint Nicholas Ave (10031-4002)
PHONE...................646 249-6200
Paul Kogan, *CEO*
EMP: 10
SALES (est): 593.6K **Privately Held**
SIC: 7372 7389 Business oriented computer software;

(G-10566)
HP INC
5 Penn Plz Ste 1912 (10001-1810)
PHONE...................212 835-1640
EMP: 52
SALES (corp-wide): 48.2B **Publicly Held**
WEB: www.3com.com
SIC: 3577 Computer peripheral equipment
PA: Hp Inc.
  1501 Page Mill Rd
  Palo Alto CA 94304
  650 857-1501

(G-10567)
HRG GROUP INC (PA)
450 Park Ave Fl 29 (10022-2640)
PHONE...................212 906-8555
Joseph S Steinberg, *Ch of Bd*
Omar M Asali, *President*
David M Maura, *Exec VP*
George Nicholson, *CFO*
EMP: 23 EST: 1954

SALES: 5.2B **Publicly Held**
WEB: www.zapatacorp.com
SIC: 3691 3634 3999 6311 Storage batteries; batteries, rechargeable; electric household cooking appliances; pet supplies; life insurance

(G-10568)
HS HOMEWORX LLC
18 E 74th St Fl 5 (10021-2612)
PHONE...................646 870-0406
Yvonne Franco, *Controller*
Harry Slatkin, *Mng Member*
EMP: 5
SALES (est): 355.8K **Privately Held**
SIC: 3999 7389 Candles;

(G-10569)
HUDSON ENVELOPE CORPORATION (PA)
Also Called: Jam Paper
135 3rd Ave (10003-2543)
PHONE...................212 473-6666
Fax: 212 473-7300
Michael Jacobs, *President*
Steve Levine, *Marketing Mgr*
Kelly Ennis, *Marketing Staff*
Caitlin Hare, *Marketing Staff*
Andrew Jacobs, *Director*
EMP: 25
SQ FT: 7,000
SALES (est): 4.6MM **Privately Held**
SIC: 2752 2759 Commercial printing, offset; envelopes: printing

(G-10570)
HUDSON NEWS INC
250 Greenwich St (10007-2140)
PHONE...................212 971-6800
Fax: 917 971-1880
EMP: 5 EST: 2011
SALES (est): 211.8K **Privately Held**
SIC: 2711 Newspapers, publishing & printing

(G-10571)
HUDSON PARK PRESS INC
232 Madison Ave Rm 1400 (10016-2918)
P.O. Box 774, Pine Plains (12567-0774)
PHONE...................212 929-8898
Gilman Park, *Ch of Bd*
▲ EMP: 5
SALES (est): 400.7K **Privately Held**
SIC: 2752 2731 Publication printing, lithographic; books: publishing only

(G-10572)
HUDSON PRINTING CO INC
747 3rd Ave Lbby 3 (10017-2810)
PHONE...................718 937-8600
Fax: 718 937-7710
Robert Bergman, *President*
Jeff Smith, *Mng Member*
Alan Bergman, *Admin Sec*
EMP: 25 EST: 1923
SQ FT: 33,000
SALES (est): 3.1MM **Privately Held**
WEB: www.hudsonprints.com
SIC: 2752 2789 Commercial printing, offset; bookbinding & related work

(G-10573)
HUDSON XINDE ENERGY INC (PA)
1 World Trade Ctr Fl 85 (10007-0103)
PHONE...................212 220-7112
David Boyd, *Ch of Bd*
Fuyan Chang, *President*
Timothy Craddock, *Senior VP*
Charles Fu, *Senior VP*
EMP: 5
SQ FT: 1,200
SALES (est): 914.6K **Privately Held**
SIC: 3589 5065 6799 Sewage treatment equipment; electronic parts & equipment; real estate investors, except property operators

(G-10574)
HUGO BOSS USA INC (HQ)
55 Water St Fl 48 (10041-3204)
PHONE...................212 940-0600
Andre Maeder, *CEO*
Anthony Lucia, *President*
Gretchen Ruoillard, *President*
Camilo Casallas, *General Mgr*

Lorena Dashnaw, *General Mgr*
◆ EMP: 75
SQ FT: 100,000
SALES (est): 293.9MM
SALES (corp-wide): 2.8B **Privately Held**
WEB: www.hugobossusa.com
SIC: 2311 2325 2337 5136 Men's & boys' suits & coats; men's & boys' trousers & slacks; women's & misses' suits & coats; suits: women's, misses' & juniors'; skirts, separate: women's, misses' & juniors'; jackets & vests, except fur & leather: women's; men's & boys' suits & trousers; men's & boys' sportswear & work clothing; men's & boys' outerwear; men's & boys' clothing stores; franchises, selling or licensing
PA: Hugo Boss Ag
  Dieselstr. 12
  Metzingen 72555
  712 394-0

(G-10575)
HUMAN CONDITION SAFETY INC
61 Broadway Fl 31 (10006-2803)
PHONE...................646 867-0644
Alexander R Baugh, *Ch of Bd*
Greg Wolyniec, *President*
Robert Price, *CFO*
Gary Foreman, *CTO*
EMP: 10
SALES (est): 1.7MM **Privately Held**
SIC: 7372 5099 Prepackaged software; safety equipment & supplies

(G-10576)
HUMAN LIFE FOUNDATION INC
271 Madison Ave Ste 1005 (10016-1006)
PHONE...................212 685-5210
Fax: 212 725-9793
Maria McFadden, *President*
Faith McFadden, *Vice Pres*
Rose Flynn, *Controller*
Ann Conlon, *Admin Sec*
EMP: 5 EST: 1974
SQ FT: 500
SALES: 628.8K **Privately Held**
WEB: www.humanlifereview.com
SIC: 2721 8399 8733 Periodicals: publishing only; social service information exchange; noncommercial research organizations

(G-10577)
HUMANA PRESS INC
233 Spring St Fl 6 (10013-1522)
PHONE...................212 460-1500
Fax: 212 807-1047
Thomas Lanigan Jr, *President*
Julia Lanigan, *Vice Pres*
Robin Weisberg, *Director*
▲ EMP: 40
SQ FT: 8,500
SALES (est): 2.2MM
SALES (corp-wide): 1.5B **Privately Held**
WEB: www.humanapr.com
SIC: 2741 2731 2721 Technical papers: publishing only, not printed on site; book clubs: publishing only, not printed on site; trade journals: publishing only, not printed on site
HQ: Springer Adis Us, Llc
  233 Spring St Fl 6
  New York NY 10013
  212 460-1500

(G-10578)
HUMANSCALE CORPORATION (PA)
11 E 26th St Fl 8 (10010-1425)
PHONE...................212 725-4749
Fax: 212 725-7545
Robert King, *CEO*
Heather Fennimore, *President*
Paul Levy, *President*
Michele Gerards, *Vice Pres*
Dave Cavanagh, *QC Mgr*
▲ EMP: 400
SQ FT: 10,000
SALES (est): 124.4MM **Privately Held**
SIC: 3577 2521 Computer peripheral equipment; wood office furniture

GEOGRAPHIC SECTION

New York - New York County (G-10608)

(G-10579)
HUMOR RAINBOW INCORPORATED
129 W 29th St Fl 10 (10001-5105)
PHONE.....................646 402-9113
Michael Maxim, *President*
EMP: 43
SALES (est): 1.6MM **Privately Held**
SIC: 2741 Miscellaneous publishing

(G-10580)
HUNTER DOUGLAS INC
979 3rd Ave (10022-1234)
PHONE.....................212 588-0564
David Shmil, *Branch Mgr*
EMP: 191 **Privately Held**
SIC: 2591 Window blinds
HQ: Hunter Douglas Inc.
  1 Blue Hill Plz Ste 1569
  Pearl River NY 10965
  845 664-7000

(G-10581)
HW HOLDINGS INC (DH)
718 5th Ave (10019-4102)
PHONE.....................212 399-1000
Nayla Hayek, *CEO*
EMP: 4
SALES (est): 60.7MM
SALES (corp-wide): 7.4B **Privately Held**
SIC: 3911 5944 6719 Jewelry, precious metal; jewelry, precious stones & precious metals; watches; investment holding companies, except banks
HQ: The Swatch Group Far East Distribution Ltd
  Seevorstadt 6
  Biel-Bienne BE 2502
  323 436-811

(G-10582)
HY GOLD JEWELERS INC
Also Called: Jj Marco
1070 Madison Ave Frnt 4 (10028-0229)
PHONE.....................212 744-3202
Mark Cohen, *President*
Julian Jaffe-Cohen, *Treasurer*
EMP: 5
SALES (est): 441.7K **Privately Held**
SIC: 3911 Jewelry, precious metal

(G-10583)
HYPERLAW INC
17 W 70th St Apt 4 (10023-4544)
PHONE.....................212 873-6982
Fax: 212 496-4138
Alan D Sugarman, *President*
EMP: 10
SALES (est): 830K **Privately Held**
WEB: www.hyperlaw.com
SIC: 7372 Publishers' computer software

(G-10584)
HYPOXICO INC
50 Lexington Ave Ste 249 (10010-2935)
PHONE.....................212 972-1009
Gary Kotliar, *President*
Yulia Soukhanova, *Vice Pres*
Brian Oe Strike, *Vice Pres*
Matt Eckert, *Manager*
▲ **EMP:** 6
SQ FT: 3,000
SALES (est): 500K **Privately Held**
WEB: www.hypoxico.com
SIC: 3949 Exercise equipment

(G-10585)
I LOVE ACCESSORIES INC
10 W 33rd St Rm 210 (10001-3326)
PHONE.....................212 239-1875
Daren Malles, *President*
▲ **EMP:** 5
SQ FT: 1,200
SALES: 5MM **Privately Held**
SIC: 3961 Costume jewelry

(G-10586)
I N K T INC
250 W 54th St Fl 9 (10019-5515)
PHONE.....................212 957-2700
Gary Winnick, *CEO*
Scott Jacobson, *COO*
Ed Ickowski, *Senior VP*
Jim Vickers, *Senior VP*
Saurabh Suri, *Vice Pres*
▲ **EMP:** 10
SALES (est): 1.6MM **Privately Held**
WEB: www.t-ink.com
SIC: 2759 5085 Commercial printing; ink, printers'

(G-10587)
I S C A CORP (PA)
Also Called: Elliot Lauren
512 7th Ave Fl 7 (10018-0862)
PHONE.....................212 719-5123
Fax: 212 719-1984
Elliot Grosovsky, *Ch of Bd*
Vijay Malani, *Controller*
▲ **EMP:** 16
SQ FT: 4,200
SALES (est): 4.7MM **Privately Held**
SIC: 2335 Women's, juniors' & misses' dresses

(G-10588)
I SPIEWAK & SONS INC
225 W 37th St Fl 15l (10018-6667)
PHONE.....................212 695-1620
Fax: 212 629-4803
Roy J Spiewak, *Ch of Bd*
Sol Jacobs, *Vice Pres*
Caron Bristol, *Manager*
Daniel Hendricks, *Manager*
▲ **EMP:** 35 **EST:** 1904
SQ FT: 10,000
SALES (est): 6.5MM **Privately Held**
SIC: 2329 Men's & boys' leather, wool & down-filled outerwear; field jackets, military; down-filled clothing: men's & boys'

(G-10589)
IAC SEARCH LLC (HQ)
555 W 18th St (10011-2822)
PHONE.....................212 314-7300
Barry Diller, *Chairman*
Ernest Wurzbach, *Senior VP*
Allan Chan, *Vice Pres*
Roman Degtyur, *Vice Pres*
Trish Lounsbury, *Vice Pres*
EMP: 41
SALES (est): 6MM
SALES (corp-wide): 3.1B **Publicly Held**
SIC: 7372 7375 Prepackaged software; information retrieval services; on-line data base information retrieval
PA: Iac/interactivecorp
  555 W 18th St
  New York NY 10011
  212 314-7300

(G-10590)
IAC/INTERACTIVECORP (PA)
555 W 18th St (10011-2822)
PHONE.....................212 314-7300
Mandy Ginsberg, *CEO*
Joseph Levin, *CEO*
Sean Moriarty, *CEO*
Sam Yagan, *CEO*
Victor A Kaufman, *Vice Ch Bd*
EMP: 3300
SQ FT: 202,500
SALES: 3.1B **Publicly Held**
WEB: www.usanetworks.com
SIC: 7372 7375 5961 Prepackaged software; information retrieval services; online data base information retrieval; catalog & mail-order houses

(G-10591)
IBIO INC
600 Madison Ave Ste 1601 (10022-1737)
PHONE.....................302 355-0650
Robert B Kay, *Ch of Bd*
Robert L Erwin, *President*
James Abbey, *Vice Pres*
Terence Ryan, *Security Dir*
EMP: 26 **EST:** 2008
SALES (est): 394K **Privately Held**
SIC: 2834 Pharmaceutical preparations

(G-10592)
IBIT INC
257 W 38th St Fl 2 (10018-4457)
PHONE.....................212 768-0292
Simon Ting, *President*
EMP: 30

SALES (est): 3.4MM **Privately Held**
WEB: www.ibit.com
SIC: 3543 7219 Industrial patterns; dressmaking service, material owned by customer

(G-10593)
IBRANDS INTERNATIONAL LLC
230 W 39th St (10018-4411)
PHONE.....................212 354-1330
Marc Garson, *Chairman*
Sylvia Lee, *Manager*
EMP: 16 **EST:** 2014
SQ FT: 4,200
SALES (est): 532.4K **Privately Held**
SIC: 2321 Polo shirts, men's & boys': made from purchased materials

(G-10594)
IBT MEDIA INC (PA)
Also Called: International Business Times
7 Hanover Sq Fl 5 (10004-2674)
PHONE.....................646 867-7100
Etienne Uzac, *President*
Alan Press, *President*
Thomas Hammer, *Senior VP*
Mitchell Caplan, *Chief Mktg Ofcr*
Emily Scheer, *Pub Rel Dir*
EMP: 40
SQ FT: 50,000
SALES (est): 32.9MM **Privately Held**
SIC: 2741

(G-10595)
IC TECHNOLOGIES LLC
475 Greenwich St (10013-1378)
PHONE.....................212 966-7895
Marcel Bekeyzer, *President*
Norah De Bekker, *Marketing Staff*
▲ **EMP:** 5
SALES (est): 577.4K **Privately Held**
SIC: 3674 Light emitting diodes

(G-10596)
ICARUS ENTERPRISES INC
568 Broadway Fl 11 (10012-3374)
PHONE.....................917 969-4461
Nicholas Hubbard, *President*
EMP: 5
SALES (est): 500K **Privately Held**
SIC: 2721 Magazines: publishing & printing

(G-10597)
ICER SCRUBS LLC
Also Called: Crocs Medical Apparel
1385 Broadway Fl 16 (10018-6041)
PHONE.....................212 221-4700
Lawrence Jemal, *Mng Member*
Iven Sandler, *Director*
▲ **EMP:** 10
SQ FT: 2,000
SALES (est): 591.2K **Privately Held**
SIC: 2335 Women's, juniors' & misses' dresses

(G-10598)
IDALIA SOLAR TECHNOLOGIES LLC
270 Lafayette St Ste 1402 (10012-3364)
PHONE.....................212 792-3913
Marc Dee,
Eric Laufer,
EMP: 9
SQ FT: 2,500
SALES (est): 500K **Privately Held**
SIC: 3674 Solar cells

(G-10599)
IDEAL BRILLIANT CO INC
580 5th Ave Ste 600 (10036-4726)
PHONE.....................212 840-2044
Meilech Fastag, *President*
Abe Fastag, *Vice Pres*
Chilly Fastag, *Manager*
EMP: 10
SQ FT: 2,000
SALES (est): 1.1MM **Privately Held**
WEB: www.idealbrilliant.com
SIC: 3915 Diamond cutting & polishing

(G-10600)
IDEAL CREATIONS INC
10 W 33rd St Rm 708 (10001-3306)
PHONE.....................212 563-5928
Moses Grunbaum, *President*
▲ **EMP:** 20

SALES (est): 1.1MM **Privately Held**
WEB: www.idealcreations.net
SIC: 2369 5136 Headwear: girls', children's & infants'; hats, men's & boys'

(G-10601)
IDENTIFYCOM INC
120 W 45th St Ste 2701 (10036-4041)
PHONE.....................212 235-0000
Debra Brown, *General Mgr*
Alexander Valcic, *Manager*
EMP: 8
SQ FT: 3,171
SALES (est): 530K **Privately Held**
SIC: 7372 Application computer software

(G-10602)
IDESCO CORP
37 W 26th St Fl 10 (10010-1097)
PHONE.....................212 889-2530
Andrew Schonzeit, *President*
EMP: 15
SALES (corp-wide): 31.5MM **Privately Held**
WEB: www.idesco.com
SIC: 2671 Packaging paper & plastics film, coated & laminated
PA: Idesco Corp.
  37 W 26th St Fl 10
  New York NY 10010
  212 889-2530

(G-10603)
IDOC SOFTWARE INC
191 Sint Nchlas Ave Apt 3 (10026)
PHONE.....................516 680-9090
EMP: 7
SALES (est): 94.4K **Privately Held**
SIC: 7372 Prepackaged software

(G-10604)
IDRA ALTA MODA LLC
200 West St 305 (10282-2102)
PHONE.....................914 644-8202
Jessica Soiser,
Adam Soiser,
EMP: 10 **EST:** 2009
SQ FT: 1,200
SALES (est): 1.1MM **Privately Held**
SIC: 2339 Women's & misses' outerwear

(G-10605)
IFG CORP
1372 Brdwy 12ae 12 Ae (10018)
PHONE.....................212 629-9600
EMP: 168
SALES (corp-wide): 43.5MM **Privately Held**
SIC: 2329 2339 Athletic (warmup, sweat & jogging) suits: men's & boys'; athletic clothing: women's, misses' & juniors'
PA: Ifg Corp.
  1400 Broadway Rm 2202
  New York NY 10018
  212 239-8615

(G-10606)
IFG CORP
463 7th Ave Fl 4 (10018-8725)
PHONE.....................212 239-8615
Ronald Adjmi, *President*
EMP: 5
SALES (corp-wide): 43.5MM **Privately Held**
SIC: 2329 Athletic (warmup, sweat & jogging) suits: men's & boys'
PA: Ifg Corp.
  1400 Broadway Rm 2202
  New York NY 10018
  212 239-8615

(G-10607)
IGC NEW YORK INC
580 5th Ave Ste 708 (10036-4725)
PHONE.....................212 764-0949
Zevi Sterling, *Principal*
EMP: 5
SALES (est): 510K **Privately Held**
WEB: www.igcgroup.com
SIC: 3915 Lapidary work & diamond cutting & polishing

(G-10608)
IGO INC (PA)
590 Madison Ave Rm 3202 (10022-8536)
PHONE.....................408 596-0061

New York - New York County (G-10609) — GEOGRAPHIC SECTION

Jack L Howard, *Ch of Bd*
Terry R Gibson, *President*
Leonard J McGill, *Vice Pres*
Christopher Rankin, *Sales Mgr*
James Doroz, *Administration*
◆ EMP: 50
SALES: 16.9MM Privately Held
WEB: www.mobilityelectronics.com
SIC: 3663 Mobile communication equipment

(G-10609)
IHEARTCOMMUNICATIONS INC
Also Called: Lite FM Radio
1133 Ave Americas Fl 34 (10036-6710)
PHONE..................212 603-4660
Fax: 212 603-4602
Robert Williams, *President*
EMP: 50 Publicly Held
SIC: 3663 Radio receiver networks
HQ: Iheartcommunications, Inc.
  200 E Basse Rd Ste 100
  San Antonio TX 78209
  210 822-2828

(G-10610)
IHI INC (HQ)
150 E 52nd St Fl 24 (10022-6246)
PHONE..................212 599-8100
Fax: 212 599-8111
Tsutomu Yoshida, *CEO*
Greg Brakefield, *Exec VP*
Jun Shigihara, *CFO*
▲ EMP: 27
SALES: 22MM
SALES (corp-wide): 13B Privately Held
WEB: www.ihiinc.ihi.co.jp
SIC: 3812 1731 Acceleration indicators & systems components, aerospace; energy management controls
PA: Ihi Corporation
  3-1-1, Toyosu
  Koto-Ku TKY 135-0
  362 047-800

(G-10611)
IKEDDI ENTERPRISES INC (PA)
1407 Brdwy Ste 2900 (10018)
PHONE..................212 302-7644
Fax: 212 302-7732
Raymond Salem, *Ch of Bd*
David Salem, *Vice Pres*
Bruce Cotter, *CFO*
▲ EMP: 12
SQ FT: 28,000
SALES (est): 4.3MM Privately Held
SIC: 2339 Sportswear, women's

(G-10612)
IKEDDI ENTERPRISES INC
1407 Broadway Rm 1805 (10018-2764)
PHONE..................212 302-7644
Raymond Salem, *Manager*
EMP: 6
SALES (corp-wide): 4.3MM Privately Held
SIC: 2339 Sportswear, women's
PA: Ikeddi Enterprises Inc.
  1407 Brdwy Ste 2900
  New York NY 10018
  212 302-7644

(G-10613)
IMAGINATION PLAYGROUND LLC
5 Union Sq W (10003-3306)
PHONE..................212 463-0334
Marc Hacker,
▲ EMP: 5
SALES (est): 576.5K Privately Held
SIC: 3949 Playground equipment

(G-10614)
IMAGINE COMMUNICATIONS CORP
Also Called: Harris Broadcast
1 Penn Plz Fl 39 (10119-0002)
PHONE..................212 303-4200
Charles Vogt, *CEO*
Ron Fehler, *Vice Pres*
Mary Mateo, *Financial Exec*
S Rosenfeld, *Branch Mgr*
Nathan Reed, *Info Tech Mgr*
EMP: 11
SALES (corp-wide): 6.6B Privately Held
SIC: 3663 Radio broadcasting & communications equipment; television broadcasting & communications equipment
HQ: Imagine Communications Corp.
  3001 Dallas Pkwy Ste 300
  Frisco TX 75034
  469 803-4900

(G-10615)
IMAGO RECORDING COMPANY (PA)
Also Called: Tigerstar Records
240 E 47th St Apt 20f (10017-2136)
PHONE..................212 751-3033
Terry Ellis, *President*
EMP: 5
SALES (est): 626.5K Privately Held
SIC: 3652 5099 Pre-recorded records & tapes; compact discs; phonograph records; tapes & cassettes, prerecorded

(G-10616)
IMEK MEDIA LLC
32 Broadway Ste 511 (10004-1665)
PHONE..................212 422-9000
Kemi Osukoya,
EMP: 20 EST: 2012
SALES (est): 1.5MM Privately Held
SIC: 2721 Magazines: publishing only, not printed on site

(G-10617)
IMENA JEWELRY MANUFACTURER INC
2 W 45th St Ste 1000 (10036-4252)
PHONE..................212 827-0073
Fax: 212 827-0418
Paul Yan, *President*
Cindy Yan, *Office Mgr*
EMP: 15
SALES (est): 1.7MM Privately Held
SIC: 3911 Jewelry, precious metal

(G-10618)
IMG THE DAILY
432 W 45th St Fl 5 (10036-3503)
PHONE..................212 541-5640
George Maier, *Principal*
Lynn Longendyke, *Vice Pres*
Justin Clements, *Consultant*
EMP: 5
SALES (est): 345.5K Privately Held
SIC: 2711 Newspapers, publishing & printing

(G-10619)
IMOBILE OF NY LLC
Also Called: Imobile of Ny-Sprint
649 Broadway (10012-2302)
PHONE..................212 505-3355
Ed Debevics, *Branch Mgr*
EMP: 5 Privately Held
SIC: 3663 Mobile communication equipment
HQ: Imobile Of Ny, Llc
  207 Terminal Dr
  Plainview NY 11803

(G-10620)
IMPERIAL-HARVARD LABEL CO
Also Called: Harvard Woven Label
236 W 40th St Fl 3 (10018-1692)
PHONE..................212 736-8420
Ira I Altfeder, *President*
Larry Saputo, *Treasurer*
EMP: 10
SQ FT: 3,000
SALES (est): 1.2MM Privately Held
SIC: 2241 Labels, woven

(G-10621)
IMPRESSIONS INC
36 W 37th St Rm 400 (10018-7497)
PHONE..................212 594-5954
Fax: 212 594-5266
John Baise, *Principal*
EMP: 5
SALES (est): 732.2K Privately Held
SIC: 2721 Periodicals: publishing only

(G-10622)
IN MOCEAN GROUP LLC (PA)
463 Fashion Ave Fl 21 (10018-7595)
PHONE..................212 944-0317
Max Anteby, *Exec VP*
Roger Gordon, *Senior VP*
Anthony Francese, *VP Sales*
Angelina Gorman, *Chief Mktg Ofcr*
Jim Zaremba, *CTO*
▲ EMP: 95 EST: 2000
SQ FT: 12,000
SALES (est): 12.3MM Privately Held
SIC: 2369 Bathing suits & swimwear: girls', children's & infants'

(G-10623)
IN MODA COM INC
241 W 37th St Rm 803 (10018-6810)
PHONE..................718 788-4466
Marco Scaba, *President*
Judy Scaba, *Vice Pres*
EMP: 23
SALES (est): 1.6MM Privately Held
SIC: 2339 Sportswear, women's

(G-10624)
IN-STEP MARKETING INC (PA)
Also Called: Z Card North America
39 Broadway Fl 32 (10006-3047)
PHONE..................212 797-3450
Fax: 212 797-1530
Tim Kunhardt, *President*
Jeremy Shaw, *CFO*
Edgar Millington, *Controller*
Magda Cygan, *Accounts Exec*
Andrzej Jamroz, *Manager*
EMP: 15
SQ FT: 6,600
SALES (est): 1.5MM Privately Held
WEB: www.zcardna.com
SIC: 2752 5199 8742 Promotional printing, lithographic; advertising specialties; marketing consulting services

(G-10625)
INCITEC PIVOT LIMITED
120 Broadway Fl 32 (10271-3299)
PHONE..................212 238-3010
EMP: 5
SALES (est): 383.5K Privately Held
SIC: 2819 Chemicals, high purity: refined from technical grade

(G-10626)
INCON GEMS INC
Also Called: Jeypore Group
2 W 46th St Ste 603 (10036-4561)
PHONE..................212 221-8560
Fax: 212 302-5404
Raju Gupta, *President*
EMP: 15
SQ FT: 2,000
SALES (est): 1.6MM Privately Held
SIC: 3911 5094 Jewelry, precious metal; precious stones (gems)

(G-10627)
INCYCLE SOFTWARE CORP (PA)
1120 Ave Of The Americas (10036-6700)
PHONE..................212 626-2608
Fredric Persoon, *President*
Claude Ramillard, *Partner*
Leo Vidosola, *Partner*
Martin Rajotte, *COO*
Julie Beaulieu, *CFO*
EMP: 9
SALES (est): 956.8K Privately Held
SIC: 7372 Prepackaged software

(G-10628)
IND REV LLC
1385 Broadway Fl 16 (10018-6041)
PHONE..................212 221-4700
Lawrence Jemal, *Mng Member*
▲ EMP: 10
SALES (est): 1.2MM Privately Held
SIC: 2331 Women's & misses' blouses & shirts

(G-10629)
INDEGY INC
154 Grand St (10013-3141)
PHONE..................866 801-5394
Barak Perelman, *CEO*
EMP: 30
SALES (est): 637.2K Privately Held
SIC: 7372 7382 Prepackaged software; security systems services

(G-10630)
INDEX MAGAZINE
526 W 26th St Rm 920 (10001-5540)
PHONE..................212 243-1428
Fax: 212 243-1603
Peter Halley, *Owner*
Scott Dixon, *Manager*
EMP: 6
SALES (est): 300K Privately Held
WEB: www.indexmagazine.com
SIC: 2721 Magazines: publishing & printing

(G-10631)
INDIA ABROAD PUBLICATIONS INC
102 Madison Ave Frnt B (10016-7592)
PHONE..................212 929-1727
Fax: 212 627-9503
Ajit Balakrishnan, *President*
Prem Panicker, *Editor*
Arti Patel, *Mktg Dir*
Gopal Raju, *Systems Mgr*
Tony Lobo, *Systems Analyst*
EMP: 59
SQ FT: 6,500
SALES (est): 4.5MM Privately Held
SIC: 2711 Newspapers: publishing only, not printed on site

(G-10632)
INDIGO HOME INC
230 5th Ave Ste 1916 (10001-7730)
PHONE..................212 684-4146
Taniya Kapoor, *Ch of Bd*
◆ EMP: 6
SALES (est): 725.5K Privately Held
WEB: www.indigohome.com
SIC: 2392 Blankets, comforters & beddings

(G-10633)
INDONESIAN IMPORTS INC (PA)
Also Called: Elliot Lucca
339 5th Ave Fl 2 (10016-5016)
PHONE..................888 800-5899
Fax: 212 545-1207
Mark A Talucchi, *CEO*
Todd Elliott, *President*
Kristin Wilcox, *Vice Pres*
Staci Battino, *Sales Staff*
Lauren Turetsky, *Info Tech Mgr*
▲ EMP: 30
SQ FT: 52,000
SALES (est): 11.4MM Privately Held
WEB: www.elliottlucca.com
SIC: 3911 5961 Earrings, precious metal; jewelry, mail order

(G-10634)
INDUSTRIAL RAW MATERIALS LLC
112 W 56th St (10019-3841)
PHONE..................212 688-8080
Keith Aufhauser,
EMP: 8 EST: 2011
SALES (est): 737.6K Privately Held
SIC: 2999 Waxes, petroleum: not produced in petroleum refineries

(G-10635)
INFINITY AUGMENTED REALITY INC
228 Park Ave S 61130 (10003-1502)
PHONE..................917 677-2084
Motti Kushnir, *CEO*
Moshe Hogeg, *Ch of Bd*
Enon Landenberg, *President*
Ortal Zanzuri, *CFO*
EMP: 6
SALES (est): 163.2K Privately Held
SIC: 7372 7371 Prepackaged software; custom computer programming services; computer software development & applications

(G-10636)
INFINITY SOURCING SERVICES LLC
224 W 35th St Ste 902 (10001-2534)
PHONE..................212 868-2900
Ray Kim, *Mng Member*
EMP: 8
SALES: 22MM Privately Held
SIC: 2335 Women's, juniors' & misses' dresses

▲ = Import ▼ = Export
◆ = Import/Export

GEOGRAPHIC SECTION

New York - New York County (G-10663)

(G-10637)
INFOBASE PUBLISHING COMPANY (PA)
Also Called: Films Media Group
132 W 31st St Fl 17 (10001-3406)
PHONE.................................212 967-8800
Mark D McDonnell, *Ch of Bd*
David Giuffre, *Editor*
Jonathan Leith, *Editor*
Jeff Soloway, *Editor*
Jared McGinley, *Regional Mgr*
EMP: 1 EST: 1999
SALES (est): 12.7MM **Privately Held**
SIC: **2731** 7372 Books: publishing only; prepackaged software

(G-10638)
INFOPRO DIGITAL INC
Also Called: Incisive Rwg, Inc.
55 Broad St Fl 22 (10004-2511)
PHONE.................................212 457-9400
Tim Weller, *President*
Ed Bean, *Editor*
Rex Bossert, *Editor*
Pamela Brownstein, *Editor*
Su A Carranza, *Editor*
EMP: 138
SQ FT: 92,000
SALES (est): 16MM **Privately Held**
WEB: www.riskwaters.com
SIC: **2731** Book publishing
HQ: Infopro Digital Limited
    Haymarket House, 28-29 Haymarket
    London
    207 316-9000

(G-10639)
INFOR GLOBAL SOLUTIONS INC (DH)
641 Avenue Of Americas (10011)
PHONE.................................646 336-1700
James Schaper, *CEO*
Bill Ellis, *President*
Justin Ali, *Project Mgr*
Luanne Jackson, *Accounting Dir*
Jodi Gilardi, *Sales Mgr*
EMP: 94
SALES: 39.5MM
SALES (corp-wide): 2.8B **Privately Held**
SIC: **7372** Prepackaged software
HQ: Infor (Us), Inc.
    13560 Morris Rd Ste 4100
    Alpharetta GA 30004
    678 319-8000

(G-10640)
INFORMA SOLUTIONS INC
Also Called: Analytics Intell
45 Rockefeller Plz # 2000 (10111-3193)
PHONE.................................516 543-3733
David Bissainthe, *President*
EMP: 48 EST: 2015
SQ FT: 200
SALES (est): 1.1MM **Privately Held**
SIC: **7372** 7373 7374 Prepackaged software; computer integrated systems design; data processing & preparation; data processing service

(G-10641)
INFORMATICA LLC
810 7th Ave Ste 1100c (10019-7597)
PHONE.................................212 845-7650
Fax: 212 845-7651
EMP: 11
SALES (corp-wide): 199.8MM **Privately Held**
SIC: **7372** Prepackaged software
HQ: Informatica Llc
    2100 Seaport Blvd
    Redwood City CA 94063

(G-10642)
INFORMERLY INC
35 Essex St (10002-4712)
PHONE.................................646 238-7137
Ranjan Roy, *CEO*
Emily Moss, *President*
EMP: 5
SALES (est): 270K **Privately Held**
SIC: **7372** Prepackaged software

(G-10643)
INKKAS LLC
38 E 29th St Rm 6r (10016-7963)
PHONE.................................646 845-9803
Daniel Ben-Mun, *Mng Member*
EMP: 6
SALES (est): 698K **Privately Held**
SIC: **3021** Canvas shoes, rubber soled

(G-10644)
INNOVANT INC
37 W 20th St Ste 209 (10011-3721)
PHONE.................................212 929-4883
Tom Navaretta, *Plant Mgr*
Antony Imbriolo, *Project Mgr*
Mark Scher, *Project Mgr*
Carl Clark, *Opers Mgr*
Eric Leclaire, *Engineer*
EMP: 100
SALES (corp-wide): 31.3MM **Privately Held**
WEB: www.innovant.com
SIC: **2521** Wood office furniture
PA: Innovant, Inc.
    135 Oval Dr
    Islandia NY 11749
    631 348-1900

(G-10645)
INNOVANT INC
37 W 20th St Ste 1101 (10011-3713)
PHONE.................................212 929-4883
Fax: 212 929-5174
Charles Braham, *Branch Mgr*
EMP: 6
SALES (corp-wide): 31.3MM **Privately Held**
WEB: www.innovant.com
SIC: **2511** Kitchen & dining room furniture
PA: Innovant, Inc.
    135 Oval Dr
    Islandia NY 11749
    631 348-1900

(G-10646)
INNOVATIVE DESIGNS LLC
141 W 36th St Fl 8 (10018-6980)
PHONE.................................212 695-0892
Warren Collin, *Human Res Mgr*
Douglas Haber, *Mng Member*
Jody Rullo, *Manager*
▲ EMP: 34
SQ FT: 8,000
SALES (est): 60MM **Privately Held**
SIC: **2678** 3944 Stationery products; craft & hobby kits & sets

(G-10647)
INO-TEX LLC
135 W 36th St Fl 6 (10018-9482)
PHONE.................................212 400-2205
Yongjun Yu, *Director*
EMP: 6
SALES (est): 406K
SALES (corp-wide): 542.5MM **Privately Held**
SIC: **2299** Batts & batting: cotton mill waste & related material; ramie yarn, thread, roving & textiles
PA: Jiangsu Lianfa Textile Co., Ltd.
    No. 88 Henglian Road, Chengdong Town, Haian County
    Nantong 22660
    513 888-6906

(G-10648)
INOLIFE TECHNOLOGIES INC (PA)
11 E 86th St Ste 19b (10028-0501)
PHONE.................................212 348-5600
Elizabeth A Cirone, *CEO*
Mark Corrao, *CFO*
EMP: 6
SALES (est): 711.5K **Publicly Held**
WEB: www.centale.com
SIC: **2834** 2835 Veterinary pharmaceutical preparations; pregnancy test kits

(G-10649)
INORI JEWELS
580 5th Ave (10036-4701)
PHONE.................................347 703-5078
Guy Israeli, *Owner*
EMP: 10 EST: 2014
SALES (est): 680.4K **Privately Held**
SIC: **3911** Jewelry, precious metal

(G-10650)
INPORA TECHNOLOGIES LLC
1501 Broadway (10036-5601)
PHONE.................................646 838-2474
Ron Siddons, *CEO*
EMP: 99
SALES (est): 5.4MM **Privately Held**
SIC: **3577** Computer peripheral equipment

(G-10651)
INPROTOPIA CORPORATION
401 W 110th St Apt 2001 (10025-2445)
PHONE.................................917 338-7501
Souyun Lee, *CEO*
WEI-Yeh Lee, *Exec VP*
EMP: 11 EST: 2011
SALES (est): 616.4K **Privately Held**
SIC: **7372** 7373 7371 Business oriented computer software; systems software development services; computer software systems analysis & design, custom

(G-10652)
INSIGHT VENTURE PARTNERS IV
1114 Avenue Of The Americ (10036-7703)
PHONE.................................212 230-9200
Alex Crisses, *Partner*
EMP: 150
SALES (est): 120.2K **Privately Held**
SIC: **7372** Prepackaged software

(G-10653)
INSPIRED ENTERTAINMENT INC (PA)
250 W 57th St Ste 2223 (10107-0013)
PHONE.................................646 565-3861
Luke L Alvarez, *CEO*
A Lorne Weil, *Ch of Bd*
David G Wilson, *COO*
Steven R Rogers, *Senior VP*
Daniel Silvers, *Security Dir*
EMP: 5
SALES (est): 525.9K **Publicly Held**
SIC: **7372** 7993 7999 Prepackaged software; arcades; gambling & lottery services

(G-10654)
INSTANT STREAM INC
Also Called: Stream Police
1271 Ave Of The Americas (10020-1300)
PHONE.................................917 438-7182
Michael Daly III, *CEO*
EMP: 32
SALES (est): 2.3MM **Privately Held**
SIC: **2752** Commercial printing, lithographic

(G-10655)
INSTITUTE OF ELECTRICAL AND EL
Ieee Communications Society
3 Park Ave Fl 17 (10016-5902)
PHONE.................................212 705-8900
Sonia Fahmy, *Vice Chairman*
Robert Heath, *Vice Chairman*
Kerrianne Sullivan, *Project Mgr*
Paul Morris, *Manager*
Suk-Chae Lee, *Senior Mgr*
EMP: 25
SALES (corp-wide): 480.3MM **Privately Held**
SIC: **2721** Trade journals: publishing & printing
PA: The Institute Of Electrical And Electronics Engineers Incorporated
    3 Park Ave Fl 17
    New York NY 10016
    212 419-7900

(G-10656)
INSTITUTIONAL INVESTER
1120 Ave Of The Amrcs Fl (10036-6700)
PHONE.................................212 224-3300
Patricia Bertucci, *Publisher*
Steve Brull, *Publisher*
Aaron Finkel, *Publisher*
Elayne Glick, *Publisher*
Kristin Hebert, *Publisher*
EMP: 5 EST: 2008
SALES (est): 387.2K **Privately Held**
SIC: **2721** Periodicals

(G-10657)
INT TRADING USA LLC
261 W 35th St Ste 1100 (10001-1900)
PHONE.................................212 760-2338
Sung Pak,
▲ EMP: 230 EST: 2004
SALES (est): 33.5MM **Privately Held**
SIC: **2325** 2339 Men's & boys' trousers & slacks; women's & misses' outerwear

(G-10658)
INTEGRATED COPYRIGHT GROUP
Also Called: Evergreen
1745 Broadway 19 (10019-4640)
PHONE.................................615 329-3999
John Barker, *President*
EMP: 22
SALES (est): 1.4MM **Privately Held**
SIC: **2741** Music, sheet: publishing only, not printed on site

(G-10659)
INTEGRATED GRAPHICS INC (PA)
Also Called: I C S
7 W 36th St Fl 12 (10018-7154)
PHONE.................................212 592-5600
James Kearns, *President*
Jay Beber, *Vice Pres*
Ronne N Carlton, *Administration*
Ann Todd,
Celeste Oria, *Social Worker*
EMP: 5
SALES (est): 3.3MM **Privately Held**
WEB: www.integratedgraphics.com
SIC: **2759** 8748 Commercial printing; business consulting

(G-10660)
INTELLICELL BIOSCIENCES INC
460 Park Ave Fl 17 (10022-1860)
PHONE.................................646 576-8700
Steven A Victor, *Ch of Bd*
Leonard Mazur, *COO*
Anna Rhodes, *Exec VP*
▼ EMP: 6
SALES (est): 712K **Privately Held**
SIC: **2834** Dermatologicals

(G-10661)
INTELLIGIZE INCORPORATED (PA)
230 Park Ave Fl 7 (10169-0935)
PHONE.................................571 612-8580
Rob Peters, *Engineer*
Mark Klinker, *Finance Mgr*
Todd Hicks, *VP Sales*
Rodrick Anderson, *Accounts Mgr*
James Batty, *Accounts Mgr*
EMP: 14
SALES (est): 2.2MM **Privately Held**
SIC: **7372** Business oriented computer software

(G-10662)
INTELLIGNC THE FTR CMPTNG NWSL
Also Called: Intelligence Newsletter
360 Central Park W (10025-6541)
P.O. Box 20008 (10025-1510)
PHONE.................................212 222-1123
Edward Rosenfeld, *Owner*
EMP: 10
SALES (est): 400K **Privately Held**
WEB: www.eintelligence.com
SIC: **2721** Periodicals

(G-10663)
INTELLITRAVEL MEDIA INC (DH)
530 Fashion Ave Rm 201 (10018-4821)
PHONE.................................646 695-6700
Nancy Telliho, *Ch of Bd*
Harold Shain, *President*
Erik Torkells, *Editor*
Monique Lewis, *Manager*
EMP: 8
SALES (est): 782.3K
SALES (corp-wide): 3.1B **Publicly Held**
SIC: **2721** Magazines: publishing only, not printed on site
HQ: The Daily Beast Company Llc
    7 Hanover Sq
    New York NY 10004
    212 445-4600

New York - New York County (G-10664)

(G-10664)
INTER PARFUMS INC (PA)
551 5th Ave (10176-0001)
PHONE.................................212 983-2640
Jean Madar, *Ch of Bd*
Philippe Benacin, *President*
Alex Canavan, *Vice Pres*
Russell Greenberg, *CFO*
Lisa Schuessling, *Asst Controller*
▲ EMP: 88
SQ FT: 16,800
SALES: 521MM **Publicly Held**
WEB: www.interparfumsinc.com
SIC: 2844 Toilet preparations; perfumes & colognes; cosmetic preparations

(G-10665)
INTERACTION INSIGHT CORP
750 3rd Ave Fl 9 (10017-2718)
PHONE.................................800 285-2950
Timothy J Feldmann, *President*
EMP: 9 EST: 2014
SQ FT: 1,000
SALES: 3MM **Privately Held**
SIC: 3651 Recording machines, except dictation & telephone answering

(G-10666)
INTERAXISSOURCINGCOM INC
41 E 11th St Fl 11 (10003-4602)
PHONE.................................212 905-6001
Donald Taffurelli, *President*
Christopher Jara, *Senior VP*
▲ EMP: 50
SQ FT: 1,000
SALES (est): 4.6MM **Privately Held**
SIC: 2231 Apparel & outerwear broadwoven fabrics

(G-10667)
INTERBRAND LLC
1 W 37th St Fl 9 (10018-5354)
PHONE.................................212 840-9595
Bob McMeekin, *President*
EMP: 9
SALES (corp-wide): 9MM **Privately Held**
WEB: www.interbrandllc.com
SIC: 2321 Men's & boys' furnishings
PA: Interbrand Llc
225 Dupont St Ste 2
Plainview NY 11803
516 349-5884

(G-10668)
INTERCEPT PHARMACEUTICALS INC (PA)
10 Hudson Yards Fl 37 (10001-2160)
PHONE.................................646 747-1000
Paolo Fundaro, *Ch of Bd*
Mark Pruzanski, *President*
Jerome B Durso, *COO*
Sandip S Kapadia, *CFO*
David Shapiro, *Chief Mktg Ofcr*
EMP: 72
SQ FT: 49,000
SALES: 24.9MM **Publicly Held**
SIC: 2834 Pharmaceutical preparations

(G-10669)
INTERCOTTON COMPANY INC
888 7th Ave Fl 29 (10106-2899)
PHONE.................................212 265-3809
Herman Landman, *President*
EMP: 3
SALES: 8.9MM **Privately Held**
SIC: 2389 Men's miscellaneous accessories

(G-10670)
INTERFACEFLOR LLC
330 5th Ave Fl 12 (10001-3213)
PHONE.................................212 686-8284
Fax: 212 213-5139
Pete Waldron, *Manager*
EMP: 25
SALES (corp-wide): 958.6MM **Publicly Held**
WEB: www.ca.interfaceinc.com
SIC: 2273 Finishers of tufted carpets & rugs
HQ: Interfaceflor, Llc
1503 Orchard Hill Rd
Lagrange GA 30240
706 882-1891

(G-10671)
INTERHELLENIC PUBLISHING INC
Also Called: Estiator
421 7th Ave Ste 810 (10001-2002)
PHONE.................................212 967-5016
Fax: 212 643-1642
Peter Makrias, *President*
EMP: 7
SQ FT: 1,500
SALES: 1.2MM **Privately Held**
WEB: www.estiator.com
SIC: 2721 Magazines: publishing only, not printed on site

(G-10672)
INTERNATIONAL AIDS VACCINE INI (PA)
125 Broad St Fl 9 (10004-2743)
PHONE.................................212 847-1111
Fax: 212 847-1112
Alex Godwin Coutinho, *Ch of Bd*
Margaret McGlynn, *President*
Thomas P Monath, *Partner*
David N Cook, *COO*
Lynn Doren, *Senior VP*
EMP: 104
SQ FT: 32,000
SALES: 72.3MM **Privately Held**
WEB: www.iavi.org
SIC: 2836 8731 Vaccines; commercial physical research

(G-10673)
INTERNATIONAL BUS MCHS CORP
Also Called: IBM
55 Broad St Fl 27 (10004-2563)
PHONE.................................212 324-5000
Jim Hertzig, *Software Engr*
Carol Moore, *Director*
EMP: 40
SALES (corp-wide): 79.9B **Publicly Held**
WEB: www.ibm.com
SIC: 3674 Computer logic modules
PA: International Business Machines Corporation
1 New Orchard Rd Ste 1
Armonk NY 10504
914 499-1900

(G-10674)
INTERNATIONAL DATA GROUP INC
Also Called: Idg Technetwork
117 E 55th St Ste 204 (10022-3502)
PHONE.................................212 331-7883
EMP: 30
SALES (corp-wide): 3.5B **Privately Held**
SIC: 2721 8732 7389 Periodicals-Publishing/Printing Commercial Nonphysical Research Business Services
PA: International Data Group, Inc.
1 Exeter Plz Fl 15
Boston MA 02116
617 534-1200

(G-10675)
INTERNATIONAL DESIGN ASSOC LTD
Also Called: Life Plus Style
747 3rd Ave Rm 218 (10017-2878)
PHONE.................................212 687-0333
Robin Nedboy, *President*
Steven Kletz, *Vice Pres*
▲ EMP: 8
SQ FT: 3,500
SALES (est): 3.5MM **Privately Held**
SIC: 2678 3999 5999 Stationery products; candles; toiletries, cosmetics & perfumes

(G-10676)
INTERNATIONAL DIRECT GROUP INC
Also Called: Idg
525 7th Ave Rm 208 (10018-5280)
PHONE.................................212 921-9036
Fax: 212 921-9038
Haynes Holding, *CEO*
Joel Ratner, *Exec VP*
Wesley Matthews, *CFO*
▲ EMP: 30

SALES (est): 6.4MM **Privately Held**
WEB: www.internationaldg.com
SIC: 2331 7389 Blouses, women's & juniors': made from purchased material; design services

(G-10677)
INTERNATIONAL INSPIRATIONS LTD (PA)
Also Called: Lux Accessories
358 5th Ave Rm 501 (10001-2228)
PHONE.................................212 465-8500
Saul Shaya Reiter, *CEO*
Maninder Kaur, *Controller*
▲ EMP: 48
SQ FT: 1,000
SALES (est): 14.3MM **Privately Held**
SIC: 3961 Costume jewelry

(G-10678)
INTERNATIONAL INSURANCE SOC
101 Murray St Fl 4 (10007-2132)
PHONE.................................212 815-9291
Fax: 212 815-9297
Douglas Leatherdale, *Ch of Bd*
Patrick W Kenny, *President*
Brian P Greig, *Partner*
Jesper D Jespersen, *Partner*
Andries Terblanche, *Partner*
EMP: 8
SALES: 2.4MM **Privately Held**
WEB: www.iisonline.org
SIC: 3825 Network analyzers

(G-10679)
INTERNATIONAL MGT NETWRK
445 Park Ave Fl 9 (10022-8606)
PHONE.................................646 401-0032
Jeff Krantz, *President*
EMP: 15
SALES: 950K **Privately Held**
SIC: 7372 Prepackaged software

(G-10680)
INTERNATIONL STUDIOS INC
108 W 39th St Rm 1300 (10018-3614)
PHONE.................................212 819-1616
Alan S Ginsberg, *President*
EMP: 5
SALES (est): 360K **Privately Held**
SIC: 2211 Apparel & outerwear fabrics, cotton

(G-10681)
INTERNTNAL FLVORS FRGRNCES INC (PA)
Also Called: IFF
521 W 57th St (10019-2929)
PHONE.................................212 765-5500
Fax: 212 708-7119
Andreas Fibig, *Ch of Bd*
Matthias Haeni, *President*
Anne Chwat, *Exec VP*
Francisco Fortanet, *Exec VP*
Gregory Yep, *Exec VP*
◆ EMP: 180 EST: 1909
SALES: 3.1B **Publicly Held**
WEB: www.iff.com
SIC: 2869 2844 2087 Flavors or flavoring materials, synthetic; perfume materials, synthetic; toilet preparations; flavoring extracts & syrups

(G-10682)
INTERNTNL PUBLCATNS MEDIA GRUP
708 3rd Ave Ste 145 (10017-4201)
PHONE.................................917 604-9602
Francois Wilson, *CEO*
EMP: 7
SQ FT: 400
SALES: 269.4K **Privately Held**
SIC: 2731 5112 5085 2721 Books: publishing & printing; laserjet supplies; ink, printers'; comic books: publishing only, not printed on site; computer software; film processing, editing & titling: motion picture

(G-10683)
INTERTEX USA INC
Also Called: B C America
131 W 35th St Fl 10 (10001-2111)
PHONE.................................212 279-3601

Fax: 212 279-3523
Yong Lee, *President*
EMP: 15
SQ FT: 6,500
SALES (est): 1MM **Privately Held**
SIC: 2221 2262 Specialty broadwoven fabrics, including twisted weaves; screen printing: manmade fiber & silk broadwoven fabrics

(G-10684)
INTERVIEW INC
Also Called: Interview Magazine
575 Broadway Fl 5 (10012-3227)
PHONE.................................212 941-2900
Fax: 212 941-2819
Sandra J Brant, *President*
David Hamilton, *Publisher*
Meghan Dailey, *Editor*
Catherine Davis, *Editor*
David Furnish, *Editor*
EMP: 29
SQ FT: 20,000
SALES (est): 3.2MM
SALES (corp-wide): 4.6MM **Privately Held**
WEB: www.interviewmagazine.com
SIC: 2721 Magazines: publishing only, not printed on site
PA: Brant Publications, Inc.
110 Greene St Ph 2
New York NY 10012
212 941-2800

(G-10685)
INTEVA PRODUCTS LLC
30 Rockefeller Plz (10112-0015)
PHONE.................................248 655-8886
Lon Offenbacher, *Branch Mgr*
EMP: 300
SALES (corp-wide): 4.1B **Privately Held**
SIC: 3089 Injection molding of plastics
HQ: Inteva Products, Llc
1401 Crooks Rd
Troy MI 48084

(G-10686)
INTIMATECO LLC
Also Called: Inteco Intimates
149 Madison Ave Rm 300 (10016-6769)
PHONE.................................212 239-4411
Gaby Sutton,
Eli Levy,
▲ EMP: 8 EST: 2008
SALES (est): 4.8MM **Privately Held**
SIC: 2341 Women's & children's underwear

(G-10687)
INTRA-CELLULAR THERAPIES INC
430 E 29th St (10016-8367)
PHONE.................................212 923-3344
Fax: 212 923-3388
Sharon Mates, *Ch of Bd*
Robert E Davis, *Senior VP*
Michael I Halstead, *Senior VP*
Kimberly E Vanover, *Senior VP*
Lawrence J Hineline, *CFO*
▲ EMP: 42
SQ FT: 16,753
SALES: 330.7K **Privately Held**
WEB: www.intracellulartherapies.com
SIC: 2834 8732 Pharmaceutical preparations; research services, except laboratory

(G-10688)
INTRALINKS HOLDINGS INC (HQ)
150 E 42nd St Fl 8 (10017-5626)
PHONE.................................212 543-7700
Michal Kimeldorfer, *Exec VP*
Dave Wareham, *Senior VP*
David Barbero, *Vice Pres*
Caulfield Brian, *Vice Pres*
SRI Chilukuri, *Vice Pres*
EMP: 30
SQ FT: 43,304
SALES: 276.1MM
SALES (corp-wide): 476.7MM **Publicly Held**
SIC: 7372 7382 Prepackaged software; security systems services

▲ = Import ▼=Export
◆ =Import/Export

GEOGRAPHIC SECTION

New York - New York County (G-10714)

PA: Synchronoss Technologies, Inc.
200 Crossing Blvd Fl 8
Bridgewater NJ 08807
866 620-3940

(G-10689)
INTRIGUING THREADS APPAREL INC (PA)
552 Fashion Ave Rm 603 (10018-3211)
PHONE..................212 768-8733
Fax: 212 768-4041
Alayne Weinstein, *President*
Frederick Demario, *Corp Secy*
Lori Kamhi, *Vice Pres*
Caryne Marinelli, *Bookkeeper*
Steve Albucher, *Sales Mgr*
▲ EMP: 13
SQ FT: 2,500
SALES (est): 3.3MM **Privately Held**
SIC: 2339 Sportswear, women's

(G-10690)
INTSTRUX LLC
Also Called: Pixacore
15 W 39th St Fl 13 (10018-0627)
PHONE..................646 688-2782
Sanjiv Mody, *President*
Alysia Antonelli, *Project Mgr*
Anisha Mody, *CPA*
Sach Jadav, *Info Tech Mgr*
EMP: 25
SQ FT: 7,500
SALES: 6.5MM **Privately Held**
SIC: 2834 Digitalis pharmaceutical preparations

(G-10691)
INTUITION PUBLISHING LIMITED
40 E 34th St Rm 1101 (10016-4501)
PHONE..................212 838-7115
Fax: 212 686-8827
David Harrison, *Manager*
EMP: 8
SALES (corp-wide): 105.9K **Privately Held**
SIC: 2741 Miscellaneous publishing
HQ: Intuition Publishing Limited
I F S C House
Dublin 1
160 543-00

(G-10692)
INVESTMENT NEWS
711 3rd Ave Fl 3 (10017-9214)
PHONE..................212 210-0100
Fax: 212 210-0444
Mary B Franklin, *Editor*
Frederick Gabriel, *Editor*
Andrew Leigh, *Regional Mgr*
Suzanne Siracuse, *Vice Pres*
Kate Costanzo, *Prdtn Mgr*
EMP: 50
SALES (est): 1.9MM **Privately Held**
WEB: www.investmentnews.net
SIC: 2711 Newspapers, publishing & printing

(G-10693)
INVESTORS BUSINESS DAILY INC
1501 Broadway Fl 12 (10036-5505)
PHONE..................212 626-7676
Fax: 212 626-7699
Janice Janendo, *Branch Mgr*
EMP: 18
SALES (corp-wide): 255MM **Privately Held**
WEB: www.investors.com
SIC: 2711 6282 Newspapers, publishing & printing; investment advice
HQ: Investor's Business Daily, Inc.
12655 Beatrice St
Los Angeles CA 90066
310 448-6000

(G-10694)
INVISION INC (HQ)
25 W 43rd St Ste 609 (10036-7422)
PHONE..................212 557-5554
Steve Marshall, *CEO*
Kami Ragsdale, *COO*
Christina Barlowe, *Senior VP*
Travis Howe, *Senior VP*
John Macdonald, *Vice Pres*
EMP: 2

SALES (est): 1.1MM
SALES (corp-wide): 126MM **Privately Held**
SIC: 7372 Prepackaged software
PA: Mediaocean Llc
45 W 18th St
New York NY 10011
212 633-8100

(G-10695)
IPC/RAZOR LLC (PA)
277 Park Ave Fl 39 (10172-2901)
PHONE..................212 551-4500
Douglas Korn, *Mng Member*
EMP: 60 EST: 2010
SALES (est): 79.5MM **Privately Held**
SIC: 3541 Machine tools, metal cutting type

(G-10696)
IPM US INC
276 5th Ave Rm 203 (10001-4509)
PHONE..................212 481-7967
Gaelle Pagy, *President*
▲ EMP: 6
SALES (est): 479.1K **Privately Held**
SIC: 2258 Lace & warp knit fabric mills

(G-10697)
IR MEDIA GROUP (USA) INC
25 Broadway Fl 9 (10004-1058)
PHONE..................212 425-9649
Ian Richman, *Ch of Bd*
Kathleen Hennessy, *Editor*
Brigitte Toledano, *Sales Staff*
EMP: 30 EST: 1995
SALES (est): 1.6MM
SALES (corp-wide): 3.3MM **Privately Held**
WEB: www.irmag.com
SIC: 2731 Books: publishing only
HQ: Cross-Border Publishing (London) Limited
111-113 Great Titchfield Street
London

(G-10698)
IRADJ MOINI COUTURE LTD
403 W 46th St (10036-3510)
PHONE..................212 594-9242
Iradj Moini, *President*
Roya Darroudi, *Director*
EMP: 12
SQ FT: 800
SALES: 500K **Privately Held**
SIC: 3911 Jewelry, precious metal

(G-10699)
IRENE GOODMAN LITERARY AGENCY
27 W 24th St Ste 700b (10010-4105)
PHONE..................212 604-0330
Irene Goodman, *President*
Beth Vesel, *Senior VP*
Miriam Kriss, *Vice Pres*
EMP: 5
SALES (est): 454.1K **Privately Held**
SIC: 7372 Publishers' computer software

(G-10700)
IRIDESSE INC
600 Madison Ave Fl 5 (10022-1615)
PHONE..................212 230-6000
Fax: 212 230-6891
Patrick B Dorsey, *President*
Judith A Baldissard, *Principal*
Michael W Connolly, *Principal*
James N Fernandez, *Principal*
Robert L Cepek, *Chairman*
EMP: 15
SALES (est): 1.9MM **Privately Held**
SIC: 3911 Necklaces, precious metal

(G-10701)
IRISH AMERICA INC
Also Called: Irish America Magazine
875 Americas Rm 2100 (10001-3586)
PHONE..................212 725-2993
Niall O'Dowd, *Publisher*
Kevin Mangan, *Controller*
Brendon Maclua, *Shareholder*
EMP: 20
SQ FT: 3,000

SALES (est): 1.7MM **Privately Held**
WEB: www.smurfitkappa.com
SIC: 2721 Magazines: publishing only, not printed on site
HQ: Smurfit Kappa Packaging Limited
Beech Hill
Dublin

(G-10702)
IRISH ECHO NEWSPAPER CORP
165 Madison Ave Rm 302 (10016-5431)
PHONE..................212 482-4818
Fax: 212 482-6569
Peter Quinn, *Ch of Bd*
EMP: 19 EST: 1928
SQ FT: 3,000
SALES (est): 1.3MM **Privately Held**
WEB: www.irishecho.com
SIC: 2711 Newspapers: publishing only, not printed on site

(G-10703)
IRISH TRIBUNE INC
Also Called: Irish Voice Newspaper
875 Avenue Of The Amerrm2 Rm 2100 (10001)
PHONE..................212 684-3366
Niell O'Dowd, *President*
Robert S Bennett, *Partner*
Sean E Crowley, *Partner*
Ann Marie Zito, *Opers Mgr*
Tracey Benson, *Manager*
EMP: 14
SALES (est): 896.1K **Privately Held**
WEB: www.smurfitkappa.com
SIC: 2711 Newspapers
HQ: Smurfit Kappa Packaging Limited
Beech Hill
Dublin

(G-10704)
IRON EAGLE GROUP INC (PA)
Also Called: (A DEVELOPMENT STAGE COMPANY)
160 W 66th St Apt 41g (10023-6565)
PHONE..................888 481-4445
Fax: 917 591-6227
Joseph E Antonini, *Ch of Bd*
Jed M Sabio, *Exec VP*
EMP: 21
SQ FT: 800
SALES (est): 30MM **Privately Held**
SIC: 1389 Construction, repair & dismantling services

(G-10705)
IRV INC
Also Called: Warshaw Jacobson Group
540 Broadway Fl 4 (10012-3953)
PHONE..................212 334-4507
Fax: 212 966-4017
Steve Warshaw, *President*
Sal Mercadante, *President*
Jay Warshaw, *Vice Pres*
Jennifer Fernandez, *Office Mgr*
Nicole Hamilton, *Director*
EMP: 23
SALES (est): 1.1MM **Privately Held**
SIC: 7372 7371 Prepackaged software; custom computer programming services

(G-10706)
IRVING FARM COFFEE CO INC (PA)
151 W 19th St Fl 6 (10011-4158)
PHONE..................212 206-0707
David Elwell, *President*
Daniel Streetman, *Vice Pres*
Clyde Miller, *Director*
Teresa Von Fuchs, *Director*
EMP: 4
SALES (est): 1.2MM **Privately Held**
WEB: www.irvingfarm.com
SIC: 2095 Roasted coffee

(G-10707)
ISABEL TOLEDO ENTERPRISES INC
1181 Broadway Fl 7 (10001-7432)
PHONE..................212 685-0948
Isabel Toledo, *President*
Ruben Toledo, *Vice Pres*
EMP: 6
SALES (est): 720K **Privately Held**
SIC: 2339 Women's & misses' outerwear

(G-10708)
ISFEL CO INC (PA)
Also Called: Top Stuff
110 W 34th St Rm 1101 (10001-2115)
PHONE..................212 736-6216
Fax: 212 465-0645
Joseph Feldman, *President*
Vivian Schwartz, *Production*
▲ EMP: 8 EST: 1948
SQ FT: 2,000
SALES (est): 3.3MM **Privately Held**
WEB: www.topstuff.com
SIC: 2369 Girls' & children's outerwear

(G-10709)
ISISNET LLC
Also Called: Isis/Koppermann
53 W 36th St Rm 502 (10018-7993)
PHONE..................212 239-1205
Fax: 212 695-9947
Michael Dematteis,
Wolfgang Koppermann,
Andreas Lachner,
EMP: 6
SQ FT: 1,200
SALES: 1MM **Privately Held**
SIC: 7372 Prepackaged software

(G-10710)
ISONICS CORPORATION (PA)
535 8th Ave Fl 3 (10018-4305)
PHONE..................212 356-7400
Christopher Toffales, *Ch of Bd*
John Sakys, *President*
Marshall Combs, *Vice Pres*
Daniel J Grady, *Vice Pres*
Gregory A Meadows, *CFO*
EMP: 4
SALES: 22.1MM **Publicly Held**
WEB: www.isonics.com
SIC: 2819 3674 Isotopes, radioactive; silicon wafers, chemically doped

(G-10711)
ITC MFG GROUP INC
109 W 38th St Rm 701 (10018-3673)
PHONE..................212 684-3696
Fax: 212 532-2097
Anthony Dadika, *President*
Irwin Jaeger, *Vice Pres*
MEI Francese, *Manager*
EMP: 10
SQ FT: 6,000
SALES (est): 900K **Privately Held**
SIC: 2241 3965 2759 Labels, woven; fasteners, buttons, needles & pins; tags: printing

(G-10712)
IZQUIERDO STUDIOS LTD
34 W 28th St 6 (10001-4201)
PHONE..................212 807-9757
Fax: 212 366-5249
Martin Izquierdo, *President*
John Inquaqiato, *Vice Pres*
Jeffrey Scherer, *Vice Pres*
EMP: 13
SQ FT: 2,000
SALES (est): 1.3MM **Privately Held**
SIC: 2389 Theatrical costumes

(G-10713)
IZUN PHARMACEUTICALS CORP (PA)
1 Rockefeller Plz Fl 11 (10020-2073)
PHONE..................212 618-6357
William Levine, *CEO*
Les Kraus, *CFO*
Aron Saffer, *Technology*
EMP: 12
SALES (est): 1.5MM **Privately Held**
WEB: www.izunpharma.com
SIC: 2834 Pharmaceutical preparations

(G-10714)
J & H CREATIONS INC
19 W 36th St Fl 3 (10018-7103)
PHONE..................212 465-0962
Fax: 212 465-0950
Jay Baek, *President*
▲ EMP: 20
SQ FT: 2,000

New York - New York County (G-10715)

SALES (est): 2.6MM **Privately Held**
WEB: www.jhcreation.com
SIC: **3961** 5094 Costume jewelry, ex. precious metal & semiprecious stones; jewelry

(G-10715)
J & M TEXTILE CO INC
505 8th Ave Rm 701 (10018-4552)
PHONE.................................212 268-8000
Fax: 212 268-2152
Maria Wiesiolek, *President*
▲ **EMP:** 11
SQ FT: 7,000
SALES (est): 1.1MM **Privately Held**
SIC: 2241 5131 Glove lining fabrics; piece goods & notions

(G-10716)
J & X PRODUCTION INC
327 W 36th St 7f (10018-6405)
PHONE.................................718 200-1228
Guo Jun Lin, *President*
EMP: 10
SALES (est): 127K **Privately Held**
SIC: 2311 Men's & boys' suits & coats

(G-10717)
J A G DIAMOND MANUFACTURERS
580 5th Ave Ste 905b (10036-4733)
PHONE.................................212 575-0660
Volf Goldrath, *President*
Sharon Fink,
EMP: 7
SALES (est): 587.5K **Privately Held**
SIC: 3915 Diamond cutting & polishing

(G-10718)
J EDLIN INTERIORS LTD
122 W 27th St Fl 2 (10001-6274)
PHONE.................................212 243-2111
Fax: 212 645-0865
Jeffrey Edlin, *President*
Joyse Edlin, *Vice Pres*
▲ **EMP:** 10
SALES (est): 1MM **Privately Held**
WEB: www.reisner.net
SIC: 2391 Curtains & draperies

(G-10719)
J H JEWELRY CO INC
12 W 32nd St Fl 12 (10001-1293)
PHONE.................................212 239-1330
Fax: 212 564-1087
Jack Leitman, *President*
Robert Hertz, *Vice Pres*
EMP: 11
SQ FT: 3,000
SALES (est): 1MM **Privately Held**
SIC: 3911 Jewelry, precious metal

(G-10720)
J KLAGSBRUN INC (PA)
25 E 86th St 6f (10028-0553)
PHONE.................................212 712-9388
Herbert Klagsbrun, *President*
Ronald Klagsbrun, *Vice Pres*
EMP: 5
SQ FT: 2,000
SALES (est): 626.5K **Privately Held**
SIC: 3915 5094 Diamond cutting & polishing; diamonds (gems)

(G-10721)
J PERCY FOR MRVIN RCHARDS LTD (HQ)
512 Fashion Ave (10018-4603)
PHONE.................................212 944-5300
Morris Goldfarb, *Ch of Bd*
Sammy Aaron, *President*
Andrew Reid, *Vice Pres*
Allan Inger, *CFO*
Tammie Hughes, *Human Resources*
◆ **EMP:** 40
SQ FT: 12,000
SALES (est): 17.7MM
SALES (corp-wide): 2.3B **Publicly Held**
SIC: 2339 2386 2371 2337 Women's & misses' outerwear; women's & misses' jackets & coats, except sportswear; coats & jackets, leather & sheep-lined; fur coats & other fur apparel; women's & misses' suits & coats

PA: G-Iii Apparel Group, Ltd.
512 7th Ave Fl 35
New York NY 10018
212 403-0500

(G-10722)
J R GOLD DESIGNS LTD
555 5th Ave Fl 19 (10017-2416)
PHONE.................................212 922-9292
Fax: 212 922-2992
Rami Uziel, *President*
Rina Uziel, *Principal*
EMP: 10
SQ FT: 2,500
SALES: 10MM **Privately Held**
WEB: www.rinalimor.com
SIC: 3911 5094 Jewelry, precious metal; jewelry

(G-10723)
J R NITES (PA)
1400 Broadway Rm 601 (10018-0728)
PHONE.................................212 354-9670
John Klein, *Principal*
EMP: 8
SALES (est): 1MM **Privately Held**
SIC: 2335 Women's, juniors' & misses' dresses

(G-10724)
J9 TECHNOLOGIES INC
25 Broadway Fl 9 (10004-1058)
PHONE.................................412 586-5038
Alan Wasserberger, *President*
Carly Campbell, *Controller*
Robert C Roach, *CTO*
EMP: 20
SALES (est): 2.5MM **Privately Held**
SIC: 7372 Operating systems computer software

(G-10725)
JAC USA INC
45 Broadway Ste 1810 (10006-3710)
PHONE.................................212 841-7430
Kazunari Okuda, *Ch of Bd*
Sinji Naka, *President*
Mary Bailey, *Manager*
EMP: 5
SQ FT: 1,400
SALES (est): 3.1MM
SALES (corp-wide): 42.5B **Privately Held**
WEB: www.jacusa.com
SIC: 3728 Aircraft parts & equipment
HQ: Japan Aerospace Corporation
1-1-1, Minamiaoyama
Minato-Ku TKY 107-0
357 855-970

(G-10726)
JACKEL INC
Also Called: Jackel International
1359 Broadway Fl 17 (10018-7117)
PHONE.................................908 359-2039
Pansy Muller, *President*
Graham Summerfield, *CFO*
Sebastien Williams, *Sales Executive*
April Wasnick, *Manager*
▲ **EMP:** 100
SQ FT: 11,800
SALES (est): 15.7MM **Privately Held**
WEB: www.jackelus.com
SIC: 2844 Cosmetic preparations

(G-10727)
JACKS AND JOKERS 52 LLC
215 E 68th St Apt 5o (10065-5720)
PHONE.................................917 740-2595
Scot Lerner,
EMP: 5
SALES (est): 631.3K **Privately Held**
SIC: 2321 Blouses, boys': made from purchased materials

(G-10728)
JACKSON DAKOTA INC (PA)
979 3rd Ave Ste 503 (10022-1393)
PHONE.................................212 838-9444
Fax: 212 758-6413
Dakota Jackson, *President*
Gwyneth Perrott, *Manager*
Daniel Brookman, *Creative Dir*
Lucas Leibman, *Creative Dir*
▲ **EMP:** 2
SQ FT: 5,500

SALES (est): 6.1MM **Privately Held**
SIC: 2512 Upholstered household furniture

(G-10729)
JACLYN INC
Also Called: Lindsay Lyn Accessories Div
330 5th Ave Rm 1305 (10001-3101)
PHONE.................................212 736-5657
Fax: 212 563-4361
Howard Rucker, *Division Mgr*
Howard Ginsburg, *Mktg Dir*
EMP: 10
SALES (corp-wide): 31.8MM **Publicly Held**
WEB: www.jaclyninc.com
SIC: 2335 Dresses, paper: cut & sewn
HQ: Jaclyn Llc
197 W Spring Valley Ave # 101
Maywood NJ 07607
201 909-6000

(G-10730)
JACMEL JEWELRY INC (PA)
1385 Broadway Fl 8 (10018-2102)
PHONE.................................718 349-4300
Fax: 718 349-4466
Jack Rahmey, *President*
Morris Dweck, *Vice Pres*
Robert Passaro, *CFO*
Evan Barkley, *Treasurer*
Bob Passaro, *Controller*
▲ **EMP:** 145 **EST:** 1977
SQ FT: 60,000
SALES: 100MM **Privately Held**
WEB: www.jacmel.com
SIC: 3911 Medals, precious or semi-precious metal

(G-10731)
JACOB HIDARY FOUNDATION INC
10 W 33rd St Rm 900 (10001-3317)
PHONE.................................212 736-6540
Abe Hidary, *President*
Jack A Hidary, *Vice Pres*
EMP: 10
SALES: 123.4K **Privately Held**
SIC: 2329 Men's & boys' sportswear & athletic clothing

(G-10732)
JACOBS & COHEN INC
Also Called: Sun Source
255 W 36th St Fl 9 (10018-7583)
PHONE.................................212 714-2702
Benjamin Cohen, *Ch of Bd*
Edward Jacobs, *President*
EMP: 25
SALES (est): 18.5K **Privately Held**
WEB: www.sunsourcejewelry.com
SIC: 3911 Jewelry, precious metal

(G-10733)
JACQUES TORRES CHOCOLATE LLC (PA)
350 Hudson St Frnt 1 (10014-4504)
PHONE.................................212 414-2462
Saida Chabla, *Mktg Dir*
Andrea Martinez, *Office Mgr*
Jacques Torres, *Mng Member*
Christine Brestlin, *Executive*
▲ **EMP:** 27
SALES (est): 2.9MM **Privately Held**
SIC: 2066 Chocolate

(G-10734)
JAGUAR CASTING CO INC
100 United Nations Plz (10017-1713)
PHONE.................................212 869-0197
Fax: 212 869-1970
Puzant Khatchadourian, *President*
Jean Khatchadourian, *Vice Pres*
EMP: 25
SQ FT: 5,000
SALES (est): 3MM **Privately Held**
SIC: 3915 3911 Jewelers' castings; jewelry, precious metal

(G-10735)
JAGUAR JEWELRY CASTING NY INC
48 W 48th St Ste 500 (10036-1713)
PHONE.................................212 768-4848
Hovig Kajajian, *President*

Kevork Vekerejian, *Owner*
Jack Hallak, *Vice Pres*
Jospeh Nakashian, *Info Tech Mgr*
EMP: 9
SQ FT: 2,500
SALES: 2MM **Privately Held**
SIC: 3911 Jewelry apparel

(G-10736)
JAKOB SCHLAEPFER INC
37 W 26th St Rm 208 (10010-1150)
PHONE.................................212 221-2323
Peter Anderegg, *President*
Shkendie Kaziu, *Vice Pres*
David Sommers, *Controller*
EMP: 3
SQ FT: 1,000
SALES (est): 1.3MM **Privately Held**
WEB: www.jakobschlaepfer.com
SIC: 2221 2241 Broadwoven fabric mills, manmade; trimmings, textile

(G-10737)
JAMES MORGAN PUBLISHING (PA)
5 Penn Plz Ste 2300 (10001-1821)
PHONE.................................212 655-5470
David L Hancock, *Chairman*
Cindy Sauer, *Vice Pres*
EMP: 1
SALES: 2MM **Privately Held**
SIC: 2731 Books: publishing & printing

(G-10738)
JAMES THOMPSON & COMPANY INC (PA)
463 7th Ave Rm 1603 (10018-7421)
PHONE.................................212 686-4242
Fax: 212 686-9528
Nicholas Griseto, *President*
Barry Garr, *Vice Pres*
Sara Loffredo, *MIS Mgr*
▲ **EMP:** 7 **EST:** 1860
SALES (est): 16.8MM **Privately Held**
WEB: www.jamesthompson.com
SIC: 2299 Burlap, jute

(G-10739)
JANE BOHAN INC
611 Broadway (10012-2608)
PHONE.................................212 529-6090
Jane Bohan, *President*
Laura Bothfeld, *Vice Pres*
▲ **EMP:** 6
SQ FT: 300
SALES: 970K **Privately Held**
SIC: 3911 Jewelry, precious metal

(G-10740)
JANES DESIGNER YRN PTTRNS INC
Also Called: Jane Knitting Kit
1745 Broadway Ste 1750 (10019-4640)
PHONE.................................347 260-3071
Jane Klein, *Principal*
EMP: 6
SQ FT: 50
SALES: 6K **Privately Held**
SIC: 2282 5949 Knitting yarn: twisting, winding or spooling; sewing, needlework & piece goods

(G-10741)
JAPAN PRINTING & GRAPHICS INC
160 Broadway Lbby D (10038-4201)
PHONE.................................212 406-2905
Fax: 212 766-0125
Hiroshi Ono, *President*
EMP: 7
SALES: 500K **Privately Held**
WEB: www.japanprint.com
SIC: 2759 2752 Commercial printing; commercial printing, lithographic

(G-10742)
JARVIK HEART INC
333 W 52nd St Ste 700 (10019-6238)
PHONE.................................212 397-3911
Robert Jarvik MD, *President*
Pamela Whitehead, *Purch Mgr*
Latha Kavala, *Engineer*
Carl McEncroe, *Engineer*
Marilyn Vos Savant, *CFO*
EMP: 36

GEOGRAPHIC SECTION
New York - New York County (G-10767)

SALES (est): 6.6MM **Privately Held**
WEB: www.jarvikheart.com
SIC: 3845 Surgical support systems: heart-lung machine, exc. iron lung

(G-10743)
JASANI DESIGNS USA INC
25 W 43rd St Ste 1014 (10036-7431)
PHONE..................................212 257-6465
Ameya Joshi, *President*
Sanjay Gokhale, *Accounts Mgr*
Abhay R Jasani, *Director*
Shyam Jasani, *Director*
Satish Joshi, *Director*
EMP: 8
SALES (est): 2.4MM **Privately Held**
SIC: 3911 Jewelry, precious metal
PA: Jasani
    Floor Hw - 6010, 6th Floor,
    Mumbai MH

(G-10744)
JAX COCO USA LLC
5 Penn Plz Ste 2300 (10001-1821)
PHONE..................................347 688-8198
John Craig, *COO*
Jason Gonzales, *Sales Mgr*
Joel McMinn, *Sales Mgr*
▲ **EMP:** 5 **EST:** 2013
SALES: 300K **Privately Held**
SIC: 2076 Coconut oil

(G-10745)
JAY STRONGWATER HOLDINGS LLC (HQ)
230 W 39th St Fl 8 (10018-4929)
PHONE..................................646 657-0558
John J Ling, *CEO*
▲ **EMP:** 1000
SALES (est): 150MM
SALES (corp-wide): 163.3MM **Privately Held**
SIC: 3499 3911 3471 3229 Picture frames, metal; jewelry, precious metal; jewelry apparel; decorative plating & finishing of formed products; glassware, art or decorative
PA: Rauch Industries, Inc.
    2408 Forbes Rd
    Gastonia NC 28056
    704 867-5333

(G-10746)
JAYA APPAREL GROUP LLC
1384 Broadway Fl 18 (10018-6122)
PHONE..................................212 764-4980
Don Lewis, *Branch Mgr*
EMP: 15
SALES (corp-wide): 110MM **Privately Held**
SIC: 2339 Women's & misses' athletic clothing & sportswear
PA: Jaya Apparel Group Llc
    5175 S Soto St
    Vernon CA 90058
    323 584-3500

(G-10747)
JAYDEN STAR LLC
385 5th Ave Rm 507 (10016-3346)
PHONE..................................212 686-0400
Maurice Mandelbaum, *Vice Pres*
Winnie Fung, *Accounts Mgr*
Jason Mandelbaum, *Mng Member*
Steven Tam, *Info Tech Dir*
EMP: 30
SQ FT: 5,000
SALES (est): 1.5MM **Privately Held**
SIC: 3911 5094 Jewelry apparel; jewelry & precious stones

(G-10748)
JAYMAR JEWELRY CO INC
69 5th Ave Apt 8d (10003-3008)
PHONE..................................212 564-4788
Fax: 212 564-2957
Jayson Levy, *President*
EMP: 5
SQ FT: 3,000
SALES (est): 551.2K **Privately Held**
SIC: 3961 Costume jewelry, ex. precious metal & semiprecious stones

(G-10749)
JBL TRADING LLC
Also Called: Crest Mills
43 W 33rd St Rm 603 (10001-3073)
PHONE..................................347 394-5592
Joey Levy, *Mng Member*
EMP: 7 **Privately Held**
SIC: 2273 Carpets & rugs
PA: Jbl Trading Llc
    43 W 33rd St Rm 201
    New York NY 10001

(G-10750)
JC CRYSTAL INC
260 W 35th St Fl 10 (10001-2528)
PHONE..................................212 594-0858
Jimmy Ping Chong Loh, *President*
Lana Hertel, *Sales Dir*
▲ **EMP:** 50
SQ FT: 5,000
SALES: 5.8MM **Privately Held**
SIC: 3911 Jewelry apparel

(G-10751)
JCDECAUX MALLSCAPE LLC (DH)
350 5th Ave Fl 73 (10118-0110)
PHONE..................................646 834-1200
Bernard Pariost,
Gabrielle Brussel, *Admin Sec*
Jean-Luc Decaux,
EMP: 11
SALES (est): 1.6MM
SALES (corp-wide): 9.3MM **Privately Held**
SIC: 2531 Benches for public buildings
HQ: Jcdecaux North America, Inc.
    350 5th Ave Fl 73
    New York NY 10118
    646 834-1200

(G-10752)
JDS GRAPHICS INC
Also Called: Jds Graphics
226 W 37th St Fl 10 (10018-9016)
PHONE..................................973 330-3300
Debra Yuran, *President*
Sheryl Heller, *Vice Pres*
Jeffery Kirschenbaum, *Vice Pres*
Robert Generale, *Controller*
EMP: 12
SQ FT: 2,500
SALES (est): 1.1MM **Privately Held**
WEB: www.jdsgraphics.com
SIC: 2752 Commercial printing, offset

(G-10753)
JDT INTERNATIONAL LLC
276 5th Ave Rm 704 (10001-4527)
PHONE..................................212 400-7570
Janet Pulley, *Mfg Staff*
Tariq Osman, *Branch Mgr*
EMP: 8
SALES (corp-wide): 1.8MM **Privately Held**
SIC: 2392 5021 Blankets, comforters & beddings; beds & bedding
PA: Jdt International, Llc
    3532 Tonkawood Rd
    Minnetonka MN 55345
    952 933-2558

(G-10754)
JEAN & ALEX JEWELRY MFG & CONS
587 5th Ave Fl 2 (10017-8757)
PHONE..................................212 935-7621
Fax: 212 935-7645
Zeng Qiang Pu, *President*
Kuofan Chen, *Vice Pres*
Michelle Tsang, *Treasurer*
EMP: 15
SQ FT: 3,000
SALES (est): 1.3MM **Privately Held**
SIC: 3911 Jewelry apparel

(G-10755)
JEAN PHILIPPE FRAGRANCES LLC
551 5th Ave Rm 1500 (10176-1599)
PHONE..................................212 983-2640
Fax: 212 983-4197
Terrence Augenbraun, *Exec VP*
Dwyane Williams, *Human Res Mgr*
Gary Roth, *VP Sales*
Jean Madar,
Russell Greenberg,
◆ **EMP:** 57
SQ FT: 7,000
SALES (est): 10.9MM
SALES (corp-wide): 521MM **Publicly Held**
WEB: www.interparfumsinc.com
SIC: 2844 Toilet preparations; perfumes & colognes; cosmetic preparations
PA: Inter Parfums, Inc.
    551 5th Ave
    New York NY 10176
    212 983-2640

(G-10756)
JEANJER LLC
Also Called: Just For Men Div
1400 Broadway Fl 15 (10018-5300)
PHONE..................................212 944-1330
Joe Nakash, *President*
AVI Naakash, *Vice Pres*
Ralph Nakash, *Treasurer*
Charles Flores, *Sales Mgr*
John Banevicius 6463838123, *Manager*
▲ **EMP:** 3000
SALES (est): 105.7MM **Privately Held**
SIC: 2331 2337 2339 2369 Blouses, women's & juniors': made from purchased material; suits: women's, misses' & juniors'; slacks: women's, misses' & juniors' girls' & children's outerwear

(G-10757)
JEANS INC
1357 Broadway Ste 411 (10018-7101)
PHONE..................................646 223-1122
Deepak Ramchandani, *CEO*
Paul Maulucci, *Controller*
EMP: 9 **EST:** 2012
SALES (est): 377.5K **Privately Held**
SIC: 2399 5136 Hand woven apparel; men's & boys' clothing

(G-10758)
JEMCAP SERVICING LLC
360 Madison Ave Rm 1902 (10017-7158)
PHONE..................................212 213-9353
Marsh Peter, *Principal*
EMP: 5
SALES (est): 278.6K **Privately Held**
SIC: 1389 Roustabout service

(G-10759)
JENALEX CREATIVE MARKETING INC
116 E 57th St Fl 3 (10022-2613)
PHONE..................................212 935-2266
Fax: 212 319-6385
Alexandra Grondahl, *President*
Ludwig J Cserhat, *Corp Secy*
Sylvia Lazzari, *Vice Pres*
Saad Bourkadi, *CFO*
▲ **EMP:** 7
SQ FT: 2,000
SALES (est): 800.2K **Privately Held**
WEB: www.jenalex.com
SIC: 3999 Boutiquing: decorating gift items with sequins, fruit, etc.

(G-10760)
JENVIE SPORT INC
255 W 36th St Ste 6 (10018-7555)
P.O. Box 856, Bethpage (11714-0017)
PHONE..................................212 967-2322
Fax: 212 239-8598
Eli Goldstein, *President*
Linda Swobe, *Vice Pres*
Neil Seiden, *Accountant*
Sandy Kanter, *Bookkeeper*
Steven Goldstein, *Admin Sec*
▲ **EMP:** 7
SQ FT: 9,000
SALES (est): 1MM **Privately Held**
WEB: www.jenvie.com
SIC: 2339 Sportswear, women's

(G-10761)
JERRY SORBARA FURS INC
39 W 32nd St Rm 1400 (10001-3841)
PHONE..................................212 594-3897
Fax: 212 643-9098
Jerry Sorbara, *President*
Sal Sorbara, *Vice Pres*
Catherine Wilson, *Treasurer*
EMP: 11
SQ FT: 4,500
SALES: 2MM **Privately Held**
SIC: 2371 Apparel, fur

(G-10762)
JEWELMAK INC
344 E 59th St Fl 1&2 (10022-1593)
PHONE..................................212 398-2999
Fax: 212 398-0721
Andy Goetz, *President*
Vincent Carotenuto, *Vice Pres*
Edgard Bayona, *Controller*
June Hardy, *Accountant*
Thanh Bui, *Human Res Dir*
EMP: 25
SQ FT: 7,240
SALES: 35MM **Privately Held**
WEB: www.jewelmak.com
SIC: 3911 Jewelry, precious metal

(G-10763)
JEWELRY ARTS MANUFACTURING
151 W 46th St Fl 12 (10036-8512)
PHONE..................................212 382-3583
Fax: 212 869-0594
Alberto Tapia, *CEO*
Ligia Tapia, *Vice Pres*
EMP: 40
SALES (est): 2.3MM **Privately Held**
WEB: www.jewelartjewelers.com
SIC: 3915 3961 3911 Jewelers' castings; jewelry polishing for the trade; jewelry soldering for the trade; costume jewelry; jewelry, precious metal

(G-10764)
JEWELS BY STAR LTD
555 5th Ave Fl 7 (10017-9267)
PHONE..................................212 308-3490
Fax: 212 486-0140
Yehuda Fouzailoff, *President*
Rafael Fouzailoff, *Vice Pres*
EMP: 20
SQ FT: 2,000
SALES (est): 2.9MM **Privately Held**
WEB: www.jewelsbystar.com
SIC: 3911 Jewelry, precious metal

(G-10765)
JEWELTEX MFG CORP
48 W 48th St Ste 507 (10036-1713)
PHONE..................................212 921-8188
Fax: 212 921-8706
Barry Rosenfeld, *President*
Joe Itzkowitx, *Admin Sec*
EMP: 13
SQ FT: 1,500
SALES (est): 2.3MM **Privately Held**
SIC: 3911 Jewelry, precious metal

(G-10766)
JEWISH WEEK INC (PA)
1501 Broadway Ste 505 (10036-5504)
PHONE..................................212 921-7822
Fax: 212 921-8420
Richard Waloff, *Publisher*
Gary Rosenblatt, *Principal*
Robert Goldblum, *Editor*
Amy Spiro, *Editor*
Jannet Hoffman, *Comptroller*
EMP: 35 **EST:** 1970
SQ FT: 6,000
SALES (est): 6.3MM **Privately Held**
WEB: www.thejewishweek.com
SIC: 2711 Newspapers: publishing only, not printed on site

(G-10767)
JFE ENGINEERING CORPORATION
350 Park Ave Fl 27th (10022-6022)
PHONE..................................212 310-9320
Moriyasu Nagae, *General Mgr*
Hedenori Tawaza, *Branch Mgr*
Shinji Kojima, *Manager*
Youji Ookawa,
EMP: 10
SALES (corp-wide): 29.3B **Privately Held**
SIC: 3312 Sheet or strip, steel, hot-rolled
HQ: Jfe Engineering Corporation
    1-8-1, Marunouchi
    Chiyoda-Ku TKY 100-0
    362 120-800

New York - New York County (G-10768)

(G-10768)
JFE STEEL AMERICA INC (HQ)
600 3rd Ave Rm 1201 (10016-1921)
PHONE..................212 310-9320
Kaoru Okamoto, *President*
Ann Fronimakas, *Admin Sec*
EMP: 7
SALES (est): 1.9MM
SALES (corp-wide): 29.1B **Privately Held**
SIC: 3312 Sheet or strip, steel, hot-rolled; sheet or strip, steel, cold-rolled: own hot-rolled; tinplate; iron & steel: galvanized, pipes, plates, sheets, etc.
PA: Jfe Holdings, Inc.
2-2-3, Uchisaiwaicho
Chiyoda-Ku TKY 100-0
335 974-321

(G-10769)
JFS INC
Also Called: Joe Fresh
531 W 26th St Unit 531 (10001-5514)
PHONE..................646 264-1200
Mario Grauso, *President*
Justin Leve, *Vice Pres*
Kari Talley, *Director*
EMP: 17 **EST:** 2010
SALES (est): 3.7MM
SALES (corp-wide): 35.5B **Privately Held**
SIC: 2253 T-shirts & tops, knit
HQ: Loblaw Companies Limited
1 Presidents Choice Cir
Brampton ON L6Y 5
905 459-2500

(G-10770)
JGX LLC
1407 Broadway Rm 1416 (10018-2842)
PHONE..................212 575-1244
Nouri Jaradeh, *Vice Pres*
Jack Grazi, *Vice Pres*
EMP: 5
SQ FT: 3,000
SALES (est): 79.1K **Privately Held**
SIC: 2369 Leggings: girls', children's & infants'

(G-10771)
JILL FAGIN ENTERPRISES INC (PA)
Also Called: Jillery
107 Avenue B (10009-6264)
PHONE..................212 674-9383
Fax: 212 674-9401
Jill Fagin, *President*
EMP: 8
SALES: 670K **Privately Held**
SIC: 3961 3262 Costume jewelry; vitreous china table & kitchenware

(G-10772)
JIM HENSON COMPANY INC
Also Called: Jim Henson Productions
117 E 69th St (10021-5004)
PHONE..................212 794-2400
Fax: 212 570-1147
Howard Sharp, *Manager*
EMP: 50
SALES (corp-wide): 10.8MM **Privately Held**
WEB: www.farscape.com
SIC: 3942 3944 2731 Dolls & stuffed toys; games, toys & children's vehicles; book publishing
PA: The Jim Henson Company Inc
1416 N La Brea Ave
Los Angeles CA 90028
323 856-6680

(G-10773)
JIM WACHTLER INC
1212 Avenue Of The Ste 2200 (10036)
PHONE..................212 755-4367
James Wachtler, *President*
EMP: 3
SALES: 3MM **Privately Held**
SIC: 3915 5094 5944 Gems, real & imitation: preparation for settings; diamond cutting & polishing; precious stones (gems); jewelry; precious stones & precious metals

(G-10774)
JIMEALE INCORPORATED
130 Church St Ste 163 (10007-2226)
P.O. Box 841, Southport CT (06890-0841)
PHONE..................917 686-5383
Jimeale Jorgensen, *Chairman*
▲ **EMP:** 6
SALES (est): 692.9K **Privately Held**
SIC: 2389 Men's miscellaneous accessories

(G-10775)
JIMMY CRYSTAL NEW YORK CO LTD
47 W 37th St Fl 3 (10018-6294)
PHONE..................212 594-0858
Fax: 212 564-0566
Ping Chong Loh, *Ch of Bd*
Alice Chui, *Vice Pres*
▲ **EMP:** 32
SQ FT: 13,500
SALES (est): 3.5MM **Privately Held**
SIC: 3231 3911 Watch crystals, glass; jewelry, precious metal

(G-10776)
JIRANIMO INDUSTRIES LTD
Also Called: Long Paige
49a W 37th St (10018-6202)
PHONE..................212 921-5106
Fax: 212 768-2835
Parviz Shirian, *President*
Aaron Ostad, *President*
Adam Ostad, *Vice Pres*
Shamouiel Ostad, *Treasurer*
Salim Panah, *Accounts Mgr*
▲ **EMP:** 12
SQ FT: 17,500
SALES (est): 1.3MM **Privately Held**
SIC: 2335 Women's, juniors' & misses' dresses

(G-10777)
JISAN TRADING CORPORATION
519 8th Ave Rm 810 (10018-4586)
PHONE..................212 244-1269
SOO Kang, *President*
EMP: 20
SALES (est): 1.2MM **Privately Held**
SIC: 2384 Dressing gowns, men's & women's: from purchased materials

(G-10778)
JJ BASICS LLC (PA)
525 7th Ave Rm 307 (10018-4930)
PHONE..................212 768-4779
Steven Bensadigh, *President*
Vivien Zhao, *Vice Pres*
Donna Klein, *Opers Mgr*
Randi Gefen, *VP Sales*
Melissa Bacs, *Marketing Staff*
▲ **EMP:** 21
SQ FT: 5,400
SALES (est): 2.6MM **Privately Held**
SIC: 2253 Sweaters & sweater coats, knit

(G-10779)
JJ FANTASIA INC
38 W 32nd St (10001-3816)
PHONE..................212 868-1198
Fax: 212 868-1195
Cheng Hsuan Wu, *Ch of Bd*
EMP: 7
SALES (est): 628.5K **Privately Held**
SIC: 3961 Jewelry apparel, non-precious metals

(G-10780)
JLM COUTURE INC (PA)
Also Called: J L M
525 Fashion Ave Rm 1703 (10018-4935)
PHONE..................212 921-7058
Fax: 212 921-7608
Daniel M Sullivan, *Ch of Bd*
Joseph L Murphy, *President*
Jerry Walkenfeld, *Controller*
Sean Abrams, *Credit Mgr*
Danielle O'Brien, *Director*
▼ **EMP:** 60
SALES (est): 16.7MM **Publicly Held**
WEB: www.jlmcouture.com
SIC: 2335 Wedding gowns & dresses

(G-10781)
JM MANUFACTURER INC
241 W 37th St Rm 924 (10018-6970)
PHONE..................212 869-0626
Liuchu Jia, *Principal*
EMP: 3
SQ FT: 700
SALES (est): 4.6MM **Privately Held**
SIC: 2221 Apparel & outerwear fabric, manmade fiber or silk

(G-10782)
JM STUDIO INC
247 W 35th St Fl 3 (10001-1926)
PHONE..................646 546-5514
Yim Lan Dong, *CEO*
▲ **EMP:** 15
SQ FT: 6,000
SALES (est): 1.9MM **Privately Held**
SIC: 2389 5699 Uniforms & vestments; sports apparel

(G-10783)
JOAN BOYCE LTD (PA)
19 W 44th St Ste 417 (10036-5900)
PHONE..................212 867-7474
Joan Boyce, *President*
Allen Boyce, *Vice Pres*
EMP: 4
SQ FT: 1,100
SALES (est): 7MM **Privately Held**
WEB: www.joanboyce.com
SIC: 3911 5944 Jewelry, precious metal; jewelry stores

(G-10784)
JOBSON MEDICAL INFORMATION LLC (PA)
440 9th Ave Fl 14 (10001-1629)
PHONE..................212 274-7000
Fax: 212 431-0500
Michael Tansey, *CEO*
Frank Bennicasa, *Publisher*
Marck Ferrera, *Publisher*
Carol Jaxel, *Publisher*
Robert Davidson, *Editor*
▲ **EMP:** 120 **EST:** 1958
SALES (est): 97.2MM **Privately Held**
WEB: www.revoptom.com
SIC: 2721 2741 Magazines: publishing & printing; miscellaneous publishing

(G-10785)
JOCKEY INTERNATIONAL INC
Also Called: Jockey Store
1411 Broadway Rm 1010 (10018-3560)
PHONE..................212 840-4900
John Brody, *Exec VP*
Janine Forgie, *Branch Mgr*
EMP: 30
SALES (corp-wide): 253.9MM **Privately Held**
SIC: 2254 Knit underwear mills
PA: Jockey International, Inc.
2300 60th St
Kenosha WI 53140
262 658-8111

(G-10786)
JOE BENBASSET INC (PA)
213 W 35th St Rm 803 (10001-1916)
PHONE..................212 268-4920
Fax: 212 268-4920
Murray Benbasset, *President*
Mila Finkelstein, *Controller*
◆ **EMP:** 25 **EST:** 1948
SQ FT: 10,000
SALES (est): 8MM **Privately Held**
SIC: 2339 Sportswear, women's

(G-10787)
JOED PRESS
242 W 36th St Fl 8 (10018-7542)
PHONE..................212 243-3620
Angela Vann, *General Mgr*
EMP: 5 **EST:** 2010
SALES (est): 243.7K **Privately Held**
SIC: 2759 Commercial printing

(G-10788)
JOHN KOCHIS CUSTOM DESIGNS
237 W 35th St Ste 702 (10001-1952)
PHONE..................212 244-6046
John Kochis, *Owner*
EMP: 7
SALES: 300K **Privately Held**
SIC: 2311 Tailored suits & formal jackets

(G-10789)
JOHN KRISTIANSEN NEW YORK INC
665 Broadway Frnt (10012-2300)
PHONE..................212 388-1097
John Kristiansen, *President*
Monroe France, *Assistant VP*
EMP: 10
SALES (est): 953.1K **Privately Held**
SIC: 2389 Costumes

(G-10790)
JOHN MARSHALL SOUND INC
630 9th Ave Ste 1108 (10036-3743)
PHONE..................212 265-6066
Cheary Marshall,
EMP: 8
SALES (est): 1.1MM **Privately Held**
SIC: 3652 Master records or tapes, preparation of

(G-10791)
JOHN N FEHLINGER CO INC (PA)
20 Vesey St Rm 1000 (10007-4225)
PHONE..................212 233-5656
Fax: 212 233-5717
Kevin Arcuri, *President*
John Capuano, *Treasurer*
Peter Sarkar, *Accountant*
James Talerico, *Manager*
Sheree Pelmen, *Admin Sec*
▲ **EMP:** 15 **EST:** 1945
SQ FT: 4,000
SALES (est): 5MM **Privately Held**
WEB: www.fehlingerco.com
SIC: 3491 3561 5084 5085 Steam traps; pumps & pumping equipment; industrial pumps & parts; industrial machinery & equipment; water pumps (industrial); valves & fittings

(G-10792)
JOHN SZOKE GRAPHICS INC
Also Called: John Szoke Editions
24 W 57th St Ste 304 (10019-3918)
PHONE..................212 219-8300
John Szoke, *President*
▲ **EMP:** 8
SQ FT: 10,000
SALES (est): 520K **Privately Held**
WEB: www.johnszokeeditions.com
SIC: 2741 Miscellaneous publishing

(G-10793)
JOHN VARVATOS COMPANY
26 W 17th St Fl 12 (10011-5710)
PHONE..................212 812-8000
John Varvatos, *President*
EMP: 30
SALES (est): 1.4MM **Privately Held**
WEB: www.nautica.com
SIC: 2329 5136 5611 6794 Men's & boys' sportswear & athletic clothing; men's & boys' sportswear & work clothing; men's & boys' robes, nightwear & undergarments; clothing, sportswear, men's & boys'; franchises, selling or licensing

(G-10794)
JOHNNY BIENSTOCK MUSIC
126 E 38th St (10016-2602)
PHONE..................212 779-7977
John Bienstock, *Owner*
EMP: 25
SALES (est): 1.3MM **Privately Held**
SIC: 2741 Music books: publishing & printing

(G-10795)
JOLIBE ATELIER LLC
325 W 38th St (10018-2915)
PHONE..................347 882-6617
EMP: 12
SALES: 917K **Privately Held**
SIC: 2389 Men's miscellaneous accessories

GEOGRAPHIC SECTION

New York - New York County (G-10821)

(G-10796)
JON TERI SPORTS INC (PA)
241 W 37th St Frnt 2 (10018-6797)
PHONE.....................212 398-0657
Fax: 212 302-2726
Rickie Freeman, *President*
Leora Platt, *Sales Staff*
Shanta Khairain, *Manager*
▲ EMP: 35 EST: 1981
SQ FT: 6,000
SALES (est): 4.5MM **Privately Held**
SIC: **2335** 2337 Women's, juniors' & misses' dresses; suits: women's, misses' & juniors'

(G-10797)
JONATHAN MEIZLER LLC
Also Called: Title of Work
37 W 26th St Ph (10010-1049)
PHONE.....................212 213-2977
Jonathan Meizler, *Mfg Staff*
EMP: 7
SQ FT: 1,500
SALES (est): 380K **Privately Held**
SIC: **2389** Men's miscellaneous accessories

(G-10798)
JONATHAN MICHAEL COAT CORP
463 Fashion Ave Rm 1502 (10018-7596)
PHONE.....................212 239-9230
Fax: 212 239-9238
Bruce Heart, *President*
Nathan Printz, *Corp Secy*
▲ EMP: 7
SQ FT: 1,500
SALES (est): 840.5K **Privately Held**
SIC: **2339** Women's & misses' jackets & coats, except sportswear

(G-10799)
JORDACHE ENTERPRISES INC
Fubu Jeans By Je Sport Co Div
1400 Broadway Rm 1415 (10018-5336)
PHONE.....................212 944-1330
AVI Nakash, *Exec VP*
Ezri Sirveb, *Branch Mgr*
EMP: 100
SALES (corp-wide): 1.3B **Privately Held**
WEB: www.jordache.com
SIC: **2339** 2325 2369 2331 Slacks: women's, misses' & juniors'; men's & boys' trousers & slacks; slacks: girls' & children's; jackets: girls, children's & infants'; shirts, women's & juniors': made from purchased materials; men's & boys' furnishings; shirts: girls', children's & infants'
PA: Jordache Enterprises Inc.
  1400 Broadway Rm 1404b
  New York NY 10018
  212 643-8400

(G-10800)
JORDACHE ENTERPRISES INC (PA)
1400 Broadway Rm 1404b (10018-5336)
PHONE.....................212 643-8400
Fax: 212 768-3096
Joe Nakash, *CEO*
Jonathan Bennett, *Managing Dir*
Ralph Nakash, *Corp Secy*
Eddie Benaderet, *Exec VP*
Bob Ross, *Exec VP*
▲ EMP: 145
SALES (est): 1.3B **Privately Held**
WEB: www.jordache.com
SIC: **2339** 2325 2369 2331 Slacks: women's, misses' & juniors'; men's & boys' trousers & slacks; slacks: girls' & children's; jackets: girls, children's & infants'; shirts, women's & juniors': made from purchased materials; men's & boys' furnishings; shirts: girls', children's & infants'

(G-10801)
JORDAN SCOTT DESIGNS LTD
Also Called: Plaza Group Creation
25 W 36th St Fl 12 (10018-7677)
PHONE.....................212 947-4250
Fax: 212 947-4247
Edward Schantz, *CEO*
EMP: 25

SQ FT: 4,500
SALES (est): 2.4MM **Privately Held**
SIC: **3911** Jewelry, precious metal

(G-10802)
JOSEPH (UK) INC
1061 Madison Ave Grnd (10028-0239)
PHONE.....................212 570-0077
Hiroaki Sumi, *Ch of Bd*
Louis Loketch, *Principal*
EMP: 5
SALES (est): 527.5K **Privately Held**
SIC: **2329** 5621 5651 Men's & boys' sportswear & athletic clothing; women's clothing stores; jeans stores

(G-10803)
JOSEPH ABBOUD MANUFACTURING
650 5th Ave Fl 20 (10019-7687)
PHONE.....................212 586-9140
Marty Staff, *Ch of Bd*
Anthony Sapienza, *President*
Eric Spiel, *Vice Pres*
Marisol Fernandez, *Asst Treas*
Brian Hrenenko, *Asst Treas*
EMP: 5
SALES (est): 230K **Privately Held**
SIC: **2326** 2339 Men's & boys' work clothing; women's & misses' athletic clothing & sportswear

(G-10804)
JOSEPH INDUSTRIES INC (PA)
Also Called: Color Fx
1410 Broadway Rm 1201 (10018-9348)
PHONE.....................212 764-0010
Prakash Joseph, *President*
▲ EMP: 5
SQ FT: 5,000
SALES (est): 3.8MM **Privately Held**
SIC: **2389** Men's miscellaneous accessories

(G-10805)
JOSEPH TREU SUCCESSORS INC
104 W 27th St Rm 5b (10001-6210)
PHONE.....................212 691-7026
Fax: 212 463-8821
Harvey Schreibman, *President*
Arlene Schreibman, *Corp Secy*
EMP: 5
SQ FT: 3,000
SALES: 700K **Privately Held**
SIC: **3953** Marking devices

(G-10806)
JOSHUA LINER GALLERY LLC
540 W 28th St Frnt (10001-5770)
PHONE.....................212 244-7415
Joshua Liner, *Owner*
EMP: 10
SALES (est): 1.2MM **Privately Held**
SIC: **3443** Liners/lining

(G-10807)
JOSIE ACCESSORIES INC (PA)
Also Called: Elrene Home Fashions
261 5th Ave Fl 10 (10016-7701)
PHONE.....................212 889-6376
Fax: 212 481-1738
Bryan Siegel, *Ch of Bd*
Craig Siegel, *Vice Pres*
Frank Giacomini, *CFO*
Richard Orent, *CFO*
▲ EMP: 75 EST: 1945
SQ FT: 20,000
SALES (est): 10.9MM **Privately Held**
SIC: **2392** Tablecloths: made from purchased materials; placemats, plastic or textile

(G-10808)
JOTALY INC
1385 Broadway Fl 12 (10018-6118)
PHONE.....................212 886-6000
Fax: 212 886-6319
Ofer Azrielant, *Ch of Bd*
John C Esposito, *Vice Pres*
Erika Dejesus, *Production*
Cristina Sousa, *Human Res Dir*
Scott Lyle, *VP Sales*
▲ EMP: 750
SQ FT: 48,000

SALES (est): 87MM
SALES (corp-wide): 223.6B **Publicly Held**
WEB: www.andin.com
SIC: **3911** Jewelry, precious metal
HQ: Richline Group, Inc.
  1385 Broadway Fl 12
  New York NY 10018

(G-10809)
JOURNAL REGISTER COMPANY (PA)
5 Hanover Sq Fl 25 (10004-4008)
PHONE.....................212 257-7212
John Paton, *CEO*
James W Hall, *Ch of Bd*
Paul Provost, *President*
Matt Derienzo, *Publisher*
Lynette Gannon, *Publisher*
EMP: 40
SQ FT: 36,443
SALES (est): 670.9MM **Privately Held**
WEB: www.journalregister.com
SIC: **2711** Newspapers, publishing & printing

(G-10810)
JOVANI FASHION LTD
1370 Broadway Fl 4 (10018-7786)
PHONE.....................212 279-0222
Fax: 212 279-0133
Saul Maslavi, *President*
Abraham Maslavi, *Vice Pres*
Carol Ramirez, *Cust Mgr*
Maria S D'Annunzio, *Sales Staff*
Agnes Rejman, *Sales Staff*
▲ EMP: 30
SQ FT: 8,000
SALES (est): 3.1MM **Privately Held**
WEB: www.jovani.com
SIC: **2335** Women's, juniors' & misses' dresses; gowns, formal

(G-10811)
JOYCE TRIMMING INC
109 W 38th St (10018-3615)
PHONE.....................212 719-3110
Fax: 212 719-2091
Hwe Young Lee, *President*
▲ EMP: 8
SQ FT: 2,000
SALES: 2MM **Privately Held**
WEB: www.ejoyce.com
SIC: **3965** Buttons & parts

(G-10812)
JRG APPAREL GROUP COMPANY LTD
Also Called: Indigo Rein
1407 Broadway Rm 817 (10018-3287)
PHONE.....................212 997-0900
Jay Gorman, *Ch of Bd*
Christina Tierney, *General Mgr*
▲ EMP: 24
SQ FT: 3,300
SALES (est): 30MM **Privately Held**
SIC: **2211** Denims

(G-10813)
JS BLANK & CO INC
112 Madison Ave Fl 7 (10016-7484)
PHONE.....................212 689-4835
Fax: 212 696-1659
Joseph S Blank, *CEO*
Barbara Blank, *Vice Pres*
EMP: 25
SQ FT: 7,500
SALES (est): 2.6MM **Privately Held**
SIC: **2323** Men's & boys' neckwear

(G-10814)
JSC DESIGNS LTD
550 Fashion Ave Fl 22 (10018-3223)
PHONE.....................212 302-1001
Mitchell Hops, *President*
Alicia Moscovitch, *Accounts Mgr*
▲ EMP: 20
SQ FT: 8,000
SALES (est): 2MM **Privately Held**
SIC: **2339** Service apparel, washable: women's

(G-10815)
JUDYS GROUP INC
1400 Broadway Rm 919 (10018-0698)
PHONE.....................212 921-0515

Fax: 212 302-5259
Howard Schlossberg, *President*
Michele Tepper, *Exec VP*
Michelle Pepper, *CFO*
▲ EMP: 50
SQ FT: 11,000
SALES (est): 9.5MM **Privately Held**
WEB: www.judysgroup.com
SIC: **2337** 2339 2335 Suits: women's, misses', misses' & juniors'; athletic clothing: women's, misses' & juniors'; women's, juniors' & misses' dresses

(G-10816)
JUICE PRESS LLC (PA)
7 W 18th St Fl 6 (10011-4663)
PHONE.....................212 777-0034
Marcus Antebi, *CEO*
Alex Jay, *Marketing Staff*
EMP: 8
SALES (est): 3.7MM **Privately Held**
SIC: **3556** Juice extractors, fruit & vegetable: commercial type

(G-10817)
JULIA JORDAN CORPORATION
530 Fashion Ave Rm 505 (10018-4890)
PHONE.....................646 214-3090
Mansour Zar, *Owner*
EMP: 10
SALES (est): 390.6K **Privately Held**
SIC: **2337** Women's & misses' suits & coats

(G-10818)
JULIUS KLEIN GROUP
580 5th Ave Ste 500 (10036-4727)
PHONE.....................212 719-1811
Julius Klein, *Owner*
Moshe Klein, *Sales Dir*
Hershy Schwartz, *Sales Executive*
Pearl Rothman, *Admin Sec*
▲ EMP: 50
SALES (est): 4.1MM **Privately Held**
SIC: **3915** Diamond cutting & polishing

(G-10819)
JULIUS LOWY FRAME RESTORING CO
232 E 59th St 4fn (10022-1464)
PHONE.....................212 861-8585
Fax: 212 988-0443
Lawrence A Shar, *President*
John Evans, *Controller*
Patty Tan, *Human Resources*
Lisa Wyer, *VP Sales*
Michael Tramis, *Manager*
EMP: 35
SQ FT: 20,000
SALES (est): 4.2MM **Privately Held**
WEB: www.lowyonline.com
SIC: **2499** 8999 Picture frame molding, finished; art restoration

(G-10820)
JUMP DESIGN GROUP INC
Also Called: Jump Design Group, The
1400 Broadway Fl 2 (10018-1075)
PHONE.....................212 869-3300
Fax: 212 869-3639
Glenn Schlossberg, *Ch of Bd*
Terry Friedman, *President*
Peter Gabbe, *Principal*
Patrick M Corrigan, *CFO*
Joann Abellar, *Office Mgr*
▲ EMP: 140
SQ FT: 18,000
SALES (est): 33.6MM **Privately Held**
WEB: www.jumpapparel.com
SIC: **2335** Women's, juniors' & misses' dresses

(G-10821)
JUMP RAMP GAMES INC
307 W 38th St Rm 1101 (10018-9528)
PHONE.....................212 500-1456
Dan Kim, *President*
Tony Vartanian, *Principal*
Alexander Betancur, *Chairman*
Ryan Safarian, *Engineer*
EMP: 45
SALES (est): 336.4K **Privately Held**
SIC: **7372** Application computer software

New York - New York County (G-10822)

(G-10822)
JUMPROPE INC
121 W 27th St Ste 1204 (10001-6261)
P.O. Box 1616 (10113-1616)
PHONE..................347 927-5867
Jesse Olsen, *CEO*
Justin Meyer, *COO*
Nathan Patton, *Engineer*
EMP: 9
SQ FT: 500
SALES (est): 580K **Privately Held**
SIC: 7372 Educational computer software

(G-10823)
JUNE JACOBS LABS LLC
460 Park Ave Fl 16 (10022-1829)
PHONE..................212 471-4830
Tiffany Cavallaro, *Vice Pres*
June Jacobs, *Human Resources*
Jessica Khani, *Marketing Mgr*
Marvin Sternlicht,
Peter T Roth,
EMP: 65
SALES (corp-wide): 16.4MM **Privately Held**
SIC: 2844 Cosmetic preparations
PA: June Jacobs Labs, Llc
  46 Graphic Pl
  Moonachie NJ 07074
  201 329-9100

(G-10824)
JUPITER CREATIONS INC
330 7th Ave Ste 901 (10001-5010)
PHONE..................917 493-9393
Michael Katina, *President*
▲ **EMP:** 2
SQ FT: 1,000
SALES: 3MM **Privately Held**
SIC: 3944 3942 Games, toys & children's vehicles; airplanes, toy; automobiles & trucks, toy; dolls & stuffed toys

(G-10825)
JUST BOTTOMS & TOPS INC (PA)
Also Called: Hot Cashews
1412 Broadway Rm 1808 (10018-9228)
PHONE..................212 564-3202
Fax: 212 564-3205
Mickey Mait, *President*
Sanders Acker, *Vice Pres*
Mitch Levy, *Vice Pres*
Aaron Feder, *Treasurer*
Jerry Hymowitz, *Admin Sec*
EMP: 10
SQ FT: 3,900
SALES (est): 915.3K **Privately Held**
SIC: 2329 2339 Sweaters & sweater jackets: men's & boys'; women's & misses' outerwear

(G-10826)
JUST BRASS INC
215 W 90th St Apt 9a (10024-1224)
PHONE..................212 724-5447
Fax: 212 875-0124
Ronald Zabinski, *President*
EMP: 5
SALES: 150K **Privately Held**
SIC: 3172 5136 2321 Personal leather goods; shirts, men's & boys'; men's & boys' furnishings

(G-10827)
JUSTPERFECTMSP LTD
48 W 48th St Ste 401 (10036-1727)
PHONE..................877 201-0005
Edward Zylka, *President*
Shirley Glumer, *Exec VP*
Ewa Zylka, *Director*
▲ **EMP:** 45 **EST:** 1994
SQ FT: 5,000
SALES (est): 1.7MM **Privately Held**
SIC: 3911 5094 Jewelry, precious metal; jewelry & precious stones
PA: Art-Tec Jewelry Designs Ltd
  48 W 48th St Ste 401
  New York NY 10036

(G-10828)
JUSTYNA KAMINSKA NY INC
1270 Broadway Rm 708 (10001-3244)
PHONE..................917 423-5527
Justyna Kaminska Cabbad, *President*
▲ **EMP:** 1

SQ FT: 800
SALES: 1MM **Privately Held**
SIC: 3911 Jewelry, precious metal

(G-10829)
JUVLY AESTHETICS INC
18 E 41st St Rm 406 (10017-6269)
PHONE..................614 686-3627
Justin Harper, *Principal*
EMP: 100
SALES (est): 3.1MM **Privately Held**
SIC: 3845 Laser systems & equipment, medical

(G-10830)
K PAT INCORPORATED
77 Columbia St (10002-2678)
PHONE..................212 688-5728
Osahon Emmanue, *CEO*
A Kings Aibangbee, *Administration*
EMP: 6
SALES (est): 239.8K **Privately Held**
SIC: 2399 5023 7389 Hand woven apparel; decorative home furnishings & supplies; styling of fashions, apparel, furniture, textiles, etc.

(G-10831)
K ROAD MOAPA SOLAR LLC
295 Madison Ave Fl 37 (10017-6343)
PHONE..................212 351-0535
William V Kriegel,
Gerrit Nicholas,
Daniel Oshea,
Thomas N Tureen,
EMP: 10
SQ FT: 4,000
SALES (est): 723.5K **Privately Held**
SIC: 3621 Power generators

(G-10832)
K ROAD POWER MANAGEMENT LLC (PA)
767 3rd Ave Fl 37 (10017-2077)
PHONE..................212 351-0535
Fax: 212 351-0530
William Kriegel, *CEO*
Mark Friedland, *Exec VP*
Carl Weatherley-White, *CFO*
Buvron Arnelle, *Office Mgr*
Amine Alami, *Director*
EMP: 15
SALES (est): 1.6MM **Privately Held**
SIC: 3612 Transformers, except electric

(G-10833)
K T P DESIGN CO INC
118 E 28th St Rm 707 (10016-8448)
PHONE..................212 481-6613
Patrick Walsh, *President*
▼ **EMP:** 15 **EST:** 1998
SALES (est): 1.6MM **Privately Held**
WEB: www.customtie.com
SIC: 2339 Neckwear & ties: women's, misses' & juniors'

(G-10834)
K2 INTERNATIONAL CORP
22 W 32nd St Fl 9 (10001-3807)
PHONE..................212 947-1734
John Hyun Kim, *President*
Jennifer Moon, *General Mgr*
Diane Kim, *Accounts Mgr*
▲ **EMP:** 5
SQ FT: 7,000
SALES (est): 390K **Privately Held**
SIC: 3961 Costume jewelry

(G-10835)
KADMON CORPORATION LLC (PA)
450 E 29th St Fl 5 (10016-8367)
PHONE..................212 308-6000
Harlan Waksal, *CEO*
Samuel D Waksal, *Chairman*
John Ryan, *Exec VP*
Zhenping Zhu, *Exec VP*
Michael Boxer, *Senior VP*
EMP: 10
SALES (est): 26.2MM **Privately Held**
SIC: 2834 Pharmaceutical preparations

(G-10836)
KADMON HOLDINGS INC
450 E 29th St (10016-8367)
PHONE..................212 308-6000
Bart M Schwartz, *Ch of Bd*
Harlan W Waksal, *President*
Lawrence K Cohen, *Exec VP*
John L Ryan, *Exec VP*
Konstantin Poukalov, *CFO*
EMP: 58
SQ FT: 48,892
SALES: 26MM **Privately Held**
SIC: 2836 2834 Biological products, except diagnostic; pharmaceutical preparations

(G-10837)
KAHN-LUCAS-LANCASTER INC
112 W 34th St Ste 600 (10120-0700)
PHONE..................212 239-2407
Justine Berndt, *Vice Pres*
Duke Marr, *Vice Pres*
Jenny Lin, *Prdtn Mgr*
Yuliya Akopova, *Production*
Linda Mulligan, *Design Engr*
EMP: 80
SALES (corp-wide): 43MM **Privately Held**
WEB: www.kahnlucas.com
SIC: 2369 Girls' & children's outerwear
PA: Kahn-Lucas-Lancaster, Inc.
  306 Primrose Ln
  Mountville PA 17554
  717 537-4140

(G-10838)
KALEIDOSCOPE IMAGING INC
251 W 39th St Fl 4 (10018-3143)
PHONE..................212 631-9947
Fax: 212 631-9948
Garo Ksparian, *Partner*
EMP: 30
SALES (corp-wide): 14.4MM **Privately Held**
SIC: 2752 Commercial printing, lithographic
PA: Kaleidoscope Imaging, Inc.
  700 N Sacramento Blvd # 2
  Chicago IL 60612
  773 722-9300

(G-10839)
KALEKO BROS
62 W 47th St Ste 1504 (10036-3249)
PHONE..................212 819-0100
Jerome Kaleko, *Partner*
EMP: 5 **EST:** 1948
SQ FT: 2,000
SALES (est): 304.2K **Privately Held**
SIC: 3915 Diamond cutting & polishing

(G-10840)
KALIKOW BROTHERS LP
34 W 33rd St Fl 4n (10001-3304)
PHONE..................212 643-0315
Fax: 212 643-0320
Marc Kalikow, *President*
Paul Levine, *Vice Pres*
Jeffrey Rosen, *Controller*
EMP: 30 **EST:** 1929
SQ FT: 8,000
SALES (est): 1.8MM **Privately Held**
WEB: www.fishmantobin.com
SIC: 2325 Trousers, dress (separate): men's, youths' & boys'
HQ: F&T Apparel Llc
  4000 Chemical Rd Ste 500
  Plymouth Meeting PA 19462
  610 828-8400

(G-10841)
KALLEN CORP
Also Called: Capstone Printing
99 Hudson St (10013-2815)
P.O. Box 516 (10014-0516)
PHONE..................212 242-1470
Alan Finkelstein, *President*
EMP: 5
SQ FT: 3,000
SALES (est): 801.6K **Privately Held**
SIC: 2759 Commercial printing

(G-10842)
KALTEX AMERICA INC
350 5th Ave Ste 7100 (10118-0110)
PHONE..................212 971-0575

Fax: 212 971-0362
Hebe Schecter, *CEO*
Rafael M Kalach, *Ch of Bd*
Jennifer Mason, *CFO*
Fred Walck, *Administration*
EMP: 18 **EST:** 1987
SQ FT: 1,000
SALES: 161MM **Privately Held**
SIC: 2339 2325 Jeans: women's, misses' & juniors'; jeans: men's, youths' & boys'
HQ: Kaltex North America, Inc.
  350 5th Ave Ste 7100
  New York NY 10118
  212 894-3200

(G-10843)
KALTEX NORTH AMERICA INC (HQ)
350 5th Ave Ste 7100 (10118-0110)
PHONE..................212 894-3200
Rafael Kalach, *Ch of Bd*
Nevolia Williams, *Finance*
▲ **EMP:** 10
SALES (est): 197.3MM **Privately Held**
WEB: www.kaltexhome.com
SIC: 2392 Comforters & quilts: made from purchased materials

(G-10844)
KANE-M INC
Also Called: Morito/Kane-M
135 W 29th St Rm 1003 (10001-5162)
PHONE..................973 777-2797
Ken Egawa, *CEO*
EMP: 7
SQ FT: 10,000
SALES (est): 490.9K
SALES (corp-wide): 388.6MM **Privately Held**
SIC: 3965 Fasteners, buttons, needles & pins
PA: Morito Co., Ltd.
  4-2-4, Minamihonmachi, Chuo-Ku
  Osaka OSK 541-0
  662 523-551

(G-10845)
KAPRIELIAN ENTERPRISES INC
Also Called: Concord Settings
207 W 25th St Fl 8 (10001-7158)
PHONE..................212 645-6623
Fax: 212 255-8128
Hratch Kaprielian, *President*
Maria Chiang, *Accountant*
Ray Mercurius, *Sales Executive*
Timothy Kilburn, *Manager*
▲ **EMP:** 70
SQ FT: 6,000
SALES (est): 9.2MM **Privately Held**
WEB: www.kaprielian.com
SIC: 3911 3915 Jewel settings & mountings, precious metal; jewelers' materials & lapidary work

(G-10846)
KARBRA COMPANY
151 W 46th St Fl 10 (10036-8512)
PHONE..................212 736-9300
Fax: 212 736-9303
Sing Ming Liu, *Partner*
Carole Roth, *Partner*
Peter Roth, *Partner*
Fiam Ildiko Roth, *Vice Pres*
George Barna, *MIS Dir*
EMP: 140 **EST:** 1940
SQ FT: 10,000
SALES (est): 13.1MM **Privately Held**
WEB: www.karbra.com
SIC: 3915 3911 3369 3341 Jewelers' castings; jewelry, precious metal; nonferrous foundries; secondary nonferrous metals

(G-10847)
KAREN KANE INC
1441 Broadway Fl 33 (10018-1905)
PHONE..................212 827-0980
Fax: 212 827-0987
Ashly Juskus, *Buyer*
Becky Blair, *Manager*
Tiffany Bowe, *Manager*
EMP: 12
SALES (corp-wide): 54.6MM **Privately Held**
SIC: 2339 Women's & misses' outerwear

GEOGRAPHIC SECTION

New York - New York County (G-10872)

PA: Karen Kane, Inc.
2275 E 37th St
Vernon CA 90058
323 588-0000

(G-10848)
KARTELL US INC
39 Greene St (10013-2605)
PHONE.................................212 966-6665
▲ EMP: 6
SALES (est): 130.3K **Privately Held**
SIC: 2392 Household furnishings

(G-10849)
KAS-RAY INDUSTRIES INC
Also Called: Kay-Ray Industries
122 W 26th St (10001-6804)
PHONE.................................212 620-3144
Fax: 212 620-4210
Tony Petrizzo, *President*
EMP: 10
SQ FT: 10,000
SALES (est): 1.9MM **Privately Held**
WEB: www.kasray.com
SIC: 2752 5112 5021 Commercial printing, offset; stationery & office supplies; office furniture

(G-10850)
KASEYA US SALES LLC
62 W 22nd St Ste 2r (10010-5147)
PHONE.................................415 694-5700
Fred Voccola, *Mng Member*
Isaac Itenberg,
EMP: 99
SALES (est): 20MM **Privately Held**
SIC: 7372 Prepackaged software

(G-10851)
KASISTO INC
43 W 24th St Rm 8b (10010-3530)
PHONE.................................917 734-4750
Zor Gorelov, *CEO*
William Mark, *Principal*
Jeffrey Seltzer, *Principal*
Ruth Brown, *Vice Pres*
Sasha Caskey, *Vice Pres*
EMP: 40 EST: 2013
SQ FT: 150
SALES (est): 327.9K **Privately Held**
SIC: 7372 Business oriented computer software

(G-10852)
KASPER GROUP LLC (HQ)
1412 Broadway Fl 5 (10018-3330)
PHONE.................................212 354-4311
EMP: 15
SALES (est): 1.7MM
SALES (corp-wide): 244.7MM **Privately Held**
SIC: 2339 Mfg Women's/Misses' Outerwear
PA: Jones Holdings Llc
1411 Brdwy
New York NY 10018
215 785-4000

(G-10853)
KASPER GROUP LLC
1412 Broadway Fl 5 (10018-3330)
PHONE.................................212 354-4311
Gregg I Marks, *CEO*
Irene Koumendouros, *President*
Daniel Fishman, *COO*
Nikki Palma, *Exec VP*
Michael Havardansky, *Controller*
◆ EMP: 250
SALES (est): 350MM
SALES (corp-wide): 2.1B **Privately Held**
SIC: 2335 Women's, juniors' & misses' dresses
PA: Nine West Holdings, Inc.
180 Rittenhouse Cir
Bristol PA 19007
215 785-4000

(G-10854)
KATE SPADE & COMPANY (HQ)
2 Park Ave Fl 8 (10016-5613)
PHONE.................................212 354-4900
Fax: 212 626-1803
Craig A Leavitt, *CEO*
George M Carrara, *President*
Timothy F Michno, *Senior VP*
Linda Yanussi, *Senior VP*
Thomas Linko, *CFO*
◆ EMP: 420
SQ FT: 135,000
SALES: 1.3B
SALES (corp-wide): 4.4B **Publicly Held**
WEB: www.lizclaiborne.com
SIC: 2331 5651 5136 5137 Women's & misses' blouses & shirts; family clothing stores; unisex clothing stores; men's & boys' clothing; women's & children's clothing; catalog & mail-order houses
PA: Coach, Inc.
10 Hudson Yards
New York NY 10001
212 594-1850

(G-10855)
KATES PAPERIE LTD
188 Lafayette St Frnt A (10013-3200)
PHONE.................................212 966-3904
Leonard Flax, *Manager*
Renee Holiday, *Manager*
Asif Iqbal, *Manager*
▲ EMP: 6
SALES (est): 330K **Privately Held**
SIC: 2759 Announcements: engraved

(G-10856)
KATHMANDO VALLEY PRESERVATION
Also Called: H THEOPHILE
36 W 25th St Fl 17 (10010-2706)
PHONE.................................212 727-0074
Erich Theophile, *Owner*
EMP: 10
SALES (est): 491.4K **Privately Held**
SIC: 3851 Temples & fronts, ophthalmic

(G-10857)
KATZ MARTELL FASHION TRDG INTL
1385 Broadway Rm 1401 (10018-6057)
PHONE.................................212 840-0070
Fax: 212 840-0110
Debbie Martell, *President*
Bonnie Katz, *Vice Pres*
▲ EMP: 7 EST: 1998
SQ FT: 2,500
SALES (est): 420K **Privately Held**
SIC: 2339 Women's & misses' athletic clothing & sportswear

(G-10858)
KAUFMAN BROTHERS PRINTING
327 W 36th St Rm 403 (10018-6971)
PHONE.................................212 563-1854
Fax: 212 268-4914
Harvey Kaufman, *Owner*
Bobby Nicol, *Vice Pres*
EMP: 5
SQ FT: 2,000
SALES (est): 2MM **Privately Held**
SIC: 2752 2759 2789 Commercial printing, offset; letterpress printing; bookbinding & related work

(G-10859)
KAWASHO FOODS USA INC
45 Broadway Fl 18 (10006-3007)
PHONE.................................212 841-7400
Tatsuya Ito, *President*
EMP: 11
SALES: 52MM
SALES (corp-wide): 29.1B **Privately Held**
SIC: 2032 Canned specialties
HQ: Kawasho Foods Corporation
2-7-1, Otemachi
Chiyoda-Ku TKY 100-0
352 031-028

(G-10860)
KAY SEE DENTAL MFG CO
777 Avenue Of The Apt 32 (10001)
PHONE.................................816 842-2817
Yachiyo Smith, *President*
Clark Y Smith, *Vice Pres*
EMP: 12
SQ FT: 15,000
SALES (est): 1.4MM **Privately Held**
WEB: www.hydrocast.com
SIC: 3843 Dental equipment; dental materials

(G-10861)
KAYMIL PRINTING COMPANY INC
140 W 30th St Frnt (10001-4005)
PHONE.................................212 594-3718
Fax: 212 594-6803
Richwar Warner, *President*
EMP: 5 EST: 1961
SQ FT: 6,000
SALES (est): 248.2K **Privately Held**
WEB: www.kaymil.com
SIC: 2759 2752 Letterpress printing; screen printing; offset & photolithographic printing

(G-10862)
KAYO OF CALIFORNIA
525 Fashion Ave Rm 309 (10018-0485)
PHONE.................................212 354-6336
Jesse Vasquez, *Office Mgr*
Steven Berman, *Manager*
EMP: 5
SALES (corp-wide): 16.4MM **Privately Held**
WEB: www.kayo.com
SIC: 2337 2339 Skirts, separate: women's, misses' & juniors'; sportswear, women's; shorts (outerwear): women's, misses' & juniors'; slacks: women's, misses' & juniors'
PA: Kayo Of California
161 W 39th St
Los Angeles CA 90037
323 233-6107

(G-10863)
KBL HEALTHCARE LP
757 3rd Ave Fl 20 (10017-2046)
PHONE.................................212 319-5555
Fax: 212 319-5591
Dr Marlene Krauss, *Manager*
EMP: 7
SALES (est): 563.6K **Privately Held**
SIC: 2834 Pharmaceutical preparations

(G-10864)
KBS COMMUNICATIONS LLC
Also Called: Mystery Scene Magazine
331 W 57th St Ste 148 (10019-3101)
PHONE.................................212 765-7124
Kathleen M Stine, *Mng Member*
Brian Skupin,
EMP: 12
SALES (est): 950.6K **Privately Held**
WEB: www.mysteryscenemag.com
SIC: 2721 Magazines: publishing & printing

(G-10865)
KC COLLECTIONS LLC
1407 Broadway Rm 1710 (10018-2789)
PHONE.................................212 302-4412
Fax: 212 840-7581
Bart Yanofsky,
Michael Carbone,
Kirk Oshan,
▲ EMP: 7
SQ FT: 4,000
SALES (est): 701.6K **Privately Held**
SIC: 2253 Cold weather knit outerwear, including ski wear

(G-10866)
KCP HOLDCO INC (PA)
603 W 50th St (10019-7029)
PHONE.................................212 265-1500
Paul Blum, *CEO*
EMP: 10
SALES (est): 678.3MM **Privately Held**
SIC: 3143 3171 5661 5632 Men's footwear, except athletic; handbags, women's; purses, women's; shoe stores; women's boots; men's shoes; women's accessory & specialty stores; apparel accessories; costume jewelry; handbags; men's & boys' clothing stores

(G-10867)
KCP OPERATING COMPANY LLC
603 W 50th St (10019-7029)
PHONE.................................212 265-1500
Kenneth Cole, *Mng Member*
EMP: 75
SALES (est): 2.6MM
SALES (corp-wide): 678.3MM **Privately Held**
SIC: 3144 3143 Women's footwear, except athletic; men's footwear, except athletic
PA: Kcp Holdco, Inc.
603 W 50th St
New York NY 10019
212 265-1500

(G-10868)
KEARNEY-NATIONAL INC (HQ)
Also Called: Coto Technology
565 5th Ave Fl 4 (10017-2424)
PHONE.................................212 661-4600
Robert R Dyson, *Ch of Bd*
Marc Feldman, *Vice Pres*
Leigh Beck, *Accounts Mgr*
John Fitzsimons, *Admin Sec*
◆ EMP: 10 EST: 1988
SALES (est): 217.9MM
SALES (corp-wide): 486.2MM **Privately Held**
WEB: www.cotorelay.com
SIC: 3679 3694 3714 3625 Electronic switches; engine electrical equipment; fuel systems & parts, motor vehicle; relays & industrial controls
PA: The Dyson-Kissner-Moran Corporation
2515 South Rd Ste 5
Poughkeepsie NY 12601
212 661-4600

(G-10869)
KEILHAUER
200 Lexington Ave Rm 1101 (10016-6255)
PHONE.................................646 742-0192
Allen Primason, *Partner*
EMP: 10
SALES (est): 828.9K **Privately Held**
WEB: www.keilhauer.com
SIC: 2522 Chairs, office: padded or plain, except wood

(G-10870)
KELLY GRACE CORP (PA)
Also Called: Danny & Nicole
49 W 37th St Fl 10 (10018-0180)
PHONE.................................212 704-9603
Fax: 212 704-0462
Jamshid Zar, *Ch of Bd*
Daniel Zar, *President*
Esshagh Zar, *Vice Pres*
Korosh Zar, *Vice Pres*
Kenneth Prizeman, *Controller*
▲ EMP: 80
SQ FT: 16,000
SALES (est): 20.5MM **Privately Held**
WEB: www.dannyandnicole.com
SIC: 2335 Women's, juniors' & misses' dresses

(G-10871)
KEMP TECHNOLOGIES INC (PA)
1540 Broadway Fl 23 (10036-4039)
PHONE.................................631 345-5292
John Becker, *Ch of Bd*
Raymond Downes, *President*
Bhargav Shukla, *Opers Staff*
John Spears, *Surgery Dir*
Delores Farrell, *Administration*
▲ EMP: 43
SQ FT: 15,000
SALES (est): 8.4MM **Privately Held**
WEB: www.kemptechnologies.com
SIC: 3571 Electronic computers

(G-10872)
KENNETH COLE PRODUCTIONS LP (DH)
603 W 50th St (10019-7051)
PHONE.................................212 265-1500
Michele Ferrandino, *Director*
EMP: 23
SALES (est): 4.1MM
SALES (corp-wide): 678.3MM **Privately Held**
SIC: 3143 Men's footwear, except athletic
HQ: Kenneth Cole Productions, Inc.
603 W 50th St
New York NY 10019
212 265-1500

New York - New York County (G-10873) GEOGRAPHIC SECTION

(G-10873)
KENNETH COLE PRODUCTIONS INC (HQ)
603 W 50th St (10019-7051)
PHONE..................212 265-1500
Fax: 212 713-6670
Marc Schneider, *CEO*
Mia Dellosso-Caputo, *President*
Chris Nakatani, *President*
Joshua Schulman, *President*
Scott Williamson, *President*
▲ **EMP:** 277
SQ FT: 119,000
SALES (est): 675.7MM
SALES (corp-wide): 678.3MM **Privately Held**
WEB: www.kennethcole.com
SIC: 3143 3144 3171 5661 Men's footwear, except athletic; women's footwear, except athletic; handbags, women's; purses, women's; shoe stores; women's boots; men's shoes; women's accessory & specialty stores; apparel accessories; costume jewelry; handbags; men's & boys' clothing stores
PA: Kcp Holdco, Inc.
603 W 50th St
New York NY 10019
212 265-1500

(G-10874)
KENNETH J LANE INC
20 W 37th St Fl 9 (10018-7367)
PHONE..................212 868-1780
Kenneth J Lane, *President*
Susan Fogelman, *Bookkeeper*
EMP: 15
SQ FT: 5,500
SALES (est): 1.6MM **Privately Held**
SIC: 3961 Jewelry apparel, non-precious metals

(G-10875)
KENSINGTON & SONS LLC
Also Called: Sir Kensington's
270 Lafayette St Ste 200 (10012-3376)
PHONE..................646 430-8298
Daniel Barber, *Opers Staff*
Christine Ramadan, *Sales Staff*
Jeannette Cornell, *VP Mktg*
Yan Sim, *Marketing Staff*
Mark Ramadan, *Mng Member*
EMP: 30
SALES (est): 2.1MM **Privately Held**
SIC: 2035 2033 5149 Mayonnaise; mustard, prepared (wet); catsup; packaged in cans, jars, etc.; condiments

(G-10876)
KENSINGTON PUBLISHING CORP
Also Called: Zebra Books
119 W 40th St Fl 21 (10018-2522)
PHONE..................212 407-1500
Fax: 212 935-0699
Steven Zacharius, *CEO*
James Abbate, *Editor*
Laurie Parkin, *Vice Pres*
Robin Cook, *Production*
Rebecca Cremonese, *Production*
EMP: 81
SQ FT: 25,000
SALES (est): 11.2MM **Privately Held**
WEB: www.kensingtonbooks.com
SIC: 2731 5192 Book publishing; books

(G-10877)
KENT ASSOCIATES INC
99 Battery Pl Apt 11p (10280-1324)
PHONE..................212 675-0722
Herman Lederfarb, *President*
EMP: 8 **EST:** 1947
SQ FT: 4,000
SALES (est): 870K **Privately Held**
SIC: 2752 Commercial printing, offset

(G-10878)
KENT CHEMICAL CORPORATION
460 Park Ave Fl 7 (10022-1841)
PHONE..................212 521-1700
John Farber, *Ch of Bd*
John Oram, *President*
Naveen Chandra, *Vice Pres*
Susan Aibinder, *Treasurer*
Jim Muller, *Controller*
◆ **EMP:** 25 **EST:** 1983
SQ FT: 15,000
SALES (est): 3.9MM
SALES (corp-wide): 1.1B **Privately Held**
SIC: 2821 2869 2911 2899 Polyvinyl chloride resins (PVC); flavors or flavoring materials, synthetic; perfume materials, synthetic; paraffin wax; fire retardant chemicals; unsupported plastics film & sheet; solutions, pharmaceutical
PA: Icc Industries Inc.
460 Park Ave Fl 7
New York NY 10022
212 521-1700

(G-10879)
KEY BRAND ENTERTAINMENT INC
104 Franklin St (10013-2923)
PHONE..................212 966-5400
EMP: 121
SALES (corp-wide): 473K **Privately Held**
SIC: 2752 Lithographic Commercial Printing
PA: Key Brand Entertainment, Inc.
1619 Broadway Fl 9
New York NY 10019
917 421-5400

(G-10880)
KEY COMPUTER SVCS OF CHELSEA
227 E 56th St (10022-3754)
PHONE..................212 206-8060
Fax: 212 206-8398
Paco Valeez, *President*
EMP: 60
SALES (est): 3.5MM **Privately Held**
SIC: 2759 7377 7372 7338 Commercial printing; computer rental & leasing; prepackaged software; resume writing service; facsimile transmission services; telephone communication, except radio

(G-10881)
KIDTELLECT INC
222 Broadway Level19 (10038-2510)
PHONE..................617 803-1456
Phylaktis Georgiou, *President*
Charles Bart Clareman, *COO*
Azadeh Jamalian, *Officer*
▲ **EMP:** 5
SALES (est): 372.3K **Privately Held**
SIC: 3944 Games, toys & children's vehicles

(G-10882)
KIDZ CONCEPTS LLC
Also Called: One Step Up Kids
1412 Brdwy Fl 3 (10018)
PHONE..................212 398-1110
Harry Adjmi,
Irwin Gindi,
▲ **EMP:** 52
SQ FT: 15,000
SALES (est): 11.4MM **Privately Held**
WEB: www.kidzconcepts.com
SIC: 2389 5137 Costumes; women's & children's sportswear & swimsuits

(G-10883)
KIDZ WORLD INC
Also Called: High Energy U. S. A.
226 W 37th St Fl 12 (10018-9850)
PHONE..................212 563-4949
Vittorio Dana, *President*
Victor Hara, *Vice Pres*
▲ **EMP:** 15
SQ FT: 2,172
SALES (est): 165.1K **Privately Held**
SIC: 2329 Men's & boys' sportswear & athletic clothing

(G-10884)
KIM EUGENIA INC
347 W 36th St Rm 502 (10018-7262)
PHONE..................212 674-1345
Fax: 212 674-1769
Eugenia Kim, *President*
Laura Burnosky, *Opers Staff*
Drew Fettner, *Production*
AVI Sanichar, *Controller*
Janice Szeto, *Accounts Exec*
▲ **EMP:** 8
SQ FT: 1,400
SALES (est): 1.6MM **Privately Held**
WEB: www.eugeniakim.com
SIC: 2353 Hats, caps & millinery

(G-10885)
KIM SEYBERT INC (PA)
37 W 37th St Fl 9 (10018-6219)
PHONE..................212 564-7850
Fax: 212 695-8803
Kim Seybert, *President*
Shirlene Asmath, *CFO*
Maloney Dyer, *Executive*
▲ **EMP:** 16
SQ FT: 10,000
SALES (est): 2.2MM **Privately Held**
WEB: www.kimseybert.com
SIC: 2392 Household furnishings

(G-10886)
KIMBALL OFFICE INC
215 Park Ave S Fl 3 (10003-1616)
PHONE..................212 753-6161
Fax: 212 593-0837
Brian Raynor, *Regional Mgr*
Michael Donahue, *Vice Pres*
EMP: 30
SALES (corp-wide): 669.9MM **Publicly Held**
SIC: 2522 Office desks & tables: except wood
HQ: Kimball Office Inc.
1600 Royal St
Jasper IN 47549
812 482-1600

(G-10887)
KIMMERIDGE ENERGY MGT CO LLC (PA)
400 Madison Ave Rm 14c (10017-1937)
PHONE..................646 517-7252
Ben Dell,
EMP: 13 **EST:** 2013
SALES (est): 2.4MM **Privately Held**
SIC: 1311 Sand & shale oil mining

(G-10888)
KIND GROUP LLC (PA)
19 W 44th St Ste 811 (10036-5901)
PHONE..................212 645-0800
Abigail Closs, *Natl Sales Mgr*
Brad Johnson, *Natl Sales Mgr*
James Arriola, *Sales Dir*
Michael Fitzgerald, *Sales Mgr*
Tom Lyons, *Sales Mgr*
EMP: 2
SQ FT: 3,000
SALES (est): 23.6MM **Privately Held**
WEB: www.20-10.com
SIC: 2844 Toilet preparations

(G-10889)
KINDLING INC
440 Park Ave S Fl 14 (10016-8012)
PHONE..................212 400-6296
Timothy Meaney, *CEO*
Daniel Summa, *President*
Alaina Jones, *Accounts Mgr*
Richard Ziade, *Admin Sec*
EMP: 17
SALES (est): 1.1MM **Privately Held**
SIC: 7372 Business oriented computer software

(G-10890)
KINETIC MARKETING INC
1133 Broadway Ste 221 (10010-8197)
PHONE..................212 620-0600
Charles Y Beyda, *Vice Pres*
▲ **EMP:** 7
SQ FT: 2,000
SALES (est): 901K **Privately Held**
WEB: www.kineticmarketing.net
SIC: 3699 5065 Household electrical equipment; electronic parts & equipment

(G-10891)
KING DISPLAYS INC
333 W 52nd St (10019-6238)
PHONE..................212 629-8455
Fax: 212 629-8457
Wayne Sapper, *President*
Joel Benton, *Prdtn Mgr*
Julie Rivkin, *Accountant*
EMP: 14 **EST:** 1938
SQ FT: 7,500
SALES (est): 1.7MM **Privately Held**
WEB: www.kingdisplays.com
SIC: 3999 3993 Theatrical scenery; displays & cutouts, window & lobby

(G-10892)
KINGLIFT ELEVATOR INC
1 Maiden Ln Fl 5 (10038-5154)
PHONE..................917 923-3517
Cem Ozalpasan, *President*
EMP: 5
SALES (est): 320.5K **Privately Held**
SIC: 3534 Elevators & moving stairways

(G-10893)
KITON BUILDING CORP
4 E 54th St (10022-4203)
PHONE..................212 486-3224
Antonio De Matteis, *Ch of Bd*
Ciro Paone, *President*
Adele Drago, *Accounting Mgr*
EMP: 20
SQ FT: 18,077
SALES (est): 2MM **Privately Held**
SIC: 2389 Costumes

(G-10894)
KKR MILLENNIUM GP LLC
9 W 57th St Ste 4150 (10019-2701)
PHONE..................212 750-8300
Lawrence J Rogers, *President*
EMP: 4850
SALES (est): 173.5MM **Privately Held**
SIC: 2515 Mattresses, innerspring or box spring

(G-10895)
KKR NTRAL RSOURCES FUND I-A LP (HQ)
9 W 57th St Ste 4200 (10019-2707)
PHONE..................212 750-8300
David J Sorkin, *General Counsel*
EMP: 7
SALES (est): 16.6MM **Publicly Held**
SIC: 1382 Oil & gas exploration services

(G-10896)
KLARA TECHNOLOGIES INC
1 State St Fl 25 (10004-1729)
PHONE..................844 215-5272
Simon Bolz, *CEO*
EMP: 17
SALES (est): 370.5K
SALES (corp-wide): 592K **Privately Held**
SIC: 7372 Business oriented computer software
PA: Klara Holdings, Inc.
1 State St Fl 25
New York NY 10004
844 215-5272

(G-10897)
KLAUBER BROTHERS INC (PA)
980 Ave Of The Ave Frnt 2 (10018)
PHONE..................212 686-2531
Fax: 212 481-7194
Roger Klauber, *President*
Mark Klauber, *Vice Pres*
Jay Marcus, *Vice Pres*
Shari Driver, *Production*
Alcillena Wilson, *Production*
▲ **EMP:** 85 **EST:** 1942
SQ FT: 11,000
SALES: 133K **Privately Held**
WEB: www.klauberlace.com
SIC: 2258 5131 Lace, knit; warp & flat knit products; textile converters

(G-10898)
KLUTZ (HQ)
Also Called: Klutz Store
568 Broadway Rm 503 (10012-3264)
PHONE..................650 687-2600
Richard Robinson, *CEO*
of Purch, *CEO*
Flora Kim, *Editor*
Dewitt Durham, *Vice Pres*
Netta Rabin, *Vice Pres*
▲ **EMP:** 26
SALES (est): 9.7MM
SALES (corp-wide): 1.7B **Publicly Held**
WEB: www.klutz.com
SIC: 2731 Books: publishing & printing

GEOGRAPHIC SECTION

New York - New York County (G-10922)

PA: Scholastic Corporation
557 Broadway Lbby 1
New York NY 10012
212 343-6100

(G-10899)
KNICKERBOCKER GRAPHICS SVCS
256 W 38th St Rm 504 (10018-5807)
PHONE...................212 244-7485
Joseph Schankweiler, *President*
Janet Schankweiler, *Vice Pres*
EMP: 14 **EST:** 1910
SQ FT: 18,000
SALES (est): 1.6MM **Privately Held**
SIC: 2752 Commercial printing, offset

(G-10900)
KNIT ILLUSTRATED INC
247 W 37th St Frnt 3 (10018-5130)
PHONE...................212 268-9054
Fax: 212 268-9073
Peter Tam, *President*
Gary Kokin, *Vice Pres*
EMP: 20
SALES: 2MM **Privately Held**
WEB: www.knitillustrated.com
SIC: 2253 Sweaters & sweater coats, knit

(G-10901)
KNIT RESOURCE CENTER LTD
250 W 39th St Rm 207 (10018-4742)
PHONE...................212 221-1990
Fax: 212 719-5344
Joseph Katz, *President*
Richard Glanzer, *Manager*
EMP: 7
SQ FT: 2,500
SALES (est): 646.5K
SALES (corp-wide): 260.8MM **Privately Held**
SIC: 2253 Sweaters & sweater coats, knit
HQ: Stoll America Knitting Machinery Inc
250 W 39th St Frnt 1
New York NY 10018
212 398-3869

(G-10902)
KNOLL INC
Also Called: Knoll Textile
1330 Ave Of The A (10019)
PHONE...................212 343-4124
Fax: 212 343-4181
Carl Magnusson, *Senior VP*
Benjamin A Pardo, *Senior VP*
Burt Staniar, *Senior VP*
Liz Needle, *VP Finance*
Mindy Rynasko, *Loan Officer*
EMP: 100
SALES (corp-wide): 1.1B **Publicly Held**
WEB: www.knoll.com
SIC: 2521 2522 2511 Wood office furniture; panel systems & partitions, office: except wood; wood household furniture
PA: Knoll, Inc.
1235 Water St
East Greenville PA 18041
215 679-7991

(G-10903)
KOBALT MUSIC PUBG AMER INC (PA)
220 W 42nd St Fl 11 (10036-7200)
PHONE...................212 247-6204
Willard Ahdritz, *President*
Vincent Clery-Melin, *Managing Dir*
Michelle Maghise, *Principal*
Jim Arnay, *Senior VP*
Al McLean, *Senior VP*
EMP: 70
SALES (est): 19.5MM **Privately Held**
WEB: www.kobaltmusic.com
SIC: 2731 Book music: publishing & printing

(G-10904)
KOBE STEEL USA HOLDINGS INC (HQ)
535 Madison Ave Fl 5 (10022-4214)
PHONE...................212 751-9400
Fax: 212 308-3116
Hiroya Kawasaki, *President*
Carrie Dugan, *Info Tech Dir*
Onuma Hideki, *Info Tech Mgr*
Kazuhiro Ono, *Info Tech Mgr*
Kazunori Yamataki, *Admin Sec*
◆ **EMP:** 8
SQ FT: 5,697
SALES (est): 210MM
SALES (corp-wide): 15.5B **Privately Held**
WEB: www.kobelco.com
SIC: 3542 3089 Extruding machines (machine tools), metal; injection molding of plastics
PA: Kobe Steel, Ltd.
2-2-4, Wakinohamakaigandori, Chuo-Ku
Kobe HYO 651-0
782 615-111

(G-10905)
KOCH SUPPLY & TRADING LP
667 Madison Ave Fl 22 (10065-8051)
PHONE...................212 319-4895
EMP: 5
SALES (corp-wide): 27.8B **Privately Held**
SIC: 2911 Petroleum refining
HQ: Koch Supply & Trading, Lp
4111 E 37th St N
Wichita KS 67220
316 828-5500

(G-10906)
KODANSHA USA INC
451 Park Ave S Fl 7 (10016-7390)
PHONE...................917 322-6200
Fax: 212 935-6929
Sawako Noma, *Ch of Bd*
Yoichi Kiyata, *Sr Exec VP*
Tokuo Kanemaru, *Manager*
▲ **EMP:** 9
SQ FT: 7,000
SALES (est): 3.6MM **Privately Held**
SIC: 2731 5192 Books: publishing only; books

(G-10907)
KOGETO INC (PA)
51 Wooster St Fl 2 (10013-2292)
PHONE...................646 490-8169
Jeff Glasse, *Ch of Bd*
John P Clark, *CFO*
EMP: 7
SQ FT: 1,000
SALES (est): 579.4K **Privately Held**
SIC: 3861 Photographic equipment & supplies

(G-10908)
KOKIN INC
247 W 38th St Rm 701 (10018-4470)
PHONE...................212 643-8225
Fax: 212 643-8284
Steven Kokin, *President*
Audrey Kokin, *Corp Secy*
Gary Kokin, *Vice Pres*
▲ **EMP:** 30
SQ FT: 6,800
SALES (est): 3.9MM **Privately Held**
SIC: 2353 2341 Hats, caps & millinery; women's & children's nightwear

(G-10909)
KOLCORP INDUSTRIES LTD (PA)
Also Called: Pro-Print
10 E 36th St (10016-3302)
PHONE...................212 354-0400
Fax: 212 768-3550
Charles Kolster, *President*
David Matos, *Bookkeeper*
EMP: 12 **EST:** 1973
SQ FT: 2,500
SALES (est): 1.6MM **Privately Held**
WEB: www.pro-print.com
SIC: 2752 Commercial printing, lithographic

(G-10910)
KOLLAGE WORK TOO LTD
261 W 35th St Ste 302 (10001-1902)
PHONE...................212 695-1821
Maria Meunier,
EMP: 7
SALES (est): 398.8K **Privately Held**
SIC: 2326 Men's & boys' work clothing

(G-10911)
KOMAR KIDS LLC (HQ)
16 E 34th St Fl 14 (10016-4360)
PHONE...................212 725-1500
Charlie Komar, *CEO*
Jay Harris, *COO*
Harry Gaffney, *CFO*
David Komar, *Admin Sec*
▲ **EMP:** 11
SQ FT: 15,000
SALES (est): 4.8MM
SALES (corp-wide): 212.2MM **Privately Held**
SIC: 2254 Nightwear (nightgowns, negligees, pajamas), knit; underwear, knit
PA: Charles Komar & Sons, Inc.
90 Hudson St Fl 9
Jersey City NJ 07302
212 725-1500

(G-10912)
KOMAR LAYERING LLC (HQ)
Also Called: O'Bryan Bros
16 E 34th St Fl 10 (10016-4360)
PHONE...................212 725-1500
Charlie Komar, *President*
David Komar, *Principal*
Allen R Bartine, *CFO*
▲ **EMP:** 40
SQ FT: 13,000
SALES (est): 10.5MM
SALES (corp-wide): 212.2MM **Privately Held**
WEB: www.cuddlduds.com
SIC: 2341 Nightgowns & negligees: women's & children's; pajamas & bedjackets: women's & children's; slips: women's, misses', children's & infants'; panties: women's, misses', children's & infants'
PA: Charles Komar & Sons, Inc.
90 Hudson St Fl 9
Jersey City NJ 07302
212 725-1500

(G-10913)
KOMAR LUXURY BRANDS
16 E 34th St Fl 10 (10016-4360)
PHONE...................646 472-0060
Charles Komar, *President*
Shelly Sosnoff, *Purchasing*
Harry Gaffney, *CFO*
Greg Holland, *Sales Mgr*
Marie Taibbi, *Admin Asst*
▲ **EMP:** 8
SALES (est): 928.4K
SALES (corp-wide): 212.2MM **Privately Held**
SIC: 2341 2384 5137 2329 Women's & children's nightwear; robes & dressing gowns; nightwear: women's, children's & infants'; sweaters & sweater jackets: men's & boys'
PA: Charles Komar & Sons, Inc.
90 Hudson St Fl 9
Jersey City NJ 07302
212 725-1500

(G-10914)
KORAL INDUSTRIES
1384 Broadway Fl 18 (10018-6122)
PHONE...................212 719-0392
Peter Crown, *Owner*
Johan Tavaris, *Office Mgr*
EMP: 10
SALES (est): 563.4K **Privately Held**
SIC: 2339 Women's & misses' athletic clothing & sportswear

(G-10915)
KORANGY PUBLISHING INC (PA)
Also Called: Real Deal, The
450 W 31st St Fl 4 (10001-4613)
PHONE...................212 260-1332
Amir Korangy, *CEO*
Doug Devine, *Real Est Agnt*
EMP: 60
SALES (est): 11.5MM **Privately Held**
SIC: 2741 Miscellaneous publishing

(G-10916)
KORIN JAPANESE TRADING CORP
57 Warren St Frnt A (10007-1018)
PHONE...................212 587-7021
Fax: 212 587-7027
Saori Kawano, *President*
John Wong, *CFO*
Sally Cen, *Asst Controller*
Mitsuko Muramatsu, *Sales Associate*
Mari Sugai, *Marketing Staff*
▲ **EMP:** 32
SQ FT: 8,000
SALES (est): 4.8MM **Privately Held**
WEB: www.korin.com
SIC: 3469 3262 3263 3421 Utensils, household: metal, except cast; vitreous china table & kitchenware; commercial tableware or kitchen articles, fine earthenware; cutlery; commercial cooking & food-warming equipment; barbecues, grills & braziers (outdoor cooking)

(G-10917)
KOSSARS BIALYS LLC
367 Grand St (10002-3951)
PHONE...................212 473-4810
Fax: 212 253-2146
Daniel Cohen, *Owner*
Juda Engelmayer, *Principal*
Debra Engel, *Director*
EMP: 8 **EST:** 1998
SQ FT: 3,000
SALES: 500K **Privately Held**
WEB: www.kossarsbialys.com
SIC: 2051 Bakery: wholesale or wholesale/retail combined

(G-10918)
KOSSARS ON GRAND LLC
367 Grand St (10002-3951)
PHONE...................212 473-4810
Evan Giniger, *CEO*
EMP: 10
SALES (est): 728.3K **Privately Held**
SIC: 2051 Rolls, bread type: fresh or frozen

(G-10919)
KOTEL IMPORTERS INC
22 W 48th St Ste 607 (10036-1803)
PHONE...................212 245-6200
Fax: 212 245-5266
Raphel Dagan, *President*
EMP: 12
SQ FT: 1,200
SALES (est): 1MM **Privately Held**
SIC: 1499 Gemstone & industrial diamond mining

(G-10920)
KOWA AMERICAN CORPORATION (DH)
55 E 59th St Fl 19 (10022-1112)
PHONE...................212 303-7800
Fax: 212 310-0101
Reid C Anthony, *Ch of Bd*
Takashi Mamemura, *Ch of Bd*
Masataka Shigenaka, *Credit Mgr*
Noriko Nagamoto, *Accountant*
Tomyouki Mase, *Manager*
◆ **EMP:** 20
SQ FT: 6,400
SALES (est): 4.6MM
SALES (corp-wide): 3.1B **Privately Held**
SIC: 2819 5032 5131 Industrial inorganic chemicals; tile, clay or other ceramic, excluding refractory; textiles, woven

(G-10921)
KOZINN+SONS MERCHANT TAILORS
Also Called: Saint Laurie
22 W 32nd St Fl 5 (10001-0590)
PHONE...................212 643-1916
Fax: 212 695-4709
Andrew Kozinn, *CEO*
Allan Stricoff, *Controller*
▲ **EMP:** 26
SQ FT: 7,500
SALES (est): 3.6MM **Privately Held**
WEB: www.saintlaurie.com
SIC: 2311 2337 5611 5621 Suits, men's & boys': made from purchased materials; suits: women's, misses' & juniors'; suits, men's; women's clothing stores

(G-10922)
KPS CAPITAL PARTNERS LP (PA)
485 Lexington Ave Fl 31 (10017-2641)
PHONE...................212 338-5100
Fax: 212 307-7100
Michael G Psaros, *Managing Prtnr*
Jay Bernstein, *Partner*
Raquel Palmer, *Partner*

New York - New York County (G-10923) GEOGRAPHIC SECTION

David Shapiro, *Partner*
Sarah Weintraub, *Asst Controller*
◆ **EMP:** 40
SQ FT: 6,000
SALES (est): 2.1B **Privately Held**
SIC: 3541 6722 3545 5084 Machine tools, metal cutting type; management investment, open-end; machine tool accessories; industrial machinery & equipment

(G-10923)
KRAINZ CREATIONS INC
589 5th Ave (10017-1923)
PHONE 212 583-1555
Roland Krainz, *President*
EMP: 35
SALES (est): 3.8MM **Privately Held**
SIC: 3961 Costume jewelry

(G-10924)
KRAMAN IRON WORKS INC
410 E 10th St (10009-4203)
PHONE 212 460-8400
Fax: 212 529-2466
Richard Kraman, *President*
EMP: 11 **EST:** 1913
SQ FT: 3,600
SALES: 1.6MM **Privately Held**
SIC: 3449 Miscellaneous metalwork

(G-10925)
KRASNER GROUP INC (PA)
40 W 37th St Ph A (10018-7415)
PHONE 212 268-4100
Al Cerbo, *Vice Pres*
Barry Ort, *Vice Pres*
David Pardington, *CFO*
▼ **EMP:** 1
SQ FT: 4,500
SALES (est): 7.9MM **Privately Held**
SIC: 3911 2339 2331 2335 Jewelry, precious metal; women's & misses' accessories; women's & misses' blouses & shirts; women's, juniors' & misses' dresses

(G-10926)
KRAUS & SONS INC
355 S End Ave Apt 10j (10280-1056)
PHONE 212 620-0408
Fax: 212 924-4081
Paul Schneider, *President*
Mildred Schneider, *Treasurer*
Saul Brown, *Director*
EMP: 15 **EST:** 1886
SQ FT: 5,000
SALES (est): 1.4MM **Privately Held**
WEB: www.krausbanners.com
SIC: 2399 3993 2394 3965 Banners, made from fabric; signs & advertising specialties; tents: made from purchased materials; buttons & parts

(G-10927)
KRAUS ORGANIZATION LIMITED (PA)
Also Called: Bernan Associates
181 Hudson St Ste 2a (10013-1812)
PHONE 212 686-5411
Frank Cermak, *President*
Herbert Gstalder, *Chairman*
Steven Gstalder, *Vice Pres*
Lisa T Provenzano, *Director*
EMP: 5
SALES (est): 7.3MM **Privately Held**
WEB: www.krausorgltd.com
SIC: 2741 7383 7389 Miscellaneous publishing; news pictures, gathering & distributing; photographic library service

(G-10928)
KRAVITZ DESIGN INC (PA)
13 Crosby St Rm 401 (10013-3145)
PHONE 212 625-1644
Lenny Kravitz, *Ch of Bd*
Bill Tannenbaum, *Manager*
Richard Feldstein, *Admin Sec*
▲ **EMP:** 8
SALES (est): 1MM **Privately Held**
SIC: 2732 Books: printing only

(G-10929)
KSE SPORTSMAN MEDIA INC (PA)
1040 Ave Of The Americas (10018-3703)
PHONE 212 852-6600

David Koff, *CEO*
Chuck Nelson, *Publisher*
Geoff Mueller, *Editor*
Richard Venola, *Editor*
Peter Kern, *Chairman*
EMP: 59
SALES (est): 38.6MM **Privately Held**
SIC: 2326 5045 Industrial garments, men's & boys'; computer software

(G-10930)
KSK INTERNATIONAL INC (PA)
Also Called: Easel
450 Park Ave Ste 2703 (10022-2646)
PHONE 212 354-7770
Neil Weiss, *CEO*
Gus Ayala, *Manager*
EMP: 25
SQ FT: 10,335
SALES (est): 2MM **Privately Held**
SIC: 2331 2339 Women's & misses' blouses & shirts; women's & misses' accessories

(G-10931)
KT GROUP INC
13 W 36th St Fl 3 (10018-7139)
PHONE 212 760-2500
Eugene Huh, *President*
Yujin Huh, *Chairman*
Delias Gonzalves, *Prdtn Mgr*
▲ **EMP:** 8
SALES (est): 973.6K **Privately Held**
SIC: 2321 Sport shirts, men's & boys': from purchased materials

(G-10932)
KURARAY AMERICA INC
33 Maiden Ln Fl 6 (10038-5152)
PHONE 212 986-2230
Yoshiki Kuroki, *General Mgr*
Larry Zeno, *Regional Mgr*
John Dennis, *Research*
Dottie Fallaw, *Engineer*
Michelle Denny, *Regl Sales Mgr*
EMP: 19
SALES (corp-wide): 4.3B **Privately Held**
SIC: 2655 Fiber cans, drums & similar products
HQ: Kuraray America, Inc.
2625 Bay Area Blvd # 600
Houston TX 77058

(G-10933)
KUREHA ADVANCED MATERIALS INC
420 Lexington Ave Rm 2510 (10170-1402)
PHONE 724 295-3352
Fred Daniell, *President*
Yoshitsugu Nishibayashi, *President*
Lee Pyfitt, *General Mgr*
Leeland Pfeifer, *Corp Secy*
Laura J Uncapher, *Manager*
▲ **EMP:** 10
SQ FT: 23,000
SALES: 1.6MM
SALES (corp-wide): 1.2B **Privately Held**
WEB: www.ttsmatl.com
SIC: 3624 Carbon & graphite products
HQ: Kureha America Inc.
420 Lexington Ave Rm 2510
New York NY 10170
212 867-7040

(G-10934)
KURT GAUM INC
Also Called: Soper Designs
580 5th Ave Ste 303 (10036-4724)
PHONE 212 719-2836
Fax: 212 719-2837
Blake Soper, *President*
Peter Boutsas, *Vice Pres*
EMP: 13 **EST:** 1954
SQ FT: 1,250
SALES (est): 1.5MM **Privately Held**
WEB: www.kurtgaum.com
SIC: 3911 Jewel settings & mountings, precious metal

(G-10935)
KWW PRODUCTIONS CORP
Also Called: American Attitude
1410 Broadway Fl 24 (10018-5007)
PHONE 212 398-8181
Izzy Pnini, *President*
EMP: 10

SALES (corp-wide): 5.7MM **Privately Held**
WEB: www.knitwork.com
SIC: 2389 Apparel for handicapped
PA: Kww Productions Corp.
1639 Centre St
Ridgewood NY 11385
718 821-2201

(G-10936)
KYBOD GROUP LLC
Also Called: Sriracha2go
222 E 34th St Apt 1005 (10016-4899)
PHONE 408 306-1657
Kyle Lewis,
Farbod Deylamian,
EMP: 2
SALES (est): 1.5MM **Privately Held**
SIC: 3085 Plastics bottles

(G-10937)
KYLE EDITING LLC
15 W 26th St Fl 8 (10010-1065)
PHONE 212 675-3464
Eytan Gutman, *General Mgr*
Nate Taylor, *Editor*
Sarah Farrand, *Producer*
Jackie Sparks, *Info Tech Mgr*
Tina Mintus,
EMP: 9 **EST:** 2010
SALES (est): 977.9K **Privately Held**
WEB: www.kyleedit.com
SIC: 3861 Editing equipment, motion picture: viewers, splicers, etc.

(G-10938)
L & M OPTICAL DISC LLC
Also Called: L & M West
65 W 36th St Fl 11 (10018-7936)
PHONE 718 649-3500
Fax: 718 649-9300
Yefit Shahar, *Controller*
Elazar Walder, *CIO*
Aaron Menche,
▲ **EMP:** 100
SALES (est): 12.7MM **Privately Held**
WEB: www.dxbind.com
SIC: 3695 Optical disks & tape, blank

(G-10939)
L F FASHION ORIENT INTL CO LTD
32 W 40th St Apt 2l (10018-3839)
PHONE 917 667-3398
Lisa LI, *President*
Angus Wong, *Controller*
▲ **EMP:** 5
SALES (est): 381.4K **Privately Held**
SIC: 2311 2335 Men's & boys' suits & coats; women's, juniors' & misses' dresses

(G-10940)
L F INTERNATIONAL INC
Also Called: Labhar - Freidman
425 Park Ave Fl 5 (10022-3506)
PHONE 212 756-5000
J Roger Friedman, *President*
▼ **EMP:** 90
SALES (est): 4.2MM
SALES (corp-wide): 108.6MM **Privately Held**
WEB: www.lf.com
SIC: 2721 Periodicals
PA: Lebhar-Friedman, Inc.
150 W 30th St Fl 19
New York NY 10001
212 756-5000

(G-10941)
L-3 CMMNCTONS FGN HOLDINGS INC (HQ)
Also Called: L3 Communication
600 3rd Ave Fl 32 (10016-2001)
PHONE 212 697-1111
Fax: 212 805-5477
Jim Parker, *President*
Larry Riddle, *President*
Michael T Strianese, *Principal*
Thomas Gallo, *Business Mgr*
Curtis B Brunson, *Exec VP*
▲ **EMP:** 45

SALES (est): 32.3MM
SALES (corp-wide): 10.5B **Publicly Held**
SIC: 3663 3669 3679 3812 Telemetering equipment, electronic; receiver-transmitter units (transceiver); amplifiers, RF power & IF; signaling apparatus, electric; intercommunication systems, electric; microwave components; search & navigation equipment; guided missile & space vehicle parts & auxiliary equipment
PA: L3 Technologies, Inc.
600 3rd Ave Fl 34
New York NY 10016
212 697-1111

(G-10942)
L-3 CMMNCTONS NTRONIX HOLDINGS
600 3rd Ave Fl 34 (10016-2001)
PHONE 212 697-1111
Michael T Strianese, *President*
Steven M Post, *Senior VP*
Scott Betchley, *Vice Pres*
Curtis Brunson, *Vice Pres*
Wendall Child, *Vice Pres*
EMP: 65
SALES (est): 18.2MM
SALES (corp-wide): 10.5B **Publicly Held**
SIC: 3625 3699 8711 Marine & navy auxiliary controls; underwater sound equipment; marine engineering
PA: L3 Technologies, Inc.
600 3rd Ave Fl 34
New York NY 10016
212 697-1111

(G-10943)
L3 TECHNOLOGIES INC (PA)
600 3rd Ave Fl 34 (10016-2001)
PHONE 212 697-1111
Michael T Strianese, *Ch of Bd*
Christopher E Kubasik, *President*
Michael Macdonald, *Business Mgr*
Neil Obright, *Business Mgr*
Ann D Davidson, *Senior VP*
▲ **EMP:** 277 **EST:** 1997
SALES: 10.5B **Publicly Held**
SIC: 3812 3663 3669 3679 Search & navigation equipment; aircraft control systems, electronic; telemetering equipment, electronic; receiver-transmitter units (transceiver); amplifiers, RF power & IF; signaling apparatus, electric; intercommunication systems, electric; microwave components; guided missile & space vehicle parts & auxiliary equipment

(G-10944)
LA COLA 1 INC
529 W 42nd St Apt 5b (10036-6228)
PHONE 917 509-6669
Thomas Dugal, *Principal*
EMP: 5
SALES (est): 270.6K **Privately Held**
SIC: 2086 Soft drinks: packaged in cans, bottles, etc.

(G-10945)
LA CREMERIA
178 Mulberry St (10012-4556)
PHONE 212 226-6758
Alessandro Tiodesam, *Managing Prtnr*
Elena Tiodesam, *Partner*
EMP: 6
SALES (est): 234.8K **Privately Held**
SIC: 2024 Ice cream, bulk

(G-10946)
LA FINA DESIGN INC
42 W 38th St Rm 1200 (10018-6212)
PHONE 212 689-6725
Fax: 212 689-5627
Chol Choi, *President*
Peter Choi, *President*
▲ **EMP:** 7
SALES (est): 1MM **Privately Held**
SIC: 3911 Jewelry, precious metal

(G-10947)
LA LAME INC
Also Called: La Lame Importers
215 W 40th St Fl 5 (10018-1602)
PHONE 212 921-9770
Fax: 212 302-4359
Benjamin Schneer, *CEO*
Edward Schneer, *Principal*

▲ = Import ▼ = Export
◆ = Import/Export

GEOGRAPHIC SECTION
New York - New York County (G-10973)

Glen Schneer, *Principal*
Alan Kerner, *Controller*
Billy Pellegrini, *Sales Staff*
▲ **EMP**: 8 **EST**: 1958
SQ FT: 7,500
SALES (est): 1.4MM **Privately Held**
WEB: www.lalame.com
SIC: 2299 2241 2282 2221 Yarns, specialty & novelty; fabrics: linen, jute, hemp, ramie; braids, textile; embroidery yarn: twisting, winding or spooling; spandex broadwoven fabrics; brocade, cotton; textile converters

(G-10948)
LABEL SOURCE INC
321 W 35th St (10001-1739)
PHONE..................212 244-1403
Stuart Rosen, *President*
EMP: 6
SQ FT: 2,000
SALES (est): 1.2MM **Privately Held**
SIC: 2241 Labels, woven

(G-10949)
LABELS INTER-GLOBAL INC
Also Called: Labels I-G
109 W 38th St Rm 701 (10018-3673)
PHONE..................212 398-0006
Fax: 212 768-8488
Steve Ziangos, *President*
Effie Ziangos, *Vice Pres*
Eric Pit, *Sls & Mktg Exec*
MEI Francese, *Sales Staff*
Juan Fernandez, *Manager*
▲ **EMP**: 14
SQ FT: 3,400
SALES (est): 2.2MM **Privately Held**
WEB: www.labelsig.com
SIC: 2759 5112 2241 Labels & seals: printing; stationery & office supplies; labels, woven

(G-10950)
LABELTEX MILLS INC
1430 Broadway Rm 1510 (10018-3368)
PHONE..................212 279-6165
Fax: 212 279-6165
Vince McGuire, *Vice Pres*
Raphaela Penn, *Vice Pres*
Ian Kantor, *Manager*
EMP: 7 **Privately Held**
WEB: www.labeltexmills.com
SIC: 2241 Narrow fabric mills
PA: Labeltex Mills, Inc.
6100 Wilmington Ave
Los Angeles CA 90001

(G-10951)
LADY ESTER LINGERIE CORP
Also Called: Sliperfection
33 E 33rd St Rm 800 (10016-5335)
PHONE..................212 689-1729
Robert T Sadock, *CEO*
M William Sadock, *President*
Karen L Sadock, *Exec VP*
Barbara Hoganson, *Purch Mgr*
Fred Adler, *CFO*
EMP: 45 **EST**: 1929
SQ FT: 15,000
SALES (est): 4.6MM **Privately Held**
SIC: 2341 2384 Women's & children's underwear; chemises, camisoles & teddies: women's & children's; slips: women's, misses', children's & infants'; robes & dressing gowns

(G-10952)
LAFAYETTE PUB INC
Also Called: Temple Bar
332 Lafayette St (10012-2739)
PHONE..................212 925-4242
Fax: 212 219-9763
George Schwartz, *President*
EMP: 25
SALES (est): 1.4MM **Privately Held**
WEB: www.templebarnyc.com
SIC: 2599 5813 Bar, restaurant & cafeteria furniture; drinking places

(G-10953)
LAGARDERE NORTH AMERICA INC (DH)
60 E 42nd St Ste 1940 (10165-6201)
PHONE..................212 477-7373
Fax: 212 767-5635

David Leckey, *Senior VP*
Richard Rabinowitz, *Vice Pres*
Thierry Auger, *Technology*
EMP: 21
SALES (est): 624.9MM
SALES (corp-wide): 62.3MM **Privately Held**
SIC: 2721 Magazines: publishing only, not printed on site
HQ: Lagardere Media
4 Rue De Presbourg
Paris 75116
140 691-600

(G-10954)
LAI APPAREL DESIGN INC
Also Called: Ella Design
209 W 38th St Rm 901 (10018-4558)
PHONE..................212 382-1075
Elaine Lai, *President*
Jacqueline Wong, *Accounts Mgr*
▲ **EMP**: 21
SQ FT: 7,000
SALES (est): 3.5MM **Privately Held**
SIC: 2339 Women's & misses' athletic clothing & sportswear

(G-10955)
LAKESTAR SEMI INC (PA)
888 7th Ave Ste 3300 (10106-3402)
PHONE..................212 974-6254
Sailesh Chittipeddi, *President*
Shiva Gowni, *President*
Shu LI, *Chairman*
Julie Hall, *Corp Secy*
Naresh Malipeddi, *COO*
▲ **EMP**: 12
SALES (est): 63.9MM **Privately Held**
WEB: www.conexant.com
SIC: 3674 5065 Semiconductors & related devices; semiconductor devices

(G-10956)
LAKEVIEW INNOVATIONS INC
112 W 34th St Ste 18030 (10120-0101)
PHONE..................212 502-6702
Scott Colquitt, *President*
Harry Mull, *CFO*
Andrew Mull, *Sales Staff*
▲ **EMP**: 10
SQ FT: 2,500
SALES (est): 3MM **Privately Held**
SIC: 2389 Cummerbunds

(G-10957)
LALI JEWELRY INC
Also Called: Lali Jewels
50 W 47th St Ste 1610 (10036-8734)
PHONE..................212 944-2277
Arun Bassalali, *President*
Adam Bassalali, *Vice Pres*
▲ **EMP**: 4 **EST**: 2015
SQ FT: 1,000
SALES: 1MM **Privately Held**
SIC: 3911 Jewelry, precious metal; pearl jewelry, natural or cultured

(G-10958)
LALIQUE NORTH AMERICA INC
Also Called: Lalique Boutique
609 Madison Ave (10022-1901)
PHONE..................212 355-6550
Fax: 212 752-6120
Maggie WEI, *Marketing Staff*
Marya Samawi, *Branch Mgr*
EMP: 20 **Privately Held**
SIC: 3231 5719 Watch crystals, glass; kitchenware
HQ: Lalique North America, Inc.
133 5th Ave Fl 3
New York NY 10003
212 355-8536

(G-10959)
LAND N SEA INC (PA)
1375 Broadway Fl 2 (10018-7073)
PHONE..................212 703-2980
Fax: 212 444-6019
Robert Sobel, *Ch of Bd*
Kirk Gellin, *Ch of Bd*
Ed Vanduzer, *Area Mgr*
Tom Schueffler, *Opers Mgr*
Heather Smith, *Opers Mgr*
◆ **EMP**: 80 **EST**: 1958
SQ FT: 21,000

SALES (est): 34.2MM **Privately Held**
SIC: 2369 2361 2331 2339 Girls' & children's outerwear; blouses: girls', children's & infants'; blouses, women's & juniors': made from purchased material; women's & misses' outerwear; family clothing stores

(G-10960)
LANDLORD GUARD INC
1 Maiden Ln Fl 7 (10038-5168)
PHONE..................212 695-6505
Christine Mathis, *President*
Tamar Ojalvo, *Manager*
EMP: 10
SALES (est): 780K **Privately Held**
SIC: 2759 Advertising literature: printing

(G-10961)
LANE PARK LITHO PLATE
155 Ave Of The Amer Fl 8 (10013-1507)
PHONE..................212 255-9100
Linda Salzhauer, *President*
Dan Salzhauer, *Vice Pres*
EMP: 30 **EST**: 1967
SQ FT: 12,500
SALES (est): 3.4MM **Privately Held**
WEB: www.parklanelitho.com
SIC: 2796 Color separations for printing

(G-10962)
LANES FLR CVRNGS INTRIORS INC
30 W 26th St Fl 11r (10010-2065)
PHONE..................212 532-5200
Fax: 212 685-7626
Lane Brettschneider, *Ch of Bd*
Kwasi Pecou, *Project Mgr*
Gary Ragin, *Sales Staff*
Umberto Aponte, *Manager*
Linda Wolstein, *Info Tech Mgr*
EMP: 25 **EST**: 1965
SQ FT: 9,000
SALES (est): 5MM **Privately Held**
WEB: www.lanes-carpets.com
SIC: 2273 Carpets & rugs

(G-10963)
LANGUAGE AND GRAPHICS INC
350 W 57th St Apt 14i (10019-3762)
PHONE..................212 315-5266
Margaret Keppler, *President*
Patricia Encinosa, *Vice Pres*
Michael Keppler, *Treasurer*
EMP: 5
SALES (est): 317.1K **Privately Held**
SIC: 2741 7389 Miscellaneous publishing; translation services

(G-10964)
LAREGENCE INC
34 W 27th St Fl 2 (10001-6901)
PHONE..................212 736-2548
Fax: 212 736-2547
Jay Perlstein, *President*
Kathy Jones, *Treasurer*
▼ **EMP**: 20
SALES (est): 2.6MM **Privately Held**
SIC: 2221 2391 Upholstery, tapestry & wall covering fabrics; curtains & draperies

(G-10965)
LARGO MUSIC INC
425 Park Ave Ste 501 (10022-3519)
PHONE..................212 756-5080
Jay Roger Friedman, *President*
EMP: 7
SQ FT: 10,000
SALES (est): 314.2K
SALES (corp-wide): 108.6MM **Privately Held**
WEB: www.largomusic.com
SIC: 2741 Music books: publishing only, not printed on site
PA: Lebhar-Friedman, Inc.
150 W 30th St Fl 19
New York NY 10001
212 756-5000

(G-10966)
LARTE DEL GELATO INC
75 9th Ave Frnt 38 (10011-4730)
PHONE..................212 366-0570
Francisco Realmuto, *Owner*
Josephine Pina, *Admin Asst*
▲ **EMP**: 9

SALES (est): 670.9K **Privately Held**
SIC: 2052 2099 Cones, ice cream; jelly, corncob (gelatin)

(G-10967)
LASER & ELECTRON BEAM INC
77 7th Ave Apt 3h (10011-6612)
PHONE..................603 626-6080
EMP: 6
SQ FT: 4,800
SALES (est): 65.9K **Privately Held**
SIC: 3599 8734 8711 Operates As A Machine Shop Testing Laboratory & Consulting Service For Hi-Tech Equipment

(G-10968)
LASVIT INC
51 Wooster St Fl 1 (10013-2292)
PHONE..................212 219-3043
Jiri Vasitek, *President*
EMP: 8
SALES (corp-wide): 1.5MM **Privately Held**
SIC: 3645 Residential lighting fixtures
PA: Lasvit Inc
28368 Constellation Rd # 350
Valencia CA 91355
661 294-6507

(G-10969)
LATCHABLE INC
450 W 33rd St Fl 12 (10001-2610)
PHONE..................646 833-0604
Luke Schoenfelder, *CEO*
EMP: 25 **EST**: 2014
SALES (est): 220.8K **Privately Held**
SIC: 7372 7389 Business oriented computer software;

(G-10970)
LATINA MEDIA VENTURES LLC (PA)
120 Broadway Fl 34 (10271-3499)
PHONE..................212 642-0200
Fax: 212 575-3088
Edward Lewis, *Ch of Bd*
James Reffler, *Production*
Stephen Liparini, *Finance*
Mattie Reyes, *Sales Staff*
Bill Toth, *Mktg Dir*
▲ **EMP**: 40
SQ FT: 11,000
SALES (est): 15MM **Privately Held**
WEB: www.latinapromotions.com
SIC: 2721 Periodicals

(G-10971)
LAUFER WIND GROUP LLC
270 Lafayette St Ste 1402 (10012-3364)
PHONE..................212 792-3912
John Knag, *Engineer*
Katherine Corle, *Office Mgr*
Eric Laufer, *Mng Member*
EMP: 15
SALES (est): 2.5MM **Privately Held**
SIC: 3812 Radar systems & equipment

(G-10972)
LAUMONT LABS INC
Also Called: Laumont Editions
333 W 52nd St Fl 14 (10019-6238)
PHONE..................212 664-0595
Philippe Laumont, *President*
Jake Guenther, *Manager*
EMP: 28
SQ FT: 18,000
SALES (est): 2.7MM **Privately Held**
WEB: www.laumont.com
SIC: 2752 Commercial printing, lithographic

(G-10973)
LAUNDRESS INC
247 W 30th St Ste 7l (10001-2824)
PHONE..................212 209-0074
Gwen Whiting, *President*
Lindsey Wieber Boyd, *Vice Pres*
Jelina Kallabaku, *Accountant*
Emily Herzig, *Manager*
▲ **EMP**: 10
SALES (est): 1.8MM **Privately Held**
SIC: 2842 Laundry cleaning preparations

New York - New York County (G-10974)   **GEOGRAPHIC SECTION**

(G-10974)
LAURICE EL BADRY RAHME LTD
Also Called: Bond No 9
399 Bleecker St (10014-2452)
PHONE................................212 633-1641
Evelyn Diaz, *Manager*
EMP: 5   **Privately Held**
SIC: 2844   Perfumes & colognes
PA: Laurice El Badry Rahme, Ltd.
9 Bond St
New York NY 10012

(G-10975)
LAZARE KAPLAN INTL INC (PA)
19 W 44th St Fl 16 (10036-6101)
PHONE................................212 972-9700
Fax: 212 972-8561
Maurice Tempelsman, *Ch of Bd*
Leon Tempelsman, *President*
Jeff Edelstein, *Vice Pres*
Charlie Rosario, *Vice Pres*
William H Moryto, *CFO*
▲ **EMP:** 56   **EST:** 1903
SQ FT: 17,351
SALES (est): 12.4MM   **Privately Held**
WEB: www.lazarediamonds.com
SIC: 3915   Diamond cutting & polishing

(G-10976)
LBG ACQUISITION LLC
Also Called: Lighting By Gregory
158 Bowery (10012-4601)
PHONE................................212 226-1276
Fax: 212 226-2705
William Skarren, *President*
EMP: 35
SALES (est): 12.7MM   **Privately Held**
SIC: 3648   Lighting equipment

(G-10977)
LE BOOK PUBLISHING INC (HQ)
552 Broadway Apt 6s (10012-3956)
PHONE................................212 334-5252
Fax: 212 941-4150
Veronique Kolasa, *President*
Michael Kazam, *Vice Pres*
▲ **EMP:** 9
SQ FT: 2,500
SALES (est): 742.6K
SALES (corp-wide): 495.4K   **Privately Held**
WEB: www.lebook.com
SIC: 2731   Books: publishing only
PA: Le Book Editions Sa
4 Rue D Enghien
Paris
147 700-330

(G-10978)
LE LABO HOLDING LLC (HQ)
Also Called: Le Labo Fragrances
233 Elizabeth St (10012-3530)
PHONE................................844 316-9319
Fabrice Penot, *Principal*
▲ **EMP:** 25
SALES (est): 7MM
SALES (corp-wide): 11.8B   **Publicly Held**
SIC: 2844   Perfumes & colognes
PA: The Estee Lauder Companies Inc
767 5th Ave Fl 37
New York NY 10153
212 572-4200

(G-10979)
LE PAVEH LTD
23 W 47th St Ste 501 (10036-2826)
PHONE................................212 736-6110
EMP: 10
SALES (est): 850K   **Privately Held**
SIC: 3911   Jewelry, precious metal

(G-10980)
LE VIAN CORP
10 W 46th St (10036-4515)
PHONE................................516 466-7200
Fax: 212 944-7734
Louis Ebrani, *President*
EMP: 36
SALES (corp-wide): 26.5MM   **Privately Held**
SIC: 3911   Jewelry, precious metal
PA: Le Vian Corp.
235 Great Neck Rd
Great Neck NY 11021
516 466-7200

(G-10981)
LEA & VIOLA INC
525 Fashion Ave Rm 1401 (10018-4914)
PHONE................................646 918-6866
Minji Kim, *President*
EMP: 6
SQ FT: 4,000
SALES (est): 900K   **Privately Held**
SIC: 2331   Women's & misses' blouses & shirts

(G-10982)
LEADERSHIP DIRECTORIES INC (PA)
Also Called: Federal Yellow Book
1407 Broadway Rm 318 (10018-3853)
PHONE................................212 627-4140
Fax: 212 645-0538
Gretchen G Teichgraeber, *CEO*
William W Cressey, *Chairman*
Thomas Silver, *Senior VP*
James Gee, *Vice Pres*
Bill Schneider, *Sales Executive*
EMP: 50   **EST:** 1965
SQ FT: 11,400
SALES (est): 6.9MM   **Privately Held**
SIC: 2741   2721   Miscellaneous publishing; directories: publishing only, not printed on site; periodicals: publishing only

(G-10983)
LEADERTEX INTL INC
Also Called: Leadertex Group
135 W 36th St Fl 12 (10018-6981)
PHONE................................212 563-2242
Fax: 212 563-0220
Joseph Delijani, *President*
▲ **EMP:** 20
SALES (est): 1.7MM   **Privately Held**
SIC: 2252   Men's, boys' & girls' hosiery

(G-10984)
LEARNINGEXPRESS LLC
224 W 29th St Fl 3 (10001-5204)
PHONE................................646 274-6454
Barry Lippman, *CEO*
Kheil McIntyre, *COO*
Steven Nolan, *Senior VP*
Steve Nolan, *Vice Pres*
Kevin Barrett, *VP Sls/Mktg*
EMP: 35
SALES (est): 5.7MM   **Privately Held**
WEB: www.learningexpressllc.com
SIC: 2731   Book publishing

(G-10985)
LEATHER IMPACT INC
525 Fashion Ave Rm 1012 (10018-0461)
PHONE................................212 382-2788
Demitri P Kermelis, *President*
Margaretha Kermelis, *Treasurer*
◆ **EMP:** 5
SQ FT: 3,650
SALES (est): 799.3K   **Privately Held**
WEB: www.leatherfacts.com
SIC: 3172   5199   Personal leather goods; leather, leather goods & furs; chamois leather

(G-10986)
LEBHAR-FRIEDMAN INC (PA)
Also Called: Chain Stores Age
150 W 30th St Fl 19 (10001-4119)
PHONE................................212 756-5000
Fax: 212 756-5270
J Roger Friedman, *President*
Daniel J Mills, *President*
Lebhar Friedman, *Publisher*
Miguel D Haro, *Publisher*
John Kenlon, *Publisher*
▲ **EMP:** 49   **EST:** 1925
SQ FT: 30,000
SALES (est): 108.6MM   **Privately Held**
WEB: www.lf.com
SIC: 2721   2711   Magazines: publishing only, not printed on site; newspapers: publishing only, not printed on site

(G-10987)
LEBHAR-FRIEDMAN INC
Also Called: Circulation Dept
425 Park Ave Fl 6 (10022-3520)
PHONE................................212 756-5000
EMP: 125
SALES (corp-wide): 105.2MM   **Privately Held**
SIC: 2721   2711   Periodicals-Publishing/Printing Newspapers-Publishing/Printing
PA: Lebhar-Friedman, Inc.
150 W 30th St Fl 19
New York NY 10001
212 756-5000

(G-10988)
LEBLON HOLDINGS LLC
33 Irving Pl Fl 3 (10003-2332)
PHONE................................212 741-2675
Jim Myers, *CFO*
Jaime Keller, *Mktg Dir*
Steven Luttmann,
▲ **EMP:** 35
SQ FT: 3,000
SALES (est): 3.8MM   **Privately Held**
SIC: 2085   Rum (alcoholic beverage)
PA: Bacardi Limited
65 Pitts Bay Road
Hamilton

(G-10989)
LEBLON LLC
Also Called: Leblon Cachaca
33 Irving Pl Fl 3 (10003-2332)
PHONE................................954 649-0148
Eric Goldman, *President*
▲ **EMP:** 11   **EST:** 2005
SALES (est): 1.2MM   **Privately Held**
SIC: 2085   Distilled & blended liquors

(G-10990)
LEBLON LLC
266 W 26th St Ste 801 (10001-6722)
PHONE................................786 281-5672
Marcio Silveira, *Dir Ops-Prd-Mfg*
Thomas Bonney, *CFO*
Steve Luttmann, *Mng Member*
Gerrard Schweitzer,
▲ **EMP:** 40
SALES (est): 2.9MM   **Privately Held**
SIC: 2085   Distilled & blended liquors

(G-10991)
LEDES GROUP INC
Also Called: Cosmetic World
85 5th Ave Fl 12 (10003-3019)
PHONE................................212 840-8800
George M Ledes, *President*
John Ledes, *Publisher*
Joseph Garces, *Vice Pres*
Sally C Ledes, *Vice Pres*
Hasu Shah, *Treasurer*
EMP: 18
SQ FT: 7,000
SALES: 25.4K   **Privately Held**
WEB: www.cosmeticworld.com
SIC: 2741   Miscellaneous publishing; newsletter publishing

(G-10992)
LEE & LOW BOOKS INCORPORATED
Also Called: Bebop Books
95 Madison Ave Rm 1205 (10016-7808)
PHONE................................212 779-4400
Fax: 212 683-1894
Thomas Low, *President*
Kandace Coston, *Editor*
Emily Hazel, *Editor*
Samantha Wolf, *Editor*
Craig Low, *Vice Pres*
▲ **EMP:** 14
SQ FT: 4,500
SALES (est): 1.4MM   **Privately Held**
WEB: www.leeandlow.com
SIC: 2731   Books: publishing only

(G-10993)
LEE WORLD INDUSTRIES LLC
150 Broadway Ste 1608 (10038-4381)
PHONE................................212 265-8866
James Lee, *CEO*
Lisa Lee, *Vice Pres*
Lydia Liu, *Project Mgr*
Jeff Lee, *Opers Mgr*
Alex Wang, *Traffic Mgr*
▲ **EMP:** 175
SQ FT: 14,500

SALES: 4MM   **Privately Held**
WEB: www.leeworld.com
SIC: 3714   Motor vehicle parts & accessories

(G-10994)
LEE YUEN FUNG TRADING CO INC (PA)
125 W 29th St Fl 5 (10001-5780)
PHONE................................212 594-9595
Fax: 212 629-0757
Moon Tong Fok, *President*
EMP: 14
SQ FT: 4,000
SALES: 8MM   **Privately Held**
SIC: 2833   5149   Drugs & herbs: grading, grinding & milling; seasonings, sauces & extracts

(G-10995)
LEFRAK ENTERTAINMENT CO LTD
Also Called: L M R
40 W 57th St Fl 4 (10019-4001)
PHONE................................212 586-3600
Samuel J Lefrak, *Ch of Bd*
Richard S Lefrak, *Vice Ch Bd*
Herbert Moelis, *President*
EMP: 9
SALES (est): 660K   **Privately Held**
SIC: 2741   3652   Music book & sheet music publishing; pre-recorded records & tapes

(G-10996)
LEGGIADRO INTERNATIONAL INC (PA)
8 W 36th St Fl 9 (10018-9772)
PHONE................................212 997-8766
Brooks Ross, *President*
Ann Ross, *Corp Secy*
Karen Degand, *Controller*
◆ **EMP:** 50
SQ FT: 6,000
SALES (est): 8.5MM   **Privately Held**
SIC: 2339   Sportswear, women's

(G-10997)
LEHMANN PRINTING COMPANY INC
247 W 37th St Rm 2a (10018-5066)
PHONE................................212 929-2395
David Lehmann, *President*
Ruth Lehmann, *Manager*
EMP: 5
SQ FT: 10,000
SALES (est): 340K   **Privately Held**
WEB: www.lehmannprinting.com
SIC: 2752   Commercial printing, lithographic; commercial printing, offset

(G-10998)
LEMETRIC HAIR CENTERS INC
124 E 40th St Rm 601 (10016-1769)
PHONE................................212 986-5620
Elline Surianello, *President*
Marvin Blender, *Vice Pres*
EMP: 15
SALES (est): 1.2MM   **Privately Held**
WEB: www.lemetric.com
SIC: 3999   7231   Hairpin mountings; beauty shops

(G-10999)
LENDING TRIMMING CO INC
179 Christopher St (10014-2815)
PHONE................................212 242-7502
John Benis, *President*
William Jarblum, *Admin Sec*
EMP: 80   **EST:** 1944
SQ FT: 7,000
SALES (est): 4.6MM   **Privately Held**
SIC: 2396   Trimming, fabric

(G-11000)
LENG UNIVERSAL INC
Also Called: Emoji
530 7th Ave Rm 1101 (10018-4868)
PHONE................................212 398-6800
Chun Pao Pleng, *CEO*
EMP: 12
SQ FT: 3,800
SALES: 1.4MM   **Privately Held**
SIC: 2369   2339   2325   Jeans: girls', children's & infants'; jeans: women's, misses' & juniors'; jeans: men's, youths' & boys'

▲ = Import   ▼ = Export
◆ = Import/Export

GEOGRAPHIC SECTION

New York - New York County (G-11028)

(G-11001)
LENON MODELS INC
236 W 27th St Rm 900 (10001-5906)
PHONE..................212 229-1581
Elise Hubsher, *President*
EMP: 5
SQ FT: 2,000
SALES (est): 480.2K **Privately Held**
SIC: 3259 Architectural clay products

(G-11002)
LENORE MARSHALL INC
231 W 29th St Frnt 1 (10001-5209)
PHONE..................212 947-5945
Fax: 212 714-1118
Leo Marshall, *President*
John Petkanas, *President*
▲ EMP: 5 EST: 1957
SALES (est): 390K **Privately Held**
SIC: 2353 Millinery

(G-11003)
LEO D BERNSTEIN & SONS INC (PA)
Also Called: Bernstein Display
151 W 25th St Frnt 1 (10001-7204)
PHONE..................212 337-9578
Fax: 516 237-5922
Roger Friedman, *Ch of Bd*
Anthony Tripoli, *President*
Edmund Bernstein, *Chairman*
Mitchell Bernstein, *COO*
Dave Howlett, *Plant Mgr*
▲ EMP: 20 EST: 1965
SQ FT: 192,000
SALES (est): 19.4MM **Privately Held**
WEB: www.bernsteindisplay.com
SIC: 3999 2541 5046 7389 Forms: display, dress & show; store & office display cases & fixtures; store fixtures; store equipment; design services

(G-11004)
LEO INGWER INC
62 W 47th St Ste 1004 (10036-3286)
PHONE..................212 719-1342
Fax: 212 869-5462
Kenneth Ingwer, *President*
Danielle I Cohen, *Vice Pres*
Rochelle Ingwer-Levine, *Vice Pres*
Sam Gross, *Sales & Mktg St*
Selochnie Persaud, *Clerk*
EMP: 42 EST: 1941
SQ FT: 3,500
SALES (est): 5.3MM **Privately Held**
WEB: www.leoingwer.com
SIC: 3911 Mountings, gold or silver: pens, leather goods, etc.

(G-11005)
LEO PAPER INC
286 5th Ave Fl 6 (10001-4512)
PHONE..................917 305-0708
Fax: 917 305-0709
Bijan Pakzada, *President*
EMP: 7
SALES (est): 426.5K **Privately Held**
SIC: 2759 Commercial printing

(G-11006)
LEO SCHACHTER & CO INC
529 5th Ave (10017-4608)
PHONE..................212 688-2000
Fax: 212 688-3345
Michael Metz, *CEO*
Sandy Marks, *VP Sales*
EMP: 100
SALES (est): 3.6MM **Privately Held**
SIC: 3911 5094 Jewelry apparel; diamonds (gems)

(G-11007)
LEO SCHACHTER DIAMONDS LLC
Also Called: Leo Diamond, The
50 W 47th St Fl 2100 (10036-8687)
PHONE..................212 688-2000
Elliot Tannenbaum, *President*
Rebecca Foerster, *Exec VP*
Jake Weinblatt, *CFO*
Andrew Doenias, *Accountant*
Shimrit Adika, *Accounts Mgr*
EMP: 100 EST: 1981
SQ FT: 11,335
SALES (est): 18.8MM **Privately Held**
WEB: www.leoschachter.com
SIC: 3915 5094 Jewelers' materials & lapidary work; jewelry & precious stones
PA: Leo Schachter Diamonds Ltd
Bezalel
Ramat Gan
357 662-23

(G-11008)
LES ATELIERS TAMALET
37 W 39th St (10018-3886)
PHONE..................929 325-7976
David, *Principal*
EMP: 20
SALES (est): 658.4K **Privately Held**
SIC: 3911 Jewelry apparel

(G-11009)
LESER ENTERPRISES LTD
Also Called: Color Story
18 E 48th St Rm 1104 (10017-1014)
PHONE..................212 644-8921
Fax: 212 308-7549
Robert Leser, *President*
Hilary Leser, *Manager*
EMP: 11
SALES (est): 1.1MM **Privately Held**
WEB: www.colorstory.com
SIC: 3911 Jewelry, precious metal

(G-11010)
LESILU PRODUCTIONS INC
Also Called: Hey Doll
60 W 38th St Rm 302 (10018-0281)
PHONE..................212 947-6419
Steven Sunshine, *CEO*
Lesli Sunshine, *President*
Luanne Trovato, *Corp Secy*
▲ EMP: 6 EST: 2000
SQ FT: 650
SALES (est): 1.1MM **Privately Held**
SIC: 3961 Costume jewelry, ex. precious metal & semiprecious stones

(G-11011)
LESLIE STUART CO INC
Also Called: Donna Degan
149 W 36th St Fl 8 (10018-9474)
PHONE..................212 629-4551
Gene Fobarty, *President*
Donna Degan, *Vice Pres*
Larry Maltzer, *Accountant*
Heshy Feldman, *Sales Mgr*
Eugene Fogarty, *Director*
▲ EMP: 17
SQ FT: 4,000
SALES (est): 2.2MM **Privately Held**
WEB: www.donnadegnan.com
SIC: 2339 Women's & misses' athletic clothing & sportswear

(G-11012)
LET WATER BE WATER LLC
Also Called: Wataah
40 W 27th St Fl 3 (10001-6908)
P.O. Box 550 (10116-0550)
PHONE..................212 627-2630
Fax: 212 627-2632
Rose Cameron, *CEO*
Christine Widga, *Mktg Dir*
EMP: 8
SALES (est): 3.6MM **Privately Held**
SIC: 2086 Water, pasteurized: packaged in cans, bottles, etc.

(G-11013)
LEVI STRAUSS & CO
1501 Broadway (10036-5601)
PHONE..................212 944-8555
Mario David, *Branch Mgr*
EMP: 19
SALES (corp-wide): 4.5B **Privately Held**
WEB: www.levistrauss.com
SIC: 2325 Jeans: men's, youths' & boys'
PA: Levi Strauss & Co.
1155 Battery St
San Francisco CA 94111
415 501-6000

(G-11014)
LEVY GROUP INC (PA)
Also Called: Liz Claiborne Coats
1333 Broadway Fl 9 (10018-1064)
PHONE..................212 398-0707
Fax: 212 719-5547
Jack Arthur Levy, *Ch of Bd*
Donald Levy, *Chairman*
Lawrence Levy, *Vice Pres*
Richard Levy, *Vice Pres*
Norah Reyes, *Manager*
▲ EMP: 150 EST: 1995
SQ FT: 27,000
SALES (est): 99.8MM **Privately Held**
WEB: www.oasisfarm.com
SIC: 2337 2385 Women's & misses' suits & coats; jackets & vests, except fur & leather: women's; raincoats, except vulcanized rubber: purchased materials

(G-11015)
LF OUTERWEAR LLC
463 7th Ave Fl 12 (10018-7499)
PHONE..................212 239-2025
Richard Kringstein,
Barry Kringstein,
▲ EMP: 80
SALES (est): 3.1MM **Privately Held**
SIC: 2337 Women's & misses' suits & coats

(G-11016)
LGB INC
Also Called: J Valdi
1410 Broadway Rm 3205 (10018-9633)
PHONE..................212 278-8280
Eduardo Snider, *President*
Peter Reidell, *Corp Secy*
Jason Schwartz, *Manager*
EMP: 20
SALES (est): 836.8K **Privately Held**
SIC: 2339 Women's & misses' outerwear

(G-11017)
LIBERTY APPAREL COMPANY INC (PA)
1407 Broadway Rm 1500 (10018-2836)
PHONE..................718 625-4000
Fax: 646 768-0660
Hagai Laniado, *President*
Albert Negri, *Principal*
Bryan Lattmen, *Vice Pres*
Jeffrey Wine, *CFO*
▲ EMP: 41
SQ FT: 38,000
SALES (est): 5.2MM **Privately Held**
WEB: www.libertyapparel.com
SIC: 2331 2339 2369 Women's & misses' blouses & shirts; women's & misses' outerwear; girls' & children's outerwear

(G-11018)
LIBRARY TALES PUBLISHING INC
244 5th Ave Ste Q222 (10001-7604)
PHONE..................347 394-2629
Usher Morgan, *CEO*
▼ EMP: 8
SQ FT: 359
SALES (est): 580K **Privately Held**
WEB: www.librarytalespublishing.com
SIC: 2731 Books: publishing & printing

(G-11019)
LICENDERS (PA)
939 8th Ave (10019-4264)
PHONE..................212 759-5200
Fax: 212 759-5250
Adie Horowitz, *Principal*
EMP: 9 EST: 2010
SALES (est): 1.3MM **Privately Held**
SIC: 3647 5087 Headlights (fixtures), vehicular; service establishment equipment

(G-11020)
LIFE STYLE DESIGN GROUP
Also Called: Sag Harbor
1441 Broadway Fl 7 (10018-1905)
PHONE..................212 391-8666
Fax: 212 730-0240
EMP: 35 EST: 1975
SQ FT: 12,000
SALES (est): 2.6MM
SALES (corp-wide): 596MM **Privately Held**
WEB: www.kellwoodco.com
SIC: 2339 Sportswear, women's
PA: Kellwood Company, Llc
600 Kellwood Pkwy Ste 200
Chesterfield MO 63017
314 576-3100

(G-11021)
LIFESTYLE DESIGN USA LTD
Also Called: Cyber Knit
315 W 39th St Rm 709 (10018-4043)
PHONE..................212 279-9400
Daniel Honig, *Principal*
Alexis Miller, *Services*
▲ EMP: 5
SALES (est): 1MM **Privately Held**
SIC: 2257 3624 5199 5949 Dyeing & finishing circular knit fabrics; brush blocks, carbon or molded graphite; art goods & supplies; fabric stores piece goods

(G-11022)
LIFESTYLE INTERNATIONAL LLC
469 7th Ave (10018-7605)
PHONE..................917 757-0067
Abraham Haber, *CEO*
EMP: 5
SALES (est): 182.8K **Privately Held**
SIC: 3263 Commercial tableware or kitchen articles, fine earthenware

(G-11023)
LIFTFORWARD INC
180 Maiden Ln Fl 10 (10038-5178)
PHONE..................917 693-4993
Jeffrey Rogers, *President*
Barbara Steinberg, *Controller*
Christine Reilly, *Officer*
EMP: 20
SALES: 25MM **Privately Held**
SIC: 7372 Business oriented computer software

(G-11024)
LIGHT HOUSE HILL MARKETING
Also Called: Signatures
38 W 39th St Fl 4l (10018-2150)
PHONE..................212 354-1338
Donald Schmidt, *President*
▲ EMP: 16
SQ FT: 2,900
SALES (est): 1.5MM **Privately Held**
WEB: www.signaturespromo.com
SIC: 2231 Apparel & outerwear broadwoven fabrics

(G-11025)
LIGHT INC
530 Fashion Ave Rm 1002 (10018-4869)
PHONE..................212 629-3255
Alice Sim, *President*
▲ EMP: 6
SALES (est): 883K **Privately Held**
WEB: www.light.com
SIC: 2339 Women's & misses' outerwear

(G-11026)
LIGHTBULB PRESS INC
39 W 28th St (10001-4203)
PHONE..................212 485-8800
Kenneth Morris, *Ch of Bd*
Rickie Kowlessar, *Info Tech Dir*
Mavis Wright, *Director*
Kara Hatch, *Art Dir*
Kara Wilson, *Creative Dir*
EMP: 30
SQ FT: 7,500
SALES (est): 2.7MM **Privately Held**
WEB: www.lightbulbpress.net
SIC: 2741 Miscellaneous publishing

(G-11027)
LIGHTHOUSE COMPONENTS
14 Wall St (10005-2101)
PHONE..................917 993-6820
Maurice Gaete, *CEO*
EMP: 25
SALES (est): 944.2K **Privately Held**
SIC: 3679 Electronic components

(G-11028)
LILY & TAYLOR INC
Also Called: Lilly Collection
247 W 37th St Frnt 6 (10018-5042)
PHONE..................212 564-5459
Fax: 212 564-2358
Sohail Elyaszadeh, *President*
Morris Elyaszadeh, *Manager*
▲ EMP: 15
SQ FT: 3,500

New York - New York County (G-11029) — GEOGRAPHIC SECTION

SALES: 6MM Privately Held
WEB: www.lilyandtaylor.com
SIC: 2339 2335 2337 Women's & misses' outerwear; slacks: women's, misses' & juniors'; gowns, formal; suits: women's, misses' & juniors'; skirts, separate: women's, misses' & juniors'

(G-11029)
LINDER NEW YORK LLC
195 Chrystie St Rm 900 (10002-1230)
PHONE..................646 678-5819
Sam Linder, Mng Member
EMP: 11 EST: 2007
SALES (est): 1.3MM Privately Held
SIC: 2329 2389 Athletic (warmup, sweat & jogging) suits: men's & boys'; men's miscellaneous accessories

(G-11030)
LINDSAY-HOENIG LTD
Also Called: Lindsay & Co
64 W 48th St Ste 1306 (10036-1746)
P.O. Box 196, Rockville Centre (11571-0196)
PHONE..................212 575-9711
Fax: 212 869-0527
David Hoenig, President
Henry F Hoenig, Vice Pres
Celeste Beckford, Office Mgr
EMP: 6
SALES (est): 604.9K Privately Held
WEB: www.lindsayco.com
SIC: 3911 Jewelry, precious metal

(G-11031)
LINRICH DESIGNS INC
Also Called: Linda Richards
256 W 38th St Fl 8 (10018-9123)
PHONE..................212 382-2257
Linda Breatti, Owner
EMP: 5
SALES (corp-wide): 699.3K Privately Held
WEB: www.lindarichards.com
SIC: 2339 2337 Women's & misses' jackets & coats, except sportswear; suits: women's, misses' & juniors'; skirts, separate: women's, misses' & juniors'
PA: Linrich Designs Inc
    256 W 38th St Fl 8
    New York NY
    212 382-2257

(G-11032)
LINTEX LINENS INC
295 5th Ave Ste 1702 (10016-7160)
PHONE..................212 679-8046
Kurt Hamburger, President
Rae Ellen Blum, Vice Pres
Glorida Matias, Bookkeeper
▲ EMP: 500
SQ FT: 6,000
SALES (est): 37.8MM Privately Held
SIC: 2299 5023 Fabrics: linen, jute, hemp, ramie; linens, table

(G-11033)
LIONEL HABAS ASSOCIATES INC
1601 3rd Ave Apt 22d (10128-0028)
PHONE..................212 860-8454
Lionel Habas, President
EMP: 10
SQ FT: 200
SALES (est): 840K Privately Held
SIC: 2652 Setup paperboard boxes

(G-11034)
LIPPINCOTT MASSIE MCQUILKIN L
27 W 20th St Ste 305 (10011-3731)
PHONE..................212 352-2055
Fax: 212 352-2059
Rob McQuilkin, Mng Member
Martin Lemelman, Professor
EMP: 10
SALES (est): 896.1K Privately Held
SIC: 2731 Book publishing

(G-11035)
LIQUOR BOTTLE PACKG INTL INC
305 Madison Ave Ste 1357 (10165-1319)
PHONE..................212 922-2813
Andy Fraser, President
▲ EMP: 5
SQ FT: 2,200
SALES (est): 1MM Privately Held
SIC: 3221 Bottles for packing, bottling & canning: glass

(G-11036)
LITERARY CLASSICS OF US
Also Called: Library of America
14 E 60th St Ste 1101 (10022-7115)
PHONE..................212 308-3360
Fax: 212 750-8352
Cheryl Hurley, President
Trish Hoard, Editor
Geoffrey G Obrien, Editor
Daniel Baker, CFO
Benjamin Ordover, Treasurer
▲ EMP: 16
SQ FT: 4,000
SALES: 5.6MM Privately Held
SIC: 2731 2732 Book publishing; book printing

(G-11037)
LITHOMATIC BUSINESS FORMS INC
233 W 18th St Frnt A (10011-4570)
PHONE..................212 255-6700
Fax: 212 242-5963
Irwin Ostrega, President
Herman Margules, Accountant
Carmin Diaz, Bookkeeper
EMP: 3
SQ FT: 5,000
SALES: 1.5MM Privately Held
SIC: 2752 Commercial printing, offset

(G-11038)
LITTLE ERIC SHOES ON MADISON
1118 Madison Ave (10028-0406)
PHONE..................212 717-1513
Robert Pansinkoff, President
Robert Pasinkoff, President
EMP: 6
SALES (est): 904.7K Privately Held
SIC: 3021 Canvas shoes, rubber soled

(G-11039)
LITTLE WOLF CABINET SHOP INC
1583 1st Ave Frnt 1 (10028-4273)
PHONE..................212 734-1116
Fax: 212 628-1966
John Wolf, President
Maureen Fritsch, Corp Secy
John Fritsch, Vice Pres
EMP: 20
SQ FT: 2,500
SALES (est): 2.8MM Privately Held
SIC: 2511 5712 Wood household furniture; furniture stores

(G-11040)
LITTLEBITS ELECTRONICS INC
601 W 26th St Ste M274 (10001-1101)
PHONE..................917 464-4577
Aya Bdeir, CEO
EMP: 95
SQ FT: 18,000
SALES (est): 18.5MM Privately Held
SIC: 3944 Electronic toys

(G-11041)
LIVE VOTE II INC ◐
105 W 86th St 322 (10024-3412)
PHONE..................646 343-9053
Michael Fellmeth, COO
EMP: 5 EST: 2017
SALES (est): 142.2K Privately Held
SIC: 7372 7371 Application computer software; computer software systems analysis & design, custom; computer software development & applications

(G-11042)
LIVERIGHT PUBLISHING CORP
Also Called: Norton, Ww & Company,
500 5th Ave Fl 6 (10110-0699)
PHONE..................212 354-5500
Drake McSeely, President
Victor Schmalzer, General Mgr
John G Benedict, Vice Pres
James Jordan, Vice Pres
Star Lawrence, Vice Pres
EMP: 9
SQ FT: 3,000
SALES (est): 888.2K Privately Held
SALES (corp-wide): 205.6MM Privately Held
WEB: www.wwnorton.com
SIC: 2731 Books: publishing only
PA: W. W. Norton & Company, Inc.
    500 5th Ave Fl 6
    New York NY 10110
    212 354-5500

(G-11043)
LIVETILES CORP
60 Madison Ave Fl 8 (10010-1676)
PHONE..................917 472-7887
Jonathan Green, Finance Dir
Alina Gertsberg, Mktg Coord
EMP: 19
SQ FT: 100
SALES (est): 928.4K Privately Held
SIC: 7372 Business oriented computer software

(G-11044)
LM MIGNON LLC
Also Called: Mignon Group, The
499 Fashion Ave Fl 4n (10018-6844)
PHONE..................212 730-9221
Vincent Mignon, Mng Member
◆ EMP: 13
SQ FT: 3,500
SALES: 6MM Privately Held
SIC: 2335 Women's, juniors' & misses' dresses; bridal & formal gowns

(G-11045)
LMR GROUP INC
463 7th Ave Fl 4 (10018-8725)
PHONE..................212 730-9221
Linlin Fang, Principal
Robi Hagooli, Principal
Steven Stuppler, Director
EMP: 5 EST: 2016
SALES (est): 247.8K Privately Held
SIC: 2335 Women's, juniors' & misses' dresses

(G-11046)
LOAR GROUP INC (PA)
450 Lexington Ave Fl 31 (10017-3925)
PHONE..................212 210-9348
Glenn Dalessandro, CFO
Jim Mullen, Sales Staff
Michael Manella, General Counsel
EMP: 144
SALES (est): 22.2MM Privately Held
SIC: 3728 Aircraft parts & equipment

(G-11047)
LOCATIONS MAGAZINE
124 E 79th St (10075-0353)
PHONE..................212 288-4745
Joel Scher, Owner
Joel Cher, Manager
Sharon Scher, Admin Sec
EMP: 5
SALES (est): 290K Privately Held
SIC: 2721 Magazines: publishing only, not printed on site

(G-11048)
LOCKHEED MARTIN CORPORATION
420 Lexington Ave Rm 2601 (10170-2602)
PHONE..................212 953-1510
Brook Awoke, Engineer
Ellen Strauss, Manager
Kimball Lau, Administration
EMP: 8 Publicly Held
WEB: www.lockheedmartin.com
SIC: 3721 Aircraft
PA: Lockheed Martin Corporation
    6801 Rockledge Dr
    Bethesda MD 20817

(G-11049)
LOCKHEED MARTIN CORPORATION
600 3rd Ave Fl 35 (10016-2001)
PHONE..................212 697-1105
Lisa McMeekin, Branch Mgr
Joe Oparesi, Info Tech Dir
EMP: 85 Publicly Held
WEB: www.lockheedmartin.com
SIC: 3812 Search & navigation equipment
PA: Lockheed Martin Corporation
    6801 Rockledge Dr
    Bethesda MD 20817

(G-11050)
LOGO
1515 Broadway (10036-8901)
PHONE..................212 846-2568
EMP: 5
SALES (est): 516.8K Privately Held
SIC: 2869 Fuels

(G-11051)
LOIS KITCHEN LLC
206 Avenue A Apt 2a (10009-3405)
PHONE..................216 308-9335
Nora O'Malley,
EMP: 5
SALES (est): 150.7K Privately Held
SIC: 3999 Manufacturing industries

(G-11052)
LOKAI HOLDINGS LLC
36 E 31st St Rm 602 (10016-6918)
PHONE..................646 979-3474
Steven Izen, CEO
Andrew Actman, CFO
▲ EMP: 10
SQ FT: 3,000
SALES: 13MM Privately Held
SIC: 3911 5199 Bracelets, precious metal; general merchandise, non-durable

(G-11053)
LOLLYTOGS LTD (PA)
Also Called: French Toast
100 W 33rd St Ste 1012 (10001-2984)
PHONE..................212 502-6000
Fax: 212 594-3030
Richard Sutton, CEO
Morris Sutton, President
Joseph Sutton, Vice Pres
Jeffrey Sutton, Treasurer
◆ EMP: 80 EST: 1958
SQ FT: 40,000
SALES (est): 2.6MM Privately Held
SIC: 2369 5137 Girls' & children's outerwear; sportswear, women's & children's

(G-11054)
LONDON THEATER NEWS LTD
12 E 86th St Apt 620 (10028-0511)
PHONE..................212 517-8608
Fax: 212 249-9371
Roger Harris, President
EMP: 19
SALES (est): 130K Privately Held
SIC: 2741 7922 Newsletter publishing; ticket agency, theatrical

(G-11055)
LONGO NEW YORK INC
444 W 17th St (10011-5893)
P.O. Box 511, Wharton NJ (07885-0511)
PHONE..................212 929-7128
Fax: 212 633-9534
Joe M Longo, President
EMP: 10
SALES (est): 485.9K Privately Held
SIC: 7694 Electric motor repair

(G-11056)
LONGTAIL STUDIOS INC
180 Varick St Rm 820 (10014-5419)
PHONE..................646 443-8146
Gerard Guillemot, President
Claude Guillemot, Vice Pres
Michelle Guillemot, Vice Pres
Yves Guillemot, Vice Pres
Sandeep Bisla, Manager
EMP: 26
SQ FT: 4,000
SALES (est): 3.3MM Privately Held
WEB: www.longtailstudios.com
SIC: 3695 Computer software tape & disks: blank, rigid & floppy

(G-11057)
LOOK BY M INC
838 Avenue Of The America (10001-4194)
PHONE..................212 213-4019
Youjung Kim, President
▲ EMP: 5
SALES (est): 398.4K Privately Held
SIC: 2252 Tights & leg warmers

▲ = Import ▼ = Export
◆ = Import/Export

GEOGRAPHIC SECTION

New York - New York County (G-11084)

(G-11058)
LOOKBOOKS MEDIA INC
208 W 30th St Rm 802 (10001-0883)
PHONE..................................646 737-3360
Adam Helfgott, *CTO*
EMP: 15
SALES (est): 1.1MM **Privately Held**
SIC: 7372 Application computer software

(G-11059)
LOOM CONCEPTS LLC
767 Lexington Ave Rm 405 (10065-8553)
PHONE..................................212 813-9586
Jorgen Lorentzen, *Vice Pres*
John O'Callaghan,
▲ EMP: 2
SQ FT: 500
SALES: 1.8MM **Privately Held**
SIC: 2273 Carpets & rugs

(G-11060)
LOOMSTATE LLC
270 Bowery Fl 3 (10012-3674)
PHONE..................................212 219-2300
Berrin Noorata, *Managing Prtnr*
Annie Graziani, *General Mgr*
Art Ryan, *Mng Member*
Kevin Ryan,
▲ EMP: 25
SALES (est): 4MM **Privately Held**
SIC: 2231 Weaving mill, broadwoven fabrics: wool or similar fabric

(G-11061)
LORAL SPACE & COMMNCTNS HOLDNG
600 5th Ave Fl 16 (10020-2324)
PHONE..................................212 697-1105
John Capogrossi, *Vice Pres*
EMP: 30
SALES (est): 1.8MM **Publicly Held**
SIC: 3663 Satellites, communications
HQ: Loral Spacecom Corporation
565 5th Ave Fl 19
New York NY 10017
212 697-1105

(G-11062)
LORAL SPACE COMMUNICATIONS INC (PA)
600 5th Ave Fl 16 (10020-2324)
PHONE..................................212 697-1105
Fax: 212 338-5662
Mark H Rachesky, *Ch of Bd*
Michael B Targoff, *Vice Ch Bd*
AVI Katz, *President*
Hampton Chan, *Vice Pres*
Ravinder S Girgla, *Vice Pres*
EMP: 425
SQ FT: 9,000
SALES (est): 60.4MM **Publicly Held**
WEB: www.ssloral.com
SIC: 3663 4899 Satellites, communications; satellite earth stations; data communication services

(G-11063)
LORAL SPACECOM CORPORATION (HQ)
565 5th Ave Fl 19 (10017-2431)
PHONE..................................212 697-1105
Michael Targoff, *CEO*
Harvey Rein, *CFO*
Richard Mastoloni, *Treasurer*
John Stack, *Asst Treas*
EMP: 30
SALES: 869.4MM **Publicly Held**
WEB: www.hq.loral.com
SIC: 3663 Satellites, communications

(G-11064)
LOREAL USA INC
Biotherm
575 5th Ave Bsmt (10017-2446)
PHONE..................................212 818-1500
Robert J Cassou, *Senior VP*
Richard Roderick, *Senior VP*
Pierre Rogers, *Senior VP*
Sarah Williams, *Vice Pres*
Bob Smith, *Controller*
EMP: 470

SALES (corp-wide): 3.2B **Privately Held**
WEB: www.lorealparisusa.com
SIC: 2844 Hair preparations, including shampoos; cosmetic preparations; perfumes & colognes
HQ: L'oreal Usa, Inc.
10 Hudson Yards Fl 30
New York NY 10001

(G-11065)
LOREAL USA INC
435 Hudson St (10014-3941)
PHONE..................................917 606-9554
Lindsay Atha, *Manager*
EMP: 373
SALES (corp-wide): 3.2B **Privately Held**
WEB: www.lorealparisusa.com
SIC: 2844 5122 Toilet preparations; cosmetics, perfumes & hair products
HQ: L'oreal Usa, Inc.
10 Hudson Yards Fl 30
New York NY 10001

(G-11066)
LOREAL USA INC
575 5th Ave Fl 20 (10017-2422)
PHONE..................................212 389-4201
Karen Czajkowski, *Branch Mgr*
EMP: 30
SALES (corp-wide): 3.2B **Privately Held**
WEB: www.lorealparisusa.com
SIC: 2844 Depilatories (cosmetic)
HQ: L'oreal Usa, Inc.
10 Hudson Yards Fl 30
New York NY 10001
212 818-1500

(G-11067)
LOREAL USA INC
Also Called: L'Oreal Paris
575 5th Ave Fl 23 (10017-2430)
PHONE..................................212 984-4704
Joseph Campinell, *Manager*
EMP: 8
SALES (corp-wide): 3.2B **Privately Held**
WEB: www.lorealparisusa.com
SIC: 2844 Hair preparations, including shampoos
HQ: L'oreal Usa, Inc.
10 Hudson Yards Fl 30
New York NY 10001
212 818-1500

(G-11068)
LOREAL USA INC
575 5th Ave Fl 25 (10017-2422)
PHONE..................................646 658-5477
Amanda Leo, *General Mgr*
EMP: 274
SALES (corp-wide): 3.2B **Privately Held**
SIC: 2844 Hair preparations, including shampoos
HQ: L'oreal Usa, Inc.
10 Hudson Yards Fl 30
New York NY 10001
212 818-1500

(G-11069)
LOREAL USA PRODUCTS INC (DH)
10 Hudson Yards (10001-2157)
PHONE..................................212 818-1500
Frederic Roze, *President*
Teresa Lopez, *General Mgr*
Rebecca Caruso, *Exec VP*
Paul Sharnsky, *Senior VP*
Wendy Charland, *Vice Pres*
▲ EMP: 5
SALES (est): 6.8MM
SALES (corp-wide): 3.2B **Privately Held**
SIC: 2844 Hair coloring preparations; shaving preparations; cosmetic preparations; toilet preparations
HQ: L'oreal Usa, Inc.
10 Hudson Yards Fl 30
New York NY 10001
212 818-1500

(G-11070)
LORELEI ORTHOTICS PROSTHETICS
19 W 21st St Rm 204 (10010-6882)
PHONE..................................212 727-2011
Brian Kilcommons, *President*

Alene Chase, *Vice Pres*
EMP: 6
SQ FT: 5,000
SALES (est): 610K **Privately Held**
SIC: 3842 Braces, orthopedic

(G-11071)
LOREMI JEWELRY INC
17 W 45th St Ste 501 (10036-4922)
PHONE..................................212 840-3429
Enzo Palmeri, *President*
EMP: 25 EST: 1987
SALES: 1MM **Privately Held**
SIC: 3911 3915 Jewelry, precious metal; jewelers' materials & lapidary work

(G-11072)
LORNAMEAD INC (DH)
175 Cooper St (10034-2331)
PHONE..................................716 874-7190
Randy Sloan, *CEO*
Brian Bradley, *President*
B Guth, *Vice Pres*
Jeff Lokken, *Vice Pres*
Colin Lorimer, *Vice Pres*
◆ EMP: 90
SQ FT: 66,000
SALES (est): 16.4MM **Privately Held**
WEB: www.lornameadna.com
SIC: 2844 3843 Toilet preparations; compounds, dental

(G-11073)
LOST WORLDS INC
920 Riverside Dr Apt 68 (10032-5468)
PHONE..................................212 923-3423
Stuart Clurman, *President*
EMP: 9
SALES (est): 670K **Privately Held**
SIC: 2386 5699 Coats & jackets, leather & sheep-lined; leather garments

(G-11074)
LOTTA LUV BEAUTY LLC
1359 Broadway Fl 17 (10018-7117)
PHONE..................................646 786-2847
Jeremy Spears, *Manager*
Sabrina Vertucci, *Executive*
Elizabeth Alli,
▲ EMP: 10
SQ FT: 20,000
SALES (est): 1MM **Privately Held**
SIC: 2834 5122 Lip balms; cosmetics
PA: Li & Fung Limited
C/O Estera Management (Bermuda) Limited
Hamilton

(G-11075)
LOU SALLY FASHIONS CORP (DH)
Also Called: S L Fashions Group
1400 Broadway Lbby 6 (10018-5371)
PHONE..................................212 354-9670
Fax: 212 719-2942
Mitchell Grabow, *President*
Bella Postelnik, *Controller*
▲ EMP: 32
SQ FT: 5,500
SALES: 35MM
SALES (corp-wide): 314MM **Privately Held**
SIC: 2335 Women's, juniors' & misses' dresses
HQ: Alex Apparel Group, Inc.
1407 Broadway Rm 1500
New York NY 10018
212 549-8510

(G-11076)
LOU SALLY FASHIONS CORP
1400 Broadway Lbby 3 (10018-5369)
PHONE..................................212 354-1283
Tony Porni, *Vice Pres*
EMP: 40
SALES (corp-wide): 314MM **Privately Held**
SIC: 2335 Women's, juniors' & misses' dresses
HQ: Lou Sally Fashions Corp
1400 Broadway Lbby 6
New York NY 10018
212 354-9670

(G-11077)
LOUIS HORNICK & CO INC
117 E 38th St (10016-2601)
P.O. Box 1584, Quogue (11959-1584)
PHONE..................................212 679-2448
Fax: 212 779-7098
Louis Hornick II, *CEO*
Louis Hornick III, *COO*
Sidney Bluming, *Counsel*
◆ EMP: 5 EST: 1918
SALES (est): 817.1K **Privately Held**
WEB: www.louishornick.com
SIC: 2391 5023 Curtains & draperies; curtains, window: made from purchased materials; curtains; draperies

(G-11078)
LOUIS TAMIS & SONS INC
10 E 38th St Fl 6 (10016-0619)
PHONE..................................212 684-1760
Fax: 212 481-3394
William Tamis, *President*
Stephen Tamis, *Corp Secy*
Jeff Tamis, *Vice Pres*
Ariella Cohen, *Admin Asst*
EMP: 25 EST: 1910
SQ FT: 4,500
SALES (est): 3.8MM **Privately Held**
WEB: www.louistamis.com
SIC: 3911 Jewelry, precious metal

(G-11079)
LOUIS VUITTON NORTH AMER INC
1000 3rd Ave (10022-1230)
PHONE..................................212 644-2574
Fax: 212 702-0795
Melina Gordon, *Branch Mgr*
EMP: 9
SALES (corp-wide): 268.1MM **Privately Held**
SIC: 2711 Newspapers, publishing & printing
HQ: Louis Vuitton North America, Inc.
1 E 57th St
New York NY 10022
212 758-8877

(G-11080)
LOUNGEHOUSE LLC
34 W 33rd St Fl 11 (10001-3304)
PHONE..................................646 524-2965
Irving Safdieh, *Mng Member*
EMP: 20
SQ FT: 10,000
SALES (est): 856.7K **Privately Held**
SIC: 2341 Nightgowns & negligees: women's & children's; women's accessory & specialty stores; family clothing stores

(G-11081)
LOVEE DOLL & TOY CO INC
39 W 38th St Rm 4w (10018-5540)
PHONE..................................212 242-1545
Fax: 212 242-4596
Sam Horowitz, *President*
▲ EMP: 5 EST: 1962
SQ FT: 40,000
SALES (est): 894.2K **Privately Held**
SIC: 3942 Dolls, except stuffed toy animals

(G-11082)
LOVELY BRIDE LLC
182 Duane St Frnt A (10013-6605)
PHONE..................................212 924-2050
Lanie List, *Owner*
EMP: 8
SALES (est): 740.3K **Privately Held**
SIC: 2335 Bridal & formal gowns

(G-11083)
LR ACQUISITION LLC ✪
1407 Broadway Rm 1207 (10018-2899)
PHONE..................................212 301-8765
Sammy Catton, *CEO*
Harry Catton, *CFO*
Wayne Lederman, *Sales Executive*
EMP: 10 EST: 2017
SALES (est): 1.1MM **Privately Held**
SIC: 2252 Hosiery

(G-11084)
LR PARIS LLC
345 7th Ave Fl 7 (10001-5052)
PHONE..................................703 652-1132

Charles Dolige, *Mng Member*
Verane Muyeed, *Manager*
Mariemma Dolige,
▲ **EMP:** 3
SALES: 1.2MM **Privately Held**
WEB: www.lrparis.com
SIC: 2389 3499 5947 5137 Masquerade costumes; giftware, brass goods; gift, novelty & souvenir shop; scarves, women's & children's; cloth cutting, bolting or winding; fabrics: linen, jute, hemp, ramie

(G-11085)
LS POWER EQUITY PARTNERS LP (PA)
1700 Broadway Fl 35 (10019-5905)
PHONE..................................212 615-3456
Mike Segal, *Ch of Bd*
Mark Brennan, *Exec VP*
Shimon Edelstein, *Exec VP*
John King, *Exec VP*
David Nanus, *Exec VP*
EMP: 1
SALES (est): 98.5MM **Privately Held**
WEB: www.ziccardi.com
SIC: 3568 1796 Power transmission equipment; power generating equipment installation

(G-11086)
LT2 LLC
Also Called: Letigre
250 Park Ave S Fl 10 (10003-1402)
PHONE..................................212 684-1510
Paul Pagano, *CFO*
Nisha Crooks, *Accountant*
Carol Wang, *Manager*
Ryan O'Sullivan,
EMP: 25
SQ FT: 1,500
SALES: 25MM **Privately Held**
WEB: www.lt2.com
SIC: 2321 2331 Men's & boys' furnishings; women's & misses' blouses & shirts

(G-11087)
LUCKY MAGAZINE
4 Times Sq Fl 22 (10036-6518)
PHONE..................................212 286-6220
EMP: 15
SALES (est): 1.2MM **Privately Held**
SIC: 2721 Periodicals-Publishing/Printing

(G-11088)
LUCKY PEACH LLC
60 E 11th St Fl 5 (10003-6009)
PHONE..................................212 228-0031
Narie Chung, *Finance*
Susan Wright,
EMP: 7
SALES (est): 693.3K **Privately Held**
SIC: 2741 Miscellaneous publishing

(G-11089)
LUDLOW MUSIC INC
266 W 37th St Fl 17 (10018-6655)
PHONE..................................212 594-9795
Larry Richmond, *President*
Allen Brackerman, *General Mgr*
Bernard Gartler, *Vice Pres*
EMP: 14 **EST:** 1949
SALES (est): 624.2K **Privately Held**
SIC: 2741 Music, sheet: publishing only, not printed on site

(G-11090)
LUKOIL AMERICAS CORPORATION (HQ)
505 5th Ave Fl 9 (10017-4921)
PHONE..................................212 421-4141
Robert Ferluga, *CEO*
Vadim Guzman, *Ch of Bd*
Linda Raynor, *Finance*
Ivan Jackson, *Sales Staff*
EMP: 125 **EST:** 1997
SALES: 128.1MM
SALES (corp-wide): 4.8B **Privately Held**
SIC: 1311 Crude petroleum & natural gas
PA: Lukoil, Pao
  11 Bulvar Sretenski
  Moscow 10100
  495 627-4444

(G-11091)
LUKOIL NORTH AMERICA LLC (DH)
505 5th Ave Fl 9 (10017-4921)
PHONE..................................212 421-4141
Vadim Gulzman, *CEO*
EMP: 23
SALES (est): 19.1MM
SALES (corp-wide): 4.8B **Privately Held**
SIC: 1381 5541 Drilling oil & gas wells; filling stations, gasoline
HQ: Lukoil-Volgogradenergo, Ooo
  17 Ul. Im Motsarta
  Volgograd 40002
  844 225-2703

(G-11092)
LULU DK LLC
245 E 60th St Apt 1 (10022-1451)
PHONE..................................212 223-4234
Pia Miranda, *Opers Staff*
Alexandra De Kwiatkowski,
Lori Prince,
▲ **EMP:** 4
SALES (est): 1MM **Privately Held**
SIC: 2679 7389 Wallpaper: made from purchased paper; interior design services

(G-11093)
LULUVISE INC
229 W 116th St Apt 5a (10026-2799)
PHONE..................................914 309-7812
Kewhyun Kelly-Yuoh, *CFO*
EMP: 25 **EST:** 2011
SQ FT: 1,000
SALES (est): 1.5MM **Privately Held**
SIC: 7372 Application computer software

(G-11094)
LUTHIER MUSICAL CORP
49 W 24th St Fl 4 (10010-3570)
PHONE..................................212 397-6038
Fax: 212 397-6048
Tony Acosta, *President*
▲ **EMP:** 6
SQ FT: 10,000
SALES (est): 112.4K **Privately Held**
WEB: www.luthiermusic.com
SIC: 3931 Guitars & parts, electric & non-electric

(G-11095)
LUXE IMAGINE CONSULTING LLC
261 W 35th St Ste 404 (10001-1906)
PHONE..................................212 273-9770
EMP: 5
SALES (est): 270K **Privately Held**
SIC: 2329 2339 Mfg Mens Children & Women's Apparel

(G-11096)
LYNX ANALYTICS INC
32 W 39th St Fl 4 (10018-2166)
PHONE..................................475 227-7347
Gyorgy Lajtai, *President*
Dan Florea, *Treasurer*
EMP: 5
SQ FT: 10,000
SALES (est): 117.2K **Privately Held**
SIC: 7372 7379 Prepackaged software; business oriented computer software; computer related consulting services

(G-11097)
M & S QUALITY CO LTD
26 W 47th St Ste 502 (10036-8603)
PHONE..................................212 302-8757
Fax: 212 302-8629
Michael Saks, *President*
EMP: 10
SALES (est): 969.5K **Privately Held**
SIC: 3911 Jewelry, precious metal

(G-11098)
M & S SCHMALBERG INC
242 W 36th St Rm 700 (10018-8965)
PHONE..................................212 244-2090
Fax: 212 244-2097
Warren Brand, *President*
Deborah Brand, *Vice Pres*
EMP: 10 **EST:** 1947
SQ FT: 2,500
SALES (est): 700K **Privately Held**
SIC: 3999 5992 Flowers, artificial & preserved; florists

(G-11099)
M G NEW YORK INC
14 E 60th St Ste 400 (10022-7146)
PHONE..................................212 371-5566
Marlyse Gros, *President*
▲ **EMP:** 10
SQ FT: 1,665
SALES (est): 28.8MM **Privately Held**
SIC: 3172 5122 Cosmetic bags; drugs, proprietaries & sundries

(G-11100)
M H MANUFACTURING INCORPORATED
50 W 47th St (10036-8621)
P.O. Box 1743 (10163-1743)
PHONE..................................212 461-6900
Judah Poupko, *Vice Pres*
EMP: 9 **EST:** 2009
SALES (est): 1.1MM **Privately Held**
WEB: www.mhdco.com
SIC: 3911 Pins (jewelry), precious metal

(G-11101)
M HESKIA COMPANY INC
98 Cutter Rd Ste 125 (10036)
PHONE..................................212 768-1845
EMP: 5
SALES (est): 450K **Privately Held**
SIC: 3911 Mfg Jewelry

(G-11102)
M HIDARY & CO INC
10 W 33rd St Rm 900 (10001-3317)
PHONE..................................212 736-6540
Fax: 212 714-9021
Morris Hidary, *Chairman*
Richard Levine, *CFO*
David Hidary, *Treasurer*
Emm McCall, *Accounting Mgr*
Jennifer Okeefe, *Credit Mgr*
▲ **EMP:** 100 **EST:** 1948
SQ FT: 20,000
SALES (est): 15.8MM **Privately Held**
SIC: 2369 2311 2325 2329 Girls' & children's outerwear; men's & boys' suits & coats; men's & boys' trousers & slacks; men's & boys' sportswear & athletic clothing; men's & boys' clothing; women's & children's clothing

(G-11103)
M I T POLY-CART CORP
211 Central Park W (10024-6020)
PHONE..................................212 724-7290
Fax: 212 721-9022
Dan Moss, *President*
Isaac Rinkewich, *Vice Pres*
Tova Moss, *Treasurer*
EMP: 5
SQ FT: 1,000
SALES (est): 300K **Privately Held**
WEB: www.mitpolycart.com
SIC: 3089 Plastic containers, except foam

(G-11104)
M L DESIGN INC (PA)
77 Ludlow St Frnt 1 (10002-3898)
PHONE..................................212 233-0213
Tommy Lam, *President*
▲ **EMP:** 9
SALES (est): 772.8K **Privately Held**
SIC: 2752 Commercial printing, offset

(G-11105)
M S B INTERNATIONAL LTD (PA)
Also Called: Nyc Design Co
1412 Broadway Rm 1210 (10018-9228)
PHONE..................................212 302-5551
Maia Chait, *President*
Robert Guttenberg, *President*
Sunny Leigh, *Vice Pres*
May Woo, *Office Mgr*
Frank Rascati, *Manager*
▲ **EMP:** 15
SALES (est): 2.6MM **Privately Held**
SIC: 2331 2321 2325 Women's & misses' blouses & shirts; men's & boys' furnishings; men's & boys' trousers & slacks

(G-11106)
M SHANKEN COMMUNICATIONS INC (PA)
825 8th Ave Fl 33 (10019-8872)
PHONE..................................212 684-4224
Fax: 212 474-5400
Marvin R Shanken, *Ch of Bd*
Michael Moaba, *Vice Ch Bd*
Michael Batterberry, *Editor*
Kimberly Carmichael, *Editor*
Alex Detoth, *Editor*
EMP: 125
SQ FT: 15,000
SALES (est): 36.7MM **Privately Held**
SIC: 2721 Magazines: publishing & printing

(G-11107)
M&S ACCESSORY NETWORK CORP
Also Called: Gabbagoods
10 W 33rd St Rm 718 (10001-3306)
PHONE..................................347 492-7790
Jack Mosseri, *CEO*
Albert Salama, *Vice Pres*
▲ **EMP:** 15 **EST:** 2011
SQ FT: 2,500
SALES (est): 2.4MM **Privately Held**
SIC: 3663 Mobile communication equipment

(G-11108)
M2 FASHION GROUP HOLDINGS INC
Also Called: M2 Apparel
153 E 87th St Apt 10d (10128-2708)
PHONE..................................917 208-2948
Ming Lee Wilcox, *President*
EMP: 6
SQ FT: 1,000
SALES (est): 2MM **Privately Held**
SIC: 2389 Apparel for handicapped

(G-11109)
M3 GRAPHIC GROUP LTD
Also Called: M3 Promotion
150 W 28th St Ste 504 (10001-6103)
PHONE..................................212 366-0863
Ross Levine, *President*
EMP: 6
SALES (est): 75.4K **Privately Held**
WEB: www.m3-promotions.com
SIC: 2752 Commercial printing, lithographic; promotional printing, lithographic

(G-11110)
MAC SWED INC
20 W 36th St Rm 5l (10018-9811)
PHONE..................................212 684-7730
Fax: 212 213-0169
Marc Shams, *President*
▲ **EMP:** 15
SQ FT: 15,000
SALES (est): 539.6K **Privately Held**
SIC: 3949 Bowling equipment & supplies

(G-11111)
MACFADDEN CMMNCTIONS GROUP LLC
Also Called: HSN
333 7th Ave Fl 11 (10001-5824)
PHONE..................................212 979-4800
Fax: 212 979-7507
Peter Callahan, *Managing Prtnr*
Jess Schesser, *Partner*
Amy Cogan, *Publisher*
Barbara Kaplan, *Publisher*
Seth Mendelson, *Vice Pres*
▲ **EMP:** 105
SQ FT: 33,000
SALES (est): 14MM **Privately Held**
SIC: 2721 Magazines: publishing only, not printed on site

(G-11112)
MACMILLAN ACADEMIC PUBG INC (HQ)
75 Varick St Fl 9 (10013-1917)
PHONE..................................212 226-1476
Richard Charkin, *Ch of Bd*
D M Bagwell, *Vice Pres*
Steve Cohen, *Vice Pres*
Roy Gainsburg, *Vice Pres*
Dominic Knight, *Vice Pres*
EMP: 18

SALES (est): 5.1MM
SALES (corp-wide): 1.5B **Privately Held**
SIC: 2741 Miscellaneous publishing
PA: Georg Von Holtzbrinck Gmbh & Co.Kg
Gansheidestr. 26
Stuttgart 70184
711 215-00

(G-11113)
MACMILLAN COLLEGE PUBG CO INC
866 3rd Ave Frnt 2 (10022-6221)
PHONE..................212 702-2000
Walter M Volpi, *CFO*
John Bender, *Manager*
United States, *Agent*
EMP: 10
SALES (corp-wide): 1.5B **Privately Held**
SIC: 2731 Book publishing
HQ: Macmillan Limited
The Macmillan Campus
London
207 833-4000

(G-11114)
MACMILLAN HOLDINGS LLC
1 New York Plz Ste 4500 (10004-1562)
PHONE..................212 576-9428
Suzannah Burywood, *Publisher*
Fritz Foy, *Principal*
Rachel Bridgewater, *Editor*
Lloyd Langman, *Editor*
Rebecca Levene, *Business Mgr*
EMP: 11
SALES (corp-wide): 1.5B **Privately Held**
SIC: 2721 Magazines: publishing only, not printed on site
HQ: Macmillan Holdings, Llc
175 5th Ave
New York NY 10010

(G-11115)
MACMILLAN PUBLISHERS INC
175 5th Ave Ste 400 (10010-7726)
PHONE..................646 307-5151
John Sargent, *CEO*
Jaime Coyne, *Editor*
Whitney Frick, *Editor*
Laurie Henderson, *Editor*
Rose Hilliard, *Editor*
▲ **EMP:** 1200
SQ FT: 81,000
SALES (est): 102.7MM
SALES (corp-wide): 1.5B **Privately Held**
SIC: 2731 5192 Books: publishing only; books
HQ: Macmillan Limited
The Macmillan Campus
London
207 833-4000

(G-11116)
MACMILLAN PUBLISHING GROUP LLC (DH)
Also Called: Palagrave Macmillan
175 5th Ave (10010-7703)
PHONE..................212 674-5151
Fax: 212 674-3179
Sally Richardson, *President*
Emily Angell, *Editor*
Nichole Argyres, *Editor*
Brenda Copeland, *Editor*
Jaime Coyne, *Editor*
▲ **EMP:** 361
SQ FT: 81,000
SALES (est): 140MM
SALES (corp-wide): 1.5B **Privately Held**
WEB: www.stmartins.com
SIC: 2731 5192 Books: publishing only; books

(G-11117)
MACROCHEM CORPORATION (HQ)
80 Broad St Ste 2210 (10004-2209)
PHONE..................212 514-8094
James M Pachence MD, *CEO*
Robert J Deluccia, *Ch of Bd*
David P Luci, *Officer*
EMP: 6
SALES (est): 107.3K
SALES (corp-wide): 889K **Publicly Held**
WEB: www.macrochem.com
SIC: 2834 8731 Pharmaceutical preparations; commercial physical research

PA: Abeona Therapeutics Inc.
3333 Lee Pkwy Ste 600
Dallas TX 75219
214 665-9495

(G-11118)
MADAME ALEXANDER DOLL CO LLC
112 W 34th St Ste 1207 (10120-1207)
PHONE..................212 244-4500
Adolfo Reynoso, *Branch Mgr*
EMP: 100
SALES (corp-wide): 43MM **Privately Held**
SIC: 3942 Dolls & stuffed toys
HQ: Madame Alexander Doll Company, Llc
306 Primrose Ln
Mountville PA 17554
717 537-4140

(G-11119)
MADE FRESH DAILY
226 Front St (10038-2009)
PHONE..................212 285-2253
Jackie Moran, *Manager*
EMP: 7
SALES (est): 373.7K **Privately Held**
SIC: 2711 Newspapers, publishing & printing

(G-11120)
MADHAT INC
149 Sullivan St Apt 3e (10012-3041)
PHONE..................518 947-0732
Jude Anasta, *CEO*
EMP: 5 **EST:** 2015
SALES (est): 149.4K **Privately Held**
SIC: 7372 Application computer software

(G-11121)
MADISON INDUSTRIES INC (PA)
295 5th Ave Ste 512 (10016-7103)
PHONE..................212 679-5110
Michael Schwartz, *Ch of Bd*
Nehemias Nieves, *Controller*
Mike Pandow, *VP Human Res*
Mary McDaniel, *Human Res Dir*
Lisa Billani, *Manager*
◆ **EMP:** 11
SQ FT: 5,800
SALES (est): 117.4MM **Privately Held**
WEB: www.madisonindustries.com
SIC: 2392 5023 Household furnishings; comforters & quilts: made from purchased materials; pillowcases: made from purchased materials; mattress protectors, except rubber; home furnishings

(G-11122)
MADOFF ENERGY III LLC
319 Lafayette St (10012-2711)
PHONE..................212 744-1918
Andy Madoff, *Mng Member*
EMP: 8
SQ FT: 3,000
SALES (est): 29.4K **Privately Held**
SIC: 1382 Oil & gas exploration services

(G-11123)
MAFCO CONSOLIDATED GROUP INC (HQ)
35 E 62nd St (10065-8014)
PHONE..................212 572-8600
Fax: 212 572-8650
Ronald O Perelman, *Ch of Bd*
EMP: 10
SALES (est): 291.6MM **Privately Held**
SIC: 2121 2131 2869 Cigars; smoking tobacco; flavors or flavoring materials, synthetic

(G-11124)
MAG BRANDS LLC
Also Called: Babydoll
463 7th Ave Fl 4 (10018-8725)
PHONE..................212 629-9600
Raymond A Dayan, *CEO*
Gerard Agoglia, *CFO*
Michael Nagurka, *Controller*
Mark Adjmi,
▲ **EMP:** 55
SALES (est): 5.9MM **Privately Held**
SIC: 2339 Service apparel, washable: women's

(G-11125)
MAGAZINE I SPECTRUM E
Also Called: I Triple E Spectrum
3 Park Ave Fl 17 (10016-5902)
PHONE..................212 419-7555
Willie Jones, *General Mgr*
James Vick, *Principal*
EMP: 38
SALES (est): 1.7MM **Privately Held**
SIC: 2721 Periodicals

(G-11126)
MAGEBA USA LLC
575 Lexington Ave Fl 4 (10022-6146)
PHONE..................212 317-1991
Thomas Spuler, *CEO*
Scott Davis, *Business Mgr*
Gianni Moor, *COO*
Robert Bradley, *Project Mgr*
Amit Kutumbale, *Project Mgr*
▲ **EMP:** 36 **EST:** 2011
SALES (est): 13.3MM **Privately Held**
SIC: 3441 3562 Expansion joints (structural shapes), iron or steel; ball bearings & parts

(G-11127)
MAGER & GOUGELMAN INC (PA)
345 E 37th St Rm 316 (10016-3256)
PHONE..................212 661-3939
Fax: 212 661-0576
Henry P Gougelman, *President*
Andrew E Gouglman, *Ophthalmology*
EMP: 7
SALES (est): 855.4K **Privately Held**
WEB: www.artificial-eyes.com
SIC: 3851 Eyes, glass & plastic

(G-11128)
MAGGY BOUTIQUE LTD
Also Called: Maggy London
530 Fashion Ave Fl 6 (10018-4878)
PHONE..................212 997-5222
Fax: 212 704-9794
Larry Lefkowitz, *President*
Lisa Leavy, *President*
Jerry Sholtz, *CFO*
Julie Monopoli, *Accounting Mgr*
Bob Jagolinzer, *Accounts Exec*
▲ **EMP:** 50
SQ FT: 5,000
SALES (est): 5.1MM **Privately Held**
SIC: 2339 5137 2337 Women's & misses' outerwear; women's & children's clothing; women's & misses' suits & coats

(G-11129)
MAGGY LONDON INTERNATIONAL LTD (PA)
Also Called: Maggy London Blouse Div
530 Fashion Ave Fl 16 (10018-4896)
PHONE..................212 944-7199
Fax: 212 840-2483
Larry Lefkowitz, *Ch of Bd*
Milton Cahn, *Chairman*
Jerry Sholtz, *Senior VP*
Devin Fitzpatrick, *Vice Pres*
Lisa West, *Vice Pres*
▲ **EMP:** 60
SQ FT: 18,000
SALES (est): 35.1MM **Privately Held**
SIC: 2331 Women's & misses' blouses & shirts

(G-11130)
MAGIC BRANDS INTERNATIONAL LLC
31 W 34th St Rm 401 (10001-3036)
PHONE..................212 563-4999
Sue Embleton, *VP Sales*
Edward J Falack,
Albert Pardo,
▲ **EMP:** 10
SALES (est): 1.1MM **Privately Held**
SIC: 2211 Apparel & outerwear fabrics, cotton

(G-11131)
MAGIC NOVELTY CO INC (PA)
308 Dyckman St (10034-5397)
PHONE..................212 304-2777
Fax: 212 567-2597
Alex Neuburger, *President*
David Neuburger, *Vice Pres*
Steven Neuburger, *Vice Pres*
Wendy Torres, *Controller*
Diana Gurevich, *Manager*
▲ **EMP:** 50 **EST:** 1940
SQ FT: 40,000
SALES (est): 10MM **Privately Held**
SIC: 3961 5094 3915 3469 Costume jewelry, ex. precious metal & semi-precious stones; jewelry; jewelers' materials & lapidary work; metal stampings; miscellaneous fabricated wire products

(G-11132)
MAGIC NUMBERS INC
Also Called: Glitter
29 Little West 12th St (10014-1393)
PHONE..................646 839-8578
EMP: 5 **EST:** 2015
SQ FT: 16,000
SALES (est): 280K **Privately Held**
SIC: 7372 Prepackaged Software Services

(G-11133)
MAGIC TANK LLC
80 Maiden Ln Rm 2204 (10038-4815)
PHONE..................877 646-2442
Steve Distritzky, *President*
EMP: 3
SQ FT: 8,000
SALES: 5MM **Privately Held**
SIC: 2865 Cyclic organic crudes

(G-11134)
MAGIC TOUCH ICEWARES INTL
220 E 72nd St Apt 11g (10021-4527)
PHONE..................212 794-2852
Susan Gitelson, *President*
◆ **EMP:** 6
SQ FT: 3,000
SALES (est): 824.7K **Privately Held**
SIC: 3069 5049 Laboratory sundries: cases, covers, funnels, cups, etc.; laboratory equipment, except medical or dental

(G-11135)
MAGNOLIA OPERATING LLC (PA)
Also Called: Magnolia Bakery
1841 Broadway (10023-7603)
PHONE..................212 265-2777
Steve Abrams, *Principal*
Sara Schoenborn, *Vice Pres*
EMP: 34
SALES (est): 9.7MM **Privately Held**
SIC: 2051 Bakery: wholesale or wholesale/retail combined

(G-11136)
MAGNUM CREATION INC
23 W 47th St Fl 5 (10036-2826)
PHONE..................212 642-0993
Fax: 212 642-0993
Nathan Cohen, *President*
Mira Cohen, *Vice Pres*
Suri Markowitz, *Bookkeeper*
EMP: 13
SQ FT: 5,500
SALES (est): 1.5MM **Privately Held**
SIC: 3911 Jewelry, precious metal

(G-11137)
MAIDENFORM LLC
260 Madison Ave Fl 6 (10016-2406)
PHONE..................201 436-9200
Fax: 212 685-1709
Maurice Reznik, *Branch Mgr*
EMP: 10
SALES (corp-wide): 6B **Publicly Held**
WEB: www.maidenform.com
SIC: 2259 2254 Girdles & other foundation garments, knit; knit underwear mills
HQ: Maidenform Llc
1000 E Hanes Mill Rd
Winston Salem NC 27105
336 519-8080

(G-11138)
MAILERS-PBLSHER WLFARE TR FUND
1501 Broadway (10036-5601)
PHONE..................212 869-5986
EMP: 1
SALES: 2.6MM **Privately Held**
SIC: 2741 Miscellaneous publishing

New York - New York County (G-11139) — GEOGRAPHIC SECTION

(G-11139)
MAIYET INC
16 Crosby St Apt Corp (10013-3108)
PHONE..................212 343-9999
Paul Van Zyl, *Ch of Bd*
Gimena Garmendia, *Marketing Staff*
Kim Coiffier, *Director*
Lisa Sages, *Director*
Rochelle Gordon, *Assistant*
EMP: 5
SALES (est): 1MM **Privately Held**
SIC: 2329 2339 Men's & boys' leather, wool & down-filled outerwear; women's & misses' outerwear

(G-11140)
MAJESTIC RAYON CORPORATION
116 W 23rd St Fl 4 (10011-2498)
PHONE..................212 929-6443
Fax: 212 929-1623
Lawrence Aibel, *President*
Richard Aibel, *Vice Pres*
Sandra Keene, *Vice Pres*
Irina Simon, *Manager*
▲ **EMP:** 25 **EST:** 1930
SQ FT: 60,000
SALES (est): 4.2MM **Privately Held**
SIC: 2282 2269 Twisting yarn; winding yarn; finishing plants

(G-11141)
MAKE MY CAKE II INC
2380 Adam Clytn Powll Jr (10030-1703)
PHONE..................212 234-2344
Fax: 212 234-2327
Joann Baylor, *President*
EMP: 7
SALES: 350K **Privately Held**
SIC: 2051 Bread, cake & related products

(G-11142)
MAKERBOT INDUSTRIES LLC
298 Mulberry St (10012-3331)
PHONE..................347 457-5758
Paul Chando, *QC Mgr*
EMP: 5
SALES (est): 799.3K **Privately Held**
SIC: 2759 Commercial printing

(G-11143)
MAKINS HATS LTD
212 W 35th St Fl 12 (10001-2508)
PHONE..................212 594-6666
Marsha Akins, *President*
EMP: 7
SQ FT: 5,000
SALES: 500K **Privately Held**
SIC: 2353 Hats, caps & millinery

(G-11144)
MALER TECHNOLOGIES INC
337 E 81st St Bsmt (10028-4068)
PHONE..................212 391-2070
Stanley Vashovsky, *Ch of Bd*
Ted Weaver, *Vice Pres*
Diane Johnson, *Mktg Dir*
EMP: 2
SQ FT: 13,617
SALES: 7.2MM **Privately Held**
WEB: www.healthsystemssolutions.com
SIC: 7372 Prepackaged software

(G-11145)
MALIN + GOETZ INC (PA)
330 7th Ave Ste 2100 (10001-5236)
PHONE..................212 244-7771
Matthew Malin, *Ch of Bd*
Andrew Goetz, *President*
Kaj Johnson, *Finance*
Alessia Thompson, *Accounts Mgr*
Amanda Michaud, *Marketing Mgr*
EMP: 12
SQ FT: 600
SALES (est): 2.3MM **Privately Held**
WEB: www.malinandgoetz.com
SIC: 2844 5999 Cosmetic preparations; cosmetics

(G-11146)
MALLORY & CHURCH LLC
552 Fashion Ave Rm 202 (10018-3247)
PHONE..................212 868-7888
Paul Weiss, *Mng Member*
EMP: 9
SALES (est): 22.2K **Privately Held**
SIC: 2323 Neckties, men's & boys': made from purchased materials

(G-11147)
MALOUF COLETTE INC
594 Broadway Rm 1216 (10012-3289)
PHONE..................212 941-9588
Fax: 212 431-9561
Colette Malouf, *President*
Lee Tam, *Prdtn Mgr*
EMP: 14
SQ FT: 2,200
SALES (est): 1.3MM **Privately Held**
WEB: www.colettemalouf.com
SIC: 3999 Hair & hair-based products

(G-11148)
MAMA LUCA PRODUCTION INC
156 W 56th St Ste 1803 (10019-3899)
PHONE..................212 582-9700
Steven Zandt, *President*
Steven Vandat, *President*
EMP: 2
SALES: 3MM **Privately Held**
SIC: 2399 Aprons, breast (harness)

(G-11149)
MAN OF WORLD
25 W 39th St Fl 5 (10018-4075)
PHONE..................212 915-0017
EMP: 5
SALES (est): 839.4K **Privately Held**
SIC: 2836 Culture media

(G-11150)
MANCHU NEW YORK INC
530 Fashion Ave Rm 1906 (10018-4853)
PHONE..................212 921-5050
▲ **EMP:** 8
SQ FT: 5,100
SALES (est): 705.4K **Privately Held**
SIC: 2361 2339 2311 Manufacturer's Rep Of Garment Manufacturer

(G-11151)
MANCHU TIMES FASHION INC
530 Sventh Ave Ste 1906 (10018)
PHONE..................212 921-5050
Michael Durbin, *CEO*
Jay Goldman, *Administration*
▲ **EMP:** 8 **EST:** 2014
SQ FT: 2,300
SALES (est): 790.6K
SALES (corp-wide): 226.3MM **Privately Held**
SIC: 2339 Women's & misses' outerwear
HQ: Manchu Times Fashion Limited
Rm 2002 20/F Park-In Coml Ctr
Mongkok KLN
278 161-88

(G-11152)
MANHATTAN CABINETS INC
1349 2nd Ave (10021-4504)
PHONE..................212 548-2436
Zaheer Akber, *President*
EMP: 3
SQ FT: 1,300
SALES: 1.7MM **Privately Held**
SIC: 2514 1751 Kitchen cabinets: metal; cabinet building & installation

(G-11153)
MANHATTAN EASTSIDE DEV CORP
Also Called: Eastside Orthotics Prosthetics
622 W 168th St Ste Vc333 (10032-3720)
PHONE..................212 305-3275
Matt D Flynn, *CEO*
Matt Flynn, *President*
EMP: 10
SALES (est): 597.3K **Privately Held**
SIC: 3841 Medical instruments & equipment, blood & bone work

(G-11154)
MANHATTAN MEDIA LLC (PA)
Also Called: Avenue Magazine
72 Madison Ave Fl 11 (10016-8731)
PHONE..................212 268-8600
Fax: 212 268-0614
Joanne Harras, *CEO*
Thomas Allon, *President*
Pamela Gross, *Editor*
Alex Schweitzer, *Sales Mgr*

Harlan Lax, *Info Tech Dir*
EMP: 23
SQ FT: 7,500
SALES (est): 12.5MM **Privately Held**
SIC: 2711 2721 Newspapers: publishing only, not printed on site; magazines: publishing only, not printed on site

(G-11155)
MANHATTAN NEON SIGN CORP
640 W 28th St Fl 2 (10001-1118)
PHONE..................212 714-0430
Fax: 212 947-3906
Marylin Tomasso, *President*
Pat Tomasso, *Vice Pres*
Debra Martinez, *Bookkeeper*
Frank Howell, *Sales Dir*
EMP: 13
SQ FT: 7,500
SALES (est): 1.9MM **Privately Held**
SIC: 3993 Neon signs

(G-11156)
MANHATTAN SCIENTIFICS INC (PA)
405 Lexington Ave Fl 26 (10174-2699)
PHONE..................212 541-2405
Emmanuel Tsoupanarias, *Ch of Bd*
Leonard Friedman, *Admin Sec*
EMP: 10
SQ FT: 300
SALES: 150K **Publicly Held**
SIC: 3699 Electrical equipment & supplies

(G-11157)
MANHATTAN SHADE & GLASS CO INC (PA)
1299 3rd Ave Frnt (10021-3397)
PHONE..................212 288-5616
Fax: 212 288-7241
Steven Schulman, *President*
Morine Shulman, *Principal*
Douglas Schulman, *Vice Pres*
Mitchell Schulman, *Vice Pres*
Sam Girgis, *Project Mgr*
▼ **EMP:** 65 **EST:** 1964
SQ FT: 3,500
SALES (est): 8.2MM **Privately Held**
WEB: www.manhattanshade.com
SIC: 2591 3211 Shade, curtain & drapery hardware; window glass, clear & colored

(G-11158)
MANHATTAN TIMES INC
5030 Broadway Ste 801 (10034-1666)
PHONE..................212 569-5800
Luis Miranda, *Chairman*
John Guttierez, *Manager*
EMP: 15
SALES (est): 570K **Privately Held**
SIC: 2711 Newspapers

(G-11159)
MANN PUBLICATIONS INC
450 Fashion Ave Ste 2306 (10123-2306)
PHONE..................212 840-6266
Jeffrey Mann, *President*
Patrick Braswell, *Associate*
EMP: 20
SQ FT: 4,000
SALES (est): 2.3MM **Privately Held**
SIC: 2721 Magazines: publishing only, not printed on site

(G-11160)
MANNESMANN CORPORATION
601 Lexington Ave Fl 56 (10022-4611)
PHONE..................212 258-4000
Peter Prinz Wittgenstein, *President*
Dr Manfred Becker, *Exec VP*
Joseph E Innamorati, *Vice Pres*
Olaf Klinger, *Treasurer*
▲ **EMP:** 100
SALES (est): 20.6MM
SALES (corp-wide): 89.6B **Privately Held**
SIC: 3536 3544 3511 3547 Hoists; cranes, industrial plant; cranes, overhead traveling; special dies, tools, jigs & fixtures; industrial molds; turbo-generators; hydraulic turbines; rolling mill machinery; steel rolling machinery; pumps & pumping equipment; internal combustion engines
HQ: Siemens Corporation
300 New Jersey Ave Nw # 10
Washington DC 20001
202 434-4800

(G-11161)
MANNINGTON MILLS INC
200 Lexington Ave Rm 430 (10016-6101)
PHONE..................212 251-0290
Fax: 212 251-0299
Austin Branscum, *District Mgr*
Joyce Cavin, *District Mgr*
Bryan Thompson, *District Mgr*
Greg Young, *District Mgr*
Anthony Faulknor, *Technical Mgr*
EMP: 5
SALES (corp-wide): 796.3MM **Privately Held**
WEB: www.mannington.com
SIC: 2273 Floor coverings, textile fiber
PA: Mannington Mills Inc.
75 Mannington Mills Rd
Salem NJ 08079
856 935-3000

(G-11162)
MANNY GRUNBERG INC
62 W 47th St Ste 703 (10036-3185)
PHONE..................212 302-6173
Fax: 212 382-1569
Manny Grunberg, *President*
EMP: 33 **EST:** 1952
SQ FT: 2,000
SALES (est): 2.4MM **Privately Held**
SIC: 3911 Jewelry, precious metal

(G-11163)
MANRICO USA INC
Also Called: Manrico Cashmere
922 Madison Ave (10021-3576)
PHONE..................212 794-4200
Virgile Verellen, *Branch Mgr*
EMP: 5
SALES (corp-wide): 8.2MM **Privately Held**
SIC: 2253 Sweaters & sweater coats, knit
PA: Manrico Usa, Inc.
922 Madison Ave
New York NY 10021
212 794-4200

(G-11164)
MANRICO USA INC (PA)
922 Madison Ave (10021-3576)
PHONE..................212 794-4200
Manrico Calzoni, *President*
▲ **EMP:** 5
SQ FT: 750
SALES (est): 8.9MM **Privately Held**
SIC: 2299 Upholstery filling, textile

(G-11165)
MANSFIELD PRESS INC
599 11th Ave Fl 3 (10036-2110)
PHONE..................212 265-5411
Fax: 212 262-7279
Stanley J Friedman, *President*
Marc Friedman, *Exec VP*
Frank J Ephraim, *Vice Pres*
Shari Friedman, *Manager*
EMP: 15 **EST:** 1935
SALES (est): 2.1MM **Privately Held**
SIC: 2752 Lithographing on metal

(G-11166)
MANSUETO VENTURES LLC
Also Called: Fast Company Magazine
7 World Trade Ctr Fl 29 (10007-2174)
PHONE..................212 389-5300
Jennifer Henkus, *Publisher*
Whelan Mahoney, *Publisher*
Jane Hazel, *Principal*
Erin Brownell, *Editor*
Leigh Buchanan, *Editor*
EMP: 210
SALES (est): 67.7MM **Privately Held**
SIC: 2721 Magazines: publishing only, not printed on site

(G-11167)
MARBLE DOCTORS LLC
244 5th Ave Ste 2608 (10001-7604)
PHONE..................203 628-8339
Sergio Gomes Da Silva, *Branch Mgr*
Kelly Dasilca,
EMP: 26
SALES (corp-wide): 425.5K **Privately Held**
SIC: 3281 1743 Marble, building: cut & shaped; marble installation, interior

PA: Marble Doctors Llc
1198 Mulberry Pl
Wellington FL 33414
203 794-1000

(G-11168)
MARCASIANO INC
296 Elizabeth St Apt 2f (10012-3590)
PHONE..................................212 614-9412
Mary Jane Marcasiano, *President*
EMP: 5 **EST:** 1977
SQ FT: 3,000
SALES (est): 501.4K **Privately Held**
SIC: 2339 Sportswear, women's

(G-11169)
MARCO HI-TECH JV LLC (PA)
475 Park Ave S Fl 10 (10016-6901)
PHONE..................................212 798-8100
Michael Barenholtz, *Treasurer*
Nick Larosa, *Controller*
Reuben Seltzer,
David Garner,
Alan Kestenbaum,
▲ **EMP:** 8
SQ FT: 4,000
SALES (est): 1.4MM **Privately Held**
WEB: www.marcohi-tech.com
SIC: 2834 Vitamin, nutrient & hematinic preparations for human use

(G-11170)
MARCONI INTL USA CO LTD
214 W 39th St Rm 1100 (10018-5533)
PHONE..................................212 391-2626
Fax: 212 391-1166
Lilian Ching, *President*
Jeremy Setol, *Bookkeeper*
John Matthes, *Director*
▲ **EMP:** 9
SQ FT: 2,500
SALES (est): 1.2MM **Privately Held**
SIC: 2339 Women's & misses' outerwear

(G-11171)
MARCUS GOLDMAN INC
Also Called: Run It Systems
37 W 39th St Rm 1201 (10018-0577)
PHONE..................................212 431-0707
Robert Marcus, *President*
Steven Treiber, *Manager*
Mark Schmidt, *Technical Staff*
Orren Grushkin, *Admin Sec*
EMP: 14
SQ FT: 5,000
SALES (est): 1.7MM **Privately Held**
WEB: www.runit.com
SIC: 7372 Prepackaged software

(G-11172)
MARI STRINGS INC
14 W 71st St (10023-4209)
PHONE..................................212 799-6781
Fax: 212 721-3932
Daniel Mari, *President*
▲ **EMP:** 15
SQ FT: 1,600
SALES: 400K **Privately Held**
SIC: 3931 Strings, musical instrument

(G-11173)
MARIE CLAIRE USA
300 W 57th St Fl 34 (10019-1497)
PHONE..................................212 841-8493
David Carey, *President*
Anne Fulenwider, *Editor*
Chris Moore, *Editor*
Glenda Bailey, *Chief*
Natalie McCray, *Business Mgr*
▲ **EMP:** 100
SALES (est): 840.1K **Privately Held**
SIC: 2721 Magazines: publishing & printing

(G-11174)
MARILYN MODEL MANAGEMENT INC
32 Union Sq E Ph 1 (10003-3220)
PHONE..................................646 556-7587
Fax: 646 260-0821
Maria Cognata, *President*
Marilyn Gauthier, *President*
Julia Kisla, *CFO*
EMP: 11
SALES (est): 980K **Privately Held**
SIC: 3999 Models, except toy

(G-11175)
MARINA JEWELRY CO INC
Also Called: Jn Marina
42 W 48th St Ste 804 (10036-1712)
PHONE..................................212 354-5027
Fax: 212 575-8086
Joseph Fontana, *President*
Anthony Barona, *Partner*
EMP: 6
SQ FT: 1,200
SALES (est): 540K **Privately Held**
WEB: www.marina-jewellery.com
SIC: 3911 3339 Jewelry, precious metal; primary nonferrous metals

(G-11176)
MARITIME ACTIVITY REPORTS (PA)
118 E 25th St Fl 2 (10010-2994)
PHONE..................................212 477-6700
John C O'Malley, *Vice Pres*
Joel Haka, *Vice Pres*
Esther Rothenberger, *Opers Mgr*
Kristen O'Malley, *Accounting Mgr*
Jocelyn Redfern, *Marketing Mgr*
EMP: 28
SQ FT: 2,500
SALES (est): 1.8MM **Privately Held**
SIC: 2721 Magazines: publishing only, not printed on site

(G-11177)
MARK KING JEWELRY INC
62 W 47th St Ste 310r (10036-3245)
PHONE..................................212 921-0746
Fax: 212 944-6345
Mark Beznicki, *President*
EMP: 1
SQ FT: 1,000
SALES (est): 570K **Privately Held**
SIC: 3911 5094 Jewelry, precious metal; jewelry & precious stones

(G-11178)
MARK LEVINE
Also Called: Kids Discover
149 5th Ave Fl 10 (10010-6832)
PHONE..................................212 677-4457
Mark Levine, *Owner*
Defi Greene, *Manager*
▲ **EMP:** 11
SQ FT: 2,500
SALES (est): 810K **Privately Held**
SIC: 2721 Magazines: publishing only, not printed on site

(G-11179)
MARK NELSON DESIGNS LLC
404 E 55th St Fl 4 (10022-5136)
PHONE..................................646 422-7020
Debra Harkl, *Office Mgr*
Mark Nelson, *Mng Member*
▲ **EMP:** 10
SALES (est): 1.3MM **Privately Held**
SIC: 2273 Rugs, hand & machine made

(G-11180)
MARK ROBINSON INC
18 E 48th St Rm 1102 (10017-1059)
PHONE..................................212 223-3515
Fax: 212 223-5133
Mark Robinson, *President*
EMP: 9
SQ FT: 200
SALES (est): 1.4MM **Privately Held**
WEB: www.markrobinson.net
SIC: 3911 Jewelry, precious metal

(G-11181)
MARKET FACTORY INC
425 Broadway Fl 3 (10013-2599)
PHONE..................................212 625-9988
James Sinclair, *CEO*
Darren Jer, *COO*
Chris Coletti, *Sales Dir*
Laura Migliozzi, *Office Mgr*
Christian Reiss, *Manager*
EMP: 19
SQ FT: 3,000
SALES (est): 5.3MM **Privately Held**
SIC: 7372 Business oriented computer software

(G-11182)
MARKET LOGIC SOFTWARE INC
80 Pine St Fl 24 (10005-1732)
PHONE..................................646 405-1041
Kay Iversen, *Director*
EMP: 19
SALES (est): 182.1K **Privately Held**
SIC: 7372 Prepackaged software

(G-11183)
MARKETING ACTION XECUTIVES INC
50 W 96th St Apt 7b (10025-6529)
P.O. Box 20356 (10025-1519)
PHONE..................................212 971-9155
Karen Korman, *President*
Barry Steinman, *Vice Pres*
EMP: 5
SALES (est): 2MM **Privately Held**
WEB: www.mactionx.com
SIC: 2241 Trimmings, textile

(G-11184)
MARKETRESEARCHCOM INC
641 Ave Of The America (10011-2014)
PHONE..................................212 807-2600
Rocco Distefano, *Branch Mgr*
Marzia Marzi, *Manager*
EMP: 15
SALES (corp-wide): 31.9MM **Privately Held**
WEB: www.marketresearch.com
SIC: 2741 Miscellaneous publishing
PA: Marketresearch.Com, Inc.
11200 Rockville Pike # 504
Rockville MD 20852
240 747-3093

(G-11185)
MARKETS MEDIA LLC
110 Wall St Fl 15 (10005-3813)
PHONE..................................646 442-4646
Mohan Virdee, *CEO*
John Antona, *Managing Dir*
Lisa Kim, *Admin Asst*
EMP: 5
SALES (est): 451.5K **Privately Held**
SIC: 2711 Newspapers, publishing & printing

(G-11186)
MARLEY SPOON INC
Also Called: Martha & Marley Spoon
601 W 26th St Rm 900 (10001-1143)
PHONE..................................646 934-6970
Fabian Siegel, *President*
EMP: 140
SALES (est): 1MM
SALES (corp-wide): 10.4MM **Privately Held**
SIC: 3411 8742 Food & beverage containers; food & beverage consultant
PA: Marley Spoon Gmbh
Paul-Lincke-Ufer 39/-40
Berlin
172 429-4851

(G-11187)
MARNIER-LAPOSTOLLE INC
Also Called: Grand Marnier
183 Madison Ave (10016-4501)
PHONE..................................212 207-4350
Fax: 212 207-4351
Elise Seignolle, *Finance Dir*
Brendan Phillips, *Manager*
Christine Yun, *Manager*
▲ **EMP:** 54
SALES: 538.7K **Privately Held**
WEB: www.grandmarnier.com
SIC: 2082 5182 2085 Malt liquors; liquor; distilled & blended liquors

(G-11188)
MARRETTI USA INC
101 Ave Of The Americas (10013-1941)
PHONE..................................212 255-5565
Marzia Marzi, *President*
EMP: 8 **EST:** 2008
SQ FT: 600
SALES (est): 467.1K **Privately Held**
SIC: 2431 Staircases, stairs & railings

(G-11189)
MARTHA STEWART LIVING (HQ)
601 W 26th St Rm 900 (10001-1143)
PHONE..................................212 827-8000
Fax: 212 827-8204
Daniel W Dienst, *CEO*
Jacqueline Landaeta, *President*
Ellen Morrissey, *Editor*
Jason Schreiber, *Editor*
Eric Pike, *Chief*
▲ **EMP:** 161
SQ FT: 176,550
SALES: 141.9MM
SALES (corp-wide): 183.7MM **Publicly Held**
WEB: www.marthastewart.com
SIC: 2721 2731 4813 7812 Magazines: publishing only, not printed on site; book publishing; ; motion picture production & distribution, television
PA: Sequential Brands Group, Inc.
601 W 26th St Rm 900
New York NY 10001
646 564-2577

(G-11190)
MARTHA STEWART LIVING OMNI LLC
20 W 43rd St (10036-7400)
PHONE..................................212 827-8000
Robin Marino, *CEO*
Laura Boberg, *Publisher*
Natalie Ermann, *General Mgr*
Jenn Andrlik, *Editor*
Alanna Fincke, *Editor*
▲ **EMP:** 350 **EST:** 1997
SALES (est): 28.1MM
SALES (corp-wide): 183.7MM **Publicly Held**
WEB: www.msliving.com
SIC: 2721 Magazines: publishing only, not printed on site
HQ: Martha Stewart Living Omnimedia, Inc.
601 W 26th St Rm 900
New York NY 10001
212 827-8000

(G-11191)
MARTIN FLYER INCORPORATED
70 W 36th St Rm 602 (10018-8049)
PHONE..................................212 840-8899
Fax: 212 768-0124
Joshua Kaufman, *COO*
Alan Flyer, *CFO*
Angie Guenther, *Accounts Exec*
Josh Kaufman, *Mng Member*
▲ **EMP:** 27
SQ FT: 8,000
SALES: 11MM **Privately Held**
WEB: www.martinflyer.com
SIC: 3911 Jewelry, precious metal

(G-11192)
MARTINEZ HAND MADE CIGARS
171 W 29th St Frnt A (10001-5100)
PHONE..................................212 239-4049
Antonio Martinez, *Owner*
EMP: 9
SALES (est): 746.3K **Privately Held**
SIC: 2121 Cigars

(G-11193)
MARVEL ENTERTAINMENT LLC (HQ)
135 W 50th St Fl 7 (10020-1201)
P.O. Box 1527, Long Island City (11101-0527)
PHONE..................................212 576-4000
Isaac Perlmutter, *CEO*
Michael Helfant, *President*
Timothy E Rothwell, *President*
Dan Buckley, *Publisher*
Bill Rahn, *Managing Dir*
▲ **EMP:** 164
SQ FT: 65,253
SALES (est): 115.6MM **Publicly Held**
SIC: 2721 6794 3944 7929 Comic books: publishing only, not printed on site; magazines: publishing only, not printed on site; patent buying, licensing, leasing; electronic games & toys; entertainment service

New York - New York County (G-11194) — GEOGRAPHIC SECTION

(G-11194)
MARVELLISSIMA INTL LTD
333 E 46th St Apt 20a (10017-7431)
PHONE..................212 682-7306
Marvel Perilla, *President*
Shanez Kollnescher, *Vice Pres*
Ellen Stutzer, *Vice Pres*
Abba Kyari, *Shareholder*
Lola Osunsade, *Shareholder*
EMP: 6
SALES (est): 615.2K **Privately Held**
SIC: **2844** 5122 Toilet preparations; cosmetics

(G-11195)
MARY BRIGHT INC
269 E 10th St Apt 7 (10009-4849)
PHONE..................212 677-1970
David Paskin, *President*
Mary Bright, *President*
EMP: 6
SALES: 367K **Privately Held**
WEB: www.marybright.com
SIC: **2258** Curtains & curtain fabrics, lace

(G-11196)
MAS CUTTING INC
257 W 39th St Rm 11e (10018-3228)
PHONE..................212 869-0826
Kitman MA, *President*
EMP: 6
SALES (est): 350K **Privately Held**
SIC: **2396** Apparel findings & trimmings

(G-11197)
MASTERPIECE COLOR LLC
12 E 46th St Fl 2 (10017-2418)
PHONE..................917 279-6056
David Markovits, *Partner*
EMP: 8
SALES: 11MM **Privately Held**
SIC: **3911** Jewelry, precious metal

(G-11198)
MASTERPIECE DIAMONDS LLC
12 E 46th St Fl 2 (10017-2418)
PHONE..................212 986-1515
David Markovits,
EMP: 19
SQ FT: 4,500
SALES (est): 2.1MM **Privately Held**
SIC: **3961** Costume jewelry

(G-11199)
MATA FASHIONS LLC
222 W 37th St Fl 4 (10018-9158)
PHONE..................917 716-7894
Maria Maglaras, *Treasurer*
Dona Elias,
EMP: 2 EST: 2014
SQ FT: 1,200
SALES: 1MM **Privately Held**
SIC: **2384** Dressing gowns, men's & women's: from purchased materials

(G-11200)
MATA IG
Also Called: Ings Mata Stone
332 Bleecker St (10014-2980)
PHONE..................212 979-7921
Ig Mata, *Owner*
EMP: 5
SALES (est): 207.3K **Privately Held**
WEB: www.igmata.com
SIC: **3229** Art, decorative & novelty glassware

(G-11201)
MATACI INC
Also Called: Lazo Setter Company
247 W 35th St Fl 15 (10001-1915)
PHONE..................212 502-1899
Adrianna Chico, *President*
▲ EMP: 60
SALES (est): 6.1MM **Privately Held**
SIC: **3961** Costume jewelry

(G-11202)
MATERNE NORTH AMERICA CORP (HQ)
Also Called: Mom Sas
20 W 22nd St Fl 12 (10010-5843)
PHONE..................212 675-7881
Michel Larroche, *CEO*
William Graham, *President*
Carole Larson, *CFO*
Sonia Sobral, *Accountant*
Anne Serrano, *Human Resources*
◆ EMP: 267
SALES: 162K **Privately Held**
SIC: **2035** 5145 Pickles, sauces & salad dressings; snack foods

(G-11203)
MATHISEN VENTURES INC
441 Lexington Ave Rm 809 (10017-3935)
PHONE..................212 986-1025
Fax: 212 986-1033
Oivind Mathisen, *President*
Timothy Beebe, *Vice Pres*
Gordon Buck, *Vice Pres*
Camille Olivere, *Vice Pres*
Monty Mathisen, *Sales Staff*
EMP: 6 EST: 1978
SALES (est): 628.9K **Privately Held**
WEB: www.cruiseindustrynews.com
SIC: **2731** 2721 2741 Book publishing; periodicals: publishing only; magazines: publishing only, not printed on site; newsletter publishing

(G-11204)
MATRIXCARE INC
Also Called: Sigmacare
575 8th Ave Fl 15 (10018-3175)
PHONE..................518 583-6400
EMP: 7
SALES (corp-wide): 92.3K **Privately Held**
SIC: **7372** 7371 Prepackaged software; custom computer programming services
HQ: Matrixcare, Inc.
10900 Hampshire Ave S # 100
Bloomington MN 55438
952 995-9800

(G-11205)
MATT TEXTILE INC
142 W 36th St Fl 3 (10018-8806)
PHONE..................212 967-6010
Firooz Fred Nili, *President*
Neda Nili, *Principal*
▲ EMP: 7
SQ FT: 8,000
SALES (est): 470K **Privately Held**
SIC: **2231** Fabric finishing: wool, mohair or similar fibers

(G-11206)
MAURICE MAX INC
Also Called: Roxanne Assoulin
49 W 27th St Fl 5 (10001-6936)
PHONE..................212 334-6573
Fax: 212 334-6152
Roxanne Assoulin, *President*
Meyer Assoulin, *Vice Pres*
Irv Dayan, *Controller*
Jose Torres, *Asst Controller*
EMP: 34
SALES (est): 5.2MM **Privately Held**
WEB: www.leeangel.com
SIC: **3961** Costume jewelry

(G-11207)
MAVEN MARKETING LLC (PA)
Also Called: Revolution Golf
349 5th Ave Fl 8 (10016-5019)
PHONE..................615 510-3248
Justin Tapper, *CEO*
Dean Strickler, *Exec Dir*
Wayne Caparas,
Jeff Evans,
EMP: 7 EST: 2008
SALES (est): 3.4MM **Privately Held**
SIC: **7372** 7371 8742 Educational computer software; software programming applications; marketing consulting services

(G-11208)
MAVERIK LACROSSE LLC
535 W 24th St Fl 5 (10011-1140)
PHONE..................516 213-3050
Fax: 516 213-3092
Dilly Pymm, *Manager*
John Gagliardi,
▲ EMP: 5022
SALES (est): 280.6K
SALES (corp-wide): 7.6B **Privately Held**
SIC: **3949** Lacrosse equipment & supplies, general
HQ: Kohlberg Sports Group, Inc.
111 Radio Circle Dr
Mount Kisco NY 10549

(G-11209)
MAVITO FINE JEWELRY LTD INC
37 W 47th St Ste 500 (10036-2861)
PHONE..................212 398-9384
Fax: 212 398-9384
Victor Scis, *President*
EMP: 11
SQ FT: 4,600
SALES: 1.8MM **Privately Held**
SIC: **3911** 7631 3915 Jewel settings & mountings, precious metal; watch, clock & jewelry repair; jewelers' materials & lapidary work

(G-11210)
MAX BRENNER UNION SQUARE LLC
841 Broadway (10003-4704)
PHONE..................646 467-8803
Ever M Elivo, *Principal*
▲ EMP: 5
SALES (est): 585.6K **Privately Held**
SIC: **2066** Chocolate bars, solid

(G-11211)
MAX KAHAN INC
20 W 47th St Ste 300 (10036-3303)
PHONE..................212 575-4646
Fax: 212 575-0888
Max Kahan, *President*
David Gluck, *Vice Pres*
Abraham Grossman, *Treasurer*
EMP: 10
SQ FT: 3,000
SALES (est): 980K **Privately Held**
SIC: **3915** Jewelers' materials & lapidary work

(G-11212)
MAXIMILLION COMMUNICATIONS LLC
245 W 17th St Fl 2 (10011-5373)
PHONE..................212 564-3945
Kathy Hipple,
EMP: 80
SALES (est): 4.7MM **Privately Held**
WEB: www.aypny.com
SIC: **2741** Telephone & other directory publishing

(G-11213)
MAXWORLD INC
Also Called: Promolines
213 W 14th St (10011-7177)
PHONE..................212 242-7588
Fax: 212 242-7512
Maximino Vazquez, *President*
Richard Garber, *Executive*
▲ EMP: 5
SQ FT: 9,000
SALES: 1.2MM **Privately Held**
WEB: www.maxworldinc.com
SIC: **3993** 7336 Signs & advertising specialties; displays & cutouts, window & lobby; displays, paint process; package design

(G-11214)
MAYBELLINE INC
575 5th Ave Bsmt Fl (10017-2446)
PHONE..................212 885-1310
Robert N Hiatt, *Ch of Bd*
John R Wendt, *President*
Gerald C Beddall, *President*
Jack J Bucher, *President*
Daniel J Coffey Jr, *President*
EMP: 4118 EST: 1915
SALES (est): 60K
SALES (corp-wide): 3.2B **Privately Held**
WEB: www.maybelline.com
SIC: **2844** 2841 Toilet preparations; cosmetic preparations; toilet preparations; perfumes & colognes; soap: granulated, liquid, cake, flaked or chip
HQ: L'oreal Usa, Inc.
10 Hudson Yards Fl 30
New York NY 10001
212 818-1500

(G-11215)
MAZ DIGITAL INC (PA)
135 W 26th St Ste 10a (10001-6809)
PHONE..................646 692-9799
Paul Canetti, *CEO*
Shouvik Paul, *President*
Paul Shouvik, *President*
Shikha Arora, *Principal*
Simon Baumer, *Principal*
EMP: 27
SALES (est): 2.3MM **Privately Held**
SIC: **7372** Publishers' computer software

(G-11216)
MBNY LLC (PA)
260 5th Ave Fl 9 (10001-6408)
PHONE..................646 467-8810
Ever Elivo, *Controller*
Yaniv Shtanger, *Mng Member*
EMP: 10
SALES (est): 1.2MM **Privately Held**
SIC: **2066** Chocolate bars, solid

(G-11217)
MC SQUARED NYC INC
Also Called: Mancum Graphics
121 Varick St Frnt B (10013-1408)
PHONE..................212 947-2260
Fax: 212 695-7985
Robert Copjec, *President*
EMP: 10
SQ FT: 1,000
SALES (est): 1.6MM **Privately Held**
SIC: **2752** Commercial printing, lithographic

(G-11218)
MCAFEE LLC
McAfee Site Advisor
1133 Avenue Of The Americ (10036-6721)
PHONE..................646 728-1440
Brian Andriolo, *Branch Mgr*
EMP: 6
SALES (corp-wide): 2.3B **Privately Held**
SIC: **7372** Prepackaged software; application computer software; business oriented computer software
PA: Mcafee, Llc
2821 Mission College Blvd
Santa Clara CA 95054
888 847-8766

(G-11219)
MCCALL PATTERN COMPANY (HQ)
Also Called: Butterck McCall Vogue Pattern
120 Broadway Fl 34 (10271-3499)
P.O. Box 3755, Manhattan KS (66505-8502)
PHONE..................212 465-6800
Fax: 212 465-6962
Frank J Rizzo, *Ch of Bd*
Robin Davies, *President*
Kathy Marrone, *Editor*
Kathleen Klausner, *Senior VP*
Nancy Dicocco, *Vice Pres*
▲ EMP: 200
SQ FT: 62,600
SALES (est): 64MM
SALES (corp-wide): 322.4MM **Publicly Held**
WEB: www.mccallpattern.com
SIC: **2335** Dresses, paper: cut & sewn; ensemble dresses: women's, misses' & juniors'
PA: Css Industries, Inc.
450 Plymouth Rd Ste 300
Plymouth Meeting PA 19462
610 729-3959

(G-11220)
MCCARTHY LLC
Also Called: Blackbook
32 Union Sq E (10003-3209)
PHONE..................646 862-5354
Jonathan Bond,
EMP: 10 EST: 2013
SALES (est): 875.1K **Privately Held**
SIC: **2721** Periodicals: publishing only

(G-11221)
MCGAW GROUP LLC
Also Called: McGaw Framed Art
233 E 93rd St (10128-3704)
PHONE..................212 876-8822
Dorris Francies, *Manager*

GEOGRAPHIC SECTION

New York - New York County (G-11248)

Bruce McGaw,
Nancy McGaw,
▲ **EMP:** 10 **EST:** 2001
SALES (est): 572.7K **Privately Held**
WEB: www.brucemcgaw.com
SIC: 3999 Framed artwork

(G-11222)
MCGRAW-HILL EDUCATION INC (PA)
2 Penn Plz Fl 20 (10121-2100)
PHONE.................646 766-2000
David Levin, *President*
Cheryl Ringer, *Editor*
Kimberly Woods, *Regional Mgr*
Chadwick Schockemoehl, *District Mgr*
Patrick Milano, *Exec VP*
EMP: 42
SALES (est): 11.1MM **Privately Held**
SIC: 2731 Books: publishing only

(G-11223)
MCGRAW-HILL GLBL EDCTN HLDNGS (PA)
2 Penn Plz Fl 20 (10121-2100)
PHONE.................646 766-2000
David Levin, *President*
Sally Shankland, *President*
Teresa Martin-Retortillo, *Senior VP*
Heath Morrison, *Senior VP*
Maryellen Valaitis, *Senior VP*
EMP: 92
SALES (est): 1.4B **Privately Held**
SIC: 2731 Textbooks: publishing & printing

(G-11224)
MCGRAW-HILL SCHOOL EDUCATION H (PA)
2 Penn Plz Fl 20 (10121-2100)
PHONE.................646 766-2000
David Levin, *President*
Teresa Martin-Retortillo, *Senior VP*
David B Stafford, *Senior VP*
Maryellen Valaitis, *Senior VP*
Patrick Milano, *CFO*
EMP: 500
SALES: 750MM **Privately Held**
SIC: 2731 Books: publishing only

(G-11225)
MCGRAW-HILL SCHOOL EDUCATN LLC
2 Penn Plz Fl 20 (10121-2100)
PHONE.................646 766-2060
David Levin, *President*
Teresa Martin-Retortillo, *Senior VP*
Maryellen Valaitis, *Senior VP*
Patrick Milano, *CFO*
David Wright, *CIO*
EMP: 599 **EST:** 2013
SALES (est): 116.8MM
SALES (corp-wide): 750MM **Privately Held**
SIC: 2731 Book publishing; books: publishing & printing
PA: Mcgraw-Hill School Education Holdings, Llc
  2 Penn Plz Fl 20
  New York NY 10121
  646 766-2000

(G-11226)
MCM PRODUCTS USA INC
681 5th Ave Fl 10 (10022-4306)
PHONE.................646 756-4090
Michael R Callahan, *CEO*
Paolo Fontanelli, *CEO*
Sung-Joo Kim, *Ch of Bd*
Patrick Valeo, *President*
Josephine Redman, *Manager*
EMP: 40 **EST:** 2007
SALES (est): 8.6MM **Privately Held**
SIC: 3171 3149 3199 Women's handbags & purses; athletic shoes, except rubber or plastic; belt laces, leather

(G-11227)
MCMAHON GROUP LLC (PA)
Also Called: MCMAHON PUBLISHING GROUP
545 W 45th St (10036-3409)
PHONE.................212 957-5300
Fax: 646 957-7230
Raymond E McMahon, *CEO*
Van N Velle, *President*

David Bronstein, *Editor*
Cynthia Gordon, *Editor*
Kristin Jannacone, *Editor*
EMP: 55
SALES: 18.5MM **Privately Held**
SIC: 2721 Trade journals: publishing only, not printed on site

(G-11228)
MDI HOLDINGS LLC
Also Called: C/O Court Sq Capitl Partners
399 Park Ave Fl 14 (10022-4614)
PHONE.................212 559-1127
Joseph M Silvestri, *President*
EMP: 2900
SALES (est): 208.8MM **Privately Held**
SIC: 2899 2842 2874 2992 Chemical preparations; plating compounds; rust resisting compounds; stencil correction compounds; cleaning or polishing preparations; phosphates; lubricating oils; offset & photolithographic printing; printers & plotters

(G-11229)
ME & RO INC (PA)
241 Elizabeth St Frnt A (10012-3544)
PHONE.................212 431-8744
Fax: 212 237-9219
Robin Renzi, *CEO*
Wu Ena, *CFO*
EMP: 7
SQ FT: 4,000
SALES (est): 2.2MM **Privately Held**
WEB: www.meandrojewelry.com
SIC: 3911 3915 Jewelry, precious metal; jewelers' materials & lapidary work

(G-11230)
MEADOWWOOD NY LLC
1 Penn Plz Ste 4000 (10119-4199)
PHONE.................212 729-5400
EMP: 6
SALES (est): 95.2K **Privately Held**
SIC: 2499 Wood products

(G-11231)
MEALPLAN CORP
203 E 4th St Apt 6 (10009-7281)
PHONE.................909 706-8398
Kevin Carter, *President*
Daniel Mao, *Vice Pres*
Vinh Thai, *Treasurer*
Helal Saleh, *Sales Mgr*
Michelle Chen, *Admin Sec*
EMP: 5
SALES (est): 141.8K **Privately Held**
SIC: 7372 Prepackaged software

(G-11232)
MED REVIEWS LLC
1370 Broadway Fl 5 (10018-7350)
PHONE.................212 239-5860
Fax: 212 201-6850
Steven Black, *Exec VP*
Charles Benaiah,
John B Simpson, *Administration*
Miichael Brawer,
Diane Gern,
EMP: 27 **EST:** 1998
SQ FT: 10,000
SALES (est): 3.6MM **Privately Held**
WEB: www.medreviews.com
SIC: 2721 Trade journals: publishing & printing

(G-11233)
MEDALLION ASSOCIATES INC
37 W 20th St Fl 4 (10011-3791)
PHONE.................212 929-9130
Fax: 212 206-7549
Donna Peters, *Principal*
Judy Melioli, *Personnel Exec*
▲ **EMP:** 50 **EST:** 1963
SALES (est): 5.9MM **Privately Held**
WEB: www.medallionltd.com
SIC: 2752 2759 2791 Commercial printing, offset; promotional printing; typesetting

(G-11234)
MEDIA PRESS CORP
55 John St 520 (10038-3752)
PHONE.................212 791-6347
Givi Topchishvili, *President*
EMP: 20

SALES (est): 1MM **Privately Held**
WEB: www.skullman.com
SIC: 2721 Periodicals

(G-11235)
MEDIA TRANSCRIPTS INC
41 W 83rd St Apt 1b (10024-5247)
PHONE.................212 362-1481
Fax: 212 362-1647
Pat King, *President*
Pat Podell, *Administration*
▲ **EMP:** 24
SALES (est): 1.5MM **Privately Held**
WEB: www.mediatranscripts.com
SIC: 2741 Miscellaneous publishing

(G-11236)
MEDIA TRUST LLC (PA)
404 Park Ave S Fl 2 (10016-8404)
PHONE.................212 802-1162
Peter Bordes, *CEO*
Keith Cohn, *President*
Dave Coburn, *COO*
Mike Stocker, *Vice Pres*
Brandon Chen, *Financial Analy*
EMP: 5
SALES (est): 4MM **Privately Held**
SIC: 2741 7311 ; advertising agencies

(G-11237)
MEDIAPLANET PUBLISHING HSE INC (PA)
350 7th Ave Fl 18 (10001-5013)
PHONE.................646 922-1400
Luciana Olson, *Managing Dir*
Shannon Pandaliano, *Business Mgr*
Timothy Rossi, *Finance Mgr*
Ramin Amili, *Accountant*
Richard Hovdsveen, *CTO*
EMP: 28
SALES (est): 13MM **Privately Held**
SIC: 2731 Book publishing

(G-11238)
MEDIAPOST COMMUNICATIONS LLC
1460 Broadway Fl 12 (10036-7306)
PHONE.................212 204-2000
Ken Fadner, *CEO*
Jeff Loechner, *President*
John Capone, *Publisher*
Nathan Pollard, *Publisher*
Phyllis Fine, *Editor*
EMP: 50
SALES (est): 5.3MM **Privately Held**
WEB: www.mediapost.com
SIC: 7372 Publishers' computer software

(G-11239)
MEDICAL DAILY INC
7 Hanover Sq Fl 6 (10004-2702)
PHONE.................646 867-7100
Johnathan Davis, *President*
Dong-Chan Kim, *Principal*
Etienne Uzac, *Treasurer*
EMP: 30
SALES (est): 2.1MM **Privately Held**
SIC: 2741

(G-11240)
MEDICAL TRANSCRIPTION BILLING
237 W 35th St Ste 1202 (10001-1950)
PHONE.................631 863-1198
EMP: 841
SALES (corp-wide): 24.4MM **Publicly Held**
SIC: 7372 Prepackaged software
PA: Medical Transcription Billing, Corp.
  7 Clyde Rd
  Somerset NJ 08873
  732 873-5133

(G-11241)
MEDIDATA SOLUTIONS INC (PA)
350 Hudson St Fl 9 (10014-4535)
PHONE.................212 918-1800
Fax: 212 918-1818
Tarek A Sherif, *Ch of Bd*
Glen M De Vries, *President*
Michael L Capone, *COO*
Julie Iskow, *Exec VP*
Michael I Otner, *Exec VP*
EMP: 432
SQ FT: 137,535

SALES: 463.3MM **Publicly Held**
WEB: www.mdsol.com
SIC: 7372 Prepackaged software; application computer software; business oriented computer software

(G-11242)
MEDIKIDZ USA INC
Also Called: Jumo
205 Lexington Ave Rm 1601 (10016-6022)
PHONE.................646 895-9319
Fax: 212 686-8138
Kevin Aniskovich, *CEO*
Kate Hersov, *Founder*
Mitzie Garland, *CFO*
Sindy Nathan, *Director*
EMP: 7 **EST:** 2013
SQ FT: 1,000
SALES (est): 3.6MM **Privately Held**
SIC: 2721 2731 Comic books: publishing & printing; books: publishing only

(G-11243)
MEDIUS SOFTWARE INC
Also Called: Medius North America
12 E 49th St Fl 11 (10017-1012)
PHONE.................877 295-0058
Dmitri Krasik, *Director*
Mattias Johansson, *Director*
Daniel Saraste, *Director*
EMP: 17
SALES (est): 186.7K **Privately Held**
SIC: 7372 Prepackaged software

(G-11244)
MEE ACCESSORIES LLC (PA)
Also Called: Mark Ecko Enterprises
475 10th Ave Fl 9 (10018-9718)
PHONE.................917 262-1000
Fax: 917 262-3519
Mark Ecko, *CEO*
Seth Gerszberg, *President*
Lee Bissonnette, *General Mgr*
Eli Reinitz, *Senior VP*
Greg Lucci, *Vice Pres*
▲ **EMP:** 189
SQ FT: 30,000
SALES (est): 37.8MM **Privately Held**
WEB: www.phys-sci.com
SIC: 2329 5136 5621 5611 Men's & boys' sportswear & athletic clothing; sportswear, men's & boys'; women's clothing stores; men's & boys' clothing stores

(G-11245)
MEEGENIUS INC
151 W 25th St Fl 3 (10001-7228)
P.O. Box 287434 (10128-0024)
PHONE.................212 283-7285
David K Park, *CEO*
EMP: 5
SALES (est): 60K **Privately Held**
SIC: 2731 Book publishing

(G-11246)
MEGA POWER SPORTS CORPORATION
1123 Broadway Ph (10010-2084)
PHONE.................212 627-3380
EMP: 6 **EST:** 1995
SALES (est): 360K **Privately Held**
SIC: 2353 5136 5137 Mfg & Whol Hats

(G-11247)
MEJ BEATS LLC ✪
Also Called: Me-J
180 E 64th St (10065-7478)
PHONE.................516 707-6655
Stephen Dabah, *Principal*
EMP: 6 **EST:** 2017
SALES (est): 218K **Privately Held**
SIC: 7372 Application computer software

(G-11248)
MEKANISM INC
80 Broad St Fl 35 (10004-2216)
PHONE.................212 226-2772
Laura Peguero, *Branch Mgr*
EMP: 40
SALES (corp-wide): 10.1MM **Privately Held**
SIC: 3993 Signs & advertising specialties

New York - New York County (G-11249)

PA: Mekanism, Inc.
640 2nd St Fl 3
San Francisco CA 94107
415 908-4000

(G-11249)
MELCHER MEDIA INC
124 W 13th St (10011-7802)
PHONE..................212 727-2322
Fax: 212 627-1973
Charles Melcher, *President*
Lauren Nathan, *Editor*
Bonnie Eldon, *VP Opers*
Susan Lynch, *Prdtn Mgr*
Kurt Andrews, *Opers Staff*
▲ EMP: 11
SQ FT: 1,500
SALES (est): 1.8MM **Privately Held**
WEB: www.melcher.com
SIC: 2731 2789 Books: publishing only; bookbinding & related work

(G-11250)
MEMORY MD INC
205 E 42nd St Fl 14 (10017-5752)
PHONE..................917 318-0215
Boris Goldstein, *Ch of Bd*
Yuriy Shirokikh, *CFO*
EMP: 5 EST: 2015
SALES (est): 240K **Privately Held**
SIC: 3841 5047 Diagnostic apparatus, medical; diagnostic equipment, medical

(G-11251)
MENS JOURNAL LLC
1290 Ave Of The Americas (10104-0295)
PHONE..................212 484-1616
Fax: 212 767-8204
Mark Healy, *Chief*
Greg Emmanuel, *Ch Credit Ofcr*
Jay Gallagher, *Risk Mgmt Dir*
EMP: 592
SALES (est): 5.5MM
SALES (corp-wide): 223MM **Privately Held**
SIC: 2741 Miscellaneous publishing
PA: American Media, Inc.
4 New York Plz Fl 2
New York NY 10004
212 545-4800

(G-11252)
MER GEMS CORP
Also Called: Romir Enterprises
62 W 47th St Ste 614 (10036-3201)
PHONE..................212 714-9129
Fax: 212 221-5743
Roshel Mirzakanzov, *President*
Nelly Mirzakanzov, *Vice Pres*
◆ EMP: 5 EST: 1998
SQ FT: 800
SALES: 1MM **Privately Held**
SIC: 3911 Jewelry, precious metal

(G-11253)
MERCHANT PUBLISHING INC
34 W 13th St Bsmt (10011-7911)
PHONE..................212 691-6666
Fax: 212 656-1568
Michael Kanbar, *CEO*
EMP: 14
SALES (est): 610K **Privately Held**
SIC: 2741 Miscellaneous publishing

(G-11254)
MEREDITH CORPORATION
125 Park Ave Fl 20 (10017-8545)
PHONE..................212 557-6600
Fax: 212 455-1444
Diane Salvatore, *Chief*
Andrea Gingold, *Branch Mgr*
SOO J Kang, *Director*
EMP: 250
SALES (corp-wide): 1.7B **Publicly Held**
WEB: www.meredith.com
SIC: 2721 Magazines: publishing & printing
PA: Meredith Corporation
1716 Locust St
Des Moines IA 50309
515 284-3000

(G-11255)
MEREDITH CORPORATION
Also Called: Meredith Corporate Solutions
805 3rd Ave Fl 22 (10022-7541)
PHONE..................212 499-2000
Joe Ceryanec, *CFO*
Noreen Rafferty, *Manager*
Drew Manroe, *Manager*
Christine Tafuri, *Manager*
Maria Caracci, *Director*
EMP: 17
SALES (corp-wide): 1.7B **Publicly Held**
WEB: www.meredith.com
SIC: 2721 Periodicals
PA: Meredith Corporation
1716 Locust St
Des Moines IA 50309
515 284-3000

(G-11256)
MEREDITH CORPORATION
Also Called: Meredith Hispanic Ventures
805 3rd Ave Fl 29 (10022-7541)
PHONE..................515 284-2157
Mike Lovell, *Branch Mgr*
Maryn Liles, *Director*
EMP: 96
SALES (corp-wide): 1.7B **Publicly Held**
SIC: 2721 2731 Magazines: publishing & printing; books: publishing only
PA: Meredith Corporation
1716 Locust St
Des Moines IA 50309
515 284-3000

(G-11257)
MERGENT INC
444 Madison Ave Ste 502 (10022-6976)
PHONE..................212 413-7700
Fax: 212 413-7670
Jonathan Worral, *CEO*
Mike Winn, *Managing Dir*
Keith Cooke, *Editor*
Bob Breslin, *Vice Pres*
Charles E Miller Jr, *CFO*
EMP: 300
SALES (est): 17.2MM **Privately Held**
SIC: 2721 Magazines: publishing only, not printed on site

(G-11258)
MERRILL COMMUNICATIONS LLC
1345 Ave Of The Amrcs 1 (10105-0199)
PHONE..................212 620-5600
Jeannette Rivera, *Research*
Matthew Young, *Accounts Exec*
Adrian Machen, *Info Tech Mgr*
EMP: 7
SALES (corp-wide): 579.3MM **Privately Held**
SIC: 2759 Commercial printing
HQ: Merrill Communications Llc
1 Merrill Cir
Saint Paul MN 55108
651 646-4501

(G-11259)
MERRILL CORPORATION
25 W 45th St Fl 10 (10036-4916)
PHONE..................917 934-7300
Fax: 212 840-7159
Anthony Giannone, *Vice Pres*
Tom Foley, *Human Res Dir*
Phyliss Salimbene, *VP Sales*
Nancy Skluth, *Sales Staff*
Kathleen Leuba, *VP Mktg*
EMP: 87
SALES (corp-wide): 579.3MM **Privately Held**
WEB: www.merrillcorp.com
SIC: 2759 Commercial printing
PA: Merrill Corporation
1 Merrill Cir
Saint Paul MN 55108
651 646-4501

(G-11260)
MERRILL CORPORATION INC
1345 Ave Of The Ave Fl 17 (10105)
PHONE..................212 620-5600
Fax: 212 229-6630
Lauren Sauter, *General Mgr*
Harold Cooney, *COO*
Grace Triolo, *COO*
Robert Chepak, *Vice Pres*
Mark Maresca, *Vice Pres*
EMP: 100

SALES (corp-wide): 691.4MM **Privately Held**
WEB: www.merrillcorp.com
SIC: 2741 Miscellaneous publishing
PA: Merrill Corporation
1 Merrill Cir
Saint Paul MN 55108
651 646-4501

(G-11261)
MERRILL NEW YORK COMPANY INC
Also Called: Merrill Communications
246 W 54th St (10019-5502)
PHONE..................212 229-6500
Tod Albright, *President*
Robert Talbot, *Controller*
EMP: 200
SALES (est): 11.9MM
SALES (corp-wide): 579.3MM **Privately Held**
WEB: www.merrillcorp.com
SIC: 2759 2752 Financial note & certificate printing & engraving; commercial printing, lithographic
PA: Merrill Corporation
1 Merrill Cir
Saint Paul MN 55108
651 646-4501

(G-11262)
MERYL DIAMOND LTD (PA)
Also Called: M D L
1375 Broadway Fl 9 (10018-7052)
PHONE..................212 730-0333
Fax: 212 730-5933
Meryl Diamond, *President*
Kim Reinle, *Financial Exec*
▲ EMP: 60
SQ FT: 13,000
SALES: 101.1MM **Privately Held**
SIC: 2339 2389 Sportswear, women's; men's miscellaneous accessories

(G-11263)
MESH LLC
350 5th Ave Lbby 9 (10118-0109)
PHONE..................646 839-7000
Richard Darling,
▲ EMP: 30
SALES (est): 1.6MM **Privately Held**
SIC: 2326 Men's & boys' work clothing
HQ: Gbg Usa Inc.
350 5th Ave Lbby 9
New York NY 10118
646 839-7000

(G-11264)
MESKITA LIFESTYLE BRANDS LLC
336 W 37th St (10018-4212)
PHONE..................212 695-5054
Alexandra Meskita, *Mng Member*
EMP: 40
SALES (est): 2.2MM **Privately Held**
SIC: 2339 Women's & misses' outerwear

(G-11265)
MESOBLAST INC
505 5th Ave Fl 3 (10017-4910)
PHONE..................212 880-2060
Silviu Itescu, *CEO*
Michael Schuster, *Top Exec*
John McMannis, *Exec VP*
Daniel Devine, *Senior VP*
Stephen Klincewicz, *Vice Pres*
EMP: 8
SALES (est): 5MM
SALES (corp-wide): 31.2MM **Privately Held**
SIC: 2834 Drugs acting on the cardiovascular system, except diagnostic
PA: Mesoblast Limited
L 38 55 Collins St
Melbourne VIC 3000
396 396-036

(G-11266)
MESSEX GROUP INC
244 5th Ave Ste D256 (10001-7604)
PHONE..................646 229-2582
Tom Carmody, *President*
Diana Popescu, *Vice Pres*
EMP: 4 EST: 2011
SQ FT: 1,000

SALES: 2MM **Privately Held**
SIC: 2325 Men's & boys' jeans & dungarees

(G-11267)
METALSIGMA USA INC
350 5th Ave (10118-0110)
PHONE..................212 731-4346
Carlo Geddo, *President*
EMP: 3 EST: 2015
SQ FT: 400
SALES: 8MM
SALES (corp-wide): 18.4MM **Privately Held**
SIC: 3449 Curtain wall, metal
PA: Metalsigma Tunesi Spa
Via Vicinale Galdina S.P. 34
Aruno MI 20010
029 015-762

(G-11268)
METRO CREATIVE GRAPHICS INC (PA)
519 8th Ave Fl 18 (10018-4577)
PHONE..................212 947-5100
Fax: 917 714-9139
Robert Zimmerman, *CEO*
Andrew Shapiro, *Ch of Bd*
Theodore Vittoria, *Vice Pres*
Millie Tricoles, *Accounting Mgr*
Ben Sandoval, *Accountant*
EMP: 38
SQ FT: 22,000
SALES (est): 6.4MM **Privately Held**
WEB: www.metroeditorialservices.com
SIC: 2731 2759 Books: publishing & printing; screen printing

(G-11269)
METROSOURCE PUBLISHING INC
498 Fashion Ave Fl 10 (10018-6957)
PHONE..................212 691-5127
Fax: 212 741-2978
Rob Davis, *President*
D'Arcy Stansberry, *Consultant*
EMP: 12
SALES (est): 1.4MM
SALES (corp-wide): 5MM **Privately Held**
SIC: 2721 Magazines: publishing & printing
PA: Davler Media Group Llc
498 Fashion Ave Fl 10
New York NY 10018
212 315-0800

(G-11270)
METTLE CONCEPT INC
545 8th Ave Rm 401 (10018-4341)
PHONE..................888 501-0680
Rex Ip, *President*
▲ EMP: 5
SQ FT: 200
SALES: 1MM **Privately Held**
SIC: 3531 Construction machinery

(G-11271)
METZGER SPECIALITY BRANDS
161 W 54th St Apt 802 (10019-5360)
PHONE..................212 957-0055
Fax: 212 957-0918
Tim Metzger, *President*
▲ EMP: 2
SQ FT: 300
SALES: 2MM **Privately Held**
SIC: 2037 2035 Frozen fruits & vegetables; pickles, sauces & salad dressings

(G-11272)
MG IMAGING
229 W 28th St Rm 300 (10001-5915)
PHONE..................212 704-4073
Mario Gambuzza, *President*
EMP: 5 EST: 2010
SALES (est): 773.3K **Privately Held**
SIC: 3577 Printers & plotters

(G-11273)
MGK GROUP INC
Also Called: Lamontage
979 3rd Ave Ste 1811 (10022-3804)
PHONE..................212 989-2732
Fax: 212 989-8246
Liora Manne, *President*
EMP: 30
SQ FT: 10,000

GEOGRAPHIC SECTION

New York - New York County (G-11299)

SALES (est): 4MM **Privately Held**
WEB: www.lamontage.com
SIC: **2273** 2211 2221 2392 Rugs, hand & machine made; upholstery fabrics, cotton; tapestry fabrics, cotton; wall covering fabrics, manmade fiber & silk; household furnishings; textile bags; nonwoven fabrics

(G-11274)
MIAMI MEDIA LLC (HQ)
72 Madison Ave Fl 11 (10016-8731)
PHONE..................................212 268-8600
Thomas Allon, *Mng Member*
EMP: 13
SALES (est): 1.6MM
SALES (corp-wide): 12.5MM **Privately Held**
SIC: **2711** 2721 Newspapers: publishing only, not printed on site; magazines: publishing only, not printed on site
PA: Manhattan Media, Llc
    72 Madison Ave Fl 11
    New York NY 10016
    212 268-8600

(G-11275)
MICHAEL ANDREWS LLC
Also Called: Michael Andrews Bespoke
680 Broadway Fl Mezz (10012-2322)
PHONE..................................212 677-1755
Michael Mantegna, *CEO*
Cory Sylvester, *VP Opers*
▲ EMP: 16
SALES (est): 848.9K **Privately Held**
SIC: **2311** 5611 Suits, men's & boys': made from purchased materials; men's & boys' clothing stores

(G-11276)
MICHAEL BONDANZA INC
10 E 38th St Fl 6 (10016-0619)
PHONE..................................212 869-0043
Fax: 212 921-2565
Michael Bondanza, *President*
Geri Bondanza, *Vice Pres*
EMP: 26
SQ FT: 2,500
SALES (est): 3.3MM **Privately Held**
WEB: www.bondanza.com
SIC: **3911** 5094 Jewelry, precious metal; jewelry

(G-11277)
MICHAEL KARP MUSIC INC
Also Called: 39th Street Music-Div
59 W 71st St Apt 7a (10023-4115)
PHONE..................................212 840-3285
Fax: 212 840-3923
Michael Karp, *President*
EMP: 6
SQ FT: 5,500
SALES (est): 490K **Privately Held**
WEB: www.michaelkarpmusic.com
SIC: **2741** 7389 Music, sheet: publishing only, not printed on site; music & broadcasting services

(G-11278)
MICHAELIAN & KOHLBERG INC
225 E 59th St (10022-1403)
PHONE..................................212 431-9009
EMP: 9
SALES (corp-wide): 4.2MM **Privately Held**
SIC: **2273** Mfg Carpets/Rugs
PA: Michaelian & Kohlberg, Inc.
    5216 Brevard Rd
    Horse Shoe NC 28742
    828 891-8511

(G-11279)
MICKELBERRY COMMUNICATIONS INC (PA)
405 Park Ave (10022-4405)
PHONE..................................212 832-0303
Fax: 212 832-0554
James C Marlas, *Ch of Bd*
Gregory J Garville, *President*
Julian Nemiropsky, *Analyst*
EMP: 8 EST: 1926
SQ FT: 4,000
SALES (est): 46.5MM **Privately Held**
WEB: www.mickelberry.com
SIC: **2752** 7311 Commercial printing, lithographic; advertising agencies

(G-11280)
MICRO PUBLISHING INC
Also Called: Micropage
71 W 23rd St Lbby A (10010-3521)
PHONE..................................212 533-9180
Fax: 212 353-1954
Kevin Boyajian, *President*
Steven Carlson, *Systems Admin*
Brian Boyajian, *Admin Sec*
EMP: 5
SQ FT: 9,000
SALES (est): 3MM **Privately Held**
WEB: www.micropage.com
SIC: **2731** 2796 Book publishing; color separations for printing

(G-11281)
MICRO SEMICDTR RESEARCHES LLC (PA)
310 W 52nd St Apt 12b (10019-6292)
PHONE..................................646 863-6070
Seiji Yamashita, *Principal*
▲ EMP: 4
SALES (est): 1.7MM **Privately Held**
SIC: **3674** 8748 Semiconductors & related devices; test development & evaluation service

(G-11282)
MICROMEM TECHNOLOGIES
245 Park Ave Fl 24 (10167-2699)
PHONE..................................212 672-1806
Steven Van Fleet, *Principal*
Janet M Garrity, *Treasurer*
Richard F Krakowski, *Director*
Audrey E Prashker, *Director*
Peter D Rutherford, *Director*
EMP: 10
SALES (est): 571.4K **Privately Held**
SIC: **3674** Semiconductors & related devices

(G-11283)
MICROSOFT CORPORATION
11 Times Sq Fl 9 (10036-6619)
PHONE..................................212 245-2100
Fax: 212 225-4479
Nancy John, *Store Mgr*
Heather Hall, *Engineer*
Peter Protan, *Engineer*
Amanda Palma, *Accounts Mgr*
Seth Amera, *Sales Staff*
EMP: 10
SALES (corp-wide): 89.9B **Publicly Held**
WEB: www.microsoft.com
SIC: **7372** Prepackaged software
PA: Microsoft Corporation
    1 Microsoft Way
    Redmond WA 98052
    425 882-8080

(G-11284)
MICROSTRATEGY INCORPORATED
5 Penn Plz Ste 901 (10001-1837)
PHONE..................................888 537-8135
Fax: 212 896-3965
John Larkin, *CEO*
EMP: 15
SALES (corp-wide): 512.1MM **Publicly Held**
WEB: www.microstrategy.com
SIC: **7372** Application computer software
PA: Microstrategy Incorporated
    1850 Towers Crescent Plz # 700
    Tysons Corner VA 22182
    703 848-8600

(G-11285)
MIDAS MDICI GROUP HOLDINGS INC (PA)
445 Park Ave Frnt 5 (10022-8603)
PHONE..................................212 792-0920
Nana Baffour, *Ch of Bd*
Johnson M Kachidza, *President*
Robert F McCarthy, *Exec VP*
Ricardo Giudice, *Vice Pres*
Mitch Lemons, *Vice Pres*
EMP: 4
SALES (est): 89.6MM **Privately Held**
SIC: **7372** Prepackaged software

(G-11286)
MIDURA JEWELS INC
36 W 47th St Ste 809i (10036-8601)
PHONE..................................213 265-8090
EMP: 2 EST: 2013
SALES: 1MM **Privately Held**
SIC: **3911** 5094 5944 Mfg Precious Metal Jewelry Whol Jewelry/Precious Stones Ret Jewelry

(G-11287)
MIGHTY QUINNS BARBEQUE LLC
103 2nd Ave Frnt 1 (10003-8336)
PHONE..................................973 777-8340
Christos Gourmos, *Managing Prtnr*
EMP: 160
SQ FT: 3,000
SALES: 10MM **Privately Held**
SIC: **2099** Food preparations

(G-11288)
MIGUELINA INC
325 W 37th St Fl 2 (10018-4817)
PHONE..................................212 925-0320
Fax: 212 218-4590
Miguelina Ganbiccini, *President*
Miguelina C Ganbiccini, *President*
Riccardo Ganbiccini, *Vice Pres*
Maria Balanta, *Sales Dir*
Patricia Butter, *Administration*
EMP: 10
SQ FT: 6,500
SALES (est): 1.2MM **Privately Held**
WEB: www.miguelina.com
SIC: **2339** Women's & misses' outerwear

(G-11289)
MIKAEL AGHAL LLC
49 W 38th St Fl 4 (10018-1913)
PHONE..................................212 596-4010
Lee Isit, *Accountant*
Michael Hakimi,
Albert Aghalarian,
◆ EMP: 11
SQ FT: 5,000
SALES (est): 786K **Privately Held**
WEB: www.mikaelaghal.com
SIC: **2339** Athletic clothing: women's, misses' & juniors'; women's & misses' athletic clothing & sportswear

(G-11290)
MIKAM GRAPHICS LLC
1440 Broadway Fl 22 (10018-3041)
PHONE..................................212 684-9393
Donald Pesce, *Vice Pres*
Jeff Getelman, *Mng Member*
EMP: 100
SQ FT: 5,000
SALES (est): 10.8MM
SALES (corp-wide): 1B **Publicly Held**
WEB: www.mikam.com
SIC: **2752** Commercial printing, offset
PA: Innerworkings, Inc.
    600 W Chicago Ave Ste 850
    Chicago IL 60654
    312 642-3700

(G-11291)
MILAAYA INC
Also Called: Milaaya Embroideries
566 Fashion Ave Rm 805 (10018-1846)
PHONE..................................212 764-6386
Fax: 212 764-3910
Gayatri Khanna, *President*
EMP: 4
SALES (est): 1.2MM **Privately Held**
SIC: **2395** Pleating & stitching

(G-11292)
MILLENNIUM MEDICAL PUBLISHING
611 Broadway Rm 310 (10012-2654)
PHONE..................................212 995-2211
Steve Kurlander, *CEO*
Devon Schuyler, *Director*
Mark Sulkowski, *Bd of Directors*
EMP: 18
SQ FT: 3,000
SALES: 6MM **Privately Held**
SIC: **2741** Miscellaneous publishing

(G-11293)
MILLENNIUM PRODUCTIONS INC
Also Called: Alice & Trixie
265 W 37th St 11 (10018-5707)
PHONE..................................212 944-6203
Andrew Oshrin, *President*
Ruth Stiefel, *Design Engr*
Lynn Harechmak, *Bookkeeper*
▲ EMP: 12
SQ FT: 2,000
SALES (est): 1.3MM **Privately Held**
WEB: www.aliceandtrixie.com
SIC: **2335** 2339 Housedresses; sportswear, women's

(G-11294)
MILLER & BERKOWITZ LTD
345 7th Ave Fl 20 (10001-5034)
PHONE..................................212 244-5459
Nathan Berkowitz, *President*
Robert Englander, *Sales Mgr*
EMP: 13 EST: 1949
SQ FT: 13,500
SALES (est): 780K **Privately Held**
SIC: **2371** Fur goods

(G-11295)
MILLER & VEIT INC
22 W 48th St Ste 703 (10036-1820)
PHONE..................................212 247-2275
Fax: 212 245-5908
Edward Ludel, *President*
Edward E Ludel, *Vice Pres*
Barbara Ludel, *Admin Sec*
EMP: 10
SQ FT: 1,566
SALES (est): 1MM **Privately Held**
SIC: **3915** 5094 Diamond cutting & polishing; diamonds (gems)

(G-11296)
MILLIORE FASHION INC
250 W 39th St Rm 506 (10018-8332)
PHONE..................................212 302-0001
Ws Min, *President*
Kyong Shin, *General Mgr*
◆ EMP: 4
SALES: 7.3MM **Privately Held**
SIC: **2335** Women's, juniors' & misses' dresses

(G-11297)
MILTON MERL & ASSOCIATES INC
647 W 174th St Bsmt B (10033-7716)
PHONE..................................212 634-9292
Fax: 212 634-9262
Milton Merl, *President*
Dan Gray, *Controller*
▲ EMP: 5
SQ FT: 2,000
SALES (est): 725.2K **Privately Held**
WEB: www.miltonmerl.com
SIC: **2542** Partitions & fixtures, except wood

(G-11298)
MILTONS OF NEW YORK INC
110 W 40th St Rm 1001 (10018-8535)
PHONE..................................212 997-3359
Fax: 212 997-3358
Kerman Minbatiwalla, *President*
Shalini Amersey, *Vice Pres*
EMP: 9
SQ FT: 600
SALES (est): 1.1MM **Privately Held**
WEB: www.miltonsny.com
SIC: **2339** 2321 2325 2369 Women's & misses' outerwear; men's & boys' furnishings; men's & boys' trousers & slacks; girls' & children's outerwear

(G-11299)
MIMEOCOM INC (PA)
3 Park Ave Fl 22 (10016-5909)
P.O. Box 654018, Dallas TX (75265-4018)
PHONE..................................212 847-3000
Adam Slutsky, *CEO*
John Delbridge, *COO*
Chuck Gehman, *COO*
Nicole P Haughey, *COO*
Kenneth Trevathan, *COO*
EMP: 277
SQ FT: 145,000

New York - New York County (G-11300) — GEOGRAPHIC SECTION

SALES (est): 243.4MM **Privately Held**
WEB: www.mimeo.com
SIC: 2759 Commercial printing

(G-11300)
MIMI SO INTERNATIONAL LLC
Also Called: Mimi So New York
22 W 48th St Ste 902 (10036-1803)
PHONE.................................212 300-8600
Nick LI, *Production*
Gregory Wong, *Controller*
Molly Conlin, *Marketing Mgr*
Karissa Basile, *Marketing Staff*
Mimi So, *Mng Member*
EMP: 20
SALES (est): 3.3MM **Privately Held**
SIC: 3911 5944 5094 Jewelry, precious metal; jewelry stores; jewelry

(G-11301)
MIN HO DESIGNS INC
425 Madison Ave Rm 1703 (10017-1150)
PHONE.................................212 838-3667
Fax: 212 838-3689
EMP: 9
SQ FT: 1,600
SALES (est): 740K **Privately Held**
SIC: 3911 Mfg Jewelry

(G-11302)
MINERALS TECHNOLOGIES INC (PA)
Also Called: MTI
622 3rd Ave Fl 38 (10017-6729)
PHONE.................................212 878-1800
Fax: 212 878-1801
Douglas T Dietrich, *CEO*
Duane R Dunham, *Ch of Bd*
Ramanathan Chandran, *Managing Dir*
D J Monagle III, *COO*
Alexander Sudnik, *Counsel*
▲ EMP: 50
SALES: 1.6B **Publicly Held**
WEB: www.mineralstech.com
SIC: 3295 2819 3274 1411 Minerals, ground or treated; minerals, ground or otherwise treated; talc, ground or otherwise treated; calcium compounds & salts, inorganic; quicklime; limestone & marble dimension stone; limestone, cut & shaped; limestone

(G-11303)
MING PAO (NEW YORK) INC
265 Canal St Ste 403 (10013-6010)
PHONE.................................212 334-2220
EMP: 10
SALES (corp-wide): 429.1MM **Privately Held**
SIC: 2711 Printing & Circulation Of Newspaper
HQ: Ming Pao (New York), Inc
    4331 33rd St
    Long Island City NY 11101

(G-11304)
MINK MART INC
345 7th Ave Fl 9 (10001-5049)
PHONE.................................212 868-2785
George J Haralabatos, *President*
EMP: 7 EST: 1960
SQ FT: 7,200
SALES (est): 680K **Privately Held**
SIC: 2371 Apparel, fur

(G-11305)
MINY GROUP INC
148 Lafayette St Fl 2 (10013-3115)
PHONE.................................212 925-6722
Shun Yen Siu, *President*
Harvey Lock, *Vice Pres*
Deirdre Quinn, *Vice Pres*
Anita Wong, *Vice Pres*
EMP: 70
SALES (est): 3.1MM **Privately Held**
SIC: 2337 Women's & misses' suits & coats

(G-11306)
MINYANVILLE MEDIA INC
708 3rd Ave Fl 6 (10017-4119)
PHONE.................................212 991-6200
Todd Harrison, *CEO*
Kevin Wassong, *President*
Allan Millstein, *CFO*
Greg Collins, *Portfolio Mgr*

Guillermo Suarez, *VP Sales*
EMP: 23
SQ FT: 6,000
SALES (est): 1.5MM **Privately Held**
SIC: 2741 Miscellaneous publishing

(G-11307)
MISS GROUP (PA)
1410 Broadway Rm 703 (10018-9365)
PHONE.................................212 391-2535
▲ EMP: 9
SALES (est): 5MM **Privately Held**
SIC: 2329 Mens And Boys Clothing, Nec, Nsk

(G-11308)
MISS JESSIES LLC
Also Called: Miss Jessies Products
441 Broadway Fl 2 (10013-2592)
PHONE.................................718 643-9016
Carissa Ballance, *Marketing Staff*
Miko Branch, *Mng Member*
Piti Branch, *Mng Member*
Furner Marquis, *Technology*
Reeves Carter, *General Counsel*
EMP: 8
SQ FT: 3,000
SALES (est): 1.3MM **Privately Held**
SIC: 3999 Hair & hair-based products

(G-11309)
MISTDODA INC (DH)
Also Called: Croscill Home Fashions
261 5th Ave Fl 25 (10016-7601)
PHONE.................................919 735-7111
Fax: 212 481-8656
Douglas Kahn, *CEO*
Marc Navarre, *President*
Bull Armpad, *Business Mgr*
Michelle L Rovere, *Senior VP*
Ken Hedrick, *Vice Pres*
▲ EMP: 50 EST: 1925
SQ FT: 35,000
SALES (est): 85.4MM
SALES (corp-wide): 4.2B **Privately Held**
WEB: www.croscill.com
SIC: 2391 5023 Curtains & draperies; decorative home furnishings & supplies

(G-11310)
MITSUBISHI CHEMICAL AMER INC (PA)
Also Called: Composite Materials Division
655 3rd Ave Fl 15 (10017-9135)
PHONE.................................212 223-3043
John Canfield, *President*
Carolyn Orner, *Human Resources*
EMP: 23
SALES (est): 5MM **Privately Held**
SIC: 3355 3444 3443 2893 Aluminum rolling & drawing; sheet metalwork; fabricated plate work (boiler shop); printing ink

(G-11311)
MJM JEWELRY CORP (PA)
Also Called: Berry Jewelry Company
29 W 38th St Rm 1601 (10018-5504)
PHONE.................................212 354-5014
Fax: 212 302-2340
Martha Berry, *President*
Anthony Katsaras, *Engineer*
Jessica Cohen, *Controller*
Joanna Underwood, *Sales Staff*
Morgan Haas, *Manager*
▲ EMP: 35
SQ FT: 10,000
SALES (est): 14.6MM **Privately Held**
WEB: www.berryjewelry.com
SIC: 3911 Jewelry, precious metal

(G-11312)
MKJ COMMUNICATIONS CORP
174 Hudson St Fl 2 (10013-2161)
PHONE.................................212 206-0072
Jennifer Herman, *President*
EMP: 11
SQ FT: 3,500
SALES: 7.2MM **Privately Held**
SIC: 3699 Security control equipment & systems

(G-11313)
MOBILE HATCH INC
555 W 18th St (10011-2822)
PHONE.................................212 314-7300
Dinesh Moorjani, *CEO*

Adam Huie, *Manager*
Jason Cowlishaw, *Director*
EMP: 6
SQ FT: 2,000
SALES (est): 343.9K
SALES (corp-wide): 3.1B **Publicly Held**
SIC: 7372 Prepackaged software
HQ: Iac Search & Media, Inc.
    555 12th St Ste 500
    Oakland CA 94607

(G-11314)
MOBO SYSTEMS INC
Also Called: Go Mobo
26 Broadway Fl 24 (10004-1840)
PHONE.................................212 260-0895
Noah H Glass, *CEO*
Matthew Tucker, *COO*
David Fellows, *Vice Pres*
Marty Hahnfeld, *Vice Pres*
Scott Lamb, *Vice Pres*
EMP: 86
SQ FT: 400
SALES (est): 12MM **Privately Held**
SIC: 7372 Business oriented computer software

(G-11315)
MODERN LANGUAGE ASSN AMER INC
Also Called: M L A
85 Broad St Fl 5 (10004-1789)
PHONE.................................646 576-5000
Fax: 646 576-5160
Margaret W Ferguson, *President*
Kwame Anthony Appiah, *Vice Pres*
Roland Greene, *Vice Pres*
Amilde Hadden, *Finance Dir*
Judith Altreuter, *Manager*
EMP: 110 EST: 1883
SQ FT: 37,500
SALES (est): 16.3MM **Privately Held**
SIC: 2731 8641 Books: publishing only; educator's association

(G-11316)
MODO RETAIL LLC
Also Called: Modo Eyeware
252 Mott St (10012-3436)
PHONE.................................212 965-4900
Sue Ng, *Controller*
Alex Lenaro,
EMP: 40
SALES (est): 3.1MM **Privately Held**
SIC: 3851 Spectacles

(G-11317)
MODULEX NEW YORK INC
Also Called: Asi Sign Systems
192 Lexington Ave Rm 1002 (10016-6823)
PHONE.................................646 742-1320
Selwyn Josset, *President*
John Jackson, *Sales Associate*
Lauren Corrigan, *Office Mgr*
EMP: 8
SQ FT: 2,200
SALES: 2.1MM **Privately Held**
SIC: 3993 Signs & advertising specialties

(G-11318)
MODULIGHTOR INC
246 E 58th St (10022-2011)
PHONE.................................212 371-0336
Fax: 212 371-0335
Ernest Wagner, *President*
Imelda Elpidma, *Bookkeeper*
▲ EMP: 12 EST: 1976
SQ FT: 7,000
SALES (est): 1.3MM **Privately Held**
WEB: www.Modulightor.com
SIC: 3646 3645 Commercial indusl & institutional electric lighting fixtures; residential lighting fixtures

(G-11319)
MOLABS INC
32 Little West 12th St (10014-1303)
PHONE.................................310 721-6828
James Payne, *CEO*
EMP: 6 EST: 2015
SALES (est): 148.8K **Privately Held**
SIC: 7372 Application computer software

(G-11320)
MOLLYS CUPCAKES NEW YORK
228 Bleecker St (10014-4420)
PHONE.................................212 255-5441
EMP: 8
SALES (est): 778.2K **Privately Held**
SIC: 2051 Bakery: wholesale or wholesale/retail combined

(G-11321)
MOM DAD PUBLISHING INC
Also Called: C/O Pdell Ndell Fine Winberger
59 Maiden Ln Fl 27 (10038-4647)
PHONE.................................646 476-9170
Bert Padell, *President*
Bruce Nadell, *CPA*
Annette Paulino, *Manager*
EMP: 30
SALES (est): 2.4MM **Privately Held**
SIC: 2741 Music, sheet: publishing only, not printed on site

(G-11322)
MOMOFUKU 171 FIRST AVENUE LLC
171 1st Ave (10003-2949)
PHONE.................................212 777-7773
David Chang, *Mng Member*
Sean Gray, *Executive*
Andrew Salmon,
Susanne Wright,
EMP: 52
SALES (est): 5.8MM **Privately Held**
SIC: 2098 Noodles (e.g. egg, plain & water), dry

(G-11323)
MONACELLI PRESS LLC
236 W 27th St Rm 4a (10001-5906)
PHONE.................................212 229-9925
Gianfranco Monacelli, *President*
Victoria Craven, *Editor*
Michael Vagnetti, *Prdtn Mgr*
Susan Enochs, *Pub Rel Dir*
Sarah Herda, *Marketing Staff*
▲ EMP: 8
SALES (est): 975.3K **Privately Held**
WEB: www.monacellipress.com
SIC: 2731 Books: publishing only

(G-11324)
MONDO PUBLISHING INC (PA)
980 Avenue Of The America (10018-7810)
PHONE.................................212 268-3560
Fax: 212 268-3561
Mark Vineis, *President*
Ellen Ungaro, *Editor*
Sallye Drinkard, *Prdtn Mgr*
Jackie Greenspan, *Sls & Mktg Exec*
Yatin Bavishi, *Controller*
▲ EMP: 20
SALES (est): 2.1MM **Privately Held**
WEB: www.mondopub.com
SIC: 2731 Books: publishing only

(G-11325)
MONELLE JEWELRY
608 5th Ave Ste 504 (10020-2303)
PHONE.................................212 977-9535
Avis Swed, *Owner*
EMP: 3
SQ FT: 600
SALES: 1.1MM **Privately Held**
WEB: www.monellejewelry.com
SIC: 3911 Jewelry, precious metal

(G-11326)
MONGODB INC
229 W 43rd St Fl 5 (10036-3982)
PHONE.................................646 727-4092
Max Schireson, *CEO*
Dwight Merriman, *Ch of Bd*
Ravi Vedantam, *Managing Dir*
Philip Carty, *Senior VP*
Matt Asay, *Vice Pres*
EMP: 826
SALES: 101.3MM **Privately Held**
SIC: 7372 Prepackaged software

(G-11327)
MONTE GOLDMAN EMBROIDERY CO
15 W 72nd St Apt 11n (10023-3440)
PHONE.................................212 874-5397
Monte Goldman, *President*

GEOGRAPHIC SECTION
New York - New York County (G-11354)

Myrna Goldman, *Corp Secy*
Steven Silverman, *Vice Pres*
EMP: 10
SQ FT: 6,000
SALES: 1MM **Privately Held**
SIC: 2395 Embroidery products, except schiffli machine

(G-11328)
MONTHLY GIFT INC
Also Called: Montly Gift
401 Park Ave S (10016-8808)
PHONE.................................888 444-9661
Lisamarie Scotti, *Vice Pres*
EMP: 6
SQ FT: 350
SALES: 500K **Privately Held**
SIC: 2676 Sanitary paper products

(G-11329)
MORELLE PRODUCTS LTD
Also Called: Philippe Adec Paris
211 E 18th St Apt 4d (10003-3624)
PHONE.................................212 391-8070
Aby Saltiel, *President*
Alexander Fronimos, *Vice Pres*
Bridgets Hutchinsn, *Accountant*
EMP: 17
SQ FT: 13,500
SALES (est): 1.4MM **Privately Held**
WEB: www.philippeadec.com
SIC: 2339 5137 Sportswear, women's; sportswear, women's & children's

(G-11330)
MORGIK METAL DESIGNS
145 Hudson St Frnt 4 (10013-2122)
P.O. Box 213, Elmwood Park NJ (07407-0213)
PHONE.................................212 463-0304
Fax: 212 463-0329
Larry Kaufman, *President*
Joe Kaufman, *Admin Sec*
EMP: 18
SQ FT: 4,000
SALES (est): 2.5MM **Privately Held**
WEB: www.morgik.com
SIC: 3446 1761 3429 Architectural metalwork; architectural sheet metal work; furniture builders' & other household hardware

(G-11331)
MORRIS BROTHERS SIGN SVC INC
37 W 20th St Ste 708 (10011-3717)
PHONE.................................212 675-9130
Fax: 212 675-7708
Peter V Bellantone, *President*
Michael Bellantone, *General Mgr*
EMP: 3
SQ FT: 4,000
SALES: 1MM **Privately Held**
WEB: www.morrisbrotherssigns.com
SIC: 3993 Signs & advertising specialties

(G-11332)
MOSBY HOLDINGS CORP (DH)
125 Park Ave (10017-5529)
PHONE.................................212 309-8100
Ron Mobed, *President*
EMP: 6
SALES (est): 82.3MM
SALES (corp-wide): 8.4B **Privately Held**
SIC: 2741 8999 Technical manuals: publishing only, not printed on site; writing for publication
HQ: Relx Inc.
230 Park Ave Ste 700
New York NY 10169
212 309-8100

(G-11333)
MOSCHOS FURS INC
345 7th Ave Rm 1501 (10001-5042)
PHONE.................................212 244-0255
Fax: 212 465-2039
George Moschos, *President*
Patricia Moschos, *Corp Secy*
Sandy Ross, *Bookkeeper*
EMP: 5
SQ FT: 4,000
SALES (est): 350K **Privately Held**
SIC: 2371 Fur coats & other fur apparel

(G-11334)
MOSCOT WHOLESALE CORP
69 W 14th St Fl 2 (10011-7417)
PHONE.................................212 647-1550
Dr Harvey Moscot, *President*
Kenny Moscot, *Shareholder*
▲ **EMP:** 6
SQ FT: 2,000
SALES (est): 847.8K **Privately Held**
SIC: 3851 5049 Frames, lenses & parts, eyeglass & spectacle; optical goods

(G-11335)
MOTEMA MUSIC LLC
8 W 127th St Apt 2 (10027-3949)
PHONE.................................212 860-6969
Jana Herzen,
Wayne More,
EMP: 7
SQ FT: 600
SALES: 700K **Privately Held**
SIC: 2782 5735 Record albums; records

(G-11336)
MP STUDIO INC
147 W 35th St Ste 1603 (10001-2100)
PHONE.................................212 302-5666
EMP: 5 **EST:** 2013
SALES (est): 300K **Privately Held**
SIC: 2337 Mfg Women's/Misses' Suits/Coats

(G-11337)
MPDRAW LLC
109 Ludlow St (10002-3240)
PHONE.................................212 228-8383
EMP: 25
SALES (est): 1.6MM **Privately Held**
SIC: 3421 Table & food cutlery, including butchers'

(G-11338)
MPL COMMUNICATIONS INC (HQ)
Also Called: Edwin H Morris & Co
41 W 54th St (10019-5404)
PHONE.................................212 246-5881
Fax: 212 977-8408
Paul McCartney, *President*
John L Eastman, *Chairman*
Bill Porricelli, *Senior VP*
Lee Estman, *Vice Pres*
Nancy Jeffries, *Marketing Mgr*
▲ **EMP:** 5 **EST:** 1942
SALES: 758.4K
SALES (corp-wide): 4.1MM **Privately Held**
SIC: 2741 Music book & sheet music publishing

(G-11339)
MRINALINI INC
Also Called: M & R Design
469 7th Ave Rm 1254 (10018-7605)
PHONE.................................646 510-2747
Mrinalini Kumari, *President*
Steven Caretsky, *Manager*
EMP: 6
SALES (est): 41.4K **Privately Held**
SIC: 2395 Embroidery & art needlework

(G-11340)
MRS JOHN L STRONG & CO LLC
Also Called: Strong Ventures
699 Madison Ave Fl 5 (10065-8039)
PHONE.................................212 838-3775
Joe Lewis, *President*
Nanette Brown,
EMP: 14
SALES (est): 1.5MM **Privately Held**
WEB: www.mrsstrong.com
SIC: 2754 Stationery: gravure printing

(G-11341)
MRT TEXTILE INC
350 5th Ave (10118-0110)
PHONE.................................800 674-1073
Ibrahim Eyidemir, *President*
David Davitoglu, *Vice Pres*
EMP: 3
SQ FT: 7,000
SALES: 4MM **Privately Held**
SIC: 2341 5137 Chemises, camisoles & teddies: women's & children's; women's & children's lingerie & undergarments

(G-11342)
MSKCC RMIPC
Also Called: Memorial Sloan Kttering Cancer
1250 1st Ave Ste S-C24 (10065-6038)
PHONE.................................212 639-6212
Aleksey Khersonskiy, *Business Mgr*
Serge Lyashchenko, *Supervisor*
Jason Lewis, *Director*
EMP: 16
SALES (est): 1.1MM **Privately Held**
SIC: 2834 Solutions, pharmaceutical

(G-11343)
MTM PUBLISHING INC
435 W 23rd St (10011-1402)
PHONE.................................212 242-6930
Valerie Tomaselli, *President*
EMP: 6
SALES (est): 507K **Privately Held**
SIC: 2741 Miscellaneous publishing

(G-11344)
MUALEMA LLC
Also Called: Sohha Savory Yogurt
128 W 112th St Apt 1a (10026-3748)
PHONE.................................609 820-6098
Angela Fout, *Mng Member*
John Fout,
EMP: 6
SALES: 600K **Privately Held**
SIC: 2026 Yogurt

(G-11345)
MUD PUDDLE BOOKS INC
36 W 25th St Fl 5 (10010-2718)
PHONE.................................212 647-9168
Gregory Boehm, *President*
▲ **EMP:** 5
SQ FT: 3,000
SALES (est): 603K **Privately Held**
WEB: www.mudpuddlebooks.com
SIC: 2731 Books: publishing only

(G-11346)
MULITEX USA INC
215 W 40th St Fl 7 (10018-1575)
PHONE.................................212 398-0440
Fax: 212 253-4017
Harry Mohinani, *CEO*
Sivaprakasham Rajakkal, *President*
Arun Mahbubani, *Director*
Vijay Mohinani, *Director*
▲ **EMP:** 6
SQ FT: 2,000
SALES: 7.1MM
SALES (corp-wide): 110MM **Privately Held**
WEB: www.mulitex.com
SIC: 2321 2325 2331 Men's & boys' furnishings; men's & boys' trousers & slacks; women's & misses' blouses & shirts
PA: Mulitex (Exports) Limited
9/F Angel Twr
Lai Chi Kok KLN
225 110-00

(G-11347)
MULTI PACKAGING SOLUTIONS INC (DH)
150 E 52nd St Ste 2800 (10022-6240)
PHONE.................................646 885-0005
Fax: 212 832-7273
Marc Shore, *CEO*
Dennis Kaltman, *President*
Nancy Smith, *President*
Arthur Kern, *Exec VP*
Rick Smith, *Exec VP*
◆ **EMP:** 20
SALES (est): 1.1B
SALES (corp-wide): 14.1B **Publicly Held**
WEB: www.ivyhill-wms.com
SIC: 2759 2731 2761 3089 Commercial printing; screen printing; letterpress printing; tags: printing; books: publishing & printing; continuous forms, office & business; identification cards, plastic; arts & crafts equipment & supplies; packaging paper & plastics film, coated & laminated
HQ: Multi Packaging Solutions International Limited
885 3rd Ave Fl 28
New York NY 10022
646 885-0005

(G-11348)
MULTI PACKG SOLUTIONS INTL LTD (HQ)
885 3rd Ave Fl 28 (10022-4834)
PHONE.................................646 885-0005
Marc Shore, *President*
Dennis Kaltman, *Exec VP*
Rick Smith, *Exec VP*
Mark Wenham, *Exec VP*
Tim Whitfield, *Exec VP*
EMP: 15 **EST:** 2005
SQ FT: 9,772
SALES: 1.6B
SALES (corp-wide): 14.1B **Publicly Held**
SIC: 2657 Folding paperboard boxes
PA: Westrock Company
504 Thrasher St
Norcross GA 30071
804 444-1000

(G-11349)
MULTIMEDIA PLUS INC
853 Broadway Ste 1605 (10003-4714)
PHONE.................................212 982-3229
Fax: 212 982-3248
David Harouche, *President*
Jodi Faye, *Exec VP*
Robert Guadalupe, *Senior VP*
Andrew Gaspar, *Director*
Andrea Weiss, *Director*
EMP: 15
SQ FT: 5,000
SALES (est): 2.5MM **Privately Held**
WEB: www.multimediaplus.com
SIC: 7372 Educational computer software

(G-11350)
MUSIC SALES CORPORATION (PA)
Also Called: Acorn
180 Madison Ave Ste 2400 (10016-5241)
PHONE.................................212 254-2100
Fax: 212 254-2013
Barrie Edwards, *President*
Susan Feder, *Exec VP*
Bob Knight, *Vice Pres*
Robert Wise, *Vice Pres*
John Castaldo, *CFO*
▲ **EMP:** 6
SQ FT: 6,800
SALES (est): 13.6MM **Privately Held**
WEB: www.msc-catalog.com
SIC: 2741 Music books: publishing only, not printed on site; music, sheet: publishing only, not printed on site

(G-11351)
MUSTANG BIO INC
2 Gansevoort St Fl 9 (10014-1667)
PHONE.................................781 652-4500
Michael S Weiss, *Ch of Bd*
Manuel Litchman, *President*
EMP: 7
SALES (est): 131.8K **Privately Held**
SIC: 2834 Pharmaceutical preparations

(G-11352)
MX SOLAR USA LLC
100 Wall St Ste 1000 (10005-3727)
PHONE.................................732 356-7300
◆ **EMP:** 150
SALES (est): 10.1MM **Privately Held**
SIC: 3433 Mfg Heating Equipment-Non-electric

(G-11353)
MY MOST FAVORITE FOOD
247 W 72nd St Frnt 1 (10023-2723)
PHONE.................................212 580-5130
Fax: 212 580-5135
Scott A Magram, *Principal*
EMP: 5
SALES (est): 271.8K **Privately Held**
SIC: 2052 2024 Bakery products, dry; ices, flavored (frozen dessert)

(G-11354)
MY PUBLISHER INC
845 3rd Ave Rm 1410 (10022-6619)
PHONE.................................212 935-5215
Fax: 212 935-3950
Katherine Lewis, *President*
Dwight Blaha, *COO*
Mark Labbe, *CTO*
EMP: 7

New York - New York County (G-11355)

SALES (est): 8.1MM
SALES (corp-wide): 1.1B **Publicly Held**
SIC: 2741 Miscellaneous publishing
PA: Shutterfly, Inc.
2800 Bridge Pkwy Ste 100
Redwood City CA 94065
650 610-5200

(G-11355)
MYCRA PAC DESIGNER WEAR INC (PA)
158 W 29th St Fl 12 (10001-5300)
PHONE.................................925 631-6878
Sharon Huebschwerlen, *President*
Jeanne Doty, *Opers Staff*
▲ EMP: 7
SQ FT: 7,000
SALES (est): 883.2K **Privately Held**
WEB: www.mycrapac.com
SIC: 2385 Raincoats, except vulcanized rubber: purchased materials

(G-11356)
MYERS GROUP LLC (PA)
Also Called: Sogimex
257 W 38th St (10018-4457)
PHONE.................................973 761-6414
Benjamin Myers, *Vice Pres*
Ted Salomon, *Sales Dir*
Bruce Bear, *Marketing Staff*
Jay Myers,
◆ EMP: 9
SQ FT: 3,200
SALES (est): 87MM **Privately Held**
SIC: 3111 Tanneries, leather

(G-11357)
MYSTIC APPAREL LLC (PA)
Also Called: Mystic Apparel Company
1333 Broadway Fl 6 (10018-7268)
PHONE.................................212 279-2466
Fax: 212 944-6478
Yasar Bashir, *Controller*
Charles Mizrahi, *Mng Member*
▲ EMP: 40
SQ FT: 24,000
SALES: 240MM **Privately Held**
WEB: www.mysticapparel.com
SIC: 3089 5137 Kitchenware, plastic; women's & children's clothing

(G-11358)
MYSTIC INC (PA)
Also Called: Herman Kay
463 7th Ave Fl 12 (10018-7499)
PHONE.................................212 239-2025
Fax: 212 643-3465
Richard Kringstein, *Ch of Bd*
Barry Kringstein, *President*
Lawrence Peltz, *CFO*
▲ EMP: 390
SQ FT: 35,000
SALES (est): 48.2MM **Privately Held**
WEB: www.mystic.com
SIC: 2339 Women's & misses' outerwear

(G-11359)
N POLOGEORGIS FURS INC
143 W 29th St Fl 8 (10001-5145)
PHONE.................................212 563-2250
Fax: 212 563-6735
Nick Pologeorgis, *President*
Joan Nathenas, *E-Business*
EMP: 11
SQ FT: 5,000
SALES (est): 1.2MM **Privately Held**
SIC: 2371 Fur coats & other fur apparel

(G-11360)
N Y BIJOUX CORP
1261 Broadway Rm 606 (10001-3539)
PHONE.................................212 244-9585
Hylong Kim, *President*
▲ EMP: 5
SALES (est): 687.6K **Privately Held**
WEB: www.nybijouxcorp.com
SIC: 3911 Jewelry, precious metal

(G-11361)
N Y WINSTONS INC
Also Called: Eko-Blu
5 W 86th St Apt 9e (10024-3664)
PHONE.................................212 665-3166
Lauren Swoszowski, *CEO*
EMP: 5

SALES (est): 212.9K **Privately Held**
SIC: 2086 Bottled & canned soft drinks

(G-11362)
NAGLE FUEL CORPORATION
265 Nagle Ave (10034-3573)
PHONE.................................212 304-4618
Johnny Arais, *Manager*
EMP: 5
SALES (est): 312.9K **Privately Held**
SIC: 2869 Fuels

(G-11363)
NAME BASE INC
172 Lexington Ave Apt 1 (10016-7481)
PHONE.................................212 545-1400
James Singer, *President*
Margaret Wolfson, *Creative Dir*
EMP: 9
SALES (est): 598.3K **Privately Held**
WEB: www.namebase.com
SIC: 3953 Irons, marking or branding

(G-11364)
NANZ CUSTOM HARDWARE INC (PA)
Also Called: Nanz Company, The
20 Vandam St Fl 5l (10013-1277)
PHONE.................................212 367-7000
Fax: 212 367-7375
Carl Sorenson, *CEO*
Samual Michaelson, *COO*
Sindhuja Chari, *Project Mgr*
Andrew Fisher, *Research*
Alex Berlingieri, *Engineer*
◆ EMP: 35
SQ FT: 7,500
SALES (est): 24.4MM **Privately Held**
WEB: www.nanz.com
SIC: 3429 5031 Door opening & closing devices, except electrical; building materials, interior

(G-11365)
NAT NAST COMPANY INC (PA)
1370 Broadway Rm 900 (10018-7309)
PHONE.................................212 575-1186
Sonny Haddad, *President*
Lawrence Deparis, *President*
Kristen O'Hara, *Office Mgr*
▲ EMP: 5
SALES (est): 1.3MM **Privately Held**
WEB: www.natnast.com
SIC: 2321 Blouses, boys': made from purchased materials

(G-11366)
NATHAN LOVE LLC
407 Broome St Rm 6r (10013-3213)
PHONE.................................212 925-7111
Joe Burrascano,
EMP: 10
SALES (est): 1.6MM **Privately Held**
SIC: 3931 Musical instruments

(G-11367)
NATION COMPANY LP
Also Called: Nation, The
520 8th Ave Rm 2100 (10018-4164)
PHONE.................................212 209-5400
Scott Klein, *President*
Katrina Vanden Heuvel, *Partner*
Teresa Stack, *Ltd Ptnr*
EMP: 30 EST: 1865
SQ FT: 11,000
SALES (est): 6MM **Privately Held**
SIC: 2721 Magazines: publishing only, not printed on site

(G-11368)
NATION MAGAZINE
33 Irving Pl Fl 8 (10003-2307)
PHONE.................................212 209-5400
Victor Navasky, *Publisher*
Ellen Bollinger, *VP Adv*
Miriam Camp, *Manager*
Amanda Hale, *Manager*
EMP: 40 EST: 2008
SALES (est): 520.3K **Privately Held**
SIC: 2721 Periodicals

(G-11369)
NATIONAL ADVERTISING & PRTG
231 W 29th St Rm 1408 (10001-5589)
P.O. Box 1775 (10001)
PHONE.................................212 629-7650
Fax: 212 629-6516
Scott Damashek, *President*
Jon Kotcher, *VP Sales*
James W Ricciardella, *VP Mktg*
EMP: 5 EST: 1923
SALES (est): 724.2K **Privately Held**
SIC: 3993 2679 Advertising novelties; novelties, paper: made from purchased material

(G-11370)
NATIONAL CONTRACT INDUSTRIES
Also Called: Nci
510 E 86th St Apt 16b (10028-7508)
P.O. Box 671 (10028-0044)
PHONE.................................212 249-0045
Maxwell J Moss, *President*
EMP: 5
SQ FT: 1,000
SALES (est): 1.5MM **Privately Held**
WEB: www.ncionline.com
SIC: 2221 Wall covering fabrics, manmade fiber & silk

(G-11371)
NATIONAL FLAG & DISPLAY CO INC (PA)
30 E 21st St Apt 2b (10010-7217)
PHONE.................................212 228-6600
Fax: 212 462-2624
Howard J Siegel, *President*
Alan R Siegel, *Vice Pres*
▲ EMP: 20
SQ FT: 8,500
SALES (est): 7.4MM **Privately Held**
WEB: www.nationalflag.com
SIC: 2399 Flags, fabric

(G-11372)
NATIONAL REPRODUCTIONS INC
229 W 28th St Fl 9 (10001-5915)
PHONE.................................212 619-3800
George Pavoides, *CEO*
John K Fitch III, *President*
EMP: 30 EST: 1946
SQ FT: 5,000
SALES (est): 2.7MM
SALES (corp-wide): 6.6MM **Privately Held**
WEB: www.fitchgroup.com
SIC: 2752 7334 Photo-offset printing; photocopying & duplicating services
PA: Francis Emory Fitch Inc
229 W 28th St Fl 9
New York NY 10001
212 619-3800

(G-11373)
NATIONAL REVIEW INC (PA)
Also Called: National Review Online
19 W 44th St Ste 1701 (10036-6101)
PHONE.................................212 679-7330
Fax: 212 696-0309
Thomas L Rhodes, *President*
James Kilbridge, *CFO*
Rose Demaio, *Treasurer*
Ray Lopez, *Manager*
Aaron Bailey, *IT/INT Sup*
EMP: 50 EST: 1955
SQ FT: 17,000
SALES: 3.2MM **Privately Held**
WEB: www.nationalreview.com
SIC: 2721 Magazines: publishing only, not printed on site; periodicals: publishing only

(G-11374)
NATIONAL SPINNING CO INC
Also Called: Caron Distribution Center
1212 Ave Of The Americ St (10036-1602)
PHONE.................................212 382-6400
Fax: 212 382-6450
Todd Browder, *Principal*
Morgan Miller, *Vice Chairman*
Kevin Whitehurst, *Technical Mgr*
EMP: 25

SALES (corp-wide): 174.5MM **Privately Held**
WEB: www.natspin.com
SIC: 2281 2269 5199 Yarn spinning mills; finishing plants; yarns
PA: National Spinning Co., Inc.
1481 W 2nd St
Washington NC 27889
252 975-7111

(G-11375)
NATIONAL TIME RECORDING EQP CO
64 Reade St Fl 2 (10007-1870)
PHONE.................................212 227-3310
Fax: 212 229-5353
Stanley A Akivis, *President*
Richard Akivis, *Vice Pres*
Ethel Akivis, *Treasurer*
Amy Kennedy, *Office Mgr*
EMP: 10 EST: 1932
SQ FT: 10,000
SALES: 1,000K **Privately Held**
WEB: www.national-pinkpages.com
SIC: 3579 7629 3873 3625 Dating & numbering devices; business machine repair, electric; watches, clocks, watchcases & parts; relays & industrial controls

(G-11376)
NATIONAL TOBACCO COMPANY LP
Also Called: North Atlantic Trading Co
257 Park Ave S Fl 7 (10010-7304)
PHONE.................................212 253-8185
Fax: 212 253-8296
Thomas Holmes, *Chairman*
Camilla Fentress, *VP Finance*
EMP: 10
SALES (corp-wide): 206.2MM **Publicly Held**
SIC: 2131 Chewing tobacco
HQ: National Tobacco Company, L.P.
5201 Interchange Way
Louisville KY 40229
800 579-0975

(G-11377)
NATIVE TEXTILES INC (PA)
411 5th Ave Rm 901 (10016-2259)
PHONE.................................212 951-5100
John Gunyan, *President*
Carl Andersen, *Vice Pres*
EMP: 6 EST: 1975
SQ FT: 7,000
SALES (est): 12.1MM **Privately Held**
SIC: 2253 2254 Knit outerwear mills; knit underwear mills

(G-11378)
NATORI COMPANY INCORPORATED (PA)
180 Madison Ave Fl 19 (10016-5267)
PHONE.................................212 532-7796
Josie Natori, *Ch of Bd*
David Leung, *Vice Pres*
Kathleen Olivieri, *Vice Pres*
Elizabeth Yee, *Vice Pres*
Pamela Stengel, *Opers Staff*
▲ EMP: 60
SQ FT: 10,500
SALES (est): 47.6MM **Privately Held**
SIC: 2384 2341 Bathrobes, men's & women's: made from purchased materials; women's & children's nightwear

(G-11379)
NATORI COMPANY INCORPORATED
Also Called: Natori Company, The
180 Madison Ave Fl 19 (10016-5267)
PHONE.................................212 532-7796
Efren Lota, *Manager*
EMP: 40
SALES (corp-wide): 47.6MM **Privately Held**
SIC: 2341 Women's & children's underwear
PA: The Natori Company Incorporated
180 Madison Ave Fl 19
New York NY 10016
212 532-7796

GEOGRAPHIC SECTION

New York - New York County (G-11405)

(G-11380)
NATURE AMERICA INC (DH)
Also Called: Nature Publishing Group
1 New York Plz Ste 4500 (10004-1562)
P.O. Box 51227, Philadelphia PA (19115-0227)
PHONE.............................212 726-9200
Fax: 212 696-9006
Steven Inchcoombe, *President*
Ruth Wilson, *Publisher*
Christian Dorbrandt, *Managing Dir*
Steve Coleman, *Editor*
Christine Gorman, *Editor*
▼ **EMP:** 380
SQ FT: 66,000
SALES: 300MM
SALES (corp-wide): 1.5B **Privately Held**
WEB: www.nature.com
SIC: 2721 Magazines: publishing only, not printed on site
HQ: Macmillan Magazines Limited
   Porters South
   London
   207 833-4000

(G-11381)
NAUTICA INTERNATIONAL INC (DH)
40 W 57th St Fl 3 (10019-4005)
PHONE.............................212 541-5757
Fax: 212 841-7154
Karen Murray, *President*
Sarah A Deckey, *President*
Harvey Sanders, *Exec VP*
Christopher Fuentes, *Vice Pres*
Ceasar Fernandez, *Purch Mgr*
▲ **EMP:** 100
SALES (est): 30.2MM
SALES (corp-wide): 12B **Publicly Held**
SIC: 2329 Men's & boys' sportswear & athletic clothing; men's & boys' leather, wool & down-filled outerwear
HQ: Vf Sportswear, Inc.
   545 Wshngton Blvd Fl 8
   Jersey City NJ 07310
   212 541-5757

(G-11382)
NAVAS DESIGNS INC
200 E 58th St Apt 17b (10022-2035)
PHONE.............................818 988-9050
Nava Writz-Shoham, *President*
Moti Shoham, *Controller*
EMP: 25
SQ FT: 4,000
SALES (est): 1.7MM **Privately Held**
WEB: www.navasdesigns.com
SIC: 2211 Linings & interlinings, cotton

(G-11383)
NAVATAR GROUP INC (HQ)
90 Broad St Ste 1703 (10004-2373)
PHONE.............................212 863-9655
Alok Misra, *President*
Bill Pinzler, *Counsel*
Bill McMonagle, *Senior VP*
Ketan Khandkar, *Vice Pres*
Allan Siegert, *VP Sales*
EMP: 40
SALES (est): 10.6MM **Privately Held**
WEB: www.navatargroup.com
SIC: 7372 Prepackaged software; business oriented computer software

(G-11384)
NBM PUBLISHING INC
Also Called: Nantier Ball Minoustchine Pubg
160 Broadway Ste 700e (10038-4201)
PHONE.............................212 643-5407
Terry Nantier, *President*
Mart Minoustchine, *Vice Pres*
Martha Samuel, *Controller*
Chris Beall, *Admin Sec*
▲ **EMP:** 6
SQ FT: 1,200
SALES (est): 510K **Privately Held**
WEB: www.nbmpub.com
SIC: 2731 2721 Books: publishing only; comic books: publishing only, not printed on site

(G-11385)
NCM PUBLISHERS INC
200 Varick St Rm 608 (10014-7486)
PHONE.............................212 691-9100
Fax: 212 645-2571
Michael Zerneck, *President*
Relisa Mitchell, *Office Mgr*
EMP: 8
SQ FT: 10,000
SALES: 1MM **Privately Held**
SIC: 2721 7812 Trade journals: publishing only, not printed on site; video tape production

(G-11386)
NEIL SAVALIA INC
15 W 47th St Ste 903 (10036-5715)
PHONE.............................212 869-0123
Neil Savalia, *President*
EMP: 10
SQ FT: 1,000
SALES: 2MM **Privately Held**
SIC: 3911 5944 5094 Jewelry, precious metal; jewelry stores; jewelry & precious stones

(G-11387)
NEMARIS INC
475 Park Ave S Fl 11 (10016-6901)
PHONE.............................646 794-8648
Fax: 646 602-6925
Frank Schwab, *CEO*
Stephen Schwab, *COO*
Raul Macule, *Engineer*
Virginie Lafage, *Info Tech Mgr*
EMP: 20
SALES (est): 1.2MM **Privately Held**
SIC: 7372 Educational computer software

(G-11388)
NEON
1400 Broadway Rm 300 (10018-1078)
PHONE.............................212 727-5628
Sabrina Prince, *Senior VP*
Julie Tripi, *Senior VP*
Kevin McHale, *Creative Dir*
EMP: 12
SALES (est): 2MM **Privately Held**
SIC: 2813 Neon

(G-11389)
NEPENTHES AMERICA INC
307 W 38th St Rm 201 (10018-3520)
PHONE.............................212 343-4262
Fax: 212 343-4261
Keizo Shimizu, *President*
Daiki Suzuki, *Corp Secy*
Akiko Shimizu, *Vice Pres*
Angelo Urritia, *Sales Mgr*
Angelo F Urrutia, *Sales Staff*
▲ **EMP:** 8 EST: 1996
SQ FT: 1,500
SALES (est): 1.4MM **Privately Held**
WEB: www.nepenthesny.com
SIC: 2329 Men's & boys' athletic uniforms

(G-11390)
NERVECOM INC
199 Lafayette St Apt 3b (10012-4279)
PHONE.............................212 625-9914
Rufus Griscom, *CEO*
Alex Michas, *Treasurer*
Gwynne Watkins, *CTO*
Yong Choi, *Web Dvlpr*
EMP: 12
SQ FT: 5,000
SALES (est): 1.5MM **Privately Held**
WEB: www.nerve.com
SIC: 2721 Periodicals

(G-11391)
NERVVE TECHNOLOGIES INC (PA)
450 Park Ave Fl 30 (10022-2637)
PHONE.............................716 800-2250
Thomas Slowe, *CEO*
Jose Cecin, *COO*
Jacob Goellner, *CTO*
Darci Hosier, *Administration*
EMP: 22
SALES (est): 3.7MM **Privately Held**
SIC: 7372 8711 Application computer software; electrical or electronic engineering

(G-11392)
NES JEWELRY INC (PA)
Also Called: Nes Costume
20 W 33rd St Fl 6 (10001-3305)
PHONE.............................212 502-0025
Nemo Gindi, *President*
Heather Goldstein, *Vice Pres*

Jack Yedid, *Vice Pres*
Jay Gassar, *CFO*
Paul Kopyt, *CFO*
▲ **EMP:** 70
SQ FT: 14,000
SALES (est): 34.5MM **Privately Held**
SIC: 3961 Costume jewelry

(G-11393)
NESHER PRINTING INC
30 E 33rd St Frnt A (10016-5337)
PHONE.............................212 760-2521
Sheldon Wrotslavsky, *President*
EMP: 6
SQ FT: 3,500
SALES: 1MM **Privately Held**
WEB: www.nesherprinting.com
SIC: 2752 Commercial printing, offset

(G-11394)
NETOLOGIC INC
Also Called: Investars
17 State St Fl 38 (10004-1537)
PHONE.............................212 269-3796
Kei Kianpoor, *CEO*
John Eagleton, *President*
William Eagleton,
Anna Aunon, *Associate*
EMP: 45
SQ FT: 1,900
SALES (est): 5.1MM **Privately Held**
WEB: www.aidworks.com
SIC: 7372 Prepackaged software

(G-11395)
NETSUITE INC
8 W 40th St 5f (10018-3902)
PHONE.............................646 652-5700
Zachary Nelson, *CEO*
Patricia McMenamin, *Sales Mgr*
Steven Lippman, *Consultant*
EMP: 9
SALES (corp-wide): 37.7B **Publicly Held**
SIC: 7372 Prepackaged software
HQ: Netsuite Inc.
   2955 Campus Dr Ste 100
   San Mateo CA 94403
   650 627-1000

(G-11396)
NETWORK INFRSTRUCTURE TECH INC
Also Called: N I T
90 John St Fl 7 (10038-3202)
PHONE.............................212 404-7340
Lior Blik, *President*
Craig Calafiore, *Exec VP*
Isaac Cohen, *Purch Mgr*
Thomas Calabria, *Technology*
Anthony Brooks, *Information Mgr*
EMP: 2
SQ FT: 3,900
SALES (est): 5.9MM
SALES (corp-wide): 8.9MM **Privately Held**
WEB: www.nitconnect.com
SIC: 7372 Business oriented computer software
PA: Exzac, Inc.
   Harborside Financial Ctr
   Jersey City NJ 07311
   201 204-5300

(G-11397)
NETWORK JOURNAL INC
39 Broadway Rm 2120 (10006-3037)
PHONE.............................212 962-3791
Fax: 212 962-3537
Aziz Adetimirin, *President*
Robert Wilkins, *Partner*
Joe Milizzo, *Editor*
Pauline Thomas, *Vice Pres*
Edward Woods, *Vice Pres*
EMP: 6
SQ FT: 250
SALES (est): 559.1K **Privately Held**
SIC: 2741 Guides: publishing only, not printed on site

(G-11398)
NEUMANN JUTTA NEW YORK INC
355 E 4th St (10009-8513)
PHONE.............................212 982-7048
Fax: 212 353-8606
Jutta Neumann, *President*

▲ **EMP:** 10
SQ FT: 750
SALES: 800K **Privately Held**
SIC: 3143 3144 3172 Sandals, men's; sandals, women's; personal leather goods

(G-11399)
NEUROTROPE INC
205 E 42nd St Fl 16 (10017-5706)
PHONE.............................973 242-0005
Susanne Wilke, *CEO*
Joshua Silverman, *Ch of Bd*
William S Singer, *Vice Ch Bd*
Daniel Alkon, *President*
David Crockford, *Vice Pres*
EMP: 5 EST: 2013
SALES (est): 524.1K **Privately Held**
SIC: 2834 8731 Pharmaceutical preparations; biological research

(G-11400)
NEVAEH JEANS COMPANY
450 W 152nd St Apt 31 (10031-1816)
PHONE.............................845 641-4255
Corey Reed, *Partner*
▲ **EMP:** 9
SALES (est): 443.9K **Privately Held**
SIC: 2329 Men's & boys' clothing

(G-11401)
NEVERWARE INC
112 W 27th St Ste 201 (10001-6242)
PHONE.............................516 302-3223
Jonathan Hefter, *CEO*
Andrew Bauer, *COO*
Emily Roiter, *Sales Staff*
EMP: 12
SQ FT: 2,000
SALES (est): 1MM **Privately Held**
SIC: 7372 Prepackaged software

(G-11402)
NEW AUDIO LLC
Also Called: Master & Dynamics
132 W 31st St Rm 701 (10001-3478)
PHONE.............................212 213-6060
Jonathan Levine, *CEO*
Michael Gonzalez, *CFO*
▲ **EMP:** 30
SQ FT: 10,000
SALES: 6MM **Privately Held**
SIC: 3651 Household audio & video equipment; microphones

(G-11403)
NEW AVON LLC (HQ)
1 Liberty Plz (10006-1404)
PHONE.............................212 282-8500
Betty Palm, *President*
Anjana Srivastava, *President*
Geralyn Drieg, *Branch Mgr*
Steven Bosson, *Mng Member*
Ginny Edwars, *Mng Member*
EMP: 2500
SQ FT: 100,000
SALES (est): 430.4MM
SALES (corp-wide): 36.1B **Publicly Held**
SIC: 2844 5122 5999 Toilet preparations; cosmetics; cosmetics
PA: Cerberus Capital Management, L.P.
   875 3rd Ave
   New York NY 10022
   212 891-2100

(G-11404)
NEW DEAL PRINTING CORP (PA)
Also Called: Altro Business Forms Div
420 E 55th St Apt Grdp (10022-5149)
PHONE.............................718 729-5800
David Ruzal, *President*
Jack Tocker, *General Mgr*
Doreen Beynders, *Corp Secy*
▲ **EMP:** 7
SALES: 9MM **Privately Held**
WEB: www.narcainus.com
SIC: 2759 Commercial printing

(G-11405)
NEW DIRECTIONS PUBLISHING
80 8th Ave Fl 19 (10011-7146)
PHONE.............................212 255-0230
Fax: 212 255-0231
Peggy Fox, *President*
Christopher Wait, *Editor*
Jeffrey Yang, *Editor*

New York - New York County (G-11406)

Jeff Clapper, *Prgrmr*
Tom Roberge, *Director*
EMP: 10 **EST:** 1936
SQ FT: 2,800
SALES (est): 1.2MM **Privately Held**
WEB: www.ndpublishing.com
SIC: 2731 Books: publishing only

(G-11406)
NEW ENERGY SYSTEMS GROUP
116 W 23rd St Fl 5 (10011-2599)
PHONE.................................917 573-0302
Weihe Yu, *Ch of Bd*
Ken Lin, *Vice Pres*
Jufeng Chen, *CFO*
EMP: 214
SALES (est): 10.1MM **Privately Held**
SIC: 3691 3433 Storage batteries; solar heaters & collectors; space heaters, except electric

(G-11407)
NEW ENGLAND ORTHOTIC & PROST
235 E 38th St (10016-2709)
PHONE.................................212 682-9313
Fax: 212 249-4633
Ryan Murphy, *Manager*
EMP: 5
SALES (corp-wide): 20.6MM **Privately Held**
WEB: www.neops.com
SIC: 3842 Prosthetic appliances
PA: New England Orthotic And Prosthetic Systems, Llc
16 Commercial St
Branford CT 06405
203 483-8488

(G-11408)
NEW GENERATION LIGHTING INC
144 Bowery Frnt 1 (10013-4288)
PHONE.................................212 966-0328
Tony Chu, *Manager*
EMP: 10
SALES (est): 880K **Privately Held**
WEB: www.newgenerationlighting.com
SIC: 3645 Residential lighting fixtures

(G-11409)
NEW GOLDSTAR 1 PRINTING CORP
63 Orchard St (10002-5414)
PHONE.................................212 343-3909
Xue Hua Xie, *President*
EMP: 8
SALES (est): 502.6K **Privately Held**
SIC: 2752 Commercial printing, lithographic

(G-11410)
NEW HAMPTON CREATIONS INC
237 W 35th St Ste 502 (10001-1905)
PHONE.................................212 244-7474
Victor Hoffman, *President*
David P Hoffman, *Corp Secy*
EMP: 5
SQ FT: 1,000
SALES (est): 430K **Privately Held**
WEB: www.nyshose.com
SIC: 2252 Hosiery

(G-11411)
NEW HOPE MEDIA LLC
Also Called: Additude Magazine
108 W 39th St Rm 805 (10018-8277)
PHONE.................................646 366-0830
Eve Macht, *General Mgr*
Susan Caughnan,
EMP: 6
SALES (est): 700.4K **Privately Held**
SIC: 2721 Magazines: publishing & printing

(G-11412)
NEW MEDIA INVESTMENT GROUP INC (PA)
1345 Avenue Of The Americ (10105-0014)
PHONE.................................212 479-3160
Michael E Reed, *CEO*
Wesley R Edens, *Ch of Bd*
Kirk Davis, *COO*
Gregory W Freiberg, *CFO*
EMP: 300

SALES: 1.2B **Publicly Held**
SIC: 2711 7373 Newspapers, publishing & printing; systems integration services

(G-11413)
NEW PRESS
120 Wall St Fl 31 (10005-4007)
PHONE.................................212 629-8802
Fax: 212 629-8617
Ellen Adler, *Publisher*
Phillip Pascascio, *Accounting Mgr*
Carline Roy, *Finance*
Paris Williams, *Human Resources*
Rachel Guidera, *Sales Staff*
EMP: 20
SQ FT: 3,500
SALES (est): 4.1MM **Privately Held**
WEB: www.thenewpress.com
SIC: 2731 Book publishing

(G-11414)
NEW STYLE SIGNS LIMITED INC
149 Madison Ave Rm 606 (10016-6765)
PHONE.................................212 242-7848
Joseph Fleischer, *President*
EMP: 10
SALES (est): 1.2MM **Privately Held**
SIC: 3993 Displays & cutouts, window & lobby; signs, not made in custom sign painting shops

(G-11415)
NEW TRIAD FOR COLLABORATIVE
205 W 86th St Apt 911 (10024-3344)
PHONE.................................212 873-9610
EMP: 24
SALES (est): 90.1K **Privately Held**
SIC: 7372 Prepackaged software

(G-11416)
NEW YORK ACCESSORY GROUP INC (PA)
Also Called: New York Accessories Group
411 5th Ave Fl 4 (10016-2272)
PHONE.................................212 532-7911
Isaac Shallom, *CEO*
Joe Tail, *Manager*
Robin Cohen, *Info Tech Dir*
▲ **EMP:** 50
SALES (est): 12.5MM **Privately Held**
SIC: 2389 2339 Men's miscellaneous accessories; women's & misses' accessories

(G-11417)
NEW YORK CT LOC246 SEIU WEL BF
217 Broadway (10007-2909)
PHONE.................................212 233-0616
Branka Stijovic, *Principal*
EMP: 4
SALES (est): 2.7MM **Privately Held**
SIC: 3011 Tires & inner tubes

(G-11418)
NEW YORK CVL SRVC EMPLYS PBLSH
Also Called: Chief, The
277 Broadway Ste 1506 (10007-2008)
PHONE.................................212 962-2690
Fax: 212 962-2556
Edward Prial, *President*
EMP: 12
SALES (est): 680K **Privately Held**
SIC: 2711 Newspapers: publishing only, not printed on site

(G-11419)
NEW YORK DAILY NEWS
4 New York Plz Fl 6 (10004-2473)
PHONE.................................212 248-2100
Nikhil Rele, *Principal*
EMP: 5
SALES (est): 371.8K **Privately Held**
SIC: 2711 Newspapers, publishing & printing

(G-11420)
NEW YORK ELEGANCE ENTPS INC
385 5th Ave Rm 709 (10016-3344)
PHONE.................................212 685-3088
Fax: 212 685-7188
Wing CHI Chung, *President*

Andrew Lupo, *VP Sales*
▲ **EMP:** 15
SQ FT: 2,000
SALES (est): 1.3MM **Privately Held**
SIC: 2342 Brassieres

(G-11421)
NEW YORK ENRGY SYNTHETICS INC
375 Park Ave Ste 2607 (10152-2600)
PHONE.................................212 634-4787
EMP: 6
SALES (est): 450K **Privately Held**
SIC: 3825 3229 Mfg Electrical Measuring Instruments Mfg Pressed/Blown Glass

(G-11422)
NEW YORK FINDINGS CORP
70 Bowery Unit 8 (10013-4607)
PHONE.................................212 925-5745
Fax: 212 925-5870
Cheryl Kerber, *President*
Mel Kerber, *Treasurer*
Wanda Holmes, *Manager*
Kim Sam, *Manager*
EMP: 15 **EST:** 1953
SQ FT: 3,000
SALES (est): 1.5MM **Privately Held**
WEB: www.newyorkfindings.com
SIC: 3915 5094 Jewelers' findings & materials; jewelers' findings

(G-11423)
NEW YORK MEDIA LLC
75 Varick St Ste 1404 (10013-1917)
PHONE.................................212 508-0700
Michael Silberman, *General Mgr*
Tara Abell, *Editor*
Joe Adalian, *Editor*
David Amsden, *Editor*
Steve Fishman, *Editor*
EMP: 250
SQ FT: 73,000
SALES (est): 87.2MM **Privately Held**
SIC: 2721 Periodicals

(G-11424)
NEW YORK NAUTICAL INC
200 Church St Frnt 4 (10013-3831)
PHONE.................................212 962-4522
Fred Walley, *CEO*
Kenneth Maisler, *President*
EMP: 7
SQ FT: 4,000
SALES (est): 989.3K **Privately Held**
WEB: www.newyorknautical.com
SIC: 3812 Nautical instruments

(G-11425)
NEW YORK PRESS INC
72 Madison Ave Fl 11 (10016-8731)
PHONE.................................212 268-8600
Fax: 212 244-9863
Russ Smith, *President*
Ingred Besak, *Human Res Dir*
Alex Schweitzer, *Sales Mgr*
Stephanie Musso, *Adv Dir*
Robynne Carroll, *Marketing Mgr*
EMP: 50
SQ FT: 10,000
SALES (est): 3.8MM **Privately Held**
WEB: www.nypress.com
SIC: 2711 Newspapers, publishing & printing

(G-11426)
NEW YORK SAMPLE CARD CO INC
151 W 26th St Fl 12 (10001-6810)
PHONE.................................212 242-1242
Fax: 212 691-8160
Kenneth Ehrlich, *President*
Roger Ehrlich, *Vice Pres*
Justin Ehrlich, *Treasurer*
EMP: 40
SQ FT: 15,000
SALES (est): 2.8MM **Privately Held**
SIC: 2759 2782 Card printing & engraving, except greeting; sample books

(G-11427)
NEW YORK SPRING WATER INC
517 W 36th St (10018-1100)
PHONE.................................212 777-4649
Richard Zakka, *President*
Luke Zakka, *VP Opers*

Mick McCay, *Mktg Dir*
Daniel Garcia, *Office Mgr*
▲ **EMP:** 28
SQ FT: 200,000
SALES (est): 37.5K **Privately Held**
SIC: 2086 Mineral water, carbonated: packaged in cans, bottles, etc.

(G-11428)
NEW YORK SWEATER COMPANY INC
141 W 36th St Rm 17 (10018-9489)
PHONE.................................845 629-9533
Leonard Keff, *President*
EMP: 30
SALES (est): 2.1MM **Privately Held**
SIC: 2253 Sweaters & sweater coats, knit

(G-11429)
NEW YORK TIMES COMPANY (PA)
620 8th Ave (10018-1618)
PHONE.................................212 556-1234
Arthur Sulzberger Jr, *Ch of Bd*
Michael Golden, *Vice Ch Bd*
Mark Thompson, *President*
James Bennet, *Editor*
Trish Hall, *Editor*
▲ **EMP:** 277
SQ FT: 828,000
SALES: 1.5B **Publicly Held**
WEB: www.nytco.com
SIC: 2711 4832 4833 7383 Newspapers, publishing & printing; radio broadcasting stations; television broadcasting stations; news feature syndicate; information retrieval services

(G-11430)
NEW YORK TIMES COMPANY
Also Called: Times Center, The
620 8th Ave Bsmt 1 (10018-1604)
PHONE.................................212 556-4300
Melanie Masserant, *Branch Mgr*
Mary Walsh, *Relations*
EMP: 12
SALES (corp-wide): 1.5B **Publicly Held**
SIC: 2711 Newspapers
PA: The New York Times Company
620 8th Ave
New York NY 10018
212 556-1234

(G-11431)
NEW YORK UNIVERSITY
Also Called: Washington Square News
7 E 12th St Ste 800 (10003-4475)
PHONE.................................212 998-4300
Fax: 212 995-4133
David Cosgrove, *General Mgr*
Sue Caporlingua, *Editor*
Jill Filipovic, *Editor*
Elizabeth Tsai, *Editor*
Jasmina Husovic, *Facilities Mgr*
EMP: 25
SQ FT: 7,410
SALES (corp-wide): 8.5B **Privately Held**
WEB: www.nyu.edu
SIC: 2711 8221 Newspapers, publishing & printing; university
PA: New York University
70 Washington Sq S
New York NY 10012
212 998-1212

(G-11432)
NEW YORK1 NEWS OPERATIONS
75 9th Ave Frnt 6 (10011-7033)
PHONE.................................212 379-3311
Steve Paulus, *CEO*
EMP: 12
SALES (est): 724.1K **Privately Held**
SIC: 2711 Newspapers, publishing & printing

(G-11433)
NEWPORT GRAPHICS INC
121 Varick St Rm 302 (10013-1408)
PHONE.................................212 924-2600
John Di Somma, *President*
Michael Paulmasano, *Vice Pres*
EMP: 30 **EST:** 1971
SQ FT: 10,000

GEOGRAPHIC SECTION

New York - New York County (G-11457)

SALES (est): 3.3MM Privately Held
WEB: www.newportgraphics.com
SIC: 2752 2789 Commercial printing, offset; bookbinding & related work

(G-11434)
NEWS COMMUNICATIONS INC (PA)
501 Madison Ave Fl 23 (10022-5608)
PHONE..................212 689-2500
Fax: 212 689-1998
James A Finkelstein, *Ch of Bd*
Jerry A Finkelstein, *Ch of Bd*
E Paul Leishman, *CFO*
Dami Cuadrado, *Director*
EMP: 11
SQ FT: 2,900
SALES (est): 8.9MM Privately Held
WEB: www.thehill.com
SIC: 2711 Newspapers: publishing only, not printed on site

(G-11435)
NEWS CORPORATION (PA)
1211 Ave Of The Americas (10036-8701)
PHONE..................212 416-3400
Fax: 212 852-7147
Robert J Thomson, *CEO*
K Rupert Murdoch, *Ch of Bd*
Lachlan K Murdoch, *Ch of Bd*
Marygrace Degrazio, *Senior VP*
Marc Frons, *Senior VP*
EMP: 183
SALES: 8.1B Publicly Held
SIC: 2711 2731 7375 Newspapers; newspapers, publishing & printing; book publishing; on-line data base information retrieval

(G-11436)
NEWS INDIA USA LLC
Also Called: News India Times
37 W 20th St Ste 1109 (10011-3749)
PHONE..................212 675-7515
Shomik Chaudhuri, *Adv Dir*
Dr Sudhir Parikh,
EMP: 8
SALES: 600K Privately Held
SIC: 2711 Newspapers, publishing & printing

(G-11437)
NEWS INDIA USA INC
Also Called: News India Times
37 W 20th St Ste 1109 (10011-3749)
PHONE..................212 675-7515
Fax: 212 675-7624
Veena Merchant, *President*
Prakash Parekh, *Mktg Dir*
Vikram Chatwal, *Director*
Dr Bhupendra Patel, *Director*
Ruba Agwani, *Mng Officer*
EMP: 15
SQ FT: 6,000
SALES (est): 720K Privately Held
SIC: 2711 2731 2791 Newspapers, publishing & printing; books: publishing & printing; typesetting

(G-11438)
NEWS/SPRTS MICROWAVE RENTL INC
Also Called: NSM Surveillance
415 Madison Ave Fl 11 (10017-7930)
PHONE..................619 670-0572
Andrew R Berdy, *President*
Tom Meaney, *General Mgr*
Carlos Arnero, *COO*
John Puetz, *Engineer*
Tony Fede, *Sales Staff*
EMP: 35
SQ FT: 10,000
SALES (est): 6.2MM Privately Held
WEB: www.nsmsurveillance.com
SIC: 3699 Security devices; security control equipment & systems
PA: Solutionpoint International, Inc.
   415 Madison Ave Fl 11
   New York NY 10017

(G-11439)
NEWSWEEK LLC
7 Hanover Sq Fl 5 (10004-2636)
PHONE..................646 867-7100
Etienne Uzac, *President*
EMP: 6 EST: 2013

SALES (est): 92.2K Privately Held
SIC: 2711 Newspapers: publishing only, not printed on site

(G-11440)
NEXT BIG SOUND INC
125 Park Ave Fl 19 (10017-8545)
PHONE..................646 657-9837
Alex White, *CEO*
David Hoffman, *Founder*
Samir Rayani, *Founder*
Yu-Ting Lin, *VP Finance*
Kris Schroder, *Sales Engr*
EMP: 6 EST: 2008
SALES (est): 1MM Privately Held
SIC: 3695 Magnetic & optical recording media

(G-11441)
NEXT POTENTIAL LLC
Also Called: Nextpotential
278 E 10th St Apt 5b (10009-4868)
PHONE..................401 742-5190
Jack Blanchette, *President*
John Blanchette, *Principal*
EMP: 6
SALES (est): 518.7K Privately Held
SIC: 2819 Catalysts, chemical

(G-11442)
NFE MANAGEMENT LLC
1345 Ave Of The Americas (10105-0302)
PHONE..................212 798-6100
Joseph Adams Jr, *President*
Demetrios Tserpelis, *Principal*
Kenneth Nicholson, *COO*
Cameron Macdougall, *Admin Sec*
Rosario Lualhati, *Administration*
EMP: 15
SQ FT: 2,038,200
SALES (est): 1MM Privately Held
SIC: 1321 Natural gas liquids

(G-11443)
NICHE MEDIA HOLDINGS LLC (HQ)
257 Park Ave S Fl 5 (10010-7304)
PHONE..................702 990-2500
Jason Binn, *Ch of Bd*
Katherine Nicholls, *Principal*
Tim Ocallaghan, *Treasurer*
Karen Whitman, *Accountant*
Jesse Taylor, *CTO*
EMP: 29
SALES (est): 26.8MM
SALES (corp-wide): 57.3MM Privately Held
SIC: 2721 Magazines: publishing & printing
PA: The Greenspun Corporation
   2275 Corp Cir Ste 300
   Henderson NV 89074
   702 259-4023

(G-11444)
NICHOLAS KIRKWOOD LLC (PA)
807 Washington St (10014-1557)
PHONE..................646 559-5239
Marell Battie, *Manager*
EMP: 8
SALES (est): 21.3MM Privately Held
SIC: 3144 3143 Women's footwear, except athletic; men's footwear, except athletic

(G-11445)
NICK LUGO INC
Also Called: La Voz Hispana
159 E 116th St Fl 2 (10029-1399)
PHONE..................212 348-2100
Nick Lugo, *President*
EMP: 12
SALES (est): 449.4K Privately Held
SIC: 2711 Newspapers

(G-11446)
NICKELODEON MAGAZINES INC (HQ)
1633 Broadway Fl 7 (10019-7637)
PHONE..................212 541-1949
Herb Scannell, *President*
Jeff Dunn, *COO*
Dan Sullivan, *Senior VP*
Noreen Rafferty, *Vice Pres*
Donna Sabino, *Vice Pres*
EMP: 3

SALES (est): 3.9MM
SALES (corp-wide): 12.4B Publicly Held
SIC: 2721 Magazines: publishing only, not printed on site
PA: Viacom Inc.
   1515 Broadway
   New York NY 10036
   212 258-6000

(G-11447)
NICOLO RAINERI
Also Called: Nicolo Raineri Jeweler
82 Bowery (10013-4656)
PHONE..................212 925-6128
Fax: 212 925-1168
Nicolo Raineri, *Owner*
Richard Komatz, *Mktg Dir*
▲ EMP: 6
SQ FT: 3,000
SALES (est): 623.4K Privately Held
WEB: www.rainerijewelers.com
SIC: 3911 5944 Jewelry, precious metal; jewelry, precious stones & precious metals

(G-11448)
NIGHTINGALE FOOD ENTPS INC
2306 1st Ave (10035-4304)
PHONE..................347 577-1630
Fax: 212 369-2262
Constantinos Kotjias, *Ch of Bd*
Evilyn Kotzias, *Manager*
▼ EMP: 4
SALES: 1.5MM Privately Held
SIC: 2051 Bread, cake & related products

(G-11449)
NIKE INC
21 Mercer St Frnt A (10013-2771)
PHONE..................212 226-5433
Wil Whitney, *Branch Mgr*
Darah Ross, *Manager*
Sharon McKee, *Senior Mgr*
EMP: 38
SALES (corp-wide): 34.3B Publicly Held
SIC: 3021 Rubber & plastics footwear
PA: Nike, Inc.
   1 Sw Bowerman Dr
   Beaverton OR 97005
   503 671-6453

(G-11450)
NIKKEI AMERICA INC (HQ)
1325 Avenue Of The Americ (10019-6055)
PHONE..................212 261-6200
Hisao Tonedachi, *President*
Hiro Aki Honda, *Exec VP*
Margaret Lim, *Manager*
Yihsuan Wu, *Asst Mgr*
EMP: 40
SQ FT: 33,000
SALES: 6.9MM
SALES (corp-wide): 3.2B Privately Held
WEB: www.nikkeius.com
SIC: 2711 Newspapers: publishing & printing
PA: Nikkei Inc.
   1-3-7, Otemachi
   Chiyoda-Ku TKY 100-0
   332 700-251

(G-11451)
NIMBLETV INC
450 Fashion Ave Fl 43 (10123-4399)
PHONE..................646 502-7010
Anand Subramanian, *CEO*
Peter Von Schlossberg, *President*
Dale Campbell, *Engineer*
Paul George, *CTO*
Daniel Szczuka, *Software Engr*
EMP: 12
SALES (est): 831.1K
SALES (corp-wide): 127.3MM Publicly Held
SIC: 2741
PA: Synacor, Inc.
   40 La Riviere Dr Ste 300
   Buffalo NY 14202
   716 853-1362

(G-11452)
NINE WEST FOOTWEAR CORPORATION (PA)
1411 Broadway Fl 20 (10018-3471)
PHONE..................800 999-1877

Rick Paterno, *President*
Ira Dansky, *Vice Pres*
Stacy Lastina, *Vice Pres*
Dora Thagouras, *Vice Pres*
John T McClain, *CFO*
▲ EMP: 400
SQ FT: 366,460
SALES (est): 36.3MM Privately Held
WEB: www.ninewest.com
SIC: 3144 3171 5661 5632 Women's footwear, except athletic; boots, canvas or leather: women's; dress shoes, women's; sandals, women's; women's handbags & purses; handbags, women's; purses, women's; shoe stores; women's shoes; women's boots; apparel accessories; handbags; footwear

(G-11453)
NINE WEST HOLDINGS INC
Jones New York
1411 Broadway Fl 38 (10018-3409)
PHONE..................212 642-3860
Gail Onorato, *Principal*
Nancy Blok-Anderson, *Senior VP*
Anna Hysore, *Hum Res Coord*
Nicole Trapani, *Marketing Staff*
UI Cho, *Director*
EMP: 6
SALES (corp-wide): 2.1B Privately Held
WEB: www.jny.com
SIC: 2339 Sportswear, women's
PA: Nine West Holdings, Inc.
   180 Rittenhouse Cir
   Bristol PA 19007
   215 785-4000

(G-11454)
NINE WEST HOLDINGS INC
Jones New York
1411 Broadway Fl 38 (10018-3409)
PHONE..................212 221-6376
Lynne Fish, *Manager*
EMP: 7
SALES (corp-wide): 2.1B Privately Held
WEB: www.jny.com
SIC: 2339 Women's & misses' athletic clothing & sportswear
PA: Nine West Holdings, Inc.
   180 Rittenhouse Cir
   Bristol PA 19007
   215 785-4000

(G-11455)
NINE WEST HOLDINGS INC
Also Called: Jones New York
1441 Broadway Fl 20 (10018-1905)
PHONE..................212 575-2571
Fax: 212 768-7759
Jack Gross, *Branch Mgr*
EMP: 7
SALES (corp-wide): 2.1B Privately Held
WEB: www.jny.com
SIC: 2329 2339 Men's & boys' sportswear & athletic clothing; women's & misses' athletic clothing & sportswear
PA: Nine West Holdings, Inc.
   180 Rittenhouse Cir
   Bristol PA 19007
   215 785-4000

(G-11456)
NINE WEST HOLDINGS INC
Jones New York
1441 Broadway (10018-1905)
PHONE..................212 822-1300
Angie Helck, *COO*
EMP: 22
SALES (corp-wide): 2.1B Privately Held
SIC: 2339 Jeans: women's, misses' & juniors'
PA: Nine West Holdings, Inc.
   180 Rittenhouse Cir
   Bristol PA 19007
   215 785-4000

(G-11457)
NINE WEST HOLDINGS INC
Also Called: Jones New York
1441 Broadway Fl 10 (10018-1905)
PHONE..................215 785-4000
Chris Lorusso, *Exec VP*
Sanjeev Savant, *Project Mgr*
Elisheva Rothstein, *Branch Mgr*
EMP: 22

New York - New York County (G-11458) — GEOGRAPHIC SECTION

SALES (corp-wide): 2.1B **Privately Held**
SIC: **2339** Women's & misses' athletic clothing & sportswear
PA: Nine West Holdings, Inc.
180 Rittenhouse Cir
Bristol PA 19007
215 785-4000

(G-11458)
NINE WEST HOLDINGS INC
1411 Broadway Fl 15 (10018-3410)
PHONE..................212 642-3860
Wesley Card, *Branch Mgr*
EMP: 120
SALES (corp-wide): 2.1B **Privately Held**
SIC: **2337** Women's & misses' suits & coats
PA: Nine West Holdings, Inc.
180 Rittenhouse Cir
Bristol PA 19007
215 785-4000

(G-11459)
NINE WEST HOLDINGS INC
Also Called: Jones New York
575 Fashion Ave Frnt 1 (10018-1886)
PHONE..................212 642-3860
Charles Hostepler, *President*
Lisa Garson, *Branch Mgr*
EMP: 22
SALES (corp-wide): 2.1B **Privately Held**
WEB: www.jny.com
SIC: **2339** Sportswear, women's
PA: Nine West Holdings, Inc.
180 Rittenhouse Cir
Bristol PA 19007
215 785-4000

(G-11460)
NLHE LLC
Also Called: Nanette Lepore
225 W 35th St (10001-1904)
PHONE..................212 594-0012
Erica Wolf, *President*
Robert Savage,
EMP: 50 EST: 2014
SALES (est): 240.9K **Privately Held**
SIC: **2339** Sportswear, women's

(G-11461)
NLR COUNTER TOPS LLC
902 E 92nd St (10128)
PHONE..................347 295-0410
AVI Harel, *Mng Member*
EMP: 5
SALES (est): 467.8K **Privately Held**
SIC: **2541** 5211 5084 Counter & sink tops; counter tops; countersinks

(G-11462)
NMNY GROUP LLC
1410 Broadway Fl 16 (10018-9339)
PHONE..................212 944-6500
Martin Schlossberg,
EMP: 25 EST: 2016
SALES (est): 673.8K **Privately Held**
SIC: **2389** Men's miscellaneous accessories

(G-11463)
NO LONGER EMPTY INC
122 W 27th St Fl 10 (10001-6227)
PHONE..................202 413-4262
Carol Stakenas, *Exec Dir*
Sara Guerrero, *Director*
Ariela Kader, *Admin Asst*
Rachel R Gugelberger, *Associate*
EMP: 6 EST: 2012
SALES: 599.6K **Privately Held**
SIC: **3812** Aircraft/aerospace flight instruments & guidance systems

(G-11464)
NOAH ENTERPRISES LTD (PA)
520 8th Ave Lbby 2 (10018-6590)
PHONE..................212 736-2888
Fax: 212 695-3545
Sam Noah, *President*
▲ EMP: 6
SQ FT: 12,000
SALES (est): 1.1MM **Privately Held**
WEB: www.noahenterprises.com
SIC: **2339** 5137 Sportswear, women's; sportswear, women's & children's

(G-11465)
NOCHAIRS INC
325 W 38th St Rm 310 (10018-9664)
PHONE..................917 748-8731
Anthony Lilore, *President*
Celeste Lilore, *Vice Pres*
EMP: 2
SQ FT: 1,100
SALES: 1MM **Privately Held**
SIC: **2211** 2259 5199 Bags & bagging, cotton; bags & bagging, knit; bags, textile

(G-11466)
NOETIC PARTNERS INC
445 Park Ave Frnt 1 (10022-8600)
PHONE..................212 836-4351
Justin Magruder, *President*
EMP: 15
SQ FT: 300
SALES: 2.7MM **Privately Held**
SIC: **7372** 5734 Business oriented computer software; software, business & non-game

(G-11467)
NOHO HEALTH INC
Also Called: Care/of
9 Great Jones St Apt 4 (10012-1164)
PHONE..................877 227-3631
David Elbert, *CEO*
EMP: 48 EST: 2015
SALES (est): 1.7MM **Privately Held**
SIC: **2834** Pharmaceutical preparations

(G-11468)
NOIR JEWELRY LLC
358 5th Ave Rm 501 (10001-2228)
PHONE..................212 465-8500
Shaya Reiter, *CEO*
Maninder Kaur, *Controller*
EMP: 6
SQ FT: 10,000
SALES (est): 580.2K
SALES (corp-wide): 14.3MM **Privately Held**
SIC: **3961** Costume jewelry
PA: International Inspirations, Ltd.
358 5th Ave Rm 501
New York NY 10001
212 465-8500

(G-11469)
NOODLE EDUCATION INC
59 Charles St Suite200 (10014-2625)
PHONE..................646 289-7800
John Katzman, *CEO*
Darwin Abella, *President*
Daniel Edmonds, *Vice Pres*
Grace Linch, *VP Mktg*
Joe Favuzzi, *Manager*
EMP: 20 EST: 2010
SALES (est): 3.2MM **Privately Held**
SIC: **2098** Noodles (e.g. egg, plain & water), dry

(G-11470)
NORDIC PRESS INC
243 E 34th St (10016-4852)
PHONE..................212 686-3356
Fax: 212 686-3356
Denis Mets, *President*
Kart Ulman, *Editor*
Anne Karu, *Administration*
EMP: 5
SALES (est): 210K **Privately Held**
WEB: www.metronome.com
SIC: **2711** Newspapers: publishing only, not printed on site

(G-11471)
NORTH AMERICAN BEAR CO INC
1261 Broadway Rm 815 (10001-3532)
PHONE..................212 388-0700
Fax: 212 388-0089
Joy Mendez, *Opers Staff*
Barbara Iserberg, *Sales/Mktg Mgr*
EMP: 10
SALES (corp-wide): 3.9MM **Privately Held**
WEB: www.nabear.com
SIC: **3942** Stuffed toys, including animals
PA: North American Bear Co., Inc.
1200 W 35th St
Chicago IL 60609
773 376-3457

(G-11472)
NORTH AMERICAN GRAPHICS INC
150 Varick St Rm 303 (10013-1218)
PHONE..................212 725-2200
Fax: 212 633-6366
Arthur Ascher, *President*
EMP: 10
SQ FT: 2,500
SALES (est): 1.2MM **Privately Held**
SIC: **2759** 7336 Commercial printing; graphic arts & related design

(G-11473)
NORTH AMERICAN MILLS INC
Also Called: Chams
1370 Broadway Rm 1101 (10018-7826)
PHONE..................212 695-6146
▲ EMP: 15
SQ FT: 6,600
SALES (est): 1MM **Privately Held**
SIC: **2329** Mfg Men's/Boy's Clothing

(G-11474)
NORTH EASTERN FABRICATORS INC
Also Called: Great Gates Etc
910 Park Ave Ph Ph (10075-0277)
PHONE..................718 542-0450
Fax: 718 328-6564
Gerald Cohen, *President*
John Fisher, *Vice Pres*
Nereida Segrra, *Manager*
▲ EMP: 20 EST: 1932
SQ FT: 10,000
SALES (est): 3.4MM **Privately Held**
SIC: **3441** Fabricated structural metal

(G-11475)
NORTH SIX INC
159 Bleecker St Frnt A (10012-1457)
PHONE..................212 463-7227
Oliver Hicks, *President*
EMP: 12
SALES (est): 10.5MM **Privately Held**
SIC: **2759** 7812 Commercial printing; motion picture & video production

(G-11476)
NORTH-SOUTH BOOKS INC
600 3rd Ave Fl 2 (10016-1919)
PHONE..................212 706-4545
Davy Sidjanski, *CEO*
David Reuther, *President*
Marianne Martens, *Vice Pres*
Heather Lennon, *Sales Staff*
Melinda Weigel, *Manager*
▲ EMP: 25
SQ FT: 11,000
SALES (est): 1.7MM **Privately Held**
WEB: www.northsouth.com
SIC: **2731** 5192 Books: publishing only; books

(G-11477)
NORTHPOINT DIGITAL LLC
1540 Broadway Fl 41 (10036-4039)
PHONE..................212 819-1700
Jeffrey Penner, *Partner*
Edwin Pacheco, *Human Res Mgr*
Elizabeth Brackett, *Mktg Coord*
Arwin Holmes, *Sr Project Mgr*
Matthew Bellantoni, *Consultant*
EMP: 8 EST: 2015
SALES (est): 191.4K **Privately Held**
SIC: **3571** Computers, digital, analog or hybrid

(G-11478)
NORTHPOINT TRADING INC (PA)
347 5th Ave (10016-5010)
PHONE..................212 481-8001
Fax: 212 481-8003
Abe Kassin, *President*
Isaac Kassin, *Vice Pres*
Joshua Kassin, *Sales Mgr*
◆ EMP: 10
SQ FT: 4,000
SALES (est): 31.8MM **Privately Held**
SIC: **2273** 2211 2392 6512 Carpets & rugs; handkerchief fabrics, cotton; blankets, comforters & beddings; shopping center, property operation only

(G-11479)
NORTHWELL HEALTH INC
521 Park Ave (10065-8140)
PHONE..................888 387-5811
EMP: 330 **Privately Held**
SIC: **3842** Cosmetic restorations
PA: Northwell Health, Inc.
2000 Marcus Ave
New Hyde Park NY 11042

(G-11480)
NOVARTIS PHARMACEUTICALS CORP
230 Park Ave (10169-0005)
PHONE..................888 669-6682
Jaclyn Feeley, *Branch Mgr*
EMP: 6
SALES (corp-wide): 48.5B **Privately Held**
SIC: **3826** Analytical instruments
HQ: Novartis Pharmaceuticals Corporation
1 Health Plz
East Hanover NJ 07936
862 778-8300

(G-11481)
NOVEN PHARMACEUTICALS INC
350 5th Ave Ste 3700 (10118-3799)
PHONE..................212 682-4420
Jeffrey F Eisenberg, *President*
Saima Siddiqui, *Project Mgr*
EMP: 32
SQ FT: 25,000
SALES (corp-wide): 1.3B **Privately Held**
SIC: **2834** Pharmaceutical preparations
HQ: Noven Pharmaceuticals, Inc.
11960 Sw 144th St
Miami FL 33186
305 964-3393

(G-11482)
NP RONIET CREATIONS INC
10 W 46th St Ste 1708 (10036-4515)
PHONE..................212 302-1847
Fax: 212 768-4172
Naftali Elias, *President*
EMP: 2
SQ FT: 2,200
SALES (est): 1MM **Privately Held**
SIC: **3911** Jewelry, precious metal

(G-11483)
NSGV INC
90 5th Ave (10011-7629)
PHONE..................212 367-3167
Timothy Forbes, *COO*
Malcolm Forbes, *Branch Mgr*
Julie Chisar, *Director*
Josh Robinson, *Director*
EMP: 20
SALES (corp-wide): 173.1MM **Privately Held**
WEB: www.forbes.com
SIC: **2721** 6282 6552 Magazines: publishing only, not printed on site; investment advisory service; subdividers & developers
HQ: Nsgv Inc.
499 Washington Blvd Fl 9
Jersey City NJ 07310

(G-11484)
NSGV INC
Also Called: American Heritage Magazine
90 5th Ave (10011-7629)
PHONE..................212 367-3100
Malcolm S Forbes Jr, *Ch of Bd*
Susan Cooney, *Advt Staff*
EMP: 50
SALES (corp-wide): 173.1MM **Privately Held**
WEB: www.forbes.com
SIC: **2721** Periodicals
HQ: Nsgv Inc.
499 Washington Blvd Fl 9
Jersey City NJ 07310

(G-11485)
NUCARE PHARMACY INC
Also Called: Nucare Pharmacy & Surgical
1789 1st Ave (10128-6901)
PHONE..................212 426-9300
Fax: 212 426-9305
Harry Wivietsky, *President*
Russell Shvartsshteyn, *Vice Pres*

GEOGRAPHIC SECTION

New York - New York County (G-11513)

Kenny Wivietsky, *Administration*
EMP: 14
SQ FT: 2,100
SALES (est): 3MM **Privately Held**
WEB: www.mynucare.com
SIC: 3842 5912 Surgical appliances & supplies; drug stores & proprietary stores

(G-11486)
NUCARE PHARMACY WEST LLC
Also Called: Nucare Pharmacy & Surgical
250 9th Ave (10001-6602)
PHONE.....................212 462-2525
Fax: 212 462-0040
Robert Marchini, *Mng Member*
Rob Marchini, *Mng Member*
Kenny Wivietsky, *Administration*
Russell Shavartsshtyn,
Harry Wivietsky,
EMP: 11
SALES (est): 1.5MM **Privately Held**
WEB: www.mynucare.com
SIC: 3842 5912 Surgical appliances & supplies; drug stores & proprietary stores

(G-11487)
NUMERIX LLC (PA)
99 Park Ave Fl 5 (10016-1360)
PHONE.....................212 302-2220
Steven R O'Hanlon, *CEO*
Gregory Whitten, *Chairman*
Andrey Itkin, *Senior VP*
Lana Chin, *Vice Pres*
James J Jockle, *Vice Pres*
EMP: 90
SQ FT: 31,650
SALES: 67.3MM **Privately Held**
SIC: 7372 Business oriented computer software

(G-11488)
NUTRACEUTICAL WELLNESS LLC
Also Called: Nutrafol
28 W 27th St Fl 2 (10001-6941)
PHONE.....................888 454-3320
Giorgos Tsetis, *CEO*
Roland Peralta, *President*
EMP: 8
SQ FT: 1,000
SALES (est): 900K **Privately Held**
SIC: 2834 Vitamin preparations

(G-11489)
NUTRAQUEEN LLC
138 E 34th St Apt 2f (10016-4773)
PHONE.....................347 368-6568
Silvia Demeter, *CEO*
EMP: 12
SALES (est): 909.2K **Privately Held**
WEB: www.nutraqueen.com
SIC: 2833 Vitamins, natural or synthetic: bulk, uncompounded

(G-11490)
NUTRIFAST LLC
244 5th Ave Ste W249 (10001-7604)
PHONE.....................347 671-3181
Andres Ballares,
EMP: 10 **EST:** 2013
SALES (est): 636.7K **Privately Held**
SIC: 2024 Ice cream & frozen desserts

(G-11491)
NV PRRCONE MD COSMECEUTICALS
1745 Broadway (10019-4640)
PHONE.....................212 734-2537
Fax: 212 734-2567
N V Perricone, *Owner*
Clinical Mirabella, *CFO*
Kella England, *Sales Dir*
EMP: 7
SALES (est): 839.5K **Privately Held**
SIC: 2834 Pharmaceutical preparations

(G-11492)
NY DENIM INC
1407 Broadway Rm 1021 (10018-3256)
PHONE.....................212 764-6668
EMP: 10
SALES (est): 720K **Privately Held**
SIC: 2253 Knit Outerwear Mills

(G-11493)
NYC DISTRICT COUNCIL UBCJA
395 Hudson St Lbby 3 (10014-7450)
PHONE.....................212 366-7500
Michael Forde, *Principal*
EMP: 2
SALES: 27.9MM **Privately Held**
SIC: 3423 Carpenters' hand tools, except saws: levels, chisels, etc.

(G-11494)
NYC IDOL APPAREL INC
214 W 39th St Rm 807 (10018-4455)
PHONE.....................212 997-9797
David Shaaya, *President*
▲ **EMP:** 4 **EST:** 2008
SQ FT: 700
SALES: 2MM **Privately Held**
SIC: 2329 2337 Down-filled clothing: men's & boys'; skirts, separate: women's, misses' & juniors'

(G-11495)
NYC KNITWEAR INC
525 Fashion Ave Rm 701 (10018-0473)
PHONE.....................212 840-1313
Fax: 212 398-3157
Jian Guo, *Chairman*
▲ **EMP:** 22
SQ FT: 13,000
SALES (est): 2.7MM **Privately Held**
SIC: 2331 Women's & misses' blouses & shirts

(G-11496)
NYCJBS LLC
Also Called: Fat Baby
112 Rivington St Frnt (10002-2259)
PHONE.....................212 533-1888
Joseph Blank, *Principal*
EMP: 15
SALES (est): 1.1MM **Privately Held**
SIC: 2064 Candy bars, including chocolate covered bars

(G-11497)
NYLON LLC
Also Called: Nylon Magazine
110 Greene St Ste 607 (10012-3838)
PHONE.....................212 226-6454
Fax: 212 226-7738
Jaclynn Jarrett, *Publisher*
Sydney Gore, *Editor*
Dana Fields, *Exec VP*
Andrew Haynes, *Manager*
Natalie Toren, *Manager*
EMP: 20
SALES (est): 3.7MM **Privately Held**
WEB: www.nylonmag.com
SIC: 2721 Magazines: publishing only, not printed on site

(G-11498)
NYLON MEDIA INC (PA)
Also Called: Nylonshop
110 Greene St Ste 607 (10012-3838)
PHONE.....................212 226-6454
Paul Greenberg, *CEO*
Marc Luzzatto, *Ch of Bd*
Jamie Elden, *President*
Carrie S Reynolds, *President*
Shruti Ganguly, *Vice Pres*
EMP: 17
SALES (est): 6.3MM **Privately Held**
SIC: 2721 Periodicals: publishing & printing

(G-11499)
NYMAN JEWELRY INC (PA)
66 W 9th St (10011-8972)
PHONE.....................212 944-1976
Fax: 212 944-5716
Corc Aydin, *President*
Gabi Gabriel, *Manager*
EMP: 6
SQ FT: 2,000
SALES (est): 558.2K **Privately Held**
SIC: 3915 5944 Gems, real & imitation: preparation for settings; jewelry stores

(G-11500)
NYP HOLDINGS INC (DH)
Also Called: New York Post
1211 Ave Of The Americas (10036-8790)
PHONE.....................212 997-9272
Fax: 212 930-8727
K Rupert Murdoch, *President*
Joe Vincent, *Exec VP*
John Ancona, *Vice Pres*
Michael Carvalhido, *Vice Pres*
Michelle Dalmeida, *Vice Pres*
▲ **EMP:** 600
SALES (est): 188.9MM
SALES (corp-wide): 8.1B **Publicly Held**
WEB: www.nypost.com
SIC: 2711 Commercial printing & newspaper publishing combined
HQ: News Preferred Holdings Inc.
20 Westport Rd
Wilton CT 06897
203 563-6483

(G-11501)
NYREV INC
Also Called: New York Review of Books
435 Hudson St Rm 300 (10014-3949)
P.O. Box 9310, Big Sandy TX (75755-3316)
PHONE.....................212 757-8070
Rae S Hederman, *Ch of Bd*
Michael Grannon, *Corp Secy*
Evan Johnston, *Prdtn Mgr*
Margerie Deblin, *Controller*
Matthew Howard, *Director*
EMP: 35
SQ FT: 12,000
SALES: 93K **Privately Held**
WEB: www.nybooks.com
SIC: 2721 Magazines: publishing only, not printed on site

(G-11502)
NYS NYU-CNTR INTL COOPERATION
418 Lafayette St (10003-6947)
PHONE.....................212 998-3680
Chris Jones, *Director*
EMP: 30
SALES (est): 1.6MM **Privately Held**
SIC: 2759 Publication printing

(G-11503)
NYT CAPITAL LLC (HQ)
620 8th Ave (10018-1618)
PHONE.....................212 556-1234
Dave Frank, *Vice Pres*
EMP: 18
SALES: 43.2K
SALES (corp-wide): 1.5B **Publicly Held**
SIC: 2711 5192 5963 7322 Newspapers, publishing & printing; commercial printing & newspaper publishing combined; newspapers; newspapers, home delivery, not by printers or publishers; collection agency, except real estate; credit reporting services
PA: The New York Times Company
620 8th Ave
New York NY 10018
212 556-1234

(G-11504)
O VAL NICK MUSIC CO INC
254 W 72nd St Apt 1a (10023-2851)
PHONE.....................212 873-2179
Fax: 212 799-6926
Nicholas Ashford, *President*
EMP: 5
SALES (est): 231.8K **Privately Held**
SIC: 2741 Miscellaneous publishing

(G-11505)
OAKHURST PARTNERS LLC
148 Madison Ave Fl 13 (10016-6772)
PHONE.....................212 502-3220
Gloria Rosenfeld, *Controller*
Boris Shlomm, *Mng Member*
Alexander Shlomm,
Daniel Shlomm,
▲ **EMP:** 5
SQ FT: 5,000
SALES (est): 689.5K **Privately Held**
SIC: 2231 Apparel & outerwear broadwoven fabrics

(G-11506)
OAKLEY INC
1515 Broadway Frnt 4 (10036-5701)
PHONE.....................212 575-0960
Jerome Stewart, *Manager*
EMP: 65 **Privately Held**
SIC: 3851 Ophthalmic goods
HQ: Oakley, Inc.
1 Icon
Foothill Ranch CA 92610
949 951-0991

(G-11507)
OCCIDENTAL ENERGY MKTG INC
1230 Av Of The Amrcs 80 (10020-1513)
PHONE.....................212 632-4950
Kenneth Huffman, *Investment Ofcr*
Francis Sheridan, *Manager*
EMP: 5
SALES (corp-wide): 10.4B **Publicly Held**
SIC: 1382 Oil & gas exploration services
HQ: Occidental Energy Marketing, Inc.
5 Greenway Plz Ste 110
Houston TX 77046
713 215-7000

(G-11508)
OCEAN WAVES SWIM LLC
231 W 39th St Rm 500 (10018-3151)
PHONE.....................212 967-4481
Eli Seruya,
Lisa Bailey,
▲ **EMP:** 7
SQ FT: 1,600
SALES (est): 419.4K **Privately Held**
SIC: 2339 Bathing suits: women's, misses' & juniors'

(G-11509)
OCIP HOLDING LLC (PA)
660 Madison Ave Fl 19 (10065-8415)
PHONE.....................646 589-6180
Kevin Struve, *Manager*
EMP: 3 **EST:** 2014
SALES (est): 258.2MM **Publicly Held**
SIC: 2861 2873 Methanol, natural (wood alcohol); ammonium nitrate, ammonium sulfate

(G-11510)
ODY ACCESSORIES INC
1239 Broadway (10001-4311)
PHONE.....................212 239-0580
Fax: 212 629-0417
Michael Weiss, *President*
▲ **EMP:** 27
SQ FT: 12,000
SALES (est): 3.5MM **Privately Held**
SIC: 2339 Women's & misses' accessories

(G-11511)
ODYSSEY MAG PUBG GROUP INC
4 New York Plz (10004-2413)
PHONE.....................212 545-4800
David J Pecker, *Principal*
Eva Elliott, *Opers Staff*
John Walberg, *Accounts Exec*
EMP: 37
SALES (est): 3.1MM
SALES (corp-wide): 223MM **Privately Held**
SIC: 2721 Magazines: publishing & printing
PA: American Media, Inc.
4 New York Plz Fl 2
New York NY 10004
212 545-4800

(G-11512)
OHR PHARMACEUTICAL INC (PA)
800 3rd Ave Fl 11 (10022-7651)
PHONE.....................212 682-8452
Jason S Slakter, *CEO*
Mike Ferguson, *Ch of Bd*
Irach Taraporewala, *President*
Sam Backenroth, *CFO*
Christine Lucus, *Accounting Mgr*
EMP: 16
SALES (est): 1.4MM **Publicly Held**
SIC: 2834 Pharmaceutical preparations

(G-11513)
OLDCASTLE BUILDING ENVELOPE (HQ)
1350 Ave Of The Americas (10019-4702)
PHONE.....................212 957-5400
Melissa Wood, *Assistant*
EMP: 9 **EST:** 2014

New York - New York County (G-11514)   **GEOGRAPHIC SECTION**

SALES (est): 134.2K
SALES (corp-wide): 28.6B Privately Held
SIC: 3231 Products of purchased glass
PA: Crh Public Limited Company
Stonemason' S Way
Dublin 16
140 410-00

(G-11514)
OLIGOMERIX INC
3960 Broadway Ste 340d (10032-1543)
PHONE...............................914 997-8877
James Moe, *CEO*
Vic Micati, *Ch of Bd*
Jack Pasini, *Ch Credit Ofcr*
Jeffrey Bluestein, *Director*
David Dantzker, *Director*
EMP: 4
SQ FT: 1,000
SALES (est): 1.1MM Privately Held
WEB: www.oligomerix.com
SIC: 2836 2834 Biological products, except diagnostic; pharmaceutical preparations

(G-11515)
OLYMPIC JEWELRY INC
62 W 47th St Ste 509 (10036-3201)
PHONE...............................212 768-7004
Roberto Ganz, *President*
Mike Genuth, *Vice Pres*
EMP: 4
SALES: 1.2MM Privately Held
SIC: 3873 5094 Watches, clocks, watchcases & parts; clocks, watches & parts

(G-11516)
OLYMPIC PRESS INC
950 3rd Ave Fl 7 (10022-2788)
PHONE...............................212 242-4934
Fax: 212 242-5727
Howard Bau, *President*
EMP: 15 EST: 1929
SALES: 1.5MM Privately Held
SIC: 2752 Commercial printing, offset

(G-11517)
OMRIX BIOPHARMACEUTICALS INC
1 Rckfller Ctr Ste 2322 (10020)
PHONE...............................908 218-0707
Robert Taub, *CEO*
Larry Ellberger, *Ch of Bd*
Nissim Mashiach, *President*
V Marc Droppert, *Exec VP*
Nanci Prado, *Vice Pres*
EMP: 212
SQ FT: 8,945
SALES: 13.7MM
SALES (corp-wide): 71.8B Publicly Held
WEB: www.omrix.com
SIC: 2836 Biological products, except diagnostic
HQ: Ethicon Inc.
Us Route 22
Somerville NJ 08876
732 524-0400

(G-11518)
OMX (US) INC
Also Called: Nasdaq Omx
140 Broadway Fl 25 (10005-1142)
PHONE...............................646 428-2800
Fax: 646 344-0079
Roland Tibell, *President*
Tor Soderquist, *Manager*
Maria Schuck, *Admin Sec*
EMP: 1500
SQ FT: 50,000
SALES (est): 55.9MM Privately Held
SIC: 7372 Application computer software

(G-11519)
ON DEMAND BOOKS LLC
939 Lexington Ave (10065-5771)
PHONE...............................212 966-2222
Andrew Pate, *Senior VP*
Thor Sigvaldason, *CTO*
Dane Neller,
Herbert Krippner,
EMP: 5
SALES (est): 923.8K Privately Held
WEB: www.ondemandbooks.com
SIC: 7372 Publishers' computer software

(G-11520)
ONE JEANSWEAR GROUP INC (HQ)
Also Called: Jones Jeanswear Group
1441 Broadway (10018-1905)
PHONE...............................212 835-3500
Fax: 212 921-2792
Jack N Gross, *CEO*
Stuart Bregman, *CEO*
Wesley Card, *Principal*
Ira Margulies, *CFO*
Christopher R Cade, *Admin Sec*
▲ EMP: 300
SALES (est): 77.1MM
SALES (corp-wide): 2.1B Privately Held
WEB: www.jny.com
SIC: 2339 2325 Jeans: women's, misses' & juniors'; men's & boys' jeans & dungarees
PA: Nine West Holdings, Inc.
180 Rittenhouse Cir
Bristol PA 19007
215 785-4000

(G-11521)
ONE STEP UP LTD
1412 Broadway Fl 3 (10018-3372)
PHONE...............................212 398-1110
Fax: 212 869-8933
Harry Adjmi, *President*
Tyrone Davis, *Principal*
Tom Wentley, *Vice Pres*
Sandy Gewercman, *CFO*
▲ EMP: 96
SALES (est): 26.1MM Privately Held
SIC: 2339 2329 Women's & misses' athletic clothing & sportswear; men's & boys' sportswear & athletic clothing

(G-11522)
ONE-BLUE LLC
1350 Broadway Rm 1406 (10018-0926)
PHONE...............................212 223-4380
Roel Kramer, *CEO*
Tom Chen, *CFO*
EMP: 7
SALES (est): 676.5K Privately Held
SIC: 7372 Application computer software

(G-11523)
ONLY HEARTS LTD (PA)
134 W 37th St Fl 9 (10018-6946)
PHONE...............................718 783-3218
Fax: 212 268-0922
Jonathan Stewart, *President*
Noel Stazko, *Opers Mgr*
Tina Vito, *Opers Staff*
Irina Geller, *Mfg Staff*
Keili Leahy, *Accounts Exec*
EMP: 40
SQ FT: 4,000
SALES (est): 7.6MM Privately Held
SIC: 2341 5137 2339 Women's & children's underwear; women's & children's clothing; lingerie; women's & misses' outerwear

(G-11524)
ONTRA PRESENTATIONS LLC
440 Park Ave S Fl 3 (10016-8012)
PHONE...............................212 213-1315
James Ontra,
Alexandra Ontra,
EMP: 6
SALES: 1MM Privately Held
SIC: 7372 7371 Prepackaged software; business oriented computer software; computer software development

(G-11525)
ONYX SOLAR GROUP LLC (PA)
1123 Broadway Ste 908 (10010-2172)
PHONE...............................917 951-9732
David Mann, *Principal*
Diego Cuevas, *Vice Pres*
▲ EMP: 6
SALES (est): 4.6MM Privately Held
SIC: 3674 Photovoltaic devices, solid state

(G-11526)
OPENFIN INC
25 Broadway Fl 9 (10004-1058)
PHONE...............................917 450-8822
Mazy Dar, *CEO*
Fred Doerr, *President*
Jen Collet, *COO*

Wenjun Che, *Vice Pres*
Steve Greenblatt, *Vice Pres*
EMP: 9
SQ FT: 1,500
SALES (est): 651K Privately Held
SIC: 7372 7371 Prepackaged software; custom computer programming services

(G-11527)
OPENROAD INTEGRATED MEDIA INC
180 Maiden Ln Ste 2803 (10038-4988)
PHONE...............................212 691-0900
Paul Slavin, *CEO*
Jane Friedman, *Ch of Bd*
Jennifer Jackson, *Vice Pres*
Daniel Shemesh, *CFO*
Mary McAveney, *Chief Mktg Ofcr*
EMP: 23
SALES (est): 3MM Privately Held
SIC: 2741 Miscellaneous publishing

(G-11528)
OPERATIVE MEDIA INC (HQ)
6 E 32nd St Fl 3 (10016-5415)
PHONE...............................212 994-8930
Lorne Brown, *President*
Venugopal Goteti, *President*
Marc Forman, *Publisher*
Brian Georgi, *Senior VP*
Sirous Wadia, *Senior VP*
EMP: 109
SALES (est): 67.8MM
SALES (corp-wide): 102.6MM Privately Held
WEB: www.operative.com
SIC: 7372 Prepackaged software
PA: Sintec Media Ltd
21 Hefetzdi Nachum
Jerusalem 95484
265 151-22

(G-11529)
OPHTHOTECH CORPORATION
1 Penn Plz Ste 1924 (10119-1924)
PHONE...............................212 845-8200
David R Guyer, *Ch of Bd*
Glenn P Sblendorio, *President*
Keith Westby, *COO*
Loni Dasilva, *Senior VP*
Barbara A Wood, *Senior VP*
EMP: 156
SQ FT: 22,400
SALES (est): 50.9MM Privately Held
SIC: 2834 Pharmaceutical preparations

(G-11530)
OPPOSUITS USA INC
228 E 45th St Ste 9e (10017-3303)
PHONE...............................917 438-8878
Jelle Van Der Zwet, *President*
Manon Lisbet, *CFO*
Edward Lenting, *Manager*
EMP: 25
SALES: 6MM Privately Held
SIC: 2311 2337 Men's & boys' suits & coats; women's & misses' suits & skirts

(G-11531)
ORACLE CORPORATION
120 Park Ave Fl 26 (10017-5511)
PHONE...............................212 508-7700
David Chow, *Project Mgr*
Tony Cassa, *Engineer*
Jamie Davis, *Sales Mgr*
Art Staple, *Accounts Exec*
Samantha Rugani, *Sr Consultant*
EMP: 250
SALES (corp-wide): 37.7B Publicly Held
WEB: www.forcecapital.com
SIC: 7372 Business oriented computer software
PA: Oracle Corporation
500 Oracle Pkwy
Redwood City CA 94065
650 506-7000

(G-11532)
ORANGENIUS INC
115 W 18th St Fl 2 (10011-4119)
PHONE...............................631 742-0648
Grace Cho, *CEO*
Robert Schlackman, *CTO*
EMP: 16 EST: 2015

SALES (est): 456.4K Privately Held
SIC: 7372 Business oriented computer software

(G-11533)
ORBIS BRYNMORE LITHOGRAPHICS
1735 2nd Ave Frnt 1 (10128-3516)
PHONE...............................212 987-2100
Fax: 212 987-1520
Ceasar Romero, *President*
Anna Romero, *Admin Sec*
EMP: 8 EST: 1932
SALES (est): 1.1MM Privately Held
SIC: 2752 Commercial printing, offset

(G-11534)
ORCAM INC
1350 Broadway Rm 1600 (10018-0904)
PHONE...............................800 713-3741
Rhys Filmer, *President*
EMP: 10
SALES (est): 623.2K Privately Held
SIC: 3842 Technical aids for the handicapped

(G-11535)
ORCHARD APPAREL GROUP LTD
212 W 35th St Fl 7 (10001-2508)
PHONE...............................212 268-8701
Robert Fox, *President*
EMP: 5
SALES (est): 308.5K
SALES (corp-wide): 51.2MM Privately Held
WEB: www.robertfox.com
SIC: 2331 Blouses, women's & juniors': made from purchased material
PA: Robert Fox Inc.
79 Main St
Mineola NY 11501
516 294-2678

(G-11536)
ORCHID MANUFACTURING CO INC
Also Called: Jessica Michelle
77 W 55th St Apt 4k (10019-4920)
PHONE...............................212 840-5700
Michael Laufer, *Ch of Bd*
Michael H Laufer, *President*
Richard Weiss, *Controller*
EMP: 10 EST: 1983
SALES (est): 980K Privately Held
SIC: 2331 Women's & misses' blouses & shirts

(G-11537)
OREGE NORTH AMERICA INC (PA)
575 Madison Ave Fl 25 (10022-8509)
PHONE...............................770 862-9388
Kevin Dunlap, *Vice Pres*
Priscilla Brooks, *Office Mgr*
Jonathan Lapin, *Admin Sec*
EMP: 1 EST: 2014
SALES: 1MM Privately Held
SIC: 3589 Sewage treatment equipment

(G-11538)
ORENS DAILY ROAST INC (PA)
12 E 46th St Fl 6 (10017-2418)
PHONE...............................212 348-5400
Oren Bloostein, *President*
Vijay Rajwani, *Human Resources*
Shirley Bethe, *Administration*
▲ EMP: 7
SQ FT: 400
SALES (est): 13.7MM Privately Held
SIC: 2095 5149 5499 Instant coffee; coffee, green or roasted; coffee

(G-11539)
ORION FASHIONS HOLDINGS LLC
390 5th Ave (10018-8104)
PHONE...............................212 764-3332
Brett Fialkoff, *Vice Chairman*
Nirmal Thapa, *Consultant*
EMP: 50
SALES (est): 1.5MM Privately Held
SIC: 3961 Costume jewelry

(G-11540)
ORPHEO USA CORP
315 Madison Ave Rm 2601 (10017-5410)
PHONE.....................212 464-8255
Alain Eisenstein, *CEO*
Jason Grassi, *Manager*
Linda Mazeyrie, *Manager*
EMP: 5
SALES (est): 674.9K **Privately Held**
SIC: 3695 7371 Audio range tape, blank; computer software development & applications

(G-11541)
ORTHO MEDICAL PRODUCTS (PA)
315 E 83rd St (10028-4301)
P.O. Box 847617, Dallas TX (75284-7617)
PHONE.....................212 879-3700
Jane Wilde, *President*
EMP: 13 **EST:** 1944
SQ FT: 7,500
SALES (est): 1.5MM **Privately Held**
SIC: 3841 3842 5999 Surgical & medical instruments; orthopedic appliances; orthopedic & prosthesis applications

(G-11542)
OS33 INC
16 W 22nd St Fl 6 (10010-5969)
PHONE.....................708 336-3466
Jacob Kazakevich, *President*
Aron Derstine, *Vice Pres*
Matt Haynes, *VP Opers*
Henry Tejada, *Technology*
James Deflumeri, *Business Dir*
EMP: 6
SALES (est): 4.3MM **Privately Held**
SIC: 7372 7371 Prepackaged software; computer software development; computer software development & applications; computer software systems analysis & design, custom
PA: Os33 Services Corp.
  120 Wood Ave S Ste 505
  Iselin NJ 08830
  866 796-0310

(G-11543)
OSCAR HEYMAN & BROS INC (PA)
501 Madison Ave Fl 15 (10022-5676)
PHONE.....................212 593-0400
Fax: 212 759-8612
Marvin Heyman, *President*
Adam Heyman, *Vice Pres*
Thomas Heyman, *Treasurer*
Whitney Wenk, *Sales Staff*
Lewis Heyman, *Admin Sec*
EMP: 28 **EST:** 1912
SQ FT: 12,000
SALES (est): 4.5MM **Privately Held**
WEB: www.oscarheyman.com
SIC: 3911 Jewelry, precious metal

(G-11544)
OSNAT GAD INC
Also Called: Ogi Limited
608 5th Ave Ste 609 (10020-2303)
PHONE.....................212 957-0535
Fax: 212 957-0534
Osnat Gad, *President*
Ed Kozin, *CPA*
EMP: 7
SQ FT: 1,450
SALES (est): 780K **Privately Held**
WEB: www.ogi-ltd.com
SIC: 3911 Jewelry, precious metal

(G-11545)
OSPREY PUBLISHING INC
1385 Broadway Fl 5 (10018-6050)
PHONE.....................212 419-5300
Rebecca Smart, *Principal*
▲ **EMP:** 9
SALES (est): 518K **Privately Held**
SIC: 2741 Miscellaneous publishing

(G-11546)
OTHER PRESS LLC
267 5th Ave Fl 6 (10016-7508)
PHONE.....................212 414-0054
Judith Gurewich, *CEO*
Paul Kozlowski, *Publisher*
Corinna Barsan, *Editor*
Amanda Glassman, *Editor*
Yvonne Cardenas, *Production*
EMP: 8
SALES (est): 1.2MM **Privately Held**
WEB: www.otherpress.com
SIC: 2731 Book publishing

(G-11547)
OTIS ELEVATOR COMPANY
1 Penn Plz Ste 410 (10119-0499)
PHONE.....................917 339-9600
Fax: 917 339-9677
Ben Petruzzella, *Manager*
EMP: 33
SALES (corp-wide): 57.2B **Publicly Held**
SIC: 3534 1796 7699 Elevators & equipment; escalators, passenger & freight; walkways, moving; installing building equipment; elevator installation & conversion; miscellaneous building item repair services; elevators: inspection, service & repair
HQ: Otis Elevator Company
  1 Carrier Pl
  Farmington CT 06032
  860 674-3000

(G-11548)
OUTERSTUFF LLC (PA)
1412 Broadway Fl 18 (10018-9258)
PHONE.....................212 594-9700
Fax: 212 239-4268
Sol Werdiger, *CEO*
Samuel Meyer, *President*
Ron Reinisch, *COO*
Gina Dinello, *Production*
Jonah Blumenfrucht, *CFO*
▲ **EMP:** 30
SALES: 304MM **Privately Held**
SIC: 2369 2339 5137 Girls' & children's outerwear; women's & misses' outerwear; women's & children's outerwear

(G-11549)
OVERTURE MEDIA INC
411 Lafayette St Ste 638 (10003-7032)
PHONE.....................917 446-7455
Jared Weiss, *CEO*
EMP: 7 **EST:** 2014
SQ FT: 153
SALES (est): 314K **Privately Held**
SIC: 7372 Prepackaged software

(G-11550)
OVID THERAPEUTICS INC
1460 Broadway Fl 4 (10036-7328)
PHONE.....................646 661-7661
Jeremy M Levin, *Ch of Bd*
Matthew During, *President*
Dirk Haasner, *Senior VP*
Ana C Ward, *Senior VP*
Yaron Werber, *CFO*
EMP: 31
SALES (est): 4.4MM **Privately Held**
SIC: 2834 Pharmaceutical preparations

(G-11551)
OXFORD BOOK COMPANY INC
9 Pine St (10005-4701)
PHONE.....................212 227-2120
William Dinger, *President*
Jim Omalley, *Info Tech Mgr*
EMP: 150
SALES (est): 5.8MM
SALES (corp-wide): 50.6MM **Privately Held**
WEB: www.sadlier.com
SIC: 2731 Textbooks: publishing only, not printed on site
PA: William H. Sadlier, Inc.
  9 Pine St
  New York NY 10005
  212 233-3646

(G-11552)
OXFORD CLEANERS
847 Lexington Ave Frnt (10065-6636)
PHONE.....................212 734-0006
Joong Lee, *Owner*
EMP: 5
SALES (est): 280K **Privately Held**
SIC: 3589 7215 Commercial cleaning equipment; coin-operated laundries & cleaning

(G-11553)
OXFORD INDUSTRIES INC
Also Called: Lanier Clothes
600 5th Ave Fl 12 (10020-2325)
PHONE.....................212 247-7712
Fax: 212 586-8825
Tracy Hunt, *Accounting Mgr*
Alan Rubin, *Branch Mgr*
Kerry Johnston, *Manager*
Elissa Golub, *Admin Asst*
EMP: 25
SALES (corp-wide): 1B **Publicly Held**
SIC: 2329 Athletic (warmup, sweat & jogging) suits: men's & boys'
PA: Oxford Industries, Inc.
  999 Peachtree St Ne # 688
  Atlanta GA 30309
  404 659-2424

(G-11554)
OXFORD INDUSTRIES INC
25 W 39th St (10018-3805)
PHONE.....................212 840-2288
Fran Hicks, *Manager*
EMP: 14
SALES (corp-wide): 1B **Publicly Held**
WEB: www.oxm.com
SIC: 2321 Men's & boys' furnishings
PA: Oxford Industries, Inc.
  999 Peachtree St Ne # 688
  Atlanta GA 30309
  404 659-2424

(G-11555)
OXFORD UNIVERSITY PRESS LLC (HQ)
Also Called: Oxford University Press, Inc.
198 Madison Ave Fl 8 (10016-4308)
PHONE.....................212 726-6000
Fax: 212 726-6457
Niko Pfund, *President*
Vineeta Gupta, *Publisher*
Sharon Sargent, *Publisher*
Laura Pearson, *General Mgr*
Ameena Saiyid, *Managing Dir*
◆ **EMP:** 265 **EST:** 1973
SQ FT: 145,000
SALES (est): 141.6MM
SALES (est): 1.5B **Privately Held**
SIC: 2731 5961 Book publishing; book & record clubs
PA: University Of Oxford
  University Offices
  Oxford OXON OX1 2
  186 527-0000

(G-11556)
OXFORD UNIVERSITY PRESS LLC
Chancellor Masters & Scholrs
198 Madison Ave Fl 8 (10016-4308)
PHONE.....................212 726-6000
Giles Kerr, *Finance*
Malcolm Fairbrother, *Manager*
EMP: 8
SALES (corp-wide): 1.5B **Privately Held**
SIC: 2731 5961 Book publishing; book & record clubs
HQ: Oxford University Press, Llc
  198 Madison Ave Fl 8
  New York NY 10016
  212 726-6000

(G-11557)
OXO INTERNATIONAL INC
601 W 26th St Rm 1050 (10001-1148)
PHONE.....................212 242-3333
Alex Lee, *President*
Michael Delevante, *Vice Pres*
Todd Cutsuries, *QC Mgr*
Tiffany Chen, *Engineer*
Matthew Dolph, *Engineer*
▲ **EMP:** 110
SQ FT: 2,500
SALES (est): 14MM **Privately Held**
SIC: 3631 3469 5099 Household cooking equipment; household cooking & kitchen utensils, metal; baby carriages, strollers & related products
PA: Helen Of Troy Limited
  C/O Conyers, Dill & Pearman
  Hamilton HM 11

(G-11558)
OZMODYL LTD
Also Called: Soho and Tribeca Map
233 Broadway Rm 707 (10279-0705)
PHONE.....................212 226-0622
EMP: 5
SALES (est): 550K **Privately Held**
SIC: 2731 Publish A Map And Guide Book Of The Soho And Tribeca Area

(G-11559)
P & I SPORTSWEAR INC
384 5th Ave (10018-8103)
PHONE.....................718 934-4587
Ignacio Bursztyn, *President*
Flora Bursztyn, *Vice Pres*
EMP: 5
SALES (est): 1.2MM **Privately Held**
SIC: 2339 2329 Women's & misses' athletic clothing & sportswear; athletic; men's & boys' sportswear & athletic clothing

(G-11560)
P & W PRESS INC
20 W 22nd St Ste 710 (10010-5877)
PHONE.....................646 486-3417
Fax: 212 929-2822
Philip Foxman, *President*
Keith Foxman, *Vice Pres*
Anita Foxman, *Sales Mgr*
EMP: 20
SQ FT: 3,000
SALES (est): 1.8MM **Privately Held**
WEB: www.pwpress.com
SIC: 2752 2759 Commercial printing, offset; letterpress printing

(G-11561)
P E GUERIN (PA)
23 Jane St (10014-1999)
PHONE.....................212 243-5270
Fax: 212 727-2290
Andrew F Ward, *President*
Martin Grubman, *General Mgr*
Candice Cudanes, *Production*
Lila Tublin, *Admin Asst*
◆ **EMP:** 69 **EST:** 1857
SALES (est): 6.5MM **Privately Held**
WEB: www.peguerin.com
SIC: 3429 5072 3432 5074 Door locks, bolts & checks; builders' hardware; plumbing fixture fittings & trim; plumbing fittings & supplies; drapery hardware & blinds & shades; window covering parts & accessories

(G-11562)
PACE EDITIONS INC (PA)
Also Called: Pace Prints
32 E 57th St Fl 3 (10022-8573)
PHONE.....................212 421-3237
Fax: 212 751-7280
Richard H Solomon, *President*
Jason Schroeder, *VP Opers*
Carlo Bella, *Director*
Kristin Heming, *Director*
Chantal Salomon-Lee, *Associate Dir*
EMP: 21 **EST:** 1968
SQ FT: 10,000
SALES (est): 2.1MM **Privately Held**
WEB: www.paceprints.com
SIC: 2741 7999 Art copy & poster publishing; art gallery, commercial

(G-11563)
PACE EDITIONS INC
44 W 18th St Fl 5 (10011-4644)
PHONE.....................212 675-7431
Richard Soloman, *President*
Kristin Heming, *Director*
Jacob Lewis, *Director*
EMP: 5
SALES (corp-wide): 2.1MM **Privately Held**
WEB: www.paceprints.com
SIC: 2752 2759 2741 Commercial printing, lithographic; commercial printing; miscellaneous publishing
PA: Pace Editions, Inc.
  32 E 57th St Fl 3
  New York NY 10022
  212 421-3237

New York - New York County (G-11564)

(G-11564)
PACIFIC ALLIANCE USA INC
350 5th Ave Fl 5 (10118-0110)
PHONE..................................336 500-8184
Jim Guido, *Regl Sales Mgr*
EMP: 8 **Privately Held**
SIC: 2339 Women's & misses' outerwear
HQ: Pacific Alliance Usa, Inc.
350 5th Ave Lbby 9
New York NY 10118

(G-11565)
PACIFIC ALLIANCE USA INC (DH)
350 5th Ave Lbby 9 (10118-0109)
PHONE..................................646 839-7000
Bruce Philip Rockowitz, *CEO*
Dow Famulak, *President*
Richard Darling, *Principal*
Ron Ventricelli, *COO*
▲ **EMP:** 40
SALES (est): 21.8MM **Privately Held**
SIC: 2339 Women's & misses' outerwear
HQ: Gbg Usa Inc.
350 5th Ave Lbby 9
New York NY 10118
646 839-7000

(G-11566)
PACIFIC CITY INTERNATIONAL
265 W 37th St (10018-5707)
PHONE..................................646 309-1250
Feng Tao, *President*
EMP: 11
SQ FT: 3,000
SALES (est): 7MM **Privately Held**
SIC: 2211 Apparel & outerwear fabrics, cotton

(G-11567)
PACIFIC WORLDWIDE INC
20 W 33rd St Fl 11 (10001-3305)
PHONE..................................212 502-3360
Martin Terzian, *President*
Ronald J Herro, *Vice Pres*
▲ **EMP:** 15
SALES (est): 2.1MM **Privately Held**
SIC: 3111 Accessory products, leather

(G-11568)
PACK AMERICA CORP (HQ)
108 W 39th St Fl 16 (10018-8255)
PHONE..................................212 508-6666
Hisao Ueda, *President*
Frank Rizzo, *Exec VP*
Haruyuki Kochi, *Vice Pres*
Steve Walker, *Prdtn Mgr*
Pam Holmes, *Financial Exec*
▲ **EMP:** 4
SQ FT: 3,100
SALES (est): 6.3MM
SALES (corp-wide): 805.8MM **Privately Held**
WEB: www.packdash.com
SIC: 2673 2679 Plastic bags: made from purchased materials; paper products, converted
PA: The Pack Corporation
2-9-9, Higashiobase, Higashinari-Ku
Osaka OSK 537-0
669 721-221

(G-11569)
PALETOT LTD
Also Called: Patricia Underwood
499 Fashion Ave Rm 25s (10018-6847)
PHONE..................................212 268-3774
Judy Hummel, *President*
Patricia Underwood, *Chairman*
EMP: 11
SQ FT: 1,500
SALES (est): 670K **Privately Held**
SIC: 2353 Hats & caps; millinery

(G-11570)
PALGRAVE MACMILLAN LTD
175 5th Ave Frnt 4 (10010-7728)
PHONE..................................646 307-5028
Fax: 212 307-5035
Ursula Gavin, *Publisher*
Peter Wolverton, *Publisher*
Gayatri Patnaik, *General Mgr*
Sarah Nathan, *Editor*
Andy Syson, *Business Mgr*
▲ **EMP:** 9
SALES (est): 1MM
SALES (corp-wide): 1.5B **Privately Held**
WEB: www.palgrave-usa.com
SIC: 2731 Book publishing
HQ: Macmillan Publishers Limited
Cromwell Place
Basingstoke HANTS RG24
125 632-9242

(G-11571)
PALLADIA INC
105 W 17th St (10011-5432)
PHONE..................................212 206-3669
Corinne Workman, *Manager*
EMP: 125
SALES (corp-wide): 46.4MM **Privately Held**
SIC: 3421 Table & food cutlery, including butchers'
PA: Palladia, Inc.
305 7th Ave Fl 10
New York NY 10001

(G-11572)
PAN AMERICAN LEATHERS INC (PA)
347 W 36th St Rm 1204 (10018-6480)
PHONE..................................978 741-4150
Mark Mendal, *President*
Abram Mendal, *Vice Pres*
Yania Halman, *Office Mgr*
▲ **EMP:** 3
SQ FT: 3,000
SALES (est): 1.3MM **Privately Held**
WEB: www.panamleathers.com
SIC: 3111 5199 Finishing of leather; leather goods, except footwear, gloves, luggage, belting

(G-11573)
PANGEA BRANDS LLC (PA)
6 W 20th St Fl 3 (10011-9270)
PHONE..................................617 638-0001
Corey Bradley, *Accounts Mgr*
Joshua Fink, *Mng Member*
Michael London,
Dan Miller,
Corey Kennedy, *Associate*
▲ **EMP:** 6
SQ FT: 5,000
SALES (est): 1.1MM **Privately Held**
SIC: 2396 Apparel & other linings, except millinery

(G-11574)
PANGEA BRANDS LLC
6 W 20th St Fl 3 (10011-9270)
PHONE..................................617 638-0001
Joshua Fink, *Branch Mgr*
EMP: 6
SALES (corp-wide): 1.1MM **Privately Held**
SIC: 2396 Apparel & other linings, except millinery
PA: Pangea Brands, Llc
6 W 20th St Fl 3
New York NY 10011
617 638-0001

(G-11575)
PAPA BUBBLE
380 Broome St Frnt A (10013-3799)
PHONE..................................212 966-2599
Ryan Grassi, *Owner*
EMP: 7
SALES (est): 496.8K **Privately Held**
SIC: 2064 Candy & other confectionery products

(G-11576)
PAPER BOX CORP
Also Called: Aaaaaa Creative Designs
1751 2nd Ave Apt 10a (10128-5377)
PHONE..................................212 226-7490
Robert Fleisig, *President*
EMP: 70 **EST:** 1900
SALES (est): 6.1MM **Privately Held**
SIC: 2631 2657 Folding boxboard; setup boxboard; folding paperboard boxes

(G-11577)
PAPER MAGIC GROUP INC
345 7th Ave Fl 6 (10001-5053)
PHONE..................................631 521-3682
Fax: 212 868-3648
Nathan Caldwell, *Manager*
Lane Fragomeli, *Exec Dir*
EMP: 450
SALES (corp-wide): 322.4MM **Publicly Held**
WEB: www.papermagic.com
SIC: 2771 2678 Greeting cards; stationery products
HQ: Paper Magic Group Inc.
54 Glenmra Ntl Blvd
Moosic PA 18507
570 961-3863

(G-11578)
PAPER PUBLISHING COMPANY INC
Also Called: Paper Magazine
15 E 32nd St (10016-5423)
PHONE..................................212 226-4405
Fax: 212 226-5929
David Hershkovits, *President*
Tom Guinness, *Editor*
Kim Hastreiter, *Treasurer*
Kim Hasreier, *Personnel Exec*
Erica Moore, *Manager*
EMP: 27
SQ FT: 3,000
SALES (est): 3.5MM **Privately Held**
WEB: www.papermag.com
SIC: 2721 Magazines: publishing only, not printed on site

(G-11579)
PAPERCUTZ INC
160 Broadway Rm 700e (10038-4201)
PHONE..................................646 559-4681
Terry Nantier, *President*
Jeff Whitman, *Editor*
Jim Salicrup, *Vice Pres*
Beth Scorzato, *Production*
Sven Larsen, *VP Mktg*
▲ **EMP:** 5
SALES (est): 4.5MM **Privately Held**
SIC: 2731 Book publishing

(G-11580)
PARACHUTE PUBLISHING LLC
322 8th Ave Ste 702 (10001-6791)
PHONE..................................212 337-6743
Arlene West, *Manager*
Joan Waricha,
Jane Stine,
▲ **EMP:** 30
SALES (est): 2.9MM **Privately Held**
WEB: www.parachuteproperties.com
SIC: 2731 Books: publishing only

(G-11581)
PARADE PUBLICATIONS INC (HQ)
Also Called: Parade Magazine
711 3rd Ave (10017-4014)
PHONE..................................212 450-7000
Fax: 212 450-7283
Carlo Vittorini, *CEO*
Susan Ollinick, *President*
Brad Dunn, *Editor*
Dave Barber, *Exec VP*
Jo Beddoe, *Vice Pres*
EMP: 46
SALES (est): 6.5MM
SALES (corp-wide): 354MM **Privately Held**
SIC: 2721 Periodicals: publishing only

(G-11582)
PARADIGM SPINE LLC
505 Park Ave Fl 14 (10022-1106)
PHONE..................................888 273-9897
Marc Viscigliosi, *CEO*
Gutmar Eisen, *President*
Jeremy Laynor, *President*
Albert Lee, *Counsel*
Gary Lowery, *Exec VP*
EMP: 23
SQ FT: 1,500
SALES (est): 6.3MM **Privately Held**
SIC: 3842 Implants, surgical

(G-11583)
PARAMOUNT TEXTILES INC
34 Walker St (10013-3514)
PHONE..................................212 966-1040
Fax: 212 941-1206
Steven Katz, *CEO*
Estate J Katz, *President*
Ronald Katz, *Vice Pres*
Alan Katz, *Admin Sec*
EMP: 10 **EST:** 1940
SQ FT: 15,000
SALES (est): 1.2MM **Privately Held**
WEB: www.paramounttextile.com
SIC: 2392 5023 5047 Household furnishings; linens & towels; linens, table; surgical equipment & supplies

(G-11584)
PARENTS GUIDE NETWORK CORP
Also Called: P G Media
419 Park Ave S Rm 505 (10016-8410)
PHONE..................................212 213-8840
Fax: 212 447-7734
Steve Elgort, *President*
Donald McDermott, *Editor*
EMP: 25
SALES (est): 2.4MM **Privately Held**
WEB: www.parentguidenews.com
SIC: 2721 8351 Magazines: publishing only, not printed on site; child day care services

(G-11585)
PARETEUM CORPORATION
100 Park Ave (10017-5516)
PHONE..................................212 984-1096
Victor Bozzo, *CEO*
Robert H Turner, *Ch of Bd*
Edward O'Donnell, *CFO*
Alexander Korff, *Ch Credit Ofcr*
Erik Kloots,
EMP: 62
SALES: 12.8MM **Privately Held**
SIC: 7372 Prepackaged software

(G-11586)
PARIS WEDDING CENTER CORP
45 E Broadway Fl 2 (10002-6804)
PHONE..................................212 267-8088
Yuki Lin, *Branch Mgr*
EMP: 26
SALES (corp-wide): 1.6MM **Privately Held**
SIC: 2335 Wedding gowns & dresses
PA: Paris Wedding Center Corp.
42-53 42 55 Main St
Flushing NY 11355
347 368-4085

(G-11587)
PARK ASSIST LLC
57 W 38th St Fl 11 (10018-1296)
PHONE..................................646 666-7525
Itay Levy, *VP Opers*
Gaby Eini, *Opers Mgr*
Lizzie Burger, *Mktg Coord*
Gary Neff, *Mng Member*
Gary Nef, *Mng Member*
▲ **EMP:** 70
SALES (est): 1.2MM **Privately Held**
WEB: www.parkassist.com
SIC: 3559 Parking facility equipment & supplies

(G-11588)
PARK WEST JEWELERY INC
565 W End Ave Apt 8b (10024-2734)
PHONE..................................646 329-6145
Fax: 212 768-8608
Dale Bearman, *President*
EMP: 6
SQ FT: 900
SALES (est): 490K **Privately Held**
SIC: 3911 Jewelry apparel

(G-11589)
PARKER WARBY RETAIL INC (PA)
Also Called: Warby Parker Eyewear
161 Ave Of The Amer Fl 6f (10013-1205)
PHONE..................................646 517-5223
Neil Blumenthal, *CEO*
Dave Gilboa, *CEO*
Andy Hunt, *Partner*
Chris Roth, *General Mgr*
Janny Wang, *Project Mgr*
▲ **EMP:** 34
SALES (est): 16.5MM **Privately Held**
SIC: 3851 5995 Eyeglasses, lenses & frames; optical goods stores

GEOGRAPHIC SECTION

New York - New York County (G-11614)

(G-11590)
PARLOR LABS INC
Also Called: Ponder
515 W 19th St (10011-2872)
PHONE..................866 801-7323
Alexander Selkirk, *President*
EMP: 5
SALES (est): 236K **Privately Held**
SIC: 7372 8748 Educational computer software; systems engineering consultant, ex. computer or professional

(G-11591)
PASABAHCE USA
41 Madison Ave Fl 7 (10010-2202)
PHONE..................212 683-1600
Neil M Orzeck, *Manager*
Martin Anderson, *Director*
▲ **EMP:** 4
SALES (est): 25MM **Privately Held**
SIC: 3229 Art, decorative & novelty glassware

(G-11592)
PASSPORT BRANDS INC (PA)
240 Madison Ave Fl 8 (10016-2878)
PHONE..................646 459-2625
Fax: 646 459-2633
Robert S Stec, *CEO*
Robert Arnot, *President*
Liviu Goldenberg, *Vice Pres*
Timothy J Tumminello, *Vice Pres*
Robert Flynn, *Security Mgr*
◆ **EMP:** 35
SQ FT: 13,500
SALES (est): 7MM **Publicly Held**
WEB: www.icisaacs.com
SIC: 2325 2339 Jeans: men's, youths' & boys'; slacks, dress: men's, youths' & boys'; shorts (outerwear): men's, youths' & boys'; jeans: women's, misses' & juniors'; slacks: women's, misses' & juniors'; shorts (outerwear): women's, misses' & juniors'

(G-11593)
PAT & ROSE DRESS INC
327 W 36th St Rm 3a (10018-7014)
PHONE..................212 279-1357
Fax: 212 279-1413
Rosalia Panebianco, *President*
Maria Milanova, *Bookkeeper*
Pat Capolupo, *Manager*
EMP: 60
SQ FT: 5,000
SALES (est): 3.6MM **Privately Held**
SIC: 2335 2331 2337 2339 Women's, juniors' & misses' dresses; blouses, women's & juniors': made from purchased material; skirts, separate: women's, misses & juniors'; women's & misses' outerwear; men's & boys' trousers & slacks; men's & boys' suits & coats

(G-11594)
PATMIAN LLC
655 Madison Ave Fl 24 (10065-8043)
PHONE..................212 758-0770
George Botis, *Chairman*
EMP: 350
SALES (est): 19.9MM **Privately Held**
SIC: 3089 3544 Plastic processing; injection molded finished plastic products; special dies, tools, jigs & fixtures

(G-11595)
PATRA LTD
Stenay
318 W 39th St Fl 2 (10018-1496)
PHONE..................212 764-6575
George Beck, *Manager*
Paul Kitos, *Manager*
EMP: 10
SALES (corp-wide): 7.3MM **Privately Held**
SIC: 2335 Gowns, formal
PA: Patra Ltd.
318 W 39th St
New York NY 10018
212 764-6575

(G-11596)
PATRA LTD
Also Called: La Nuit Collection
318 W 39th St (10018-1407)
PHONE..................212 764-6575
Fax: 212 768-7862
Pat Dipietroantonio, *President*
EMP: 10
SALES (corp-wide): 7.3MM **Privately Held**
SIC: 2335 Women's, juniors' & misses' dresses
PA: Patra Ltd.
318 W 39th St
New York NY 10018
212 764-6575

(G-11597)
PATRA LTD (PA)
318 W 39th St (10018-1407)
PHONE..................212 764-6575
Fax: 212 268-6838
Paquale Di Pietrantonio, *CEO*
Pat Di Pietrantonio, *President*
Timothy M Sinatro, *Treasurer*
George C Beck, *Admin Sec*
▲ **EMP:** 20
SALES (est): 7.3MM **Privately Held**
SIC: 2335 Gowns, formal

(G-11598)
PATRON TECHNOLOGY INC
850 7th Ave Ste 704 (10019-5230)
PHONE..................212 271-4328
Eugene Carr, *President*
Lily Traub, *President*
Lorna Dolci, *General Mgr*
Robert Friend, *Vice Pres*
Ling Leung, *Bookkeeper*
EMP: 7
SQ FT: 800
SALES (est): 1.1MM **Privately Held**
WEB: www.patrontech.com
SIC: 7372 Prepackaged software

(G-11599)
PAUL DAVID ENTERPRISES INC
19 W 34th St Rm 1018 (10001-3006)
PHONE..................646 667-5530
Daniel Koroiev, *Vice Pres*
EMP: 9 EST: 2013
SALES (est): 356.2K **Privately Held**
SIC: 2431 Jalousies, glass, wood frame

(G-11600)
PAULA DORF COSMETICS INC
850 7th Ave Ste 801 (10019-5446)
PHONE..................212 582-0073
Sandy Dekovnick, *CEO*
Sandy De Kovnick, *CEO*
Paula Dorf, *President*
Lindsay Santlas, *Manager*
▲ **EMP:** 30
SALES (est): 4.2MM **Privately Held**
WEB: www.pauladorf.com
SIC: 2844 5122 Toilet preparations; cosmetics, perfumes & hair products

(G-11601)
PAULA VARSALONA LTD
552 Fashion Ave Rm 602 (10018-3239)
PHONE..................212 570-9100
Fax: 212 869-9566
Paula Varsalona, *President*
EMP: 15
SQ FT: 5,000
SALES (est): 1.3MM **Privately Held**
WEB: www.paulavarsalona.com
SIC: 2335 2396 Wedding gowns & dresses; veils & veiling: bridal, funeral, etc.

(G-11602)
PAVANA USA INC
10 W 33rd St Rm 408 (10001-3306)
P.O. Box 237191 (10023-0033)
PHONE..................646 833-8811
Avisha Uttamchandani, *President*
Toni Hazzard, *Vice Pres*
Bhavik Patel, *Accountant*
◆ **EMP:** 5
SALES (est): 1MM **Privately Held**
SIC: 3873 Watches, clocks, watchcases & parts

(G-11603)
PAVMED INC
60 E 42nd St Fl 46 (10165-0043)
PHONE..................212 401-1951
Dennis M McGrath, *CFO*

EMP: 5
SALES (est): 347.2K **Privately Held**
SIC: 3841 Surgical & medical instruments

(G-11604)
PEANUT BUTTER & CO INC
119 W 57th St Ste 300 (10019-2302)
P.O. Box 2000 (10101-2000)
PHONE..................212 757-3130
Lee E Zalben, *President*
Paul Prusienky, *Accounts Mgr*
▲ **EMP:** 25
SALES (est): 5.5MM **Privately Held**
WEB: www.ilovepeanutbutter.com
SIC: 2099 Peanut butter

(G-11605)
PEARL ERWIN INC (PA)
389 5th Ave Rm 1100 (10016-3350)
PHONE..................212 889-7410
Fax: 212 889-3076
Erwin Pearl, *President*
Michael Elswit, *Vice Pres*
Joel Weinstein, *CFO*
Anita Rosenberg, *Manager*
EMP: 30
SALES (est): 31.6MM **Privately Held**
SIC: 3961 3911 Costume jewelry; jewelry, precious metal

(G-11606)
PEARL ERWIN INC
300 Madison Ave Frnt 1 (10017-6250)
PHONE..................212 883-0650
Erwin Pearl, *President*
EMP: 33
SALES (corp-wide): 31.6MM **Privately Held**
SIC: 3961 Costume jewelry
PA: Pearl Erwin Inc
389 5th Ave Rm 1100
New York NY 10016
212 889-7410

(G-11607)
PEARSON EDUCATION INC
1185 Avenue Of The Americ (10036-2601)
PHONE..................212 782-3337
Fax: 212 782-3394
Roth Wilkofsky, *President*
EMP: 16
SALES (corp-wide): 5.6B **Privately Held**
WEB: www.phgenit.com
SIC: 2731 Book publishing
HQ: Pearson Education, Inc.
221 River St
Hoboken NJ 07030
201 236-7000

(G-11608)
PEARSON EDUCATION INC
375 Hudson St (10014-3658)
PHONE..................212 366-2000
Tom Altier, *Branch Mgr*
EMP: 27
SALES (corp-wide): 5.6B **Privately Held**
WEB: www.phgenit.com
SIC: 2731 Book publishing
HQ: Pearson Education, Inc.
221 River St
Hoboken NJ 07030
201 236-7000

(G-11609)
PEARSON EDUCATION HOLDINGS INC (HQ)
330 Hudson St Fl 9 (10013-1048)
PHONE..................201 236-6716
Will Ethridge, *President*
Jim Tognolini, *Managing Dir*
Paul Crockett, *Editor*
Steve Temblett, *Editor*
Michelle West, *Editor*
▲ **EMP:** 2000 EST: 1998
SQ FT: 475,000
SALES (est): 3.7B
SALES (corp-wide): 5.6B **Privately Held**
WEB: www.pearsoned.com
SIC: 2731 Textbooks: publishing & printing
PA: Pearson Plc
80 Strand
London WC2R
207 010-2000

(G-11610)
PEARSON INC (HQ)
1330 Hudson St (10013)
PHONE..................212 641-2400
Fax: 212 641-2500
John Fallon, *CEO*
Fred Becker, *General Mgr*
Boone Novy, *Principal*
Glen Moreno, *Chairman*
Christopher Howard, *Business Mgr*
▼ **EMP:** 58
SALES (est): 2.3B
SALES (corp-wide): 5.6B **Privately Held**
SIC: 2711 2731 Newspapers; books: publishing & printing; textbooks: publishing & printing
PA: Pearson Plc
80 Strand
London WC2R
207 010-2000

(G-11611)
PEARSON LONGMAN LLC
51 Madison Ave Fl 27 (10010-1609)
PHONE..................917 981-2200
Bruce Styron, *Facilities Mgr*
Roth Wilkofsky, *Manager*
EMP: 120
SALES (corp-wide): 5.6B **Privately Held**
SIC: 2731 Books: publishing & printing
HQ: Pearson Longman Llc
10 Bank St Ste 1030
White Plains NY 10606
212 641-2400

(G-11612)
PEEK A BOO USA INC
Also Called: Beaba USA
555 8th Ave Rm 403 (10018-4383)
PHONE..................201 533-8700
Lisa Speransky, *CEO*
Isabel Martinez, *Manager*
▲ **EMP:** 5
SQ FT: 1,200
SALES (est): 633.7K
SALES (corp-wide): 104.4MM **Privately Held**
SIC: 3089 3634 Plastic kitchenware, tableware & houseware; electric household cooking appliances
HQ: Beaba
31 Avenue De L Opera
Paris 75001
474 120-910

(G-11613)
PEER INTERNATIONAL CORP (HQ)
Also Called: 3239603400 La Head Quarters
250 W 57th St Ste 820 (10107-0814)
PHONE..................212 265-3910
Ralph Peer II, *President*
Elizabeth W Peer, *Vice Pres*
Cecile Russo, *Vice Pres*
Kathryn Spanberger, *Vice Pres*
Todd Vunderink, *Vice Pres*
▲ **EMP:** 30
SQ FT: 11,448
SALES (est): 2.9MM
SALES (corp-wide): 10.1MM **Privately Held**
SIC: 2741 Music books: publishing only, not printed on site
PA: Southern Music Publishing Co., Inc.
810 7th Ave Fl 36
New York NY 10019
212 265-3910

(G-11614)
PEER-SOUTHERN PRODUCTIONS INC (HQ)
250 W 57th St (10107-0001)
PHONE..................212 265-3910
Ralph Peer II, *President*
Mariano Hegi, *Marketing Staff*
Marilyn La Vine, *Admin Sec*
EMP: 30 EST: 1961
SALES (est): 1.7MM
SALES (corp-wide): 10.1MM **Privately Held**
SIC: 3652 Master records or tapes, preparation of
PA: Southern Music Publishing Co., Inc.
810 7th Ave Fl 36
New York NY 10019
212 265-3910

New York - New York County (G-11615) — GEOGRAPHIC SECTION

(G-11615)
PEERMUSIC III LTD (PA)
250 W 57th St Ste 820 (10107-0814)
PHONE 212 265-3910
EMP: 15 EST: 2013
SALES (est): 1.1MM **Privately Held**
SIC: 2741 Music books: publishing only, not printed on site

(G-11616)
PEERMUSIC LTD (HQ)
250 W 57th St Ste 820 (10107-0814)
PHONE 212 265-3910
Ralph Peer II, *President*
Elizabeth W Peer, *Vice Pres*
Cecile Russo, *Vice Pres*
Katheryn Spanberger, *Vice Pres*
Craig Currier, *Director*
EMP: 10
SQ FT: 1,000
SALES (est): 4MM
SALES (corp-wide): 10.1MM **Privately Held**
WEB: www.digitalpressure.com
SIC: 2741 7922 Music books: publishing only, not printed on site; theatrical producers & services
PA: Southern Music Publishing Co., Inc.
810 7th Ave Fl 36
New York NY 10019
212 265-3910

(G-11617)
PEFIN TECHNOLOGIES LLC
39 W 32nd St Rm 1500 (10001-3841)
PHONE 917 715-3720
Ramya Joseph, *CEO*
Catherine Flax, *CEO*
EMP: 10
SALES (est): 322.7K **Privately Held**
SIC: 7372 Application computer software

(G-11618)
PEGASUS BOOKS NY LTD
148 W 37th St Fl 13 (10018-6976)
PHONE 646 343-9502
EMP: 5
SALES: 500K **Privately Held**
SIC: 2731 Book publishing

(G-11619)
PEGASYSTEMS INC
1120 Ave Of The Americas (10036-6700)
PHONE 212 626-6550
Fax: 212 626-6966
Beth Saperstein, *Branch Mgr*
EMP: 25
SALES (corp-wide): 750.2MM **Publicly Held**
WEB: www.pega.com
SIC: 7372 7379 Business oriented computer software; computer related consulting services
PA: Pegasystems Inc.
1 Rogers St
Cambridge MA 02142
617 374-9600

(G-11620)
PELOTON INTERACTIVE INC (PA)
125 W 25th St Fl 11 (10001-7232)
PHONE 866 650-1996
John Foley, *CEO*
William Lynch, *President*
Graham Stanton, *President*
Thomas Cortese, *COO*
Ben Holstein, *Vice Pres*
▲ EMP: 50
SQ FT: 9,000
SALES (est): 15.2MM **Privately Held**
SIC: 3949 Gymnasium equipment

(G-11621)
PENGUIN RANDOM HOUSE LLC
1540 Broadway (10036-4039)
PHONE 212 782-1000
Markus Dohle, *CEO*
Jurand Honisch, *Senior VP*
Henrik Pahls, *Senior VP*
Jacqueline Chasey, *Vice Pres*
Peter Muller, *Vice Pres*
EMP: 25
SALES (corp-wide): 17.9B **Privately Held**
SIC: 2731 Book publishing
HQ: Penguin Random House Llc
1745 Broadway
New York NY 10019
212 782-9000

(G-11622)
PENGUIN RANDOM HOUSE LLC (HQ)
1745 Broadway (10019-4640)
PHONE 212 782-9000
Markus Dohle, *CEO*
Madeline McIntosh, *President*
Coram Williams, *CFO*
Emily Bestler, *Director*
Devin Guinn, *Director*
EMP: 277
SALES (est): 1.4B
SALES (corp-wide): 17.9B **Privately Held**
SIC: 2731 Books: publishing only
PA: Bertelsmann Se & Co. Kgaa
Carl-Bertelsmann-Str. 270
Gutersloh 33335
524 180-0

(G-11623)
PENGUIN RANDOM HOUSE LLC
1745 Broadway Frnt 3 (10019-4641)
PHONE 212 572-6162
Markus Dohle, *CEO*
EMP: 513
SALES (corp-wide): 17.9B **Privately Held**
SIC: 2731 5942 Books: publishing only; book stores
HQ: Penguin Random House Llc
1745 Broadway
New York NY 10019
212 782-9000

(G-11624)
PENGUIN RANDOM HOUSE LLC
1745 Broadway Frnt 3 (10019-4641)
PHONE 212 782-9000
Markus Dohle, *CEO*
EMP: 1000
SALES (corp-wide): 17.9B **Privately Held**
SIC: 2731 Books: publishing only
HQ: Penguin Random House Llc
1745 Broadway
New York NY 10019
212 782-9000

(G-11625)
PENHOUSE MEDIA GROUP INC (PA)
11 Penn Plz Fl 12 (10001-2027)
PHONE 212 702-6000
Fax: 212 702-6262
John Prebich, *President*
Claude Bertin, *Exec VP*
Nina Guccione, *Exec VP*
Hal Halpner, *Exec VP*
Hope Brick, *Vice Pres*
▲ EMP: 150
SALES (est): 11.5MM **Privately Held**
SIC: 2721 5999 6512 6794 Magazines: publishing only, not printed on site; art dealers; commercial & industrial building operation; copyright buying & licensing

(G-11626)
PENSIONS & INVESTMENTS
Also Called: P&I, Pper P I Daily P I People
711 3rd Ave (10017-4014)
PHONE 212 210-0763
William T Bisson Jr, *Principal*
EMP: 43
SALES (est): 3.7MM **Privately Held**
SIC: 2721 Magazines: publishing & printing

(G-11627)
PENTON MEDIA INC (DH)
Also Called: Penton Media - Aviation Week
1166 Avenue Of The Americ (10036-2743)
PHONE 212 204-4200
Fax: 212 206-3622
David Kieselstein, *Ch of Bd*
Sandi Brown, *President*
Paul Miller, *President*
Francine Brasseur, *Publisher*
Bill Rodman, *Publisher*
▲ EMP: 500 EST: 1976
SQ FT: 189,000
SALES (est): 225.1MM
SALES (corp-wide): 501.3K **Privately Held**
WEB: www.penton.com
SIC: 2721 7389 7313 7375 Periodicals; periodicals: publishing & printing; magazines: publishing & printing; advertising, promotional & trade show services; printed media advertising representatives; on-line data base information retrieval
HQ: Penton Business Media, Inc.
1166 Avenue Of The Americ
New York NY 10036
212 204-4200

(G-11628)
PENTON MEDIA INC
Also Called: Used Equipment Directory
1166 Avenue Of The Americ (10036-2743)
PHONE 212 204-4200
James Mack, *Principal*
Angela Daunis, *Editor*
Olivia Labarre, *Editor*
Andrew Zvonek, *Personnel Exec*
Dan Elm, *Accounts Exec*
EMP: 9
SALES (corp-wide): 501.3K **Privately Held**
WEB: www.penton.com
SIC: 2721 Magazines: publishing & printing
HQ: Penton Media, Inc.
1166 Avenue Of The Americ
New York NY 10036
212 204-4200

(G-11629)
PEPE CREATIONS INC
2 W 45th St Ste 1003 (10036-4212)
PHONE 212 391-1514
Fax: 212 391-4445
Frank Gomez, *President*
EMP: 12
SALES: 1.5MM **Privately Held**
WEB: www.pepecreations.com
SIC: 3961 Costume jewelry

(G-11630)
PER ANNUM INC
555 8th Ave Rm 202 (10018-4386)
PHONE 212 647-8700
Fax: 212 647-8716
Alicia Settle, *President*
Tom Settle, *Corp Secy*
Lauren Romero, *Sls & Mktg Exec*
Ben Deutsch, *Director*
▲ EMP: 25
SQ FT: 14,000
SALES (est): 2MM **Privately Held**
WEB: www.perannum.com
SIC: 2741 Miscellaneous publishing

(G-11631)
PERCEPTIVE PIXEL INC (HQ)
641 Avenue Of The Ste 7 (10011)
PHONE 701 367-5845
Jefferson Y Han, *CEO*
Fred Allman, *Vice Pres*
Diane Carlson, *Vice Pres*
Bob Pette, *Vice Pres*
Natalie Vien, *Project Mgr*
EMP: 28
SALES (est): 11.3MM
SALES (corp-wide): 89.9B **Publicly Held**
WEB: www.perceptivepixel.com
SIC: 3577 Computer peripheral equipment
PA: Microsoft Corporation
1 Microsoft Way
Redmond WA 98052
425 882-8080

(G-11632)
PEREGRINE INDUSTRIES INC
40 Wall St (10005-1304)
PHONE 631 838-2870
Richard Rubin, *CEO*
EMP: 5
SALES (est): 513K
SALES (corp-wide): 2.3MM **Privately Held**
SIC: 3569 Filters
PA: Dolomite Holdings Ltd
7 Jabotinsky
Ramat Gan 52520
368 455-00

(G-11633)
PEREIRA & ODELL LLC
5 Crosby St Rm 5h (10013-3154)
PHONE 212 897-1000
Cory Berger, *Director*
EMP: 22
SALES (corp-wide): 18MM **Privately Held**
SIC: 3993 Advertising artwork
PA: Pereira & O'dell Llc
215 2nd St Ste 100
San Francisco CA 94105
415 284-9916

(G-11634)
PERFUME AMERICANA INC (PA)
Also Called: Perfume Americana Wholesale
1216 Broadway (10001-4301)
PHONE 212 683-8029
Fax: 212 779-2383
Mukstar Cheema, *Principal*
▼ EMP: 8
SALES (est): 5.2MM **Privately Held**
SIC: 2844 Perfumes & colognes

(G-11635)
PERFUME AMRCANA WHLESALERS INC
11 W 30th St Betwe Broad Between (10001)
PHONE 212 683-8029
Mukhtar S Cheema, *President*
Bharati Cheema, *President*
Oscar Singh, *Sales Mgr*
▼ EMP: 10
SALES (est): 1.3MM **Privately Held**
SIC: 2844 Perfumes & colognes

(G-11636)
PERFUMERS WORKSHOP INTL LTD (PA)
350 7th Ave Rm 802 (10001-1941)
PHONE 212 644-8950
Donald G Bauchner, *President*
Steven Levenson, *Exec VP*
▲ EMP: 8
SQ FT: 1,800
SALES (est): 1MM **Privately Held**
SIC: 2844 Perfumes & colognes

(G-11637)
PERIMONDO LLC
331 W 84th St Apt 2 (10024-4215)
P.O. Box 200 (10024-0200)
PHONE 212 749-0721
Matthias Rebmann, *Mng Member*
▲ EMP: 6
SALES (est): 896.3K **Privately Held**
SIC: 2074 Lecithin, cottonseed

(G-11638)
PERMA GLOW LTD INC
48 W 48th St Ste 301 (10036-1713)
PHONE 212 575-9677
Fax: 212 575-9733
Richard Scandaglia, *President*
Joseph Scandaglia, *Vice Pres*
▲ EMP: 15
SQ FT: 2,000
SALES: 400K **Privately Held**
SIC: 3915 Jewel cutting, drilling, polishing, recutting or setting

(G-11639)
PERMIT FASHION GROUP INC
135 W 36th St Fl 16 (10018-7172)
PHONE 212 912-0988
Zhouping Zheng, *CEO*
▲ EMP: 8 EST: 2012
SALES (est): 870K **Privately Held**
SIC: 2331 2337 2339 Blouses, women's & juniors': made from purchased material; skirts, separate: women's, misses' & juniors'; jackets & vests, except fur & leather: women's; slacks: women's, misses' & juniors'

(G-11640)
PERNOD RICARD USA LLC (DH)
250 Park Ave Ste 17a (10177-1702)
PHONE 212 372-5400
Fax: 914 848-4777
Bryan Fry, *President*
Mathieu Lambotte, *President*
Lauren Simkin, *General Mgr*

▲ = Import ▼ = Export
◆ = Import/Export

John Bensen, *District Mgr*
Matt Aeppli, *Senior VP*
◆ **EMP:** 100
SALES (est): 471.1MM
SALES (corp-wide): 156.6MM **Privately Held**
WEB: www.pernod-ricard-usa.com
SIC: 2085 Distilled & blended liquors
HQ: Pernod Ricard North America
12 Place Des Etats Unis
Paris
141 004-100

(G-11641)
PERRY ELLIS INTERNATIONAL INC
1126 Avenue Of The Americ (10036-6708)
PHONE..................212 536-5400
Fax: 212 536-5870
Matthew Cronin, *Vice Pres*
John Griffin, *Branch Mgr*
EMP: 12
SALES (corp-wide): 861MM **Publicly Held**
SIC: 2321 2325 6794 Men's & boys' sports & polo shirts; men's & boys' trousers & slacks; trousers, dress (separate); men's, youths' & boys' shorts (outerwear); men's, youths' & boys' franchises, selling or licensing
PA: Perry Ellis International Inc
3000 Nw 107th Ave
Doral FL 33172
305 592-2830

(G-11642)
PERRY ELLIS INTERNATIONAL INC
42 W 39th St Fl 4 (10018-3841)
PHONE..................212 536-5499
Hope Wright, *VP Finance*
Kevin Kiley, *Branch Mgr*
EMP: 9
SALES (corp-wide): 861MM **Publicly Held**
WEB: www.cubabera.com
SIC: 2321 Men's & boys' sports & polo shirts
PA: Perry Ellis International Inc
3000 Nw 107th Ave
Doral FL 33172
305 592-2830

(G-11643)
PERRY ELLIS MENSWEAR LLC (HQ)
Also Called: Perry Ellis America
1120 Ave Of The Americas (10036-6700)
PHONE..................212 221-7500
Doug Jakubowski, *Ch of Bd*
Awadhesh K Sinha, *COO*
Elliot M Lavigne, *Exec VP*
Brian Root, *Senior VP*
Felice Schulaner, *Senior VP*
◆ **EMP:** 150 **EST:** 1893
SQ FT: 27,000
SALES (est): 110.2MM
SALES (corp-wide): 861MM **Publicly Held**
WEB: www.perryellis.com
SIC: 2325 5611 2321 2387 Slacks, dress: men's, youths' & boys'; jeans: men's, youths' & boys'; men's & boys' clothing stores; men's & boys' furnishings; apparel belts; suspenders; neckties, men's & boys': made from purchased materials
PA: Perry Ellis International Inc
3000 Nw 107th Ave
Doral FL 33172
305 592-2830

(G-11644)
PERRY STREET SOFTWARE INC
489 5th Ave Rm 2900 (10017-6115)
PHONE..................415 935-1429
John Skandros, *President*
Eric Silverberg, *Admin Sec*
EMP: 5 **EST:** 2011
SALES (est): 430K **Privately Held**
SIC: 7372 Prepackaged software

(G-11645)
PERSEUS FISHER BOOKS LLC
387 Park Ave S Fl 12 (10016-8810)
PHONE..................212 340-8100
EMP: 54
SALES (est): 5.9K
SALES (corp-wide): 173.4MM **Privately Held**
SIC: 2731 Book publishing
PA: Clp Pb, Llc
1290 Ave Of The Amrcas
New York NY 10104
212 340-8100

(G-11646)
PERSISTENT SYSTEMS LLC
303 5th Ave Rm 306 (10016-6635)
PHONE..................212 561-5895
Herbert B Rubens, *CEO*
Louis Sutherland, *President*
Edward Leopold, *Project Mgr*
Ruben Neira, *Production*
Helson Maria, *QC Mgr*
EMP: 50
SQ FT: 5,000
SALES (est): 22.2MM **Privately Held**
SIC: 3663 Radio broadcasting & communications equipment

(G-11647)
PERSONAL ALARM SEC SYSTEMS
379 5th Ave Fl 3 (10016-3324)
PHONE..................212 448-1944
Leonard Meyerson, *President*
Sam Minzer, *Vice Pres*
Richard Burton, *Sales Mgr*
Jay Black, *Office Mgr*
EMP: 12
SQ FT: 3,000
SALES (est): 1.2MM **Privately Held**
SIC: 3669 5999 Emergency alarms; alarm signal systems

(G-11648)
PESSELNIK & COHEN INC
82 Bowery Unit 10 (10013-4656)
PHONE..................212 925-0287
Salvatore Diadema, *President*
Stephen De Angelo, *Admin Sec*
EMP: 7
SALES (est): 550K **Privately Held**
SIC: 3911 5094 Jewelry, precious metal; jewelry; watches & parts

(G-11649)
PET PROTEINS LLC
347 W 36th St Rm 1204 (10018-6480)
PHONE..................888 293-1029
Steven Mendal,
Jayme Mendal,
Mark Mendal,
◆ **EMP:** 7
SQ FT: 500
SALES: 1MM **Privately Held**
SIC: 2047 Dog & cat food

(G-11650)
PETER ATMAN INC
6 E 45th St Rm 1100 (10017-2475)
PHONE..................212 644-8882
Fax: 212 644-3888
Peter Philipakos, *Ch of Bd*
Peter Phillips, *President*
EMP: 10
SALES (est): 1.3MM **Privately Held**
WEB: www.peteratman.com
SIC: 3911 5944 Jewelry, precious metal; jewelry, precious stones & precious metals

(G-11651)
PETER LANG PUBLISHING INC (DH)
29 Broadway Rm 1800 (10006-3221)
PHONE..................212 647-7700
Fax: 212 647-7707
Alessandra Anzani, *Editor*
Richard Breitenbach, *Editor*
Laurel Plapp, *Editor*
Christabel Scaife, *Editor*
Sebastian Schmitt, *Editor*
EMP: 12
SQ FT: 8,000
SALES (est): 1.1MM
SALES (corp-wide): 274.9K **Privately Held**
WEB: www.peterlangusa.com
SIC: 2731 Textbooks: publishing only, not printed on site
HQ: Peter Lang Ag Internationaler Verlag Der Wissenschaften
Wabernstrasse 40
Bern BE
313 061-717

(G-11652)
PETER MAYER PUBLISHERS INC
Also Called: Overlook Press, The
141 Wooster St Fl 4 (10012-3163)
PHONE..................212 673-2210
Peter Mayer, *President*
George Davidson, *Production*
Maura Diamond, *Manager*
▲ **EMP:** 13
SQ FT: 5,000
SALES: 1MM **Privately Held**
WEB: www.overlookpress.com
SIC: 2731 Books: publishing only

(G-11653)
PETER THOMAS ROTH LABS LLC (PA)
460 Park Ave Fl 16 (10022-1829)
PHONE..................212 581-5800
Peter Thomasroth, *Vice Pres*
June Jacobs,
June Jacbos,
Peter Roth,
▲ **EMP:** 40
SQ FT: 5,500
SALES (est): 29.3MM **Privately Held**
SIC: 2844 Cosmetic preparations

(G-11654)
PETNET SOLUTIONS INC
660 1st Ave Rm 140 (10016-3295)
PHONE..................865 218-2000
Barry Scott, *CEO*
EMP: 6
SALES (corp-wide): 89.6B **Privately Held**
SIC: 2834 Solutions, pharmaceutical
HQ: Petnet Solutions, Inc.
810 Innovation Dr
Knoxville TN 37932
865 218-2000

(G-11655)
PEXIP INC (HQ)
240 W 35th St Ste 1002 (10001-2506)
PHONE..................703 338-3544
Adam Marlin, *Vice Pres*
Richard Coder, *Vice Pres*
Matt Hansen, *VP Opers*
Per-Arne Olausson, *Sales Staff*
Darik Rude, *Technology*
EMP: 23 **EST:** 2012
SQ FT: 3,000
SALES (est): 2.8MM
SALES (corp-wide): 15.1MM **Privately Held**
SIC: 7372 Application computer software

(G-11656)
PFIZER HCP CORPORATION (HQ)
235 E 42nd St (10017-5703)
PHONE..................212 733-2323
Fax: 212 573-7851
Ian C Read, *CEO*
Geno Germano, *President*
Frank D'Amelio, *Exec VP*
Rady Johnson, *Exec VP*
Freda C Lewis-Hall, *Exec VP*
▲ **EMP:** 12
SALES (est): 4.3MM
SALES (corp-wide): 52.8B **Publicly Held**
WEB: www.pfizer.com
SIC: 2834 Pharmaceutical preparations
PA: Pfizer Inc.
235 E 42nd St
New York NY 10017
212 733-2323

(G-11657)
PFIZER INC (PA)
235 E 42nd St (10017-5703)
PHONE..................212 733-2323
Fax: 212 309-0896
Ian C Read, *Ch of Bd*
Albert Bourla, *President*
Mikael Dolsten, *President*
John D Young, *President*
Charles H Hill III, *Exec VP*
◆ **EMP:** 2500 **EST:** 1942
SALES: 52.8B **Publicly Held**
WEB: www.pfizer.com
SIC: 2834 2833 Pharmaceutical preparations; drugs acting on the cardiovascular system, except diagnostic; drugs affecting parasitic & infective diseases; veterinary pharmaceutical preparations; antibiotics

(G-11658)
PFIZER INC
150 E 42nd St Fl 38 (10017-5612)
PHONE..................937 746-3603
Daniel Reardon, *Principal*
Gavin Cronin, *Business Mgr*
Dianbo Cao, *Project Mgr*
Sarah Cate, *Accountant*
Maritza Rosener, *Hum Res Coord*
EMP: 214
SALES (corp-wide): 52.8B **Publicly Held**
SIC: 2834 Pharmaceutical preparations
PA: Pfizer Inc.
235 E 42nd St
New York NY 10017
212 733-2323

(G-11659)
PFIZER INC
150 E 42nd St Bsmt 2 (10017-5642)
PHONE..................212 733-6276
Hugh Oconnor, *Vice Pres*
Macdara Lynch, *Plant Mgr*
Anthony P Carcich, *Engineer*
Delano F Randolph, *Controller*
William Waldin, *Persnl Mgr*
EMP: 70
SALES (corp-wide): 52.8B **Publicly Held**
WEB: www.pfizer.com
SIC: 2834 Pharmaceutical preparations
PA: Pfizer Inc.
235 E 42nd St
New York NY 10017
212 733-2323

(G-11660)
PFIZER INC
235 E 42nd St (10017-5703)
PHONE..................804 257-2000
Lucile Callahan, *President*
Michael Mead, *Vice Pres*
Robert Hunter, *VP Opers*
Victor Perez, *QC Mgr*
EMP: 146
SALES (corp-wide): 52.8B **Publicly Held**
WEB: www.wyeth.com
SIC: 2834 Pharmaceutical preparations
PA: Pfizer Inc.
235 E 42nd St
New York NY 10017
212 733-2323

(G-11661)
PFIZER INC
235 E 42nd St (10017-5703)
PHONE..................212 733-2323
EMP: 146
SALES (corp-wide): 52.8B **Publicly Held**
SIC: 2834 Pharmaceutical preparations
PA: Pfizer Inc.
235 E 42nd St
New York NY 10017
212 733-2323

(G-11662)
PFIZER OVERSEAS LLC
235 E 42nd St (10017-5703)
PHONE..................212 733-2323
Ian C Read, *Ch of Bd*
Mikael Dolsten, *President*
Frank D'Amelio, *Exec VP*
Chuck Hill, *Exec VP*
Rady Johnson, *Exec VP*
EMP: 7
SALES (est): 440.5K
SALES (corp-wide): 52.8B **Publicly Held**
SIC: 2834 2833 Pharmaceutical preparations; antibiotics
PA: Pfizer Inc.
235 E 42nd St
New York NY 10017
212 733-2323

(G-11663)
PGS MILLWORK INC (PA)
535 8th Ave Rm 20n (10018-4493)
PHONE..................212 244-6610

New York - New York County (G-11664)   GEOGRAPHIC SECTION

Fax: 212 244-0587
Thomas Spurge, CEO
Mara Lopez, Counsel
Nick Ference, Marketing Staff
▲ EMP: 65
SQ FT: 44,000
SALES (est): 12.9MM Privately Held
WEB: www.pgsmillwork.com
SIC: 2431 2434 2499 5211 Millwork; wood kitchen cabinets; decorative wood & woodwork; millwork & lumber

(G-11664)
PHAIDON PRESS INC
65 Bleecker St Fl 8 (10012-2420)
PHONE....................212 652-5400
Fax: 212 652-5410
Keith Fox, CEO
Bridget McCarthy, Editor
Deborah Aaronson, Vice Pres
Andrew Price, Vice Pres
Rob Mounty, Warehouse Mgr
▲ EMP: 20
SALES (est): 2.6MM
SALES (corp-wide): 33.7MM Privately Held
SIC: 2731 Book publishing
HQ: Phaidon Press Limited
    Regent's Wharf
    London N1 9P
    207 843-1000

(G-11665)
PHC RESTORATION HOLDINGS LLC
Also Called: Philip Crangi
147 W 29th St Fl 4 (10001-5107)
PHONE....................212 643-0517
Courtney Crangi, Mng Member
Jeffry Aronsson,
Philip Crangi,
EMP: 10
SQ FT: 2,000
SALES: 1.5MM Privately Held
SIC: 3911 Jewelry, precious metal
PA: Phc Restoration, Inc.
    147 W 29th St Ste 4e
    New York NY 10001
    212 643-0517

(G-11666)
PHILIP MORRIS INTL INC (PA)
120 Park Ave Fl 6 (10017-5592)
PHONE....................917 663-2000
Fax: 212 907-5430
Andre Calantzopoulos, CEO
Louis C Camilleri, Ch of Bd
Drago Azinovic, President
Frederic De Wilde, President
Martin King, President
◆ EMP: 94
SALES: 74.9B Publicly Held
SIC: 2111 Cigarettes

(G-11667)
PHILIPS LIGHTING N AMER CORP
267 5th Ave (10016-7503)
PHONE....................646 265-7170
Jeffrey Cassis, CEO
Leverda Wallace, Surgery Dir
EMP: 190
SALES (corp-wide): 7.5B Privately Held
SIC: 3646 Commercial indusl & institutional electric lighting fixtures
HQ: Philips Lighting North America Corporation
    3 Burlington Woods Dr # 4
    Burlington MA 01803
    617 423-9999

(G-11668)
PHILLIPS-VAN HEUSEN EUROPE
Also Called: Pvh Europe
200 Madison Ave Bsmt 1 (10016-3913)
PHONE....................212 381-3500
Ellen Constantinides, President
Dominic Catalfamo, Vice Pres
Marcela Manubens, Vice Pres
Carlos Heredia, Project Mgr
Richard Alfonso, Technical Mgr
EMP: 12

SALES: 20MM
SALES (corp-wide): 8.2B Publicly Held
SIC: 2321 2331 2253 3143 Men's & boys' dress shirts; blouses, women's & juniors': made from purchased material; sweaters & sweater coats, knit; men's footwear, except athletic; ready-to-wear apparel, women's; men's & boys' clothing stores
PA: Pvh Corp.
    200 Madison Ave Bsmt 1
    New York NY 10016
    212 381-3500

(G-11669)
PHOEBE COMPANY LLC
Also Called: Kay Unger
230 W 38th St Fl 11 (10018-9053)
PHONE....................212 302-5556
Fax: 212 302-5965
Richard Honig, CFO
Rob Fineberg, Mng Member
▲ EMP: 55
SQ FT: 8,000
SALES (est): 4.6MM Privately Held
SIC: 2335 Women's, juniors' & misses' dresses

(G-11670)
PHOENIX RIBBON CO INC
20 W 36th St Fl 7 (10018-8086)
PHONE....................212 239-0155
Fax: 212 268-1897
Irving Besterman, President
Anne Besterman, Treasurer
Astill Matt, Manager
▲ EMP: 8
SQ FT: 6,500
SALES (est): 659.2K Privately Held
SIC: 2396 Ribbons & bows, cut & sewed

(G-11671)
PHOENIX USA LLC
315 W 33rd St Apt 30h (10001-2795)
PHONE....................646 351-6598
Roger Garcia,
▲ EMP: 2
SALES (est): 4.5MM Privately Held
SIC: 2211 7389 Apparel & outerwear fabrics, cotton;

(G-11672)
PHOENIX VENTURE FUND LLC
70 E 55th St Fl 10 (10022-3334)
PHONE....................212 759-1909
Philip S Sassower, Ch of Bd
EMP: 21
SALES (est): 1.8MM Privately Held
SIC: 3577 Computer peripheral equipment

(G-11673)
PHREESIA NEW YORK
432 Park Ave S Fl 12 (10016-8013)
PHONE....................888 654-7473
Chaim Indig, CEO
Michael Davidoff, Vice Pres
Evan Roberts, Vice Pres
Thomas Altier, CFO
EMP: 275
SQ FT: 18,000
SALES: 60MM Privately Held
SIC: 3695 Computer software tape & disks: blank, rigid & floppy

(G-11674)
PHYSICALMIND INSTITUTE
84 Wooster St Ste 605 (10012-4363)
PHONE....................212 343-2150
Joan Breibart, General Mgr
▲ EMP: 10
SALES (est): 600K Privately Held
SIC: 3949 7812 8621 Exercise equipment; video tape production; professional membership organizations

(G-11675)
PIAGET
663 5th Ave Fl 7 (10022-5353)
PHONE....................212 355-6444
Fax: 212 355-6996
Thomas Bouillonnec, General Mgr
Eduardo Tartalo, General Mgr
Adriana Gravier, Area Mgr
Wong Lyn, Sls & Mktg Exec
Brandi McCoy, Accounts Mgr
EMP: 15 EST: 2010

SALES (est): 1.5MM Privately Held
SIC: 2329 Men's & boys' clothing

(G-11676)
PIAGGIO GROUP AMERICAS INC
257 Park Ave S Fl 4 (10010-7304)
PHONE....................212 380-4400
Miguel Martinez, President
Mauro Prignoli, Vice Pres
Roland Delongoria, Regl Sales Mgr
◆ EMP: 22
SALES (est): 6MM
SALES (corp-wide): 4.5MM Privately Held
WEB: www.piaggiousa.com
SIC: 3751 Motor scooters & parts
PA: Immsi Spa
    Piazza Vilfredo Pareto 3
    Mantova MN 46100
    027 621-261

(G-11677)
PIANO SOFTWARE INC
1 World Trade Ctr Ste 46d (10007-0092)
PHONE....................646 350-1999
Kweli Washington, COO
Alex Franta, CFO
EMP: 100
SALES (est): 1.3MM Privately Held
SIC: 7372 Application computer software

(G-11678)
PICADOR USA
175 5th Ave (10010-7703)
PHONE....................646 307-5629
Frances Coady, Vice Pres
Kelsey Smith, Manager
EMP: 12
SALES (est): 923.7K
SALES (corp-wide): 1.5B Privately Held
SIC: 2731 Book publishing
HQ: Macmillan Holdings, Llc
    175 5th Ave
    New York NY 10010

(G-11679)
PIDYON CONTROLS INC (PA)
141 W 24th St Apt 4 (10011-1958)
PHONE....................212 683-9523
Yochi Cohen, CEO
EMP: 1
SQ FT: 10,000
SALES: 10MM Privately Held
SIC: 3944 3751 Child restraint seats, automotive; gears, motorcycle & bicycle

(G-11680)
PIEMONTE HOME MADE RAVIOLI CO
190 Grand St (10013-3712)
PHONE....................212 226-0475
Fax: 212 226-0476
Mario Bertorelli, President
EMP: 6
SALES (corp-wide): 1.6MM Privately Held
WEB: www.piemonteravioli.com
SIC: 2098 Macaroni & spaghetti
PA: Piemonte Home Made Ravioli Co, Inc
    3436 65th St
    Woodside NY 11377
    718 429-1972

(G-11681)
PILOT INC (PA)
421 W 24th St Apt 4c (10011-1244)
PHONE....................212 951-1133
Ben Brooks, President
EMP: 8
SALES (est): 439.1K Privately Held
SIC: 7372 7389 Business oriented computer software;

(G-11682)
PILOT INC
110 E 25th St (10010-2913)
PHONE....................212 951-1133
Ben Brooks, Manager
EMP: 8
SALES (corp-wide): 439.1K Privately Held
SIC: 7372 7389 Business oriented computer software;

PA: Pilot, Inc.
    421 W 24th St Apt 4c
    New York NY 10011
    212 951-1133

(G-11683)
PIN PHARMA INC
3960 Broadway Fl 2 (10032-1543)
PHONE....................212 543-2583
Hestaline Reynolds, Principal
Colin Bier, Executive
EMP: 8
SALES (est): 894.3K Privately Held
SIC: 3452 Pins

(G-11684)
PINGMD INC
136 Madison Ave Fl 6 (10016-6795)
PHONE....................212 632-2665
Susan Driscoll, CEO
Lawrence Sosnow, Ch of Bd
EMP: 6 EST: 2009
SALES (est): 492.9K Privately Held
SIC: 7372 Application computer software

(G-11685)
PINK INC
23 E 10th St Apt 1b (10003-6114)
PHONE....................212 352-8282
Debra Roth, President
EMP: 22
SQ FT: 2,000
SALES: 1.6MM Privately Held
WEB: www.pinkinc.org
SIC: 2395 Quilted fabrics or cloth

(G-11686)
PINK CRUSH LLC
1410 Broadway Rm 1002 (10018-9359)
PHONE....................718 788-6978
Rori Nadrich, President
Raymond Kassin, Vice Pres
EMP: 4
SQ FT: 1,800
SALES: 2MM Privately Held
SIC: 2369 Girls' & children's outerwear

(G-11687)
PINS N NEEDLES
1045 Lexington Ave (10021-3252)
PHONE....................212 535-6222
Rachel Low, CEO
EMP: 9
SALES (est): 1MM Privately Held
SIC: 3452 Pins

(G-11688)
PITNEY BOWES INC
637 W 27th St Fl 8 (10001-1019)
PHONE....................212 564-7548
Fax: 917 351-2965
Giberti Alberti, Exec VP
James Euchner, Vice Pres
Gregory Forbes, Project Mgr
Benjamin Dock, Engineer
Joseph Guiles, Engineer
EMP: 35
SALES (corp-wide): 3.4B Publicly Held
SIC: 3579 7359 Postage meters; business machine & electronic equipment rental services
PA: Pitney Bowes Inc.
    3001 Summer St Ste 3
    Stamford CT 06905
    203 356-5000

(G-11689)
PITNEY BOWES INC
90 Park Ave Rm 1110 (10016-1301)
PHONE....................203 356-5000
Michael Levitan, Principal
EMP: 35
SALES (corp-wide): 3.4B Publicly Held
SIC: 3579 7359 Postage meters; business machine & electronic equipment rental services
PA: Pitney Bowes Inc.
    3001 Summer St Ste 3
    Stamford CT 06905
    203 356-5000

(G-11690)
PIWIK PRO LLC
222 Broadway Fl 19 (10038-2550)
PHONE....................888 444-0049
Maiciej Zawadski, CEO

GEOGRAPHIC SECTION

New York - New York County (G-11717)

EMP: 30
SALES (est): 897.5K **Privately Held**
SIC: 7372 Application computer software

(G-11691)
PJ DESIGNS INC
Also Called: Peggy Jennings Designs
100 E 50th St Ste 38a (10022-6844)
PHONE 212 355-3100
Herbert Kosterlitz, *Manager*
EMP: 40
SALES (corp-wide): 5.1MM **Privately Held**
SIC: 2335 Dresses, paper: cut & sewn
PA: P.J. Designs, Inc.
2830 46th Ave N
Saint Petersburg FL 33714
727 525-0599

(G-11692)
PKG GROUP
560 Broadway Rm 406 (10012-3946)
PHONE 212 965-0112
Edward Csaszar, *Manager*
EMP: 7
SALES (est): 702.1K **Privately Held**
SIC: 2631 Container, packaging & boxboard

(G-11693)
PLACE VENDOME HOLDING CO INC
Also Called: R & F Marketing
230 5th Ave Ste 1107 (10001-7823)
PHONE 212 696-0765
Rhonda Finkelstein, *Ch of Bd*
Arnold Finkelstein, *President*
Mark Engel, *Vice Pres*
Jibreel Champion, *Project Mgr*
▲ **EMP:** 110
SQ FT: 3,500
SALES (est): 13.3MM **Privately Held**
WEB: www.rfmarketing.com
SIC: 2392 Household furnishings; pillows, bed: made from purchased materials

(G-11694)
PLASCOLINE INC
275 Madison Ave Fl 14th (10016-1101)
PHONE 917 410-5754
Rafael Faramand, *CEO*
EMP: 18
SQ FT: 2,000
SALES: 7MM **Privately Held**
SIC: 3089 Organizers for closets, drawers, etc.: plastic; plastic kitchenware, tableware & houseware

(G-11695)
PLAYBILL INCORPORATED (PA)
729 7th Ave Fl 4 (10019-6827)
PHONE 212 557-5757
Fax: 212 682-2932
Philip S Birsh, *President*
Khadijah Rentas, *Editor*
Arthur T Birsh, *Chairman*
Joan Alleman-Birsh, *Exec VP*
Susan Ludlow, *Accounts Mgr*
EMP: 20 **EST:** 1882
SQ FT: 4,500
SALES (est): 21.6MM **Privately Held**
SIC: 2721 Periodicals: publishing & printing

(G-11696)
PLAYLIFE LLC
297 Church St Fl 5 (10013-5716)
PHONE 646 207-9082
Mattias Stanghed,
EMP: 5
SALES (est): 250K **Privately Held**
SIC: 2741 7389 ;

(G-11697)
PLEASURE CHEST SALES LTD
156 7th Ave S (10014-2727)
PHONE 212 242-4185
Brian Robinson, *President*
EMP: 10
SALES (est): 800K **Privately Held**
WEB: www.pleasurewipes.com
SIC: 3089 Novelties, plastic

(G-11698)
PLECTICA LLC
175 Varick St (10014-4604)
PHONE 917 304-7052
Adam Riggs, *Partner*
Derek Cabrera, *Partner*
Laura Cabrera, *Partner*
EMP: 9
SQ FT: 300
SALES (est): 236.6K **Privately Held**
SIC: 7372 Application computer software

(G-11699)
PLEXI CRAFT QUALITY PRODUCTS
200 Lexington Ave Rm 914 (10016-6255)
PHONE 212 924-3244
George Frechter, *President*
EMP: 15
SQ FT: 10,000
SALES (est): 2.3MM **Privately Held**
WEB: www.plexi-craft.com
SIC: 2821 Thermoplastic materials

(G-11700)
PLUGG LLC
Also Called: Coliseum
1410 Broadway Frnt 2 (10018-9302)
PHONE 212 840-6655
Fax: 212 840-3078
Laureen Emilius, *Sales Staff*
John Kiplani, *Branch Mgr*
Triven Thadhani, *Director*
EMP: 10
SALES (corp-wide): 13.7MM **Privately Held**
WEB: www.coliseum.com
SIC: 2331 2335 2339 Women's & misses' blouses & shirts; women's, juniors' & misses' dresses; slacks: women's, misses' & juniors'
PA: Plugg Llc
250 Moonachie Rd Ste 501
Moonachie NJ 07074
201 662-8200

(G-11701)
PMI GLOBAL SERVICES INC
120 Park Ave Fl 6 (10017-5579)
PHONE 917 663-2000
James R Mortensen, *President*
Patrick Murphy, *Analyst*
EMP: 24
SALES (est): 4.9MM
SALES (corp-wide): 74.9B **Publicly Held**
SIC: 2111 Cigarettes
PA: Philip Morris International Inc.
120 Park Ave Fl 6
New York NY 10017
917 663-2000

(G-11702)
POETS HOUSE INC
10 River Ter (10282-1240)
PHONE 212 431-7920
Margo Viscusi, *President*
Frank Platt, *Vice Pres*
Martin Gomez, *Treasurer*
Amanda Glassman, *Librarian*
Carlin Wragg, *Manager*
EMP: 14 **EST:** 1985
SALES: 1.3MM **Privately Held**
SIC: 2731 8231 Book publishing; libraries

(G-11703)
POLLACK GRAPHICS INC
601 W 26th St Ste M204 (10001-1101)
PHONE 212 727-8400
Fax: 212 727-1056
Glenn Pollack, *President*
Peter Mirenda, *Sales Mgr*
EMP: 5
SQ FT: 1,600
SALES (est): 450K **Privately Held**
SIC: 2752 Commercial printing, offset

(G-11704)
POLYMER SLUTIONS GROUP FIN LLC (PA)
100 Park Ave Fl 31 (10017-5584)
PHONE 212 771-1717
Mike Ivany, *CEO*
EMP: 4 **EST:** 2015
SALES (est): 40.4MM **Privately Held**
SIC: 2869 Industrial organic chemicals

(G-11705)
POP BAR LLC
5 Carmine St Frnt 6 (10014-4440)
PHONE 212 255-4874
Daniel Yaghoubi,
◆ **EMP:** 6 **EST:** 2010
SALES (est): 383.4K **Privately Held**
SIC: 2024 Ice cream & frozen desserts

(G-11706)
POPNYC 1 LLC
Also Called: Pop Nyc
75 Saint Nicholas Pl 2e (10032-8030)
PHONE 646 684-4600
Gina Panella, *Mng Member*
Joseph Peraino,
▲ **EMP:** 5
SQ FT: 1,000
SALES: 2MM **Privately Held**
SIC: 2339 Women's & misses' accessories

(G-11707)
POPPIN INC
Also Called: Www.poppin.com
1115 Broadway Fl 3 (10010-3457)
PHONE 212 391-7200
Randy Nicolau, *CEO*
Chris Robison, *General Mgr*
Michael Chauliac, *Principal*
Andrew Benoit, *COO*
Jimmy Abbott, *Vice Pres*
▲ **EMP:** 52
SALES (est): 14.8MM **Privately Held**
SIC: 2521 2522 Cabinets, office: wood; tables, office: wood; chairs, office: padded or plain, except wood

(G-11708)
PORTFOLIO MEDIA INC
Also Called: Law360
111 W 19th St Fl 5 (10011-4166)
PHONE 646 783-7100
Fax: 646 783-7161
Scott Roberts, *CEO*
Jocelyn Allison, *Editor*
Kerry Benn, *Editor*
John Blakeley, *Editor*
Patricia Cole, *Editor*
EMP: 200
SQ FT: 46,000
SALES (est): 16.1MM
SALES (corp-wide): 8.4B **Privately Held**
WEB: www.portfoliomedia.com
SIC: 2741 Business service newsletters: publishing & printing
HQ: Relx Inc.
230 Park Ave Ste 700
New York NY 10169
212 309-8100

(G-11709)
PORTWARE LLC (HQ)
233 Broadway Fl 24 (10279-2502)
PHONE 212 425-5233
Fax: 212 571-4634
Alfred Eskandar, *CEO*
Scott Depetris, *President*
Eric Goldberg, *Founder*
Ary Khatchikian, *Founder*
Michael Steinberg, *Controller*
EMP: 73
SALES (est): 15.7MM
SALES (corp-wide): 1.1B **Publicly Held**
SIC: 7372 Prepackaged software
PA: Factset Research Systems Inc.
601 Merritt 7
Norwalk CT 06851
203 810-1000

(G-11710)
POSITIVE PRINT LITHO OFFSET
121 Varick St Rm 204 (10013-1461)
PHONE 212 431-4850
Fax: 212 431-0414
Garry Koppel, *President*
EMP: 8
SQ FT: 2,000
SALES (est): 1MM **Privately Held**
SIC: 2752 Commercial printing, offset

(G-11711)
POST MODERN PRODUCTIONS INC (PA)
Also Called: Sylvia Heisel
20 Orchard St Apt 2f (10002-6264)
PHONE 212 719-3916

Fax: 212 719-4651
Sylvia Heisel, *President*
Anouchka Orenzow, *Bookkeeper*
EMP: 3
SALES (est): 1.1MM **Privately Held**
WEB: www.sylviaheisel.com
SIC: 2335 Women's, juniors' & misses' dresses

(G-11712)
POST ROAD
101 E 16th St Apt 4b (10003-2150)
PHONE 203 545-2122
David Ryan, *President*
John Todd, *Managing Prtnr*
EMP: 14 **EST:** 2001
SALES (est): 833.3K **Privately Held**
SIC: 2752 7371 Publication printing, lithographic; computer software development & applications

(G-11713)
POWA TECHNOLOGIES INC
1 Bryant Park Ste 39 (10036-6747)
PHONE 347 344-7848
Jeff Dumbrell, *CEO*
Jeff Max, *President*
Ilan Levine, *COO*
Paul Rasori, *Exec VP*
EMP: 40
SQ FT: 10,000
SALES (est): 3.8MM
SALES (corp-wide): 328.1K **Privately Held**
SIC: 7372 3578 Business oriented computer software; point-of-sale devices
HQ: Powa Technologies Group Plc
Heron Tower 35th Floor
London

(G-11714)
POWERCOMPLETE LLC
636 Broadway Rm 300 (10012-2623)
PHONE 212 228-4129
Fax: 917 591-2831
Jason Feingold,
Ben Boyd,
EMP: 6
SALES (est): 961.3K **Privately Held**
WEB: www.powercomplete.com
SIC: 3621 Motors & generators

(G-11715)
PRAGER METIS CPAS LLC
225 W 34th St Ste 1800 (10122-1800)
PHONE 212 972-7555
Fax: 212 370-1532
Smadar Rinat, *Manager*
Michael Lang, *Senior Mgr*
Stewart Berger, *Director*
Ira Levine, *Director*
EMP: 12
SALES (corp-wide): 34.5MM **Privately Held**
SIC: 3661 Communication headgear, telephone
HQ: Prager Metis Cpas, Llc
14 Penn Plz Ste 1800
New York NY 10122
212 643-0099

(G-11716)
PRC LIQUIDATING COMPANY
Also Called: New York Running Co
10 Columbus Cir (10019-1158)
PHONE 212 823-9626
Eugene Mitchell, *Bd of Directors*
EMP: 30
SALES (corp-wide): 1.8B **Publicly Held**
SIC: 3949 Sporting & athletic goods
HQ: Prc Liquidating Company
632 Overhill Rd
Ardmore PA 19003
610 649-1876

(G-11717)
PRECISION CUSTOM COATINGS LLC
234 W 39th St (10018-4412)
PHONE 212 868-5770
Peter Longo, *Branch Mgr*
EMP: 242
SALES (corp-wide): 137.2MM **Privately Held**
SIC: 2295 Coated fabrics, not rubberized

New York - New York County (G-11718) — GEOGRAPHIC SECTION

PA: Precision Custom Coatings Llc
200 Maltese Dr
Totowa NJ 07512
973 785-4390

(G-11718)
PRECISION DIAMOND CUTTERS INC
2 W 46th St Ste 1007 (10036-4502)
PHONE...........................212 719-4438
Fax: 212 719-4582
David Lew, *President*
Kathy Paykany, *Vice Pres*
EMP: 6
SALES (est): 500K **Privately Held**
WEB: www.bellnor.com
SIC: 3915 Diamond cutting & polishing

(G-11719)
PRECISION INTERNATIONAL CO INC
Also Called: Cenere
201 E 28th St 9n (10016-8538)
PHONE...........................212 268-9090
Fax: 212 268-9094
Michelle Kim, *President*
▲ EMP: 6
SQ FT: 4,200
SALES (est): 410K **Privately Held**
SIC: 3873 5094 Watches, clocks, watch-cases & parts; jewelry & precious stones

(G-11720)
PREMIER GROUP NY
18 W 23rd St Fl 3 (10010-5233)
PHONE...........................212 229-1200
Tania Cetto, *President*
EMP: 10
SALES (est): 655.4K **Privately Held**
SIC: 3281 1741 Marble, building: cut & shaped; masonry & other stonework

(G-11721)
PREMIUM 5 KIDS LLC
Also Called: AG Kids
31 W 34th St (10001-3009)
PHONE...........................212 563-4999
Albert Pardo,
EMP: 15
SALES (est): 526K **Privately Held**
SIC: 2211 Apparel & outerwear fabrics, cotton

(G-11722)
PREPLAY INC
33 W 17th St Ste 901 (10011-5520)
PHONE...........................917 297-7428
Andrew Daines, *CEO*
Scott Neff, *Admin Sec*
EMP: 8
SALES (est): 548.4K
SALES (corp-wide): 21MM **Privately Held**
SIC: 7372 Application computer software
PA: Fanvision Entertainment Llc
33 W 17th St Ste 901
New York NY 10011
917 297-7428

(G-11723)
PRESCRIBING REFERENCE INC
275 7th Ave Fl 10 (10001-6756)
PHONE...........................646 638-6000
William Pecover, *Ch of Bd*
Lee Maniscalco, *President*
John Harrington, *Editor*
Sam James, *Editor*
Frank Washkuch, *Editor*
EMP: 85
SQ FT: 18,000
SALES: 3.5MM
SALES (corp-wide): 270.3MM **Privately Held**
SIC: 2721 Magazines: publishing only, not printed on site
HQ: Haymarket Media, Inc.
275 7th Ave Fl 10
New York NY 10001
646 638-6000

(G-11724)
PRESS OF FREMONT PAYNE INC
55 Broad St Frnt 3 (10004-2569)
PHONE...........................212 966-6570
Charles J Esposito, *President*
John Esposito, *Vice Pres*

Logan Ripley, *Systems Analyst*
Thomas D Esposito, *Admin Sec*
EMP: 8 EST: 1890
SQ FT: 3,500
SALES (est): 610K **Privately Held**
SIC: 2752 Commercial printing, offset

(G-11725)
PRESTEL PUBLISHING LLC
900 Broadway Ste 603 (10003-1237)
PHONE...........................212 995-2720
Fax: 212 995-2733
Stephen Hulburt, *Vice Pres*
Raya Thoma, *Marketing Staff*
▲ EMP: 8
SQ FT: 1,620
SALES: 764.6K
SALES (corp-wide): 17.9B **Privately Held**
SIC: 2731 Books: publishing only
HQ: Verlagsgruppe Random House Gmbh
Neumarkter Str. 28
Munchen 81673
894 136-0

(G-11726)
PRESTIGE GLOBAL NY SLS CORP
102 W 38th St Fl 8 (10018-3685)
PHONE...........................212 776-4322
Linda Tencek, *President*
Catherine Sierra, *Office Mgr*
EMP: 7 EST: 2015
SALES (est): 271.1K **Privately Held**
SIC: 2329 Riding clothes:, men's, youths' & boys'

(G-11727)
PRETLIST
545 W 110th St Apt 2b (10025-2016)
PHONE...........................646 368-1849
Rashid Altayer, *President*
EMP: 5 EST: 2013
SALES (est): 351.7K **Privately Held**
SIC: 7372 Prepackaged software

(G-11728)
PRICING ENGINE INC
175 Varick St Fl 4 (10014-7412)
P.O. Box 221 (10276-0221)
PHONE...........................917 549-3289
Jeremy Kagan, *CEO*
Shobu Filho, *Accounts Mgr*
Yagmur Coker, *CTO*
EMP: 10
SALES (est): 244K **Privately Held**
SIC: 7372 Business oriented computer software

(G-11729)
PRIDE & JOYS INC
Also Called: OLIVEA MATHEWS
1400 Broadway Rm 503 (10018-1044)
PHONE...........................212 594-9820
Fax: 212 594-7767
Eli Rousso, *Ch of Bd*
Rochelle Reis, *Corp Secy*
Neil Rousso, *Vice Pres*
EMP: 15
SQ FT: 4,000
SALES: 7.2MM **Privately Held**
SIC: 2339 2329 Sportswear, women's; knickers, dress (separate): men's & boys'

(G-11730)
PRIMARY WAVE PUBLISHING LLC
116 E 16th St Fl 9 (10003-2123)
PHONE...........................212 661-6990
Winston Simone, *Principal*
Robert Dippold, *VP Sls/Mktg*
Ranon Villa, *CFO*
Erica Emerson, *Controller*
Adam Lowenberg, *Chief Mktg Ofcr*
EMP: 9
SALES (est): 660K **Privately Held**
SIC: 2741 Miscellaneous publishing

(G-11731)
PRIME GARMENTS INC
1407 Broadway Rm 1200 (10018-2850)
PHONE...........................212 354-7294
Joseph Hamdar, *President*
Beth Matran, *Bookkeeper*
▲ EMP: 15
SALES (est): 2.6MM **Privately Held**
SIC: 2342 Bras, girdles & allied garments

(G-11732)
PRIME PACK LLC
Also Called: Prime Pharmaceutical
303 5th Ave Rm 1007 (10016-6681)
PHONE...........................732 253-7734
Sreedara Nagarajan, *Mng Member*
Amrita Gupta,
Lakshmi Nagarajan,
▲ EMP: 10
SQ FT: 13,598
SALES (est): 870K **Privately Held**
SIC: 2834 Pharmaceutical preparations

(G-11733)
PRIME VIEW USA INC
36 W 44th St Ste 812 (10036-8105)
PHONE...........................212 730-4905
Shay Giuili, *CEO*
Elinor Bain, *Office Mgr*
▲ EMP: 5
SALES: 2MM **Privately Held**
SIC: 3663 Television broadcasting & communications equipment

(G-11734)
PRINCESS MUSIC PUBLISHING CO
1650 Broadway Ste 701 (10019-6966)
PHONE...........................212 586-0240
Fax: 212 586-4306
Hal Webman, *Owner*
EMP: 20
SALES (est): 1MM **Privately Held**
SIC: 2741 Music books: publishing & printing

(G-11735)
PRINCIPIA PARTNERS LLC
140 Broadway Fl 46 (10005-1155)
PHONE...........................212 480-2270
Dan Smith, *CFO*
Theresa Adams, *Mng Member*
Suzanne Brower, *Sr Software Eng*
Mark Kovach, *Administration*
Brian Donnally,
EMP: 55
SALES (est): 4MM **Privately Held**
WEB: www.ppllc.com
SIC: 7372 8742 Business oriented computer software; financial consultant

(G-11736)
PRINT BY PREMIER LLC
Also Called: Premier Supplies
212 W 35th St Fl 2 (10001-2508)
PHONE...........................212 947-1365
Sheldon Lehman, *Mng Member*
EMP: 6
SALES (est): 1.7MM **Privately Held**
SIC: 2752 Publication printing, lithographic

(G-11737)
PRINT CITY CORP
165 W 29th St (10001-5101)
PHONE...........................212 487-9778
Anna Wadolowska-Panagoda, *Ch of Bd*
Walter Panagoda, *President*
EMP: 16
SALES (est): 545K **Privately Held**
SIC: 2759 Commercial printing

(G-11738)
PRINT MANAGEMENT GROUP INC
33 E 33rd St Fl 3 (10016-5335)
PHONE...........................212 213-1555
John Scalli, *President*
Tony Santaniello, *Prdtn Mgr*
EMP: 7
SALES (est): 1.4MM **Privately Held**
SIC: 2752 Commercial printing, lithographic

(G-11739)
PRINT MEDIA INC
350 7th Ave Fl 12 (10001-5013)
PHONE...........................212 563-4040
Fax: 212 563-4041
Jordan H Wachtell, *Ch of Bd*
Kady Myers, *Accountant*
▲ EMP: 100
SQ FT: 2,000
SALES (est): 11.7MM **Privately Held**
SIC: 2752 Commercial printing, lithographic

(G-11740)
PRINTECH BUSINESS SYSTEMS INC
519 8th Ave Fl 3 (10018-4594)
PHONE...........................212 290-2542
Fax: 212 290-2541
Frank Passantino, *President*
Marc Zaransky, *Vice Pres*
Ralph Pantuso, *Senior Engr*
Sue Teraghty, *Office Mgr*
Howard Widensky, *Webmaster*
EMP: 18
SQ FT: 15,000
SALES (est): 3.2MM **Privately Held**
WEB: www.printechny.com
SIC: 2789 2752 7374 2759 Binding only: books, pamphlets, magazines, etc.; commercial printing, lithographic; commercial printing, offset; optical scanning data service; promotional printing

(G-11741)
PRINTFACILITY INC
225 Broadway Fl 3 (10007-3001)
PHONE...........................212 349-4009
Fax: 212 406-5575
Farah Khan, *CEO*
Sarah Shabbir, *Manager*
EMP: 8
SQ FT: 2,000
SALES (est): 670K **Privately Held**
WEB: www.printfacility.com
SIC: 2759 Commercial printing

(G-11742)
PRINTINGHOUSE PRESS LTD
10 E 39th St Rm 700 (10016-0111)
PHONE...........................212 719-0990
Fax: 212 398-9253
Myron Schonfeld, *Chairman*
EMP: 6
SALES (est): 1MM **Privately Held**
WEB: www.phpny.com
SIC: 2752 Commercial printing, lithographic

(G-11743)
PRIORITY PRINTING ENTPS INC
Also Called: Priority Enterprise
315 W 36th St (10018-6404)
PHONE...........................646 285-0684
Ronald Bright, *President*
EMP: 12
SALES (est): 3.5MM **Privately Held**
WEB: www.priorityenterpriseinc.com
SIC: 2759 Commercial printing

(G-11744)
PRO DRONES USA LLC
115 E 57th St Fl 11 (10022-2120)
PHONE...........................718 530-3558
Vivien Heriard Dubreuil,
EMP: 12 EST: 2015
SALES (est): 590.2K **Privately Held**
SIC: 3721 Aircraft

(G-11745)
PRO LINE MANUFACTURING CO LLC
Also Called: Top Line
500 Fashion Ave Fl 16 (10018-4613)
PHONE...........................973 692-9696
Peter Ryu, *CEO*
Tae Kim, *COO*
Sue Ryu, *CFO*
Jennifer Kang, *Manager*
▲ EMP: 40
SQ FT: 710,000
SALES: 29MM **Privately Held**
WEB: www.prolineboots.com
SIC: 3021 Rubber & plastics footwear

(G-11746)
PRO PUBLICA INC
155 Ave Of The Americas (10013-1507)
PHONE...........................212 514-5250
Richard Tofel, *President*
Stephen Engelberg, *Editor*
Robin Fields, *Editor*
Adam Harris, *Editor*
Terry Parris, *Editor*
EMP: 52
SALES: 17MM **Privately Held**
SIC: 2731 Book publishing

▲ = Import ▼ = Export
◆ = Import/Export

GEOGRAPHIC SECTION

New York - New York County (G-11776)

(G-11747)
PROCTER & GAMBLE COMPANY
120 W 45th St Fl 3 (10036-4041)
PHONE..................646 885-4201
Brandon Lane, *Treasurer*
Nancy Medici, *Branch Mgr*
EMP: 150
SALES (corp-wide): 65B **Publicly Held**
SIC: **2676** 2844 Towels, napkins & tissue paper products; diapers, paper (disposable; made from purchased paper); feminine hygiene paper products; toilet preparations; hair preparations, including shampoos; oral preparations; deodorants, personal
PA: The Procter & Gamble Company
1 Procter And Gamble Plz
Cincinnati OH 45202
513 983-1100

(G-11748)
PRODUCT DEVELOPMENT INTL LLC
215 W 40th St Fl 8 (10018-1575)
PHONE..................212 279-6170
Sue Sun, *Accountant*
Donald L Foss, *Mng Member*
Eric Chu,
▲ EMP: 9
SQ FT: 5,000
SALES (est): 1MM **Privately Held**
SIC: **2335** Women's, juniors' & misses' dresses

(G-11749)
PROFESSNAL SPT PBLICATIONS INC (PA)
Also Called: Touchdown
519 8th Ave (10018-6506)
PHONE..................212 697-1460
Fax: 212 286-8154
Mitchell Zeifman, *President*
John Martin, *Editor*
Ryan Mattos, *Editor*
Steven Fox, *Exec VP*
Martin Lewis, *Exec VP*
EMP: 120 EST: 1990
SALES (est): 19.4MM **Privately Held**
WEB: www.pspsports.com
SIC: **2721** 7941 Magazines: publishing only, not printed on site; sports promotion

(G-11750)
PROGENICS PHARMACEUTICALS INC (PA)
1 World Trade Ctr Fl 47 (10007-0089)
PHONE..................646 975-2500
Fax: 914 789-2817
Mark R Baker, *CEO*
Peter J Crowley, *Ch of Bd*
Vivien Wong, *Exec VP*
Ann Assumma, *Vice Pres*
Jeff Summer, *Vice Pres*
EMP: 66
SALES (est): 69.4MM **Publicly Held**
WEB: www.progenics.com
SIC: **2834** Pharmaceutical preparations

(G-11751)
PROGRESSIVE FIBRE PRODUCTS CO
160 Broadway Rm 1105 (10038-4212)
PHONE..................212 566-2720
Fax: 212 566-2726
Elliot Kozer, *President*
EMP: 40
SALES (est): 3.7MM **Privately Held**
WEB: www.fibrecase.com
SIC: **3161** Sample cases

(G-11752)
PROLINK INDUSTRIES INC
1407 Broadway Rm 3605 (10018-2364)
PHONE..................212 354-5690
▲ EMP: 10
SALES (est): 1.1MM **Privately Held**
SIC: **2389** Mfg Apparel/Accessories

(G-11753)
PROMOTIONAL SALES BOOKS LLC
30 W 26th St Frnt (10010-2011)
PHONE..................212 675-0364
EMP: 5

SQ FT: 2,500
SALES (est): 410K **Privately Held**
SIC: **2732** Publisher

(G-11754)
PROMPT BINDERY CO INC
350 W 38th St (10018-5206)
PHONE..................212 675-5181
Fax: 212 255-5925
Louis Levine, *President*
EMP: 12
SQ FT: 5,800
SALES (est): 759.3K **Privately Held**
SIC: **2789** Bookbinding & related work

(G-11755)
PRONOVIAS USA INC
14 E 52nd St (10022-5308)
PHONE..................212 897-6393
Alberto Palatchi, *Ch of Bd*
Joseluis Perez Herrero, *President*
Jordi Morral, *Exec VP*
Llouis Sole, *Opers Mgr*
Nuria Salazar, *Credit Mgr*
▲ EMP: 30
SQ FT: 20,000
SALES (est): 4.5MM **Privately Held**
WEB: www.pronoviasusa.com
SIC: **2335** Gowns, formal
PA: Pronovias SI
Poligono Industrial Mas Mateu, S/N
El Prat De Llobregat
934 799-700

(G-11756)
PRONTO JEWELRY INC
23 W 47th St (10036-2826)
PHONE..................212 719-9455
Fax: 212 302-5413
Misak Terjinian, *President*
EMP: 23
SALES (est): 1.8MM **Privately Held**
SIC: **3911** Jewelry, precious metal

(G-11757)
PROOF 7 LTD
121 Varick St Rm 301 (10013-1408)
PHONE..................212 680-1843
Joshua Cooper, *President*
Laurence Chandler, *Vice Pres*
Kadeem Buckham, *Production*
Sergio Bello, *Accounts Exec*
Max Cantatore, *Sales Staff*
EMP: 10
SQ FT: 3,000
SALES (est): 1.1MM **Privately Held**
SIC: **2759** 7336 7299 Card printing & engraving, except greeting; advertising literature: printing; catalogs: printing; announcements: engraved; graphic arts & related design; party planning service

(G-11758)
PROPER CLOTH LLC
495 Broadway Fl 6 (10012-4457)
PHONE..................646 964-4221
Joseph Skerritt, *Mng Member*
EMP: 8
SQ FT: 3,000
SALES (est): 856.9K **Privately Held**
SIC: **2311** Men's & boys' suits & coats

(G-11759)
PROPS DISPLAYS & INTERIORS
Also Called: Pdi
132 W 18th St (10011-5403)
PHONE..................212 620-3840
Fax: 212 620-5472
Stephen Sebbane, *President*
Wendy Isaacson, *President*
EMP: 15
SALES (est): 950K **Privately Held**
SIC: **3993** 3999 2431 Displays, paint process; stage hardware & equipment, except lighting; interior & ornamental woodwork & trim

(G-11760)
PROSPECT NEWS
6 Maiden Ln Fl 9 (10038-5134)
PHONE..................212 374-2800
Bernard Dankowski, *Principal*
Janene Geiss, *Editor*
Tali Rackner, *Editor*
Zhaniece Springer, *Admin Asst*
EMP: 14 EST: 2007

SALES (est): 654K **Privately Held**
SIC: **2711** Newspapers, publishing & printing

(G-11761)
PROSPECTOR NETWORK
350 5th Ave Fl 59 (10118-5999)
PHONE..................212 601-2781
Claude Duhamel, *President*
EMP: 50
SALES (est): 1.5MM **Privately Held**
SIC: **7372** Application computer software

(G-11762)
PROSTHODONTIC & IMPLANT DEN
693 5th Ave (10022-3110)
PHONE..................212 319-6363
Fax: 212 319-4995
Dean Vafiadis, *President*
EMP: 8
SALES (est): 1.2MM **Privately Held**
SIC: **3842** Implants, surgical

(G-11763)
PS38 LLC
Also Called: Public School
545 8th Ave Rm 350 (10018-4647)
PHONE..................212 819-1123
Alan Mak,
EMP: 12 EST: 2012
SALES (est): 761.7K **Privately Held**
SIC: **2329** Men's & boys' sportswear & athletic clothing

(G-11764)
PSYCHONOMIC SOCIETY INC
233 Spring St Fl 7 (10013-1522)
PHONE..................512 381-1494
EMP: 26
SQ FT: 6,000
SALES: 954.7K **Privately Held**
SIC: **2721** 2789 2752 Periodical-Publish/Print Bookbinding/Related Work Lithographic Coml Print

(G-11765)
PTI-PACIFIC INC
166 5th Ave Fl 4t (10010-5909)
PHONE..................212 414-8495
Simon Chong, *President*
▲ EMP: 5 EST: 2009
SQ FT: 2,000
SALES: 10MM **Privately Held**
SIC: **2329** 2339 2369 Men's & boys' athletic uniforms; women's & misses' outerwear; girls' & children's outerwear

(G-11766)
PTS FINANCIAL TECHNOLOGY LLC
1001 Ave Of The Americas (10018-5460)
PHONE..................844 825-7634
Farid Naib, *CEO*
EMP: 40 EST: 1999
SALES (est): 969.8K **Privately Held**
SIC: **7372** Application computer software

(G-11767)
PUBLIC RELATIONS SOC AMER INC (PA)
Also Called: PRSA
120 Wall St Fl 21 (10005-4024)
PHONE..................212 460-1400
Joseph P Truncale, *CEO*
William Murray, *President*
Jeffrey P Julin, *Principal*
Haley Higgs, *Vice Pres*
Sarah Johnson, *Vice Pres*
EMP: 50
SQ FT: 22,000
SALES (est): 11.6MM **Privately Held**
WEB: www.newyorkcity.com
SIC: **2721** 8621 Trade journals: publishing only, not printed on site; professional membership organizations

(G-11768)
PUBLIC SCHOOL
209 W 38th St Rm 501 (10018-0498)
PHONE..................212 302-1108
EMP: 5 EST: 2014
SALES (est): 248.9K **Privately Held**
SIC: **2311** 2337 Men's & boys' suits & coats; suits: women's, misses' & juniors'

(G-11769)
PUBLISHING GROUP AMERICA INC
Also Called: American Profile Magazine
60 E 42nd St Ste 1146 (10165-1146)
PHONE..................646 658-0550
Fax: 646 865-1921
Peggy Bosco, *Branch Mgr*
EMP: 18
SALES (corp-wide): 6.5MM **Privately Held**
WEB: www.pubgroupofamerica.com
SIC: **2711** Newspapers: publishing only, not printed on site
PA: Publishing Group Of America, Inc.
1200 Clinton St Ste 219
Nashville TN 37203
615 468-6000

(G-11770)
PUBLISHING SYNTHESIS LTD
39 Crosby St Apt 2n (10013-3254)
PHONE..................212 219-0135
Fax: 212 219-0136
Otto H Barz, *Partner*
Ellen Small, *Vice Pres*
George Ernsberger, *Manager*
EMP: 6
SQ FT: 1,000
SALES (est): 420K **Privately Held**
WEB: www.pubsyn.com
SIC: **2791** Typesetting

(G-11771)
PUIG USA INC (PA)
40 E 34th St Fl 19 (10016-4501)
PHONE..................212 271-5940
Marc Puig, *President*
Kaatje Noens, *General Mgr*
Jean Huang, *Vice Pres*
Gary Ragusa, *CFO*
Pascal Jodra, *Sales Staff*
▲ EMP: 15
SALES (est): 2.2MM **Privately Held**
SIC: **2844** Toilet preparations

(G-11772)
PULSE INSIGHTS LLC
175 Varick St Fl 4 (10014-7412)
PHONE..................888 718-6860
EMP: 8
SALES (est): 120.1K **Privately Held**
SIC: **7372** Business oriented computer software

(G-11773)
PUNCH FASHIONS LLC
3 W 35th St (10001-2204)
PHONE..................646 519-7333
Fax: 212 736-7456
David Cleary, *CEO*
John Higgins, *COO*
EMP: 5
SALES (est): 60K **Privately Held**
SIC: **3911** Jewelry, precious metal

(G-11774)
PURE TRADE US INC
347 5th Ave Rm 604 (10016-5031)
PHONE..................212 256-1600
Stefane Ladous, *CEO*
▲ EMP: 40
SALES (est): 3.2MM **Privately Held**
SIC: **2652** 3171 Setup paperboard boxes; women's handbags & purses

(G-11775)
PUREBASE NETWORKS INC
37 Wall St Apt 9a (10005-2019)
PHONE..................646 670-8964
Steven Ridder, *CEO*
EMP: 8
SALES (est): 204.7K **Privately Held**
SIC: **7372** Business oriented computer software

(G-11776)
PURELY MAPLE INC
159 Bleecker St Apt 2b (10012-1490)
P.O. Box 20784 (10025-1523)
PHONE..................646 524-7135
William Finkelstein, *CFO*
EMP: 10
SALES (est): 311.7K **Privately Held**
SIC: **2037** Fruit juices

New York - New York County (G-11777) — GEOGRAPHIC SECTION

(G-11777)
PURELY MAPLE LLC
902 Broadway Fl 6 (10010-6039)
P.O. Box 20784 (10025-1523)
PHONE 203 997-9309
ARI Tolwin, *CEO*
EMP: 15 **EST:** 2013
SALES (est): 851.2K **Privately Held**
SIC: 2086 Fruit drinks (less than 100% juice); packaged in cans, etc.

(G-11778)
PUREOLOGY RESEARCH LLC
565 5th Ave (10017-2413)
PHONE 212 984-4360
Pat Parenty, *General Mgr*
EMP: 18
SALES (est): 1.4MM
SALES (corp-wide): 3.2B **Privately Held**
WEB: www.pureology.com
SIC: 2844 Hair preparations, including shampoos
HQ: L'oreal Usa, Inc.
10 Hudson Yards Fl 30
New York NY 10001
212 818-1500

(G-11779)
PUTNAM ROLLING LADDER CO INC (PA)
32 Howard St (10013-3112)
PHONE 212 226-5147
Fax: 212 941-1836
Warren R Monsees, *President*
Lloyd Javois, *Sales Staff*
K Laura Monsees, *Director*
Gregg Monsees, *Admin Sec*
▲ **EMP:** 15 **EST:** 1897
SQ FT: 45,000
SALES (est): 3.6MM **Privately Held**
WEB: www.putnamrollingladder.com
SIC: 2499 5084 Ladders, wood; woodworking machinery

(G-11780)
PVH CORP (PA)
200 Madison Ave Bsmt 1 (10016-3913)
P.O. Box 64945, Saint Paul MN (55164-0945)
PHONE 212 381-3500
Fax: 212 381-3950
Francis K Duane, *CEO*
Daniel Grieder, *CEO*
Steven B Shiffman, *CEO*
Emanuel Chirico, *Ch of Bd*
Michael A Shaffer, *COO*
▲ **EMP:** 100 **EST:** 1881
SQ FT: 209,000
SALES: 8.2B **Publicly Held**
WEB: www.pvh.com
SIC: 2321 2331 2253 3143 Men's & boys' dress shirts; sport shirts, men's & boys': from purchased materials; blouses, women's & juniors': made from purchased material; shirts, women's & juniors': made from purchased materials; sweaters & sweater coats, knit; shirts (outerwear), knit; men's footwear, except athletic; ready-to-wear apparel, women's; men's & boys' clothing stores

(G-11781)
PVH CORP
Van Heusen
200 Madison Ave Bsmt 1 (10016-3913)
PHONE 212 381-3800
Ken Duane, *Branch Mgr*
John Hayes, *Executive*
EMP: 7
SALES (corp-wide): 8.2B **Publicly Held**
WEB: www.pvh.com
SIC: 2329 2339 Men's & boys' sportswear & athletic clothing; sportswear, women's
PA: Pvh Corp.
200 Madison Ave Bsmt 1
New York NY 10016
212 381-3500

(G-11782)
PVH CORP
Also Called: Van Heusen
404 5th Ave Fl 4 (10018-7566)
PHONE 212 502-6300
Allain Russo, *President*
EMP: 60
SALES (corp-wide): 8.2B **Publicly Held**
WEB: www.pvh.com
SIC: 2339 Women's & misses' outerwear
PA: Pvh Corp.
200 Madison Ave Bsmt 1
New York NY 10016
212 381-3500

(G-11783)
PVH CORP
Also Called: Van Heusen
205 W 39th St Fl 4 (10018-3102)
PHONE 212 719-2600
Barb Nykolichuk, *District Mgr*
Sherrie Seymour, *District Mgr*
Richard Deck, *Exec VP*
David F Kozel, *Exec VP*
Pamela Bradford, *Senior VP*
EMP: 9
SALES (corp-wide): 8.2B **Publicly Held**
SIC: 2321 2331 Men's & boys' dress shirts; sport shirts, men's & boys': from purchased materials; blouses, women's & juniors': made from purchased material; shirts, women's & juniors': made from purchased materials
PA: Pvh Corp.
200 Madison Ave Bsmt 1
New York NY 10016
212 381-3500

(G-11784)
PVI SOLAR INC
599 11th Ave Bby (10036-2110)
PHONE 212 280-2100
Paul Mladineo, *Managing Dir*
Ted Hasenstaub, *Exec VP*
Ed Shenker, *Exec VP*
EMP: 8
SALES (est): 642.1K **Privately Held**
SIC: 3674 3679 Integrated circuits, semiconductor networks, etc.; electronic loads & power supplies

(G-11785)
PWXYZ LLC
Also Called: Publishers Weekly
71 W 23rd St Ste 1608 (10010-4186)
PHONE 212 377-5500
George W Slowik Jr, *President*
Carl Pritzkat, *President*
Cevin Bryerman, *Publisher*
Andrew Albanese, *Editor*
Adam Boretz, *Editor*
EMP: 5
SALES (est): 480K **Privately Held**
SIC: 2721 2731 Trade journals: publishing only, not printed on site; books: publishing only

(G-11786)
Q COMMUNICATIONS INC
Also Called: Passport Magazine
247 W 35th St Rm 1200 (10001-1917)
PHONE 212 594-6520
Don Tuthill, *President*
Andrew Mersmann, *Editor*
Robert Adams, *Treasurer*
Brett Caldwell, *Mktg Dir*
EMP: 7
SALES (est): 890K **Privately Held**
WEB: www.passportmagazine.net
SIC: 2721 Magazines: publishing only, not printed on site

(G-11787)
Q ED CREATIONS
Also Called: Savoritefactory
2 W 46th St Ste 1408 (10036-4502)
PHONE 212 391-1155
Ariel Assaf, *Owner*
Daniel Assaf, *Co-Owner*
◆ **EMP:** 1
SQ FT: 1,400
SALES: 3.7MM **Privately Held**
SIC: 3911 5094 Jewelry, precious metal; jewelry

(G-11788)
Q SQUARED DESIGN LLC
41 Madison Ave Ste 1905 (10010-2343)
P.O. Box 1550, Sanibel FL (33957-1550)
PHONE 212 686-8860
Shannon McAlpine, *Sales Dir*
Nancy Mosny, *Mng Member*
Rudolf Mosny,
▲ **EMP:** 25
SALES (est): 2.6MM **Privately Held**
SIC: 3089 2392 Tableware, plastic; household furnishings

(G-11789)
QHI GROUP INCORPORATED
40 Wall St Ste 2866 (10005-1304)
PHONE 646 512-5727
Steven Quinn, *President*
EMP: 5 **EST:** 2010
SALES (est): 658.5K **Privately Held**
SIC: 3829 Thermometers & temperature sensors

(G-11790)
QLOGIX ENTERTAINMENT LLC
600 W 113th St 7b4 (10025-7952)
PHONE 215 459-6315
Shyno Mathew, *CEO*
Jennifer Appawu, *President*
EMP: 5
SALES (est): 117.2K **Privately Held**
SIC: 7372 7371 Educational computer software; custom computer programming services

(G-11791)
QUAD/GRAPHICS INC
60 5th Ave Low Level (10011-8868)
PHONE 212 206-5535
EMP: 509
SALES (corp-wide): 4.3B **Publicly Held**
SIC: 2752 Commercial printing, lithographic
PA: Quad/Graphics Inc.
N61w23044 Harrys Way
Sussex WI 53089
414 566-6000

(G-11792)
QUAD/GRAPHICS INC
375 Hudson St (10014-3658)
PHONE 212 741-1001
Fax: 212 741-1077
Mike Horton, *Branch Mgr*
EMP: 509
SALES (corp-wide): 4.3B **Publicly Held**
SIC: 2752 Commercial printing, lithographic
PA: Quad/Graphics Inc.
N61w23044 Harrys Way
Sussex WI 53089
414 566-6000

(G-11793)
QUALITY IMPRESSIONS INC
163 Varick St Fl 6 (10013-1108)
PHONE 646 613-0002
Fax: 646 613-0002
Brennan Ganga, *President*
EMP: 6
SALES: 600K **Privately Held**
SIC: 2759 Commercial printing

(G-11794)
QUALITY PATTERNS INC
246 W 38th St Fl 9 (10018-9076)
PHONE 212 704-0355
Fax: 212 921-0568
Mario Lipari, *President*
Joe Lipari, *Vice Pres*
EMP: 70
SQ FT: 14,000
SALES (est): 5.8MM **Privately Held**
WEB: www.qualitypatterns.com
SIC: 2335 2741 Women's, juniors' & misses' dresses; miscellaneous publishing

(G-11795)
QUARTET FINANCIAL SYSTEMS INC (PA)
1412 Broadway Rm 2300 (10018-9240)
PHONE 845 358-6071
Kathleen Perrotte, *President*
Xavier Bellouard, *Managing Dir*
Georges Bory, *Managing Dir*
David Cassonnet, *Managing Dir*
Zevier Dellouard, *Managing Dir*
EMP: 14
SALES (est): 5.9MM **Privately Held**
SIC: 7372 Prepackaged software

(G-11796)
QUARTO GROUP INC (DH)
276 5th Ave Rm 205 (10001-8308)
PHONE 212 779-0700
Lawrence Orbach, *Chairman*
Marcus Leaver, *COO*
Vessela Antonova, *Manager*
Carine Delagrave, *Director*
Ben Heywood, *Director*
▲ **EMP:** 30
SALES (est): 62.1MM
SALES (corp-wide): 9MM **Privately Held**
WEB: www.quarto.com
SIC: 2731 Books: publishing only
HQ: Quarto Group Inc(The)
The Old Brewery
London
207 700-6700

(G-11797)
QUEST BEAD & CAST INC
Also Called: Quest Beads
49 W 37th St Fl 16 (10018-6226)
PHONE 212 354-1737
Fax: 212 354-0978
Marcelle Rosenstrauch, *President*
Josephine Polizzi, *Manager*
▼ **EMP:** 8
SQ FT: 2,000
SALES (est): 510K **Privately Held**
WEB: www.questbeads.com
SIC: 3914 Pewter ware

(G-11798)
QUEST MEDIA LLC
Also Called: Quest Magazine
920 3rd Ave Fl 6 (10022-3627)
PHONE 646 840-3404
Fax: 212 840-3408
Lily Hoagland, *Editor*
Alex Travers, *Assoc Editor*
Christopher Meigher,
EMP: 19
SQ FT: 9,000
SALES (est): 2.6MM **Privately Held**
SIC: 2721 Magazines: publishing only, not printed on site

(G-11799)
QUILTED KOALA LTD
1384 Broadway Ste 15 (10018-6108)
PHONE 800 223-5678
Stephanie Oppenheim, *CEO*
David Weinstein, *President*
EMP: 11 **EST:** 2007
SALES (est): 148.2K **Privately Held**
SIC: 3171 5137 5632 Women's handbags & purses; handbags; handbags

(G-11800)
QUINN AND CO OF NY LTD
48 W 38th St Ph (10018-6248)
PHONE 212 868-1900
Florence Quinn, *President*
Morgan Painvin, *Exec VP*
Gregory McGunagle, *Vice Pres*
Suzanne Rosnowski, *Real Estate*
EMP: 70
SALES: 10MM **Privately Held**
SIC: 2084 5141 7011 4724 Wines, brandy & brandy spirits; food brokers; resort hotel; travel agencies

(G-11801)
QUOGUE CAPITAL LLC
1285 Ave Of The Ave Fl 35 (10019)
PHONE 212 554-4475
Wayne Rothbaum, *Mng Member*
EMP: 5 **EST:** 2001
SALES (est): 406.8K **Privately Held**
SIC: 2834 Pharmaceutical preparations

(G-11802)
QUOTABLE CARDS INC
611 Broadway Rm 810 (10012-2648)
PHONE 212 420-7552
Gillian Simon, *CEO*
Carol Monte, *Opers Staff*
Lauren Dopkin, *Sales Mgr*
Kris Ohlsen, *Director*
▲ **EMP:** 6
SALES: 500K **Privately Held**
WEB: www.quotablecards.com
SIC: 2771 2782 Greeting cards; memorandum books, printed

▲ = Import ▼ = Export
◆ = Import/Export

GEOGRAPHIC SECTION
New York - New York County (G-11828)

(G-11803)
QUOVO INC
29 W 30th St Fl 2 (10001-4615)
PHONE.................................646 216-9437
Lowell Putnam, *CEO*
Anne Buckel, *Analyst*
EMP: 20
SALES (est): 1.5MM **Privately Held**
SIC: 7372 Application computer software

(G-11804)
QUVA PHARMA INC
135 Central Park W (10023-2413)
PHONE.................................973 224-7795
Stuart Hinchen, *President*
EMP: 5
SALES (est): 355K **Privately Held**
SIC: 2834 Pharmaceutical preparations

(G-11805)
QWORLDSTAR INC
200 Park Ave S Fl 8 (10003-1526)
PHONE.................................212 768-4500
EMP: 8 EST: 2013
SALES (est): 470.7K **Privately Held**
SIC: 2741 Internet Publishing And Broadcasting

(G-11806)
R & M GRAPHICS OF NEW YORK
121 Varick St Fl 9 (10013-1408)
PHONE.................................212 929-0294
Mario Balzano, *President*
Ron Balzano, *Vice Pres*
EMP: 15 EST: 1991
SQ FT: 10,000
SALES: 1.5MM **Privately Held**
SIC: 2759 Commercial printing

(G-11807)
R & M INDUSTRIES INC
111 Broadway Rm 1112 (10006-1933)
PHONE.................................212 366-6414
Erik Van Kreuninger, *CEO*
Metje Saffir, *Principal*
Robert Van Kreuninger, *Vice Pres*
Sherry Moore, *Controller*
▲ EMP: 14
SQ FT: 198,000
SALES (est): 1MM **Privately Held**
SIC: 2392 Pillows, bed: made from purchased materials; tablecloths: made from purchased materials

(G-11808)
R & M RICHARDS INC (PA)
1400 Broadway Fl 9 (10018-5300)
PHONE.................................212 921-8820
Fax: 212 398-1813
Mario Dellanno, *CEO*
Richard Dellanno, *President*
Robert Dellanno, *Vice Pres*
Robert Dellano, *Vice Pres*
Stephanie Louis, *Production*
▲ EMP: 65
SQ FT: 19,000
SALES (est): 33.1MM **Privately Held**
WEB: www.rmrich.com
SIC: 2337 2335 Women's & misses' suits & skirts; women's, juniors' & misses' dresses

(G-11809)
R & R GROSBARD INC
1156 Avenue Of The Americ (10036-2702)
PHONE.................................212 575-0077
Robert Grosbard, *Ch of Bd*
Amish Shah, *COO*
Grendy Raymonds, *Controller*
Fran Laucella, *Relations*
EMP: 30
SALES (est): 3.2MM **Privately Held**
SIC: 3911 Jewelry apparel

(G-11810)
R-PAC INTERNATIONAL CORP (PA)
132 W 36th St Fl 7 (10018-8825)
PHONE.................................212 465-1818
Daniel Teitelbaum, *CEO*
Michael Teitelbaum, *President*
Peter D Amico, *CFO*
Aaron Glatman, *VP Sales*
▲ EMP: 40
SQ FT: 15,000
SALES (est): 11.1MM **Privately Held**
SIC: 2241 Labels, woven

(G-11811)
R-S RESTAURANT EQP MFG CORP (PA)
Also Called: Preferred Wholesale
272 Bowery (10012-3674)
PHONE.................................212 925-0335
Chekee Ho, *President*
Fu Ho, *Vice Pres*
▲ EMP: 10
SQ FT: 2,500
SALES (est): 1.8MM **Privately Held**
SIC: 3589 5046 Commercial cooking & foodwarming equipment; restaurant equipment & supplies

(G-11812)
RADICLE FARM LLC
Also Called: Radicle Farm Company
394 Broadway Fl 5 (10013-6023)
P.O. Box 7361, Newark NJ (07107-0361)
PHONE.................................315 226-3294
Christopher Washington, *CEO*
Jenna Blumenfeld, *Principal*
Tony Gibbons, *Principal*
Silvia Huerta, *Principal*
James Livengood, *Principal*
EMP: 5
SALES (est): 183K **Privately Held**
SIC: 2099 Salads, fresh or refrigerated

(G-11813)
RAFFETTOS CORP
144 W Houston St (10012-2546)
PHONE.................................212 777-1261
Fax: 212 777-1429
Richard Raffetto, *President*
Andrew Raffetto, *Vice Pres*
EMP: 20
SQ FT: 7,000
SALES (est): 2.5MM **Privately Held**
SIC: 2098 5499 Macaroni & spaghetti; noodles (e.g. egg, plain & water), dry; gourmet food stores

(G-11814)
RAG & BONE INDUSTRIES LLC
416 W 13th St (10014-1117)
PHONE.................................212 249-3331
Shannon Overman, *Area Mgr*
Rachel Zacharias, *Store Mgr*
Chris Vieth, *CFO*
Pamela Yueh, *Controller*
Litisha Daring, *Branch Mgr*
EMP: 42
SALES (corp-wide): 52.4MM **Privately Held**
SIC: 2326 Men's & boys' work clothing
PA: Rag & Bone Industries Llc
425 W 13th St Ofc 2
New York NY 10014
212 278-8214

(G-11815)
RAG & BONE INDUSTRIES LLC (PA)
425 W 13th St Ofc 2 (10014-1123)
PHONE.................................212 278-8214
Marissa Kraxberger, *Vice Pres*
John Gram, *Store Mgr*
Krystin Vandervort, *Store Mgr*
Jamie Steingold, *Human Res Mgr*
Stefan Ayon, *Accounts Exec*
▲ EMP: 70
SALES (est): 52.4MM **Privately Held**
SIC: 2326 Men's & boys' work clothing

(G-11816)
RAILWORKS TRANSIT SYSTEMS INC (DH)
5 Penn Plz (10001-1810)
PHONE.................................212 502-7900
Jeffrey M Levy, *President*
Daniel Brown, *Principal*
Gene Cellini, *Senior VP*
John August, *Vice Pres*
Geane Jospeh Celoini, *Vice Pres*
EMP: 21
SALES (est): 73.8MM
SALES (corp-wide): 1.4B **Privately Held**
SIC: 3531 Railway track equipment
HQ: Railworks Corporation
5 Penn Plz
New York NY 10001
212 502-7900

(G-11817)
RAINFOREST APPAREL LLC
1385 Broadway Fl 24 (10018-6009)
PHONE.................................212 840-0880
Jack Wo, *President*
▲ EMP: 8
SALES (est): 547.3K **Privately Held**
SIC: 2389 Disposable garments & accessories

(G-11818)
RALEIGH AND DRAKE PBC
110 E 25th St Fl 3 (10010-2913)
PHONE.................................212 625-8212
Fax: 212 625-8211
Patrick Sarkissian, *CEO*
Gilad Goren,
EMP: 15
SALES (est): 860K **Privately Held**
SIC: 7372 Application computer software

(G-11819)
RALPH LAUREN CORPORATION (PA)
650 Madison Ave Fl C1 (10022-1070)
PHONE.................................212 318-7000
Fax: 212 318-7180
Ralph Lauren, *Ch of Bd*
David Lauren, *Vice Ch Bd*
Patrice Louvet, *President*
Valerie Hermann, *President*
Kristen Bowman, *Vice Pres*
◆ EMP: 500 EST: 1967
SQ FT: 270,000
SALES: 6.6B **Publicly Held**
WEB: www.polo.com
SIC: 2325 2321 2253 2323 Men's & boys' trousers & slacks; men's & boys' dress shirts; men's & boys' sports & polo shirts; shirts (outerwear), knit; sweaters & sweater coats, knit; ties, handsewn: made from purchased materials; topcoats, men's & boys': made from purchased materials; men's & boys' sportswear & athletic clothing; sweaters & sweater jackets: men's & boys'

(G-11820)
RALPH LAUREN CORPORATION
979 3rd Ave Ste 404 (10022-1270)
PHONE.................................212 421-1570
Brittany Atlas, *Marketing Staff*
Lauren Atlas, *Marketing Staff*
Megan Forlines, *Marketing Staff*
Thao Ngo, *Marketing Staff*
Sarah Cappy, *Manager*
EMP: 9
SALES (corp-wide): 6.6B **Publicly Held**
SIC: 2321 Men's & boys' furnishings
PA: Ralph Lauren Corporation
650 Madison Ave Fl C1
New York NY 10022
212 318-7000

(G-11821)
RALPH LAUREN CORPORATION
205 W 39th St Fl 13 (10018-3532)
PHONE.................................917 934-4200
EMP: 7
SALES (corp-wide): 6.6B **Publicly Held**
SIC: 2339 Women's & misses' outerwear
PA: Ralph Lauren Corporation
650 Madison Ave Fl C1
New York NY 10022
212 318-7000

(G-11822)
RALPH LAUREN CORPORATION
25 W 39th St Fl 8 (10018-4073)
PHONE.................................212 221-7751
Michael Arahill, *Branch Mgr*
Patrick McCombb, *Technician*
EMP: 10
SALES (corp-wide): 6.6B **Publicly Held**
SIC: 2335 Women's, juniors' & misses' dresses
PA: Ralph Lauren Corporation
650 Madison Ave Fl C1
New York NY 10022
212 318-7000

(G-11823)
RAMSBURY PROPERTY US INC (DH)
Also Called: Benetton Services
601 5th Ave Fl 4 (10017-8258)
P.O. Box 6020, Somerset NJ (08875-6020)
PHONE.................................212 223-6250
Fax: 212 371-1438
Carlo Tunioli, *Vice Pres*
Diane Mravcak, *Vice Pres*
Kurt Andersen, *Manager*
Robyn Forest, *Manager*
Angie Maximo, *Manager*
▲ EMP: 13
SQ FT: 10,000
SALES (est): 4.4MM
SALES (corp-wide): 9.1MM **Privately Held**
SIC: 2329 2339 5651 8742 Men's & boys' sportswear & athletic clothing; sportswear, women's; family clothing stores; marketing consulting services
HQ: Benetton Group Srl
Via Villa Minelli 1
Ponzano Veneto TV 31050
042 251-9111

(G-11824)
RAMY BROOK LLC
231 W 39th St Rm 720 (10018-1089)
PHONE.................................212 744-2789
Ira Rosenfeld, *COO*
Peter Macri, *Senior VP*
Nellie Roch, *Opers Mgr*
Kristina Aquino, *Design Engr*
Aryeh Melaris, *CFO*
▲ EMP: 30
SQ FT: 5,000
SALES (est): 4.1MM **Privately Held**
SIC: 2331 Women's & misses' blouses & shirts

(G-11825)
RANDA ACCESSORIES LEA GDS LLC
417 5th Ave Fl 11 (10016-2238)
PHONE.................................212 354-5100
John Hastings, *Branch Mgr*
EMP: 100
SALES (corp-wide): 126.8MM **Privately Held**
SIC: 2387 3161 3172 2389 Apparel belts; attache cases; briefcases; suitcases; wallets; suspenders; neckties, men's & boys': made from purchased materials
PA: Randa Accessories Leather Goods Llc
5600 N River Rd Ste 500
Rosemont IL 60018
847 292-8300

(G-11826)
RANDALL LOEFFLER INC
588 Broadway Rm 1203 (10012-5237)
PHONE.................................212 226-8787
Jessica L Randall, *CEO*
Amanda Thomas, *COO*
Brian Murphy, *CFO*
▲ EMP: 30
SQ FT: 2,500
SALES (est): 4.6MM **Privately Held**
SIC: 3131 7371 5699 Boot & shoe accessories; computer software development & applications; designers, apparel

(G-11827)
RANDGOLD RESOURCES LTD
101 Barclay St (10007-2550)
PHONE.................................212 815-2129
Graham Shuttleworth, *CFO*
Ted De Villiers, *Manager*
EMP: 5
SALES (est): 235.7K **Privately Held**
SIC: 1241 Coal mining services

(G-11828)
RASCO GRAPHICS INC
519 8th Ave Fl 18 (10018-4577)
PHONE.................................212 206-0447
Fax: 212 242-2818
Howard Frank, *President*
Jackie Romano, *Bookkeeper*
EMP: 6
SQ FT: 2,000
SALES (est): 570K **Privately Held**
SIC: 2752 Commercial printing, offset

New York - New York County (G-11829) GEOGRAPHIC SECTION

(G-11829)
RAVEN NEW YORK LLC
450 W 15th St (10011-7097)
PHONE..................................212 584-9690
Fax: 212 466-1808
▲ EMP: 6
SQ FT: 2,500
SALES (est): 710K Privately Held
SIC: 2331 2335 Womens And Misses Blouses And Shirts, Nsk

(G-11830)
RAXON FABRICS CORP (HQ)
261 5th Ave (10016-7701)
PHONE..................................212 532-6816
Fax: 212 481-9361
Joe Berasi, *President*
Ruud Averson, *President*
Harry Ellis, *Vice Pres*
Kevin Michael, *Plant Mgr*
Connie Loftis, *QA Dir*
▲ EMP: 13 EST: 1947
SQ FT: 7,400
SALES (est): 4.4MM Privately Held
WEB: www.raxon.com
SIC: 2262 Silk broadwoven fabric finishing
PA: Vescom B.V.
  V Diepenheim Scheltusln 32
  Leusden
  334 944-010

(G-11831)
RAY GRIFFITHS INC
303 5th Ave Rm 1901 (10016-6658)
PHONE..................................212 689-7209
Ray Griffiths, *Principal*
Kirsten Geary, *Marketing Staff*
EMP: 7
SALES (est): 457.8K Privately Held
SIC: 1499 Gem stones (natural) mining

(G-11832)
RAY MEDICA INC
505 Park Ave Ste 1400 (10022-9315)
PHONE..................................952 885-0500
Todd Johnson, *Vice Pres*
Mary Fuller, *CFO*
Monique Priest, *Supervisor*
EMP: 45
SALES (est): 1.9MM Privately Held
SIC: 3845 Electromedical equipment

(G-11833)
RAYDOOR INC
134 W 29th St Rm 909 (10001-5304)
PHONE..................................212 421-0641
Fax: 212 349-1856
Luke Sigel, *President*
Craig Weidhorn, *General Mgr*
Lana Abraham, *Vice Pres*
Justin Brownell, *Project Mgr*
Ted Fotopoulos, *Opers Mgr*
EMP: 6
SALES (est): 1MM Privately Held
WEB: www.raydoor.com
SIC: 3442 Metal doors, sash & trim

(G-11834)
RAZORFISH LLC
1440 Broadway Fl 18 (10018-2312)
PHONE..................................212 798-6600
Lorna Colgan, *Publisher*
Maggie Boyer, *General Mgr*
Paul Brownlow, *Project Mgr*
Melanie Bean, *Buyer*
Nate Carlson, *Buyer*
EMP: 10
SALES (corp-wide): 28.2MM Privately Held
WEB: www.avenuea.com
SIC: 7372 Prepackaged software
HQ: Razorfish, Llc
  424 2nd Ave W
  Seattle WA 98119
  206 816-8800

(G-11835)
RB DIAMOND INC
22 W 48th St Ste 904 (10036-1803)
PHONE..................................212 398-4560
Fax: 866 266-0078
Rafael Inoyatov, *Principal*
EMP: 5
SALES (est): 396.3K Privately Held
SIC: 3356 Gold & gold alloy bars, sheets, strip, etc.

(G-11836)
RD INTRNTNL STYLE
275 W 39th St Fl 7 (10018-0748)
PHONE..................................212 382-2360
Kenneth Hollinger, *Ch of Bd*
▲ EMP: 8
SALES (est): 750K Privately Held
SIC: 2339 Women's & misses' outerwear

(G-11837)
RDA HOLDING CO (PA)
Also Called: Rittlewood Holding Co
750 3rd Ave (10017-2703)
PHONE..................................914 238-1000
Harvey Golub, *CEO*
Fredric G Reynolds, *Ch of Bd*
Bonnie Kintzer, *President*
Randall Curran, *Chairman*
Albert L Perruzza, *Exec VP*
EMP: 17
SQ FT: 445,193
SALES (est): 1.3B Privately Held
SIC: 2721 2731 5961 2741 Periodicals; book publishing; catalog & mail-order houses; miscellaneous publishing

(G-11838)
RDD PHARMA INC
3 Columbus Cir Fl 15 (10019-8716)
PHONE..................................302 319-9970
Nir Barak, *Principal*
Arie Giniger, *Bd of Directors*
EMP: 5
SQ FT: 150
SALES (est): 260.3K Privately Held
SIC: 3841 Surgical & medical instruments

(G-11839)
READERS DIGEST ASSN INC THE
16 E 34th St Fl 14 (10016-4360)
PHONE..................................414 423-0100
Diane Jones, *Branch Mgr*
EMP: 16
SALES (corp-wide): 1.3B Privately Held
WEB: www.rd.com
SIC: 2721 Magazines: publishing only, not printed on site
HQ: Trusted Media Brands, Inc.
  750 3rd Ave Fl 3
  New York NY 10017
  914 238-1000

(G-11840)
READING ROOM INC (PA)
48 Wall St Fl 5 (10005-2911)
PHONE..................................212 463-1029
EMP: 6
SALES (est): 1.8MM Privately Held
SIC: 2731 Book publishing

(G-11841)
REAL ESTATE MEDIA INC
120 Broadway Fl 5 (10271-1100)
PHONE..................................212 929-6976
Jonathan Schein, *President*
Jessica Dume, *Human Resources*
EMP: 45
SALES (est): 3.9MM Privately Held
SIC: 2721 Magazines: publishing only, not printed on site

(G-11842)
REAL INDUSTRY INC (PA)
17 State St Ste 3811 (10004-1728)
PHONE..................................805 435-1255
William K Hall, *Ch of Bd*
Kyle Ross, *President*
Terrance Hogan, *President*
Kelly G Howard, *Exec VP*
John Miller, *Exec VP*
EMP: 12
SALES: 1.2B Publicly Held
SIC: 3341 3313 3613 Secondary nonferrous metals; alloys, additive, except copper: not made in blast furnaces; ferromanganese, not made in blast furnaces; power circuit breakers; circuit breakers, air

(G-11843)
REALITY ANALYTICS INC
Also Called: Reality Ai
157 Columbus Ave (10023-6082)
PHONE..................................347 363-2200

Stuart Feffer, *CEO*
Jeff Sieracki, *Chief Engr*
EMP: 5
SALES (est): 540.2K Privately Held
SIC: 7372 Business oriented computer software

(G-11844)
REASON SOFTWARE COMPANY INC
228 Park Ave S Unit 74122 (10003-1502)
PHONE..................................646 664-1038
Andrew Newman, *CEO*
EMP: 10
SQ FT: 2,000
SALES (est): 244K Privately Held
SIC: 7372 Operating systems computer software

(G-11845)
REDBOOK MAGAZINE
224 W 57th St Lbby Fl22 (10019-3212)
PHONE..................................212 649-3331
Fax: 212 581-8114
Daniel Zucchi, *Principal*
Ellen Kumes, *Chief*
EMP: 12
SALES (est): 1.4MM Privately Held
SIC: 2721 7313 Magazines: publishing & printing; radio, television, publisher representatives

(G-11846)
REDKEN 5TH AVENUE NYC LLC
565 5th Ave (10017-2413)
PHONE..................................212 984-5113
Lynn Winsell, *Manager*
Claire Buxton, *Director*
EMP: 8
SALES (est): 1.1MM Privately Held
SIC: 2844 Cosmetic preparations

(G-11847)
REEBOK INTERNATIONAL LTD
1185 Av Of The Amrcs Lbby (10036-2601)
PHONE..................................212 221-6375
EMP: 7
SALES (corp-wide): 20.4B Privately Held
SIC: 3149 Athletic shoes, except rubber or plastic
HQ: Reebok International Ltd.
  1895 J W Foster Blvd
  Canton MA 02021
  781 401-5000

(G-11848)
REENTRY GAMES INC
215 E 5th St (10003-8563)
PHONE..................................646 421-0080
Andrew Kutruff, *President*
EMP: 5
SALES (est): 251.2K Privately Held
SIC: 7372 Home entertainment computer software

(G-11849)
REFINERY 29 INC (PA)
225 Broadway Fl 23 (10007-3728)
PHONE..................................212 966-3112
Philippe Von Borries, *Principal*
Christene Barberich, *Principal*
Piera Gelardi, *Principal*
Melissa Goidel, *Principal*
Justin Stesano, *Principal*
EMP: 73
SALES (est): 4.5MM Privately Held
SIC: 2741 Miscellaneous publishing

(G-11850)
REFUEL INC (PA)
Also Called: Refuel Jeans
1384 Broadway Rm 407 (10018-6140)
PHONE..................................917 645-2974
Srinivas RAO, *President*
Greg Anthony, *Natl Sales Mgr*
▲ EMP: 8
SQ FT: 1,800
SALES: 4MM Privately Held
SIC: 2211 5091 5699 Apparel & outerwear fabrics, cotton; sporting & recreation goods; sports apparel

(G-11851)
REGAL EMBLEM CO INC
250 W Broadway Fl 2 (10013-2431)
P.O. Box 230695 (10023-0012)
PHONE..................................212 925-8833
Fax: 212 925-3413
Judith Nadelson, *President*
Michael Bottino, *Vice Pres*
EMP: 15 EST: 1931
SQ FT: 5,000
SALES (est): 1.7MM Privately Held
SIC: 2399 Emblems, badges & insignia: from purchased materials

(G-11852)
REGAL JEWELRY INC
39 W 32nd St Rm 1004 (10001-3842)
PHONE..................................212 382-1695
Isaac Fraiwa, *President*
▲ EMP: 6
SQ FT: 10,000
SALES: 6MM Privately Held
SIC: 3911 Jewelry, precious metal

(G-11853)
REGAN ARTS LLC
65 Bleecker St Fl 8 (10012-2420)
PHONE..................................646 488-6610
Judith Regan, *CEO*
EMP: 12
SALES (est): 1.5MM
SALES (corp-wide): 33.7MM Privately Held
SIC: 2741 Miscellaneous publishing
HQ: Phaidon Press Limited
  Regent's Wharf
  London N1 9P
  207 843-1000

(G-11854)
REINHOLD BROTHERS INC
799 Park Ave (10021-3275)
PHONE..................................212 867-8310
John Reinhold, *President*
EMP: 20
SALES (est): 1.5MM Privately Held
SIC: 3911 5944 Jewel settings & mountings, precious metal; pearl jewelry, natural or cultured; jewelry, precious stones & precious metals

(G-11855)
RELAVIS CORPORATION
40 Wall St Ste 3300 (10005-1463)
PHONE..................................212 995-2900
Robert De Maio, *President*
Michael Baum, *President*
Jean-Pierre Ducondi, *Vice Pres*
EMP: 45
SQ FT: 2,500
SALES (est): 3MM Privately Held
SIC: 7372 Business oriented computer software

(G-11856)
RELIANT SECURITY
450 Fashion Ave Ste 503 (10123-0591)
PHONE..................................917 338-2200
Richard Newman, *CEO*
Mark Weiner, *Principal*
Jason Anderson, *VP Opers*
Thom Holland, *Project Mgr*
Charles Obrien, *Senior Engr*
EMP: 23
SALES: 2.8MM Privately Held
SIC: 7372 Prepackaged software

(G-11857)
RELMADA THERAPEUTICS INC
750 3rd Ave Fl 9 (10017-2718)
PHONE..................................646 677-3853
Sergio Traversa, *CEO*
Danny KAO, *Senior VP*
Michael D Becker, *CFO*
Richard M Mangano, *Security Dir*
EMP: 18 EST: 2007
SALES (est): 3.5MM Privately Held
SIC: 2834 Pharmaceutical preparations

(G-11858)
RELX INC (DH)
Also Called: Reed Business Information
230 Park Ave Ste 700 (10169-0005)
PHONE..................................212 309-8100
Fax: 212 309-5480
Mark Kelsey, *CEO*

Dominic Feltham, *President*
Michael Kaplun, *President*
Nicholas Luff, *President*
Koos Admiraal, *Publisher*
◆ **EMP:** 40
SQ FT: 30,000
SALES (est): 4.4B
SALES (corp-wide): 8.4B **Privately Held**
WEB: www.lexis-nexis.com
SIC: 2721 2731 7389 7374 Trade journals: publishing only, not printed on site; books: publishing only; trade show arrangement; data processing & preparation; systems analysis or design
HQ: Reed Elsevier Us Holdings, Inc.
1105 N Market St Ste 501
Wilmington DE 19801
302 427-2672

(G-11859)
RELX INC
249 W 17th St (10011-5390)
PHONE.............................212 463-6644
Cheryl Miller, *Manager*
EMP: 35
SALES (corp-wide): 8.4B **Privately Held**
WEB: www.lexis-nexis.com
SIC: 2721 Magazines: publishing only, not printed on site
HQ: Relx Inc.
230 Park Ave Ste 700
New York NY 10169
212 309-8100

(G-11860)
RELX INC
655 6th Ave (10010-5107)
PHONE.............................212 633-3900
Russell White, *President*
Jay Katzen, *Managing Dir*
Lisa Layton, *Manager*
EMP: 260
SALES (corp-wide): 8.4B **Privately Held**
WEB: www.lexis-nexis.com
SIC: 2721 Periodicals
HQ: Relx Inc.
230 Park Ave Ste 700
New York NY 10169
212 309-8100

(G-11861)
REMAINS LIGHTING
130 W 28th St Frnt 1 (10001-6151)
PHONE.............................212 675-8051
Fax: 212 675-8052
David Calligeros, *Owner*
Jimmy Kaston, *General Mgr*
Katie Brennan, *Sales Dir*
Hayley Mace, *Sales Staff*
Lauren Reed, *Sales Staff*
EMP: 20
SQ FT: 1,500
SALES (est): 2.8MM **Privately Held**
SIC: 3646 3645 Commercial indusl & institutional electric lighting fixtures; residential lighting fixtures

(G-11862)
RENAISSANCE BIJOU LTD
20 W 47th St Ste 18 (10036-3303)
PHONE.............................212 869-1969
Fax: 212 869-1371
Elias Theodoropoulos, *President*
EMP: 8
SQ FT: 3,000
SALES (est): 680K **Privately Held**
SIC: 3911 Jewelry, precious metal

(G-11863)
RENAISSNCE CRPT TAPESTRIES INC
Also Called: Renaissance Global
200 Lexington Ave Rm 1006 (10016-6255)
PHONE.............................212 696-0080
Fax: 212 696-4248
Jan Soleimani, *President*
Jeffrey Soleimani, *Vice Pres*
John Lally, *Office Mgr*
Bergi Andonian, *Admin Sec*
▲ **EMP:** 12
SQ FT: 7,000
SALES (est): 1.5MM **Privately Held**
SIC: 2273 2211 Rugs, hand & machine made; tapestry fabrics, cotton

(G-11864)
RENCO GROUP INC (PA)
1 Rockefeller Plz Fl 29 (10020-2021)
PHONE.............................212 541-6000
Fax: 212 541-6197
Ira Leon Rennert, *President*
ARI Rennert, *Chairman*
Marvin Koenig, *Exec VP*
Diana Sadykova, *Assistant VP*
Roger L Fay, *Vice Pres*
◆ **EMP:** 4
SQ FT: 10,000
SALES (est): 4.1B **Privately Held**
WEB: www.rencogroup.net
SIC: 3312 3316 2514 2511 Sheet or strip, steel, cold-rolled: own hot-rolled; corrugating iron & steel, cold-rolled; metal kitchen & dining room furniture; wood household furniture; kitchen & dining room furniture; handbags, women's; cages, wire

(G-11865)
RENEGADE NATION LTD
434 Av Of The Amercs Fl 6 (10011-8411)
PHONE.............................212 868-9000
Jerry Eisner, *Principal*
Gloria Winter, *Office Mgr*
Mike Dimino, *Info Tech Dir*
Louis Arzonico, *Art Dir*
Dennis Mortensen, *Executive*
EMP: 15 **EST:** 1993
SQ FT: 4,400
SALES (est): 1.4MM **Privately Held**
WEB: www.renegadenation.com
SIC: 2782 Record albums

(G-11866)
RENEGADE NATION ONLINE LLC
434 Ave Of The Americas # 6 (10011-8411)
PHONE.............................212 868-9000
Jerome Eisner, *Accountant*
EMP: 8
SQ FT: 2,400
SALES (est): 265K **Privately Held**
SIC: 2741

(G-11867)
REPERTOIRE INTERNATIONAL DE LI
Also Called: RILM
365 5th Ave Fl 3 (10016-4309)
PHONE.............................212 817-1990
Jason Oakes, *Editor*
Lori Rothstein, *Editor*
Michele Smith, *Editor*
Naomi Perley, *Office Mgr*
Rachael Brungard, *Assoc Editor*
EMP: 25
SALES: 3MM **Privately Held**
SIC: 2731 2741 Book publishing; miscellaneous publishing

(G-11868)
REPUBLIC CLOTHING CORPORATION
Also Called: Republic Clothing Group
1411 Broadway Fl 37 (10018-3413)
PHONE.............................212 719-3000
Fax: 212 719-3057
Steven M Sall, *Ch of Bd*
Michael Warner, *President*
Jerry Kau, *Office Mgr*
▲ **EMP:** 30
SQ FT: 7,500
SALES (est): 10.7MM **Privately Held**
SIC: 2339 Women's & misses' outerwear

(G-11869)
REPUBLIC CLOTHING GROUP INC
1411 Broadway Fl 37 (10018-3413)
PHONE.............................212 719-3000
Michael Warner, *President*
Steven M Sall, *Chairman*
Alison Cho, *Controller*
EMP: 150
SQ FT: 7,500
SALES (est): 1.8MM **Privately Held**
SIC: 2339 Aprons, except rubber or plastic: women's, misses', juniors'

(G-11870)
RES MEDIA GROUP INC
Also Called: RES Magazine
601 W 26th St Fl 11 (10001-1101)
PHONE.............................212 320-3750
Fax: 212 937-7134
David Beal, *CEO*
Les Garland, *President*
Jonathan Wells, *Vice Pres*
EMP: 12
SALES (est): 801.7K **Privately Held**
WEB: www.res.com
SIC: 2721 8742 Periodicals; management consulting services
PA: Sputnik7.Com Llc
601 W 26th St Fl 11
New York NY

(G-11871)
RESERVOIR MEDIA MANAGEMENT INC (PA)
225 Varick St Fl 6 (10014-4388)
PHONE.............................212 675-0541
Golnar Khosrowshahi, *CEO*
Rell Lafargue, *COO*
Faith Newman, *Senior VP*
Steven Storch, *CFO*
Tom Barnhart, *Office Admin*
EMP: 12
SQ FT: 8,000
SALES (est): 1.5MM **Privately Held**
SIC: 2741 Music book & sheet music publishing

(G-11872)
RESONANT LEGAL MEDIA LLC
1040 Av Of The Amrcs 18 (10018-3703)
PHONE.............................212 687-7100
Patrick Swart, *Branch Mgr*
EMP: 20
SALES (corp-wide): 34.9MM **Privately Held**
SIC: 2752 7336 8748 Commercial printing, lithographic; commercial art & graphic design; business consulting
PA: Resonant Legal Media, Llc
1 Penn Plz Ste 1514
New York NY 10119
800 781-3591

(G-11873)
RESONANT LEGAL MEDIA LLC (PA)
Also Called: Trialgraphix
1 Penn Plz Ste 1514 (10119-1514)
PHONE.............................800 781-3591
Fax: 212 687-0411
Richard S Pennell, *CEO*
Steven Stolberg, *President*
Luis E Otero, *Vice Pres*
Patrick Paulin, *Vice Pres*
Elizabeth Noble, *Prdtn Mgr*
EMP: 90
SQ FT: 35,000
SALES (est): 34.9MM **Privately Held**
SIC: 2752 7336 3993 2761 Commercial printing, offset; graphic arts & related design; signs & advertising specialties; manifold business forms

(G-11874)
RESOURCE PTRLM&PTROCHMCL INTL
3 Columbus Cir Fl 15 (10019-8716)
PHONE.............................212 537-3856
Damon Lee, *Ch of Bd*
Daunette Lee, *Vice Pres*
Akpan Ekpo, *Director*
EMP: 20
SALES (est): 384.9K **Privately Held**
SIC: 1311 Crude petroleum production

(G-11875)
RESTAURANT 570 8TH AVENUE LLC
Also Called: Wok To Walk
213 W 40th St Fl 3 (10018-1627)
PHONE.............................646 722-8191
Aviv Schwietzer,
EMP: 15 **EST:** 2013
SALES (est): 1.5MM **Privately Held**
SIC: 2599 Food wagons, restaurant

(G-11876)
RETROPHIN LLC
777 3rd Ave Fl 22 (10017-1401)
PHONE.............................646 564-3680
Martin Shkreli, *CEO*
Alvin Shih, *Exec VP*
Jennifer Hunt, *Vice Pres*
Nils Olsson, *Vice Pres*
Jesse Shefferman, *Vice Pres*
EMP: 8
SALES (est): 832.1K **Privately Held**
SIC: 2834 Pharmaceutical preparations

(G-11877)
RETURN TEXTILES LLC
187 Lafayette St Fl 5 (10013-3221)
PHONE.............................646 408-0108
Pinothy Coombs, *Mng Member*
Tyson Toussaint, *Mng Member*
Pharrell Williams,
EMP: 6
SALES (est): 273.9K **Privately Held**
SIC: 2299 Apparel filling: cotton waste, kapok & related material; upholstery filling, textile

(G-11878)
REVLON INC (PA)
1 New York Plz (10004-1901)
PHONE.............................212 527-4000
Fax: 212 527-4130
Ronald O Perelman, *Ch of Bd*
E Scott Beattie, *Vice Ch Bd*
Fabian T Garcia, *President*
Chris Peterson, *COO*
Giovanni Pieraccini, *COO*
▲ **EMP:** 277
SQ FT: 91,000
SALES: 2.3B **Publicly Held**
WEB: www.revlon.com
SIC: 2844 Toilet preparations; perfumes & colognes; deodorants, personal; hair coloring preparations

(G-11879)
REVLON CONSUMER PRODUCTS CORP (HQ)
1 New York Plz (10004-1901)
PHONE.............................212 527-4000
Ronald O Perelman, *Ch of Bd*
Fabian T Garcia, *President*
Gianni Pieraccioni, *COO*
Juan R Figuereo, *CFO*
▲ **EMP:** 277
SQ FT: 91,000
SALES: 2.3B **Publicly Held**
SIC: 2844 3421 Toilet preparations; cosmetic preparations; perfumes & colognes; hair preparations, including shampoos; clippers, fingernail & toenail; scissors, hand
PA: Revlon, Inc.
1 New York Plz
New York NY 10004
212 527-4000

(G-11880)
REVMAN INTERNATIONAL INC (DH)
350 5th Ave Fl 70 (10118-7000)
PHONE.............................212 894-3100
Richard Roman, *President*
Normand Savaria, *Senior VP*
Brad Comisar, *Vice Pres*
Tom Derosa, *Vice Pres*
Diane Piemonte, *Vice Pres*
◆ **EMP:** 40
SQ FT: 20,000
SALES (est): 36.3MM **Privately Held**
WEB: www.revman.com
SIC: 2391 2392 Draperies, plastic & textile: from purchased materials; comforters & quilts: made from purchased materials
HQ: Kaltex North America, Inc.
350 5th Ave Ste 7100
New York NY 10118
212 894-3200

(G-11881)
REVOLUTIONWEAR INC
1745 Broadway Fl 17 (10019-4642)
PHONE.............................617 669-9191
Mathias Ingvarsson, *President*
Kinda Youmes, *Manager*
▲ **EMP:** 5

New York - New York County (G-11882)   GEOGRAPHIC SECTION

SALES (est): 368.2K **Privately Held**
SIC: 2322 Men's & boys' underwear & nightwear

(G-11882)
REYNOLDS METALS COMPANY LLC (HQ)
390 Park Ave (10022-4608)
PHONE..................212 518-5400
Tomas Mar Sigurdsson, *President*
Julian Taylor, *Exec VP*
Francesco Bassoli, *Vice Pres*
Robert Bear, *Vice Pres*
Amador Cardenas, *Vice Pres*
◆ EMP: 1 EST: 1928
SALES (est): 1.2B
SALES (corp-wide): 9.3B **Publicly Held**
SIC: 3411 Aluminum cans; beverage cans, metal: except beer; beer cans, metal; food containers, metal
PA: Alcoa Corporation
  201 Isabella St Ste 500
  Pittsburgh PA 15212
  412 992-5450

(G-11883)
RFP LLC
Also Called: Bridal Guide
228 E 45th St Fl 11 (10017-3345)
PHONE..................212 838-7733
Fax: 212 308-7165
Barry Rosenbloom, *Partner*
Jeremy Bucovetsky, *Partner*
Yelena Malinovskaya, *Partner*
Mike Rosenbloom, *Partner*
Mary Clarke, *Editor*
EMP: 35
SQ FT: 11,000
SALES (est): 5.3MM **Privately Held**
WEB: www.bridalguide.com
SIC: 2721 4724 Magazines: publishing only, not printed on site; travel agencies

(G-11884)
RG BARRY CORPORATION
Also Called: Dearfoams Div
9 E 37th St Fl 11 (10016-2822)
PHONE..................212 244-3145
Howard Eisenberg, *Manager*
EMP: 10
SALES (corp-wide): 29.1MM **Privately Held**
WEB: www.rgbarry.com
SIC: 3142 House slippers
HQ: R.G. Barry Corporation
  13405 Yarmouth Rd Nw
  Pickerington OH 43147
  614 864-6400

(G-11885)
RG GLASS CREATIONS INC
Also Called: R G Glass
1441 Broadway 28 (10018-1905)
PHONE..................212 675-0030
Edward Geyman, *President*
EMP: 38
SALES (est): 8.7MM **Privately Held**
SIC: 3211 Construction glass

(G-11886)
RHODA LEE INC
77 W 55th St Apt 4k (10019-4920)
PHONE..................212 840-5700
Fax: 212 819-1269
Michael Laufer, *President*
Henry Alcalay, *Vice Pres*
Audrey Laufer, *Vice Pres*
▲ EMP: 75
SQ FT: 11,000
SALES (est): 6.2MM **Privately Held**
SIC: 2331 2337 2339 Blouses, women's & juniors': made from purchased material; skirts, separate: women's, misses & juniors'; slacks: women's, misses' & juniors'

(G-11887)
RIBZ LLC
1407 Broadway Rm 1402 (10018-2838)
PHONE..................212 764-9595
EMP: 5
SALES (est): 330K **Privately Held**
SIC: 2389 Mfg Apparel/Accessories

(G-11888)
RICHARD LEEDS INTL INC (PA)
Also Called: True Colors
135 Madison Ave Fl 10 (10016-6739)
PHONE..................212 532-4546
Fax: 212 696-8450
Marcia L Leeds, *President*
Richard M Leeds, *Chairman*
Beth Shindelman, *CFO*
Sudesh Chonkar, *Controller*
Mary Petrolino, *Human Res Dir*
▲ EMP: 49
SQ FT: 12,500
SALES (est): 13.6MM **Privately Held**
WEB: www.richardleeds.com
SIC: 2339 2384 2341 Women's & misses athletic clothing & sportswear; bathrobes, men's & women's: made from purchased materials; women's & children's nightwear

(G-11889)
RICHEMONT NORTH AMERICA INC
Also Called: A. Lange & Sohne Corporate
645 5th Ave Fl 6 (10022-5923)
PHONE..................212 891-2440
EMP: 5
SALES (corp-wide): 12.3B **Privately Held**
SIC: 3873 Watches, clocks, watchcases & parts
HQ: Richemont North America, Inc.
  645 5th Ave Fl 5
  New York NY 10022
  212 891-2440

(G-11890)
RICHLINE GROUP INC
Eclipse Design Div
245 W 29th St Rm 900 (10001-5396)
PHONE..................212 643-2908
Eric Frid, *Branch Mgr*
EMP: 45
SALES (corp-wide): 223.6B **Publicly Held**
WEB: www.aurafin.net
SIC: 3911 Earrings, precious metal
HQ: Richline Group, Inc.
  1385 Broadway Fl 12
  New York NY 10018

(G-11891)
RICHLINE GROUP INC
1385 Broadway Fl 12 (10018-6118)
PHONE..................212 764-8454
EMP: 194
SALES (corp-wide): 194.6B **Publicly Held**
SIC: 3911 5094 Mfg Precious Metal Jewelry Whol Jewelry/Precious Stones
HQ: Richline Group, Inc.
  1385 Broadway Fl 12
  New York NY 10018
  212 886-6000

(G-11892)
RICHLINE GROUP INC
Also Called: Aurafin Oroamerica
1385 Broadway Fl 12 (10018-6118)
PHONE..................914 699-0000
EMP: 177
SALES (corp-wide): 194.6B **Publicly Held**
SIC: 3911 Mfg Precious Metal Jewelry
HQ: Richline Group, Inc.
  1385 Broadway Fl 12
  New York NY 10018
  212 886-6000

(G-11893)
RICHLOOM CORP
Also Called: Richloom Home Fashion
261 5th Ave Fl 12 (10016-7794)
PHONE..................212 685-5400
James Richman, *President*
Richard Wold, *Finance Dir*
▲ EMP: 10 EST: 1995
SALES (est): 6MM **Privately Held**
SIC: 2392 Bedspreads & bed sets: made from purchased materials

(G-11894)
RICHLOOM FABRICS CORP (PA)
261 5th Ave Fl 12 (10016-7794)
PHONE..................212 685-5400
Fax: 212 696-4407
James Richman, *Ch of Bd*
Fred M Richman, *President*
Ralph Geller, *Vice Pres*
Marvin Karp, *CFO*
Sidney J Silverman, *Admin Sec*
▲ EMP: 10
SQ FT: 12,000
SALES (est): 48.4MM **Privately Held**
SIC: 2391 5131 2392 Curtains & draperies; drapery material, woven; household furnishings

(G-11895)
RICHLOOM FABRICS GROUP INC (HQ)
Also Called: Berkshire Weaving
261 5th Ave Fl 12 (10016-7794)
PHONE..................212 685-5400
Fax: 212 689-0230
Great Neck Richman, *CEO*
James Richman, *Ch of Bd*
Michael Saivetz, *COO*
Louise C Robinson, *Vice Pres*
Marci Cohen, *Sls & Mktg Exec*
▲ EMP: 10
SQ FT: 1,500
SALES (est): 47.2MM
SALES (corp-wide): 48.4MM **Privately Held**
SIC: 2392 2391 Blankets, comforters & beddings; curtains & draperies
PA: Richloom Fabrics Corp.
  261 5th Ave Fl 12
  New York NY 10016
  212 685-5400

(G-11896)
RICHLOOM HOME FASHIONS CORP
Also Called: Coham/Rvrdale Dcrative Fabrics
261 5th Ave Fl 12 (10016-7794)
PHONE..................212 685-5400
Ralph Geller, *President*
Fred Richman, *Treasurer*
Michel Spaniel, *Manager*
▲ EMP: 10 EST: 1966
SQ FT: 1,500
SALES (est): 713.9K
SALES (corp-wide): 48.4MM **Privately Held**
WEB: www.richloom.com
SIC: 2391 2211 2221 Curtains & draperies; draperies & drapery fabrics, cotton; draperies & drapery fabrics, manmade fiber & silk
PA: Richloom Fabrics Corp.
  261 5th Ave Fl 12
  New York NY 10016
  212 685-5400

(G-11897)
RINGS WIRE INC
Also Called: Rome Fastener
246 W 38th St Rm 501 (10018-9089)
PHONE..................212 741-9779
Fax: 212 741-9774
Dr Stanley Reiter, *President*
Stanley Rieter, *Manager*
EMP: 10
SALES (corp-wide): 2.4MM **Privately Held**
SIC: 3965 Fasteners, snap; buckles & buckle parts
PA: Rings Wire Inc
  257 Depot Rd
  Milford CT 06460
  203 874-6719

(G-11898)
RIO APPAREL USA INC
237 W 37th St Rm 13l (10018-6768)
PHONE..................212 869-9150
Tong Kyoon Lee, *President*
▲ EMP: 5
SALES (est): 640K **Privately Held**
SIC: 2331 Women's & misses' blouses & shirts

(G-11899)
RIRI USA INC (DH)
350 5th Ave Ste 6700 (10118-6704)
PHONE..................212 268-3866
L Benjamin Howell II, *Ch of Bd*
Mitch Kupinsky, *Regional Mgr*
Mark Teel, *Vice Pres*
▲ EMP: 6
SQ FT: 5,000

SALES (est): 521K **Privately Held**
SIC: 3965 Zipper
HQ: Riri Sa
  Via Della Regione Veneto 3
  Padova PD
  049 899-6611

(G-11900)
RISION INC
306 E 78th St Apt 1b (10075-2243)
PHONE..................212 987-2628
Kate Cornick, *CEO*
Earle Harper, *COO*
Ryan O'Donnell, *Vice Pres*
Steven Salsberg, *General Counsel*
EMP: 7 EST: 2015
SALES (est): 272.5K **Privately Held**
SIC: 7372 7389 Business oriented computer software;

(G-11901)
RISK SOCIETY MANAGEMENT PUBG
Also Called: Risk Management Magazine
655 3rd Ave Fl 2 (10017-9130)
PHONE..................212 286-9364
Fax: 212 922-0716
Jack Hampton, *Exec Dir*
Colin Ferenbach, *Administration*
EMP: 43
SALES (est): 1.5MM
SALES (corp-wide): 15.3MM **Privately Held**
SIC: 2721 Magazines: publishing only, not printed on site
PA: Risk And Insurance Management Society, Inc.
  1065 Ave Of The Amrcs 1
  New York NY 10018
  212 286-9292

(G-11902)
RITCHIE CORP
263 W 38th St Fl 13 (10018-0280)
PHONE..................212 768-0083
Fax: 212 768-7773
Lynn Ritchie, *President*
Andre Tirenin, *Design Engr*
▲ EMP: 16 EST: 1990
SQ FT: 3,000
SALES (est): 1.4MM **Privately Held**
WEB: www.lynn-ritchie.com
SIC: 2339 Sportswear, women's

(G-11903)
RIZZOLI INTL PUBLICATIONS INC (DH)
300 Park Ave S Fl 4 (10010-5399)
PHONE..................212 387-3400
Fax: 212 387-3434
Antonio Polito, *President*
Margaret Chace, *Publisher*
Caitlin Leffel, *Editor*
Loren Olson, *Editor*
Anthony Petrillose, *Editor*
◆ EMP: 40
SALES (est): 19.6MM
SALES (corp-wide): 185.4K **Privately Held**
WEB: www.rizzoliusa.com
SIC: 2731 5192 5942 5961 Books: publishing only; books; book stores; books, mail order (except book clubs)

(G-11904)
RIZZOLI INTL PUBLICATIONS INC
Also Called: Universe Publishing
300 Park Ave S Fl 3 (10010-5399)
PHONE..................212 387-3572
Fax: 212 387-3644
Antonio Polito, *President*
EMP: 15
SALES (corp-wide): 185.4K **Privately Held**
SIC: 2731 Book publishing
HQ: Rizzoli International Publications, Inc.
  300 Park Ave S Fl 4
  New York NY 10010
  212 387-3400

GEOGRAPHIC SECTION
New York - New York County (G-11931)

(G-11905)
RIZZOLI INTL PUBLICATIONS INC
Also Called: Amica Magazine
300 Park Ave Frnt 4 (10022-7404)
PHONE..................212 308-2000
Fax: 212 308-4308
Imma Vaccaro, *Manager*
Pietro Banas, *Correspondent*
EMP: 12
SALES (corp-wide): 185.4K Privately Held
SIC: 2711 Newspapers
HQ: Rizzoli International Publications, Inc.
300 Park Ave S Fl 4
New York NY 10010
212 387-3400

(G-11906)
RJM2 LTD
241 W 37th St Rm 926 (10018-6963)
PHONE..................212 944-1660
Richard Weinsieder, *President*
Meryl Weinsieder, *Vice Pres*
▲ EMP: 5
SALES (est): 487.2K Privately Held
WEB: www.rjm2ltd.com
SIC: 2389 Men's miscellaneous accessories

(G-11907)
RND ENTERPRISES INC
Also Called: Next Magazine
446 W 33rd St (10001-2601)
PHONE..................212 627-0165
David Moyal, *President*
Roberto Buckley, *Accounts Exec*
EMP: 4
SALES (est): 1MM Privately Held
SIC: 2721 Magazines: publishing & printing

(G-11908)
ROADRUNNER RECORDS INC (PA)
1290 Avenue Of The Americ (10104-0101)
PHONE..................212 274-7500
Fax: 212 505-7469
Jones Nachsin, *President*
Mark Abramson, *Vice Pres*
John Boulos, *Vice Pres*
Rodney King, *Vice Pres*
Jeffery Teldman, *Personnel Exec*
EMP: 35
SQ FT: 8,000
SALES (est): 2.9MM Privately Held
WEB: www.roadrunnerrecords.com
SIC: 3652 Pre-recorded records & tapes; magnetic tape (audio): prerecorded; phonograph records, prerecorded

(G-11909)
ROBELL RESEARCH INC
Also Called: Supersmile
635 Madison Ave Fl 13 (10022-1009)
PHONE..................212 755-6577
Irwin Smigel, *CEO*
Lucia Smigel, *President*
Joel Levy, *COO*
Meredith Johnson, *Sales Executive*
▲ EMP: 8
SQ FT: 1,500
SALES (est): 1.8MM Privately Held
SIC: 2844 5122 Oral preparations; mouthwashes; toiletries

(G-11910)
ROBERT DANES DANES INC (PA)
481 Greenwich St Apt 5b (10013-1398)
PHONE..................212 226-1351
Rachel Danes, *President*
Robert Danes, *Treasurer*
EMP: 4
SQ FT: 1,500
SALES (est): 1.6MM Privately Held
WEB: www.robertdanes.com
SIC: 2331 Women's & misses' blouses & shirts

(G-11911)
ROBERT EHRLICH
Also Called: Blackswirl
75 Saint Marks Pl (10003-7944)
PHONE..................516 353-4617
Robert Ehrlich, *Owner*

EMP: 5
SALES (est): 194.1K Privately Held
SIC: 7372 Application computer software

(G-11912)
ROBERTO COIN INC (PA)
579 5th Ave Fl 17 (10017-8760)
PHONE..................212 486-4545
Fax: 212 486-0111
Anthony Peter Webster, *Ch of Bd*
Sophia Macris, *Vice Pres*
Amy Lane, *VP Sales*
Alessandra Savo, *VP Sales*
▲ EMP: 13
SQ FT: 3,500
SALES (est): 3.3MM Privately Held
WEB: www.robertocoin.com
SIC: 3911 Jewelry, precious metal

(G-11913)
ROBESPIERRE INC
Also Called: Nanette Lepore Showroom
214 W 39th St Ph Ste 602 (10018-4404)
PHONE..................212 764-8810
Fax: 212 764-8796
Megan Darling, *Manager*
EMP: 8
SALES (corp-wide): 19.6MM Privately Held
WEB: www.nanettelepore.com
SIC: 2339 Women's & misses' athletic clothing & sportswear
PA: Robespierre, Inc.
225 W 35th St Ste 600
New York NY 10001
212 594-0012

(G-11914)
ROBESPIERRE INC (PA)
Also Called: Nanette Lepore
225 W 35th St Ste 600 (10001-1904)
PHONE..................212 594-0012
Fax: 212 594-0038
Robert Savage, *President*
Nanette Lepore, *Vice Pres*
Jenny Rodriguez, *Accountant*
▲ EMP: 115
SQ FT: 39,000
SALES (est): 19.6MM Privately Held
WEB: www.nanettelepore.com
SIC: 2339 Sportswear, women's

(G-11915)
ROBIN STANLEY INC
Also Called: Pearltek
1212 Avenue Of The Americ (10036-1600)
PHONE..................212 871-0007
Stanley Robin, *President*
EMP: 6 EST: 1975
SALES (est): 510K Privately Held
SIC: 3911 Pearl jewelry, natural or cultured

(G-11916)
ROBLY DIGITAL MARKETING LLC
93 Leonard St Apt 6 (10013-3459)
PHONE..................917 238-0730
Adam Robinson, *Mng Member*
EMP: 40
SALES (est): 966.9K Privately Held
SIC: 7372 Prepackaged software

(G-11917)
ROCCO BORMIOLI GLASS CO INC (PA)
41 Madison Ave Ste 1603 (10010-2236)
PHONE..................212 719-0606
Fax: 212 719-3606
Davide Sereni, *Ch of Bd*
Rocco Bormioli, *President*
Maurizio Amari, *Treasurer*
Jose Perez, *VP Sales*
▲ EMP: 20 EST: 1978
SALES (est): 3MM Privately Held
SIC: 3221 Glass containers

(G-11918)
ROCKEFELLER UNIVERSITY
Press Office
950 3rd Ave Fl 2 (10022-2705)
PHONE..................212 327-8568
Fax: 212 327-8587
Michael Rossner, *General Mgr*
Lorna Petersen, *Advt Staff*
Michael Held, *Branch Mgr*
David W Greene, *Manager*

Torsten N D, *Director*
EMP: 6
SQ FT: 3,000
SALES (corp-wide): 537MM Privately Held
SIC: 2741 Miscellaneous publishing
PA: The Rockefeller University
1230 York Ave
New York NY 10065
212 327-8078

(G-11919)
ROCKET FUEL INC
195 Broadway Fl 10 (10007-3140)
PHONE..................212 594-8888
Fax: 212 594-8889
Yasmine Decosterd, *Vice Pres*
Scott Spaulding, *VP Sales*
Doug Herko, *Sales Dir*
Jennifer Stein, *Sales Staff*
Peter Sulick, *Manager*
EMP: 14
SALES (corp-wide): 172.7MM Privately Held
SIC: 3993 Advertising artwork
HQ: Rocket Fuel Inc.
2000 Seaport Blvd Ste 400
Redwood City CA 94063

(G-11920)
ROCKPORT PA LLC
477 Madison Ave Fl 18 (10022-5831)
PHONE..................212 482-8580
William Trepp, *Principal*
EMP: 10
SALES (est): 886.2K Privately Held
SIC: 7372 Prepackaged software

(G-11921)
RODALE INC
Also Called: Women's Health Magazine
733 3rd Ave Fl 15 (10017-3293)
PHONE..................212 697-2040
Fax: 212 949-9455
Debbie McHugh, *Editor*
Tom Reifinger, *COO*
Stephen Borkowski, *Production*
Jessica Sokol, *Design Engr*
Jamie Amsel, *Accounts Mgr*
EMP: 300
SALES (corp-wide): 228.8MM Privately Held
WEB: www.rodale.com
SIC: 2721 Magazines: publishing & printing
PA: Rodale Inc.
400 S 10th St
Emmaus PA 18049
800 848-4735

(G-11922)
RODEM INCORPORATED
Also Called: Galian Handbags
120 W 29th St Frnt A (10001-5596)
PHONE..................212 779-7122
John Woo, *General Mgr*
▲ EMP: 10
SALES (est): 670.9K Privately Held
SIC: 3171 Women's handbags & purses

(G-11923)
RODEO OF NY INC
62 W 47th St (10036-3201)
PHONE..................212 730-0744
Joseph Janfar, *President*
Christine Chang, *Bookkeeper*
▲ EMP: 20
SQ FT: 1,200
SALES (est): 18MM Privately Held
SIC: 3366 Castings (except die)

(G-11924)
ROFFE ACCESSORIES INC (PA)
833 Broadway Apt 4 (10003-4700)
PHONE..................212 213-1440
Murray Roffe, *Ch of Bd*
Mark Ptak, *Vice Pres*
▲ EMP: 15
SQ FT: 50,000
SALES (est): 2.6MM Privately Held
SIC: 2321 2323 5136 Men's & boys' furnishings; men's & boys' neckwear; neckwear, men's & boys'

(G-11925)
ROGAN LLC
330 Bowery (10012-2414)
PHONE..................212 680-1407
Kevin Ryan, *Branch Mgr*
EMP: 5
SALES (corp-wide): 2.3MM Privately Held
WEB: www.roganandcompany.com
SIC: 2335 Women's, juniors' & misses' dresses
PA: Rogan, Llc
270 Bowery 3
New York NY 10012
646 496-9339

(G-11926)
ROGAN LLC (PA)
270 Bowery 3 (10012-3674)
PHONE..................646 496-9339
Dulce Camacho, *Credit Mgr*
Rogan Gregory, *Creative Dir*
Kevin Ryan, *President*
Roger Gregory,
▲ EMP: 25
SALES (est): 2.4MM Privately Held
WEB: www.roganandcompany.com
SIC: 2335 Women's, juniors' & misses' dresses

(G-11927)
ROGER & SONS INC (PA)
268 Bowery Frnt 6 (10012-3992)
PHONE..................212 226-4734
Carl Saitta, *Ch of Bd*
Anthony Saitta, *Ch of Bd*
Maria Saitta, *President*
Joe Cirone, *Vice Pres*
EMP: 8
SQ FT: 15,000
SALES (est): 2.1MM Privately Held
SIC: 3589 5046 5719 Commercial cooking & foodwarming equipment; restaurant equipment & supplies; kitchenware

(G-11928)
ROGERS GROUP INC
Also Called: Ferrara Manufacturing
318 W 39th St Fl 4 (10018-1493)
PHONE..................212 643-9292
Joe Ferrara, *Ch of Bd*
Carolyn Ferrara, *President*
Joseph Ferrara, *Vice Pres*
Alva Lama, *Manager*
EMP: 50
SQ FT: 25,000
SALES (est): 4MM Privately Held
SIC: 2369 2339 Girls' & children's outerwear; women's & misses' outerwear

(G-11929)
ROLI USA INC
100 5th Ave (10011-6903)
PHONE..................412 600-4840
Danny Siger, *Manager*
EMP: 15 EST: 2015
SALES (est): 626.7K Privately Held
SIC: 3931 Musical instruments

(G-11930)
ROLLING STONE MAGAZINE
1290 Ave Of The Amer Fl 2 (10104-0295)
PHONE..................212 484-1616
Fax: 212 767-8205
Steven Deluca, *Publisher*
Jill Thiry, *Publisher*
R Brownridge, *Principal*
John Gruber, *Controller*
Ed Needham, *Manager*
EMP: 9
SALES (est): 832.5K Privately Held
WEB: www.rollingstone.com
SIC: 2741 2721 Miscellaneous publishing; periodicals

(G-11931)
ROMA INDUSTRIES LLC
12 W 37th St Fl 10 (10018-7379)
PHONE..................212 268-0723
Paul Aglietti, *Vice Pres*
Kristin Franz, *Manager*
EMP: 8
SALES (corp-wide): 49.5MM Privately Held
WEB: www.watchstraps.com
SIC: 3172 Watch straps, except metal

New York - New York County (G-11932)   GEOGRAPHIC SECTION

PA: Roma Industries Llc
12821 Starkey Rd Ste 4500
Largo FL 33773
727 545-9009

(G-11932)
ROMANCE & CO INC
2 W 47th St Ste 1111 (10036-3329)
PHONE..................................212 382-0337
Uriel Kaykov, CEO
EMP: 5
SALES (est): 262.5K **Privately Held**
SIC: 1499 5094 Diamond mining, industrial; diamonds (gems)

(G-11933)
RONNI NICOLE GROUP LLC
1400 Broadway Rm 2102 (10018-0649)
PHONE..................................212 764-1000
Ronnie Russell, President
David Brokman, Prdtn Mgr
Andy Hilowitz, Controller
Cindy Garcia, Manager
Merrill Bernstein,
◆ EMP: 35
SQ FT: 2,500
SALES (est): 4.1MM **Privately Held**
SIC: 2335 Women's, juniors' & misses' dresses

(G-11934)
ROOMACTUALLY LLC
175 Varick St (10014-4604)
PHONE..................................646 388-1922
William Keck,
EMP: 5
SALES (est): 278K **Privately Held**
SIC: 7372 7373 7371 Prepackaged software; business oriented computer software; systems software development services; computer software development

(G-11935)
ROSEMONT PRESS INCORPORATED (PA)
253 Church St Apt 2 (10013-3438)
PHONE..................................212 239-4770
Fax: 212 268-8619
James J Reardon, Ch of Bd
Patricia Reardon, Manager
Anthony Romano, Manager
EMP: 39 EST: 1963
SQ FT: 12,800
SALES (est): 9.6MM **Privately Held**
WEB: www.rosemontpress.com
SIC: 2752 2789 Commercial printing, offset; bookbinding & related work

(G-11936)
ROSEN MANDELL & IMMERMAN INC
Also Called: Rmi Printing
121 Varick St Rm 301 (10013-1408)
PHONE..................................212 691-2277
Fax: 212 675-4243
Steve Visoky, President
Joel Kubie, VP Finance
Bobbi Peters, Manager
EMP: 24
SQ FT: 3,500
SALES (est): 2.6MM **Privately Held**
WEB: www.rmiprinting.com
SIC: 2789 2752 Bookbinding & related work; commercial printing, lithographic

(G-11937)
ROSEN PUBLISHING GROUP INC
29 E 21st St Fl 2 (10010-6256)
P.O. Box 29278 (10087-9278)
PHONE..................................212 777-3017
Fax: 212 777-0277
Roger C Rosen, President
Holly Cefrey, Editor
Gina Hayn, Vice Pres
Nancy Nelson, Human Resources
Christopher Brand, Mktg Dir
▲ EMP: 150
SQ FT: 12,000
SALES (est): 37.9MM **Privately Held**
WEB: www.rosenpublishing.com
SIC: 2731 Book publishing

(G-11938)
ROSENAU BECK INC
135 W 36th St Rm 10l (10018-9473)
PHONE..................................212 279-6202
Fax: 212 563-4786
Thomas Rosenau, President
EMP: 12
SALES (corp-wide): 2.5MM **Privately Held**
SIC: 2361 Dresses: girls', children's & infants'
PA: Beck Rosenau Inc
1310 Industrial Blvd # 201
Southampton PA 18966
215 364-1714

(G-11939)
ROSETTI HANDBAGS AND ACC (DH)
1333 Broadway Fl 9 (10018-1064)
PHONE..................................212 273-3765
Jane Thompson, President
Lisa Ayoob, Vice Pres
Nanette Acost, Office Mgr
▲ EMP: 45
SQ FT: 4,000
SALES (est): 6.1MM **Privately Held**
SIC: 2389 Men's miscellaneous accessories
HQ: Gbg Usa Inc.
350 5th Ave Lbby 9
New York NY 10118
646 839-7000

(G-11940)
ROUGH DRAFT PUBLISHING LLC
Also Called: Proof Magazine
1916 Old Chelsea Sta (10113)
PHONE..................................212 741-4773
Stephen Davis,
EMP: 15
SALES (est): 1.2MM **Privately Held**
SIC: 2721 Periodicals

(G-11941)
ROUGH GUIDES US LTD
345 Hudson St Fl 4 (10014-4536)
PHONE..................................212 414-3635
Anna Paynton, Top Exec
Martin Dunford, Exec Dir
▲ EMP: 75 EST: 1982
SALES (est): 3.9MM **Privately Held**
WEB: www.roughguides.com
SIC: 2741 Miscellaneous publishing

(G-11942)
ROYAL HOME FASHIONS INC (DH)
261 5th Ave Fl 25 (10016-7601)
PHONE..................................212 689-7222
Myron Kahn, CEO
Douglas Kahn, President
Stanley Kahn, Corp Secy
David Kahn, Exec VP
Anthony Cassella, CFO
▲ EMP: 2
SALES (est): 64.3MM
SALES (corp-wide): 4.2B **Privately Held**
SIC: 2391 2392 Curtains & draperies; comforters & quilts: made from purchased materials
HQ: Mistdoda, Inc.
261 5th Ave Fl 25
New York NY 10016
919 735-7111

(G-11943)
ROYAL MIRACLE CORP
2 W 46th St Rm 9209 (10036-4811)
PHONE..................................212 921-5797
Edmond Elyassian, President
EMP: 30
SQ FT: 5,000
SALES (est): 22.5MM **Privately Held**
WEB: www.royalmiracle.com
SIC: 3911 Jewelry, precious metal

(G-11944)
ROYAL NEWS CORP
Also Called: Royal Media Group
8 W 38th St Rm 901 (10018-6239)
PHONE..................................212 564-8972
Fax: 212 564-8973
Jonathan Hornblass, President

EMP: 12
SQ FT: 2,000
SALES (est): 1.1MM **Privately Held**
WEB: www.momentic.com
SIC: 2711 Newspapers

(G-11945)
ROYAL PROMOTION GROUP INC
Also Called: Rpg
119 W 57th St Ste 906 (10019-2401)
PHONE..................................212 246-3780
Fax: 212 399-9135
Bruce E Teitelbaum, CEO
Ellen L Friedman, Exec VP
Andrea Millner, Exec VP
Eric Williams, Exec VP
Ajay Khanna, CFO
▲ EMP: 60
SQ FT: 20,000
SALES (est): 10.4MM **Privately Held**
WEB: www.royalpromo.com
SIC: 3993 Signs & advertising specialties; displays & cutouts, window & lobby; displays, paint process

(G-11946)
ROYALTY NETWORK INC (PA)
224 W 30th St Rm 1007 (10001-1077)
PHONE..................................212 967-4300
Fax: 212 967-3447
Frank Liwall, President
Renato Olivari, Vice Pres
Lawson Higgins, Admin Asst
Ben Gray, Administration
EMP: 7
SQ FT: 2,500
SALES (est): 754.9K **Privately Held**
WEB: www.roynet.com
SIC: 2741 Patterns, paper: publishing & printing

(G-11947)
RP55 INC
230 W 39th St Fl 7 (10018-4977)
PHONE..................................212 840-4035
Fax: 212 840-7684
Lisa Blumenthal, Vice Pres
Sabai Burnett, VP Mktg
Ron Poisson, Manager
EMP: 6
SALES (corp-wide): 15.1MM **Privately Held**
SIC: 2329 Men's & boys' sportswear & athletic clothing
PA: Rp55, Inc.
520 Viking Dr
Virginia Beach VA 23452
757 428-0300

(G-11948)
RR DONNELLEY & SONS COMPANY
Also Called: Studio 26
250 W 26th St Rm 402 (10001-6737)
PHONE..................................646 755-8125
Fax: 646 336-5165
Mike James, Manager
EMP: 8
SALES (corp-wide): 6.9B **Publicly Held**
WEB: www.rrdonnelley.com
SIC: 2759 Commercial printing
PA: R. R. Donnelley & Sons Company
35 W Wacker Dr Ste 3650
Chicago IL 60601
312 326-8000

(G-11949)
RSL MEDIA LLC
Also Called: New York Enterprise Report
1001 Ave Of The Ave Fl 11 (10018)
PHONE..................................212 307-6760
Robert Lebin,
EMP: 9
SALES (est): 934K **Privately Held**
SIC: 2721 2741 Magazines: publishing only, not printed on site; miscellaneous publishing

(G-11950)
RTR BAG & CO LTD
27 W 20th St (10011-3707)
PHONE..................................212 620-0011
Ron Raznick, President
▲ EMP: 7

SALES (est): 503.4K **Privately Held**
SIC: 2673 2674 Plastic bags: made from purchased materials; shopping bags: made from purchased materials

(G-11951)
RUBY NEWCO LLC
1211 Ave Of The Americas (10036-8701)
PHONE..................................212 852-7000
Keith Rupert Murdoch, CEO
EMP: 6
SALES (est): 228.2K
SALES (corp-wide): 8.1B **Publicly Held**
SIC: 2711 2721 6289 Newspapers, publishing & printing; magazines: publishing only, not printed on site (periodicals): publishing & printing; financial reporting; stock quotation service
HQ: News Preferred Holdings Inc.
20 Westport Rd
Wilton CT 06897
203 563-6483

(G-11952)
RUDOLF FRIEDMAN INC
42 W 48th St Ste 1102 (10036-1701)
PHONE..................................212 869-5070
Fax: 212 944-7114
Alexander Nadaner, President
Glenn Nadaner, Vice Pres
Fay Nadaner, Treasurer
Celena Hecht, Admin Sec
EMP: 12 EST: 1946
SQ FT: 1,200
SALES (est): 940K **Privately Held**
WEB: www.rudolffriedmann.com
SIC: 3911 Jewelry, precious metal

(G-11953)
RULEVILLE MANUFACTURING CO INC (PA)
469 Fashion Ave Fl 10 (10018-7640)
PHONE..................................212 695-1620
Gerald Spiewak, Ch of Bd
Roy Spiewak, President
Pat Cunningham, Controller
▲ EMP: 2
SQ FT: 10,000
SALES (est): 16.1MM **Privately Held**
WEB: www.spiewak.com
SIC: 2326 2329 Men's & boys' work clothing; men's & boys' sportswear & athletic clothing

(G-11954)
RUMSON ACQUISITION LLC
Also Called: Stephen Dweck
1385 Broadway Fl 9 (10018-6001)
PHONE..................................718 349-4300
Jack Rahmey, President
EMP: 18
SQ FT: 4,500
SALES: 3MM **Privately Held**
SIC: 3911 Jewelry, precious metal

(G-11955)
RUSSIAN STANDARD VODKA USA INC
Also Called: Roust USA
232 Madison Ave Fl 16 (10016-2909)
PHONE..................................212 679-1894
Leonid Yangarber, CEO
John Palatella, President
Michael Stoner, President
Steve Ballard, Division Mgr
Nelia Nuriakhmetova, Principal
◆ EMP: 5
SALES (est): 731.5K **Privately Held**
SIC: 2085 Vodka (alcoholic beverage)

(G-11956)
RUTHYS CHEESECAKE RUGELACH BKY
Also Called: Ruthy's Bakery & Cafe
300 E 54th St Apt 31b (10022-5037)
PHONE..................................212 463-8800
Patrizia Alessi, President
Patricia Alessi, President
EMP: 18
SQ FT: 7,000
SALES (est): 2MM **Privately Held**
WEB: www.ruthys.com
SIC: 2051 5461 Bread, cake & related products; bakery: wholesale or wholesale/retail combined; bakeries

GEOGRAPHIC SECTION

New York - New York County (G-11985)

(G-11957)
RVC ENTERPRISES LLC (PA)
Also Called: Dereon/24 K Style
1384 Broadway Fl 17 (10018-0508)
P.O. Box 607 (10150-0607)
PHONE..................212 391-4600
Michael Alestra, Credit Staff
Victor Azrak, Mng Member
Ryan Steele, Info Tech Dir
Charles Azrak,
Reuben Azrak,
▲ EMP: 29
SALES (est): 8.3MM **Privately Held**
SIC: 2339 Women's & misses' outerwear

(G-11958)
RYAN GEMS INC
20 E 46th St Rm 200 (10017-9287)
PHONE..................212 697-0149
Edison Akhavan, President
Jeffrey Eischen, Vice Pres
Simon Eliassi, Marketing Staff
▲ EMP: 38
SQ FT: 4,500
SALES (est): 9MM **Privately Held**
WEB: www.ryangems.com
SIC: 3911 Jewelry, precious metal

(G-11959)
RYLAND PETERS & SMALL INC
341 E 116th St (10029-1502)
PHONE..................646 791-5410
David Peters, President
Jeremy Scholl, CFO
▲ EMP: 6
SALES (est): 586.9K **Privately Held**
WEB: www.rylandpeters.com
SIC: 2731 Books: publishing only

(G-11960)
S & C BRIDALS LLC (PA)
Also Called: US Angels
1407 Broadway Fl 41 (10018-2348)
PHONE..................212 789-7000
Diane O'Brien, Controller
Stanley Cayre, Mng Member
Amin Cayre,
Hank Shalom,
▲ EMP: 11
SQ FT: 10,000
SALES (est): 5.8MM **Privately Held**
WEB: www.usangels.com
SIC: 2361 5641 Girls' & children's dresses, blouses & shirts; children's wear

(G-11961)
S & S MANUFACTURING CO INC (PA)
1375 Broadway Fl 2 (10018-7073)
PHONE..................212 444-6000
Kirk Gellin, Co-President
Robert Sobel, Co-President
Robert Frederick, Vice Pres
▲ EMP: 75
SQ FT: 21,000
SALES (est): 5.7MM **Privately Held**
SIC: 2331 2339 Blouses, women's & juniors': made from purchased material; sportswear, women's

(G-11962)
S G I
40 E 52nd St Frnt A (10022-5911)
PHONE..................917 386-0385
Richard L Miller, Principal
EMP: 5 EST: 2010
SALES (est): 260K **Privately Held**
SIC: 3577 Computer peripheral equipment

(G-11963)
S P BOOKS INC
99 Spring St Fl 3 (10012-3929)
PHONE..................212 431-5011
Pearson Allen, President
EMP: 6
SALES: 1.5MM **Privately Held**
WEB: www.spibooks.com
SIC: 2731 5192 Book publishing; books

(G-11964)
S ROTHSCHILD & CO INC (PA)
Also Called: Rothschild Mens Div
1407 Broadway Fl 10 (10018-3271)
PHONE..................212 354-8550
Fax: 212 921-5564
Isidore Friedman, CEO
Mark Friedman, President
Zac Greene, Mfg Staff
William Mitchell, CFO
Nancy Tassoni, Sales Mgr
▼ EMP: 110 EST: 1881
SQ FT: 50,000
SALES (est): 7.3MM **Privately Held**
SIC: 2369 Girls' & children's outerwear

(G-11965)
S1 BIOPHARMA INC
7 World Trade Ctr 250g (10007-2140)
PHONE..................201 839-0941
John Kaufmann, CFO
EMP: 5 EST: 2013
SALES (est): 518.4K **Privately Held**
SIC: 2834 Pharmaceutical preparations

(G-11966)
SAAD COLLECTION INC (PA)
1165 Broadway Ste 305 (10001-7450)
PHONE..................212 937-0341
Farzana Younus, President
Mohammad Younus, Manager
EMP: 9
SALES (est): 1.3MM **Privately Held**
SIC: 2321 2331 Men's & boys' furnishings; women's & misses' blouses & shirts

(G-11967)
SABIN ROBBINS PAPER COMPANY
455 E 86th St (10028-6400)
PHONE..................513 874-5270
Thomas Roberts, President
EMP: 30
SALES (est): 10.4MM **Privately Held**
SIC: 2621 Building paper, sheathing

(G-11968)
SABON MANAGEMENT LLC
123 Prince St Frnt A (10012-5312)
PHONE..................212 982-0968
Irina Stepanova, Branch Mgr
EMP: 16
SALES (corp-wide): 17.8MM **Privately Held**
SIC: 2841 Soap & other detergents
PA: Sabon Management, Llc
    38 Greene St Fl 5
    New York NY 10013
    212 473-1009

(G-11969)
SACKS AND COMPANY NEW YORK (PA)
119 W 57th St Ph N (10019-2303)
PHONE..................212 741-1000
Fax: 212 741-9007
Carla Sacks, President
Samantha Tillman, Director
Ethan Stuber, Personnel Assit
Cami Opere,
Chris Schimpf, Relations
EMP: 9
SALES (est): 837.1K **Privately Held**
SIC: 2741 Miscellaneous publishing

(G-11970)
SAFE SKIES LLC (PA)
Also Called: TSA Luggage Locks
954 3rd Ave Ste 504 (10022-2013)
PHONE..................888 632-5027
David Tropp, Mng Member
▲ EMP: 9
SQ FT: 70,000
SALES (est): 106.4MM **Privately Held**
SIC: 3429 Locks or lock sets

(G-11971)
SAKONNET TECHNOLOGY LLC
11 E 44th St Fl 1000 (10017-0058)
PHONE..................212 849-9267
Fax: 212 343-3103
Alarik Myrin, Partner
Melanie Penachio, Vice Pres
Angela Santos, Finance
Melanie Tenachio, Finance
Bethany Kalmanson, Admin Asst
EMP: 30
SALES (est): 2.7MM **Privately Held**
WEB: www.sknt.com
SIC: 7372 Prepackaged software

(G-11972)
SALE 121 CORP
1324 Lexington Ave # 111 (10128-1145)
PHONE..................240 855-8988
Mohammad Naz, Branch Mgr
EMP: 99
SALES (corp-wide): 3.5MM **Privately Held**
SIC: 3572 8748 7371 7373 Disk drives, computer; systems engineering consultant, ex. computer or professional; computer software development; systems software development services; office computer automation systems integration
PA: Sale 121 Corp
    1467 68th Ave
    Sacramento CA 95822
    888 233-7667

(G-11973)
SALENTICA SYSTEMS INC
245 Park Ave Fl 39 (10167-4000)
PHONE..................212 672-1777
Bil Rourke, Principal
Dave Ireland, Vice Pres
EMP: 20
SALES (est): 1MM **Privately Held**
SIC: 7372 Prepackaged software

(G-11974)
SALES TAX ASSET RCEIVABLE CORP
255 Greenwich St Fl 6 (10007-2422)
PHONE..................212 788-5874
Allan Anders, President
Jay Olson, Treasurer
Lawrance Glantz, Controller
EMP: 3
SALES: 170.4MM **Privately Held**
SIC: 3953 Embossing seals, corporate & official

(G-11975)
SALMCO JEWELRY CORP
Also Called: Bay Sales Company
22 W 32nd St Fl 16 (10001-1698)
PHONE..................212 695-8792
Fax: 212 564-5609
Errol Salm, President
Morton Salm, Principal
Jarred Salm, Manager
Lance Salm, Manager
▲ EMP: 17 EST: 1980
SQ FT: 6,000
SALES (est): 2.6MM **Privately Held**
WEB: www.baysalesinc.com
SIC: 3961 Costume jewelry, ex. precious metal & semiprecious stones

(G-11976)
SALONCLICK LLC
Also Called: Min New York
117 Crosby St (10012-3301)
PHONE..................718 643-6793
Chad Muranczyk,
EMP: 12
SQ FT: 2,000
SALES (est): 2.1MM **Privately Held**
SIC: 2844 Hair coloring preparations; hair preparations, including shampoos

(G-11977)
SALUTEM GROUP LLC
44 Wall St Fl 12 (10005-2433)
PHONE..................347 620-2640
Mikhail Abarshalin, Principal
EMP: 6
SALES (est): 595.7K **Privately Held**
SIC: 2834 Pharmaceutical preparations

(G-11978)
SAM HEE INTERNATIONAL INC
213 W 35th St Ste 503 (10001-1903)
PHONE..................212 594-7815
Fax: 212 594-7844
Hoon Lee, CEO
Caroline Lee, Accountant
Eric Chong, Manager
▲ EMP: 7
SQ FT: 3,000
SALES (est): 1.8MM **Privately Held**
SIC: 2339 Athletic clothing: women's, misses' & juniors'

(G-11979)
SAM SALEM & SON LLC
302 5th Ave Fl 4 (10001-3604)
PHONE..................212 695-6020
Fax: 212 695-6303
Jesse Salem, Mng Member
Sam Salem,
Carey Sutton,
▲ EMP: 13
SQ FT: 1,800
SALES (est): 3.4MM **Privately Held**
SIC: 2299 Linen fabrics

(G-11980)
SAMUEL FRENCH INC (PA)
235 Park Ave S Fl 5 (10003-1405)
PHONE..................212 206-8990
Fax: 212 206-1429
Nathan Collins, Ch of Bd
Charles Nostrand, President
Merle Cosgrove, Vice Pres
John Graham, Vice Pres
Casey McLain, Opers Spvr
EMP: 45 EST: 1830
SQ FT: 17,000
SALES (est): 7.1MM **Privately Held**
WEB: www.samuelfrench.com
SIC: 2731 5942 5192 Books: publishing & printing; book stores; books

(G-11981)
SAMUEL SCHULMAN FURS INC
Also Called: Alexandre Furs
150 W 30th St Fl 13 (10001-4185)
PHONE..................212 736-5550
Fax: 212 564-8079
Edwin L Schulman, President
Larry Schulman, Vice Pres
Stanley R Schulman, Treasurer
EMP: 25 EST: 1940
SQ FT: 12,000
SALES (est): 1.4MM **Privately Held**
SIC: 2371 Fur coats & other fur apparel; jackets, fur

(G-11982)
SANCTUARY BRANDS LLC (PA)
Also Called: Tailorbyrd
70 W 40th St Fl 5 (10018-2626)
PHONE..................212 704-4014
Traci Young, Senior VP
Larry Stemerman,
EMP: 6
SALES (est): 699.8K **Privately Held**
SIC: 2329 5136 5611 Riding clothes:, men's, youths' & boys'; men's & boys' clothing; men's & boys' clothing stores

(G-11983)
SANDBOX BRANDS INC
26 W 17th St Lbby (10011-5710)
PHONE..................212 647-8877
David Barber, President
Tom Hubben, Vice Pres
EMP: 7
SALES: 490K **Privately Held**
WEB: www.sandboxbrands.com
SIC: 3944 Games, toys & children's vehicles

(G-11984)
SANDOW MEDIA LLC
1271 Ave Of The Ave Fl 17 (10020)
PHONE..................646 805-0200
Arlyn Hernandez, Editor
Jim Toomey, Business Mgr
Jessica Kleiman, Exec VP
Robyn Fingerman, Vice Pres
Pamela McNally, Vice Pres
EMP: 10
SALES (corp-wide): 98.9MM **Privately Held**
SIC: 2721 Magazines: publishing only, not printed on site
PA: Sandow Media, Llc
    3651 Nw 8th Ave Ste 200
    Boca Raton FL 33431
    561 961-7700

(G-11985)
SANDY DALAL LTD
220 Central Park S 10f (10019-1417)
PHONE..................212 532-5822
Michael Agashiwala, President
Loma Agashiwala, Admin Sec
EMP: 5

New York - New York County (G-11986)

SQ FT: 1,200
SALES (est): 330K **Privately Held**
WEB: www.sandydalal.com
SIC: 2329 Men's & boys' sportswear & athletic clothing

(G-11986)
SANGUINE GAS EXPLORATION LLC
152 W 57th St Fl 4100 (10019-3322)
PHONE.....................212 582-8555
EMP: 26
SALES (corp-wide): 115.9MM **Privately Held**
SIC: 1382 Oil & gas exploration services
PA: Sanguine Gas Exploration, L.L.C.
110 W 7th St Ste 2700
Tulsa OK 74119
918 494-6070

(G-11987)
SANOY INC
Also Called: Bonnie J
19 W 36th St Fl 11 (10018-7699)
PHONE.....................212 695-6384
Larry Jonas, *President*
Bonnie Jonas, *Vice Pres*
Peter Feil, *Human Res Mgr*
EMP: 28
SQ FT: 5,000
SALES (est): 4.1MM **Privately Held**
SIC: 3911 3961 Jewelry, precious metal; costume jewelry

(G-11988)
SANTEE PRINT WORKS (PA)
58 W 40th St Fl 11 (10018-2638)
PHONE.....................212 997-1570
Fax: 212 869-7230
Martin Barocas, *Chairman*
Joe Turbeville, *Human Res Mgr*
Furman Dominick, *MIS Mgr*
Leon Barocas, *Admin Sec*
▲ EMP: 15 EST: 1949
SQ FT: 1,500,000
SALES (est): 56.3MM **Privately Held**
WEB: www.classiccottons.com
SIC: 2261 Finishing plants, cotton; printing of cotton broadwoven fabrics

(G-11989)
SAPPHIRE SYSTEMS INC (PA)
405 Lexington Ave Fl 49 (10174-0002)
PHONE.....................212 905-0100
Uys Moller, *Vice Pres*
Lorenzo Zecca, *Vice Pres*
Derek Dieringer, *Finance*
George Powers, *Accounts Mgr*
Giancarlo Fransvea, *Consultant*
EMP: 10
SALES (est): 1.8MM **Privately Held**
SIC: 7372 Business oriented computer software

(G-11990)
SARATOGA LIGHTING HOLDINGS LLC (PA)
535 Madison Ave Fl 4 (10022-4291)
PHONE.....................212 906-7800
Christian L Oberbeck,
Damon H Ball,
Richard A Petrocelli,
▲ EMP: 3
SALES (est): 180MM **Privately Held**
SIC: 3641 3645 3646 3648 Electric lamps & parts for generalized applications; residential lighting fixtures; commercial indusl & institutional electric lighting fixtures; lighting equipment

(G-11991)
SARGENT MANUFACTURING INC
120 E 124th St (10035-1933)
P.O. Box 740607, Bronx (10474-9425)
PHONE.....................212 722-7000
Richard Oswald, *President*
Robert Oswald, *Vice Pres*
Andrew Geraci, *Engineer*
Roland McNary, *Engineer*
Jacqueline Bacha, *Manager*
EMP: 2 EST: 1973
SQ FT: 5,000

SALES: 1.4MM
SALES (corp-wide): 3.4MM **Privately Held**
SIC: 3443 Chutes & troughs
PA: H. C. Oswald Supply Co., Inc.
725 Whittier St
Bronx NY 10474
718 620-1400

(G-11992)
SARGENTO FOODS INC
498 7th Ave (10018-6798)
PHONE.....................920 893-8484
EMP: 120
SALES (corp-wide): 1.8B **Privately Held**
SIC: 2022 Natural cheese; processed cheese
PA: Sargento Foods Inc.
1 Persnickety Pl
Plymouth WI 53073
920 893-8484

(G-11993)
SARINA ACCESSORIES LLC
15 W 36th St Fl 5 (10018-7130)
PHONE.....................212 239-8106
Marc Faham, *Mng Member*
▲ EMP: 12
SQ FT: 4,000
SALES (est): 3.4MM **Privately Held**
SIC: 3961 2339 3873 Costume jewelry; scarves, hoods, headbands, etc.: women's; watches, clocks, watchcases & parts

(G-11994)
SARKISIANS JEWELRY CO
17 W 45th St Ste 201 (10036-4922)
PHONE.....................212 869-1060
Fax: 212 398-4045
Vazgen Sarkisian, *President*
EMP: 5
SALES (est): 360K **Privately Held**
WEB: www.sarkisiansjewelry.com
SIC: 3911 Medals, precious or semi-precious metal

(G-11995)
SAS INSTITUTE INC
787 Seventh Ave Fl 47 (10019-6018)
PHONE.....................212 757-3826
Fax: 212 757-4086
Michael Rosenthal, *Partner*
Kristie Collins, *Principal*
Fiona McNeill, *Principal*
Wes Strom, *Principal*
Tim Fairchlld, *Business Mgr*
EMP: 15
SALES (corp-wide): 2.9B **Privately Held**
WEB: www.sas.com
SIC: 7372 Prepackaged software
PA: Sas Institute Inc.
100 Sas Campus Dr
Cary NC 27513
919 677-8000

(G-11996)
SATELLITE INCORPORATED
43 W 46th St Ste 503 (10036-4121)
PHONE.....................212 221-6687
Paula STA Cruz, *General Mgr*
EMP: 5
SALES (est): 316.3K **Privately Held**
SIC: 3911 Jewelry, precious metal

(G-11997)
SAVEUR MAGAZINE
304 Park Ave S Fl 8 (10010-4310)
PHONE.....................212 219-7400
Fax: 212 219-1260
Russ Cherami, *Publisher*
Kylie Hill, *Sales Mgr*
Coleman Andrews, *Manager*
Stefanie McNamara, *Associate Dir*
EMP: 32
SALES (est): 2.2MM **Privately Held**
SIC: 2721 Periodicals

(G-11998)
SAVWATT USA INC (PA)
475 Park Ave S Fl 30 (10016-6901)
PHONE.....................646 478-2676
Michael Haug, *CEO*
Isaac H Sutton, *Ch of Bd*
EMP: 8
SQ FT: 2,000

SALES (est): 715.8K **Publicly Held**
SIC: 3646 3645 Commercial indusl & institutional electric lighting fixtures; residential lighting fixtures

(G-11999)
SB CORPORATION
114 W 41st St Fl 4 (10036-7308)
PHONE.....................212 822-3166
Rob Cohen, *Principal*
Eric Olmsted, *Info Tech Dir*
▼ EMP: 5
SALES (est): 360K **Privately Held**
SIC: 2329 Men's & boys' sportswear & athletic clothing

(G-12000)
SB NEW YORK INC (HQ)
Also Called: Metro New York
120 Broadway (10271-0002)
PHONE.....................212 457-7790
Fax: 212 952-1505
Oskar Bjorner, *CFO*
Michele Earl, *Accounting Dir*
Al Romei, *Credit Mgr*
Juliano Michael, *Sales Executive*
Lisa Dell, *Senior Mgr*
EMP: 57
SALES (est): 12.5MM **Privately Held**
WEB: www.metronewyork.com
SIC: 2711 Newspapers

(G-12001)
SC SUPPLY CHAIN MANAGEMENT LLC
Also Called: SCM
90 Broad St Ste 1504 (10004-2276)
PHONE.....................212 344-3322
Anan Bishara, *Mng Member*
Denise Barrel, *Manager*
▲ EMP: 6
SQ FT: 2,600
SALES: 3MM **Privately Held**
SIC: 3569 Filters

(G-12002)
SCALAMANDRE SILKS INC (PA)
979 3rd Ave Ste 202 (10022-1294)
PHONE.....................212 980-3888
▲ EMP: 65 EST: 1927
SALES (est): 62.1MM **Privately Held**
SIC: 2221 2241 5131 2273 Manmad Brdwv Fabric Mill Narrow Fabric Mill Whol Piece Goods/Notions

(G-12003)
SCH DPX CORPORATION
22 W 21st St Ste 700 (10010-6982)
PHONE.....................917 405-5377
Joe Schoenfelder, *President*
Ricardo Hurtado, *Sales Mgr*
EMP: 7
SALES (est): 510K **Privately Held**
WEB: www.schoenfelder.com
SIC: 2369 Girls' & children's outerwear

(G-12004)
SCHALLER MANUFACTURING CORP (PA)
Also Called: Schaller & Weber
1654 2nd Ave Apt 2n (10028-3109)
PHONE.....................718 721-5480
Fax: 212 879-9260
Ralph Schaller, *Ch of Bd*
Marianne Schaller, *Vice Pres*
Harold Nagel, *Plant Mgr*
George Nici, *Engineer*
Maryanne Karis, *Controller*
EMP: 70 EST: 1937
SQ FT: 16,000
SALES (est): 8.8MM **Privately Held**
WEB: www.schallerweber.com
SIC: 2013 5421 Prepared pork products from purchased pork; meat & fish markets

(G-12005)
SCHINDLER ELEVATOR CORPORATION
620 12th Ave Fl 4 (10036-1016)
PHONE.....................212 708-1000
Fax: 212 582-4092
John Soutar, *Superintendent*
John Frank, *Project Mgr*
Michael Joseph, *Project Mgr*
Jack Walsh, *Manager*

Claude Brun, *Manager*
EMP: 250
SALES (corp-wide): 9.5B **Privately Held**
WEB: www.us.schindler.com
SIC: 3534 1796 Elevators & moving stairways; installing building equipment
HQ: Schindler Elevator Corporation
20 Whippany Rd
Morristown NJ 07960
973 397-6500

(G-12006)
SCHINDLER ELEVATOR CORPORATION
1211 6th Ave Ste 2950 (10036-8705)
PHONE.....................800 225-3123
Fax: 212 398-8222
Timothy Whalen, *Project Mgr*
James Iannaccone, *Manager*
EMP: 30
SALES (corp-wide): 9.5B **Privately Held**
WEB: www.us.schindler.com
SIC: 3534 1796 Elevators & equipment; elevator installation & conversion
HQ: Schindler Elevator Corporation
20 Whippany Rd
Morristown NJ 07960
973 397-6500

(G-12007)
SCHLESINGER SIEMANS ELEC LLC
527 Madison Ave Fl 8 (10022-4376)
PHONE.....................718 386-6230
Anthony Kim, *General Mgr*
Ralph Scotti, *Manager*
Lana Petrocelli, *Manager*
EMP: 10
SALES (est): 1.6MM
SALES (corp-wide): 89.6B **Privately Held**
SIC: 3634 Electric housewares & fans
PA: Siemens Ag
Werner-Von-Siemens-Str. 1
Munchen 80333
896 360-0

(G-12008)
SCHNEEMAN STUDIO LIMITED
330 W 38th St Rm 505 (10018-8639)
PHONE.....................212 244-3330
John Schneeman, *President*
EMP: 5
SQ FT: 2,000
SALES: 500K **Privately Held**
SIC: 2389 Theatrical costumes

(G-12009)
SCHNEIDER AMALCO INC
600 3rd Ave Fl 2 (10016-1919)
PHONE.....................917 470-9674
Thomas Schneider, *CEO*
EMP: 10
SQ FT: 3,500
SALES (est): 515.8K **Privately Held**
SIC: 1381 1389 6792 Drilling oil & gas wells; oil field services; oil royalty traders; oil leases, buying & selling on own account

(G-12010)
SCHNEIDER ELC SYSTEMS USA INC
7 E 8th St (10003-5901)
PHONE.....................214 527-3099
EMP: 10
SALES (corp-wide): 241K **Privately Held**
SIC: 3823 Industrial instrmnts msrmnt display/control process variable; flow instruments, industrial process type; pressure measurement instruments, industrial; liquid level instruments, industrial process type
HQ: Schneider Electric Systems Usa, Inc.
38 Neponset Ave
Foxboro MA 02035
508 543-8750

(G-12011)
SCHNEIDER ELECTRIC IT CORP
Also Called: APC-Mge
520 8th Ave Rm 2103 (10018-6507)
PHONE.....................646 335-0216
George Chappas, *Manager*
Tanya Tomlin, *Manager*
EMP: 10

GEOGRAPHIC SECTION

New York - New York County (G-12037)

SALES (corp-wide): 241K **Privately Held**
WEB: www.apcc.com
SIC: 3612 Power & distribution transformers
HQ: Schneider Electric It Corporation
  132 Fairgrounds Rd
  West Kingston RI 02892
  401 789-5735

(G-12012)
SCHNEIDER ELECTRIC USA INC
112 W 34th St Ste 908 (10120-0999)
PHONE.................................646 335-0220
James Montemarano, *Principal*
EMP: 136
SALES (corp-wide): 241K **Privately Held**
SIC: 3613 Switchgear & switchboard apparatus
HQ: Schneider Electric Usa, Inc.
  800 Federal St
  Andover MA 01810
  978 975-9600

(G-12013)
SCHNEIDER MILLS INC
Also Called: Wilkesboro Road
1430 Broadway Rm 1202 (10018-3390)
P.O. Box 519, Taylorsville NC (28681-0519)
PHONE.................................828 632-0801
Harry McPherson, *VP Admin*
Josh Schneider, *Vice Pres*
Tim Little, *Opers Staff*
Bill Brinkley, *Purch Mgr*
Mark Cochran, *QC Dir*
EMP: 250
SALES (corp-wide): 51.2MM **Privately Held**
SIC: 2211 2221 Broadwoven fabric mills, cotton; broadwoven fabric mills, man-made
PA: Schneider Mills, Inc.
  170 Hwy 16 N
  Taylorsville NC 28681
  212 768-7500

(G-12014)
SCHOEN TRIMMING & CORD CO INC
151 W 25th St Fl 10 (10001-7250)
PHONE.................................212 255-3949
Fax: 212 924-4945
Martin Silver, *President*
▲ EMP: 17 EST: 1939
SQ FT: 6,000
SALES: 2.7MM **Privately Held**
SIC: 2241 Cords, fabric

(G-12015)
SCHOLASTIC CORPORATION (PA)
557 Broadway Lbby 1 (10012-3999)
PHONE.................................212 343-6100
Fax: 212 343-6737
Richard Robinson, *Ch of Bd*
Alan Boyko, *President*
Jane Nussbaum, *Editor*
Andrew S Hedden, *Exec VP*
Judith A Newman, *Exec VP*
▲ EMP: 9
SQ FT: 500,000
SALES: 1.7B **Publicly Held**
WEB: www.scholastic.com
SIC: 2731 2721 7372 7812 Book publishing; books: publishing only; textbooks: publishing only, not printed on site; magazines: publishing only, not printed on site; educational computer software; non-theatrical motion picture production, television; video production; motion picture production; copyright buying & licensing; advertising agencies

(G-12016)
SCHOLASTIC INC (HQ)
557 Broadway Lbby 1 (10012-3999)
PHONE.................................800 724-6527
Fax: 212 343-4638
Richard Robinson, *Ch of Bd*
Neal Goff, *President*
John Cassidy, *Publisher*
Rosamund Else-Mitchell, *Publisher*
Wayne Friedman, *Publisher*
◆ EMP: 2000 EST: 1920
SQ FT: 300,000

SALES (est): 1.6B
SALES (corp-wide): 1.7B **Publicly Held**
WEB: www.scholasticdealer.com
SIC: 2731 2721 7372 7812 Books: publishing only; textbooks: publishing only, not printed on site; magazines: publishing only, not printed on site; statistical reports (periodicals): publishing only; educational computer software; video production; television film production; motion picture production & distribution
PA: Scholastic Corporation
  557 Broadway Lbby 1
  New York NY 10012
  212 343-6100

(G-12017)
SCHOLASTIC INC
Also Called: Scholastic Copy Center
557 Broadway Lbby 1 (10012-3999)
PHONE.................................212 343-6100
Richard Robinson, *CEO*
EMP: 25
SALES (corp-wide): 1.7B **Publicly Held**
WEB: www.scholasticdealer.com
SIC: 2731 Book publishing
HQ: Scholastic Inc.
  557 Broadway Lbby 1
  New York NY 10012
  800 724-6527

(G-12018)
SCHOLASTIC INC
568 Broadway Rm 809 (10012-3253)
PHONE.................................212 343-7100
Fax: 212 343-4951
Chris Lick, *Vice Pres*
Natnaree Junboonta, *Production*
Barb Ballard, *Accounts Exec*
Seth Radwell, *Branch Mgr*
Norah Forman, *Senior Mgr*
EMP: 100
SALES (corp-wide): 1.7B **Publicly Held**
WEB: www.scholasticdealer.com
SIC: 2741 Business service newsletters: publishing & printing
HQ: Scholastic Inc.
  557 Broadway Lbby 1
  New York NY 10012
  800 724-6527

(G-12019)
SCHOOLNET INC (DH)
525 Fashion Ave Fl 4 (10018-4940)
PHONE.................................646 496-9000
Fax: 212 675-0815
Jonathan D Harber, *CEO*
Mark Chernis, *President*
Jane Lockett, *Senior VP*
Diane Malanowski, *Senior VP*
Susan Aspey, *Vice Pres*
EMP: 116
SQ FT: 11,500
SALES: 10.4MM
SALES (corp-wide): 5.6B **Privately Held**
WEB: www.schoolnet.com
SIC: 7372 7373 Educational computer software; systems software development services
HQ: Pearson Education, Inc.
  221 River St
  Hoboken NJ 07030
  201 236-7000

(G-12020)
SCHURMAN FINE PAPERS
275 7th Ave Frnt 6 (10001-5821)
PHONE.................................212 206-0067
Nhan Truong, *Branch Mgr*
EMP: 158
SALES (corp-wide): 1.3B **Privately Held**
SIC: 2771 Greeting cards
PA: Schurman Fine Papers
  500 Chadbourne Rd
  Fairfield CA 94534
  707 425-8006

(G-12021)
SCI BORE INC
70 Irving Pl Apt 5c (10003-2218)
PHONE.................................212 674-7128
Robert Olsen, *Partner*
Nadiya D Jinnah, *Partner*
EMP: 7

SALES (est): 550K **Privately Held**
SIC: 3496 Miscellaneous fabricated wire products

(G-12022)
SCIENTIFIC PLASTICS INC
243 W 30th St Fl 8 (10001-2812)
PHONE.................................212 967-1199
Fax: 212 967-9609
Steven Stegman, *President*
Jeffrey Stegman, *Vice Pres*
EMP: 12 EST: 1940
SALES (est): 1.1MM **Privately Held**
WEB: www.scientificplastics.com
SIC: 3842 Surgical appliances & supplies

(G-12023)
SCITERRA LLC
244 5th Ave Ste L280 (10001-7604)
PHONE.................................646 883-3724
Alexandra Litvinov, *CEO*
Astrid Androsch, *COO*
EMP: 5
SALES: 200K **Privately Held**
SIC: 7372 Educational computer software

(G-12024)
SCOOPS R US INCORPORATED
1514 Broadway (10036-4002)
PHONE.................................212 730-7959
EMP: 8
SALES (est): 652.9K **Privately Held**
SIC: 2024 Mfg Ice Cream/Frozen Desert

(G-12025)
SCOTT KAY INC
154 W 14th St Fl 6 (10011-7334)
PHONE.................................201 287-0100
David Minster, *CEO*
Scott Kay, *President*
Jeffrey Simon, *CFO*
Elaine Ye, *Controller*
EMP: 120
SQ FT: 12,000
SALES (est): 18.5MM **Privately Held**
WEB: www.scottkay.com
SIC: 3911 5944 Jewelry, precious metal; jewelry stores

(G-12026)
SCREEN GEMS-EMI MUSIC INC (DH)
Also Called: EMI Music Publishing
150 5th Ave Fl 7 (10011-4372)
PHONE.................................212 786-8000
Martin Bandier, *CEO*
Santiago Men Ndez-Pidal, *Managing Dir*
Joanne Boris, *Exec VP*
EMP: 60
SQ FT: 45,000
SALES (est): 47.6MM **Privately Held**
SIC: 2741 Music, sheet: publishing only, not printed on site

(G-12027)
SCROLL MEDIA INC
235 W 102nd St Apt 14i (10025-8432)
PHONE.................................617 395-8904
Samir Patil, *President*
EMP: 5 EST: 2013
SALES: 660K **Privately Held**
SIC: 3577 Data conversion equipment, media-to-media: computer

(G-12028)
SEABAY MEDIA HOLDINGS LLC (PA)
Also Called: Metro Nespaper
120 Broadway Fl 6 (10271-0034)
PHONE.................................212 457-7790
Pelle Tornberg, *CEO*
EMP: 1
SALES (est): 15.4MM **Privately Held**
SIC: 2711 2741 Newspapers; miscellaneous publishing

(G-12029)
SEAN JOHN CLOTHING INC
1710 Broadway Frnt 1 (10019-5254)
PHONE.................................212 500-2200
Sean John, *Manager*
EMP: 28 **Privately Held**
SIC: 2325 Men's & boys' trousers & slacks

PA: Sean John Clothing, Inc.
  1440 Broadway Frnt 3
  New York NY 10018

(G-12030)
SEAN JOHN CLOTHING INC (PA)
1440 Broadway Frnt 3 (10018-2301)
PHONE.................................212 500-2200
Jeff Tweedy, *President*
Derek Ferguson, *CFO*
EMP: 25
SALES (est): 6.3MM **Privately Held**
SIC: 2325 Men's & boys' trousers & slacks

(G-12031)
SECRET CELEBRITY LICENSING LLC
1431 Broadway Fl 10 (10018-1910)
PHONE.................................212 812-9277
Kathryn Sio, *Mng Member*
EMP: 5
SALES (est): 912.7K **Privately Held**
SIC: 3648 5023 Decorative area lighting fixtures; decorative home furnishings & supplies

(G-12032)
SECURED SERVICES INC (PA)
110 William St Fl 14 (10038-3901)
PHONE.................................866 419-3900
King T Moore, *President*
EMP: 4
SALES (est): 3.2MM **Privately Held**
WEB: www.secured-services.com
SIC: 7372 Prepackaged software

(G-12033)
SECURITIES DATA PUBLISHING INC (PA)
Also Called: Venture Economics
11 Penn Plz Fl 17 (10001-2006)
PHONE.................................212 631-1411
Bruce Morris, *President*
Wendi Winshall, *Vice Pres*
William Johnston, *CFO*
▲ EMP: 4
SALES (est): 17.1MM **Privately Held**
SIC: 2721 Magazines: publishing & printing

(G-12034)
SECURITY LETTER
166 E 96th St Apt 3b (10128-2512)
PHONE.................................212 348-1553
Fax: 212 534-2957
Robert McCrie, *Owner*
EMP: 5 EST: 1970
SALES: 270K **Privately Held**
SIC: 2721 8742 Trade journals: publishing only, not printed on site; business consultant

(G-12035)
SEED MEDIA GROUP LLC
405 Greenwich St Apt 2 (10013-2047)
P.O. Box 2092 (10013-0875)
PHONE.................................646 502-7050
Vera Savcic, *CFO*
Adam Bly, *Mng Member*
Franchesca Arkus, *Manager*
Gita Linkeviciute, *Info Tech Mgr*
EMP: 40
SALES (est): 3.8MM **Privately Held**
SIC: 7372 8748 Application computer software; business consulting

(G-12036)
SEEDLNGS LF SCNCE VENTURES LLC
230 E 15th St Apt 1a (10003-3941)
PHONE.................................917 913-8511
Keith Rubin, *CEO*
Ken Solovay, *Manager*
EMP: 7
SALES (est): 546.8K **Privately Held**
SIC: 3841 Surgical & medical instruments

(G-12037)
SEFAIRA INC
135 E 57th St Fl 6 (10022-2185)
PHONE.................................855 733-2472
Mads Jensen, *CEO*
Sandeep Menon, *Vice Pres*
Stephen Grist, *CFO*
Scott Stelzer, *Accounts Mgr*

New York - New York County (G-12038)

GEOGRAPHIC SECTION

Annette Burgard, *VP Mktg*
EMP: 35
SALES (est): 2.6MM **Privately Held**
SIC: 7372 Business oriented computer software
HQ: Sefaira Limited
Sefaira Uk Ltd, Queens House, 55-56
London
207 269-8500

(G-12038)
SEGOVIA TECHNOLOGY CO
115 W 18th St Fl 2 (10011-4113)
PHONE..................212 868-4412
Michael Faye, *CEO*
EMP: 10
SQ FT: 1,500
SALES (est): 583.1K **Privately Held**
SIC: 7372 Prepackaged software

(G-12039)
SEIDLIN CONSULTING
580 W End Ave (10024-1723)
PHONE..................212 496-2043
Mindell Seidlin, *Owner*
EMP: 1
SALES: 1MM **Privately Held**
SIC: 2834 Pharmaceutical preparations

(G-12040)
SEKAS INTERNATIONAL LTD
345 7th Ave Fl 9 (10001-5049)
PHONE..................212 629-6095
Fax: 212 629-6097
Nicholas Sekas, *President*
Gus Sekas, *Director*
Athina Orthodoxou, *Admin Sec*
EMP: 10
SQ FT: 2,500
SALES (est): 3.1MM **Privately Held**
SIC: 2371 Fur goods

(G-12041)
SELECT INDUSTRIES NEW YORK INC
450 Fashion Ave Ste 3002 (10123-3002)
PHONE..................800 723-5333
Jerry Friedman, *Principal*
▲ **EMP:** 13 **EST:** 2011
SALES (est): 2.2MM **Privately Held**
SIC: 3999 Manufacturing industries

(G-12042)
SELECT INFORMATION EXCHANGE
175 W 79th St 3a (10024-6450)
PHONE..................212 496-6435
Fax: 212 787-4269
George H Wein, *Owner*
Alex Wein, *Manager*
Dan Lam, *Prgrmr*
Terri Chiodo, *Director*
EMP: 18
SQ FT: 2,200
SALES (est): 1.1MM **Privately Held**
WEB: www.siecom.com
SIC: 2741 7331 Catalogs: publishing only, not printed on site; mailing list compilers

(G-12043)
SELECTIVE BEAUTY CORPORATION
315 Bleecker St 109 (10014-3427)
PHONE..................585 336-7600
Sylvie Ganter, *President*
EMP: 10
SALES (est): 980K **Privately Held**
WEB: www.selective-beauty.com
SIC: 2844 Perfumes & colognes

(G-12044)
SELINI NECKWEAR INC
248 W 37th St (10018-6603)
PHONE..................212 268-5488
Fax: 212 725-6595
Paul Park, *President*
▲ **EMP:** 8
SQ FT: 3,500
SALES (est): 990K **Privately Held**
SIC: 2323 Men's & boys' neckwear

(G-12045)
SEMI-LINEAR INC
1123 Broadway Ste 718 (10010-2097)
PHONE..................212 243-2108
Linda Holliday, *CEO*
Michael Kostadinovich, *CTO*
EMP: 5
SALES (est): 526.6K **Privately Held**
SIC: 3599 Industrial machinery

(G-12046)
SENDYNE CORP
250 W Broadway Fl 6 (10013-2431)
PHONE..................212 966-0663
John Milios, *CEO*
Aakar Patel, *Vice Pres*
Victor Marten, *Engineer*
Marcin Ziemianowicz, *Engineer*
Michele Decaprio, *Corp Comm Staff*
EMP: 6
SALES (est): 550K **Privately Held**
SIC: 3674 Semiconductors & related devices

(G-12047)
SENSATIONAL COLLECTION INC (PA)
1410 Broadway Rm 505 (10018-9372)
PHONE..................212 840-7388
Azar Kada, *Owner*
Jeff Matalon, *VP Sales*
▲ **EMP:** 3
SQ FT: 5,600
SALES (est): 3.8MM **Privately Held**
SIC: 2339 5137 Women's & misses' athletic clothing & sportswear; women's & children's sportswear & swimsuits

(G-12048)
SENSUAL INC
Also Called: Icy Hot Lingerie
463 7th Ave (10018-7448)
PHONE..................212 869-1450
Sami Souid, *CEO*
Avraham Cohen, *Accountant*
EMP: 20
SQ FT: 4,000
SALES (est): 2.1MM
SALES (corp-wide): 2.3MM **Privately Held**
SIC: 2342 Bras, girdles & allied garments
PA: Usa Apparel Group Inc
183 Madison Ave Rm 401
New York NY 10016
212 869-1450

(G-12049)
SENTIMENTAL INC
Also Called: Sentimental NY
214 W 39th St Rm 504a (10018-5585)
PHONE..................212 221-0282
Sam Hourani, *CEO*
EMP: 8 **EST:** 2012
SALES: 5MM **Privately Held**
SIC: 2339 Women's & misses' outerwear

(G-12050)
SERRAVIEW AMERICA INC
2 Wall St Fl 10 (10005-2004)
PHONE..................800 903-3716
Stephen Macnee, *CEO*
Ian Morley, *Principal*
EMP: 70
SQ FT: 1,000
SALES (est): 1.2MM **Privately Held**
SIC: 7372 Business oriented computer software

(G-12051)
SERVICENOW INC
60 E 42nd St Ste 1230 (10165-1203)
PHONE..................914 318-1168
Tom Moore, *Branch Mgr*
EMP: 10
SALES (corp-wide): 1.3B **Publicly Held**
SIC: 7372 Prepackaged software
PA: Servicenow, Inc.
2225 Lawson Ln
Santa Clara CA 95054
408 501-8550

(G-12052)
SEVEN STORIES PRESS INC
140 Watts St (10013-1738)
PHONE..................212 226-8760
Daniel Simon, *President*
Dennis Loo, *COO*
Ria Julien, *Mfg Spvr*
Jon Gilbert, *Sls & Mktg Exec*
Ruth Weiner, *Mktg Dir*
▲ **EMP:** 7
SQ FT: 2,500
SALES (est): 1MM **Privately Held**
WEB: www.sevenstories.com
SIC: 2731 Book publishing

(G-12053)
SG NYC LLC
28 W 27th St Fl 12 (10001-6906)
PHONE..................310 210-1837
Daniel Chiu, *Managing Prtnr*
Stephanie Garcia, *Managing Prtnr*
Tiffany Chang, *Manager*
EMP: 20
SQ FT: 4,000
SALES (est): 4.2MM **Privately Held**
SIC: 2335 Women's, juniors' & misses' dresses

(G-12054)
SGD NORTH AMERICA
900 3rd Ave Fl 4 (10022-4998)
PHONE..................212 753-4200
Peter Acerra, *President*
Sheherazade Chamlou, *Marketing Staff*
Eleonor Sylio, *Administration*
▲ **EMP:** 33 **EST:** 2007
SALES (est): 3.5MM **Privately Held**
SIC: 3221 Glass containers

(G-12055)
SGD PHARMA PACKAGING INC
900 3rd Ave Fl 4 (10022-4998)
PHONE..................212 223-7100
Nadir Lahneur, *President*
Nadir Lahmeur, *Vice Pres*
EMP: 8
SQ FT: 2,500
SALES (est): 122K **Publicly Held**
SIC: 3221 Glass containers
HQ: Sgd S.A.
14 B Terrasse Bellini
Puteaux 92800
140 903-600

(G-12056)
SGL SERVICES CORP
1221 Ave Of Americas 42 (10020)
PHONE..................718 630-0392
Rudolph Jones, *Managing Dir*
Erwin Lontok, *Principal*
Lauren Jones, *Opers Staff*
▲ **EMP:** 8 **EST:** 2007
SALES (est): 1.6MM **Privately Held**
SIC: 3534 Elevators & moving stairways

(G-12057)
SHADAL LLC
Also Called: Sermoneta Gloves
609 Madison Ave Ste 611 (10022-1901)
PHONE..................212 319-5946
Aldo Sermonetta, *Manager*
EMP: 6
SALES (est): 18.1K **Privately Held**
SIC: 3111 Glove leather

(G-12058)
SHADOWTV INC
630 9th Ave Ste 202 (10036-4752)
PHONE..................212 445-2540
Joachim Kim, *President*
Carl Rischar, *President*
Tracy Fred, *Bookkeeper*
Kevin Riley, *Sales Mgr*
Phil Gove, *Director*
EMP: 6
SALES (est): 855K **Privately Held**
WEB: www.shadowtv.com
SIC: 3575 Computer terminals, monitors & components

(G-12059)
SHAH DIAMONDS INC
Also Called: Venus
22 W 48th St Ste 600 (10036-1820)
PHONE..................212 888-9393
Natwar Shah, *President*
Danny Gagasia, *Business Mgr*
Harshit Shah, *Sales Staff*
Gita Shah, *Admin Sec*
▲ **EMP:** 19
SQ FT: 4,000
SALES (est): 3.2MM **Privately Held**
WEB: www.hoc.com
SIC: 3911 3915 5094 Jewelry, precious metal; diamond cutting & polishing; jewelry; diamonds (gems)

(G-12060)
SHAHIN DESIGNS LTD
766 Madison Ave Fl 3 (10065-6563)
PHONE..................212 737-7225
Samouhi Shahin, *President*
EMP: 5
SALES (est): 390K **Privately Held**
SIC: 2211 Apparel & outerwear fabrics, cotton

(G-12061)
SHAKE INC
175 Varick St Fl 4 (10014-7412)
PHONE..................650 544-5479
Abraham Geiger, *CEO*
EMP: 13 **EST:** 2012
SQ FT: 1,000
SALES (est): 922.9K **Privately Held**
SIC: 7372 Business oriented computer software

(G-12062)
SHAMRON MILLS LTD
242 W 38th St Fl 14 (10018-9062)
PHONE..................212 354-0430
Fax: 212 302-7776
Ronnye Shamron, *President*
▲ **EMP:** 3
SQ FT: 3,000
SALES (est): 3MM **Privately Held**
WEB: www.shamron.com
SIC: 2389 Hospital gowns

(G-12063)
SHANU GEMS INC
1212 Ave Of The Americas (10036-1602)
P.O. Box 680, New City (10956-0680)
PHONE..................212 921-4470
Fax: 212 921-4522
Pramod Agrawal, *President*
Manensha Agrawal, *Vice Pres*
EMP: 10
SALES (est): 840K **Privately Held**
WEB: www.shanugems.com
SIC: 3911 5094 Jewelry, precious metal; jewelry

(G-12064)
SHAPEWAYS INC (PA)
419 Park Ave S Fl 9 (10016-8409)
PHONE..................914 356-5816
Peter Weijmarshausen, *CEO*
Pieter Limburg, *President*
Erkowitz Hobbs, *Production*
Martin Meyer, *CFO*
Jay Kiecolt-Wahl, *Accountant*
EMP: 94
SALES (est): 22.8MM **Privately Held**
SIC: 2759 Commercial printing

(G-12065)
SHAPIRO BERNSTEIN & CO INC
488 Madison Ave Fl 1201 (10022-5708)
PHONE..................212 588-0878
Micheal Brettler, *President*
Alexa Cabellon, *Manager*
Jacob Maletsky, *Manager*
Chris Thompson, *Manager*
Laura Sodders, *Consultant*
▲ **EMP:** 12
SALES (est): 850K **Privately Held**
WEB: www.shapirobernstein.com
SIC: 2741 Music, sheet: publishing only, not printed on site

(G-12066)
SHAREDBOOK INC
110 William St Fl 30 (10038-3901)
PHONE..................646 442-8840
Fax: 646 442-8841
Caroline Vanderlip, *CEO*
Josef Hollander, *President*
Caroline Weng, *Accountant*
EMP: 30
SQ FT: 8,000
SALES (est): 361.4K **Privately Held**
WEB: www.sharedbook.com
SIC: 2741 5942 Miscellaneous publishing; book stores

GEOGRAPHIC SECTION

(G-12067)
SHAW CONTRACT FLRG SVCS INC
521 5th Ave Fl 37 (10175-0094)
PHONE..................212 953-7429
Fax: 212 953-2589
Joe Sulima, *Manager*
Richard Butrym, *Manager*
Leon Martin, *Manager*
Kyle Golombos, *Commercial*
Laura Mahadeo, *Commercial*
EMP: 8
SALES (corp-wide): 223.6B **Publicly Held**
SIC: 2273 Carpets & rugs
HQ: Shaw Contract Flooring Services, Inc.
616 E Walnut Ave
Dalton GA 30721
706 278-3812

(G-12068)
SHAWMUT WOODWORKING & SUP INC
Also Called: Shawmutdesign and Construction
3 E 54th St Fl 8 (10022-3141)
PHONE..................212 920-8900
Jack Fickes, *Superintendent*
Leszek Piotrowski, *Superintendent*
Michael Simon, *Branch Mgr*
Hes Abdollahi, *Manager*
Felicia Bua, *Manager*
EMP: 6
SALES (corp-wide): 957.6MM **Privately Held**
WEB: www.shawmut.com
SIC: 2431 Millwork
PA: Shawmut Woodworking & Supply, Inc.
560 Harrison Ave Ste 200
Boston MA 02118
617 338-6200

(G-12069)
SHELLEY PROMOTIONS INC
87 5th Ave (10003)
PHONE..................212 924-4987
James Scott Shelley, *President*
EMP: 5
SALES (est): 370K **Privately Held**
SIC: 3861 Photographic film, plate & paper holders

(G-12070)
SHENNONG PHARMACEUTICALS INC
110 Wall St (10005-3801)
PHONE..................347 422-2200
Jason Frankovich, *Manager*
EMP: 20
SALES (est): 846.9K **Privately Held**
SIC: 2834 Pharmaceutical preparations

(G-12071)
SHIELD PRESS INC
9 Lispenard St Fl 1 (10013-2290)
PHONE..................212 431-7489
Bryan Shield, *President*
Stephen Shield, *Treasurer*
Ellen Shield, *Admin Sec*
EMP: 6 EST: 1940
SQ FT: 1,500
SALES: 750K **Privately Held**
SIC: 2752 7389 Commercial printing, offset; printers' services: folding, collating

(G-12072)
SHIELD SECURITY DOORS LTD
124 W 60th St (10023-7451)
PHONE..................202 468-3308
EMP: 5
SALES (est): 524.2K **Privately Held**
SIC: 3699 5072 Security control equipment & systems; security devices, security devices, locks

(G-12073)
SHIMADA SHOJI (HK) LIMITED
501 5th Ave Rm 1105 (10017-7879)
PHONE..................212 268-0465
Toshio Shimada, *Branch Mgr*
EMP: 7
SALES (corp-wide): 19.3MM **Privately Held**
SIC: 3965 Buttons & parts

PA: Shimada Shoji (H.K.) Limited
Rm 507-11 5/F Cheung Sha Wan Plz Twr 1
Cheung Sha Wan KLN
273 933-19

(G-12074)
SHINDO USA INC
162 W 36th St (10018-6901)
PHONE..................212 868-9311
Tadashi Shindo, *CEO*
Shingo Nagai, *Principal*
Brian Tedesco, *Sales Dir*
Junichiro Tanaka, *Regl Sales Mgr*
Masako Yasuda, *Wholesale*
EMP: 7
SALES (est): 429.3K **Privately Held**
SIC: 2211 Stretch fabrics, cotton

(G-12075)
SHIRA ACCESSORIES LTD
30 W 36th St Rm 504 (10018-9791)
PHONE..................212 594-4455
Fax: 212 594-4466
Barry Shapiro, *President*
EMP: 15
SQ FT: 2,000
SALES (est): 1.5MM **Privately Held**
SIC: 3961 Costume jewelry

(G-12076)
SHIRO LIMITED
928 Broadway Ste 806 (10010-8128)
PHONE..................212 780-0007
Fax: 212 614-8526
Gary Mandel, *President*
▲ EMP: 5
SQ FT: 2,000
SALES (est): 390.8K **Privately Held**
SIC: 3911 Jewelry, precious metal

(G-12077)
SHISEIDO AMERICAS CORPORATION (HQ)
Also Called: Shiseido Cosmetics
900 3rd Ave Fl 15 (10022-4792)
PHONE..................212 805-2300
Edward W Klause, *Vice Pres*
Tatsuya Toda, *Vice Pres*
Elias Meza, *Opers Mgr*
George Grossi Jr, *CFO*
Pankaj Gupta, *CFO*
◆ EMP: 7
SQ FT: 108,000
SALES (est): 405.1MM
SALES (corp-wide): 7.6B **Privately Held**
SIC: 2844 5122 Cosmetic preparations; toilet preparations; cosmetics; toilet preparations
PA: Shiseido Company, Limited
7-5-5, Ginza
Chuo-Ku TKY 104-0
335 725-111

(G-12078)
SHRINEETA PHARMACY
1749 Amsterdam Ave Frnt (10031-4618)
PHONE..................212 234-7959
Robby Annamaneni, *Principal*
EMP: 5
SALES (est): 812.6K **Privately Held**
SIC: 2834 Pharmaceutical preparations

(G-12079)
SHRINEETA PHARMACY INC
Also Called: Amsterdam Pharmacy
1743 Amsterdam Ave (10031-4614)
PHONE..................212 234-7959
Fax: 212 234-7969
Sreenivasa R Gade, *Ch of Bd*
Ravinder Annamaneni, *Director*
EMP: 21
SQ FT: 1,600
SALES (est): 8.1MM **Privately Held**
SIC: 2834 Pharmaceutical preparations

(G-12080)
SHYAM AHUJA LIMITED
201 E 56th St Frnt A (10022-3724)
PHONE..................212 644-5910
Fax: 212 644-5787
Azmina Merali, *Branch Mgr*
EMP: 7

SALES (corp-wide): 1.4MM **Privately Held**
WEB: www.shyamahujahome.com
SIC: 2391 2273 3999 Curtains & draperies; carpets & rugs; atomizers, toiletry
PA: Shyam Ahuja Private Limited
Floor A - 6 Poonam Appartment
Mumbai MH 40001
226 524-6967

(G-12081)
SHYK INTERNATIONAL CORP
258 Riverside Dr Apt 7b (10025-6160)
PHONE..................212 663-3302
Steven Kline, *President*
EMP: 2
SQ FT: 2,500
SALES (est): 75MM **Privately Held**
SIC: 3651 Home entertainment equipment, electronic

(G-12082)
SIDE HUSTLE MUSIC GROUP LLC
600 3rd Ave Fl 2 (10016-1919)
PHONE..................800 219-4003
Fabian Cummings,
EMP: 10
SQ FT: 574,000
SALES (est): 1.2MM **Privately Held**
WEB: www.sidehustlemusicgroup.com
SIC: 3652 Pre-recorded records & tapes

(G-12083)
SIEGEL & STOCKMAN INC
126 W 25th St Frnt 1 (10001-7413)
PHONE..................212 633-1508
Chris Israel, *President*
Tess Tobias, *Comptroller*
▲ EMP: 5
SALES (est): 374.2K **Privately Held**
SIC: 3999 Mannequins

(G-12084)
SIEMENS CORPORATION
527 Madison Ave Fl 8 (10022-4376)
PHONE..................202 434-7800
Terry Heath, *Senior VP*
Alison Taylor, *Vice Pres*
Klaus P Stegemann, *CFO*
Dina Dougherty, *Sales Staff*
Al Robertson, *Marketing Staff*
EMP: 10
SALES (corp-wide): 89.6B **Privately Held**
SIC: 3661 3641 3844 3612 Telephones & telephone apparatus; electric lamps; radiographic X-ray apparatus & tubes; distribution transformers, electric; voltage regulators, transmission & distribution; nonferrous wiredrawing & insulating
HQ: Siemens Corporation
300 New Jersey Ave Nw # 10
Washington DC 20001
202 434-4800

(G-12085)
SIEMENS ELECTRO INDUSTRIAL SA
527 Madison Ave Fl 8 (10022-4376)
PHONE..................212 258-4000
Kees Smaling, *Managing Dir*
Steffen Meyer, *Principal*
Pete Tubolino, *Business Mgr*
Julie Brunett, *Counsel*
Thomas Leubner, *Senior VP*
EMP: 785
SALES (est): 63.5MM
SALES (corp-wide): 89.6B **Privately Held**
SIC: 3648 Lighting equipment
PA: Siemens Ag
Werner-Von-Siemens-Str. 1
Munchen 80333
896 360-0

(G-12086)
SIEMENS USA HOLDINGS INC
601 Lexington Ave Fl 56 (10022-4611)
PHONE..................212 258-4000
Fax: 212 258-4370
George C Nolan, *President*
James Harris, *General Mgr*
Christopher J Flynn, *Counsel*
Joseph N Gunn, *Counsel*
Frank Helminski, *Counsel*
EMP: 300

SALES (est): 44.4MM
SALES (corp-wide): 89.6B **Privately Held**
SIC: 3612 3844 3641 3357 Distribution transformers, electric; voltage regulators, transmission & distribution; radiographic X-ray apparatus & tubes; electric lamps; nonferrous wiredrawing & insulating; telephones & telephone apparatus
PA: Siemens Ag
Werner-Von-Siemens-Str. 1
Munchen 80333
896 360-0

(G-12087)
SIFONYA INC
Also Called: Cego Custom Shirts
303 Park Ave S Frnt 2 (10010-3677)
PHONE..................212 620-4512
Carl Goldberg, *President*
EMP: 6
SQ FT: 300
SALES: 600K **Privately Held**
WEB: www.cego.com
SIC: 2321 5131 Men's & boys' furnishings; piece goods & other fabrics

(G-12088)
SIGA TECHNOLOGIES INC (PA)
27 E 62nd St Apt 5a (10065-8091)
PHONE..................212 672-9100
Phil Gomez, *CEO*
Eric A Rose, *Ch of Bd*
William J Haynes II, *Exec VP*
Dennis E Hruby, *Vice Pres*
Daniel Luckshire, *CFO*
EMP: 34
SALES: 14.9MM **Privately Held**
WEB: www.siga.com
SIC: 2834 2836 Pharmaceutical preparations; vaccines & other immunizing products

(G-12089)
SIGMA WORLDWIDE LLC (PA)
65 W 83rd St Apt 5 (10024-5237)
PHONE..................646 217-0629
Jeffrey Muti, *CEO*
Peter Devries, *Opers Staff*
EMP: 8
SALES: 15MM **Privately Held**
SIC: 3161 5099 3089 Cases, carrying; cases, carrying; cases, plastic

(G-12090)
SIGN CENTER INC
Also Called: Sign Company, The
15 W 39th St Fl 7 (10018-0633)
PHONE: 212 967-2113
Fax: 212 967-4119
Mark Dressman, *President*
James Kelly, *Vice Pres*
EMP: 10
SQ FT: 2,000
SALES (est): 897.7K **Privately Held**
SIC: 3993 Signs, not made in custom sign painting shops; displays & cutouts, window & lobby

(G-12091)
SIGN COMPANY
Also Called: Sjm Interface
15 W 39th St Fl 7 (10018-0633)
PHONE..................212 967-2113
James Kelly, *Owner*
EMP: 9
SALES (est): 544.6K **Privately Held**
SIC: 3993 5812 Signs & advertising specialties; eating places

(G-12092)
SIGNA CHEMISTRY INC (PA)
400 Madison Ave Fl 21 (10017-8901)
PHONE..................212 933-4101
Michael Lefenfeld, *President*
Paul F Vogt, *Vice Pres*
Peter Cash, *Mfg Mgr*
Paul Krumrine, *Engineer*
Kate Carney, *Marketing Staff*
EMP: 14
SQ FT: 7,000
SALES (est): 7.8MM **Privately Held**
WEB: www.signachem.com
SIC: 2819 3511 Catalysts, chemical; hydraulic turbine generator set units, complete

New York - New York County (G-12093)   **GEOGRAPHIC SECTION**

(G-12093)
SIGNATURE DIAMOND ENTPS LLC
15 W 47th St Ste 203 (10036-5708)
PHONE.................................212 869-5115
Jeremy S Hill,
EMP: 40
SQ FT: 3,000
SALES (est): 3.2MM Privately Held
SIC: 1499 Diamond mining, industrial

(G-12094)
SIGNATURE SYSTEMS GROUP LLC
38 E 29th St Fl 3l (10016-7911)
PHONE.................................800 569-2751
EMP: 10
SALES (corp-wide): 60.9MM Privately Held
SIC: 3996 Hard surface floor coverings
HQ: Signature Systems Group, Llc
   1201 Lkeside Pkwy Ste 150
   Flower Mound TX 75028
   972 684-5736

(G-12095)
SIGNEXPO ENTERPRISES INC (PA)
Also Called: Sign Expo
127 W 26th St Rm 401 (10001-6870)
PHONE.................................212 925-8585
Offer Sharaby, CEO
Frayda Sharaby, Ch of Bd
Michelle Shapiro, General Mgr
Evan Swartz, CFO
EMP: 14
SALES (est): 1.5MM Privately Held
SIC: 3993 Signs & advertising specialties

(G-12096)
SIGNPOST INC
127 W 26th St Fl 2 (10001-6881)
PHONE.................................877 334-2837
Stuart Wall, CEO
Seth Purcell, President
Chrissy Ewell, Accounts Mgr
Matthew June, Accounts Exec
Erik Bromley, Sales Executive
EMP: 250
SALES (est): 2.2MM Privately Held
SIC: 7372 Application computer software

(G-12097)
SILVATRIM CORP
Also Called: Silvatrim Corporation America
324 W 22nd St (10011-2602)
PHONE.................................212 675-0933
William Shanok, President
Daniel Shanok, Vice Pres
Frederick Shanok, Vice Pres
Victor Shanok, Treasurer
EMP: 120 EST: 1931
SQ FT: 120,000
SALES (est): 8MM Privately Held
SIC: 3089 Plastic processing; molding primary plastic

(G-12098)
SIMCO MANUFACTURING JEWELERS
62 W 47th St Ste 903 (10036-3271)
PHONE.................................212 575-8390
Fax: 212 768-0376
David Unger, President
EMP: 10 EST: 1953
SALES: 1.5MM Privately Held
SIC: 3911 Jewelry, precious metal

(G-12099)
SIMILARWEB INC
50 W 17th St Fl 9 (10011-5702)
PHONE.................................347 685-5422
Jason Schwartz, CFO
EMP: 18
SALES (est): 468.9K Privately Held
SIC: 7372 Prepackaged software

(G-12100)
SIMKA DIAMOND CORP
580 5th Ave Ste 709 (10036-4728)
PHONE.................................212 921-4420
Philip Katz, President
Isaac Friedman, Vice Pres
Surie Friedman, Admin Sec
Raizel Katz, Admin Sec
EMP: 15
SQ FT: 3,000
SALES (est): 1.4MM Privately Held
WEB: www.simkadiamond.com
SIC: 3911 Jewelry, precious metal

(G-12101)
SIMMONS-BOARDMAN PUBG CORP (HQ)
55 Broad St Fl 26 (10004-2580)
PHONE.................................212 620-7200
Arthur J Mc Ginnis Jr, President
Carol Franklin, Manager
Morene Cooney, Director
EMP: 3 EST: 1928
SQ FT: 10,000
SALES (est): 8.8MM Privately Held
WEB: www.marinelog.com
SIC: 2721 2731 8249 Periodicals: publishing only; book music: publishing only, not printed on site; correspondence school

(G-12102)
SIMON & SCHUSTER INC
Pocket Books
1230 Ave Of The Americas (10020-1586)
PHONE.................................212 698-7000
Carolyn Kroll Reidy, Branch Mgr
EMP: 51
SALES (corp-wide): 13.1B Publicly Held
SIC: 2731 Book publishing
HQ: Simon & Schuster, Inc.
   1230 Ave Of The Americas
   New York NY 10020
   212 698-7000

(G-12103)
SIMON & SIMON LLC
Also Called: Magic Maestro Music
1745 Broadway Fl 17 (10019-4642)
PHONE.................................202 419-0490
Bonnie Simon, Mng Member
Stephen Simon,
EMP: 5
SALES: 10K Privately Held
SIC: 2782 Record albums

(G-12104)
SIMON SCHUSTER DIGITAL SLS INC
51 W 52d St (10019)
PHONE.................................212 698-4391
Carolyn Reidy, Chairman
Robert Riger, Vice Pres
EMP: 53
SALES (est): 3.2MM
SALES (corp-wide): 13.1B Publicly Held
SIC: 2731 Book publishing
HQ: Simon & Schuster, Inc.
   1230 Ave Of The Americas
   New York NY 10020
   212 698-7000

(G-12105)
SIMPLICITY CREATIVE GROUP INC (DH)
261 Madison Ave Fl 4 (10016-3906)
PHONE.................................212 686-7676
J Cary Findlay, Ch of Bd
Konstance J K Findlay, Senior VP
William M Stewart, VP Mfg
David Sears, VP Sales
Jennifer Pegram, Marketing Mgr
◆ EMP: 725
SQ FT: 220,000
SALES (est): 126.5MM Privately Held
WEB: www.conso.com
SIC: 2241 2221 2396 2298 Narrow fabric mills; fringes, woven; trimmings, textile; fabric tapes; jacquard woven fabrics, manmade fiber & silk; automotive & apparel trimmings; cordage & twine

(G-12106)
SIMPLY GUM INC
270 Lafayette St Ste 1301 (10012-3327)
PHONE.................................917 721-8032
Caron Proschan, CEO
Ken Seiff, Officer
Craig Shapiro, Officer
EMP: 35
SALES (est): 955K Privately Held
SIC: 2067 Chewing gum

(G-12107)
SING TAO NEWSPAPERS NY LTD (PA)
Also Called: Sing Tao Daily
188 Lafayette St (10013-3200)
PHONE.................................212 699-3800
Fax: 212 699-3828
Robin Mui, CEO
Rick Ho, General Mgr
Alice Lee, Corp Secy
Jerry Du, Accounts Exec
Charles Fu, Manager
▲ EMP: 20
SALES: 22.5MM Privately Held
WEB: www.nysingtao.com
SIC: 2711 2741 Newspapers: publishing only, not printed on site; miscellaneous publishing

(G-12108)
SING TRIX
118 W 22nd St Fl 3 (10011-2416)
PHONE.................................212 352-1500
Al Roque, Principal
John Devecka, Vice Pres
Eric Berkowitz, Mng Member
EMP: 10
SALES (est): 894.2K Privately Held
SIC: 3651 Home entertainment equipment, electronic

(G-12109)
SINO PRINTING INC
30 Allen St Frnt A (10002-5363)
PHONE.................................212 334-6896
Craig Marsden, Principal
◆ EMP: 15
SALES (est): 1.1MM Privately Held
SIC: 2759 Commercial printing

(G-12110)
SISTER SISTER INC (PA)
463 7th Ave Fl 4 (10018-8725)
PHONE.................................212 629-9600
Fax: 212 629-6699
Jack Adjmi, Ch of Bd
Joseph Dwek, President
Joseph Dweck, President
Mark Adjmi, Vice Pres
Terry Dwek, Vice Pres
▲ EMP: 6
SQ FT: 15,000
SALES (est): 4.9MM Privately Held
SIC: 2369 2329 Headwear: girls', children's & infants'; men's & boys' sportswear & athletic clothing

(G-12111)
SITECOMPLI LLC
53 W 23rd St Fl 12 (10010-4313)
PHONE.................................800 564-1152
Ross Goldenberg,
Jason Griffith,
EMP: 21
SALES (est): 2.4MM Privately Held
SIC: 7372 Application computer software

(G-12112)
SIX BORO PUBLISHING
221 E 122nd St Apt 1703 (10035-2015)
P.O. Box 1811 (10035-0816)
PHONE.................................347 589-6756
Danielle Sullivan, Principal
EMP: 5
SALES: 26K Privately Held
SIC: 2731 Book publishing

(G-12113)
SIXTEEN MARKETS INC
110 Wall St Ste 1502 (10005-3801)
PHONE.................................347 759-1024
Minjin Chen, Director
EMP: 10
SALES: 800K Privately Held
SIC: 7372 7389 Business oriented computer software; financial services

(G-12114)
SKETCH STUDIO TRADING INC
221 W 37th St Ste 600 (10018-5782)
PHONE.................................212 244-2875
ARI Merabi, President
Isaac Merabi, Manager
Arry Miraly, Manager
Priscilla Chan, Administration
EMP: 3
SQ FT: 2,500
SALES (est): 9MM Privately Held
SIC: 2384 Bathrobes, men's & women's: made from purchased materials

(G-12115)
SKILLS ALLIANCE INC
135 W 29th St Rm 201 (10001-5188)
PHONE.................................646 492-5300
Joseph Wolf CPA, Principal
EMP: 8
SALES (est): 896.2K Privately Held
SIC: 2834 Pharmaceutical preparations

(G-12116)
SKIN NUTRITION INTL INC
410 Park Ave Fl 15 (10022-4407)
PHONE.................................212 231-8355
Richard Purvis, CEO
EMP: 21
SQ FT: 400
SALES (est): 2.2MM Privately Held
SIC: 2844 Cosmetic preparations

(G-12117)
SKINCARE PRODUCTS INC
118 E 57th St (10022-2663)
PHONE.................................917 837-5255
Allan Vanhoven, CEO
EMP: 9
SALES: 900K Privately Held
SIC: 2834 7991 7389 Dermatologicals; spas; design services

(G-12118)
SKIP HOP INC
50 W 23rd St Fl 10 (10010-5383)
PHONE.................................646 902-9874
Fax: 646 607-1989
Michael Damant, CEO
Michael Damiant, CEO
Janet Villano, President
Ellen Damiant, COO
Michael Fox, CFO
◆ EMP: 40
SALES: 28MM
SALES (corp-wide): 3.2B Publicly Held
WEB: www.skiphop.com
SIC: 2361 3942 2676 Girls' & children's dresses, blouses & shirts; stuffed toys, including animals; infant & baby paper products
HQ: Skip Hop Holdings, Inc.
   50 W 23rd St Fl 10
   New York NY 10010
   212 868-9850

(G-12119)
SKIP HOP HOLDINGS INC (HQ)
50 W 23rd St Fl 10 (10010-5383)
PHONE.................................212 868-9850
Michael Diamant, CEO
EMP: 3
SALES (est): 28MM
SALES (corp-wide): 3.2B Publicly Held
SIC: 2361 3942 2676 6719 Girls' & children's dresses, blouses & shirts; stuffed toys, including animals; infant & baby paper products; investment holding companies, except banks
PA: Carter's, Inc.
   3438 Peachtree Rd Ne # 1800
   Atlanta GA 30326
   678 791-1000

(G-12120)
SKY FRAME & ART INC (PA)
Also Called: Pop A2z
141 W 28th St Fl 12 (10001-6115)
PHONE.................................212 925-7856
Fax: 212 941-6048
Robert Benrimon, President
Sheila Benrimon, Vice Pres
Stephanie Rich, Vice Pres
Jonny Benrimon, Marketing Staff
EMP: 23
SQ FT: 7,000 Privately Held
SIC: 2499 Picture frame molding, finished

(G-12121)
SKYHORSE PUBLISHING INC
307 W 36th St Fl 11 (10018-6592)
PHONE.................................212 643-6816
Tony Lyons, President
Bill Wolfsthal, Publisher

▲ = Import ▼=Export
◆ =Import/Export

GEOGRAPHIC SECTION

New York - New York County (G-12149)

Joseph Sverchek, *Editor*
Katrina Enright, *Sales Staff*
Tad Crawford, *Manager*
▲ **EMP:** 40
SALES (est): 7.6MM **Privately Held**
WEB: www.skyhorsepublishing.com
SIC: 2731 Book publishing

(G-12122)
SKYLER BRAND VENTURES LLC
590 Madison Ave Fl 19 (10022-2544)
PHONE 646 979-5904
Betsy Schmalz Ferguson, *President*
Paul Wahlgren, *Managing Dir*
Konstantinos M Lahanas, *Vice Pres*
Jules Zecchino, *Officer*
EMP: 5 **EST:** 2013
SALES: 1MM **Privately Held**
SIC: 3841 Skin grafting equipment

(G-12123)
SKYSTEM LLC
100 W 92nd St Apt 20d (10025-7504)
PHONE 877 778-3320
Shagun Malhotra, *CEO*
EMP: 5
SALES (est): 228.6K **Privately Held**
SIC: 7372 Prepackaged software

(G-12124)
SL INDUSTRIES INC (DH)
590 Madison Ave Fl 32 (10022-2524)
PHONE 212 520-2300
Fax: 856 727-1683
William Fejes Jr, *President*
Louis Belardi, *CFO*
Steve Kochanski, *Controller*
Ryan Heal, *Accountant*
Craig Reynolds, *Assistant*
▲ **EMP:** 80 **EST:** 1956
SALES: 199.8MM
SALES (corp-wide): 1.1B **Publicly Held**
WEB: www.slpdq.com
SIC: 3679 3643 Power supplies, all types: static; electric connectors

(G-12125)
SLEEPABLE SOFAS LTD
Also Called: Lodi Down & Feather
600 3rd Ave Fl 15 (10016-1928)
PHONE 973 546-4502
Fax: 973 546-9347
Donna De Matteo, *President*
Darren Dematteo, *Vice Pres*
Susan Marino, *Purch Agent*
Robert Randall, *Marketing Staff*
EMP: 80
SQ FT: 28,000
SALES (est): 12.2MM
SALES (corp-wide): 15.4MM **Privately Held**
WEB: www.sleepablesofas.com
SIC: 2515 2512 2392 Sofa beds (convertible sofas); wood upholstered chairs & couches; household furnishings; comforters & quilts: made from purchased materials
PA: Carlyle Custom Convertibles Ltd
6 Empire Blvd
Moonachie NJ 07074
973 546-4502

(G-12126)
SLEEPWEAR HOLDINGS INC
Also Called: Knothe Apparel Group
1372 Broadway Fl 18 (10018-6107)
PHONE 516 466-4738
Brian Minkoff, *CEO*
Richard N Bern, *Ch of Bd*
Jim Callahan, *Vice Pres*
David Ford, *Vice Pres*
Richard Bern, *CFO*
▲ **EMP:** 125
SQ FT: 11,500
SALES (est): 81.6K **Privately Held**
WEB: www.knothe.com
SIC: 2322 2341 Nightwear, men's & boys': from purchased materials; pajamas & bedjackets: women's & children's

(G-12127)
SLIDEBEAN INCORPORATED
25 Broadway (10004-1010)
PHONE 866 365-0588
Jose Cayasso, *CEO*
EMP: 15
SALES: 500K **Privately Held**
SIC: 7372 Prepackaged software

(G-12128)
SM NEWS PLUS INCORPORATED
346 E 59th St Frnt 1 (10022-1527)
PHONE 212 888-0153
EMP: 5
SALES (est): 141.1K **Privately Held**
SIC: 2711 Newspapers

(G-12129)
SMART & STRONG LLC
Also Called: Poz Publishing
212 W 35th St Fl 8 (10001-2508)
PHONE 212 938-2051
Brad Peebles, *Partner*
Sean O'Brien Strub, *Founder*
Tom Doyle, *COO*
Michelle Lopez, *Admin Sec*
EMP: 25
SALES (est): 2.4MM **Privately Held**
WEB: www.poz.com
SIC: 2721 Magazines: publishing only, not printed on site

(G-12130)
SMART SPACE PRODUCTS LLC (PA)
244 5th Ave Ste 2487 (10001-7604)
PHONE 877 777-2441
Adam Rozen, *Mng Member*
EMP: 5
SQ FT: 1,200
SALES: 1MM **Privately Held**
SIC: 2599 5712 Hotel furniture; furniture stores

(G-12131)
SMILE SPECIALISTS
236 E 36th St (10016-3777)
PHONE 877 337-6135
Marvin Lagstein, *Principal*
EMP: 9
SALES (est): 1.3MM **Privately Held**
SIC: 3843 Cutting instruments, dental

(G-12132)
SMITH & WATSON
200 Lexington Ave Rm 805 (10016-6111)
PHONE 212 686-6444
Fax: 212 686-6606
Robert Ryan, *President*
John P Ryan, *Chairman*
Barbara R Pilcher, *Vice Pres*
Jeffrey Soleimani, *Vice Pres*
Teresa Hoang, *Finance Mgr*
▲ **EMP:** 20 **EST:** 1907
SQ FT: 8,000
SALES: 2MM **Privately Held**
WEB: www.smith-watson.com
SIC: 2512 Upholstered household furniture

(G-12133)
SMITH INTERNATIONAL INC
601 Lexington Ave Fl 57 (10022-4627)
PHONE 212 350-9400
Fax: 212 350-9547
Chris Hanson, *Vice Pres*
Ann Marie Copo, *Office Mgr*
William T McCormick Jr, *Director*
EMP: 89 **Privately Held**
SIC: 1382 1389 Geophysical exploration, oil & gas field; well logging
HQ: Smith International, Inc.
1310 Rankin Rd
Houston TX 77073
281 443-3370

(G-12134)
SMK WINES & LIQUORS LLC
23 E 28th St (10016-7921)
PHONE 212 685-7651
Steve Kaiden, *Mng Member*
EMP: 5
SALES (est): 342.9K **Privately Held**
SIC: 2084 Wines, brandy & brandy spirits

(G-12135)
SML USA INC (PA)
5 Penn Plz Ste 1500 (10001-1810)
PHONE 212 736-8800
Paul Gnieser, *CEO*

Thomas Blaze, *Manager*
Gary Moskovciak, *Manager*
▲ **EMP:** 50
SQ FT: 16,000
SALES (est): 12.8MM **Privately Held**
SIC: 2679 2241 2269 5131 Tags & labels, paper; building, insulating & packaging paper; labels, woven; labels, cotton: printed; labels; textile machinery & equipment

(G-12136)
SMM - NORTH AMERICA TRADE CORP
Also Called: Sims Metal Management
16 W 22nd St Fl 10 (10010-5967)
PHONE 212 604-0710
Robert A Kelman, *President*
Michael S Collins, *Vice Pres*
Marian Arnold, *Manager*
Chrystelle Ball, *Manager*
Nina Goryntseva, *Manager*
EMP: 5
SALES (est): 1.2MM **Privately Held**
SIC: 3291 Grit, steel

(G-12137)
SMOKE N VAPE
644 9th Ave Frnt 1 (10036-3626)
PHONE 212 390-1654
EMP: 7
SALES (est): 120.7K **Privately Held**
SIC: 3999 Cigar & cigarette holders

(G-12138)
SMOOTH INDUSTRIES INCORPORATED
1411 Broadway Rm 3000 (10018-3496)
PHONE 212 869-1080
Fax: 212 302-5699
Celeste Chan, *President*
Alice Kalenial, *Accountant*
▲ **EMP:** 25
SQ FT: 7,000
SALES (est): 1.8MM **Privately Held**
WEB: www.smoothny.com
SIC: 2339 Women's & misses' outerwear

(G-12139)
SMOOTH MAGAZINE
55 John St Ste 800 (10038-3752)
PHONE 212 925-1150
Sandra Vasceannie, *President*
EMP: 10
SALES (est): 730K **Privately Held**
SIC: 2721 Periodicals

(G-12140)
SNEAKER NEWS INC
41 Elizabeth St Ste 301 (10013-4637)
PHONE 347 687-1588
Yu-Ming Wu, *President*
EMP: 9
SALES (est): 1.8MM **Privately Held**
SIC: 2741 Shopping news: publishing only, not printed on site

(G-12141)
SNEAKERS SOFTWARE INC
Also Called: Dvmax
519 8th Ave Rm 812 (10018-4588)
PHONE 800 877-9221
Paul R Greenman, *CEO*
Larry White, *Engineer*
EMP: 18
SQ FT: 800
SALES: 3MM **Privately Held**
WEB: www.DVMAX.com
SIC: 7372 Prepackaged software

(G-12142)
SNOWMAN
1181 Broadway Fl 6 (10001-7433)
PHONE 212 239-8818
Jennifer Suh, *Vice Pres*
Baekkyu Suh, *Mng Member*
EMP: 5
SALES (est): 557.2K **Privately Held**
SIC: 2339 Sportswear, women's

(G-12143)
SOCIAL REGISTER ASSOCIATION
14 Wall St Ste 3f (10005-2141)
PHONE 646 612-7314

Matthew Campbell, *President*
EMP: 18
SALES (est): 92.8K **Privately Held**
WEB: www.socialregisterassociation.com
SIC: 2731 Books: publishing only

(G-12144)
SOCIETY FOR THE STUDY
Also Called: PARABOLA
20 W 20th St Fl 2 (10011-9260)
PHONE 212 822-8806
Steven Schiff, *President*
Joseph Kulin, *Publisher*
Bob Doto, *Manager*
Erynn Sosinski, *Assistant*
EMP: 7
SQ FT: 1,500
SALES: 432.3K **Privately Held**
SIC: 2721 5735 5942 Magazines: publishing only, not printed on site; video tapes, prerecorded; audio tapes, prerecorded; book stores

(G-12145)
SOFT SHEEN PRODUCTS INC (DH)
575 5th Ave (10017-2422)
PHONE 212 818-1500
Patricia Cumberland, *President*
Candace Matthews, *Principal*
Gut Peyrelongue, *Div Sub Head*
Adu Darkwa, *Vice Pres*
Amy Hilliard, *Vice Pres*
▼ **EMP:** 1
SALES (est): 4MM
SALES (corp-wide): 3.2B **Privately Held**
WEB: www.softsheen-carson.com
SIC: 2844 Shampoos, rinses, conditioners: hair
HQ: L'oreal Usa, Inc.
10 Hudson Yards Fl 30
New York NY 10001
212 818-1500

(G-12146)
SOHO APPAREL LTD
Also Called: Flirtatious
525 Fashion Ave Fl 6 (10018-4960)
PHONE 212 840-1109
Nikou Achouri, *President*
Jeffrey Stein, *Exec VP*
EMP: 5
SQ FT: 3,140
SALES (est): 550.2K **Privately Held**
SIC: 2331 5137 Women's & misses' blouses & shirts; women's & children's clothing

(G-12147)
SOHO PRESS INC
853 Broadway Ste 1402 (10003-4716)
PHONE 212 260-1900
Fax: 212 260-1902
Juris Jurjevics, *President*
Bronwen Hruska, *Publisher*
Mark Doten, *Editor*
Amara Hoshijo, *Editor*
Laura Hruska, *Vice Pres*
EMP: 5
SQ FT: 1,250
SALES (est): 510K **Privately Held**
WEB: www.sohopress.com
SIC: 2731 5942 Books: publishing only; book stores

(G-12148)
SOLABIA USA INC
28 W 44th St (10036-7406)
PHONE 212 847-2397
Michael J Conti, *President*
▲ **EMP:** 7
SQ FT: 1,100
SALES (est): 6.6MM **Privately Held**
SIC: 2844 Cosmetic preparations

(G-12149)
SOLARPATH INC
Also Called: Solarpath Sun Solutions
415 Madison Ave Fl 14 (10017-7935)
PHONE 201 490-4499
Ori Aldubi, *CEO*
Amir Warshazsky, *President*
Scott Marquartt, *Manager*
EMP: 6
SQ FT: 5,000

New York - New York County (G-12150)   **GEOGRAPHIC SECTION**

SALES (est): 900.6K **Privately Held**
SIC: 3646 Commercial indusl & institutional electric lighting fixtures

(G-12150)
SOLO LICENSING CORP
358 5th Ave Rm 1205 (10001-2209)
PHONE..............................212 244-5505
Fax: 212 244-5535
David Freed, *President*
Fern Pochtar, *Vice Pres*
Barbara Freed, *Admin Sec*
▲ EMP: 8
SQ FT: 2,200
SALES (est): 1MM **Privately Held**
SIC: 2341 2322 Women's & children's underwear; men's & boys' underwear & nightwear

(G-12151)
SOLSTARS INC
Also Called: Solstarny
575 Madison Ave Ste 1006 (10022-8511)
PHONE..............................212 605-0430
Haim Hassin, *President*
▲ EMP: 7
SALES (est): 642.2K **Privately Held**
SIC: 2084 Wine cellars, bonded: engaged in blending wines

(G-12152)
SOLSTISS INC
561 Fashion Ave Fl 16 (10018-1816)
PHONE..............................212 719-9194
Fax: 212 302-8109
Francois Damide, *President*
Sandrine Bernard, *Exec VP*
Ahsan Masood, *Controller*
Kaitlyn J Neumann, *Accounts Exec*
Sara Campos, *Sales Staff*
EMP: 6
SQ FT: 3,500
SALES (est): 624.7K **Privately Held**
SIC: 2241 2258 Silk narrow fabrics; lace & lace products

(G-12153)
SOLUDOS LLC
520 Broadway Fl 5 (10012-4436)
PHONE..............................212 219-1101
Manish Karna, *Controller*
Caroline Savitt, *Accounts Mgr*
Bob Perkins, *Director*
Nick Brown,
Jim Altieri,
EMP: 13 EST: 2010
SALES (est): 1.9MM **Privately Held**
SIC: 3021 7389 Shoes, rubber or plastic molded to fabric; shoe designers

(G-12154)
SOLUTIA BUSINESS ENTPS INC
111 8th Ave (10011-5201)
PHONE..............................314 674-1000
Timothy J Spihlman, *Ch of Bd*
Charles Petracra, *Credit Mgr*
EMP: 15
SALES (est): 1MM **Publicly Held**
SIC: 2824 Organic fibers, noncellulosic
HQ: Solutia Inc.
    575 Maryville Centre Dr
    Saint Louis MO 63141
    423 229-2000

(G-12155)
SONTEK INDUSTRIES INC (PA)
36 E 12th St Fl 6 (10003-4604)
PHONE..............................781 749-3055
Garry A Prime, *President*
Gary Prime, *President*
James Gerson, *Chairman*
Donald I McCarthy, *Treasurer*
David H Drohan, *Clerk*
EMP: 6
SQ FT: 3,000
SALES (est): 8.1MM **Privately Held**
SIC: 3842 5047 Respiratory protection equipment, personal; medical equipment & supplies

(G-12156)
SONY BROADBAND ENTERTAINMENT (DH)
550 Madison Ave Fl 6 (10022-3211)
PHONE..............................212 833-6800
Howard Stringer, *Ch of Bd*
Peter Jensen, *Senior VP*
Janel Clausen, *Vice Pres*
Robert Wiesenthal, *CFO*
Steven Kober, *Controller*
▲ EMP: 12
SQ FT: 20,000
SALES (est): 1.4B
SALES (corp-wide): 66.9B **Privately Held**
SIC: 3652 7812 5734 7832 Pre-recorded records & tapes; motion picture production & distribution; motion picture production & distribution, television; software, computer games; motion picture theaters, except drive-in; video discs & tapes, pre-recorded
HQ: Sony Corporation Of America
    25 Madison Ave Fl 27
    New York NY 10010
    212 833-8000

(G-12157)
SONY CORPORATION OF AMERICA (HQ)
Also Called: Sony Music Entertainment
25 Madison Ave Fl 27 (10010-8601)
PHONE..............................212 833-8000
Fax: 212 833-7392
Kazuo Hirai, *Ch of Bd*
Howard Stringer, *President*
Peter Viot, *General Mgr*
Hironori Wada, *General Mgr*
Michelle McManus, *Principal*
◆ EMP: 250
SQ FT: 20,000
SALES (est): 12B
SALES (corp-wide): 66.9B **Privately Held**
WEB: www.sony.com
SIC: 3695 3652 3651 3577 Optical disks & tape, blank; compact laser discs, prerecorded; household audio & video equipment; computer peripheral equipment; computer storage devices
PA: Sony Corporation
    1-7-1, Konan
    Minato-Ku TKY 108-0
    367 482-111

(G-12158)
SONY DADC US INC
Also Called: Sony Style
550 Madison Ave (10022-3211)
PHONE..............................212 833-8000
David Rubenstein, *Branch Mgr*
Catherine Wozney, *Manager*
EMP: 386
SALES (corp-wide): 66.9B **Privately Held**
SIC: 3695 Optical disks & tape, blank
HQ: Sony Dadc Us Inc.
    1800 N Fruitridge Ave
    Terre Haute IN 47804
    812 462-8100

(G-12159)
SONY MUSIC ENTERTAINMENT (DH)
Also Called: Sony Wonder
25 Madison Ave Fl 19 (10010-8601)
PHONE..............................212 833-8500
Fax: 212 833-4082
Hartwig Masuch, *CEO*
Antonio Reid, *CEO*
Robert Sorrentino, *Ch of Bd*
Colin Currie, *Managing Dir*
Jong R Kim, *Managing Dir*
▲ EMP: 2000
SQ FT: 500,000
SALES (est): 1.4B
SALES (corp-wide): 66.9B **Privately Held**
WEB: www.sonymusic.com
SIC: 3652 5064 Pre-recorded records & tapes; electrical appliances, television & radio
HQ: Sony Broadband Entertainment Corp
    550 Madison Ave Fl 6
    New York NY 10022
    212 833-6800

(G-12160)
SONY MUSIC ENTERTAINMENT INC
Also Called: Sony Music Holdings
25 Madison Ave Fl 19 (10010-8601)
PHONE..............................212 833-8000
Fax: 212 833-8338
Thomas Mottola, *CEO*
Catherine Wozney, *Manager*
Kevin Kiernan, *Director*
EMP: 2000
SALES (corp-wide): 66.9B **Privately Held**
WEB: www.sonymusic.com
SIC: 3652 Pre-recorded records & tapes
HQ: Sony Music Entertainment
    25 Madison Ave Fl 19
    New York NY 10010
    212 833-8500

(G-12161)
SONY MUSIC ENTERTAINMENT INC
Tristar Music
79 5th Ave Fl 16 (10003-3034)
PHONE..............................212 833-5057
Rich Isaacson, *President*
Jeff Swierk, *Manager*
Catherine Wozney, *Manager*
EMP: 45
SALES (corp-wide): 66.9B **Privately Held**
WEB: www.sonymusic.com
SIC: 3652 Pre-recorded records & tapes
HQ: Sony Music Entertainment
    25 Madison Ave Fl 19
    New York NY 10010
    212 833-8500

(G-12162)
SONY MUSIC HOLDINGS INC (DH)
25 Madison Ave Fl 26 (10010-8601)
PHONE..............................212 833-8000
Douglas P Morris, *CEO*
Steven E Kober, *President*
Charles Goldstuck, *President*
Richard Griffiths, *President*
Robert Jamieson, *President*
◆ EMP: 800
SQ FT: 300,000
SALES (est): 424.4MM
SALES (corp-wide): 66.9B **Privately Held**
WEB: www.bmgentertainment.com
SIC: 3652 5099 2741 Pre-recorded records & tapes; phonograph records; tapes & cassettes, prerecorded; compact discs; miscellaneous publishing
HQ: Sony Corporation Of America
    25 Madison Ave Fl 27
    New York NY 10010
    212 833-8000

(G-12163)
SONY/ATV MUSIC PUBLISHING LLC (DH)
25 Madison Ave Fl 24 (10010-8601)
PHONE..............................212 833-7730
Martin N Bandier, *CEO*
Peter Brodsky, *Exec VP*
▲ EMP: 20 EST: 1995
SALES (est): 22.7MM
SALES (corp-wide): 66.9B **Privately Held**
SIC: 2741 Music book & sheet music publishing
HQ: Sony Corporation Of America
    25 Madison Ave Fl 27
    New York NY 10010
    212 833-8000

(G-12164)
SOS CHEFS OF NEW YORK INC
104 Avenue B Apt 1 (10009-6286)
P.O. Box 517 (10021-0011)
PHONE..............................212 505-5813
Fax: 212 505-5815
Atef Boulaabi, *President*
▲ EMP: 5
SALES (est): 503.6K **Privately Held**
WEB: www.sos-chefs.com
SIC: 2099 Seasonings & spices

(G-12165)
SOS INTERNATIONAL LLC
40 Fulton St Fl 26 (10038-5007)
PHONE..............................212 742-2410
Mark Burgess, *CFO*
Bjorn Delaney, *Program Mgr*
EMP: 309
SALES (corp-wide): 76.3MM **Privately Held**
SIC: 3724 Aircraft engines & engine parts
PA: Sos International Llc
    1881 Campus Commons Dr
    Reston VA 20191
    703 391-9680

(G-12166)
SOS INTERNATIONAL LLC
Also Called: Sosi
40 Fulton St Fl 26 (10038-5007)
PHONE..............................212 742-2410
EMP: 111
SALES (corp-wide): 76.3MM **Privately Held**
SIC: 3724 8711 8732 7389 Aircraft engines & engine parts; engineering services; opinion research; translation services
PA: Sos International Llc
    1881 Campus Commons Dr
    Reston VA 20191
    703 391-9680

(G-12167)
SOTERIX MEDICAL INC
Also Called: Soterix Medical Technologies
237 W 35th St Ste 1401 (10001-1950)
PHONE..............................888 990-8327
Lucas Parra, *President*
Pragya Bista, *Engineer*
Rakshya Bista, *Engineer*
Rabinson Shakya, *Engineer*
Marco Martinez, *Design Engr*
▲ EMP: 12
SALES (est): 595.9K **Privately Held**
SIC: 3845 Electromedical equipment

(G-12168)
SOURCE MEDIA LLC (HQ)
1 State St Fl 27 (10004-1561)
PHONE..............................212 803-8200
Douglas J Manoni, *CEO*
Tim Whiting, *Publisher*
Benjamin Felix, *General Mgr*
Victor Kuo, *General Mgr*
Robert Barba, *Editor*
▲ EMP: 208
SQ FT: 60,000
SALES (est): 185MM **Privately Held**
WEB: www.sourcemedia.com/
SIC: 2721 Magazines: publishing & printing

(G-12169)
SOUTH BRIDGE PRESS INC
122 W 26th St Fl 3 (10001-6804)
PHONE..............................212 233-4047
Mitch Nochlin, *President*
EMP: 8
SALES (est): 946.9K **Privately Held**
SIC: 2752 Commercial printing, lithographic

(G-12170)
SOUTINE INC
104 W 70th St Frnt 1 (10023-4454)
PHONE..............................212 496-1450
Fax: 212 496-1791
Madge Rosenberg, *President*
Barry Rosenberg, *Vice Pres*
EMP: 6
SQ FT: 600
SALES (est): 497.2K **Privately Held**
WEB: www.soutine.com
SIC: 2051 5812 Bakery: wholesale or wholesale/retail combined; caterers

(G-12171)
SOVEREIGN BRANDS LLC (PA)
81 Greene St Apt 2 (10012-5349)
PHONE..............................212 343-8366
Brett R Berish, *CEO*
Allison Kolos, *Area Mgr*
Scott Cohen, *VP Opers*
Shannon Bullinger, *Opers Staff*
Dan Thurston, *Regl Sales Mgr*
▲ EMP: 6
SQ FT: 1,800
SALES (est): 1MM **Privately Held**
WEB: www.sovereignbrands.com
SIC: 2085 Distilled & blended liquors

(G-12172)
SPARK CREATIONS INC
10 W 46th St Fl 9 (10036-4515)
PHONE..............................212 575-8385
Fax: 212 764-5455
Eli Aviram, *President*
Benjamin Aviram, *Vice Pres*
▲ EMP: 17
SQ FT: 4,000

New York - New York County (G-12198)

SALES (est): 1.8MM Privately Held
WEB: www.sparkcreations.com
SIC: 3911 Jewelry, precious metal

(G-12173)
SPARTACIST PUBLISHING CO
48 Warren St (10007-1017)
P.O. Box 1377 (10116-1377)
PHONE 212 732-7860
Fax: 212 406-2210
Elizabeth R Gordis, *CEO*
James M Robertson, *President*
A Robinson Hunt, *Treasurer*
Robinson A Hunt, *Treasurer*
EMP: 20
SALES (est): 1.8MM Privately Held
SIC: 2731 2711 Pamphlets: publishing only, not printed on site; newspapers: publishing only, not printed on site

(G-12174)
SPARTAN BRANDS INC (PA)
451 Park Ave S Fl 5 (10016-7390)
PHONE 212 340-0320
Fax: 212 684-0625
Gary Grey, *President*
Eli Motovich, *CFO*
Cynthia Murphy, *Manager*
◆ **EMP:** 12 EST: 1946
SQ FT: 2,500
SALES (est): 12.7MM Privately Held
WEB: www.spartanbrands.com
SIC: 3999 Hair & hair-based products

(G-12175)
SPARTAN BRANDS INC
451 Park Ave S Fl 5 (10016-7390)
PHONE 212 340-0320
Bill Moser, *Manager*
EMP: 11
SALES (corp-wide): 12.7MM Privately Held
WEB: www.spartanbrands.com
SIC: 2252 2254 Hosiery; knit underwear mills
PA: Spartan Brands, Inc.
  451 Park Ave S Fl 5
  New York NY 10016
  212 340-0320

(G-12176)
SPATULA LLC
2165 Broadway (10024-6629)
PHONE 917 582-8684
Nicolo Derienzo, *Mng Member*
Stesano Ciravegna,
▲ **EMP:** 17
SALES (est): 780K Privately Held
SIC: 2024 Ice cream & frozen desserts

(G-12177)
SPC GLOBAL LLC
1270 Broadway Rm 710 (10001-3224)
PHONE 646 723-3238
EMP: 6
SALES (est): 555.4K Privately Held
SIC: 2337 Pantsuits: women's, misses' & juniors'

(G-12178)
SPECIALTY MINERALS INC (HQ)
Also Called: S M I
622 3rd Ave Fl 38 (10017-6729)
PHONE 212 878-1800
Paul R Saueracker, *Ch of Bd*
Timothy South, *Managing Prtnr*
Dj Monagle, *Principal*
Kenneth Mueller, *Business Mgr*
Scott McDougal, *Production*
◆ **EMP:** 50
SQ FT: 42,000
SALES (est): 904.2MM
SALES (corp-wide): 1.6B Publicly Held
WEB: www.specialtyminerals.com
SIC: 2819 5032 1422 5169 Industrial inorganic chemicals; calcium carbide; lime building products; crushed & broken limestone; chemical additives; chemical preparations
PA: Minerals Technologies Inc.
  622 3rd Ave Fl 38
  New York NY 10017
  212 878-1800

(G-12179)
SPECIALTY SIGNS CO INC
15 W 39th St Fl 7 (10018-0633)
PHONE 212 243-8521
Fax: 212 243-6457
Marc Frankel, *President*
Edna Batounis, *Project Mgr*
EMP: 13 EST: 1971
SQ FT: 6,000
SALES (est): 850K Privately Held
SIC: 3993 Signs & advertising specialties

(G-12180)
SPECILTY BUS MCHS HOLDINGS LLC
260 W 35th St Fl 11 (10001-2528)
PHONE 212 587-9600
Steven Schaps, *Mng Member*
EMP: 26
SALES (est): 3.6MM Privately Held
SIC: 3555 Printing trades machinery

(G-12181)
SPECTRUM APPAREL INC
463 Fashion Ave Fl 12 (10018-7499)
PHONE 212 239-2025
Richard Kringstein, *President*
EMP: 85
SALES (est): 5.7MM Privately Held
SIC: 2339 Women's & misses' jackets & coats, except sportswear

(G-12182)
SPECTRUM PRTG LITHOGRAPHY INC
Also Called: Earth Spectrum
505 8th Ave Rm 1802 (10018-4707)
PHONE 212 255-3131
Peter Mandelkern, *President*
Karen Targrove, *Vice Pres*
Lauren Moore, *Manager*
EMP: 10
SQ FT: 5,000
SALES (est): 1.9MM Privately Held
SIC: 2752 2789 2759 2675 Color lithography; bookbinding & related work; commercial printing; die-cut paper & board

(G-12183)
SPEKTRIX INC
115 W 30th St Rm 501 (10001-4071)
PHONE 646 741-5110
Steven Walsh, *Project Mgr*
Rebecca Kahn, *Mng Member*
Emily Childs, *Training Spec*
EMP: 6
SQ FT: 1,200
SALES (est): 148.8K Privately Held
SIC: 7372 Publishers' computer software

(G-12184)
SPENCER AB INC
265 W 37th St Rm 2388 (10018-5757)
PHONE 646 831-3728
Tommy Tsui, *President*
Joel Glentz, *VP Sales*
Lisa Tsui, *Admin Asst*
EMP: 7
SALES (est): 1.5MM Privately Held
SIC: 2335 2331 Women's, juniors' & misses' dresses; women's & misses' blouses & shirts

(G-12185)
SPF HOLDINGS II LLC (HQ)
9 W 57th St Ste 4200 (10019-2707)
PHONE 212 750-8300
Dave West, *President*
EMP: 9
SALES (est): 2.1B
SALES (corp-wide): 7.3B Publicly Held
SIC: 2033 5149 6719 2099 Fruits & fruit products in cans, jars, etc.; vegetables & vegetable products in cans, jars, etc.; tomato products: packaged in cans, jars, etc.; canned goods: fruit, vegetables, seafood, meats, etc.; pet foods; personal holding companies, except banks; syrups; frosting, ready-to-use; sandwiches, assembled & packaged: for wholesale market; peanut butter
PA: The J M Smucker Company
  1 Strawberry Ln
  Orrville OH 44667
  330 682-3000

(G-12186)
SPH GROUP HOLDINGS LLC (HQ)
590 Madison Ave Fl 32 (10022-2524)
PHONE 212 520-2300
Jack L Howard, *CEO*
EMP: 13 EST: 2013
SALES (est): 938.8MM
SALES (corp-wide): 1.1B Publicly Held
SIC: 3339 3011 3312 Precious metals; tire & inner tube materials & related products; wire products, steel or iron
PA: Steel Partners Holdings L.P.
  590 Madison Ave Rm 3202
  New York NY 10022
  212 520-2300

(G-12187)
SPIN MAGAZINE MEDIA
276 5th Ave Rm 800 (10001-4509)
PHONE 212 231-7400
Fax: 212 231-7312
Nion McEvoy, *CEO*
Jack Jensen, *President*
Malcom Kimball, *Publisher*
Mary Howard, *General Mgr*
Tom Fernald, *Vice Pres*
EMP: 9
SALES (est): 198.3K
SALES (corp-wide): 6.1MM Privately Held
WEB: www.spinmag.com
SIC: 2721 Periodicals
PA: Buzz Media Inc.
  6464 W Sunset Blvd # 650
  Los Angeles CA 90028
  213 252-8999

(G-12188)
SPIRIT MUSIC GROUP INC (HQ)
235 W 23rd St Fl 4 (10011-2371)
PHONE 212 533-7672
Fax: 212 979-8566
Mark Fried, *President*
David Renzer, *Chairman*
Jennifer Scher, *CFO*
David Fedon, *Manager*
EMP: 20
SALES (est): 1.4MM Privately Held
WEB: www.spiritmusicgroup.com
SIC: 2741 Music books: publishing & printing

(G-12189)
SPORT ATHLEISURE LTD ✪
16 W 36th St Rm 1205 (10018-9754)
PHONE 212 868-6505
Shalom Asher, *President*
Steven Goldfarb, *Vice Pres*
EMP: 10 EST: 2017
SALES: 12MM Privately Held
SIC: 2339 2329 Women's & misses' athletic clothing & sportswear; men's & boys' sportswear & athletic clothing

(G-12190)
SPORTS ILLUSTRATED FOR KIDS
1271 Ave Of The Americas (10020-1300)
PHONE 212 522-1212
Fax: 212 522-0926
Don Logan, *CEO*
Paul Caine, *Publisher*
Sherrill Clarke, *Publisher*
Charles Kammer, *Publisher*
Diane Oshin, *Publisher*
▲ **EMP:** 50
SALES (est): 5.1MM
SALES (corp-wide): 3B Publicly Held
WEB: www.siphoto.com
SIC: 2721 Magazines: publishing only, not printed on site
PA: Time Inc.
  225 Liberty St Ste C2
  New York NY 10281
  212 522-1212

(G-12191)
SPORTS PBLICATIONS PROD NY LLC
708 3rd Ave Fl 12 (10017-4129)
PHONE 212 366-7700
Brent Diamond,
EMP: 80

SALES (est): 2.3MM Privately Held
SIC: 2711 Newspapers, publishing & printing

(G-12192)
SPORTS PRODUCTS AMERICA LLC
Popsicle Playwear
34 W 33rd St Fl 2 (10001-3304)
PHONE 212 594-5511
Fax: 212 564-0174
Richard Adjmi, *Sales Associate*
EMP: 50
SALES (corp-wide): 32.7MM Privately Held
SIC: 2361 Girls' & children's dresses, blouses & shirts; girls' & children's blouses & shirts
HQ: Sports Products Of America Llc
  463 7th Ave
  New York NY 10018
  212 629-9600

(G-12193)
SPORTS REPORTER INC
527 3rd Ave Ste 327 (10016-4168)
PHONE 212 737-2750
Lindsay Hamilton, *President*
EMP: 6
SALES (est): 280K Privately Held
WEB: www.sportsreporter.com
SIC: 2711 Newspapers, publishing & printing

(G-12194)
SPRING INC
41 E 11th St Fl 11 (10003-4602)
PHONE 646 732-0323
Ofer Leidner, *President*
EMP: 6
SALES (est): 448.2K Privately Held
SIC: 7372 Application computer software

(G-12195)
SPRINGER ADIS US LLC (DH)
233 Spring St Fl 6 (10013-1578)
PHONE 212 460-1500
Derk Haank, *CEO*
Tom Lee, *Finance*
EMP: 18
SALES (est): 3MM
SALES (corp-wide): 1.5B Privately Held
SIC: 2721 2731 Trade journals: publishing only, not printed on site; magazines: publishing only, not printed on site; books: publishing only
HQ: Springer Science + Business Media, Llc
  233 Spring St Fl 6
  New York NY 10013
  781 871-6600

(G-12196)
SPRINGER CUSTOMER SVC CTR LLC
233 Spring St Fl 6 (10013-1578)
PHONE 212 460-1500
Edward Woods, *CFO*
EMP: 400
SQ FT: 80,000
SALES (est): 19.5MM Privately Held
SIC: 2731 Book publishing

(G-12197)
SPRINGER HEALTHCARE LLC
233 Spring St Fl 6 (10013-1578)
PHONE 212 460-1500
Fax: 212 460-1575
Rick Werdann, *Principal*
Martin Mos, *COO*
Jan De Boer, *Exec VP*
Myrtle Bannis, *Facilities Mgr*
Ulrich Vest, *CFO*
EMP: 25
SALES: 950K Privately Held
SIC: 2721 Periodicals

(G-12198)
SPRINGER PUBLISHING CO LLC
11 W 42nd St Ste 15a (10036-8007)
PHONE 212 431-4370
Fax: 212 941-7842
Ursula Springer, *President*
Lindsay Claire, *Editor*
Christina Morgan, *Editor*
Joseph Morita, *Editor*

New York - New York County (G-12199)

Jeffrey Meltzer, *Vice Pres*
EMP: 38 **EST:** 1950
SQ FT: 9,000
SALES (est): 7.1MM **Privately Held**
WEB: www.springerpub.com
SIC: 2731 2721 Books: publishing only; trade journals: publishing only, not printed on site

(G-12199)
SPRINGER SCNCE + BUS MEDIA LLC (DH)
Also Called: Springer Business Media
233 Spring St Fl 6 (10013-1578)
PHONE.................................781 871-6600
Jeff Davis, *Editor*
Daniel Dominguez, *Editor*
Herma Drees, *Editor*
Jennifer Evans, *Editor*
Melissa Fearon, *Editor*
◆ **EMP:** 83 **EST:** 1964
SQ FT: 40,000
SALES (est): 109.1MM
SALES (corp-wide): 1.5B **Privately Held**
WEB: www.telospub.com
SIC: 2721 2731 Trade journals: publishing only, not printed on site; books: publishing only
HQ: Springer Science+Business Media Gmbh
Heidelberger Platz 3
Berlin 14197
308 278-70

(G-12200)
SPUTNICK 84 LLC
Also Called: Out of Print
127 W 26th St Rm 400 (10001-0119)
PHONE.................................844 667-7468
Todd Lawton, *Principal*
Jeffrey Leblanc, *Principal*
EMP: 5
SALES (est): 544K
SALES (corp-wide): 17.9B **Privately Held**
SIC: 2752 Commercial printing, lithographic
HQ: Penguin Random House Llc
1745 Broadway
New York NY 10019
212 782-9000

(G-12201)
SRP APPAREL GROUP INC
525 7th Ave Rm 1808 (10018-5274)
PHONE.................................212 764-4810
Scott Pianin, *President*
▲ **EMP:** 5
SALES (est): 905.3K **Privately Held**
SIC: 2339 Women's & misses' outerwear

(G-12202)
SSA TRADING LTD
226 W 37th St Fl 6 (10018-9020)
PHONE.................................646 465-9500
Gary Cohen, *President*
Robert Klein, *CFO*
Bernard Stern, *CFO*
Marc Klein, *Treasurer*
EMP: 12
SQ FT: 5,000
SALES (est): 1.4MM **Privately Held**
SIC: 2339 Sportswear, women's

(G-12203)
SSG FASHIONS LTD
27 E 37th St Frnt 1 (10016-3004)
PHONE.................................212 221-0933
William Seng, *President*
Tim Burman, *Controller*
▲ **EMP:** 6
SQ FT: 3,000
SALES (est): 1MM **Privately Held**
WEB: www.ssgfashions.com
SIC: 2339 2335 Sportswear, women's; women's, juniors' & misses' dresses

(G-12204)
ST TROPEZ INC
530 Broadway Fl 10 (10012-3920)
PHONE.................................800 366-6383
Isaac Naim, *President*
EMP: 7
SQ FT: 4,300
SALES (est): 300K
SALES (corp-wide): 1.1B **Privately Held**
SIC: 2844 Suntan lotions & oils

PA: Pz Cussons Plc
3500 Aviator Way Manchester Business Park
Manchester M22 5
161 435-1000

(G-12205)
STANDARD ANALYTICS IO INC
7 World Trade Ctr 46th (10007-2140)
PHONE.................................917 882-5422
Tiffany Bogich, *COO*
EMP: 6
SALES (est): 219.1K **Privately Held**
SIC: 2721 2741 7371 7374 Periodicals; ; computer software development; data processing & preparation; distribution channels consultant

(G-12206)
STANDARD SCREEN SUPPLY CORP (PA)
Also Called: Active Process Supply
121 Varick St Rm 200 (10013-1408)
PHONE.................................212 627-2727
Fax: 212 627-2710
Arthur Gononsky, *President*
Sue Gonosky, *Vice Pres*
Susan Gononsky, *Treasurer*
▼ **EMP:** 11 **EST:** 1951
SALES (est): 1.2MM **Privately Held**
WEB: www.standardscreen.com
SIC: 2893 Screen process ink

(G-12207)
STANMARK JEWELRY INC
64 W 48th St Ste 1303 (10036-1708)
PHONE.................................212 730-2557
Stanley Krukowski, *President*
EMP: 6
SQ FT: 10,000
SALES (est): 510K **Privately Held**
WEB: www.stanmark.com
SIC: 3911 5944 Jewelry, precious metal; jewelry stores

(G-12208)
STAR CHILDRENS DRESS CO INC (PA)
Also Called: Rare Editions
1250 Broadway Fl 18 (10001-3749)
PHONE.................................212 279-1524
Fax: 212 594-7532
Edward Rosen, *Ch of Bd*
Andy Brown, *General Mgr*
Dominique Carter, *Production*
Aletha Mercer, *Sales Executive*
Julie Shellman, *Business Anlyst*
▲ **EMP:** 60 **EST:** 1953
SQ FT: 12,000
SALES (est): 53MM **Privately Held**
WEB: www.rareeditions.com
SIC: 2361 Dresses: girls', children's & infants'

(G-12209)
STAR WIRE MESH FABRICATORS
518 E 119th St (10035-4432)
P.O. Box 678 (10035-0678)
PHONE.................................212 831-4133
Fax: 212 876-0634
Alex Pavur, *President*
Anistasia Pavur, *Treasurer*
EMP: 5
SQ FT: 2,500
SALES (est): 510K **Privately Held**
WEB: www.starwiremesh.com
SIC: 3496 Screening, woven wire: made from purchased wire; mesh, made from purchased wire

(G-12210)
STARK SCALAMANDRE FABRIC LLC
942 3rd Ave (10022-2701)
PHONE.................................212 376-2900
Doris Farno, *Branch Mgr*
EMP: 70
SALES (corp-wide): 135.2MM **Privately Held**
SIC: 2221 Upholstery fabrics, manmade fiber & silk

HQ: Stark Scalamandre Fabric Llc
979 3rd Ave Ste 1002
New York NY 10022
212 355-7186

(G-12211)
STARLITE MEDIA LLC (PA)
118 E 28th St Rm 601 (10016-8447)
PHONE.................................212 909-7700
Fax: 212 838-4533
Harold Lueken, *CEO*
Tim Daly,
Karen Jolicoeur,
Bruce Seidel,
EMP: 4
SQ FT: 1,000
SALES (est): 3.7MM **Privately Held**
WEB: www.starlitemedia.com
SIC: 3993 Signs & advertising specialties

(G-12212)
STEEL PARTNERS HOLDINGS LP (PA)
590 Madison Ave Rm 3202 (10022-8536)
PHONE.................................212 520-2300
Jack L Howard, *President*
Warren G Lichtenstein, *Chairman*
Douglas B Woodworth, *CFO*
Andrew Azzara, *Controller*
Michele A Giglietta, *Benefits Mgr*
EMP: 32
SALES (est): 1.1B **Publicly Held**
SIC: 3479 3497 1381 6141 Etching & engraving; copper foil; gold foil or leaf; nickel foil; silver foil or leaf; drilling oil & gas wells; consumer finance companies

(G-12213)
STEEZYS LLC
80 8th Ave 202 (10011-5126)
PHONE.................................646 276-5333
Robert Lebowitz, *Mng Member*
Edina Sultanik,
EMP: 7
SALES (est): 592.2K **Privately Held**
SIC: 3961 Costume jewelry, ex. precious metal & semiprecious stones

(G-12214)
STEFAN FURS INC
150 W 30th St Fl 15 (10001-4138)
PHONE.................................212 594-2788
Alex Amanatides, *President*
EMP: 5
SQ FT: 800
SALES (est): 382.1K **Privately Held**
SIC: 2371 Fur goods

(G-12215)
STEINWAY MUSICAL INSTRS INC (HQ)
1133 Ave Of The Americas (10036-6710)
PHONE.................................781 894-9770
Michael T Sweeney, *President*
Ron Losby, *President*
John Stoner Jr, *President*
Donna M Lucente, *Vice Pres*
Dennis M Hanson, *Treasurer*
◆ **EMP:** 37
SALES (est): 338MM
SALES (corp-wide): 41.1MM **Privately Held**
WEB: www.steinwaymusical.com
SIC: 3931 Musical instruments; pianos, all types: vertical, grand, spinet, player, etc.; string instruments & parts; woodwind instruments & parts
PA: Paulson & Co. Inc.
1251 Avenue Of The Americ
New York NY 10020
212 956-2221

(G-12216)
STEMLINE THERAPEUTICS INC
750 Lexington Ave Fl 11 (10022-9817)
PHONE.................................646 502-2311
Ivan Bergstein, *Ch of Bd*
Kenneth Hoberman, *COO*
David G Gionco,
EMP: 29
SALES: 1MM **Privately Held**
WEB: www.stemline.com
SIC: 2834 Pharmaceutical preparations

(G-12217)
STENSUL INC
150 W 25th St Fl 3 (10001-7404)
PHONE.................................212 380-8620
Noah Dinkin, *CEO*
Gabriel Sosa, *Vice Pres*
Jonathan Travin, *Vice Pres*
EMP: 33
SQ FT: 5,500
SALES (est): 567.6K **Privately Held**
SIC: 7372 Prepackaged software

(G-12218)
STEPHAN & COMPANY ACC LTD (PA)
10 E 38th St Fl 9 (10016-0616)
PHONE.................................212 481-3888
Fax: 212 481-4244
Stephan Rubin, *President*
Shellie Rubin, *VP Sales*
Lella Anceschi, *MIS Dir*
▲ **EMP:** 20
SQ FT: 2,400
SALES (est): 31.5K **Privately Held**
WEB: www.stephanco.com
SIC: 3961 Costume jewelry, ex. precious metal & semiprecious stones

(G-12219)
STEPHEN GOULD CORPORATION
450 7th Ave Fl 32 (10123-3299)
PHONE.................................212 497-8180
Rachel Golden, *Office Mgr*
Mike Garcia, *Branch Mgr*
EMP: 15
SALES (corp-wide): 665.1MM **Privately Held**
WEB: www.stephengould.com
SIC: 3086 Packaging & shipping materials, foamed plastic
PA: Stephen Gould Corporation
35 S Jefferson Rd
Whippany NJ 07981
973 428-1500

(G-12220)
STEPHEN SINGER PATTERN CO INC
Also Called: Popular Pattern
340 W 39th St Fl 4 (10018-1345)
PHONE.................................212 947-2902
Fax: 212 643-0025
Stephen Singer, *President*
EMP: 12
SQ FT: 7,000
SALES (est): 1.9MM **Privately Held**
SIC: 2621 2741 Pattern tissue; miscellaneous publishing

(G-12221)
STERLING POSSESSIONS LTD
251 W 39th St (10018-3105)
PHONE.................................212 594-0418
Fax: 212 594-2529
William Callaghan, *Ch of Bd*
Richard Castagna, *President*
▲ **EMP:** 8
SQ FT: 3,000
SALES (est): 740K **Privately Held**
WEB: www.sterlingposs.com
SIC: 3911 5094 2329 2339 Jewelry apparel; jewelry; men's & boys' sportswear & athletic clothing; sportswear, women's; sportswear, men's & boys'; sportswear, women's & children's

(G-12222)
STERLING SOUND INC
88 10th Ave Frnt 6 (10011-4745)
PHONE.................................212 604-9433
Fax: 212 604-9964
Murat Aktar, *President*
Justin Guip, *Facilities Mgr*
EMP: 30
SALES (est): 4.7MM **Privately Held**
SIC: 3652 Master records or tapes, preparation of

(G-12223)
STEVEN GALAPO DIAMONDS LLC
15 W 47th St Ste 1204 (10036-3305)
PHONE.................................212 221-3000
EMP: 6 **EST:** 2011

GEOGRAPHIC SECTION

New York - New York County (G-12250)

SALES (est): 388.4K **Privately Held**
SIC: 3915 5094 Diamond cutting & polishing; diamonds (gems)

(G-12224)
STEVEN MADDEN LTD
41 W 34th St (10001-3081)
PHONE....................212 736-3283
Kelly Paytner, *Branch Mgr*
EMP: 25
SALES (corp-wide): 1.4B **Publicly Held**
SIC: 3143 Men's footwear, except athletic
PA: Steven Madden, Ltd.
 5216 Barnett Ave
 Long Island City NY 11104
 718 446-1800

(G-12225)
STEVEN MADDEN LTD
Also Called: Madden Zone
19 W 34th St Fl 4 (10001-3006)
PHONE....................212 695-5545
Jeff Goldstein, *Branch Mgr*
EMP: 75
SALES (corp-wide): 1.4B **Publicly Held**
SIC: 3144 Women's footwear, except athletic; boots, canvas or leather: women's
PA: Steven Madden, Ltd.
 5216 Barnett Ave
 Long Island City NY 11104
 718 446-1800

(G-12226)
STEVENS BANDES GRAPHICS CORP
333 Hudson St Fl 3 (10013-1006)
PHONE....................212 675-1128
Fax: 212 924-6362
Stephen Kilduff, *President*
Kevin Roach, *Admin Sec*
EMP: 10
SQ FT: 2,500
SALES: 1.5MM **Privately Held**
WEB: www.stevensbandes.com
SIC: 2752 Commercial printing, lithographic

(G-12227)
STEVES ORIGINAL FURS INC
345 7th Ave Fl 9 (10001-5049)
PHONE....................212 967-8007
Steve Panaretos, *President*
Aspasia Panaretos, *Admin Sec*
EMP: 20
SALES (est): 2MM **Privately Held**
WEB: www.stevesoriginalfurs.com
SIC: 2371 Fur finishers & liners for the fur goods trade

(G-12228)
STICKY SOCKS LLC
200 W 60th St Apt 7g (10023-8504)
PHONE....................212 541-5927
Eva Di Nardo, *President*
EMP: 5
SALES (est): 309K **Privately Held**
SIC: 2252 Socks

(G-12229)
STITCH & COUTURE INC (PA)
Also Called: Lela Rose
224 W 30th St Fl 14 (10001-1493)
PHONE....................212 947-9204
Lela Rose, *Ch of Bd*
Chanelle Smith, *Production*
Nandini Amrrit, *Finance*
Caroline Faulkner, *Accounts Exec*
Caitlin Costello, *Marketing Staff*
EMP: 25
SQ FT: 3,000
SALES: 11MM **Privately Held**
WEB: www.lelarose.com
SIC: 2331 2335 Blouses, women's & juniors': made from purchased material; shirts, women's & juniors': made from purchased materials; bridal & formal gowns

(G-12230)
STONE HOUSE ASSOCIATES INC
37 W 47th St Ste 910 (10036-2809)
PHONE....................212 221-7447
Elaine Wong, *President*
EMP: 5

SALES: 450K **Privately Held**
WEB: www.theidea-network.com
SIC: 3911 Jewelry, precious metal

(G-12231)
STONESONG PRESS LLC
270 W 39th St Rm 201 (10018-0137)
PHONE....................212 929-4600
Emmanuelle Morgen, *Principal*
Katherine Latshaw, *Editor*
Jessica Rosen, *Editor*
Judy Linden, *Exec VP*
Alison Fargis, *Mng Member*
EMP: 6 **EST:** 1978
SALES (est): 450K **Privately Held**
SIC: 2731 Book publishing

(G-12232)
STONY APPAREL CORP
Also Called: Eye Shadow
1407 Broadway Rm 3300 (10018-2395)
PHONE....................212 391-0022
Fax: 212 819-9456
Shaun Jackson, *Manager*
Charity Fox, *Manager*
EMP: 5 **Privately Held**
SIC: 2339 Women's & misses' athletic clothing & sportswear
PA: Stony Apparel Corp.
 1500 S Evergreen Ave
 Los Angeles CA 90023

(G-12233)
STRAIGHT ARROW PUBLISHING CO
Also Called: Mens Journal
1290 Ave Of The Amer Fl 2 (10104-0298)
PHONE....................212 484-1616
Fax: 212 767-8209
John Gruber, *CFO*
Hugh T Scogin Jr, *General Counsel*
John F Walsh Jr, *Officer*
Frank Janoscak, *Administration*
EMP: 200
SALES: 11.8MM
SALES (corp-wide): 89.1MM **Privately Held**
WEB: www.mensjournal.com
SIC: 2741 Miscellaneous publishing
PA: Wenner Media Llc
 1290 Ave Of The Amer Fl 2
 New York NY 10104
 212 484-1616

(G-12234)
STRATCONGLOBAL INC
685 3rd Ave Fl 4 (10017-8408)
PHONE....................212 989-2355
Joanna Peters, *Principal*
Tatum Pursell, *Opers Staff*
EMP: 5 **EST:** 2008
SALES (est): 215.4K **Privately Held**
SIC: 2711 Newspapers

(G-12235)
STREET KING LLC
Also Called: Sk Energy Shots
575 Madison Ave Fl 24 (10022-8538)
PHONE....................212 400-2200
Sabrina Peterson, *President*
Rosie Jonker, *Manager*
EMP: 8
SALES: 1MM **Privately Held**
SIC: 2086 Bottled & canned soft drinks

(G-12236)
STREET SMART DESIGNS INC
29 W 35th St Fl 6 (10001-2299)
PHONE....................646 865-0056
Fax: 646 865-0052
Richard H Bienen, *Ch of Bd*
Dera Jairam, *Manager*
▲ **EMP:** 6
SALES (est): 888.8K **Privately Held**
WEB: www.streetsmartdesigns.com
SIC: 3111 5137 Handbag leather; handbags

(G-12237)
STRIATA INC
48 Wall St Ste 1100 (10005-2903)
PHONE....................212 918-4677
Michael Wright, *President*
Garin Toren, *COO*
Natasha Felski, *Project Mgr*
Renee Hart, *Project Mgr*

Katrina Scott, *QA Dir*
EMP: 85
SQ FT: 6,000
SALES (est): 6.3MM **Privately Held**
WEB: www.striata.com
SIC: 7372 Application computer software

(G-12238)
STRIDER GLOBAL LLC
261 W 28th St Apt 6a (10001-5936)
PHONE....................212 726-1302
EMP: 5
SALES: 100K **Privately Held**
SIC: 3648 Mfg Lighting Equipment

(G-12239)
STRUCTURED RETAIL PRODUCTS
Also Called: SRP
225 Park Ave S Fl 8 (10003-1604)
PHONE....................212 224-3692
Sunny Singh, *Principal*
Joe Burris, *Principal*
EMP: 5
SQ FT: 60,000
SALES (est): 259.7K
SALES (corp-wide): 522.6MM **Privately Held**
SIC: 7372 Prepackaged software; business oriented computer software
HQ: Euromoney Global Limited
 6-8 Bouverie Street
 London EC4Y
 207 779-8888

(G-12240)
STRUCTUREDWEB INC
20 W 20th St Ste 402 (10011-9258)
PHONE....................201 325-3110
Daniel Nissan, *President*
Yotam Hadass, *Vice Pres*
Adam Krapish, *Vice Pres*
Michael Coscetta, *VP Sales*
Sam Oliff, *Sales Associate*
EMP: 40
SQ FT: 7,500
SALES (est): 5.1MM **Privately Held**
WEB: www.structuredweb.com
SIC: 7372 7371 Business oriented computer software; computer software development; software programming applications

(G-12241)
STUDIO ASSOCIATES OF NEW YORK
242 W 30th St Rm 604 (10001-4913)
P.O. Box 4306 (10163-4306)
PHONE....................212 268-1163
Fax: 212 268-2646
Edward Jenner, *President*
Joseph Perilla, *Corp Secy*
EMP: 6
SALES (est): 450K **Privately Held**
WEB: www.sanylaser.com
SIC: 3299 Architectural sculptures: gypsum, clay, papier mache, etc.

(G-12242)
STUDIO KRP LLC
210 11th Ave Rm 500 (10001-1210)
PHONE....................310 589-5777
Carol Rosenstein, *CEO*
EMP: 13
SQ FT: 1,500
SALES: 3MM **Privately Held**
SIC: 2335 Women's, juniors' & misses' dresses

(G-12243)
STUDIO ONE LEATHER DESIGN INC
270 W 39th St Rm 505 (10018-0334)
PHONE....................212 760-1701
Fax: 212 760-1702
Arthur Coines, *President*
EMP: 12
SQ FT: 2,500
SALES (est): 888.7K **Privately Held**
SIC: 2386 3543 Garments, leather; industrial patterns

(G-12244)
STUFF MAGAZINE
1040 Ave Of The Amrcas (10018-3703)
PHONE....................212 302-2626
Steven Collvin, *President*
EMP: 5
SALES (est): 500K **Privately Held**
SIC: 2721 Magazines: publishing & printing

(G-12245)
STYLE PARTNERS INC
Also Called: Jana Kos Collection, The
318 W 39th St Fl 7 (10018-1465)
PHONE....................212 904-1499
Jana Kos, *President*
Victor Ruiz, *Controller*
▲ **EMP:** 15
SALES (est): 965K **Privately Held**
WEB: www.janakos.com
SIC: 2335 2331 2337 Women's, juniors' & misses' dresses; women's & misses' blouses & shirts; women's & misses' suits & coats

(G-12246)
STYLECLICK INC (HQ)
810 7th Ave Fl 18 (10019-5879)
PHONE....................212 329-0300
Lisa Brown, *CEO*
Robert Halper, *President*
Bruce Goldstein, *Exec VP*
Barry W Hall, *CFO*
EMP: 52
SALES (est): 3.6MM
SALES (corp-wide): 3.1B **Publicly Held**
WEB: www.styleclick.com
SIC: 7372 Business oriented computer software
PA: Iac/Interactivecorp
 555 W 18th St
 New York NY 10011
 212 314-7300

(G-12247)
STYLISTIC PRESS INC
99 Battery Pl Apt 11p (10280-1324)
PHONE....................212 675-0797
Jeff Lederfarb, *President*
EMP: 15
SQ FT: 2,500
SALES (est): 1.5MM **Privately Held**
SIC: 2752 Commercial printing, offset

(G-12248)
SUCCESS APPAREL LLC
19 W 34th St Fl 7 (10001-0055)
PHONE....................212 502-1890
Gila Goodman, *CEO*
Ewan Mendis, *Admin Sec*
EMP: 5 **EST:** 2015
SALES (est): 215.5K **Privately Held**
SIC: 2211 Apparel & outerwear fabrics, cotton

(G-12249)
SUGAR FOODS CORPORATION (PA)
950 3rd Ave Fl 21 (10022-2786)
PHONE....................212 753-6900
Fax: 212 753-6988
Donald G Tober, *Ch of Bd*
Marty Wilson, *President*
Stephen Odell, *President*
Myron Stein, *Vice Pres*
Brian Thomson, *Opers Mgr*
▼ **EMP:** 34
SQ FT: 10,000
SALES (est): 295.1MM **Privately Held**
WEB: www.sugarfoods.com
SIC: 2869 2023 2099 2068 Sweeteners, synthetic; cream substitutes; sugar; seasonings & spices; packaged combination products: pasta, rice & potato; bread crumbs, not made in bakeries; salted & roasted nuts & seeds; packaging & labeling services

(G-12250)
SULLIVAN ST BKY - HLLS KIT INC
533 W 47th St (10036-7903)
PHONE....................212 265-5580
James Lahey, *Principal*
Daniel Solbany, *Manager*
▲ **EMP:** 29

New York - New York County (G-12251) — GEOGRAPHIC SECTION

SALES (est): 4.4MM **Privately Held**
SIC: 2051 Bread, cake & related products

(G-12251)
SULPHUR CREATIONS INC
71 W 47th St Ste 402 (10036-2819)
PHONE 212 719-2223
Elliott Delshad, *President*
EMP: 5
SQ FT: 1,240
SALES (est): 374.5K **Privately Held**
SIC: 3911 Jewelry, precious metal

(G-12252)
SUMA INDUSTRIES INC
345 E 52nd St Apt 9d (10022-6344)
PHONE 646 436-5202
Arthur Forst, *President*
Robert Katz, *Exec VP*
Christopher Patterson, *Vice Pres*
Myra Hyman, *Executive*
EMP: 5
SALES (est): 420K **Privately Held**
WEB: www.sumaindustries.com
SIC: 3993 Signs, not made in custom sign painting shops

(G-12253)
SUMER GOLD LTD
33 W 46th St Fl 4 (10036-4103)
PHONE 212 354-8677
Fax: 212 354-8697
Juan Merchan, *President*
Suzanna Merchan, *Treasurer*
EMP: 6
SQ FT: 700
SALES (est): 634.5K **Privately Held**
SIC: 3911 Jewelry, precious metal

(G-12254)
SUMITOMO ELC USA HOLDINGS INC (HQ)
600 5th Ave Fl 18 (10020-2320)
PHONE 212 490-6610
Yoshitomo Kasui, *President*
Hideo Takahashi, *President*
David Saleeby, *Editor*
Jim Pierce, *Plant Mgr*
Kim Dawkins, *Materials Mgr*
▲ **EMP:** 8
SALES: 46MM
SALES (corp-wide): 24.7B **Privately Held**
WEB: www.engsin.com
SIC: 3674 Semiconductors & related devices
PA: Sumitomo Electric Industries, Ltd.
4-5-33, Kitahama, Chuo-Ku
Osaka OSK 541-0
662 204-141

(G-12255)
SUMMIT FINCL DISCLOSURE LLC
216 E 45th St Fl 15 (10017-3304)
PHONE 212 913-0510
James W Palmiter, *Owner*
Kenneth M McClure, *Owner*
Scott Damico, *COO*
EMP: 40
SQ FT: 15,000
SALES (est): 7.8MM **Privately Held**
SIC: 2621 Printing paper

(G-12256)
SUMMIT PROFESSIONAL NETWORKS
469 Fashion Ave Fl 10 (10018-7640)
PHONE 212 557-7480
EMP: 60
SALES (corp-wide): 235.3MM **Privately Held**
SIC: 2721 Magazines: publishing & printing
HQ: Summit Professional Networks
4157 Olympic Blvd Ste 225
Erlanger KY 41018
859 692-2100

(G-12257)
SUNA BROS INC
10 W 46th St Fl 5 (10036-4515)
PHONE 212 869-5670
Aron Suna, *President*
Wendy Schwartz, *Cust Mgr*
Jonathan Suna, *Admin Sec*
EMP: 30 **EST:** 1934

SQ FT: 5,000
SALES (est): 4.2MM **Privately Held**
WEB: www.sunabros.com
SIC: 3911 5944 Jewelry, precious metal; jewelry stores

(G-12258)
SUNHAM HOME FASHIONS LLC (PA)
136 Madison Ave Fl 16 (10016-6786)
PHONE 212 695-1218
Howard Yung, *CEO*
Jane Bognacki, *President*
Arthur Coubanou, *COO*
Gregory Chletsos, *Vice Pres*
Simpi Singh, *Opers Mgr*
◆ **EMP:** 58
SQ FT: 15,000
SALES (est): 200MM **Privately Held**
WEB: www.sunham.com
SIC: 2392 Blankets, comforters & beddings

(G-12259)
SUNNY SCUBA INC (PA)
Also Called: Sunny Sports
454 9th Ave (10018-5617)
PHONE 212 333-4915
Leo Kline, *Manager*
EMP: 2
SALES (est): 1.1MM **Privately Held**
SIC: 3949 Skin diving equipment, scuba type; camping equipment & supplies

(G-12260)
SUNSHINE DIAMOND CUTTER INC
38 W 48th St Ste 905 (10036-1805)
PHONE 212 221-1028
Manglaben Dhanani, *President*
EMP: 7
SALES (est): 484K **Privately Held**
SIC: 3915 Lapidary work & diamond cutting & polishing

(G-12261)
SUNWIN GLOBAL INDUSTRY INC
295 5th Ave Ste 515 (10016-7103)
PHONE 646 370-6196
Sophie Cheng, *President*
Lily Zhang, *General Mgr*
Susan Rybnick, *Director*
EMP: 5
SQ FT: 850
SALES: 423.6K
SALES (corp-wide): 125.1MM **Privately Held**
SIC: 2258 5137 Lace & warp knit fabric mills; baby goods; apparel belts, women's & children's
PA: Shanghai Sunwin Investment Holding Group Co.,Ltd.
No.17,Lane 688, Hengnan Road, Minhang District
Shanghai 20111
216 036-0260

(G-12262)
SUNYNAMS FASHIONS LTD
Also Called: Sunny Names
270 W 38th St Fl 2 (10018-1563)
PHONE 212 268-5200
Fax: 212 268-4842
Sunny Neman, *President*
▲ **EMP:** 7
SQ FT: 5,000
SALES (est): 1.3MM **Privately Held**
SIC: 2339 Women's & misses' outerwear

(G-12263)
SUPER-TRIM INC
30 W 24th St Fl 4 (10010-3558)
PHONE 212 255-2370
Fax: 212 243-8414
Daniel Noy, *President*
Rafael Noy, *Vice Pres*
EMP: 20
SQ FT: 5,000
SALES (est): 1.1MM **Privately Held**
WEB: www.supertrim.com
SIC: 2258 5131 Lace & lace products; lace fabrics

(G-12264)
SUPERCHAT LLC
310 E 70th St Apt 6lm (10021-8609)
PHONE 212 352-8581
Kevin Koplin, *Principal*
EMP: 6
SQ FT: 500
SALES (est): 136.3K **Privately Held**
SIC: 7372 Application computer software

(G-12265)
SUPERMEDIA LLC
Also Called: Verizon
2 Penn Plz Fl 22 (10121-2299)
PHONE 212 513-9700
Jeanne Ryans, *Manager*
EMP: 100
SALES (corp-wide): 1.8B **Privately Held**
WEB: www.verizon.superpages.com
SIC: 2741 8741 Directories: publishing only, not printed on site; administrative management
HQ: Supermedia Llc
2200 W Airfield Dr
Dfw Airport TX 75261
972 453-7000

(G-12266)
SURE FIT INC
58 W 40th St Rm 2a (10018-2658)
PHONE 212 395-9340
Fax: 212 869-6644
Dean Smith, *Opers Staff*
EMP: 25 **Privately Held**
SIC: 2392 Household furnishings
HQ: Sure Fit Home Products, Llc
8000 Quarry Rd Ste C
Alburtis PA 18011
610 264-7300

(G-12267)
SUREPURE INC
405 Lexington Ave Fl 25 (10174-0002)
PHONE 917 368-8480
Guy Kebble, *President*
Stephen Robinson, *CFO*
EMP: 6
SALES: 1.2MM **Privately Held**
SIC: 3559 Chemical machinery & equipment; refinery, chemical processing & similar machinery

(G-12268)
SURFACE MAGAZINE
Also Called: Surface Publishing
134 W 26th St Frnt 1 (10001-6803)
PHONE 646 805-0200
Richard Klein, *Owner*
Lance Crapo, *Principal*
Spencer Bailey, *Editor*
Miles Bingham, *Controller*
Adriana Gelves, *Adv Dir*
EMP: 25
SALES (est): 1.9MM **Privately Held**
SIC: 2721 Periodicals

(G-12269)
SUSSEX PUBLISHERS LLC (PA)
Also Called: Psychology Today
115 E 23rd St Fl 9 (10010-4559)
PHONE 212 260-7210
Fax: 212 260-7445
John P Colman, *President*
Lybi MA, *Editor*
Jennifer Redmond, *Med Doctor*
EMP: 20
SQ FT: 7,400 **Privately Held**
WEB: www.blues-buster.com
SIC: 2721 Magazines: publishing only, not printed on site

(G-12270)
SWANK INC
90 Park Ave Rm 1302 (10016-1395)
PHONE 212 867-2600
Fax: 212 370-1039
John A Tulin, *Ch of Bd*
Eric P Luft, *President*
Paul Duckett, *Senior VP*
James E Tulin, *Senior VP*
Christophe Wolf, *Senior VP*
▲ **EMP:** 256 **EST:** 1936
SQ FT: 242,000

SALES (est): 352.9K
SALES (corp-wide): 126.8MM **Privately Held**
WEB: www.swankaccessories.com
SIC: 2389 5611 Men's miscellaneous accessories; clothing accessories: men's & boys'
PA: Randa Accessories Leather Goods Llc
5600 N River Rd Ste 500
Rosemont IL 60018
847 292-8300

(G-12271)
SWAPS MONITOR PUBLICATIONS INC
29 Broadway Rm 1315 (10006-3252)
PHONE 212 742-8550
Paul Spraos, *President*
EMP: 10
SALES (est): 1.1MM **Privately Held**
WEB: www.financialcalendar.com
SIC: 2721 6282 Periodicals; investment advice

(G-12272)
SWAROVSKI NORTH AMERICA LTD
1 Penn Plz Frnt 4 (10119-0202)
PHONE 212 695-1502
EMP: 7
SALES (corp-wide): 3.7B **Privately Held**
SIC: 3961 Costume jewelry
HQ: Swarovski North America Limited
1 Kenney Dr
Cranston RI 02920
401 463-6400

(G-12273)
SWATFAME INC
530 Fashion Ave Rm 1204 (10018-4862)
PHONE 212 944-8022
Marcy Olin, *Branch Mgr*
EMP: 6
SALES (corp-wide): 136.8MM **Privately Held**
WEB: www.swatfame.com
SIC: 2339 2369 Women's & misses' athletic clothing & sportswear; girls' & children's outerwear
PA: Swat.Fame, Inc.
16425 Gale Ave
City Of Industry CA 91745
626 961-7928

(G-12274)
SWED MASTERS WORKSHOP LLC
214 E 82nd St Frnt 1 (10028-2723)
PHONE 212 644-8822
Eyal Fogelnest, *Store Mgr*
Lee Fogelnest, *Manager*
Yossi Swed,
EMP: 11
SALES (est): 1.3MM **Privately Held**
WEB: www.swedllc.com
SIC: 3914 Silversmithing

(G-12275)
SWEET APPAREL INC
525 7th Ave Rm 513 (10018-0642)
PHONE 212 221-3321
Yoself Abrohmara, *Principal*
EMP: 9
SALES (est): 329.8K **Privately Held**
SIC: 2331 Women's & misses' blouses & shirts

(G-12276)
SWEET MOUTH INC
244 5th Ave Ste L243 (10001-7604)
PHONE 800 433-7758
Lucas Dawson, *President*
EMP: 20
SQ FT: 2,000
SALES (est): 720.6K **Privately Held**
SIC: 2731 Book publishing

(G-12277)
SWEETRIOT INC
131 Varick St Ste 936 (10013-1443)
P.O. Box 140441, Brooklyn (11214-0441)
PHONE 212 431-7468
Sarah Endline, *President*
Andy Neiterman, *Controller*
▲ **EMP:** 5

▲ = Import ▼ = Export ◆ = Import/Export

GEOGRAPHIC SECTION

New York - New York County (G-12305)

SALES (est): 726K Privately Held
SIC: 2066 Chocolate & cocoa products

(G-12278)
SYMANTEC CORPORATION
1 Penn Plz Ste 5420 (10119-5420)
PHONE..................646 487-6000
Chris Klein, Natl Sales Mgr
Robert Zampolin, Sales Executive
Ken Lowe, Manager
EMP: 65
SALES (corp-wide): 4B Publicly Held
WEB: www.symantec.com
SIC: 7372 Prepackaged software
PA: Symantec Corporation
   350 Ellis St
   Mountain View CA 94043
   650 527-8000

(G-12279)
SYMPHONY TALENT LLC (PA)
19 W 34th St Fl 10 (10001-3006)
PHONE..................212 999-9000
Roopesh Nair, CEO
Sal Apuzzio, Senior VP
Samantha Loveland, Senior VP
Gayleen Robinson, Senior VP
Ben Camacho, Vice Pres
EMP: 75 EST: 2007
SALES: 50MM Privately Held
SIC: 7372 7361 Business oriented computer software; employment agencies

(G-12280)
SYMRISE INC
505 Park Ave Fl 15 (10022-9333)
PHONE..................646 459-5000
Fax: 646 459-5020
Lawrence Garro, Mfg Dir
Blagovest Kotsev, Production
Anh Ngo, Engineer
Rekha Rana, Accountant
Magali Leogrande, Sales Staff
EMP: 25
SALES (corp-wide): 3B Privately Held
WEB: www.symriseinc.com
SIC: 2869 Perfume materials, synthetic; flavors or flavoring materials, synthetic
HQ: Symrise Inc.
   300 North St
   Teterboro NJ 07608
   201 462-5559

(G-12281)
SYNCED INC
120 Walker St Ste 4 (10013-4117)
PHONE..................917 565-5591
Andrew Ferenci, CEO
Scott Paladini, COO
Michael Paladini, Risk Mgmt Dir
EMP: 5
SALES: 5MM Privately Held
SIC: 7372 Application computer software

(G-12282)
SYNCO TECHNOLOGIES INC
54 W 21st St Rm 602 (10010-7347)
P.O. Box 976 (10113-0976)
PHONE..................212 255-2031
Fax: 212 255-1464
John Rau, President
Terry Cook, Vice Pres
Steve Schimmele, Controller
Carly Cadet, Manager
EMP: 6
SQ FT: 1,250
SALES: 1MM Privately Held
WEB: www.syncotec.com
SIC: 7372 Prepackaged software

(G-12283)
SYNERGY PHARMACEUTICALS INC (HQ)
420 Lexington Ave Rm 2500 (10170-0020)
PHONE..................212 227-8611
EMP: 6
SQ FT: 1,750
SALES (est): 992.3K Publicly Held
SIC: 2836 8731 Mfg Biological Products Commercial Physical Research

(G-12284)
SYNERGY PHARMACEUTICALS INC (PA)
420 Lexington Ave Rm 2012 (10170-2099)
PHONE..................212 297-0020

Fax: 212 297-0019
Gary S Jacob, Ch of Bd
Marino Garcia, Exec VP
Scott Brunetto, Vice Pres
Chhaya Shah, Vice Pres
Ken Holick, Opers Staff
EMP: 44
SQ FT: 8,500
SALES (est): 26.3MM Publicly Held
SIC: 2834 Pharmaceutical preparations

(G-12285)
SYNTEL INC
1 Exchange Plz Ste 2001 (10006-3736)
PHONE..................212 785-9810
Fax: 212 785-9811
Bhares Bissa, President
EMP: 14
SALES (corp-wide): 966.5MM Publicly Held
SIC: 7372 8748 Prepackaged software; systems analysis & engineering consulting services
PA: Syntel, Inc.
   525 E Big Beaver Rd # 300
   Troy MI 48083
   248 619-2800

(G-12286)
T & M PLATING INC
357 W 36th St Fl 7 (10018-6455)
PHONE..................212 967-1110
Joseph AMI, President
Steve Amiriam, Director
EMP: 30
SQ FT: 24,000
SALES (est): 3.2MM Privately Held
SIC: 3471 Electroplating of metals or formed products; polishing, metals or formed products

(G-12287)
T & R KNITTING MILLS INC
Also Called: Direct Alliance
214 W 39th St (10018-4404)
PHONE..................212 840-8665
Rocco Marini, Branch Mgr
EMP: 16
SALES (corp-wide): 20MM Privately Held
SIC: 2253 Knit outerwear mills
PA: T & R Knitting Mills Inc.
   8000 Cooper Ave Ste 6
   Glendale NY 11385
   718 497-4017

(G-12288)
T L DIAMOND & COMPANY INC (PA)
Also Called: Eagle Zinc Co Div
116 E 68th St Apt 5a (10065-5995)
PHONE..................212 249-6660
Fax: 212 582-3412
Theodore L Diamond, President
C W Diamond, Corp Secy
EMP: 9 EST: 1950
SQ FT: 5,000
SALES (est): 6.7MM Privately Held
SIC: 3356 Lead & zinc

(G-12289)
T M W DIAMONDS MFG CO (PA)
15 W 47th St Ste 302 (10036-3442)
PHONE..................212 869-8444
Leibis Morgenstern, President
Jonah Morgenstern, Vice Pres
EMP: 9 EST: 1973
SALES: 1.5MM Privately Held
SIC: 3915 5094 Diamond cutting & polishing; diamonds (gems)

(G-12290)
T O DEY SERVICE CORP
Also Called: To Dey
151 W 46th St Fl 3 (10036-8512)
PHONE..................212 683-6300
Fax: 212 683-3445
Rose Bifulco, President
Thomas Bifulco, Vice Pres
Gino Fulco, Vice Pres
Ciro Bifulco, Treasurer
EMP: 16
SQ FT: 6,700
SALES (est): 1.7MM Privately Held
SIC: 3144 3143 Orthopedic shoes, women's; men's footwear, except athletic

(G-12291)
T O GRONLUND COMPANY INC
200 Lexington Ave Rm 1515 (10016-6112)
PHONE..................212 679-3535
Fax: 212 725-3847
Robert L Gronlund, President
Brooks Gronlund, Corp Secy
EMP: 18
SQ FT: 3,600
SALES (est): 2.1MM Privately Held
SIC: 2599 Cabinets, factory

(G-12292)
T V TRADE MEDIA INC
Also Called: TV Executive
216 E 75th St Apt 1w (10021-2921)
PHONE..................212 288-3933
Fax: 212 734-9033
Dom Serafini, President
Sara Alessi, Editor
EMP: 12
SQ FT: 2,000
SALES (est): 890K Privately Held
SIC: 2721 Magazines: publishing & printing

(G-12293)
TABRISSE COLLECTIONS INC
Also Called: Oberon
1412 Broadway (10018-9228)
PHONE..................212 921-1014
Fax: 212 869-8608
Mark Naim, President
Ebi Shaer, Vice Pres
Sam Naim, Treasurer
Jeannine Simpson, Sales Staff
EMP: 10
SQ FT: 5,500
SALES (est): 790K Privately Held
SIC: 2335 Women's, juniors' & misses' dresses

(G-12294)
TACTICA INTERNATIONAL INC (PA)
11 W 42nd St (10036-8002)
PHONE..................212 575-0500
Fax: 212 354-5323
Prem Ramchandani, President
Kurt Streams, CFO
AVI Sivan, Director
Paul Greenfield, Admin Sec
▲ EMP: 15
SQ FT: 11,500
SALES (est): 1.6MM Privately Held
SIC: 3999 3634 Hair & hair-based products; electric housewares & fans

(G-12295)
TAHARI ASL LLC
Also Called: Tahari Arthur S Levine
1114 Ave Of The Americas (10036-7703)
PHONE..................212 763-2800
Lester Schreiber, Manager
EMP: 299
SALES (corp-wide): 76.5MM Privately Held
SIC: 2331 2335 2339 Blouses, women's & juniors': made from purchased material; women's, juniors' & misses' dresses; slacks: women's, misses' & juniors'
PA: Tahari A.S.L. Llc
   16 Bleeker St
   Millburn NJ 07041
   888 734-7459

(G-12296)
TAIKOH USA INC
369 Lexington Ave Fl 2 (10017-6516)
PHONE..................646 556-6652
Masaki Nomura, President
Gen Sato, Vice Pres
▲ EMP: 11
SALES (est): 1.4MM
SALES (corp-wide): 449.6K Privately Held
SIC: 2211 Canvas
HQ: Futamura Chemical Co.,Ltd.
   2-29-16, Meieki, Nakamura-Ku
   Nagoya AIC 450-0
   525 651-212

(G-12297)
TAILORED SPORTSMAN LLC
Also Called: Ogulnick Uniforms
230 W 38th St Fl 6 (10018-9058)
PHONE..................646 366-8733

Fax: 646 366-0590
Peter Loferfo, General Mgr
Van Isaacs, Info Tech Mgr
▲ EMP: 12
SALES (est): 1.8MM Privately Held
WEB: www.thetailoredsportsman.com
SIC: 2339 Neckwear & ties: women's, misses' & juniors'; riding habits: women's, misses' & juniors'

(G-12298)
TAMBER KNITS INC
Also Called: Gilber Braid
231 W 39th St Fl 8 (10018-1070)
PHONE..................212 730-1121
Fax: 212 730-8484
Richard Lansey, President
EMP: 20
SQ FT: 6,000
SALES (est): 1.6MM Privately Held
SIC: 2241 3965 Trimmings, textile; braids, textile; fasteners, buttons, needles & pins

(G-12299)
TAMBETTI INC
48 W 48th St Ste 501 (10036-1713)
PHONE..................212 751-9584
Fax: 212 751-9698
Dvora Horvitz, President
Joseph Segal, Corp Secy
EMP: 5
SQ FT: 1,612
SALES (est): 340K Privately Held
SIC: 3911 Jewelry, precious metal

(G-12300)
TAMSEN Z LLC
350 Park Ave Fl 4 (10022-6067)
PHONE..................212 292-6412
Tamsen Ziff, Mng Member
Victoria Wallace, Manager
EMP: 5
SALES (est): 348.3K Privately Held
SIC: 3911 Jewelry, precious metal

(G-12301)
TANAGRO JEWELRY CORP
36 W 44th St Ste 1101 (10036-8104)
PHONE..................212 753-2817
Fax: 212 753-1328
Pietro Dibenedetto, President
Antonio Dibenedetto, Vice Pres
EMP: 20
SQ FT: 2,200
SALES: 4.3MM Privately Held
WEB: www.tanagro.com
SIC: 3911 Jewelry, precious metal

(G-12302)
TANDUS CENTIVA INC
71 5th Ave Fl 2 (10003-3004)
PHONE..................212 206-7170
EMP: 171
SALES (corp-wide): 528.7K Privately Held
SIC: 2273 Carpets & rugs
HQ: Tandus Centiva Inc.
   311 Smith Industrial Blvd
   Dalton GA 30721
   706 259-9711

(G-12303)
TAO GROUP LLC
355 W 16th St (10011-5902)
PHONE..................646 625-4818
EMP: 6
SALES (est): 132.4K Privately Held
SIC: 2599 5963 Food wagons, restaurant; beverage services, direct sales

(G-12304)
TAP2PLAY LLC
110 W 40th St Rm 1902 (10018-3699)
PHONE..................914 960-6232
Ilya Nikolayev, CEO
EMP: 5
SALES (est): 117.2K Privately Held
SIC: 7372 Prepackaged software

(G-12305)
TARSIER LTD
655 Madison Ave Frnt 3 (10065-8043)
PHONE..................212 401-6181
Isaac H Sutton, Ch of Bd
EMP: 106

New York - New York County (G-12306) — GEOGRAPHIC SECTION

SALES (est): 9.6MM **Privately Held**
SIC: **3648** 3645 3674 Lighting equipment; public lighting fixtures; residential lighting fixtures; light emitting diodes

(G-12306)
TAYLOR & FRANCIS GROUP LLC
711 3rd Ave Fl 8 (10017-9209)
PHONE..................................212 216-7800
Linda Bathgate, *Publisher*
Naomi Silverman, *Publisher*
Len Cornacchia, *Principal*
Kate Bracaglia, *Editor*
Iris Fahrer, *Editor*
EMP: 133
SALES (corp-wide): 501.3K **Privately Held**
HQ: Taylor & Francis Group, Llc
 6000 Broken Sound Pkwy Nw # 300
 Boca Raton FL 33487
 561 994-0555

(G-12307)
TBHL INTERNATIONAL LLC
Also Called: Globe-Tex Apparel
252 W 38th St Fl 11 (10018-5806)
PHONE..................................212 799-2007
Stuart Hurvitz, *Principal*
Jodi Gallagher, *Production*
Robert Hurvitz,
Joel Limenes,
EMP: 10 EST: 1995
SQ FT: 1,400
SALES (est): 1MM **Privately Held**
SIC: **2329** 2339 Men's & boys' sportswear & athletic clothing; women's & misses' outerwear

(G-12308)
TC TRANSCONTINENTAL USA INC
Also Called: Transcontinental Ross-Ellis
67 Irving Pl Fl 2 (10003-2202)
PHONE..................................818 993-4767
Nina Sheldon, *Director*
EMP: 6
SALES (corp-wide): 1.5B **Privately Held**
SIC: **2759** Commercial printing
HQ: Tc Transcontinental U.S.A. Inc.
 8550 Balboa Blvd Ste 240
 Northridge CA 91325
 818 993-4767

(G-12309)
TDG OPERATIONS LLC
200 Lexington Ave Rm 1314 (10016-6201)
PHONE..................................212 779-4300
Mark Nestler, *Owner*
EMP: 8
SALES (corp-wide): 397.4MM **Publicly Held**
SIC: **2273** Carpets & rugs
HQ: Tdg Operations, Llc
 716 Bill Myles Dr
 Saraland AL 36571
 251 675-9080

(G-12310)
TE NEUES PUBLISHING COMPANY (PA)
350 7th Ave Rm 301 (10001-1957)
PHONE..................................212 627-9090
Hendrik Teneues, *Managing Prtnr*
Hendrik Te Neues, *Partner*
Sebastian Te Neues, *Partner*
Harold Thieck, *Managing Dir*
Audrey Barr, *Sales Dir*
▲ EMP: 11
SQ FT: 5,000
SALES (est): 1.3MM **Privately Held**
WEB: www.teneues-usa.com
SIC: **2741** 5192 Miscellaneous publishing; books

(G-12311)
TEACHERGAMING LLC
809 W 181st St 231 (10033-4516)
PHONE..................................866 644-9323
Joel Levin, *Principal*
Santeri Koivisto, *Principal*
Carl Syren, *Principal*
EMP: 12 EST: 2012
SQ FT: 200

SALES (est): 281.6K **Privately Held**
SIC: **7372** Educational computer software

(G-12312)
TEACHERS COLLEGE COLUMBIA UNIV
Also Called: Teachers College Press
1234 Amsterdam Ave (10027-6602)
PHONE..................................212 678-3929
Fax: 212 678-4149
Leyli Shayegan, *Sales Executive*
Carole Saltz, *Director*
Emily Spangler, *Teacher*
EMP: 25
SALES (corp-wide): 228.3MM **Privately Held**
WEB: www.teacherscollege.edu
SIC: **2731** Book publishing
PA: Teachers College, Columbia University
 525 W 120th St
 New York NY 10027
 212 678-3000

(G-12313)
TEACHLEY LLC
25 Broadway Fl 13 (10004-1081)
PHONE..................................347 552-1272
Rachael Labrecque, *Partner*
Kara Carpenter, *Partner*
Dana Pagar, *Partner*
EMP: 6
SALES (est): 480.2K **Privately Held**
SIC: **7372** Educational computer software

(G-12314)
TECHGRASS
77 Water St (10005-4401)
PHONE..................................646 719-2000
Susan Aexander, *Mng Member*
EMP: 10
SALES (est): 479.9K **Privately Held**
SIC: **3999** Grasses, artificial & preserved

(G-12315)
TECHNOLOGY DESKING INC
39 Broadway Rm 1640 (10006-3057)
PHONE..................................212 257-6998
Lee Markwick, *President*
Kallita Phipps, *Administration*
▲ EMP: 26
SQ FT: 6,100
SALES (est): 4.1MM **Privately Held**
SIC: **2521** Wood office furniture

(G-12316)
TECTONIC FLOORING USA LLC
1140 1st Ave Frnt 1 (10065-7961)
PHONE..................................212 686-2700
Mondo Pallon,
Rupert Dowd,
▲ EMP: 4
SQ FT: 2,100
SALES (est): 7MM **Privately Held**
SIC: **2426** Flooring, hardwood

(G-12317)
TED-STEEL INDUSTRIES LTD
Also Called: Ted-Steel Indstries
361 W 36th St Frnt A (10018-6408)
PHONE..................................212 279-3878
Fax: 212 279-3878
Charles Desimone, *President*
Joseph Desimone, *Vice Pres*
Saml T Grayburn,
EMP: 6 EST: 1959
SQ FT: 10,000
SALES (est): 530K **Privately Held**
SIC: **2542** Garment racks: except wood

(G-12318)
TELEPHONE SALES & SERVICE CO (PA)
132 W Broadway (10013-3396)
PHONE..................................212 233-8505
Fax: 212 233-8507
William Bradley, *President*
Neil Bradley, *Vice Pres*
James Woods, *Engineer*
EMP: 23
SQ FT: 4,000
SALES (est): 3MM **Privately Held**
SIC: **3612** 1731 Transmission & distribution voltage regulators; sound equipment specialization

(G-12319)
TELESCA-HEYMAN INC
304 E 94th St 6 (10128-5688)
PHONE..................................212 534-3442
Mario Dire, *President*
Remo Dire, *Vice Pres*
EMP: 15
SQ FT: 14,500
SALES (est): 805.2K **Privately Held**
SIC: **2541** 7641 Cabinets, except refrigerated: show, display, etc.: wood; furniture refinishing; antique furniture repair & restoration

(G-12320)
TELMAR INFORMATION SERVICES (PA)
711 3rd Ave Rm 1500 (10017-9201)
PHONE..................................212 725-3000
Stanley Federman, *Ch of Bd*
Corey V Panno, *President*
Corey Panno, *President*
Jennfer Potter, *Sr Corp Ofcr*
Susan Lanzetta, *Exec VP*
EMP: 30 EST: 1968
SQ FT: 4,400
SALES (est): 19.1MM **Privately Held**
WEB: www.telmar.com
SIC: **7372** Business oriented computer software

(G-12321)
TEMPLE ST CLAIR LLC
594 Broadway Rm 306 (10012-3234)
PHONE..................................212 219-8664
Fax: 212 219-8740
Frank Trent, *CFO*
Temple S Carr, *Human Resources*
Jamie McGrath, *Sales Staff*
Logan Gough, *Marketing Staff*
Melanie Oswald, *Marketing Staff*
▲ EMP: 27
SALES: 13MM **Privately Held**
SIC: **3911** Jewelry, precious metal

(G-12322)
TENBY LLC
344 W 38th St Fl 3 (10018-8414)
PHONE..................................646 863-5890
Toni Palmarini, *Manager*
EMP: 101 EST: 2016
SALES (est): 2.1MM
SALES (corp-wide): 221.6MM **Privately Held**
SIC: **2337** Skirts, separate: women's, misses' & juniors'
PA: The Kittrich Corporation
 1585 W Mission Blvd
 Pomona CA 91766
 714 736-1000

(G-12323)
TERRA ENRGY RESOURCE TECH INC (PA)
99 Park Ave Ph A (10016-1340)
PHONE..................................212 286-9197
Fax: 917 591-5988
Dmitry Vilbaum, *CEO*
Alexandre Agaian PHD, *Ch of Bd*
EMP: 10
SALES (est): 3.3MM **Publicly Held**
WEB: www.terrainsight.com
SIC: **1389** Testing, measuring, surveying & analysis services

(G-12324)
TERRANUA US CORP
535 5th Ave Fl 4 (10017-8020)
PHONE..................................212 852-9028
Brian Fahey, *CEO*
Frank Hourihane, *CFO*
EMP: 16
SALES (est): 1.7MM **Privately Held**
SIC: **7372** Prepackaged software
PA: Terranua Limited
 Unit 2c
 Dublin

(G-12325)
TESLA MOTORS INC
10 Columbus Cir Ste 102d (10019-1215)
PHONE..................................212 206-1204
EMP: 663

SALES (corp-wide): 4B **Publicly Held**
SIC: **3711** 3714 Mfg Motor Vehicle/Car Bodies & Components
PA: Tesla Motors, Inc.
 3500 Deer Creek Rd
 Palo Alto CA 94304
 650 681-5000

(G-12326)
TEXPORT FABRICS CORP
Also Called: Rose-Ann Division
495 Broadway Fl 7 (10012-4457)
PHONE..................................212 226-6066
Fax: 212 966-6785
Sonia Essebag, *President*
EMP: 10
SQ FT: 48,000
SALES (est): 1.1MM **Privately Held**
SIC: **2335** Women's, juniors' & misses' dresses

(G-12327)
TEXWOOD INC (U S A)
850 7th Ave Ste 1000 (10019-5438)
PHONE..................................212 262-8383
Fax: 212 262-9787
Herbert Tam, *President*
Herbert Tam Shiu, *President*
Jeanette Shi, *Exec VP*
EMP: 5
SQ FT: 3,000
SALES (est): 361.2K **Privately Held**
SIC: **2339** 5136 Jeans: women's, misses' & juniors'; trousers, men's & boys'
HQ: Texwood Limited
 3/F Texwood Plz
 Kwun Tong KLN
 279 773-33

(G-12328)
TG THERAPEUTICS INC
2 Gansevoort St Fl 9 (10014-1667)
PHONE..................................212 554-4484
Fax: 212 582-3957
Michael S Weiss, *Ch of Bd*
Sean A Power, *CFO*
▲ EMP: 64
SALES: 152.3K **Privately Held**
WEB: www.manhattanpharma.com
SIC: **2834** Pharmaceutical preparations

(G-12329)
TGP FLYING CLOUD HOLDINGS LLC
565 5th Ave Fl 27 (10017-2478)
PHONE..................................646 829-3900
James Pagano, *Principal*
Ashlynn Smith, *Principal*
EMP: 25
SALES: 500K **Privately Held**
SIC: **3511** Turbines & turbine generator sets

(G-12330)
THE DESIGN GROUP INC
Also Called: J.hoaglund
240 Madison Ave Fl 8 (10016-2878)
PHONE..................................212 681-1548
Robert Rosen, *President*
Daniel Cohen, *Chairman*
▲ EMP: 10
SALES: 3MM **Privately Held**
SIC: **2339** Women's & misses' outerwear

(G-12331)
THE SWATCH GROUP U S INC
56 Grand Central Terminal (10017-5622)
PHONE..................................212 297-9192
Kyle Hoffman, *Manager*
EMP: 6
SALES (corp-wide): 7.4B **Privately Held**
WEB: www.mcrystal.com
SIC: **3423** Jewelers' hand tools
HQ: The Swatch Group U S Inc
 703 Nw 62nd Ave Ste 450
 Miami FL 33126
 201 271-1400

(G-12332)
THEHUFFINGTONPOSTCOM INC (DH)
Also Called: Huffington Post, The
770 Broadway Fl 4 (10003-9558)
PHONE..................................212 245-7844
Eric Hippeau, *CEO*
Rowaida Abdelaziz, *Editor*

▲ = Import ▼ = Export ◆ = Import/Export

GEOGRAPHIC SECTION
New York - New York County (G-12355)

Robyn Baitcher, *Editor*
William Bradley, *Editor*
James Cave, *Editor*
EMP: 33
SALES (est): 4.9MM
SALES (corp-wide): 125.9B **Publicly Held**
SIC: 2741

(G-12333)
THEIRAPP LLC
Also Called: Apprise Mobile
880 3rd Ave (10022-4730)
PHONE..........................212 896-1255
Ben Gholian, *Partner*
Jeff Corbin, *Mng Member*
Jeffrey Corbin, *Mng Member*
EMP: 35
SALES (est): 2.2MM
SALES (corp-wide): 5.4MM **Privately Held**
SIC: 7372 Application computer software
PA: Kanan, Corbin, Schupak & Aronow, Inc.
880 3rd Ave Fl 6
New York NY 10022
212 682-6300

(G-12334)
THEORY LLC
1114 Avenue Of The Americ (10036-7703)
PHONE..........................212 762-2300
Fax: 212 997-7409
Pamela Meany, *Human Res Dir*
Andrew Rosen, *Manager*
Rudolph Gopie, *Supervisor*
Alexander Rakovsky, *Info Tech Dir*
Leanne Fremar, *Director*
EMP: 100
SALES (corp-wide): 17.4B **Privately Held**
SIC: 2337 Suits: women's, misses' & juniors'
HQ: Theory Llc
38 Gansevoort St
New York NY 10014
212 300-0800

(G-12335)
THEORY LLC
1157 Madison Ave (10028-0409)
PHONE..........................212 879-0265
Sylke Cunha, *Branch Mgr*
EMP: 7
SALES (corp-wide): 17.4B **Privately Held**
SIC: 2337 Suits: women's, misses' & juniors'
HQ: Theory Llc
38 Gansevoort St
New York NY 10014
212 300-0800

(G-12336)
THESKIMM INC
49 W 23rd St Fl 10 (10010-4224)
PHONE..........................212 228-4628
Carly Zakin, *CEO*
Dheerja Kaur, *Prdtn Mgr*
EMP: 15
SQ FT: 1,500
SALES (est): 1.1MM **Privately Held**
SIC: 2741 Miscellaneous publishing

(G-12337)
THESTREET INC (PA)
14 Wall St Fl 15 (10005-2139)
PHONE..........................212 321-5000
Fax: 212 321-5016
Lawrence S Kramer, *Ch of Bd*
David Callaway, *President*
Jeffrey Davis, *President*
Eric Lundberg, *CFO*
Cameron Ireland, *CTO*
EMP: 77
SQ FT: 35,000
SALES: 37MM **Publicly Held**
WEB: www.thestreet.com
SIC: 2711 2721 Newspapers: publishing only, not printed on site; periodicals: publishing only

(G-12338)
THING DAEMON INC
Also Called: Fancy
96 Spring St Fl 5 (10012-3923)
PHONE..........................917 746-9895
Joseph Einhorn, *CEO*
Jack Einhorn, *President*

Michael Silverman, *COO*
Andrew Tuch, *Vice Pres*
Gilah Elul, *Director*
EMP: 25 **EST:** 2010
SALES (est): 4.9MM **Privately Held**
SIC: 7372 Application computer software

(G-12339)
THINKTREK INC
Also Called: Complystream
420 Lexington Ave Rm 300 (10170-0399)
PHONE..........................212 884-8399
Jyoti Prasanna, *Principal*
Tridib Majumder, *Director*
Prasanna Kumar, *Director*
EMP: 10
SQ FT: 1,000
SALES (est): 385.8K **Privately Held**
SIC: 7372 Business oriented computer software

(G-12340)
THOMAS GROUP INC
Also Called: Thomas Group, The
131 Varick St Rm 1016 (10013-1417)
PHONE..........................212 947-6400
Fax: 212 947-6462
Jamie H Tomashoff, *President*
Charlene Schoen, *Controller*
Vera Caras, *Manager*
Gheen Stephen, *Manager*
EMP: 10
SQ FT: 18,000
SALES (est): 1.8MM **Privately Held**
WEB: www.thethomasgroup.com
SIC: 2752 2791 2789 Commercial printing, offset; typesetting; bookbinding & related work

(G-12341)
THOMAS INTERNATIONAL PUBG CO (HQ)
5 Penn Plz Fl 15 (10001-1810)
PHONE..........................212 613-3441
Fax: 212 629-1542
John L Lindsey, *President*
Bonnie Kantor, *Manager*
Keith Biondo, *Director*
EMP: 10
SALES (est): 769K
SALES (corp-wide): 200.6MM **Privately Held**
SIC: 2721 Trade journals: publishing only, not printed on site
PA: Thomas Publishing Company Llc
5 Penn Plz Fl 9
New York NY 10001
212 695-0500

(G-12342)
THOMAS PUBLISHING COMPANY LLC (PA)
Also Called: Thomas Enterprise Solutions
5 Penn Plz Fl 9 (10001-1860)
PHONE..........................212 695-0500
Fax: 212 290-7389
Jos E Andrade, *Ch of Bd*
Tony Uphoff, *President*
Robert Ferguson, *Publisher*
Heather Holst-Knudsen, *Publisher*
Matt Campbell, *Editor*
EMP: 300 **EST:** 1898
SQ FT: 100,000
SALES (est): 200.6MM **Privately Held**
WEB: www.inboundlogistics.com
SIC: 2741 2721 7374 7331 Directories: publishing only, not printed on site; catalogs: publishing only, not printed on site; trade journals: publishing only, not printed on site; data processing service; direct mail advertising services

(G-12343)
THOMAS PUBLISHING COMPANY LLC
5 Penn Plz Fl 9 (10001-1860)
PHONE..........................212 695-0500
Fax: 212 290-7307
Sandra Batzel, *Engineer*
Ed Edwards, *Sales Staff*
Tom Marren, *Marketing Staff*
Delimar Melendez, *Manager*
EMP: 70

SALES (corp-wide): 200.6MM **Privately Held**
WEB: www.inboundlogistics.com
SIC: 2741 Catalogs: publishing & printing
PA: Thomas Publishing Company Llc
5 Penn Plz Fl 9
New York NY 10001
212 695-0500

(G-12344)
THOMAS PUBLISHING COMPANY LLC
Also Called: Magazine Group
5 Penn Plz Fl 8 (10001-1851)
PHONE..........................212 695-0500
Ralph Richardson, *Manager*
EMP: 9
SALES (corp-wide): 200.6MM **Privately Held**
WEB: www.inboundlogistics.com
SIC: 2721 Magazines: publishing only, not printed on site
PA: Thomas Publishing Company Llc
5 Penn Plz Fl 9
New York NY 10001
212 695-0500

(G-12345)
THOMAS PUBLISHING COMPANY LLC
Managing Automation Magazine
5 Penn Plz Fl 9 (10001-1860)
PHONE..........................212 695-0500
Fax: 212 629-1170
Karen Molitz, *Marketing Staff*
Margret Bresto, *Manager*
EMP: 9
SALES (corp-wide): 200.6MM **Privately Held**
WEB: www.inboundlogistics.com
SIC: 2721 Magazines: publishing & printing
PA: Thomas Publishing Company Llc
5 Penn Plz Fl 9
New York NY 10001
212 695-0500

(G-12346)
THOMAS SASSON CO INC
555 5th Ave Rm 1900 (10017-9250)
PHONE..........................212 697-4998
Jeffery Thomas, *President*
Lois Dianne Sasson, *Vice Pres*
EMP: 2
SQ FT: 1,000
SALES: 1MM **Privately Held**
SIC: 3911 Jewelry apparel

(G-12347)
THOMPSON FERRIER LLC
230 5th Ave Ste 1004 (10001-7834)
PHONE..........................212 244-2212
Pauline Dana, *COO*
Essie Gonzales, *Bookkeeper*
Raffi Arslanian,
▲ **EMP:** 9
SQ FT: 2,000
SALES (est): 1.2MM **Privately Held**
SIC: 3999 2844 Candles; concentrates, perfume

(G-12348)
THOMSON REUTERS CORPORATION
500 Pearl St (10007-1316)
PHONE..........................212 393-9461
Gail Appleson, *Principal*
Bill Dickinson, *Manager*
EMP: 15
SALES (corp-wide): 3.1B **Publicly Held**
SIC: 2741 Miscellaneous publishing
HQ: Thomson Reuters Corporation
3 Times Sq
New York NY 10036
646 223-4000

(G-12349)
THOMSON REUTERS CORPORATION (DH)
3 Times Sq (10036-6564)
PHONE..........................646 223-4000
David Thomson, *Ch of Bd*
James C Smith, *President*
Vin Caraher, *President*
David W Craig, *President*
Gonzalo Lissarrague, *President*

▲ **EMP:** 16600
SQ FT: 558,500
SALES: 12.2B
SALES (corp-wide): 3.1B **Publicly Held**
WEB: www.thomsonreuters.com
SIC: 2741 8111 7372 7383 Miscellaneous publishing; legal services; prepackaged software; news syndicates
HQ: Woodbridge Company Limited, The
65 Queen St W Suite 2400
Toronto ON M5H 2
416 364-8700

(G-12350)
THORNWILLOW PRESS LTD
57 W 58th St Ste 11e (10019-1630)
P.O. Box 1202 (10028-0048)
PHONE..........................212 980-0738
Luke Pontifell, *President*
EMP: 3
SALES: 1MM **Privately Held**
WEB: www.thornwillow.com
SIC: 2731 5942 Book publishing; book stores

(G-12351)
THREAD LLC (PA)
26 W 17th St Rm 301 (10011-5730)
PHONE..........................212 414-8844
Fax: 212 414-9169
Beth Blake,
Melissa Akey,
▲ **EMP:** 5 **EST:** 1999
SALES (est): 482.1K **Privately Held**
WEB: www.threaddesign.com
SIC: 2335 Bridal & formal gowns

(G-12352)
THREE FIVE III-V MATERIALS INC
19 W 21st St Rm 203 (10010-6866)
PHONE..........................212 213-8290
Thomas Guan, *President*
Peter Wong, *Manager*
EMP: 10
SALES (est): 860.9K **Privately Held**
SIC: 3679 Electronic loads & power supplies

(G-12353)
THYSSENKRUPP ELEVATOR CORP
519 8th Ave Fl 6 (10018-4591)
PHONE..........................212 268-2020
Fax: 212 344-2090
Ben Siano, *Branch Mgr*
EMP: 58
SALES (corp-wide): 44.2B **Privately Held**
WEB: www.tyssnkrupp.com
SIC: 3534 Elevators & moving stairways
HQ: Thyssenkrupp Elevator Corporation
11605 Haynes Bridge Rd # 650
Alpharetta GA 30009
678 319-3240

(G-12354)
THYSSENKRUPP MATERIALS NA INC
Thyssnkrupp Mtllrgcal Pdts USA
489 5th Ave Fl 20 (10017-6125)
PHONE..........................212 972-8800
Herr Thorsten Sorje, *Branch Mgr*
EMP: 10
SALES (corp-wide): 44.2B **Privately Held**
SIC: 3499 3313 Fire- or burglary-resistive products; ferroalloys
HQ: Thyssenkrupp Materials Na, Inc.
22355 W 11 Mile Rd
Southfield MI 48033
248 233-5600

(G-12355)
TIE KING INC
Jimmy's Sales
42 W 38th St Rm 1200 (10018-6212)
PHONE..........................212 714-9611
Jimmy Azizo, *President*
EMP: 5
SALES (corp-wide): 4.6MM **Privately Held**
WEB: www.thetieking.com
SIC: 2323 Ties, handsewn: made from purchased materials

New York - New York County (G-12356)   **GEOGRAPHIC SECTION**

PA: The Tie King Inc
243 44th St
Brooklyn NY 11232
718 768-8484

(G-12356)
TIGER 21 LLC
1995 Broadway Fl 6 (10023-5882)
PHONE.................................212 360-1700
Michael Sonnenfeldt, *Principal*
Ellen Breslau, *Senior VP*
EMP: 7
SALES (est): 1.7MM **Privately Held**
SIC: 2273 Carpets & rugs

(G-12357)
TIGER FASHION INC
20 W 36th St Frnt (10018-9781)
PHONE.................................212 244-1175
John Joo, *President*
▲ **EMP:** 20
SALES (est): 1.4MM **Privately Held**
SIC: 2337 5137 Women's & misses' suits & skirts; suits: women's, children's & infants'

(G-12358)
TIGER J LLC (PA)
1430 Broadway Rm 1900 (10018-3308)
PHONE.................................212 465-9300
Fax: 212 435-7412
Jeffrey Steinberg, *Ch of Bd*
Mark Locks, *President*
Arnold Brodsky, *CFO*
Andrew Steinberg, *Info Tech Dir*
Guillaume Poupart, *Director*
▲ **EMP:** 44
SQ FT: 15,600
SALES: 39.5MM **Privately Held**
WEB: www.terrytiger.com
SIC: 2339 2337 Women's & misses' outerwear; sportswear, women's; jackets & vests, except fur & leather: women's; women's & misses' suits & skirts; skirts, separate: women's, misses' & juniors'

(G-12359)
TIKA MOBILE INC (PA)
Also Called: Tikamobile
902 Broadway Fl 6 (10010-6039)
PHONE.................................646 650-5545
Anthony Bowden, *Principal*
Manish Sharma, *Principal*
Amin Torabkhani, *Director*
EMP: 7
SQ FT: 500
SALES (est): 1.5MM **Privately Held**
SIC: 7372 Business oriented computer software

(G-12360)
TILLSONBURG COMPANY USA INC
37 W 39th St Rm 1101 (10018-3894)
PHONE.................................267 994-8096
Tony Cooper, *CEO*
Ramaswamy Arakoni, *Ch of Bd*
Indira Sukdeo, *Office Mgr*
Sandy Jabaly, *Director*
Alex Lam, *Director*
▲ **EMP:** 50
SQ FT: 3,000
SALES (est): 5MM **Privately Held**
SIC: 2339 2329 Women's & misses' athletic clothing & sportswear; men's & boys' sportswear & athletic clothing
PA: Tillsonburg Company Limited
18/F Corporation Sq
Kowloon Bay KLN
233 138-84

(G-12361)
TIME HOME ENTERTAINMENT INC
1271 Ave Of The Americas (10020-1300)
PHONE.................................212 522-1212
Jim Childs, *Publisher*
Barbara Kaczynski, *Officer*
EMP: 32
SALES (est): 2.5MM
SALES (corp-wide): 3B **Publicly Held**
SIC: 2731 Book publishing
PA: Time Inc.
225 Liberty St Ste C2
New York NY 10281
212 522-1212

(G-12362)
TIME INC
Sports Illustrated Magazine
1271 Avenue Of The Americ (10020-1300)
PHONE.................................212 522-1212
Fax: 212 522-0392
David Morris, *Publisher*
Bradford Wallick, *Principal*
Paul Cacciato, *Director*
Liana Zamora, *Director*
Sarah McCarrick, *Associate*
EMP: 31
SALES (corp-wide): 3B **Publicly Held**
SIC: 2721 2731 Magazines: publishing & printing; book publishing
PA: Time Inc.
225 Liberty St Ste C2
New York NY 10281
212 522-1212

(G-12363)
TIME INC (PA)
225 Liberty St Ste C2 (10281-1088)
PHONE.................................212 522-1212
Fax: 212 522-0096
Joseph A Ripp, *Ch of Bd*
Richard Battista, *President*
Erik Moreno, *President*
Rupert Turnbull, *Publisher*
Melanie Lieberman, *Editor*
◆ **EMP:** 2800
SQ FT: 696,000
SALES: 3B **Publicly Held**
WEB: www.timeinc.com
SIC: 2721 Magazines: publishing only, not printed on site

(G-12364)
TIME INC
Time/Fortune Money Group
1271 Ave Of The Amer Sb7 (10020-1393)
PHONE.................................212 522-0361
Fax: 212 522-0841
Ann Moore, *CEO*
EMP: 28
SALES (corp-wide): 3B **Publicly Held**
SIC: 2721 Magazines: publishing only, not printed on site
PA: Time Inc.
225 Liberty St Ste C2
New York NY 10281
212 522-1212

(G-12365)
TIME INC AFFLUENT MEDIA GROUP (HQ)
Also Called: American Express Publishing
1120 Ave Of The Americas (10036-6700)
PHONE.................................212 382-5600
Fax: 212 382-5878
Edward F Kelly Jr, *President*
Dana Cowin, *Senior VP*
Michael Crotty, *Senior VP*
Nikki Upshaw, *Senior VP*
Simon Taylor, *Vice Pres*
▲ **EMP:** 300 **EST:** 1938
SALES (est): 35.9MM
SALES (corp-wide): 3B **Publicly Held**
WEB: www.fwmediakit.com
SIC: 2721 Magazines: publishing only, not printed on site
PA: Time Inc.
225 Liberty St Ste C2
New York NY 10281
212 522-1212

(G-12366)
TIME INC AFFLUENT MEDIA GROUP (DH)
Also Called: Travel Leisure Magazine
1120 Ave Of The Americas (10036-6700)
PHONE.................................212 382-5600
Fax: 212 382-5788
Ted Kelly, *President*
EMP: 5
SALES (est): 404.8K
SALES (corp-wide): 3B **Publicly Held**
SIC: 2721 7389 Magazines: publishing only, not printed on site; subscription fulfillment services: magazine, newspaper, etc.
HQ: Southern Progress Corporation
2100 Lakeshore Dr
Birmingham AL 35209
205 445-6000

(G-12367)
TIME OUT NEW YORK PARTNERS LP
475 10th Ave Fl 12 (10018-1175)
PHONE.................................646 432-3000
Alison Tocci, *President*
Tony Elliott, *Partner*
Marisa Fari A, *Publisher*
Michael Freidson, *Principal*
Raven Snook, *Editor*
▲ **EMP:** 91
SALES (est): 17.8MM
SALES (corp-wide): 43.9MM **Privately Held**
SIC: 2721 Periodicals
HQ: Time Out Digital Limited
4th Floor
London
207 813-3000

(G-12368)
TIME TO KNOW INC
655 3rd Ave Fl 21 (10017-5621)
PHONE.................................212 230-1210
Yonit Tzadok, *CFO*
Bryan Fryer, *Controller*
Jamie Iesner, *Director*
Lawrence Malkin, *Director*
EMP: 10
SALES (est): 875K **Privately Held**
SIC: 7372 Educational computer software

(G-12369)
TIME WARNER COMPANIES INC (DH)
1 Time Warner Ctr Bsmt B (10019-6010)
PHONE.................................212 484-8000
Jeff Bewkes, *Ch of Bd*
Howard M Averill, *Exec VP*
Paul T Cappuccio, *Exec VP*
Gary L Ginsberg, *Exec VP*
Karen Magee, *Exec VP*
EMP: 67
SQ FT: 451,000
SALES (est): 42.4MM
SALES (corp-wide): 29.3B **Publicly Held**
SIC: 3652 6794 2741 7812 Compact laser discs, prerecorded; magnetic tape (audio): prerecorded; music licensing to radio stations; performance rights, publishing & licensing; music royalties, sheet & record; music, sheet: publishing only, not printed on site; music books: publishing only, not printed on site; motion picture production & distribution; television film production; motion picture production & distribution, television; video tape production; cable television services; magazines: publishing only, not printed on site

(G-12370)
TIMELESS FASHIONS LLC
100 United Nations Plz (10017-1713)
PHONE.................................212 730-9328
Syed Sajid, *CFO*
Navin Mahtani, *Mng Member*
Ravi Datwani,
▲ **EMP:** 7
SQ FT: 2,900
SALES: 10MM **Privately Held**
SIC: 2389 Apparel for handicapped

(G-12371)
TIMES SQUARE STUDIOS LTD
Also Called: ABC Television Network
1500 Broadway Fl 2 (10036-4055)
PHONE.................................212 930-7720
Fax: 212 930-7790
Ruth Anne Alsop, *Senior VP*
Jeff Braet, *Vice Pres*
Jeff Hartnett, *Manager*
EMP: 200
SALES (est): 28.7MM **Publicly Held**
WEB: www.go.com
SIC: 3663 Studio equipment, radio & television broadcasting
PA: The Walt Disney Company
500 S Buena Vista St
Burbank CA 91521

(G-12372)
TIMING GROUP LLC
237 W 37th St Ste 1100 (10018-6770)
P.O. Box 275, Tallman (10982-0275)
PHONE.................................646 878-2600

AVI Schwebel, *Mng Member*
Michelle Jacobs, *Manager*
Alan Friedman,
▲ **EMP:** 15
SALES (est): 1.7MM **Privately Held**
SIC: 3021 Rubber & plastics footwear

(G-12373)
TIO FOODS LLC
Also Called: Tio Gazpacho
115 W 18th St Fl 2 (10011-4113)
PHONE.................................305 672-6645
Austin V Allan, *Mng Member*
EMP: 10
SQ FT: 150
SALES: 500K **Privately Held**
SIC: 3411 Food & beverage containers

(G-12374)
TITAN CONTROLS INC
122 W 27th St Fl 5 (10001-6227)
PHONE.................................516 358-2407
Paul Deronde, *President*
Gary Sefcheck, *Vice Pres*
EMP: 11
SQ FT: 2,000
SALES (est): 820K **Privately Held**
WEB: www.titancontrols.com
SIC: 3829 Temperature sensors, except industrial process & aircraft

(G-12375)
TLC-LC INC (PA)
115 E 57th St Bsmt (10022-2090)
PHONE.................................212 756-8900
Loida Nicolas Lewis, *Ch of Bd*
Reynaldo R Glover, *President*
▲ **EMP:** 27
SQ FT: 2,500
SALES (est): 62.1MM **Privately Held**
SIC: 2024 2096 5149 5411 Ice cream & ice milk; dairy based frozen desserts; potato chips & similar snacks; potato chips & other potato-based snacks; beverages, except coffee & tea; grocery stores

(G-12376)
TM MUSIC INC
Also Called: Casablanca Records
9 E 63rd St Apt 2-3 (10065-7236)
PHONE.................................212 471-4000
Fax: 212 471-4090
Thomas Mottola, *President*
Susan Steinsapir, *Business Mgr*
Kamal Darraz, *Business Anlyst*
EMP: 10
SQ FT: 12,000
SALES: 5MM **Privately Held**
SIC: 2782 Record albums

(G-12377)
TOHO SHOJI (NEW YORK) INC
990 Avenue Of The America (10018-5419)
PHONE.................................212 868-7466
Fax: 212 868-7464
T Mishide, *President*
▲ **EMP:** 15
SALES (est): 1.1MM
SALES (corp-wide): 24.3MM **Privately Held**
SIC: 3961 Costume jewelry
PA: Toho Shoji Co., Ltd.
5-29-8, Asakusabashi
Taito-Ku TKY 111-0
338 613-274

(G-12378)
TOLTEC FABRICS INC
437 5th Ave Fl 10 (10016-2205)
PHONE.................................212 706-9310
Fax: 212 684-2522
Barbara Nymark, *President*
Judy Lester, *Vice Pres*
Claudia Rycz, *Vice Pres*
EMP: 155
SQ FT: 6,000
SALES (est): 8.7MM
SALES (corp-wide): 71.5K **Privately Held**
WEB: www.interfacefabricsgroup.com
SIC: 2262 2221 Finishing plants, manmade fiber & silk fabrics; decorative finishing of manmade broadwoven fabrics; broadwoven fabric mills, manmade

HQ: True Textiles, Inc.
5300 Corprte Grv Dr Se
Grand Rapids MI 49512
616 301-7540

(G-12379)
TOM & LINDA PLATT INC
29 W 38th St Rm 6l (10018-2174)
PHONE..................................212 221-7208
Fax: 212 727-1912
Linda Platt, *President*
Tom Platt, *Treasurer*
EMP: 13
SALES (est): 1.4MM **Privately Held**
WEB: www.tomandlindaplatt.com
SIC: 2335 Women's, juniors' & misses' dresses

(G-12380)
TOM DOHERTY ASSOCIATES INC
Also Called: Tor Books
175 5th Ave Frnt 1 (10010-7704)
PHONE..................................212 388-0100
Fax: 212 388-0191
Tom Doherty, *President*
Elayne Becker, *Editor*
Bess Cozby, *Editor*
Liz Gorinsky, *Editor*
Marco Palmieri, *Editor*
EMP: 44
SQ FT: 7,000
SALES (est): 8.6MM
SALES (corp-wide): 1.5B **Privately Held**
WEB: www.stmartins.com
SIC: 2731 Books: publishing only
HQ: Macmillan Holdings, Llc
175 5th Ave
New York NY 10010

(G-12381)
TOM JAMES COMPANY
641 Lexington Ave Fl 19 (10022-4503)
PHONE..................................212 581-6968
John Minhain, *Branch Mgr*
EMP: 10
SALES (corp-wide): 422.6MM **Privately Held**
WEB: www.englishamericanco.com
SIC: 2311 Suits, men's & boys': made from purchased materials
PA: Tom James Company
263 Seaboard Ln
Franklin TN 37067
615 771-1122

(G-12382)
TOM JAMES COMPANY
717 5th Ave (10022-8101)
PHONE..................................212 593-0204
George Mattos, *Branch Mgr*
EMP: 10
SALES (corp-wide): 422.6MM **Privately Held**
WEB: www.englishamericanco.com
SIC: 2311 Suits, men's & boys': made from purchased materials
PA: Tom James Company
263 Seaboard Ln
Franklin TN 37067
615 771-1122

(G-12383)
TOM MORIBER FURS INC
345 7th Ave Fl 19 (10001-5035)
PHONE..................................212 244-2180
Tom Moriber, *President*
EMP: 10
SQ FT: 15,000
SALES (est): 760K **Privately Held**
SIC: 2371 Fur goods

(G-12384)
TOMAS MAIER
956 Madison Ave Frnt 1 (10021-2635)
PHONE..................................212 988-8686
Tomas Maier, *Owner*
EMP: 7
SALES (est): 511K **Privately Held**
SIC: 2253 Bathing suits & swimwear, knit; jerseys, knit
HQ: B.V. Servizi Srl
Viale Della Scienza 9/11
Vicenza VI 36100

(G-12385)
TOMIA BEAUTY BRANDS LLC
Also Called: Tomia Beauty Supply
38 W 21st St (10010-6906)
PHONE..................................917 301-0125
Jack Bensason,
▲ **EMP:** 5 **EST:** 2014
SALES (est): 131.8K **Privately Held**
SIC: 2844 Toilet preparations

(G-12386)
TOMMY BOY ENTERTAINMENT LLC
220 E 23rd St Ste 400 (10010-4669)
PHONE..................................212 388-8300
Thomas Silverman,
EMP: 12
SQ FT: 5,500
SALES (est): 1.3MM **Privately Held**
WEB: www.tommyboy.com
SIC: 2782 Record albums

(G-12387)
TOMMY JOHN INC
100 Broadway Ste 1101 (10005-4504)
PHONE..................................800 708-3490
Thomas J Patterson, *President*
John Wu, *COO*
Al Valdes, *Vice Pres*
Margaret Breitton, *Opers Staff*
Al Valdez, *Controller*
▲ **EMP:** 50
SQ FT: 17,500
SALES (est): 31MM **Privately Held**
SIC: 2322 Men's & boys' underwear & nightwear

(G-12388)
TONIX PHRMCEUTICALS HOLDG CORP (PA)
509 Madison Ave Rm 306 (10022-5583)
PHONE..................................212 980-9155
Fax: 212 923-5700
Seth Lederman, *Ch of Bd*
Bradley Saenger, *CFO*
Gregory Sullivan, *Chief Mktg Ofcr*
EMP: 28
SQ FT: 4,800
SALES (est): 2.8MM **Publicly Held**
SIC: 2834 Pharmaceutical preparations

(G-12389)
TOP COPI REPRODUCTIONS INC
Also Called: Hard Copy Printing
160 Broadway Fl 3 (10038-4237)
PHONE..................................212 571-4141
Fax: 212 571-4154
Abraham Faerberg, *President*
Gene R Ruscigno, *Vice Pres*
Thihira S Mangal, *VP Mktg*
EMP: 10 **EST:** 1967
SQ FT: 4,000
SALES (est): 2.4MM **Privately Held**
WEB: www.hardcopyprinting.com
SIC: 2752 2759 Commercial printing, offset; commercial printing

(G-12390)
TOP QUALITY PRODUCTS INC
1173 Broadway (10001-7505)
PHONE..................................212 213-1988
Phu Thanh Nguyen, *Principal*
▲ **EMP:** 6
SALES (est): 735.4K **Privately Held**
SIC: 3081 Unsupported plastics film & sheet

(G-12391)
TOPPAN PRINTING CO AMER INC (HQ)
747 3rd Ave Fl 7 (10017-2821)
PHONE..................................212 596-7747
Fax: 212 246-3067
Toru Moriyama, *Ch of Bd*
James Violette, *Corp Secy*
Minoru Kamigahira, *Senior VP*
John Lee, *Senior VP*
Brian Healy, *Accounts Exec*
▲ **EMP:** 20
SQ FT: 12,000
SALES (est): 22.6MM
SALES (corp-wide): 12.6B **Privately Held**
WEB: www.toppan.com
SIC: 2752 7384 Commercial printing, offset; film processing & finishing laboratory
PA: Toppan Printing Co., Ltd.
1, Kandaizumicho
Chiyoda-Ku TKY 101-0
338 355-111

(G-12392)
TOPPAN VINTAGE INC (PA)
747 3rd Ave Fl 7 (10017-2821)
PHONE..................................212 596-7747
Jeff Riback, *President*
Lee Asher, *Senior VP*
Glen Buchbaum, *Senior VP*
Bill Lee, *Senior VP*
Ernest J Verrico, *Senior VP*
EMP: 70
SALES (est): 19.1MM **Privately Held**
SIC: 2759 8732 Commercial printing; merger, acquisition & reorganization research

(G-12393)
TORAY HOLDING (USA) INC (HQ)
461 5th Ave Fl 9 (10017-7730)
PHONE..................................212 697-8150
Akihiro Nikkaku, *President*
Yasuke Orito, *Principal*
K Nakajima, *Admin Sec*
◆ **EMP:** 50
SALES (est): 619.1MM
SALES (corp-wide): 17.8B **Privately Held**
SIC: 2821 Plastics materials & resins
PA: Toray Industries,Inc.
2-1-1, Nihombashimuromachi
Chuo-Ku TKY 103-0
332 455-111

(G-12394)
TORAY INDUSTRIES INC
600 3rd Ave Fl 5 (10016-1919)
PHONE..................................212 697-8150
Fax: 212 972-4279
Yvette Kosar, *Branch Mgr*
EMP: 8
SALES (corp-wide): 17.8B **Privately Held**
WEB: www.toray.co.jp
SIC: 2221 2821 3089 3081 Broadwoven fabric mills, manmade; plastics materials & resins; plastic processing; unsupported plastics film & sheet
PA: Toray Industries,Inc.
2-1-1, Nihombashimuromachi
Chuo-Ku TKY 103-0
332 455-111

(G-12395)
TORCH GRAPHICS INC
1001 Ave Of The Americas (10018-5460)
PHONE..................................212 679-4334
Gary Handis, *President*
Rosemary Johnson, *Info Tech Dir*
EMP: 20
SALES (est): 873.9K **Privately Held**
SIC: 2796 Color separations for printing

(G-12396)
TORRE PRODUCTS CO INC
479 Washington St (10013-1381)
PHONE..................................212 925-8989
Liberty F Raho, *President*
Peter N Raho, *Treasurer*
Philip Raho, *Admin Sec*
EMP: 9 **EST:** 1917
SALES (est): 1MM **Privately Held**
SIC: 2899 2087 Essential oils; flavoring extracts & syrups

(G-12397)
TOSHIBA AMER INFO SYSTEMS INC (DH)
1251 Ave Of The Ste 4110 (10020)
P.O. Box 19724, Irvine CA (92623-9724)
PHONE..................................949 583-3000
Fax: 949 587-6280
Mark Simons, *CEO*
Ted Flati, *Vice Pres*
Scott Moore, *Purch Mgr*
Michael Bone, *Engineer*
Erik Monisera, *Engineer*
▲ **EMP:** 277
SQ FT: 446,000
SALES (est): 287.4MM
SALES (corp-wide): 42.8B **Privately Held**
WEB: www.toshiba-components.com
SIC: 3571 3577 3572 3661 Electronic computers; computer peripheral equipment; disk drives, computer; telephones & telephone apparatus; facsimile equipment; computers, peripherals & software
HQ: Toshiba America Inc
1251 Ave Of Ameri Ste 4100
New York NY 10020
212 596-0600

(G-12398)
TOSHIBA AMERICA INC (HQ)
1251 Ave Of Ameri Ste 4100 (10020)
PHONE..................................212 596-0600
Fax: 212 593-3875
Hideo Ito, *CEO*
Takeshi Okatomi, *Ch of Bd*
Hiromitsu Igarashi, *President*
Hisashi Izumi, *President*
Toru Uchiike, *President*
◆ **EMP:** 28
SALES (est): 4.3B
SALES (corp-wide): 42.8B **Privately Held**
SIC: 3651 3631 5064 5075 Television receiving sets; video cassette recorders/players & accessories; microwave ovens, including portable; household; video cassette recorders & accessories; high fidelity equipment; compressors, air conditioning; personal computers (microcomputers); multiplex equipment, telephone & telegraph
PA: Toshiba Corporation
1-1-1, Shibaura
Minato-Ku TKY 105-0
334 574-511

(G-12399)
TOTAL CONCEPT GRAPHIC INC
519 8th Ave Rm 805a (10018-5182)
PHONE..................................212 229-2626
Fax: 212 229-2677
Joe Ferrara, *President*
John Chessa, *Vice Pres*
EMP: 4
SQ FT: 500
SALES (est): 2MM **Privately Held**
SIC: 2752 Commercial printing, offset

(G-12400)
TOTAL OFFSET INC
Also Called: Total Offset Graphic
200 Hudson St Fl 11 (10013-1807)
PHONE..................................212 966-4482
Fax: 212 219-3009
Phil Deluca, *President*
George Stern, *Treasurer*
EMP: 11
SQ FT: 3,600
SALES (est): 1.1MM **Privately Held**
SIC: 3555 Plates, offset

(G-12401)
TOTO USA INC
20 W 22nd St Frnt 2 (10010-5887)
PHONE..................................917 237-0665
Kazuo Sako, *Principal*
EMP: 5
SALES (corp-wide): 5B **Privately Held**
SIC: 3432 Plumbing fixture fittings & trim
HQ: Toto U.S.A., Inc.
1800 Murphy Ave Sw
Atlanta GA 30310
404 752-8998

(G-12402)
TOTO USA INC
20 W 22nd St Frnt 2 (10010-5887)
PHONE..................................770 282-8686
Fax: 917 237-0654
Kazuo Sako, *Principal*
Lori Peterson, *Human Res Mgr*
Ivette Cardenas, *Sales Staff*
EMP: 5
SALES (est): 483.1K **Privately Held**
SIC: 3432 Plumbing fixture fittings & trim

(G-12403)
TOUCHTUNES MUSIC CORPORATION (HQ)
Also Called: Touch Tunes
850 3rd Ave Ste 15c (10022-7263)
PHONE..................................847 419-3300

New York - New York County (G-12404) **GEOGRAPHIC SECTION**

Fax: 646 365-0011
Charles Goldstuck, *CEO*
Ross Honey, *President*
Heather S Aguirre, *Counsel*
Marc Felsen, *Senior VP*
Vicki Saunders, *Senior VP*
EMP: 60
SALES (est): 8.5MM
SALES (corp-wide): 8.5MM **Privately Held**
SIC: 3651 Household audio & video equipment; audio electronic systems
PA: Searchlight Capital Partners, L.P.
745 5th Ave Fl 27
New York NY 10151
212 293-3730

(G-12404)
TOWNLEY INC
Also Called: Townley Cosmetics
10 W 33rd St Rm 418 (10001-3324)
PHONE..................................212 779-0544
Abraham Safdieh, *President*
Joe Gindi, *Vice Pres*
Wandy Abreau, *Controller*
Felena Jagarnauth, *VP Finance*
▲ **EMP:** 30
SQ FT: 9,000
SALES (est): 5.8MM **Privately Held**
SIC: 3915 Jewelers' materials & lapidary work

(G-12405)
TOYMAX INC (DH)
Also Called: Candy Planet Division
200 5th Ave (10010-3302)
PHONE..................................212 633-6611
David Ki Kwan Chu, *Ch of Bd*
Steven Lebensfeld, *President*
Carmine Russo, *COO*
Harvey Goldberg, *Exec VP*
Kenneth Price, *Senior VP*
EMP: 8
SQ FT: 30,000
SALES (est): 3.6MM **Publicly Held**
WEB: www.toymax.com
SIC: 3944 5092 Games, toys & children's vehicles; toys

(G-12406)
TR APPAREL LLC
609 Greenwich St Fl 3 (10014-3610)
PHONE..................................310 595-4337
Andrew Wong, *Branch Mgr*
EMP: 40
SALES (corp-wide): 10.3MM **Privately Held**
SIC: 2389 Academic vestments (caps & gowns)
HQ: Tr Apparel, Llc
609 Greenwich St Fl 3
New York NY 10014

(G-12407)
TR APPAREL LLC (HQ)
Also Called: Row, The
609 Greenwich St Fl 3 (10014-3610)
PHONE..................................646 358-3888
Francois Kress, *President*
Ashley Olsen, *Owner*
Mary Kate Olsen, *Owner*
Isabella Isbiroglu, *Pub Rel Mgr*
Greg Eyink, *CFO*
EMP: 9
SALES (est): 10.9MM **Privately Held**
WEB: www.therow.com
SIC: 2389 Academic vestments (caps & gowns)
PA: Dualstar Entertainment Group Llc
3525 Hayden Ave
Culver City CA 10014
310 945-3705

(G-12408)
TR DESIGNS INC
Also Called: Tracy Reese
260 W 39th St Fl 19 (10018-0360)
PHONE..................................212 398-9300
ADI Kandel, *President*
Tracy Reese, *Principal*
Om Batheja, *Vice Pres*
▲ **EMP:** 32
SQ FT: 11,000
SALES (est): 4.1MM **Privately Held**
SIC: 2339 Sportswear, women's

(G-12409)
TRADER JOES COMPANY
Also Called: Trader Joe's 541
138 E 14th St (10003-4170)
PHONE..................................212 529-6326
John Martinelli, *Manager*
EMP: 40 **Privately Held**
SIC: 2084 Wines
HQ: Trader Joe's Company
800 S Shamrock Ave
Monrovia CA 91016
626 599-3700

(G-12410)
TRADING SERVICES INTERNATIONAL
Also Called: Tsi Technologies
133 W 72nd St Rm 601 (10023-3236)
PHONE..................................212 501-0142
Joel Darr, *President*
Judy Darr, *Vice Pres*
▲ **EMP:** 14
SQ FT: 2,000
SALES (est): 24MM **Privately Held**
WEB: www.tsitec.com
SIC: 3679 5013 Electronic circuits; motor vehicle supplies & new parts

(G-12411)
TRAFALGAR COMPANY LLC (HQ)
417 5th Ave Fl 11 (10016-2238)
PHONE..................................212 768-8800
Jeffrey Spiegel, *Mng Member*
John Hastings,
▲ **EMP:** 5 **EST:** 2003
SQ FT: 6,500
SALES (est): 626.9K
SALES (corp-wide): 126.8MM **Privately Held**
WEB: www.ghurka.com
SIC: 2387 3172 3161 2389 Apparel belts; wallets; attache cases; briefcases; suitcases; suspenders
PA: Randa Accessories Leather Goods Llc
5600 N River Rd Ste 500
Rosemont IL 60018
847 292-8300

(G-12412)
TRANS-HIGH CORPORATION
250 W 57th St Ste 920 (10107-0003)
PHONE..................................212 387-0500
Mary McCvoy, *Principal*
EMP: 22 **EST:** 2013
SALES (est): 2.7MM **Privately Held**
SIC: 2721 Magazines: publishing & printing

(G-12413)
TRANS-LUX CORPORATION (PA)
445 Park Ave Ste 2001 (10022-8613)
PHONE..................................800 243-5544
George W Schiele, *Ch of Bd*
Jean-Marc Allain, *President*
Alberto Shaio, *COO*
Alexandro Gomez, *Senior VP*
Todd Dupee, *Vice Pres*
EMP: 80 **EST:** 1920
SALES: 21.1MM **Publicly Held**
WEB: www.trans-lux.com
SIC: 3993 Electric signs

(G-12414)
TRANSPARENCY LIFE SCIENCES LLC
225 W 60th St Apt 15d (10023-7430)
PHONE..................................862 252-1216
Alex Greenberg, *Marketing Mgr*
Jen Nwankwo, *Marketing Staff*
Lisa Abrams, *Director*
Tomasz Sablinski,
Marc Foster,
EMP: 10
SALES (est): 771.7K **Privately Held**
SIC: 2834 Pharmaceutical preparations

(G-12415)
TRASH AND VAUDEVILLE INC
96 E 7th St Frnt A (10009-8042)
PHONE..................................212 777-1727
Diana Otoole, *Manager*
EMP: 6
SALES (corp-wide): 1MM **Privately Held**
SIC: 2389 Men's miscellaneous accessories
PA: Trash And Vaudeville, Inc.
5200 W Side Ave
North Bergen NJ 07047
201 520-0420

(G-12416)
TRAVIS AYERS INC
Also Called: Isabel and Nina
1412 Broadway Fl 8 (10018-3528)
PHONE..................................212 921-5165
Fax: 212 921-5068
Maia Chiat, *President*
Fred Chill, *Vice Pres*
Cheryl Feld, *Vice Pres*
Karen Wilson, *Accounting Dir*
Frank Rascati, *Manager*
EMP: 21
SQ FT: 4,000
SALES (est): 1.3MM **Privately Held**
SIC: 2337 5137 Suits: women's, misses' & juniors'; suits: women's, children's & infants'

(G-12417)
TREAUU INC
60 E 120th St Fl 2 (10035-3571)
PHONE..................................703 731-0196
Tahira White, *Principal*
Marcus Scott, *Principal*
EMP: 6
SALES (est): 340K **Privately Held**
SIC: 7372 7389 Application computer software;

(G-12418)
TREBBIANNO LLC (PA)
Also Called: Lucky Brand
19 W 34th St Fl 7 (10001-0055)
PHONE..................................212 868-2770
Terry McCormick, *President*
Victoria Maresco, *CFO*
Richard Schaefer, *CFO*
▲ **EMP:** 49
SQ FT: 25,000
SALES (est): 29.9MM **Privately Held**
SIC: 3111 Handbag leather

(G-12419)
TRENDSFORMERS LTD LIABILITY CO
Also Called: Trensdformers
150 W 56th St Apt 6406 (10019-3848)
PHONE..................................888 700-2423
David Klar,
EMP: 4
SQ FT: 5,000
SALES (est): 2MM **Privately Held**
SIC: 3999 8748 Atomizers, toiletry; business consulting

(G-12420)
TRI-FORCE SALES LLC
767 3rd Ave Rm 35b (10017-2082)
PHONE..................................732 261-5507
Robert Bracebic, *President*
Scp Crusader LLC, *Principal*
Matthew Marone, *Vice Pres*
Hemang Mehta, *Vice Pres*
▼ **EMP:** 24 **EST:** 2008
SQ FT: 5,500
SALES: 12MM **Privately Held**
SIC: 3999 8742 Models, except toy; marketing consulting services

(G-12421)
TRI-LON CLOR LITHOGRAPHERS LTD
Also Called: Trilon Color Lithographers
233 Spring St Frnt 9th (10013-1522)
PHONE..................................212 255-6140
Fax: 212 929-1690
Marc Strickler, *President*
David Strickler, *Chairman*
Esther Strickler, *Corp Secy*
Dave Strickler, *Vice Pres*
EMP: 26 **EST:** 1964
SQ FT: 10,000
SALES (est): 3.4MM **Privately Held**
SIC: 2752 2791 2789 2759 Commercial printing, lithographic; typesetting; bookbinding & related work; commercial printing

(G-12422)
TRI-PLEX PACKAGING CORPORATION
307 5th Ave Fl 7 (10016-6574)
PHONE..................................212 481-6070
Fax: 212 481-1550
Ken Golden, *President*
Barry Walsh, *Opers Staff*
Ron Verblaauw, *CFO*
Adam Caraher, *Director*
▲ **EMP:** 26
SALES (est): 10MM **Privately Held**
WEB: www.lieberman-nyc.com
SIC: 3999 2671 Advertising display products; paper coated or laminated for packaging

(G-12423)
TRI-STATE BRICK & STONE NY INC (PA)
333 7th Ave Fl 5 (10001-5829)
PHONE..................................212 366-0300
Fax: 212 366-0339
Robert Turzilli, *President*
Michael Falcone, *Vice Pres*
Vincent Falcone, *Vice Pres*
Louis J Formica, *Vice Pres*
▲ **EMP:** 60
SQ FT: 6,500
SALES (est): 24.4MM **Privately Held**
SIC: 2421 5031 Building & structural materials, wood; building materials, exterior

(G-12424)
TRIANON COLLECTION INC
16 W 46th St Fl 10 (10036-4503)
PHONE..................................212 921-9450
Fax: 212 921-9454
Anthony Hopenka JM, *CEO*
Joseph Bauer, *President*
Anthony Hopenhajm, *Vice Pres*
Manny Walia, *Accountant*
▲ **EMP:** 24
SQ FT: 3,390
SALES (est): 3MM **Privately Held**
WEB: www.trianonnet.com
SIC: 3911 Jewelry, precious metal
PA: Banisa Corporation
21860 Masters Cir
Estero FL 33928
239 949-2309

(G-12425)
TRIBUNE ENTERTAINMENT CO DEL
220 E 42nd St Fl 26 (10017-5806)
PHONE..................................203 866-2204
Milan Chilla, *Sales Mgr*
Michael Fischer, *Manager*
EMP: 40
SALES (corp-wide): 1.9B **Publicly Held**
SIC: 2711 2741 4833 Newspapers, publishing & printing; miscellaneous publishing; television broadcasting stations
HQ: Tribune Entertainment Company (Del)
435 N Michigan Ave Fl 19
Chicago IL 60611
312 222-4441

(G-12426)
TRICYCLE FOUNDATION INC
89 5th Ave Ste 301 (10003-3020)
PHONE..................................800 873-9871
Fax: 212 645-1493
Elizabeth Lees, *President*
Emma Varvaloucas, *Editor*
Alyssa Snow, *Controller*
Joellen Sommer, *Controller*
James Shaheen, *Exec Dir*
EMP: 9
SQ FT: 2,500
SALES: 1.5MM **Privately Held**
SIC: 2711 Newspapers: publishing only, not printed on site

(G-12427)
TRIMASTER/HTECH HOLDING LLC (HQ)
590 Madison Ave Fl 27 (10022-2544)
PHONE..................................212 257-6772
EMP: 4
SALES (est): 18.7MM **Privately Held**
SIC: 3544 3545 Special dies, tools, jigs & fixtures; precision tools, machinists'

GEOGRAPHIC SECTION

New York - New York County (G-12452)

(G-12428)
TRITON INFOSYS INC
1230 Avenue Of The Americ (10020-1513)
PHONE...................................877 308-2388
Mike Patel, *President*
Babubhai Patel, *Shareholder*
EMP: 30
SALES (est): 3.2MM **Privately Held**
SIC: 3699 Security devices; security control equipment & systems

(G-12429)
TRIUMPH APPAREL CORPORATION (PA)
530 Fashion Ave Ste M1 (10018-4878)
PHONE...................................212 302-2606
Carol Hockman, *President*
Donald Schupak, *Principal*
Philip Davis, *Vice Pres*
John A Sarto, *CFO*
Henry T Mortmer Jr, *Director*
▲ **EMP:** 42
SALES (est): 87.7MM **Privately Held**
WEB: www.danskin.com
SIC: 2331 Women's & misses' blouses & shirts

(G-12430)
TRIUMPH LEARNING LLC (DH)
Also Called: Options Publishing
136 Madison Ave (10016-6711)
PHONE...................................212 652-0200
Fax: 212 652-0277
Rick Noble, *President*
Thomas Emrick, *President*
Brad Peters, *President*
Amy Goodale, *Editor*
Marilyn Locker, *Editor*
▲ **EMP:** 50 **EST:** 1963
SALES (est): 20.7MM
SALES (corp-wide): 96.4MM **Privately Held**
SIC: 2741 Miscellaneous publishing
HQ: Haights Cross Operating Company
10 New King St Ste 102
White Plains NY 10604
914 289-9400

(G-12431)
TROPP PRINTING CORP
Also Called: Tropp Prntng
181 Broadway Fl 3 (10007-3129)
PHONE...................................212 233-4519
Fax: 212 791-2953
Lee Tropp, *President*
William Tropp, *Vice Pres*
EMP: 6
SQ FT: 4,000
SALES (est): 757.5K **Privately Held**
SIC: 2752 Commercial printing, offset; lithographing on metal

(G-12432)
TRUEEX LLC
162 5th Ave Ste 900 (10010-5972)
PHONE...................................646 786-8526
Sunil Hirani, *CEO*
Karen O'Connor, *COO*
Christina Landry, *Project Mgr*
Diane Bartone, *Opers Mgr*
Raymond Jeong, *Engineer*
EMP: 48
SALES (est): 381.9K **Privately Held**
SIC: 7372 Business oriented computer software

(G-12433)
TRUNK & TROLLEY LLC
15 W 34th St (10001-3215)
PHONE...................................212 947-9001
Jade Corff, *Manager*
Sammy Sitt,
Steven Russo,
▲ **EMP:** 5
SQ FT: 25,000
SALES (est): 290K **Privately Held**
SIC: 3161 Luggage

(G-12434)
TRUST OF COLUM UNIVE IN THE CI
Also Called: Columbia Univ Publications
2929 Broadway Fl 3 (10025-7819)
PHONE...................................212 854-2793
Fax: 212 854-9509

Sandy Kaufman, *Director*
EMP: 19
SALES (corp-wide): 3.8B **Privately Held**
WEB: www.columbia.edu
SIC: 2754 8221 Labels: gravure printing; letter, circular & form: gravure printing; university
PA: The Trustees Of Columbia University In The City Of New York
116th And Bdwy Way
New York NY 10027
212 854-9970

(G-12435)
TRUSTED MEDIA BRANDS INC (HQ)
Also Called: Reader's Digest
750 3rd Ave Fl 3 (10017-2723)
PHONE...................................914 238-1000
Fax: 914 238-4559
Randall Curran, *Ch of Bd*
Bonnie Kintzer, *President*
Lorraine Burton, *Editor*
Lee Dashiell, *Editor*
Spencer Mary, *Editor*
◆ **EMP:** 1100 **EST:** 1922
SQ FT: 445,193
SALES (est): 1.3B **Privately Held**
WEB: www.rd.com
SIC: 2721 2731 5961 2741 Magazines: publishing only, not printed on site; books: publishing only; books, mail order (except book clubs); record &/or tape (music or video) club, mail order; miscellaneous publishing
PA: Rda Holding Co.
750 3rd Ave
New York NY 10017
914 238-1000

(G-12436)
TRUSTED MEDIA BRANDS INC
Reader's Digest
750 3rd Ave Fl 4 (10017-2723)
PHONE...................................646 293-6025
Fax: 212 696-9608
Linda Vaughan, *Publisher*
Randee Cohen, *Editor*
Richard Hessney, *Editor*
Jennifer Lenhart, *Editor*
Patricia Nolan, *Prdtn Mgr*
EMP: 16
SQ FT: 30,000
SALES (corp-wide): 1.3B **Privately Held**
WEB: www.rd.com
SIC: 2721 2731 Magazines: publishing only, not printed on site; books: publishing only
HQ: Trusted Media Brands, Inc.
750 3rd Ave Fl 3
New York NY 10017
914 238-1000

(G-12437)
TRYP TIMES SQUARE
234 W 48th St (10036-1540)
PHONE...................................212 246-8800
EMP: 6
SALES (est): 111.5K **Privately Held**
SIC: 2711 Newspapers

(G-12438)
TSAR USA LLC
99 Madison Ave Fl 5 (10016-7419)
PHONE...................................646 415-7968
Lucy Tupu, *General Mgr*
David Sharpley, *Mng Member*
▲ **EMP:** 12 **EST:** 2011
SALES (est): 1.4MM
SALES (corp-wide): 1.5MM **Privately Held**
SIC: 2273 Carpets, hand & machine made
PA: Dakee Australia Pty. Ltd.
3 Wellington Street
St Kilda VIC 3182
395 250-488

(G-12439)
TSS-TRANSPORT SNLTN SSTMS
20 W 22nd St Ste 612 (10010-6067)
PHONE...................................917 267-8534
Alex Gerodimos, *President*
Alejandro Molina, *Managing Dir*
Josep Aymami, *Sr Project Mgr*
Nadia Feddo, *Officer*
EMP: 5

SALES (est): 593.1K **Privately Held**
SIC: 7372 Prepackaged software
PA: Tss Transport Simulation Systems Sl
Ronda Universitat, 22 - At
Barcelona 08007

(G-12440)
TTG LLC
Also Called: Titan Technology Group
115 W 30th St Rm 209 (10001-4218)
PHONE...................................917 777-0959
Jessica Densky, *Marketing Staff*
Mark Liebmam, *Mng Member*
Paula Deverse, *Manager*
Tom Skovran, *Manager*
Danny Keren,
EMP: 9
SQ FT: 1,600
SALES (est): 968.9K **Privately Held**
WEB: www.titantechgroup.com
SIC: 7372 Prepackaged software

(G-12441)
TUCANO USA INC
77 Bleecker St Apt C212 (10012-1586)
PHONE...................................212 966-9211
Franco Luini, *President*
Sergio Musati, *Exec VP*
Mattia Cesco, *Manager*
◆ **EMP:** 6
SQ FT: 1,200
SALES (est): 4.8MM **Privately Held**
SIC: 3199 Leather garments

(G-12442)
TUDOR ELECTRICAL SUPPLY CO INC
137 W 24th St (10011-1901)
PHONE...................................212 867-7550
Jay Wittner, *President*
Steve Kramer, *Vice Pres*
EMP: 8
SQ FT: 8,500
SALES (est): 1.4MM **Privately Held**
SIC: 3645 5063 Residential lighting fixtures; electrical supplies

(G-12443)
TULA LIFE LLC
660 Madison Ave Ste 1600 (10065-8418)
PHONE...................................201 895-3309
Julia Strauss, *Mng Member*
Andi Christian,
Julia Straus,
EMP: 6 **EST:** 2013
SALES (est): 349.9K **Privately Held**
SIC: 2844 Toilet preparations

(G-12444)
TUMI INC
261 5th Ave Rm 2010 (10016-7704)
PHONE...................................212 447-8747
Jamie Webb, *Vice Pres*
EMP: 160 **Privately Held**
SIC: 3161 Hat boxes
HQ: Tumi, Inc.
1001 Durham Ave Ste 1b
South Plainfield NJ 07080
908 756-4400

(G-12445)
TUMI INC
Also Called: Tumi Stores
67 Wall St Frnt 3 (10005-3101)
PHONE...................................212 742-8020
Larry Holmes, *Branch Mgr*
EMP: 160 **Privately Held**
SIC: 3161 Traveling bags; attache cases; cases, carrying; briefcases
HQ: Tumi, Inc.
1001 Durham Ave Ste 1b
South Plainfield NJ 07080
908 756-4400

(G-12446)
TURN ON PRODUCTS INC (PA)
Also Called: Almost Famous Clothing
270 W 38th St Rm 1200 (10018-1573)
PHONE...................................212 764-2121
Peter Kossoy, *President*
Robert Regina, *Vice Pres*
Marc Wasserman, *CFO*
Desiree Reghubeer, *Controller*
▲ **EMP:** 80
SQ FT: 20,000

SALES (est): 123.9MM **Privately Held**
WEB: www.youniqueclothing.com
SIC: 2339 2331 Sportswear, women's; women's & misses' blouses & shirts

(G-12447)
TURN ON PRODUCTS INC
Also Called: Younique Clothing
525 7th Ave Rm 1403 (10018-4967)
PHONE...................................212 764-4545
Fax: 212 768-1289
Peter Kossoy, *President*
EMP: 12
SALES (corp-wide): 123.9MM **Privately Held**
WEB: www.youniqueclothing.com
SIC: 2331 2339 2337 2335 Blouses, women's & juniors': made from purchased material; slacks: women's, misses' & juniors'; skirts, separate: women's, misses' & juniors'; women's, juniors' & misses' dresses
PA: Turn On Products Inc.
270 W 38th St Rm 1200
New York NY 10018
212 764-2121

(G-12448)
TV GUIDE MAGAZINE LLC (HQ)
50 Rockefeller Plz Fl 14 (10020-1617)
P.O. Box 37360 (10020)
PHONE...................................800 866-1400
Fax: 212 852-7323
David J Fishman, *CEO*
Angel Gonzalez, *Opers Staff*
Michell Lindquist, *CFO*
Mark Gudewitz, *Manager*
Nerina Rammairone, *Senior Editor*
EMP: 5
SALES (est): 115.2MM
SALES (corp-wide): 117.4MM **Privately Held**
SIC: 2721 Magazines: publishing & printing
PA: Ntvb Media, Inc.
209 Park Dr
Troy MI 48083
248 583-4190

(G-12449)
TV GUIDE MAGAZINE GROUP INC (DH)
1211 Ave Of The Americas (10036-8701)
PHONE...................................212 852-7500
John Loughlin, *CEO*
Stacy Jolna, *Senior VP*
Danila Koverman, *Senior VP*
Kayne Lanahan, *Senior VP*
Stacy Lifton, *Senior VP*
▲ **EMP:** 100 **EST:** 2008
SQ FT: 40,000
SALES (est): 10.6MM
SALES (corp-wide): 117.4MM **Privately Held**
SIC: 2721 Magazines: publishing only, not printed on site; television schedules: publishing only, not printed on site

(G-12450)
TWCC PRODUCT AND SALES
122 5th Ave (10011-5605)
PHONE...................................212 614-9364
Katrina Hanritty, *Vice Pres*
EMP: 50
SALES (est): 2.7MM **Privately Held**
SIC: 2389 7389 Apparel & accessories; design services

(G-12451)
TWIST INTIMATE GROUP LLC (PA)
Also Called: Twist Intimate Apparel
35 W 35th St Rm 903 (10001-2238)
PHONE...................................212 695-5990
David Sutton, *VP Sales*
Jack Saldar, *Mng Member*
David Sutone,
◆ **EMP:** 7
SQ FT: 5,000
SALES (est): 1.1MM **Privately Held**
SIC: 2322 Underwear, men's & boys': made from purchased materials

(G-12452)
TWO PALMS PRESS INC
476 Broadway Ste 3f (10013-2641)
PHONE...................................212 965-8598

New York - New York County (G-12453)

David Lasry, *President*
Abelan Lasry, *Co-Owner*
EMP: 10
SALES: 950K **Privately Held**
WEB: www.twopalmspress.com
SIC: 2741 Miscellaneous publishing

(G-12453)
TWP AMERICA INC (DH)
Also Called: Tien Wah Press
299 Broadway Ste 720 (10007-1987)
PHONE.................................212 274-8090
Fax: 212 274-0771
Christina Hockin, *Vice Pres*
Bella Lukovsky, *Sales Dir*
Gary Watson, *Manager*
Deah Gerard, *Officer*
◆ **EMP:** 7
SQ FT: 4,500
SALES (est): 508.8K
SALES (corp-wide): 12.4B **Privately Held**
WEB: www.twpny.com
SIC: 2732 Books: printing only
HQ: Tien Wah Press (Pte.) Limited
  4 Pandan Crescent
  Singapore 12847
  646 662-22

(G-12454)
TYCOON INTERNATIONAL INC
3436 W 32nd St Fl 4 (10001)
PHONE.................................212 563-7107
Young Eun Kin, *President*
▲ **EMP:** 6
SALES (est): 682.8K **Privately Held**
SIC: 3961 Costume jewelry

(G-12455)
TYME GLOBAL TECHNOLOGIES LLC
Also Called: Hotelexpert
60 W 66th St Apt 15a (10023-6288)
PHONE.................................212 796-1950
David Cristescu, *CFO*
Ryan Levin,
EMP: 21
SALES (est): 437.5K **Privately Held**
SIC: 7372 Business oriented computer software

(G-12456)
TYME TECHNOLOGIES INC (PA)
44 Wall St Fl 12 (10005-2433)
PHONE.................................646 205-1603
Steve Hoffman, *CEO*
Michael Demurjian, *COO*
Robert Dickey IV, *CFO*
Giuseppe Del Priore, *Chief Mktg Ofcr*
EMP: 9
SALES (est): 849.8K **Publicly Held**
SIC: 2834 Pharmaceutical preparations

(G-12457)
U S JAPAN PUBLICATION NY INC
147 W 35th St Ste 1705 (10001-2100)
PHONE.................................212 252-8833
Nobuo Ijichi, *Ch of Bd*
Yoshimi Kiyoshi, *Editor*
Akiko Omori, *Marketing Staff*
Kazuyo Nakagawa, *Manager*
Naoki Hishida, *Art Dir*
▲ **EMP:** 7
SQ FT: 2,500
SALES (est): 760K **Privately Held**
SIC: 2721 Magazines: publishing only, not printed on site

(G-12458)
UBM INC
2 Penn Plz (10121-0101)
PHONE.................................212 600-3000
David Levin, *CEO*
Kevin Cronin, *Editor*
Norbert Sparrow, *Editor*
Tim Wilson, *Editor*
Greg McDonald, *Business Mgr*
EMP: 3500
SALES: 228.8MM
SALES (corp-wide): 1B **Privately Held**
WEB: www.unm.com
SIC: 2721 2711 8732 2741 Periodicals; newspapers; commercial nonphysical research; business research service; business service newsletters: publishing & printing
PA: Ubm Plc
  240 Blackfriars Road
  London SE1 8
  207 921-5000

(G-12459)
UBM LLC
Also Called: Cmp Media
2 Penn Plz Fl 15 (10121-1700)
PHONE.................................516 562-5000
Fax: 516 562-5131
Michael Duck, *Senior VP*
Pamala McGlinchey, *Vice Pres*
Jason Kates, *Technical Mgr*
Maureen Passaro, *Accounting Mgr*
Edwin Lothrock, *Director*
EMP: 10
SALES (corp-wide): 1B **Privately Held**
WEB: www.cmp.com
SIC: 2711 2721 Commercial printing & newspaper publishing combined; magazines: publishing & printing
HQ: Ubm Llc
  1983 Marcus Ave Ste 250
  New Hyde Park NY 11042
  516 562-7800

(G-12460)
UDISENSE INC
Also Called: Nannit
620 8th Ave Fl 38 (10018-1442)
PHONE.................................858 442-9875
Assaf Glazer, *CEO*
Andrew Berman, *COO*
Tor Ivry, *Officer*
EMP: 8
SQ FT: 10,000
SALES (est): 670.9K **Privately Held**
SIC: 7372 Home entertainment computer software

(G-12461)
UFO CONTEMPORARY INC
42 W 38th St Rm 1204 (10018-0054)
P.O. Box 20505 (10017-0005)
PHONE.................................212 226-5400
Fax: 212 219-8928
Lorna Brody, *President*
▲ **EMP:** 10
SALES (est): 1.1MM **Privately Held**
WEB: www.ufojeans.com
SIC: 2389 Men's miscellaneous accessories

(G-12462)
UFX HOLDING I CORPORATION (HQ)
55 E 52nd St Fl 35 (10055-0110)
PHONE.................................212 644-5900
Vincent MAI, *Principal*
▲ **EMP:** 1
SALES (est): 61.3MM
SALES (corp-wide): 2.5B **Privately Held**
SIC: 3299 Ceramic fiber
PA: Aea Investors Lp
  666 5th Ave Fl 36
  New York NY 10103
  212 644-5900

(G-12463)
UFX HOLDING II CORPORATION (DH)
55 E 52nd St Fl 35 (10055-0110)
PHONE.................................212 644-5900
Vincent MAI, *Principal*
EMP: 1
SALES (est): 61.3MM
SALES (corp-wide): 2.5B **Privately Held**
SIC: 3299 Ceramic fiber

(G-12464)
UIPATH
311 W 43rd St Fl 13 (10036-6003)
PHONE.................................844 432-0455
Daniel Dines, *Owner*
Coenraad Van Der Poel, *Managing Dir*
EMP: 245
SALES: 5.8MM **Privately Held**
SIC: 3569 Robots, assembly line: industrial & commercial

(G-12465)
UNCHARTED PLAY INC
246 Lenox Ave (10027-5543)
PHONE.................................646 675-7783
Jessica O Matthews, *Ch of Bd*
Christopher Strunk, *Finance*
Nicholas Navarro, *Director*
▲ **EMP:** 25
SALES (est): 4.3MM **Privately Held**
SIC: 3699 Generators, ultrasonic

(G-12466)
UNCO UNITED OIL HOLDINGS LLC
100 Park Ave Fl 16 (10017-5538)
PHONE.................................212 481-1003
Paulette Long, *President*
John C Long, *Treasurer*
EMP: 10 **EST:** 2006
SQ FT: 2,400
SALES: 1.4MM **Privately Held**
SIC: 1382 Oil & gas exploration services

(G-12467)
UNDERLINE COMMUNICATIONS LLC
12 W 27th St Fl 14 (10001-6903)
PHONE.................................212 994-4340
Fax: 212 686-8224
Monika Gmochowska, *President*
Liyo Hsieh, *Project Mgr*
Ariella Raviv, *Production*
Michelle Duda, *Director*
Joshua McFarren, *Director*
EMP: 10
SALES (est): 1.3MM **Privately Held**
WEB: www.underlinecom.com
SIC: 2741 Miscellaneous publishing

(G-12468)
UNI JEWELRY INC
48 W 48th St Ste 1401 (10036-1718)
PHONE.................................212 398-1818
Frank Lee, *President*
▲ **EMP:** 7
SQ FT: 1,000
SALES (est): 540K **Privately Held**
SIC: 3911 5094 Jewelry, precious metal; jewelry

(G-12469)
UNICOM GRAPHIC COMMUNICATIONS
230 Park Ave Rm 1000 (10169-1001)
PHONE.................................212 221-2456
Khaled Sawaf, *President*
Karim Sawaf, *Vice Pres*
EMP: 7
SQ FT: 1,500
SALES: 3MM
SALES (corp-wide): 452.3K **Privately Held**
SIC: 2752 Commercial printing, offset
PA: Unicom Communications Graphiques Inc
  5000 Rue Jean-Talon O Bureau 100
  Montreal QC H4P 1

(G-12470)
UNIFIED INC IED
35 W 36th St (10018-7906)
PHONE.................................646 370-4650
EMP: 10
SALES (est): 500K **Privately Held**
SIC: 2389 Mfg Apparel/Accessories

(G-12471)
UNIFIED MEDIA INC
180 Madison Ave Lbby L (10016-5267)
PHONE.................................917 595-2710
Sheldon Owen, *CEO*
Pushp Kumar, *COO*
Roger Clark, *CFO*
Amanda Baldauf, *Accounts Mgr*
Adam Ops, *Manager*
EMP: 19
SALES (est): 1.2MM **Privately Held**
SIC: 2711 Newspapers, publishing & printing

(G-12472)
UNIFOR INC
149 5th Ave Ste 3r (10010-6899)
PHONE.................................212 673-3434
Fax: 212 673-7317
Gianfranco Marinelli, *President*
Mersiha Makota, *Project Mgr*
Shannon Devine, *Comms Dir*
Matthew Pych, *Manager*
▲ **EMP:** 19
SALES (est): 3MM **Privately Held**
SIC: 2531 Public building & related furniture

(G-12473)
UNIFRAX HOLDING CO (DH)
55 E 52nd St Fl 35 (10055-0110)
PHONE.................................212 644-5900
Joseph D Carrabino, *Managing Dir*
Martin C Eltrich, *Managing Dir*
Daniel H Klebes, *Managing Dir*
Vincent MAI, *Principal*
EMP: 1
SALES (est): 61.3MM
SALES (corp-wide): 2.5B **Privately Held**
SIC: 3299 Ceramic fiber
HQ: Ufx Holding Ii Corporation
  55 E 52nd St Fl 35
  New York NY 10055
  212 644-5900

(G-12474)
UNILEVER UNITED STATES INC
390 Park Ave (10022-4608)
PHONE.................................212 546-0200
Fax: 212 906-4666
Anil Dhiman, *Manager*
Amanda Koval, *Manager*
EMP: 10
SALES (corp-wide): 55.5B **Privately Held**
SIC: 2035 2086 2024 2038 Pickles, sauces & salad dressings; dressings, salad: raw & cooked (except dry mixes); mayonnaise; spreads, sandwich: salad dressing base; bottled & canned soft drinks; ice cream & frozen desserts; frozen specialties; toilet preparations; toothpastes or powders, dentifrices; hair preparations, including shampoos; cosmetic preparations; detergents, synthetic organic or inorganic alkaline; dishwashing compounds; soap: granulated, liquid, cake, flaked or chip
HQ: Unilever United States, Inc.
  700 Sylvan Ave
  Englewood Cliffs NJ 07632
  201 894-4000

(G-12475)
UNILEVER UNITED STATES INC
Also Called: Elizabeth Arden
663 5th Ave Fl 8 (10022-5328)
PHONE.................................212 546-0200
Fax: 212 546-0304
Teresa McKee, *Manager*
EMP: 250
SALES (corp-wide): 55.5B **Privately Held**
WEB: www.unilever.com
SIC: 2035 2086 2024 2038 Pickles, sauces & salad dressings; dressings, salad: raw & cooked (except dry mixes); mayonnaise; spreads, sandwich: salad dressing base; bottled & canned soft drinks; ice cream & frozen desserts; frozen specialties; toilet preparations; toothpastes or powders, dentifrices; hair preparations, including shampoos; cosmetic preparations; detergents, synthetic organic or inorganic alkaline; dishwashing compounds; soap: granulated, liquid, cake, flaked or chip
HQ: Unilever United States, Inc.
  700 Sylvan Ave
  Englewood Cliffs NJ 07632
  201 894-4000

(G-12476)
UNIMAX SUPPLY CO INC (PA)
269 Canal St (10013-3568)
PHONE.................................212 925-1051
Fax: 646 925-7424
Westley Wood, *President*
▲ **EMP:** 27
SQ FT: 10,000
SALES (est): 2.8MM **Privately Held**
WEB: www.unimaxsupply.com
SIC: 3911 Earrings, precious metal

(G-12477)
UNIMEX CORPORATION (PA)
Also Called: Lee Spring Company Div
54 E 64th St (10065-7306)
PHONE.................................212 755-8800
Fax: 212 486-5737
Arthur L Carter, *Ch of Bd*
Tom Scheinman, *President*

GEOGRAPHIC SECTION

New York - New York County (G-12503)

Vincent A Bohn Jr, *Vice Pres*
Brian G Kempner, *Vice Pres*
Ezra Berger, *Treasurer*
EMP: 100
SQ FT: 10,000
SALES (est): 43.6MM **Privately Held**
SIC: 3495 Wire springs

(G-12478)
UNIPHARM INC (PA)
350 5th Ave Ste 6701 (10118-6708)
PHONE.................................212 564-3634
Victor Sapritsky, *President*
Robert D Sires, *President*
Chris Adamo, *General Mgr*
Bernie Hubert, *Buyer*
Rozalia Gandelman, *QC Dir*
▼ **EMP:** 30
SALES (est): 15.1MM **Privately Held**
WEB: www.unipharmus.com
SIC: 2834 5122 Vitamin preparations; vitamins & minerals

(G-12479)
UNIQLO USA LLC
546 Broadway (10012-3912)
PHONE.................................877 486-4756
Andrew Rosen, *Mng Member*
▲ **EMP:** 17
SALES (est): 1.9MM
SALES (corp-wide): 17.4B **Privately Held**
SIC: 2329 2337 5621 Sweaters & sweater jackets: men's & boys'; women's & misses' capes & jackets; women's clothing stores
PA: Fast Retailing Co., Ltd.
  9-7-1, Akasaka
  Minato-Ku TKY 107-0
  368 650-050

(G-12480)
UNIQUE DESIGNS INC
521 5th Ave Rm 820 (10175-0800)
PHONE.................................212 575-7701
Tejas Shah, *CEO*
Ben Yep, *President*
Chai Lin, *Vice Pres*
Karen Lin, *Controller*
Dolly Ng, *Office Mgr*
EMP: 19
SQ FT: 1,000
SALES (est): 52.6MM
SALES (corp-wide): 1.1B **Privately Held**
WEB: www.uniquedesigns.com
SIC: 3911 Jewelry, precious metal
PA: Kiran Gems Private Limited
  Fe-5011, G Block, Bandra Kurla Complex,
  Mumbai MH 40005
  224 050-4444

(G-12481)
UNIQUE PETZ LLC
10 W 33rd St Rm 220 (10001-3306)
PHONE.................................212 714-1800
Adam Ash, *President*
▲ **EMP:** 25
SALES: 20MM **Privately Held**
SIC: 3999 Pet supplies

(G-12482)
UNISYSTEMS INC (PA)
Also Called: Modern Publishing
155 E 55th St Apt 203 (10022-4051)
PHONE.................................212 826-0850
Fax: 212 759-9069
Larry Steinberg, *Ch of Bd*
Andrew Steinberg, *President*
Warren Cohen, *Exec VP*
Fill Lapinig, *Controller*
Shini Parker, *Administration*
▲ **EMP:** 34
SQ FT: 8,200
SALES (est): 3.6MM **Privately Held**
WEB: www.modernpublishing.com
SIC: 2731 Books: publishing only

(G-12483)
UNITED BROTHERS JEWELRY INC
Also Called: U B J
48 W 48th St Ste 700 (10036-1703)
PHONE.................................212 921-2558
Fax: 212 398-9482
Gabriel Nisanov, *CEO*
Roman Nisanov, *Vice Pres*

Israel Nisanov, *Treasurer*
Nadya Nisanov, *Manager*
Katanov Rafi, *Manager*
EMP: 50
SQ FT: 6,000
SALES (est): 4.4MM **Privately Held**
SIC: 3911 Jewelry, precious metal

(G-12484)
UNITED KNITWEAR INTERNATIONAL (PA)
1384 Broadway Rm 1210 (10018-0509)
PHONE.................................212 354-2920
Fax: 212 354-2921
Carlos Hausner, *President*
Winter Evans, *Sales Staff*
Shy Efter, *Manager*
▲ **EMP:** 3
SQ FT: 860
SALES (est): 4.4MM **Privately Held**
WEB: www.unitedknitwear.com
SIC: 2253 5136 5137 Sweaters & sweater coats, knit; men's & boys' clothing; women's & children's clothing

(G-12485)
UNITED RETAIL II
Also Called: Happy Sock
436 W Broadway (10012-3752)
PHONE.................................212 966-9692
EMP: 5 **EST:** 2013
SALES (est): 364.5K **Privately Held**
SIC: 2252 Socks

(G-12486)
UNITED STRUCTURE SOLUTION INC
240 W 65th St Apt 26c (10023-6412)
PHONE.................................347 227-7526
Ying Lu, *President*
Tc Yuan, *Project Mgr*
EMP: 15 **EST:** 2010
SALES (est): 2MM **Privately Held**
SIC: 3441 Fabricated structural metal

(G-12487)
UNITED SYNGGUE CNSRVTIVE JDISM (PA)
120 Broadway Ste 1540 (10271-0032)
PHONE.................................212 533-7800
Rabbi Steven Wernick, *CEO*
Rabbi Jerome Epstein, *Exec VP*
Abe Fried-Tanzer, *Project Dir*
Mark Gapski, *CFO*
Jeffrey S Krasnick, *Treasurer*
▲ **EMP:** 50
SQ FT: 50,000
SALES (est): 16.3MM **Privately Held**
WEB: www.uscj.org
SIC: 2731 8661 Books: publishing only; religious organizations

(G-12488)
UNITONE COMMUNICATION SYSTEMS
220 E 23rd St Ste 411 (10010-4659)
PHONE.................................212 777-9090
Fax: 212 777-9094
Lucien Bohbot, *President*
Preya Khusial, *Vice Pres*
Andrew Doilodov, *Manager*
EMP: 6
SALES (est): 983.4K **Privately Held**
WEB: www.unitonecom.com
SIC: 3669 7622 Burglar alarm apparatus, electric; fire alarm apparatus, electric; intercommunication systems, electric; communication equipment repair

(G-12489)
UNIVERSAL CMMNCATIONS OF MIAMI
Also Called: Elite Traveler Magazine
801 2nd Ave Lbby (10017-4706)
PHONE.................................212 986-5100
Geoffrey Lurie, *CEO*
Carl Reuderman, *Ch of Bd*
Douglas Gollan, *President*
Mikki Dorsey, *Exec VP*
Mikki Dosey, *Exec VP*
EMP: 125
SALES (est): 10.7MM **Privately Held**
SIC: 2721 Magazines: publishing & printing

(G-12490)
UNIVERSAL EDITION INC
Also Called: Ue Music
331 W 57th St Ste 380 (10019-3101)
PHONE.................................917 213-2177
Robert Thompson, *President*
Wolfgang Schaufler, *Manager*
▲ **EMP:** 65
SQ FT: 5,000
SALES: 8MM **Privately Held**
WEB: www.roxannapanufnik.com
SIC: 2741 Music books: publishing & printing

(G-12491)
UNIVERSAL ELLIOT CORP
327 W 36th St Rm 700 (10018-6929)
PHONE.................................212 736-8877
Fax: 212 736-8611
Mike Gadh, *President*
Ush Gadh, *Vice Pres*
Gurpal Gadh, *Admin Sec*
EMP: 9
SALES (est): 550K **Privately Held**
SIC: 2387 Apparel belts

(G-12492)
UNIVERSAL MUSIC GROUP INC
825 8th Ave Fl C2b (10019-7472)
PHONE.................................212 333-8237
Fax: 212 603-3971
Bill Evans, *Regional Mgr*
Greg Thompson, *Exec VP*
Chrisopher Atlas, *Senior VP*
Sheryl L Gold, *Senior VP*
Bob Schnieders, *Senior VP*
EMP: 10
SALES (corp-wide): 48.6MM **Privately Held**
SIC: 3652 Pre-recorded records & tapes
HQ: Universal Music Group, Inc.
  2220 Colorado Ave
  Santa Monica CA 90404
  310 865-4000

(G-12493)
UNLIMITED JEANS CO INC
401 Broadway Frnt A (10013-3005)
PHONE.................................212 661-6355
EMP: 12
SALES (corp-wide): 2MM **Privately Held**
SIC: 2253 Pants, slacks or trousers, knit
PA: Unlimited Jeans Co., Inc.
  850 2nd Ave
  New York NY 10017
  212 661-6355

(G-12494)
UNTUCKIT LLC
220 Lafayette St (10012-4079)
PHONE.................................201 214-9054
Chris Riccobono, *CEO*
Aaron Sanandres, *Co-CEO*
Gabrielle Gerstley, *Manager*
▲ **EMP:** 165
SALES (est): 450.3K **Privately Held**
SIC: 2326 2339 Men's & boys' work clothing; athletic clothing: women's, misses' & juniors'

(G-12495)
UPPER NINTY LLC
Also Called: Upper Ninty Soccer and Sport
697 Amsterdam Ave (10025-6933)
PHONE.................................646 863-3105
Jonathan Bennett, *Sales Executive*
Zac Rubin, *Manager*
Jack Rubin,
Douglas Gatanis,
Walker Latham, *Cashier*
EMP: 9
SALES (est): 2.7MM **Privately Held**
SIC: 3131 Uppers

(G-12496)
UPTOWN MEDIA GROUP LLC
113 E 125th St Frnt 1 (10035-1661)
PHONE.................................212 360-5073
Brett Wright,
Leonard Burnett,
EMP: 36
SALES (est): 4MM **Privately Held**
SIC: 2721 Magazines: publishing & printing

(G-12497)
UPTOWN NAILS LLC
500 5th Ave (10110-0002)
P.O. Box 20456 (10021-0067)
PHONE.................................800 748-1881
Fax: 212 398-7198
Larry G Kapfer, *Principal*
EMP: 106
SALES (est): 461.8K **Privately Held**
SIC: 3999 Fingernails, artificial

(G-12498)
URBAN APPAREL GROUP INC
226 W 37th St Fl 17 (10018-9011)
PHONE.................................212 947-7009
Fax: 212 947-7218
Karen Camporeale, *President*
Noreen Camporeale, *Vice Pres*
David A Dulinski, *CFO*
Glenn M, *VP Sales*
Anna Imperati, *Manager*
▲ **EMP:** 37
SQ FT: 9,000
SALES (est): 4.5MM **Privately Held**
WEB: www.urbanapparel.com
SIC: 2339 Sportswear, women's

(G-12499)
URBAN GREEN ENERGY INC
Also Called: Uge
330 W 38th St Rm 1103 (10018-8446)
PHONE.................................917 720-5681
Nick Blitterswyk, *CEO*
Joshua Rogol, *President*
Henry Hatch, *Business Mgr*
Mateo Chaskel, *Vice Pres*
Anthony Ditietro, *Vice Pres*
◆ **EMP:** 31
SQ FT: 35,000
SALES: 5MM **Privately Held**
SIC: 3825 Energy measuring equipment, electrical

(G-12500)
URBAN MAPPING INC
Also Called: Umi
295 Madison Ave Rm 1010 (10017-6340)
PHONE.................................415 946-8170
Ian White, *President*
John Marshall, *CTO*
Timothy Caro-Bruce, *Prgrmr*
Amy Ocasio, *Admin Sec*
EMP: 11
SALES (est): 1.1MM **Privately Held**
WEB: www.urbanmapping.com
SIC: 2741 Atlas, map & guide publishing

(G-12501)
URBAN TEXTILES INC
Also Called: Forest Uniforms
49 Elizabeth St Fl 6 (10013-4636)
PHONE.................................212 777-1900
Fax: 212 777-1980
Michael Schackett, *President*
Maria Pino, *Accounting Mgr*
Mary Cuevas, *Manager*
▲ **EMP:** 10
SQ FT: 5,000
SALES (est): 1.4MM **Privately Held**
SIC: 2311 Men's & boys' uniforms

(G-12502)
URBANDADDY INC
900 Broadway Ste 1003 (10003-1215)
PHONE.................................212 929-7905
Lance Broumand, *CEO*
Sam Eichner, *Editor*
Chris Lamorte, *Editor*
Geoff Rynex, *Editor*
Sarah Sung, *Editor*
EMP: 14
SALES (est): 3.7MM **Privately Held**
SIC: 2721 Magazines: publishing & printing

(G-12503)
URTHWORX INC
320 W 106th St Apt 2f (10025-3470)
PHONE.................................646 373-7535
Michael Fox, *CEO*
EMP: 5 **EST:** 2014
SALES (est): 277K **Privately Held**
SIC: 7372 7389 Home entertainment computer software;

New York - New York County (G-12504) — GEOGRAPHIC SECTION

(G-12504)
US CHINA MAGAZINE
200 W 95th St Apt 21 (10025-6315)
PHONE..................................212 663-4333
Zhong Vhan, *President*
Angila Chan, *Vice Pres*
Andrew Heermans, *Exec Dir*
Andrew Jee, *Director*
EMP: 25 **EST:** 1994
SALES: 500K **Privately Held**
SIC: 2721 Periodicals

(G-12505)
US DESIGN GROUP LTD
Also Called: Request Jeans
1385 Broadway Rm 1905 (10018-6001)
PHONE..................................212 354-4070
Fax: 212 354-4418
Frank Jbara, *President*
Frank Jebara, *President*
Assad Charles Jebara, *Vice Pres*
Imad Jebara, *Admin Sec*
▲ **EMP:** 18
SQ FT: 10,000
SALES (est): 1.2MM **Privately Held**
SIC: 2211 Apparel & outerwear fabrics, cotton

(G-12506)
US DIAGNOSTICS INC
Also Called: Vertaloc
711 3rd Ave Rm 1502 (10017-9200)
PHONE..................................866 216-5308
Edward Letko, *President*
Marwa Elkholyhttp, *Sales Mgr*
▲ **EMP:** 20
SALES (est): 3.2MM **Privately Held**
SIC: 2835 In vitro & in vivo diagnostic substances

(G-12507)
US FRONTLINE NEWS INC
228 E 45th St Rm 700 (10017-3336)
PHONE..................................212 922-9090
Fax: 212 922-9119
Ryu Fujiwara, *President*
Yuri Yamane, *Vice Pres*
EMP: 30
SQ FT: 5,000
SALES (est): 3.5MM **Privately Held**
WEB: www.usfl.com
SIC: 2721 Magazines: publishing only, not printed on site

(G-12508)
US HOME TEXTILES GROUP LLC
1400 Broadway Fl 18 (10018-5300)
PHONE..................................212 768-3030
▲ **EMP:** 6
SALES (est): 570K **Privately Held**
SIC: 2221 Manmade Broadwoven Fabric Mill

(G-12509)
US NEWS & WORLD REPORT INC (PA)
4 New York Plz Fl 6 (10004-2473)
PHONE..................................212 716-6800
Fax: 212 916-7400
Mortimer B Zuckerman, *CEO*
Shelbi Austin, *Editor*
Brian Duffy, *Editor*
Fred Drasner, *Co-COB*
Bill Frischling, *Vice Pres*
▲ **EMP:** 150 **EST:** 1933
SQ FT: 100,000
SALES (est): 110.4MM **Privately Held**
WEB: www.usnews.com
SIC: 2721 Magazines: publishing & printing

(G-12510)
US WEEKLY LLC
1290 Ave Of The Americas (10104-0295)
PHONE..................................212 484-1616
David J Pecker, *CEO*
Will Schenck, *Publisher*
Kent Brownridge, *General Mgr*
Will Brownrigeg, *General Mgr*
Abby Feiner, *Editor*
EMP: 75
SQ FT: 15,000
SALES (est): 10.6MM
SALES (corp-wide): 223MM **Privately Held**
WEB: www.usweekly.com
SIC: 2721 Magazines: publishing only, not printed on site
PA: American Media, Inc.
4 New York Plz Fl 2
New York NY 10004
212 545-4800

(G-12511)
USA FURS BY GEORGE INC
212 W 30th St (10001-4901)
PHONE..................................212 643-1415
George Chrisomalides, *President*
Johanna Chrisomalides, *Vice Pres*
EMP: 4
SQ FT: 2,500
SALES: 1MM **Privately Held**
SIC: 2371 Fur coats & other fur apparel

(G-12512)
USA TODAY INTERNATIONAL CORP
535 Madison Ave Fl 27 (10022-4216)
PHONE..................................703 854-3400
Fax: 212 371-0241
David Mazzarella, *Manager*
EMP: 8
SALES (corp-wide): 3B **Publicly Held**
SIC: 2711 Newspapers
HQ: Usa Today International Corp
7950 Jones Branch Dr
Mc Lean VA 22102
703 854-3400

(G-12513)
USPA ACCESSORIES LLC
Also Called: Concept One Accessories
119 W 40th St Fl 3 (10018-2526)
PHONE..................................212 868-2590
Fax: 212 868-2595
Margaret Close, *Vice Pres*
Israel Roman, *Opers Mgr*
Christopher Graham, *Production*
Bernie Hafif, *CFO*
Darlene Warren, *Controller*
▲ **EMP:** 150
SQ FT: 38,000
SALES (est): 22.6MM **Privately Held**
SIC: 2339 Women's & misses' accessories

(G-12514)
USQ GROUP LLC
222 Broadway Fl 19 (10038-2550)
PHONE..................................212 777-7751
Shanto Goswami, *CEO*
EMP: 5
SALES (est): 189.3K **Privately Held**
SIC: 7372 Application computer software; home entertainment computer software

(G-12515)
UTRECHT MANUFACTURING CORP
Also Called: Utrecht Art Supplies
237 W 23rd St (10011-2302)
PHONE..................................212 675-8699
Fax: 212 675-8654
Jeffrey Pratt, *Branch Mgr*
EMP: 5
SALES (corp-wide): 160.8MM **Privately Held**
SIC: 3952 Lead pencils & art goods
HQ: Utrecht Manufacturing Corporation
6 Corp Dr Ste 1
Cranbury NJ 08512
609 409-8001

(G-12516)
VALENTIN & KALICH JWLY MFG LTD
Also Called: Valentin Magro
42 W 48th St Ste 903 (10036-1712)
PHONE..................................212 575-9044
Valente Magro, *President*
Terry Magro, *Vice Pres*
EMP: 24
SALES (est): 3.1MM **Privately Held**
SIC: 3911 Jewelry, precious metal

(G-12517)
VALENTINE JEWELRY MFG CO INC
31 W 47th St Ste 602 (10036-2833)
PHONE..................................212 382-0606
Fax: 212 382-0608
Emil Feiger, *President*
EMP: 20 **EST:** 1969
SQ FT: 2,000
SALES (est): 1.9MM **Privately Held**
SIC: 3911 Jewelry, precious metal

(G-12518)
VALIANT ENTERTAINMENT LLC
350 7th Ave Rm 300 (10001-1957)
PHONE..................................212 972-0361
Peter Cuneo, *Ch of Bd*
Walter Black, *Vice Pres*
EMP: 20
SQ FT: 4,000
SALES: 5MM **Privately Held**
SIC: 2721 Comic books: publishing only, not printed on site

(G-12519)
VALMONT INC (PA)
1 W 34th St Rm 303 (10001-3011)
PHONE..................................212 685-1653
Fax: 212 689-6325
Nicholas Vales, *President*
Nicholas Vale, *President*
Nick Vale, *VP Opers*
Errol Lewis, *Mfg Mgr*
David Klein, *Accountant*
▲ **EMP:** 15 **EST:** 1944
SQ FT: 1,000
SALES (est): 3.1MM **Privately Held**
SIC: 2342 5961 Brassieres; catalog & mail-order houses

(G-12520)
VALUE LINE INC (HQ)
551 5th Ave Rm 300 (10176-0399)
PHONE..................................212 907-1500
Fax: 212 682-5778
Howard A Brecher, *Ch of Bd*
Howard Brecher, *COO*
Stephen R Anastasio, *CFO*
Mary Bernstein, *Accountant*
EMP: 65
SQ FT: 44,493
SALES: 34.5MM
SALES (corp-wide): 36MM **Publicly Held**
SIC: 2721 6282 2741 Periodicals: publishing only; investment advisory service; miscellaneous publishing
PA: Bernhard Arnold & Company Inc
485 Lexington Ave Fl 9
New York NY 10017
212 907-1500

(G-12521)
VALUE LINE PUBLISHING LLC
551 5th Ave Rm 300 (10176-0399)
PHONE..................................201 842-8054
Howard Brether, *CEO*
George Moy, *Manager*
Christine Gould, *CTO*
Ted Krismann, *Director*
EMP: 175
SQ FT: 80,000
SALES (est): 33.9MM
SALES (corp-wide): 36MM **Publicly Held**
SIC: 2721 Periodicals: publishing only
HQ: Value Line, Inc.
551 5th Ave Rm 300
New York NY 10176
212 907-1500

(G-12522)
VANDAM INC
121 W 27th St Ste 1102 (10001-6261)
PHONE..................................212 929-0416
Fax: 212 929-0426
Stephan Muth Vandam, *President*
Jacob Benjamin, *Editor*
Jessy Cerda, *Opers Staff*
Bob Troast, *VP Sales*
Gail Grant, *Corp Comm Staff*
▲ **EMP:** 12
SQ FT: 2,500
SALES: 1.5MM **Privately Held**
SIC: 2741 2731 6794 Maps: publishing only, not printed on site; books: publishing only; patent buying, licensing, leasing

(G-12523)
VANDER HEYDEN WOODWORKING
Also Called: Tapestries Etc
151 W 25th St Fl 8 (10001-7204)
PHONE..................................212 242-0525
Fax: 212 242-0988
Marcia Vander Heyden, *President*
EMP: 6
SQ FT: 3,000
SALES (est): 480K **Privately Held**
WEB: www.metookids.com
SIC: 2431 0742 Interior & ornamental woodwork & trim; veterinary services, specialties

(G-12524)
VANITY FAIR
4 Times Sq Bsmt C1b (10036-6518)
PHONE..................................212 286-6052
Fax: 212 286-6916
Graydon Carter, *Chief*
Edward Menicheschi, *Vice Pres*
Susan White, *Director*
◆ **EMP:** 15
SALES (est): 2MM **Privately Held**
WEB: www.vf.com
SIC: 2721 Magazines: publishing & printing

(G-12525)
VANITY FAIR BRANDS LP
25 W 39th St (10018-3805)
PHONE..................................212 548-1548
Pat Lager, *Manager*
EMP: 250
SALES (corp-wide): 223.6B **Publicly Held**
SIC: 2341 Nightgowns & negligees: women's & children's
HQ: Vanity Fair Brands, Lp
1 Fruit Of The Loom Dr
Bowling Green KY 42103
270 781-6400

(G-12526)
VANITY ROOM INC
Also Called: Four Star
230 W 39th St Fl 9 (10018-4411)
PHONE..................................212 921-7154
Fax: 212 391-5520
Geneva Goldsmith, *President*
Kelsi Klatzky, *VP Prdtn*
Teresa Boanco, *Assistant*
EMP: 10
SALES (est): 2.8MM **Privately Held**
SIC: 2331 2335 Women's & misses' blouses & shirts; women's, juniors' & misses' dresses

(G-12527)
VANTAGE PRESS INC
419 Park Ave S Fl 18 (10016-8410)
PHONE..................................212 736-1767
Fax: 212 736-2273
Martin Kleinwald, *President*
Mark Skelton, *Opers Mgr*
Martin Littlefield, *Controller*
Donna Kempe, *Bd of Directors*
Susanne Camilleri, *Admin Sec*
▲ **EMP:** 26 **EST:** 1949
SQ FT: 8,000
SALES (est): 3.2MM **Privately Held**
WEB: www.vantagepress.com
SIC: 2731 Books: publishing only

(G-12528)
VARIABLE GRAPHICS LLC
15 W 36th St Rm 601 (10018-7122)
PHONE..................................212 691-2323
Keneth Ratskin,
Arthur Raskin,
Kenneth Ratskin,
▲ **EMP:** 6
SALES (est): 540K **Privately Held**
WEB: www.variablegraphics.com
SIC: 2752 Commercial printing, lithographic

(G-12529)
VARICK STREET LITHO INC
121 Varick St (10013-1408)
PHONE..................................646 843-0800
EMP: 6
SALES (est): 653.6K **Privately Held**
SIC: 2759 Commercial printing

▲ = Import ▼ = Export
◆ = Import/Export

GEOGRAPHIC SECTION

New York - New York County (G-12558)

(G-12530)
VARNISH SOFTWARE INC
85 Broad St Fl 18 (10004-2783)
PHONE.....................201 857-2832
Lars Larsson, *President*
Lina Gunhamre, *Finance Mgr*
Daniel Jacobs, *Sales Mgr*
Alexandra Lehner, *Marketing Staff*
Hugo Cruz, *Manager*
EMP: 5
SALES (est): 121K **Privately Held**
SIC: 7372 Prepackaged software

(G-12531)
VARONIS SYSTEMS INC (PA)
1250 Broadway Fl 29 (10001-3720)
PHONE.....................877 292-8767
Yakov Faitelson, *Ch of Bd*
Eric Mann, *COO*
James O'Boyle, *Senior VP*
Seth Gerson, *Vice Pres*
Ken Spiegel, *Vice Pres*
EMP: 947
SQ FT: 31,000
SALES: 127.2MM **Publicly Held**
SIC: 7372 Prepackaged software

(G-12532)
VARSITY MONITOR LLC
50 5th Ave Fl 3 (10011)
PHONE.....................212 691-6292
Sam Carnahan, *Managing Prtnr*
Farrah Carnahan, *Managing Dir*
EMP: 9
SALES (est): 470K **Privately Held**
SIC: 7372 Business oriented computer software

(G-12533)
VASQUEZ TITO
Also Called: Tito Moldmaker Co
36 W 47th St Ste 206 (10036-8636)
PHONE.....................212 944-0441
Tito Vasquez, *Owner*
EMP: 10
SALES (est): 789.9K **Privately Held**
SIC: 2822 Silicone rubbers

(G-12534)
VAUGHAN DESIGNS INC (HQ)
979 3rd Ave Ste 1511 (10022-3804)
PHONE.....................212 319-7070
Michael Vaughan, *President*
Chris Chadwick, *Human Resources*
▲ **EMP:** 3
SQ FT: 1,700
SALES (est): 1MM
SALES (corp-wide): 19MM **Privately Held**
WEB: www.vaughandesigns.com
SIC: 3645 5021 Residential lighting fixtures; tables, occasional
PA: Vaughan Limited
Unit 1 Chelsea Harbour Design Centre, Chelsea Harbour
London SW10
207 349-4600

(G-12535)
VAULTCOM INC (PA)
Also Called: Vault.com, Vault Media
132 W 31st St Rm 1501 (10001-3406)
PHONE.....................212 366-4212
Fax: 212 366-6712
Eric Ober, *President*
Samer Hamadeh, *Chairman*
Hussam Hamadeh, *Vice Pres*
Mark Oldman, *Vice Pres*
Chad A Coon, *Accounts Exec*
EMP: 50 **EST:** 1992
SALES (est): 6.1MM **Privately Held**
WEB: www.vaultmatch.com
SIC: 2731 7361 Books: publishing only; employment agencies

(G-12536)
VECTOR GROUP LTD
712 5th Ave (10019-4108)
PHONE.....................212 409-2800
Ellen Jorgenson, *Manager*
EMP: 256
SALES (corp-wide): 1.6B **Publicly Held**
SIC: 2111 Cigarettes

PA: Vector Group Ltd.
4400 Biscayne Blvd Fl 10
Miami FL 33137
305 579-8000

(G-12537)
VEERHOUSE VODA HAITI LLC
Also Called: Veerhouse Voda Haiti SA
42 Broadway Fl 12 (10004-3892)
PHONE.....................917 353-5944
Farooq Hassan,
Brendon Brewster,
EMP: 25
SALES (est): 1.4MM **Privately Held**
SIC: 3448 Buildings, portable: prefabricated metal

(G-12538)
VEGA COFFEE INC
325 N End Ave Apt 4b (10282-1027)
PHONE.....................415 881-7969
William Deluca, *Co-Owner*
Noushin Ketabi, *Co-Owner*
Robert Terenzi, *Co-Owner*
EMP: 5
SALES (est): 169.2K **Privately Held**
SIC: 2095 Roasted coffee

(G-12539)
VELOCITY OUTSOURCING LLC
750 3rd Ave (10017-2703)
PHONE.....................212 891-4043
Charles Weinstein, *Manager*
EMP: 24
SALES (est): 2.2MM **Privately Held**
SIC: 7372 Business oriented computer software

(G-12540)
VENDOME GROUP LLC
216 E 45th St Fl 6 (10017-3304)
PHONE.....................646 795-3899
Fax: 212 228-1308
Jane Butler, *CEO*
Mark Fried, *President*
Gary Enos, *Editor*
Daniel Gross, *Exec VP*
Ann Hendrich, *Vice Pres*
EMP: 89
SQ FT: 10,000
SALES (est): 16MM **Privately Held**
SIC: 2741 Miscellaneous publishing

(G-12541)
VENTURA ENTERPRISE CO INC
512 Fashion Ave Fl 38 (10018-0827)
PHONE.....................212 391-0170
Saul Tawil, *Ch of Bd*
Shelley Rindner, *Exec VP*
Henry Dweck, *Vice Pres*
Kim Spencer, *Controller*
Phil Horowitz, *VP Sales*
▲ **EMP:** 40
SQ FT: 8,000
SALES (est): 4.7MM **Privately Held**
SIC: 2326 2331 Men's & boys' work clothing; women's & misses' blouses & shirts

(G-12542)
VERA WANG GROUP LLC (PA)
Also Called: V E W
15 E 26th St Fl 4 (10010-1536)
PHONE.....................212 575-6400
Vera W Becker, *Ch of Bd*
Taryn Thomas, *Vice Pres*
Dennis Johnson, *Opers Staff*
Kathy Yen, *Production*
Pamela Anthony, *Accountant*
▲ **EMP:** 190 **EST:** 2004
SQ FT: 14,000
SALES (est): 59.6MM **Privately Held**
WEB: www.verawang.com
SIC: 2335 5621 Bridal & formal gowns; wedding gowns & dresses; gowns, formal; bridal shops; dress shops

(G-12543)
VERANDA PUBLICATIONS INC
Also Called: Veranda Magazine
300 W 57th St Fl 28 (10019-5288)
PHONE.....................212 903-5206
Lisa Newsom, *President*
Katie Brockman, *Publisher*
EMP: 8

SALES (est): 510.1K
SALES (corp-wide): 6.4B **Privately Held**
WEB: www.hearstcorp.com
SIC: 2721 Magazines: publishing only, not printed on site
PA: The Hearst Corporation
300 W 57th St Fl 42
New York NY 10019
212 649-2000

(G-12544)
VERATEX INC (PA)
254 5th Ave Fl 3 (10001-6406)
P.O. Box 682 (10108-0682)
PHONE.....................212 683-9300
Fax: 212 889-5573
Claude Simon, *President*
John Simon, *Vice Pres*
▲ **EMP:** 10
SQ FT: 2,500
SALES (est): 2MM **Privately Held**
SIC: 2258 Tricot fabrics

(G-12545)
VERDONETTE INC
270 W 39th St Fl 5 (10018-4409)
PHONE.....................212 719-2003
EMP: 5
SALES (est): 310K **Privately Held**
SIC: 2395 Pleating/Stitching Services

(G-12546)
VERILED INC
100 Church St Ste 871 (10007-2601)
PHONE.....................877 521-5520
Michael Handerhan, *CEO*
EMP: 6 **EST:** 2013
SQ FT: 2,000
SALES (est): 881.2K **Privately Held**
SIC: 3674 Light emitting diodes

(G-12547)
VERRAGIO LTD (PA)
132 W 36th St Bsmt (10018-6903)
PHONE.....................212 868-8181
Barry Nisguretsky, *President*
Randy Green, *Regional Mgr*
Jeff Sullivan, *Natl Sales Mgr*
Tab Judd, *Regl Sales Mgr*
Neha Shah, *Accounts Exec*
▲ **EMP:** 22
SQ FT: 8,000
SALES (est): 4.1MM **Privately Held**
WEB: www.verragio.com
SIC: 3911 Jewelry apparel

(G-12548)
VERRIS INC ✪
99 Wall St Unit 236 (10005-4301)
PHONE.....................201 565-1648
John Paris, *CEO*
Scott Berchin, *Senior VP*
EMP: 2 **EST:** 2017
SALES: 2MM **Privately Held**
SIC: 7372 7389 Prepackaged software;

(G-12549)
VERSAILLES INDUSTRIES LLC
485 Fashion Ave Rm 500 (10018-6804)
PHONE.....................212 792-9615
Freddy Hamra, *Mng Member*
▲ **EMP:** 6
SALES (est): 579.6K **Privately Held**
SIC: 2329 Riding clothes:, men's, youths' & boys'

(G-12550)
VERSO CORPORATION
370 Lexington Ave Rm 802 (10017-6510)
PHONE.....................212 599-2700
Gerhard Nussbaumer, *Principal*
Jennifer Young, *Mktg Dir*
Chip Ernst, *Director*
EMP: 400 **Publicly Held**
SIC: 2621 3554 Paper mills; paper industries machinery
PA: Verso Corporation
8540 Gander Creek Dr
Miamisburg OH 45342

(G-12551)
VERSO PAPER MANAGEMENT LP
370 Lexington Ave Rm 802 (10017-6510)
PHONE.....................781 320-8660
Alvin Smart, *Branch Mgr*

EMP: 1449 **Privately Held**
SIC: 2621 Paper mills
PA: Verso Paper Management Lp
60 W 42nd Ste 1942
New York NY 10165

(G-12552)
VERSO PAPER MANAGEMENT LP (PA)
60 W 42nd Ste 1942 (10165)
PHONE.....................212 599-2700
Michael A Jackson, *President*
Susan Frye, *Manager*
Jesse Rothfork, *Network Mgr*
Patricia Oetken, *Analyst*
EMP: 3
SALES (est): 817.3MM **Privately Held**
SIC: 2621 Paper mills

(G-12553)
VERTANA GROUP LLC (PA)
Also Called: Killer Motor Sports
37 W 20th St Ste 804 (10011-3716)
PHONE.....................646 430-8226
Emmanuel Tesone, *President*
EMP: 5 **EST:** 2012
SALES (est): 2.3MM **Privately Held**
SIC: 7372 Prepackaged software

(G-12554)
VERTICAL RESEARCH PARTNERS LLC
52 Vanderbilt Ave Rm 200 (10017-3860)
PHONE.....................212 257-6499
EMP: 18
SALES (corp-wide): 4.4MM **Privately Held**
SIC: 2591 Drapery Hardware And Blinds And Shades
PA: Vertical Research Partners Llc
1 Landmark Sq Fl 4
Stamford CT 06901
203 276-5680

(G-12555)
VETROELITE INC
115 W 30th St Rm 402 (10001-4179)
PHONE.....................925 724-7900
Daniele Feletto, *Ch of Bd*
▲ **EMP:** 5
SALES (est): 497.3K **Privately Held**
SIC: 3565 Packing & wrapping machinery

(G-12556)
VETTA JEWELRY INC (PA)
Also Called: Spring Street Design Group
70 W 36th St Fl 9 (10018-1798)
PHONE.....................212 564-8250
Edwin Peissis, *Ch of Bd*
Mary Walsh, *President*
▲ **EMP:** 50
SALES (est): 7.4MM **Privately Held**
WEB: www.cosmotronics.com
SIC: 3961 Costume jewelry

(G-12557)
VF SPORTSWEAR INC
Nautica Womens Sportswear
40 W 57th St Fl 3 (10019-4001)
PHONE.....................212 541-5757
Fax: 212 841-7291
Christopher Young, *President*
Kathy Hines, *Vice Pres*
Lisa Whitney, *Vice Pres*
Marla Baldassare, *VP Sales*
Sara Hiller, *Marketing Mgr*
EMP: 21
SALES (corp-wide): 12B **Publicly Held**
SIC: 2339 Athletic clothing: women's, misses' & juniors'
HQ: Vf Sportswear, Inc.
545 Wshngton Blvd Fl 8
Jersey City NJ 07310
212 541-5757

(G-12558)
VGG HOLDING LLC
590 Madison Ave Fl 41 (10022-2524)
PHONE.....................212 415-6700
EMP: 6
SALES (est): 653.1K **Privately Held**
SIC: 3674 Semiconductors & related devices

New York - New York County (G-12559) — GEOGRAPHIC SECTION

(G-12559)
VHX CORPORATION
555 W 18th St (10011-2822)
PHONE..................347 689-1446
Jamie Wilkinson, CEO
Katleen Barrett, Finance
Kevin Sheurs, CTO
EMP: 13 **EST:** 2013
SALES (est): 1.2MM
SALES (corp-wide): 3.1B **Publicly Held**
SIC: 7372 Prepackaged software
PA: Iac/Interactivecorp
555 W 18th St
New York NY 10011
212 314-7300

(G-12560)
VIA AMERICA FINE JEWELRY INC
578 5th Ave Unit 26 (10036-4836)
PHONE..................212 302-1218
Fax: 212 768-2731
Mary Yogurtco, President
Sadik Yogurtco, Vice Pres
Harutyn Temurco, Admin Sec
EMP: 5
SQ FT: 3,000
SALES (est): 420K **Privately Held**
SIC: 3915 Jewelers' materials & lapidary work

(G-12561)
VIBE MEDIA GROUP LLC
Also Called: Vibe Magazine
120 Wall St Fl 21 (10005-4024)
P.O. Box 618180, Chicago IL (60661-8180)
PHONE..................212 448-7300
Fax: 212 448-7400
Danyel Smith, Vice Pres
Nicky Booth, Manager
Gary R Lewis, Officer
Steve Aaron,
EMP: 65
SALES (est): 4.7MM **Privately Held**
SIC: 2721 Periodicals

(G-12562)
VICKERS STOCK RESEARCH CORP (HQ)
61 Broadway Rm 1910 (10006-2761)
PHONE..................212 425-7500
Fax: 516 945-0030
Fern Dorsey, President
Kathy Kareseboom, Human Resources
EMP: 40
SQ FT: 5,000
SALES (est): 2.6MM
SALES (corp-wide): 12.8MM **Privately Held**
WEB: www.vickers-stock.com
SIC: 2721 Periodicals
PA: Argus Research Group Inc Del
61 Broadway Rm 1702
New York NY 10006
212 425-7500

(G-12563)
VICTORIA ALBI INTL INC
Also Called: Makari
1178 Broadway Fl 5 (10001-5404)
PHONE..................212 689-2600
Raquel Aini, CEO
Leah Hollender, Sales Executive
▲ **EMP:** 10
SALES (est): 2.4MM **Privately Held**
SIC: 2844 Cosmetic preparations

(G-12564)
VICTORY GARDEN
31 Carmine St Frnt A (10014-4327)
PHONE..................212 206-7273
Sophia Brittain, Owner
EMP: 7
SALES (est): 385.3K **Privately Held**
SIC: 2024 Ice cream, bulk

(G-12565)
VIDAL CANDIES USA INC
845 3rd Ave Fl 6 (10022-6630)
PHONE..................609 781-8169
Mitchell Bernstein, Director
▲ **EMP:** 9
SALES (est): 988.2K
SALES (corp-wide): 93.8MM **Privately Held**
SIC: 2064 Candy & other confectionery products
PA: Vidal Golosinas Sa
Avenida Gutierrez Mellado, S/N
Molina De Segura 30500
968 647-100

(G-12566)
VIEW COLLECTIONS INC
265 W 37th St Rm 5w (10018-5750)
PHONE..................212 944-4030
David Shavolian, President
Nathan Shavolian, Chairman
EMP: 12
SQ FT: 6,000
SALES (est): 910K **Privately Held**
SIC: 2337 Suits: women's, misses' & juniors'

(G-12567)
VIEWFINDER INC
Also Called: First View
101 W 23rd St Ste 2303 (10011-2490)
PHONE..................212 831-0939
Donald Asbey, President
Marcio Moraes, Vice Pres
EMP: 5
SALES (est): 522.6K **Privately Held**
WEB: www.firstview.com
SIC: 2741 Miscellaneous publishing

(G-12568)
VIKTOR GOLD ENTERPRISE CORP
58 W 47th St Unit 36 (10036-8610)
PHONE..................212 768-8885
Boris Yakutilov, Principal
EMP: 3 **EST:** 1996
SALES (est): 1MM **Privately Held**
SIC: 3911 Jewelry, precious metal

(G-12569)
VILLEROY & BOCH USA INC
41 Madison Ave Ste 1801 (10010-2226)
PHONE..................212 213-8149
Macha McQueen, Accounting Mgr
EMP: 5
SALES (corp-wide): 867.1MM **Privately Held**
SIC: 3089 Plastic kitchenware, tableware & houseware
HQ: Villeroy & Boch Usa, Inc.
3a S Middlesex Ave
Monroe Township NJ 08831
800 536-2284

(G-12570)
VINCI ENTERPRISE CORP
110 W 40th St Rm 209 (10018-8585)
PHONE..................212 768-7888
Tom Sun, CEO
Felix Liu, Office Mgr
EMP: 11
SQ FT: 2,000
SALES (est): 1.1MM **Privately Held**
SIC: 2311 Men's & boys' suits & coats

(G-12571)
VINOUS GROUP LLC
Also Called: Delectable
54 W 40th St (10018-2602)
PHONE..................917 275-5184
EMP: 6 **EST:** 2016
SQ FT: 100
SALES (est): 170.5K **Privately Held**
SIC: 2741 Internet Publishing And Broadcasting

(G-12572)
VIOLIFE LLC
3 W 35th St Fl 7 (10001-2204)
PHONE..................914 207-1820
Joel Pinsky, Ch of Bd
Jonathan Pinsky, Ch of Bd
Jonathan Pinksy, Vice Pres
Richard Walter, Vice Pres
Steven Raptis, Controller
▲ **EMP:** 9
SQ FT: 2,500
SALES (est): 959.1K **Privately Held**
SIC: 3991 Toothbrushes, except electric

(G-12573)
VIP PAPER TRADING INC
1140 Ave Of The (10036)
PHONE..................212 382-4642
Rebecca Silver, President
▼ **EMP:** 20
SALES (est): 2.3MM **Privately Held**
SIC: 2679 Paper products, converted

(G-12574)
VIRGIL MOUNTAIN INC (PA)
1 E 28th St Fl 4 (10016-7432)
PHONE..................212 378-0007
Fax: 212 779-4066
Stephen Dignam, President
Edmund Mandrala, Corp Secy
Gerard Glenn, Vice Pres
▲ **EMP:** 8
SQ FT: 5,000
SALES (est): 1MM **Privately Held**
SIC: 2752 Commercial printing, lithographic

(G-12575)
VIRIDIS LEARNING INC
2 Gold St Apt 4005 (10038-4862)
PHONE..................347 420-9181
Felix Ortiz, CEO
Felix W Ortiz III, Principal
Alex Carstens, COO
EMP: 6
SALES (est): 33.2K **Privately Held**
SIC: 7372 Prepackaged software

(G-12576)
VIROPRO INC
49 W 38th St Fl 11 (10018-1933)
PHONE..................650 300-5190
Bruce A Cohen, Ch of Bd
Joseph J Vallner, President
Scott M Brown, Security Dir
EMP: 34
SALES (est): 1.8MM **Privately Held**
SIC: 2834 Pharmaceutical preparations

(G-12577)
VIRTUAL FRAMEWORKS INC
841 Broadway Ste 504 (10003-4704)
PHONE..................646 690-8207
Tomer Benami, Vice Pres
EMP: 16
SALES (est): 353.2K **Privately Held**
SIC: 7372 Application computer software

(G-12578)
VIRTUAL SUPER LLC
116 E 27th St Fl 3 (10016-8942)
PHONE..................212 685-6400
Joshua Smith,
EMP: 5
SALES (est): 50K **Privately Held**
SIC: 3822 Building services monitoring controls, automatic

(G-12579)
VIRTUVENT INC
1221 Av Of The Amrcas 4200 (10020-1001)
PHONE..................646 845-0387
Saul Sutcher, COO
EMP: 7 **EST:** 2012
SALES (est): 417K **Privately Held**
SIC: 7372 7389 Business oriented computer software;

(G-12580)
VISAGE SWISS WATCH LLC
Also Called: Visage Watches
29 W 30th St Rm 701 (10001-4463)
PHONE..................212 594-7991
Richa Patel,
▲ **EMP:** 9 **EST:** 2014
SALES (est): 392.9K **Privately Held**
SIC: 3873 Watches & parts, except crystals & jewels

(G-12581)
VISIONAIRE PUBLISHING LLC
Also Called: V Magazine
30 W 24th St (10010-3207)
PHONE..................646 434-6091
Fax: 212 343-2595
Donald Hearn, Prdtn Dir
Sooraya Pariag, Controller
Stephen Gan,
Farzana Khan, Admin Sec
Cecilia Dean,
▲ **EMP:** 20
SALES (est): 3.1MM **Privately Held**
WEB: www.visionaireworld.com
SIC: 2721 Magazines: publishing only, not printed on site

(G-12582)
VITAFEDE (PA)
25 W 26th St Fl 5 (10010-1039)
PHONE..................213 488-0136
▲ **EMP:** 10
SALES (est): 4.9MM **Privately Held**
SIC: 3961 Mfg Costume Jewelry

(G-12583)
VITALIS LLC
902 Broadway Fl 6 (10010-6039)
PHONE..................646 831-7338
Joseph Habboushe,
EMP: 5 **EST:** 2012
SALES (est): 58.7K **Privately Held**
SIC: 2834 Pharmaceutical preparations

(G-12584)
VITALIZE LABS LLC
Also Called: Eboost
134 Spring St Ste 502 (10012-3886)
PHONE..................212 966-6130
Christine Cummings, Opers Staff
Malijian Sjam, CFO
Thomas Ortis, Marketing Staff
Blake Sheridan, Marketing Staff
John McDonald,
EMP: 5
SQ FT: 1,000
SALES: 3MM **Privately Held**
SIC: 2833 Vitamins, natural or synthetic: bulk, uncompounded

(G-12585)
VITRA INC (DH)
29 9th Ave (10014-1205)
PHONE..................212 463-5700
Fax: 212 929-6424
Stefan Golinski, President
Patrick Guntzburger, Managing Dir
Rolf Fehlbaum, Chairman
Andrew Caliente, Senior VP
Alan Severance, Senior VP
◆ **EMP:** 16
SALES (est): 12.6MM **Privately Held**
SIC: 2522 Chairs, office: padded or plain, except wood
HQ: Vitra Collections Ag
Klunenfeldstrasse 22
Muttenz BL
418 111-327

(G-12586)
VIZBEE INC
120 E 23rd St Fl 5 (10010-4519)
PHONE..................650 787-1424
Darren Feher, CEO
Prashanth Pappu, Principal
EMP: 8
SALES (est): 200K **Privately Held**
SIC: 7372 7371 Home entertainment computer software; computer software systems analysis & design, custom

(G-12587)
VIZIO MEDICAL DEVICES LLC
200 Chambers St Apt 28a (10007-1350)
PHONE..................646 845-7382
EMP: 10
SALES (est): 600K **Privately Held**
SIC: 3841 Mfg Surgical/Medical Instruments

(G-12588)
VNOVOM SVETE
55 Broad St Fl 20 (10004-2501)
PHONE..................212 302-9480
Helen Brusilovski, Principal
EMP: 9 **EST:** 2012
SALES (est): 280K **Privately Held**
SIC: 2711 Newspapers, publishing & printing

(G-12589)
VOGEL APPLIED TECHNOLOGIES
Also Called: Brainwave Toys-New York
36 E 12th St Fl 7 (10003-4604)
PHONE..................212 677-3136
Fax: 212 677-4346

▲ = Import ▼ = Export
◆ = Import/Export

GEOGRAPHIC SECTION
New York - New York County (G-12615)

David Vogel, *President*
EMP: 1
SQ FT: 500
SALES: 1MM **Privately Held**
WEB: www.brainwavetoys.com
SIC: 3944 Games, toys & children's vehicles

(G-12590)
VOGUE MAGAZINE
1 World Trade Ctr Fl 25 (10007-0090)
PHONE.................212 286-2860
Fax: 212 286-8169
Taylor Antrim, *General Mgr*
Charles Townsend, *Principal*
Edward Barsamian, *Editor*
Jillian Demling, *Editor*
Rebecca Johnson, *Editor*
EMP: 61
SALES (est): 5.9MM **Privately Held**
SIC: 2721 Periodicals

(G-12591)
VOGUE TOO PLTING STITCHING EMB
265 W 37th St Fl 14 (10018-5707)
PHONE.................212 354-1022
Fax: 212 704-0038
Larry Geffner, *President*
EMP: 13 **EST:** 2001
SALES (est): 1.1MM **Privately Held**
SIC: 2395 Pleating & tucking, for the trade

(G-12592)
VOICE ANALYSIS CLINIC
326 W 55th St Apt 4d (10019-5112)
PHONE.................212 245-3803
James Lynn, *Owner*
EMP: 6
SALES (est): 310K **Privately Held**
SIC: 3829 Vibration meters, analyzers & calibrators

(G-12593)
VON MUSULIN PATRICIA
148 W 24th St Fl 10 (10011-1951)
PHONE.................212 206-8345
Fax: 212 627-7216
Patricia Von Musulin, *President*
EMP: 8
SALES (est): 610K **Privately Held**
SIC: 3911 3961 Jewelry, precious metal; jewelry apparel, non-precious metals

(G-12594)
VON POK & CHANG NEW YORK INC
4 E 43rd St Fl 7 (10017-4607)
PHONE.................212 599-0556
Omega Chang, *Ch of Bd*
Bernd Guhl, *Finance Mgr*
▲ **EMP:** 6
SQ FT: 1,000
SALES: 4.8MM **Privately Held**
WEB: www.vonpok.com
SIC: 3993 Advertising novelties

(G-12595)
VONDOM LLC
979 3rd Ave Ste 1532 (10022-3806)
PHONE.................212 207-3252
Olga Tomas, *CFO*
Antonio Esteve,
▲ **EMP:** 4
SALES: 1.6MM **Privately Held**
SIC: 2519 Furniture, household: glass, fiberglass & plastic

(G-12596)
VOSS USA INC
236 W 30th St Rm 900 (10001-0900)
PHONE.................212 995-2255
Fax: 212 995-2425
Jack Baelsito, *CEO*
Joe Bayern, *COO*
Patrick Larkin, *Senior VP*
Jan Saboe, *CFO*
Jan Eystein Saeboe, *CFO*
◆ **EMP:** 150
SQ FT: 1,000
SALES (est): 40.1MM **Privately Held**
SIC: 3561 Pumps & pumping equipment
HQ: Voss Of Norway As
Vatnestrom Industriomrade 5
Vatnestrom 4730
231 316-16

(G-12597)
VSM INVESTORS LLC (PA)
245 Park Ave Fl 41 (10167-0002)
PHONE.................212 351-1600
John Magliana, *Managing Dir*
Anna McGoldrick, *Accountant*
Norm Alpert, *Director*
Susan Hoffman, *Assistant*
▲ **EMP:** 1
SALES (est): 396.7MM **Privately Held**
SIC: 3842 2599 2515 Wheelchairs; personal safety equipment; respirators; hospital beds; hospital furniture, except beds; mattresses & foundations

(G-12598)
VUUM LLC
249 W 34th St Rm 703 (10001-2867)
PHONE.................212 868-3459
Mary Ellen Carroll,
EMP: 6
SALES (est): 251.5K **Privately Held**
SIC: 3663 Radio & TV communications equipment

(G-12599)
VVS INTERNATIONAL INC
2 W 46th St (10036-4811)
PHONE.................212 302-5410
EMP: 5
SALES (est): 252.8K **Privately Held**
SIC: 2834 Pharmaceutical preparations

(G-12600)
VYERA PHARMACEUTICALS LLC
600 3rd Ave Fl 10 (10016-1923)
PHONE.................646 356-5577
Ron Tilles, *Ch of Bd*
Eliseo Salinas, *President*
Adam Brockman, *Top Exec*
Howard L Dorfman, *Senior VP*
Nicholas Pelliccione, *Vice Pres*
EMP: 25
SALES (est): 9.2MM
SALES (corp-wide): 1.1MM **Privately Held**
SIC: 2836 5122 Biological products, except diagnostic; pharmaceuticals
PA: Turing Pharmaceuticals Ag
Haldenstrasse 5
Baar ZG 6340
417 602-424

(G-12601)
W B BOW TIE CORP
Also Called: Bentley Cravats
521 W 26th St Fl 6 (10001-5531)
PHONE.................212 683-6130
Fax: 212 779-2108
Walter Schick, *President*
Marion Schick, *Admin Sec*
EMP: 10 **EST:** 1948
SQ FT: 10,000
SALES (est): 572.1K **Privately Held**
SIC: 2323 Men's & boys' neckwear; neckties, men's & boys': made from purchased materials

(G-12602)
W W NORTON & COMPANY INC (PA)
500 5th Ave Fl 6 (10110-0054)
PHONE.................212 354-5500
Fax: 212 869-0856
W Drake McFeely, *President*
Amber Watkins, *Publisher*
Melissa Atkin, *Editor*
Jennifer Barnhardt, *Editor*
Danielle R Belfiore, *Editor*
▲ **EMP:** 130 **EST:** 1923
SQ FT: 30,000
SALES (est): 205.6MM **Privately Held**
WEB: www.wwnorton.com
SIC: 2731 5192 Textbooks: publishing only, not printed on site; books: publishing only; books

(G-12603)
W W NORTON & COMPANY INC
Countryman Press, The
500 5th Ave Lbby 1 (10110-0105)
PHONE.................212 354-5500
Ann Treistman, *Branch Mgr*
Kermit Hummel, *Director*
EMP: 8
SALES (corp-wide): 205.6MM **Privately Held**
SIC: 2731 Book publishing
PA: W. W. Norton & Company, Inc.
500 5th Ave Fl 6
New York NY 10110
212 354-5500

(G-12604)
WACOAL AMERICA INC
Also Called: Dkny Underwear
136 Madison Ave Fl 15 (10016-6787)
PHONE.................212 743-9600
Fax: 212 696-5608
Susan Malinowski, *Vice Pres*
Maribel Dominguez, *Production*
Virginia Grudichak, *Sales Associate*
Rich Murray, *Branch Mgr*
Sandra Lopez, *Consultant*
EMP: 30
SALES (corp-wide): 1.7B **Privately Held**
WEB: www.wacoal-america.com
SIC: 2342 Bras, girdles & allied garments
HQ: Wacoal America, Inc.
1 Wacoal Plz
Lyndhurst NJ 07071
201 933-8400

(G-12605)
WACOAL INTERNATIONAL CORP
136 Madison Ave Fl 15 (10016-6787)
PHONE.................212 532-6100
Richard C Murray, *President*
EMP: 100
SALES (corp-wide): 1.7B **Privately Held**
SIC: 2341 Women's & children's undergarments
HQ: Wacoal International Corp
1 Wacoal Plz
Lyndhurst NJ 07071
201 933-8400

(G-12606)
WALDMAN ALEXANDER M DIAMOND CO
Also Called: Waldman Diamond Company
30 W 47th St Ste 805 (10036-8644)
PHONE.................212 921-8098
Fax: 212 869-8238
Alexander M Waldman, *President*
Leon Waldman, *Admin Sec*
Rose Lafurge, *Technician*
EMP: 35
SQ FT: 3,500
SALES (est): 4.6MM **Privately Held**
WEB: www.wdcgroup.com
SIC: 3915 5094 Diamond cutting & polishing; diamonds (gems)

(G-12607)
WALDMAN PUBLISHING CORPORATION (PA)
570 Fashion Ave Rm 800 (10018-1603)
P.O. Box 1587 (10028-0013)
PHONE.................212 730-9590
Rachel Waldman, *Ch of Bd*
▲ **EMP:** 10 **EST:** 1961
SQ FT: 3,200
SALES (est): 2.4MM **Privately Held**
SIC: 2731 Books: publishing only

(G-12608)
WALL STREET BUSINESS PDTS INC
151 W 30th St Fl 8 (10001-4026)
PHONE.................212 563-4014
Steven Altman, *President*
Ed Walker, *Vice Pres*
EMP: 31
SQ FT: 7,500
SALES (est): 3.3MM **Privately Held**
WEB: www.wallmail.com
SIC: 2752 Commercial printing, offset

(G-12609)
WALL STREET REPORTER MAGAZINE
419 Lafayette St Fl 2 (10003-7033)
PHONE.................212 363-2600
Jack Marks, *President*
Nadejda Bojinova, *Research*
Alan Wolski, *Treasurer*
EMP: 62 **EST:** 1993

SQ FT: 9,000
SALES: 4MM **Privately Held**
WEB: www.wallstreetreporter.com
SIC: 2721 Magazines: publishing & printing

(G-12610)
WALLACE REFINERS INC
15 W 47th St Ste 808 (10036-5703)
PHONE.................212 391-2649
EMP: 5
SQ FT: 1,500
SALES (est): 510K **Privately Held**
SIC: 3339 5094 Refine Buys And Wholesales Precious Metals

(G-12611)
WALLICO SHOES CORP
32 E 57th St Fl 14 (10022-8566)
PHONE.................212 826-7171
Fax: 212 826-7720
Walter Steiger, *Owner*
Antonia Trimarchi, *Manager*
EMP: 5
SALES (est): 461.4K **Privately Held**
SIC: 3021 5139 5661 Rubber & plastics footwear; footwear; shoe stores

(G-12612)
WALTER EDBRIL INC
10 E 38th St Fl 6 (10016-0014)
PHONE.................212 532-3253
Clifford Tamis, *President*
Jeffrey Tamis, *Vice Pres*
EMP: 30
SQ FT: 4,500
SALES (est): 3MM **Privately Held**
SIC: 3911 Jewelry, precious metal

(G-12613)
WARM
181 Mott St Frnt 1 (10012-4581)
PHONE.................212 925-1200
EMP: 9 **EST:** 2014
SALES (est): 388.2K **Privately Held**
SIC: 2253 Warm weather knit outerwear, including beachwear

(G-12614)
WARNACO GROUP INC (HQ)
501 Fashion Ave (10018-5903)
PHONE.................212 287-8000
Fax: 212 287-8297
Helen McCluskey, *CEO*
James B Gerson, *President*
Joanne Kaye, *President*
Martha Olson, *President*
Michael Prendergast, *President*
◆ **EMP:** 40
SALES (est): 781.7MM
SALES (corp-wide): 8.2B **Publicly Held**
SIC: 2322 2329 2339 2369 Underwear, men's & boys': made from purchased materials; men's & boys' sportswear & athletic clothing; women's & misses' outerwear; bathing suits: women's, misses' & juniors'; beachwear: women's, misses' & juniors'; children's bathing suits & beachwear; bras, girdles & allied garments; brassieres; girdles & panty girdles; panties: women's, misses', children's & infants'; women's & children's nightwear
PA: Pvh Corp.
200 Madison Ave Bsmt 1
New York NY 10016
212 381-3500

(G-12615)
WARNACO INC (DH)
Also Called: Warner S
501 Fashion Ave Fl 14 (10018-5942)
PHONE.................212 287-8000
Joseph R Gromek, *Ch of Bd*
Charles R Perrin, *Ch of Bd*
Helen McCluskey, *President*
Les Hall, *President*
Larry Rutkowski, *Exec VP*
◆ **EMP:** 300 **EST:** 1874
SQ FT: 25,000

New York - New York County (G-12616) — GEOGRAPHIC SECTION

SALES (est): 731.2MM
SALES (corp-wide): 8.2B **Publicly Held**
WEB: www.warnaco.com
SIC: **2342** 2341 2321 2329 Bras, girdles & allied garments; brassieres; girdles & panty girdles; panties: women's, misses', children's & infants'; women's & children's nightwear; men's & boys' dress shirts; men's & boys' sportswear & athletic clothing; underwear, men's & boys': made from purchased materials; men's & boys' neckwear
HQ: The Warnaco Group Inc
  501 Fashion Ave
  New York NY 10018
  212 287-8000

(G-12616)
WARNER MUSIC GROUP CORP (DH)
1633 Broadway (10019-6708)
PHONE..........................212 275-2000
Fax: 212 757-3985
Stephen Cooper, *CEO*
Stu Bergen, *CEO*
Cameron Strang, *CEO*
Len Blavatnik, *Vice Ch Bd*
Michael Fleisher, *Vice Chairman*
EMP: 277
SALES: 3.2B **Privately Held**
SIC: **3652** 6794 Pre-recorded records & tapes; music licensing & royalties

(G-12617)
WARNER MUSIC INC (DH)
75 Rockefeller Plz Bsmt 1 (10019-0011)
PHONE..........................212 275-2000
Fax: 212 275-4760
Paul Rene' Albertini, *President*
David H Johnson, *Exec VP*
Olafur Olafsson, *Exec VP*
Jim Noonan, *Senior VP*
Liz Rosenberg, *Vice Pres*
▼ EMP: 100
SQ FT: 333,500
SALES (est): 769.4MM **Privately Held**
SIC: **3652** 2741 Pre-recorded records & tapes; phonograph records, prerecorded; magnetic tape (audio): prerecorded; compact laser discs, prerecorded; music, sheet: publishing & printing
HQ: Wmg Acquisition Corp.
  75 Rockefeller Plz
  New York NY 10019
  212 275-2000

(G-12618)
WARREN CORPORATION (DH)
711 5th Ave Fl 11 (10022-3113)
PHONE..........................917 379-3434
Pier Guerci, *President*
Guy Birkhead, *Senior VP*
Lisa Cornish, *Vice Pres*
Richard Anderman, *Admin Sec*
Giuseppe Monteoeone, *Maintence Staff*
◆ EMP: 180 EST: 1853
SQ FT: 330,000
SALES (est): 22.8MM
SALES (corp-wide): 268.1MM **Privately Held**
WEB: www.warrencorp.com
SIC: **2231** Overcoatings: wool, mohair or similar fibers; suitings: wool, mohair or similar fibers
HQ: Loro Piana Spa
  Corso Pietro Rolandi 10
  Quarona VC 13017
  016 320-1111

(G-12619)
WARREN ENERGY SERVICES LLC
1114 Ave Of The Americas (10036-7703)
PHONE..........................212 697-9660
Fax: 212 697-9466
Saema Somalya, *Senior VP*
Robert Wimbush, *Accountant*
Isaac Dt, *Info Tech Mgr*
James A Watt,
EMP: 10
SQ FT: 4,200
SALES (est): 409.7K
SALES (corp-wide): 88.3MM **Publicly Held**
SIC: **1382** Oil & gas exploration services
PA: Warren Resources, Inc.
  5420 Lbj Fwy Ste 600
  Dallas TX 75240
  214 393-9688

(G-12620)
WASTECORP PUMPS LLC (PA)
345 W 85th St Apt 23 (10024-3834)
P.O. Box 70, Grand Island (14072-0070)
PHONE..........................888 829-2783
Dan Starr,
◆ EMP: 10
SQ FT: 2,000,000
SALES (est): 1.1MM **Privately Held**
SIC: **3561** Pumps & pumping equipment

(G-12621)
WATCH JOURNAL LLC
110 E 25th St Fl 4 (10010-2913)
PHONE..........................212 229-1500
Marc Lotenberg,
EMP: 7
SALES (est): 1.7MM **Privately Held**
SIC: **2721** Magazines: publishing & printing

(G-12622)
WATCHANISH LLC
1 Rockefeller Plz Fl 11 (10020-2073)
PHONE..........................917 558-0404
Anish Bhatt, *Principal*
EMP: 10
SALES (est): 229.1K **Privately Held**
SIC: **2741** Miscellaneous publishing

(G-12623)
WATCHITOO INC
24 W 40th St Fl 14 (10018-1093)
PHONE..........................212 354-5888
Eyal Hillman, *General Mgr*
Eric Lipkind, *Principal*
Tom Clark, *Exec VP*
Omer Sali, *Vice Pres*
Michael Marsico, *Research*
EMP: 5
SALES (est): 532.7K **Privately Held**
SIC: **7372** Prepackaged software

(G-12624)
WATER ENERGY SYSTEMS LLC
1 Maiden Ln (10038-4015)
PHONE..........................844 822-7665
EMP: 8 EST: 2015
SALES (est): 431K **Privately Held**
SIC: **3589** Mfg Service Industry Machinery

(G-12625)
WATERBURY GARMENT LLC
Also Called: Jackie's Girls
16 E 34th St Fl 10 (10016-4360)
PHONE..........................212 725-1500
Daniel Livingston, *President*
Harry Gaffney, *CFO*
▲ EMP: 30 EST: 1921
SQ FT: 19,000
SALES (est): 1.6MM
SALES (corp-wide): 212.2MM **Privately Held**
WEB: www.waterburygarment.com
SIC: **2341** 2369 2322 Women's & children's nightwear; children's robes & housecoats; men's & boys' underwear & nightwear
HQ: Komar Kids, L.L.C.
  16 E 34th St Fl 14
  New York NY 10016
  212 725-1500

(G-12626)
WATSON ADVENTURES LLC
330 W 38th St Rm 407 (10018-8307)
PHONE..........................212 564-8293
Stacy King, *General Mgr*
Daniel Maranon, *Principal*
Tara Melvin, *Accounts Mgr*
Ryan Greene, *Marketing Mgr*
EMP: 6
SALES (est): 550.2K **Privately Held**
SIC: **3949** Sporting & athletic goods

(G-12627)
WAY OUT TOYS INC
230 5th Ave Ste 800 (10001-7857)
PHONE..........................212 689-9094
Eddie Mishan, *President*
Al Mishan, *Vice Pres*
Jeffrey Mishan, *Vice Pres*
Morris Mishan, *Vice Pres*
Steven Mishan, *Vice Pres*
EMP: 6
SALES (est): 660K **Privately Held**
SIC: **3944** 5092 Games, toys & children's vehicles; toys & games

(G-12628)
WE WORK
1 Little West 12th St (10014-1302)
PHONE..........................877 673-6628
Adam Wacenske, *Associate*
EMP: 6
SALES (est): 493.2K **Privately Held**
SIC: **2011** Meat packing plants

(G-12629)
WEA INTERNATIONAL INC (DH)
75 Rockefeller Plz (10019-6908)
PHONE..........................212 275-1300
Keith Bruce, *Senior VP*
Ramon Lopez, *Vice Pres*
EMP: 100
SQ FT: 3,500
SALES (est): 123.6MM **Privately Held**
SIC: **3652** Master records or tapes, preparation of

(G-12630)
WEAR ABOUTS APPAREL INC
260 W 36th St Rm 602 (10018-7603)
PHONE..........................212 827-0888
Kim Yu, *President*
Geri Nelson, *Executive*
▲ EMP: 12 EST: 1998
SQ FT: 4,500
SALES (est): 4.1MM **Privately Held**
SIC: **2335** Women's, juniors' & misses' dresses

(G-12631)
WEEKLY BUSINESS NEWS CORP
274 Madison Ave Rm 1101 (10016-0700)
PHONE..........................212 689-5888
Yoshiaki Takahashi, *President*
Akiko Kudo, *Editor*
Akiko Kido, *Office Mgr*
EMP: 6
SALES (est): 202.2K **Privately Held**
SIC: **2711** Newspapers

(G-12632)
WEIDER PUBLICATIONS LLC
Also Called: A M I
1 Park Ave Fl 10 (10016-5818)
PHONE..........................212 545-4800
Mike Kahane, *Senior VP*
Stuart Zakim, *Senior VP*
David Obey, *Vice Pres*
Beverly Levy, *Branch Mgr*
Robin Berstein, *Art Dir*
EMP: 200
SALES (corp-wide): 223MM **Privately Held**
WEB: www.fitnessonline.com
SIC: **2721** Magazines: publishing only, not printed on site
HQ: Weider Publications, Llc
  3699 Wilshire Blvd # 1220
  Los Angeles CA 90010

(G-12633)
WEISCO INC
246 W 38th St Fl 6 (10018-5854)
PHONE..........................212 575-8989
Alex Weiss, *President*
Edward Weiss, *Vice Pres*
Peter Weiss, *Treasurer*
EMP: 15
SQ FT: 7,000
SALES (est): 1.5MM **Privately Held**
WEB: www.weisco.com
SIC: **3911** Jewelry, precious metal

(G-12634)
WELCOME RAIN PUBLISHERS LLC
Also Called: South Brooklyn Book Company
230 5th Ave (10001-7704)
PHONE..........................212 686-1909
John Weber,
EMP: 2
SALES: 1.5MM **Privately Held**
SIC: **2741** Miscellaneous publishing

(G-12635)
WELDING CHAPTER OF NEW YORK
44 W 28th St Fl 12 (10001-4291)
PHONE..........................212 481-1496
Ray Hopkins, *President*
EMP: 5
SALES (est): 345.1K **Privately Held**
SIC: **7692** Welding repair

(G-12636)
WELLQUEST INTERNATIONAL INC (PA)
230 5th Ave Ste 800 (10001-7851)
PHONE..........................212 689-9094
Eddie Mishan, *President*
Al Mishan, *Vice Pres*
Isaac Mishan, *Vice Pres*
Morris Mishan, *Vice Pres*
▲ EMP: 6
SQ FT: 2,000
SALES (est): 847.4K **Privately Held**
WEB: www.wellquestinternational.com
SIC: **2833** 5122 Vitamins, natural or synthetic: bulk, uncompounded; vitamins & minerals

(G-12637)
WELLSPRING CORP (PA)
54a Ludlow St (10002)
PHONE..........................212 529-5454
Fax: 212 979-6779
Yon K Lai, *Ch of Bd*
Danny Lai, *President*
EMP: 5
SQ FT: 1,000
SALES (est): 741.4K **Privately Held**
WEB: www.wellspringcorp.com
SIC: **2064** 5149 Candy & other confectionery products; groceries & related products; chocolate; mineral or spring water bottling; crackers, cookies & bakery products

(G-12638)
WELLSPRING OMNI HOLDINGS CORP
390 Park Ave (10022-4608)
PHONE..........................212 318-9800
William F Dawson Jr, *President*
Joshua C Cascade, *Corp Secy*
EMP: 950
SALES (est): 12.1MM **Privately Held**
SIC: **1382** 1389 7349 Seismograph surveys; lease tanks, oil field: erecting, cleaning & repairing; cleaning service, industrial or commercial

(G-12639)
WENNER MEDIA LLC (PA)
Also Called: Rolling Stone
1290 Ave Of The Amer Fl 2 (10104-0295)
P.O. Box 30895 (10087-0895)
PHONE..........................212 484-1616
Fax: 212 767-8203
Hugh Scogin, *CEO*
Dana L Fields, *Publisher*
Steven Schwartz, *Chairman*
Katey Distefano, *COO*
Daniel Shearer, *Assistant VP*
▲ EMP: 300 EST: 1967
SQ FT: 75,000
SALES (est): 89.1MM **Privately Held**
SIC: **2721** Magazines: publishing & printing

(G-12640)
WEST INTERNET TRADING COMPANY
Also Called: Idonethis
47 Great Jones St Fl 5 (10012-1196)
PHONE..........................415 484-5848
EMP: 6
SALES (est): 320K **Privately Held**
SIC: **7372** Prepackaged Software Services

(G-12641)
WEST PACIFIC ENTERPRISES CORP
260 W 39th St Rm 5w (10018-4432)
PHONE..........................212 564-6800
Daniel Kwok Sui Chuen, *Vice Pres*
Jackie Lee, *Manager*
▲ EMP: 5
SQ FT: 700

▲ = Import ▼ = Export
◆ = Import/Export

GEOGRAPHIC SECTION

New York - New York County (G-12668)

SALES: 17MM
SALES (corp-wide): 134.4MM Privately Held
SIC: 2339 Sportswear, women's
PA: Tungtex (Holdings) Company Limited
12/F Tungtex Bldg
Kwun Tong KLN
279 770-00

(G-12642)
WEST PUBLISHING CORPORATION
Also Called: West Information Center
530 5th Ave Fl 7 (10036-5118)
PHONE.................212 922-1920
Fax: 212 548-7401
Dan Zawislak, *General Mgr*
Allen Hobbs, *Pub Rel Mgr*
Doug French, *Chief Mktg Ofcr*
EMP: 40
SALES (corp-wide): 3.1B Publicly Held
WEB: www.ruttergroup.com
SIC: 2711 Newspapers, publishing & printing
HQ: West Publishing Corporation
610 Opperman Dr
Eagan MN 55123
651 687-7000

(G-12643)
WESTPOINT HOME LLC (DH)
28 E 28th St Cncrse Level (10016)
PHONE.................212 930-2074
Fax: 212 930-2525
Christopher N Baker, *Senior VP*
Billy Harris, *Vice Pres*
Justin Coffey, *Opers Mgr*
Cindy Norman, *Senior Buyer*
Mike Smith, *VP Human Res*
◆ **EMP:** 800
SALES (est): 921.7MM
SALES (corp-wide): 16.3B Publicly Held
SIC: 2211 2221 Broadwoven fabric mills, cotton; sheets, bedding & table cloths: cotton; towels, dishcloths & washcloths: cotton; bedding, manmade or silk fabric
HQ: Westpoint International, Inc.
28 E 28th St Bsmt 2
New York NY 10016
212 930-2044

(G-12644)
WESTPOINT INTERNATIONAL INC (HQ)
28 E 28th St Bsmt 2 (10016-7914)
PHONE.................212 930-2044
Joseph Pennacchio, *CEO*
EMP: 15
SALES (est): 947.5MM
SALES (corp-wide): 16.3B Publicly Held
SIC: 2211 Broadwoven fabric mills, cotton
PA: Icahn Enterprises L.P.
767 5th Ave Ste 4700
New York NY 10153
212 702-4300

(G-12645)
WESTROCK MWV LLC
299 Park Ave Fl 13 (10171-3800)
PHONE.................212 688-5000
Luke John, *Trustee*
Jeff Jensen, *Vice Pres*
Tony Milikin, *Vice Pres*
John Cherry, *Sales Staff*
John A Luke, *Branch Mgr*
EMP: 227
SALES (est): 14.1B Publicly Held
WEB: www.meadwestvaco.com
SIC: 2631 2671 2678 2677 Linerboard; packaging paper & plastics film, coated & laminated; stationery products; envelopes; gum & wood chemicals
HQ: Westrock Mwv, Llc
501 S 5th St
Richmond VA 23219
804 444-1000

(G-12646)
WESTSIDE CLOTHING CO INC
240 W 35th St Ste 1000 (10001-2514)
P.O. Box 220394, Great Neck (11022-0394)
PHONE.................212 273-9898
Jeff Borer, *President*
EMP: 4

SALES: 1.7MM Privately Held
WEB: www.westsideclothingco.com
SIC: 2331 Women's & misses' blouses & shirts

(G-12647)
WETPAINTCOM INC
Also Called: Wet Paint
902 Broadway Fl 11 (10010-6034)
PHONE.................206 859-6300
Ben Elowitz, *CEO*
Bert Hogue, *CFO*
Ji Mun, *Software Dev*
EMP: 38
SALES (est): 3MM
SALES (corp-wide): 4.5MM Publicly Held
WEB: www.wetpaint.com
SIC: 7372 7371 Prepackaged software; custom computer programming services
PA: X Function Inc
902 Broadway Fl 11
New York NY 10010
212 231-0092

(G-12648)
WEY INC
21 W 39th St Fl 6 (10018-0614)
PHONE.................212 532-3299
Matt Zierdniewski, *President*
Armin Klingler, *Managing Dir*
Giuseppe Zaccaria, *Managing Dir*
EMP: 7
SALES (est): 645.5K Privately Held
SIC: 3575 Keyboards, computer, office machine

(G-12649)
WHEELER/RINSTAR LTD
242 W 30th St (10001-4903)
PHONE.................212 244-1130
Fax: 212 594-4697
Noel Shavzin, *President*
Anatol Shavzin, *Vice Pres*
EMP: 10
SQ FT: 2,400
SALES (est): 1.2MM Privately Held
SIC: 2759 Commercial printing

(G-12650)
WHENTECH LLC (DH)
55 E 52nd St Fl 40 (10055-0005)
PHONE.................212 571-0042
David Wender,
EMP: 10
SALES (est): 2.8MM
SALES (corp-wide): 4.5B Publicly Held
WEB: www.whentech.com
SIC: 7372 Business oriented computer software

(G-12651)
WHISPR GROUP INC
72 Allen St Fl 3 (10002-5366)
PHONE.................212 924-3979
Joakim Leijon, *President*
John Studer, *Finance*
EMP: 13 **EST:** 2009
SQ FT: 4,000
SALES (est): 1.1MM Privately Held
SIC: 3993 5199 7389 7311 Advertising artwork; advertising specialties; ; advertising consultant

(G-12652)
WHITE GATE HOLDINGS INC (PA)
22 W 38th St Fl 6 (10018-0107)
PHONE.................212 564-3266
Michael Nolan, *President*
Kevin Joss, *Vice Pres*
Stephi Ruben, *Vice Pres*
Jamie Locastro, *Assoc VP*
Ellen Lipkin, *CFO*
▲ **EMP:** 20
SALES (est): 4.5MM Privately Held
WEB: www.nolanglove.com
SIC: 2339 Women's & misses' accessories

(G-12653)
WHITE LABEL PARTNERS LLC
250 Mercer St Apt B1205 (10012-6125)
PHONE.................917 445-6750
Benedict Aitkenhead, *Business Mgr*
Mark Kaplan,
EMP: 5

SALES (est): 277.2K Privately Held
SIC: 7372 Application computer software

(G-12654)
WHITE WORKROOM INC
40 W 27th St Fl 11 (10001-6944)
PHONE.................212 941-5910
Vivian White, *Partner*
Gary Weisner, *Partner*
EMP: 6
SQ FT: 1,000
SALES (est): 280K Privately Held
SIC: 2391 Curtains & draperies

(G-12655)
WHITEBOARD VENTURES INC
Also Called: Xpand
315 W 36th St Fl 10 (10018-6527)
PHONE.................855 972-6346
Deb Bardhan, *CEO*
Kalyan Anumula, *President*
EMP: 16
SALES (est): 51.6K Privately Held
SIC: 7372 Application computer software

(G-12656)
WHITTALL & SHON (PA)
1201 Broadway Ste 904a (10001-5656)
PHONE.................212 594-2626
Fax: 212 268-2862
Elliot Whittall, *President*
Richard Shon, *Vice Pres*
Charlaine Bivens, *Sales Mgr*
EMP: 3
SALES (est): 14.2MM Privately Held
SIC: 2353 2321 Hats: cloth, straw & felt; millinery; men's & boys' furnishings

(G-12657)
WICKED SPOON INC
127 W 24th St Fl 6 (10011-1943)
PHONE.................646 335-2890
Alex Rozhitsky, *President*
EMP: 11
SALES: 750K Privately Held
SIC: 2024 Ice cream & frozen desserts

(G-12658)
WIDMER TIME RECORDER COMPANY
27 Park Pl Rm 219 (10007-2526)
PHONE.................212 227-0405
Fax: 212 489-3478
Robert Widmer, *President*
Robert Reese, *Vice Pres*
Walter Szymanski, *Prdtn Mgr*
EMP: 10
SALES (corp-wide): 8.8MM Privately Held
WEB: www.widmertime.com
SIC: 3579 Time clocks & time recording devices
PA: Widmer Time Recorder Company Inc
228 Park St
Hackensack NJ 07601
201 489-3810

(G-12659)
WILLCO FINE ART LTD
145 Nassau St Apt 9c (10038-1514)
PHONE.................718 935-9567
William Wolod, *President*
EMP: 10
SALES: 700K Privately Held
SIC: 2759 Commercial printing

(G-12660)
WILLIAM GOLDBERG DIAMOND CORP
589 5th Ave Fl 14 (10017-7293)
PHONE.................212 980-4343
Fax: 212 980-6120
Saul Goldberg, *Ch of Bd*
Benjamin Goldberg, *President*
Eve Goldberg, *Vice Pres*
Lili Goldberg, *CFO*
EMP: 20 **EST:** 1954
SQ FT: 6,000
SALES (est): 3.8MM Privately Held
SIC: 3915 3911 5094 Diamond cutting & polishing; jewelry, precious metal; jewelry & precious stones

(G-12661)
WILLIAM H SADLIER INC (PA)
9 Pine St (10005-4701)
P.O. Box 5685, Hicksville (11802-5685)
PHONE.................212 233-3646
Fax: 212 312-6080
Frank S Dinger, *Ch of Bd*
Ray Fagan, *President*
William S Dinger, *President*
Rosemary Calicchio, *Exec VP*
John Bonenberger, *Vice Pres*
◆ **EMP:** 191 **EST:** 1928
SQ FT: 56,000
SALES (est): 50.6MM Privately Held
WEB: www.sadlier.com
SIC: 2731 Book publishing

(G-12662)
WILLIAM H SHAPIRO
Also Called: Shapiro Wlliam NY Univ Med Ctr
530 1st Ave Ste 3e (10016-6402)
PHONE.................212 263-7037
William H Shapiro, *Owner*
EMP: 5 **EST:** 1999
SALES (est): 424.9K Privately Held
SIC: 3842 Hearing aids

(G-12663)
WILLIAM SOMERVILLE MAINTENANCE
166 E 124th St (10035-1712)
PHONE.................212 534-4600
Merna Miller, *President*
EMP: 68
SQ FT: 40,000
SALES (est): 5.3MM Privately Held
SIC: 2511 Wood household furniture

(G-12664)
WILLIAMS-SONOMA STORES INC
Also Called: Williams-Sonoma Store 154
110 7th Ave (10011-1801)
PHONE.................212 633-2203
Donnie Cassell, *Manager*
EMP: 13
SALES (corp-wide): 5B Publicly Held
SIC: 3263 Cookware, fine earthenware
HQ: Williams-Sonoma Stores, Inc.
3250 Van Ness Ave
San Francisco CA 94109
415 421-7900

(G-12665)
WILLIS MC DONALD CO INC
44 W 62nd St Ph A (10023-7039)
PHONE.................212 366-1526
Jerry Dennehy, *President*
EMP: 15
SQ FT: 10,000
SALES: 1.3MM Privately Held
SIC: 2759 2732 Periodicals: printing; pamphlets: printing only, not published on site

(G-12666)
WILMAX USA LLC
315 5th Ave Rm 505 (10016-6592)
PHONE.................917 388-2790
Maksym Kyrylov,
EMP: 15
SQ FT: 1,500
SALES (est): 1MM Privately Held
SIC: 3469 Cooking ware, porcelain enameled

(G-12667)
WINDIAM USA INC
580 5th Ave Ste 2907 (10036-4724)
PHONE.................212 542-0949
Sacha Zaidman, *CEO*
EMP: 6
SALES (est): 19.3K Privately Held
SIC: 3915 Diamond cutting & polishing

(G-12668)
WINDOW TECHNOLOGIES LLC
555 5th Ave Fl 14 (10017-9257)
PHONE.................402 464-0202
Craig Anderson,
EMP: 9
SQ FT: 135,000
SALES (est): 1.4MM Privately Held
SIC: 2431 Windows, wood

New York - New York County (G-12669)

(G-12669)
WINE & SPIRITS MAGAZINE INC (PA)
2 W 32nd St Ste 601 (10001-3834)
PHONE.....................212 695-4660
Joshua Greene, *President*
Marcy Crimmins, *Vice Pres*
Roy Schneider, *Finance Dir*
Stephanie Johnson, *Director*
Mike Rush, *Art Dir*
EMP: 6
SQ FT: 2,300
SALES (est): 1MM **Privately Held**
WEB: www.wineandspiritsmagazine.com
SIC: 2721 Magazines: publishing only, not printed on site

(G-12670)
WING HEUNG NOODLE INC
144 Baxter St (10013-3605)
PHONE.....................212 966-7496
Fax: 212 966-7496
Ng Shoong Kwong, *Ch of Bd*
Tippy T Yuan Gong, *Vice Pres*
EMP: 13
SQ FT: 2,000
SALES (est): 910K **Privately Held**
WEB: www.chicago-chinatown.com
SIC: 2098 Noodles (e.g. egg, plain & water), dry

(G-12671)
WING KEI NOODLE INC
102 Canal St (10002-6004)
PHONE.....................212 226-1644
Yik Pui Kong, *Ch of Bd*
EMP: 17
SQ FT: 1,200
SALES (est): 1.6MM **Privately Held**
SIC: 2098 Macaroni products (e.g. alphabets, rings & shells), dry

(G-12672)
WINK INC
606 W 28th St Fl 6 (10001-1108)
PHONE.....................212 389-1382
EMP: 45 **EST:** 2013
SALES (est): 2.2MM
SALES (corp-wide): 19.5MM **Privately Held**
SIC: 7372 5961 Prepackaged Software Services Ret Mail-Order House
PA: Quirky, Inc.
606 W 28th St Fl 7
New York NY 10001
212 389-4759

(G-12673)
WINK LABS INC (DH)
Also Called: Wink Acquisition Corp.
606 W 28th St Fl 7 (10001-1108)
PHONE.....................916 717-0437
Nathan Smith, *President*
EMP: 30
SQ FT: 6,000
SALES (est): 14.2MM
SALES (corp-wide): 24.4B **Privately Held**
SIC: 7372 Application computer software

(G-12674)
WINSIGHT LLC
90 Broad St Ste 402 (10004-3312)
PHONE.....................646 708-7309
EMP: 5
SALES (corp-wide): 15.9MM **Privately Held**
SIC: 2721 Periodicals
HQ: Winsight, Llc
300 S Riverside Plz # 1600
Chicago IL 60606
312 876-0004

(G-12675)
WIZQ INC
307 5th Ave Fl 8 (10016-6573)
PHONE.....................586 381-9048
Marcus Kay, *CEO*
Wing Tung LI, *Controller*
EMP: 10 **EST:** 2011
SQ FT: 3,000
SALES (est): 358.3K **Privately Held**
SIC: 7372 Prepackaged software

(G-12676)
WMG ACQUISITION CORP (DH)
75 Rockefeller Plz (10019-6908)
PHONE.....................212 275-2000
Stephen F Cooper, *President*
Mark Ansorge, *Exec VP*
Paul M Robinson, *Exec VP*
Will Tanous, *Exec VP*
Steven Macri, *CFO*
EMP: 15
SALES (est): 769.4MM **Privately Held**
SIC: 2782 2741 7929 Record albums; music books: publishing & printing; music, sheet: publishing & printing; musical entertainers
HQ: Warner Music Group Corp.
1633 Broadway
New York NY 10019
212 275-2000

(G-12677)
WMG HOLDING COMPANY INC
75 Rockefeller Plz (10019-6908)
PHONE.....................212 275-2000
Edgar Bronfman Jr, *Ch of Bd*
David S Johnson, *Vice Pres*
Michael Ward, *CFO*
EMP: 7810
SALES (est): 162.2MM **Privately Held**
SIC: 3652 2741 Pre-recorded records & tapes; music books: publishing & printing; music, sheet: publishing & printing
HQ: Warner Music Group Corp.
1633 Broadway
New York NY 10019
212 275-2000

(G-12678)
WOBBLEWORKS INC (PA)
Also Called: 3doodler
89 5th Ave Ste 802 (10003-3020)
PHONE.....................718 618-9904
Maxwell Bogue, *CEO*
Daniel Cowen, *COO*
Amanda Sekulow, *Manager*
Peter Dilworth, *CTO*
EMP: 14
SALES (est): 2.7MM **Privately Held**
SIC: 3944 Electronic toys

(G-12679)
WOCHIT INC (PA)
12 E 33rd St Fl 4 (10016-5090)
PHONE.....................212 979-8343
Dror Ginzberg, *CEO*
Christoph Pleitgen, *Senior VP*
Drew Berkowitz, *Vice Pres*
Elizabeth Hellman, *Vice Pres*
Ron Maayan, *Vice Pres*
EMP: 5
SALES (est): 3.2MM **Privately Held**
SIC: 7372 7812 Business oriented computer software; publishers' computer software; video production

(G-12680)
WOLTERS KLUWER US INC
111 8th Ave Fl 13 (10011-5213)
PHONE.....................212 894-8920
Susan Chazin, *Publisher*
Kenneth Litt, *Editor*
Shawn McKinney, *Editor*
Gloria Moran, *Editor*
Lora West, *Business Mgr*
EMP: 12
SALES (corp-wide): 4.5B **Privately Held**
SIC: 2731 Book publishing
HQ: Wolters Kluwer United States Inc.
2700 Lake Cook Rd
Riverwoods IL 60015
847 580-5000

(G-12681)
WOMENS E NEWS INC
6 Barclay St Fl 6 (10007-2721)
PHONE.....................212 244-1720
Fax: 212 244-2320
Rita Henley Jensen, *President*
Kristen Elechko, *Exec Dir*
Lori Sokol, *Exec Dir*
EMP: 7
SALES (est): 840.9K **Privately Held**
WEB: www.womensenews.org
SIC: 2721 Periodicals

(G-12682)
WONTON FOOD INC
183 E Broadway (10002-5503)
PHONE.....................212 677-8865
Fax: 212 777-6308
Chan Wai, *Principal*
Michael Chua, *Sales Executive*
EMP: 15
SALES (corp-wide): 76.5MM **Privately Held**
WEB: www.wontonfood.com
SIC: 2099 2098 Noodles, fried (Chinese); noodles (e.g. egg, plain & water), dry
PA: Wonton Food Inc.
220 Moore St 222
Brooklyn NY 11206
718 628-6868

(G-12683)
WOOD FLOOR EXPO INC
Also Called: Scerri Quality Wood Floors
426 E 73rd St Frnt 1 (10021-3866)
PHONE.....................212 472-0671
Fax: 212 737-4280
Joseph Scerri, *President*
Edward Laboy, *Vice Pres*
Peter Palagian, *Controller*
EMP: 5
SALES (est): 510K **Privately Held**
WEB: www.woodfloorexpo.com
SIC: 2426 Flooring, hardwood

(G-12684)
WOODMERE FABRICS INC
35 W 35th St (10001-2205)
PHONE.....................212 695-0144
Ira Schantz, *President*
EMP: 5
SQ FT: 2,000
SALES: 5MM **Privately Held**
SIC: 2311 Men's & boys' suits & coats

(G-12685)
WOOLMARK AMERICAS INC
Also Called: WOOLMARK COMPANY, THE
110 E 25th St Fl 3 (10010-2913)
PHONE.....................347 767-3160
Velma George, *Principal*
EMP: 1
SALES (est): 2.6MM **Privately Held**
SIC: 2231 Cloth, wool: mending

(G-12686)
WORKING MOTHER MEDIA INC
Also Called: Diversity Best Practices
2 Park Ave Fl 10 (10016-5604)
PHONE.....................212 351-6400
Carol Evans, *President*
Suzanne Richards, *Vice Pres*
Nancy Colter, *CFO*
Laquanda Murray, *Sales Dir*
Ayesha Mahmood, *Sales Staff*
EMP: 51 **EST:** 2001
SQ FT: 15,000
SALES (est): 5.5MM
SALES (corp-wide): 2.8B **Privately Held**
WEB: www.workingmother.com
SIC: 2721 4813 Magazines: publishing only, not printed on site;
HQ: Bonnier Corporation
460 N Orlando Ave Ste 200
Winter Park FL 32789
407 628-4802

(G-12687)
WORKMAN PUBLISHING CO INC (PA)
Also Called: Algonquin Books Chapel Hl Div
225 Varick St Fl 9 (10014-4381)
PHONE.....................212 254-5900
Fax: 212 614-7783
Dan Reynolds, *CEO*
Elisabeth Scharlatt, *Publisher*
Chuck Adams, *Editor*
Sarah Brady, *Editor*
Elise Howard, *Editor*
◆ **EMP:** 200
SQ FT: 57,000
SALES (est): 103.1MM **Privately Held**
WEB: www.pageaday.com
SIC: 2731 Books: publishing only

(G-12688)
WORKMAN PUBLISHING CO INC
Artisan House Div
708 Broadway Fl 6 (10003-9508)
PHONE.....................212 254-5900
Fax: 212 254-8098
Richard Petry, *Controller*
Trent Duffy, *Manager*
Mairead Duffy, *Technical Staff*
Elizabeth Hermann, *Director*
Peter Workman, *Director*
EMP: 150
SALES (corp-wide): 103.1MM **Privately Held**
WEB: www.pageaday.com
SIC: 2731 Books: publishing only
PA: Workman Publishing Co. Inc.
225 Varick St Fl 9
New York NY 10014
212 254-5900

(G-12689)
WORLD GUIDE PUBLISHING
1271 Ave Of The Americas (10020-1300)
PHONE.....................800 331-7840
Tina Threston, *CEO*
EMP: 40
SQ FT: 600
SALES (est): 1.5MM **Privately Held**
SIC: 2721 Periodicals: publishing only

(G-12690)
WORLD JOURNAL LLC
205 E 78th St (10075-1243)
PHONE.....................212 879-3933
EMP: 7
SALES (est): 94.4K **Privately Held**
SIC: 2711 Newspapers

(G-12691)
WORTH COLLECTION LTD (PA)
520 8th Ave Rm 2301 (10018-4108)
PHONE.....................212 268-0312
Francine Della Badia, *CEO*
David Defeo, *CEO*
Seth Grossman, *COO*
Alain Tiangco, *VP Prdtn*
Janet Nagy, *Buyer*
▲ **EMP:** 50
SQ FT: 8,000
SALES (est): 45.2MM **Privately Held**
WEB: www.worthny.com
SIC: 2335 Women's, juniors' & misses' dresses

(G-12692)
WORTH PUBLISHERS INC
1 New York Plz Ste 4500 (10004-1562)
PHONE.....................212 475-6000
Fax: 212 505-9570
Elizabeth Widdicombe, *President*
Michael Ross, *Treasurer*
Jeff Harris, *VP Finance*
Danielle Bartholemew, *Manager*
Michael McNamara, *MIS Dir*
EMP: 110
SQ FT: 14,000
SALES (est): 24MM
SALES (corp-wide): 1.5B **Privately Held**
WEB: www.hbpubny.com
SIC: 2731 Textbooks: publishing only, not printed on site
HQ: Macmillan Holdings, Llc
175 5th Ave
New York NY 10010

(G-12693)
WORZALLA PUBLISHING COMPANY
222 W 37th St Fl 10 (10018-9001)
PHONE.....................212 967-7909
Lynn Carroll, *Branch Mgr*
EMP: 189
SALES (corp-wide): 90MM **Privately Held**
SIC: 2732 Book printing
PA: Worzalla Publishing Company
3535 Jefferson St
Stevens Point WI 54481
715 344-9600

(G-12694)
WP LAVORI USA INC (DH)
597 Broadway Fl 2 (10012-3211)
PHONE.....................212 244-6074
Cristina Calori, *President*

Ethem Gungor, *Vice Pres*
Arianna Marcollo, *Manager*
▲ **EMP:** 5
SALES (est): 1.2MM **Privately Held**
SIC: 2311 5136 Men's & boys' suits & coats; men's & boys' clothing
HQ: W.P. Lavori In Corso Srl
Via Dell'arcoveggio 59/5
Bologna BO 40129
051 416-1411

(G-12695)
WR DESIGN CORP
Also Called: Wr9000
230 W 39th St Fl 5f (10018-4933)
PHONE 212 354-9000
Sunny Lam, *President*
EMP: 20
SALES: 8.4MM **Privately Held**
SIC: 2253 Sweaters & sweater coats, knit

(G-12696)
WSN INC
Also Called: World Screen News
1123 Broadway Ste 1207 (10010-2007)
PHONE 212 924-7620
Fax: 212 924-6940
Ricardo Guise, *President*
Marissa Graziadio, *Editor*
Jeff Bewkes, *Vice Pres*
Nathalie Jaspar, *Vice Pres*
Jamie LI, *Vice Pres*
EMP: 6
SQ FT: 500
SALES (est): 540K **Privately Held**
WEB: www.worldscreen.com
SIC: 2721 Magazines: publishing only, not printed on site

(G-12697)
WYETH LLC (HQ)
235 E 42nd St (10017-5703)
PHONE 973 660-5000
Ian Reid, *CEO*
Etienne N Attar, *President*
Richard R Deluca, *President*
Michael Kamarck, *President*
Joseph Mahady, *President*
◆ **EMP:** 850 **EST:** 1926
SALES (est): 4.7B
SALES (corp-wide): 52.8B **Publicly Held**
WEB: www.wyeth.com
SIC: 2834 2836 Analgesics; cough medicines; veterinary pharmaceutical preparations; biological products, except diagnostic; allergens, allergenic extracts; vaccines; veterinary biological products
PA: Pfizer Inc.
235 E 42nd St
New York NY 10017
212 733-2323

(G-12698)
X FUNCTION INC (PA)
902 Broadway Fl 11 (10010-6034)
PHONE 212 231-0092
Robert F X Sillerman, *Ch of Bd*
Mitchell J Nelson, *Exec VP*
Olga Bashkatova, *CFO*
EMP: 21
SQ FT: 16,500
SALES: 4.5MM **Publicly Held**
SIC: 7372 7371 Prepackaged software; custom computer programming services

(G-12699)
X MYLES MAR INC
Also Called: Marx Myles Graphic Services
875 Av Of The Americas (10001-3507)
PHONE 212 683-2015
Fax: 212 213-0015
Arthur Marx, *President*
Sheldon Marx, *Vice Pres*
Nancy Lupton, *Controller*
Barry Heaney, *Sales Dir*
Craig Liebowitz, *Accounts Exec*
EMP: 40
SQ FT: 7,000
SALES (est): 6.1MM **Privately Held**
WEB: www.marxmyles.com
SIC: 2759 2791 2789 2752 Commercial printing; typesetting; bookbinding & related work; commercial printing, lithographic

(G-12700)
XANADU
150 W 30th St Rm 702 (10001-4155)
PHONE 212 465-0580
Gus Xanthoudakis, *Owner*
EMP: 5
SQ FT: 5,000
SALES: 750K **Privately Held**
SIC: 2371 Apparel, fur

(G-12701)
XEROX CORPORATION
245 Park Ave Fl 21 (10167-2900)
PHONE 212 716-4000
Alfonso Lopez, *Principal*
David Lezinsky, *Vice Pres*
Ann Smith, *Vice Pres*
Jeff Fowler, *Engineer*
Glenn Keenan, *Engineer*
EMP: 260
SALES (corp-wide): 10.7B **Publicly Held**
WEB: www.xerox.com
SIC: 3861 Photographic equipment & supplies
PA: Xerox Corporation
201 Merritt 7
Norwalk CT 06851
203 968-3000

(G-12702)
XEROX CORPORATION
485 Lexington Ave Fl 10 (10017-2652)
PHONE 212 330-1386
EMP: 80
SALES (corp-wide): 10.7B **Publicly Held**
SIC: 3861 Photocopy machines
PA: Xerox Corporation
201 Merritt 7
Norwalk CT 06851
203 968-3000

(G-12703)
XING LIN USA INTL CORP
1410 Broadway (10018-5007)
PHONE 212 947-4846
Wen Y Wu, *President*
Richard Jacobs, *General Mgr*
Maggie Yeoh, *Opers Mgr*
Glenn Barnett, *VP Sales*
▲ **EMP:** 5
SQ FT: 900
SALES: 6.5MM **Privately Held**
SIC: 2211 Denims

(G-12704)
XINYA INTERNATIONAL TRADING CO
Also Called: Polly Treating
115 W 30th St Rm 1109 (10001-4056)
PHONE 212 216-9681
Fax: 212 216-9681
Peng Sen Liu, *President*
EMP: 6
SALES: 700K **Privately Held**
SIC: 2387 3851 Apparel belts; glasses, sun or glare

(G-12705)
XL GRAPHICS INC
121 Varick St Rm 300 (10013-1408)
PHONE 212 929-8700
Jeff Baltimore, *Ch of Bd*
Michelle Darpa, *Office Mgr*
Hank Briody, *Manager*
EMP: 5
SQ FT: 4,000
SALES (est): 610.9K **Privately Held**
SIC: 2759 Commercial printing

(G-12706)
XOMOX JEWELRY INC
151 W 46th St Fl 15 (10036-8512)
PHONE 212 944-8428
Mark Bugnacki, *President*
EMP: 7
SQ FT: 1,200
SALES (est): 850K **Privately Held**
WEB: www.xomoxjewelry.com
SIC: 3911 Jewelry, precious metal

(G-12707)
XSTELOS HOLDINGS INC
630 5th Ave Ste 2600 (10111-2697)
PHONE 212 729-4962
Jonathan M Couchman, *President*
EMP: 3
SALES: 28.7MM **Privately Held**
SIC: 2834 Pharmaceutical preparations

(G-12708)
YACOUBIAN JEWELERS INC
2 W 45th St Ste 1104 (10036-4248)
PHONE 212 302-6729
Fax: 212 302-3439
Mike Yacoubian, *President*
EMP: 30
SALES (est): 2.7MM **Privately Held**
SIC: 3961 Costume jewelry

(G-12709)
YALE ROBBINS INC
Also Called: Manhattan Map Co
205 Lexington Ave Fl 12 (10016-6022)
PHONE 212 683-5700
Fax: 212 545-0764
Yale Robbins, *President*
Debra Estock, *Editor*
Henry Robbins, *Vice Pres*
Victor Marcos, *Research*
Sofia Sapeg, *Research*
EMP: 60
SQ FT: 4,000
SALES (est): 8.9MM **Privately Held**
WEB: www.yalerobbins.com
SIC: 2721 8742 6531 Periodicals: publishing & printing; business consultant; real estate brokers & agents

(G-12710)
YAM TV LLC
144 W 23rd St Apt 8e (10011-9403)
PHONE 917 932-5418
Matan Koren,
EMP: 2
SALES: 5MM **Privately Held**
SIC: 2741 7819 Miscellaneous publishing; services allied to motion pictures

(G-12711)
YARNZ INTERNATIONAL INC
260 W 36th St Rm 201 (10018-7524)
PHONE 212 868-5883
Mujadid Shah, *Chairman*
▲ **EMP:** 6
SALES (est): 654.6K **Privately Held**
WEB: www.yarnz.com
SIC: 2231 Apparel & outerwear broadwoven fabrics

(G-12712)
YEOHLEE INC
12 W 29th St (10001-4516)
PHONE 212 631-8099
Fax: 212 631-0918
Yeohlee Teng, *President*
Arthur Laurel, *Manager*
EMP: 13 **EST:** 1975
SQ FT: 6,000
SALES (est): 1.5MM **Privately Held**
WEB: www.yeohlee.com
SIC: 2331 2335 2337 Women's & misses' blouses & shirts; women's, juniors' & misses' dresses; women's & misses' suits & coats

(G-12713)
YIGAL-AZROUEL INC
225 W 39th St Fl 5 (10018-3498)
PHONE 212 302-1194
Fax: 212 221-3870
Yigal Azrouel, *President*
Flora Cervantes, *Principal*
Andre Edwards, *Accounts Exec*
Susan Wetts, *Office Mgr*
Kristen Caruso, *Director*
EMP: 30
SALES (est): 5.2MM **Privately Held**
WEB: www.yigal-azrouel.com
SIC: 2369 2339 Girls' & children's outerwear; women's & misses' outerwear

(G-12714)
YINGLI GREEN ENRGY AMRICAS INC (DH)
Also Called: Yingli Solar
33 Irving Pl Fl 3 (10003-2332)
PHONE 888 686-8820
Robert Petrina, *Ch of Bd*
Liansheng Miao, *Chairman*
Brian Grenko, *Director*
Matthew Sachs, *Director*
▲ **EMP:** 20
SALES (est): 3.4MM **Privately Held**
SIC: 3674 Solar cells
HQ: Baoding Tianwei Yingli New Energy Resources Co., Ltd.
No.3399, North Chaoyang Avenue, Gaokai Dist.
Baoding 07100
312 892-9787

(G-12715)
YIWEN USA INC
60 E 42nd St Ste 1030 (10165-1030)
PHONE 212 370-0828
You Chang, *President*
John Morr, *Opers Staff*
Candy Tan, *Human Res Mgr*
EMP: 10
SALES (est): 1.3MM **Privately Held**
SIC: 2899 Chemical preparations

(G-12716)
YOMIURI INTERNATIONAL INC
747 3rd Ave Fl 28 (10017-2832)
PHONE 212 752-2196
Fax: 212 752-2575
Michiro Okamoto, *Principal*
EMP: 7
SALES (est): 653.2K
SALES (corp-wide): 18.1MM **Privately Held**
SIC: 3714 Motor vehicle parts & accessories
HQ: Yomiuri Shinbun Tokyo Honsha, The
1-7-1, Otemachi
Chiyoda-Ku TKY 100-0
332 421-111

(G-12717)
YONG XIN KITCHEN SUPPLIES INC
50 Delancey St Frnt A (10002-2967)
PHONE 212 995-8908
Chang Wang, *President*
Yvette Lang, *Accountant*
▲ **EMP:** 18
SALES (est): 179.9K **Privately Held**
SIC: 3993 Signs & advertising specialties

(G-12718)
YOU AND ME LEGWEAR LLC
10 W 33rd St Rm 300 (10001-3306)
PHONE 212 279-9292
Fax: 212 268-0543
Sam Hemaoui, *Controller*
Albert Cohen,
▲ **EMP:** 18
SQ FT: 5,000
SALES: 6.7MM **Privately Held**
SIC: 2252 Hosiery

(G-12719)
YS PUBLISHING CO INC
228 E 45th St Rm 700 (10017-3336)
PHONE 212 682-9360
Fax: 212 682-3916
Hitoshi Yoshida, *President*
Miyuki Hanakoshi, *Accountant*
▲ **EMP:** 9
SALES (est): 1.2MM **Privately Held**
WEB: www.us-benricho.com
SIC: 2731 Book publishing

(G-12720)
YURMAN RETAIL INC
Also Called: David Yurman
712 Madison Ave (10065-7207)
PHONE 888 398-7626
David Yurman, *President*
Scott Vogel, *Vice Pres*
Laurie Adorno, *Site Mgr*
Jaime Quinn, *Finance*
EMP: 8
SQ FT: 1,000
SALES (est): 1.2MM
SALES (corp-wide): 276.9MM **Privately Held**
WEB: www.davidyurman.com
SIC: 3911 Jewelry, precious metal
PA: David Yurman Enterprises Llc
24 Vestry St
New York NY 10013
212 896-1550

New York - New York County (G-12721)

(G-12721)
Z-PLY CORP
Also Called: Texray
213 W 35th St Ste 5w (10001-1903)
PHONE..................................212 398-7011
Fax: 212 398-7647
Timothy Chung, *Ch of Bd*
J J Hou, *Exec VP*
Sharon Grosso, *Prdtn Mgr*
Sam Chang, *CFO*
▲ **EMP:** 40
SQ FT: 5,000
SALES (est): 5.1MM Privately Held
WEB: www.z-ply.com
SIC: 2339 2369 Women's & misses' athletic clothing & sportswear; girls' & children's outerwear

(G-12722)
ZAK JEWELRY TOOLS INC
55 W 47th St Fl 2 (10036-2812)
PHONE..................................212 768-8122
Roman Zak, *President*
Robert Zak, *Vice Pres*
◆ **EMP:** 14
SQ FT: 7,500
SALES (est): 1.7MM Privately Held
SIC: 3915 5251 Jewel preparing: instruments, tools, watches & jewelry; tools

(G-12723)
ZAR GROUP LLC (PA)
Also Called: Zar Apparel Group
1375 Broadway Fl 12 (10018-7044)
PHONE..................................212 944-2510
Bobby Zar, *CEO*
Bruce Bond, *President*
Mansour Zar, *Chairman*
Michael Namdar, *Director*
AVI Zukerman, *Director*
▼ **EMP:** 8 **EST:** 1985
SQ FT: 20,000
SALES: 100MM Privately Held
SIC: 2339 Women's & misses' outerwear

(G-12724)
ZARALO LLC
Also Called: Shugaray Division of Zaralo
500 7th Ave Fl 18 (10018-4502)
PHONE..................................212 764-4590
David Lomita, *Principal*
EMP: 8
SALES (corp-wide): 138MM Privately Held
SIC: 2337 Women's & misses' suits & skirts
HQ: Zaralo, Llc
    1 Cape May St Ste 3
    Harrison NJ 07029

(G-12725)
ZARO BAKE SHOP INC
Also Called: Zaro's Bread Basket
370 Lexington Ave (10017-6503)
PHONE..................................212 292-0175
Fax: 212 292-0188
Joseph Zaro, *Manager*
EMP: 59
SALES (corp-wide): 77.8MM Privately Held
WEB: www.zaro.com
SIC: 3556 Ovens, bakery
PA: Zaro Bake Shop, Inc.
    138 Bruckner Blvd
    Bronx NY 10454
    718 993-7327

(G-12726)
ZAZOOM LLC (PA)
Also Called: Zazoom Media Group
1 Exchange Plz Ste 801 (10006-3008)
PHONE..................................212 321-2100
Tim Minton, *CEO*
Chris Green, *Editor*
Greg Morey, *Exec VP*
Steve Charlier, *Vice Pres*
Michaelle Antoine, *Finance Mgr*
EMP: 14
SALES (est): 1.9MM Privately Held
SIC: 2741

(G-12727)
ZEDGE INC
22 Cortlandt St Fl 14 (10007-3152)
PHONE..................................330 577-3424
Tom Arnoy, *CEO*

Jonathan Reich, *COO*
EMP: 53
SQ FT: 500
SALES: 11.1MM Privately Held
SIC: 7372 Prepackaged software

(G-12728)
ZEEBA JEWELRY MFG INC
Also Called: Zeeba Jewelry Manufacturing
36 W 47th St Ste 902 (10036-8641)
PHONE..................................212 997-1009
Fred Navi, *President*
Ray Lavi, *Vice Pres*
EMP: 3
SQ FT: 2,000
SALES: 1MM Privately Held
SIC: 3911 Jewelry, precious metal

(G-12729)
ZETEK CORPORATION
Also Called: Zeteck
13 E 37th St Ste 701 (10016-2841)
PHONE..................................212 668-1485
Fax: 212 668-1487
Bertrand Dorfman, *President*
Raymond McKee, *Director*
EMP: 10
SQ FT: 1,500
SALES (est): 1.1MM Privately Held
WEB: www.zetek.com
SIC: 3663 3669 7622 7629 Radio & TV communications equipment; fire detection systems, electric; communication equipment repair; electrical equipment repair services

(G-12730)
ZG APPAREL GROUP LLC
1375 Broadway Fl 12 (10018-7044)
PHONE..................................212 944-2510
Maurice Salama, *Finance*
Babak Zar, *Mng Member*
Mansur Zar,
◆ **EMP:** 40 **EST:** 2014
SALES (est): 27MM Privately Held
SIC: 2339 Women's & misses' athletic clothing & sportswear; athletic clothing: women's, misses' & juniors'

(G-12731)
ZIA POWER INC
116 E 27th St (10016-8942)
PHONE..................................845 661-8388
Nathaniel Thompkins, *President*
EMP: 36
SQ FT: 2,000
SALES (est): 1.4MM Privately Held
SIC: 2339 Women's & misses' outerwear

(G-12732)
ZINEPAK LLC
349 5th Ave (10016-5019)
PHONE..................................212 706-8621
Amanda Fishman, *Project Mgr*
Carly Prakapas, *Project Mgr*
Brittney Hodak, *Mng Member*
Brittany Hodak, *Mng Member*
Abby Downing, *Creative Dir*
EMP: 10
SALES: 2.9MM Privately Held
SIC: 2731 Book publishing

(G-12733)
ZIRCONIA CREATIONS INTL
134 W 29th St Rm 801 (10001-0107)
PHONE..................................212 239-3730
Fax: 212 239-3733
Michael Halpert, *President*
Yisha Weber, *Vice Pres*
EMP: 8
SQ FT: 3,000
SALES: 1.1MM Privately Held
SIC: 3915 Jewelers' materials & lapidary work

(G-12734)
ZITOMER LLC
969 Madison Ave Fl 1 (10021-2763)
PHONE..................................212 737-5560
Thanh Tran, *Principal*
Sharmin Rai, *Marketing Mgr*
▲ **EMP:** 9 **EST:** 1997
SALES (est): 1.5MM Privately Held
SIC: 2834 Solutions, pharmaceutical

(G-12735)
ZIVA GEM LLC (PA)
200 Madison Ave Ste 2225 (10016-4000)
PHONE..................................646 416-5828
Marc Klein, *President*
Ronnie Dushey, *Vice Pres*
EMP: 10 **EST:** 2015
SALES: 1MM Privately Held
SIC: 3961 Costume jewelry

(G-12736)
ZOE SAKOUTIS LLC
Also Called: Blueprint Cleanse
135 W 29th St Rm 704 (10001-5172)
PHONE..................................212 414-5741
Zoe Sakoutis, *Principal*
Erica Huss, *Principal*
Patrick Burlingham, *Manager*
EMP: 15
SALES (est): 2.4MM Publicly Held
SIC: 2037 Fruit juices
PA: The Hain Celestial Group Inc
    1111 Marcus Ave Ste 100
    New Hyde Park NY 11042

(G-12737)
ZOGRAPHOS DESIGNS LTD
300 E 33rd St Apt 9m (10016-9412)
PHONE..................................212 545-0227
Nicos Zographos, *President*
Terry Lapining, *Marketing Staff*
EMP: 8
SQ FT: 2,250
SALES (est): 961.6K Privately Held
WEB: www.zographos.com
SIC: 2521 2522 Wood office furniture; office furniture, except wood

(G-12738)
ZOLA BOOKS INC (PA)
242 W 38th St Fl 2 (10018-5820)
PHONE..................................917 822-4950
Michael Strong, *CEO*
Amanda McPherson, *Design Engr*
Lynda Radosevich, *Chief Mktg Ofcr*
Tad Floridis, *Director*
Phil Hanrahan, *Director*
EMP: 6
SALES (est): 1.2MM Privately Held
SIC: 2731 Book publishing

(G-12739)
ZORLU USA INC (PA)
295 5th Ave Ste 503 (10016-7103)
PHONE..................................212 689-4622
Fax: 212 689-4380
Vedat Aydin, *President*
Sevket Celikkanat, *Vice Pres*
Filiz Ozpicak, *Vice Pres*
Alihan Altunbas, *Controller*
Salih Poyraz, *Accounts Mgr*
▲ **EMP:** 10
SALES (est): 8.8MM Privately Held
WEB: www.zorluusa.com
SIC: 2221 5131 Textile mills, broadwoven: silk & manmade, also glass; textiles, woven

---

New York Mills
Oneida County

(G-12740)
DELFT BLUE LLC
36 Garden St A (13417-1301)
PHONE..................................315 768-7100
Fax: 315 768-7992
John Gorea, *Plant Mgr*
Kimberly Milller, *Accountant*
Jerry Bartelsi,
EMP: 108
SQ FT: 3,000
SALES (est): 19.3MM Privately Held
SIC: 2011 Veal from meat slaughtered on site

(G-12741)
DI HIGHWAY SIGN STRUCTURE CORP
40 Greenman Ave (13417-1004)
P.O. Box 123 (13417-0123)
PHONE..................................315 736-8312
Fax: 315 736-7172
Steven Mulvihill, *General Mgr*

Jane Mulvihill, *Principal*
Jeff Welch, *Production*
Alex Baisley, *QC Mgr*
Joel Sims, *QC Mgr*
EMP: 40
SQ FT: 35,000
SALES (est): 12.8MM Privately Held
SIC: 3499 Metal household articles; trophies, metal, except silver

(G-12742)
FOUNTAINHEAD GROUP INC (PA)
Also Called: Burgess Products Division
23 Garden St (13417-1318)
PHONE..................................315 736-0037
John F Romano, *CEO*
John O'Toole, *President*
George Mitchell, *Vice Pres*
Linda E Romano, *Vice Pres*
James Siepiola, *Vice Pres*
◆ **EMP:** 150 **EST:** 1973
SQ FT: 40,000
SALES (est): 34.9MM Privately Held
WEB: www.thefountainheadgroup.com
SIC: 3563 3523 3569 Spraying outfits: metals, paints & chemicals (compressor); sprayers & spraying machines, agricultural; fertilizing, spraying, dusting & irrigation machinery; firefighting apparatus

(G-12743)
FOUNTAINHEAD GROUP INC
Bridgeview Aerosol
3 Graden St (13417)
PHONE..................................708 598-7100
Jack Young, *COO*
Richard Bannon, *Controller*
Carol Nelson, *Human Res Mgr*
EMP: 170
SALES (corp-wide): 34.9MM Privately Held
SIC: 3563 2813 Spraying outfits: metals, paints & chemicals (compressor); aerosols
PA: The Fountainhead Group Inc
    23 Garden St
    New York Mills NY 13417
    315 736-0037

(G-12744)
HERMOSA CORP
102 Main St (13417-1103)
P.O. Box 274 (13417-0274)
PHONE..................................315 768-4320
Fax: 315 768-3818
Steven Mulvihill, *President*
Michael Sheridan Pe, *Vice Pres*
Alan Morgan, *Opers Mgr*
Patrick Sullivan, *QC Mgr*
Keith Polisse, *Engineer*
EMP: 20
SQ FT: 40,000
SALES (est): 3.7MM Privately Held
WEB: www.hermosacorp.com
SIC: 3993 Signs, not made in custom sign painting shops

(G-12745)
MOHAWK VALLEY KNT MCHY CO INC
561 Main St (13417-1431)
P.O. Box 120 (13417-0120)
PHONE..................................315 736-3038
Thomas P Firsching, *President*
EMP: 19
SQ FT: 40,000
SALES (est): 3.6MM Privately Held
SIC: 3552 Textile machinery

(G-12746)
QUALITY MACHINING SERVICE INC
70 Sauquoit St (13417-1018)
PHONE..................................315 736-5774
Tom Ostrander, *President*
EMP: 5
SQ FT: 3,000
SALES: 150K Privately Held
SIC: 3599 Machine shop, jobbing & repair

Newburgh - Orange County (G-12771)

(G-12747)
TRANSCOLUX CORP
Also Called: 24-Hour Heating & Cooling Svc
587 Main St Ste 303 (13417-1486)
P.O. Box 587, Herkimer (13350-0587)
PHONE.............................315 768-1500
Yuri Zaikoff, *Ch of Bd*
EMP: 6
SALES (est): 117.1K Privately Held
SIC: 3585 Parts for heating, cooling & refrigerating equipment

Newark
Wayne County

(G-12748)
ADDEX INC
251 Murray St (14513-1216)
PHONE.............................315 331-7700
Barb Cree, *Owner*
Robert Cree, *Exec VP*
Dan Carey, *Manager*
EMP: 9
SALES (corp-wide): 1.6MM Privately Held
WEB: www.addexinc.com
SIC: 3625 Control equipment, electric
PA: Addex, Inc.
   251 Murray St
   Newark NY 14513
   781 344-5800

(G-12749)
ADDEX INC (PA)
251 Murray St (14513-1216)
PHONE.............................781 344-5800
Rudiger Von Kraus, *President*
Robert E Cree, *Exec VP*
Bill Randolph, *Engineer*
Kathy McCluskey, *Manager*
▲ **EMP:** 5
SQ FT: 10,000
SALES (est): 1.6MM Privately Held
WEB: www.addexinc.com
SIC: 3559 Plastics working machinery

(G-12750)
C&C AUTOMATICS INC
127 W Shore Blvd (14513-1259)
PHONE.............................315 331-1436
Craig T Parsons, *President*
Craig Halstead, *Vice Pres*
EMP: 20
SQ FT: 9,000
SALES (est): 2.3MM Privately Held
WEB: www.ccautomatics.com
SIC: 3451 Screw machine products

(G-12751)
HALLAGAN MANUFACTURING CO INC
500 Hoffman St (14513-1858)
P.O. Box 268 (14513-0268)
PHONE.............................315 331-4640
Charles W Hallagan, *Ch of Bd*
Stephen Hallagan, *President*
Walter Hallagan, *Vice Pres*
EMP: 80
SQ FT: 97,000
SALES (est): 10.3MM Privately Held
SIC: 2512 Living room furniture: upholstered on wood frames

(G-12752)
IEC ELECTRONICS CORP (PA)
105 Norton St (14513-1298)
P.O. Box 271 (14513-0271)
PHONE.............................315 331-7742
Fax: 315 331-3547
Jeremy R Nowak, *Ch of Bd*
Jeffery T Schlarbaum, *President*
Jens Hauvn, *Senior VP*
Dj Dugger, *Facilities Mgr*
Thomas Giuliani, *Purch Mgr*
▲ **EMP:** 634 **EST:** 1966
SQ FT: 235,000
SALES: 127MM Publicly Held
WEB: www.iec-electronics.com
SIC: 3672 3679 Printed circuit boards; electronic circuits

(G-12753)
IEC ELECTRONICS WIRE CABLE INC
105 Norton St (14513-1218)
P.O. Box 271 (14513-0271)
PHONE.............................585 924-9010
Jeffrey T Schlarbaum, *President*
Donald S Doody, *Vice Pres*
Debbie Bridger, *Prdtn Mgr*
Vincent Leo, *CFO*
Christi Rollo, *Credit Mgr*
EMP: 100
SQ FT: 19,000
SALES (est): 12.2MM
SALES (corp-wide): 127MM Publicly Held
WEB: www.val-u-tech.com
SIC: 3672 Printed circuit boards
PA: Iec Electronics Corp.
   105 Norton St
   Newark NY 14513
   315 331-7742

(G-12754)
LEGENDARY AUTO INTERIORS LTD
121 W Shore Blvd (14513-1259)
PHONE.............................315 331-1212
Fax: 315 331-2244
Martin J Beckenbach, *Ch of Bd*
▲ **EMP:** 40
SQ FT: 12,000
SALES (est): 5.8MM Privately Held
WEB: www.legendaryautointeriors.com
SIC: 2396 5013 5531 3429 Automotive trimmings, fabric; automotive trim; automotive accessories; manufactured hardware (general); leather tanning & finishing; nonwoven fabrics

(G-12755)
MACO BAG CORPORATION
412 Van Buren St (14513-9205)
PHONE.............................315 226-1000
Fax: 315 226-1050
J Scott Miller, *Ch of Bd*
Craig Miller, *President*
Susan Miller, *Corp Secy*
Bob Finley, *Safety Dir*
Robert Finley, *Safety Dir*
▲ **EMP:** 140 **EST:** 1929
SQ FT: 60,000
SALES (est): 38MM Privately Held
WEB: www.macobag.com
SIC: 3081 2673 Plastic film & sheet; plastic & pliofilm bags

(G-12756)
MCDOWELL RESEARCH CO INC (HQ)
2000 Technology Pkwy (14513-2175)
PHONE.............................315 332-7100
John D Kavazanjian, *President*
Julius Cirin, *Vice Pres*
Dede Emery, *Senior Buyer*
Molly Hedges, *Controller*
Jeff Luke, *Chief Mktg Ofcr*
▲ **EMP:** 100
SQ FT: 54,000
SALES (est): 88.2MM
SALES (corp-wide): 82.4MM Publicly Held
WEB: www.mrc-power.com
SIC: 3669 Intercommunication systems, electric
PA: Ultralife Corporation
   2000 Technology Pkwy
   Newark NY 14513
   315 332-7100

(G-12757)
MICRO-TECH MACHINE INC
301 W Shore Blvd (14513-1261)
PHONE.............................315 331-6671
Fax: 315 331-0142
Michael R Davis, *President*
Lance Mebb, *General Mgr*
Lori Ramsey, *Purchasing*
Bill Guinup, *Engineer*
Amy Davis, *CFO*
EMP: 44
SQ FT: 13,000
SALES (est): 7.4MM Privately Held
WEB: www.microtechmachine.com
SIC: 3599 Machine shop, jobbing & repair

(G-12758)
MOOSEBERRY SOAP CO LLC
513 W Union St Ste B (14513-1365)
PHONE.............................315 332-8913
Mary Bartolotta, *Mng Member*
EMP: 7 **EST:** 2011
SQ FT: 5,000
SALES (est): 896.5K Privately Held
SIC: 2841 Soap: granulated, liquid, cake, flaked or chip

(G-12759)
NEWCHEM INC
Also Called: Newcut
434 E Union St (14513-1610)
PHONE.............................315 331-7680
Fax: 315 331-0313
Sean Whittaker, *President*
Pete Engel, *Engineer*
Illa Burbank, *CFO*
Richard Boerman, *Human Res Dir*
EMP: 22
SALES (est): 4MM Privately Held
SIC: 3479 Etching, photochemical

(G-12760)
NORTH AMERICAN FILTER CORP (PA)
Also Called: Nafco
200 W Shore Blvd (14513-1258)
PHONE.............................800 265-8943
Fax: 315 331-4750
Steve Taylor, *President*
Jerry Dusharm, *Opers Staff*
▼ **EMP:** 74
SQ FT: 75,000
SALES (est): 14.3MM Privately Held
WEB: www.nafcoinc.com
SIC: 3569 3564 Filters, general line: industrial; blowers & fans

(G-12761)
P V C MOLDING TECHNOLOGIES
122 W Shore Blvd (14513-1258)
PHONE.............................315 331-1212
Martin Beckenbach, *President*
EMP: 12
SQ FT: 14,198
SALES (est): 1MM Privately Held
SIC: 3089 Plastic processing

(G-12762)
PROGRESSIVE GRAPHICS & PRTG
1171 E Union St (14513-9201)
P.O. Box 492 (14513-0492)
PHONE.............................315 331-3635
Robert Kelly, *President*
Dennis Chasse, *Vice Pres*
EMP: 6
SQ FT: 10,000
SALES (est): 418K Privately Held
SIC: 2752 2791 2789 Commercial printing, offset; typesetting; bookbinding & related work

(G-12763)
SMITH METAL WORKS NEWARK INC
1000 E Union St (14513-1643)
PHONE.............................315 331-1651
Fax: 315 331-0910
Wayne F Smith, *President*
Janice Smith, *Treasurer*
Barbara Jones, *Manager*
Joe Cosentino, *IT/INT Sup*
EMP: 27 **EST:** 1942
SQ FT: 5,000
SALES (est): 7.5MM Privately Held
WEB: www.smithspreaders.com
SIC: 3714 3599 Sanders, motor vehicle safety; machine shop, jobbing & repair; custom machinery

(G-12764)
SPINCO METAL PRODUCTS INC
1 Country Club Dr (14513-1250)
PHONE.............................315 331-6285
Fax: 315 331-9535
C Robert Straubing Jr, *Ch of Bd*
Thurlow Hammond, *Controller*
John Bulger, *Admin Sec*
▲ **EMP:** 80
SQ FT: 48,000
SALES (est): 24MM Privately Held
WEB: www.spincometal.com
SIC: 3498 Tube fabricating (contract bending & shaping)

(G-12765)
SUPERGEN PRODUCTS LLC
320 Hoffman St (14513-1830)
PHONE.............................315 573-7887
Paul Cole, *Mng Member*
EMP: 9
SALES: 140K Privately Held
SIC: 3621 Motors & generators

(G-12766)
ULTRALIFE CORPORATION (PA)
2000 Technology Pkwy (14513-2175)
PHONE.............................315 332-7100
Bradford T Whitmore, *Ch of Bd*
Michael D Popielec, *President*
Philip A Fain, *CFO*
▲ **EMP:** 552
SQ FT: 250,000
SALES: 82.4MM Publicly Held
WEB: www.ulbi.com
SIC: 3691 3679 Storage batteries; alkaline cell storage batteries; batteries, rechargeable; electronic loads & power supplies; harness assemblies for electronic use: wire or cable; parametric amplifiers

(G-12767)
UPSTATE REFRACTORY SVCS INC
100 Erie Blvd (14513-1163)
PHONE.............................315 331-2955
Fax: 315 364-4594
David Wetmore, *President*
Diane Wetmore, *Vice Pres*
Bryan Wetmore, *Warehouse Mgr*
Bill Wilck, *Senior Engr*
Diana Harder, *Manager*
EMP: 29
SQ FT: 18,000
SALES (est): 5.5MM Privately Held
WEB: www.upstaterefractoryservices.com
SIC: 3255 5085 Clay refractories; refractory material

(G-12768)
VAN LAEKEN RICHARD
Also Called: Harris Machine
2680 Parker Rd (14513-9750)
PHONE.............................315 331-0289
Richard Van Laeken, *Owner*
EMP: 5 **EST:** 1995
SQ FT: 2,600
SALES: 450K Privately Held
SIC: 3599 Machine shop, jobbing & repair

Newburgh
Orange County

(G-12769)
ALUMIL FABRICATION INC
1900 Corporate Blvd (12550-6412)
PHONE.............................845 469-2874
Kyt Bazenikas, *Ch of Bd*
▲ **EMP:** 14
SALES (est): 2.9MM Privately Held
SIC: 3442 Screens, window, metal

(G-12770)
AMERICAN ICON INDUSTRIES INC
392 N Montgomery St Ste 2 (12550-6802)
PHONE.............................845 561-1299
Fax: 845 913-9067
Robert Kucharek, *CEO*
Andrew Abate, *General Mgr*
Gary Rausenberger, *Principal*
Drew Abate, *COO*
Roger Conant, *COO*
EMP: 6
SALES (est): 991.4K Privately Held
SIC: 2752 Commercial printing, lithographic

(G-12771)
ARCTIC GLACIER NEWBURGH INC (HQ)
225 Lake St (12550-5242)
PHONE.............................845 561-0549

Newburgh - Orange County (G-12772)

Robert Nagy, *President*
Al Feller, *General Mgr*
Keith McMahon, *Vice Pres*
Scott Hinson, *Manager*
Hugh Adams, *Admin Sec*
EMP: 15
SQ FT: 40,000
SALES (est): 3.1MM
SALES (corp-wide): 240.7MM **Privately Held**
SIC: 2097 Manufactured ice
PA: Arctic Glacier Inc
   625 Henry Ave
   Winnipeg MB R3A 0
   204 772-2473

(G-12772)
BIG SHINE WORLDWIDE INC
Also Called: Big Shine Energy
300 Corporate Blvd (12550-6402)
PHONE..................845 444-5255
Dong IL Lee, *CEO*
Merealess Ferreira, *Director*
Bong Hee Lee Kim, *Admin Sec*
EMP: 6
SALES: 30MM **Privately Held**
SIC: 3646 Commercial indusl & institutional electric lighting fixtures

(G-12773)
BIMBO BAKERIES USA INC
98 Scobie Dr (12550-3257)
PHONE..................845 568-0943
Michael D'Adamo, *Director*
EMP: 53 **Privately Held**
SIC: 2051 Bread, cake & related products
HQ: Bimbo Bakeries Usa, Inc
   255 Business Center Dr # 200
   Horsham PA 19044
   215 347-5500

(G-12774)
COMMODORE CHOCOLATIER USA INC
482 Broadway (12550-5333)
PHONE..................845 561-3960
John Courtsunis, *President*
EMP: 10 **EST**: 1935
SQ FT: 5,000
SALES: 1MM **Privately Held**
SIC: 2066 5149 5441 Chocolate; chocolate; candy

(G-12775)
E & O MARI INC
Also Called: La Bella Strings
256 Broadway (12550-5487)
P.O. Box 869 (12551-0869)
PHONE..................845 562-4400
Fax: 845 562-4491
Richard Cocco Jr, *President*
Robert Archigian, *Sales/Mktg Dir*
Lorenza Cocco, *Director*
▲ **EMP**: 89 **EST**: 1915
SQ FT: 29,000
SALES (est): 12.8MM **Privately Held**
SIC: 3931 Strings, musical instrument

(G-12776)
FRAGRANCE ACQUISITIONS LLC
1900 Corporate Blvd (12550-6412)
PHONE..................845 534-9172
Glenn Palmer, *Partner*
▲ **EMP**: 70 **EST**: 2011
SALES (est): 10.2MM **Privately Held**
SIC: 2844 Perfumes & colognes

(G-12777)
GASOFT EQUIPMENT INC
231 Dubois St (12550-3410)
PHONE..................845 863-1010
Tony M Colandrea, *President*
Nick Gurlakis, *Vice Pres*
◆ **EMP**: 14
SQ FT: 5,000
SALES: 5.6MM **Privately Held**
SIC: 3577 5045 Computer peripheral equipment; computers, peripherals & software

(G-12778)
GENERAL ELECTRIC COMPANY
169 New York 17k 17 K (12550)
PHONE..................845 567-7410
Dan Melvin, *Manager*

EMP: 21
SALES (corp-wide): 123.6B **Publicly Held**
WEB: www.gecapital.com
SIC: 3743 Train cars & equipment, freight or passenger
PA: General Electric Company
   41 Farnsworth St
   Boston MA 02210
   617 443-3000

(G-12779)
GENERAL TRAFFIC EQUIPMENT CORP
259 Broadway (12550-5452)
PHONE..................845 569-9000
Fax: 845 569-1800
Raymond Staffon, *President*
Eileen Staffon, *Sales Mgr*
Jackie Deleon, *Office Mgr*
▲ **EMP**: 15
SQ FT: 15,000
SALES (est): 2.4MM **Privately Held**
WEB: www.generaltrafficequip.com
SIC: 3669 Traffic signals, electric

(G-12780)
GLASBAU HAHN AMERICA LLC
15 Little Brook Ln Ste 2 (12550-1687)
PHONE..................845 566-3331
Jamie Ponton, *Principal*
Cathy Lima, *Manager*
▲ **EMP**: 5
SALES (est): 390K **Privately Held**
SIC: 2542 Counters or counter display cases: except wood

(G-12781)
GTI GRAPHIC TECHNOLOGY INC (PA)
211 Dupont Ave (12550-4019)
P.O. Box 3138 (12550-0651)
PHONE..................845 562-7066
Fax: 845 562-2543
Robert Mc Curdy, *President*
Louis Chappo, *Vice Pres*
Robert McCurdy, *Vice Pres*
Elizabeth Mc Curdy, *Treasurer*
Bruce Sparrow, *Sales Staff*
EMP: 32
SQ FT: 40,000
SALES: 5MM **Privately Held**
WEB: www.graphiclite.com
SIC: 3648 Lighting equipment

(G-12782)
HOME DEPOT USA INC
Also Called: Home Depot, The
1220 New York 300 (12550)
PHONE..................845 561-6540
Fax: 845 563-9016
Michael J Pleskach, *Manager*
Scott Procia, *Manager*
EMP: 240
SALES (corp-wide): 94.6B **Publicly Held**
WEB: www.homerentalsdepot.com
SIC: 3699 Electrical equipment & supplies
HQ: Home Depot U.S.A., Inc.
   2455 Paces Ferry Rd Se
   Atlanta GA 30339
   770 433-8211

(G-12783)
HUDSON VALLEY BLACK PRESS
343 Broadway (12550-5301)
P.O. Box 2160 (12550-0332)
PHONE..................845 562-1313
Charles Stewart, *President*
John Callahan, *Accounts Exec*
EMP: 7
SQ FT: 4,000
SALES (est): 378.6K **Privately Held**
SIC: 2711 Newspapers: publishing only, not printed on site

(G-12784)
HUDSON VALLEY OFFICE FURN INC
7 Wisner Ave (12550-5133)
PHONE..................845 565-6673
Fax: 845 565-7269
Tom Chickery, *Owner*
EMP: 8

SALES (corp-wide): 4MM **Privately Held**
WEB: www.thewowguys.com
SIC: 2522 Office furniture, except wood
PA: Hudson Valley Office Furniture, Inc.
   375 Main St
   Poughkeepsie NY 12601
   845 471-7910

(G-12785)
HUDSON VALLEY PAPER WORKS INC
8 Lander St 15 (12550-4938)
PHONE..................845 569-8883
Luke Pontifell, *President*
▲ **EMP**: 15
SALES (est): 1.2MM **Privately Held**
SIC: 2732 Book printing

(G-12786)
LA ESCONDIDA INC
129 Lake St (12550-5242)
PHONE..................845 562-1387
Andres Garcia, *President*
Emigdio Carrera, *Vice Pres*
EMP: 8
SQ FT: 2,000
SALES (est): 850.5K **Privately Held**
WEB: www.laescondida.com
SIC: 2099 Tortillas, fresh or refrigerated

(G-12787)
MAGNETIC AIDS INC
201 Ann St (12550-5417)
P.O. Box 2502 (12550-0610)
PHONE..................845 863-1400
Joe Formoso, *President*
George Klapiscak, *Sales Staff*
Eve Formoso, *Manager*
Stacy Pecka, *Manager*
Daniel Formoso, *Master*
▲ **EMP**: 8 **EST**: 1958
SQ FT: 12,000
SALES: 750K **Privately Held**
WEB: www.magneticaids.com
SIC: 3499 3429 Magnets, permanent: metallic; manufactured hardware (general); hangers, wall hardware

(G-12788)
MIXTURE SCREEN PRINTING
1607 Route 300 100 (12550-1738)
PHONE..................845 561-2857
Christopher D Fahrbach, *Owner*
EMP: 8
SALES (est): 515.6K **Privately Held**
SIC: 2759 3993 5099 Screen printing; signs & advertising specialties; signs, except electric

(G-12789)
MOKAI MANUFACTURING INC
13 Jeanne Dr (12550-1788)
PHONE..................845 566-8287
Rick Murray, *President*
Justin Bruyn, *Design Engr*
Misses Jones, *Manager*
EMP: 6
SALES (est): 999.5K **Privately Held**
WEB: www.mokai.com
SIC: 3732 Boat building & repairing

(G-12790)
MONDELEZ GLOBAL LLC
Also Called: Nabisco
800 Corporate Blvd (12550-6407)
PHONE..................845 567-4701
Patrick Sherman, *General Mgr*
EMP: 6 **Publicly Held**
SIC: 2022 Cheese, natural & processed
HQ: Mondelez Global Llc
   3 Parkway N Ste 300
   Deerfield IL 60015
   847 943-4000

(G-12791)
NEWBURGH BREWING COMPANY LLC
88 S Colden St (12550-5640)
Rural Route 72, Salisbury Mills (12577)
PHONE..................845 569-2337
Paul Halayko,
Beth Laub, *Assistant*
EMP: 14 **EST**: 2012
SALES (est): 2.2MM **Privately Held**
SIC: 2082 Beer (alcoholic beverage)

(G-12792)
NEWBURGH ENVELOPE CORP
1720 Route 300 (12550-8930)
PHONE..................845 566-4211
Fax: 845 566-4212
Carl Stillwaggon, *President*
Stuart Stillwaggon, *Vice Pres*
EMP: 7
SQ FT: 1,800
SALES (est): 640K **Privately Held**
SIC: 2752 Commercial printing, offset

(G-12793)
ORANGE COUNTY CHOPPERS INC
Also Called: O C Choppers
14 Crossroads Ct (12550-5064)
PHONE..................845 522-5200
Fax: 845 522-5227
Paul Teutul Sr, *President*
Jason Pohl, *Design Engr*
Jessica Miller, *Executive*
EMP: 6
SALES: 1MM **Privately Held**
SIC: 3751 Motorcycles & related parts

(G-12794)
ORANGE DIE CUTTING CORP
Also Called: Orange Packaging
1 Favoriti Ave (12550-4015)
P.O. Box 2295 (12550-0441)
PHONE..................845 562-0900
Fax: 845 562-1020
Anthony Esposito Sr, *Ch of Bd*
Anthony Esposito Jr, *President*
Hector Torres, *General Mgr*
Brenda Benevides, *Sales Staff*
Tom Pederson, *Mktg Dir*
▲ **EMP**: 120 **EST**: 1950
SQ FT: 40,000
SALES (est): 29.9MM **Privately Held**
SIC: 2675 Die-cut paper & board

(G-12795)
ORNAMETAL INC
216 S William St (12550-5845)
PHONE..................845 562-5151
Richard Cohen, *Owner*
EMP: 5
SALES (est): 387K **Privately Held**
SIC: 3446 Stairs, staircases, stair treads: prefabricated metal

(G-12796)
PECKHAM MATERIALS CORP
322 Walsh Ave (12553-6748)
P.O. Box 4074, New Windsor (12553-0074)
PHONE..................845 562-5370
EMP: 5
SALES (corp-wide): 200.6MM **Privately Held**
SIC: 2951 Asphalt & asphaltic paving mixtures (not from refineries)
HQ: Peckham Materials Corp
   20 Haarlem Ave Ste 200
   White Plains NY 10603
   914 686-2045

(G-12797)
PEPSI-COLA NEWBURGH BTLG INC
Also Called: Pepsico
1 Pepsi Way (12550-3921)
PHONE..................845 562-5400
Fax: 845 562-7480
Charles T Tenney Jr, *President*
Tom Strahle, *COO*
Joseph McDonald, *CFO*
Toni L Taylor, *Payroll Mgr*
Topher Black, *Director*
EMP: 150 **EST**: 1939
SALES (est): 29.7MM **Privately Held**
SIC: 2086 Carbonated soft drinks, bottled & canned

(G-12798)
PRISMATIC DYEING & FINSHG INC
40 Wisner Ave (12550-5132)
P.O. Box 2456 (12550-0732)
PHONE..................845 561-1800
Gary Innocenti, *President*
Deborah Emerick, *Manager*
EMP: 60
SQ FT: 110,000

SALES (est): 11.7MM **Privately Held**
WEB: www.prismaticdyeing.com
SIC: 2861 2269 2262 2261 Dyeing materials, natural; finishing plants; finishing plants, manmade fiber & silk fabrics; finishing plants, cotton

(G-12799)
PROKOSCH AND SONN SHEET METAL
772 South St (12550-4149)
PHONE...............................845 562-4211
Fax: 845 562-8782
Alfred Prokosch Jr, *Ch of Bd*
Annunciata Prokosch, *President*
John F Prokosch, *Vice Pres*
EMP: 21
SQ FT: 2,400
SALES (est): 4.2MM **Privately Held**
SIC: 3444 1711 Sheet metalwork; heating & air conditioning contractors

(G-12800)
PROSTHETIC REHABILITATION CTR (PA)
2 Winding Ln (12550-2223)
PHONE...............................845 565-8255
Fax: 845 565-4409
Andrew Carubia, *President*
Carol Hatcher, *Admin Sec*
EMP: 8
SALES (est): 750.9K **Privately Held**
SIC: 3842 5999 Limbs, artificial; artificial limbs

(G-12801)
RUSSIN LUMBER CORP
Also Called: Staining Plant
75 Pierces Rd (12550-3263)
PHONE...............................845 457-4000
Barry Russin, *President*
EMP: 10
SALES (corp-wide): 47.6MM **Privately Held**
WEB: www.russinlumber.com
SIC: 2431 Millwork
PA: Russin Lumber Corp.
   21 Leonards Dr
   Montgomery NY 12549
   800 724-0010

(G-12802)
SANDY LITTMAN INC
Also Called: American Glass Light
420 N Montgomery St (12550-3680)
P.O. Box 11089, Greenwich CT (06831-1089)
PHONE...............................845 562-1112
Fax: 212 371-4874
Sandy Littman, *President*
Kim Gabriel, *Manager*
Irene Higgins, *Manager*
EMP: 6
SQ FT: 800
SALES (est): 1.2MM **Privately Held**
WEB: www.americanglasslight.com
SIC: 3646 3645 Commercial indusl & institutional electric lighting fixtures; residential lighting fixtures

(G-12803)
SOLATA FOODS LLC ✪
20 Governor Dr (12550-8338)
PHONE...............................845 245-4812
EMP: 20 **EST:** 2017
SALES (est): 671.8K **Privately Held**
SIC: 2099 Ready-to-eat meals, salads & sandwiches

(G-12804)
STEELWAYS INC
Also Called: Steelways Shipyard
401 S Water St (12553-6038)
PHONE...............................845 562-0860
David Plotkins, *Ch of Bd*
Brian Plotkin, *Exec VP*
Brian Plotkins, *Exec VP*
Steve Laker, *CFO*
EMP: 29
SQ FT: 15,000
SALES (est): 7.5MM **Privately Held**
WEB: www.steelwaysinc.com
SIC: 3731 3443 Commercial cargo ships, building & repairing; tanks, standard or custom fabricated: metal plate

PA: Steelways Holdings Group, Inc.
   401 S Water St
   Newburgh NY 12553

(G-12805)
TELECHEMISCHE INC
222 Dupont Ave (12550-4060)
PHONE...............................845 561-3237
Mary Mallavarapu, *Ch of Bd*
Leo Mallavarapu PHD, *President*
Anita Soares, *Admin Sec*
EMP: 6
SALES: 100K **Privately Held**
WEB: www.telechemische.en.ecplaza.net
SIC: 2821 2869 Plastics materials & resins; industrial organic chemicals

(G-12806)
UNICO INC
25 Renwick St (12550-6029)
PHONE...............................845 562-9255
Fax: 845 562-7759
Michael Guarneri, *President*
Joseph Guarneri Jr, *Vice Pres*
Regina Guarneri, *Vice Pres*
Edward Guarneri, *Treasurer*
EMP: 15 **EST:** 1948
SQ FT: 12,000
SALES (est): 2.1MM **Privately Held**
SIC: 3431 3231 2821 2541 Metal sanitary ware; doors, glass: made from purchased glass; plastics materials & resins; wood partitions & fixtures

(G-12807)
UNICO SPECIAL PRODUCTS INC
25 Renwick St (12550-6029)
PHONE...............................845 562-9255
Joseph Guarneri Jr, *President*
Edward Guarneri, *Corp Secy*
Michael Guarneri, *Vice Pres*
▲ **EMP:** 50
SQ FT: 44,000
SALES: 250K **Privately Held**
SIC: 3083 Plastic finished products, laminated

(G-12808)
UNIVERSAL THIN FILM LAB CORP
232 N Plank Rd (12550-1775)
PHONE...............................845 562-0601
Carmelo Comito, *President*
Christopher Infante, *Engineer*
Mike Middleton, *Engineer*
Alison Comito, *Treasurer*
Michael Straub, *Manager*
EMP: 7 **EST:** 1997
SQ FT: 3,000
SALES: 1MM **Privately Held**
SIC: 3559 Optical lens machinery

(G-12809)
WAGNER TECHNICAL SERVICES INC
1658 Route 300 (12550-1757)
PHONE...............................845 566-4018
Gerald L Wagner, *President*
Gerald Wagner, *President*
Edward Busse, *Manager*
EMP: 17
SALES (est): 3.4MM **Privately Held**
WEB: www.wagnertech.com
SIC: 7372 Utility computer software

(G-12810)
WALLKILL VALLEY PUBLICATIONS
Also Called: Wallkill Valley Times
300 Stony Brook Ct Ste B (12550-6535)
PHONE...............................845 561-0170
Carl Aiello, *President*
EMP: 20
SQ FT: 1,500
SALES (est): 1.1MM **Privately Held**
WEB: www.tcnewspapers.com
SIC: 2711 2791 2752 2721 Newspapers: publishing only, not printed on site; typesetting; commercial printing, lithographic; periodicals

Newfane
Niagara County

(G-12811)
KSM GROUP LTD
2905 Beebe Rd (14108-9655)
PHONE...............................716 751-6006
Fax: 716 751-6335
Daniel King, *President*
Judith M King, *Vice Pres*
EMP: 5
SQ FT: 18,000
SALES (est): 430K **Privately Held**
WEB: www.ksmgroup.org
SIC: 3444 Sheet metalwork

(G-12812)
SAVACO INC
2905 Beebe Rd (14108-9655)
PHONE...............................716 751-9455
Judith King, *President*
Kevin King, *Opers Mgr*
Brad Few, *Info Tech Mgr*
EMP: 7
SQ FT: 18,000
SALES: 500K **Privately Held**
WEB: www.savacoinc.com
SIC: 3444 Sheet metalwork

(G-12813)
VANTE INC
Also Called: Plasticweld Systems
3600 Coomer Rd (14108-9651)
PHONE...............................716 778-7691
Fax: 716 778-5671
Brian Strini, *CEO*
Norman Strobel, *President*
Scott Dewitt, *General Mgr*
Ziggy Franusiak, *Electrical Engi*
Pete Strobel, *Manager*
▲ **EMP:** 10
SQ FT: 4,800
SALES (est): 1.9MM
SALES (corp-wide): 19MM **Privately Held**
WEB: www.plasticweldsystems.com
SIC: 3841 3548 Catheters; welding apparatus
PA: Machine Solutions, Inc.
   2951 W Shamrell Blvd # 107
   Flagstaff AZ 86005
   928 556-3109

Newport
Herkimer County

(G-12814)
FULLER TOOL INCORPORATED
225 Platform Rd (13416-2217)
PHONE...............................315 891-3183
Rodney Fuller, *CEO*
EMP: 10
SQ FT: 2,800
SALES: 500K **Privately Held**
WEB: www.fullertool.com
SIC: 3312 3544 Tool & die steel & alloys; special dies, tools, jigs & fixtures

(G-12815)
NEWPORT MAGNETICS INC
396 Old State Rd (13416)
P.O. Box 533 (13416-0533)
PHONE...............................315 845-8878
Fax: 315 845-8876
Ronald Fusco, *President*
▲ **EMP:** 9
SQ FT: 5,000
SALES: 500K **Privately Held**
WEB: www.newportmagnetics.com
SIC: 3493 Coiled flat springs

(G-12816)
REYNOLDS DRAPERY SERVICE INC
Also Called: Country Coin-Op
7440 Main St (13416-7707)
PHONE...............................315 845-8632
Fax: 315 845-8645
Richard Reynolds, *President*
Michael Moody, *Vice Pres*
EMP: 10 **EST:** 1964
SQ FT: 6,500
SALES (est): 964.8K **Privately Held**
SIC: 2391 5023 5714 7216 Draperies, plastic & textile: from purchased materials; draperies; draperies; curtain cleaning & repair; fire resistance finishing of cotton broadwoven fabrics; laundry, coin-operated

Niagara Falls
Niagara County

(G-12817)
AAVID NIAGARA LLC (DH)
3315 Haseley Dr (14304-1460)
PHONE...............................716 297-0652
Barry Heckman, *CEO*
Alan Wong, *President*
Tana Laskowski, *General Mgr*
Scott Mowry, *Vice Pres*
Donald Hall, *Plant Mgr*
▲ **EMP:** 31
SQ FT: 45,000
SALES (est): 30.8MM
SALES (corp-wide): 437.6MM **Privately Held**
WEB: www.niagarathermal.com
SIC: 3443 5084 Heat exchangers, condensers & components; heat exchange equipment, industrial
HQ: Aavid Thermalloy, Llc
   1 Aavid Cir
   Laconia NH 03246
   603 528-3400

(G-12818)
ADVANTAGE MACHINING INC
6421 Wendt Dr (14304-1100)
PHONE...............................716 731-6418
Scott Ranney, *President*
EMP: 10
SALES (est): 1MM **Privately Held**
SIC: 3441 Fabricated structural metal

(G-12819)
ANGUS CHEMICAL COMPANY
Also Called: Angus Buffers & Biochemicals
2236 Liberty Dr (14304-3756)
PHONE...............................716 283-1434
Fred Dlugos, *CFO*
Mark Deuble, *Manager*
Bill Brewer, *Manager*
EMP: 23
SALES (corp-wide): 7.1B **Privately Held**
SIC: 2836 Culture media
HQ: Angus Chemical Company
   1500 E Lake Cook Rd
   Buffalo Grove IL 60089
   847 215-8600

(G-12820)
APOLLO STEEL CORPORATION
4800 Tomson Ave (14304-2150)
PHONE...............................716 283-8758
Fax: 716 283-1136
George E Merkling III, *President*
Bill Crissy, *Business Mgr*
EMP: 16
SQ FT: 15,000
SALES (est): 5.7MM **Privately Held**
SIC: 3441 Bridge sections, prefabricated highway; bridge sections, prefabricated railway; expansion joints (structural shapes), iron or steel; floor jacks, metal

(G-12821)
BRAUN HORTICULTURE INC
3302 Highland Ave (14305-2013)
P.O. Box 260 (14305-0260)
PHONE...............................716 282-6101
Peter Braun, *President*
Ken Young, *Controller*
Pam Lord, *Data Proc Dir*
▲ **EMP:** 7
SQ FT: 31,500
SALES (est): 1.3MM
SALES (corp-wide): 202.9K **Privately Held**
WEB: www.braungroup.com
SIC: 3315 Baskets, steel wire

Niagara Falls - Niagara County (G-12822)

GEOGRAPHIC SECTION

HQ: Braun Nursery Limited
2004 Glancaster Rd
Mount Hope ON L0R 1
905 648-1911

(G-12822)
BRODA MACHINE CO INC
8745 Packard Rd (14304-1497)
PHONE 716 297-3221
Fax: 716 297-0270
Matthew Broda, *President*
Thomas J Broda, *President*
Lillian Broda, *Corp Secy*
Mark Broda, *Vice Pres*
EMP: 13
SQ FT: 10,000
SALES (est): 3.5MM **Privately Held**
WEB: www.brodamachine.com
SIC: 3451 Screw machine products

(G-12823)
CALSPAN CORPORATION
Also Called: Calspan Flight Research Center
2041 Niagara Falls Blvd (14304-1617)
PHONE 716 236-1040
Paul Nafziger, *Branch Mgr*
EMP: 11
SALES (corp-wide): 16.3MM **Privately Held**
WEB: www.windtunnel.com
SIC: 3721 Research & development on aircraft by the manufacturer
HQ: Calspan Corporation
4455 Genesee St
Buffalo NY 14225
716 631-6955

(G-12824)
CASCADES NEW YORK INC
4001 Packard Rd (14303-2202)
PHONE 716 285-3681
Craig Griffith, *General Mgr*
Mary Malone, *Manager*
EMP: 115
SALES (corp-wide): 2.9B **Privately Held**
SIC: 2631 Linerboard
HQ: Cascades New York Inc.
1845 Emerson St
Rochester NY 14606
585 527-8110

(G-12825)
CCT (US) INC
2221 Niagara Falls Blvd # 5 (14304-5709)
PHONE 716 297-7509
Fax: 716 297-3262
Yves Therrien, *President*
Jacques Chevrette, *Admin Sec*
▲ EMP: 15
SQ FT: 20,000
SALES (est): 595.4K
SALES (corp-wide): 4.3MM **Privately Held**
SIC: 2679 Building, insulating & packaging paper; building, insulating & packaging paperboard
PA: Papiers C.C.T. Inc
830 Rue Saint-Viateur
Berthierville QC J0K 1
450 836-3846

(G-12826)
CHEMOURS COMPANY FC LLC
3181 Buffalo Ave (14303-2158)
P.O. Box 787 (14302-0787)
PHONE 716 278-5100
Fax: 716 278-5195
Kelly Kober, *Human Res Dir*
Tim Reece, *Manager*
Jeffrey Manning, *Manager*
Marie Kandt, *Supervisor*
Esther Lorence, *Director*
EMP: 50
SALES (corp-wide): 5.4B **Publicly Held**
WEB: www.dupont.com
SIC: 2819 2865 2812 Industrial inorganic chemicals; cyclic crudes & intermediates; alkalies & chlorine
HQ: The Chemours Company Fc Llc
1007 Market St
Wilmington DE 19298
302 774-1000

(G-12827)
COMMUNITY NEWSPPR HOLDINGS INC
Also Called: Tonanwanda News
473 3rd St Ste 201 (14301-1500)
PHONE 716 693-1000
Wayne Lowman, *Branch Mgr*
EMP: 100
SQ FT: 21,892 **Privately Held**
WEB: www.clintonnc.com
SIC: 2711 Newspapers: publishing only, not printed on site
PA: Community Newspaper Holdings, Inc.
445 Dexter Ave Ste 7000
Montgomery AL 36104

(G-12828)
COMMUNITY NEWSPPR HOLDINGS INC
Also Called: Niagara Gazette
473 3rd St Ste 201 (14301-1500)
PHONE 716 282-2311
Fax: 716 285-5610
Steve Braver, *Principal*
Samantha Dreverman, *Manager*
Cheryl Phillips, *Director*
EMP: 55
SQ FT: 21,534 **Privately Held**
WEB: www.clintonnc.com
SIC: 2711 2741 Newspapers; miscellaneous publishing
PA: Community Newspaper Holdings, Inc.
445 Dexter Ave Ste 7000
Montgomery AL 36104

(G-12829)
COSTANZOS WELDING INC (PA)
Also Called: Cataract Steel Industries
22nd Allen St (14302)
P.O. Box 862 (14302-0862)
PHONE 716 282-0845
Scott Costanzo, *President*
Thomas Costanzo, *Vice Pres*
Jim Willett, *Manager*
Rich Winchel, *Maintence Staff*
▼ EMP: 36
SQ FT: 100,000
SALES: 8MM **Privately Held**
WEB: www.cataractsteel.com
SIC: 3443 Heat exchangers, plate type

(G-12830)
CRYSTAL CERES INDUSTRIES INC
2250 Liberty Dr (14304-3756)
PHONE 716 283-0445
Michael Lynch, *Vice Pres*
▲ EMP: 58
SALES (est): 8.2MM **Privately Held**
WEB: www.cerescrystal.com
SIC: 1481 7631 Nonmetallic mineral services; diamond setter

(G-12831)
CSI INTERNATIONAL INC
1001 Main St (14301-1111)
PHONE 800 441-2895
Fax: 716 285-6332
Steven Brown, *President*
Erika Lorange, *Opers Mgr*
Maria Vapri, *Controller*
Jim Drakakis, *VP Sales*
Theresa Ventry, *Sales Staff*
▲ EMP: 40
SQ FT: 37,000
SALES (est): 6.9MM **Privately Held**
SIC: 3911 3914 5947 Jewelry, precious metal; trophies, plated (all metals); gift shop

(G-12832)
DELFINGEN US-NEW YORK INC
Also Called: Sofanou
2221 Niagara Falls Blvd # 12 (14304-5709)
PHONE 716 215-0300
Fax: 716 215-0304
Bernard Streit, *President*
Olivier Mathieu, *General Mgr*
David Streit, *Vice Pres*
Mark Blanke, *Treasurer*
Daniel Margrave, *Director*
▲ EMP: 25
SALES (est): 5.3MM
SALES (corp-wide): 3.8MM **Privately Held**
SIC: 3643 Caps & plugs, electric: attachment
HQ: Delfingen Us, Inc.
3985 W Hamlin Rd
Rochester Hills MI 48309

(G-12833)
DONNA KARAN COMPANY LLC
1900 Military Rd (14304-1737)
PHONE 716 297-0752
Fax: 716 298-5724
Elizabeth Carroll, *Branch Mgr*
EMP: 157
SALES (corp-wide): 2.3B **Publicly Held**
SIC: 2335 Women's, juniors' & misses' dresses
HQ: The Donna Karan Company Llc
240 W 40th St
New York NY 10018
212 789-1500

(G-12834)
DUREZ CORPORATION
5000 Packard Rd (14304-1510)
PHONE 716 286-0100
John W Fisher, *CEO*
EMP: 15
SALES (corp-wide): 1.7B **Privately Held**
SIC: 2865 2821 Cyclic crudes & intermediates; plastics materials & resins
HQ: Durez Corporation
46820 Magellan Dr Ste C
Novi MI 48377
248 313-7000

(G-12835)
EASTERN MACHINE AND ELECTRIC
1041 Niagara Ave (14305-2639)
PHONE 716 284-8271
Fax: 716 284-0277
Louis Destino, *President*
Daniel Destino, *Corp Secy*
EMP: 6 EST: 1957
SQ FT: 7,200
SALES (est): 514.2K **Privately Held**
SIC: 3599 Machine shop, jobbing & repair

(G-12836)
ENSIL TECHNICAL SERVICES INC
1901 Maryland Ave (14305-1722)
PHONE 716 282-1020
Farsad Kiani, *President*
Lewi Koykas, *General Mgr*
Louis Koikas, *Principal*
EMP: 50
SALES (est): 7.3MM **Privately Held**
SIC: 3728 Aircraft parts & equipment

(G-12837)
EUROTEX INC
Also Called: Eurotex North America
4600 Witmer Rd (14305-1217)
PHONE 716 205-8861
Sasha Mitic, *President*
▲ EMP: 12
SALES (est): 1.3MM **Privately Held**
SIC: 2295 Coated fabrics, not rubberized

(G-12838)
EYE DEAL EYEWEAR INC
4611 Military Rd (14305-1337)
PHONE 716 297-1500
Mike Trombley, *President*
▲ EMP: 5
SALES (est): 516.4K **Privately Held**
WEB: www.eyedealeyewear.com
SIC: 3851 3229 Frames, lenses & parts, eyeglass & spectacle; pressed & blown glass

(G-12839)
FELICETTI CONCRETE PRODUCTS
4129 Hyde Park Blvd (14305-1711)
PHONE 716 284-5740
Fax: 716 284-5751
Gene Felicetti, *Corp Secy*
Henry Felicetti, *Vice Pres*
Frank M Felicetti, *Shareholder*
Phillip Felicetti, *Shareholder*
Richard B Felicetti, *Shareholder*
EMP: 7
SQ FT: 1,750
SALES (est): 1.1MM **Privately Held**
SIC: 3271 Blocks, concrete or cinder: standard; brick, concrete

(G-12840)
FELTON MACHINE CO INC
2221 Niagara Falls Blvd (14304-5709)
P.O. Box 239 (14304-0239)
PHONE 716 215-9001
Fax: 716 731-9048
Robert J Schroeder, *President*
Jeff Gorney, *Mfg Staff*
Bridget M Schroeder, *Treasurer*
Lindsay Schroeder, *Clerk*
EMP: 38
SQ FT: 42,000
SALES (est): 6.3MM **Privately Held**
WEB: www.feltonmachine.com
SIC: 3599 Machine shop, jobbing & repair

(G-12841)
FERRO ELECTRONICS MATERIALS
4511 Hyde Park Blvd (14305-1215)
PHONE 716 278-9400
Lyndon La Brake, *Branch Mgr*
Pat Jones, *Branch Mgr*
EMP: 200
SALES (corp-wide): 1.1B **Publicly Held**
SIC: 3264 2819 Porcelain electrical supplies; industrial inorganic chemicals
HQ: Ferro Electronics Materials Inc
1789 Transelco Dr
Penn Yan NY 14527
315 536-3357

(G-12842)
FLAME CONTROL COATINGS LLC
4120 Hyde Park Blvd (14305-1793)
PHONE 716 282-1399
Fax: 716 285-6303
Tim Walker, *Prdtn Mgr*
Jeff Fallon,
Jonathan Hatch,
▼ EMP: 26 EST: 1976
SQ FT: 26,000
SALES (est): 7.3MM **Privately Held**
WEB: www.flamecontrol.com
SIC: 2899 Fire retardant chemicals

(G-12843)
FROSS INDUSTRIES INC
Also Called: Niagara Development & Mfg Div
3315 Haseley Dr (14304-1460)
PHONE 716 297-0652
Fax: 716 297-2550
Silvio Derubeis, *President*
Robert Schultz, *Vice Pres*
Donald H Smith, *Treasurer*
Mark Parisi, *Business Dir*
Gordon Smith, *Admin Sec*
EMP: 50 EST: 1981
SQ FT: 16,000
SALES (est): 6.2MM **Privately Held**
SIC: 3443 3599 Heat exchangers, plate type; machine shop, jobbing & repair

(G-12844)
GLOBE METALLURGICAL INC
Also Called: Globe Specialty Metals
3807 Highland Ave (14305-1723)
PHONE 716 804-0862
Fax: 716 278-6199
David Nau, *Plant Mgr*
David Shaw, *Prdtn Mgr*
Tammy Mack, *Controller*
Paul Kwapiszeski, *Branch Mgr*
Richard Schmidt, *Security Mgr*
EMP: 90
SALES (corp-wide): 1.5B **Privately Held**
WEB: www.globemetallurgical.com
SIC: 3339 3313 Silicon refining (primary, over 99% pure); ferromanganese, not made in blast furnaces
HQ: Globe Metallurgical Inc.
County Road 32
Waterford OH 45786
740 984-2361

Niagara Falls - Niagara County

(G-12845)
GRAPHICOMM INC
Also Called: Insty-Prints
7703 Niagara Falls Blvd (14304-1739)
P.O. Box 543, Grand Island (14072-0543)
PHONE..................716 283-0830
Fax: 716 283-2217
John Jones, *President*
Stephen Perry, *Prdtn Mgr*
Jill Welsby, *Graphic Designe*
EMP: 5
SQ FT: 2,200
SALES (est): 687.4K **Privately Held**
SIC: 2752 7334 2791 2789 Commercial printing, lithographic; photocopying & duplicating services; typesetting; bookbinding & related work

(G-12846)
GREATER NIAGARA BLDG CTR INC
9540 Niagara Falls Blvd (14304-4909)
PHONE..................716 299-0543
Bill Burg, *CEO*
EMP: 12
SALES (est): 2.1MM **Privately Held**
SIC: 2421 Building & structural materials, wood

(G-12847)
GREEN GLOBAL ENERGY INC
2526 Niagara Falls Blvd (14304-4519)
PHONE..................716 501-9770
Dan Schriber, *President*
EMP: 6
SALES (est): 850K **Privately Held**
SIC: 2911 Fuel additives

(G-12848)
GREENPAC MILL LLC (DH)
4400 Royal Ave (14303-2128)
PHONE..................716 299-0560
Veronique Dion, *Manager*
Rhonda Perry, *Manager*
Luc Nadeau,
▲ EMP: 101 **EST:** 2010
SALES (est): 47.5MM
SALES (corp-wide): 2.9B **Privately Held**
SIC: 2631 Linerboard
HQ: Cascades New York Inc.
1845 Emerson St
Rochester NY 14606
585 527-8110

(G-12849)
GUESS INC
1826 Military Rd Spc 113 (14304-1772)
PHONE..................716 298-3561
Danielle Guetta, *Manager*
EMP: 25
SALES (corp-wide): 2.2B **Publicly Held**
WEB: www.guess.com
SIC: 2325 Men's & boys' jeans & dungarees
PA: Guess , Inc.
1444 S Alameda St
Los Angeles CA 90021
213 765-3100

(G-12850)
HEAVEN FRESH USA INC
4600 Witmer Industrial Es (14305-1364)
PHONE..................800 642-0367
Mohammad Kamal Anwar, *President*
Imran Bashir, *Vice Pres*
Taoufik Lahrache, *Treasurer*
Abrar Shaikh, *Supervisor*
▲ EMP: 5
SALES (est): 521.4K **Privately Held**
SIC: 3634 3585 5722 Air purifiers, portable; humidifiers & dehumidifiers; electric household appliances, small

(G-12851)
HELMEL ENGINEERING PDTS INC
6520 Lockport Rd (14305-3512)
PHONE..................716 297-8644
Fax: 716 297-9405
Erwin Helmel, *President*
Arthur Whistler, *Marketing Staff*
Robert Cliffe, *Asst Mgr*
Dora Helmel, *Admin Sec*
▲ EMP: 22
SQ FT: 23,000
SALES: 2.9MM **Privately Held**
WEB: www.helmel.com
SIC: 3829 Measuring & controlling devices

(G-12852)
IMERYS FSED MNRL NGARA FLS INC (DH)
2000 College Ave (14305-1734)
P.O. Box 1438 (14302-1438)
PHONE..................716 286-1250
Fax: 716 286-1224
Christian Pfeifer, *CEO*
Laura Nowak, *Manager*
Sandi Polanski, *Executive*
▲ EMP: 35
SQ FT: 4,950
SALES (est): 7.9MM
SALES (corp-wide): 1.7MM **Privately Held**
SIC: 3291 Abrasive products
HQ: Imerys Usa, Inc.
100 Mansell Ct E Ste 300
Roswell GA 30076
770 645-3300

(G-12853)
IMERYS STEELCASTING USA INC (DH)
4111 Witmer Rd (14305-1720)
P.O. Box 368 (14302-0368)
PHONE..................716 278-1634
Fax: 716 284-8753
Gilles Michel, *CEO*
Jurgen Sardemann, *Ch of Bd*
Manfred Beck, *President*
Tim Wilson, *Corp Secy*
Michael Monberg, *Vice Pres*
▲ EMP: 73
SALES (est): 17.9MM **Privately Held**
WEB: www.stollberg.com
SIC: 3399 Powder, metal
HQ: Imerys Metalcasting Germany Gmbh
Duisburger Str. 69-73
Oberhausen 46049
208 850-0500

(G-12854)
INDUSTRIAL SERVICES OF WNY
7221 Niagara Falls Blvd (14304-1715)
Rural Route 7221 Niaga (14304)
PHONE..................716 799-7788
Georgena Dinieri, *Owner*
EMP: 5
SALES (est): 210K **Privately Held**
SIC: 3599 Machine & other job shop work

(G-12855)
J D CALATO MANUFACTURING CO (PA)
Also Called: Regal Tip
4501 Hyde Park Blvd (14305-1215)
PHONE..................716 285-3546
Fax: 716 285-2710
Carol Calato, *CEO*
Joseph D Calato, *CEO*
Catherine Calato, *Vice Pres*
Sharon Schaal, *Purch Agent*
Matthew Carrier, *QC Dir*
EMP: 35 EST: 1961
SQ FT: 17,000
SALES (est): 4.1MM **Privately Held**
WEB: www.calato.com
SIC: 3931 Musical instruments; drums, parts & accessories (musical instruments)

(G-12856)
JOHNNIE RYAN CO INC
3084 Niagara St (14303-2030)
PHONE..................716 282-1606
Fax: 716 282-6737
Paul Janik, *Vice Pres*
Kathy Tedesco, *Office Mgr*
EMP: 15
SQ FT: 10,000
SALES (est): 2.1MM **Privately Held**
WEB: www.johnnieryan.com
SIC: 2086 Soft drinks: packaged in cans, bottles, etc.

(G-12857)
KINTEX INC
Also Called: Niagara Thermo Products
3315 Haseley Dr (14304-1460)
PHONE..................716 297-0652
Barry Heckman, *Owner*
Donald Hall, *Engineer*
Frank Yang, *Manager*
EMP: 90
SALES (est): 6.3MM **Privately Held**
SIC: 3443 Heat exchangers, condensers & components

(G-12858)
L A R ELECTRONICS CORP
2733 Niagara St (14303-2027)
PHONE..................716 285-0555
Lawrence Kutner, *President*
EMP: 7 EST: 1980
SQ FT: 3,500
SALES: 150K **Privately Held**
WEB: www.laraudio.com
SIC: 3651 5065 1731 Speaker systems; sound equipment, electronic; sound equipment specialization

(G-12859)
LIDDELL CORPORATION
4600 Witmer Ind Est 5 (14305-1364)
PHONE..................716 297-8557
Lon Flick, *President*
EMP: 14
SALES: 1.3MM **Privately Held**
WEB: www.nicel.com
SIC: 2844 Cosmetic preparations

(G-12860)
LIQUID INDUSTRIES INC
7219 New Jersey Ave (14305)
PHONE..................716 628-2999
Hamish Shaw, *President*
EMP: 6
SALES (est): 694.3K **Privately Held**
SIC: 3589 Car washing machinery

(G-12861)
LOCKHEED MARTIN CORPORATION
2221 Niagara Falls Blvd (14304-5709)
PHONE..................716 297-1000
Mike Davis, *Safety Mgr*
Donald Kellner, *QC Dir*
Clive A Affleck, *Engineer*
David Savini, *Engineer*
H M Neeson, *Sales/Mktg Dir*
EMP: 40 **Publicly Held**
WEB: www.lockheedmartin.com
SIC: 3721 3812 3769 Motorized aircraft; search & navigation equipment; guided missile & space vehicle parts & auxiliary equipment
PA: Lockheed Martin Corporation
6801 Rockledge Dr
Bethesda MD 20817

(G-12862)
MARIPHARM LABORATORIES
2045 Niagara Falls Blvd (14304-1675)
PHONE..................716 984-6520
Christopher Dean, *Owner*
EMP: 10
SALES (est): 564.9K **Privately Held**
SIC: 3821 Laboratory apparatus & furniture

(G-12863)
METAL PRODUCTS INTL LLC
7510 Porter Rd Ste 4 (14304-1692)
PHONE..................716 215-1930
Laurine Stamborski, *Controller*
Thomas Fleckestien,
Kenneth Koedinger,
▲ EMP: 5
SALES: 12MM **Privately Held**
WEB: www.metalproducts.com
SIC: 3449 Miscellaneous metalwork

(G-12864)
METRO MATTRESS CORP
2212 Military Rd (14304-1760)
PHONE..................716 205-2300
Randy Pegan, *Branch Mgr*
EMP: 28
SALES (corp-wide): 38MM **Privately Held**
SIC: 2515 5712 5719 Mattresses & bedsprings; beds & accessories; beddings & linens
PA: Metro Mattress Corp.
3545 John Glenn Blvd
Syracuse NY 13209
315 218-1200

(G-12865)
MOOG INC
Also Called: Moog - Isp
6686 Walmore Rd (14304-1638)
PHONE..................716 731-6300
Fax: 716 731-6329
James Zappa, *Engineer*
Donna Lough, *Accountant*
Jerry Fritz, *Branch Mgr*
Cheryl Gray, *Manager*
EMP: 100
SALES (corp-wide): 2.4B **Publicly Held**
SIC: 2819 Industrial inorganic chemicals
PA: Moog Inc.
400 Jamison Rd Plant26
Elma NY 14059
716 652-2000

(G-12866)
NATIONAL MAINT CONTG CORP
Also Called: Nmcc
5600 Niagara Falls Blvd (14304-1532)
P.O. Box 258 (14304-0258)
PHONE..................716 285-1583
Samuel D Lehr, *President*
John Shubbuck, *Project Mgr*
Linda Lehr, *Office Mgr*
EMP: 54
SALES: 5MM **Privately Held**
SIC: 3499 Welding tips, heat resistant: metal

(G-12867)
NIAGARA SAMPLE BOOK CO INC
1717 Mackenna Ave (14303-1715)
PHONE..................716 284-6151
Fax: 716 284-7117
Joseph P Pinzotti, *President*
Marsha A Pinzotti, *Vice Pres*
Mary B Pinzotti, *Treasurer*
Marcella Pinzotti, *Admin Sec*
EMP: 15 EST: 1945
SQ FT: 20,000
SALES (est): 1.3MM **Privately Held**
WEB: www.niagarasample.com
SIC: 2782 2759 Sample books; commercial printing

(G-12868)
NIKE INC
1886 Military Rd (14304-1772)
PHONE..................716 298-5615
EMP: 6
SALES (corp-wide): 34.3B **Publicly Held**
SIC: 3021 Rubber & plastics footwear
PA: Nike, Inc.
1 Sw Bowerman Dr
Beaverton OR 97005
503 671-6453

(G-12869)
NORTH AMERICAN HOGANAS INC
5950 Packard Rd (14304-1584)
P.O. Box 310 (14304-0310)
PHONE..................716 285-3451
Avinash Gore, *President*
Terry Heinrich, *Corp Secy*
Nagarjuna Nandivada, *Vice Pres*
Patricia Burkstone, *Purchasing*
Eric Reynolds, *Accountant*
◆ EMP: 41
SALES (est): 14MM
SALES (corp-wide): 784.2MM **Privately Held**
SIC: 2819 Iron (ferric/ferrous) compounds or salts
HQ: North American Hoganas Holdings, Inc.
111 Hoganas Way
Hollsopple PA 15935
814 479-2551

(G-12870)
NORTHEAST WIRE AND CABLE CO
8635 Packard Rd (14304-5612)
P.O. Box 503, Grand Island (14072-0503)
PHONE..................716 297-8483
Fax: 716 297-1412
Gregory Barker, *President*
EMP: 5
SQ FT: 15,000

Niagara Falls - Niagara County (G-12871)

SALES (est): 750.4K **Privately Held**
WEB: www.northeastwire.com
SIC: 3315 Cable, steel: insulated or armored

(G-12871)
NORTHKNIGHT LOGISTICS INC
7724 Buffalo Ave (14304-4134)
PHONE 716 283-3090
John Rendle, *CEO*
◆ **EMP:** 15 **EST:** 2007
SQ FT: 14,000
SALES (est): 2MM **Privately Held**
SIC: 3429 Builders' hardware

(G-12872)
NUTTALL GEAR L L C (HQ)
Also Called: Delroyd Worm Gear
2221 Niagara Falls Blvd # 17 (14304-5710)
PHONE 716 298-4100
Fax: 716 298-4101
Michael Hurt, *CEO*
Scott Jimbroni, *General Mgr*
Greg Klein, *Project Mgr*
Jeannine Jackson, *Purch Mgr*
Makrk Rawls, *Controller*
▲ **EMP:** 50
SQ FT: 107,000
SALES (est): 14.9MM
SALES (corp-wide): 708.9MM **Publicly Held**
WEB: www.nuttallgear.com
SIC: 3566 Speed changers, drives & gears
PA: Altra Industrial Motion Corp.
   300 Granite St Ste 201
   Braintree MA 02184
   781 917-0600

(G-12873)
OCCIDENTAL CHEMICAL CORP
4700 Buffalo Ave (14304-3821)
P.O. Box 344 (14302-0344)
PHONE 716 278-7795
Fax: 716 278-7880
Joseph G Dewey, *Human Res Mgr*
Tom Feeney, *Branch Mgr*
James Czapla, *Technology*
EMP: 35
SALES (corp-wide): 10.4B **Publicly Held**
WEB: www.oxychem.com
SIC: 2812 Alkalies & chlorine
HQ: Occidental Chemical Corporation
   5005 Lyndon B Johnson Fwy # 2200
   Dallas TX 75244
   972 404-3800

(G-12874)
OCCIDENTAL CHEMICAL CORP
56 Street & Energy Blvd (14302)
P.O. Box 344 (14302-0344)
PHONE 716 278-7794
Herb Jones, *General Mgr*
EMP: 200
SALES (corp-wide): 10.4B **Publicly Held**
SIC: 2812 2874 Alkalies & chlorine; chlorine, compressed or liquefied; caustic soda, sodium hydroxide; potassium carbonate; phosphatic fertilizers
HQ: Occidental Chemical Corporation
   5005 Lyndon B Johnson Fwy # 2200
   Dallas TX 75244
   972 404-3800

(G-12875)
OLIN CHLOR ALKALI LOGISTICS
Also Called: Chlor Alkali Products & Vinyls
2400 Buffalo Ave (14304-1959)
P.O. Box 748 (14320-0748)
PHONE 716 278-6411
Fax: 716 278-6495
Brian Vain, *COO*
J Murphy, *Purchasing*
Daniel Palermo, *Engineer*
Erich Ely, *Electrical Engi*
Mike Bentley, *Human Res Dir*
EMP: 150
SALES (corp-wide): 5.5B **Publicly Held**
WEB: www.olin.com
SIC: 2812 2842 Alkalies & chlorine; specialty cleaning, polishes & sanitation goods
HQ: Olin Chlor Alkali Logistics Inc
   490 Stuart Rd Ne
   Cleveland TN 37312
   423 336-4850

(G-12876)
OXAIR LTD
8320 Quarry Rd (14304-1068)
P.O. Box 4039 (14304-8039)
PHONE 716 298-8288
Fax: 716 298-8889
Flavio Zeni, *President*
▼ **EMP:** 5
SQ FT: 10,000
SALES (est): 550K **Privately Held**
WEB: www.oxair.com
SIC: 2813 Oxygen, compressed or liquefied

(G-12877)
PENETRADAR CORPORATION
2509 Niagara Falls Blvd (14304-4518)
PHONE 716 731-2629
Fax: 716 731-5040
Anthony J Alongi, *President*
Jacqueline Joaquin, *General Mgr*
Rick Geltz, *Purch Agent*
Kevin Lewis, *Mktg Dir*
James Vogt, *Manager*
EMP: 15
SQ FT: 15,000
SALES (est): 2.1MM **Privately Held**
WEB: www.penetradar.com
SIC: 3812 Radar systems & equipment

(G-12878)
PLIOTRON COMPANY AMERICA LLC
4650 Witmer Indus Est (14305-1360)
PHONE 716 298-4457
Fax: 716 298-4459
Robert Leiathton, *Plant Mgr*
Richard Rohm, *Manager*
Albert E Matthews,
Linda Matthews,
EMP: 5 **EST:** 1962
SQ FT: 8,125
SALES (est): 330K **Privately Held**
WEB: www.pliotron.com
SIC: 3564 Filters, air: furnaces, air conditioning equipment, etc.

(G-12879)
PRAXAIR INC
4501 Royal Ave (14303-2121)
PHONE 716 286-4600
Fax: 716 286-4619
Elizabeth Casciani, *Safety Mgr*
Brian McKie, *Branch Mgr*
EMP: 50
SALES (corp-wide): 10.5B **Publicly Held**
SIC: 2813 Industrial gases
PA: Praxair, Inc.
   10 Riverview Dr
   Danbury CT 06810
   203 837-2000

(G-12880)
PRECIOUS PLATE INC
2124 Liberty Dr (14304-3799)
PHONE 716 283-0690
Fax: 716 283-9185
David R Hurst, *President*
William Copping, *Vice Pres*
Scott Law, *Vice Pres*
David Miller, *Vice Pres*
Ken Russell, *Safety Mgr*
▲ **EMP:** 75
SQ FT: 65,000
SALES (est): 13.9MM **Privately Held**
SIC: 3471 Plating & polishing

(G-12881)
PRECISION ELCTRO MNRL PMCO INC
150 Portage Rd (14303-1535)
P.O. Box 8 (14302-0008)
PHONE 716 284-2484
Fax: 716 284-2483
Abdul Labi, *President*
Manny Trinidad, *Office Mgr*
EMP: 25
SQ FT: 40,000
SALES (est): 2MM **Privately Held**
WEB: www.pemco-niagara.com
SIC: 2819 3291 1446 Silica compounds; abrasive products; industrial sand

(G-12882)
PRECISION PROCESS INC (PA)
2111 Liberty Dr (14304-3744)
PHONE 716 731-1587
Fax: 716 236-7802
David Hurst, *CEO*
Bill Copping, *Vice Pres*
Jeannine Jackson, *Purchasing*
Roger Hartley, *QC Mgr*
Joe Hoyt, *VP Finance*
▲ **EMP:** 83
SQ FT: 65,000
SALES (est): 17.3MM **Privately Held**
WEB: www.precisionprocess.com
SIC: 3559 Electroplating machinery & equipment

(G-12883)
QUANTUM COLOR INC
Also Called: Niagara Printing
8742 Buffalo Ave (14304-4342)
PHONE 716 283-8700
Fax: 716 283-3527
Darry Finn, *President*
David Finn, *Vice Pres*
Jack Birkman, *Accounts Exec*
Bob Edwards, *Accounts Exec*
Mary Gibson, *Accounts Exec*
EMP: 40
SQ FT: 41,000
SALES (est): 4.4MM **Privately Held**
SIC: 2752 Periodicals, lithographed

(G-12884)
RANNEY PRECISION
Also Called: Ranney Precision Machining
6421 Wendt Dr (14304-1100)
PHONE 716 731-6418
Fax: 716 731-6521
David Ranney, *Owner*
Joanne Ranney, *Co-Owner*
EMP: 17
SQ FT: 10,000
SALES (est): 1.3MM **Privately Held**
WEB: www.ranneyprecision.com
SIC: 3451 Screw machine products

(G-12885)
RELIANCE FLUID TECH LLC
3943 Buffalo Ave (14303-2136)
PHONE 716 332-0988
John Garguiolo, *President*
Ryan Sanders, *Clerk*
EMP: 40
SALES (est): 1.7MM **Privately Held**
SIC: 2899 Corrosion preventive lubricant

(G-12886)
RT MACHINED SPECIALTIES
2221 Niagara Falls Blvd (14304-5709)
PHONE 716 731-2055
Fax: 716 731-2055
Rebecca Christie, *President*
Jon Christie, *Manager*
EMP: 5
SALES: 300K **Privately Held**
SIC: 3599 Machine shop, jobbing & repair

(G-12887)
RUS INDUSTRIES INC
3255 Lockport Rd (14305-2398)
PHONE 716 284-7828
Fax: 716 284-0514
Alice G Carlson, *Ch of Bd*
James A Ryding, *Vice Pres*
Greg Robinson, *VP Sales*
Erik Davis, *Marketing Mgr*
Eric Carlson, *Manager*
▲ **EMP:** 32
SQ FT: 29,000
SALES (est): 4.8MM **Privately Held**
WEB: www.rusindustries.com
SIC: 3441 3661 Fabricated structural metal; communication headgear, telephone

(G-12888)
SAINT GOBAIN GRAINS & POWDERS
6600 Walmore Rd (14304-1638)
PHONE 716 731-8200
Tom Vincent, *Principal*
Annie Marcantonio, *Administration*
▲ **EMP:** 1196
SALES (est): 83MM
SALES (corp-wide): 185.8MM **Privately Held**
SIC: 3221 3269 2891 Glass containers; food containers, glass; bottles for packing, bottling & canning: glass; vials, glass; laboratory & industrial pottery; chemical porcelain; adhesives: adhesives, plastic; cement, except linoleum & tile; epoxy adhesives
HQ: Saint-Gobain Corporation
   20 Moores Rd
   Malvern PA 19355

(G-12889)
SAINT-GBAIN ADVNCED CRMICS LLC (HQ)
Also Called: Structural Ceramics Division
23 Acheson Dr (14303-1555)
PHONE 716 278-6066
Ron Lambright, *CEO*
Jean Louis Beffa, *Ch of Bd*
Curtis Schmit, *General Mgr*
Michael J Fricano, *Controller*
Diana Tierney, *Human Res Mgr*
▲ **EMP:** 150
SQ FT: 1,064
SALES (est): 29.2MM
SALES (corp-wide): 185.8MM **Privately Held**
WEB: www.hexoloy.com
SIC: 3269 Laboratory & industrial pottery
PA: Compagnie De Saint-Gobain
   Les Miroirs La Defense 3
   Courbevoie 92400
   147 623-000

(G-12890)
SAINT-GOBAIN DYNAMICS INC
Also Called: Structural Ceramics Group
23 Acheson Dr (14303-1555)
PHONE 716 278-6007
Curtis M Schmit, *President*
EMP: 10
SALES (est): 1MM **Privately Held**
SIC: 3297 Nonclay refractories

(G-12891)
SAINT-GOBAIN STRL CERAMICS
23 Acheson Dr (14303-1555)
PHONE 716 278-6233
John T Crowe, *CEO*
Lawrence Banach, *Engineer*
John Bevilacqua, *Manager*
◆ **EMP:** 1793
SALES (est): 139.8MM
SALES (corp-wide): 185.8MM **Privately Held**
SIC: 3255 Brick, clay refractory
HQ: Saint-Gobain Corporation
   20 Moores Rd
   Malvern PA 19355

(G-12892)
SATURN SALES INC
4500 Witmer Indstrl 202 (14305-1386)
PHONE 519 658-5125
Zafar Syed, *President*
EMP: 20
SALES (est): 1.1MM
SALES (corp-wide): 7.3MM **Privately Held**
SIC: 2522 Office furniture, except wood
PA: Saturn Sales Inc
   130 Guelph Ave
   Cambridge ON N3C 1
   519 658-6263

(G-12893)
SHIPMAN PRINTING INDS INC
Also Called: Shipman Print Solutions
2424 Niagara Falls Blvd (14304-4562)
P.O. Box 357 (14304-0357)
PHONE 716 504-7700
Fax: 716 504-7710
Gary Blum, *Ch of Bd*
Richard Faiola, *Exec VP*
Randy Duncan, *Vice Pres*
Michael Fiore, *Vice Pres*
Diane Donner, *Accounts Mgr*
EMP: 34 **EST:** 1905
SQ FT: 20,000

GEOGRAPHIC SECTION

Norfolk - St. Lawrence County (G-12915)

SALES (est): 6.8MM **Privately Held**
WEB: www.shipmanprint.com
SIC: **2752** 2789 2759 Commercial printing, offset; bookbinding & related work; envelopes: printing

(G-12894)
SILIPOS HOLDING LLC
7049 Williams Rd (14304-3731)
PHONE 716 283-0700
Fax: 212 818-9873
Richard Margolis, *President*
Peter Bickel, *Exec VP*
Ian Shaw, *Director*
◆ EMP: 40 EST: 2015
SQ FT: 35,000
SALES (est): 2.5MM **Privately Held**
SIC: **3842** Surgical appliances & supplies

(G-12895)
STEPHENSON CUSTOM CASE COMPANY
Also Called: Portequip Work Stations
1623 Military Rd (14304-1745)
PHONE 905 542-8762
John Stephenson, *Owner*
EMP: 30
SALES: 950K **Privately Held**
SIC: **3949** Sporting & athletic goods

(G-12896)
SWISSMAR INC
6391 Walmore Rd (14304-1613)
PHONE 905 764-1121
Daniel Oehy, *President*
George Hobson, *VP Finance*
Paula Schrader, *Manager*
EMP: 8 EST: 1990
SQ FT: 15,000
SALES (est): 758.2K **Privately Held**
SIC: **3262** 5719 China cookware; housewares

(G-12897)
TAM CERAMICS GROUP OF NY LLC
4511 Hyde Park Blvd (14305-1298)
PHONE 716 278-9400
George Bilkey, *President*
Mike Chu,
EMP: 62
SQ FT: 3,750
SALES: 30MM **Privately Held**
SIC: **3399** Powder, metal

(G-12898)
TAM CERAMICS LLC
4511 Hyde Park Blvd (14305-1298)
PHONE 716 278-9480
Fax: 716 278-9571
Eric Hanson, *Vice Pres*
John Hess, *Engineer*
Matthew Szarleta, *Engineer*
Chris Merry, *Controller*
George H Bilkey IV, *Mng Member*
▲ EMP: 52
SQ FT: 373,593
SALES (est): 20.2MM **Privately Held**
SIC: **2899** Chemical preparations
PA: All American Holdings, Llc
3714 W End Ave
Nashville TN 37205

(G-12899)
TECMOTIV (USA) INC
1500 James Ave (14305-1222)
PHONE 905 669-5911
Arthur Hayden, *President*
Lorna Earrett, *Vice Pres*
Gary Sheedy, *Vice Pres*
Sally L Yan, *CFO*
◆ EMP: 31
SQ FT: 27,000
SALES: 9MM
SALES (corp-wide): 2.6MM **Privately Held**
WEB: www.tecmotiv.com
SIC: **3795** Tanks & tank components
PA: Tecmotiv Corporation
131 Saramia Cres 2nd Fl
Concord ON L4K 4
905 669-5911

(G-12900)
TORONTO METAL SPINNING AND LTG
4500 Witmer Indus Ests (14305-1386)
PHONE 905 793-1174
EMP: 32
SALES (est): 107.5K **Privately Held**
SIC: **3469** Spinning metal for the trade

(G-12901)
TRANSCEDAR INDUSTRIES LTD
Also Called: Motorad of America
6292 Walmore Rd (14304-5703)
PHONE 716 731-6442
Fax: 716 731-6436
Kelly Runkle, *Branch Mgr*
Juan Saldivar, *Director*
EMP: 7
SALES (corp-wide): 3.1MM **Privately Held**
SIC: **3714** Air conditioner parts, motor vehicle
PA: Transcedar Industries Ltd
120 Silver Star Blvd Unit A
Scarborough ON M1V 4

(G-12902)
TULIP MOLDED PLASTICS CORP
Also Called: Niagara Falls Plant
3123 Highland Ave (14305-2051)
PHONE 716 282-1261
Fax: 716 285-6075
James Carter, *Vice Pres*
S Shoecraft, *Research*
David Delange, *Personnel*
G Moran, *Personnel*
John Signore, *Manager*
EMP: 80 **Privately Held**
WEB: www.tulipcorp.com
SIC: **3089** Plastic processing
HQ: Tulip Molded Plastics Corporation
714 E Keefe Ave
Milwaukee WI 53212
414 963-3120

(G-12903)
UNIFRAX CORPORATION
2351 Whirlpool St (14305-2413)
PHONE 716 278-3800
Fax: 716 278-3900
Mark Travers, *COO*
Matt W Colbert, *Senior VP*
Paul Boymel, *Vice Pres*
Paul Viola, *Vice Pres*
Bruce Zoitos, *Facilities Mgr*
EMP: 34
SALES (est): 5MM **Privately Held**
SIC: **3296** Mineral wool insulation products

(G-12904)
US DRIVES INC
2221 Niagara Falls Blvd # 41 (14304-5711)
P.O. Box 281 (14304-0281)
PHONE 716 731-1606
Fax: 716 731-1524
Kader Laroussi, *President*
Dick Torbenson, *President*
James S Grisante, *Vice Pres*
Paul Wizner, *VP Prdtn*
Theodore G Nuding, *VP Finance*
EMP: 60
SQ FT: 70,000
SALES (est): 10.5MM **Privately Held**
WEB: www.usdrivesinc.com
SIC: **3625** Motor controls, electric

(G-12905)
VIOLA CABINET CORPORATION
Also Called: Viola Construction
4205 Hyde Park Blvd (14305-1709)
PHONE 716 284-6327
Fax: 716 284-6336
Pat Viola, *President*
EMP: 6
SQ FT: 3,500
SALES: 1MM **Privately Held**
SIC: **2434** Wood kitchen cabinets

(G-12906)
VISHAY THIN FILM LLC
2160 Liberty Dr (14304-3727)
PHONE 716 283-4025
Fax: 716 283-3205
Dr Felix Zandman, *President*

Rachel Corulli, *Purch Mgr*
Rachel Bricca, *Purchasing*
Ray Chotkowski, *Design Engr Mgr*
Robert A Freece, *Treasurer*
▲ EMP: 154
SQ FT: 33,000
SALES (est): 23.9MM
SALES (corp-wide): 2.3B **Publicly Held**
SIC: **3676** 3861 3577 Electronic resistors; photographic equipment & supplies; computer peripheral equipment
HQ: Dale Vishay Electronics Llc
1122 23rd St
Columbus NE 68601
605 665-9301

(G-12907)
WASHINGTOM MILLS ELEC MNRLS (HQ)
1801 Buffalo Ave (14303-1528)
P.O. Box 423 (14302-0423)
PHONE 716 278-6600
Fax: 716 278-6654
Don McLeod, *President*
Jef Perry, *Plant Mgr*
Lew Mangin, *Opers Mgr*
Marie Hinds, *Safety Mgr*
Scott Timme, *Mfg Spvr*
◆ EMP: 100
SALES (est): 32.7MM
SALES (corp-wide): 176.3MM **Privately Held**
WEB: www.washingtonmills.com
SIC: **3291** 2819 Abrasive grains; industrial inorganic chemicals
PA: Washington Mills Group, Inc.
20 N Main St
North Grafton MA 01536
508 839-6511

(G-12908)
YORKVILLE SOUND INC
4625 Witmer Indus Est (14305-1390)
PHONE 716 297-2920
Fax: 716 297-3689
Steven Long, *Owner*
Jack Long, *Founder*
Terry Sherwood, *Controller*
Tim Marshall, *Marketing Mgr*
Todd Michael, *Manager*
▲ EMP: 7
SALES (est): 1.3MM **Privately Held**
SIC: **3651** Audio electronic systems

Nichols
Tioga County

(G-12909)
WOODS MACHINE AND TOOL LLC
150 Howell St (13812-2146)
PHONE 607 699-3253
Fax: 607 699-3725
Ricky E Woods,
Michael Woods,
Richard Woods,
EMP: 16
SQ FT: 2,400
SALES (est): 1.4MM **Privately Held**
SIC: **3599** Machine shop, jobbing & repair

Niskayuna
Schenectady County

(G-12910)
ADC ACQUISITION COMPANY
Also Called: Automated Dynamics
2 Commerce Park Rd (12309-3545)
PHONE 518 377-6471
Fax: 518 377-5628
Robert Langone, *President*
Hauber David, *Vice Pres*
Ralph Marcario, *Vice Pres*
Becker Robert, *Vice Pres*
James Mondo, *Engineer*
▼ EMP: 34
SQ FT: 30,000
SALES: 5.7MM **Privately Held**
WEB: www.automateddynamics.com
SIC: **3083** Thermoplastic laminates: rods, tubes, plates & sheet

(G-12911)
GE GLOBAL RESEARCH
1 Research Cir (12309-1027)
PHONE 518 387-5000
George Dalakos, *Managing Dir*
Victor R Abate, *Senior VP*
Donald Wilcox, *Opers Mgr*
Doug Dinon, *Mfg Mgr*
Xianglei Chen, *Research*
EMP: 8 EST: 2016
SALES (est): 272.3K
SALES (corp-wide): 123.6B **Publicly Held**
SIC: **3511** 8742 Turbines & turbine generator sets; industrial consultant
PA: General Electric Company
41 Farnsworth St
Boston MA 02210
617 443-3000

(G-12912)
GENERAL ELECTRIC COMPANY
2690 Balltown Rd Bldg 600 (12309-1004)
PHONE 518 385-7620
Doug Wood, *Branch Mgr*
Matthew Mattson, *Manager*
Phil Tolbert, *Manager*
Steve Fo, *CIO*
EMP: 50
SALES (corp-wide): 123.6B **Publicly Held**
SIC: **3724** 3511 3612 Aircraft engines & engine parts; research & development on aircraft engines & parts; steam turbines; gas turbines, mechanical drive; autotransformers, electric (power transformers)
PA: General Electric Company
41 Farnsworth St
Boston MA 02210
617 443-3000

(G-12913)
SILICON IMAGING INC
25 Covington Ct (12309-1323)
PHONE 518 374-3367
ARI Presler, *President*
Tom Gielow, *Vice Pres*
Mark Kolvites, *Vice Pres*
Steve Nordhauser, *Vice Pres*
Allison Russell, *Manager*
EMP: 8
SQ FT: 5,000
SALES (est): 982.6K **Privately Held**
WEB: www.siliconimaging.com
SIC: **3663** Cameras, television

Norfolk
St. Lawrence County

(G-12914)
APC PAPER COMPANY INC
100 Remington Ave (13667-4136)
P.O. Box 756 (13667-0756)
PHONE 315 384-4225
Kyle Dansereau, *Safety Dir*
Al Ames, *Manager*
EMP: 55
SALES (corp-wide): 14.2MM **Privately Held**
WEB: www.apcpaper.com
SIC: **2621** 4953 2674 2611 Kraft paper; refuse systems; bags: uncoated paper & multiwall; pulp mills
PA: Apc Paper Company, Inc.
130 Sullivan St
Claremont NH 03743
603 542-0411

(G-12915)
CRANESVILLE BLOCK CO INC
Also Called: Cranesville Concrete
8405 State Highway 56 (13667-4221)
PHONE 315 384-4000
Fax: 315 384-3419
Randy Braul, *Manager*
EMP: 6
SALES (corp-wide): 45.4MM **Privately Held**
SIC: **3273** 5211 Ready-mixed concrete; masonry materials & supplies
PA: Cranesville Block Co., Inc.
1250 Riverfront Ctr
Amsterdam NY 12010
518 684-6154

Norfolk - St. Lawrence County (G-12916)

(G-12916)
LENCORE ACOUSTICS CORP
1 S Main St (13667-3111)
P.O. Box 616 (13667-0616)
PHONE..................................315 384-9114
Fax: 315 384-4974
Brian Leonard, *Branch Mgr*
EMP: 10
SALES (corp-wide): 5.6MM **Privately Held**
WEB: www.lencore.com
SIC: 3296 Acoustical board & tile, mineral wool
PA: Lencore Acoustics Corp.
1 Crossways Park Dr W
Woodbury NY 11797
516 682-9292

(G-12917)
NORTHERN MACHINING INC
2a N Main St (13667-4154)
PHONE..................................315 384-3189
Fax: 315 384-4164
Ted Ashley, *President*
Kathie Ashley, *Vice Pres*
Marie Delosh, *Admin Sec*
EMP: 10
SQ FT: 7,000
SALES: 1.1MM **Privately Held**
WEB: www.northernmachininginc.com
SIC: 3599 Machine shop, jobbing & repair

North Babylon
Suffolk County

(G-12918)
GO BLUE TECHNOLOGIES LTD
325 August Rd (11703-1014)
PHONE..................................631 404-6285
Carlo Drago, *CEO*
EMP: 1
SALES: 1MM **Privately Held**
SIC: 3624 3842 Carbon & graphite products; gas masks

(G-12919)
PMB PRECISION PRODUCTS INC
Also Called: Spartan Instruments
725 Mount Ave (11703)
PHONE..................................631 491-6753
Michael Belesis, *President*
Jan Craw, *Principal*
Richard Jackson, *Sales Mgr*
EMP: 16
SALES (est): 2.8MM **Privately Held**
SIC: 3399 Metal fasteners

(G-12920)
QUALITY FUEL 1 CORPORATION
1235 Deer Park Ave (11703-3112)
PHONE..................................631 392-4090
EMP: 6
SALES (est): 664.8K **Privately Held**
SIC: 2869 Fuels

North Baldwin
Nassau County

(G-12921)
DURA SPEC INC
Also Called: Jamaica Electroplating
1239 Village Ct (11510-1138)
PHONE..................................718 526-3053
Fax: 718 657-8867
C Samuel Williams, *President*
Violet Williams, *Vice Pres*
EMP: 18
SQ FT: 5,000
SALES (est): 1.5MM **Privately Held**
SIC: 3471 Electroplating of metals or formed products

(G-12922)
GENESIS MACHINING CORP
725 Brooklyn Ave (11510-2708)
PHONE..................................516 377-1197
Michael A Chin, *President*
EMP: 12
SQ FT: 4,000
SALES (est): 1.7MM **Privately Held**
SIC: 3599 Machine & other job shop work

(G-12923)
GUOSA LIFE SCIENCES INC
846 Center Dr (11510-1104)
PHONE..................................718 813-7806
Charles Oviawe, *Principal*
Edema Oviawe,
EMP: 12 **EST:** 2012
SALES (est): 850K **Privately Held**
SIC: 2834 8999 Solutions, pharmaceutical; tablets, pharmaceutical; scientific consulting

(G-12924)
HUBRAY INC
Also Called: Stu-Art Supplies
2045 Grand Ave (11510-2915)
PHONE..................................800 645-2855
Fax: 516 377-3512
Lisa Hubley, *President*
Andrew Ray, *Vice Pres*
EMP: 12
SQ FT: 10,000
SALES: 1MM **Privately Held**
WEB: www.stu-artsupplies.com
SIC: 2675 2499 5961 Panels, cardboard, die-cut: made from purchased materials; picture & mirror frames, wood; mail order house

(G-12925)
SANDY DUFTLER DESIGNS LTD
775 Brooklyn Ave Ste 105 (11510-2948)
PHONE..................................516 379-3084
Fax: 516 379-4156
Irwin Duftler, *CEO*
Sandra Duftler, *Ch of Bd*
Gregg Duftler, *President*
EMP: 12
SALES (est): 1.2MM **Privately Held**
SIC: 2387 Apparel belts

(G-12926)
SPLIT SYSTEMS CORP (PA)
Also Called: Johnson Contrls Authorized Dlr
1593 Grand Ave (11510-1849)
PHONE..................................516 223-5511
Charles Solon, *President*
Mike Solon, *Vice Pres*
EMP: 1
SALES (est): 1.8MM **Privately Held**
SIC: 3585 5075 Air conditioning equipment, complete; refrigeration equipment, complete; warm air heating & air conditioning

(G-12927)
SWIRL BLISS LLC
1777 Grand Ave (11510-2429)
PHONE..................................516 867-9475
Jeanette Reed,
EMP: 5
SALES (est): 331.9K **Privately Held**
SIC: 2024 Yogurt desserts, frozen

(G-12928)
V C N GROUP LTD INC
1 Clifton St (11510-2114)
PHONE..................................516 223-4812
Florence Abate, *President*
Vincent Abate, *Vice Pres*
Anthony Abate, *Admin Sec*
EMP: 5
SQ FT: 500
SALES (est): 523.6K **Privately Held**
SIC: 2752 Advertising posters, lithographed

(G-12929)
VORTEX VENTURES INC
857 Newton Ave (11510-2826)
PHONE..................................516 946-8345
Kevin Walters, *President*
EMP: 5
SALES (est): 193.4K **Privately Held**
SIC: 7372 7389 Publishers' computer software;

(G-12930)
W & B MAZZA & SONS INC
Also Called: Mazza Co, The
2145 Marion Pl (11510-2921)
PHONE..................................516 379-4130
Fax: 516 379-4152
William Mazza, *President*
William Mazza Jr, *Treasurer*
Steven Mazza, *VP Mktg*
Jeffrey Mazza, *Admin Sec*
EMP: 28
SQ FT: 8,000
SALES (est): 3MM **Privately Held**
WEB: www.mazzajewelry.com
SIC: 3911 Jewelry, precious metal; rings, finger: precious metal; pins (jewelry), precious metal; earrings, precious metal

North Bellmore
Nassau County

(G-12931)
21ST CENTURY FINISHES INC
1895 Newbridge Rd (11710)
P.O. Box 471, Bellmore (11710-0471)
PHONE..................................516 221-7000
Al Doerbecker, *President*
EMP: 14
SALES (est): 1.4MM **Privately Held**
SIC: 3471 Finishing, metals or formed products

(G-12932)
CAPITOL RESTORATION CORP
2473 Belmond Ave (11710-1205)
PHONE..................................516 783-1425
Seeme Rizvi, *President*
EMP: 6
SALES (est): 627.6K **Privately Held**
SIC: 3297 1771 1521 Brick refractories; concrete repair; new construction, single-family houses

(G-12933)
CHERRY HOLDING LTD
Also Called: Cherry Metal Works
1536 Broad St (11710-2146)
PHONE..................................516 679-3748
Michale Kersch, *President*
EMP: 5
SALES (est): 630.7K **Privately Held**
SIC: 3444 Sheet metalwork

(G-12934)
COSTANZA READY MIX INC
1345 Newbridge Rd (11710-1629)
PHONE..................................516 783-4444
Frank Costanza, *President*
Dawn Night, *Accountant*
EMP: 5
SALES (est): 540.3K **Privately Held**
SIC: 3273 Ready-mixed concrete

(G-12935)
CUPCAKE CONTESSAS CORPORATION
1242 Julia Ln (11710-1925)
PHONE..................................516 307-1222
Laura Andreacchi, *Chairman*
EMP: 6
SALES (est): 412K **Privately Held**
SIC: 2051 Cakes, bakery: except frozen

(G-12936)
CUSTOM DISPLAY MANUFACTURE
1686 Logan St (11710-2528)
PHONE..................................516 783-6491
Paul Kassbaum, *President*
EMP: 5
SQ FT: 8,000
SALES (est): 440K **Privately Held**
SIC: 2511 3993 Chairs, household, except upholstered: wood; signs & advertising specialties

(G-12937)
GEORGE BASCH CO INC
1554 Peapond Rd (11710-2925)
P.O. Box 188, Freeport (11520-0188)
PHONE..................................516 378-8100
Fax: 516 378-8140
Laurie Basch-Levy, *President*
Mildred Basch, *Treasurer*
Rhonda Ax, *Admin Sec*
EMP: 10 **EST:** 1929
SQ FT: 6,800
SALES (est): 1MM **Privately Held**
WEB: www.nevrdull.com
SIC: 2842 Cleaning or polishing preparations

(G-12938)
KP INDUSTRIES INC
Also Called: K P Signs
2481 Charles Ct Ste 1 (11710-2761)
P.O. Box 1000, Bethpage (11714-0019)
PHONE..................................516 679-3161
Fax: 516 679-3668
Karen A Puchacz, *President*
Dee Smith, *Admin Sec*
EMP: 11 **EST:** 1997
SQ FT: 3,600
SALES (est): 1.5MM **Privately Held**
SIC: 3993 Signs & advertising specialties

(G-12939)
TOWER INSULATING GLASS LLC
2485 Charles Ct (11710-2733)
PHONE..................................516 887-3300
Fax: 516 887-3323
Barry Litt, *Principal*
EMP: 22
SQ FT: 12,000
SALES (est): 3.5MM **Privately Held**
SIC: 3211 Insulating glass, sealed units

North Chili
Monroe County

(G-12940)
ALBERT GATES INC
3434 Union St (14514-9731)
PHONE..................................585 594-9401
Fax: 585 594-4305
Andrew J Laniak, *Ch of Bd*
Robert J Brinkman, *President*
Dan Ferries, *General Mgr*
James Adams, *Vice Pres*
Dan Helfrich, *QC Mgr*
EMP: 75
SQ FT: 26,000
SALES (est): 17.4MM
SALES (corp-wide): 112.8MM **Privately Held**
WEB: www.gatesalbert.com
SIC: 3451 Screw machine products
PA: Brinkman International Group, Inc.
167 Ames St
Rochester NY 14611
585 429-5000

(G-12941)
P TOOL & DIE CO INC
3535 Union St (14514-9709)
P.O. Box 369 (14514-0369)
PHONE..................................585 889-1340
Fax: 585 889-4636
Michael J Sucese, *President*
Pam McCormick, *Office Mgr*
James Allen, *Manager*
Paul Bradler, *Manager*
Mike Carr, *Manager*
EMP: 22
SQ FT: 18,000
SALES (est): 3.8MM **Privately Held**
SIC: 3544 Special dies, tools, jigs & fixtures

North Collins
Erie County

(G-12942)
AMERICAN WIRE TIE INC (PA)
2073 Franklin St (14111-9636)
P.O. Box 696 (14111-0696)
PHONE..................................716 337-2412
Fax: 716 337-3728
James W Smith, *President*
Ronald Lehnortt, *Sales Staff*
Amelia Jarzynski, *Sales Associate*
Gregory C Mumbach, *Admin Sec*
▲ **EMP:** 30
SQ FT: 54,000

GEOGRAPHIC SECTION

North Syracuse - Onondaga County (G-12963)

SALES (est): 12.4MM **Privately Held**
WEB: www.americanwiretie.com
SIC: **3599** 3496 3315 2631 Ties, form: metal; miscellaneous fabricated wire products; steel wire & related products; paperboard mills

(G-12943)
CRESCENT MARKETING INC (PA)
Also Called: Crescent Manufacturing
10285 Eagle Dr (14111)
P.O. Box 1500 (14111-1500)
PHONE..................716 337-0145
Fax: 716 337-0146
Richard Frazer Jr, *President*
Bruce Penn, *Vice Pres*
Paul Mosher, *Safety Dir*
Emily Frazer, *Purch Dir*
Linda Kempf, *QC Mgr*
▲ EMP: 123
SQ FT: 110,000
SALES (est): 17.1MM **Privately Held**
SIC: **2842** Specialty cleaning, polishes & sanitation goods; specialty cleaning preparations; polishing preparations & related products

(G-12944)
E & D SPECIALTY STANDS INC
2081 Franklin St (14111-9636)
P.O. Box 700 (14111-0700)
PHONE..................716 337-0161
Fax: 716 337-2903
David A Metzger, *President*
Ryan Zahm, *Vice Pres*
Dean Metzger, *Treasurer*
Charlene Heppel, *Accountant*
Dee Pelz, *Human Res Dir*
EMP: 50 EST: 1956
SQ FT: 85,000
SALES (est): 9MM **Privately Held**
WEB: www.edstands.com
SIC: **2531** Bleacher seating, portable

(G-12945)
NITRO MANUFACTURING LLC
440 Shirley Rd (14111)
PHONE..................716 646-9900
Christine Frascella, *Mng Member*
Tim Frascella,
William Frascella,
Dave Kota,
EMP: 5
SALES (est): 576.8K **Privately Held**
SIC: **3599** Machine & other job shop work

(G-12946)
NITRO WHEELS INC
4440 Shirley Rd (14111-9783)
PHONE..................716 337-0709
Louis Frascella, *Principal*
EMP: 10
SALES (est): 1MM **Privately Held**
SIC: **3312** Wheels, locomotive & car: iron & steel

(G-12947)
RENALDOS SALES AND SERVICE CTR
1770 Milestrip Rd (14111-9753)
P.O. Box 820 (14111-0820)
PHONE..................716 337-3760
James V Renaldo, *President*
Joan E Renaldo, *Vice Pres*
EMP: 8
SQ FT: 3,800
SALES: 2.1MM **Privately Held**
SIC: **3523** 3713 Trailers & wagons, farm; planting machines, agricultural; truck bodies (motor vehicles)

(G-12948)
WINTERS RAILROAD SERVICE INC
11309 Sisson Hwy (14111-9729)
PHONE..................716 337-2668
Fax: 716 337-2503
David Winter, *President*
Michael Winter, *Corp Secy*
EMP: 6
SQ FT: 15,000
SALES: 530K **Privately Held**
SIC: **3423** 3441 Hand & edge tools; fabricated structural metal

North Creek
Warren County

(G-12949)
CREATIVE STAGE LIGHTING CO INC
Also Called: C S L
149 State Route 28n (12853-2707)
P.O. Box 567 (12853-0567)
PHONE..................518 251-3302
Fax: 518 251-2908
George B Studnicky III, *President*
Darrell Barnes, *Business Mgr*
Jason Lemery, *Financial Exec*
Phil Heid, *Sales Staff*
Tim Ellifritz, *Manager*
◆ EMP: 43
SQ FT: 32,000
SALES: 8MM **Privately Held**
WEB: www.creativestagelighting.com
SIC: **3648** 5063 7922 Lighting equipment; lighting fixtures, commercial & industrial; lighting, theatrical

North Java
Wyoming County

(G-12950)
SELECT INTERIOR DOOR LTD
Also Called: Select Door
2074 Perry Rd (14113-9722)
P.O. Box 178 (14113-0178)
PHONE..................585 535-9900
Fax: 585 535-9923
John Angelbeck, *President*
Maureen Ronan, *CFO*
EMP: 40
SQ FT: 25,000
SALES (est): 5.7MM **Privately Held**
WEB: www.sidl.com
SIC: **2431** 3231 Doors, wood; products of purchased glass

North Lawrence
St. Lawrence County

(G-12951)
UPSTATE NIAGARA COOP INC
Also Called: North Country Dairy
22 County Route 52 (12967-9539)
PHONE..................315 389-5111
Tim Gominiack, *Branch Mgr*
EMP: 59
SALES (corp-wide): 228.8MM **Privately Held**
SIC: **2026** Fluid milk; milk & cream, except fermented, cultured & flavored; fermented & cultured milk products
PA: Upstate Niagara Cooperative, Inc.
25 Anderson Rd
Buffalo NY 14225
716 892-3156

North Rose
Wayne County

(G-12952)
FLEISCHMANNS VINEGAR CO INC
Also Called: Fleischman Vinegar
4754 State Route 414 (14516-9704)
PHONE..................315 587-4414
John Wilson, *Manager*
EMP: 20
SALES (corp-wide): 3.4B **Publicly Held**
WEB: www.breadworld.com
SIC: **2099** Vinegar
HQ: Fleischmann's Vinegar Company, Inc.
12604 Hiddencreek Way A
Cerritos CA 90703
562 483-4619

(G-12953)
GARGRAVES TRACKAGE CORPORATION (PA)
Also Called: Gardner The Train Doctor
8967 Ridge Rd (14516-9753)
PHONE..................315 483-6577
Fax: 315 483-2425
Michael Roder, *President*
Thomas Roder, *Vice Pres*
EMP: 5
SQ FT: 5,000
SALES: 500K **Privately Held**
WEB: www.gargraves.com
SIC: **3944** 5945 Trains & equipment, toy: electric & mechanical; hobby, toy & game shops

(G-12954)
OLMSTEAD MACHINE INC
10399 Warehouse Ave (14516-9537)
P.O. Box 331 (14516-0331)
PHONE..................315 587-9864
Fax: 315 587-9110
Dale Liechti, *President*
EMP: 10
SQ FT: 10,000
SALES (est): 1.4MM **Privately Held**
SIC: **3599** Machine shop, jobbing & repair

North Salem
Westchester County

(G-12955)
METROPOLITAN FINE MLLWK CORP
Also Called: Metro Millwork
230 Hardscrabble Rd (10560-1019)
PHONE..................914 669-4900
Fax: 914 669-4904
Robert Sposato, *President*
Michael Duignan, *Vice Pres*
Linda Dengler, *Office Mgr*
EMP: 18
SQ FT: 5,000
SALES: 250K **Privately Held**
SIC: **2431** Millwork; doors, wood

(G-12956)
TOTAL ENERGY FABRICATION CORP
2 Hardscrabble Rd (10560-1014)
PHONE..................580 363-1500
Robert Armentano, *CEO*
Gary Harvey, *Principal*
Frank Kovacs, *Principal*
▲ EMP: 6
SALES (est): 1.3MM **Privately Held**
SIC: **3491** Pressure valves & regulators, industrial

North Syracuse
Onondaga County

(G-12957)
CLEANROOM SYSTEMS INC
7000 Performance Dr (13212-3439)
PHONE..................315 452-7400
Larry Wetzel, *President*
Bruce Meissner, *Engineer*
Scott Toukatly, *Engineer*
Deb Emery, *CFO*
Ann Tindall, *Human Res Dir*
EMP: 42
SQ FT: 48,378
SALES (est): 191.9K
SALES (corp-wide): 8.9MM **Privately Held**
WEB: www.cleanroomsystems.com
SIC: **3585** Refrigeration equipment, complete
PA: Air Innovations, Inc.
7000 Performance Dr
North Syracuse NY 13212
315 452-7400

(G-12958)
DISPLAYS BY RIOUX INC
6090 E Taft Rd (13212-3303)
P.O. Box 3008, Syracuse (13220-3008)
PHONE..................315 458-3639
Fax: 315 458-3722
Robert A Rioux Jr, *President*
EMP: 7
SQ FT: 12,200
SALES (est): 972.5K **Privately Held**
WEB: www.displaysbyrioux.com
SIC: **3083** 3089 Laminated plastics plate & sheet; cases, plastic

(G-12959)
DL MANUFACTURING INC
340 Gateway Park Dr (13212-3758)
PHONE..................315 432-8977
Donald L Metz, *Ch of Bd*
Rick Woytan, *Controller*
Lee Eslicker, *Human Res Mgr*
Michael Rivizzigno, *Regl Sales Mgr*
EMP: 30
SQ FT: 22,000
SALES: 12MM **Privately Held**
WEB: www.dlmanufacturing.com
SIC: **3537** 5084 5031 5075 Loading docks: portable, adjustable & hydraulic; industrial machinery & equipment; doors; ventilating equipment & supplies

(G-12960)
G A BRAUN INC (PA)
79 General Irwin Blvd (13212-5279)
P.O. Box 3029, Syracuse (13220-3029)
PHONE..................315 475-3123
JB Werner, *Ch of Bd*
Joe Gudenburr, *President*
David Welsh, *General Mgr*
David Clark, *Vice Pres*
Jim Corrigan, *Vice Pres*
▲ EMP: 90
SQ FT: 75,000
SALES: 29.1MM **Privately Held**
WEB: www.gabraun.com
SIC: **3582** 5087 Washing machines, laundry: commercial, incl. coin-operated; laundry equipment & supplies

(G-12961)
GAYLORD BROS INC
Also Called: Gaylord Archival
7282 William Barry Blvd (13212-3347)
P.O. Box 4901, Syracuse (13221-4901)
PHONE..................315 457-5070
Fax: 315 457-9655
R Keith George, *CEO*
Gony Green, *Credit Staff*
Mark Anderson, *Manager*
Danny McCartin, *Manager*
Courtney McEvoy, *Manager*
◆ EMP: 60
SQ FT: 80,000
SALES (est): 18.3MM
SALES (corp-wide): 117MM **Privately Held**
WEB: www.gaylord.com
SIC: **2679** 2657 2542 Adding machine rolls, paper: made from purchased material; folding paperboard boxes; fixtures: display, office or store: except wood
PA: Demco, Inc.
4810 Forest Run Rd
Madison WI 53704
800 356-1200

(G-12962)
GEDDES BAKERY CO INC
421 S Main St (13212-2800)
PHONE..................315 437-8084
Fax: 315 410-1971
Vasilios Pappas, *President*
Bill Pappas, *Office Mgr*
EMP: 24
SQ FT: 5,600
SALES (est): 3.3MM **Privately Held**
WEB: www.geddesbakery.com
SIC: **2051** 5461 Bakery: wholesale or wholesale/retail combined; bakeries

(G-12963)
GRYPHON SENSORS LLC
7351 Round Pond Rd (13212-2552)
PHONE..................315 452-8882
Anthony Albanese, *President*
EMP: 15
SQ FT: 1,000
SALES (est): 2.4MM **Privately Held**
SIC: **3812** Antennas, radar or communications

North Syracuse - Onondaga County (G-12964)

(G-12964)
ICM CONTROLS CORP
7313 William Barry Blvd (13212-3384)
PHONE................................315 233-5266
Hassan B Kadah, *Ch of Bd*
Andrew Kadah, *President*
Laurie Kadah, *Treasurer*
▲ **EMP:** 16
SALES (est): 3.5MM
SALES (corp-wide): 50MM **Privately Held**
SIC: 3625 Electric controls & control accessories, industrial
PA: International Controls & Measurements Corp.
7313 William Barry Blvd
North Syracuse NY 13212
315 233-5266

(G-12965)
INTERNTNAL CNTRLS MSRMNTS CORP (PA)
Also Called: ICM
7313 William Barry Blvd (13212-3384)
PHONE................................315 233-5266
Hassan B Kadah, *Ch of Bd*
Andrew Kadah, *President*
Christina Staniec, *Purch Dir*
Laurie Kadah, *Treasurer*
Joe Nappi, *Accounting Mgr*
▲ **EMP:** 194
SQ FT: 85,000
SALES: 50MM **Privately Held**
WEB: www.icmcontrols.com
SIC: 3625 Electric controls & control accessories, industrial

(G-12966)
JADAK LLC (HQ)
7279 William Barry Blvd (13212-3349)
PHONE................................315 701-0678
Jeffrey Pine, *President*
Jan Douma, *Managing Dir*
John Pettinelli, *Engineer*
Jim Wellington, *Sales Staff*
John Prior, *Marketing Mgr*
EMP: 15
SALES (est): 123.5K
SALES (corp-wide): 384.7MM **Publicly Held**
SIC: 3577 3845 Optical scanning devices; ultrasonic scanning devices, medical
PA: Novanta Inc.
125 Middlesex Tpke
Bedford MA 01730
781 266-5700

(G-12967)
JADAK TECHNOLOGIES INC (DH)
7279 William Barry Blvd (13212-3349)
PHONE................................315 701-0678
Fax: 315 701-0679
David Miller, *President*
Frank J Borghese, *Vice Pres*
Jennifer Cruse, *Purch Mgr*
James Bowden, *QC Mgr*
Michael Desocio, *Engineer*
EMP: 100
SALES (est): 21.8MM
SALES (corp-wide): 384.7MM **Publicly Held**
WEB: www.jadaktech.com
SIC: 3577 Bar code (magnetic ink) printers
HQ: Novanta Corporation
125 Middlesex Tpke
Bedford MA 01730
781 266-5700

(G-12968)
KELLOGG COMPANY
7350 Round Pond Rd (13212-2553)
PHONE................................315 452-0310
Nick Carlucci, *Manager*
EMP: 30
SALES (corp-wide): 13B **Publicly Held**
WEB: www.kelloggs.com
SIC: 2043 Cereal breakfast foods
PA: Kellogg Company
1 Kellogg Sq
Battle Creek MI 49017
269 961-2000

(G-12969)
TERRYS TRANSMISSION
6217 E Taft Rd (13212-2527)
PHONE................................315 458-4333
Terry Bish, *President*
Charlene Bish, *Vice Pres*
EMP: 6
SQ FT: 5,500
SALES (est): 862.2K **Privately Held**
WEB: www.terrystransmission.com
SIC: 3714 Motor vehicle transmissions, drive assemblies & parts

North Tonawanda
Niagara County

(G-12970)
369 RIVER ROAD INC
369 River Rd (14120-7108)
PHONE................................716 694-5001
Michael Deakin, *President*
EMP: 25 **EST:** 2007
SQ FT: 25,000
SALES (est): 942.6K **Privately Held**
SIC: 3496 Miscellaneous fabricated wire products

(G-12971)
AMERI-CUT TOOL GRINDING INC
Also Called: Superior Tool Company
1020 Oliver St (14120-2710)
PHONE................................716 692-3900
Fax: 716 692-3937
Todd Brosius Jr, *President*
EMP: 5
SQ FT: 10,000
SALES: 500K **Privately Held**
WEB: www.superiortoolllc.com
SIC: 3545 Cutting tools for machine tools

(G-12972)
AN-COR INDUSTRIAL PLASTICS INC
900 Niagara Falls Blvd (14120-2096)
PHONE................................716 695-3141
Fax: 716 695-0465
Merrill W Arthur, *President*
Joseph Gates, *Vice Pres*
Paul Biondi, *CFO*
Rob Spiesz, *Sales Associate*
Ronald Hughes, *Manager*
EMP: 83
SQ FT: 96,000
SALES (est): 26.7MM **Privately Held**
WEB: www.an-cor.com
SIC: 3089 3088 Plastic & fiberglass tanks; plastics plumbing fixtures

(G-12973)
ARMSTRONG PUMPS INC
93 East Ave (14120-6594)
PHONE................................716 693-8813
Fax: 716 693-8970
J A C Armstrong, *CEO*
Bruce V Nus, *Managing Dir*
Bruce Van Nus, *Managing Dir*
Mike Dumais, *Materials Mgr*
Steven Yung, *Controller*
◆ **EMP:** 100
SQ FT: 150,000
SALES (est): 51.6MM
SALES (corp-wide): 51.9MM **Privately Held**
WEB: www.armstrongpumps.com
SIC: 3561 Pumps & pumping equipment
PA: S. A. Armstrong Limited
23 Bertrand Ave
Toronto ON M1L 2
416 755-2291

(G-12974)
ASCENSION INDUSTRIES INC (PA)
1254 Erie Ave (14120-3036)
PHONE................................716 693-9381
Fax: 716 693-9381
Jack Kopczynski Jr, *Ch of Bd*
Donald Naab, *President*
Gary Vincent, *Regional Mgr*
Cliff Post, *VP Opers*
Michael Conti, *Project Mgr*
▲ **EMP:** 85 **EST:** 1975
SQ FT: 140,000
SALES (est): 23.5MM **Privately Held**
WEB: www.asmfab.com
SIC: 3544 3541 3444 Special dies, tools, jigs & fixtures; machine tools, metal cutting type; sheet metalwork

(G-12975)
AUDUBON MACHINERY CORPORATION (PA)
Also Called: Oxygen Generating Systems Intl
814 Wurlitzer Dr (14120-3042)
PHONE................................716 564-5165
Joseph M McMahon, *President*
Robert Schlehr, *Vice Pres*
Dave White, *Prdtn Mgr*
Bob Schlehr, *VP Sls/Mktg*
Timothy Blach, *CFO*
▲ **EMP:** 60
SQ FT: 40,000
SALES (est): 13.7MM **Privately Held**
WEB: www.ogsi.com
SIC: 3569 Gas producers, generators & other gas related equipment

(G-12976)
BAKER TOOL & DIE
48 Industrial Dr (14120-3244)
PHONE................................716 694-2025
EMP: 8
SALES (est): 690K **Privately Held**
SIC: 3312 Blast furnaces & steel mills

(G-12977)
BAKER TOOL & DIE & DIE
48 Industrial Dr (14120-3244)
PHONE................................716 694-2025
Fax: 716 694-2026
Jon C Olstad, *President*
Dottie Harvey, *Bookkeeper*
EMP: 6
SQ FT: 6,000
SALES (est): 480K **Privately Held**
SIC: 3312 Tool & die steel

(G-12978)
BATTENFELD GREASE OIL CORP NY
1174 Erie Ave (14120-3036)
P.O. Box 728 (14120-0728)
PHONE................................716 695-2100
Fax: 716 695-0367
Barbara A Bellanti, *Ch of Bd*
John A Bellanti, *President*
Paul Carpenter, *Plant Mgr*
Don Bowen, *Sales Executive*
Mark Swanson, *CTO*
▲ **EMP:** 40
SALES (est): 11.8MM **Privately Held**
SIC: 2992 Lubricating oils & greases

(G-12979)
BROADWAY KNITTING MILLS INC
1333 Strad Ave Ste 216 (14120-3061)
PHONE................................716 692-4421
Craig Boyce, *President*
Russell Boyce, *Vice Pres*
Susan Boyce, *Treasurer*
Molly Boyce, *Admin Sec*
EMP: 5 **EST:** 1932
SQ FT: 8,400
SALES: 210K **Privately Held**
WEB: www.broadwayknitting.com
SIC: 2329 5611 2326 Jackets (suede, leatherette, etc.), sport: men's & boys'; clothing accessories: men's & boys'; men's & boys' work clothing

(G-12980)
BUFFALO ABRASIVES INC (PA)
960 Erie Ave (14120-3503)
PHONE................................716 693-3856
Fax: 716 693-4092
Arthur A Russ Jr, *President*
Jeffrey J Binkley, *Chairman*
Tim Wagner, *Vice Pres*
Fred Williams, *Vice Pres*
Frank Pawlik, *Safety Mgr*
▲ **EMP:** 45
SQ FT: 65,000
SALES (est): 14.1MM **Privately Held**
WEB: www.buffaloabrasives.com
SIC: 3291 Abrasive products

(G-12981)
BUFFALO PUMPS INC (HQ)
Also Called: A Division A & Liquid Systems
874 Oliver St (14120-3298)
PHONE................................716 693-1850
Fax: 716 693-6303
Robert Paul, *Ch of Bd*
Charles Kistner, *President*
Kathy Kalczynski, *Plant Mgr*
Marty Kraft, *QC Dir*
Terrence Kenny, *Treasurer*
▲ **EMP:** 120
SQ FT: 140,000
SALES (est): 39.5MM
SALES (corp-wide): 331.8MM **Publicly Held**
WEB: www.buffalopumps.com
SIC: 3561 Pumps & pumping equipment
PA: Ampco-Pittsburgh Corporation
726 Bell Ave Ste 301
Carnegie PA 15106
412 456-4400

(G-12982)
CALGON CARBON CORPORATION
830 River Rd (14120-6557)
PHONE................................716 531-9113
EMP: 9
SALES (est): 1.2MM **Privately Held**
SIC: 2819 Charcoal (carbon), activated

(G-12983)
CANALSIDE CREAMERY INC
985 Ruie Rd (14120-1727)
PHONE................................716 695-2876
Barbara Labruna, *Owner*
EMP: 8
SALES (est): 604K **Privately Held**
SIC: 2021 Creamery butter

(G-12984)
COMMERCIAL FABRICS INC
908 Niagara Falls Blvd (14120-2019)
PHONE................................716 694-0641
Fax: 716 694-3803
Michel Senecal, *President*
James Senecal, *Corp Secy*
EMP: 15
SQ FT: 30,000
SALES (est): 1.7MM **Privately Held**
WEB: www.commercialfabrics.com
SIC: 3999 Hot tub & spa covers

(G-12985)
CONFER PLASTICS INC
97 Witmer Rd (14120-2421)
PHONE................................800 635-3213
Fax: 716 694-3102
Douglas C Confer, *President*
Bob Confer, *Vice Pres*
Peter Miller, *Plant Mgr*
Timothy Sudezko, *Opers Mgr*
Cliff Hoover, *QC Mgr*
◆ **EMP:** 130
SQ FT: 100,000
SALES (est): 35.3MM **Privately Held**
WEB: www.conferladders.com
SIC: 3089 Blow molded finished plastic products

(G-12986)
DELAWARE MFG INDS CORP (PA)
3776 Commerce Ct (14120-2024)
PHONE................................716 743-4360
Fax: 716 743-4370
Renzo Mestieri, *Ch of Bd*
Michelle Lattuca, *Vice Pres*
Eric Stanczyk, *Opers Mgr*
Mike Cotterell, *Purch Mgr*
Chuck Wolski, *Info Tech Mgr*
▼ **EMP:** 58
SQ FT: 55,000
SALES (est): 11MM **Privately Held**
WEB: www.dmic.com
SIC: 3494 Valves & pipe fittings

(G-12987)
DMIC INC
Also Called: Delaware Manufacturing Inds
3776 Commerce Ct (14120-2024)
PHONE................................716 743-4360
Chuck Wolski, *Principal*
Eric Stanczyk, *Engineer*

▲ = Import ▼ = Export
◆ = Import/Export

GEOGRAPHIC SECTION

North Tonawanda - Niagara County (G-13012)

EMP: 10
SALES (est): 1.5MM **Privately Held**
SIC: 3492 3714 Fluid power valves for aircraft; motor vehicle parts & accessories

(G-12988)
EXPEDIENT HEAT TREATING CORP
61 Dale Dr (14120-4201)
PHONE 716 433-1177
Paul Waild, *President*
EMP: 5 **EST:** 1979
SQ FT: 2,000
SALES (est): 400K **Privately Held**
SIC: 3398 Metal heat treating

(G-12989)
FAIRVIEW FITTING & MFG INC
3777 Commerce Ct (14120-2024)
PHONE 716 614-0320
Fax: 716 614-0327
Leslie Woodward, *Ch of Bd*
Joseph B Kozak, *General Mgr*
Jack Alley, *Branch Mgr*
Ron Hageman, *Manager*
Gordon Shanor, *Manager*
▲ **EMP:** 53
SQ FT: 50,000
SALES (est): 9.6MM **Privately Held**
SIC: 3599 Flexible metal hose, tubing & bellows

(G-12990)
FEI PRODUCTS LLC (PA)
825 Wurlitzer Dr (14120-3041)
PHONE 716 693-6230
Fax: 716 693-6368
Charles S Craig, *President*
Paul Wasielewski, *Opers Staff*
Lance Bronnenkant, *Research*
Jennifer Gates, *CFO*
Paul G Baldetti, *Manager*
EMP: 35
SQ FT: 23,500
SALES (est): 5.2MM **Privately Held**
SIC: 3089 Plastic processing

(G-12991)
GARDEI INDUSTRIES LLC (PA)
Also Called: F K Williams Division
1087 Erie Ave (14120-3532)
PHONE 716 693-7100
Lori Ferraraccio, *Mng Member*
Jordon Lizy,
▲ **EMP:** 17 **EST:** 1936
SQ FT: 25,000
SALES (est): 1.6MM **Privately Held**
WEB: www.gardei.net
SIC: 2679 3545 Paper products, converted; machine tool accessories

(G-12992)
GLI-DEX SALES CORP
Also Called: Glidden Machine & Tool
855 Wurlitzer Dr (14120-3041)
PHONE 716 692-6501
Fax: 716 692-6551
James Gerace, *President*
Marcia Gerace, *Corp Secy*
Robert Gerace, *Vice Pres*
EMP: 35 **EST:** 1946
SQ FT: 12,000
SALES (est): 2.3MM **Privately Held**
WEB: www.glidex.biz
SIC: 3599 Machine shop, jobbing & repair

(G-12993)
GRIFFIN CHEMICAL COMPANY LLC
Also Called: W.O.w Brand Products
889 Erie Ave Ste 1 (14120-3533)
PHONE 716 693-2465
Gregory Robinson, *Mng Member*
Bernard Zysman,
EMP: 9
SQ FT: 15,000
SALES: 500K **Privately Held**
SIC: 2842 Specialty cleaning preparations

(G-12994)
IMPRESSIVE IMPRINTS
601 Division St (14120-4461)
PHONE 716 692-0905
Fax: 716 693-8997
Robert Albert, *Owner*
Kyle Crotty, *Vice Pres*
Cathy Piciulo, *Marketing Staff*
Judy Albert, *Manager*
EMP: 12
SQ FT: 3,000
SALES (est): 1MM **Privately Held**
SIC: 2759 Commercial printing

(G-12995)
INTERNATIONAL FIBER CORP (PA)
50 Bridge St (14120-6842)
PHONE 716 693-4040
Ron Evans, *Senior VP*
Jit Ang, *Vice Pres*
Lawrence A McKee, *Vice Pres*
Scott Olick, *Safety Mgr*
Stevie Short, *Maint Spvr*
EMP: 11
SALES (est): 13.7MM **Privately Held**
SIC: 2823 Cellulosic manmade fibers

(G-12996)
ISLAND STREET LUMBER CO INC
11 Felton St (14120-6503)
PHONE 716 692-4127
James Le Blanc, *President*
Joan Le Blanc, *Vice Pres*
EMP: 5 **EST:** 1949
SQ FT: 11,500
SALES (est): 600.8K **Privately Held**
SIC: 2431 5211 Millwork; millwork & lumber

(G-12997)
ISOLATION SYSTEMS INC
889 Erie Ave Ste 1 (14120-3533)
PHONE 716 694-6390
Ted Arts, *President*
John Richmond, *Vice Pres*
Susan Arts, *Comptroller*
EMP: 10
SQ FT: 98,000
SALES (est): 2.3MM **Privately Held**
WEB: www.isolation-systems.com
SIC: 3564 Filters, air: furnaces, air conditioning equipment, etc.

(G-12998)
L & S METALS INC
111 Witmer Rd (14120-2443)
PHONE 716 692-6865
Gary Schade, *President*
Steven Oslen, *Purchasing*
Tiffany Shaffer, *Controller*
Dave Orth, *Sales Staff*
Becky Beutel, *Manager*
EMP: 23
SQ FT: 17,000
SALES (est): 4MM **Privately Held**
WEB: www.ls-metals.com
SIC: 3599 7692 Machine shop, jobbing & repair; welding repair

(G-12999)
LISTON MANUFACTURING INC
421 Payne Ave (14120-6987)
P.O. Box 178 (14120-0178)
PHONE 716 695-2111
Fax: 716 695-0443
Theodore Pyrak, *Ch of Bd*
Joseph Laduca, *President*
Russell Laduca, *Vice Pres*
Charles E Pyrak, *Treasurer*
Edward Pyrak, *Treasurer*
EMP: 50 **EST:** 1954
SQ FT: 60,000
SALES (est): 10.7MM **Privately Held**
WEB: www.listonmfg.com
SIC: 3568 Bearings, bushings & blocks

(G-13000)
MODU-CRAFT INC
337 Payne Ave (14120-7236)
PHONE 716 694-0709
Kenneth Babka, *President*
EMP: 7
SALES (corp-wide): 1MM **Privately Held**
SIC: 2599 3821 Factory furniture & fixtures; laboratory furniture
PA: Modu-Craft Inc
  276 Creekside Dr
  Tonawanda NY 14150
  716 694-0709

(G-13001)
NIAGARA SHEETS LLC
7393 Shawnee Rd (14120-1325)
PHONE 716 692-1129
Fax: 716 799-8320
John Bolender, *President*
Skip Polowy, *Vice Pres*
Kurt Schuler, *Controller*
▲ **EMP:** 75 **EST:** 2007
SALES (est): 31.8MM
SALES (corp-wide): 136.3MM **Privately Held**
SIC: 2653 Corrugated boxes, partitions, display items, sheets & pad
PA: Jamestown Container Corp
  14 Deming Dr
  Falconer NY 14733
  716 665-4623

(G-13002)
OCCIDENTAL CHEMICAL CORP
3780 Commerce Ct Ste 600 (14120-2025)
PHONE 716 694-3827
Rose Zenturin, *General Mgr*
EMP: 5
SALES (corp-wide): 10.4B **Publicly Held**
WEB: www.oxychem.com
SIC: 2874 Phosphatic fertilizers
HQ: Occidental Chemical Corporation
  5005 Lyndon B Johnson Fwy # 2200
  Dallas TX 75244
  972 404-3800

(G-13003)
PELLETS LLC
63 Industrial Dr Ste 3 (14120-3248)
PHONE 716 693-1750
Fax: 716 693-1880
Mike Deakin, *President*
Kevin Deakin, *General Mgr*
Kathy Reitz, *Admin Asst*
▲ **EMP:** 6
SQ FT: 7,500
SALES (est): 1MM
SALES (corp-wide): 2.7MM **Privately Held**
WEB: www.pelletsllc.com
SIC: 3291 Abrasive metal & steel products
PA: Val-Kro, Inc.
  369 River Rd
  North Tonawanda NY
  716 694-5001

(G-13004)
PIONEER PRINTERS INC
Also Called: Gardei Manufacturing
1087 Erie Ave (14120-3532)
PHONE 716 693-7100
Fax: 716 692-8671
Carl Hoover, *CEO*
Courtney Frank, *Manager*
EMP: 16
SQ FT: 7,000
SALES (est): 2.7MM **Privately Held**
WEB: www.pioneerprinters.com
SIC: 2752 Commercial printing, offset

(G-13005)
PROTOTYPE MANUFACTURING CORP
836 Wurlitzer Dr (14120-3042)
PHONE 716 695-1700
Fax: 716 695-2735
Richard A Christie, *President*
Timothy G Christie, *Vice Pres*
EMP: 10
SQ FT: 8,000
SALES (est): 1.4MM **Privately Held**
SIC: 3544 Special dies & tools

(G-13006)
RECORD ADVERTISER
435 River Rd (14120-6809)
P.O. Box 668 (14120-0668)
PHONE 716 693-1000
Fax: 716 693-8573
Wayne Lowman, *President*
Robert Kazeangin, *Manager*
EMP: 40
SALES (est): 2MM **Privately Held**
SIC: 2711 Newspapers

(G-13007)
RILEY GEAR CORPORATION
61 Felton St (14120-6598)
PHONE 716 694-0900
Fax: 716 694-9094
David Sambuchi, *Vice Pres*
Ted Galeza, *Plant Mgr*
Donn Neffke, *Manager*
Douglas Caswell, *Manager*
EMP: 20
SALES (corp-wide): 27.8MM **Privately Held**
WEB: www.rileygear.com
SIC: 3462 Gears, forged steel
PA: Riley Gear Corporation
  1 Precision Dr
  Saint Augustine FL 32092
  904 829-5652

(G-13008)
RIVERFRONT COSTUME DESIGN
Also Called: A D M
200 River Rd (14120-5708)
PHONE 716 693-2501
Fax: 716 693-2502
Paul Tucker, *President*
Barbara Tucker, *Vice Pres*
EMP: 9
SQ FT: 12,500
SALES (est): 1MM **Privately Held**
SIC: 2521 2522 Cabinets, office: wood; cabinets, office: except wood

(G-13009)
ROEMAC INDUSTRIAL SALES INC
Also Called: Buffalo Snowmelter
27 Fredericka St (14120-6590)
PHONE 716 692-7332
Fax: 716 692-7366
Mitchell Roemer, *President*
Greg Roemer, *Corp Secy*
Nicholas B Roemer, *Vice Pres*
EMP: 9 **EST:** 1947
SQ FT: 7,000
SALES: 900K **Privately Held**
WEB: www.roemac.com
SIC: 3443 3585 Fabricated plate work (boiler shop); evaporative condensers, heat transfer equipment

(G-13010)
ROGER L URBAN INC (PA)
Also Called: Platter's Chocolates
908 Niagara Falls Blvd # 107 (14120-2021)
PHONE 716 693-5391
Fax: 716 693-2055
Joseph Urban, *President*
Sherry Di Guiseppe, *Vice Pres*
Sherry Diguiseppe, *Vice Pres*
Sherry Guiseppe, *Comms Dir*
Michael Urban, *Shareholder*
EMP: 21
SQ FT: 11,000
SALES (est): 2.7MM **Privately Held**
WEB: www.platterschocolate.com
SIC: 2066 5441 5145 2064 Chocolate candy, solid; candy; confectionery; candy & other confectionery products

(G-13011)
SHANNON ENTPS WSTN NY INC
Also Called: Insultech
75 Main St (14120-5903)
P.O. Box 199 (14120-0199)
PHONE 716 693-7954
Fax: 716 693-1647
Frank Kovacs, *President*
Dennis Dombrowski, *Controller*
Joseph Moran, *Sales Dir*
Robert Weir, *Admin Sec*
▼ **EMP:** 58
SQ FT: 20,000
SALES (est): 6.7MM **Privately Held**
WEB: www.corian-countertop.com
SIC: 2299 Insulating felts

(G-13012)
SOLID SURFACE ACRYLICS INC
800 Walck Rd Ste 14 (14120-3500)
PHONE 716 743-1870
John Linde,
Bob Barenthaler,
EMP: 10
SQ FT: 60,000
SALES (est): 1.3MM **Privately Held**
SIC: 3083 Plastic finished products, laminated

(PA)=Parent Co (HQ)=Headquarters (DH)=Div Headquarters
✪ = New Business established in last 2 years

North Tonawanda - Niagara County (G-13013)

(G-13013)
SOLID SURFACE ACRYLICS LLC
800 Walck Rd Ste 14 (14120-3500)
PHONE..................716 743-1870
Fax: 716 743-0475
Paul Biondi, *Controller*
Jack Tillotsom,
Merrill Arthur,
EMP: 16
SQ FT: 76,000
SALES (est): 3.8MM **Privately Held**
WEB: www.ssacrylics.com
SIC: 2824 Acrylic fibers

(G-13014)
SOLIVAIRA SPECIALTIES INC
4 Detroit St (14120)
PHONE..................716 693-4009
Jerry Bianchi, *Manager*
EMP: 58
SALES (corp-wide): 130.8MM **Privately Held**
WEB: www.ifcfiber.com
SIC: 2023 2299 2823 Dry, condensed, evaporated dairy products; flock (recovered textile fibers); cellulosic manmade fibers
PA: Solvaira Specialties Inc.
 50 Bridge St
 North Tonawanda NY 14120
 716 693-4040

(G-13015)
SOLVAIRA SPECIALTIES INC (PA)
50 Bridge St (14120-6842)
PHONE..................716 693-4040
L J Baillargeon, *CEO*
Dean Newby, *Exec VP*
Ron Evans, *Senior VP*
Jit Ang, *Vice Pres*
Lawrence A McKee, *Vice Pres*
◆ EMP: 110 EST: 1917
SQ FT: 270,000
SALES (est): 130.8MM **Privately Held**
WEB: www.ifcfiber.com
SIC: 2823 2299 Cellulosic manmade fibers; flock (recovered textile fibers)

(G-13016)
STRASSBURG MEDICAL LLC
525 Wheatfield St (14120-7034)
P.O. Box 1213, Lockport (14095-1213)
PHONE..................716 433-9368
David Strassburg,
Amanda Bunn,
EMP: 4
SALES: 1.3MM **Privately Held**
WEB: www.thesock.com
SIC: 2252 Socks

(G-13017)
T-S-K ELECTRONICS INC
908 Niagara Falls Blvd # 122 (14120-2016)
PHONE..................716 693-3916
Fax: 716 692-6433
Kevin Kedzierski, *President*
Michael Kedzierski, *Vice Pres*
EMP: 5 EST: 1958
SQ FT: 15,000
SALES (est): 727.7K **Privately Held**
SIC: 3679 Electronic circuits

(G-13018)
TABER ACQUISITION CORP
Also Called: Taber Industries
455 Bryant St (14120-7043)
PHONE..................716 694-4000
Fax: 716 694-1450
Daniel Slawson, *Ch of Bd*
Martin Slawson, *President*
Kenneth L Slawson, *COO*
Rocer Foore, *Vice Pres*
James Stawitzky, *Vice Pres*
EMP: 60
SQ FT: 72,000
SALES (est): 19.1MM **Privately Held**
WEB: www.taberindustries.com
SIC: 3823 Pressure measurement instruments, industrial

(G-13019)
TAYLOR DEVICES INC (PA)
90 Taylor Dr (14120-6894)
P.O. Box 748 (14120-0748)
PHONE..................716 694-0800
Fax: 716 695-6015
Douglas P Taylor, *Ch of Bd*
Richard G Hill, *Vice Pres*
Mark V McDonough, *CFO*
▲ EMP: 110 EST: 1955
SALES: 25.5MM **Publicly Held**
WEB: www.taylordevices.com
SIC: 3569 Industrial shock absorbers

(G-13020)
TEVA WOMENS HEALTH INC
825 Wurlitzer Dr (14120-3041)
PHONE..................716 693-6230
Paul Wasielewski, *Opers Staff*
Jennifer Gates, *Branch Mgr*
Paul McCarthy, *Info Tech Mgr*
EMP: 17
SALES (corp-wide): 19.7B **Privately Held**
WEB: www.barrlabs.com
SIC: 3089 Plastic processing
HQ: Teva Women's Health, Inc.
 5040 Duramed Rd
 Cincinnati OH 45213
 513 731-9900

(G-13021)
TRINITY TOOLS INC
261 Main St (14120-7106)
PHONE..................716 694-1111
Fax: 716 692-0959
Mitchell Banas, *President*
Chris Wein, *Vice Pres*
Michael Ostrowski, *Admin Sec*
EMP: 20
SQ FT: 18,000
SALES (est): 2.2MM **Privately Held**
WEB: www.trinitytoolrentals.com
SIC: 3544 3545 Special dies & tools; jigs & fixtures; gauges (machine tool accessories)

(G-13022)
UNITED MATERIALS LLC (PA)
3949 Frest Pk Way Ste 400 (14120)
PHONE..................716 683-1432
Ross Eckert, *Ch of Bd*
Peter Romano, *President*
Roger Ball, *CFO*
EMP: 57 EST: 1997
SQ FT: 15,000
SALES (est): 17.3MM **Privately Held**
SIC: 3273 Ready-mixed concrete

(G-13023)
WESTROCK CP LLC
51 Robinson St (14120-6805)
PHONE..................716 694-1000
Dave Hromowyk, *Safety Mgr*
Don Laurie, *Branch Mgr*
Mark Savre, *Manager*
EMP: 165
SALES (corp-wide): 14.1B **Publicly Held**
WEB: www.sto.com
SIC: 2653 3412 Boxes, corrugated: made from purchased materials; metal barrels, drums & pails
HQ: Westrock Cp, Llc
 504 Thrasher St
 Norcross GA 30071

(G-13024)
WESTROCK CP LLC
51 Robinson St (14120-6805)
PHONE..................716 692-6510
Fax: 716 694-9262
Mike McGugan, *Branch Mgr*
EMP: 101
SALES (corp-wide): 14.1B **Publicly Held**
WEB: www.smurfit-stone.com
SIC: 2653 Corrugated boxes, partitions, display items, sheets & pad
HQ: Westrock Cp, Llc
 504 Thrasher St
 Norcross GA 30071

Northport
Suffolk County

(G-13025)
BIO-CHEM BARRIER SYSTEMS LLC
11 W Scudder Pl (11768-3040)
PHONE..................631 261-2682
Patricia J Maloney,
Raymond Maloney,
EMP: 8
SQ FT: 1,200
SALES: 1.6MM **Privately Held**
WEB: www.bio-chembarriersystemllc.com
SIC: 3842 Personal safety equipment

(G-13026)
CADDELL BURNS MANUFACTURING CO
247 Asharoken Ave (11768-1120)
PHONE..................631 757-1772
Fax: 516 742-2416
Vincent Burns, *President*
Caryl Burns, *Vice Pres*
EMP: 20 EST: 1946
SQ FT: 14,000
SALES (est): 2.6MM **Privately Held**
WEB: www.caddell-burns.com
SIC: 3677 3612 Coil windings, electronic; transformers, except electric

(G-13027)
CHASE CORPORATION
Also Called: Chase Partners
7 Harbour Point Dr (11768-1556)
PHONE..................631 827-0476
EMP: 11
SALES (corp-wide): 238MM **Publicly Held**
SIC: 3644 Noncurrent-carrying wiring services
PA: Chase Corporation
 295 University Ave
 Westwood MA 02090
 508 819-4200

(G-13028)
CYPRESS SEMICONDUCTOR CORP
Also Called: Sales Office
34 Rowley Dr (11768-3246)
PHONE..................631 261-1358
Carl Finke, *Branch Mgr*
EMP: 14
SALES (corp-wide): 1.9B **Publicly Held**
WEB: www.cypress.com
SIC: 3674 5065 Semiconductors & related devices; electronic parts & equipment
PA: Cypress Semiconductor Corporation
 5883 Rue Ferrari Ste 100
 San Jose CA 95138
 408 943-2600

(G-13029)
FRANKLIN PACKAGING INC (PA)
96 Sea Cove Rd (11768-1847)
PHONE..................631 582-8900
Steven Lincon, *CEO*
Joan Lincoln, *Treasurer*
EMP: 6
SQ FT: 1,500
SALES: 800K **Privately Held**
SIC: 2759 Commercial printing

(G-13030)
HAMMER COMMUNICATIONS INC
Also Called: Hammer Magazine
28 Sunken Meadow Rd (11768-2719)
PHONE..................631 261-5806
John Rigrod, *President*
Michaelina Rigrod, *Vice Pres*
Michalina Rigrod, *Vice Pres*
EMP: 10
SALES: 1.5MM **Privately Held**
SIC: 2721 Periodicals

(G-13031)
KEEP HEALTHY INC
1019 Fort Salonga Rd (11768-2270)
PHONE..................631 651-9090
Ronald Sowa, *President*
EMP: 12 EST: 2014
SALES: 500K **Privately Held**
SIC: 2064 Breakfast bars

(G-13032)
LEDAN INC
Also Called: Ledan Design Group
6 Annetta Ave (11768-1802)
PHONE..................631 239-1226
Fax: 516 747-5933
Daniel Leo Sr, *CEO*
Steven Leo, *President*
Dan Leo Jr, *Vice Pres*
Carla Polizzi, *Sales Staff*
EMP: 25
SQ FT: 20,000
SALES (est): 3.1MM **Privately Held**
WEB: www.ledan.com
SIC: 2542 Office & store showcases & display fixtures

(G-13033)
LIK LLC
6 Bluff Point Rd (11768-1516)
PHONE..................516 848-5135
Laura Kampa, *President*
EMP: 10
SALES (est): 761.8K **Privately Held**
SIC: 3669 Communications equipment

(G-13034)
MARKETING GROUP INTERNATIONAL
Also Called: Mgi
1 Stargazer Ct (11768-1054)
PHONE..................631 754-8095
Bruce Chautin, *Partner*
Linda Kupcewicz, *Partner*
▲ EMP: 7
SALES (est): 1.1MM **Privately Held**
SIC: 2679 Paper products, converted

(G-13035)
WACF ENTERPRISE INC
275 Asharoken Ave (11768-1120)
PHONE..................631 745-5841
Richard Orofino, *Owner*
Jim Peterson, *General Mgr*
EMP: 50
SQ FT: 4,000
SALES (est): 5.2MM **Privately Held**
SIC: 2833 Botanical products, medicinal: ground, graded or milled

Northville
Fulton County

(G-13036)
BEST TINSMITH SUPPLY INC
4 Zetta Dr (12134-5322)
PHONE..................518 863-2541
John Crawford Jr, *President*
Claudia Hutchins, *Treasurer*
EMP: 5
SQ FT: 6,000
SALES: 507.1K **Privately Held**
SIC: 3444 Sheet metalwork

Norwich
Chenango County

(G-13037)
BYTHEWAY PUBLISHING SERVICES
365 Follett Hill Rd (13815-3378)
PHONE..................607 334-8365
Betty Bytheway, *Owner*
Lori Holland, *Office Mgr*
EMP: 17
SALES (est): 1.4MM **Privately Held**
WEB: www.bytheway.com
SIC: 2791 Typesetting

(G-13038)
CHENANGO ASPHALT PRODUCTS
23 State St (13815-1400)
P.O. Box 270 (13815-0270)
PHONE..................607 334-3117

GEOGRAPHIC SECTION   Nunda - Livingston County (G-13059)

Fax: 607 334-4843
Barry Christophgrsen, *Manager*
EMP: 10
SALES (est): 431.2K **Privately Held**
SIC: 1442 Construction sand & gravel

(G-13039)
CHENANGO CONCRETE CORP
Also Called: Boeing Medcl Trtmnt Mltry Arcr
County Rd 32 E River Rd (13815)
PHONE..........................607 334-2545
Darryl Davis, *Vice Pres*
Patrick Shanahan, *Vice Pres*
Milt Sheppler, *Manager*
Mike Dwyer, *Director*
EMP: 10
SQ FT: 3,264
SALES (corp-wide): 6.5MM **Privately Held**
SIC: 3271 Concrete block & brick
PA: Chenango Concrete Corp.
145 Podpadic Rd
Richmondville NY 12149
518 294-9964

(G-13040)
CHENANGO UNION PRINTING INC
15 American Ave (13815-1834)
P.O. Box 149 (13815-0149)
PHONE..........................607 334-2112
Fax: 607 334-9205
Andrew Phelps, *President*
David Phelps, *Shareholder*
EMP: 8
SALES (est): 1.2MM **Privately Held**
WEB: www.chenangounion.com
SIC: 2759 2752 Letterpress printing; commercial printing, offset

(G-13041)
CHENTRONICS CORPORATION
115 County Rd 45 (13815)
PHONE..........................607 334-5531
Fax: 607 336-7447
John Killean, *President*
Stephen Biviano, *Vice Pres*
Mary P Lanfair, *Sales Executive*
Allen Pardon, *Admin Sec*
▲ **EMP:** 22
SALES (est): 4.5MM
SALES (corp-wide): 27.8B **Privately Held**
WEB: www.chentronics.com
SIC: 3433 Heating equipment, except electric
PA: Koch Industries, Inc.
4111 E 37th St N
Wichita KS 67220
316 828-5500

(G-13042)
CHOBANI LLC (HQ)
147 State Highway 320 (13815-3561)
PHONE..........................607 337-1246
Hamdi Ulukaya, *CEO*
Tim Brown, *President*
Michael Forrar, *President*
Michael Gonda, *President*
Kurt Atkinson, *Division Mgr*
▲ **EMP:** 120
SQ FT: 60,000
SALES (est): 893.6MM
SALES (corp-wide): 203.8MM **Privately Held**
SIC: 2026 Yogurt
PA: Chobani Global Holdings, Llc
147 State Highway 320
Norwich NY 13815
607 847-6181

(G-13043)
CHOBANI IDAHO LLC
147 State Highway 320 (13815-3561)
PHONE..........................208 432-2248
Zach Lorcher, *Manager*
Randy Sabin, *Supervisor*
Emily Acee, *Administration*
EMP: 7
SALES (est): 100.4K **Privately Held**
SIC: 2024 Dairy based frozen desserts

(G-13044)
COMMERCIAL DISPLAY DESIGN LLC
120 Kemper Ln (13815-3579)
PHONE..........................607 336-7353

Fax: 607 336-7357
Bernard Freudenmann, *Sales Executive*
W Russell Hurd,
Thomas G Naughton,
Gregory C Yungbluth,
EMP: 15
SALES (est): 100K
SALES (corp-wide): 19.6MM **Privately Held**
SIC: 2521 Cabinets, office: wood
PA: Burt Rigid Box, Inc.
58 Browne St
Oneonta NY 13820
607 433-2510

(G-13045)
DAN WESSON CORP
Also Called: Cz USA Dwf Dan Wesson Firearm
65 Borden Ave (13815)
PHONE..........................607 336-1174
Robert W Serva, *President*
EMP: 18
SQ FT: 24,000
SALES (est): 1.4MM **Privately Held**
WEB: www.danwessonfirearms.com
SIC: 3484 Small arms

(G-13046)
ELECTRON COIL INC
Also Called: Eci
141 Barr Rd (13815)
P.O. Box 71 (13815-0071)
PHONE..........................607 336-7414
Douglas Marchant, *CEO*
John Barnett, *General Mgr*
Richard Marchant, *Vice Pres*
Paula McCall, *Purch Agent*
Jeff Cola, *QC Mgr*
EMP: 55
SQ FT: 10,000
SALES (est): 10.7MM **Privately Held**
WEB: www.electroncoil.com
SIC: 3621 3612 3675 3677 Coils, for electric motors or generators; power & distribution transformers; electronic capacitors; electronic coils, transformers & other inductors

(G-13047)
GOLUB CORPORATION
Also Called: Price Chopper Pharmacy
5631 State Highway 12 (13815-3205)
PHONE..........................607 336-2588
Vincent Mainella, *Branch Mgr*
EMP: 74
SALES (corp-wide): 3.4B **Privately Held**
SIC: 3751 Motorcycles & related parts
PA: The Golub Corporation
461 Nott St
Schenectady NY 12308
518 355-5000

(G-13048)
KERRY BFNCTNAL INGREDIENTS INC (DH)
Also Called: Kerry Bio-Science
158 State Highway 320 (13815-3561)
PHONE..........................607 334-1700
Stan McCarthy, *CEO*
Gerry Behan, *Chairman*
Kelly Anderson, *Controller*
Crystal Dunninger, *Manager*
Michael Woods, *Manager*
◆ **EMP:** 69
SQ FT: 127,353
SALES (est): 17.3MM **Privately Held**
SIC: 2099 2079 2023 Food preparations; seasonings: dry mixes; edible fats & oils; dry, condensed, evaporated dairy products
HQ: Kerry Inc.
3330 Millington Rd
Beloit WI 53511
608 363-1200

(G-13049)
LABEL GALLERY INC
1 Lee Ave 11 (13815-1108)
PHONE..........................607 334-3244
Fax: 607 334-4815
Christopher Ulatowski, *President*
Anna Ulatowski, *Vice Pres*
Michael Gladstone, *Plant Mgr*
Walt Reid, *Opers Staff*
Gail Lawrence, *Human Res Dir*

EMP: 30
SQ FT: 15,000
SALES (est): 6.5MM **Privately Held**
WEB: www.labelgallery.net
SIC: 2672 2752 Labels (unprinted), gummed: made from purchased materials; commercial printing, lithographic

(G-13050)
NEW BERLIN GAZETTE
29 Lackawanna Ave (13815-1404)
PHONE..........................607 847-6131
Dick Snyder, *Owner*
EMP: 20
SQ FT: 2,400
SALES (est): 799.5K **Privately Held**
SIC: 2711 Commercial printing & newspaper publishing combined

(G-13051)
NORWICH AERO PRODUCTS INC (HQ)
50 Ohara Dr (13815-2029)
P.O. Box 109 (13815-0109)
PHONE..........................607 336-7636
Fax: 607 336-2610
Curtis Reusser, *CEO*
Roger Alan Ross, *President*
Christoper Ainsworth, *VP Opers*
Michael Crandell, *Engineer*
Robert D George, *CFO*
EMP: 58
SQ FT: 56,000
SALES (est): 13.9MM
SALES (corp-wide): 1.9B **Publicly Held**
WEB: www.norwichaero.com
SIC: 3812 3829 3823 Search & navigation equipment; measuring & controlling devices; temperature instruments: industrial process type
PA: Esterline Technologies Corp
500 108th Ave Ne Ste 1500
Bellevue WA 98004
425 453-9400

(G-13052)
NORWICH PHARMACEUTICALS INC
Also Called: Norwich Pharma Services
6826 State Highway 12 (13815-3335)
PHONE..........................607 335-3000
Chris Calhoun, *President*
Darren Alkins, *President*
Lisa Graver, *Exec VP*
Carolyn Gerardi, *Vice Pres*
Tami Watson, *Opers Staff*
▲ **EMP:** 375
SQ FT: 375,000
SALES (est): 66.5MM **Privately Held**
SIC: 2834 Pharmaceutical preparations
PA: Alvogen Group, Inc.
10 Bloomfield Ave
Pine Brook NJ 07058

(G-13053)
PRECISION BUILT TOPS LLC
89 Borden Ave (13815-1105)
PHONE..........................607 336-5417
Fax: 607 336-7585
Steven Serafan,
EMP: 6
SALES (est): 654.5K **Privately Held**
WEB: www.precisionbuilttops.com
SIC: 2541 Counter & sink tops

(G-13054)
PRIME TOOL & DIE LLC
6277 County Road 32 (13815-3560)
P.O. Box 83 (13815-0083)
PHONE..........................607 334-5435
George H Prime Jr, *Mng Member*
Steve Prime, *Manager*
EMP: 6
SALES: 400K **Privately Held**
SIC: 3544 Jigs & fixtures

(G-13055)
SUN PRINTING INCORPORATED
57 Borden Ave 65 (13815-1105)
P.O. Box 151 (13815-0151)
PHONE..........................607 337-3034
Fax: 607 334-5136
Bradford R Dick, *Principal*
EMP: 29 **EST:** 2001

SALES (est): 2.5MM **Privately Held**
SIC: 2752 Commercial printing, lithographic

(G-13056)
SURESEAL CORPORATION
Also Called: Norwich Aero
50 Ohara Dr (13815-2029)
P.O. Box 109 (13815-0109)
PHONE..........................607 336-6676
Randy Mohr, *President*
Mike Crandell, *Engineer*
Terry Keister, *CFO*
Edward Campbell, *Executive*
EMP: 7
SQ FT: 56,000
SALES (est): 844.7K
SALES (corp-wide): 1.9B **Publicly Held**
WEB: www.norwichaero.com
SIC: 3678 Electronic connectors
HQ: Norwich Aero Products, Inc.
50 Ohara Dr
Norwich NY 13815
607 336-7636

(G-13057)
UNISON INDUSTRIES LLC
5345 State Highway 12 (13815-1246)
P.O. Box 310 (13815-0310)
PHONE..........................607 335-5000
Steve Logan, *Purch Agent*
Debbie Morgan, *Buyer*
Mike Terzo, *Engineer*
Timothy Carr, *Project Engr*
Raj Nair, *Sales Staff*
EMP: 350
SALES (corp-wide): 123.6B **Publicly Held**
WEB: www.unisonindustries.com
SIC: 3679 3769 Electronic circuits; guided missile & space vehicle parts & auxiliary equipment
HQ: Unison Industries, Llc
7575 Baymeadows Way
Jacksonville FL 32256
904 739-4000

Norwood
St. Lawrence County

(G-13058)
BARRETT PAVING MATERIALS INC
Also Called: Norwood Quar Btmnous Con Plnts
Rr 56 (13668)
P.O. Box 203 (13668-0203)
PHONE..........................315 353-6611
Fax: 315 353-2768
David R Wright, *Superintendent*
EMP: 25
SALES (corp-wide): 77.1MM **Privately Held**
WEB: www.barrettpaving.com
SIC: 2951 5032 1611 2952 Concrete, bituminous; paving materials; surfacing & paving; asphalt felts & coatings
HQ: Barrett Paving Materials Inc.
3 Becker Farm Rd Ste 307
Roseland NJ 07068
973 533-1001

Nunda
Livingston County

(G-13059)
ONCE AGAIN NUT BUTTER COLLECTV (PA)
12 S State St (14517)
P.O. Box 429 (14517-0429)
PHONE..........................585 468-2535
Fax: 585 468-5995
Robert Gelser, *President*
Franklin Lew, *Production*
Jake Rawleigh, *QC Mgr*
Lawrence Filipski, *CFO*
Gael Orr, *Comms Mgr*
▲ **EMP:** 64
SQ FT: 20,000

Nunda - Livingston County (G-13060)

SALES (est): 12.6MM **Privately Held**
WEB: www.onceagainnutbutter.com
SIC: 2099 Peanut butter; almond pastes; honey, strained & bottled

(G-13060)
SEATING INC
60 N State St (14517)
P.O. Box 898 (14517-0898)
PHONE..................800 468-2475
Fax: 585 468-2804
Judy Hart, *President*
Doug Hart, *Vice Pres*
Christine Woodard, *Natl Sales Mgr*
Tammy Everts, *Manager*
EMP: 31
SQ FT: 65,000
SALES (est): 3.7MM **Privately Held**
WEB: www.seatinginc.com
SIC: 2522 2531 Office chairs, benches & stools, except wood; public building & related furniture

Nyack
Rockland County

(G-13061)
BECTON DICKINSON AND COMPANY
Also Called: Bd Initiative-Hlthcare Wrkr SA
1 Main St Apt 3307 (10960-3236)
PHONE..................845 353-3371
Johannes Gustafsson, *Engineer*
Amit Limaye, *Engineer*
John Manocchio, *Senior Engr*
Jill Garnette, *Manager*
EMP: 379
SALES (corp-wide): 12.4B **Publicly Held**
SIC: 3841 Surgical & medical instruments
PA: Becton, Dickinson And Company
1 Becton Dr
Franklin Lakes NJ 07417
201 847-6800

(G-13062)
BERRY INDUSTRIAL GROUP INC (PA)
30 Main St (10960-3202)
PHONE..................845 353-8338
Debra Berry, *CEO*
Peter Berry, *President*
Lori Lichtig, *General Mgr*
EMP: 5
SQ FT: 1,800
SALES (est): 915.7K **Privately Held**
WEB: www.berryindustrial.com
SIC: 2448 5031 Wood pallets & skids; lumber: rough, dressed & finished

(G-13063)
CHARLES PERRELLA INC
78 S Broadway (10960-6802)
PHONE..................845 348-4777
Marie Somos, *President*
Richard Townsend, *Corp Secy*
Phyllis Townsend, *Vice Pres*
EMP: 20
SQ FT: 7,500
SALES (est): 1.5MM **Privately Held**
WEB: www.perrellainc.com
SIC: 3911 5944 Jewelry, precious metal; jewelry stores

(G-13064)
CONCEPT PRINTING INC
Also Called: Concept Printing and Promotion
40 Lydecker St (10960-2104)
PHONE..................845 353-4040
Kerry Gaughan Monahan, *President*
▲ EMP: 4
SALES: 1.3MM **Privately Held**
WEB: www.conceptprintinginc.com
SIC: 2752 5199 Commercial printing, offset; advertising specialties

(G-13065)
DESIGNPLEX LLC
107 Cedar Hill Ave (10960-3705)
PHONE..................845 358-6647
Loren Bloom, *President*
EMP: 5
SQ FT: 1,500
SALES: 200K **Privately Held**
WEB: www.designplex.org
SIC: 3993 Signs & advertising specialties

(G-13066)
EASTERN PRECISION MFG
76 S Franklin St 78 (10960-3734)
PHONE..................845 358-1951
Harold Hill, *President*
EMP: 6 EST: 1973
SQ FT: 600
SALES (est): 418.8K **Privately Held**
SIC: 3569 Firefighting apparatus

(G-13067)
EDROY PRODUCTS CO INC
245 N Midland Ave (10960-1949)
P.O. Box 998 (10960-0998)
PHONE..................845 358-6600
Fax: 845 358-4098
Steven Stoltze, *President*
EMP: 7 EST: 1937
SQ FT: 4,700
SALES (est): 606.2K **Privately Held**
WEB: www.edroyproducts.com
SIC: 3851 Magnifiers (readers & simple magnifiers)

(G-13068)
GLOBAL BRANDS INC
1031 Route 9w S (10960-4907)
PHONE..................845 358-1212
Ralph Ferrante, *CEO*
Herbert M Paul, *President*
Lawrence Ackemern, *Office Mgr*
EMP: 8
SQ FT: 1,250
SALES (est): 802.1K **Privately Held**
SIC: 2086 Mineral water, carbonated: packaged in cans, bottles, etc.

(G-13069)
LUGO NUTRITION INC
51 N Broadway Unit 2b (10960-2643)
PHONE..................302 573-2503
Richard Lugo, *President*
Nicholas Lugo, *Vice Pres*
Karen Logu, *CFO*
EMP: 6
SALES (est): 348.4K **Privately Held**
SIC: 2099 Food preparations

(G-13070)
SARAVAL INDUSTRIES
348 N Midland Ave (10960-1531)
PHONE..................516 768-9033
Fax: 845 323-4010
Dave Schwartz, *Owner*
Maria Vestal, *Managing Dir*
EMP: 9
SALES (est): 480K **Privately Held**
SIC: 2521 Wood office furniture

(G-13071)
TANDY LEATHER FACTORY INC
298 Main St (10960-2418)
PHONE..................845 480-3588
Kelly Perini, *Manager*
EMP: 5
SALES (corp-wide): 82.9MM **Publicly Held**
SIC: 3111 5199 5948 Accessory products, leather; lace leather; leather, leather goods & furs; leather goods, except luggage & shoes
PA: Tandy Leather Factory, Inc.
1900 Se Loop 820
Fort Worth TX 76140
817 872-3200

(G-13072)
TEKA PRECISION INC
251 Mountainview Ave (10960-1700)
PHONE..................845 753-1900
Fax: 845 727-4040
Helen Roderick, *President*
EMP: 7
SQ FT: 1,500
SALES (est): 660K **Privately Held**
SIC: 3496 3541 3495 3452 Miscellaneous fabricated wire products; machine tools, metal cutting type; wire springs; bolts, nuts, rivets & washers

(G-13073)
WIRELESS COMMUNICATIONS INC
4 Chemong Ct (10960-2307)
PHONE..................845 353-5921
Robert H Colten, *Owner*
EMP: 5
SALES (est): 317.7K **Privately Held**
SIC: 3663 Radio broadcasting & communications equipment

Oakdale
Suffolk County

(G-13074)
CJ COMPONENT PRODUCTS LLC
624 Tower Mews (11769-2449)
PHONE..................631 567-3733
David Howe, *CEO*
Kevin Lee, *Vice Pres*
▼ EMP: 5
SQ FT: 880
SALES (est): 798.9K **Privately Held**
WEB: www.cjcomponents.com
SIC: 3663 Radio & TV communications equipment

(G-13075)
GALAXY SOFTWARE LLC
154 Middlesex Ave (11769-1975)
P.O. Box 229 (11769-0229)
PHONE..................631 244-8405
Andrew Cohen, *Sales Executive*
Cathline Cohen,
EMP: 8
SALES (est): 664.9K **Privately Held**
WEB: www.galaxy-software.com
SIC: 7372 7371 Application computer software; software programming applications

(G-13076)
GSA UPSTATE NY (PA)
755 Montauk Hwy (11769-1801)
PHONE..................631 244-5744
John Beaver, *CEO*
EMP: 2
SQ FT: 1,000
SALES (est): 5.5MM **Privately Held**
WEB: www.gsasales.com
SIC: 3699 Electrical equipment & supplies

(G-13077)
MODERN ITLN BKY OF W BABYLON
301 Locust Ave (11769-1652)
PHONE..................631 589-7300
Fax: 631 589-7383
James Turco, *Principal*
Kevin Connors, *Controller*
Bridgette Johnston, *Controller*
Mike Sable, *Controller*
Jerry Yllanes, *Persnl Mgr*
EMP: 170
SQ FT: 54,000
SALES (est): 43.9MM **Privately Held**
WEB: www.modernbakedprod.com
SIC: 2051 5142 5149 Bread, all types (white, wheat, rye, etc): fresh or frozen; bakery products, frozen; bakery products

(G-13078)
MORELAND HOSE & BELTING CORP
4118 Sunrise Hwy (11769-1013)
PHONE..................631 563-7071
Fax: 631 563-3457
William Delmore, *Manager*
EMP: 8
SALES (corp-wide): 6.4MM **Privately Held**
WEB: www.morelandhose.com
SIC: 3052 Hose, pneumatic: rubber or rubberized fabric
PA: Moreland Hose & Belting Corp
135 Adams Ave
Hempstead NY 11550
516 485-9898

(G-13079)
PUPELLOS ORGANIC CHIPS INC
509 Ockers Dr (11769-1410)
P.O. Box 542, Bohemia (11716-0542)
PHONE..................718 710-9154
John Adam Pupello, *CEO*
EMP: 15
SALES: 950K **Privately Held**
SIC: 2096 Potato sticks

(G-13080)
SPECIALTY FABRICATORS
4120 Sunrise Hwy (11769-1079)
PHONE..................631 256-6982
Charlie Aguilera, *Principal*
EMP: 10
SALES (est): 1.1MM **Privately Held**
SIC: 3399 Primary metal products

(G-13081)
SPEEDZONE INC
Also Called: Speedzone Raceway Hobbies
937 Montauk Hwy (11769-1733)
PHONE..................631 750-1973
EMP: 6 EST: 2007
SALES (est): 70.8K **Privately Held**
SIC: 3644 Raceways

(G-13082)
STEEL-BRITE LTD
Also Called: September Associates
2 Dawn Dr (11769-1624)
PHONE..................631 589-4044
Marilyn Cohen, *President*
Susan McCarthy, *Managing Dir*
EMP: 10
SQ FT: 2,500
SALES (est): 770K **Privately Held**
SIC: 3993 5072 Displays & cutouts, window & lobby; hardware

Oakfield
Genesee County

(G-13083)
BONDUELLE USA INC
40 Stevens St (14125-1227)
PHONE..................585 948-5252
Daniel Vielfaure, *CEO*
EMP: 32
SALES (est): 9.1MM **Privately Held**
SIC: 3556 Smokers, food processing equipment

(G-13084)
KEEBLER COMPANY
2999 Judge Rd (14125-9771)
PHONE..................585 948-8010
Fax: 585 948-8023
Ed Watson, *Manager*
EMP: 17
SALES (corp-wide): 13B **Publicly Held**
WEB: www.keebler.com
SIC: 2052 Cookies
HQ: Keebler Company
1 Kellogg Sq
Battle Creek MI 49017
269 961-2000

(G-13085)
UNITED STATES GYPSUM COMPANY
2750 Maple Ave (14125-9722)
PHONE..................585 948-5221
Fax: 585 948-5018
Jim Perry, *Plant Mgr*
Jim Roz, *Opers Staff*
Debbie Rich, *Purchasing*
Ray Dunlevy, *Personnel*
Gregg Diefenbacher, *Branch Mgr*
EMP: 123
SALES (corp-wide): 3B **Publicly Held**
WEB: www.usg.com
SIC: 3275 Gypsum products
HQ: United States Gypsum Company Inc
550 W Adams St Ste 1300
Chicago IL 60661
312 606-4000

Oakland Gardens
Queens County

(G-13086)
SLIMS BAGELS UNLIMITED INC (PA)
22118 Horace Harding Expy (11364-2390)
P.O. Box 640206 (11364-0206)
PHONE..................................718 229-1140
Fax: 718 225-0514
Joseph Dvir, *President*
David Katz, *Vice Pres*
EMP: 27 **EST:** 1999
SQ FT: 5,000
SALES (est): 1.5MM **Privately Held**
SIC: 2051 5641 Bakery: wholesale or wholesale/retail combined; children's & infants' wear stores

(G-13087)
SRTECH INDUSTRY CORP
5022 201st St (11364-1014)
PHONE..................................718 496-7001
S Chung, *President*
EMP: 25
SQ FT: 5,000
SALES: 3MM **Privately Held**
SIC: 3663 Amplifiers, RF power & IF

Oaks Corners
Ontario County

(G-13088)
ELDERLEE INCORPORATED (HQ)
729 Cross Rd (14518)
P.O. Box 10 (14518-0010)
PHONE..................................315 789-6670
Fax: 315 789-4262
Basil A Shorb III, *Ch of Bd*
William J Shorb, *President*
David Dejohn, *Vice Pres*
Robert Rook, *Vice Pres*
Paul R Strain, *Vice Pres*
EMP: 120
SQ FT: 240,000
SALES (est): 48.4MM
SALES (corp-wide): 80.9MM **Privately Held**
WEB: www.elderlee.com
SIC: 3312 1611 3444 3993 Iron & steel: galvanized, pipes, plates, sheets, etc.; guardrail construction, highways; guard rails, highway: sheet metal; signs & advertising specialties; concrete products
PA: Reh Holdings, Inc
150 S Sumner St
York PA 17404
717 843-0021

(G-13089)
HANSON AGGREGATES PA LLC
2026 County Rd Ste 6 (14518)
PHONE..................................315 789-6202
Fax: 315 789-1030
Kenny Thurston, *Opers-Prdtn-Mfg*
Mike Cool, *Personnel Exec*
EMP: 25
SALES (corp-wide): 16B **Privately Held**
SIC: 1442 3281 1422 Gravel mining; stone, quarrying & processing of own stone products; crushed & broken limestone
HQ: Hanson Aggregates Pennsylvania, Llc
7660 Imperial Way
Allentown PA 18195
610 366-4626

Oceanside
Nassau County

(G-13090)
3KRF LLC
3516 Hargale Rd (11572-5820)
PHONE..................................516 208-6824
Timothy Hopper, *Managing Prtnr*
Mark Gruenspecht, *Mng Member*
EMP: 5
SALES (est): 410K **Privately Held**
SIC: 3699 Electrical welding equipment

(G-13091)
AHW PRINTING CORP
Also Called: PIP Printing
2920 Long Beach Rd (11572-3114)
PHONE..................................516 536-3600
Fax: 516 536-9290
Alan Waldman, *President*
Harriet Waldman, *Treasurer*
EMP: 11
SQ FT: 1,900
SALES (est): 1.6MM **Privately Held**
SIC: 2752 Commercial printing, offset

(G-13092)
ASTRODYNE INC
18 Neil Ct (11572-5816)
P.O. Box 354, Rockville Centre (11571-0354)
PHONE..................................516 536-5755
Fax: 516 536-5063
David J Salwen, *CEO*
Ira M Salwen, *President*
Barbara Salwen, *Admin Sec*
EMP: 6
SQ FT: 5,000
SALES (est): 931.1K **Privately Held**
SIC: 3861 5045 5734 Photographic equipment & supplies; computers, peripherals & software; computer software; computer & software stores; computer software & accessories

(G-13093)
BAGELS BY BELL LTD
Also Called: B & S Bialy
3333 Royal Ave (11572-3625)
PHONE..................................718 272-2780
Fax: 718 272-2789
Warren Bell, *President*
Marvin Wolsy, *Manager*
▼ **EMP:** 34
SALES (est): 5.8MM **Privately Held**
SIC: 2051 Bagels, fresh or frozen

(G-13094)
CHUDNOW MANUFACTURING CO INC
3055 New St (11572-2743)
PHONE..................................516 593-4222
Fax: 516 593-4156
Richard B Cohen, *President*
Ralph Pierro, *General Mgr*
EMP: 45 **EST:** 1934
SQ FT: 28,000
SALES: 5MM **Privately Held**
SIC: 3585 Soda fountain & beverage dispensing equipment & parts; soda fountains, parts & accessories

(G-13095)
D & M CUSTOM CABINETS INC
2994 Long Beach Rd (11572-3205)
P.O. Box 37 (11572-0037)
PHONE..................................516 678-2818
Fax: 516 678-0042
Michael J Lastella, *President*
Doris Lastella, *Admin Sec*
EMP: 12
SQ FT: 7,500
SALES (est): 1.3MM **Privately Held**
WEB: www.d-mcc.com
SIC: 2434 Wood kitchen cabinets

(G-13096)
DDC TECHNOLOGIES INC
311 Woods Ave (11572-2128)
PHONE..................................516 594-1533
Dimitri Donskoy, *President*
Alex Chernovets, *Marketing Mgr*
EMP: 5
SALES (est): 872.9K **Privately Held**
WEB: www.ddctech.com
SIC: 3845 Laser systems & equipment, medical

(G-13097)
DRILL AMERICA INC
3574 Lawson Blvd (11572-4909)
PHONE..................................516 764-5700
▲ **EMP:** 6
SALES (est): 420K **Privately Held**
SIC: 3545 Mfg Machine Tool Accessories

(G-13098)
EAST COAST MOLDERS INC
3001 New St Ste F (11572-2747)
PHONE..................................516 240-6000
Richard Mandell, *President*
EMP: 225
SQ FT: 7,000
SALES (est): 9.5MM **Privately Held**
SIC: 2342 Brassieres

(G-13099)
EXPRESS BUILDING SUPPLY INC
Also Called: Wholesale Window Warehouse
3550 Lawson Blvd (11572-4908)
PHONE..................................516 608-0379
Robert Freedman, *President*
Justin Freedman, *Vice Pres*
EMP: 25 **EST:** 1996
SQ FT: 9,000
SALES (est): 2.5MM **Privately Held**
SIC: 3211 5031 5211 Window glass, clear & colored; windows; windows, storm: wood or metal

(G-13100)
FIVE BORO DOORS MOULDINGS INC
3569 Maple Ct (11572-4821)
PHONE..................................718 865-9371
Usher Krasne, *Principal*
EMP: 6
SALES (est): 130.2K **Privately Held**
SIC: 3442 Metal doors, sash & trim

(G-13101)
HENNIG CUSTOM WOODWORK CORP
Also Called: Hennig Custom Woodworking
2497 Long Beach Rd (11572-1321)
PHONE..................................516 536-3460
James Hennig, *President*
EMP: 5
SALES: 500K **Privately Held**
SIC: 2421 7389 5031 2499 Furniture dimension stock, softwood; laminating service; kitchen cabinets; decorative wood & woodwork; cabinet & finish carpentry

(G-13102)
IP MED INC
3571 Hargale Rd (11572-5821)
PHONE..................................516 766-3800
Judah Isaacs, *President*
EMP: 7
SALES (est): 346K **Privately Held**
SIC: 2836 3841 2834 5122 Bacterial vaccines; inhalators, surgical & medical; proprietary drug products; drugs & drug proprietaries

(G-13103)
JONDEN MANUFACTURING CO INC
3069 Lawson Blvd (11572-2939)
P.O. Box 401, Hewlett (11557-0401)
PHONE..................................516 442-4895
Linda Smilowitz, *CEO*
Jon Smilowitz, *President*
Linda Leal, *Principal*
John Smilowitz, *Chairman*
Denise Smilowitz, *Exec VP*
▲ **EMP:** 18
SALES (est): 3.3MM **Privately Held**
WEB: www.jonden.com
SIC: 2339 Sportswear, women's

(G-13104)
JQ WOODWORKING INC
3085 New St (11572-2743)
PHONE..................................516 766-3424
John Quinn, *Ch of Bd*
EMP: 5
SQ FT: 10,000
SALES: 1MM **Privately Held**
SIC: 3259 1751 Architectural clay products; cabinet & finish carpentry

(G-13105)
KANTEK INC
Also Called: Spectrum
3460a Hampton Rd (11572-4803)
PHONE..................................516 594-4600
Fax: 516 594-1555
Herman Kappel, *President*

AVI Kappel, *General Mgr*
▲ **EMP:** 30
SQ FT: 25,000
SALES (est): 15MM **Privately Held**
WEB: www.kantek.com
SIC: 3577 5045 Computer peripheral equipment; computers, peripherals & software

(G-13106)
L N D INCORPORATED
Also Called: Lnd
3230 Lawson Blvd (11572-3796)
PHONE..................................516 678-6141
Fax: 516 678-6704
Peter T Neyland, *President*
Spencer B Neyland, *Vice Pres*
Robert Sears, *Purchasing*
Bill Chatfield, *Controller*
William J Lehnert, *VP Sales*
EMP: 45 **EST:** 1964
SQ FT: 14,000
SALES (est): 10.7MM **Privately Held**
WEB: www.lndinc.com
SIC: 3829 Nuclear radiation & testing apparatus

(G-13107)
LOVE BRIGHT JEWELRY INC
Also Called: Lovebrightjewelry.com
3446 Frederick St (11572-4713)
PHONE..................................516 620-2509
Bhupen Kapadia, *President*
EMP: 25
SQ FT: 2,000
SALES (est): 1.4MM **Privately Held**
SIC: 3911 5094 5944 Jewelry apparel; jewelry; jewelry stores

(G-13108)
MARK PERI INTERNATIONAL
3516 Hargale Rd (11572-5820)
PHONE..................................516 208-6824
Mark Gruenspecht, *Director*
EMP: 10
SALES (est): 797.8K **Privately Held**
SIC: 3663 Radio & TV communications equipment

(G-13109)
MARKPERICOM
3516 Hargale Rd (11572-5820)
PHONE..................................516 208-6824
Mark Gruenspecht, *President*
EMP: 9
SALES (est): 711.8K **Privately Held**
SIC: 3569 General industrial machinery

(G-13110)
ONLY NATURAL INC
Also Called: Bio Nutrition
3580 Oceanside Rd Unit 5 (11572-5825)
PHONE..................................516 897-7001
Fax: 516 897-9332
Robert Lomacchio, *President*
EMP: 15
SQ FT: 3,600
SALES (est): 2.1MM **Privately Held**
WEB: www.onlynaturalinc.com
SIC: 2833 5499 Vitamins, natural or synthetic: bulk, uncompounded; health & dietetic food stores

(G-13111)
PIER-TECH INC
7 Hampton Rd (11572-4808)
PHONE..................................516 442-5420
Robert Sackaris, *Ch of Bd*
Jennifer Sackaris, *Manager*
Irene Sackaris, *Admin Sec*
EMP: 42
SALES (est): 8.8MM **Privately Held**
SIC: 3531 Construction machinery

(G-13112)
POETRY MAILING LIST MARSH HAWK
2823 Rockaway Ave (11572-1018)
P.O. Box 206, East Rockaway (11518-0206)
PHONE..................................516 766-1891
Jane Augustine, *President*
EMP: 5
SALES: 45.4K **Privately Held**
SIC: 2731 Book publishing

Oceanside - Nassau County (G-13113)   GEOGRAPHIC SECTION

(G-13113)
RADAR SPORTS LLC
Also Called: Radarsport.com
2660 Washington Ave (11572-1540)
PHONE...................516 678-1919
Barbara Schure,
Allen Web,
EMP: 4
SQ FT: 1,500
SALES: 1.2MM **Privately Held**
SIC: 3949 Sporting & athletic goods

(G-13114)
RADIANT PRO LTD
245 Merrick Rd (11572-1428)
PHONE...................516 763-5678
John Cioento, *Owner*
EMP: 7 **EST:** 2000
SALES (est): 655.7K **Privately Held**
SIC: 3567 Radiant heating systems, industrial process

(G-13115)
ROSE TRUNK MFG CO INC
3935 Sally Ln (11572-5934)
PHONE...................516 766-6686
Melvin Lapidus, *President*
Mark Lapidus, *Vice Pres*
▼ **EMP:** 15 **EST:** 1945
SQ FT: 15,000
SALES (est): 1.4MM **Privately Held**
WEB: www.rosetrunk.com
SIC: 3161 Luggage; trunks

(G-13116)
ROYAL MARBLE & GRANITE INC
3295 Royal Ave (11572-3625)
PHONE...................516 536-5900
Richard Tafuri, *President*
Anthony Tafuri, *Vice Pres*
▲ **EMP:** 8
SQ FT: 8,000
SALES (est): 738.4K **Privately Held**
SIC: 3281 3272 Granite, cut & shaped; art marble, concrete

(G-13117)
RUSSCO METAL SPINNING CO INC
3064 Lawson Blvd (11572-2711)
PHONE...................516 872-6055
Fax: 516 872-8199
William Russ, *President*
Mary Russ, *Corp Secy*
Michael Byrne, *Plant Mgr*
EMP: 10
SQ FT: 5,300
SALES (est): 1.2MM **Privately Held**
SIC: 3469 Spinning metal for the trade

(G-13118)
SEA WAVES INC (PA)
2425 Long Beach Rd (11572-1320)
PHONE...................516 766-4201
Brian Corhan, *President*
Harold Corhan, *Vice Pres*
▲ **EMP:** 5
SQ FT: 2,000
SALES (est): 660.1K **Privately Held**
SIC: 2339 Bathing suits: women's, misses' & juniors'; beachwear: women's, misses' & juniors'

(G-13119)
STRONG GROUP INC
222 Atlantic Ave Unit B (11572-2045)
PHONE...................516 766-6300
Fax: 516 766-6307
Walter Bistrong, *President*
Ann Sigel, *Corp Secy*
EMP: 8
SALES (est): 550K **Privately Held**
SIC: 2311 Policemen's uniforms: made from purchased materials

(G-13120)
STYLES MANUFACTURING CORP
3571 Hargale Rd (11572-5821)
PHONE...................516 763-5303
Louis Fuchs, *President*
Ron Keyes, *Vice Pres*
Irene Sassaman, *Manager*
▲ **EMP:** 5

SALES (est): 5MM **Privately Held**
SIC: 3315 Hangers (garment), wire

(G-13121)
SUM SUM LLC
3595 Lawson Blvd Whse D Warehouse D (11572)
PHONE...................516 812-3959
Jaymie Dahan, *CEO*
David Dahan, *Vice Pres*
EMP: 5
SQ FT: 1,000
SALES: 250K **Privately Held**
SIC: 2035 Dressings, salad: raw & cooked (except dry mixes)

(G-13122)
TAG FLANGE & MACHINING INC
3375 Royal Ave (11572-4812)
PHONE...................516 536-1300
Theodore A Gallucci III, *President*
Sean F Gallucci, *Vice Pres*
EMP: 6
SQ FT: 10,000
SALES (est): 500K **Privately Held**
SIC: 3498 Fabricated pipe & fittings

(G-13123)
THE NUGENT ORGANIZATION INC
Also Called: Nugent Printing Company
3433 Ocean Harbor Dr (11572-3516)
PHONE...................212 645-6600
Fax: 212 645-6605
Antonino Longo, *President*
Vincent Longo, *Vice Pres*
EMP: 18
SQ FT: 10,000
SALES (est): 2.3MM **Privately Held**
WEB: www.nugentprint.com
SIC: 2752 7331 2732 Commercial printing, offset; mailing service; book printing

(G-13124)
UNITED THREAD MILLS CORP (PA)
3530 Lawson Blvd Gf (11572-4908)
P.O. Box 766, Rockville Centre (11571-0766)
PHONE...................516 536-3900
Fax: 516 536-3547
Ira Henkus, *President*
▼ **EMP:** 6 **EST:** 1948
SQ FT: 66,000
SALES (est): 54.2MM **Privately Held**
SIC: 2284 2281 Thread mills; yarn spinning mills

(G-13125)
VENEER ONE INC
3415 Hampton Rd (11572-4835)
PHONE...................516 536-6480
Victor Giaime, *Ch of Bd*
Arnold Lanzillotta, *President*
Steve Horan, *Admin Sec*
▲ **EMP:** 28 **EST:** 2000
SQ FT: 19,000
SALES (est): 4.1MM **Privately Held**
WEB: www.veneer1.com
SIC: 2435 Hardwood veneer & plywood

(G-13126)
VIANA SIGNS CORP
3520 Lawson Blvd (11572-4908)
PHONE...................516 887-2000
Leo Viana, *President*
EMP: 10
SALES (est): 750K **Privately Held**
SIC: 3993 Signs & advertising specialties

(G-13127)
WESTRON CORPORATION
Also Called: Westron Lighting
18 Neil Ct (11572-5816)
PHONE...................516 678-2300
Irving Allerhand, *Ch of Bd*
Hershel Allerhand, *President*
Les Deutsch, *Sales/Mktg Dir*
Rosary Holmes, *Manager*
▲ **EMP:** 50
SQ FT: 25,000
SALES (est): 5.4MM **Privately Held**
WEB: www.westronlighting.com
SIC: 3641 Electric lamps

(G-13128)
YALE TROUSER CORPORATION
Also Called: Smokey Joes
3670 Oceanside Rd W Ste 6 (11572-5961)
PHONE...................516 255-0700
Arnold Bloom, *President*
Gary Bloom, *Vice Pres*
EMP: 10 **EST:** 1950
SALES (est): 1.1MM **Privately Held**
WEB: www.yaletrouser.com
SIC: 2325 2321 Slacks, dress: men's, youths' & boys'; trousers, dress (separate): men's, youths' & boys'; men's & boys' furnishings

Odessa
Schuyler County

(G-13129)
FINGER LAKES CHEESE TRAIL
4970 County Road 14 (14869-9730)
PHONE...................607 857-5726
Carmella Hoffman, *Treasurer*
EMP: 13
SALES (est): 718.6K **Privately Held**
SIC: 2026 Fluid milk

Ogdensburg
St. Lawrence County

(G-13130)
ACCO BRANDS USA LLC
Also Called: Acco North America
941 Acco Way (13669-4438)
PHONE...................847 541-9500
Fax: 315 393-7887
Chad Kiah, *Controller*
Michele McFee, *Corp Comm Staff*
Sandra Fazio, *Manager*
Kyle Foster, *Manager*
Jeffery Almasian, *Director*
EMP: 120
SALES (corp-wide): 1.5B **Publicly Held**
WEB: www.accobrands.com
SIC: 2782 Looseleaf binders & devices
HQ: Acco Brands Usa Llc
4 Corporate Dr
Lake Zurich IL 60047
800 222-6462

(G-13131)
ALGONQUIN POWER
19 Mill St (13669-1304)
PHONE...................315 393-5595
Walter Bracy, *Manager*
EMP: 7
SALES (est): 886.8K **Privately Held**
SIC: 3634 Electric housewares & fans

(G-13132)
ANSEN CORPORATION (PA)
100 Chimney Point Dr (13669-2206)
PHONE...................315 393-3573
James Kingman, *CEO*
Jerry W Slusser, *Vice Pres*
Kenneth Emter, *Corp Secy*
Nadia Cutler, *Senior Buyer*
Jason W Slusser, *Director*
▲ **EMP:** 1
SQ FT: 72,000
SALES (est): 97MM **Privately Held**
WEB: www.ansencorp.com
SIC: 3672 Printed circuit boards

(G-13133)
ANSEN CORPORATION
100 Chimney Point Dr (13669-2206)
PHONE...................315 393-3573
Craig D Kelley, *Vice Pres*
Don McCormick, *Vice Pres*
Jeff Hilk, *Sales Staff*
Rodney Bush, *Branch Mgr*
EMP: 110
SQ FT: 71,000
SALES (corp-wide): 97MM **Privately Held**
WEB: www.ansencorp.com
SIC: 3672 Printed circuit boards

PA: Ansen Corporation
100 Chimney Point Dr
Ogdensburg NY 13669
315 393-3573

(G-13134)
CANARM LTD (HQ)
808 Commerce Park Dr (13669-2208)
PHONE...................800 267-4427
David Beatty, *CEO*
James Cooper, *President*
▲ **EMP:** 2
SQ FT: 1,500
SALES: 75MM
SALES (corp-wide): 59.3MM **Privately Held**
SIC: 3564 3645 3646 5064 Blowing fans: industrial or commercial; exhaust fans: industrial or commercial; ventilating fans: industrial or commercial; residential lighting fixtures; commercial indusl & institutional electric lighting fixtures; fans, household: electric; fans, industrial; lighting fixtures, commercial & industrial; lighting fixtures, residential
PA: Canarm Ltd
2157 Parkedale Ave
Brockville ON K6V 0
613 342-5424

(G-13135)
DEFELSKO CORPORATION
800 Proctor Ave (13669-2205)
PHONE...................315 393-4450
Fax: 315 393-8471
Frank Koch, *President*
Terry Larue, *General Mgr*
David Beamish, *Chairman*
Linda K Beamish, *Vice Pres*
Steven Nowell, *QC Mgr*
◆ **EMP:** 60 **EST:** 1965
SQ FT: 15,000
SALES (est): 17.5MM **Privately Held**
WEB: www.defelsko.com
SIC: 3823 3829 Industrial instrmnts msrmnt display/control process variable; measuring & controlling devices

(G-13136)
HANSON AGGREGATES PA LLC
701 Cedar St (13669-3000)
P.O. Box 250 (13669-0250)
PHONE...................315 393-3743
Daniel O'Connor, *Manager*
Robert Bismarck, *Manager*
Mark Macklen, *Manager*
EMP: 14
SQ FT: 2,196
SALES (corp-wide): 16B **Privately Held**
SIC: 1429 1422 Grits mining (crushed stone); limestones, ground
HQ: Hanson Aggregates Pennsylvania, Llc
7660 Imperial Way
Allentown PA 18195
610 366-4626

(G-13137)
HOOSIER MAGNETICS INC
110 Denny St (13669-1797)
PHONE...................315 323-5832
Fax: 315 393-0017
B Thomas Shirk, *President*
Joe Vierno, *Manager*
Mary Alice Shirk, *Admin Sec*
◆ **EMP:** 50
SQ FT: 30,000
SALES (est): 8.7MM **Privately Held**
WEB: www.hoosiermagnetics.com
SIC: 3264 Ferrite & ferrite parts

(G-13138)
LAWTONS ELECTRIC MOTOR SERVICE
Also Called: Lawton Electric Co
148 Cemetery Rd (13669-4179)
PHONE...................315 393-2728
Bernard Lawton, *Partner*
Timothy Lawton, *Partner*
EMP: 7 **EST:** 1968
SALES: 500K **Privately Held**
SIC: 7694 Electric motor repair

(G-13139)
MAXAM NORTH AMERICA INC
3 Cemetary Dr (13669-4528)
PHONE...................313 322-8651

▲ = Import ▼ = Export
◆ = Import/Export

GEOGRAPHIC SECTION

Olean - Cattaraugus County (G-13160)

EMP: 6
SALES (corp-wide): 37.8MM Privately Held
SIC: 2892 5169 Explosives; explosives
HQ: Maxam North America, Inc.
433 Las Colinas Blvd E # 900
Irving TX 75039
801 233-6000

(G-13140)
MED-ENG LLC
103 Tulloch Dr (13669-2215)
PHONE..................................315 713-0103
Scott Obrien, *CEO*
Dennis Morris, *President*
Aris Makris, *CTO*
Maureen Mackie, *Info Tech Mgr*
EMP: 40
SALES (est): 3.7MM
SALES (corp-wide): 881.4MM Privately Held
WEB: www.allen-vanguard.com
SIC: 2311 Military uniforms, men's & youths': purchased materials
HQ: Safariland, Llc
13386 International Pkwy
Jacksonville FL 32218
904 741-5400

(G-13141)
QUEENAIRE TECHNOLOGIES INC
9483 State Highway 37 (13669-4467)
PHONE..................................315 393-5454
Susan Duffy, *President*
Paul McGrath, *Opers Dir*
Richard Luscombe-Mills, *Research*
Nicole Plumley, *Finance*
Tom Coplen, *Sales Staff*
▼ **EMP:** 6
SQ FT: 6,600
SALES (est): 1.3MM Privately Held
SIC: 3559 Ozone machines

(G-13142)
RIVER RAT DESIGN
Also Called: Roethel
1801 Ford St Ste A (13669-1980)
PHONE..................................315 393-4770
Laurel Roethel, *Owner*
EMP: 15
SQ FT: 6,600
SALES (est): 712.7K Privately Held
SIC: 2395 Embroidery & art needlework

(G-13143)
ST LAWRENCE COUNTY NEWSPAPERS (HQ)
Also Called: Courier Observer
230 Caroline St Ste 1 (13669-1629)
PHONE..................................315 393-1003
Fax: 315 393-5108
Charles Kelly, *Publisher*
Chuck Kelley, *General Mgr*
Eileen Kast, *Purch Agent*
Brenda L Brake, *VP Finance*
Cindy Ford, *Accounts Exec*
▲ **EMP:** 60
SQ FT: 15,000
SALES (est): 6.3MM
SALES (corp-wide): 32MM Privately Held
WEB: www.courierobserver.com
SIC: 2711 2752 Newspapers, publishing & printing; commercial printing, lithographic
PA: Johnson Newspaper Corporation
260 Washington St
Watertown NY
315 782-1000

(G-13144)
T-BASE COMMUNICATIONS USA INC
806 Commerce Park Dr (13669-2208)
PHONE..................................315 713-0013
Sharylyn Ayotte, *President*
Bruce Moszcelt, *Managing Dir*
Christine Roy, *Human Res Dir*
Paula Woods, *Manager*
Sommer Friot, *Supervisor*
EMP: 40
SALES (est): 3.2MM Privately Held
SIC: 2759 Commercial printing

Old Bethpage
Nassau County

(G-13145)
ALJO PRECISION PRODUCTS INC
205 Bethpge Sweet Holw (11804-1309)
PHONE..................................516 420-4419
Fax: 516 756-1995
John Adelmann, *President*
Albert Adelmann, *Vice Pres*
Michael Mattern, *Vice Pres*
Gary Settaeucto, *Sales Mgr*
Marilyn Platz, *Office Mgr*
EMP: 35 **EST:** 1953
SQ FT: 24,000
SALES (est): 4.8MM Privately Held
WEB: www.aljogefa.com
SIC: 3599 Machine shop, jobbing & repair

(G-13146)
ALJO-GEFA PRECISION MFG LLC
205 Bethpage Sweet Holw (11804-1309)
PHONE..................................516 420-4419
John Addleman, *Partner*
Michael Mattern, *General Mgr*
Albert Adelmann, *Senior VP*
Suanne Hippner, *Office Mgr*
EMP: 33 **EST:** 1999
SQ FT: 26,000
SALES (est): 6.4MM Privately Held
SIC: 3674 Integrated circuits, semiconductor networks, etc.

(G-13147)
BARSON COMPOSITES CORPORATION (PA)
Also Called: Hitemco
160 Bethpage Sweet (11804)
PHONE..................................516 752-7882
Fax: 516 752-7951
Terrell Barnard, *CEO*
Edwin Garofalo, *Vice Pres*
Doug Kowaczek, *Opers Mgr*
Dana Barnard, *CFO*
Kristen Larson, *Supervisor*
EMP: 50
SQ FT: 32,500
SALES (est): 16MM Privately Held
WEB: www.hitemco.com
SIC: 3479 2899 2851 Painting, coating & hot dipping; chemical preparations; paints & allied products

(G-13148)
GEFA INSTRUMENT CORP
205 Bethpage Sweet (11804)
PHONE..................................516 420-4419
Gunther Faas, *President*
Tyrone Faas, *Treasurer*
Susan Hippner, *Office Mgr*
Collette Faas, *Shareholder*
EMP: 12 **EST:** 1966
SQ FT: 10,000
SALES (est): 1.2MM Privately Held
SIC: 3599 Machine shop, jobbing & repair

(G-13149)
HITEMCO MEDICAL APPLICATIONS
Also Called: Hi-Med
160 Sweet Hollow Rd (11804-1315)
PHONE..................................516 752-7882
Terrill E Barnard, *Ch of Bd*
Edwin Garofalo, *President*
John Lagaros, *Vice Pres*
Dana Barnard, *CFO*
EMP: 134
SQ FT: 5,000
SALES (est): 12.3MM
SALES (corp-wide): 16MM Privately Held
WEB: www.hitemco.com
SIC: 3479 Painting, coating & hot dipping
PA: Barson Composites Corporation
160 Bethpage Sweet
Old Bethpage NY 11804
516 752-7882

(G-13150)
INTELLIGEN POWER SYSTEMS LLC
301 Winding Rd (11804-1322)
PHONE..................................212 750-0373
David H Lesser,
Stephen Bellone,
EMP: 8
SALES (est): 990K Privately Held
SIC: 3621 Power generators

(G-13151)
SEVILLE CENTRAL MIX CORP
495 Wining Rd (11804)
PHONE..................................516 293-6190
Peter Scalamandre, *Vice Pres*
Peter Buck, *Branch Mgr*
EMP: 60
SALES (corp-wide): 13.1MM Privately Held
WEB: www.sevillecentralmix.com
SIC: 3273 3531 Ready-mixed concrete; concrete plants
PA: Seville Central Mix Corp.
157 Albany Ave
Freeport NY 11520
516 868-3000

Old Forge
Herkimer County

(G-13152)
ADIRONDACK OUTDOOR CENTER LLC (PA)
2839 State Route 28 (13420)
P.O. Box 1146 (13420-1146)
PHONE..................................315 369-2300
John Nemjo,
EMP: 8
SALES (est): 2.3MM Privately Held
SIC: 3949 5091 Camping equipment & supplies; camping equipment & supplies

Old Westbury
Nassau County

(G-13153)
DE ORIGINALS LTD
22 Laurel Ln (11568-1544)
PHONE..................................516 474-6544
Daniel Kalu, *President*
EMP: 8
SQ FT: 2,000
SALES (est): 6MM Privately Held
SIC: 2821 Polyvinyl chloride resins (PVC)

(G-13154)
NU LIFE RESTORATIONS OF L I
Also Called: Nu-Life Long Island
51 Valley Rd (11568-1015)
PHONE..................................516 489-5200
Fax: 516 481-9791
Mark Marinbach, *President*
EMP: 84
SQ FT: 8,500
SALES (est): 10.2MM Privately Held
WEB: www.nulifeli.com
SIC: 3843 Dental laboratory equipment

Olean
Cattaraugus County

(G-13155)
AVX CORPORATION
Also Called: Olean Advanced Products
1695 Seneca Ave (14760-9532)
PHONE..................................716 372-6611
Fax: 585 372-6635
Wayne Floyd, *Vice Pres*
Richard Gerringer, *Purch Agent*
Stan Cygan, *Engineer*
Norman J Malick, *Senior Engr*
Martin McGuigan, *Finance*
EMP: 95

SALES (corp-wide): 12.5B Publicly Held
WEB: www.avxcorp.com
SIC: 3675 5065 Electronic capacitors; capacitors, electronic
HQ: Avx Corporation
1 Avx Blvd
Fountain Inn SC 29644
864 967-2150

(G-13156)
BIMBO BAKERIES USA INC
Also Called: Stroehmann Bakeries 56
111 N 2nd St (14760-2501)
PHONE..................................716 372-8444
Fax: 716 372-7808
Nancy Fox, *Human Res Dir*
Frank Catarisano, *Sales Staff*
Ted Lipeowski, *Branch Mgr*
EMP: 140 Privately Held
SIC: 2051 Bakery: wholesale or wholesale/retail combined
HQ: Bimbo Bakeries Usa, Inc
255 Business Center Dr # 200
Horsham PA 19044
215 347-5500

(G-13157)
BRADFORD PUBLICATIONS INC
Also Called: Times Herald, The
639 W Norton Dr (14760-1402)
PHONE..................................716 373-2500
Fax: 585 372-0740
Rick Miller, *Editor*
Jeff Cole, *Accountant*
Jim Bonn, *Mktg Dir*
Lori Coffman, *Manager*
Bill Fitzpatrick, *Manager*
EMP: 130
SQ FT: 22,300 Privately Held
WEB: www.oleantimesherald.com
SIC: 2711 7313 Newspapers, publishing & printing; newspaper advertising representative
HQ: Bradford Publishing Company
43 Main St
Bradford PA 16701
814 368-3173

(G-13158)
CITY OF OLEAN
Also Called: Olean Waste Water Treatment
174 S 19th St (14760-3326)
PHONE..................................716 376-5694
Fax: 585 376-5629
William Quinlan, *Mayor*
Jeremy Meerdink, *Manager*
John Anastasia, *Hlthcr Dir*
EMP: 9
SQ FT: 1,080 Privately Held
SIC: 3589 9111 Water treatment equipment, industrial; mayors' offices
PA: City Of Olean
101 E State St Ste 1
Olean NY 14760
716 376-5683

(G-13159)
CONCRETE MIXER SUPPLYCOM INC (PA)
1721 Cornell Dr (14760-9753)
PHONE..................................716 375-5565
Fax: 716 701-6747
Audrey D Pavia, *President*
Mike Jones, *Sales Mgr*
Rick Pavia, *Manager*
◆ **EMP:** 9
SQ FT: 3,000
SALES (est): 1.6MM Privately Held
SIC: 3713 Truck bodies & parts

(G-13160)
COOPER POWER SYSTEMS LLC
1648 Dugan Rd (14760-9527)
PHONE..................................716 375-7100
Fax: 585 375-7202
Cindy Peterson, *Buyer*
Wayne E Traugh, *Purchasing*
Herce Alcocer, *Engineer*
Jim Lee, *Engineer*
Jennifer Noll, *Human Res Mgr*
EMP: 300 Privately Held
WEB: www.cooperpower.com

Olean - Cattaraugus County (G-13161)

SIC: 3612 3699 3674 3643 Transformers, except electric; electrical equipment & supplies; semiconductors & related devices; current-carrying wiring devices; switchgear & switchboard apparatus
HQ: Cooper Power Systems, Llc
2300 Badger Dr
Waukesha WI 53188
262 524-4227

(G-13161)
CUTCO CUTLERY CORPORATION (HQ)
1116 E State St (14760-3814)
P.O. Box 810 (14760-0810)
PHONE 716 372-3111
Fax: 585 373-6145
James E Stitt, *Ch of Bd*
James M Stitt, *President*
Carey F Litteer, *Exec VP*
Larry Penman, *Opers Staff*
Dan Wenke, *Opers Staff*
▲ EMP: 300
SQ FT: 226,370
SALES (est): 67MM
SALES (corp-wide): 144.6MM Privately Held
WEB: www.campusrelations.com
SIC: 3421 Cutlery
PA: Cutco Corporation
1116 E State St
Olean NY 14760
716 372-3111

(G-13162)
CYTEC INDUSTRIES INC
Also Called: Cytec Solvay Group
1405 Buffalo St (14760-1197)
PHONE 716 372-9650
Fax: 716 372-1594
Jeff Maley, *Site Mgr*
David Lilley, *Branch Mgr*
John Clarke, *Manager*
Gerret Peters, *Manager*
Leonard Riker, *Manager*
EMP: 66
SALES (corp-wide): 11.4MM Privately Held
SIC: 2899 2821 2672 2851 Water treating compounds; plastics materials & resins; adhesive backed films, foams & foils; paints & allied products; cellulosic manmade fibers
HQ: Cytec Industries Inc.
5 Garret Mountain Plz
Woodland Park NJ 07424

(G-13163)
CYTEC OLEAN INC
1405 Buffalo St (14760-1197)
PHONE 716 372-9650
William Work, *Purch Mgr*
Leonard Riker, *Manager*
Maureen Dearmitt, *Info Tech Mgr*
Marsha Topor, *Administration*
▼ EMP: 75
SQ FT: 105,000
SALES (est): 14.8MM
SALES (corp-wide): 11.4MM Privately Held
WEB: www.conap.com
SIC: 2821 5169 Plastics materials & resins; thermoplastic materials; chemicals & allied products
HQ: Cytec Industries Inc.
5 Garret Mountain Plz
Woodland Park NJ 07424

(G-13164)
DRESSER-RAND GROUP INC
500 Paul Clark Dr (14760-9560)
PHONE 716 375-3000
Fax: 585 375-3178
Jean Chevrier, *Vice Pres*
Dwight D Everetts, *Vice Pres*
Edmund Reybitz, *Project Dir*
Glenn Grosso, *Technical Mgr*
Job Barboza, *Engineer*
EMP: 66
SALES (corp-wide): 89.6B Privately Held
SIC: 3563 3511 Air & gas compressors; turbines & turbine generator sets
HQ: Dresser-Rand Group Inc
10205 Westheimer Rd # 1000
Houston TX 77042
713 354-6100

(G-13165)
DSTI INC
Also Called: Scott Rotary Seals
301 W Franklin St (14760-1211)
PHONE 716 557-2362
Fax: 716 557-8613
Jeffrey Meister, *President*
Scott Ilstrup, *Vice Pres*
John Knoll, *Vice Pres*
Lynne Humphrey, *CFO*
Patrick Pastoors, *Controller*
EMP: 7
SQ FT: 13,000
SALES (est): 1.8MM
SALES (corp-wide): 12.5MM Privately Held
WEB: www.scottrotaryseals.com
SIC: 3492 Control valves, fluid power: hydraulic & pneumatic
PA: Dynamic Sealing Technologies, Inc.
13829 Jay St Nw
Andover MN 55304
763 786-3758

(G-13166)
DYNAMIC SEALING TECH INC
Also Called: Scott Rotary Seals
301 W Franklin St (14760-1211)
PHONE 716 376-0708
Jeffrey Meister, *Branch Mgr*
EMP: 6
SQ FT: 15,000
SALES (corp-wide): 12.5MM Privately Held
SIC: 3492 Control valves, fluid power: hydraulic & pneumatic
PA: Dynamic Sealing Technologies, Inc.
13829 Jay St Nw
Andover MN 55304
763 786-3758

(G-13167)
DZ9 POWER LLC
408 Wayne St (14760-2462)
P.O. Box 862 (14760-0862)
PHONE 877 533-5530
Brian Benka, *President*
EMP: 7
SALES (est): 296.1K Privately Held
SIC: 3499 Target drones, for use by ships: metal

(G-13168)
EATON HYDRAULICS LLC
1648 Dugan Rd (14760-9527)
PHONE 716 375-7132
William Sorokes, *Manager*
EMP: 9 Privately Held
SIC: 3625 Motor controls & accessories
HQ: Eaton Hydraulics Llc
14615 Lone Oak Rd
Eden Prairie MN 55344
952 937-9800

(G-13169)
G & H WOOD PRODUCTS LLC
Also Called: Pallets Plus
2427 N Union Street Ext (14760-1529)
PHONE 716 372-5510
Terrance Grant,
EMP: 10
SQ FT: 4,343
SALES (est): 1.1MM Privately Held
SIC: 2448 Pallets, wood

(G-13170)
KAMERYS WHOLESALE MEATS INC
322 E Riverside Dr (14760-3964)
PHONE 716 372-6756
David A Kamery, *President*
EMP: 6
SALES (est): 564.1K Privately Held
SIC: 2011 5147 Meat packing plants; meats, fresh

(G-13171)
L AMERICAN LTD
Also Called: Swatt Baking Co
222 Homer St (14760-1132)
PHONE 716 372-9480
Fax: 716 373-6019
Leonard Anzivine, *President*
Lee Anzivine, *Vice Pres*
EMP: 16
SQ FT: 9,400

SALES (est): 2MM Privately Held
WEB: www.lamerican.com
SIC: 2051 5461 Bread, all types (white, wheat, rye, etc): fresh or frozen; rolls, bread type: fresh or frozen; bakeries

(G-13172)
MONEYSAVER ADVERTISING INC
Also Called: Moneysaver Shopping News
639 W Norton Dr (14760-1402)
PHONE 585 593-1275
Fax: 585 928-2191
William W Jones, *President*
Deborah J Jones, *Vice Pres*
Carol Perrin, *Sales Mgr*
EMP: 15
SALES (est): 906.3K Privately Held
SIC: 2711 Newspapers: publishing only, not printed on site

(G-13173)
NES BEARING COMPANY INC
1601 Johnson St (14760-1127)
PHONE 716 372-6532
Fax: 585 372-1448
Christopher Napoleon, *President*
Jim Hardy, *QC Mgr*
Colby Austin, *Engineer*
Heather Franz-Piatt, *Office Mgr*
Jane Chew, *Manager*
▲ EMP: 48
SALES (est): 13.6MM Privately Held
WEB: www.nesbearings.com
SIC: 3562 8711 Ball bearings & parts; sanitary engineers

(G-13174)
PIERCE STEEL FABRICATORS
430 N 7th St (14760-2330)
P.O. Box 504 (14760-0504)
PHONE 716 372-7652
Fax: 716 372-3102
Michael Derose, *President*
Daniel Derose, *Vice Pres*
Janice Bronson, *Manager*
EMP: 11
SQ FT: 20,000
SALES (est): 2.4MM Privately Held
WEB: www.piercesteel.com
SIC: 3449 Curtain wall, metal

(G-13175)
SOLEPOXY INC
211 W Franklin St (14760-1211)
PHONE 716 372-6300
Jeff Belt, *Ch of Bd*
Kaitlyn Penston, *QC Mgr*
Melissa Wiegand, *Engineer*
Barry Goodin, *Director*
◆ EMP: 55 EST: 2010
SQ FT: 250,000
SALES (est): 12.3MM Privately Held
SIC: 3087 Custom compound purchased resins

(G-13176)
TOTAL PIPING SOLUTIONS INC
1760 Haskell Rd (14760-9756)
P.O. Box 525 (14760-0525)
PHONE 716 372-0160
Daryl Piontek, *President*
Mark Langenhan, *President*
▲ EMP: 10
SQ FT: 35,000
SALES (est): 1.9MM Privately Held
WEB: www.tps.us
SIC: 3494 Pipe fittings

Oneida
Madison County

(G-13177)
GOLUB CORPORATION
Also Called: Price Chopper Pharmacy
142 Genesee St (13421-2704)
PHONE 315 363-0679
Nena Crowne, *Branch Mgr*
EMP: 99
SALES (corp-wide): 3.4B Privately Held
SIC: 3751 Motorcycles & related parts

PA: The Golub Corporation
461 Nott St
Schenectady NY 12308
518 355-5000

(G-13178)
HARTMAN ENTERPRISES INC
455 Elizabeth St (13421-2438)
P.O. Box 360 (13421-0360)
PHONE 315 363-7300
Fax: 315 363-0314
Robert E Sweet Jr, *CEO*
Bob Sweep, *President*
Merry Dailey, *Manager*
Dave Stastny, *Executive*
EMP: 55
SQ FT: 18,000
SALES (est): 8.4MM Privately Held
WEB: www.hartmanenterprisesinc.com
SIC: 3599 7692 Machine shop, jobbing & repair; welding repair

(G-13179)
HP HOOD LLC
252 Genesee St (13421-2709)
P.O. Box 491 (13421-0491)
PHONE 315 363-3870
Fax: 315 363-9534
Gary Musial, *Vice Pres*
Ray Johnson, *Safety Mgr*
Brandon Cook, *Warehouse Mgr*
Ed Hickey, *Warehouse Mgr*
Ross Hasty, *Production*
EMP: 200
SALES (corp-wide): 1.7B Privately Held
WEB: www.hphood.com
SIC: 2026 5143 Fluid milk; dairy products, except dried or canned
PA: Hp Hood Llc
6 Kimball Ln Ste 400
Lynnfield MA 01940
617 887-8441

(G-13180)
M M WELDING
558 Lenox Ave (13421-1522)
PHONE 315 363-3980
Michael Marley, *Owner*
Denice Marley, *Partner*
EMP: 20
SALES (est): 425.1K Privately Held
SIC: 7692 Welding repair

(G-13181)
ONEIDA FOUNDRIES INC
559 Fitch St (13421-1515)
PHONE 315 363-4570
Fax: 315 363-4692
John Albanse, *President*
Harry Hood, *Vice Pres*
Shelly Albanse, *Office Mgr*
EMP: 20 EST: 1900
SQ FT: 30,000
SALES (est): 5.4MM Privately Held
SIC: 3321 Gray iron castings; ductile iron castings

(G-13182)
ONEIDA INTERNATIONAL INC
163-181 Kenwood Ave (13421)
PHONE 315 361-3000
Fax: 315 361-3745
Terry G Westbrook, *President*
EMP: 6
SALES (est): 301.7K
SALES (corp-wide): 228.8MM Privately Held
WEB: www.oneida.net
SIC: 3262 3231 3914 3421 Vitreous china table & kitchenware; ornamental glass: cut, engraved or otherwise decorated; silverware & plated ware; cutlery
HQ: Oneida Ltd.
163 Kenwood Ave Ste 181
Oneida NY 13421
315 361-3000

(G-13183)
ONEIDA MOLDED PLASTICS LLC (PA)
104 S Warner St (13421-1510)
PHONE 315 363-7980
Barry Uber, *Ch of Bd*
Kevin McGreevy, *Business Mgr*
Raymond E Randall Jr, *Business Mgr*
James Seipola, *Vice Pres*

Richard Harrington, *Plant Mgr*
▲ **EMP:** 130 **EST:** 2006
SQ FT: 82,000
SALES (est): 36.7MM **Privately Held**
WEB: oneidamoldedplastics.com
SIC: 3089 Injection molding of plastics

(G-13184)
ONEIDA MOLDED PLASTICS LLC
104 S Warner St (13421-1510)
PHONE.................................315 363-7990
Joe Kiah, *CEO*
David Harrington, *President*
Tim Mc Cullough, *Vice Pres*
Kenneth Morey, *Vice Pres*
Robert Wiehl, *VP Finance*
EMP: 72
SQ FT: 41,000
SALES (est): 4.5MM
SALES (corp-wide): 36.7MM **Privately Held**
SIC: 3089 Plastic containers, except foam
PA: Oneida Molded Plastics, Llc
104 S Warner St
Oneida NY 13421
315 363-7980

(G-13185)
ONEIDA PUBLICATIONS INC
Also Called: Oneida Dispatch
130 Broad St (13421-1684)
PHONE.................................315 363-5100
Fax: 315 363-9832
Phil Austin, *CEO*
Perry L Novak, *Editor*
Maryann Hawthorne, *Accounting Dir*
Janice Collins, *Sales Associate*
Bradley Markowski, *Sales Associate*
EMP: 40 **EST:** 1851
SQ FT: 10,000
SALES (est): 2.4MM **Privately Held**
SIC: 2711 Newspapers

(G-13186)
ONEIDA SILVERSMITHS INC
163 Kenwood Ave 181 (13421-2829)
PHONE.................................315 361-3000
Fax: 315 361-3290
James E Joseph, *Ch of Bd*
EMP: 7
SALES (est): 783.5K
SALES (corp-wide): 228.8MM **Privately Held**
WEB: www.oneida.net
SIC: 3262 3231 3914 3421 Vitreous china table & kitchenware; ornamental glass: cut, engraved or otherwise decorated; silverware & plated ware; cutlery
HQ: Oneida Ltd.
163 Kenwood Ave Ste 181
Oneida NY 13421
315 361-3000

(G-13187)
PATHFINDER 103 INC
229 Park Ave (13421-2021)
PHONE.................................315 363-4260
Larry Manser, *President*
EMP: 8
SALES (est): 961.4K **Privately Held**
SIC: 3589 Sewer cleaning equipment, power

(G-13188)
S K CIRCUITS INC (PA)
483 Foxwood Ter (13421-2609)
PHONE.................................703 376-8718
Vijay K Kodali, *President*
EMP: 14
SALES (est): 1.8MM **Privately Held**
SIC: 3672 Printed circuit boards

(G-13189)
SHIRL-LYNN OF NEW YORK (PA)
266 Wilson St (13421-1722)
PHONE.................................315 363-5898
Fax: 315 363-5936
Shirley Thurston, *Partner*
Mary Blau, *Partner*
EMP: 12
SQ FT: 4,300

SALES: 1MM **Privately Held**
SIC: 2339 5699 5632 Women's & misses' athletic clothing & sportswear; bathing suits: women's, misses' & juniors'; bathing suits; sports apparel; costumes, masquerade or theatrical; dancewear

(G-13190)
THOMAS FOUNDRY LLC
559 Fitch St (13421-1515)
P.O. Box 175 (13421-0175)
PHONE.................................315 361-9048
John D Albanese III,
Shelly M Albanese,
John Albanse III,
EMP: 8
SQ FT: 7,400
SALES: 600K **Privately Held**
WEB: www.thomasfoundry.com
SIC: 3471 3364 Sand blasting of metal parts; nonferrous die-castings except aluminum

(G-13191)
V & J GRAPHICS INC
153 Phelps St (13421-1708)
PHONE.................................315 363-1933
Vernon Waters, *President*
Janice Waters, *Treasurer*
Sandy Harrison,
EMP: 8
SQ FT: 4,960
SALES (est): 989.5K **Privately Held**
SIC: 2752 Commercial printing, offset

(G-13192)
VISIBLE SYSTEMS CORPORATION (PA)
248 Main St Ste 2 (13421-2100)
PHONE.................................508 628-1510
Fax: 315 363-7488
George Cagliuso, *President*
Michael Paul, *Vice Pres*
Mike Cesino, *Sls & Mktg Exec*
Ellen Shoner, *CFO*
EMP: 20
SQ FT: 6,000
SALES (est): 4MM **Privately Held**
SIC: 7372 5045 8748 Prepackaged software; computer software; systems analysis or design

Oneonta
Otsego County

(G-13193)
AMERICAN BLADE MFG LLC (PA)
Also Called: G C Casting
138 Roundhouse Rd (13820-1200)
PHONE.................................607 432-4518
Raymond Harvey,
EMP: 12 **EST:** 1946
SQ FT: 1,500
SALES (est): 1.3MM **Privately Held**
WEB: www.charleslay.com
SIC: 3365 3366 Aluminum foundries; bronze foundry

(G-13194)
ARNAN DEVELOPMENT CORP (PA)
Also Called: PICKETT BUILDING MATERIALS
6459 State Highway 23 (13820-6542)
PHONE.................................607 432-8391
Fax: 607 433-6284
Robert A Harlem Jr, *Ch of Bd*
Rebecca Lloyd, *Vice Pres*
Kevin Curnalia, *Store Mgr*
Larry Covell, *Purchasing*
Tom Ballard, *Sales Staff*
EMP: 52
SQ FT: 40,000
SALES (est): 14.9MM **Privately Held**
WEB: www.oneontablock.com
SIC: 3271 3272 5082 5211 Architectural concrete: block, split, fluted, screen, etc.; concrete products; septic tanks, concrete; masonry equipment & supplies; lumber & other building materials; management services

(G-13195)
ASTROCOM ELECTRONICS INC
115 Dk Lifgren Dr (13820-3682)
PHONE.................................607 432-1930
Fax: 607 432-1286
Terry D Lifgren, *President*
Kim Roseboom, *General Mgr*
Doug Lifgren, *COO*
Dan Berard, *Vice Pres*
Kenny Morrell, *Safety Mgr*
▲ **EMP:** 93 **EST:** 1961
SQ FT: 65,000
SALES (est): 16.3MM **Privately Held**
WEB: www.astrocom-electronics.com
SIC: 3661 Communication headgear, telephone

(G-13196)
BK ASSOCIATES INTL INC
127 Commerce Rd (13820-3539)
P.O. Box 1238 (13820-5238)
PHONE.................................607 432-1499
Fax: 607 432-1592
Paul Karabinis, *President*
Eugene Bettiol Sr, *Treasurer*
Steve Palmer, *Office Mgr*
EMP: 15
SQ FT: 20,000
SALES (est): 2.1MM **Privately Held**
SIC: 2095 Coffee roasting (except by wholesale grocers)

(G-13197)
BROOKS BOTTLING CO LLC
5560 State Highway 7 (13820-3699)
PHONE.................................607 432-1782
Wendy Hunter, *Accountant*
Ryan Brooks, *Mng Member*
Angelina Shultis, *Admin Asst*
EMP: 10
SALES (est): 1.4MM **Privately Held**
SIC: 3565 Bottling machinery: filling, capping, labeling

(G-13198)
BURT RIGID BOX INC
58 Browne St (13820-1092)
PHONE.................................607 433-2510
Ron Bolaird, *Managing Dir*
William Howard, *Vice Pres*
Ralph Underwood, *Plant Mgr*
Penny Timer, *Production*
Dave Van Pelt, *Purch Agent*
EMP: 52
SQ FT: 77,280
SALES (corp-wide): 19.6MM **Privately Held**
WEB: www.burtbox.com
SIC: 2653 2657 2652 Boxes, solid fiber: made from purchased materials; folding paperboard boxes; setup paperboard boxes
PA: Burt Rigid Box, Inc.
58 Browne St
Oneonta NY 13820
607 433-2510

(G-13199)
BURT RIGID BOX INC (PA)
58 Browne St (13820-1092)
P.O. Box 1883, Buffalo (14225-8883)
PHONE.................................607 433-2510
Fax: 607 433-2512
W Russell Hurd, *President*
Laura Brodie, *Vice Pres*
William Howard, *Vice Pres*
Greg Ward, *Opers Mgr*
Bill Howard, *Safety Mgr*
▲ **EMP:** 10
SQ FT: 500,000
SALES (est): 19.6MM **Privately Held**
WEB: www.burtbox.com
SIC: 2631 Folding boxboard; setup boxboard

(G-13200)
CITY OF ONEONTA
Also Called: Oneonta City Wtr Trtmnt Plant
110 East St (13820-1304)
PHONE.................................607 433-3470
Fax: 607 433-3486
Stanley Shaffer, *Manager*
EMP: 5 **Privately Held**
SIC: 3589 9111 Water treatment equipment, industrial; mayors' offices

PA: City Of Oneonta
258 Main St Ste 1
Oneonta NY 13820
607 432-6450

(G-13201)
CO-OPTICS AMERICA LAB INC
Also Called: Co-Optics Groups, The
297 River Street Svc Rd Service (13820)
PHONE.................................607 432-0557
Fax: 607 432-1668
Paul Strenn, *President*
Israel Soto, *Vice Pres*
EMP: 20
SQ FT: 3,300
SALES (est): 3MM **Privately Held**
WEB: www.co-optics.com
SIC: 3851 3229 Lenses, ophthalmic; pressed & blown glass

(G-13202)
COBLESKILL STONE PRODUCTS INC
Also Called: Oneonta Asphalt
57 Ceperley Ave (13820)
PHONE.................................607 432-8321
Fax: 607 432-7960
Lennie Goodspeed, *Branch Mgr*
Cliff Cooper, *Manager*
EMP: 10
SQ FT: 1,353
SALES (corp-wide): 115.2MM **Privately Held**
WEB: www.cobleskillstone.com
SIC: 2951 Asphalt & asphaltic paving mixtures (not from refineries)
PA: Cobleskill Stone Products, Inc.
112 Rock Rd
Cobleskill NY 12043
518 234-0221

(G-13203)
COMMUNITY NEWSPAPER GROUP LLC
Daily Star, The
102 Chestnut St (13820-2584)
P.O. Box 250 (13820-0250)
PHONE.................................607 432-1000
Fax: 607 432-5847
David Kiehm, *Editor*
Daniel Swift, *Editor*
Peter Hill, *Counsel*
Kay Helms, *Finance Mgr*
Rocky Jackson, *Finance Mgr*
EMP: 18 **Privately Held**
WEB: www.clintonnc.com
SIC: 2711 2752 Newspapers: publishing only, not printed on site; commercial printing, lithographic
HQ: Community Newspaper Group, Llc
3500 Colonnade Pkwy # 600
Birmingham AL 35243

(G-13204)
COOPERSTOWN BREWING CO LLC
41 Browne St (13820-1472)
PHONE.................................607 286-9330
Dennis Haeley, *Partner*
Jewel Hall, *Partner*
Stanley Hall,
EMP: 5
SQ FT: 5,000
SALES (est): 394.4K **Privately Held**
WEB: www.cooperstownbrewing.com
SIC: 2082 Malt beverages

(G-13205)
CORNING INCORPORATED
275 River St (13820-2299)
PHONE.................................607 433-3100
Fax: 607 433-3161
Marla Kelly, *Engineer*
Mark Maroz, *Engineer*
Teri Mauk, *Enginr/R&D Mgr*
Don Capelluto, *Senior Mgr*
William Petrizze, *Supervisor*
EMP: 25
SQ FT: 20,106
SALES (corp-wide): 9.3B **Publicly Held**
WEB: www.corning.com
SIC: 3229 Pressed & blown glass
PA: Corning Incorporated
1 Riverfront Plz
Corning NY 14831
607 974-9000

Oneonta - Otsego County (G-13206)

(G-13206)
CREATIVE ORTHOTICS PROSTHETICS
Also Called: Hanger Clinic
37 Associate Dr (13820-2266)
PHONE..................607 431-2526
Chris German, *Manager*
Sheryl Price, *Director*
EMP: 7
SALES (corp-wide): 451.4MM **Publicly Held**
WEB: www.creativeoandp.com
SIC: 3842 Surgical appliances & supplies
HQ: Creative Orthotics & Prosthetics, Inc.
1300 College Ave Ste 1
Elmira NY 14901
607 734-7215

(G-13207)
CUSTOM ELECTRONICS INC
87 Browne St (13820-1096)
PHONE..................607 432-3880
Fax: 607 432-3913
Peter Dokuchitz, *Ch of Bd*
Michael Pentaris, *President*
Carroll Brower, *Vice Pres*
Jonathan Dokuchitz, *VP Opers*
Laura Raner, *Opers Mgr*
▲ **EMP:** 62 **EST:** 1964
SQ FT: 27,500
SALES (est): 13MM **Privately Held**
WEB: www.customelec.com
SIC: 3675 Electronic capacitors

(G-13208)
EQUISSENTIALS LLC
3200 Chestnut St Ste 5 (13820-1072)
PHONE..................607 432-2856
Fax: 607 432-2951
Joseph Creighton,
Tracie Jones,
EMP: 12 **EST:** 1999
SQ FT: 5,000
SALES (est): 1.4MM **Privately Held**
WEB: www.equissentials.net
SIC: 2231 Apparel & outerwear broadwoven fabrics

(G-13209)
FOTIS ONEONTA ITALIAN BAKERY
42 River St (13820-4320)
PHONE..................607 432-3871
James Tomaino, *Owner*
EMP: 6
SALES (est): 508.7K **Privately Held**
SIC: 2051 Bakery: wholesale or wholesale/retail combined

(G-13210)
MEDICAL COACHES INCORPORATED (PA)
399 County Highway 58 (13820-3422)
P.O. Box 129 (13820-0129)
PHONE..................607 432-1333
Fax: 607 432-8190
Geoffrey A Smith, *President*
Ian Smith, *Founder*
Leonard W Marsh, *COO*
Jim Brownell, *Vice Pres*
Joseph Fazio, *Opers Staff*
◆ **EMP:** 50 **EST:** 1952
SQ FT: 100,000
SALES: 10MM **Privately Held**
WEB: www.medcoach.com
SIC: 3711 Automobile assembly, including specialty automobiles

(G-13211)
MOLD-A-MATIC CORPORATION
Also Called: Mamco
147 River St (13820-2276)
PHONE..................607 433-2121
Fax: 607 432-7861
Siro Vergari, *Ch of Bd*
Mark Vergari, *Vice Pres*
William Giese, *Finance Mgr*
Francis Colone, *Director*
▲ **EMP:** 45 **EST:** 1964
SQ FT: 31,000
SALES: 4MM **Privately Held**
WEB: www.mamcomolding.com
SIC: 3549 3089 Assembly machines, including robotic; plastic processing

(G-13212)
ONEONTA FENCE
2 Washburn St (13820-2721)
PHONE..................607 433-6707
EMP: 6
SALES (est): 506.7K **Privately Held**
SIC: 3089 3315 Fences, gates & accessories: plastic; fence gates posts & fittings: steel

(G-13213)
OTSEGO READY MIX INC
2 Wells Ave (13820-2723)
PHONE..................607 432-3400
Fax: 607 433-6287
Robert Harlem Jr, *President*
EMP: 16
SQ FT: 8,000
SALES (est): 3.4MM **Privately Held**
SIC: 3273 Ready-mixed concrete

(G-13214)
PONY FARM PRESS & GRAPHICS
Also Called: Village Print Room
330 Pony Farm Rd (13820-3591)
PHONE..................607 432-9020
Edward May, *President*
Chris Chase, *IT/INT Sup*
EMP: 7
SQ FT: 12,000
SALES (est): 594.5K **Privately Held**
WEB: www.ponyfarmpress.com
SIC: 2759 Commercial printing

(G-13215)
RJ MILLWORKERS INC
12 Lewis St (13820-2652)
PHONE..................607 433-0525
Fax: 607 433-0478
Randy J Morley, *President*
Ellen Morley, *Vice Pres*
EMP: 20
SALES (est): 3.6MM **Privately Held**
WEB: www.rjmillworkers.com
SIC: 2431 Millwork

(G-13216)
T S PINK CORP
Also Called: TS Pink
139 Pony Farm Rd (13820-3537)
PHONE..................607 432-1100
Fax: 607 433-0500
Todd Pink, *President*
Diana Colone, *Vice Pres*
▲ **EMP:** 16
SQ FT: 15,000
SALES (est): 2MM **Privately Held**
WEB: www.tspink.com
SIC: 2841 Textile soap

Ontario
Wayne County

(G-13217)
ARIEL OPTICS INC
261 David Pkwy (14519-8955)
PHONE..................585 265-4820
Frederick Koch, *President*
EMP: 8
SALES: 525K **Privately Held**
WEB: www.arieloptics.com
SIC: 3827 Prisms, optical

(G-13218)
AVALANCHE FABRICATION INC
6314 Dean Pkwy (14519-9011)
PHONE..................585 545-4000
Paul Duerr, *President*
Thad Spaulding, *Vice Pres*
EMP: 14 **EST:** 1998
SQ FT: 5,500
SALES: 1.1MM **Privately Held**
WEB: www.afinc.biz
SIC: 3444 Sheet metalwork

(G-13219)
CLAUDE TRIBASTONE INC
6367 Dean Pkwy (14519-8939)
PHONE..................585 265-3776
Claude Tribastone, *President*
Tom Kelly, *Controller*
EMP: 6

SALES (est): 611.8K
SALES (corp-wide): 33.7MM **Privately Held**
WEB: www.photonicsolutionsusa.com
SIC: 3827 Lenses, optical: all types except ophthalmic
PA: Optimax Systems, Inc.
6367 Dean Pkwy
Ontario NY 14519
585 265-1020

(G-13220)
CS AUTOMATION INC
Also Called: C S Welding
518 Berg Rd (14519-9376)
PHONE..................315 524-5123
Craig Schieven, *Principal*
EMP: 10
SALES (est): 480K **Privately Held**
SIC: 7692 7389 8742 Welding repair; inspection & testing services; automation & robotics consultant

(G-13221)
DATA CONTROL INC
277 David Pkwy (14519-8955)
PHONE..................585 265-2980
Lori Ferguson, *President*
EMP: 4
SQ FT: 12,712
SALES: 1MM **Privately Held**
WEB: www.datacontrolinc.com
SIC: 2542 Fixtures: display, office or store: except wood

(G-13222)
DJ ACQUISITION MANAGEMENT CORP
Also Called: Weco Metal Products
6364 Dean Pkwy (14519-8970)
PHONE..................585 265-3000
Fax: 585 265-3447
Donald Cornwell, *President*
John R Gillan, *Vice Pres*
Bill Connor, *Purch Agent*
Christopher Sherland, *Human Resources*
▲ **EMP:** 75
SQ FT: 55,000
SALES (est): 18MM **Privately Held**
WEB: www.wecometal.com
SIC: 3444 Sheet metalwork

(G-13223)
FRED A NUDD CORPORATION (PA)
1743 State Route 104 (14519-8935)
P.O. Box 577 (14519-0577)
PHONE..................315 524-2531
Fax: 315 524-4249
Thomas Nudd, *President*
Frederick Nudd, *Vice Pres*
Bonnie Judware, *Accountant*
Tim Wilson, *Sales Mgr*
Lyle Nudd, *Manager*
EMP: 32
SQ FT: 40,000
SALES (est): 7.1MM **Privately Held**
WEB: www.nuddtowers.com
SIC: 3444 3441 1799 1622 Sheet metalwork; tower sections, radio & television transmission; antenna installation; bridge, tunnel & elevated highway

(G-13224)
G&G SEALCOATING AND PAVING INC
1449 Ontario (14519)
PHONE..................585 787-1500
Fax: 585 265-9016
Manny Giudice, *President*
EMP: 23
SALES (est): 3.1MM **Privately Held**
SIC: 2951 Asphalt paving mixtures & blocks

(G-13225)
HARBEC INC
358 Timothy Ln (14519-9012)
PHONE..................585 265-0010
Fax: 585 265-1306
Robert Bechtold, *President*
Gerald Wahl, *Counsel*
Brad Miller, *Project Mgr*
John Hoefen, *Opers Staff*
Jeffrey Eisenhauer, *Engineer*

EMP: 100
SQ FT: 15,000
SALES (est): 24.5MM **Privately Held**
WEB: www.harbec.com
SIC: 3089 Injection molded finished plastic products

(G-13226)
INTEGRITY TOOL INCORPORATED
6485 Furnace Rd (14519-8920)
PHONE..................315 524-4409
Mike Freidler, *President*
Les Saiers, *Plant Mgr*
Terri Nichols, *Manager*
EMP: 13 **EST:** 1996
SQ FT: 6,000
SALES (est): 1.5MM **Privately Held**
SIC: 3449 Miscellaneous metalwork

(G-13227)
LAKE IMMUNOGENICS INC
348 Berg Rd (14519-9374)
PHONE..................585 265-1973
Fax: 585 265-2306
James Bowman, *President*
Barbara Bowman, *Vice Pres*
Anne Rowlands, *Cust Mgr*
Ginger Sullivan, *Manager*
EMP: 15
SQ FT: 8,000
SALES (est): 3.1MM **Privately Held**
WEB: www.lakeimmunogenics.com
SIC: 2836 Plasmas; veterinary biological products

(G-13228)
NORTHERN BIODIESEL INC
317 State Route 104 (14519-8958)
PHONE..................585 545-4534
Jason Masters, *Ch of Bd*
Robert Bethold, *Vice Pres*
Jeff Frank, *Technician*
EMP: 5
SALES (est): 690K **Privately Held**
WEB: www.northernbiodiesel.com
SIC: 2911 Diesel fuels

(G-13229)
OPTIMAX SYSTEMS INC (PA)
6367 Dean Pkwy (14519-8939)
PHONE..................585 265-1020
Fax: 585 265-1033
Rick Plympton, *CEO*
Michael P Mandina, *Ch of Bd*
Robert Sawyer, *Managing Dir*
Richard Plympton, *Vice Pres*
John Rohrbaugh, *Facilities Mgr*
EMP: 164
SQ FT: 40,000
SALES (est): 33.7MM **Privately Held**
WEB: www.optimaxsi.com
SIC: 3827 Lenses, optical: all types except ophthalmic; prisms, optical

(G-13230)
OPTIPRO SYSTEMS LLC
6368 Dean Pkwy (14519-8970)
PHONE..................585 265-0160
Fax: 585 265-9416
Tim Ansalvi, *Controller*
Mike Bechtold, *Mng Member*
◆ **EMP:** 54
SQ FT: 20,000
SALES (est): 13MM
SALES (corp-wide): 9.4MM **Privately Held**
WEB: www.optipro.com
SIC: 3559 3827 Optical lens machinery; optical instruments & lenses
PA: Brightside 09 Inc.
6368 Dean Pkwy
Ontario NY 14519
585 265-0160

(G-13231)
PHOTON GEAR INC
245 David Pkwy (14519-8955)
PHONE..................585 265-3360
Fax: 315 524-2681
Gary Blough, *President*
EMP: 11
SQ FT: 5,400

GEOGRAPHIC SECTION

SALES (est): 2.4MM **Privately Held**
WEB: www.photongear.com
SIC: 3827 8711 Optical elements & assemblies, except ophthalmic; engineering services

(G-13232)
R C KOLSTAD WATER CORP
73 Lake Rd (14519-9311)
PHONE..................................585 216-2230
William Kolstad, *President*
EMP: 5
SALES: 2MM **Privately Held**
SIC: 3589 Water treatment equipment, industrial

(G-13233)
RANGER DESIGN US INC
6377 Dean Pkwy (14519-8939)
PHONE..................................800 565-5321
Derek Cowie, *President*
Randal Cowie, *Chairman*
Katie Stearns, *Human Resources*
Glenn Brothers, *Accounts Exec*
Paul Rogers, *Manager*
▲ EMP: 20
SQ FT: 80,000
SALES (est): 3.6MM **Privately Held**
SIC: 3711 Motor vehicles & car bodies

(G-13234)
ROCHESTER INDUSTRIAL CTRL INC (PA)
6400 Furnace Rd (14519-9744)
PHONE..................................315 524-4555
Fax: 315 524-5733
John Little, *Ch of Bd*
Mike Clancy, *Plant Mgr*
Heather Glanzel, *Purch Mgr*
Donna Perry, *Purch Mgr*
Peter Blum, *QC Mgr*
▲ EMP: 99
SQ FT: 23,600
SALES: 10MM **Privately Held**
SIC: 3625 3679 3672 Relays & industrial controls; electronic circuits; printed circuit boards

(G-13235)
ROCHESTER INDUSTRIAL CTRL INC
Also Called: R I C
6345 Furnace Rd (14519-9744)
PHONE..................................315 524-4555
Eric Albert, *President*
EMP: 100
SQ FT: 8,050
SALES (corp-wide): 10MM **Privately Held**
SIC: 3679 Electronic circuits
PA: Rochester Industrial Control, Inc.
    6400 Furnace Rd
    Ontario NY 14519
    315 524-4555

(G-13236)
SCIENTIFIC POLYMER PRODUCTS
6265 Dean Pkwy (14519-8997)
PHONE..................................585 265-0413
Fax: 585 265-1390
Bret Vanzo, *Ch of Bd*
Leslie Twist, *Manager*
EMP: 5
SQ FT: 10,000
SALES (est): 1.2MM **Privately Held**
WEB: www.scientificpolymer.com
SIC: 2819 Industrial inorganic chemicals

(G-13237)
SMITH INTERNATIONAL INC
Also Called: Smith Service Corps
1915 Lake Rd (14519-9792)
PHONE..................................585 265-2330
Fax: 315 524-6369
Drew Smith, *Principal*
EMP: 12 **Privately Held**
WEB: www.smith-intl.com
SIC: 3533 Oil & gas field machinery
HQ: Smith International, Inc.
    1310 Rankin Rd
    Houston TX 77073
    281 443-3370

Orangeburg
Rockland County

(G-13238)
AALBORG INSTRS & CONTRLS INC
20 Corporate Dr (10962-2616)
PHONE..................................845 398-3160
Fax: 845 770-3010
T J Baan, *CEO*
Karen Baan, *Admin Sec*
EMP: 54 EST: 1972
SQ FT: 33,000
SALES (est): 11.4MM **Privately Held**
WEB: www.aalborg.com
SIC: 3823 3824 3577 3494 Primary elements for process flow measurement; fluid meters & counting devices; computer peripheral equipment; valves & pipe fittings; fluid power valves & hose fittings

(G-13239)
API INDUSTRIES INC (PA)
Also Called: Aluf Plastics Division
2 Glenshaw St (10962-1207)
PHONE..................................845 365-2200
Fax: 845 365-2294
Susan Rosenberg, *CEO*
Reuven Rosenberg, *President*
Gabriel Kahana, *General Mgr*
Ezra Majerowitz, *Safety Mgr*
Tito Obado, *Purchasing*
▲ EMP: 280
SQ FT: 300,000
SALES (est): 122.8MM **Privately Held**
SIC: 2673 3081 Plastic bags: made from purchased materials; unsupported plastics film & sheet

(G-13240)
API INDUSTRIES INC
Base Plastics
2 Glenshaw St (10962-1207)
PHONE..................................845 365-2200
Fax: 845 680-0421
Susan Rosenberg, *CEO*
Angela Pendleton, *Cust Mgr*
Robert Lazarus, *Accounts Exec*
David Sabo, *Marketing Mgr*
Gary Schmertz, *Marketing Staff*
EMP: 125
SALES (corp-wide): 122.8MM **Privately Held**
SIC: 2673 3081 Plastic bags: made from purchased materials; unsupported plastics film & sheet
PA: Api Industries, Inc.
    2 Glenshaw St
    Orangeburg NY 10962
    845 365-2200

(G-13241)
ARON STREIT INC
Also Called: Streit Matzoh Co
171 Route 303 (10962-2209)
PHONE..................................212 475-7000
Fax: 212 505-7650
Aron S Yagoda, *Ch of Bd*
Isabella Dinatale, *Exec VP*
Alan Adler, *Vice Pres*
Malka Kubersky, *Controller*
Carmine V Minichino, *Controller*
▲ EMP: 45
SQ FT: 100,000
SALES (est): 8.2MM **Privately Held**
WEB: www.streitsmatzos.com
SIC: 2052 5149 Matzos; bakery products

(G-13242)
AVERY DENNISON CORPORATION
524 Route 303 (10962-1309)
PHONE..................................845 680-3873
EMP: 116
SALES (corp-wide): 6B **Publicly Held**
SIC: 2672 Adhesive papers, labels or tapes: from purchased material
PA: Avery Dennison Corporation
    207 N Goode Ave Fl 6
    Glendale CA 91203
    626 304-2000

(G-13243)
CEROVENE INC
10 Corporate Dr (10962-2614)
PHONE..................................845 359-1101
Manish Shah, *President*
EMP: 10
SALES (corp-wide): 8MM **Privately Held**
SIC: 2834 Pharmaceutical preparations
PA: Cerovene Inc.
    612 Corporate Way Ste 10
    Valley Cottage NY 10989
    845 267-2055

(G-13244)
CHROMALLOY AMERICAN LLC (DH)
330 Blaisdell Rd (10962-2510)
PHONE..................................845 230-7355
Armand F Lauzon Jr, *CEO*
EMP: 24 EST: 1986
SALES (est): 26.2MM
SALES (corp-wide): 2.2B **Publicly Held**
SIC: 3724 7699 Aircraft engines & engine parts; engine repair & replacement, non-automotive
HQ: Chromalloy Gas Turbine Llc
    3999 Rca Blvd
    Palm Beach Gardens FL 33410
    561 935-3571

(G-13245)
CHROMALLOY GAS TURBINE LLC
Also Called: Chromalloy New York
330 Blaisdell Rd (10962-2510)
PHONE..................................845 359-2462
Fax: 845 359-4409
Vince Martling, *General Mgr*
Zenon Piatnyczka, *General Mgr*
Tim Ulles, *General Mgr*
Keith Chessum, *Vice Pres*
Peter Howard, *Vice Pres*
EMP: 200
SALES (corp-wide): 2.2B **Publicly Held**
WEB: www.chromalloysatx.com
SIC: 3724 Aircraft engines & engine parts
HQ: Chromalloy Gas Turbine Llc
    3999 Rca Blvd
    Palm Beach Gardens FL 33410
    561 935-3571

(G-13246)
DHS SYSTEMS LLC (HQ)
560 Route 303 Ste 206 (10962-1329)
PHONE..................................845 359-6066
Samuel R Marrone, *CEO*
A Jon Prusmack, *President*
Samuel Marrone, *COO*
Brian Mindich, *Mfg Dir*
Mike Hall, *Prdtn Mgr*
▲ EMP: 15
SQ FT: 75,000
SALES: 80MM **Privately Held**
WEB: www.drash.com
SIC: 2394 Tents: made from purchased materials

(G-13247)
EMMI USA INC
100 Dutch Hill Rd Ste 220 (10962-2198)
PHONE..................................845 268-9990
Fax: 845 268-9991
Steven Millard, *President*
Paul Schilt, *President*
Jim Delaurentis, *General Mgr*
Mattaias Kinz, *Chairman*
Carol Nicolay, *Manager*
▲ EMP: 19
SQ FT: 12,000
SALES (est): 3.7MM
SALES (corp-wide): 220.3MM **Privately Held**
WEB: www.emmiusa.com
SIC: 2096 Cheese curls & puffs
HQ: Emmi International Ag
    Landenbergstrasse 1
    Luzern LU 6005

(G-13248)
ESSILOR LABORATORIES AMER INC
Also Called: Nova Optical
165 Route 303 (10962-2209)
PHONE..................................845 365-6700
EMP: 50

SALES (corp-wide): 100.9MM **Privately Held**
SIC: 3851 Mfg Ophthalmic Goods
HQ: Essilor Laboratories Of America, Inc.
    13515 N Stemmons Fwy
    Dallas TX 75234
    972 241-4141

(G-13249)
EUROMED INC
25 Corporate Dr (10962-2615)
PHONE..................................845 359-4039
Richard Wildnauer, *Ch of Bd*
Thomas E Gardner, *President*
Stephen Powell, *COO*
Brian Coughlin, *Vice Pres*
Ravi Ramjit, *Vice Pres*
◆ EMP: 95
SQ FT: 42,000
SALES (est): 22.8MM
SALES (corp-wide): 348.6MM **Privately Held**
WEB: www.euromedinc.com
SIC: 3842 Bandages & dressings
PA: Scapa Group Public Limited Company
    994 Manchester Road
    Ashton-Under-Lyne LANCS OL7 0
    161 301-7400

(G-13250)
FERRO MACHINE CO INC
70 S Greenbush Rd (10962-1323)
PHONE..................................845 398-3641
John Ferrogari, *President*
Susan Ferrogari, *Vice Pres*
EMP: 5
SQ FT: 4,500
SALES (est): 490K **Privately Held**
SIC: 3599 Machine shop, jobbing & repair

(G-13251)
INERTIA SWITCH INC
70 S Greenbush Rd (10962-1323)
PHONE..................................845 359-8300
Fax: 845 359-6227
Ruth Fischer, *President*
Brian Digirolamo, *Vice Pres*
Nadine Nodhturft, *Controller*
EMP: 25 EST: 1959
SQ FT: 9,500
SALES (est): 5.4MM **Privately Held**
WEB: www.inertiaswitch.com
SIC: 3625 3812 3643 3613 Control circuit devices, magnet & solid state; acceleration indicators & systems components, aerospace; current-carrying wiring devices; switchgear & switchboard apparatus

(G-13252)
INNOVATIVE PLASTICS CORP (PA)
400 Route 303 (10962-1340)
PHONE..................................845 359-7500
Fax: 845 359-0237
Judith Hershaft, *Ch of Bd*
Jim Parrish, *President*
Steve Fairbanks, *Regional Mgr*
Stephen Hershaft, *Vice Pres*
Rick Colton, *VP Opers*
▼ EMP: 150 EST: 1982
SQ FT: 100,000
SALES: 39MM **Privately Held**
WEB: www.innovative-plastics.com
SIC: 3089 Plastic processing; thermoformed finished plastic products; molding primary plastic

(G-13253)
INSTRUMENTATION LABORATORY CO
526 Route 303 (10962-1309)
PHONE..................................845 680-0028
Fax: 845 365-8031
Doug Ward, *General Mgr*
Maryann Kocubinski, *Senior Buyer*
Lori Bailey, *Buyer*
Kathy Ottinger, *QC Dir*
Andre Surprenant, *QC Mgr*
EMP: 180
SQ FT: 54,883

Orangeburg - Rockland County (G-13254)

SALES (corp-wide): 49.2MM **Privately Held**
WEB: www.ilww.com
SIC: **2836** 3842 3821 2899 Blood derivatives; surgical appliances & supplies; laboratory apparatus & furniture; chemical preparations
HQ: Instrumentation Laboratory Company
    180 Hartwell Rd
    Bedford MA 01730
    781 861-0710

(G-13254)
KEEBLER COMPANY
29 Corporate Dr (10962-2615)
PHONE.................................845 365-5200
Fax: 845 365-5286
Joseph Aidio, *Manager*
EMP: 40
SALES (corp-wide): 13B **Publicly Held**
WEB: www.keebler.com
SIC: **2052** Cookies
HQ: Keebler Company
    1 Kellogg Sq
    Battle Creek MI 49017
    269 961-2000

(G-13255)
KELLOGG COMPANY
29 Corporate Dr (10962-2615)
PHONE.................................845 365-5284
Joseph Aidio, *Branch Mgr*
EMP: 699
SALES (corp-wide): 13B **Publicly Held**
WEB: www.kelloggs.com
SIC: **2043** Cereal breakfast foods
PA: Kellogg Company
    1 Kellogg Sq
    Battle Creek MI 49017
    269 961-2000

(G-13256)
LTS (CHEMICAL) INC
37 Ramland Rd 2 (10962-2606)
PHONE.................................845 494-2940
Hirak Aarmaker, *President*
Slava Kogan, *Treasurer*
▲ **EMP:** 12
SQ FT: 1,400
SALES (est): 1.7MM **Privately Held**
WEB: www.ltschem.com
SIC: **2865** Chemical indicators

(G-13257)
MACHIDA INCORPORATED
Also Called: Vision-Sciences
40 Ramland Rd Ste 1 (10962-2698)
PHONE.................................845 365-0600
Fax: 845 365-0620
Ron Hadani, *CEO*
Jitu Patel, *Vice Pres*
Don McPhail, *Purchasing*
Yoav M Cohen, *CFO*
Kerry Bunn, *Human Resources*
EMP: 7
SQ FT: 10,000
SALES (est): 2.1MM
SALES (corp-wide): 51.8MM **Publicly Held**
WEB: www.visionsciences.com
SIC: **3827** Boroscopes
PA: Cogentix Medical, Inc.
    5420 Feltl Rd
    Minnetonka MN 55343
    952 426-6140

(G-13258)
NICE-PAK PRODUCTS INC (PA)
2 Nice Pak Park (10962-1376)
PHONE.................................845 365-2772
Fax: 845 365-1717
Robert Julius, *President*
John Culligan, *President*
Jon Kupperman, *President*
Zachary Julius, *Exec VP*
William E Dwan, *Senior VP*
◆ **EMP:** 400
SQ FT: 168,000
SALES (est): 416.3MM **Privately Held**
WEB: www.nicepak.com
SIC: **2621** 7389 2676 Towels, tissues & napkins: paper & stock; sanitary tissue paper; packaging & labeling services; sanitary paper products

(G-13259)
OCTAGON PROCESS LLC (DH)
30 Ramland Rd S Ste 103 (10962-2626)
PHONE.................................845 680-8800
Joe McGrail, *President*
Jeff B Crevoiserat, *President*
Michael Beraota, *Controller*
EMP: 5 **EST:** 1940
SALES (est): 1.1MM
SALES (corp-wide): 5.7B **Privately Held**
SIC: **2899** Chemical preparations; deicing or defrosting fluid
HQ: Clariant Corporation
    4000 Monroe Rd
    Charlotte NC 28205
    704 331-7000

(G-13260)
PAXAR CORPORATION (HQ)
Also Called: Avery Dennison
524 Route 303 (10962-1397)
PHONE.................................845 398-3229
Fax: 845 359-0380
Susan C Miller, *Ch of Bd*
Robert Van Der Merwe, *President*
John J Fitzgerald, *Senior VP*
Joseph Fetzner, *Vice Pres*
Paul S Huyffer, *Vice Pres*
◆ **EMP:** 50
SQ FT: 30,000
SALES (est): 20.9MM
SALES (corp-wide): 6B **Publicly Held**
WEB: www.paxar.com
SIC: **2269** 2752 3555 3577 Labels, cotton: printed; tags, lithographed; printing trades machinery; bar code (magnetic ink) printers
PA: Avery Dennison Corporation
    207 N Goode Ave Fl 6
    Glendale CA 91203
    626 304-2000

(G-13261)
PHOTOMEDEX INC (DH)
Also Called: PHOTOMEDEX SURGICAL PRODUCTS
40 Ramland Rd S Fl 2 (10962-2623)
PHONE.................................888 966-1010
Dolev Rafaeli, *CEO*
Dennis M McGrath, *President*
Barbara Onraet, *Business Mgr*
Albert Intintoli, *Research*
Courtney Colwell, *Sales Mgr*
▲ **EMP:** 30 **EST:** 1980
SALES: 38.4MM
SALES (corp-wide): 16.7MM **Publicly Held**
WEB: www.photomedex.com
SIC: **2834** 3845 3699 Pharmaceutical preparations; laser systems & equipment, medical; laser systems & equipment
HQ: Ictv Holdings, Inc.
    489 Devon Park Dr Ste 315
    Wayne PA 19087
    484 598-2300

(G-13262)
PICCINI INDUSTRIES LTD
37 Ramland Rd (10962-2606)
PHONE.................................845 365-0614
John Piccininni, *Ch of Bd*
Senolisa Santos, *Admin Asst*
EMP: 30
SQ FT: 23,000
SALES (est): 3.2MM **Privately Held**
WEB: www.piccini.net
SIC: **2421** 2522 2521 2511 Sawmills & planing mills, general; office furniture, except wood; wood office furniture; wood household furniture; wood kitchen cabinets; millwork

(G-13263)
PRAXAIR INC
542 Route 303 (10962-1309)
PHONE.................................845 359-4200
Mark Murphy, *President*
Nicole Mitchell, *Human Res Dir*
Paul Gilman, *Info Tech Dir*
David Strauss, *Director*
EMP: 150
SALES (corp-wide): 10.5B **Publicly Held**
SIC: **2813** Industrial gases
PA: Praxair, Inc.
    10 Riverview Dr
    Danbury CT 06810
    203 837-2000

(G-13264)
PRAXAIR SURFACE TECH INC
560 Route 303 (10962-1329)
PHONE.................................845 398-8322
Nicole Mitchell, *Human Res Dir*
David Strauff, *Manager*
Mark Nestle, *Director*
EMP: 160
SALES (corp-wide): 10.5B **Publicly Held**
SIC: **3471** Plating & polishing
HQ: Praxair Surface Technologies, Inc.
    1500 Polco St
    Indianapolis IN 46222
    317 240-2500

(G-13265)
PRODUCTO ELECTRIC CORP
Also Called: Peco Conduit Fittings
11 Kings Hwy (10962-1897)
PHONE.................................845 359-4900
Fax: 845 359-4978
Arthur Lemay, *President*
John Fischer, *Vice Pres*
Nancy Jaccoi, *Administration*
▲ **EMP:** 30 **EST:** 1935
SQ FT: 54,000
SALES (est): 5.2MM **Privately Held**
WEB: www.pecoelect.com
SIC: **3644** Electric conduits & fittings

(G-13266)
PROFESSIONAL DISPOSABLES INC
2 Nice Pak Park (10962-1317)
PHONE.................................845 365-1700
Robert P Julius, *President*
William E Dwan, *Senior VP*
Ed Ostendorf, *Project Mgr*
Frank Gagliano, *Maint Spvr*
Rich Eberle, *Purch Agent*
◆ **EMP:** 590
SALES (est): 157.1MM **Privately Held**
SIC: **2676** 7389 2621 Sanitary paper products; packaging & labeling services; towels, tissues & napkins: paper & stock; sanitary tissue paper

(G-13267)
RADIANCY INC (DH)
40 Ramland Rd S Ste 200 (10962-2623)
PHONE.................................845 398-1647
Fax: 845 398-1648
Dolev Rafaeli, *CEO*
Therese Joyce, *Assistant VP*
AVI Hanin, *Controller*
Linda Merxhushi, *Accountant*
Miki Van Soest, *Office Mgr*
▲ **EMP:** 10
SQ FT: 5,000
SALES (est): 1.8MM
SALES (corp-wide): 16.7MM **Publicly Held**
WEB: www.radiancy.com
SIC: **3845** Electromedical equipment
HQ: Ictv Holdings, Inc.
    489 Devon Park Dr Ste 315
    Wayne PA 19087
    484 598-2300

(G-13268)
SENSORMATIC ELECTRONICS LLC
10 Corporate Dr (10962-2614)
PHONE.................................845 365-3125
Per-Olof Loof, *President*
Gareth McClean, *Engineer*
Larry Matteson, *Manager*
Mike Tabola, *Manager*
Kelly Schwedland, *Consultant*
EMP: 15 **Privately Held**
WEB: www.sensormatic.com
SIC: **3812** Detection apparatus: electronic/magnetic field, light/heat
HQ: Sensormatic Electronics, Llc
    6600 Congress Ave
    Boca Raton FL 33487
    561 912-6000

(G-13269)
SEQUA CORPORATION
300 Blaisdell Rd (10962-2506)
PHONE.................................201 343-1122
John Lansdale, *President*
Mitchell Bittman, *Counsel*
Peter Howard, *Vice Pres*
William Johnson, *Purch Mgr*
Roberto Santilli, *Design Engr*
EMP: 50
SQ FT: 367,000
SALES (corp-wide): 2.2B **Publicly Held**
WEB: www.sequa.com
SIC: **3479** Coating of metals & formed products
HQ: Sequa Corporation
    3999 Rca Blvd
    Palm Beach Gardens FL 33410
    201 343-1122

(G-13270)
ZACKS ENTERPRISES INC
Also Called: Zagwear
33 Corporate Dr (10962-2615)
PHONE.................................800 366-4924
Fax: 845 398-0303
Toby Zacks, *CEO*
Judd Karofsky, *President*
Nick Piscitelli, *COO*
Lenny Polakoff, *Exec VP*
Bob Hay, *Senior VP*
▲ **EMP:** 50
SQ FT: 48,000
SALES (est): 15.6MM **Privately Held**
SIC: **2759** 8742 Screen printing; marketing consulting services

Orchard Park
Erie County

(G-13271)
303 CONTRACTING INC (HQ)
5486 Powers Rd (14127-3111)
P.O. Box 831, Buffalo (14240-0831)
PHONE.................................716 896-2122
Edward Janowski, *Ch of Bd*
Henry Van Mollenberg, *President*
Joseph Kilijanski, *Exec VP*
James P Camarre, *CFO*
EMP: 43
SQ FT: 10,000
SALES (est): 5MM
SALES (corp-wide): 65.2MM **Privately Held**
SIC: **3444** 1799 7692 3699 Sheet metalwork; ducts, sheet metal; welding on site; welding repair; electrical equipment & supplies
PA: Mollenberg-Betz Holdings Llc
    300 Scott St
    Buffalo NY 14204
    716 614-7473

(G-13272)
A LUNT DESIGN INC
5755 Big Tree Rd (14127-4115)
P.O. Box 247 (14127-0247)
PHONE.................................716 662-0781
Fax: 716 662-0784
Audrey Lunt, *President*
Thomas Lunt, *Vice Pres*
Nicholas Buccieri CPA, *Accountant*
Robert Kresse, *Shareholder*
▲ **EMP:** 16
SQ FT: 15,000
SALES (est): 1.4MM **Privately Held**
WEB: www.alunt.com
SIC: **2389** Disposable garments & accessories

(G-13273)
ACCIPITER RADAR CORPORATION
40 Centre Dr Ste 3 (14127-4100)
PHONE.................................716 508-4432
Dr Tim Nohara, *President*
Carl Krasnor, *Vice Pres*
Darryl Nohara, *Vice Pres*
Jeffrey Ogden, *Vice Pres*
Josey V Melick, *Sales Staff*
EMP: 5

SALES (est): 509.1K
SALES (corp-wide): 576.3K **Privately Held**
SIC: 3812 Search & navigation equipment
HQ: Accipiter Radar Technologies Inc
576 Hwy 20 W
Fenwick ON L0S 1
905 228-6888

(G-13274)
ADVAN-TECH MANUFACTURING INC
3645 California Rd (14127-1715)
PHONE 716 667-1500
Fax: 716 667-2860
Peter Munschauer, *President*
Mathew Weierheiser, *QC Mgr*
Denise Dietz, *Manager*
Tim Smith, *Consultant*
EMP: 23
SQ FT: 7,750
SALES (est): 3.7MM **Privately Held**
SIC: 3599 Machine shop, jobbing & repair

(G-13275)
AURORA INDUS MACHINING INC
3380 N Benzing Rd (14127-1538)
PHONE 716 826-7911
Fax: 716 827-1041
Robert T Hesse, *President*
Mary C Hesse, *Vice Pres*
John Breen, *Treasurer*
EMP: 25
SQ FT: 20,000
SALES (est): 4.8MM
SALES (corp-wide): 34.2MM **Privately Held**
WEB: www.auroraheatexchangers.com
SIC: 3443 Heat exchangers, condensers & components; vessels, process or storage (from boiler shops); metal plate
PA: Hesse Industrial Sales, Inc.
3370 N Benzing Rd
Orchard Park NY 14127
716 827-4951

(G-13276)
BOS-HATTEN INC
Also Called: Ipe
50 Cobham Dr (14127-4121)
PHONE 716 662-7030
Fax: 716 662-6548
Warner G Martin, *Ch of Bd*
Anthony Paliwoda, *Vice Pres*
Shirley Martin, *Admin Sec*
EMP: 10
SQ FT: 5,500
SALES (est): 747.9K
SALES (corp-wide): 417MM **Publicly Held**
WEB: www.bos-hatten.com
SIC: 3443 Heat exchangers, condensers & components
HQ: Peerless Mfg. Co.
14651 Dallas Pkwy Ste 500
Dallas TX 75254
214 357-6181

(G-13277)
BOSTON VALLEY POTTERY INC (PA)
Also Called: Boston Valley Terra Cotta
6860 S Abbott Rd (14127-4707)
PHONE 716 649-7490
Fax: 716 649-7688
John B Krouse, *Principal*
Gretchen E Krouse, *Vice Pres*
Richard O Krouse, *Vice Pres*
William D Krouse, *Vice Pres*
Desiree Wisser, *Project Mgr*
▲ **EMP:** 95
SQ FT: 95,300
SALES (est): 52.2MM **Privately Held**
SIC: 3259 Architectural terra cotta; roofing tile, clay

(G-13278)
BUCKLEY QC FASTENERS INC
3874 California Rd (14127-2262)
PHONE 716 662-1490
Fax: 716 662-0669
Ruth M Kohl, *General Mgr*
Kris Furjanic, *Sales Staff*
EMP: 32
SQ FT: 11,000
SALES (est): 4.5MM **Privately Held**
SIC: 3452 Nuts, metal; bolts, metal; screws, metal

(G-13279)
BUFFALO CIRCUITS INC
105 Mid County Dr (14127-1773)
PHONE 716 662-2113
Fax: 716 662-2696
Peter Messina Sr, *President*
Liz Bever, *Manager*
EMP: 7
SQ FT: 4,920
SALES (est): 760K **Privately Held**
SIC: 3672 7336 Printed circuit boards; silk screen design

(G-13280)
BURGESS-MANNING INC (DH)
Also Called: Skimovex USA
50 Cobham Dr (14127-4121)
PHONE 716 662-6540
Warner G Martin, *Ch of Bd*
Robert Sherman, *President*
Philip Otto, *Plant Mgr*
Edward Rucker, *Controller*
Anthony Paliwoda, *VP Finance*
▲ **EMP:** 60
SQ FT: 5,500
SALES (est): 21.7MM
SALES (corp-wide): 417MM **Publicly Held**
WEB: www.burgessmanning.com
SIC: 3625 Noise control equipment
HQ: Peerless Mfg. Co.
14651 Dallas Pkwy Ste 500
Dallas TX 75254
214 357-6181

(G-13281)
CARBON ACTIVATED CORPORATION
336 Stonehenge Dr (14127-2841)
PHONE 716 662-2005
Chris Allen, *Branch Mgr*
EMP: 8 **Privately Held**
WEB: www.carbonactivatedcorp.com
SIC: 2819 Charcoal (carbon), activated
PA: Carbon Activated Corporation
2250 S Central Ave
Compton CA 90220

(G-13282)
CARLETON TECHNOLOGIES INC (HQ)
10 Cobham Dr (14127-4195)
PHONE 716 662-0006
Fax: 716 662-0747
Kenneth Kota, *Ch of Bd*
Kelly Coffield, *President*
Nicholas Dziama, *General Mgr*
Kenneth A Kota, *General Mgr*
Jeffrey Carriero, *Business Mgr*
EMP: 277
SQ FT: 93,000
SALES (est): 236.3MM
SALES (corp-wide): 2.3B **Privately Held**
SIC: 3728 Aircraft parts & equipment
PA: Cobham Plc
Brook Road
Wimborne BH21
120 288-2020

(G-13283)
CENVEO INC
Mail-Well
100 Centre Dr (14127-4122)
PHONE 716 662-2800
Sheryl McFeely, *HR Admin*
Mike A Zaietar, *Manager*
EMP: 67 **Publicly Held**
SIC: 2677 Envelopes
PA: Cenveo, Inc.
200 First Stamford Pl # 200
Stamford CT 06902

(G-13284)
CHET KRUSZKAS SERVICE INC
Also Called: Chet Kruszka's Svce
3536 Southwestern Blvd (14127-1707)
PHONE 716 662-7450
Fax: 716 662-9593
Michael Kruszka, *President*
Rose Kruszka, *Office Mgr*
Jan Hoelscher, *Manager*
EMP: 12

SQ FT: 18,000
SALES: 1MM **Privately Held**
SIC: 3493 5013 5531 7538 Steel springs, except wire; automobile springs; truck parts & accessories; truck equipment & parts; general truck repair; body shop, automotive; body shop, trucks; collision shops, automotive

(G-13285)
COBHAM HOLDINGS (US) INC
10 Cobham Dr (14127-4121)
PHONE 716 662-0006
Betty Bible, *President*
Bob Murphy, *Principal*
Scott Manecke, *Finance Mgr*
Jeff Ehret, *Manager*
EMP: 3700
SALES (est): 228.8MM
SALES (corp-wide): 2.3B **Privately Held**
SIC: 3679 3812 Microwave components; acceleration indicators & systems components, aerospace
HQ: Lockman Investments Limited
Brook Road
Wimborne

(G-13286)
COBHAM HOLDINGS INC (DH)
10 Orchard Park Dr (14127)
PHONE 716 662-0006
Bob Murphy, *CEO*
Walt Stierhoff, *General Mgr*
Robert Atkins, *Business Mgr*
Michael Odonnell, *Business Mgr*
Rob Schaeffer, *Business Mgr*
EMP: 20
SALES (est): 959.5MM
SALES (corp-wide): 2.3B **Privately Held**
SIC: 3679 3812 Microwave components; acceleration indicators & systems components, aerospace

(G-13287)
COBHAM MANAGEMENT SERVICES INC
Also Called: Cobham Mission Systems Div
10 Cobham Dr (14127-4121)
PHONE 716 662-0006
Warren Tucker, *President*
Adreanne Lippa, *Opers Mgr*
Tim Thommen, *Opers Mgr*
Mike Rapp, *Production*
Barbara Walters, *Buyer*
◆ **EMP:** 2650
SQ FT: 37,024
SALES (est): 228.8MM
SALES (corp-wide): 2.3B **Privately Held**
SIC: 3568 Couplings, shaft: rigid, flexible, universal joint, etc.
HQ: Cobham Holdings Inc.
10 Orchard Park Dr
Orchard Park NY 14127
716 662-0006

(G-13288)
CONTECH ENGNERED SOLUTIONS LLC
34 Birdsong Pkwy (14127-3067)
PHONE 716 870-9091
Gene Majchrzack, *Principal*
EMP: 12 **Privately Held**
SIC: 3443 Fabricated plate work (boiler shop)
HQ: Contech Engineered Solutions Llc
9025 Ctr Pinte Dr Ste 400
West Chester OH 45069
513 645-7000

(G-13289)
CURBELL MEDICAL PRODUCTS INC
20 Centre Dr (14127-4102)
PHONE 716 667-2520
Craig Fenske, *Senior Buyer*
Rick Crandall, *Engineer*
Dave Zavah, *Branch Mgr*
Thomas Rutherford, *Technology*
EMP: 12
SALES (corp-wide): 187.3MM **Privately Held**
SIC: 3669 Intercommunication systems, electric

HQ: Curbell Medical Products, Inc.
7 Cobham Dr
Orchard Park NY 14127
716 667-2520

(G-13290)
CURBELL MEDICAL PRODUCTS INC (HQ)
7 Cobham Dr (14127-4180)
PHONE 716 667-2520
Thomas E Leone, *Ch of Bd*
Christine L Sabuda, *Vice Ch Bd*
Abdulkadir Sarac, *President*
Shawn Heeter, *Mfg Dir*
Stephanie Booker, *Production*
▲ **EMP:** 159
SALES: 50.4MM
SALES (corp-wide): 187.3MM **Privately Held**
WEB: www.curbell.com
SIC: 3669 Intercommunication systems, electric
PA: Curbell, Inc.
7 Cobham Dr
Orchard Park NY 14127
716 667-3377

(G-13291)
CUSTOM COUNTERTOPS INC
5260 Armor Duells Rd (14127-4409)
PHONE 716 646-1579
Gloria Marino, *President*
EMP: 5
SQ FT: 7,588
SALES (corp-wide): 750K **Privately Held**
WEB: www.customcountertops.com
SIC: 3131 Counters
PA: Custom Countertops Inc
3192 Walden Ave
Depew NY 14043
716 685-2871

(G-13292)
DESMI-AFTI INC
227 Thorn Ave Bldg C (14127-2600)
P.O. Box 575 (14127-0575)
PHONE 716 662-0632
Fax: 716 662-0636
Peter Lane, *President*
Andy Nash, *Business Mgr*
Carole Lane, *Production*
David Kuczma, *Engineer*
Charlene Cousineau, *Accountant*
▼ **EMP:** 20
SQ FT: 26,131
SALES (est): 5MM **Privately Held**
WEB: www.afti.com
SIC: 3533 3535 Oil field machinery & equipment; belt conveyor systems, general industrial use

(G-13293)
FLOW-SAFE INC
3865 Taylor Rd (14127-2297)
PHONE 716 662-2585
Warner Martin, *Ch of Bd*
Kevin Martin, *President*
Edward Rucker, *Controller*
Dawn Hawell, *Accounts Mgr*
Rita Williams, *Technology*
▲ **EMP:** 40
SQ FT: 25,000
SALES (est): 8.5MM **Privately Held**
SIC: 3491 5074 Industrial valves; plumbing & heating valves

(G-13294)
GAYMAR INDUSTRIES INC
10 Centre Dr (14127-2280)
PHONE 800 828-7341
Fax: 716 662-8785
Bradford L Saar, *CEO*
Kent J Davies, *Principal*
Pradeep Gupta, *QA Dir*
Timothy Bialek, *Engineer*
Carrie Herdman, *Human Res Mgr*
▲ **EMP:** 350 EST: 1956
SQ FT: 110,000
SALES (est): 42.9MM
SALES (corp-wide): 11.3B **Publicly Held**
WEB: www.gaymar.com
SIC: 3841 Surgical & medical instruments
PA: Stryker Corporation
2825 Airview Blvd
Portage MI 49002
269 385-2600

Orchard Park - Erie County (G-13295)

(G-13295)
GENIUS TOOLS AMERICAS CORP
Also Called: Genius Tool Americas
15 Cobham Dr (14127-4101)
PHONE..................716 662-6872
Winni Chang, *Branch Mgr*
EMP: 10
SALES (corp-wide): 2.4MM **Privately Held**
WEB: www.geniustoolsusa.com
SIC: 3545 Tools & accessories for machine tools
PA: Genius Tools Americas Corp
   1440 E Cedar St
   Ontario CA 91761
   909 230-9588

(G-13296)
GOODNATURE PRODUCTS INC (PA)
3860 California Rd (14127-2262)
PHONE..................716 855-3325
Fax: 716 667-3328
Dale Wettlaufer, *President*
Larry Colucci, *Engineer*
Diane Massett, *Finance*
Lori Sonnenfeld, *Human Res Mgr*
Pete Whitehead, *VP Sales*
EMP: 12
SQ FT: 18,000
SALES: 5MM **Privately Held**
WEB: www.goodnature.com
SIC: 3634 3556 Juice extractors, electric; pasteurizing equipment, dairy machinery

(G-13297)
GRASERS DENTAL CERAMICS
5020 Armor Duells Rd # 2 (14127-4441)
PHONE..................716 649-5100
Thomas John Graser Jr, *Owner*
EMP: 6
SQ FT: 600
SALES: 60K **Privately Held**
SIC: 3843 Dental materials

(G-13298)
IMPACT JOURNALS LLC
Also Called: Publishing Medical Journals
6666 E Quaker St Ste 1 (14127-2547)
PHONE..................800 922-0957
Zoya Demidenko, *Mng Member*
EMP: 8
SALES: 100K **Privately Held**
SIC: 2721 Periodicals: publishing & printing

(G-13299)
ITT ENIDINE INC (DH)
Also Called: Enivate - Aerospace Division
7 Centre Dr (14127-2281)
PHONE..................716 662-1900
Fax: 716 662-1909
Dennise Ramos, *CEO*
Munish Nanda, *Ch of Bd*
Dennis Schully, *President*
David Snowberger, *Business Mgr*
Christophe Lee, *Vice Pres*
▲ **EMP:** 275
SQ FT: 85,000
SALES (est): 121.6MM
SALES (corp-wide): 2.4B **Publicly Held**
WEB: www.enidine.com
SIC: 3724 3714 3593 Aircraft engines & engine parts; motor vehicle parts & accessories; fluid power cylinders & actuators
HQ: Itt Llc
   1133 Westchester Ave N-100
   White Plains NY 10604
   914 641-2000

(G-13300)
J H BUSCHER INC
227 Thorn Ave Ste 30 (14127-2671)
PHONE..................716 667-2003
John H Buscher, *President*
Margaret G Buscher, *Vice Pres*
EMP: 5
SQ FT: 3,000
SALES: 700K **Privately Held**
WEB: www.jhbi.com
SIC: 3491 Industrial valves

(G-13301)
JARACZ JR JOSEPH PAUL
64 Ferndale Dr (14127-1644)
PHONE..................716 533-1377
Joseph Paul Jaracz Jr, *Owner*
Kyle Gooding, *CFO*
EMP: 8
SALES (est): 293.5K **Privately Held**
SIC: 3845 3841 Electromedical equipment; surgical & medical instruments

(G-13302)
KELSON PRODUCTS INC
3300 N Benzing Rd (14127-1538)
PHONE..................716 825-2585
Joseph P Merz, *President*
EMP: 7
SQ FT: 10,864
SALES: 700K **Privately Held**
WEB: www.kelsonproducts.com
SIC: 3069 Rubberized fabrics

(G-13303)
KINEDYNE INC
Also Called: Engineered Lifting Tech
3566 S Benzing Rd (14127-1703)
PHONE..................716 667-6833
William Hanes, *President*
Andrew Reardon, *VP Opers*
Matthew Filion, *Project Engr*
Jeremy Inda, *Design Engr*
Bob Delong, *Marketing Staff*
EMP: 18
SQ FT: 17,000
SALES (est): 4.4MM **Privately Held**
SIC: 3531 Cranes

(G-13304)
LAKE REGION MEDICAL INC
3902 California Rd (14127-2275)
P.O. Box 637 (14127-0637)
PHONE..................716 662-5025
Fax: 716 662-5772
Lisa Kull, *Vice Pres*
Michael Ekstrum, *Opers Staff*
Andrew Aube, *QC Mgr*
Alexander Nastevski, *Engineer*
Michael Clayback, *Director*
EMP: 110
SALES (corp-wide): 1.3B **Publicly Held**
SIC: 3841 Surgical instruments & apparatus; medical instruments & equipment, blood & bone work
HQ: Lake Region Medical, Inc.
   100 Fordham Rd Ste 3
   Wilmington MA 01887
   978 570-6900

(G-13305)
LD MCCAULEY LLC
3875 California Rd (14127-2239)
PHONE..................716 662-6744
Durham McCauley, *President*
Peter McCauley, *Vice Pres*
David Powers, *Vice Pres*
Darryl Rieger, *Manager*
EMP: 120
SALES (est): 15.5MM **Privately Held**
SIC: 3452 Bolts, nuts, rivets & washers

(G-13306)
MANZELLA KNITTING
3345 N Benzing Rd (14127-1539)
PHONE..................716 825-0808
Ed Masanovic, *Owner*
▲ **EMP:** 7
SALES (est): 608.3K **Privately Held**
SIC: 2381 Gloves, work: woven or knit, made from purchased materials

(G-13307)
MARATHON ROOFING PRODUCTS INC
3310 N Benzing Rd (14127-1538)
PHONE..................716 685-3340
Tod Cislo, *President*
Tim Krawczyk, *Sales Dir*
Tony Venturoli, *Sales Associate*
Cindy Fiordaliso, *Manager*
◆ **EMP:** 10
SQ FT: 30,000
SALES (est): 3MM **Privately Held**
WEB: www.marathondrains.com
SIC: 2952 5033 Roofing materials; roofing & siding materials

(G-13308)
MEDSOURCE TECHNOLOGIES LLC
3902 California Rd (14127-2275)
PHONE..................716 662-5025
Jim Hillman, *General Mgr*
Mark Lee, *Plant Mgr*
Jim Clark, *Manager*
EMP: 100
SALES (corp-wide): 1.3B **Publicly Held**
WEB: www.medsourcetech.com
SIC: 3841 Surgical & medical instruments
HQ: Medsource Technologies, Llc
   100 Fordham Rd Ste 1
   Wilmington MA 01887
   978 570-6900

(G-13309)
MENTHOLATUM COMPANY (DH)
707 Sterling Dr (14127-1587)
PHONE..................716 677-2500
Fax: 716 677-9531
Akiyoshi Yoshida PHD, *CEO*
Kunio Yamada, *President*
Barbara Regan, *Regional Mgr*
Randal Beard, *Business Mgr*
David Moore, *Sr Corp Ofcr*
◆ **EMP:** 34 EST: 1889
SQ FT: 102,000
SALES (est): 60.4MM
SALES (corp-wide): 1.4B **Privately Held**
WEB: www.mentholatum.com
SIC: 2834 2844 Pharmaceutical preparations; analgesics; lip balms; toilet preparations
HQ: Rohto Usa Inc
   707 Sterling Dr
   Orchard Park NY 14127
   716 677-2500

(G-13310)
NITRAM ENERGY INC
Also Called: Alco Products Div
50 Cobham Dr (14127-4121)
PHONE..................716 662-6540
Peter J Burlage, *CEO*
Robert Sherman, *President*
Bob Wicher, *Engineer*
Joe Hasler, *Controller*
John Buczynskyj, *Sales Staff*
EMP: 50
SQ FT: 5,500
SALES (est): 4.5MM
SALES (corp-wide): 417MM **Publicly Held**
SIC: 3625 3443 Control equipment, electric; heat exchangers: coolers (after, inter), condensers, etc.
HQ: Peerless Mfg. Co.
   14651 Dallas Pkwy Ste 500
   Dallas TX 75254
   214 357-6181

(G-13311)
P M PLASTICS INC
1 Bank St Ste 1 (14127-2997)
PHONE..................716 662-1255
Paul Sparks, *President*
Mark Zybert, *Corp Secy*
EMP: 25
SQ FT: 46,000
SALES: 3.5MM **Privately Held**
SIC: 3089 Injection molding of plastics

(G-13312)
PANAGRAPHICS INC
Also Called: Polish American Journal
30 Quail Run (14127-4611)
P.O. Box 198, Bowmansville (14026-0198)
PHONE..................716 312-8088
Mark A Cohan, *President*
Christopher Misztal, *Vice Pres*
Caroline Szczepanski, *Treasurer*
Scott Oziemek, *Manager*
Barbara Pinkowski, *Director*
EMP: 5
SQ FT: 1,200
SALES (est): 462K **Privately Held**
SIC: 2791 2711 Typesetting; newspapers

(G-13313)
PARATUS INDUSTRIES INC
6659 E Quaker St (14127-2503)
PHONE..................716 826-2000
Stephen Idziur, *President*
Thomas Zimmermann, *Vice Pres*
Trish Kernitz, *Controller*
EMP: 30
SQ FT: 20,000
SALES (est): 5.3MM **Privately Held**
WEB: www.paratusindustries.com
SIC: 3553 Woodworking machinery

(G-13314)
PEERLESS MFG CO
Also Called: Alco Products USA
50 Cobham Dr (14127-4121)
PHONE..................716 539-7400
Peter J Burlage, *Branch Mgr*
Tom Platek, *Technology*
EMP: 40
SALES (corp-wide): 417MM **Publicly Held**
WEB: www.peerlessmfg.com
SIC: 3569 Separators for steam, gas, vapor or air (machinery)
HQ: Peerless Mfg. Co.
   14651 Dallas Pkwy Ste 500
   Dallas TX 75254
   214 357-6181

(G-13315)
POLYMER CONVERSIONS INC
5732 Big Tree Rd (14127-4196)
PHONE..................716 662-8550
Jack E Bertsch, *CEO*
Joan Bertsch, *Corp Secy*
Benjamin Harp, *COO*
Ken Cook, *Maint Spvr*
Tom Rybicki, *Opers Staff*
EMP: 70
SQ FT: 35,000
SALES (est): 19.7MM **Privately Held**
WEB: www.polymerconversions.com
SIC: 3089 Molding primary plastic

(G-13316)
PRECISION ABRASIVES CORP
3176 Abbott Rd (14127-1069)
PHONE..................716 826-5833
Kevin Wyckoff, *President*
Pam Vogel, *Exec VP*
Jeff Kraatz, *Plant Mgr*
Craig Young, *Prdtn Mgr*
David Menzer, *Treasurer*
▲ **EMP:** 50
SQ FT: 25,000
SALES (est): 6.7MM
SALES (corp-wide): 32.3MM **Privately Held**
WEB: www.wesand.com
SIC: 3291 Coated abrasive products
PA: Sopark Corp.
   3300 S Park Ave
   Buffalo NY 14218
   716 822-0434

(G-13317)
QUAKER BOY INC (PA)
Also Called: Quaker Boy Turkey Calls
5455 Webster Rd (14127-1742)
PHONE..................716 662-3979
Fax: 716 662-9426
Richard C Kirby, *President*
Laurie Rizzo, *Manager*
▲ **EMP:** 50
SQ FT: 13,000
SALES (est): 4.9MM **Privately Held**
WEB: www.quakerboy.com
SIC: 3949 5961 Game calls; hunting equipment; mail order house

(G-13318)
QUAKER MILLWORK & LUMBER INC
77 S Davis St (14127-2684)
PHONE..................716 662-3388
Fax: 716 662-2220
Robert J Raber, *President*
Lyn Raber, *Office Mgr*
Joan Siarek, *Manager*
EMP: 40
SQ FT: 36,000
SALES (est): 6.9MM **Privately Held**
WEB: www.quakermills.com
SIC: 2431 Millwork; doors & door parts & trim, wood; staircases, stairs & railings

Oriskany - Oneida County (G-13341)

(G-13319)
QUALITY INDUSTRIAL SERVICES
Also Called: Bws Specialty Fabrication
75 Bank St (14127-2908)
PHONE....................716 667-7703
John E Sisson, *CEO*
Cindee Fahey, *Accounting Mgr*
EMP: 14
SQ FT: 52,800
SALES (est): 2.9MM **Privately Held**
SIC: **3496** 7692 Miscellaneous fabricated wire products; welding repair

(G-13320)
ROHTO USA INC (HQ)
707 Sterling Dr (14127-1557)
PHONE....................716 677-2500
Eugene Khitrik, *Manager*
Peter Arena, *Supervisor*
James W Ingham, *Admin Sec*
◆ EMP: 1
SALES (est): 60.4MM
SALES (corp-wide): 1.4B **Privately Held**
SIC: **2834** 8731 Pharmaceutical preparations; analgesics; lip balms; medical research, commercial
PA: Rohto Pharmaceutical Co., Ltd.
1-8-1, Tatsuminishi, Ikuno-Ku
Osaka OSK 544-0
667 581-231

(G-13321)
S & K COUNTER TOPS INC
4708 Duerr Rd (14127-3141)
PHONE....................716 662-7986
Fax: 716 648-4776
Bob Hayes, *President*
Tim Huwes, *Vice Pres*
EMP: 7
SQ FT: 2,400
SALES: 500K **Privately Held**
SIC: **2542** 5211 Cabinets: show, display or storage; except wood; counters or counter display cases; except wood; cabinets, kitchen; counter tops

(G-13322)
STI-CO INDUSTRIES INC
11 Cobham Dr Ste A (14127-4187)
PHONE....................716 662-2680
Fax: 716 662-5150
Antoinette Kaiser, *CEO*
Antoinette P Kaiser, *CEO*
Kyle Sawiat, *President*
Kyle Swiat, *Business Mgr*
Joseph M Collura, *Prdtn Mgr*
EMP: 48
SQ FT: 10,000
SALES (est): 13.6MM **Privately Held**
WEB: www.sti-co.com
SIC: **3663** Radio & TV communications equipment

(G-13323)
TAYLOR METALWORKS INC
3925 California Rd (14127-2276)
PHONE....................716 662-3113
Peter G Taylor, *President*
Gary Lumley, *Managing Dir*
Jason Taylor, *Vice Pres*
Paul Johnson, *Engineer*
Keith McFadden, *Engineer*
EMP: 110
SQ FT: 37,000
SALES (est): 21.8MM **Privately Held**
WEB: www.taylorcnc.com
SIC: **3451** 3365 Screw machine products; aluminum & aluminum-based alloy castings

(G-13324)
TRANSPORT NATIONAL DEV INC (PA)
Also Called: North American Carbide
5720 Ellis Rd (14127-2223)
PHONE....................716 662-0270
Robert E Gralke, *CEO*
Carl Dischner, *Plant Mgr*
Paul Johnson, *CFO*
Elizabeth Liebich, *Treasurer*
Debby Oconnor, *VP Finance*
EMP: 50
SQ FT: 30,000
SALES (est): 14.5MM **Privately Held**
SIC: **3541** Machine tools, metal cutting type

(G-13325)
TRANSPORT NATIONAL DEV INC
Also Called: North American Carbide of NY
5720 Ellis Rd (14127-2223)
PHONE....................716 662-0270
Marsha Gralke, *Opers Mgr*
Robert Gralke, *Enginr/R&D Mgr*
Cindy Donnelly, *Office Mgr*
EMP: 50
SALES (corp-wide): 14.5MM **Privately Held**
SIC: **2819** 3545 Carbides; machine tool accessories
PA: Transport National Development, Inc.
5720 Ellis Rd
Orchard Park NY 14127
716 662-0270

(G-13326)
UNITED MATERIALS LLC
Also Called: Frey Concrete Incoporated
75 Bank St (14127-2908)
PHONE....................716 662-0564
EMP: 6
SALES (corp-wide): 19.2MM **Privately Held**
SIC: **3273** 1442 Mfg Ready-Mixed Concrete Construction Sand/Gravel
PA: United Materials, L.L.C.
3949 Frest Pk Way Ste 400
North Tonawanda NY 14120
716 683-1432

(G-13327)
VIBRATION & NOISE ENGRG CORP
Also Called: Vanec
3374 N Benzing Rd (14127-1538)
PHONE....................716 827-4959
Art Cagney, *President*
Thomas Lowe, *President*
Jim McGrath, *Cust Mgr*
Charlie Dias, *Manager*
EMP: 3
SQ FT: 2,000
SALES (est): 1.6MM **Privately Held**
WEB: www.vanec.com
SIC: **3625** 5084 Noise control equipment; industrial machinery & equipment

Oriskany
Oneida County

(G-13328)
ALFRED PUBLISHING CO INC
Also Called: Alfred Music
123 Dry Rd (13424-4312)
PHONE....................315 736-1572
Michelle Major, *General Mgr*
Daniel Mayack, *Branch Mgr*
Brian Simpson, *Info Tech Mgr*
EMP: 70
SALES (corp-wide): 72MM **Privately Held**
WEB: www.alfred.com
SIC: **2731** 5192 Book music: publishing & printing; books, periodicals & newspapers
PA: The Full Void 2 Inc
16320 Roscoe Blvd Ste 100
Van Nuys CA 91406
818 891-5999

(G-13329)
BONIDE PRODUCTS INC
6301 Sutliff Rd (13424-4326)
PHONE....................315 736-8231
James J Wurz, *CEO*
Edward T Wurz, *Vice Pres*
Tom Wurz, *Vice Pres*
Nancy Long, *Technical Mgr*
Michael Klein, *Human Res Mgr*
▲ EMP: 200 EST: 1926
SQ FT: 27,000
SALES (est): 65MM **Privately Held**
WEB: www.bonideproducts.com
SIC: **2899** Chemical preparations

(G-13330)
CALDWELL BENNETT INC
Also Called: C B I
6152 County Seat Rd (13424-4308)
P.O. Box 610, Rome (13442-0610)
PHONE....................315 337-8540
Fax: 315 337-0215
Douglas Brazinski, *President*
Brian Branzinski, *Vice Pres*
Brian Brazinski, *Vice Pres*
Joan Brazinski, *Vice Pres*
Paul Brazinski, *Vice Pres*
EMP: 45
SQ FT: 40,000
SALES (est): 9.1MM **Privately Held**
WEB: www.cbicables.com
SIC: **3357** Communication wire

(G-13331)
CPP - STEEL TREATERS
100 Furnace St (13424-4816)
PHONE....................315 736-3081
Fax: 315 736-8849
Joseph Weber, *President*
Pat Fonner, *Vice Pres*
Kevin Thomas, *Vice Pres*
Rob Thompson, *QC Dir*
Ronald Russell, *Treasurer*
EMP: 29 EST: 1957
SQ FT: 4,000
SALES (est): 6.5MM
SALES (corp-wide): 6.3B **Privately Held**
SIC: **3398** Metal heat treating
HQ: Cpp-Syracuse, Inc.
901 E Genesee St
Chittenango NY 13037
315 687-0014

(G-13332)
DAIMLER BUSES NORTH AMER INC
165 Base Rd (13424)
P.O. Box 748 (13424-0748)
PHONE....................315 768-8101
Fax: 315 768-3513
Bernd Voigt, *Ch of Bd*
Andreas Strecker, *President*
Harry Rendel, *CFO*
▲ EMP: 560
SQ FT: 40,000
SALES (est): 68.3MM
SALES (corp-wide): 162B **Privately Held**
WEB: www.orionbus.com
SIC: **3713** 3711 Truck & bus bodies; motor buses, except trackless trollies, assembly of
HQ: Daimler Trucks North America Llc
4555 N Channel Ave
Portland OR 97217
503 745-8000

(G-13333)
FIBER INSTRUMENT SALES INC (PA)
Also Called: F I S
161 Clear Rd (13424-4339)
PHONE....................315 736-2206
Fax: 315 736-2285
Frank Giotto, *President*
Susan Grabinsky, *President*
Kim Teesdale, *President*
Kirk Donley, *Senior VP*
Donley Kirk, *Senior VP*
◆ EMP: 150
SQ FT: 90,000
SALES (est): 57.2MM **Privately Held**
WEB: www.fisfiber.com
SIC: **3661** 3643 2298 3699 Fiber optics communications equipment; connectors & terminals for electrical devices; cable, fiber; security devices

(G-13334)
GOLD MEDAL PACKING INC
8301 Old River Rd (13424)
PHONE....................315 337-1911
Fax: 315 339-5854
Joseph Rocco III, *President*
Nancy Stilwell, *Controller*
Liz Shapano, *Admin Sec*
EMP: 60
SQ FT: 10,000
SALES (est): 9MM **Privately Held**
WEB: www.goldmedalpacking.com
SIC: **2011** Meat packing plants

(G-13335)
INDUSTRIAL OIL TANK SERVICE
120 Dry Rd (13424-4311)
PHONE....................315 736-6080
John E Hitchings Jr, *President*
John E Hitchings Sr, *Admin Sec*
EMP: 10
SQ FT: 11,580
SALES (est): 1.1MM **Privately Held**
SIC: **2992** Re-refining lubricating oils & greases

(G-13336)
ORISKANY ARMS INC
175 Clear Rd (13424-4301)
PHONE....................315 737-2196
Frank Giotto, *CEO*
Jim Rabbia, *President*
EMP: 13
SQ FT: 10,000
SALES (est): 5MM **Privately Held**
SIC: **3484** Guns (firearms) or gun parts, 30 mm. & below

(G-13337)
SEIFERT GRAPHICS INC
Also Called: Seifert Transit Graphics
6133 Judd Rd (13424-4220)
PHONE....................315 736-2744
Fax: 315 736-6602
Karen M Seifert, *President*
Robert J Dunn, *COO*
Emmett Seifert, *Accounts Exec*
Todd Stern, *Manager*
EMP: 15
SQ FT: 20,000
SALES (est): 2.8MM **Privately Held**
WEB: www.seifertgraphics.com
SIC: **2752** Commercial printing, lithographic

(G-13338)
SUIT-KOTE CORPORATION
Also Called: Central Asphalt
191 Dry Rd (13424-4312)
PHONE....................315 735-8501
Fax: 315 735-4604
Lee Wall, *Branch Mgr*
EMP: 13
SALES (corp-wide): 226MM **Privately Held**
WEB: www.suit-kote.com
SIC: **2951** Asphalt paving mixtures & blocks
PA: Suit-Kote Corporation
1911 Lorings Crossing Rd
Cortland NY 13045
607 753-1100

(G-13339)
SUMAX CYCLE PRODUCTS INC
122 Clear Rd (13424-4300)
PHONE....................315 768-1058
Fax: 315 768-1046
Linda Van Scoten, *President*
Kirk Van Scotten, *Vice Pres*
EMP: 16
SQ FT: 11,000
SALES (est): 611.4K **Privately Held**
WEB: www.sumax.com
SIC: **3751** Motorcycles & related parts; motorcycle accessories

(G-13340)
TERAHERTZ TECHNOLOGIES INC
Also Called: T T I
169 Clear Rd (13424-4301)
PHONE....................315 736-3642
John Gentile, *President*
Donald Biron, *Director*
Donna Gentile, *Admin Sec*
EMP: 6
SQ FT: 28,000
SALES: 1.8MM **Privately Held**
WEB: www.terahertztechnologies.com
SIC: **3661** 8742 8731 Fiber optics communications equipment; industrial & labor consulting services; electronic research

(G-13341)
TLC-THE LIGHT CONNECTION INC
132 Base Rd (13424-4204)
PHONE....................315 736-7384

Oriskany Falls - Oneida County (G-13342)

Fax: 315 736-1927
Brian Mohar, *President*
Brain Mohar, *President*
Fritz Barns, *Principal*
Doug Rouse, *Principal*
Keith Vanderzell, *Principal*
EMP: 70
SQ FT: 19,500
SALES (est): 19.5MM
SALES (corp-wide): 57.2MM **Privately Held**
WEB: www.thelightconnection.com
SIC: 3357 Fiber optic cable (insulated)
PA: Fiber Instrument Sales, Inc.
  161 Clear Rd
  Oriskany NY 13424
  315 736-2206

Oriskany Falls
Oneida County

(G-13342)
HANSON AGGREGATES PA LLC
1780 State Route 12b (13425)
PHONE.................315 821-7222
Donald Hennings, *Plant Mgr*
Donald Henings, *Manager*
EMP: 15
SALES (corp-wide): 16B **Privately Held**
SIC: 1442 1429 1422 Common sand mining; grits mining (crushed stone); crushed & broken limestone
HQ: Hanson Aggregates Pennsylvania, Llc
  7660 Imperial Way
  Allentown PA 18195
  610 366-4626

(G-13343)
ZIELINSKIS ASPHALT INC
4989 State Route 12b (13425-4541)
PHONE.................315 306-4057
Kevin J Zielinski, *Principal*
EMP: 12
SALES (est): 2.4MM **Privately Held**
SIC: 2951 Asphalt paving mixtures & blocks

Ossining
Westchester County

(G-13344)
ALLIANCE MAGNETIC LLC
100 Executive Blvd # 202 (10562-2557)
PHONE.................914 944-1690
Martin Kuo,
▲ **EMP:** 5
SALES (est): 527.2K **Privately Held**
WEB: www.alliancemagnetics.net
SIC: 3571 Electronic computers

(G-13345)
CATARACT HOSE CO
Also Called: Cataract Hose Co No 2
6 Waller Ave (10562-4711)
PHONE.................914 941-9019
Louie Diloreto, *President*
EMP: 40
SALES (est): 2.7MM **Privately Held**
SIC: 3052 Fire hose, rubber

(G-13346)
CLEAR CAST TECHNOLOGIES INC (PA)
99 N Water St (10562-3255)
PHONE.................914 945-0848
Fax: 914 945-0436
Peter Goldstein, *President*
Jerry Brown, *General Mgr*
Chris Beigie, *VP Sales*
Janice McAlevy, *Accounts Mgr*
Andy Ramey, *Manager*
▲ **EMP:** 30
SQ FT: 28,000
SALES (est): 6.2MM **Privately Held**
WEB: www.clearcasttech.com
SIC: 3083 Laminated plastics plate & sheet

(G-13347)
METALLIZED CARBON CORPORATION (PA)
Also Called: Metcar Products
19 S Water St (10562-4633)
PHONE.................914 941-3738
Fax: 914 941-4050
Matt Brennan, *Ch of Bd*
Bruce Hard, *General Mgr*
Manuel Debarros, *Prdtn Mgr*
Frank Puentes, *Opers Staff*
Donald Destefano, *Purchasing*
EMP: 140
SQ FT: 50,000
SALES (est): 21.5MM **Privately Held**
WEB: www.carbongraphite.net
SIC: 3624 3568 Electric carbons; carbon specialties for electrical use; fibers, carbon & graphite; power transmission equipment

(G-13348)
OSSINING BAKERY LMP INC
50 N Highland Ave (10562-3432)
PHONE.................914 941-2654
Tony Martins, *President*
EMP: 7 **EST:** 1973
SQ FT: 3,000
SALES: 490K **Privately Held**
SIC: 2051 Bread, cake & related products

(G-13349)
OSSINING VILLAGE OF INC
Also Called: Indian Water Treatment Plant
25 Fowler Ave (10562-1919)
P.O. Box 1166 (10562-0996)
PHONE.................914 202-9668
Fax: 914 923-6239
George Gibson, *Chief*
EMP: 5 **Privately Held**
SIC: 3589 Water treatment equipment, industrial
PA: Ossining, Village Of Inc
  16 Croton Ave Ste 2
  Ossining NY 10562
  914 941-3554

(G-13350)
PAN AMERICAN ROLLER INC
5 Broad Ave (10562-4601)
P.O. Box 1225 (10562-0057)
PHONE.................914 762-8700
Fax: 914 762-8700
Gertrude Wolf, *Corp Secy*
Michael Wolf, *Vice Pres*
Jean Black, *Office Mgr*
EMP: 10
SQ FT: 15,000
SALES: 1MM **Privately Held**
SIC: 3991 Paint rollers

(G-13351)
REMUS INDUSTRIES
11 Oakbrook Rd (10562-2650)
PHONE.................914 906-1544
Robert Leggio, *Principal*
EMP: 8
SALES (est): 839.4K **Privately Held**
SIC: 3999 Manufacturing industries

(G-13352)
SABRA DENTAL PRODUCTS
24 Quail Hollow Rd (10562-2545)
PHONE.................914 945-0836
Adrian Avram, *Owner*
EMP: 2
SALES (est): 1.5MM **Privately Held**
SIC: 3843 Dental equipment & supplies

Oswego
Oswego County

(G-13353)
BATTERY RESEARCH AND TSTG INC
1313 County Route 1 (13126-5999)
Rural Route 1313 Rt1 (13126)
PHONE.................315 342-2373
Fax: 315 342-0797
Patricia I Demar, *CEO*
Petter Demar, *Vice Pres*
Pam Shatrau, *Finance Dir*
Dennis Barber, *Natl Sales Mgr*
Steve Johnson, *Natl Sales Mgr*
EMP: 10
SQ FT: 3,600
SALES: 2MM **Privately Held**
WEB: www.batteryresearch.com
SIC: 3691 Storage batteries

(G-13354)
DESIGNER HARDWOOD FLRG CNY INC
193 E Seneca St (13126-1644)
PHONE.................315 207-0044
Joseph Marmon, *Vice Pres*
EMP: 10 **EST:** 2014
SALES (est): 608.8K **Privately Held**
SIC: 2426 Flooring, hardwood

(G-13355)
DOTTO WAGNER
Also Called: Local News
185 E Seneca St (13126-1600)
P.O. Box 276 (13126-0276)
PHONE.................315 342-8020
Wagner Dotto, *Owner*
Anand Shivnani,
EMP: 6
SALES (est): 664.5K **Privately Held**
WEB: www.cnyfall.com
SIC: 2721 Magazines: publishing only, not printed on site

(G-13356)
ENERGY NUCLEAR OPERATIONS
Also Called: Chemistry Department
268 Lake Rd (13126-6325)
P.O. Box 110, Lycoming (13093-0110)
PHONE.................315 342-0055
Ted Sullivan, *Vice Pres*
EMP: 30
SALES (est): 8.7MM **Privately Held**
SIC: 3443 Nuclear reactors, military or industrial

(G-13357)
HEALTHWAY PRODUCTS COMPANY
249a Mitchell St (13126-1279)
PHONE.................315 207-1410
William O'Hara, *President*
Michael Daly, *Vice Pres*
EMP: 25
SQ FT: 33,000
SALES (est): 3.8MM **Privately Held**
SIC: 3564 3585 Blowers & fans; refrigeration & heating equipment

(G-13358)
INDUSTRIAL PRECISION PDTS INC
350 Mitchell St (13126-1270)
PHONE.................315 343-4421
Fax: 315 342-5662
William J Gallagher, *Chairman*
George Savas, *Controller*
Steve Standish, *Sales Staff*
Chris Fregale, *Office Mgr*
Kevin Doovan, *Manager*
EMP: 20 **EST:** 1951
SQ FT: 26,000
SALES: 1.7MM **Privately Held**
WEB: www.indprecision.com
SIC: 3599 Machine & other job shop work; custom machinery

(G-13359)
LAZAREK INC
209 Erie St (13126-2459)
PHONE.................315 343-1242
Fax: 315 343-2916
Walter Lazarek Jr, *President*
Jean Lararek, *Vice Pres*
Stanley Lazarek, *Admin Sec*
EMP: 5 **EST:** 1936
SQ FT: 950
SALES (est): 705.8K **Privately Held**
SIC: 3273 5032 1442 Ready-mixed concrete; concrete & cinder block; construction sand mining; gravel mining

(G-13360)
MITCHELL PRTG & MAILING INC (PA)
1 Burkle St (13126-3261)
P.O. Box 815 (13126-0815)
PHONE.................315 343-3531
Fax: 315 343-3577
John Henry, *President*
Kathleen Henry, *Vice Pres*
Helen Henry, *Office Mgr*
EMP: 10 **EST:** 1930
SQ FT: 2,112
SALES: 400K **Privately Held**
WEB: www.mpcny.com
SIC: 2752 Commercial printing, offset

(G-13361)
NORTHLAND FILTER INTL LLC
249a Mitchell St (13126-1279)
PHONE.................315 207-1410
Gilles Morin,
◆ **EMP:** 20
SALES (est): 4.5MM **Privately Held**
WEB: www.northlandfilter.com
SIC: 3564 Filters, air: furnaces, air conditioning equipment, etc.

(G-13362)
NOVELIS CORPORATION
448 County Route 1a (13126-5962)
P.O. Box 28 (13126-0028)
PHONE.................315 342-1036
Thomas Walpole, *Engineer*
Larry Hudson, *Engineer*
Gordon Barkley, *Controller*
Mark Dawson, *Personnel*
Bernard Sanders, *Systems Mgr*
EMP: 300
SALES (corp-wide): 5B **Privately Held**
SIC: 3353 Aluminum sheet, plate & foil
HQ: Novelis Corporation
  3560 Lenox Rd Ne Ste 2000
  Atlanta GA 30326
  404 760-4000

(G-13363)
NOVELIS CORPORATION
72 Alcan W Entrance Rd (13126)
P.O. Box 28 (13126-0028)
PHONE.................315 349-0121
Jack Morrison, *Principal*
EMP: 300
SALES (corp-wide): 5B **Privately Held**
SIC: 3353 Aluminum sheet, plate & foil
HQ: Novelis Corporation
  3560 Lenox Rd Ne Ste 2000
  Atlanta GA 30326
  404 760-4000

(G-13364)
NOVELIS INC
448 County Route 1a (13126-5963)
P.O. Box 28 (13126-0028)
PHONE.................315 349-0121
Steve Fisher, *CEO*
Philip Robert Martens, *Ch of Bd*
Michael Herron, *Purch Mgr*
James Brown, *Technology*
▲ **EMP:** 21
SALES (est): 2.8MM **Privately Held**
SIC: 3355 Aluminum rolling & drawing; aluminum ingot

(G-13365)
SAMPLE NEWS GROUP LLC
Also Called: Palladium Times
140 W 1st St (13126-1514)
PHONE.................315 343-3800
Fax: 315 343-0273
John Spalding, *Manager*
Ron Waer, *Manager*
Sarah McCrobie, *Relations*
EMP: 55
SQ FT: 9,620
SALES (corp-wide): 8MM **Privately Held**
WEB: www.gatehousemedia.com
SIC: 2711 2752 Newspapers; commercial printing, lithographic
PA: Sample News Group, L.L.C.
  28 W South St
  Corry PA 16407
  814 665-8291

GEOGRAPHIC SECTION

(G-13366)
SPEEDWAY PRESS INC
Also Called: Mitchell's Speedway Press
1 Burkle St (13126-3271)
P.O. Box 2006 (13126-0606)
PHONE..............................315 343-3531
Fax: 315 342-1363
George Caruso Jr, *President*
Romeo Caruso, *Corp Secy*
Douglas Caruso, *Vice Pres*
Kathy Henry, *VP Sales*
EMP: 9
SQ FT: 9,000
SALES (est): 360K
SALES (corp-wide): 400K **Privately Held**
WEB: www.speedwaypress.com
SIC: 2752 Commercial printing, offset
PA: Mitchell Printing & Mailing, Inc.
1 Burkle St
Oswego NY 13126
315 343-3531

(G-13367)
STONES HOMEMADE CANDIES INC
145 W Bridge St (13126-1440)
PHONE..............................315 343-8401
Margaret Stanchowicz, *President*
Margaret Stachowicz, *President*
EMP: 7 **EST:** 1946
SQ FT: 3,000
SALES (est): 650.3K **Privately Held**
SIC: 2064 Candy & other confectionery products

(G-13368)
SURE-LOCK INDUSTRIES LLC
193 E Seneca St (13126-1644)
PHONE..............................315 207-0044
Fax: 315 207-0400
Art Brown,
Barbara Brown,
Irving Brown,
EMP: 13
SALES (est): 1.6MM **Privately Held**
SIC: 2435 Hardwood veneer & plywood

Otisville
Orange County

(G-13369)
FEDERAL PRISON INDUSTRIES
Also Called: Unicor
2 Mile Dr (10963)
PHONE..............................845 386-6819
William Bondy, *Superintendent*
EMP: 150 **Publicly Held**
WEB: www.unicor.gov
SIC: 3795 Tanks, military, including factory rebuilding
HQ: Federal Prison Industries, Inc
320 1st St Nw
Washington DC 20534
202 305-3500

Ovid
Seneca County

(G-13370)
CROSSWINDS FARM & CREAMERY
6762 Log City Rd (14521-9789)
PHONE..............................607 327-0363
Sarah B Vanorden, *Owner*
EMP: 5
SALES (est): 236.8K **Privately Held**
SIC: 2022 5451 Natural cheese; dairy products stores

(G-13371)
HOSMER INC
Also Called: Hosmer's Winery
6999 State Route 89 (14521-9569)
PHONE..............................888 467-9363
Cameron Hosmer, *President*
Maren Hosmer, *Vice Pres*
Virginia Graber, *Manager*
EMP: 15
SALES: 500K **Privately Held**
WEB: www.hosmerwinery.com
SIC: 2084 Wines

(G-13372)
SENECA COUNTY AREA SHOPPER
1885 State Route 96a (14521-9712)
PHONE..............................607 532-4333
Joan E Hendrix, *Principal*
EMP: 5
SALES (est): 261.9K **Privately Held**
SIC: 2711 Newspapers, publishing & printing

(G-13373)
SHELDRAKE POINT VINEYARD LLC
Also Called: Sheldrake Point Winery
7448 County Road 153 (14521-9564)
PHONE..............................607 532-8967
Fax: 607 532-8967
Robert Madill, *General Mgr*
EMP: 10
SQ FT: 4,063
SALES: 800K **Privately Held**
SIC: 2084 Wines

(G-13374)
THIRSTY OWL WINE COMPANY
6861 State Route 89 (14521-9599)
PHONE..............................607 869-5805
Fax: 607 869-5851
Jonathan C Cupp, *President*
John Cupp, *President*
Mary Dauber, *Manager*
EMP: 7
SALES (est): 628K **Privately Held**
WEB: www.thirstyowl.com
SIC: 2084 Wines

Owego
Tioga County

(G-13375)
APPLIED TECHNOLOGY MFG CORP
71 Temple St (13827-1338)
P.O. Box 189 (13827-0189)
PHONE..............................607 687-2200
Fax: 607 687-8145
Stephen M Lounsberry III, *President*
Peter C Lounsberry, *Vice Pres*
Doug Bidwell, *QC Mgr*
Steve Bean, *Manager*
EMP: 30 **EST:** 1927
SQ FT: 25,000
SALES (est): 7.9MM **Privately Held**
WEB: www.appliedtechmfg.com
SIC: 3531 3599 Railway track equipment; railroad related equipment; machine & other job shop work

(G-13376)
C & C READY-MIX CORPORATION
3818 Rt 17 C (13827)
P.O. Box 174 (13827-0174)
PHONE..............................607 687-1690
Fax: 607 687-7152
Andy Cerretani, *Enginr/R&D Mgr*
EMP: 16
SALES (corp-wide): 5.3MM **Privately Held**
WEB: www.ccreadymix.com
SIC: 3273 2951 Ready-mixed concrete; asphalt paving mixtures & blocks
PA: C & C Ready-Mix Corporation
3112 Vestal Rd
Vestal NY 13850
607 797-5108

(G-13377)
INDUSTRIAL PAINT SERVICES CORP
60 W Main St 62 (13827-1537)
PHONE..............................607 687-0107
Fax: 607 687-0208
Jean Chapman, *President*
John Spencer, *General Mgr*
Margo Padgett, *Supervisor*
EMP: 17
SQ FT: 20,000
SALES (est): 1.7MM **Privately Held**
WEB: www.ipsowego.com
SIC: 3479 Painting of metal products

(G-13378)
KYOCERA PRECISION TOOLS INC
Also Called: New York Division
1436 Taylor Rd (13827-1833)
PHONE..............................607 687-0012
Stephen Hansen, *Branch Mgr*
EMP: 14
SALES (corp-wide): 12.5B **Publicly Held**
WEB: www.tycom.com
SIC: 3541 Machine tools, metal cutting type
HQ: Kyocera Precision Tools, Inc
102 Industrial Park Rd
Hendersonville NC 28792
800 823-7284

(G-13379)
LOCKHEED MARTIN CORPORATION
1801 State Route 17 (13827)
PHONE..............................607 751-2000
Dustin Vantassel, *Engineer*
Bryan Ruskavich, *Mktg Dir*
Joseph Trench, *Manager*
Martin Patchett, *Manager*
Mike McNeil, *Senior Mgr*
EMP: 1261 **Publicly Held**
WEB: www.lockheedmartin.com
SIC: 3812 3761 Search & navigation equipment; guided missiles & space vehicles
PA: Lockheed Martin Corporation
6801 Rockledge Dr
Bethesda MD 20817

(G-13380)
LOCKHEED MARTIN CORPORATION
Also Called: Mission Systems & Training
1801 State Rd 17c 17 C (13827)
PHONE..............................607 751-7434
Deborah Zacharias, *Manager*
EMP: 100 **Publicly Held**
WEB: www.lockheedmartin.com
SIC: 3812 3761 Search & navigation equipment; guided missiles & space vehicles
PA: Lockheed Martin Corporation
6801 Rockledge Dr
Bethesda MD 20817

(G-13381)
NATIONAL PAPER CONVERTING INC
207 Corporate Dr (13827-3249)
PHONE..............................607 687-6049
Eric Kretzmer, *President*
EMP: 5
SQ FT: 8,000
SALES (est): 837.5K **Privately Held**
WEB: www.nationaladh.com
SIC: 2621 Absorbent paper

(G-13382)
NORWESCO INC
263 Corporate Dr (13827-3249)
PHONE..............................607 687-8081
Fax: 607 687-7585
Rich Barto, *Manager*
EMP: 11
SALES (corp-wide): 44.1MM **Privately Held**
WEB: www.ncmmolding.com
SIC: 3089 Plastic & fiberglass tanks
PA: Norwesco, Inc.
4365 Steiner St
Saint Bonifacius MN 55375
952 446-1945

(G-13383)
OWEGO PENNYSAVER PRESS INC
181 Front St (13827-1520)
PHONE..............................607 687-2434
Fax: 607 687-6858
George V Lynett, *President*
EMP: 10
SALES (est): 534.5K
SALES (corp-wide): 11.8MM **Privately Held**
WEB: www.sundayreview.com
SIC: 2711 Newspapers, publishing & printing
PA: Towanda Printing Co Inc
116 N Main St
Towanda PA 18848
570 265-2151

(G-13384)
SANMINA CORPORATION
1200 Taylor Rd (13827-1292)
PHONE..............................607 689-5000
Fax: 607 689-5903
James Griffin, *Vice Pres*
Ed Fisher, *Purch Agent*
Brian Barber, *Purchasing*
Chuck Pigos, *Senior Engr*
Theresa Nugent, *Human Res Mgr*
EMP: 500
SALES (corp-wide): 6.4B **Publicly Held**
WEB: www.sanmina.com
SIC: 3672 Printed circuit boards
PA: Sanmina Corporation
2700 N 1st St
San Jose CA 95134
408 964-3500

(G-13385)
TIOGA COUNTY COURIER
59 Church St (13827-1439)
PHONE..............................607 687-0108
Mary Jones, *Owner*
EMP: 5
SALES (est): 224.6K **Privately Held**
SIC: 2711 Newspapers: publishing only, not printed on site

(G-13386)
WAGNER MILLWORK INC
Also Called: Wagner Lumber
4060 Gaskill Rd (13827-4741)
PHONE..............................607 687-5362
Fax: 607 687-2633
Steven Schaeffer, *Vice Pres*
Terry Bouck, *Buyer*
Ernie Creeden, *Buyer*
Rob Humphrey, *Buyer*
Steve Houseknecht, *Sales Staff*
▼ **EMP:** 70
SQ FT: 60,000
SALES (est): 21.5MM **Privately Held**
WEB: www.wagnerlumber.com
SIC: 2421 2431 2426 Sawmills & planing mills, general; millwork; hardwood dimension & flooring mills

(G-13387)
WHOLESALE MULCH & SAWDUST INC
Also Called: Tioga County Waste Wood Recycl
3711 Waverly Rd (13827-2860)
PHONE..............................607 687-2637
Fax: 607 687-1907
Philip Nestor, *President*
Cynthia Nestor, *Vice Pres*
EMP: 5
SQ FT: 1,624
SALES (est): 460K **Privately Held**
SIC: 2499 Mulch or sawdust products, wood

Oxford
Chenango County

(G-13388)
AUTOMECHA INTERNATIONAL LTD (PA)
48 S Canal St (13830-4318)
P.O. Box 660 (13830-0660)
PHONE..............................607 843-2235
Fax: 607 843-7075
Kenneth E St John, *President*
Kevin Gates, *Controller*
Mike Sawyer, *Manager*
Norell Bates, *Admin Sec*
Sonjia Strobach, *Admin Sec*
EMP: 28
SQ FT: 23,000

Oxford - Chenango County (G-13389)

SALES (est): 4.8MM **Privately Held**
WEB: www.asmarc.com
SIC: 3579 5044 3565 3554 Addressing machines, plates & plate embossers; address labeling machines; mailing, letter handling & addressing machines; office equipment; packaging machinery; paper industries machinery

(G-13389)
RAPID REPRODUCTIONS LLC
4511 State Hwy 12 (13830)
PHONE 607 843-2221
Fax: 607 843-6487
Barbara Blackman, *General Mgr*
Bryant Latourette, *Mng Member*
EMP: 8
SQ FT: 11,000
SALES (est): 680K **Privately Held**
SIC: 2752 Commercial printing, lithographic

Oyster Bay
Nassau County

(G-13390)
AMERICAN TRANS-COIL CORP
Also Called: A T C
69 Hamilton Ave Ste 3 (11771-1573)
P.O. Box 629 (11771-0629)
PHONE 516 922-9640
Fax: 516 922-3361
Mark Masin, *President*
William Rogers, *Principal*
Robert Booker, *Purch Agent*
Ken Winheim, *Design Engr*
Stewart Goldberg, *Analyst*
EMP: 15 **EST:** 1960
SQ FT: 5,000
SALES (est): 2.3MM **Privately Held**
WEB: www.atc-us.com
SIC: 3677 Electronic coils, transformers & other inductors

(G-13391)
APOTHECUS PHARMACEUTICAL CORP (PA)
220 Townsend Sq (11771-2339)
PHONE 516 624-8200
Thomas Leon, *Ch of Bd*
Daniel Leon, *President*
Jonathan Leon, *Vice Pres*
Paul Gabel, *VP Opers*
Michael Lesser, *CFO*
EMP: 14
SQ FT: 7,000
SALES (est): 4.6MM **Privately Held**
WEB: www.apothecus.com
SIC: 2834 5122 Pharmaceutical preparations; proprietary (patent) medicines

(G-13392)
ART LEATHER MFG CO INC
69 Hamilton Ave Ste 2 (11771-1573)
PHONE 516 867-4716
Mark Roberts, *President*
Mitchell Lubow, *CFO*
▲ **EMP:** 569 **EST:** 1929
SQ FT: 240,000
SALES (est): 36.4MM **Privately Held**
WEB: www.eframe.com
SIC: 2782 3199 3172 Albums; novelties, leather; personal leather goods

(G-13393)
CIRCO FILE CORP
Also Called: Circo-O-File
69 Hamilton Ave Ste 1 (11771-1573)
PHONE 516 922-1848
Thomas Carrella, *President*
Ralph Carrella, *Shareholder*
EMP: 7 **EST:** 1955
SQ FT: 2,000
SALES (est): 1MM **Privately Held**
WEB: www.circofile.com
SIC: 3423 3545 Hand & edge tools; machine tool accessories

(G-13394)
COMANDER TERMINALS LLC
1 Commander Sq (11771-1536)
PHONE 516 922-7600
Abrham Prznaski, *President*
EMP: 14
SALES (est): 1.4MM **Privately Held**
SIC: 2843 Oils & greases

(G-13395)
ENGINEERING MAINT PDTS INC
Also Called: Hippo Industries
250 Berry Hill Rd (11771-3121)
P.O. Box 548 (11771-0548)
PHONE 516 624-9774
Fax: 516 624-9860
Ansuya Dave, *President*
Peter Dave, *Vice Pres*
Shashidhar H Dave, *Vice Pres*
EMP: 14
SQ FT: 4,000
SALES (est): 4MM **Privately Held**
SIC: 2899 5169 Corrosion preventive lubricant; anti-corrosion products

(G-13396)
IMREX LLC (PA)
55 Sandy Hill Rd (11771-3110)
P.O. Box 154 (11771-0154)
PHONE 516 479-3675
Jacob Armon, *Mng Member*
Harry Armon,
Alan J Weiss,
EMP: 350
SQ FT: 32,000
SALES (est): 53.5MM **Privately Held**
WEB: www.imrex.com
SIC: 3679 Electronic circuits

(G-13397)
MILL-MAX MFG CORP
190 Pine Hollow Rd (11771-4711)
P.O. Box 300 (11771-0300)
PHONE 516 922-6000
Fax: 516 922-9253
Roger L Bahnik, *Ch of Bd*
James W Litke, *President*
Claude A Bahnik, *Vice Pres*
Bradley E Kuczinski, *Vice Pres*
Marge Ruzicka, *Purchasing*
▲ **EMP:** 190
SQ FT: 135,000
SALES (est): 49.2MM **Privately Held**
WEB: www.mil-max.com
SIC: 3678 5065 Electronic connectors; electronic parts & equipment

(G-13398)
MIRODDI IMAGING INC (PA)
Also Called: M Squared Graphics
27 Centre View Dr (11771-2815)
PHONE 516 624-6898
Cherrise Miroddi, *Ch of Bd*
EMP: 2
SQ FT: 8,000
SALES (est): 1MM **Privately Held**
WEB: www.msquaredgraphics.com
SIC: 2796 Gravure printing plates or cylinders, preparation of

(G-13399)
PRINTERY
Also Called: Printing House of W S Miller
43 W Main St (11771-2215)
PHONE 516 922-3250
Fax: 516 922-2823
William Miller, *President*
Mary Abbene, *Vice Pres*
EMP: 5 **EST:** 1973
SALES (est): 522.7K **Privately Held**
SIC: 2759 2791 Card printing & engraving, except greeting; typesetting

(G-13400)
R F GIARDINA CO
200 Lexington Ave Apt 3a (11771-2114)
P.O. Box 562 (11771-0562)
PHONE 516 922-1364
Robert Giardina, *President*
EMP: 10
SALES (est): 753.2K **Privately Held**
WEB: www.rfgco.com
SIC: 3944 Craft & hobby kits & sets

Ozone Park
Queens County

(G-13401)
ABIGAL PRESS INC
9735 133rd Ave (11417-2119)
P.O. Box 170704 (11417-0704)
PHONE 718 641-5350
Salvatore Stratis, *CEO*
Jeff Gaines, *President*
Jeffrey Gaines, *President*
Lois Berl, *Vice Pres*
Angela Zuniga, *Purchasing*
◆ **EMP:** 98 **EST:** 1956
SQ FT: 30,000
SALES (est): 13.5MM **Privately Held**
WEB: www.abigal.com
SIC: 2759 Card printing & engraving, except greeting

(G-13402)
CENTRE INTERIORS WDWKG CO INC
10001 103rd Ave (11417-1712)
PHONE 718 323-1343
Fax: 718 323-1856
Alex Lee, *President*
EMP: 20
SALES (est): 3.5MM **Privately Held**
SIC: 2521 Wood office desks & tables

(G-13403)
ELEVATOR VENTURES CORPORATION
Also Called: Ver-Tech Elevator
9720 99th St (11416-2602)
PHONE 212 375-1900
Fax: 718 850-9533
Don Gelestino, *Owner*
Don Celestino, *General Mgr*
Jonathan Gatmaitan, *Manager*
EMP: 99
SALES (est): 10.2MM **Privately Held**
SIC: 3534 Elevators & moving stairways

(G-13404)
FASTENER DIMENSIONS INC
9403 104th St (11416-1723)
PHONE 718 847-6321
Fax: 718 847-8414
Darryl A Hinkle, *President*
Debbie Blizzard, *Manager*
EMP: 35
SQ FT: 24,000
SALES (est): 3.2MM **Privately Held**
WEB: www.fastdim.com
SIC: 3429 5085 5088 3452 Aircraft hardware; fasteners, industrial: nuts, bolts, screws, etc.; aircraft equipment & supplies; bolts, nuts, rivets & washers

(G-13405)
FOOD GEMS LTD
8423 Rockaway Blvd (11416-1249)
PHONE 718 296-7788
Fax: 718 296-7788
Bradley Stroll, *President*
Frank Kurt, *Vice Pres*
Jean Walker, *Manager*
EMP: 24
SQ FT: 10,000
SALES (est): 1.2MM **Privately Held**
WEB: www.foodgems.com
SIC: 2051 5812 Bread, cake & related products; eating places

(G-13406)
JOLDESON ONE AEROSPACE INDS
Also Called: Joldeson One Aerospace Inds
10002 103rd Ave (11417-1713)
PHONE 718 848-7396
Fax: 718 848-7396
Ecatarina Joldeson, *President*
George Joldeson, *Vice Pres*
Richard Joldeson, *Admin Sec*
EMP: 93
SALES: 8.5MM **Privately Held**
SIC: 3728 3496 3812 3643 Aircraft parts & equipment; woven wire products; search & navigation equipment; current-carrying wiring devices; conveyors & conveying equipment; partitions & fixtures, except wood

(G-13407)
JULIA KNIT INC
8050 Pitkin Ave (11417-1211)
PHONE 718 848-1900
Avraham Lip, *President*
▲ **EMP:** 6
SALES (est): 1.3MM **Privately Held**
SIC: 2253 Sweaters & sweater coats, knit

(G-13408)
KW DISTRIBUTORS GROUP INC
9018 Liberty Ave (11417-1350)
PHONE 718 843-3500
Vito Altesi, *President*
Daniel Altesi, *Corp Secy*
Riccardo Altesi, *Vice Pres*
▲ **EMP:** 10
SQ FT: 3,600
SALES (est): 820K **Privately Held**
SIC: 2434 Wood kitchen cabinets

(G-13409)
MAMITAS ICES LTD
10411 100th St (11417-2206)
PHONE 718 738-3238
Fax: 718 738-0784
Javier Morel, *Partner*
◆ **EMP:** 10
SALES (est): 780K **Privately Held**
SIC: 2097 Manufactured ice

(G-13410)
PREMIER KNITS LTD
9735 133rd Ave (11417-2119)
PHONE 718 323-8264
Fax: 718 323-8274
Panta Ardeljan, *President*
Petar Ardeljan Jr, *Vice Pres*
EMP: 10
SQ FT: 35,000
SALES (est): 610K **Privately Held**
WEB: www.premierknits.com
SIC: 2253 5199 Sweaters & sweater coats, knit; knit goods

(G-13411)
ROBERT COHEN
Also Called: Allied Orthopedics
10540 Rockaway Blvd Ste A (11417-2304)
PHONE 718 789-0996
Fax: 718 789-3716
Robert F Cohen, *Owner*
EMP: 6
SQ FT: 4,000
SALES (est): 587.9K **Privately Held**
SIC: 3842 Limbs, artificial; braces, orthopedic

(G-13412)
WALL TOOL & TAPE CORP
Also Called: Wall Tool Manufacturing
8111 101st Ave (11416-2008)
P.O. Box 20637, Floral Park (11002-0637)
PHONE 718 641-6813
Fax: 718 641-6758
Dorothy Kaliades, *President*
Steven Kaliades, *Sales Mgr*
EMP: 20
SQ FT: 12,000
SALES (est): 3.2MM **Privately Held**
SIC: 3423 Edge tools for woodworking: augers, bits, gimlets, etc.

(G-13413)
WORKSMAN TRADING CORP
Also Called: Worksman Cycles
9415 100th St (11416-1707)
PHONE 718 322-2000
Jeffrey A Mishkin, *President*
Wayne Sosin, *President*
Donnalee Quintana, *General Mgr*
Al Venditti, *General Mgr*
Brian Mishkin, *Vice Pres*
▲ **EMP:** 50 **EST:** 1898
SQ FT: 100,000

GEOGRAPHIC SECTION

SALES (est): 15MM **Privately Held**
SIC: 3751 5962 5091 5941 Motorcycles, bicycles & parts; merchandising machine operators; bicycle equipment & supplies; bicycle & bicycle parts

(G-13414)
ZONE FABRICATORS INC
10780 101st St (11417-2609)
PHONE..................718 272-0200
Peter Scaminaci, *President*
Frances Hultin, *Vice Pres*
James Matera, *Opers Mgr*
Matt Vowell, *Manager*
EMP: 16
SQ FT: 8,000
SALES (est): 1.7MM **Privately Held**
WEB: www.zonefabinc.com
SIC: 3089 3443 Plastic processing; metal parts

Painted Post
Steuben County

(G-13415)
AUTOMATED CELLS & EQP INC
9699 Enterprise Dr (14870-9166)
PHONE..................607 936-1341
James Morris, *President*
Charlie Claes, *Engineer*
Dylan Kephart, *Engineer*
Eric Mahon, *Design Engr*
Mindi McCann, *Controller*
EMP: 38
SQ FT: 27,000
SALES (est): 10.9MM **Privately Held**
WEB: www.autocells.com
SIC: 3569 5084 Robots, assembly line: industrial & commercial; robots, industrial

(G-13416)
CORNING INCORPORATED
905 Addison Rd (14870-9726)
PHONE..................607 974-1274
Julie Frey, *Engineer*
John Rector, *Project Engr*
Richard Jack, *Branch Mgr*
EMP: 50
SALES (corp-wide): 9.3B **Publicly Held**
WEB: www.corning.com
SIC: 3229 3264 Pressed & blown glass; porcelain electrical supplies
PA: Corning Incorporated
    1 Riverfront Plz
    Corning NY 14831
    607 974-9000

(G-13417)
CORNING INCORPORATED
9261 Addison Rd (14870-9650)
PHONE..................607 974-6729
Jim Blade, *Principal*
Thomas Moag, *Engineer*
EMP: 5
SALES (corp-wide): 9.3B **Publicly Held**
WEB: www.corning.com
SIC: 3357 3661 3211 3229 Fiber optic cable (insulated); telephone & telegraph apparatus; flat glass; pressed & blown glass; semiconductors & related devices; analytical instruments
PA: Corning Incorporated
    1 Riverfront Plz
    Corning NY 14831
    607 974-9000

(G-13418)
PACE MANUFACTURING COMPANY
894 Addison Rd (14870-9726)
PHONE..................607 936-0431
Dennis Friends, *Branch Mgr*
EMP: 5
SALES (corp-wide): 7.4MM **Privately Held**
SIC: 2048 5191 Prepared feeds; animal feeds
HQ: Pace Manufacturing Company Inc
    30 N Harrison St Ste 2
    Easton MD 21601

(G-13419)
SCHULER-HAAS ELECTRIC CORP
598 Ritas Way (14870-8546)
PHONE..................607 936-3514
EMP: 7
SALES (corp-wide): 21MM **Privately Held**
SIC: 3699 1731 Electrical equipment & supplies; electrical work
PA: Schuler-Haas Electric Corp.
    240 Commerce Dr
    Rochester NY 14623
    585 325-1060

(G-13420)
SIRIANNI HARDWOODS INC
912 Addison Rd (14870-9729)
PHONE..................607 962-4688
Fax: 607 936-6237
James Sirianni, *CEO*
Mary Sirianni, *Corp Secy*
Tom Armentano, *Purch Agent*
Keith McPherson, *Sales Mgr*
Ann Short, *Manager*
EMP: 24
SQ FT: 69,024
SALES (est): 3.5MM **Privately Held**
WEB: www.siriannihardwoods.com
SIC: 2426 Lumber, hardwood dimension

Palatine Bridge
Montgomery County

(G-13421)
LEE NEWSPAPERS INC
6113 State Highway 5 (13428)
PHONE..................518 673-3237
Fred Lee, *Principal*
EMP: 11
SALES (est): 734K **Privately Held**
SIC: 2711 Newspapers

(G-13422)
LEE PUBLICATIONS INC (PA)
Also Called: Waste Management
6113 State Highway 5 (13428-2809)
P.O. Box 121 (13428-0121)
PHONE..................518 673-3237
Fax: 518 673-2322
Fred Lee, *President*
Bruce Button, *Division Mgr*
Janet Lee Button, *Treasurer*
Robert Moyer, *Controller*
John Snyder, *Sales Mgr*
EMP: 99
SQ FT: 25,000
SALES (est): 10.8MM **Privately Held**
WEB: www.leepub.com
SIC: 2711 Newspapers, publishing & printing

Palenville
Greene County

(G-13423)
NATIONAL PARACHUTE INDUSTRIES
Also Called: National Parachute Industry
78 White Rd Extensio (12463)
P.O. Box 245 (12463-0245)
PHONE..................908 782-1646
Larry Krueger, *President*
Jeanette Krueger, *Admin Sec*
EMP: 20 **EST:** 1976
SQ FT: 6,000
SALES (est): 1.2MM **Privately Held**
SIC: 2399 Parachutes

(G-13424)
PRECISION TOOL AND MFG
314 Pennsylvania Ave (12463-2615)
P.O. Box 160 (12463-0160)
PHONE..................518 678-3130
Fax: 518 678-3570
Alan Schneck, *President*
EMP: 27
SALES (est): 3.2MM **Privately Held**
SIC: 3599 Machine shop, jobbing & repair

Palisades
Rockland County

(G-13425)
ADVANCED DISTRIBUTION SYSTEM
275 Oak Tree Rd (10964-1003)
PHONE..................845 848-2357
Jean Higgins, *Manager*
Ron Gittens, *Manager*
Chris Sheldon, *Manager*
Tomaj Vadasz, *Info Tech Dir*
▲ EMP: 80
SALES (est): 5.4MM **Privately Held**
SIC: 3084 Plastics pipe

(G-13426)
HISTORY PUBLISHING COMPANY LLC
173 Route 9w (10964-1616)
P.O. Box 700 (10964-0700)
PHONE..................845 398-8161
Carolyn Winter, *Publisher*
Don Bracken, *Mng Member*
EMP: 6
SALES (est): 459.1K **Privately Held**
WEB: www.historypublishingco.com
SIC: 2741 Posters: publishing only, not printed on site

(G-13427)
SKAE POWER SOLUTIONS LLC (PA)
348 Route 9w (10964-1200)
P.O. Box 615 (10964-0615)
PHONE..................845 365-9103
Chris Morzello, *Engineer*
Michael Patrizio, *Engineer*
Anthony Russo, *Engineer*
Jason Ketcham, *Electrical Engi*
Daniel Taylor, *Electrical Engi*
EMP: 30
SQ FT: 6,000
SALES (est): 7.9MM **Privately Held**
WEB: www.skaepower.com
SIC: 3699 8711 Electrical equipment & supplies; consulting engineer

(G-13428)
TRI VALLEY IRON INC
700 Oak Tree Rd (10964-1533)
P.O. Box 234 (10964-0234)
PHONE..................845 365-1013
Nancy Bucciarelli, *President*
James McCarthy, *Vice Pres*
EMP: 15
SALES: 1.5MM **Privately Held**
SIC: 3312 Bars, iron: made in steel mills

(G-13429)
VELL COMPANY INC
700 Oak Tree Rd (10964-1533)
P.O. Box 622 (10964-0622)
PHONE..................845 365-1013
Larry Bucciarelli, *Principal*
EMP: 8
SALES (est): 1MM **Privately Held**
SIC: 3312 Bars & bar shapes, steel, hot-rolled

Palmyra
Wayne County

(G-13430)
FARADYNE MOTORS LLC
Also Called: Juan Motors
2077 Division St (14522-9211)
PHONE..................315 331-5985
Mellisa Kidd, *Mng Member*
Juan Lugo, *Mng Member*
Kathy Cox, *Manager*
Colin R Sabol, *Director*
▲ EMP: 14
SQ FT: 28,000
SALES (est): 4.3MM **Privately Held**
WEB: www.faradynemotors.com
SIC: 3621 Motors & generators

(G-13431)
FINZER HOLDING LLC
Also Called: Finzer Roller New York
2085 Division St (14522-9211)
PHONE..................315 597-1147
David Finzer, *President*
Kevin Byer, *Plant Mgr*
Grace Devito, *Accountant*
Brian La Due, *Financial Exec*
EMP: 27
SALES (corp-wide): 13.2MM **Privately Held**
SIC: 3069 3061 Roll coverings, rubber; mechanical rubber goods
PA: Finzer Holding Llc
    129 Rawls Rd
    Des Plaines IL 60018
    847 390-6200

(G-13432)
GARLOCK SEALING TECH LLC
1666 Division St (14522-9350)
PHONE..................315 597-4811
Paul Baldetti, *President*
Ray Davis, *Vice Pres*
James Erven, *Vice Pres*
Al Lariviere, *Vice Pres*
K B Schoenfelder, *Vice Pres*
EMP: 950
SALES (corp-wide): 1.1B **Publicly Held**
SIC: 3053 Gaskets, packing & sealing devices
HQ: Garlock Sealing Technologies Llc
    1666 Division St
    Palmyra NY 14522
    315 597-4811

(G-13433)
GENTNER PRECISION COMPONENTS
406 Stafford Rd (14522-9426)
PHONE..................315 597-5734
Richard Genter, *President*
John E Gentner Jr, *Principal*
EMP: 5
SALES (est): 421.3K **Privately Held**
SIC: 3599 Machine & other job shop work

(G-13434)
JRLON INC
4344 Fox Rd (14522-9423)
P.O. Box 244 (14522-0244)
PHONE..................315 597-4067
Fax: 315 597-9781
James F Redmond, *President*
Lindsey Redmond, *Corp Secy*
Jerry Sprague, *Engineer*
Brandon Redmond, *Marketing Mgr*
Chad Redmond, *Manager*
▲ EMP: 80 **EST:** 1981
SQ FT: 60,000
SALES (est): 18.1MM **Privately Held**
WEB: www.jrlon.com
SIC: 2821 3566 3479 3462 Molding compounds, plastics; gears, power transmission, except automotive; painting, coating & hot dipping; iron & steel forgings; paints & allied products

(G-13435)
KYLE R LAWRENCE ELECTRIC INC
101 Hyde Pkwy (14522-1209)
PHONE..................315 502-4181
Kyle R Lawrence, *Ch of Bd*
EMP: 5
SALES (est): 361.7K **Privately Held**
SIC: 3699 Electrical equipment & supplies

(G-13436)
LABCO OF PALMYRA INC
904 Canandaigua Rd (14522-9701)
P.O. Box 216 (14522-0216)
PHONE..................315 597-5202
Fax: 315 597-2112
Gary Laberge, *President*
Lynette McTigue, *Vice Pres*
Sharyl Digiovanni, *Treasurer*
Marybeth Laberge, *Admin Sec*
EMP: 12 **EST:** 1956
SQ FT: 7,800
SALES (est): 1.7MM **Privately Held**
WEB: www.labco-ny.com
SIC: 3599 Machine shop, jobbing & repair

Palmyra - Wayne County (G-13437)

(G-13437)
MODERN COATING AND RESEARCH
400 E Main St (14522-1132)
PHONE.................................315 597-3517
Fax: 315 597-6045
James Deagman, *President*
Jae Chatfield, *Office Mgr*
Ed Meyer, *Director*
James Hollingsworth, *Shareholder*
Kevin Marvin, *Administration*
EMP: 11
SQ FT: 26,000
SALES: 700K **Privately Held**
WEB: www.moderncoatings.com
SIC: 3479 Coating of metals & formed products

(G-13438)
PAUL T FREUND CORPORATION (PA)
216 Park Dr (14522-1114)
P.O. Box 475 (14522-0475)
PHONE.................................315 597-4873
Fax: 315 597-4188
Dennis Baron, *President*
Paul T Freund Jr, *Corp Secy*
Thomas Farnham, *Vice Pres*
▲ **EMP:** 85
SQ FT: 126,000
SALES (est): 7.2MM **Privately Held**
WEB: www.freundcarton.com
SIC: 2652 Filing boxes, paperboard: made from purchased materials

Parish
Oswego County

(G-13439)
BIOSPHERIX LTD
Also Called: Biospherix Medical
25 Union St (13131)
PHONE.................................315 387-3414
Randy Yerden, *Ch of Bd*
Mark Simpson, *Human Res Dir*
Ray Gould, *Sales Mgr*
Krystal Ketnourath, *Sales Staff*
Kayla Nolan, *Sales Associate*
EMP: 50
SQ FT: 30,000
SALES (est): 10.6MM **Privately Held**
WEB: www.biospherix.com
SIC: 3821 Laboratory equipment: fume hoods, distillation racks, etc.

Patchogue
Suffolk County

(G-13440)
BAKERY INNOVATIVE TECH CORP
139 N Ocean Ave (11772-2018)
PHONE.................................631 758-3081
Fax: 631 758-3779
Robert White, *President*
Robert Andersen, *Engineer*
Maryann Rose, *Manager*
EMP: 15
SQ FT: 8,000
SALES: 1.5MM **Privately Held**
WEB: www.bit-corp.com
SIC: 3625 Motor control accessories, including overload relays

(G-13441)
BAYSHORE ELECTRIC MOTORS
Also Called: Bayshore Motors
33 Suffolk Ave (11772-1651)
PHONE.................................631 475-1397
Paul Phillips, *Owner*
EMP: 5
SALES (est): 220.1K **Privately Held**
SIC: 7694 Electric motor repair

(G-13442)
CLASSIC LABELS INC
217 River Ave (11772-3312)
PHONE.................................631 467-2300
Fax: 718 358-3262
John Orta, *President*
EMP: 21 **EST:** 1978
SQ FT: 29,000
SALES (est): 2.4MM **Privately Held**
WEB: www.classiclabels.com
SIC: 2759 2891 2672 2671 Labels & seals: printing; adhesives & sealants; coated & laminated paper; packaging paper & plastics film, coated & laminated

(G-13443)
DEPOT LABEL COMPANY INC
Also Called: Colonial Label
217 River Ave (11772-3312)
PHONE.................................631 467-2952
Mike Juliano, *President*
Russell England, *Branch Mgr*
EMP: 7
SALES (est): 1.8MM **Privately Held**
SIC: 2679 5013 2671 2241 Tags & labels, paper; automotive supplies & parts; packaging paper & plastics film, coated & laminated; narrow fabric mills

(G-13444)
EQUICHECK LLC
20 Medford Ave Ste 7 (11772-1220)
PHONE.................................631 987-6356
Fax: 631 447-0084
Warren Rothstein, *Owner*
EMP: 5
SALES (est): 300K **Privately Held**
WEB: www.equicheck.com
SIC: 3851 Lens coating, ophthalmic

(G-13445)
GEM WEST INC
Also Called: Cya Action Funwell
433 E Main St Unit 1 (11772-3177)
PHONE.................................631 567-4228
Sylvia Stephanie, *President*
EMP: 6
SALES (est): 261.6K **Privately Held**
SIC: 2759 Commercial printing

(G-13446)
GROVER ALUMINUM PRODUCTS INC
Also Called: Grover Home Headquarters
577 Medford Ave (11772-1307)
PHONE.................................631 475-3500
Fax: 631 475-3569
Arthur R Spencer, *President*
Irving Fine, *Corp Secy*
Lorrine Heuthe, *Bookkeeper*
EMP: 20 **EST:** 1956
SQ FT: 20,000
SALES (est): 3.3MM **Privately Held**
WEB: www.groverhome.com
SIC: 3442 Louver windows, metal; metal doors

(G-13447)
HIGH TIMES VAPE
500 Medford Ave Ste 1 (11772-1854)
PHONE.................................631 569-5322
EMP: 9
SALES (est): 112.3K **Privately Held**
SIC: 3999 Cigar & cigarette holders

(G-13448)
HOPTRON BREWTIQUE
22 W Main St Ste 11 (11772-3007)
PHONE.................................631 438-0296
Amanda Danielsen, *Owner*
EMP: 8
SALES (est): 578.5K **Privately Held**
SIC: 2082 5182 Beer (alcoholic beverage); wine coolers, alcoholic

(G-13449)
INNER-PAK CONTAINER INC
116 West Ave (11772-3525)
PHONE.................................631 289-9700
Fax: 631 289-9797
Judith M Nadler, *Ch of Bd*
EMP: 15
SALES (est): 2.9MM **Privately Held**
SIC: 2653 5113 Boxes, corrugated: made from purchased materials; corrugated & solid fiber boxes

(G-13450)
JABO AGRICULTURAL INC
9 Northwood Ln (11772-2228)
PHONE.................................631 475-1800
Robert Muchnick, *CEO*
Jacob Gurewich, *President*
EMP: 5
SQ FT: 1,000
SALES (est): 226.8K **Privately Held**
SIC: 2452 Farm & agricultural buildings, prefabricated wood

(G-13451)
JOHN LOR PUBLISHING LTD
Also Called: Islip Bulletin
20 Medford Ave Ste 1 (11772-1220)
P.O. Box 780 (11772-0780)
PHONE.................................631 475-1000
Fax: 631 589-2460
John Tuthill III, *President*
Lorerir Mary Lou Cohalon, *Vice Pres*
EMP: 20 **EST:** 1950
SALES (est): 930.7K **Privately Held**
WEB: www.islipbulletin.net
SIC: 2711 Newspapers: publishing only, not printed on site

(G-13452)
KEVIN FREEMAN
Also Called: Rf Inter Science Co
414 S Service Rd Ste 119 (11772-2254)
PHONE.................................631 447-5321
Kevin Freeman, *President*
EMP: 5
SALES (est): 398.6K **Privately Held**
SIC: 3827 Optical instruments & apparatus

(G-13453)
L3 TECHNOLOGIES INC
L3 Communications Narda - Atm
49 Rider Ave (11772-3915)
PHONE.................................631 289-0363
Geoffrey Smith, *Branch Mgr*
EMP: 50
SALES (corp-wide): 10.5B **Publicly Held**
SIC: 3679 Microwave components
PA: L3 Technologies, Inc.
600 3rd Ave Fl 34
New York NY 10016
212 697-1111

(G-13454)
NEW LIVING INC
99 Waverly Ave Apt 6d (11772-1922)
PHONE.................................631 751-8819
Christine Harvey, *Principal*
EMP: 7
SALES (est): 267K **Privately Held**
SIC: 2711 Newspapers, publishing & printing

(G-13455)
PARIS ART LABEL CO INC
217 River Ave (11772-3312)
PHONE.................................631 467-2300
Fax: 631 467-1729
Ronald P Tarantino, *Ch of Bd*
John Raguso, *Sales Mgr*
▲ **EMP:** 100 **EST:** 1925
SQ FT: 20,000
SALES (est): 26.2MM
SALES (corp-wide): 14.1B **Publicly Held**
WEB: www.parisartlabel.com
SIC: 2672 Labels (unprinted), gummed: made from purchased materials
HQ: Multi Packaging Solutions International Limited
885 3rd Ave Fl 28
New York NY 10022
646 885-0005

(G-13456)
PATCHOGUE ADVANCE INC
Also Called: Long Island Advance
20 Medford Ave Ste 1 (11772-1220)
PHONE.................................631 475-1000
Fax: 631 475-1565
John T Tuthill III, *President*
Joanne Labarca, *General Mgr*
Mark Nolan, *Chief*
Lorelei T Tuthill, *Admin Sec*
EMP: 35 **EST:** 1821
SQ FT: 7,000
SALES (est): 1.8MM **Privately Held**
WEB: www.longislandadvance.net
SIC: 2711 Newspapers: publishing only, not printed on site

(G-13457)
PEPSI BOTTLING VENTURES LLC
Also Called: Pepsi-Cola
4141 Parklane Ave Ste 600 (11772)
PHONE.................................631 772-6144
Theresa Dunton, *Manager*
Wes Krupp, *Administration*
EMP: 53
SALES (corp-wide): 2.2B **Privately Held**
SIC: 2086 Bottled & canned soft drinks
HQ: Pepsi Bottling Ventures Llc
4141 Parklake Ave Ste 600
Raleigh NC 27612
919 865-2300

(G-13458)
PRINCETON LABEL & PACKAGING
217 River Ave (11772-3312)
PHONE.................................609 490-0800
Donald J Guli, *President*
John Muccino, *Sales Staff*
EMP: 35
SQ FT: 7,800
SALES (est): 6.3MM **Privately Held**
WEB: www.princetonlabel.com
SIC: 2672 7389 Coated & laminated paper; packaging & labeling services

(G-13459)
RELIABLE WELDING & FABRICATION
214 W Main St (11772-3004)
PHONE.................................631 758-2637
EMP: 7
SALES (est): 490K **Privately Held**
SIC: 7692 5051 5021 1799 Welding Repair Metals Service Center Whol Furniture Special Trade Contractor

(G-13460)
SUFFOLK MCHY & PWR TL CORP (PA)
Also Called: Gschwind Group
12 Waverly Ave (11772-1902)
PHONE.................................631 289-7153
Fax: 631 289-7156
Arthur F Gschwind Sr, *President*
Debbie Freyre, *General Mgr*
Tom Davies, *Director*
▼ **EMP:** 3
SQ FT: 4,000
SALES (est): 1.2MM **Privately Held**
WEB: www.timberwolf1.com
SIC: 3425 Saw blades & handsaws

(G-13461)
T & SMOOTHIE INC
499 N Service Rd Ste 83 (11772-2290)
PHONE.................................631 804-6653
Tiffany Wirth, *Principal*
EMP: 6
SALES (est): 316.5K **Privately Held**
SIC: 2037 Frozen fruits & vegetables

Patterson
Putnam County

(G-13462)
DICAMILLO MARBLE AND GRANITE
20 Jon Barrett Rd (12563-2164)
PHONE.................................845 878-0078
Fax: 845 878-2250
EMP: 20 **EST:** 1991
SALES (est): 1.6MM **Privately Held**
SIC: 3281 Mfg Cut Stone/Products

(G-13463)
EAST HUDSON WATERSHED CORP
2 Route 164 (12563-2813)
PHONE.................................845 319-6349
Peter Parsons, *President*
EMP: 5
SQ FT: 1,000
SALES: 2.7MM **Privately Held**
SIC: 3822 Auto controls regulating residntl & coml environmt & applncs

GEOGRAPHIC SECTION

Pearl River - Rockland County (G-13485)

(G-13464)
GOLDEN GROUP INTERNATIONAL LTD
305 Quaker Rd (12563-2191)
P.O. Box 407, Brewster (10509-0407)
PHONE.................................845 440-1025
Jacqueline Transue, *President*
Kevin Hanna, *Info Tech Mgr*
EMP: 6
SALES (est): 530K **Privately Held**
SIC: 2673 5113 3444 5199 Trash bags (plastic film); made from purchased materials; food storage & trash bags (plastic); bags, paper & disposable plastic; bins, prefabricated sheet metal; art goods & supplies

(G-13465)
JRS PHARMA LP (DH)
2981 Route 22 Ste 1 (12563-2359)
PHONE.................................845 878-8300
Josef Rettenmaier, *Partner*
J Rettenmaier America, *Partner*
Josef Otto Rettenmaier, *Partner*
J Rettenmaier Holding USA, *Partner*
Jennifer Good, *Vice Pres*
▲ **EMP:** 48
SQ FT: 46,000
SALES (est): 23.5MM **Privately Held**
SIC: 2834 Pharmaceutical preparations
HQ: Jrs Pharma Gmbh & Co. Kg
Holzmuhle 1
Rosenberg 73494
796 715-2312

(G-13466)
LANE PARK GRAPHICS INC
93 Mcmanus Rd S (12563-2900)
PHONE.................................914 273-5898
Susan Scholer, *President*
Rich Harmon, *Manager*
Kris Smith, *Manager*
EMP: 7
SQ FT: 1,000
SALES (est): 866.5K **Privately Held**
SIC: 2754 7336 Commercial printing, gravure; commercial art & graphic design

(G-13467)
REELEX PACKAGING SOLUTIONS INC
39 Jon Barrett Rd (12563-2165)
PHONE.................................845 878-7878
Thomas R Copp, *President*
Frank Kotzur, *Vice Pres*
Ronald Zajac, *Vice Pres*
Gregory Kotzur, *Engineer*
Scott Kotzur, *Engineer*
▲ **EMP:** 40
SQ FT: 50,000
SALES (est): 9.2MM **Privately Held**
SIC: 3549 6794 Metalworking machinery; patent buying, licensing, leasing
PA: Da Capo Al Fine Ltd
81 Stone Crop Ln
Cold Spring NY 10516
845 265-2011

(G-13468)
SPANISH ARTISAN WINE GROUP LLC
Also Called: Spanish Artisan Wine Group Ltd
370 Cushman Rd (12563-2638)
PHONE.................................914 414-6982
Gerry Dawes, *Principal*
Gerald Dawes, *Mng Member*
EMP: 5
SALES: 1MM **Privately Held**
SIC: 2084 5182 7389 Wines; neutral spirits; brokers, business: buying & selling business enterprises

(G-13469)
TAUMEL METALFORMING CORP
Also Called: Taumel Assembly Systems
25 Jon Barrett Rd (12563-2165)
PHONE.................................845 878-3100
Ernest Bodmer, *President*
Tony A Huber, *Vice Pres*
Werner Stutz, *Vice Pres*
Peter Bodmer, *Treasurer*
Phil Huber, *Manager*
EMP: 8
SQ FT: 10,000
SALES (est): 853K **Privately Held**
WEB: www.taumel.com
SIC: 3542 Machine tools, metal forming type

(G-13470)
WERLATONE INC
17 Jon Barrett Rd (12563-2165)
P.O. Box 47, Brewster (10509-0047)
PHONE.................................845 278-2220
Fax: 845 279-7404
Glen C Werlau, *Ch of Bd*
Diane Wolpert, *General Mgr*
Austin Kile, *Corp Secy*
Eric Kowalik, *Opers Staff*
James Kakadeles, *Buyer*
EMP: 38 **EST:** 1965
SQ FT: 7,000
SALES (est): 7.6MM **Privately Held**
WEB: www.werlatone.com
SIC: 3679 Electronic circuits

Pattersonville
Schenectady County

(G-13471)
DJ PIRRONE INDUSTRIES INC
8865 Mariaville Rd (12137-3007)
PHONE.................................518 864-5496
David Pirrone, *Principal*
EMP: 5
SALES (est): 234.2K **Privately Held**
SIC: 3999 Manufacturing industries

Pavilion
Genesee County

(G-13472)
HANSON AGGREGATES NEW YORK LLC
6895 Ellicott Street Rd (14525-9614)
PHONE.................................585 638-5841
Daniel M Meehan, *Principal*
Scott Wheaton, *Plant Mgr*
Craig Green, *Opers Staff*
Doug Fuess, *Sales Dir*
EMP: 15
SALES (corp-wide): 16B **Privately Held**
SIC: 3273 Ready-mixed concrete
HQ: Hanson Aggregates New York Llc
8505 Freport Pkwy Ste 500
Irving TX 75063

Pawling
Dutchess County

(G-13473)
JOE PIETRYKA INCORPORATED (PA)
85 Charles Colman Blvd (12564-1160)
PHONE.................................845 855-1201
Joseph W Pietryka, *Ch of Bd*
John Drake, *Sales Staff*
EMP: 49
SQ FT: 65,000
SALES (est): 13.1MM **Privately Held**
WEB: www.dwconcepts.net
SIC: 3089 Injection molded finished plastic products

(G-13474)
PAWLING CORPORATION (PA)
Also Called: Pawling Engineered Products
157 Charles Colman Blvd (12564-1188)
PHONE.................................845 855-1000
Fax: 845 855-1937
Craig Busby, *President*
Roger W Smith, *Chairman*
Gregory S Holen, *Vice Pres*
John C Rickert, *Vice Pres*
Jason W Smith, *Vice Pres*
▼ **EMP:** 180
SQ FT: 250,000

(G-13475)
PAWLING ENGINEERED PDTS INC
157 Charles Colman Blvd (12564-1121)
PHONE.................................845 855-1000
Craig Busby, *President*
John Rickert, *Vice Pres*
EMP: 120
SQ FT: 250,000
SALES (est): 10MM **Privately Held**
SIC: 3061 3089 Mechanical rubber goods; extruded finished plastic products

Pearl River
Rockland County

(G-13476)
21ST CENTURY FOX AMERICA INC
Also Called: Corporate News
1 Blue Hill Plz Ste 1525 (10965-3129)
PHONE.................................845 735-1116
EMP: 8
SALES (corp-wide): 27.3B **Publicly Held**
SIC: 2711 Newspapers: publishing only, not printed on site
HQ: 21st Century Fox America, Inc.
1211 Ave Of The Americas
New York NY 10036
212 852-7000

(G-13477)
C B MANAGEMENT SERVICES INC
Also Called: Beitals Aquarium Sales & Svc
73 S Pearl St (10965-2235)
PHONE.................................845 735-2300
Craig Beital, *President*
Craig Beital, *President*
EMP: 13
SQ FT: 5,000
SALES (est): 970K **Privately Held**
WEB: www.cbmanagementservices.com
SIC: 3231 5999 7389 Aquariums & reflectors, glass; aquarium supplies; aquarium design & maintenance

(G-13478)
FIVE STAR MILLWORK LLC
6 E Dexter Plz (10965-2360)
PHONE.................................845 920-0247
Marco Santos,
Dario Fonseca,
Tiago Fonseca,
EMP: 12
SQ FT: 15,000
SALES (est): 4MM **Privately Held**
SIC: 2431 Millwork

(G-13479)
FUJITSU NTWRK CMMNICATIONS INC
2 Blue Hill Plz Ste 1609 (10965-3115)
PHONE.................................845 731-2000
Henry Chang, *Engineer*
Bob Demarco, *Manager*
EMP: 18
SALES (corp-wide): 39.6B **Privately Held**
WEB: www.fnc.fujitsu.com
SIC: 3661 8731 3663 Fiber optics communications equipment; commercial physical research; radio & TV communications equipment
HQ: Fujitsu Network Communications, Inc.
2801 Telecom Pkwy
Richardson TX 75082
972 479-6000

(G-13480)
HEARTLAND COMMERCE INC
Also Called: Pcamerica
1 Blue Hill Plz Ste 16 (10965-3100)
PHONE.................................845 920-0800
David J Gosman, *CEO*
Tony Scarpa, *Sales Mgr*
Ronny Polo, *Software Engr*
EMP: 21
SALES (corp-wide): 2.9B **Publicly Held**
SIC: 7372 Business oriented computer software
HQ: Heartland Commerce, Inc.
90 Nassau St Fl 2
Princeton NJ 08542
609 683-3831

(G-13481)
HUDSON TECHNOLOGIES COMPANY (PA)
1 Blue Hill Plz Ste 1541 (10965-3110)
P.O. Box 1541 (10965)
PHONE.................................845 735-6000
Kevin Zugibe, *Ch of Bd*
Briann Coleman, *President*
Stephen Mandracchia, *Vice Pres*
Marylyn Hu, *Accountant*
EMP: 38
SQ FT: 4,500
SALES: 48.6MM **Privately Held**
SIC: 2869 Fluorinated hydrocarbon gases

(G-13482)
HUNTER DOUGLAS INC (DH)
1 Blue Hill Plz Ste 1569 (10965-6101)
PHONE.................................845 664-7000
Ralph Sonnenberg, *Ch of Bd*
Marvin B Hopkins, *President*
David H Sonnenberg, *President*
Marko H Sonnenberg, *President*
Bryan Clabeaux, *General Mgr*
▲ **EMP:** 100
SQ FT: 32,000
SALES (est): 2.4B **Privately Held**
WEB: www.hunterdouglas.com
SIC: 2591 3444 5084 Window blinds; window shades; venetian blinds; sheet metalwork; industrial machinery & equipment
HQ: Hunter Douglas N.V.
Piekstraat 2
Rotterdam 3071
104 869-911

(G-13483)
HUNTS POINT CLEAN ENERGY LLC
Also Called: Hpce
401 N Middletown Rd (10965-1298)
PHONE.................................203 451-5143
Alfredo Forte,
Steven Switzen,
EMP: 6
SQ FT: 63,000
SALES (est): 267.4K **Privately Held**
SIC: 2869 Methyl alcohol, synthetic methanol

(G-13484)
KRAFT HAT MANUFACTURERS INC
7 Veterans Pkwy (10965-1328)
PHONE.................................845 735-6200
Israel Rosenzweig, *President*
Steven Rosenzweig, *Corp Secy*
Lawrence Rosenzweig, *Vice Pres*
Stacey Fromowitz, *Systems Mgr*
▲ **EMP:** 100
SQ FT: 34,000
SALES (est): 9.3MM **Privately Held**
WEB: www.krafthat.com
SIC: 2353 Hats, caps & millinery; millinery

(G-13485)
LEVOLOR WINDOW FURNISHINGS INC (DH)
1 Blue Hill Plz (10965-3104)
PHONE.................................845 664-7000
Marvin B Hopkins, *President*
Mark Carroll, *Vice Pres*
Jim Morando, *Vice Pres*
Craig York, *Vice Pres*
Ryan Mohre, *Manager*
▲ **EMP:** 300
SALES (est): 56.2MM **Privately Held**
SIC: 2591 Window blinds; blinds vertical
HQ: Hunter Douglas Inc.
1 Blue Hill Plz Ste 1569
Pearl River NY 10965
845 664-7000

Pearl River - Rockland County (G-13486)

GEOGRAPHIC SECTION

(G-13486)
NEXBEV INDUSTRIES LLC
1 Blue Hill Plz Ste 1564 (10965-3123)
PHONE..................917 626-5255
Charles Sessoms IV,
Antonio Johnson,
EMP: 10
SQ FT: 750
SALES (est): 444K **Privately Held**
SIC: 2086 Carbonated beverages, nonalcoholic; bottled & canned

(G-13487)
PIEZO ELECTRONICS RESEARCH
Also Called: Peri
30 Walter St (10965-1722)
PHONE..................845 735-9349
David Marsh, *President*
EMP: 12 **EST:** 1946
SQ FT: 3,000
SALES: 1MM **Privately Held**
SIC: 3674 7389 Solid state electronic devices; packaging & labeling services

(G-13488)
POLY SOFTWARE INTERNATIONAL
7 Kerry Ct (10965-3034)
P.O. Box 60 (10965-0060)
PHONE..................845 735-9301
Xiaowu Wang, *CEO*
Linda Hu, *Office Mgr*
EMP: 6
SALES (est): 448.8K **Privately Held**
WEB: www.polysoftware.com
SIC: 7372 Prepackaged software

(G-13489)
QUALITY GRAPHICS TRI STATE
171 Center St (10965-1630)
PHONE..................845 735-2523
Fax: 845 735-0182
Phyllis Schweizer, *President*
Bruce Schweizer, *Vice Pres*
EMP: 5
SALES (est): 779.2K **Privately Held**
SIC: 2752 Commercial printing, lithographic

(G-13490)
SKIN PRINTS INC
63 Walter St (10965-1723)
PHONE..................845 920-8756
Diane Kaufman, *President*
EMP: 3
SQ FT: 10,000
SALES (est): 1.2MM **Privately Held**
SIC: 2269 Finishing plants

(G-13491)
STRATEGIC MKTG PROMOTIONS INC (PA)
Also Called: S M P
1 Blue Hill Plz Ste 1561 (10965-3194)
PHONE..................845 623-7777
Jennifer Pagels-Caglione, *Ch of Bd*
Robert Russo, *President*
Greg Caglione, *Vice Pres*
Jennifer Caglione, *Director*
▼ **EMP:** 15
SQ FT: 3,000
SALES (est): 1.8MM **Privately Held**
SIC: 3999 Advertising display products

(G-13492)
UTILITY ENGINEERING CO
40 Walter St (10965-1795)
PHONE..................845 735-8900
Fax: 845 735-0363
George Huston, *President*
Mike Taylor, *Engineer*
EMP: 10
SQ FT: 7,400
SALES (est): 620K **Privately Held**
WEB: www.utilitydisplays.com
SIC: 3496 Miscellaneous fabricated wire products

(G-13493)
WYETH HOLDINGS LLC
Also Called: Wyeth Pharmaceutical Division
401 N Middletown Rd (10965-1298)
PHONE..................845 602-5000
Fax: 845 602-5599
David Zisa, *Principal*
Andy Schaschl, *Engineer*
James S Morrissey, *Project Leader*
Clive Pepper, *IT/INT Sup*
Debbie Bertero, *Director*
EMP: 100
SALES (corp-wide): 52.8B **Publicly Held**
SIC: 2834 2836 3842 3841 Pharmaceutical preparations; biological products, except diagnostic; surgical appliances & supplies; surgical & medical instruments; ophthalmic goods; chemical preparations
HQ: Wyeth Holdings Llc
5 Giralda Farms
Madison NJ 07940

Peconic
Suffolk County

(G-13494)
DORSET FARMS INC
Also Called: Lenz
38355 Main Rd (11958-1515)
P.O. Box 28 (11958-0028)
PHONE..................631 734-6010
Fax: 631 734-6069
Peter Carroll, *President*
Deborah Carroll, *Vice Pres*
▲ **EMP:** 10
SALES (est): 1MM **Privately Held**
SIC: 2084 Wines

(G-13495)
J PETROCELLI WINE CELLARS LLC
Also Called: Raphael
39390 Route 25 (11958-1501)
P.O. Box 17 (11958-0017)
PHONE..................631 765-1100
Chip Cheek, *Sales Mgr*
Joann Deangelo, *Sales Staff*
Jack Petrocelli, *Mng Member*
Diane Ferruzzi, *Manager*
▲ **EMP:** 25
SALES: 450K **Privately Held**
SIC: 2084 5921 Wines; wine

(G-13496)
PINDAR VINEYARDS LLC
37645 Route 25 (11958-1514)
P.O. Box 332 (11958-0332)
PHONE..................631 734-6200
Fax: 631 734-6205
Kathy Krejci, *Business Mgr*
Steve Ciuffo, *Sales Mgr*
Elizabeth Rolison, *Marketing Staff*
Herdotes Damianos, *Mng Member*
Alethea Conroy, *Manager*
EMP: 20
SQ FT: 5,000
SALES (est): 2.4MM **Privately Held**
WEB: www.pindar.net
SIC: 2084 Wines

Peekskill
Westchester County

(G-13497)
BASF CORPORATION
1057 Lower South St (10566-5302)
PHONE..................914 737-2554
Daniel S Gulley, *Branch Mgr*
Rick King, *Info Tech Mgr*
EMP: 344
SALES (corp-wide): 60.8B **Privately Held**
WEB: www.basf.com
SIC: 2816 Inorganic pigments
HQ: Basf Corporation
100 Park Ave
Florham Park NJ 07932
973 245-6000

(G-13498)
BASF CORPORATION
1057 Lower South St (10566-5302)
PHONE..................914 788-1627
EMP: 368
SALES (corp-wide): 60.8B **Privately Held**
WEB: www.basf.com
SIC: 2819 Industrial inorganic chemicals
HQ: Basf Corporation
100 Park Ave
Florham Park NJ 07932
973 245-6000

(G-13499)
CANDLES BY FOSTER
810 South St (10566-3431)
P.O. Box 89 (10566-0089)
PHONE..................914 739-9226
Donald Foster, *Owner*
EMP: 6
SQ FT: 6,500
SALES (est): 355.5K **Privately Held**
SIC: 3999 5999 Candles; candle shops

(G-13500)
ECONOMY ENERGY LLC
500 Highland Ave (10566-2320)
PHONE..................845 222-3384
Henry E Seger,
Patricia V McGrath,
EMP: 5
SALES (est): 652.4K **Privately Held**
SIC: 2869 Fuels

(G-13501)
ELEVATOR ACCESSORIES MFG
Also Called: Paxton Metal Craft Division
1035 Howard St 37 (10566-2819)
P.O. Box 430 (10566-0430)
PHONE..................914 739-7004
Fax: 914 736-3366
Alan Messing, *President*
John Johnson, *Vice Pres*
Vicki Messing, *Admin Sec*
EMP: 12
SALES (est): 2.2MM **Privately Held**
SIC: 3534 3441 3446 3444 Elevators & equipment; fabricated structural metal; architectural metalwork; sheet metalwork

(G-13502)
GIULIANTE MACHINE TOOL INC
12 John Walsh Blvd (10566-5323)
PHONE..................914 835-0008
Martha Giuliante, *President*
Armando Giuliante, *Vice Pres*
Marcelo Giuliante, *Vice Pres*
EMP: 25
SQ FT: 27,000
SALES: 4.5MM **Privately Held**
WEB: www.gmtgear.com
SIC: 3599 Machine shop, jobbing & repair

(G-13503)
HAT FACTORY FURNITURE CO
Also Called: Hudson Cabinetry Design
1000 N Division St Ste 8 (10566-1830)
PHONE..................914 788-6288
Douglas Bialor, *Owner*
EMP: 6 **EST:** 1998
SALES (est): 119.7K **Privately Held**
SIC: 3553 Cabinet makers' machinery

(G-13504)
HUDSON MIRROR LLC
Also Called: Mirrorlite Superscript
710 Washington St (10566-5418)
PHONE..................914 930-8906
Dwayne Reith, *Vice Pres*
Gary Reith,
EMP: 25
SQ FT: 2,000
SALES (est): 4MM **Privately Held**
SIC: 3827 Mirrors, optical

(G-13505)
RESCUESTUFF INC
962 Washington St (10566-5816)
PHONE..................718 318-7570
Greg Grimaldi, *President*
Seth Porter, *CFO*
EMP: 5
SQ FT: 2,000
SALES: 250K **Privately Held**
WEB: www.rescuestuff.net
SIC: 2395 2262 Embroidery products, except schiffli machine; screen printing: manmade fiber & silk broadwoven fabrics

(G-13506)
RMS PACKAGING INC
Also Called: Aurora Sef
1050 Lower South St (10566-5313)
PHONE..................914 205-2070

Sheldon Rosenberg, *President*
Ernest Peiffer, *VP Opers*
Stacy Christensen, *Manager*
▲ **EMP:** 16
SALES (est): 4.8MM **Privately Held**
SIC: 2671 Plastic film, coated or laminated for packaging

(G-13507)
SD CHRISTIE ASSOCIATES INC
424 Central Ave Ste 5 (10566-2056)
P.O. Box 5158, Cary NC (27512-5158)
PHONE..................914 734-1800
Thomas Christie, *President*
EMP: 5
SALES (est): 503.9K **Privately Held**
SIC: 3069 5085 Molded rubber products; mattress protectors, rubber; fasteners, industrial: nuts, bolts, screws, etc.; rubber goods, mechanical

(G-13508)
VIVID RGB LIGHTING LLC
824 Main St Ste 1 (10566-2052)
PHONE..................718 635-0817
Brian Fassett, *Managing Dir*
EMP: 7
SQ FT: 3,000
SALES (est): 721.8K **Privately Held**
SIC: 3648 Lighting equipment

(G-13509)
W DESIGNE INC
Also Called: Wood Design
5 John Walsh Blvd (10566-5307)
PHONE..................914 736-1058
Alex Bernabo, *President*
Gladys Pagan, *Manager*
▲ **EMP:** 20
SQ FT: 25,000
SALES (est): 3.1MM **Privately Held**
SIC: 2434 2517 Wood kitchen cabinets; wood television & radio cabinets

(G-13510)
WALTER G LEGGE COMPANY INC
Also Called: Legge System
444 Central Ave (10566-2003)
PHONE..................914 737-5040
Fax: 800 332-2636
Elizabeth Bauer, *President*
Jane Fejes, *General Mgr*
Ihor Wowtschuk, *Marketing Mgr*
▲ **EMP:** 9 **EST:** 1936
SQ FT: 10,000
SALES (est): 1.6MM **Privately Held**
WEB: www.leggesystems.com
SIC: 2842 3272 3679 Sanitation preparations, disinfectants & deodorants; tile, precast terrazzo or concrete; power supplies, all types: static

(G-13511)
WESTCHESTER TECHNOLOGIES INC
8 John Walsh Blvd Ste 311 (10566-5347)
PHONE..................914 736-1034
Fax: 914 736-1217
Roger Prahl, *CEO*
Carol Townley, *Office Mgr*
Thomas Ross, *Manager*
EMP: 23
SQ FT: 4,000
SALES: 4.1MM **Privately Held**
WEB: www.microoptics.com
SIC: 3827 Optical instruments & apparatus

(G-13512)
WESTYPO PRINTERS INC
540 Harrison Ave (10566-2318)
PHONE..................914 737-7394
Fax: 914 739-7717
Mike Mc Guggart, *President*
Teri Mc Gugart, *Treasurer*
EMP: 6 **EST:** 1964
SQ FT: 8,000
SALES (est): 535.1K **Privately Held**
SIC: 2752 2759 Commercial printing, offset; commercial printing

▲ = Import ▼ = Export
◆ = Import/Export

GEOGRAPHIC SECTION

Penn Yan - Yates County (G-13537)

Pelham
Westchester County

(G-13513)
ARCHIE COMIC PUBLICATIONS INC
Also Called: Archie Comics Publishers
629 Fifth Ave Ste 100 (10803-3714)
PHONE..................914 381-5155
Fax: 914 381-2335
Michael Silberkleit, *Chairman*
Victor Gorelick, *Vice Pres*
Ed Spallone, *Controller*
Joe Morciglio, *Assoc Editor*
Harold Buchholz, *Exec Dir*
EMP: 75 EST: 1939
SQ FT: 10,000
SALES (est): 12.1MM **Privately Held**
WEB: www.archiecomics.com
SIC: 2721 Comic books: publishing only, not printed on site

(G-13514)
BANK-MILLER CO INC
333 Fifth Ave (10803-1203)
PHONE..................914 227-9357
Steven Bank, *President*
Anna Paljuski, *Manager*
▲ EMP: 20
SQ FT: 5,500
SALES (est): 2.6MM **Privately Held**
WEB: www.bankmiller.com
SIC: 2259 2339 5131 Convertors, knit goods; women's & misses' outerwear; textile converters

(G-13515)
EASTCO MANUFACTURING CORP
Also Called: K & S & East
323 Fifth Ave (10803-1203)
PHONE..................914 738-5667
Fax: 914 738-1859
Jack Koff, *President*
Philip Schwartzman, *Vice Pres*
Adam Sanchez, *Engineer*
Stanley Rothman, *Sales Mgr*
EMP: 12
SQ FT: 5,000
SALES (est): 2.4MM **Privately Held**
SIC: 3699 Electrical equipment & supplies

(G-13516)
ENVENT SYSTEMS INC
62 Harmon Ave (10803-1708)
PHONE..................646 294-6980
Michael Curtin, *President*
EMP: 6
SALES (est): 2MM **Privately Held**
SIC: 3571 7389 Electronic computers;

(G-13517)
IMPERIA MASONRY SUPPLY CORP (PA)
57 Canal Rd (10803-2706)
PHONE..................914 738-0900
Fax: 914 738-0243
Joseph Imperia, *President*
Janice Piszczatowski, *CFO*
Joe Lombardozzi, *Sales Associate*
Lisa Carabello, *Admin Sec*
▲ EMP: 30 EST: 1927
SQ FT: 8,400
SALES (est): 2.6MM **Privately Held**
WEB: www.imperiabros.com
SIC: 3271 5031 5032 5211 Concrete block & brick; lumber, plywood & millwork; brick, stone & related material; brick, except refractory; stone, crushed or broken; lumber & other building materials; lumber products; brick; masonry materials & supplies

(G-13518)
MANACRAFT PRECISION INC
945 Spring Rd (10803-2714)
PHONE..................914 654-0967
Fax: 914 654-9006
Richard Osterer, *President*
EMP: 10 EST: 1946
SQ FT: 3,000
SALES (est): 1.1MM **Privately Held**
SIC: 3451 Screw machine products

(G-13519)
SHORELINE PUBLISHING INC
629 Fifth Ave Ste B01 (10803-3708)
PHONE..................914 738-7869
Fax: 914 738-7876
Edward Shapiro, *President*
EMP: 7
SQ FT: 1,000
SALES (est): 911K **Privately Held**
WEB: www.shorelinepub.com
SIC: 2721 2752 Periodicals; commercial printing, offset

(G-13520)
TALYARPS CORPORATION (PA)
143 Sparks Ave (10803-1810)
PHONE..................914 699-3030
Michael E Borner, *CEO*
Raymond Chlodney, *President*
James E Borner, *Chairman*
William J Borner, *Vice Pres*
Al Sarnotsky, *Vice Pres*
◆ EMP: 85 EST: 1936
SQ FT: 9,000
SALES (est): 30.2MM **Privately Held**
WEB: www.spraylat.com
SIC: 2851 Paints & paint additives

Penfield
Monroe County

(G-13521)
ALUMI-TECH LLC
1640 Harris Rd (14526-1816)
PHONE..................585 663-7010
Elizabeth Pantalo, *Manager*
James Putnam,
EMP: 8
SQ FT: 2,500
SALES (est): 103.5K **Privately Held**
WEB: www.saddlestackers.com
SIC: 3354 Aluminum extruded products

(G-13522)
DOLOMITE PRODUCTS COMPANY INC
746 Whalen Rd (14526-1022)
PHONE..................585 586-2568
Fax: 585 389-1577
Don Hosensele, *Manager*
EMP: 20
SQ FT: 2,280
SALES (corp-wide): 28.6B **Privately Held**
WEB: www.dolomitegroup.com
SIC: 2951 1429 Paving mixtures; trap rock, crushed & broken-quarrying
HQ: Dolomite Products Company Inc.
1150 Penfield Rd
Rochester NY 14625
315 324-1998

(G-13523)
IRPENSCOM
4 Katsura Ct (14526-2612)
PHONE..................585 507-7997
Sabatino Agnitti Jr, *Owner*
EMP: 5
SALES (est): 343.2K **Privately Held**
SIC: 3571 Electronic computers

(G-13524)
NIFTY BAR GRINDING & CUTTING
450 Whitney Rd (14526-2326)
PHONE..................585 381-0450
Fax: 585 381-4712
John Raimondi, *President*
EMP: 23 EST: 1967
SQ FT: 24,000
SALES (est): 5MM **Privately Held**
WEB: www.niftybar.com
SIC: 3541 Machine tools, metal cutting type

(G-13525)
RANGE REPAIR WAREHOUSE
421 Penbrooke Dr Ste 2 (14526-2045)
PHONE..................585 235-0980
Paul V Ciminelli, *Owner*
EMP: 5
SALES (est): 274.5K **Privately Held**
SIC: 3499 Fabricated metal products

(G-13526)
ROBINSON TOOLS LLC
Also Called: Garco
477 Whitney Rd (14526-2328)
PHONE..................585 586-5432
James D Keppel, *President*
Judy Haley, *Plant Mgr*
Philip Decaire, *Manager*
EMP: 7 EST: 1836
SQ FT: 5,000
SALES (est): 650K **Privately Held**
WEB: www.robinsontools.com
SIC: 3423 Hand & edge tools

(G-13527)
SCHNEIDER ELECTRIC USA INC
441 Penbrooke Dr Ste 9 (14526-2046)
PHONE..................585 377-1313
Brian Hoffman, *Manager*
EMP: 11
SALES (corp-wide): 241K **Privately Held**
WEB: www.squared.com
SIC: 3612 Transformers, except electric
HQ: Schneider Electric Usa, Inc.
800 Federal St
Andover MA 01810
978 975-9600

(G-13528)
VIEWSPORT INTERNATIONAL INC
11 Feathery Cir (14526-2816)
PHONE..................585 259-1562
Benjamin Wood, *President*
Gregory Wood, *Opers Staff*
EMP: 3
SALES (est): 5.7MM **Privately Held**
SIC: 2396 7389 Screen printing on fabric articles;

Penn Yan
Yates County

(G-13529)
BIRKETT MILLS (PA)
163 Main St Ste 2 (14527-1284)
PHONE..................315 536-3311
Fax: 315 536-6740
Wayne W Wagner, *President*
Jeffrey S Gifford, *Exec VP*
Cliff Orr, *Sls & Mktg Exec*
Wayne Agner, *Manager*
Bill Fitzwater, *Manager*
◆ EMP: 5 EST: 1797
SQ FT: 12,018
SALES (est): 7.4MM **Privately Held**
WEB: www.thebirkettmills.com
SIC: 2041 5999 5261 Flour & other grain mill products; farm equipment & supplies; nurseries & garden centers; lawn & garden supplies

(G-13530)
BIRKETT MILLS
163 Main St Ste 3 (14527-1284)
PHONE..................315 536-4112
Jeff Gifford, *Manager*
EMP: 32
SQ FT: 60,455
SALES (corp-wide): 7.4MM **Privately Held**
WEB: www.thebirkettmills.com
SIC: 2041 Flour & other grain mill products
PA: The Birkett Mills
163 Main St Ste 2
Penn Yan NY 14527
315 536-3311

(G-13531)
CHRONICLE EXPRESS
138 Main St (14527-1299)
PHONE..................315 536-4422
Fax: 315 536-0682
George Barnes, *President*
Irene Vanderlinder, *Sales/Mktg Mgr*
Robert Corey, *Manager*
Michael Hansen, *Graphic Designe*
EMP: 15
SALES (est): 640K **Privately Held**
WEB: www.chronicleexpress.com
SIC: 2711 5994 Newspapers; news dealers & newsstands

(G-13532)
FERRO CORPORATION
1789 Transelco Dr (14527-9752)
PHONE..................315 536-3357
Fax: 315 536-8091
Gary Braun, *General Mgr*
John Prendergast, *Business Mgr*
Terry Fennelly, *Opers Mgr*
Michael O'Loughlin, *Facilities Mgr*
Richard Rickman, *Controller*
EMP: 200
SALES (corp-wide): 1.1B **Publicly Held**
WEB: www.ferro.com
SIC: 2819 Industrial inorganic chemicals
PA: Ferro Corporation
6060 Parkland Blvd # 250
Mayfield Heights OH 44124
216 875-5600

(G-13533)
FERRO ELECTRONICS MATERIALS (HQ)
Also Called: Ferro Electronic Mtl Systems
1789 Transelco Dr (14527-9752)
PHONE..................315 536-3357
Lyn Labrake, *Manager*
Bob Gage, *Manager*
Mary Champln, *Admin Asst*
◆ EMP: 2
SALES (est): 17MM
SALES (corp-wide): 1.1B **Publicly Held**
SIC: 3264 Porcelain electrical supplies
PA: Ferro Corporation
6060 Parkland Blvd # 250
Mayfield Heights OH 44124
216 875-5600

(G-13534)
FERRO ELECTRONICS MATERIALS
Also Called: Ferro Electronic Mtl Systems
1789 Transelco Dr (14527-9752)
PHONE..................315 536-3357
EMP: 101
SALES (corp-wide): 1.1B **Publicly Held**
SIC: 3264 Porcelain electrical supplies
HQ: Ferro Electronics Materials Inc
1789 Transelco Dr
Penn Yan NY 14527
315 536-3357

(G-13535)
FOX RUN VINEYARDS INC
670 State Route 14 (14527-9622)
PHONE..................315 536-4616
Fax: 315 536-1383
Scott Osbourne, *President*
Ruth Osborn, *Vice Pres*
Dan Mitchell, *Sales Mgr*
Marisa Indelicato, *Marketing Staff*
Michelle Eades, *Manager*
EMP: 12
SQ FT: 8,000
SALES (est): 3.7MM **Privately Held**
WEB: www.foxrunvineyards.com
SIC: 2084 Wines

(G-13536)
HANSON AGGREGATES EAST LLC
131 Garfield Ave (14527-1655)
P.O. Box 168 (14527-0168)
PHONE..................315 536-9391
Kenny Thurston, *Manager*
EMP: 6
SALES (corp-wide): 16B **Privately Held**
WEB: www.hansonaggeast.com
SIC: 1442 Common sand mining
HQ: Hanson Aggregates East Llc
3131 Rdu Center Dr
Morrisville NC 27560
919 380-2500

(G-13537)
HOFFMAN & HOFFMAN
Also Called: Rooster Hill Vineyards
489 State Route 54 (14527-9595)
P.O. Box 11 (14527-0011)
PHONE..................315 536-4773
David W Hoffman, *Partner*
Amy E Hoffman, *Partner*
Ron Reals, *Director*
EMP: 7

(PA)=Parent Co (HQ)=Headquarters (DH)=Div Headquarters
◎ = New Business established in last 2 years

Penn Yan - Yates County (G-13538)

SALES (est): 620.3K **Privately Held**
WEB: www.roosterhill.com
SIC: 2084 Wines, brandy & brandy spirits

(G-13538)
JASPER TRANSPORT LLC
1680 Flat St (14527-9024)
P.O. Box 441 (14527-0441)
PHONE.................................315 729-5760
Ross Newcomb,
EMP: 6
SALES (est): 570K **Privately Held**
SIC: 3537 Trucks, tractors, loaders, carriers & similar equipment

(G-13539)
PREJEAN WINERY INC
2634 State Route 14 (14527-9735)
PHONE.................................315 536-7524
Fax: 315 536-7635
Elizabeth Prejean, *President*
Thomas Prejean, *Vice Pres*
EMP: 11
SQ FT: 6,000
SALES (est): 1.2MM **Privately Held**
WEB: www.prejeanwinery.com
SIC: 2084 Wines

(G-13540)
RED TAIL RIDGE INC
Also Called: Red Tail Ridge Winery
846 State Route 14 (14527-9622)
PHONE.................................315 536-4580
Nancy Irelan, *Ch of Bd*
Mike Schnelle, *President*
EMP: 5
SALES (est): 441.1K **Privately Held**
SIC: 2084 Wines

(G-13541)
RIBBLE LUMBER INC
249 1/2 Lake St (14527-1812)
PHONE.................................315 536-6221
Roger C Ribble, *President*
Roger A Ribble Sr, *Corp Secy*
EMP: 5
SALES (est): 360K **Privately Held**
SIC: 2434 1794 4212 Wood kitchen cabinets; excavation work; dump truck haulage

(G-13542)
ROTO SALT COMPANY INC
118 Monell St (14527-1404)
PHONE.................................315 536-3742
Fax: 315 536-7273
Brett M Oakes, *President*
Susan Ettinger, *Vice Pres*
Ann Olney, *Controller*
EMP: 32
SQ FT: 20,000
SALES (est): 7.8MM **Privately Held**
SIC: 2899 3281 Salt; building stone products

(G-13543)
SILGAN PLASTICS LLC
40 Powell Ln (14527-1072)
PHONE.................................315 536-5690
Taylor Stratton, *Mfg Mgr*
Rodney Olevnik, *Senior Engr*
Donald Oakleas, *Controller*
Diana Brown, *HR Admin*
Joseph Pollhein, *Manager*
EMP: 250
SQ FT: 100,000
SALES (corp-wide): 3.6B **Publicly Held**
WEB: www.silganplastics.com
SIC: 3089 Plastics containers, except foam
HQ: Silgan Plastics Llc
14515 North Outer 40 Rd # 210
Chesterfield MO 63017
800 274-5426

(G-13544)
WARRIOR SPORTS INC
Also Called: In The Crease
26 Powell Ln (14527-1072)
PHONE.................................315 536-0937
Fax: 315 536-3128
Steve Trombley, *Branch Mgr*
EMP: 5

SALES (corp-wide): 1.4B **Privately Held**
SIC: 3949 2329 2339 Team sports equipment; lacrosse equipment & supplies, general; soccer equipment & supplies; men's & boys' athletic uniforms; sportswear, women's
HQ: Warrior Sports, Inc.
32125 Hollingsworth Ave
Warren MI 48092
586 978-2595

Perry
Wyoming County

(G-13545)
CREATIVE FOOD INGREDIENTS INC
Also Called: CFI
1 Lincoln Ave (14530-1605)
PHONE.................................585 237-2213
Andrew W O'Flaherty, *CEO*
Dave Goodwin, *Prdtn Mgr*
Jeffrey Arcand, *CFO*
Mike Casey, *Controller*
Debra Bevans, *Human Res Dir*
▼ EMP: 140
SALES (est): 25.4MM **Privately Held**
SIC: 2052 Bakery products, dry

(G-13546)
EAST HILL CREAMERY LLC
346 Main St S (14530-9551)
PHONE.................................585 237-3622
Gary Burley, *Mng Member*
EMP: 6
SALES (est): 203.6K **Privately Held**
SIC: 2022 Cheese spreads, dips, pastes & other cheese products

(G-13547)
J N WHITE ASSOCIATES INC
Also Called: J.N. White Designs
129 N Center St (14530-9701)
P.O. Box 219 (14530-0219)
PHONE.................................585 237-5191
Fax: 585 237-2115
Randy White, *President*
Ken Boss, *Vice Pres*
John Steff, *Vice Pres*
Susan C White, *Vice Pres*
Jerome Dellapietra, *Opers Mgr*
EMP: 95
SQ FT: 25,000
SALES (est): 17.5MM **Privately Held**
WEB: www.jnwhitedesigns.com
SIC: 2759 7389 Screen printing; printed circuitry graphic layout

(G-13548)
R J LIEBE ATHLETIC COMPANY
Also Called: Liebe NY
200 Main St N (14530-1211)
PHONE.................................585 237-6111
Jim Liebe, *Mng Member*
Rob Knoll,
EMP: 95
SQ FT: 200,000
SALES (est): 7.5MM **Privately Held**
WEB: www.americanclassicoutfitters.com
SIC: 2329 Men's & boys' athletic uniforms

(G-13549)
SIGN LANGUAGE INC
Also Called: Sign Language Custom WD Signs
6491 State Route 20a (14530-9758)
PHONE.................................585 237-2620
Fax: 585 237-5868
Dave Caito, *President*
Jeff Fitch, *Corp Secy*
EMP: 8
SQ FT: 3,000
SALES (est): 570K **Privately Held**
WEB: www.signlanguageinc.com
SIC: 3993 Signs, not made in custom sign painting shops

Peru
Clinton County

(G-13550)
ROBERT W BUTTS LOGGING CO
420 Mannix Rd (12972-4529)
PHONE.................................518 643-2897
Robert Butts, *Owner*
EMP: 6
SALES (est): 625.6K **Privately Held**
SIC: 2411 Logging camps & contractors

Petersburg
Rensselaer County

(G-13551)
TONOGA INC (PA)
Also Called: Taconic
136 Coon Brook Rd (12138)
P.O. Box 69 (12138-0069)
PHONE.................................518 658-3202
Fax: 518 658-3988
Andrew G Russell, *Chairman*
Lawrence Carroll, *Exec VP*
Sharon Goodermote, *Vice Pres*
Manfred Huschka, *Vice Pres*
Scott Schulz, *Vice Pres*
▲ EMP: 180 EST: 1961
SQ FT: 150,000
SALES (est): 125.6MM **Privately Held**
WEB: www.taconic-afd.com
SIC: 2295 3629 Resin or plastic coated fabrics; electronic generation equipment

Phelps
Ontario County

(G-13552)
AMERICAN CRMIC PROCESS RES LLC
835 Mcivor Rd (14532-9535)
P.O. Box 213 (14532-0213)
PHONE.................................315 828-6268
Jesse Sheckler,
EMP: 6
SQ FT: 18,670
SALES (est): 279.8K **Privately Held**
SIC: 3299 Nonmetallic mineral products

(G-13553)
BENEMY WELDING & FABRICATION
8 Pleasant Ave (14532-1100)
PHONE.................................315 548-8500
Fax: 315 548-8550
Dave Suhr, *President*
Christine Suhr, *Vice Pres*
EMP: 6
SQ FT: 1,852
SALES (est): 675.2K **Privately Held**
SIC: 7692 Welding repair

(G-13554)
DORGAN WELDING SERVICE
1378 White Rd (14532-9502)
PHONE.................................315 462-9030
Bob Dorgan, *Owner*
EMP: 5
SQ FT: 7,000
SALES: 450K **Privately Held**
SIC: 7692 1799 Welding repair; welding on site

(G-13555)
GW LISK COMPANY INC
Also Called: Lisk Coils
1369 Phelps Junction Rd (14532-9747)
PHONE.................................315 548-2165
EMP: 40
SALES (corp-wide): 113.1MM **Privately Held**
SIC: 3629 Mfg Electrical Industrial Apparatus
PA: G.W. Lisk Company, Inc.
2 South St
Clifton Springs NY 14432
315 462-2611

(G-13556)
HANSON AGGREGATES EAST LLC
392 State Route 96 (14532-9531)
PHONE.................................315 548-2911
Mike Cool, *Manager*
Bob Clapp, *Manager*
EMP: 26
SQ FT: 6,756
SALES (corp-wide): 16B **Privately Held**
SIC: 3273 1442 Ready-mixed concrete; construction sand & gravel
HQ: Hanson Aggregates East Llc
3131 Rdu Center Dr
Morrisville NC 27560
919 380-2500

(G-13557)
MAGNUS PRECISION MFG INC
1912 State Route 96 (14532-9705)
PHONE.................................315 548-8032
Fax: 315 548-8041
Thomas Shepard, *Principal*
Alfred Mustardo, *Vice Pres*
Ron Kosmider, *Plant Mgr*
Eric Galens, *QC Mgr*
John Hallett, *Engineer*
EMP: 68
SQ FT: 55,000
SALES (est): 14.1MM
SALES (corp-wide): 83.7MM **Privately Held**
WEB: www.magnuscnc.com
SIC: 3625 3544 Relays & industrial controls; special dies & tools
PA: Floturn, Inc.
4236 Thunderbird Ln
West Chester OH 45014
513 860-8040

(G-13558)
PHELPS CEMENT PRODUCTS INC
5 S Newark St (14532-9708)
P.O. Box 40 (14532-0040)
PHONE.................................315 548-9415
Fax: 315 548-2235
Gerald Haers, *Ch of Bd*
Michael Haers, *President*
Philip Haers, *Manager*
Chris Wheelers, *Manager*
Gerry Haers, *Admin Sec*
EMP: 23
SQ FT: 4,000
SALES (est): 4.4MM **Privately Held**
WEB: www.phelpscement.com
SIC: 3271 5211 5032 Concrete block & brick; lumber & other building materials; brick, stone & related material

(G-13559)
SENECA CERAMICS CORP
835 Mcivor Rd (14532-9535)
P.O. Box 213 (14532-0213)
PHONE.................................315 781-0100
Chad Scheckler, *President*
Howard Hersey, *Treasurer*
Larisa Scheckler, *Admin Sec*
EMP: 6
SALES: 300K **Privately Held**
SIC: 3469 Utensils, household: porcelain enameled

(G-13560)
SHEPPARD GRAIN ENTERPRISES LLC
1615 Maryland Rd (14532-9507)
PHONE.................................315 548-9271
Fax: 315 548-7669
Mark Santoro, *Controller*
Susan Allens, *Accountant*
Steve Sheppard, *Mng Member*
John Sheppard, *Manager*
◆ EMP: 35
SQ FT: 3,600
SALES: 40MM **Privately Held**
SIC: 2041 Flour & other grain mill products

(G-13561)
TRIPLETT MACHINE INC
1374 Phelps Junction Rd (14532-9747)
PHONE.................................315 548-3198
Fax: 315 548-4143
Douglas A Triplett Jr, *CEO*
Jeffrey Triplett, *Vice Pres*

Grant Abrams, *Engineer*
James Cheney, *Manager*
Douglas Triplett Sr, *Shareholder*
EMP: 65
SQ FT: 30,000
SALES (est): 16.5MM **Privately Held**
WEB: www.triplettmachine.com
SIC: 3599 Machine & other job shop work

(G-13562)
VALVETECH INC
1391 Phelps Junction Rd (14532-9747)
P.O. Box 118 (14532-0118)
PHONE......................315 548-4551
Fax: 315 548-4200
Michael Mullally, *President*
Russell Williams Jr, *Vice Pres*
Mary Edwards, *Treasurer*
Timothy Mullally, *Sales Mgr*
EMP: 35
SQ FT: 1,000
SALES (est): 7.1MM
SALES (corp-wide): 165.7MM **Privately Held**
WEB: www.valvetech.net
SIC: 3592 Valves, aircraft
PA: G.W. Lisk Company, Inc.
 2 South St
 Clifton Springs NY 14432
 315 462-2611

(G-13563)
Z-AXIS INC
Also Called: Boundless Technologies
1916 State Route 96 (14532-9705)
PHONE......................315 548-5000
Fax: 315 548-5100
Michael Allen, *President*
John Bartolotto, *Mfg Mgr*
Chris Friel, *Purch Mgr*
Donna Smith, *Purch Mgr*
Chet Gridley, *Finance Mgr*
▲ **EMP:** 55
SQ FT: 30,000
SALES (est): 15.3MM **Privately Held**
WEB: www.zaxis.net
SIC: 3699 3845 3577 Electrical equipment & supplies; electromedical equipment; computer peripheral equipment

Philadelphia
Jefferson County

(G-13564)
NATURES WAREHOUSE
55 Main St (13673-4189)
PHONE......................800 215-4372
Carl L Laudon, *Partner*
Daniel Laudon, *Partner*
Dennis Yoder, *Office Mgr*
EMP: 10
SALES (est): 1.2MM **Privately Held**
SIC: 2899 2841 5499 Essential oils; soap & other detergents; vitamin food stores

Philmont
Columbia County

(G-13565)
FALLS MANUFACTURING INC (PA)
95 Main St (12565)
P.O. Box 798 (12565-0798)
PHONE......................518 672-7189
Fax: 518 672-7195
Frederick A Meyer, *President*
EMP: 8
SQ FT: 4,800
SALES (est): 2.3MM **Privately Held**
SIC: 2381 2339 Fabric dress & work gloves; women's & misses' outerwear

(G-13566)
PVC CONTAINER CORPORATION
Also Called: Nova Pack
370 Stevers Crossing Rd (12565)
P.O. Box 784 (12565-0784)
PHONE......................518 672-7721
Fax: 518 672-7351
Gary Gendron, *Plant Mgr*

Edna Hover, *Manager*
Sharad Prasad, *Technology*
EMP: 160 **Privately Held**
WEB: www.airopak.com
SIC: 3085 3089 Plastics bottles; molding primary plastic
HQ: Pvc Container Corporation
 15450 South Outer 40 Rd # 120
 Chesterfield MO 63017
 732 542-0060

Phoenix
Oswego County

(G-13567)
AMERICAN MATERIAL PROCESSING
126 Bankrupt Rd (13135-2193)
P.O. Box 643, Newark (14513-0643)
PHONE......................315 318-0017
Lawson Whiting, *President*
Matthew Eddy, *COO*
Jason McKinney, *Vice Pres*
EMP: 11 **EST:** 2013
SQ FT: 800
SALES (est): 1.2MM **Privately Held**
SIC: 3532 3569 3532 3535 Crushing, pulverizing & screening equipment; feeders, ore & aggregate; ice crushers (machinery); crushing, pulverizing & screening machinery; belt conveyor systems, general industrial use; bulk handling conveyor systems

(G-13568)
AMERICAN MATERIAL PROCESSING
126 Bankrupt Rd (13135-2193)
P.O. Box 643, Newark (14513-0643)
PHONE......................315 695-6204
Matt Eddy, *Admin Sec*
EMP: 10
SALES (est): 123.7K **Privately Held**
SIC: 3536 3339 5082 Monorail systems; precious metals; construction & mining machinery

(G-13569)
MAJESTIC MOLD & TOOL INC
177 Volney St (13135-3116)
PHONE......................315 695-2079
Fax: 315 695-3493
Timothy King, *President*
Dennis Lyons, *Vice Pres*
Stephen Corsette, *Treasurer*
Pam Najdul, *Manager*
EMP: 16
SQ FT: 8,000
SALES (est): 4MM **Privately Held**
WEB: www.majesticmold.com
SIC: 2821 Molding compounds, plastics

(G-13570)
PHOENIX WELDING & FABG INC
Also Called: Phoenix Material Handling
10 County Route 6 (13135-2118)
PHONE......................315 695-2223
Fax: 315 695-3437
Brian D Dates, *Ch of Bd*
Michelle Wagner, *Office Mgr*
EMP: 5
SQ FT: 2,500
SALES (est): 882.1K **Privately Held**
SIC: 7692 Welding repair

(G-13571)
SOUTHERN GRAPHIC SYSTEMS LLC
67 County Route 59 (13135-2116)
PHONE......................315 695-7079
Fax: 315 695-3160
Vic Baranowski, *Mng Member*
Frank Palmieri, *Manager*
Ginny Paparo, *Manager*
Jennifer Shutts, *Technology*
EMP: 27
SALES (corp-wide): 301.9MM **Privately Held**
SIC: 3555 Printing trades machinery
HQ: Southern Graphic Systems, Llc
 626 W Main St Ste 500
 Louisville KY 40202
 502 637-5443

Piermont
Rockland County

(G-13572)
ROCKLAND COLLOID CORP (PA)
Also Called: Rockaloid
44 Franklin St (10968-1010)
P.O. Box 3120, Oregon City OR (97045-0306)
PHONE......................845 359-5559
Robert Cone, *President*
Francis Cooper, *Corp Secy*
Robert Cone Jr, *Vice Pres*
EMP: 5
SQ FT: 3,000
SALES (est): 697.4K **Privately Held**
WEB: www.rockloid.com
SIC: 3861 5043 Photographic equipment & supplies; photographic equipment & supplies

Piffard
Livingston County

(G-13573)
ARKEMA INC
Also Called: Genesee Plant
3289 Genesee St (14533-9745)
P.O. Box 188, Geneseo (14454-0188)
PHONE......................585 243-6359
Richard Gahagan, *Safety Mgr*
Joe Marcin, *Safety Mgr*
Jamie Mullen, *Opers Staff*
Daryl Roberts, *Mfg Staff*
Jake Zimmerman, *Engineer*
EMP: 170
SALES (corp-wide): 20MM **Privately Held**
SIC: 2869 2819 Industrial organic chemicals; industrial inorganic chemicals
HQ: Arkema Inc.
 900 First Ave
 King Of Prussia PA 19406
 610 205-7000

(G-13574)
EXXELIA-RAF TABTRONICS LLC
2854 Genesee St (14533-9749)
P.O. Box 128, Geneseo (14454-0128)
PHONE......................585 243-4331
Mark Stevens, *Safety Mgr*
James Charles Tabbi, *Manager*
EMP: 43
SALES (corp-wide): 15.8MM **Privately Held**
SIC: 3677 3643 3612 Electronic transformers; coil windings, electronic; current-carrying wiring devices; transformers, except electric
PA: Exxelia-Raf Tabtronics, Llc
 1221 N Us Highway 17 92
 Longwood FL 32750
 386 736-1698

Pine Bush
Orange County

(G-13575)
MOBILE MEDIA INC (PA)
24 Center St (12566-6004)
P.O. Box 177 (12566-0177)
PHONE......................845 744-8080
Fax: 845 744-8090
Lance Pennington, *Principal*
Nancy Pennington, *Vice Pres*
Antoinette Fitzpatrick, *Controller*
Angela Ruggiero, *Accounts Mgr*
Robin Vitacco, *Accounts Mgr*
▲ **EMP:** 23
SQ FT: 31,000
SALES: 10.9MM **Privately Held**
WEB: www.rolleasy.com
SIC: 2542 Partitions & fixtures, except wood

(G-13576)
P & B WOODWORKING INC
2415 State Route 52 (12566-7041)
P.O. Box 225 (12566-0225)
PHONE......................845 744-2508
Fax: 845 744-5548
Jake Donnell, *President*
Steven Reinhardt, *Vice Pres*
EMP: 10
SQ FT: 11,000
SALES: 1.1MM **Privately Held**
SIC: 2541 Cabinets, lockers & shelving

Pine City
Chemung County

(G-13577)
DALRYMPLE GRAV & CONTG CO INC (HQ)
2105 S Broadway (14871-9700)
PHONE......................607 739-0391
Fax: 607 737-1056
David J Dalrymple, *Ch of Bd*
Robert H Dalrymple, *President*
Edward C Dalrymple Jr, *Vice Pres*
Roger Burris, *Plant Mgr*
Al Murphy, *Controller*
EMP: 18 **EST:** 1890
SQ FT: 10,000
SALES (est): 40.9MM
SALES (corp-wide): 108.4MM **Privately Held**
SIC: 1442 3273 Construction sand & gravel; ready-mixed concrete
PA: Dalrymple Holding Corp
 2105 S Broadway
 Pine City NY 14871
 607 737-6200

(G-13578)
DALRYMPLE HOLDING CORP (PA)
2105 S Broadway (14871-9700)
PHONE......................607 737-6200
David J Dalrymple, *President*
Edward C Dalrymple Jr, *Vice Pres*
Robert H Dalrymple, *Admin Sec*
EMP: 20
SQ FT: 5,000
SALES (est): 108.4MM **Privately Held**
SIC: 3273 1611 1442 1622 Ready-mixed concrete; highway & street construction; construction sand & gravel; bridge construction; stone, quarrying & processing of own stone products

(G-13579)
SENECA STONE CORPORATION (HQ)
2105 S Broadway (14871-9700)
PHONE......................607 737-6200
David J Dalrymple, *President*
Edward C Dalrymple Jr, *Vice Pres*
Robert H Dalrymple, *Vice Pres*
Edward C Dalrymple Sr, *Treasurer*
Sandy Strong, *Manager*
EMP: 4
SQ FT: 800
SALES (est): 1.6MM
SALES (corp-wide): 108.4MM **Privately Held**
SIC: 3281 1771 1442 Cut stone & stone products; concrete work; construction sand & gravel
PA: Dalrymple Holding Corp
 2105 S Broadway
 Pine City NY 14871
 607 737-6200

Pine Island
Orange County

(G-13580)
REELCOLOGY INC
39 Transport Ln (10969-1223)
P.O. Box 305 (10969-0305)
PHONE......................845 258-1880
Kenneth H Smith, *President*
EMP: 15
SQ FT: 7,000

Pine Plains - Dutchess County (G-13581) GEOGRAPHIC SECTION

SALES (est): 1.8MM **Privately Held**
SIC: 3496 3499 Cable, uninsulated wire: made from purchased wire; reels, cable: metal

Pine Plains
Dutchess County

(G-13581)
ABRA MEDIA INC
Also Called: Live Oak Media
2773 W Church St (12567-5421)
P.O. Box 652 (12567-0652)
PHONE..................................518 398-1010
Arnold Cardillo, *President*
Debra Cardillo, *Admin Sec*
EMP: 6
SALES (est): 480K **Privately Held**
WEB: www.liveoakmedia.com
SIC: 2741 7812 Miscellaneous publishing; audio-visual program production

(G-13582)
DUTCH SPIRITS LLC
Also Called: Dutch's Spirits
98 Ryan Rd (12567-5022)
PHONE..................................518 398-1022
Ariel Schlein, *Mng Member*
John Adams,
Ronit Schlein,
▲ EMP: 17
SQ FT: 7,424,000
SALES: 250K **Privately Held**
SIC: 2084 5999 2085 Neutral spirits, fruit; alcoholic beverage making equipment & supplies; cocktails, alcoholic

Pine Valley
Chemung County

(G-13583)
AMES COMPANIES INC
114 Smith Rd (14872)
P.O. Box 126 (14872-0126)
PHONE..................................607 739-4544
Fax: 607 739-0030
John Stoner, *Owner*
Mark Schrage, *Manager*
EMP: 20
SQ FT: 13,235
SALES (corp-wide): 1.9B **Publicly Held**
WEB: www.ames.com
SIC: 3423 Hand & edge tools
HQ: The Ames Companies Inc
   465 Railroad Ave
   Camp Hill PA 17011
   717 737-1500

Pittsford
Monroe County

(G-13584)
AD PUBLICATIONS INC
8 Greenwood Park (14534-2912)
PHONE..................................585 248-2888
Donald Stahl, *President*
Cheryl Stahl, *Vice Pres*
Patricia Stahl, *Admin Sec*
EMP: 10
SQ FT: 450
SALES (est): 786.8K **Privately Held**
SIC: 2759 Coupons: printing

(G-13585)
BRIGHT LINE ETING SLUTIONS LLC
18 Brickston Dr (14534-3627)
PHONE..................................585 245-2956
Julia Harold,
EMP: 26
SALES: 6MM **Privately Held**
SIC: 2741

(G-13586)
COMET INFORMATICS LLC
642 Kreag Rd Ste 300 (14534-3736)
PHONE..................................585 385-2310
Thomas Guhl, *Sales Mgr*

Dirk Hightower,
Daniel Draper,
Leonard Gingello,
Serge Lossa,
EMP: 5 EST: 2011
SALES (est): 279.6K **Privately Held**
SIC: 7372 Educational computer software; publishers' computer software

(G-13587)
EASTMAN KODAK COMPANY
1818 W Jefferson Rd (14534-1033)
PHONE..................................585 722-9695
Dawn Schweitze, *Principal*
EMP: 67
SALES (corp-wide): 1.8B **Publicly Held**
SIC: 3861 Film, sensitized motion picture, X-ray, still camera, etc.
PA: Eastman Kodak Company
   343 State St
   Rochester NY 14650
   585 724-4000

(G-13588)
FLUOROLOGIC INC
33 Bishops Ct (14534-2882)
PHONE..................................585 248-2796
Laura Weller-Brophy, *CEO*
EMP: 7
SALES (est): 407K **Privately Held**
SIC: 3841 Surgical & medical instruments

(G-13589)
GATEHOUSE MEDIA LLC (HQ)
175 Sullys Trl Ste 300 (14534-4560)
PHONE..................................585 598-0030
Adam Reinebach, *CEO*
Rick Daniels, *President*
Peter Newton, *President*
Paul Ameden, *Principal*
Walter Belback, *Editor*
▲ EMP: 105
SQ FT: 15,000
SALES (est): 147.1MM
SALES (corp-wide): 1.2B **Publicly Held**
WEB: www.gatehousemedia.com
SIC: 2711 7311 2759 Newspapers, publishing & printing; advertising agencies; commercial printing
PA: New Media Investment Group Inc.
   1345 Avenue Of The Americ
   New York NY 10105
   212 479-3160

(G-13590)
GATEHOUSE MEDIA MO HOLDINGS
Also Called: Rolla Daily News Plus
175 Sullys Trl Ste 300 (14534-4560)
PHONE..................................530 846-3661
Michael E Reed, *CEO*
EMP: 8 EST: 2013
SALES (est): 415.7K **Privately Held**
SIC: 2711 Newspapers, publishing & printing

(G-13591)
GATEHUSE MEDIA PA HOLDINGS INC (HQ)
175 Sullys Trl Fl 3 (14534-4560)
PHONE..................................585 598-0030
Kirk Davis, *CEO*
EMP: 45
SALES (est): 9.2MM
SALES (corp-wide): 1.2B **Publicly Held**
SIC: 2711 Commercial printing & newspaper publishing combined
PA: New Media Investment Group Inc.
   1345 Avenue Of The Americ
   New York NY 10105
   212 479-3160

(G-13592)
IMAGINANT INC
Also Called: Jsr Ultrasonics Division
3800 Monroe Ave Ste 29 (14534-1330)
PHONE..................................585 264-0480
Fax: 585 264-9642
Todd Jackson, *CEO*
Samuel Rosenberg, *President*
Robert Hibbard, *Corp Secy*
Valerie Sill, *Engineer*
Steve Smith, *Engineer*
EMP: 32
SQ FT: 10,000

SALES (est): 5.9MM **Privately Held**
WEB: www.jsrultrasonics.com
SIC: 3829 Measuring & controlling devices

(G-13593)
INFIMED INC
15 Fishers Rd (14534-9544)
PHONE..................................585 383-1710
Pat Rox, *Branch Mgr*
Jack Mooney, *Manager*
Tim Seeler, *Manager*
EMP: 7
SALES (corp-wide): 8.3MM **Privately Held**
SIC: 3845 Electromedical equipment
PA: Infimed, Inc.
   121 Metropolitan Park Dr
   Liverpool NY 13088
   315 453-4545

(G-13594)
KERNOW NORTH AMERICA
5 Park Forest Dr (14534-3557)
PHONE..................................585 586-3590
Bosy Colak, *Owner*
Craig Surette, *Info Tech Mgr*
EMP: 11 EST: 2010
SALES (est): 1.1MM **Privately Held**
SIC: 3089 Plastic containers, except foam

(G-13595)
LIFE JUICE BRANDS LLC
115 Brook Rd (14534-1144)
PHONE..................................585 944-7982
Peter Schulick, *CEO*
EMP: 4
SQ FT: 1,400
SALES: 1.7MM **Privately Held**
SIC: 2033 Vegetable juices: packaged in cans, jars, etc.

(G-13596)
MAGNUM SHIELDING CORPORATION
3800 Monroe Ave Ste 14f (14534-1330)
P.O. Box 827 (14534-0827)
PHONE..................................585 381-9957
Fax: 585 381-9956
Scott Hurwitz, *President*
Tom Vierthaler, *General Mgr*
Chad Conklin, *Manager*
Sue Myer, *Manager*
Jeremy Austin, *Senior Mgr*
▲ EMP: 50
SQ FT: 15,000
SALES (est): 9.1MM **Privately Held**
WEB: www.magnumshielding.com
SIC: 3694 Ignition apparatus & distributors

(G-13597)
MARDEK LLC
73 N Wilmarth Rd (14534-9775)
P.O. Box 134, North Hero VT (05474-0134)
PHONE..................................585 735-9333
Charles Dekar, *President*
Nick Dekar, *President*
▲ EMP: 5
SALES: 2MM **Privately Held**
SIC: 3312 Rods, iron & steel: made in steel mills

(G-13598)
MILLERCOORS LLC
1000 Pittsford Victor Rd (14534-3822)
PHONE..................................585 385-0670
Dennis Perreault, *Branch Mgr*
EMP: 25
SALES (corp-wide): 4.8B **Publicly Held**
SIC: 2082 Malt beverages
HQ: Millercoors Llc
   250 S Wacker Dr Ste 800
   Chicago IL 60606
   312 496-2700

(G-13599)
OPTICS TECHNOLOGY INC
3800 Monroe Ave Ste 3 (14534-1330)
PHONE..................................585 586-0950
Fax: 585 248-2371
John Warda, *President*
Ben Piatt, *Prdtn Mgr*
Sia Mullen, *Admin Asst*
EMP: 6
SQ FT: 6,000

SALES (est): 1.3MM **Privately Held**
WEB: www.opticstechnology.com
SIC: 3827 3599 8711 Lenses, optical: all types except ophthalmic; lens mounts; optical elements & assemblies, except ophthalmic; machine & other job shop work; machine shop, jobbing & repair; engineering services

(G-13600)
PA PELLETS LLC (HQ)
1 Fischers Rd Ste 160 (14534)
PHONE..................................814 848-9970
Dan Wetzel, *Principal*
▼ EMP: 14 EST: 2010
SALES (est): 2.8MM
SALES (corp-wide): 24.5MM **Privately Held**
SIC: 2421 Fuelwood, from mill waste
PA: Biomaxx, Inc.
   1160 Pittsford Victor Rd F
   Pittsford NY 14534
   585 314-7304

(G-13601)
PACTIV LLC
1169 Pittsford Victor Rd (14534-3809)
P.O. Box 5032, Lake Forest IL (60045-5032)
PHONE..................................585 248-1213
EMP: 50 **Privately Held**
WEB: www.pactiv.com
SIC: 2631 2653 Paperboard mills; container board; folding boxboard; corrugated & solid fiber boxes
HQ: Pactiv Llc
   1900 W Field Ct
   Lake Forest IL 60045
   847 482-2000

(G-13602)
ROCKWELL AUTOMATION INC
1000 Pittsford Victor Rd # 17 (14534-3822)
PHONE..................................585 487-2700
Brian Blaisdell, *Area Mgr*
Kevin Phelps, *Vice Pres*
Brian Kress, *Sales Engr*
Scott Turling, *Manager*
Dave Cicero, *Technical Staff*
EMP: 27 **Publicly Held**
SIC: 3625 Relays & industrial controls
PA: Rockwell Automation, Inc.
   1201 S 2nd St
   Milwaukee WI 53204

(G-13603)
UNITED TECHNOLOGIES CORP
Lenel
1212 Pittsford Victor Rd (14534-3820)
PHONE..................................866 788-5095
Mark Kozik, *Sales Engr*
Diego Ponti, *Sales Engr*
Ewa Pigna, *CTO*
John Merlino, *Director*
Brian Beideman, *Director*
EMP: 500
SALES (corp-wide): 57.2B **Publicly Held**
SIC: 3699 Electrical equipment & supplies
PA: United Technologies Corporation
   10 Farm Springs Rd
   Farmington CT 06032
   860 728-7000

(G-13604)
XELIC INCORPORATED
1250 Pittsford Victor Rd # 370 (14534-9541)
PHONE..................................585 415-2764
Mark Gibson, *President*
Doug Bush, *Vice Pres*
Kenny Chung, *Design Engr*
Jamie Howard, *Design Engr*
Richard Wanzenried, *Design Engr*
EMP: 18
SQ FT: 2,400
SALES: 3MM **Privately Held**
WEB: www.xelic.com
SIC: 3825 Integrated circuit testers

▲ = Import ▼ = Export
◆ = Import/Export

Plainview
Nassau County

(G-13605)
5YZ LOGISTICS LLC
Also Called: U2o Usa, LLC
206 Terminal Dr (11803-2312)
PHONE.................................516 813-9500
Kavir Sra, *General Mgr*
Sam Lamba, *Chairman*
Dennis Dantes, *Vice Pres*
EMP: 1000
SALES: 6MM
SALES (corp-wide): 6.7MM **Privately Held**
SIC: 3661 5065 Headsets, telephone; mobile telephone equipment
PA: U2o Global Co.,Ltd.
4f U2o Building, No.385, Huanzhu Rd.,
Jimei District
Xiamen 36102
159 594-5208

(G-13606)
ADART POLYETHYLENE BAG MFG
Also Called: Adart Poly Bag Mfg
1 W Ames Ct Ste 201 (11803-2328)
P.O. Box 615 (11803-0019)
PHONE.................................516 932-1001
Robert Wolk, *President*
Gabriella Grama, *Manager*
EMP: 6 **EST:** 1968
SQ FT: 13,500
SALES (est): 1.1MM **Privately Held**
SIC: 2673 Bags: plastic, laminated & coated

(G-13607)
AEROFLEX HOLDING CORP
35 S Service Rd (11803-4117)
P.O. Box 6022 (11803-0622)
PHONE.................................516 694-6700
Hugh Evans, *Ch of Bd*
Leonard Borow, *President*
John Buyko, *Exec VP*
Andrew F Kaminsky, *Senior VP*
Edward Wactlar, *Senior VP*
▼ **EMP:** 2700
SQ FT: 90,000
SALES (est): 203MM
SALES (corp-wide): 2.3B **Privately Held**
SIC: 3674 Semiconductors & related devices
HQ: Cobham Holdings Inc.
10 Orchard Park Dr
Orchard Park NY 14127
716 662-0006

(G-13608)
AEROFLEX INCORPORATED (HQ)
35 S Service Rd (11803-4117)
P.O. Box 6022 (11803-0622)
PHONE.................................516 694-6700
Fax: 516 694-0658
Robert B McKeon, *Ch of Bd*
Leonard J Borow, *President*
Bill Burrows, *General Mgr*
Matt Gordon, *Area Mgr*
Carlos Rojas, *Area Mgr*
▲ **EMP:** 450
SQ FT: 69,000
SALES (est): 492.6MM
SALES (corp-wide): 2.3B **Privately Held**
WEB: www.aeroflex.com
SIC: 3812 3621 3677 3674 Acceleration indicators & systems components, aerospace; torque motors, electric; electronic coils, transformers & other inductors; microcircuits, integrated (semiconductor); mesh, made from purchased wire; optical instruments & apparatus
PA: Cobham Plc
Brook Road
Wimborne BH21
120 288-2020

(G-13609)
AEROFLEX PLAINVIEW INC (DH)
35 S Service Rd (11803-4117)
P.O. Box 6022 (11803-0622)
PHONE.................................516 694-6700
Fax: 516 694-6715
Jill Kale, *CEO*
Leonard Borow, *Ch of Bd*
Joseph Castaldo, *General Mgr*
Carl Caruso, *Senior VP*
William Brown, *Vice Pres*
EMP: 422
SQ FT: 69,000
SALES (est): 199.9MM
SALES (corp-wide): 2.3B **Privately Held**
SIC: 3679 3621 3674 3827 Electronic circuits; motors, electric; microcircuits, integrated (semiconductor); microprocessors; optical instruments & lenses

(G-13610)
ALCATEL-LUCENT USA INC
1 Fairchild Ct Ste 340 (11803-1720)
PHONE.................................516 349-4900
Arthur Betz, *Sales Staff*
EMP: 58
SALES (corp-wide): 884MM **Privately Held**
SIC: 3661 Telephone & telegraph apparatus
HQ: Alcatel-Lucent Usa Inc.
600 Mountain Ave Ste 700
New Providence NJ 07974

(G-13611)
AMERICAN CASTING AND MFG CORP (PA)
51 Commercial St (11803-2490)
PHONE.................................800 342-0333
Fax: 516 349-8389
Norman Wenk III, *President*
H L Christian Wenk IV, *Corp Secy*
Joseph Wenk, *Vice Pres*
Carlos Cuadros, *Manager*
◆ **EMP:** 70 **EST:** 1916
SQ FT: 40,000
SALES: 16.1MM **Privately Held**
WEB: www.americancasting.com
SIC: 3089 3364 2759 5085 Injection molding of plastics; lead die-castings; labels & seals: printing, seals, industrial

(G-13612)
AMERICAN CASTING AND MFG CORP
65 S Terminal Dr (11803-2310)
PHONE.................................516 349-7010
Jim Wenk, *Mktg Dir*
Norman Wenk, *Branch Mgr*
EMP: 5
SALES (corp-wide): 16.1MM **Privately Held**
WEB: www.americancasting.com
SIC: 3089 3364 3429 Injection molding of plastics; lead die-castings; manufactured hardware (general)
PA: American Casting And Manufacturing Corporation
51 Commercial St
Plainview NY 11803
800 342-0333

(G-13613)
AUDIO VIDEO INVASION INC
Also Called: AVI
53 Werman Ct (11803-4507)
PHONE.................................516 345-2636
Panos Anassis, *Principal*
Christina Anassis, *Manager*
EMP: 15
SALES (est): 1.9MM **Privately Held**
SIC: 3651 5999 Household audio & video equipment; audio-visual equipment & supplies

(G-13614)
AUFHAUSER CORPORATION (PA)
Also Called: I R M
39 West Mall (11803-4209)
PHONE.................................516 694-8696
Fax: 516 694-8690
R K Aufhauser, *CEO*
Pl Tsang Wu, *Vice Pres*
Edgar Torres, *Manager*
▲ **EMP:** 18
SQ FT: 28,000
SALES: 30MM **Privately Held**
WEB: www.aufhauser.net
SIC: 3356 2899 5051 Welding rods; solder: wire, bar, acid core, & rosin core; fluxes: brazing, soldering, galvanizing & welding; metals service centers & offices

(G-13615)
AUFHAUSER MANUFACTURING CORP
Also Called: Aufhauser Corp Canada
39 West Mall (11803-4209)
PHONE.................................516 694-8696
R Keith Aufhauser, *President*
Wu Pl Tsang, *Vice Pres*
Fred Wu, *Treasurer*
EMP: 20
SQ FT: 25,000
SALES: 25MM **Privately Held**
WEB: www.brazing.com
SIC: 3356 Welding rods

(G-13616)
CENTROID INC
111 E Ames Ct Unit 1 (11803-2311)
PHONE.................................516 349-0070
Fax: 516 349-9141
Gerald I Starr, *Ch of Bd*
Marc A Starr, *President*
Nancy Budd, *Purch Agent*
Steve Apelman, *Engineer*
Peggy Carey, *Controller*
EMP: 23 **EST:** 1965
SQ FT: 8,000
SALES (est): 4.5MM **Privately Held**
WEB: www.centroidinc.com
SIC: 3679 Oscillators

(G-13617)
CHERRY LANE LITHOGRAPHING CORP
15 E Bethpage Rd Unit A (11803-4217)
PHONE.................................516 293-9294
William Citterbart Jr, *President*
Joann Citterbart, *Corp Secy*
William Citterbart III, *Vice Pres*
Bill Fuchf, *Safety Mgr*
Jo A Citterbrt, *Treasurer*
EMP: 48 **EST:** 1962
SQ FT: 54,000
SALES (est): 10.1MM **Privately Held**
WEB: www.cherrylanelitho.com
SIC: 2752 Lithographing on metal

(G-13618)
COINMACH SERVICE CORP
303 Sunnyside Blvd # 70 (11803-1598)
PHONE.................................516 349-8555
Robert M Doyle, *Ch of Bd*
Carol A Siebuhr, *President*
Adrian Verquer, *President*
VA Richmond, *Regional Mgr*
NC Charlotte, *Vice Pres*
EMP: 805
SQ FT: 11,600
SALES: 116.5MM
SALES (corp-wide): 369.9MM **Privately Held**
SIC: 3633 5087 Household laundry equipment; laundry equipment & supplies
HQ: Spin Holdco Inc.
303 Sunnyside Blvd # 70
Plainview NY 11803

(G-13619)
COLONIAL GROUP LLC
150 Express St Ste 2 (11803-2421)
PHONE.................................516 349-8010
Pierre Lavi,
EMP: 25
SALES (est): 1.9MM **Privately Held**
SIC: 3724 Aircraft engines & engine parts

(G-13620)
CONRAD BLASIUS EQUIPMENT CO
Also Called: Cbe/New York
199 Newtown Rd (11803-4308)
PHONE.................................516 753-1200
Fax: 516 756-1209
Richard Fiordelisi Sr, *President*
Richard C Fiordelisi Jr, *President*
EMP: 6
SQ FT: 10,000
SALES (est): 630K **Privately Held**
SIC: 3599 3291 2842 5084 Tubing, flexible metallic; coated abrasive products; metal polish; industrial machinery & equipment

(G-13621)
CONTROLLED CASTINGS CORP
31 Commercial Ct (11803-2403)
PHONE.................................516 349-1718
Fax: 516 349-1126
Carmella Fratello, *Ch of Bd*
Peter Fratello Jr, *President*
Clifford Fratello, *Vice Pres*
EMP: 30 **EST:** 1961
SQ FT: 32,500
SALES (est): 4.3MM **Privately Held**
SIC: 3369 Castings, except die-castings, precision

(G-13622)
CORAL CAST LLC
31 Commercial Ct (11803-2403)
PHONE.................................516 349-1300
Joseph Marden,
EMP: 21
SALES (est): 3.5MM **Privately Held**
SIC: 3272 Precast terrazo or concrete products

(G-13623)
COX & COMPANY INC
1664 Old Country Rd (11803-5013)
PHONE.................................212 366-0200
Fax: 212 366-0222
John Smith, *Ch of Bd*
Thomas Ferguson, *Senior VP*
Kevin Pierce, *Buyer*
Kamel Al-Khalil, *Engineer*
Tom Arcati, *Engineer*
▲ **EMP:** 185 **EST:** 1944
SQ FT: 90,000
SALES (est): 53MM **Privately Held**
SIC: 3625 3743 3822 3812 Relays & industrial controls; railroad equipment; auto controls regulating residntl & coml environmt & applncs; search & navigation equipment; current-carrying wiring devices; aircraft parts & equipment; deicing equipment, aircraft

(G-13624)
CSC SERVICEWORKS INC (HQ)
303 Sunnyside Blvd # 70 (11803-1597)
PHONE.................................516 349-8555
Mark Hjelle, *CEO*
Stacy Weaver, *President*
Tim Guido, *Regional Mgr*
Hector Acosta, *Area Mgr*
Brian Bass, *Area Mgr*
EMP: 63
SALES (est): 219.8MM
SALES (corp-wide): 369.9MM **Privately Held**
SIC: 3633 5087 Household laundry equipment; laundry equipment & supplies
PA: Csc Serviceworks Holdings, Inc
303 Sunnyside Blvd # 70
Plainview NY 11803
516 349-8555

(G-13625)
CSC SERVICEWORKS HOLDINGS (PA)
303 Sunnyside Blvd # 70 (11803-1597)
PHONE.................................516 349-8555
EMP: 32 **EST:** 2013
SALES (est): 369.9MM **Privately Held**
SIC: 3633 5087 Household laundry equipment; laundry equipment & supplies

(G-13626)
DERM/BURO INC (PA)
229 Newtown Rd (11803-4309)
PHONE.................................516 694-8300
Frank Guthart, *President*
Kathy Daponce, *Manager*
EMP: 2
SQ FT: 1,100

Plainview - Nassau County (G-13627) — GEOGRAPHIC SECTION

SALES (est): 3.4MM **Privately Held**
WEB: www.gforces.com
SIC: **3841** 5122 5047 3842 Surgical & medical instruments; pharmaceuticals; instruments, surgical & medical; surgical appliances & supplies

(G-13627)
DIE-MATIC PRODUCTS LLC
130 Express St (11803-2477)
PHONE 516 433-7900
Fax: 516 433-7966
Arnold Klein, *President*
Bill Oehrlein, *Opers Mgr*
Evelyn Martinez, *Controller*
Dan Farber, *Info Tech Mgr*
Sheldon Fox,
EMP: 30 **EST:** 1944
SQ FT: 30,000
SALES (est): 5.3MM **Privately Held**
WEB: www.diematicproducts.com
SIC: **3469** Stamping metal for the trade

(G-13628)
EBY ELECTRO INC
210 Express St (11803-2423)
PHONE 516 576-7777
Fax: 516 576-1414
Mitchell Solomon, *President*
Charles Louie, *Opers Mgr*
Jim Fennell, *Opers Staff*
John Mancini, *Opers Staff*
Margo Schein, *Purch Mgr*
▲ **EMP:** 28
SQ FT: 20,000
SALES (est): 5.7MM **Privately Held**
WEB: www.ebyelectro.com
SIC: **3678** Electronic connectors

(G-13629)
EVANS & PAUL LLC
140 Dupont St (11803-1603)
PHONE 516 576-0800
Jeffrey Evans, *Mng Member*
EMP: 50
SQ FT: 30,000
SALES: 5.1MM **Privately Held**
SIC: **2599** 2542 1799 Hospital furniture, except beds; fixtures, office: except wood; office furniture installation

(G-13630)
FACTORY WHEEL WAREHOUSE INC
30 W Ames Ct (11803-2319)
PHONE 516 605-2131
EMP: 9 **EST:** 2012
SALES (est): 1MM **Privately Held**
SIC: **3714** 5013 5015 5085 Motor vehicle wheels & parts; wheel rims, motor vehicle; wheels, motor vehicle; wheels, motor vehicle; wheels, used: motor vehicle; bearings, bushings, wheels & gears

(G-13631)
FIBRE MATERIALS CORP
40 Dupont St (11803-1679)
PHONE 516 349-1660
Fax: 516 349-1671
Glenn Fellows, *CEO*
Brian Grossberg, *President*
Elvira Minerva, *Controller*
▲ **EMP:** 27 **EST:** 1963
SQ FT: 34,000
SALES (est): 4.7MM **Privately Held**
WEB: www.fibrematerials.com
SIC: **3089** 5162 Washers, plastic; plastics materials & basic shapes

(G-13632)
FULL MOTION BEVERAGE INC (PA)
998 Old Country Rd (11803-4928)
PHONE 631 585-1100
Peter Frazzetto, *CEO*
Vincent Butta, *President*
Chris Mollica, *President*
Paul Dua, *Vice Pres*
Tim Mayette, *CFO*
EMP: 6
SALES: 396.4K **Publicly Held**
WEB: www.web2corp.com
SIC: **2869** Alcohols, non-beverage

(G-13633)
HOSHIZAKI NRTHEASTERN DIST CTR
150 Dupont St Ste 100 (11803-1603)
PHONE 516 605-1411
Toshio Mase, *President*
Mitsuhiro Nomura, *CFO*
Ron Podolsky, *Accounts Mgr*
Artic Rade, *Admin Sec*
▲ **EMP:** 6
SALES (est): 1.1MM
SALES (corp-wide): 2.4B **Privately Held**
WEB: www.hoshizaki.com
SIC: **3585** Ice making machinery
HQ: Hoshizaki America, Inc.
618 Highway 74 S
Peachtree City GA 30269
770 487-2331

(G-13634)
HOT LINE INDUSTRIES INC (PA)
Also Called: Castle Harbor
28 South Mall (11803-4208)
PHONE 516 764-0400
Fax: 516 764-6009
Howard Negrin, *President*
Jeff Negrin, *Corp Secy*
Elliot Negrin, *Vice Pres*
▲ **EMP:** 14
SQ FT: 9,000
SALES (est): 983.3K **Privately Held**
WEB: www.hotlineindustries.com
SIC: **2339** Women's & misses' outerwear

(G-13635)
HOWARD J MOORE COMPANY INC
Also Called: Morco
210 Terminal Dr Ste B (11803-2322)
PHONE 631 351-8467
Eric Moore, *President*
Spencer Moore, *Sales Mgr*
Margaret Bram, *Director*
EMP: 28 **EST:** 1945
SQ FT: 17,000
SALES (est): 5.5MM **Privately Held**
WEB: www.morcofab.com
SIC: **3082** 2679 Unsupported plastics profile shapes; building, insulating & packaging paper

(G-13636)
INDUSTRIAL RAW MATERIALS LLC
Also Called: Industrial Wax
39 West Mall (11803-4209)
PHONE 212 688-8080
Keith Aufhauser, *Mng Member*
▲ **EMP:** 19
SQ FT: 6,000
SALES (est): 4.6MM
SALES (corp-wide): 30MM **Privately Held**
WEB: www.industrialwax.com
SIC: **2911** 5172 Paraffin wax; petroleum products
PA: Aufhauser Corporation
39 West Mall
Plainview NY 11803
516 694-8696

(G-13637)
INTELLIDYNE LLC
303 Sunnyside Blvd # 75 (11803-1508)
PHONE 516 676-0777
Michelle David, *Manager*
Jack Hammer,
EMP: 17
SQ FT: 4,500
SALES (est): 3.5MM **Privately Held**
WEB: www.intellidynellc.com
SIC: **3822** Temperature controls, automatic

(G-13638)
INTERNATIONAL PATTERNS INC
8 Arthur Ct (11803-3708)
PHONE 631 952-2000
Fax: 631 952-7602
Paul Kaplan, *Ch of Bd*
Shelley Beckwith, *President*
Keith Huntington, *Vice Pres*
Leona Weiner, *Treasurer*
▲ **EMP:** 100
SQ FT: 37,000

SALES (est): 13.7MM **Privately Held**
WEB: www.internationalpatterns.com
SIC: **3993** Signs & advertising specialties

(G-13639)
INTERPARTS INTERNATIONAL INC (PA)
190 Express St (11803-2405)
PHONE 516 576-2000
Hung Da Yang, *President*
Frank Buquicchio, *Controller*
Andrew Feng, *Asst Controller*
Dauphine Yang, *Director*
▲ **EMP:** 20
SQ FT: 40,000
SALES (est): 3.2MM **Privately Held**
SIC: **3714** 5013 3566 Motor vehicle brake systems & parts; automotive brakes; speed changers, drives & gears

(G-13640)
JEM CONTAINER CORP
151 Fairchild Ave Ste 1 (11803-1716)
P.O. Box 456, Farmingdale (11735-0456)
PHONE 800 521-0145
Ohn C Mc Laughlin, *Ch of Bd*
EMP: 10
SALES (est): 1.4MM **Privately Held**
SIC: **3086** Packaging & shipping materials, foamed plastic

(G-13641)
KAREY KASSL CORP
Also Called: Karey Products
180 Terminal Dr (11803-2324)
PHONE 516 349-8484
Fax: 516 349-9329
Gary J Kassl, *CEO*
Ronald Kassl, *President*
Carlos Gomez, *Info Tech Mgr*
▲ **EMP:** 30
SQ FT: 40,000
SALES (est): 2.5MM **Privately Held**
SIC: **3442** Storm doors or windows, metal

(G-13642)
KENSTAN LOCK & HARDWARE CO INC
Also Called: Kenstan Lock Co.
101 Commercial St Ste 100 (11803-2408)
PHONE 631 423-1977
Fax: 516 576-0100
Hans E R Bosch, *President*
Bob Harrison, *Executive*
▲ **EMP:** 38 **EST:** 1964
SQ FT: 10,000
SALES (est): 8.4MM **Privately Held**
WEB: www.kenstan.com
SIC: **3429** Cabinet hardware

(G-13643)
LIFETIME CHIMNEY SUPPLY LLC
171 E Ames Ct (11803-2332)
PHONE 516 576-8144
Fax: 516 576-8145
Abraham J Finkler, *President*
Deborah Grandison, *General Mgr*
Dennis Martinez, *Vice Pres*
Susan Esswein, *Controller*
Joshua Lang, *Director*
▲ **EMP:** 5
SQ FT: 6,000
SALES (est): 1.2MM **Privately Held**
WEB: www.lifetimechimneysupply.com
SIC: **3443** 5023 Liners, industrial: metal plate; kitchenware

(G-13644)
MACHINE COMPONENTS CORP
70 Newtown Rd (11803-4382)
PHONE 516 694-7222
Fax: 516 694-7252
Joseph Kaplan, *President*
Miriam Kaplan, *President*
Jay Kaplan, *Corp Secy*
Gregory Ahmad, *Engineer*
Rana Klein, *Administration*
EMP: 25 **EST:** 1959
SQ FT: 10,000
SALES (est): 5MM **Privately Held**
WEB: www.machinecomp.com
SIC: **3568** 3625 Clutches, except vehicular; switches, electronic applications

(G-13645)
MARCEL FINISHING CORP
4 David Ct (11803-6009)
PHONE 718 381-2889
Marcel Brenka, *President*
Floarea Brenka, *Admin Sec*
EMP: 30
SQ FT: 7,000
SALES (est): 1.9MM **Privately Held**
SIC: **2269** 2261 2262 Finishing plants; finishing plants, cotton; finishing plants, manmade fiber & silk fabrics

(G-13646)
METAL TEK PRODUCTS
100 Express St (11803-2405)
PHONE 516 586-4514
Chris Loften, *Principal*
EMP: 8
SALES (est): 347.6K **Privately Held**
SIC: **3444** Sheet metal specialties, not stamped

(G-13647)
METROFAB PIPE INCORPORATED
15 Fairchild Ct (11803-1701)
PHONE 516 349-7373
Elizabeth Ficken, *President*
Joe Magliato, *Vice Pres*
Cathy Karp, *Manager*
EMP: 10
SALES (est): 2.6MM **Privately Held**
SIC: **3462** 3443 Flange, valve & pipe fitting forgings, ferrous; pipe, standpipe & culverts

(G-13648)
MGD BRANDS INC
Also Called: Finesse Accessories
30 Commercial Ct (11803-2415)
PHONE 516 545-0150
Arthur Damast, *CEO*
Scott Damast, *Vice Pres*
▲ **EMP:** 50
SALES (est): 25MM **Privately Held**
WEB: www.finessenovelty.com
SIC: **3911** 3999 5094 5131 Jewelry, precious metal; hair & hair-based products; jewelry; hair accessories; ribbons; novelties

(G-13649)
MICRO CENTRIC CORPORATION (PA)
25 S Terminal Dr (11803-2314)
PHONE 800 573-1139
Fax: 516 349-9354
Nicholas Fink, *Ch of Bd*
Dan Olsen, *VP Opers*
Eva Fink, *Treasurer*
Maria Koski, *Controller*
Tim Croan, *Sales Staff*
◆ **EMP:** 28
SQ FT: 14,000
SALES (est): 4.1MM **Privately Held**
WEB: www.microcentric.com
SIC: **3545** 5084 Machine tool accessories; collets (machine tool accessories); industrial machinery & equipment

(G-13650)
N & G OF AMERICA INC
28 W Lane Dr (11803-5436)
PHONE 516 428-3414
Najmi Hussain, *President*
EMP: 12
SALES: 500K **Privately Held**
SIC: **3571** Electronic computers

(G-13651)
NASH PRINTING INC
Also Called: Sir Speedy
101 Dupont St Ste 2 (11803-1612)
PHONE 516 935-4567
Fax: 516 935-4736
Noor Baqueri, *President*
Hussain Baqueri, *CFO*
Ali Baqueri, *Manager*
EMP: 10
SQ FT: 4,500
SALES (est): 1.6MM **Privately Held**
SIC: **2752** Commercial printing, lithographic

▲ = Import ▼ = Export
◆ = Import/Export

Plainview - Nassau County (G-13676)

(G-13652)
NASTEL TECHNOLOGIES INC (PA)
88 Sunnyside Blvd Ste 101 (11803-1507)
PHONE..................631 761-9100
Fax: 631 761-9101
David Mavashev, *CEO*
Scott Corrigan, *Vice Pres*
Larry Jeshiva, *Vice Pres*
Richard Nikula, *Vice Pres*
Michael Ragusa, *Vice Pres*
EMP: 120
SQ FT: 7,500
SALES (est): 15MM **Privately Held**
WEB: www.nastel.com
SIC: 7372 Prepackaged software

(G-13653)
NUCLEAR DIAGNOSTIC PDTS NY INC
130 Commercial St (11803-2414)
PHONE..................516 575-4201
Wayne Wong, *Ch of Bd*
Tom Poland, *Manager*
EMP: 7
SALES (est): 986.7K **Privately Held**
SIC: 3829 Medical diagnostic systems, nuclear

(G-13654)
OMEGA INDUSTRIES & DEVELOPMENT
Also Called: Turbo Dynamics
150 Express St Ste 2 (11803-2421)
PHONE..................516 349-8010
Fax: 516 349-0677
Pierre Lavi, *President*
Edward Lavi, *Treasurer*
EMP: 26
SQ FT: 25,000
SALES (est): 2.9MM **Privately Held**
SIC: 3519 3511 3728 6512 Jet propulsion engines; gas turbines, mechanical drive; aircraft parts & equipment; nonresidential building operators; aircraft engines & engine parts; motor vehicle parts & accessories

(G-13655)
P D R INC
Also Called: Sir Speedy
101 Dupont St (11803-1608)
PHONE..................516 829-5300
Fax: 516 829-5650
Pat Riccardi, *President*
EMP: 8
SQ FT: 4,500
SALES (est): 1.1MM **Privately Held**
SIC: 2752 2791 Commercial printing, lithographic; typesetting

(G-13656)
PETER DIGIOIA
Also Called: Medsurg Direct
7 Sherwood Dr (11803-3218)
PHONE..................516 644-5517
Peter Digioia, *Owner*
EMP: 5
SALES (est): 424.1K **Privately Held**
SIC: 3841 5047 Surgical & medical instruments; medical equipment & supplies

(G-13657)
PETRO INC
3 Fairchild Ct (11803-1701)
PHONE..................516 686-1717
Brian Boschert, *Branch Mgr*
EMP: 8 **Publicly Held**
SIC: 1389 Gas field services
HQ: Petro, Inc.
9 W Broad St Ste 3
Stamford CT 06902
203 325-5400

(G-13658)
PORT EVERGLADES MACHINE WORKS
Also Called: P E Machine Works
57 Colgate Dr (11803-1803)
PHONE..................516 367-2280
Steven Bellask, *President*
John Schaefer, *Vice Pres*
EMP: 10
SQ FT: 10,000
SALES (est): 966K **Privately Held**
SIC: 3599 3731 Machine shop, jobbing & repair; shipbuilding & repairing

(G-13659)
PURITY PRODUCTS INC
200 Terminal Dr (11803-2312)
PHONE..................516 767-1967
Jahn Levin, *President*
Dorothy Brown, *Purch Mgr*
Richard Conant, *QA Dir*
Michael Iwanciw, *Controller*
Phyllis Levin, *Human Resources*
▲ EMP: 61
SALES (est): 14.2MM **Privately Held**
SIC: 2834 Vitamin, nutrient & hematinic preparations for human use

(G-13660)
ROMAC ELECTRONICS INC
155 E Ames Ct Unit 1 (11803-2383)
PHONE..................516 349-7900
Fax: 516 349-7573
Jerome Bloomberg, *President*
Al Debello, *General Mgr*
Lee Bloomberg, *Vice Pres*
Michael Bloomberg, *Vice Pres*
Ronald Bloomberg, *Vice Pres*
EMP: 49 EST: 1952
SQ FT: 42,000
SALES (est): 9.9MM **Privately Held**
WEB: www.romacelectronics.com
SIC: 3499 Shims, metal

(G-13661)
S E A SUPPLIES LTD
Also Called: S E A Supls
1670 Old Country Rd # 104 (11803-5000)
PHONE..................516 694-6677
Martin Reynolds, *Vice Pres*
Paul Hastings, *Manager*
EMP: 15
SQ FT: 1,400
SALES (est): 1.5MM **Privately Held**
WEB: www.seasupplies.com
SIC: 2819 3646 Industrial inorganic chemicals; commercial indusl & institutional electric lighting fixtures

(G-13662)
SPIN HOLDCO INC (DH)
303 Sunnyside Blvd # 70 (11803-1597)
PHONE..................516 349-8555
Bob Doyl, *Principal*
Russ Harrison, *Finance*
EMP: 1
SALES (est): 148.2MM
SALES (corp-wide): 369.9MM **Privately Held**
SIC: 3633 5087 Household laundry equipment; laundry equipment & supplies
HQ: Csc Serviceworks, Inc
303 Sunnyside Blvd # 70
Plainview NY 11803
516 349-8555

(G-13663)
STEVAL GRAPHICS CONCEPTS INC
Also Called: Graphic Concepts
7 Fairchild Ct Ste 200 (11803-1701)
PHONE..................516 576-0220
Fax: 516 576-2002
Stephen Trigg, *CEO*
EMP: 12
SQ FT: 5,000
SALES (est): 760K **Privately Held**
SIC: 2752 Commercial printing, offset

(G-13664)
SUPREME SCREW PRODUCTS INC
10 Skyline Dr Unit B (11803-2517)
PHONE..................718 293-6600
Fax: 718 293-6602
Misha Migdal, *President*
Gerald Lopez, *Manager*
Reinaldo Lopez, *Manager*
Lurise Napolitano, *Executive Asst*
Wendy Sosa, *Administration*
EMP: 65 EST: 1963
SQ FT: 11,000
SALES (est): 5.2MM **Privately Held**
SIC: 3451 Screw machine products

(G-13665)
TECHNIC INC
Also Called: Advanced Technology Division
111 E Ames Ct Unit 2 (11803-2311)
PHONE..................516 349-0700
Rob Sheddy, *Branch Mgr*
EMP: 15
SALES (corp-wide): 165.7MM **Privately Held**
WEB: www.technic.com
SIC: 2899 3559 Metal treating compounds; electroplating machinery & equipment
PA: Technic, Inc.
47 Molter St
Cranston RI 02910
401 781-6100

(G-13666)
TRANE US INC
245 Newtown Rd Ste 500 (11803-4300)
PHONE..................631 952-9477
Fax: 631 269-3601
Steve Wey, *District Mgr*
Eric Barkowitz, *Branch Mgr*
Richard Halley, *Manager*
Deborah Hole, *Manager*
EMP: 20 **Privately Held**
SIC: 3585 Refrigeration & heating equipment
HQ: Trane U.S. Inc.
1 Centennial Ave Ste 101
Piscataway NJ 08854
732 652-7100

(G-13667)
ULTRA FINE JEWELRY MFG
180 Dupont St Unit C (11803-1616)
PHONE..................516 349-2848
Benjamin Matalon, *President*
Sandra Matalon, *Vice Pres*
▲ EMP: 20 EST: 1978
SALES (est): 2.3MM **Privately Held**
SIC: 3911 Jewelry, precious metal

(G-13668)
VASOMEDICAL INC (PA)
137 Commercial St Ste 200 (11803-2410)
PHONE..................516 997-4600
Fax: 516 997-2299
Joshua Markowitz, *Ch of Bd*
David Lieberman, *Vice Ch Bd*
Jun MA, *President*
Peter C Castle, *COO*
Hong Chen, *Senior Engr*
▲ EMP: 281
SQ FT: 8,700
SALES: 72.5MM **Publicly Held**
WEB: www.vasomedical.com
SIC: 3845 3841 Electromedical equipment; surgical & medical instruments

(G-13669)
VASOMEDICAL SOLUTIONS INC
137 Commercial St Ste 200 (11803-2410)
PHONE..................516 997-4600
Jai Daodat, *Accountant*
EMP: 99
SALES (est): 5.8MM
SALES (corp-wide): 72.5MM **Publicly Held**
SIC: 3841 Diagnostic apparatus, medical
PA: Vasomedical, Inc.
137 Commercial St Ste 200
Plainview NY 11803
516 997-4600

(G-13670)
VEECO INSTRUMENTS INC
Also Called: Veeco Process Equipment
1 Terminal Dr (11803-2313)
PHONE..................516 349-8300
Susan Troncale, *Engineer*
Emmanuel Lakios, *Branch Mgr*
Jim Hopkins, *Network Enginr*
EMP: 150
SALES (corp-wide): 332.4MM **Publicly Held**
WEB: www.veeco.com
SIC: 3612 5932 Transformers, except electric; building materials, secondhand
PA: Veeco Instruments Inc.
1 Terminal Dr
Plainview NY 11803
516 677-0200

(G-13671)
VEECO INSTRUMENTS INC (PA)
1 Terminal Dr (11803-2313)
PHONE..................516 677-0200
Fax: 516 349-6232
John R Peeler, *Ch of Bd*
William J Miller, *President*
John P Kiernan, *Senior VP*
John Kiernan, *Senior VP*
Kathy Damiani, *Vice Pres*
▲ EMP: 277
SQ FT: 80,000
SALES: 332.4MM **Publicly Held**
WEB: www.veeco.com
SIC: 3559 Semiconductor manufacturing machinery

(G-13672)
VEECO PROCESS EQUIPMENT INC (HQ)
1 Terminal Dr (11803-2313)
PHONE..................516 677-0200
John R Peeler, *CEO*
Russell Low, *President*
Gerry Blumenstock, *General Mgr*
Derek Derosia, *Regional Mgr*
David Glass, *Exec VP*
EMP: 122
SQ FT: 18,000
SALES (est): 141.4MM
SALES (corp-wide): 332.4MM **Publicly Held**
SIC: 3569 Assembly machines, non-metalworking
PA: Veeco Instruments Inc.
1 Terminal Dr
Plainview NY 11803
516 677-0200

(G-13673)
VERTIV SERVICES INC
79 Express St Fl 14 (11803-2419)
PHONE..................516 349-8500
Tammy Burns, *Branch Mgr*
Jay Mohr, *Network Mgr*
EMP: 8 **Privately Held**
SIC: 3823 Industrial instrmnts msrmnt display/control process variable
HQ: Vertiv Services, Inc.
610 Executive Campus Dr
Westerville OH 43082
614 841-6400

(G-13674)
WILLIAM CHARLES PRTG CO INC
7 Fairchild Ct Ste 100 (11803-1701)
PHONE..................516 349-0900
Fax: 516 349-0935
Chris Pellegrini, *President*
Joseph Pelligrini, *President*
Jamie Foster, *Managing Dir*
Charles Pelligrini, *Principal*
Ed Simon, *Cust Mgr*
EMP: 35 EST: 1935
SQ FT: 17,000
SALES (est): 6.3MM **Privately Held**
WEB: www.williamcharlesprinting.com
SIC: 2752 2759 2789 Commercial printing, offset; letterpress printing; bookbinding & related work

(G-13675)
XPRESS PRINTING INC
Also Called: T L X
7 Fairchild Ct Ste 100 (11803-1701)
PHONE..................516 605-1000
Chris Moscatl, *President*
EMP: 8
SQ FT: 60,000
SALES (est): 885K **Privately Held**
SIC: 2759 Promotional printing

(G-13676)
Y & Z PRECISION INC
Also Called: Y & Z Precision Machine Shop
155 E Ames Ct Unit 4 (11803-2300)
PHONE..................516 349-8243
Fax: 516 349-7615
Zoltan Vays, *President*
Ryszard Dobrogowski, *Admin Sec*
EMP: 15
SQ FT: 7,400
SALES (est): 2.5MM **Privately Held**
SIC: 3671 Electron tubes

Plattsburgh
Clinton County

(G-13677)
A D K DENTAL LAB
87 Hammond Ln (12901-2000)
PHONE...................518 563-6093
Robert Squire, *Owner*
EMP: 5
SQ FT: 7,000
SALES (est): 250K **Privately Held**
SIC: 3843 Dental laboratory equipment

(G-13678)
ADIRONDACK PENNYSAVER INC
177 Margaret St (12901-1837)
PHONE...................518 563-0100
Fax: 518 562-0303
Corinne Rigby, *President*
Mark Rigby, *Corp Secy*
EMP: 25
SQ FT: 5,000
SALES (est): 2.2MM **Privately Held**
WEB: www.adkpennysaver.com
SIC: 2741 2759 Shopping news: publishing & printing; commercial printing

(G-13679)
APGN INC
Also Called: Apg Neuros
160 Banker Rd (12901-7309)
PHONE...................518 324-4150
Omar Hammoud, *President*
EMP: 30
SALES (corp-wide): 27.4MM **Privately Held**
SIC: 3564 Blowing fans: industrial or commercial
HQ: Apgn Inc
1270 Boul Michele-Bohec
Blainville QC J7C 5
450 939-0799

(G-13680)
AWR ENERGY INC
35 Melody Ln (12901-6414)
P.O. Box 3027 (12901-0298)
PHONE...................585 469-7750
Steve Baiocchi, *President*
George Klemann, *Treasurer*
EMP: 10
SALES (est): 911.9K **Privately Held**
SIC: 3511 Turbines & turbine generator sets

(G-13681)
B3CG INTERCONNECT USA INC
18 Northern Ave 100 (12903-3905)
PHONE...................450 491-4040
Stefan Baumans, *President*
Marc Brosseau, *Vice Pres*
EMP: 19 **EST:** 2008
SALES (est): 3.8MM
SALES (corp-wide): 35.7MM **Privately Held**
SIC: 3679 Harness assemblies for electronic use: wire or cable
HQ: B3cg Interconnect Inc
310 Boul Industriel
Saint-Eustache QC J7R 5
450 491-4040

(G-13682)
BIOTECH ENERGY INC
Also Called: Biotech Energy Systems
100 Clinton Point Dr (12901-6002)
PHONE...................800 340-1387
Stan Kinsman, *CEO*
EMP: 6 **EST:** 2015
SALES (est): 316.4K **Privately Held**
SIC: 3433 Burners, furnaces, boilers & stokers

(G-13683)
BOMBARDIER MASS TRANSIT CORP
71 Wall St (12901-3755)
PHONE...................518 566-0150
Fax: 518 566-0052
William Spurr, *President*
Serge Planchet, *General Mgr*
Rene Lalande, *Vice Pres*
James Tooley, *Vice Pres*
Mike Mitchell, *Opers Staff*
▲ **EMP:** 380
SALES (est): 60.3MM
SALES (corp-wide): 2.7B **Privately Held**
SIC: 3743 Railroad equipment
HQ: Brp Us Inc.
10101 Science Dr
Sturtevant WI 53177
715 842-8886

(G-13684)
BRUSHTECH (DISC) INC
4 Matt Ave (12901-3736)
P.O. Box 1130 (12901-0068)
PHONE...................518 563-8420
Fax: 518 563-0581
Nora Gunjian, *President*
Zaven Gunjian, *Vice Pres*
Ralph Downey, *Plant Mgr*
▲ **EMP:** 18
SQ FT: 34,000
SALES (est): 3.3MM **Privately Held**
WEB: www.brushtech.com
SIC: 3991 Brushes, household or industrial

(G-13685)
CAMSO MANUFACTURING USA LTD (HQ)
1 Martina Cir (12901-7421)
PHONE...................518 561-7528
Fax: 518 561-7651
Ivan Warmuth, *Ch of Bd*
Mario Bouchard, *Treasurer*
Wanda Haby, *Human Res Mgr*
▲ **EMP:** 70
SALES (est): 16.2MM
SALES (corp-wide): 785MM **Privately Held**
SIC: 3061 Oil & gas field machinery rubber goods (mechanical)
PA: Camso Inc
2633 Rue Macpherson
Magog QC J1X 0
819 823-1777

(G-13686)
CEIT CORP
625 State Route 3 Unit 2 (12901-6530)
PHONE...................518 825-0649
Fax: 518 825-0651
▲ **EMP:** 10
SQ FT: 15,000
SALES (est): 950K **Privately Held**
SIC: 3648 Mfg Lighting Equipment

(G-13687)
CINTUBE LTD
139 Distribution Way (12901-3734)
PHONE...................518 324-3333
EMP: 11
SALES (est): 1.4MM **Privately Held**
SIC: 3399 Primary metal products

(G-13688)
COMMUNITY NEWSPAPER GROUP LLC
Also Called: Plattsburgh Press-Republican
170 Margaret St (12901-1838)
P.O. Box 459 (12901-0459)
PHONE...................518 565-4114
Fax: 518 561-3362
Kevin Richard, *President*
Bob Parks, *Branch Mgr*
Jim Dynko, *Manager*
EMP: 21 **Privately Held**
WEB: www.clintonnc.com
SIC: 2711 Newspapers: publishing only, not printed on site
HQ: Community Newspaper Group, Llc
3500 Colonnade Pkwy # 600
Birmingham AL 35243

(G-13689)
DENTON PUBLICATIONS INC
Also Called: Free Trader
21 Mckinley Ave Ste 3 (12901-3800)
PHONE...................518 561-9680
Cindy Tucker, *General Mgr*
James Fields, *Manager*
EMP: 20
SALES (corp-wide): 6MM **Privately Held**
WEB: www.denpubs.com
SIC: 2711 2721 Commercial printing & newspaper publishing combined; periodicals
PA: Denton Publications, Inc.
14 Hand Ave
Elizabethtown NY 12932
518 873-6368

(G-13690)
EURO GEAR (USA) INC
1 Cumberland Ave (12901-1833)
PHONE...................518 578-1775
Eloise Beauche, *Branch Mgr*
EMP: 8
SALES (corp-wide): 5.4MM **Privately Held**
SIC: 3241 3599 Natural cement; machine & other job shop work
PA: Euro Gear (Usa), Inc.
1395 Brickell Ave Ste 800
Miami FL 33131
518 578-1775

(G-13691)
FEDEX GROUND PACKAGE SYS INC
82 Gateway Dr (12901-5371)
PHONE...................800 463-3339
William Battle, *General Mgr*
EMP: 5
SALES (corp-wide): 60.3B **Publicly Held**
SIC: 3086 Packaging & shipping materials, foamed plastic
HQ: Fedex Ground Package System, Inc.
1000 Fed Ex Dr
Coraopolis PA 15108
800 463-3339

(G-13692)
GEORGIA-PACIFIC LLC
327 Margaret St (12901-1719)
PHONE...................518 561-3500
Fax: 518 562-6598
Kirk Stallsmith, *Vice Pres*
Michael Penfield, *Facilities Mgr*
Mike Bell, *Maint Spvr*
Ray Desso, *QC Dir*
Gary Frenia, *Manager*
EMP: 540
SQ FT: 14,464
SALES (corp-wide): 27.8B **Privately Held**
WEB: www.gp.com
SIC: 2621 2676 Paper mills; sanitary paper products
HQ: Georgia-Pacific Llc
133 Peachtree St Ne # 4810
Atlanta GA 30303
404 652-4000

(G-13693)
GRAYMONT MATERIALS INC
Also Called: Plattsburgh Quarry
111 Quarry Rd (12901-6215)
PHONE...................518 561-5200
Todd Kempainen, *President*
Dennis Tsuchida, *General Mgr*
Mark Coombs, *Sales Mgr*
Rick Maguire, *Manager*
Diane Nichols, *Manager*
EMP: 28
SALES (est): 922.1K **Privately Held**
SIC: 3281 2951 Stone, quarrying & processing of own stone products; asphalt paving mixtures & blocks

(G-13694)
HANET PLASTICS USA INC
139 Distribution Way (12901-3734)
PHONE...................518 324-5850
EMP: 5
SALES (est): 370K **Privately Held**
SIC: 2821 Mfg Plastic Materials/Resins

(G-13695)
HERITAGE PRINTING CENTER
94 Margaret St (12901-2925)
PHONE...................518 563-8240
Fax: 518 563-9377
Roger A Conant, *Partner*
Roger W Conant, *Partner*
EMP: 7 **EST:** 1976
SQ FT: 2,200
SALES (est): 730.2K **Privately Held**
WEB: www.heritageprint.com
SIC: 2752 Commercial printing, offset

(G-13696)
IEC HOLDEN CORPORATION
51 Distribution Way (12901-3731)
PHONE...................518 213-3991
Robert Briscoe, *Ch of Bd*
▲ **EMP:** 17
SALES (est): 3.5MM **Privately Held**
SIC: 3621 Inverters, rotating: electrical

(G-13697)
INTRAPAC INTERNATIONAL CORP
4 Plant St (12901-3771)
PHONE...................518 561-2030
Steve Braido, *Plant Mgr*
Tony Searing, *Plant Mgr*
Robert Thiessen, *Plant Mgr*
Christina Baker, *Human Res Mgr*
Anthony Staring, *Manager*
EMP: 150
SALES (corp-wide): 120MM **Privately Held**
SIC: 3085 3221 Plastics bottles; glass containers
PA: Intrapac International Corporation
136 Fairview Rd Ste 320
Mooresville NC 28117
704 360-8910

(G-13698)
ISLAND MACHINE INC
86 Boynton Ave (12901-1236)
PHONE...................518 562-1232
Fax: 518 561-0307
Marvin C Benton, *President*
Marvin Benton, *President*
Bonnie Benton, *Vice Pres*
EMP: 9
SQ FT: 2,100
SALES: 600K **Privately Held**
SIC: 3599 Machine & other job shop work

(G-13699)
JOHNS MANVILLE CORPORATION
1 Kaycee Loop Rd (12901-2010)
PHONE...................518 565-3000
Fax: 518 565-3010
David Hardway, *Production*
Steve Kuhn, *Manager*
David Berglund, *Maintence Staff*
EMP: 28
SALES (corp-wide): 223.6B **Publicly Held**
WEB: www.jm.com
SIC: 2952 Roofing materials
HQ: Johns Manville Corporation
717 17th St Ste 800
Denver CO 80202
303 978-2000

(G-13700)
KNORR BRAKE COMPANY LLC
613 State Route 3 Unit 1 (12901-6530)
PHONE...................518 561-1387
Fax: 518 561-1344
Phil Rockwell, *Site Mgr*
EMP: 6 **Privately Held**
WEB: www.knorrbrakecorp.com
SIC: 3743 Brakes, air & vacuum: railway; rapid transit cars & equipment
HQ: Knorr Brake Company Llc
1 Arthur Peck Dr
Westminster MD 21157
410 875-0900

(G-13701)
LAKESIDE CONTAINER CORP (PA)
299 Arizona Ave (12903-4429)
P.O. Box 845 (12901-0845)
PHONE...................518 561-6150
George Bouyea, *President*
Paige Raville, *Vice Pres*
Darrin Campbell, *Design Engr*
Carol Hollenbeck, *Marketing Staff*
Miki Worden, *Program Mgr*
EMP: 19 **EST:** 1958
SQ FT: 65,000
SALES (est): 2.2MM **Privately Held**
WEB: www.lakesidecontainer.com
SIC: 2653 Boxes, corrugated: made from purchased materials

GEOGRAPHIC SECTION

Plattsburgh - Clinton County (G-13726)

(G-13702)
LEROUX FUELS
994 Military Tpke (12901-5926)
PHONE.....................518 563-3653
Nicholas Leroux, *Principal*
EMP: 10
SALES (est): 1.5MM **Privately Held**
SIC: 2869 Fuels

(G-13703)
MATROX GRAPHICS INC
625 State Route 3 1/2 (12901-6530)
PHONE.....................518 561-4417
Robert Lasalle Jr, *Manager*
Benoit Lachance, *Senior Mgr*
EMP: 8
SALES (corp-wide): 11.3MM **Privately Held**
SIC: 3572 Computer tape drives & components
PA: Graphiques Matrox Inc
1055 Boul Saint-Regis
Dorval QC H9P 2
514 822-6000

(G-13704)
MOLD-RITE PLASTICS LLC
1 Plant St (12901-3788)
PHONE.....................518 561-1812
Fax: 518 561-0017
Dennis Houpt, *Senior VP*
Barry Daggett, *Vice Pres*
Bhojraj Naveen, *Vice Pres*
Keith Kelble, *Opers Mgr*
Tim Boshart, *Opers Staff*
EMP: 6 **Privately Held**
SIC: 3544 Industrial molds
HQ: Mold-Rite Plastics, Llc
30 N La Salle St Ste 2425
Chicago IL 60602
518 561-1812

(G-13705)
MONAGHAN MEDICAL CORPORATION (PA)
5 Latour Ave Ste 1600 (12901-7271)
PHONE.....................518 561-7330
Fax: 518 561-5660
Gerald Slemko, *President*
Dominic Coppolo, *Vice Pres*
William Seitz, *Vice Pres*
Dick Thayer, *Purchasing*
Ronald Grahm, *Controller*
▲ **EMP:** 52
SALES (est): 10.9MM **Privately Held**
WEB: www.monaghanmed.com
SIC: 3841 Surgical & medical instruments

(G-13706)
NORSK TITANIUM US INC (DH)
44 Martina Cir (12901-7420)
PHONE.....................949 735-9463
Warren Boley, *Ch of Bd*
Bart V Aalst, *CFO*
Gunnar Aasbo-Skinderhaug, *Bd of Directors*
EMP: 9
SQ FT: 5,000
SALES (est): 584.9K
SALES (corp-wide): 341.7K **Privately Held**
SIC: 3728 Aircraft assemblies, subassemblies & parts

(G-13707)
NORTH AMERICAN DOOR CORP
Also Called: Nadcor
1471 Military Tpke (12901-7453)
PHONE.....................518 566-0161
Fax: 518 566-6172
Antonio Gervasi, *President*
Anna Montesano, *Corp Secy*
Bruno Gervasi, *Vice Pres*
Connie Carrozza, *Office Mgr*
Patrick McCall, *Manager*
▼ **EMP:** 12
SQ FT: 20,000
SALES (est): 3.6MM **Privately Held**
WEB: www.nadcor.com
SIC: 3442 Metal doors, sash & trim

(G-13708)
NORTHEAST CONCRETE PDTS INC
1024 Military Tpke (12901-5959)
PHONE.....................518 563-0700
Arthur Spiegel, *President*
James L Neverett, *Senior VP*
Darren C Babbie, *Vice Pres*
Suzanne Arlt, *Finance Dir*
Jill Friedrich, *Administration*
EMP: 15 **EST:** 1938
SQ FT: 31,500
SALES (est): 1.4MM **Privately Held**
WEB: www.concretebuildingsupply.com
SIC: 3272 Precast terrazo or concrete products

(G-13709)
NORTHEAST GROUP
Also Called: Strictly Business
12 Nepco Way (12903-3961)
PHONE.....................518 563-8214
Herb Carpenter, *Partner*
Mary Carpenter, *Partner*
Mike Carpenter, *Partner*
▲ **EMP:** 55
SALES (est): 6.6MM **Privately Held**
WEB: www.sbmonthly.com
SIC: 2721 Periodicals

(G-13710)
NORTHEAST PRTG & DIST CO INC
163 Idaho Ave (12903-3987)
PHONE.....................514 577-3545
EMP: 7
SALES (corp-wide): 6MM **Privately Held**
SIC: 2721 Periodicals
PA: Northeast Printing & Distribution Company, Inc.
12 Nepco Way
Plattsburgh NY 12903
518 563-8214

(G-13711)
NORTHEAST PRTG & DIST CO INC (PA)
Also Called: Northeast Group, The
12 Nepco Way (12903-3961)
PHONE.....................518 563-8214
Fax: 518 563-3320
Herb Carpenter, *President*
Mary E Carpenter, *Vice Pres*
Michael Carpenter, *Vice Pres*
Kelly Miller, *Facilities Mgr*
Marcia Vicencio, *Purch Mgr*
▲ **EMP:** 37
SQ FT: 115,000
SALES (est): 6MM **Privately Held**
WEB: www.thenortheastgroup.com
SIC: 2752 Commercial printing, offset

(G-13712)
PACTIV LLC
74 Weed St (12901-1260)
PHONE.....................518 562-6101
Michael Petit, *Plant Mgr*
Tony Scaring, *Plant Mgr*
Matt Labombard, *QC Mgr*
Mark Lowther, *Engineer*
Damijan Vujanovic, *Engineer*
EMP: 200
SQ FT: 64,904 **Privately Held**
WEB: www.pactiv.com
SIC: 2656 2657 2671 Plates, paper: made from purchased material; food containers, folding: made from purchased material; packaging paper & plastics film, coated & laminated
HQ: Pactiv Llc
1900 W Field Ct
Lake Forest IL 60045
847 482-2000

(G-13713)
PACTIV LLC
74 Weed St (12901-1260)
PHONE.....................518 562-6120
Anthony Searing, *Manager*
EMP: 120 **Privately Held**
WEB: www.pactiv.com
SIC: 3089 Plastic containers, except foam

HQ: Pactiv Llc
1900 W Field Ct
Lake Forest IL 60045
847 482-2000

(G-13714)
PERFORMANCE DIESEL SERVICE LLC
24 Latour Ave (12901-7206)
PHONE.....................315 854-5269
Scott Roketenetz,
EMP: 11
SALES (est): 1.8MM **Privately Held**
SIC: 2911 Diesel fuels

(G-13715)
PLATTCO CORPORATION (PA)
7 White St (12901-3471)
PHONE.....................518 563-4640
Fax: 518 563-4892
Douglas J Crozierm, *Ch of Bd*
Dean Surprenant, *Production*
Stacie Chapman, *Purch Mgr*
Logan Miller, *Design Engr*
Danielle Ross, *Sales Mgr*
◆ **EMP:** 50 **EST:** 1897
SQ FT: 60,000
SALES (est): 7.3MM **Privately Held**
WEB: www.plattco.com
SIC: 3369 3491 3322 Machinery castings, nonferrous: ex. alum., copper, die, etc.; industrial valves; malleable iron foundries

(G-13716)
PLATTSBURGH SHEET METAL INC
95 Sailly Ave (12901-1726)
PHONE.....................518 561-4930
Sandra Carlo, *President*
EMP: 5
SALES (est): 1MM **Privately Held**
SIC: 3444 Sheet metalwork

(G-13717)
PREVOST CAR US INC
Also Called: Nova Bus Lfs, A Division of PR
260 Banker Rd (12901-7310)
PHONE.....................518 957-2052
Corrine Govinden, *Controller*
Mathew Nadal, *Sales Mgr*
▲ **EMP:** 202
SQ FT: 140,000
SALES (est): 109.6MM **Privately Held**
SIC: 3711 Buses, all types, assembly of

(G-13718)
PRICE CHOPPER OPERATING CO
19 Centre Dr (12901-6553)
PHONE.....................518 562-3565
Tom Tsounis, *Manager*
Lori L Duprey, *Manager*
Sharon Wood, *Manager*
EMP: 10
SALES (corp-wide): 3.4B **Privately Held**
SIC: 3751 Motorcycles & related parts
HQ: Price Chopper Operating Co., Inc
501 Duanesburg Rd
Schenectady NY 12306
518 379-1600

(G-13719)
PRIM HALL ENTERPRISES INC
11 Spellman Rd (12901-5326)
PHONE.....................518 561-7408
Fax: 518 563-1472
John Prim, *President*
David Hall, *Vice Pres*
Thomas Venne, *Engineer*
Bill Kelting, *Accounts Mgr*
Mat Demers, *Manager*
EMP: 12
SQ FT: 43,000
SALES (est): 1.4MM **Privately Held**
WEB: www.primhall.com
SIC: 3555 7699 3542 7389 Printing trades machinery; industrial machinery & equipment repair; machine tools, metal forming type; design, commercial & industrial

(G-13720)
R & S MACHINE CENTER INC
Also Called: R&S Machine
4398 Route 22 (12901-5851)
P.O. Box 40 (12901-0040)
PHONE.....................518 563-4016
Robert Davenport, *President*
EMP: 10
SQ FT: 7,000
SALES: 1.9MM **Privately Held**
SIC: 3599 5051 Machine shop, jobbing & repair; steel

(G-13721)
RAILTECH COMPOSITES INC
80 Montana Dr (12903-4933)
PHONE.....................518 324-6190
John Natale, *President*
Nestor Lewyckyj, *Vice Pres*
Mark Beaudoin, *Manager*
EMP: 14
SQ FT: 10,000
SALES (est): 1.9MM
SALES (corp-wide): 19.3MM **Privately Held**
WEB: www.railtechcomposites.com
SIC: 2439 Structural wood members
HQ: Skyfold Inc
325 Av Lee
Baie-D'urfe QC H9X 3
514 457-4767

(G-13722)
RAMBACHS INTERNATIONAL BAKERY
65 S Peru St (12901-3834)
PHONE.....................518 563-1721
Gerard Rambach, *President*
Joan Rambach, *Treasurer*
EMP: 18
SQ FT: 3,500
SALES (est): 830K **Privately Held**
SIC: 2051 Bakery: wholesale or wholesale/retail combined

(G-13723)
RAPA INDEPENDENT NORTH AMERICA
Also Called: Rina
124 Connecticut Rd (12903-4955)
PHONE.....................518 561-0513
Manil Whig, *President*
▲ **EMP:** 6
SQ FT: 5,000
SALES: 200K **Privately Held**
SIC: 2013 Sausage casings, natural

(G-13724)
SALERNO PACKAGING INC (HQ)
Also Called: Salerno Plastic Film and Bags
14 Gus Lapham Ln (12901-6534)
PHONE.....................518 563-3636
Fax: 518 563-3839
Kurt Strater, *President*
Roger Sullivan, *Senior VP*
Mac Elgin, *Vice Pres*
Matt Ramsey, *Marketing Staff*
Greg Crites, *Manager*
EMP: 12
SALES (est): 38.7MM
SALES (corp-wide): 1B **Privately Held**
SIC: 2673 Plastic bags: made from purchased materials
PA: Inteplast Group Corporation
9 Peach Tree Hill Rd
Livingston NJ 07039
973 994-8000

(G-13725)
SEMEC CORP
20 Gateway Dr (12901-5371)
PHONE.....................518 825-0160
Mario Babin, *Manager*
Deborah Wells, *Admin Mgr*
▲ **EMP:** 15
SALES (est): 2.1MM **Privately Held**
SIC: 3743 Railroad equipment

(G-13726)
SSF PRODUCTION LLC
194 Pleasant Ridge Rd (12901-5841)
PHONE.....................518 324-3407
Tilo Hildebrand, *Plant Mgr*
Frank Filbir, *Mng Member*
Tilo Hilderbrand,

Plattsburgh - Clinton County (G-13727)

▲ EMP: 10
SQ FT: 17,000
SALES (est): 1.8MM **Privately Held**
SIC: 3296 Acoustical board & tile, mineral wool

(G-13727)
STEELE TRUSS COMPANY INC
118 Trade Rd (12901-6259)
PHONE..................518 562-4663
Robert Steele, *CEO*
Joel C Steele, *President*
Thomas E Steele Sr, *President*
Loretta Steele, *Corp Secy*
Marvin Hooper, *VP Engrg*
EMP: 25
SQ FT: 80,000
SALES: 2MM **Privately Held**
WEB: www.steeltrusses.net
SIC: 2439 1541 Trusses, wooden roof; steel building construction

(G-13728)
STERRX LLC (PA)
141 Idaho Ave (12903-3987)
PHONE..................518 324-7879
Terry Wiley, *VP Mfg*
Gary Hanley,
EMP: 22
SALES (est): 5.7MM **Privately Held**
SIC: 2834 Solutions, pharmaceutical

(G-13729)
STERRX LLC
Also Called: Sterrx Cmo
141 Idaho Ave Ste 1 (12903-3987)
PHONE..................518 324-7879
Terry Wiley, *VP Mfg*
EMP: 10
SALES (corp-wide): 5.7MM **Privately Held**
SIC: 2834 Water, sterile: for injections
PA: Sterrx, Llc
141 Idaho Ave
Plattsburgh NY 12903
518 324-7879

(G-13730)
STUDLEY PRINTING & PUBLISHING
Also Called: Lake Champlain Weekly
4701 State Route 9 (12901-6036)
PHONE..................518 563-1414
Fax: 518 563-7060
William Studley, *President*
Caroline Kehne, *Editor*
Lynn Roberts-Devins, *Accounts Exec*
Kim Mousseau, *Director*
EMP: 18
SALES (est): 2.9MM **Privately Held**
WEB: www.studleyprinting.com
SIC: 2752 8743 Commercial printing, lithographic; public relations & publicity

(G-13731)
SWAROVSKI LIGHTING LTD (PA)
Also Called: Schonbek
61 Industrial Blvd (12901-1908)
PHONE..................518 563-7500
Fax: 518 563-4228
John Simms, *CEO*
Andrew Schonbek, *President*
Tania Patone, *Project Mgr*
Mike Stratte, *Project Mgr*
Deborah Buskey, *Engineer*
◆ EMP: 267
SQ FT: 200,000
SALES (est): 59.4MM **Privately Held**
SIC: 3645 Residential lighting fixtures

(G-13732)
SWAROVSKI LIGHTING LTD
Also Called: Schonbek Shipping Bldg
1483 Military Tpke Ste B (12901-7453)
PHONE..................518 324-6378
PR Llier, *Principal*
EMP: 400
SALES (corp-wide): 59.4MM **Privately Held**
SIC: 3645 Chandeliers, residential
PA: Swarovski Lighting, Ltd.
61 Industrial Blvd
Plattsburgh NY 12901
518 563-7500

(G-13733)
TITHERINGTON DESIGN & MFG
102 Sharron Ave Unit 1 (12901-3828)
PHONE..................518 324-2205
Philip D Titherington, *CEO*
EMP: 11
SALES (est): 1.9MM **Privately Held**
SIC: 3089 7336 Injection molding of plastics; package design

(G-13734)
UMS MANUFACTURING LLC
194 Pleasant Ridge Rd (12901-5841)
PHONE..................518 562-2410
Ed Martin, *Controller*
Mark Schulter,
Udo Schulter,
EMP: 10
SQ FT: 57,000
SALES: 1.2MM **Privately Held**
SIC: 2675 Waterproof cardboard: made from purchased materials

(G-13735)
UPSTONE MATERIALS INC (DH) ⊙
111 Quarry Rd (12901-6215)
PHONE..................518 561-5321
Sylvan Gross, *President*
EMP: 90 EST: 2017
SQ FT: 5,000
SALES: 40MM
SALES (corp-wide): 77.1MM **Privately Held**
SIC: 1429 3273 2951 Grits mining (crushed stone); ready-mixed concrete; asphalt & asphaltic paving mixtures (not from refineries)
HQ: Barrett Industries Corporation
73 Headquarters Plz
Morristown NJ 07960
973 533-1001

(G-13736)
UPSTONE MATERIALS INC
Also Called: Potsdam Stone Concrete
111 Quarry Rd (12901-6215)
PHONE..................315 265-8036
Fax: 315 265-3402
Judy Fuhr, *Superintendent*
Dave Gordon, *Plant Mgr*
Donny Smith, *Manager*
EMP: 17
SQ FT: 3,769
SALES (corp-wide): 77.1MM **Privately Held**
WEB: www.graymont-ab.com
SIC: 3273 5083 Ready-mixed concrete; landscaping equipment
HQ: Upstone Materials Inc.
111 Quarry Rd
Plattsburgh NY 12901
518 561-5321

(G-13737)
VIDEOTEC SECURITY INC
35 Gateway Dr Ste 100 (12901-5382)
PHONE..................518 825-0020
Gianni Viero, *President*
Marta Stocchero, *Sales Staff*
Martina Panighel, *Corp Comm Staff*
Maureen Carlo, *Marketing Staff*
Michael Bedard, *Technical Staff*
▲ EMP: 5
SALES (est): 773.8K
SALES (corp-wide): 173.1K **Privately Held**
SIC: 3699 Security devices
HQ: Videotec Spa
Via Friuli 6
Schio VI 36015
044 569-7411

(G-13738)
WEBER INTL PACKG CO LLC
318 Cornelia St (12901-2300)
PHONE..................518 561-8282
K Heinz Weber, *CEO*
Michael Hanley, *Engineer*
Alice Barcomb, *Finance*
Tihamer Monostori,
EMP: 54
SQ FT: 44,000
SALES (est): 11.8MM **Privately Held**
WEB: www.weberintl.com
SIC: 3085 Plastics bottles

(G-13739)
WESTINGHOUSE A BRAKE TECH CORP
72 Arizona Ave (12903-4427)
PHONE..................518 561-0044
Bob Brassee, *Manager*
Alisa Langille, *Administration*
EMP: 70
SALES (corp-wide): 2.9B **Publicly Held**
WEB: www.wabtecglobalservices.com
SIC: 3743 Brakes, air & vacuum: railway; locomotives & parts; freight cars & equipment; rapid transit cars & equipment
PA: Westinghouse Air Brake Technologies Corporation
1001 Airbrake Ave
Wilmerding PA 15148
412 825-1000

(G-13740)
WOODFALLS INDUSTRIES
434 Burke Rd (12901-5214)
PHONE..................518 236-7201
Tammy Deyo, *Owner*
EMP: 10 EST: 2010
SALES (est): 450K **Privately Held**
SIC: 3999 Manufacturing industries

(G-13741)
XBORDER ENTERTAINMENT LLC
568 State Route 3 (12901-6526)
PHONE..................518 726-7036
Casey Spiegel, *Mng Member*
EMP: 7
SQ FT: 35,000
SALES (est): 193.4K **Privately Held**
SIC: 7372 Application computer software

Pleasant Valley
Dutchess County

(G-13742)
DETECTOR PRO
Also Called: Hudson River Met Detector Sls
1447 Route 44 (12569-7832)
PHONE..................845 635-3488
Gary Storm, *Owner*
EMP: 5
SALES (est): 300K **Privately Held**
WEB: www.detectorpro.com
SIC: 3669 Metal detectors

(G-13743)
SIMMONS FABRICATING SVC INC
1558 Main St (12569-7817)
P.O. Box 690 (12569-0690)
PHONE..................845 635-3755
Robert Lalonde, *President*
Colleen Lalonde, *President*
EMP: 5
SQ FT: 5,000
SALES: 250K **Privately Held**
SIC: 3444 Sheet metalwork

Pleasantville
Westchester County

(G-13744)
CARLARA GROUP LTD
Also Called: Sir Speedy
467 Bedford Rd (10570-2928)
PHONE..................914 769-2020
Fax: 914 769-4680
Carlos Bernard, *President*
Susana Lara, *Vice Pres*
EMP: 5
SQ FT: 3,000
SALES (est): 580K **Privately Held**
SIC: 2752 2791 2789 Commercial printing, lithographic; typesetting; bookbinding & related work

(G-13745)
COUNTY FABRICATORS
175 Marble Ave (10570-3421)
PHONE..................914 741-0219
Michael Gomes, *Bookkeeper*
Kristina Benza, *Mng Member*
Robert Benza, *Manager*
Mike Husband, *Director*
Phillip R Benza, *President*
EMP: 18
SQ FT: 13,200
SALES: 1.5MM **Privately Held**
WEB: www.countyfabricators.com
SIC: 3441 Fabricated structural metal

(G-13746)
HOME SERVICE PUBLICATIONS (DH)
1 Readers Digest Rd (10570-7000)
PHONE..................914 238-1000
Bonnie Dachar, *President*
Clifford Dupree, *Admin Sec*
Peggy Cassin,
EMP: 5
SALES (est): 1.4MM
SALES (corp-wide): 1.3B **Privately Held**
SIC: 2741 Miscellaneous publishing
HQ: Rd Publications, Inc.
1 Readers Digest Rd
Pleasantville NY 10570
914 238-1000

(G-13747)
OPTIMIZED DEVICES INC
220 Marble Ave (10570-3465)
PHONE..................914 769-6100
Fax: 914 769-6102
Arthur Zuch, *President*
Robert Zuch, *Vice Pres*
EMP: 13
SQ FT: 6,000
SALES (est): 2MM **Privately Held**
WEB: www.optdev.com
SIC: 3825 Instruments to measure electricity

(G-13748)
RD PUBLICATIONS INC (DH)
1 Readers Digest Rd (10570-7000)
PHONE..................914 238-1000
Thomas O Ryder, *President*
Robert J Krefting, *Senior VP*
Michael Geltzeiler, *Vice Pres*
Eric Gruseke, *Vice Pres*
George Scimone, *CFO*
EMP: 120
SQ FT: 50,000
SALES (est): 21.7MM
SALES (corp-wide): 1.3B **Privately Held**
WEB: www.rdpublications.com
SIC: 2721 Magazines: publishing only, not printed on site
HQ: Trusted Media Brands, Inc.
750 3rd Ave Fl 3
New York NY 10017
914 238-1000

(G-13749)
READERS DGEST YUNG FMILIES INC
Readers Digest Rd (10570)
PHONE..................914 238-1000
Thomas O Ryder, *Ch of Bd*
EMP: 25
SALES (est): 868.4K
SALES (corp-wide): 1.3B **Privately Held**
WEB: www.rd.com
SIC: 2731 Book publishing
HQ: Trusted Media Brands, Inc.
750 3rd Ave Fl 3
New York NY 10017
914 238-1000

(G-13750)
SAW MILL PEDIATRICS PLLC
95 Locust Rd (10570-3333)
PHONE..................914 449-6064
Maryann Hammel, *Principal*
Maryann Hammel, *Office Mgr*
Jeanne M Wilson, *Pediatrics*
Jeannie Leclere, *Nurse Practr*
EMP: 9
SALES (est): 996.9K **Privately Held**
SIC: 2421 Sawmills & planing mills, general

(G-13751)
STAUB USA INC
270 Marble Ave (10570-3464)
PHONE..................914 747-0300
Francis Staub, *President*
Alain Stammur, *Vice Pres*

▲ **EMP:** 5
SALES (est): 466.9K
SALES (corp-wide): 3.5B **Privately Held**
WEB: www.staubusa.com
SIC: 3321 Cooking utensils, cast iron
HQ: Zwilling J.A. Henckels, Llc
270 Marble Ave
Pleasantville NY 10573
800 777-4308

Poestenkill
Rensselaer County

(G-13752)
CANTON BIO-MEDICAL INC (PA)
Also Called: Saint-Gobain Performance Plas
11 Sicho Rd (12140-3102)
PHONE..................518 283-5963
Fax: 518 283-1418
John Bedell, *Principal*
Bob Pellerin, *Controller*
EMP: 36
SQ FT: 36,000
SALES (est): 2.4MM **Privately Held**
SIC: 2822 Silicone rubbers

(G-13753)
DYNAMIC SYSTEMS INC
Also Called: D S I
323 Rte 355 (12140)
P.O. Box 1234 (12140-1234)
PHONE..................518 283-5350
Fax: 518 283-3160
David Ferguson, *President*
Jean Jacon, *Vice Pres*
Emily Warren, *Materials Mgr*
Todd Bonesteel, *Production*
Mark Budesheim, *Purchasing*
▲ **EMP:** 38 **EST:** 1957
SQ FT: 29,000
SALES (est): 11.8MM **Privately Held**
WEB: www.gleeble.com
SIC: 3829 Measuring & controlling devices

(G-13754)
INTER STATE LAMINATES INC
44 Main St (12140)
P.O. Box 270 (12140-0270)
PHONE..................518 283-8355
Fax: 518 283-8358
Harold Crandall, *President*
Cheryl Littlefield, *Sales Staff*
Debbie Crandall, *Admin Sec*
EMP: 46
SALES (est): 6.1MM **Privately Held**
WEB: www.isltops.com
SIC: 3083 2541 Plastic finished products, laminated; wood partitions & fixtures

(G-13755)
SAINT-GOBAIN PRFMCE PLAS CORP
11 Sicho Rd (12140-3102)
PHONE..................518 283-5963
Lynn Monrow, *General Mgr*
Tammy L Teal, *Manager*
EMP: 41
SALES (corp-wide): 185.8MM **Privately Held**
SIC: 3089 Spouting, plastic & glass fiber reinforced
HQ: Saint-Gobain Performance Plastics Corporation
31500 Solon Rd
Solon OH 44139
440 836-6900

(G-13756)
VAN SLYKE BELTING LLC
606 Snyders Corners Rd (12140-2914)
PHONE..................518 283-5479
H Van, *Principal*
EMP: 6
SALES (est): 652.2K **Privately Held**
SIC: 3052 Rubber belting

Poland
Herkimer County

(G-13757)
PERFEX CORPORATION
32 Case St (13431)
PHONE..................315 826-3600
Fax: 315 826-7471
Michael E Kubick, *President*
Mike Dougherty, *Sales Staff*
Cynthia Chmielewski, *Manager*
▲ **EMP:** 13 **EST:** 1924
SQ FT: 24,000
SALES (est): 2.3MM **Privately Held**
WEB: www.perfexonline.com
SIC: 3991 2392 Brooms & brushes; mops, floor & dust

Pomona
Rockland County

(G-13758)
CAMBRIDGE SECURITY SEALS LLC
1 Cambridge Plz (10970-2676)
PHONE..................845 520-4111
Brian Lyle, *VP Sales*
Jill Nilsson, *Sales Associate*
Elisha Tropper, *Mng Member*
▲ **EMP:** 20
SQ FT: 25,000
SALES (est): 5.4MM **Privately Held**
SIC: 3089 Injection molding of plastics

(G-13759)
NUTRA-SCIENTIFICS LLC
108 Overlook Rd (10970-2115)
PHONE..................917 238-8510
Patrice Mouehla,
EMP: 9 **EST:** 2012
SALES (est): 575K **Privately Held**
SIC: 2834 5122 Pharmaceutical preparations; pharmaceuticals

(G-13760)
PARKWAY BREAD DISTRIBUTORS INC
15 Conklin Rd (10970-3601)
PHONE..................845 362-1221
Debra L Smith, *Principal*
EMP: 8
SALES (est): 428.3K **Privately Held**
SIC: 2051 Bread, cake & related products

(G-13761)
SAN JAE EDUCATIONAL RESOU
9 Chamberlain Ct (10970-2837)
PHONE..................845 364-5458
James Butler, *CEO*
Sandy Butler, *President*
EMP: 4
SALES (est): 1MM **Privately Held**
WEB: www.sanjaeco.com
SIC: 7372 Educational computer software

Port Byron
Cayuga County

(G-13762)
MARTENS COUNTRY KIT PDTS LLC
1323 Towpath Rd (13140)
P.O. Box 428 (13140-0428)
PHONE..................315 776-8821
Jill Skrupa, *Sales Staff*
Timothy Martens,
▲ **EMP:** 10
SALES (est): 859.8K **Privately Held**
SIC: 2099 Potatoes, dried: packaged with other ingredients

(G-13763)
MAX 200 PERFORMANCE DOG EQP
2113 State Route 31 (13140-9423)
PHONE..................315 776-9588
Fax: 315 776-9603
Irene Lamphere, *President*
Alfred Lamphere, *Vice Pres*
EMP: 22
SQ FT: 18,000
SALES (est): 1.5MM **Privately Held**
WEB: www.max200.com
SIC: 3199 Dog furnishings: collars, leashes, muzzles, etc.: leather

(G-13764)
PRECISION DIECUTTING INC
1381 Spring Lake Rd (13140-3375)
PHONE..................315 776-8465
Norma Compson, *President*
Jamie Compson, *Vice Pres*
EMP: 6
SALES (est): 300K **Privately Held**
SIC: 2675 Die-cut paper & board; stencil board, die-cut: made from purchased materials; stencil cards, die-cut: made from purchased materials

Port Chester
Westchester County

(G-13765)
AIR STRUCTURES AMERCN TECH INC
211 S Ridge St Ste 3 (10573-3445)
PHONE..................914 937-4500
Fax: 914 937-6331
Donato A Fraioli, *CEO*
Jan Ligas Jr, *Vice Pres*
Robert Tornquist, *CFO*
Rosemarie Fraioli, *Admin Sec*
▼ **EMP:** 50
SQ FT: 2,500
SALES (est): 10MM **Privately Held**
WEB: www.asati.com
SIC: 2394 Tents: made from purchased materials

(G-13766)
ALBUMX CORP
Also Called: Renanssance The Book
21 Grace Church St (10573-4911)
PHONE..................914 939-6878
Fax: 914 939-5874
Terry Huang, *President*
Albert Huang, *Prdtn Mgr*
Yung Kwong, *Treasurer*
Victor Huang, *Human Resources*
Tasha Homyak, *Manager*
▲ **EMP:** 80
SQ FT: 27,000
SALES (est): 7.9MM **Privately Held**
WEB: www.renaissancealbums.com
SIC: 2782 Albums

(G-13767)
ALWAYS PRINTING
149 Highland St (10573-3301)
PHONE..................914 481-5209
Jodi McCredo, *Owner*
EMP: 5
SALES (est): 483.6K **Privately Held**
SIC: 2759 Commercial printing

(G-13768)
COMPOSITE FORMS INC
7 Merritt St (10573-3502)
PHONE..................914 937-1808
Fax: 914 937-1952
Frank J Madonia, *CEO*
Frank Madonia Jr, *President*
Frank Madonia Sr, *Director*
EMP: 10
SQ FT: 6,500
SALES (est): 930K **Privately Held**
WEB: www.sidingsolutions.com
SIC: 2752 5112 Commercial printing, offset; business forms

(G-13769)
D & M ENTERPRISES INCORPORATED
Also Called: A W S
1 Mill St Ste 2 (10573-6301)
PHONE..................914 937-6430
Dino Alampi, *President*
Mary Alampi, *Vice Pres*
Angie Glosser, *Consultant*
Alison Bayer, *Supervisor*
EMP: 8
SQ FT: 5,000
SALES (est): 327K **Privately Held**
SIC: 3088 3999 Hot tubs, plastic or fiberglass; hot tubs

(G-13770)
DESIGNS BY NOVELLO INC
505 N Main St (10573-3360)
PHONE..................914 934-7711
George Bulger, *Owner*
▲ **EMP:** 5 **EST:** 1997
SALES (est): 594.8K **Privately Held**
SIC: 3449 Miscellaneous metalwork

(G-13771)
EAGLE INSTRUMENTS INC
35 Grove St (10573-4501)
PHONE..................914 939-6843
Robert Schneider, *President*
EMP: 7
SQ FT: 4,000
SALES (est): 970.2K **Privately Held**
SIC: 3599 Machine shop, jobbing & repair

(G-13772)
EHS GROUP LLC
69 Townsend St (10573-4311)
PHONE..................914 937-6162
Fax: 914 937-6365
Steven Kennedy, *President*
Lisa Cartolano, *Corp Secy*
EMP: 8
SQ FT: 6,000
SALES (est): 1.6MM **Privately Held**
SIC: 2759 Envelopes: printing

(G-13773)
EMPIRE COFFEE COMPANY INC
106 Purdy Ave (10573-4624)
PHONE..................914 934-1100
Fax: 914 934-1190
Steven Dunefsky, *President*
Laura Thoden, *Manager*
Robert Richter, *Admin Sec*
Tasha Alicea, *Admin Asst*
▲ **EMP:** 35
SQ FT: 30,000
SALES (est): 6.6MM **Privately Held**
WEB: www.empire-coffee.com
SIC: 2095 Coffee roasting (except by wholesale grocers)

(G-13774)
GMP LLC
Also Called: Graphic Management Partners
47 Purdy Ave (10573-5028)
PHONE..................914 939-0571
Fax: 914 939-1670
Jim Berger, *VP Human Res*
Rosanna Burgio, *Human Res Mgr*
Jim Ritch, *Accounts Mgr*
James Coyman, *Mng Member*
Anthony Corrado,
EMP: 86
SQ FT: 20,000
SALES (est): 12.6MM **Privately Held**
SIC: 2752 Promotional printing, lithographic

(G-13775)
GOOD BREAD BAKERY
Also Called: Best Bread
33 New Broad St Ste 1 (10573-4651)
PHONE..................914 939-3900
Fax: 914 939-2513
Michael Beldotti, *Owner*
Chris Beldotti, *Owner*
EMP: 15
SALES (est): 1.4MM **Privately Held**
SIC: 2051 Bakery: wholesale or wholesale/retail combined

(G-13776)
INTEGRATED SOLAR TECH LLC
181 Westchester Ave # 409 (10573-4534)
PHONE..................914 249-9364
Oliver Koehler, *CEO*
▲ **EMP:** 5
SQ FT: 500
SALES (est): 350.4K **Privately Held**
SIC: 3433 Solar heaters & collectors

Port Chester - Westchester County (G-13777)

(G-13777)
JJ CASSONE BAKERY INC
202 S Regent St (10573-4791)
PHONE..............................914 939-1568
Fax: 914 939-3811
Mary Lou Cassone, *President*
Dominic Ambrose, *Vice Pres*
Tony Crusco, *Vice Pres*
Jack Guarcello, *Vice Pres*
Greg Mancuso, *Vice Pres*
▲ **EMP:** 280
SQ FT: 180,000
SALES (est): 53.8MM **Privately Held**
WEB: www.jjcassone.com
SIC: 2051 5461 Bread, cake & related products; bread, all types (white, wheat, rye, etc); fresh or frozen; bakeries

(G-13778)
LANZA CORP
Also Called: Sign Design
404 Willett Ave (10573-3132)
PHONE..............................914 937-6360
Fax: 914 937-0105
Joseph Lanza, *President*
Ray Carpenter, *General Mgr*
EMP: 9
SQ FT: 4,000
SALES (est): 1.4MM **Privately Held**
WEB: www.clicksignage.com
SIC: 3993 2394 7389 5999 Signs & advertising specialties; electric signs; neon signs; canvas awnings & canopies; sign painting & lettering shop; awnings; carved & turned wood; sign installation & maintenance

(G-13779)
MATTHEW SHIVELY LLC
28 Bulkley Ave (10573-3902)
PHONE..............................914 937-3531
Matthew Shively,
EMP: 7
SQ FT: 5,000
SALES (est): 330.5K **Privately Held**
SIC: 2519 Household furniture

(G-13780)
PARSONS & WHITTEMORE INC
4 International Dr # 300 (10573-1064)
PHONE..............................914 937-9009
Arthur L Schwartz, *President*
George F Landegger, *Chairman*
Robert H Masson, *Vice Pres*
Steve Sweeney, *Vice Pres*
Jose Alvelo, *Treasurer*
EMP: 40 **EST:** 1853
SQ FT: 16,650
SALES (est): 66.1MM
SALES (corp-wide): 84.6MM **Privately Held**
SIC: 2611 Pulp mills
PA: Parsons & Whittemore Enterprises Corp.
4 International Dr # 300
Port Chester NY 10573
914 937-9009

(G-13781)
PARSONS WHITTEMORE ENTPS CORP (PA)
4 International Dr # 300 (10573-1064)
PHONE..............................914 937-9009
George F Landegger, *Ch of Bd*
Carl C Landegger, *Vice Ch Bd*
Steven Sweeney, *CFO*
Frank Grasso, *Treasurer*
EMP: 25
SQ FT: 16,650
SALES (est): 84.6MM **Privately Held**
SIC: 2611 Pulp mills

(G-13782)
QUEMERE INTERNATIONAL LLC
330 N Main St (10573-3307)
PHONE..............................914 934-8366
Fax: 914 934-8401
Celine Quemere, *Owner*
EMP: 8
SALES (est): 692K **Privately Held**
SIC: 3253 Ceramic wall & floor tile

(G-13783)
STEILMANN EUROPEAN SELECTIONS
354 N Main St (10573-3307)
PHONE..............................914 997-0015
Bruni Butschek, *President*
Paul Knerr, *VP Sales*
EMP: 60
SALES (est): 1.9MM
SALES (corp-wide): 1.4B **Privately Held**
SIC: 2339 Sportswear, women's
HQ: Klaus Steilmann Gmbh & Co. Kg
Industriestr. 24
Bergkamen 59192
238 990-070

(G-13784)
SWISSBIT NA INC
18 Willett Ave 202 (10573-4326)
PHONE..............................914 935-1400
Anthony Cerreta, *President*
Grady Lambert, *Business Mgr*
Roland Ochoa, *Engineer*
Witold Wrotek, *Design Engr*
Theresa Gaudreau, *Sales Staff*
EMP: 3
SQ FT: 2,050
SALES (est): 20MM **Privately Held**
WEB: www.swissbitna.com
SIC: 3674 Semiconductors & related devices
HQ: Swissbit Ag
Industriestrasse 4-8
Bronschhofen SG 9552
719 130-303

(G-13785)
ZYLOWARE CORPORATION (PA)
Also Called: Zyloware Eyewear
8 Slater St Ste 1 (10573-4984)
PHONE..............................914 708-1200
Christopher Shyer, *President*
Robert Shyer, *Principal*
Jennifer Derryberry, *Vice Pres*
James Shyer, *Vice Pres*
Lisa Mulqueen, *Opers Mgr*
▲ **EMP:** 66
SQ FT: 21,000
SALES (est): 12.1MM **Privately Held**
WEB: www.zyloware.com
SIC: 3851 Frames & parts, eyeglass & spectacle

Port Jeff STA
Suffolk County

(G-13786)
BILTRON AUTOMOTIVE PRODUCTS
509 Bicycle Path Unit Q (11776-3491)
PHONE..............................631 928-8613
Fax: 631 928-5028
Ron Stoll, *President*
David Gayle, *Controller*
▲ **EMP:** 30
SQ FT: 21,000
SALES (est): 4.4MM **Privately Held**
WEB: www.biltronauto.com
SIC: 3714 3566 3462 Steering mechanisms, motor vehicle; speed changers, drives & gears; iron & steel forgings

(G-13787)
CABLE YOUR WORLD INC
1075 Route 112 Ste 4 (11776-8050)
P.O. Box 1214, Miller Place (11764-1154)
PHONE..............................631 509-1180
Eric Levy, *President*
EMP: 4
SQ FT: 3,000
SALES (est): 1MM **Privately Held**
SIC: 3357 Fiber optic cable (insulated)

(G-13788)
COLUMBIA METAL FABRICATORS
801 Hallock Ave (11776-1226)
PHONE..............................631 476-7527
Dean T Hough, *Ch of Bd*
Don Hoeffner, *General Mgr*
EMP: 6 **EST:** 1997
SALES (est): 644.5K **Privately Held**
SIC: 3441 Fabricated structural metal

(G-13789)
DESIGN/OL INC
200 Wilson St Unit D2 (11776-1150)
PHONE..............................631 474-5536
Fax: 631 474-9310
William Delongis, *President*
August Oetting, *Vice Pres*
Chris Siemes, *Finance Mgr*
EMP: 16
SQ FT: 12,500
SALES (est): 2.5MM **Privately Held**
WEB: www.design-ol.com
SIC: 3728 Aircraft assemblies, subassemblies & parts

(G-13790)
NORTH SHORE HOME IMPROVER
200 Wilson St (11776-1100)
PHONE..............................631 474-2824
David Kielhurn, *CEO*
EMP: 16
SALES (est): 910K **Privately Held**
WEB: www.lihomeshows.com
SIC: 2731 Books; publishing only

(G-13791)
NORTH SHORE ORTHTICS PRSTHTICS
591 Bicycle Path Ste D (11776-3421)
PHONE..............................631 928-3040
Fax: 631 474-8020
Robert Biaggi, *President*
EMP: 7
SQ FT: 1,000
SALES (est): 994.5K **Privately Held**
WEB: www.nsop.com
SIC: 3842 5999 Limbs, artificial; artificial limbs

(G-13792)
OCCUNOMIX INTERNATIONAL LLC
585 Bicycle Path Ste 52 (11776-3431)
PHONE..............................631 741-1940
Richard Hauser, *President*
Joel Cooper, *Business Mgr*
Mike Monte, *Opers Staff*
Christine Hadjigeorge, *CFO*
Jim Preston, *Controller*
▲ **EMP:** 45
SQ FT: 48,500
SALES (est): 9.7MM **Privately Held**
WEB: www.occunomix.com
SIC: 3842 2311 2326 5047 Personal safety equipment; men's & boys' uniforms; men's & boys' work clothing; medical & hospital equipment

(G-13793)
ST GERARD ENTERPRISES INC
Also Called: St Gerard Printing
507 Bicycle Path (11776-3446)
P.O. Box 834, East Setauket (11733-0644)
PHONE..............................631 473-2003
Fax: 631 473-2025
Eugene Gerrard, *CEO*
Paul Gerrard, *Vice Pres*
EMP: 11 **EST:** 1965
SQ FT: 7,100
SALES (est): 1.3MM **Privately Held**
WEB: www.stgerardprinting.com
SIC: 2752 Commercial printing, offset

(G-13794)
STARGATE COMPUTER CORP
24 Harmony Dr (11776-3168)
P.O. Box 11161, Hauppauge (11788-0702)
PHONE..............................516 474-4799
EMP: 5
SALES (est): 400K **Privately Held**
SIC: 3571 Mfg Electronic Computers

(G-13795)
T EASON LAND SURVEYOR
27 Poplar St (11776-1415)
PHONE..............................631 474-2200
Treimane Eason, *Owner*
Pam Easton, *Controller*
EMP: 6
SALES (est): 414.8K **Privately Held**
WEB: www.teasonlandsurveyor.com
SIC: 2499 Surveyors' stakes, wood

(G-13796)
TKM TECHNOLOGIES INC
623 Bicycle Path Ste 5 (11776-3444)
P.O. Box 665, Mount Sinai (11766-0665)
PHONE..............................631 474-4700
Fax: 631 736-7991
Mike Moroff, *President*
Monika Moroff, *Vice Pres*
EMP: 6
SQ FT: 1,200
SALES (est): 950K **Privately Held**
WEB: www.tkmtechnologies.com
SIC: 3651 8711 Household audio & video equipment; electrical or electronic engineering

Port Jefferson
Suffolk County

(G-13797)
CHIP IT ALL LTD
366 Sheep Pasture Rd (11777-2059)
P.O. Box 959, Port Jeff STA (11776-0812)
PHONE..............................631 473-2040
Richard Edgar, *President*
Linda Edgar, *Admin Sec*
EMP: 7
SQ FT: 720
SALES (est): 885.9K **Privately Held**
SIC: 2411 Wood chips, produced in the field

(G-13798)
LONG ISLAND GEOTECH
6 Berkshire Ct (11777-1906)
PHONE..............................631 473-1044
Micheal Verruto, *President*
EMP: 5
SALES (est): 308.6K **Privately Held**
SIC: 3272 Concrete products

(G-13799)
M H MANDELBAUM ORTHOTIC
116 Oakland Ave (11777-2172)
PHONE..............................631 473-8668
Fax: 631 473-8691
Martin H Mandelbaum, *President*
Marc Werner, *Vice Pres*
Terri Conigliaro, *Office Mgr*
EMP: 10
SQ FT: 5,300
SALES (est): 890K **Privately Held**
WEB: www.mhmoandp.com
SIC: 3842 5999 8011 Orthopedic appliances; prosthetic appliances; artificial limbs; offices & clinics of medical doctors

(G-13800)
PACE WALKERS OF AMERICA INC
Also Called: Thomas Jefferson Press
105 Washington Ave (11777-2003)
P.O. Box 843, East Setauket (11733-0653)
PHONE..............................631 444-2147
Steven Jonas, *President*
EMP: 12
SALES (est): 907.2K **Privately Held**
SIC: 2731 Book publishing

(G-13801)
SARTEK INDUSTRIES INC (PA)
Also Called: Snr Cctv Systems Division
34 Jamaica Ave Ste 1 (11777-2270)
PHONE..............................631 473-3555
Carl Saieva, *President*
EMP: 6
SQ FT: 5,200
SALES (est): 950.3K **Privately Held**
WEB: www.sarind.com
SIC: 3663 1731 Television closed circuit equipment; closed circuit television installation

(G-13802)
WHITFORD DEVELOPMENT INC
646 Main St Ste 301 (11777-2230)
PHONE..............................631 471-7711
Fax: 631 471-0332
Victor Irizarry, *President*
EMP: 11
SALES (est): 1.1MM **Privately Held**
WEB: www.whitfordhomes.com
SIC: 2789 Trade binding services

Port Jervis
Orange County

(G-13803)
CERAMATERIALS LLC
226 Route 209 (12771-5124)
PHONE...........................518 701-6722
Jerry Weinstein, *Mng Member*
▲ **EMP:** 5
SQ FT: 3,000
SALES (est): 571.2K **Privately Held**
SIC: 3624 8748 5945 3297 Carbon & graphite products; business consulting; ceramics supplies; nonclay refractories

(G-13804)
CONIC SYSTEMS INC
11 Rebel Ln (12771-3547)
PHONE...........................845 856-4053
Fax: 845 858-2824
Vincent Genovese, *President*
◆ **EMP:** 10
SQ FT: 12,000
SALES (est): 1.6MM **Privately Held**
WEB: www.conicsystems.com
SIC: 3625 Control equipment, electric

(G-13805)
DATATRAN LABS INC
Also Called: Nireco America
11 Rebel Ln (12771-3547)
PHONE...........................845 856-4313
Fax: 845 858-2384
Vincent Genovesse, *President*
EMP: 7 **EST:** 1969
SQ FT: 11,000
SALES (est): 1MM **Privately Held**
WEB: www.datatranlabs.com
SIC: 3625 3577 Industrial controls: push button, selector switches, pilot; computer peripheral equipment

(G-13806)
FLANAGANS CREATIVE DISP INC
55 Jersey Ave (12771-2514)
P.O. Box 98 (12771-0098)
PHONE...........................845 858-2542
Fax: 845 856-5931
Michael Flanagan, *President*
Kelly Flanagan, *Office Mgr*
EMP: 35
SQ FT: 30,000
SALES (est): 6.9MM **Privately Held**
SIC: 3496 Miscellaneous fabricated wire products

(G-13807)
GILLINDER BROTHERS INC
Also Called: Gillinder Glass
39 Erie St 55 (12771-2809)
P.O. Box 1007 (12771-0187)
PHONE...........................845 856-5375
Fax: 845 858-2687
Charles E Gillinder, *Ch of Bd*
Dave Fox, *General Mgr*
Susan Gillinder, *Corp Secy*
Ken Moore, *Plant Mgr*
Walter Kozlowski, *Controller*
▲ **EMP:** 70 **EST:** 1912
SQ FT: 120,000
SALES (est): 7MM **Privately Held**
WEB: www.gillinderglass.com
SIC: 3229 Pressed & blown glass

(G-13808)
HORNET GROUP INC
Also Called: Hgi Skydyne
100 River Rd (12771-2931)
PHONE...........................845 858-6400
Jay Benson, *CEO*
EMP: 70
SALES (est): 8MM **Privately Held**
WEB: www.hornetgroup.com
SIC: 3089 3449 7336 3412 Boxes, plastic; miscellaneous metalwork; package design; metal barrels, drums & pails; metal cans; luggage

(G-13809)
KALTEC FOOD PACKAGING INC
36 Center St 40 (12771)
PHONE...........................845 856-9888
Nick Mascarra, *CEO*
Ed Mascara, *President*
Harriet L Mascara, *Shareholder*
▲ **EMP:** 30
SQ FT: 20,000
SALES (est): 5.7MM **Privately Held**
SIC: 2052 Cookies & crackers

(G-13810)
KALTECH FOOD PACKAGING INC
3640 Center St (12771)
PHONE...........................845 856-1210
Harriet L Mascara, *CEO*
Frank Mascara, *Exec VP*
Edward Mascara, *Vice Pres*
Debra Salazar, *Office Mgr*
EMP: 26
SQ FT: 70,000
SALES: 2.2MM **Privately Held**
SIC: 2033 Spaghetti & other pasta sauce: packaged in cans, jars, etc.

(G-13811)
KLG USA LLC
20 W King St (12771-3061)
P.O. Box 1111 (12771-0154)
PHONE...........................845 856-5311
Joseph Healey, *Ch of Bd*
Rob Edmonds, *President*
James Skelton, *COO*
Jack Fallon, *Vice Pres*
Robert Jaegly, *Vice Pres*
▲ **EMP:** 1000
SQ FT: 4,210
SALES (est): 183.3MM **Privately Held**
WEB: www.kolmar.com
SIC: 2844 7389 2834 Toilet preparations; packaging & labeling services; pharmaceutical preparations

(G-13812)
MORGAN FUEL & HEATING CO INC
6 Sleepy Hollow Rd (12771-5308)
PHONE...........................845 856-7831
Dave Wood, *Branch Mgr*
EMP: 44
SALES (corp-wide): 48MM **Privately Held**
SIC: 2869 Fuels
PA: Morgan Fuel & Heating Co., Inc.
2785 W Main St
Wappingers Falls NY 12590
845 297-5580

(G-13813)
PARAMOUNT GRAPHIX
26 Hill St (12771-2024)
PHONE...........................845 367-5003
Daniel King, *Principal*
EMP: 5 **EST:** 2010
SALES (est): 310.2K **Privately Held**
SIC: 2499 Signboards, wood

(G-13814)
PORT JERVIS MACHINE CORP
176 1/2 Jersey Ave (12771-2612)
PHONE...........................845 856-6210
Sal Spiezio, *Manager*
EMP: 8
SALES (corp-wide): 737K **Privately Held**
SIC: 3599 Machine shop, jobbing & repair
PA: Port Jervis Machine Corporation
180 Jersey Ave
Port Jervis NY
845 856-3333

(G-13815)
SAMAKI INC
62 Jersey Ave (12771-2513)
P.O. Box 554, Westbrookville (12785-0554)
PHONE...........................845 858-1012
Simon Marrian, *President*
Laura Marrian, *Treasurer*
EMP: 7
SQ FT: 2,800
SALES (est): 880.8K **Privately Held**
WEB: www.samaki.com
SIC: 2091 Fish, smoked; fish, cured

(G-13816)
SKYDYNE COMPANY
100 River Rd (12771-2997)
PHONE...........................845 858-6400
Peter A Keay, *President*
Peter A Siebert, *Corp Secy*
▲ **EMP:** 70
SALES (est): 18.8MM **Privately Held**
WEB: www.skydyne.com
SIC: 2655 Containers, laminated phenolic & vulcanized fiber

(G-13817)
SWIMWEAR ANYWHERE INC
Also Called: Finals, The
21 Minisink Ave (12771-2320)
PHONE...........................845 858-4141
Fax: 845 858-4193
Art Conway, *Exec VP*
Brenda Blackman, *VP Sales*
Nancy Piccolo, *Manager*
EMP: 40
SALES (corp-wide): 43.4MM **Privately Held**
SIC: 2329 2339 Bathing suits & swimwear: men's & boys'; athletic (warmup, sweat & jogging) suits: men's & boys'; bathing suits: women's, misses' & juniors'; athletic clothing: women's, misses' & juniors'
PA: Swimwear Anywhere, Inc.
85 Sherwood Ave
Farmingdale NY 11735
631 420-1400

Port Washington
Nassau County

(G-13818)
ACTIONCRAFT PRODUCTS INC
2 Manhasset Ave (11050-2008)
PHONE...........................516 883-6423
Fax: 516 883-7447
Nina Straus, *President*
EMP: 8 **EST:** 1951
SQ FT: 4,000
SALES (est): 381.6K **Privately Held**
WEB: www.industrialtest.com
SIC: 2759 Tags: printing

(G-13819)
ADVANCED POLYMER SOLUTIONS LLC
99 Seaview Blvd Ste 1a (11050-4632)
PHONE...........................516 621-5800
Rita Ryan, *Senior VP*
Purushoth Kesavan, *Prdtn Mgr*
John M Ryan,
Rita N Ryan,
EMP: 9
SQ FT: 10,000
SALES (est): 1.6MM **Privately Held**
WEB: www.advancedpolymersolutions.com
SIC: 2891 8731 Adhesives & sealants; chemical laboratory, except testing

(G-13820)
ALAN F BOURGUET
63 Essex Ct (11050-4222)
PHONE...........................516 883-4315
Alan F Bourguet, *President*
EMP: 15 **EST:** 2001
SALES (est): 842.1K **Privately Held**
SIC: 2844 Perfumes & colognes

(G-13821)
ALMOND JEWELERS INC
Also Called: Almond Group
16 S Maryland Ave (11050-2913)
P.O. Box 471 (11050-0135)
PHONE...........................516 933-6000
Jonathan Mandelbaum, *President*
Maurice Mandelbaum, *Vice Pres*
Jason Mandelbaum, *Mfg Staff*
Henry Bubrow, *CFO*
Barbara Schmidt, *Persnl Mgr*
▲ **EMP:** 15
SQ FT: 3,500
SALES: 100MM **Privately Held**
SIC: 3911 Jewelry, precious metal

(G-13822)
APPLE & EVE LLC (DH)
2 Seaview Blvd Ste 100 (11050-4634)
PHONE...........................516 621-1122
Gordon Crane, *President*
John Emerson, *President*
Sol Jacobs, *General Mgr*
Robert Mortati, *Senior VP*
David Yarmoff, *Senior VP*
◆ **EMP:** 65
SQ FT: 14,000
SALES (est): 52.7MM
SALES (corp-wide): 261.9MM **Privately Held**
WEB: www.appleandeve.com
SIC: 2033 Fruit juices: packaged in cans, jars, etc.
HQ: Us Juice Partners, Llc
2 Seaview Blvd
Port Washington NY 11050
516 621-1122

(G-13823)
ARENA GRAPHICS INC
Also Called: Arena Sports Center
52 Main St Frnt (11050-2952)
PHONE...........................516 767-5108
Fax: 516 944-5626
Christopher J Avazis, *President*
Steven Avazis, *Vice Pres*
EMP: 9
SQ FT: 4,700
SALES (est): 1.2MM **Privately Held**
WEB: www.arenagraphics.com
SIC: 2759 5941 2395 Screen printing; sporting goods & bicycle shops; embroidery products, except schiffli machine

(G-13824)
BEVILACQUE GROUP LLC
Also Called: Bevilacque Group LLC By Profor
19 Norwood Rd (11050-1423)
PHONE...........................212 414-8858
Mark Bevilacque,
EMP: 11
SQ FT: 2,750
SALES (est): 1.3MM **Privately Held**
WEB: www.bevilacque.com
SIC: 2752 7389 Commercial printing, lithographic; advertising, promotional & trade show services

(G-13825)
BOMBAY KITCHEN FOODS INC
76 S Bayles Ave (11050-3729)
PHONE...........................516 767-7401
Fax: 516 767-7402
Sanjiv Mody, *President*
Ajit Mody, *Treasurer*
Sachin Mody, *Admin Sec*
▲ **EMP:** 15
SQ FT: 18,000
SALES (est): 2.5MM **Privately Held**
SIC: 2099 Food preparations

(G-13826)
CARNELS PRINTING INC
Also Called: Carnel Printing and Copying
22 Main St Frnt A (11050-2933)
PHONE...........................516 883-3355
Fax: 516 883-0085
Kay W Ray, *President*
EMP: 6
SQ FT: 2,500
SALES (est): 758.9K **Privately Held**
SIC: 2752 2791 2789 Commercial printing, offset; typesetting; bookbinding & related work

(G-13827)
CHANNEL MANUFACTURING INC (PA)
55 Channel Dr (11050-2216)
PHONE...........................516 944-6271
Jordan Klein, *President*
Carol Caplen, *Controller*
Peter Contomanolis, *Marketing Staff*
Carole Kaplan, *Manager*
Bill Koines, *Manager*
▲ **EMP:** 25 **EST:** 2000
SALES (est): 2.9MM **Privately Held**
WEB: www.channelmfg.com
SIC: 2499 3537 Food handling & processing products, wood; industrial trucks & tractors

Port Washington - Nassau County (G-13828)   GEOGRAPHIC SECTION

(G-13828)
CHOICE MAGAZINE LISTENING INC
85 Channel Dr Ste 3 (11050-2278)
PHONE..................516 883-8280
Fax: 516 944-5849
William O'Conner, *Chairman*
Lois Miller, *Manager*
Sondra Mochson, *Director*
EMP: 7
SALES (est): 520K Privately Held
WEB: www.choicemagazinelistening.org
SIC: 2721 8322 Periodicals; social services for the handicapped

(G-13829)
COMPOZ A PUZZLE INC
2 Secatoag Ave (11050-2107)
PHONE..................516 883-2311
Robert F Krisch, *Chairman*
Richard Hinchey, *Vice Pres*
Livon Bailey, *Manager*
EMP: 5
SQ FT: 4,000
SALES: 500K Privately Held
WEB: www.compozapuzzle.com
SIC: 3944 5945 Puzzles; hobby, toy & game shops

(G-13830)
DATA PALETTE INFO SVCS LLC
35 Marino Ave (11050-4207)
PHONE..................718 433-1060
Fax: 718 433-1074
Walter Reinhardt, *Manager*
Fred Disalvatore, *Consultant*
Ramil Cargullo, *Software Dev*
Joel Ronis,
Joseph Aronne,
▲ EMP: 75
SQ FT: 35,000
SALES (est): 11.2MM Privately Held
SIC: 2759 7331 7374 7389 Laser printing; mailing service; data processing & preparation;

(G-13831)
DIAMOND BOUTIQUE
77 Main St (11050-2929)
PHONE..................516 444-3373
Joseph Daniel, *Owner*
EMP: 6
SALES: 2.5MM Privately Held
SIC: 3915 5944 Jewel cutting, drilling, polishing, recutting or setting; jewelry stores

(G-13832)
DJ PUBLISHING INC
25 Willowdale Ave (11050-3716)
PHONE..................516 767-2500
Vincent P Testa, *President*
Tom McCarty, *Sales Mgr*
Chris Caruso, *Assoc Editor*
EMP: 50
SALES (est): 2.8MM Privately Held
WEB: www.testabags.com
SIC: 2721 Magazines: publishing only, not printed on site

(G-13833)
DOMA MARKETING INC
28 Haven Ave Ste 226 (11050-3646)
PHONE..................516 684-1111
Doron Katz, *Owner*
EMP: 5 EST: 2012
SQ FT: 2,000
SALES: 100K Privately Held
SIC: 2066 Chocolate

(G-13834)
E GLOBAL SOLUTIONS INC
Also Called: E G S
8 Haven Ave Ste 221 (11050-3636)
P.O. Box 771 (11050-0771)
PHONE..................516 767-5138
Anthony Straggi, *Ch of Bd*
EMP: 6
SQ FT: 9,000
SALES (est): 690K Privately Held
SIC: 3822 Auto controls regulating residntl & coml environmt & applncs

(G-13835)
ELCO MANUFACTURING CO INC (PA)
26 Ivy Way (11050-3802)
P.O. Box 1759 (11050-7759)
PHONE..................516 767-3577
Eric Weintraub, *President*
Stanley Weintraub, *Vice Pres*
E Nash, *Admin Sec*
EMP: 19 EST: 1904
SQ FT: 10,000
SALES: 1.5MM Privately Held
WEB: www.elcomfg.com
SIC: 3172 5199 Personal leather goods; advertising specialties

(G-13836)
EVOLVE GUEST CONTROLS LLC (PA)
16 S Maryland Ave (11050-2913)
PHONE..................855 750-9090
Staffan Encrantz, *Ch of Bd*
Len Horowitz, *President*
David Korcz, *CFO*
Robert Kaye, *Controller*
▲ EMP: 15
SQ FT: 10,000
SALES (est): 4.1MM Privately Held
SIC: 3822 7371 2591 1731 Auto controls regulating residntl & coml environmt & applncs; building services monitoring controls, automatic; computer software development; shade, curtain & drapery hardware; electronic controls installation; energy management controls

(G-13837)
FINER TOUCH PRINTING CORP
4 Yennicock Ave (11050-2131)
PHONE..................516 944-8000
Fax: 516 944-9439
Kenny Cummings, *President*
Sharon Verity, *Office Mgr*
EMP: 10
SQ FT: 2,500
SALES: 1.1MM Privately Held
WEB: www.comiccastle.com
SIC: 2752 Commercial printing, offset

(G-13838)
FRANKLIN-DOUGLAS INC
Also Called: Omnimusic
52 Main St Side (11050-2965)
PHONE..................516 883-0121
Fax: 516 883-0271
Douglas Wood, *President*
Patricia Wood, *Vice Pres*
EMP: 12 EST: 1975
SQ FT: 4,000
SALES (est): 1MM Privately Held
WEB: www.omnimusic.com
SIC: 2741 Music book & sheet music publishing

(G-13839)
G & C WELDING CO INC
39 Annette Dr (11050-2803)
PHONE..................516 883-3228
Carmine Meluzio, *President*
EMP: 5
SALES (est): 179.5K Privately Held
SIC: 7692 1799 Welding repair; welding on site

(G-13840)
GANNETT CO INC
Also Called: U S A Today
99 Seaview Blvd Ste 200 (11050-4632)
PHONE..................516 484-7510
Fax: 516 621-5307
Peter Donohue, *Branch Mgr*
EMP: 40
SALES (corp-wide): 3B Publicly Held
WEB: www.gannett.com
SIC: 2711 Newspapers, publishing & printing
PA: Gannett Co., Inc.
7950 Jones Branch Dr
Mc Lean VA 22102
703 854-6000

(G-13841)
GE HEALTHCARE INC
Also Called: Medi-Physics
80 Seaview Blvd Ste E (11050-4618)
PHONE..................516 626-2799
Fax: 516 621-5807
Franklyn Robinson, *Manager*
EMP: 14
SALES (corp-wide): 123.6B Publicly Held
SIC: 2833 Medicinals & botanicals
HQ: Ge Healthcare Inc.
100 Results Way
Marlborough MA 01752
800 292-8514

(G-13842)
HERCULES GROUP INC
27 Seaview Blvd (11050-4610)
PHONE..................212 813-8000
Fax: 212 899-5559
Sara Amani, *President*
Jennifer Ryder, *Controller*
Rosan Jesdine, *Manager*
▲ EMP: 20
SQ FT: 2,000
SALES (est): 4.2MM Privately Held
WEB: www.herculesgroup.com
SIC: 2385 Diaper covers, waterproof: made from purchased materials

(G-13843)
HURRYWORKS LLC
990 Seaview Blvd (11050)
PHONE..................516 998-4600
Richard Kolodny, *CEO*
EMP: 99
SQ FT: 10,000
SALES (est): 2.5MM Privately Held
SIC: 3841 Surgical & medical instruments

(G-13844)
IDENTFICATION DATA IMAGING LLC
Also Called: IDI
26 Harbor Park Dr (11050-4602)
PHONE..................516 484-6500
Fax: 516 484-4486
Mohammed Abu-Khraybeh, *Vice Pres*
Pat Schrenzel, *Accounts Exec*
Pat Screnzel,
Jeffrey Brodsky,
▼ EMP: 6
SQ FT: 1,300
SALES (est): 590.7K Privately Held
WEB: www.idius.com
SIC: 3999 Identification badges & insignia

(G-13845)
IDEOLI GROUP INC
938 Port Washington Blvd # 1 (11050-2932)
PHONE..................212 705-8769
George Stroumboulis, *CEO*
Chris Hartswick,
EMP: 10
SQ FT: 2,000
SALES: 213K Privately Held
SIC: 2599 3646 Bar, restaurant & cafeteria furniture; commercial indusl & institutional electric lighting fixtures

(G-13846)
INDUSTRIAL TEST EQP CO INC
2 Manhasset Ave (11050-2008)
PHONE..................516 883-6423
Fax: 516 883-7155
Jay Monroe, *President*
Hugo Harnella, *Purch Dir*
Barbara Assa, *Persnl Dir*
Sam Lou, *Marketing Staff*
Barbara Monroe, *Admin Sec*
EMP: 20
SQ FT: 8,000
SALES: 1MM Privately Held
WEB: www.rf-pwr-amps.com
SIC: 3621 3829 2759 Generating apparatus & parts, electrical; gas detectors; tags: printing

(G-13847)
INTECH 21 INC
21 Harbor Park Dr (11050-4658)
PHONE..................516 626-7221
Fax: 516 626-7021
George Y Bilenko, *President*
Joe Adinolfi, *General Mgr*
Victor Zelmanovich, *Exec VP*
Aleksandr Baranov, *Software Engr*
Jules Leibman, *Shareholder*
▲ EMP: 12
SQ FT: 8,000
SALES (est): 1.8MM Privately Held
WEB: www.intech21.com
SIC: 3674 Computer logic modules

(G-13848)
IVY ENTERPRISES INC (HQ)
3 Seaview Blvd (11050-4610)
PHONE..................516 621-9779
Fax: 516 621-9779
Hee J Chang, *President*
David Kim, *Finance*
Belle Park, *Manager*
Jin Kim, *Director*
Robert Kim, *Director*
◆ EMP: 500
SALES (est): 16.7MM
SALES (corp-wide): 32.3MM Privately Held
SIC: 3999 5087 Fingernails, artificial; beauty parlor equipment & supplies
PA: Kiss Nail Products, Inc.
57 Seaview Blvd
Port Washington NY 11050
516 625-9292

(G-13849)
JAIDAN INDUSTRIES INC
Also Called: Absolute Business Products
16 Capi Ln (11050-3410)
PHONE..................516 944-3650
Richard Sussman, *President*
Louise Feliciano, *Manager*
▲ EMP: 16
SALES (est): 3.6MM Privately Held
WEB: www.jaidan.com
SIC: 3442 Window & door frames; moldings & trim, except automobile: metal

(G-13850)
JESCO LIGHTING INC
15 Harbor Park Dr (11050-4604)
PHONE..................718 366-3211
Richard Kurtz, *Chairman*
Edward MA, *Chairman*
Joan Miller, *Accounts Exec*
Maria Olivas, *Accounts Exec*
Mike Wright, *Sales Associate*
▲ EMP: 50
SQ FT: 70,000
SALES (est): 11.9MM Privately Held
SIC: 3646 Commercial indusl & institutional electric lighting fixtures

(G-13851)
JESCO LIGHTING GROUP LLC (PA)
15 Harbor Park Dr (11050-4604)
PHONE..................718 366-3211
Richard Kurtz, *President*
Mike Yung, *Sales Staff*
Shelley Leiter, *Office Mgr*
Jack Chang, *Manager*
▲ EMP: 60 EST: 2008
SQ FT: 70,000
SALES (est): 10.9MM Privately Held
SIC: 3646 Commercial indusl & institutional electric lighting fixtures

(G-13852)
JWIN ELECTRONICS CORP (PA)
Also Called: Iluv
2 Harbor Park Dr (11050-4602)
PHONE..................516 626-7188
Fax: 516 533-8766
Justin Kim, *Ch of Bd*
David Dunn, *Warehouse Mgr*
Sangyub Choo, *Design Engr*
Kevin Vinlim, *Controller*
Jay Han, *Asst Controller*
▲ EMP: 100
SQ FT: 132,000
SALES (est): 15.5MM Privately Held
WEB: www.jwin.com
SIC: 3651 Television receiving sets; radio receiving sets; home entertainment equipment, electronic

GEOGRAPHIC SECTION — Port Washington - Nassau County

(G-13853)
KELLER INTERNATIONAL PUBG LLC (PA)
150 Main St Ste 10 (11050-2849)
PHONE...................516 829-9210
Fax: 516 829-5414
Terry Beirne, *Publisher*
Felicia M Morales, *Editor*
Carel Letschert, *Vice Pres*
Kelly Keller, *Sales Dir*
Brad Berger, *Sales Mgr*
EMP: 40 EST: 1882
SQ FT: 7,000
SALES (est): 2.8MM Privately Held
WEB: www.glscs.com
SIC: 2721 Magazines: publishing only, not printed on site

(G-13854)
KITTYWALK SYSTEMS INC
10 Farmview Rd (11050-4511)
PHONE...................516 627-8418
Jeff King, *CEO*
Lise King, *President*
▲ EMP: 2
SALES: 1MM Privately Held
SIC: 3999 Pet supplies

(G-13855)
KLEARBAR INC
8 Graywood Rd (11050-1516)
PHONE...................516 684-9892
Mark Klein, *President*
Scott Bercu, *Admin Sec*
▲ EMP: 5
SALES (est): 413.3K Privately Held
SIC: 3585 Soda fountain & beverage dispensing equipment & parts

(G-13856)
KRAUS USA INC
12 Harbor Park Dr (11050-4649)
PHONE...................800 775-0703
Russel Levi, *President*
Russell Levi, *President*
Michael Rukhlin, *Principal*
Dmitry Rukhlin, *COO*
Daniel Lusby, *CFO*
▲ EMP: 10
SQ FT: 37,500
SALES (est): 2.5MM Privately Held
SIC: 3431 3261 Bathroom fixtures, including sinks; sinks: enameled iron, cast iron or pressed metal; sinks, vitreous china

(G-13857)
KRUG PRECISION INC
7 Carey Pl (11050-2421)
PHONE...................516 944-9350
Fax: 516 944-5841
Michael Krug, *President*
Rosemarie Krug, *Corp Secy*
EMP: 9
SQ FT: 6,500
SALES: 1.3MM Privately Held
SIC: 3599 Machine shop, jobbing & repair

(G-13858)
LIF INDUSTRIES INC (PA)
Also Called: Long Island Fireproof Door
5 Harbor Park Dr Ste 1 (11050-4698)
PHONE...................516 390-6800
Fax: 516 390-6848
Vincent Gallo, *Ch of Bd*
Joseph Gallo Jr, *President*
Anthony Gallo, *Vice Pres*
Mark Farina, *Project Mgr*
Ian Ostrager, *Project Mgr*
EMP: 76
SQ FT: 85,000
SALES (est): 22.9MM Privately Held
WEB: www.lifi.net
SIC: 3442 5031 Metal doors; window & door frames; door frames, all materials

(G-13859)
LIFC CORP
101 Haven Ave (11050-3936)
PHONE...................516 426-5737
Brian Kenny, *President*
EMP: 5
SALES (est): 410K Privately Held
SIC: 3569 5812 Firefighting apparatus & related equipment; caterers

(G-13860)
M R C INDUSTRIES INC
Also Called: Mason Medical Products
99 Seaview Blvd Ste 210 (11050-4632)
P.O. Box 609 (11050-0609)
PHONE...................516 328-6900
Fax: 516 328-6622
Leonard Horowitz, *CEO*
Brian Goldstein, *Vice Pres*
Bernice Wien, *Treasurer*
◆ EMP: 200
SQ FT: 60,000
SALES (est): 22.2MM Privately Held
WEB: www.masonmedical.com
SIC: 2515 Mattresses & foundations

(G-13861)
MEDER TEXTILE CO INC
20 Lynn Rd (11050-4437)
PHONE...................516 883-0409
Bruce T Lindemann, *President*
EMP: 4 EST: 1936
SQ FT: 500
SALES: 1MM Privately Held
SIC: 2211 Broadwoven fabric mills, cotton; upholstery fabrics, cotton

(G-13862)
MEDICAL DEPOT INC (PA)
Also Called: Drive / Devilbiss Healthcare
99 Seaview Blvd Ste 210 (11050-4632)
P.O. Box 842450, Boston MA (02284-2450)
PHONE...................516 998-4600
Fax: 631 420-4468
Harvey P Diamond, *CEO*
Barry Fink, *President*
Richard S Kolodny, *President*
Thomas Reynolds, *President*
Jeffery Schwartz, *Exec VP*
◆ EMP: 262
SQ FT: 43,159
SALES (est): 123.7MM Privately Held
WEB: www.drivemedical.com
SIC: 3841 Surgical & medical instruments

(G-13863)
MEDICAL INFORMATION SYSTEMS
2 Seaview Blvd Ste 104 (11050-4634)
PHONE...................516 621-7200
Fax: 516 423-0161
Irving Silverberg, *President*
Roy Silverberg, *Vice Pres*
Neshea Smith, *Marketing Staff*
Hazel Silverberg, *Admin Sec*
EMP: 5
SQ FT: 5,000
SALES: 2.3MM Privately Held
WEB: www.medinfosystems.com
SIC: 2741 Miscellaneous publishing

(G-13864)
MEDSAFE SYSTEMS INC
46 Orchard Farm Rd (11050-3338)
PHONE...................516 883-8222
Bernard Shore, *President*
EMP: 6
SQ FT: 1,000
SALES: 1.2MM Privately Held
SIC: 3823 Telemetering instruments, industrial process type

(G-13865)
MEKATRONICS INCORPORATED
85 Channel Dr Ste 2 (11050-2248)
PHONE...................516 883-6805
Jack Bendror, *President*
Kenneth Lines, *Engineer*
▲ EMP: 24
SQ FT: 30,000
SALES (est): 4MM Privately Held
SIC: 3679 3555 3861 Electronic circuits; printing trades machinery; microfilm equipment: cameras, projectors, readers, etc.

(G-13866)
MUSIC & SOUND RETAILER INC
Also Called: Retailer, The
25 Willowdale Ave (11050-3716)
PHONE...................516 767-2500
Vincent Testa, *President*
EMP: 28
SQ FT: 1,500
SALES (est): 1.7MM Privately Held
SIC: 2721 Magazines: publishing only, not printed on site

(G-13867)
OSWALD MANUFACTURING CO INC
65 Channel Dr (11050-2216)
PHONE...................516 883-8850
Fax: 516 883-7857
Fred Oswald, *President*
Angella Oswald, *Vice Pres*
▲ EMP: 30
SQ FT: 22,000
SALES (est): 3.9MM Privately Held
SIC: 3531 Construction machinery

(G-13868)
OZTECK INDUSTRIES INC
65 Channel Dr (11050-2216)
PHONE...................516 883-8857
Fred Oswald, *President*
Angella Oswald, *Vice Pres*
Tiffany Shackatano, *Vice Pres*
Joanna Stupar, *Bookkeeper*
◆ EMP: 40
SQ FT: 22,000
SALES (est): 10MM Privately Held
WEB: www.oztec.com
SIC: 3531 Vibrators for concrete construction; surfacers, concrete grinding

(G-13869)
PALL BIOMEDICAL INC
Also Called: Pall Medical
25 Harbor Park Dr (11050-4605)
PHONE...................516 484-3600
Fax: 516 484-3637
Ricardo Alfonso, *President*
Eric Kransnoff, *Principal*
Stella Rivera, *Human Res Mgr*
Tim Lynch, *Manager*
▲ EMP: 200
SALES (est): 32.2MM
SALES (corp-wide): 16.8B Publicly Held
WEB: www.pall.com
SIC: 3842 Surgical appliances & supplies
HQ: Pall Corporation
    25 Harbor Park Dr
    Port Washington NY 11050
    516 484-5400

(G-13870)
PALL CORPORATION (HQ)
25 Harbor Park Dr (11050-4664)
PHONE...................516 484-5400
Fax: 516 484-3633
Rainer Blair, *President*
Yves Baratelli, *President*
Michael Egholm, *President*
Naresh Narasimhan, *President*
Brian Burnett, *Senior VP*
◆ EMP: 1200 EST: 2015
SQ FT: 25,000
SALES: 2.7B
SALES (corp-wide): 16.8B Publicly Held
WEB: www.pall.com
SIC: 3569 3599 3714 2834 Filters; filters, general line: industrial; filter elements, fluid, hydraulic line; separators for steam, gas, vapor or air (machinery); air intake filters, internal combustion engine, except auto; gasoline filters, internal combustion engine, except auto; oil filters, internal combustion engine, except automotive; filters: oil, fuel & air, motor vehicle; solutions, pharmaceutical; surgical & medical instruments; IV transfusion apparatus
PA: Danaher Corporation
    2200 Penn Ave Nw Ste 800w
    Washington DC 20037
    202 828-0850

(G-13871)
PALL CORPORATION
Also Called: Pall Life Sciences
25 Harbor Park Dr (11050-4664)
PHONE...................516 484-2818
Keitha Buckingham, *Vice Pres*
Dan Dhanraj, *Vice Pres*
Jamie Marchand, *Vice Pres*
Carl Chamberlain, *Opers Staff*
Doreen Stillman, *Senior Buyer*
EMP: 750
SALES (corp-wide): 16.8B Publicly Held
WEB: www.pall.com
SIC: 3842 Surgical appliances & supplies
HQ: Pall Corporation
    25 Harbor Park Dr
    Port Washington NY 11050
    516 484-5400

(G-13872)
PARAGON CORPORATION
21 Forest Dr (11050-1910)
PHONE...................516 484-6090
Serena Jen, *President*
▲ EMP: 12
SQ FT: 4,466
SALES (est): 1MM Privately Held
WEB: www.paradigmsw.com
SIC: 2399 3911 5199 Emblems, badges & insignia; jewelry, precious metal; badges

(G-13873)
PLAY-IT PRODUCTIONS INC
735 Port Washington Blvd (11050-3735)
PHONE...................212 695-6530
Fax: 212 695-4304
Terri Tyler, *Vice Pres*
EMP: 10
SQ FT: 3,000
SALES (est): 1.2MM Privately Held
WEB: www.play-itproductions.net
SIC: 2752 7336 7812 7819 Commercial printing, lithographic; graphic arts & related design; audio-visual program production; video tape or disk reproduction

(G-13874)
PROFICIENT SURGICAL EQP INC
99 Seaview Blvd Ste 1c (11050-4632)
PHONE...................516 487-1175
Steven Baum, *President*
Harold Mondschein, *Sales Mgr*
Chris Fiengo, *Sales Staff*
Michael Albano, *Sales Executive*
Alicia Mamarella, *Office Mgr*
▲ EMP: 6 EST: 1996
SALES (est): 710K Privately Held
WEB: www.proficientsurgical.com
SIC: 3842 Surgical appliances & supplies

(G-13875)
RADNOR-WALLACE (PA)
921 Port Washington Blvd # 1 (11050-2976)
PHONE...................516 767-2131
Michael O'Beirne, *Director*
EMP: 5
SQ FT: 600
SALES: 500K Privately Held
WEB: www.radnorwallace.com
SIC: 7372 Prepackaged software

(G-13876)
ROBERT BARTHOLOMEW LTD
Also Called: Magnus Sands Point Shop
15 Main St (11050-2916)
PHONE...................516 767-7774
Fax: 516 767-7774
Robert C Mazza, *President*
Robert S Mazza, *President*
Donai Keogh, *Vice Pres*
Bob Mazza, *Manager*
Laura Mazza, *Admin Sec*
EMP: 32
SQ FT: 12,000
SALES (est): 5.3MM Privately Held
WEB: www.robertbartholomew.com
SIC: 3911 Jewelry, precious metal

(G-13877)
SAFAVIEH INC
40 Harbor Park Dr (11050-4602)
PHONE...................516 945-1900
Mohsen Yaraghi, *Ch of Bd*
Kevin Yaraghi, *Payroll Mgr*
EMP: 525
SALES: 350MM Privately Held
SIC: 2273 5712 Rugs, hand & machine made; furniture stores

(G-13878)
SAINT HONORE PASTRY SHOP INC
993 Port Washington Blvd (11050-2910)
PHONE...................516 767-2555
Jacques Leguelaf, *President*

EMP: 5
SQ FT: 1,500
SALES (est): 270K Privately Held
SIC: 2051 5461 Bread, cake & related products; bakeries

(G-13879)
SAMMBA PRINTING INC
Also Called: Minuteman Press
437 Port Washington Blvd (11050-4225)
PHONE..............................516 944-4449
Fax: 516 944-4428
Mark Gutner, President
Susan Spira, Vice Pres
EMP: 6
SQ FT: 1,700
SALES: 900K Privately Held
SIC: 2752 2759 Commercial printing, lithographic; invitation & stationery printing & engraving

(G-13880)
SCHOLIUM INTERNATIONAL INC
151 Cow Neck Rd (11050-1143)
PHONE..............................516 883-8032
Fax: 516 944-9824
Arthur A Candido, President
Elena M Candido, Vice Pres
EMP: 5 EST: 1970
SQ FT: 1,800
SALES (est): 319.2K Privately Held
WEB: www.scholium.com
SIC: 2731 5192 Book publishing; books

(G-13881)
SHAKE-N-GO FASHION INC
83 Harbor Rd (11050-2535)
PHONE..............................516 944-7777
EMP: 47
SALES (corp-wide): 315.2MM Privately Held
SIC: 3999 Hairpin mountings
PA: Shake-N-Go Fashion, Inc.
  85 Harbor Rd
  Port Washington NY 11050
  516 944-7777

(G-13882)
SHAKE-N-GO FASHION INC (PA)
85 Harbor Rd (11050-2535)
PHONE..............................516 944-7777
James K Kim, Ch of Bd
Mike Kim, Vice Pres
Young Ryoo, Opers Mgr
Betty Kim, Treasurer
Jessica Cho, Controller
◆ EMP: 56
SQ FT: 75,000
SALES: 315.2MM Privately Held
WEB: www.shake-n-gofashions.com
SIC: 3999 Hairpin mountings; wigs, including doll wigs, toupees or wiglets

(G-13883)
SHARODINE INC
18 Haven Ave Frnt 2 (11050-3642)
PHONE..............................516 767-3548
Ron Sharoni, President
EMP: 9
SALES (est): 1.3MM Privately Held
SIC: 3911 Jewelry, precious metal

(G-13884)
SOUND COMMUNICATIONS INC
25 Willowdale Ave (11050-3716)
PHONE..............................516 767-2500
Vincent Testa, President
John Carr, Publisher
John Beresford, Editor
Dan Ferrisi, Editor
Shonan Noronha, Editor
EMP: 40
SALES (est): 2.2MM Privately Held
SIC: 2721 Magazines: publishing only, not printed on site

(G-13885)
SWITCH BEVERAGE COMPANY LLC
2 Seaview Blvd Fl 3 (11050-4634)
PHONE..............................203 202-7383
Brian Boyd, CEO
Maura Mottolese, President
Richard Beswick, Sales Staff
EMP: 11
SQ FT: 1,200

SALES (est): 767.3K
SALES (corp-wide): 261.9MM Privately Held
WEB: www.switchbev.com
SIC: 2096 2086 Potato chips & similar snacks; carbonated beverages, nonalcoholic: bottled & canned
HQ: Apple & Eve, Llc
  2 Seaview Blvd Ste 100
  Port Washington NY 11050
  516 621-1122

(G-13886)
TESTA COMMUNICATIONS INC
Also Called: Sound & Communication
25 Willowdale Ave (11050-3716)
PHONE..............................516 767-2500
Vincent Testa, President
Steve Thorakos, Prdtn Mgr
EMP: 40
SQ FT: 1,500
SALES (est): 4.6MM Privately Held
WEB: www.testa.com
SIC: 2721 Magazines: publishing only, not printed on site

(G-13887)
THETA INDUSTRIES INC
26 Valley Rd Ste 1 (11050-2498)
PHONE..............................516 883-4088
Fax: 516 883-4599
Gerhard Clusener, President
Brigette Clusener, Admin Sec
EMP: 10
SQ FT: 10,000
SALES (est): 2.1MM Privately Held
WEB: www.theta-us.com
SIC: 3821 7699 Laboratory apparatus & furniture; laboratory equipment: fume hoods, distillation racks, etc.; laboratory instrument repair

(G-13888)
US JUICE PARTNERS LLC (DH)
Also Called: Apple
2 Seaview Blvd (11050-4614)
PHONE..............................516 621-1122
Pierre-Paul Lassonde, Ch of Bd
EMP: 5
SALES (est): 52.7MM
SALES (corp-wide): 261.9MM Privately Held
SIC: 2033 Fruit juices: packaged in cans, jars, etc.
HQ: Industries Lassonde Inc
  755 Rue Principale
  Rougemont QC J0L 1
  450 469-4926

(G-13889)
WELL-MADE TOY MFG CORPORATION
146 Soundview Dr (11050-1751)
PHONE..............................718 381-4225
Fax: 718 381-5532
Fred F Catapano, President
Susan Cook, Vice Pres
Gilbert Edovas, Controller
Susan Small, Sales Staff
▲ EMP: 20
SALES (est): 2.8MM Privately Held
WEB: www.wellmadetoy.com
SIC: 3942 Stuffed toys, including animals

Portageville
Wyoming County

(G-13890)
FILLMORE GREENHOUSES INC
11589 State Route 19a (14536-9611)
PHONE..............................585 567-2678
Fax: 585 567-2247
Mario Van Logten, Chairman
▲ EMP: 45
SALES (est): 6.6MM Privately Held
SIC: 3448 Greenhouses: prefabricated metal

Portland
Chautauqua County

(G-13891)
OLDE CHTQUA VNEYARDS LTD LBLTY
Also Called: Twentyone Brix Winery
6654 W Main Rd (14769-9621)
PHONE..............................716 792-2749
Marion Jordan, General Mgr
Kris Kane,
Bryan Jordan,
Michael Jordan,
EMP: 12
SQ FT: 10,000
SALES (est): 910K Privately Held
SIC: 2084 5921 Wines; wine

Portville
Cattaraugus County

(G-13892)
FIBERCEL PACKAGING LLC (HQ)
46 Brooklyn St (14770-9529)
P.O. Box 610 (14770-0610)
PHONE..............................716 933-8703
Fax: 585 933-6948
Bruce E Olson,
Richard Flanagan,
Gale Hastings,
Robert T Hinett,
Cheryl A Leblanc,
EMP: 28
SQ FT: 7,200
SALES (est): 8.6MM
SALES (corp-wide): 16.2MM Privately Held
SIC: 2621 Molded pulp products
PA: Orcon Industries Corp.
  8715 Lake Rd
  Le Roy NY 14482
  585 768-7000

(G-13893)
IA CONSTRUCTION CORPORATION
Also Called: Portville Sand & Gravel Div
Rr 305 Box S (14770)
PHONE..............................716 933-8787
Fax: 585 933-8787
John Taylor, Sales/Mktg Mgr
EMP: 5
SQ FT: 1,800
SALES (corp-wide): 77.1MM Privately Held
WEB: www.iaconstruction.com
SIC: 1442 Gravel mining
HQ: Ia Construction Corporation
  24 Gibb Rd
  Franklin PA 16323
  814 432-3184

Potsdam
St. Lawrence County

(G-13894)
3 BEARS GLUTEN FREE BAKERY
51 Market St (13676-1744)
PHONE..............................315 323-0277
Christopher Durand, President
Faye Ori, Vice Pres
EMP: 11 EST: 2014
SALES (est): 1MM Privately Held
SIC: 2051 Bakery: wholesale or wholesale/retail combined

(G-13895)
ATLANTIS SOLAR INC
Also Called: Atlantis Solar and Wind
2302 River Rd (13676-3491)
PHONE..............................916 226-9183
Lance Thomas, President
Michael Becker, Manager
EMP: 12
SQ FT: 47,000

SALES (est): 926.7K
SALES (corp-wide): 3.6MM Publicly Held
SIC: 3433 Solar heaters & collectors
PA: Solar Thin Films Inc
  1136 Rxr Plz
  Uniondale NY 11556
  516 341-7787

(G-13896)
DONALD SNYDER JR
Also Called: Donald Snyder Jr Logging
528 Allen Falls Rd (13676-4032)
PHONE..............................315 265-4485
Donald Snyder Jr, Owner
EMP: 15
SALES (est): 1.1MM Privately Held
SIC: 2411 Logging

(G-13897)
LCDRIVES CORP
65 Main St Pytn Hl 3204 Rm 3204 Peyton Hall (13676)
PHONE..............................860 712-8926
Russel Marvin, CEO
EMP: 13 EST: 2012
SALES (est): 2.1MM Privately Held
SIC: 3621 Motors & generators

(G-13898)
NORTH COUNTRY THIS WEEK
19 Depot St Ste 1 (13676-1143)
P.O. Box 975 (13676-0975)
PHONE..............................315 265-1000
Fax: 315 268-8701
William C Shumway, President
Craig Freilich, Assoc Editor
Julie Spadaccini, Relations
EMP: 9
SQ FT: 2,000
SALES: 850K Privately Held
WEB: www.northcountrynow.com
SIC: 2711 Newspapers

(G-13899)
POTSDAM SPECIALTY PAPER INC (HQ)
Also Called: Potsdam Specialty Paper, Inc.
547a Sissonville Rd (13676-3549)
PHONE..............................315 265-4000
Fax: 315 265-4005
Mike Huth, CEO
WEI Qun Zhang, President
Ronald Charette, General Mgr
Roxanne Kilgore, Senior Buyer
Joel Behm, Technical Mgr
◆ EMP: 70
SQ FT: 18,400
SALES (est): 32.4MM
SALES (corp-wide): 13.8MM Privately Held
SIC: 2621 Specialty papers

(G-13900)
POTTERS INDUSTRIES LLC
72 Reynolds Rd (13676-3588)
P.O. Box 697 (13676-0697)
PHONE: 315 265-4920
Fax: 315 265-2474
Andy Gray, Manager
Andrew Gray, Manager
Jim Casella, Info Tech Mgr
EMP: 40
SALES (corp-wide): 1B Publicly Held
WEB: www.flexolite.com
SIC: 3231 Reflector glass beads, for highway signs or reflectors
HQ: Potters Industries, Llc
  300 Lindenwood Dr
  Malvern PA 19355
  610 651-4700

(G-13901)
RANDY SIXBERRY
Also Called: Great Northern Printing Co
6 Main St Ste 101 (13676-2066)
P.O. Box 270 (13676-0270)
PHONE..............................315 265-6211
Randy Sixberry, Owner
Ranah Matott, Corp Secy
EMP: 7
SQ FT: 3,800
SALES: 700K Privately Held
SIC: 2396 5699 Screen printing on fabric articles; T-shirts, custom printed

(G-13902)
SNYDER LOGGING
528 Allen Falls Rd (13676-4032)
PHONE.................................315 265-1462
Donald Snyder, *Owner*
EMP: 12
SALES (est): 605.6K **Privately Held**
SIC: 2411 Logging camps & contractors

(G-13903)
SUNFEATHER NATURAL SOAP CO INC
Also Called: Sunfeather Herbal Soap
1551 State Highway 72 (13676-4031)
PHONE.................................315 265-1776
Fax: 315 265-2902
Sandra Maine, *CEO*
Kelly Deshaw, *Vice Pres*
Winona Crump, *Production*
EMP: 8
SQ FT: 6,000
SALES (est): 930K **Privately Held**
WEB: www.sunsoap.com
SIC: 2841 Soap & other detergents

Poughkeepsie
Dutchess County

(G-13904)
AMERICAN HORMONES INC
69 W Cedar St Ste 2 (12601-1351)
PHONE.................................845 471-7272
Salvatore J Rubino, *Principal*
Ashok Kadambi, *Principal*
Debbie Carey, *Office Mgr*
EMP: 12
SALES (est): 2.6MM **Privately Held**
WEB: www.americanhormones.com
SIC: 2834 Hormone preparations

(G-13905)
APPARATUS MFG INC
13 Commerce St (12603-2608)
PHONE.................................845 471-5116
Norman Murley, *President*
EMP: 6
SQ FT: 7,500
SALES (est): 600K **Privately Held**
WEB: www.apparatusmfg.com
SIC: 3444 Sheet metalwork

(G-13906)
ARCHITECTURAL DCTG CO LLC
Also Called: Hyde Park
130 Salt Point Tpke (12603-1016)
PHONE.................................845 483-1340
Fax: 845 483-1343
Eli Nassim, *President*
EMP: 20
SALES (est): 1.6MM **Privately Held**
SIC: 2499 Carved & turned wood

(G-13907)
ATLANTIS ENERGY SYSTEMS INC (PA)
7 Industry St (12603-2617)
PHONE.................................845 486-4052
Frank Pao, *Principal*
Joe Morrissey, *Vice Pres*
Jack Kennedy, *Plant Mgr*
Keith Mack, *Manager*
Dohn Paditsone, *Manager*
▲ **EMP:** 13
SALES (est): 2.3MM **Privately Held**
SIC: 3674 Solar cells

(G-13908)
ATLANTIS ENERGY SYSTEMS INC (PA)
7 Industry St (12603-2617)
PHONE.................................916 438-2930
Frank Pao, *President*
Joe Morrissey, *Vice Pres*
Carolyn Courtney, *Accounts Mgr*
Terri Lucas, *Admin Mgr*
Eleanor Pao, *Director*
EMP: 3
SQ FT: 10,000
SALES (est): 1.4MM **Privately Held**
SIC: 3674 3433 Semiconductors & related devices; solar heaters & collectors

(G-13909)
AW MACK MANUFACTURING CO INC
1098 Dutchess Tpke (12603-1150)
PHONE.................................845 452-4050
Fax: 845 452-4057
Albert Mack, *CEO*
John Mack, *Vice Pres*
Diane Conners, *Office Mgr*
EMP: 16
SQ FT: 19,000
SALES (est): 1.6MM **Privately Held**
SIC: 3599 Machine shop, jobbing & repair

(G-13910)
BRIDGE CITY VAPE CO LLC
106 Van Wagner Rd Apt 6f (12603-1311)
PHONE.................................845 625-7962
Michael Tori, *Principal*
EMP: 7
SALES (est): 103.9K **Privately Held**
SIC: 3999 Cigar & cigarette holders

(G-13911)
CETEK INC (PA)
19 Commerce St (12603-2608)
PHONE.................................845 452-3510
Fayiz Hilal, *President*
John Hilal, *Vice Pres*
▲ **EMP:** 25
SQ FT: 20,000
SALES (est): 3.2MM **Privately Held**
SIC: 3299 3599 3444 3825 Ceramic fiber; machine shop, jobbing & repair; forming machine work, sheet metal; instruments to measure electricity; porcelain electrical supplies

(G-13912)
CHOCOVISION CORPORATION
14 Catharine St (12601-3104)
PHONE.................................845 473-4970
Babu Mandava, *CEO*
Abubaker Shagan, *Manager*
◆ **EMP:** 10
SALES (est): 1.8MM **Privately Held**
WEB: www.chocovision.com
SIC: 3599 Custom machinery

(G-13913)
CREATIVE COUNTER TOPS INC
17 Van Kleeck Dr (12601-2163)
PHONE.................................845 471-6480
Andrew Schor, *President*
EMP: 12
SALES (est): 600K **Privately Held**
SIC: 2541 Counters or counter display cases, wood; cabinets, except refrigerated: show, display, etc.: wood

(G-13914)
DORSEY METROLOGY INTL INC
53 Oakley St (12601-2004)
PHONE.................................845 229-2929
Fax: 845 454-3888
Devon Luty, *President*
Peter Klepp, *President*
Mark Swenson, *Vice Pres*
Ronald Moore, *Mfg Staff*
Nancy J Drugan, *QC Mgr*
EMP: 40
SQ FT: 18,000
SALES: 6MM **Privately Held**
WEB: www.dorseymetrology.com
SIC: 3545 5084 3827 3699 Gauges (machine tool accessories); precision tools, machinists'; industrial machinery & equipment; optical instruments & lenses; optical comparators; electrical equipment & supplies

(G-13915)
DYSON-KISSNER-MORAN CORP (PA)
2515 South Rd Ste 5 (12601-5474)
PHONE.................................212 661-4600
Fax: 212 986-2268
Robert R Dyson, *Ch of Bd*
Michael J Harris, *President*
Steve Colantonio, *Accountant*
Linda Portner, *Manager*
Henry Beinstein, *Director*
◆ **EMP:** 30

(G-13916)
EAW ELECTRONIC SYSTEMS INC
16 Victory Ln Ste 3 (12603-1563)
PHONE.................................845 471-5290
Victoria Winiarski, *President*
Edward Winiarski, *Vice Pres*
Adam Secovnie, *Design Engr*
Anna Tastro, *Sales Mgr*
Ana Castro, *Admin Asst*
EMP: 7
SALES (est): 820K **Privately Held**
WEB: www.eawelectro.com
SIC: 3568 Power transmission equipment

(G-13917)
EMPIRE BUSINESS FORMS INC (PA)
Also Called: Forms For You Division
15 Olympic Way (12603-1923)
P.O. Box 3480 (12603-0480)
PHONE.................................845 471-5666
John Vincent Rice, *President*
Louise Rice, *Corp Secy*
EMP: 12
SQ FT: 10,000
SALES (est): 2.2MM **Privately Held**
SIC: 2759 5112 Business forms: printing; business forms

(G-13918)
FACES MAGAZINE INC (PA)
46 Violet Ave (12601-1521)
PHONE.................................201 843-4004
Scott Figman, *President*
Adrianne Moore, *Editor*
▲ **EMP:** 18
SALES (est): 3.3MM **Privately Held**
SIC: 2721 Magazines: publishing only, not printed on site

(G-13919)
FACES MAGAZINE INC
40 Violet Ave (12601-1521)
PHONE.................................845 454-7420
Timothy Perretta, *Manager*
EMP: 100
SALES (corp-wide): 3.3MM **Privately Held**
SIC: 2731 Book music: publishing & printing
PA: Faces Magazine Inc
46 Violet Ave
Poughkeepsie NY 12601
201 843-4004

(G-13920)
GANNETT STLLITE INFO NTWRK LLC
Also Called: Poughkeepsie Journal
85 Civic Center Plz (12601-2498)
P.O. Box 1231 (12602-1231)
PHONE.................................845 454-2000
Fax: 845 437-4903
James Konrad, *Editor*
Ellen Smith, *Adv Dir*
Barry Rothfeld, *Branch Mgr*
Richard L Kleban, *Manager*
J Bainbridge, *Systems Dir*
EMP: 250
SALES (corp-wide): 3B **Publicly Held**
WEB: www.usatoday.com
SIC: 2711 Newspapers, publishing & printing
HQ: Gannett Satellite Information Network, Llc
7950 Jones Branch Dr
Mc Lean VA 22102
703 854-6000

(G-13921)
GET REAL SURFACES INC (PA)
121 Washington St (12601-1806)
PHONE.................................845 337-4483
Fax: 845 483-9580
George Bishop, *President*
Avis Bishop, *Vice Pres*
▼ **EMP:** 15
SQ FT: 19,800
SALES (est): 3.9MM **Privately Held**
WEB: www.getrealsurfaces.com
SIC: 3271 3272 Architectural concrete: block, split, fluted, screen, etc.; concrete products

(G-13922)
GLOEDE NEON SIGNS LTD INC
97 N Clinton St (12601-2032)
PHONE.................................845 471-4366
Fax: 845 471-0987
Barbara Fitzgerald, *President*
Todd Lanthier, *Opers Mgr*
Lori Giustino, *Office Mgr*
EMP: 12 **EST:** 1922
SQ FT: 9,500
SALES (est): 1.7MM **Privately Held**
WEB: www.gloedesigns.com
SIC: 3993 1799 Electric signs; neon signs; sign installation & maintenance

(G-13923)
GREAT EASTERN COLOR LITH (PA)
46 Violet Ave (12601-1599)
PHONE.................................845 454-7420
Lawrence Perretta, *President*
Louis Perretta Jr, *Vice Pres*
EMP: 100 **EST:** 1949
SQ FT: 115,000
SALES (est): 13.9MM **Privately Held**
WEB: www.magnapublishing.com
SIC: 2752 Commercial printing, lithographic

(G-13924)
GREY HOUSE PUBLISHING INC
Also Called: Greyhouse Publshng
84 Patrick Ln Stop 3 (12603-2950)
PHONE.................................845 483-3535
Fax: 845 483-3542
Jennifer Patrick, *Manager*
EMP: 25
SALES (corp-wide): 5.5MM **Privately Held**
WEB: www.greyhouse.com
SIC: 2731 2741 Book publishing; miscellaneous publishing
PA: Grey House Publishing, Inc.
4919 Route 22
Amenia NY 12501
518 789-8700

(G-13925)
HARMON AND CASTELLA PRINTING
164 Garden St (12601-1934)
PHONE.................................845 471-9163
Fax: 845 471-2590
Frank Castella, *President*
Karen Castella, *Vice Pres*
EMP: 13
SQ FT: 4,500
SALES (est): 2.1MM **Privately Held**
WEB: www.hcprinting.com
SIC: 2752 2759 Commercial printing, offset; letterpress printing

(G-13926)
HATFIELD METAL FAB INC
16 Hatfield Ln (12603-6250)
PHONE.................................845 454-9078
Fax: 845 454-9036
Ann Hatfield, *Ch of Bd*
Christopher Hatfield, *Vice Pres*
Henry Hatfield, *Vice Pres*
Ann Schwarzbarg, *Bookkeeper*
EMP: 45
SQ FT: 60,000
SALES (est): 11MM **Privately Held**
WEB: www.hatfieldmetal.com
SIC: 3444 5051 3479 3499 Sheet metalwork; sheets, metal; painting, coating & hot dipping; metal household articles

(G-13927)
INTERNATIONAL BUS MCHS CORP
Also Called: IBM
2455 South Rd (12601-5463)
PHONE.................................845 433-1234
Dave Turek, *President*
Kevin Cleary, *General Mgr*
Dino Quintero, *General Mgr*
Leon Stok, *Vice Pres*

Poughkeepsie - Dutchess County (G-13928) GEOGRAPHIC SECTION

Tim Curtiss, *Project Mgr*
EMP: 4500
SALES (corp-wide): 79.9B **Publicly Held**
WEB: www.ibm.com
SIC: 3575 Computer terminals
PA: International Business Machines Corporation
  1 New Orchard Rd Ste 1
  Armonk NY 10504
  914 499-1900

(G-13928)
JABIL CIRCUIT INC
2455 South Rd (12601-5463)
PHONE..............................845 471-9237
Daniel Whalen, *Manager*
EMP: 421
SALES (corp-wide): 18.3B **Publicly Held**
SIC: 3672 Printed circuit boards
PA: Jabil Inc.
  10560 Dr Martin Luther
  Saint Petersburg FL 33716
  727 577-9749

(G-13929)
JAMES L TAYLOR MFG CO (PA)
Also Called: James L. Taylor Mfg.
130 Salt Point Tpke (12603-1016)
PHONE..............................845 452-3780
Fax: 845 452-0764
Michael Burdis, *CEO*
Joseph Burdis, *Editor*
Bradley Quick, *Vice Pres*
Gordon Burdis, *Engineer*
Judi Paolillow, *Office Mgr*
◆ **EMP:** 21 EST: 1911
SALES (est): 4MM **Privately Held**
WEB: www.jltclamps.com
SIC: 3553 Woodworking machinery

(G-13930)
JAMES L TAYLOR MFG CO
Also Called: Jlt Lancaster Clamps Div
130 Salt Point Tpke (12603-1016)
PHONE..............................845 452-3780
Michael Burdis, *President*
Emily Burdis, *Marketing Staff*
EMP: 9
SALES (corp-wide): 4MM **Privately Held**
WEB: www.jltclamps.com
SIC: 3553 Woodworking machinery
PA: James L. Taylor Manufacturing Co.
  130 Salt Point Tpke
  Poughkeepsie NY 12603
  845 452-3780

(G-13931)
KOSHII MAXELUM AMERICA INC
12 Van Kleeck Dr (12601-2164)
P.O. Box 352 (12602-0352)
PHONE..............................845 471-0500
Mick Morita, *Ch of Bd*
Stan Posluszny, *Business Mgr*
Michelle Niles, *Controller*
Stanley Poluesny, *Sales Executive*
▲ **EMP:** 34
SQ FT: 60,000
SALES (est): 7.5MM
SALES (corp-wide): 85.3MM **Privately Held**
WEB: www.kmamax.com
SIC: 3743 Railway maintenance cars
PA: Koshii & Co., Ltd.
  1-2-158, Hirabayashikita, Suminoe-Ku
  Osaka OSK 559-0
  666 852-061

(G-13932)
LJMM INC
Also Called: Nilda Desserts
188 Washington St (12601-1357)
PHONE..............................845 454-5876
Linda Tritto, *President*
Jason Tritto, *Vice Pres*
EMP: 20
SQ FT: 4,000
SALES (est): 1.2MM **Privately Held**
SIC: 2051 Bakery: wholesale or wholesale/retail combined

(G-13933)
MACHINE TECHNOLOGY INC
104 Bushwick Rd (12603-3813)
PHONE..............................845 454-4030
Fax: 845 454-4031

Klaus Greinacher, *President*
EMP: 5
SQ FT: 3,500
SALES (est): 430K **Privately Held**
SIC: 3829 Measuring & controlling devices

(G-13934)
MARCO MANUFACTURING INC
55 Page Park Dr (12603-2583)
P.O. Box 3733 (12603-0733)
PHONE..............................845 485-1571
Fax: 845 485-1649
Michael Ratliff, *President*
Brian Lowe, *Opers Mgr*
Jim Burger, *Materials Mgr*
Patty Jessup, *QC Mgr*
Timothy McMorris, *Sales Mgr*
EMP: 40
SQ FT: 10,000
SALES (est): 12MM **Privately Held**
WEB: www.marcomanf.com
SIC: 3577 Computer peripheral equipment

(G-13935)
MID HDSON WKSHP FOR THE DSBLED
188 Washington St (12601-1357)
PHONE..............................845 471-3820
Fax: 845 452-3407
Robert Nellis, *President*
Richard Stark, *Vice Pres*
▲ **EMP:** 25
SQ FT: 52,000
SALES (est): 709.7K **Privately Held**
WEB: www.midhudsonworkshop.com
SIC: 3679 Electronic circuits

(G-13936)
MODERN CABINET COMPANY INC
Also Called: Kitchen Cabinet Co
17 Van Kleeck Dr (12601-2163)
PHONE..............................845 473-4900
Andrew Schor, *President*
Lisa Turner, *Vice Pres*
Maxine Schor, *Treasurer*
EMP: 45
SQ FT: 21,000
SALES (est): 6.2MM **Privately Held**
SIC: 2434 Wood kitchen cabinets

(G-13937)
MPI INCORPORATED
165 Smith St Stop 5 (12601-2108)
PHONE..............................845 471-7630
Bruce S Phipps, *Principal*
Chris Dyson, *Vice Pres*
Jeffrey Rich, *Vice Pres*
Bill Nicholas, *Plant Mgr*
Chris Chmura, *Project Mgr*
▼ **EMP:** 65 EST: 1951
SQ FT: 30,000
SALES (est): 17.1MM **Privately Held**
WEB: www.mpi-systems.com
SIC: 3542 Pressing machines

(G-13938)
MR SMOOTHIE
207 South Ave Ste F102 (12601-4815)
PHONE..............................845 296-1686
Aaron S Goldberg, *Vice Pres*
Robert Botllieri, *Branch Mgr*
EMP: 5
SALES (corp-wide): 696.9K **Privately Held**
SIC: 2087 Concentrates, drink
PA: Mr Smoothie
  1000 Ross Park Mall Dr Vc13
  Pittsburgh PA 15237
  412 630-9065

(G-13939)
NEW BGNNNGS WIN DOOR DSTRS LLC
28 Willowbrook Hts (12603-5708)
PHONE..............................845 214-0698
Domenica Haines, *Mng Member*
EMP: 10
SALES (est): 1.2MM **Privately Held**
SIC: 3442 5031 Window & door frames; windows

(G-13940)
NILDAS DESSERTS LIMITED
188 Washington St (12601-1357)
PHONE..............................845 454-5876
Fax: 845 471-9479
James Milano, *President*
EMP: 10 EST: 1989
SQ FT: 5,000
SALES (est): 500K **Privately Held**
SIC: 2051 Bakery: wholesale or wholesale/retail combined

(G-13941)
NUTRA-VET RESEARCH CORP
201 Smith St (12601-2198)
PHONE..............................845 473-1900
Robert Abady, *President*
EMP: 10 EST: 1971
SQ FT: 14,000
SALES (est): 822.8K **Privately Held**
SIC: 2048 Mineral feed supplements

(G-13942)
OPTIMUM APPLIED SYSTEMS INC
16 Victory Ln Ste 5 (12601-1563)
P.O. Box 3572 (12603-0572)
PHONE..............................845 471-3333
Edward Awiniarski, *President*
Jonathan Walters, *Cust Mgr*
EMP: 19
SALES (est): 950K **Privately Held**
SIC: 3699 Electrical equipment & supplies

(G-13943)
PERRETTA GRAPHICS CORP
46 Violet Ave (12601-1521)
PHONE..............................845 473-0550
Fax: 845 473-2919
Lawrence Perretta, *President*
Neil Rockwell, *Publisher*
Christopher Perretta, *Vice Pres*
Louis Perretta Jr, *Vice Pres*
Bruce Quilliam Sr, *Vice Pres*
EMP: 40
SQ FT: 115,000
SALES (est): 8.8MM **Privately Held**
SIC: 3555 Printing trades machinery

(G-13944)
PROTECTIVE POWER SYSTMS & CNTR
Also Called: AC DC Power Systems & Contrls
259 N Grand Ave (12603-1007)
P.O. Box 119, Staatsburg (12580-0119)
PHONE..............................845 773-9016
Andrea Patierno, *CEO*
John Patierno, *Vice Pres*
Joe Szabo, *Sales Mgr*
Chris Brodeur, *Sales Staff*
EMP: 11
SALES (est): 2.7MM **Privately Held**
WEB: www.protectivepowersystems.com
SIC: 3621 Motors & generators

(G-13945)
QUENCH IT INC
Also Called: Half Time
2290 South Rd (12601-5586)
PHONE..............................845 462-5400
Fax: 845 462-5401
Allan Daniels, *Ch of Bd*
▲ **EMP:** 20
SALES (est): 2.5MM **Privately Held**
WEB: www.halftimebeverage.com
SIC: 2086 Bottled & canned soft drinks

(G-13946)
ROBERT ABADY DOG FOOD CO LTD
201 Smith St (12601-2198)
PHONE..............................845 473-1900
Robert Abady, *President*
EMP: 12
SALES (est): 1.5MM **Privately Held**
SIC: 2047 Dog food; cat food

(G-13947)
ROYAL COPENHAGEN INC (PA)
63 Page Park Dr (12603-2583)
P.O. Box 610, Belmar NJ (07719-0610)
PHONE..............................845 454-4442
Nicolai Lindhardt, *President*
Lisa Roberson, *Controller*
Karin Skipper-Ulstrup, *Marketing Mgr*

Niels Bastrup, *Creative Dir*
▲ **EMP:** 10
SQ FT: 6,000
SALES (est): 722.9K **Privately Held**
SIC: 2392 Tablecloths & table settings

(G-13948)
SCHATZ BEARING CORPORATION
10 Fairview Ave (12601-1312)
PHONE..............................845 452-6000
Dr Stephen D E Pomeroy, *CEO*
Bob Lanser, *Plant Mgr*
John Forbes, *Buyer*
Paul Biondi, *QC Mgr*
Pearl Scherf, *Financial Exec*
▲ **EMP:** 75
SQ FT: 50,000
SALES (est): 21.2MM **Privately Held**
WEB: www.schatzbearing.com
SIC: 3562 Ball bearings & parts

(G-13949)
SCIANE ENTERPRISES INC
Also Called: Emdroidme
2600 South Rd Ste 37 (12601-7004)
PHONE..............................845 452-2400
Diane Pawenski, *Ch of Bd*
Patricia Skokan, *Vice Pres*
Ralph Skokan, *Vice Pres*
Gerald Vansteenburg, *Vice Pres*
Jessica McKeown, *Manager*
EMP: 7
SALES (est): 136.2K **Privately Held**
SIC: 2395 2261 Embroidery & art needlework; screen printing of cotton broadwoven fabrics

(G-13950)
SPECTRA VISTA CORPORATION
29 Firemens Way Stop 3 (12603-6523)
PHONE..............................845 471-7007
Fax: 845 471-7020
William G Goffe, *Ch of Bd*
Tom Corl, *President*
Larry Slomer, *Senior Engr*
Ward Duffield, *Manager*
EMP: 6
SQ FT: 2,000
SALES (est): 1.2MM **Privately Held**
SIC: 3826 Spectrometers

(G-13951)
STANFORDVILLE MCH & MFG CO INC (PA)
Also Called: Kent Gage & Tool Company
29 Victory Ln (12603-1562)
P.O. Box B, Stanfordville (12581)
PHONE..............................845 868-2266
Fax: 845 868-7259
Neal Johnsen, *Ch of Bd*
Ann Marie Johnsen, *Corp Secy*
Peter Johnsen, *Vice Pres*
Joe La Falce, *CFO*
Bob Jones, *Manager*
EMP: 57 EST: 1975
SALES (est): 10.5MM **Privately Held**
WEB: www.stanfordville.com
SIC: 3599 Machine shop, jobbing & repair

(G-13952)
STEBE SHCJHJFF
18 Lynbrook Rd (12603-4608)
PHONE..............................839 383-9833
EMP: 10
SALES (est): 480K **Privately Held**
SIC: 2051 Mfg Bread/Related Products

(G-13953)
SUPERIOR WLLS OF HDSON VLY INC
Also Called: Superior Walls of Hudson Vly
68 Violet Ave (12601-1521)
PHONE..............................845 485-4033
Fax: 845 485-2501
Karen Ackert, *President*
Arthur Ackert Sr, *General Mgr*
Tammi Ackert, *Treasurer*
Louis Foscaldi, *Controller*
EMP: 50
SALES (est): 5.9MM **Privately Held**
WEB: www.superiorwallshv.com
SIC: 3272 Precast terrazo or concrete products; concrete products, precast

GEOGRAPHIC SECTION

(G-13954)
VANTAGE MFG & ASSEMBLY LLC
Also Called: Vma
900 Dutchess Tpke (12603-1554)
P.O. Box 3623 (12603-0623)
PHONE.................................845 471-5290
Edward Winiarski, *President*
Micheal Sterbenz, *Finance*
Scott Syska, *Sales Dir*
Ana Castro, *Manager*
Greg Devine, *Manager*
EMP: 48
SALES: 19.6MM **Privately Held**
SIC: 3824 Electromechanical counters

(G-13955)
VETERINARY BIOCHEMICAL LTD
201 Smith St (12601-2110)
PHONE.................................845 473-1900
Robert Abady, *President*
EMP: 5
SQ FT: 14,000
SALES (est): 650K **Privately Held**
SIC: 2048 Feed supplements

(G-13956)
VIKING IRON WORKS INC
37 Hatfield Ln (12603-6249)
PHONE.................................845 471-5010
Fax: 845 471-7925
Richard J Kunkel, *Ch of Bd*
Richard J Kunke, *President*
Paul Kunkel, *Vice Pres*
Jennifer George, *Accounts Mgr*
David Labadie, *Marketing Staff*
EMP: 14
SQ FT: 6,000
SALES (est): 3.3MM **Privately Held**
WEB: www.vikingironworks.com
SIC: 3462 Iron & steel forgings

Poughquag
Dutchess County

(G-13957)
FRED SCHULZ INC
Also Called: Schulz Interiors
4 Jordan Ct (12570-5039)
PHONE.................................845 724-3409
Fax: 845 724-3681
Fred Schulz, *President*
Mary Schulz, *Corp Secy*
EMP: 6
SALES (est): 549.6K **Privately Held**
WEB: www.fredschulz.com
SIC: 2511 Wood household furniture

Pound Ridge
Westchester County

(G-13958)
BIORESEARCH INC (PA)
4 Sunset Ln (10576-2318)
PHONE.................................212 734-5315
Fax: 631 249-8027
Leonard Kirth, *President*
EMP: 9
SQ FT: 7,000
SALES (est): 928.8K **Privately Held**
WEB: www.bioresearch.com
SIC: 3841 Surgical & medical instruments

(G-13959)
DYNAX CORPORATION
79 Westchester Ave (10576-1702)
P.O. Box 285 (10576-0285)
PHONE.................................914 764-0202
Fax: 914 764-0553
Eduard K Kleiner PHD, *President*
Chang Jho, *Vice Pres*
Bryan Rambo, *VP Sales*
Istvan Borsody, *Consultant*
▲ **EMP:** 6
SQ FT: 3,600
SALES (est): 1.3MM **Privately Held**
WEB: www.dynaxcorp.com
SIC: 2822 2824 Fluoro rubbers; fluorocarbon fibers

(G-13960)
LLOYD PRICE ICON FOOD BRANDS
Also Called: Lawdy Miss Clawdy
95 Horseshoe Hill Rd (10576-1636)
PHONE.................................914 764-8624
Lloyd Price, *Ch of Bd*
Bill Waller, *COO*
Jacqueline Battle, *Admin Sec*
EMP: 15
SQ FT: 2,500
SALES (est): 950K **Privately Held**
WEB: www.lawdymissclawdy.com
SIC: 2052 Cookies

Prattsville
Greene County

(G-13961)
COBLESKILL STONE PRODUCTS INC
Also Called: Falke's Quarry
395 Falke Rd (12468-5811)
P.O. Box 268 (12468-0268)
PHONE.................................518 299-3066
Fax: 518 299-3067
Richard Mahar, *Branch Mgr*
EMP: 10
SALES (corp-wide): 115.2MM **Privately Held**
WEB: www.cobleskillstone.com
SIC: 1422 Crushed & broken limestone
PA: Cobleskill Stone Products, Inc.
112 Rock Rd
Cobleskill NY 12043
518 234-0221

Pulaski
Oswego County

(G-13962)
FELIX SCHOELLER NORTH AMER INC
179 County Route 2a (13142-2546)
P.O. Box 250 (13142-0250)
PHONE.................................315 298-8425
Michael Szidat, *Ch of Bd*
Thomas Scheck, *Vice Pres*
Steve Evans, *Controller*
Pam Helinger, *Accounts Mgr*
EMP: 75 EST: 1961
SQ FT: 150,000
SALES (est): 1.4MM
SALES (corp-wide): 482.3MM **Privately Held**
WEB: www.felix-schoeller.com
SIC: 2672 5113 Coated & laminated paper; industrial & personal service paper
HQ: Schoeller Beteiligungen Gmbh
Burg Gretesch 1
Osnabruck
541 380-00

(G-13963)
FELIX SCHOELLER NORTH AMER INC
Also Called: Felix Schoeller Technical Pprs
179 County Route 2a (13142-2546)
P.O. Box 250 (13142-0250)
PHONE.................................315 298-5133
Fax: 315 298-4337
Michael Szidat, *President*
Steve Evans, *Controller*
Arthur Steinbrecher, *Administration*
▲ **EMP:** 110
SQ FT: 500,000
SALES: 168MM
SALES (corp-wide): 482.3MM **Privately Held**
WEB: www.felix-schoeller.com
SIC: 2679 Paper products, converted
HQ: Schoeller Beteiligungen Gmbh
Burg Gretesch 1
Osnabruck
541 380-00

(G-13964)
FULTON BOILER WORKS INC (PA)
3981 Port St (13142-4604)
P.O. Box 257 (13142-0257)
PHONE.................................315 298-5121
Fax: 315 298-6390
Ronald B Palm, *Ch of Bd*
Nathan F Fulton, *General Mgr*
Nelson Lewis, *Engineer*
Scott Redden, *Info Tech Dir*
Fred Farnarier, *Info Tech Mgr*
▲ **EMP:** 60
SQ FT: 120,000
SALES (est): 91.2MM **Privately Held**
WEB: www.fulton.com
SIC: 3443 Boilers: industrial, power, or marine

(G-13965)
FULTON BOILER WORKS INC
972 Centerville Rd (13142-2595)
PHONE.................................315 298-5121
Ronald Palm, *Manager*
EMP: 250
SALES (corp-wide): 91.2MM **Privately Held**
SIC: 3443 Fabricated plate work (boiler shop)
PA: Fulton Boiler Works, Inc.
3981 Port St
Pulaski NY 13142
315 298-5121

(G-13966)
FULTON HEATING SOLUTIONS INC
972 Centerville Rd (13142-2595)
P.O. Box 257 (13142-0257)
PHONE.................................315 298-5121
Ronald B Palm Jr, *Ch of Bd*
Karen Currier, *Credit Mgr*
▲ **EMP:** 55
SQ FT: 200,000
SALES (est): 5.7MM
SALES (corp-wide): 19.1MM **Privately Held**
SIC: 3433 Burners, furnaces, boilers & stokers
PA: Hangzhou Fulton Thermal Equipment Co., Ltd.
No.09,Street 18, Xiasha Economic And Technological Development Z
Hangzhou 31001
571 867-2589

(G-13967)
FULTON VOLCANIC INC (PA)
Also Called: Fulton Companies
3981 Port St (13142-4604)
P.O. Box 257 (13142-0257)
PHONE.................................315 298-5121
Ronald B Palm, *President*
Kathy Sega, *Exec VP*
Julie Hemingway, *Production*
Fran Hicks, *QC Mgr*
Alireza Bahrami, *Research*
▼ **EMP:** 70
SQ FT: 20,000
SALES (est): 31.1MM **Privately Held**
WEB: www.volcanic-heater.com
SIC: 3433 3567 3634 Heating equipment, except electric; heating units & devices, industrial: electric; electric housewares & fans

(G-13968)
HEALTHWAY HOME PRODUCTS INC
3420 Maple Ave (13142-4502)
P.O. Box 485 (13142-0485)
PHONE.................................315 298-2904
Vincent G Lobdell Sr, *Ch of Bd*
Jeffrey Herberger, *Vice Pres*
Vince Lobdell Jr, *Vice Pres*
Yinyin C Blodgett, *Opers Mgr*
Terri Moot, *Hum Res Coord*
▲ **EMP:** 30
SQ FT: 20,000
SALES (est): 8.5MM **Privately Held**
WEB: www.healthway.com
SIC: 3564 Filters, air: furnaces, air conditioning equipment, etc.

(G-13969)
SOLITEC INCORPORATED
3981 Port St (13142-4614)
P.O. Box 257 (13142-0257)
PHONE.................................315 298-4213
R Bramley Palm Jr, *President*
Ronald B Palm, *Vice Pres*
EMP: 19
SQ FT: 14,400
SALES (est): 1.5MM **Privately Held**
SIC: 3585 Refrigeration & heating equipment

Purchase
Westchester County

(G-13970)
BOVIE MEDICAL CORPORATION (PA)
4 Manhattanville Rd # 106 (10577-2119)
PHONE.................................914 468-4009
Robert Gershon, *CEO*
Robert L Gershon, *CEO*
Andrew Makrides, *Ch of Bd*
John Andres, *Vice Ch Bd*
Moshe Citronowicz, *Senior VP*
EMP: 217
SQ FT: 3,650
SALES: 36.6MM **Publicly Held**
WEB: www.boviemedical.com
SIC: 3841 Surgical & medical instruments

(G-13971)
CENTRAL NAT PULP & PPR SLS INC
3 Manhattanville Rd (10577-2116)
PHONE.................................914 696-9000
Kenneth L Wallach, *Chairman*
EMP: 2500
SALES (est): 67.3MM
SALES (corp-wide): 4.4B **Privately Held**
SIC: 2611 Pulp mills; pulp mills, mechanical & recycling processing
PA: Central National Gottesman Inc.
3 Manhattanville Rd # 301
Purchase NY 10577
914 696-9000

(G-13972)
FMC INTERNATIONAL LTD
Also Called: Biologic Solutions
2975 Westchester Ave (10577-2518)
PHONE.................................914 935-0918
Harvey Fishman, *President*
Peter Blumenthal, *CFO*
EMP: 2
SALES (est): 2MM **Privately Held**
WEB: www.biologicsolutions.com
SIC: 2844 Toilet preparations

(G-13973)
HITACHI CABLE AMERICA INC (DH)
2 Manhattanville Rd # 301 (10577-2118)
PHONE.................................914 694-9200
Fax: 914 993-0997
Toro Aoki, *CEO*
Bob Sebesto, *Business Mgr*
Tatsuo Kinoshita, *Corp Secy*
John Gibson, *Senior VP*
Katsura Ishikawa, *Vice Pres*
▲ **EMP:** 13
SQ FT: 6,000
SALES (est): 165.2MM
SALES (corp-wide): 80.6B **Privately Held**
WEB: www.hitachi-cable.com
SIC: 3052 Rubber & plastics hose & beltings
HQ: Hitachi Metals America, Ltd.
2 Manhattanville Rd # 301
Purchase NY 10577
914 694-9200

(G-13974)
HITACHI METALS AMERICA LTD
HI Specialties America Div
2 Manhattanville Rd # 301 (10577-2103)
PHONE.................................914 694-9200
Ernie Striscsck, *President*
David Whigham, *Manager*
EMP: 24

Purchase - Westchester County (G-13975)

SALES (corp-wide): 80.6B **Privately Held**
SIC: **3312** 3496 3316 3315 Rods, iron & steel: made in steel mills; miscellaneous fabricated wire products; cold finishing of steel shapes; steel wire & related products
HQ: Hitachi Metals America, Ltd.
2 Manhattanville Rd # 301
Purchase NY 10577
914 694-9200

(G-13975)
HITACHI METALS AMERICA LTD (DH)
2 Manhattanville Rd # 301 (10577-2103)
PHONE..................914 694-9200
Fax: 914 694-9279
Hideaki Takahashi, *CEO*
Tomoyasu Kubota, *Ch of Bd*
Tomoyuki Hatano, *President*
Hiroaki Nakanishi, *President*
Barb Arakelian, *General Mgr*
▲ **EMP:** 45 **EST:** 1965
SQ FT: 25,000
SALES (est): 984.4MM
SALES (corp-wide): 80.6B **Privately Held**
SIC: **3264** 3577 3365 5051 Magnets, permanent: ceramic or ferrite; computer peripheral equipment; aluminum & aluminum-based alloy castings; steel; castings, rough: iron or steel; ductile iron castings; gray iron castings; automotive related machinery
HQ: Hitachi Metals, Ltd.
1-2-70, Konan
Minato-Ku TKY 108-0
367 743-001

(G-13976)
LIGHTING HOLDINGS INTL LLC (PA)
4 Manhattanville Rd (10577-2139)
PHONE..................845 306-1850
Dionne Gadsden, *CEO*
Steve Imgham, *CEO*
Jan Germis, *Exec VP*
Tom Mullally, *Exec VP*
Marcos Paganini, *Exec VP*
◆ **EMP:** 1400
SQ FT: 1,700
SALES (est): 141.7MM **Privately Held**
WEB: www.sli-lighting.com
SIC: **3641** 5719 5063 4225 Electric lamps & parts for generalized applications; lamps & lamp shades; lighting fixtures; general warehousing; current-carrying wiring devices; lamp sockets & receptacles (electric wiring devices); pressed & blown glass

(G-13977)
MAM USA CORPORATION
2700 Westchester Ave # 315 (10577-2554)
PHONE..................914 269-2500
Jennifer Mitchell, *CEO*
Fritz Hirsch, *CEO*
Niklaus Schertenlieb, *President*
Stefan Roehrig, *Vice Pres*
Denis Campbell, *Accounting Mgr*
▲ **EMP:** 10
SALES (est): 2.1MM **Privately Held**
SIC: **3069** 5999 Baby pacifiers, rubber; infant furnishings & equipment
HQ: Mam Babyartikel Gesellschaft M.B.H.
Lorenz Mandl-Gasse 50
Wien 1160
149 141-0

(G-13978)
NXXI INC
4 Manhattanville Rd # 205 (10577-2139)
PHONE..................914 701-4500
Michael A Zeher, *President*
Alan J Kirschbaum, *CFO*
Alpha Jallow, *Accountant*
Robert E Pollack, *Director*
Robert Pollack, *President*
EMP: 11
SQ FT: 5,383
SALES: 6.6MM **Privately Held**
WEB: www.nutrition21.com
SIC: **2836** 8733 Biological products, except diagnostic; noncommercial biological research organization; biotechnical research, noncommercial

(G-13979)
PEPSI-COLA METRO BTLG CO INC
700 Anderson Hill Rd (10577-1444)
PHONE..................914 253-2000
Robert K Biggart, *President*
David Cummings, *General Mgr*
La'mont Jackson, *District Mgr*
Ruchi Modi, *Opers Mgr*
Ashley Rahaim, *Opers Mgr*
EMP: 31
SALES (est): 2.7MM **Privately Held**
SIC: **2086** Carbonated soft drinks, bottled & canned

(G-13980)
PEPSI-COLA SALES AND DIST INC (HQ)
700 Anderson Hill Rd (10577-1444)
PHONE..................914 253-2000
Kirk Tanner, *CEO*
EMP: 6
SALES (est): 787.2K
SALES (corp-wide): 62.8B **Publicly Held**
SIC: **2086** 5149 Soft drinks: packaged in cans, bottles, etc.; beverages, except coffee & tea
PA: Pepsico, Inc.
700 Anderson Hill Rd
Purchase NY 10577
914 253-2000

(G-13981)
PEPSICO INC (PA)
700 Anderson Hill Rd (10577-1444)
PHONE..................914 253-2000
Fax: 914 253-2203
Laxman Narasimhan, *CEO*
Indra K Nooyi, *Ch of Bd*
Silviu Popvici, *President*
Hugh F Johnston, *Vice Chairman*
Kim Baker, *Exec VP*
◆ **EMP:** 1500 **EST:** 1919
SALES: 62.8B **Publicly Held**
WEB: www.pepsico.com
SIC: **2096** 2087 2086 2037 Potato chips & similar snacks; corn chips & other corn-based snacks; potato chips & other potato-based snacks; cheese curls & puffs; flavoring extracts & syrups; syrups, drink; fruit juices: concentrated for fountain use; concentrates, drink; bottled & canned soft drinks; iced tea & fruit drinks, bottled & canned; soft drinks: packaged in cans, bottles, etc.; carbonated beverages, non-alcoholic: bottled & canned; fruit juices; cookies & crackers; cereal breakfast foods; oatmeal: prepared as cereal breakfast food

(G-13982)
PEPSICO INC
Anderson Hill Rd (10577)
PHONE..................914 253-2000
D Wayne Calloway, *Ch of Bd*
Joseph Sim, *Vice Pres*
EMP: 700
SALES (corp-wide): 62.8B **Publicly Held**
SIC: **2086** Carbonated soft drinks, bottled & canned
PA: Pepsico, Inc.
700 Anderson Hill Rd
Purchase NY 10577
914 253-2000

(G-13983)
PEPSICO INC
700 Anderson Hill Rd (10577-1444)
PHONE..................914 253-2713
Denise Passarella, *Branch Mgr*
EMP: 10
SALES (corp-wide): 62.8B **Publicly Held**
SIC: **2086** Carbonated soft drinks, bottled & canned
PA: Pepsico, Inc.
700 Anderson Hill Rd
Purchase NY 10577
914 253-2000

(G-13984)
PEPSICO CAPITAL RESOURCES INC
700 Anderson Hill Rd (10577-1444)
PHONE..................914 253-2000
Judy Germano, *Principal*
EMP: 6
SALES (est): 395.2K **Privately Held**
SIC: **2086** Bottled & canned soft drinks

(G-13985)
PEPSICO SALES INC
700 Anderson Hill Rd (10577-1444)
PHONE..................914 253-2000
Charles F Mueller, *Principal*
EMP: 5 **EST:** 2003
SALES (est): 83K
SALES (corp-wide): 62.8B **Publicly Held**
SIC: **2086** 5149 Soft drinks: packaged in cans, bottles, etc.; beverages, except coffee & tea
PA: Pepsico, Inc.
700 Anderson Hill Rd
Purchase NY 10577
914 253-2000

(G-13986)
REGAL TRADING INC
Also Called: Regal Commodities
2975 Westchester Ave # 210 (10577-2500)
PHONE..................914 694-6100
Joseph Apuzzo Jr, *CEO*
Sid Abramowitz, *Vice Pres*
Arlene Zimmer, *Accounts Mgr*
▲ **EMP:** 35
SALES (est): 5.9MM **Privately Held**
SIC: **2095** Coffee roasting (except by wholesale grocers)

(G-13987)
RIGHT WORLD VIEW
2900 Purchase St 528 (10577-2131)
PHONE..................914 406-2994
Daniel Parzow, *Owner*
Andrew Berman, *Chief*
Logan Osberg, *Manager*
EMP: 30
SALES (est): 1.3MM **Privately Held**
SIC: **2711** Newspapers, publishing & printing

Purdys
Westchester County

(G-13988)
DATA INTERCHANGE SYSTEMS INC
Also Called: Peltrix
9 Ridge Way (10578-1405)
PHONE..................914 277-7775
Amit Peleg, *President*
EMP: 8
SQ FT: 8,000
SALES (est): 3MM **Privately Held**
SIC: **3651** Audio electronic systems

Putnam Valley
Putnam County

(G-13989)
ARGOS INC
58 Seifert Ln (10579-1707)
PHONE..................845 528-0576
Fax: 845 278-6769
Steven A Roy, *President*
Roger Eriksen, *Vice Pres*
Dennis Klubnick, *Admin Sec*
EMP: 24
SQ FT: 10,000
SALES (est): 3.7MM **Privately Held**
WEB: www.argos.net
SIC: **3366** 3369 Bronze foundry; nonferrous foundries

Queens Village
Queens County

(G-13990)
ALL TIME PRODUCTS INC
21167 Jamaica Ave (11428-1621)
PHONE..................718 464-1400
Fax: 718 464-4967
Junior Lindo, *President*
Vinton Lindo, *Admin Sec*
EMP: 6
SALES (est): 660K **Privately Held**
SIC: **2752** Commercial printing, lithographic

(G-13991)
COLGATE-PALMOLIVE COMPANY
21818 100th Ave (11429-1209)
PHONE..................718 506-3961
Ian M Cook, *President*
EMP: 279
SALES (corp-wide): 15.2B **Publicly Held**
SIC: **2844** Toothpastes or powders, dentifrices
PA: Colgate-Palmolive Company
300 Park Ave Fl 5
New York NY 10022
212 310-2000

(G-13992)
EAST END VINEYARDS LLC
Also Called: Clovis Point
21548 Jamaica Ave (11428-1716)
P.O. Box 669, Jamesport (11947-0669)
PHONE..................718 468-0500
Hal R Ginsburg, *Mng Member*
▲ **EMP:** 7
SQ FT: 5,000
SALES: 300K **Privately Held**
SIC: **2084** Wines

(G-13993)
GM ICE CREAM INC
8911 207th St (11427-2238)
P.O. Box 5064, Astoria (11105-5064)
PHONE..................646 236-7383
George Mylonas, *President*
EMP: 6
SALES (est): 406.7K **Privately Held**
SIC: **2024** Ice cream & frozen desserts

(G-13994)
GRAY GLASS INC
21744 98th Ave Ste C (11429-1252)
PHONE..................718 217-2943
Fax: 718 217-0280
Christopher A Viggiano, *Ch of Bd*
William O Bryan, *Vice Pres*
Kenneth Rutowicz, *Site Mgr*
Val Krejci, *Financial Exec*
Jim Valenti, *VP Sales*
▲ **EMP:** 49
SQ FT: 50,000
SALES: 7.8MM **Privately Held**
WEB: www.grayglass.net
SIC: **3229** 3231 Glass tubes & tubing; products of purchased glass

(G-13995)
IGNELZI INTERIORS INC
9805 217th St (11429-1234)
PHONE..................718 464-0279
Fax: 718 464-1986
Paul Ignelzi, *President*
Hugo Pomies, *Vice Pres*
EMP: 20
SQ FT: 16,000
SALES (est): 3.1MM **Privately Held**
WEB: www.ignelziinteriors.com
SIC: **2431** 2434 Woodwork, interior & ornamental; wood kitchen cabinets

(G-13996)
JAMAICA LAMP CORP
21220 Jamaica Ave (11428-1618)
PHONE..................718 776-5039
Irving Shernock, *President*
Norman Weiselberg, *Manager*
▲ **EMP:** 30 **EST:** 1955
SQ FT: 20,000
SALES (est): 2.8MM **Privately Held**
SIC: **3999** 3645 Shades, lamp or candle; residential lighting fixtures

(G-13997)
LAMS FOODS INC
9723 218th St (11429-1251)
PHONE..................718 217-0476
Fax: 718 217-0655
Sherlock Lam, *President*
Cleveland Lam, *Vice Pres*
Shervin Lam, *Vice Pres*
Trevor Lam, *Vice Pres*
Cesar Cercado, *Accountant*
▲ **EMP:** 17

SQ FT: 20,000
SALES (est): 3.3MM **Privately Held**
WEB: www.lamsnacks.com
SIC: 2099 Noodles, fried (Chinese)

(G-13998)
MSQ CORPORATION
21504 Hempstead Ave (11429-1222)
PHONE.................................718 465-0900
Craig Zoly, *President*
EMP: 7
SALES (est): 268.7K **Privately Held**
SIC: 2024 Ice cream & frozen desserts; ice cream & ice milk

(G-13999)
VOLKERT PRECISION TECH INC
22240 96th Ave Ste 3 (11429-1330)
PHONE.................................718 464-9500
Fax: 718 464-8536
Kenneth J Heim, *Ch of Bd*
Jerome Bloomberg, *Vice Pres*
Omadai Laljit, *Manager*
EMP: 47
SQ FT: 50,000
SALES (est): 9.1MM **Privately Held**
WEB: www.volkertprecision.com
SIC: 3469 Stamping metal for the trade; machine parts, stamped or pressed metal

(G-14000)
XEDIT CORP
Also Called: Servo Reeler System
21831 97th Ave (11429-1232)
PHONE.................................718 380-1592
Fax: 718 464-9435
Claude Karczmer, *President*
Eileen Karczmer, *Sales Staff*
EMP: 7
SQ FT: 1,800
SALES (est): 660K **Privately Held**
WEB: www.servoreelers.com
SIC: 3679 Electronic circuits

Queensbury
Warren County

(G-14001)
ADIRONDACK PRECISION CUT STONE (PA)
536 Queensbury Ave (12804-7612)
PHONE.................................518 681-3060
Kris Johnston, *Owner*
EMP: 11
SALES (est): 1MM **Privately Held**
SIC: 3281 Cut stone & stone products

(G-14002)
AMSTERDAM PRINTING & LITHO INC
Resource One
428 Corinth Rd (12804-7816)
P.O. Box 267, Hagaman (12086-0267)
PHONE.................................518 792-6501
Kevin Kirbey, *Manager*
EMP: 10
SQ FT: 24,000
SALES (corp-wide): 4.3B **Privately Held**
WEB: www.amsterdamprinting.com
SIC: 2752 Commercial printing, offset
HQ: Amsterdam Printing & Litho, Inc.
166 Wallins Corners Rd
Amsterdam NY 12010
518 842-6000

(G-14003)
AMSTERDAM PRINTING & LITHO INC
Also Called: Web Graphics
428 Corinth Rd (12804-7816)
PHONE.................................518 792-6501
Michael Hart, *Mfg Dir*
Bill Matte, *Purch Agent*
Bob Mongin, *Natl Sales Mgr*
Connie Marcotte, *Cust Mgr*
Tim Taylor, *Branch Mgr*
EMP: 12
SALES (corp-wide): 4.3B **Privately Held**
WEB: www.amsterdamprinting.com
SIC: 2759 Laser printing

HQ: Amsterdam Printing & Litho, Inc.
166 Wallins Corners Rd
Amsterdam NY 12010
518 842-6000

(G-14004)
ANGIODYNAMICS INC
603 Queensbury Ave (12804-7619)
PHONE.................................518 975-1400
Lynn Wadleigh, *Controller*
EMP: 400
SALES (corp-wide): 349.6MM **Publicly Held**
SIC: 3841 Surgical & medical instruments
PA: Angiodynamics, Inc.
14 Plaza Dr
Latham NY 12110
518 795-1400

(G-14005)
ANGIODYNAMICS INC
543 Queensbury Ave (12804-7629)
PHONE.................................518 742-4430
Christina Bolduc, *Supervisor*
EMP: 275
SALES (corp-wide): 353.8MM **Publicly Held**
SIC: 3841 Surgical & medical instruments
PA: Angiodynamics, Inc.
14 Plaza Dr
Latham NY 12110
518 795-1400

(G-14006)
ARLINGTON EQUIPMENT CORP
588 Queensbury Ave (12804-7612)
P.O. Box 4557 (12804-0557)
PHONE.................................518 798-5867
Pauline Burnett, *President*
Debbie Burnett, *Vice Pres*
EMP: 8
SALES (est): 700K **Privately Held**
SIC: 3537 Industrial trucks & tractors

(G-14007)
C R BARD INC
289 Bay Rd (12804-2015)
PHONE.................................518 793-2531
Fax: 518 793-1012
David Freeman, *President*
Chris Melton, *President*
Ronald Greene, *Vice Pres*
Brian Battease, *Warehouse Mgr*
David Walls, *Buyer*
EMP: 485
SALES (corp-wide): 3.7B **Publicly Held**
SIC: 3841 Surgical & medical instruments
PA: C. R. Bard, Inc.
730 Central Ave
New Providence NJ 07974
908 277-8000

(G-14008)
DUKE CONCRETE PRODUCTS INC
50 Duke Dr (12804-2048)
PHONE.................................518 793-7743
Fax: 518 793-0179
O E S Hedbring, *Ch of Bd*
John Hedbring, *President*
Gary Hukey, *Vice Pres*
Joanne Major, *Info Tech Dir*
Richard Schumaker, *Admin Sec*
EMP: 25
SQ FT: 9,000
SALES (est): 5.2MM
SALES (corp-wide): 156.8MM **Privately Held**
WEB: www.dukeconcrete.com
SIC: 3271 5211 5082 Blocks, concrete or cinder: standard; concrete & cinder block; masonry materials & supplies; masonry equipment & supplies
PA: The Fort Miller Service Corp
688 Wilbur Ave
Greenwich NY 12834
518 695-5000

(G-14009)
GLENS FALLS BUSINESS FORMS INC
Also Called: G F Labels
10 Ferguson Ln (12804-7641)
PHONE.................................518 798-6643
Fax: 518 798-0741
Robert Gray, *CEO*
Steve Badera, *General Mgr*
Jacob Vanness, *Vice Pres*
Betsy Carney, *Admin Sec*
EMP: 14
SQ FT: 12,000
SALES (est): 3.3MM **Privately Held**
WEB: www.gflabels.com
SIC: 2675 Die-cut paper & board

(G-14010)
GLENS FALLS READY MIX INC
Also Called: Crainville Block Co
112 Big Boom Rd (12804-7861)
PHONE.................................518 793-1695
Fax: 518 684-6141
John Tesiero, *President*
EMP: 12
SQ FT: 195
SALES (est): 770K **Privately Held**
SIC: 3272 3273 Concrete products, pre-cast; ready-mixed concrete

(G-14011)
HARRIS LOGGING INC
39 Mud Pond Rd (12804-7313)
PHONE.................................518 792-1083
Fax: 518 639-8351
Keith L Harris, *President*
Pamela Harris, *Corp Secy*
EMP: 30
SALES (est): 2.2MM **Privately Held**
SIC: 2411 Logging

(G-14012)
HJE COMPANY INC
820 Quaker Rd (12804-3811)
PHONE.................................518 792-8733
Joseph Tunick Strauss, *President*
Dan James, *CIO*
EMP: 5
SQ FT: 4,500
SALES (est): 605K **Privately Held**
SIC: 3549 3399 Metalworking machinery; powder, metal

(G-14013)
JAMES KING WOODWORKING INC
656 County Line Rd (12804-7621)
PHONE.................................518 761-6091
Scott Kingsley, *President*
James Morris, *Vice Pres*
Wandi Abbote, *Office Mgr*
EMP: 6
SQ FT: 76,230
SALES (est): 410K **Privately Held**
SIC: 2499 Decorative wood & woodwork

(G-14014)
JE MONAHAN FABRICATIONS LLC
559 Queensbury Ave 1/2 (12804-7613)
PHONE.................................518 761-0414
Lois Bennett, *Office Mgr*
Harold A Smith,
Joe E Monahan,
Walter R Smith,
EMP: 11
SQ FT: 25,000
SALES (est): 1.2MM **Privately Held**
SIC: 3499 Welding tips, heat resistant: metal

(G-14015)
KINGSBURY PRINTING CO INC
813 Bay Rd (12804-5906)
PHONE.................................518 747-6606
Robert Bombard, *President*
Victoria Bombard-Bushey, *Director*
EMP: 6
SALES (est): 600K **Privately Held**
WEB: www.kingsburyprinting.com
SIC: 2752 Commercial printing, offset

(G-14016)
KOKE INC
582 Queensbury Ave (12804-7612)
PHONE.................................800 535-5303
Richard Koke, *President*
Michael Nelson, *CFO*
Tom Miksch, *Mktg Dir*
◆ **EMP:** 20 **EST:** 1972
SQ FT: 36,000
SALES (est): 5.2MM **Privately Held**
SIC: 3537 5084 Trucks, tractors, loaders, carriers & similar equipment; materials handling machinery

(G-14017)
M & S PRECISION MACHINE CO LLC
27 Casey Rd (12804-7627)
PHONE.................................518 747-1193
Dave Mc Donald, *Mng Member*
Joyllen Sporiwski, *Manager*
Michael Spirowski,
▲ **EMP:** 10
SALES (est): 1.2MM **Privately Held**
SIC: 3545 3599 Machine tool accessories; machine & other job shop work

(G-14018)
MORRIS PRODUCTS INC
53 Carey Rd (12804-7880)
PHONE.................................518 743-0523
Jeff Schwartz, *President*
Yani Cruz, *General Mgr*
Mike Mensler, *Manager*
▲ **EMP:** 10
SQ FT: 20,000
SALES (est): 1.9MM **Privately Held**
WEB: www.morrisproducts.com
SIC: 3625 5063 Electric controls & control accessories, industrial; electrical construction materials

(G-14019)
NORTHERN DESIGN & BLDG ASSOC
Also Called: Hamilton Design Kit Homes
100 Park Rd (12804-7616)
P.O. Box 47, Hudson Falls (12839-0047)
PHONE.................................518 747-2200
Fax: 518 747-8032
Richard Kent McNairy, *CEO*
Douglas Thayer, *Exec VP*
Bob Niedermeyer, *Vice Pres*
Brian Thayer, *Consultant*
EMP: 21
SQ FT: 20,000
SALES (est): 3.4MM **Privately Held**
SIC: 2452 7389 Prefabricated wood buildings; design services

(G-14020)
PRAXIS POWDER TECHNOLOGY INC
604 Queensbury Ave (12804-7618)
PHONE.................................518 812-0112
Joseph A Grohowski, *President*
Piemme Jobe, *President*
Harold Mapes, *COO*
Tracy Macneal, *Vice Pres*
Susan Purinton, *Office Mgr*
EMP: 24
SQ FT: 8,400
SALES (est): 5.3MM **Privately Held**
SIC: 3841 Surgical & medical instruments

(G-14021)
PRIME WOOD PRODUCTS
1288 Vaughn Rd (12804-7356)
PHONE.................................518 792-1407
Fax: 518 792-4357
Richard Caravaggio, *Owner*
EMP: 6
SALES (est): 364.6K **Privately Held**
SIC: 2499 Decorative wood & woodwork

(G-14022)
RWS MANUFACTURING INC
22 Ferguson Ln (12804-7641)
PHONE.................................518 361-1657
Eric Fortin, *President*
Yvin Fortin, *Vice Pres*
EMP: 5
SALES (est): 839.2K
SALES (corp-wide): 4.9MM **Privately Held**
SIC: 2429 Shavings & packaging, excelsior
PA: Litiere Royal Inc
2327 Boul Du Versant-Nord Bureau 250
Quebec QC
418 780-3373

Queensbury - Warren County (G-14023)

(G-14023)
S & H ENTERPRISES INC
Also Called: Nationwide Lifts
10b Holden Ave (12804-3316)
PHONE.................................888 323-8755
Andrew Darnley, *President*
EMP: 5
SALES (est): 465.9K **Privately Held**
SIC: **3534** 3999 Stair elevators, motor powered; wheelchair lifts

(G-14024)
SEELEY MACHINE INC
Also Called: Seeley Machine & Fabrication
75 Big Boom Rd (12804-7858)
PHONE.................................518 798-9510
Fax: 518 798-0687
Daryl W Pechtel, *Ch of Bd*
Craig Seeley, *President*
Barbara Seeley, *Corp Secy*
Charles Seeley, *Vice Pres*
EMP: 25
SQ FT: 14,000
SALES (est): 5.1MM **Privately Held**
WEB: www.seeleymachine.com
SIC: **3599** Machine shop, jobbing & repair

(G-14025)
SINCLAIR INTERNATIONAL COMPANY (PA)
85 Boulevard (12804-3903)
PHONE.................................518 798-2361
Fax: 518 798-3028
David H Sinclair Jr, *President*
Mark Havens, *Engineer*
Jason Viele, *Manager*
Donald Weaver, *Manager*
EMP: 48 EST: 1925
SQ FT: 28,000
SALES (est): 5.9MM **Privately Held**
SIC: **3496** 3554 3569 Wire cloth & woven wire products; paper industries machinery; filters

(G-14026)
TRIBUNE MEDIA SERVICES INC (HQ)
Also Called: TV Data
40 Media Dr (12804-4086)
PHONE.................................518 792-9914
Fax: 518 792-4671
Daniel Kazan, *CEO*
John B Kelleher, *President*
Richard Cusick, *General Mgr*
John Kelleher, *General Mgr*
Kathleen Tolstrup, *General Mgr*
EMP: 300
SQ FT: 38,000
SALES (est): 47.4MM
SALES (corp-wide): 1.9B **Publicly Held**
WEB: www.tvdata.com
SIC: **2741** Miscellaneous publishing
PA: Tribune Media Company
    435 N Michigan Ave Fl 2
    Chicago IL 60611
    212 210-2786

(G-14027)
WF LAKE CORP
65 Park Rd (12804-7615)
P.O. Box 4214 (12804-0214)
PHONE.................................518 798-9934
Fax: 518 798-9936
Jim Meyer, *President*
John L Hodgkins III, *Corp Secy*
▲ EMP: 25
SQ FT: 33,000
SALES (est): 5.5MM **Privately Held**
WEB: www.wflake.com
SIC: **3052** Rubber & plastics hose & beltings

Quogue
Suffolk County

(G-14028)
PECONIC PLASTICS INC
6062 Old Country Rd (11959)
P.O. Box 1425 (11959-1425)
PHONE.................................631 653-3676
Fax: 631 653-3649
Ralph Ponto, *President*
Gerhart Ponto, *Vice Pres*
Elizabeth Ponto, *Manager*
EMP: 10
SALES (est): 786.7K **Privately Held**
WEB: www.peconicplastics.com
SIC: **3089** Molding primary plastic

Randolph
Cattaraugus County

(G-14029)
METALLIC LADDER MFG CORP
Also Called: Alumidock
41 S Washington St (14772-1326)
PHONE.................................716 358-6201
Fax: 716 358-4736
William Wadsworth, *President*
Christian Monroe, *Sls & Mktg Exec*
Daryl Wadsworth, *Admin Sec*
▼ EMP: 15
SQ FT: 12,000
SALES (est): 3.2MM **Privately Held**
WEB: www.alumidock.com
SIC: **3448** 3499 Docks: prefabricated metal; ladders, portable: metal

(G-14030)
RANDOLPH DIMENSION CORPORATION
216 Main St Ste 216 (14772)
PHONE.................................716 358-6901
EMP: 10 EST: 1965
SQ FT: 72,000
SALES (est): 130.2K **Privately Held**
SIC: **2426** 2431 Hardwood Dimension/Floor Mill Mfg Millwork

(G-14031)
REGISTER GRAPHICS INC
220 Main St (14772-1213)
P.O. Box 98 (14772-0098)
PHONE.................................716 358-2921
Fax: 716 358-5695
Robert G Beach, *President*
Tim Beach, *President*
Mark Hinman, *Corp Secy*
Jean D Beach, *Vice Pres*
Sandra Simmons, *Manager*
EMP: 23 EST: 1865
SQ FT: 13,000
SALES (est): 3.7MM **Privately Held**
WEB: www.registergraphics.com
SIC: **2752** Commercial printing, offset

Ransomville
Niagara County

(G-14032)
J F MACHINING COMPANY INC
2382 Balmer Rd (14131-9787)
P.O. Box 249 (14131-0249)
PHONE.................................716 791-3910
Fax: 716 791-3913
Joseph Fleckenstein, *President*
Kelly Fleckenstein, *Vice Pres*
EMP: 10
SQ FT: 2,000
SALES (est): 800K **Privately Held**
SIC: **3599** Machine shop, jobbing & repair

Ravena
Albany County

(G-14033)
BLEEZARDE PUBLISHING INC
Also Called: Greenville Local
164 Main St (12143-1112)
PHONE.................................518 756-2030
Fax: 518 756-8555
Richard G Bleezarde, *President*
Keith Shoemaker, *Advt Staff*
EMP: 8 EST: 1880
SQ FT: 5,400
SALES: 305K **Privately Held**
SIC: **2711** Commercial printing & newspaper publishing combined

(G-14034)
HOOTZ FAMILY BOWLING INC
100 Main St (12143-1709)
PHONE.................................518 756-4668
Brian Hotaoing, *President*
EMP: 10
SALES (est): 704.9K **Privately Held**
SIC: **3949** Bowling alleys & accessories

(G-14035)
LAFARGE BUILDING MATERIALS INC
Rr (12143)
PHONE.................................518 756-5000
Martin Turecky, *Manager*
EMP: 14
SALES (corp-wide): 26.6B **Privately Held**
SIC: **3241** Masonry cement
HQ: Lafarge Building Materials Inc.
    8700 W Bryn Mawr Ave 300n
    Chicago IL 60631
    678 746-2000

(G-14036)
LAFARGE NORTH AMERICA INC
1916 Route 9 W (12143)
P.O. Box 3 (12143-0003)
PHONE.................................518 756-5000
Bernie Dushane, *Maint Spvr*
Martin Turecky, *Branch Mgr*
Sarah Sweeney, *Manager*
Morgan Huffman, *Supervisor*
EMP: 27
SALES (corp-wide): 26.6B **Privately Held**
WEB: www.lafargenorthamerica.com
SIC: **3241** 3273 3272 3271 Cement, hydraulic; portland cement; ready-mixed concrete; concrete products; precast terrazo or concrete products; prestressed concrete products; cylinder pipe, prestressed or pretensioned concrete; blocks, concrete or cinder: standard; construction sand & gravel; construction sand mining; gravel mining; asphalt paving mixtures & blocks; paving mixtures; asphalt & asphaltic paving mixtures (not from refineries)
HQ: Lafarge North America Inc.
    8700 W Bryn Mawr Ave Ll
    Chicago IL 60631
    703 480-3600

Ray Brook
Essex County

(G-14037)
FEDERAL PRISON INDUSTRIES
Also Called: Unicor
Old Ray Brook Rd (12977)
PHONE.................................518 897-4000
Steve Priddell, *Principal*
Jon Hensley, *Principal*
Diane Klusman, *Principal*
EMP: 99 **Publicly Held**
WEB: www.unicor.gov
SIC: **2299** Textile mill waste & remnant processing
HQ: Federal Prison Industries, Inc
    320 1st St Nw
    Washington DC 20534
    202 305-3500

Red Creek
Wayne County

(G-14038)
RED CREEK COLD STORAGE LLC (PA)
14127 Keeley St (13143-9513)
P.O. Box 622 (13143-0622)
PHONE.................................315 576-2069
Joel Daugherty, *President*
Joseph Dougherty, *CFO*
EMP: 5
SALES: 500K **Privately Held**
SIC: **2022** Natural cheese

(G-14039)
SMOOTHBORE INTERNATIONAL INC
13881 Westbury Cutoff Rd (13143)
PHONE.................................315 754-8124
Jason Smith, *President*
EMP: 7
SALES (est): 793.4K **Privately Held**
SIC: **2411** Logging camps & contractors

(G-14040)
WAYUGA COMMUNITY NEWSPAPERS (PA)
Also Called: Wayuga News
6784 Main St (13143)
PHONE.................................315 754-6229
Fax: 315 594-6331
Angelo Palermo, *President*
Carol Palermo, *Vice Pres*
Pat Scutt, *Purch Agent*
EMP: 20
SQ FT: 9,520
SALES (est): 2.5MM **Privately Held**
WEB: www.wayuga.com
SIC: **2711** 2741 Newspapers, publishing & printing; miscellaneous publishing

Red Hook
Dutchess County

(G-14041)
CORT CONTRACTING
188 W Market St (12571-2710)
PHONE.................................845 758-1190
Ralph Cort, *Owner*
EMP: 10
SALES (est): 680K **Privately Held**
WEB: www.cortcontracting.com
SIC: **2452** Prefabricated wood buildings

(G-14042)
UNIVERSAL BUILDERS SUPPLY INC
45 Ocallaghan Ln (12571-1776)
PHONE.................................845 758-8801
Fax: 845 758-5510
Paul Grenon, *Purch Agent*
Dave Rice, *CFO*
EMP: 16
SALES (corp-wide): 20MM **Privately Held**
WEB: www.ubs1.com
SIC: **3357** Nonferrous wiredrawing & insulating
PA: Universal Builders Supply Inc
    27 Horton Ave Ste 5
    New Rochelle NY 10801
    914 699-2400

Rego Park
Queens County

(G-14043)
CARMONA NYC LLC
9830 67th Ave Apt 1d (11374-4942)
PHONE.................................718 227-6662
Tammy Carmona,
Steve Bistritzky, *Administration*
EMP: 5
SALES (est): 410K **Privately Held**
SIC: **3262** Tableware, vitreous china

(G-14044)
DIDCO INC
8570 67th Ave (11374-5225)
PHONE.................................212 997-5022
Malcolm Doyle, *President*
EMP: 12 EST: 2012
SALES (est): 831.8K **Privately Held**
SIC: **1499** Gemstone & industrial diamond mining

(G-14045)
J I INTRNTNAL CONTACT LENS LAB
6352 Saunders St Ste A (11374-2000)
PHONE.................................718 997-1212
Joseph Itzkowitz, *President*
EMP: 7 EST: 1964

GEOGRAPHIC SECTION

SQ FT: 2,000
SALES: 750K **Privately Held**
SIC: 3851 Contact lenses

(G-14046)
KEFA INDUSTRIES GROUP INC
9219 63rd Dr (11374-2926)
PHONE.................................718 568-9297
Keyan Xing, *Principal*
Huicong Cong, *Manager*
▲ EMP: 7
SALES (est): 461K **Privately Held**
SIC: 3499 Machine bases, metal

(G-14047)
METRO LUBE (PA)
9110 Metropolitan Ave (11374-5328)
PHONE.................................718 947-1167
Fernando Magalhaes, *Principal*
EMP: 5
SALES (est): 1.4MM **Privately Held**
SIC: 3589 Car washing machinery

(G-14048)
MILESTONE CONSTRUCTION CORP
9229 Queens Blvd Ste C2 (11374-1099)
PHONE.................................718 459-8500
Mike S Lee, *Ch of Bd*
EMP: 6
SALES (est): 570K **Privately Held**
SIC: 1442 Construction sand & gravel

(G-14049)
PCB COACH BUILDERS CORP
Also Called: Picasso Coach Builders
6334 Austin St (11374-2923)
PHONE.................................718 897-7606
Gualberto Diaz, *President*
Laura Diaz, *Treasurer*
EMP: 6
SQ FT: 20,000
SALES (est): 1.6MM **Privately Held**
WEB: www.picassocoachbuilders.com
SIC: 3711 Automobile assembly, including specialty automobiles

(G-14050)
PROFESSIONAL PAVERS CORP
6605 Woodhaven Blvd Bsmt (11374-5235)
P.O. Box 790186, Middle Village (11379-0186)
PHONE.................................718 784-7853
Duarte N Lopes, *Ch of Bd*
Nunu Lopes, *President*
Joseph Foley, *Vice Pres*
Veronica Garcia, *Manager*
Melissa Rodriguez, *Manager*
▲ EMP: 30
SALES (est): 6.6MM **Privately Held**
SIC: 3531 Road construction & maintenance machinery

(G-14051)
SPECTACLE OPTICAL INC
9801 67th Ave Apt 7f (11374-4903)
PHONE.................................646 706-1015
Elizabeth Geheran, *CEO*
EMP: 5
SALES (est): 283.3K **Privately Held**
SIC: 3851 Spectacles

Remsen
Oneida County

(G-14052)
GRAPHICS OF UTICA
10436 Dustin Rd (13438-4241)
PHONE.................................315 797-4868
Elaine B Kovach, *CEO*
EMP: 5
SQ FT: 3,319
SALES (est): 460K **Privately Held**
SIC: 2752 7334 Commercial printing, offset; photocopying & duplicating services

Rensselaer
Rensselaer County

(G-14053)
ALBANY INTERNATIONAL CORP
Press Fabrics Division
253 Troy Rd (12144-9473)
P.O. Box 1907, Albany (12201-1907)
PHONE: 518 445-2200
Fax: 518 285-4253
Steve Sassaman, *General Mgr*
Andy Dolan, *Vice Pres*
Jack Taffe, *Marketing Staff*
Gard Emond, *MIS Dir*
Thomas Curry, *Director*
EMP: 180
SALES (corp-wide): 779.8MM **Publicly Held**
WEB: www.albint.com
SIC: 2221 2297 2241 Paper broadwoven fabrics; nonwoven fabrics; narrow fabric mills
PA: Albany International Corp.
216 Airport Dr
Rochester NH 03867
603 330-5850

(G-14054)
ALBANY MOLECULAR RESEARCH INC
Also Called: Amri Rensselaer
81 Columbia Tpke (12144-3411)
PHONE.................................518 433-7700
Thomas E D'Ambra, *Ch of Bd*
Gerry Wilcox, *Purch Mgr*
EMP: 10
SALES (corp-wide): 77.1MM **Privately Held**
SIC: 2833 Medicinals & botanicals
HQ: Albany Molecular Research, Inc.
26 Corporate Cir
Albany NY 12203
518 512-2000

(G-14055)
ALBANY MOLECULAR RESEARCH INC
Also Called: Amri
33 Riverside Ave (12144-2951)
PHONE.................................518 512-2000
Norberto Cintron, *Facilities Mgr*
Lauren Boltz, *Engineer*
Venkat Chikkala, *Human Res Mgr*
Steven R Hagen, *Branch Mgr*
George Rickert, *Manager*
EMP: 10
SALES (corp-wide): 77.1MM **Privately Held**
SIC: 2833 Medicinals & botanicals
HQ: Albany Molecular Research, Inc.
26 Corporate Cir
Albany NY 12203
518 512-2000

(G-14056)
BASF CORPORATION
Chemicals Division
70 Riverside Ave (12144-2938)
PHONE.................................518 465-6534
Fax: 518 472-8370
Michael Murphy, *Safety Mgr*
Dave Wos, *Production*
Wayne Sinclair, *Manager*
Mike Pietrko, *Manager*
Jim Kois, *Director*
EMP: 280
SALES (corp-wide): 60.8B **Privately Held**
WEB: www.basf.com
SIC: 2869 Industrial organic chemicals
HQ: Basf Corporation
100 Park Ave
Florham Park NJ 07932
973 245-6000

(G-14057)
GRAPES & GRAINS
279 Troy Rd Ste 4 (12144-9752)
PHONE.................................518 283-9463
Andrew Stasky, *Owner*
EMP: 9
SQ FT: 3,000
SALES: 2.1MM **Privately Held**
SIC: 2084 Wines

(G-14058)
GREAT 4 IMAGE INC
Also Called: G4i
5 Forest Hills Blvd (12144-5831)
PHONE.................................518 424-2058
Daren Arakelian, *President*
▲ EMP: 32
SALES: 1MM **Privately Held**
WEB: www.g4i.com
SIC: 2311 Men's & boys' suits & coats

(G-14059)
INTEGRATED LINER TECH INC (PA)
45 Discovery Dr (12144-3466)
PHONE.................................518 621-7422
Fax: 518 432-9146
Paul Petrosino, *Ch of Bd*
Ken Greene, *Project Engr*
Dee Vandyke, *Accountant*
Michele Slade, *Sales Mgr*
▲ EMP: 48
SQ FT: 30,000
SALES (est): 9.7MM **Privately Held**
WEB: www.integratedliner.com
SIC: 3821 2822 Chemical laboratory apparatus; synthetic rubber

(G-14060)
POCONO POOL PRODUCTS-NORTH
15 Krey Blvd (12144-9746)
PHONE.................................518 283-1023
Fax: 518 283-1059
Mark Vultaggio, *President*
Charles Boomhower, *Vice Pres*
EMP: 25
SQ FT: 10,000
SALES: 1MM **Privately Held**
WEB: www.completepoolsource.com
SIC: 3081 3949 Vinyl film & sheet; sporting & athletic goods

(G-14061)
REGENERON PHARMACEUTICALS INC
81 Columbia Tpke (12144-3423)
PHONE.................................518 488-6000
Fax: 518 488-6030
Dr Randall Rupp, *General Mgr*
Deborah Teggan, *Purch Mgr*
Carol Jones, *Engineer*
Diane Yocum, *Supervisor*
EMP: 40
SALES (corp-wide): 4.8B **Publicly Held**
WEB: www.regeneron.com
SIC: 2833 Medicinals & botanicals
PA: Regeneron Pharmaceuticals Inc
777 Old Saw Mill River Rd # 10
Tarrytown NY 10591
914 847-7000

(G-14062)
STEMCULTURES LLC
1 Discovery Dr (12144-3448)
PHONE.................................518 621-0848
Jeffrey Stern, *CEO*
William Price, *COO*
Christopher Fasano, *Bd of Directors*
EMP: 7
SALES (est): 368K **Privately Held**
SIC: 2836 Biological products, except diagnostic; culture media

(G-14063)
ULTRADIAN DIAGNOSTICS LLC
5 University Pl A324 (12144-3461)
PHONE.................................518 618-0046
Douglas Pickard, *CFO*
John P Willis,
EMP: 5
SQ FT: 2,000
SALES (est): 600.5K **Privately Held**
SIC: 3845 Electromedical equipment

Retsof
Livingston County

(G-14064)
AMERICAN ROCK SALT COMPANY LLC (PA)
3846 Retsof Rd (14539)
P.O. Box 190, Mount Morris (14510-0190)
PHONE.................................585 991-6878
Fax: 585 243-7676
Gunther Buerman, *Ch of Bd*
Justin Curley, *General Mgr*
Joseph G Bucci, *Principal*
Lee McKinney, *Safety Dir*
Greg Norris, *Plant Mgr*
▲ EMP: 20
SALES (est): 971.9MM **Privately Held**
WEB: www.americanrocksalt.com
SIC: 1479 5169 Rock salt mining; salts, industrial

Rexford
Saratoga County

(G-14065)
MOBIUS LABS INC
37 Vischer Ferry Rd (12148-1617)
PHONE.................................518 961-2600
Frank Lipowitz, *Principal*
EMP: 5
SALES (est): 239.7K **Privately Held**
SIC: 3829 Hydrometers, except industrial process type

(G-14066)
WERNER BROTHERS ELECTRIC INC
677 Riverview Rd (12148-1427)
PHONE.................................518 377-3056
Craig Werner, *Owner*
EMP: 8
SALES (est): 1.1MM **Privately Held**
SIC: 3699 Electrical equipment & supplies

Rhinebeck
Dutchess County

(G-14067)
CORE GROUP DISPLAYS INC
41 Pitcher Rd (12572-1035)
PHONE.................................845 876-5109
Dan Riso, *President*
◆ EMP: 21 EST: 2007
SALES: 1.2MM **Privately Held**
SIC: 2542 Partitions & fixtures, except wood

(G-14068)
DUTCHESS WINES LLC
Also Called: Alison Wine & Vineyard
39 Lorraine Dr (12572-1203)
P.O. Box 619 (12572-0619)
PHONE.................................845 876-1319
Richard Lewit, *President*
EMP: 5
SALES: 280K **Privately Held**
WEB: www.alisonwine.com
SIC: 2084 Wines, brandy & brandy spirits

(G-14069)
PDQ MANUFACTURING CO INC
29 Hilee Rd (12572-2349)
PHONE.................................845 889-3123
Fax: 845 889-8241
Scott Hutchins, *Ch of Bd*
Kristin Hutchins, *President*
Kerri Tiano, *Opers Mgr*
Brian Hutchins, *Facilities Mgr*
EMP: 45 EST: 1975
SQ FT: 40,000
SALES (est): 8.7MM **Privately Held**
WEB: www.pdqmfg.com
SIC: 3444 Sheet metalwork

(G-14070)
SMITHERS TOOLS & MCH PDTS INC
Also Called: Stamp
3718 Route 9g (12572-1139)
P.O. Box 391 (12572-0391)
PHONE..................845 876-3063
Roland Jennings, *Ch of Bd*
Gary L Hosey, *President*
Robert Nevins, *Vice Pres*
Joann Russell, *Vice Pres*
EMP: 63 **EST:** 1947
SQ FT: 35,000
SALES (est): 10.7MM **Privately Held**
WEB: www.stampinc.com
SIC: 3699 3469 7692 3599 Electrical equipment & supplies; stamping metal for the trade; welding repair; machine shop, jobbing & repair

(G-14071)
UMBRO MACHINE & TOOL CO INC
3811 Route 9g (12572-1042)
PHONE..................845 876-4669
Fax: 845 876-0720
Gerald Umbro, *President*
Claire Umbro, *Vice Pres*
Rosemary Kavanaugh, *Admin Sec*
EMP: 12 **EST:** 1959
SQ FT: 1,800
SALES (est): 1MM **Privately Held**
SIC: 3451 Screw machine products

(G-14072)
WARREN CUTLERY CORP
3584 Route 9g (12572-3309)
P.O. Box 289 (12572-0289)
PHONE..................845 876-3444
Fax: 845 876-5664
James Zitz, *President*
Richard Von Husen, *Vice Pres*
EMP: 10
SQ FT: 3,500
SALES (est): 1.5MM **Privately Held**
WEB: www.warrencutlery.com
SIC: 3421 3291 5072 5085 Cutlery; abrasive products; cutlery; abrasives

(G-14073)
WATER ORACLE
41 E Market St (12572-1634)
PHONE..................845 876-8327
Stacey Held, *Principal*
EMP: 5
SALES (est): 82.7K **Privately Held**
SIC: 7372 Prepackaged software

Richfield Springs
Otsego County

(G-14074)
ANDELA TOOL & MACHINE INC
Also Called: Andela Products
493 State Route 28 (13439-3739)
PHONE..................315 858-0055
Fax: 315 858-2669
Cynthia Andela, *President*
James Andela, *Vice Pres*
Janice Arkema, *Admin Sec*
▼ **EMP:** 8
SQ FT: 10,000
SALES (est): 1.9MM **Privately Held**
WEB: www.andelaproducts.com
SIC: 3559 Recycling machinery

(G-14075)
WELDING AND BRAZING SVCS INC
2761 County Highway 26 (13439-3049)
PHONE..................607 397-1009
David R Parker, *President*
Kay Parker, *Vice Pres*
Carter Cook, *Manager*
EMP: 5
SALES (est): 412K **Privately Held**
SIC: 7692 Welding repair; brazing

Richford
Tioga County

(G-14076)
MARATHON HEATER CO INC
13 Town Barn Rd (13835)
P.O. Box 58 (13835-0058)
PHONE..................607 657-8113
Fax: 607 657-8114
Thomas J Parker, *President*
EMP: 6
SQ FT: 16,000
SALES (est): 500K **Privately Held**
WEB: www.marathonheaterco.com
SIC: 3585 3433 Furnaces, warm air: electric; burners, furnaces, boilers & stokers

Richmond Hill
Queens County

(G-14077)
131-11 ATLANTIC RE INC
Also Called: Premier
13111 Atlantic Ave Ste 1 (11418-3305)
PHONE..................718 441-7700
Kevin Leichter, *CEO*
Harry Leichter, *President*
Sari Nathan, *COO*
Peter Vasile, *Sales Executive*
◆ **EMP:** 75
SQ FT: 250,000
SALES (est): 12.5MM **Privately Held**
WEB: www.premierpaintroller.com
SIC: 3991 Paint rollers

(G-14078)
ALL AMERICAN STAIRS & RAILING
13023 91st Ave (11418-3320)
PHONE..................718 441-8400
Fax: 718 850-3080
Marie Bottari, *President*
EMP: 12
SALES (est): 2.4MM **Privately Held**
SIC: 3446 Stairs, fire escapes, balconies, railings & ladders

(G-14079)
ATLANTIC FARM & FOOD INC
11415 Atlantic Ave (11418-3139)
PHONE..................718 441-3152
Gurcharn Singh, *Principal*
EMP: 13
SALES (est): 1.7MM **Privately Held**
SIC: 2037 8611 Frozen fruits & vegetables; growers' marketing advisory service

(G-14080)
BARALAN USA INC (DH)
Also Called: Arrowpak
12019 89th Ave (11418-3235)
PHONE..................718 849-5768
Fax: 718 849-1343
Roland Baranes, *President*
Ellis Rudman, *Corp Secy*
Chris Llamas, *Opers Mgr*
Luisa Kamelhar, *Human Res Dir*
Joe Payne, *Sales Staff*
◆ **EMP:** 35 **EST:** 1980
SQ FT: 70,000
SALES: 4.9MM
SALES (corp-wide): 849.4K **Privately Held**
WEB: www.arrowpak.com
SIC: 3221 3089 Cosmetic jars, glass; plastic containers, except foam
HQ: Baralan International Spa
Via Nicolo' Copernico 34
Trezzano Sul Naviglio MI 20090
024 844-961

(G-14081)
BELLE MAISON USA LTD
Also Called: Stylemaster
8950 127th St (11418-3323)
PHONE..................718 805-0200
Elizabeth Romano, *Ch of Bd*
Ethel Romano, *Vice Pres*
◆ **EMP:** 30
SALES (est): 3.5MM **Privately Held**
WEB: www.stylemasterusa.com
SIC: 2392 2391 Bedspreads & bed sets: made from purchased materials; curtains, window: made from purchased materials

(G-14082)
BEST TIME PROCESSOR LLC
8746 Van Wyck Expy (11418-1958)
PHONE..................917 455-4126
Charlie Bachu,
Somdat Bachu,
EMP: 5
SALES (est): 384.5K **Privately Held**
SIC: 2679 Paper products, converted

(G-14083)
CARLOS & ALEX ATELIER INC
Also Called: C & A Atelier
10010 91st Ave Fl 2 (11418-2118)
PHONE..................718 441-8911
Carlos Queiroz, *CEO*
Claudio Goncalves, *COO*
EMP: 24
SQ FT: 22,000
SALES (est): 2MM **Privately Held**
SIC: 2434 2511 Wood kitchen cabinets; wood household furniture

(G-14084)
ELECTRON TOP MFG CO INC
12615 89th Ave (11418-3337)
PHONE..................718 846-7400
Fax: 718 846-8426
Craig Strauss, *President*
Frederick W Strauss III, *Vice Pres*
Kimberly S Hess, *Treasurer*
EMP: 41 **EST:** 1947
SQ FT: 20,000
SALES (est): 6.4MM **Privately Held**
WEB: www.electrontop.com
SIC: 3714 Tops, motor vehicle

(G-14085)
EMPIRE STATE METAL PDTS INC
10110 Jamaica Ave (11418-2007)
PHONE..................718 847-1617
Fax: 718 805-1189
David Millshauser, *President*
▲ **EMP:** 20 **EST:** 1946
SQ FT: 20,475
SALES (est): 2MM **Privately Held**
SIC: 3965 Buttons & parts; buckles & buckle parts

(G-14086)
GAUGHAN CONSTRUCTION CORP
13034 90th Ave (11418-3309)
PHONE..................718 850-9577
Anthony Gaughan, *President*
Margaret Gaughan, *Admin Sec*
EMP: 5
SQ FT: 6,000
SALES (est): 731.1K **Privately Held**
SIC: 2541 Wood partitions & fixtures

(G-14087)
HILL KNITTING MILLS INC
10005 92nd Ave Ste Mgmt (11418-2910)
PHONE..................718 846-5000
Jeff Rosen, *President*
Peter Cruciata, *Corp Secy*
EMP: 23
SQ FT: 30,000
SALES (est): 2.1MM **Privately Held**
SIC: 2257 Pile fabrics, circular knit

(G-14088)
J & E TALIT INC
13011 Atlantic Ave Fl 2 (11418-3304)
PHONE..................718 850-1333
Fax: 718 850-1666
Eitan Talit, *President*
EMP: 8
SQ FT: 6,000
SALES (est): 1MM **Privately Held**
WEB: www.jandetalit.com
SIC: 2253 2339 T-shirts & tops, knit; sportswear, women's

(G-14089)
OLYMPIC ICE CREAM CO INC (PA)
Also Called: Marinos Italian Ices
12910 91st Ave (11418-3317)
PHONE..................718 849-6200
Fax: 718 805-0455
Michael Barone Sr, *President*
Frank Barone, *Vice Pres*
Frank Stracucca, *Sales Staff*
▲ **EMP:** 35
SQ FT: 50,000
SALES (est): 12.9MM **Privately Held**
WEB: www.marinositalianices.com
SIC: 2024 Ice cream & frozen desserts; ices, flavored (frozen dessert)

(G-14090)
PREMIER PAINT ROLLER CO LLC
13111 Atlantic Ave (11418-3397)
PHONE..................718 441-7700
Kevin Leichter, *CEO*
EMP: 11 **EST:** 2004
SALES (est): 483.9K **Privately Held**
SIC: 3991 5198 Paint rollers; paint brushes, rollers, sprayers

(G-14091)
RESEARCH CENTRE OF KABBALAH
Also Called: Kabbalah Centre
8384 115th St (11418-1303)
PHONE..................718 805-0380
Philip Berg, *President*
Beatrice Cohen, *Treasurer*
Karen Berg, *Admin Sec*
EMP: 6
SQ FT: 40,000
SALES (est): 536.6K **Privately Held**
WEB: www.kabbalahcentre.com
SIC: 2731 Books: publishing only; pamphlets: publishing only, not printed on site

(G-14092)
RN FURNITURE CORP
11409 Atlantic Ave (11418-3139)
PHONE..................347 960-9622
Tamesh Nankumar, *President*
EMP: 5 **EST:** 2009
SALES (est): 460K **Privately Held**
SIC: 3231 Furniture tops, glass: cut, beveled or polished

(G-14093)
RUBIES COSTUME COMPANY INC (PA)
12008 Jamaica Ave (11418-2521)
PHONE..................718 846-1008
Marc P Beige, *Ch of Bd*
Joanne Rudis, *Division Mgr*
Howard Beige, *Vice Pres*
Frank Deluca, *Controller*
David Beige, *Sales Staff*
◆ **EMP:** 400
SQ FT: 55,000
SALES (est): 429.9MM **Privately Held**
SIC: 2389 7299 Costumes; costume rental

(G-14094)
RUBIES COSTUME COMPANY INC
12017 Jamaica Ave (11418-2522)
PHONE..................718 441-0834
Charlie Flohr, *Credit Mgr*
Jenn Deseve, *Sales Staff*
Arthur Savarese, *Branch Mgr*
Frank Cangelosi, *CTO*
Francine Robinson, *Admin Asst*
EMP: 148
SALES (corp-wide): 428MM **Privately Held**
SIC: 2389 Costumes
PA: Rubie's Costume Company, Inc.
12008 Jamaica Ave
Richmond Hill NY 11418
718 846-1008

(G-14095)
RUBIES COSTUME COMPANY INC
1 Rubie Plz (11418)
PHONE..................718 846-1008
Catherine Zubrovich, *Prdtn Mgr*

GEOGRAPHIC SECTION

Ridgewood - Queens County (G-14121)

Maryann Depaola, *Purchasing*
Heather Mathiesen, *Design Engr*
Virginia Szczepanski, *Accounting Mgr*
Michael Laimo, *Sales Mgr*
EMP: 148
SALES (corp-wide): 429.9MM Privately Held
SIC: 2389 7299 Costumes; costume rental
PA: Rubie's Costume Company, Inc.
12008 Jamaica Ave
Richmond Hill NY 11418
718 846-1008

(G-14096)
RUBIES MASQUERADE COMPANY LLC (PA)
1 Rubie Plz (11418)
PHONE.................................718 846-1008
Dick Roche,
EMP: 5
SALES (est): 13.9MM Privately Held
SIC: 2389 Masquerade costumes

(G-14097)
STAIRWORLD INC
10114 Jamaica Ave (11418-2007)
PHONE.................................718 441-9722
John Franklin, *President*
Kenneth Franklin, *President*
EMP: 5
SQ FT: 3,000
SALES (est): 390K Privately Held
WEB: www.stairworld.com
SIC: 2431 Stair railings, wood; staircases & stairs, wood

(G-14098)
SUPER EXPRESS USA PUBG CORP
8410 101st St Apt 4l (11418-1150)
PHONE.................................212 227-5800
Fax: 212 227-5910
Ana Gierzphall, *President*
EMP: 12
SALES (est): 801.2K Privately Held
SIC: 2741 Miscellaneous publishing

(G-14099)
TERBO LTD
Also Called: Interiors By Robert
8905 130th St (11418-3328)
PHONE.................................718 847-2860
Fax: 718 847-2826
Robert Boccard, *President*
EMP: 9
SQ FT: 3,400
SALES (est): 893.1K Privately Held
SIC: 2391 2392 7641 Curtains & draperies; household furnishings; upholstery work

(G-14100)
WOMENS HEALTH CARE PC (PA)
Also Called: Park Avenue Nutrition
11311 Jamaica Ave Ste C (11418-2476)
PHONE.................................718 850-0009
Rehana Sajjad, *CEO*
EMP: 4
SALES (est): 1.1MM Privately Held
SIC: 3842 7991 7299 Gynecological supplies & appliances; physical fitness facilities; personal appearance services

Richmondville
Schoharie County

(G-14101)
CHENANGO CONCRETE CORP (PA)
145 Podpadic Rd (12149-2205)
PHONE.................................518 294-9964
Martin Galasso, *President*
Timothy Gaffney Sr, *CFO*
Emil Galasso, *Treasurer*
Cathy Manchester, *Manager*
EMP: 12
SALES (est): 6.5MM Privately Held
SIC: 3273 Ready-mixed concrete

(G-14102)
TRI-CITY HIGHWAY PRODUCTS INC
145 Podpadic Rd (12149-2205)
PHONE.................................518 294-9964
Martin Galasso, *CEO*
David Black, *Chairman*
Martin A Galasso Jr, *Chairman*
Warner Hodddon, *Manager*
EMP: 23
SALES (est): 5.3MM Privately Held
SIC: 2951 1442 Asphalt paving mixtures & blocks; construction sand & gravel

Ridge
Suffolk County

(G-14103)
AIRWELD INC
1740 Middle Country Rd (11961-2407)
PHONE.................................631 924-6366
John Zak, *Branch Mgr*
EMP: 5
SALES (corp-wide): 29.7MM Privately Held
SIC: 7692 Welding repair
PA: Airweld, Inc.
94 Marine St
Farmingdale NY 11735
631 694-4343

(G-14104)
AMERICAN PHYSICAL SOCIETY
Also Called: Physical Review
1 Research Rd (11961-2701)
PHONE.................................631 591-4025
Fax: 631 591-4155
Joe Ignacio, *Persnl Mgr*
Jeanette Russo, *Manager*
Mark Kryder, *CTO*
Charles Muller, *Director*
Harvey Yau, *Executive*
EMP: 95
SALES (corp-wide): 56.6MM Privately Held
WEB: www.phystec.net
SIC: 2721 Trade journals: publishing only, not printed on site
PA: American Physical Society
1 Physics Ellipse
College Park MD 20740
301 209-3200

(G-14105)
OCEANS CUISINE LTD
367 Sheffield Ct (11961-2028)
PHONE.................................631 209-9200
Fax: 631 209-9630
Philip Melfi, *President*
Linda Melfi, *Admin Sec*
EMP: 15
SQ FT: 1,000
SALES (est): 1.7MM Privately Held
WEB: www.oceanscuisine.com
SIC: 2092 Seafoods, frozen: prepared

(G-14106)
QUALITY AND ASRN TECH CORP
Also Called: Qna Tech
18 Marginwood Dr (11961-2902)
PHONE.................................646 450-6762
Marcos Merced, *CEO*
Antonio Cefalo, *Engineer*
Daniel Corozza, *Engineer*
Jean Machado, *Engineer*
EMP: 7
SALES (est): 500K Privately Held
SIC: 7372 7379 Business oriented computer software; computer hardware requirements analysis

(G-14107)
RESIDENTIAL FENCES CORP
1760 Middle Country Rd (11961-2415)
PHONE.................................631 205-9758
John Gulino, *Branch Mgr*
EMP: 30
SALES (corp-wide): 13.4MM Privately Held
SIC: 3273 Ready-mixed concrete

PA: Residential Fences Corp.
1775 Middle Country Rd
Ridge NY 11961
631 924-3011

(G-14108)
WEATHER TIGHT EXTERIORS
8 Woodbrook Dr (11961-2132)
PHONE.................................631 375-5108
Rick Dandria, *Owner*
EMP: 8
SALES (est): 550K Privately Held
SIC: 2421 Siding (dressed lumber)

Ridgewood
Queens County

(G-14109)
333 J & M FOOD CORP
Also Called: Allsupermarkets
333 Seneca Ave (11385-1338)
PHONE.................................718 381-1493
Jose Espinal, *Ch of Bd*
EMP: 12 EST: 2011
SALES (est): 2.4MM Privately Held
SIC: 2674 Grocers' bags: made from purchased materials

(G-14110)
AABCO SHEET METAL CO INC (PA)
Also Called: Asm Mechanical Systems
47 40 Metropolitan Ave (11385)
PHONE.................................718 821-1166
Ronald J Palmerick, *President*
Richard Minieri, *President*
Edmund MEI, *President*
Tom Brady, *Purchasing*
George Quattlander, *Information Mgr*
EMP: 75
SQ FT: 85,000
SALES (est): 51.2MM Privately Held
SIC: 3444 1711 1761 Ducts, sheet metal; metal housings, enclosures, casings & other containers; ventilation & duct work contractor; sheet metalwork

(G-14111)
ABR MOLDING ANDY LLC
1624 Centre St (11385-5336)
PHONE.................................212 576-1821
Andy Skoczek, *Owner*
▲ **EMP:** 15
SALES (est): 2.5MM Privately Held
SIC: 3089 Molding primary plastic

(G-14112)
ALPINE BUILDING SUPPLY INC
4626 Metropolitan Ave (11385-1045)
PHONE.................................718 456-2522
Marcangelo Cotoia, *President*
EMP: 7
SALES (est): 86.3K Privately Held
SIC: 3272 Concrete products

(G-14113)
ARAMSCO INC
1819 Flushing Ave Ste 2 (11385-1002)
PHONE.................................718 361-7540
Toll Free:.................................888 -
Mike Dambrosio, *Manager*
EMP: 10
SALES (corp-wide): 229.6MM Privately Held
SIC: 3842 Personal safety equipment
HQ: Aramsco, Inc.
1480 Grandview Ave
Paulsboro NJ 08066
856 686-7700

(G-14114)
BARKER BROTHERS INCORPORATED
1666 Summerfield St Ste 1 (11385-5748)
PHONE.................................718 456-6400
Kenneth A Doyle, *Ch of Bd*
Edwin Doyle, *Ch of Bd*
Walter Doyle, *Vice Pres*
David Thomas, *Vice Pres*
Thomas Vissichelli, *Vice Pres*
▲ **EMP:** 100 EST: 1911
SQ FT: 50,000

SALES (est): 17.2MM Privately Held
WEB: www.bardoabrasives.com
SIC: 3291 Buffing or polishing wheels, abrasive or nonabrasive

(G-14115)
BEST ADHESIVES COMPANY INC
4702 Metropolitan Ave (11385-1047)
PHONE.................................718 417-3800
Sholm Singer, *President*
EMP: 6
SQ FT: 10,000
SALES (est): 670K Privately Held
SIC: 2891 Adhesives

(G-14116)
BRICK & BALLERSTEIN INC
1085 Irving Ave (11385-5745)
P.O. Box 1158, Yorktown Heights (10598-8158)
PHONE.................................718 497-1400
Fax: 718 366-0149
Robert Levinson, *Ch of Bd*
Gary Levinson, *President*
Bruce Levinson, *Vice Pres*
Gladys Kaplan, *Purchasing*
▲ **EMP:** 82
SQ FT: 54,000
SALES (est): 15.1MM Privately Held
WEB: www.brickandballerstein.com
SIC: 2652 Setup paperboard boxes

(G-14117)
COSCO ENTERPRISES INC
Also Called: Cosco Soap & Detergent
1930 Troutman St (11385-1020)
PHONE.................................718 383-4488
Andrew Cook, *President*
Lawrence McGreevy, *Vice Pres*
Pat Loy, *Office Mgr*
EMP: 7 EST: 1966
SQ FT: 10,000
SALES (est): 1.4MM Privately Held
SIC: 2841 Soap & other detergents

(G-14118)
ELECTRO-OPTICAL PRODUCTS CORP
6240 Forest Ave Fl 2 (11385-1929)
P.O. Box 650441, Fresh Meadows (11365-0441)
PHONE.................................718 456-6000
Fax: 718 456-6050
Ziva Tuchman, *President*
EMP: 6
SQ FT: 1,600
SALES: 1MM Privately Held
WEB: www.eopc.com
SIC: 3829 Measuring & controlling devices

(G-14119)
FIVE STAR AWNINGS INC
5923 Decatur St (11385-5942)
PHONE.................................718 860-6070
Christopher Rice, *Principal*
EMP: 12
SALES (est): 1.4MM Privately Held
SIC: 3444 Awnings & canopies

(G-14120)
GENERAL COATINGS TECH INC (PA)
24 Woodward Ave (11385-1022)
PHONE.................................718 821-1232
Fax: 718 381-6935
Michael Ghitelman, *President*
Robert Ghitelman, *Vice Pres*
EMP: 25
SQ FT: 160,000
SALES (est): 8.3MM Privately Held
SIC: 2851 Paints & paint additives; varnishes

(G-14121)
GRIMALDIS HOME BREAD INC
Also Called: Grimaldi Bakery
2101 Menahan St (11385-2046)
PHONE.................................718 497-1425
Fax: 718 366-0590
Vito J Grimaldi, *President*
Joseph Anobile, *COO*
Joseph Grimaldi, *Vice Pres*
Joseph Anovile, *Purch Agent*
John Lamonaca, *Sales Executive*

(PA)=Parent Co (HQ)=Headquarters (DH)=Div Headquarters
✪ = New Business established in last 2 years

2018 Harris
New York Manufacturers Directory

Ridgewood - Queens County (G-14122)

EMP: 85
SQ FT: 30,000
SALES (est): 12.2MM **Privately Held**
WEB: www.grimaldibakery.com
SIC: 2051 Bread, cake & related products

(G-14122)
GW MANUFACTURING
Also Called: G W Manufacturing
24a Woodward Ave (11385-1175)
PHONE...................................718 386-8078
Fax: 718 386-7950
George Stavilla, *President*
▲ EMP: 32
SALES (est): 5.4MM **Privately Held**
SIC: 2431 Millwork

(G-14123)
J & C FINISHING
1067 Wyckoff Ave (11385-5751)
PHONE...................................718 456-1087
Jose Hernandez, *President*
EMP: 20
SALES (est): 1.2MM **Privately Held**
SIC: 2389 Apparel & accessories

(G-14124)
JULIAN A MCDERMOTT CORPORATION
Also Called: McDermott Light & Signal
1639 Stephen St (11385-5345)
PHONE...................................718 456-3606
Fax: 718 381-0229
Vernon McDermott, *Ch of Bd*
Andrea McDermott, *Vice Pres*
Resa Thomsan, *Manager*
▲ EMP: 45 EST: 1943
SQ FT: 25,000
SALES: 6MM **Privately Held**
WEB: www.mcdermottlight.com
SIC: 3648 Lighting equipment

(G-14125)
L S SIGN CO INC
1030 Wyckoff Ave (11385-5355)
PHONE...................................718 469-8600
Anthony Fodera, *President*
Joseph Fodera, *Vice Pres*
Christian Tomas, *Treasurer*
EMP: 19
SQ FT: 10,000
SALES (est): 1.6MM **Privately Held**
SIC: 3993 Signs, not made in custom sign painting shops

(G-14126)
LONG ISLAND STAMP & SEAL CO
Also Called: L I Stamp
5431 Myrtle Ave Ste 2 (11385-3403)
P.O. Box 863990 (11386-3990)
PHONE...................................718 628-8550
Fax: 718 628-8560
Harriet Pollak, *President*
Harry Pollak, *Vice Pres*
EMP: 15
SQ FT: 4,000
SALES (est): 980K **Privately Held**
SIC: 3953 Date stamps, hand: rubber or metal

(G-14127)
LYRIC LIGHTING LTD INC
4825 Metro Ave Ste 3 (11385-1008)
PHONE...................................718 497-0109
Fax: 718 497-2351
Chester Mudick, *President*
EMP: 6 EST: 1962
SQ FT: 25,000
SALES (est): 570K **Privately Held**
SIC: 3645 Residential lighting fixtures

(G-14128)
NULUX INC
1717 Troutman St (11385-1034)
PHONE...................................718 383-1112
Fax: 718 383-1118
Delia Price, *President*
Frank Conti, *Vice Pres*
Karen Jackson, *Manager*
EMP: 33
SQ FT: 4,500
SALES (est): 6.5MM **Privately Held**
WEB: www.nulux.com
SIC: 3645 3646 Residential lighting fixtures; commercial indusl & institutional electric lighting fixtures

(G-14129)
ON THE SPOT BINDING INC
4805 Metropolitan Ave (11385-1007)
P.O. Box 863104 (11386-3104)
PHONE...................................718 497-2200
Isaac Mutzen, *President*
Nathan Hirsch, *Corp Secy*
Jerry Josefson, *Vice Pres*
EMP: 26
SQ FT: 10,000
SALES (est): 2MM **Privately Held**
SIC: 2789 Binding & repair of books, magazines & pamphlets

(G-14130)
PLANET EMBROIDERY
6695 Forest Ave (11385-3839)
PHONE...................................718 381-4827
Edwin Sotto, *Owner*
EMP: 12
SALES (est): 111.4K **Privately Held**
SIC: 2395 Embroidery & art needlework

(G-14131)
PRINT BETTER INC
5939 Myrtle Ave (11385-5657)
PHONE...................................347 348-1841
Ayman Naguib, *Ch of Bd*
▲ EMP: 6
SALES (est): 534.4K **Privately Held**
SIC: 2752 Commercial printing, lithographic

(G-14132)
PRISMA GLASS & MIRROR INC
1815 Decatur St (11385-6017)
PHONE...................................718 366-7191
Fax: 718 628-5444
Candice Tonkowich, *President*
Teresa Oneil, *Principal*
EMP: 5 EST: 1947
SQ FT: 5,000
SALES (est): 330K **Privately Held**
SIC: 3231 Mirrors, truck & automobile: made from purchased glass

(G-14133)
PUBLIMAX PRINTING CORP
6615 Traffic Ave (11385-3307)
PHONE...................................718 366-7133
Patricia Flores, *President*
Taniya Flores, *Office Mgr*
▲ EMP: 6
SALES (est): 881.9K **Privately Held**
WEB: www.publimaxprinting.com
SIC: 2759 Commercial printing

(G-14134)
RIDGEWOOD TIMES PRTG & PUBG
Also Called: Times News Weekly
6071 Woodbine St Fl 1 (11385-3242)
PHONE...................................718 821-7500
Fax: 718 456-0125
Maureen E Walthers, *President*
William Mitchell, *Manager*
EMP: 30
SQ FT: 3,500
SALES (est): 1.6MM **Privately Held**
WEB: www.timesnewsweekly.com
SIC: 2711 Newspapers, publishing & printing

(G-14135)
SARUG INC
Also Called: Sarug Knitwear
1616 Summerfield St (11385-5748)
PHONE...................................718 381-7300
Steve Virbasthe, *President*
EMP: 6
SALES (est): 549K **Privately Held**
SIC: 2253 Sweaters & sweater coats, knit

(G-14136)
SCHNEIDER M SOAP & CHEMICAL CO
1930 Troutman St (11385-1020)
PHONE...................................718 389-1000
Andrew Cook, *President*

EMP: 8 EST: 1969
SQ FT: 10,000
SALES (est): 740K **Privately Held**
SIC: 2841 Soap: granulated, liquid, cake, flaked or chip

(G-14137)
SPARCLEAN MBL REFINISHING INC
6915 64th Pl (11385-5251)
PHONE...................................718 445-2351
Rafa Colman, *President*
EMP: 5
SALES (est): 277.7K **Privately Held**
SIC: 1429 Marble, crushed & broken-quarrying

(G-14138)
STUDIO SILVERSMITHS INC
6315 Traffic Ave (11385-2629)
PHONE...................................718 418-6785
Fax: 718 418-6863
Arnold Godinger, *Ch of Bd*
Issac Godinger, *President*
Larry Lack, *Vice Pres*
Max Harris, *Manager*
▲ EMP: 40
SQ FT: 300,000
SALES (est): 3.8MM **Privately Held**
SIC: 3914 5199 Silverware; gifts & novelties

(G-14139)
TEC - CRETE TRANSIT MIX CORP
4673 Metropolitan Ave (11385-1044)
PHONE...................................718 657-6880
Linda Gisond, *Ch of Bd*
Dale Lahman, *Bookkeeper*
EMP: 25
SQ FT: 20,000
SALES (est): 3.8MM **Privately Held**
SIC: 3273 Ready-mixed concrete

(G-14140)
TIBANA FINISHING INC
1630 Cody Ave (11385-5734)
PHONE...................................718 417-5375
Fax: 718 417-0372
Tiberija Miksa, *President*
◆ EMP: 20
SQ FT: 21,000
SALES (est): 2.5MM **Privately Held**
WEB: www.tibana.com
SIC: 2329 2331 Men's & boys' sportswear & athletic clothing; women's & misses' blouses & shirts

(G-14141)
TRADING EDGE LTD
1923 Bleecker St Apt 1r (11385-9200)
PHONE...................................347 699-7079
Michael Oniszczuk, *Purch Mgr*
EMP: 5
SALES (est): 130.5K **Privately Held**
SIC: 2741

(G-14142)
TRI-BORO SHLVING PRTITION CORP
1940 Flushing Ave (11385-1043)
PHONE...................................718 782-8527
Fax: 718 963-0457
Fred Demaio, *President*
A P Demaio, *Vice Pres*
Stan Covington, *Plant Mgr*
John De Maio, *Sales/Mktg Mgr*
Nelson Cantillo, *Mktg Dir*
EMP: 15
SQ FT: 11,950
SALES (corp-wide): 10.7MM **Privately Held**
WEB: www.triboroshelving.com
SIC: 2542 5046 5084 Shelving, office & store: except wood; shelving, commercial & industrial; materials handling machinery
PA: Tri-Boro Shelving, Inc.
300 Dominion Dr
Farmville VA 23901
434 315-5600

(G-14143)
VIP FOODS INC
1080 Wyckoff Ave (11385-5757)
PHONE...................................718 821-5330

Edward Fruend, *President*
Mendel Fruend, *Vice Pres*
Esther Fruend, *Purchasing*
Tobias Fruend, *Treasurer*
▲ EMP: 25
SQ FT: 13,000
SALES (est): 4MM **Privately Held**
WEB: www.vipfoodsinc.com
SIC: 2099 Dessert mixes & fillings; gelatin dessert preparations

Rifton
Ulster County

(G-14144)
COMMUNITY PRODUCTS LLC (PA)
Also Called: Community Plythings Rifton Eqp
2032 Route 213 St (12471-7700)
P.O. Box 260 (12471-0260)
PHONE...................................845 658-8799
John Rhodes, *CEO*
Peter Alexander, *General Mgr*
Carol Kleinsasser, *Manager*
Eric Nelson, *Manager*
Nancy Voll, *Manager*
▲ EMP: 120
SQ FT: 5,000
SALES: 88.5MM **Privately Held**
WEB: www.communityplaythings.com
SIC: 3842 2511 3844 Orthopedic appliances; children's wood furniture; therapeutic X-ray apparatus & tubes

(G-14145)
COMMUNITY PRODUCTS LLC
2032 Route 213 St (12471-7700)
P.O. Box 903 (12471-0903)
PHONE...................................845 658-8351
Christoph Meier,
EMP: 30
SALES (corp-wide): 88.5MM **Privately Held**
SIC: 3993 Signs & advertising specialties
PA: Community Products, Llc
2032 Route 213 St
Rifton NY 12471
845 658-8799

(G-14146)
KEITH LEWIS STUDIO INC
35 Rifton Ter (12471)
P.O. Box 357 (12471-0357)
PHONE...................................845 339-5629
EMP: 9
SQ FT: 2,000
SALES: 375K **Privately Held**
SIC: 3911 5094 Jewelry, precious metal; jewelry

Ripley
Chautauqua County

(G-14147)
CHROMA LOGIC
6651 Wiley Rd (14775-9527)
PHONE...................................716 736-2458
Jason W Peterson, *President*
Jhon Mara, *Vice Pres*
EMP: 2
SQ FT: 5,000
SALES: 1.5MM **Privately Held**
SIC: 3552 Dyeing, drying & finishing machinery & equipment

(G-14148)
RIPLEY MACHINE & TOOL CO INC
9825 E Main Rd (14775-9504)
PHONE...................................716 736-3205
Fax: 716 736-3215
Andrew Reinwald, *President*
Quenti Besink, *Vice Pres*
EMP: 17 EST: 1944
SQ FT: 15,000
SALES (est): 2.6MM **Privately Held**
SIC: 3599 Machine shop, jobbing & repair

Riverhead
Suffolk County

(G-14149)
AUTO-MATE TECHNOLOGIES LLC
34 Hinda Blvd (11901-4804)
PHONE..................................631 727-8886
Fax: 631 369-3903
Kenneth Herzog,
▼ EMP: 12
SALES (est): 1.9MM **Privately Held**
WEB: www.automatech.com
SIC: 3365 Machinery castings, aluminum

(G-14150)
BERRY SPECIALTY TAPES LLC
1852 Old Country Rd (11901-3144)
PHONE..................................631 727-6000
John Pufahl, *Vice Pres*
Robert Pufahl, *Vice Pres*
Joseph M Pufahl,
EMP: 110 EST: 2002
SQ FT: 180,000
SALES (est): 3.6MM
SALES (corp-wide): 6.4B **Publicly Held**
SIC: 2672 Tape, pressure sensitive: made from purchased materials; coated paper, except photographic, carbon or abrasive
HQ: Berry Global, Inc.
101 Oakley St
Evansville IN 47710
812 424-2904

(G-14151)
CUSTOM WOODWORK LTD
Also Called: Heritage Wide Plank Flooring
205 Marcy Ave (11901-3029)
PHONE..................................631 727-5260
Cathaleen Lanieri, *President*
John Bullis, *Project Mgr*
Genie Rindfuss, *Manager*
EMP: 16
SQ FT: 3,500
SALES (est): 3.2MM **Privately Held**
WEB: www.heritagewideplankflooring.com
SIC: 2426 Flooring, hardwood

(G-14152)
DUNE WOODWORKING
723 Pulaski St (11901-3039)
PHONE..................................631 996-2482
Carl Schaffer, *Owner*
EMP: 5 EST: 2015
SALES (est): 87.1K **Privately Held**
SIC: 2431 Millwork

(G-14153)
DYNASTY METAL WORKS INC
787 Raynor Ave (11901-2949)
PHONE..................................631 284-3719
John Harold Jr, *President*
John Harold Sr, *Treasurer*
▲ EMP: 7
SALES (est): 1MM **Privately Held**
SIC: 3272 3441 Concrete products, precast; fabricated structural metal

(G-14154)
EASTERN WELDING INC
274 Mill Rd (11901-3145)
PHONE..................................631 727-0306
Fax: 631 727-4682
William Stubelek, *President*
Brian Stubelek, *Vice Pres*
EMP: 6
SQ FT: 10,000
SALES: 228.4K **Privately Held**
SIC: 3713 3523 3732 4226 Truck bodies (motor vehicles); farm machinery & equipment; boat building & repairing; special warehousing & storage; fabricated structural metal

(G-14155)
FREDERICK COWAN & COMPANY INC
48 Kroemer Ave (11901-3108)
PHONE..................................631 369-0360
Fax: 631 369-0637
Thomas L Cowan, *President*
Mildred Cowan, *Corp Secy*
EMP: 14
SQ FT: 20,000
SALES (est): 2.4MM **Privately Held**
WEB: www.fcowan.com
SIC: 3612 3433 Ignition transformers, for use on domestic fuel burners; gas burners, industrial

(G-14156)
HALLOCK FABRICATING CORP
324 Doctors Path (11901-1509)
PHONE..................................631 727-2441
Corey Hallock, *President*
Doreen Hallock, *Admin Sec*
EMP: 6
SQ FT: 10,000
SALES (est): 1MM **Privately Held**
SIC: 3312 3599 3441 1799 Stainless steel; machine shop, jobbing & repair; fabricated structural metal; welding on site

(G-14157)
KAPS-ALL PACKAGING SYSTEMS
200 Mill Rd (11901-3125)
PHONE..................................631 574-8778
Fax: 631 369-5939
Kenneth Herzog, *Ch of Bd*
◆ EMP: 61
SQ FT: 60,000
SALES (est): 16.2MM **Privately Held**
WEB: www.kapsall.com
SIC: 3565 Bottling machinery: filling, capping, labeling

(G-14158)
LA FORGE FRANCAISE LTD INC
100 Kroemer Ave (11901-3117)
P.O. Box 1322, Boulder UT (84716-1322)
PHONE..................................631 591-0572
Patrice Humbert, *President*
Marlyse Humbert, *Vice Pres*
EMP: 6
SQ FT: 1,000
SALES (est): 579.6K **Privately Held**
SIC: 2514 Metal household furniture

(G-14159)
LEHNEIS ORTHOTICS PROSTHETIC
518 E Main St (11901-2529)
PHONE..................................631 369-3115
EMP: 7
SALES (corp-wide): 5MM **Privately Held**
SIC: 3842 5047 5999 Mfg Surgical Appliances/Supplies Whol Medical/Hospital Equipment Ret Misc Merchandise
PA: Lehneis Orthotics & Prosthetic Associates Ltd
13 Bedells Landing Rd
Roslyn NY
516 621-7277

(G-14160)
LONG IRELAND BREWING LLC
723 Pulaski St (11901-3039)
PHONE..................................631 403-4303
Gregory Martin, *President*
EMP: 5
SALES: 668K **Privately Held**
SIC: 2082 Malt beverages

(G-14161)
LONG ISLAND GREEN GUYS
26 Silverbrook Dr (11901-4269)
PHONE..................................631 664-4306
Martin Hand, *Principal*
EMP: 5
SALES (est): 473.9K **Privately Held**
SIC: 3272 Grease traps, concrete

(G-14162)
LUXFER MAGTECH INC
680 Elton St (11901-2555)
PHONE..................................631 727-8600
Brian Purves, *CEO*
Marc Lamensdorf, *President*
Deepak Madan, *Vice Pres*
Deborah Simsen, *Treasurer*
James Gardella, *Exec Dir*
EMP: 80
SALES (est): 13.4MM
SALES (corp-wide): 414.8MM **Privately Held**
SIC: 2899 5149 Desalter kits, sea water; oxidizers, inorganic; groceries & related products
PA: Luxfer Holdings Plc
Ancorage Gateway
Salford LANCS M50 3
161 300-0611

(G-14163)
MAHIN IMPRESSIONS INC
30 W Main St Ste 301 (11901-2806)
PHONE..................................212 871-9777
Fax: 212 871-5530
Sharon Mahin, *President*
Brian Mahin, *Treasurer*
EMP: 3
SALES: 1MM **Privately Held**
WEB: www.mahinimpressions.com
SIC: 2752 Commercial printing, lithographic

(G-14164)
NORTH COAST OUTFITTERS LTD
1015 E Main St Ste 1 (11901-2678)
PHONE..................................631 727-5580
Charles Darling III, *President*
Horst Ehinger, *Vice Pres*
Maria Lafrance, *Office Mgr*
▼ EMP: 20 EST: 1996
SQ FT: 30,000
SALES (est): 2.2MM **Privately Held**
WEB: www.charlieshorse.com
SIC: 3949 3444 3354 Sporting & athletic goods; sheet metalwork; aluminum extruded products

(G-14165)
PHOENIX WOOD WRIGHTS LTD
132 Kroemer Ave 3 (11901-3117)
PHONE..................................631 727-9691
James Gleason, *President*
EMP: 14 EST: 2007
SALES (est): 2.3MM **Privately Held**
SIC: 3553 Bandsaws, woodworking

(G-14166)
QUANTUM KNOWLEDGE LLC
356 Reeves Ave (11901-1109)
PHONE..................................631 727-6111
Alexander Pozamantir,
EMP: 6
SALES (est): 848.5K **Privately Held**
SIC: 3572 Computer storage devices

(G-14167)
ROBERT & WILLIAM INC (PA)
224 Griffing Ave (11901-3214)
PHONE..................................631 727-5780
Wil S Field, *CEO*
William Schofield Sr, *CEO*
Robert Frankel, *President*
Julie Brooke, *Manager*
Kim Curry, *Administration*
▼ EMP: 5 EST: 1997
SQ FT: 3,200
SALES: 30.1MM **Privately Held**
WEB: www.randw.com
SIC: 2011 Meat by-products from meat slaughtered on site

(G-14168)
SCHILLER STORES INC (PA)
Also Called: Le Creuset
509 Tanger Mall Dr (11901-6405)
PHONE..................................631 208-9400
Michael Kryivski, *Manager*
EMP: 5
SALES (est): 491K **Privately Held**
SIC: 3469 Cooking ware, porcelain enameled

(G-14169)
SENTRY AUTOMATIC SPRINKLER
735 Flanders Rd (11901-3828)
PHONE..................................631 723-3095
Thomas Andracchi, *President*
EMP: 10
SALES (est): 980K **Privately Held**
SIC: 3569 Sprinkler systems, fire: automatic

(G-14170)
SPIRENT INC (HQ)
303 Griffing Ave (11901-3010)
PHONE..................................631 208-0680
L John Knox, *President*
Frank V Pizzi, *Treasurer*
▲ EMP: 7
SQ FT: 51,000
SALES: 87.2MM
SALES (corp-wide): 457.9MM **Privately Held**
SIC: 3699 High-energy particle physics equipment
PA: Spirent Communications Plc
Northwood Park
Crawley W SUSSEX RH10
129 376-7676

(G-14171)
TIKI INDUSTRIES INC
8 Tree Haven Ln (11901-4908)
PHONE..................................516 779-3629
Kalani Aiwohi, *President*
EMP: 5
SALES (est): 261.3K **Privately Held**
SIC: 3999 1611 1622 1741 Manufacturing industries; general contractor, highway & street construction; sidewalk construction; bridge construction; masonry & other stonework; waterproofing

(G-14172)
TUTHILL CORPORATION
75 Kings Dr (11901-6202)
PHONE..................................631 727-1097
EMP: 467
SALES (corp-wide): 469.3MM **Privately Held**
SIC: 3511 Mfg Steel Turbines
PA: Tuthill Corporation
8500 S Madison St
Burr Ridge IL 60527
630 382-4900

(G-14173)
WEDEL SIGN COMPANY INC
705 W Main St (11901-2843)
PHONE..................................631 727-4577
Fax: 631 727-4578
Barry Wedel, *President*
EMP: 5
SQ FT: 2,000
SALES: 276.8K **Privately Held**
SIC: 3993 Signs & advertising specialties

(G-14174)
WINE SERVICES INC
1129 Cross River Dr Ste A (11901-1703)
PHONE..................................631 722-3800
John White, *President*
John Flock, *Director*
EMP: 5
SQ FT: 21,000
SALES (est): 420.1K **Privately Held**
WEB: www.wineservices.com
SIC: 2084 Wine cellars, bonded: engaged in blending wines

Rochester
Monroe County

(G-14175)
A Q P INC
Also Called: Advanced Quickprinting
2975 Brighton Henrietta T (14623-2787)
PHONE..................................585 256-1690
Fax: 585 256-1694
James L Roach, *President*
Kim Dodson, *Office Mgr*
EMP: 7
SQ FT: 3,700
SALES (est): 1MM **Privately Held**
SIC: 2752 7334 Commercial printing, offset; photocopying & duplicating services

(G-14176)
A R ARENA PRODUCTS INC
2101 Mount Read Blvd (14615-3708)
PHONE..................................585 277-1680
Fax: 585 254-1046
Anthony R Arena, *CEO*
Charles Arena, *Vice Pres*
Jeff Reeves, *Mfg Mgr*

Rochester - Monroe County (G-14177)

Richard Hasenauer, *Engineer*
Chris Mabry, *Engineer*
▲ **EMP:** 20
SQ FT: 30,000
SALES (est): 7.8MM **Privately Held**
WEB: www.arenaproducts.com
SIC: 3089 7359 Plastic containers, except foam; shipping container leasing

(G-14177)
AAA WELDING AND FABRICATION OF
1085 Lyell Ave (14606-1935)
PHONE 585 254-2830
Fax: 585 254-7951
Sam Dinch, *President*
Steven Stadtmiller, *Corp Secy*
EMP: 9
SQ FT: 16,000
SALES (est): 2MM **Privately Held**
WEB: www.aaawelding.com
SIC: 3441 1623 7692 Fabricated structural metal; pipe laying construction; welding repair

(G-14178)
AARON TOOL & MOLD INC
620 Trolley Blvd (14606-4215)
PHONE 585 426-5100
Daniel Morgan, *President*
Ellen Morgan, *Vice Pres*
EMP: 8
SQ FT: 6,000
SALES (est): 1MM **Privately Held**
WEB: www.aaronmold.com
SIC: 3544 Industrial molds

(G-14179)
ACAD DESIGN CORP
975 Mount Read Blvd (14606-2829)
PHONE 585 254-6960
Fax: 585 254-6967
Thomas Sheen, *President*
Karen Sheen, *Vice Pres*
Jo Menaldino, *Office Mgr*
EMP: 13
SQ FT: 20,000
SALES: 2MM **Privately Held**
WEB: www.acaddesigncorp.com
SIC: 3599 7389 8711 Machine & other job shop work; design services; engineering services

(G-14180)
ACCEDE MOLD & TOOL CO INC
1125 Lexington Ave (14606-2995)
PHONE 585 254-6490
Fax: 585 254-0954
Roger Fox, *CEO*
Alton L Fox, *President*
Nancy Fox, *Vice Pres*
Brett Lindenmuth, *VP Opers*
John Nelson, *Purch Mgr*
▲ **EMP:** 58
SQ FT: 38,000
SALES (est): 12.4MM **Privately Held**
WEB: www.accedemold.com
SIC: 3544 3599 Forms (molds), for foundry & plastics working machinery; custom machinery

(G-14181)
ACCU COAT INC
111 Humboldt St Ste 8 (14609-7415)
PHONE 585 288-2330
Paul Meier-Wang, *President*
Patrick Iuliamello, *Vice Pres*
EMP: 7
SQ FT: 4,500
SALES (est): 1.1MM **Privately Held**
WEB: www.accucoatinc.com
SIC: 3851 Ophthalmic goods

(G-14182)
ACCURATE PNT POWDR COATING INC
606 Hague St (14606-1214)
PHONE 585 235-1650
Fax: 585 235-3884
Christopher Ralph, *President*
Jeremy Seaver, *General Mgr*
Gina Sorokti, *Opers Mgr*
EMP: 17
SQ FT: 40,000
SALES: 1.2MM **Privately Held**
SIC: 3479 3999 Etching & engraving; coating of metals & formed products; barber & beauty shop equipment

(G-14183)
ACCURATE TOOL & DIE LLC
1085 Lyell Ave (14606-1935)
PHONE 585 254-2830
Sam Dinch, *Mng Member*
Mark Drewiega,
Steve Drewiega,
Gene Lippa,
EMP: 15
SQ FT: 15,000
SALES (est): 1.1MM **Privately Held**
SIC: 3544 Special dies, tools, jigs & fixtures

(G-14184)
ACES OVER EIGHTS INC
Also Called: Woodcraft
1100 Jefferson Rd Ste 22 (14623-3135)
PHONE 585 292-9690
Sean Clayton, *President*
Andrea Clayton, *Admin Sec*
EMP: 8 **EST:** 2001
SQ FT: 7,600
SALES (est): 1.2MM **Privately Held**
SIC: 2499 Decorative wood & woodwork

(G-14185)
ACME PRECISION SCREW PDTS INC
623 Glide St (14606-1345)
P.O. Box 60649 (14606-0649)
PHONE 585 328-2028
Fax: 585 235-0601
Rodney Czudak, *President*
Barbara Czudak, *Manager*
EMP: 18
SQ FT: 10,000
SALES (est): 3.5MM **Privately Held**
SIC: 3451 Screw machine products

(G-14186)
ACRO INDUSTRIES INC
554 Colfax St (14606-3112)
PHONE 585 254-3661
Fax: 585 254-0415
Joseph A Noto, *President*
Robert Coyne, *COO*
John H Gefell, *Vice Pres*
James Francisco, *Opers Mgr*
Brian Gefell, *Production*
▲ **EMP:** 148
SQ FT: 150,000
SALES (est): 56.2MM **Privately Held**
WEB: www.acroind.com
SIC: 3444 3599 3443 3469 Culverts, flumes & pipes; amusement park equipment; fabricated plate work (boiler shop); metal stampings

(G-14187)
ACUITY POLYMERS INC
1667 Lake Ave Ste 303 (14615-3047)
PHONE 585 458-8409
James Bonafini, *President*
EMP: 8
SALES (est): 614.1K **Privately Held**
SIC: 3851 Contact lenses

(G-14188)
ADDISON PRECISION MFG CORP
500 Avis St (14615-3308)
P.O. Box 15393 (14615-0393)
PHONE 585 254-1386
Fax: 585 254-5342
Robert E Champagne, *CEO*
Rodney C Champagne, *President*
Roger C Champagne, *Vice Pres*
Laura Caraballo, *Production*
Eric Caudill, *Manager*
EMP: 72 **EST:** 1950
SQ FT: 40,000
SALES (est): 15.3MM **Privately Held**
WEB: www.addisonprec.com
SIC: 3599 Machine & other job shop work

(G-14189)
ADFLEX CORPORATION
300 Ormond St (14605-3090)
PHONE 585 454-2950
Fax: 585 454-5583
Joseph Andolora, *Ch of Bd*
Jeffery Andolora, *President*
Christopher Andolora, *Vice Pres*
Daniel Valentine, *Controller*
EMP: 36
SQ FT: 25,000
SALES (est): 7.7MM **Privately Held**
WEB: www.adflexcorp.com
SIC: 2796 7336 2754 2672 Platemaking services; engraving platemaking services; art design services; labels: gravure printing; coated & laminated paper; commercial printing

(G-14190)
ADRIAN JULES LTD
Also Called: Adrian-Jules Custom Tailor
1392 E Ridge Rd (14621-2005)
PHONE 585 342-5886
Fax: 585 342-0345
Adriano P Roberti, *Ch of Bd*
Arnald J Roberti, *President*
Peter E Roberti, *President*
Angela Lolas, *Human Res Dir*
Scotti Gaylor, *Manager*
▲ **EMP:** 80 **EST:** 1964
SQ FT: 14,000
SALES (est): 7.7MM **Privately Held**
WEB: www.adrianjules.com
SIC: 2311 5699 2325 Men's & boys' suits & coats; custom tailor; men's & boys' trousers & slacks

(G-14191)
ADVANCE CIRCUIT TECHNOLOGY INC
19 Jetview Dr (14624-4903)
PHONE 585 328-2000
Fax: 585 328-2019
James Morrison, *Ch of Bd*
Robert Drozdowski, *Business Mgr*
Robert Kajfasz, *Vice Pres*
Kalman Zsamboky, *Vice Pres*
▲ **EMP:** 42 **EST:** 1998
SQ FT: 35,000
SALES (est): 10.5MM **Privately Held**
WEB: www.advcircuit.com
SIC: 3679 3672 Electronic circuits; printed circuit boards

(G-14192)
ADVANCED COATING SERVICE LLC
15 Hytec Cir (14606-4255)
P.O. Box 60387 (14606-0387)
PHONE 585 247-3970
Donald Titus, *Mng Member*
Donald E Titus Jr, *Mng Member*
EMP: 7
SALES (est): 1MM **Privately Held**
WEB: www.acscoating.com
SIC: 3479 Etching & engraving

(G-14193)
ADVANCED GLASS INDUSTRIES INC
Also Called: A G I
1335 Emerson St (14606-3006)
P.O. Box 60467 (14606-0467)
PHONE 585 458-8040
Anthony Marino, *President*
H John Fischer, *Vice Pres*
Bill Neylor, *Engrg Mgr*
Alicia Gionta, *Marketing Mgr*
Henry Louis, *Marketing Staff*
▲ **EMP:** 51
SQ FT: 42,000
SALES (est): 19.1MM **Privately Held**
WEB: www.agi.com
SIC: 3827 Lenses, optical: all types except ophthalmic

(G-14194)
ADVANCED MACHINE INC
439 Central Ave Ste 108 (14605-3016)
PHONE 585 423-8255
Fax: 585 423-9804
John Bauman, *President*
Jacqueline De Mario, *Treasurer*
Dana Byron, *Admin Sec*
EMP: 10
SQ FT: 5,600
SALES (est): 1.3MM **Privately Held**
SIC: 3599 Machine shop, jobbing & repair

(G-14195)
ADVANTAGE METALWORK FINSHG LLC
1000 University Ave # 700 (14607-1286)
PHONE 585 454-0160
Fax: 585 454-0173
Chet Wester, *CEO*
Arthur Carroll, *Exec VP*
Dale Campbell, *Vice Pres*
Greg Miller, *Opers Mgr*
Thomas Coburn, *Engineer*
EMP: 86
SALES (est): 19.5MM **Privately Held**
SIC: 3542 Machine tools, metal forming type

(G-14196)
ADVANTECH INDUSTRIES INC
3850 Buffalo Rd (14624-1104)
PHONE 585 247-0701
Fax: 585 247-0745
James Gizzi, *Ch of Bd*
EMP: 115
SALES (est): 26.4MM **Privately Held**
WEB: www.advantechindustries.com
SIC: 3399 3444 Laminating steel; sheet metalwork

(G-14197)
AIRGAS INC
77 Deep Rock Rd (14624-3519)
PHONE 585 436-7780
Fax: 585 436-8907
Bob Hewitt, *CEO*
EMP: 23
SALES (corp-wide): 163.9MM **Privately Held**
SIC: 2813 Industrial gases
HQ: Airgas, Inc.
  259 N Radnor Chester Rd # 100
  Radnor PA 19087
  610 687-5253

(G-14198)
AIRGAS USA LLC
77 Deep Rock Rd (14624-3519)
PHONE 585 436-7781
Robert Gross, *Opers Mgr*
Bob Hewitt, *Branch Mgr*
EMP: 15
SQ FT: 12,330
SALES (corp-wide): 163.9MM **Privately Held**
WEB: www.airgas.com
SIC: 2813 Industrial gases
HQ: Airgas Usa, Llc
  259 N Radnor Chester Rd # 100
  Radnor PA 19087
  610 687-5253

(G-14199)
AJL MANUFACTURING INC
100 Holleder Pkwy (14615-3800)
PHONE 585 254-1128
David Zink, *General Mgr*
Albert F Porter, *Chairman*
Mark Burch, *Facilities Dir*
Joe Frillici, *Plant Mgr*
Patrick Palermo, *Opers Mgr*
▲ **EMP:** 112
SQ FT: 165,000
SALES (est): 31.1MM **Privately Held**
WEB: www.ajlmfg.com
SIC: 3469 Stamping metal for the trade

(G-14200)
ALCOA FASTENING SYSTEMS
181 Mckee Rd (14611-2011)
PHONE 585 368-5049
Vitaliy Rusakov, *CEO*
EMP: 8 **EST:** 2015
SALES (est): 672.1K **Privately Held**
SIC: 3353 Aluminum sheet & strip

(G-14201)
ALKEMY MACHINE LLC
Also Called: Aurora Machine
1600 Lexington Ave 103c (14606-3000)
PHONE 585 436-8730
Jonathan Amoia, *General Mgr*
Jordan Kowalczyk, *General Mgr*
EMP: 8
SALES (est): 1.5MM **Privately Held**
SIC: 3444 3599 Sheet metalwork; machine shop, jobbing & repair

GEOGRAPHIC SECTION

Rochester - Monroe County (G-14224)

(G-14202)
ALLESON OF ROCHESTER INC (PA)
Also Called: Alleson Athletic
2921 Brighton Henrietta (14623-2798)
PHONE..................................800 641-0041
Fax: 585 272-9639
Elena Oliveri, *Ch of Bd*
Todd Levine, *President*
Sam Green, *Vice Pres*
Michael J Kretovic, *Vice Pres*
Peter Palermo, *Vice Pres*
▲ **EMP:** 100 **EST:** 1935
SQ FT: 128,000
SALES (est): 58MM **Privately Held**
SIC: 2329 2339 Athletic (warmup, sweat & jogging) suits: men's & boys'; women's & misses' outerwear

(G-14203)
ALLIANCE AUTOMATION SYSTEMS
400 Trabold Rd (14624-2529)
PHONE..................................585 426-2700
Fax: 585 426-3788
Arthur Anderson, *CEO*
Stewart H Rodman, *Ch of Bd*
Donald Doell, *Vice Pres*
Graham Hippworth, *Plant Mgr*
Chuck Melia, *Plant Mgr*
▲ **EMP:** 125
SQ FT: 120,000
SALES: 15MM **Privately Held**
SIC: 3549 3569 Assembly machines, including robotic; assembly machines, non-metalworking

(G-14204)
ALLIANCE PRECISION PLAS CORP (PA)
1220 Lee Rd (14606-4252)
PHONE..................................585 426-5310
Walter C Butler Jr, *CEO*
Bradley C Scott, *President*
Diana Smalley, *Purchasing*
Paul Cooper, *Project Engr*
Clarke Gould, *CFO*
▲ **EMP:** 200 **EST:** 1998
SQ FT: 80,000
SALES (est): 64.7MM **Privately Held**
WEB: www.allianceppc.com
SIC: 3089 3544 Injection molded finished plastic products; dies, plastics forming

(G-14205)
ALLIANCE PRECISION PLAS CORP
105 Elmore Dr (14606-3429)
PHONE..................................585 426-5310
Joe Zinni, *Purchasing*
Michael Rice, *QC Mgr*
John Oakes, *Engineer*
Sara Bruzda, *Human Resources*
Brad Scott, *Branch Mgr*
EMP: 41
SALES (corp-wide): 64.7MM **Privately Held**
SIC: 3089 3544 Injection molded finished plastic products; dies, plastics forming
PA: Alliance Precision Plastics Corporation
1220 Lee Rd
Rochester NY 14606
585 426-5310

(G-14206)
ALLSTATE TOOL AND DIE INC
Also Called: Atd Precision Machining
15 Coldwater Cres (14624-2590)
PHONE..................................585 426-0400
Fax: 585 426-2121
Paul Held Sr, *President*
Paul Held Jr, *President*
Elizabeth Held, *Vice Pres*
Stacey Costello, *Purchasing*
Richard Huber, *Sales Mgr*
▲ **EMP:** 68
SQ FT: 37,000
SALES (est): 8.8MM **Privately Held**
WEB: www.atdprecision.com
SIC: 3544 Special dies, tools, jigs & fixtures

(G-14207)
ALOI SOLUTIONS LLC (PA)
Also Called: Aloi Materials Handling
140 Commerce Dr (14623-3504)
PHONE..................................585 292-0920
Fax: 585 292-1740
Jeff Gambrill, *President*
Robert Manion, *Vice Pres*
Trish Hedeen, *Controller*
Daniel Cavanaugh, *Accounts Mgr*
▲ **EMP:** 30 **EST:** 1987
SQ FT: 16,500
SALES (est): 7.9MM **Privately Held**
WEB: www.aloi.com
SIC: 3599 3999 Custom machinery; atomizers, toiletry

(G-14208)
ALPHA IRON WORKS LLC
65 Goodway Dr S (14623-3018)
PHONE..................................585 424-7260
Evangelos Economides, *Mng Member*
Maria Economides,
EMP: 16
SQ FT: 13,000
SALES (est): 3.2MM **Privately Held**
WEB: www.alphairon.com
SIC: 3446 Architectural metalwork

(G-14209)
ALTON MANUFACTURING INC
825 Lee Rd (14606-4290)
PHONE..................................585 458-2600
Fax: 585 458-8524
George Chornobil, *Ch of Bd*
Andrew Chornobil, *President*
Dale Green, *Engineer*
Karnail Singh, *Manager*
Connie Coia, *Info Tech Mgr*
EMP: 90
SQ FT: 150,000
SALES (est): 16.4MM **Privately Held**
WEB: www.altonmfg.com
SIC: 3469 3544 3541 Stamping metal for the trade; special dies, tools, jigs & fixtures; machine tools, metal cutting type

(G-14210)
AMARR COMPANY
Also Called: Amarr Garage Doors
550 Mile Crssing Blvd 1 (14624)
PHONE..................................585 426-8290
Fax: 585 426-8299
Demetrius Scott, *Site Mgr*
Philip Bordelen, *Manager*
Mark Fiorella, *Manager*
EMP: 10
SALES (corp-wide): 7.7B **Privately Held**
WEB: www.amarr.com
SIC: 3442 5211 Garage doors, overhead: metal; garage doors, sale & installation
HQ: Amarr Company
165 Carriage Ct
Winston Salem NC 27105
336 744-5100

(G-14211)
AMERICAN AEROGEL CORPORATION
460 Buffalo Rd Ste 200a (14611-2026)
PHONE..................................585 328-2140
Michael Hone, *CEO*
Jay McHarg, *President*
David Abruzzese, *Vice Pres*
Nick Fusilli, *Opers Mgr*
Tanner King, *QC Mgr*
EMP: 34
SQ FT: 40,000
SALES (est): 12.1MM **Privately Held**
WEB: www.americanaerogel.com
SIC: 3441 Fabricated structural metal

(G-14212)
AMERICAN FUEL CELL LLC
1200 Ridgeway Ave Ste 123 (14615-3758)
PHONE..................................585 474-3993
Daniel O'Connell,
David Wetter,
EMP: 6
SQ FT: 1,500
SALES (est): 444.7K **Privately Held**
SIC: 3629 3674 Electrochemical generators (fuel cells); fuel cells, solid state

(G-14213)
AMERICAN PACKAGING CORPORATION
1555 Lyell Ave (14606-2145)
PHONE..................................585 254-2002
Peter Scottland, *President*
Dave Hebberecht, *General Mgr*
EMP: 7
SALES (corp-wide): 185.6MM **Privately Held**
SIC: 2673 3497 2671 Bags: plastic, laminated & coated; metal foil & leaf; paper coated or laminated for packaging
PA: American Packaging Corporation
777 Driving Park Ave
Rochester NY 14613
585 254-9500

(G-14214)
AMERICAN PACKAGING CORPORATION (PA)
Also Called: Flexographic Printing
777 Driving Park Ave (14613-1591)
PHONE..................................585 254-9500
Fax: 585 254-5801
Peter B Schottland, *President*
Steven Schottland, *Chairman*
Jeffery R Koch, *Exec VP*
Raymond Graham, *Vice Pres*
Dylan Gaudineer, *Safety Dir*
▲ **EMP:** 150
SQ FT: 150,000
SALES (est): 185.6MM **Privately Held**
WEB: www.ampkcorp.com
SIC: 2673 3497 2671 2754 Bags: plastic, laminated & coated; metal foil & leaf; paper coated or laminated for packaging; rotogravure printing; bags: uncoated paper & multiwall

(G-14215)
AMERICAN SPECIALTY MFG CO
Also Called: Boss Sauce
272 Hudson Ave (14605-2124)
P.O. Box 31344 (14603-1344)
PHONE..................................585 544-5600
Fax: 585 544-5691
Eddie Harris, *President*
Loreta Pope, *Vice Pres*
Regina Harris, *Treasurer*
EMP: 11
SQ FT: 6,500
SALES (est): 400K **Privately Held**
SIC: 2035 Seasonings, meat sauces (except tomato & dry)

(G-14216)
AMERICAN SPORTS MEDIA LLC (PA)
2604 Elmwood Ave Ste 343 (14618-2213)
PHONE..................................585 377-9636
Fax: 585 292-0035
David Jones,
David Aultman,
Brian Spindler,
EMP: 1
SQ FT: 3,000
SALES (est): 1.2MM **Privately Held**
WEB: www.americansportsmedia.com
SIC: 2711 Newspapers: publishing only, not printed on site

(G-14217)
AMERICAN TIME MFG LTD
Also Called: American Products
1600 N Clinton Ave Ste 1 (14621-2200)
PHONE..................................585 266-5120
Fax: 585 266-7223
Clifford Charlson, *President*
Micheal Caston, *Controller*
▲ **EMP:** 18
SQ FT: 7,000
SALES (est): 1.8MM **Privately Held**
WEB: www.americanproducts-ny.com
SIC: 3873 Watchcases

(G-14218)
AMETEK INC
Also Called: Ametek Power Instruments
255 Union St N (14605-2699)
P.O. Box 1764, Paoli PA (19301-0801)
PHONE..................................585 263-7700
Fax: 585 238-7805
Carlos Saavedra, *Facilities Mgr*
Paul Parsons, *Opers Staff*
John Sotack, *Design Engr*
Steven Bleier, *Sales Mgr*
Jim Bates, *Sales Staff*
EMP: 68
SALES (corp-wide): 3.8B **Publicly Held**
SIC: 3621 3823 3825 3812 Motors & generators; industrial instrmnts msrmnt display/control process variable; instruments to measure electricity; search & navigation equipment; electrical equipment & supplies
PA: Ametek, Inc.
1100 Cassatt Rd
Berwyn PA 19312
610 647-2121

(G-14219)
ANALOG DIGITAL TECHNOLOGY LLC
Also Called: Adtech
95 Mount Read Blvd # 149 (14611-1923)
PHONE..................................585 698-1845
Tom Crumlish, *President*
Eric Hauptmann, *Vice Pres*
EMP: 9
SQ FT: 6,500
SALES (est): 1.1MM **Privately Held**
WEB: www.adtech-inst.com
SIC: 3699 5084 Chimes, electric; industrial machinery & equipment

(G-14220)
ANDEX CORP
69 Deep Rock Rd (14624-3575)
PHONE..................................585 328-3790
Fax: 585 328-3792
Andrew J Cherre, *President*
EMP: 30 **EST:** 1962
SQ FT: 17,000
SALES (est): 6.6MM **Privately Held**
SIC: 2621 Filter paper

(G-14221)
ANDROS MANUFACTURING CORP
30 Hojack Park (14612-1994)
PHONE..................................585 663-5700
Fax: 585 663-1212
Russell Steenhoff, *President*
Nancy Commanda, *Vice Pres*
Fred Steenhoff, *Director*
EMP: 10
SQ FT: 12,000
SALES: 700K **Privately Held**
WEB: www.androsmfg.com
SIC: 3451 3643 Screw machine products; solderless connectors (electric wiring devices)

(G-14222)
ANMAR ACQUISITION LLC (HQ)
35 Vantage Point Dr (14624-1142)
PHONE..................................585 352-7777
Lee Rudow, *CEO*
John Zimmer, *CFO*
EMP: 5
SALES (est): 2.5MM
SALES (corp-wide): 143.9MM **Publicly Held**
SIC: 3825 Radar testing instruments, electric
PA: Transcat, Inc.
35 Vantage Point Dr
Rochester NY 14624
585 352-7777

(G-14223)
ANTAB MCH SPRFINISHING LAB INC
46 Latta Rd (14612-4708)
PHONE..................................585 865-8290
Araxie Aintablian, *President*
John Aintablian, *Manager*
▲ **EMP:** 7
SALES (est): 470K **Privately Held**
SIC: 3599 Machine shop, jobbing & repair

(G-14224)
APPLIED COATINGS HOLDING CORP (PA)
1653 E Main St Ste 1 (14609-7000)
PHONE..................................585 482-0300
Bruno Glavich, *President*
Lois Mooney, *Controller*
Candice Moran, *Accounts Mgr*

Rochester - Monroe County (G-14225)

Omer Yilbiz, *Manager*
◆ **EMP:** 8 **EST:** 1998
SQ FT: 5,000
SALES (est): 5MM **Privately Held**
SIC: 3827 Optical elements & assemblies, except ophthalmic

(G-14225)
APPLIED IMAGE INC
1653 E Main St Ste 1 (14609-7090)
PHONE..................................585 482-0300
Fax: 585 224-0402
Dave Doubledee, *President*
Katie Caccamise, *General Mgr*
Glenn Jackling, *General Mgr*
Luke Hobson, *Vice Pres*
Greg Peck, *VP Opers*
EMP: 20
SQ FT: 20,000
SALES (est): 4.7MM
SALES (corp-wide): 5MM **Privately Held**
WEB: www.appliedimage.net
SIC: 3826 3827 7335 Analytical optical instruments; optical instruments & apparatus; color separation, photographic & movie film
PA: Applied Coatings Holding Corp.
1653 E Main St Ste 1
Rochester NY 14609
585 482-0300

(G-14226)
ARM GLOBAL SOLUTIONS INC
138 Joseph Ave (14605-1938)
PHONE..................................844 276-4525
Joe Meindl, *President*
Jim Knauf, *Vice Pres*
Joe Jim Groh, *CFO*
Brian Meindl, *Manager*
Alan Wallace, *Administration*
EMP: 5 **EST:** 2014
SALES (est): 222.7K **Privately Held**
SIC: 2671 Plastic film, coated or laminated for packaging

(G-14227)
ARM ROCHESTER INC
138 Joseph Ave (14605-1938)
PHONE..................................585 354-5077
Armando Santiago, *President*
James Jacus, *Director*
Robert Vavrina, *Director*
EMP: 15
SQ FT: 15,000
SALES (est): 1.5MM **Privately Held**
SIC: 3086 7389 Padding, foamed plastic;

(G-14228)
ARNOLD MAGNETIC TECH CORP (HQ)
Also Called: Magnetic Technology
770 Linden Ave (14625-2716)
PHONE..................................585 385-9010
Fax: 585 385-3868
Gordon H McNeil, *President*
Roy Hollon, *General Mgr*
Michael Stachura, *General Mgr*
Jim Sotelo, *Business Mgr*
Michael Calzada, *Engineer*
▲ **EMP:** 202
SQ FT: 70,000
SALES (est): 290.5MM
SALES (corp-wide): 978.3MM **Publicly Held**
WEB: www.arnoldmagnetics.com
SIC: 3264 3499 Magnets, permanent: ceramic or ferrite; magnets, permanent: metallic
PA: Compass Diversified Holdings
301 Riverside Ave
Westport CT 06880
203 221-1703

(G-14229)
ARNPRIOR RPID MFG SLUTIONS INC (PA)
2400 Mount Read Blvd # 112 (14615-2744)
PHONE..................................585 617-6301
Leonard M Levie, *Ch of Bd*
John Wilbur, *President*
Pamela Barnard, *Principal*
Thomas Palumbo, *Principal*
Carol Rath, *Principal*
EMP: 143
SALES (est): 20MM **Privately Held**
SIC: 3999 Advertising display products

(G-14230)
ARNPRIOR RPID MFG SLUTIONS INC
2400 Mount Read Blvd # 1124 (14615-2744)
PHONE..................................585 617-6301
Thomas Palumbo, *Manager*
EMP: 9 **Privately Held**
SIC: 3999 Advertising display products
PA: Arnprior Rapid Manufacturing Solutions, Inc.
2400 Mount Read Blvd # 112
Rochester NY 14615

(G-14231)
ART-CRAFT OPTICAL COMPANY INC
57 Goodway Dr S (14623-3018)
PHONE..................................585 546-6640
Fax: 585 546-5133
C Thomas Eagle, *President*
Norman Radziwon, *Division Mgr*
Michael D Franz, *Exec VP*
Martin Gullen, *Exec VP*
Christopher Eagle, *VP Opers*
EMP: 49
SQ FT: 90,000
SALES (est): 9.1MM **Privately Held**
WEB: www.artcraftoptical.com
SIC: 3851 Frames & parts, eyeglass & spectacle

(G-14232)
ARYZTA LLC
Rochester Div
64 Chester St (14611-2110)
PHONE..................................310 417-4700
John Menne, *Branch Mgr*
EMP: 87
SALES (corp-wide): 4.3B **Privately Held**
WEB: www.pennantfoods.com
SIC: 2045 2099 2051 Prepared flour mixes & doughs; food preparations; bread, cake & related products
HQ: Aryzta Llc
6080 Center Dr Ste 900
Los Angeles CA 90045
310 417-4700

(G-14233)
ARYZTA LLC
Also Called: Pennant Foods
235 Buffalo Rd (14611-1905)
PHONE..................................585 235-8160
Steven Smith, *Branch Mgr*
Stan Fisher, *Manager*
EMP: 218
SALES (corp-wide): 4.3B **Privately Held**
WEB: www.pennantfoods.com
SIC: 2051 2052 Bread, cake & related products; bakery products, dry
HQ: Aryzta Llc
6080 Center Dr Ste 900
Los Angeles CA 90045
310 417-4700

(G-14234)
ASCRIBE INC
383 Buell Rd (14624-3123)
PHONE..................................585 413-0298
Fax: 585 425-1605
Mark Shaw, *Ch of Bd*
Dean Saklis, *President*
EMP: 50
SALES (est): 3.6MM **Privately Held**
SIC: 3999 7389 3479 Atomizers, toiletry; grinding, precision: commercial or industrial; etching & engraving

(G-14235)
ASP INDUSTRIES INC
9 Evelyn St (14606-5533)
PHONE..................................585 254-9130
Fax: 585 254-9139
Suzanne M Phillips, *President*
Douglas Muller, *Engineer*
Susan Allen, *Controller*
Michael Garner, *Manager*
EMP: 20
SQ FT: 23,000
SALES: 2.8MM **Privately Held**
WEB: www.aspindustries.com
SIC: 3444 3441 Sheet metalwork; fabricated structural metal

(G-14236)
AYCAN MEDICAL SYSTEMS LLC
693 East Ave Ste 102 (14607-2160)
PHONE..................................585 271-3078
Fax: 585 473-1596
Steven Wagner, *General Mgr*
Lin McKernan, *Sales Mgr*
Ana Tindal, *Sales Staff*
Frank Burkhardt, *Marketing Mgr*
EMP: 15 **EST:** 2003
SQ FT: 4,000
SALES (est): 1.8MM **Privately Held**
SIC: 7372 Business oriented computer software

(G-14237)
BAGEL LAND
1896 Monroe Ave (14618-1918)
PHONE..................................585 442-3080
Robert Juliano, *Owner*
EMP: 20
SALES (est): 1.1MM **Privately Held**
SIC: 2051 5461 Bagels, fresh or frozen; bakeries

(G-14238)
BAGS UNLIMITED INC
7 Canal St (14608-1910)
PHONE..................................585 436-6282
Fax: 585 328-8526
Michael Macaluso, *President*
Marion Oyer, *Controller*
Kris Schofield, *Manager*
Ken Seen, *Manager*
▲ **EMP:** 20
SQ FT: 90,000
SALES (est): 5MM **Privately Held**
WEB: www.bagsunlimited.com
SIC: 2673 2759 Plastic bags: made from purchased materials; bags, plastic: printing

(G-14239)
BAKER COMMODITIES INC
Rochester Division
2268 Browncroft Blvd (14625-1000)
PHONE..................................585 482-1880
Fax: 585 654-7070
Francis Renzaneth, *Division Mgr*
Herbert Bietry, *Controller*
William Schmieder, *Manager*
EMP: 40
SALES (corp-wide): 200.8MM **Privately Held**
WEB: www.bakercommodities.com
SIC: 2077 2048 Tallow rendering, inedible; prepared feeds
PA: Baker Commodities, Inc.
4020 Bandini Blvd
Vernon CA 90058
323 268-2801

(G-14240)
BALIVA CONCRETE PRODUCTS INC
245 Paul Rd (14624-4923)
P.O. Box 24581 (14624-0581)
PHONE..................................585 328-8442
Fax: 585 328-8384
Richard Baliva, *President*
EMP: 6 **EST:** 1943
SQ FT: 3,000
SALES: 1MM **Privately Held**
SIC: 3272 Concrete products

(G-14241)
BAUM CHRISTINE AND JOHN CORP
Also Called: Minuteman Press
1577 W Ridge Rd (14615-2520)
PHONE..................................585 621-8910
Fax: 585 663-8832
John Baum, *President*
Christine Baum, *Vice Pres*
EMP: 9
SQ FT: 2,500
SALES (est): 1.3MM **Privately Held**
SIC: 2752 2791 2789 Commercial printing, lithographic; typesetting; bookbinding & related work

(G-14242)
BAUSCH & LOMB INCORPORATED (DH)
1400 N Goodman St (14609-3596)
P.O. Box 25169, Lehigh Valley PA (18002-5169)
PHONE..................................585 338-6000
Fax: 585 338-5594
Fred Hassan, *Ch of Bd*
Brenton L Saunders, *Ch of Bd*
Robert Bertolini, *President*
Alan H Farnsworth, *Exec VP*
Robert D Bailey, *Vice Pres*
◆ **EMP:** 400
SALES (est): 2.5B
SALES (corp-wide): 9.6B **Privately Held**
WEB: www.bausch.com
SIC: 3851 2834 3841 Ophthalmic goods; contact lenses; magnifiers (readers & simple magnifiers); pharmaceutical preparations; solutions, pharmaceutical; druggists' preparations (pharmaceuticals); vitamin preparations; ophthalmic instruments & apparatus
HQ: Bausch & Lomb Holdings Incorporated
450 Lexington Ave
New York NY 10017
585 338-6000

(G-14243)
BAUSCH & LOMB INCORPORATED
1400 N Goodman St (14609-3596)
PHONE..................................585 338-6000
Bert Dipaola, *Vice Pres*
Paul Erickson, *Vice Pres*
Michael Rowe, *Vice Pres*
Julie Marletta, *Project Mgr*
Larry Kraatz, *Research*
EMP: 400
SQ FT: 2,336
SALES (corp-wide): 9.6B **Privately Held**
WEB: www.bausch.com
SIC: 3851 Ophthalmic goods
HQ: Bausch & Lomb Incorporated
1400 N Goodman St
Rochester NY 14609
585 338-6000

(G-14244)
BEASTONS BUDGET PRINTING
Also Called: Sir Speedy
1260 Scttsvlle Rd Ste 300 (14624)
PHONE..................................585 244-2721
Fax: 585 244-6018
Nancy Beaston, *President*
Shel Beaston, *Vice Pres*
EMP: 9
SALES (est): 1.1MM **Privately Held**
SIC: 2752 2791 2789 Commercial printing, lithographic; typesetting; bookbinding & related work

(G-14245)
BEETS LOVE PRODUCTION LLC
1150 Lee Rd (14606-4251)
PHONE..................................585 270-2471
Dave Stocklosa, *Finance Dir*
EMP: 35
SQ FT: 98,500
SALES: 1.5MM **Privately Held**
SIC: 2063 Beet sugar

(G-14246)
BEREZA IRON WORKS INC
87 Dewey Ave (14608-1289)
PHONE..................................585 254-6311
Fax: 585 254-2533
William Goy, *President*
Irene E Gratton, *Vice Pres*
Terry Baumbarger, *Accounts Mgr*
Lon Nadelen, *Sales Executive*
EMP: 18
SQ FT: 15,000
SALES: 4.4MM **Privately Held**
SIC: 3441 Fabricated structural metal

(G-14247)
BETTER POWER INC
Also Called: Better Light & Power
508 White Spruce Blvd (14623-1613)
PHONE..................................585 475-1321
Fax: 585 424-1193
Catherine Henn, *Owner*
EMP: 6

GEOGRAPHIC SECTION

Rochester - Monroe County (G-14271)

SQ FT: 4,000
SALES (est): 1.5MM **Privately Held**
WEB: www.betterlighting.com
SIC: 3569 Gas generators

(G-14248)
BFGG INVESTORS GROUP LLC
1900 University Ave (14610-2621)
PHONE 585 424-3456
Chris Guider, *Mng Member*
EMP: 5
SALES (est): 530K **Privately Held**
SIC: 3081 Film base, cellulose acetate or nitrocellulose plastic

(G-14249)
BIGSKY TECHNOLOGIES LLC
1600 N Clinton Ave Ste 11 (14621-2200)
PHONE 585 218-9499
Kent Tapper, *Controller*
Cathy A Fleischer, *Mng Member*
EMP: 7
SQ FT: 2,000
SALES (est): 1.3MM **Privately Held**
SIC: 2843 Surface active agents

(G-14250)
BIRDS EYE HOLDINGS INC
90 Linden Park (14625)
PHONE 585 383-1850
David M Hooper, *Author*
Brian Ratzan, *Author*
EMP: 2960
SALES (est): 140.7MM
SALES (corp-wide): 321.9MM **Privately Held**
SIC: 2033 2013 2035 2096 Fruits & fruit products in cans, jars, etc.; fruit pie mixes & fillings: packaged in cans, jars, etc.; canned meats (except baby food) from purchased meat; beef stew from purchased meat; pickles, vinegar; dressings, salad: raw & cooked (except dry mixes); potato chips & other potato-based snacks; cheese curls & puffs
HQ: Vestar/Agrilink Holdings Llc
90 Linden Park
Rochester NY

(G-14251)
BITTNER COMPANY LLC
Also Called: AlphaGraphics
75 Goodway Dr Ste 3 (14623-3000)
PHONE 585 214-1790
EMP: 13
SALES (est): 1.5MM **Privately Held**
SIC: 2752 Comm Prtg Litho

(G-14252)
BLACKBOX BIOMETRICS INC
125 Tech Park Dr Ste 1131 (14623-2438)
PHONE 585 329-3399
Joseph V Bridgeford, *Ch of Bd*
Ryan Ramplin, *Engineer*
David Gillette, *Electrical Engi*
Michael Ostertag, *Electrical Engi*
Scott Featherman, *Sales Staff*
EMP: 22
SALES (est): 2.2MM **Privately Held**
SIC: 3999 Barber & beauty shop equipment

(G-14253)
BLOCH INDUSTRIES LLC
140 Commerce Dr (14623-3504)
P.O. Box 25806 (14625-0806)
PHONE 585 334-9600
Fax: 585 334-9636
Diane Miller, *Office Mgr*
Brian Geary, *Mng Member*
EMP: 60
SQ FT: 54,000
SALES (est): 6.4MM **Privately Held**
WEB: www.blochindustries.com
SIC: 2434 2541 2431 2521 Wood kitchen cabinets, counters or counter display cases, wood; millwork; wood office furniture

(G-14254)
BLUE CHIP MOLD INC
95 Lagrange Ave (14613-1509)
PHONE 585 647-1790
Fax: 585 647-2138
Paul A Engert, *President*
Danielle Champeney, *Manager*

EMP: 13
SQ FT: 10,250
SALES (est): 1.3MM **Privately Held**
SIC: 3544 Industrial molds

(G-14255)
BLUE TOAD HARD CIDER
120 Mushroom Blvd (14623-3263)
PHONE 585 424-5508
Todd Rath, *Co-Owner*
EMP: 20
SALES (est): 2.1MM **Privately Held**
SIC: 3556 Presses, food: cheese, beet, cider & sugarcane

(G-14256)
BMA MEDIA SERVICES INC
Also Called: Spinergy
1655 Lyell Ave (14606-2311)
PHONE 585 385-2060
EMP: 29 EST: 2013
SQ FT: 79,000
SALES (est): 1.7MM **Privately Held**
SIC: 3695 Mfg Magnetic/Optical Recording Media

(G-14257)
BOB PERANI SPORT SHOPS INC
1225 Jefferson Rd (14623-3163)
PHONE 585 427-2930
Raymund House, *Branch Mgr*
EMP: 8
SALES (corp-wide): 12.7MM **Privately Held**
SIC: 3949 Sporting & athletic goods
PA: Bob Perani Sport Shops, Inc.
3600 S Dort Hwy Ste 19
Flint MI 48507
810 744-3338

(G-14258)
BODYCOTE THERMAL PROC INC
620 Buffalo Rd (14611-2006)
PHONE 585 436-7876
Keith Stewart, *Div Sub Head*
Milton Cage, *Opers Mgr*
Christian Miller, *QC Mgr*
Tony Schaut, *Branch Mgr*
EMP: 24
SQ FT: 10,000
SALES (corp-wide): 739.3MM **Privately Held**
SIC: 3398 Metal heat treating
HQ: Bodycote Thermal Processing, Inc.
12700 Park Central Dr # 700
Dallas TX 75251
214 904-2420

(G-14259)
BOEHM SURGICAL INSTRUMENT
966 Chili Ave Ste 3 (14611-2896)
PHONE 585 436-6584
Fax: 585 436-6428
Paul Boehm, *President*
Mary L Cooper, *Corp Secy*
Jean Sullivan, *Treasurer*
EMP: 11 EST: 1915
SQ FT: 13,000
SALES (est): 1MM **Privately Held**
SIC: 3841 3843 3429 3641 Surgical & medical instruments; dental equipment; keys, locks & related hardware; electric lamps & parts for specialized applications

(G-14260)
BOOK1ONE LLC
655 Driving Park Ave (14613-1566)
PHONE 585 458-2101
Peter Pape, *CEO*
Jim Gleason, *Credit Mgr*
Marc Bardeen,
EMP: 7
SALES (est): 1MM **Privately Held**
WEB: www.book1one.com
SIC: 2732 Books: printing & binding

(G-14261)
BOYDELL & BREWER INC
Also Called: Camden House
668 Mount Hope Ave (14620-2731)
PHONE 585 275-0419
Fax: 585 271-8778

Sue Smit, *President*
Sue Miller, *Marketing Staff*
Sue Smith, *Exec Dir*
Eloise Puls, *Director*
Richard Barber, *Intl Dir*
EMP: 12
SQ FT: 1,500
SALES (est): 1.3MM **Privately Held**
SIC: 2731 Book music: publishing only, not printed on site
PA: Boydell & Brewer Group Limited
Bridge Farm Business Park
Woodbridge
139 461-0600

(G-14262)
BRAYLEY TOOL & MACHINE INC
1685 Lyell Ave (14606-2311)
PHONE 585 342-7190
Fax: 585 342-0972
Stephen Roeger, *President*
Rena Roeger, *Vice Pres*
EMP: 8
SQ FT: 6,500
SALES: 700K **Privately Held**
WEB: www.brayleytool.com
SIC: 3544 Special dies, tools, jigs & fixtures

(G-14263)
BRINKMAN INTL GROUP INC (PA)
167 Ames St (14611-1701)
PHONE 585 429-5000
Andrew J Laniak, *CEO*
Robert Brinkman, *Ch of Bd*
Daniel Bavineau, *Mfg Dir*
Dan Robinson, *Engineer*
Ella Gardner, *Controller*
EMP: 1
SQ FT: 12,000
SALES (est): 112.8MM **Privately Held**
WEB: www.brinkmanig.com
SIC: 3545 3451 3325 3542 Thread cutting dies; screw machine products; steel foundries; machine tools, metal forming type

(G-14264)
BRINKMAN PRODUCTS INC (HQ)
Also Called: Davenport
167 Ames St (14611-1701)
PHONE 585 235-4545
Andrew Laniak, *Ch of Bd*
Andrew J Laniak, *President*
Robert J Brinkman, *Principal*
Paul Francia, *Engineer*
Jim Henderson, *Plant Engr*
▲ **EMP:** 290
SQ FT: 118,000
SALES (est): 62MM
SALES (corp-wide): 112.8MM **Privately Held**
WEB: www.davenportmachine.com
SIC: 3541 5084 Machine tools, metal cutting type; industrial machinery & equipment
PA: Brinkman International Group, Inc.
167 Ames St
Rochester NY 14611
585 429-5000

(G-14265)
BRISTOL BOARDING INC
1336 Culver Rd (14609-5336)
PHONE 585 271-7860
Fax: 585 271-3679
Bille McDonald, *President*
Mary McDonald, *Vice Pres*
EMP: 6 EST: 1974
SALES (est): 1MM **Privately Held**
WEB: www.bristolcase.com
SIC: 2441 5099 Shipping cases, wood: nailed or lock corner; cases, carrying

(G-14266)
BUFFALO SPREE PUBLISHING INC
100 Allens Creek Rd Ste 8 (14618-3303)
PHONE 585 413-0040
Laurence Levite, *Branch Mgr*
EMP: 5
SALES (corp-wide): 2.3MM **Privately Held**
SIC: 2721 Periodicals: publishing only

PA: Buffalo Spree Publishing, Inc.
1738 Elmwood Ave Ste 103
Buffalo NY 14207
716 783-9119

(G-14267)
BURKE & BANNAYAN
2465 W Ridge Rd Ste 2 (14626-3046)
PHONE 585 723-1010
Fax: 585 723-1070
Vic Bannayan, *President*
EMP: 5
SQ FT: 2,480
SALES (est): 370K **Privately Held**
SIC: 3911 7631 5944 Jewelry, precious metal; jewelry repair services; jewelry stores

(G-14268)
BURKE FRGING HEAT TREATING INC
30 Sherer St (14611-1618)
PHONE 585 235-6060
Fax: 585 235-6068
Ronald Thompson, *Ch of Bd*
James Granville, *Vice Pres*
Martha Vanderhoof, *Treasurer*
Suzanne Adam, *Credit Mgr*
James Warner, *Sales Mgr*
EMP: 24
SQ FT: 58,000
SALES (est): 5.4MM **Privately Held**
SIC: 3462 3398 Iron & steel forgings; metal heat treating

(G-14269)
BURNETT PROCESS INC (HQ)
545 Colfax St (14606-3111)
PHONE 585 254-8080
Jack Cannon, *Ch of Bd*
Scott Peters, *Senior Engr*
Peat Howlard, *Assistant*
▲ **EMP:** 1
SQ FT: 60,000
SALES (est): 5.4MM
SALES (corp-wide): 38.7MM **Privately Held**
WEB: www.burnettprocessinc.com
SIC: 3296 3086 7699 Fiberglass insulation; plastics foam products; industrial equipment services
PA: Cannon Industries, Inc.
525 Lee Rd
Rochester NY 14606
585 254-8080

(G-14270)
BURNETT PROCESS INC
545 Colfax St (14606-3111)
PHONE 585 277-1623
Paul Campbell, *Purchasing*
Ronald Salayda, *Manager*
Gerhard Drechsler, *Manager*
EMP: 30
SALES (corp-wide): 43MM **Privately Held**
WEB: www.burnettprocessinc.com
SIC: 3569 Filters
HQ: Burnett Process, Inc.
545 Colfax St
Rochester NY 14606
585 254-8080

(G-14271)
C J WINTER MACHINE TECH (HQ)
167 Ames St (14611-1701)
PHONE 585 429-5000
Robert Brinkman, *President*
Dave Ostrander, *Plant Mgr*
Liberato Pietrantoni, *Research*
Philip Daggar, *Treasurer*
Connie Tribotte, *Personnel*
EMP: 20 EST: 1933
SQ FT: 118,000
SALES (est): 4MM
SALES (corp-wide): 112.8MM **Privately Held**
WEB: www.cjwinter.com
SIC: 3545 3542 3325 Thread cutting dies; machine tools, metal forming type; steel foundries
PA: Brinkman International Group, Inc.
167 Ames St
Rochester NY 14611
585 429-5000

Rochester - Monroe County (G-14272)

GEOGRAPHIC SECTION

(G-14272)
C R C MANUFACTURING INC
37 Curlew St (14606-2535)
PHONE.................................585 254-8820
Fax: 585 254-8859
Todd Chapman, *CEO*
Brian Van Ocker, *Admin Sec*
EMP: 10
SQ FT: 7,000
SALES (est): 1.1MM **Privately Held**
SIC: 3599 3451 Machine shop, jobbing & repair; screw machine products

(G-14273)
CALIBER IMGING DIAGNOSTICS INC (PA)
50 Methodist Hill Dr (14623-4267)
PHONE.................................585 239-9800
L Michael Hone, *CEO*
William J Shea, *Ch of Bd*
Marcy K Davis-Mchugh, *COO*
Robert P Fischmann, *Vice Pres*
William J Fox, *Vice Pres*
EMP: 35
SQ FT: 20,000
SALES: 3.3MM **Publicly Held**
WEB: www.lucid-tech.com
SIC: 3827 3845 3841 Optical instruments & lenses; electromedical equipment; surgical & medical instruments

(G-14274)
CAMPUS CRAFTS INC
160 Murray St (14606-1151)
P.O. Box 60650 (14606-0650)
PHONE.................................585 328-6780
Fax: 585 328-0898
Greg Weinrieb, *President*
Kathleen Weinrieb, *Corp Secy*
▲ **EMP:** 6 **EST:** 1970
SQ FT: 7,000
SALES (est): 840.7K **Privately Held**
WEB: www.campuscrafts.com
SIC: 3231 Strengthened or reinforced glass; mirrored glass

(G-14275)
CANFIELD & TACK INC
Also Called: Dellas Graphics
925 Exchange St (14608-2802)
PHONE.................................585 235-7710
Fax: 585 235-4166
Michael Guche, *CEO*
Ray Brown, *President*
Gary Cvejic, *COO*
EMP: 85 **EST:** 1926
SQ FT: 45,000
SALES (est): 25.9MM **Privately Held**
WEB: www.canfieldtack.com
SIC: 2752 4225 Commercial printing, offset; general warehousing & storage

(G-14276)
CANNON INDUSTRIES INC (PA)
525 Lee Rd (14606-4236)
PHONE.................................585 254-8080
Jack Cannon, *CEO*
Reggie Cannon, *President*
Scott Thomas, *VP Opers*
Kiet Tran, *Plant Mgr*
Bruce Canon, *Prdtn Mgr*
▲ **EMP:** 97
SQ FT: 100,000
SALES (est): 43MM **Privately Held**
WEB: www.cannonind.com
SIC: 3444 3469 5051 3861 Sheet metalwork; metal stampings; metals service centers & offices; photocopy machines

(G-14277)
CAPS TEAMWEAR INC
65 Milburn St (14607-2914)
PHONE.................................585 663-1750
Roy Brewer Jr, *Manager*
EMP: 5
SALES (est): 320.9K **Privately Held**
SIC: 2329 Men's & boys' sportswear & athletic clothing

(G-14278)
CARESTREAM HEALTH INC
1669 Lake Ave (14652-0001)
PHONE.................................585 627-1800
EMP: 300
SALES (corp-wide): 22.5B **Publicly Held**
SIC: 3861 Photographic equipment & supplies
HQ: Carestream Health, Inc.
150 Verona St
Rochester NY 14608
585 627-1800

(G-14279)
CARTA USA LLC
1600 Lexington Ave # 116 (14606-3061)
PHONE.................................585 436-3012
Fax: 585 436-3018
Mike Welch, *General Mgr*
Jake Carey, *Vice Pres*
Josh Cummings, *Sales Mgr*
Connie Jarosinski, *Sales Associate*
▲ **EMP:** 20
SALES (est): 465.1K
SALES (corp-wide): 95.4MM **Privately Held**
SIC: 2621 Paper mills
PA: Flower City Printing, Inc.
1725 Mount Read Blvd
Rochester NY 14606
585 663-9000

(G-14280)
CARTER STREET BAKERY INC
580 Child St (14606-1158)
PHONE.................................585 749-7104
Takele Delnesa, *President*
EMP: 8 **EST:** 2015
SALES (est): 371.1K **Privately Held**
SIC: 2051 Bakery: wholesale or wholesale/retail combined

(G-14281)
CARTERS INC
3349 Monroe Ave (14618-5513)
PHONE.................................585 387-9043
EMP: 5
SALES (corp-wide): 3.2B **Publicly Held**
SIC: 2361 Girls' & children's dresses, blouses & shirts
PA: Carter's, Inc.
3438 Peachtree Rd Ne # 1800
Atlanta GA 30326
678 791-1000

(G-14282)
CASUAL FRIDAY INC
1561 Lyell Ave (14606-2123)
PHONE.................................585 544-9470
Anthony Germano, *President*
John Lansdown, *Manager*
Renee Yell, *Art Dir*
EMP: 12
SQ FT: 6,000
SALES (est): 1.6MM **Privately Held**
SIC: 2396 Fabric printing & stamping

(G-14283)
CDJ STAMPING INC
146 Halstead St Ste 123 (14610-1954)
PHONE.................................585 224-8120
Fax: 585 224-8201
Timothy Merklinger, *President*
Jason Schulmerich, *Vice Pres*
EMP: 5
SQ FT: 4,000
SALES (est): 366K **Privately Held**
WEB: www.cdjstamping.com
SIC: 3089 Plastic processing

(G-14284)
CEIPAL LLC
722 Weiland Rd (14626-3957)
PHONE.................................585 351-2934
EMP: 5 **EST:** 2014
SQ FT: 3,000
SALES (est): 300K **Privately Held**
SIC: 7372 Prepackaged Software Services

(G-14285)
CEIPAL LLC
687 Lee Rd Ste 208a (14606-4257)
PHONE.................................585 584-1316
Deepika Nampally, *Sales Staff*
Sameer Penakalapati, *Mng Member*
Mitch Meller,
EMP: 5
SALES (est): 193.8K **Privately Held**
SIC: 7372 Prepackaged software; application computer software; business oriented computer software

(G-14286)
CELLEC TECHNOLOGIES INC
125 Tech Park Dr Ste 2111 (14623-2448)
PHONE.................................585 454-9166
Christopher Schauerman, *President*
Brian Landi, *Vice Pres*
Ryne Raffaelle, *Vice Pres*
Matthew Ganter, *Treasurer*
EMP: 5
SALES (est): 229.9K **Privately Held**
SIC: 3691 Storage batteries

(G-14287)
CENTURY MOLD COMPANY INC (PA)
25 Vantage Point Dr (14624-1142)
PHONE.................................585 352-8600
Fax: 585 352-8609
Ron Ricotta, *CEO*
John Buckley, *Plant Mgr*
Richard Liberte, *Plant Mgr*
Terry Hog, *Purchasing*
Gavin Simpson, *Purchasing*
▲ **EMP:** 100 **EST:** 1978
SQ FT: 80,000
SALES (est): 203.7MM **Privately Held**
WEB: www.centurymold.com
SIC: 3089 3544 Injection molding of plastics; industrial molds

(G-14288)
CENTURY MOLD MEXICO LLC (HQ)
25 Vantage Point Dr (14624-1142)
PHONE.................................585 352-8600
Melissa Hayes, *Controller*
Ronald Ricotta,
▲ **EMP:** 6
SALES (est): 46MM
SALES (corp-wide): 203.7MM **Privately Held**
SIC: 3089 Injection molding of plastics
PA: Century Mold Company, Inc.
25 Vantage Point Dr
Rochester NY 14624
585 352-8600

(G-14289)
CERION ENERGY INC
1 Blossom Rd (14610-1009)
PHONE.................................585 271-5630
George M Stadler, *CEO*
Landon Mertz, *Ch of Bd*
Bruce Brown, *VP Sales*
Garner Corby, *VP Sales*
▼ **EMP:** 25
SALES (est): 5MM **Privately Held**
SIC: 2819 Industrial inorganic chemicals

(G-14290)
CERION LLC
1 Blossom Rd (14610-1009)
PHONE.................................585 271-5630
Matt Winslow, *COO*
Dana Black, *Accounts Mgr*
Jan Back, *Marketing Staff*
George M Stadler,
EMP: 15
SALES (est): 2.8MM **Privately Held**
SIC: 2819 Industrial inorganic chemicals

(G-14291)
CHAMBERLIN RUBBER COMPANY INC
3333 Brighton Henrietta (14623-2842)
P.O. Box 22700 (14692-2700)
PHONE.................................585 427-7780
Fax: 585 427-2429
Philip Collins, *President*
Stephen Anderson, *Vice Pres*
Jerome Stomper, *Vice Pres*
John Giancursio, *Opers Mgr*
Scott Bready, *Opers Staff*
▲ **EMP:** 31
SQ FT: 30,000
SALES: 8.6MM **Privately Held**
WEB: www.crubber.com
SIC: 3069 Rubber automotive products

(G-14292)
CHAMPION PHOTOCHEMISTRY INC
1669 Lake Ave (14615)
PHONE.................................585 760-6444
R Fraser Mason, *Ch of Bd*
Peter Newton, *President*
Brian Bingaman, *Finance Mgr*
◆ **EMP:** 65
SQ FT: 375,000
SALES: 10.5MM
SALES (corp-wide): 207.3K **Privately Held**
WEB: www.championphotochemistry.com
SIC: 3861 Photographic processing chemicals
HQ: Champion Photochemistry Limited
1760 Meyerside Dr
Mississauga ON L5T 1
905 670-7900

(G-14293)
CHAMTEK MFG INC
123 Louise St (14606-1321)
PHONE.................................585 328-4900
Fax: 585 328-2938
Donald Zenkel, *President*
Franklin Chamberlain, *Corp Secy*
Thomas Williams, *Vice Pres*
Derick Samson, *Sales Staff*
Kathy Johnson, *Office Mgr*
EMP: 27
SQ FT: 18,000
SALES: 2.3MM **Privately Held**
WEB: www.chamtek.com
SIC: 3544 3444 Special dies, tools, jigs & fixtures; sheet metalwork

(G-14294)
CHECKLIST BOARDS CORPORATION
763 Linden Ave Ste 2 (14625-2725)
PHONE.................................585 586-0152
Rick Taylor, *President*
Jim Wemett, *Vice Pres*
EMP: 5
SALES: 500K **Privately Held**
SIC: 3993 Signs, not made in custom sign painting shops

(G-14295)
CHINA IMPRINT LLC
750 Saint Paul St (14605-1737)
PHONE.................................585 563-3391
Christopher Adams, *CFO*
William A Dolan II,
▲ **EMP:** 5
SQ FT: 20,000
SALES: 2MM **Privately Held**
SIC: 2752 Promotional printing, lithographic

(G-14296)
CHRISTI PLASTICS INC
215 Tremont St (14608-2393)
PHONE.................................585 436-8510
Fax: 585 436-8519
Earl Martin, *President*
Deborah Scally, *Corp Secy*
EMP: 4
SQ FT: 10,500
SALES: 1.1MM **Privately Held**
SIC: 3089 Extruded finished plastic products

(G-14297)
CITY NEWSPAPER
250 N Goodman St Ste 1 (14607-1199)
PHONE.................................585 244-3329
Fax: 585 244-1126
Mary Towler, *Publisher*
Bill Towler, *Publisher*
Jake Clapp, *Editor*
Chris Fien, *Editor*
Eric Rezsnyak, *Editor*
EMP: 6
SALES (est): 420.9K **Privately Held**
SIC: 2711 Newspapers, publishing & printing

(G-14298)
CJK MANUFACTURING LLC
160 Commerce Dr (14623-3504)
PHONE.................................585 663-6370
Keith Woodward,
Charles Tutty,
EMP: 14
SQ FT: 20,000
SALES (est): 3.1MM **Privately Held**
WEB: www.cjkmanufacturing.com
SIC: 3089 Thermoformed finished plastic products

▲ = Import ▼=Export
◆ =Import/Export

GEOGRAPHIC SECTION
Rochester - Monroe County (G-14322)

(G-14299)
CLARSONS CORP
Also Called: Express Press
215 Tremont St Ste 8 (14608-2366)
PHONE 585 235-8775
Fax: 585 235-7847
David Clar, *President*
Robert M Clar, *President*
Michael Cwikinski, *VP Prdtn*
Joan Clar, *Admin Sec*
EMP: 11
SQ FT: 4,000
SALES (est): 1MM **Privately Held**
WEB: www.expresspress.com
SIC: 2752 2791 7334 Commercial printing, offset; typesetting; photocopying & duplicating services

(G-14300)
CLERIO VISION INC
312 Susquehanna Rd (14618-2940)
PHONE 617 216-7881
Mikael Totterman, *President*
EMP: 12
SQ FT: 2,000
SALES (est): 860K **Privately Held**
SIC: 3841 Surgical lasers

(G-14301)
CLUB 1100
1100 Jay St (14611-1131)
PHONE 585 235-3478
Louis Vertiz, *Owner*
EMP: 5
SQ FT: 4,112
SALES (est): 230K **Privately Held**
WEB: www.1100club.com
SIC: 2033 5813 Fruit juices: fresh; tavern (drinking places)

(G-14302)
COAST TO COAST CIRCUITS INC
Metro Circuits
205 Lagrange Ave (14613-1562)
PHONE 585 254-2980
Walter Stender, *CEO*
Walt Stender, *CEO*
Cheryl Covert, *Principal*
Burhen Capar, *Opers-Prdtn-Mfg*
Kevin Jacobus, *Engineer*
EMP: 45
SALES (corp-wide): 19.7MM **Privately Held**
WEB: www.speedycircuits.com
SIC: 3672 Wiring boards
PA: Coast To Coast Circuits, Inc.
5331 Mcfadden Ave
Huntington Beach CA 92649
585 254-2980

(G-14303)
COATING TECHNOLOGY INC
800 Saint Paul St (14605-1032)
PHONE 585 546-7170
Fax: 585 546-7202
Stanley Dahle, *Ch of Bd*
Ronald L Feeley, *President*
Bryant Dunham, *QC Mgr*
EMP: 30
SQ FT: 40,000
SALES (est): 3.6MM
SALES (corp-wide): 17.1MM **Privately Held**
WEB: www.coatingtechnologyinc.com
SIC: 3471 Plating of metals or formed products
PA: The Metal Arts Company Inc
800 Saint Paul St
Rochester NY

(G-14304)
COLOR ME MINE
3349 Monroe Ave Ste 32 (14618-5513)
PHONE 585 383-8420
Fax: 585 383-8425
Joe Maxon, *Owner*
Lynn Maxon, *Co-Owner*
EMP: 15
SALES (est): 660.7K **Privately Held**
SIC: 3479 Painting, coating & hot dipping

(G-14305)
CONDOR ELECTRONICS CORP
295 Mount Read Blvd (14611-1931)
P.O. Box 60590 (14606-0590)
PHONE 585 235-1500
Fax: 585 235-0552
Wayne S Corso, *President*
Lisa Corso, *Corp Secy*
Margaret Fox, *Purchasing*
▲ **EMP:** 30
SQ FT: 18,000
SALES (est): 4.3MM **Privately Held**
WEB: www.condorelectronics.com
SIC: 3679 Harness assemblies for electronic use: wire or cable

(G-14306)
CONE BUDDY SYSTEM INC
3495 Winton Pl Ste E290 (14623-2819)
PHONE 585 427-9940
Fax: 585 427-2403
Robert Sotile, *President*
EMP: 15 EST: 1994
SALES (est): 1.4MM **Privately Held**
WEB: www.buddysystemusa.com
SIC: 2052 Cones, ice cream

(G-14307)
CONNECTION MOLD INC
585 Ling Rd (14612-1936)
PHONE 585 458-6463
Fax: 585 254-7825
Thomas Strecker, *President*
Reiner Strecker, *Vice Pres*
Tom Hockborn, *Design Engr*
David Schwenger, *Design Engr*
EMP: 7
SQ FT: 6,800
SALES (est): 1MM **Privately Held**
WEB: www.connectionmold.com
SIC: 3965 Button blanks & molds

(G-14308)
CONOPCO INC
28 Mansfield St (14606-2327)
PHONE 585 647-8322
John Frank, *Branch Mgr*
EMP: 35
SALES (corp-wide): 55.5B **Privately Held**
SIC: 2844 Toilet preparations
HQ: Conopco, Inc.
700 Sylvan Ave
Englewood Cliffs NJ 07632
201 894-2727

(G-14309)
CONSOLIDATED CONTAINER CO LLC
Also Called: Liquitane
18 Champeney Ter (14605-2711)
PHONE 585 262-6470
Fax: 585 262-3521
Jerry Zaklick, *Plant Mgr*
Peter Schulick, *Mfg Staff*
Brian Avery, *Executive*
EMP: 150
SALES (corp-wide): 13.1B **Publicly Held**
WEB: www.ccclllc.com
SIC: 2655 2656 Fiber cans, drums & containers; sanitary food containers
HQ: Consolidated Container Company, Llc
3101 Towercreek Pkwy Se
Atlanta GA 30339
678 742-4600

(G-14310)
CORBETT STVES PTTERN WORKS INC
80 Lowell St (14605-1831)
PHONE 585 546-7109
Fax: 585 546-6157
John K Steeves Jr, *President*
Kevin Steeves, *Vice Pres*
George Williams, *Controller*
Jorge Williams, *Controller*
Sandy Erickson, *Manager*
EMP: 20 EST: 1914
SQ FT: 20,000
SALES (est): 3.6MM **Privately Held**
WEB: www.corbett-steeves.com
SIC: 3365 3599 3553 3469 Machinery castings, aluminum; machine shop, jobbing & repair; pattern makers' machinery, woodworking; patterns on metal

(G-14311)
COUNTY WD APPLNC & TV SRVC OF
95 Mount Read Blvd Ste 14 (14611-1936)
PHONE 585 328-7417
Fax: 585 328-0983
Stephen Greczyn, *President*
Judy Greczyn, *Vice Pres*
EMP: 10
SQ FT: 2,600
SALES (est): 1.6MM **Privately Held**
SIC: 3357 Appliance fixture wire, nonferrous

(G-14312)
CRAFTSMAN MANUFACTURING CO IN
1279 Mount Read Blvd (14606-2817)
PHONE 585 426-5780
Fax: 585 426-2617
Kevin Contestabile, *President*
EMP: 5
SQ FT: 3,000
SALES (est): 320K **Privately Held**
SIC: 3599 Machine shop, jobbing & repair

(G-14313)
CRYOVAC INC
1525 Brooks Ave (14624-3545)
PHONE 585 436-3211
Antonio Ramon, *Human Resources*
Mark Davis, *Manager*
Faith Foo, *Manager*
Diane Vongelis, *Manager*
EMP: 150
SALES (corp-wide): 6.7B **Publicly Held**
WEB: www.cryovac.com
SIC: 3087 Custom compound purchased resins
HQ: Cryovac, Inc.
2415 Cascade Pointe Blvd
Charlotte NC 28208
980 430-7000

(G-14314)
CRYSTAL LINTON TECHNOLOGIES
2180 Brigh Henri Town Lin (14623)
PHONE 585 444-8784
Rick Webb, *COO*
Gary Goyette, *Engineer*
Thanasis Gkourlias, *Electrical Engi*
Melissa Logan, *Manager*
Brian Repman, *Manager*
EMP: 11 EST: 2013
SQ FT: 15,713
SALES (est): 2.6MM **Privately Held**
SIC: 3821 Furnaces, laboratory

(G-14315)
CSW INC
Also Called: Diegraphics Group
70 Pixley Industrial Pkwy (14624-2377)
PHONE 585 247-4010
Ann Lukasik, *General Mgr*
Ed Begy, *Prdtn Mgr*
Mark Buchanan, *Prdtn Mgr*
Tom Harris, *Prdtn Mgr*
James Mootz, *Production*
EMP: 15
SALES (corp-wide): 16MM **Privately Held**
WEB: www.citystamp.com
SIC: 3555 2796 2791 Printing plates; platemaking services; typesetting
PA: Csw, Inc.
45 Tyburski Rd
Ludlow MA 01056
413 589-1311

(G-14316)
CURAEGIS TECHNOLOGIES INC (PA)
1999 Mount Read Blvd # 3 (14615-3700)
PHONE 585 254-1100
Richard A Kaplan, *CEO*
Gary A Siconolfi, *Ch of Bd*
Keith E Gleasman, *President*
Kathleen A Browne, *CFO*
Colette Christen, *Accounts Mgr*
EMP: 24
SQ FT: 13,650

SALES: 26K **Publicly Held**
WEB: www.torvec.com
SIC: 7372 3561 Business oriented computer software; pumps & pumping equipment

(G-14317)
CUSTOM SOUND AND VIDEO
Also Called: Casco Security
40 Rutter St (14606-1806)
PHONE 585 424-5000
Casimer S Plonczynski, *President*
Rosa F Ladelfa, *Business Mgr*
Bee Ong, *Accountant*
Cecelia Percle, *Finance*
EMP: 20
SQ FT: 6,500
SALES (est): 2.2MM **Privately Held**
SIC: 3699 5731 7629 Security devices; radio, television & electronic stores; electronic equipment repair

(G-14318)
CVI LASER LLC
Also Called: Melles Griot
55 Science Pkwy (14620-4258)
PHONE 585 244-7220
David Durfee, *Engineer*
Carrie Royer, *Engineer*
David Stephenson, *Engineer*
William Polito, *Controller*
Chuck Synborski, *Branch Mgr*
EMP: 100
SALES (corp-wide): 2.1B **Publicly Held**
SIC: 3827 3699 Optical instruments & lenses; laser systems & equipment
HQ: Cvi Laser, Llc
200 Dorado Pl Se
Albuquerque NM 87123
505 296-9541

(G-14319)
DAGOSTINO IRON WORKS INC
10 Deep Rock Rd (14624-3520)
PHONE 585 235-8850
Fax: 585 328-5710
Kenneth J D'Agostino Jr, *President*
Kenneth Dagostino, *Project Mgr*
Amy King, *Manager*
EMP: 9
SQ FT: 4,000
SALES (est): 750K **Privately Held**
SIC: 3312 Blast furnaces & steel mills

(G-14320)
DAILY RECORD (PA)
Also Called: Daily Media
16 W Main St Ste G9 (14614-1604)
PHONE 585 232-2035
Fax: 585 232-2740
Jim Dolan, *President*
Tracy Bartlett, *Advt Staff*
EMP: 10 EST: 1908
SQ FT: 36,000
SALES (est): 654K **Privately Held**
WEB: www.dailyrecord.com
SIC: 2752 2711 Commercial printing, lithographic; newspapers, publishing & printing

(G-14321)
DANISCO US INC
Also Called: Genencor Division Danisco US
3490 Winton Pl (14623-2829)
PHONE 585 256-5200
Randy Fisher, *Production*
Robert Villas, *Manager*
Andrea Logan, *Supervisor*
David Charest, *Director*
EMP: 75
SALES (corp-wide): 72.7B **Publicly Held**
SIC: 2835 8731 2899 2869 In vitro & in vivo diagnostic substances; commercial physical research; chemical preparations; industrial organic chemicals
HQ: Danisco Us Inc.
925 Page Mill Rd
Palo Alto CA 94304
650 846-7500

(G-14322)
DANISCO US INC
Also Called: Genencor International
1700 Lexington Ave (14606-3140)
PHONE 585 277-4300
Nancy Ritz, *Human Resources*

Rochester - Monroe County (G-14323)   GEOGRAPHIC SECTION

Cindy Boston, *Marketing Staff*
Thomas Mitchell, *Branch Mgr*
Peggy Kriger, *Manager*
Robert Villas, *Manager*
EMP: 100
SALES (corp-wide): 72.7B **Publicly Held**
SIC: 2819 2087 Industrial inorganic chemicals; flavoring extracts & syrups
HQ: Danisco Us Inc.
  925 Page Mill Rd
  Palo Alto CA 94304
  650 846-7500

(G-14323)
DAYTON ROGERS NEW YORK LLC
150 Fedex Way (14624-1174)
PHONE..................585 349-4040
Fax: 585 349-4049
Ron Lowry, *CEO*
Rich Vanaernum, *General Mgr*
Thomas A Pilon, *Vice Pres*
Jesse Wolfanger, *Mfg Mgr*
David Buccini, *Engineer*
EMP: 60
SQ FT: 38,000
SALES (est): 10.7MM
SALES (corp-wide): 76.6MM **Privately Held**
SIC: 3469 Metal stampings
PA: Dayton Rogers Manufacturing Co.
  8401 W 35w Service Dr Ne
  Minneapolis MN 55449
  763 717-6450

(G-14324)
DEAD RINGER LLC
2100 Brghton Hnrtta St375 Ste 375 (14623)
PHONE..................585 355-4685
Kristian Meyer, *Vice Pres*
Jesse Erdle,
▲ **EMP:** 2 **EST:** 2011
SALES: 2.6MM **Privately Held**
SIC: 3423 5091 Hand & edge tools; sharpeners, sporting goods

(G-14325)
DEAL INTERNATIONAL INC
110 Halstead St Ste 1 (14610-1952)
P.O. Box 10088 (14610-0088)
PHONE..................585 288-4444
Menish Damani, *President*
Alice Barbarito, *Manager*
▲ **EMP:** 26
SQ FT: 6,000
SALES (est): 5.1MM **Privately Held**
WEB: www.diihq.com
SIC: 2891 Sealants

(G-14326)
DEES AUDIO & VISION
347 Seneca Pkwy (14613-1416)
PHONE..................585 719-9256
EMP: 5
SALES (est): 150K **Privately Held**
SIC: 3571 Electronics/Audio/Sales

(G-14327)
DIAMOND PACKAGING HOLDINGS LLC
111 Commerce Dr (14623-3503)
PHONE..................585 334-8030
Dave Rydell, *Vice Pres*
Keith Robinson,
EMP: 8
SALES (est): 1MM **Privately Held**
SIC: 2657 3089 Food containers, folding: made from purchased material; air mattresses, plastic

(G-14328)
DIEMAX OF ROCHESTER INC
1555 Lyell Ave Ste 141 (14606-2148)
PHONE..................585 288-3912
Richard J Oliver, *President*
Wayne Rotella, *Vice Pres*
Ryan Prue, *Treasurer*
▲ **EMP:** 7
SQ FT: 900
SALES (est): 998.2K **Privately Held**
WEB: www.diemax.com
SIC: 3544 Special dies & tools

(G-14329)
DIGITRONIK DEV LABS INC
181 Saint Paul St Apt 6d (14604-1127)
PHONE..................585 360-0043
Shawn Mott, *Ch of Bd*
Christopher Coon, *Vice Pres*
Stephan Mokey, *Treasurer*
Darren Dewispelaere, *Marketing Staff*
David Coon, *Admin Sec*
EMP: 12
SQ FT: 1,000
SALES: 350K **Privately Held**
SIC: 3823 8731 8711 7371 Controllers for process variables, all types; computer (hardware) development; engineering services; custom computer programming services

(G-14330)
DIMENSION TECHNOLOGIES INC
Also Called: D T I
315 Mount Read Blvd Ste 5 (14611-1900)
PHONE..................585 436-3530
Fax: 585 436-3280
Arnold Lagergren, *CEO*
Arnold D Lagergren, *President*
Michael Casciano, *President*
Jesse B Eichenlaub, *Vice Pres*
Michael Farrell, *Purch Mgr*
EMP: 5
SQ FT: 3,400
SALES (est): 1MM **Privately Held**
WEB: www.dti3d.com
SIC: 3679 Liquid crystal displays (LCD)

(G-14331)
DIPAOLO BAKING CO INC
598 Plymouth Ave N (14608-1691)
PHONE..................585 303-5013
Fax: 585 423-5975
Dominick P Massa, *President*
Stephen Woerner, *Vice Pres*
EMP: 80 **EST:** 1910
SQ FT: 30,000
SALES (est): 12.7MM **Privately Held**
WEB: www.dipaolobread.com
SIC: 2051 5461 Bread, all types (white, wheat, rye, etc): fresh or frozen; rolls, bread type: fresh or frozen; bakeries; bread

(G-14332)
DISTECH SYSTEMS INC (HQ)
1000 University Ave # 400 (14607-1286)
PHONE..................585 254-7020
Fax: 585 254-1905
John J Perrotti, *CEO*
Dan Schwab, *President*
Thomas Fitzsimmons, *VP Opers*
Jason Snell, *Project Mgr*
Loreen Deperna, *Buyer*
▲ **EMP:** 3
SQ FT: 12,900
SALES (est): 7.6MM
SALES (corp-wide): 1B **Privately Held**
WEB: www.distechsystems.com
SIC: 3569 Assembly machines, non-metalworking
PA: Gleason Corporation
  1000 University Ave
  Rochester NY 14607
  585 473-1000

(G-14333)
DIVERSIFIED ENVELOPE LTD
95 Mount Read Blvd # 103 (14611-1923)
PHONE..................585 615-4697
Fax: 585 527-8106
Robert Eckert, *President*
EMP: 10
SQ FT: 13,000
SALES: 1MM **Privately Held**
WEB: www.diversifiedenvelope.com
SIC: 2759 2752 5112 Envelopes: printing; commercial printing, lithographic; envelopes

(G-14334)
DIXON TOOL AND MANUFACTURING
240 Burrows St (14606-2637)
PHONE..................585 235-1352
Fax: 585 235-8465
Rober Hyder, *President*
EMP: 10
SQ FT: 5,224
SALES (est): 1.2MM **Privately Held**
SIC: 3544 Special dies & tools

(G-14335)
DOCK HARDWARE INCORPORATED
Also Called: Rogers Enterprises
24 Seneca Ave Ste 4 (14621-2387)
P.O. Box 17266 (14617-0266)
PHONE..................585 266-7920
Garry Rogers, *President*
Mike Chiumento, *Director*
EMP: 10
SALES (est): 960K **Privately Held**
WEB: www.dockhardware.com
SIC: 3545 Machine tool accessories

(G-14336)
DOCUMENT STRATEGIES LLC
185 Gibbs St (14605-2907)
PHONE..................585 506-9000
James Bowen, *Principal*
Jeremy Hutchinson, *Software Dev*
EMP: 12
SALES (est): 536.9K **Privately Held**
SIC: 7372 Application computer software

(G-14337)
DOLOMITE PRODUCTS COMPANY INC (DH)
Also Called: Shadow Lake Golf & Racquet CLB
1150 Penfield Rd (14625-2202)
PHONE..................315 524-1998
John M Odenbach Jr, *President*
John Siel, *Chairman*
Russ Larocca, *Senior VP*
Gardner Odenbach, *Treasurer*
Mike Bagne, *Manager*
EMP: 25 **EST:** 1920
SQ FT: 5,000
SALES (est): 26.2MM
SALES (corp-wide): 28.6B **Privately Held**
WEB: www.dolomitegroup.com
SIC: 2951 1422 5031 8741 Paving mixtures; dolomite, crushed & broken-quarrying; building materials, exterior; building materials, interior; circuit management for motion picture theaters; golf club, membership; golf, tennis & ski shops

(G-14338)
DRAPERY INDUSTRIES INC
175 Humboldt St Ste 222 (14610-1060)
PHONE..................585 232-2992
Fax: 585 325-6290
Mark Kosinski, *President*
David Geen, *Vice Pres*
Diane Russell, *Manager*
EMP: 14
SQ FT: 8,000
SALES (est): 1.6MM **Privately Held**
WEB: www.draperyindustries.com
SIC: 2391 2591 1799 Curtains, window: made from purchased materials; draperies, plastic & textile: from purchased materials; window blinds; home/office interiors finishing, furnishing & remodeling; drapery track installation

(G-14339)
DYNA-TECH QUALITY INC
1570 Emerson St (14606-3118)
PHONE..................585 458-9970
Andy Masters, *President*
EMP: 5 **EST:** 1998
SALES (est): 362.4K **Privately Held**
SIC: 3599 Machine shop, jobbing & repair

(G-14340)
DYNAMASTERS INC
1570 Emerson St (14606-3118)
PHONE..................585 458-9970
Andy Mastrodonato Sr, *President*
EMP: 5 **EST:** 2008
SALES (est): 440K **Privately Held**
SIC: 3569 Assembly machines, non-metalworking

(G-14341)
DYNAMIC DIES INC
70 Pixley Industrial Pkwy (14624-2377)
PHONE..................585 247-4010
Fax: 585 247-7203
EMP: 14
SALES (corp-wide): 22.2MM **Privately Held**
SIC: 3544 Mfg Dies/Tools/Jigs/Fixtures
PA: Dynamic Dies, Inc.
  1705 Commerce Rd
  Holland OH 43528
  419 865-0249

(G-14342)
E I DU PONT DE NEMOURS & CO
Also Called: Dupont
69 Seneca Ave (14621-2316)
PHONE..................585 339-4200
Thomas Walter, *Engineer*
Donna Newhart, *Human Res Mgr*
Shona Fullerton, *Marketing Staff*
Frank Pinkosky, *Planning Mgr*
EMP: 50
SQ FT: 24,546
SALES (corp-wide): 72.7B **Publicly Held**
WEB: www.dupont.com
SIC: 2819 2899 Industrial inorganic chemicals; chemical preparations
HQ: E. I. Du Pont De Nemours And Company
  974 Centre Rd
  Wilmington DE 19805
  302 774-1000

(G-14343)
EAGLE GRAPHICS INC
149 Anderson Ave (14607-1106)
PHONE..................585 244-5006
Fax: 585 244-5884
Nancy Powell, *President*
Michael W Powell, *Vice Pres*
EMP: 9 **EST:** 1977
SQ FT: 10,000
SALES (est): 1.5MM **Privately Held**
WEB: www.eaglegraphicsinc.com
SIC: 2752 Commercial printing, lithographic

(G-14344)
EAST RIDGE QUICK PRINT
1249 Ridgeway Ave Ste Y (14615-3761)
PHONE..................585 266-4911
Fax: 585 266-2721
Richard San Angelo, *President*
Janice San Angelo, *Vice Pres*
EMP: 15
SQ FT: 6,000
SALES (est): 1.5MM **Privately Held**
WEB: www.eastridgequickprint.com
SIC: 2752 Commercial printing, offset

(G-14345)
EAST SIDE DEVELOPMENT CORP
Also Called: Arctic Wholesale Refrigeration
274 N Goodman St (14607-1154)
PHONE..................585 242-9219
William E Stong, *President*
Alex Primakov, *Manager*
EMP: 6
SQ FT: 13,000
SALES (est): 1MM **Privately Held**
SIC: 3699 7629 5064 Household electrical equipment; electrical household appliance repair; electric household appliances

(G-14346)
EASTMAN CHEMICAL COMPANY
2255 Mount Read Blvd (14615-2712)
PHONE..................585 722-2905
Brian Bennett, *Research*
Anthony Debboli, *Manager*
EMP: 60 **Publicly Held**
WEB: www.eastman.com
SIC: 2869 Industrial organic chemicals
PA: Eastman Chemical Company
  200 S Wilcox Dr
  Kingsport TN 37660

(G-14347)
EASTMAN KODAK COMPANY
233 Olde Harbour Trl (14612-2936)
PHONE..................585 722-2187
Fax: 585 726-2700
Gus Gleichauf, *Principal*
Dale Lipscomb, *Human Res Mgr*
EMP: 65

GEOGRAPHIC SECTION

Rochester - Monroe County (G-14372)

SALES (corp-wide): 1.8B **Publicly Held**
SIC: 3861 Film, sensitized motion picture, X-ray, still camera, etc.
PA: Eastman Kodak Company
343 State St
Rochester NY 14650
585 724-4000

(G-14348)
EASTMAN KODAK COMPANY
(PA)
343 State St (14650-0001)
PHONE 585 724-4000
Fax: 585 724-9700
Jeffrey J Clarke, *CEO*
James V Continenza, *Ch of Bd*
Jason Ho, *Business Mgr*
Joyce Haag, *Senior VP*
Sharon E Underberg, *Senior VP*
◆ **EMP:** 277 **EST:** 1880
SALES: 1.8B **Publicly Held**
SIC: 3861 3577 7384 Film, sensitized motion picture, X-ray, still camera, etc.; cameras, still & motion picture (all types); photographic paper & cloth, all types; computer peripheral equipment; graphic displays, except graphic terminals; optical scanning devices; photofinish laboratories

(G-14349)
EASTMAN KODAK COMPANY
1669 Lake Ave Bldg 31-4 (14652-0001)
PHONE 585 724-5600
Fax: 585 588-5040
Jerome Johnson, *Exec VP*
Patricia Parisi, *Buyer*
Thomas McKeehan, *Senior Engr*
Tim Kiehle, *Branch Mgr*
John Chiazza, *MIS Dir*
EMP: 60
SALES (corp-wide): 1.8B **Publicly Held**
SIC: 3861 Film, sensitized motion picture, X-ray, still camera, etc.
PA: Eastman Kodak Company
343 State St
Rochester NY 14650
585 724-4000

(G-14350)
EASTMAN KODAK COMPANY
39 Kaywood Dr (14626-3753)
PHONE 585 726-6261
Ed Schranz, *Design Engr*
Raul Santiago, *Branch Mgr*
Larry Wolfe, *Manager*
EMP: 65
SALES (corp-wide): 1.8B **Publicly Held**
SIC: 3861 Film, sensitized motion picture, X-ray, still camera, etc.
PA: Eastman Kodak Company
343 State St
Rochester NY 14650
585 724-4000

(G-14351)
EASTMAN KODAK COMPANY
2600 Manitou Rd (14650-0001)
PHONE 585 724-4000
EMP: 74
SALES (corp-wide): 1.8B **Publicly Held**
SIC: 3861 Film, sensitized motion picture, X-ray, still camera, etc.
PA: Eastman Kodak Company
343 State St
Rochester NY 14650
585 724-4000

(G-14352)
EASTMAN KODAK COMPANY
343 State St (14650-0001)
PHONE 800 698-3324
Vahaaj Khan, *VP Sales*
Lori Perez, *Branch Mgr*
EMP: 15
SALES (corp-wide): 1.8B **Publicly Held**
SIC: 3861 Film, sensitized motion picture, X-ray, still camera, etc.
PA: Eastman Kodak Company
343 State St
Rochester NY 14650
585 724-4000

(G-14353)
EASTMAN KODAK COMPANY
1999 Lake Ave 6/83/RI (14650-0001)
PHONE 585 722-4385
Rudy Hicks, *Division Mgr*
Dennis Butterfield, *Research*
Frances Schantz, *Research*
Duane Courtney, *Electrical Engi*
Mary J Hellyar, *Branch Mgr*
EMP: 99
SALES (corp-wide): 1.8B **Publicly Held**
SIC: 3861 Film, sensitized motion picture, X-ray, still camera, etc.
PA: Eastman Kodak Company
343 State St
Rochester NY 14650
585 724-4000

(G-14354)
EASTMAN KODAK COMPANY
300 Weiland Road (14650-0001)
PHONE 585 588-5598
EMP: 78
SALES (corp-wide): 1.8B **Publicly Held**
SIC: 3861 Film, sensitized motion picture, X-ray, still camera, etc.
PA: Eastman Kodak Company
343 State St
Rochester NY 14650
585 724-4000

(G-14355)
EASTMAN KODAK COMPANY
343 State St (14650-0001)
PHONE 585 726-7000
Baerbel Post, *CFO*
Robert Yelencsics, *Sales Mgr*
Kathy Meyer, *Manager*
Donna Gozia, *Technology*
Bonnie Saravullo, *Administration*
EMP: 130
SALES (corp-wide): 1.8B **Publicly Held**
SIC: 3861 Film, sensitized motion picture, X-ray, still camera, etc.
PA: Eastman Kodak Company
343 State St
Rochester NY 14650
585 724-4000

(G-14356)
EASTMAN KODAK COMPANY
2400 Mount Read Blvd (14615-2744)
PHONE 585 722-4007
Tomas McHugh, *Plant Mgr*
Dennis Boldt, *Project Mgr*
Susan Shattuck, *Purch Agent*
David Bishop, *Engineer*
John Milazzo, *CIO*
EMP: 5
SQ FT: 14,909
SALES (corp-wide): 1.8B **Publicly Held**
SIC: 3861 Film, sensitized motion picture, X-ray, still camera, etc.
PA: Eastman Kodak Company
343 State St
Rochester NY 14650
585 724-4000

(G-14357)
EASTMAN KODAK COMPANY
100 Latona Rd Gate 340 (14652-0001)
PHONE 585 588-3896
Jack Kosoff, *Branch Mgr*
EMP: 78
SALES (corp-wide): 1.8B **Publicly Held**
SIC: 3861 Film, sensitized motion picture, X-ray, still camera, etc.
PA: Eastman Kodak Company
343 State St
Rochester NY 14650
585 724-4000

(G-14358)
EASTMAN KODAK COMPANY
343 State St (14650-0001)
P.O. Box 15399 (14615-0399)
PHONE 585 724-4000
EMP: 39
SALES (corp-wide): 1.8B **Publicly Held**
SIC: 3861 Photographic equipment & supplies
PA: Eastman Kodak Company
343 State St
Rochester NY 14650
585 724-4000

(G-14359)
EASTMAN PARK MICROGRAPHICS INC
100 Latona Rd Bldg 318 (14652-0001)
PHONE 866 934-4376
William D Oates, *President*
Domenic Masiello, *Mfg Staff*
Robert Breslawski, *Manager*
Richard McDaniel, *Manager*
Susanna Records, *Info Tech Mgr*
EMP: 36 **Privately Held**
SIC: 3861 Film, sensitized motion picture, X-ray, still camera, etc.
PA: Park Eastman Micrographics Inc
6300 Cedar Springs Rd
Dallas TX 75235

(G-14360)
EBERHARDT ENTERPRISES INC
1325 Mount Read Blvd (14606-2819)
PHONE 585 458-7681
Fax: 585 458-6018
Peter Eberhardt, *President*
Carla Madau, *Office Mgr*
▲ **EMP:** 10
SQ FT: 18,000
SALES (est): 1.5MM **Privately Held**
SIC: 3544 Special dies, tools, jigs & fixtures

(G-14361)
EIS INC
Also Called: Light Fabrications
40 Hytec Cir (14606-4255)
PHONE 585 426-5330
Jim Cucinelli, *Principal*
Doreen Demchock, *Purch Mgr*
Ernesto Torres, *QC Mgr*
Scott Vara, *QC Mgr*
Donna Biondi, *Human Resources*
EMP: 53
SALES (corp-wide): 15.3B **Publicly Held**
SIC: 2672 3842 7699 Adhesive backed films, foams & foils; adhesive papers, labels or tapes: from purchased material; adhesive tape & plasters, medicated or non-medicated; industrial equipment services
HQ: Eis, Inc.
2018 Powers Ferry Rd Se # 500
Atlanta GA 30339
678 255-3600

(G-14362)
ELAB SMOKERS BOUTIQUE
4373 Lake Ave (14612-4864)
PHONE 585 865-4513
Steve J Glover, *Partner*
Steve Glover, *Partner*
Mark Landon, *Partner*
EMP: 5
SALES (est): 621.1K **Privately Held**
SIC: 2131 5621 Chewing & smoking tobacco; boutiques

(G-14363)
ELECTRONICS & INNOVATION LTD
150 Research Blvd (14623-3436)
PHONE 585 214-0598
Fax: 585 214-0580
Tony Harris, *President*
John Andrews, *Vice Pres*
▼ **EMP:** 10
SALES (est): 1.8MM **Privately Held**
WEB: www.electronicsandinnovation.com
SIC: 3679 Parametric amplifiers

(G-14364)
ELO TOUCH SOLUTIONS INC
2245 Brdgtn Hnrtta Twn Ln (14623)
PHONE 585 427-2802
Craig Witsoe, *CEO*
Jim Melton, *Vice Pres*
Sean Miller, *Vice Pres*
Dave Renner, *Vice Pres*
Bruno Thuillier, *Vice Pres*
▲ **EMP:** 21 **EST:** 2012
SALES (est): 4.6MM **Privately Held**
SIC: 3571 Computers, digital, analog or hybrid

(G-14365)
EMERSON & OLIVER LLC
44 Elton St (14607-1216)
PHONE 585 775-9929
Laura Bascomb-Werth, *Principal*
EMP: 5 **EST:** 2015
SALES (est): 412.5K **Privately Held**
SIC: 2339 Women's & misses' outerwear

(G-14366)
EMPIRE FABRICATORS INC
Also Called: Cusimano, Michael
95 Saginaw Dr (14623-3131)
PHONE 585 235-3050
Fax: 585 235-3055
Michael Cusimano, *President*
EMP: 7
SQ FT: 10,000
SALES (est): 1.1MM **Privately Held**
WEB: www.empirefabricators.com
SIC: 2541 5084 Counter & sink tops; countersinks

(G-14367)
EMPIRE METAL FABRICATORS INC
1385 Empire Blvd Ste 3 (14609-5915)
PHONE 585 288-2140
Fax: 585 288-2145
John Singer, *President*
EMP: 7
SQ FT: 4,000
SALES (est): 520K **Privately Held**
SIC: 3441 Fabricated structural metal

(G-14368)
EMPIRE OPTICAL INC
1249 Ridgeway Ave Ste P (14615-3761)
P.O. Box 40320 (14604-0820)
PHONE 585 454-4470
Fax: 585 454-3128
James Willoth, *President*
Barbara Willoth, *Treasurer*
Elaine Kleehammer, *Manager*
EMP: 12
SQ FT: 2,400
SALES (est): 1MM **Privately Held**
SIC: 3851 Lens grinding, except prescription: ophthalmic

(G-14369)
ENBI INDIANA INC
1661 Lyell Ave (14606-2311)
PHONE 585 647-1627
Jim Maulucci, *Plant Mgr*
Mike McMindes, *Branch Mgr*
EMP: 25
SALES (corp-wide): 44.9MM **Privately Held**
SIC: 3069 Printers' rolls & blankets: rubber or rubberized fabric
PA: Indiana Enbi Inc
1703 Mccall Dr
Shelbyville IN 46176
317 398-3267

(G-14370)
ENCORE CHOCOLATES INC
147 Pattonwood Dr (14617-1409)
PHONE 585 266-2970
Nancy Stiebitz, *President*
EMP: 5
SALES (est): 410K **Privately Held**
WEB: www.encorechocolates.com
SIC: 2066 Chocolate candy, solid

(G-14371)
ENERGY HARVESTERS LLC
Also Called: Walking Charger, The
63 Garden Dr (14609-4342)
PHONE 617 325-9852
Lawrence Grumer, *CEO*
Sherry Handel, *COO*
EMP: 5
SALES (est): 46.6K **Privately Held**
SIC: 3629 Electrical industrial apparatus

(G-14372)
ENGRAV-O-TYPE PRESS INC
Also Called: Epi Printing & Finishing
30 Bermar Park Ste 2 (14624-1541)
PHONE 585 262-7590
Fax: 585 262-7594
Rick Speciale, *President*
Emile L Speciale Jr, *Treasurer*

Rochester - Monroe County (G-14373)   GEOGRAPHIC SECTION

EMP: 17
SQ FT: 12,000
SALES (est): 3.5MM **Privately Held**
WEB: www.epiprinting.com
SIC: 2752 Commercial printing, offset

(G-14373)
ENI MKS PRODUCTS GROUP
100 Highpower Rd (14623-3498)
PHONE.....................585 427-8300
Paul Eyerman, *Principal*
▲ **EMP:** 11
SALES (est): 1.6MM
SALES (corp-wide): 1.3B **Publicly Held**
SIC: 3663 Airborne radio communications equipment
PA: Mks Instruments, Inc.
  2 Tech Dr Ste 201
  Andover MA 01810
  978 645-5500

(G-14374)
ENI TECHNOLOGY INC (HQ)
100 Highpower Rd (14623-3498)
PHONE.....................585 427-8300
John R Bertucci, *CEO*
Edward Maier, *General Mgr*
Cristiano Salino, *General Mgr*
Michael Laska, *Engineer*
Jon Smyka, *Engineer*
▲ **EMP:** 500
SQ FT: 160,000
SALES (est): 24.9MM
SALES (corp-wide): 1.3B **Publicly Held**
WEB: www.enipower.com
SIC: 3679 3677 3663 3621 Electronic loads & power supplies; electronic coils, transformers & other inductors; radio & TV communications equipment; motors & generators
PA: Mks Instruments, Inc.
  2 Tech Dr Ste 201
  Andover MA 01810
  978 645-5500

(G-14375)
EPP TEAM INC
Also Called: Empire Precision Plastics
500 Lee Rd Ste 400 (14606-4260)
PHONE.....................585 454-4995
Neal P Elli, *Ch of Bd*
Bob Zygulski, *COO*
Rick Wilson, *Vice Pres*
Mark Ward, *Project Mgr*
Steve Steinmetz, *Prdtn Mgr*
▲ **EMP:** 82
SQ FT: 45,000
SALES (est): 17.2MM **Privately Held**
WEB: www.empireprecision.com
SIC: 3089 Injection molded finished plastic products; injection molding of plastics

(G-14376)
ERDLE PERFORATING HOLDINGS INC (PA)
100 Pixley Indus Pkwy (14624-2325)
PHONE.....................585 247-4700
Fax: 585 247-4716
Frank Pfau, *President*
Thomas J Pariso, *Exec VP*
Chuck Gartley, *Opers Mgr*
Clint Stevens, *Safety Mgr*
Jim Garand, *Opers Staff*
EMP: 100 **EST:** 1870
SQ FT: 92,000
SALES (est): 25.3MM **Privately Held**
SIC: 3469 Perforated metal, stamped

(G-14377)
ERNIE GREEN INDUSTRIES INC
85 Pixley Industrial Pkwy (14624-2322)
PHONE.....................585 295-8951
Fax: 585 295-8956
Lubomira Rochet, *Manager*
EMP: 100
SALES (corp-wide): 521.4MM **Privately Held**
SIC: 3089 Injection molding of plastics
PA: Ernie Green Industries, Inc.
  2030 Dividend Dr
  Columbus OH 43228
  614 219-1423

(G-14378)
ERNIE GREEN INDUSTRIES INC
Also Called: Eg Industries
1667 Emerson St (14606-3119)
PHONE.....................585 647-2300
Rob Lannon, *Purch Agent*
Aaron Leighton, *Controller*
Nartign Vanmanen, *Manager*
EMP: 240
SALES (corp-wide): 521.4MM **Privately Held**
SIC: 3089 Injection molding of plastics; blow molded finished plastic products
PA: Ernie Green Industries, Inc.
  2030 Dividend Dr
  Columbus OH 43228
  614 219-1423

(G-14379)
ERNIE GREEN INDUSTRIES INC
Also Called: Eg Indsturies
460 Buffalo Rd Ste 220 (14611-2022)
PHONE.....................585 647-2300
Diane Crispino, *VP Opers*
Mark Hurlbut, *Technology*
EMP: 100
SALES (corp-wide): 521.4MM **Privately Held**
SIC: 3089 Injection molding of plastics; blow molded finished plastic products
PA: Ernie Green Industries, Inc.
  2030 Dividend Dr
  Columbus OH 43228
  614 219-1423

(G-14380)
ESTEBANIA ENTERPRISES INC
Also Called: Aries Precision Products
15 Mcardle St Ste A (14611-1513)
PHONE.....................585 529-9330
Jose L Suro, *President*
EMP: 7
SQ FT: 9,600
SALES (est): 1.1MM **Privately Held**
WEB: www.connectorindustry.com
SIC: 3599 Machine shop, jobbing & repair

(G-14381)
ET PRECISION OPTICS INC
33 Curlew St (14606-2535)
PHONE.....................585 254-2560
Fax: 585 254-2966
Thomas R Eckler, *President*
Vanessa Distrul, *Manager*
EMP: 71
SQ FT: 3,000
SALES (est): 12.6MM **Privately Held**
WEB: www.etprecision.com
SIC: 3599 Machine shop, jobbing & repair

(G-14382)
EVOLUTION IMPRESSIONS INC
160 Commerce Dr (14623-3504)
P.O. Box 12788 (14612-0788)
PHONE.....................585 473-6600
Thomas A Gruber, *President*
Craig Miller, *Principal*
Mike Buell, *Vice Pres*
Thomas Kelly, *Vice Pres*
EMP: 60
SQ FT: 28,000
SALES (est): 6.8MM **Privately Held**
WEB: www.evolutionimpressions.com
SIC: 2752 7334 Commercial printing, lithographic; photocopying & duplicating services

(G-14383)
EXACT MACHINING & MFG
305 Commerce Dr Ste 7 (14623-3538)
PHONE.....................585 334-7090
Dan Bleier, *President*
Tim Bleier, *Corp Secy*
Jay Pryor, *Vice Pres*
EMP: 5
SQ FT: 3,600
SALES (est): 638.2K **Privately Held**
SIC: 3599 Machine shop, jobbing & repair

(G-14384)
EXCELSUS SOLUTIONS LLC
300b Commerce Dr (14623-3508)
PHONE.....................585 533-0003
Mark Laniak, *CEO*
Chris Laniak, *Production*
Gene Snyder, *Purchasing*
John Bennett, *CFO*
David Miller, *Cust Mgr*
EMP: 24
SQ FT: 18,000
SALES (est): 4.5MM **Privately Held**
WEB: www.excelsussolutions.com
SIC: 2759 Commercial printing

(G-14385)
EXECUPRINT INC
111 Humboldt St (14609-7463)
PHONE.....................585 288-5570
Anthony J Finazzo III, *Principal*
EMP: 7
SALES (est): 94.4K **Privately Held**
SIC: 2752 Commercial printing, lithographic

(G-14386)
EXIGO PRECISION INC
190 Murray St (14606-1126)
P.O. Box 60917 (14606-0917)
PHONE.....................585 254-5818
EMP: 7
SALES (est): 499.5K **Privately Held**
SIC: 3599 Mfg Industrial Machinery

(G-14387)
EXPOSITOR NEWSPAPERS INC
Also Called: Rochester Golf Week
2535 Brighton Henrietta (14623-2711)
PHONE.....................585 427-2468
Fax: 585 427-8521
Barbara Morgenstern, *President*
Dave Eaton, *Editor*
George Morgenstern, *Editor*
EMP: 6
SALES (est): 270K **Privately Held**
SIC: 2711 Newspapers: publishing only, not printed on site

(G-14388)
EYEWORKS INC
1249 Ridgeway Ave Ste M (14615-3761)
PHONE.....................585 454-4470
Mark Keehammer, *President*
Elaine Kleehammer, *Vice Pres*
▲ **EMP:** 7
SALES: 950K **Privately Held**
SIC: 3851 Ophthalmic goods

(G-14389)
F OLIVERS LLC
747 Park Ave (14607-3020)
PHONE.....................585 244-2585
Leah Wolanski, *Branch Mgr*
EMP: 5
SALES (corp-wide): 377.3K **Privately Held**
SIC: 2079 Olive oil
PA: F. Oliver's Llc
  129 S Main St
  Canandaigua NY 14424
  585 396-2585

(G-14390)
FARO INDUSTRIES INC
340 Lyell Ave (14606-1697)
PHONE.....................585 647-6000
Fax: 585 647-2886
Matthew Mc Conville, *President*
William Bashford, *General Mgr*
Ray Fitcher, *Engineer*
Matt McConville, *Info Tech Mgr*
Chuck Zimmerman, *Director*
EMP: 17
SQ FT: 26,000
SALES (est): 3.3MM **Privately Held**
WEB: www.faroindustries.com
SIC: 3089 Injection molding of plastics; plastic processing

(G-14391)
FIELDTEX PRODUCTS INC
3055 Brighton Henrietta (14623-2749)
PHONE.....................585 427-2940
Fax: 585 427-8666
Sanford R Abbey, *President*
Jonathan Abbey, *General Mgr*
Patricia Draper, *General Mgr*
Mike Ferris, *Plant Mgr*
Cynthia Helander, *Plant Mgr*
▲ **EMP:** 130
SQ FT: 40,000
SALES (est): 27.1MM **Privately Held**
WEB: www.e-firstaidsupplies.com
SIC: 3151 3161 Leather gloves & mittens; cases, carrying

(G-14392)
FINGER LAKES CHEMICALS INC (PA)
Also Called: Finger Lakes/Castle
420 Saint Paul St (14605-1734)
PHONE.....................585 454-4760
Ewald Blatter, *President*
Hans Blatter, *Vice Pres*
Mark Schroeder, *Safety Mgr*
Andy Santerre, *Director*
Ron Wells, *Executive*
EMP: 50
SQ FT: 100,000
SALES: 10MM **Privately Held**
WEB: www.castlepackspower.com
SIC: 2842 5169 Specialty cleaning preparations; chemicals & allied products

(G-14393)
FIRTH RIXSON INC (DH)
Also Called: Firth Rixson Monroe
181 Mckee Rd (14611-2011)
PHONE.....................585 328-1383
Fax: 585 328-2885
David C Mortimer, *CEO*
Michael Belmont, *General Mgr*
Shawn Gould, *General Mgr*
Chris Gratton, *General Mgr*
Brian Hoover, *General Mgr*
▲ **EMP:** 80
SQ FT: 23,821
SALES: 121.6MM
SALES (corp-wide): 12.3B **Publicly Held**
WEB: www.firthrixson.com
SIC: 3462 Iron & steel forgings; aircraft forgings, ferrous
HQ: Firth Rixson Limited
  Centre Court Building
  Sheffield S4 7Q
  114 219-3000

(G-14394)
FIVE STAR TOOL CO INC
125 Elmgrove Park (14624-1359)
PHONE.....................585 328-9580
Fax: 585 328-0106
Kenneth Klalonde, *President*
Julio Ahumada, *President*
Joanne Rizziteno, *General Mgr*
Mark Schaefer, *Design Engr*
Alicia Hunt, *Accounting Mgr*
EMP: 23 **EST:** 1965
SQ FT: 9,200
SALES (est): 4.5MM **Privately Held**
SIC: 3451 3541 Screw machine products; milling machines

(G-14395)
FLINT GROUP INCORPORATED
Also Called: Flint Ink North America Div
1128 Lexington Ave Bldg 3 (14606-2909)
PHONE.....................585 458-1223
Fax: 585 458-7569
Kathy Marx, *Vice Pres*
Robert Heath, *Purchasing*
Harry Reeves, *Manager*
EMP: 26
SALES (corp-wide): 3.8B **Privately Held**
WEB: www.flintink.com
SIC: 2893 Printing ink
PA: Flint Group Us Llc
  14909 N Beck Rd
  Plymouth MI 48170
  734 781-4600

(G-14396)
FLOWER CITY PRINTING INC (PA)
1725 Mount Read Blvd (14606-2827)
P.O. Box 60680 (14606-0680)
PHONE.....................585 663-9000
Fax: 585 663-4908
George Scharr, *CEO*
Matt Bryant, *Controller*
Carrie Stewart, *Credit Mgr*
Scott Fox, *Accounts Mgr*
Tina Beauchemin, *Mktg Dir*
EMP: 197
SQ FT: 135,000

GEOGRAPHIC SECTION

Rochester - Monroe County (G-14421)

SALES (est): 95.4MM **Privately Held**
WEB: www.flowercityprinting.com
SIC: 2657 2752 Folding paperboard boxes; commercial printing, offset

(G-14397)
FLOWER CITY PRINTING INC
1001 Lee Rd (14606-4243)
PHONE................................585 512-1235
Matt Bryant, *Principal*
EMP: 5
SALES (corp-wide): 95.4MM **Privately Held**
SIC: 2752 Commercial printing, lithographic
PA: Flower City Printing, Inc.
  1725 Mount Read Blvd
  Rochester NY 14606
  585 663-9000

(G-14398)
FLOWER CY TISSUE MILLS CO INC (PA)
700 Driving Park Ave (14613-1506)
P.O. Box 13497 (14613-0497)
PHONE................................585 458-9200
Fax: 585 458-3812
William F Shafer III, *Ch of Bd*
William F Shafer IV, *Vice Pres*
Thomas Myers, *Treasurer*
Don Macdonald, *Sales Dir*
Luke Schafer, *Accounts Mgr*
▲ **EMP:** 50
SQ FT: 46,000
SALES (est): 8.7MM **Privately Held**
WEB: www.flowercitytissue.com
SIC: 2621 Wrapping paper

(G-14399)
FLUXDATA INCORPORATED
176 Anderson Ave Ste F304 (14607-1169)
PHONE................................800 425-0176
Pano Spiliotis, *President*
Lawrence Taplin, *CTO*
Tracie Spiliotis, *Officer*
EMP: 6
SQ FT: 4,665
SALES (est): 1.3MM
SALES (corp-wide): 1.2B **Privately Held**
SIC: 3861 Aerial cameras
PA: Halma Public Limited Company
  Misbourne Court
  Amersham BUCKS HP7 0
  149 472-1111

(G-14400)
FORBES PRECISION INC
100 Boxart St Ste 105 (14612-5658)
PHONE................................585 865-7069
Michael Forbes, *Ch of Bd*
EMP: 11
SQ FT: 3,000
SALES (est): 1MM **Privately Held**
SIC: 3599 Machine shop, jobbing & repair

(G-14401)
FORWARD ENTERPRISES INC
Also Called: Brewer & Newell Printing
215 Tremont St Ste 8 (14608-2366)
PHONE................................585 235-7670
Fax: 585 235-7789
Gerald Ward, *President*
Lisa Fairchild, *General Mgr*
Dick Shellman, *Vice Pres*
Melinda Ward, *Vice Pres*
Stan Phillips, *Representative*
EMP: 10
SQ FT: 4,000
SALES (est): 1.1MM **Privately Held**
SIC: 2759 2752 Letterpress printing; commercial printing, offset

(G-14402)
FRAMING TECHNOLOGY INC
137 Syke St (14611-1738)
PHONE................................585 464-8470
Fax: 585 464-8471
Chris Hill, *President*
Jim Hartke, *Vice Pres*
John Bryce, *Engineer*
Daniel Johnstone, *Manager*
Nicole King, *Office Admin*
▲ **EMP:** 20
SALES: 2.2MM **Privately Held**
WEB: www.framingtech.com
SIC: 3448 Prefabricated metal buildings

(G-14403)
FRANK J MARTELLO
Also Called: Countertop Creations
1227 Maple St (14611-1545)
PHONE................................585 235-2780
Fax: 585 235-2788
Frank J Martello, *Owner*
Cynthia Martello, *Manager*
EMP: 6 **EST:** 1996
SQ FT: 6,000
SALES (est): 620.9K **Privately Held**
WEB: www.countertop-creations.com
SIC: 2541 Counter & sink tops

(G-14404)
FREETIME MAGAZINE INC
1255 University Ave # 270 (14607-1643)
PHONE................................585 473-2266
Fax: 585 473-5214
Thomas Cannon, *President*
EMP: 8
SQ FT: 1,000
SALES (est): 430K **Privately Held**
WEB: www.freetime.com
SIC: 2711 Newspapers: publishing only, not printed on site

(G-14405)
FRESHOP INC
3246 Monroe Ave Ste 1 (14618-4628)
PHONE................................585 738-6035
Brian Moyer, *CEO*
Karthik Balasubramanian, *President*
▼ **EMP:** 35
SQ FT: 20,000
SALES (est): 446.9K **Privately Held**
SIC: 7372 Application computer software

(G-14406)
FTT MEDICAL INC
Also Called: Electrosurgical Instrument Co
275 Commerce Dr (14623-3505)
PHONE................................585 444-0980
Fax: 585 235-1438
John Longuil, *CEO*
EMP: 8
SQ FT: 9,000
SALES (est): 1.3MM **Privately Held**
WEB: www.electrosurgicalinstrument.com
SIC: 3841 Surgical & medical instruments

(G-14407)
GADABOUT USA WHEELCHAIRS INC
892 E Ridge Rd (14621-1718)
P.O. Box 17890 (14617-0890)
PHONE................................585 338-2110
Fax: 585 338-7578
Michael Fonte, *President*
EMP: 15
SALES (est): 853.6K **Privately Held**
SIC: 3842 Wheelchairs

(G-14408)
GANNETT CO INC
Also Called: Democrat & Chronicle
245 E Main St (14604-2103)
PHONE................................585 232-7100
Fax: 585 258-2734
Eric Gustavs, *Opers Mgr*
Linda Baird, *VP Human Res*
Brian Ambor, *Branch Mgr*
Dick Moss, *Director*
EMP: 76
SALES (corp-wide): 3B **Publicly Held**
SIC: 2711 Newspapers, publishing & printing
PA: Gannett Co., Inc.
  7950 Jones Branch Dr
  Mc Lean VA 22102
  703 854-6000

(G-14409)
GATTI TOOL & MOLD INC
997 Beahan Rd (14624-3548)
PHONE................................585 328-1350
Fax: 585 328-1679
Gino Gatti, *President*
EMP: 12
SALES (est): 1.2MM **Privately Held**
WEB: www.gattitool.com
SIC: 3544 Industrial molds

(G-14410)
GE MDS LLC (HQ)
Also Called: Aferge Mds
175 Science Pkwy (14620-4260)
PHONE................................585 242-9600
Heather Gatley, *Vice Pres*
Henry Garcia, *Opers Mgr*
Stephen Cyran, *Engineer*
Bradford Laundry, *Engineer*
Ken Robson, *Engineer*
◆ **EMP:** 200
SALES (est): 25.6MM
SALES (corp-wide): 123.6B **Publicly Held**
WEB: www.microwavedata.com
SIC: 3663 Radio & TV communications equipment
PA: General Electric Company
  41 Farnsworth St
  Boston MA 02210
  617 443-3000

(G-14411)
GEM MANUFACTURING INC
853 West Ave Bldg 17a (14611-2413)
PHONE................................585 235-1670
Fax: 585 235-3666
Scott Keller, *President*
Thad Spaulding, *Vice Pres*
Stuart Kristensen, *Engineer*
Daniel Frankenberger, *Manager*
EMP: 5
SQ FT: 7,000
SALES (est): 737.6K **Privately Held**
WEB: www.gemmachine.com
SIC: 3599 Machine shop, jobbing & repair

(G-14412)
GENERAL PLATING LLC
850 Saint Paul St Ste 10 (14605-1065)
PHONE................................585 423-0830
Fax: 585 423-2257
Tom Schenkel, *Partner*
Don Schenkel, *Partner*
John Schenkel, *Partner*
Richard Schenkel, *Partner*
Roger Schenkel, *Partner*
EMP: 20 **EST:** 1890
SQ FT: 35,000
SALES (est): 598.9K **Privately Held**
SIC: 3471 Finishing, metals or formed products

(G-14413)
GENERAL WELDING & FABG INC
60 Saginaw Dr Ste 4 (14623-3159)
PHONE................................585 697-7660
Fax: 585 697-7660
Cheryl Lis, *Vice Pres*
EMP: 7
SALES (corp-wide): 5.9MM **Privately Held**
WEB: www.gwfab.com
SIC: 3713 5531 7539 Truck bodies & parts; trailer hitches, automotive; trailer repair
PA: General Welding & Fabricating, Inc.
  991 Maple Rd
  Elma NY 14059
  716 652-0033

(G-14414)
GENESCO INC
Also Called: Hat World & Lids
271 Greece Rdg 69a (14626-2818)
PHONE................................585 227-3080
Matthew Toor, *Manager*
EMP: 5
SALES (corp-wide): 2.8B **Publicly Held**
WEB: www.genesco.com
SIC: 2353 Hats & caps
PA: Genesco Inc.
  1415 Murfreesboro Pike
  Nashville TN 37217
  615 367-7000

(G-14415)
GENESEE MANUFACTURING CO INC
566 Hollenbeck St (14621-2288)
PHONE................................585 266-3201
Kevin Hite, *President*
Donald A Kohler Jr, *Vice Pres*
EMP: 9 **EST:** 1905
SQ FT: 8,000
SALES: 558.3K **Privately Held**
WEB: www.geneseemfg.com
SIC: 3545 5084 Cutting tools for machine tools; industrial machinery & equipment

(G-14416)
GENESEE VLY MET FINSHG CO INC
244 Verona St (14608-1708)
PHONE................................585 232-4412
Fax: 585 232-2106
Peter N Dresser, *President*
Salvatore Vittozzi, *Corp Secy*
Cathy Heuft, *Manager*
EMP: 6 **EST:** 1948
SQ FT: 11,400
SALES (est): 568.3K **Privately Held**
SIC: 3471 Electroplating of metals or formed products; finishing, metals or formed products

(G-14417)
GENESIS DIGITAL IMAGING INC
150 Verona St (14608-1733)
PHONE................................310 305-7358
Joseph Eliafan, *President*
EMP: 9
SALES (est): 1MM
SALES (corp-wide): 22.5B **Publicly Held**
WEB: www.genesisdigitalimaging.com
SIC: 3844 Radiographic X-ray apparatus & tubes
HQ: Carestream Health, Inc.
  150 Verona St
  Rochester NY 14608
  585 627-1800

(G-14418)
GENESIS VISION INC
Also Called: Rochester Optical
1260 Lyell Ave (14606-2040)
PHONE................................585 254-0193
Jeremy Ho, *CEO*
Patrick Ho, *Ch of Bd*
Steve Asch, *Controller*
▲ **EMP:** 25
SQ FT: 22,500
SALES (est): 6MM **Privately Held**
SIC: 3827 Optical instruments & lenses

(G-14419)
GERMAN MACHINE & ASSEMBLY INC
226 Jay St (14608-1623)
PHONE................................585 546-4200
Fax: 585 546-4400
Kim Beasley, *Ch of Bd*
Scott Boheen, *President*
Margaret Blair, *Bookkeeper*
EMP: 25
SALES (est): 3.5MM **Privately Held**
WEB: www.germanmach.com
SIC: 3469 Machine parts, stamped or pressed metal

(G-14420)
GERMANOW-SIMON CORPORATION
Also Called: G-S Plastic Optics
408 Saint Paul St (14605-1788)
PHONE................................585 232-1440
Fax: 585 232-3866
Andrew Germanow, *Ch of Bd*
Kathye Simon, *General Mgr*
Lori Steffenilla, *Mfg Dir*
Chris Smock, *Plant Mgr*
Don Seames, *Materials Mgr*
◆ **EMP:** 40 **EST:** 1916
SQ FT: 125,000
SALES (est): 9MM **Privately Held**
WEB: www.gsoptics.com
SIC: 3089 3559 3829 3545 Plastic processing; plastics working machinery; thermometers, liquid-in-glass & bimetal type; machine tool accessories; pressed & blown glass

(G-14421)
GETINGE SOURCING LLC
1777 E Henrietta Rd (14623-3133)
PHONE................................585 475-1400
Fax: 585 272-5291
John Aymong, *President*
Darren Soudan, *CFO*

Rochester - Monroe County (G-14422) GEOGRAPHIC SECTION

Camille Majewski, *Planning Mgr*
▲ **EMP**: 174
SALES (est): 25.9MM
SALES (corp-wide): 3.2B **Privately Held**
SIC: 3842 Sterilizers, hospital & surgical
PA: Getinge Ab
  Lindholmspiren 7a
  Goteborg 417 5
  103 350-000

(G-14422)
GETINGE USA INC (HQ)
1777 E Henrietta Rd (14623-3133)
PHONE..................800 475-9040
Andrew Ray, *Ch of Bd*
Charles Carrier, *President*
Charles Dacey, *Area Mgr*
Harald Castler, *Vice Pres*
Terry D Cooke, *Vice Pres*
▲ **EMP**: 150 **EST**: 1971
SQ FT: 250,000
SALES (est): 154.1MM
SALES (corp-wide): 3.2B **Privately Held**
SIC: 3842 3841 Sterilizers, hospital & surgical; surgical & medical instruments
PA: Getinge Ab
  Lindholmspiren 7a
  Goteborg 417 5
  103 350-000

(G-14423)
GH INDUCTION ATMOSPHERES LLC
35 Industrial Park Cir (14624-2403)
PHONE..................585 368-2120
Fax: 585 368-2123
Becky Sheldon, *Manager*
Rebecca Sheldon, *Info Tech Mgr*
Steven Skewes,
Dale Wilcox,
▲ **EMP**: 35
SQ FT: 19,000
SALES (est): 7.9MM **Privately Held**
WEB: www.inductionatmospheres.com
SIC: 3542 Machine tools, metal forming type
HQ: Gh Electrotermia Sa
  Calle Vereda Real, S/N
  San Antonio De Benageber 46184
  961 352-020

(G-14424)
GIZMO PRODUCTS INC
205 Seneca Pkwy (14613-1414)
PHONE..................585 301-0970
EMP: 5
SALES (est): 828.5K **Privately Held**
SIC: 3823 Mfg Process Control Instruments

(G-14425)
GLASSFAB INC
257 Ormond St (14605-3024)
P.O. Box 31880 (14603-1880)
PHONE..................585 262-4000
Fax: 585 454-4305
Robert Saltzman, *Ch of Bd*
Daniel Saltzman, *President*
Wayne Leon, *General Mgr*
Tom Kirk, *COO*
Mary Leach, *Controller*
▲ **EMP**: 30
SQ FT: 30,000
SALES (est): 6.1MM **Privately Held**
WEB: www.glassfab.com
SIC: 3231 Products of purchased glass

(G-14426)
GLASTEEL PARTS & SERVICES INC (DH)
1000 West Ave (14611-2442)
P.O. Box 23600 (14692-3600)
PHONE..................585 235-1010
Gary Brewer, *President*
EMP: 50
SQ FT: 18,000
SALES (est): 9.2MM
SALES (corp-wide): 7.2B **Publicly Held**
SIC: 3229 Pressed & blown glass
HQ: Pfaudler, Inc.
  1000 West Ave
  Rochester NY 14611
  585 464-5663

(G-14427)
GLAXOSMITHKLINE LLC
1177 Winton Rd S (14618-2240)
PHONE..................585 738-9025
EMP: 26
SALES (corp-wide): 34.3B **Privately Held**
SIC: 2834 Pharmaceutical preparations
HQ: Glaxosmithkline Llc
  5 Crescent Dr
  Philadelphia PA 19112
  215 751-4000

(G-14428)
GLEASON CORPORATION (PA)
1000 University Ave (14607-1286)
P.O. Box 22970 (14692-2970)
PHONE..................585 473-1000
Fax: 585 461-4092
Maria Austria, *President*
John J Perrotti, *President*
Johannes Becker, *General Mgr*
He Bo, *General Mgr*
Klaus Kremmin, *General Mgr*
◆ **EMP**: 800
SQ FT: 721,400
SALES (est): 1B **Privately Held**
SIC: 3541 3829 Machine tools, metal cutting type; gear cutting & finishing machines; numerically controlled metal cutting machine tools; machine tool replacement & repair parts, metal cutting types; physical property testing equipment

(G-14429)
GLEASON WORKS (HQ)
1000 University Ave (14607-1286)
PHONE..................585 473-1000
Fax: 585 461-4348
James S Gleason, *Ch of Bd*
John J Perrotti, *President*
Nanci Malin Peck, *Vice Pres*
Edward J Pelta, *Vice Pres*
John W Pysnack, *Vice Pres*
◆ **EMP**: 925 **EST**: 1865
SQ FT: 721,000
SALES (est): 281.9MM
SALES (corp-wide): 1B **Privately Held**
WEB: www.gleason.com
SIC: 3714 3728 3566 3541 Gears, motor vehicle; gears, aircraft power transmission; gears, power transmission, except automotive; gear cutting & finishing machines; numerically controlled metal cutting machine tools; machine tool replacement & repair parts, metal cutting types; physical property testing equipment; metal stampings
PA: Gleason Corporation
  1000 University Ave
  Rochester NY 14607
  585 473-1000

(G-14430)
GM COMPONENTS HOLDINGS LLC
Also Called: Gmch Rochester
1000 Lexington Ave (14606-2810)
P.O. Box 92700 (14692-8800)
PHONE..................585 647-7000
Chuck Gifford, *Principal*
Eugene Bovenzi, *Engineer*
John Butler, *Engineer*
Andrew White, *Engineer*
Chris Kiellach, *Manager*
EMP: 350
SQ FT: 2,250 **Publicly Held**
SIC: 3714 Motor vehicle parts & accessories
HQ: Gm Components Holdings, Llc
  300 Renaissance Ctr
  Detroit MI 48243

(G-14431)
GOLD PRIDE PRESS INC
12 Pixley Industrial Pkwy # 40 (14624-2364)
PHONE..................585 224-8800
Fax: 585 224-9633
Ted Rhodes, *Vice Pres*
Gloria Cambisi, *Office Mgr*
Tom Steele, *Supervisor*
EMP: 20
SQ FT: 30,000

SALES (est): 4.4MM **Privately Held**
WEB: www.goldpride.com
SIC: 2789 Trade binding services

(G-14432)
GRADIENT LENS CORPORATION
207 Tremont St Ste 1 (14608-2398)
PHONE..................585 235-2620
Fax: 585 235-6645
Douglas Kindred, *President*
Linda Plate, *Business Mgr*
Leland Atkinson, *Vice Pres*
Kenneth Harrington, *Marketing Staff*
Duncan Moore, *Director*
EMP: 35
SQ FT: 9,500
SALES (est): 4.4MM **Privately Held**
WEB: www.gradientlens.com
SIC: 3827 Optical instruments & lenses; interferometers

(G-14433)
GRAYWOOD COMPANIES INC (PA)
Also Called: Jasco Cutting Tools
1390 Mount Read Blvd (14606-2820)
P.O. Box 60497 (14606-0497)
PHONE..................585 254-7000
Fax: 585 254-2655
John M Summers, *Ch of Bd*
Eugene Baldino, *President*
Dave Krigeer, *Vice Pres*
Mary Schiltz, *Purchasing*
Diane Simon, *CFO*
▲ **EMP**: 40 **EST**: 2005
SQ FT: 36,000
SALES (est): 102.4MM **Privately Held**
SIC: 3541 3545 3544 3398 Machine tools, metal cutting type; boring mills; countersinking machines; deburring machines; machine tool accessories; drill bits, metalworking; taps, machine tool; reamers, machine tool; special dies, tools, jigs & fixtures; metal heat treating

(G-14434)
GSP COMPONENTS INC
1190 Brooks Ave (14624-3112)
PHONE..................585 436-3377
Fax: 585 436-5123
Ronald J Motsay, *CEO*
Tim Lynn, *Opers Mgr*
Pedeville Glenn, *QC Mgr*
Eric Aldridge, *Manager*
Rick Palmer, *Manager*
EMP: 62 **EST**: 1951
SQ FT: 34,000
SALES (est): 17.1MM **Privately Held**
WEB: www.gspcomponents.com
SIC: 3451 Screw machine products

(G-14435)
H RISCH INC
44 Saginaw Dr (14623-3132)
PHONE..................585 442-0110
Fax: 585 442-0189
Sara Tartaglia, *CEO*
Michael Pauly, *President*
Tammy Omay, *Sales Staff*
Laurie Mannhardt, *Manager*
Ned Meddaugh, *Manager*
EMP: 60 **EST**: 1935
SQ FT: 15,000
SALES (est): 9.5MM **Privately Held**
WEB: www.hrisch.com
SIC: 3089 Floor coverings, plastic

(G-14436)
H S ASSEMBLY INC
570 Hollanback (14605)
PHONE..................585 266-4287
David Marcellus, *President*
EMP: 5
SALES (est): 550K **Privately Held**
WEB: www.hsassembly.com
SIC: 3541 8711 Machine tools, metal cutting type; engineering services

(G-14437)
H T SPECIALTY INC
70 Bermar Park (14624-1541)
PHONE..................585 458-4060
Fax: 585 458-7592
Russel W Thiel, *President*
Donna Thiel, *Vice Pres*

Susan Thomas, *Office Mgr*
Judy Thiel, *Manager*
EMP: 18
SQ FT: 8,400
SALES (est): 2.2MM **Privately Held**
SIC: 3599 Machine shop, jobbing & repair

(G-14438)
HAMTRONICS INC
39 Willnick Cir (14626-4748)
PHONE..................585 392-9430
Fax: 585 392-9420
G Francis Vogt, *President*
Joan Vogt, *Sales Executive*
EMP: 7
SALES: 500K **Privately Held**
SIC: 3663 5961 Radio broadcasting & communications equipment; mail order house

(G-14439)
HANGER PRSTHETCS & ORTHO INC
333 Metro Park Ste F200 (14623-2632)
PHONE..................585 292-9510
Zoltan Pallagi, *Branch Mgr*
Zulfiqar Ahmed, *Executive*
EMP: 7
SALES (corp-wide): 451.4MM **Publicly Held**
SIC: 3842 Surgical appliances & supplies
HQ: Hanger Prosthetics & Orthotics, Inc.
  10910 Domain Dr Ste 300
  Austin TX 78758
  512 777-3800

(G-14440)
HANSON AGGREGATES PA LLC
1535 Scottsville Rd (14623-1934)
PHONE..................585 436-3250
Jeff Kramarz, *Branch Mgr*
EMP: 15
SALES (corp-wide): 16B **Privately Held**
SIC: 2899 1442 Concrete curing & hardening compounds; gravel mining
HQ: Hanson Aggregates Pennsylvania, Llc
  7660 Imperial Way
  Allentown PA 18195
  610 366-4626

(G-14441)
HARRIS CORPORATION
Harris Long Range Radio
1680 University Ave (14610-1887)
PHONE..................585 244-5830
Fax: 585 242-4755
Madjid Abdi, *Principal*
Janice Lenzy, *Exec VP*
Bob Griffith, *Opers Staff*
Steven Trumpiniski, *Engineer*
Mark Turner, *Engineer*
EMP: 2600
SALES (corp-wide): 5.9B **Publicly Held**
SIC: 3663 Radio & TV communications equipment
PA: Harris Corporation
  1025 W Nasa Blvd
  Melbourne FL 32919
  321 727-9100

(G-14442)
HARRIS CORPORATION
Also Called: Exelis Geospatial Systems
400 Initiative Dr (14624-6219)
P.O. Box 60488 (14606-0488)
PHONE..................585 269-6600
Christopher Young, *CEO*
William Brown, *President*
William Gattle, *President*
David Melcher, *President*
Conrad Cierniak, *Vice Pres*
EMP: 800
SALES (corp-wide): 5.9B **Publicly Held**
SIC: 3812 Space vehicle guidance systems & equipment
PA: Harris Corporation
  1025 W Nasa Blvd
  Melbourne FL 32919
  321 727-9100

(G-14443)
HARRIS CORPORATION
Also Called: Exelis Geospatial Systems
800 Lee Rd Bldg 601 (14606-4248)
P.O. Box 60488 (14606-0488)
PHONE..................585 269-5001

GEOGRAPHIC SECTION

Rochester - Monroe County (G-14467)

William Brown, *CEO*
William Gattle, *President*
David Melcher, *President*
Richard W Wambach, *Branch Mgr*
Kathryn Lloyd, *MIS Mgr*
EMP: 400
SALES (corp-wide): 5.9B **Publicly Held**
SIC: 3812 Space vehicle guidance systems & equipment
PA: Harris Corporation
1025 W Nasa Blvd
Melbourne FL 32919
321 727-9100

(G-14444)
HARRIS CORPORATION
Also Called: Exelis
800 Lee Rd (14606-4248)
P.O. Box 60488 (14606-0488)
PHONE...........................413 263-6200
Christopher Young, *CEO*
William Gattle, *President*
David McCaffrey, *Branch Mgr*
Kathryn Lloyd, *MIS Mgr*
EMP: 509
SALES (corp-wide): 5.9B **Publicly Held**
SIC: 3669 Burglar alarm apparatus, electric
PA: Harris Corporation
1025 W Nasa Blvd
Melbourne FL 32919
321 727-9100

(G-14445)
HARRIS CORPORATION
2696 Manitou Rd Bldg 101 (14624-1173)
PHONE...........................585 269-5000
Robert Golightly, *Business Mgr*
Tommy Brazie, *Vice Pres*
Michael Ognenovski, *Vice Pres*
Joe Westbay, *Vice Pres*
Joan Gardner, *Project Mgr*
EMP: 163
SALES (corp-wide): 5.9B **Publicly Held**
SIC: 3812 Space vehicle guidance systems & equipment
PA: Harris Corporation
1025 W Nasa Blvd
Melbourne FL 32919
321 727-9100

(G-14446)
HARRIS CORPORATION
Also Called: Rf Communications
570 Culver Rd (14609-7442)
PHONE...........................585 244-5830
Dana Mehnert, *Manager*
Melissa Revilla, *Manager*
Bill Fisher, *MIS Dir*
EMP: 20
SALES (corp-wide): 5.9B **Publicly Held**
SIC: 3661 3671 Telephone & telegraph apparatus; electron tubes
PA: Harris Corporation
1025 W Nasa Blvd
Melbourne FL 32919
321 727-9100

(G-14447)
HARRIS CORPORATION
50 Carlson Rd (14610-1021)
PHONE...........................585 244-5830
Holland Brown, *Vice Pres*
EMP: 441
SALES (corp-wide): 5.9B **Publicly Held**
SIC: 3663 Radio & TV communications equipment
PA: Harris Corporation
1025 W Nasa Blvd
Melbourne FL 32919
321 727-9100

(G-14448)
HARRIS CORPORATION
Also Called: Harris Rf Communications
1350 Jefferson Rd (14623-3106)
PHONE...........................585 244-5830
Frank Connolly, *Exec VP*
EMP: 441
SALES (corp-wide): 5.9B **Publicly Held**
SIC: 3663 Radio & TV communications equipment
PA: Harris Corporation
1025 W Nasa Blvd
Melbourne FL 32919
321 727-9100

(G-14449)
HAWVER DISPLAY INC (PA)
140 Carter St (14621-5136)
PHONE...........................585 544-2290
Fax: 585 544-2292
Timothy Culver, *President*
Cindy Bauman, *Purch Mgr*
EMP: 29
SQ FT: 44,000
SALES (est): 3.7MM **Privately Held**
WEB: www.hawver.com
SIC: 2542 Fixtures: display, office or store: except wood

(G-14450)
HAZLOW ELECTRONICS INC
49 Saint Bridgets Dr (14605-1899)
PHONE...........................585 325-5323
Fax: 585 325-4308
Alma Publow, *President*
David Publow, *Admin Sec*
EMP: 25
SQ FT: 40,000
SALES (est): 5.7MM **Privately Held**
WEB: www.hazlow.com
SIC: 3679 3672 Harness assemblies for electronic use: wire or cable; printed circuit boards

(G-14451)
HEALTH CARE ORIGINALS INC
1 Pleasant St Ste 442 (14604-1455)
PHONE...........................585 471-8215
Jared Dwarika, *Owner*
EMP: 7
SALES (est): 330.5K **Privately Held**
SIC: 3845 8731 Electromedical apparatus; medical research, commercial

(G-14452)
HEDONIST ARTISAN CHOCOLATES
674 South Ave Ste B (14620-1378)
PHONE...........................585 461-2815
Jennifer Posey, *Partner*
Zahra Langford, *Partner*
EMP: 11
SALES (est): 1.3MM **Privately Held**
SIC: 2064 Candy & other confectionery products

(G-14453)
HICKEY FREEMAN TAILORED CL INC
1155 N Clinton Ave (14621-4454)
PHONE...........................585 467-7240
Fax: 585 467-1315
Stephen Granovsky, *CEO*
Alan Abramowicz, *President*
Mark Donovan, *CFO*
EMP: 423
SQ FT: 224,874
SALES: 45MM **Privately Held**
SIC: 2311 Men's & boys' suits & coats; jackets, tailored suit-type: men's & boys'; suits, men's & boys': made from purchased materials; tuxedos: made from purchased materials
PA: Luxury Men's Apparel Group Ltd
6930 Av Du Parc
Montreal QC H3N 1
514 273-7741

(G-14454)
HIGH FALLS BREWING COMPANY LLC (DH)
Also Called: North Americas Breweries
445 Saint Paul St (14605-1726)
P.O. Box 30762 (14603-0762)
PHONE...........................585 546-1030
Michael Gaesser, *Vice Pres*
Andrew Yeager, *Treasurer*
Jessica Chatterton, *Info Tech Mgr*
Samuel T Hubbard Jr,
Michael C Atseff,
▲ **EMP:** 115
SQ FT: 900,000
SALES (est): 62.3MM **Privately Held**
WEB: www.highfalls.com
SIC: 2082 Beer (alcoholic beverage); ale (alcoholic beverage)

(G-14455)
HIGH FALLS OPERATING CO LLC
445 Saint Paul St (14605-1726)
PHONE...........................585 546-1030
Katie Blahowicz, *Controller*
Kenneth Yartz, *Mng Member*
EMP: 800
SALES (est): 98.1MM **Privately Held**
SIC: 2082 Malt beverage products
HQ: North American Breweries, Inc.
445 Saint Paul St
Rochester NY 14605

(G-14456)
HIGH SPEED HAMMER COMPANY INC
Also Called: Assembly Equipment Division
313 Norton St (14621-3331)
PHONE...........................585 266-4287
Fax: 585 544-8921
David Marcellus, *President*
Richard Marcellus, *Corp Secy*
EMP: 15 **EST:** 1917
SQ FT: 12,000
SALES: 1MM **Privately Held**
SIC: 3542 3541 Riveting machines; machine tools, metal cutting: exotic (explosive, etc.); machine tool replacement & repair parts, metal cutting types

(G-14457)
HIS VISION INC
1260 Lyell Ave (14606-2040)
PHONE...........................585 254-0022
Patrick Ho, *President*
Wayne Ohl, *Admin Sec*
▲ **EMP:** 48 **EST:** 1941
SQ FT: 21,000
SALES: 3.5MM **Privately Held**
WEB: www.rochesteroptical.com
SIC: 3851 Frames & parts, eyeglass & spectacle

(G-14458)
HOBART CORPORATION
3495 Winton Pl (14623-2824)
PHONE...........................585 427-9000
Fax: 585 427-8818
Pat Allen, *Manager*
EMP: 50
SALES (corp-wide): 13.6B **Publicly Held**
SIC: 3589 Dishwashing machines, commercial
HQ: Hobart Corporation
701 S Ridge Ave
Troy OH 45374
937 332-3000

(G-14459)
HOVER-DAVIS INC (DH)
100 Paragon Dr (14624-1129)
PHONE...........................585 352-9590
John Hover, *President*
Peter Davis, *Vice Pres*
Chris Bennette, *Controller*
Kraig Cotter, *Director*
▲ **EMP:** 125
SQ FT: 66,000
SALES (est): 15.6MM **Privately Held**
WEB: www.hoverdavis.com
SIC: 3549 Assembly machines, including robotic
HQ: Ui Holding Company
33 Broome Corporate Pkwy
Conklin NY 13748
607 779-7522

(G-14460)
HUDSON STEEL FABRICATORS
444 Hudson Ave (14605-1359)
P.O. Box 31547 (14603-1547)
PHONE...........................585 454-3923
Fax: 585 454-6141
Rosario La Delfa, *President*
Russ La Delfa, *Purch Agent*
Don Brown, *Controller*
EMP: 40
SQ FT: 18,000
SALES (est): 7.4MM **Privately Held**
SIC: 3441 Fabricated structural metal

(G-14461)
HY-TECH MOLD INC
60 Elmgrove Park (14624-1363)
PHONE...........................585 247-2450
Fax: 585 247-2461
Donald Philipp, *President*
Patricia Philipp, *Vice Pres*
Stuart Norris, *Treasurer*
EMP: 10
SQ FT: 10,000
SALES: 800K **Privately Held**
WEB: www.hy-techmold.com
SIC: 3544 Industrial molds

(G-14462)
ID SIGNSYSTEMS INC
410 Atlantic Ave (14609-7356)
PHONE...........................585 266-5750
Fax: 585 266-5798
Katrina Beatty, *CEO*
Paul Dudley, *President*
Jeff Ureles, *COO*
◆ **EMP:** 48
SQ FT: 15,000
SALES (est): 5.2MM **Privately Held**
WEB: www.idsignsystems.com
SIC: 3993 Signs & advertising specialties

(G-14463)
IDEX CORPORATION
2883 Brghtn Hnretta Tl Rd (14623-2790)
PHONE...........................585 292-8121
Michael Bonomo, *Manager*
EMP: 5
SALES (corp-wide): 2.1B **Publicly Held**
SIC: 3563 Air & gas compressors
PA: Idex Corporation
1925 W Field Ct Ste 200
Lake Forest IL 60045
847 498-7070

(G-14464)
IEC ELECTRONICS CORP
Celmet
1365 Emerson St (14606-3006)
PHONE...........................585 647-1760
Fax: 585 647-2308
Rich Ramell, *Marketing Staff*
Tom Guiliani, *Director*
EMP: 155
SALES (corp-wide): 127MM **Publicly Held**
SIC: 3444 Sheet metalwork
PA: Iec Electronics Corp.
105 Norton St
Newark NY 14513
315 331-7742

(G-14465)
IHEARTCOMMUNICATIONS INC
Also Called: Wham 1180 AM
100 Chestnut St Ste 1700 (14604-2418)
PHONE...........................585 454-4884
Fax: 585 262-9426
Karen Carey, *President*
Nick Francesco, *Social Dir*
EMP: 120 **Publicly Held**
SIC: 3663 4832 Radio receiver networks; radio broadcasting stations
HQ: Iheartcommunications, Inc.
200 E Basse Rd Ste 100
San Antonio TX 78209
210 822-2828

(G-14466)
IMAGE360
Also Called: Signs Now
275 Marketplace Dr (14623-6001)
PHONE...........................585 272-1234
Fax: 585 272-1252
Julie St Germaine, *President*
Jackie Ciresi, *Treasurer*
EMP: 5
SALES (est): 712.9K **Privately Held**
WEB: www.signsnow405.com
SIC: 3993 Signs & advertising specialties

(G-14467)
IMPRESSIONS INTERNATIONAL INC
1255 University Ave # 150 (14607-1643)
PHONE...........................585 442-5240
Terry Gersey, *President*
Harry Gersey, *Vice Pres*
▲ **EMP:** 7
SQ FT: 2,500

Rochester - Monroe County (G-14468)

SALES (est): 969.7K Privately Held
WEB: www.checkfraud.com
SIC: 3555 Printing plates

(G-14468)
INDEPENDENT BREWERS UNTD CORP
445 Saint Paul St (14605-1726)
PHONE.................................585 263-9308
EMP: 7
SALES (est): 94.4K Privately Held
SIC: 2082 Malt beverages

(G-14469)
INNEX INDUSTRIES INC
6 Marway Dr (14624-2349)
PHONE.................................585 247-3575
Fax: 585 247-1903
Luka Gakovic, *President*
Helen J Gakovic, *Vice Pres*
▼ EMP: 28
SQ FT: 20,000
SALES (est): 6.9MM Privately Held
WEB: www.innexind.com
SIC: 3545 Milling machine attachments (machine tool accessories)

(G-14470)
INSTANT AGAIN LLC
1277 Mount Read Blvd # 2 (14606-2850)
PHONE.................................585 436-8003
Fax: 585 436-8012
James Webster, *Sales Executive*
Andrew Gross III,
EMP: 20
SALES (est): 3MM Privately Held
WEB: www.instantagain.com
SIC: 2752 Commercial printing, lithographic

(G-14471)
INSTANT MONOGRAMMING INC
1150 University Ave Ste 5 (14607-1647)
PHONE.................................585 654-5550
Fax: 585 654-5554
Daniel Bloom, *President*
Deborah Bloom, *Corp Secy*
EMP: 7
SALES (est): 683.1K Privately Held
SIC: 2395 Embroidery & art needlework; emblems, embroidered

(G-14472)
INTELLIMETAL INC
2025 Brighton Henrietta (14623-2509)
PHONE.................................585 424-3260
Kim Lazzara Zapiach, *President*
Linda Brockett, *General Mgr*
Scott Lazzara, *General Mgr*
Tony Delvecchio, *Opers Mgr*
Shannon Pryce, *Accountant*
EMP: 57
SALES (est): 11.9MM Privately Held
SIC: 3444 Sheet metalwork

(G-14473)
INTERNATIONAL PAPER COMPANY
200 Boxart St (14612-5646)
PHONE.................................585 663-1000
Mike Rougeux, *Mfg Mgr*
Pam Hayes, *Safety Mgr*
John McCormick, *Purch Mgr*
Les Senft, *Manager*
Rex Roy, *Maintence Staff*
EMP: 150
SALES (corp-wide): 21B Publicly Held
WEB: www.internationalpaper.com
SIC: 2653 2671 Boxes, corrugated: made from purchased materials; packaging paper & plastics film, coated & laminated
PA: International Paper Company
  6400 Poplar Ave
  Memphis TN 38197
  901 419-9000

(G-14474)
INTERNATIONAL TOOL & MCH INC
121 Lincoln Ave (14611-2444)
PHONE.................................585 654-6955
Fax: 585 654-8919
Eric Moore, *President*
▲ EMP: 10
SQ FT: 8,000

SALES: 800K Privately Held
SIC: 3599 Machine shop, jobbing & repair

(G-14475)
INTRINSIQ MATERIALS INC
1200 Ridgeway Ave Ste 110 (14615-3758)
PHONE.................................585 301-4432
Robert Cournoyer, *President*
Sujatha Ramanujan, *Vice Pres*
EMP: 7 EST: 2011
SALES (est): 1.2MM Privately Held
WEB: www.intrinsiqmaterials.com
SIC: 2893 8731 Printing ink; electronic research

(G-14476)
IROQUOIS ROCK PRODUCTS INC (DH)
1150 Penfield Rd (14625-2202)
PHONE.................................585 381-7010
John Odenbach Jr, *President*
Richard E Williams, *President*
David Fingar, *Vice Pres*
Frederick J Odenbach, *Vice Pres*
Gerard Odenbach, *Vice Pres*
EMP: 10
SQ FT: 5,000
SALES (est): 2.6MM
SALES (corp-wide): 28.6B Privately Held
SIC: 3281 2951 3273 Stone, quarrying & processing of own stone products; paving mixtures; asphalt & asphaltic paving mixtures (not from refineries); road materials, bituminous (not from refineries); ready-mixed concrete
HQ: Dolomite Products Company Inc.
  1150 Penfield Rd
  Rochester NY 14625
  315 524-1998

(G-14477)
J MACKENZIE LTD
234 Wallace Way (14624-6216)
P.O. Box 22678 (14692-2678)
PHONE.................................585 321-1770
Fax: 585 321-3277
James E Hammer, *President*
John Fischer, *Manager*
Christopher F Wieser, *Admin Sec*
▲ EMP: 39
SQ FT: 56,000
SALES (est): 3.5MM
SALES (corp-wide): 119.2MM Privately Held
WEB: www.jmackenzie.com
SIC: 2789 Paper cutting
PA: Hammer Packaging Corp.
  200 Lucius Gordon Dr
  West Henrietta NY 14586
  585 424-3880

(G-14478)
J VOGLER ENTERPRISE LLC
15 Evelyn St (14606-5533)
P.O. Box 24361 (14624-0361)
PHONE.................................585 247-1625
Fax: 585 247-1637
James Vogler,
EMP: 10
SQ FT: 6,000
SALES (est): 1.7MM Privately Held
WEB: www.jvogler.com
SIC: 3541 Machine tools, metal cutting type

(G-14479)
JAM INDUSTRIES INC
Also Called: Ace Manufacturing
9 Marway Cir (14624-2320)
PHONE.................................585 458-9830
Fax: 585 458-7696
Eric L Johnson, *Ch of Bd*
Todd Hallquist, *General Mgr*
Martha Moriarty, *Vice Pres*
Bill Farrell, *Purchasing*
Scott Brownstein, *Branch Mgr*
▲ EMP: 45
SQ FT: 25,000
SALES (est): 7.4MM Privately Held
WEB: www.jamindustries.com
SIC: 3599 Machine & other job shop work

(G-14480)
JAMES CONOLLY PRINTING CO
72 Marway Cir (14624-2380)
PHONE.................................585 426-4150

Fax: 585 426-4198
Robert Conolly, *President*
Luke Burnahy, *Manager*
Beth Calkins, *Manager*
EMP: 21 EST: 1968
SQ FT: 13,000
SALES (est): 3.3MM Privately Held
SIC: 2752 2789 2791 Commercial printing, offset; bookbinding & related work; typesetting

(G-14481)
JAMESTOWN CONT OF ROCHESTER
82 Edwards Deming Dr (14606-2842)
PHONE.................................585 254-9190
Bruce Janowsky, *Ch of Bd*
Lou Petitti, *General Mgr*
Dick P Weimer, *Corp Secy*
Joseph R Palmeri, *Vice Pres*
EMP: 70
SALES (est): 19.1MM
SALES (corp-wide): 136.3MM Privately Held
WEB: www.jamestowncontainer.com
SIC: 2653 Corrugated & solid fiber boxes
PA: Jamestown Container Corp
  14 Deming Dr
  Falconer NY 14733
  716 665-4623

(G-14482)
JAVLYN PROCESS SYSTEMS LLC
3136 Winton Rd S Ste 102 (14623-2928)
PHONE.................................585 424-5580
Victor Tifone, *President*
EMP: 23
SQ FT: 8,000
SALES (est): 1.4MM
SALES (corp-wide): 225.8K Privately Held
SIC: 3569 8742 Liquid automation machinery & equipment; automation & robotics consultant; food & beverage consultant
HQ: Krones, Inc.
  9600 S 58th St
  Franklin WI 53132
  414 409-4000

(G-14483)
JK JEWELRY INC
Also Called: J K J
1500 Brighton Henrietta (14623-2340)
PHONE.................................585 292-0770
John S Kaupp, *President*
Joni Lucas, *COO*
Jeff Glover, *Mfg Spvr*
John Berg, *Sales Staff*
Ron Koenigs, *Sales Staff*
▲ EMP: 70
SQ FT: 18,000
SALES (est): 19.2MM Privately Held
WEB: www.jkfindings.com
SIC: 3911 Jewelry, precious metal

(G-14484)
JML OPTICAL INDUSTRIES LLC
Also Called: Gregg Sadwick
820 Linden Ave (14625-2710)
PHONE.................................585 248-8900
Bob Bicksler, *CEO*
Joseph Lobozzo II, *President*
Trett Sadwick, *COO*
Graldine Lynch, *Vice Pres*
Michael McCusker, *Vice Pres*
▲ EMP: 86
SQ FT: 72,000
SALES (est): 14.1MM Privately Held
SIC: 3827 Lenses, optical: all types except ophthalmic; mirrors, optical; prisms, optical

(G-14485)
JOHNSON CONTROLS INC
1669 Lake Ave Bldg 333 (14652-0001)
PHONE.................................585 724-2232
Lee Arbagast, *Branch Mgr*
EMP: 120 Privately Held

SIC: 2531 3714 3691 3822 Seats, automobile; motor vehicle body components & frame; instrument board assemblies, motor vehicle; lead acid batteries (storage batteries); building services monitoring controls, automatic; facilities support services
HQ: Johnson Controls, Inc.
  5757 N Green Bay Ave
  Milwaukee WI 53209
  414 524-1200

(G-14486)
JORDAN MACHINE INC
1241 Ridgeway Ave Ste I (14615-3757)
PHONE.................................585 647-3585
Thomas Lacey, *President*
Christine Lacey, *Principal*
Jordan Kesselring, *Vice Pres*
EMP: 5 EST: 2016
SALES (est): 202.8K Privately Held
SIC: 3599 Machine & other job shop work

(G-14487)
JTEKT TORSEN NORTH AMERICA
2 Jetview Dr (14624-4904)
PHONE.................................585 464-5000
Fax: 585 328-5477
Hiroyuki Kaijima, *President*
Y Kataoka, *President*
Gary Lynch, *Controller*
Christine Stokes, *Accountant*
Joseph Parisi, *Admin Sec*
▲ EMP: 10
SQ FT: 30,000
SALES: 2MM
SALES (corp-wide): 11.6B Privately Held
SIC: 3714 3711 Motor vehicle parts & accessories; motor vehicles & car bodies
HQ: Jtekt North America, Inc.
  47771 Halyard Dr
  Plymouth MI 48170
  734 454-1500

(G-14488)
JUST PRESS PRINT LLC
304 Whitney St (14606-1110)
PHONE.................................585 783-1300
Fax: 585 464-9632
Raphael Coccia, *President*
EMP: 5
SALES (est): 372.2K Privately Held
SIC: 2752 Commercial printing, lithographic

(G-14489)
K BARTHELMES MFG CO INC
61 Brooklea Dr (14624-2701)
PHONE.................................585 328-8140
Fax: 585 328-5932
John Wischmeyer, *President*
Janet Wischmeyer, *Admin Sec*
EMP: 15 EST: 1917
SQ FT: 55,000
SALES: 1.9MM Privately Held
WEB: www.barthelmes.com
SIC: 3444 Sheet metalwork

(G-14490)
KAMAN AUTOMATION INC
1000 University Ave (14607-1286)
PHONE.................................585 254-8840
EMP: 60
SALES (corp-wide): 1.8B Publicly Held
SIC: 3625 Relays & industrial controls; motor controls & accessories
HQ: Kaman Automation, Inc.
  1 Vision Way
  Bloomfield CT 06002
  860 687-5000

(G-14491)
KEVIN J KASSMAN
Also Called: Uniform Express
1408 Buffalo Rd (14624-1827)
PHONE.................................585 529-4245
Fax: 585 529-4247
Kevin J Kassman, *Owner*
EMP: 6
SQ FT: 4,500
SALES: 600K Privately Held
SIC: 2395 2396 Embroidery & art needlework; screen printing on fabric articles

GEOGRAPHIC SECTION

Rochester - Monroe County (G-14516)

(G-14492)
KLEE CORP
Also Called: Klees Car Wash and Detailing
340 Jefferson Rd (14623-2644)
PHONE.....................585 272-0320
Daniel Edelman, *Manager*
EMP: 7
SQ FT: 5,625
SALES (corp-wide): 9.9MM **Privately Held**
SIC: 3589 Car washing machinery
PA: Klee Corp
  3044 E Henrietta Rd
  Henrietta NY 14467
  585 321-1510

(G-14493)
KODAK ALARIS INC (HQ)
2400 Mount Read Blvd # 1175 (14615-2744)
PHONE.....................585 290-2891
Marc Jourlait, *CEO*
Rick Costanzo, *President*
Rick Costanzom, *President*
Dennis Olbrich, *President*
Nicki Zongrone, *President*
◆ **EMP:** 277
SQ FT: 340,000
SALES (est): 298.7MM
SALES (corp-wide): 812.9MM **Privately Held**
SIC: 3861 Photographic equipment & supplies
PA: Kodak Alaris Holdings Limited
  Hemel One Boundary Way
  Hemel Hempstead HERTS HP2 7
  845 757-3175

(G-14494)
KURZ AND ZOBEL INC
688 Colfax St (14606-3193)
PHONE.....................585 254-9060
Fax: 585 254-0123
Michael Zobel Jr, *President*
Sandy Rosengrant, *Office Mgr*
EMP: 8
SQ FT: 15,000
SALES (est): 867.9K **Privately Held**
SIC: 3599 3462 Machine shop, jobbing & repair; gear & chain forgings

(G-14495)
LAGOE-OSWEGO CORP
429 Antlers Dr (14618-2103)
PHONE.....................315 343-3160
Fax: 315 343-5882
David A Falk, *President*
Bertram Falk, *Vice Pres*
Ben Bailey, *Manager*
Glenn Sharkey, *Manager*
EMP: 30
SQ FT: 19,000
SALES (est): 4.5MM **Privately Held**
SIC: 3599 7692 Machine shop, jobbing & repair; welding repair

(G-14496)
LASERMAX INC
Also Called: Lasermaxdefense
3495 Winton Pl Ste A37 (14623-2898)
PHONE.....................585 272-5420
Fax: 585 272-5427
Susan H Walter, *President*
Will H Walter, *Exec VP*
James Bunnell, *Opers Staff*
Daniel J Maier, *CFO*
Joyce Worboys, *Accounts Mgr*
EMP: 54
SQ FT: 10,250
SALES (est): 11MM **Privately Held**
WEB: www.lasermax.com
SIC: 3699 3674 Laser systems & equipment; semiconductors & related devices

(G-14497)
LAZER INCORPORATED (PA)
Also Called: Lazer Photo Engraving
1465 Jefferson Rd Ste 110 (14623-3149)
PHONE.....................336 744-8047
Fax: 585 247-9647
Gary Stafford, *President*
Ken Smoker, *Manager*
Bill Eaton, *Information Mgr*
Lesia Telega, *Director*
EMP: 50
SQ FT: 10,000
SALES (est): 3.5MM **Privately Held**
WEB: www.lazerinc.com
SIC: 2796 Color separations for printing

(G-14498)
LENS TRIPTAR CO INC
439 Monroe Ave Ste 1 (14607-3787)
PHONE.....................585 473-4470
Fax: 585 473-3945
Allen Krisiloff, *President*
EMP: 5
SQ FT: 3,300
SALES (est): 821.4K **Privately Held**
WEB: www.triptar.com
SIC: 3827 Lenses, optical: all types except ophthalmic

(G-14499)
LEXINGTON MACHINING LLC
677 Buffalo Rd (14611-2014)
PHONE.....................585 235-0880
Ken Vivlamore, *Vice Pres*
Rick Donofrio, *Controller*
Kathi Horch, *Systems Staff*
EMP: 100 **Privately Held**
SIC: 3451 Screw machine products
PA: Lexington Machining Llc
  677 Buffalo Rd
  Rochester NY 14611

(G-14500)
LEXINGTON MACHINING LLC (PA)
677 Buffalo Rd (14611-2014)
PHONE.....................585 235-0880
Michael Lubin, *Ch of Bd*
Warren Deiano, *President*
Timothy Duemmel, *General Mgr*
Robert S Ducharme, *Engineer*
William Serow, *Engineer*
EMP: 174
SALES (est): 24MM **Privately Held**
WEB: www.lexingtonmachining.com
SIC: 3451 Screw machine products

(G-14501)
LMT TECHNOLOGY SOLUTIONS ✪
4 Commercial St Ste 400 (14614-1000)
PHONE.....................585 784-7470
Lillian Sandvik,
EMP: 10 **EST:** 2017
SALES (est): 221.8K **Privately Held**
SIC: 7372 Prepackaged software

(G-14502)
LOAD/N/GO BEVERAGE CORP (PA)
Also Called: Fiz Beverages
355 Portland Ave (14605-1565)
PHONE.....................585 218-4019
Fax: 585 467-7114
Paul Johnson, *President*
Linda Povlock, *Office Mgr*
EMP: 10 **EST:** 1964
SQ FT: 11,000
SALES (est): 1.6MM **Privately Held**
SIC: 2086 5181 5149 5921 Soft drinks: packaged in cans, bottles, etc.; beer & other fermented malt liquors; soft drinks; beer (packaged)

(G-14503)
LOGICAL OPERATIONS INC
3535 Winton Pl (14623-2803)
PHONE.....................585 350-7000
Fax: 585 288-7411
Bill Rosenthal, *President*
Michelle Mattick, *CFO*
▲ **EMP:** 110
SALES (est): 18.8MM **Privately Held**
SIC: 2732 Books: printing & binding

(G-14504)
LOUIS HEINDL & SON INC
Also Called: Heindl Printers
306 Central Ave (14605-3007)
P.O. Box 31121 (14603-1121)
PHONE.....................585 454-5080
Fax: 585 454-5350
P J Heindl, *President*
Debra Heindl, *Vice Pres*
Craig Schinsing, *Manager*
EMP: 6 **EST:** 1873
SQ FT: 3,500

SALES (est): 540K **Privately Held**
SIC: 2752 2759 2791 2789 Commercial printing, offset; letterpress printing; typesetting; bookbinding & related work

(G-14505)
LUMETRICS INC
1565 Jefferson Rd Ste 420 (14623-3190)
PHONE.....................585 214-2455
John Hart, *President*
Filipp Ignatovich, *General Mgr*
Todd Blalock, *Vice Pres*
Steve Heveron-Smith, *Vice Pres*
Steve Kelly, *Vice Pres*
▼ **EMP:** 17
SQ FT: 4,416
SALES (est): 4.4MM **Privately Held**
WEB: www.lumetrics.com
SIC: 3827 Optical instruments & apparatus

(G-14506)
MACAUTO USA INC
80 Excel Dr (14621-3470)
PHONE.....................585 342-2060
Fax: 585 342-2085
J J Liao, *President*
Jerry Hsu, *QC Mgr*
Douglas Chang, *Treasurer*
▲ **EMP:** 30
SQ FT: 15,000
SALES (est): 4.8MM
SALES (corp-wide): 141.8MM **Privately Held**
SIC: 3089 Automotive parts, plastic
PA: Macauto Industrial Co., Ltd.
  No. 6, Yongke 5th Rd.,
  Tainan City 71041
  623 310-88

(G-14507)
MACHINECRAFT INC
1645 Lyell Ave Ste 125 (14606-2331)
PHONE.....................585 436-1070
Alan D Lintz, *Ch of Bd*
EMP: 25
SQ FT: 8,750
SALES (est): 2.4MM **Privately Held**
SIC: 3544 Special dies & tools

(G-14508)
MACINNES TOOL CORPORATION
1700 Hudson Ave Ste 3 (14617-5155)
PHONE.....................585 467-1920
Fax: 585 467-7807
Gary Haines, *President*
Sherry Haines, *Treasurer*
Janet Lawson, *Office Mgr*
EMP: 20 **EST:** 1953
SQ FT: 6,000
SALES (est): 2.8MM **Privately Held**
WEB: www.macto.com
SIC: 3545 5085 Cutting tools for machine tools; industrial supplies

(G-14509)
MADISON & DUNN
850 Saint Paul St Ste 29 (14605-1065)
PHONE.....................585 563-7760
Christine Baliva, *Owner*
EMP: 6
SALES (est): 834K **Privately Held**
SIC: 2426 Flooring, hardwood

(G-14510)
MAGNA PRODUCTS CORP
777 Mount Read Blvd (14606-2129)
PHONE.....................585 647-2280
Fax: 585 647-2155
Kenneth Morrow, *President*
Pat Morrow, *Vice Pres*
Brian Reeves, *Accounting Mgr*
Norene Bauer, *Financial Exec*
Andrew Bolton, *Sales Staff*
EMP: 20
SALES (est): 4.2MM **Privately Held**
WEB: www.magnaproducts.com
SIC: 3621 3566 Servomotors, electric; drives, high speed industrial, except hydrostatic

(G-14511)
MAGNETIC TECHNOLOGIES CORP (DH)
770 Linden Ave (14625-2764)
PHONE.....................585 385-9010

Fax: 585 385-5625
Gordon H McNeil, *Ch of Bd*
Jeremy Morgan, *Vice Pres*
Steve Gleckler, *Facilities Mgr*
Kathleen Palia, *Controller*
Greg Daly, *Accounting Mgr*
▲ **EMP:** 60
SQ FT: 70,000
SALES (est): 11.2MM
SALES (corp-wide): 978.3MM **Publicly Held**
WEB: www.arnoldmagnetics.com
SIC: 3579 Typing & word processing machines
HQ: Arnold Magnetic Technologies Corporation
  770 Linden Ave
  Rochester NY 14625
  585 385-9010

(G-14512)
MAIDSTONE COFFEE CO
60 Mushroom Blvd (14623-3202)
PHONE.....................585 272-1040
Fax: 585 272-8495
Garrett Dobesh, *CEO*
EMP: 38
SALES (est): 5.9MM
SALES (corp-wide): 34.4MM **Privately Held**
SIC: 2095 Roasted coffee
HQ: Restaurant Brands International Inc
  226 Wyecroft Rd
  Oakville ON L6K 3
  905 845-6511

(G-14513)
MANITOU CONCRETE
1260 Jefferson Rd (14623-3104)
PHONE.....................585 424-6040
Fax: 585 424-1846
John Topping, *Sales Engr*
John Pelrier, *Manager*
J McCarthy, *Manager*
Jim Wagner, *Director*
EMP: 65
SQ FT: 2,536
SALES (est): 6.6MM **Privately Held**
SIC: 3273 Ready-mixed concrete

(G-14514)
MANUFACTURING RESOURCES INC
2392 Innovation Way # 4 (14624-6225)
PHONE.....................631 481-0041
Fax: 585 473-0099
James Wildman, *Ch of Bd*
James Widman, *Ch of Bd*
EMP: 40 **EST:** 2002
SQ FT: 30,000
SALES (est): 805.7K **Privately Held**
WEB: www.mfgresource.com
SIC: 3444 3549 Sheet metalwork; assembly machines, including robotic

(G-14515)
MANUFACTURING SOLUTIONS INC
850 Saint Paul St Ste 11 (14605-1065)
PHONE.....................585 235-3320
Fax: 585 235-3324
Oscar Wilson, *President*
Jane Murray, *Manager*
EMP: 25
SQ FT: 5,000
SALES (est): 3.8MM **Privately Held**
WEB: www.mfgsolonline.com
SIC: 3699 Electrical equipment & supplies

(G-14516)
MARACLE INDUSTRIAL FINSHG CO
93 Kilbourn Rd (14618-3607)
PHONE.....................585 387-9077
Fax: 585 872-0285
Thomas Maracle, *President*
Nelson Maracle, *Vice Pres*
Valerie Eaton, *Office Mgr*
EMP: 30 **EST:** 1960
SQ FT: 30,000
SALES (est): 3MM **Privately Held**
SIC: 3471 Finishing, metals or formed products

Rochester - Monroe County (G-14517) GEOGRAPHIC SECTION

(G-14517)
MARDON TOOL & DIE CO INC
19 Lois St (14606-1801)
PHONE..................585 254-4545
Fax: 585 254-8258
Donald Fox, *President*
EMP: 13 EST: 1981
SQ FT: 4,000
SALES (est): 1.8MM Privately Held
SIC: 3599 Machine shop, jobbing & repair

(G-14518)
MAREX AQUISITION CORP
1385 Emerson St (14606-3027)
PHONE..................585 458-3940
Gary Baxter, *Ch of Bd*
John Olivieri Sr, *Ch of Bd*
Leonard Olivieri, *Vice Pres*
▲ EMP: 115
SQ FT: 55,000
SALES (est): 9.6MM
SALES (corp-wide): 51MM Privately Held
WEB: www.martecindustries.com
SIC: 3469 3444 3443 3441 Metal stampings; sheet metalwork; fabricated plate work (boiler shop); fabricated structural metal
PA: Peko Precision Products, Inc.
    1400 Emerson St
    Rochester NY 14606
    585 647-3010

(G-14519)
MARTEC INDUSTRIES
1385 Emerson St (14606-3027)
PHONE..................585 458-3940
Fax: 585 458-5412
John Olivieri, *Principal*
Craig Tallman, *Mfg Staff*
EMP: 16
SALES (est): 2.2MM Privately Held
SIC: 3999 Manufacturing industries

(G-14520)
MASTRO GRAPHIC ARTS INC
67 Deep Rock Rd (14624-3519)
PHONE..................585 436-7570
Fax: 585 436-4245
Rae Mastrofilippo, *Ch of Bd*
Ms Rae Mastrofilippo, *Ch of Bd*
William Betteridge, *President*
Thomas Tortora, *CFO*
Nick Mastro, *Treasurer*
EMP: 34
SQ FT: 23,000
SALES (est): 8.1MM Privately Held
WEB: www.mastrographics.com
SIC: 2759 2754 Screen printing; rotary photogravure printing

(G-14521)
MCALPIN INDUSTRIES INC (PA)
255 Hollenbeck St (14621-3294)
PHONE..................585 266-3060
Kenneth McAlpin, *CEO*
John Rowe, *General Mgr*
Mike McAlpin, *Exec VP*
Dave Krieger, *Plant Mgr*
Patti Clossom, *Mfg Mgr*
▲ EMP: 150 EST: 1964
SQ FT: 140,000
SALES (est): 29.2MM Privately Held
WEB: www.mcalpin-ind.com
SIC: 3444 Sheet metalwork

(G-14522)
MCALPIN INDUSTRIES INC
Also Called: Monroe Plating Div
265 Hollenbeck St (14621-3294)
PHONE..................585 544-5335
Fax: 585 266-8091
Mike Mumm, *Branch Mgr*
EMP: 45
SQ FT: 8,000
SALES (corp-wide): 29.2MM Privately Held
WEB: www.mcalpin-ind.com
SIC: 3471 Plating & polishing
PA: Mcalpin Industries, Inc.
    255 Hollenbeck St
    Rochester NY 14621
    585 266-3060

(G-14523)
MCM NATURAL STONE INC
860 Linden Ave Ste 1 (14625-2718)
PHONE..................585 586-6510
Marilyn Valle, *President*
EMP: 12
SALES (est): 1.5MM Privately Held
WEB: www.mcmstone.com
SIC: 3281 5032 1423 Granite, cut & shaped; limestone, cut & shaped; granite building stone; limestone; crushed & broken granite

(G-14524)
MELIORUM TECHNOLOGIES INC
620 Park Ave 145 (14607-2943)
PHONE..................585 313-0616
Jason Rama, *President*
John Gibson, *Bd of Directors*
▼ EMP: 5
SALES (est): 487.3K Privately Held
SIC: 2821 2819 Silicone resins; aluminum oxide

(G-14525)
MERCURY PRINT PRODUCTIONS INC (PA)
2332 Innovation Way 4 (14624-6225)
PHONE..................585 458-7900
Fax: 585 458-2896
John Place, *CEO*
Christian Schamberger, *President*
Dean McDonough, *Dean*
Scott Fox, *Vice Pres*
Christian Schaumburger, *Vice Pres*
▲ EMP: 181
SQ FT: 80,000
SALES (est): 68.2MM Privately Held
WEB: www.mercuryprint.com
SIC: 2752 7334 2791 2789 Commercial printing, offset; photocopying & duplicating services; typesetting; bookbinding & related work

(G-14526)
METROPOLITAN GRANITE & MBL INC
860 Maple St Ste 100 (14611-1612)
PHONE..................585 342-7020
Fax: 585 342-7032
Helmettin Cakir, *President*
Melissa Zeaso, *Manager*
EMP: 5
SALES (est): 450K Privately Held
SIC: 2541 Counter & sink tops

(G-14527)
MICHAEL TODD STEVENS
Also Called: Rochester Screen Printing
95 Mount Read Blvd # 125 (14611-1923)
PHONE..................585 436-9957
Michael Stevens, *Owner*
EMP: 5
SALES (est): 317K Privately Held
SIC: 3953 Screens, textile printing

(G-14528)
MICRO INSTRUMENT CORP
Also Called: Automated Systems Group
1199 Emerson St (14606-3038)
P.O. Box 60619 (14606-0619)
PHONE..................585 458-3150
John Pfeffer, *Ch of Bd*
Anthony De Salvo, *President*
William Gunther, *President*
Chris Lindstrom, *Project Mgr*
Steve Hakes, *Materials Mgr*
EMP: 100 EST: 1944
SQ FT: 56,000
SALES (est): 23.7MM Privately Held
WEB: www.microinst.com
SIC: 3599 3613 7389 6552 Machine & other job shop work; control panels, electric; grinding, precision; commercial or industrial; land subdividers & developers, commercial; special dies, tools, jigs & fixtures; aluminum foundries

(G-14529)
MICRO THREADED PRODUCTS INC
325 Mount Read Blvd Ste 4 (14611-1928)
PHONE..................585 288-0080
Robert Osipovitch, *President*
EMP: 5
SALES (est): 500K Privately Held
SIC: 3451 Screw machine products

(G-14530)
MICROERA PRINTERS INC
304 Whitney St (14606-1110)
PHONE..................585 783-1300
Bruno Coccia, *Ch of Bd*
Raphael Coccia, *Vice Pres*
EMP: 22
SQ FT: 20,000
SALES (est): 4.4MM Privately Held
WEB: www.microera.com
SIC: 2752 Commercial printing, lithographic

(G-14531)
MICROMOD AUTOMATION INC
3 Townline Cir Ste 4 (14623-2537)
PHONE..................585 321-9200
Fax: 585 321-9291
Richard Keane, *President*
Carol McNelly, *Vice Pres*
Sharon Masseth, *Prdtn Mgr*
Nancy Gilbride, *Treasurer*
Juan Ruiz, *Regl Sales Mgr*
EMP: 20
SALES (est): 4.2MM Privately Held
WEB: www.micmod.com
SIC: 3625 Industrial controls: push button, selector switches, pilot

(G-14532)
MICROMOD AUTOMTN & CONTRLS INC
3 Townline Cir Ste 4 (14623-2537)
PHONE..................585 321-9209
Wayne France, *General Mgr*
Nancy Gilbride, *CFO*
Rochelle Pettijohn, *Sales Staff*
EMP: 13
SALES (est): 2.2MM Privately Held
SIC: 3823 Industrial process control instruments

(G-14533)
MICRON INDS ROCHESTER INC
31 Industrial Park Cir (14624-2403)
PHONE..................585 247-6130
Fax: 585 247-0783
Stephen K Schmidt, *President*
Kirk Schmidt, *Vice Pres*
Eric Schmidt, *Admin Sec*
EMP: 9
SQ FT: 20,000
SALES (est): 1.3MM Privately Held
WEB: www.micronindustries.com
SIC: 3544 Special dies & tools; industrial molds

(G-14534)
MILLER METAL FABRICATING INC
315 Commerce Dr (14623-3507)
PHONE..................585 359-3400
Steven Mertz, *President*
EMP: 9
SQ FT: 10,500
SALES (est): 1.3MM Privately Held
SIC: 3443 3441 3545 7692 Weldments; fabricated structural metal for bridges; precision tools, machinists'; welding repair; sandblasting of building exteriors

(G-14535)
MINORITY REPORTER INC (PA)
19 Borrowdale Dr (14626-1751)
P.O. Box 26352 (14626-0352)
PHONE..................585 225-3628
Dave McCleary, *Principal*
EMP: 8
SALES (est): 568.2K Privately Held
SIC: 2711 Newspapers, publishing & printing

(G-14536)
MITCHELL MACHINE TOOL LLC
190 Murray St (14606-1126)
PHONE..................585 254-7520
Michael Mitchell,
Maryland Mitchell,
EMP: 5
SALES (est): 330K Privately Held
WEB: www.mitchellmachinetool.com
SIC: 3599 Machine & other job shop work

(G-14537)
MKS INSTRUMENTS INC
100 Highpower Rd (14623-3498)
PHONE..................585 292-7472
Paul Eyerman, *General Mgr*
Bill Schumacher, *Opers Mgr*
Mary Hoopes, *Senior Buyer*
Karen Savastano, *Senior Buyer*
Ana Espinoza, *Buyer*
EMP: 20
SALES (corp-wide): 1.3B Publicly Held
WEB: www.mksinst.com
SIC: 3823 Industrial instrmnts msrmnt display/control process variable
PA: Mks Instruments, Inc.
    2 Tech Dr Ste 201
    Andover MA 01810
    978 645-5500

(G-14538)
MKS MEDICAL ELECTRONICS
Also Called: M K S
100 Highpower Rd (14623-3498)
PHONE..................585 292-7400
Paul M Eyerman, *General Mgr*
Yogendra Chawla, *Engng Exec*
Kemble Morrison, *Controller*
Jonna Gearry, *Office Mgr*
Don Fowler, *Director*
EMP: 112 EST: 1970
SQ FT: 20,000
SALES (est): 11.3MM
SALES (corp-wide): 1.3B Publicly Held
WEB: www.mksinst.com
SIC: 3621 3663 Generating apparatus & parts, electrical; amplifiers, RF power & IF
PA: Mks Instruments, Inc.
    2 Tech Dr Ste 201
    Andover MA 01810
    978 645-5500

(G-14539)
MOLECULAR GLASSES INC
1667 Lake Ave Ste 278b (14615-3047)
PHONE..................585 210-2861
Michel Molaire, *CEO*
Mark Juba, *COO*
EMP: 8 EST: 2015
SQ FT: 1,000
SALES (est): 279.7K Privately Held
SIC: 2869 High purity grade chemicals, organic

(G-14540)
MONROE COUNTY AUTO SVCS INC (PA)
Also Called: Ziebart
1505 Lyell Ave (14606-2109)
PHONE..................585 764-3741
Fax: 585 458-0614
Anthony Mattiacio, *President*
Mark Porter, *Real Est Agnt*
EMP: 36
SALES: 7MM Privately Held
SIC: 3479 5012 Coating, rust preventive; automotive brokers

(G-14541)
MOONEY-KEEHLEY INC
38 Saginaw Dr (14623-3132)
PHONE..................585 271-1573
Fax: 585 271-1579
David Hedges, *President*
Kenneth Hempson, *Owner*
Elihu Hedges Jr, *Vice Pres*
Judith Gessner, *Treasurer*
Elizabeth Hedges, *Admin Sec*
EMP: 6 EST: 1944
SQ FT: 12,000
SALES (est): 910.3K Privately Held
WEB: www.mooneykeehley.com
SIC: 2752 7389 Cards, lithographed; engraving service
PA: 22 Winston, Inc.
    22 Winston Pl
    Rochester NY 14607
    585 271-1573

(G-14542)
MORGOOD TOOLS INC
940 Millstead Way (14624-5108)
P.O. Box 24997 (14624-0997)
PHONE..................585 436-8828
Fax: 585 436-2426
Virginia L Marshall, *CEO*
Doug Meier, *President*

GEOGRAPHIC SECTION

Rochester - Monroe County (G-14567)

James Faas, *Engineer*
Diane Soper, *CFO*
Janet Garrison, *Bookkeeper*
EMP: 60 **EST:** 1945
SQ FT: 30,000
SALES (est): 9MM **Privately Held**
WEB: www.morgood.com
SIC: 3545 Cutting tools for machine tools; cams (machine tool accessories)

(G-14543)
MORRIS MACHINING SERVICE INC
95 Mount Read Blvd (14611-1923)
PHONE.................585 527-8100
James Morris, *President*
EMP: 5
SQ FT: 4,000
SALES (est): 220K **Privately Held**
SIC: 3599 Machine shop, jobbing & repair

(G-14544)
MULLERS CIDER HOUSE LLC
1344 University Ave # 180 (14607-1656)
PHONE.................585 287-5875
Samuel Conjerti, *Mng Member*
EMP: 5 **EST:** 2015
SALES (est): 322.3K **Privately Held**
SIC: 2099 Cider, nonalcoholic

(G-14545)
MULTIPLE IMPRSSONS OF RCHESTER (PA)
Also Called: Minuteman Press
41 Chestnut St (14604-2303)
PHONE.................585 546-1160
William Malone Sr, *President*
Jay Malone, *Corp Secy*
Brad Amedeo, *Prdtn Mgr*
EMP: 8
SQ FT: 3,600
SALES (est): 719.8K **Privately Held**
WEB: www.dtmmp.com
SIC: 2752 7334 2791 2789 Commercial printing, lithographic; photocopying & duplicating services; typesetting; bookbinding & related work

(G-14546)
MWI INC (PA)
1269 Brighton Henrietta T (14623-2485)
PHONE.................585 424-4200
David Mc Mahon, *Ch of Bd*
Kevin Mc Mahon, *President*
Brian Mc Mahon, *COO*
John DOD, *Exec VP*
Ryan Mc Mahon, *Vice Pres*
▲ **EMP:** 100
SQ FT: 28,000
SALES (est): 22.9MM **Privately Held**
WEB: www.mwiedm.com
SIC: 3624 Carbon & graphite products

(G-14547)
NALGE NUNC INTERNATIONAL CORP (DH)
1600 Lexington Ave # 107 (14606-3000)
PHONE.................585 498-2661
Fax: 585 264-3709
Michaeline Reed, *Principal*
Ken Bunn, *VP Opers*
Paul Crane, *Engineer*
Gregory Pankratz, *Engineer*
David Sauter, *Engineer*
▲ **EMP:** 903
SQ FT: 275,000
SALES (est): 219.5MM
SALES (corp-wide): 18.2B **Publicly Held**
WEB: www.nuncbrand.com
SIC: 3089 3949 3821 3085 Plastic processing; plastic & fiberglass tanks; sporting & athletic goods; laboratory apparatus & furniture; plastics bottles; laminated plastics plate & sheet
HQ: Fisher Scientific International Llc
81 Wyman St
Waltham MA 02451
781 622-1000

(G-14548)
NATIONWIDE CIRCUITS INC
1444 Emerson St (14606-3009)
PHONE.................585 328-0791
Fax: 585 328-9152
Alan Austin, *President*
Judith Austin, *Vice Pres*
Tim Sauer, *Vice Pres*
Brett Austin, *Human Res Mgr*
David Ciufo, *Sales Mgr*
EMP: 28 **EST:** 1971
SQ FT: 20,000
SALES (est): 3.9MM **Privately Held**
WEB: www.nciproto.com
SIC: 3672 Wiring boards

(G-14549)
NATIONWIDE PRECISION PDTS CORP
Also Called: Hn Precision-Ny
200 Tech Park Dr (14623-2445)
PHONE.................585 272-7100
Fax: 585 272-0171
Dan Nash, *CEO*
Dan Brooks, *Vice Pres*
Rick Menaldino, *Vice Pres*
Sharon Pierce, *Vice Pres*
Cleve Claudill, *Engng Exec*
▲ **EMP:** 425 **EST:** 1999
SQ FT: 160,000
SALES (est): 109.9MM **Privately Held**
WEB: www.nationwideprecision.com
SIC: 3356 Nonferrous rolling & drawing

(G-14550)
NAVITAR INC
200 Commerce Dr (14623-3589)
PHONE.................585 359-4000
Julian Goldstein, *Ch of Bd*
Robert Prato, *General Mgr*
Donna Backus, *COO*
Thomas McCune, *COO*
Craig Fitzgerald, *Vice Pres*
▼ **EMP:** 71
SQ FT: 19,000
SALES (est): 16MM **Privately Held**
WEB: www.navitar.com
SIC: 3699 3651 3827 3674 Laser systems & equipment; household audio & video equipment; optical instruments & lenses; semiconductors & related devices; radio & TV communications equipment; pressed & blown glass

(G-14551)
NBN TECHNOLOGIES LLC
136 Wilshire Rd (14618-1221)
PHONE.................585 355-5556
Shimon Miamon PHD,
Joseph Wodenscheck,
EMP: 6
SALES (est): 698.4K **Privately Held**
SIC: 3699 Electrical equipment & supplies

(G-14552)
NEW YORK MANUFACTURED PRODUCTS
6 Cairn St (14611-2416)
PHONE.................585 254-9353
Salvatore Anselmo, *Partner*
Boubane Aselmo, *Partner*
EMP: 10
SALES: 2MM **Privately Held**
SIC: 3441 3499 3089 Fabricated structural metal; metal household articles; injection molding of plastics

(G-14553)
NEW YORK MANUFACTURING CORP
6 Cairn St (14611-2416)
PHONE.................585 254-9353
Salvatore Anselmo,
Bouabane Anselmo,
EMP: 6
SQ FT: 20,000
SALES (est): 1.1MM **Privately Held**
WEB: www.newyorkmanufacturing.com
SIC: 7692 Welding repair

(G-14554)
NEW YORK MARKING DEVICES CORP
C H Morse Stamp Co
700 Clinton Ave S Ste 2 (14620-1383)
PHONE.................585 454-5188
Fax: 585 454-5446
Joseph Stummer, *President*
Peter Stummer, *Vice Pres*
Peter J Stummer, *Branch Mgr*
EMP: 6
SALES (corp-wide): 1.7MM **Privately Held**
WEB: www.nymarking.com
SIC: 3953 Marking devices
PA: New York Marking Devices Corp
2207 Teall Ave
Syracuse NY 13206
315 463-8641

(G-14555)
NEWPORT CORPORATION
705 Saint Paul St (14605-1730)
PHONE.................585 248-4246
Linda Nittolo, *Purchasing*
Jeff Olson, *Engineer*
Ann M Brennan, *Human Resources*
Christophe Palmer, *Manager*
Paula Gullo, *Manager*
EMP: 20
SALES (corp-wide): 1.3B **Publicly Held**
WEB: www.newport.com
SIC: 3821 Laboratory apparatus & furniture
HQ: Newport Corporation
1791 Deere Ave
Irvine CA 92606
949 863-3144

(G-14556)
NEWPORT ROCHESTER INC
705 Saint Paul St (14605-1730)
PHONE.................585 262-1325
Chris Palmer, *General Mgr*
▲ **EMP:** 60
SALES: 19.3MM
SALES (corp-wide): 1.3B **Publicly Held**
WEB: www.newport.com
SIC: 3827 Gratings, diffraction
HQ: Newport Corporation
1791 Deere Ave
Irvine CA 92606
949 863-3144

(G-14557)
NICOFORM INC
72 Cascade Dr Ste 12 (14614-1109)
PHONE.................585 454-5530
Fax: 585 454-5167
Berl Stein, *President*
Richard Kraynik, *Vice Pres*
Chris Reynolds, *QC Mgr*
John Contino, *Engineer*
Joe Jachlewski, *Engineer*
▼ **EMP:** 20
SQ FT: 12,000
SALES: 2.4MM **Privately Held**
WEB: www.nicoform.com
SIC: 3544 3599 Industrial molds; bellows, industrial: metal

(G-14558)
NORDON INC (PA)
691 Exchange St (14608-2714)
PHONE.................585 546-6200
Fax: 585 546-7748
Terry J Donovan, *CEO*
John Buck, *Project Mgr*
Jenni Smith, *Purchasing*
Richard Sullivan, *Sales Engr*
Sara Bruzda, *Manager*
◆ **EMP:** 100
SQ FT: 64,000
SALES (est): 25.2MM **Privately Held**
WEB: www.nordon.org
SIC: 3089 3544 Injection molding of plastics; industrial molds

(G-14559)
NORTH AMERICAN BREWERIES INC (DH)
Also Called: Northamerican Breweries
445 Saint Paul St (14605-1726)
PHONE.................585 546-1030
Kris Sirchio, *CEO*
Richard Lozyniak, *Ch of Bd*
Raquel Vargas, *President*
Larry Cornish, *District Mgr*
Justin Horvatin, *District Mgr*
▼ **EMP:** 10
SALES (est): 357MM **Privately Held**
SIC: 2082 Beer (alcoholic beverage)

(G-14560)
NORTH AMERICAN MINT INC
1600 Lexington Ave 240a (14606-3062)
PHONE.................585 654-8500
William La Mere Jr, *President*
Brad La Mere, *Principal*
Michael La Mere, *Principal*
EMP: 6
SQ FT: 1,200
SALES (est): 727.6K **Privately Held**
SIC: 3911 Medals, precious or semi-precious metal

(G-14561)
NORTH AMERICAN STONE INC
1358 E Ridge Rd (14621-2005)
PHONE.................585 266-4020
Fax: 585 266-4042
Dave Julian, *President*
EMP: 7
SALES (est): 1MM **Privately Held**
SIC: 3281 Cut stone & stone products

(G-14562)
NORTH AMRCN BRWRIES HLDNGS LLC (PA)
445 Saint Paul St (14605-1726)
PHONE.................585 546-1030
Rich Lozyniak, *CEO*
Katie Blahowicz, *Controller*
EMP: 26
SALES (est): 76.7MM **Privately Held**
SIC: 2082 Beer (alcoholic beverage)

(G-14563)
NORTHEASTERN SEALCOAT INC
470 Hollenbeck St Bldg 3 (14621-2213)
PHONE.................585 544-4372
Shawn Grimes, *President*
EMP: 10
SQ FT: 4,000
SALES (est): 1.9MM **Privately Held**
SIC: 2951 2952 4959 Asphalt paving mixtures & blocks; asphalt felts & coatings; snowplowing

(G-14564)
NORTHERN AIR SYSTEMS INC (PA)
3605 Buffalo Rd (14624-1120)
PHONE.................585 594-5050
Fax: 585 594-8888
Timothy Confer, *President*
Garland Beasley, *Vice Pres*
Joseph Denninger, *Vice Pres*
Gerald Christie, *Project Mgr*
Kirk Hoak, *Mfg Staff*
EMP: 46
SQ FT: 45,000
SALES (est): 11.2MM **Privately Held**
SIC: 3585 Heating & air conditioning combination units

(G-14565)
NORTHERN AIR TECHNOLOGY INC (PA)
3605 Buffalo Rd (14624-1120)
PHONE.................585 594-5050
Timothy J Confer, *President*
Joseph Denninger, *Vice Pres*
EMP: 1 **EST:** 2000
SQ FT: 1,000
SALES (est): 1.1MM **Privately Held**
SIC: 3648 Outdoor lighting equipment

(G-14566)
NORTHERN KING LURES INC (PA)
167 Armstrong Rd (14616-2703)
P.O. Box 12482 (14612-0482)
PHONE.................585 865-3373
Fax: 585 865-7176
Patsy Distaffen, *President*
Etta Distaffen, *Treasurer*
Beverly Cahill, *Bookkeeper*
EMP: 5
SALES (est): 733K **Privately Held**
WEB: www.northernkinglures.com
SIC: 3949 Lures, fishing: artificial

(G-14567)
NU WAYS INC
655 Pullman Ave (14615-3334)
PHONE.................585 254-7510
Edward A Coleman, *President*
Richard Albert, *Treasurer*
Michael Bater, *Finance*
EMP: 6 **EST:** 1996

Rochester - Monroe County (G-14568)

SALES: 1.2MM **Privately Held**
SIC: 2591 Window blinds

(G-14568)
OLEDWORKS LLC (PA)
1645 Lyell Ave Ste 140 (14606-2331)
PHONE..................................585 287-6802
David Dejoy, *CEO*
Joh Hamer, *COO*
Ralph Young, *Consultant*
Michael Boroson, *CTO*
Giana Phelan,
EMP: 27
SALES (est): 4.6MM **Privately Held**
SIC: 3641 3646 3999 3674 Electric lamps; commercial indusl & institutional electric lighting fixtures; barber & beauty shop equipment; light emitting diodes

(G-14569)
OMG DESSERTS INC
1227 Ridgeway Ave Ste J (14615-3759)
PHONE..................................585 698-1561
Mary E Graham, *President*
Mary Graham, *President*
EMP: 10
SALES (est): 1MM **Privately Held**
SIC: 2099 Desserts, ready-to-mix

(G-14570)
OMNI-ID USA INC
1200 Ridgeway Ave Ste 106 (14615-3758)
PHONE..................................585 697-9913
George E Daddis Jr, *President*
Tony Kington, *COO*
Ed Nabrotzky, *Exec VP*
Andre Cote, *Senior VP*
Tracy Gay, *Vice Pres*
EMP: 37
SALES (est): 5.6MM **Privately Held**
WEB: www.omni-id.com
SIC: 3825 Radio frequency measuring equipment

(G-14571)
ON SEMICONDUCTOR CORPORATION
1964 Lake Ave (14615-2316)
PHONE..................................585 784-5770
Brett Nicholson, *Business Mgr*
David Sackett, *Manager*
Joe Blakely, *Info Tech Dir*
Wilson Weir, *Network Tech*
Cindy Van Buren, *Director*
EMP: 8
SALES (est): 1.1MM **Privately Held**
SIC: 3674 Semiconductors & related devices

(G-14572)
ONTARIO PLASTICS INC
2503 Dewey Ave (14616-4728)
PHONE..................................585 663-2644
Fax: 585 865-7774
Gerard Reynolds, *President*
Jim Beifus, *Principal*
Ralph E Barnes, *Vice Pres*
Dorraine Coughlin, *Asst Controller*
M Lambert, *Director*
▲ EMP: 35 EST: 1945
SQ FT: 40,000
SALES (est): 7.8MM **Privately Held**
WEB: www.ontario-plastics.com
SIC: 3082 3089 Unsupported plastics profile shapes; plastic containers, except foam; boxes, plastic

(G-14573)
ORMEC SYSTEMS CORP (PA)
19 Linden Park (14625-2776)
PHONE..................................585 385-3520
Fax: 585 385-6833
Edward J Krasnicki, *CEO*
David Goodwin, *Research*
Robert McMillen, *Engineer*
Dennis Morrow, *VP Sls/Mktg*
John Greve, *Controller*
EMP: 35
SQ FT: 15,600
SALES (est): 6MM **Privately Held**
WEB: www.ormec.com
SIC: 3823 3672 Controllers for process variables, all types; printed circuit boards

(G-14574)
OROLIA USA INC
Also Called: Spectracom
1565 Jefferson Rd Ste 460 (14623-3190)
PHONE..................................585 321-5800
Elizabeth Withers, *President*
John Fischer, *Vice Pres*
Josh Harris, *Sls & Mktg Exec*
Philip Teece, *Sls & Mktg Exec*
Tony Diflorio, *Marketing Staff*
EMP: 55 EST: 1972
SQ FT: 26,000
SALES (est): 16.2MM **Privately Held**
WEB: www.spectracomcorp.com
SIC: 3829 Measuring & controlling devices
HQ: Orolia Holding Sas
Drakkar Batiment D
Valbonne 06560
492 907-040

(G-14575)
ORTHO-CLINICAL DIAGNOSTICS INC
100 Latona Rd Bldg 313 (14626)
PHONE..................................585 453-4771
EMP: 400
SALES (corp-wide): 916.5MM **Privately Held**
SIC: 3841 Diagnostic apparatus, medical
PA: Ortho-Clinical Diagnostics, Inc.
1001 Us Highway 202
Raritan NJ 08869
908 218-8000

(G-14576)
ORTHO-CLINICAL DIAGNOSTICS INC
Also Called: Ortho/Rochester Tech
2402 Innovation Way # 3 (14624-6226)
PHONE..................................585 453-5200
EMP: 14
SALES (corp-wide): 916.5MM **Privately Held**
SIC: 3841 Diagnostic apparatus, medical
PA: Ortho-Clinical Diagnostics, Inc.
1001 Us Highway 202
Raritan NJ 08869
908 218-8000

(G-14577)
ORTHO-CLINICAL DIAGNOSTICS INC
1000 Lee Rd (14626)
PHONE..................................585 453-3000
Linda Farr, *Manager*
EMP: 33
SALES (corp-wide): 916.5MM **Privately Held**
WEB: www.orthoclinical.com
SIC: 2835 Blood derivative diagnostic agents
PA: Ortho-Clinical Diagnostics, Inc.
1001 Us Highway 202
Raritan NJ 08869
908 218-8000

(G-14578)
ORTHOGONAL
1999 Lake Ave (14650-0001)
PHONE..................................585 254-2775
John Defranco, *CEO*
Fox Holt, *Principal*
Victor Hsia, *Vice Pres*
Terrence O'Toole, *Vice Pres*
EMP: 5
SALES (est): 684.6K **Privately Held**
SIC: 3679 Liquid crystal displays (LCD)

(G-14579)
ORTHOTICS & PROSTHETICS DEPT
Also Called: Strong Hospital
4901 Lac De Ville Blvd (14618-5647)
PHONE..................................585 341-9299
Rob Brown, *Manager*
EMP: 15
SALES (est): 978.4K **Privately Held**
SIC: 3842 Orthopedic appliances

(G-14580)
OTEX PROTECTIVE INC
2180 Brighton Henrietta (14623-2704)
PHONE..................................585 232-7160
Jacob Weidert, *CEO*
EMP: 6

SALES (est): 738.8K **Privately Held**
SIC: 2311 Men's & boys' uniforms

(G-14581)
OZIPKO ENTERPRISES INC
Also Called: Printing Plus
125 White Spruce Blvd # 5 (14623-1607)
PHONE..................................585 424-6740
Rita Ozipko, *President*
Carl Ozipko, *Vice Pres*
Jim Ozipko, *Admin Sec*
EMP: 8
SQ FT: 3,000
SALES (est): 890K **Privately Held**
SIC: 2752 2791 2789 Commercial printing, offset; typesetting; bookbinding & related work

(G-14582)
P & H MACHINE SHOP INC
40 Industrial Park Cir (14624-2404)
PHONE..................................585 247-5500
Fax: 585 247-5572
EMP: 5
SQ FT: 3,000
SALES (est): 360K **Privately Held**
SIC: 3544 Mfg Dies/Tools/Jigs/Fixtures

(G-14583)
P & R INDUSTRIES INC (PA)
1524 N Clinton Ave (14621-2206)
PHONE..................................585 266-6725
Fax: 585 266-0075
Lawrence F Coyle, *President*
Charles Sheelar, *Vice Pres*
Donna Stein, *Purch Agent*
Bob Brawn, *Engineer*
Brian Stein, *Sls & Mktg Exec*
EMP: 50
SQ FT: 22,000
SALES (est): 16.7MM **Privately Held**
SIC: 3544 3541 Special dies, tools, jigs & fixtures; machine tools, metal cutting type

(G-14584)
P & R INDUSTRIES INC
1524 N Clinton Ave (14621-2206)
PHONE..................................585 544-1811
Nick Natali, *Branch Mgr*
EMP: 10
SALES (corp-wide): 16.7MM **Privately Held**
SIC: 3544 Special dies & tools
PA: P & R Industries, Inc.
1524 N Clinton Ave
Rochester NY 14621
585 266-6725

(G-14585)
P K G EQUIPMENT INCORPORATED
367 Paul Rd (14624-4925)
PHONE..................................585 436-4650
Fax: 585 436-3751
Stephen Pontarelli, *CEO*
Stephen T Pontarelli, *Ch of Bd*
Timothy Brunke, *Engineer*
Maria Parker, *Treasurer*
Eddie Hebra, *Manager*
EMP: 30
SQ FT: 35,000
SALES (est): 8.3MM **Privately Held**
WEB: www.pkgequipment.com
SIC: 3559 3441 Metal finishing equipment for plating, etc.; fabricated structural metal

(G-14586)
P3 TECHNOLOGIES
383 Buell Rd (14624-3123)
PHONE..................................585 730-7340
Mark Shaw, *President*
EMP: 6 EST: 2012
SQ FT: 10,000
SALES (est): 674.6K **Privately Held**
SIC: 3471 Anodizing (plating) of metals or formed products

(G-14587)
PACTECH PACKAGING LLC
2605 Manitou Rd (14624-1109)
PHONE..................................585 458-8008
Fax: 585 647-9116
John Ferber, *Vice Pres*
Jennifer Englert, *Purch Agent*
Alicia Buchta, *Human Res Mgr*
Chad Buchta, *Mng Member*

Pat Morris, *Administration*
▲ EMP: 65
SALES (est): 21.9MM **Privately Held**
WEB: www.pactechpackaging.com
SIC: 2671 Packaging paper & plastics film, coated & laminated
PA: Barrier Packaging, Inc.
2605 Manitou Rd 200
Rochester NY

(G-14588)
PALEY STUDIOS LTD
1677 Lyell Ave A (14606-2311)
PHONE..................................585 232-5260
Fax: 585 232-5507
Albert Paley, *President*
Frances Welley-Paley, *Treasurer*
▲ EMP: 16
SQ FT: 18,000
SALES: 1.4MM **Privately Held**
WEB: www.albertpaley.com
SIC: 3446 8412 Architectural metalwork; ornamental metalwork; museums & art galleries

(G-14589)
PALLET DIVISION INC
40 Silver St (14611-2208)
PHONE..................................585 328-3780
Fax: 585 227-2766
Bernie Mangold, *President*
EMP: 7
SALES (est): 922.9K **Privately Held**
SIC: 2448 Pallets, wood & metal combination

(G-14590)
PALLET SERVICES INC
1681 Lyell Ave (14606-2311)
PHONE..................................585 647-4020
Fax: 585 647-1756
Donald Matre, *Branch Mgr*
EMP: 40
SALES (corp-wide): 9.2MM **Privately Held**
SIC: 2448 Wood pallets & skids
PA: Pallet Services, Inc.
4055 Casillio Pkwy
Clarence NY 14031
716 873-7700

(G-14591)
PANTHER GRAPHICS INC (PA)
465 Central Ave (14605-3012)
PHONE..................................585 546-7163
Fax: 585 325-3943
Daryll A Jackson Sr, *President*
Josh Cummings, *General Mgr*
Carolyn Stewart, *Accountant*
Henry Ehindero, *Sales Staff*
Rachael Hudson-Rodvik, *Office Mgr*
▲ EMP: 39
SQ FT: 12,000
SALES (est): 48.2MM **Privately Held**
WEB: www.panthergraphics.net
SIC: 2752 Commercial printing, offset

(G-14592)
PARAGON STEEL RULE DIES INC
979 Mount Read Blvd (14606-2829)
PHONE..................................585 254-3395
Fax: 585 254-8839
Michael McDeid, *President*
Teresa McDeid, *Manager*
EMP: 13
SQ FT: 13,000
SALES (est): 1.9MM **Privately Held**
WEB: www.paragonsrd.com
SIC: 3544 Dies, steel rule

(G-14593)
PARK ENTERPRISES ROCHESTER INC
226 Jay St (14608-1623)
PHONE..................................585 546-4200
Fax: 585 546-7088
Sook Cha Park, *President*
Rob Brunskill, *Principal*
Hyo Sang Park, *Principal*
Tom Sydeski, *Principal*
Patricia Favilli, *Accounts Mgr*
▲ EMP: 200
SQ FT: 60,000

GEOGRAPHIC SECTION

Rochester - Monroe County (G-14615)

SALES (est): 33.1MM **Privately Held**
WEB: www.parkent.com
SIC: 3545 Precision tools, machinists'

(G-14594)
PEKO PRECISION PRODUCTS INC
70 Holworthy St (14606-1313)
PHONE 585 301-1386
Scott H Baube, *Project Mgr*
Donald Delaney, *Project Mgr*
Timothy Knox, *Project Mgr*
Sonny Sok, *Manager*
Louis E Emerson, *Manager*
EMP: 12
SALES (corp-wide): 51MM **Privately Held**
WEB: www.pekoprecision.com
SIC: 3599 Crankshafts & camshafts, machining
PA: Peko Precision Products, Inc.
1400 Emerson St
Rochester NY 14606
585 647-3010

(G-14595)
PENNANT INGREDIENTS INC (DH)
64 Chester St (14611-2110)
PHONE 585 235-8160
Simon Teel, *President*
Karel Zimmermann, *President*
EMP: 90 EST: 2015
SALES (est): 61.7MM **Privately Held**
SIC: 2099 Food preparations

(G-14596)
PERFORMANCE TECHNOLOGIES INC (HQ)
3500 Winton Pl Ste 4 (14623-2860)
PHONE 585 256-0200
Fax: 585 256-0791
John M Slusser, *Ch of Bd*
John J Peters, *Senior VP*
J Patrick Rice, *Senior VP*
Dorrance W Lamb, *CFO*
Bob Appolito, *Sales Staff*
EMP: 39
SQ FT: 32,000
SALES (est): 17MM
SALES (corp-wide): 252.5MM **Publicly Held**
WEB: www.pt.com
SIC: 3672 3661 3577 7373 Printed circuit boards; telephone & telegraph apparatus; computer peripheral equipment; computer integrated systems design
PA: Sonus Networks, Inc.
4 Technology Park Dr
Westford MA 01886
978 614-8100

(G-14597)
PERI-FACTS ACADEMY
601 Elmwood Ave (14642-0001)
PHONE 585 275-6037
Dr James Woods, *Senior Editor*
EMP: 5
SALES (est): 273.1K **Privately Held**
SIC: 2731 Textbooks: publishing & printing

(G-14598)
PFAUDLER INC (HQ)
Also Called: Glassteel Parts and Services
1000 West Ave (14611-2442)
P.O. Box 23600 (14692-3600)
PHONE 585 464-5663
Fax: 585 423-9644
Micheal F Powers, *Principal*
Christine Winter, *Materials Mgr*
Philip McGrath, *Engineer*
William Rowe, *Engineer*
Bob Waddell, *Human Res Dir*
◆ EMP: 300
SQ FT: 500,000
SALES (est): 122.2MM
SALES (corp-wide): 7.2B **Publicly Held**
SIC: 3559 Refinery, chemical processing & similar machinery; pharmaceutical machinery
PA: National Oilwell Varco, Inc.
7909 Parkwood Circle Dr
Houston TX 77036
713 346-7500

(G-14599)
PFAUDLER US INC
1000 West Ave (14611-2442)
PHONE 585 235-1000
Bob Waddell, *Vice Pres*
Pat Coleman, *Vice Pres*
Donald Cornwell, *Vice Pres*
Russ Bennett, *Plant Mgr*
Bob Polvino, *Design Engr Mgr*
▲ EMP: 200 EST: 1883
SALES (est): 24.7K **Privately Held**
SIC: 3443 Fabricated plate work (boiler shop)

(G-14600)
PHARMA-SMART INTERNATIONAL INC
Also Called: Pharmasmart
Rochester Tech Park 773 E (14624)
PHONE 585 427-0730
Fax: 585 427-8165
Frederick W Sarkis II, *CEO*
Drew Knopfel, *President*
Ashton S Maaraba, *COO*
Lisa M Goodwin, *Exec VP*
Joseph O Sarkis, *Senior VP*
▼ EMP: 39
SQ FT: 52,000
SALES (est): 7MM **Privately Held**
SIC: 3841 5047 8099 Diagnostic apparatus, medical; diagnostic equipment, medical; health screening service

(G-14601)
PHOENIX GRAPHICS INC
464 State St 470 (14608-1739)
PHONE 585 232-4040
Fax: 585 232-5642
Sal De Biase III, *President*
Mark Stavalone, *Vice Pres*
Kim Randall, *Human Resources*
Mike Curran, *Accounts Mgr*
Keith Boas, *Manager*
EMP: 20
SALES (est): 5.9MM **Privately Held**
WEB: www.phoenix-graphics.com
SIC: 2752 Commercial printing, lithographic

(G-14602)
PHOTONAMICS INC
Also Called: Elmgrove Technologies Div
558 Elmgrove Rd (14606-3348)
PHONE 585 426-3774
Fax: 585 426-3754
Ross Cooley, *President*
Eric Johengen, *Vice Pres*
Kay Carducci, *Manager*
EMP: 10
SQ FT: 4,000
SALES (est): 1.9MM **Privately Held**
WEB: www.elmgrovetechnologies.com
SIC: 3679 Electronic circuits

(G-14603)
PIERCE INDUSTRIES LLC
465 Paul Rd (14624-4779)
PHONE 585 458-0888
Dick Webb, *CEO*
Rick Schopinsky, *President*
Pat Sennett, *Opers Staff*
Elaine Deacon, *Engineer*
Craig Neubauer, *Engineer*
▲ EMP: 40
SQ FT: 60,000
SALES (est): 15.2MM **Privately Held**
WEB: www.pierceindustries.com
SIC: 3441 Fabricated structural metal

(G-14604)
PIERREPONT VISUAL GRAPHICS
15 Elser Ter (14611-1607)
PHONE 585 305-9672
Fax: 585 235-8376
Scott Zappia, *President*
Terence Zappia, *Vice Pres*
Mark Matyjakowski, *Info Tech Mgr*
EMP: 2 EST: 1958
SQ FT: 15,000
SALES: 1MM **Privately Held**
WEB: www.pierrepont.com
SIC: 2759 Screen printing

(G-14605)
PMI INDUSTRIES LLC
350 Buell Rd (14624-3124)
PHONE 585 464-8050
Fax: 585 328-6509
V Sheldon Alfiero, *President*
Roger Reiner, *General Mgr*
◆ EMP: 30
SQ FT: 48,500
SALES (est): 8.9MM
SALES (corp-wide): 43.3MM **Privately Held**
WEB: www.pro-moldinc.com
SIC: 3544 3089 Industrial molds; injection molded finished plastic products
PA: Bam Enterprises, Inc.
2937 Alt Blvd
Grand Island NY 14072
716 773-7634

(G-14606)
POLYMAG TEK INC
215 Tremont St Ste 2 (14608-2371)
PHONE 585 235-8390
Gary Larsen, *President*
Brian Giardino, *Engineer*
Ronald W Sweet, *Treasurer*
Jennifer Sweet, *Manager*
Pete Byam, *Executive*
EMP: 12
SALES (est): 2.4MM **Privately Held**
WEB: www.polymagtek.com
SIC: 3547 7389 Rolling mill machinery; design services

(G-14607)
POLYMER ENGINEERED PDTS INC
23 Moonlanding Rd (14624-2505)
PHONE 585 426-1811
Fax: 585 426-1444
George Peroutka, *President*
Sharon Niederschmiet, *Accounting Mgr*
Dan Dicicco, *Manager*
Mike Bruno, *Analyst*
EMP: 100
SQ FT: 55,000
SALES (corp-wide): 13.6MM **Privately Held**
SIC: 3089 Injection molding of plastics
PA: Polymer Engineered Products, Inc.
595 Summer St Ste 2
Stamford CT 06901
203 324-3737

(G-14608)
POSEIDON SYSTEMS LLC
200 Canal View Blvd # 300 (14623-2851)
PHONE 585 239-6025
Ryan Brewer, *President*
Nikhil Beke, *Engineer*
Robert Livolsi, *Engineer*
Alexander Pelkey, *Engineer*
Theodore Meyer, *Project Engr*
EMP: 11
SQ FT: 6,000
SALES (est): 2.2MM **Privately Held**
SIC: 3829 3823 Measuring & controlling devices; industrial instrmnts msrmnt display/control process variable; flow instruments, industrial process type; data loggers, industrial process type

(G-14609)
POWER-FLO TECHNOLOGIES INC
Also Called: Auburn Armature
62 Marway Cir (14624-2321)
PHONE 585 426-4607
Joe Santasia, *Manager*
EMP: 36
SALES (corp-wide): 32.2MM **Privately Held**
SIC: 7694 Armature rewinding shops
PA: Power-Flo Technologies, Inc.
270 Park Ave
New Hyde Park NY 11040
516 812-6800

(G-14610)
PPG ARCHITECTURAL FINISHES INC
Also Called: Glidden Professional Paint Ctr
566 Clinton Ave S (14620-1135)
PHONE 585 271-1363
Fax: 716 271-2449
Rochard Puzzolo, *Branch Mgr*
EMP: 5
SALES (corp-wide): 14.7B **Publicly Held**
WEB: www.gliddenpaint.com
SIC: 2891 Adhesives
HQ: Ppg Architectural Finishes, Inc.
1 Ppg Pl
Pittsburgh PA 15272
412 434-3131

(G-14611)
PPI CORP
Also Called: Ftt Manufacturing
275 Commerce Dr (14623-3505)
PHONE 585 880-7277
John Longuil, *President*
Darrell Gibson, *Mfg Mgr*
Mike Cianciola, *Purch Mgr*
Paul Opela, *Controller*
Janet Oliviari, *Human Resources*
EMP: 42
SALES (est): 361.2K **Privately Held**
SIC: 3541 3449 3599 3544 Numerically controlled metal cutting machine tools; miscellaneous metalwork; machine shop, jobbing & repair; special dies, tools, jigs & fixtures

(G-14612)
PPI CORP
Also Called: Ftt Mfg
275 Commerce Dr (14623-3505)
PHONE 585 243-0300
John Longuil, *CEO*
Paul Opela, *Vice Pres*
Darrel Gibson, *Mfg Mgr*
Steve Norsen, *QA Dir*
Don Vogler, *Manager*
▲ EMP: 60
SQ FT: 47,000
SALES (est): 13.5MM **Privately Held**
WEB: www.fttmfg.com
SIC: 3545 Precision tools, machinists'; screw machine products; instruments, surgical & medical; numerically controlled metal cutting machine tools; electrical discharge machining (EDM); machinery castings, aluminum

(G-14613)
PRECISE TOOL & MFG INC
9 Coldwater Cres (14624-2512)
PHONE 585 247-0700
Fax: 585 247-0746
John S Gizzi, *President*
John P Gizzi, *President*
Rose A Poirier, *Corp Secy*
Gary Mastro, *Vice Pres*
Dale Sloan, *Controller*
▲ EMP: 100
SQ FT: 150,000
SALES (est): 22.2MM **Privately Held**
WEB: www.precisetool.com
SIC: 3541 Numerically controlled metal cutting machine tools; milling machines; boring mills

(G-14614)
PRECISION DESIGN SYSTEMS INC
1645 Lyell Ave Ste 136 (14606-2386)
PHONE 585 426-4500
William J West, *President*
Jeff Sutton, *Vice Pres*
EMP: 20
SQ FT: 18,000
SALES (est): 3.5MM **Privately Held**
SIC: 3829 3479 Measuring & controlling devices; name plates: engraved, etched, etc.

(G-14615)
PRECISION GRINDING & MFG CORP (PA)
Also Called: P G M
1305 Emerson St (14606-3098)
PHONE 585 458-4300
Fax: 585 458-6465
Michael Hockenberger, *CEO*
William C Hockenberger, *Ch of Bd*
Nick Baldassaia, *General Mgr*
Nick Baldassara, *General Mgr*
Todd Hockenberger, *Vice Pres*
▲ EMP: 126
SQ FT: 62,000

Rochester - Monroe County (G-14616)

SALES: 19.3MM **Privately Held**
WEB: www.pgmcorp.com
SIC: 3545 3544 Precision tools, machinists'; special dies & tools

(G-14616)
PRECISION LASER TECHNOLOGY LLC
Also Called: Plt
1001 Lexington Ave Ste 4 (14606-2847)
PHONE.................................585 458-6208
Ron Natale Jr,
James Garcia,
EMP: 10
SQ FT: 7,000
SALES (est): 798K **Privately Held**
SIC: 3479 Etching & engraving

(G-14617)
PRECISION MACHINE TECH LLC
Also Called: Spex
85 Excel Dr (14621-3471)
PHONE.................................585 467-1840
Michael Nolan, *President*
Lisa Fess, *Manager*
▲ **EMP:** 60
SQ FT: 16,000
SALES (est): 15.9MM **Privately Held**
WEB: www.spex1.com
SIC: 3451 Screw machine products

(G-14618)
PRECISION MAGNETICS LLC
770 Linden Ave (14625-2716)
PHONE.................................585 385-9010
Yhuang Wang, *Controller*
Andrew Albers,
Terence R Loughrey,
▲ **EMP:** 50
SQ FT: 12,000
SALES (est): 5.9MM **Privately Held**
WEB: www.precisionmagnetics.com
SIC: 3499 Magnets, permanent: metallic

(G-14619)
PREMIER METALS GROUP
11 Cairn St (14611-2415)
PHONE.................................585 436-4020
Fax: 585 436-4021
Marc Olgin, *CEO*
Mike Diamond, *Principal*
Steve Olgin, *Exec VP*
Ed Czemeryck, *CFO*
Sharna Larson, *Controller*
EMP: 32
SALES (est): 5.1MM **Privately Held**
SIC: 3469 Metal stampings
HQ: Scholz Holding Gmbh
   Berndt-Ulrich-Scholz-Str. 1
   Essingen 73457
   736 584-0

(G-14620)
PREMIER SIGN SYSTEMS LLC
10 Excel Dr (14621-3470)
PHONE.................................585 235-0390
Fax: 585 235-0392
Jeff Sherwood, *Owner*
James Peacock, *Principal*
Jamie Rawleigh, *Project Mgr*
Lori Herold, *Controller*
EMP: 28
SALES (est): 4.5MM **Privately Held**
SIC: 3993 Signs & advertising specialties

(G-14621)
PRESSTEK PRINTING LLC
521 E Ridge Rd (14621-1203)
PHONE.................................585 467-8140
Fax: 585 467-0550
Dennis Collins, *President*
EMP: 10
SQ FT: 1,400
SALES (est): 459.7K **Privately Held**
SIC: 2752 2791 Commercial printing, offset; typesetting

(G-14622)
PRESSTEK PRINTING LLC
Also Called: Washburn Litho Envirgo Prtg
20 Balfour Dr (14621-3202)
P.O. Box 67211 (14617-7211)
PHONE.................................585 266-2770
Fax: 585 266-6065
Antony Disalvo, *President*
Dennis Collins, *Vice Pres*
Stephanie Weber, *Office Mgr*
EMP: 14
SQ FT: 6,600
SALES (est): 1.7MM **Privately Held**
SIC: 2759 2752 Commercial printing; commercial printing, lithographic

(G-14623)
PRINT ON DEMAND INITIATIVE INC
1240 Jefferson Rd (14623-3104)
PHONE.................................585 239-6044
Gaurav Govil, *President*
Tracy Burkovich, *Manager*
EMP: 19
SQ FT: 900
SALES: 159.9K **Privately Held**
SIC: 2752 Commercial printing, lithographic

(G-14624)
PRINTROC INC
620 South Ave (14620-1316)
PHONE.................................585 461-2556
Fax: 585 461-3673
Ronald Schutt, *President*
Daniel McCarthy, *Vice Pres*
Jesse McCarthy, *Director*
EMP: 12
SQ FT: 6,000
SALES (est): 1.2MM **Privately Held**
WEB: www.pinnacleprinters.com
SIC: 2752 Commercial printing, offset

(G-14625)
PRIVATE LBEL FODS RCHESTER INC
1686 Lyell Ave (14606-2312)
P.O. Box 60805 (14606-0805)
PHONE.................................585 254-9205
Fax: 585 254-0186
Bonnie Lavorato, *Ch of Bd*
Frank Lavorato III, *Vice Pres*
Russ Eliason, *CFO*
EMP: 30
SQ FT: 125,000
SALES (est): 11.4MM **Privately Held**
WEB: www.privatelabelfoods.com
SIC: 2033 Tomato products: packaged in cans, jars, etc.

(G-14626)
PRO-TECH WLDG FABRICATION INC
Also Called: Pro-Tech Sno Pusher
711 West Ave (14611-2412)
PHONE.................................585 436-9855
Fax: 585 436-5645
Michael P Weagley, *President*
EMP: 35
SQ FT: 30,000
SALES (est): 8.3MM **Privately Held**
SIC: 3531 7692 Snow plow attachments; welding repair

(G-14627)
PRO-VALUE DISTRIBUTION INC
1547 Lyell Ave Ste 3 (14606-2123)
PHONE.................................585 783-1461
Thomas W Mayberry, *President*
EMP: 6
SQ FT: 4,000
SALES (est): 839.3K **Privately Held**
SIC: 3714 Motor vehicle parts & accessories

(G-14628)
PRODUCT INTEGRATION & MFG INC
55 Fessenden St (14611-2815)
PHONE.................................585 436-6260
Tyrone Reaves, *Ch of Bd*
Tom Bare, *General Mgr*
Brenda Wilson, *Human Res Mgr*
Long Nguyen, *Manager*
Lorriane Reeve, *Manager*
EMP: 22
SQ FT: 25,000
SALES (est): 4.8MM **Privately Held**
SIC: 3444 Sheet metalwork; forming machine work, sheet metal

(G-14629)
PRODUCTION METAL CUTTING INC
1 Curlew St (14606-2535)
P.O. Box 60535 (14606-0535)
PHONE.................................585 458-7136
Fax: 585 458-1215
Leo T Glogowski, *President*
▲ **EMP:** 12
SQ FT: 34,000
SALES (est): 2.1MM
SALES (corp-wide): 2.4MM **Privately Held**
WEB: www.zedcomachinery.com
SIC: 3545 Machine tool accessories
PA: Zedco Machinery Inc
   1 Curlew St
   Rochester NY 14606
   585 458-6920

(G-14630)
PSB LTD
543 Atlantic Ave Ste 2 (14609-7396)
PHONE.................................585 654-7078
Robert Armitage, *President*
EMP: 13
SQ FT: 30,000
SALES (est): 2.5MM **Privately Held**
WEB: www.psb.net
SIC: 3471 Electroplating & plating

(G-14631)
PULLMAN MFG CORPORATION
77 Commerce Dr (14623-3501)
PHONE.................................585 334-1350
Fax: 585 359-4460
Chris Biegel, *CEO*
William A Palmer, *Shareholder*
▼ **EMP:** 6 **EST:** 1886
SQ FT: 36,000
SALES (est): 1.2MM **Privately Held**
WEB: www.pullmanmfg.com
SIC: 3495 Sash balances, spring

(G-14632)
PULSAFEEDER INC (HQ)
Also Called: Engineered Products Oper Epo
2883 Brighton Henrietta T (14623-2790)
PHONE.................................585 292-8000
Fax: 585 424-6268
Richard C Morgan, *Ch of Bd*
John Carter, *Ch of Bd*
Dieter Sauer, *President*
Todd Hanson, *Prdtn Dir*
Joe Patarino, *Prdtn Mgr*
◆ **EMP:** 122
SQ FT: 45,000
SALES (est): 25.5MM
SALES (corp-wide): 2.1B **Publicly Held**
WEB: www.pulsa.com
SIC: 3561 3825 3823 3822 Pumps & pumping equipment; measuring instruments & meters, electric; industrial instrmnts msrmnt display/control process variable; auto controls regulating residntl & coml environmt & applncs; relays & industrial controls; measuring & dispensing pumps
PA: Idex Corporation
   1925 W Field Ct Ste 200
   Lake Forest IL 60045
   847 498-7070

(G-14633)
QED TECHNOLOGIES INTL INC
Also Called: Q.E.d
1040 University Ave (14607-1282)
PHONE.................................585 256-6540
Fax: 585 256-3211
Andrew Kulawiec, *CEO*
Ralph Scialo, *Facilities Mgr*
Al Deeley, *Buyer*
Chris Hoyng, *QC Mgr*
Michael Natkin, *Research*
▲ **EMP:** 45
SALES (est): 13.2MM
SALES (corp-wide): 430.4MM **Publicly Held**
WEB: www.qedmrf.com
SIC: 3577 Computer peripheral equipment
PA: Cabot Microelectronics Corporation
   870 N Commons Dr
   Aurora IL 60504
   630 375-6631

(G-14634)
QES SOLUTIONS INC (PA)
1547 Lyell Ave (14606-2123)
PHONE.................................585 783-1455
Thomas W Mayberry, *Chairman*
Karen Knapp, *Accounts Mgr*
◆ **EMP:** 98
SQ FT: 15,000
SALES (est): 13.2MM **Privately Held**
SIC: 3559 Metal finishing equipment for plating, etc.

(G-14635)
QUADRISTI LLC
275 Mount Read Blvd (14611-1924)
PHONE.................................585 279-3318
Marc Iacona,
▲ **EMP:** 11
SQ FT: 10,000
SALES: 500K **Privately Held**
SIC: 3644 Electric conduits & fittings

(G-14636)
QUALITY CONTRACT ASSEMBLIES
Also Called: Qca
100 Boxart St Ste 251 (14612-5656)
P.O. Box 12868 (14612-0868)
PHONE.................................585 663-9030
Fax: 585 663-1432
Richard Frank, *President*
Lynn Gongwer, *Bookkeeper*
Dawn Moore, *Manager*
John Newton, *Lab Dir*
▲ **EMP:** 12
SQ FT: 5,500
SALES (est): 1.9MM **Privately Held**
WEB: www.qcacorp.com
SIC: 3679 Electronic circuits; harness assemblies for electronic use: wire or cable

(G-14637)
QUALITY VISION INTL INC (PA)
Also Called: Optical Gaging Products Div
850 Hudson Ave (14621-4839)
PHONE.................................585 544-0400
Fax: 585 544-4998
Edward T Polidor, *CEO*
Bob Scheidt, *VP Mfg*
Tim Tieppo, *Traffic Mgr*
Lars Avery, *Engineer*
George Guarino, *Controller*
▲ **EMP:** 3
SALES (est): 108.6MM **Privately Held**
SIC: 3827 Optical test & inspection equipment

(G-14638)
QUALITY VISION SERVICES INC
Also Called: Quality Vision International
1175 North St (14621-4942)
PHONE.................................585 544-0450
Fax: 585 506-4307
Timothy Moriarty, *President*
Raymond Go, *Regional Mgr*
Tim Sladden, *Regional Mgr*
Joe Soistman, *Regional Mgr*
Frank Opett, *Opers Staff*
▲ **EMP:** 56
SALES (est): 10.3MM
SALES (corp-wide): 108.6MM **Privately Held**
SIC: 3827 8734 Optical comparators; optical test & inspection equipment; calibration & certification
PA: Quality Vision International Inc.
   850 Hudson Ave
   Rochester NY 14621
   585 544-0400

(G-14639)
QUANTUM MEDICAL IMAGING LLC
150 Verona St (14608-1733)
PHONE.................................631 567-5800
Fax: 631 567-5074
Scott Matovich, *President*
Shalom Cohen, *President*
Keith Matovich, *Vice Pres*
Gerbert Garcia, *Production*
Tom Currie, *Senior Buyer*
▲ **EMP:** 100
SQ FT: 55,000

GEOGRAPHIC SECTION

Rochester - Monroe County (G-14664)

SALES (est): 26.9MM
SALES (corp-wide): 22.5B **Publicly Held**
WEB: www.qmiteam.com
SIC: **3844** 5047 Radiographic X-ray apparatus & tubes; medical equipment & supplies
HQ: Carestream Health, Inc.
150 Verona St
Rochester NY 14608
585 627-1800

(G-14640)
QUANTUM SAILS ROCHESTER LLC
1461 Hudson Ave (14621-1716)
PHONE.....................585 342-5200
Kristofer Werner, *President*
EMP: 5 EST: 2015
SALES (est): 325K **Privately Held**
SIC: **2394** 7532 Convertible tops, canvas or boat: from purchased materials; sails: made from purchased materials; canvas boat seats; liners & covers, fabric: made from purchased materials; tops (canvas or plastic), installation or repair: automotive

(G-14641)
QUB9 INC
181 Saint Paul St Apt 3a (14604-1192)
PHONE.....................585 484-1808
Amy Jerman, *Principal*
EMP: 6 EST: 2015
SALES (est): 245.2K **Privately Held**
SIC: **3448** 7389 Buildings, portable: prefabricated metal;

(G-14642)
QUINTEL USA INC
1200 Ridgeway Ave Ste 132 (14615-3758)
PHONE.....................585 420-8364
Alastair Westgarth, *CEO*
Bob Fishback, *CFO*
▲ EMP: 50
SALES (est): 8MM **Privately Held**
SIC: **3663** Radio & TV communications equipment

(G-14643)
R P FEDDER CORP (PA)
740 Driving Park Ave B (14613-1596)
PHONE.....................585 288-1600
Fax: 585 288-2481
Stephen Quinn, *Ch of Bd*
Joseph Vancura, *President*
Joseph Pennise, *Vice Pres*
Gordon Leonard, *Engineer*
Tammy Giosefﬁ, *Controller*
▲ EMP: 28 EST: 1958
SQ FT: 65,000
SALES: 15MM **Privately Held**
WEB: www.rpfedder.com
SIC: **3564** 5075 2674 Filters, air: furnaces, air conditioning equipment, etc.; air filters; bags: uncoated paper & multi-wall

(G-14644)
R V DOW ENTERPRISES INC
Also Called: B J Long Co
466 Central Ave (14605-3011)
PHONE.....................585 454-5862
Fax: 585 454-2836
Richard V Dow, *President*
▲ EMP: 17
SQ FT: 9,000
SALES: 700K **Privately Held**
WEB: www.bjlong.com
SIC: **3999** Pipe cleaners

(G-14645)
RAPID PRECISION MACHINING INC
Also Called: Quality Plus
50 Lafayette Rd (14609-3119)
PHONE.....................585 467-0780
John Nolan, *President*
EMP: 70
SQ FT: 51,000
SALES: 6.6MM **Privately Held**
SIC: **3541** Mfg Machine Tools-Cutting

(G-14646)
RED OAK SOFTWARE INC
3349 Monroe Ave Ste 175 (14618-5513)
PHONE.....................585 454-3170
Greg Waffen, *Branch Mgr*
EMP: 5
SALES (corp-wide): 2.1MM **Privately Held**
WEB: www.redoaksw.com
SIC: **7372** Prepackaged software
PA: Red Oak Software Inc
115 Us Highway 46 F1000
Mountain Lakes NJ 07046
973 316-6064

(G-14647)
RHINO TRUNK & CASE INC
Also Called: Trunk Outlet
565 Blossom Rd Ste J (14610-1859)
PHONE.....................585 244-4553
Gregory Hurwitz, *President*
Bob Eastwood, *Manager*
EMP: 15
SALES: 5MM **Privately Held**
WEB: www.trunkoutlet.com
SIC: **3161** Luggage

(G-14648)
RID LOM PRECISION MFG
50 Regency Oaks Blvd (14624-5901)
P.O. Box 64473 (14624-6873)
PHONE.....................585 594-8600
Fax: 585 594-5550
John D Rider, *President*
Jack Trimer, *Manager*
EMP: 20
SQ FT: 7,100
SALES (est): 2.9MM **Privately Held**
WEB: www.ridlom.com
SIC: **3544** Special dies & tools

(G-14649)
RIDGE CABINET & SHOWCASE INC
1545 Mount Read Blvd # 2 (14606-2848)
PHONE.....................585 663-0560
Fax: 585 663-1445
Steve Lader, *Ch of Bd*
EMP: 20
SQ FT: 6,200
SALES (est): 3.6MM **Privately Held**
SIC: **2541** Counter & sink tops

(G-14650)
RIVERSIDE MFG ACQUISITION LLC
655 Driving Park Ave (14613-1566)
PHONE.....................585 458-2090
Fax: 585 458-2123
Mike Hill, *President*
Dannie Simons, *General Mgr*
Gerard Shafer, *Vice Pres*
Jerry Shafer, *Accounting Dir*
EMP: 110 EST: 1973
SQ FT: 120,000
SALES (est): 16.5MM **Privately Held**
SIC: **2789** Bookbinding & related work; bookbinding & repairing: trade, edition, library, etc.; paper cutting; display mounting

(G-14651)
RIVERVIEW ASSOCIATES INC
Also Called: Riverside Automation
1040 Jay St (14611-1110)
PHONE.....................585 235-5980
Fax: 585 235-8626
John A Christopher, *Ch of Bd*
Jeremey Duell, *Controller*
EMP: 13
SQ FT: 20,000
SALES: 2.5MM **Privately Held**
WEB: www.riversideautomation.com
SIC: **3559** Automotive related machinery

(G-14652)
RMB EMBROIDERY SERVICE
176 Anderson Ave Ste F110 (14607-1169)
PHONE.....................585 271-5560
Ruta Szabo, *Partner*
Birute Collier, *Partner*
Maria Stankus, *Partner*
EMP: 7 EST: 1995
SQ FT: 850
SALES: 140K **Privately Held**
SIC: **2397** Schifﬂi machine embroideries

(G-14653)
ROBERT J FARAONE
Also Called: O Tex
1600 N Clinton Ave (14621-2200)
PHONE.....................585 232-7160
Robert J Faraone, *Owner*
EMP: 7
SALES: 500K **Privately Held**
WEB: www.otex.com
SIC: **3545** Tool holders

(G-14654)
ROCCERA LLC
771 Elmgrove Rd Bldg No2 (14624-6200)
PHONE.....................585 426-0887
Syamal Ghosh, *President*
Frank Kaduc, *Vice Pres*
EMP: 18
SQ FT: 10,000
SALES (est): 2.2MM **Privately Held**
SIC: **3297** 3432 3599 Heat resistant mixtures; alumina fused refractories; plumbing ﬁxture ﬁttings & trim; machine & other job shop work; custom machinery

(G-14655)
ROCHESTER 100 INC
40 Jefferson Rd (14623-2132)
P.O. Box 92801 (14692-8901)
PHONE.....................585 475-0200
Fax: 585 475-0340
Nicholas Sﬁkas, *President*
Catherine Sﬁkas, *Principal*
Geraldine E Warner, *Corp Secy*
William Fish, *Vice Pres*
Allen Michael, *Opers Mgr*
▲ EMP: 129 EST: 1962
SQ FT: 100,000
SALES: 19.6MM **Privately Held**
WEB: www.rochester100.com
SIC: **2677** 2672 Adhesive papers, labels or tapes: from purchased material; envelopes

(G-14656)
ROCHESTER ASPHALT MATERIALS (DH)
1150 Penﬁeld Rd (14625-2202)
PHONE.....................585 381-7010
John M Odenbach Jr, *President*
Gardner Odenbach, *Treasurer*
Mary Swierkos, *Admin Sec*
EMP: 8
SQ FT: 5,000
SALES (est): 11.7MM
SALES (corp-wide): 28.6B **Privately Held**
SIC: **2951** 3273 Road materials, bituminous (not from reﬁneries); ready-mixed concrete

(G-14657)
ROCHESTER ATOMATED SYSTEMS INC
40 Regency Oaks Blvd (14624-5901)
PHONE.....................585 594-3222
Fax: 585 594-5810
Jerrold Potter, *President*
Frank Denaro, *Vice Pres*
George Gamer, *Vice Pres*
Bob Conklin, *Engineer*
EMP: 20
SQ FT: 12,000
SALES (est): 3.8MM **Privately Held**
WEB: www.rochauto.com
SIC: **3599** Machine & other job shop work; custom machinery

(G-14658)
ROCHESTER BUSINESS JOURNAL
16 W Main St Ste 341 (14614-1604)
PHONE.....................585 546-8303
Fax: 585 546-3398
Susan Holliday, *President*
Cynthia Belzl, *Vice Pres*
John Bouchard, *Vice Pres*
Karen Martin, *Vice Pres*
Daniel Peck, *Sls & Mktg Exec*
EMP: 35
SALES (est): 2.8MM **Privately Held**
WEB: www.rbj.net
SIC: **2711** Newspapers: publishing only, not printed on site

(G-14659)
ROCHESTER CATHOLIC PRESS (PA)
Also Called: CATHOLIC COURIER
1150 Buffalo Rd (14624-1823)
P.O. Box 24379 (14624-0379)
PHONE.....................585 529-9530
Fax: 585 529-9532
Bishop Salvatore R Matano, *President*
Karen M Franz, *General Mgr*
William H Kedley, *Treasurer*
Arlene Gall, *Manager*
Rev Daniel Condon, *Admin Sec*
EMP: 14
SQ FT: 3,188
SALES: 1.3MM **Privately Held**
WEB: www.catholiccourier.com
SIC: **2711** Newspapers: publishing only, not printed on site

(G-14660)
ROCHESTER COCA COLA BOTTLING
Also Called: Coca-Cola
123 Upper Falls Blvd (14605-2156)
PHONE.....................585 546-3900
Fax: 585 325-1816
George Keim, *Manager*
Jeff Alchowiak, *IT/INT Sup*
EMP: 65
SALES (corp-wide): 41.8B **Publicly Held**
SIC: **2086** 5149 Bottled & canned soft drinks; groceries & related products
HQ: Rochester Coca Cola Bottling Corp
300 Oak St
Pittston PA 18640
570 655-2874

(G-14661)
ROCHESTER COLONIAL MFG CORP (PA)
1794 Lyell Ave (14606-2316)
PHONE.....................585 254-8191
Fax: 585 254-1768
Mark S Gionta, *CEO*
Norm Dix, *President*
Paul Gionta, *Plant Mgr*
Chris Gionta, *Project Mgr*
Ed Johnson, *Opers Staff*
EMP: 100
SQ FT: 100,000
SALES (est): 14.1MM **Privately Held**
WEB: www.rochestercolonial.com
SIC: **2431** 3442 3231 3444 Windows & window parts & trim, wood; metal doors, sash & trim; strengthened or reinforced glass; sheet metalwork

(G-14662)
ROCHESTER COUNTERTOP INC (PA)
Also Called: Premier Cabinet Wholesalers
3300 Monroe Ave Ste 212 (14618-4621)
PHONE.....................585 338-2260
Fax: 585 338-2265
Dean Pelletier, *President*
Dean Pelleiter, *Controller*
EMP: 10
SQ FT: 9,000
SALES (est): 1MM **Privately Held**
WEB: www.premiercabinetwholesalers.com
SIC: **2541** 1799 Counter & sink tops; counter top installation; kitchen cabinets

(G-14663)
ROCHESTER DEMOCRAT & CHRONICLE
55 Exchange Blvd (14614-2001)
PHONE.....................585 232-7100
Fax: 585 258-2734
EMP: 26
SALES (est): 2.1MM **Privately Held**
SIC: **2711** Newspapers-Publishing/Printing

(G-14664)
ROCHESTER GEAR INC
213 Norman St (14613-1875)
PHONE.....................585 254-5442
Fax: 585 254-0427
Anthony J Fedor, *President*
Scott Caccamise, *Exec VP*
Robert Eckelberger, *Mfg Mgr*
Walt Steele, *QC Mgr*
Jim Horan, *Sales Executive*
EMP: 37

(PA)=Parent Co (HQ)=Headquarters (DH)=Div Headquarters
✪ = New Business established in last 2 years

Rochester - Monroe County (G-14665)

SQ FT: 25,000
SALES (est): 5.9MM **Privately Held**
WEB: www.rochestergear.com
SIC: 3566 Speed changers, drives & gears

(G-14665)
ROCHESTER MIDLAND CORPORATION (PA)
155 Paragon Dr (14624-1167)
P.O. Box 64462 (14624-6862)
PHONE..................585 336-2200
Fax: 585 266-8919
H Bradley Calkins, *CEO*
Harlan D Calkins, *Ch of Bd*
Kevin McCormick, *President*
Glenn A Paynter, *President*
Cathy Lindahl, *Co-CEO*
◆ EMP: 170
SQ FT: 190,000
SALES (est): 125.6MM **Privately Held**
WEB: www.rochestermidland.com
SIC: 2842 2676 2899 Specialty cleaning, polishes & sanitation goods; floor waxes; cleaning or polishing preparations; disinfectants, household or industrial plant; feminine hygiene paper products; chemical preparations

(G-14666)
ROCHESTER ORTHOPEDIC LABS (PA)
300 Airpark Dr Ste 100 (14624-5723)
PHONE..................585 272-1060
Fax: 585 272-0871
David Forbes, *President*
Gerald Tendall, *Vice Pres*
Eric Ober, *Admin Sec*
EMP: 8 EST: 1962
SQ FT: 12,000
SALES (est): 1.9MM **Privately Held**
WEB: www.rochesterorthopediclabs.com
SIC: 3842 Limbs, artificial; braces, elastic; braces, orthopedic

(G-14667)
ROCHESTER OVERNIGHT PLTG LLC
2 Cairn St (14611-2416)
PHONE..................585 328-4590
Fax: 585 328-1984
Catherine Hurd, *President*
Kathy Hurd, *COO*
Donna Bennett, *Office Mgr*
Shirley Tallman, *Office Mgr*
EMP: 60
SQ FT: 40,000
SALES (est): 5.9MM **Privately Held**
WEB: www.rochesterplatingworks.com
SIC: 3471 Plating of metals or formed products

(G-14668)
ROCHESTER PHOTONICS CORP
115 Canal Landing Blvd (14626-5105)
PHONE..................585 387-0674
Michael Morris, *CEO*
Paul Marx, *President*
EMP: 60
SQ FT: 52,000
SALES (est): 4.5MM
SALES (corp-wide): 9.3B **Publicly Held**
WEB: www.corning.com
SIC: 3827 Optical instruments & lenses
PA: Corning Incorporated
    1 Riverfront Plz
    Corning NY 14831
    607 974-9000

(G-14669)
ROCHESTER SEAL PRO LLC
53 Northwind Way (14624-2473)
PHONE..................585 594-3818
Joshua Piron, *President*
EMP: 5
SALES: 500K **Privately Held**
SIC: 2951 0781 Asphalt paving mixtures & blocks; landscape services

(G-14670)
ROCHESTER SILVER WORKS LLC
100 Latona Rd Bldg 110 (14652-0001)
P.O. Box 15397 (14615-0397)
PHONE..................585 477-9501
William Stewart, *General Mgr*

David Dix, *Opers Mgr*
Bob Surash, *Technical Mgr*
Chuck Hirbour, *Regl Sales Mgr*
Eileen Cear, *Manager*
▲ EMP: 50
SALES (est): 13.2MM **Privately Held**
SIC: 1044 Silver ores processing

(G-14671)
ROCHESTER SILVER WORKS LLC
240 Aster St (14615)
P.O. Box 15397 (14615-0397)
PHONE..................585 743-1610
Ralph Holmes, *Purch Mgr*
EMP: 9
SALES (est): 914.2K **Privately Held**
SIC: 3339 Silver refining (primary)

(G-14672)
ROCHESTER STAMPINGS INC
400 Trade Ct (14624-4773)
PHONE..................585 467-5241
Fax: 585 467-2518
L Charles Hicks, *President*
Charles Hicks, *Engineer*
EMP: 16 EST: 1958
SQ FT: 15,000
SALES (est): 3MM **Privately Held**
WEB: www.rochstamp.com
SIC: 3544 3469 3452 Special dies & tools; metal stampings; bolts, nuts, rivets & washers

(G-14673)
ROCHESTER STEEL TREATING WORKS
962 E Main St (14605-2780)
PHONE..................585 546-3348
Fax: 585 546-1684
Eugene Miller, *President*
Bryan Miller, *Production*
EMP: 18
SQ FT: 13,000
SALES (est): 2MM **Privately Held**
WEB: www.rstwinc.com
SIC: 3398 Metal heat treating

(G-14674)
ROCHESTER STRUCTURAL LLC
961 Lyell Ave Bldg 5 (14606-1956)
PHONE..................585 436-1250
David Yelle, *President*
Justin Yelle, *Project Mgr*
Brian Carmer,
EMP: 25
SQ FT: 15,000
SALES (est): 7.1MM **Privately Held**
SIC: 3312 1791 Structural shapes & pilings, steel; structural steel erection

(G-14675)
ROCHESTER TOOL AND MOLD INC
515 Lee Rd (14606-4236)
PHONE..................585 464-9336
Fax: 585 464-8043
Al Kapoor, *President*
Paul Tolley, *Vice Pres*
Elise Engelberger, *Office Mgr*
Franky Arndt, *Manager*
EMP: 11
SQ FT: 5,600
SALES (est): 1.8MM **Privately Held**
WEB: www.rochestertoolandmold.com
SIC: 3544 3599 Industrial molds; machine shop, jobbing & repair

(G-14676)
ROCHESTER TUBE FABRICATORS
1128 Lexington Ave 5d (14606-2909)
PHONE..................585 254-0290
James R Bunting, *Principal*
EMP: 10
SALES (est): 1.3MM **Privately Held**
SIC: 3498 Fabricated pipe & fittings

(G-14677)
ROCHLING ADVENT TOOL & MOLD LP
999 Ridgeway Ave (14615-3819)
PHONE..................585 254-2000
Ken Desrosiers, *General Ptnr*
Rich Feldman, *Sales Engr*

Douglas Gresens, *Sales Engr*
EMP: 57
SALES (est): 19.4MM
SALES (corp-wide): 1.7B **Privately Held**
SIC: 3089 3544 3545 Injection molding of plastics; industrial molds; tools & accessories for machine tools
HQ: Rochling Engineering Plastics Se & Co. Kg
    Rochlingstr. 1
    Haren (Ems) 49733
    593 470-10

(G-14678)
ROESSEL & CO INC
199 Lagrange Ave (14613-1593)
PHONE..................585 458-5560
Fax: 585 458-6074
William R Laitenberger, *President*
Kathy Laitenberger, *President*
Alfred P Laitenberger, *Treasurer*
Patrick Mulrooney, *Manager*
EMP: 8 EST: 1952
SQ FT: 6,000
SALES (est): 2MM **Privately Held**
WEB: www.roessel.com
SIC: 3823 Water quality monitoring & control systems

(G-14679)
ROMOLD INC
5 Moonlanding Rd (14624-2505)
PHONE..................585 529-4440
Louis Romano, *President*
Diane Romano, *Corp Secy*
▲ EMP: 16
SQ FT: 11,500
SALES (est): 1.3MM **Privately Held**
WEB: www.romold.net
SIC: 3544 Industrial molds

(G-14680)
ROTORK CONTROLS INC
Also Called: Jordon Controls
675 Mile Crossing Blvd (14624-6212)
PHONE..................585 328-1550
Brian Hennig, *Info Tech Dir*
EMP: 12
SALES (corp-wide): 726.4MM **Privately Held**
SIC: 3625 Actuators, industrial
HQ: Rotork Controls Inc.
    675 Mile Crossing Blvd
    Rochester NY 14624
    585 328-1550

(G-14681)
ROTORK CONTROLS INC (DH)
675 Mile Crossing Blvd (14624-6212)
PHONE..................585 328-1550
Fax: 585 247-2308
Robert H Arnold, *Ch of Bd*
William H Whiteley, *President*
Rand Underwood, *General Mgr*
Terry Pettit, *Area Mgr*
Fred Dowdeswell, *Vice Pres*
▲ EMP: 160 EST: 1967
SALES (est): 48.8MM
SALES (corp-wide): 726.4MM **Privately Held**
SIC: 3625 Actuators, industrial
HQ: Rotork Overseas Limited
    Rotork House
    Bath
    122 573-3200

(G-14682)
RPC PHOTONICS INC
330 Clay Rd (14623-3227)
PHONE..................585 272-2840
Fax: 585 272-5845
Dr G Michael Morris, *CEO*
Laura Weller-Brophy, *General Mgr*
Mark A Hirschler, *Facilities Mgr*
Sam Ward, *Engineer*
Jeffrey Shaw, *Design Engr*
EMP: 19
SALES (est): 4.4MM **Privately Held**
SIC: 3827 Optical instruments & lenses

(G-14683)
RT SOLUTIONS LLC
Also Called: Worm Power
80 Linden Oaks Ste 210 (14625-2809)
PHONE..................585 245-3456
Thomas Herlihy, *President*

Shawn Ferro, *Manager*
EMP: 8
SQ FT: 80,000
SALES (est): 1.3MM **Privately Held**
SIC: 2873 8711 Nitrogenous fertilizers; engineering services

(G-14684)
RY-GAN PRINTING INC
111 Humboldt St (14609-7463)
PHONE..................585 482-7770
Fax: 585 482-7039
Craig Schinsing, *President*
EMP: 9
SQ FT: 8,000
SALES (est): 1.4MM **Privately Held**
WEB: www.rygan.com
SIC: 2752 Commercial printing, lithographic

(G-14685)
S C T
3000 E Ridge Rd (14622-3028)
PHONE..................585 467-7740
Fax: 585 339-2550
Nancy Keucher, *Principal*
EMP: 12
SALES (est): 1.1MM **Privately Held**
SIC: 7372 Prepackaged software

(G-14686)
SAFE PASSAGE INTERNATIONAL INC
333 Metro Park Ste F204 (14623-2632)
PHONE..................585 292-4910
Andrew Figiel, *Owner*
Michael Rooksby, *COO*
Lew Pulvino, *Sales Executive*
Gregory Wahl, *Sales Executive*
Vicki Tran, *Mktg Coord*
EMP: 14
SQ FT: 3,500
SALES (est): 1.2MM **Privately Held**
WEB: www.safe-passage.com
SIC: 7372 7371 Prepackaged software; custom computer programming services

(G-14687)
SAMCO SCIENTIFIC CORPORATION
75 Panorama Creek Dr (14625-2303)
PHONE..................800 522-3359
Tuyen Nguyen, *Manager*
Sandy McKinsey, *Manager*
EMP: 167
SQ FT: 80,000
SALES (est): 13.9MM
SALES (corp-wide): 18.2B **Publicly Held**
WEB: www.samcosci.com
SIC: 3085 Plastics bottles
HQ: Fisher Scientific International Llc
    81 Wyman St
    Waltham MA 02451
    781 622-1000

(G-14688)
SANDSTONE TECHNOLOGIES CORP (PA)
2117 Buffalo Rd 245 (14624-1507)
PHONE..................585 785-5537
Timothy Williams, *President*
Matthew Brodie, *Manager*
◆ EMP: 1
SALES: 1MM **Privately Held**
SIC: 3661 Fiber optics communications equipment

(G-14689)
SANDSTONE TECHNOLOGIES CORP
2117 Buffalo Rd Unit 245 (14624-1507)
PHONE..................585 785-5537
Matthew Brodie, *Branch Mgr*
EMP: 7
SALES (corp-wide): 1MM **Privately Held**
SIC: 3661 Fiber optics communications equipment
PA: Sandstone Technologies Corp.
    2117 Buffalo Rd 245
    Rochester NY 14624
    585 785-5537

GEOGRAPHIC SECTION

Rochester - Monroe County (G-14715)

(G-14690)
SASSY SAUCE INC
740 Driving Park Ave F (14613-1534)
PHONE.....................585 621-1050
Fax: 585 621-1099
Salvatore Nalbone, *President*
Sal Nalbone, *President*
Terry O'Brien, *Vice Pres*
EMP: 7
SALES (est): 572.2K **Privately Held**
SIC: 2035 Seasonings & sauces, except tomato & dry

(G-14691)
SATISPIE LLC
155 Balta Dr (14623-3142)
PHONE.....................716 982-4600
Dan Mulvaney, *CFO*
Vernon Miller, *Controller*
Ann Pasqual, *Controller*
Mike Pinkowski,
▲ EMP: 20
SALES (est): 5.5MM **Privately Held**
WEB: www.satispie.com
SIC: 2051 Cakes, pies & pastries

(G-14692)
SAVAGE & SON INSTALLATIONS LLC
676 Pullman Ave (14615-3335)
P.O. Box 12647 (14612-0647)
PHONE.....................585 342-7533
Gerald Champman,
EMP: 30 EST: 2008
SALES (est): 4.1MM **Privately Held**
SIC: 2952 Mastic roofing composition

(G-14693)
SCAIFE ENTERPRISES INC
Also Called: Petrillo's Bakery
67 Lyell Ave (14608-1414)
PHONE.....................585 454-5231
Richard Scaife, *President*
EMP: 18
SALES (est): 1.6MM **Privately Held**
SIC: 2051 Cakes, bakery: except frozen

(G-14694)
SCHLEGEL ELECTRONIC MTLS INC (PA)
1600 Lexington Ave 236a (14606-3000)
PHONE.....................585 295-2030
Johnny C C Lo, *President*
Christina Pachett, *Manager*
Lorrie Fairey, *Admin Asst*
EMP: 15
SQ FT: 25,000
SALES (est): 2.1MM **Privately Held**
SIC: 3053 Gaskets & sealing devices

(G-14695)
SCHLEGEL SYSTEMS INC (DH)
Also Called: S S I
1555 Jefferson Rd (14623-3109)
PHONE.....................585 427-7200
Fax: 585 427-7216
Jeff Grady, *CEO*
Jonathan Petromelis, *Ch of Bd*
Paula Toland, *Accounts Mgr*
Santiago Garcia, *Sales Staff*
Susan Sim, *Office Mgr*
▲ EMP: 200 EST: 1885
SQ FT: 150,000
SALES (est): 282.3MM
SALES (corp-wide): 563.3MM **Privately Held**
WEB: www.schlegel.com
SIC: 3053 3089 3069 Gaskets, packing & sealing devices; plastic hardware & building products; pillows, sponge rubber

(G-14696)
SCHWAB CORP (DH)
900 Linden Ave (14625-2700)
PHONE.....................585 381-4900
James Brush, *President*
Denise Booream, *Partner*
Tony Lucido, *General Mgr*
Ellen Boesner, *Counsel*
Linn Ferguson, *Senior VP*
▼ EMP: 30 EST: 1872
SQ FT: 10,000
SALES (est): 12.2MM
SALES (corp-wide): 4.9B **Publicly Held**
WEB: www.schwabcorp.com
SIC: 3499 3442 2522 Safes & vaults, metal; fire doors, metal; file drawer frames: except wood
HQ: Sentry Safe, Inc.
137 W Forest Hill Ave
Oak Creek WI 53154
585 381-4900

(G-14697)
SCJ ASSOCIATES INC
60 Commerce Dr (14623-3502)
PHONE.....................585 359-0600
Fax: 585 359-0856
Scott Sutherland, *Ch of Bd*
Jone Holdforth, *Purch Mgr*
Gary Brusdal, *Engineer*
Richard Figueras, *Engineer*
David Sutherland, *Controller*
EMP: 40
SQ FT: 15,000
SALES (est): 11.4MM **Privately Held**
WEB: www.scjassociates.com
SIC: 3825 Test equipment for electronic & electric measurement

(G-14698)
SDJ MACHINE SHOP INC
1215 Mount Read Blvd # 1 (14606-2895)
PHONE.....................585 458-1236
Fax: 585 254-0912
Don Celestino, *President*
Aggie Polny, *Office Mgr*
EMP: 11
SQ FT: 20,000
SALES (est): 2MM **Privately Held**
WEB: www.sdjmachine.com
SIC: 3599 Machine shop, jobbing & repair

(G-14699)
SEABREEZE PAVEMENT OF NY LLC
14 Maryknoll Park (14622-1542)
PHONE.....................585 338-2333
Keruin Negron, *CEO*
Kelly Mahoney,
EMP: 8 EST: 2015
SALES (est): 547.8K **Privately Held**
SIC: 2951 Concrete, asphaltic (not from refineries)

(G-14700)
SECUPRINT INC
1560 Emerson St (14606-3118)
PHONE.....................585 341-3100
Patrick White, *Ch of Bd*
Tiffany Carthen, *Office Mgr*
EMP: 9
SALES (est): 1.6MM
SALES (corp-wide): 19.1MM **Publicly Held**
SIC: 3577 Printers & plotters
PA: Document Security Systems Inc
200 Canal View Blvd # 300
Rochester NY 14623
585 325-3610

(G-14701)
SEISENBACHER INC
175 Humboldt St Ste 250 (14610-1058)
PHONE.....................585 730-4960
Ken Biggins, *CEO*
Werner Pumhosel, *Director*
Lisa Testa, *Admin Sec*
EMP: 10 EST: 2016
SALES (est): 125K **Privately Held**
SIC: 3743 Rapid transit cars & equipment

(G-14702)
SEMROK INC (HQ)
Also Called: Semrock
3625 Buffalo Rd Ste 6 (14624-1179)
PHONE.....................585 594-7050
Fax: 585 594-3898
Victor Mizrahi, *President*
Jim Cutaia, *Engineer*
Craig Hodgson, *Engineer*
Brian O'Flaherty, *Engineer*
Jeremy Grace, *Design Engr*
▲ EMP: 79
SQ FT: 22,000
SALES (est): 13.8MM
SALES (corp-wide): 2.1B **Publicly Held**
WEB: www.semrock.com
SIC: 3229 Optical glass
PA: Idex Corporation
1925 W Field Ct Ste 200
Lake Forest IL 60045
847 498-7070

(G-14703)
SERI SYSTEMS INC
172 Metro Park (14623-2610)
PHONE.....................585 272-5515
Ron Lablanc, *Vice Pres*
Martin Sondervan, *Vice Pres*
Dan Wagner, *Vice Pres*
Robert McJury, *VP Sales*
EMP: 20
SQ FT: 6,000
SALES (est): 2MM **Privately Held**
SIC: 2759 Decals: printing; labels & seals: printing; screen printing

(G-14704)
SHAMROCK PLASTIC CORPORATION
95 Mount Read Blvd (14611-1923)
PHONE.....................585 328-6040
Timothy Kelly, *President*
EMP: 5
SALES (est): 1.2MM **Privately Held**
SIC: 3089 Plastic processing

(G-14705)
SHAMROCK PLASTICS & TOOL INC
95 Mount Read Blvd # 149 (14611-1933)
PHONE.....................585 328-6040
Timothy Kelly, *President*
EMP: 5
SQ FT: 10,000
SALES (est): 1.2MM **Privately Held**
SIC: 3089 Plastic processing

(G-14706)
SHORETEL INC
300 State St Ste 100 (14614-1047)
PHONE.....................877 654-3573
Don Joos, *Branch Mgr*
EMP: 9 **Publicly Held**
SIC: 3661 3663 7372 Telephone & telegraph apparatus; radio & TV communications equipment; prepackaged software
PA: Shoretel, Inc.
960 Stewart Dr
Sunnyvale CA 94085

(G-14707)
SIEMENS INDUSTRY INC
50 Methodist Hill Dr # 1500 (14623-4269)
PHONE.....................585 797-2300
Fax: 585 797-2320
Karen Demeester, *Financial Exec*
Greg Aiken, *Branch Mgr*
EMP: 40
SALES (corp-wide): 89.6B **Publicly Held**
WEB: www.sibt.com
SIC: 3822 7629 1731 5075 Temperature controls, automatic; electrical equipment repair services; electrical work; warm air heating & air conditioning; plumbing & hydronic heating supplies
HQ: Siemens Industry, Inc.
1000 Deerfield Pkwy
Buffalo Grove IL 60089
847 215-1000

(G-14708)
SIGN IMPRESSIONS INC
2590 W Ridge Rd Ste 6 (14626-3041)
PHONE.....................585 723-0420
Fax: 585 723-0535
Gerald Mallaber, *President*
EMP: 8
SQ FT: 3,000
SALES (est): 1.1MM **Privately Held**
WEB: www.signimpressions.com
SIC: 3993 Signs, not made in custom sign painting shops

(G-14709)
SIGNATURE NAME PLATE CO INC
292 Commerce Dr (14623-3506)
PHONE.....................585 321-9960
William Monell, *President*
Harry T Bain Jr, *Vice Pres*
EMP: 7
SQ FT: 9,000
SALES (est): 784.9K **Privately Held**
WEB: www.signaturenp.com
SIC: 3993 Name plates: except engraved, etched, etc.: metal

(G-14710)
SIKORSKY AIRCRAFT CORPORATION
Also Called: Impact Tech A Skrsky Innvtions
300 Canal View Blvd (14623-2811)
PHONE.....................585 424-1990
Fax: 585 424-1177
James Cycon, *General Mgr*
EMP: 68 **Publicly Held**
SIC: 3721 Aircraft
HQ: Sikorsky Aircraft Corporation
6900 Main St
Stratford CT 06614

(G-14711)
SIMPLEXGRINNELL LP
90 Goodway Dr (14623-3039)
PHONE.....................585 288-6200
Tom Deveronica, *Opers Mgr*
Kerry Maier, *Human Res Dir*
Gary Gokey, *Branch Mgr*
Kevin Fady, *Manager*
Ruth Sardone, *Traffic Dir*
EMP: 74 **Privately Held**
WEB: www.simplexgrinnell.com
SIC: 3669 Emergency alarms
HQ: Simplexgrinnell Lp
4700 Exchange Ct
Boca Raton FL 33431
561 988-7200

(G-14712)
SKILLSOFT CORPORATION
Also Called: Element K
500 Canal View Blvd (14623-2800)
PHONE.....................585 240-7500
Bruce Barnes, *Chairman*
Dan Cleveland, *Vice Pres*
Christopher Harte, *Vice Pres*
Michele Delass, *Accounts Mgr*
Todd Marino, *Accounts Mgr*
EMP: 6 **Privately Held**
SIC: 7372 Educational computer software
HQ: Skillsoft Corporation
300 Innovative Way # 201
Nashua NH 03062
603 324-3000

(G-14713)
SLIM LINE CASE CO INC
64 Spencer St (14608-1423)
PHONE.....................585 546-3639
Bette Thomas, *CEO*
Andrea Coulter, *President*
EMP: 15
SQ FT: 14,000
SALES (est): 560K **Privately Held**
WEB: www.slimlinecase.com
SIC: 3172 Leather cases

(G-14714)
SOCIAL SCIENCE ELECTRONIC PUBG
1239 University Ave (14607-1636)
PHONE.....................585 442-8170
Fax: 585 442-8171
Greg Gordon, *President*
Robert McCormick, *Research*
EMP: 16
SALES (est): 1.3MM **Privately Held**
WEB: www.ssrn.com
SIC: 2741 8299 Miscellaneous publishing; educational services

(G-14715)
SOLID CELL INC (PA)
771 Elmgrove Rd (14624-6200)
PHONE.....................585 426-5000
Sergey Somov, *Engineer*
Zachary Rosen, *CFO*
EMP: 5
SALES (est): 975.6K **Privately Held**
SIC: 3674 Semiconductors & related devices

Rochester - Monroe County (G-14716) GEOGRAPHIC SECTION

(G-14716)
SOLID SURFACES INC
1 Townline Cir (14623-2513)
PHONE..................585 292-5340
Fax: 585 292-5344
Gregg Sadwick, *President*
EMP: 100
SQ FT: 7,800
SALES (est): 4.1MM
SALES (corp-wide): 109.7MM **Privately Held**
WEB: www.solidsurfacesinc.net
SIC: 2541 2821 Counter & sink tops; table or counter tops, plastic laminated; plastics materials & resins
PA: Clio Holdings Llc
  300 Park St Ste 380
  Birmingham MI

(G-14717)
SOUND SOURCE INC
161 Norris Dr (14610-2422)
PHONE..................585 271-5370
Fax: 585 271-5373
John Castronova, *President*
Robert Storms, *Vice Pres*
EMP: 7
SQ FT: 7,500
SALES (est): 570K **Privately Held**
SIC: 3931 5731 Musical instruments; consumer electronic equipment

(G-14718)
SPECTRACOM CORPORATION (DH)
1565 Jefferson Rd Ste 460 (14623-3190)
PHONE..................585 321-5800
Jan-Yves Courtois, *President*
Theodore Tarsici, *General Mgr*
Jose Toledo, *Sales Staff*
EMP: 32
SALES (est): 12.4MM **Privately Held**
SIC: 3663 Radio & TV communications equipment
HQ: Orolia Holding Sas
  Drakkar Batiment D
  Valbonne 06560
  492 907-040

(G-14719)
SPECTRUM CABLE CORPORATION
295 Mount Read Blvd Ste 2 (14611-1967)
PHONE..................585 235-7714
Fax: 585 235-7739
Marc Iacona, *CEO*
Mark Philip, *President*
Simon Braitman, *Corp Secy*
EMP: 6
SQ FT: 17,000
SALES: 1.3MM **Privately Held**
WEB: www.spectrumcablecorp.com
SIC: 3315 1731 Wire & fabricated wire products; electrical work

(G-14720)
SPIN-RITE CORPORATION
30 Dubelbeiss Ln (14622-2402)
P.O. Box 67184 (14617-7184)
PHONE..................585 266-5200
Gary Bohrer, *President*
EMP: 16
SQ FT: 1,400
SALES (est): 3.2MM **Privately Held**
SIC: 3312 Tool & die steel & alloys

(G-14721)
SPX CORPORATION
SPX Flow Technology
135 Mount Read Blvd (14611-1921)
P.O. Box 31370 (14603-1370)
PHONE..................585 436-5550
Fax: 585 527-1712
Andrwe Creathorn, *General Mgr*
Hock Teoh, *General Mgr*
Tom Kaufman, *Business Mgr*
Laura Dwyer, *Vice Pres*
James Stanton, *Vice Pres*
EMP: 480
SALES (corp-wide): 1.4B **Publicly Held**
WEB: www.spx.com
SIC: 3443 Cooling towers, metal plate
PA: Spx Corporation
  13320a Balntyn Corp Pl
  Charlotte NC 28277
  980 474-3700

(G-14722)
SPX FLOW US LLC
Also Called: SPX Flow Technology
135 Mount Read Blvd (14611-1921)
PHONE..................585 436-5550
Andrew Creathorn, *General Mgr*
Jim Myers, *General Mgr*
Paul Santiago, *Facilities Mgr*
Terrance Wiseman, *Buyer*
Rosemary Fabian, *QC Mgr*
EMP: 8
SALES (est): 287.5K
SALES (corp-wide): 2B **Publicly Held**
SIC: 3824 7699 Impeller & counter driven flow meters; cash register repair
PA: Spx Flow, Inc.
  13320 Balntyn Corp Pl
  Charlotte NC 28277
  704 752-4400

(G-14723)
ST VINCENT PRESS INC
250 Cumberland St Ste 260 (14605-2811)
PHONE..................585 325-5320
Fax: 585 325-2571
Barbara Anzalone, *President*
Ken Holeperl, *Vice Pres*
Vincent Anzalone, *CFO*
EMP: 15
SQ FT: 18,000
SALES (est): 2.5MM **Privately Held**
WEB: www.stvincentpress.com
SIC: 2752 Commercial printing, offset

(G-14724)
STAMPER TECHNOLOGY INC
232 Wallace Way (14624-6216)
PHONE..................585 247-8370
Bruce Ha, *President*
▲ EMP: 7
SQ FT: 5,000
SALES (est): 1.2MM **Privately Held**
SIC: 3695 Magnetic & optical recording media

(G-14725)
STEEL WORK INC
340 Oak St (14608-1727)
PHONE..................585 232-1555
Tim Grove, *President*
EMP: 9
SQ FT: 7,000
SALES (est): 1.4MM **Privately Held**
WEB: www.steelwork.com
SIC: 3446 3444 Architectural metalwork; sheet metalwork

(G-14726)
STEFAN SYDOR OPTICS INC
31 Jetview Dr (14624-4903)
P.O. Box 20001 (14602-0001)
PHONE..................585 271-7300
Fax: 585 271-7309
James Sydor, *President*
Michael Naselaris, *General Mgr*
John Escolas, *Opers Mgr*
Sam Ezzezew, *Prdtn Mgr*
Nicole Cafolla, *QA Dir*
▼ EMP: 43
SQ FT: 40,000
SALES (est): 10MM **Privately Held**
WEB: www.sydor.com
SIC: 3827 3229 3211 Optical instruments & lenses; pressed & blown glass; flat glass

(G-14727)
STERILIZ LLC
150 Linden Oaks (14625-2802)
PHONE..................585 415-5411
James T Townsend,
Samuel R Trapani,
EMP: 5
SALES (est): 691.9K **Privately Held**
SIC: 3821 3842 Sterilizers; sterilizers, hospital & surgical

(G-14728)
STEVEN COFFEY PALLET S INC
3376 Edgemere Dr (14612-1128)
PHONE..................585 261-6783
Steven Coffey, *Principal*
EMP: 8
SALES (est): 917.6K **Privately Held**
SIC: 2448 Pallets, wood & wood with metal

(G-14729)
STRAUSS EYE PROSTHETICS INC
360 White Spruce Blvd (14623-1604)
PHONE..................585 424-1350
James V Strauss, *President*
Josie Strauss, *Admin Sec*
EMP: 5
SQ FT: 2,024
SALES (est): 310K **Privately Held**
WEB: www.strausseye.com
SIC: 3851 Eyes, glass & plastic

(G-14730)
SUIT-KOTE CORPORATION
Also Called: Western Bituminous
2 Rockwood St Frnt (14610-2611)
PHONE..................585 473-6321
Fax: 585 473-1774
Tom Hackwelder, *Vice Pres*
Frank Suits, *Vice Pres*
Steve Rebman, *Sales & Mktg St*
EMP: 25
SALES (corp-wide): 226MM **Privately Held**
WEB: www.suit-kote.com
SIC: 2951 5032 Asphalt & asphaltic paving mixtures (not from refineries); asphalt mixture
PA: Suit-Kote Corporation
  1911 Lorings Crossing Rd
  Cortland NY 13045
  607 753-1100

(G-14731)
SUPERIOR TECHNOLOGY INC
200 Paragon Dr (14624-1159)
PHONE..................585 352-6556
Fax: 585 352-6559
John P Shortino, *President*
Barbara Dawkins, *COO*
Anthony J Shortino, *Vice Pres*
Joseph Shortino, *Vice Pres*
Sam Goz, *Purch Mgr*
▲ EMP: 50 EST: 1987
SQ FT: 36,500
SALES (est): 10.3MM **Privately Held**
WEB: www.superiortech.org
SIC: 3599 Machine shop, jobbing & repair

(G-14732)
SWEETWATER ENERGY INC
500 Lee Rd Ste 200 (14606-4261)
PHONE..................585 647-5760
Jack Baron, *CEO*
Ron Boillat, *Exec VP*
Nina Pearlmutter, *Vice Pres*
Jonathan Sherwood, *Vice Pres*
Sharon Samjitsingh, *Project Mgr*
▲ EMP: 7
SALES (est): 750K **Privately Held**
SIC: 2046 Corn sugar

(G-14733)
SWIFT MULTIGRAPHICS LLC
55 Southwood Ln (14618-4019)
PHONE..................585 442-8000
Kenneth Stahl, *Principal*
EMP: 2
SQ FT: 200
SALES: 1MM **Privately Held**
SIC: 2759 3999 Promotional printing; advertising display products

(G-14734)
SYNAPTICS INCORPORATED
90 Linden Oaks Ste 100 (14625-2830)
PHONE..................585 899-4300
Rick Bergman, *President*
Joe Muczynski, *Manager*
Murat Ozbas, *Manager*
EMP: 16
SALES (corp-wide): 1.7B **Publicly Held**
SIC: 3577 Computer peripheral equipment
PA: Synaptics Incorporated
  1251 Mckay Dr
  San Jose CA 95131
  408 904-1100

(G-14735)
SYNERGY FLAVORS NY COMPANY LLC
Also Called: Vanlab
86 White St (14608-1435)
PHONE..................585 232-6648
Bob Strassner, *Branch Mgr*
Jim Abraham, *Manager*
Paulete Lanzoff, *Manager*
EMP: 9 **Privately Held**
SIC: 2087 Flavoring extracts & syrups
HQ: Synergy Flavors (Ny) Company Llc
  1500 Synergy Dr
  Wauconda IL 60084
  585 232-6648

(G-14736)
SYNTEC TECHNOLOGIES INC (PA)
Also Called: Syntec Optics
515 Lee Rd (14606-4236)
PHONE..................585 768-2513
Alok Kapoor, *President*
Terry Phelix, *President*
Richard Arndt, *Vice Pres*
Steve Polvinen, *Vice Pres*
Tim Vorndran, *Opers Mgr*
EMP: 50 EST: 1981
SQ FT: 25,000
SALES (est): 16.1MM **Privately Held**
WEB: www.syntecoptics.com
SIC: 3089 Injection molding of plastics

(G-14737)
SYNTEC TECHNOLOGIES INC
Also Called: Syntec Optics
515 Lee Rd (14606-4236)
PHONE..................585 464-9336
Phil Race, *Branch Mgr*
EMP: 11
SALES (corp-wide): 16.1MM **Privately Held**
WEB: www.syntecoptics.com
SIC: 3544 3599 Industrial molds; machine shop, jobbing & repair
PA: Syntec Technologies, Inc.
  515 Lee Rd
  Rochester NY 14606
  585 768-2513

(G-14738)
T & C POWER CONVERSION INC
132 Humboldt St (14610-1046)
PHONE..................585 482-5551
Fax: 585 482-8487
Tomasz Mokrzan, *President*
Joe Reminder, *General Mgr*
Noam Sarfati, *Opers Staff*
Golan Jacob, *Engineer*
Andrzej Marcinkowski, *Project Engr*
EMP: 13
SQ FT: 3,000
SALES (est): 2.5MM **Privately Held**
WEB: www.tcpowerconversion.com
SIC: 3825 Radio frequency measuring equipment

(G-14739)
T & L AUTOMATICS INC
770 Emerson St (14613-1895)
PHONE..................585 647-3717
Fax: 585 647-1126
Thomas W Hassett, *President*
Vincent Buzzelli, *Senior VP*
David Murphy, *Vice Pres*
Vince Vuzzelli, *VP Opers*
William Green, *Marketing Staff*
EMP: 120 EST: 1975
SQ FT: 120,000
SALES (est): 23.3MM **Privately Held**
WEB: www.tandlautomatics.com
SIC: 3451 Screw machine products

(G-14740)
T L F GRAPHICS INC
Also Called: Tlf Graphics
235 Metro Park (14623-2618)
PHONE..................585 272-5500
Fax: 585 272-5525
Ronald Leblanc, *Ch of Bd*
Dan Wagner, *Vice Pres*
Rich Cromwell, *Materials Mgr*
Tom Crowley, *Materials Mgr*
Ray McHargue, *Safety Mgr*
EMP: 59

GEOGRAPHIC SECTION

Rochester - Monroe County (G-14765)

SQ FT: 12,000
SALES (est): 26.5MM *Privately Held*
SIC: 2672 2759 Tape, pressure sensitive: made from purchased materials; labels (unprinted), gummed: made from purchased materials; screen printing

(G-14741)
TAC SCREW PRODUCTS INC
170 Bennington Dr (14616-4754)
PHONE.................585 663-5840
Fax: 585 663-8221
Julius Papp, *President*
Mark Laisure, *Vice Pres*
EMP: 10
SQ FT: 4,000
SALES (est): 1.4MM *Privately Held*
SIC: 3451 Screw machine products

(G-14742)
TCS INDUSTRIES INC
400 Trabold Rd (14624-2529)
PHONE.................585 426-1160
Fax: 585 426-1162
Manoj Shekar, *President*
Dan McElligott, *QC Mgr*
Bill Rankin, *Manager*
▲ EMP: 80
SQ FT: 110,000
SALES: 17MM *Privately Held*
WEB: www.tcsindustries.com
SIC: 3444 Sheet metalwork

(G-14743)
TE CONNECTIVITY CORPORATION
2245 Brighton Henrta Twn (14623-2705)
PHONE.................585 785-2500
John Rowe, *Manager*
EMP: 50
SALES (corp-wide): 12.2B *Privately Held*
WEB: www.raychem.com
SIC: 3679 Electronic circuits
HQ: Te Connectivity Corporation
 1050 Westlakes Dr
 Berwyn PA 19312
 610 893-9800

(G-14744)
TEALE MACHINE COMPANY INC
1425 University Ave (14607-1617)
P.O. Box 10340 (14610-0340)
PHONE.................585 244-6700
Fax: 585 473-1271
Ronald E Larock, *Ch of Bd*
Aimee Ciulla, *Vice Pres*
Michael E Larock, *Vice Pres*
Aimee R Larock, *Treasurer*
Jackie Iwasko, *Admin Asst*
EMP: 70
SQ FT: 22,000
SALES (est): 18.1MM *Privately Held*
WEB: www.tealemachine.com
SIC: 3451 3625 Screw machine products; numerical controls

(G-14745)
TECH PARK FOOD SERVICES LLC
Also Called: Rochester Technology Park
789 Elmgrove Rd (14624-6200)
PHONE.................585 295-1250
Naresh Ramarathnan, *CFO*
EMP: 5
SALES (est): 310.9K *Privately Held*
SIC: 3721 1541 Research & development on aircraft by the manufacturer; warehouse construction

(G-14746)
TEL-TRU INC (PA)
Also Called: Tel-Tru Manufacturing Company
408 Saint Paul St (14605-1734)
PHONE.................585 295-0225
Andrew Germanow, *President*
Felisha Bostick, *Purchasing*
Paul Marchand, *Engineer*
Catherine Staudmyer, *Financial Exec*
Steve Deweese, *Manager*
EMP: 56
SALES (est): 11.1MM *Privately Held*
SIC: 3823 Temperature measurement instruments, industrial; resistance thermometers & bulbs, industrial process type

(G-14747)
TELEDYNE OPTECH INC
1046 University Ave # 147 (14607-1672)
PHONE.................585 427-8310
Maxime Elbaz, *President*
Michel Stanier, *Exec VP*
Paul Larocque, *Vice Pres*
Ed Sluys, *Vice Pres*
EMP: 13
SALES (est): 2.3MM
SALES (corp-wide): 2.1B *Publicly Held*
SIC: 3699 3845 Laser systems & equipment; laser systems & equipment, medical
HQ: Teledyne Optech Incorporated
 300 Interchange Way
 Vaughan ON L4K 5
 905 660-0808

(G-14748)
THE CALDWELL MANUFACTURING CO (PA)
2605 Manitou Rd Ste 100 (14624-1199)
P.O. Box 92891 (14692-8991)
PHONE.................585 352-3790
Fax: 585 352-3729
Edward A Boucher, *CEO*
Eric W Mertz, *Ch of Bd*
James Boucher, *Ch of Bd*
Carmen Berretta, *District Mgr*
Peter M Egberts, *Vice Pres*
◆ EMP: 100 EST: 1888
SQ FT: 126,000
SALES: 50MM *Privately Held*
WEB: www.caldwellmfgco.com
SIC: 3495 Wire springs

(G-14749)
THERMO FISHER SCIENTIFIC INC
1999 Mnt Rd Blvd 1-3 Bldg 13 (14615)
PHONE.................585 458-8008
Chad Buchta, *Technical Mgr*
Helene Diederich, *Branch Mgr*
EMP: 307
SALES (corp-wide): 18.2B *Publicly Held*
WEB: www.thermo.com
SIC: 3826 Analytical instruments
PA: Thermo Fisher Scientific Inc.
 168 3rd Ave
 Waltham MA 02451
 781 622-1000

(G-14750)
THERMO FISHER SCIENTIFIC INC
75 Panorama Creek Dr (14625-2385)
PHONE.................585 899-7610
Dan Biggs, *Vice Pres*
David Eddy, *Opers Staff*
Peter Baird, *Engineer*
Karen A Dally, *Sls & Mktg Exec*
Guy Lachance, *Manager*
EMP: 900
SALES (corp-wide): 18.2B *Publicly Held*
SIC: 3826 Analytical instruments
PA: Thermo Fisher Scientific Inc.
 168 3rd Ave
 Waltham MA 02451
 781 622-1000

(G-14751)
THREE POINT VENTURES LLC
Also Called: Skooba Design
3495 Winton Pl Ste E120 (14623-2838)
PHONE.................585 697-3444
Fax: 585 697-3447
Nancy Laniak, *Manager*
Michael J Hess,
▲ EMP: 10
SQ FT: 20,000
SALES (est): 640K *Privately Held*
WEB: www.roadwired.com
SIC: 3161 Cases, carrying

(G-14752)
THREE R ENTERPRISES INC
Also Called: Jason Manufacturing Company
447 Adirondack St (14606-2213)
PHONE.................585 254-5050
Richard Wallenhorst II, *President*
Patty Wallenhorst, *Admin Sec*
EMP: 30 EST: 1981
SQ FT: 10,000
SALES (est): 3.8MM *Privately Held*
SIC: 2431 2541 2521 Millwork; store fixtures, wood; office fixtures, wood; cabinets, office: wood

(G-14753)
THYSSENKRUPP MATERIALS NA INC
Copper & Brass Sales
1673 Lyell Ave (14606-2311)
PHONE.................585 279-0000
Fax: 585 279-0052
Dick Blake, *Branch Mgr*
EMP: 7
SALES (corp-wide): 44.2B *Privately Held*
SIC: 3317 3465 Tubes, wrought: welded or lock joint; automotive stampings
HQ: Thyssenkrupp Materials Na, Inc.
 22355 W 11 Mile Rd
 Southfield MI 48033
 248 233-5600

(G-14754)
TILE SHOP INC
420 Jefferson Rd Ste 3 (14623-2447)
PHONE.................585 424-2180
Tara Yost, *Manager*
EMP: 5 EST: 2010
SALES (est): 383.7K *Privately Held*
SIC: 3253 Floor tile, ceramic

(G-14755)
TODD WALBRIDGE
Also Called: T M Design Screen Printing
1916 Lyell Ave (14606-2306)
PHONE.................585 254-3018
Fax: 585 254-8657
Todd Walbridge, *Owner*
EMP: 7
SQ FT: 3,500
SALES (est): 605.6K *Privately Held*
WEB: www.tmdesigncorp.com
SIC: 2759 3993 2396 2395 Screen printing; signs & advertising specialties; automotive & apparel trimmings; pleating & stitching

(G-14756)
TOUCHSTONE TECHNOLOGY INC
350 Mile Crossing Blvd (14624-6207)
PHONE.................585 458-2690
Fax: 585 458-2733
Eric B Snavely, *Ch of Bd*
Todd Sheehan, *Design Engr*
David J Meisenzahl, *CFO*
Kelly Fairchild, *Controller*
Courtney Armstrong, *Cust Mgr*
▲ EMP: 16
SQ FT: 13,000
SALES (est): 5.5MM *Privately Held*
WEB: www.touchstn.com
SIC: 3575 Computer terminals, monitors & components; keyboards, computer, office machine

(G-14757)
TRANE US INC
75 Town Centre Dr Ste I (14623-4259)
PHONE.................585 256-2500
Fax: 585 256-0067
Vincent Ferrer, *Engineer*
Dan Wendo, *Systems Staff*
EMP: 47 *Privately Held*
SIC: 3585 Refrigeration & heating equipment
HQ: Trane U.S. Inc.
 1 Centennial Ave Ste 101
 Piscataway NJ 08854
 732 652-7100

(G-14758)
TREAD QUARTERS (PA)
200 Holleder Pkwy (14615-3808)
PHONE.................800 876-6676
EMP: 8
SALES (est): 1.7MM *Privately Held*
SIC: 3131 Quarters

(G-14759)
TRIPLEX INDUSTRIES INC
100 Boxart St Ste 27 (14612-5659)
PHONE.................585 621-6920
Fax: 585 621-7068
Christa Roesner, *President*
Patrick Moran, *Opers Staff*
Scott Patrick, *QC Mgr*
Jeff Jones, *Regl Sales Mgr*
EMP: 10 EST: 1981
SQ FT: 8,500
SALES (est): 1.5MM *Privately Held*
SIC: 3599 Machine shop, jobbing & repair

(G-14760)
TROYER INC
4555 Lyell Rd (14606-4316)
PHONE.................585 352-5590
Fax: 585 352-5593
William Colton, *President*
Kris Kettlewell, *Manager*
EMP: 15
SQ FT: 18,000
SALES (est): 1.7MM *Privately Held*
SIC: 3711 3714 5531 Motor vehicles & car bodies; motor vehicle parts & accessories; speed shops, including race car supplies

(G-14761)
TRUESENSE IMAGING INC
1964 Lake Ave (14615-2316)
PHONE.................585 784-5500
Fax: 585 784-5602
Chris McNiffe, *CEO*
Michael Miller, *Opers Dir*
David Nichols, *Research*
Rachel Kielon, *CFO*
Stephanie Newman, *Info Tech Mgr*
EMP: 207 EST: 2011
SQ FT: 260,000
SALES (est): 27.3MM
SALES (corp-wide): 3.9B *Publicly Held*
SIC: 3861 Film, sensitized motion picture, X-ray, still camera, etc.
HQ: Semiconductor Components Industries, Llc
 5005 E Mcdowell Rd
 Phoenix AZ 85008
 602 244-6600

(G-14762)
TRUFORM MANUFACTURING CORP
1500 N Clinton Ave (14621-2206)
PHONE.................585 458-1090
Fax: 585 458-1155
Tyrone Reaves, *Ch of Bd*
Bryan Putt, *General Mgr*
Stuart Kristensen, *Engineer*
Pat Small, *Engineer*
Sharon McCullough, *Manager*
EMP: 70
SQ FT: 45,000
SALES (est): 14.8MM *Privately Held*
WEB: www.truformmfg.com
SIC: 3444 Sheet metalwork

(G-14763)
TURNER BELLOWS INC
Also Called: Tb
526 Child St Ste 1 (14606-1187)
PHONE.................585 235-4456
Fax: 585 235-4593
Marilyn Yeager, *CEO*
Amanda Pontaella, *Ch of Bd*
Phyllis Rosenhack, *General Mgr*
▲ EMP: 45
SQ FT: 85,000
SALES (est): 8.3MM *Privately Held*
WEB: www.turnerbellows.com
SIC: 3081 3069 3861 Unsupported plastics film & sheet; foam rubber; photographic sensitized goods

(G-14764)
TURNING POINT TOOL LLC
135 Dodge St (14606-1503)
PHONE.................585 288-7380
Rob Kirby, *Opers Mgr*
Connie Pezzulo, *Office Mgr*
Frank Pezzulo,
Robert Kirby,
EMP: 6
SALES (est): 778.5K *Privately Held*
WEB: www.turningpointtool.com
SIC: 3544 Special dies, tools, jigs & fixtures

(G-14765)
UCB PHARMA INC (PA)
755 Jefferson Rd (14623-3233)
PHONE.................919 767-2555

Rochester - Monroe County (G-14766)

GEOGRAPHIC SECTION

Roch Doliveux, *CEO*
Lisa Pisenti, *Top Exec*
Lindsay Wills, *Counsel*
Fabrice Enderlin, *Exec VP*
Ismail Kola, *Exec VP*
▲ **EMP:** 400
SQ FT: 556,000
SALES (est): 46.9MM **Privately Held**
SIC: 2833 2834 5122 Anesthetics, in bulk form; drugs & herbs: grading, grinding & milling; pharmaceutical preparations; pharmaceuticals

(G-14766)
ULTRA TOOL AND MANUFACTURING
159 Lagrange Ave (14613-1511)
P.O. Box 17860 (14617-0860)
PHONE..........................585 467-3700
Daniel E Herzog, *President*
James M Schmeer, *Vice Pres*
Carol Herzog, *Office Mgr*
EMP: 13
SQ FT: 4,000
SALES: 1.3MM **Privately Held**
SIC: 3599 Machine & other job shop work; machine shop, jobbing & repair

(G-14767)
UNICELL BODY COMPANY INC
1319 Brighton Henrietta (14623-2408)
PHONE..........................585 424-2660
Fax: 585 424-2782
Steven Bones, *Manager*
EMP: 14
SQ FT: 7,200
SALES (corp-wide): 20MM **Privately Held**
WEB: www.unicell.com
SIC: 3713 Truck & bus bodies
PA: Unicell Body Company, Inc
  571 Howard St
  Buffalo NY 14206
  716 853-8628

(G-14768)
UNIFAB INC
215 Tremont St Ste 31 (14608-2370)
PHONE..........................585 235-1760
Fax: 585 235-1762
Brian Malark, *President*
William S Martin, *Vice Pres*
EMP: 7
SQ FT: 2,500
SALES: 1MM **Privately Held**
SIC: 3089 Plastic processing

(G-14769)
UNITHER MANUFACTURING LLC
755 Jefferson Rd (14623-3233)
PHONE..........................585 475-9000
Kevin Haehl, *General Mgr*
Gerbino Jennifer, *Engineer*
Amy Gould, *Human Resources*
Ted Collins, *Director*
▲ **EMP:** 250
SALES (est): 63.7MM **Privately Held**
SIC: 2834 Pharmaceutical preparations
HQ: Unither Pharmaceuticals
  Espace Industriel Nord
  Amiens 80080
  322 547-300

(G-14770)
UNITHER MANUFACTURING LLC
331 Clay Rd (14623-3226)
PHONE..........................585 274-5430
EMP: 10
SALES (est): 1MM **Privately Held**
SIC: 3999 Manufacturing industries

(G-14771)
UNIVERSAL PRECISION CORP
40 Commerce Dr (14623-3502)
PHONE..........................585 321-9760
Fax: 585 321-9828
Michael J Schmitt, *President*
Michael Domenico, *Vice Pres*
Dana Goodman, *Opers Mgr*
Jason Mansfield, *Purchasing*
Sonya Dotson, *QA Dir*
EMP: 24
SQ FT: 12,000
SALES (est): 4.5MM **Privately Held**
WEB: www.universalprecision.com
SIC: 3444 Sheet metalwork

(G-14772)
UNIVERSITY OF ROCHESTER
Also Called: Labortory For Laser Energetics
250 E River Rd (14623-1212)
PHONE..........................585 275-3483
Fax: 585 275-5353
Steven Verbridge, *Research*
Robert Jungquist, *Engineer*
Alex Maltsev, *Engineer*
Sam Morse, *Engineer*
Brian Rice, *Engineer*
EMP: 400
SALES (corp-wide): 3B **Privately Held**
WEB: www.rochester.edu
SIC: 3845 8221 Laser systems & equipment, medical; university
PA: University Of Rochester
  500 Joseph C Wilson Blvd
  Rochester NY 14627
  585 275-2121

(G-14773)
UPSTATE CABINET CO INC
32 Marway Cir (14624-2321)
PHONE..........................585 429-5090
Fax: 585 429-5096
Todd Whelehan, *President*
Vincenzo Delucia, *Vice Pres*
Jon Ingrick, *Sales Executive*
Annette Whelehan, *Manager*
Donna Demanchick, *Admin Asst*
EMP: 14
SQ FT: 30,000
SALES (est): 1.9MM **Privately Held**
WEB: www.upstatecabinet.com
SIC: 2434 Wood kitchen cabinets

(G-14774)
UPSTATE INCRETE INCORPORATED
49 Adelaide St (14606-2205)
PHONE..........................585 254-2010
Jeff Barlette, *Principal*
EMP: 9
SALES (est): 1.1MM **Privately Held**
SIC: 2421 Building & structural materials, wood

(G-14775)
UPSTATE NIAGARA COOP INC
Also Called: Sealtest Dairy Products
45 Fulton Ave (14608-1032)
PHONE..........................585 458-1880
Fax: 585 458-2887
John Gould, *Vice Pres*
Christine Krawczyk, *Safety Dir*
Stephan Hranjec, *Plant Mgr*
Roger Grove, *Opers Mgr*
Terry Wihlen, *Maint Spvr*
EMP: 150
SQ FT: 40,000
SALES (corp-wide): 228.8MM **Privately Held**
SIC: 2026 Milk processing (pasteurizing, homogenizing, bottling)
PA: Upstate Niagara Cooperative, Inc.
  25 Anderson Rd
  Buffalo NY 14225
  716 892-3156

(G-14776)
USAIRPORTS SERVICES INC
Also Called: US Airports Flight Support Svc
1295 Scottsville Rd (14624-5125)
PHONE..........................585 527-6835
Fax: 585 529-5581
Anthony Castillo, *President*
Patrick Smelt, *Controller*
Barbara Marianetti, *Human Res Dir*
EMP: 22
SQ FT: 29,800 **Privately Held**
WEB: www.usairportsflight.com
SIC: 3728 Refueling equipment for use in flight, airplane
PA: Usairports Services, Inc
  1 Airport Way Ste 300
  Rochester NY 14624

(G-14777)
VA INC
Also Called: Vincent Associates
803 Linden Ave Ste 1 (14625-2723)
PHONE..........................585 385-5930
Kevin Farrell, *Ch of Bd*
Stephen Pasquarella, *Vice Pres*
EMP: 25
SQ FT: 6,500
SALES (est): 4.3MM **Privately Held**
WEB: www.uniblitz.com
SIC: 3861 3827 Shutters, camera; optical instruments & lenses

(G-14778)
VALASSIS COMMUNICATIONS INC
Also Called: Printed Deals
5 Marway Cir Ste 8 (14624-2362)
PHONE..........................585 627-4138
EMP: 5 **Privately Held**
SIC: 2721 Magazines: publishing & printing
HQ: Valassis Communications, Inc.
  19975 Victor Pkwy
  Livonia MI 48152
  734 591-3000

(G-14779)
VAN REENEN TOOL & DIE INC
350 Commerce Dr 4 (14623-3508)
PHONE..........................585 288-6000
Fax: 585 288-6889
Richard Van Reenen, *President*
Richard V Reenen, *President*
Zack V Reenen, *Managing Dir*
Amy V Reenen, *Vice Pres*
Amy Reenen, *Vice Pres*
EMP: 12
SQ FT: 35,000
SALES (est): 1.9MM **Privately Held**
WEB: www.vanreenentoolanddieinc.com
SIC: 3469 3544 3599 Metal stampings; special dies, tools, jigs & fixtures; machine shop, jobbing & repair

(G-14780)
VAN THOMAS INC
Also Called: Ruggeri Manufacturing
740 Driving Park Ave G1 (14613-1594)
PHONE..........................585 426-1414
Fax: 585 247-0661
Charles E Thomas, *President*
Gary Vander Mallie, *Vice Pres*
Lisa Rutenberg, *Bookkeeper*
Dale Palmer, *Sales Mgr*
▲ **EMP:** 35
SQ FT: 37,000
SALES (est): 850K **Privately Held**
SIC: 3599 3544 Machine & other job shop work; special dies, tools, jigs & fixtures

(G-14781)
VETERANS OFFSET PRINTING INC
Also Called: Veteran Offset Printing
500 N Goodman St (14609-6136)
PHONE..........................585 288-2900
Fax: 585 288-2908
Louie Difilippo, *President*
John Dukay, *Vice Pres*
John Duque, *Vice Pres*
EMP: 3 **EST:** 1940
SALES: 2MM **Privately Held**
SIC: 2752 2759 Commercial printing, offset; commercial printing

(G-14782)
VIGNERI CHOCOLATE INC
810 Emerson St (14613-1804)
PHONE..........................585 254-6160
Alex Vigneri, *CEO*
◆ **EMP:** 7
SQ FT: 10,000
SALES: 500K **Privately Held**
SIC: 2064 Candy bars, including chocolate covered bars; chocolate candy, except solid chocolate

(G-14783)
W M T PUBLICATIONS INC
250 N Goodman St Ste 1 (14607-1150)
PHONE..........................585 244-3329
Mary Anna Towler, *President*
Michael Alo, *Vice Pres*
William J Towler, *Treasurer*
EMP: 16
SALES (est): 879.5K **Privately Held**
SIC: 2711 Newspapers, publishing & printing

(G-14784)
WATER WISE OF AMERICA INC
90 Canal St (14608-1958)
PHONE..........................585 232-1210
Bob Beach, *Branch Mgr*
EMP: 7 **Privately Held**
WEB: www.waterwiseofamerica.com
SIC: 2899 Water treating compounds
PA: Water Wise Of America, Inc
  75 Bermar Park Ste 5
  Rochester NY 14624

(G-14785)
WATER WISE OF AMERICA INC (PA)
75 Bermar Park Ste 5 (14624-1500)
PHONE..........................585 232-1210
Fax: 585 232-1263
Michael Bromley, *President*
Anne Jefferson, *Corp Secy*
EMP: 7
SQ FT: 2,500
SALES (est): 857.6K **Privately Held**
WEB: www.waterwiseofamerica.com
SIC: 2899 5169 Water treating compounds; chemicals & allied products

(G-14786)
WEB SEAL INC (PA)
15 Oregon St (14605-3094)
PHONE..........................585 546-1320
Fax: 585 546-5746
John F Hurley, *President*
Betty A Hurley, *Treasurer*
Marie Martin, *Finance*
Nick Riola, *Regl Sales Mgr*
Cheryl Schreiner, *Director*
EMP: 20 **EST:** 1960
SQ FT: 13,000
SALES (est): 4.7MM **Privately Held**
WEB: www.websealinc.com
SIC: 3053 5085 Gaskets & sealing devices; seals, industrial

(G-14787)
WELCH MACHINE INC
961 Lyell Ave Bldg 1-6 (14606-1956)
PHONE..........................585 647-3578
Martin Welch, *President*
EMP: 5
SQ FT: 5,000
SALES (est): 633.4K **Privately Held**
SIC: 3541 Machine tool replacement & repair parts, metal cutting types

(G-14788)
WELDRITE CLOSURES INC
2292 Innovation Way (14624-6224)
PHONE..........................585 429-8790
Jason Nelson, *President*
Richard Knapp, *General Mgr*
Greg Scace, *Vice Pres*
Marc Longbine, *Project Mgr*
Mary J Maier, *Manager*
EMP: 40
SALES (est): 9.6MM **Privately Held**
SIC: 3731 Offshore supply boats, building & repairing

(G-14789)
WERE FORMS INC
500 Helendale Rd Ste 190 (14609-3125)
PHONE..........................585 482-4400
Fax: 585 482-5243
Kim Hostutler, *President*
Chris Accorso, *Accounts Mgr*
John Duggan, *Accounts Mgr*
Julie Mandelaro, *Director*
EMP: 6
SQ FT: 2,000
SALES (est): 480K **Privately Held**
WEB: www.wereforms.com
SIC: 2759 Commercial printing

(G-14790)
WHIRLWIND MUSIC DISTRS INC
99 Ling Rd (14612-1965)
PHONE..........................800 733-9473
Fax: 585 865-8930
Al Keltz, *General Mgr*
Michael Laiacona, *Principal*
Scott Harvey, *Prdtn Mgr*
Debbie Noble, *Prdtn Mgr*
Holly Bryan, *Purch Agent*
▲ **EMP:** 100
SQ FT: 28,000

GEOGRAPHIC SECTION

Rockaway Park - Queens County (G-14812)

SALES (est): 21.3MM **Privately Held**
WEB: www.whirlwindusa.com
SIC: 3651 3678 3663 3643 Audio electronic systems; amplifiers: radio, public address or musical instrument; public address systems; electronic connectors; radio & TV communications equipment; current-carrying wiring devices; nonferrous wiredrawing & insulating

(G-14791)
WIKOFF COLOR CORPORATION
686 Pullman Ave (14615-3335)
PHONE...................585 458-0653
EMP: 16
SALES (corp-wide): 148.3MM **Privately Held**
SIC: 2893 Printing ink
PA: Wikoff Color Corporation
1886 Merritt Rd
Fort Mill SC 29715
803 548-2210

(G-14792)
WINDSOR TECHNOLOGY LLC
1527 Lyell Ave (14606-2121)
PHONE...................585 461-2500
Grant Randall, *President*
Julie Sullivan, *General Mgr*
Douglas Green, *Vice Pres*
Ann Shattuck, *QA Dir*
Chad Notebaert, *Engineer*
EMP: 10
SQ FT: 40,000
SALES: 10MM **Privately Held**
WEB: www.windsortec.com
SIC: 3672 Printed circuit boards

(G-14793)
WOERNER INDUSTRIES INC
Also Called: Wizer Equipment
485 Hague St (14606-1296)
PHONE...................585 436-1934
Philip Collins, *President*
EMP: 40
SALES (corp-wide): 4.4MM **Privately Held**
WEB: www.lasscowizer.com
SIC: 3555 Printing trades machinery
PA: Woerner Industries, Llc
485 Hague St
Rochester NY
585 235-1991

(G-14794)
WORDINGHAM MACHINE CO INC
Also Called: Wordingham Technologies
515 Lee Rd (14606-4236)
PHONE...................585 924-2294
Fax: 585 924-7660
Alok Kapoor, *CEO*
Mark Hurlbut, *CFO*
Bob Orcutt, *VP Sales*
Tim Bechtold, *Accounts Mgr*
Tony Phillips, *Sales Staff*
EMP: 45
SQ FT: 26,000
SALES (est): 9MM **Privately Held**
SIC: 3599 Machine & other job shop work

(G-14795)
XACTRA TECHNOLOGIES INC
105 Mcloughlin Rd Ste F (14615-3762)
PHONE...................585 426-2030
David W Binn, *President*
Michael Binn, *Manager*
John Bartlett, *Supervisor*
EMP: 55
SQ FT: 33,000
SALES (est): 7.7MM **Privately Held**
WEB: www.prestigeprecision.com
SIC: 3545 Precision tools, machinists'

(G-14796)
XEROX CORPORATION
100 S Clinton Ave Fl 4 (14604-1877)
PHONE...................585 423-4711
Fax: 585 423-5620
Carl Langsenkamp, *Principal*
John M Kelly, *Exec VP*
Munish Agrawal, *Vice Pres*
Anne Blaber, *Vice Pres*
Michael Frey, *Vice Pres*
EMP: 10

SALES (corp-wide): 10.7B **Publicly Held**
WEB: www.xerox.com
SIC: 3861 Photographic equipment & supplies
PA: Xerox Corporation
201 Merritt 7
Norwalk CT 06851
203 968-3000

(G-14797)
XEROX CORPORATION
225 Tech Park Dr (14623-2444)
PHONE...................585 427-4500
Dave Kreienberg, *Project Mgr*
Marcello Vince, *Project Mgr*
Dante Pietrantoni, *Project Engr*
Russ Laymen, *Manager*
Timothy Irving, *Sr Sys Analyst*
EMP: 125
SALES (corp-wide): 10.7B **Publicly Held**
WEB: www.xerox.com
SIC: 3861 3577 7629 7378 Photocopy machines; computer peripheral equipment; business machine repair, electric; computer peripheral equipment repair & maintenance; fine paper; property damage insurance; fire, marine & casualty insurance: mutual
PA: Xerox Corporation
201 Merritt 7
Norwalk CT 06851
203 968-3000

(G-14798)
XEROX CORPORATION
100 S Clinton Ave (14604-1877)
PHONE...................585 423-3538
James Danylyshyn, *Manager*
Stella Naugle, *Officer*
EMP: 25
SALES (corp-wide): 10.7B **Publicly Held**
WEB: www.xerox.com
SIC: 3577 Computer peripheral equipment
PA: Xerox Corporation
201 Merritt 7
Norwalk CT 06851
203 968-3000

(G-14799)
XEROX CORPORATION
80 Linden Oaks (14625-2809)
PHONE...................585 264-5584
EMP: 200
SALES (corp-wide): 21.4B **Publicly Held**
SIC: 3861 Mfg Photographic Equipment/Supplies
PA: Xerox Corporation
45 Glover Ave Ste 700
Norwalk CT 06851
203 968-3000

(G-14800)
XLI CORPORATION
55 Vanguard Pkwy (14606-3101)
PHONE...................585 436-2250
Peter Schott, *Ch of Bd*
Camille Declerck, *Project Mgr*
Curt Hampton, *Safety Mgr*
Vlade Kordovich, *Engineer*
Jim Ours, *Engineer*
EMP: 60 EST: 1967
SQ FT: 35,000
SALES (est): 10.6MM **Privately Held**
WEB: www.xlionline.com
SIC: 3544 Special dies, tools, jigs & fixtures

(G-14801)
XMH-HFI INC (PA)
Also Called: Bobby Jones Sportswear
1155 N Clinton Ave (14621-4454)
PHONE...................585 467-7240
Fax: 585 467-1485
Walter Hickey, *Ch of Bd*
Mike Cohen, *President*
Paulette Garafalo, *President*
Fruno Castagna, *Exec VP*
Sean C Fresco, *Vice Pres*
▲ EMP: 700 EST: 1899
SQ FT: 200,000
SALES (est): 187.2MM **Privately Held**
WEB: www.hickeyfreeman.com
SIC: 2311 2325 Suits, men's & boys': made from purchased materials; tailored dress & sport coats: men's & boys'; slacks, dress: men's, youths' & boys'

(G-14802)
YELLOWPAGECITYCOM
280 Kenneth Dr Ste 300 (14623-5263)
PHONE...................585 410-6688
Jamie Boyd, *Opers Mgr*
Michelle Quilitzsch, *Consultant*
Mark Brightenfield, *Associate*
EMP: 15
SALES (est): 2MM **Privately Held**
SIC: 3993 Signs & advertising specialties

(G-14803)
ZELLER WOODWORKS LLC
35 Norman St (14613-1809)
PHONE...................585 254-7607
Fritz Zeller, *Mng Member*
Jason Cudzilo,
Daniel Fallon,
EMP: 10 EST: 2012
SQ FT: 10,000
SALES: 1MM **Privately Held**
SIC: 2431 Woodwork, interior & ornamental

(G-14804)
ZEROVALENT NANOMETALS INC
693 East Ave Ste 103 (14607-2160)
PHONE...................585 298-8592
Joseph Fargnoli, *Principal*
EMP: 7
SALES (est): 286.2K **Privately Held**
SIC: 3339 Antimony refining (primary); cobalt refining (primary); babbitt metal (primary); beryllium metal

(G-14805)
ZIP PRODUCTS INC
565 Blossom Rd Ste E (14610-1873)
PHONE...................585 482-0044
Fax: 585 482-0040
Nikolay Petukhov, *President*
Iosif Zinger, *Vice Pres*
EMP: 14 EST: 1998
SQ FT: 8,000
SALES: 800K **Privately Held**
SIC: 3599 Machine & other job shop work

(G-14806)
ZWEIGLES INC
651 Plymouth Ave N (14608-1689)
PHONE...................585 546-1740
Fax: 585 546-8721
Julie E Camardo-Steron, *Ch of Bd*
Roberta Camardo, *President*
John Scott, *Plant Mgr*
Tina Steinmetz, *Purch Mgr*
Dominic Lippa, *CFO*
EMP: 55 EST: 1880
SQ FT: 37,000
SALES (est): 10.4MM **Privately Held**
WEB: www.zweigles.com
SIC: 2013 Sausages & other prepared meats; sausages from purchased meat

Rock City Falls
Saratoga County

(G-14807)
COTTRELL PAPER COMPANY INC
1135 Rock City Rd (12863-1208)
P.O. Box 35 (12863-0035)
PHONE...................518 885-1702
Fax: 518 885-0741
Jack L Cottrell, *Ch of Bd*
Ben Cottrell, *Vice Pres*
Darren Costanzo, *Purchasing*
Donna Hatch, *Bookkeeper*
Kathy Vandyk, *Manager*
▲ EMP: 36 EST: 1926
SQ FT: 40,000
SALES (est): 9.2MM **Privately Held**
WEB: www.cottrellpaper.com
SIC: 2621 Specialty papers; insulation siding, paper

Rock Stream
Schuyler County

(G-14808)
ROCK STREAM VINEYARDS
162 Fir Tree Point Rd (14878-9700)
PHONE...................607 243-8322
Mark Karasz, *Owner*
EMP: 7
SALES (est): 682.6K **Privately Held**
SIC: 2084 Wines

Rock Tavern
Orange County

(G-14809)
CREATIVE DESIGN AND MCH INC
197 Stone Castle Rd (12575-5000)
PHONE...................845 778-9001
Fax: 845 778-9086
Clifford Broderick, *CEO*
Mark Pugh, *Project Engr*
Brian Robertson, *Sales Mgr*
Alan Gelb, *Technical Staff*
Honorine Messersmith, *Admin Asst*
◆ EMP: 25
SQ FT: 24,000
SALES (est): 5.3MM **Privately Held**
SIC: 3469 Machine parts, stamped or pressed metal

Rockaway Beach
Queens County

(G-14810)
MADELAINE CHOCOLATE NOVLT INC (PA)
Also Called: Madelaine Chocolate Company
9603 Beach Channel Dr (11693-1398)
PHONE...................718 945-1500
Fax: 718 318-4607
Jorge Farber, *CEO*
Scott Wright, *COO*
Vivian Farber, *Exec VP*
Norman Gold, *Vice Pres*
David Reifer, *CFO*
▲ EMP: 100 EST: 1949
SQ FT: 200,000
SALES (est): 22MM **Privately Held**
WEB: www.madelainechocolate.com
SIC: 2066 Chocolate candy, solid

(G-14811)
WAVE PUBLISHING CO INC
Also Called: Wave of Long Island, The
8808 Rockaway Beach Blvd (11693-1608)
PHONE...................718 634-4000
Fax: 718 945-0913
Susan Locke, *President*
Howie Schwach, *Editor*
Sanford Bernstein, *Treasurer*
Felisha Edwards, *Adv Mgr*
Daniel Offner, *Assoc Editor*
EMP: 15
SQ FT: 4,500
SALES: 850K **Privately Held**
SIC: 2711 8111 Newspapers: publishing only, not printed on site; legal services

Rockaway Park
Queens County

(G-14812)
A-1 STAMPING & SPINNING CORP
225 Beach 143rd St (11694-1106)
PHONE...................718 388-2626
Fax: 718 486-8317
Ira Zapolsky, *President*
▲ EMP: 15 EST: 1947
SQ FT: 14,000

Rockaway Park - Queens County (G-14813)

(G-14813)
EVELO INC
327 Beach 101st St (11694-2831)
PHONE..............................917 251-8743
Yevgeniy Morekovic, *President*
Boris Morekovic, *Vice Pres*
▲ **EMP:** 2
SALES: 1MM **Privately Held**
SIC: 3751 Bicycles & related parts

(G-14814)
NICKEL GROUP LLC
212 Beach 141st St (11694-1230)
PHONE..............................212 706-7906
EMP: 5
SALES (est): 538.1K **Privately Held**
SIC: 3356 Nickel

(G-14815)
RELIANCE MICA CO INC
336 Beach 149th St (11694-1027)
PHONE..............................718 788-0282
Fax: 718 768-2593
Peter Yanello Jr, *President*
Michael Parrella, *Div Sub Head*
Frank Callahan, *Vice Pres*
▲ **EMP:** 6 **EST:** 1924
SQ FT: 10,000
SALES (est): 480K **Privately Held**
SIC: 3299 Mica products

Rockville Centre
Nassau County

(G-14816)
BIANCA BURGERS LLC
Also Called: Janowski Hamburger
15 S Long Beach Rd (11570-5621)
PHONE..............................516 764-9591
Fax: 516 764-1908
William Vogelsberg, *President*
EMP: 12
SALES (est): 2MM **Privately Held**
SIC: 2013 Prepared beef products from purchased beef

(G-14817)
CHAMPION CUTTING TOOL CORP
11-15 Saint Marks Ave (11570-4244)
P.O. Box 368 (11571-0368)
PHONE..............................516 536-8200
Lowell Frey, *President*
Diane Ruggiero, *Controller*
Andy Lebrecque, *Regl Sales Mgr*
Frank Suarez, *Sales Staff*
Marlene Ostroff, *Marketing Mgr*
▲ **EMP:** 50
SQ FT: 15,000
SALES (est): 6.8MM
SALES (corp-wide): 17.9MM **Privately Held**
WEB: www.championcuttingtool.com
SIC: 3545 Cutting tools for machine tools
PA: The Frey Company Inc
  190 Madison Ave
  Rockville Centre NY 11572
  516 536-8200

(G-14818)
CREATION BAUMANN USA INC
114 N Centre Ave (11570-3948)
PHONE..............................516 764-7431
George Baumann, *President*
Gloria Mastranni, *Human Res Mgr*
Harry Persaus, *Executive*
EMP: 30
SALES (est): 1.9MM **Privately Held**
SIC: 2211 2221 5949 5131 Apparel & outerwear fabrics, cotton; broadwoven fabric mills, manmade; fabric stores piece goods; piece goods & other fabrics

(G-14819)
GRAPHIC FABRICATIONS INC
Also Called: Minuteman Press
488a Sunrise Hwy (11570-5037)
PHONE..............................516 763-3222
Fax: 516 764-9334
George Dormani, *President*
EMP: 6
SQ FT: 4,000
SALES (est): 843.4K **Privately Held**
SIC: 2752 7334 2791 Commercial printing, lithographic; photocopying & duplicating services; typesetting

(G-14820)
HANGER INC
556 Merrick Rd Ste 101 (11570-5545)
PHONE..............................516 678-3650
EMP: 33
SALES (corp-wide): 451.4MM **Publicly Held**
SIC: 3841 Surgical & medical instruments
PA: Hanger, Inc.
  10910 Domain Dr Ste 300
  Austin TX 78758
  512 777-3800

(G-14821)
J SOEHNER CORPORATION
200 Brower Ave (11570-2603)
PHONE..............................516 599-2534
Fax: 516 599-2718
James Soehner, *President*
William F Soehner, *Vice Pres*
EMP: 17 **EST:** 1948
SQ FT: 18,000
SALES (est): 1.9MM **Privately Held**
SIC: 3599 Custom machinery

(G-14822)
LONG ISLAND CATHOLIC NEWSPAPER
50 N Park Ave (11570-4129)
PHONE..............................516 594-1212
Liz O'Conner, *Principal*
Cathy Casanova, *Purchasing*
Marianne Sheridan, *Director*
EMP: 30
SALES (est): 1.9MM **Privately Held**
SIC: 2721 2711 Periodicals; newspapers

(G-14823)
MEGAMATT INC
Also Called: Whistle Stop Bakery
35 Vassar Pl (11570-2830)
PHONE..............................516 536-3541
Jeff Tierney, *President*
Mary Tierney, *Treasurer*
EMP: 10
SQ FT: 4,600
SALES (est): 530K **Privately Held**
WEB: www.megamatt.com
SIC: 2051 5461 Bread, cake & related products; cakes, bakery: except frozen; bakeries; cakes

(G-14824)
MERCURY ENVELOPE CO INC
Also Called: Mercury Envelope Printing
100 Merrick Rd Ste 204e (11570-4801)
P.O. Box 200 (11571-0200)
PHONE..............................516 678-6744
Fax: 516 678-6764
Maurice Deutsch, *Ch of Bd*
Scott Deutsch, *President*
Maury Dautsch, *Vice Pres*
Maury Deutsch, *Vice Pres*
Colleen Cunningham, *CFO*
EMP: 75
SQ FT: 2,500
SALES (est): 18.8MM **Privately Held**
SIC: 2677 Envelopes

(G-14825)
PROGRESSUS COMPANY INC
100 Merrick Rd Ste 510w (11570-4825)
PHONE..............................516 255-0245
Fax: 516 255-0243
Lawrence Hutzler, *President*
Lillian Ehrenhaus, *Vice Pres*
Glenn Ehrenhaus, *VP Sales*
▲ **EMP:** 10
SQ FT: 60,000
SALES (est): 1.2MM **Privately Held**
WEB: www.progressus.com
SIC: 3469 Household cooking & kitchen utensils, metal

(G-14826)
QUALITY METAL STAMPING LLC (PA)
100 Merrick Rd Ste 310w (11570-4884)
PHONE..............................516 255-9000
Robert Serling, *Owner*
Joe Austin, *Engineer*
Steven White, *Engineer*
Joe Downing, *Senior Engr*
Jerry Flecker, *Controller*
EMP: 3
SQ FT: 2,000
SALES (est): 9.2MM **Privately Held**
SIC: 3469 Metal stampings

(G-14827)
SLEEP IMPROVEMENT CENTER INC
178 Sunrise Hwy Fl 2 (11570-4704)
PHONE..............................516 536-5799
Reza Naghavi, *President*
EMP: 12
SALES (est): 1MM **Privately Held**
SIC: 2515 Sleep furniture

(G-14828)
SOLVE ADVISORS INC
265 Sunrise Hwy Ste 22 (11570-4912)
PHONE..............................646 699-5041
Yevgeniy Grinberg, *President*
Gerard Nealon, *President*
Keenan Marshall, *CTO*
William Yu, *Prgrmr*
EMP: 8 **EST:** 2011
SQ FT: 2,000
SALES (est): 687.2K **Privately Held**
SIC: 7372 Business oriented computer software

(G-14829)
SOUTHBAY FUEL INJECTORS
566 Merrick Rd Ste 3 (11570-5547)
PHONE..............................516 442-4707
EMP: 7
SALES (est): 721.3K **Privately Held**
SIC: 2869 Fuels

(G-14830)
TRUEFORGE GLOBAL MCHY CORP
100 Merrick Rd Ste 208e (11570-4817)
PHONE..............................516 825-7040
Ronald E Jaggie, *President*
▲ **EMP:** 3
SQ FT: 2,500
SALES: 9MM **Privately Held**
WEB: www.trueforge.com
SIC: 3542 Forging machinery & hammers

(G-14831)
VENDING TIMES INC
55 Maple Ave Ste 304 (11570-4267)
PHONE..............................516 442-1850
Alicia Lavay, *President*
Nicolas Montano, *Vice Pres*
Frances Lavay, *Treasurer*
EMP: 11 **EST:** 1961
SQ FT: 4,000
SALES (est): 1.1MM **Privately Held**
SIC: 2721 2741 Magazines: publishing only, not printed on site; miscellaneous publishing

Rome
Oneida County

(G-14832)
ALLIANCE PAVING MATERIALS INC
846 Lawrence St (13440-8102)
PHONE..............................315 337-0795
Kimberly Ocuto, *President*
Roger Krol, *Manager*
Mark Tibbetts, *Manager*
Daniel Armstrong, *Director*
James Fahey, *Director*
EMP: 6
SQ FT: 4,000
SALES (est): 820K **Privately Held**
SIC: 2951 1771 Road materials, bituminous (not from refineries); driveway, parking lot & blacktop contractors

(G-14833)
BARTELL MACHINERY SYSTEMS LLC (DH)
6321 Elmer Hill Rd (13440-9325)
PHONE..............................315 336-7600
Pat Morocco, *President*
Rick Foland, *Engineer*
Thomas Lazzaro, *Engineer*
John Swift, *Engineer*
Dave Weiler, *Engineer*
▲ **EMP:** 140
SQ FT: 115,000
SALES (est): 31.5MM
SALES (corp-wide): 1.5B **Privately Held**
WEB: www.bartellmachinery.com
SIC: 3549 Metalworking machinery
HQ: Pettibone L.L.C.
  27501 Bella Vista Pkwy
  Warrenville IL 60555
  630 353-5000

(G-14834)
BAUMS CASTORINE COMPANY INC
200 Matthew St (13440-6533)
PHONE..............................315 336-8154
Fax: 315 336-3854
Charles F Mowry, *President*
Paul H Berger Jr, *Chairman*
Theodore Mowry, *Vice Pres*
Kathy Cardinal, *Manager*
▼ **EMP:** 7 **EST:** 1879
SQ FT: 22,000
SALES (est): 1.4MM **Privately Held**
WEB: www.baumscastorine.com
SIC: 2992 2841 Lubricating oils & greases; soap & other detergents

(G-14835)
BECK VAULT COMPANY
6648 Shank Ave (13440-9357)
PHONE..............................315 337-7590
EMP: 5 **EST:** 1946
SQ FT: 4,500
SALES: 500K **Privately Held**
SIC: 3272 7359 Mfg Concrete Burial Vaults & Rents Burial Equipment

(G-14836)
CAPTECH INDUSTRIES LLC
6 Revere Park (13440-5567)
PHONE..............................347 374-1182
Asher Wagh,
EMP: 9
SALES (est): 950K **Privately Held**
SIC: 3398 Brazing (hardening) of metal

(G-14837)
CATHEDRAL CORPORATION (PA)
632 Ellsworth Rd (13441-4808)
PHONE..............................315 338-0021
Fax: 315 338-5874
Marianne W Gaige, *President*
Lucie Shoen, *President*
Tom Wetjen, *Senior VP*
Aart Knyff, *Vice Pres*
Emery Tondreau, *Vice Pres*
EMP: 138
SQ FT: 58,000
SALES: 34.4MM **Privately Held**
WEB: www.cathedralcorporation.com
SIC: 2752 Commercial printing, lithographic

(G-14838)
COLD POINT CORPORATION
Also Called: Adirondack-Aire
7500 Cold Point Dr (13440-1852)
PHONE..............................315 339-2331
Gary F Brockett, *President*
Terry L Crawford, *Vice Pres*
▲ **EMP:** 30
SQ FT: 18,000
SALES (est): 7.1MM **Privately Held**
WEB: www.coldpointcorp.com
SIC: 3585 Air conditioning condensers & condensing units

GEOGRAPHIC SECTION

Rome - Oneida County (G-14862)

(G-14839)
ENVIROMASTER INTERNATIONAL LLC
Also Called: E M I
5780 Success Dr (13440-1769)
P.O. Box 4729, Utica (13504-4729)
PHONE.................................315 336-3716
Fax: 315 336-3981
Joe Hughes, *Engineer*
Thomas Stull, *Info Tech Dir*
Earl C Reed,
Earl Reed,
Timothy Reed,
▲ EMP: 100
SQ FT: 52,000
SALES (est): 14MM
SALES (corp-wide): 100.9MM **Privately Held**
WEB: www.ecrinternational.com
SIC: 3585 Heating & air conditioning combination units
PA: Ecr International, Inc.
  2201 Dwyer Ave
  Utica NY 13501
  315 797-1310

(G-14840)
GOODRICH CORPORATION
104 Otis St (13441-4714)
PHONE.................................315 838-1200
Jeff Meredith, *Managing Prtnr*
Steve Croke, *Vice Pres*
Joshua Clark, *Engineer*
Frank Kucerak, *Engineer*
Craig Matzeck, *Engineer*
EMP: 200
SALES (corp-wide): 5.7B **Publicly Held**
WEB: www.bfgoodrich.com
SIC: 3728 Aircraft parts & equipment
HQ: Goodrich Corporation
  2730 W Tyvola Rd
  Charlotte NC 28217
  704 423-7000

(G-14841)
HARRIS CORPORATION
474 Phoenix Dr (13441-4911)
PHONE.................................703 668-6239
Dave Melcher, *Principal*
EMP: 143
SALES (corp-wide): 5.9B **Publicly Held**
SIC: 3823 3812 Industrial instrmnts msrmnt display/control process variable; search & navigation equipment
PA: Harris Corporation
  1025 W Nasa Blvd
  Melbourne FL 32919
  321 727-9100

(G-14842)
HCI ENGINEERING
5880 Bartlett Rd (13440-1111)
PHONE.................................315 336-3450
Jim Carrol, *General Mgr*
James Carroll, *Engineer*
Staurt Hatzinder, *Manager*
EMP: 3
SALES: 1MM **Privately Held**
SIC: 3829 Measuring & controlling devices

(G-14843)
HUBBARD TOOL AND DIE CORP
Rome Indus Ctr Bldg 5 (13440)
PHONE.................................315 337-7840
Fax: 315 337-7865
Eric Hubbard, *President*
Randall Hubbard, *Treasurer*
Robin Yaworski, *Manager*
EMP: 22 EST: 1957
SQ FT: 12,000
SALES: 3MM **Privately Held**
SIC: 3599 3545 Machine shop, jobbing & repair; precision tools, machinists'

(G-14844)
J DAVIS MANUFACTURING CO INC
Also Called: R-Tronics
222 Erie Blvd E (13440-6814)
PHONE.................................315 337-7574
Fax: 315 337-0804
Lucille Kroeger, *CEO*
Rocco Garro, *Principal*
William Abrams, *Webmaster*
EMP: 20
SQ FT: 8,000
SALES (est): 4.6MM **Privately Held**
WEB: www.r-tronics.com
SIC: 3496 Cable, uninsulated wire: made from purchased wire

(G-14845)
KRIS-TECH WIRE COMPANY INC (PA)
80 Otis St (13441-4712)
P.O. Box 4377 (13442-4377)
PHONE.................................315 339-5268
Fax: 315 339-5277
Jon C Brodock, *CEO*
Cheryl Ingersoll, *COO*
Chuck Dillman, *Plant Mgr*
Steven Benjamin, *Mfg Spvr*
▲ EMP: 32
SQ FT: 50,000
SALES (est): 6.6MM **Privately Held**
WEB: www.kristechwire.com
SIC: 3357 Nonferrous wiredrawing & insulating; appliance fixture wire, nonferrous; building wire & cable, nonferrous

(G-14846)
L & L TRUCKING INC
1 Revere Park (13440-5568)
PHONE.................................315 339-2550
Joe Mammone, *President*
Mike Barrilo, *Sales Staff*
Bob Galbraith, *Sales Staff*
Andrew Hovest, *Sales Staff*
Dan Karley, *Sales Staff*
EMP: 20
SALES (est): 727.1K **Privately Held**
SIC: 2741 Miscellaneous publishing

(G-14847)
LEONARD BUS SALES INC
730 Ellsworth Rd (13441-4309)
PHONE.................................607 467-3100
Mike Leonard, *President*
EMP: 6
SALES (corp-wide): 36.8MM **Privately Held**
SIC: 3711 5012 Buses, all types, assembly of; buses
PA: Leonard Bus Sales, Inc.
  4 Leonard Way
  Deposit NY 13754
  607 467-3100

(G-14848)
MCINTOSH BOX & PALLET CO INC
200 6th St (13440-6069)
PHONE.................................315 446-9350
Fax: 315 337-4196
Dan Balitz, *Manager*
Vayeli Rivera, *Manager*
EMP: 26
SALES (corp-wide): 26.9MM **Privately Held**
WEB: www.mcintoshbox.com
SIC: 2499 2448 2441 5085 Spools, wood; wood pallets & skids; nailed wood boxes & shook; bins & containers, storage
PA: Mcintosh Box & Pallet Co., Inc.
  5864 Pyle Dr
  East Syracuse NY 13057
  315 446-9350

(G-14849)
MGS MANUFACTURING INC (PA)
Also Called: Mgs Group, The
122 Otis St (13441-4714)
P.O. Box 4259 (13442-4259)
PHONE.................................315 337-3350
Fax: 315 483-5391
Robert Johnson, *Ch of Bd*
Scott Stephan, *COO*
Tom Comiskey, *Vice Pres*
William Gurecki, *Vice Pres*
Joe Davis, *Plant Mgr*
▲ EMP: 50 EST: 1957
SQ FT: 20,000
SALES (est): 18.4MM **Privately Held**
SIC: 3549 Wiredrawing & fabricating machinery & equipment, ex. die

(G-14850)
MSI-MOLDING SOLUTIONS INC
6247 State Route 233 (13440-1037)
PHONE.................................315 736-2412
Frank Giotto, *Ch of Bd*
Thomas Bashant, *President*
Cindy Waterman, *Manager*
▲ EMP: 20
SALES: 2.8MM
SALES (corp-wide): 57.2MM **Privately Held**
SIC: 3089 Molding primary plastic
PA: Fiber Instrument Sales, Inc.
  161 Clear Rd
  Oriskany NY 13424
  315 736-2206

(G-14851)
NASH METALWARE CO INC
Also Called: American Metal
200 Railroad St (13440-6951)
PHONE.................................315 339-5794
Fax: 315 339-0933
Donald Beebe, *Manager*
EMP: 11
SALES (corp-wide): 11.4MM **Privately Held**
SIC: 3469 5719 Household cooking & kitchen utensils, metal; kitchenware
PA: Nash Metalware Co Inc
  72 N 15th St
  Brooklyn NY 11222
  718 384-1500

(G-14852)
NCI GROUP INC
Metal Building Components Mbci
6168 State Route 233 (13440-1033)
P.O. Box 4141 (13442-4141)
PHONE.................................315 339-1245
Fax: 315 339-6284
Chuck Glady, *Branch Mgr*
EMP: 100
SALES (corp-wide): 1.6B **Publicly Held**
SIC: 3448 3444 3441 Prefabricated metal buildings; prefabricated metal components; sheet metalwork; fabricated structural metal
HQ: Nci Group, Inc.
  10943 N Sam Huston Pkwy W
  Houston TX 77064
  281 897-7500

(G-14853)
NORAS CANDY SHOP
Also Called: Candy Land
321 N Doxtator St (13440-3121)
PHONE.................................315 337-4530
Spiro Haritatos, *Owner*
EMP: 14
SALES (est): 1.2MM **Privately Held**
SIC: 2064 5441 2066 Candy & other confectionery products; candy; chocolate & cocoa products

(G-14854)
NORTEK POWDER COATING LLC
5900 Success Dr (13440-1743)
PHONE.................................315 337-2339
Bunrith Lach, *Vice Pres*
Tom Serwatka, *Sales Mgr*
Borin Chea, *Mng Member*
Borin Keith,
▲ EMP: 16
SALES (est): 3.2MM **Privately Held**
SIC: 2851 Paints & allied products

(G-14855)
NORTHROP GRUMMAN SYSTEMS CORP
Rr 26 Box N (13440)
PHONE.................................315 336-0500
Steve Maiser, *Manager*
EMP: 25 **Publicly Held**
WEB: www.logicon.com
SIC: 7372 Operating systems computer software
HQ: Northrop Grumman Systems Corporation
  2980 Fairview Park Dr
  Falls Church VA 22042
  703 280-2900

(G-14856)
OMEGA WIRE INC
900 Railroad St (13440-6900)
PHONE.................................315 337-4300
James A Spargo IV, *Manager*
EMP: 50
SQ FT: 50,980
SALES (corp-wide): 432.1MM **Privately Held**
WEB: www.omegawire.com
SIC: 3366 Copper foundries
HQ: Omega Wire, Inc.
  12 Masonic Ave
  Camden NY 13316
  315 245-3800

(G-14857)
PERATON INC
Also Called: Harris Corporation
474 Phoenix Dr (13441-4911)
PHONE.................................315 838-7000
Fax: 315 334-4964
John Cappelli, *Marketing Mgr*
Vic Choo, *Branch Mgr*
Elizabeth Shea, *Senior Mgr*
Scot Tucker, *Info Tech Dir*
Liz Palumbo, *Executive*
EMP: 40
SALES (corp-wide): 582.3MM **Privately Held**
WEB: www.ittind.com
SIC: 3625 Control equipment, electric
HQ: Peraton Inc.
  12975 Worldgate Dr # 7322
  Herndon VA 20170
  703 668-6000

(G-14858)
PROFESSIONAL TECHNOLOGY INC
Also Called: Professional Technologies
5433 Lowell Rd (13440-7815)
PHONE.................................315 337-4156
John Puleo, *President*
EMP: 5
SALES (est): 540K **Privately Held**
SIC: 3651 1731 Speaker systems; communications specialization

(G-14859)
R&S STEEL LLC
412 Canal St (13440-6835)
PHONE.................................315 281-0123
Fax: 315 281-0124
Paul Raulli, *Mng Member*
Patty Huey, *Manager*
Richie T Raulli,
Thomas Raulli,
EMP: 21
SQ FT: 5,600
SALES (est): 3.9MM **Privately Held**
SIC: 3441 Fabricated structural metal

(G-14860)
RAULLI IRON WORKS INC
133 Mill St (13440-6945)
PHONE.................................315 337-8070
Fax: 315 337-3960
Agostino Raulli, *President*
Mark Raulli, *Vice Pres*
EMP: 10 EST: 1938
SQ FT: 3,600
SALES: 900K **Privately Held**
WEB: www.raulliandsonsincornamental.com
SIC: 3446 Architectural metalwork

(G-14861)
ROME SIGN & DISPLAY CO
510 Erie Blvd W (13440-4806)
PHONE.................................315 336-0550
Randall Denton, *President*
Terrance Denton, *Vice Pres*
EMP: 7
SQ FT: 1,000
SALES (est): 917.3K **Privately Held**
SIC: 3993 Signs, not made in custom sign painting shops

(G-14862)
ROME SPECIALTY COMPANY INC
Also Called: Rosco Div
501 W Embargo St (13440-4061)
P.O. Box 109 (13442-0109)
PHONE.................................315 337-8200
Fax: 315 339-2523
Judith Kieman, *President*
Michael Bleem, *Finance Dir*
John Butts, *Supervisor*
◆ EMP: 20 EST: 1926
SQ FT: 35,000

Rome - Oneida County (G-14863)

SALES (est): 2MM **Privately Held**
WEB: www.roscoinc.com
SIC: 3949 Fishing equipment; fishing tackle, general

(G-14863)
RTD MANUFACTURING INC
6273 State Route 233 (13440-1037)
PHONE..................315 337-3151
Brian P Getbehead, *President*
Robert Getbehead, *Vice Pres*
Sandra Vanslyke, *Office Mgr*
Mike Waterman, *Executive*
Iva S Getbehead, *Admin Sec*
EMP: 7
SQ FT: 3,500
SALES (est): 600K **Privately Held**
WEB: www.rtdmfg.com
SIC: 3599 Machine shop, jobbing & repair

(G-14864)
SERWAY BROS INC (PA)
Also Called: Serway Cabinet Trends
Plant 2 Rome Indus Ctr (13440)
PHONE..................315 337-0601
Christine N Serway, *Ch of Bd*
Dorothy Alexander, *Manager*
James Pacific, *Director*
Sophia Pelose, *Admin Sec*
EMP: 22
SQ FT: 20,800
SALES (est): 2.3MM **Privately Held**
WEB: www.serway.com
SIC: 2541 5211 3648 5719 Counters or counter display cases, wood; cabinets, kitchen; lighting fixtures, except electric: residential; lighting fixtures; wood kitchen cabinets

(G-14865)
TIPS & DIES INC
505 Rome Industrial Park (13440-6948)
PHONE..................315 337-4161
Randall Hubbard, *President*
Gary Johnson, *Sales Staff*
Peter Scribner, *Sales Staff*
EMP: 12
SALES: 2.3MM **Privately Held**
WEB: www.tipsanddies.com
SIC: 3544 Special dies & tools

(G-14866)
TONYS ORNAMENTAL IR WORKS INC
6757 Martin St (13440-7106)
P.O. Box 4425 (13442-4425)
PHONE..................315 337-3730
Fax: 315 337-0213
Anthony J Pettinelli Jr, *President*
Toni Olejarczyk, *Corp Secy*
EMP: 20
SQ FT: 13,800
SALES (est): 3.4MM **Privately Held**
SIC: 3449 3446 Miscellaneous metalwork; architectural metalwork

(G-14867)
VARFLEX CORPORATION
512 W Court St (13440-4000)
P.O. Box 551 (13442-0551)
PHONE..................315 336-4400
Fax: 315 336-0005
Daniel J Burgdorf, *President*
William L Griffin, *Vice Pres*
Christine Ruben, *Safety Mgr*
Charles J Schoff, *Treasurer*
Lisa Dombrowski, *Sales Associate*
▲ EMP: 150 EST: 1924
SQ FT: 144,000
SALES (est): 12.1MM **Privately Held**
WEB: www.varflex.com
SIC: 3644 Insulators & insulation materials, electrical

(G-14868)
WORTHINGTON INDUSTRIES INC
530 Henry St (13440-5639)
PHONE..................315 336-5500
Roger Pratt, *Plant Mgr*
Jerry Tomassi, *Safety Mgr*
James Obrien, *Human Res Dir*
EMP: 72
SALES (corp-wide): 2.8B **Publicly Held**
SIC: 3316 Strip steel, cold-rolled: from purchased hot-rolled

PA: Worthington Industries, Inc.
200 W Old Wlson Bridge Rd
Worthington OH 43085
614 438-3210

Romulus
Seneca County

(G-14869)
COBBLESTONE FRM WINERY VINYRD
5102 State Route 89 (14541-9779)
PHONE..................315 549-1004
Jennifer Clark, *Principal*
EMP: 10
SALES (est): 840.1K **Privately Held**
SIC: 2084 Wines, brandy & brandy spirits

(G-14870)
SCHRADER MEAT MARKET
1937 Summerville Rd (14541-9800)
PHONE..................607 869-6328
Keith Schrader, *Owner*
EMP: 19
SALES: 600K **Privately Held**
SIC: 3421 2013 Table & food cutlery, including butchers'; sausages & other prepared meats

(G-14871)
SOUTH SENECA VINYL LLC
1585 Yale Farm Rd (14541-9761)
PHONE..................315 585-6050
Nelson Sensenig,
EMP: 9
SQ FT: 5,000
SALES (est): 1.1MM **Privately Held**
SIC: 3211 Window glass, clear & colored

(G-14872)
SWEDISH HILL VINEYARD INC
Also Called: Swedish Hill Winery
4565 State Route 414 (14541-9769)
PHONE..................607 403-0029
Fax: 315 549-8477
David Peterson, *CEO*
Richard Peterson, *President*
Cynthia Peterson, *Vice Pres*
Lindsay Case, *Marketing Staff*
Derek Wilber, *Manager*
EMP: 70
SALES: 6MM **Privately Held**
SIC: 2084 0721 Wines; vines, cultivation of

Ronkonkoma
Suffolk County

(G-14873)
A A TECHNOLOGY INC
101 Trade Zone Dr (11779-7363)
PHONE..................631 913-0400
Fax: 631 563-3994
Henry Tang, *CEO*
Chris Leone, *Business Mgr*
Frank Rosselli, *Vice Pres*
James Stapleton, *Vice Pres*
James Unser, *QC Mgr*
◆ EMP: 85
SQ FT: 15,700
SALES (est): 8.6MM **Privately Held**
SIC: 3672 Printed circuit boards

(G-14874)
ACCELA INC
100 Comac St Ste 2 (11779-6928)
PHONE..................631 563-5005
Daryl Blowes, *General Mgr*
EMP: 10
SALES (corp-wide): 80MM **Privately Held**
SIC: 7372 Prepackaged software
PA: Accela, Inc.
2633 Camino Ramon Ste 500
San Ramon CA 94583
925 659-3200

(G-14875)
ACCENT LABEL & TAG CO INC (PA)
348 Woodlawn Ave (11779-5055)
PHONE..................631 244-7066
Fax: 631 244-7108
Larry Gutman, *President*
EMP: 6
SALES (est): 592.2K **Privately Held**
WEB: www.accentlabelandtag.com
SIC: 2679 7336 Labels, paper: made from purchased material; graphic arts & related design

(G-14876)
ACE CANVAS & TENT CORP
155 Raynor Ave (11779-6666)
PHONE..................631 648-0614
Fax: 631 981-4430
Vincent Cardillo, *Vice Pres*
▲ EMP: 10
SQ FT: 5,500
SALES (est): 1.5MM **Privately Held**
SIC: 3081 2394 7359 Vinyl film & sheet; canvas & related products; tent & tarpaulin rental

(G-14877)
ACME INDUSTRIES OF W BABYLON
125 Gary Way Ste 2 (11779-6576)
PHONE..................631 737-5231
John Landrio, *President*
EMP: 10
SQ FT: 3,000
SALES (est): 1.8MM **Privately Held**
SIC: 3599 7389 Machine shop, jobbing & repair; grinding, precision: commercial or industrial

(G-14878)
ADAPTIVE MFG TECH INC
181 Remington Blvd (11779-6911)
PHONE..................631 580-5400
Terence Larocca, *Ch of Bd*
EMP: 32
SQ FT: 18,000
SALES (est): 7.9MM **Privately Held**
WEB: www.amtautomation.com
SIC: 3542 3599 Machine tools, metal forming type; custom machinery

(G-14879)
ADVANCE MICRO POWER CORP
2190 Smithtown Ave (11779-7355)
PHONE..................631 471-6157
Jasbir Mahajan, *President*
▲ EMP: 15
SQ FT: 14,000
SALES (est): 1.6MM **Privately Held**
SIC: 3672 Printed circuit boards

(G-14880)
ADVANCED MANUFACTURING SVC INC
100 13th Ave Ste 2 (11779-6820)
PHONE..................631 676-5210
John Nucatola, *President*
Laura Patanella, *Buyer*
Alan Kaufman, *Purchasing*
EMP: 28
SALES (est): 6.5MM **Privately Held**
SIC: 3672 Printed circuit boards

(G-14881)
ADVANCED PHOTONICS INC
151 Trade Zone Dr (11779-7384)
PHONE..................631 471-3693
Fax: 631 471-3750
Robert Turner, *President*
Richard Turner, *Vice Pres*
Jack Raybin, *CFO*
EMP: 14
SQ FT: 5,000
SALES: 1.4MM **Privately Held**
WEB: www.advancedphotonicsusa.com
SIC: 3699 5084 Laser systems & equipment; industrial machinery & equipment

(G-14882)
AERO-DATA METAL CRAFTERS INC
2085 5th Ave (11779-6903)
PHONE..................631 471-7733
Fax: 631 471-9161

Robert De Luca, *President*
David Rubinstein, *Project Mgr*
Chris Behr, *Purch Agent*
Andrea Savino, *Human Res Mgr*
Ed Fiance, *Sales Executive*
EMP: 110
SQ FT: 100,000
SALES (est): 23.3MM **Privately Held**
WEB: www.metal-crafters.com
SIC: 3444 3446 3443 3441 Sheet metal specialties, not stamped; architectural metalwork; fabricated plate work (boiler shop); fabricated structural metal; cold finishing of steel shapes

(G-14883)
AIR CRAFTERS INC
2085 5th Ave (11779-6903)
PHONE..................631 471-7788
Fax: 631 471-9161
Robert Deluca, *President*
Ed Fiance, *General Mgr*
Michael Hennessey, *Vice Pres*
Chris Behr, *Manager*
William Mabanta, *Admin Sec*
EMP: 105
SQ FT: 40,000
SALES: 12MM **Privately Held**
WEB: www.air-crafters.com
SIC: 2542 5085 3625 3564 Fixtures, office: except wood; clean room supplies; relays & industrial controls; blowers & fans

(G-14884)
AIRGLE CORPORATION
711 Koehler Ave Ste 3 (11779-7410)
PHONE..................866 501-7750
Fax: 718 395-2376
Yang Lo, *President*
Mike Anderson, *Vice Pres*
▲ EMP: 20 EST: 2006
SQ FT: 7,300
SALES (est): 184.5K **Privately Held**
SIC: 3589 3564 Water purification equipment, household type; air purification equipment

(G-14885)
AKSHAR EXTRACTS INC
59 Remington Blvd (11779-6954)
PHONE..................631 588-9727
Jay Patel, *President*
Nat Patel, *Vice Pres*
Dee Patel, *Treasurer*
▲ EMP: 5
SQ FT: 3,000
SALES: 500K **Privately Held**
WEB: www.pureextracts.com
SIC: 2836 Extracts

(G-14886)
ALKEN INDUSTRIES INC
2175 5th Ave (11779-6217)
PHONE..................631 467-2000
Fax: 631 467-2877
Kimberly Senior, *President*
Anthony Landisi, *President*
Tricia Voigt, *General Mgr*
Tami Senior-Humanitizki, *Vice Pres*
Amanda Cartwright, *Purch Mgr*
EMP: 70
SQ FT: 52,000
SALES (est): 22.9MM **Privately Held**
WEB: www.alkenind.com
SIC: 3728 Aircraft parts & equipment

(G-14887)
ALL AROUND SPIRAL INC
10 Fleetwood Ct (11779-6907)
PHONE..................631 588-0220
Richard Kern, *Ch of Bd*
EMP: 9
SALES (est): 1.2MM **Privately Held**
SIC: 3444 Sheet metalwork

(G-14888)
ALL PACKAGING MCHY & SUPS CORP
90 13th Ave Unit 11 (11779-6818)
PHONE..................631 588-7310
Fax: 631 467-4690
Albert Bolla, *President*
Joel Busel, *Vice Pres*
Samul Posner, *Vice Pres*
Eric Wassing, *Controller*

EMP: 10
SQ FT: 10,000
SALES: 2.4MM
SALES (corp-wide): 2.6MM Privately Held
WEB: www.triopackaging.com
SIC: 3565 Packaging machinery
PA: Trio Packaging Corp.
90 13th Ave Unit 11
Ronkonkoma NY 11779
631 588-0800

(G-14889)
ALL PHASES ASP & LDSCPG DSGN
60 18th Ave (11779-6204)
PHONE.................................631 588-1372
Vincent Schlosser, Principal
EMP: 10
SALES (est): 883K Privately Held
SIC: 2951 Asphalt paving mixtures & blocks

(G-14890)
ALLIANT TCHSYSTEMS OPRTONS LLC
77 Raynor Ave (11779-6649)
PHONE.................................631 737-6100
Robert Bakos, Vice Pres
John Tilleli, Finance
EMP: 20
SALES (corp-wide): 4.4B Publicly Held
WEB: www.mrcwdc.com
SIC: 3721 Research & development on aircraft by the manufacturer
HQ: Alliant Techsystems Operations Llc
4700 Nathan Ln N
Plymouth MN 55442

(G-14891)
ALLURE METAL WORKS INC
71 Hoffman Ln (11749-5007)
PHONE.................................631 588-0220
Jillian Guido, Principal
EMP: 10
SALES (est): 1.5MM Privately Held
SIC: 3444 1711 Sheet metalwork; plumbing, heating, air-conditioning contractors

(G-14892)
ALROD ASSOCIATES INC
710 Union Pkwy Ste 9 (11779-7428)
PHONE.................................631 981-2193
Fax: 631 981-2197
Evan Alrod, President
Peggy Axelrod, Vice Pres
Evan Axelrod, Treasurer
EMP: 10
SQ FT: 6,000
SALES (est): 1.3MM Privately Held
SIC: 2541 2542 5046 Store fixtures, wood; fixtures, store: except wood; store fixtures

(G-14893)
ALTAQUIP LLC
200 13th Ave Unit 6 (11779-6815)
PHONE.................................631 580-4740
EMP: 8
SALES (corp-wide): 194.6B Publicly Held
SIC: 3699 Mfg Electrical Equipment/Supplies
HQ: Altaquip Llc
100 Production Dr
Harrison OH 45030
513 674-6464

(G-14894)
AMERICAN BOTTLING COMPANY
Also Called: Snapple Distributors
2004 Orville Dr N (11779-7645)
PHONE.................................516 714-0002
Ray Russo, Manager
EMP: 19 Publicly Held
SIC: 2086 Bottled & canned soft drinks
HQ: The American Bottling Company
5301 Legacy Dr
Plano TX 75024

(G-14895)
AMERICAN QUALITY EMBROIDERY (PA)
740 Koehler Ave (11779-7406)
PHONE.................................631 467-3200
Fax: 631 467-0273
Robert Kalinowski, President
EMP: 1
SQ FT: 1,600
SALES (est): 17.8MM Privately Held
SIC: 2284 2395 Embroidery thread; embroidery products, except schiffli machine

(G-14896)
AMETEK INC
903 S 2nd St (11779-7201)
PHONE.................................631 467-8400
EMP: 6
SALES (corp-wide): 3.8B Publicly Held
SIC: 3621 Motors & generators
PA: Ametek, Inc.
1100 Cassatt Rd
Berwyn PA 19312
610 647-2121

(G-14897)
AMETEK CTS US INC
Also Called: Instruments For Industry, Inc.
903 S 2nd St (11779-7201)
PHONE.................................631 467-8400
Mark Swanson, President
Leon Benatar, Vice Pres
Bernie Papocchia, Manager
Dennis Tucker, Manager
Mike Yantez, Director
EMP: 25 EST: 1953
SQ FT: 10,600
SALES (est): 7.5MM
SALES (corp-wide): 3.8B Publicly Held
WEB: www.ifi.com
SIC: 3663 Amplifiers, RF power & IF
PA: Ametek, Inc.
1100 Cassatt Rd
Berwyn PA 19312
610 647-2121

(G-14898)
AMRON ELECTRONICS INC
160 Gary Way (11779-6509)
PHONE.................................631 737-1234
Rick Foora, CEO
James Flora, Vice Pres
EMP: 50
SALES (est): 2.9MM Privately Held
SIC: 3679 Commutators, electronic

(G-14899)
APOLLO DISPLAY TECH CORP (PA)
87 Raynor Ave Ste 1 (11779-6667)
PHONE.................................631 580-4360
Fax: 631 580-4370
Bernhard Staller, President
Werner Schubert, Managing Dir
Joanne Sottile, Senior VP
Jim Rossi, Opers Staff
Adam Larkinith, Engineer
▲ EMP: 35
SQ FT: 15,000
SALES (est): 6.5MM Privately Held
WEB: www.apollodisplays.com
SIC: 3679 5065 Liquid crystal displays (LCD); electronic parts & equipment

(G-14900)
ARTISAN MACHINING INC
49 Remington Blvd (11779-6909)
PHONE.................................631 589-1416
John Caccavale, President
EMP: 7
SALES (est): 800K Privately Held
WEB: www.artisanmachining.com
SIC: 3599 Machine shop, jobbing & repair

(G-14901)
ASSOCIATED MATERIALS LLC
Also Called: Alside Supply Center
1830 Lakeland Ave (11779-7404)
PHONE.................................631 467-4535
Debbie Gittleman, Site Mgr
William Prush, Manager
EMP: 10 Privately Held
WEB: www.associatedmaterials.com
SIC: 3089 Plastic hardware & building products

HQ: Associated Materials, Llc
3773 State Rd
Cuyahoga Falls OH 44223
330 929-1811

(G-14902)
ATK GASL INC
77 Raynor Ave (11779-6649)
PHONE.................................631 737-6100
John Tilleli, Principal
EMP: 19
SALES (est): 3.1MM Privately Held
SIC: 3721 Research & development on aircraft by the manufacturer

(G-14903)
AZTEC INDUSTRIES INC
200 13th Ave Unit 5 (11779-6815)
PHONE.................................631 585-1331
Phil Del Giudice, President
Randyll Brooks, Financial Analy
EMP: 6
SQ FT: 2,500
SALES: 500K Privately Held
SIC: 2522 Panel systems & partitions, office: except wood

(G-14904)
B & B PRECISION COMPONENTS INC
301 Christopher St # 303 (11779-6922)
PHONE.................................631 273-3321
Fax: 631 273-3936
Lucille Bricker, President
August Bricker, COO
Kathryn Richichi, Manager
EMP: 5
SQ FT: 12,000
SALES (est): 1.6MM Privately Held
WEB: www.bbprecisioncomponents.com
SIC: 3728 Aircraft parts & equipment

(G-14905)
B H AIRCRAFT COMPANY INC (PA)
2230 Smithtown Ave (11779-7329)
PHONE.................................631 580-9747
Vincent E Kearns, Ch of Bd
Daniel Kearns, President
Sebastian F Digiacomo, Principal
Dan Fugua, Principal
Paul Goggi, Principal
EMP: 90 EST: 1933
SQ FT: 100,000
SALES (est): 14.7MM Privately Held
WEB: www.bhaircraft.com
SIC: 3724 Aircraft engines & engine parts

(G-14906)
BANNER METALCRAFT INC
300 Trade Zone Dr (11779-7345)
PHONE.................................631 563-7303
Fax: 631 563-7655
Kenneth R Bednar, President
Nancy E Bednar, Corp Secy
Richard Martin, Foreman/Supr
Kurt Butcher, Engineer
Michael Berg, Sls & Mktg Exec
EMP: 70
SQ FT: 32,000
SALES: 12.1MM Privately Held
WEB: www.bannermetalcraft.com
SIC: 3444 Sheet metalwork

(G-14907)
BECKER ELECTRONICS INC
50 Alexander Ct Ste 2 (11779-6568)
PHONE.................................631 619-9100
Fax: 631 699-0138
David M Sosnow, CEO
Sharon Becker, Vice Pres
Patrick Spagnuolo, Treasurer
Frank Spagnuolo, Administration
EMP: 80
SQ FT: 14,000
SALES: 12MM Privately Held
WEB: www.beckerelectronicsinc.com
SIC: 3679 5065 Harness assemblies for electronic use: wire or cable; electronic parts & equipment

(G-14908)
BOBLEY-HARMANN CORPORATION
Also Called: Gift Valleys.com
200 Trade Zone Dr Unit 2 (11779-7359)
PHONE.................................516 433-3800
Mark Bobley, President
Barbara Monks, Opers Mgr
Fred Auer, Finance Mgr
Bob Hagenburger, Executive
▲ EMP: 8
SQ FT: 500
SALES (est): 912.1K Privately Held
WEB: www.bobley.com
SIC: 2731 2759 Book publishing; promotional printing

(G-14909)
BROADWAY NATIONAL GROUP LLC
Also Called: Broadway National Sign & Ltg
1900 Ocean Ave (11779-6520)
PHONE.................................800 797-4467
Diane Belkin, Controller
William Paparella, Mng Member
Jen Keppler, Office Admin
EMP: 80
SALES (est): 14.2MM Privately Held
SIC: 3993 1711 7349 3648 Signs & advertising specialties; plumbing, heating, air-conditioning contractors; building maintenance services; lighting equipment

(G-14910)
BROADWAY NEON SIGN CORP
Also Called: Broadway National
1900 Ocean Ave (11779-6520)
PHONE.................................908 241-4177
William Paparella, President
Joy Sparano, Manager
Phil Varca, Manager
EMP: 18
SQ FT: 50,000
SALES (est): 3MM Privately Held
WEB: www.broadwaynational.com
SIC: 3993 3444 2431 2394 Neon signs; sheet metalwork; millwork; canvas & related products

(G-14911)
C TO C DESIGN & PRINT INC
1850 Pond Rd Unit B (11779-7210)
PHONE.................................631 885-4020
Anthony Aceto, Ch of Bd
EMP: 10
SALES (est): 1.3MM Privately Held
SIC: 2752 Commercial printing, lithographic

(G-14912)
CALCHEM CORPORATION (PA)
2001 Ocean Ave (11779-6500)
P.O. Box 4258, Huntington (11743-0777)
PHONE.................................631 423-5696
John H Chen, President
Molly Chen, Exec VP
▲ EMP: 7
SQ FT: 12,000
SALES (est): 1.9MM Privately Held
WEB: www.calchemcorp.com
SIC: 2893 Printing ink

(G-14913)
CANFIELD AEROSPACE & MAR INC
90 Remington Blvd (11779-6910)
PHONE.................................631 648-1050
Lynn Zaun, President
EMP: 20 EST: 2000
SALES (est): 1.2MM Privately Held
WEB: www.canfieldam.com
SIC: 3728 Aircraft parts & equipment

(G-14914)
CAROLINA PRECISION PLAS LLC
Also Called: Cpp Global
115 Comac St (11779-6931)
PHONE.................................631 981-0743
Fax: 631 585-1405
EMP: 94
SALES (corp-wide): 74.8MM Privately Held
SIC: 3089 Injection molding of plastics

Ronkonkoma - Suffolk County (G-14915)

PA: Carolina Precision Plastics Llc
405 Commerce Pl
Asheboro NC 27203
336 498-2654

(G-14915)
CEDAR WEST INC (PA)
1700 Ocean Ave Ste 1 (11779-6570)
PHONE 631 467-1444
Joanne D Herman, *President*
Michael Clark, *Vice Pres*
Robert Herman, *Vice Pres*
Gloria J Smalley, *CFO*
EMP: 2
SALES (est): 3.6MM **Privately Held**
WEB: www.cedarwest.com
SIC: 2752 Commercial printing, offset

(G-14916)
COPY X/PRESS LTD
Also Called: Ocean Printing
700 Union Pkwy Ste 5 (11779-7427)
PHONE 631 585-2200
Fax: 631 585-0071
John Harkins, *President*
David Milano, *Vice Pres*
Terri Bligh, *Human Resources*
Kristyn Hovanec, *Marketing Mgr*
Margaret Morales, *Manager*
EMP: 63
SQ FT: 30,000
SALES (est): 9.3MM **Privately Held**
WEB: www.oceanprinting.com
SIC: 2759 Commercial printing

(G-14917)
CORNING RUBBER COMPANY INC
Also Called: Corning Wax
1744 Julia Goldbach Ave (11779-6413)
PHONE 631 738-0041
Fax: 631 738-0045
Robert Schiemel, *President*
Claudio Acquafredda, *Vice Pres*
▲ **EMP:** 14 **EST:** 1946
SQ FT: 10,000
SALES: 1.2MM **Privately Held**
WEB: www.corningwax.com
SIC: 3843 Wax, dental

(G-14918)
COSMOPOLITAN CABINET COMPANY
40 Fleetwood Ct Ste 1 (11779-6944)
P.O. Box 2797, North Babylon (11703-0797)
PHONE 631 467-4960
Fax: 631 467-0869
James M Harvell, *CEO*
EMP: 8 **EST:** 2000
SALES (est): 670K **Privately Held**
SIC: 2434 Wood kitchen cabinets

(G-14919)
CRYSTALONICS INC
2805 Veterans Mem Hwy 14 (11779-7680)
PHONE 631 981-6140
Paul Weinstein, *President*
Brian Gomes, *Treasurer*
Joseph Plescia, *Treasurer*
Fred Boening, *Controller*
EMP: 12
SQ FT: 14,000
SALES (est): 1.5MM **Privately Held**
WEB: www.crystalonics.com
SIC: 3674 Semiconductors & related devices; hybrid integrated circuits; transistors

(G-14920)
DAK MICA AND WOOD PRODUCTS
Also Called: Coronet Kitchen & Bath
2147 5th Ave (11779-6908)
PHONE 631 467-0749
Fax: 631 467-6137
David Kaplan, *President*
Micheline Auchenbaugh, *Office Mgr*
EMP: 5
SQ FT: 5,800
SALES: 1MM **Privately Held**
SIC: 2434 5031 1751 Wood kitchen cabinets; kitchen cabinets; cabinet & finish carpentry

(G-14921)
DELLA SYSTEMS INC
951 S 2nd St (11779-7203)
PHONE 631 580-0010
Fax: 631 567-0040
John Della Croce, *President*
John Odella, *Purch Agent*
Melissa Gordon, *Purchasing*
EMP: 14
SQ FT: 3,000
SALES (est): 2.5MM **Privately Held**
WEB: www.dellasystems.com
SIC: 3672 8711 Printed circuit boards; engineering services

(G-14922)
DESIGNS FOR VISION INC
760 Koehler Ave (11779-7405)
PHONE 631 585-3300
Fax: 631 585-3404
Richard Feinbloom, *Chairman*
Herb Schwartz, *Vice Pres*
Judy Bowers, *Purchasing*
Ken Braganca, *Engineer*
Peter Murphy, *Treasurer*
▲ **EMP:** 130
SQ FT: 30,000
SALES (est): 28.4MM **Privately Held**
WEB: www.designsforvision.com
SIC: 3841 3851 Surgical & medical instruments; ophthalmic goods

(G-14923)
DYNAMIC LABORATORIES INC
Also Called: Dynamic Labs
30 Haynes Ct (11779-7220)
PHONE 631 231-7474
David Beauchamp, *President*
Steven Zwerman, *Vice Pres*
Rick Beauchamp, *Production*
Chris Cabal, *Engineer*
▲ **EMP:** 38
SQ FT: 18,000
SALES: 8.7MM **Privately Held**
SIC: 3827 5049 Optical instruments & lenses; optical goods

(G-14924)
EAST/WEST INDUSTRIES INC
2002 Orville Dr N (11779-7661)
PHONE 631 981-5900
Fax: 631 981-5990
Teresa Ferraro, *President*
Mary Spinosa, *Corp Secy*
Joseph Spinosa, *Vice Pres*
David Guterman, *Purchasing*
Jeff Walsh, *Engineer*
EMP: 45
SQ FT: 38,000
SALES (est): 11.2MM **Privately Held**
WEB: www.eastwestindustries.com
SIC: 3728 2531 Seat ejector devices, aircraft; oxygen systems, aircraft; seats, aircraft

(G-14925)
EASTERN STOREFRONTS & MTLS INC
1739 Julia Goldbach Ave (11779-6412)
P.O. Box 431, Bohemia (11716-0431)
PHONE 631 471-7065
Timothy Dittmeier, *Ch of Bd*
EMP: 14
SALES (est): 2.3MM **Privately Held**
SIC: 3442 Store fronts, prefabricated, metal

(G-14926)
EASTLAND ELECTRONICS CO INC
700 Union Pkwy Ste 9 (11779-7427)
PHONE 631 580-3800
William Mercurio, *President*
Prem Dally, *Admin Asst*
▲ **EMP:** 7
SQ FT: 2,000
SALES (est): 1.1MM **Privately Held**
WEB: www.eastlandny.com
SIC: 3679 Electronic circuits

(G-14927)
ES BETA INC
125 Comac St (11779-6931)
PHONE 631 582-6740
Wayne Demmons, *Principal*
John Karcher, *Principal*
EMP: 43 **EST:** 2006
SALES (est): 2.1MM
SALES (corp-wide): 94.4MM **Privately Held**
SIC: 3677 Electronic coils, transformers & other inductors
PA: Electro Switch Business Trust
775 Pleasant St Ste 1
Weymouth MA 02189
781 335-1195

(G-14928)
EXECUTIVE MIRROR DOORS INC
1 Comac Loop Unit 7 (11779-6816)
PHONE 631 234-1090
Fax: 631 234-6939
Robert Cozzie, *President*
Carol Cozzie, *Vice Pres*
EMP: 7
SQ FT: 5,400
SALES (est): 720K **Privately Held**
WEB: www.executivemirror.com
SIC: 3231 5211 5085 Doors, glass: made from purchased glass; door & window products; industrial supplies

(G-14929)
FIRST IMPRESSIONS FINISHING
132 Remington Blvd (11779-6912)
PHONE 631 467-2244
Fax: 631 467-0368
Scott Shapiro, *President*
Laura Shapiro, *Vice Pres*
EMP: 6
SQ FT: 4,000
SALES: 351.9K **Privately Held**
SIC: 3471 Finishing, metals or formed products

(G-14930)
FORMATIX CORP
9 Colt Ct (11779-6949)
PHONE 631 467-3399
Radjesh Guptar, *CEO*
Carmine Russo, *Accountant*
Aviska Dabiveen, *Bookkeeper*
EMP: 20
SALES (est): 3.7MM **Privately Held**
SIC: 3089 Blister or bubble formed packaging, plastic

(G-14931)
FOUR PAWS PRODUCTS LTD
3125 Vtrans Mem Hwy Ste 1 (11779-7644)
PHONE 631 436-7421
Allen Simon, *President*
Perry Krewson, *Area Mgr*
Barry Askin, *Vice Pres*
Hector Melgar, *Purchasing*
Tony Mirabella, *Purchasing*
▲ **EMP:** 85 **EST:** 1970
SQ FT: 50,000
SALES (est): 8.5MM
SALES (corp-wide): 1.8B **Publicly Held**
WEB: www.fourpaws.com
SIC: 3999 2844 Pet supplies; toilet preparations
PA: Central Garden & Pet Company
1340 Treat Blvd Ste 600
Walnut Creek CA 94597
925 948-4000

(G-14932)
GENERAL CUTTING INC
90 13th Ave Unit 10 (11779-6818)
PHONE 631 580-5011
Fax: 631 585-3712
Ralph Viteritti, *President*
EMP: 12
SQ FT: 8,000
SALES (est): 946K **Privately Held**
SIC: 3599 Machine shop, jobbing & repair

(G-14933)
GLIPTONE MANUFACTURING INC
Also Called: Camco
1740 Julia Goldbach Ave (11779-6409)
PHONE 631 285-7250
Rocco Coparaso Jr, *President*
▲ **EMP:** 10
SQ FT: 6,500
SALES (est): 1.7MM **Privately Held**
WEB: www.gliptone.com
SIC: 2842 Specialty cleaning preparations; automobile polish

(G-14934)
GLOBAL ENTITY MEDIA INC
2090 5th Ave Ste 2 (11779-6958)
PHONE 631 580-7772
Michael J Cutino, *Principal*
EMP: 5
SALES (est): 600.5K **Privately Held**
SIC: 2721 Periodicals: publishing only

(G-14935)
GOT POWER INC
5 Campus Ln (11779-1924)
PHONE 631 767-9493
Luis Duarte, *Owner*
EMP: 5
SALES (est): 100K **Privately Held**
SIC: 3621 Motors & generators

(G-14936)
H & H TECHNOLOGIES INC
10 Colt Ct (11779-6948)
PHONE 631 567-3526
Henry J Kleitsch, *President*
Georgette Adora, *Controller*
David Puckett, *Manager*
Frank Dimato, *Supervisor*
EMP: 40
SQ FT: 14,000
SALES (est): 7.3MM **Privately Held**
WEB: www.hhtech.com
SIC: 3599 Machine shop, jobbing & repair

(G-14937)
H A GUDEN COMPANY INC
99 Raynor Ave (11779-6634)
PHONE 631 737-2900
Fax: 631 737-2933
Paul A Guden, *President*
Kirby D Moyers, *Vice Pres*
Elyse Levine, *Executive*
Mary L Schwarz, *Admin Sec*
▲ **EMP:** 25
SQ FT: 20,000
SALES: 8.5MM **Privately Held**
SIC: 3429 5072 Manufactured hardware (general); hardware

(G-14938)
HADFIELD INC
840 S 2nd St (11779-7202)
PHONE 631 981-4314
Charles Hadfield, *President*
EMP: 10
SALES (est): 980K **Privately Held**
SIC: 7692 1799 Welding repair; welding on site

(G-14939)
HASTINGS TILE & BATH INC (PA)
711 Koehler Ave Ste 8 (11779-7410)
PHONE 516 379-3500
Lee Kohrman, *President*
Michael Homola, *President*
Richard Kucera, *Corp Secy*
Charlene Hymes, *Accounting Mgr*
Cary Hergenrother, *Manager*
▲ **EMP:** 18
SQ FT: 36,000
SALES: 5.4MM **Privately Held**
WEB: www.hastingstilebath.com
SIC: 3253 Ceramic wall & floor tile

(G-14940)
IMPALA PRESS LTD
931 S 2nd St (11779-7203)
PHONE 631 588-4262
Fax: 631 588-4029
Peter Wolf, *President*
EMP: 8
SQ FT: 6,000
SALES (est): 850K **Privately Held**
WEB: www.impalapress.com
SIC: 2752 Commercial printing, lithographic

(G-14941)
INGENIOUS DESIGNS LLC
Also Called: Idl
2060 9th Ave (11779-6253)
PHONE 631 254-3376

GEOGRAPHIC SECTION

Ronkonkoma - Suffolk County (G-14967)

Joy Mangano, *Ch of Bd*
Ronni Fauci, *Vice Pres*
Alan Mandell, *Finance*
Myleen Hanlon, *Director*
▲ **EMP:** 110
SQ FT: 63,000
SALES (est): 36.9MM **Publicly Held**
WEB: www.ingeniousdesigns.com
SIC: 2392 5199 3089 5099 Mops, floor & dust; broom, mop & paint handles; plastic containers, except foam; containers: glass, metal or plastic
PA: Hsn, Inc.
    1 Hsn Dr
    Saint Petersburg FL 33729

(G-14942)
ISINE INC (PA)
4155 Veterans Memorial Hw (11779-6063)
PHONE 631 913-4400
Louis J Morales, *President*
Barry Eckstein, *Vice Pres*
Louis A Morales, *Vice Pres*
Gary Stevens, *Vice Pres*
Robert Gross, *Senior Engr*
▲ **EMP:** 7
SQ FT: 1,800
SALES (est): 1.4MM **Privately Held**
WEB: www.isine.com
SIC: 3672 3674 Printed circuit boards; semiconductors & related devices

(G-14943)
ISLAND RESEARCH AND DEV CORP
Also Called: Island Technology
200 13th Ave Unit 12 (11779-6815)
PHONE 631 471-7100
Robert Guy Ward, *President*
Lavonia Scaggs, *Human Res Dir*
EMP: 75
SQ FT: 10,000
SALES (est): 9.8MM **Privately Held**
WEB: www.islandresearch.net
SIC: 3679 Electronic circuits

(G-14944)
J F M SHEET METAL INC
2090 Pond Rd (11779-7216)
PHONE 631 737-8494
Joseph Magri, *President*
Jeff Stern, *Manager*
EMP: 5
SALES: 450K **Privately Held**
SIC: 3441 Fabricated structural metal

(G-14945)
J R S PRECISION MACHINING
40 Raynor Ave Ste 2 (11779-6623)
PHONE 631 737-1330
Fax: 631 737-3065
Scott Sopko, *President*
EMP: 8
SQ FT: 2,000
SALES (est): 737K **Privately Held**
SIC: 3599 Machine shop, jobbing & repair

(G-14946)
JAAB PRECISION INC
180 Gary Way (11779-6509)
PHONE 631 218-3725
Joseph W Aloi, *President*
Josephine Blasso, *Office Mgr*
EMP: 9
SALES (est): 2.3MM **Privately Held**
SIC: 3441 Fabricated structural metal

(G-14947)
JET REDI MIX CONCRETE INC
Also Called: J E T
2101 Pond Rd Ste 1 (11779-7213)
PHONE 631 580-3640
Fax: 631 580-3641
Steve Jensen, *President*
Harold Jensen, *President*
Linda Lavzaro, *Office Mgr*
EMP: 14
SQ FT: 15,000
SALES (est): 2.2MM **Privately Held**
WEB: www.jetredimixconcrete.com
SIC: 3273 Ready-mixed concrete

(G-14948)
JMG FUEL INC
3 Fowler Ave (11779-4105)
PHONE 631 579-4319

Brian Gauci, *Principal*
EMP: 6 **EST:** 2010
SALES (est): 681.1K **Privately Held**
SIC: 2869 Fuels

(G-14949)
KELTRON ELECTRONICS (DE CORP)
Also Called: Keltron Connector Co.
3385 Vtrans Mem Hwy Ste E (11779-7660)
PHONE 631 567-6300
Fax: 631 567-6363
David Levison, *President*
Joanne Perks, *Mfg Staff*
Elaine Carucci, *Controller*
Diane Kearns, *Sales Staff*
▲ **EMP:** 15
SALES (est): 2.4MM **Privately Held**
WEB: www.keltronconnectors.com
SIC: 3679 Electronic circuits

(G-14950)
KETCHAM MEDICINE CABINETS
3505 Vtrans Mem Hwy Ste L (11779-7613)
PHONE 631 615-6151
Tracey Bonham, *General Mgr*
Gina Lacarrubba, *Vice Pres*
EMP: 25
SALES (est): 10MM **Privately Held**
SIC: 3431 Bathroom fixtures, including sinks

(G-14951)
KNF CLEAN ROOM PRODUCTS CORP
1800 Ocean Ave (11779-6532)
PHONE 631 588-7000
Philip J Carcara, *Ch of Bd*
Chuck McAteer, *Sls & Mktg Exec*
John Stuerzel, *Human Res Dir*
Patricia Floro, *Mktg Dir*
Chris Marx, *Manager*
EMP: 50
SQ FT: 22,000
SALES (est): 9.1MM **Privately Held**
SIC: 3699 1541 3081 5085 Electrical equipment & supplies; pharmaceutical manufacturing plant construction; unsupported plastics film & sheet; clean room supplies

(G-14952)
KONDOR TECHNOLOGIES INC
206 Christopher St (11779-6921)
PHONE 631 471-8832
Fax: 631 471-8834
Nils Youngwall, *President*
Carie Lanarca, *Manager*
EMP: 7
SQ FT: 3,500
SALES (est): 990K **Privately Held**
SIC: 3599 Machine shop, jobbing & repair

(G-14953)
L W S INC
125 Gary Way Ste 1 (11779-6576)
PHONE 631 580-0472
Leon Shapiro, *President*
EMP: 15
SQ FT: 3,000
SALES (est): 1.4MM **Privately Held**
SIC: 3471 Finishing, metals or formed products; polishing, metals or formed products

(G-14954)
LAB CRAFTERS INC
2085 5th Ave (11779-6903)
PHONE 631 471-7755
Bob Deluca Sr, *President*
Robert Deluca, *Principal*
Edward Fiance, *Principal*
David Rubinstein, *Project Mgr*
Coryn Skolnick, *Project Mgr*
EMP: 25
SQ FT: 90,000
SALES (est): 6.9MM **Privately Held**
SIC: 3821 5049 Laboratory apparatus & furniture; laboratory equipment, except medical or dental

(G-14955)
LAB-AIDS INC
17 Colt Ct (11779-6949)
PHONE 631 737-1133
Fax: 631 737-1286

Morton Frank, *President*
David M Frank, *President*
Lori Massucci, *Controller*
John Garrett, *Regl Sales Mgr*
Amy Kezman, *Regl Sales Mgr*
▲ **EMP:** 49 **EST:** 1963
SQ FT: 41,000
SALES (est): 9MM **Privately Held**
WEB: www.lab-aid.com
SIC: 3999 Education aids, devices & supplies

(G-14956)
LAKELAND INDUSTRIES INC (PA)
3555 Vtrans Mem Hwy Ste C (11779-7636)
PHONE 631 981-9700
Fax: 631 981-9751
A John Kreft, *Ch of Bd*
Christopher J Ryan, *President*
Daniel L Edwards, *Senior VP*
Charles D Roberson, *Senior VP*
Teri W Hunt, *CFO*
▲ **EMP:** 187
SALES: 86.1MM **Publicly Held**
WEB: www.lakeland-ind.com
SIC: 3842 2389 Personal safety equipment; clothing, fire resistant & protective; gloves, safety; disposable garments & accessories

(G-14957)
LANCO CORPORATION
Also Called: Brijon
2905 Vtrans Mem Hwy Ste 3 (11779-7655)
PHONE 631 231-2300
Fax: 631 231-2731
Brian Landow, *President*
Tom Kronberger, *Regional Mgr*
Irwin Landow, *Vice Pres*
Dan Ventola, *Vice Pres*
John Whitaker, *Vice Pres*
◆ **EMP:** 250
SQ FT: 40,000
SALES (est): 48.5MM **Privately Held**
WEB: www.lancopromo.com
SIC: 3993 2066 5149 2064 Signs & advertising specialties; chocolate & cocoa products; chocolate; candy & other confectionery products

(G-14958)
LANGER BIOMECHANICS INC
2905 Vtrans Mem Hwy Ste 2 (11779-7655)
PHONE 800 645-5520
Bruce Marrison, *CEO*
Jason Kraus, *President*
Terence Fitzmaurice, *Controller*
Karen Strebel, *Info Tech Mgr*
EMP: 71
SALES (est): 9.5MM
SALES (corp-wide): 647.1K **Privately Held**
SIC: 3842 Orthopedic appliances
PA: Orthotic Holdings, Inc.
    2905 Veterans Mem Hwy
    Ronkonkoma NY 11779
    416 479-8609

(G-14959)
LEE PHILIPS PACKAGING INC
750 Union Pkwy (11779-7413)
PHONE 631 580-3306
Fax: 631 580-3298
Lee Schnitzer, *President*
▲ **EMP:** 14
SQ FT: 26,000
SALES (est): 3.4MM **Privately Held**
WEB: www.leephilipspackaging.com
SIC: 2653 Corrugated & solid fiber boxes

(G-14960)
LINK CONTROL SYSTEMS INC
16 Colt Ct (11779-6948)
PHONE 631 471-3950
Fax: 631 471-2390
William F Bowden, *President*
David Cotte, *Engineer*
Francine Abramowitz, *Manager*
Clive Dillon, *Info Tech Mgr*
EMP: 15
SQ FT: 12,000
SALES (est): 3.3MM **Privately Held**
WEB: www.linkconsys.com
SIC: 3613 Control panels, electric

(G-14961)
LONG ISLAND BUSINESS NEWS
2150 Smithtown Ave Ste 7 (11779-7348)
PHONE 631 737-1700
Fax: 631 737-1890
Jordan Zeigler, *Partner*
Scott Schoen, *Vice Pres*
Mike Gates, *Adv Dir*
Tim Carini, *Manager*
Peggy Jaeger, *Director*
EMP: 22 **EST:** 1953
SQ FT: 6,000
SALES (est): 1.5MM
SALES (corp-wide): 478.5MM **Privately Held**
WEB: www.libn.com
SIC: 2711 Newspapers
HQ: Dolan Llc
    222 S 9th St Ste 2300
    Minneapolis MN 55402

(G-14962)
LUX MUNDI CORP
10 Colt Ct (11779-6948)
PHONE 631 244-4596
Henry Kleitsch, *President*
EMP: 8
SALES (est): 803.8K **Privately Held**
SIC: 3999 Candles

(G-14963)
MAHARLIKA HOLDINGS LLC
Also Called: Atis Colojet
111 Trade Zone Ct Unit A (11779-7367)
PHONE 631 319-6203
Erez Shoshoni, *General Mgr*
▲ **EMP:** 14
SALES: 3MM **Privately Held**
SIC: 3559 Chemical machinery & equipment

(G-14964)
MANTEL & MANTEL STAMPING CORP
802 S 4th St (11779-7200)
PHONE 631 467-1916
Fax: 631 467-1916
Edward Mantel, *President*
EMP: 8 **EST:** 1977
SQ FT: 7,500
SALES: 1MM **Privately Held**
SIC: 3544 3469 Special dies & tools; metal stampings

(G-14965)
MARCOVICCI-WENZ ENGINEERING
33 Comac Loop Unit 10 (11779-6856)
PHONE 631 467-9040
Ted Wenz, *President*
Peter Marcovicci, *Vice Pres*
EMP: 6
SQ FT: 4,000
SALES (est): 490K **Privately Held**
SIC: 3714 5531 3711 Motor vehicle engines & parts; speed shops, including race car supplies; automobile assembly, including specialty automobiles

(G-14966)
MASTER-HALCO INC
54 Union Ave Ste B (11779-5850)
PHONE 631 585-8150
Bob Locurto, *Manager*
EMP: 14
SALES (corp-wide): 42.5B **Privately Held**
WEB: www.fenceonline.com
SIC: 3315 5039 5031 1799 Chain link fencing; wire fence, gates & accessories; fencing, wood; fence construction
HQ: Master-Halco, Inc.
    3010 Lbj Fwy Ste 800
    Dallas TX 75234
    972 714-7300

(G-14967)
MAYFAIR MACHINE COMPANY INC
128 Remington Blvd (11779-6912)
PHONE 631 981-6644
EMP: 6
SQ FT: 1,500
SALES (est): 610K **Privately Held**
SIC: 3599 Machine Shop

(PA)=Parent Co (HQ)=Headquarters (DH)=Div Headquarters
◯ = New Business established in last 2 years

Ronkonkoma - Suffolk County (G-14968)

(G-14968)
MICRO PHOTO ACOUSTICS INC
105 Comac St (11779-6931)
PHONE..................631 750-6035
Xiaojie Zhao, *President*
EMP: 5
SALES (est): 754.7K
SALES (corp-wide): 6MM **Privately Held**
SIC: 3826 Laser scientific & engineering instruments
PA: Advanced Optowave Corporation
 105 Comac St
 Ronkonkoma NY 11779
 631 750-6035

(G-14969)
MIN-MAX MACHINE LTD
1971 Pond Rd (11779-7244)
PHONE..................631 585-4378
Fax: 631 585-4610
Randy Neubauer, *Ch of Bd*
Rodney Neubauer, *Corp Secy*
Ralph Neubauer, *Vice Pres*
EMP: 18
SQ FT: 18,000
SALES: 4MM **Privately Held**
SIC: 3728 Aircraft parts & equipment; aircraft assemblies, subassemblies & parts

(G-14970)
MINUTEMEN PRECSN MCHNING TOOL
Also Called: Minutemen Precision Mch & Tl
135 Raynor Ave (11779-6666)
PHONE..................631 467-4900
Fax: 631 467-6850
Michael Castoro, *Ch of Bd*
Michael Lane, *Vice Pres*
Carlo J Castoro, *Treasurer*
EMP: 37
SQ FT: 14,900
SALES (est): 8.1MM **Privately Held**
SIC: 3728 3599 Aircraft parts & equipment; machine shop, jobbing & repair

(G-14971)
MNS FUEL CORP
2154 Pond Rd (11779-7216)
P.O. Box 344, East Islip (11730-0344)
PHONE..................516 735-3835
Irene F Walsh, *Principal*
EMP: 12
SALES (est): 2.5MM **Privately Held**
SIC: 2869 Fuels

(G-14972)
MULTIMATIC PRODUCTS INC
900 Marconi Ave (11779-7212)
PHONE..................800 767-7633
Hyman Jack Kipnes, *President*
Rohit C Chodha, *Managing Dir*
Irving Kipnes, *Corp Secy*
Bart Kipnes, *Opers Staff*
EMP: 74 **EST:** 1962
SQ FT: 20,000
SALES: 3MM **Privately Held**
WEB: www.multimaticproducts.com
SIC: 3451 3541 Screw machine products; machine tools, metal cutting type

(G-14973)
N & L INSTRUMENTS INC
90 13th Ave Unit 1 (11779-6818)
PHONE..................631 471-4000
Fax: 631 471-0339
John Walz, *President*
Anthony Kearney, *Treasurer*
Teresa Smith, *Manager*
EMP: 17
SQ FT: 20,000
SALES (est): 2MM **Privately Held**
WEB: www.namf.com
SIC: 3571 3444 Electronic computers; sheet metalwork

(G-14974)
NATECH PLASTICS INC
85 Remington Blvd (11779-6923)
PHONE..................631 580-3506
Fax: 631 580-5448
Gerd Nagler, *Ch of Bd*
Thomas Nagler, *President*
Carol Nagler, *Vice Pres*
Ray Schneider, *Engineer*
Jennifer Nagler, *Manager*
EMP: 45 **EST:** 1998
SQ FT: 10,000
SALES (est): 10.1MM **Privately Held**
WEB: www.natechplastics.com
SIC: 3089 Injection molding of plastics

(G-14975)
NATURES BOUNTY (NY) INC (DH)
Also Called: Nature's Bounty, Inc.
2100 Smithtown Ave (11779-7347)
PHONE..................631 580-6137
Dipak Golechha, *Ch of Bd*
Harvey Kamil, *President*
Jim Flaherty, *Senior VP*
Joe Franzino, *Controller*
Adrianne Delaraba, *Director*
▲ **EMP:** 800
SQ FT: 15,000
SALES (est): 1.3MM **Publicly Held**
WEB: www.nbty.com
SIC: 2834 Vitamin preparations
HQ: The Nature's Bounty Co
 2100 Smithtown Ave
 Ronkonkoma NY 11779
 631 200-2000

(G-14976)
NATURES BOUNTY CO
Also Called: Accounts Payable Department
2100 Smithtown Ave (11779-7347)
P.O. Box 9011 (11779-9011)
PHONE..................631 244-2065
Jeff Nagel, *Branch Mgr*
Michelle Tahir, *Director*
EMP: 12 **Publicly Held**
SIC: 2833 Vitamins, natural or synthetic: bulk, uncompounded
HQ: The Nature's Bounty Co
 2100 Smithtown Ave
 Ronkonkoma NY 11779
 631 200-2000

(G-14977)
NATURES BOUNTY CO
2100 Smithtown Ave (11779-7347)
PHONE..................631 244-2021
Fax: 631 244-1777
Dorie Greenblatt, *Principal*
EMP: 90 **Publicly Held**
SIC: 2833 5122 5499 5961 Vitamins, natural or synthetic: bulk, uncompounded; vitamins & minerals; health & dietetic food stores; vitamin food stores; health foods; pharmaceuticals, mail order
HQ: The Nature's Bounty Co
 2100 Smithtown Ave
 Ronkonkoma NY 11779
 631 200-2000

(G-14978)
NATURES BOUNTY CO (HQ)
2100 Smithtown Ave (11779-7347)
P.O. Box 9014 (11779-9014)
PHONE..................631 200-2000
Paul Sturman, *CEO*
Andre Branch, *President*
Kevin Warren, *President*
Rita Dubowski, *General Mgr*
Ahmed Raza, *General Mgr*
◆ **EMP:** 800 **EST:** 1979
SQ FT: 110,000
SALES: 2MM **Publicly Held**
WEB: www.nbty.com
SIC: 2833 5122 5499 5961 Vitamins, natural or synthetic: bulk, uncompounded; vitamins & minerals; health & dietetic food stores; vitamin food stores; health foods; dietetic foods; pharmaceuticals, mail order

(G-14979)
NATURES BOUNTY CO
2145 9th Ave (11779-6280)
PHONE..................631 200-7338
Laura Bode, *Marketing Staff*
EMP: 90 **Publicly Held**
SIC: 2833 Vitamins, natural or synthetic: bulk, uncompounded
HQ: The Nature's Bounty Co
 2100 Smithtown Ave
 Ronkonkoma NY 11779
 631 200-2000

(G-14980)
NBTY MANUFACTURING LLC (DH)
2100 Smithtown Ave (11779-7347)
PHONE..................631 567-9500
Joe Looney, *Vice Pres*
Harvey Kamil, *Mng Member*
◆ **EMP:** 39
SQ FT: 6,000,000
SALES (est): 500K **Publicly Held**
SIC: 2833 5122 Vitamins, natural or synthetic: bulk, uncompounded; vitamins & minerals
HQ: The Nature's Bounty Co
 2100 Smithtown Ave
 Ronkonkoma NY 11779
 631 200-2000

(G-14981)
NEW AGE PRECISION TECH INC
151 Remington Blvd (11779-6911)
PHONE..................631 471-4000
Mario Costa, *President*
Robert Flower, *Sales Mgr*
EMP: 20
SALES (est): 1MM **Privately Held**
SIC: 3599 Machine & other job shop work

(G-14982)
OAKDALE INDUSTRIAL ELEC CORP
1995 Pond Rd (11779-7259)
PHONE..................631 737-4090
Fax: 631 737-4349
Abraham Mamoor, *President*
Allen Mamoor, *Vice Pres*
▼ **EMP:** 15
SQ FT: 5,000
SALES (est): 4MM **Privately Held**
SIC: 3679 3672 5065 Electronic circuits; printed circuit boards; electronic parts

(G-14983)
OAKLEE INTERNATIONAL INC
Also Called: Pro-Tek Packaging Group
125 Raynor Ave (11779-6666)
PHONE..................631 436-7900
Leo Lee, *President*
Alice Zebrowski, *Exec VP*
Wayne Lorick, *Opers Mgr*
Donna Neumann, *Exec Dir*
EMP: 75
SALES (est): 9.7MM **Privately Held**
WEB: www.oaklee.com
SIC: 2672 3081 Adhesive papers, labels or tapes: from purchased material; unsupported plastics film & sheet

(G-14984)
OMEGA HEATER COMPANY INC
2059 9th Ave (11779-6233)
PHONE..................631 588-8820
Fax: 631 588-8953
Alfred Gaudio, *President*
Gina Gaudio, *Manager*
▲ **EMP:** 60 **EST:** 1970
SQ FT: 30,000
SALES: 3MM **Privately Held**
WEB: www.omegaheater.com
SIC: 3433 Heating equipment, except electric

(G-14985)
OMNTEC MFG INC
1993 Pond Rd (11779-7259)
P.O. Box 30 (11779-0030)
PHONE..................631 981-2001
Fax: 631 981-2007
Lee J Nicholson, *President*
Tom Dalessandro, *Exec VP*
Tom D'Alessandro, *Vice Pres*
▲ **EMP:** 34
SQ FT: 13,600
SALES (est): 7.3MM **Privately Held**
WEB: www.omntec.com
SIC: 3625 5065 Relays & industrial controls; electronic parts & equipment

(G-14986)
P R B METAL PRODUCTS INC
200 Christopher St (11779-6921)
PHONE..................631 467-1800
Fax: 631 467-1894
Ronald Breunig, *President*
Peter Breunig, *Vice Pres*
EMP: 10
SQ FT: 10,000
SALES: 1MM **Privately Held**
SIC: 3444 3465 3469 Sheet metal specialties, not stamped; automotive stampings; metal stampings

(G-14987)
PAAL TECHNOLOGIES INC
152 Remington Blvd Ste 1 (11779-6964)
PHONE..................631 319-6262
Latha Chandran, *Ch of Bd*
Prem Chandran, *Vice Pres*
EMP: 5
SALES: 300K **Privately Held**
WEB: www.paaltech.com
SIC: 3679 Harness assemblies for electronic use: wire or cable

(G-14988)
PARAMOUNT EQUIPMENT INC
Also Called: O P I Industries
201 Christopher St (11779-6956)
PHONE..................631 981-4422
Jerome Bernzweig, *President*
Matt Barbaro, *Vice Pres*
Steve Bearman, *Vice Pres*
Ken Muller, *Vice Pres*
Tony Buttonow, *Graphic Designe*
▲ **EMP:** 20
SQ FT: 10,000
SALES (est): 4.7MM **Privately Held**
SIC: 2673 5113 Plastic bags: made from purchased materials; bags, paper & disposable plastic

(G-14989)
PARSLEY APPAREL CORP
2153 Pond Rd (11779-7214)
PHONE..................631 981-7181
Ronald Colnick, *President*
EMP: 50
SQ FT: 5,000
SALES (est): 3MM **Privately Held**
SIC: 2335 Wedding gowns & dresses

(G-14990)
PAUL MICHAEL GROUP INC
Also Called: PMG
460 Hawkins Ave (11779-4248)
P.O. Box 1493 (11779-0426)
PHONE..................631 585-5700
Vincent Gennaro, *President*
▲ **EMP:** 7
SQ FT: 1,500
SALES (est): 974.9K **Privately Held**
SIC: 2752 7389 Commercial printing, offset; packaging & labeling services

(G-14991)
PCX AEROSTRUCTURES LLC
70 Raynor Ave (11779-6650)
PHONE..................631 249-7901
Paul Iannotta, *Branch Mgr*
EMP: 50
SALES (corp-wide): 100MM **Privately Held**
SIC: 3441 Fabricated structural metal
PA: Pcx Aerostructures, Llc
 300 Fenn Rd
 Newington CT 06111
 860 666-2471

(G-14992)
PHOTONICS INDUSTRIES INTL INC (PA)
1800 Ocean Ave Unit A (11779-6532)
PHONE..................631 218-2240
Fax: 631 218-2275
Yusong Yin, *Ch of Bd*
Serena Zhao, *Controller*
Joe Echolitc, *Manager*
Jim Raftery, *Director*
Laura Bjorke, *Assistant*
▲ **EMP:** 60
SQ FT: 184,000
SALES (est): 10.8MM **Privately Held**
WEB: www.photonix.com
SIC: 3845 Laser systems & equipment, medical

(G-14993)
PHYSIOLOGICS LLC
2100 Smithtown Ave (11779-7347)
PHONE..................800 765-6775
Chris De Petris, *Manager*

EMP: 14
SALES (est): 1.4MM Privately Held
WEB: www.physiologics.com
SIC: 2023 Dietary supplements, dairy & non-dairy based

(G-14994)
PIC A POC ENTERPRISES INC
53 Union Ave (11779-5814)
P.O. Box 338, Holbrook (11741-0338)
PHONE 631 981-2094
Fax: 631 981-2105
Nicholas J Ullrich II, *President*
Marilyn Ullrich, *Principal*
EMP: 5
SQ FT: 2,000
SALES: 500K Privately Held
SIC: 2752 7336 Commercial printing, lithographic; graphic arts & related design

(G-14995)
PRINTCORP INC
2050 Ocean Ave (11779-6536)
PHONE 631 696-0641
Joseph C Fazzingo Jr, *CEO*
Arthur Foti, *Marketing Staff*
EMP: 18 EST: 1994
SALES (est): 2.7MM Privately Held
SIC: 2752 Commercial printing, lithographic

(G-14996)
PROFITS DIRECT INC
Also Called: Sundial Editions
200 Trade Zone Dr Unit 2 (11779-7359)
PHONE 631 851-4083
Rakesh Gilani, *President*
Edward Hughes, *Vice Pres*
▲ **EMP:** 2 EST: 2012
SALES (est): 1.7MM Privately Held
SIC: 2731 5961 Book publishing; books, mail order (except book clubs)

(G-14997)
PRONTO TOOL & DIE CO INC
50 Remington Blvd (11779-6910)
PHONE 631 981-8920
Fax: 631 981-8344
Michael Silvestri, *President*
Donna Schecker, *Corp Secy*
Marion Silvestri, *Vice Pres*
Linda Young, *Manager*
EMP: 30 EST: 1980
SQ FT: 10,000
SALES (est): 4.7MM Privately Held
SIC: 3544 3599 3469 Special dies & tools; machine & other job shop work; metal stampings

(G-14998)
QUALITY KING DISTRIBUTORS INC
201 Comac St (11779-6950)
PHONE 631 439-2027
Glenn H Nussdorf, *CEO*
EMP: 147
SALES (corp-wide): 634MM Privately Held
SIC: 2844 5122 Toilet preparations; toilet preparations
PA: Quality King Distributors, Inc.
35 Sawgrass Dr Ste 3
Bellport NY 11713
631 439-2000

(G-14999)
QUALITY ONE WIRELESS LLC
2127 Lakeland Ave Unit 2 (11779-7431)
PHONE 631 233-3337
John Chiorando, *CEO*
EMP: 250
SALES (corp-wide): 297.4MM Privately Held
SIC: 3661 Headsets, telephone
PA: Quality One Wireless, Llc
1500 Tradeport Dr Ste B
Orlando FL 32824
407 857-3737

(G-15000)
R S T CABLE AND TAPE INC
2130 Pond Rd Ste B (11779-7239)
PHONE 631 981-0096
Fax: 631 981-0130
David M Rothert, *President*
William Hilder, *Vice Pres*

Stephen Thomas, *Director*
EMP: 8
SQ FT: 6,500
SALES (est): 2MM Privately Held
SIC: 3479 Painting, coating & hot dipping; coating of metals with plastic or resins

(G-15001)
RATAN RONKONKOMA
3055 Veterans Mem Hwy (11779-7612)
PHONE 631 588-6800
Mahesh Ratanji, *Administration*
EMP: 8 EST: 2011
SALES (est): 1MM Privately Held
SIC: 3421 Table & food cutlery, including butchers'

(G-15002)
RESONANCE TECHNOLOGIES INC
109 Comac St (11779-6931)
PHONE 631 237-4901
George Szenczy, *President*
Mark Anatov, *Director*
EMP: 35
SALES (est): 5MM Privately Held
WEB: www.res-tek.com
SIC: 3678 Electronic connectors

(G-15003)
RICK-MIC INDUSTRIES INC
1951 Ocean Ave Ste 6 (11779-6564)
PHONE 631 563-8389
Rod Dimiano, *President*
EMP: 6
SALES (est): 420K Privately Held
SIC: 3599 Machine shop, jobbing & repair

(G-15004)
ROGER LATARI
Also Called: Island Precision
30 Raynor Ave Ste 1 (11779-6628)
PHONE 631 580-2422
Roger Licari, *Owner*
EMP: 5
SALES (est): 300K Privately Held
WEB: www.rogerblench.info
SIC: 3599 Machine shop, jobbing & repair

(G-15005)
RONA PRECISION INC
Also Called: Rona Precision Mfg
142 Remington Blvd Ste 2 (11779-6960)
PHONE 631 737-4034
Fax: 631 737-4064
Ronald Alber, *President*
Marie Alber, *Treasurer*
EMP: 6
SQ FT: 3,500
SALES (est): 752.4K Privately Held
SIC: 3599 Machine shop, jobbing & repair

(G-15006)
SENTRY TECHNOLOGY CORPORATION
Also Called: Knogo
1881 Lakeland Ave (11779-7416)
PHONE 631 739-2000
Peter Murdoch, *CEO*
Joane Miller, *CFO*
Maryanne Owens, *Credit Mgr*
Elizabeth Heyder, *Admin Sec*
▲ **EMP:** 30
SQ FT: 20,000
SALES (est): 3.4MM Publicly Held
SIC: 3812 7359 Detection apparatus: electronic/magnetic field, light/heat; electronic equipment rental, except computers
PA: Sentry Technology Corporation
1881 Lakeland Ave
Ronkonkoma NY 11779

(G-15007)
SENTRY TECHNOLOGY CORPORATION (PA)
Also Called: Sentry Funding Partnership
1881 Lakeland Ave (11779-7416)
PHONE 800 645-4224
Fax: 631 232-2812
Peter L Murdoch, *Ch of Bd*
Joseph Ryan, *Vice Pres*
Nelson Hocker, *Project Dir*
Renny Dindyal, *Opers Staff*
Matt Eckert, *Senior Engr*
▲ **EMP:** 13

SQ FT: 20,000
SALES (est): 9.6MM Publicly Held
SIC: 3812 3663 Detection apparatus: electronic/magnetic field, light/heat; television closed circuit equipment

(G-15008)
SETAUKET MANUFACTURING CO
202 Christopher St (11779-6921)
PHONE 631 231-7272
Michael Horrigan, *President*
Linda Horrigan, *Vice Pres*
EMP: 5
SQ FT: 4,000
SALES: 500K Privately Held
SIC: 2833 5499 Medicinals & botanicals; health & dietetic food stores

(G-15009)
SHERRY-MICA PRODUCTS INC
45 Remington Blvd Ste D (11779-9500)
PHONE 631 471-7513
Fax: 631 471-2675
Anthony Villano, *President*
EMP: 5
SQ FT: 2,000
SALES (est): 578.6K Privately Held
SIC: 2434 5031 Wood kitchen cabinets; vanities, bathroom: wood; kitchen cabinets

(G-15010)
SOC AMERICA INC
3505 Veterans Memorial Hw (11779-7613)
PHONE 631 472-6666
Neil Sato, *President*
Karl Lindquist, *Vice Pres*
Yuichi Sato, *Vice Pres*
Sharon Terry, *Electrical Engi*
Dawn Minichello, *Executive Asst*
EMP: 15
SQ FT: 3,200
SALES (est): 2.6MM
SALES (corp-wide): 35.2MM Privately Held
WEB: www.san-o.com
SIC: 3613 Fuses, electric
PA: Soc Corporation
3-16-17, Takanawa
Minato-Ku TKY 108-0
354 201-011

(G-15011)
SPECIALTY MICROWAVE CORP
120 Raynor Ave (11779-6655)
PHONE 631 737-2175
Fax: 631 737-2175
Stephen Faber, *President*
EMP: 18
SQ FT: 7,500
SALES (est): 3.4MM Privately Held
WEB: www.specialtymicrowave.com
SIC: 3663 Microwave communication equipment

(G-15012)
ST JAMES PRINTING INC
656 Rosevale Ave (11779-3098)
PHONE 631 981-2095
Fax: 631 981-4646
Gert Kuehnel, *President*
EMP: 5
SQ FT: 5,000
SALES (est): 300K Privately Held
SIC: 2759 2752 Commercial printing; commercial printing, lithographic

(G-15013)
SWITCHING POWER INC
3601 Veterans Mem Hwy (11779-7691)
PHONE 631 981-7231
Fax: 631 981-7266
Melvin Kravitz, *President*
John Bellone, *Vice Pres*
Carmen Midiri, *Purch Mgr*
Peter Herringer, *Engineer*
David Kravitz, *Engineer*
▲ **EMP:** 65
SQ FT: 30,000
SALES (est): 14.2MM Privately Held
WEB: www.switchpwr.com
SIC: 3613 5065 3643 3612 Power switching equipment; electronic parts & equipment; current-carrying wiring devices; transformers, except electric

(G-15014)
SYNERGY INTRNTNAL OPTRNICS LLC
101 Comac St (11779-6931)
P.O. Box 1422 (11779-0899)
PHONE 631 277-0500
Richard Heathcote, *President*
Robert Tartaglia, *Vice Pres*
Lydia Bozymowski, *Manager*
Lori Pflug, *Teacher*
EMP: 36
SQ FT: 12,500
SALES (est): 5.8MM Privately Held
WEB: www.siollc.com
SIC: 3827 Optical instruments & lenses

(G-15015)
TRANSISTOR DEVICES INC
125 Comac St (11779-6931)
PHONE 631 471-7492
Fax: 631 471-7497
Ron Deluca, *Manager*
Martin Goheen, *Info Tech Dir*
EMP: 27 Privately Held
WEB: www.transdev.com
SIC: 3625 3612 3672 3812 Switches, electric power; power transformers, electric; printed circuit boards; search & navigation equipment
HQ: Transistor Devices, Inc.
36 Newburgh Rd
Hackettstown NJ 07840
908 850-5088

(G-15016)
TRUEMADE PRODUCTS INC
910 Marconi Ave (11779-7212)
PHONE 631 981-4755
Carmen Yvonne Mender, *President*
EMP: 5
SQ FT: 4,000
SALES: 400K Privately Held
SIC: 3541 Machine tools, metal cutting type

(G-15017)
U S AIR TOOL CO INC (PA)
Also Called: U S Air Tool International
60 Fleetwood Ct (11779-6907)
PHONE 631 471-3300
Fax: 631 471-3308
Geoffrey J Percz, *Ch of Bd*
Laurence Percz, *Vice Pres*
David Lombardo, *Controller*
▲ **EMP:** 14 EST: 1951
SQ FT: 14,000
SALES (est): 4.6MM Privately Held
SIC: 3423 5084 3542 Hand & edge tools; pneumatic tools & equipment; sheet metalworking machines; riveting machines

(G-15018)
UCR STEEL GROUP LLC
90 Trade Zone Ct (11779-7369)
PHONE 718 764-3414
Charles Starace, *Mng Member*
EMP: 15
SALES (corp-wide): 4.5MM Privately Held
SIC: 3444 Sheet metalwork
PA: Ucr Steel Group Llc
405 Rxr Plz
Uniondale NY 11556
718 764-3414

(G-15019)
ULTRAFLEX POWER TECHNOLOGIES
158 Remington Blvd Ste 2 (11779-6966)
PHONE 631 467-6814
Mario Metodiev, *President*
Nedelina Metodieva, *Treasurer*
Kira Schmitt, *Consultant*
EMP: 5
SQ FT: 3,000
SALES (est): 519.2K Privately Held
SIC: 3567 Induction heating equipment

(G-15020)
ULTRAVOLT INC
1800 Ocean Ave Unit A (11779-6532)
PHONE 631 471-4444
Fax: 631 471-4696
James Morrison, *CEO*
Cheryl Broesler, *Purch Mgr*

Carlos Alicea, *Engineer*
Stephen Schutter, *Engineer*
Daniel Bartley, *Controller*
EMP: 100
SQ FT: 20,000
SALES (est): 21.7MM
SALES (corp-wide): 483.7MM **Publicly Held**
WEB: www.ultravolt.com
SIC: 3679 5065 5084 Power supplies, all types: static; electronic parts & equipment; power plant machinery
PA: Advanced Energy Industries, Inc.
1625 Sharp Point Dr
Fort Collins CO 80525
970 221-4670

(G-15021)
VACUUM INSTRUMENT CORPORATION (PA)
Also Called: Vic Leak Detection
2101 9th Ave Ste A (11779-6282)
PHONE..................631 737-0900
Fax: 631 737-0949
Frederick Ewing II, *CEO*
John Schreiner, *Vice Pres*
Vivian Russo, *Purch Agent*
Art Hoffmann, *Engineer*
Phyllis Smith, *Manager*
EMP: 100
SQ FT: 48,000
SALES (est): 25.4MM **Privately Held**
WEB: www.vacuuminst.com
SIC: 3823 3829 3812 Industrial instrmnts msrmnt display/control process variable; measuring & controlling devices; search & navigation equipment

(G-15022)
VISION QUEST LIGHTING INC
Also Called: E-Quest Lighting
90 13th Ave Unit 1 (11779-6818)
PHONE..................631 737-4800
Larry Lieberman, *Ch of Bd*
Torrey Bievenour, *Vice Pres*
Janelle Norton, *Vice Pres*
▲ **EMP:** 33
SQ FT: 2,500
SALES (est): 8.7MM **Privately Held**
WEB: www.vql.com
SIC: 3646 3645 Commercial indusl & institutional electric lighting fixtures; fluorescent lighting fixtures, commercial; ornamental lighting fixtures, commercial; residential lighting fixtures; fluorescent lighting fixtures, residential; garden, patio, walkway & yard lighting fixtures: electric

(G-15023)
VORMITTAG ASSOCIATES INC (PA)
Also Called: V A I
120 Comac St Ste 1 (11779-6941)
PHONE..................800 824-7776
Fax: 631 588-9770
Robert Vormittag, *President*
Russ Cereola, *Vice Pres*
Ira Dannenberg, *Vice Pres*
Larry Murphy, *Vice Pres*
Joe Scioscia, *Vice Pres*
EMP: 5
SQ FT: 15,000
SALES (est): 35.4MM **Privately Held**
WEB: www.vaihome.com
SIC: 7372 7371 5045 Prepackaged software; computer software systems analysis & design, custom; computers, peripherals & software

(G-15024)
VOSKY PRECISION MACHINING CORP
70 Air Park Dr (11779-7360)
PHONE..................631 737-3200
Mourad Voskinarian, *President*
Eddy Voskinarian, *Manager*
EMP: 18
SQ FT: 11,000
SALES (est): 4.1MM **Privately Held**
WEB: www.voskyprecision.com
SIC: 3728 3469 3599 Aircraft parts & equipment; machine parts, stamped or pressed metal; machine shop, jobbing & repair

(G-15025)
WILCO INDUSTRIES INC
788 Marconi Ave (11779-7230)
P.O. Box 277 (11779-0277)
PHONE..................631 676-2593
Fax: 631 588-5578
Otto Wildmann, *President*
Robert Fischer, *QC Mgr*
EMP: 9
SQ FT: 8,000
SALES (est): 970K **Privately Held**
WEB: www.wilcoindustries.com
SIC: 3728 Aircraft assemblies, subassemblies & parts

(G-15026)
ZETA MACHINE CORP
206 Christopher St (11779-6921)
PHONE..................631 471-8832
Frank Castelli, *President*
Carol Castelli, *Vice Pres*
EMP: 8 **EST:** 1975
SQ FT: 8,000
SALES (est): 660K **Privately Held**
SIC: 3469 Machine parts, stamped or pressed metal

Roosevelt
Nassau County

(G-15027)
AUTOSTAT CORPORATION
209 Nassau Rd 11 (11575-1756)
P.O. Box 170 (11575-0170)
PHONE..................516 379-9447
Fax: 516 868-5568
Arthur Baer, *President*
▲ **EMP:** 10 **EST:** 1955
SQ FT: 9,000
SALES (est): 1.2MM **Privately Held**
SIC: 3549 Marking machines, metalworking

(G-15028)
GENERAL DIE AND DIE CUTNG INC
151 Babylon Tpke (11575-2122)
PHONE..................516 665-3584
Fax: 516 623-5142
Peter Vallone Sr, *CEO*
Peter Vallone Jr, *President*
Louann Vallone Pepi, *Vice Pres*
Richard Vallone, *Treasurer*
▲ **EMP:** 55 **EST:** 1961
SQ FT: 30,000
SALES (est): 47.6K **Privately Held**
WEB: www.gendiecut.com
SIC: 2653 2675 3544 Display items, corrugated: made from purchased materials; boxes, corrugated: made from purchased materials; corrugated boxes, partitions, display items, sheets & pad; die-cut paper & board; special dies, tools, jigs & fixtures

(G-15029)
INTRIGUE CONCEPTS INC
8 Gilbert Pl Ste 8 (11575-1718)
PHONE..................800 424-8170
Dennis Barclift, *President*
EMP: 6
SALES (est): 429.2K **Privately Held**
SIC: 2326 Work shirts: men's, youths' & boys'

(G-15030)
K F I INC
33 Debevoise Ave (11575-1711)
PHONE..................516 546-2904
Sion Elalouf, *President*
Jeff Denecke, *Opers Staff*
▲ **EMP:** 8
SALES (est): 491.7K **Privately Held**
WEB: www.euroyarns.com
SIC: 2299 Yarns, specialty & novelty

(G-15031)
PARABIT SYSTEMS INC
35 Debevoise Ave (11575-1711)
P.O. Box 481 (11575-0481)
PHONE..................516 378-4800
Fax: 516 378-4843
Robert Leiponis, *President*
Pat Zajicek, *General Mgr*
Bob Hricisak, *VP Sales*
Ted Joseph, *Accounts Exec*
Charles Bunker, *Technology*
▲ **EMP:** 50
SQ FT: 25,000
SALES (est): 11.8MM **Privately Held**
SIC: 3699 3661 3578 2542 Security devices; telephone & telegraph apparatus; telephone station equipment & parts, wire; automatic teller machines (ATM); telephone booths: except wood

(G-15032)
SOUTH SHORE ICE CO INC
89 E Fulton Ave (11575-2212)
PHONE..................516 379-2056
Al Farina, *President*
EMP: 10
SQ FT: 4,500
SALES (est): 1MM **Privately Held**
SIC: 2097 5999 5169 Manufactured ice; ice; dry ice

(G-15033)
TROPICAL DRIFTWOOD ORIGINALS
Also Called: Tdo Sandblasting
499 Nassau Rd (11575-1019)
PHONE..................516 623-0980
John O'Brien Sr, *President*
EMP: 5
SQ FT: 4,000
SALES (est): 270K **Privately Held**
SIC: 3441 3446 3471 Fabricated structural metal; architectural metalwork; sand blasting of metal parts

Roscoe
Sullivan County

(G-15034)
PROHIBITION DISTILLERY LLC
10 Union St (12776-5210)
PHONE..................917 685-8989
Brian Facquet, *Mng Member*
EMP: 8
SALES (est): 423K **Privately Held**
SIC: 2085 Distilled & blended liquors

(G-15035)
ROSCOE LITTLE STORE INC
Also Called: Little Store, The
59 Stewart Ave (12776)
PHONE..................607 498-5553
Elwin Wood, *President*
Deborah Gabry, *Corp Secy*
EMP: 9
SQ FT: 3,200
SALES (est): 982.3K **Privately Held**
SIC: 3949 Sporting & athletic goods

Rosedale
Queens County

(G-15036)
CARPET BEATERS LLC
12163 235th St (11422-1030)
P.O. Box 38372, Elmont (11003-8372)
PHONE..................877 375-9336
Peace J Blessings, *Principal*
T Mitchell, *Principal*
EMP: 5 **EST:** 2016
SALES (est): 259.3K **Privately Held**
SIC: 2899 Fluxes: brazing, soldering, galvanizing & welding

(G-15037)
LARRY KINGS CORPORATION
13708 250th St (11422-2110)
PHONE..................718 481-8741
Fax: 718 481-9859
Larry Yoen, *President*
Clara Wong, *Treasurer*
Ken Klein, *Systems Mgr*
Johnny Yoen, *Shareholder*
Penny Yoen, *Admin Sec*
EMP: 6
SALES (est): 663.4K **Privately Held**
SIC: 3825 Instruments to measure electricity

(G-15038)
MASTRO CONCRETE INC
15433 Brookville Blvd (11422-3163)
PHONE..................718 528-6788
Tony Mastronardi, *President*
Mario Mastronardi, *Vice Pres*
EMP: 8
SQ FT: 10,000
SALES (est): 1.4MM **Privately Held**
SIC: 3273 Ready-mixed concrete

(G-15039)
WATER COOLING CORP
24520 Merrick Blvd (11422-1464)
P.O. Box 220056 (11422-0056)
PHONE..................718 723-6500
Elliott Miller, *President*
Robert Miller, *Consultant*
EMP: 7 **EST:** 1939
SQ FT: 5,500
SALES (est): 1.3MM **Privately Held**
WEB: www.watcopumps.com
SIC: 3443 3561 Water tanks, metal plate; tanks, standard or custom fabricated: metal plate; pumps, domestic: water or sump; industrial pumps & parts

Roslyn
Nassau County

(G-15040)
BEACON SPCH LNGE PTHLGY PHYS
Also Called: Beacon Therapy Services
1441 Old Northern Blvd (11576-2146)
PHONE..................516 626-1635
Barbar Lehrer, *Partner*
Barbara Lehrer, *Partner*
EMP: 16
SQ FT: 5,500
SALES: 7MM **Privately Held**
SIC: 3841 Inhalation therapy equipment

(G-15041)
CLOUD ROCK GROUP LLC
525 Bryant Ave (11576-1146)
PHONE..................516 967-6023
Leon Hedvat, *Manager*
EMP: 5
SALES (est): 350K **Privately Held**
SIC: 7372 7389 Application computer software;

(G-15042)
CUSTOM ECO FRIENDLY LLC (PA)
Also Called: Custom Eco Friendly Bags
50 Spruce Dr (11576-2330)
PHONE..................347 227-0229
Matthew Kesten, *CEO*
Jonathon Wollman, *President*
▲ **EMP:** 9
SQ FT: 250
SALES: 2.4MM **Privately Held**
SIC: 2674 Shopping bags: made from purchased materials

(G-15043)
DYNAMIC PHOTOGRAPHY INC
Also Called: Daisy Memory Products
48 Flamingo Rd N (11576-2606)
PHONE..................516 381-2951
Robert M Deangelo Jr, *President*
Richard J Deangelo, *Vice Pres*
EMP: 5
SALES: 7MM **Privately Held**
SIC: 3674 7336 7221 Magnetic bubble memory device; commercial art & graphic design; photographer, still or video

(G-15044)
HAND CARE INC
42 Sugar Maple Dr (11576-3207)
P.O. Box 331, Albertson (11507-0331)
PHONE..................516 747-5649
Harrison Fuller, *President*
Patricia Fuller, *Admin Sec*
▲ **EMP:** 2
SQ FT: 15,000
SALES: 2MM **Privately Held**
WEB: www.handcare.net
SIC: 3842 Gloves, safety; adhesive tape & plasters, medicated or non-medicated

GEOGRAPHIC SECTION

Rouses Point - Clinton County (G-15067)

(G-15045)
NEW YORK LASER & AESTHETICKS
1025 Nthrn Blvd Ste 206 (11576)
PHONE..................516 627-7777
Ofra Grinbaum, *Owner*
EMP: 5
SALES (est): 445.8K **Privately Held**
SIC: 3845 Laser systems & equipment, medical

(G-15046)
NORTHWEST TEXTILE HOLDING INC (PA)
Also Called: Wilmington Products USA
49 Bryant Ave (11576-1123)
P.O. Box 263 (11576-0263)
PHONE..................516 484-6996
Ross Auerbach, *President*
Marc Friedman, *COO*
Glenn Auerbach, *Exec VP*
Kim Rizzardi, *Vice Pres*
Tim Darnell, *Warehouse Mgr*
▲ EMP: 80
SQ FT: 15,000
SALES (est): 150MM **Privately Held**
WEB: www.thenorthwest.com
SIC: 2211 Blankets & blanketings, cotton

(G-15047)
ROVEL MANUFACTURING CO INC
52 Wimbledon Dr (11576-3082)
PHONE..................516 365-2752
William Levor, *President*
Andrew A Levor, *Vice Pres*
EMP: 5
SQ FT: 10,000
SALES: 400K **Privately Held**
SIC: 2299 Batts & batting: cotton mill waste & related material; batting, wadding, padding & fillings

(G-15048)
WM E MARTIN AND SONS CO INC
55 Bryant Ave Ste 300 (11576-1158)
PHONE..................516 605-2444
Fax: 718 291-0331
William Martin Jr, *President*
William S Martin, *Vice Pres*
Martin Spencer, *Accounting Mgr*
Abby Zeifman, *Director*
Spencer Martin, *Administration*
▲ EMP: 22 EST: 1954
SQ FT: 60,000
SALES (est): 7.6MM **Privately Held**
SIC: 2099 2034 Spices, including grinding; vegetables, dried or dehydrated (except freeze-dried)

Roslyn Heights
Nassau County

(G-15049)
CABOT COACH BUILDERS INC
Also Called: Royale Limousine Manufacturers
77 Carriage Ln (11577-2615)
PHONE..................516 625-4000
Lucy Berritto, *Manager*
EMP: 8
SALES (corp-wide): 11.1MM **Privately Held**
WEB: www.royalelimo.com
SIC: 3711 5511 Automobile assembly, including specialty automobiles; automobiles, new & used
PA: Cabot Coach Builders Inc.
99 Newark St
Haverhill MA 01832
978 374-4530

(G-15050)
ERGUN INC
10 Mineola Ave Unit B (11577-1067)
PHONE..................631 721-0049
Omer Eguner, *President*
EMP: 2
SQ FT: 200
SALES: 15.9MM **Privately Held**
SIC: 2911 Oils, fuel

(G-15051)
HIGHWAY TOLL ADM LLC
66 Powerhouse Rd Ste 301 (11577-1372)
P.O. Box 30 (11577-0030)
PHONE..................516 684-9584
David Centner, *CEO*
Keith Baylor, *CTO*
Jonathan Schweiger,
▲ EMP: 15
SALES (est): 4.6MM
SALES (corp-wide): 1MM **Privately Held**
SIC: 3829 Toll booths, automatic
PA: Hta Holdings, Inc.
66 Powerhouse Rd Ste 301
Roslyn Heights NY

(G-15052)
IET LABS INC (PA)
1 Expressway Plz Ste 120 (11577-2031)
PHONE..................516 334-5959
Fax: 516 334-5988
Sam Sheena, *President*
David Sheena, *Vice Pres*
Ben Sheena, *VP Sales*
▲ EMP: 12
SQ FT: 11,000
SALES (est): 5.2MM **Privately Held**
SIC: 3825 Test equipment for electronic & electrical circuits

(G-15053)
KIM JAE PRINTING CO INC
249 Parkside Dr (11577-2211)
PHONE..................212 691-6289
Jae Kye Kim, *President*
Yun Kim, *Vice Pres*
EMP: 5
SQ FT: 6,000
SALES (est): 500K **Privately Held**
SIC: 2759 2752 Newspapers: printing; commercial printing, lithographic

(G-15054)
MASON SCOTT INDUSTRIES LLC
159 Westwood Cir (11577-1844)
PHONE..................516 349-1800
Scott Fishkind, *Mng Member*
EMP: 13
SQ FT: 20,000
SALES: 12MM **Privately Held**
SIC: 3444 Sheet metalwork

(G-15055)
NATIONAL MARKETING SERVICES
Also Called: Cars Magazine
200 S Service Rd Ste 203 (11577-2118)
P.O. Box 206, Franklin Square (11010-0206)
PHONE..................516 942-9595
Bryan Flyn, *President*
EMP: 12
SALES (est): 1.3MM **Privately Held**
SIC: 2721 Periodicals

(G-15056)
ROSLYN BREAD COMPANY INC
190 Mineola Ave (11577-2093)
PHONE..................516 625-1470
EMP: 35
SQ FT: 3,500
SALES: 1.1MM **Privately Held**
SIC: 2051 5149 5461 5812 Mfg Whol Ret Bread & Restaurant

(G-15057)
SOMERSET MANUFACTURERS INC
36 Glen Cove Rd (11577-1703)
PHONE..................516 626-3832
Jacob Ambalu, *President*
Esther Ambalu, *Vice Pres*
EMP: 20
SALES (est): 1.6MM **Privately Held**
SIC: 3911 Jewelry, precious metal

(G-15058)
US CONCRETE INC
Also Called: Kings Ready Mix
10 Powerhouse Rd (11577-1311)
PHONE..................718 853-4644
EMP: 50
SALES (corp-wide): 1.1B **Publicly Held**
SIC: 3273 Ready-mixed concrete
PA: U.S. Concrete, Inc.
331 N Main St
Euless TX 76039
817 835-4105

Rotterdam Junction
Schenectady County

(G-15059)
SI GROUP INC
Also Called: Si Group Global Manufacturing
1000 Main St (12150-9702)
PHONE..................518 347-4200
David Dawood, *VP Opers*
EMP: 200
SALES (corp-wide): 1.1B **Privately Held**
SIC: 2865 Phenol, alkylated & cumene
PA: Si Group, Inc.
2750 Balltown Rd
Schenectady NY 12309
518 347-4200

(G-15060)
SI GROUP INC
Rr 5 Box South (12150)
P.O. Box 1046, Schenectady (12301-1046)
PHONE..................518 347-4200
Andy Barrett, *General Mgr*
EMP: 150
SALES (corp-wide): 1.1B **Privately Held**
WEB: www.schenectadyinternational.com
SIC: 2851 Varnishes
PA: Si Group, Inc.
2750 Balltown Rd
Schenectady NY 12309
518 347-4200

Round Lake
Saratoga County

(G-15061)
DEATH WISH COFFEE COMPANY LLC
19 Wood Rd Ste 500 (12151-1718)
PHONE..................518 400-1050
Michael Brown, *CEO*
EMP: 11 EST: 2015
SALES (est): 1.6MM **Privately Held**
SIC: 2095 5499 Coffee extracts; coffee roasting (except by wholesale grocers); coffee

(G-15062)
USHERS MACHINE AND TOOL CO INC
180 Ushers Rd (12151-1806)
PHONE..................518 877-5501
Fax: 518 877-8575
Don Lincoln, *President*
Joseph Hopeck, *President*
Patte Prevost, *Manager*
Nick Jones, *Senior Mgr*
EMP: 20
SQ FT: 5,000
SALES (est): 4.3MM
SALES (corp-wide): 2.6B **Privately Held**
WEB: www.ushersm.com
SIC: 3599 Machine shop, jobbing & repair
PA: Aalberts Industries N.V.
Sandenburgerlaan 4
Langbroek
343 565-080

(G-15063)
WYRESTORM TECHNOLOGIES LLC
23 Wood Rd (12151-1708)
PHONE..................518 289-1293
Derek Hulbert, *President*
Hal Truax, *VP Sales*
Ken Vanier, *Sales Associate*
Todd Akins, *Marketing Staff*
Ken Kingdon, *Marketing Staff*
▲ EMP: 15
SQ FT: 2,500
SALES (est): 2.9MM **Privately Held**
SIC: 3651 Household audio & video equipment

HQ: Wyrestorm Technologies Europe Limited
Unit 22 Kelvin Road
Swindon WILTS
179 323-0343

Round Top
Greene County

(G-15064)
ROUND TOP KNIT & SCREENING
Rr 31 (12473)
P.O. Box 188 (12473-0188)
PHONE..................518 622-3600
Fax: 518 622-9041
Manny Voss, *Owner*
Dolly Cavicchioni, *Office Mgr*
EMP: 5
SQ FT: 6,000
SALES: 750K **Privately Held**
SIC: 2759 5651 2395 2396 Screen printing; family clothing stores; embroidery & art needlework; automotive & apparel trimmings

Rouses Point
Clinton County

(G-15065)
CHAMPLAIN PLASTICS INC
Also Called: Champlain Hanger
87 Pillsbury Rd (12979-1701)
P.O. Box 2947, Plattsburgh (12901-0269)
PHONE..................518 297-3700
Fax: 518 297-3777
Alan L Taveroff, *Ch of Bd*
Joe Zalter, *President*
Joanne Palliotti, *Accounting Mgr*
Monique Perez, *Accountant*
Beverly McKernan, *Accounts Mgr*
▲ EMP: 85 EST: 1998
SALES (est): 14.7MM
SALES (corp-wide): 2.7MM **Privately Held**
WEB: www.olympicpoolaccessories.com
SIC: 3089 Injection molding of plastics
PA: Canadian Buttons Limited
7020 Boul Newman
Lasalle QC H8N 3
514 363-0210

(G-15066)
PFIZER INC
Also Called: Wyeth
64 Maple St (12979-1424)
P.O. Box 697 (12979-0697)
PHONE..................518 297-6611
Fax: 518 297-8122
John Nichols, *Opers Mgr*
Tony Pilcher, *Engineer*
Thomas Trombley, *Engineer*
Lynn Jock, *Corp Comm Staff*
William Brooks, *Branch Mgr*
EMP: 440
SALES (corp-wide): 52.8B **Publicly Held**
WEB: www.wyeth.com
SIC: 2834 Pharmaceutical preparations
PA: Pfizer Inc.
235 E 42nd St
New York NY 10017
212 733-2323

(G-15067)
POWERTEX INC (PA)
1 Lincoln Blvd Ste 101 (12979-1087)
PHONE..................518 297-4000
Fax: 518 297-2634
Stephen Podd, *President*
Victor I Podd, *Vice Pres*
Karen M Lamberton, *Treasurer*
Kelly Timmons, *Human Resources*
Heather Laforest, *Accounts Mgr*
▲ EMP: 34 EST: 1977
SQ FT: 65,900
SALES: 3.6MM **Privately Held**
WEB: www.powertex.com
SIC: 3089 Plastic containers, except foam

Rouses Point - Clinton County (G-15068)

(G-15068)
SANDYS DELI INC
Also Called: Last Resort, The
90 Montgomery St (12979-1018)
PHONE 518 297-6951
Carolyn Reid, *President*
EMP: 6 **EST:** 2016
SQ FT: 1,000
SALES: 145K
SALES (corp-wide): 450K **Privately Held**
SIC: 2599 Bar, restaurant & cafeteria furniture
PA: Sandy's Deli Inc
133 Lake St
Rouses Point NY 12979
518 297-6951

(G-15069)
VWR CHEMICALS LLC (DH)
3 Lincoln Blvd (12979-1037)
PHONE 518 297-4444
Fax: 518 297-2960
Theodore Pulkownick, *President*
Doug Crossman, *General Mgr*
Tom Caramia, *Production*
Tom Parrott, *Purchasing*
Meredith Earnest, *Accounts Mgr*
▲ **EMP:** 30
SQ FT: 30,000
SALES (est): 20.8MM
SALES (corp-wide): 4.5B **Publicly Held**
WEB: www.anachemiachemicals.com
SIC: 2819 Industrial inorganic chemicals
HQ: Vwr Funding, Inc.
100 W Matsonford Rd
Radnor PA 19087
610 386-1700

Rush
Monroe County

(G-15070)
CONVERGENT AUDIO TECH INC
85 High Tech Dr (14543-9746)
PHONE 585 359-2700
Ken Stevens, *President*
Truddy Stevens, *Vice Pres*
Cheri Milliman, *Office Mgr*
EMP: 5
SQ FT: 3,300
SALES (est): 842.4K **Privately Held**
SIC: 3651 Household audio equipment

(G-15071)
EMPIRE STATE PIPELINE (HQ)
6685 W Henrietta Rd (14543-9735)
P.O. Box 409 (14543-0409)
PHONE 585 321-1560
Fax: 716 857-7648
Randy Goodman, *Superintendent*
David Sword, *Manager*
EMP: 3
SQ FT: 3,600
SALES (est): 1.6MM
SALES (corp-wide): 1.4B **Publicly Held**
WEB: www.natfuel.com
SIC: 1389 Gas field services
PA: National Fuel Gas Company
6363 Main St
Williamsville NY 14221
716 857-7000

(G-15072)
EXTEK INC
7500 W Henrietta Rd (14543-9790)
PHONE 585 533-1672
John Demanaco, *Engineer*
Caroline Eastman, *Branch Mgr*
Glen Crast, *Branch Mgr*
Tom Bienias, *Manager*
Anne Rowlinds, *Manager*
EMP: 50
SALES (corp-wide): 5.5MM **Privately Held**
WEB: www.sts.ethoxint.com
SIC: 3841 Surgical & medical instruments
PA: Extek, Inc.
370 Summit Point Dr
Henrietta NY
585 321-5000

(G-15073)
G & G WINDOW REPAIR INC
6710 W Henrietta Rd Ste 4 (14543-9770)
PHONE 585 334-3370
Gary Donald Larzelere, *President*
EMP: 11
SALES (est): 1.5MM **Privately Held**
SIC: 2431 Windows & window parts & trim, wood

(G-15074)
GPM ASSOCIATES LLC
Graphik Promotional Products
45 High Tech Dr Ste 100 (14543-9746)
PHONE 585 359-1770
Sean Fraser, *Sales Dir*
Kevin Webster, *Marketing Mgr*
Lauren A Wrobel, *Marketing Staff*
Jim McDermott,
EMP: 6
SALES (corp-wide): 15.8MM **Privately Held**
SIC: 2393 Textile bags
PA: Gpm Associates Llc
45 High Tech Dr
Rush NY 14543
585 334-4800

(G-15075)
GPP POST-CLOSING INC
Also Called: Global Precision Products
90 High Tech Dr (14543-9746)
PHONE 585 334-4640
Fax: 585 334-2815
Mark Labell, *CEO*
Doug Labell, *Vice Pres*
Charles Cornelius, *Engineer*
EMP: 22
SQ FT: 250,000
SALES (est): 4.1MM **Privately Held**
WEB: www.globalppi.com
SIC: 3599 Machine & other job shop work

(G-15076)
KEUKA STUDIOS INC
1011 Rush Henrietta Townl (14543-9763)
PHONE 585 624-5960
Dan White, *President*
Jeanne White, *Corp Secy*
▼ **EMP:** 8
SQ FT: 10,000
SALES (est): 740K **Privately Held**
WEB: www.keuka-studios.com
SIC: 3446 Architectural metalwork

(G-15077)
SPS MEDICAL SUPPLY CORP (DH)
6789 W Henrietta Rd (14543-9797)
PHONE 585 359-0130
Gary Steinberg, *President*
Charles A Hughes, *General Mgr*
John Hughes, *General Mgr*
Rex Norton, *Opers Mgr*
Gavin Burke, *Mfg Mgr*
◆ **EMP:** 73
SQ FT: 40,000
SALES (est): 20.3MM
SALES (corp-wide): 770.1MM **Publicly Held**
WEB: www.spsmedical.com
SIC: 3842 Surgical appliances & supplies
HQ: Crosstex International, Inc.
10 Ranick Rd
Hauppauge NY 11788
631 582-6777

Rushville
Yates County

(G-15078)
RUSH MACHINERY INC
4761 State Route 364 (14544-9721)
PHONE 585 554-3070
Fax: 585 554-4077
William P Freese, *President*
David Burdett, *General Mgr*
Bill Freese, *Sales Mgr*
Maggie Atkins, *Admin Mgr*
▲ **EMP:** 9
SQ FT: 7,000
SALES (est): 2.1MM **Privately Held**
SIC: 3541 Centering machines

Rye
Westchester County

(G-15079)
ALEX AND ANI LLC
52 Purchase St (10580-3009)
PHONE 914 481-1506
EMP: 9 **Privately Held**
SIC: 3915 Jewelers' materials & lapidary work
PA: Alex And Ani, Llc
2000 Chapel View Blvd # 360
Cranston RI 02920

(G-15080)
AUXILIUM PHARMACEUTICALS INC
70 High St (10580-1506)
PHONE 484 321-2022
Brian Wogram, *Director*
EMP: 10
SALES (est): 870K **Privately Held**
SIC: 2834 Pharmaceutical preparations

(G-15081)
CONSOLIDATED EDISON CO NY INC
511 Theodore Fremd Ave (10580-1432)
PHONE 914 933-2936
William McGrath, *Principal*
EMP: 17
SALES (corp-wide): 12B **Publicly Held**
SIC: 2869 Fuels
HQ: Consolidated Edison Company Of New York, Inc.
4 Irving Pl
New York NY 10003
212 460-4600

(G-15082)
GAZETTE PRESS INC
2 Clinton Ave (10580-1629)
PHONE 914 963-8300
Richard Martinelli, *CEO*
Angelo R Martinelli, *President*
Angelo Martinelli, *Chairman*
Carol Martinelli, *Treasurer*
EMP: 20 **EST:** 1864
SQ FT: 10,000
SALES (est): 2.8MM **Privately Held**
SIC: 2759 2796 2791 2789 Letterpress printing; platemaking services; typesetting; bookbinding & related work; commercial printing, lithographic

(G-15083)
GB AERO ENGINE LLC
555 Theodore Fremd Ave (10580-1451)
PHONE 914 925-9600
Raynard D Benvenuti,
Noah Roy,
Rob Wolf,
EMP: 390
SALES (est): 20.4MM **Privately Held**
SIC: 3724 3541 3769 Aircraft engines & engine parts; machine tools, metal cutting type; guided missile & space vehicle parts & auxiliary equipment

(G-15084)
GLOBAL GOLD CORPORATION (PA)
555 Theodore Fremd Ave C208 (10580-1451)
PHONE 914 925-0020
Fax: 203 422-2330
Van Z Krikorian, *Ch of Bd*
W E S Urquhart, *Vice Pres*
Jan Dulman, *CFO*
Drury J Gallagher, *Treasurer*
EMP: 12
SALES (est): 3.4MM **Publicly Held**
WEB: www.globalgoldcorp.com
SIC: 1021 1041 1094 1044 Copper ores; gold ores; uranium ore mining; silver ores

(G-15085)
HIBERT PUBLISHING LLC
222 Purchase St (10580-2101)
PHONE 914 381-7474
Jean Sheff, *Editor*
Nina Spiegelman, *Accounts Mgr*
Lynnmarie Hanley, *Accounts Exec*
Gary Hibert, *Branch Mgr*
EMP: 5
SALES (corp-wide): 1.1MM **Privately Held**
SIC: 2741 Miscellaneous publishing
PA: Hibert Publishing Llc
7555 E Hampden Ave # 405
Denver CO 80231
303 312-1000

(G-15086)
HYDRIVE ENERGY
350 Theodore Fremd Ave (10580-1573)
PHONE 914 925-9100
Michael F Weinstein, *Chairman*
EMP: 6
SALES (est): 451.8K **Privately Held**
SIC: 2086 Carbonated beverages, nonalcoholic: bottled & canned

(G-15087)
JUDITH N GRAHAM INC
Also Called: Pink and Palmer
64 Halls Ln (10580-3124)
PHONE 914 921-5446
James Graham, *Principal*
EMP: 7
SALES (est): 537.5K **Privately Held**
SIC: 2844 Toilet preparations

(G-15088)
MARTINELLI HOLDINGS LLC
Also Called: Today Media
2 Clinton Ave (10580-1629)
PHONE 302 504-1361
Dianne Green, *Controller*
EMP: 50
SALES (corp-wide): 15K **Privately Held**
SIC: 2721 Magazines: publishing only, not printed on site
PA: Martinelli Holdings Llc
3301 Lancaster Pike 5c
Wilmington DE 19805
302 656-1809

(G-15089)
MASON & GORE INC
Also Called: Gazette & Press
2 Clinton Ave (10580-1629)
PHONE 914 921-1025
Fax: 914 476-1052
Angelo R Martinelli, *President*
EMP: 20 **EST:** 1956
SQ FT: 4,500
SALES (est): 2MM **Privately Held**
WEB: www.gazettepress.com
SIC: 2752 7331 7311 Commercial printing, offset; mailing service; advertising consultant

(G-15090)
MONEYPAPER INC
411 Theodore Fremd Ave # 132 (10580-1410)
P.O. Box 451 (10580-0451)
PHONE 914 925-0022
Fax: 914 921-9318
Vita Nelson, *President*
EMP: 12
SALES (est): 807.6K **Privately Held**
WEB: www.giftsofstock.com
SIC: 2711 6282 Newspapers, publishing & printing; investment advice

(G-15091)
O C TANNER COMPANY
27 Park Dr S (10580-1826)
PHONE 914 921-2025
Thomas Rosato, *Manager*
EMP: 5
SALES (corp-wide): 351.1MM **Privately Held**
WEB: www.octanner.com
SIC: 3911 5944 Pins (jewelry), precious metal; jewelry, precious stones & precious metals
PA: O. C. Tanner Company
1930 S State St
Salt Lake City UT 84115
801 486-2430

GEOGRAPHIC SECTION

Saint James - Suffolk County (G-15114)

(G-15092)
QUOIN LLC
555 Theodore Fremd Ave B302
(10580-1451)
PHONE 914 967-9400
Martin Franklin, *CEO*
EMP: 1402
SALES (est): 709.4MM
SALES (corp-wide): 13.2B **Publicly Held**
WEB: www.jarden.com
SIC: 3089 Plastic containers, except foam
HQ: Jarden Corporation
221 River St
Hoboken NJ 07030

(G-15093)
RYE RECORD
14 Elm Pl Ste 200 (10580-2951)
PHONE 914 713-3213
Dolores Eyler, *Partner*
Allen Clarck, *Partner*
Robin Jovanovich, *Partner*
Susan Bontempo, *Marketing Staff*
Sylke Schuster, *Agent*
EMP: 8
SALES (est): 500K **Privately Held**
SIC: 2721 Periodicals

(G-15094)
SMN MEDICAL PC
Also Called: Docchat
2 Allendale Dr (10580-2402)
PHONE 844 362-2428
Michael Okhravi, *CEO*
Steve Okhravi, *President*
EMP: 10
SALES (est): 739.5K **Privately Held**
SIC: 7372 8011 7389 Application computer software; offices & clinics of medical doctors;

(G-15095)
WESTERN OIL AND GAS JV INC
Also Called: Michael Neuman
7 Mccullough Pl (10580-2934)
PHONE 914 967-4758
Michael Neuman, *President*
Richard Neuman, *Vice Pres*
EMP: 3 EST: 2008
SALES: 2.1MM **Privately Held**
SIC: 1321 8748 1381 Natural gas liquids; energy conservation consultant; drilling oil & gas wells

Rye Brook
Westchester County

(G-15096)
ELIAS FRAGRANCES INC (PA)
3 Hunter Dr (10573-1406)
PHONE 718 693-6400
Fax: 718 856-8061
Robert Elias, *President*
Barbara Elias, *Corp Secy*
Lewis Elias, *Exec VP*
Jackie James, *Bookkeeper*
EMP: 17 EST: 1972
SQ FT: 8,000
SALES (est): 1.3MM **Privately Held**
SIC: 2844 5122 Perfumes, natural or synthetic; perfumes

(G-15097)
FLOW CONTROL LLC (HQ)
1 International Dr (10573-1058)
PHONE 914 323-5700
Sonia Hollies, *Mng Member*
EMP: 250
SALES: 25MM **Publicly Held**
SIC: 3561 Pumps, domestic: water or sump

(G-15098)
MITSUI CHEMICALS AMERICA INC (HQ)
800 Westchester Ave N607 (10573-1328)
PHONE 914 253-0777
Naoto Tani, *President*
Masaharu Kubo, *General Mgr*
Ken Migita, *General Mgr*
Kenji Miyachi, *General Mgr*
Keiichi Sano, *Managing Dir*
◆ **EMP:** 40

SQ FT: 13,000
SALES: 329.7MM
SALES (corp-wide): 10.6B **Privately Held**
SIC: 2821 2865 3082 8731 Plastics materials & resins; plasticizer/additive based plastic materials; cyclic crudes & intermediates; unsupported plastics profile shapes; computer (hardware) development; chemical additives; loan institutions, general & industrial
PA: Mitsui Chemicals, Inc.
1-5-2, Higashishimbashi
Minato-Ku TKY 105-0
362 532-100

(G-15099)
PARACO GAS CORPORATION (PA)
800 Westchester Ave S604 (10573-1397)
PHONE 800 647-4427
Joseph Armentano, *CEO*
Michael Gioffre, *President*
Peter Teresi, *Regional Mgr*
Frank Carlone, *Business Mgr*
Dave Muscato, *COO*
EMP: 21
SALES (est): 214.3MM **Privately Held**
SIC: 1321 Propane (natural) production

(G-15100)
PROGRESSIVE PRODUCTS LLC
Also Called: Wipesplus
4 International Dr # 224 (10573-1065)
PHONE 914 417-6022
Jason Englander, *CEO*
Gabby Hunter, *Bookkeeper*
Michael Glenn, *Sales Staff*
Mary Delsranco, *Manager*
Carol Lugo, *Administration*
▲ **EMP:** 8
SQ FT: 2,000
SALES: 12MM **Privately Held**
SIC: 2842 Cleaning or polishing preparations

(G-15101)
SNAPPLE BEVERAGE CORP (DEL) (HQ)
900 King St (10573-1226)
PHONE 914 612-4000
Larry D Young, *CEO*
Ernie Cavallo, *President*
Bryan Mazur, *Vice Pres*
Scott Miller, *Vice Pres*
Michael Sandes, *Vice Pres*
EMP: 70
SQ FT: 55,000
SALES (est): 71.5MM **Publicly Held**
SIC: 2086 Bottled & canned soft drinks

(G-15102)
XYLEM INC (PA)
1 International Dr (10573-1058)
PHONE 914 323-5700
Fax: 914 323-5800
Markos I Tambakeras, *Ch of Bd*
Patrick K Decker, *President*
Tomas Brannemo, *President*
David Flinton, *President*
Pak Steven Leung, *President*
EMP: 277
SQ FT: 67,000
SALES: 3.7B **Publicly Held**
SIC: 3561 Pumps & pumping equipment

Sag Harbor
Suffolk County

(G-15103)
CAM TOUCHVIEW PRODUCTS INC
51 Division St (11963-3162)
P.O. Box 1980 (11963-0067)
PHONE 631 842-3400
Emanuel Cardinale, *President*
EMP: 15 EST: 2013
SQ FT: 4,000
SALES: 1.2MM **Privately Held**
SIC: 3674 Thin film circuits

(G-15104)
COASTAL PUBLICATIONS INC
22 Division St (11963)
P.O. Box 1620 (11963-0058)
PHONE 631 725-1700
Gavin Menu, *Principal*
EMP: 10
SALES (est): 663.1K **Privately Held**
SIC: 2741 Miscellaneous publishing

(G-15105)
DORTRONICS SYSTEMS INC
1668 Bhmpton Sag Hbr Tpke (11963-3706)
PHONE 631 725-0505
Fax: 631 725-8148
Paul R Scheerer, *CEO*
John Fitzpaprick, *President*
John Fitzpatrick, *President*
John Fitzgerald, *Vice Pres*
Mary Scheerer, *Vice Pres*
EMP: 21
SQ FT: 10,000
SALES: 3.9MM
SALES (corp-wide): 16.7MM **Privately Held**
WEB: www.dortronics.com
SIC: 3429 3679 3625 3089 Locks or lock sets; electronic switches; switches, electronic applications; timing devices, electronic; plastic hardware & building products
PA: Sag Harbor Industries, Inc.
1668 Bhmpton Sag Hbr Tpke
Sag Harbor NY 11963
631 725-0440

(G-15106)
SAG HARBOR EXPRESS
35 Main St (11963-3012)
P.O. Box 1620 (11963-0058)
PHONE 631 725-1700
Fax: 631 725-1584
Bryan Boyhan, *Manager*
EMP: 7
SALES (est): 507.4K **Privately Held**
WEB: www.sagharboronline.com
SIC: 2741 2711 Miscellaneous publishing; newspapers

(G-15107)
SAG HARBOR INDUSTRIES INC (PA)
1668 Bhmpton Sag Hbr Tpke (11963-3714)
PHONE 631 725-0440
Fax: 631 725-4234
Paul R Scheerer Jr, *Ch of Bd*
Mary Scheerer, *President*
John Fitzpatrick, *Vice Pres*
Dave Leeney, *Vice Pres*
Rhonda Baker, *Purch Mgr*
EMP: 50 EST: 1946
SQ FT: 50,000
SALES: 16.7MM **Privately Held**
WEB: www.sagharborind.com
SIC: 3621 3672 3677 5065 Coils, for electric motors or generators; printed circuit boards; electronic coils, transformers & other inductors; electronic parts & equipment; transformers, except electric

(G-15108)
SECOND CHANCE PRESS INC
Also Called: Permanent Press
4170 Noyac Rd (11963-2809)
PHONE 631 725-1101
Martin Shepard, *President*
Rania Graetz, *Editor*
Cathy Suter, *Editor*
Judith Shepard, *Vice Pres*
EMP: 6
SALES (est): 420K **Privately Held**
WEB: www.thepermanentpress.com
SIC: 2731 5942 Books: publishing only; book stores

Sagaponack
Suffolk County

(G-15109)
WOLFFER ESTATE VINEYARD INC
Also Called: Wolffer Estate Winery
139 Sagg Rd (11962-2006)
P.O. Box 9002 (11962-9002)
PHONE 631 537-5106
Christian Wolffer, *President*
Judy Malone, *Comms Dir*
Roman Roth, *Technical Staff*
▲ **EMP:** 50
SALES (est): 8.2MM **Privately Held**
WEB: www.wolffer.com
SIC: 2084 5813 Wines, brandy & brandy spirits; wine bar

Saint Albans
Queens County

(G-15110)
HOUSE OF THE FOAMING CASE INC
110 08 Dunkirk St (11412)
PHONE 718 454-0101
Mark Levy, *Principal*
EMP: 7
SALES (est): 1MM **Privately Held**
SIC: 3523 Farm machinery & equipment

(G-15111)
INTEGRATED TECH SUPPORT SVCS
Also Called: Itss
18616 Jordan Ave (11412-2308)
PHONE 718 454-2497
Gerald Cortez, *President*
Damon Kinebrew, *Sales/Mktg Dir*
Michael Greaves, *Admin Mgr*
EMP: 7 EST: 2001
SQ FT: 1,000
SALES: 150K **Privately Held**
SIC: 2522 Office furniture, except wood

(G-15112)
ZZZ MATTRESS MANUFACTURING
Also Called: Purest of America
11080 Dunkirk St (11412-1950)
PHONE 718 454-1468
Charlie Jad, *Ch of Bd*
EMP: 30 EST: 2012
SQ FT: 40,000
SALES: 3MM **Privately Held**
SIC: 2515 5719 Mattresses & bedsprings; beddings & linens

Saint James
Suffolk County

(G-15113)
2600 ENTERPRISES INC
Also Called: The Hacker Quarterly
2 Flowerfield Ste 30 (11780-1507)
P.O. Box 848, Middle Island (11953-0848)
PHONE 631 474-2677
Emmanuel Goldstein, *Principal*
Eric Corley, *Editor*
▲ **EMP:** 10
SALES (est): 1MM **Privately Held**
WEB: www.2600.net
SIC: 2721 Magazines: publishing only, not printed on site

(G-15114)
CREATE-A-CARD INC
16 Brasswood Rd (11780-3410)
PHONE 631 584-2273
Arthur Messina, *President*
Marian Abrilz, *Marketing Staff*
EMP: 5

Saint James - Suffolk County (G-15115)

SALES: 375K **Privately Held**
WEB: www.createacardinc.com
SIC: 2752 2759 Color lithography; post cards, picture; lithographed; visiting cards (including business); printing

(G-15115)
DESIGN SOLUTIONS LI INC
711 Middle Country Rd (11780-3209)
PHONE..............................631 656-8700
Mario Adragna, *Owner*
EMP: 1
SQ FT: 6,000
SALES: 4MM **Privately Held**
SIC: 3639 Major kitchen appliances, except refrigerators & stoves

(G-15116)
IMAGE SPECIALISTS INC
80 Elderwood Dr (11780-3445)
PHONE..............................631 475-0867
Fax: 631 475-2244
Doris Costello, *Ch of Bd*
Joseph P Costello, *Vice Pres*
Stephen J Costello Sr, *Vice Pres*
Tom Domino, *Plant Mgr*
Bryan Ford, *Warehouse Mgr*
▲ EMP: 18
SQ FT: 30,000
SALES (est): 3.4MM **Privately Held**
WEB: www.imagespecialists.com
SIC: 2893 Printing ink

(G-15117)
SMITHTOWN CONCRETE PRODUCTS
441 Middle Country Rd (11780-3201)
P.O. Box 612, Smithtown (11787-0612)
PHONE..............................631 265-1815
Neil Spevak, *President*
Barbara Spevak, *Treasurer*
Rob Barttlett, *Adv Mgr*
EMP: 16 EST: 1940
SALES: 950K **Privately Held**
WEB: www.smithtownconcrete.com
SIC: 3271 Concrete block & brick

Saint Johnsville
Montgomery County

(G-15118)
CELLECT LLC
10 New St (13452-1313)
PHONE..............................508 744-6906
Kevin Hoffman, *Opers Staff*
Richard Bambara, *Manager*
Michael Tuza, *Manager*
Carl Ursi, *Manager*
Scott Smith,
▲ EMP: 140
SQ FT: 200,000
SALES (est): 14.7MM **Privately Held**
WEB: www.cellectfoam.com
SIC: 3086 Packaging & shipping materials, foamed plastic

(G-15119)
CELLECT PLASTICS LLC
12 New St (13452-1313)
PHONE..............................518 568-7036
Scott Smith, *CEO*
▲ EMP: 100
SQ FT: 197,952
SALES: 4.7MM **Privately Held**
SIC: 3086 Plastics foam products

(G-15120)
HANSON AGGREGATES PA INC
7904 St Hwy 5 (13452-3514)
PHONE..............................518 568-2444
Don Sheldon, *Superintendent*
EMP: 10
SALES (corp-wide): 16B **Privately Held**
SIC: 1442 1422 Common sand mining; limestones, ground
HQ: Hanson Aggregates Pennsylvania, Llc
7660 Imperial Way
Allentown PA 18195
610 366-4626

(G-15121)
HELMONT MILLS INC (HQ)
15 Lion Ave (13452-1398)
PHONE..............................518 568-7913
Fax: 518 568-7866
George G Gehring Jr, *CEO*
John Davidson, *Controller*
John Geesler, *Maintence Staff*
EMP: 1 EST: 1992
SALES (est): 9.8MM
SALES (corp-wide): 60.9MM **Privately Held**
SIC: 2258 Lace & warp knit fabric mills
PA: Gehring Tricot Corporation
1225 Franklin Ave Ste 300
Garden City NY 11530
315 429-8551

(G-15122)
HIGHWAY GARAGE
110 State Highway 331 (13452-2818)
PHONE..............................518 568-2837
Rich Crum, *Manager*
EMP: 7 EST: 2011
SALES (est): 412.3K **Privately Held**
SIC: 3531 Drags, road (construction & road maintenance equipment)

(G-15123)
RC ENTPS BUS & TRCK INC
5895 State Highway 29 (13452-2413)
P.O. Box 193 (13452-0193)
PHONE..............................518 568-5753
Robert Crum, *Ch of Bd*
EMP: 6
SALES (est): 460K **Privately Held**
SIC: 7694 Motor repair services

(G-15124)
SENTINEL PRODUCTS CORP
12 New St (13452-1396)
PHONE..............................518 568-7036
Fax: 518 568-2614
Michael Tuza, *Manager*
Michael Bambara, *Manager*
EMP: 14
SALES (corp-wide): 1MM **Privately Held**
WEB: www.sentinelproducts.net
SIC: 3081 Polyethylene film
PA: Sentinel Products Corp
1550 Falmouth Rd
Centerville MA
508 775-5220

Salamanca
Cattaraugus County

(G-15125)
ALICE PERKINS
Also Called: A & F Trucking & Excavating
148 Washington St (14779-1045)
PHONE..............................716 378-5100
Alice Perkins, *Co-Owner*
Fred Perkins, *Co-Owner*
EMP: 6
SQ FT: 3,212
SALES: 1.5MM **Privately Held**
SIC: 1389 4212 1411 Excavating slush pits & cellars; dump truck haulage; granite dimension stone

(G-15126)
CAPSTREAM TECHNOLOGIES LLC
16 Main St (14779-1528)
PHONE..............................716 945-7100
Dale M Wymer, *Project Mgr*
Michael Krysick,
EMP: 6
SALES (est): 900.6K **Privately Held**
SIC: 3669 Intercommunication systems, electric

(G-15127)
HIGHLAND INJECTION MOLDING
Also Called: Ubec
175 Rochester St (14779-1508)
PHONE..............................716 945-2424
Fax: 716 945-5772
Joseph G Collins, *President*
Lew Jewell, *Purch Agent*
Lewis Jewel, *Treasurer*
Ron Johnson, *Controller*
Richard Guthrie, *CIO*
EMP: 100
SALES (est): 9.6MM **Privately Held**
WEB: www.highland-plastics.com
SIC: 3089 Injection molding of plastics; trays, plastic

(G-15128)
MCHONE INDUSTRIES INC
110 Elm St (14779-1500)
P.O. Box 69 (14779-0069)
PHONE..............................716 945-3380
Fax: 716 945-3780
Arnold McHone, *President*
Eva Hone, *Vice Pres*
Eva McHone, *Vice Pres*
Marlin Robbins, *Vice Pres*
Mike Robbins, *Manager*
EMP: 75 EST: 1952
SQ FT: 75,000
SALES (est): 17.7MM **Privately Held**
WEB: www.mchoneind.com
SIC: 3469 3317 3569 3444 Metal stampings; steel pipe & tubes; robots, assembly line: industrial & commercial; sheet metalwork

(G-15129)
MONROE TABLE COMPANY INC
255 Rochester St Ste 15 (14779-1563)
PHONE..............................716 945-7700
Douglas Kirchner, *CEO*
Orville Johnston, *President*
EMP: 10
SALES (est): 1MM **Privately Held**
SIC: 2599 Bar, restaurant & cafeteria furniture

(G-15130)
NORTON-SMITH HARDWOODS INC (PA)
Also Called: Arbor Valley Flooring
25 Morningside Ave (14779-1210)
PHONE..............................716 945-0346
Art Smith, *Co-President*
Dan Smith, *Co-President*
Dorothy Jacoby, *Office Mgr*
▼ EMP: 7
SQ FT: 18,000
SALES (est): 2MM **Privately Held**
SIC: 2426 Dimension, hardwood

(G-15131)
SALAMANCA LUMBER COMPANY INC
59 Rochester St (14779-1508)
P.O. Box 416 (14779-0416)
PHONE..............................716 945-4810
Fax: 716 945-1531
Reinier Taapken, *CEO*
Rinus Vollenberg, *Vice Pres*
Mike Gilbert, *Safety Mgr*
Susan Rockwell, *Financial Exec*
▼ EMP: 45
SQ FT: 3,000
SALES (est): 6.9MM **Privately Held**
WEB: www.salamancalumber.com
SIC: 2421 Kiln drying of lumber
PA: Leyenaar Taapken Lamaker Holding B.V.
Kamerlingh Onnesweg 7
Vianen Ut 4131
347 374-844

(G-15132)
SALAMANCA PRESS PENNY SAVER
Also Called: Salamanca Penny Saver
36 River St (14779-1495)
PHONE..............................716 945-1500
Fax: 716 945-4285
F David Radler, *President*
Kevin Burleson, *Principal*
Ernie Sage, *Sales/Mktg Mgr*
John H Satterwhite, *Treasurer*
Ellen Dougherty, *Office Mgr*
EMP: 30
SALES (est): 1.7MM **Privately Held**
SIC: 2741 2759 2711 Shopping news; publishing & printing; commercial printing; newspapers

(G-15133)
SENECA MANUFACTURING COMPANY
175 Rochester St (14779-1508)
P.O. Box 496 (14779-0496)
PHONE..............................716 945-4400
Gary Sanden, *Partner*
Travis Heron, *Partner*
Dave Sanden, *Office Mgr*
▲ EMP: 8
SQ FT: 40,000
SALES (est): 1.7MM **Privately Held**
SIC: 2111 Cigarettes

(G-15134)
SNYDER MANUFACTURING INC
Also Called: SMI
255 Rochester St Unit 1 (14779-1563)
PHONE..............................716 945-0354
James F Snyder, *President*
Cynthia Snyder, *Corp Secy*
Bob Barnes, *Mfg Staff*
John Doyle, *VP Mktg*
▲ EMP: 25 EST: 2000
SQ FT: 40,000
SALES (est): 4.7MM **Privately Held**
WEB: www.snyder-mfg.com
SIC: 3423 Hand & edge tools

(G-15135)
STRATEGIES NORTH AMERICA INC
Also Called: Ellicottville Kitchen Eqp
150 Elm St (14779-2002)
P.O. Box 1549, Ellicottville (14731-1549)
PHONE..............................716 945-6053
John Karassik, *President*
EMP: 5
SQ FT: 4,000
SALES (est): 885.7K **Privately Held**
SIC: 3589 Dishwashing machines, commercial

(G-15136)
SUN-TIMES MEDIA GROUP INC
Also Called: Salamanca Daily Reporter
36 River St (14779-1474)
P.O. Box 111 (14779-0111)
PHONE..............................716 945-1644
Kevin Burleson, *Manager*
EMP: 32
SALES (corp-wide): 304.8MM **Privately Held**
SIC: 2711 Newspapers
HQ: Sun-Times Media Group, Inc.
350 N Orleans St Fl 10
Chicago IL 60654
312 321-2299

Salem
Washington County

(G-15137)
CAROLINA EASTERN-VAIL INC
Also Called: Carol Vail
4134 State Route 22 (12865)
PHONE..............................518 854-9785
Charles Tucker, *Branch Mgr*
EMP: 25
SALES (corp-wide): 74.9MM **Privately Held**
SIC: 2875 Fertilizers, mixing only
PA: Carolina Eastern-Vail, Inc.
831 County Rte 28
Niverville NY 12130
518 784-9166

(G-15138)
MAPLELAND FARMS LLC
647 Bunker Hill Rd (12865-1716)
PHONE..............................518 854-7669
David Campbell, *President*
Terry Campbell, *Vice Pres*
EMP: 7
SALES (est): 210.5K **Privately Held**
SIC: 2087 0191 Syrups, flavoring (except drink); general farms, primarily crop

Salisbury Mills
Orange County

(G-15139)
CALLAHAN & NANNINI QUARRY INC
276 Clove Rd (12577-5224)
P.O. Box 164 (12577-0164)
PHONE..................................845 496-4323
Fax: 845 496-8910
Robert Nannini, *President*
Bob Nannini, *Vice Pres*
Jay Nannini, *Vice Pres*
Leigh Nannini, *Pub Rel Mgr*
Leslie Nannini, *Admin Sec*
EMP: 5
SQ FT: 3,600
SALES (est): 4.8MM **Privately Held**
SIC: 1459 5032 Shale (common) quarrying; stone, crushed or broken

Sanborn
Niagara County

(G-15140)
BRIDGE COMPONENTS INC
2122 Cory Dr (14132-9338)
PHONE..................................716 731-1184
Silvio G Derubeis, *Principal*
EMP: 6
SALES (est): 628.8K **Privately Held**
SIC: 3399 Primary metal products

(G-15141)
BRIDGESTONE APM COMPANY
6350 Inducon Dr E (14132-9015)
PHONE..................................419 423-9552
Duke Kawai, *Manager*
EMP: 60
SALES (corp-wide): 30.1B **Privately Held**
SIC: 3061 Automotive rubber goods (mechanical)
HQ: Bridgestone Apm Company
    2030 Production Dr
    Findlay OH 45840
    419 423-9552

(G-15142)
BRUCE PIERCE
Also Called: Core Welding
2386 Lockport Rd (14132-9011)
P.O. Box 209 (14132-0209)
PHONE..................................716 731-9310
Fax: 716 731-9310
Bruce Pierce, *Owner*
Coreen Froman, *Admin Sec*
EMP: 5
SQ FT: 4,080
SALES (est): 500K **Privately Held**
WEB: www.brucepierce.com
SIC: 3443 3599 7692 1799 Fabricated plate work (boiler shop); machine shop, jobbing & repair; welding repair; sandblasting of building exteriors

(G-15143)
BUFFALO GEAR INC
3635 Lockport Rd (14132-9704)
PHONE..................................716 731-2100
Fax: 716 731-2553
Daniel Szczygiel, *President*
Gail Nichols, *Vice Pres*
John Jerge, *Manager*
Allan Monich, *Manager*
▲ EMP: 20 EST: 1962
SQ FT: 22,000
SALES (est): 4MM **Privately Held**
WEB: www.buffalogear.com
SIC: 3566 Speed changers, drives & gears

(G-15144)
CERTIFIED FABRICATIONS INC
2127 Cory Dr (14132-9338)
PHONE..................................716 731-8123
Fax: 716 731-8123
Christopher Karnavas, *President*
EMP: 15
SQ FT: 12,000
SALES (est): 1.3MM **Privately Held**
SIC: 7692 3599 Welding repair; machine shop, jobbing & repair

(G-15145)
EDWARDS VACUUM LLC (DH)
6416 Inducon Dr W (14132-9019)
PHONE..................................800 848-9800
Matthew Taylor, *CEO*
John O'Sullivan, *Ch of Bd*
Butch Paddock, *President*
Michael Allison, *Vice Pres*
Nigel Wenden, *Vice Pres*
▲ EMP: 100
SALES (est): 166.5MM
SALES (corp-wide): 10.9B **Privately Held**
SIC: 3563 Vacuum (air extraction) systems, industrial
HQ: Edwards Limited
    Innovation Drive
    Burgess Hill W SUSSEX RH15
    144 425-3000

(G-15146)
FINGER FOOD PRODUCTS INC
6400 Inducon Dr W (14132-9019)
P.O. Box 560, Niagara Falls (14304-0560)
PHONE..................................716 297-4888
Fax: 716 297-4944
Jason Cordova, *CEO*
Darlene Valente, *Office Mgr*
EMP: 48
SQ FT: 34,000
SALES (est): 7MM **Privately Held**
WEB: www.fingerfoodproducts.com
SIC: 2038 Frozen specialties

(G-15147)
GAMBLE & GAMBLE INC (PA)
Also Called: Unit Step Company
5890 West St (14132-9245)
PHONE..................................716 731-3239
Fax: 716 731-3239
Ronald H Gamble, *President*
EMP: 4
SQ FT: 2,500
SALES (est): 1.3MM **Privately Held**
SIC: 3272 Concrete products, precast

(G-15148)
INNOVATIVE CLEANING SOLUTIONS
2990 Carney Dr (14132-9305)
PHONE..................................716 731-4408
EMP: 5
SQ FT: 1,600
SALES (est): 727.2K **Privately Held**
SIC: 3559 Mfg Misc Industry Machinery

(G-15149)
KATZ GROUP AMERICAS INC (DH)
Also Called: Katz Americas
3685 Lockport Rd (14132-9404)
PHONE..................................716 995-3059
Tammy Gorzka, *President*
Michael Elbers, *COO*
Scott Townsend, *Production*
Michael Dimartino, *CFO*
Craig Erisman, *Controller*
▲ EMP: 50
SQ FT: 70,000
SALES (est): 13.4MM
SALES (corp-wide): 783.1MM **Privately Held**
WEB: www.american-coaster.com
SIC: 2679 Paper products, converted
HQ: Katz Gmbh & Co. Kg
    Hauptstr. 2
    Weisenbach 76599
    722 464-70

(G-15150)
KINSHOFER USA INC
6420 Inducon Dr W Ste G (14132-9025)
PHONE..................................716 731-4333
Martin Francois, *General Mgr*
Francois Martin, *General Mgr*
▲ EMP: 22
SALES (est): 4.7MM
SALES (corp-wide): 4.8B **Privately Held**
SIC: 3531 Excavators: cable, clamshell, crane, derrick, dragline, etc.; cranes

HQ: Kinshofer Gmbh
    Hauptstr. 76
    Waakirchen 83666
    802 188-990

(G-15151)
MYLES TOOL COMPANY INC
6300 Inducon Corporate Dr (14132-9346)
PHONE..................................716 731-1300
Fax: 716 731-9140
Myles Barraclough, *President*
Tim Barraclough, *Vice Pres*
James Thiel, *Vice Pres*
Paul Reding, *Prdtn Mgr*
Joe Adams, *Manager*
EMP: 42 EST: 1977
SQ FT: 4,500
SALES (est): 9.9MM **Privately Held**
WEB: www.mylestool.com
SIC: 3545 3541 Machine tool accessories; machine tools, metal cutting type

(G-15152)
PRECISION PLUS VACUUM PARTS
6416 Inducon Dr W (14132-9019)
PHONE..................................716 297-2039
Joe Miller, *President*
Joseph Miller, *Superintendent*
Sarah De, *Accounts Mgr*
Micheal Willis, *Marketing Mgr*
Ron Aloisio, *Manager*
▲ EMP: 62
SQ FT: 20,000
SALES (est): 11.4MM
SALES (corp-wide): 10.9B **Privately Held**
WEB: www.precisionplus.com
SIC: 3563 Vacuum pumps, except laboratory
HQ: Edwards Vacuum Llc
    6416 Inducon Dr W
    Sanborn NY 14132
    800 848-9800

(G-15153)
PYROTEK INCORPORATED
Metaullics Systems Division
2040 Cory Dr (14132-9388)
PHONE..................................716 731-3221
Fax: 716 731-4943
George Bitler, *Principal*
Kevin Scott, *Manager*
Dave Burkholder, *Manager*
EMP: 50
SALES (corp-wide): 582MM **Privately Held**
SIC: 3624 3569 3999 Carbon & graphite products; filters; chairs, hydraulic, barber & beauty shop
PA: Pyrotek Incorporated
    705 W 1st Ave
    Spokane WA 99201
    509 926-6212

(G-15154)
SHARP PRINTING INC
3477 Lockport Rd (14132-9491)
PHONE..................................716 731-3994
Slade Sharpsteen, *President*
EMP: 7
SQ FT: 1,200
SALES (est): 715K **Privately Held**
WEB: www.sharpprinting.com
SIC: 2759 Commercial printing

(G-15155)
SHIPMAN PRINTING INDS INC
6120 Lendell Dr (14132-9455)
PHONE..................................716 504-7700
Fax: 716 731-9620
Gary E Blum, *Ch of Bd*
EMP: 5
SALES (est): 322K **Privately Held**
SIC: 2752 Commercial printing, lithographic

(G-15156)
UNITED BIOCHEMICALS LLC
6351 Inducon Dr E (14132-9016)
PHONE..................................716 731-5161
Fax: 716 731-5163
Mahmud Hashmi, *Vice Pres*
Dr Duane Mazur, *Vice Pres*
Paul Parwulski, *VP Opers*
Nicholas Bell, *Buyer*
Joanne Hussain, *Controller*

▲ EMP: 41
SALES (est): 12.5MM
SALES (corp-wide): 4.5B **Publicly Held**
SIC: 2869 Industrial organic chemicals
HQ: Vwr International, Llc
    100 W Matsonford Rd # 1
    Radnor PA 19087
    610 386-1700

(G-15157)
UNITED MATERIALS LLC
2186 Cory Dr (14132-9338)
PHONE..................................716 731-2332
Jim Pierce, *Mfg Staff*
Lean Guilinan, *Manager*
Leon Juiliani, *Manager*
Jeff Whalen, *Manager*
EMP: 22
SALES (corp-wide): 17.3MM **Privately Held**
SIC: 3273 Ready-mixed concrete
PA: United Materials, L.L.C.
    3949 Frest Pk Way Ste 400
    North Tonawanda NY 14120
    716 683-1432

(G-15158)
VOSS MANUFACTURING INC
2345 Lockport Rd (14132-9636)
PHONE..................................716 731-5062
Fax: 716 731-5868
Rita Voss Kammerer, *President*
Thomas Kammerer, *Vice Pres*
Mark Targus, *Engineer*
Ursula Voss, *Admin Sec*
◆ EMP: 73
SQ FT: 55,000
SALES (est): 24.6MM **Privately Held**
WEB: www.vossmfg.com
SIC: 3444 3599 7389 3549 Sheet metalwork; custom machinery; design, commercial & industrial; metalworking machinery

Sandy Creek
Oswego County

(G-15159)
CASTERS CUSTOM SAWING
6323 Us Route 11 (13145-2191)
PHONE..................................315 387-5104
Fax: 315 387-5104
Edith Caster, *Principal*
EMP: 7
SALES (est): 771.9K **Privately Held**
SIC: 2421 Sawmills & planing mills, general

Sangerfield
Oneida County

(G-15160)
CHAMPION HOME BUILDERS INC
951 Rte 12 S (13455)
P.O. Box 177 (13455-0177)
PHONE..................................315 841-4122
Fax: 315 841-4660
John Copeletti, *General Mgr*
Lloyd Black, *Div Sub Head*
Ed Ostrander, *Purchasing*
James Sigsbee, *Engineer*
Jack Susanburger, *Personnel*
EMP: 150
SQ FT: 115,000 **Privately Held**
WEB: www.championaz.com
SIC: 2451 Mobile homes
HQ: Champion Home Builders, Inc.
    755 W Big Beaver Rd # 1000
    Troy MI 48084
    248 614-8200

Saranac
Clinton County

(G-15161)
OPTIC SOLUTION LLC
133 Standish Rd (12981-2630)
PHONE...................518 293-4034
Darrell McGee,
Gregory Gibbons, *Administration*
EMP: 13
SALES: 675K **Privately Held**
SIC: 3652 3812 Compact laser discs, pre-recorded; aircraft flight instruments

Saranac Lake
Franklin County

(G-15162)
ADIRONDACK PUBLISHING CO INC (HQ)
Also Called: Adirondack Daily Enterprise
54 Broadway (12983-1704)
P.O. Box 318 (12983-0318)
PHONE...................518 891-2600
Fax: 518 891-2756
George Ogden Nutting, *President*
Cathy Moore, *Publisher*
Peter Crowley, *Editor*
Morgan Ryan, *Editor*
EMP: 32 **EST:** 1904
SQ FT: 5,000
SALES (est): 2.9MM
SALES (corp-wide): 627.3MM **Privately Held**
SIC: 2711 2752 Job printing & newspaper publishing combined; commercial printing, lithographic
PA: The Ogden Newspapers Inc
1500 Main St
Wheeling WV 26003
304 233-0100

(G-15163)
COMPASS PRINTING PLUS
42 Main St (12983-1708)
PHONE...................518 891-7050
John Gagnon, *Branch Mgr*
EMP: 11 **Privately Held**
SIC: 2752 Commercial printing, lithographic
PA: Compass Printing Plus
42 Main St
Saranac Lake NY 12983

(G-15164)
COMPASS PRINTING PLUS (PA)
42 Main St (12983-1708)
PHONE...................518 523-3308
Tom Connors, *Owner*
EMP: 7
SALES (est): 986K **Privately Held**
SIC: 2752 Commercial printing, lithographic

(G-15165)
GETTING THE WORD OUT INC
Also Called: ADIRONDACK EXPLORER
36 Church St Apt 106 (12983-1850)
PHONE...................518 891-9352
Dick Beamish, *President*
Richard Beamish, *Publisher*
Thomas Woodman, *Publisher*
Debra Stover, *Office Mgr*
Andreas Mowka, *Director*
EMP: 5
SALES: 843K **Privately Held**
SIC: 2721 Magazines: publishing only, not printed on site

(G-15166)
NORTHERN NEW YORK RURAL
Also Called: NORTH COUNTRY BEHAVIORAL HEALT
126 Kiwassa Rd (12983-2357)
P.O. Box 891 (12983-0891)
PHONE...................518 891-9460
Fax: 518 891-9461
Samantha Dashnaw, *Manager*
Samantha Denshaw, *Manager*
Barry Brogan, *Director*
EMP: 5
SALES: 431.7K **Privately Held**
SIC: 3999 Education aids, devices & supplies

(G-15167)
UPSTONE MATERIALS INC
909 State Route 3 (12983-5109)
PHONE...................518 891-0236
Stephane Godin, *Vice Pres*
Phil Marquis, *Plant Mgr*
Nathan Dutil, *Project Mgr*
Shawn Stedman, *Human Res Dir*
Julie King, *Human Resources*
EMP: 22
SALES (corp-wide): 77.1MM **Privately Held**
WEB: www.graymont-ab.com
SIC: 1422 Crushed & broken limestone
HQ: Upstone Materials Inc.
111 Quarry Rd
Plattsburgh NY 12901
518 561-5321

Saratoga Springs
Saratoga County

(G-15168)
09 FLSHY BLL/DSERT SUNRISE LLC
2 Smith Bridge Rd (12866-5617)
PHONE...................518 583-6638
Lindsey Heumann CPA, *Principal*
EMP: 5
SALES (est): 326.1K **Privately Held**
SIC: 3291 Hones

(G-15169)
ADIRONDACK SIGN PERFECT INC
72 Ballston Ave (12866-4427)
PHONE...................518 409-7446
Adam Wakulenko, *Managing Prtnr*
John Natale, *Principal*
Adam Wakalenko, *Principal*
EMP: 8 **EST:** 2007
SQ FT: 3,500
SALES: 740K **Privately Held**
SIC: 3993 Signs & advertising specialties

(G-15170)
ADVANTAGE PRESS INC
74 Warren St (12866-2534)
PHONE...................518 584-3405
Fax: 518 583-2763
Mark Sutton, *President*
Kimberly Sutton, *Corp Secy*
EMP: 12
SQ FT: 4,800
SALES (est): 900K **Privately Held**
WEB: www.myadvantagepress.com
SIC: 2752 Commercial printing, offset

(G-15171)
AGROCHEM INC
26 Freedom Way Saratoga Springs (12866-9075)
PHONE...................518 226-4850
Robert J Demarco, *Principal*
John Demarco, *Vice Pres*
Amiee Trader, *Manager*
EMP: 20
SQ FT: 38,000
SALES (est): 6MM **Privately Held**
WEB: www.agrocheminc.com
SIC: 2879 Agricultural chemicals

(G-15172)
BALL METAL BEVERAGE CONT CORP
Also Called: Ball Metal Beverage Cont Div
11 Adams Rd (12866-9061)
PHONE...................518 587-6030
Fax: 518 587-5272
Steve Di Loreto, *Plant Mgr*
Steven Di Lorto, *Plant Mgr*
Eileen Holzwarth, *Purch Mgr*
Andy Sharp, *Purch Agent*
Tracy Ellis, *Accounting Dir*
EMP: 225
SALES (corp-wide): 9B **Publicly Held**
SIC: 3411 Metal cans
HQ: Ball Metal Beverage Container Corp.
9300 W 108th Cir
Westminster CO 80021

(G-15173)
BIG JOHNS ADIRONDACK INC
Also Called: Big John's Beef Jerky
45 N Milton Rd (12866-6137)
PHONE...................518 587-3680
John Ponessa, *President*
EMP: 5
SALES: 60K **Privately Held**
SIC: 2013 Snack sticks, including jerky: from purchased meat

(G-15174)
C C INDUSTRIES INC
344 Burgoyne Rd (12866-5493)
PHONE...................518 581-7633
Charles Carlstrom, *President*
EMP: 13
SQ FT: 9,500
SALES: 450K **Privately Held**
SIC: 2754 Imprinting, gravure

(G-15175)
CAPITAL STONE SARATOGA LLC
4295 Route 50 (12866-2962)
PHONE...................518 226-8677
Paul Sicluna,
EMP: 6
SALES (est): 599.9K **Privately Held**
SIC: 3281 Granite, cut & shaped

(G-15176)
CAPITOL EQ 2 LLC
376 Broadway Ste 27 (12866-3115)
PHONE...................518 886-8341
Daniel Grignon,
EMP: 3
SALES: 5MM **Privately Held**
SIC: 3531 Construction machinery

(G-15177)
CHEQUEDCOM INC
513 Broadway Ste 1 (12866-6730)
PHONE...................888 412-0699
Greg Moran, *CEO*
John Tobison, *COO*
George Ehinger, *Vice Pres*
Gary Ito, *CFO*
Kevin Williams, *Security Dir*
EMP: 30
SALES (est): 3MM **Privately Held**
SIC: 7372 8742 Business oriented computer software; human resource consulting services
PA: Chequed Holdings, Llc
513 Broadway Ste 1
Saratoga Springs NY 12866
888 412-0699

(G-15178)
COLUMBIA CABINETS LLC
489 Broadway (12866-6734)
PHONE...................518 283-1700
EMP: 10
SALES (corp-wide): 1.1MM **Privately Held**
SIC: 2434 Wood kitchen cabinets
PA: Columbia Cabinets, Llc
332 E Main St
Mount Kisco NY 10549
212 972-7550

(G-15179)
ENCORE ELECTRONICS INC
4400 Route 50 (12866-2924)
PHONE...................518 584-5354
Fax: 518 584-5963
Thomas J Barrett, *General Mgr*
Brian Crowe, *COO*
Nancy Zucchino, *Vice Pres*
Rosemary Lafreniere, *Mfg Staff*
Jim Frederick, *Sales Mgr*
EMP: 25
SQ FT: 15,000
SALES (est): 5.8MM **Privately Held**
WEB: www.encore-elec.com
SIC: 3824 Mechanical & electromechanical counters & devices; electromechanical counters

(G-15180)
ESPEY MFG & ELECTRONICS CORP (PA)
233 Ballston Ave (12866-4767)
PHONE...................518 584-4100
Fax: 518 245-4421
Howard Pinsley, *Ch of Bd*
Patrick T Enright Jr, *President*
David A O'Neil, *CFO*
Katrina L Sparano,
Peggy A Murphy, *Admin Sec*
EMP: 138 **EST:** 1928
SQ FT: 151,000
SALES: 22.5MM **Publicly Held**
WEB: www.espey.com
SIC: 3679 Power supplies, all types: static

(G-15181)
FREEDOM MFG LLC
3 Duplainville Rd Apt C (12866-9074)
PHONE...................518 584-0441
Scott Mummert, *Principal*
EMP: 13
SALES (est): 1.4MM **Privately Held**
SIC: 3999 Manufacturing industries

(G-15182)
FRIENDLY FUEL INCORPORATED
54 Church St (12866-2007)
PHONE...................518 581-7036
Manjinder Grewal, *Principal*
EMP: 5
SALES (est): 491.8K **Privately Held**
SIC: 2869 Fuels

(G-15183)
GOLUB CORPORATION
3045 Route 50 (12866-2919)
PHONE...................518 583-3697
Fax: 518 583-3110
Paul R Flately, *Manager*
EMP: 99
SALES (corp-wide): 3.4B **Privately Held**
SIC: 3751 Motorcycles & related parts
PA: The Golub Corporation
461 Nott St
Schenectady NY 12308
518 355-5000

(G-15184)
GREAT AMERICAN BICYCLE LLC
41 Geyser Rd (12866-9038)
PHONE...................518 584-8100
Ben Serotta, *Mng Member*
Rick Laspesa, *IT/INT Sup*
Brendan Quirk, *IT/INT Sup*
EMP: 50
SQ FT: 15,000
SALES (est): 6.9MM **Privately Held**
WEB: www.serotta.com
SIC: 3751 5941 Bicycles & related parts; frames, motorcycle & bicycle; sporting goods & bicycle shops

(G-15185)
GREENFIELD MANUFACTURING INC
25 Freedom Way (12866-9076)
PHONE...................518 581-2368
Duane R Palmateer, *President*
Dan O'Rourke, *General Mgr*
Mary McChesney, *Bookkeeper*
▲**EMP:** 11
SQ FT: 40,000
SALES (est): 2.2MM **Privately Held**
WEB: www.greenfieldmfg.com
SIC: 2899 Acid resist for etching

(G-15186)
GUYSON CORPORATION OF USA (DH)
13 Grande Blvd (12866-9090)
PHONE...................518 587-7894
Fax: 518 587-7840
Steve Byrnes, *President*
Mark Butler, *Engineer*
Stephen M Donohue, *VP Sales*
◆**EMP:** 46
SQ FT: 78,000

SALES (est): 10.2MM
SALES (corp-wide): 26.7MM **Privately Held**
WEB: www.guyson.com
SIC: 3569 Blast cleaning equipment, dustless

(G-15187)
HAPPY SOFTWARE INC
11 Federal St (12866-4111)
PHONE.................................518 584-4668
Fax: 518 584-5388
Joseph Mastrianni, *President*
Beth Lee, *Manager*
EMP: 7 EST: 1994
SQ FT: 1,500
SALES (est): 969.9K **Privately Held**
WEB: www.happysoftware.com
SIC: 7372 Prepackaged software

(G-15188)
HUNTINGTON INGALLS INC
33 Cady Hill Blvd (12866-9047)
PHONE.................................518 884-3834
Peter Wedesky, *Branch Mgr*
Benjamin England, *Associate*
EMP: 50 **Publicly Held**
SIC: 3731 Shipbuilding & repairing
HQ: Huntington Ingalls Incorporated
4101 Washington Ave
Newport News VA 23607
757 380-2000

(G-15189)
INCENTIVATE HEALTH LLC
60 Railroad Pl Ste 101 (12866-3045)
PHONE.................................518 469-8491
J Lawrence Toole, *President*
Patricia Hasbrouck, *Co-Owner*
Robert Legrande II, *Co-Owner*
EMP: 5
SALES (est): 128.9K **Privately Held**
SIC: 7372 Application computer software

(G-15190)
INSTRUMENTAL SOFTWARE TECH
77 Van Dam St Ste 9 (12866-2056)
PHONE.................................518 602-0001
Sidney Hellman, *Branch Mgr*
Eileen Calabrese, *Info Tech Mgr*
Alexander Schnackenberg, *Software Dev*
Stefan Lisowski, *Instructor*
EMP: 7
SALES (corp-wide): 750K **Privately Held**
SIC: 7372 Prepackaged software
PA: Instrumental Software Technologies
70 Cereus Way
New Paltz NY 12561
845 256-9290

(G-15191)
JOURNAL REGISTER COMPANY
Also Called: Saratogian USA Today
20 Lake Ave (12866-2314)
PHONE.................................518 584-4242
Fax: 518 583-8014
Bob O'Leary, *General Mgr*
Charlie Krabel, *Editor*
Christopher Brown, *Traffic Mgr*
Sean Fagan, *Accounts Exec*
Jaclyn Grady, *Accounts Exec*
EMP: 80
SALES (corp-wide): 670.9MM **Privately Held**
SIC: 2711 Newspapers: publishing only, not printed on site
PA: Journal Register Company
5 Hanover Sq Fl 25
New York NY 10004
212 257-7212

(G-15192)
LYONS & SULLIVAN INC
376 Caroline St (12866-3739)
PHONE.................................518 584-1523
Charles Sullivan, *President*
EMP: 5
SALES (est): 334.5K **Privately Held**
SIC: 2421 Sawmills & planing mills, general

(G-15193)
NALCO COMPANY LLC
6 Butler Pl 2 (12866-2155)
PHONE.................................518 796-1985
Joseph Fitzhenry, *Manager*
EMP: 20
SALES (corp-wide): 13.1B **Publicly Held**
WEB: www.nalco.com
SIC: 2899 5169 Chemical preparations; chemicals & allied products
HQ: Nalco Company Llc
1601 W Diehl Rd
Naperville IL 60563
630 305-1000

(G-15194)
NANOBIONOVUM LLC
117 Grand Ave (12866-4118)
P.O. Box 4434 (12866-8026)
PHONE.................................518 581-1171
Lance Bell, *CEO*
EMP: 10
SQ FT: 5,000
SALES (est): 708.6K **Privately Held**
SIC: 3841 Diagnostic apparatus, medical

(G-15195)
OLDE SARATOGA BREWING
131 Excelsior Ave (12866-8545)
PHONE.................................518 581-0492
Colleen Clark, *Owner*
Lindsey Murray, *Manager*
Meg Thompson, *Manager*
EMP: 12
SALES (est): 1.5MM **Privately Held**
SIC: 2082 5181 Malt beverages; beer & ale

(G-15196)
PHYTOFILTER TECHNOLOGIES INC
9 Kirby Rd Apt 19 (12866-9287)
PHONE.................................518 507-6399
Martin Mittelmark, *CEO*
EMP: 5 EST: 2010
SALES (est): 400K **Privately Held**
SIC: 3564 Air purification equipment

(G-15197)
PRIME TURBINE PARTS LLC
85 Railroad Pl (12866-2124)
PHONE.................................518 306-7306
Martin Harr,
◆ EMP: 3
SALES: 2MM **Privately Held**
SIC: 3511 Turbines & turbine generator sets

(G-15198)
QUAD/GRAPHICS INC
56 Duplainville Rd (12866-9050)
PHONE.................................518 581-4000
Fax: 518 583-0810
Dave Calmes, *General Mgr*
Davida Scripter, *Buyer*
Tom Kazda, *Engineer*
John Atkinson, *Human Res Mgr*
Janette Spieldenner, *Accounts Mgr*
EMP: 900
SALES (corp-wide): 4.3B **Publicly Held**
WEB: www.qg.com
SIC: 2752 2791 2789 Commercial printing, offset; typesetting; bookbinding & related work
PA: Quad/Graphics Inc.
N61w23044 Harrys Way
Sussex WI 53089
414 566-6000

(G-15199)
RECORD
Also Called: Sunday Record, The
20 Lake Ave (12866-2314)
PHONE.................................518 270-1200
Fax: 518 270-1202
Chad Beatty, *President*
Fred Degesco, *Publisher*
Genette Brookshire, *Editor*
David Johnson, *Editor*
Linda Gunther, *Human Res Dir*
EMP: 1
SQ FT: 35,000
SALES (est): 1.6MM
SALES (corp-wide): 670.9MM **Privately Held**
WEB: www.troyrecord.com
SIC: 2711 Newspapers, publishing & printing

PA: Journal Register Company
5 Hanover Sq Fl 25
New York NY 10004
212 257-7212

(G-15200)
REDSPRING COMMUNICATIONS INC
125 High Rock Ave (12866-2307)
PHONE.................................518 587-0547
James Hill, *President*
EMP: 44
SQ FT: 10,500
SALES (est): 2.7MM **Privately Held**
WEB: www.redspring.com
SIC: 2741 Newsletter publishing; posters: publishing only, not printed on site

(G-15201)
SARATOGA CHIPS LLC
63 Putnam St Ste 202 (12866-3285)
PHONE.................................877 901-6950
James R Schneider, *President*
David Boff, *Vice Pres*
Joseph Boff, *Vice Pres*
Danny Jameson, *Vice Pres*
Joel I Bobrow, *Vice Pres*
EMP: 7
SQ FT: 1,500
SALES: 1MM **Privately Held**
SIC: 2096 Potato chips & similar snacks; popcorn, already popped (except candy covered)

(G-15202)
SARATOGA SPRING WATER COMPANY
11 Geyser Rd (12866-9038)
PHONE.................................518 584-6363
Fax: 518 584-0380
Adam Madkour, *CEO*
Steve Gilbank, *Principal*
Mark Horwitz, *Controller*
Shanon Green, *Human Res Mgr*
John Madkour, *Sales Mgr*
EMP: 22
SQ FT: 40,000
SALES (est): 6MM **Privately Held**
WEB: www.saratogaspringwater.com
SIC: 2086 Mineral water, carbonated: packaged in cans, bottles, etc.

(G-15203)
SCA TISSUE NORTH AMERICA LLC
49 Geyser Rd (12866-9038)
PHONE.................................518 583-2785
Tim Cutler, *Manager*
EMP: 219
SALES (corp-wide): 12.6B **Privately Held**
SIC: 2621 Paper mills
HQ: Sca Tissue North America, Llc
984 Winchester Rd
Neenah WI 54956
920 727-3770

(G-15204)
STRATEGIC SIGNAGE SOURCING LLC
2 Gilbert Rd (12866-9701)
PHONE.................................518 450-1093
Robert L Keyser, *President*
Kenneth W Wasson, *Vice Pres*
Amber-Lee Ranalli, *Project Mgr*
Carole Van Buren, *Project Mgr*
Suzanne K Nelson, *Marketing Staff*
EMP: 10
SALES (est): 1.2MM **Privately Held**
SIC: 3993 Signs & advertising specialties

(G-15205)
TMC USA LLC (PA)
60 Railroad Pl Ste 501 (12866-3048)
PHONE.................................518 587-8920
John Halnan,
EMP: 7
SALES (est): 4.5MM **Privately Held**
WEB: www.tmcusallc.com
SIC: 2721 Periodicals

(G-15206)
WARD LAFRANCE TRUCK CORP
26 Congress St Ste 259f (12866-4168)
PHONE.................................518 893-1865
Daniel Olszansky, *President*
EMP: 15 EST: 1978
SALES: 12.8MM **Privately Held**
SIC: 3537 Trucks: freight, baggage, etc.: industrial, except mining

Saugerties
Ulster County

(G-15207)
ADIRONDACK STAIRS INC
990 Kings Hwy (12477-4373)
P.O. Box 419 (12477-0419)
PHONE.................................845 246-2525
Fax: 845 246-3131
Karl H Neumann, *President*
Mattie Anttila, *Vice Pres*
EMP: 12 EST: 1966
SALES (est): 1.3MM **Privately Held**
SIC: 2431 Staircases & stairs, wood

(G-15208)
AMETEK TECHNICAL & INDUS PDTS
Also Called: Rotron
75 North St (12477-1039)
PHONE.................................845 246-3401
Mark Dwyer, *Plant Mgr*
Edward Hopp, *Plant Mgr*
David Cade, *Engineer*
Jeremy Roberts, *Engineer*
Stephen Woodard, *Accounts Mgr*
EMP: 26
SALES (corp-wide): 3.8B **Publicly Held**
WEB: www.rotronmilaero.com
SIC: 3564 Blowers & fans
HQ: Ametek Technical & Industrial Products, Inc
100 E Erie St Ste 130
Kent OH 44240
330 677-3754

(G-15209)
ARISTA FLAG CORPORATION
157 W Saugerties Rd (12477-3532)
P.O. Box 319 (12477-0319)
PHONE.................................845 246-7700
Fax: 845 246-7786
Stephen Suma, *President*
Susan Suma, *Corp Secy*
Rita Mary Suma, *Vice Pres*
EMP: 12
SQ FT: 5,500
SALES (est): 1.1MM **Privately Held**
WEB: www.aristaflag.com
SIC: 2399 Banners, made from fabric; flags, fabric; pennants

(G-15210)
CERES TECHNOLOGIES INC
5 Tower Dr (12477-4386)
P.O. Box 209 (12477-0209)
PHONE.................................845 247-4701
Fax: 845 247-4707
Kevin Brady, *President*
Sharon Burton, *General Mgr*
Petra Klein, *Vice Pres*
Kira Cozzolino, *Project Mgr*
Terry Brady, *Opers Mgr*
EMP: 70
SQ FT: 50,000
SALES: 21.1MM **Privately Held**
SIC: 3674 3823 3826 Semiconductors & related devices; industrial instrmnts msrmnt display/control process variable; analytical instruments

(G-15211)
CVD EQUIPMENT CORPORATION
1117 Kings Hwy (12477-4343)
PHONE.................................845 246-3631
Kevin Collions, *Manager*
EMP: 20
SALES (corp-wide): 20.9MM **Publicly Held**
WEB: www.cvdequipment.com
SIC: 3559 Sewing machines & hat & zipper making machinery
PA: Cvd Equipment Corporation
355 S Technology Dr
Central Islip NY 11722
631 981-7081

Saugerties - Ulster County (G-15212)

(G-15212)
DE LUXE PACKAGING CORP
63 North St (12477-1039)
PHONE..............................416 754-4633
Richard Goulet, *President*
Paul Fischer, *Plant Supt*
EMP: 50 **EST:** 2003
SALES (est): 7.7MM
SALES (corp-wide): 2.6B **Privately Held**
SIC: 2671 3497 Packaging paper & plastics film, coated & laminated; paper coated or laminated for packaging; plastic film, coated or laminated for packaging; waxed paper; made from purchased material; foil containers for bakery goods & frozen foods
HQ: Packaging Dynamics Corporation
3900 W 43rd St
Chicago IL 60632
773 254-8000

(G-15213)
DELUXE PACKAGING CORP
63 North St (12477-1039)
P.O. Box 269 (12477-0269)
PHONE..............................845 246-6090
Fax: 845 246-0511
Jim Tarrant, *Sales Staff*
Franco Petronio, *Sales Executive*
Richard Goulet, *Branch Mgr*
Paul Fischer, *Manager*
Lisa Gardner, *Relations*
EMP: 19
SQ FT: 32,740
SALES (corp-wide): 16.5MM **Privately Held**
WEB: www.deluxepack.com
SIC: 2676 Toilet paper; made from purchased paper
PA: De Luxe Paper Products Inc
120 Nugget Ave
Scarborough ON M1S 3
416 291-0598

(G-15214)
INQUIRING MINDS INC (PA)
65 S Partition St (12477-1413)
PHONE..............................845 246-5775
Bryan Donahue, *President*
EMP: 10 **EST:** 2012
SALES (est): 1MM **Privately Held**
SIC: 3421 Table & food cutlery, including butchers'

(G-15215)
KENBENCO INC
Also Called: Benson Steel Fabricators
437 Route 212 (12477-4620)
P.O. Box 480 (12477-0480)
PHONE..............................845 246-3066
Myron E Benson, *Owner*
Jeniffer Benson, *Manager*
EMP: 15
SQ FT: 12,000
SALES (est): 3.1MM **Privately Held**
WEB: www.bensonsteelfabricators.com
SIC: 3312 3431 Blast furnaces & steel mills; metal sanitary ware

(G-15216)
LODOLCE MACHINE CO INC
196 Malden Tpke (12477-5015)
PHONE..............................845 246-7017
Michael Lodolce, *President*
Dennis Barringer, *Engineer*
Robin Charlton, *Office Mgr*
Joseph Fisco, *Manager*
▲ **EMP:** 38 **EST:** 1963
SQ FT: 65,000
SALES (est): 8.1MM **Privately Held**
WEB: www.lodolce.com
SIC: 3599 1761 3479 Machine shop, jobbing & repair; sheet metalwork; painting, coating & hot dipping

(G-15217)
MORGAN FUEL & HEATING CO INC
240 Ulster Ave (12477-1221)
PHONE..............................845 246-4931
EMP: 26
SALES (corp-wide): 48MM **Privately Held**
SIC: 2869 Fuels

PA: Morgan Fuel & Heating Co., Inc.
2785 W Main St
Wappingers Falls NY 12590
845 297-5580

(G-15218)
NORTHEAST SOLITE CORPORATION (PA)
1135 Kings Hwy (12477-4343)
P.O. Box 437, Mount Marion (12456-0437)
PHONE..............................845 246-2646
Fax: 845 246-3356
John W Roberts, *Ch of Bd*
Philip M Nesmith, *President*
Jessica Eng, *Senior VP*
James Gregory, *Vice Pres*
Bruce Jones, *Vice Pres*
EMP: 40
SALES (est): 16.2MM **Privately Held**
WEB: www.nesolite.com
SIC: 3295 Minerals, ground or treated

(G-15219)
PAPER HOUSE PRODUCTIONS INC
160 Malden Tpke Bldg 2 (12477-5015)
P.O. Box 259 (12477-0259)
PHONE..............................845 246-7261
Donald A Guidi, *CEO*
Pam Gardeski, *Vice Pres*
Linda Vansteenburg, *CFO*
Pam Gardski, *Financial Exec*
Sarah Ardila, *VP Sales*
▲ **EMP:** 25
SQ FT: 16,000
SALES: 3.7MM **Privately Held**
WEB: www.paperhouseproductions.com
SIC: 2771 2752 5112 5945 Greeting cards; decals, lithographed; greeting cards; hobby & craft supplies

(G-15220)
PESCES BAKERY INC
Also Called: Pesce Bakery
20 Pesce Ct (12477-5054)
PHONE..............................845 246-4730
Richard Pesce, *President*
Rich Pesce, *President*
EMP: 6 **EST:** 1946
SQ FT: 3,000
SALES (est): 626.8K **Privately Held**
SIC: 2051 5461 Bakery: wholesale or wholesale/retail combined; bakeries

(G-15221)
PETE LEVIN MUSIC INC
598 Schoolhouse Rd (12477-3325)
PHONE..............................845 247-9211
Peter Levin, *President*
Theresa Levin, *Vice Pres*
EMP: 5
WEB: www.petelevin.com
SIC: 3652 Pre-recorded records & tapes

(G-15222)
ROTHE WELDING INC
1455 Route 212 (12477-3040)
PHONE..............................845 246-3051
Fax: 845 246-6351
Dorothy L Fauci, *Chairman*
Raymond Scally, *Corp Secy*
EMP: 8
SQ FT: 11,500
SALES (est): 1.8MM **Privately Held**
WEB: www.hvaccess.com
SIC: 3441 7692 Fabricated structural metal; welding repair

(G-15223)
SIMULAIDS INC
16 Simulaids Dr (12477-5067)
P.O. Box 1289 (12477-8289)
PHONE..............................845 679-2475
Dean T Johnson, *CEO*
J Boyce, *Vice Pres*
Jack McNeff, *Vice Pres*
Gus Hof, *Plant Mgr*
Patricia Stockman, *Human Res Mgr*
EMP: 93 **EST:** 1963
SQ FT: 50,000

SALES (est): 18.1MM
SALES (corp-wide): 317.3MM **Privately Held**
WEB: www.simulaids.com
SIC: 3841 7841 3699 Surgical & medical instruments; video tape rental; electrical equipment & supplies
HQ: Nasco Healthcare Inc.
901 Janesville Ave
Fort Atkinson WI 53538
920 568-5600

(G-15224)
STAINLESS DESIGN CONCEPTS LTD
Also Called: SDC
1117 Kings Hwy (12477-4343)
P.O. Box 514, Smithtown (11787-0514)
PHONE..............................845 246-3631
Fax: 845 246-1595
Len Rosenbaum, *Ch of Bd*
Kevin Collins, *General Mgr*
Bill Iacobellis, *Purch Mgr*
Glen Charles, *CFO*
Mary Sauer, *Human Res Mgr*
EMP: 35 **EST:** 1986
SQ FT: 25,000
SALES (est): 7.2MM
SALES (corp-wide): 20.9MM **Publicly Held**
WEB: www.stainlessdesign.com
SIC: 3559 Chemical machinery & equipment
PA: Cvd Equipment Corporation
355 S Technology Dr
Central Islip NY 11722
631 981-7081

(G-15225)
STUART SPECTOR DESIGNS LTD
1450 Route 212 (12477-3028)
PHONE..............................845 246-6124
Fax: 845 246-0833
Stuart Spector, *President*
Darryl Ford, *General Mgr*
▲ **EMP:** 9
SQ FT: 4,500
SALES: 850K **Privately Held**
WEB: www.ssdbass.com
SIC: 3931 Guitars & parts, electric & non-electric

(G-15226)
THE SMOKE HOUSE OF CATSKILLS
724 Route 212 (12477-4617)
PHONE..............................845 246-8767
Charles Rothe, *President*
EMP: 7 **EST:** 1952
SQ FT: 2,400
SALES (est): 242K **Privately Held**
SIC: 2011 5421 Meat packing plants; meat markets, including freezer provisioners

(G-15227)
WORKING FAMILY SOLUTIONS INC
359 Washington Avenue Ext (12477-5221)
P.O. Box 88, Malden On Hudson (12453-0088)
PHONE..............................845 802-6182
Danielle N Heller, *CEO*
EMP: 5
SALES (est): 360.9K **Privately Held**
SIC: 2835 Pregnancy test kits

Sauquoit
Oneida County

(G-15228)
CUSTOM STAIR & MILLWORK CO
Also Called: Kitchen Design Center
6 Gridley Pl (13456-3416)
PHONE..............................315 839-5793
John Dweyer, *President*
EMP: 9
SQ FT: 10,000
SALES (est): 750K **Privately Held**
SIC: 2431 Millwork; staircases & stairs, wood

(G-15229)
LEATHERSTOCKING MOBILE HOME PA
2089 Doolittle Rd (13456-2409)
PHONE..............................315 839-5691
Jane W Brennan, *Ch of Bd*
EMP: 5
SALES (est): 613.7K **Privately Held**
SIC: 2451 Mobile homes

(G-15230)
PARKS PAVING & SEALING INC
Also Called: Parks TRUcking&paving
3220 Valley Pl (13456-2808)
P.O. Box 508 (13456-0508)
PHONE..............................315 737-5761
Tadd Aparks, *President*
Marietha Parks, *Office Mgr*
EMP: 11
SALES (est): 900K **Privately Held**
SIC: 2951 Asphalt & asphaltic paving mixtures (not from refineries)

Savannah
Wayne County

(G-15231)
PEARL TECHNOLOGIES INC
13297 Seneca St (13146-9663)
P.O. Box 196 (13146-0196)
PHONE..............................315 365-2632
Fax: 315 365-3433
Robert Tewksbury, *President*
Linda Gillette, *VP Opers*
Bill Gillette, *Mfg Mgr*
Gary Stover, *Purch Agent*
Andrew Prudhomme, *Engineer*
EMP: 35
SQ FT: 35,000
SALES (est): 8.2MM **Privately Held**
SIC: 3559 Plastics working machinery
HQ: Gloucester Engineering Co., Inc.
11 Dory Rd
Gloucester MA 01930
978 281-1800

Sayville
Suffolk County

(G-15232)
AQUARIUM PUMP & PIPING SYSTEMS
528 Chester Rd (11782-1808)
PHONE..............................631 567-5555
Fax: 631 589-0154
Charles Eckstein, *Owner*
Virginia Eckstein, *Finance Other*
EMP: 11
SQ FT: 2,500
SALES (est): 619.4K **Privately Held**
SIC: 3499 3089 Aquarium accessories, metal; aquarium accessories, plastic

(G-15233)
BRAINWORKS SOFTWARE DEV CORP (PA)
100 S Main St Ste 102 (11782-3148)
PHONE..............................631 563-5000
John Barry, *President*
Richard Kitzmiller, *General Mgr*
Elly Barry, *Office Mgr*
EMP: 9
SQ FT: 4,000
SALES (est): 9.7MM **Privately Held**
SIC: 7372 Publishers' computer software

(G-15234)
BUNGERS SURF SHOP
Also Called: Bunger Sayville
247 W Main St (11782-2522)
PHONE..............................631 244-3646
Sammy Hito, *Principal*
EMP: 8 **EST:** 2012
SALES (est): 481.4K **Privately Held**
SIC: 3949 Surfboards; water sports equipment

(G-15235)
CNA SPECIALTIES INC
226 Mcneil St (11782-2249)
PHONE..................631 567-7929
Carolyn Ward, *CEO*
EMP: 5
SALES (est) 537.6K **Privately Held**
SIC: 2541 3431 5046 Cabinets, lockers & shelving; shower stalls, metal; partitions

(G-15236)
ESC CONTROL ELECTRONICS LLC
Also Called: Control Elec Div Fil-Coil
98 Lincoln Ave (11782-2711)
PHONE..................631 467-5328
Syed Zaidi, *Accountant*
Paul Alessandrini,
▲ **EMP:** 35
SQ FT: 2,000
SALES (est) 4.8MM **Privately Held**
SIC: 3677 3679 3841 3851 Electronic transformers; filtration devices, electronic; delay lines; surgical & medical instruments; ophthalmic goods
PA: Fil-Coil (Fc) Corp.
98 Lincoln Ave
Sayville NY 11782

(G-15237)
FIL-COIL (FC) CORP (PA)
Also Called: Custom Power System
98 Lincoln Ave (11782-2711)
PHONE..................631 467-5328
Carrol Trust, *CEO*
Paul Alessandrini Sr, *Ch of Bd*
Batt Trust, *Vice Pres*
Dan Barnett Jr, *Director*
▲ **EMP:** 25
SQ FT: 6,000
SALES (est) 4.8MM **Privately Held**
SIC: 3677 Filtration devices, electronic

(G-15238)
FIL-COIL INTERNATIONAL LLC
98 Lincoln Ave (11782-2711)
PHONE..................631 467-5328
Laura Ritter, *Vice Chairman*
EMP: 14
SQ FT: 1,500
SALES (est) 527.2K **Privately Held**
SIC: 3677 Transformers power supply, electronic type

(G-15239)
FIRE ISLAND TIDE PUBLICATION
Also Called: Fire Island Tide The
40 Main St (11782-2552)
P.O. Box 70 (11782-0070)
PHONE..................631 567-7470
Fax: 631 567-1271
Patricia E King, *President*
Warren McDowell, *Publisher*
John Lee, *Editor*
EMP: 12
SALES 500K **Privately Held**
SIC: 2711 7313 Newspapers; newspaper advertising representative

(G-15240)
KKW CORP
Also Called: Koster Keunen Waxes
90 Bourne Blvd (11782-3307)
PHONE..................631 589-5454
Richard B Koster, *Ch of Bd*
▲ **EMP:** 40
SQ FT: 60,000
SALES (est) 6.8MM **Privately Held**
WEB: www.paramold.com
SIC: 3999 Candles

(G-15241)
KOSTER KEUNEN WAXES LTD
90 Bourne Blvd (11782-3307)
PHONE..................631 589-0400
Fax: 631 589-1232
Richard Koster, *President*
Kathryn Koster, *QC Dir*
James Bullwinkle, *Plant Engr*
Randolph Bruckner, *CFO*
Joanne Whitney, *Bookkeeper*
▲ **EMP:** 15
SQ FT: 45,000
SALES (est): 2MM **Privately Held**
SIC: 2911 Mineral waxes, natural

(G-15242)
OPTIKA EYES LTD
153 Main St Unit 1 (11782-2566)
PHONE..................631 567-8852
Nancy Pacella, *President*
EMP: 8
SQ FT: 1,000
SALES (est) 610K **Privately Held**
SIC: 3851 5995 Frames, lenses & parts, eyeglass & spectacle; contact lenses; optical goods stores

(G-15243)
REDDI CAR CORP
174 Greeley Ave (11782-2396)
PHONE..................631 589-3141
Kenneth Johnson, *President*
EMP: 7 **EST:** 1957
SQ FT: 5,000
SALES (est) 538K **Privately Held**
SIC: 2851 2899 5085 Paints & paint additives; chemical preparations; fasteners, industrial: nuts, bolts, screws, etc.

(G-15244)
WEEKS & REICHEL PRINTING INC
131 Railroad Ave (11782-2799)
PHONE..................631 589-1443
Fax: 631 589-2723
John A Weeks, *President*
Robert Reichel, *Corp Secy*
EMP: 5
SQ FT: 2,400
SALES (est) 537.1K **Privately Held**
SIC: 2759 2752 Letterpress printing; commercial printing, offset

---

Scarsdale
Westchester County

(G-15245)
AMERICAN EPOXY AND METAL INC
83 Cushman Rd (10583-3403)
PHONE..................718 828-7828
Samer Daniel, *President*
Ralph Maccarino, *Vice Pres*
EMP: 8
SALES (est): 996.7K **Privately Held**
WEB: www.americanepoxy.com
SIC: 2821 2511 Epoxy resins; whatnot shelves: wood; tables, household: wood

(G-15246)
CRANIAL TECHNOLOGIES INC
495 Central Park Ave (10583-1068)
PHONE..................914 472-0975
Tammy Jones, *Manager*
EMP: 10 **Privately Held**
SIC: 3842 Orthopedic appliances
PA: Cranial Technologies, Inc.
1395 W Auto Dr
Tempe AZ 85284

(G-15247)
GOTHAM CITY INDUSTRIES INC
372 Fort Hill Rd (10583-2411)
PHONE..................914 713-0979
Barbara Chalton, *Ch of Bd*
Jay Chalson, *Vice Pres*
Todd Petre, *Vice Pres*
Lucia Silva, *Office Mgr*
Roger Nafziger, *Director*
▲ **EMP:** 20
SQ FT: 17,000
SALES (est): 3.4MM **Privately Held**
WEB: www.gothamind.com
SIC: 2541 Wood partitions & fixtures

(G-15248)
JAPAN AMERICA LEARNING CTR INC (PA)
Also Called: Enjoy
81 Montgomery Ave (10583-5104)
P.O. Box 606, Hartsdale (10530-0606)
PHONE..................914 723-7600
Fax: 914 723-1515
Kazuko Maeda, *President*
EMP: 10
SQ FT: 2,000
SALES: 300K **Privately Held**
SIC: 2721 8299 Trade journals: publishing only, not printed on site; language school

(G-15249)
LAND PACKAGING CORP
7 Black Birch Ln (10583-7456)
PHONE..................914 472-5976
Lawrence Rosefeld, *President*
Lawrence Rosenfeld, *President*
EMP: 10
SQ FT: 3,000
SALES: 5MM **Privately Held**
SIC: 2653 Corrugated boxes, partitions, display items, sheets & pad

(G-15250)
NATHAN PRINTING EXPRESS INC
740 Central Park Ave (10583-2504)
PHONE..................914 472-0914
Fax: 914 472-5398
Nathan Wong, *President*
Neil Moreton, *Vice Pres*
Alex Wong, *Vice Pres*
EMP: 7
SQ FT: 1,600
SALES (est): 871.5K **Privately Held**
SIC: 2759 Commercial printing

(G-15251)
PERFORMANCE SOURCING GROUP INC
109 Montgomery Ave (10583-5531)
PHONE..................914 636-2100
S Shwartz, *President*
Sanjay Tillu, *CFO*
EMP: 40
SALES: 35MM **Privately Held**
SIC: 2392 Household furnishings

(G-15252)
PLAIN DIGITAL INC
235 Garth Rd Apt D6a (10583-3949)
PHONE..................914 310-0280
Stuart Pekowsky, *President*
EMP: 6 **EST:** 1999
SALES: 250K **Privately Held**
SIC: 7372 7389 Prepackaged software;

(G-15253)
S I COMMUNICATIONS INC
Also Called: Scarsdale Inquirer
8 Harwood Ct (10583-4104)
P.O. Box 418 (10583-0418)
PHONE..................914 725-2500
Fax: 914 725-1552
Deborah White, *President*
Eileen Farrell, *Director*
EMP: 13
SALES (est): 1MM **Privately Held**
WEB: www.scarsdaleinquirer.com
SIC: 2711 Newspapers: publishing only, not printed on site

(G-15254)
SHERIDAN HOUSE INC
230 Nelson Rd (10583-5908)
PHONE..................914 725-5431
Fax: 914 693-0776
Lothar Simon, *President*
Jeannine Simon, *Vice Pres*
▲ **EMP:** 5
SQ FT: 4,000
SALES (est): 709.7K **Privately Held**
WEB: www.sheridanhouse.com
SIC: 2731 Book publishing

(G-15255)
ZANZANO WOODWORKING INC
91 Locust Ave (10583-6230)
PHONE..................914 725-6025
Michael Zanzano, *Principal*
EMP: 13
SALES (est): 1.6MM **Privately Held**
SIC: 2431 Millwork

Schenectady
Schenectady County

(G-15256)
A W HAMEL STAIR MFG INC
3111 Amsterdam Rd (12302-6328)
PHONE..................518 346-3031
Fax: 518 346-3523
Joseph Lucarelli, *President*
Donald Lucarelli, *Vice Pres*
Scott Ressel, *Manager*
EMP: 16
SQ FT: 30,000
SALES (est): 1.3MM **Privately Held**
SIC: 2431 Staircases & stairs, wood; stair railings, wood

(G-15257)
ALSTOM SIGNALING INC (DH)
Also Called: Alstrom Trnspt Info Solutions
1 River Rd (12345-6000)
PHONE..................585 783-2000
Fax: 585 783-2009
Ulisses Camillo, *CEO*
Ellen Oneill, *President*
Jamie Van Scoter, *General Mgr*
William Wilson, *Managing Dir*
Gian-Luca Erbacci, *Vice Pres*
▲ **EMP:** 270
SALES (est): 77.6MM
SALES (corp-wide): 123.6B **Publicly Held**
WEB: www.alstomsignalingsolutions.com
SIC: 3669 Railroad signaling devices, electric; signaling apparatus, electric

(G-15258)
ALSTOM SIGNALING INC
1 River Rd (12345-6000)
PHONE..................585 274-8700
John Desmond, *Opers Mgr*
Ken Witt, *Electrical Engi*
Lisa Critchly, *Human Res Mgr*
Ian Desousa, *Manager*
EMP: 50
SALES (corp-wide): 123.6B **Publicly Held**
WEB: www.alstomsignalingsolutions.com
SIC: 3669 3743 3643 Railroad signaling devices, electric; signaling apparatus, electric; railroad equipment; current-carrying wiring devices
HQ: Alstom Signaling Inc.
1 River Rd
Schenectady NY 12345
585 783-2000

(G-15259)
AMERICAN HSPTALS PATIENT GUIDE
1890 Maxon Rd Ext (12308-1140)
P.O. Box 1031 (12301-1031)
PHONE..................518 346-1099
Fax: 518 346-1461
Robert J Kosineski Sr, *President*
EMP: 10
SALES (est): 630K **Privately Held**
SIC: 2741 Miscellaneous publishing

(G-15260)
AUTERRA INC
2135 Technology Dr (12308-1143)
PHONE..................518 382-9600
Eric Burnett, *President*
Steven T Jackson, *Vice Pres*
EMP: 9 **EST:** 2006
SALES (est): 2MM **Privately Held**
SIC: 2819 Industrial inorganic chemicals

(G-15261)
AXLE EXPRESS
729 Broadway (12305-2703)
PHONE..................518 347-2220
Samuel Caldarazzo, *President*
EMP: 25
SALES (est): 2.2MM **Privately Held**
SIC: 3714 Motor vehicle parts & accessories

Schenectady - Schenectady County (G-15262) — GEOGRAPHIC SECTION

(G-15262)
BENCHEMARK PRINTING INC
1890 Maxon Rd Ext (12308-1149)
P.O. Box 1031 (12301-1031)
PHONE..................................518 393-1361
Fax: 518 372-1336
Robert Kosineski, *President*
Denise Hecker, *Human Resources*
Joe Prock, *Accounts Exec*
Betsy Saltsman, *Accounts Exec*
Doug Fiorillo, *Sales Staff*
▲ EMP: 55
SQ FT: 75,000
SALES (est): 14MM **Privately Held**
SIC: 2752 2791 2789 2759 Commercial printing, lithographic; typesetting; bookbinding & related work; commercial printing

(G-15263)
BESTLINE INTERNATIONAL RES INC
224 State St (12305-1806)
PHONE..................................518 631-2177
John Polster, *Principal*
EMP: 8
SALES (est): 1.1MM **Privately Held**
SIC: 2992 Lubricating oils & greases

(G-15264)
CALLANAN INDUSTRIES INC
145 Cordell Rd (12303-2701)
P.O. Box 40, Selkirk (12158-0040)
PHONE..................................518 382-5354
Joe Decelle, *Branch Mgr*
EMP: 8
SALES (corp-wide): 28.6B **Privately Held**
SIC: 3999 Barber & beauty shop equipment
HQ: Callanan Industries, Inc.
8 Southwoods Blvd Ste 4
Albany NY 12211
518 374-2222

(G-15265)
CAPITAL DST PRINT & IMAGING
Also Called: Allegra Print & Imaging
2075 Central Ave (12304-4426)
PHONE..................................518 456-6773
Jim Cazavilan, *President*
EMP: 7
SQ FT: 2,500
SALES (est): 1MM **Privately Held**
WEB: www.allegraalbany.com
SIC: 2752 7334 Commercial printing, offset; photocopying & duplicating services

(G-15266)
CAPITAL STONE LLC
2241 Central Ave (12304-4379)
PHONE..................................518 382-7588
James Nass, *President*
Caron Beggan, *General Mgr*
Carmine Petti, *Manager*
Paul Sicluna, *Manager*
EMP: 9
SQ FT: 5,000
SALES: 1MM **Privately Held**
SIC: 3281 Granite, cut & shaped

(G-15267)
CASCADE TECHNICAL SERVICES LLC
2846 Curry Rd Ste B (12303-3463)
PHONE..................................518 355-2201
Matthew Ednie, *Manager*
EMP: 5
SALES (corp-wide): 399.2MM **Privately Held**
WEB: www.teamzebra.com
SIC: 3822 Auto controls regulating residntl & coml environmt & applncs
HQ: Cascade Technical Services Llc
30 N Prospect Ave
Lynbrook NY 11563
516 596-6300

(G-15268)
CASCADES NEW YORK INC
801 Corporation Park (12302-1061)
PHONE..................................518 346-6151
Marc Andre Depin, *President*
EMP: 150
SALES (corp-wide): 2.9B **Privately Held**
SIC: 2653 Corrugated & solid fiber boxes
HQ: Cascades New York Inc.
1845 Emerson St
Rochester NY 14606
585 527-8110

(G-15269)
CDS PRODUCTIONS INC
108 Erie Blvd Ste 400 (12305-2223)
PHONE..................................518 385-8255
Fax: 518 385-8290
Anthony Casapullo, *President*
James Fuller, *Vice Pres*
EMP: 16
SQ FT: 15,000
SALES: 937.7K **Privately Held**
SIC: 2752 2791 7334 Commercial printing, lithographic; typesetting; computer controlled; photocopying & duplicating services

(G-15270)
CHURCH & DWIGHT CO INC
Also Called: Arm & Hammer
706 Ennis Rd (12306-7420)
PHONE..................................518 887-5109
Douglas Waddell, *Branch Mgr*
EMP: 12
SALES (corp-wide): 3.4B **Publicly Held**
WEB: www.churchdwight.com
SIC: 2812 Sodium bicarbonate
PA: Church & Dwight Co., Inc.
500 Charles Ewing Blvd
Ewing NJ 08628
609 806-1200

(G-15271)
CLEMENTE LATHAM CONCRETE CORP
Also Called: Clemente Latham North Div
1245 Kings Rd (12303-2831)
P.O. Box 15097, Albany (12212-5097)
PHONE..................................518 374-2222
Frank A Clemente, *Ch of Bd*
EMP: 100 EST: 1993
SALES (est): 14.1MM
SALES (corp-wide): 28.6B **Privately Held**
SIC: 3273 5032 Ready-mixed concrete; brick, stone & related material
HQ: Oldcastle Materials, Inc.
900 Ashwood Pkwy Ste 700
Atlanta GA 30338

(G-15272)
CODINOS LIMITED INC
704 Corporation Park # 5 (12302-1091)
PHONE..................................518 372-3308
Scott Devantier, *President*
Glen Brown, *Plant Mgr*
Rita Vose, *Shareholder*
EMP: 33
SQ FT: 33,000
SALES (corp-wide): 6.1MM **Privately Held**
SIC: 2038 Frozen specialties

(G-15273)
CON REL AUTO ELECTRIC INC
3637 Carman Rd (12303-5401)
PHONE..................................518 356-1646
Fax: 518 356-9080
Kevin Relyea, *President*
Michael Relyea, *Corp Secy*
David O'Connell, *Vice Pres*
Gloria Mc Cue, *Financial Exec*
Gloria McCue, *Office Mgr*
EMP: 35
SQ FT: 9,000
SALES: 3.9MM **Privately Held**
SIC: 3621 3694 3625 Starters, for motors; alternators, automotive; relays & industrial controls

(G-15274)
DAILY GAZETTE COMPANY (PA)
2345 Maxon Rd Ext (12308-1150)
P.O. Box 1090 (12301-1090)
PHONE..................................518 374-4141
Fax: 518 395-3089
John Hume, *President*
Tom Boggie, *Editor*
Steven Yansak, *District Mgr*
Elizabeth Lind, *Vice Pres*
Ernest Grandy, *Treasurer*
EMP: 325 EST: 1894
SQ FT: 111,000
SALES (est): 79.1MM **Privately Held**
WEB: www.dailygazette.com
SIC: 2711 Newspapers, publishing & printing

(G-15275)
DAILY GAZETTE COMPANY
2345 Maxon Rd Ext (12308-1150)
P.O. Box 1090 (12301-1090)
PHONE..................................518 395-3060
Lance Geda, *VP Finance*
Richard Dwyer, *Branch Mgr*
Steve Amedio, *Manager*
Lee Brill, *Manager*
Victoria Spagnoli, *Manager*
EMP: 110
SALES (corp-wide): 79.1MM **Privately Held**
SIC: 2711 Newspapers, publishing & printing
PA: Daily Gazette Company
2345 Maxon Rd Ext
Schenectady NY 12308
518 374-4141

(G-15276)
DSM NUTRITIONAL PRODUCTS LLC
2105 Technology Dr (12308-1143)
PHONE..................................518 372-5155
EMP: 152
SALES (corp-wide): 8.3B **Privately Held**
SIC: 2834 3295 2087 Vitamin, nutrient & hematinic preparations for human use; vitamin preparations; minerals, ground or treated; flavoring extracts & syrups
HQ: Dsm Nutritional Products, Llc
45 Waterview Blvd
Parsippany NJ 07054
800 526-0189

(G-15277)
ENER-G-ROTORS INC
17 Fern Ave (12306-2708)
PHONE..................................518 372-2608
Michael Newell, *Ch of Bd*
Edward Zampella III, *President*
EMP: 5
SALES (est): 946K **Privately Held**
SIC: 3621 7694 5084 5063 Motors & generators; armature rewinding shops; hydraulic systems equipment & supplies; electrical apparatus & equipment

(G-15278)
ENERGY PANEL STRUCTURES INC
Also Called: Fingerlakes Construction
864 Burdeck St (12306-1218)
PHONE..................................518 355-6708
Kirt Burghdorf, *Vice Pres*
EMP: 7
SALES (corp-wide): 700K **Privately Held**
SIC: 3448 2452 Prefabricated metal buildings; prefabricated wood buildings
HQ: Energy Panel Structures, Inc.
603 N Van Gordon Ave
Graettinger IA 51342
712 859-3219

(G-15279)
ENVIRONMENT-ONE CORPORATION
Also Called: E/One Utility Systems
2773 Balltown Rd (12309-1090)
PHONE..................................518 346-6161
Fax: 518 346-6188
Eric Lacoppola, *President*
Irwin Hyman, *Exec VP*
David M Doin, *Vice Pres*
Mark Stasko, *Vice Pres*
Tony Sims, *Mfg Dir*
▲ EMP: 135
SQ FT: 78,000
SALES (est): 48.3MM
SALES (corp-wide): 223.6B **Publicly Held**
WEB: www.eone.com
SIC: 3589 3824 Sewage treatment equipment; mechanical & electromechanical counters & devices
HQ: Precision Castparts Corp.
4650 Sw Mcdam Ave Ste 300
Portland OR 97239
503 946-4800

(G-15280)
EPICOR SOFTWARE CORPORATION
Docstar
2165 Technology Dr (12308-1143)
PHONE..................................805 496-6789
Ray Emirzian, *VP Opers*
Phil Meredith, *Sales Engr*
Suren Pai, *Branch Mgr*
Mark Sanges, *Manager*
Tim Bishop, *Director*
EMP: 45 **Publicly Held**
SIC: 7372 Application computer software
HQ: Epicor Software Corporation
804 Las Cimas Pkwy
Austin TX 78746

(G-15281)
F CAPPIELLO DAIRY PDTS INC
115 Van Guysling Ave (12305-2708)
PHONE..................................518 374-5064
Fax: 518 374-4015
Peter Cappiello, *President*
Ken Lakich, *General Mgr*
Brian Carr, *Manager*
EMP: 40
SALES (est): 5.3MM **Privately Held**
WEB: www.cappiello.com
SIC: 2022 Cheese, natural & processed

(G-15282)
GE TRANSPORTATION ENG SYSTEMS
Also Called: GE Transportation Energy
1 River Rd Bldg 2-333d (12345-6000)
PHONE..................................518 258-9276
EMP: 8
SALES (corp-wide): 123.6B **Publicly Held**
SIC: 3511 Turbines & turbine generator sets
HQ: Ge Transportation Engine Systems Company
6 Northway Ln
Latham NY

(G-15283)
GENERAL ELECTRIC COMPANY
1 River Rd Bldg 55 (12305-2551)
PHONE..................................518 385-4022
Teddy Schiopu, *Buyer*
Andrew Crapo, *Engineer*
Brian Fahrenkopf, *Engineer*
Cynthia O'Connor, *Marketing Staff*
Teal Reeves, *Program Mgr*
EMP: 603
SQ FT: 23,808
SALES (corp-wide): 123.6B **Publicly Held**
SIC: 3724 3511 3612 3641 Aircraft engines & engine parts; research & development on aircraft engines & parts; steam turbines; gas turbines, mechanical drive; autotransformers, electric (power transformers); electric lamps & parts for generalized applications; electric light bulbs, complete; lamps, incandescent filament, electric; lamps, fluorescent, electric; refrigerators, mechanical & absorption: household; freezers, home & farm; television broadcasting stations
PA: General Electric Company
41 Farnsworth St
Boston MA 02210
617 443-3000

(G-15284)
GENERAL ELECTRIC COMPANY
1 River Rd Bldg 33 (12305-2551)
PHONE..................................518 385-2211
John G Rice, *Branch Mgr*
EMP: 500
SALES (corp-wide): 123.6B **Publicly Held**
SIC: 3511 Turbines & turbine generator sets
PA: General Electric Company
41 Farnsworth St
Boston MA 02210
617 443-3000

(G-15285)
GENERAL ELECTRIC COMPANY
1 River Rd Bldg 43 (12345-6000)
PHONE..................................203 373-2756

Steve Bolze, *President*
EMP: 458
SALES (corp-wide): 123.6B **Publicly Held**
SIC: 3511 Turbines & turbine generator sets
PA: General Electric Company
41 Farnsworth St
Boston MA 02210
617 443-3000

(G-15286)
GENERAL ELECTRIC COMPANY
1 River Rd (12345-6000)
PHONE.................518 385-3716
Damian D Foti, *Principal*
EMP: 491
SALES (corp-wide): 123.6B **Publicly Held**
SIC: 3511 Gas turbine generator set units, complete
PA: General Electric Company
41 Farnsworth St
Boston MA 02210
617 443-3000

(G-15287)
GENERAL ELECTRIC COMPANY
1 River Rd Bldg 37 (12345-6000)
PHONE.................518 385-2211
John G Rice, *President*
Tom Saddlemeyer, *Finance*
John C Loomis, *Human Resources*
Jim Suciu, *Sales Staff*
Dell Williamson, *Marketing Staff*
EMP: 500
SALES (corp-wide): 123.6B **Publicly Held**
SIC: 3511 3621 Gas turbine generator set units, complete; steam turbine generator set units, complete; motors & generators
PA: General Electric Company
41 Farnsworth St
Boston MA 02210
617 443-3000

(G-15288)
GENERAL ELECTRIC COMPANY
1 Research Cir (12309-1027)
P.O. Box 8 (12301-0008)
PHONE.................518 387-5000
Marguerite Catanzaro, *Managing Dir*
Tom Shaginaw, *Business Mgr*
Mark M Little, *Vice Pres*
Dharmender Kumar, *Project Mgr*
Christopher Kapusta, *Opers Staff*
EMP: 500
SALES (corp-wide): 123.6B **Publicly Held**
SIC: 3511 Turbines & turbine generator sets
PA: General Electric Company
41 Farnsworth St
Boston MA 02210
617 443-3000

(G-15289)
GENERAL ELECTRIC COMPANY
705 Corporation Park (12302-1092)
PHONE.................518 385-3439
Robert Flag, *Branch Mgr*
EMP: 8
SALES (corp-wide): 123.6B **Publicly Held**
SIC: 3511 Turbines & turbine generator sets
PA: General Electric Company
41 Farnsworth St
Boston MA 02210
617 443-3000

(G-15290)
GEORGIA-PACIFIC LLC
801 Corporation Park (12302-1097)
PHONE.................518 346-6151
Fax: 518 346-8504
Sheri Nolan, *Human Res Mgr*
P J Hand, *Manager*
EMP: 180
SALES (corp-wide): 27.8B **Privately Held**
WEB: www.gp.com
SIC: 2653 Boxes, corrugated: made from purchased materials
HQ: Georgia-Pacific Llc
133 Peachtree St Ne # 4810
Atlanta GA 30303
404 652-4000

(G-15291)
GOTTAVAPE
1870 Altamont Ave (12303-3837)
PHONE (12303-3837) 518 945-8273
EMP: 9
SALES (est): 138.3K **Privately Held**
SIC: 3999 Cigar & cigarette holders

(G-15292)
GRANDVIEW BLOCK & SUPPLY CO
1705 Hamburg St (12304-4699)
PHONE.................518 346-7981
Fax: 518 374-3908
Salvatore Salamone, *President*
Samuel Salamone, *Vice Pres*
James Salamone, *Admin Sec*
EMP: 20 **EST:** 1946
SQ FT: 22,500
SALES (est): 3.3MM **Privately Held**
SIC: 3271 5032 Blocks, concrete or cinder: standard; masons' materials

(G-15293)
GRANDVIEW CONCRETE CORP
1705 Hamburg St (12304-4673)
PHONE.................518 346-7981
George Salamone, *President*
Attilio A Salamone, *Shareholder*
Frank J Salamone, *Shareholder*
EMP: 24
SQ FT: 22,500
SALES (est): 3.1MM **Privately Held**
SIC: 3273 Ready-mixed concrete

(G-15294)
GUARDIAN CONCRETE INC
Also Called: Guardian Concrete Steps
2140 Maxon Rd Ext (12308-1102)
PHONE.................518 372-0080
Fax: 518 372-6729
W K Stanton, *President*
EMP: 12
SQ FT: 13,000
SALES (est): 1.8MM **Privately Held**
SIC: 3272 5211 5039 Concrete products, precast; masonry materials & supplies; septic tanks

(G-15295)
HOHMANN & BARNARD INC
Sandell Moisture
310 Wayto Rd (12304-4538)
PHONE.................518 357-9757
Fax: 518 357-9636
Paul Napora, *Plant Mgr*
EMP: 21
SALES (corp-wide): 223.6B **Publicly Held**
SIC: 3496 3462 Clips & fasteners, made from purchased wire; iron & steel forgings
HQ: Hohmann & Barnard, Inc.
30 Rasons Ct
Hauppauge NY 11788
631 234-0600

(G-15296)
IGT GLOBAL SOLUTIONS CORP
1 Broadway Ctr Fl 2 (12305-2554)
PHONE.................518 382-2900
Ed Bourghan, *Branch Mgr*
Paul Stelmaszyk, *Manager*
EMP: 70
SALES (corp-wide): 5.1B **Privately Held**
WEB: www.gtech.com
SIC: 3575 Computer terminals
HQ: Igt Global Solutions Corporation
10 Memorial Blvd
Providence RI 02903
401 392-1000

(G-15297)
JIM QUINN
Also Called: Jim Quinn and Associates
12 Morningside Dr (12303-5610)
PHONE.................518 356-0398
Jim Quinn, *Owner*
EMP: 10
SALES (est): 634.7K **Privately Held**
SIC: 2426 7641 Carvings, furniture: wood; office furniture repair & maintenance

(G-15298)
JOHN C DOLPH COMPANY INC
200 Von Roll Dr (12306-2443)
PHONE.................732 329-2333
Jack Hasson, *President*
▲ **EMP:** 26 **EST:** 1910
SQ FT: 50,000
SALES (est): 8.3MM
SALES (corp-wide): 3.8MM **Privately Held**
WEB: www.johncdolph.com
SIC: 2851 2821 Varnishes; epoxy resins
PA: Von Roll Holding Ag
Passwangstrasse 20
Breitenbach SO
442 043-000

(G-15299)
KATES KAKES
987 Kings Rd (12303-2718)
PHONE.................518 466-8671
G Crandall, *Principal*
EMP: 5
SALES (est): 234.9K **Privately Held**
SIC: 2053 Cakes, bakery: frozen

(G-15300)
KERYAKOS INC
1080 Catalyn St Fl 2 (12303-1835)
PHONE.................518 344-7092
Fax: 518 344-7096
Charles Contompasis, *President*
Marika Contompasis, *Principal*
Laurie Ives, *Vice Pres*
EMP: 15
SALES (est): 1.9MM **Privately Held**
SIC: 2253 5137 Sweaters & sweater coats, knit; sweaters, women's & children's

(G-15301)
KING ROAD MATERIALS INC
145 Cordell Rd (12303-2701)
PHONE.................518 382-5354
Fax: 518 382-5442
Chris Hensler, *Manager*
EMP: 11
SQ FT: 500
SALES (corp-wide): 28.6B **Privately Held**
SIC: 2951 Asphalt & asphaltic paving mixtures (not from refineries)
HQ: King Road Materials, Inc.
8 Southwoods Blvd
Albany NY 12211
518 381-9995

(G-15302)
LATHAM INTERNATIONAL INC
Also Called: Latham Manufacturing
706 Corporation Park 1 (12302-1047)
PHONE.................518 346-5292
Tony Pagano, *Branch Mgr*
EMP: 11
SALES (corp-wide): 218.9MM **Privately Held**
WEB: www.pacificpools.com
SIC: 3081 Vinyl film & sheet
PA: Latham International, Inc.
787 Watervliet Shaker Rd
Latham NY 12110
518 783-7776

(G-15303)
LUCIDEON
2210 Technology Dr (12308-1145)
PHONE.................518 382-0082
Steve Newman, *Manager*
EMP: 12
SALES (est): 1.6MM **Privately Held**
SIC: 3297 Nonclay refractories

(G-15304)
METAL COATED FIBERS INC
679 Mariaville Rd (12306-6806)
PHONE.................518 280-8514
Robert Duval, *President*
EMP: 22 **EST:** 2012
SALES (est): 1.4MM **Privately Held**
SIC: 3624 Fibers, carbon & graphite

(G-15305)
MILLIVAC INSTRUMENTS INC
2818 Curry Rd (12303-3463)
PHONE.................518 355-8300
Imek Metzger, *President*
Pola Metzger, *Corp Secy*
Jan Metzger, *Vice Pres*
EMP: 7
SQ FT: 12,000
SALES (est): 600K **Privately Held**
WEB: www.millivacinstruments.com
SIC: 3825 Test equipment for electronic & electric measurement

(G-15306)
MISCELLNOUS IR FABRICATORS INC
1404 Dunnsville Rd (12306-5509)
PHONE.................518 355-1822
Fax: 518 355-2337
Helmut Giesselmann, *Ch of Bd*
Gunther Giesselmann, *President*
Daniel Eaton, *Financial Exec*
Tom Giesselmann, *Sales Staff*
Reinhart Giesselmann, *Admin Sec*
EMP: 22 **EST:** 1966
SQ FT: 22,000
SALES (est): 5.6MM **Privately Held**
SIC: 3441 1791 7699 Fabricated structural metal; iron work, structural; metal reshaping & replating services

(G-15307)
NEW MOUNT PLEASANT BAKERY
941 Crane St (12303-1140)
PHONE.................518 374-7577
Fax: 518 374-5548
Joe Riitano, *President*
Debra Riitano, *Vice Pres*
Ann Moore, *Manager*
EMP: 50 **EST:** 1932
SQ FT: 15,000
SALES (est): 4.8MM **Privately Held**
SIC: 2051 5461 2052 Bread, cake & related products; bakeries; cookies & crackers

(G-15308)
NORAMPAC NEW ENGLAND INC
Also Called: Norampac Thompson Inc.
801 Corporation Park (12302-1061)
PHONE.................860 923-9563
Bryan Fagan, *General Mgr*
Joe Distesano, *Plant Mgr*
Bryan Sagan, *Plant Mgr*
Lee Kozlowski, *Controller*
Firas Mando, *Controller*
EMP: 120 **EST:** 1958
SQ FT: 150,000
SALES (est): 2MM
SALES (corp-wide): 2.9B **Privately Held**
SIC: 2653 Boxes, corrugated: made from purchased materials; pads, corrugated: made from purchased materials; sheets, corrugated: made from purchased materials
HQ: Cascades Canada Ulc
404 Boul Marie-Victorin
Kingsey Falls QC J0A 1
819 363-5100

(G-15309)
OLSON SIGN COMPANY INC
Also Called: Olson Signs & Graphics
1750 Valley Rd Ext (12302)
PHONE.................518 370-2118
Fax: 518 370-3873
Richard Olson, *President*
Kelly Lee Olson, *Vice Pres*
EMP: 8
SQ FT: 6,200
SALES: 580K **Privately Held**
SIC: 3993 Electric signs; displays & cutouts, window & lobby

(G-15310)
PACKAGE ONE INC (PA)
414 Union St (12305-1107)
P.O. Box 414 (12301-0414)
PHONE.................518 344-5425
David W Dussault, *President*
Lawrence Pigliavento, *CFO*
Rick Greminger, *Manager*
▲ **EMP:** 61
SQ FT: 30,000
SALES (est): 20.8MM **Privately Held**
SIC: 3568 Power transmission equipment

Schenectady - Schenectady County (G-15311) — GEOGRAPHIC SECTION

(G-15311)
PRINTZ AND PATTERNZ LLC
Also Called: Printz Pttrnz Scrn-Prnting EMB
1550 Altamont Ave (12303-2147)
PHONE.................................518 944-6020
Mike Crowley, *Vice Pres*
Daniel Crowley, *Mng Member*
Kristie Crowley, *Administration*
EMP: 6 **EST:** 2009
SALES (est): 778.1K **Privately Held**
SIC: 2752 2281 2396 Commercial printing, lithographic; embroidery yarn, spun; screen printing on fabric articles

(G-15312)
RAND PRODUCTS MANUFACTURING CO
Also Called: Rand Mfg
1602 Van Vranken Ave (12308-2239)
PHONE.................................518 374-9871
Henry W Frick, *President*
Karen Frick Connlly, *Manager*
Karen Lewis, *Manager*
EMP: 5 **EST:** 1977
SQ FT: 7,000
SALES (est): 470K **Privately Held**
WEB: www.randmfg.com
SIC: 3444 Radiator shields or enclosures, sheet metal

(G-15313)
RAY SIGN INC
Also Called: Color Pro Sign
28 Colonial Ave (12304-4122)
PHONE.................................518 377-1371
Fax: 518 377-2704
Russell Hazen, *President*
EMP: 13 **EST:** 1980
SQ FT: 5,000
SALES (est): 1.6MM **Privately Held**
SIC: 3993 1799 7389 Electric signs; sign installation & maintenance; sign painting & lettering shop

(G-15314)
REN TOOL & MANUFACTURING CO
1801 Chrisler Ave (12303-1517)
PHONE.................................518 377-2123
Fax: 518 393-8986
Renato Belletti, *President*
Ellen Belletti, *Corp Secy*
EMP: 10 **EST:** 1949
SQ FT: 7,000
SALES (est): 1.5MM **Privately Held**
SIC: 3599 Machine shop, jobbing & repair

(G-15315)
SAMPSONS PRSTHTIC ORTHOTIC LAB
Also Called: Sampsons Prsthtic Orthotic Lab
1737 State St (12304-1832)
PHONE.................................518 374-6011
Fax: 518 393-3292
William Sampson, *President*
Pat Johnson, *Manager*
EMP: 24
SQ FT: 3,500
SALES (est): 2.4MM **Privately Held**
WEB: www.sampsons.com
SIC: 3842 5999 Prosthetic appliances; orthopedic & prosthesis applications

(G-15316)
SANZDRANZ LLC
388 Broadway (12305-2520)
PHONE.................................518 894-8625
Sandro Gerbini, *Branch Mgr*
EMP: 6
SALES (corp-wide): 210K **Privately Held**
SIC: 2043 Cereal breakfast foods
PA: Sanzdranz Llc
   83 Dumbarton Dr
   Delmar NY 12054
   518 894-8625

(G-15317)
SCHENECTADY STEEL CO INC
18 Mariaville Rd (12306-1398)
PHONE.................................518 355-3220
Fax: 518 355-3284
Claudio Zullo, *President*
Charles Chamulak, *Vice Pres*
Jeffrey Hoffmann, *Treasurer*
John Sportman, *Controller*
Sandra Anderson, *Human Resources*
EMP: 44
SQ FT: 77,700
SALES: 18.5MM **Privately Held**
SIC: 3441 Fabricated structural metal

(G-15318)
SCOTIA BEVERAGES INC
Also Called: Adirondack Beverage Co Inc
701 Corporation Park (12302-1060)
PHONE.................................518 370-3621
Ralph Crowley Jr, *President*
Angelo Mastrangelo, *Chairman*
Michael Mulrain, *Corp Secy*
Christopher Crowley, *Vice Pres*
Douglas Martin, *Vice Pres*
▲ **EMP:** 1000
SQ FT: 240,000
SALES (est): 180MM
SALES (corp-wide): 404.9MM **Privately Held**
WEB: www.adirondackbeverages.com
SIC: 2086 Soft drinks: packaged in cans, bottles, etc.; pasteurized & mineral waters, bottled & canned
PA: Polar Corp.
   1001 Southbridge St
   Worcester MA 01610
   508 753-6383

(G-15319)
SI GROUP INC (PA)
2750 Balltown Rd (12309-1006)
P.O. Box 1046 (12301-1046)
PHONE.................................518 347-4200
Fax: 518 346-6908
Wallace A Graham, *CEO*
Frank Bozich, *Ch of Bd*
Paul Tilley, *Senior VP*
Richard Barlow, *Vice Pres*
Emmanuel Hess, *Vice Pres*
◆ **EMP:** 150 **EST:** 1906
SALES (est): 1.1B **Privately Held**
WEB: www.schenectadyinternational.com
SIC: 2865 3087 2851 Phenol, alkylated & cumene; custom compound purchased resins; enamels

(G-15320)
SIERRA PROCESSING LLC
2 Moyer Ave (12306-1308)
PHONE.................................518 433-0020
Fax: 518 356-1720
William Wilczak,
Dave Fusco,
EMP: 15
SALES (est): 41.5K
SALES (corp-wide): 3.3B **Privately Held**
SIC: 2611 Pulp manufactured from waste or recycled paper
HQ: Waste Connections Us, Inc.
   3 Waterway Square Pl # 110
   The Woodlands TX 77380
   832 442-2200

(G-15321)
SKYTRAVEL (USA) LLC
20 Talon Dr (12309-1839)
PHONE.................................518 888-2610
Hongwei Jin, *Owner*
EMP: 10 **EST:** 2015
SALES (est): 575.6K **Privately Held**
SIC: 3593 Fluid power cylinders, hydraulic or pneumatic

(G-15322)
SQP INC
Also Called: Speciality Quality Packaging
602 Potential Pkwy (12302-1041)
PHONE.................................518 831-6800
Fax: 518 374-8542
Barbara Slaming, *President*
Maria Gutierrez, *Manager*
Tim Odell, *Manager*
Bryan Griffith, *Maintence Staff*
▲ **EMP:** 140
SALES (est): 27.6MM **Publicly Held**
WEB: www.usfoodservice.com
SIC: 2676 2656 Sanitary paper products; straws, drinking: made from purchased material
HQ: Us Foods, Inc.
   9399 W Higgins Rd Ste 500
   Rosemont IL 60018
   847 720-8000

(G-15323)
STARFIRE SYSTEMS INC
8 Sarnowski Dr (12302-3504)
PHONE.................................518 899-9336
Andrew Skinner, *CEO*
Richard M Saburro, *Ch of Bd*
Caron Buresh, *Controller*
▲ **EMP:** 12
SALES (est): 2MM **Privately Held**
WEB: www.starfiresystems.com
SIC: 3299 8731 Ceramic fiber; commercial physical research

(G-15324)
STS STEEL INC
301 Nott St Ste 2 (12305-1053)
PHONE.................................518 370-2693
Fax: 518 370-2696
James A Stori, *Ch of Bd*
Jim Stori, *President*
Glenn Tabolt, *Vice Pres*
David McDermott, *Project Mgr*
Debbie Clements, *Finance Mgr*
EMP: 65
SQ FT: 85,000
SALES (est): 16.4MM **Privately Held**
WEB: www.stssteel.com
SIC: 3441 Fabricated structural metal; fabricated structural metal for bridges

(G-15325)
SUPERPOWER INC
450 Duane Ave Ste 1 (12304-2631)
PHONE.................................518 346-1414
Fax: 518 346-6080
Toru Fukushima, *CEO*
John Dackow, *COO*
Hisaki Sakamoto, *Vice Pres*
Ross B McClure, *Opers Mgr*
Erin Corcuera, *Purch Mgr*
▲ **EMP:** 29
SALES (est): 8.9MM
SALES (corp-wide): 7.4B **Privately Held**
SIC: 3643 Current-carrying wiring devices
PA: Furukawa Electric Co.,Ltd.
   2-2-3, Marunouchi
   Chiyoda-Ku TKY 100-0
   332 863-001

(G-15326)
TABLECLOTHS FOR GRANTED LTD
510 Union St (12305-1117)
PHONE.................................518 370-5481
Fax: 518 723-2009
Rudolph R Grant, *President*
Gary Lombardi, *Vice Pres*
David Siders, *Vice Pres*
Richard Walsh, *Admin Sec*
EMP: 11
SALES (est): 890K **Privately Held**
SIC: 2392 Tablecloths: made from purchased materials; towels, dishcloths & dust cloths

(G-15327)
TATTERSALL INDUSTRIES LLC
Also Called: Frank Murken Products
2125 Technology Dr (12308-1143)
PHONE.................................518 381-4270
Fax: 518 381-4351
Derek Sutherland, *Plant Mgr*
James Dominelli, *Sales Mgr*
Donna Compton, *Accounts Mgr*
John Tattersall, *Mng Member*
▼ **EMP:** 20 **EST:** 1963
SQ FT: 35,000
SALES (est): 7.6MM **Privately Held**
WEB: www.fmproducts.com
SIC: 3429 5085 5169 Manufactured hardware (general); rubber goods, mechanical; chemicals & allied products

(G-15328)
THERESE THE CHILDRENS COLLECTN
301 Nott St (12305-1039)
PHONE.................................518 346-2315
Fax: 518 377-3351
Marie Guidarelli, *President*
Sally Racicot, *Bookkeeper*
EMP: 1
SQ FT: 4,000
SALES: 1.2MM **Privately Held**
SIC: 2369 5137 2353 2335 Girls' & children's outerwear; women's & children's clothing; hats, caps & millinery; women's, juniors' & misses' dresses; men's & boys' suits & coats

(G-15329)
TRAC MEDICAL SOLUTIONS INC
2165 Technology Dr (12308-1143)
PHONE.................................518 346-7799
John Botti, *Ch of Bd*
Jeff Frankel, *President*
Brad Pivar, *Vice Pres*
EMP: 7
SALES: 500K
SALES (corp-wide): 20.2MM **Publicly Held**
WEB: www.tracmed.com
SIC: 7372 Application computer software
PA: Authentidate Holding Corp.
   2225 Centennial Dr
   Gainesville GA 30504
   888 661-0225

(G-15330)
UNICELL BODY COMPANY INC
170 Cordell Rd (12303-2702)
PHONE.................................716 853-8628
Dale Wunsch, *Purch Mgr*
James Motler, *Sales Staff*
Brad Worthington, *Sales Staff*
Carmin Sperduti, *Branch Mgr*
EMP: 14
SALES (corp-wide): 20MM **Privately Held**
WEB: www.unicell.com
SIC: 3713 5084 Truck bodies & parts; industrial machinery & equipment
PA: Unicell Body Company, Inc
   571 Howard St
   Buffalo NY 14206
   716 853-8628

(G-15331)
UNILUX ADVANCED MFG LLC
30 Commerce Park Rd (12309-3545)
PHONE.................................518 344-7490
Fax: 518 344-7495
Lawrence Farrelly,
EMP: 50
SQ FT: 70,000
SALES: 11MM **Privately Held**
SIC: 3433 Heating equipment, except electric; boilers, low-pressure heating: steam or hot water

(G-15332)
VAN ALPHEN & DORAN CORP
3098 Guilderland Ave (12306-3655)
PHONE.................................518 782-9242
Teresa M Van Alphen, *Principal*
EMP: 5
SALES (est): 305.2K **Privately Held**
SIC: 2024 Ice cream & frozen desserts

(G-15333)
VINCYS PRINTING LTD
1832 Curry Rd (12306-4237)
PHONE.................................518 355-4363
Fax: 518 355-2416
Evelyn L Vincinguerra, *President*
EMP: 10 **EST:** 1967
SQ FT: 3,000
SALES (est): 1.5MM **Privately Held**
WEB: www.vincysprinting.com
SIC: 2752 2741 Commercial printing, offset; miscellaneous publishing

(G-15334)
VON ROLL USA INC (HQ)
200 Von Roll Dr (12306-2443)
PHONE.................................518 344-7100
Fax: 518 344-7286
Jon Roberts, *CEO*
Eran Rosenzweig, *Ch of Bd*
Andrew T Harrin, *President*
Jurg Brunner, *Vice Pres*
Lawrence Ostwald, *Controller*
▲ **EMP:** 130
SQ FT: 200,000
SALES (est): 47.8MM
SALES (corp-wide): 3.8MM **Privately Held**
SIC: 3644 Insulators & insulation materials, electrical

GEOGRAPHIC SECTION

Scottsville - Monroe County (G-15355)

PA: Von Roll Holding Ag
Passwangstrasse 20
Breitenbach SO
442 043-000

(G-15335)
WHITE EAGLE PACKING CO INC
922 Congress St (12303-1728)
PHONE..........................518 374-4366
Gary Markiewicz, *President*
George Markiewicz, *Vice Pres*
EMP: 12 **EST:** 1951
SQ FT: 15,000
SALES (est): 1.4MM **Privately Held**
SIC: 2013 Sausages & other prepared meats; frankfurters from purchased meat; sausages from purchased meat; bologna from purchased meat

Schenevus
Otsego County

(G-15336)
A AND L HOME FUEL LLC
601 Smokey Ave (12155-4012)
PHONE..........................607 638-1994
Frank Competiello, *Principal*
EMP: 9
SALES (est): 1.2MM **Privately Held**
SIC: 2869 Fuels

(G-15337)
SCEHENVUS FIRE DIST
Also Called: Scehenvus Gram Hose Co
40 Main St (12155-2020)
PHONE..........................607 638-9017
Chief Pete Comion, *CEO*
EMP: 65 **EST:** 1900
SALES (est): 3.8MM **Privately Held**
SIC: 3711 Fire department vehicles (motor vehicles), assembly of

Schoharie
Schoharie County

(G-15338)
COBLESKILL STONE PRODUCTS INC
Also Called: Schoharie Quarry/Asphalt
163 Eastern Ave (12157-3209)
P.O. Box 220, Cobleskill (12043-0220)
PHONE..........................518 295-7121
Shae Adams, *Vice Pres*
Tim Adams, *Vice Pres*
Mike Moore, *Vice Pres*
Pete Gray, *Manager*
EMP: 12
SQ FT: 1,104
SALES (corp-wide): 115.2MM **Privately Held**
WEB: www.cobleskillstone.com
SIC: 1422 Crushed & broken limestone
PA: Cobleskill Stone Products, Inc.
112 Rock Rd
Cobleskill NY 12043
518 234-0221

(G-15339)
MASICK SOIL CONSERVATION CO
Also Called: Carver Sand & Gravel
4860 State Route 30 (12157-2906)
PHONE..........................518 827-5354
Fax: 518 827-5307
Carver Laraway, *Owner*
EMP: 11
SQ FT: 800
SALES (est): 500K **Privately Held**
SIC: 3274 0711 Agricultural lime; lime spreading services

Schuylerville
Saratoga County

(G-15340)
EMPIRE BUILDING PRODUCTS INC
12 Spring St (12871-1049)
PHONE..........................518 695-6094
Thomas R Harrison, *President*
Derek Harrison, *General Mgr*
Paul J Martin, *Vice Pres*
Melinda O'Neill, *Sales Staff*
Dave Jenkins, *Marketing Staff*
EMP: 5
SQ FT: 1,500
SALES (est): 584.8K **Privately Held**
WEB: www.vtf.com
SIC: 2439 2431 Timbers, structural: laminated lumber; panel work, wood
PA: Vermont Timber Frames, Inc
458 Morse Rd
Bennington VT 05201

(G-15341)
GASSHO BODY & MIND INC
76 Broad St (12871-1301)
P.O. Box 910, Saratoga Springs (12866-0836)
PHONE..........................518 695-9991
Louis Hotchkiss, *President*
Junko Kobori, *Vice Pres*
▼ **EMP:** 5
SALES (est): 815.8K **Privately Held**
SIC: 2844 2044 5122 Face creams or lotions; bran, rice; toiletries

Scio
Allegany County

(G-15342)
HYDRAMEC INC
4393 River St (14880-9702)
P.O. Box 69 (14880-0069)
PHONE..........................585 593-5190
Fax: 585 593-5194
Gregg D Shear, *President*
James Vossler, *Vice Pres*
Ruth Coats, *Treasurer*
Karen Jandrew, *Finance Mgr*
Erik Potter, *Manager*
▲ **EMP:** 23 **EST:** 1924
SQ FT: 23,000
SALES (est): 4.6MM **Privately Held**
WEB: www.hydrameconline.com
SIC: 3423 3542 Hand & edge tools; machine tools, metal forming type

Scipio Center
Cayuga County

(G-15343)
CUSTOM CONTROLS
2804 Skillett Rd (13147-3127)
PHONE..........................315 253-4785
Fax: 315 253-7970
Jay Horst, *Owner*
EMP: 6
SALES (est): 702.2K **Privately Held**
SIC: 3613 Control panels, electric

(G-15344)
VANSRIDGE DAIRY LLC
2831 Black St (13147-3173)
PHONE..........................315 364-8569
Sharon Vannostrand, *Partner*
EMP: 30
SALES (est): 1.3MM **Privately Held**
SIC: 3523 Barn, silo, poultry, dairy & livestock machinery

Scotia
Schenectady County

(G-15345)
ARCHITCTRAL SHETMETAL PDTS INC
1329 Amsterdam Rd (12302-6306)
P.O. Box 2150 (12302-0150)
PHONE..........................518 381-6144
Toll Free:..........................888 -
Gary Curcio, *President*
William Donnan, *Vice Pres*
EMP: 6
SQ FT: 8,000
SALES (est): 640K **Privately Held**
SIC: 3444 Sheet metalwork; metal roofing & roof drainage equipment

(G-15346)
DIMENSION FABRICATORS INC
2000 7th St (12302-1051)
PHONE..........................518 374-1936
Fax: 518 374-4830
Scott Stevens, *President*
Joel C Patrie, *Principal*
Coleen Stevens, *Corp Secy*
Scott A Mushaw, *Vice Pres*
Valerie M Borst, *Manager*
▲ **EMP:** 50
SQ FT: 46,000
SALES (est): 18.8MM **Privately Held**
WEB: www.dimensionfab.com
SIC: 3449 Bars, concrete reinforcing: fabricated steel

(G-15347)
GRENO INDUSTRIES INC (PA)
2820 Amsterdam Rd (12302-6323)
P.O. Box 542, Schenectady (12301-0542)
PHONE..........................518 393-4195
Fax: 518 393-4182
Robert W Golden, *CEO*
Eileen Guarino, *President*
Joe Vainauskas, *VP Opers*
Dan Reid, *Maint Spvr*
Bill Slocum, *QC Mgr*
▲ **EMP:** 6
SQ FT: 70,000
SALES: 8.4MM **Privately Held**
WEB: www.greno.com
SIC: 3599 Machine shop, jobbing & repair

(G-15348)
HADP LLC
602 Potential Pkwy (12302-1041)
PHONE..........................518 831-6824
Maria Dallas, *Controller*
Paul Epstein,
Adam Epstein,
David Epstein,
EMP: 11
SALES (est): 1.2MM **Privately Held**
SIC: 2656 Plates, paper: made from purchased material

(G-15349)
INTERACTIVE INSTRUMENTS INC
704 Corporation Park # 1 (12302-1078)
PHONE..........................518 347-0955
Robert Skala, *President*
James Hutchison, *Vice Pres*
EMP: 6
SQ FT: 9,000
SALES (est): 920.3K **Privately Held**
WEB: www.interactiveinstruments.com
SIC: 3599 Custom machinery; machine shop, jobbing & repair

(G-15350)
JBS LLC
Also Called: J B S
6 Maple Ave (12302-4612)
PHONE..........................518 346-0001
Tommy Bouck, *Engineer*
John Busino, *Mng Member*
EMP: 20
SQ FT: 18,000
SALES (est): 3.7MM **Privately Held**
SIC: 3441 Fabricated structural metal

(G-15351)
NEFAB PACKAGING NORTH EAST LLC
203 Glenville Indus Park (12302-1072)
PHONE..........................518 346-9105
Fax: 518 382-9931
Paul Frisch, *General Mgr*
Jerry Dolly, *Sales Staff*
Brad Lawyer, *Manager*
EMP: 37
SALES (corp-wide): 359.1MM **Privately Held**
SIC: 2448 Wood pallets & skids
HQ: Nefab Packaging, Inc.
204 Airline Dr Ste 100
Coppell TX 75019
469 444-5264

(G-15352)
OAK-BARK CORPORATION
Also Called: Silar Laboratories Division
37 Maple Ave (12302-4613)
PHONE..........................518 372-5691
Fax: 518 372-5720
Bob Ruskino, *Manager*
Mike Hewitt, *Manager*
EMP: 8
SQ FT: 256
SALES (corp-wide): 12.7MM **Privately Held**
WEB: www.wrightcorp.com
SIC: 2869 Industrial organic chemicals; formaldehyde (formalin)
PA: Oak-Bark Corporation
1224 Old Nc Highway 87
Riegelwood NC 28456
910 655-9225

(G-15353)
SHIPMTES/PRINTMATES HOLDG CORP (PA)
Also Called: Velocity Print Solutions
705 Corporation Park # 2 (12302-1092)
PHONE..........................518 370-1158
James Stiles, *CEO*
David Benny, *General Mgr*
Michael Mello, *CFO*
Gail Jefts, *Human Res Mgr*
Gail Jeste, *Persnl Mgr*
EMP: 85
SQ FT: 60,000
SALES (est): 33.2MM **Privately Held**
WEB: www.sm-pm.com
SIC: 2752 5111 7334 7319 Commercial printing, lithographic; printing & writing paper; photocopying & duplicating services; distribution of advertising material or sample services; direct mail advertising services

(G-15354)
SPECIALTY QUALITY PACKG LLC
Also Called: Sqp
602 Potential Pkwy (12302-1041)
PHONE..........................914 580-3200
Maria Gutierrez, *Controller*
Peter Stull, *Credit Mgr*
Paul Epstein, *Mng Member*
▲ **EMP:** 81
SQ FT: 267,000
SALES (est): 30.2MM **Privately Held**
SIC: 2679 Papier mache articles, except statuary & art goods

Scottsville
Monroe County

(G-15355)
ADRIA MACHINE & TOOL INC
966 North Rd (14546-9770)
P.O. Box 208 (14546-0208)
PHONE..........................585 889-3360
Fax: 585 889-3365
Janos Poloznik, *President*
John Hehnen, *Opers Mgr*
EMP: 4
SQ FT: 7,000
SALES: 1MM **Privately Held**
WEB: www.adriamachine.com
SIC: 3541 Machine tool replacement & repair parts, metal cutting types

Scottsville - Monroe County (G-15356)

GEOGRAPHIC SECTION

(G-15356)
AMBRELL CORPORATION (HQ)
39 Main St (14546-1356)
PHONE.....................585 889-0236
Fax: 585 889-2066
Tony Mazzullo, *President*
Girish Dahake, *Vice Pres*
Bill Heist, *Vice Pres*
Skip Thompson, *Vice Pres*
Steve Enes, *Mfg Staff*
▲ **EMP:** 13
SQ FT: 25,000
SALES: 21.4MM
SALES (corp-wide): 40.2MM **Publicly Held**
WEB: www.ameritherm.com
SIC: 3567 Induction heating equipment
PA: Intest Corporation
   804 E Gate Dr Ste 200
   Mount Laurel NJ 08054
   856 505-8800

(G-15357)
COOPERVISION INC
711 North Rd (14546-1238)
PHONE.....................585 889-3301
Fax: 585 385-6145
Michael Schaenen, *Vice Chairman*
Mona Swanson, *COO*
Robert Steen, *Prdtn Mgr*
Dennis Snyder, *Mfg Staff*
Jim Galloway, *Purch Dir*
EMP: 660
SALES (corp-wide): 1.9B **Publicly Held**
SIC: 3851 Contact lenses
HQ: Coopervision, Inc.
   209 High Point Dr
   Victor NY 14564
   585 385-6810

(G-15358)
HEANY INDUSTRIES INC
249 Briarwood Ln (14546-1244)
P.O. Box 38 (14546-0038)
PHONE.....................585 889-2700
Fax: 585 889-2708
S Scott Zolnier, *Ch of Bd*
Charles Aldridge, *Vice Pres*
Brian Roberts, *Safety Mgr*
Theresa Dunn, *Purchasing*
Joan Smith, *Accounts Mgr*
▲ **EMP:** 58 **EST:** 1937
SQ FT: 18,000
SALES (est): 10MM **Privately Held**
WEB: www.heany.com
SIC: 3299 3479 2851 2816 Ceramic fiber; coating of metals with plastic or resins; paints & allied products; inorganic pigments

(G-15359)
JACK W MILLER
Also Called: Miller Truck Rental
2339 North Rd (14546-9737)
PHONE.....................585 538-2399
Fax: 585 538-2107
Jack W Miller, *Owner*
EMP: 9
SQ FT: 13,000
SALES (est): 1.3MM **Privately Held**
SIC: 3519 7538 Diesel engine rebuilding; diesel engine repair: automotive

(G-15360)
POWER AND CNSTR GROUP INC
Also Called: Livingston Lighting and Power
86 River Rd (14546-9503)
PHONE.....................585 889-6020
Fax: 585 889-1194
John Cleveland, *Vice Pres*
Philip Brooks, *Branch Mgr*
EMP: 26
SALES (corp-wide): 43.4MM **Privately Held**
WEB: www.valleysandandgravel.com
SIC: 3648 3647 Street lighting fixtures; streetcar lighting fixtures
PA: Power And Construction Group, Inc.
   119 River Rd
   Scottsville NY 14546
   585 889-8500

(G-15361)
SABIN METAL CORPORATION
1647 Wheatland Center Rd (14546-9709)
P.O. Box 905 (14546-0905)
PHONE.....................585 538-2194
Fax: 585 538-2593
John Waldon, *Maint Spvr*
Mike Nichols, *Research*
David Petishnok, *Engineer*
Vicki Strong, *Accounting Dir*
Sherrye Cook, *Human Res Dir*
EMP: 125
SALES (corp-wide): 43.2MM **Privately Held**
WEB: www.sabinmetal.com
SIC: 3341 3339 Secondary precious metals; primary nonferrous metals
PA: Sabin Metal Corporation
   300 Pantigo Pl Ste 102
   East Hampton NY 11937
   631 329-1695

(G-15362)
SWAIN TECHNOLOGY INC
963 North Rd (14546-1228)
PHONE.....................585 889-2786
Fax: 585 889-5218
Daniel Swain, *President*
Richard Tucker, *General Mgr*
Linda Swain, *Vice Pres*
EMP: 15
SQ FT: 11,000
SALES (est): 1.6MM **Privately Held**
WEB: www.swaintech.com
SIC: 3479 Coating of metals & formed products

Sea Cliff
Nassau County

(G-15363)
GOTHAM T-SHIRT CORP
211 Glen Cove Ave Unit 5 (11579-1432)
PHONE.....................516 676-0900
Howard Zwang, *Ch of Bd*
EMP: 5
SALES (est): 504.6K **Privately Held**
SIC: 2211 Shirting fabrics, cotton

(G-15364)
ROBS REALLY GOOD LLC
100 Roslyn Ave (11579-1274)
P.O. Box 355 (11579-0355)
PHONE.....................516 671-4411
Robert Ehrlich, *Mng Member*
EMP: 10
SALES (est): 1.5MM **Privately Held**
SIC: 2096 Potato chips & similar snacks

Seaford
Nassau County

(G-15365)
A & A GRAPHICS INC II
615 Arlington Dr (11783-1135)
PHONE.....................516 735-0078
Eli P Pandolfi, *President*
EMP: 3
SQ FT: 5,000
SALES (est): 1.2MM **Privately Held**
SIC: 2759 Commercial printing

(G-15366)
KYRA COMMUNICATIONS CORP
3864 Bayberry Ln (11783-1503)
PHONE.....................516 783-6244
Fax: 516 679-8167
Richard Doherty, *President*
Carol Doherty, *Vice Pres*
William Taczak, *Vice Pres*
Richard Dougherty, *Manager*
Elise Tanaka, *Director*
EMP: 14
SALES (est): 928.6K **Privately Held**
SIC: 2741 8734 Miscellaneous publishing; testing laboratories

(G-15367)
LUCAS ELECTRIC
3524 Merrick Rd (11783-2824)
PHONE.....................516 809-8619
EMP: 7
SALES (est): 146.9K **Privately Held**
SIC: 3699 Electrical equipment & supplies

(G-15368)
MEETHAPPY INC
2122 Bit Path (11783-2402)
PHONE.....................917 903-0591
Joana Gutierrez, *CEO*
EMP: 18
SALES (est): 352.3K **Privately Held**
SIC: 7372 7389 7375 Application computer software; ; information retrieval services

Selden
Suffolk County

(G-15369)
BLUE TORTILLA LLC
1070 Middle Country Rd # 4 (11784-2529)
PHONE.....................631 451-0100
Eric Gorber, *Owner*
EMP: 6
SALES (est): 492.4K **Privately Held**
SIC: 2099 Tortillas, fresh or refrigerated

(G-15370)
CENTRAL GARDEN & PET COMPANY
1100 Middle Country Rd (11784-2513)
PHONE.....................631 451-8021
Stacey Rossi, *Manager*
EMP: 9
SALES (corp-wide): 1.8B **Publicly Held**
WEB: www.centralgardenandpet.com
SIC: 2048 Prepared feeds
PA: Central Garden & Pet Company
   1340 Treat Blvd Ste 600
   Walnut Creek CA 94597
   925 948-4000

(G-15371)
CREATIVE STONE & CABINETS
448 Middle Country Rd # 1 (11784-2657)
PHONE.....................631 772-6548
Juan Cuzco, *President*
EMP: 6 **EST:** 2010
SALES (est): 1MM **Privately Held**
SIC: 2599 Cabinets, factory

(G-15372)
DATORIB INC
Also Called: Minuteman Press
974 Middle Country Rd (11784-2535)
PHONE.....................631 698-6222
Fax: 631 698-6153
William J Passeggio, *President*
Rita Passeggio, *Sales Mgr*
EMP: 5
SQ FT: 1,850
SALES (est): 657.4K **Privately Held**
SIC: 2752 Commercial printing, lithographic

(G-15373)
ILAB AMERICA INC
45 Hemlock St (11784-1327)
PHONE.....................631 615-5053
Wayne Boyle, *President*
EMP: 6
SALES (est): 800K **Privately Held**
WEB: www.ilabamerica.com
SIC: 3651 Amplifiers: radio, public address or musical instrument

(G-15374)
NORTHERN METALWORKS CORP
15 King Ave (11784-2314)
PHONE.....................646 523-1689
Shakir Qureshi, *President*
EMP: 5
SALES (est): 233.9K **Privately Held**
SIC: 3449 Miscellaneous metalwork

(G-15375)
PROGRESSIVE ORTHOTICS LTD (PA)
280 Middle Country Rd G (11784-2532)
PHONE.....................631 732-5556
Fax: 631 732-0218
Bruce Goodman, *President*
EMP: 9
SQ FT: 2,400
SALES (est): 905.9K **Privately Held**
WEB: www.progressiveorthotics.com
SIC: 3842 3841 5999 5047 Limbs, artificial; orthopedic appliances; surgical & medical instruments; orthopedic & prosthesis applications; medical & hospital equipment

Selkirk
Albany County

(G-15376)
CQ TRAFFIC CONTROL DEVICES LLC
Also Called: Cq Traffic Control Products
1521 Us Rte 9w (12158)
P.O. Box 192 (12158-0192)
PHONE.....................518 767-0057
Fax: 518 767-0058
William Quattrochi,
Frank Conrad,
Carol Quattrochi,
Douglas Robbins,
EMP: 5
SALES (est): 881K **Privately Held**
SIC: 3669 Pedestrian traffic control equipment

(G-15377)
GE PLASTICS
1 Noryl Ave (12158-9784)
PHONE.....................518 475-5011
Fax: 518 475-5650
Jeffery Immelt, *Principal*
Massimo Spiezia, *Safety Mgr*
Dave Ehlinger, *IT/INT Sup*
◆ **EMP:** 5
SALES (est): 860.2K **Privately Held**
SIC: 2821 Plastics materials & resins

(G-15378)
OLDCASTLE PRECAST INC
Also Called: Oldcastle Precast Bldg Systems
123 County Route 101 (12158-2606)
PHONE.....................518 767-2112
Edward Soler, *Manager*
Sheila Conners, *Manager*
Christopher Mueller, *Manager*
EMP: 40
SALES (corp-wide): 28.6B **Privately Held**
WEB: www.oldcastle-precast.com
SIC: 3272 Concrete products, precast
HQ: Oldcastle Precast, Inc.
   1002 15th St Sw Ste 110
   Auburn WA 98001
   253 833-2777

(G-15379)
PALPROSS INCORPORATED
Also Called: L P Transportation
Maple Ave Rr 396 (12158)
P.O. Box 95 (12158-0095)
PHONE.....................845 469-2188
Andrew Palmer, *Manager*
EMP: 10
SQ FT: 2,400
SALES (corp-wide): 14.7MM **Privately Held**
SIC: 3537 Trucks, tractors, loaders, carriers & similar equipment
PA: Palpross Incorporated
   Rr Box 17m
   Chester NY 10918
   845 469-2188

(G-15380)
SABIC INNOVATIVE PLAS US LLC
1 Noryl Ave (12158-9765)
PHONE.....................518 475-5011
Charlie Crew, *Manager*
EMP: 258 **Privately Held**
WEB: www.sabic-ip.com
SIC: 2821 Plastics materials & resins
HQ: Sabic Innovative Plastics Us Llc
   2500 City W Blvd Ste 100
   Houston TX 77042
   713 430-2300

Seneca Castle
Ontario County

(G-15381)
CASTLE HARVESTER CO INC
Also Called: Castle Harvstr Met Fabricators
3165 Seneca Castle Rd (14547)
P.O. Box 167 (14547-0167)
PHONE.................................585 526-5884
Michael Kunes, *President*
Linda Gulvin, *Office Mgr*
EMP: 9
SQ FT: 10,000
SALES (est): 1.1MM **Privately Held**
SIC: 3441 Fabricated structural metal

Seneca Falls
Seneca County

(G-15382)
GOULDS PUMPS LLC (HQ)
Also Called: Goulds Pumps Incorporated
240 Fall St (13148-1573)
PHONE.................................315 568-2811
Fax: 315 568-5737
Robert Pagano, *Ch of Bd*
Aris Chicles, *President*
Ken Napolitano, *President*
Stan Knecht, *Opers Mgr*
Narda Romero, *Senior Buyer*
◆ **EMP:** 1100 **EST:** 1984
SALES (est): 37.2MM
SALES (corp-wide): 2.4B **Publicly Held**
WEB: www.gouldspumps.com
SIC: 3561 5084 Pumps & pumping equipment; industrial pumps & parts; pumps, oil well & field; pumps, domestic: water or sump; industrial machinery & equipment
PA: Itt Inc.
   1133 Westchester Ave N-100
   White Plains NY 10604
   914 641-2000

(G-15383)
ITT CORPORATION
A-C Pump Division
240 Fall St (13148-1590)
PHONE.................................315 568-2811
Kris Nuich, *Materials Mgr*
Aaron Hagen, *Purch Agent*
Dave Menapace, *Buyer*
Joe Christofferson, *Engineer*
Steve Durham, *Engineer*
EMP: 58
SALES (corp-wide): 2.4B **Publicly Held**
SIC: 3625 3823 3363 3812 Control equipment, electric; fluidic devices, circuits & systems for process control; aluminum die-castings; radar systems & equipment; infrared object detection equipment; fluid power pumps & motors; pumps & pumping equipment
HQ: Itt Llc
   1133 Westchester Ave N-100
   White Plains NY 10604
   914 641-2000

(G-15384)
ITT ENGINEERED VALVES LLC (DH)
240 Fall St (13148-1590)
Rural Route 750 (13148)
PHONE.................................662 257-6982
Randy Garman, *General Mgr*
Fred Bose, *General Mgr*
▲ **EMP:** 40
SALES (est): 10.1MM
SALES (corp-wide): 2.4B **Publicly Held**
SIC: 2611 Pulp mills
HQ: Itt Llc
   1133 Westchester Ave N-100
   White Plains NY 10604
   914 641-2000

(G-15385)
ITT GOULDS PUMPS INC
240 Fall St (13148-1573)
PHONE.................................914 641-2129
Michael J Savinelli, *Principal*
EMP: 4500
SALES (est): 37.2MM
SALES (corp-wide): 2.4B **Publicly Held**
SIC: 3561 5084 Pumps & pumping equipment; industrial machinery & equipment
PA: Itt Inc.
   1133 Westchester Ave N-100
   White Plains NY 10604
   914 641-2000

(G-15386)
ITT LLC
Also Called: ITT Monitoring Control
240 Fall St (13148-1590)
PHONE.................................315 568-4733
Doug Brown, *Manager*
EMP: 5
SALES (corp-wide): 2.4B **Publicly Held**
SIC: 3491 Automatic regulating & control valves
HQ: Itt Llc
   1133 Westchester Ave N-100
   White Plains NY 10604
   914 641-2000

(G-15387)
ITT LLC
2881 E Bayard Street Ext (13148-8745)
PHONE.................................914 641-2000
Peter Verdehem, *Engineer*
Don Radford, *Branch Mgr*
EMP: 58
SALES (corp-wide): 2.4B **Publicly Held**
WEB: www.ittind.com
SIC: 3625 3823 3363 3812 Control equipment, electric; fluidic devices, circuits & systems for process control; aluminum die-castings; radar systems & equipment; infrared object detection equipment
HQ: Itt Llc
   1133 Westchester Ave N-100
   White Plains NY 10604
   914 641-2000

(G-15388)
ITT WATER TECHNOLOGY INC
Also Called: Goulds Pumps
2881 E Bayard Street Ext (13148-8745)
PHONE.................................315 568-2811
Fax: 315 568-2046
Douglas Bingler, *President*
Robert T Butera, *Vice Pres*
Douglas M Lawrence, *Vice Pres*
Maria Tzortzatos, *Treasurer*
Robert Kilmer, *VP Mktg*
▲ **EMP:** 350
SALES (est): 69.8MM
SALES (corp-wide): 2.4B **Publicly Held**
SIC: 3561 Pumps & pumping equipment
HQ: Itt Llc
   1133 Westchester Ave N-100
   White Plains NY 10604
   914 641-2000

(G-15389)
MONTEZUMA WINERY LLC
2981 Us Route 20 (13148-9423)
PHONE.................................315 568-8190
Bill Martin,
▲ **EMP:** 9
SALES (est): 826.5K **Privately Held**
WEB: www.montezumawinery.com
SIC: 2084 Wines

(G-15390)
SCEPTER INC
Also Called: Scepter New York
11 Lamb Rd (13148-8432)
PHONE.................................315 568-4225
Fax: 315 568-4240
Garney Scott III, *Manager*
EMP: 30
SALES (corp-wide): 71.9MM **Privately Held**
WEB: www.scepterinc.com
SIC: 3341 Secondary nonferrous metals
PA: Scepter, Inc.
   1485 Scepter Ln
   Waverly TN 37185
   931 535-3565

(G-15391)
SENECA FALLS CAPITAL INC (PA)
Also Called: Seneca Falls Machine
314 Fall St (13148-1543)
PHONE.................................315 568-5804
Fax: 315 568-5800
Attila Libertiny, *President*
EMP: 2
SQ FT: 115,000
SALES (est): 4.7MM **Privately Held**
SIC: 3541 Machine tools, metal cutting type

(G-15392)
SENECA FALLS MACHINE TOOL CO
Also Called: Seneca Falls Technology Group
314 Fall St (13148-1543)
PHONE.................................315 568-5804
Attila Libertiny, *President*
Dave Matteson, *Senior VP*
EMP: 60
SQ FT: 115,000
SALES: 3MM **Privately Held**
WEB: www.sftg.com
SIC: 3541 3545 Machine tools, metal cutting type; machine tool accessories
PA: Seneca Falls Capital, Inc.
   314 Fall St
   Seneca Falls NY 13148

(G-15393)
SENECA FLS SPC & LOGISTICS CO (PA)
50 Johnston St (13148-1235)
PHONE.................................315 568-4139
Fax: 315 568-9082
Stephen M Bregande, *President*
Bruce Chilton, *General Mgr*
Bruce Hilton, *Vice Pres*
Christopher Woods, *Vice Pres*
Matthew Dukat, *Opers Mgr*
▲ **EMP:** 80 **EST:** 1880
SALES (est): 37.8MM **Privately Held**
SIC: 2653 2652 Boxes, corrugated: made from purchased materials; setup paperboard boxes

(G-15394)
TI GROUP AUTO SYSTEMS LLC
240 Fall St (13148-1590)
PHONE.................................315 568-7042
Danielle Roetting, *Manager*
EMP: 5
SALES (corp-wide): 15.1B **Privately Held**
WEB: www.tiautomotive.com
SIC: 3317 3312 3599 3052 Tubes, seamless steel; tubes, steel & iron; hose, flexible metallic; plastic hose; fuel systems & parts, motor vehicle
HQ: Ti Group Automotive Systems, Llc
   2020 Taylor Rd
   Auburn Hills MI 48326
   248 296-8000

(G-15395)
WILSON PRESS LLC
56 Miller St (13148-1585)
PHONE.................................315 568-9693
Fax: 315 568-9693
Don Johnson, *Sales Staff*
Richard Ricci, *Manager*
Sharon Tyler, *Manager*
Nora Ricci,
EMP: 20
SQ FT: 5,500
SALES: 2MM **Privately Held**
SIC: 2752 2791 2789 2759 Commercial printing, lithographic; typesetting; bookbinding & related work; commercial printing

(G-15396)
XYLEM INC
2881 E Bayard Street Ext (13148-8745)
P.O. Box 750 (13148-0750)
PHONE.................................716 862-4123
Douglas Bingler, *Branch Mgr*
Marlene Fingar, *Info Tech Dir*
Linda Lynch, *Director*
Liz Coakley, *Executive Asst*
EMP: 15 **Publicly Held**
SIC: 3561 Pumps & pumping equipment
PA: Xylem Inc.
   1 International Dr
   Rye Brook NY 10573

(G-15397)
XYLEM INC
Also Called: Global Financial Shared Svcs
2881 E Bayard Street Ext (13148-8745)
PHONE.................................315 239-2499
Linda Lynch, *Branch Mgr*
EMP: 84 **Publicly Held**
SIC: 3561 Pumps & pumping equipment
PA: Xylem Inc.
   1 International Dr
   Rye Brook NY 10573

Setauket
Suffolk County

(G-15398)
ADVANCED RESEARCH MEDIA INC
60 Route 25a Ste 1 (11733-2872)
PHONE.................................631 751-9696
Fax: 631 751-9699
Steve Blechman, *CEO*
Elyse Blechman, *President*
Benise Gehring, *Controller*
Denise Gehring, *Controller*
Angela Frizalone, *Sales Executive*
EMP: 17
SALES (est): 5MM **Privately Held**
SIC: 2721 Magazines: publishing only, not printed on site

(G-15399)
BC SYSTEMS INC
200 N Belle Mead Ave # 2 (11733-3463)
PHONE.................................631 751-9370
Fax: 631 751-9378
Gus Blazek, *President*
Gustav Blazek, *President*
Dennis Carrigan, *Vice Pres*
Art Charych, *Vice Pres*
Carl Balk, *Mfg Staff*
EMP: 50
SQ FT: 16,000
SALES (est): 11.7MM **Privately Held**
WEB: www.bcpowersys.com
SIC: 3679 Power supplies, all types: static

(G-15400)
EATINGEVOLVED LLC
10 Technology Dr Unit 4 (11733-4063)
PHONE.................................631 675-2440
Christine Cusano, *CEO*
Richard Gusmano, *COO*
EMP: 16
SALES (est): 674.9K **Privately Held**
SIC: 2064 Candy bars, including chocolate covered bars

(G-15401)
ELIMA-DRAFT INCORPORATED
3 Bancroft St (11733-2005)
PHONE.................................631 375-2830
Robert W Viggers, *Ch of Bd*
EMP: 5
SQ FT: 2,100
SALES: 125K **Privately Held**
SIC: 3585 5075 Air conditioning equipment, complete; air conditioning & ventilation equipment & supplies

(G-15402)
MAUSNER EQUIPMENT CO INC
8 Heritage Ln (11733-3018)
PHONE.................................631 689-7358
Seymour Mausner, *President*
Dorothy Mausner, *Corp Secy*
Leonard Mausner, *Vice Pres*
EMP: 137
SQ FT: 17,000
SALES: 27.5MM **Privately Held**
SIC: 3545 5084 3823 Precision measuring tools; measuring & testing equipment, electrical; industrial instrmnts msrmnt display/control process variable

(G-15403)
MT FUEL CORP
7 Bridge Rd (11733-3021)
PHONE.................................631 445-2047

Sharon Springs - Schoharie County (G-15404)

Robert Trivigno, *Principal*
EMP: 5
SALES (est): 413.8K **Privately Held**
SIC: 2869 Fuels

Sharon Springs
Schoharie County

(G-15404)
ADELPHI PAPER HANGINGS
102 Main St (13459-3136)
P.O. Box 135 (13459-0135)
PHONE 518 284-9066
Fax: 518 284-3011
Chris Ohrstrom, *President*
Steve Larson, *Manager*
EMP: 5
SALES: 380K **Privately Held**
WEB: www.adelphipaperhangings.com
SIC: 2679 Wallpaper

(G-15405)
AMT INCORPORATED
883 Chestnut St (13459-2131)
P.O. Box 338 (13459-0338)
PHONE 518 284-2910
Fax: 518 284-2911
Lanning Brandel, *President*
Beth Brandel, *Corp Secy*
Yana Bolins, *Officer*
EMP: 33
SQ FT: 22,000
SALES (est): 7.9MM **Privately Held**
WEB: www.amtcastings.com
SIC: 3366 3365 3354 3341 Bushings & bearings, copper (nonmachined); aluminum foundries; aerospace castings, aluminum; machinery castings, aluminum; aluminum extruded products; secondary nonferrous metals; steel foundries; miscellaneous nonferrous products; ferrous metals

(G-15406)
MONOLITHIC COATINGS INC
916 Highway Route 20 (13459-3108)
PHONE 914 621-2765
EMP: 5
SALES (est): 566.1K **Privately Held**
SIC: 3674 Read-only memory (ROM)

(G-15407)
TIMOTHY L SIMPSON
5819 State Route 145 (13459-3205)
PHONE 518 234-1401
Timothy L Simpson, *Principal*
EMP: 6
SALES (est): 492.5K **Privately Held**
SIC: 2411 Logging

Shelter Island
Suffolk County

(G-15408)
COECLES HBR MARINA & BOAT YARD
68 Cartwright Rd (11964)
PHONE 631 749-0856
John Needham, *President*
EMP: 15
SALES (corp-wide): 1.2MM **Privately Held**
SIC: 3732 Boat building & repairing
PA: Coecles Harbor Marina & Boat Yard Inc
18 Hudson Ave
Shelter Island NY 11964
631 749-0700

(G-15409)
GOODING & ASSOCIATES INC
15 Dinah Rock Rd (11964)
P.O. Box 1690 (11964-1690)
PHONE 631 749-3313
A Gordon Gooding Jr, *President*
Joy Strasser, *Office Mgr*
EMP: 14
SALES (est): 1.3MM **Privately Held**
SIC: 2741 Catalogs: publishing & printing

(G-15410)
SHELTER ISLAND REPORTER INC
Also Called: Shelter Island Cmnty Nwspapers
50 N Ferry Rd (11964)
P.O. Box 756 (11964-0756)
PHONE 631 749-1000
Troy Gustavson, *President*
Andrew Olsen, *Vice Pres*
◆ **EMP:** 8
SALES (est): 490K **Privately Held**
SIC: 2711 Newspapers, publishing & printing

Sherburne
Chenango County

(G-15411)
CHENANGO VALLEY TECH INC
328 Route 12b (13460)
P.O. Box 1038 (13460-1038)
PHONE 607 674-4115
Fax: 607 674-4953
Lloyd Baker, *CEO*
Lucille Baker, *President*
John Davis, *President*
John Clark, *Plant Mgr*
Norman Wynn, *Production*
EMP: 35 **EST:** 1997
SQ FT: 30,000
SALES (est): 6.7MM **Privately Held**
WEB: www.chenangovalleytech.com
SIC: 3544 3089 Industrial molds; injection molding of plastics

(G-15412)
COLUMBUS WOODWORKING INC
164 Casey Cheese Fctry Rd (13460-5006)
PHONE 607 674-4546
Michael Tomaselli, *President*
Stacy Tomaselli, *Corp Secy*
EMP: 5
SQ FT: 15,000
SALES (est): 653.2K **Privately Held**
SIC: 2431 Millwork

(G-15413)
EGG LOW FARMS INC
35 W State St (13460-9424)
PHONE 607 674-4653
Fax: 607 674-9216
Helen Dunckel, *President*
David Dunckel, *Vice Pres*
Thena Russell, *Manager*
EMP: 10
SQ FT: 38,000
SALES: 850K **Privately Held**
SIC: 2015 Egg substitutes made from eggs

(G-15414)
KENYON PRESS INC
1 Kenyon Press Dr (13460-5670)
P.O. Box 710 (13460-0710)
PHONE 607 674-9066
Fax: 607 674-4952
Ray Kenyon, *President*
Debra Ford, *General Mgr*
Donald Washburn, *Prdtn Mgr*
Carrie Guyer, *Opers Staff*
Heather Norton, *Production*
EMP: 50
SQ FT: 75,000
SALES (est): 10MM **Privately Held**
SIC: 2752 Commercial printing, offset

(G-15415)
MID-YORK PRESS INC
2808 State Highway 80 (13460-4549)
P.O. Box 733 (13460-0733)
PHONE 607 674-4491
Fax: 607 674-9482
Robert W Tenney, *Ch of Bd*
Jane Eaton, *Principal*
Mary Mahoney, *Principal*
Cynthia Tenney, *Principal*
Pat Dowdall, *COO*
EMP: 70 **EST:** 1946
SQ FT: 56,000
SALES (est): 27.8MM **Privately Held**
WEB: www.midyorkpress.com
SIC: 2679 2752 2711 Paperboard products, converted; commercial printing, offset; newspapers, publishing & printing
PA: Media Tenney Group
28 Robinson Rd
Clinton NY 13323
315 853-5569

(G-15416)
READY EGG FARMS INC
35 W State St (13460-9424)
P.O. Box 843, Silverton OR (97381-0843)
PHONE 607 674-4653
Patrick Green, *President*
EMP: 9
SQ FT: 40,000
SALES: 1.5MM **Privately Held**
WEB: www.readyeggfarms.com
SIC: 2015 Egg processing

(G-15417)
SHERBURNE METAL SALES INC (PA)
40 S Main St (13460-9804)
PHONE 607 674-4441
Fax: 607 674-9576
David Harvey, *President*
Gregory Panagiotakis, *Vice Pres*
EMP: 19
SQ FT: 60,000
SALES (est): 36.6MM **Privately Held**
WEB: www.sherburnemetals.com
SIC: 3331 3351 Primary copper; rolled or drawn shapes: copper & copper alloy

(G-15418)
SMITH TOOL & DIE INC
714 Pleasant Valley Rd (13460-3101)
P.O. Box 205 (13460-0205)
PHONE 607 674-4165
Fax: 607 674-4335
Kenneth Smith, *President*
EMP: 6
SQ FT: 2,000
SALES (est): 340K **Privately Held**
WEB: www.cncsurfacegrinding.com
SIC: 3599 Machine shop, jobbing & repair

(G-15419)
STEEL SALES INC
8085 New York St Hwy 12 (13460)
P.O. Box 539 (13460-0539)
PHONE 607 674-6363
Fax: 607 674-9706
Brenda Westcott, *Ch of Bd*
Barbie Joe, *Sales Mgr*
EMP: 20
SQ FT: 20,000
SALES (est): 6.1MM **Privately Held**
WEB: www.steelsalesinc.com
SIC: 3446 3444 3449 5051 Architectural metalwork; sheet metalwork; bars, concrete reinforcing: fabricated steel; metals service centers & offices; steel

(G-15420)
TECNOFIL CHENANGO SAC
40 S Main St (13460-9804)
PHONE 607 674-4441
Jose Babadia, *Principal*
Marcelo Quinones, *Plant Mgr*
Belinda Fairess, *Human Resources*
◆ **EMP:** 30
SALES (est): 10.4MM **Privately Held**
SIC: 3331 Primary copper

(G-15421)
WHITE HOUSE CABINET SHOP LLC
11 Knapp St (13460-9791)
P.O. Box 877 (13460-0877)
PHONE 607 674-9358
Jeff Webster, *Mng Member*
Bruce Webster,
Mike Webster,
EMP: 8
SQ FT: 5,112
SALES (est): 797.9K **Privately Held**
SIC: 2434 Wood kitchen cabinets

Sheridan
Chautauqua County

(G-15422)
COTTON WELL DRILLING CO INC
Center Rd (14135)
P.O. Box 203 (14135-0203)
PHONE 716 672-2788
Fax: 716 672-6183
Donald D Cotton, *President*
Mollie Cotton, *Office Mgr*
EMP: 8
SQ FT: 2,400
SALES (est): 916K **Privately Held**
SIC: 1389 Oil & gas wells: building, repairing & dismantling

Sherman
Chautauqua County

(G-15423)
BISSEL-BABCOCK MILLWORK INC
3866 Kendrick Rd (14781-9628)
PHONE 716 761-6976
James Babcock, *President*
Paula Babcock, *Admin Sec*
EMP: 11
SQ FT: 5,000
SALES: 1.1MM **Privately Held**
SIC: 2421 Sawmills & planing mills, general

(G-15424)
FIRE APPARATUS SERVICE TECH
7895 Lyons Rd (14781-9657)
PHONE 716 753-3538
Danny Karges, *Executive*
EMP: 7
SALES (est): 962.8K **Privately Held**
SIC: 3669 Fire alarm apparatus, electric

(G-15425)
TRIPLE E MANUFACTURING
117 Osborn St (14781-9790)
P.O. Box 438 (14781-0438)
PHONE 716 761-6996
Fax: 716 761-6688
Richard Watrous, *Partner*
Pamela Watrous, *Partner*
▲ **EMP:** 18
SQ FT: 12,000
SALES (est): 1.8MM **Privately Held**
SIC: 2399 Horse & pet accessories, textile

Sherrill
Oneida County

(G-15426)
BRIGGS & STRATTON CORPORATION
4245 Highbridge Rd (13461)
PHONE 315 495-0100
Philip Wenzel, *Manager*
EMP: 15
SALES (corp-wide): 1.7B **Publicly Held**
SIC: 3519 Internal combustion engines
PA: Briggs & Stratton Corporation
12301 W Wirth St
Wauwatosa WI 53222
414 259-5333

(G-15427)
DLR ENTERPRISES LLC
Also Called: Noble Wood Shavings
104 E Seneca St (13461-1008)
PHONE 315 813-2911
EMP: 5
SALES (est): 793.5K **Privately Held**
SIC: 2421 Sawmill/Planing Mill

(G-15428)
DUTCHLAND PLASTICS LLC
102 E Seneca St (13461-1008)
PHONE 315 280-0247

Daven Claerbout, *Branch Mgr*
EMP: 223
SALES (corp-wide): 109.9MM **Privately Held**
SIC: 3089 Molding primary plastic
PA: Dutchland Plastics, Llc
  54 Enterprise Ct
  Oostburg WI 53070
  920 564-3633

(G-15429)
PATLA ENTERPRISES INC
190 E State St (13461-1232)
PHONE..................................315 790-0143
Jodie-Lynn Patla, *Ch of Bd*
EMP: 6
SALES (est): 445.5K **Privately Held**
SIC: 2013 1541 Beef, dried; from purchased meat; food products manufacturing or packing plant construction

(G-15430)
SHERRILL MANUFACTURING INC
102 E Seneca St (13461-1008)
PHONE..................................315 280-0727
Gregory L Owens, *CEO*
Matthew A Roberts, *President*
Gina M Connelly, *Technology*
EMP: 140
SQ FT: 1,000,000
SALES (est): 26.4MM **Privately Held**
WEB: www.sherrillmfg.com
SIC: 3421 3914 3471 Cutlery; silverware, silver plated; gold plating

(G-15431)
SILVER CITY GROUP INC
Also Called: Silver City Metals
27577 W Seneca St (13461)
PHONE..................................315 363-0344
Fax: 315 361-1125
Dennis Tormey, *President*
Cliff Wittman, *Vice Pres*
EMP: 5
SQ FT: 2,500
SALES (est): 400K **Privately Held**
SIC: 3914 Pewter ware

(G-15432)
TIBRO WATER TECHNOLOGIES LTD
106 E Seneca St Unit 25 (13461-1008)
PHONE..................................647 426-3415
Dhiren Chandaria, *President*
Dharmendra Variya, *Controller*
EMP: 15
SQ FT: 7,000
SALES: 1.2MM
SALES (corp-wide): 1.2MM **Privately Held**
SIC: 2819 Sodium & potassium compounds, exc. bleaches, alkalies, alum.
PA: Tibro International Ltd
  1 Scarsdale Rd Unit 300
  North York ON M3B 2
  647 426-3415

(G-15433)
WESTMOOR LTD
Also Called: Conde Pumps Div
906 W Hamilton Ave (13461-1366)
P.O. Box 99 (13461-0099)
PHONE..................................315 363-1500
Fax: 315 363-0193
James R Hendry, *Ch of Bd*
EMP: 10 **EST:** 1939
SQ FT: 18,000
SALES (est): 2.6MM **Privately Held**
WEB: www.westmoorltd.com
SIC: 3561 3523 Pumps & pumping equipment; milking machines

Shirley
Suffolk County

(G-15434)
AMERICAN REGENT INC
Also Called: American Regent Laboratories
5 Ramsey Rd (11967-4701)
P.O. Box 9001 (11967-9001)
PHONE..................................631 924-4000
Fax: 631 924-1731
Ralf Lange, *President*
Bobby Kniffin, *Managing Prtnr*
Jean Poulos, *Vice Pres*
Joe Puglisi, *Facilities Mgr*
Anna Kirk, *Purch Agent*
EMP: 425
SQ FT: 95,000
SALES (est): 52.1MM
SALES (corp-wide): 8.4B **Privately Held**
WEB: www.osteohealth.com
SIC: 2834 Pharmaceutical preparations
HQ: Luitpold Pharmaceuticals, Inc.
  5 Ramsey Rd
  Shirley NY 11967
  631 924-4000

(G-15435)
ANTHONY GIGI INC
Also Called: Russo's Gluten Free Gourmet
45 Ramsey Rd Unit 28 (11967-4712)
PHONE..................................860 964-1943
Neil Russo, *President*
EMP: 5
SQ FT: 2,000
SALES: 300K **Privately Held**
SIC: 2046 Gluten meal

(G-15436)
ATLANTIC COLOR CORP
14 Ramsey Rd (11967-4704)
PHONE..................................631 345-3800
Richard Reina, *Ch of Bd*
EMP: 20
SALES (est): 3.1MM **Privately Held**
WEB: www.atlanticcolor.com
SIC: 2752 Commercial printing, offset

(G-15437)
ATLANTIC INDUSTRIAL TECH INC
90 Precision Dr (11967-4702)
PHONE..................................631 234-3131
Robert Ferrara, *Ch of Bd*
Thomas Ferrara, *Vice Pres*
Laura Roppelt, *Purchasing*
Thomas Behling, *Engineer*
Jennifer Wines, *Accounting Mgr*
EMP: 35
SQ FT: 20,000
SALES (est): 12.2MM **Privately Held**
WEB: www.aitzone.com
SIC: 3443 8711 7699 3594 Fabricated plate work (boiler shop); engineering services; industrial machinery & equipment repair; fluid power pumps & motors

(G-15438)
B V M ASSOCIATES
999-32 Montrell 414 (11967)
PHONE..................................631 254-6220
Mike Lucyk, *Owner*
EMP: 8
SQ FT: 5,000
SALES (est): 510K **Privately Held**
SIC: 3577 Computer peripheral equipment

(G-15439)
BIODEX MEDICAL SYSTEMS INC (PA)
20 Ramsey Rd (11967-4704)
PHONE..................................631 924-9000
Fax: 631 924-9338
James Reiss, *Ch of Bd*
Allyson Scerri, *President*
Kate Dimeglio, *Vice Pres*
Bob Ranieri, *Vice Pres*
Carlos Dragovich, *VP Opers*
▲ **EMP:** 170
SQ FT: 83,000
SALES (est): 28.9MM **Privately Held**
WEB: www.biodex.com
SIC: 3842 3841 3844 Radiation shielding aprons, gloves, sheeting, etc.; muscle exercise apparatus, ophthalmic; X-ray apparatus & tubes

(G-15440)
BIODEX MEDICAL SYSTEMS INC
49 Natcon Dr (11967-4700)
PHONE..................................631 924-3146
John Ryan, *Manager*
EMP: 30
SALES (corp-wide): 28.9MM **Privately Held**
WEB: www.biodex.com
SIC: 3842 3841 Radiation shielding aprons, gloves, sheeting, etc.; muscle exercise apparatus, ophthalmic
PA: Biodex Medical Systems, Inc.
  20 Ramsey Rd
  Shirley NY 11967
  631 924-9000

(G-15441)
FIRE ISLAND FUEL
106 Parkwood Dr (11967-3918)
PHONE..................................631 772-1482
Joseph Intravaia, *Principal*
EMP: 6
SALES (est): 587.3K **Privately Held**
SIC: 2869 Fuels

(G-15442)
FRANK LOWE RBR & GASKET CO INC
44 Ramsey Rd (11967-4704)
PHONE..................................631 777-2707
Ira M Warren, *Ch of Bd*
Judy Rosalez, *Vice Pres*
Ruth Lyons, *Purch Dir*
Azhar Chishti, *Manager*
Ruth Kowalski, *Manager*
▲ **EMP:** 35
SQ FT: 60,000
SALES (est): 8.3MM **Privately Held**
WEB: www.franklowe.com
SIC: 3053 Gaskets, all materials

(G-15443)
INNOVATION MGT GROUP INC
999 Montauk Hwy (11967-2130)
PHONE..................................800 889-0987
Jerry Hussong, *Vice Pres*
EMP: 10
SALES (corp-wide): 950K **Privately Held**
WEB: www.imgpresents.com
SIC: 7372 Prepackaged software
PA: Innovation Management Group, Inc.
  5348 Vegas Dr Ste 285
  Las Vegas NV 89108
  800 889-0987

(G-15444)
J & M FEED CORPORATION
675 Montauk Hwy (11967-2105)
PHONE..................................631 281-2152
John Colondona, *President*
EMP: 6
SQ FT: 7,500
SALES (est): 843.2K **Privately Held**
SIC: 2048 5999 Prepared feeds; feed supplements; pet food

(G-15445)
L I F PUBLISHING CORP (PA)
Also Called: The Fisherman
14 Ramsey Rd (11967-4704)
PHONE..................................631 345-5200
Richard Reina Sr, *President*
Fred Galofaro, *Publisher*
Richard S Reina, *Vice Pres*
Mihai Margineanu, *Prdtn Mgr*
Madalyn Lechner, *Finance Other*
EMP: 20
SQ FT: 14,000
SALES (est): 5.1MM **Privately Held**
SIC: 2721 2752 Periodicals; commercial printing, offset

(G-15446)
LUITPOLD PHARMACEUTICALS INC (HQ)
5 Ramsey Rd (11967-4701)
P.O. Box 9001 (11967-9001)
PHONE..................................631 924-4000
Mary Jane Helenek, *Chairman*
Alicia L Shepard, *Business Mgr*
Joel Steckler, *Business Mgr*
Gopal Anyarambhatla, *Vice Pres*
Jackie Beltrani, *Vice Pres*
▲ **EMP:** 500 **EST:** 1946
SALES (est): 220.5MM
SALES (corp-wide): 8.4B **Privately Held**
WEB: www.osteohealth.com
SIC: 2834 Pharmaceutical preparations
PA: Daiichi Sankyo Company, Limited
  3-5-1, Nihombashihoncho
  Chuo-Ku TKY 103-0
  362 251-111

(G-15447)
LUITPOLD PHARMACEUTICALS INC
Osteohealth Company
5 Ramsey Rd (11967-4701)
PHONE..................................631 924-4000
Mary Jane Helenek, *President*
Gary Coughlen, *CFO*
Matthew Banisch, *Sales Mgr*
Bethany Dudley, *Sales Mgr*
Ryan Hayes, *Sales Mgr*
EMP: 20
SALES (corp-wide): 8.4B **Privately Held**
WEB: www.osteohealth.com
SIC: 3843 Dental equipment & supplies
HQ: Luitpold Pharmaceuticals, Inc.
  5 Ramsey Rd
  Shirley NY 11967
  631 924-4000

(G-15448)
MID ATLANTIC GRAPHICS CORP
14 Ramsey Rd (11967-4704)
PHONE..................................631 345-3800
Fax: 631 345-5304
Madaline Lechner, *CEO*
Richard Reina Sr, *President*
Richard S Reina, *Vice Pres*
EMP: 20
SQ FT: 14,000
SALES (est): 2.4MM
SALES (corp-wide): 5.1MM **Privately Held**
SIC: 2752 Commercial printing, offset
PA: L I F Publishing Corp
  14 Ramsey Rd
  Shirley NY 11967
  631 345-5200

(G-15449)
MODULAR DEVICES INC
Also Called: M D I
1 Roned Rd (11967-4706)
PHONE..................................631 345-3100
Fax: 631 345-3106
Steven E Summer, *President*
Henry Striegl, *Regional Mgr*
Greg Mink, *COO*
Henry Striegl, *Vice Pres*
Henry F Striegl Jr, *Vice Pres*
▲ **EMP:** 55
SQ FT: 20,000
SALES (est): 12.1MM **Privately Held**
WEB: www.modev.com
SIC: 3621 Motors & generators

(G-15450)
NJF PUBLISHING CORP
Also Called: The Fisherman
14 Ramsey Rd (11967-4704)
PHONE..................................631 345-5200
EMP: 6
SQ FT: 1,800
SALES (est): 680K **Privately Held**
SIC: 2721 8412 Periodicals-Publishing/Printing Museum/Art Gallery

(G-15451)
POWR-UPS CORP
1 Roned Rd (11967-4707)
PHONE..................................631 345-5700
Fax: 631 345-0060
Steven Summer, *President*
D Wheeler, *General Mgr*
Debbie Wheeler, *Mktg Dir*
EMP: 25 **EST:** 1981
SQ FT: 20,000
SALES: 2.7MM **Privately Held**
WEB: www.powrupscorp.com
SIC: 3625 5063 Motor controls & accessories; electrical apparatus & equipment

(G-15452)
PRMS INC
Also Called: Prms Electronic Components
45 Ramsey Rd Unit 26 (11967-4712)
PHONE..................................631 851-7945
Ron Roybal, *Owner*
Linda Roybal, *Vice Pres*
Mary Palmer, *VP Sales*
EMP: 6

Shirley - Suffolk County (G-15453) **GEOGRAPHIC SECTION**

SQ FT: 5,000
SALES (est): 1.7MM Privately Held
WEB: www.prmsinc.com
SIC: 3677 Filtration devices, electronic

(G-15453)
UNCLE WALLYS LLC
41 Natcon Dr (11967-4700)
PHONE...................................631 205-0455
Lou Avignone, *President*
Jerry Ceccio, *Vice Pres*
Michael Petrucelli, *CFO*
Denise Weber, *Controller*
Kathy Lennon, *Sales Mgr*
EMP: 35
SQ FT: 60,000
SALES (est): 1.5MM Privately Held
WEB: www.unclewallys.com
SIC: 2051 Bread, cake & related products
HQ: Give And Go Prepared Foods Corp
6650 Finch Ave W Suite 1
Etobicoke ON M9W 5
416 674-8944

(G-15454)
UNITED BAKING CO INC (PA)
41 Natcon Dr (11967-4700)
PHONE...................................631 205-0455
Fax: 631 205-9691
Louis Avignone, *Ch of Bd*
David Nemer, *VP Opers*
Jim Magorrian, *Plant Supt*
Susan Vizzi, *Controller*
Kim Massa, *Accountant*
EMP: 3
SQ FT: 60,000
SALES (est): 34.6MM Privately Held
SIC: 2052 Cookies & crackers

Shokan
Ulster County

(G-15455)
MACK WOOD WORKING
Also Called: General Specialties
2792 State Route 28 (12481-5002)
PHONE...................................845 657-6625
Fax: 845 657-6630
Ben Mack, *Owner*
EMP: 8
SQ FT: 8,000
SALES (est): 500K Privately Held
SIC: 2431 Millwork

Shortsville
Ontario County

(G-15456)
GLK FOODS LLC
Curtice Burns Foods
11 Clark St (14548-9755)
P.O. Box 450 (14548-0450)
PHONE...................................585 289-4414
Dave Flanagan, *Opers-Prdtn-Mfg*
David Pico, *Controller*
EMP: 40
SALES (corp-wide): 37MM Privately Held
SIC: 2035 2033 Sauerkraut, bulk; sauerkraut: packaged in cans, jars, etc.
PA: Glk Foods, Llc
158 E Northland Ave
Appleton WI 54911
715 752-4105

Sidney
Delaware County

(G-15457)
AMERICAN BLUESTONE LLC
760 Quarry Rd (13838)
P.O. Box 117 (13838-0117)
PHONE...................................607 369-2235
Robert McDuffey, *Mng Member*
Deborah McDuffey,
EMP: 12
SALES (est): 1.5MM Privately Held
SIC: 3281 Cut stone & stone products

(G-15458)
AMPHENOL CORPORATION
Also Called: Amphenol Aerospace Industrial
40-60 Delaware Ave (13838-1395)
PHONE...................................607 563-5364
Rick Aiken, *General Mgr*
Mark Tompkins, *Superintendent*
Archie Stockwell, *Facilities Mgr*
Jan Mancini, *Purch Agent*
Dan Williams, *QC Mgr*
EMP: 345
SQ FT: 675,000
SALES (corp-wide): 6.2B Publicly Held
SIC: 3678 Electronic connectors
PA: Amphenol Corporation
358 Hall Ave
Wallingford CT 06492
203 265-8900

(G-15459)
AMPHENOL CORPORATION
Amphenol Aerospace Operations
40-60 Delaware Ave (13838-1395)
PHONE...................................607 563-5011
Fax: 607 563-5107
Bill Doherty, *General Mgr*
Stan Backus, *District Mgr*
Mark Philpott, *Opers Mgr*
Paul Moran, *Opers Staff*
Christopher Sheldon, *Purch Mgr*
EMP: 1500
SALES (corp-wide): 6.2B Publicly Held
SIC: 3678 Electronic connectors
PA: Amphenol Corporation
358 Hall Ave
Wallingford CT 06492
203 265-8900

(G-15460)
DECKER FOREST PRODUCTS INC
New York State Rte 8 (13838)
P.O. Box 205 (13838-0205)
PHONE...................................607 563-2345
Floyd Decker, *President*
Mark Decker, *Vice Pres*
Carol Decker, *Admin Sec*
EMP: 5
SQ FT: 15,000
SALES (est): 330K Privately Held
SIC: 2411 Logging camps & contractors

(G-15461)
EGLI MACHINE COMPANY INC
240 State Highway 7 (13838-2716)
PHONE...................................607 563-3663
Fax: 607 563-1160
Denis Egli, *President*
Charles Howand, *Engineer*
Ellen Egli, *Treasurer*
Dorthea Christensen, *Admin Sec*
EMP: 28
SQ FT: 18,000
SALES: 3.5MM Privately Held
WEB: www.eglimachine.com
SIC: 3545 3544 3089 Precision tools, machinists'; special dies, tools, jigs & fixtures; molding primary plastic

(G-15462)
JP OIL GROUP INC
49 Union St (13838-1442)
PHONE...................................607 563-1360
John Tal, *President*
EMP: 5
SALES (est): 306.7K Privately Held
SIC: 1382 Oil & gas exploration services

(G-15463)
REFILL SERVICES LLC
16 Winkler Rd (13838-1056)
PHONE...................................607 369-5864
Austin Wilson, *Mng Member*
EMP: 5
SALES (est): 320K Privately Held
SIC: 2621 Stationery, envelope & tablet papers

(G-15464)
TRI-TOWN NEWS INC (PA)
Also Called: Sidney Favorite Printing Div
74 Main St (13838-1134)
PHONE...................................607 561-3515
Fax: 607 563-1716
Paul Hamilton Sr, *President*
Wiley Vincent, *Vice Pres*

EMP: 25 EST: 1925
SQ FT: 10,080
SALES (est): 1.7MM Privately Held
WEB: www.powerofprint.com
SIC: 2752 2711 Commercial printing, off-set; newspapers, publishing & printing

(G-15465)
UFP NEW YORK LLC
13 Winkler Rd (13838-1057)
PHONE...................................607 563-1556
William Conner, *Plant Mgr*
Kirk Weaver, *Sales Staff*
James Brennan, *Manager*
EMP: 45
SQ FT: 14,988
SALES (corp-wide): 3.2B Publicly Held
WEB: www.ufpinc.com
SIC: 2439 Structural wood members
HQ: Ufp New York, Llc
11 Allen St
Auburn NY 13021
315 253-2758

(G-15466)
UNADILLA SILO COMPANY INC
Also Called: Unadilla Laminated Products
100 West Rd (13838)
PHONE...................................607 369-9341
Barb Deblasio, *Human Res Mgr*
Phillip Holowacz, *VP Sales*
Floyd Spencer, *Manager*
Zoe Dandermeulen, *CIO*
EMP: 62
SALES (corp-wide): 6.8MM Privately Held
SIC: 2431 3444 2439 Silo staves, wood; sheet metalwork; structural wood members
PA: Unadilla Silo Company, Inc.
18 Clifton St
Unadilla NY 13849
607 369-9341

(G-15467)
USA CUSTOM PAD CORP (PA)
16 Winkler Rd (13838-1056)
PHONE...................................607 563-9550
Fax: 607 563-9553
Eric T Wilson, *Chairman*
Marcia Wilson, *Admin Sec*
▲ EMP: 29
SQ FT: 20,000
SALES (est): 7MM Privately Held
WEB: www.memopads.com
SIC: 2678 2759 2741 Tablets & pads, book & writing: from purchased materials; commercial printing; miscellaneous publishing

Silver Bay
Warren County

(G-15468)
HACKER BOAT COMPANY INC (PA)
8 Delaware Ave (12874-1815)
PHONE...................................518 543-6731
Fax: 518 543-6732
Ernest George Badcock III, *Ch of Bd*
Lynn R Wagemann, *President*
Dolores Kunker, *Sales Mgr*
Mike Bonn, *Director*
▲ EMP: 20
SALES (est): 5.5MM Privately Held
WEB: www.hackerboatco.com
SIC: 3732 Boat building & repairing

Silver Creek
Chautauqua County

(G-15469)
CHAUTAUQUA WINE COMPANY INC
Also Called: Willow Creek Winery
2627 Chapin Rd (14136-9760)
PHONE...................................716 934-9463
Fax: 716 934-9463
Holly Metzger, *President*
Holly Metzter, *President*
Dawn Ellis, *Manager*

EMP: 5 EST: 2000
SALES (est): 459K Privately Held
WEB: www.willowcreekwinery.com
SIC: 2084 Wines

(G-15470)
EXCELCO DEVELOPMENTS INC
65 Main St (14136-1467)
P.O. Box 230 (14136-0230)
PHONE...................................716 934-2651
Christopher J Lanski, *President*
Douglas A Newman, *Exec VP*
Eric Niedbalski, *QC Mgr*
Philip J Azzarella, *CFO*
Paul Rozewicz, *Finance Mgr*
EMP: 37
SQ FT: 40,000
SALES (est): 7MM Privately Held
SIC: 3728 3731 3429 Aircraft assemblies, subassemblies & parts; shipbuilding & repairing; manufactured hardware (general)

(G-15471)
EXCELCO/NEWBROOK INC
16 Mechanic St (14136-1202)
P.O. Box 231 (14136-0231)
PHONE...................................716 934-2644
Fax: 716 934-2646
Christopher J Lanski, *CEO*
Geoff Rondeau, *General Mgr*
Paul Narraway, *Engineer*
P J Azzarella, *CFO*
Gary Willert, *Admin Asst*
EMP: 85 EST: 1952
SQ FT: 93,000
SALES (est): 13.4MM Privately Held
WEB: www.excelco.net
SIC: 3728 3731 7692 Aircraft assemblies, subassemblies & parts; shipbuilding & repairing; welding repair

Silver Springs
Wyoming County

(G-15472)
MORTON SALT INC
45 Ribaud Ave (14550-9805)
P.O. Box 342 (14550-0342)
PHONE...................................585 493-2511
Fax: 585 493-2067
Matt Ashley, *Project Engr*
Norbert Fuest, *Human Res Dir*
Steve Hull, *Human Res Mgr*
Daniel Border, *Branch Mgr*
Marlene Bassett, *Manager*
EMP: 12
SALES (corp-wide): 3.6B Privately Held
SIC: 1479 Salt & sulfur mining
HQ: Morton Salt, Inc.
444 W Lake St Ste 3000
Chicago IL 60606

Sinclairville
Chautauqua County

(G-15473)
CARLSON WOOD PRODUCTS INC (PA)
1705 Bates Rd (14782-9726)
PHONE...................................716 287-2923
Fax: 716 287-2657
William Carlson, *President*
Ivetta Carlson, *Vice Pres*
EMP: 6
SQ FT: 4,000
SALES: 1.3MM Privately Held
SIC: 2426 2421 Lumber, hardwood dimension; kiln drying of lumber

(G-15474)
CONTAINER TSTG SOLUTIONS LLC (PA)
17 Lester St (14782-9724)
PHONE...................................716 487-3300
Brian Johnson, *Ch of Bd*
EMP: 10
SALES (est): 1.7MM Privately Held
SIC: 2834 Solutions, pharmaceutical

(G-15475)
RAND MACHINE PRODUCTS INC
Spartan Tool Division
5035 Route 60 (14782-9731)
P.O. Box 72, Falconer (14733-0072)
PHONE..................................716 985-4681
Fax: 716 985-4683
Herman C Ruhlman, *Sales/Mktg Mgr*
Chad Ruhlman, *Manager*
EMP: 9
SALES (corp-wide): 22.7MM Privately Held
WEB: www.randmachine.com
SIC: **3544** 2865 Special dies, tools, jigs & fixtures; dyes & pigments
PA: Rand Machine Products, Inc.
2072 Allen Street Ext
Falconer NY 14733
716 665-5217

Skaneateles
Onondaga County

(G-15476)
ANYELAS VINEYARDS LLC
2433 W Lake Rd (13152-9471)
PHONE..................................315 685-3797
Patti Nocek, *Manager*
James Nocek,
EMP: 13
SQ FT: 5,000
SALES: 200K Privately Held
SIC: **2084** Wines

(G-15477)
BURDICK PUBLICATIONS INC
Also Called: EB&I Marketing
2352 E Lake Rd (13152-8924)
P.O. Box 977 (13152-0977)
PHONE..................................315 685-9500
Elaina K Burdick, *CEO*
EMP: 6
SQ FT: 1,200
SALES (est): 900K Privately Held
WEB: www.burdickpubs.com
SIC: **2741** Miscellaneous publishing

(G-15478)
CHOHEHCO LLC
78 State St (13152-1218)
PHONE..................................315 420-4624
Vedran Psenicnik,
EMP: 7 EST: 2014
SALES (est): 355.4K Privately Held
SIC: **2086** Carbonated beverages, nonalcoholic: bottled & canned

(G-15479)
DIGITAL ANALYSIS CORPORATION
716 Visions Dr (13152)
P.O. Box 95 (13152-0095)
PHONE..................................315 685-0760
Fax: 315 685-0766
Richard Pinkowski, *President*
Joe Pinkowski, *Vice Pres*
Sherri Springer, *Accounting Mgr*
Michael Johnson, *Manager*
Kathleen Pinkowski, *Manager*
EMP: 19
SQ FT: 12,000
SALES: 4.4MM Privately Held
WEB: www.digital-analysis.com
SIC: **3823** Industrial instrmnts msrmnt display/control process variable

(G-15480)
DIVINE PHOENIX LLC
Also Called: Divine Phoenix Books
2985 Benson Rd (13152-9638)
P.O. Box 1001 (13152-5001)
PHONE..................................585 737-1482
Laura Ponticello, *Principal*
EMP: 585
SQ FT: 850
SALES: 30K Privately Held
SIC: **2731** Book publishing

(G-15481)
G E INSPECTION TECHNOLOGIES LP
721 Visions Dr (13152-6475)
PHONE..................................315 554-2000
Todd Brugger, *Branch Mgr*
Maureen Omeara, *Associate*
EMP: 175
SALES (corp-wide): 123.6B Publicly Held
SIC: **3829** 8734 7359 3651 Physical property testing equipment; testing laboratories; equipment rental & leasing; household audio & video equipment
HQ: G E Inspection Technologies, Lp
721 Visions Dr
Skaneateles NY 13152
315 554-2000

(G-15482)
GENERAL ELECTRIC COMPANY
721 Visions Dr (13152-6475)
PHONE..................................315 554-2000
Melissa Lainhart, *General Mgr*
William Kelly, *Design Engr*
Dennis McEnery, *Engng Exec*
Jeff Anderson, *Branch Mgr*
Jeff Register, *Manager*
EMP: 8
SALES (corp-wide): 123.6B Publicly Held
WEB: www.gecommercialfinance.com
SIC: **3699** 3651 3634 Electrical equipment & supplies; household audio & video equipment; electric housewares & fans
PA: General Electric Company
41 Farnsworth St
Boston MA 02210
617 443-3000

(G-15483)
HABA USA
4407 Jordan Rd (13152-9371)
PHONE..................................800 468-6873
Hugh Reed, *Vice Pres*
Alison Barron, *Sales Staff*
Ashley Ware, *Sales Staff*
▲ EMP: 5
SALES (est): 60K Privately Held
SIC: **3944** Games, toys & children's vehicles

(G-15484)
HABERMAASS CORPORATION
Also Called: T C Timber
4407 Jordan Rd (13152-8300)
P.O. Box 42 (13152-0042)
PHONE..................................315 685-8919
Fax: 315 685-3792
Klaus Habermaass, *President*
Rolf Sievers, *Vice Pres*
Janet Walker, *Accounts Mgr*
Ashley Ware, *Sales Staff*
▲ EMP: 12
SQ FT: 150,000
SALES (est): 2.3MM
SALES (corp-wide): 100.2MM Privately Held
SIC: **3944** 5092 Games, toys & children's vehicles; toys & hobby goods & supplies
PA: Habermaass Gmbh
August-Grosch-Str. 28-38
Bad Rodach 96476
956 492-9601

(G-15485)
HANSON AGGREGATES PA LLC
Rr 321 (13152)
PHONE..................................315 685-3321
Dirk Field, *Vice Pres*
Ken Slater, *Plant Mgr*
Phil Wheeler, *Manager*
EMP: 25
SQ FT: 2,160
SALES (corp-wide): 16B Privately Held
SIC: **1442** 1422 Common sand mining; crushed & broken limestone
HQ: Hanson Aggregates Pennsylvania, Llc
7660 Imperial Way
Allentown PA 18195
610 366-4626

(G-15486)
PATIENCE BREWSTER INC
3872 Jordan Rd (13152-9317)
P.O. Box 689 (13152-0689)
PHONE..................................315 685-8336
Patience Brewster Gregg, *CEO*
Holland Gregg, *President*
▲ EMP: 15
SALES: 5MM Privately Held
SIC: **3999** Christmas tree ornaments, except electrical & glass

(G-15487)
SCALE-TRONIX INC (PA)
4341 State Street Rd (13152-9338)
PHONE..................................914 948-8117
Fax: 914 948-0581
Carolyn Lepler, *President*
David C Hale, *Principal*
EMP: 10
SQ FT: 5,000
SALES (est): 4.1MM Privately Held
SIC: **3596** Baby scales; bathroom scales; weighing machines & apparatus

(G-15488)
TESSY PLASTICS CORP (PA)
700 Visions Dr (13152-6475)
PHONE..................................315 689-3924
Fax: 315 689-6595
Roland Beck, *President*
Joseph Raffa, *General Mgr*
Greg Levengood, *COO*
Barry Carson, *Plant Mgr*
Russ Marsh, *Plant Mgr*
◆ EMP: 260
SQ FT: 240,000
SALES (est): 274.2MM Privately Held
WEB: www.tessy.com
SIC: **3089** 3549 Injection molding of plastics; assembly machines, including robotic

Skaneateles Falls
Onondaga County

(G-15489)
CLEAR EDGE CROSIBLE INC
Also Called: Clear Edge Filtration
4653 Jordan Rd (13153-7704)
PHONE..................................315 685-3466
Michael Kriever, *Branch Mgr*
Steve Coghlan, *Manager*
Mike Reichert, *Supervisor*
EMP: 100
SALES (corp-wide): 26.8MM Privately Held
WEB: www.crosible.com
SIC: **2393** Textile bags
PA: Clear Edge Crosible Inc
11607 E 43rd St N
Tulsa OK 74116
918 984-6000

(G-15490)
HAND HELD PRODUCTS INC (HQ)
Also Called: Honeywell Imaging and Mobility
700 Visions Dr (13153-5312)
P.O. Box 208 (13153-0208)
PHONE..................................315 554-6000
Kevin Jost, *CEO*
John F Waldron, *Ch of Bd*
Darius Adamczyk, *Chairman*
Michael A Ehrhart, *Vice Pres*
David Guido, *Vice Pres*
▲ EMP: 500
SQ FT: 120,000
SALES (est): 148.6MM
SALES (corp-wide): 39.3B Publicly Held
WEB: www.handheld.com
SIC: **3577** 3571 3663 3578 Magnetic ink & optical scanning devices; electronic computers; radio & TV communications equipment; calculating & accounting equipment
PA: Honeywell International Inc.
115 Tabor Rd
Morris Plains NJ 07950
973 455-2000

(G-15491)
HAND HELD PRODUCTS INC
Also Called: Honeywell Scanning & Mobility
700 Visions Dr (13153-5312)
PHONE..................................315 554-6000
Ej Riley, *Regional Mgr*
Bill Coleman, *Purch Mgr*
Rick Witkowski, *Engineer*
Dave Guido, *CFO*
Joe Henningan, *CFO*
EMP: 7
SALES (corp-wide): 39.3B Publicly Held
SIC: **3577** Magnetic ink & optical scanning devices
HQ: Hand Held Products, Inc.
700 Visions Dr
Skaneateles Falls NY 13153
315 554-6000

(G-15492)
HONEYWELL INTERNATIONAL INC
700 Visions Dr (13153-5311)
PHONE..................................315 554-6643
Kevin Jost, *President*
Joanne Plis, *Sales Associate*
Eileen Clancy, *Technical Staff*
EMP: 657
SALES (corp-wide): 39.3B Publicly Held
SIC: **3724** Aircraft engines & engine parts
PA: Honeywell International Inc.
115 Tabor Rd
Morris Plains NJ 07950
973 455-2000

(G-15493)
WELCH ALLYN INC
Data Collection Division
4341 State Street Rd (13153-5301)
P.O. Box 220 (13153-0220)
PHONE..................................315 685-4100
Tim McGilloway, *Sales Mgr*
Mary Adams, *Marketing Staff*
Dewey Shimer, *Branch Mgr*
EMP: 1000
SALES (corp-wide): 2.6B Publicly Held
SIC: **3841** 3577 Diagnostic apparatus, medical; computer peripheral equipment
HQ: Welch Allyn Inc
4341 State Street Rd
Skaneateles Falls NY 13153
315 685-4100

(G-15494)
WELCH ALLYN INC (HQ)
4341 State Street Rd (13153-5301)
P.O. Box 220 (13153-0220)
PHONE..................................315 685-4100
Fax: 315 685-4091
Stephen Meyer, *President*
Naveen Velagapudi, *General Mgr*
Chris Bragg, *Business Mgr*
Tom Pelchy, *Business Mgr*
Mike Ehrhart, *Exec VP*
◆ EMP: 1400
SALES (est): 684.6MM
SALES (corp-wide): 2.6B Publicly Held
SIC: **3841** 2835 3827 Diagnostic apparatus, medical; otoscopes, except electromedical; ophthalmic instruments & apparatus; blood pressure apparatus; in vitro & in vivo diagnostic substances; optical instruments & lenses
PA: Hill-Rom Holdings, Inc.
2 Prudential Plz Ste 4100
Chicago IL 60601
312 819-7200

(G-15495)
WELCH ALLYN INC
Also Called: Lighting Products Division
4619 Jordan Rd (13153-5313)
P.O. Box 187 (13153-0187)
PHONE..................................315 685-4347
Fax: 315 685-2854
William Allyn, *Research*
Troy Perkins, *Engineer*
Jan Slodlkowski, *Engineer*
Gregory Vanepps, *Engineer*
Tiffany Moon, *Marketing Staff*
EMP: 1000
SALES (corp-wide): 1.9B Publicly Held
SIC: **3841** 3641 Diagnostic apparatus, medical; electric lamps

Slate Hill - Orange County (G-15496) — GEOGRAPHIC SECTION

HQ: Welch Allyn Inc
4341 State Street Rd
Skaneateles Falls NY 13153
315 685-4100

Slate Hill
Orange County

(G-15496)
RICHARD ROTHBARD INC
1866 Route 284 (10973-4208)
P.O. Box 480 (10973-0480)
PHONE..................845 355-2300
Richard Rothbard, *President*
Joanna Rothbard, *Admin Sec*
EMP: 9
SQ FT: 1,500
SALES (est): 675.2K **Privately Held**
SIC: 2499 Decorative wood & woodwork

Sleepy Hollow
Westchester County

(G-15497)
TRADER INTERNTNAL PUBLICATIONS
50 Fremont Rd (10591-1118)
P.O. Box 687, Tarrytown (10591-0687)
PHONE..................914 631-6856
Jean Sudol, *President*
Edward R Sudol, *Corp Secy*
EMP: 6
SALES: 500K **Privately Held**
SIC: 2741 2721 Miscellaneous publishing; periodicals: publishing only; trade journals: publishing only, not printed on site

(G-15498)
VALERIE BOHIGIAN
Also Called: Valian Associates
225 Hunter Ave (10591-1316)
PHONE..................914 631-8866
Valerie Bohigian, *Owner*
EMP: 6
SALES (est): 230K **Privately Held**
WEB: www.valianassociates.com
SIC: 3914 Trophies, pewter

Slingerlands
Albany County

(G-15499)
LONG LUMBER AND SUPPLY CORP
2100 New Scotland Rd (12159-3419)
PHONE..................518 439-1661
Fax: 518 439-8832
Richard L Long Jr, *President*
Robert P Long, *Vice Pres*
EMP: 10 **EST:** 1945
SQ FT: 10,000
SALES (est): 912.3K **Privately Held**
SIC: 2511 2499 5712 5211 Wood lawn & garden furniture; fencing, wood; furniture stores; fencing

(G-15500)
SABRE ENERGY SERVICES LLC
1891 New Scotland Rd (12159-3628)
PHONE..................518 514-1572
Steven D Oesterle, *CEO*
John Y Mason, *Ch of Bd*
Michael Cecchini, *Info Tech Mgr*
Gillian Webster, *Administration*
EMP: 14
SALES (est): 3.5MM **Privately Held**
SIC: 2819 1389 Sulfur chloride; cementing oil & gas well casings

Sloansville
Schoharie County

(G-15501)
FLORIDA NORTH INC
134 Vanderwerken Rd (12160-2211)
PHONE..................518 868-2888
Fax: 518 868-4888
Daniel Nelson, *President*
EMP: 15
SQ FT: 85,000
SALES: 650K **Privately Held**
WEB: www.makarioscondos.com
SIC: 3949 Swimming pools, plastic

Sloatsburg
Rockland County

(G-15502)
CUSTOM EUROPEAN IMPORTS INC
100 Sterling Mine Rd (10974-2502)
PHONE..................845 357-5718
Martin Lichtman, *President*
▲ **EMP:** 20
SALES (est): 1.7MM **Privately Held**
SIC: 2394 Canvas & related products

Smithtown
Suffolk County

(G-15503)
A & G HEAT SEALING
1 Albatross Ln (11787-3301)
PHONE..................631 724-7764
George Ciunga, *President*
EMP: 8
SQ FT: 12,000
SALES (est): 790.8K **Privately Held**
WEB: www.agheatsealing.com
SIC: 3089 3565 Plastic processing; packaging machinery

(G-15504)
ALL PRODUCTS DESIGNS
227a Route 111 (11787-4754)
PHONE..................631 748-6901
Xiurong Liu, *Owner*
EMP: 7
SALES (est): 346.7K **Privately Held**
SIC: 3669 Communications equipment

(G-15505)
ANCHOR CANVAS LLC
556 W Jericho Tpke (11787-2601)
PHONE..................631 265-5602
Fax: 631 265-5632
Jo A Hnsen, *Finance Mgr*
Jon Hansen,
Rita Zelig, *Administration*
EMP: 6
SQ FT: 8,000
SALES (est): 675.7K **Privately Held**
SIC: 2394 Canvas & related products

(G-15506)
CERTIFIED FLAMEPROOFING CORP
17 N Ingelore Ct (11787-1544)
PHONE..................631 265-4824
Edwards Fallom, *President*
EMP: 6
SALES (est): 436.1K **Privately Held**
SIC: 3251 Fireproofing tile, clay

(G-15507)
DIGITAL ASSOCIATES LLC
50 Karl Ave Ste 303 (11787-2744)
PHONE..................631 983-6075
Vincent RE,
EMP: 8
SALES (est): 225.2K **Privately Held**
SIC: 7372 Publishers' computer software

(G-15508)
DUKE OF IRON INC
1039 W Jericho Tpke (11787-3205)
PHONE..................631 543-3600
Fax: 631 543-3629
Paul Montelbano, *President*
EMP: 6
SQ FT: 8,000
SALES: 1MM **Privately Held**
WEB: www.dukeofiron.com
SIC: 3446 Ornamental metalwork

(G-15509)
G N R PLASTICS INC
Also Called: G N R Co
11 Wandering Way (11787-1147)
PHONE..................631 724-8758
EMP: 9
SQ FT: 10,000
SALES (est): 760K **Privately Held**
SIC: 3544 3089 Mfg Dies/Tools/Jigs/Fixtures Mfg Plastic Products

(G-15510)
HOTELINTERACTIVE INC
155 E Main St Ste 140 (11787-2853)
PHONE..................631 424-7755
Richard Viola, *President*
Joseph Viola, *COO*
Diane Viola, *CFO*
Kelly Arbia, *Office Mgr*
Mike Lemoine, *Director*
EMP: 15
SQ FT: 3,000
SALES (est): 2.3MM **Privately Held**
WEB: www.hotelinteractive.com
SIC: 2721 7389 Trade journals: publishing & printing; decoration service for special events

(G-15511)
IGAMBIT INC (PA)
1050 W Jericho Tpke Ste A (11787-3242)
PHONE..................631 670-6777
Fax: 631 670-6780
John Salerno, *Ch of Bd*
Elisa Luqman, *Exec VP*
Elisa Lugman, *CFO*
EMP: 20
SQ FT: 1,000
SALES (est): 1.9MM **Publicly Held**
SIC: 7372 Business oriented computer software

(G-15512)
IRON WORKER
1039 W Jericho Tpke (11787-3205)
PHONE..................516 338-2756
Fax: 516 543-3629
Paul Montelbano, *President*
EMP: 14
SALES (est): 1.1MM **Privately Held**
SIC: 3446 Stairs, staircases, stair treads: prefabricated metal

(G-15513)
JERIC KNIT WEAR
61 Hofstra Dr (11787-2053)
PHONE..................631 979-8827
Jerry Lobel, *Owner*
EMP: 5
SALES (est): 452.3K **Privately Held**
SIC: 2253 Sweaters & sweater coats, knit

(G-15514)
KANTIAN SKINCARE LLC
496 Smithtown Byp (11787-5005)
PHONE..................631 780-4711
Jonathan Klein,
Richard Klein,
EMP: 5 **EST:** 2012
SALES (est): 492.4K **Privately Held**
SIC: 2844 Cosmetic preparations

(G-15515)
NATURALLY FREE FOOD INC
35 Roundabout Rd (11787-1822)
P.O. Box 1365 (11787-0896)
PHONE..................631 361-9710
Christine Mitchell, *Principal*
EMP: 6
SALES (est): 429.6K **Privately Held**
SIC: 2099 Food preparations

(G-15516)
PBL INDUSTRIES CORP
49 Dillmont Dr (11787-1635)
PHONE..................631 979-4266
William Loffman, *President*
EMP: 10
SALES: 950K **Privately Held**
SIC: 3499 Fabricated metal products

(G-15517)
PERFECT FORMS AND SYSTEMS INC
35 Riverview Ter (11787-1155)
PHONE..................631 462-1100
Fax: 631 382-4976
Joseph Messana, *President*
Jacquelyn Cully, *Business Dir*
EMP: 15
SALES (est): 1.6MM **Privately Held**
SIC: 2752 Business form & card printing, lithographic

(G-15518)
PRECISION DENTAL CABINETS INC (PA)
900 W Jericho Tpke (11787-3206)
PHONE..................631 543-3870
Fax: 631 543-1609
Peter Loscialpo, *President*
Joseph Pisk, *Vice Pres*
Antoinette Frumusa, *Bookkeeper*
EMP: 13 **EST:** 1965
SQ FT: 12,000
SALES (est): 2.3MM **Privately Held**
SIC: 3843 2434 1751 Cabinets, dental; wood kitchen cabinets; cabinet building & installation

(G-15519)
PSI TRANSIT MIX CORP
34 E Main St (11787-2804)
P.O. Box 178 (11787-0178)
PHONE..................631 382-7930
Albino Almeida, *President*
EMP: 5
SALES (est): 478K **Privately Held**
SIC: 2951 Concrete, asphaltic (not from refineries); concrete, bituminous

(G-15520)
QUALTRONIC DEVICES INC
130 Oakside Dr (11787-1132)
PHONE..................631 360-0859
Peter A Ferentinos, *CEO*
Steven Ferentinos, *Ch of Bd*
Antoine Dominic, *Project Mgr*
EMP: 18
SQ FT: 3,000
SALES (est): 2.2MM **Privately Held**
SIC: 3571 Electronic computers

(G-15521)
SMITHTOWN NEWS INC
Also Called: North Shore News Group
1 Brooksite Dr (11787-3493)
P.O. Box 805 (11787-0805)
PHONE..................631 265-2100
Fax: 631 265-6237
Bernard Paley, *President*
Mary Lavecchia, *Office Mgr*
EMP: 32
SQ FT: 7,000
SALES (est): 1.9MM **Privately Held**
WEB: www.thesmithtownnews.com
SIC: 2711 Newspapers

(G-15522)
T-COMPANY LLC
16 Monitor Rd (11787-1867)
PHONE..................646 290-6365
Mark Grottano, *Mng Member*
Lisa Frizol,
Agatha Grottano,
EMP: 5
SQ FT: 2,100
SALES (est): 400K **Privately Held**
SIC: 2599 Factory furniture & fixtures

(G-15523)
TRADEWINS PUBLISHING CORP
19 Bellemeade Ave Ste B (11787-1877)
PHONE..................631 361-6916
Steve Schmidt, *President*
Jane Schmidt, *Admin Sec*
EMP: 5

▲ = Import ▼ = Export
◆ = Import/Export

SQ FT: 1,000
SALES (est): 440K **Privately Held**
WEB: www.tradewinspublishing.com
SIC: 7372 Publishers' computer software

(G-15524)
VITAKEM NUTRACEUTICAL INC
811 W Jericho Tpke (11787-3232)
PHONE 631 956-8343
EMP: 250
SQ FT: 35,000
SALES: 15MM **Privately Held**
SIC: 2023 Mfg Dietary Supplements Products

Sodus
Wayne County

(G-15525)
MIZKAN AMERICAS INC
7673 Sodus Center Rd (14551-9539)
PHONE 315 483-6944
Carlos Mansinho, *Plant Mgr*
Kevin Perry, *Opers Staff*
Ted Pouley, *Manager*
EMP: 10 **Privately Held**
SIC: 2099 Vinegar
HQ: Mizkan America, Inc.
    1661 Feehanville Dr # 200
    Mount Prospect IL 60056
    847 590-0059

(G-15526)
NYKON INC
Also Called: Ramco Arts
8175 Stell Rd (14551-9530)
PHONE 315 483-0504
Alice Cuvelier, *Principal*
Craig Cuvelier, *Controller*
EMP: 9
SQ FT: 5,000
SALES (est): 793.3K **Privately Held**
WEB: www.nykon.net
SIC: 3651 Music distribution apparatus

(G-15527)
TERMATEC MOLDING INC
28 Foley Dr (14551-1044)
P.O. Box 96 (14551-0096)
PHONE 315 483-4150
Fax: 315 483-6365
Brad Cuvelier, *President*
James Peerson, *Plant Mgr*
James Peterson, *Plant Mgr*
EMP: 15
SQ FT: 6,500
SALES (est): 2.4MM **Privately Held**
SIC: 3089 Molding primary plastic

Solvay
Onondaga County

(G-15528)
BERRY GLOBAL INC
1500 Milton Ave (13209-1622)
PHONE 315 484-0397
David Heigel, *Manager*
Peter Miller, *Manager*
Tom Taylor, *Info Tech Mgr*
EMP: 178
SALES (corp-wide): 6.4B **Publicly Held**
SIC: 3089 Bottle caps, molded plastic; unsupported plastics film & sheet
HQ: Berry Global, Inc.
    101 Oakley St
    Evansville IN 47710
    812 424-2904

(G-15529)
EASTERN COMPANY
Also Called: Frazer & Jones Division
3000 Milton Ave (13209)
P.O. Box 4955, Syracuse (13221-4955)
PHONE 315 468-6251
Stan Newsome, *Plant Supt*
Sadmir Brkanovic, *QC Mgr*
Michael Reilley, *Technical Mgr*
Thomas Giannone, *Controller*
A T Giannone, *Comptroller*
EMP: 100

SALES (corp-wide): 137.6MM **Publicly Held**
WEB: www.easterncompany.com
SIC: 3322 Malleable iron foundries
PA: The Eastern Company
    112 Bridge St
    Naugatuck CT 06770
    203 729-2255

(G-15530)
EVENT SERVICES CORPORATION
6171 Airport Rd (13209-9754)
P.O. Box 587 (13209-0587)
PHONE 315 488-9357
Kevin Jankiewicz, *President*
EMP: 6
SALES (est): 440K **Privately Held**
SIC: 2099 Food preparations

Somers
Westchester County

(G-15531)
GENERAL CINEMA BEVS OF OHIO
Also Called: Pepsi Bottle and Group
1 Pepsi Way Ste 1 (10589-2212)
PHONE 914 767-6000
Craig Weatherup, *President*
Mike Becker, *Senior Mgr*
Christian Luther, *Info Tech Mgr*
Chris Knox, *Director*
EMP: 1200
SALES (est): 63.4MM
SALES (corp-wide): 62.8B **Publicly Held**
WEB: www.joy-of-cola.com
SIC: 2086 Soft drinks: packaged in cans, bottles, etc.
HQ: Pepsi-Cola Metropolitan Bottling Company, Inc.
    1111 Westchester Ave
    White Plains NY 10604
    914 767-6000

(G-15532)
GRAYHAWK LEASING LLC (HQ)
1 Pepsi Way (10589-2212)
PHONE 914 767-6000
Saad Abdul-Latif, *CEO*
EMP: 7
SALES (est): 2.1MM
SALES (corp-wide): 62.8B **Publicly Held**
SIC: 2086 7359 Bottled & canned soft drinks; rental store, general
PA: Pepsico, Inc.
    700 Anderson Hill Rd
    Purchase NY 10577
    914 253-2000

(G-15533)
PEPSI BTLG GROUP GLOBL FIN LLC (DH)
1 Pepsi Way Ste 1 (10589-2212)
PHONE 914 767-6000
Eric J Ross, *President*
EMP: 6
SALES (est): 2.5MM
SALES (corp-wide): 62.8B **Publicly Held**
SIC: 2086 Carbonated soft drinks, bottled & canned
HQ: Pepsi-Cola Metropolitan Bottling Company, Inc.
    1111 Westchester Ave
    White Plains NY 10604
    914 767-6000

(G-15534)
RICHARD C OWEN PUBLISHERS INC
243 Route 100 (10589-3203)
P.O. Box 585, Katonah (10536-0585)
PHONE 914 232-3903
Fax: 914 232-3977
Richard C Owen, *President*
Phyllis Morrison, *Office Mgr*
▲ **EMP:** 11
SQ FT: 5,000
SALES (est): 1.5MM **Privately Held**
WEB: www.rcowen.com
SIC: 2731 Books: publishing only

Sound Beach
Suffolk County

(G-15535)
PREFAB CONSTRUCTION INC
16 Jackson Ave (11789-2623)
PHONE 631 821-9613
Charles Kapp, *Ch of Bd*
EMP: 12 **EST:** 2001
SALES: 800K **Privately Held**
WEB: www.prefabconstruction.com
SIC: 1389 Construction, repair & dismantling services

South Bethlehem
Albany County

(G-15536)
OLDCASTLE PRECAST INC
100 S County Rte 101 (12161)
PHONE 518 767-2116
Fax: 518 767-2183
Sheila Connor, *Manager*
EMP: 10
SALES (corp-wide): 28.6B **Privately Held**
WEB: www.oldcastle-precast.com
SIC: 3272 3446 3273 Concrete products, precast; pipe, concrete or lined with concrete; open flooring & grating for construction; ready-mixed concrete
HQ: Oldcastle Precast, Inc.
    1002 15th St Sw Ste 110
    Auburn WA 98001
    253 833-2777

South Colton
St. Lawrence County

(G-15537)
J & S LOGGING INC
3860 State Highway 56 (13687-3403)
PHONE 315 262-2112
Stephen Poste, *President*
Patricia Poste, *Vice Pres*
Teresa Fisher, *Director*
Jerry Poste, *Director*
EMP: 20
SALES (est): 2.3MM **Privately Held**
SIC: 2411 4212 Logging camps & contractors; local trucking, without storage

(G-15538)
NORTHEASTERN SIGN CORP
102 Cold Brook Dr (13687)
P.O. Box 340 (13687-0340)
PHONE 315 265-6657
Anne Clarkson, *President*
EMP: 8
SQ FT: 1,600
SALES (est): 983.3K **Privately Held**
SIC: 3993 Signs & advertising specialties

South Dayton
Cattaraugus County

(G-15539)
BIRDS EYE FOODS INC
Also Called: Comstock Foods Division
Mechanic St (14138)
PHONE 716 988-3218
Sam Chiavetta, *Branch Mgr*
EMP: 4
SALES (corp-wide): 2.5B **Publicly Held**
SIC: 2037 Vegetables, quick frozen & cold pack, excl. potato products
HQ: Birds Eye Foods, Inc.
    121 Woodcrest Rd
    Cherry Hill NJ 08003
    585 383-1850

(G-15540)
CHERRY CREEK WOODCRAFT INC (PA)
Also Called: Great Impressions
1 Cherry St (14138-9736)
P.O. Box 267 (14138-0267)
PHONE 716 988-3211
Fax: 716 988-3109
Michael Lord, *Ch of Bd*
Martin Goldman, *President*
Jennifer Brown, *Finance Dir*
Jennifer Morey, *Director*
Charlene Sterlace, *Executive*
EMP: 34
SQ FT: 60,000
SALES (est): 4.4MM **Privately Held**
SIC: 2499 Trophy bases, wood

(G-15541)
COUNTRY SIDE SAND & GRAVEL
8458 Route 62 (14138-9756)
PHONE 716 988-3271
Fax: 716 988-3272
Mark Smith, *Vice Pres*
Jason Rosier, *Manager*
EMP: 10
SALES (corp-wide): 27.5MM **Privately Held**
SIC: 1442 Construction sand mining; gravel mining
HQ: Country Side Sand & Gravel Inc
    Taylor Hollow Rd
    Collins NY 14034
    716 988-3271

South Fallsburg
Sullivan County

(G-15542)
ALLIED WINE CORP
Also Called: Rosedub
121 Main St (12779-5104)
P.O. Box 88, Ellenville (12428-0088)
PHONE 845 796-4160
Fax: 845 434-4086
Moshe Schwartz, *President*
Abe Schwartz, *Vice Pres*
EMP: 10 **EST:** 1992
SQ FT: 18,000
SALES (est): 265.1K **Privately Held**
SIC: 2084 Wines; brandy & brandy spirits

(G-15543)
MB FOOD PROCESSING INC
5190 S Fallsburg Main St (12779)
P.O. Box 13 (12779-0013)
PHONE 845 436-5001
Fax: 845 436-5001
Dean Koplik, *President*
EMP: 350
SALES (est): 1.8MM **Privately Held**
WEB: www.murrayschicken.com
SIC: 2015 Poultry slaughtering & processing
PA: M.B. Consulting Group, Ltd.
    5190 S Fallsburg Main
    South Fallsburg NY 12779
    845 434-5050

(G-15544)
MURRAY BRESKY CONSULTANTS LTD (PA)
Also Called: Murray's Chicken
5190 Main St (12779)
P.O. Box P (12779-2015)
PHONE 845 436-5001
Murray Bresky, *President*
Ellen Gold, *Corp Secy*
Dean Koplik, *Vice Pres*
Allen Schwartz, *Opers Mgr*
Maureen J Pinto, *Human Res Dir*
EMP: 299
SQ FT: 40,000
SALES (est): 47MM **Privately Held**
SIC: 2015 Poultry slaughtering & processing

South Glens Falls
Saratoga County

(G-15545)
AMES ADVANCED MATERIALS CORP (HQ)
50 Harrison Ave (12803-4912)
PHONE..................518 792-5808
Frank Barber, *President*
EMP: 63
SALES (est): 27.7MM
SALES (corp-wide): 35.6MM **Privately Held**
SIC: 3399 Silver powder; flakes, metal
PA: Ames Goldsmith Corp.
50 Harrison Ave
South Glens Falls NY 12803
518 792-5808

(G-15546)
ARCA INK LLC
30 Bluebird Rd (12803-5707)
PHONE..................518 798-0100
Robert Chadwick, *Mng Member*
Wendy Lafountain-Chadwick, *Mng Member*
EMP: 6
SQ FT: 9,000
SALES (est): 828.2K **Privately Held**
SIC: 2759 Screen printing

(G-15547)
CASTLE POWER SOLUTIONS LLC
22 Hudson Falls Rd Ste D (12803-5067)
PHONE..................518 743-1000
Maureen Losito, *President*
▲ **EMP:** 14
SQ FT: 3,200
SALES: 3MM **Privately Held**
SIC: 3699 Electrical equipment & supplies

(G-15548)
HEXION INC
64 Fernan Rd (12803-5047)
P.O. Box B (12803)
PHONE..................518 792-8040
Mike Karpinski, *Purchasing*
Kathleen Ervine, *Manager*
EMP: 20 **Privately Held**
SIC: 2821 2869 2891 Melamine resins, melamine-formaldehyde; formaldehyde (formalin); adhesives & sealants
HQ: Hexion Inc.
180 E Broad St Fl 26
Columbus OH 43215
614 225-4000

(G-15549)
MDI EAST INC
Also Called: Bates Industries
22 Hudson Falls Rd Ste 6 (12803-5069)
PHONE..................518 747-8730
Fax: 518 747-8392
Randy Bodkin, *Plant Mgr*
Tom Pendergrass, *Plant Mgr*
Rhonda Sharp, *Materials Mgr*
Dale Jenks, *Engineer*
Michael Siano, *Engineer*
EMP: 50
SALES (corp-wide): 13.6MM **Privately Held**
SIC: 3841 Surgical & medical instruments
HQ: Mdi East, Inc.
6918 Ed Perkic St
Riverside CA 92504
951 509-6918

(G-15550)
NORTHEAST PROMOTIONAL GROUP IN
75 Main St (12803-4706)
PHONE..................518 793-1024
Deana Endieveri, *President*
Jim Chamberlin, *Vice Pres*
Mike Endieveri, *Vice Pres*
Kindra Chamberlin, *Treasurer*
Kate Cochran, *Representative*
EMP: 5
SALES (est): 666.9K **Privately Held**
WEB: www.nepromo.com
SIC: 3993 7389 Advertising novelties; embroidering of advertising on shirts, etc.

(G-15551)
NORTHEAST STITCHES & INK INC
Also Called: Sperry Advertising
95 Main St (12803-4706)
PHONE..................518 798-5549
Deana Endieveri, *President*
Kindra Chamberlin, *Corp Secy*
James Chamberlin, *Vice Pres*
Michael Endieveri, *Vice Pres*
Jeremy Terry, *Manager*
EMP: 34
SQ FT: 20,000
SALES (est): 2.8MM **Privately Held**
WEB: www.nestitchesink.com
SIC: 2395 2396 Embroidery & art needlework; automotive & apparel trimmings

(G-15552)
O RAMA LIGHT INC
22 Hudson Falls Rd Ste 52 (12803-5067)
PHONE..................518 539-9000
John N Potochnak, *CEO*
Dan Baldwin, *Co-Owner*
EMP: 20 EST: 2009
SALES (est): 2.6MM **Privately Held**
SIC: 3577 Computer peripheral equipment

South Hempstead
Nassau County

(G-15553)
ACCESSORIES FOR ELECTRONICS
Also Called: Afe
620 Mead Ter (11550-8011)
PHONE..................631 847-0158
William J Epstein, *President*
Peter Wright, *Treasurer*
EMP: 26
SQ FT: 3,000
SALES (est): 5.4MM **Privately Held**
WEB: www.afeaccess.com
SIC: 3678 3679 Electronic connectors; electronic circuits

(G-15554)
MIRANDY PRODUCTS LTD
1078 Grand Ave (11550-7902)
PHONE..................516 489-6800
Ira Breiter, *President*
Mike Glassman, *Treasurer*
EMP: 28
SQ FT: 5,000
SALES (est): 3.5MM **Privately Held**
WEB: www.mirandy.com
SIC: 2842 5087 Industrial plant disinfectants or deodorants; service establishment equipment

South Otselic
Chenango County

(G-15555)
GLADDING BRAIDED PRODUCTS LLC
1 Gladding St (13155)
P.O. Box 164 (13155-0164)
PHONE..................315 653-7211
Fax: 315 653-4492
Sparky Christakos, *President*
Mike Radziwon, *Vice Pres*
Charles Bishop, *VP Prdtn*
Rick Burt, *Manager*
▲ **EMP:** 45
SQ FT: 85,000
SALES (est): 7.5MM **Privately Held**
WEB: www.gladdingbraid.com
SIC: 2298 Rope, except asbestos & wire; cordage: abaca, sisal, henequen, hemp, jute or other fiber; cord, braided

South Ozone Park
Queens County

(G-15556)
CONTINENTAL LIFT TRUCK INC
12718 Foch Blvd (11420-2824)
PHONE..................718 738-4738
Giuseppe Donofrio, *CEO*
Julia Adeleke, *Analyst*
▲ **EMP:** 16
SALES (est): 4.4MM **Privately Held**
SIC: 3537 Forklift trucks

(G-15557)
EXTREME AUTO ACCESSORIES CORP (PA)
Also Called: Rennen International
12019 Rockaway Blvd (11420-2423)
PHONE..................718 978-6722
Fax: 718 504-9637
Takang Lee, *Ch of Bd*
Weizrung Lee, *COO*
Rich Sha, *Vice Pres*
Tony Lao, *Manager*
Linda Liu, *Administration*
▲ **EMP:** 15
SQ FT: 15,000
SALES (est): 3.6MM **Privately Held**
WEB: www.renneninternational.com
SIC: 3714 5013 Wheel rims, motor vehicle; automotive supplies

South Richmond Hill
Queens County

(G-15558)
MAIZTECA FOODS INC
13005 Liberty Ave (11419-3121)
PHONE..................718 641-3933
Sixto Reyes, *CEO*
Carlos Reyes, *President*
EMP: 40
SQ FT: 10,000
SALES: 3.5MM **Privately Held**
SIC: 2099 Tortillas, fresh or refrigerated

South Salem
Westchester County

(G-15559)
GUITAR SPECIALIST INC
219 Oakridge Cmn (10590)
PHONE..................914 533-5589
EMP: 5
SQ FT: 2,400
SALES (est): 310K **Privately Held**
SIC: 3931 7699 Mfg Musical Instruments Repair Services

(G-15560)
SERENDIPITY CONSULTING CORP
48 Twin Lakes Rd (10590-1009)
PHONE..................914 763-8251
Senia E Feiner, *President*
Mark Feiner, *Info Tech Mgr*
EMP: 10
SQ FT: 3,200
SALES (est): 601.5K **Privately Held**
WEB: www.sccny.com
SIC: 7372 8742 Application computer software; training & development consultant

(G-15561)
THE CENTRO COMPANY INC
215 Silver Spring Rd (10590-2525)
PHONE..................914 533-2200
Alan Greene, *Ch of Bd*
Susan Green, *President*
EMP: 5
SALES (est): 508.6K **Privately Held**
SIC: 3061 Mechanical rubber goods

Southampton
Suffolk County

(G-15562)
AMERICAN COUNTRY QUILTS & LIN
Also Called: Judi Boisson American Country
134 Mariner Dr Unit C (11968-3482)
PHONE..................631 283-5466
Judi Boisson, *President*
Erin Boisson, *Vice Pres*
EMP: 8
SQ FT: 4,000
SALES (est): 567.9K **Privately Held**
SIC: 2395 2269 3269 5023 Quilted fabrics or cloth; linen fabrics: dyeing, finishing & printing; art & ornamental ware, pottery; linens & towels; linens, table; decorative home furnishings & supplies; mail order house; antiques

(G-15563)
BEST MDLR HMS AFRBE P Q& S IN
495 County Road 39 (11968-5236)
PHONE..................631 204-0049
Fax: 631 204-1534
John Distefano, *Ch of Bd*
Laureiann Distefano, *Vice Pres*
Susan Ehrlich, *Manager*
EMP: 14
SALES (est): 1.6MM **Privately Held**
SIC: 2452 Modular homes, prefabricated, wood

(G-15564)
CENTRAL KITCHEN CORP
871 County Road 39 (11968-5227)
PHONE..................631 283-1029
Fax: 631 283-1138
Robert Grigo, *President*
Doreen Grigo, *Corp Secy*
William Grigo, *Real Est Agnt*
EMP: 10
SQ FT: 4,000
SALES (est): 1.4MM **Privately Held**
WEB: www.centralkitchenscorp.com
SIC: 2434 5712 1751 5031 Wood kitchen cabinets; cabinet work, custom; cabinets, except custom made: kitchen; cabinet & finish carpentry; cabinet building & installation; kitchen cabinets

(G-15565)
DANS PAPER INC
Also Called: South of The Highway
158 County Road 39 (11968-5252)
PHONE..................631 537-0500
Fax: 631 537-3330
Jean Lynch, *Publisher*
Margo C Abrams, *General Mgr*
Roy E Brown, *Chairman*
Allison Bourquin, *Sales Staff*
Leslie Ernst, *Sales Staff*
EMP: 68
SQ FT: 2,500
SALES (est): 5.3MM
SALES (corp-wide): 8.9MM **Privately Held**
WEB: www.danspapers.com
SIC: 2711 Newspapers: publishing only, not printed on site
PA: News Communications Inc
501 Madison Ave Fl 23
New York NY 10022
212 689-2500

(G-15566)
FRONTIERS UNLIMITED INC
Also Called: Homes Land Eastrn Long Island
52 Jagger Ln (11968-4822)
PHONE..................631 283-4663
Fax: 631 283-4018
James Miller, *President*
EMP: 8
SQ FT: 1,300
SALES: 1.5MM **Privately Held**
WEB: www.hamptonshomes.com
SIC: 2721 Periodicals

GEOGRAPHIC SECTION

(G-15567)
GABANI INC
81 Lee Ave (11968-4518)
PHONE..................................631 283-4930
Gabrielle Sampietro, *President*
Miguel Sampietro, *Treasurer*
EMP: 6
SQ FT: 900
SALES (est): 42.6K Privately Held
SIC: 2253 Knit outerwear mills

(G-15568)
HAMPTONS MAGAZINE
67 Hampton Rd Unit 5 (11968-4962)
PHONE..................................631 283-7125
Randy Schindler, *President*
Jason Binn, *Publisher*
Debra Halpert, *Publisher*
Samantha Yanks, *Publisher*
Avery Andon, *Editor*
EMP: 50
SQ FT: 2,400
SALES: 3.5MM Privately Held
SIC: 2721 2791 2752 Periodicals-Publishing/Printing Typesetting Services Lithographic Commercial Printing

(G-15569)
HAMPTONS MEDIA LLC
Also Called: Hamptons Magazine
67 Hampton Rd Unit 5 (11968-4962)
PHONE..................................631 283-6900
Fax: 631 283-7854
Jason Binn,
EMP: 5
SALES: 149.3K
SALES (corp-wide): 57.3MM Privately Held
SIC: 2721 Periodicals
HQ: Niche Media Holdings, L.L.C
    257 Park Ave S Fl 5
    New York NY 10010
    702 990-2500

(G-15570)
LTB MEDIA (USA) INC
Also Called: Louise Blouin Media
376 Gin Ln (11968-5077)
PHONE..................................212 447-9555
Louise B Macbain, *President*
Nicolai Hartvig, *Editor*
Derek Page, *Vice Pres*
Jonny Leather, *Prdtn Mgr*
Aasia Idris, *Accounting Mgr*
EMP: 100
SQ FT: 16,000
SALES (est): 14MM Privately Held
SIC: 2721 Magazines: publishing & printing

(G-15571)
MORRIS GOLF VENTURES
Sebonac Inlet Rd (11968)
PHONE..................................631 283-0559
James Morris, *Owner*
EMP: 25
SALES (est): 1.7MM Privately Held
SIC: 3949 Golf equipment

(G-15572)
PAULPAC LLC
104 Foster Xing (11968-4955)
PHONE..................................631 283-7610
Michela Keszlies,
EMP: 6
SALES: 500K Privately Held
WEB: www.paulpac.com
SIC: 2393 Textile bags

(G-15573)
PECONIC IRONWORKS LTD
33 Flying Point Rd # 108 (11968-5280)
PHONE..................................631 204-0323
Patrick Grace, *President*
Thomas Berglin, *Vice Pres*
Don Gauthir, *Manager*
EMP: 13 **EST:** 1997
SALES (est): 2.4MM Privately Held
SIC: 3446 Architectural metalwork

(G-15574)
ROCKWELL VIDEO SOLUTIONS LLC
10 Koral Dr (11968-4307)
PHONE..................................631 745-0582
Adam Cusack,
EMP: 15
SALES (est): 950K Privately Held
SIC: 3999 Manufacturing industries

(G-15575)
SHADE & SHUTTER SYSTEMS OF NY
260 Hampton Rd (11968-5028)
PHONE..................................631 208-0275
EMP: 6
SALES (est): 630K Privately Held
SIC: 3442 Louvers, shutters, jalousies & similar items

(G-15576)
SOUTHAMPTON TOWN NEWSPAPERS (PA)
Also Called: Press of Manorville & Moriches
135 Windmill Ln (11968-4840)
PHONE..................................631 283-4100
Fax: 631 283-4927
Joseph Louchheim, *President*
Nick Thomas, *Business Mgr*
Scott Enstine, *Prdtn Mgr*
Paul Conroy, *Sales Mgr*
David Macmillan, *Sales Executive*
EMP: 30
SQ FT: 1,500
SALES (est): 3.9MM Privately Held
WEB: www.southamptonpress.com
SIC: 2711 2741 Newspapers: publishing only, not printed on site; miscellaneous publishing

(G-15577)
THEORY LLC
98 Main St (11968-4834)
PHONE..................................631 204-0231
EMP: 5
SALES (corp-wide): 17.4B Privately Held
SIC: 2337 Suits: women's, misses' & juniors'
HQ: Theory Llc
    38 Gansevoort St
    New York NY 10014
    212 300-0800

(G-15578)
THOMAS MATTHEWS WDWKG LTD
15 Powell Ave (11968)
PHONE..................................631 287-3657
Thomas Matthews, *Branch Mgr*
EMP: 14 Privately Held
SIC: 2499 Woodenware, kitchen & household
PA: Thomas Matthews Woodworking Ltd.
    225 Ocean View Pkwy
    Southampton NY 11968

(G-15579)
THOMAS MATTHEWS WDWKG LTD (PA)
225 Ocean View Pkwy (11968-5523)
P.O. Box 520, Bridgehampton (11932-0520)
PHONE..................................631 287-2023
Thomas Matthew, *President*
EMP: 6
SALES (est): 1.1MM Privately Held
SIC: 2499 Woodenware, kitchen & household

Southfields
Orange County

(G-15580)
KARLYN INDUSTRIES INC
16 Spring St (10975-2614)
P.O. Box 310 (10975-0310)
PHONE..................................845 351-2249
Fax: 845 351-2256
Hans Bierdumpfel, *President*
Margaret Bierdumpfel, *Vice Pres*
Joyce Lasalle, *Treasurer*
▲ **EMP:** 15
SQ FT: 10,000
SALES (est): 1.3MM Privately Held
WEB: www.karlynsti.com
SIC: 3714 3694 Motor vehicle parts & accessories; spark plugs for internal combustion engines

Southold
Suffolk County

(G-15581)
ACADEMY PRINTING SERVICES INC
Also Called: Peconic B Shopper
42 Hortons Ln (11971-1686)
P.O. Box 848 (11971-0848)
PHONE..................................631 765-3346
Fax: 631 765-3369
Michael Hagerman, *President*
Rita Hagerman, *Vice Pres*
EMP: 6
SQ FT: 4,000
SALES (est): 866.4K Privately Held
SIC: 2752 2759 Photo-offset printing; commercial printing

(G-15582)
FUTURE SCREW MACHINE PDTS INC
41155 County Road 48 (11971-5041)
PHONE..................................631 765-1610
Fax: 631 765-2683
Ellen Hufe, *President*
Glen Grathwhol, *Manager*
EMP: 10
SQ FT: 2,700
SALES (est): 1.8MM Privately Held
SIC: 3599 Machine shop, jobbing & repair

(G-15583)
INTERNODAL INTERNATIONAL INC
54800 Route 25 (11971-4648)
P.O. Box 606 (11971-0606)
PHONE..................................631 765-0037
Fax: 631 765-2337
Rosemary Verrecchio, *President*
Joe Stadler, *Vice Pres*
EMP: 25
SALES (est): 1.4MM Privately Held
WEB: www.internodalinternational.com
SIC: 7372 7389 Prepackaged software; design services

(G-15584)
NEW ENGLAND BARNS INC
45805 Route 25 (11971-4670)
P.O. Box 1447, Mattituck (11952-0925)
PHONE..................................631 445-1461
William Gorman, *Owner*
EMP: 22
SALES (est): 1.7MM Privately Held
SIC: 2439 Timbers, structural: laminated lumber

(G-15585)
WALLACE HOME DESIGN CTR
44500 County Road 48 (11971-5034)
P.O. Box 181, Peconic (11958-0181)
PHONE..................................631 765-3890
George Wallace, *President*
Rene Lisowy, *Owner*
EMP: 6
SQ FT: 2,400
SALES (est): 839.5K Privately Held
SIC: 2211 2511 2512 5713 Draperies & drapery fabrics, cotton; wood household furniture; upholstered household furniture; carpets; window furnishings

Sparrow Bush
Orange County

(G-15586)
ETERNAL LINE
1237 State Route 42 (12780-5042)
PHONE..................................845 856-1999
Marius Winograd, *Owner*
Agnes Winograd, *Co-Owner*
EMP: 2
SALES: 1.2MM Privately Held
SIC: 3911 Jewelry, precious metal

Speculator
Hamilton County

(G-15587)
STEPHENSON LUMBER COMPANY INC
Rr 8 (12164)
PHONE..................................518 548-7521
John Shaw, *Manager*
EMP: 5
SALES (corp-wide): 6MM Privately Held
WEB: www.riversidetruss.com
SIC: 2439 5211 Arches, laminated lumber; millwork & lumber
PA: Stephenson Lumber Company, Inc.
    Riverside Station Rd
    Riparius NY 12862
    518 494-4733

Spencer
Tioga County

(G-15588)
STARFIRE SWORDS LTD INC
74 Railroad Ave (14883-9543)
PHONE..................................607 589-7244
Fax: 607 589-6630
Maciej Zakrzewski, *President*
Sandy Russell, *Vice Pres*
Alexandra White, *Vice Pres*
EMP: 20
SALES (est): 2.5MM Privately Held
WEB: www.starfireswords.com
SIC: 3421 Swords

Spencerport
Monroe County

(G-15589)
AZTEC MFG OF ROCHESTER
19 Hickory Ln (14559-2511)
PHONE..................................585 352-8152
James Monsees, *Ch of Bd*
Mary Monsees, *Manager*
EMP: 7
SQ FT: 5,382
SALES (est): 903.8K Privately Held
SIC: 3541 Machine tools, metal cutting type

(G-15590)
BOSS PRECISION LTD
2440 S Union St (14559-2230)
PHONE..................................585 352-7070
Fax: 585 352-7059
Gerd Herrman, *Ch of Bd*
Paul Dugan, *Vice Pres*
Alec Ollies, *Treasurer*
EMP: 60
SQ FT: 45,000
SALES (est): 11.8MM Privately Held
SIC: 3444 Sheet metalwork

(G-15591)
BSV METAL FINISHERS INC
Also Called: Bsv Enterprises
11 Aristocrat Cir (14559-1042)
PHONE..................................585 349-7072
Benjamin S Vasquez, *President*
EMP: 26
SQ FT: 13,000
SALES (est): 5.4MM Privately Held
SIC: 3398 Metal heat treating

(G-15592)
BULLET INDUSTRIES INC
Also Called: Coyote Motorsports
7 Turner Dr (14559-1930)
PHONE..................................585 352-0836
Mark Lipari, *CEO*
EMP: 6 **EST:** 2007
SALES (est): 451.8K Privately Held
SIC: 3799 7539 Recreational vehicles; machine shop, automotive

Spencerport — Monroe County

(G-15593)
DOLOMITE PRODUCTS COMPANY INC
2540 S Union St (14559-2232)
PHONE..................585 352-0460
Wally Przybcien, *Principal*
EMP: 16
SALES (corp-wide): 28.6B **Privately Held**
SIC: 2951 Asphalt paving mixtures & blocks
HQ: Dolomite Products Company Inc.
 1150 Penfield Rd
 Rochester NY 14625
 315 524-1998

(G-15594)
IMCO INC
15 Turner Dr (14559-1930)
PHONE..................585 352-7810
Fax: 585 352-7809
David Demallie, *Principal*
John Stresz, *Marketing Staff*
Susan Rinere, *Manager*
Audrey Mair, *Director*
EMP: 47
SQ FT: 25,000
SALES (est): 9.1MM **Privately Held**
SIC: 3089 Injection molding of plastics

(G-15595)
KLEIN REINFORCING SERVICES INC
11 Turner Dr (14559-1930)
PHONE..................585 352-9433
Fax: 585 352-4474
Mark Kulzer, *President*
EMP: 15
SQ FT: 15,000
SALES (est): 3.7MM **Privately Held**
SIC: 3449 Bars, concrete reinforcing: fabricated steel

(G-15596)
MANUFACTURERS TOOL & DIE CO
3 Turner Dr (14559-1930)
P.O. Box 139 (14559-0139)
PHONE..................585 352-1080
Fax: 585 352-1086
Douglas Sullivan, *President*
Dan Sullivan, *Vice Pres*
Gail Sullivan, *Office Mgr*
EMP: 5 **EST:** 1918
SQ FT: 10,000
SALES: 300K **Privately Held**
SIC: 3544 Special dies, tools, jigs & fixtures

(G-15597)
ROTATION DYNAMICS CORPORATION
Rotadyne
3581 Big Ridge Rd (14559-1709)
PHONE..................585 352-9023
Dave Baldwin, *Plant Mgr*
Scott Bleier, *Opers Staff*
EMP: 36
SALES (corp-wide): 155.8MM **Privately Held**
SIC: 3069 2796 Rolls, solid or covered rubber; platemaking services
PA: Rotation Dynamics Corporation
 8140 Cass Ave
 Darien IL 60561
 630 769-9255

(G-15598)
WESTSIDE NEWS INC
Also Called: Suburban News
1835 N Union St (14559-1153)
P.O. Box 106 (14559-0106)
PHONE..................585 352-3411
Fax: 585 352-4811
Keith Ryan, *Ch of Bd*
Evelyn Dow, *Advt Staff*
Barbara Burke, *Manager*
EMP: 18
SQ FT: 1,000
SALES (est): 1.4MM **Privately Held**
SIC: 2711 Newspapers: publishing only, not printed on site

Speonk
Suffolk County

(G-15599)
HENPECKED HUSBAND FARMS CORP
1212 Speonk Riverhead Rd (11972)
PHONE..................631 728-2800
Raayah Churgin, *Principal*
Jennifer Roberts, *Administration*
EMP: 6
SQ FT: 12,000
SALES (est): 348K **Privately Held**
SIC: 2869 Industrial organic chemicals

(G-15600)
JOHN T MONTECALVO INC
1233 Speonk River Head Rd (11972)
PHONE..................631 325-1492
Margaret Fig, *Branch Mgr*
EMP: 5
SALES (corp-wide): 4.2MM **Privately Held**
SIC: 2951 1611 Asphalt paving mixtures & blocks; surfacing & paving
PA: John T. Montecalvo, Inc.
 48 Railroad Ave
 Center Moriches NY
 631 325-1492

Sprakers
Montgomery County

(G-15601)
BILL LAKE HOMES CONSTRUCTION
188 Flanders Rd (12166-4519)
P.O. Box 105 (12166-0105)
PHONE..................518 673-2424
Fax: 518 673-5039
William Lake, *President*
John Connolly, *Purchasing*
Cindy Jackland, *Manager*
EMP: 56
SALES (est): 8MM **Privately Held**
WEB: www.billlakehomes.com
SIC: 2452 Modular homes, prefabricated, wood

Spring Valley
Rockland County

(G-15602)
CITATION MANUFACTURING CO INC
42 Harmony Rd (10977-2328)
P.O. Box 418 (10977-0418)
PHONE..................845 425-6868
Margo Nelson, *CEO*
Phil Nelson, *President*
EMP: 5
SQ FT: 900
SALES (est): 625K **Privately Held**
SIC: 3651 Sound reproducing equipment

(G-15603)
DELUXE CORPORATION
9 Lincoln Ave (10977-8938)
PHONE..................845 362-4054
Yakov Breuer, *Branch Mgr*
EMP: 267
SALES (corp-wide): 1.8B **Publicly Held**
SIC: 2782 Checkbooks
PA: Deluxe Corporation
 3680 Victoria St N
 Shoreview MN 55126
 651 483-7111

(G-15604)
EAGLE REGALIA CO INC
Also Called: Abbot Flag Co Div
747 Chestnut Ridge Rd # 101 (10977-6225)
PHONE..................845 425-2245
Fax: 845 425-2637
Michael Kartzmer, *President*
Norma Kartzmer, *Vice Pres*
J Cohen, *Mfg Staff*
▲ **EMP:** 10 **EST:** 1910
SQ FT: 4,000
SALES (est): 730K **Privately Held**
SIC: 2399 3999 2395 3911 Flags, fabric; banners, made from fabric; badges, metal: policemen, firemen, etc.; plaques, picture, laminated; emblems, embroidered; medals, precious or semiprecious metal

(G-15605)
ECKERSON DRUGS INC
275 N Main St Ste 12 (10977-2917)
PHONE..................845 352-1800
Ashish Amin, *Principal*
EMP: 14
SALES (est): 2.2MM **Privately Held**
SIC: 2834 Tablets, pharmaceutical

(G-15606)
EZ LIFT OPERATOR CORP
Also Called: EZ Lift Garage Door Service
111 S Main St (10977-5617)
PHONE..................845 356-1676
EMP: 10
SALES: 870K **Privately Held**
SIC: 3699 5084 5211 1751 Mfg Elec Mach/Equip/Supp Whol Industrial Equip Ret Lumber/Building Mtrl Carpentry Contractor

(G-15607)
FINAL TOUCH PRINTING INC
29 Decatur Ave Unit 1 (10977-4782)
PHONE..................845 352-2677
Shmiel Elger, *Chairman*
EMP: 13
SALES (est): 1.3MM **Privately Held**
SIC: 2752 Commercial printing, lithographic

(G-15608)
FROZEN PASTRY PRODUCTS CORP
41 Lincoln Ave (10977-1918)
PHONE..................845 364-9833
Fax: 845 364-9833
Dov Sandburg, *President*
Michael Schwartz, *Manager*
EMP: 33
SQ FT: 8,000
SALES (est): 3.1MM **Privately Held**
SIC: 2041 Doughs, frozen or refrigerated

(G-15609)
GOLDEN TASTE INC
318 Roosevelt Ave (10977-5824)
PHONE..................845 356-4133
Fax: 845 356-4231
Rachel Perlmutter, *President*
Rafiel Perlmutter, *Vice Pres*
Jacob Taub, *Manager*
EMP: 32
SQ FT: 20,000
SALES (est): 6MM **Privately Held**
SIC: 2099 Salads, fresh or refrigerated

(G-15610)
GUARDIAN BOOTH LLC
29 Roosevelt Ave Ste 301 (10977-7844)
PHONE..................844 992-6684
Abraham Taub, *Owner*
▲ **EMP:** 10
SQ FT: 10,000
SALES (est): 636.6K **Privately Held**
SIC: 3448 Docks: prefabricated metal

(G-15611)
HOLY COW KOSHER LLC
750 Chestnut Ridge Rd (10977-6438)
PHONE..................347 788-8620
Gilead Mooseek,
Gabi Harkham,
EMP: 5 **EST:** 2010
SALES: 400K **Privately Held**
SIC: 2013 Snack sticks, including jerky: from purchased meat

(G-15612)
JAY BAGS INC
55 Union Rd Ste 107 (10977-3900)
PHONE..................845 459-6500
Gitty Rubin, *Principal*
Joseph Pultman, *Manager*
▲ **EMP:** 3 **EST:** 2010
SQ FT: 20,000
SALES: 2MM **Privately Held**
SIC: 2673 Bags: plastic, laminated & coated

(G-15613)
LECHLER LABORATORIES INC
Also Called: Lechler Labs
100 Red Schoolhse Rd C2 (10977-7049)
PHONE..................845 426-6800
Fax: 845 426-1515
Martin Melik, *President*
Jimmy Varghese, *Research*
Thomas Miller, *Accountant*
Denise Viola, *Office Mgr*
EMP: 25 **EST:** 1957
SALES (est): 4.1MM **Privately Held**
WEB: www.lechlerlabs.com
SIC: 2844 5961 Cosmetic preparations; colognes; catalog & mail-order houses

(G-15614)
LIPTIS PHARMACEUTICALS USA INC
110 Red Schoolhouse Rd (10977-7032)
PHONE..................845 627-0260
Sherin Awad, *CEO*
Dick Klaus, *President*
Jenny Avalos, *Vice Pres*
▲ **EMP:** 1022
SALES (est): 115.6MM **Privately Held**
WEB: www.liptis.com
SIC: 2834 Pharmaceutical preparations

(G-15615)
LOUIS SCHWARTZ
Also Called: Supreme Leather Products
28 Lawrence St (10977-5038)
PHONE..................845 356-6624
Louis Schwartz, *Owner*
EMP: 6 **EST:** 1949
SQ FT: 7,500
SALES (est): 220K **Privately Held**
SIC: 2386 Garments, leather

(G-15616)
MASTER ART CORP
131 Clinton Ln Ste E (10977-8918)
PHONE..................845 362-6430
Tzipprah Austerlitz, *Principal*
▲ **EMP:** 8
SALES (est): 1.1MM **Privately Held**
SIC: 3944 Craft & hobby kits & sets

(G-15617)
MBH FURNITURE INNOVATIONS INC
28 Lincoln Ave (10977-1915)
P.O. Box 28 (10977-0028)
PHONE..................845 354-8202
Simcha Greenberg, *Ch of Bd*
EMP: 6
SALES (est): 578.4K **Privately Held**
SIC: 2519 Household furniture, except wood or metal: upholstered

(G-15618)
MEASUPRO INC (PA)
Also Called: Smart Weigh
1 Alpine Ct (10977-5647)
PHONE..................845 425-8777
EMP: 13
SALES (est): 3.7MM **Privately Held**
SIC: 3596 Weighing machines & apparatus

(G-15619)
PALISADES PAPER INC
13 Jackson Ave (10977-1910)
PHONE..................845 354-0333
Jochanan Schwaite, *President*
EMP: 6
SALES: 2MM **Privately Held**
SIC: 2621 Parchment paper

(G-15620)
RAMI SHEET METAL INC
25 E Hickory St (10977-3709)
PHONE..................845 426-2948
Nathan Gdanski, *President*
EMP: 6
SALES (est): 489.8K **Privately Held**
SIC: 3444 Sheet metalwork

Stamford - Delaware County (G-15644)

(G-15621)
REGAL SCREEN PRINTING INTL
Also Called: Shirt Shack
42 Grove St (10977-4852)
PHONE..................................845 356-8181
Fax: 845 352-8575
Stan Mesnick, *President*
Barbara Mesnick, *Vice Pres*
EMP: 6
SQ FT: 2,200
SALES (est): 717.8K Privately Held
SIC: 2759 Letterpress & screen printing

(G-15622)
RESERVE CONFECTIONS INC
Also Called: Reserve Confections Chocolate
3 Perlman Dr Ste 105 (10977-5281)
P.O. Box 186, Monsey (10952-0186)
PHONE..................................845 371-7744
Juda Fisch, *President*
▲ EMP: 11 EST: 2014
SALES (est): 1MM Privately Held
SIC: 2066 Chocolate

(G-15623)
STRATIVA PHARMACEUTICALS
1 Ram Ridge Rd (10977-6714)
PHONE..................................201 802-4000
Paul V Campanelli, *CEO*
Terrance J Coughlin, *COO*
Michael A Tropiano, *Exec VP*
EMP: 13
SALES (est): 1MM Privately Held
SIC: 2834 Pharmaceutical preparations

(G-15624)
TRAFFIC LOGIX CORPORATION
3 Harriet Ln (10977-1302)
PHONE..................................866 915-6449
Louis Newman, *CEO*
Mindy N Cohen, *General Mgr*
James Weatherall, *General Mgr*
Ben Cohen, *Treasurer*
George Dobilas, *Sales Mgr*
▼ EMP: 7
SQ FT: 100
SALES (est): 1.2MM Privately Held
SIC: 3812 3069 5084 Radar systems & equipment; molded rubber products; safety equipment

(G-15625)
ULTRA CLARITY CORP
3101 Parkview Dr (10977-4979)
PHONE..................................719 470-1010
Goldie Halpert, *CEO*
Samuel Halpert, *Principal*
EMP: 5 EST: 2014
SALES (est): 289.2K Privately Held
SIC: 3496 5051 Cable, uninsulated wire; made from purchased wire; cable, wire

(G-15626)
UNEEDA ENTERPRIZES INC
640 Chestnut Ridge Rd (10977-5653)
P.O. Box 209 (10977-0209)
PHONE..................................800 431-2494
Fax: 845 426-2810
Bruce Fuchs, *President*
Herman Fuchs, *President*
Richard Caporusso, *Vice Pres*
Kenneth Chilson, *Plant Mgr*
Mina Fuchs, *Treasurer*
▲ EMP: 110 EST: 1967
SQ FT: 58,000
SALES (est): 22MM Privately Held
WEB: www.uneeda.com
SIC: 3291 5084 5085 Abrasive products; industrial machinery & equipment; abrasives

(G-15627)
UNIVERSITY TABLE CLOTH COMPANY
10 Centre St (10977-5025)
PHONE..................................845 371-3876
Debra Timco, *President*
Lu Temco, *Manager*
▲ EMP: 11 EST: 1998
SQ FT: 5,000
SALES (est): 949.1K Privately Held
SIC: 2392 Tablecloths: made from purchased materials

(G-15628)
US POLYCHEMICAL HOLDING CORP
584 Chestnut Ridge Rd (10977-5648)
PHONE..................................845 356-5530
David Cherry, *CEO*
Mark Paul, *Director*
EMP: 21 EST: 2012
SALES (est): 4.1MM Privately Held
SIC: 2842 Cleaning or polishing preparations

Springfield Gardens
Queens County

(G-15629)
DUNDY GLASS & MIRROR CORP
12252 Montauk St (11413-1034)
PHONE..................................718 723-5800
Eric Latin, *President*
Florence Latin, *Treasurer*
Angelique Beamon, *Manager*
Ellen Latin, *Admin Sec*
▲ EMP: 25 EST: 1900
SQ FT: 17,000
SALES (est): 4.2MM Privately Held
WEB: www.dundyglass.com
SIC: 3231 Mirrored glass; furniture tops, glass; cut, beveled or polished

Springville
Erie County

(G-15630)
DELOCON WHOLESALE INC
270 W Main St (14141-1070)
P.O. Box 4 (14141-0004)
PHONE..................................716 592-2711
Sherwin Lape, *President*
Laurel Swartz, *Sales Mgr*
Ryan Beebe, *Sales Staff*
Theresa Chase, *Consultant*
EMP: 15
SALES (est): 2.2MM Privately Held
WEB: www.delocon.com
SIC: 2541 5211 Counter & sink tops; lumber & other building materials

(G-15631)
GERNATT ASPHALT PRODUCTS INC
Benz Dr (14141)
PHONE..................................716 496-5111
Fax: 716 592-7352
Mark Smith, *Vice Pres*
EMP: 7
SALES (corp-wide): 27.5MM Privately Held
WEB: www.gernatt.com
SIC: 2951 Asphalt paving mixtures & blocks
PA: Gernatt Asphalt Products, Inc.
13870 Taylor Hollow Rd
Collins NY 14034
716 532-3371

(G-15632)
GRAMCO INC (PA)
299 Waverly St (14141-1055)
P.O. Box 68 (14141-0068)
PHONE..................................716 592-2845
Fax: 716 592-2091
Robert D Mattison, *President*
Nancy J Human, *Vice Pres*
Torrance H Brooks, *Admin Sec*
EMP: 3
SQ FT: 800
SALES (est): 5.2MM Privately Held
WEB: www.gramcoonline.com
SIC: 2048 5999 Feed concentrates; feed & farm supply

(G-15633)
HEARY BROS LGHTNING PROTECTION
11291 Moore Rd (14141-9614)
PHONE..................................716 941-6141
Fax: 716 941-6141
Kenneth Heary, *President*
Edwin Heary, *Vice Pres*
EMP: 40
SQ FT: 22,800
SALES (est): 3MM Privately Held
WEB: www.hearybros.com
SIC: 3643 Lightning protection equipment

(G-15634)
PEERLESS-WINSMITH INC
172 Eaton St (14141-1197)
PHONE..................................716 592-9311
Fax: 716 592-9311
Paul Hardaway, *Plant Mgr*
Boyd Thomas, *Opers Staff*
Tom Stahley, *Buyer*
H Koelbel, *Purchasing*
Bruce Demont, *QC Dir*
EMP: 225
SALES (corp-wide): 230.1MM Privately Held
WEB: www.peerlesswinsmith.com
SIC: 3566 5063 Speed changers, drives & gears; power transmission equipment, electric
HQ: Peerless-Winsmith, Inc.
5200 Upper Metro Pl # 110
Dublin OH 43017
614 526-7000

(G-15635)
PERFECTION GEAR INC
172 Eaton St (14141-1165)
PHONE..................................716 592-9310
Kim Neyrett, *Manager*
EMP: 150
SALES (corp-wide): 255MM Privately Held
SIC: 3566 Reduction gears & gear units for turbines, except automotive
HQ: Perfection Gear, Inc.
9 N Bear Creek Rd
Asheville NC 28806
828 253-0000

(G-15636)
SPRINGVILLE MFG CO INC
8798 North St (14141-9648)
P.O. Box 367 (14141-0367)
PHONE..................................716 592-4957
Fax: 716 592-9834
Daniel J Schmauss, *President*
William Kneeland, *Counsel*
Carol Chowaniec, *Accountant*
Mary Boberg, *Director*
Joseph Schmauss, *Shareholder*
EMP: 31 EST: 1958
SQ FT: 28,000
SALES (est): 7MM Privately Held
WEB: www.springvillemfg.com
SIC: 3593 3599 Fluid power cylinders, hydraulic or pneumatic; machine shop, jobbing & repair

Staatsburg
Dutchess County

(G-15637)
CURRANT COMPANY LLC
Also Called: Currantc
59 Walnut Ln (12580-6346)
PHONE..................................845 266-8999
Greg Quinn,
▲ EMP: 5
SALES (est): 540.1K Privately Held
WEB: www.currantc.com
SIC: 2026 Yogurt

(G-15638)
DUTCHESS PLUMBING & HEATING
28 Reservoir Rd (12580-5317)
PHONE..................................845 889-8255
Fax: 845 876-2986
Steven Eckelman, *President*
Maryanne Eckelman, *Vice Pres*
EMP: 5
SALES (est): 420K Privately Held
SIC: 2759 Commercial printing

(G-15639)
UNIFUSE LLC
2092 Route 9g (12580-5426)
PHONE..................................845 889-4000
Jeff Bookstein, *Managing Dir*
Dan Aiello, *Principal*
Andrew Flynn, *Manager*
EMP: 15
SQ FT: 50,000
SALES (est): 3.1MM Privately Held
WEB: www.unifuse.com
SIC: 3089 Plastic processing

Stafford
Genesee County

(G-15640)
GENESEE BUILDING PRODUCTS LLC
7982 Byron Stafford Rd (14143)
PHONE..................................585 548-2726
Ronald Wheeler, *President*
EMP: 7
SQ FT: 20,000
SALES (est): 820.4K Privately Held
SIC: 3444 Gutters, sheet metal

(G-15641)
HANSON AGGREGATES EAST LLC
5870 Main Rd (14143-9519)
PHONE..................................585 343-1787
Scott Wheaton, *Plant Mgr*
Kelly Kinney, *Office Mgr*
Jeff Curry, *Manager*
EMP: 22
SALES (corp-wide): 16B Privately Held
SIC: 2951 Asphalt paving mixtures & blocks
HQ: Hanson Aggregates East Llc
3131 Rdu Center Dr
Morrisville NC 27560
919 380-2500

(G-15642)
RJ PRECISION LLC
6662 Main Rd (14143-9554)
PHONE..................................585 768-8030
Kathleen Johns, *Partner*
Robert Johns,
EMP: 5
SQ FT: 5,300
SALES (est): 820K Privately Held
SIC: 3441 Fabricated structural metal

Stamford
Delaware County

(G-15643)
AUDIO-SEARS CORP
2 South St (12167-1211)
PHONE..................................607 652-7305
Fax: 607 652-3653
David Hartwell, *President*
Shawn Hartwell, *Vice Pres*
Nicholas Knoll, *Purch Mgr*
Glenn Bertrand, *QC Dir*
Karen Chichester, *Controller*
▲ EMP: 81 EST: 1956
SQ FT: 25,000
SALES (est): 14.3MM Privately Held
WEB: www.audiosears.com
SIC: 3661 Telephones & telephone apparatus

(G-15644)
CATSKILL CRAFTSMEN INC
15 W End Ave (12167-1296)
PHONE..................................607 652-7321
Fax: 607 652-7293
Duncan Axtell, *Ch of Bd*
Henry Cioccari, *Purchasing*
Ken Smith, *CFO*
Kate Rowlison, *Info Tech Mgr*
▲ EMP: 55
SQ FT: 94,000
SALES (est): 7.7MM Privately Held
WEB: www.catskillcraftsmen.com
SIC: 2434 2499 2511 Wood kitchen cabinets; woodenware, kitchen & household; kitchen & dining room furniture

Stamford - Delaware County (G-15645)

(G-15645)
MACADOODLES
26 River St (12167-1014)
PHONE..................................607 652-9019
Michelle Caiazza, *Owner*
EMP: 6
SALES (est): 524.6K **Privately Held**
WEB: www.macadoodles.com
SIC: 2024 Ice cream & frozen desserts

(G-15646)
STONE CREST INDUSTRIES INC
Also Called: Generic Compositors
152 Starheim Rd (12167-1757)
PHONE..................................607 652-2665
Fax: 607 652-2416
Gerald Stoner, *President*
Ellen Thorn, *CFO*
EMP: 5
SALES (est): 302.5K **Privately Held**
WEB: www.genericcomp.com
SIC: 2791 Typesetting

Stanfordville
Dutchess County

(G-15647)
GALLANT GRAPHICS LTD
242 Attlebury Hill Rd (12581-5635)
PHONE..................................845 868-1166
Melvin Eiger, *President*
Ralph Brunks, *Vice Pres*
Julian Thorn, *Vice Pres*
▲ EMP: 26
SALES (est): 4.7MM **Privately Held**
WEB: www.gallantgraphics.com
SIC: 2752 2796 2791 2759 Commercial printing, offset; platemaking services; typesetting; commercial printing

Star Lake
St. Lawrence County

(G-15648)
CLEARLAKE LAND CO INC
Hanks Rd (13690)
PHONE..................................315 848-2427
Gordon Gardner, *President*
Lynn Gardner, *Treasurer*
EMP: 10
SALES: 900K **Privately Held**
SIC: 2411 Logging

Staten Island
Richmond County

(G-15649)
828 EXPRESS INC
619 Elbe Ave (10304-3412)
PHONE..................................917 577-9019
Nelson Liu, *President*
EMP: 9 EST: 2011
SALES (est): 1.1MM **Privately Held**
SIC: 3443 Containers, shipping (bombs, etc.): metal plate

(G-15650)
A K A COMPUTER CONSULTING INC
1412 Richmond Rd (10304-2312)
PHONE..................................718 351-5200
Alex Kleyff, *Founder*
Eva Kleyff, *Vice Pres*
Leonardo Vasquez, *Prgrmr*
EMP: 5
SQ FT: 1,200
SALES (est): 812.6K **Privately Held**
WEB: www.akaconsulting.com
SIC: 7372 Prepackaged software

(G-15651)
A&B MCKEON GLASS INC
69 Roff St (10304-1856)
PHONE..................................718 525-2152
Charles Bell, *President*
Terri Barbato, *Manager*
EMP: 5 EST: 1976
SQ FT: 750

SALES (est): 560K **Privately Held**
SIC: 3449 1542 1793 1761 Curtain wall, metal; store front construction; glass & glazing work; architectural sheet metal work

(G-15652)
A/C DESIGN & FABRICATION CORP
638 Sharrotts Rd (10309-1992)
PHONE..................................718 227-8100
Fax: 718 227-8100
Jeff Arcello, *President*
▲ EMP: 5
SALES (est): 828.6K **Privately Held**
SIC: 3441 Fabricated structural metal

(G-15653)
ADVANCE PUBLICATIONS INC (PA)
Also Called: Staten Island Advance
950 W Fingerboard Rd (10305-1453)
PHONE..................................718 981-1234
Samuel I Newhouse III, *President*
Michael A Newhouse, *President*
Steven O Newhouse, *President*
Keith Dawn, *Publisher*
Carmine Angioli, *Editor*
▲ EMP: 100 EST: 1924
SQ FT: 40,000
SALES (est): 6.2B **Privately Held**
WEB: www.advance.net
SIC: 2711 2731 2721 2791 Newspapers, publishing & printing; book publishing; magazines: publishing & printing; typesetting; commercial printing, lithographic

(G-15654)
ALBA HOUSE PUBLISHERS
2187 Victory Blvd (10314-6603)
PHONE..................................718 698-2759
Ignatius Staniszewski, *CEO*
▲ EMP: 25
SALES (est): 1.2MM **Privately Held**
SIC: 2731 Book publishing

(G-15655)
ALL SHORE INDUSTRIES INC
1 Edgewater St Ste 215 (10305-4900)
PHONE..................................718 720-0018
Fax: 718 720-0225
Sandor Goldner, *CEO*
Norman Goldner, *President*
Hannah Goldner, *Corp Secy*
Elizabeth Torres, *Accountant*
Jean Steinmetz, *Info Tech Mgr*
▲ EMP: 10
SQ FT: 5,000
SALES (est): 890K **Privately Held**
SIC: 3679 3677 3699 Electronic circuits; electronic coils, transformers & other inductors; appliance cords for household electrical equipment

(G-15656)
ALL SIGNS
Also Called: Woodside Decorator
63 Bridgetown St (10314-6211)
PHONE..................................973 736-2113
Vincent Iannuzzelli, *Owner*
EMP: 7
SALES: 600K **Privately Held**
SIC: 3993 Signs & advertising specialties

(G-15657)
ALPHA MARINE REPAIR
88 Coursen Pl (10304-2506)
PHONE..................................718 816-7150
Eutrice Robinson, *Principal*
Heather Robinson, *Principal*
EMP: 45
SALES: 950K **Privately Held**
SIC: 3731 Shipbuilding & repairing

(G-15658)
AMERICAN ROLLING DOOR LTD
40 Dolson Pl (10303-1402)
PHONE..................................718 273-0485
Ed Simone, *President*
Peter Paloscio, *Vice Pres*
EMP: 8
SQ FT: 7,600
SALES (est): 992.1K **Privately Held**
SIC: 3442 Garage doors, overhead: metal

(G-15659)
ARC TEC WLDG & FABRICATION INC
15 Harrison Ave (10302-1328)
PHONE..................................718 982-9274
Kim R Genduso, *President*
EMP: 5
SALES (est): 673.3K **Privately Held**
SIC: 7692 Welding repair

(G-15660)
ARIMED ORTHOTICS PROSTHETICS P
235 Dongan Hills Ave 2d (10305-1224)
PHONE..................................718 979-6155
Fax: 718 668-9431
Steven Mirones, *Branch Mgr*
EMP: 13
SALES (corp-wide): 3.7MM **Privately Held**
SIC: 3842 Braces, orthopedic
PA: Arimed Orthotics Prosthetics Pedorthics
302 Livingston St
Brooklyn NY 11217
718 875-8754

(G-15661)
ATHLETIC CAP CO INC
123 Fields Ave (10314-5066)
PHONE..................................718 398-1300
Fax: 718 399-0999
Arthur Farkas, *Ch of Bd*
Ira Farkas, *Vice Pres*
EMP: 40
SQ FT: 9,000
SALES (est): 1.2MM **Privately Held**
SIC: 2353 2396 2395 Hats & caps; automotive & apparel trimmings; pleating & stitching

(G-15662)
B & R TOOL INC
955 Rensselaer Ave (10309-2227)
PHONE..................................718 948-2729
William Nobile, *President*
EMP: 6
SALES (est): 567K **Privately Held**
SIC: 3469 Metal stampings

(G-15663)
BANDS N BOWS
34 Fieldway Ave (10308-2930)
PHONE..................................718 984-4316
Ted Mazola, *Principal*
EMP: 5
SALES (est): 285.1K **Privately Held**
SIC: 2339 Scarves, hoods, headbands, etc.: women's

(G-15664)
BARBERA TRANSDUSER SYSTEMS
21 Louis St (10304-2111)
PHONE..................................718 816-3025
Richard Barbera, *Partner*
Katherine Sanfilippo, *Partner*
EMP: 10
SALES (est): 520K **Privately Held**
SIC: 3931 5736 String instruments & parts; musical instrument stores

(G-15665)
BEETINS WHOLESALE INC
125 Ravenhurst Ave (10310-2633)
PHONE..................................718 524-0899
Gamade Perera, *CEO*
EMP: 13
SALES (est): 1.5MM **Privately Held**
SIC: 2679 Paper products, converted

(G-15666)
BEST LINE INC
101 Manila Ave Fl 2 (10306-5605)
PHONE..................................917 670-6210
Andrey Kanevsky, *President*
▼ EMP: 6
SALES (est): 189.4K **Privately Held**
WEB: www.mozga.net
SIC: 2711 5192 Newspapers; newspapers

(G-15667)
BILLING BLOCKS INC
147 North Ave (10314-2653)
PHONE..................................718 442-5006

Fax: 718 504-6015
Dan Kuper, *President*
EMP: 10
SALES (est): 338.2K **Privately Held**
WEB: www.billingblocks.com
SIC: 7372 7371 Prepackaged software; custom computer programming services

(G-15668)
BLINDS TO GO (US) INC
2845 Richmond Ave (10314-5883)
PHONE..................................718 477-9523
Fax: 718 477-9525
Bill Forte, *Manager*
Shawna Bodemer, *Manager*
EMP: 30
SALES (corp-wide): 77.7MM **Privately Held**
SIC: 2591 5719 Drapery hardware & blinds & shades; window furnishings
HQ: Blinds To Go (U.S.) Inc.
101 E State Rt 4
Paramus NJ 07652
201 441-9260

(G-15669)
BLOOD MOON PRODUCTIONS LTD
75 Saint Marks Pl (10301-1606)
PHONE..................................718 556-9410
Danforth Prince, *CEO*
EMP: 7
SALES (est): 494.9K **Privately Held**
WEB: www.bloodmoonproductions.com
SIC: 2741 Miscellaneous publishing

(G-15670)
BORO PARK CUTTING TOOL CORP
106b Wakefield Ave (10314-3624)
PHONE..................................718 720-0610
Fax: 718 720-1084
Vito Rubino, *President*
Steven Bruzese, *General Mgr*
Vincent Bruzese, *Treasurer*
EMP: 21
SQ FT: 10,000
SALES: 1MM **Privately Held**
SIC: 3545 5251 Cutting tools for machine tools; tools

(G-15671)
BRAZE ALLOY INC
3075 Richmond Ter (10303-1303)
PHONE..................................718 815-5757
Princie Sevaratnam, *President*
EMP: 5
SALES (est): 554.8K **Privately Held**
SIC: 3356 Solder: wire, bar, acid core, & rosin core

(G-15672)
BRITISH SCIENCE CORPORATION (PA)
100 Wheeler Ave (10314-4018)
PHONE..................................212 980-8700
David H Kingsley, *President*
Yvonne Kingsley, *Corp Secy*
EMP: 8
SALES (est): 744K **Privately Held**
SIC: 2844 7299 Shampoos, rinses, conditioners: hair; scalp treatment service

(G-15673)
C & R DE SANTIS INC
Also Called: Royal Press
2645 Forest Ave Ste 2 (10303-1503)
PHONE..................................718 447-5076
Fax: 718 448-7573
Robert De Santis, *President*
Lucille Chazanoff, *COO*
Janet Sher, *Office Mgr*
Beth Cotroneo, *Art Dir*
EMP: 22 EST: 1926
SQ FT: 5,000
SALES: 83.9K **Privately Held**
WEB: www.royalpress.com
SIC: 2752 2672 Commercial printing, lithographic; commercial printing, offset; coated & laminated paper

GEOGRAPHIC SECTION

Staten Island - Richmond County (G-15702)

(G-15674)
CADDELL DRY DOCK & REPR CO INC
Also Called: Caddell Ship Yards
Foot Of Broadway 1 W New (10310)
P.O. Box 100327 (10310-0327)
PHONE.................................718 442-2112
Fax: 718 981-7493
John B Caddell, *CEO*
Steven P Kalil, *President*
Cynthia Patelli, *Corp Secy*
Luc Vaval, *Sr Corp Ofcr*
Brian Donato, *Safety Mgr*
EMP: 180 **EST:** 1903
SQ FT: 100,000
SALES (est): 34.2MM Privately Held
WEB: www.caddelldrydock.com
SIC: 3731 Shipbuilding & repairing

(G-15675)
CALIA TECHNICAL INC
Also Called: Calia Consultants
420 Jefferson Blvd (10312-2334)
PHONE.................................718 447-3928
Fax: 718 815-2887
Anthony Calia, *President*
Robert Santagata, *Vice Pres*
EMP: 6
SALES: 650K Privately Held
SIC: 3625 8742 Control equipment, electric; training & development consultant

(G-15676)
CARMINE STREET BAGELS INC
Also Called: Bagels On The Square
107 Park Dr N (10314-5702)
PHONE.................................212 691-3041
Joseph Turchiano, *Ch of Bd*
Neil Guy, *President*
EMP: 10
SQ FT: 2,000
SALES (est): 870.7K Privately Held
SIC: 2051 Bakery: wholesale or wholesale/retail combined

(G-15677)
CARTERS INC
430 New Dorp Ln (10306-4946)
PHONE.................................718 980-1759
EMP: 9
SALES (corp-wide): 3.2B Publicly Held
SIC: 2361 Dresses: girls', children's & infants'
PA: Carter's, Inc.
3438 Peachtree Rd Ne # 1800
Atlanta GA 30326
678 791-1000

(G-15678)
CHEESE EXPERTS USA LTD LBLTY
14 Notus Ave (10312-3123)
PHONE.................................908 275-3889
Richard Falcone, *President*
Joseph Pastorello, *Principal*
EMP: 9
SALES (est): 577K Privately Held
SIC: 2022 Cheese spreads, dips, pastes & other cheese products

(G-15679)
COCA-COLA BTLG CO OF NY INC
400 Western Ave (10303-1199)
PHONE.................................718 420-6800
Fax: 718 420-6801
Susan Stavan, *Branch Mgr*
Sam Campanello, *Manager*
EMP: 12
SALES (corp-wide): 41.8B Publicly Held
SIC: 2086 Bottled & canned soft drinks
HQ: The Coca-Cola Bottling Company Of New York Inc
2500 Windy Ridge Pkwy Se
Atlanta GA 30339
770 989-3000

(G-15680)
COFFEE HOLDING CO INC (PA)
3475 Victory Blvd Ste 4 (10314-6785)
PHONE.................................718 832-0800
Andrew Gordon, *President*
David Gordon, *Exec VP*
Mike Ruiz, *Safety Dir*
Derek Hutton, *Opers Mgr*
◆ **EMP:** 69
SALES: 78.9MM Publicly Held
WEB: www.coffeeholding.com
SIC: 2095 5149 5499 Roasted coffee; coffee, green or roasted; coffee

(G-15681)
CONTEMPRA DESIGN INC
20 Grille Ct (10309-1400)
PHONE.................................718 984-8586
Fax: 718 356-9813
James Pelligrino, *President*
Dominique Bifiory, *Corp Secy*
EMP: 6
SQ FT: 4,000
SALES: 800K Privately Held
SIC: 2541 1799 Table or counter tops, plastic laminated; showcases, except refrigerated: wood; counter top installation

(G-15682)
CORMAN USA INC
1140 Bay St Ste 2c (10305-4910)
PHONE.................................718 727-7455
Giorgio Mantovani, *Ch of Bd*
EMP: 8
SALES (est): 1.1MM
SALES (corp-wide): 79.4MM Privately Held
SIC: 2676 Feminine hygiene paper products
PA: Corman Spa
Via Amatore Antonio Sciesa 10
Lacchiarella MI 20084
029 008-097

(G-15683)
CRAFT PAK INC
67 Gateway Dr (10304-4440)
PHONE.................................718 257-2700
Anthony Deviasi, *Owner*
EMP: 8
SALES (est): 412.8K Privately Held
SIC: 2673 Bags: plastic, laminated & coated

(G-15684)
CYCLONE AIR POWER INC
Also Called: Four Wheel Drive
12 Van St (10310-1311)
PHONE.................................718 447-3038
Robert J Meeker, *President*
Veronica Larney, *Manager*
Demaira Vontana, *Administration*
▲ **EMP:** 9
SALES (est): 1MM Privately Held
WEB: www.cycloneair.com
SIC: 3599 3563 7539 Machine shop, jobbing & repair; air & gas compressors; automotive repair shops

(G-15685)
DI DOMENICO PACKAGING CO INC
304 Bertram Ave (10312-5200)
PHONE.................................718 727-5454
Fax: 718 727-5577
Vincent A Di Domenico, *President*
Michael A Di Domenico, *President*
Steven M Di Domenico, *Vice Pres*
Lisa Marchase, *Manager*
EMP: 6
SQ FT: 21,000
SALES (est): 1.2MM Privately Held
SIC: 2631 3089 Folding boxboard; setup boxboard; blister or bubble formed packaging, plastic

(G-15686)
DIMARZIO INC
1388 Richmond Ter (10310-1115)
P.O. Box 100387 (10310-0387)
PHONE.................................718 442-6655
Fax: 718 720-5296
Lawrence Dimarzio, *President*
Steven Blucher II, *Vice Pres*
Marina Levit, *Export Mgr*
Louis Butera, *Engineer*
Glenn Simmons, *Director*
▲ **EMP:** 30
SQ FT: 2,000
SALES (est): 4.9MM Privately Held
WEB: www.dimarzio.com
SIC: 3931 Guitars & parts, electric & non-electric

(G-15687)
DOUG LAMBERTSON OD
2555 Richmond Ave Ste 4 (10314-5848)
PHONE.................................718 698-9300
Doug Lambertson, *Principal*
EMP: 5
SALES (est): 132.3K Privately Held
SIC: 3851 Ophthalmic goods

(G-15688)
E I DU PONT DE NEMOURS & CO
10 Teleport Dr (10311-1001)
PHONE.................................718 761-0043
Jennifer Dupont, *Branch Mgr*
EMP: 182
SALES (corp-wide): 72.7B Publicly Held
SIC: 2879 Agricultural chemicals
HQ: E. I. Du Pont De Nemours And Company
974 Centre Rd
Wilmington DE 19805
302 774-1000

(G-15689)
EAG ELECTRIC INC
496 Mosel Ave (10304-1621)
PHONE.................................201 376-5103
Christopher Todd, *Vice Pres*
EMP: 6
SALES: 500K Privately Held
SIC: 3534 Elevators & moving stairways

(G-15690)
EASTERN ENTERPRISE CORP
Also Called: Vinyl Tech Window
465 Bay St Ste 2 (10304-3842)
PHONE.................................718 727-8600
Fax: 718 727-8684
Al Gargiulo Jr, *President*
Mary Waller, *Manager*
EMP: 15
SALES (est): 1.6MM Privately Held
SIC: 3089 Windows, plastic

(G-15691)
EASTERN GRANITE INC
6228 Amboy Rd (10309-3117)
PHONE.................................718 356-9139
Brian W Hall, *Ch of Bd*
EMP: 6
SALES (est): 235.3K Privately Held
WEB: www.easterngranite.com
SIC: 3272 Monuments, concrete

(G-15692)
ENVIRO SERVICE & SUPPLY CORP
45b Marble Loop (10309-1326)
PHONE.................................347 838-6500
Dom Guercio, *President*
Christopher Lorippo, *Vice Pres*
EMP: 10
SALES (est): 1.1MM Privately Held
SIC: 2842 2869 2841 Specialty cleaning preparations; sanitation preparations, disinfectants & deodorants; disinfectants, household or industrial plant; industrial organic chemicals; soap & other detergents

(G-15693)
F & D SERVICES INC
Also Called: F & D Printing
34 E Augusta Ave (10308-1323)
PHONE.................................718 984-1635
Fax: 718 987-8075
Frank Sisino, *President*
Donald Marcus, *Vice Pres*
EMP: 14
SQ FT: 2,400
SALES (est): 1.2MM Privately Held
SIC: 2752 Letters, circular or form: lithographed; commercial printing, offset

(G-15694)
FEDEX OFFICE & PRINT SVCS INC
2456 Richmond Ave Ste C (10314-5804)
PHONE.................................718 982-5223
Fax: 718 982-8310
Sandy Sneiderman, *Manager*
Julee Cruz, *Manager*
EMP: 6
SALES (corp-wide): 50.3B Publicly Held
WEB: www.kinkos.com
SIC: 2759 5099 7334 Commercial printing; signs, except electric; photocopying & duplicating services
HQ: Fedex Office And Print Services, Inc.
7900 Legacy Dr
Plano TX 75024
214 550-7000

(G-15695)
FRANK TORRONE & SONS INC
Also Called: Torrone Outdoor Displays
400 Broadway (10310-2036)
PHONE.................................718 273-7600
Fax: 718 447-5103
Arthur Torrone Jr, *President*
EMP: 15 **EST:** 1944
SQ FT: 9,000
SALES (est): 1.2MM Privately Held
SIC: 3993 Neon signs

(G-15696)
FRESH TORTILLAS SI INC
304 New Dorp Ln (10306-3036)
PHONE.................................718 979-6666
Chun Qi Chen, *Ch of Bd*
EMP: 6
SALES (est): 276.8K Privately Held
SIC: 2099 Tortillas, fresh or refrigerated

(G-15697)
GANGI DISTRIBUTORS INC
Also Called: Snapple Distributors
135 Mcclean Ave (10305-4655)
PHONE.................................718 442-5745
Santo Spallina, *President*
EMP: 12
SQ FT: 5,000
SALES (est): 890K Privately Held
SIC: 2086 Bottled & canned soft drinks

(G-15698)
GENERAL TRADE MARK LA
31 Hylan Blvd Apt 14c (10305-2079)
PHONE.................................718 979-7261
Fax: 718 448-9808
Richard Capuozzo, *President*
Virginia Kruse, *Corp Secy*
EMP: 30 **EST:** 1924
SQ FT: 20,000
SALES (est): 3.4MM Privately Held
WEB: www.incrediblelabels.com
SIC: 2759 2671 Labels & seals: printing; tags: printing; packaging paper & plastics film, coated & laminated

(G-15699)
GLENDA INC
Also Called: Victory Sports
1732 Victory Blvd (10314-3510)
PHONE.................................718 442-8981
Fax: 718 442-2730
George Siller, *President*
Glenda Siller, *Corp Secy*
EMP: 5
SQ FT: 2,500
SALES: 500K Privately Held
SIC: 2395 5941 Emblems, embroidered; sporting goods & bicycle shops

(G-15700)
GOTTLIEB SCHWARTZ FAMILY
724 Collfield Ave (10314-4253)
PHONE.................................718 761-2010
Michael Gottlieb, *Owner*
EMP: 50 **EST:** 1973
SALES (est): 4.5MM Privately Held
SIC: 3444 Skylights, sheet metal

(G-15701)
GRADO GROUP INC
66 Willow Ave (10305-1829)
PHONE.................................718 556-4200
Richard Grado, *President*
Nadiane Cintia, *Admin Asst*
EMP: 7 **EST:** 2000
SQ FT: 2,900
SALES (est): 782.6K Privately Held
SIC: 2759 Advertising literature: printing

(G-15702)
GRAPHIC SIGNS & AWNINGS LTD
165 Industrial Loop Ste 1 (10309-1109)
PHONE.................................718 227-6000

Fax: 718 227-2057
Mike Demarco, *Vice Pres*
EMP: 5
SALES: 355K **Privately Held**
SIC: 3993 5999 Signs & advertising specialties; awnings

(G-15703)
GREAT ATL PR-CAST CON STATUARY
225 Ellis St (10307-1128)
PHONE.................................718 948-5677
Frank Fresca, *President*
EMP: 4
SQ FT: 5,000
SALES: 4MM **Privately Held**
SIC: 3272 Concrete products

(G-15704)
HENRY MORGAN
Also Called: Pensrus
433 Tennyson Dr (10312-6545)
P.O. Box 90219 (10309-0219)
PHONE.................................718 317-5013
Henry Morgan, *Owner*
Christine Voltaggio, *Sls & Mktg Exec*
Sandy Aubry, *Sales Staff*
Amanda Carbone, *Technology*
Christine Voltaggio, *Executive Asst*
EMP: 11
SALES: 5MM **Privately Held**
WEB: www.pensrus.com
SIC: 3951 Pens & mechanical pencils

(G-15705)
HOMESELL INC
4010 Hylan Blvd (10308-3331)
PHONE.................................718 514-0346
Frank Lopa, *CEO*
Paul Lopa, *General Mgr*
Tracy Hardyal, *Admin Sec*
EMP: 10
SQ FT: 1,200
SALES (est): 620K **Privately Held**
WEB: www.homesell.com
SIC: 2721 Magazines: publishing & printing

(G-15706)
I D TEL CORP
Also Called: Metro Tel Communications
55 Canal St (10304-3809)
PHONE.................................718 876-6000
Fax: 718 876-6003
Anthony Giammanco, *President*
Edward Pavia, *Vice Pres*
Steven Giammanco, *Technical Mgr*
Barbara Syracuse, *Sales Staff*
▲ **EMP:** 12
SQ FT: 4,000
SALES: 1MM **Privately Held**
SIC: 3661 Telephones & telephone apparatus

(G-15707)
IADC INC
845 Father Capodanno Blvd (10305-4039)
PHONE.................................718 238-0623
EMP: 10
SALES (est): 690K **Privately Held**
SIC: 3089 Mfg Plastic Products

(G-15708)
INFINITE SOFTWARE SOLUTIONS
Also Called: Md-Reports
1110 South Ave Ste 303 (10314-3411)
PHONE.................................718 982-1315
Fax: 718 477-3692
Srikanth Gosike, *President*
Hari Gandham, *Vice Pres*
Naina Gosike, *Vice Pres*
Sagarika Ramanan, *Sales Executive*
Mahesh Muthyala, *Marketing Staff*
EMP: 12
SALES (est): 1.4MM **Privately Held**
WEB: www.infinitesoftsol.com
SIC: 3695 5045 Computer software tape & disks: blank, rigid & floppy; computer software

(G-15709)
INTERNTIONAL GOURMET SOUPS INC
Also Called: Famous Manhattan Soup Chef
1110 South Ave Ste 300 (10314-3414)
PHONE.................................212 768-7687
Jamieson Karson, *CEO*
Robert Bertrand, *President*
Jessy Parez, *Admin Sec*
EMP: 20
SALES (est): 1.9MM **Privately Held**
WEB: www.manhattansoupchef.com
SIC: 2034 5499 Dried & dehydrated soup mixes; soups, dehydrated; gourmet food stores

(G-15710)
ISLAND STAIRS CORP
178 Industrial Loop (10309-1145)
PHONE.................................347 645-0560
Fax: 347 967-1708
Vassili Lijnev, *President*
EMP: 6
SQ FT: 5,000
SALES (est): 484.5K **Privately Held**
WEB: www.islandstairs.com
SIC: 2431 Staircases & stairs, wood

(G-15711)
ITTS INDUSTRIAL INC
165 Industrial Loop Ste C (10309-1109)
PHONE.................................718 605-6934
Harvey Itts, *CEO*
Felix Tricoche, *Vice Pres*
▲ **EMP:** 8
SQ FT: 8,000
SALES (est): 1.4MM **Privately Held**
SIC: 3354 Aluminum extruded products

(G-15712)
J T PRINTING 21
304 Broad St (10304-2045)
PHONE.................................718 484-3939
EMP: 6
SALES (est): 127.3K **Privately Held**
SIC: 2759 Publication printing

(G-15713)
J V HARING & SON
Also Called: Haring, J V & Son
1277 Clove Rd Ste 2 (10301-4339)
PHONE.................................718 720-1947
Fax: 718 448-0608
Connie Mauro, *President*
EMP: 6
SQ FT: 1,000
SALES (est): 760K **Privately Held**
SIC: 2752 Commercial printing, lithographic

(G-15714)
JMS ICES INC
Also Called: Ralph's Ices
501 Port Richmond Ave (10302-1720)
PHONE.................................718 448-0853
Michael Scolaro, *President*
Larry Silvestro, *Corp Secy*
John Scolaro, *Vice Pres*
EMP: 15
SQ FT: 5,000
SALES (est): 4.5MM **Privately Held**
SIC: 2024 Ices, flavored (frozen dessert)

(G-15715)
JOSEPH A FILIPPAZZO SOFTWARE
106 Lovell Ave (10314-4905)
PHONE.................................718 987-1626
EMP: 5 EST: 2010
SALES (est): 230K **Privately Held**
SIC: 7372 Prepackaged Software Services

(G-15716)
JOSEPH FEDELE
Also Called: Rainbow Custom Counter Tops
1950b Richmond Ter (10302)
PHONE.................................718 448-3658
Fax: 718 273-4368
Joseph Fedele, *Owner*
Rachael Fedele, *Bookkeeper*
EMP: 6
SQ FT: 5,000
SALES (est): 580K **Privately Held**
SIC: 2541 5211 5031 1799 Counter & sink tops; cabinets, lockers & shelving; cabinets, kitchen; kitchen cabinets; counter top installation

(G-15717)
JPMORGAN CHASE BANK NAT ASSN
1690 Hylan Blvd (10305-1930)
PHONE.................................718 668-0346
EMP: 6
SALES (corp-wide): 105.4B **Publicly Held**
SIC: 3578 Automatic teller machines (ATM)
HQ: Jpmorgan Chase Bank, National Association
1111 Polaris Pkwy
Columbus OH 43240
614 436-3055

(G-15718)
KLEEN STIK INDUSTRIES INC
44 Lenzie St (10312-6118)
PHONE.................................718 984-5031
Edwin Wallace, *President*
Rosalie Wallace, *Admin Sec*
▲ **EMP:** 17
SQ FT: 20,000
SALES (est): 1.8MM **Privately Held**
WEB: www.kleenstik.net
SIC: 2672 Tape, pressure sensitive: made from purchased materials

(G-15719)
LAROSA CUPCAKES
314 Lake Ave (10303-2610)
PHONE.................................347 866-3920
EMP: 8
SALES (est): 443.4K **Privately Held**
SIC: 2051 Bread, cake & related products

(G-15720)
LASER AND VARICOSE VEIN TRTMNT
500 Seaview Ave Ste 240 (10305-3403)
PHONE.................................718 667-1777
Inam Haq, *Principal*
EMP: 8
SALES (est): 963.8K **Privately Held**
SIC: 3845 Laser systems & equipment, medical

(G-15721)
LOFFRENO CSTM INTERIORS CONTG
33 Ada Pl (10301-3801)
PHONE.................................718 981-0319
Frank Loffreno, *President*
EMP: 25
SALES (est): 2.9MM **Privately Held**
SIC: 2521 2517 Cabinets, office: wood; wood television & radio cabinets

(G-15722)
LOOBRICA INTERNATIONAL CORP
41 Darnell Ln (10309-1933)
PHONE.................................347 997-0296
Marshall Weinberg, *Principal*
Jason Weinberg, *Administration*
▲ **EMP:** 8 EST: 2012
SALES (est): 960K **Privately Held**
SIC: 2992 8733 Lubricating oils & greases; scientific research agency

(G-15723)
M & L STEEL & ORNAMENTAL IRON
27 Housman Ave (10303-2701)
PHONE.................................718 816-8660
Fax: 718 815-6104
Lubomir P Svoboda, *President*
Pete Svoboda, *Executive*
▲ **EMP:** 14
SALES (est): 3.4MM **Privately Held**
SIC: 3441 1791 Fabricated structural metal; iron work, structural

(G-15724)
MADISONS DELIGHT LLC
711 Forest Ave (10310-2506)
PHONE.................................718 720-8900
David Saraf, *Mng Member*
Danny Saraf, *Manager*
EMP: 10
SQ FT: 2,200
SALES (est): 496.7K **Privately Held**
SIC: 2066 Chocolate

(G-15725)
MAXINE DENKER INC (PA)
Also Called: Tokens
212 Manhattan St (10307-1805)
PHONE.................................212 689-1440
Fax: 212 689-1517
Maxine Denker, *President*
Carla Elson, *Vice Pres*
EMP: 1
SALES (est): 1.2MM **Privately Held**
SIC: 3911 3965 Jewelry, precious metal; buckles & buckle parts; hair curlers

(G-15726)
MAY SHIP REPAIR CONTG CORP
3075 Richmond Ter Ste 3 (10303-1300)
PHONE.................................718 442-9700
Fax: 718 494-4499
Mohamed M Adam, *President*
Omar Abouelellac, *Project Engr*
Yvonne Heredia, *Office Mgr*
Angel Heredia, *Supervisor*
▲ **EMP:** 45
SQ FT: 1,800
SALES (est): 9.9MM **Privately Held**
WEB: www.mayship.com
SIC: 3731 3732 Shipbuilding & repairing; boat building & repairing

(G-15727)
MILANO GRANITE AND MARBLE CORP
3521 Victory Blvd (10314-6763)
PHONE.................................718 477-7200
Fax: 718 477-3910
Joseph Moreale, *President*
EMP: 12
SALES (est): 1.7MM **Privately Held**
SIC: 3272 Art marble, concrete

(G-15728)
MORAN SHIPYARD CORPORATION (DH)
2015 Richmond Ter (10302-1298)
PHONE.................................718 981-5600
Fax: 718 448-4147
Malcolm W McLeod, *President*
Peter Keyes, *Vice Pres*
Brian Burtner, *Purchasing*
Lee Christensen, *Treasurer*
Joseph De'angelo, *Treasurer*
▲ **EMP:** 187
SQ FT: 26,400
SALES (est): 11.7MM **Privately Held**
SIC: 3731 Shipbuilding & repairing
HQ: Moran Towing Corporation
50 Locust Ave Ste 10
New Canaan CT 06840
203 442-2800

(G-15729)
MORAN TOWING CORPORATION
Also Called: Moran Ship Yard
2015 Richmond Ter (10302-1298)
PHONE.................................718 981-5600
Fax: 718 447-4076
Patty Boncoraglio, *Branch Mgr*
EMP: 9 **Privately Held**
WEB: www.morantug.com
SIC: 3731 Shipbuilding & repairing
HQ: Moran Towing Corporation
50 Locust Ave Ste 10
New Canaan CT 06840
203 442-2800

(G-15730)
MOTHER MOUSSE LTD (PA)
3767 Victory Blvd Ste D (10314)
PHONE.................................718 983-8366
Fax: 718 698-5282
Theresa Rutigilano, *President*
Joan Ingrisani, *Vice Pres*
EMP: 9
SQ FT: 3,500
SALES (est): 1.5MM **Privately Held**
WEB: www.mamamousse.com
SIC: 2051 Bakery: wholesale or wholesale/retail combined

GEOGRAPHIC SECTION

Staten Island - Richmond County (G-15761)

(G-15731)
NEWSPAPER DELIVERY SOLUTIONS
309 Bradley Ave (10314-5154)
PHONE 718 370-1111
Peter Priolo, *CEO*
EMP: 5 **EST:** 2011
SALES (est): 235.2K **Privately Held**
SIC: 2711 Newspapers

(G-15732)
NORTH AMERICAN DF INC (PA)
280 Watchogue Rd (10314-3100)
PHONE 718 698-2500
Chrissy Mazzola, *President*
EMP: 8
SQ FT: 5,000
SALES (est): 2MM **Privately Held**
SIC: 2759 Advertising literature: printing

(G-15733)
NORTH AMERICAN MFG ENTPS INC (PA)
Also Called: Mht Lighting
1961 Richmond Ter (10302-1201)
PHONE 718 524-4370
Thomas Spinelli, *Ch of Bd*
Mark Shotton, *Vice Pres*
▲ **EMP:** 32 **EST:** 2009
SQ FT: 56,000
SALES (est): 3.9MM **Privately Held**
SIC: 3646 Commercial indusl & institutional electric lighting fixtures

(G-15734)
NORTH AMERICAN MFG ENTPS INC
1961 Richmond Ter (10302-1201)
PHONE 718 524-4370
Joe Scalice, *Director*
EMP: 15
SALES (corp-wide): 3.9MM **Privately Held**
SIC: 3646 Commercial indusl & institutional electric lighting fixtures
PA: North American Manufacturing Enterprises, Inc.
1961 Richmond Ter
Staten Island NY 10302
718 524-4370

(G-15735)
NORTH EAST FUEL GROUP INC
51 Stuyvesant Ave (10312-3721)
PHONE 718 984-6774
Richard D Auria, *Principal*
EMP: 7
SALES (est): 724.9K **Privately Held**
SIC: 2869 Fuels

(G-15736)
NORTHEASTERN FUEL CORP
51 Stuyvesant Ave (10312-3721)
PHONE 917 560-6241
Richard Dauria, *Principal*
EMP: 6
SALES (est): 832.9K **Privately Held**
SIC: 2869 Fuels

(G-15737)
NY TITANIUM INC
63 Robin Ct (10309-1923)
PHONE 718 227-4244
Mark Kaplan, *Chairman*
EMP: 5 **EST:** 2009
SALES (est): 386.3K **Privately Held**
SIC: 3356 Titanium

(G-15738)
OCCHIOEROSSO JOHN
Also Called: All Gone Restoration
75 Santa Monica Ln (10309-2833)
PHONE 718 541-7025
John Occhiogrosso, *Owner*
EMP: 10
SALES (est): 284.4K **Privately Held**
SIC: 1389 Construction, repair & dismantling services

(G-15739)
OH HOW CUTE INC
38 Androvette St (10309-1302)
PHONE 347 838-6031
Margaret Delia, *President*
EMP: 6
SQ FT: 800
SALES: 80K **Privately Held**
SIC: 2064 5199 5092 5145 Cake ornaments, confectionery; gifts & novelties; balloons, novelty, candy

(G-15740)
PHILLIP JUAN
9 Union Ave (10303-2424)
PHONE 800 834-4543
Philip Juan, *Owner*
Fu-Chang Juan, *Maintence Staff*
EMP: 7
SQ FT: 2,500
SALES (est): 340K **Privately Held**
WEB: www.juanscorp.com
SIC: 2032 Chinese foods: packaged in cans, jars, etc.

(G-15741)
PHOTOGRAVE CORPORATION
Also Called: Www.picturesongold.com
1140 S Railroad Ave (10306-3371)
PHONE 718 667-4825
Bernard Schifter, *CEO*
Daniel Schifter, *President*
▲ **EMP:** 23
SQ FT: 3,000
SALES: 10.5MM **Privately Held**
WEB: www.photograve.com
SIC: 3911 Jewelry, precious metal

(G-15742)
PIAZZAS ICE CREAM ICE HSE INC
41 Housman Ave (10303-2701)
PHONE 718 818-8811
Salvatore J Piazz, *Ch of Bd*
Sam Conte, *Manager*
EMP: 16 **EST:** 2010
SALES (est): 2.4MM **Privately Held**
SIC: 2024 Ice cream & frozen desserts

(G-15743)
PLAYFITNESS CORP
27 Palisade St (10305-4711)
PHONE 917 497-5443
Pavel Asanov, *CEO*
EMP: 5
SALES (est): 351.8K **Privately Held**
SIC: 7372 7999 7389 Educational computer software; physical fitness instruction;

(G-15744)
PORT AUTHORITY OF NY & NJ
2777 Goethals Rd N Fl 2 (10303-1107)
PHONE 718 390-2534
Jerry Deltufo, *Manager*
EMP: 90
SALES (corp-wide): 4.8B **Privately Held**
WEB: www.portnynj.com
SIC: 3441 Bridge sections, prefabricated highway
PA: The Port Authority Of New York & New Jersey
4 World Trade Ctr 150
New York NY 10007
212 435-7000

(G-15745)
PREPARATORY MAGAZINE GROUP
1200 South Ave Ste 202 (10314-3424)
PHONE 718 761-4800
Luciano Rammairone, *President*
Gina Biancardi, *President*
EMP: 55
SQ FT: 9,000
SALES: 2.5MM **Privately Held**
SIC: 2721 Magazines: publishing only, not printed on site

(G-15746)
QPS DIE CUTTERS FINISHERS CORP
140 Alverson Ave (10309-1776)
PHONE 718 966-1811
Eva Choina, *President*
Semion Goldsman, *Vice Pres*
EMP: 42
SQ FT: 35,000
SALES (est): 3.2MM **Privately Held**
SIC: 3999 Advertising display products

(G-15747)
R & L PRESS INC
896 Forest Ave (10310-2413)
PHONE 718 447-8557
Fax: 718 448-4261
Ron Patterson, *President*
EMP: 5
SQ FT: 4,000
SALES (est): 776.8K **Privately Held**
SIC: 2752 Promotional printing, lithographic; commercial printing, offset

(G-15748)
R & L PRESS OF SI INC
Also Called: Luke's Copy Shop
2506 Hylan Blvd (10306-4366)
PHONE 718 667-3258
Fax: 718 667-7815
Luke Callas, *President*
Kim Catanese, *Manager*
EMP: 3
SQ FT: 1,200
SALES: 2.3MM **Privately Held**
SIC: 2752 7334 Commercial printing, offset; photocopying & duplicating services

(G-15749)
RAMHOLTZ PUBLISHING INC
Also Called: Collegebound Teen Magazine
1200 South Ave Ste 202 (10314-3424)
PHONE 718 761-4800
Luciano Rammairone, *CEO*
Gina Biancardi, *Vice Pres*
Mario Lupia, *VP Opers*
Aleks Danilov, *Accounts Mgr*
Joseph Cardinale, *Accounts Exec*
EMP: 60
SQ FT: 10,000
SALES (est): 6.1MM **Privately Held**
SIC: 2721 Magazines: publishing only, not printed on site

(G-15750)
RD2 CONSTRUCTION & DEM LLC
63 Trossach Rd (10304-2131)
PHONE 718 980-1650
Kathleen Cloppse, *Controller*
Peter Dagostino,
EMP: 15
SALES (est): 2.2MM **Privately Held**
SIC: 1442 Construction sand & gravel

(G-15751)
REEBOK INTERNATIONAL LTD
2655 Richmond Ave (10314-5821)
PHONE 718 370-0471
EMP: 205
SALES (corp-wide): 20.4B **Privately Held**
SIC: 3149 Athletic shoes, except rubber or plastic
HQ: Reebok International Ltd.
1895 J W Foster Blvd
Canton MA 02021
781 401-5000

(G-15752)
REMSEN FUEL INC
4668 Amboy Rd (10312-4150)
PHONE 718 984-9551
Natha Singh, *President*
EMP: 6 **EST:** 2012
SALES (est): 595.4K **Privately Held**
SIC: 2869 Fuels

(G-15753)
REYNOLDS SHIPYARD CORPORATION
200 Edgewater St (10305-4996)
P.O. Box 50010 (10305-0010)
PHONE 718 981-2800
Fax: 718 447-2710
Michael Reynolds, *President*
▲ **EMP:** 10
SQ FT: 30,000
SALES (est): 1.3MM **Privately Held**
SIC: 3731 Cargo vessels, building & repairing; tugboats, building & repairing; barges, building & repairing; scows, building & repairing

(G-15754)
RGM SIGNS INC
Also Called: Blue Boy
1234 Castleton Ave (10310-1717)
PHONE 718 442-0598
Fax: 718 442-2343
Ron Malanga, *President*
EMP: 6
SQ FT: 684
SALES (est): 593.9K **Privately Held**
WEB: www.rgmsigns.com
SIC: 3993 2752 5999 1799 Signs & advertising specialties; offset & photolithographic printing; awnings; sign installation & maintenance

(G-15755)
RICHMOND READY MIX CORP
328 Park St (10306-1859)
PHONE 917 731-8400
EMP: 7 **EST:** 2015
SALES (est): 740.6K **Privately Held**
SIC: 3273 Ready-mixed concrete

(G-15756)
SCARA-MIX INC
2537 Richmond Ter (10303-2390)
P.O. Box 30313 (10303-0313)
PHONE 718 442-7357
Fax: 718 948-7198
Philip Castellano, *President*
Peter Mauro, *Manager*
EMP: 45 **EST:** 1981
SQ FT: 17,000
SALES (est): 5.2MM **Privately Held**
SIC: 3273 Ready-mixed concrete

(G-15757)
SECOND GENERATION WOOD STAIRS
2581 Richmond Ter Ste 3 (10303-2323)
PHONE 718 370-0085
EMP: 10
SALES (est): 740K **Privately Held**
SIC: 2431 Staircases, stairs & railings

(G-15758)
SPECIAL TEES
250 Buel Ave (10305-1204)
PHONE 718 980-0987
Fax: 718 980-1048
Tom Siniscalchi, *Programmer Anys*
Joanne Homsey, *Prgrmr*
Vicent Bonomi, *Program Dir*
Gary Rando, *Administration*
EMP: 24
SALES (est): 1.4MM **Privately Held**
WEB: www.specialtees-si.com
SIC: 2396 Screen printing on fabric articles

(G-15759)
SPEEDWAY LLC
951 Bay St (10305-4938)
PHONE 718 815-6897
Antonio Balle, *Manager*
EMP: 10 **Publicly Held**
WEB: www.hess.com
SIC: 1389 Gas field services
HQ: Speedway Llc
500 Speedway Dr
Enon OH 45323
937 864-3000

(G-15760)
ST JOHN
229 Morrison Ave (10310-2836)
PHONE 718 720-8367
Barbara A Logan, *Principal*
EMP: 5 **EST:** 2011
SALES (est): 241.5K **Privately Held**
SIC: 2339 Sportswear, women's

(G-15761)
STATED ISLAND STAIR INC
439 Sharrotts Rd (10309-1414)
PHONE 718 317-9276
Fran Imber, *President*
EMP: 5
SQ FT: 4,500
SALES: 450K **Privately Held**
SIC: 2431 Staircases & stairs, wood; stair railings, wood

Staten Island - Richmond County (G-15762)

(G-15762)
STATEN ISLAND PARENT MAGAZINE
16 Shenandoah Ave Ste 2 (10314-3652)
PHONE.................................718 761-4800
Orlando Frank, *Owner*
Mario Lupia, *COO*
Giulio Rammairone, *Vice Pres*
Nicole Puglia, *Manager*
Patrick Mok, *Info Tech Mgr*
EMP: 5
SALES (est): 373.2K **Privately Held**
SIC: 2721 Periodicals

(G-15763)
STATEN ISLAND STAIR INC
439 Sharrotts Rd (10309-1414)
PHONE.................................718 317-9276
Fax: 718 966-8176
Fran Imber, *President*
Benjamin Imber, *Manager*
Fran Imber, *Executive*
EMP: 5
SALES: 500K **Privately Held**
SIC: 2431 Staircases & stairs, wood

(G-15764)
STONEY CROFT CONVERTERS INC
Also Called: Alltek Labeling Systems
364 Sharrotts Rd (10309-1990)
PHONE.................................718 608-9800
Fax: 718 608-9200
John Conti, *President*
Ann Conti, *Vice Pres*
EMP: 16
SQ FT: 7,000
SALES: 3.9MM **Privately Held**
WEB: www.allteklabeling.com
SIC: 2672 2679 Adhesive papers, labels or tapes: from purchased material; labels, paper: made from purchased material

(G-15765)
STRADA SOFT INC
20 Clifton Ave (10305-4912)
PHONE.................................718 556-6940
Lou Esposito, *Principal*
EMP: 8
SALES: 300K **Privately Held**
WEB: www.stradasoft.com
SIC: 7372 Prepackaged software

(G-15766)
SUPERIOR CONFECTIONS INC
1150 South Ave (10314-3404)
PHONE.................................718 698-3300
Fax: 718 494-4576
George Kaye, *President*
Michael K Katsoris, *Exec VP*
Peter Kaye, *Vice Pres*
▲ **EMP:** 100 **EST:** 1951
SQ FT: 40,000
SALES (est): 10.1MM **Privately Held**
SIC: 2066 Chocolate candy, solid

(G-15767)
SUPREME CHOCOLATIER LLC
1150 South Ave Fl 1 (10314-3404)
PHONE.................................718 761-9600
Fax: 718 761-5279
George Kaye, *Info Tech Dir*
Kraichen Tracey, *Administration*
▲ **EMP:** 50 **EST:** 1999
SALES: 10.1MM **Privately Held**
WEB: www.supremechocolatier.com
SIC: 2061 Raw cane sugar

(G-15768)
TDS WOODWORKING INC
Also Called: TDS Woodcraft
104 Port Richmond Ave (10302-1334)
PHONE.................................718 442-5298
Fax: 718 816-8403
Salvatore Piscicelli, *President*
Diane Steoppiell, *Admin Sec*
EMP: 10
SALES (est): 1.2MM **Privately Held**
SIC: 2431 Millwork

(G-15769)
TEAM BUILDERS INC
Also Called: Team Builders Management
88 New Dorp Plz S Ste 303 (10306-2902)
P.O. Box 778 (10302)
PHONE.................................718 979-1005
Christine B Fasier, *President*
Daniel Harris, *Manager*
EMP: 11
SQ FT: 1,100
SALES: 2MM **Privately Held**
SIC: 7372 Business oriented computer software

(G-15770)
TECH PRODUCTS INC
105 Willow Ave (10305-1896)
PHONE.................................718 442-4900
Fax: 718 442-2124
Kenneth Nelson Sr, *President*
Carey Nelson, *Corp Secy*
Robert Rosenbaum, *CFO*
Daniel Oconnor, *VP Sales*
Richard Failla, *Sales Engr*
▼ **EMP:** 44 **EST:** 1948
SQ FT: 1,600
SALES (est): 7.7MM **Privately Held**
WEB: www.techproducts.com
SIC: 3953 3993 Marking devices; signs & advertising specialties

(G-15771)
TODT HILL AUDIOLOGICAL SVCS
78 Todt Hill Rd Ste 202 (10314-4528)
PHONE.................................718 816-1952
Theresa Cannon, *President*
EMP: 5
SALES (est): 660.1K **Privately Held**
SIC: 3842 8049 Hearing aids; audiologist

(G-15772)
ULTIMATE PAVERS CORP
659 Quincy Ave (10305-4100)
PHONE.................................917 417-2652
EMP: 27
SALES (est): 4.9MM **Privately Held**
SIC: 2951 Asphalt paving mixtures & blocks

(G-15773)
VCP MOBILITY INC
4131 Richmond Ave (10312-5633)
PHONE.................................718 356-7827
EMP: 400
SALES (corp-wide): 396.7MM **Privately Held**
SIC: 3842 Wheelchairs
HQ: Vcp Mobility, Inc.
6899 Winchester Cir # 200
Boulder CO 80301
303 218-4500

(G-15774)
VEZ INC
Also Called: Fastsigns
1209 Forest Ave (10310-2416)
PHONE.................................718 273-7002
Fax: 718 273-7006
Rich Vezzuto, *President*
Kurt Kracsun, *Vice Pres*
EMP: 6
SQ FT: 1,400
SALES: 900K **Privately Held**
WEB: www.veztek.com
SIC: 3993 2759 Signs & advertising specialties; business forms: printing

(G-15775)
VF OUTDOOR INC
2655 Richmond Ave # 1570 (10314-5821)
PHONE.................................718 698-6215
EMP: 46
SALES (corp-wide): 12B **Publicly Held**
SIC: 2329 Men's & boys' leather, wool & down-filled outerwear
HQ: Vf Outdoor, Llc
2701 Harbor Bay Pkwy
Alameda CA 94502
510 618-3500

(G-15776)
WELSH GOLD STAMPERS INC
44 Lenzie St (10312-6118)
PHONE.................................718 984-5031

Fax: 212 505-9206
Edwin Wallace, *President*
▲ **EMP:** 27
SALES (est): 1.6MM **Privately Held**
SIC: 3999 2759 2675 2796 Gold stamping, except books; embossing on paper; die-cut paper & board; platemaking services; bookbinding & related work

(G-15777)
YPIS OF STATEN ISLAND INC
130 Stuyvesant Pl Ste 5 (10301-1900)
PHONE.................................718 815-4557
Dominick Brancato, *Exec Dir*
EMP: 2
SALES: 5.5MM **Privately Held**
SIC: 7372 Business oriented computer software

Stephentown
Rensselaer County

(G-15778)
ATLANTIS EQUIPMENT CORPORATION (PA)
16941 Ny 22 (12168)
PHONE.................................518 733-5910
Fax: 518 733-6834
Louis Schroeter, *President*
Richard W Keeler Jr, *Vice Pres*
Kate Beach, *Manager*
Catherine Beach, *Technology*
EMP: 18
SQ FT: 40,000
SALES: 5MM **Privately Held**
SIC: 3599 3441 7692 3444 Machine shop, jobbing & repair; fabricated structural metal; welding repair; sheet metalwork

(G-15779)
FOUR FAT FOWL INC
324 State Route 43 Stop B (12168-2933)
PHONE.................................518 733-5230
Willard Bridgham IV, *President*
Josie Madison, *Opers Mgr*
Shaleena Bridgham, *Sales Mgr*
EMP: 5
SALES: 325K **Privately Held**
SIC: 2022 Natural cheese

(G-15780)
ZWACK INCORPORATED
15875 Ny 22 (12168)
P.O. Box 100 (12168-0100)
PHONE.................................518 733-5135
Fax: 518 733-6135
Frank J Zwack, *President*
Mike Zwack, *Manager*
Maria Zwack, *Admin Sec*
EMP: 50 **EST:** 1971
SQ FT: 30,000
SALES (est): 9.2MM **Privately Held**
WEB: www.zwackinc.com
SIC: 3541 3714 5082 Machine tools, metal cutting type; sanders, motor vehicle safety; general construction machinery & equipment

Stillwater
Saratoga County

(G-15781)
FANTASY FIREWORKS DISPLAY
28 Flike Rd (12170-1231)
PHONE.................................518 664-1809
Scott Demarco, *Owner*
EMP: 5
SALES: 400K **Privately Held**
SIC: 2899 Fireworks

(G-15782)
H2O SOLUTIONS INC
61 Major Dickinson Ave (12170-7729)
P.O. Box 721 (12170-0721)
PHONE.................................518 527-0915
Daniel Reilly, *Principal*
EMP: 15
SALES (est): 953.8K **Privately Held**
SIC: 3589 Water filters & softeners, household type

(G-15783)
STILLWATER WOOD & IRON
114 N Hudson Ave (12170)
P.O. Box 736 (12170-0736)
PHONE.................................518 664-4501
Charles Robert Hallum, *Owner*
C Robert Hallum, *Owner*
Bob Hallum, *Partner*
EMP: 5
SQ FT: 13,000
SALES: 650K **Privately Held**
WEB: www.stillwaterfdny.com
SIC: 2511 Wood household furniture; unassembled or unfinished furniture, household: wood

Stittville
Oneida County

(G-15784)
DYNA-VAC EQUIPMENT INC
8963 State Route 365 (13469-1021)
PHONE.................................315 865-8084
Hal Reigi, *President*
Laurie Reigi, *Vice Pres*
Mike Simpson, *Sales Mgr*
EMP: 11
SQ FT: 6,000
SALES: 1.8MM **Privately Held**
WEB: www.dynavacequipment.com
SIC: 3589 Sewer cleaning equipment, power

Stone Ridge
Ulster County

(G-15785)
FTS SYSTEMS INC (DH)
3538 Main St (12484-5601)
PHONE.................................845 687-5300
Fax: 845 687-7481
Claus Kinder, *Principal*
Thomas Verdey, *Technology*
EMP: 85 **EST:** 1971
SQ FT: 34,000
SALES (est): 7.6MM
SALES (corp-wide): 1.4B **Privately Held**
WEB: www.ftssystems.com
SIC: 3821 3823 3585 Laboratory equipment: fume hoods, distillation racks, etc.; industrial instrmnts msrmnt display/control process variable; refrigeration & heating equipment
HQ: S P Industries, Inc.
935 Mearns Rd
Warminster PA 18974
215 672-7800

(G-15786)
PK30 SYSTEM LLC
3607 Atwood Rd (12484-5446)
P.O. Box 656 (12484-0656)
PHONE.................................212 473-8050
Philip Kerzner, *Owner*
EMP: 13
SALES (est): 2MM **Privately Held**
SIC: 3442 3446 3429 Store fronts, prefabricated, metal; architectural metalwork; builders' hardware

Stony Brook
Suffolk County

(G-15787)
BABY UV/KIDS UV INC (PA)
11 Hawks Nest Rd (11790-1103)
PHONE.................................917 301-9020
Francesann Dipietro, *President*
Chris Zanaty, *Principal*
EMP: 12
SALES (est): 633.6K **Privately Held**
SIC: 2369 Bathing suits & swimwear: girls', children's & infants'

GEOGRAPHIC SECTION

(G-15788)
BASF BEAUTY CARE SOLUTIONS LLC
50 Health Sciences Dr (11790-3349)
PHONE 631 689-0200
John Marchese, *Safety Mgr*
Steve Palmberg, *Purchasing*
Kevin Regan, *QC Mgr*
James Haywood, *Manager*
EMP: 8
SALES (est): 1.1MM
SALES (corp-wide): 60.8B **Privately Held**
SIC: 2816 Inorganic pigments
HQ: Basf Catalysts Llc
25 Middlesex Tpke
Iselin NJ 08830
732 205-5000

(G-15789)
COGNITIVEFLOW SENSOR TECH
9 Melville Ct (11790-1851)
PHONE 631 513-9369
Mitchell Fourman, *CEO*
EMP: 9 **EST:** 2011
SALES (est): 775K **Privately Held**
SIC: 3841 Surgical & medical instruments

(G-15790)
CREATIVE CABINET CORP AMERICA
3 Onyx Dr (11790-3013)
PHONE 631 751-5768
Arthur A Daniels, *President*
Barbara Giordano, *Bookkeeper*
Mark Daniels, *Sales Mgr*
Tony Peterford, *Info Tech Dir*
EMP: 25 **EST:** 1975
SQ FT: 40,000
SALES: 3.2MM **Privately Held**
SIC: 2434 5031 5211 Wood kitchen cabinets; kitchen cabinets; cabinets, kitchen

(G-15791)
INTELIBS INC
1500 Stony Brook Rd Ste 3 (11794-4600)
PHONE 877 213-2640
Seyong Park, *President*
Dorene Weiland, *Executive*
EMP: 5
SALES (est): 929K **Privately Held**
SIC: 3663

(G-15792)
SAFINA CENTER
118 Administration (11794-0001)
PHONE 808 888-9440
Mayra Marino, *Manager*
EMP: 9 **EST:** 2015
SQ FT: 564
SALES (est): 550K **Privately Held**
SIC: 3545 Mandrels

(G-15793)
STONY BROOK UNIVERSITY
Also Called: University Advertising Agency
310 Administration Bldg (11794-0001)
PHONE 631 632-6434
Richard Fine, *Dean*
Suzanne Shane, *Counsel*
Bruce Schroffel, *Exec VP*
Michael Teta, *Facilities Mgr*
Samantha Thomas, *Transportation*
EMP: 40 **Privately Held**
WEB: www.sunysb.edu
SIC: 2752 8221 9411 Commercial printing, lithographic; colleges universities & professional schools; administration of educational programs;
HQ: Stony Brook University
100 Nicolls Rd
Stony Brook NY 11794
631 632-6000

Stony Point
Rockland County

(G-15794)
FANTASY GLASS COMPAN
61 Beach Rd (10980-2035)
PHONE 845 786-5818
Greggory Barbutl, *Owner*

EMP: 5
SALES (est): 339.5K **Privately Held**
SIC: 3732 Boats, fiberglass: building & repairing

(G-15795)
GOTHAM INK & COLOR CO INC
19 Holt Dr (10980-1919)
PHONE 845 947-4000
Fax: 845 947-4007
William Olson, *General Mgr*
Joseph Simons, *Vice Pres*
Bill Olsen, *Manager*
EMP: 20
SQ FT: 25,000
SALES (est): 3.4MM **Privately Held**
SIC: 2893 Printing ink

(G-15796)
KEON OPTICS INC
30 John F Kennedy Dr (10980-3207)
PHONE 845 429-7103
Kevin McKeon, *President*
EMP: 10
SQ FT: 1,300
SALES (est): 815.2K **Privately Held**
SIC: 3827 Optical instruments & lenses

(G-15797)
LIGHTING SERVICES INC (PA)
2 Holt Dr (10980-1920)
PHONE 845 942-2800
Fax: 914 942-2392
Daniel Gelman, *President*
Ken Kane, *Exec VP*
Daniel Lareau, *VP Opers*
Rose Miller, *Purch Agent*
Joe Mazzurco, *Buyer*
▲ **EMP:** 100 **EST:** 1958
SQ FT: 50,000
SALES (est): 17.9MM **Privately Held**
WEB: www.lightingservicesinc.com
SIC: 3646 Commercial indusl & institutional electric lighting fixtures

(G-15798)
PRECISION TECHNIQUES INC
25 Holt Dr (10980-1919)
PHONE 718 991-1440
Fax: 718 991-1447
Paul Mangione, *President*
Joseph De Savage, *Corp Secy*
▲ **EMP:** 85
SQ FT: 70,000
SALES (est): 11.4MM **Privately Held**
WEB: www.precisiontechniquesinc.com
SIC: 3089 4783 Injection molding of plastics; packing & crating

(G-15799)
STONY POINT GRAPHICS LTD
Also Called: Shell Ann Printing
1 S Liberty Dr (10980-1811)
PHONE 845 786-3322
Fax: 845 786-2122
Phillip Laquidara, *President*
Felix Laquidara, *Vice Pres*
Loraine Laquidara, *Admin Sec*
EMP: 5
SQ FT: 4,000
SALES: 300K **Privately Held**
SIC: 2752 2759 Commercial printing, offset; letterpress printing

(G-15800)
TIMES SQUARE STAGE LTG CO INC
Also Called: Time Square Lighting
5 Holt Dr (10980-1919)
PHONE 845 947-3034
Fax: 845 947-3047
Robert Riccadelli, *President*
Bruce Tyler, *General Mgr*
Thomas Tyler, *Engineer*
Eric Leskin, *Accounting Dir*
Bruce M Farlane, *Finance Mgr*
▲ **EMP:** 50 **EST:** 1938
SQ FT: 32,000
SALES (est): 11MM **Privately Held**
WEB: www.tslight.com
SIC: 3648 Lighting equipment

Stormville
Dutchess County

(G-15801)
GALLI SHIRTS AND SPORTS AP
246 Judith Dr (12582-5262)
PHONE 845 226-7305
Fax: 845 227-6984
Vincent Gallipani, *President*
Erika Gallipani, *Vice Pres*
EMP: 5
SALES: 300K **Privately Held**
WEB: www.gallishirts.com
SIC: 2396 7311 Screen printing on fabric articles; advertising consultant

(G-15802)
PACKAGE PAVEMENT COMPANY INC
3530 Route 52 (12582-5651)
P.O. Box 408 (12582-0408)
PHONE 845 221-2224
Fax: 845 221-0433
Darren Doherty, *Ch of Bd*
Frank J Doherty, *President*
Paul Doherty, *General Mgr*
Gary Lancour, *General Mgr*
Eileen Doherty, *Vice Pres*
▲ **EMP:** 95 **EST:** 1951
SQ FT: 5,000
SALES (est): 26.9MM **Privately Held**
SIC: 2951 Asphalt paving mixtures & blocks; asphalt & asphaltic paving mixtures (not from refineries); concrete, asphaltic (not from refineries); concrete, bituminous

Stottville
Columbia County

(G-15803)
IRV SCHRODER & SONS INC
2906 Atlantic Ave (12172-7700)
P.O. Box 300 (12172-0300)
PHONE 518 828-0194
Fax: 518 828-2402
Jim Schroder, *President*
EMP: 20
SQ FT: 6,000
SALES (est): 3.8MM **Privately Held**
SIC: 3441 1791 Fabricated structural metal; structural steel erection

Stuyvesant
Columbia County

(G-15804)
MAPLE HILL CREAMERY LLC (PA)
285 Allendale Rd W (12173-2611)
P.O. Box 323, Kinderhook (12106-0323)
PHONE 518 758-7777
Peter Meck, *Vice Pres*
Charles Zentay, *CFO*
Peter T Joseph, *Mng Member*
EMP: 20
SQ FT: 6,000
SALES: 8MM **Privately Held**
SIC: 2026 Yogurt

Stuyvesant Falls
Columbia County

(G-15805)
BETHS FARM KITCHEN
504 Rte 46 (12174)
P.O. Box 113 (12174-0113)
PHONE 518 799-3414
Fax: 518 799-2042
Beth Linskey, *Owner*
EMP: 8
SALES (est): 556.3K **Privately Held**
WEB: www.bethsfarmkitchen.com
SIC: 2033 Jams, jellies & preserves: packaged in cans, jars, etc.

Suffern
Rockland County

(G-15806)
ADVANCED MEDICAL MFG CORP
Also Called: Crown Medical Products
7-11 Suffern Pl Ste 2 (10901-5501)
PHONE 845 369-7535
Ron Resnick, *Owner*
Carol Wynee, *Controller*
Linda Montemarano, *Cust Svc Dir*
EMP: 20
SALES (est): 1.4MM **Privately Held**
SIC: 2393 Cushions, except spring & carpet: purchased materials

(G-15807)
AMERICAN BEST CABINETS INC
Also Called: Malibu Cabinets
397 Spook Rock Rd (10901-5319)
PHONE 845 369-6666
Fax: 845 369-7777
Sam Blum, *President*
Aron Feldman, *Vice Pres*
Gitty Samet, *Sales Mgr*
▲ **EMP:** 39
SQ FT: 26,000
SALES (est): 3.9MM **Privately Held**
WEB: www.malibucabinets.com
SIC: 2514 Kitchen cabinets: metal

(G-15808)
BEER MARKETERS INSIGHTS INC
49 E Maple Ave (10901-5507)
PHONE 845 507-0040
Benj Steinman, *President*
Robin Steinman, *Vice Pres*
Irene Steinman, *Treasurer*
Christopher Shepard, *Assoc Editor*
EMP: 8
SALES (est): 969.1K **Privately Held**
WEB: www.beerinsights.com
SIC: 2721 8742 Trade journals: publishing & printing; management consulting services

(G-15809)
CLASSIC CABINETS
375 Spook Rock Rd (10901-5314)
PHONE 845 357-4331
John Cheman, *Owner*
EMP: 10
SALES (est): 767.5K **Privately Held**
WEB: www.classcabs.com
SIC: 2434 Wood kitchen cabinets

(G-15810)
DYNAMIC INTL MFRS & DISTRS INC
78 Lafayette Ave Ste 201 (10901-5551)
PHONE 347 993-1914
Avery Engel, *President*
▲ **EMP:** 10
SALES (est): 745.6K **Privately Held**
SIC: 2678 Stationery products

(G-15811)
E-FFINERGY GROUP LLC
Also Called: Day One Lighting
355 Spook Rock Rd (10901-5314)
PHONE 845 547-2424
Mendel Hecht, *Mng Member*
EMP: 5
SQ FT: 1,000
SALES: 1.3MM **Privately Held**
SIC: 3646 Commercial indusl & institutional electric lighting fixtures

(G-15812)
EMPIRE COACHWORKS INTL LLC
475 Haverstraw Rd (10901-3135)
PHONE 732 257-7981
Ron Dubiel, *Controller*
Edward Vergopia, *Mng Member*
Micheal Misseri,
EMP: 70
SQ FT: 88,000

Suffern - Rockland County (G-15813)

SALES (est): 5.3MM **Privately Held**
SIC: 3711 Automobile bodies, passenger car, not including engine, etc.

(G-15813)
HUDSON ENERGY SERVICES LLC (PA)
4 Executive Blvd Ste 301 (10901-4190)
PHONE..................................630 300-0013
Fax: 845 228-3422
Holly Hopper, *Business Mgr*
Diana Kreppelt, *Business Mgr*
Joanna Magnani, *Business Mgr*
Susan Persson, *Business Mgr*
Robert Vera, *Business Mgr*
EMP: 6
SQ FT: 1,500
SALES (est): 1.3MM **Privately Held**
WEB: www.hudsonenergyservices.com
SIC: 2911 Gases & liquefied petroleum gases

(G-15814)
I TRADE TECHNOLOGY LTD
400 Rella Blvd Ste 165 (10901-8114)
PHONE..................................615 348-7233
Andy Gordon, *Branch Mgr*
EMP: 6
SALES (corp-wide): 1.5MM **Privately Held**
SIC: 3678 5999 5065 Electronic connectors; electronic parts & equipment; connectors, electronic
PA: I Trade Technology, Ltd.
115 Franklin Tpke Ste 144
Mahwah NJ 07430
615 348-7233

(G-15815)
LA VITA HEALTH FOODS LTD
257 Route 59 (10901-5303)
PHONE..................................845 368-4101
Zina Minz, *President*
Eli Minz, *Vice Pres*
▼ EMP: 6
SQ FT: 6,000
SALES: 500K **Privately Held**
SIC: 2052 Cookies

(G-15816)
LE CHOCOLATE OF ROCKLAND LLC
1 Ramapo Ave (10901-5805)
PHONE..................................845 533-4125
Simon Rottenburg,
▲ EMP: 25
SALES (est): 4.6MM **Privately Held**
SIC: 2066 Chocolate

(G-15817)
OUTLOOK NEWSPAPER
145 College Rd (10901-3620)
PHONE..................................845 356-6261
Fax: 845 574-4476
Ian Newman, *Director*
EMP: 25
SALES (est): 609.2K **Privately Held**
SIC: 2711 2741 Newspapers, publishing & printing; miscellaneous publishing

(G-15818)
PRIME FEATHER INDUSTRIES LTD
7-11 Suffern Pl (10901-5501)
PHONE..................................718 326-8701
Fax: 718 326-8436
Justin J Shipper, *President*
EMP: 10
SQ FT: 5,500
SALES (est): 760K **Privately Held**
SIC: 2392 Cushions & pillows

(G-15819)
RADIATION SHIELDING SYSTEMS
415 Spook Rock Rd (10901-5308)
PHONE..................................888 631-2278
Ed Delia, *CEO*
Seth Warnock, *Vice Pres*
Brenda Velez, *Manager*
EMP: 11

SALES (est): 1.9MM **Privately Held**
WEB: www.radiationshieldingsystems.com
SIC: 3444 3271 Radiator shields or enclosures, sheet metal; blocks, concrete: radiation-proof

(G-15820)
ROYAL TEES INC
29 Lafayette Ave (10901-5405)
PHONE..................................845 357-9448
Fax: 845 357-9490
Al Rosenblatt, *President*
EMP: 5
SQ FT: 8,000
SALES: 750K **Privately Held**
WEB: www.royaltees.com
SIC: 2759 2395 2752 5611 Screen printing; embroidery & art needlework; transfers, decalcomania or dry: lithographed; clothing, sportswear, men's & boys'; women's sportswear

(G-15821)
SUPER CONDUCTOR MATERIALS INC
Also Called: SCM
391 Spook Rock Rd (10901-5319)
P.O. Box 701, Tallman (10982-0701)
PHONE..................................845 368-0240
Fax: 845 368-0250
Aftab Dar, *President*
Neelam Dar, *Corp Secy*
▼ EMP: 14
SQ FT: 10,000
SALES (est): 2.3MM **Privately Held**
WEB: www.scm-inc.com
SIC: 3674 Semiconductors & related devices

(G-15822)
UNITED ROCKLAND HOLDING CO INC
9 N Airmont Rd (10901-5101)
P.O. Box 68, Tallman (10982-0068)
PHONE..................................845 357-1900
Paul Wishnoff, *President*
Stanley Wishnoff, *Chairman*
Mitchell Kolata, *Treasurer*
Linda Olivo, *Manager*
EMP: 20 EST: 1961
SQ FT: 20,000
SALES (est): 1.6MM **Privately Held**
WEB: www.unitedrocklandstairs.com
SIC: 2431 Staircases & stairs, wood; stair railings, wood

(G-15823)
XEROX CORPORATION
30 Dunnigan Dr Ste 3 (10901-4185)
PHONE..................................845 918-3147
Norb Stampfel, *Manager*
Michael Feeney, *Manager*
EMP: 50
SALES (corp-wide): 10.7B **Publicly Held**
WEB: www.xerox.com
SIC: 3861 Photographic equipment & supplies
PA: Xerox Corporation
201 Merritt 7
Norwalk CT 06851
203 968-3000

Sugar Loaf
Orange County

(G-15824)
IRINIRI DESIGNS LTD
1358 Kings Hwy (10981)
P.O. Box 378 (10981-0378)
PHONE..................................845 469-7934
Rit Goldman, *Ch of Bd*
Nirit Rechtman, *President*
EMP: 12
SQ FT: 1,653
SALES (est): 1MM **Privately Held**
SIC: 3911 5944 Jewelry, precious metal; jewelry stores

Sunnyside
Queens County

(G-15825)
ANOTHER 99 CENT PARADISE
4206 Greenpoint Ave (11104-3004)
PHONE..................................718 786-4578
Ali Gohar, *Principal*
Gohar Ali, *Manager*
EMP: 5
SALES (est): 411.4K **Privately Held**
SIC: 3643 Outlets, electric: convenience

(G-15826)
DEANCO DIGITAL PRINTING LLC
Also Called: NY Print Partners
4545 39th St (11104-4401)
PHONE..................................212 371-2025
Joe Aziz, *Mng Member*
Pete Lamba,
EMP: 10
SQ FT: 2,500
SALES: 1.2MM **Privately Held**
SIC: 2752 Commercial printing, lithographic

(G-15827)
DEELKA VISION CORP
Also Called: New York Style Eats
4502 Queens Blvd (11104-2304)
PHONE..................................718 937-4121
Fax: 718 937-1338
Mark Stroubosm, *Ch of Bd*
Mark Stroubos, *Principal*
EMP: 20
SALES (est): 2.3MM **Privately Held**
SIC: 2091 Canned & cured fish & seafoods

(G-15828)
EASTERN CONCEPTS LTD
Also Called: Green Mountain Graphics
4125 39th St (11104-4201)
P.O. Box 1417, Long Island City (11101-0417)
PHONE..................................718 472-3377
Fax: 718 472-4040
Eric Greenberg, *President*
Yugnik Singh, *General Mgr*
Elsie Gerena, *Purch Mgr*
Brian Berg, *Sales Executive*
Steve Goldman, *Sales Executive*
EMP: 11
SQ FT: 6,000
SALES (est): 980K **Privately Held**
WEB: www.gm-graphics.com
SIC: 3993 Signs & advertising specialties

(G-15829)
NODUS NOODLE CORPORATION
4504 Queens Blvd (11104-2304)
PHONE..................................718 309-3725
Thomas SAE Tang, *CEO*
EMP: 8
SALES (est): 335.2K **Privately Held**
SIC: 2098 Noodles (e.g. egg, plain & water), dry

(G-15830)
S DONADIC WOODWORKING INC
4525 39th St (11104-4401)
PHONE..................................718 361-9888
Steven Donadic, *President*
EMP: 60
SQ FT: 7,000
SALES: 2MM **Privately Held**
SIC: 2434 2431 2426 2421 Wood kitchen cabinets; millwork; hardwood dimension & flooring mills; sawmills & planing mills, general

(G-15831)
T S B A GROUP INC (PA)
3830 Woodside Ave (11104-1004)
PHONE..................................718 565-6000
Samuel Brown, *Chairman*
Duane Fuller, *Purchasing*
Mark Grossman, *Controller*
Anthony Difiglia, *Marketing Mgr*
EMP: 30
SQ FT: 70,000

SALES (est): 19.4MM **Privately Held**
SIC: 3822 1731 Temperature controls, automatic; energy management controls

Surprise
Greene County

(G-15832)
ROYAL METAL PRODUCTS INC
463 West Rd (12176-1709)
PHONE..................................518 966-4442
Fax: 518 966-5148
David M Johannesen, *President*
Steven Johannesen, *Vice Pres*
Robert Johannesen, *Treasurer*
EMP: 40 EST: 1956
SQ FT: 49,600
SALES (est): 4.5MM **Privately Held**
WEB: www.royalmetalproducts.com
SIC: 2514 3446 2522 3444 Metal household furniture; architectural metalwork; office furniture, except wood; sheet metalwork; products of purchased glass

Syosset
Nassau County

(G-15833)
ANDOR DESIGN CORP
20 Pond View Dr (11791-4409)
PHONE..................................516 364-1619
Fax: 516 364-5428
Ralph Silvera, *President*
EMP: 7
SALES: 800K **Privately Held**
WEB: www.andordesign.com
SIC: 3829 Tensile strength testing equipment; testing equipment: abrasion, shearing strength, etc.

(G-15834)
ANNA B INC
391 Cold Spring Rd (11791-1805)
PHONE..................................516 680-6609
Anna Blumenfeld, *President*
EMP: 5
SALES: 250K **Privately Held**
SIC: 2335 Bridal & formal gowns

(G-15835)
BEKTROM FOODS INC (PA)
Also Called: Lots O' Luv
6800 Jericho Tpke 207w (11791-4445)
PHONE..................................516 802-3800
Thomas Barbella, *President*
Marguerite Barbella, *Office Mgr*
▲ EMP: 6
SALES (est): 11.4MM **Privately Held**
SIC: 2045 2099 Prepared flour mixes & doughs; packaged combination products: pasta, rice & potato

(G-15836)
BUFFALO DENTAL MFG CO INC
Also Called: Bdm
159 Lafayette Dr (11791-3933)
P.O. Box 678 (11791-0678)
PHONE..................................516 496-7200
Fax: 516 496-7751
Donald Nevin, *President*
Marshall Nevin, *Chairman*
Doris Nevin, *Admin Sec*
▲ EMP: 50 EST: 1869
SQ FT: 25,000
SALES (est): 8.6MM **Privately Held**
SIC: 3843 Dental equipment & supplies

(G-15837)
CONTI AUTO BODY CORP
44 Jericho Tpke (11791)
PHONE..................................516 921-6435
Liam Martin, *Principal*
EMP: 7
SALES (est): 775.7K **Privately Held**
SIC: 3711 3713 7532 Automobile bodies, passenger car, not including engine, etc.; truck & bus bodies; top & body repair & paint shops

GEOGRAPHIC SECTION
Syosset - Nassau County (G-15861)

(G-15838)
COSENSE INC
125 Coachman Pl W (11791-3059)
PHONE.....................516 364-9161
Fax: 631 231-0838
Naim Dam, *President*
Sal Stiperi, *Vice Pres*
Melt Boyatan, *Purchasing*
Howard Austerlitz, *Engineer*
Shamine Dam, *Controller*
EMP: 35
SQ FT: 10,000
SALES (est): 6.6MM
SALES (corp-wide): 12.2B **Privately Held**
WEB: www.cosense.com
SIC: 3829 Measuring & controlling devices
HQ: Measurement Specialties, Inc.
   1000 Lucas Way
   Hampton VA 23666
   757 766-1500

(G-15839)
DANDREA INC
115 Eileen Way Ste 106 (11791-5314)
P.O. Box 391, Port Washington (11050-0392)
PHONE.....................516 496-2200
Fax: 516 496-2425
Anthony J D'Andrea, *President*
Rosemary D'Andrea, *Corp Secy*
Terry Day, *Manager*
▲ **EMP:** 40 **EST:** 1922
SQ FT: 12,000
SALES (est): 5MM **Privately Held**
SIC: 3931 5736 Musical instruments; musical instrument stores

(G-15840)
DELANEY BOOKS INC
212 Michael Dr (11791-5379)
PHONE.....................516 921-8888
Michael Rudman, *President*
Frances Rudman, *Vice Pres*
EMP: 15 **EST:** 1968
SQ FT: 5,000
SALES (est): 1.5MM **Privately Held**
WEB: www.passbooks.com
SIC: 2731 Books: publishing only
PA: National Learning Corp
   212 Michael Dr
   Syosset NY 11791
   516 921-8888

(G-15841)
ETERNAL LOVE PARFUMS CORP
Also Called: Eternal Love Perfumes
485 Underhill Blvd # 207 (11791-3434)
PHONE.....................516 921-6100
Fax: 516 921-6142
Mahender Sabhnani, *President*
◆ **EMP:** 4
SALES: 4.2MM **Privately Held**
WEB: www.eternalloveparfums.com
SIC: 2844 5122 Toilet preparations; perfumes

(G-15842)
FLUID METERING INC (HQ)
5 Aerial Way Ste 500 (11791-5593)
PHONE.....................516 922-6050
Harry E Pinkerton III, *President*
Robert A Warren Jr, *Vice Pres*
Anthony Mennella, *Purch Mgr*
Daniel Lee, *Design Engr*
EMP: 50 **EST:** 1959
SALES (est): 15.2MM
SALES (corp-wide): 3.7B **Publicly Held**
WEB: www.fmipump.com
SIC: 3825 Meters: electric, pocket, portable, panelboard, etc.
PA: Roper Technologies, Inc.
   6901 Prof Pkwy E Ste 200
   Sarasota FL 34240
   941 556-2601

(G-15843)
FRANK MERRIWELL INC
212 Michael Dr (11791-5305)
PHONE.....................516 921-8888
Jack Rudman, *President*
Frances Rudman, *Vice Pres*
EMP: 15
SQ FT: 5,000
SALES (est): 737.9K
SALES (corp-wide): 1.5MM **Privately Held**
WEB: www.frankmerriwell.com
SIC: 2731 Books: publishing only
PA: National Learning Corp
   212 Michael Dr
   Syosset NY 11791
   516 921-8888

(G-15844)
GENERAL MICROWAVE CORPORATION (HQ)
227a Michael Dr (11791-5306)
PHONE.....................516 802-0900
Deanna Lund, *CEO*
Eric Demarco, *President*
Michael Fink, *Vice Pres*
Michael W Fink, *Vice Pres*
Nola Hess, *Manager*
EMP: 11 **EST:** 1960
SQ FT: 3,000
SALES: 10MM **Publicly Held**
SIC: 3674 5065 3825 6794 Hybrid integrated circuits; electronic parts & equipment; electronic parts; test equipment for electronic & electrical circuits; patent owners & lessors; microwave components; analytical instruments

(G-15845)
GOTHAM INK CORP
19 Teibrook Ave (11791-3831)
PHONE.....................516 677-1969
Edward Feldstein, *President*
Paul Weinstein, *Vice Pres*
EMP: 7 **EST:** 2001
SQ FT: 5,000
SALES: 925K **Privately Held**
SIC: 2752 7331 Commercial printing, lithographic; direct mail advertising services

(G-15846)
KNOLL PRINTING & PACKAGING INC
Also Called: Knoll Worldwide
149 Eileen Way (11791-5302)
PHONE.....................516 621-0100
Jeremy Cohen, *Ch of Bd*
Linda Drew, *Vice Pres*
Coleen Corporal, *Prdtn Mgr*
▲ **EMP:** 24
SALES: 5MM **Privately Held**
WEB: www.knollpack.com
SIC: 2657 3081 3086 Folding paperboard boxes; packing materials, plastic sheet; packaging & shipping materials, foamed plastic

(G-15847)
KUSH OASIS ENTERPRISES LLC
228 Martin Dr (11791-5406)
PHONE.....................516 513-1316
Jyoti Jaiswal,
▲ **EMP:** 5
SALES (est): 210K **Privately Held**
SIC: 2393 Textile bags

(G-15848)
MESTEL BROTHERS STAIRS & RAILS
11 Gary Rd Ste 102 (11791-6211)
PHONE.....................516 496-4127
Fax: 516 496-4127
Barry Mestel, *President*
EMP: 236
SALES (est): 14.5MM **Privately Held**
WEB: www.mestelbrothersstairs.com
SIC: 2431 3446 1751 Staircases & stairs, wood; architectural metalwork; carpentry work

(G-15849)
NASCO ENTERPRISES INC
95 Woodcrest Dr (11791-3037)
PHONE.....................516 921-9696
Naimish P Shah, *President*
▲ **EMP:** 1
SALES: 1MM **Privately Held**
SIC: 3841 Catheters

(G-15850)
NATIONAL LEARNING CORP (PA)
212 Michael Dr (11791-5379)
PHONE.....................516 921-8888
Fax: 516 921-8743
Michael Rudman, *President*
Frances Rudman, *Vice Pres*
EMP: 15
SQ FT: 15,000
SALES: 1.5MM **Privately Held**
WEB: www.delaneybooks.com
SIC: 2731 Book clubs: publishing & printing

(G-15851)
NATIONAL RDING STYLES INST INC
Also Called: N R S I
179 Lafayette Dr (11791-3933)
P.O. Box 737 (11791-0737)
PHONE.....................516 921-5500
Fax: 516 921-5591
Marie Carbo, *President*
Juliet Ditroia, *Corp Secy*
Gail Banks, *Bookkeeper*
EMP: 12
SQ FT: 6,400
SALES: 1.5MM **Privately Held**
WEB: www.nrsi.com
SIC: 2741 8748 Miscellaneous publishing; educational consultant

(G-15852)
NEW JERSEY PULVERIZING CO INC (PA)
4 Rita St (11791-5918)
PHONE.....................516 921-9595
Fax: 516 921-9575
Martin Tanzer, *President*
Barbara Tanzer, *Vice Pres*
Barbara Deegan, *Treasurer*
EMP: 19 **EST:** 1915
SQ FT: 2,500
SALES (est): 2.1MM **Privately Held**
SIC: 1446 Industrial sand

(G-15853)
NORTH HILLS SIGNAL PROC CORP (HQ)
6851 Jericho Tpke Ste 170 (11791-4454)
PHONE.....................516 682-7700
Fax: 516 682-7750
Estro Vitantonio, *CEO*
Warren Esanu, *Ch of Bd*
Richard Schwarz, *General Mgr*
Ralph Depascale, *Opers Staff*
Agnieszka Koziel, *Project Engr*
▲ **EMP:** 1
SQ FT: 12,000
SALES (est): 5.7MM
SALES (corp-wide): 544.5K **Privately Held**
WEB: www.northhills-sp.com
SIC: 3679 Harness assemblies for electronic use: wire or cable
PA: North Hills Holding Company Llc
   6851 Jericho Tpke Ste 170
   Syosset NY 11791
   516 682-7705

(G-15854)
NORTH HILLS SIGNAL PROC CORP
North Hill Signal Prossesing
6851 Jericho Tpke Ste 170 (11791-4454)
PHONE.....................516 682-7740
Richard Schwartz, *General Mgr*
Renee Taylor, *Administration*
EMP: 10
SALES (corp-wide): 544.5K **Privately Held**
SIC: 3669 Signaling apparatus, electric
HQ: North Hills Signal Processing Corp.
   6851 Jericho Tpke Ste 170
   Syosset NY 11791
   516 682-7700

(G-15855)
PARADIGM MKTG CONSORTIUM INC
Also Called: United Supply Systems
350 Michael Dr (11791-5307)
PHONE.....................516 677-6012
Fax: 516 677-6013
Ralph Bianculli Jr, *CEO*
Pamela Bianculli, *President*
Thomas Bathe, *VP Sales*
Marsha Pearl, *Administration*
▲ **EMP:** 50
SQ FT: 100,000
SALES (est): 15.5MM **Privately Held**
SIC: 2679 5087 Paper products, converted; cleaning & maintenance equipment & supplies

(G-15856)
QUALBUYS LLC
6800 Jericho Tpke 120w (11791-4436)
PHONE.....................855 884-3274
Amy Kajiya, *COO*
EMP: 5 **EST:** 2011
SALES (est): 177.7K **Privately Held**
SIC: 3999 Barber & beauty shop equipment

(G-15857)
RAMLER INTERNATIONAL LTD
485 Underhill Blvd # 100 (11791-3434)
PHONE.....................516 353-3106
Garry Ramler, *President*
Gail Gordon, *Director*
▲ **EMP:** 24 **EST:** 2010
SALES: 12MM **Privately Held**
SIC: 2599 Hotel furniture

(G-15858)
REAL EST BOOK OF LONG ISLAND
575 Underhill Blvd # 110 (11791-3426)
PHONE.....................516 364-5000
Bryan Flynn, *President*
Julie Lindh, *Office Mgr*
EMP: 10
SQ FT: 1,600
SALES: 2MM **Privately Held**
SIC: 2721 7319 Periodicals: publishing only; magazines: publishing only, not printed on site; distribution of advertising material or sample services

(G-15859)
ROTA FILE CORPORATION
Also Called: Rota Tool
159 Lafayette Dr (11791-3933)
P.O. Box 678 (11791-0678)
PHONE.....................516 496-7200
Don Nevin, *President*
Richard Byalick, *General Mgr*
EMP: 20
SALES (est): 2.2MM **Privately Held**
WEB: www.rotafile.com
SIC: 3545 Cutting tools for machine tools

(G-15860)
SDS BUSINESS CARDS INC
Also Called: B C T
170 The Vale (11791-4312)
PHONE.....................516 747-3131
Fax: 516 746-3425
Todd Peters, *President*
Sharon Peters, *Vice Pres*
EMP: 10
SQ FT: 3,000
SALES: 1.2MM **Privately Held**
SIC: 2752 2759 Commercial printing, lithographic; commercial printing

(G-15861)
VIDEO TECHNOLOGY SERVICES INC
5 Aerial Way Ste 300 (11791-5594)
PHONE.....................516 937-9700
Andres Sierra, *President*
Philip Lapierre, *Engineer*
Phillip Pierre, *Engineer*
Richard Rouse, *Engineer*
Lisa Morreale, *Manager*
EMP: 12
SQ FT: 7,200
SALES (est): 1.9MM **Privately Held**
WEB: www.videotechnologyservices.com
SIC: 3651 7622 5099 Household video equipment; video repair; video & audio equipment

Syosset - Nassau County (G-15862) — GEOGRAPHIC SECTION

(G-15862)
VIVONA BUSINESS PRINTERS INC
Also Called: PIP Printing
343 Jackson Ave (11791-4123)
PHONE...............................516 496-3453
Fax: 516 496-8949
Joseph Vivonia, *CEO*
Joe Vivona, *President*
Anne Marie Bono, *Vice Pres*
Fran Galligan, *Office Mgr*
EMP: 8
SALES (est): 1.2MM **Privately Held**
SIC: 2752 Commercial printing, offset

(G-15863)
ZASTECH INC
15 Ryan St (11791-2129)
PHONE...............................516 496-4777
Raymond Zhou, *CEO*
▲ **EMP:** 20
SALES (est): 1.5MM **Privately Held**
SIC: 3674 Semiconductors & related devices

Syracuse
Onondaga County

(G-15864)
219 SOUTH WEST
219 S West St (13202-1874)
PHONE...............................315 474-2065
EMP: 8
SALES (est): 560K **Privately Held**
SIC: 2448 Mfg Wood Pallets/Skids

(G-15865)
A NUCLIMATE QULTY SYSTEMS INC
1 General Motors Dr Ste 5 (13206-1122)
PHONE...............................315 431-0226
Edward Campagna Jr, *President*
John Dimillo, *Vice Pres*
James Miller, *VP Engrg*
William Shultes, *VP Sales*
EMP: 19
SALES (est): 2.6MM **Privately Held**
SIC: 3585 3433 Heating equipment, complete; heating & air conditioning combination units; heating equipment, except electric

(G-15866)
A ZIMMER LTD
Also Called: Syracuse New Times
W Tenesee St (13204)
PHONE...............................315 422-7011
Arthur Zimmer, *President*
Bill Brod, *Publisher*
Gregg Gambell, *General Mgr*
Shirley Zimmer, *CFO*
Jill Hutchinson, *Finance*
EMP: 84
SQ FT: 24,000
SALES (est): 5.2MM **Privately Held**
WEB: www.syracusenewtimes.com
SIC: 2711 5521 Newspapers; used car dealers

(G-15867)
AIRGAS USA LLC
121 Boxwood Ln (13206-1802)
PHONE...............................315 433-1295
Fax: 315 463-7346
Bill Hartsock, *Branch Mgr*
EMP: 20
SALES (corp-wide): 163.9MM **Privately Held**
SIC: 2813 Industrial gases
HQ: Airgas Usa, Llc
   259 N Radnor Chester Rd # 100
   Radnor PA 19087
   610 687-5253

(G-15868)
ALL TIMES PUBLISHING LLC
Also Called: Syracuse New Times
1415 W Genesee St (13204-2119)
PHONE...............................315 422-7011
Fax: 315 422-1721
William Brod, *CEO*
Art Zimmer, *Publisher*
James Coleman, *Vice Pres*

EMP: 24
SALES: 2MM **Privately Held**
SIC: 2741 Miscellaneous publishing

(G-15869)
ALL-STATE DIVERSIFIED PDTS INC
8 Dwight Park Dr (13209-1034)
PHONE...............................315 472-4728
EMP: 50
SALES (est): 5.3MM **Privately Held**
SIC: 3443 Mfg Fabricated Plate Work

(G-15870)
ALLIED DECORATIONS CO INC
Also Called: Allied Sign Co
720 Erie Blvd W (13204-2226)
PHONE...............................315 637-0273
Fax: 315 476-3756
Michael E Pfohl, *President*
Ken Colton, *Natl Sales Mgr*
Kim Charette, *Office Mgr*
EMP: 15
SQ FT: 45,000
SALES (est): 1.8MM **Privately Held**
WEB: www.alliedsigncompany.com
SIC: 3993 7389 Signs & advertising specialties; decoration service for special events; trade show arrangement

(G-15871)
ALPHA DC MOTORS INC
5949 E Molloy Rd (13211-2125)
P.O. Box 3166 (13220-3166)
PHONE...............................315 432-9039
Fax: 315 432-9085
Elton Mantle, *CEO*
Josh Rauscher, *Manager*
EMP: 10
SALES (est): 890K **Privately Held**
WEB: www.alphadcmotors.com
SIC: 7694 Electric motor repair

(G-15872)
ALPHA PRINTING CORP
131 Falso St (13211-2106)
P.O. Box 26 (13211-0026)
PHONE...............................315 454-5507
Stephen Larose, *President*
Chris Graney, *Sales Staff*
Castro Dyane, *Manager*
Sally Godkin, *Manager*
EMP: 12
SQ FT: 5,000
SALES (est): 1.5MM **Privately Held**
SIC: 2752 Commercial printing, offset

(G-15873)
ALTIUS AVIATION LLC
113 Tuskegee Rd Ste 2 (13211-1332)
PHONE...............................315 455-7555
Vaughn J Crawford, *Mng Member*
Vaughn Crawford, *Exec Dir*
EMP: 6
SALES (est): 860.2K **Privately Held**
SIC: 3721 6722 8742 Aircraft; management investment, open-end; management consulting services

(G-15874)
ANSUN GRAPHICS INC
6392 Deere Rd Ste 4 (13206-1317)
PHONE...............................315 437-6869
Fax: 315 437-6979
Jeff Schoenfeld, *President*
Jim Mahon, *VP Sales*
Patricia Craine, *Manager*
Joe Marrinan, *Shareholder*
Todd Thomas, *Admin Sec*
EMP: 12
SALES (est): 1.7MM **Privately Held**
WEB: www.ansun.biz
SIC: 2759 Commercial printing

(G-15875)
ANTHONY RIVER INC
116 Granger St (13202-2388)
PHONE...............................315 475-1315
Fax: 315 475-6341
Ken Abramson, *President*
EMP: 15
SQ FT: 21,500
SALES: 2MM **Privately Held**
SIC: 3471 3083 2851 Finishing, metals or formed products; plastic finished products, laminated; paints & allied products

(G-15876)
ARCOM AUTOMATICS LLC
185 Ainsley Dr (13210-4202)
P.O. Box 6729 (13217-6729)
PHONE...............................315 422-1230
Fax: 315 422-2963
Gregory A Tresness, *President*
Barbara Beckner, *Vice Pres*
William Warwick, *Engineer*
EMP: 8
SALES (est): 1.4MM **Privately Held**
WEB: www.arcomlabs.com
SIC: 3663 Cable television equipment

(G-15877)
ARO-GRAPH CORPORATION
Also Called: Aro-Graph Displays
847 North Ave (13206-1630)
PHONE...............................315 463-8693
Fax: 315 463-0026
Neal Burrei, *President*
Carol Burrei, *Vice Pres*
EMP: 5 **EST:** 1946
SQ FT: 7,000
SALES (est): 786.6K **Privately Held**
WEB: www.arograph.com
SIC: 2752 2396 Decals, lithographed; screen printing on fabric articles

(G-15878)
ARPAC LLC
6581 Townline Rd (13206-1175)
PHONE...............................315 471-5103
EMP: 10
SALES (corp-wide): 61.6MM **Privately Held**
SIC: 3537 Palletizers & depalletizers
PA: Arpac, Llc
   9555 Irving Park Rd
   Schiller Park IL 60176
   847 678-9034

(G-15879)
ARROW-COMMUNICATION LABS INC
Also Called: Arcom Labs
185 Ainsley Dr (13210-4202)
P.O. Box 6729 (13217-6729)
PHONE...............................315 422-1230
Andrew Tresness, *President*
David Dixon, *Vice Pres*
Michael Thayer, *Safety Dir*
David Dickson, *Controller*
Barb Beckner, *VP Sales*
▲ **EMP:** 300
SQ FT: 30,000
SALES (est): 52.6MM
SALES (corp-wide): 52.8MM **Privately Held**
SIC: 3663 Cable television equipment
PA: Northern Catv Sales Inc
   185 Ainsley Dr
   Syracuse NY
   315 422-1230

(G-15880)
ATLAS BITUMINOUS CO INC
173 Farrell Rd (13209-1823)
PHONE...............................315 457-2394
Charmaine Jones, *President*
Robert Shattel, *Treasurer*
Robert Shattell Sr, *Treasurer*
James Shattel, *Admin Sec*
EMP: 11 **EST:** 1963
SQ FT: 2,500
SALES (est): 1.9MM **Privately Held**
SIC: 2951 6513 Asphalt & asphaltic paving mixtures (not from refineries); apartment hotel operation

(G-15881)
AUTOMATION CORRECT LLC
Also Called: Automationcorrect.com
405 Parrish Ln (13205-3323)
PHONE...............................315 299-3589
Neil Waelder, *Manager*
EMP: 5
SALES (est): 530K **Privately Held**
WEB: www.automationcorrect.com
SIC: 3825 Test equipment for electronic & electrical circuits

(G-15882)
AUTOMATION PAPERS INC
Also Called: National Pad & Paper
6361 Thompson Rd Stop 1 (13206-1412)
P.O. Box 572, Fayetteville (13066-0572)
PHONE...............................315 432-0565
David T Carroll, *President*
Donald T Carroll, *Vice Pres*
Jean Carroll, *Admin Sec*
▼ **EMP:** 7
SQ FT: 17,000
SALES (est): 1.1MM **Privately Held**
SIC: 2621 Writing paper

(G-15883)
AVALON COPY CENTERS AMER INC (PA)
Also Called: Avalon Document Services
901 N State St (13208-2515)
PHONE...............................315 471-3333
Fax: 315 471-3334
John P Midgley, *CEO*
Shawn Thrall, *President*
Jon Willette, *COO*
Jason Schroeder, *Vice Pres*
Matthew Malburg, *CFO*
EMP: 65
SQ FT: 13,000
SALES (est): 19.6MM **Privately Held**
SIC: 2741 7375 7336 7334 Art copy; publishing & printing; information retrieval services; commercial art & graphic design; photocopying & duplicating services

(G-15884)
BABBITT BEARINGS INC (PA)
Also Called: Babbitt Bearings
734 Burnet Ave (13203-2999)
PHONE...............................315 479-6603
Fax: 315 479-5103
Tracy S Stevenson, *CEO*
H Thomas Wart, *Vice Pres*
Charles R Wat, *Plant Mgr*
John Cerrone, *Treasurer*
Marian Wart, *Admin Sec*
EMP: 90 **EST:** 1943
SQ FT: 34,000
SALES (est): 14.3MM **Privately Held**
SIC: 3599 Machine shop, jobbing & repair

(G-15885)
BABBITT BEARINGS INCORPORATED
734 Burnet Ave (13203-2999)
PHONE...............................315 479-6603
Charles R Wart Jr, *President*
Jeffrey Rossman, *Purchasing*
John Cerrone, *Treasurer*
Marian Wart, *Admin Sec*
EMP: 75 **EST:** 1970
SQ FT: 60,000
SALES (est): 6.4MM
SALES (corp-wide): 14.3MM **Privately Held**
WEB: www.babbitt-inc.com
SIC: 3599 3568 Machine shop, jobbing & repair; power transmission equipment
PA: Babbitt Bearings, Inc.
   734 Burnet Ave
   Syracuse NY 13203
   315 479-6603

(G-15886)
BADOUD COMMUNICATIONS INC
Also Called: Scotsman Press
750 W Genesee St (13204-2306)
P.O. Box 130, Camillus (13031-0130)
PHONE...............................315 472-7821
John Badoud, *President*
Nancy Badoud, *Admin Sec*
EMP: 225
SQ FT: 51,682
SALES (est): 14.1MM **Privately Held**
SIC: 2752 2741 Commercial printing, lithographic; shopping news: publishing & printing

(G-15887)
BARNES GROUP INC
Associated Spring
1225 State Fair Blvd (13209-1011)
PHONE...............................315 457-9200
Fax: 315 457-9228
Kenneth Martin, *Division Mgr*

▲ = Import ▼ = Export ◆ = Import/Export

Malinda Peterman, *Sales Executive*
Larry Johnson, *Branch Mgr*
Sean Foran, *Manager*
Eric Condreay, *Executive*
EMP: 8
SQ FT: 22,448
SALES (corp-wide): 1.2B **Publicly Held**
WEB: www.barnesgroupinc.com
SIC: 3495 3469 Wire springs; metal stampings
PA: Barnes Group Inc.
123 Main St
Bristol CT 06010
860 583-7070

(G-15888)
BENCHMARK MEDIA SYSTEMS INC
203 E Hampton Pl Ste 2 (13206-1676)
PHONE 315 437-6300
Fax: 315 437-8119
Ruth S Burdick, *CEO*
Allen H Burdick, *President*
Peter Depuy, *Prdtn Mgr*
Richard Kalinowski, *Purch Mgr*
Rory Rall, *Sales Mgr*
EMP: 14
SQ FT: 5,500
SALES (est): 2.4MM **Privately Held**
WEB: www.benchmarkmedia.com
SIC: 3663 Radio & TV communications equipment

(G-15889)
BILLY BEEZ USA LLC
9090 Destiy Usa Dr L301 Unit L 301 (13204)
PHONE 315 741-5099
EMP: 6
SALES (corp-wide): 14.2MM **Privately Held**
SIC: 3949 5137 7999 Playground equipment; women's & children's dresses, suits, skirts & blouses; amusement ride
PA: Billy Beez Usa, Llc
3 W 35th St Fl 3
New York NY 10001
646 606-2249

(G-15890)
BITZER SCROLL INC
6055 Court Street Rd (13206-1749)
PHONE 315 463-2101
Peter P Narreau, *CEO*
Richard Kobor, *President*
Peter Schaufler, *Principal*
Dolores Cotroneo, *Purch Mgr*
Tom O'Donnell, *Engineer*
▲ **EMP:** 97
SALES (est): 42.6MM
SALES (corp-wide): 195.3K **Privately Held**
SIC: 3822 Air conditioning & refrigeration controls
HQ: Bitzer Se
Eschenbrunnlestr. 15
Sindelfingen 71065
703 193-20

(G-15891)
BODYCOTE SYRACUSE HEAT TREATIN
7055 Interstate Island Rd (13209-9750)
PHONE 315 451-0000
Fax: 315 451-3895
John H Mac Allister, *Ch of Bd*
Dave Stopera, *General Mgr*
George Stupp, *Vice Pres*
John Macalister, *CFO*
EMP: 23 **EST:** 1932
SQ FT: 30,000
SALES (est): 5.6MM
SALES (corp-wide): 739.3MM **Privately Held**
WEB: www.syracuseheattreating.com
SIC: 3398 Metal heat treating; brazing (hardening) of metal
HQ: Bodycote Usa, Inc.
12700 Park Central Dr # 700
Dallas TX 75201
214 904-2420

(G-15892)
BOMAC INC
6477 Ridings Rd (13206-1110)
PHONE 315 433-9181
Fax: 315 433-1910
Kevin T Knecht, *President*
Mark Pauls, *Vice Pres*
William Decoursey, *Foreman/Supr*
Thomas Pauls, *Purchasing*
Jeff Allen, *Engineer*
EMP: 18 **EST:** 1959
SQ FT: 22,000
SALES (est): 4.7MM **Privately Held**
WEB: www.bomacinc.com
SIC: 3625 Electric controls & control accessories, industrial

(G-15893)
BOXCAR PRESS INCORPORATED
509 W Fayette St Ste 135 (13204-2987)
PHONE 315 473-0930
Harold Kyle, *Ch of Bd*
Debbi Urbanski, *Vice Pres*
Alison Cotsonas, *Project Mgr*
Adriana Sosnowski, *Opers Mgr*
Sam Drori, *Software Engr*
EMP: 30
SALES (est): 5.6MM **Privately Held**
WEB: www.boxcarpress.com
SIC: 2752 5084 Commercial printing, lithographic; printing trades machinery, equipment & supplies

(G-15894)
BRIGHTON BAKERY
335 E Brighton Ave (13210-4141)
PHONE 315 475-2948
Mark Stefanski, *Owner*
EMP: 7
SQ FT: 3,000
SALES (est): 240K **Privately Held**
SIC: 2051 5461 Bread, all types (white, wheat, rye, etc): fresh or frozen; pastries, e.g. danish: except frozen; rolls, bread type: fresh or frozen; bakeries

(G-15895)
BROADNET TECHNOLOGIES INC
2-212 Center For Science (13244-0001)
PHONE 315 443-3694
Michael Sun, *CEO*
Humenn Polar, *Web Proj Mgr*
EMP: 15 **EST:** 2000
SQ FT: 2,000
SALES (est): 1.2MM **Privately Held**
SIC: 3577 Optical scanning devices

(G-15896)
BURR & SON INC
Also Called: Dover Enterprises
119 Seeley Rd (13224-1113)
PHONE 315 446-1550
Fax: 315 446-9976
J Peter Burr, *President*
EMP: 5 **EST:** 1973
SQ FT: 3,000
SALES (est): 360K **Privately Held**
WEB: www.doverent.com
SIC: 2759 Imprinting; engraving

(G-15897)
BUSCH PRODUCTS INC
110 Baker St (13206-1701)
PHONE 315 474-8422
Robert Brown Sr, *President*
Darlene Brown, *Vice Pres*
Paul Conley, *Engineer*
Lisa Verrillo, *Cust Mgr*
Ryan Labrake, *Sales Staff*
EMP: 50
SALES (est): 6.4MM **Privately Held**
WEB: www.buschproducts.com
SIC: 3281 Cut stone & stone products

(G-15898)
BYRNE DAIRY INC
Also Called: Byrne Distribution Center
275 Cortland Ave (13202)
PHONE 315 475-2111
Mike Haldane, *Manager*
EMP: 20
SQ FT: 54,928
SALES (corp-wide): 278.8MM **Privately Held**
WEB: www.byrnedairy.com
SIC: 2024 Ice cream, bulk
PA: Byrne Dairy Inc.
2394 Us Route 11
La Fayette NY 13084
315 475-2121

(G-15899)
C & M PRODUCTS INC
1209 N Salina St Ste 1 (13208-1581)
PHONE 315 471-3303
Fax: 315 471-4406
Charles Mott, *President*
EMP: 6 **EST:** 1965
SQ FT: 5,600
SALES (est): 579.5K **Privately Held**
SIC: 3479 3499 3089 Name plates: engraved, etched, etc.; trophies, metal, except silver; laminating of plastic

(G-15900)
C M E CORP
Also Called: Central Marking Equipment
1005 W Fayette St Ste 3c (13204-2840)
PHONE 315 451-7101
Leedom Kettell, *President*
Andrew Kettell, *General Mgr*
Elena Brusa, *Office Mgr*
Heather Finn, *Office Mgr*
EMP: 11
SQ FT: 12,000
SALES: 1MM **Privately Held**
SIC: 3555 3953 Printing plates; marking devices

(G-15901)
CAFE KUBAL
202 Lockwood Rd (13214-2035)
PHONE 315 278-2812
Matthew Godard, *Branch Mgr*
EMP: 12
SALES (corp-wide): 1MM **Privately Held**
SIC: 2095 Roasted coffee
PA: Cafe Kubal
3501 James St Ste 2
Syracuse NY 13206
315 278-2812

(G-15902)
CALTEX INTERNATIONAL LTD
60 Presidential Plz # 1405 (13202-2444)
PHONE 315 425-1040
Kapil Kevin Sodhi, *President*
Jennifer Hetherington, *Vice Pres*
EMP: 39
SQ FT: 26,000
SALES: 6.4MM **Privately Held**
WEB: www.iscbiostrat.com
SIC: 2869 2842 3826 Industrial organic chemicals; specialty cleaning preparations; environmental testing equipment

(G-15903)
CAMFIL USA INC
6600 Deere Rd (13206-1311)
PHONE 518 456-6085
EMP: 8
SALES (est): 1.3MM **Privately Held**
SIC: 3564 Blowers & fans

(G-15904)
CAROLS POLAR PARLOR
3800 W Genesee St (13219-1928)
PHONE 315 468-3404
Carol Franceschetti, *Owner*
EMP: 5
SALES (est): 358.5K **Privately Held**
SIC: 2024 Ice cream & frozen desserts

(G-15905)
CARPENTER INDUSTRIES INC
1 General Motors Dr # 10 (13206-1129)
P.O. Box 888 (13206-0888)
PHONE 315 463-4284
Fax: 315 463-4051
Edward Tibbits, *President*
Brian Wersinger, *Sales Associate*
Ed Downs, *Manager*
EMP: 11
SQ FT: 25,000
SALES (est): 1.3MM **Privately Held**
WEB: www.carpenterindustries.com
SIC: 3471 3441 Sand blasting of metal parts; fabricated structural metal

(G-15906)
CARRIER CORPORATION
Also Called: Carrier Globl Engrg Conference
Carrier Pkwy Trl 20 (13221)
P.O. Box 4808 (13221-4808)
PHONE 315 432-6000
EMP: 48
SALES (corp-wide): 57.2B **Publicly Held**
WEB: www.carrier.com
SIC: 3585 Air conditioning equipment, complete
HQ: Carrier Corporation
13995 Pasteur Blvd
Jupiter FL 33458
561 796-2000

(G-15907)
CARRIER CORPORATION
Carrier Pkwy Tr 20 (13221)
P.O. Box 4808 (13221-4808)
PHONE 315 432-6000
Randall J Hogan, *President*
Nassem Shaikh, *Vice Pres*
Bruce Poplawski, *Engineer*
Dick Ferguson, *Accounting Mgr*
Patrick Preux, *VP Human Res*
EMP: 400
SALES (corp-wide): 57.2B **Publicly Held**
WEB: www.carrier.com
SIC: 3822 3585 3433 Refrigeration/air-conditioning defrost controls; refrigeration & heating equipment, except electric
HQ: Carrier Corporation
13995 Pasteur Blvd
Jupiter FL 33458
561 796-2000

(G-15908)
CARRIER CORPORATION
Carrier Global Account (13221)
P.O. Box 4808 (13221-4808)
PHONE 315 432-6000
Geraud Darnis, *Branch Mgr*
EMP: 1200
SALES (corp-wide): 57.2B **Publicly Held**
WEB: www.carrier.com
SIC: 3585 Refrigeration & heating equipment
HQ: Carrier Corporation
13995 Pasteur Blvd
Jupiter FL 33458
561 796-2000

(G-15909)
CATHEDRAL CANDLE CO
510 Kirkpatrick St (13208-2100)
PHONE 315 422-9119
Fax: 315 478-1610
Louis J Steigerwald III, *Ch of Bd*
Mark Steigerwald, *Vice Pres*
John Hogan, *Treasurer*
Linda D Rohde, *Admin Sec*
▲ **EMP:** 52 **EST:** 1897
SQ FT: 17,000
SALES (est): 7.2MM **Privately Held**
WEB: www.cathedralcandle.com
SIC: 3999 5049 Candles; religious supplies

(G-15910)
CAVALRY SOLUTIONS
449 E Wshngtn St Ste 100 (13202-1965)
PHONE 315 422-1699
John Devendorf, *Owner*
EMP: 5
SALES (est): 260.5K **Privately Held**
SIC: 7372 Prepackaged software

(G-15911)
CHAMPION MILLWORK INC
140 Hiawatha Pl (13208-1268)
PHONE 315 463-0711
Fax: 315 463-0655
Micheal Duffy, *President*
Mark J Zapisek, *Co-Owner*
EMP: 25
SALES (est): 4.4MM **Privately Held**
SIC: 2541 Wood partitions & fixtures

Syracuse - Onondaga County (G-15912)

(G-15912)
CHEMTRADE CHEMICALS US LLC
Also Called: General Chemical
1421 Willis Ave (13204-1051)
P.O. Box 16 (13209-0016)
PHONE..................315 430-7650
Fax: 315 478-6247
Biagio Vavala, Plant Mgr
Biagio Bavala, Opers-Prdtn-Mfg
Kathleen Nese, Technology
EMP: 40
SALES (corp-wide): 789.3MM **Privately Held**
SIC: 2819 Industrial inorganic chemicals
HQ: Chemtrade Chemicals Us Llc
90 E Halsey Rd
Parsippany NJ 07054
973 515-0900

(G-15913)
CHEMTRADE CHEMICALS US LLC
Also Called: Syracuse Technical Center
344 W Genesee St Ste 100 (13202-1010)
PHONE..................315 478-2323
Joseph Hurd, Manager
Ben Shultes, Manager
EMP: 5
SALES (corp-wide): 789.3MM **Privately Held**
SIC: 2819 Sodium compounds or salts, inorg., ex. refined sod. chloride
HQ: Chemtrade Chemicals Us Llc
90 E Halsey Rd
Parsippany NJ 07054
973 515-0900

(G-15914)
CITY PATTERN SHOP INC
4052 New Court Ave (13206-1639)
P.O. Box 6 (13206-0006)
PHONE..................315 463-5239
Fax: 315 463-1138
Paul M Clisson, President
Robert Leonard, Vice Pres
Mike Davrany, Manager
EMP: 10 **EST:** 1961
SQ FT: 7,500
SALES (est): 1.2MM **Privately Held**
WEB: www.citypatternshop.com
SIC: 3543 Industrial patterns

(G-15915)
CLARK CONCRETE CO INC (PA)
Also Called: Clark Trucking Co Div
434 E Brighton Ave (13210-4144)
PHONE..................315 478-4101
Fax: 315 452-3150
Donald W Clark, President
Lyndon S Clark, Vice Pres
Stephen Clark, Vice Pres
John Wehrle, Sales Staff
EMP: 6 **EST:** 1920
SQ FT: 8,000
SALES (est): 1.8MM **Privately Held**
SIC: 3273 4212 Ready-mixed concrete; local trucking, without storage

(G-15916)
CLEAN ALL OF SYRACUSE LLC
838 Erie Blvd W (13204-2228)
PHONE..................315 472-9189
Fax: 315 472-3904
Severino Gonnella, President
Angela Gonnella, Vice Pres
EMP: 9
SQ FT: 40,000
SALES (est): 980K **Privately Held**
SIC: 2842 5999 Cleaning or polishing preparations; swimming pool chemicals, equipment & supplies

(G-15917)
CNY BUSINESS REVIEW INC
Also Called: Business Journal
269 W Jefferson St (13202-2334)
PHONE..................315 472-3104
Fax: 315 472-3644
Norman Poltenson, President
Marny Nesher, COO
Vance Marriner, Engineer
Mary Lamacchia, Accounts Mgr
Kurt Bramer, Manager
EMP: 14

SQ FT: 3,000
SALES (est): 1MM **Privately Held**
WEB: www.cnybj.com
SIC: 2711 2721 Newspapers; periodicals

(G-15918)
COASTEL CABLE TOOLS INC
Also Called: Coastel Cable Tools Intl
344 E Brighton Ave (13210-4142)
PHONE..................315 471-5361
Edward Dale, President
Mary Shaver, Vice Pres
John Lumia, Manager
EMP: 21
SQ FT: 42,000
SALES (est): 2MM **Privately Held**
WEB: www.coasteltools.com
SIC: 3541 3423 Machine tools, metal cutting type; hand & edge tools

(G-15919)
COCA-COLA BTLG CO OF NY INC
298 Farrell Rd (13209-1876)
PHONE..................315 457-9221
Lucky Wyrick, Sales/Mktg Mgr
Heaven Donner, Manager
EMP: 10
SQ FT: 117,740
SALES (corp-wide): 41.8B **Publicly Held**
SIC: 2086 Bottled & canned soft drinks
HQ: The Coca-Cola Bottling Company Of New York Inc
2500 Windy Ridge Pkwy Se
Atlanta GA 30339
770 989-3000

(G-15920)
COLD SPRINGS R & D INC
1207 Van Vleck Rd Ste A (13209-1017)
PHONE..................315 413-1237
Fax: 315 413-0456
Scott Grimshaw, President
Valerie Grimshaw, Vice Pres
EMP: 10
SQ FT: 10,000
SALES (est): 1.3MM **Privately Held**
WEB: www.csrdinc.com
SIC: 3674 Semiconductors & related devices

(G-15921)
COMMERCIAL MILLWORKS INC
221 W Division St (13204-1411)
PHONE..................315 475-7479
John Tortorello, Ch of Bd
Theodore Kinder, Vice Pres
EMP: 9
SQ FT: 10,000
SALES (est): 850.7K **Privately Held**
SIC: 2434 Wood kitchen cabinets

(G-15922)
COMMUNICATIONS & ENERGY CORP
204 Ambergate Rd (13214-2204)
PHONE..................315 446-5723
Emily Bostick, Ch of Bd
Christopher Bostick, President
EMP: 10
SQ FT: 5,500
SALES (est): 2MM **Privately Held**
WEB: www.cefilter.com
SIC: 3679 8742 2741 Electronic circuits; foreign trade consultant; miscellaneous publishing

(G-15923)
CONCEPTS IN WOOD OF CNY
4021 New Court Ave (13206-1640)
PHONE..................315 463-8084
Fax: 315 463-1157
David Fuleihan, President
EMP: 25
SQ FT: 16,000
SALES (est): 3.4MM **Privately Held**
SIC: 2521 2511 2431 Cabinets, office: wood; filing cabinets (boxes), office: wood; wood household furniture; millwork

(G-15924)
CONSTAS PRINTING CORPORATION
Also Called: Taylor Copy Services
1120 Burnet Ave (13203-3210)
PHONE..................315 474-2176
Fax: 315 474-2079
Diane M Brindak, Ch of Bd
Diane Constas, President
Claudia Constas, Vice Pres
EMP: 7
SQ FT: 2,400
SALES (est): 798.5K **Privately Held**
SIC: 2752 7334 Commercial printing, offset; photocopying & duplicating services

(G-15925)
COOKIE CONNECTION INC
705 Park Ave (13204-2223)
PHONE..................315 422-2253
Kathleen Sniezak, President
Elizabeth Johnson, Vice Pres
EMP: 5
SQ FT: 1,500
SALES (est): 305.8K **Privately Held**
SIC: 2051 Bakery: wholesale or wholesale/retail combined

(G-15926)
COOPER & CLEMENT INC
1840 Lemoyne Ave (13208-1367)
PHONE..................315 454-8135
Fax: 315 455-9490
John Clement, President
Inga Clement, Vice Pres
Ole Westergaard, Vice Pres
EMP: 29
SQ FT: 35,000
SALES (est): 4.6MM **Privately Held**
SIC: 2759 2396 Promotional printing; automotive & apparel trimmings

(G-15927)
COOPER CROUSE-HINDS LLC (HQ)
Also Called: Cooper Crouse Hinds Elec Pdts
1201 Wolf St (13208-1376)
P.O. Box 4999 (13221-4999)
PHONE..................866 764-5454
Fax: 315 477-5717
Alexander M Cutler, CEO
Grant L Gawronski, President
Vincent Dejoseph, Business Mgr
Chris Cooney, Vice Pres
John Dinger, Vice Pres
▲ **EMP:** 500
SQ FT: 1,000,000
SALES (est): 438MM **Privately Held**
WEB: www.coopercrouse-hinds.com
SIC: 3699 Fire control or bombing equipment, electronic

(G-15928)
COOPER INDUSTRIES LLC
Also Called: Cooper Molded Products
Wolf & 7th North St (13208)
PHONE..................315 477-7000
Christopher Cooney, Vice Pres
Hays Lengyel, Vice Pres
Nancy Gianni, Project Mgr
Pat Blincoe, Engineer
Darren Rutland, Sales Mgr
EMP: 21 **Privately Held**
SIC: 3646 3648 3613 5063 Commercial indusl & institutional electric lighting fixtures; lighting equipment; switchgear & switchgear accessories; electrical supplies; electrical equipment & supplies; construction machinery
HQ: Cooper Industries, Llc
600 Travis St Ste 5400
Houston TX 77002
713 209-8400

(G-15929)
COOPER LIGHTING LLC
125 E Jefferson St (13202-2020)
PHONE..................315 579-2873
EMP: 30 **Privately Held**
SIC: 3645 Fluorescent lighting fixtures, residential
HQ: Cooper Lighting, Llc
1121 Highway 74 S
Peachtree City GA 30269
770 486-4800

(G-15930)
COUNTERTOPS & CABINETS INC
4073 New Court Ave (13206-1646)
PHONE..................315 433-1038
Emil Henry, President
Nick Henry, Admin Sec
EMP: 5
SQ FT: 3,200
SALES (est): 752K **Privately Held**
WEB: www.cnytops.com
SIC: 2541 1799 Counter & sink tops; counter top installation

(G-15931)
CREATIVE LAMINATES INC
4003 Eastbourne Dr (13206-1631)
PHONE..................315 463-7580
Fax: 315 463-0509
Dennis N Brackly, President
Melody Brough, Manager
EMP: 19
SQ FT: 12,000
SALES (est): 133.1K **Privately Held**
WEB: www.creativelaminates.com
SIC: 2431 Millwork

(G-15932)
CRITICAL LINK LLC
6712 Brooklawn Pkwy # 203 (13211-2110)
PHONE..................315 425-4045
Neha Chopra, Project Mgr
Anna Higgs, Production
Alex Block, Engineer
Tom Catalino, Engineer
Adam Dziedzic, Engineer
EMP: 20
SQ FT: 8,000
SALES (est): 6MM **Privately Held**
SIC: 3571 8711 Electronic computers; engineering services

(G-15933)
CRUCIBLE INDUSTRIES LLC
575 State Fair Blvd (13209-1560)
PHONE..................800 365-1180
Jim Beckman, President
James Beckman, President
Lorna Carpenter, Vice Pres
Lorna E Carpenter, Vice Pres
Joe Nadzan, Vice Pres
◆ **EMP:** 290
SALES (est): 92MM **Privately Held**
SIC: 3312 Bars, iron: made in steel mills

(G-15934)
CRYOMECH INC
113 Falso Dr (13211-2106)
PHONE..................315 455-2555
Fax: 315 455-2544
Peter Gifford, President
Rudolph Capella, General Mgr
Rich Dausman, COO
Todd Cooper, Production
Lindsay Hoage, Production
▲ **EMP:** 100
SQ FT: 24,000
SALES (est): 32.2MM **Privately Held**
WEB: www.cryomech.com
SIC: 3559 Cryogenic machinery, industrial

(G-15935)
CUMMINS NORTHEAST LLC
6193 Eastern Ave (13211-2208)
PHONE..................315 437-2296
Fax: 315 437-6596
Robin Riewaldt, Opers-Prdtn-Mfg
EMP: 36
SQ FT: 13,760
SALES (corp-wide): 17.5B **Publicly Held**
SIC: 3519 5013 Internal combustion engines; automotive engines & engine parts
HQ: Cummins Northeast Llc
30 Braintree Hill Park # 101
Braintree MA 02184

(G-15936)
CUSTOM SHEET METAL CORP
1 General Motors Dr Ste 5 (13206-1122)
PHONE..................315 463-9105
Fax: 315 463-6664
Wilson C Brown, President
Shaun Mills, Manager
EMP: 8
SQ FT: 5,000

GEOGRAPHIC SECTION

Syracuse - Onondaga County (G-15961)

(G-15937)
CYANDIA INC
843 Malden Rd (13211)
PHONE 315 679-4268
Michael Wetzer, *CEO*
Christine Wetzer, *Vice Pres*
EMP: 15
SQ FT: 4,800
SALES (est): 1.2MM **Privately Held**
SIC: 7372 Prepackaged Software As A Services

(G-15938)
D & D MOTOR SYSTEMS INC
215 Park Ave (13204-2459)
PHONE 315 701-0861
Mike Dearoff, *President*
Eric Dearoff, *Vice Pres*
Eric Dieroff, *Vice Pres*
Robert Breen, *Engineer*
Jeff Boylan, *Manager*
▲ **EMP:** 20
SALES (est): 4.8MM **Privately Held**
WEB: www.ddmotorsystems.com
SIC: 3621 Motors & generators

(G-15939)
D N GANNON FABRICATING INC
404 Wavel St (13206-1728)
P.O. Box 6572 (13217-6572)
PHONE 315 463-7466
Fax: 315 432-8110
Frank Deuel, *President*
John Noel, *Vice Pres*
EMP: 5
SQ FT: 15,000
SALES (est): 500K **Privately Held**
SIC: 3441 Fabricated structural metal

(G-15940)
DAILY ORANGE CORPORATION
744 Ostrom Ave (13210-2942)
PHONE 315 443-2314
Dave Seal, *Editor*
Nancy Peck, *Adv Dir*
Peter Waack, *Manager*
Ryne Gery, *Relations*
Trevor Hass, *Relations*
EMP: 50
SALES: 282K **Privately Held**
WEB: www.dailyorange.com
SIC: 2711 Newspapers: publishing only, not printed on site

(G-15941)
DARCO MANUFACTURING INC
6756 Thompson Rd (13211-2122)
P.O. Box 6304 (13217-6304)
PHONE 315 432-8905
Fax: 315 432-9241
David A Redding, *President*
Laura Miller, *General Mgr*
Debbie Gray, *Software Dev*
EMP: 42
SQ FT: 22,000
SALES (est): 10.5MM **Privately Held**
SIC: 3599 Machine shop, jobbing & repair

(G-15942)
DAVID FEHLMAN
Also Called: Rollers Unlimited
6729 Pickard Dr (13211-2123)
P.O. Box 5059 (13220-5059)
PHONE 315 455-8888
Fax: 315 454-8600
David Fehlman, *Owner*
EMP: 5
SQ FT: 3,200
SALES (est): 341.9K **Privately Held**
SIC: 3599 3562 3366 3312 Machine & other job shop work; ball & roller bearings; copper foundries; blast furnaces & steel mills; synthetic rubber; platemaking services

(G-15943)
DECORATED COOKIE COMPANY LLC
314 Lakeside Rd (13209-9729)
PHONE 315 487-2111
Peter Hess, *Mng Member*
EMP: 30
SQ FT: 13,000
SALES (est): 4.9MM **Privately Held**
SIC: 2052 Cookies

(G-15944)
DEPENDABLE TOOL & DIE CO INC
129 Dwight Park Cir # 2 (13209-1010)
PHONE 315 453-5696
Fax: 315 453-2810
Anthony D Dantuono, *President*
Maria Ancona, *VP Sls/Mktg*
Lorraine Ryan, *Manager*
Andrea Tarolli, *Admin Sec*
EMP: 8
SQ FT: 20,000
SALES (est): 1.1MM **Privately Held**
SIC: 3599 Machine shop, jobbing & repair

(G-15945)
DUPLI GRAPHICS CORPORATION (HQ)
Also Called: Dupli Envelope & Graphics
6761 Thompson Rd (13211-2119)
P.O. Box 11500 (13218-1500)
PHONE 315 234-7286
J Kemper Matt, *Ch of Bd*
J Kemper Matt Jr, *President*
Thomas Booth, *Vice Pres*
Rob Slate, *Opers Mgr*
Todd Luchsinger, *CFO*
EMP: 117
SQ FT: 150,000
SALES (est): 25.5MM
SALES (corp-wide): 27.2MM **Privately Held**
WEB: www.duplionline.com
SIC: 2759 2752 Commercial printing; envelopes: printing; commercial printing, lithographic
PA: Matt Industries Inc.
6761 Thompson Rd
Syracuse NY 13211
315 472-1316

(G-15946)
DUPLI GRAPHICS CORPORATION
Grafek Direct
Dupli Park Dr (13218)
P.O. Box 11500 (13218-1500)
PHONE 315 422-4732
Kemper J Matt, *President*
Fred Kocher, *Sales Mgr*
EMP: 8
SALES (corp-wide): 27.2MM **Privately Held**
WEB: www.duplionline.com
SIC: 2759 2752 Envelopes: printing; commercial printing, offset
HQ: Dupli Graphics Corporation
6761 Thompson Rd
Syracuse NY 13211
315 234-7286

(G-15947)
DYNAMIC HYBIRDS INC
1201 E Fayette St Ste 11 (13210-1933)
PHONE 315 426-8110
Don Hazelmyer, *President*
Jackie Kowaleski, *Marketing Staff*
EMP: 7
SQ FT: 2,500
SALES (est): 1MM **Privately Held**
WEB: www.hybridcircuit.com
SIC: 3679 Electronic circuits

(G-15948)
EAGLE ENVELOPE COMPANY INC (DH)
1 Dupli Park Dr (13204-1436)
P.O. Box 236, Ithaca (14851-0236)
PHONE 607 387-3195
Fax: 607 387-3196
J Kemper Matt Sr, *CEO*
Richard Spingarn, *President*
Dave Martin, *Manager*
EMP: 9
SQ FT: 3,000
SALES (est): 1.1MM
SALES (corp-wide): 27.2MM **Privately Held**
WEB: www.eagleprint.com
SIC: 2759 Commercial printing; envelopes: printing
HQ: Dupli Graphics Corporation
6761 Thompson Rd
Syracuse NY 13211
315 234-7286

(G-15949)
EAGLE MEDIA PARTNERS LP (PA)
Also Called: Eagle Newspapers
2501 James St Ste 100 (13206-2996)
PHONE 315 434-8889
H Douglas Barclay, *Partner*
Edward S Green, *Partner*
Stewart Hancock, *Partner*
David Northrup, *Partner*
David Tyler, *Editor*
EMP: 33
SQ FT: 7,000
SALES (est): 3.3MM **Privately Held**
WEB: www.cnylink.com
SIC: 2711 Commercial printing & newspaper publishing combined

(G-15950)
EASTWOOD LITHO INC
4020 New Court Ave (13206-1663)
P.O. Box 131 (13206-0131)
PHONE 315 437-2626
Fax: 315 432-9227
Justin F Mohr, *CEO*
Mark J Mohr, *President*
Betty E Mohr, *Vice Pres*
Patrick H Mohr, *Treasurer*
Mark Lowry, *Manager*
EMP: 30
SQ FT: 15,000
SALES (est): 4.8MM **Privately Held**
WEB: www.eastwoodlitho.com
SIC: 2759 2752 2791 2789 Letterpress printing; commercial printing, lithographic; typesetting; bookbinding & related work

(G-15951)
EATON CORPORATION
Also Called: Ephesus Lighting
125 E Jefferson St (13202-2020)
PHONE 315 579-2872
Brian Wilson, *Engineer*
EMP: 30 **Privately Held**
SIC: 3645 Fluorescent lighting fixtures, residential
HQ: Eaton Corporation
1000 Eaton Blvd
Cleveland OH 44122
216 523-5000

(G-15952)
EATON CROUSE-HINDS
500 7th North St (13208)
PHONE 315 477-7000
Scott Hearn, *Principal*
EMP: 200
SALES (est): 16.6MM **Privately Held**
SIC: 3699 Electrical equipment & supplies

(G-15953)
EATONS CROUSE HINDS BUSINESS
1201 Wolf St (13208-1375)
PHONE 315 477-7000
Jacquiline Townshend, *Sales Mgr*
Matt Hyder, *Marketing Staff*
Kathleen Mills, *Manager*
EMP: 17
SALES (est): 2.9MM **Privately Held**
SIC: 3625 Motor controls & accessories

(G-15954)
ELIZABETH WOOD
Also Called: Endoscopic Procedure Center
4900 Broad Rd (13215-2265)
PHONE 315 492-5470
Elizabeth Wood, *Principal*
EMP: 5
SALES (est): 905.2K **Privately Held**
SIC: 3845 Endoscopic equipment, electromedical

(G-15955)
ELTON EL MANTLE INC
6072 Court Street Rd (13206-1711)
P.O. Box 3166 (13220-3166)
PHONE 315 432-9067
Elton Mantle, *President*
EMP: 5
SALES (est): 356.3K **Privately Held**
SIC: 3621 Motors, electric

(G-15956)
EMPIRE BREWING COMPANY INC
120 Walton St (13202-1571)
PHONE 315 925-8308
Fax: 315 475-4413
David Katleski, *President*
Lisa Shoen, *Human Res Dir*
Tricia Little, *Mktg Dir*
Monica Palmer, *Mktg Dir*
Olivia Cerio, *Marketing Mgr*
EMP: 64
SALES: 3MM **Privately Held**
SIC: 2082 5812 Ale (alcoholic beverage); American restaurant

(G-15957)
EMPIRE DIVISION INC
201 Kirkpatrick St # 207 (13208-2075)
PHONE 315 476-6273
Vincent Williams, *President*
EMP: 72
SQ FT: 9,000
SALES (est): 5MM **Privately Held**
SIC: 3589 3621 5063 5064 Vacuum cleaners & sweepers, electric: industrial; water purification equipment, household type; motors, electric; motors, electric; vacuum cleaners, household; water purification equipment; cleaning equipment & supplies; motors, electric; water purification equipment

(G-15958)
ERHARD & GILCHER INC
235 Cortland Ave (13202-3825)
P.O. Box 84 (13209-0084)
PHONE 315 474-1072
Fax: 315 475-0751
Peter Coyne, *President*
Rosemary Coyne, *Corp Secy*
Lance McGee, *Vice Pres*
EMP: 35 **EST:** 1913
SQ FT: 25,000
SALES (est): 3.6MM **Privately Held**
SIC: 2789 Bookbinding & related work

(G-15959)
EVERGREEN CORP CENTRAL NY
Also Called: Evergreen Manufacturing
235 Cortland Ave (13202-3825)
PHONE 315 454-4175
Fax: 315 454-4177
Rene Musso, *President*
EMP: 18
SQ FT: 4,500
SALES (est): 2.9MM **Privately Held**
SIC: 3544 2759 Paper cutting dies; commercial printing

(G-15960)
EXCEL ALUMINUM PRODUCTS INC
563 N Salina St (13208-2530)
PHONE 315 471-0925
Frank Tafel Jr, *President*
Raymond Tafel, *Admin Sec*
EMP: 5
SQ FT: 2,000
SALES: 250K **Privately Held**
SIC: 3442 5031 Storm doors or windows, metal; windows; doors

(G-15961)
FALSO INDUSTRIES INC
Also Called: Falso Metal Fabricating
4100 New Court Ave (13206-1698)
PHONE 315 463-0266
Fax: 315 463-5193
Raymond Falso, *President*
Dean Sharron, *General Mgr*
Richard Iorio, *Corp Secy*
Norb Kieffer, *Plant Mgr*
Dennis McGough, *Engineer*
EMP: 20
SQ FT: 19,000
SALES (est): 4.4MM **Privately Held*
WEB: www.falsoindustries.com
SIC: 3469 Metal stampings

Syracuse - Onondaga County (G-15962)

GEOGRAPHIC SECTION

(G-15962)
FAYETTE STREET COATINGS INC (DH)
Also Called: Strathmore Products, Inc.
1970 W Fayette St (13204-1740)
P.O. Box 151 (13201-0151)
PHONE..................................315 488-5401
Fax: 315 488-2715
Eric T Burr, *Ch of Bd*
Ricky Reider, *Plant Supt*
Liza Adamitz, *Purch Mgr*
Kurt Engel, *Research*
Jim Rogers, *Research*
EMP: 6
SQ FT: 50,000
SALES (est): 6.4MM
SALES (corp-wide): 23.4MM **Publicly Held**
WEB: www.publicsafety.com
SIC: 2851 Paints & allied products
HQ: The Whitmore Manufacturing Company
930 Whitmore Dr
Rockwall TX 75087
972 771-1000

(G-15963)
FELDMEIER EQUIPMENT INC (PA)
6800 Townline Rd (13211-1325)
P.O. Box 474 (13211-0474)
PHONE..................................315 823-2000
Fax: 315 454-3701
Robert E Feldmeier, *CEO*
Jean Jackson, *Vice Pres*
Denny Davis, *Plant Mgr*
James Hulbert, *Project Mgr*
Ron Lamanna, *Purch Mgr*
EMP: 100 EST: 1953
SQ FT: 60,000
SALES (est): 90.5MM **Privately Held**
WEB: www.feldmeier.com
SIC: 3443 Fabricated plate work (boiler shop)

(G-15964)
FRAZER & JONES CO
Also Called: Frasier and Jones
3000 Milton Ave (13209)
P.O. Box 4955 (13221-4955)
PHONE..................................315 468-6251
Fax: 315 468-3676
Mark Novakowski, *Principal*
Noel Ebner, *Director*
EMP: 90
SQ FT: 182,784
SALES (est): 9.7MM **Privately Held**
WEB: www.frazerandjones.com
SIC: 3325 Steel foundries

(G-15965)
FUTON CITY DISCOUNTERS INC
Also Called: Sleep Master
6361 Thompson Rd (13206-1448)
PHONE..................................315 437-1328
Fax: 315 446-3013
Charles Vanpatten, *President*
EMP: 18
SALES (est): 3.4MM **Privately Held**
SIC: 2599 5712 Factory furniture & fixtures; furniture stores

(G-15966)
G A BRAUN INC
461 E Brighton Ave (13210-4143)
P.O. Box 3029 (13220-3029)
PHONE..................................315 475-3123
Fax: 315 475-4130
Steve Bregande, *Principal*
Jeffrey Hohman, *Project Mgr*
Ed Bidwell, *Purchasing*
Jim Massey, *Natl Sales Mgr*
Pamela Simonetti, *Corp Comm Staff*
EMP: 25
SALES (corp-wide): 29.1MM **Privately Held**
SIC: 3582 Commercial laundry equipment
PA: G. A. Braun, Inc.
79 General Irwin Blvd
North Syracuse NY 13212
315 475-3123

(G-15967)
G C HANFORD MANUFACTURING CO (PA)
Also Called: Hanford Pharmaceuticals
304 Oneida St (13202-3433)
P.O. Box 1017 (13201-1017)
PHONE..................................315 476-7418
Fax: 315 476-7434
George R Hanford, *Principal*
Joseph J Heath, *Principal*
Peter Ward, *Principal*
Bill Snook, *Opers Mgr*
Gail Goson, *Safety Mgr*
EMP: 186 EST: 1846
SQ FT: 80,000
SALES (est): 48.4MM **Privately Held**
WEB: www.hanford.com
SIC: 2834 2833 5122 Penicillin preparations; antibiotics; pharmaceuticals

(G-15968)
GARDALL SAFE CORPORATION
219 Lamson St Ste 1 (13206-2879)
P.O. Box 240 (13206-0240)
PHONE..................................315 432-9115
Fax: 315 434-9422
Edward Baroody, *Ch of Bd*
Kris Ruffos, *Purch Mgr*
Larry Galster, *Engineer*
David A Patton, *Treasurer*
David A Ptton, *Treasurer*
◆ EMP: 25 EST: 1950
SQ FT: 85,000
SALES (est): 4.9MM **Privately Held**
WEB: www.gardall.com
SIC: 3499 Safes & vaults, metal

(G-15969)
GARDNER DNVER OBERDORFER PUMPS
5900 Firestone Dr (13206-1103)
PHONE..................................315 437-0361
Robin Watkins, *Principal*
Michael Walker, *Chief Mktg Ofcr*
▲ EMP: 30
SQ FT: 50,000
SALES (est): 5.1MM
SALES (corp-wide): 1.9B **Publicly Held**
SIC: 3561 Pumps & pumping equipment
HQ: Gardner Denver, Inc.
222 E Erie St Ste 500
Milwaukee WI 53202

(G-15970)
GEAR MOTIONS INCORPORATED (PA)
Also Called: Nixon Gear
1750 Milton Ave (13209-1626)
PHONE..................................315 488-0100
Fax: 315 488-0196
Samuel R Haines, *President*
Dean Burroes, *President*
Ron Wright, *Sales Engr*
EMP: 50
SQ FT: 45,000
SALES (est): 18MM **Privately Held**
WEB: www.gearmotions.com
SIC: 3462 Gears, forged steel

(G-15971)
GENERAL ELECTRIC COMPANY
5990 E Molloy Rd (13211-2130)
PHONE..................................315 456-3304
Matthew J Battle, *Branch Mgr*
Jeff Martin, *Info Tech Mgr*
EMP: 20
SQ FT: 8,000
SALES (corp-wide): 123.6B **Publicly Held**
SIC: 7694 Electric motor repair
PA: General Electric Company
41 Farnsworth St
Boston MA 02210
617 443-3000

(G-15972)
GENERATION POWER LLC
238 W Division St (13204-1412)
PHONE..................................315 234-2451
Steve Starrantino, *Vice Pres*
Frank Besio, *Manager*
Darren Otis, *Manager*
Bob Zywicki,
Jay Bernhardt,
EMP: 9

SALES (est): 1.8MM **Privately Held**
SIC: 3621 Motors & generators

(G-15973)
GEORGE RETZOS
Also Called: Columbus Baking Co
502 Pearl St (13203-1702)
PHONE..................................315 422-2913
James Retzos, *Owner*
EMP: 5 EST: 1934
SALES (est): 480.8K **Privately Held**
SIC: 2051 Bread, all types (white, wheat, rye, etc): fresh or frozen

(G-15974)
GREENLEAF CABINET MAKERS LLC
6691 Pickard Dr (13211-2114)
PHONE..................................315 432-4600
Gerard Davis, *Mng Member*
Kevin Davis, *Manager*
Dave Morrison, *Manager*
EMP: 10 EST: 2001
SQ FT: 3,000
SALES (est): 1.5MM **Privately Held**
SIC: 2541 Wood partitions & fixtures

(G-15975)
H C YOUNG TOOL & MACHINE CO
3700 New Court Ave (13206-1674)
PHONE..................................315 463-0663
Fax: 315 463-0663
Gordon K Young, *President*
EMP: 5 EST: 1935
SQ FT: 1,000
SALES (est): 553K **Privately Held**
WEB: www.hcyoung.com
SIC: 3599 Machine shop, jobbing & repair

(G-15976)
HANGER PRSTHETCS & ORTHO INC
910 Erie Blvd E Ste 3 (13210-1060)
PHONE..................................315 472-5200
Roy Ostrander, *Manager*
EMP: 5
SALES (corp-wide): 451.4MM **Publicly Held**
SIC: 3842 Limbs, artificial
HQ: Hanger Prosthetics & Orthotics, Inc.
10910 Domain Dr Ste 300
Austin TX 78758
512 777-3800

(G-15977)
HARRISON BAKERY WEST
1306 W Genesee St (13204-2184)
PHONE..................................315 422-1468
Fax: 315 422-4083
James Rothfeld, *President*
Michael Rothfeld, *Vice Pres*
EMP: 30
SQ FT: 15,000
SALES (est): 5.2MM **Privately Held**
SIC: 2051 5461 Bread, all types (white, wheat, rye, etc): fresh or frozen; cakes, bakery: except frozen; doughnuts, except frozen; bread; cakes; doughnuts

(G-15978)
HART RIFLE BARREL INC
1680 Jamesville Ave (13214-4236)
P.O. Box 182, La Fayette (13084-0182)
PHONE..................................315 677-9841
Fax: 315 677-9610
Jack Sutton, *Partner*
James Hart, *Partner*
EMP: 7 EST: 1955
SQ FT: 2,000
SALES (est): 750K **Privately Held**
WEB: www.hartbarrels.com
SIC: 3484 Rifles or rifle parts, 30 mm. & below

(G-15979)
HOLISTIC BLENDS INC
6726 Townline Rd Stop 1 (13211-1915)
PHONE..................................315 468-4300
Sherry Brescia, *President*
EMP: 8
SALES (est): 892.9K **Privately Held**
SIC: 2834 Vitamin, nutrient & hematinic preparations for human use

(G-15980)
HY-GRADE METAL PRODUCTS CORP
906 Burnet Ave (13203-3206)
PHONE..................................315 475-4221
Fax: 315 472-3101
Michael Donegan, *President*
EMP: 7
SQ FT: 10,000
SALES (est): 495K **Privately Held**
WEB: www.hy-grademetal.com
SIC: 3469 Spinning metal for the trade

(G-15981)
INDEPENDENT FIELD SVC LLC (PA)
6744 Pickard Dr (13211-2115)
PHONE..................................315 559-9243
Aaron Barbaro, *Owner*
EMP: 6
SQ FT: 8,000
SALES (est): 1.2MM **Privately Held**
SIC: 3621 Power generators

(G-15982)
INGLIS CO INC
116 Granger St (13202-2315)
P.O. Box 401, Manlius (13104-0401)
PHONE..................................315 475-1315
Kenneth Abramson, *President*
Anthony River, *Vice Pres*
EMP: 7
SQ FT: 5,000
SALES (est): 768.8K **Privately Held**
SIC: 2893 2851 5084 Printing ink; paints & paint additives; lacquers, varnishes, enamels & other coatings; removers & cleaners; paint spray equipment, industrial

(G-15983)
J & J PRINTING INC (PA)
500 Cambridge Ave (13208-1415)
PHONE..................................315 458-7411
Fax: 315 454-0912
Matthew Joseph Farr, *President*
Charlie Dalley, *General Mgr*
Betty Farr, *Vice Pres*
EMP: 8 EST: 1969
SQ FT: 3,000
SALES (est): 719.8K **Privately Held**
SIC: 2752 Commercial printing, offset

(G-15984)
JACOBS WOODWORKING LLC
801 W Fayette St (13204-2805)
PHONE..................................315 427-8999
Jacob Gerros, *Mng Member*
EMP: 7
SALES (est): 632.5K **Privately Held**
SIC: 2431 Millwork

(G-15985)
JAQUITH INDUSTRIES INC
600 E Brighton Ave (13210-4248)
P.O. Box 780 (13205-0780)
PHONE..................................315 478-5700
Fax: 315 478-5707
D Scott Jaquith, *President*
Rob Loughlin, *General Mgr*
Joe Antczak, *Opers Mgr*
Adam Antczak, *Buyer*
Bill Schai, *VP Sales*
◆ EMP: 50
SQ FT: 120,000
SALES (est): 10.1MM **Privately Held**
WEB: www.jaquith.com
SIC: 3312 3648 3728 3444 Blast furnaces & steel mills; lighting equipment; aircraft parts & equipment; sheet metalwork; fabricated plate work (boiler shop); manufactured hardware (general)

(G-15986)
JOHN A EBERLY INC
136 Beattie St (13224-1102)
P.O. Box 8047 (13217-8047)
PHONE..................................315 449-3034
John Lee, *President*
EMP: 7
SQ FT: 6,000

GEOGRAPHIC SECTION

Syracuse - Onondaga County (G-16011)

SALES (est): 1.1MM **Privately Held**
WEB: www.jaeberly.com
SIC: 3421 5084 Scissors, shears, clippers, snips & similar tools; textile machinery & equipment

(G-15987)
JOHN F KRELL JR
Also Called: Syracuse Hvac
4046 W Seneca Trpk (13215)
PHONE 315 492-3201
John F Krell, *Partner*
Andrew Krell, *Partner*
EMP: 5
SALES (est): 609.8K **Privately Held**
SIC: 3585 Heating & air conditioning combination units

(G-15988)
JOHNSTON DANDY COMPANY
Cook, E F Co
100 Dippold Ave (13208-1320)
PHONE 315 455-5773
Fax: 315 454-9357
Michael Myers, *General Mgr*
Don Wilson, *Store Mgr*
Debbie Warback, *Safety Mgr*
Kimberly Pinkham, *Controller*
EMP: 7
SQ FT: 12,540
SALES (corp-wide): 6.6MM **Privately Held**
WEB: www.johnstondandy.com
SIC: 3547 3554 Rolling mill machinery; paper industries machinery
PA: Johnston Dandy Company
148 Main St
Lincoln ME 04457
207 794-6571

(G-15989)
JORDON BOX COMPANY INC
Also Called: Jordan Box Co
140 Dickerson St (13202-2309)
P.O. Box 1054 (13201-1054)
PHONE 315 422-3419
Fax: 315 422-0318
Rick Casper, *President*
EMP: 20
SQ FT: 30,000
SALES (est): 700K **Privately Held**
WEB: www.jordanboxco.com
SIC: 2652 Setup paperboard boxes

(G-15990)
JPW STRUCTURAL CONTRACTING INC
Also Called: Jpw Riggers & Erectors
6376 Thompson Rd (13206-1406)
PHONE 315 432-1111
Fax: 315 432-8202
John P Wozniczka III, *Ch of Bd*
Patricia Wozniczka, *Corp Secy*
Jeffery Exner, *Vice Pres*
Jody Wozniczka, *Vice Pres*
Jody Wozniczka, *Opers Mgr*
EMP: 25
SQ FT: 70,000
SALES (est): 8.1MM **Privately Held**
SIC: 3441 Fabricated structural metal

(G-15991)
K&G OF SYRACUSE INC
2500 Erie Blvd E (13224-1110)
PHONE 315 446-1921
Karamjit Grewal, *Principal*
EMP: 5
SALES (est): 526.1K **Privately Held**
SIC: 3578 Automatic teller machines (ATM)

(G-15992)
KASSIS SUPERIOR SIGN CO INC
6699 Old Thompson Rd (13211-2118)
PHONE 315 463-7446
Fax: 315 463-7449
Joseph Kassis, *CEO*
Anthony Sklaney, *CFO*
Kim Malone, *Office Mgr*
Betty Clute, *Manager*
Edda Kassis, *Admin Sec*
EMP: 19
SALES (est): 4.5MM **Privately Held**
WEB: www.kassissigns.com
SIC: 3444 5039 Sheet metalwork; awnings

(G-15993)
KILIAN MANUFACTURING CORP (HQ)
1728 Burnet Ave (13206-3340)
P.O. Box 6974 (13217-6974)
PHONE 315 432-0700
Fax: 315 432-1312
Don Wierbinski, *President*
William Duff, *General Mgr*
Lorenzo Spinelli, *Plant Mgr*
Keith Austin, *Purchasing*
David Bourdeau, *Engineer*
▲ **EMP:** 73 **EST:** 1921
SQ FT: 100,000
SALES (est): 70.2MM
SALES (corp-wide): 708.9MM **Publicly Held**
SIC: 3562 3429 Ball bearings & parts; manufactured hardware (general)
PA: Altra Industrial Motion Corp.
300 Granite St Ste 201
Braintree MA 02184
781 917-0600

(G-15994)
KINANECO INC (PA)
Also Called: Kinaneco Printing Systems
2925 Milton Ave (13209-2519)
PHONE 315 468-6201
Fax: 315 468-6202
Greg Kinane, *Chairman*
Peter T Kinane, *Chairman*
Sue Sgarlata, *Production*
Judy Soliday, *CFO*
Paul Manganiello, *Office Mgr*
EMP: 20 **EST:** 1973
SQ FT: 6,000
SALES (est): 3.9MM **Privately Held**
WEB: www.kinaneco.com
SIC: 2759 2752 7311 2754 Business forms: printing; commercial printing, offset; advertising agencies; color printing, gravure

(G-15995)
KNISE & KRICK INC
324 Pearl St (13203-1998)
PHONE 315 422-3516
Fax: 315 422-3594
John P Extrom, *President*
Terry Bunch, *Vice Pres*
Bettty Clute, *Office Mgr*
Beth Moore, *Admin Sec*
EMP: 20 **EST:** 1926
SQ FT: 30,000
SALES (est): 3.7MM **Privately Held**
WEB: www.knisekrick.com
SIC: 3544 Jigs & fixtures

(G-15996)
LEMOYNE MACHINE PRODUCTS CORP
106 Evelyn Ter (13208-1321)
PHONE 315 454-0708
Marvin Kisselstein, *President*
Robert Grandinetti, *Vice Pres*
EMP: 5
SQ FT: 5,000
SALES (est): 643.1K **Privately Held**
SIC: 3562 Ball & roller bearings

(G-15997)
LIBERTY FOOD AND FUEL
1131 N Salina St (13208-2027)
PHONE 315 299-4039
Anwa Nagnaji, *Manager*
EMP: 6
SALES (est): 803.6K **Privately Held**
SIC: 2869 Fuels

(G-15998)
LIFT SAFE - FUEL SAFE INC
212 W Seneca Tpke (13205-2709)
PHONE 315 423-7702
Daniel Sorber, *CEO*
EMP: 10
SALES (est): 1.4MM **Privately Held**
SIC: 2869 Fuels

(G-15999)
LINDE GAS NORTH AMERICA LLC
Also Called: Lifegas
147 Midler Park Dr (13206-1817)
PHONE 315 431-4081
Fax: 315 431-4082
Richard Kelley, *Branch Mgr*
Dick Kelly, *Manager*
EMP: 19
SALES (corp-wide): 17.9B **Privately Held**
SIC: 2813 Nitrogen; oxygen, compressed or liquefied
HQ: Linde Gas North America Llc
200 Somerset Corp Blvd # 7000
Bridgewater NJ 08807

(G-16000)
LOCKHEED MARTIN
497 Electronics Pkwy (13221)
P.O. Box 4840 (13221-4840)
PHONE 315 456-3333
Kenneth George, *Personnel Exec*
Ronald Pacini, *Info Tech Dir*
Keith Speidel, *Technical Staff*
David Svendsen, *Data Proc Exec*
EMP: 26 **Publicly Held**
SIC: 3577 Data conversion equipment, media-to-media: computer
HQ: Lockheed Martin Integrated Systems, Llc
6801 Rockledge Dr
Bethesda MD 20817

(G-16001)
LOCKHEED MARTIN CORPORATION
6060 Tarbell Rd (13206-1301)
PHONE 315 456-6604
Mark Schmidt, *Branch Mgr*
EMP: 45 **Publicly Held**
WEB: www.lockheedmartin.com
SIC: 3812 Sonar systems & equipment; radar systems & equipment
PA: Lockheed Martin Corporation
6801 Rockledge Dr
Bethesda MD 20817

(G-16002)
LOUIS IANNETTONI
1841 Lemoyne Ave (13208-1328)
PHONE 315 454-3231
Louis Iannettoni, *Owner*
Jim Iannettoni, *Vice Pres*
EMP: 65
SALES (est): 4.5MM **Privately Held**
SIC: 3363 Aluminum die-castings

(G-16003)
M & W ALUMINUM PRODUCTS INC
321 Wavel St (13206-1726)
PHONE 315 414-0005
Uriah P Montclair, *President*
EMP: 16
SQ FT: 12,330
SALES (est): 2.7MM **Privately Held**
WEB: www.mwalum.com
SIC: 3465 Body parts, automobile: stamped metal

(G-16004)
MARZULLO ELECTRIC LLC
103 Oliva Dr (13211-1902)
PHONE 315 455-1050
Joseph Marzullo, *Owner*
EMP: 6
SALES (est): 714.8K **Privately Held**
SIC: 3699 Electrical equipment & supplies

(G-16005)
MATT INDUSTRIES INC (PA)
Also Called: Grphics Grafek
6761 Thompson Rd (13211-2119)
P.O. Box 11500 (13218-1500)
PHONE 315 472-1316
J Kemper Matt, *President*
David Martin, *Division Mgr*
Thomas Booth, *Vice Pres*
John Mather, *Vice Pres*
J Kemper Matt Jr, *Vice Pres*
EMP: 120
SQ FT: 150,000
SALES (est): 27.2MM **Privately Held**
SIC: 2759 5112 Envelopes: printing; envelopes

(G-16006)
MELOON FOUNDRIES LLC
1841 Lemoyne Ave (13208-1389)
PHONE 315 454-3231
Fax: 315 454-8559
Robert Evans, *President*
Raymond King, *Division Mgr*
Cecelia Bleich, *Office Mgr*
EMP: 42
SQ FT: 90,000
SALES (est): 10.5MM
SALES (corp-wide): 28.2MM **Privately Held**
SIC: 3365 3366 3291 Aluminum foundries; copper foundries; brass foundry; bronze foundry; abrasive products
HQ: Evans Industries, Inc.
249 Boston St
Detroit MI 48243
313 259-2266

(G-16007)
METALICO ALUMINUM RECOVERY INC
6223 Thompson Rd (13206-1405)
P.O. Box 88, East Syracuse (13057-0088)
PHONE 315 463-9500
Fax: 315 463-9290
Carlos E Aguero, *President*
Dennis Flanagan, *General Mgr*
Michael J Drury, *COO*
Arnold S Graber, *Exec VP*
David Delbianco, *Vice Pres*
▲ **EMP:** 40
SALES (est): 12MM
SALES (corp-wide): 476MM **Privately Held**
SIC: 3341 5093 Aluminum smelting & refining (secondary); scrap & waste materials
PA: Metalico, Inc.
135 Dermody St
Cranford NJ 07016
908 497-9610

(G-16008)
MIDDLE AGES BREWING COMPANY
120 Wilkinson St Ste 3 (13204-2490)
PHONE 315 476-4250
Fax: 315 476-4264
Mary Rubenstein, *President*
Isaac Rubenstein, *Vice Pres*
Marc Rubenstein, *Treasurer*
Matt Vogelsang, *Marketing Mgr*
▲ **EMP:** 6
SQ FT: 10,000
SALES (est): 450K **Privately Held**
SIC: 2082 Beer (alcoholic beverage)

(G-16009)
MIDGLEY PRINTING CORP
433 W Onondaga St Ste B (13202-3277)
PHONE 315 475-1864
Fax: 315 475-8325
Lena Midgley, *President*
David Midgley, *Vice Pres*
Robert Midgley, *Vice Pres*
Walter Midgley, *Vice Pres*
John Midgley, *Treasurer*
EMP: 9 **EST:** 1955
SQ FT: 10,000
SALES (est): 830K **Privately Held**
SIC: 2752 2759 2791 2789 Commercial printing, lithographic; letterpress printing; typesetting; bookbinding & related work

(G-16010)
MIDSTATE SPRING INC
Also Called: Syracuse Midstate Spring
4054 New Court Ave (13206-1639)
P.O. Box 850 (13206-0850)
PHONE 315 437-2623
Fax: 315 437-0796
Walter Melnikow, *President*
Paul S Bernet, *Vice Pres*
Richard Raus, *Plant Mgr*
Keith Miller, *Opers Staff*
Krystal Alger, *Engineer*
▲ **EMP:** 41
SQ FT: 13,000
SALES (est): 10.2MM **Privately Held**
WEB: www.midstatespring.com
SIC: 3493 3495 Steel springs, except wire; wire springs

(G-16011)
MINIMILL TECHNOLOGIES INC
5792 Widewaters Pkwy # 1 (13214-1847)
PHONE 315 692-4557

Syracuse - Onondaga County (G-16012)

Kamala G Rajan, *President*
Joseph Gasperetti, *Senior VP*
Srinivasan Balaji, *Vice Pres*
Donnie Parks, *Vice Pres*
George Rice, *Vice Pres*
EMP: 14
SALES: 6MM **Privately Held**
SIC: 2621 Paper mills

(G-16012)
MITTEN MANUFACTURING INC
5960 Court Street Rd (13206-1706)
PHONE.................................315 437-7564
John P Mitten Jr, *CEO*
Jack Mitten, *Principal*
Ron Pfaff, *Systs Engr*
David Bennett, *Sales Mgr*
Tim Reiss, *Manager*
EMP: 40
SALES (est): 5.2MM **Privately Held**
SIC: 3999 Atomizers, toiletry

(G-16013)
MONAGHAN MEDICAL CORPORATION
Also Called: Sales & Marketing Office
327 W Fayette St Ste 212 (13202-1331)
PHONE.................................315 472-2136
Michael Amato, *Vice Pres*
EMP: 8
SALES (corp-wide): 10.9MM **Privately Held**
WEB: www.monaghanmed.com
SIC: 3842 Respiratory protection equipment, personal
PA: Monaghan Medical Corporation
5 Latour Ave Ste 1600
Plattsburgh NY 12901
518 561-7330

(G-16014)
MUENCH-KREUZER CANDLE COMPANY (PA)
Also Called: Emkay Candle Company
617 Hiawatha Blvd E (13208-1228)
PHONE.................................315 471-4515
Fax: 315 471-4581
John P Brogan, *Ch of Bd*
Shawn Lynch, *Purchasing*
Greg Kiesinger, *VP Mktg*
▲ **EMP:** 80
SQ FT: 100,000
SALES (est): 9.9MM **Privately Held**
WEB: www.emkaycandle.com
SIC: 3999 Candles

(G-16015)
MUZET INC
104 S Main St (13212-3104)
PHONE.................................315 452-0050
Fax: 315 452-1996
Frank Crawford, *Manager*
EMP: 10
SALES (corp-wide): 2.2MM **Privately Held**
SIC: 3931 Musical instruments
PA: Muzet Inc
219 W Commercial St
East Rochester NY 14445
585 586-5320

(G-16016)
N E CONTROLS LLC
7048 Interstate Island Rd (13209-9712)
PHONE.................................315 626-2480
Evan Weaver, *Engineer*
Brad Stone-Sales, *Sales Mgr*
Al Weaver,
Herb Smith,
Harvey Stone,
EMP: 12
SQ FT: 6,000
SALES: 950K **Privately Held**
WEB: www.necontrols.com
SIC: 3625 5084 Control equipment, electric; industrial machinery & equipment

(G-16017)
NEPTUNE SOFT WATER INC
1201 E Fayette St Ste 6 (13210-1896)
PHONE.................................315 446-5151
Fax: 315 445-9094
William Olivieri, *President*
EMP: 15 **EST:** 1963
SQ FT: 4,500

SALES (est): 2.4MM **Privately Held**
SIC: 3589 5999 5074 Water treatment equipment, industrial; water purification equipment, household type; water purification equipment; water purification equipment

(G-16018)
NEW YORK MARKING DEVICES CORP (PA)
Also Called: Jessel Marking Equipment
2207 Teall Ave (13206-1544)
P.O. Box 234 (13206-0234)
PHONE.................................315 463-8641
Fax: 315 463-8363
Joseph L Stummer Jr, *President*
Amy Stummer, *Vice Pres*
Ellen Stummer, *Vice Pres*
Peter J Stummer, *Vice Pres*
Kathy Stummer, *Office Mgr*
EMP: 7
SQ FT: 7,800
SALES: 1.7MM **Privately Held**
WEB: www.nymarking.com
SIC: 3953 Marking devices

(G-16019)
NOLL REYNOLDS MET FABRICATION
554 E Brighton Ave Ste 1 (13210-4265)
PHONE.................................315 422-3333
Kurt Noll, *Owner*
Tarren Reynolds, *Principal*
EMP: 7
SALES: 750K **Privately Held**
SIC: 3499 Furniture parts, metal

(G-16020)
NOVANTA INC
Also Called: Photo Research
7279 William Barry Blvd (13212-3349)
PHONE.................................818 341-5151
EMP: 24
SALES (corp-wide): 384.7MM **Publicly Held**
SIC: 3827 Optical instruments & lenses
PA: Novanta Inc.
125 Middlesex Tpke
Bedford MA 01730
781 266-5700

(G-16021)
OBERDORFER PUMPS INC
5900 Firestone Dr (13206-1103)
PHONE.................................315 437-0361
Fax: 315 463-9561
Kevin Digney, *CEO*
Timothy C Brown, *President*
Phillip J Stuecker, *Vice Pres*
Gary Young, *Technology*
EMP: 43
SQ FT: 46,000
SALES (est): 10MM
SALES (corp-wide): 1.9B **Publicly Held**
WEB: www.oberdorfer-pumps.com
SIC: 3561 Pumps & pumping equipment; industrial pumps & parts
HQ: Gardner Denver, Inc.
222 E Erie St Ste 500
Milwaukee WI 53202

(G-16022)
OESTREICH METAL WORKS INC
6131 Court Street Rd (13206-1302)
PHONE.................................315 463-4268
Fax: 315 463-4459
Steve Tallman, *President*
EMP: 5
SQ FT: 4,000
SALES (est): 588.2K **Privately Held**
SIC: 3564 Blowing fans: industrial or commercial; ventilating fans: industrial or commercial; exhaust fans: industrial or commercial

(G-16023)
OMEGA FURNITURE MANUFACTURING
102 Wavel St (13206-1303)
PHONE.................................315 463-7428
Fax: 315 463-8740
George Sakellariou, *President*
EMP: 12
SQ FT: 10,000

SALES: 600K **Privately Held**
WEB: www.omegafmi.com
SIC: 2521 5712 Wood office furniture; furniture stores

(G-16024)
ONE TREE DIST
200 Midler Park Dr (13206-1819)
P.O. Box 373 (13206-0373)
PHONE.................................315 701-2924
EMP: 6
SALES (est): 690.9K **Privately Held**
SIC: 2421 Building & structural materials, wood

(G-16025)
ONEIDA AIR SYSTEMS INC
1001 W Fayette St Ste 2a (13204-2873)
PHONE.................................315 476-5151
Fax: 315 476-5044
Robert Witter, *President*
Jen McManus, *Controller*
Jeffrey Hill, *Manager*
◆ **EMP:** 50
SQ FT: 60,000
SALES (est): 13.5MM **Privately Held**
WEB: www.oneida-air.com
SIC: 3553 3564 Woodworking machinery; purification & dust collection equipment

(G-16026)
OPTOGENICS OF SYRACUSE INC
2840 Erie Blvd E (13224-1304)
P.O. Box 4894 (13221-4894)
PHONE.................................315 446-3000
Fax: 315 446-5742
Kurt Schrantz, *President*
Marybeth Busch, *Accounting Mgr*
Sheri Niedens, *Human Res Mgr*
Yani Alvarez, *Marketing Staff*
Jarrid Pearson, *Manager*
EMP: 100
SQ FT: 7,000
SALES (est): 13.2MM
SALES (corp-wide): 938.9MM **Privately Held**
WEB: www.optogenics.com
SIC: 3851 Eyeglasses, lenses & frames
HQ: Essilor Laboratories Of America, Inc.
13515 N Stemmons Fwy
Dallas TX 75234
972 241-4141

(G-16027)
P C I PAPER CONVERSIONS INC (PA)
3584 Walters Rd (13209-9700)
PHONE.................................315 437-1641
Fax: 315 437-3634
Lloyd M Withers, *President*
Darcy Lewis, *General Mgr*
Peter McDermott, *General Mgr*
Matthew Withers, *Vice Pres*
Robert Liedka, *Production*
▲ **EMP:** 120 **EST:** 1973
SQ FT: 121,300
SALES (est): 22MM **Privately Held**
WEB: www.riverleaf.com
SIC: 2679 2678 2672 Paper products, converted; stationery products; coated & laminated paper

(G-16028)
P C I PAPER CONVERSIONS INC
Stik-Withit Printworks
6761 Thompson Rd (13211-2119)
PHONE.................................315 703-8300
Howard Kaye, *Managing Dir*
EMP: 100
SALES (corp-wide): 22MM **Privately Held**
SIC: 2891 Adhesives & sealants
PA: P. C. I. Paper Conversions, Inc.
3584 Walters Rd
Syracuse NY 13209
315 437-1641

(G-16029)
P C I PAPER CONVERSIONS INC
Coated Products Division
6761 Thompson Rd (13211-2119)
PHONE.................................315 634-3317
Howard Kaye, *Managing Dir*
Theresa Brown, *Mfg Mgr*
Tim Byrne, *Sales Mgr*

Jill Ladd, *Manager*
EMP: 25
SALES (corp-wide): 22MM **Privately Held**
SIC: 2891 Adhesives & sealants
PA: P. C. I. Paper Conversions, Inc.
3584 Walters Rd
Syracuse NY 13209
315 437-1641

(G-16030)
P C I PAPER CONVERSIONS INC
Notes
6761 Thompson Rd (13211-2119)
PHONE.................................315 437-1641
Pete Langdon, *Sales Mgr*
Peter McDermott, *Manager*
EMP: 10
SALES (corp-wide): 22MM **Privately Held**
SIC: 2679 Novelties, paper: made from purchased material
PA: P. C. I. Paper Conversions, Inc.
3584 Walters Rd
Syracuse NY 13209
315 437-1641

(G-16031)
PARATORE SIGNS INC
1551 Brewerton Rd (13208-1403)
PHONE.................................315 455-5551
Fax: 315 455-5920
John Paratore, *CEO*
Valoree Paratore, *VP Sls/Mktg*
Paige J Paratore, *Treasurer*
EMP: 6 **EST:** 1950
SQ FT: 13,000
SALES (est): 845.6K **Privately Held**
WEB: www.paratoresigns.com
SIC: 2759 7389 Screen printing; sign painting & lettering shop

(G-16032)
PASS & SEYMOUR INC (DH)
50 Boyd Ave (13209-2313)
P.O. Box 4822 (13221-4822)
PHONE.................................315 468-6211
Fax: 315 487-3907
Halsey Cook, *CEO*
Steve Schoffstall, *Principal*
Robert P Smith, *Exec VP*
Phil Leroux, *Senior VP*
Robert Julian, *Vice Pres*
◆ **EMP:** 353 **EST:** 1901
SQ FT: 300,000
SALES (est): 378.9MM
SALES (corp-wide): 16.3MM **Privately Held**
WEB: www.passandseymour.com
SIC: 3643 5731 Current-carrying wiring devices; consumer electronic equipment
HQ: Legrand Holding, Inc.
60 Woodlawn St
West Hartford CT 06110
860 233-6251

(G-16033)
PILKINGTON NORTH AMERICA INC
6412 Deere Rd Ste 1 (13206-1133)
PHONE.................................315 438-3341
EMP: 225
SALES (corp-wide): 5.1B **Privately Held**
SIC: 3211 Flat glass
HQ: Pilkington North America, Inc.
811 Madison Ave Fl 1
Toledo OH 43604
419 247-4955

(G-16034)
PINOS PRESS INC
201 E Jefferson St (13202-2644)
PHONE.................................315 935-0110
Maria Marzocchi, *President*
Michael Marzocchi, *Vice Pres*
EMP: 6
SQ FT: 15,000
SALES: 467K **Privately Held**
SIC: 2079 Olive oil

(G-16035)
PRINTING PRMTNAL SOLUTIONS LLC
Also Called: Printing Promotional Solutions
2320 Milton Ave Ste 5 (13209-2197)
PHONE.................................315 474-1110

Todd Ruetsch,
EMP: 17
SALES (est): 2.9MM **Privately Held**
SIC: 2759 Commercial printing

(G-16036)
PRINTWORKS PRINTING & DESIGN
5982 E Molloy Rd (13211-2130)
PHONE..................315 433-8587
Fax: 315 433-5102
Michael Kinsella, *President*
EMP: 5
SALES (est): 475K **Privately Held**
SIC: 2759 Commercial printing

(G-16037)
QUADRANT BIOSCIENCES INC
505 Irving Ave Ste 3100ab (13210-1718)
PHONE..................315 614-2325
Richard Uhlig, *CEO*
EMP: 18
SQ FT: 2,600
SALES (est): 563K **Privately Held**
SIC: 3845 Patient monitoring apparatus

(G-16038)
R K B OPTO-ELECTRONICS INC (PA)
6677 Moore Rd (13211-2112)
PHONE..................315 455-6636
Fax: 315 455-8216
Bruce Dobbie, *President*
William Dobbie, *Chairman*
Sonhui Dobbie, *Purchasing*
Alex Fern Ndez, *Sales Dir*
Chris Wu, *Sales Dir*
EMP: 10
SQ FT: 12,500
SALES (est): 1.6MM **Privately Held**
WEB: www.rkbopto.com
SIC: 3823 3825 Industrial instrmnts msrmnt display/control process variable; instruments to measure electricity

(G-16039)
RAM FABRICATING LLC
412 Wavel St (13206-1728)
PHONE..................315 437-6654
Fax: 315 437-4101
Angela Pitts, *Regional Mgr*
Charlie Meakin, *Vice Pres*
Brian Garrett, *QA Dir*
Mike Skowron, *Research*
Drew Lopitz, *Accounts Mgr*
EMP: 30
SQ FT: 15,000
SALES (est): 7.2MM **Privately Held**
SIC: 3498 Tube fabricating (contract bending & shaping)

(G-16040)
RAULLI AND SONS INC (PA)
213 Teall Ave (13210-1291)
PHONE..................315 479-6693
Fax: 315 479-5514
Richie Raulli, *President*
Paul Raulli, *Corp Secy*
Thomas Raulli, *Vice Pres*
Debbie Kuepper, *Manager*
EMP: 60
SQ FT: 40,000
SALES (est): 17.9MM **Privately Held**
WEB: www.raulliandsons.com
SIC: 3441 3446 Fabricated structural metal; architectural metalwork; gates, ornamental metal; railings, prefabricated metal; stairs, staircases, stair treads: prefabricated metal

(G-16041)
RAULLI AND SONS INC
660 Burnet Ave (13203-2404)
PHONE..................315 474-1370
Fax: 315 478-4030
Dennis Raulli, *Manager*
EMP: 15
SQ FT: 9,276
SALES (corp-wide): 17.9MM **Privately Held**
WEB: www.raulliandsons.com
SIC: 3446 Stairs, staircases, stair treads: prefabricated metal

PA: Raulli And Sons, Inc.
213 Teall Ave
Syracuse NY 13210
315 479-6693

(G-16042)
RAULLI AND SONS INC
920 Canal St (13210-1204)
PHONE..................315 479-2515
Joseph Ruscitto, *Branch Mgr*
EMP: 30
SALES (corp-wide): 17.9MM **Privately Held**
SIC: 3291 Abrasive metal & steel products
PA: Raulli And Sons, Inc.
213 Teall Ave
Syracuse NY 13210
315 479-6693

(G-16043)
RB WOODCRAFT INC
1860 Erie Blvd E Ste 1 (13210-1255)
PHONE..................315 474-2429
Fax: 315 474-2734
Raymond A Brooks, *President*
Gary Fritz, *Project Mgr*
Edward Vancott, *Purch Mgr*
Matthew Bush, *Engineer*
Dave Nicoll, *Engineer*
EMP: 50
SQ FT: 40,000
SALES (est): 10.3MM **Privately Held**
WEB: www.rbwoodcraft.com
SIC: 2431 Millwork; interior & ornamental woodwork & trim

(G-16044)
REHABLITATION TECH OF SYRACUSE
Also Called: Rehab Tech
1101 Erie Blvd E Ste 209 (13210-1144)
PHONE..................315 426-9920
Michael T Hall, *President*
Theresa Hall, *Vice Pres*
EMP: 5
SQ FT: 3,000
SALES (est): 692.7K **Privately Held**
SIC: 3842 Orthopedic appliances; prosthetic appliances

(G-16045)
REVONATE MANUFACTURING LLC
7401 Round Pond Rd (13212-2515)
PHONE..................315 433-1160
Jeff Purdy, *Controller*
Kevin P Conley,
EMP: 50
SALES (est): 736.3K **Privately Held**
SIC: 3571 Electronic computers

(G-16046)
ROBOSHOP INC
226 Midler Park Dr (13206-1819)
PHONE..................315 437-6454
Frank Giovinazzo, *President*
Matthew Eddy, *Vice Pres*
EMP: 7 **EST:** 1997
SQ FT: 4,500
SALES (est): 500K **Privately Held**
SIC: 3599 Custom machinery

(G-16047)
ROBS CYCLE SUPPLY
613 Wolf St (13208-1141)
PHONE..................315 292-6878
Robert Woodward, *President*
EMP: 9
SALES (est): 1MM **Privately Held**
SIC: 3751 Motorcycles & related parts

(G-16048)
ROTH GLOBAL PLASTICS INC
Also Called: Fralo
1 General Motors Dr (13206-1117)
P.O. Box 245 (13211-0245)
PHONE..................315 475-0100
Fax: 315 475-0200
Jochen Drewniok, *Ch of Bd*
Tim Hall, *Regional Mgr*
Joseph Brown, *Senior VP*
Theresa Lauer, *Senior VP*
John Pezzi, *Vice Pres*
▲ **EMP:** 20
SQ FT: 100,000

SALES (est): 5.5MM **Privately Held**
WEB: www.fralo.net
SIC: 3089 Septic tanks, plastic

(G-16049)
ROYAL ADHESIVES & SEALANTS LLC
Also Called: Advanced Polymers Intl
3584 Walters Rd Rsd (13209-9700)
PHONE..................315 451-1755
Fax: 315 451-9442
Ted Clark, *CEO*
EMP: 15
SALES (corp-wide): 582.2MM **Privately Held**
SIC: 2891 Adhesives & sealants
PA: Royal Adhesives And Sealants Llc
2001 W Washington St
South Bend IN 46628
574 246-5000

(G-16050)
SAAKSHI INC
Also Called: North Salina Cigar Store
851 N Salina St (13208-2512)
PHONE..................315 475-3988
Fax: 315 426-1143
Jay Vave, *Principal*
EMP: 6
SALES (est): 903K **Privately Held**
SIC: 3999 Cigarette & cigar products & accessories

(G-16051)
SABRE ENTERPRISES INC
1813 Lemoyne Ave (13208-1328)
P.O. Box 68 (13211-0068)
PHONE..................315 430-3127
Bob Dumas, *President*
Gerald Vecchiarelli, *Vice Pres*
Scott Wilkinson, *Treasurer*
John White, *Admin Sec*
EMP: 7 **EST:** 2009
SQ FT: 10,000
SALES (est): 589.3K **Privately Held**
SIC: 3711 Snow plows (motor vehicles), assembly of

(G-16052)
SAGELIFE PARENTING LLC
Also Called: Sagemylife
235 Harrison St Ste 2 (13202-3119)
PHONE..................315 299-5713
Glenna Crooks, *CEO*
EMP: 5 **EST:** 2014
SQ FT: 34,000
SALES (est): 188.5K **Privately Held**
SIC: 2741

(G-16053)
SANDYS BUMPER MART INC
120 Wall St (13204-2182)
PHONE..................315 472-8149
Sandor Bozo, *President*
Romana Bozo, *Vice Pres*
Alex Bozo, *Sales Executive*
EMP: 7 **EST:** 1970
SQ FT: 10,500
SALES (est): 870.4K **Privately Held**
SIC: 3471 Electroplating of metals or formed products

(G-16054)
SCANCORP INC
1840 Lemoyne Ave (13208-1329)
PHONE..................315 454-5596
Fax: 315 454-8903
John Clement, *President*
Ole Westergaard, *Vice Pres*
EMP: 16
SQ FT: 35,000
SALES (est): 1.3MM **Privately Held**
WEB: www.scancorp.com
SIC: 2759 Promotional printing

(G-16055)
SCHILLING FORGE INC
606 Factory Ave (13208-1437)
PHONE..................315 454-4421
Fax: 315 455-8115
Brent A Driscoll, *CEO*
James E Stitt, *Ch of Bd*
Douglas S Pelsue, *President*
John W Whelpley, *Corp Secy*
Linda Roby, *Controller*
▲ **EMP:** 26 **EST:** 1975

SQ FT: 30,000
SALES (est): 3.2MM
SALES (corp-wide): 144.6MM **Privately Held**
WEB: www.schillingforge.com
SIC: 3841 3843 3462 3423 Surgical instruments & apparatus; dental equipment & supplies; iron & steel forgings; hand & edge tools; cutlery
PA: Cutco Corporation
1116 E State St
Olean NY 14760
716 372-3111

(G-16056)
SCHNEIDER BROTHERS CORPORATION
7371 Eastman Rd (13212-2504)
PHONE..................315 458-8369
Fax: 315 458-0358
William D Schneider, *President*
Chris C Schneider, *Corp Secy*
Robert Schneider, *Vice Pres*
Julie Schneider, *Manager*
EMP: 35
SQ FT: 11,000
SALES (est): 7.2MM **Privately Held**
SIC: 3441 Fabricated structural metal

(G-16057)
SCIENTIFIC TOOL CO INC (PA)
101 Arterial Rd (13206-1585)
PHONE..................315 431-4243
Fax: 315 431-4247
Duane Krull, *President*
Chuck Gorman, *President*
Dave Spies, *Vice Pres*
▲ **EMP:** 18
SQ FT: 16,000
SALES (est): 3.2MM **Privately Held**
SIC: 3599 Machine shop, jobbing & repair

(G-16058)
SEAL & DESIGN INC
Higbee Division
6741 Thompson Rd (13211-2119)
PHONE..................315 432-8021
Fax: 315 432-0227
Larry Higbee, *President*
EMP: 40
SALES (corp-wide): 49.8MM **Privately Held**
SIC: 3053 Gaskets & sealing devices
PA: Seal & Design Inc.
4015 Casillio Pkwy
Clarence NY 14031
716 759-2222

(G-16059)
SECUREIT TACTICAL INC (PA)
6691 Commerce Blvd (13211-2211)
PHONE..................800 651-8835
Thomas Kubiniec, *President*
EMP: 15
SALES (est): 1.6MM **Privately Held**
SIC: 3499 Locks, safe & vault: metal

(G-16060)
SELFLOCK SCREW PRODUCTS CO INC
Also Called: SSP
461 E Brighton Ave (13210-4143)
PHONE..................315 541-4464
Fax: 315 475-1093
David M Freund, *President*
Daniel H Kuhns, *Vice Pres*
Carmen Russo, *Prdtn Mgr*
EMP: 30 **EST:** 1920
SQ FT: 50,000
SALES (est): 7.7MM **Privately Held**
WEB: www.selflockscrew.com
SIC: 3451 3541 Screw machine products; machine tools, metal cutting type

(G-16061)
SENECA SIGNS LLC
102 Headson Dr (13214-1102)
PHONE..................315 446-9420
Steve Warner, *Mng Member*
EMP: 7
SALES (est): 55.6K **Privately Held**
WEB: www.signartwork.com
SIC: 3993 Signs & advertising specialties

Syracuse - Onondaga County (G-16062) — GEOGRAPHIC SECTION

(G-16062)
SHARENET INC
214 Solar St Ste 110 (13204-1426)
PHONE 315 477-1100
Ray Davis, *President*
Susan Richardson, *Vice Pres*
Kathleen Reichard, *VP Opers*
EMP: 6
SALES (est): 1.6MM **Privately Held**
SIC: 3578 Automatic teller machines (ATM)

(G-16063)
SHENFIELD STUDIO LLC
Also Called: Shenfield Studio Tile
6361 Thompson Rd Stop 12 (13206-1412)
PHONE 315 436-8869
Robert C Shenfield, *Mng Member*
EMP: 10
SALES: 930K **Privately Held**
SIC: 3292 Floor tile, asphalt

(G-16064)
SIGN A RAMA OF SYRACUSE
Also Called: Sign-A-Rama
3060 Erie Blvd E Ste 1 (13224-1404)
PHONE 315 446-9420
Steve Werner, *Partner*
EMP: 9
SALES (est): 740.9K **Privately Held**
SIC: 3993 Signs & advertising specialties

(G-16065)
SPAULDING LAW PRINTING INC
231 Walton St Ste 103 (13202-1230)
PHONE 315 422-4805
Alexander Douglas, *President*
EMP: 3
SQ FT: 1,000
SALES: 1MM **Privately Held**
SIC: 2759 Commercial printing

(G-16066)
SPECIALTY WLDG & FABG NY INC (PA)
1025 Hiawatha Blvd E (13208-1359)
P.O. Box 145 (13211-0145)
PHONE 315 426-1807
Fax: 315 426-1805
Michael P Murphy, *Ch of Bd*
Randal Stier, *President*
Jack Griffiths, *Vice Pres*
Bill Colclough, *Research*
Leslie McNeil, *Controller*
EMP: 61
SQ FT: 135,000
SALES (est): 27.8MM **Privately Held**
WEB: www.specweld.com
SIC: 3441 Fabricated structural metal

(G-16067)
SRCTEC LLC
5801 E Taft Rd Ste 6 (13212-3275)
PHONE 315 452-8700
Drew James, *President*
Deborah Sabella, *Treasurer*
Robert Young, *Accountant*
Dan Andress, *Info Tech Mgr*
Mary Pat Hartnett, *Admin Sec*
EMP: 150
SALES (est): 33.3MM
SALES (corp-wide): 141.4MM **Privately Held**
WEB: www.srctecinc.com
SIC: 3812 Antennas, radar or communications
PA: Src, Inc.
7502 Round Pond Rd
North Syracuse NY 13212
315 452-8000

(G-16068)
STEPS PLUS INC
6375 Thompson Rd (13206-1495)
PHONE 315 432-0885
Fax: 315 432-0612
Richard R Kopp, *Ch of Bd*
Judy Taylor, *Vice Pres*
Robert H Kopp, *Treasurer*
Brian Deacan, *Manager*
Bert Kopp, *Admin Sec*
EMP: 100
SQ FT: 18,000
SALES (est): 14.7MM **Privately Held**
WEB: www.steps-plus.com
SIC: 3446 Architectural metalwork

(G-16069)
STERI-PHARMA LLC
429 S West St (13202-2326)
PHONE 315 473-7180
Andrew Mather, *Prdtn Mgr*
Nick Walip, *Branch Mgr*
Yasser Alejo, *Manager*
John Connelly, *Senior Mgr*
Lisa Bukowski, *Director*
EMP: 25
SQ FT: 775 **Privately Held**
WEB: www.hanford.com
SIC: 2834 Pharmaceutical preparations
PA: Steri-Pharma, Llc
120 N State Rt 17
Paramus NJ 07652

(G-16070)
SULLIVAN BAZINET BONGIO INC
Also Called: S B B
1 General Motors Dr Ste 5 (13206-1122)
PHONE 315 437-6500
John Bazinet, *Partner*
Vincent Bongio, *Partner*
Mike Sullivan, *Partner*
Brandon Bogart, *General Mgr*
Sheila Cooperider, *Manager*
EMP: 30
SQ FT: 9,000
SALES (est): 7.4MM **Privately Held**
WEB: www.sbbinc.com
SIC: 3564 Air purification equipment

(G-16071)
SUPER COMPANY INC
235 Harrison St Mail Drop (13202)
PHONE 315 569-5153
EMP: 7
SALES (est): 94.4K **Privately Held**
SIC: 7372 Business oriented computer software

(G-16072)
SYRACO PRODUCTS INC
Also Called: Syracuse Stamping Company
1054 S Clinton St (13202-3409)
PHONE 315 476-5306
Fax: 315 474-8876
Fred V Honnold, *Ch of Bd*
Elizabeth Hartnett, *Treasurer*
Steve Quigley, *Finance Dir*
EMP: 14 EST: 1993
SQ FT: 103,000
SALES (est): 7.7MM **Privately Held**
WEB: www.syraco.com
SIC: 3429 3491 2655 Manufactured hardware (general); industrial valves; spools, fiber; made from purchased material

(G-16073)
SYRACUSE CASING CO INC
528 Erie Blvd W (13204-2423)
PHONE 315 475-0309
Fax: 315 475-8536
Peter Frey Jr, *President*
Christine Frey, *Corp Secy*
▲ **EMP:** 16
SQ FT: 150,000
SALES (est): 1.7MM **Privately Held**
SIC: 2013 Sausages & other prepared meats; prepared pork products from purchased pork

(G-16074)
SYRACUSE CATHOLIC PRESS ASSN
Also Called: Catholic Sun, The
421 S Warren St Fl 2 (13202-2640)
P.O. Box 511 (13201-0511)
PHONE 315 422-8153
Fax: 315 422-7549
Connie Berry, *Publisher*
Rev Donald Bourgeois, *Manager*
Doug Ross, *Manager*
L D Costanza, *Associate*
EMP: 6
SALES: 850K **Privately Held**
SIC: 2711 Newspapers

(G-16075)
SYRACUSE COMPUTER FORMS INC
Also Called: Hansen & Hansen Qulty Prtg Div
216 Burnet Ave (13203-2335)
P.O. Box 6761 (13217-6761)
PHONE 315 478-0108
Fax: 315 475-7234
Ted Hansen, *CEO*
Michael Hansen, *President*
Ric Clark, *Prdtn Mgr*
Toni Hansen, *Treasurer*
Mary Hansen, *Admin Sec*
EMP: 20
SQ FT: 38,172
SALES (est): 3.3MM **Privately Held**
WEB: www.hansenqp.com
SIC: 2761 2752 2796 2791 Computer forms, manifold or continuous; commercial printing, lithographic; commercial printing, offset; platemaking services; typesetting

(G-16076)
SYRACUSE CULTURAL WORKERS PRJ
400 Lodi St (13203-2069)
P.O. Box 6367 (13217-6367)
PHONE 315 474-1132
Fax: 315 475-1277
Teresa Florack, *Principal*
John Faley, *Business Mgr*
Andy Mager, *Sales Mgr*
Marie Summerwood, *Mktg Coord*
Karen Kerney, *Director*
▲ **EMP:** 10
SQ FT: 1,800
SALES (est): 780K **Privately Held**
WEB: www.syracuseculturalworkers.com
SIC: 2732 5961 Books: printing & binding; pamphlets: printing & binding, not published on site; books, mail order (except book clubs); mail order house

(G-16077)
SYRACUSE INDUSTRIAL SLS CO LTD
1850 Lemoyne Ave (13208-1282)
PHONE 315 478-5751
Fax: 315 472-0855
EMP: 11
SQ FT: 4,500
SALES (est): 1.8MM **Privately Held**
SIC: 2431 5251 Mfg Millwork Ret Hardware

(G-16078)
SYRACUSE LABEL CO INC
Also Called: Syracuse Label & Surround Prtg
200 Stewart Dr (13212-3426)
PHONE 315 422-1037
Fax: 315 422-6763
Peter Rhodes, *Ch of Bd*
Kathy Alaimo, *President*
Mark Howard, *Vice Pres*
Paul Roux, *Vice Pres*
Kevin Ekbom, *VP Mfg*
EMP: 86 EST: 1974
SQ FT: 35,000
SALES (est): 23.7MM **Privately Held**
WEB: www.syrlabel.com
SIC: 2672 2759 Labels (unprinted), gummed: made from purchased materials; commercial printing

(G-16079)
SYRACUSE PROSTHETIC CENTER INC
1124 E Fayette St (13210-1922)
PHONE 315 476-9697
Fax: 315 476-9694
John Tyo, *President*
Sheila Harrington, *Vice Pres*
EMP: 5
SQ FT: 2,000
SALES (est): 682.8K **Privately Held**
WEB: www.cnyprocenter.com
SIC: 3842 Surgical appliances & supplies

(G-16080)
SYRACUSE UNIVERSITY PRESS INC
621 Skytop Rd Ste 110 (13244-0001)
PHONE 315 443-5534
Victoria Lane, *Design Engr*
Theresa A Litz, *Sls & Mktg Exec*
Enid Darby, *Supervisor*
Alice Pfeiffer, *Director*
Vikki Mossotti, *Admin Sec*
▲ **EMP:** 21
SALES (est): 2.4MM
SALES (corp-wide): 513MM **Privately Held**
SIC: 2731 Books: publishing only
PA: Syracuse University
900 S Crouse Ave Ste 620
Syracuse NY 13244
315 443-1870

(G-16081)
TERRELLS POTATO CHIP CO INC
218 Midler Park Dr (13206-1819)
PHONE 315 437-2786
Fax: 315 437-2069
Jack Terrell, *President*
Jim Cashin, *Division Mgr*
Jane Kelsey, *Office Mgr*
Brenda Terrell, *Admin Sec*
EMP: 70 EST: 1946
SQ FT: 30,000
SALES (est): 12.2MM **Privately Held**
SIC: 2096 5145 Potato chips & other potato-based snacks; popcorn & supplies; pretzels; potato chips

(G-16082)
THERMOPATCH CORPORATION (PA)
2204 Erie Blvd E (13224-1100)
P.O. Box 8007 (13217-8007)
PHONE 315 446-8110
Fax: 315 445-8046
Tom Depuit, *Ch of Bd*
Edward Gublo, *Opers Staff*
Mark Matteson, *Production*
Vic Simons, *Purch Mgr*
E Zeltmann, *Research*
EMP: 100
SQ FT: 52,000
SALES (est): 36.3MM **Privately Held**
WEB: www.thermopatch.com
SIC: 3953 3582 7359 Figures (marking devices), metal; drycleaning equipment & machinery, commercial; laundry equipment leasing

(G-16083)
TOMPKINS SRM LLC
Also Called: Tomkins USA
623 Oneida St (13202-3414)
PHONE 315 422-8763
Mike Mosher, *General Mgr*
William Savage, *Bd of Directors*
EMP: 6
SQ FT: 31,705
SALES (est): 1MM **Privately Held**
SIC: 3559 Sewing machines & attachments, industrial

(G-16084)
TONY BAIRD ELECTRONICS INC
461 E Brighton Ave (13210-4143)
PHONE 315 422-4430
Tony Jeffrey Baird, *CEO*
Khaliph A Bey, *Manager*
Sal Damelio, *Manager*
Robert Leuzzi, *Manager*
B J Meltzie, *Manager*
EMP: 4
SQ FT: 1,060
SALES (est): 1.4MM **Privately Held**
WEB: tonybairdelectronics.com
SIC: 3679 5999 Harness assemblies for electronic use: wire or cable; liquid crystal displays (LCD); audio-visual equipment & supplies

(G-16085)
TRI KOLOR PRINTING & STY
1035 Montgomery St (13202-3507)
P.O. Box 669 (13201-0669)
PHONE 315 474-6753
Fax: 315 478-6723
Charles De Wolf, *Owner*
Shannon Brown, *Supervisor*
Jim Verrette, *Supervisor*
Mike Albanese, *Representative*
EMP: 10
SQ FT: 12,000

SALES: 580K **Privately Held**
SIC: 2752 2759 2791 7336 Commercial printing, offset; letterpress printing; typesetting; graphic arts & related design

(G-16086)
TV GUILFOIL & ASSOCIATES INC (PA)
121 Dwight Park Cir (13209-1005)
P.O. Box 187, Solvay (13209-0187)
PHONE...................................315 453-0920
Fax: 315 453-5091
Phillip H Allen III, *President*
Tim Allen, *Admin Sec*
▲ **EMP:** 7
SQ FT: 10,000
SALES (est): 816.6K **Privately Held**
WEB: www.tvguilfoil.com
SIC: 3999 Candles

(G-16087)
UNIMAR INC
3195 Vickery Rd (13212-4574)
PHONE...................................315 699-4400
Michael Marley, *President*
Beth Andrews, *General Mgr*
Thad Fink, *General Mgr*
Michelle Bovee, *Accountant*
Chris Phelps, *Sales Staff*
◆ **EMP:** 14
SQ FT: 21,000
SALES (est): 4.8MM **Privately Held**
SIC: 3625 5084 5063 Relays & industrial controls; controlling instruments & accessories; lighting fixtures, commercial & industrial

(G-16088)
UPSTATE PRINTING INC
433 W Onondaga St (13202-3209)
PHONE...................................315 475-6140
Fax: 315 475-0169
Jack Rotondo, *President*
Debi Rotondo, *Treasurer*
Patti Vinciguerra, *Marketing Staff*
EMP: 14
SALES (est): 2.1MM **Privately Held**
SIC: 2752 Commercial printing, lithographic

(G-16089)
US BEVERAGE NET INC
225 W Jefferson St (13202-2457)
PHONE...................................315 579-2025
Mark Young, *President*
EMP: 12
SALES (est): 1.2MM **Privately Held**
SIC: 3556 7371 Beverage machinery; custom computer programming services

(G-16090)
VEHICLE SAFETY DEPT
5801 E Taft Rd Ste 4 (13212-3273)
PHONE...................................315 458-6683
Fax: 315 458-8468
James Donnery, *Manager*
EMP: 18
SALES (est): 1.2MM **Privately Held**
SIC: 3714 Sanders, motor vehicle safety

(G-16091)
VERTEX INNOVATIVE SOLUTIONS IN
6671 Commerce Blvd (13211-2211)
PHONE...................................315 437-6711
Paul Snow, *Chairman*
Bill Roberge, *Sales Associate*
EMP: 18
SALES (est): 3.4MM **Privately Held**
SIC: 3648 Lighting equipment

(G-16092)
VETERAN AIR LLC
Also Called: Veteran Air Filtration
7174 State Fair Blvd (13209-1835)
PHONE...................................315 720-1101
Christopher Clark, *Vice Pres*
David Clark, *Vice Pres*
Lawrence Clark, *Vice Pres*
Steven Clark, *Vice Pres*
Alexandra Johnsin,
EMP: 5 **Privately Held**
SIC: 3564 Air cleaning systems

(G-16093)
WARD SALES CO INC
1117 W Fayette St Ste 1 (13204-2733)
PHONE...................................315 476-5276
Fax: 315 476-2056
Richard Hayko, *President*
Joseph Hayko, *Vice Pres*
EMP: 6
SQ FT: 30,000
SALES (est): 648.6K **Privately Held**
WEB: www.wardsalescompany.com
SIC: 2261 3953 3942 5199 Screen printing of cotton broadwoven fabrics; screens, textile printing; stuffed toys, including animals; advertising specialties

(G-16094)
WEATHER PRODUCTS CORPORATION
Also Called: Dynamic Pak
102 W Division St Fl 1 (13204-1470)
PHONE...................................315 474-8593
Fax: 315 474-8795
W Davies Birchenough Jr, *Ch of Bd*
Herman Garcia, *Vice Pres*
EMP: 8
SQ FT: 30,000
SALES (est): 1.4MM **Privately Held**
SIC: 3089 7389 Thermoformed finished plastic products; packaging & labeling services; labeling bottles, cans, cartons, etc.

(G-16095)
WESTROCK - SOLVAY LLC (DH)
53 Indl Dr (13204)
PHONE...................................315 484-9050
Fax: 315 484-9434
Peter Tantalo, *General Mgr*
Tom Stigers, *Vice Pres*
George Turner, *Vice Pres*
Matt Wadach, *Purch Mgr*
Cris Machano, *Controller*
▲ **EMP:** 150
SQ FT: 300,000
SALES: 71.8MM
SALES (corp-wide): 14.1B **Publicly Held**
WEB: www.solvaypaperboard.com
SIC: 2631 Container board
HQ: Westrock Rkt Company
504 Thrasher St
Norcross GA 30071
770 448-2193

(G-16096)
WESTROCK CP LLC
53 Industrial Dr (13204-1035)
PHONE...................................315 484-9050
EMP: 86
SALES (corp-wide): 14.1B **Publicly Held**
SIC: 2631 Container board
HQ: Westrock Cp, Llc
504 Thrasher St
Norcross GA 30071

(G-16097)
WIZARD EQUIPMENT INC
Also Called: Bob's Signs
10 Dwight Park Dr Ste 3 (13209-1098)
PHONE...................................315 414-9999
Bob Reilly, *President*
Robert Barnes, *Vice Pres*
EMP: 5
SALES: 200K **Privately Held**
SIC: 3993 Signs & advertising specialties

(G-16098)
WOLFF & DUNGEY INC
325 Temple St (13202-3417)
P.O. Box 3673 (13220-3673)
PHONE...................................315 475-2105
Fax: 315 475-8369
Maurice Birchmeyer, *CEO*
Charles M Reschke, *Vice Pres*
John Birchmeyer, *Admin Sec*
EMP: 30
SQ FT: 20,000
SALES (est): 4.5MM **Privately Held**
SIC: 3365 3543 Aluminum foundries; industrial patterns

(G-16099)
WOOD ETC INC
1175 State Fair Blvd # 3 (13209-1082)
PHONE...................................315 484-9663
Fax: 315 484-9098

Kathleen Schmidt, *President*
Arnold Schmidt, *Vice Pres*
Jesse Schmidt, *Vice Pres*
EMP: 18
SQ FT: 30,000
SALES (est): 2.4MM **Privately Held**
SIC: 2521 2599 2434 Cabinets, office: wood; cabinets, factory; wood kitchen cabinets

Taberg
Oneida County

(G-16100)
TYCO SIMPLEXGRINNELL
4057 Wilson Rd E (13471-2037)
PHONE...................................315 337-6333
EMP: 92
SALES (corp-wide): 1.4B **Privately Held**
SIC: 3569 Sprinkler systems, fire: automatic
PA: Tyco Simplexgrinnell
1501 Nw 51st St
Boca Raton FL 33431
561 988-3658

Tallman
Rockland County

(G-16101)
KRAMARTRON PRECISION INC
2 Spook Rock Rd Unit 107 (10982)
PHONE...................................845 368-3668
Brian Kramer, *President*
EMP: 5 **EST:** 1974
SQ FT: 3,000
SALES: 500K **Privately Held**
SIC: 3599 Machine shop, jobbing & repair

Tappan
Rockland County

(G-16102)
AG TECH WELDING CORP
238 Oak Tree Rd (10983-2812)
PHONE...................................845 398-0005
Martin De Joia, *President*
Agnes De Joia, *Corp Secy*
EMP: 6
SQ FT: 5,000
SALES (est): 69.3K **Privately Held**
SIC: 3599 1799 Machine shop, jobbing & repair; welding on site

(G-16103)
CARIBBEAN FOODS DELIGHT INC
117 Route 303 Ste B (10983-2136)
PHONE...................................845 398-3000
Fax: 845 398-3001
Vincent Hosang, *President*
Jeanette Hosang, *Vice Pres*
Raquel Pasquel, *Safety Mgr*
Allen Cartanini, *Controller*
Jose Siguroa, *CTO*
◆ **EMP:** 80
SQ FT: 100,000
SALES (est): 17.5MM **Privately Held**
WEB: www.caribbeanfooddelights.com
SIC: 2013 2011 Frozen meats from purchased meat; meat packing plants

(G-16104)
EN TECH CORP
375 Western Hwy (10983-1317)
PHONE...................................845 398-0776
EMP: 15
SALES (corp-wide): 7.8MM **Privately Held**
SIC: 3321 Gray & ductile iron foundries
PA: En Tech Corp
91 Ruckman Rd
Closter NJ 07624
718 389-2058

(G-16105)
NATIONWIDE CUSTOM SERVICES
Also Called: Custom Studio Division
77 Main St (10983-2400)
PHONE...................................845 365-0414
Fax: 845 365-0864
Norman Shaifer, *President*
Helen Newman, *Vice Pres*
Grant Venneo, *Manager*
EMP: 8 **EST:** 1961
SQ FT: 2,000
SALES (est): 590K **Privately Held**
SIC: 2731 8661 Books: publishing & printing; religious organizations

(G-16106)
PULMUONE FOODS USA INC
30 Rockland Park Ave (10983-2629)
PHONE...................................845 365-3300
Fax: 845 365-3311
Chang Hwang, *Branch Mgr*
EMP: 25
SALES (corp-wide): 48.8MM **Privately Held**
SIC: 2024 Tofu desserts, frozen
HQ: Pulmuone Foods Usa, Inc.
2315 Moore Ave
Fullerton CA 92833
714 578-2800

(G-16107)
RJ HARVEY INSTRUMENT CORP
Also Called: Romark Diagnostics
11 Jane St (10983-2503)
PHONE...................................845 359-3943
Fax: 845 359-0264
Robert Maines, *President*
Angelo D'Imperio, *Vice Pres*
EMP: 10
SQ FT: 3,600
SALES (est): 1.1MM **Privately Held**
WEB: www.rjharveyinst.com
SIC: 3841 3829 Diagnostic apparatus, medical; measuring & controlling devices

Tarrytown
Westchester County

(G-16108)
AEROLASE CORPORATION
777 Old Saw Mill River Rd # 2 (10591-6717)
PHONE...................................914 345-8300
Pavel Efremkin, *CEO*
Joseph Hurley, *COO*
Yuri Vladagin, *Project Mgr*
Ryan McFadden, *Project Engr*
Edward Zubek, *Project Engr*
EMP: 100
SQ FT: 3,000
SALES (est): 14.1MM **Privately Held**
WEB: www.friendlylight.com
SIC: 3841 Surgical lasers

(G-16109)
ALTARO CORP
Also Called: Kaffeto Gourmet
520 White Plains Rd (10591-5102)
PHONE...................................855 674-2455
Rafael Arturo Almanzar, *Officer*
EMP: 18
SALES (est): 649.9K **Privately Held**
SIC: 2095 Instant coffee

(G-16110)
AMPACET CORPORATION (PA)
660 White Plains Rd # 360 (10591-5171)
PHONE...................................914 631-6600
Fax: 914 631-0556
Robert A Defalco, *Ch of Bd*
Christian Carnevali, *General Mgr*
Giuseppe Giusto, *General Mgr*
Alvaro Mendoza, *General Mgr*
Tom Phiffer, *Business Mgr*
◆ **EMP:** 948
SQ FT: 36,000
SALES (est): 639.6MM **Privately Held**
WEB: www.ampacet.com
SIC: 3087 Custom compound purchased resins

Tarrytown - Westchester County (G-16111)   GEOGRAPHIC SECTION

(G-16111)
BASF CORPORATION
500 White Plains Rd (10591-5102)
PHONE..................914 785-2000
Stephen Zlock, *Business Mgr*
Loretta Czereeki, *Vice Pres*
Eric Finkelman, *Vice Pres*
Linda Repaci, *Vice Pres*
Michael Hoey, *Technical Mgr*
EMP: 400
SALES (corp-wide): 60.8B **Privately Held**
WEB: www.cibasc.com
SIC: 2869 2819 2899 2843 Industrial organic chemicals; industrial inorganic chemicals; antifreeze compounds; surface active agents; pharmaceutical preparations; vitamin preparations; agricultural chemicals
HQ: Basf Corporation
  100 Park Ave
  Florham Park NJ 07932
  973 245-6000

(G-16112)
BASF CORPORATION
560 White Plains Rd (10591-5113)
PHONE..................973 245-6000
Stefan Koenig, *Branch Mgr*
EMP: 5
SALES (corp-wide): 60.8B **Privately Held**
WEB: www.cibasc.com
SIC: 2819 Industrial inorganic chemicals
HQ: Basf Corporation
  100 Park Ave
  Florham Park NJ 07932
  973 245-6000

(G-16113)
CROSS BORDER TRANSACTIONS LLC
580 White Plains Rd # 660 (10591-5198)
PHONE..................646 767-7342
David Bukovac, *CEO*
Donald Scherer, *Ch of Bd*
Mimi Song, *Vice Pres*
Lisa Zimbalist, *Vice Pres*
Alyssa Dorfman, *CFO*
EMP: 50 **EST:** 2015
SALES (est): 156K **Privately Held**
SIC: 7372 Business oriented computer software

(G-16114)
DENTEK ORAL CARE INC (HQ)
660 White Plains Rd # 250 (10591-5171)
PHONE..................865 983-1300
John M Jansheski, *CEO*
David Fox, *President*
▲ **EMP:** 65
SQ FT: 64,000
SALES (est): 10.6MM
SALES (corp-wide): 882MM **Publicly Held**
WEB: www.usdentek.com
SIC: 3843 Dental equipment & supplies
PA: Prestige Brands Holdings, Inc.
  660 White Plains Rd
  Tarrytown NY 10591
  914 524-6800

(G-16115)
FOSECO INC
777 Old Saw Mill River Rd (10591-6717)
PHONE..................914 345-4760
EMP: 10
SALES (corp-wide): 2.3B **Privately Held**
SIC: 2899 3569 Mfg Exorterneic Compunds Fluxes And Ceramic Filters
HQ: Foseco, Inc.
  20200 Sheldon Rd
  Cleveland OH 44142
  440 826-4548

(G-16116)
KRAFT HEINZ FOODS COMPANY
555 S Broadway (10591-6301)
PHONE..................914 335-2500
Fax: 914 335-6774
Jean Spence, *Vice Pres*
Ralph Warren, *Opers Staff*
David Crowley, *Engineer*
John Mitchell, *Engineer*
Stella Marinelli, *Manager*
EMP: 610

SALES (corp-wide): 26.4B **Publicly Held**
WEB: www.kraftfoods.com
SIC: 2099 2095 2086 2043 Food preparations; roasted coffee; bottled & canned soft drinks; cereal breakfast foods
HQ: Kraft Heinz Foods Company
  1 Ppg Pl Ste 3200
  Pittsburgh PA 15222
  412 456-5700

(G-16117)
MAIN STREET SWEETS
35 Main St (10591-3627)
PHONE..................914 332-5757
Merlina Bertolacci, *Partner*
EMP: 10 **EST:** 2008
SALES (est): 738.4K **Privately Held**
SIC: 2024 Ice cream & frozen desserts

(G-16118)
MARSHALL CAVENDISH CORP
Also Called: Benchmark Books
99 White Plains Rd (10591-5502)
PHONE..................914 332-8888
Fax: 914 332-1082
Richard Farley, *President*
Dovan Chia, *Sales Executive*
Lee C Peng, *Info Tech Mgr*
▲ **EMP:** 40
SQ FT: 30,000
SALES (est): 3.5MM
SALES (corp-wide): 1.4B **Privately Held**
WEB: www.marshallcavendish.com
SIC: 2731 Books: publishing only
HQ: Marshall Cavendish Limited
  32-38 Saffron Hill
  London EC1N

(G-16119)
MEDTECH PRODUCTS INC (HQ)
Also Called: New Skin
660 White Plains Rd (10591-5139)
PHONE..................914 524-6810
Fax: 914 366-6405
Matthew Mannelly, *President*
Timothy J Connors, *Exec VP*
Jean A Boyko PHD, *Senior VP*
John Parkinson, *Senior VP*
Samuel C Cowley, *Vice Pres*
▲ **EMP:** 16
SQ FT: 7,000
SALES (est): 16.6MM
SALES (corp-wide): 882MM **Publicly Held**
SIC: 2841 2834 Soap & other detergents; pharmaceutical preparations
PA: Prestige Brands Holdings, Inc.
  660 White Plains Rd
  Tarrytown NY 10591
  914 524-6800

(G-16120)
MICRO POWDERS INC (PA)
Also Called: M P I
580 White Plains Rd # 400 (10591-5198)
PHONE..................914 332-6400
Fax: 914 472-7098
James Strauss, *President*
Gary Strauss, *General Mgr*
David Gittleman, *Manager*
Phyllis Strauss, *Admin Sec*
◆ **EMP:** 26
SQ FT: 2,500
SALES (est): 8.4MM **Privately Held**
WEB: www.micropowders.com
SIC: 3952 3555 2899 2893 Wax, artists'; printing trades machinery; chemical preparations; printing ink; cyclic crudes & intermediates; specialty cleaning, polishes & sanitation goods

(G-16121)
MOMENTIVE PERFORMANCE MTLS INC
Also Called: OSI Specialties
769 Old Saw Mill River Rd (10591-6732)
PHONE..................914 784-4807
Michael Pigeon, *Manager*
EMP: 80
SALES (corp-wide): 2.2B **Privately Held**
WEB: www.gewaterford.com
SIC: 2843 2099 2821 8731 Surface active agents; emulsifiers, food; plastics materials & resins; commercial physical research; chemical preparations

HQ: Momentive Performance Materials Inc.
  260 Hudson River Rd
  Waterford NY 12188
  518 237-3330

(G-16122)
NOVARTIS CORPORATION
711 Old Saw Mill River Rd (10591-6701)
PHONE..................914 592-7476
John King, *Branch Mgr*
EMP: 25
SALES (corp-wide): 48.5B **Privately Held**
WEB: www.novartis.com
SIC: 2834 Pharmaceutical preparations
HQ: Novartis Corporation
  1 S Ridgedle Ave 122
  East Hanover NJ 07936
  212 307-1122

(G-16123)
NUK USA LLC
303 S Broadway Ste 450 (10591-5484)
PHONE..................914 366-2820
Ian Bukzin, *Branch Mgr*
EMP: 9
SALES (corp-wide): 13.2B **Publicly Held**
SIC: 2676 Infant & baby paper products
HQ: Nuk Usa Llc
  728 Booster Blvd
  Reedsburg WI 53959

(G-16124)
OPEN-XCHANGE INC
303 S Broadway Ste 224 (10591-5410)
P.O. Box 143, Ardsley On Hudson (10503-0143)
PHONE..................914 332-5720
Richard Seibt, *Ch of Bd*
Rafael Laguna, *President*
Carsten Dirks, *COO*
Monika Schroeder, *CFO*
Daniel M Kusnetzky, *Manager*
EMP: 10
SALES (est): 798K **Privately Held**
SIC: 2741 Guides: publishing & printing

(G-16125)
POLICY ADM SOLUTIONS INC
505 White Plains Rd (10591-5101)
PHONE..................914 332-4320
Peter Pantelides, *President*
EMP: 45
SALES: 7.5MM **Privately Held**
SIC: 3571 Mainframe computers

(G-16126)
PRESTIGE BRANDS INTL LLC
660 White Plains Rd (10591-5139)
PHONE..................914 524-6810
Matthew Mannelly, *President*
Timothy J Connors, *Exec VP*
Jean A Boyko PHD, *Senior VP*
Samuel C Cowley, *Vice Pres*
Ronald M Lombardi, *CFO*
◆ **EMP:** 16
SALES (est): 169.5K
SALES (corp-wide): 882MM **Publicly Held**
SIC: 2834 Pharmaceutical preparations
PA: Prestige Brands Holdings, Inc.
  660 White Plains Rd
  Tarrytown NY 10591
  914 524-6800

(G-16127)
RAUCH INDUSTRIES INC
828 S Broadway (10591-6600)
PHONE..................704 867-5333
Bruce Charbeck, *Branch Mgr*
EMP: 41
SALES (corp-wide): 163.3MM **Privately Held**
SIC: 3231 Christmas tree ornaments: made from purchased glass
PA: Rauch Industries, Inc.
  2408 Forbes Rd
  Gastonia NC 28056
  704 867-5333

(G-16128)
REGENERON PHARMACEUTICALS INC (PA)
777 Old Saw Mill River Rd # 10 (10591-6707)
PHONE..................914 847-7000
Fax: 914 347-5045

P Roy Vagelos, *Ch of Bd*
Leonard S Schleifer, *President*
Neil Stahl, *Exec VP*
Daniel P Van Plew, *Exec VP*
Michael Aberman, *Senior VP*
▲ **EMP:** 277
SQ FT: 1,108,000
SALES: 4.8B **Publicly Held**
WEB: www.regeneron.com
SIC: 2834 Pharmaceutical preparations

(G-16129)
REGENRON HLTHCARE SLUTIONS INC
745 Old Saw Mill River Rd (10591-6701)
PHONE..................914 847-7000
Robert Terifay, *General Mgr*
David Robinson, *Vice Pres*
Melissa Giliberti, *Systems Staff*
Joseph Larosa, *Admin Sec*
EMP: 603
SALES (est): 14.4MM **Privately Held**
SIC: 2834 Pharmaceutical preparations

(G-16130)
SIEMENS HLTHCARE DGNOSTICS INC
511 Benedict Ave (10591-5005)
PHONE..................914 631-0475
EMP: 39
SALES (corp-wide): 89.6B **Privately Held**
SIC: 2835 8734 Mfg Diagnostic Substances Testing Laboratory
HQ: Siemens Healthcare Diagnostics Inc.
  511 Benedict Ave
  Tarrytown NY 10591
  914 631-8000

(G-16131)
SNEAKY CHEF FOODS LLC
520 White Plains Rd (10591-5102)
PHONE..................914 301-3277
Missy Chase Lapine, *CEO*
Helen Spanjer, *COO*
Laurence Chase, *Vice Pres*
▲ **EMP:** 10 **EST:** 2012
SALES (est): 1MM **Privately Held**
SIC: 2033 2099 Spaghetti & other pasta sauce: packaged in cans, jars, etc.; peanut butter

(G-16132)
SPIC AND SPAN COMPANY
660 White Plains Rd # 250 (10591-5171)
PHONE..................914 524-6823
Fax: 914 524-6815
Matthew M Mannelly, *CEO*
Mark Pettie, *Ch of Bd*
Peter Anderson, *CFO*
Harris Semegram, *Director*
EMP: 12 **EST:** 2000
SQ FT: 6,000
SALES (est): 2MM
SALES (corp-wide): 882MM **Publicly Held**
SIC: 2842 Cleaning or polishing preparations
PA: Prestige Brands Holdings, Inc.
  660 White Plains Rd
  Tarrytown NY 10591
  914 524-6800

(G-16133)
TARRYTOWN BAKERY INC
150 Wildey St (10591-2910)
PHONE..................914 631-0209
Michael J Birrittella, *President*
EMP: 10
SQ FT: 5,000
SALES (est): 1MM **Privately Held**
WEB: www.plazaview.com
SIC: 2051 5461 Bread, all types (white, wheat, rye, etc): fresh or frozen; bakeries

(G-16134)
TRADEPAQ CORPORATION
220 White Plains Rd # 360 (10591-7800)
PHONE..................914 332-9174
Elena Serova, *Technical Mgr*
Donald Gross, *Branch Mgr*
EMP: 11 **Privately Held**
WEB: www.tradepaq.com
SIC: 7372 Prepackaged software
PA: Tradepaq Corporation
  33 Maiden Ln Fl 8
  New York NY

▲ = Import ▼ = Export
◆ = Import/Export

GEOGRAPHIC SECTION

(G-16135)
YES DENTAL LABORATORY INC
155 White Plains Rd # 223 (10591-5523)
PHONE..................914 333-7550
Robin Michaels, *President*
Evan Krouse, *Vice Pres*
Karen Lariccia, *Controller*
Kirk Fereira, *Info Tech Mgr*
Jason Gleason, *Director*
EMP: 25
SALES (est): 3.2MM **Privately Held**
SIC: 3843 Teeth, artificial (not made in dental laboratories)

(G-16136)
ZIP-JACK INDUSTRIES LTD
Also Called: Zip Jack Custom Umbrellas
73 Carrollwood Dr (10591-5210)
PHONE..................914 592-2000
Fax: 914 592-3023
Emanuel Dubinsky, *President*
Martha Dubinsky, *Info Tech Mgr*
Charlotte L Dubinsky, *Treasurer*
▲ **EMP:** 25 **EST:** 1950
SQ FT: 20,000
SALES (est): 2MM **Privately Held**
WEB: www.zipjack.com
SIC: 3999 5699 Garden umbrellas; umbrellas

Thiells
Rockland County

(G-16137)
STEEL TECH SA LLC
7 Hillside Dr (10984-1431)
P.O. Box 361 (10984-0361)
PHONE..................845 786-3691
Allen Klein,
EMP: 5
SALES: 430K **Privately Held**
SIC: 3441 Fabricated structural metal

Thompsonville
Sullivan County

(G-16138)
MONTICELLO BLACK TOP CORP
80 Patio Dr (12784)
P.O. Box 95 (12784-0095)
PHONE..................845 434-7280
Joseph Gottlieb, *President*
EMP: 5 **EST:** 1964
SQ FT: 4,000
SALES (est): 729.9K **Privately Held**
SIC: 2951 5032 Concrete, asphaltic (not from refineries); sand, construction; gravel

Thornwood
Westchester County

(G-16139)
AUTOMATED CONTROL LOGIC INC
Also Called: Acl
578 Commerce St (10594-1327)
PHONE..................914 769-8880
Fax: 203 769-2753
Preston Bruenn, *President*
Joe Escaravage, *Info Tech Mgr*
EMP: 12
SALES (est): 3.4MM **Privately Held**
WEB: www.automatedcontrollogic.com
SIC: 3674 3825 1711 Solid state electronic devices; test equipment for electronic & electrical circuits; heating & air conditioning contractors

(G-16140)
CARL ZEISS INC (DH)
1 Zeiss Dr (10594-1996)
P.O. Box 5943, New York (10087-5943)
PHONE..................914 747-1800
Fax: 914 681-7443
Cheryl Sarli, *President*
Abdel Barraj, *General Mgr*
Edward Mancini, *Managing Dir*
Dr Michael Kaschke, *Principal*
Bernd Ayernschmalz, *Editor*
▲ **EMP:** 120 **EST:** 1925
SQ FT: 124,000
SALES (est): 306.4MM **Privately Held**
SIC: 3827 5049 3829 5084 Optical instruments & apparatus; optical goods; measuring & controlling devices; instruments & control equipment; analytical instruments
HQ: Carl Zeiss Ag
  Carl-Zeiss-Str. 22
  Oberkochen 73447
  736 420-0

(G-16141)
COMMERCE OFFSET LTD
657 Commerce St (10594-1399)
PHONE..................914 769-6671
Fax: 914 769-7845
EMP: 5
SQ FT: 8,400
SALES (est): 540K **Privately Held**
SIC: 2752 Lithographic Commercial Printing

(G-16142)
FENBAR PRCISION MACHINISTS INC
633 Commerce St (10594-1302)
PHONE..................914 769-5506
Fax: 914 769-5602
Leonard Vallender, *President*
Gloria Vallender, *Corp Secy*
Mike Allen, *Plant Mgr*
Louanne Gambino, *Manager*
EMP: 18
SQ FT: 6,500
SALES (est): 3.3MM **Privately Held**
WEB: www.fenbar.com
SIC: 3599 Machine shop, jobbing & repair

(G-16143)
HOUGHTON MIFFLIN HARCOURT PUBG
28 Claremont Ave (10594-1042)
PHONE..................914 747-2709
Glenn Polin, *Owner*
EMP: 124
SALES (corp-wide): 1.3B **Publicly Held**
WEB: www.hmco.com
SIC: 2731 Books: publishing only
HQ: Houghton Mifflin Harcourt Publishing Company
  125 High St Ste 900
  Boston MA 02110
  617 351-5000

(G-16144)
THORNWOOD PRODUCTS LTD
Also Called: All Star Fabricators
401 Claremont Ave Ste 7 (10594-1038)
PHONE..................914 769-9161
Fax: 914 747-4038
Peter Cuneo, *President*
Lew Tischler, *Sales Executive*
EMP: 30
SALES (est): 3.7MM **Privately Held**
SIC: 2599 1799 Cabinets, factory; counter top installation

Three Mile Bay
Jefferson County

(G-16145)
ST LAWRENCE LUMBER INC
27140 County Route 57 (13693-7205)
PHONE..................315 649-2990
Gregory L Hoppel, *President*
Julie Hoppel, *Vice Pres*
EMP: 7
SALES: 1MM **Privately Held**
WEB: www.stlawrencelumber.com
SIC: 2421 Sawmills & planing mills, general

Ticonderoga
Essex County

(G-16146)
ADIRONDACK MEAT COMPANY INC
30 Commerce Dr (12883-3823)
PHONE..................518 585-2333
Peter Ward, *President*
Denise Ward, *Vice Pres*
Joshua Titus, *Office Mgr*
Taylor Ward, *Asst Mgr*
EMP: 13 **EST:** 2012
SALES (est): 1.8MM **Privately Held**
SIC: 2011 2013 Hides, cured or uncured: from carcasses slaughtered on site; sausages & other prepared meats

(G-16147)
ADIRONDACK WASTE MGT INC
Also Called: Adirondack Sanitary Service
963 New York State 9n (12883)
PHONE..................518 585-2224
Fax: 518 585-2224
R D Seargent Condit, *President*
Cindy Condit, *Vice Pres*
Doran Rockhill, *Treasurer*
EMP: 7
SQ FT: 1,000
SALES (est): 300K **Privately Held**
SIC: 2842 Sanitation preparations

(G-16148)
INTERNATIONAL PAPER COMPANY
568 Shore Airport Rd (12883-2890)
PHONE..................518 585-6761
Fax: 518 585-5358
Kevin Harkonen, *Plant Mgr*
Bob Ballard, *Buyer*
Eugene Fox, *Engineer*
Stephen Treat, *Controller*
Chris Mallon, *Branch Mgr*
EMP: 650
SQ FT: 1,920
SALES (corp-wide): 21B **Publicly Held**
WEB: www.internationalpaper.com
SIC: 2621 Paper mills
PA: International Paper Company
  6400 Poplar Ave
  Memphis TN 38197
  901 419-9000

(G-16149)
LIBBYS BAKERY CAFE LLC
92 Montcalm St (12883-1352)
P.O. Box 61 (12883-0061)
PHONE..................603 918-8825
Andrew Rasmus, *Principal*
Claire Brown, *Principal*
Katherine Lewis, *Principal*
EMP: 5
SALES (est): 395.1K **Privately Held**
SIC: 2051 Cakes, pies & pastries

(G-16150)
SPECIALTY MINERALS INC
35 Highland St (12883-1520)
PHONE..................518 585-7982
Fax: 518 585-7930
Elaine Bertrand, *General Mgr*
Robert Dorr, *Plant Mgr*
EMP: 6
SALES (corp-wide): 1.6B **Publicly Held**
WEB: www.specialtyminerals.com
SIC: 2819 Industrial inorganic chemicals
HQ: Specialty Minerals Inc.
  622 3rd Ave Fl 38
  New York NY 10017
  212 878-1800

(G-16151)
TICONDEROGA MCH & WLDG CORP
55 Race Track Rd (12883-4003)
PHONE..................518 585-7444
EMP: 5 **EST:** 1954
SQ FT: 980
SALES (est): 36.3K **Privately Held**
SIC: 3599 Machine Shop

Tillson
Ulster County

(G-16152)
WINERACKSCOM INC
819 Route 32 (12486-1724)
PHONE..................845 658-7181
Michael Babcock, *President*
Howard Babcock, *Vice Pres*
EMP: 26 **EST:** 1990
SQ FT: 20,000
SALES (est): 4.1MM **Privately Held**
SIC: 2541 Wood partitions & fixtures

Tomkins Cove
Rockland County

(G-16153)
TILCON NEW YORK INC
Fort Of Elm (10986)
P.O. Box 217 (10986-0217)
PHONE..................845 942-0602
Rich Moon, *Superintendent*
Nathalie Boboshko, *Credit Mgr*
EMP: 22
SQ FT: 2,184
SALES (corp-wide): 28.6B **Privately Held**
WEB: www.tilconny.com
SIC: 1442 Sand mining; gravel & pebble mining
HQ: Tilcon New York Inc.
  162 Old Mill Rd
  West Nyack NY 10994
  845 358-4500

Tonawanda
Erie County

(G-16154)
3M COMPANY
305 Sawyer Ave (14150-7718)
PHONE..................716 876-1596
Roy Zimmerman, *Plant Mgr*
Kathren Kaspar, *Project Engr*
Mike Dolan, *Human Res Dir*
Mike Mazur, *Manager*
Daniel O'Brien, *Manager*
EMP: 400
SALES (corp-wide): 30.1B **Publicly Held**
WEB: www.mmm.com
SIC: 3089 2823 Sponges, plastic; cellulosic manmade fibers
PA: 3m Company
  3m Center
  Saint Paul MN 55144
  651 733-1110

(G-16155)
54321 US INC (DH)
295 Fire Tower Dr (14150-5833)
PHONE..................716 695-0258
Morris Goodman, *President*
Moe Cahill, *Vice Pres*
Ted Wise, *Treasurer*
Cynthia Todd, *Accounts Mgr*
▲ **EMP:** 10
SALES (est): 1.5MM
SALES (corp-wide): 184MM **Privately Held**
WEB: www.54321answer.com
SIC: 3842 Sponges, surgical; surgical appliances & supplies
HQ: Pharmascience Inc
  6111 Av Royalmount Bureau 100
  Montreal QC H4P 2
  514 340-1114

(G-16156)
ACE SPECIALTY CO INC
695 Ensminger Rd (14150-6698)
PHONE..................716 874-3670
Fax: 716 876-7418
Patrick J Allen, *President*
Patti Post, *Office Mgr*
EMP: 9 **EST:** 1947
SQ FT: 25,000

Tonawanda - Erie County (G-16157)

GEOGRAPHIC SECTION

SALES: 1.1MM **Privately Held**
WEB: www.acespecialtycompany.com
SIC: 3544 Special dies & tools

(G-16157)
ADAMS SFC INC (HQ)
225 E Park Dr (14150-7813)
P.O. Box 963, Buffalo (14240-0963)
PHONE 716 877-2608
Jack H Berg, *President*
Glenn Mountain, *General Mgr*
Scott Kroon, *Research*
Karen Pochylski, *Prgrmr*
Carole L Berg, *Admin Sec*
▲ **EMP:** 40
SQ FT: 39,152
SALES (est): 6.6MM
SALES (corp-wide): 62.5MM **Privately Held**
WEB: www.pacerpumps.com
SIC: 3569 3563 Filters, general line: industrial; vacuum (air extraction) systems, industrial
PA: Service Filtration Corp.
2900 Macarthur Blvd
Northbrook IL 60062
847 509-2900

(G-16158)
ALFA LAVAL KATHABAR INC
91 Sawyer Ave (14150-7716)
PHONE 716 875-2000
EMP: 6
SALES (est): 117.1K **Privately Held**
SIC: 3585 Humidifiers & dehumidifiers

(G-16159)
ALRY TOOL AND DIE CO INC
386 Fillmore Ave (14150-2417)
P.O. Box 43 (14151-0043)
PHONE 716 693-2419
Fax: 716 693-5971
Michael J Allen, *President*
Daniel T Allen, *Corp Secy*
Francis D Allen Jr, *Vice Pres*
Thomas Allen, *Vice Pres*
Patricia King, *Manager*
EMP: 20 **EST:** 1944
SQ FT: 23,500
SALES (est): 2.6MM **Privately Held**
WEB: www.alry.com
SIC: 3462 3544 Machinery forgings, ferrous; dies & die holders for metal cutting, forming, die casting

(G-16160)
ANDERSON EQUIPMENT COMPANY
2140 Military Rd (14150-6002)
PHONE 716 877-1992
David McDermott, *Inv Control Mgr*
Don Geis, *Financial Exec*
John Park, *Manager*
John Zappia, *Info Tech Dir*
EMP: 70
SALES (corp-wide): 98MM **Privately Held**
SIC: 3531 Construction machinery
PA: Anderson Equipment Company
1000 Washington Pike
Bridgeville PA 15017
412 343-2300

(G-16161)
ARROW GRINDING INC
525 Vicke St Tonaw Ctr (14150)
PHONE 716 693-3333
John C Goller, *President*
Kathy Goller, *Corp Secy*
Doug Deschamps, *Mfg Staff*
Jim Whistler, *Sales Executive*
EMP: 25
SQ FT: 25,000
SALES (est): 4.1MM **Privately Held**
SIC: 3599 Machine shop, jobbing & repair

(G-16162)
AVANTI U S A LTD
412 Young St (14150-4037)
PHONE 716 695-5800
Fax: 716 695-0855
G J Caruso, *Principal*
Gregory J Van Norman, *Vice Pres*
A P Caruso, *Controller*
EMP: 15
SQ FT: 4,863

SALES (est): 1.7MM **Privately Held**
SIC: 3842 2386 3089 Surgical appliances & supplies; garments, leather; injection molding of plastics

(G-16163)
AWNINGS PLUS INC
363 Delaware St (14150-3951)
PHONE 716 693-3690
Fax: 716 693-3767
Dan R Gagliardo, *President*
EMP: 15
SQ FT: 20,000
SALES (est): 998.5K **Privately Held**
WEB: www.awningsplus.com
SIC: 2394 1799 Awnings, fabric: made from purchased materials; awning installation

(G-16164)
B & W HEAT TREATING COMPANY
2780 Kenmore Ave (14150-7775)
PHONE 716 876-8184
Clifford Calvello, *President*
EMP: 8
SQ FT: 14,000
SALES (est): 1.3MM **Privately Held**
SIC: 3398 3471 Metal heat treating; cleaning, polishing & finishing

(G-16165)
BCO INDUSTRIES WESTERN NY INC
77 Oriskany Dr (14150-6722)
P.O. Box 100 (14151-0100)
PHONE 716 877-2800
Janet Soltzman, *President*
Douglas Saltzman, *President*
Theresa Subsara, *Bookkeeper*
EMP: 31
SALES (est): 4.5MM **Privately Held**
WEB: www.bcoworld.com
SIC: 2759 2791 Thermography; visiting cards (including business): printing; facsimile letters: printing; stationery: printing; typesetting

(G-16166)
BIMBO BAKERIES USA INC
Also Called: Best Foods Baking Group
1960 Niagara Falls Blvd (14150-5542)
PHONE 716 692-9140
Catherine E Irish, *Branch Mgr*
EMP: 5 **Privately Held**
WEB: www.gwbakeries.com
SIC: 2051 Bread, cake & related products
HQ: Bimbo Bakeries Usa, Inc
255 Business Center Dr # 200
Horsham PA 19044
215 347-5500

(G-16167)
BONCRAFT INC
777 E Park Dr (14150-6708)
PHONE 716 662-9720
Fax: 716 662-9578
Timothy Bubar, *CEO*
James Bubar Jr, *President*
Bryan McMullen, *Prdtn Mgr*
Mike Ruda, *Maint Spvr*
Robert Reis, *Opers Staff*
EMP: 75 **EST:** 1952
SQ FT: 20,400
SALES (est): 9.3MM **Privately Held**
WEB: www.boncraft.com
SIC: 2752 2791 2789 Commercial printing, lithographic; typesetting; bookbinding & related work

(G-16168)
BOULEVARD PRINTING
1330 Niagara Falls Blvd # 2 (14150-8900)
PHONE 716 837-3800
Fax: 716 837-0500
John Battistella, *Owner*
EMP: 6
SALES (est): 620.2K **Privately Held**
SIC: 2752 Commercial printing, lithographic

(G-16169)
BRIGHTON TOOL & DIE DESIGNERS (PA)
Also Called: Brighton Design
463 Brighton Rd (14150-6966)
PHONE 716 876-0879
Fax: 716 876-8341
Chris Banas, *President*
Chris Eanas, *President*
EMP: 15
SQ FT: 2,000
SALES (est): 1.7MM **Privately Held**
SIC: 3544 Special dies & tools

(G-16170)
BROTHERS-IN-LAWN PROPERTY
176 Vulcan (14150)
PHONE 716 279-6191
Rodney Koeppen, *President*
EMP: 9 **EST:** 2012
SALES (est): 783.8K **Privately Held**
SIC: 3711 0781 Snow plows (motor vehicles), assembly of; landscape services

(G-16171)
BULOW & ASSOCIATES INC
317 Wheeler St (14150-3828)
P.O. Box 35 (14151-0035)
PHONE 716 838-0298
Fax: 716 838-0299
William A Bulow, *President*
William A Bullow, *President*
Dennis Wilcox, *Vice Pres*
Neal Wilcox, *Admin Sec*
EMP: 5
SALES: 100K **Privately Held**
SIC: 3993 Signs & advertising specialties

(G-16172)
CENTRAL REDE SIGN CO INC
317 Wheeler St (14150-3828)
PHONE 716 213-0797
Neal Wilcox, *Principal*
John Wilcox, *VP Sales*
EMP: 5
SALES (est): 698.5K **Privately Held**
SIC: 3993 Signs & advertising specialties

(G-16173)
CENTRISOURCE INC
777 E Park Dr (14150-6708)
PHONE 716 871-1105
Fax: 716 505-4354
David Zenger, *President*
Joseph Zenger, *Treasurer*
EMP: 5
SALES (est): 440K **Privately Held**
SIC: 2732 Book printing

(G-16174)
CLIFFORD H JONES INC
608 Young St (14150-4195)
PHONE 716 693-2444
Fax: 716 693-2598
Phillip Jones, *President*
David Jones, *Vice Pres*
Jamie Mawson, *Opers Mgr*
EMP: 15
SQ FT: 18,000
SALES (est): 4MM **Privately Held**
WEB: www.chjones.com
SIC: 3544 3089 Forms (molds), for foundry & plastics working machinery; injection molding of plastics

(G-16175)
COCA-COLA BTLG CO BUFFALO INC
200 Milens Rd (14150-6795)
PHONE 716 874-4610
Fax: 716 874-7739
John F Bitzer III, *President*
Rick Horn Jr, *General Mgr*
Horn Rick, *Sls & Mktg Exec*
Flora Torina, *Controller*
David Moden, *Manager*
▲ **EMP:** 170
SQ FT: 75,000
SALES: 908.8K
SALES (corp-wide): 361.4MM **Privately Held**
SIC: 2086 Bottled & canned soft drinks

PA: Abarta, Inc.
200 Alpha Dr
Pittsburgh PA 15238
412 963-6226

(G-16176)
DIGITAL INSTRUMENTS INC
580 Ensminger Rd (14150-6668)
PHONE 716 874-5848
Fax: 716 874-5954
John Swanson, *President*
Amy Betz, *Office Mgr*
▲ **EMP:** 10
SQ FT: 6,000
SALES (est): 2MM **Privately Held**
WEB: www.digitalinstruments.com
SIC: 3625 Relays & industrial controls; industrial controls: push button, selector switches, pilot

(G-16177)
E-ZOIL PRODUCTS INC
234 Fillmore Ave (14150-2340)
PHONE 716 213-0103
Glenn Miller, *President*
Christopher Miller, *Vice Pres*
Arnette Rauh, *Office Mgr*
▲ **EMP:** 25
SQ FT: 10,000
SALES (est): 6.1MM **Privately Held**
WEB: www.ezoil.com
SIC: 2911 Fuel additives

(G-16178)
EMULSO CORP
2750 Kenmore Ave (14150-7707)
PHONE 716 854-2889
William Breeser, *President*
Brian Williams, *Opers Dir*
EMP: 6
SQ FT: 30,000
SALES (est): 550K **Privately Held**
WEB: www.emulso.com
SIC: 2842 2841 5087 Soap: granulated, liquid, cake, flaked or chip; waxes for wood, leather & other materials; furniture polish or wax; janitors' supplies

(G-16179)
FCMP INC
230 Fire Tower Dr (14150-5832)
PHONE 716 692-4623
David Callendrier, *President*
Toni Clark, *Manager*
▲ **EMP:** 17 **EST:** 2000
SQ FT: 20,000
SALES (est): 3.7MM **Privately Held**
WEB: www.fcmp.com
SIC: 3714 3592 Bearings, motor vehicle; pistons & piston rings

(G-16180)
FIBER LAMINATIONS LIMITED
Also Called: C/O M&M Fowarding
600 Main St (14150-3723)
PHONE 716 692-1825
Fax: 716 692-0056
William Neal, *Branch Mgr*
EMP: 13
SALES (corp-wide): 2.9MM **Privately Held**
SIC: 3089 Automotive parts, plastic
PA: Fibre Laminations Ltd
651 Burlington St E
Hamilton ON L8L 4
905 312-9152

(G-16181)
FMC CORPORATION
Also Called: F M C Peroxygen Chemicals Div
78 Sawyer Ave Ste 1 (14150-7751)
PHONE 716 879-0400
Fax: 716 879-0474
Daryl Largis, *Plant Mgr*
Greg Campo, *Engineer*
James Heigl, *Engineer*
Edward Rzadkiwwicz, *Engineer*
Robert Service, *Manager*
EMP: 200
SALES (corp-wide): 3.2B **Publicly Held**
WEB: www.fmc.com
SIC: 2869 Industrial organic chemicals
PA: Fmc Corporation
2929 Walnut St
Philadelphia PA 19104
215 299-6668

GEOGRAPHIC SECTION

Tonawanda - Erie County (G-16207)

(G-16182)
GERALD FRD PACKG DISPLAY LLC (PA)
550 Fillmore Ave (14150-2520)
PHONE...............716 692-2705
Fax: 716 692-5458
Karen Goraj, *Human Res Mgr*
Val Sracine, *Mng Member*
▲ EMP: 14 EST: 1946
SQ FT: 50,000
SALES (est): 2.3MM Privately Held
SIC: 2542 Counters or counter display cases: except wood

(G-16183)
GREAT LAKES GEAR CO INC
126 E Niagara St Ste 2 (14150-1215)
PHONE...............716 694-0715
Fax: 716 694-7241
Donald Eggleston, *President*
Robert Rees, *President*
Timothy Rees, *Vice Pres*
Susan Guenther, *Human Res Dir*
Mathew Dubin, *Information Mgr*
EMP: 8
SQ FT: 4,500
SALES: 900K Privately Held
SIC: 3462 Gears, forged steel

(G-16184)
GREAT LAKES METAL TREATING
300 E Niagara St (14150-1218)
P.O. Box 118 (14151-0118)
PHONE...............716 694-1240
Thomas Snyder, *President*
EMP: 10
SQ FT: 18,000
SALES (est): 966.9K Privately Held
SIC: 3398 Metal heat treating

(G-16185)
GREEN BUFFALO FUEL LLC
Also Called: Gbf
720 Riverview Blvd (14150-7824)
PHONE...............716 768-0600
Peter Coleman, *CEO*
EMP: 10 EST: 2012
SALES (est): 1.2MM Privately Held
SIC: 1311 1321 Natural gas production; butane (natural) production

(G-16186)
GREIF INC
2122 Colvin Blvd (14150-6908)
PHONE...............716 836-4200
Alco Drost, *Opers Mgr*
Pat Wolfe, *Maint Spvr*
Clinton Gathins, *Opers-Prdtn-Mfg*
Doug Lingrel, *Financial Exec*
Karen Muranyi, *Financial Exec*
EMP: 70
SALES (corp-wide): 3.3B Publicly Held
WEB: www.greif.com
SIC: 2655 Drums, fiber: made from purchased material
PA: Greif, Inc.
425 Winter Rd
Delaware OH 43015
740 549-6000

(G-16187)
HDM HYDRAULICS LLC
125 Fire Tower Dr (14150-5880)
PHONE...............716 694-8004
William Anderson, *President*
Ron Wojthkowski, *Controller*
Heckman Barry, *CTO*
▲ EMP: 100
SQ FT: 46,560
SALES (est): 27.7MM
SALES (corp-wide): 557.2MM Privately Held
WEB: www.ligonindustries.com
SIC: 3511 Hydraulic turbine generator set units, complete
PA: Ligon Industries, Llc
1927 1st Ave N Ste 500
Birmingham AL 35203
205 322-3302

(G-16188)
HEBELER LLC (PA)
2000 Military Rd (14150-6704)
PHONE...............716 873-9300
Fax: 716 873-7538
Ken Snyder, *President*
Paul Forkey, *Project Mgr*
Zeke Gray, *Project Mgr*
Gino Kellerhouse, *Project Mgr*
Nick Leibring, *Project Mgr*
▲ EMP: 140 EST: 1929
SQ FT: 100,000
SALES (est): 40MM Privately Held
WEB: www.hebeler.com
SIC: 3599 Custom machinery

(G-16189)
HEBELER PROCESS SOLUTIONS LLC
2000 Military Rd (14150-6704)
PHONE...............716 873-9300
Kenneth Snyder, *President*
Kenneth Snyder, *President*
EMP: 20 EST: 2016
SALES (est): 1.5MM Privately Held
SIC: 3599 Custom machinery

(G-16190)
HERR MANUFACTURING CO INC
17 Pearce Ave (14150-6711)
PHONE...............716 874-6066
Fax: 716 874-4341
Bruce Mc Lean, *President*
Rick Wahl, *Sales Staff*
EMP: 25 EST: 1913
SALES (est): 3.1MM Privately Held
SIC: 3552 Textile machinery

(G-16191)
IMA LIFE NORTH AMERICA INC
2175 Military Rd (14150-6001)
PHONE...............716 695-6354
Giovanni Pecchioli, *President*
Sergio Marzo, *Corp Secy*
Jose Ruiz, *Exec VP*
Laura Opera, *Vice Pres*
Ernesto Renzi, *Vice Pres*
◆ EMP: 150
SQ FT: 43,000
SALES: 70MM Privately Held
SIC: 2834 Druggists' preparations (pharmaceuticals)
HQ: I.M.A. Industria Macchine Automatiche Spa
Via Bruno Tosarelli 182/184
Castenaso BO 40055
051 651-4111

(G-16192)
INPRO CORPORATION
Fireline 520
250 Cooper Ave Ste 102 (14150-6633)
PHONE...............716 332-4699
Aj Shaw, *Manager*
EMP: 5
SALES (corp-wide): 141.5MM Privately Held
SIC: 3499 Barricades, metal
PA: Inpro Corporation
S80w18766 Apollo Dr
Muskego WI 53150
262 679-9010

(G-16193)
INTEGUMENT TECHNOLOGIES INC
72 Pearce Ave (14150-6711)
PHONE...............716 873-1199
Fax: 716 873-1303
Terrence G Vargo, *President*
Jeff Gruszka, *Controller*
Jennifer Smyth, *Marketing Staff*
EMP: 16
SALES (est): 2.4MM Privately Held
WEB: www.integument.com
SIC: 3081 Unsupported plastics film & sheet

(G-16194)
KELLER TECHNOLOGY CORPORATION (PA)
2320 Military Rd (14150-6005)
P.O. Box 103, Buffalo (14217-0103)
PHONE...............716 693-3840
Fax: 716 693-0512
Michael A Keller, *Ch of Bd*
Arthur Keller Jr, *Ch of Bd*
Peter Keller, *Vice Pres*
Pam Iamunno, *Project Mgr*
Chris Sansone, *Prdtn Mgr*
▲ EMP: 175 EST: 1947
SQ FT: 200,000
SALES (est): 58.5MM Privately Held
WEB: www.kellertechnology.com
SIC: 3599 Custom machinery

(G-16195)
LAFARGE NORTH AMERICA INC
4001 River Rd (14150-6513)
PHONE...............716 876-8788
Mark Joslin, *Branch Mgr*
EMP: 13
SALES (corp-wide): 26.6B Privately Held
SIC: 1422 Crushed & broken limestone
HQ: Lafarge North America Inc.
8700 W Bryn Mawr Ave Ll
Chicago IL 60631
703 480-3600

(G-16196)
LORNAMEAD INC
175 Cooper Ave (14150-6656)
PHONE...............716 874-7190
James Carney, *VP Opers*
EMP: 76 Privately Held
SIC: 2844 Hair preparations, including shampoos
HQ: Lornamead, Inc
175 Cooper St
New York NY 10034
716 874-7190

(G-16197)
MANTH MFG INC
131 Fillmore Ave (14150-2337)
P.O. Box 866 (14151-0866)
PHONE...............716 693-6525
Fax: 716 693-6560
Duane Manth, *President*
Ron McCarthy, *Plant Mgr*
EMP: 35
SQ FT: 14,000
SALES: 1.9MM Privately Held
SIC: 3599 Machine shop, jobbing & repair

(G-16198)
MAY TOOL & DIE INC
9 Hackett Dr (14150-3797)
PHONE...............716 695-1033
Fax: 716 695-1090
Martin J May, *President*
Frederick J May, *Vice Pres*
Joseph O May, *Vice Pres*
Mary Kreher, *Admin Sec*
EMP: 5 EST: 1970
SQ FT: 8,000
SALES: 500K Privately Held
SIC: 3544 Special dies & tools

(G-16199)
MIDLAND MACHINERY CO INC
101 Cranbrook Road Ext Exd (14150-4110)
PHONE...............716 692-1200
Fax: 716 731-1924
Barre W Banks, *President*
Lalit Kumar, *Engineer*
Dave Reinard, *Engineer*
Darrell Banks, *Sls & Mktg Exec*
▲ EMP: 59 EST: 1969
SQ FT: 15,000
SALES (est): 14.8MM Privately Held
WEB: www.midlandmachinery.com
SIC: 3531 Asphalt plant, including gravel-mix type; mixers, concrete; pavers

(G-16200)
MODU-CRAFT INC (PA)
276 Creekside Dr (14150-1435)
PHONE...............716 694-0709
Fax: 716 694-0709
Kenneth Babka, *President*
EMP: 5
SQ FT: 30,000
SALES: 1MM Privately Held
SIC: 3821 2599 2542 Laboratory furniture; factory furniture & fixtures; partitions & fixtures, except wood

(G-16201)
MORNINGSTAR CONCRETE PRODUCTS
528 Young St (14150-4107)
PHONE...............716 693-4020
Fax: 716 693-4021
Juanita Morningstar, *President*
Ray D Morningstar, *Vice Pres*
▲ EMP: 14 EST: 1913
SQ FT: 120,000
SALES (est): 1.7MM Privately Held
WEB: www.morningstarturf.com
SIC: 3271 Blocks, concrete or cinder: standard

(G-16202)
NEW YORK IMAGING SERVICE INC
255 Cooper Ave (14150-6641)
PHONE...............716 834-8022
Rob Muzzio, *Branch Mgr*
EMP: 11
SALES (corp-wide): 15.6MM Privately Held
SIC: 3844 X-ray apparatus & tubes
PA: New York Imaging Service Inc.
1 Dalfonso Rd
Newburgh NY 12550
845 561-6947

(G-16203)
NIABRAZE LLC
675 Ensminger Rd (14150-6609)
PHONE...............716 447-1082
Fax: 716 447-1084
Albert Bluemle Sr, *President*
Thomas Bluemle, *Treasurer*
EMP: 14
SALES (est): 2.2MM Privately Held
SIC: 3421 3425 Cutlery; saw blades for hand or power saws

(G-16204)
NIAGARA BLOWER COMPANY (DH)
91 Sawyer Ave (14150-7716)
PHONE...............800 426-5169
Fax: 716 875-1077
Peter G Demakos, *President*
Craig D Boyce, *Vice Pres*
Thomas Nicholas, *Project Engr*
Sally Santor, *Accountant*
Mark Vogel, *Manager*
▼ EMP: 108 EST: 1904
SQ FT: 60,000
SALES (est): 34MM
SALES (corp-wide): 3.8B Privately Held
WEB: www.niagarablower.com
SIC: 3585 Refrigeration & heating equipment; air conditioning units, complete: domestic or industrial; humidifying equipment, except portable

(G-16205)
NOCO INCORPORATED (PA)
2440 Sheridan Dr Ste 202 (14150-9416)
PHONE...............716 833-6626
James D Newman, *Ch of Bd*
R J Stapell, *Ch of Bd*
Michael Newman, *Exec VP*
Michael L Bradley, *CFO*
Scott Ernst, *Director*
EMP: 5
SQ FT: 15,000
SALES (est): 420.2MM Privately Held
SIC: 2992 6719 5172 4924 Lubricating oils & greases; investment holding companies, except banks; petroleum products; natural gas distribution

(G-16206)
NORTH DELAWARE PRINTING INC
645 Delaware St Ste 1 (14150-5390)
PHONE...............716 692-0576
Michael J Brown, *President*
Steven Brown, *Vice Pres*
EMP: 9
SQ FT: 3,200
SALES (est): 1.5MM Privately Held
WEB: www.northdelawareprinting.com
SIC: 2752 7334 Commercial printing, lithographic; photocopying & duplicating services

(G-16207)
ODEN MACHINERY INC (PA)
600 Ensminger Rd (14150-6637)
PHONE...............716 874-3000
Ronald Sarto, *CEO*
Tony Fwedersky, *President*
Gregory E Simsa, *CFO*

Tonawanda - Erie County (G-16208)

GEOGRAPHIC SECTION

Dave Carroll, *Sales Mgr*
EMP: 20
SQ FT: 25,000
SALES: 4.5MM **Privately Held**
SIC: 3823 Thermometers, filled system: industrial process type

(G-16208)
OPTICS PLUS INC
4291 Delaware Ave (14150-6129)
PHONE....................716 744-2636
Forrest Reukauf, *Principal*
▲ **EMP:** 9
SALES (est): 1.1MM **Privately Held**
SIC: 3827 Optical instruments & lenses

(G-16209)
PADDOCK CHEVROLET GOLF DOME
175 Brompton Rd (14150-4534)
PHONE....................716 504-4059
Fax: 716 504-4060
Jeff Rainey, *Director*
EMP: 25
SALES (est): 1.2MM **Privately Held**
WEB: www.tonawanda.ny.us
SIC: 3949 7999 Driving ranges, golf, electronic; tennis services & professionals

(G-16210)
PDM STUDIOS INC
510 Main St (14150-3853)
PHONE....................716 694-8337
Paul Michalski, *President*
Samantha Crocker, *Admin Asst*
EMP: 6
SALES (est): 519.3K **Privately Held**
SIC: 2759 Screen printing

(G-16211)
PINE PHARMACEUTICALS LLC
100 Colvin Woods Pkwy (14150-6974)
PHONE....................716 248-1025
Alfonse Muto, *Mng Member*
EMP: 5
SALES (est): 1.1MM **Privately Held**
SIC: 2834 Druggists' preparations (pharmaceuticals)

(G-16212)
PRAXAIR INC
175 E Park Dr (14150-7891)
P.O. Box 44 (14151-0044)
PHONE....................716 879-2000
Fax: 716 879-4720
Joel Emmet, *Principal*
Tim Howley, *Senior VP*
Dennis Conroy, *Vice Pres*
William Therrien, *Vice Pres*
Karen Ginnane, *Plant Mgr*
EMP: 15
SALES (corp-wide): 10.5B **Publicly Held**
SIC: 2819 Industrial inorganic chemicals
PA: Praxair, Inc.
  10 Riverview Dr
  Danbury CT 06810
  203 837-2000

(G-16213)
PRAXAIR INC
135 E Park Dr (14150-7844)
PHONE....................716 879-4000
John Lewendowski, *Principal*
EMP: 50
SALES (corp-wide): 10.5B **Publicly Held**
SIC: 2813 Industrial gases
PA: Praxair, Inc.
  10 Riverview Dr
  Danbury CT 06810
  203 837-2000

(G-16214)
R J REYNOLDS TOBACCO COMPANY
275 Cooper Ave Ste 116 (14150-6643)
PHONE....................716 871-1553
Tracy Wozniak, *Principal*
EMP: 226
SALES (corp-wide): 18.1B **Publicly Held**
SIC: 2111 Cigarettes
HQ: R. J. Reynolds Tobacco Company
  401 N Main St
  Winston Salem NC 27101
  336 741-5000

(G-16215)
REGULUS ENERGY LLC
250 Cooper Ave Ste 106 (14150-6633)
PHONE....................716 200-7417
Glenn Thomas, *Principal*
Christine Bird, *Vice Pres*
EMP: 12
SALES (est): 546.3K **Privately Held**
SIC: 2911 Jet fuels; diesel fuels; oils, fuel

(G-16216)
S R INSTRUMENTS INC (PA)
600 Young St (14150-4188)
PHONE....................716 693-5977
Fax: 716 693-5854
John Siegel, *President*
Brandon Darnell, *Engineer*
Teresa Eyring, *Sls & Mktg Exec*
Peter Adolf, *Human Res Mgr*
Janelle Heimgartner, *Accounts Mgr*
EMP: 48
SQ FT: 25,000
SALES (est): 6.2MM **Privately Held**
WEB: www.srinstruments.com
SIC: 3825 3596 Measuring instruments & meters, electric; weighing machines & apparatus

(G-16217)
SAFESPAN PLATFORM SYSTEMS INC
237 Fillmore Ave (14150-2339)
PHONE....................716 694-1100
Lambros Apostolopoulos, *President*
Thomas Lauber, *Executive*
EMP: 40 **Privately Held**
SIC: 3312 Slabs, steel; structural shapes & pilings, steel
PA: Safespan Platform Systems, Inc.
  252 Fillmore Ave
  Tonawanda NY 14150

(G-16218)
SAFESPAN PLATFORM SYSTEMS INC (PA)
252 Fillmore Ave (14150-2408)
PHONE....................716 694-3332
Fax: 716 694-1100
Lambros Aposto, *CEO*
Davy Passucci, *Vice Pres*
Dimitris Oktapodas, *Admin Sec*
▲ **EMP:** 60
SQ FT: 6,400
SALES (est): 20.4MM **Privately Held**
SIC: 3446 1799 Architectural metalwork; scaffolds, mobile or stationary: metal; rigging & scaffolding; scaffolding construction

(G-16219)
SCHWABEL FABRICATING CO INC (PA)
349 Sawyer Ave (14150-7796)
PHONE....................716 876-2086
Fax: 716 876-5042
Gerald Schwabel, *President*
Paul Schwabel, *Vice Pres*
Janice Malburg, *Office Mgr*
Dave Purcell, *Director*
William Schwabel, *Admin Sec*
EMP: 23
SQ FT: 30,000
SALES (est): 3.1MM **Privately Held**
WEB: www.schwabelfab.com
SIC: 3443 3599 3552 Heat exchangers, plate type; vessels, process or storage (from boiler shops): metal plate; tanks, standard or custom fabricated: metal plate; machine shop, jobbing & repair; textile machinery

(G-16220)
SCIENTIFICS DIRECT INC
532 Main St (14150-3853)
PHONE....................716 773-7500
Paul Gerspach, *Ch of Bd*
Linda Nogle, *General Mgr*
Ann Palka, *Purchasing*
▲ **EMP:** 17 **EST:** 2012
SALES (est): 2.3MM **Privately Held**
SIC: 3229 5049 5961 Scientific glassware; scientific & engineering equipment & supplies; scientific instruments;

(G-16221)
SERVICE FILTRATION CORP
225 E Park Dr (14150-7813)
P.O. Box 963, Buffalo (14240-0963)
PHONE....................716 877-2608
EMP: 30
SALES (corp-wide): 62.5MM **Privately Held**
WEB: www.pacerpumps.com
SIC: 3569 3677 Filters, general line: industrial; filtration devices, electronic
PA: Service Filtration Corp.
  2900 Macarthur Blvd
  Northbrook IL 60062
  847 509-2900

(G-16222)
SNYDER INDUSTRIES INC (PA)
340 Wales Ave (14150-2513)
P.O. Box 586, North Tonawanda (14120-0586)
PHONE....................716 694-1240
Fax: 716 693-4623
Thomas W Snyder, *Ch of Bd*
Thomas Dunch, *Vice Pres*
Charlie Rudolph, *Vice Pres*
Marie Snyder, *Vice Pres*
Bill Snyder, *Plant Mgr*
EMP: 55 **EST:** 1971
SQ FT: 24,000
SALES (est): 14.2MM **Privately Held**
WEB: www.snyderindustriesinc.com
SIC: 3599 Machine shop, jobbing & repair

(G-16223)
SUMITOMO RUBBER USA LLC (HQ)
Also Called: Goodyear
10 Sheridan Dr (14150-7752)
P.O. Box 1109, Buffalo (14240-1109)
PHONE....................716 879-8200
Fax: 716 879-8222
Jennifer Budd, *Regional Mgr*
Timothy Noe, *Senior VP*
William Jackson, *Vice Pres*
Tim Frossell, *Plant Mgr*
Joe Hinkle, *Safety Mgr*
◆ **EMP:** 1190
SQ FT: 14,000
SALES: 350MM
SALES (corp-wide): 6.8B **Privately Held**
WEB: www.gdtna.com
SIC: 3011 Tires & inner tubes
PA: Sumitomo Rubber Industries, Ltd.
  3-6-9, Wakinohamacho, Chuo-Ku
  Kobe HYO 651-0
  782 653-000

(G-16224)
SURE FLOW EQUIPMENT INC
250 Cooper Ave Ste 102 (14150-6633)
P.O. Box 321 (14151-0321)
PHONE....................800 263-8251
John Wordsworth, *President*
EMP: 50
SALES (est): 14MM **Privately Held**
SIC: 3494 5072 Valves & pipe fittings; hardware

(G-16225)
SWIFT RIVER ASSOCIATES INC (PA)
4051 River Rd (14150-6513)
PHONE....................716 875-0902
Kenneth Rawe Sr, *President*
Tony Pariso, *Corp Secy*
Carmen Pariso, *Vice Pres*
Kenneth Rawe Jr, *Vice Pres*
Jessica Toohey, *Sr Consultant*
EMP: 7
SALES (est): 667.3K **Privately Held**
SIC: 2951 Concrete, asphaltic (not from refineries)

(G-16226)
TONAWANDA COKE CORPORATION (PA)
3875 River Rd (14150-6591)
P.O. Box 5007 (14151-5007)
PHONE....................716 876-6222
Fax: 716 876-4400
J D Crane, *CEO*
Ugene Wilkowski, *General Mgr*
Donna Pallas, *Buyer*
Christian Kaderabeck, *QC Mgr*

Ron Hostler, *Engineer*
▲ **EMP:** 100
SQ FT: 150,000
SALES (est): 33.7MM **Privately Held**
WEB: www.tonawandacoke.com
SIC: 3312 Coke produced in chemical recovery coke ovens

(G-16227)
TONAWANDA LIMB & BRACE INC
545 Delaware St (14150-5301)
PHONE....................716 695-1131
Fax: 716 695-0016
Robert Catipovic, *President*
Richard C Catipovic, *Vice Pres*
Nancy Sardina, *Manager*
EMP: 5
SQ FT: 14,000
SALES (est): 659.7K **Privately Held**
SIC: 3842 Prosthetic appliances

(G-16228)
TREEHOUSE PRIVATE BRANDS INC
570 Fillmore Ave (14150-2509)
PHONE....................716 693-4715
EMP: 175
SALES (corp-wide): 6.1B **Publicly Held**
SIC: 2052 Cookies
HQ: Treehouse Private Brands, Inc.
  800 Market St Ste 2600
  Saint Louis MO 63101

(G-16229)
TREYCO PRODUCTS CORP
131 Fillmore Ave (14150-2396)
P.O. Box 866 (14150-0866)
PHONE....................716 693-6525
Duane Manth, *President*
▲ **EMP:** 5 **EST:** 1961
SQ FT: 10,000
SALES (est): 520.8K **Privately Held**
WEB: www.treyco.com
SIC: 3421 Scissors, shears, clippers, snips & similar tools; shears, hand; clippers, fingernail & toenail; snips, tinners'

(G-16230)
UNIFRAX I LLC
Fiberfrax Manufacturing
360 Fire Tower Dr (14150-5893)
PHONE....................716 696-3000
Scott Penman, *Production*
John Di Matteo, *Engineer*
Barbara Chasser, *Personnel*
William Hanley, *CTO*
EMP: 165 **Publicly Held**
WEB: www.insulfrax.com
SIC: 3297 3299 3296 Nonclay refractories; ceramic fiber; mineral wool
HQ: Unifrax I Llc
  600 Rverwalk Pkwy Ste 120
  Tonawanda NY 14150

(G-16231)
UNIFRAX I LLC (HQ)
600 Rverwalk Pkwy Ste 120 (14150)
PHONE....................716 768-6500
Fax: 716 768-6400
David E Brooks, *President*
Kevin J Gorman, *Senior VP*
Joseph Kuchera, *Vice Pres*
Kevin O'Gorman, *Vice Pres*
Dan Fitch, *Facilities Mgr*
▲ **EMP:** 110
SALES (est): 418.1MM **Publicly Held**
WEB: www.insulfrax.com
SIC: 3299 Ceramic fiber

(G-16232)
UOP LLC
175 E Park Dr (14150-7844)
P.O. Box 986 (14151-0986)
PHONE....................716 879-7600
Charles J Schorr, *General Mgr*
EMP: 21
SALES (corp-wide): 39.3B **Publicly Held**
WEB: www.uop.com
SIC: 2819 Catalysts, chemical
HQ: Uop Llc
  25 E Algonquin Rd
  Des Plaines IL 60016
  847 391-2000

▲ = Import ▼ = Export
◆ = Import/Export

GEOGRAPHIC SECTION

(G-16233)
VIATRAN CORPORATION (DH)
199 Fire Tower Dr (14150-5813)
PHONE..................716 564-7813
George A Fraas, *CEO*
Kenneth H Brown, *Ch of Bd*
Carol Starck, *Opers Mgr*
Todd Avery, *QC Mgr*
Bill Blazejewski, *Engineer*
EMP: 50 **EST:** 1965
SQ FT: 18,000
SALES (est): 7MM
SALES (corp-wide): 3.7B **Publicly Held**
WEB: www.viatran.com
SIC: 3823 3825 5084 Pressure measurement instruments, industrial; instruments to measure electricity; industrial machinery & equipment

(G-16234)
WASHINGTON MILLS TONAWANDA INC (HQ)
1000 E Niagara St (14150-1306)
PHONE..................716 693-4550
Ronald Campbell, *Chairman*
Kersi Dordi, *Vice Pres*
Armand Ladage, *Vice Pres*
Melvin Dashineau, *QC Dir*
Michael Pagano, *CFO*
▲ **EMP:** 30
SQ FT: 273,000
SALES (est): 47.2MM
SALES (corp-wide): 176.3MM **Privately Held**
WEB: www.exolon.com
SIC: 3291 Abrasive products; aluminum oxide (fused) abrasives; silicon carbide abrasive
PA: Washington Mills Group, Inc.
20 N Main St
North Grafton MA 01536
508 839-6511

(G-16235)
WGB INDUSTRIES INC
233 Fillmore Ave Ste 23 (14150-2316)
PHONE..................716 693-5527
Daniel Woodward, *President*
Daniel R Woodward, *President*
Scott Smith, *Managing Dir*
Renee Gagnon, *Manager*
Erik Woodward, *Manager*
EMP: 16
SQ FT: 6,000
SALES: 2MM **Privately Held**
SIC: 3365 Aluminum foundries

(G-16236)
WOODWARD INDUSTRIES INC
233 Fillmore Ave Ste 23 (14150-2316)
P.O. Box 410 (14151-0410)
PHONE..................716 692-2242
Daniel Woodward, *President*
Linda Higgins, *Office Mgr*
EMP: 16 **EST:** 1953
SQ FT: 18,845
SALES (est): 1.4MM **Privately Held**
WEB: www.woodwardind.com
SIC: 3543 Industrial patterns

(G-16237)
WSF INDUSTRIES INC
7 Hackett Dr (14150-3798)
P.O. Box 400, Buffalo (14217-0400)
PHONE..................716 692-4930
Fax: 716 692-4135
John Hettrick Jr, *CEO*
Gary Fornasiero, *President*
Pat Barrett, *Plant Mgr*
Nancy Warner, *Buyer*
Curtis Smith, *QC Mgr*
EMP: 25 **EST:** 1941
SQ FT: 66,000
SALES: 2.8MM **Privately Held**
WEB: www.wsf-inc.com
SIC: 3443 Autoclaves, industrial

(G-16238)
ZENGER GROUP INC
777 E Park Dr (14150-6708)
PHONE..................716 871-1058
Stephen Zenger, *Ch of Bd*
EMP: 44

SALES (est): 4.1MM
SALES (corp-wide): 18.6MM **Privately Held**
SIC: 2752 Commercial printing, lithographic
PA: Zenger Group Inc.
777 E Park Dr
Tonawanda NY 14150
716 871-1058

Troy
Albany County

(G-16239)
ALBANY NIPPLE AND PIPE MFG
60 Cohoes Ave Ste 100a (12183-1518)
PHONE..................518 270-2162
Fax: 518 270-2169
Robert Moss, *President*
Mark Wentland, *Info Tech Dir*
EMP: 20
SALES (est): 2.7MM **Privately Held**
SIC: 3498 Fabricated pipe & fittings

(G-16240)
CRYSTAL IS INC (HQ)
70 Cohoes Ave Ste 1b (12183-1531)
PHONE..................518 271-7375
Fax: 518 271-7394
Larry Felton, *CEO*
Steven Berger, *President*
Keith Evans, *Vice Pres*
Shwan Gibb, *Vice Pres*
Ben Jamison, *Vice Pres*
EMP: 45
SQ FT: 10,500
SALES (est): 9.9MM
SALES (corp-wide): 16.5B **Privately Held**
WEB: www.crystal-is.com
SIC: 3679 Electronic crystals
PA: Asahi Kasei Corporation
1-105, Kandajimbocho
Chiyoda-Ku TKY 101-0
332 963-000

(G-16241)
HONEYWELL INTERNATIONAL INC
3 Tibbits Ave (12183-1433)
PHONE..................518 270-0200
Gary Andrews, *Purch Mgr*
Patricia Marzinsky, *Finance Mgr*
Twila Harrison, *Human Res Mgr*
Steve Kratz, *Branch Mgr*
Steve Katz, *Manager*
EMP: 80
SALES (corp-wide): 39.3B **Publicly Held**
WEB: www.honeywell.com
SIC: 3052 Air line or air brake hose, rubber or rubberized fabric
PA: Honeywell International Inc.
115 Tabor Rd
Morris Plains NJ 07950
973 455-2000

(G-16242)
KAYS CAPS INC (PA)
65 Arch St (12183-1599)
PHONE..................518 273-6079
Fax: 518 791-8529
Roberta Fine, *Ch of Bd*
EMP: 8
SQ FT: 1,000
SALES (est): 608.1K **Privately Held**
WEB: www.kayscaps.com
SIC: 2353 Uniform hats & caps

(G-16243)
LONG ISLAND PIPE SUPPLY INC
60 Cohoes Ave (12183-1555)
PHONE..................518 270-2159
Fax: 518 270-8384
Bob Moss, *President*
Keith Cowan, *Sales Associate*
EMP: 6
SALES (corp-wide): 59.6MM **Privately Held**
SIC: 3498 Fabricated pipe & fittings
PA: Long Island Pipe Supply Inc
586 Commercial Ave
Garden City NY 11530
516 222-8008

(G-16244)
SEALY MATTRESS CO ALBANY INC
30 Veterans Memorial Dr (12183-1517)
PHONE..................518 880-1600
Fax: 518 880-1600
David J McIlquham, *President*
Gregg Tanis, *Superintendent*
Tony Vivenzio, *Mfg Dir*
Bill Oryell, *Maint Spvr*
Caroline Feester, *Human Res Dir*
EMP: 300
SQ FT: 265,000
SALES (est): 44.5MM
SALES (corp-wide): 3.1B **Publicly Held**
SIC: 2515 Mattresses, innerspring or box spring
HQ: Sealy Mattress Company
1 Office Parkway Rd
Trinity NC 27370
336 861-3500

Troy
Rensselaer County

(G-16245)
A I T COMPUTERS INC
157 Hoosick St (12180-2375)
PHONE..................518 266-9010
Fax: 518 266-9012
Ahmed Ali, *President*
EMP: 3
SQ FT: 2,000
SALES: 1MM **Privately Held**
WEB: www.aitcomputers.com
SIC: 3577 5734 Computer peripheral equipment; computer & software stores

(G-16246)
APPLIED BIOPHYSICS INC
185 Jordan Rd Ste 7 (12180-7611)
PHONE..................518 880-6860
Fax: 518 880-6865
Charles Keese, *President*
Christian Dehnert, *Vice Pres*
Ivar Giaever, *Vice Pres*
Christian Renken, *Vice Pres*
Noreen Coughlin, *Controller*
EMP: 8
SALES: 950K **Privately Held**
WEB: www.biophysics.com
SIC: 3826 Laser scientific & engineering instruments

(G-16247)
APPRENDA INC (PA)
433 River St Fl 4 (12180-2250)
PHONE..................518 383-2130
Fax: 518 533-3898
Sinclair Schuller, *CEO*
Matthew Ammerman, *Vice Pres*
Rakesh Malhotra, *Vice Pres*
Abraham Sultan, *Vice Pres*
Dan Domkowski, *Project Mgr*
EMP: 59 **EST:** 2007
SALES (est): 11.7MM **Privately Held**
SIC: 7372 Prepackaged software

(G-16248)
ARDEX COSMETICS OF AMERICA
744 Pawling Ave (12180-6212)
PHONE..................518 283-6700
Nubar Sukljian, *President*
▲ **EMP:** 20
SQ FT: 250,000
SALES (est): 2.1MM **Privately Held**
SIC: 2844 Cosmetic preparations

(G-16249)
BATTERY ENERGY STORAGE SYSTEMS
Also Called: Besstech
291 River St Ste 318 (12180-3218)
PHONE..................518 256-7029
Bruce Toyama, *Vice Pres*
Brian Butcher,
Benjamin Backes,
Fernando Gomez-Baquero,
Jae Ho Lee,
EMP: 6
SALES (est): 553.5K **Privately Held**
SIC: 3691 Storage batteries

(G-16250)
BROWN PRINTERS OF TROY INC
Also Called: Brown Printing Co
363 5th Ave (12182-3119)
P.O. Box 388 (12182-0388)
PHONE..................518 235-4080
Fax: 518 235-0884
John H Parry III, *President*
Dawn Parry, *Vice Pres*
Patti Kane, *Office Mgr*
EMP: 14
SQ FT: 9,000
SALES (est): 1.5MM **Privately Held**
WEB: www.brownprinters.com
SIC: 2752 Commercial printing, offset

(G-16251)
CHARLES V WEBER MACHINE SHOP
Also Called: Weber's Mach Shop
2 Campbell Ave (12180-6004)
PHONE..................518 272-8033
Fax: 518 272-8034
Charles H Weber, *President*
EMP: 5 **EST:** 1942
SQ FT: 8,800
SALES (est): 603.5K **Privately Held**
SIC: 3599 Machine shop, jobbing & repair

(G-16252)
CHART INC
Also Called: Clever Fellows I
302 10th St (12180-1617)
PHONE..................518 272-3565
Fax: 518 272-3582
Sam Thomas, *CEO*
John Corey, *President*
EMP: 12
SALES (corp-wide): 859.1MM **Publicly Held**
SIC: 3599 3621 3585 Custom machinery; electric motor & generator parts; parts for heating, cooling & refrigerating equipment
HQ: Chart Inc
407 7th St Nw
New Prague MN 56071
952 758-4484

(G-16253)
CHOPPY V M & SONS LLC
Also Called: V M Choppy & Sons
4 Van Buren St (12180-5550)
PHONE..................518 266-1444
Vincent J Choppy, *Purchasing*
Anne F Choppy, *Mng Member*
Vincent M Choppy,
EMP: 30
SQ FT: 35,000
SALES (est): 5.2MM **Privately Held**
WEB: www.vmchoppyandsons.com
SIC: 3444 Sheet metal specialties, not stamped

(G-16254)
COOKIE FACTORY LLC
520 Congress St (12180-4332)
PHONE..................518 268-1060
Fax: 518 268-1063
Chris Alverino,
EMP: 40
SALES (est): 6MM **Privately Held**
SIC: 2052 Cookies

(G-16255)
DEAKON HOMES AND INTERIORS
Also Called: Troy Cabinet Manufacturing Div
16 Industrial Park Rd (12180-6197)
PHONE..................518 271-0342
Diane F Decurtis, *President*
John De Curtis, *General Mgr*
Margo Jordan, *Bookkeeper*
EMP: 15
SQ FT: 7,000
SALES (est): 1.4MM **Privately Held**
WEB: www.troycabinet.com
SIC: 2434 2541 1521 2522 Wood kitchen cabinets; wood partitions & fixtures; general remodeling, single-family houses; office furniture, except wood; wood office furniture; wood household furniture

Troy - Rensselaer County (G-16256)   GEOGRAPHIC SECTION

(G-16256)
DOWD - WITBECK PRINTING CORP
Also Called: SCHENECTADY HERALD PRINTING CO
599 Pawling Ave (12180-5823)
PHONE..................518 274-2421
Toll Free:..........................877 -
Denise Padula, *President*
John E Hupe, *Vice Pres*
Steve Bowes, *Production*
Chip Kress, *Sales Staff*
Colleen Mooney, *Marketing Staff*
EMP: 18
SQ FT: 10,200
SALES: 2.3MM **Privately Held**
WEB: www.alchar.com
SIC: 2752 2796 2791 2789 Commercial printing, offset; platemaking services; typesetting; bookbinding & related work; commercial art & graphic design

(G-16257)
FLOAT TECH INC
216 River St Ste 1 (12180-3848)
PHONE..................518 266-0964
Cecilia Domingos, *President*
Harald Warelius, *Managing Dir*
EMP: 6
SALES (est): 480K **Privately Held**
SIC: 2385 Waterproof outerwear

(G-16258)
GEORGE M DUJACK
Also Called: Du Serv Development Co
80 Town Office Rd (12180-8817)
PHONE..................518 279-1303
George M Dujack, *Owner*
EMP: 5 **EST:** 1973
SALES: 400K **Privately Held**
SIC: 2821 Silicone resins

(G-16259)
GURLEY PRECISION INSTRS INC
514 Fulton St (12180-3315)
PHONE..................518 272-6300
O Patrick Brady, *Ch of Bd*
Rick Evans, *Vice Pres*
Yuiry Benderskiy, *Mfg Dir*
Tom Reed, *Safety Mgr*
Shish Arya, *Engineer*
EMP: 105
SQ FT: 78,000
SALES (est): 27MM **Privately Held**
WEB: www.gurley.com
SIC: 3827 3824 3829 3823 Optical instruments & lenses; water meters; physical property testing equipment; industrial instrmnts msrmnt display/control process variable; semiconductors & related devices; radio & TV communications equipment

(G-16260)
HAMILTON PRINTING COMPANY INC
22 Hamilton Ave (12180-7863)
PHONE..................518 732-2161
Fax: 518 732-7714
John Paeglow, *CEO*
William Greenawalt, *Vice Pres*
Brian F Payne, *Vice Pres*
Mike Hart, *VP Finance*
▲ **EMP:** 140 **EST:** 1912
SQ FT: 100,000
SALES (est): 16.9MM **Privately Held**
WEB: www.hamprint.com
SIC: 2732 2789 Books: printing & binding; binding only: books, pamphlets, magazines, etc.

(G-16261)
HOFFMANS TRADE GROUP LLC
64 2nd St (12180-3927)
PHONE..................518 250-5556
Gael Coakley,
▼ **EMP:** 6
SALES (est): 680K **Privately Held**
SIC: 3255 Plastic refractories

(G-16262)
INDUSTRIAL TOOL & DIE CO INC
14 Industrial Park Rd (12180-6197)
PHONE..................518 273-7383
Paul V Cacciotti, *President*
Loretta Williams, *Finance Mgr*
Denise Blaire, *Office Mgr*
▲ **EMP:** 14
SQ FT: 17,000
SALES (est): 1.4MM **Privately Held**
SIC: 3544 Special dies, tools, jigs & fixtures

(G-16263)
INTERNTNAL ELCTRONIC MCHS CORP
Also Called: I E M
850 River St (12180-1239)
PHONE..................518 268-1636
Zack Mian, *President*
Peter Hayes, *Engineer*
Bill Peabody, *Design Engr*
Valerie Alexander, *Manager*
Robert Foss, *Manager*
◆ **EMP:** 29
SQ FT: 35,000
SALES: 5MM **Privately Held**
WEB: www.iem.net
SIC: 3825 8711 Instruments to measure electricity; engineering services

(G-16264)
MATERIALS RECOVERY COMPANY
8000 Main St (12180-5963)
P.O. Box 11150, Albany (12211-0150)
PHONE..................518 274-3681
Fax: 518 274-3976
James Ricardi, *Owner*
Marc Perez, *Manager*
▼ **EMP:** 16
SALES (est): 1.4MM **Privately Held**
WEB: www.mrecovery.com
SIC: 3559 Recycling machinery

(G-16265)
NEXT ADVANCE INC (PA)
2113 Ny 7 (12180-9188)
PHONE..................518 674-3510
Ian Glasgow, *President*
EMP: 15
SALES (est): 212.3K **Privately Held**
WEB: www.nextadvance.com
SIC: 3821 Clinical laboratory instruments, except medical & dental

(G-16266)
NIBBLE INC BAKING CO
451 Broadway Apt 5 (12180-3355)
PHONE..................518 334-3950
EMP: 8
SALES (est): 475K **Privately Held**
SIC: 2051 Bread, cake & related products

(G-16267)
NORTHEAST PALLET & CONT CO INC
1 Mann Ave Bldg 300 (12180-5547)
PHONE..................518 271-0535
James F Price, *President*
EMP: 16
SQ FT: 18,000
SALES (est): 1.4MM **Privately Held**
SIC: 2449 2448 Rectangular boxes & crates, wood; pallets, wood

(G-16268)
OLD WORLD PROVISIONS INC (PA)
12 Industrial Park Rd (12180-6197)
PHONE..................518 465-7307
Mark Shuket, *Ch of Bd*
EMP: 63
SALES: 25MM **Privately Held**
SIC: 2011 Meat packing plants

(G-16269)
PB MAPINFO CORPORATION
1 Global Vw (12180-8371)
PHONE..................518 285-6000
Murray Martin, *CEO*
John E O'Hara, *Ch of Bd*
Michael J Hickey, *COO*
Brian Lants, *Senior VP*
Barret Johnson, *Vice Pres*
EMP: 903
SQ FT: 150,000
SALES (est): 668.1K
SALES (corp-wide): 3.4B **Publicly Held**
WEB: www.mapinfo.com
SIC: 7372 Business oriented computer software
PA: Pitney Bowes Inc.
    3001 Summer St Ste 3
    Stamford CT 06905
    203 356-5000

(G-16270)
PERROTTAS BAKERY INC
766 Pawling Ave (12180-6294)
PHONE..................518 283-4711
Charles A Perrotta, *President*
Louis Perrotta, *Corp Secy*
EMP: 9 **EST:** 1962
SQ FT: 5,000
SALES (est): 925.9K **Privately Held**
SIC: 2051 5461 Bakery: wholesale or wholesale/retail combined; bakeries

(G-16271)
PITNEY BOWES INC
350 Jordan Rd Ste 1 (12180-8358)
PHONE..................518 283-0345
Bob Weber, *Division VP*
Jim Gully, *Branch Mgr*
EMP: 130
SALES (corp-wide): 3.4B **Publicly Held**
SIC: 3579 Mailing machines
PA: Pitney Bowes Inc.
    3001 Summer St Ste 3
    Stamford CT 06905
    203 356-5000

(G-16272)
PITNEY BOWES SOFTWARE INC
Also Called: Thompson Group
350 Jordan Rd Ste 1 (12180-8358)
PHONE..................518 272-0014
John Hobson, *General Mgr*
Michael Cooper, *General Mgr*
Nathan Lobban, *Accounting Dir*
Alex Yamane, *Info Tech Mgr*
EMP: 14
SALES (corp-wide): 3.4B **Publicly Held**
WEB: www.mapinfo.com
SIC: 7372 7371 Business oriented computer software; computer software development & applications
HQ: Pitney Bowes Software Inc.
    27 Waterview Dr
    Shelton CT 06484
    855 839-5119

(G-16273)
PLACID BAKER
250 Broadway (12180-3235)
PHONE..................518 326-2657
Margaret Obert, *Principal*
EMP: 8
SALES (est): 588.5K **Privately Held**
SIC: 2051 Cakes, bakery: except frozen

(G-16274)
RAITH AMERICA INC
Also Called: Vistec Lithography
300 Jordan Rd (12180-8346)
PHONE..................518 874-3000
Rainer Schmid, *Branch Mgr*
EMP: 33
SALES (corp-wide): 25MM **Privately Held**
SIC: 2752 Color lithography
PA: Raith America, Inc.
    1377 Long Iisland Motor P Ste 101
    Islandia NY 11749
    518 874-3020

(G-16275)
ROSS VALVE MFG
75 102nd St (12180-1125)
PHONE..................518 274-0961
EMP: 7
SALES (est): 672.9K **Privately Held**
SIC: 3494 Valves & pipe fittings

(G-16276)
S/N PRECISION ENTERPRISES INC
Also Called: Pacamor/Kubar Bearings
145 Jordan Rd Ste 1 (12180-8390)
PHONE..................518 283-8002
Augustine J Sperrazza Jr, *CEO*
Edward Osta, *Exec VP*
Steve Angrisano, *Controller*
Chris Lake, *Manager*
EMP: 45
SQ FT: 13,250
SALES (est): 9.9MM **Privately Held**
WEB: www.pacamor.com
SIC: 3562 Ball bearings & parts

(G-16277)
SCRIVEN DUPLICATING SERVICE
Also Called: Scriven Press
100 Eastover Rd (12182-1108)
PHONE..................518 233-8180
Fax: 518 233-8780
Kevin Rafferty, *President*
Brian Rafferty, *Vice Pres*
EMP: 6
SQ FT: 4,800
SALES: 750K **Privately Held**
SIC: 2752 Photo-offset printing

(G-16278)
SIGN STUDIO INC
1 Ingalls Ave (12180-1220)
PHONE..................518 266-0877
Ronald Levesque, *CEO*
Jazmin Low, *Executive Asst*
EMP: 12
SQ FT: 2,500
SALES (est): 1.1MM **Privately Held**
SIC: 3993 Signs & advertising specialties

(G-16279)
SILVER GRIFFIN INC
691 Hoosick Rd (12180-8818)
PHONE..................518 272-7771
Fax: 518 272-7773
Paul Noonan, *President*
Geoff Scarchilli, *Graphic Designe*
EMP: 15
SALES (est): 1.2MM **Privately Held**
SIC: 2759 7299 7334 Commercial printing; wedding chapel, privately operated; ; photocopying & duplicating services

(G-16280)
STANDARD MANUFACTURING CO INC (PA)
Also Called: Sportsmaster Apparel
750 2nd Ave (12182-2290)
P.O. Box 380 (12182-0380)
PHONE..................518 235-2200
Fax: 518 235-2668
George Arakelian, *CEO*
Dorothy King, *Corp Secy*
Christian Arakelian, *Vice Pres*
Thomas Thalmann, *Controller*
George Bean, *Info Tech Mgr*
▲ **EMP:** 65
SQ FT: 250,000
SALES (est): 8.9MM **Privately Held**
SIC: 2337 2339 2329 Jackets & vests, except fur & leather: women's; women's & misses' outerwear; jackets (suede, leatherette, etc.), sport: men's & boys'; men's & boys' leather, wool & down-filled outerwear

(G-16281)
SUNWARD ELECTRONICS INC
Also Called: Dog Guard
258 Broadway Ste 2a (12180-3235)
Rural Route 258 Broadw (12180)
PHONE..................518 687-0030
Fax: 518 687-0037
Rose Watkins, *President*
William Drew, *General Mgr*
Richard Dawson, *Marketing Staff*
EMP: 11
SQ FT: 5,000
SALES (est): 1.8MM **Privately Held**
WEB: www.teacherspetproducts.com
SIC: 3496 3612 Fencing, made from purchased wire; transformers, except electric

(G-16282)
TROY BOILER WORKS INC
2800 7th Ave (12180-1587)
PHONE..................518 274-2650
Fax: 518 274-5454
Louis E Okonski, *President*
John E Okonski Sr, *President*
Brian Maxwell, *General Mgr*
Richard Okonski, *Corp Secy*
Kenneth Erskin, *Manager*

GEOGRAPHIC SECTION

Tuxedo Park - Orange County (G-16307)

EMP: 50 **EST:** 1863
SQ FT: 25,000
SALES (est): 14.6MM **Privately Held**
WEB: www.troyboilerworks.com
SIC: 3443 7699 Vessels, process or storage (from boiler shops): metal plate; tanks, standard or custom fabricated: metal plate; boiler & boiler shop work; boiler repair shop

(G-16283)
VICARIOUS VISIONS INC
350 Jordan Rd (12180-8352)
PHONE 518 283-4090
Karthik Bala, *CEO*
Guha Bala, *President*
Steve Derrick, *Manager*
EMP: 60
SQ FT: 5,751
SALES (est): 3MM
SALES (corp-wide): 6.6B **Publicly Held**
WEB: www.vvisions.com
SIC: 7372 Prepackaged software
PA: Activision Blizzard, Inc.
3100 Ocean Park Blvd
Santa Monica CA 90405
310 255-2000

(G-16284)
VISTEC LITHOGRAPHY INC
300 Jordan Rd (12180-8346)
PHONE 518 874-3184
Ken Diekroeger, *President*
Susan Adams, *Manager*
Steve Casella, *Info Tech Mgr*
EMP: 15
SALES (est): 1.5MM **Privately Held**
WEB: www.visteclithography.com
SIC: 3674 Semiconductors & related devices

(G-16285)
VITA RARA INC
Also Called: Enable Labs
415 River St Ste 4 (12180-2834)
PHONE 518 369-7356
Mark Menard, *President*
John Fitzpatrick, *Opers Staff*
Patrick McConnell, *Software Engr*
Jonathan Chapman, *Software Dev*
EMP: 5
SALES (est): 750K **Privately Held**
WEB: www.vitarara.net
SIC: 7372 Business oriented computer software

(G-16286)
VITAL VIO INC
185 Jordan Rd Ste 1 (12180-7611)
PHONE 914 245-6048
Colleen Costello, *CEO*
EMP: 10
SALES (est): 245.6K **Privately Held**
SIC: 3646 7342 Commercial indusl & institutional electric lighting fixtures; disinfecting services

(G-16287)
WANT-AD DIGEST INC
Also Called: Classified Advertising
870 Hoosick Rd Ste 1 (12180-6622)
PHONE 518 279-1181
Fax: 518 279-1991
William Engelke, *President*
Rose Engelke, *Vice Pres*
Paul Engelke, *Office Mgr*
Rose Hastings, *Director*
EMP: 18
SQ FT: 2,000
SALES (est): 175.4K **Privately Held**
WEB: www.wantaddigest.com
SIC: 2741 5521 Directories: publishing & printing; used car dealers

(G-16288)
WEIGHING & SYSTEMS TECH INC
274 2nd St (12180-4616)
PHONE 518 274-2797
EMP: 7
SALES (corp-wide): 695K **Privately Held**
SIC: 3596 Mfg Scales/Balances-Nonlaboratory

PA: Weighing & Systems Technology, Inc.
4558 Morgan Pl
Liverpool NY 13090
315 451-7940

(G-16289)
WELDCOMPUTER CORPORATION
105 Jordan Rd Ste 1 (12180-7612)
PHONE 518 283-2897
Fax: 518 283-2907
Robert Cohen, *President*
Dr Keith Strain, *Vice Pres*
Lisa Matter, *Manager*
EMP: 13
SQ FT: 4,000
SALES: 1.5MM **Privately Held**
WEB: www.weldcomputer.com
SIC: 3625 Control equipment, electric

Trumansburg
Tompkins County

(G-16290)
FLO-TECH ORTHOTIC & PROSTHETIC
7325 Halseyville Rd (14886)
P.O. Box 462 (14886-0462)
PHONE 607 387-3070
Fax: 607 387-3176
Robert N Brown Sr, *CEO*
Kathleen Brown, *President*
EMP: 8
SALES (est): 900K **Privately Held**
WEB: www.1800flo-tech.com
SIC: 3842 Prosthetic appliances

(G-16291)
FORCE DYNAMICS INC
4995 Voorhies Rd (14886-9435)
PHONE 607 546-5023
Micheal D Wiernicki, *Principal*
EMP: 19
SALES (est): 2.4MM **Privately Held**
WEB: www.force-dynamics.com
SIC: 3559 Special industry machinery

(G-16292)
WASHBURN MANUFACTURING TECH
9828 State Route 96 (14886-9327)
PHONE 607 387-3991
Thomas Washburn, *President*
EMP: 8
SQ FT: 2,000
SALES: 1MM **Privately Held**
SIC: 3599 Custom machinery

Tuckahoe
Westchester County

(G-16293)
AUTOMTIVE UPHL CNVERTIBLE TOPS
170 Marbledale Rd (10707-3118)
PHONE 914 961-4242
Fax: 914 961-5155
Frank Ackermann, *President*
Ron Ackermann, *Vice Pres*
EMP: 5
SQ FT: 5,000
SALES (est): 370K **Privately Held**
SIC: 2394 2399 Convertible tops, canvas or boat: from purchased materials; automotive covers, except seat & tire covers

(G-16294)
GLOBAL FOOD SOURCE & CO INC
114 Carpenter Ave (10707-2104)
PHONE 914 320-9615
Albert J Savarese, *President*
Teresa Belvedere, *Vice Pres*
▲ **EMP:** 4
SALES (est): 5MM **Privately Held**
SIC: 2032 Canned specialties

(G-16295)
MEDI-RAY INC
150 Marbledale Rd (10707-3197)
PHONE 877 898-3003
Fax: 914 337-4620
Ralph F Farella, *President*
Barry N Dansky, *Treasurer*
Diane Smith, *Manager*
▲ **EMP:** 63
SQ FT: 23,000
SALES (est): 11.5MM **Privately Held**
WEB: www.mediray.com
SIC: 3412 3842 5063 7623 Metal barrels, drums & pails; orthopedic appliances; electrical apparatus & equipment; refrigeration service & repair; nonferrous foundries; nonferrous rolling & drawing

(G-16296)
STOFFEL POLYGON SYSTEMS INC
199 Marbledale Rd (10707-3117)
PHONE 914 961-2000
Fax: 914 961-7231
John F Stoffel, *President*
Arlene M Gruber, *Admin Sec*
Reda Riad, *Administration*
EMP: 10
SQ FT: 22,180
SALES (est): 1.2MM **Privately Held**
WEB: www.stoffelpolygon.com
SIC: 3462 Iron & steel forgings

Tully
Onondaga County

(G-16297)
APPLIED CONCEPTS INC
397 State Route 281 (13159-2486)
P.O. Box 1175 (13159-1175)
PHONE 315 696-6676
Fax: 315 696-9923
Kurt Shaffer, *CEO*
Stephen C Soos, *President*
Brian Poole, *Purch Mgr*
Jim Canale, *Engineer*
Lucas Zimmerman, *Design Engr*
EMP: 28
SQ FT: 16,000
SALES (est): 5.2MM **Privately Held**
WEB: www.acipower.com
SIC: 3679 Power supplies, all types: static

(G-16298)
BARBER & DELINE ENRGY SVCS LLC
10 Community Dr (13159)
PHONE 315 696-8961
Eva Deline, *Mng Member*
EMP: 10
SALES (est): 674.7K **Privately Held**
SIC: 1381 1389 Drilling oil & gas wells; drilling water intake wells; service well drilling; spudding in oil & gas wells; construction, repair & dismantling services

(G-16299)
BARBER & DELINE LLC
995 State Route 11a (13159-2426)
PHONE 607 749-2619
Frank Lap, *Manager*
Eva Deline,
EMP: 10
SQ FT: 3,000
SALES (est): 2.5MM **Privately Held**
WEB: www.barber-deline.com
SIC: 1381 1781 Drilling oil & gas wells; water well drilling

Tupper Lake
Franklin County

(G-16300)
LIZOTTE LOGGING INC
50 Haymeadow Rd (12986-1069)
PHONE 518 359-2200
Fax: 518 359-9253
Jeannel Lizotte, *President*
Cynthia Lizotte, *Admin Sec*
EMP: 15

SALES (est): 2MM **Privately Held**
SIC: 2411 Logging camps & contractors

(G-16301)
MITCHELL STONE PRODUCTS LLC
161 Main St (12986-1023)
Rural Route 15 (12986)
PHONE 518 359-7029
Paul Mitchell, *Principal*
EMP: 6
SALES (est): 152.7K **Privately Held**
SIC: 1442 Construction sand & gravel

(G-16302)
PAUL J MITCHELL LOGGING INC
15 Mitchell Ln (12986-1056)
PHONE 518 359-7029
Fax: 518 359-3707
Paul J Mitchell, *President*
Mary Michell, *Admin Sec*
EMP: 26
SQ FT: 7,000
SALES (est): 3.6MM **Privately Held**
SIC: 2411 Logging camps & contractors

(G-16303)
RICHARDS LOGGING LLC
201 State Route 3 (12986-7705)
PHONE 518 359-2775
Fax: 518 359-2779
Bruce Richards, *Mng Member*
Lawrence Richards,
EMP: 15
SALES (est): 2.3MM **Privately Held**
SIC: 2411 Logging camps & contractors

(G-16304)
TRILAKE THREE PRESS CORP
136 Park St (12986-1818)
PHONE 518 359-2462
Dan McClelland, *President*
Judy McClelland, *Vice Pres*
Chantel Skiff, *Advt Staff*
John Morris, *Director*
EMP: 6
SQ FT: 3,500
SALES (est): 340K **Privately Held**
SIC: 2711 Newspapers, publishing & printing

(G-16305)
TUPPER LAKE HARDWOODS INC
167 Pitchfork Pond Rd (12986-1047)
P.O. Box 748 (12986-0748)
PHONE 518 359-8248
Fax: 518 259-8337
Greg Paneaudeau, *President*
Robert Gibeault, *General Mgr*
EMP: 32 **EST:** 1994
SQ FT: 21,356
SALES (est): 3.8MM **Privately Held**
SIC: 2421 2426 Sawmills & planing mills, general; hardwood dimension & flooring mills

Tuxedo Park
Orange County

(G-16306)
I & I SYSTEMS
66 Table Rock Rd (10987-4720)
PHONE 845 753-9126
Shan Custello, *President*
EMP: 7
SALES (est): 701.6K **Privately Held**
SIC: 3953 Letters (marking devices), metal

(G-16307)
INTERNATIONAL PAPER COMPANY
1422 Long Meadow Rd (10987-3500)
PHONE 845 986-6409
Fax: 845 577-7307
Virginia Rizzo, *Manager*
Donald G Scott, *Systems Mgr*
David Eurich, *Gnrl Med Prac*
EMP: 140

Ulster Park - Ulster County (G-16308)

GEOGRAPHIC SECTION

SALES (corp-wide): 21B **Publicly Held**
WEB: www.internationalpaper.com
SIC: 2621 8731 Paper mills; commercial physical research
PA: International Paper Company
6400 Poplar Ave
Memphis TN 38197
901 419-9000

Ulster Park
Ulster County

(G-16308)
DYNO NOBEL INC
161 Ulster Ave (12487-5019)
PHONE.....................845 338-2144
Margie Seeger, *Production*
Margaret Seeger, *Opers-Prdtn-Mfg*
Frank Knapp, *Purchasing*
Tom Gaffney, *Human Res Dir*
Fred Jardinico, *Manager*
EMP: 55
SALES (corp-wide): 2.5B **Privately Held**
SIC: 2892 3489 Explosives; ordnance & accessories
HQ: Dyno Nobel Inc.
2795 E Cottonwood Pkwy # 500
Salt Lake City UT 84121
801 364-4800

(G-16309)
MORESCA CLOTHING AND COSTUME
361 Union Center Rd (12487-5232)
PHONE.....................845 331-6012
Lena Dun, *President*
EMP: 10
SQ FT: 11,000
SALES (est): 1.4MM **Privately Held**
WEB: www.moresca.com
SIC: 2389 5699 5136 5137 Costumes; costumes, masquerade or theatrical; men's & boys' clothing; women's & children's clothing

Unadilla
Otsego County

(G-16310)
AMES COMPANIES INC
196 Clifton St (13849-2418)
P.O. Box 644 (13849-0644)
PHONE.....................607 369-9595
Fax: 607 369-9595
Jay Gerber, *Controller*
Alexander Miller, *Branch Mgr*
EMP: 61
SQ FT: 25,000
SALES (corp-wide): 2B **Publicly Held**
WEB: www.ames.com
SIC: 3423 Garden & farm tools, including shovels
HQ: The Ames Companies Inc
465 Railroad Ave
Camp Hill PA 17011
717 737-1500

Uniondale
Nassau County

(G-16311)
AITHACA CHEMICAL CORP
50 Charles Lindbergh Blvd # 400 (11553-3600)
PHONE.....................516 229-2330
Fax: 516 229-2350
Eric Kastens, *President*
EMP: 10
SQ FT: 300
SALES: 1.3MM **Privately Held**
WEB: www.aithaca.com
SIC: 2819 5169 Chemicals, high purity: refined from technical grade; chemicals & allied products

(G-16312)
CAMBRIDGE WHOS WHO PUBG INC (PA)
498 Rxr Plz Fl 4 (11556-0400)
PHONE.....................516 833-8440
Mitchel Robbins, *CEO*
Randy Narod, *President*
Eric Lee, *COO*
Awilda Cruz, *Engineer*
Ken Ampel, *Account Dir*
EMP: 45
SALES (est): 20.3MM **Privately Held**
SIC: 2741 8748 Miscellaneous publishing; business consulting

(G-16313)
COTY US LLC
726 Eab Plz (11556-0726)
PHONE.....................212 389-7000
Rich Garzon, *Branch Mgr*
EMP: 284 **Publicly Held**
SIC: 2844 Perfumes & colognes; cosmetic preparations
HQ: Coty Us Llc
350 5th Ave
New York NY 10118
212 389-7000

(G-16314)
ELIZABETH WILSON
Also Called: Elizabeth's
579 Edgemere Ave (11553-2517)
PHONE.....................516 486-2157
Elizabeth Wilson, *Owner*
EMP: 4
SQ FT: 1,200
SALES (est): 2.2MM **Privately Held**
WEB: www.elizabethwilson.com
SIC: 2339 Aprons, except rubber or plastic: women's, misses', juniors'

(G-16315)
FEI COMMUNICATIONS INC
55 Charles Lindbergh Blvd (11553-3689)
PHONE.....................516 794-4500
Martin B Bloch, *President*
Harry Newman, *VP Finance*
EMP: 180
SALES (est): 27.8MM
SALES (corp-wide): 60.3MM **Publicly Held**
WEB: www.freqelec.com
SIC: 3679 Electronic circuits
PA: Frequency Electronics, Inc.
55 Charles Lindbergh Blvd # 2
Uniondale NY 11553
516 794-4500

(G-16316)
FEI-ZYFER INC
55 Charles Lindbergh Blvd (11553-3689)
PHONE.....................714 933-4045
EMP: 8
SALES (corp-wide): 60.3MM **Publicly Held**
SIC: 3663 Antennas, transmitting & communications
HQ: Fei-Zyfer, Inc.
7321 Lincoln Way
Garden Grove CA 92841
714 933-4000

(G-16317)
FREQUENCY ELECTRONICS INC (PA)
55 Charles Lindbergh Blvd # 2 (11553-3699)
PHONE.....................516 794-4500
Fax: 516 794-4340
Joel Girsky, *Ch of Bd*
Martin B Bloch, *President*
James Davis, *President*
Steven Strang, *President*
Stanton Sloane, *COO*
EMP: 390 **EST:** 1961
SALES: 50.3MM **Publicly Held**
WEB: www.freqelec.com
SIC: 3825 3812 3669 3679 Elapsed time meters, electronic; frequency meters: electrical, mechanical & electronic; search & detection systems & instruments; detection apparatus: electronic/magnetic field, light/heat; intercommunication systems, electric; microwave components

(G-16318)
HEARST BUSINESS MEDIA (HQ)
Also Called: F C W Division
50 Charles Lindbergh Blvd # 100 (11553-3600)
PHONE.....................516 227-1300
Rich Malloch, *CEO*
Kathy Chacana, *VP Human Res*
Carolyn Giroux, *Technology*
EMP: 63
SALES (est): 10.1MM
SALES (corp-wide): 6.4B **Privately Held**
SIC: 2721 2741 Magazines: publishing only, not printed on site; directories: publishing only, not printed on site
PA: The Hearst Corporation
300 W 57th St Fl 42
New York NY 10019
212 649-2000

(G-16319)
JPM AND ASSOCIATES
639 Nostrand Ave (11553-3026)
PHONE.....................516 483-4699
Sterling Michel, *Vice Pres*
EMP: 10
SALES (est): 860K **Privately Held**
SIC: 7372 Application computer software

(G-16320)
LOCKHEED MARTIN CORPORATION
55 Charles Lindbergh Blvd # 1 (11553-3682)
PHONE.....................516 228-2000
Fax: 516 228-3035
Michael Stein, *General Mgr*
John Piccirillo, *Managing Dir*
Hugh Rice, *Research*
Joseph Cappiello, *Engineer*
Michael Chen, *Engineer*
EMP: 225 **Publicly Held**
WEB: www.lockheedmartin.com
SIC: 3571 Electronic computers
PA: Lockheed Martin Corporation
6801 Rockledge Dr
Bethesda MD 20817

(G-16321)
MERCHANT SERVICE PYMNT ACCESS ◆
626 Rxr Plz (11556-0626)
PHONE.....................212 561-5516
Sean Ellis, *President*
EMP: 5 **EST:** 2017
SALES: 10MM **Privately Held**
SIC: 3578 Calculating & accounting equipment

(G-16322)
SOLAR THIN FILMS INC (PA)
Also Called: Stf
1136 Rxr Plz (11556-1100)
PHONE.....................516 341-7787
Jim Solano, *CEO*
James J Solano Jr, *CEO*
▲ **EMP:** 16
SALES (est): 3.6MM **Publicly Held**
SIC: 3674 Photovoltaic devices, solid state

(G-16323)
TDK USA CORPORATION (HQ)
455 Rxr Plz (11556-3811)
PHONE.....................516 535-2600
Francis J Sweeney Jr, *Ch of Bd*
Susan Sparks, *Vice Pres*
Iesha Brown, *Administration*
◆ **EMP:** 68
SQ FT: 60,000
SALES (est): 213.7MM
SALES (corp-wide): 10.3B **Privately Held**
SIC: 3679 8741 Recording & playback apparatus, including phonograph; administrative management; financial management for business
PA: Tdk Corporation
3-9-1, Shibaura
Minato-Ku TKY 108-0
368 527-300

(G-16324)
UCR STEEL GROUP LLC (PA)
405 Rxr Plz (11556-3811)
PHONE.....................718 764-3414
Tomas Cruze, *Vice Pres*

Charlie Starce, *Mng Member*
Justin Schire, *General Counsel*
EMP: 15
SQ FT: 33,000
SALES (est): 4.5MM **Privately Held**
SIC: 3444 Sheet metalwork

(G-16325)
VALLE SIGNS AND AWNINGS
889 Nassau Rd (11553-3131)
PHONE.....................516 408-3440
Fax: 516 408-3441
Oscar Valle, *Owner*
Neal McLendon, *CFO*
EMP: 10
SALES (est): 929.1K **Privately Held**
SIC: 3993 Signs & advertising specialties

Unionville
Orange County

(G-16326)
ROYAL FIREWORKS PRINTING CO
First Ave (10988)
PHONE.....................845 726-3333
Thomas Kemnitz, *President*
EMP: 13
SQ FT: 66,000
SALES (est): 1.8MM **Privately Held**
SIC: 2732 5942 Book printing; book stores

Upper Jay
Essex County

(G-16327)
AMSTUTZE WOODWORKING (PA)
246 Springfield Rd (12987-3200)
PHONE.....................518 946-8206
Steve Amstutz, *Principal*
EMP: 5
SALES (est): 456.5K **Privately Held**
SIC: 2431 Millwork

Utica
Oneida County

(G-16328)
A&P MASTER IMAGES LLC
205 Water St (13502-3101)
PHONE.....................315 793-1934
Amanda L Potter,
Howard A Potter,
EMP: 15
SALES (est): 428.3K **Privately Held**
SIC: 2759 Promotional printing

(G-16329)
ADVANCE ENERGY SYSTEMS NY LLC
17 Tilton Rd (13501-6411)
PHONE.....................315 735-5125
Duane Farr, *President*
EMP: 5
SALES (est): 649.2K **Privately Held**
SIC: 3699 High-energy particle physics equipment

(G-16330)
AEROMED INC
1821 Broad St Ste 1 (13501-1115)
P.O. Box 768, Amsterdam (12010-0768)
PHONE.....................518 843-9144
William E Palmer, *President*
EMP: 5
SALES (est): 721.5K **Privately Held**
WEB: www.aeromed.com
SIC: 3564 Air purification equipment

(G-16331)
AUSTIN MOHAWK AND COMPANY LLC
2175 Beechgrove Pl (13501-1705)
PHONE.....................315 793-3000
Hayes Barnard, *General Mgr*
John B Millet, *Plant Mgr*

GEOGRAPHIC SECTION

Utica - Oneida County (G-16355)

Ted Flint, *Safety Mgr*
Richard Davies, *Controller*
Richard Davis, *Controller*
▲ **EMP:** 29
SQ FT: 20,000
SALES: 5.5MM **Privately Held**
WEB: www.austinmohawk.com
SIC: 3448 3444 Prefabricated metal buildings; canopies, sheet metal

(G-16332)
BAGEL GROVE INC
7 Burrstone Rd (13502-5405)
PHONE...............................315 724-8015
Anne Wadsworth, *President*
Maggie McCarty, *Manager*
EMP: 25
SQ FT: 2,600
SALES: 450K **Privately Held**
WEB: www.bagelgrove.com
SIC: 2051 5149 5461 Bagels, fresh or frozen; crackers, cookies & bakery products; bagels

(G-16333)
BRODOCK PRESS INC (PA)
502 Court St Ste G (13502-4233)
PHONE...............................315 735-9577
Fax: 315 624-0597
Craig S Brodock, *Chairman*
Donald Weagley, *Vice Pres*
Dick Phillips, *Plant Mgr*
EMP: 74 **EST:** 1960
SQ FT: 80,000
SALES: 12MM **Privately Held**
WEB: www.brodock.com
SIC: 2759 2752 2791 2789 Letterpress printing; commercial printing, lithographic; typesetting; bookbinding & related work

(G-16334)
CLARA PAPA
Also Called: Kennel Klub
1323 Blandina St 1 (13501-1915)
PHONE...............................315 733-2660
Clara Papa, *Owner*
EMP: 5
SQ FT: 15,000
SALES (est): 237.2K **Privately Held**
SIC: 3999 5199 Pet supplies; pet supplies

(G-16335)
CNY BUSINESS SOLUTIONS
502 Court St Ste 206 (13502-0001)
PHONE...............................315 733-5031
Jennifer Racquet, *President*
Wendy Aiello, *Principal*
EMP: 5
SALES (est): 472.6K **Privately Held**
SIC: 3577 Printers & plotters

(G-16336)
COLLINITE CORPORATION
1520 Lincoln Ave (13502-5200)
PHONE...............................315 732-2282
Fax: 315 732-2816
Michael Taylor, *President*
Chris Curley, *Manager*
Ronald Yoddow, *Manager*
Christine Taylor, *Admin Sec*
EMP: 5 **EST:** 1912
SQ FT: 6,000
SALES (est): 831.5K **Privately Held**
WEB: www.collinite.com
SIC: 2842 5087 5169 5999 Cleaning or polishing preparations; polishing preparations & related products; janitors' supplies; waxes, except petroleum; cleaning equipment & supplies; mail order house

(G-16337)
CONMED ANDOVER MEDICAL INC (HQ)
525 French Rd Ste 3 (13502-5994)
PHONE...............................315 797-8375
Fax: 315 732-5267
Joseph J Corasanti, *CEO*
Paul Sandock, *Sls & Mktg Exec*
EMP: 12
SALES (est): 6.3MM
SALES (corp-wide): 763.5MM **Publicly Held**
SIC: 3845 Electromedical apparatus
PA: Conmed Corporation
525 French Rd
Utica NY 13502
315 797-8375

(G-16338)
CONMED CORPORATION
Endoscopic Technologies Div
525 French Rd (13502-5994)
PHONE...............................315 797-8375
Robert Shaw Jr, *Plant Mgr*
Dennis Werger, *Manager*
Mike Giordano, *IT/INT Sup*
EMP: 83
SALES (corp-wide): 763.5MM **Publicly Held**
SIC: 3845 8731 3841 Electromedical equipment; commercial physical research; surgical & medical instruments
PA: Conmed Corporation
525 French Rd
Utica NY 13502
315 797-8375

(G-16339)
CONMED CORPORATION (PA)
525 French Rd (13502-5994)
PHONE...............................315 797-8375
Fax: 315 797-0321
Mark E Tryniski, *Ch of Bd*
Curt R Hartman, *President*
Patrick J Beyer, *President*
Heather L Cohen, *Exec VP*
Daniel S Jonas, *Exec VP*
◆ **EMP:** 277
SQ FT: 500,000
SALES: 763.5MM **Publicly Held**
SIC: 3845 3841 Electromedical apparatus; electrocardiographs; patient monitoring apparatus; surgical instruments & apparatus; trocars; suction therapy apparatus; probes, surgical

(G-16340)
CRANESVILLE BLOCK CO INC
Also Called: Cranesville Concrete Co
895 Catherine St (13501-1409)
PHONE...............................315 732-2135
Fax: 315 732-8418
John Abdo, *District Mgr*
Mark Smith, *Branch Mgr*
EMP: 25
SQ FT: 3,462
SALES (corp-wide): 45.4MM **Privately Held**
SIC: 3273 Ready-mixed concrete
PA: Cranesville Block Co., Inc.
1250 Riverfront Ctr
Amsterdam NY 12010
518 684-6154

(G-16341)
CRITICAL IMAGING LLC
2428 Chenango Rd (13502-5909)
PHONE...............................315 732-5020
Harold Wood, *Electrical Engi*
Richard Evans,
EMP: 23
SALES (est): 3.9MM **Privately Held**
WEB: www.infraredcomponents.com
SIC: 3861 Cameras, still & motion picture (all types)

(G-16342)
CYBERSPORTS INC (PA)
11 Avery Pl (13502-5401)
PHONE...............................315 737-7150
Todd Hobin, *President*
Candice Hobin, *Vice Pres*
EMP: 7
SALES (est): 726.3K **Privately Held**
WEB: www.cybersportsinc.com
SIC: 7372 Prepackaged software

(G-16343)
DACOBE ENTERPRISES LLC
325 Lafayette St (13502-4228)
PHONE...............................315 368-0093
Geoff Thorp, *President*
EMP: 10
SQ FT: 20,000
SALES: 5MM **Privately Held**
SIC: 3089 Plastic processing

(G-16344)
DARMAN MANUFACTURING CO INC
1410 Lincoln Ave (13502-5019)
PHONE...............................315 724-9632
Fax: 315 724-8099
Pamela Darman, *CEO*
Cynthia J Lane, *Controller*
Gail Yakuboski, *Office Mgr*
James Henrickson, *CTO*
Michael Swiercz, *CTO*
▼ **EMP:** 16 **EST:** 1936
SQ FT: 20,800
SALES: 2MM **Privately Held**
WEB: www.darmanco.com
SIC: 3429 Cabinet hardware

(G-16345)
DEIORIO FOODS INC (PA)
Also Called: De Iorio's Bakery
2200 Bleecker St (13501-1739)
PHONE...............................315 732-7612
Fax: 315 724-6964
Robert J Ragusa, *CEO*
Richard Viti, *President*
Larry Evans, *Vice Pres*
Robert Horth, *Vice Pres*
Scott Hoke, *Facilities Mgr*
EMP: 25 **EST:** 1924
SALES (est): 17.4MM **Privately Held**
WEB: www.deiorios.com
SIC: 2053 Frozen bakery products, except bread

(G-16346)
DICO PRODUCTS CORPORATION
200 Seward Ave (13502-5750)
PHONE...............................315 797-0470
Bradford Lees Divine, *President*
Dan Beligel, *Treasurer*
▲ **EMP:** 15
SALES (est): 1.2MM **Privately Held**
WEB: www.dicoproducts.com
SIC: 3496 3429 3291 2392 Hardware cloth, woven wire; manufactured hardware (general); abrasive products; household furnishings

(G-16347)
DIMANCO INC (PA)
Also Called: Divine Bros
200 Seward Ave (13502-5750)
PHONE...............................315 797-0470
Fax: 315 797-0058
B Lees Divine, *President*
Thomas B Dalton, *COO*
Brian Carpenter, *Plant Mgr*
Mike Plescia, *Purch Mgr*
Thomas Banks, *CFO*
◆ **EMP:** 3
SQ FT: 170,000
SALES (est): 28.4MM **Privately Held**
WEB: www.dimanco.com
SIC: 3291 3562 Buffing or polishing wheels, abrasive or nonabrasive; casters

(G-16348)
DINOS SAUSAGE & MEAT CO INC
722 Catherine St (13501-1304)
PHONE...............................315 732-2661
Fax: 315 732-3094
Anthony Ferrucci, *President*
Carman Bossone, *Manager*
EMP: 11
SQ FT: 6,300
SALES (est): 1.9MM **Privately Held**
SIC: 2013 Sausages & other prepared meats; sausages & related products, from purchased meat; prepared beef products from purchased beef

(G-16349)
DIVA FARMS LTD
1301 Broad St (13501-1605)
PHONE...............................315 735-4397
Margherita Schuller, *President*
EMP: 7
SQ FT: 2,000
SALES: 550K **Privately Held**
SIC: 2099 Seasonings & spices

(G-16350)
DIVINE BROTHERS COMPANY
Also Called: Dico Products
200 Seward Ave (13502-5750)
PHONE...............................315 797-0470
Bradford W Divine, *President*
Charles H Divine, *Vice Pres*
Thomas Banks, *CFO*
Michael Plecia, *Director*
◆ **EMP:** 112 **EST:** 1892
SQ FT: 112,000
SALES: 9.8MM
SALES (corp-wide): 28.4MM **Privately Held**
WEB: www.divinebrothers.com
SIC: 3291 Buffing or polishing wheels, abrasive or nonabrasive
PA: Dimanco Inc.
200 Seward Ave
Utica NY 13502
315 797-0470

(G-16351)
ECR INTERNATIONAL INC (PA)
Also Called: Utica Boilers
2201 Dwyer Ave (13501-1101)
P.O. Box 4729 (13504-4729)
PHONE...............................315 797-1310
Fax: 315 797-3762
Ronald J Passafaro, *President*
Timothy R Reed, *President*
Earle C Reed, *Vice Chairman*
Donald Fedor, *COO*
James Benson, *Vice Pres*
◆ **EMP:** 100 **EST:** 1928
SQ FT: 190,000
SALES (est): 100.9MM **Privately Held**
WEB: www.ecrinternational.com
SIC: 3433 3443 Boilers, low-pressure heating: steam or hot water; fabricated plate work (boiler shop)

(G-16352)
ELG UTICA ALLOYS HOLDINGS INC
91 Wurz Ave (13502-2533)
PHONE...............................315 733-0475
Anthony Moreno, *President*
EMP: 5
SALES (est): 526.1K
SALES (corp-wide): 3.8B **Privately Held**
SIC: 3599 Industrial machinery
HQ: Elg Utica Alloys International Gmbh
Kremerskamp 16
Duisburg
203 450-10

(G-16353)
FALVO MANUFACTURING CO INC
20 Harbor Point Rd (13502-2502)
PHONE...............................315 738-7682
Eugene T Falvo, *President*
EMP: 15
SQ FT: 26,000
SALES (est): 2.3MM **Privately Held**
SIC: 2441 2512 2522 2541 Packing cases, wood: nailed or lock corner; upholstered household furniture; office cabinets & filing drawers: except wood; store fixtures, wood

(G-16354)
FARRINGTON PACKAGING CORP
2007 Beechgrove Pl (13501-1703)
PHONE...............................315 733-4600
Raymond Mele, *President*
Brendan Jenkins, *Vice Pres*
Gerard Morrissey, *Controller*
Kevin Siembab, *Sales Mgr*
Bill Richardson, *Manager*
EMP: 40
SALES (est): 5MM **Privately Held**
SIC: 2631 2541 Packaging board; wood partitions & fixtures

(G-16355)
FEDERAL SHEET METAL WORKS INC
1416 Dudley Ave (13501-4611)
P.O. Box 273 (13503-0273)
PHONE...............................315 735-4730
Fax: 315 735-0729
Leonard A Capuana, *President*

Utica - Oneida County (G-16356)

Michael Capuana, *Treasurer*
EMP: 12
SQ FT: 7,500
SALES: 1.5MM **Privately Held**
SIC: 3444 Sheet metalwork

(G-16356)
FOURTEEN ARNOLD AVE CORP
Also Called: PROGRESS INDUSTRIES SALES
14 Arnold Ave (13502-5602)
PHONE 315 272-1700
Fax: 315 735-4800
Angela Van Derhoof, *President*
Russell Bell, *Manager*
James Coffin, *Business Dir*
EMP: 13
SALES: 312.3K **Privately Held**
SIC: 3565 Packing & wrapping machinery

(G-16357)
G W CANFIELD & SON INC
600 Plant St (13502-4712)
PHONE 315 735-5522
Fax: 315 735-4945
Mark W Canfield, *President*
Anne C Kuhn, *Vice Pres*
Sharyn Woods, *Manager*
EMP: 6
SQ FT: 5,000
SALES (est): 921.4K **Privately Held**
WEB: www.gwcanfield.com
SIC: 2752 Commercial printing, lithographic; commercial printing, offset

(G-16358)
GAMETIME SPORTSWEAR PLUS LLC
1206 Belle Ave (13501-2614)
PHONE 315 724-5893
Michael Macchione,
EMP: 6
SQ FT: 3,200
SALES (est): 460K **Privately Held**
SIC: 2329 5699 Men's & boys' sportswear & athletic clothing; sports apparel

(G-16359)
GATEHOUSE MEDIA LLC
Also Called: Observer Dispatch
350 Willowbrook Office Pa (13501)
PHONE 315 792-5000
Fax: 315 792-4973
Terry Cascioli, *Publisher*
Donna Donnovan, *Principal*
Ben Birnell, *Editor*
Rob Booth, *Editor*
Barbara Laible, *Editor*
EMP: 34
SALES (corp-wide): 1.2B **Publicly Held**
WEB: www.gatehousemedia.com
SIC: 2711 Newspapers
HQ: Gatehouse Media, Llc
   175 Sullys Trl Ste 300
   Pittsford NY 14534
   585 598-0030

(G-16360)
GERMANIUM CORP AMERICA INC
1634 Lincoln Ave (13502-5312)
PHONE 315 732-3744
Bill McOrney, *President*
▲ **EMP:** 5
SALES (est): 433.7K
SALES (corp-wide): 193.5MM **Privately Held**
WEB: www.indium.com
SIC: 3339 Germanium refining (primary)
PA: Indium Corporation Of America
   34 Robinson Rd
   Clinton NY 13323
   800 446-3486

(G-16361)
H F BROWN MACHINE CO INC
708 State St (13502-3458)
PHONE 315 732-6129
James F Chubbuck, *President*
Joseph Chubbuck, *Vice Pres*
George Chubbuck, *Treasurer*
EMP: 10 **EST:** 1946
SQ FT: 26,000
SALES (est): 1.3MM **Privately Held**
SIC: 3599 Machine shop, jobbing & repair

(G-16362)
HPK INDUSTRIES LLC
1208 Broad St (13501-1604)
P.O. Box 4682 (13504-4682)
PHONE 315 724-0196
Fax: 315 724-0197
Mike Liberatore, *Director*
Michael A Liberatore,
▲ **EMP:** 15
SQ FT: 11,000
SALES (est): 1.3MM **Privately Held**
WEB: www.hpkindustries.com
SIC: 2389 5131 Disposable garments & accessories; piece goods & notions

(G-16363)
HUMAN ELECTRONICS INC
155 Genesee St (13501-2105)
PHONE 315 724-9850
Philip Szeliga, *President*
EMP: 5 **EST:** 1999
SQ FT: 16,000
SALES (est): 568K **Privately Held**
WEB: www.humanelectronics.com
SIC: 3571 4813 Electronic computers; telephone communication, except radio

(G-16364)
HUMAN TECHNOLOGIES CORPORATION
Also Called: Graphtex A Div of Htc
2260 Dwyer Ave (13501-1193)
PHONE 315 735-3532
Fax: 315 735-2699
Tom Keller, *Manager*
Richard E Sebastian, *Manager*
Michael Kowiatek, *Info Tech Mgr*
EMP: 10
SQ FT: 7,600
SALES (corp-wide): 17.4MM **Privately Held**
WEB: www.htcorp.net
SIC: 2396 2759 2395 Screen printing on fabric articles; screen printing; embroidery products, except schiffli machine
PA: Human Technologies Corporation
   2260 Dwyer Ave
   Utica NY 13501
   315 724-9891

(G-16365)
IDG LLC
Also Called: Microfoam
31 Faass Ave (13502-3350)
PHONE 315 797-1000
Fax: 315 724-8427
W S Ingersoll, *Corp Comm Staff*
Kevin Sharrow, *Manager*
Steve Bednarz, *Manager*
Scott Ingersoll, *Manager*
Mark Ingersoll, *Director*
EMP: 49
SALES (corp-wide): 255.8MM **Privately Held**
SIC: 3069 Rolls, solid or covered rubber
HQ: Idg, Llc
   1480 Gould Dr
   Cookeville TN 38506
   931 432-4000

(G-16366)
INDIUM CORPORATION OF AMERICA
1676 Lincoln Ave (13502-5398)
PHONE 315 793-8200
Fax: 315 853-1000
Ning Lee, *Vice Pres*
John Sovinsky, *Opers Staff*
David Hu, *Technical Mgr*
Geoff Beckwith, *Engineer*
Larry Schram, *Engineer*
EMP: 30
SQ FT: 31,210
SALES (corp-wide): 193.5MM **Privately Held**
WEB: www.indium.com
SIC: 3356 2899 Solder: wire, bar, acid core, & rosin core; chemical preparations
PA: Indium Corporation Of America
   34 Robinson Rd
   Clinton NY 13323
   800 446-3486

(G-16367)
INDIUM CORPORATION OF AMERICA
111 Business Park Dr (13502-6303)
PHONE 315 381-2330
Anthony Lanza, *Engineer*
EMP: 38
SALES (corp-wide): 193.5MM **Privately Held**
SIC: 3356 Solder: wire, bar, acid core, & rosin core
PA: Indium Corporation Of America
   34 Robinson Rd
   Clinton NY 13323
   800 446-3486

(G-16368)
INFRARED COMPONENTS CORP
2306 Bleecker St (13501-1746)
PHONE 315 732-1544
Thomas Clynne, *President*
Don Darling, *Plant Mgr*
Dick Evans, *Sales Staff*
EMP: 20
SQ FT: 17,000
SALES (est): 3.1MM **Privately Held**
SIC: 3812 Infrared object detection equipment; detection apparatus: electronic/magnetic field, light/heat

(G-16369)
INTERNATIONAL PAPER COMPANY
50 Harbor Point Rd (13502-2502)
PHONE 315 797-5120
Dale Seaton, *Info Tech Mgr*
EMP: 160
SALES (corp-wide): 21B **Publicly Held**
SIC: 2621 Paper mills
PA: International Paper Company
   6400 Poplar Ave
   Memphis TN 38197
   901 419-9000

(G-16370)
KELLY FOUNDRY & MACHINE CO
300 Hubbell St Ste 308 (13501-1404)
PHONE 315 732-8313
Fax: 315 732-8364
Geoia M Kelley, *President*
Marsha J Kelly, *Corp Secy*
James S Kelly III, *Vice Pres*
Mark James Kelly, *Vice Pres*
EMP: 48 **EST:** 1892
SQ FT: 14,632
SALES (est): 7.5MM **Privately Held**
WEB: www.kellyfoundry.com
SIC: 3369 3999 3953 Nonferrous foundries; plaques, picture, laminated; marking devices

(G-16371)
METAL SOLUTIONS INC
1821 Broad St Ste 5 (13501-1115)
PHONE 315 732-6271
Joseph Cattadoris Jr, *President*
Cathy Cattadoris, *Vice Pres*
John Kulis, *Shareholder*
EMP: 50 **EST:** 1954
SQ FT: 110,000
SALES (est): 13.7MM **Privately Held**
WEB: www.nhsmetal.com
SIC: 3444 Sheet metalwork

(G-16372)
MILLENNIUM ANTENNA CORP
1001 Broad St Ste 401 (13501-1545)
PHONE 315 798-9374
David Schroeter, *President*
Paul King, *Manager*
EMP: 10
SQ FT: 2,000
SALES (est): 950K **Privately Held**
WEB: www.millenniumantenna.com
SIC: 3663 8711 8731 Antennas, transmitting & communications; engineering services; electronic research

(G-16373)
MOBILE MINI INC
2222 Oriskany St W Ste 3 (13502-2925)
PHONE 315 732-4555
Marc Allen, *Branch Mgr*
EMP: 10
SALES (corp-wide): 508.6MM **Publicly Held**
WEB: www.mobilemini.com
SIC: 3448 3441 3412 7359 Prefabricated metal buildings; fabricated structural metal; metal barrels, drums & pails; equipment rental & leasing
PA: Mobile Mini, Inc.
   4646 E Van Buren St # 400
   Phoenix AZ 85008
   480 894-6311

(G-16374)
MUNSON MACHINERY COMPANY INC
210 Seward Ave (13502-5750)
PHONE 315 797-0090
Fax: 315 797-5582
Charles H Divine, *CEO*
Josh Kelly, *Production*
Jackie Miller, *Purch Agent*
Robert Batson, *Engineer*
Dier Vinnie, *Engineer*
▲ **EMP:** 40 **EST:** 1828
SQ FT: 45,000
SALES (est): 11.3MM
SALES (corp-wide): 28.4MM **Privately Held**
WEB: www.munsonmachinery.com
SIC: 3532 3531 3559 3541 Crushing, pulverizing & screening equipment; mixers: ore, plaster, slag, sand, mortar, etc.; refinery, chemical processing & similar machinery; machine tools, metal cutting type; buffing & polishing machines; grinding machines, metalworking; metalworking machinery
PA: Dimanco Inc.
   200 Seward Ave
   Utica NY 13502
   315 797-0470

(G-16375)
NATHAN STEEL CORP
36 Wurz Ave (13502-2534)
P.O. Box 299 (13503-0299)
PHONE 315 797-1335
Fax: 315 797-1536
Edward Kowalsky, *President*
Wade Wells, *Warehouse Mgr*
Helen Evans, *Manager*
Peter Morgan, *Manager*
EMP: 15
SQ FT: 12,000
SALES (est): 4.1MM **Privately Held**
SIC: 3441 5051 Fabricated structural metal; steel

(G-16376)
NORTH COUNTRY BOOKS INC
220 Lafayette St (13502-4312)
PHONE 315 735-4877
Fax: 315 738-4342
Robert Igoe, *President*
▲ **EMP:** 5 **EST:** 1965
SQ FT: 5,000
SALES: 1.1MM **Privately Held**
WEB: www.northcountrybooks.com
SIC: 2732 5192 Books: printing only; books

(G-16377)
NOVA HEALTH SYSTEMS INC
1001 Broad St Ste 3 (13501-1546)
P.O. Box 212, Forestport (13338-0212)
PHONE 315 798-9018
Fax: 315 798-9337
Wade Abraham, *President*
▲ **EMP:** 6
SQ FT: 4,000
SALES (est): 847.1K **Privately Held**
WEB: www.novahealthsystems.com
SIC: 3842 5047 Surgical appliances & supplies; medical & hospital equipment

(G-16378)
OHIO BAKING COMPANY INC
Also Called: Spano's Bread
10585 Cosby Manor Rd (13502-1207)
PHONE 315 724-2033
Fax: 315 735-7419
Joseph A Spano, *President*
EMP: 20 **EST:** 1930
SQ FT: 4,000

GEOGRAPHIC SECTION

Valley Cottage - Rockland County (G-16404)

SALES (est): 3.5MM **Privately Held**
SIC: **2041** 2051 5149 5461 Pizza dough, prepared; pizza mixes; bread, all types (white, wheat, rye, etc); fresh or frozen; bakery products; bakeries

(G-16379)
ORBCOMM INC
125 Business Park Dr (13502-6304)
PHONE 703 433-6396
EMP: 11
SALES (corp-wide): 186.7MM **Publicly Held**
SIC: **3663** Satellites, communications
PA: Orbcomm Inc.
395 W Passaic St Ste 325
Rochelle Park NJ 07662
703 433-6361

(G-16380)
PRINT SHOPPE
311 Turner St Ste 310 (13501-1766)
PHONE 315 792-9585
Fax: 315 732-3200
Steven Finch, *Partner*
Thomas Stewart, *Partner*
EMP: 7
SALES (est): 725.4K **Privately Held**
SIC: **2759** Screen printing

(G-16381)
ROBERT BOSCH LLC
2118 Beechgrove Pl (13501-1706)
PHONE 315 733-3312
EMP: 25
SALES (corp-wide): 268.9MM **Privately Held**
SIC: **3841** Mfg Surgical/Medical Instruments
HQ: Robert Bosch Llc
2800 S 25th Ave
Broadview IL 60155
708 865-5200

(G-16382)
SCOOBY RENDERING & INC
Also Called: Scooby Dog Food
1930 Oriskany St W (13502-2920)
PHONE 315 793-1014
Fax: 315 793-0043
Michael P Dote, *President*
EMP: 5
SQ FT: 3,000
SALES (est): 654.4K **Privately Held**
SIC: **2047** Dog food

(G-16383)
SHIPRITE SOFTWARE INC
1312 Genesee St (13502-4700)
PHONE 315 733-6191
J Mark Ford, *President*
EMP: 9
SQ FT: 8,400
SALES (est): 1.1MM **Privately Held**
SIC: **7372** 7334 7359 Prepackaged software; photocopying & duplicating services; shipping container leasing

(G-16384)
STURGES MANUFACTURING CO INC
2030 Sunset Ave (13502-5500)
P.O. Box 59 (13503-0059)
PHONE 315 732-6159
Fax: 315 732-2314
Bruce T Brach, *General Mgr*
Richard R Griffith, *Principal*
Tyler Griffith, *Vice Pres*
Norma Jean Rice, *Vice Pres*
Norma Rice, *QC Mgr*
▲ **EMP:** 75 EST: 1909
SQ FT: 58,000
SALES (est): 15.7MM **Privately Held**
WEB: www.sturgesmfg.com
SIC: **2241** Strapping webs; webbing, woven

(G-16385)
T C PETERS PRINTING CO INC
2336 W Whitesboro St (13502-3235)
PHONE 315 724-4149
Fax: 315 738-8983
Richard Peters, *CEO*
Douglas Peters, *President*
EMP: 9
SQ FT: 13,200

SALES (est): 1.4MM **Privately Held**
SIC: **2752** Commercial printing, offset

(G-16386)
USA SEWING INC
901 Broad St Ste 2 (13501-1500)
PHONE 315 792-8017
John D Inserra, *President*
Lisa Bates, *Manager*
Linda Taglimonte, *Manager*
EMP: 49
SALES (est): 4MM **Privately Held**
SIC: **3151** Leather gloves & mittens

(G-16387)
UTICA CUTLERY COMPANY
Also Called: Walco Stainless
820 Noyes St (13502-5053)
P.O. Box 10527 (13503-1527)
PHONE 315 733-4663
Fax: 315 733-6602
A Edward Allen Jr, *Ch of Bd*
David S Allen, *Ch of Bd*
Phil Benbenek, *Exec VP*
Roy Gonzales, *Vice Pres*
David Barr, *Engineer*
▲ **EMP:** 60
SQ FT: 90,000
SALES (est): 13MM **Privately Held**
WEB: www.kutmaster.com
SIC: **3914** 3421 5023 5072 Flatware, stainless steel; cutlery, stainless steel; knives: butchers', hunting, pocket, etc.; stainless steel flatware; cutlery

(G-16388)
UTICA METAL PRODUCTS INC
1526 Lincoln Ave (13502-5298)
PHONE 315 732-6163
Fax: 315 732-0234
Charles J Fields, *Ch of Bd*
Monte L Craig, *Vice Ch Bd*
Robert Moore, *COO*
Justin Shade, *Engineer*
Lou Rabbia, *Controller*
EMP: 73 EST: 1956
SQ FT: 30,000
SALES (est): 13.8MM **Privately Held**
WEB: www.uticametals.com
SIC: **3465** 3471 Automotive stampings; hub caps, automobile: stamped metal; anodizing (plating) of metals or formed products

(G-16389)
WHERE IS UTICA COF RASTING INC
92 Genesee St (13502-3519)
PHONE 315 269-8898
Frank Ilias, *President*
EMP: 15 EST: 2005
SQ FT: 1,000
SALES: 300K **Privately Held**
SIC: **2095** 0161 Coffee roasting (except by wholesale grocers); green lima bean farm

Valatie
Columbia County

(G-16390)
WEISS INDUSTRIES INC
Also Called: Precision Machine Parts
27 Blossom Ln (12184-9201)
PHONE 518 784-9643
Michael Weiss, *President*
EMP: 7
SALES (est): 778.3K **Privately Held**
SIC: **3599** Machine shop, jobbing & repair

Valhalla
Westchester County

(G-16391)
CHESTER SHRED-IT/WEST
420 Columbus Ave Ste 100 (10595-1382)
PHONE 914 407-2502
Greg Brophy, *President*
EMP: 20 EST: 1994
SALES (est): 1.4MM **Privately Held**
SIC: **3589** Shredders, industrial & commercial

(G-16392)
CONSTRUCTION TECHNOLOGY INC (PA)
400 Columbus Ave Ste 110s (10595-3320)
PHONE 914 747-8900
Richard Levine, *President*
Deborah Jillson, *Exec Dir*
EMP: 5
SQ FT: 1,000
SALES (est): 2MM **Privately Held**
SIC: **7372** Prepackaged software

(G-16393)
EPOCH MICROELECTRONICS INC
420 Columbus Ave Ste 204 (10595-1382)
PHONE 914 332-8570
Ken Suyama, *President*
Aleksander Dec, *Vice Pres*
Sachiko Tokai, *Manager*
EMP: 9
SALES (est): 1.1MM **Privately Held**
WEB: www.epochmicro.com
SIC: **3825** Integrated circuit testers

(G-16394)
LEGACY VALVE LLC
14 Railroad Ave (10595-1609)
P.O. Box 107 (10595-0107)
PHONE 914 403-5075
Charles Cassidy, *President*
EMP: 13
SALES (est): 2.6MM **Privately Held**
SIC: **3494** Pipe fittings

(G-16395)
PEPSICO
100 Summit Lake Dr # 103 (10595-2318)
PHONE 914 801-1500
Rene Lammers, *COO*
Heidi Dubois, *Counsel*
Larry D Thompson, *Exec VP*
Nicolas Nicolaou, *CFO*
Lindsay Carroll, *Finance Mgr*
▲ **EMP:** 31
SALES (est): 4.8MM **Privately Held**
SIC: **2086** Carbonated soft drinks, bottled & canned

(G-16396)
PEPSICO INC
100 E Stevens Ave (10595-1299)
PHONE 914 742-4500
Fax: 914 749-3330
Noel E Anderson, *Vice Pres*
Lee French, *Project Mgr*
Onna Burleson, *Research*
Raymond McGarvey, *Research*
Kevin Doyle, *Engineer*
EMP: 380
SALES (corp-wide): 62.8B **Publicly Held**
WEB: www.pepsico.com
SIC: **2086** Carbonated soft drinks, bottled & canned
PA: Pepsico, Inc.
700 Anderson Hill Rd
Purchase NY 10577
914 253-2000

(G-16397)
PRESBREY-LELAND INC
Also Called: Presbrey- Leland Memorials
250 Lakeview Ave (10595-1618)
PHONE 914 949-2264
Fax: 914 949-7846
Nancy Dylan, *President*
EMP: 5 EST: 1982
SALES (est): 630.2K **Privately Held**
SIC: **3272** 5999 Monuments, concrete; monuments, finished to custom order; monuments & tombstones

(G-16398)
RUHLE COMPANIES INC
Also Called: Farrand Controls Division
99 Wall St (10595-1462)
PHONE 914 287-4000
Fax: 914 761-0405
Frank S Ruhle, *Ch of Bd*
Robert E Ruhle, *Exec VP*
Richard Babcock, *Production*
William Moore, *QC Mgr*
Robert Baer, *Manager*
EMP: 50
SQ FT: 33,000

SALES (est): 9.2MM **Privately Held**
WEB: www.ruhle.com
SIC: **3679** 3625 3577 3674 Transducers, electrical; control equipment, electric; computer peripheral equipment; semiconductors & related devices; radio & TV communications equipment; motors & generators

(G-16399)
VTB HOLDINGS INC (HQ)
100 Summit Lake Dr (10595-1339)
PHONE 914 345-2255
Juergen Stark, *CEO*
John Hanson, *CFO*
EMP: 6
SALES: 207.1MM **Publicly Held**
SIC: **3651** Sound reproducing equipment

Valley Cottage
Rockland County

(G-16400)
ACCESS 24
570 Kings Hwy Fl 4 (10989-1231)
PHONE 845 358-5397
John Sindelar, *Owner*
EMP: 6
SALES (est): 600K **Privately Held**
SIC: **3661** Telephones & telephone apparatus

(G-16401)
AERO HEALTHCARE (US) LLC
616 Corporate Way Ste 6 (10989-2047)
PHONE 855 225-2376
Brian Parker, *General Mgr*
EMP: 5
SALES: 912.5K
SALES (corp-wide): 4.4MM **Privately Held**
SIC: **3842** 5099 Bandages & dressings; tape, adhesive: medicated or non-medicated; lifesaving & survival equipment (non-medical)
PA: Aero Healthcare Partnership
63 Seaton St
Armidale NSW 2350
267 767-200

(G-16402)
AREMCO PRODUCTS INC
707 Executive Blvd Ste B (10989-2025)
P.O. Box 517 (10989-0517)
PHONE 845 268-0039
Peter Schwartz, *President*
David Heinl, *Manager*
Esther Schwartz, *Admin Sec*
▲ **EMP:** 15
SQ FT: 15,500
SALES: 3.9MM **Privately Held**
WEB: www.aremco.com
SIC: **3559** 2891 2952 3253 Refinery, chemical processing & similar machinery; adhesives; cement, except linoleum & tile; coating compounds, tar; ceramic wall & floor tile

(G-16403)
CEROVENE INC (PA)
612 Corporate Way Ste 10 (10989-2027)
PHONE 845 267-2055
Manish Shah, *President*
Ray Difalco, *Vice Pres*
Lisa Rinaldi, *Manager*
EMP: 10
SQ FT: 40,000
SALES: 8MM **Privately Held**
WEB: www.cerovene.com
SIC: **2834** Pharmaceutical preparations

(G-16404)
FIRST SBF HOLDING INC (PA)
Also Called: Gevril
9 Pinecrest Rd Ste 101 (10989-1443)
PHONE 845 425-9882
Samuel Friedman, *President*
Steven Pachtinger, *Vice Pres*
Keith Burns, *Opers Mgr*
Perla Hershkowitz, *Buyer*
Rachel Itzkowitz, *Bookkeeper*
▼ **EMP:** 10

Valley Cottage - Rockland County (G-16405)

SALES: 16.1MM **Privately Held**
WEB: www.gevril.com
SIC: 3873 Watches & parts, except crystals & jewels

(G-16405)
INNOTECH GRAPHIC EQP CORP
614 Corporate Way Ste 5 (10989-2026)
PHONE..................................845 268-6900
EMP: 8
SQ FT: 7,500
SALES (est): 800K **Privately Held**
SIC: 3555 5084 Mfg Printing Trades Machinery Whol Industrial Equipment

(G-16406)
LANDMARK GROUP INC
Also Called: National Ramp
709 Executive Blvd Ste A (10989-2024)
PHONE..................................845 358-0350
Garth Walker, *Ch of Bd*
EMP: 40
SALES (est): 9.2MM **Privately Held**
SIC: 3448 Ramps: prefabricated metal

(G-16407)
LEXAR GLOBAL LLC
711 Executive Blvd Ste K (10989-2006)
PHONE..................................845 352-9700
Guy Jacobs, *President*
▲ EMP: 9
SQ FT: 18,000
SALES: 4.9MM **Privately Held**
SIC: 3555 Printing trade parts & attachments

(G-16408)
MOUNT VERNON MACHINE INC
614 Corporate Way Ste 8 (10989-2026)
PHONE..................................845 268-9400
Fax: 845 268-9486
Karl Wallburg, *President*
EMP: 20
SQ FT: 16,000
SALES (est): 2.2MM **Privately Held**
WEB: www.mountvernonmachine.com
SIC: 3599 3555 Machine & other job shop work; printing trades machinery

(G-16409)
MP DISPLAYS LLC
704 Executive Blvd Ste 1 (10989-2010)
PHONE..................................845 268-4113
Michael Parkes, *Mng Member*
Marilyn Glisci, *Manager*
▲ EMP: 9
SQ FT: 5,300
SALES (est): 1.7MM **Privately Held**
WEB: www.mpdisplays.com
SIC: 2653 3577 Display items, corrugated: made from purchased materials; display items, solid fiber: made from purchased materials; graphic displays, except graphic terminals

(G-16410)
NORTH SUNSHINE LLC
616 Corporate Way Ste 2-3 (10989-2044)
PHONE..................................307 027-1634
EMP: 15 EST: 2016
SALES: 800K **Privately Held**
SIC: 2273 5713 Mfg Carpets/Rugs Ret Floor Covering

(G-16411)
PRAXAIR INC
614 Corporate Way Ste 4 (10989-2026)
PHONE..................................845 267-2337
Robert Berkey, *Branch Mgr*
EMP: 20
SALES (corp-wide): 10.5B **Publicly Held**
SIC: 2813 Industrial gases
PA: Praxair, Inc.
10 Riverview Dr
Danbury CT 06810
203 837-2000

(G-16412)
REAL CO INC
616 Corporate Way (10989-2044)
PHONE..................................347 433-8549
Raphaele Chartrand, *Principal*
Muhammad Elkateb, *COO*
▲ EMP: 8 EST: 2014

SALES (est): 258.8K **Privately Held**
SIC: 2044 2099 2899 Rice milling; sugar; salt

(G-16413)
ROSSI TOOL & DIES INC
161 Route 303 (10989-1922)
PHONE..................................845 267-8246
Fax: 845 268-4966
James Veltidi, *President*
EMP: 6 EST: 1952
SQ FT: 4,000
SALES (est): 699.7K **Privately Held**
SIC: 3544 3599 Dies & die holders for metal cutting, forming, die casting; machine shop, jobbing & repair

(G-16414)
SCIENTA PHARMACEUTICALS LLC
612 Corporate Way Ste 9 (10989-2027)
PHONE..................................845 589-0774
EMP: 2
SQ FT: 2,000
SALES (est): 320K **Privately Held**
SIC: 2834 Mfg Pharmaceutical Preparations

(G-16415)
STAR PRESS PEARL RIVER INC
614 Corporate Way Ste 8 (10989-2026)
PHONE..................................845 268-2294
Marino Nicolich, *President*
EMP: 6 EST: 1969
SALES (est): 1MM **Privately Held**
SIC: 2752 2759 Commercial printing, lithographic; letterpress printing

(G-16416)
STATEWIDE FIREPROOF DOOR CO
178 Charles Blvd (10989-2437)
PHONE..................................845 268-6043
Fax: 718 596-4591
Joseph Caneiro, *President*
Carmen Caraballo, *Bookkeeper*
EMP: 11 EST: 1965
SQ FT: 11,000
SALES (est): 1.1MM **Privately Held**
SIC: 3442 Fire doors, metal

(G-16417)
STROMBERG BRAND CORPORATION
Also Called: Stormberg Brand
12 Ford Products Rd (10989-1238)
PHONE..................................914 739-7410
Richard Stromberg, *CEO*
Helen Stromberg, *President*
EMP: 10
SQ FT: 9,000
SALES (est): 600K **Privately Held**
WEB: www.strombergbrand.com
SIC: 2759 Screen printing

(G-16418)
SUPPLYNET INC (PA)
706 Executive Blvd Ste B (10989-2039)
PHONE..................................800 826-0279
Fax: 845 267-2420
Robert Berkey, *President*
Beverly Lewis, *CFO*
Marcia Kalmus, *Accountant*
EMP: 6
SQ FT: 7,500
SALES: 7.3MM **Privately Held**
WEB: www.thesupplynet.com
SIC: 3678 Electronic connectors

(G-16419)
THOR MARKETING CORP
616 Corporate Way Ste 2 (10989-2047)
PHONE..................................201 247-7103
Igor Poluyko, *CEO*
▲ EMP: 8 EST: 2015
SQ FT: 5,800
SALES (est): 299.7K **Privately Held**
SIC: 2392 Blankets, comforters & beddings

(G-16420)
UNIVERSAL STRAPPING INC
630 Corporate Way (10989-2002)
PHONE..................................845 268-2500
Fax: 845 268-7999
Sol Oberlander, *President*

Gedalia Oberlander, *Corp Secy*
▲ EMP: 20
SQ FT: 100,000
SALES (est): 3.6MM **Privately Held**
WEB: www.universalstrapping.com
SIC: 3089 Bands, plastic

(G-16421)
ZEO HEALTH LTD
159 Route 303 (10989-1922)
PHONE..................................845 353-5185
Micah Portney, *President*
EMP: 16
SQ FT: 5,000
SALES: 500K **Privately Held**
SIC: 2834 Vitamin, nutrient & hematinic preparations for human use

Valley Falls
Rensselaer County

(G-16422)
STEPHEN BADER COMPANY INC
10 Charles St (12185-3437)
P.O. Box 297 (12185-0297)
PHONE..................................518 753-4456
Fax: 518 753-4962
Daniel W Johnson, *President*
Rosemarie Johnson, *Vice Pres*
Carrie Johnson, *Admin Sec*
▼ EMP: 10 EST: 1951
SQ FT: 14,000
SALES (est): 1.5MM **Privately Held**
WEB: www.stephenbader.com
SIC: 3541 Grinding machines, metalworking

Valley Stream
Nassau County

(G-16423)
5TH AVENUE CHOCOLATIERE LTD
396 Rockaway Ave (11581-1938)
PHONE..................................516 561-1570
Joseph E Whaley, *Branch Mgr*
EMP: 10
SALES (corp-wide): 1.6MM **Privately Held**
SIC: 2064 5441 2066 Candy & other confectionery products; candy; chocolate & cocoa products
PA: 5th Avenue Chocolatiere Ltd
114 Church St
Freeport NY 11520
212 935-5454

(G-16424)
ADC INDUSTRIES INC (PA)
181a E Jamaica Ave (11580-6069)
PHONE..................................516 596-1304
Joseph Mannino, *President*
Jennifer Krific, *Manager*
EMP: 25
SQ FT: 2,000
SALES: 4.5MM **Privately Held**
WEB: www.airlockdoor.com
SIC: 3491 Valves, automatic control

(G-16425)
ANSA SYSTEMS OF USA INC
145 Hook Creek Blvd B6a1 (11581-2293)
PHONE..................................718 835-3743
John Olusoga, *President*
Fola Olusoga, *Office Mgr*
EMP: 5
SALES: 500K **Privately Held**
SIC: 7372 Prepackaged software

(G-16426)
AUTOMATED OFFICE SYSTEMS INC
Also Called: Aos
71 S Central Ave (11580-5495)
PHONE..................................516 396-5555
Larry Sachs, *President*
Kirill Khazan, *Manager*
EMP: 10
SQ FT: 5,000

SALES (est): 483.5K **Privately Held**
WEB: www.aosdata.com
SIC: 7372 Business oriented computer software

(G-16427)
BRAUN BROS BRUSHES INC
35 4th St (11581-1231)
P.O. Box 2822, Babylon (11703-0822)
PHONE..................................631 667-2179
Fax: 516 825-2222
James Braun, *President*
Pamela Sue Gagas, *Purch Mgr*
EMP: 5 EST: 1946
SQ FT: 1,400
SALES (est): 554.8K **Privately Held**
WEB: www.braunbrosbrushes.com
SIC: 3991 5085 Brushes, household or industrial; brushes, industrial

(G-16428)
CITY REAL ESTATE BOOK INC
9831 S Franklin Ave (11580)
PHONE..................................516 593-2949
Charles Danas, *President*
EMP: 8
SALES: 500K **Privately Held**
SIC: 2721 Magazines: publishing & printing

(G-16429)
CLIQUE APPAREL INC
2034 Green Acres Mall (11581-1545)
PHONE..................................516 375-7969
Naveen Shikapuri, *Ch of Bd*
EMP: 3 EST: 2011
SQ FT: 3,000
SALES: 1MM **Privately Held**
SIC: 2329 Knickers, dress (separate): men's & boys'

(G-16430)
CNI MEAT & PRODUCE INC
Also Called: Key Foods
500 W Merrick Rd (11580-5233)
PHONE..................................516 599-5929
▲ EMP: 5
SALES (est): 225K **Privately Held**
SIC: 2011 2013 Meat by-products from meat slaughtered on site; canned meats (except baby food), meat slaughtered on site; sausages & other prepared meats

(G-16431)
ELLIS PRODUCTS CORP (PA)
Also Called: Style Plus Hosiery Mills
628 Golf Dr (11581-3550)
PHONE..................................516 791-3732
Seymour Ellis, *President*
EMP: 4 EST: 1954
SALES (est): 6.1MM **Privately Held**
SIC: 2251 3944 Women's hosiery, except socks; panty hose; electronic game machines, except coin-operated

(G-16432)
FACILAMATIC INSTRUMENT CORP
39 Clinton Ave (11580-6024)
PHONE..................................516 825-6300
Fax: 516 825-6324
Dennis West, *President*
John E Bergquist, *Vice Pres*
EMP: 15
SQ FT: 15,000
SALES: 1.8MM **Privately Held**
SIC: 3812 Aircraft/aerospace flight instruments & guidance systems; gyro gimbals; gyrocompasses; gyropilots

(G-16433)
FREQUENCY SELECTIVE NETWORKS
12 N Cottage St (11580-4647)
PHONE..................................718 424-7500
Julius Tischkewitsch, *President*
Michael Izzolo, *Vice Pres*
Mike Izzolo, *Sales Staff*
Christine Wingate, *Office Mgr*
EMP: 10
SQ FT: 10,000
SALES (est): 1.9MM **Privately Held**
SIC: 3677 Electronic coils, transformers & other inductors; filtration devices, electronic

GEOGRAPHIC SECTION

Vernon Center - Oneida County (G-16460)

(G-16434)
GLOBAL PAYMENT TECH INC
20 E Sunrise Hwy (11581-1260)
PHONE 516 887-0700
Fax: 516 256-1620
Sue Comple, *Human Res Mgr*
Stephen Katz, *Branch Mgr*
EMP: 10
SALES (corp-wide): 11.8MM **Publicly Held**
WEB: www.gptx.com
SIC: 3581 Mechanisms & parts for automatic vending machines
PA: Global Payment Technologies, Inc.
170 Wilbur Pl Ste 600
Bohemia NY 11716
631 563-2500

(G-16435)
HETEROCHEMICAL CORPORATION
111 E Hawthorne Ave (11580-6319)
PHONE 516 561-8225
Fax: 516 561-8413
Lynne Galler, *President*
Beatrice Galler, *Corp Secy*
Raymond Berruti, *Vice Pres*
EMP: 10 EST: 1946
SQ FT: 18,000
SALES (est): 876.5K **Privately Held**
SIC: 2899 Chemical preparations

(G-16436)
HIGH PERFORMANCE SFTWR USA INC
Also Called: Zuant
145 Hook Creek Blvd (11581-2299)
PHONE 866 616-4958
Pete Gillett, *Director*
EMP: 30
SALES (est): 159.2K **Privately Held**
SIC: 7372 Prepackaged software

(G-16437)
JERRYS BAGELS
Also Called: Jerry's Bagels & Bakery
951 Rosedale Rd (11581-2318)
PHONE 516 791-0063
Jerry Jacobs, *Owner*
EMP: 8
SALES (est): 571.4K **Privately Held**
SIC: 2051 Bakery: wholesale or wholesale/retail combined

(G-16438)
L M N PRINTING COMPANY INC
23 W Merrick Rd Ste A (11580-5757)
P.O. Box 696 (11582-0696)
PHONE 516 285-8526
Fax: 516 285-9268
Nora Aly, *President*
Noreen Carro, *Vice Pres*
EMP: 25
SQ FT: 5,200
SALES (est): 3.8MM **Privately Held**
WEB: www.lmnprinting.com
SIC: 2752 2791 Commercial printing, offset; typesetting

(G-16439)
LELAB DENTAL LABORATORY INC
Also Called: Le Lab
550 W Merrick Rd Ste 8 (11580-5101)
PHONE 516 561-5050
Edmond Mardirossia, *President*
Maronlyn Mardirossian, *Vice Pres*
EMP: 5
SQ FT: 1,000
SALES (est): 612.7K **Privately Held**
SIC: 3843 Dental equipment & supplies

(G-16440)
MICHAEL FIORE LTD
126 E Fairview Ave (11580-5930)
PHONE 516 561-8238
Michael Fiore, *President*
EMP: 6
SQ FT: 6,000
SALES: 2MM **Privately Held**
SIC: 3545 Machine tool accessories

(G-16441)
ONE IN A MILLION INC
51 Franklin Ave (11580-2847)
P.O. Box 234111, Great Neck (11023-4111)
PHONE 516 829-1111
Sasan Shavanson, *President*
Yaso Soleimani, *Admin Sec*
EMP: 6
SQ FT: 2,000
SALES (est): 800K **Privately Held**
SIC: 2759 5112 2284 Screen printing; stationery; embroidery thread

(G-16442)
PARNASA INTERNATIONAL INC
Also Called: C-Air International
181 S Franklin Ave # 400 (11581-1138)
PHONE 516 394-0400
Glenn Schacher, *President*
Lucille Schacher, *Admin Sec*
▲ EMP: 8
SALES (est): 520K **Privately Held**
SIC: 2099 Food preparations

(G-16443)
PRECISELED INC
52 Railroad Ave (11580-6031)
PHONE 516 418-5337
Daniel Machlis, *President*
▲ EMP: 10 EST: 2015
SQ FT: 13,000
SALES (est): 502.6K **Privately Held**
SIC: 3646 3645 Commercial indusl & institutional electric lighting fixtures; residential lighting fixtures

(G-16444)
PRECISION TL DIE & STAMPING CO
Also Called: G & W Tool & Die Co
68 Franklin Ave (11580-2845)
PHONE 516 561-0041
Fax: 516 561-5197
William Heath, *President*
Deborah Bruno, *Office Mgr*
EMP: 10 EST: 1955
SQ FT: 6,000
SALES: 900K **Privately Held**
SIC: 3469 3544 Metal stampings; special dies & tools

(G-16445)
PRO METAL OF NY CORP
814 W Merrick Rd (11580-4829)
PHONE 516 285-0440
Michael Marin, *President*
EMP: 5
SALES (est): 701.3K **Privately Held**
SIC: 3585 1761 Heating & air conditioning combination units; sheet metalwork

(G-16446)
PSG INNOVATIONS INC
924 Kilmer Ln (11581-3130)
PHONE 917 299-8986
Philip Green, *CEO*
EMP: 15 EST: 2010
SQ FT: 2,500
SALES: 16MM **Privately Held**
SIC: 3648 Flashlights

(G-16447)
RAYS ITALIAN BAKERY INC
Also Called: Roma Ray Bakery
45 Railroad Ave (11580-6030)
PHONE 516 825-9170
Fax: 516 599-9340
Robert Degiovanni, *President*
Vincent Giovanni, *Vice Pres*
Dario Degiovanni, *Admin Sec*
EMP: 12
SQ FT: 10,000
SALES (est): 1.2MM **Privately Held**
SIC: 2051 Bread, cake & related products

(G-16448)
READY TO ASSEMBLE COMPANY INC
Also Called: Debra Fisher
115 S Corona Ave (11580-6217)
PHONE 516 825-4397
Bruce Wulwick, *CEO*
Phyllis Wulwick, *Treasurer*
EMP: 20
SALES (est): 2.1MM **Privately Held**
SIC: 2519 7389 Household furniture, except wood or metal: upholstered;

(G-16449)
ROMA BAKERY INC
45 Railroad Ave (11580-6030)
PHONE 516 825-9170
Jacoui Digiovanni, *President*
EMP: 17
SQ FT: 10,000
SALES (est): 1.8MM **Privately Held**
SIC: 2051 Bread, cake & related products

(G-16450)
SENERA CO INC
834 Glenridge Ave (11581-3019)
PHONE 516 639-3774
Seema Gupta, *President*
EMP: 10
SALES: 100K **Privately Held**
SIC: 3674 Switches, silicon control

(G-16451)
SOUTH SHORE READY MIX INC
116 E Hawthorne Ave (11580-6331)
PHONE 516 872-3049
Joseph Dilemme, *President*
EMP: 5
SQ FT: 10,000
SALES (est): 712.7K **Privately Held**
SIC: 3273 Ready-mixed concrete

(G-16452)
TASTE AND SEE ENTRMT INC
Also Called: Taqa Entertainment
255 Dogwood Rd (11580-4039)
P.O. Box 367 (11582-0367)
PHONE 516 285-3010
Barry Whipple, *CEO*
Patricia Whipple, *General Mgr*
EMP: 5
SALES (est): 863.1K **Privately Held**
SIC: 3652 7812 5734 7832 Pre-recorded records & tapes; motion picture & video production; computer & software stores; motion picture theaters, except drive-in; record & prerecorded tape stores

(G-16453)
TOTAL DNTL IMPLANT SLTIONS LLC
Also Called: Tag Dental Implant Solutions
260 W Sunrise Hwy (11581-1011)
PHONE 212 877-3777
Ariel Goldschlag,
EMP: 5
SALES: 750K **Privately Held**
SIC: 3843 Dental equipment & supplies

(G-16454)
UNIVERSAL 3D INNOVATION INC
1085 Rockaway Ave (11581-2137)
PHONE 516 837-9423
Tomer Yariz, *President*
Adam Gansky, *Marketing Staff*
Noa Gansky, *Manager*
EMP: 10
SQ FT: 5,000
SALES: 2.5MM **Privately Held**
SIC: 3993 Signs, not made in custom sign painting shops

Van Hornesville
Herkimer County

(G-16455)
OGD V-HVAC INC
174 Pumkinhook Rd (13475)
PHONE 315 858-1002
Ormonde G Drham III, *President*
Linda Bowers, *Administration*
EMP: 20
SALES: 400K **Privately Held**
SIC: 3999 Manufacturing industries

Vernon
Oneida County

(G-16456)
CHEPAUME INDUSTRIES LLC
6201 Cooper St (13476-4022)
PHONE 315 829-6400
Fax: 315 768-0270
Chester Poplaski,
Melissa Foppes,
EMP: 6
SQ FT: 17,114
SALES (est): 569.1K **Privately Held**
WEB: www.chepaume.com
SIC: 3479 Coating electrodes

(G-16457)
FOUR DIRECTIONS INC
4677 State Route 5 (13476-3525)
PHONE 315 829-8388
Fax: 315 361-8621
Peter Wiezalis, *Director*
Kelli Bradley, *Administration*
EMP: 20
SALES (est): 760.1K **Privately Held**
WEB: www.fourdirectionsmedia.com
SIC: 2711 Newspapers: publishing only, not printed on site
HQ: Oneida Nation Enterprises
5218 Patrick Rd
Verona NY 13478

(G-16458)
HP HOOD LLC
19 Ward St (13476-4415)
P.O. Box 930 (13476-0930)
PHONE 315 829-3339
Fax: 315 829-3108
Phil Campbell, *Plant Mgr*
Howard Holdridge, *QC Dir*
EMP: 100
SQ FT: 800
SALES (corp-wide): 1.7B **Privately Held**
WEB: www.hphood.com
SIC: 2026 2024 2022 Fluid milk; cream, sweet; yogurt; ice cream & frozen desserts; processed cheese
PA: Hp Hood Llc
6 Kimball Ln Ste 400
Lynnfield MA 01940
617 887-8441

(G-16459)
J H RHODES COMPANY INC
10 Ward St (13476-4416)
PHONE 315 829-3600
J Rhodes, *Principal*
EMP: 11
SALES (corp-wide): 61.6MM **Privately Held**
SIC: 3674 Semiconductors & related devices
HQ: J H Rhodes Company Inc.
2800 N 44th St Ste 675
Phoenix AZ 85008
602 449-8689

Vernon Center
Oneida County

(G-16460)
MCDONOUGH HARDWOODS LTD
6426 Skinner Rd (13477-3840)
PHONE 315 829-3449
Daniel McDonough, *CEO*
James McDonough, *Treasurer*
EMP: 25
SALES: 1.1MM **Privately Held**
SIC: 2421 Sawmills & planing mills, general

Vestal
Broome County

(G-16461)
ADVANCED MTL ANALYTICS LLC
85 Murray HI Rd Ste 2115 (13850)
PHONE 321 684-0528
Swastisharan Dey,
EMP: 5
SQ FT: 500
SALES (est): 350K **Privately Held**
SIC: 3826 Analytical instruments

(G-16462)
BARNEY & DICKENSON INC (PA)
520 Prentice Rd (13850-2197)
PHONE 607 729-1536
Fax: 607 797-3931
Robert S Murphy Jr, *President*
Mary M Harrison, *Vice Pres*
Brian Taylor, *Engineer*
EMP: 49
SQ FT: 100,000
SALES (est): 8.2MM **Privately Held**
SIC: 3273 5032 1771 Ready-mixed concrete; concrete mixtures; sand, construction; gravel; concrete pumping

(G-16463)
BIMBO BAKERIES USA INC
Also Called: Stroehmann Bakeries 90
1624 Castle Gardens Rd (13850-1102)
PHONE 800 856-8544
Fax: 607 748-8790
Michael Hicks, *Area Mgr*
Bruce Gross, *Manager*
EMP: 20 **Privately Held**
SIC: 2051 5149 Breads, rolls & buns; groceries & related products
HQ: Bimbo Bakeries Usa, Inc
255 Business Center Dr # 200
Horsham PA 19044
215 347-5500

(G-16464)
BOB MURPHY INC
3127 Vestal Rd (13850-2109)
PHONE 607 729-3553
Fax: 607 770-8064
Robert S Murphy Jr, *President*
Mary Murphy Harrison, *Vice Pres*
EMP: 17
SQ FT: 130,000
SALES: 2MM **Privately Held**
SIC: 3441 5031 Fabricated structural metal; building materials, exterior; building materials, interior

(G-16465)
C & C READY-MIX CORPORATION (PA)
3112 Vestal Rd (13850-2110)
P.O. Box 157 (13851-0157)
PHONE 607 797-5108
Fax: 607 770-1940
Nicholas D Cerretani Jr, *President*
Nichols Cerretani Jr, *President*
Anthony Cerretani, *Vice Pres*
Lanny Kipp, *Sales Mgr*
EMP: 25
SQ FT: 1,500
SALES: 5.3MM **Privately Held**
WEB: www.ccreadymix.com
SIC: 3273 2951 Ready-mixed concrete; asphalt & asphaltic paving mixtures (not from refineries)

(G-16466)
CARR COMMUNICATIONS GROUP LLC
Also Called: Carr Printing
513 Prentice Rd (13850-2105)
P.O. Box 8409, Endwell (13762-8409)
PHONE 607 748-0481
Holly Reyan, *General Mgr*
Kris Osborn, *Purchasing*
Marilyn Maney, *Financial Exec*
Dorothy Wells, *Human Resources*
Mike Zeitz, *Sales Staff*
EMP: 18
SQ FT: 11,000
SALES: 1.5MM **Privately Held**
SIC: 2752 Commercial printing, offset

(G-16467)
CHROMANANOTECH LLC
85 Murray Hill Rd (13850)
PHONE 607 239-9626
William Bernier,
EMP: 5 **EST:** 2014
SQ FT: 100
SALES (est): 299.1K **Privately Held**
SIC: 2899 Household tints or dyes

(G-16468)
DEAN MANUFACTURING INC
413 Commerce Rd (13850-2238)
PHONE 607 770-1300
Fax: 607 770-1309
Karl E Hughes Jr, *President*
EMP: 10
SALES (est): 921.8K **Privately Held**
WEB: www.centerlessgrinder.com
SIC: 3546 7389 Grinders, portable: electric or pneumatic; grinding, precision: commercial or industrial

(G-16469)
DETEKION SECURITY SYSTEMS INC
200 Plaza Dr Ste 1 (13850-3680)
PHONE 607 729-7179
James Walsh, *President*
Alexander Haker, *Vice Pres*
Kevin Kelly, *Engineer*
Baruch Koren, *VP Sls/Mktg*
Bill Walsh, *Accounts Mgr*
EMP: 18
SQ FT: 7,200
SALES (est): 3.7MM **Privately Held**
SIC: 3699 5063 1731 Security control equipment & systems; burglar alarm systems; fire detection & burglar alarm systems specialization

(G-16470)
GANNETT CO INC
Also Called: Binghamton Press
4421 Vestal Pkwy E (13850-3556)
P.O. Box 1270, Binghamton (13902-1270)
PHONE 607 798-1234
Fax: 607 798-1113
Sherman Bodner, *President*
Richard J Romano, *Personnel*
Sharon A Houghton, *Marketing Mgr*
Donna Bell, *Director*
Nancy Warner, *Executive*
EMP: 77
SQ FT: 100,498
SALES (corp-wide): 3B **Publicly Held**
WEB: www.gannett.com
SIC: 2711 Newspapers
PA: Gannett Co., Inc.
7950 Jones Branch Dr
Mc Lean VA 22102
703 854-6000

(G-16471)
GEOWEB3D INC
4104 Vestal Rd Ste 202 (13850-3554)
P.O. Box 2019, Binghamton (13902-2019)
PHONE 607 323-1114
Robert Holicky, *CEO*
Vincent Autieri, *COO*
Christian Maire, *Vice Pres*
George Davis, *Business Dir*
EMP: 15
SQ FT: 3,300
SALES (est): 417K **Privately Held**
WEB: www.geoweb3d.com
SIC: 7372 7371 Prepackaged software; computer software development

(G-16472)
GREAT AMERICAN INDUSTRIES INC (DH)
300 Plaza Dr (13850-3647)
PHONE 607 729-9331
Fax: 607 798-1079
Burton I Koffman, *Ch of Bd*
Richard E Koffman, *Senior VP*
Bert Kaufman, *Manager*
Stphen Fisher,
Paul Garginkle,
◆ **EMP:** 1 **EST:** 1928
SQ FT: 2,000
SALES (est): 80.7MM
SALES (corp-wide): 4MM **Privately Held**
SIC: 3086 5031 5074 3442 Plastics foam products; building materials, interior; plumbing fittings & supplies; metal doors, sash & trim; metal doors; wet suits, rubber; watersports equipment & supplies; diving equipment & supplies
HQ: Public Loan Company Inc
300 Plaza Dr
Vestal NY 13850
607 584-5274

(G-16473)
K HEIN MACHINES INC
341 Vestal Pkwy E (13850-1631)
PHONE 607 748-1546
Fax: 607 748-0734
Walter C Hein Sr, *CEO*
W Charles Hein Jr, *President*
Steven W Hein, *Vice Pres*
EMP: 9
SQ FT: 15,000
SALES (est): 591.1K **Privately Held**
WEB: www.kheinmachines.com
SIC: 3599 Machine shop, jobbing & repair

(G-16474)
NATIONAL PIPE & PLASTICS INC (PA)
Also Called: Nppi
3421 Vestal Rd (13850-2188)
PHONE 607 729-9381
Fax: 607 729-6130
David J Culbertson, *CEO*
Charles E Miller, *Vice Pres*
Matt Siegel, *Vice Pres*
Michael Westover, *Plant Mgr*
Debbie Belknap, *Purch Dir*
◆ **EMP:** 170
SQ FT: 157,000
SALES (est): 92.9MM **Privately Held**
WEB: www.nationalpipe.com
SIC: 3084 Plastics pipe

(G-16475)
NORANDEX INC VESTAL
2300 Vestal Rd (13850-1937)
PHONE 607 786-0778
Fax: 607 786-0814
Richard Riesen, *Principal*
EMP: 6
SALES (est): 832.2K **Privately Held**
SIC: 3442 5031 5211 Screens, window, metal; windows; lumber & other building materials

(G-16476)
SCORPION SECURITY PRODUCTS INC
330 N Jensen Rd (13850-2132)
PHONE 607 724-9999
Pete Gulick, *President*
▲ **EMP:** 5 **EST:** 2008
SQ FT: 4,700
SALES (est): 200K **Privately Held**
SIC: 3699 Security devices

(G-16477)
SPST INC
Also Called: Embroidery Screen Prtg Netwrk
119b Rano Blvd (13850-2729)
PHONE 607 798-6952
James Porter, *President*
EMP: 5
SALES (est): 450K **Privately Held**
SIC: 2759 Screen printing

(G-16478)
SUPERIOR PRINT ON DEMAND
165 Charles St (13850-2431)
PHONE 607 240-5231
Jeff Valent, *Principal*
EMP: 8 **EST:** 2011
SALES (est): 596.1K **Privately Held**
SIC: 2752 2759 7389 Offset & photolithographic printing; financial note & certificate printing & engraving; personal service agents, brokers & bureaus

(G-16479)
TRUEBITE INC
Also Called: Fotofiles
2590 Glenwood Rd (13850-6115)
PHONE 607 785-7664
Edward J Calafut, *President*
◆ **EMP:** 23
SQ FT: 6,000
SALES (est): 4.5MM **Privately Held**
WEB: www.truebite.com
SIC: 3499 3674 Magnets, permanent: metallic; photoelectric magnetic devices

(G-16480)
VESTAL ASPHALT INC (PA)
201 Stage Rd (13850-1608)
PHONE 607 785-3393
Fax: 607 785-3396
Neil I Guiles, *President*
Jim Unkel, *Vice Pres*
Garrett Guiles, *VP Opers*
Kim Hickok, *Office Mgr*
Timothy Howell, *Manager*
EMP: 14
SQ FT: 3,000
SALES (est): 3.7MM **Privately Held**
WEB: www.vestalasphalt.com
SIC: 2951 Asphalt & asphaltic paving mixtures (not from refineries)

(G-16481)
XEKU CORPORATION
2520 Vestal Pkwy E222 (13850-2078)
PHONE 607 761-1447
Charles S Jakaitis, *Principal*
EMP: 12
SALES (est): 830K **Privately Held**
SIC: 3829 Measuring & controlling devices

Victor
Ontario County

(G-16482)
331 HOLDING INC
Also Called: U S TEC
100 Rawson Rd Ste 205 (14564-1100)
PHONE 585 924-1740
Fax: 585 924-7498
William H Thompson, *President*
Dominic Piazza, *Treasurer*
Linda Stellman, *Controller*
EMP: 32
SALES (est): 4MM **Privately Held**
WEB: www.ustecnet.com
SIC: 3699 7373 1731 Electrical equipment & supplies; computer integrated systems design; electrical work

(G-16483)
ADVANCED INTERCONNECT MFG INC (HQ)
Also Called: A I M
780 Canning Pkwy (14564-8983)
PHONE 585 742-2220
Fax: 585 742-8818
John Durst, *President*
Diane Pepe, *Treasurer*
Gretchen Dunfey, *Human Res Mgr*
Jerry Kearns, *Manager*
▲ **EMP:** 62
SQ FT: 50,000
SALES (est): 14MM
SALES (corp-wide): 83.7MM **Privately Held**
SIC: 3679 Harness assemblies for electronic use: wire or cable
PA: Floturn, Inc.
4236 Thunderbird Ln
West Chester OH 45014
513 860-8040

(G-16484)
AMERICAN SPORTS MEDIA
106 Cobblestone Court Dr # 323 (14564-1045)
PHONE 585 924-4250
David Aultman, *Principal*
EMP: 6
SALES (est): 403K **Privately Held**
SIC: 2711 Newspapers, publishing & printing

(G-16485)
AVCOM OF VIRGINIA INC
Also Called: Ramsey Electronics
590 Fishers Station Dr (14564-9744)
PHONE 585 924-4560
Fax: 585 924-4555
Jay Evans, *Ch of Bd*

John G Ramsey, *President*
EMP: 53
SQ FT: 10,000
SALES (est): 7.2MM
SALES (corp-wide): 30MM **Privately Held**
WEB: www.brynavon.com
SIC: 3825 5961 8331 3651 Test equipment for electronic & electrical circuits; catalog & mail-order houses; job training & vocational rehabilitation services; household audio & video equipment
PA: Brynavon Group, Inc
 2000 Montgomery Ave
 Villanova PA 19085
 610 525-2102

(G-16486)
BIOREM ENVIRONMENTAL INC
100 Rawson Rd Ste 230 (14564-1177)
PHONE..................................585 924-2220
Fax: 585 924-8280
Peter Bruijns, *CEO*
Rick Williams, *Prdtn Mgr*
Brian Jensen, *Engineer*
Patrick Barr, *Manager*
David Pieczarka, *Manager*
▲ **EMP:** 40
SALES (est): 7.9MM
SALES (corp-wide): 12.6MM **Privately Held**
SIC: 3822 Electric air cleaner controls, automatic
HQ: Biorem Technologies Inc
 7496 Wellington Road 34
 Guelph ON N1H 6
 519 767-9100

(G-16487)
BIOWORKS INC (PA)
100 Rawson Rd Ste 205 (14564-1100)
PHONE..................................585 924-4362
Bill Foster, *President*
Chris Hayes, *Engineer*
Doug Oneil, *Controller*
Joe Gionta, *Finance Dir*
Jeff Distasio, *Natl Sales Mgr*
▲ **EMP:** 3
SQ FT: 1,380
SALES (est): 4.5MM **Privately Held**
WEB: www.bioworksinc.com
SIC: 2879 Fungicides, herbicides

(G-16488)
BRISTOL INSTRUMENTS INC
50 Victor Heights Pkwy (14564-9010)
PHONE..................................585 924-2620
Brian Samoriski, *President*
Michael Houk, *Vice Pres*
John Theodorsen, *Vice Pres*
Zachary Houk, *Project Mgr*
Peter Battisti, *CFO*
EMP: 6
SQ FT: 2,000
SALES (est): 1.5MM **Privately Held**
WEB: www.bristol-inst.com
SIC: 3826 Analytical instruments

(G-16489)
BUCKEYE CORRUGATED INC
Also Called: Koch Container Div
797 Old Dutch Rd (14564-8972)
PHONE..................................585 924-1600
Fax: 585 924-7040
Robert Harris, *President*
Karen Schafer, *Safety Dir*
Philip Trautman, *Prdtn Mgr*
EMP: 80
SALES (corp-wide): 196.7MM **Privately Held**
WEB: www.buckeyecorrugated.com
SIC: 2653 3993 Boxes, corrugated; made from purchased materials; signs & advertising specialties
PA: Buckeye Corrugated, Inc
 822 Kumho Dr Ste 400
 Fairlawn OH 44333
 330 576-0590

(G-16490)
CHARLES A ROGERS ENTPS INC
Also Called: Car Engineering and Mfg
51 Victor Heights Pkwy (14564-8926)
P.O. Box 627 (14564-0627)
PHONE..................................585 924-6400
Fax: 585 924-6408
Charles A Rogers, *CEO*
Yvette Rogers Pagano, *President*
Brian Rumsey, *Vice Pres*
Stephen Weilert, *Project Mgr*
John Alliet, *Engineer*
EMP: 45
SQ FT: 40,000
SALES (est): 16.3MM **Privately Held**
WEB: www.car-eng.com
SIC: 3469 3549 3544 Stamping metal for the trade; metalworking machinery; special dies & tools

(G-16491)
CLEARCOVE SYSTEMS INC
7910 Rae Blvd (14564-8820)
PHONE..................................585 734-3012
Gregory Westbrook, *CEO*
Gary Miller, *President*
Terry Wright, *Chief Engr*
EMP: 10 **EST:** 2014
SQ FT: 750
SALES (est): 2.5MM **Privately Held**
SIC: 3589 Sewage & water treatment equipment

(G-16492)
COACH INC
7979 Pittsford Victor Rd (14564)
PHONE..................................585 425-7720
Fax: 585 425-9678
Kelly Lazore, *Manager*
EMP: 15
SALES (corp-wide): 4.4B **Publicly Held**
WEB: www.coach.com
SIC: 3171 Handbags, women's
PA: Coach, Inc.
 10 Hudson Yards
 New York NY 10001
 212 594-1850

(G-16493)
CONSTELLATION BRANDS INC (PA)
207 High Point Dr # 100 (14564-1061)
PHONE..................................585 678-7100
Richard Sands, *Ch of Bd*
Robert Sands, *President*
William A Newlands, *COO*
Thomas J Mullin, *Exec VP*
David Klein, *CFO*
EMP: 95
SALES: 7.3B **Publicly Held**
WEB: www.cbrands.com
SIC: 2084 5182 5181 2082 Wines, brandy & brandy spirits; wine & distilled beverages; wine; neutral spirits; beer & other fermented malt liquors; beer (alcoholic beverage); distilled & blended liquors; concentrates, drink

(G-16494)
COOPERVISION INC
209 High Point Dr (14564-1061)
PHONE..................................585 385-6810
▲ **EMP:** 250
SQ FT: 35,000
SALES (est): 31.2MM
SALES (corp-wide): 1.8B **Publicly Held**
SIC: 3851 Mfg Ophthalmic Goods
HQ: Coopervision, Inc.
 209 High Point Dr
 Victor NY 14564
 585 385-6810

(G-16495)
COOPERVISION INC (HQ)
Also Called: Ocular Sciences A Coopervision
209 High Point Dr (14564-1061)
PHONE..................................585 385-6810
Thomas Bender, *Ch of Bd*
Bob Ferrigno, *President*
Andrew Sedweg, *President*
Steve Hill, *General Mgr*
Steve Mathieson, *Managing Dir*
▲ **EMP:** 65
SQ FT: 20,000
SALES: 329.5MM
SALES (corp-wide): 1.9B **Publicly Held**
SIC: 3851 Contact lenses
PA: The Cooper Companies Inc
 6140 Stoneridge Mall Rd # 590
 Pleasanton CA 94588
 925 460-3600

(G-16496)
DAY AUTOMATION SYSTEMS INC (PA)
7931 Rae Blvd (14564-9017)
PHONE..................................585 924-4630
Eric J Orban, *CEO*
Bob Ormsby, *Business Mgr*
Robert Ormsby, *Vice Pres*
Charlie Loucks, *Project Mgr*
Kenneth Reukauf, *Project Mgr*
EMP: 74
SALES (est): 29.6MM **Privately Held**
WEB: www.dayasi.com
SIC: 3822 Temperature controls, automatic

(G-16497)
DICE AMERICA INC
7676 Netlink Dr (14564-9419)
P.O. Box 360 (14564-0360)
PHONE..................................585 869-6200
Jeff Shufelt, *President*
EMP: 8
SALES: 650K **Privately Held**
WEB: www.diceamerica.com
SIC: 2821 Plastics materials & resins

(G-16498)
ELECTRICAL CONTROLS LINK
100 Rawson Rd Ste 220 (14564-1100)
PHONE..................................585 924-7010
Jim Flynn, *Controller*
EMP: 42
SALES (est): 3.2MM **Privately Held**
WEB: www.han-tek.com
SIC: 3829 Measuring & controlling devices

(G-16499)
ENETICS INC
830 Canning Pkwy (14564-8940)
PHONE..................................585 924-5010
Fax: 585 924-7271
William C Bush, *President*
Travis Downs, *Opers Mgr*
Michael Wowzynski, *Engineer*
EMP: 6
SQ FT: 6,000
SALES (est): 1MM **Privately Held**
WEB: www.enetics.com
SIC: 3625 Relays & industrial controls

(G-16500)
EXHIBITS & MORE
7615 Omnitech Pl Ste 4a (14564-9767)
PHONE..................................585 924-4040
Fax: 585 924-4056
Brian Pitre, *Principal*
EMP: 5
SALES (est): 188.6K **Privately Held**
SIC: 2711 5999 7319 Newspapers, publishing & printing; miscellaneous retail stores; display advertising service

(G-16501)
FLEX ENTERPRISES INC
820 Canning Pkwy (14564-8940)
PHONE..................................585 742-1000
Fax: 585 742-1037
Linda Murphy, *CEO*
Guy Murphy, *President*
▲ **EMP:** 30
SQ FT: 15,000
SALES (est): 5.1MM **Privately Held**
WEB: www.flexenterprises.com
SIC: 3052 5085 Rubber & plastics hose & beltings; industrial supplies; hose, belting & packing; gaskets

(G-16502)
FLIGHTLINE ELECTRONICS INC (DH)
Also Called: Ultra Elec Flightline Systems
7625 Omnitech Pl (14564-9816)
PHONE..................................585 742-5340
Fax: 585 742-5397
Paul Fardellone, *President*
Tom Cooper, *President*
Carlos Santiago, *Principal*
Anthony Diduro, *Vice Pres*
Tony Diduro, *VP Opers*
EMP: 100
SQ FT: 33,000
SALES (est): 43MM
SALES (corp-wide): 967.3MM **Privately Held**
WEB: www.ultra-fei.com
SIC: 3812 Search & navigation equipment
HQ: Ultra Electronics Defense Inc.
 4101 Smith School Rd
 Austin TX 78744
 512 327-6795

(G-16503)
GOOD HEALTH HEALTHCARE NEWSPPR
106 Cobblestone Court Dr (14564-1045)
PHONE..................................585 421-8109
Fax: 585 421-8129
Wagner Dotto, *Owner*
EMP: 10
SALES (est): 264.3K **Privately Held**
WEB: www.cnyhealth.com
SIC: 2711 Newspapers: publishing only, not printed on site

(G-16504)
GORBEL INC
600 Fishers Run (14564-9732)
PHONE..................................800 821-0086
Brian Reh, *President*
Bruce Stevenson, *Facilities Mgr*
Laura Herd, *Production*
Krista Compton, *Buyer*
Jim Gill, *QC Mgr*
EMP: 15 **EST:** 2011
SALES (est): 1.8MM **Privately Held**
SIC: 3536 Hoists, cranes & monorails

(G-16505)
HUNTER MACHINE INC
6551 Anthony Dr (14564-1400)
P.O. Box 50 (14564-0050)
PHONE..................................585 924-7480
Fax: 585 924-8305
John D Vouros, *President*
Lynne Vouros, *Accountant*
EMP: 20
SQ FT: 11,600
SALES: 5MM **Privately Held**
WEB: www.hmicncmachining.com
SIC: 3599 Machine & other job shop work

(G-16506)
INDUSTRIAL INDXYING SYSTEMS INC
626 Fishers Run (14564-9732)
PHONE..................................585 924-9181
Fax: 585 924-2169
William Schnaufer, *President*
Jon Cassano, *Vice Pres*
Chris Draper, *Purch Agent*
Debbie Seibert, *Purchasing*
Peter Drexel, *Engineer*
EMP: 22 **EST:** 1977
SQ FT: 13,000
SALES (est): 5.2MM **Privately Held**
WEB: www.iis-servo.com
SIC: 3625 Relays & industrial controls

(G-16507)
JOHN RAMSEY ELEC SVCS LLC
Also Called: Jre Test
7940 Rae Blvd (14564-8933)
PHONE..................................585 298-9596
Donna Dedes, *General Mgr*
John G Ramsey,
Bruce Sidari,
EMP: 8
SALES: 2.8MM **Privately Held**
SIC: 3825 Instruments to measure electricity

(G-16508)
JOHNSON CONTROLS INC
7612 Main Street Fishers (14564-9601)
PHONE..................................585 924-9346
Fax: 585 924-7086
Todd Mancuso, *Sales Executive*
Joe Knight, *Manager*
EMP: 37 **Privately Held**
SIC: 3822 Temperature controls, automatic
HQ: Johnson Controls, Inc.
 5757 N Green Bay Ave
 Milwaukee WI 53209
 414 524-1200

Victor - Ontario County (G-16509)

GEOGRAPHIC SECTION

(G-16509)
JRE TEST LLC
7940 Rae Blvd (14564-8933)
P.O. Box 182, Mendon (14506-0182)
PHONE................................585 298-9736
Donna Dedes, *Opers Mgr*
Bruce Sidari, *Mng Member*
John Ramsey,
EMP: 7
SQ FT: 2,000
SALES: 2.8MM **Privately Held**
SIC: 3825 Test equipment for electronic & electric measurement

(G-16510)
KIRTAS INC
749 Phillips Rd Ste 300 (14564-9434)
PHONE................................585 924-5999
EMP: 6
SALES (corp-wide): 401.2K **Privately Held**
SIC: 3678 Electronic connectors
PA: Ristech Information Systems Inc
5115 Harvester Rd Unit 8
Burlington ON L7L 0
905 631-7451

(G-16511)
KIRTAS INC
7620 Omnitech Pl (14564-9428)
P.O. Box 729, Bolton MA (01740-0729)
PHONE................................585 924-2420
Fax: 585 924-2441
Robb Richardson, *CEO*
▼ **EMP:** 27
SQ FT: 12,000
SALES (est): 4MM
SALES (corp-wide): 401.2K **Privately Held**
WEB: www.kirtastech.com
SIC: 3678 Electronic connectors
PA: Ristech Information Systems Inc
5115 Harvester Rd Unit 8
Burlington ON L7L 0
905 631-7451

(G-16512)
LIFETIME STAINLESS STEEL CORP
7387 Ny 96 850 (14564)
PHONE................................585 924-9393
Stephen Foti, *President*
EMP: 6
SALES: 900K **Privately Held**
SIC: 3263 Cookware, fine earthenware

(G-16513)
LOGICAL CONTROL SOLUTIONS INC
829 Phillips Rd Ste 100 (14564-9341)
PHONE................................585 424-5340
James Urbanczyk, *President*
Susan Lampi, *General Mgr*
EMP: 18
SQ FT: 45,000
SALES (est): 4.2MM **Privately Held**
SIC: 3824 Temperature controls, automatic

(G-16514)
MAGNET-NDCTIVE SYSTEMS LTD USA
Also Called: Ultra Electronics Inc
7625 Omnitech Pl (14564-9816)
PHONE................................585 924-4000
Russell Greenway, *President*
Bill Gill, *Treasurer*
Colin Frame, *Software Engr*
Nancy Como, *Admin Sec*
▲ **EMP:** 22
SQ FT: 10,000
SALES (est): 4.6MM
SALES (corp-wide): 967.3MM **Privately Held**
SIC: 3663 Receiver-transmitter units (transceiver)
HQ: Ultra Electronics Inc
107 Church Hill Rd
Sandy Hook CT 06482
203 270-3695

(G-16515)
MINITEC FRAMING SYSTEMS LLC
100 Rawson Rd Ste 228 (14564-1151)
PHONE................................585 924-4690
Fax: 585 924-4821
Susan Gijanto-Paeth, *General Mgr*
Susan Paeth, *General Mgr*
Jason Cooley, *Foreman/Supr*
Matt Hoad, *Engineer*
Mike Taylor, *Sales Engr*
▲ **EMP:** 14
SQ FT: 40,000
SALES: 3.5MM **Privately Held**
SIC: 3354 Aluminum extruded products

(G-16516)
NEW SCALE TECHNOLOGIES INC
121 Victor Heights Pkwy (14564-8938)
PHONE................................585 924-4450
Fax: 585 924-4468
David Henderson, *CEO*
Allison Leet, *Vice Pres*
Daniele Piazza, *Vice Pres*
Steven Mowers, *CFO*
Susan Henderson, *Accountant*
EMP: 25
SQ FT: 10,000
SALES: 4MM **Privately Held**
WEB: www.newscaletech.com
SIC: 3823 Controllers for process variables, all types

(G-16517)
NEWTEX INDUSTRIES INC (PA)
Also Called: Trident Partners III
8050 Victor Mendon Rd (14564-9109)
PHONE................................585 924-9135
Fax: 585 924-4645
Jerome Joliet, *CEO*
Douglas Bailey, *President*
Mat Krempl, *VP Opers*
Kelly Goforth, *Controller*
Kathie Laduca, *Accounting Mgr*
▲ **EMP:** 45 **EST:** 1978
SQ FT: 103,000
SALES: 9MM **Privately Held**
WEB: www.newtex.com
SIC: 2221 2295 2241 Fiberglass fabrics; coated fabrics, not rubberized; narrow fabric mills

(G-16518)
NEXT STEP PUBLISHING INC
Also Called: Next Step Magazine, The
2 W Main St Ste 200 (14564-1153)
PHONE................................585 742-1260
Fax: 585 742-1263
David Mammano, *President*
Vincent Crapanzano, *Vice Pres*
Jessica Stein, *Accounts Exec*
Diana Fisher, *Marketing Staff*
Renee Bates, *Manager*
EMP: 15
SQ FT: 1,500
SALES (est): 2.6MM **Privately Held**
SIC: 2721 8748 Periodicals; business consulting

(G-16519)
PACE WINDOW AND DOOR CORP (PA)
Also Called: Pace Window & Door
7224 State Route 96 (14564-9754)
PHONE................................585 924-8350
Fax: 716 942-4837
Robert Mehalso, *Ch of Bd*
Steven Abramson, *President*
Sara Colunio, *Purch Mgr*
Kelly Beer, *Purchasing*
Mark Jacobs, *Controller*
EMP: 50
SQ FT: 21,000
SALES (est): 8.7MM **Privately Held**
WEB: www.pacewindows.com
SIC: 3089 1751 Plastic hardware & building products; window & door (prefabricated) installation

(G-16520)
PREMIER PACKAGING CORPORATION
6 Framark Dr (14564-1136)
P.O. Box 352 (14564-0352)
PHONE................................585 924-8460
Fax: 585 924-8753
Robert B Bzdick, *Principal*
Joe Plummer, *Prdtn Mgr*
Joan T Bzdick, *Treasurer*
Chris Winfield, *Sales Mgr*
Brett Jump, *Accounts Mgr*
EMP: 32
SQ FT: 40,000
SALES (est): 5.9MM
SALES (corp-wide): 19.1MM **Publicly Held**
WEB: www.premiercustompkg.com
SIC: 2657 2675 2677 Folding paperboard boxes; die-cut paper & board; envelopes
PA: Document Security Systems Inc
200 Canal View Blvd # 300
Rochester NY 14623
585 325-3610

(G-16521)
PROGRESSIVE MCH & DESIGN LLC (PA)
Also Called: Pmd
727 Rowley Rd (14564-9728)
PHONE................................585 924-5250
Fax: 585 924-3580
Ron Richards, *Project Mgr*
Tony Silipini, *Project Mgr*
Joseph Costello, *Opers Mgr*
Bruce Allison, *Safety Mgr*
Lori Herold, *Purch Agent*
EMP: 110
SQ FT: 26,000
SALES: 39MM **Privately Held**
WEB: www.pmdautomation.com
SIC: 3599 Machine & other job shop work

(G-16522)
RAMSEY ELECTRONICS LLC
590 Fishers Station Dr (14564-9744)
PHONE................................585 924-4560
Michael Leo, *General Mgr*
Dick Pache, *Engineer*
Richard Oddo, *CFO*
EMP: 20
SALES (est): 5.5MM **Privately Held**
SIC: 3825 5065 Test equipment for electronic & electric measurement; electronic parts & equipment

(G-16523)
RAPID PRINT AND MARKETING INC
8 High St (14564-1105)
PHONE................................585 924-1520
Fax: 585 924-1584
David Gaudieri, *Owner*
EMP: 5
SQ FT: 3,000
SALES (est): 916.9K **Privately Held**
SIC: 2752 7334 Commercial printing, lithographic; commercial printing, offset; photocopying & duplicating services

(G-16524)
REDCOM LABORATORIES INC
1 Redcom Ctr (14564-9785)
PHONE................................585 924-6567
Fax: 585 924-6572
Klaus Gueldenpfennig, *President*
Charles Breidenstein, *President*
Dinah Weisberg, *Vice Pres*
Jennifer Triftshauser, *Project Mgr*
Steve Husband, *Opers Staff*
▲ **EMP:** 200 **EST:** 1978
SQ FT: 140,000
SALES (est): 53.6MM **Privately Held**
WEB: www.redcom.com
SIC: 3661 8748 Switching equipment, telephone; communications consulting

(G-16525)
SENSOR FILMS INCORPORATED
687 Rowley Rd (14564-9728)
PHONE................................585 738-3500
Peter Hessney, *Principal*
EMP: 25
SALES: 1.6MM **Privately Held**
SIC: 3699 Sound signaling devices, electrical

(G-16526)
SERVICE EDUCATION INCORPORATED
790 Canning Pkwy Ste 1 (14564-9019)
PHONE................................585 264-9240
Terence Wolfe, *President*
EMP: 6
SQ FT: 2,100
SALES (est): 300K **Privately Held**
WEB: www.serviceed.com
SIC: 2741 Technical manuals: publishing & printing

(G-16527)
SURMOTECH LLC
7676 Netlink Dr (14564-9419)
PHONE................................585 742-1220
Fax: 585 742-1221
Jerry F Valentine, *CEO*
Arthur Kaempffe, *Vice Pres*
Vince Andrews, *Opers Staff*
Steven Faulkner, *Opers Staff*
David Rizzo, *Opers Staff*
▲ **EMP:** 100
SQ FT: 20,000
SALES: 33.7MM **Privately Held**
WEB: www.surmotech.com
SIC: 3679 Electronic circuits

(G-16528)
SYCAMORE HILL DESIGNS INC
7585 Modock Rd (14564-9104)
PHONE................................585 820-7322
Frank Vallone, *President*
EMP: 5
SALES (est): 300K **Privately Held**
SIC: 3484 Small arms

(G-16529)
SYRACUSA SAND AND GRAVEL INC
1389 Malone Rd (14564-9147)
P.O. Box 2 (14564-0002)
PHONE................................585 924-7146
Scott Syracusa, *President*
Mark Syracusa, *Vice Pres*
EMP: 10
SQ FT: 1,000
SALES (est): 1.6MM **Privately Held**
SIC: 1442 Construction sand mining; gravel mining

(G-16530)
TEKNIC INC
115 Victor Heights Pkwy (14564-8938)
PHONE................................585 784-7454
Fax: 585 784-7460
Alan Fullerton, *CEO*
Thomas Bucella, *Ch of Bd*
David Sewhuk, *President*
Warren God, *Exec VP*
Mark Deangelo, *Engineer*
▲ **EMP:** 35
SQ FT: 10,000
SALES (est): 6.4MM **Privately Held**
WEB: www.teknic.com
SIC: 3625 Motor controls & accessories

(G-16531)
TELOG INSTRUMENTS INC
830 Canning Pkwy (14564-8940)
PHONE................................585 742-3000
Fax: 585 742-3006
Barry L Ceci, *President*
Greg Desantis, *Vice Pres*
Carlton Quallo, *Vice Pres*
Charlene Donofrio, *Buyer*
Everett Lago, *Engineer*
EMP: 30
SQ FT: 20,000
SALES: 5.7MM
SALES (corp-wide): 2.3B **Publicly Held**
WEB: www.telog.com
SIC: 3829 3823 Measuring & controlling devices; industrial instrmnts msrmnt display/control process variable
PA: Trimble Inc.
935 Stewart Dr
Sunnyvale CA 94085
408 481-8000

(G-16532)
THE CALDWELL MANUFACTURING CO
Advantage Mfg
Holland Industrial Park (14564)
PHONE................................585 352-2803
Michelle McCorry, *Manager*
EMP: 35
SALES (corp-wide): 50MM **Privately Held**
SIC: 3495 Wire springs

GEOGRAPHIC SECTION   Walden - Orange County (G-16556)

PA: The Caldwell Manufacturing Company
2605 Manitou Rd Ste 100
Rochester NY 14624
585 352-3790

(G-16533)
TRIAD NETWORK TECHNOLOGIES
75b Victor Heights Pkwy (14564-8926)
PHONE..................................585 924-8505
Fax: 585 924-8507
Pete Sweltz, *President*
Frank Carusone, *Vice Pres*
Don Munn, *Accounts Exec*
Michelle Carusone, *Office Mgr*
EMP: 20
SQ FT: 3,500
SALES (est): 3.3MM Privately Held
WEB: www.triadnt.com
SIC: 2298 Cable, fiber

(G-16534)
VICTOR INSULATORS INC
280 Maple Ave (14564-1385)
PHONE..................................585 924-2127
Fax: 585 924-7906
Ira Knickerbocker, *Ch of Bd*
Andrew E Schwalm, *President*
Chris Rishel, *Safety Mgr*
Peggy Volpe, *Purchasing*
Troy Sebring, *Engineer*
▲ EMP: 105
SQ FT: 327,000
SALES: 17MM Privately Held
WEB: www.victorinsulatorsinc.com
SIC: 3264 Insulators, electrical; porcelain

(G-16535)
W STUART SMITH INC
Also Called: Heritage Packaging
625 Fishers Run (14564-8905)
PHONE..................................585 742-3310
William S Smith, *Ch of Bd*
Kristin J Smith, *Vice Pres*
Scott Floyd, *Sales Engr*
Joseph Benzer, *Marketing Staff*
Jason Tuccio, *Manager*
◆ EMP: 40
SQ FT: 50,000
SALES (est): 8.7MM Privately Held
WEB: www.heritagepackaging.com
SIC: 3086 Packaging & shipping materials, foamed plastic

(G-16536)
WASHER SOLUTIONS INC
760 Canning Pkwy Ste A (14564-9018)
PHONE..................................585 742-6388
Mickie T Pitts, *CEO*
EMP: 10 EST: 2001
SQ FT: 1,200
SALES (est): 2.2MM Privately Held
WEB: www.washersolutions.com
SIC: 3519 Gas engine rebuilding

(G-16537)
WILLIAMSON LAW BOOK CO
790 Canning Pkwy Ste 2 (14564-9019)
PHONE..................................585 924-3400
Fax: 585 924-4153
Greg Chwiecko, *President*
Thomas Osborne, *Treasurer*
EMP: 12 EST: 1870
SQ FT: 10,800
SALES (est): 1.2MM Privately Held
WEB: www.wlbonline.com
SIC: 2761 7371 Manifold business forms; computer software development

Voorheesville
Albany County

(G-16538)
ATLAS COPCO COMPTEC LLC (HQ)
46 School Rd (12186-9696)
PHONE..................................518 765-3344
Fax: 518 765-3357
Peter Wagner, *President*
Holly Simboli, *Principal*
Dan Drescher, *VP Mfg*
Mike Babin, *Safety Dir*
Bill Volk, *Plant Mgr*
◆ EMP: 330 EST: 1970
SQ FT: 100,000
SALES (est): 148.5MM
SALES (corp-wide): 10.9B Privately Held
WEB: www.atlascopco-act.com
SIC: 3563 Air & gas compressors including vacuum pumps
PA: Atlas Copco Ab
Sickla industrivag 3
Nacka 131 5
874 380-00

(G-16539)
SPAULDING & ROGERS MFG INC
3252 New Scotland Rd (12186-4332)
PHONE..................................518 768-2070
Fax: 518 768-2240
Huck Spaulding, *Ch of Bd*
Josephine Spaulding, *President*
Jeff Lawyer, *Vice Pres*
Bobbi Defranco, *Financial Exec*
Jon Schwalb, *Consultant*
▲ EMP: 70
SALES (est): 8.9MM Privately Held
WEB: www.spaulding-rogers.com
SIC: 3952 Artists' equipment

(G-16540)
STANDARD STEEL FABRICATORS
Dutch Hill Rd (12186)
PHONE..................................518 765-4820
David Meixner, *President*
EMP: 18
SALES (est): 2.9MM Privately Held
SIC: 3441 Fabricated structural metal

Waccabuc
Westchester County

(G-16541)
MANN CONSULTANTS LLC
67 Chapel Rd (10597-1001)
PHONE..................................914 763-0512
Stuart Mann,
Jeffrey Mandelbaum,
EMP: 22
SALES (est): 1MM Privately Held
SIC: 2253 2329 T-shirts & tops, knit; men's & boys' sportswear & athletic clothing

Waddington
St. Lawrence County

(G-16542)
STRUCTURAL WOOD CORPORATION
Also Called: Roll Lock Truss
243 Lincoln Ave (13694-3203)
P.O. Box 339 (13694-0339)
PHONE..................................315 388-4442
Michael McGee, *CEO*
Peter Rieter, *President*
Jim Lyon, *Finance Mgr*
Jim Lion, *Finance*
Bernard Shorett, *Sales Mgr*
EMP: 32
SQ FT: 20,000
SALES (est): 4.9MM Privately Held
WEB: www.rolllocktruss.com
SIC: 2439 5031 5211 Structural wood members; doors & windows; lumber & other building materials

Wading River
Suffolk County

(G-16543)
A I P PRINTING & STATIONERS
Also Called: Airport Printing & Stationers
6198 N Country Rd (11792-1625)
PHONE..................................631 929-5529
George A Waldemar, *President*
Chris Waldemar, *Sales Mgr*
Debra Waldemar, *Administration*
EMP: 8
SALES (est): 760K Privately Held
SIC: 2752 Lithographing on metal

(G-16544)
LO-CO FUEL CORP
10 Stephen Dr (11792-2126)
PHONE..................................631 929-5086
Michael Lopez, *Principal*
EMP: 5
SALES (est): 538.6K Privately Held
SIC: 2869 Fuels

(G-16545)
SAFEGUARD INC
578 Sound Ave (11792)
P.O. Box 922 (11792-0922)
PHONE..................................631 929-3273
Charlie Zimmerman, *President*
EMP: 15
SALES (est): 2.5MM Privately Held
SIC: 2899 Fire retardant chemicals

(G-16546)
SPLIT ROCK TRADING CO INC
22 Creek Rd (11792-2501)
P.O. Box 841, Shoreham (11786-0841)
PHONE..................................631 929-3261
Jim Loscalzo, *President*
Peggy Vonbernewitz, *Corp Secy*
EMP: 7
SQ FT: 13,000
SALES (est): 480K Privately Held
WEB: www.splitrockvideo.com
SIC: 3499 5012 5013 5531 Novelties & specialties, metal; automobiles; motorcycles; automotive supplies & parts; automotive accessories; automobiles, new & used; motorcycles

(G-16547)
SWISS SPECIALTIES INC
15 Crescent Ct (11792-3004)
PHONE..................................631 567-8800
Fax: 631 567-8850
Daniel J George, *President*
EMP: 14
SQ FT: 5,000
SALES: 1.9MM Privately Held
SIC: 3541 Screw machines, automatic

Wainscott
Suffolk County

(G-16548)
MAPEASY INC
54 Industrial Rd (11975-2001)
P.O. Box 80 (11975-0080)
PHONE..................................631 537-6213
Fax: 631 537-4541
Gary Bradhering, *President*
Chris Harris, *Vice Pres*
▲ EMP: 12
SQ FT: 11,000
SALES (est): 980.4K Privately Held
WEB: www.mapeasy.com
SIC: 2741 4724 Maps: publishing & printing; travel agencies

Walden
Orange County

(G-16549)
AMPAC PAPER LLC (PA)
30 Coldenham Rd (12586-2036)
P.O. Box 271 (12586-0271)
PHONE..................................845 778-5511
John Q Baumann, *Ch of Bd*
Robert Tillis, *President*
Leland Lewis, *Chairman*
Robert De Gregorio, *Senior VP*
Robert D Gregorio, *Senior VP*
▲ EMP: 470
SQ FT: 200,000
SALES (est): 101.5MM Privately Held
WEB: www.ampaconline.com
SIC: 2674 2621 5162 Shopping bags: made from purchased materials; paper mills, plastics materials

(G-16550)
C & C ATHLETIC INC
Also Called: Viking Jackets & Athletic Wear
11 Myrtle Ave (12586-2340)
PHONE..................................845 713-4670
Andrea Conklin, *President*
EMP: 5
SQ FT: 4,000
SALES (est): 318.7K Privately Held
WEB: www.vikingathletic.com
SIC: 2759 2339 Screen printing; athletic clothing: women's, misses' & juniors'

(G-16551)
CALFONEX COMPANY
121 Orchard St (12586-1707)
PHONE..................................845 778-2212
Terrance Donovan, *Owner*
EMP: 15
SALES (est): 836.8K Privately Held
SIC: 2899 Chemical preparations

(G-16552)
DWYER FARM LLC
40 Bowman Ln (12586-2100)
PHONE..................................914 456-2742
Brian Dwyer, *Principal*
Christopher Dwyer, *Principal*
Jeannie Dwyer, *Principal*
Joseph Dwyer, *Principal*
Mel Dwyer, *Principal*
EMP: 6
SALES (est): 185.1K Privately Held
SIC: 2026 Farmers' cheese

(G-16553)
PACIFIC DIE CAST INC
Also Called: Qssi
827 Route 52 Ste 2 (12586-2747)
PHONE..................................845 778-6374
Fax: 845 778-6380
Melissa Durant, *Principal*
EMP: 15
SALES (corp-wide): 11.6MM Privately Held
SIC: 3544 Special dies & tools
PA: Pacific Die Cast, Inc.
12802 Commodity Pl
Tampa FL 33626
813 316-2221

(G-16554)
POLICH TALLIX INC
39 Edmunds Ln (12586-1538)
PHONE..................................845 567-9464
Richard Polich, *President*
Adam D Pe, *General Mgr*
Adam Demchak, *Vice Pres*
Chris McGrath, *Project Mgr*
Andrew Pharmer, *Site Mgr*
▲ EMP: 63
SALES (est): 14.8MM Privately Held
SIC: 3369 3499 Nonferrous foundries; novelties & specialties, metal

(G-16555)
ROMAR CONTRACTING INC
630 State Route 52 (12586-2709)
P.O. Box 658 (12586-0658)
PHONE..................................845 778-2737
Rod Winchell, *President*
Kyle Winchell, *Technology*
EMP: 5
SALES: 500K Privately Held
SIC: 3441 Fabricated structural metal

(G-16556)
SPENCE ENGINEERING COMPANY INC
Also Called: Nicholson Steam Trap
150 Coldenham Rd (12586-2909)
PHONE..................................845 778-5566
Fax: 845 778-7123
A William Higgins, *Ch of Bd*
David A Bloss Sr, *President*
Alan R Carlsen, *Vice Pres*
Douglas Frank, *Vice Pres*
Kenneth Smith, *Vice Pres*
▲ EMP: 150
SQ FT: 79,000

Walden - Orange County (G-16557)

SALES (est): 26.1MM
SALES (corp-wide): 590.2MM **Publicly Held**
WEB: www.spenceengineering.com
SIC: 3491 3444 3612 3494 Pressure valves & regulators, industrial; metal ventilating equipment; transformers, except electric; valves & pipe fittings
PA: Circor International, Inc.
30 Corporate Dr Ste 200
Burlington MA 01803
781 270-1200

(G-16557)
TILCON NEW YORK INC
272 Berea Rd (12586-2906)
PHONE.................................845 778-5591
Reinis Siplls, *Branch Mgr*
EMP: 27
SALES (corp-wide): 28.6B **Privately Held**
WEB: www.tilconny.com
SIC: 1429 Trap rock, crushed & broken-quarrying; dolomitic marble, crushed & broken-quarrying
HQ: Tilcon New York Inc.
162 Old Mill Rd
West Nyack NY 10994
845 358-4500

(G-16558)
WALLKILL LODGE NO 627 F&AM
61 Main St (12586-1824)
P.O. Box 311 (12586-0311)
PHONE.................................845 778-7148
Mark Balck, *President*
EMP: 14 **EST:** 2001
SQ FT: 7,326
SALES (est): 564.6K **Privately Held**
SIC: 2711 Newspapers

Wales Center
Erie County

(G-16559)
AM BICKFORD INC
12318 Big Tree Rd (14169)
P.O. Box 201 (14169-0201)
PHONE.................................716 652-1590
Fax: 716 652-2046
John Bickford, *President*
Jane Keohane, *Sls & Mktg Exec*
Laureen Stevenson, *Sales Mgr*
EMP: 12
SQ FT: 5,000
SALES: 2MM **Privately Held**
WEB: www.ambickford.com
SIC: 3841 Surgical & medical instruments

(G-16560)
HALE ELECTRICAL DIST SVCS INC
12088 Big Tree Rd (14169)
P.O. Box 221 (14169-0221)
PHONE.................................716 818-7595
David Neveaux, *President*
EMP: 6
SALES: 1.5MM **Privately Held**
SIC: 3612 Distribution transformers, electric

Wallkill
Ulster County

(G-16561)
ARTCRAFT BUILDING SERVICES
85 Old Hoagerburgh Rd (12589-3419)
PHONE.................................845 895-3893
Pasqual J Petrucci, *President*
Janice A Petrucci, *Vice Pres*
EMP: 5
SQ FT: 3,000
SALES (est): 660.6K **Privately Held**
SIC: 3537 Platforms, stands, tables, pallets & similar equipment; dollies (hand or power trucks), industrial except mining

(G-16562)
CATSMO LLC
Also Called: Solex Catsmo Fine Foods
25 Myers Rd (12589-3516)
PHONE.................................845 895-2296
Fax: 845 895-1232
Markus Draxler, *CEO*
Jeff Craig, *CFO*
Frederic Pothier, *CFO*
◆ **EMP:** 12 **EST:** 1995
SQ FT: 15,000
SALES (est): 2.6MM **Privately Held**
WEB: www.catsmo.com
SIC: 2091 Salmon, smoked

(G-16563)
FAIR-RITE PRODUCTS CORP (PA)
1 Commercial Row (12589-4438)
P.O. Box 288 (12589-0288)
PHONE.................................845 895-2055
Fax: 845 895-2629
Richard Parker, *Ch of Bd*
Carole U Parker, *President*
Larry Surrells, *Division Mgr*
Mike Eanni, *Purchasing*
Rocco Conklin, *Engineer*
▲ **EMP:** 125 **EST:** 1952
SQ FT: 80,000
SALES (est): 21.2MM **Privately Held**
WEB: www.fair-rite.com
SIC: 3679 Cores, magnetic

(G-16564)
JAMES B CROWELL & SONS INC
242 Lippincott Rd (12589-3643)
PHONE.................................845 895-3464
Fax: 845 895-9701
James Crowell III, *President*
Wendy Sutherland, *Vice Pres*
EMP: 9 **EST:** 1872
SQ FT: 4,800
SALES (est): 1MM **Privately Held**
SIC: 3544 Industrial molds

(G-16565)
RICHTER METALCRAFT CORPORATION
Also Called: Charles Richter
80 Cottage St (12589-3128)
P.O. Box 297 (12589-0297)
PHONE.................................845 895-2025
David Richter, *President*
Carol Morgan, *Vice Pres*
Carl Ulrich, *Maint Spvr*
Louise Tancriedi, *Admin Sec*
EMP: 35 **EST:** 1934
SQ FT: 50,000
SALES (est): 4MM **Privately Held**
WEB: www.charlesrichter.com
SIC: 3469 Metal stampings; stamping metal for the trade; spinning metal for the trade

(G-16566)
SELECT-TECH INC
3050 State Route 208 (12589-4431)
P.O. Box 259 (12589-0259)
PHONE.................................845 895-8111
Fax: 845 895-8112
William Diener, *President*
Thomas Diener, *Treasurer*
▲ **EMP:** 5
SQ FT: 25,000
SALES (est): 600K **Privately Held**
WEB: www.select-tech.com
SIC: 3291 Abrasive products

(G-16567)
WASH QUARTERS LLC
680 Hoagerburgh Rd (12589-3424)
PHONE.................................989 802-2017
Jeffrey I Maynard, *Administration*
EMP: 6
SALES (est): 162.7K **Privately Held**
SIC: 3131 Quarters

Walton
Delaware County

(G-16568)
BEYOND DESIGN INC
807 Pines Brook Rd (13856-2381)
PHONE.................................607 865-7487
Barbara A Salvatore, *President*
EMP: 7
SALES (est): 638.4K **Privately Held**
SIC: 3299 Architectural sculptures: gypsum, clay, papier mache, etc.

(G-16569)
KRAFT HEINZ FOODS COMPANY
261 Delaware St (13856-1099)
PHONE.................................607 865-7131
Fax: 607 865-5830
Thomas Kuhrt, *Opers Staff*
Cynthia Waggoner, *Opers-Prdtn-Mfg*
Greg Higby, *Engineer*
Claudia Gonus, *Manager*
Keith Ormsby, *Executive*
EMP: 200
SALES (corp-wide): 26.4B **Publicly Held**
WEB: www.kraftfoods.com
SIC: 2026 2022 Fermented & cultured milk products; cheese, natural & processed
HQ: Kraft Heinz Foods Company
1 Ppg Pl Ste 3200
Pittsburgh PA 15222
412 456-5700

(G-16570)
NORTHEAST FABRICATORS LLC
30-35 William St (13856-1497)
P.O. Box 65 (13856-0065)
PHONE.................................607 865-4031
Steve Schick, *Purch Mgr*
Judy Beardslee, *Human Res Mgr*
Kathy Cole, *Office Mgr*
William Brodeur,
John Phraner,
EMP: 70 **EST:** 1997
SQ FT: 80,000
SALES (est): 20.6MM **Privately Held**
SIC: 3444 3441 Sheet metalwork; fabricated structural metal

Walworth
Wayne County

(G-16571)
MEDCO MACHINE LLC
2320 Walworth Marion Rd (14568-9501)
P.O. Box 454 (14568-0454)
PHONE.................................315 986-2109
Mark Medyn,
EMP: 6
SQ FT: 4,800
SALES (est): 700K **Privately Held**
SIC: 3599 Machine shop, jobbing & repair

(G-16572)
ROCHESTER ASPHALT MATERIALS
Also Called: Dolomite Group
1200 Atlantic Ave (14568-9792)
PHONE.................................315 524-4619
Harvey Smeatin, *Manager*
EMP: 7
SALES (corp-wide): 28.6B **Privately Held**
SIC: 3531 Asphalt plant, including gravel-mix type
HQ: Rochester Asphalt Materials Inc
1150 Penfield Rd
Rochester NY 14625
585 381-7010

(G-16573)
SOFTWARE & GENERAL SERVICES CO
Also Called: S and G Imaging
1365 Fairway 5 Cir (14568-9444)
PHONE.................................315 986-4184
John Larysz, *Owner*
EMP: 6

SALES (est): 480K **Privately Held**
WEB: www.softwareandgeneral.com
SIC: 7372 Prepackaged software

Wampsville
Madison County

(G-16574)
DIEMOLDING CORPORATION (PA)
100 Donald Hicks Dew Dr (13163)
P.O. Box 26 (13163-0026)
PHONE.................................315 363-4710
Donald H Dew, *CEO*
Mark Vanderveen, *Ch of Bd*
Dennis O'Brien, *President*
Jim Morin, *Vice Pres*
Carl Cook, *Plant Mgr*
▲ **EMP:** 6 **EST:** 1920
SQ FT: 50,000
SALES (est): 17.2MM **Privately Held**
WEB: www.diemolding.com
SIC: 2655 Containers, laminated phenolic & vulcanized fiber

(G-16575)
DIEMOLDING CORPORATION
Also Called: Dietooling
N Court St (13163)
PHONE.................................315 363-7747
Fax: 315 363-7747
Tom Pavente, *General Mgr*
EMP: 17
SALES (corp-wide): 17.2MM **Privately Held**
WEB: www.diemolding.com
SIC: 3544 Special dies & tools
PA: Diemolding Corporation
100 Donald Hicks Dew Dr
Wampsville NY 13163
315 363-4710

Wantagh
Nassau County

(G-16576)
1/2 OFF CARDS WANTAGH INC
1162 Wantagh Ave (11793-2110)
PHONE.................................516 809-9832
Steven Bodenstein, *CEO*
EMP: 5
SALES (est): 544K **Privately Held**
SIC: 2771 Greeting cards

(G-16577)
CHRISTOPHER ANTHONY PUBG CO
Also Called: Christiny
2225 Wantagh Ave (11793-3917)
PHONE.................................516 826-9205
Anthony Fannin, *President*
Jo Ann Fannin, *Admin Sec*
▼ **EMP:** 19 **EST:** 1978
SQ FT: 6,000
SALES: 2.5MM **Privately Held**
WEB: www.christony.com
SIC: 2741 Catalogs: publishing only, not printed on site

(G-16578)
GREENVALE BAGEL INC
3060 Merrick Rd (11793-4395)
PHONE.................................516 221-8221
Cesidia Facchini, *President*
Claudio Facchini, *Corp Secy*
Ralph Facchini, *Vice Pres*
EMP: 30
SQ FT: 1,200
SALES (est): 3MM **Privately Held**
SIC: 2051 Bagels, fresh or frozen; bakery: wholesale or wholesale/retail combined

(G-16579)
HERSHEY KISS 203 INC
3536 Bunker Ave (11793-3439)
PHONE.................................516 503-3740
Brian Deluca, *Chairman*
EMP: 5 **EST:** 2010
SALES (est): 261.4K **Privately Held**
SIC: 2066 Chocolate & cocoa products

GEOGRAPHIC SECTION

(G-16580)
LIFESCAN INC
15 Tardy Ln N (11793-1928)
PHONE....................516 557-2693
EMP: 258
SALES (corp-wide): 71.8B Publicly Held
SIC: 2835 Blood derivative diagnostic agents
HQ: Lifescan, Inc.
　965 Chesterbrook Blvd
　Chesterbrook PA 19087
　800 227-8862

(G-16581)
MORTGAGE PRESS LTD
1220 Wantagh Ave (11793-2202)
PHONE....................516 409-1400
Russell Sickmen, CEO
Joel M Berman, President
Andrew Berman, Exec VP
EMP: 22
SQ FT: 4,000
SALES (est): 1.3MM Privately Held
WEB: www.mortgagepress.com
SIC: 2711 2741 Newspapers; miscellaneous publishing

(G-16582)
NBETS CORPORATION
Also Called: Wantagh 5 & 10
1901 Wantagh Ave (11793-3930)
PHONE....................516 785-1259
Fax: 516 785-1294
John Norris, Ch of Bd
EMP: 8 EST: 2010
SALES (est): 855.8K Privately Held
SIC: 2392 Household furnishings

(G-16583)
R M F HEALTH MANAGEMENT L L C
Also Called: Professional Health Imaging
3361 Park Ave (11793-3735)
PHONE....................718 854-5400
Syndney Bernstein, Executive
Robyn Feldstein,
EMP: 21
SQ FT: 9,600
SALES (est): 3.2MM Privately Held
SIC: 3844 X-ray apparatus & tubes; nuclear irradiation equipment

(G-16584)
WANTAGH COMPUTER CENTER
10 Stanford Ct (11793-1863)
PHONE....................516 826-2189
Sidney B Nudelman, CEO
EMP: 14
SQ FT: 4,000
SALES (est): 1.3MM
SALES (corp-wide): 1.4MM Privately Held
SIC: 3577 3571 Computer peripheral equipment; electronic computers
PA: S B Nudelman Inc
　10 Stanford Ct
　Wantagh NY 11793
　516 826-2189

(G-16585)
ZUCKERBAKERS INC
2845 Jerusalem Ave (11793-2016)
PHONE....................516 785-6900
Andrew Greenstein, Principal
EMP: 11
SALES (est): 1.2MM Privately Held
SIC: 2051 Bread, cake & related products

Wappingers Falls
Dutchess County

(G-16586)
DRA IMAGING PC
169 Myers Corners Rd # 250 (12590-3868)
PHONE....................845 296-1057
Richard Friedland, CEO
EMP: 27
SALES (est): 5.1MM Privately Held
SIC: 3844 X-ray apparatus & tubes

(G-16587)
FLAVORMATIC INDUSTRIES INC
90 Brentwood Dr (12590-3344)
PHONE....................845 297-9100
Fax: 845 297-2881
Judith Back, President
Ron Back, Exec VP
Ronald Back, Exec VP
Robert Back, Vice Pres
Rick Febles, QC Dir
▼ EMP: 20 EST: 1887
SQ FT: 21,000
SALES (est): 4.6MM Privately Held
WEB: www.flavormatic.com
SIC: 2087 5169 2844 Beverage bases, concentrates, syrups, powders & mixes; beverage bases; extracts, flavoring; essential oils; perfumes, natural or synthetic

(G-16588)
FRESH HARVEST INCORPORATED
1574 Route 9 (12590-2846)
PHONE....................845 296-1024
Jin Chul Lee, President
EMP: 9
SALES (est): 1.7MM Privately Held
SIC: 3556 Bakery machinery

(G-16589)
G BOPP USA INC
4 Bill Horton Way (12590-2018)
P.O. Box 393, Hopewell Junction (12533-0393)
PHONE....................845 296-1065
Andrew Moss, General Mgr
George Baker, COO
▲ EMP: 7
SALES (est): 1.2MM Privately Held
SIC: 3496 Wire cloth & woven wire products
PA: G. Bopp & Co Ag
　Bachmannweg 21
　ZUrich ZH
　443 776-666

(G-16590)
GEM REPRODUCTION SERVICES CORP
Also Called: Signal Graphics Printing
1299 Route 9 Ste 105 (12590-4918)
PHONE....................845 298-0172
Fax: 845 298-0307
Gary Mensching, President
Elizabeth Mensching, Admin Sec
EMP: 5
SQ FT: 3,300
SALES (est): 956.9K Privately Held
SIC: 2752 2759 Commercial printing, offset; commercial printing

(G-16591)
GLAXOSMITHKLINE LLC
6 Alpert Dr (12590-4602)
PHONE....................845 797-3259
EMP: 26
SALES (corp-wide): 34.3B Privately Held
SIC: 2834 Pharmaceutical preparations
HQ: Glaxosmithkline Llc
　5 Crescent Dr
　Philadelphia PA 19112
　215 751-4000

(G-16592)
HIGHLAND VALLEY SUPPLY INC
30 Airport Dr (12590-6164)
PHONE....................845 849-2863
Raymond Marsella, President
David Caparaso, Vice Pres
Jan Caparaso, Treasurer
EMP: 15
SQ FT: 11,000
SALES (est): 3.6MM Privately Held
WEB: www.highlandvalleysupply.com
SIC: 3644 Electric conduits & fittings

(G-16593)
HUDSON VALLEY LIGHTING INC
151 Airport Dr (12590-6161)
P.O. Box 10775, Newburgh (12552-0775)
PHONE....................845 561-0300
Fax: 845 561-6848
David Littman, President
Brent Fields, Vice Pres
◆ EMP: 75 EST: 1960
SQ FT: 65,000
SALES (est): 17.7MM Privately Held
WEB: www.hudsonvalleylighting.com
SIC: 3646 3645 Commercial indusl & institutional electric lighting fixtures; residential lighting fixtures

(G-16594)
JPMORGAN CHASE BANK NAT ASSN
1460 Route 9 (12590-4425)
PHONE....................845 298-2461
Rick Mendes, Branch Mgr
EMP: 12
SALES (corp-wide): 105.4B Publicly Held
SIC: 3644 Insulators & insulation materials, electrical
HQ: Jpmorgan Chase Bank, National Association
　1111 Polaris Pkwy
　Columbus OH 43240
　614 436-3055

(G-16595)
MONEAST INC
Also Called: Sir Speedy
1708 Route 9 Ste 3 (12590-1367)
P.O. Box 679 (12590-0679)
PHONE....................845 298-8898
David Monto, President
Randall J Easter, Treasurer
Mary Alice Monto, Admin Sec
EMP: 6
SQ FT: 2,800
SALES (est): 825K Privately Held
SIC: 2752 2791 2789 Commercial printing, lithographic; typesetting; bookbinding & related work

(G-16596)
SONNEMAN-A WAY OF LIGHT
151 Airport Dr (12590-6161)
P.O. Box 7458, Newburgh (12550)
PHONE....................845 926-5469
Sonny Park, Owner
▲ EMP: 5
SALES (est): 800.2K Privately Held
SIC: 3646 Commercial indusl & institutional electric lighting fixtures

(G-16597)
THINK GREEN JUNK REMOVAL INC
29 Meadow Wood Ln (12590-5937)
PHONE....................845 297-7771
George Makris, Owner
EMP: 7
SALES (est): 842.5K Privately Held
SIC: 3089 Garbage containers, plastic

(G-16598)
WAPPINGERS FALLS SHOPPER INC
Also Called: Beacon Press News
84 E Main St (12590-2504)
PHONE....................845 297-3723
Fax: 845 297-6810
Albert M Osten, President
Curtis Schmidt, General Mgr
Pat Roza, Director
Jothi Vaidyalingan, Director
EMP: 50 EST: 1959
SQ FT: 12,000
SALES (est): 3.6MM Privately Held
SIC: 2711 2752 Newspapers: publishing only, not printed on site; commercial printing, lithographic

Warnerville
Schoharie County

(G-16599)
ZMZ MFG INC
300 Mickle Hollow Rd (12187-2507)
PHONE....................518 234-4336
Lisa Zaba Miller, Principal
EMP: 8
SALES (est): 634.1K Privately Held
SIC: 3999 Manufacturing industries

Warrensburg
Warren County

(G-16600)
LUMAZU LLC
141 Garnet Lake Rd (12885-5907)
PHONE....................518 623-3372
Sheila Flanagan,
EMP: 5 Privately Held
SIC: 2022 2024 Cheese spreads, dips, pastes & other cheese products; sherbets, dairy based
PA: Lumazu, Llc
　484 S Johnsburg Rd
　Warrensburg NY 12885

(G-16601)
LUMAZU LLC (PA)
Also Called: Nettle Meadow Farm
484 S Johnsburg Rd (12885-5944)
PHONE....................518 623-3372
Sheila Flanagan,
Lorraine Lambiase,
EMP: 15
SQ FT: 7,500
SALES (est): 1.4MM Privately Held
SIC: 2022 2024 Cheese spreads, dips, pastes & other cheese products; sherbets, dairy based

(G-16602)
NORTHEASTERN PRODUCTS CORP (PA)
Also Called: Nepco
115 Sweet Rd (12885-4754)
P.O. Box 98 (12885-0098)
PHONE....................518 623-3161
Fax: 518 623-3803
Paul Schiavi, CEO
Gary Schiavi, President
Mark Stauber, Plant Mgr
Richard Morgan, Sales Mgr
Lee Schiavi, Exec Dir
EMP: 23
SQ FT: 2,400
SALES (est): 11MM Privately Held
WEB: www.nep-co.com
SIC: 2493 Reconstituted wood products

(G-16603)
TUMBLEHOME BOATSHOP
684 State Route 28 (12885-5301)
PHONE....................518 623-5050
Reuben Smith, Owner
EMP: 6
SALES (est): 534.6K Privately Held
SIC: 3732 Boat building & repairing

Warsaw
Wyoming County

(G-16604)
FAIRVIEW PAPER BOX CORP
200 Allen St (14569-1562)
PHONE....................585 786-5230
Fax: 585 786-5711
Donald Zaas, Ch of Bd
Joel Zaas, President
Mark Cassese, COO
John L Asimakopoulos, CFO
EMP: 31
SQ FT: 55,000
SALES (est): 6.8MM
SALES (corp-wide): 58.5MM Privately Held
WEB: www.boxit.com
SIC: 2652 Setup paperboard boxes
PA: The Apex Paper Box Company
　5555 Walworth Ave
　Cleveland OH 44102
　216 631-4000

(G-16605)
MORTON BUILDINGS INC
5616 Route 20a E (14569-9302)
PHONE....................585 786-8191
Fax: 585 786-5116
John Edmunds, Opers-Prdtn-Mfg
Ed Neudeck, Sales Mgr
EMP: 40

SQ FT: 5,122
SALES (corp-wide): 521.8MM Privately Held
WEB: www.mortonbuildings.com
SIC: 3448 5039 Prefabricated metal buildings; prefabricated structures
PA: Morton Buildings, Inc.
252 W Adams St
Morton IL 61550
800 447-7436

(G-16606)
UNIDEX CORPORATION WESTERN NY
Also Called: Unidex Company
2416 State Route 19 N (14569-9336)
PHONE.................585 786-3170
Arthur Crater, President
Don Cunningham, General Mgr
Susan M Gardner, Vice Pres
Thomas Baldwin, Treasurer
EMP: 16
SQ FT: 21,000
SALES (est): 3.1MM Privately Held
WEB: www.unidex-inc.com
SIC: 3549 Assembly machines, including robotic

(G-16607)
UPSTATE DOOR INC
26 Industrial St (14569-1550)
PHONE.................585 786-3880
Robert J Fontaine, CEO
Brock Beckstrand, Safety Mgr
Craig Smith, Engineer
Matt Nelson, Controller
Jason Hurley, Sales Mgr
▲ EMP: 75
SQ FT: 55,000
SALES (est): 7.6MM Privately Held
WEB: www.upstatedoor.com
SIC: 2431 Interior & ornamental woodwork & trim

Warwick
Orange County

(G-16608)
AMERICAN TOWMAN NETWORK INC
Also Called: American Towman Expeditions
7 West St (10990-1447)
PHONE.................845 986-4546
Fax: 845 986-5181
Steven L Calitri, President
Neila Smith, President
Brendan Dooley, Editor
Miriam Ortiz, Manager
Annmarie Nitti, Art Dir
EMP: 12
SALES (est): 940K Privately Held
WEB: www.towman.com
SIC: 2721 7549 Periodicals; towing services; towing service, automotive

(G-16609)
DANGELO HOME COLLECTIONS INC
Also Called: Victoria Dngelo Intr Cllctions
39 Warwick Tpke (10990-3632)
P.O. Box 271 (10990-0271)
PHONE.................917 267-8920
Victoria D'Angelo, President
Stuart Morrison, Vice Pres
▲ EMP: 7
SQ FT: 16,000
SALES (est): 750K Privately Held
WEB: www.dangelohome.com
SIC: 2431 Woodwork, interior & ornamental

(G-16610)
DIGITAL UNITED COLOR PRTG INC
Also Called: Warwick Press
33 South St (10990-1624)
P.O. Box 708 (10990-0708)
PHONE.................845 986-9846
Scott J Lieberman, Ch of Bd
EMP: 9
SALES (est): 1.3MM Privately Held
SIC: 2752 Color lithography

(G-16611)
DREAM GREEN PRODUCTIONS
Also Called: Dream Fabric Printing
39 Warwick Tpke (10990-3632)
P.O. Box 271 (10990-0271)
PHONE.................917 267-8920
Victoria D'Angelo, Principal
EMP: 5
SALES (est): 220K Privately Held
SIC: 2399 Fabricated textile products

(G-16612)
GARDEN STATE SHAVINGS INC
16 Almond Tree Ln (10990-2442)
PHONE.................845 544-2835
Kimberlee Martin, CEO
Barry Luyster, Vice Pres
▼ EMP: 15
SQ FT: 60,000
SALES (est): 1.4MM Privately Held
SIC: 2421 Sawdust, shavings & wood chips

(G-16613)
KECK GROUP INC (PA)
314 State Route 94 S (10990-3379)
PHONE.................845 988-5757
Fax: 845 343-0428
Robert Koeck, CEO
Terry Yungman, Manager
EMP: 12
SQ FT: 20,000
SALES (est): 904.6K Privately Held
WEB: www.keckgroup.com
SIC: 2531 Pews, church

(G-16614)
KINGS QUARTET CORP
270 Kings Hwy (10990-3417)
PHONE.................845 986-9090
Gary Bernstein, President
David Bernstein, Treasurer
Bernard Bernstein, Admin Sec
Kenneth Bernstein, Admin Sec
EMP: 5
SALES (est): 309.8K Privately Held
SIC: 2435 Plywood, hardwood or hardwood faced

(G-16615)
KNG CONSTRUCTION CO INC
19 Silo Ln (10990-2872)
PHONE.................212 595-1451
Mark V Azzopardi, President
EMP: 10
SALES (est): 1.2MM Privately Held
SIC: 2431 1542 1521 Woodwork, interior & ornamental; commercial & office buildings, renovation & repair; general remodeling, single-family houses

(G-16616)
MECHANICAL RUBBER PDTS CO INC
Also Called: Minisink Rubber
77 Forester Ave Ste 1 (10990-1107)
P.O. Box 593 (10990-0593)
PHONE.................845 986-2271
Fax: 845 986-0399
Cedric Glasper, President
Dan Wayman, COO
Nicole Cosimano, Purchasing
Steve Kelley, Sales Staff
Barry Moellman, Marketing Staff
EMP: 15
SQ FT: 53,000
SALES (est): 2.8MM Privately Held
SIC: 3061 3089 Mechanical rubber goods; molding primary plastic

(G-16617)
MEECO SULLIVAN LLC
3 Chancellor Ln (10990-3411)
PHONE.................800 232-3625
EMP: 225
SQ FT: 50,000
SALES: 22MM Privately Held
SIC: 2499 4493 Mfg Wood Products Marina Operation

(G-16618)
TRACK 7 INC
3 Forester Ave (10990-1129)
PHONE.................845 544-1810
Betsy Mitchell, Principal

EMP: 6
SALES (est): 990.8K Privately Held
SIC: 2653 Corrugated & solid fiber boxes

(G-16619)
TRANSPRTTION COLLABORATIVE INC
Also Called: Trans Tech Bus
7 Lake Station Rd (10990-3426)
PHONE.................845 988-2333
Danny Daniels, President
EMP: 39
SALES (est): 9.7MM Privately Held
SIC: 3711 Motor vehicles & car bodies

Washingtonville
Orange County

(G-16620)
BRISTOL GIFT CO INC
8 North St (10992-1113)
PHONE.................845 496-2821
Fax: 845 496-2859
Matthew A Ropiecki Sr, President
Ellen Martarano, Corp Secy
Matthew M Ropiecki Jr, Vice Pres
EMP: 15
SQ FT: 7,000
SALES (est): 2.3MM Privately Held
WEB: www.bristolgift.net
SIC: 3499 Picture frames, metal

(G-16621)
BROTHERHOOD AMERICAS
Also Called: Vinevrest Co
100 Brotherhood Plaza Dr (10992-2262)
P.O. Box 190 (10992-0190)
PHONE.................845 496-3661
Fax: 845 496-8720
Hernan Donoso, President
Cesar Baeza, Corp Secy
Robert Liberto, Finance Dir
Carol Tepper, Manager
▲ EMP: 35
SALES (est): 6.9MM Privately Held
WEB: www.brotherhoodwinery.net
SIC: 2084 Wines

Wassaic
Dutchess County

(G-16622)
PAWLING CORPORATION
Also Called: Standard Products Division
32 Nelson Hill Rd (12592-2121)
P.O. Box 200 (12592-0200)
PHONE.................845 373-9300
Fax: 845 373-8712
Greg Holen, Vice Pres
Lou Musella, Prdtn Mgr
Ron Peck, Purch Mgr
Warren Rozelle, Purch Mgr
Deborah Barbanti, Purch Agent
EMP: 65
SALES (corp-wide): 44MM Privately Held
WEB: www.pawling.com
SIC: 3061 3446 2273 Mechanical rubber goods; architectural metalwork; carpets & rugs
PA: Pawling Corporation
157 Charles Colman Blvd
Pawling NY 12564
845 855-1000

(G-16623)
PRESRAY CORPORATION
Also Called: Door Dam
32 Nelson Hill Rd (12592-2121)
P.O. Box 200 (12592-0200)
PHONE.................845 373-9300
Theodore C Hollander, Ch of Bd
Jason Smith, President
Kevin Harris, General Mgr
Jered Tuberville, Opers Mgr
Michael McGregor, Controller
▲ EMP: 25 EST: 1955
SQ FT: 50,000

SALES (est): 6.1MM
SALES (corp-wide): 44MM Privately Held
WEB: www.presray.com
SIC: 3442 Metal doors
PA: Pawling Corporation
157 Charles Colman Blvd
Pawling NY 12564
845 855-1000

(G-16624)
WALL PROTECTION PRODUCTS LLC
Also Called: Wallguard.com
32 Nelson Hill Rd (12592-2121)
P.O. Box 1109, Dover Plains (12522-1109)
PHONE.................877 943-6826
Fax: 845 373-7761
Rose Davis, General Mgr
Ralph Skokan, CFO
Rose Benson, Manager
EMP: 30
SALES (est): 3.1MM Privately Held
SIC: 3069 Rubber floor coverings, mats & wallcoverings

Water Mill
Suffolk County

(G-16625)
CAR DOCTOR MOTOR SPORTS LLC
Also Called: Car Doctor, The
610 Scuttle Hole Rd (11976-2520)
P.O. Box 1384, Amagansett (11930-1384)
PHONE.................631 537-1548
Fax: 631 267-3514
Ryan Pilla, Owner
EMP: 6
SALES (est): 450K Privately Held
SIC: 3949 Cartridge belts, sporting type

(G-16626)
DEERFIELD MILLWORK INC
58 Deerfield Rd Unit 2 (11976-2151)
PHONE.................631 726-9663
Keith Dutcher, President
Michelle Dutcher, Finance
Adam Schmidt, Manager
Jeanette Camara, Info Tech Dir
EMP: 11
SQ FT: 5,000
SALES (est): 1.7MM Privately Held
WEB: www.deerfieldmillwork.com
SIC: 2431 8712 Millwork; architectural services

(G-16627)
DUCK WALK VINYARDS
231 Montauk Hwy (11976-2639)
P.O. Box 962 (11976-0962)
PHONE.................631 726-7555
Fax: 631 726-4395
Herodotus Damianos, President
Alexander Damianos, Vice Pres
EMP: 20
SQ FT: 22,470
SALES (est): 1.6MM Privately Held
WEB: www.duckwalk.com
SIC: 2084 Wines

(G-16628)
WALPOLE WOODWORKERS INC
779 Montauk Hwy (11976-2607)
P.O. Box 1281 (11976-1281)
PHONE.................631 726-2859
Fax: 631 726-2861
Lou Maglio, President
EMP: 8
SALES (corp-wide): 103.2MM Privately Held
WEB: www.walpolewoodworkers.com
SIC: 2499 5211 5712 2452 Fencing, wood; fencing; outdoor & garden furniture; prefabricated wood buildings; prefabricated metal buildings; wood household furniture
PA: Walpole Woodworkers, Inc.
767 East St
Walpole MA 02081
508 668-2800

GEOGRAPHIC SECTION

Waterloo - Seneca County (G-16651)

(G-16629)
WONDER NATURAL FOODS CORP (PA)
30 Blank Ln (11976-2134)
PHONE..................631 726-4433
Lloyd Lasdon, *CEO*
Stuart Lasdon, *COO*
▲ **EMP:** 6
SQ FT: 3,000
SALES (est): 1.1MM **Privately Held**
WEB: www.peanutwonder.com
SIC: 2099 Peanut butter

Waterford
Saratoga County

(G-16630)
CASCADES TSSUE GROUP-SALES INC
148 Hudson River Rd (12188-1908)
PHONE..................518 238-1900
Andre Lair, *Manager*
EMP: 100
SALES (corp-wide): 2.9B **Privately Held**
SIC: 2676 Towels, napkins & tissue paper products
HQ: Cascades Tissue Group-Sales Inc.
148 Hudson River Rd
Waterford NY 12188
819 363-5100

(G-16631)
CASCADES TSSUE GROUP-SALES INC (HQ)
148 Hudson River Rd (12188-1908)
P.O. Box 369 (12188-0369)
PHONE..................819 363-5100
Fax: 518 238-1919
Daniel Morneau, *President*
Gary A Hayden, *Chairman*
Maryse Fernet, *Vice Pres*
Stephanie Croto, *Controller*
Brad Winchell, *Marketing Staff*
▲ **EMP:** 40
SALES (est): 28.1MM
SALES (corp-wide): 2.9B **Privately Held**
SIC: 2621 Absorbent paper
PA: Cascades Inc
404 Boul Marie-Victorin
Kingsey Falls QC J0A 1
819 363-5100

(G-16632)
EVONIK CORPORATION
7 Schoolhouse Ln (12188-1931)
P.O. Box 188 (12188-0188)
PHONE..................518 233-7090
Fax: 518 237-0478
Carlos Araujo, *Business Mgr*
Terri Owens, *Plant Mgr*
Chuck Wilpers, *Warehouse Mgr*
Robert Blackman, *Engineer*
Dan Miller, *Plant Engr*
EMP: 32
SALES (corp-wide): 2.3B **Privately Held**
SIC: 2869 Industrial organic chemicals
HQ: Evonik Corporation
299 Jefferson Rd
Parsippany NJ 07054
973 929-8000

(G-16633)
HALFMOON TOWN WATER DEPARTMENT
8 Brookwood Rd (12188-1206)
PHONE..................518 233-7489
Fax: 518 233-1705
Frank Tironi, *Director*
EMP: 9 **EST:** 2007
SALES (est): 603.6K **Privately Held**
SIC: 2899 Water treating compounds

(G-16634)
MAXIMUM SECURITY PRODUCTS CORP
Also Called: Hillside Iron Works
3 Schoolhouse Ln (12188-1931)
PHONE..................518 233-1800
Fax: 518 233-8069
Joseph Burch, *President*
Harold Hatfield, *Corp Secy*
Robert Magee, *Vice Pres*
▲ **EMP:** 50
SQ FT: 100,000
SALES (est): 11.9MM **Privately Held**
WEB: www.maximumsecuritycorp.com
SIC: 3446 3499 2542 2531 Architectural metalwork; stairs, fire escapes, balconies, railings & ladders; fences, gates, posts & flagpoles; fire- or burglary-resistive products; partitions & fixtures, except wood; public building & related furniture

(G-16635)
MILLWOOD INC
430 Hudson River Rd (12188-1916)
PHONE..................518 233-1475
Mike Cusack, *Branch Mgr*
EMP: 17 **Privately Held**
SIC: 3565 5084 Packaging machinery; packaging machinery & equipment
PA: Millwood, Inc.
3708 International Blvd
Vienna OH 44473

(G-16636)
MOMENTIVE PERFORMANCE (DH)
260 Hudson River Rd (12188-1910)
PHONE..................281 325-3536
Douglas A Johns, *Vice Pres*
EMP: 1
SALES (est): 1MM
SALES (corp-wide): 2.2B **Privately Held**
SIC: 2899 Chemical preparations
HQ: Momentive Performance Materials Inc.
260 Hudson River Rd
Waterford NY 12188
518 237-3330

(G-16637)
MOMENTIVE PERFORMANCE MTLS INC
260 Hudson River Rd (12188-1910)
PHONE..................614 986-2495
Steve Delarge, *Opers Staff*
EMP: 1500
SALES (corp-wide): 2.2B **Privately Held**
WEB: www.gewaterford.com
SIC: 2869 Silicones
HQ: Momentive Performance Materials Inc.
260 Hudson River Rd
Waterford NY 12188
518 237-3330

(G-16638)
MOMENTIVE PERFORMANCE MTLS INC (DH)
260 Hudson River Rd (12188-1910)
PHONE..................518 237-3330
John G Boss, *President*
Nathan E Fisher, *Exec VP*
John Moran, *Senior VP*
Brian Berger, *Vice Pres*
Craig R Branchfield, *Vice Pres*
◆ **EMP:** 20
SALES: 2.2B **Privately Held**
WEB: www.gewaterford.com
SIC: 2869 3479 3679 Silicones; coating of metals with silicon; electronic crystals; quartz crystals, for electronic application
HQ: Mpm Intermediate Holdings Inc.
260 Hudson River Rd
Waterford NY 12188
518 237-3330

(G-16639)
MPM HOLDINGS INC (PA)
260 Hudson River Rd (12188-1910)
PHONE..................518 237-3330
John G Boss, *President*
Douglas A Johns, *Exec VP*
John D Moran, *Senior VP*
George F Knight, *Vice Pres*
Erick R Asmussen, *CFO*
EMP: 5
SALES (est): 2.2B **Privately Held**
SIC: 2869 3479 3679 Silicones; coating of metals with silicon; electronic crystals; quartz crystals, for electronic application

(G-16640)
MPM INTERMEDIATE HOLDINGS INC (HQ)
260 Hudson River Rd (12188-1910)
PHONE..................518 237-3330
John G Boss, *President*
Brian D Berger, *CFO*
EMP: 2 **EST:** 2014
SALES (est): 2.2B **Privately Held**
SIC: 2869 3479 3679 Silicones; coating of metals with silicon; electronic crystals; quartz crystals, for electronic application
PA: Mpm Holdings Inc
260 Hudson River Rd
Waterford NY 12188
518 237-3330

(G-16641)
MPM SILICONES LLC
Also Called: Momentive
260 Hudson River Rd (12188-1910)
PHONE..................518 233-3330
Fax: 518 233-3866
Rick Schumacher, *Vice Pres*
Mary Krenceski, *Research*
Jacob Weinreb, *Engineer*
Brian D Berger, *CFO*
Kimberly Barnett, *Auditor*
EMP: 4600
SALES (est): 228.8MM
SALES (corp-wide): 2.2B **Privately Held**
SIC: 2869 Silicones
HQ: Momentive Performance Materials Inc.
260 Hudson River Rd
Waterford NY 12188
518 237-3330

(G-16642)
SOFT-TEX INTERNATIONAL INC
Also Called: Soft-Tex Manufacturing Co
428 Hudson River Rd (12188-1916)
P.O. Box 278 (12188-0278)
PHONE..................800 366-2324
T Arthur Perry, *President*
Robert O'Connell, *Exec VP*
Jeff Chilton, *Senior VP*
Keith Bolton, *Vice Pres*
Harold J Perry Jr, *Vice Pres*
▲ **EMP:** 90
SQ FT: 120,000
SALES (est): 20.2MM **Privately Held**
WEB: www.bedpillows.com
SIC: 2392 Cushions & pillows

(G-16643)
STEPPING STONES ONE DAY SIGNS
105 Broad St (12188-2313)
P.O. Box 128 (12188-0128)
PHONE..................518 237-5774
Fax: 518 237-1410
John Matson, *President*
Paul Matson, *Vice Pres*
EMP: 5
SQ FT: 3,000
SALES (est): 517.4K **Privately Held**
SIC: 3993 Signs & advertising specialties

(G-16644)
UPSTATE PIPING PRODUCTS INC
95 Hudson River Rd (12188-1937)
P.O. Box 321 (12188-0321)
PHONE..................518 238-3457
Bob Lafountain, *President*
EMP: 3
SQ FT: 7,500
SALES: 2MM **Privately Held**
SIC: 3462 Flange, valve & pipe fitting forgings, ferrous

(G-16645)
URSULA OF SWITZERLAND INC (PA)
Also Called: Ursula Company Store
31 Mohawk Ave (12188-2290)
PHONE..................518 237-2580
Fax: 518 237-3038
Ursula G Rickenbacher, *President*
Lou Pingatore, *COO*
Douglas Randancco, *Vice Pres*
Beth Easly, *Purchasing*
Meinrad Rickenbacher, *Treasurer*
EMP: 22 **EST:** 1965
SQ FT: 35,000
SALES (est): 2.8MM **Privately Held**
WEB: www.ursula.com
SIC: 2335 2337 2331 Gowns, formal; ensemble dresses: women's, misses' & juniors'; women's & misses' suits & coats; women's & misses' blouses & shirts

Waterloo
Seneca County

(G-16646)
EVANS CHEMETICS LP
228 E Main St (13165-1534)
PHONE..................315 539-9221
Fax: 315 539-9627
Barb Guthrie, *Purch Mgr*
Jeff Mooneyhan, *Engineer*
Pat Wrobel, *Engineer*
Bernie Souza, *Sales Mgr*
Frank Dipasquale, *Branch Mgr*
EMP: 55
SALES (corp-wide): 29.7MM **Privately Held**
WEB: www.evanschemetics.com
SIC: 2899 Acids
PA: Evans Chemetics Lp
Glenpointe Center West 4
Teaneck NJ 07666
201 992-3100

(G-16647)
FINGER LAKES CONVEYORS INC
2359 State Route 414 E (13165-9633)
PHONE..................315 539-9246
Fax: 315 539-0879
Michael J Gelder, *Ch of Bd*
Nancy Gelder, *Vice Pres*
EMP: 9
SQ FT: 37,000
SALES: 806.5K **Privately Held**
WEB: www.flconveyors.com
SIC: 3499 1796 Fire- or burglary-resistive products; machinery installation

(G-16648)
FRAZIER INDUSTRIAL COMPANY
1291 Waterloo Geneva Rd (13165-1201)
PHONE..................315 539-9256
Staci Predicho, *Human Resources*
EMP: 55
SQ FT: 62,116
SALES (corp-wide): 254.6MM **Privately Held**
WEB: www.ecologic.com
SIC: 2542 3441 Pallet racks: except wood; fabricated structural metal
PA: Frazier Industrial Company
91 Fairview Ave
Long Valley NJ 07853
908 876-3001

(G-16649)
GHARANA INDUSTRIES LLC
Also Called: Ganesh Foods
61 Swift St (13165-1124)
PHONE..................315 651-4004
◆ **EMP:** 6
SQ FT: 122,000
SALES (est): 420K **Privately Held**
SIC: 2022 Mfg Cheese

(G-16650)
GUESS INC
655 State Route 318 # 96 (13165-5632)
PHONE..................315 539-5634
Lisa Kuney, *Principal*
EMP: 25
SALES (corp-wide): 2.2B **Publicly Held**
SIC: 2325 Men's & boys' jeans & dungarees
PA: Guess, Inc.
1444 S Alameda St
Los Angeles CA 90021
213 765-3100

(G-16651)
HAMPSHIRE CHEMICAL CORP
228 E Main St (13165-1529)
P.O. Box 700 (13165-0700)
PHONE..................315 539-9221
Richard Babiarz, *Partner*
Romaine Dutcher, *Maint Spvr*
Gary Horvath, *QC Dir*
Lori Bentley, *Human Res Mgr*
EMP: 100

Waterloo - Seneca County (G-16652)

GEOGRAPHIC SECTION

SALES (corp-wide): 72.7B Publicly Held
SIC: 2869 2899 2819 Industrial organic chemicals; chemical preparations; industrial inorganic chemicals
HQ: Hampshire Chemical Corp
2 E Spit Brook Rd
Nashua NH

(G-16652)
MARROS EQUIPMENT & TRUCKS
2354 State Route 414 (13165-8473)
PHONE..................315 539-8702
John Marro Jr, *President*
EMP: 14 EST: 1946
SQ FT: 14,400
SALES (est): 1.4MM Privately Held
SIC: 3713 3536 Truck bodies (motor vehicles); hoists

(G-16653)
PETER PRODUCTIONS DEVIVI INC
2494 Kingdom Rd (13165-9400)
PHONE..................315 568-8484
Fax: 315 568-6041
Peter Devivi, *President*
EMP: 10
SQ FT: 9,000
SALES (est): 1.5MM Privately Held
WEB: www.tapertite.com
SIC: 2431 Millwork

(G-16654)
ZYP PRECISION LLC
1098 Birdsey Rd (13165-9404)
PHONE..................315 539-3667
Edward Huff,
EMP: 5
SALES (est): 399.8K Privately Held
SIC: 3541 Lathes, metal cutting & polishing

Watertown
Jefferson County

(G-16655)
A & K EQUIPMENT INCORPORATED
407 Sherman St (13601-3958)
PHONE..................705 428-3573
Jim Lowe, *President*
Kevin Lowe, *Principal*
Cathy Lowe, *Corp Secy*
Andrew Lowe, *Vice Pres*
EMP: 5
SALES (est): 425.8K Privately Held
SIC: 3596 5046 Scales & balances, except laboratory; scales, except laboratory

(G-16656)
ALLIED MOTION TECHNOLOGIES INC
Also Called: Stature Electric
22543 Fisher Rd (13601-1090)
P.O. Box 6660 (13601-6660)
PHONE..................315 782-5910
Bill Stout, *General Mgr*
Lenissa Chenoweth, *Materials Mgr*
Ron Wenzen, *Branch Mgr*
Jeff Shearer, *Technology*
EMP: 200
SALES (corp-wide): 245.8MM Publicly Held
WEB: www.alliedmotion.com
SIC: 3621 3546 Electric motor & generator parts; motors, electric; power-driven handtools
PA: Allied Motion Technologies Inc.
495 Commerce Dr Ste 3
Amherst NY 14228
716 242-8634

(G-16657)
ATOMIC SIGNWORKS
1040 Bradley St Ste 3 (13601-1224)
P.O. Box 6103 (13601-6103)
PHONE..................315 779-7446
Fax: 315 779-7479
Daniel Gill, *Owner*
EMP: 5
SALES: 250K Privately Held
WEB: www.atomicsignworks.com
SIC: 3993 Signs & advertising specialties

(G-16658)
BARRETT PAVING MATERIALS INC
26572 State Route 37 (13601-5789)
PHONE..................315 788-2037
Fax: 315 786-0748
Sylvain Gross, *General Mgr*
Patrick O'Bryan, *General Mgr*
Dave Putnam, *Plant Supt*
Scott Lockerbie, *Site Mgr*
Tammy Causey, *Financial Exec*
EMP: 12
SQ FT: 820
SALES (corp-wide): 77.1MM Privately Held
WEB: www.barrettpaving.com
SIC: 3273 2951 1611 Ready-mixed concrete; asphalt paving mixtures & blocks; highway & street construction
HQ: Barrett Paving Materials Inc.
3 Becker Farm Rd Ste 307
Roseland NJ 07068
973 533-1001

(G-16659)
BIMBO BAKERIES USA INC
144 Eastern Blvd (13601-3132)
PHONE..................315 785-7060
George Weston, *Branch Mgr*
EMP: 18 Privately Held
WEB: www.gwbakeries.com
SIC: 2051 Bread, cake & related products
HQ: Bimbo Bakeries Usa, Inc
255 Business Center Dr # 200
Horsham PA 19044
215 347-5500

(G-16660)
BIMBO BAKERIES USA INC
1100 Water St (13601-2146)
PHONE..................315 782-4189
Rick Kimbell, *Manager*
EMP: 165 Privately Held
SIC: 2051 Bread, cake & related products
HQ: Bimbo Bakeries Usa, Inc
255 Business Center Dr # 200
Horsham PA 19044
215 347-5500

(G-16661)
BLACK RIVER BREWING CO INC
500 Newell St (13601-2428)
PHONE..................315 755-2739
Michael Niezabytoski, *Owner*
EMP: 5
SALES (est): 330.7K Privately Held
SIC: 2082 Malt beverages

(G-16662)
BOTTLING GROUP LLC
Also Called: Pepsi Beverages Company
1035 Bradley St (13601-1248)
PHONE..................315 788-6751
Fax: 315 788-6756
Eric Foss, *CEO*
Dan Wiseman, *General Mgr*
Casey Jones, *Engineer*
Darel Jones, *Info Tech Dir*
Winnie Parker, *Administration*
EMP: 39 EST: 1999
SALES (est): 4MM Privately Held
SIC: 2086 Carbonated soft drinks, bottled & canned

(G-16663)
CAR-FRESHNER CORPORATION (HQ)
Also Called: Little Trees
21205 Little Tree Dr (13601-5861)
P.O. Box 719 (13601-0719)
PHONE..................315 788-6250
Fax: 315 788-7467
Richard O Flechtner, *Chairman*
Tami Petrus, *Opers Mgr*
Richard Stancato, *Opers Mgr*
Amber Geidel, *Safety Mgr*
Lindsay Sparacino, *Research*
◆ EMP: 250 EST: 1952
SQ FT: 30,000
SALES (est): 83.2MM Privately Held
WEB: www.little-trees.com
SIC: 2842 Deodorants, nonpersonal

(G-16664)
CAR-FRESHNER CORPORATION
22569 Fisher Cir (13601-1058)
P.O. Box 719 (13601-0719)
PHONE..................315 788-6250
Fax: 315 782-0140
Robert Swank, *Principal*
Walter Humphrey, *Engineer*
Theresa Jewett, *Human Resources*
Travis Washburn, *Sales Mgr*
Mary Crooker, *Asst Director*
EMP: 59 Privately Held
WEB: www.little-trees.com
SIC: 2842 Specialty cleaning, polishes & sanitation goods
HQ: Car-Freshner Corporation
21205 Little Tree Dr
Watertown NY 13601
315 788-6250

(G-16665)
CHRISTIAN BUS ENDEAVORS INC (PA)
Also Called: Coughlin Printing Group
210 Court St Ste 10 (13601-4546)
PHONE..................315 788-8560
Michael A Biolsi, *President*
Brian Peck, *Principal*
Gary Ingram, *Corp Secy*
Laura Biolsi, *Accounts Mgr*
Dan Kelebes, *Manager*
EMP: 10
SALES (est): 1.2MM Privately Held
WEB: www.amfcoughlin.com
SIC: 2759 7374 Commercial printing; computer graphics service

(G-16666)
CLEMENTS BURRVILLE SAWMILL
18181 Van Allen Rd N (13601-5711)
PHONE..................315 782-4549
Fax: 315 782-4549
Philip Clement, *President*
Betty Clement, *Vice Pres*
EMP: 9
SQ FT: 8,820
SALES: 700K Privately Held
SIC: 2448 2426 2421 Pallets, wood; hardwood dimension & flooring mills; sawmills & planing mills, general

(G-16667)
COCA-COLA REFRESHMENTS USA INC
22614 County Route 51 (13601-5064)
PHONE..................315 785-8907
Fax: 315 785-6841
Jess Duck, *Manager*
EMP: 33
SALES (corp-wide): 41.8B Publicly Held
WEB: www.cokecce.com
SIC: 2086 Bottled & canned soft drinks
HQ: Coca-Cola Refreshments Usa, Inc.
2500 Windy Ridge Pkwy Se
Atlanta GA 30339
770 989-3000

(G-16668)
COUGHLIN PRINTING GROUP
Also Called: A M F/Coughlin Printing
210 Court St Ste 10 (13601-4546)
PHONE..................315 788-8560
Fax: 315 836-0043
Doug Bockstanz, *President*
Brian Peck, *General Mgr*
William Barden, *Vice Pres*
Nance Bockstanz, *Vice Pres*
Gary Ingram, *Vice Pres*
EMP: 7
SQ FT: 1,500
SALES (est): 792.7K Privately Held
SIC: 2752 Commercial printing, lithographic; commercial printing, offset

(G-16669)
CURRENT APPLICATIONS INC
275 Bellew Ave S (13601-2381)
P.O. Box 321 (13601-0321)
PHONE..................315 788-4689
George M Anderson, *President*
Roger Snyder, *Corp Secy*
Christopher Gilbert, *Vice Pres*
Robert Olin, *Vice Pres*
▲ EMP: 49

SQ FT: 20,000
SALES (est): 10.9MM Privately Held
WEB: www.currentapps.com
SIC: 3621 Motors, electric

(G-16670)
CYCLOTHERM OF WATERTOWN INC
787 Pearl St (13601-9111)
PHONE..................315 782-1100
Charles E Stafford, *President*
EMP: 25
SQ FT: 20,000
SALES (est): 805.2K Privately Held
SIC: 3443 3554 Boiler shop products: boilers, smokestacks, steel tanks; paper industries machinery

(G-16671)
DOCO QUICK PRINT INC
808 Huntington St (13601-2864)
PHONE..................315 782-6623
Fax: 315 782-6623
Carolyn Osborne, *President*
Daniel Osborne, *Treasurer*
EMP: 6
SQ FT: 3,000
SALES (est): 768.1K Privately Held
SIC: 2752 Commercial printing, offset

(G-16672)
E AND V ENERGY CORPORATION
22925 State Route 12 (13601-5034)
PHONE..................315 786-2067
Fax: 315 786-0733
Bill Austin, *Branch Mgr*
EMP: 16
SALES (corp-wide): 19.7MM Privately Held
SIC: 2911 Still oil
PA: E. And V. Energy Corporation
2737 Erie Dr
Weedsport NY 13166
315 594-8076

(G-16673)
GERTRUDE HAWK CHOCOLATES INC
21182 Salmon Run Mall Loo (13601-2248)
EMP: 20
SALES (corp-wide): 240.6MM Privately Held
SIC: 2064 Mfg Candy/Confectionery
PA: Gertrude Hawk Chocolates, Inc.
9 Keystone Industrial Par
Dunmore PA 18512
570 342-7556

(G-16674)
HANSON AGGREGATES PA LLC
25133 Nys Rt 3 (13601-1718)
P.O. Box 130 (13601-0130)
PHONE..................315 782-2300
Dan O'Connor, *Manager*
Roger Hutchinson, *Manager*
EMP: 10
SALES (corp-wide): 16B Privately Held
SIC: 1442 5032 Gravel mining; stone, crushed or broken
HQ: Hanson Aggregates Pennsylvania, Llc
7660 Imperial Way
Allentown PA 18195
610 366-4626

(G-16675)
HENDERSON PRODUCTS INC
Also Called: Henderson Truck Equipment
22686 Fisher Rd Ste A (13601-1088)
PHONE..................315 785-0994
Dave O'Brien, *Manager*
Dave Obrien, *Manager*
EMP: 22 Publicly Held
WEB: www.henderson-mfg.com
SIC: 3822 Ice maker controls
HQ: Henderson Products, Inc.
1085 S 3rd St
Manchester IA 52057
563 927-2828

(G-16676)
JAIN IRRIGATION INC
740 Water St (13601-2114)
PHONE..................315 755-4400
Aric Olson, *President*

GEOGRAPHIC SECTION
Watertown - Jefferson County (G-16698)

EMP: 70
SALES (corp-wide): 577.4MM **Privately Held**
SIC: 3052 3523 Plastic hose; fertilizing, spraying, dusting & irrigation machinery
HQ: Jain Irrigation, Inc.
2060 E Francis St
Ontario CA 91761
909 395-5200

(G-16677)
JEFFERSON CONCRETE CORP
22850 County Route 51 (13601-5081)
PHONE..................................315 788-4171
Mark Thompson, *CEO*
Mark Losee, *General Mgr*
Barbara Belcher, *Human Res Dir*
Donna Borkland, *Manager*
EMP: 55
SQ FT: 37,000
SALES (est): 9.8MM **Privately Held**
WEB: www.jeffconcrete.com
SIC: 3272 Manhole covers or frames, concrete; septic tanks, concrete; tanks, concrete; burial vaults, concrete or precast terrazzo

(G-16678)
JOHN VESPA INC (PA)
Also Called: Vespa Sand & Stone
19626 Overlook Dr (13601-5443)
PHONE..................................315 788-6330
Fax: 315 788-7360
John Vespa Jr, *President*
Dorothy Vespa, *Admin Sec*
EMP: 13 **EST:** 1941
SQ FT: 2,400
SALES: 1.5MM **Privately Held**
SIC: 1422 1442 Crushed & broken limestone; construction sand mining; gravel mining

(G-16679)
KENAL SERVICES CORP
Also Called: Metal Man Services
1109 Water St (13601-2147)
PHONE..................................315 788-9226
Fax: 315 788-9440
Kenneth Moseley, *President*
Michael Vecchio, *CFO*
Victor Scott, *Manager*
EMP: 7
SQ FT: 15,272
SALES: 600K **Privately Held**
WEB: www.metalmanservices.com
SIC: 3446 Architectural metalwork

(G-16680)
KENT NUTRITION GROUP INC
810 Waterman Dr (13601-2371)
PHONE..................................315 788-0032
Fax: 315 788-6033
Brad Coolidge, *Opers-Prdtn-Mfg*
Jeremy Ruckman, *QA Dir*
Dave Moorhead, *Engineer*
Bob Spindell, *Systems Staff*
EMP: 10
SQ FT: 13,608
SALES (corp-wide): 604.1MM **Privately Held**
WEB: www.blueseal.com
SIC: 2048 Prepared feeds
HQ: Kent Nutrition Group, Inc.
1600 Oregon St
Muscatine IA 52761
866 647-1212

(G-16681)
KNORR BRAKE HOLDING CORP (DH)
748 Starbuck Ave (13601-1620)
PHONE..................................315 786-5356
Heinz Hermann Thiele, *President*
Jerry Autry, *Senior Mgr*
▲ **EMP:** 1
SALES (est): 1.2B **Privately Held**
SIC: 3743 5013 Railroad equipment; motor vehicle supplies & new parts
HQ: Knorr-Bremse Ag
Moosacher Str. 80
Munchen 80809
893 547-0

(G-16682)
KNORR BRAKE TRUCK SYSTEMS CO (DH)
Also Called: New York Air Brake
748 Starbuck Ave (13601-1620)
P.O. Box 6760 (13601-6760)
PHONE..................................315 786-5200
Peter Riedlinger, *Vice Ch Bd*
Heinz Hermann Thiele, *President*
Mike Hawthorne, *President*
Jamie Perkins, *Editor*
Jason Connell, *Senior VP*
▲ **EMP:** 445
SQ FT: 250,000
SALES (est): 1.1B **Privately Held**
SIC: 3743 Brakes, air & vacuum: railway
HQ: Knorr Brake Holding Corporation
748 Starbuck Ave
Watertown NY 13601
315 786-5356

(G-16683)
KNOWLTON TECHNOLOGIES LLC
213 Factory St (13601-2748)
PHONE..................................315 782-0600
Frederick G Rudmann, *CEO*
James Ganter, *Exec VP*
James Lee, *Vice Pres*
Nick Cassoni, *Plant Mgr*
Jamie Ganter, *Plant Mgr*
▲ **EMP:** 130
SQ FT: 287,000
SALES (est): 59.9MM **Publicly Held**
SIC: 2621 Filter paper; specialty papers
PA: Eastman Chemical Company
200 S Wilcox Dr
Kingsport TN 37660

(G-16684)
LCO DESTINY LLC
Also Called: Timeless Frames
22476 Fisher Rd (13601-1090)
P.O. Box 28 (13601-0028)
PHONE..................................315 782-3302
Fax: 315 782-4825
Kevin Davis, *Opers Staff*
Sandy Durgan, *Opers Staff*
Liana Newton, *Buyer*
Greg Gaston, *CFO*
Jackie George, *Human Res Dir*
◆ **EMP:** 300
SQ FT: 235,000
SALES (est): 45.5MM **Privately Held**
WEB: www.timelessframes.com
SIC: 2499 Picture & mirror frames, wood

(G-16685)
LERAY HOMES INC
22732 Duffy Rd (13601-1794)
PHONE..................................315 788-6087
Daniel Tontarski, *President*
Geraldine Tontarski, *Admin Sec*
EMP: 5
SQ FT: 169
SALES: 4MM **Privately Held**
SIC: 3441 Building components, structural steel

(G-16686)
MARTINS DENTAL STUDIO
Also Called: Martin Dental Studio
162 Sterling St (13601-3311)
P.O. Box 228 (13601-0228)
PHONE..................................315 788-0800
Richard Martin Jr, *President*
EMP: 7
SQ FT: 1,400
SALES (est): 951.7K **Privately Held**
SIC: 3843 8072 Teeth, artificial (not made in dental laboratories); dental laboratories

(G-16687)
MEXICO INDEPENDENT INC (PA)
Also Called: Salmon River News
260 Washington St (13601-4669)
PHONE..................................315 963-3763
Mark Backus, *President*
Roseann Parsons, *Editor*
R Charles Backus, *Vice Pres*
Horace Backus, *Treasurer*
James Homa, *Accounts Exec*
EMP: 20 **EST:** 1924
SQ FT: 6,139
SALES (est): 1.9MM **Privately Held**
SIC: 2711 2741 Job printing & newspaper publishing combined; catalogs: publishing & printing

(G-16688)
NEW YORK AIR BRAKE LLC (DH)
748 Starbuck Ave (13601-1620)
P.O. Box 6760 (13601-6760)
PHONE..................................315 786-5219
Fax: 315 786-5676
Heinz Thiele, *Ch of Bd*
Frank Henderson, *President*
J Paul Morgan, *President*
Marshall G Beck, *Senior VP*
Eric Wright, *Engineer*
▲ **EMP:** 140
SALES: 22.5MM **Privately Held**
SIC: 3743 Brakes, air & vacuum: railway
HQ: Knorr Brake Holding Corporation
748 Starbuck Ave
Watertown NY 13601
315 786-5356

(G-16689)
NORTH COUNTRY WELDING INC
904 Leray St (13601-1315)
PHONE..................................315 788-9718
Fax: 315 788-7182
Timothy Shawl, *President*
EMP: 6
SQ FT: 3,000
SALES (est): 626.2K **Privately Held**
SIC: 7692 Welding repair

(G-16690)
NORTHERN AWNING & SIGN COMPANY
Also Called: N A S C O
22891 County Route 51 (13601-5005)
PHONE..................................315 782-8515
Fax: 315 782-4859
Michael Fitzgerald, *President*
Donna Yang, *Treasurer*
Barbara Raftrey, *Business Anlyst*
EMP: 5
SQ FT: 4,000
SALES (est): 598K **Privately Held**
WEB: www.nascosigns.com
SIC: 2394 3993 3444 Canvas & related products; awnings, fabric: made from purchased materials; signs & advertising specialties; sheet metalwork

(G-16691)
NORTHERN NY NEWSPAPERS CORP
Also Called: Watertown Daily Times
260 Washington St (13601-4669)
PHONE..................................315 782-1000
Fax: 315 782-1040
John B Johnson Jr, *CEO*
Harold B Johnson II, *President*
Amy Durant, *Editor*
Ken Eysaman, *Editor*
Rich Fyle, *Editor*
EMP: 210
SQ FT: 30,000
SALES: 13.2MM
SALES (corp-wide): 32MM **Privately Held**
WEB: www.lowville.com
SIC: 2711 2752 Newspapers; commercial printing, lithographic
PA: Johnson Newspaper Corporation
260 Washington St
Watertown NY
315 782-1000

(G-16692)
PACKAGING CORPORATION AMERICA
Also Called: Pca/Watertown 393
20480 Old Rome State Rd (13601-5514)
PHONE..................................315 785-9083
Fax: 315 786-8796
Beth Hogue, *Manager*
EMP: 15
SALES (corp-wide): 5.7B **Publicly Held**
WEB: www.packagingcorp.com
SIC: 2653 Boxes, corrugated: made from purchased materials
PA: Packaging Corporation Of America
1955 W Field Ct
Lake Forest IL 60045
847 482-3000

(G-16693)
PETRE ALII PETROLEUM
Also Called: Express Mart
1268 Arsenal St (13601-2214)
PHONE..................................315 785-1037
EMP: 6
SALES: 200K **Privately Held**
SIC: 2911 Petroleum Refiner

(G-16694)
SEMCO CERAMICS INC (HQ)
363 Eastern Blvd (13601-3140)
PHONE..................................315 782-3000
Alfred E Calligaris, *President*
Tony Marra, *Vice Pres*
Joe Branch, *CFO*
Douglas E Miller, *Asst Controller*
Douglas Millr, *Asst Controller*
EMP: 3
SQ FT: 30,000
SALES (est): 4.3MM
SALES (corp-wide): 171.8MM **Privately Held**
SIC: 3253 3251 Ceramic wall & floor tile; structural brick & blocks
PA: The Stebbins Engineering And Manufacturing Company
363 Eastern Blvd
Watertown NY 13601
315 782-3000

(G-16695)
STATURE ELECTRIC INC
22543 Fisher Rd (13601-1090)
P.O. Box 6660 (13601-6660)
PHONE..................................315 782-5910
Fax: 315 782-1917
Roger Ormsby, *President*
Michael Weaver, *QC Mgr*
Lori Ruckar, *Manager*
▲ **EMP:** 332
SQ FT: 112,000
SALES (est): 39.7MM
SALES (corp-wide): 245.8MM **Publicly Held**
WEB: www.statureelectric.com
SIC: 3621 3546 Electric motor & generator parts; motors, electric; power-driven handtools
PA: Allied Motion Technologies Inc.
495 Commerce Dr Ste 3
Amherst NY 14228
716 242-8634

(G-16696)
TAYLOR CONCRETE PRODUCTS INC
20475 Old Rome Rd (13601-5509)
PHONE..................................315 788-2191
Thomas O'Connor, *President*
Ellen O'Connor, *Vice Pres*
Richard O'Connor, *Vice Pres*
Pat Hayes, *Sales Staff*
EMP: 21 **EST:** 1932
SQ FT: 2,500
SALES: 4.1MM **Privately Held**
WEB: www.taylorconcrete.com
SIC: 3271 5032 5211 3272 Blocks, concrete or cinder: standard; concrete & cinder block; concrete & cinder block; concrete products

(G-16697)
TIMELESS DECOR LLC
22419 Fisher Rd (13601-1090)
P.O. Box 28 (13601-0028)
PHONE..................................315 782-5759
Kathy Watson, *Human Res Dir*
Sandra Cesario, *Product Mgr*
Lisa Weber,
EMP: 118
SALES (est): 13MM **Privately Held**
SIC: 2599 3231 3952 7699 Hotel furniture; framed mirrors; frames for artists' canvases; picture framing, custom; art, picture frames & decorations

(G-16698)
WATERTOWN CONCRETE INC
24471 State Route 12 (13601-5784)
PHONE..................................315 788-1040

Fax: 315 788-2649
Joseph Belcher, *President*
Jason Belcher, *Vice Pres*
Chris Gregory, *Finance Mgr*
Bill Hallon, *Sales Mgr*
EMP: 16
SQ FT: 10,000
SALES (est): 2MM **Privately Held**
SIC: 3273 Ready-mixed concrete

(G-16699)
ZIEGLER TRUCK & DIESL REPR INC
22249 Fabco Rd (13601-1775)
PHONE.................................315 782-7278
Charles E Ziegler, *President*
Helen Ziegler, *Admin Sec*
EMP: 5
SALES: 425K **Privately Held**
SIC: 3531 Construction machinery

Waterville
Oneida County

(G-16700)
CENTER STATE PROPANE LLC (PA)
1130 Mason Rd (13480-2102)
PHONE.................................315 841-4044
Karen Kelly, *Manager*
James Wratten,
Mike Buell,
EMP: 4
SALES (est): 1.1MM **Privately Held**
SIC: 1321 Butane (natural) production

(G-16701)
F & R ENTERPRISES INC (PA)
Also Called: Pumilia's Pizza Shell
1594 State Route 315 (13480-1516)
P.O. Box 345 (13480-0345)
PHONE.................................315 841-8189
John Pumilia, *President*
Richard Viti, *CFO*
EMP: 7
SALES (est): 1.1MM **Privately Held**
SIC: 2038 Pizza, frozen

Watervliet
Albany County

(G-16702)
ACTASYS INC
805 25th St (12189)
PHONE.................................617 834-0666
Michael Amitay, *President*
Daniele Gallardo, *President*
David Menicovich, *President*
◆ **EMP:** 6
SQ FT: 230,000
SALES: 1.3MM **Privately Held**
SIC: 3714 Motor vehicle parts & accessories

(G-16703)
BIGBEE STEEL AND TANK COMPANY
Also Called: New York Tank Co
958 19th St (12189-1752)
PHONE.................................518 273-0801
Fax: 518 273-1365
Chad O'Brien, *Plant Mgr*
Steven Mapes, *Finance Mgr*
Tim Duffy, *Credit Mgr*
Brian Kostelnik, *Sales Associate*
Tim Silvi, *Manager*
EMP: 25
SALES (corp-wide): 44.8MM **Privately Held**
WEB: www.highlandtank.com
SIC: 3443 3714 Farm storage tanks, metal plate; motor vehicle parts & accessories
PA: Bigbee Steel And Tank Company Inc
4535 Elizabethtown Rd
Manheim PA 17545
814 893-5701

(G-16704)
BONDED CONCRETE INC (PA)
303 Watervliet Shaker Rd (12189-3424)
P.O. Box 189 (12189-0189)
PHONE.................................518 273-5800
Fax: 518 273-0848
Salvatore O Clemente, *Ch of Bd*
Thomas A Clemente, *President*
Philip Clemente, *Vice Pres*
Scott Face, *Safety Dir*
Jude Clemente, *Treasurer*
EMP: 25 **EST:** 1964
SQ FT: 10,000
SALES (est): 10.8MM **Privately Held**
WEB: www.bondedconcrete.com
SIC: 3273 Ready-mixed concrete

(G-16705)
CARDISH MACHINE WORKS INC
7 Elm St (12189-1826)
PHONE.................................518 273-2329
Fax: 518 273-0016
Eugene J Cardish Jr, *President*
Charles Cardish, *Vice Pres*
EMP: 33 **EST:** 1933
SALES: 6.3MM **Privately Held**
WEB: www.cardishmachineworks.com
SIC: 3599 Machine shop, jobbing & repair

(G-16706)
CLEVELAND POLYMER TECH LLC (PA)
125 Monroe St Bldg 125 (12189-4019)
P.O. Box 9340, Schenectady (12309-0340)
PHONE.................................518 326-9146
Sam McLafferty, *CEO*
Harry Adler, *Plant Mgr*
Michele Kennedy, *Office Mgr*
Jen Angelopoulos,
Panos Angelopoulos,
EMP: 8
SQ FT: 3,000
SALES (est): 1.5MM **Privately Held**
SIC: 3499 Machine bases, metal

(G-16707)
COMFORTEX CORPORATION (DH)
Also Called: Comfortex Window Fashions
21 Elm St (12189-1770)
PHONE.................................518 273-3333
Fax: 518 273-4079
Thomas Marusak, *President*
Suk-Joung Kahng, *Principal*
Ray Rusch, *Senior Buyer*
Rod Akers, *Engineer*
Chris Ogrady, *Controller*
◆ **EMP:** 168
SQ FT: 100,000
SALES (est): 42.6MM **Privately Held**
WEB: www.comfortex.com
SIC: 2591 Window blinds; window shades
HQ: Hunter Douglas Inc.
1 Blue Hill Plz Ste 1569
Pearl River NY 10965
845 664-7000

(G-16708)
EXTREME MOLDING LLC
25 Gibson St Ste 2 (12189-3375)
PHONE.................................518 326-9319
Fax: 518 266-6263
Lynn Momrow,
Joanne Moon,
▲ **EMP:** 50
SQ FT: 13,500
SALES (est): 4MM **Privately Held**
WEB: www.extrememolding.com
SIC: 3089 Injection molding of plastics

(G-16709)
GENERAL BUSINESS SUPPLY INC
Also Called: Tech Valley Printing
2550 9th Ave (12189-1962)
PHONE.................................518 720-3939
Fax: 518 720-3938
John Smith, *President*
EMP: 55
SALES (est): 5.3MM **Privately Held**
SIC: 2759 2752 Business forms: printing; commercial printing, offset

(G-16710)
HARTCHROM INC
25 Gibson St Ste 1 (12189-3342)
PHONE.................................518 880-0411
Fax: 518 880-0450
Edgar Oehler, *CEO*
Michael Flaherty, *General Mgr*
EMP: 18
SQ FT: 33,000
SALES: 4.9MM
SALES (corp-wide): 983.9MM **Privately Held**
WEB: www.hartchrom.com
SIC: 3471 3541 Plating & polishing; anodizing (plating) of metals or formed products; grinding, polishing, buffing, lapping & honing machines
PA: Arbonia Ag
Amriswilerstrasse 50
Arbon TG
714 474-141

(G-16711)
LWA WORKS INC
2622 7th Ave Ste 50s (12189-1963)
PHONE.................................518 271-8360
Lance Weinheimer, *President*
▲ **EMP:** 5
SALES (est): 500K **Privately Held**
WEB: www.lanartworks.com
SIC: 3599 Machine shop, jobbing & repair

(G-16712)
SAINT-GOBAIN ABRASIVES INC
Also Called: Coated Abrasive Division
2600 10th Ave (12189-1766)
PHONE.................................518 266-2200
Paul Valle, *Vice Pres*
Pat Acker, *Purch Agent*
Judy Alison, *Manager*
John Snyder, *MIS Mgr*
Frederick Villoutreix, *MIS Mgr*
EMP: 400
SQ FT: 1,880
SALES (corp-wide): 185.8MM **Privately Held**
WEB: www.sgabrasives.com
SIC: 3291 Abrasive products
HQ: Saint-Gobain Abrasives, Inc.
1 New Bond St
Worcester MA 01606
508 795-5000

(G-16713)
SOLID SEALING TECHNOLOGY INC
44 Dalliba Ave Ste 240 (12189-4017)
PHONE.................................518 266-6019
Gary L Balfour, *Ch of Bd*
Alan Fuierer, *COO*
Thomas Forbes, *Mfg Mgr*
Jennifer Salamack, *Design Engr*
Denise Balfour, *Human Res Mgr*
EMP: 25
SQ FT: 10,000
SALES (est): 5.7MM **Privately Held**
WEB: www.solidsealing.com
SIC: 3629 Rectifiers (electrical apparatus)

(G-16714)
STRECKS INC
Also Called: Streck's Machinery
800 1st St (12189-3501)
PHONE.................................518 273-4410
Lloyd Demaranville, *President*
Christine Demaranville, *Vice Pres*
Emmy Obrien, *Treasurer*
▲ **EMP:** 20 **EST:** 1952
SQ FT: 50,000
SALES (est): 3.3MM **Privately Held**
SIC: 3599 7692 7629 Machine shop, jobbing & repair; welding repair; electrical repair shops

(G-16715)
TROY BELTING AND SUPPLY CO
70 Cohoes Rd (12189-1895)
PHONE.................................518 272-4920
Fax: 518 272-0531
Jason W Smith, *Ch of Bd*
David R Barcomb, *General Mgr*
Jason Smith, *Vice Pres*
Matt Lapoint, *Project Mgr*
Doug Rogers, *Warehouse Mgr*
EMP: 67
SQ FT: 55,000
SALES (est): 17.5MM **Privately Held**
WEB: www.troybelting.com
SIC: 7694 3052 5084 5085 Electric motor repair; rubber & plastics hose & beltings; industrial machinery & equipment; industrial supplies; conveyors & conveying equipment; motors & generators

(G-16716)
UTILITY SYSTEMS TECH INC
70 Cohoes Rd (12189-1829)
P.O. Box 110, Latham (12110-0110)
PHONE.................................518 326-4142
Robert Degeneff, *President*
Mark Degeneffe, *General Mgr*
David Wightman, *General Mgr*
Jeff Foran, *Engineer*
Hung Nguyen, *Engineer*
EMP: 13
SALES (est): 2.7MM **Privately Held**
WEB: www.ustpower.com
SIC: 3643 Current-carrying wiring devices

(G-16717)
WICKED SMART LLC
700 5th Ave (12189-3610)
PHONE.................................518 459-2855
Todd Van Epps, *Mng Member*
Marcie Van Epps,
EMP: 15
SALES: 1.1MM **Privately Held**
SIC: 2396 2395 Screen printing on fabric articles; embroidery & art needlework

Watkins Glen
Schuyler County

(G-16718)
BMS MANUFACTURING CO INC
2857 County Line Rd (14891-9615)
PHONE.................................607 535-2426
Fax: 607 535-9793
William C Meehan Jr, *CEO*
Norm Macwilliams, *Manager*
Beth Meehan, *Manager*
EMP: 45
SQ FT: 50,000
SALES (est): 7.2MM **Privately Held**
WEB: www.bmsmanufacturing.com
SIC: 7692 3599 3441 Welding repair; machine & other job shop work; fabricated structural metal

(G-16719)
CARGILL INCORPORATED
518 E 4th St (14891-1219)
PHONE.................................607 535-6300
Fax: 607 535-6348
Rene Osorio, *Marketing Staff*
Greg Meyer, *Manager*
Jameson Becker, *Manager*
Michael Schmit, *MIS Mgr*
EMP: 93
SQ FT: 10,840
SALES (corp-wide): 109.7B **Privately Held**
WEB: www.cargill.com
SIC: 2899 Salt
PA: Cargill, Incorporated
15407 Mcginty Rd W
Wayzata MN 55391
952 742-7575

(G-16720)
LAKEWOOD VINEYARDS INC
4024 State Route 14 (14891-9630)
PHONE.................................607 535-9252
Fax: 607 535-6656
Christopher Lamont Stamp, *President*
David A Stamp, *Vice Pres*
Beverly Stamp, *Treasurer*
Teresa Knapp, *Shareholder*
Michael E Stamp, *Shareholder*
▲ **EMP:** 12
SQ FT: 7,500
SALES (est): 930K **Privately Held**
WEB: www.lakewoodvineyards.com
SIC: 2084 Wines

GEOGRAPHIC SECTION

(G-16721)
SKYLARK PUBLICATIONS LTD
Also Called: Hi-Lites
217 N Franklin St (14891-1201)
PHONE..................607 535-9866
Damir Lazaric, *Managing Prtnr*
Flyod Vlajic, *Partner*
Millie Gernold, *Sales Mgr*
Bridgette Goodman, *Software Engr*
EMP: 5
SQ FT: 3,184
SALES (est): 385K **Privately Held**
SIC: 2741 Shopping news: publishing only, not printed on site

(G-16722)
SUIT-KOTE CORPORATION
Also Called: Central Asphalt
20 Fairgrounds Ln (14891-1632)
PHONE..................607 535-2743
Kevin Suits, *Branch Mgr*
EMP: 30
SQ FT: 11,524
SALES (corp-wide): 226MM **Privately Held**
WEB: www.suit-kote.com
SIC: 2951 1611 2952 Asphalt paving mixtures & blocks; highway & street construction; asphalt felts & coatings
PA: Suit-Kote Corporation
1911 Lorings Crossing Rd
Cortland NY 13045
607 753-1100

(G-16723)
US SALT LLC
Salt Point Rd (14891)
PHONE..................607 535-2721
Fax: 607 535-2953
Traver Bob, *Safety Dir*
Bob Traver, *Safety Dir*
Sue Oliver, *QA Dir*
Alan Parry, *Manager*
Susan Forshee, *Manager*
EMP: 100
SALES (corp-wide): 2.5B **Publicly Held**
SIC: 2899 Salt
HQ: Us Salt, Llc
2440 Pershing Rd Ste 260
Kansas City MO 64108
816 842-8181

Waverly
Tioga County

(G-16724)
CHARM MFG CO INC
Also Called: Charm Pools
251 State Route 17c (14892-9507)
P.O. Box 294 (14892-0294)
PHONE..................607 565-8161
Fax: 607 565-3212
Jane Spicer, *President*
Linda Spicer, *Corp Secy*
Kay Onofre, *Vice Pres*
Richard Spicer, *Vice Pres*
EMP: 50
SQ FT: 50,000
SALES: 2.1MM **Privately Held**
WEB: www.charmpools.com
SIC: 3949 5091 5999 Swimming pools, except plastic; hot tubs; spa equipment & supplies; hot tub & spa chemicals, equipment & supplies; sauna equipment & supplies

(G-16725)
CHEMITE INC
407 County Road 60 (14892-9833)
P.O. Box 271 (14892-0271)
PHONE..................607 529-3218
George D Howell, *President*
Jana Howell, *Vice Pres*
Tim Gable, *Purch Mgr*
Gloria Smith, *Manager*
Eric Howell, *Shareholder*
EMP: 9
SQ FT: 38,000
SALES: 3.3MM **Privately Held**
WEB: www.chemiteinc.com
SIC: 2841 Soap & other detergents

(G-16726)
DORY ENTERPRISES INC
184 Sr 17c (14892)
PHONE..................607 565-7079
Fax: 607 565-4794
Robert Rynone, *President*
Frederick Douglas, *Sales Staff*
Jackie Cole, *Office Mgr*
EMP: 10
SQ FT: 3,000
SALES (est): 1.3MM **Privately Held**
SIC: 2653 5113 Corrugated boxes, partitions, display items, sheets & pad; bags, paper & disposable plastic

(G-16727)
GRANITE WORKS LLC
133 William Donnelly (14892-1547)
PHONE..................607 565-7012
Rai Leigh, *Sales Staff*
Mary Wilcox, *Manager*
Fred Elias, *Admin Mgr*
Jason Vandyk,
▲ **EMP:** 20
SALES (est): 3.3MM **Privately Held**
SIC: 3281 Curbing, granite or stone

(G-16728)
HANCOR INC
1 William Donnly Inds (14892-1599)
PHONE..................607 565-3033
Fax: 607 565-2339
Dave Markie, *Manager*
EMP: 80
SALES (corp-wide): 1.2B **Publicly Held**
SIC: 3082 3084 Tubes, unsupported plastic; plastics pipe
HQ: Hancor, Inc.
4640 Trueman Blvd
Hilliard OH 43026
614 658-0050

(G-16729)
LEPRINO FOODS COMPANY
400 Leprino Ave (14892-1351)
PHONE..................570 888-9658
Fax: 570 888-6612
Neil Brown, *Manager*
EMP: 230
SALES (corp-wide): 1.9B **Privately Held**
WEB: www.leprinofoods.com
SIC: 2022 Cheese, natural & processed
PA: Leprino Foods Company
1830 W 38th Ave
Denver CO 80211
303 480-2600

(G-16730)
RYNONE MANUFACTURING CORP
229 Howard St (14892-1519)
PHONE..................607 565-8187
Fax: 607 565-2905
Chuck Lawson, *Manager*
EMP: 15
SALES (corp-wide): 37.8MM **Privately Held**
WEB: www.rynone.com
SIC: 3089 Plastic containers, except foam
PA: Rynone Manufacturing Corp.
N Thomas Ave
Sayre PA 18840
570 888-5272

(G-16731)
RYNONE PACKAGING CORP
184 State Route 17c (14892-9504)
PHONE..................607 565-8173
Robert F Rynone, *Ch of Bd*
▼ **EMP:** 8
SALES (est): 886.3K **Privately Held**
SIC: 2671 Packaging paper & plastics film, coated & laminated

Wawarsing
Ulster County

(G-16732)
PRECISION MACHINING AND MFG
190 Port Ben Rd (12489)
P.O. Box 104 (12489-0104)
PHONE..................845 647-5380

Nick Gajdcz, *President*
Wasyl Gajdycz, *President*
Lisia Gajdycz, *Admin Sec*
EMP: 5
SQ FT: 6,500
SALES: 270K **Privately Held**
SIC: 3544 Special dies & tools

Wayland
Steuben County

(G-16733)
BELANGERS GRAVEL & STONE INC
10184 State Route 21 (14572-9544)
PHONE..................585 728-3906
Norb Belanger, *Ch of Bd*
EMP: 6
SALES (est): 605.3K **Privately Held**
SIC: 1442 Construction sand & gravel

(G-16734)
GUNLOCKE COMPANY LLC (HQ)
1 Gunlocke Dr (14572-9515)
PHONE..................585 728-5111
Fax: 585 728-8353
Aron Fehr, *Business Mgr*
Jason Thomas, *Business Mgr*
Michael Moffett, *Mfg Dir*
Christopher Harrison, *Opers Staff*
Floyd Sharp, *Opers Staff*
▲ **EMP:** 155
SQ FT: 720,000
SALES: 178.9MM
SALES (corp-wide): 2.2B **Publicly Held**
WEB: www.gunlocke.com
SIC: 2521 Wood office furniture
PA: Hni Corporation
600 E 2nd St
Muscatine IA 52761
563 272-7400

(G-16735)
SPECIALTY SERVICES
Also Called: Accent Printing &GRaphics
2631e Naples St (14572)
P.O. Box 397 (14572-0397)
PHONE..................585 728-5650
Fax: 585 728-5782
Randall Bergvall, *Owner*
EMP: 5
SQ FT: 12,000
SALES (est): 432.4K **Privately Held**
SIC: 2541 2431 Display fixtures, wood; millwork

Wayne
Schuyler County

(G-16736)
NEW MARKET PRODUCTS CO INC
9671 Back St (14893)
P.O. Box 135 (14893-0135)
PHONE..................607 292-6226
Fax: 607 293-6858
Gary Oborne, *President*
EMP: 12 EST: 1967
SQ FT: 10,500
SALES (est): 740K **Privately Held**
WEB: www.nmpco.com
SIC: 3545 Tool holders

Webster
Monroe County

(G-16737)
ASHLY AUDIO INC
847 Holt Rd Ste 1 (14580-9193)
PHONE..................585 872-0010
Fax: 585 872-0739
David Parse, *CEO*
J P Boucher, *General Mgr*
William Thompson, *Chairman*
John Sexton, *Vice Pres*
Michael Mosher, *Engineer*
▲ **EMP:** 42
SQ FT: 25,000

SALES (est): 10.8MM **Privately Held**
WEB: www.ashly.com
SIC: 3651 3663 Household audio equipment; radio & TV communications equipment

(G-16738)
CALVARY DESIGN TEAM INC (PA)
Also Called: Calvary Robotics
855 Publishers Pkwy (14580-2587)
PHONE..................585 347-6127
Fax: 585 321-5054
Mark Chaney, *President*
Ken Strittmatter, *Managing Dir*
Jim Diederich, *Business Mgr*
Jose Oliver, *Business Mgr*
James Gardner, *Mfg Dir*
▲ **EMP:** 200
SQ FT: 375,000
SALES: 65.4MM **Privately Held**
WEB: www.calvauto.com
SIC: 3599 8711 Custom machinery; mechanical engineering; industrial engineers

(G-16739)
CDA MACHINE INC
514 Vosburg Rd (14580-1043)
PHONE..................585 671-5959
Fax: 585 671-5903
William Crosby, *President*
Laurie Maggio, *Office Mgr*
EMP: 9
SQ FT: 13,400
SALES (est): 1MM **Privately Held**
WEB: www.cdamachine.com
SIC: 3599 Machine shop, jobbing & repair

(G-16740)
CGS FABRICATION LLC
855 Publishers Pkwy (14580-2587)
PHONE..................585 347-6127
Mark Chaney, *Owner*
EMP: 15 EST: 2012
SALES: 21.6MM **Privately Held**
SIC: 3469 Machine parts, stamped or pressed metal

(G-16741)
CLARK RIGGING & RENTAL CORP
680 Basket Rd (14580-9764)
PHONE..................585 265-2910
David Clark, *Branch Mgr*
Dave Baran, *Manager*
EMP: 11
SALES (corp-wide): 8.5MM **Privately Held**
SIC: 3731 Marine rigging
PA: Clark Rigging & Rental Corp
500 Ohio St
Lockport NY 14094
716 433-4600

(G-16742)
CLASSIC AUTOMATION LLC (PA)
800 Salt Rd (14580-9666)
PHONE..................585 241-6010
Margaret Nichols, *Vice Pres*
Fritz Ruebeck, *Mng Member*
▲ **EMP:** 40
SQ FT: 17,000
SALES: 10MM **Privately Held**
SIC: 3823 Controllers for process variables, all types; boiler controls: industrial, power & marine type

(G-16743)
CLINTON SIGNS INC
1407 Empire Blvd (14580-2101)
PHONE..................585 482-1620
Fax: 585 482-3384
Michael S Mammano III, *President*
Kim Mammano, *Controller*
EMP: 6 EST: 1938
SQ FT: 5,700
SALES: 400K **Privately Held**
WEB: www.clintonsigns.com
SIC: 3993 7389 1799 7336 Electric signs; sign painting & lettering shop; sign installation & maintenance; commercial art & graphic design

Webster - Monroe County (G-16744)

(G-16744)
DATA-PAC MAILING SYSTEMS CORP
1217 Bay Rd Ste 12 (14580-1958)
PHONE..................585 671-0210
Fax: 585 671-1409
Richard A Yankloski, *President*
Ana Yankloski, *Vice Pres*
Mary Smith, *Administration*
EMP: 10
SQ FT: 3,000
SALES (est): 2.5MM **Privately Held**
WEB: www.data-pac.com
SIC: 3571 Electronic computers

(G-16745)
DIGITAL HOME CREATIONS INC
350 Shadowbrook Dr (14580-9108)
PHONE..................585 576-7070
Ryan J Hills, *CEO*
EMP: 5
SALES: 1.4MM **Privately Held**
SIC: 3491 3651 Automatic regulating & control valves; household audio & video equipment

(G-16746)
EAST SIDE MACHINE INC
625 Phillips Rd (14580-9786)
PHONE..................585 265-4560
Fax: 585 265-4569
Paul Derleth, *President*
Lou Rossetti, *Vice Pres*
Pat Latona, *Office Mgr*
EMP: 26
SQ FT: 16,000
SALES (est): 5.9MM **Privately Held**
WEB: www.esm1.com
SIC: 3545 Precision tools, machinists'

(G-16747)
EMPIRE STATE WEEKLIES INC
Also Called: Wayne County Mail
46 North Ave (14580-3008)
PHONE..................585 671-1533
Fax: 585 671-7067
David Young, *President*
EMP: 20
SQ FT: 5,100
SALES (est): 1.5MM **Privately Held**
WEB: www.empirestateweeklies.com
SIC: 2711 Job printing & newspaper publishing combined

(G-16748)
GRIFFIN MANUFACTURING COMPANY
1656 Ridge Rd (14580-3697)
P.O. Box 308 (14580-0308)
PHONE..................585 265-1991
Fax: 585 265-2621
Angelo Papia, *President*
Kristin P Papia, *Managing Dir*
Darryl Papia, *Vice Pres*
Gary Papia, *Vice Pres*
Terry Papia, *Vice Pres*
▲ **EMP:** 20 **EST:** 1946
SQ FT: 6,000
SALES (est): 3.7MM **Privately Held**
WEB: www.grifhold.com
SIC: 3545 Machine tool accessories

(G-16749)
HEARING SPECH CTR OF ROCHESTER
Also Called: Sonus-USA
1170 Ridge Rd Ste 2 (14580-2977)
PHONE..................585 286-9373
EMP: 31
SALES (corp-wide): 6.4MM **Privately Held**
SIC: 3842 Hearing aids
PA: Hearing And Speech Center Of Rochester Inc
1000 Elmwood Ave Ste 400
Rochester NY 14620
585 271-0680

(G-16750)
JOHNSON CONTROLS INC
237 Birch Ln (14580-1301)
PHONE..................585 671-1930
Peter Baranello, *Manager*
EMP: 25 **Privately Held**
SIC: 2531 Seats, automobile
HQ: Johnson Controls, Inc.
5757 N Green Bay Ave
Milwaukee WI 53209
414 524-1200

(G-16751)
KAL MANUFACTURING CORPORATION
657 Basket Rd (14580-9764)
PHONE..................585 265-4310
Fax: 585 265-4854
Alan Liwush, *President*
Richard Liwush, *Ch of Bd*
Tim Lindsay, *Sales Mgr*
Brian Hooker, *Manager*
Erika Muscato, *Manager*
EMP: 37 **EST:** 1943
SQ FT: 50,000
SALES (est): 9.5MM **Privately Held**
WEB: www.kal-mfg.com
SIC: 3444 3845 3599 3441 Sheet metalwork; electromedical equipment; machine & other job shop work; fabricated structural metal

(G-16752)
KATHLEEN B MEAD
Also Called: Automatic Bar Machining Co
393 Coastal View Dr (14580-9037)
PHONE..................585 247-0146
Fax: 585 247-2141
Kathleen B Mead, *Owner*
EMP: 5 **EST:** 1957
SQ FT: 16,800
SALES (est): 284.3K **Privately Held**
SIC: 3451 Screw machine products

(G-16753)
OPTICOOL SOLUTIONS LLC
Also Called: Opticool Technologies
855 Publishers Pkwy (14580-2587)
PHONE..................585 347-6127
David Brown, *Director*
EMP: 17
SALES (est): 4.6MM **Privately Held**
SIC: 3585 Parts for heating, cooling & refrigerating equipment

(G-16754)
PLANAR OPTICS INC
858 Hard Rd (14580-8950)
PHONE..................585 671-0100
Fax: 585 671-1303
Horst Koch, *President*
Otto Wolsgoot, *Vice Pres*
EMP: 7
SQ FT: 5,400
SALES (est): 939.7K **Privately Held**
SIC: 3827 Optical instruments & lenses

(G-16755)
PRACTICAL INSTRUMENT ELEC INC
Also Called: Pie
82 E Main St Ste 3 (14580-3243)
PHONE..................585 872-9350
Ronald P Clarridge, *CEO*
EMP: 10
SALES (est): 1.2MM **Privately Held**
WEB: www.piecal.com
SIC: 3825 Instruments to measure electricity; engine electrical test equipment

(G-16756)
R D SPECIALTIES INC
560 Salt Rd (14580-9718)
PHONE..................585 265-0220
Fax: 585 265-1132
Douglas R Krasucki, *President*
Jim Mottlet, *Opers Staff*
Grace Krasucki, *Treasurer*
EMP: 15
SQ FT: 8,000
SALES (est): 1.1MM **Privately Held**
WEB: www.rdspecialties.com
SIC: 3312 Bar, rod & wire products

(G-16757)
R P M MACHINE CO
755 Gravel Rd (14580-1715)
PHONE..................585 671-3744
Timothy Mangus, *Partner*
Richard P Mangus, *Partner*
EMP: 5
SALES: 160K **Privately Held**
SIC: 3451 Screw machine products

(G-16758)
RADAX INDUSTRIES INC
700 Basket Rd Ste A (14580-1718)
PHONE..................585 265-2055
Fax: 585 265-0072
Rocco Sacco, *Ch of Bd*
Richard Sacco, *President*
Jefferson Treadwell, *Sales Mgr*
Amy Years Formicola, *Admin Sec*
EMP: 27
SQ FT: 55,000
SALES (est): 6.3MM **Privately Held**
WEB: www.radax.com
SIC: 3452 Screws, metal

(G-16759)
RESPONSE CARE INC
38 Commercial St (14580-3106)
PHONE..................585 671-4144
Myron Kowal, *President*
Richard Moore, *Co-Owner*
EMP: 7
SQ FT: 6,500
SALES (est): 1MM **Privately Held**
SIC: 3669 Intercommunication systems, electric

(G-16760)
SCHUTT CIDER MILL
1063 Plank Rd (14580-9399)
PHONE..................585 872-2924
Martin Schutt, *Owner*
EMP: 10
SQ FT: 3,308
SALES (est): 765.8K **Privately Held**
WEB: www.schuttsapplemill.com
SIC: 2099 5499 5149 Cider, nonalcoholic; juices, fruit or vegetable; juices

(G-16761)
SICK INC
Lazerdata Division
855 Publishers Pkwy (14580-2587)
P.O. Box 448 (14580-0448)
PHONE..................585 347-2000
EMP: 50 **Privately Held**
SIC: 3599 Mfg General Industrial Machinery
HQ: Sick, Inc
6900 W 110th St
Minneapolis MN 55438
952 941-6780

(G-16762)
STUDCO BUILDING SYSTEMS US LLC
1700 Boulter Indus Park (14580-9763)
PHONE..................585 545-3000
Joan Congdon, *Accounts Mgr*
Allan Parr, *Mng Member*
▲ **EMP:** 30
SQ FT: 65,000
SALES (est): 8.9MM **Privately Held**
WEB: www.studcosystems.com
SIC: 3444 Studs & joists, sheet metal

(G-16763)
TRICON MACHINE LLC
820 Coventry Dr (14580-8422)
PHONE..................585 671-0679
Gary German,
EMP: 7
SQ FT: 10,000
SALES: 1MM **Privately Held**
WEB: www.triconmachine.com
SIC: 3599 Custom machinery

(G-16764)
TRIDENT PRECISION MFG INC
734 Salt Rd (14580-9718)
PHONE..................585 265-2010
Fax: 585 265-2304
Nicholas Juskiw, *President*
Dan Nuijens, *Plant Mgr*
Peter Collins, *Opers Mgr*
Kelly Brayer, *Purch Agent*
Diane Cialini, *Buyer*
▲ **EMP:** 95
SQ FT: 60,000
SALES (est): 31.6MM **Privately Held**
WEB: www.tridentprecision.com
SIC: 3469 3545 3569 7373 Stamping metal for the trade; machine tool accessories; assembly machines, non-metalworking; computer-aided design (CAD) systems service; computer-aided manufacturing (CAM) systems service; laser welding, drilling & cutting equipment; sheet metalwork

(G-16765)
UNISEND LLC
249 Gallant Fox Ln (14580-9034)
PHONE..................585 414-9575
Sheikh Wasim Khaled, *Principal*
Steve Muratore, *Principal*
EMP: 5 **EST:** 2012
SALES (est): 380.3K **Privately Held**
SIC: 3822 Building services monitoring controls, automatic

(G-16766)
UNISTEL LLC
860 Hard Rd (14580-8825)
PHONE..................585 341-4600
Ana Nikolovska, *Principal*
Sankar Sewnauth,
▲ **EMP:** 99
SALES (est): 8.2MM **Privately Held**
SIC: 3999 Manufacturing industries

(G-16767)
WEBSTER ONTRIO WLWRTH PNNYSVER
164 E Main St (14580-3230)
P.O. Box 1135 (14580-7835)
PHONE..................585 265-3620
Geoffrey Mohr, *Partner*
Mary Jill Mohr, *Partner*
EMP: 12
SQ FT: 1,000
SALES (est): 770.7K **Privately Held**
WEB: www.websterpennysaver.com
SIC: 2711 Newspapers

(G-16768)
WEBSTER PRINTING CORPORATION
46 North Ave (14580-3008)
PHONE..................585 671-1533
W David Young, *President*
Leslie Young, *Admin Sec*
EMP: 18
SQ FT: 2,500
SALES (est): 1.5MM **Privately Held**
SIC: 2759 2791 2789 2752 Newspapers: printing; typesetting; bookbinding & related work; commercial printing, lithographic

(G-16769)
XEROX CORPORATION
800 Phillips Rd Ste 20599 (14580-9791)
PHONE..................585 422-4564
Fax: 585 422-8576
Bernard Blocchi, *General Mgr*
Patricia Cusick, *Vice Pres*
Scott Frame, *Vice Pres*
Robert Wagner, *Vice Pres*
Peter Zehler, *Vice Pres*
EMP: 700
SALES (corp-wide): 10.7B **Publicly Held**
WEB: www.xerox.com
SIC: 3861 Reproduction machines & equipment
PA: Xerox Corporation
201 Merritt 7
Norwalk CT 06851
203 968-3000

(G-16770)
XEROX CORPORATION
800 Phillips Rd (14580-9791)
PHONE..................585 423-5090
Fax: 585 423-4848
Pankaj Kalra, *General Mgr*
Frederick Debolt, *Vice Pres*
Rich Jarry, *Production*
Robert Arnold, *Purchasing*
Manuel Ortiz, *Engineer*
EMP: 75
SALES (corp-wide): 10.7B **Publicly Held**
WEB: www.xerox.com
SIC: 3861 Photographic equipment & supplies

GEOGRAPHIC SECTION

West Babylon - Suffolk County (G-16794)

PA: Xerox Corporation
201 Merritt 7
Norwalk CT 06851
203 968-3000

(G-16771)
ZOMEGA TERAHERTZ CORPORATION
806 Admiralty Way (14580-3912)
PHONE..................585 347-4337
Thomas Tongue, *CEO*
Wendy Zhang, *CFO*
EMP: 15
SALES (est): 3MM **Privately Held**
SIC: 3829 Measuring & controlling devices

Weedsport
Cayuga County

(G-16772)
BARBER WELDING INC
Also Called: Alpha Boats Unlimited
2517 Rte 31 W (13166)
P.O. Box 690 (13166-0690)
PHONE..................315 834-6645
Stephen L Walczyk, *President*
Dave Dunham, *Plant Mgr*
▲ **EMP:** 20
SQ FT: 18,000
SALES (est): 2.6MM **Privately Held**
WEB: www.barberweldinginc.com
SIC: 7692 3441 Welding repair; fabricated structural metal

Wellsburg
Chemung County

(G-16773)
ELMIRA GRINDING WORKS INC
311 Main St (14894-9781)
PHONE..................607 734-1579
Fax: 607 734-7593
Jon Bauer, *President*
Kim Hancock, *Manager*
EMP: 10 **EST:** 1964
SQ FT: 7,500
SALES: 500K **Privately Held**
SIC: 3541 3451 Grinding, polishing, buffing, lapping & honing machines; screw machine products

Wellsville
Allegany County

(G-16774)
ANNIES ICE
35 Herman Ave (14895-9513)
PHONE..................585 593-5605
Laurie Hennessey, *Partner*
Joseph Hennessy, *Partner*
EMP: 5
SALES (est): 191.7K **Privately Held**
SIC: 2097 Manufactured ice

(G-16775)
ARVOS INC (DH)
Also Called: Air Preheater
3020 Truax Rd (14895-9531)
P.O. Box 372 (14895-0372)
PHONE..................585 593-2700
David Breckinridge, *President*
Brent Beachy, *President*
Karsten Stckrath, *President*
Ludger Heuberg, *CFO*
Guillaume Boutillot, *Marketing Staff*
EMP: 340
SALES (est): 342.7MM **Privately Held**
SIC: 3443 Fabricated plate work (boiler shop); air preheaters, nonrotating: plate type
HQ: Arvos Raymond Bartlett Snow Holding Llc
3020 Truax Rd
Wellsville NY 14895
630 393-1000

(G-16776)
CURRENT CONTROLS INC
353 S Brooklyn Ave (14895-1446)
PHONE..................585 593-1544
Fax: 585 593-1713
Robert Landon, *President*
Carl Baxter, *Engineer*
Jeremy McNaughton, *Engineer*
Jason Hamer, *Sales Mgr*
Angela Dunham, *Office Mgr*
EMP: 150
SQ FT: 25,000
SALES (est): 30.6MM **Privately Held**
WEB: www.currentcontrols.com
SIC: 3612 Control transformers

(G-16777)
DRESSER-RAND COMPANY
37 Coats St (14895-1003)
P.O. Box 592 (14895-0592)
PHONE..................585 596-3100
Fax: 585 596-3647
Terah Soule, *Business Mgr*
Jason Mattison, *Project Mgr*
Joe Menichino, *Engineer*
Al Schmidt, *Engineer*
Clay Hale, *CFO*
EMP: 650
SALES (corp-wide): 89.6B **Privately Held**
WEB: www.dresser-rand.com
SIC: 3491 3511 Industrial valves; turbines & turbine generator sets; turbines & turbine generator sets & parts
HQ: Dresser-Rand Company
500 Paul Clark Dr
Olean NY 14760
716 375-3000

(G-16778)
GENERAL ELECTRIC COMPANY
372 Andover Rd (14895)
PHONE..................585 593-2700
Pierre Gauthier, *CEO*
EMP: 5
SALES (corp-wide): 123.6B **Publicly Held**
SIC: 3443 Air preheaters, nonrotating: plate type
PA: General Electric Company
41 Farnsworth St
Boston MA 02210
617 443-3000

(G-16779)
GENESEE METAL PRODUCTS INC
106 Railroad Ave (14895-1143)
PHONE..................585 968-6000
Fax: 585 968-7000
Michael P Oleksiak, *President*
EMP: 20
SQ FT: 28,000
SALES (est): 3.2MM **Privately Held**
SIC: 3449 Miscellaneous metalwork

(G-16780)
MATTESON LOGGING INC
2808 Beech Hill Rd (14895-9779)
PHONE..................585 593-3037
Brian Matteson, *President*
Pammy Matteson, *Vice Pres*
EMP: 5
SALES (est): 411.3K **Privately Held**
SIC: 2411 Logging camps & contractors

(G-16781)
NORTHERN LIGHTS ENTPS INC
Also Called: Northern Lights Candles
3474 Andover Rd (14895-9525)
PHONE..................585 593-1200
Fax: 585 593-6481
Andrew Glanzman, *President*
Jeannie Skiffington, *Principal*
Christina Glanzman, *Vice Pres*
Leslie Belsito, *Buyer*
Teri Shaughnessy, *Engineer*
✪ **EMP:** 120 **EST:** 1977
SQ FT: 20,000
SALES (est): 14.3MM **Privately Held**
WEB: www.northernlightscandles.com
SIC: 3999 5999 Candles; candle shops

(G-16782)
RELEASE COATINGS NEW YORK INC
125 S Brooklyn Ave (14895-1453)
PHONE..................585 593-2335
Fax: 585 593-4912
Ralph A Naples, *President*
Dennis T Harris, *Vice Pres*
EMP: 5
SQ FT: 7,200
SALES (est): 1MM **Privately Held**
SIC: 2822 Synthetic rubber

(G-16783)
SANDLE CUSTOM BEARING CORP
1110 State Route 19 (14895-9120)
PHONE..................585 593-7000
Fax: 585 593-7027
Eric Sandle, *President*
Lisa Lindsay, *Manager*
Nancy Reiman, *Manager*
Diana Sandle, *Admin Sec*
▼ **EMP:** 9
SQ FT: 4,000
SALES (est): 1.6MM **Privately Held**
SIC: 3562 Ball & roller bearings

(G-16784)
SENECA MEDIA INC
Also Called: Wellsville Daily Reporter
159 N Main St (14895-1149)
PHONE..................585 593-5300
Oak Duke, *Branch Mgr*
EMP: 12
SALES (corp-wide): 6.2MM **Privately Held**
WEB: www.eveningtribune.com
SIC: 2711 Newspapers: publishing only, not printed on site
PA: Seneca Media Inc
32 Broadway Mall
Hornell NY 14843
607 324-1425

(G-16785)
SIEMENS GOVERNMENT TECH INC
Also Called: Sgt Dresser-Rand
37 Coats St (14895-1003)
P.O. Box 592 (14895-0592)
PHONE..................585 593-1234
Barbara Humrton, *CEO*
Jim Chalker, *Engineer*
Joe Lamberson, *Engineer*
John Meehan, *Engineer*
Clay Hale, *CFO*
EMP: 405
SALES (corp-wide): 89.6B **Privately Held**
WEB: www.dresser-rand.com
SIC: 3511 Turbines & turbine generator sets; turbines & turbine generator sets & parts
HQ: Siemens Government Technologies, Inc.
2231 Crystal Dr Ste 700
Arlington VA 22202
703 860-1574

West Babylon
Suffolk County

(G-16786)
110 SAND COMPANY
170 Cabot St (11704-1102)
PHONE..................631 694-2822
Tom Murphy, *Manager*
EMP: 17
SALES (corp-wide): 8MM **Privately Held**
SIC: 1442 Construction sand & gravel
PA: 110 Sand Company
136 Spagnoli Rd
Melville NY 11747
631 694-2822

(G-16787)
A-MARK MACHINERY CORP
101 Lamar St (11704-1301)
PHONE..................631 643-6300
Fax: 631 643-9069
Marcel Edelstein, *President*
Shelly Edelstein, *Corp Secy*
Paul Schwartz, *Vice Pres*
EMP: 15
SQ FT: 24,000
SALES (est): 5.7MM **Privately Held**
SIC: 3555 Printing trades machinery

(G-16788)
A-QUICK BINDERY LLC
30 Gleam St Unit C (11704-1207)
PHONE..................631 491-1110
Fax: 631 491-0388
Nick Koutsoliontos, *Owner*
John Liontos,
EMP: 5
SALES (est): 758.6K **Privately Held**
SIC: 2789 Bookbinding & related work

(G-16789)
ABERDEEN BLOWER & SHTMTL WORKS
401 Columbus Ave (11704-5541)
P.O. Box 1134 (11704-0134)
PHONE..................631 661-6100
Fax: 631 661-0624
Peter Levine, *President*
John Rolleri, *Partner*
EMP: 7
SALES: 1.5MM **Privately Held**
SIC: 3444 Sheet metalwork

(G-16790)
ADCOMM GRAPHICS INC
21 Lamar St (11704-1301)
PHONE..................212 645-1298
Guy Leibstein, *President*
Raymond Muccioli, *Vice Pres*
Nancy Leibstein, *Controller*
Paul Leibstein, *Admin Sec*
EMP: 25
SQ FT: 5,000
SALES (est): 2.1MM **Privately Held**
SIC: 2741 7336 Miscellaneous publishing; graphic arts & related design

(G-16791)
ADVANCE PRECISION INDUSTRIES
9 Mahan St Unit A (11704-1319)
PHONE..................631 491-0910
Fax: 631 491-0911
Anton Korconkiewicz, *President*
EMP: 6 **EST:** 1963
SQ FT: 4,000
SALES (est): 435.6K **Privately Held**
SIC: 3599 Machine shop, jobbing & repair

(G-16792)
AIRCRAFT FINISHING CORP (PA)
100 Field St Unit A (11704-5550)
PHONE..................631 422-5000
Fax: 631 422-0815
Sam Serigano, *President*
John Serigano, *Vice Pres*
Kathleen Serigano, *Treasurer*
Ann Serigano, *Admin Sec*
EMP: 16
SQ FT: 18,000
SALES (est): 2MM **Privately Held**
SIC: 3471 3479 Plating of metals or formed products; painting of metal products

(G-16793)
ALLMETAL CHOCOLATE MOLD CO INC
135 Dale St (11704-1103)
PHONE..................631 752-2888
Fax: 718 752-2885
Joseph Micelli, *President*
Teresa Puma, *Office Mgr*
John Micelli, *Admin Sec*
EMP: 10 **EST:** 1947
SQ FT: 10,000
SALES (est): 1.3MM **Privately Held**
WEB: www.micelli.com
SIC: 3544 Industrial molds

(G-16794)
AMACON CORPORATION
49 Alder St Unit A (11704-1093)
PHONE..................631 293-1888
Fax: 631 293-1868
Costas Antoniou, *President*
John Mateus, *Superintendent*
Ted Antoniou, *Vice Pres*
Henry Mancura, *Vice Pres*

West Babylon - Suffolk County (G-16795)

Donald O'Day, *Vice Pres*
EMP: 11
SALES (est): 1.2MM **Privately Held**
WEB: www.amacon.com
SIC: 3599 Machine shop, jobbing & repair

(G-16795)
AMERICAN ACRYLIC CORPORATION
400 Sheffield Ave (11704-5333)
PHONE 631 422-2200
Fax: 631 422-2811
Mandell Ziegler, *CEO*
Thomas C Ziegler, *President*
Ken Bauhof, *General Mgr*
Jennifer Meaney, *General Mgr*
Charlie Ziegler, *Treasurer*
◆ **EMP:** 20
SQ FT: 20,000
SALES: 1.8MM **Privately Held**
WEB: www.americanacrylic.com
SIC: 3083 3081 2821 Laminated plastics plate & sheet; unsupported plastics film & sheet; plastics materials & resins

(G-16796)
AMERICAN METAL SPINNING PDTS
21 Eads St (11704-1125)
PHONE 631 454-6276
Fax: 516 454-4867
Clark Morse, *President*
Michelle Morse, *Office Mgr*
EMP: 9
SQ FT: 8,000
SALES (est): 726K **Privately Held**
WEB: www.amermetalspinning.com
SIC: 3469 Spinning metal for the trade

(G-16797)
AUTOMATION SOURCE TECHNOLOGIES (PA)
21 Otis St Unit B (11704-1440)
PHONE 631 643-1678
Peter Dougherty,
▲ **EMP:** 12 **EST:** 2012
SALES (est): 2MM **Privately Held**
SIC: 3621 Phase or rotary converters (electrical equipment)

(G-16798)
BABYLON IRON WORKS INC
205 Edison Ave (11704-1030)
PHONE 631 643-3311
Fax: 631 253-0950
Raymond Zahralban, *President*
EMP: 16
SQ FT: 14,000
SALES (est): 3.2MM **Privately Held**
SIC: 3446 Architectural metalwork

(G-16799)
BARTOLOMEO PUBLISHING INC
Also Called: Northport Printing
100 Cabot St Unit A (11704-1133)
PHONE 631 420-4949
Dan Bartolomeo, *President*
Patricia Bartolomeo, *Vice Pres*
EMP: 5
SQ FT: 17,200
SALES (est): 1.5MM **Privately Held**
SIC: 2759 2752 Commercial printing; letterpress printing; flexographic printing; commercial printing, offset

(G-16800)
BEAM MANUFACTURING CORP
Also Called: Sigro Precision
107 Otis St Unit A (11704-1444)
PHONE 631 253-2724
Fax: 631 253-2246
Ernie Lampeter, *President*
EMP: 6
SQ FT: 4,000
SALES (est): 856K **Privately Held**
SIC: 3599 Machine shop, jobbing & repair

(G-16801)
BROOKVALE RECORDS INC
Also Called: Looney Tunes CD Store
31 Brookvale Ave (11704-7901)
PHONE 631 587-7722
Kral Groger, *President*
EMP: 11

SALES (est): 950K **Privately Held**
SIC: 2782 Record albums

(G-16802)
BSD TOP DIRECT INC
68 Route 109 (11704-6208)
PHONE 646 468-0156
Elisha Mishael, *CEO*
EMP: 5
SALES (est): 330K **Privately Held**
SIC: 2096 Potato chips & similar snacks

(G-16803)
BURTON INDUSTRIES INC
243 Wyandanch Ave Ste A (11704-1593)
PHONE 631 643-6660
Fax: 631 643-6665
Charles Seelinger, *CEO*
Richard Santos, *President*
Dariusz Siniakowicz, *Exec VP*
Warren Hartman, *Vice Pres*
Thomas Seelinger, *Vice Pres*
EMP: 35
SQ FT: 38,000
SALES (est): 7.8MM **Privately Held**
WEB: www.burtonheat.com
SIC: 3398 Metal heat treating

(G-16804)
BUSINESS CARD EXPRESS INC
300 Farmingdale Rd (11704)
PHONE 631 669-3400
Fax: 631 669-1222
William Richards, *President*
Jerry Peirano, *Treasurer*
EMP: 40
SQ FT: 11,000
SALES (est): 5.4MM **Privately Held**
SIC: 2759 2752 Thermography; commercial printing, lithographic

(G-16805)
C J & C SHEET METAL CORP
433 Falmouth Rd (11704-5654)
PHONE 631 376-9425
James Thurau, *President*
EMP: 12
SALES (est): 970K **Privately Held**
SIC: 3444 Sheet metalwork

(G-16806)
CENTURY READY MIX INC
615 Cord Ave (11704)
P.O. Box 1065 (11704-0065)
PHONE 631 888-2200
Nicolina Nicolia, *President*
Liliana Legarreta, *Accountant*
EMP: 6
SALES (est): 510K **Privately Held**
SIC: 3273 5039 Ready-mixed concrete; mobile homes

(G-16807)
CHECK-MATE INDUSTRIES INC
370 Wyandanch Ave (11704-1524)
PHONE 631 491-1777
Fax: 631 491-1745
Regina M Vieweg, *CEO*
Edward Tracy, *CFO*
Jackie Viewig, *Chief Mktg Ofcr*
Jacquelyn Santoro, *Director*
Lucille Scavone, *Admin Asst*
EMP: 45
SQ FT: 23,000
SALES (est): 11.7MM **Privately Held**
SIC: 3469 Metal stampings

(G-16808)
CHEM-TAINER INDUSTRIES INC (PA)
Also Called: Todd Enterprises
361 Neptune Ave (11704-5800)
PHONE 631 422-8300
Fax: 631 661-8923
Stuart Pivar, *Ch of Bd*
James Glen, *President*
Anthony Lamb, *Vice Pres*
Joe Maiello, *Vice Pres*
Joseph Distefano, *Controller*
◆ **EMP:** 50 **EST:** 1961
SQ FT: 20,000
SALES (est): 49.9MM **Privately Held**
WEB: www.chemtainer.com
SIC: 3089 Plastic containers, except foam

(G-16809)
CHURCH BULLETIN INC
200 Dale St (11704-1124)
P.O. Box 1659, Massapequa (11758-0911)
PHONE 631 249-4994
Fax: 631 293-8354
George Keenan Jr, *President*
EMP: 15
SALES (est): 1.4MM **Privately Held**
WEB: www.thechurchbulletininc.com
SIC: 2741 Business service newsletters: publishing & printing

(G-16810)
COMPUTERIZED METAL BENDING SER
91 Cabot St Unit A (11704-1132)
PHONE 631 249-1177
Kenneth Rosner, *President*
EMP: 16
SALES (est): 980.2K **Privately Held**
SIC: 3441 Fabricated structural metal

(G-16811)
CUSTOM FRAME & MOLDING CO
97 Lamar St 101 (11704-1308)
PHONE 631 491-9091
Nick Maminakis, *President*
Dr Steven Lewen, *Vice Pres*
Michelle Lewen, *Admin Sec*
EMP: 12
SQ FT: 15,000
SALES (est): 1.5MM **Privately Held**
SIC: 3499 Picture frames, metal

(G-16812)
CUSTOM METAL INCORPORATED
Also Called: Custom Metal Fabrication
72 Otis St (11704-1406)
PHONE 631 643-4075
Stephen Pratt, *President*
Nancy Pratt, *Corp Secy*
Jackie Smith, *Office Mgr*
EMP: 11
SQ FT: 11,300
SALES: 1.4MM **Privately Held**
WEB: www.custommetalfabrication.com
SIC: 3469 Machine parts, stamped or pressed metal

(G-16813)
DBS INTERIORS CORP
Also Called: Island Interiors
81 Otis St (11704-1405)
P.O. Box 1780 (11704-0780)
PHONE 631 491-3013
Fax: 631 491-4112
Robert Laurie, *President*
Ed Bundock, *Vice Pres*
Richard Mills, *Purch Agent*
John Bemonte, *Marketing Mgr*
Susan Laurie, *Office Mgr*
EMP: 12
SQ FT: 7,000
SALES (est): 2MM **Privately Held**
SIC: 2519 2541 2517 2511 Furniture, household: glass, fiberglass & plastic; wood partitions & fixtures; wood television & radio cabinets; wood household furniture; wood kitchen cabinets; millwork

(G-16814)
DISPLAY COMPONENTS MFG INC
Also Called: D C M
267 Edison Ave (11704-1020)
PHONE 631 420-0600
Fax: 516 420-1049
James P Devine III, *President*
Julie Braga, *Controller*
Barbara Jones, *Manager*
Donna Devine, *Admin Sec*
EMP: 30
SQ FT: 25,000
SALES (est): 5.1MM **Privately Held**
WEB: www.displaycomponents.com
SIC: 2542 Fixtures: display, office or store: except wood

(G-16815)
EAST CAST CLOR COMPOUNDING INC
Also Called: Linli Color
15 Kean St (11704-1208)
PHONE 631 491-9000
Fax: 631 491-9008
George Benz, *CEO*
Tony Arra, *President*
Kevin Rigoulot, *General Mgr*
Jon Shuman, *Vice Pres*
EMP: 9
SQ FT: 10,000
SALES (est): 1.6MM **Privately Held**
WEB: www.linlicolor.com
SIC: 2865 3089 Dyes & pigments; extruded finished plastic products

(G-16816)
EXCEL COMMERCIAL SEATING
Also Called: Dine Right Seating
190 Field St (11704-1214)
PHONE 828 428-8338
Phil Breisen, *Owner*
EMP: 50
SALES (est): 2.8MM **Privately Held**
SIC: 2599 Restaurant furniture, wood or metal

(G-16817)
FAMOUS BOX SCOOTER CO
75 Rogers Ct (11704-6540)
PHONE 631 943-2013
Charles Rubino, *Owner*
EMP: 5
SALES (est): 217.8K **Privately Held**
SIC: 3944 Scooters, children's

(G-16818)
FLEXENE CORP
Also Called: Edge-Craft Process Co
108 Lamar St (11704-1312)
P.O. Box 1457 (11704-0457)
PHONE 631 491-0580
Kurt Godigkeit, *President*
Walter Ploeger, *Manager*
EMP: 20 **EST:** 1946
SQ FT: 11,000
SALES (est): 2.3MM **Privately Held**
WEB: www.flexenedgecraft.com
SIC: 2269 Finishing plants

(G-16819)
GAMMA ENTERPRISES LLC
Also Called: Gamma Lab
113 Alder St (11704-1001)
PHONE 631 755-1080
Clifford Morgan, *CEO*
Matthew Alvarez, *Controller*
▼ **EMP:** 30
SQ FT: 19,000
SALES: 7.9MM **Privately Held**
SIC: 2834 Vitamin, nutrient & hematinic preparations for human use

(G-16820)
GREAT EASTERN PASTA WORKS LLC
Also Called: Pasta People
385 Sheffield Ave (11704-5326)
PHONE 631 956-0889
Kambiz Morakkabi,
EMP: 20
SQ FT: 1,500
SALES: 2.1MM **Privately Held**
SIC: 2099 5149 Pasta, uncooked: packaged with other ingredients; pasta & rice

(G-16821)
HEALTHCARE CONSULTING SVCS INC
974 Little East Neck Rd (11704-4623)
PHONE 860 740-8660
Eric Rogan,
EMP: 15
SALES: 2.5MM **Privately Held**
SIC: 2899

(G-16822)
INFINITLINK CORPORATION
455 Sunrise Hwy Ste 2r (11704-5910)
PHONE 934 777-0180
Ryan Vigorito, *President*
Tracy Hanley, *Vice Pres*
Gianni Vigorito, *Shareholder*

▲ = Import ▼=Export
◆ =Import/Export

GEOGRAPHIC SECTION

West Babylon - Suffolk County (G-16848)

Ruthan Douglas, *Admin Sec*
EMP: 9 **EST:** 2016
SQ FT: 2,600
SALES: 200K **Privately Held**
SIC: 2721 7374 2741 Statistical reports (periodicals): publishing & printing; data processing service;

(G-16823)
ISOLATION DYNAMICS CORP
Also Called: Idc
66 Otis St Unit A (11704-1427)
P.O. Box 361, Merrick (11566-0361)
PHONE 631 491-5670
Fax: 516 785-6484
Max Borrasino, *President*
EMP: 20
SQ FT: 4,000
SALES (est): 3.4MM **Privately Held**
WEB: www.isolator.com
SIC: 3493 Steel springs, except wire

(G-16824)
ISOLATION TECHNOLOGY INC
73 Nancy St Unit A (11704-1428)
P.O. Box 460, Massapequa (11758-0460)
PHONE 631 253-3314
Fax: 631 253-3316
Bob Grefe, *President*
Robert Joyner, *Corp Secy*
▲ **EMP:** 6
SQ FT: 4,000
SALES (est): 1.1MM **Privately Held**
WEB: www.isolationtech.com
SIC: 3699 Electric sound equipment

(G-16825)
J & T METAL PRODUCTS CO INC
89 Eads St (11704-1105)
PHONE 631 226-7400
Thomas Lander, *President*
EMP: 20 **EST:** 1964
SQ FT: 18,000
SALES (est): 1.9MM **Privately Held**
SIC: 3443 Industrial vessels, tanks & containers; tanks, standard or custom fabricated: metal plate

(G-16826)
J C INDUSTRIES INC
89 Eads St (11704-1186)
PHONE 631 420-1920
Fax: 516 420-0467
Joseph V Celano, *Ch of Bd*
James Celano, *Vice Pres*
Durwood Woodall, *Vice Pres*
Steve Erwin, *Accountant*
EMP: 30 **EST:** 1973
SQ FT: 14,000
SALES (est): 5.4MM **Privately Held**
WEB: www.jcindustries.com
SIC: 3411 Metal cans

(G-16827)
J T D STAMPING CO INC
403 Wyandanch Ave (11704-1599)
PHONE 631 643-4144
Fax: 631 643-4016
Giovanni Bianco, *President*
Aldo D'Adamo, *Vice Pres*
Aldo Dadamo, *Vice Pres*
Tania Malbonavo, *Bookkeeper*
EMP: 39
SQ FT: 20,000
SALES: 3.5MM **Privately Held**
WEB: www.jtdstamping.com
SIC: 3452 Spring washers, metal

(G-16828)
JALEX INDUSTRIES LTD
86 Nancy St (11704-1404)
PHONE 631 491-5072
Fax: 631 491-5201
Alexander Jedynski, *President*
Richard Goldsmith, *Vice Pres*
Michele Jedynski, *Vice Pres*
Woon Lee, *Engineer*
EMP: 15
SQ FT: 7,000
SALES (est): 1.8MM **Privately Held**
SIC: 3541 Machine tools, metal cutting type

(G-16829)
JAVIN MACHINE CORP
31 Otis St (11704-1405)
PHONE 631 643-3322
Fax: 631 643-3340
Geri Spiezio, *CEO*
Sal Spiezio, *President*
Vincent Spiezio, *President*
John Zielinski, *QC Mgr*
Carol Bertolo, *Office Mgr*
EMP: 15
SQ FT: 16,000
SALES (est): 3MM **Privately Held**
WEB: www.javinmachine.net
SIC: 3599 Machine shop, jobbing & repair

(G-16830)
JF MACHINE SHOP INC
89 Otis St Unit A (11704-1442)
PHONE 631 491-7273
Fax: 631 491-7221
Anthony Schiavone, *President*
EMP: 10
SQ FT: 9,000
SALES (est): 1.6MM **Privately Held**
WEB: www.jfmachine.com
SIC: 3599 Machine shop, jobbing & repair

(G-16831)
JOHNNYS MACHINE SHOP
81 Mahan St (11704-1303)
PHONE 631 338-9733
Juan Campos, *Owner*
EMP: 5
SALES: 200K **Privately Held**
SIC: 3599 Machine & other job shop work; machine shop, jobbing & repair

(G-16832)
KESSLER THERMOMETER CORP
40 Gleam St (11704-1205)
PHONE 631 841-5500
Fax: 631 841-5553
Robert Peyser, *President*
▲ **EMP:** 9
SALES (est): 1MM **Privately Held**
SIC: 3823 Thermometers, filled system: industrial process type

(G-16833)
KING ALBUM INC
20 Kean St (11704-1209)
PHONE 631 253-9500
Warren King, *President*
EMP: 20
SQ FT: 7,700
SALES: 2.2MM **Privately Held**
SIC: 2782 Albums

(G-16834)
L K MANUFACTURING CORP
56 Eads St (11704-1106)
P.O. Box 167, Huntington Station (11746-0137)
PHONE 631 243-6910
Fax: 516 420-9506
Robert Lutzker, *President*
Kay Kelly, *Vice Pres*
Samuel Martin, *Vice Pres*
EMP: 22
SQ FT: 15,000
SALES (est): 1.9MM **Privately Held**
WEB: www.lkmfg.com
SIC: 3089 5065 Kitchenware, plastic; electronic parts & equipment

(G-16835)
LETTERAMA INC (PA)
111 Cabot St (11704-1100)
PHONE 516 349-0800
Mark Costa, *President*
Kevin Hardiman, *Controller*
▼ **EMP:** 7 **EST:** 1959
SQ FT: 30,000
SALES: 3MM **Privately Held**
SIC: 3993 Signs & advertising specialties

(G-16836)
LINZER PRODUCTS CORP (DH)
248 Wyandanch Ave (11704-1506)
PHONE 631 253-3333
Brent Swenson, *President*
Mark Saji, *Treasurer*
Len Zichlin, *Controller*
Brendan Jones, *Accountant*
Joe Dichiria, *Natl Sales Mgr*
▲ **EMP:** 200 **EST:** 1892
SQ FT: 166,000
SALES: 120MM
SALES (corp-wide): 12.9MM **Privately Held**
SIC: 3991 5198 Paint & varnish brushes; paint brushes, rollers, sprayers

(G-16837)
M T D CORPORATION
41 Otis St (11704-1405)
PHONE 631 491-3905
Matthew Turnbull, *President*
Michael Deletto, *Vice Pres*
Lisa Muford, *Bookkeeper*
EMP: 10
SQ FT: 6,500
SALES (est): 1.2MM **Privately Held**
WEB: www.makeupart.net
SIC: 2521 2511 Wood office furniture; wood household furniture

(G-16838)
MAGELLAN AEROSPACE PROCESSING
Also Called: Ripak Aerospace Processing
165 Field St (11704-1210)
PHONE 631 694-1818
Phillip Underwood, *President*
Jason Addis, *Vice Pres*
Mark Allcock, *Vice Pres*
Jo-Ann Ball, *Vice Pres*
Konrad Hahnelt, *Vice Pres*
EMP: 8
SQ FT: 72,000
SALES (est): 217.6K
SALES (corp-wide): 742.4MM **Privately Held**
SIC: 3724 3429 Aircraft engines & engine parts; aircraft hardware
PA: Magellan Aerospace Corporation
3160 Derry Rd E
Mississauga ON L4T 1
905 677-1889

(G-16839)
MATRIX MACHINING CORP
69 B Nancy St Unitb (11704)
PHONE 631 643-6690
Fax: 631 643-2310
Joseph Abdale, *President*
Ray Abdale, *Corp Secy*
EMP: 6
SQ FT: 4,700
SALES (est): 999.8K **Privately Held**
SIC: 3599 Machine shop, jobbing & repair

(G-16840)
MATRIX RAILWAY CORP
69 Nancy St Unit A (11704-1425)
PHONE 631 643-1483
Nelson Rivas, *Ch of Bd*
▲ **EMP:** 9
SQ FT: 4,000
SALES (est): 1.9MM **Privately Held**
WEB: www.matrixrailway.com
SIC: 3621 Railway motors & control equipment, electric

(G-16841)
METRO DYNMC SCNTIFIC INSTR LAB
20 Nancy St (11704-1448)
PHONE 631 842-4300
Steve Plaener, *President*
EMP: 15
SQ FT: 6,000
SALES (est): 1.5MM **Privately Held**
SIC: 3812 Search & navigation equipment

(G-16842)
MILLWRIGHT WDWRK INSTALLETION
991 Peconic Ave (11704-5629)
PHONE 631 587-2635
Fax: 631 587-1573
Martin Sherlock, *President*
Peggy Mauro, *Office Mgr*
Jim Orlando, *Executive*
EMP: 20
SQ FT: 16,000
SALES (est): 2.1MM **Privately Held**
SIC: 2431 1751 Millwork; finish & trim carpentry

(G-16843)
MPI CONSULTING INCORPORATED
Also Called: Wal Machine
87 Jersey St (11704-1206)
PHONE 631 253-2377
Fax: 631 253-2286
William A Toscano, *CEO*
Jennifer Luizzi, *Vice Pres*
EMP: 13 **EST:** 1966
SQ FT: 8,000
SALES: 7MM **Privately Held**
SIC: 3429 Aircraft hardware

(G-16844)
MPI CONSULTING INCORPORATED
Also Called: Wal Machine
87 Jersey St (11704-1206)
PHONE 631 253-2377
William Toscano, *President*
EMP: 3 **EST:** 2011
SQ FT: 12,000
SALES: 5MM **Privately Held**
SIC: 3365 Aerospace castings, aluminum

(G-16845)
NASSAU TOOL WORKS INC
34 Lamar St (11704-1309)
PHONE 631 328-7031
Fax: 631 643-3432
Vincent Di Carlo Jr, *President*
Marisol Arroyo, *General Mgr*
Robert Hunt, *Corp Secy*
Elona Maturo, *Manager*
EMP: 50
SQ FT: 60,000
SALES (est): 9.1MM
SALES (corp-wide): 66.9MM **Publicly Held**
SIC: 3728 3599 Aircraft parts & equipment; aircraft landing assemblies & brakes; machine shop, jobbing & repair
PA: Air Industries Group
3609 Motor Pkwy Ste 100
Hauppauge NY 11788
631 881-4920

(G-16846)
NEWMAT NORTHEAST CORP
81b Mahan St (11704-1303)
PHONE 631 253-9277
Timothy T Greco, *President*
EMP: 11
SQ FT: 8,000
SALES (est): 2.8MM **Privately Held**
SIC: 2821 1742 Polyvinyl chloride resins (PVC); acoustical & ceiling work

(G-16847)
OUR TERMS FABRICATORS INC
48 Cabot St (11704-1109)
PHONE 631 752-1517
John Friese, *President*
Greg D'Arrigo, *Vice Pres*
Terry Connolly, *Manager*
EMP: 32
SQ FT: 18,000
SALES (est): 4.5MM **Privately Held**
WEB: www.ourtermsfabricators.com
SIC: 3231 Furniture tops, glass: cut, beveled or polished

(G-16848)
PEYSER INSTRUMENT CORPORATION
Also Called: Chase Instrument Co
40 Gleam St (11704-1205)
PHONE 631 841-3600
Fax: 516 841-5553
Robert Peyser, *President*
Leonard Peyser, *Vice Pres*
John Lewis, *Executive*
▲ **EMP:** 20
SQ FT: 1,500
SALES (est): 2.5MM **Privately Held**
SIC: 3829 5049 Hydrometers, except industrial process type; analytical instruments

West Babylon - Suffolk County (G-16849)

(G-16849)
PREMIUM WOODWORKING LLC
108 Lamar St (11704-1312)
PHONE..................................631 485-3133
Bhevendra Persaud,
EMP: 5
SQ FT: 5,000
SALES: 2MM **Privately Held**
SIC: 2434 Wood kitchen cabinets

(G-16850)
QUALITY SAW & KNIFE INC
115 Otis St (11704-1429)
PHONE..................................631 491-4747
Fredrick Luberto, *President*
Paul Siegfried, *Vice Pres*
EMP: 10
SQ FT: 3,000
SALES (est): 800K **Privately Held**
SIC: 3425 7699 Saw blades, chain type; saw blades for hand or power saws; knife, saw & tool sharpening & repair

(G-16851)
R & J DISPLAYS INC
96 Otis St (11704-1430)
PHONE..................................631 491-3500
Fax: 631 491-8566
Lance Landau, *President*
Phyllis Lazar, *Office Mgr*
EMP: 30
SQ FT: 20,000
SALES (est): 3.2MM **Privately Held**
SIC: 3993 Displays & cutouts, window & lobby

(G-16852)
RGH ASSOCIATES INC
Also Called: Richards Screw Machine
86 Nancy St (11704-1404)
PHONE..................................631 643-1111
Richard Honan, *President*
Richard Goldsmith, *Corp Secy*
EMP: 19
SQ FT: 7,200
SALES: 6.5MM **Privately Held**
SIC: 3599 Machine shop, jobbing & repair

(G-16853)
RICHARD MANNO & COMPANY INC
42 Lamar St (11704-1302)
PHONE..................................631 643-2200
Fax: 631 643-2215
Vincent Manno, *President*
Ilian Dimitrov, *General Mgr*
Vincent Chiappone, *Exec VP*
Jason Wagner, *Exec VP*
Christine Burns, *Vice Pres*
▲ **EMP:** 54
SQ FT: 18,000
SALES (est): 10.4MM **Privately Held**
WEB: www.richardmanno.com
SIC: 3599 Machine shop, jobbing & repair

(G-16854)
ROSE GRAPHICS LLC
109 Kean St (11704-1208)
PHONE..................................516 547-6142
Jeannie Bissert, *Manager*
Anthony F Severino,
EMP: 10
SQ FT: 8,000
SALES: 2MM **Privately Held**
SIC: 2759 Commercial printing

(G-16855)
S & D WELDING CORP
Also Called: S&D Welding
229 Edison Ave Ste A (11704-1042)
PHONE..................................631 454-0383
Fax: 516 454-0802
Mark Dubicki, *President*
Lucia Dubicki, *Treasurer*
EMP: 5
SALES: 275K **Privately Held**
SIC: 7692 1799 5046 Welding repair; welding on site; commercial cooking & food service equipment

(G-16856)
SAGE KNITWEAR INC
103 Jersey St Unit D (11704-1219)
P.O. Box 748231, Rego Park (11374-8231)
PHONE..................................718 628-7902
Payam Ebrani, *President*
EMP: 5
SQ FT: 3,500
SALES (est): 604.1K **Privately Held**
SIC: 2253 Sweaters & sweater coats, knit; dresses, knit; skirts, knit

(G-16857)
SAV THERMO INC
133 Cabot St (11704-1101)
PHONE..................................631 249-9444
Vincent Caputi, *President*
Anthony Bangaroo, *Vice Pres*
EMP: 10
SQ FT: 10,000
SALES (est): 1.6MM **Privately Held**
SIC: 3089 Trays, plastic

(G-16858)
SINN- TECH INDUSTRIES INC
48 Gleam St (11704-1205)
PHONE..................................631 643-1171
Fax: 631 643-1176
Daniel Tierney, *Owner*
Robert Becker, *Director*
EMP: 10
SQ FT: 7,000
SALES: 1MM **Privately Held**
WEB: www.sinn-tech.com
SIC: 3545 Machine tool accessories

(G-16859)
SINN-TECH INDUSTRIES INC
48 Gleam St (11704-1205)
PHONE..................................631 643-1171
Daniel Tierney, *President*
EMP: 8 **EST:** 2015
SALES (est): 311.7K **Privately Held**
SIC: 3449 Miscellaneous metalwork

(G-16860)
SONAER INC
68 Lamar St Unit D (11704-1316)
PHONE..................................631 756-4780
Donald Cierco, *Ch of Bd*
Donald Ciervo, *Ch of Bd*
EMP: 8
SQ FT: 3,000
SALES (est): 1.1MM **Privately Held**
WEB: www.sonozap.com
SIC: 3679 Electronic circuits

(G-16861)
SONICOR INC
82 Otis St (11704-1406)
PHONE..................................631 920-6555
Michael J Parker, *President*
Edmond J Parker, *Vice Pres*
Augusto D' Agostino, *Manager*
▲ **EMP:** 12 **EST:** 1966
SQ FT: 3,500
SALES (est): 2.4MM **Privately Held**
WEB: www.sonicor.com
SIC: 3569 3559 3554 3699 Separators for steam, gas, vapor or air (machinery); electroplating machinery & equipment; paper mill machinery: plating, slitting, waxing, etc.; welding machines & equipment, ultrasonic; cleaning equipment, ultrasonic, except medical & dental; medical cleaning equipment, ultrasonic

(G-16862)
SPARTAN PRECISION MACHINING
56 Cabot St (11704-1109)
PHONE..................................516 546-5171
Fax: 516 546-8359
George Pappas, *President*
Mabel Pappas, *Bookkeeper*
William Draffen, *Sales Staff*
EMP: 35 **EST:** 1966
SQ FT: 5,000
SALES (est): 3.7MM **Privately Held**
SIC: 3599 Machine shop, jobbing & repair

(G-16863)
SPECIALTY BLDG SOLUTIONS INC
Eads St Ste 165a (11704)
PHONE..................................631 393-6918
John Pearson, *Owner*
Jeanne Demaio, *Office Mgr*
EMP: 8 **EST:** 2009
SALES (est): 535K **Privately Held**
SIC: 3479 Coating or wrapping steel pipe

(G-16864)
STERLING TOGGLE INC
99 Mahan St (11704-1303)
PHONE..................................631 491-0500
Fax: 631 491-3401
William Horne Jr, *President*
Susan Horne, *Vice Pres*
Debra Irving, *Vice Pres*
Emily Williams, *Manager*
EMP: 12
SALES (est): 2.1MM **Privately Held**
WEB: www.sterlingtoggle.com
SIC: 3555 Printing trades machinery

(G-16865)
STRAHL & PITSCH INC
230 Great East Neck Rd (11704-7602)
P.O. Box 1098 (11704-0098)
PHONE..................................631 669-0175
Fax: 631 587-9120
William France, *Ch of Bd*
William Deluca, *President*
John Gomes, *Vice Pres*
Hans Kestler, *Vice Pres*
Bill Schnabel, *Plant Mgr*
◆ **EMP:** 40 **EST:** 1904
SALES (est): 18.2MM **Privately Held**
WEB: www.spwax.com
SIC: 2842 Waxes for wood, leather & other materials

(G-16866)
SUPER WEB INC
97 Lamar St (11704-1308)
PHONE..................................631 643-9100
Fax: 631 643-9069
Marcel Edelstein, *Ch of Bd*
Paul Schwartz, *Vice Pres*
Shelly Edelstein, *Admin Sec*
▲ **EMP:** 30
SQ FT: 27,000
SALES (est): 7.6MM **Privately Held**
WEB: www.superwebusa.com
SIC: 3555 5084 Printing trades machinery; printing trades machinery, equipment & supplies

(G-16867)
SWEET TOOTH ENTERPRISES LLC
Also Called: Micelli Chocalate Mold Co
135 Dale St (11704-1103)
PHONE..................................631 752-2888
Tim Goddeau, *Opers Mgr*
Paul Hamilton,
EMP: 20
SALES (est): 4.6MM **Privately Held**
SIC: 3089 Molding primary plastic

(G-16868)
TRIANGLE GRINDING MACHINE CORP
66 Nancy St Unit A (11704-1436)
PHONE..................................631 643-3636
Santo Turano, *President*
Domingo Turano, *Vice Pres*
George Turano, *Vice Pres*
EMP: 5
SQ FT: 800
SALES (est): 634.7K **Privately Held**
SIC: 3599 Machine shop, jobbing & repair

(G-16869)
US ELECTROPLATING CORP
100 Field St Unit A (11704-1294)
PHONE..................................631 293-1998
Fax: 516 293-7742
Robert Birnbaum, *President*
EMP: 6 **EST:** 1971
SQ FT: 3,000
SALES (est): 520K **Privately Held**
SIC: 3471 Plating of metals or formed products; polishing, metals or formed products

(G-16870)
VANDILAY INDUSTRIES INC
Also Called: Dualtron Manufacturing
60 Bell St Unit A (11704-1038)
PHONE..................................631 226-3064
Don Ehrlich, *President*
Chris Schleimer, *Vice Pres*
EMP: 22 **EST:** 1997
SQ FT: 22,000
SALES (est): 4.1MM **Privately Held**
SIC: 3545 Machine tool accessories

(G-16871)
VILLAGE VIDEO PRODUCTIONS INC
Also Called: Village Video News
107 Alder St (11704-1001)
PHONE..................................631 752-9311
Robert Wolf, *President*
Doreen Wolf, *Manager*
EMP: 6
SQ FT: 2,000
SALES (est): 876.3K **Privately Held**
WEB: www.vvn.com
SIC: 3663 Satellites, communications

(G-16872)
WEICRO GRAPHICS INC
Also Called: Able Printing
95 Mahan St (11704-1303)
PHONE..................................631 253-3360
Fax: 631 253-3369
Sanford Weiss, *President*
Lucyna Mleczko, *Vice Pres*
EMP: 22
SQ FT: 5,500
SALES (est): 3.5MM **Privately Held**
WEB: www.lemontreestationery.com
SIC: 2752 2759 Commercial printing, offset; commercial printing

(G-16873)
YANKEE FUEL INC
780 Sunrise Hwy (11704-6105)
PHONE..................................631 880-8810
Ibrahim Sergi, *Principal*
EMP: 5
SALES (est): 387.2K **Privately Held**
SIC: 2869 Fuels

West Burlington
Otsego County

(G-16874)
CONTROL LOGIC CORPORATION
2533 State Highway 80 (13482-9717)
PHONE..................................607 965-6423
Fax: 607 965-6426
Randy Holdredge, *President*
Joanne Holdredge, *Admin Sec*
EMP: 6
SALES (est): 460K **Privately Held**
WEB: www.controllogic.com
SIC: 3577 Printers, computer

West Edmeston
Madison County

(G-16875)
SCULLY SANITATION
11146 Skaneateles Tpke (13485-3060)
PHONE..................................315 899-8996
Timothy Scully, *Partner*
Kevin Scully, *Partner*
EMP: 8
SALES: 300K **Privately Held**
SIC: 2842 Sanitation preparations, disinfectants & deodorants

West Falls
Erie County

(G-16876)
BUTTERWOOD DESSERTS INC
Also Called: Swamp Island Dessert Co
1863 Davis Rd (14170-9701)
PHONE..................................716 652-0131
Fax: 585 652-1759
EMP: 40
SQ FT: 15,000
SALES: 3.4MM **Privately Held**
SIC: 2099 2053 2052 Mfg Food Preparations Mfg Frozen Bakery Prdts Mfg Cookies/Crackers

GEOGRAPHIC SECTION

(G-16877)
TEAM FABRICATION INC
1055 Davis Rd (14170-9734)
P.O. Box 32 (14170-0032)
PHONE..................716 655-4038
Robert Hopkins, *President*
William Emhof, *Director*
EMP: 8
SQ FT: 2,376
SALES (est): 1.5MM **Privately Held**
WEB: www.teamfabrication.com
SIC: 3441 Fabricated structural metal

West Haverstraw
Rockland County

(G-16878)
VIN-CLAIR INC
Also Called: Vin-Clair Bindery
132 E Railroad Ave (10993-1418)
PHONE..................845 429-4998
Fax: 845 429-5747
Lou Maiello, *President*
Florence Maiello, *Vice Pres*
Claire Blaha, *Bookkeeper*
EMP: 10
SQ FT: 17,000
SALES (est): 77.3K **Privately Held**
SIC: 2789 Bookbinding & related work

(G-16879)
YOUR FURNITURE DESIGNERS INC
Also Called: Yfd Cabinetry
118 E Railroad Ave (10993-1416)
PHONE..................845 947-3046
Jose A Mata, *President*
Cristina Matha, *Manager*
EMP: 5
SALES (est): 725.4K **Privately Held**
SIC: 2511 2521 2434 2542 Wood household furniture; wood bedroom furniture; kitchen & dining room furniture; wood office furniture; wood kitchen cabinets; vanities, bathroom: wood; shelving, office & store: except wood

West Hempstead
Nassau County

(G-16880)
ARTISAN WOODWORKING LTD
Also Called: Artisan Custom Interiors
163 Hempstead Tpke (11552-1622)
PHONE..................516 486-0818
Michael Aiello, *President*
Janet Aiello, *Corp Secy*
EMP: 6
SQ FT: 6,500
SALES (est): 834.8K **Privately Held**
WEB: www.artisancustominteriors.com
SIC: 2511 Wood household furniture

(G-16881)
AUTOMOTION PARKING SYSTEMS LLC
411 Hempstead Tpke # 200 (11552-1350)
PHONE..................516 565-5600
Perry Finkelman, *Managing Dir*
Daniel McCrossin, *Opers Mgr*
EMP: 2
SQ FT: 1,000
SALES: 2.1MM **Privately Held**
SIC: 3559 Parking facility equipment & supplies

(G-16882)
CENTAR FUEL CO INC
700 Nassau Blvd (11552-3531)
PHONE..................516 538-2424
John Skei, *Principal*
EMP: 5 **EST:** 2007
SALES (est): 563.8K **Privately Held**
SIC: 2869 Fuels

(G-16883)
D-BEST EQUIPMENT CORP
77 Hempstead Gardens Dr (11552-2643)
PHONE..................516 358-0965
Marc Cali, *CEO*
EMP: 24
SALES (est): 5MM **Privately Held**
SIC: 2869 Enzymes

(G-16884)
GARDEN CITY PRINTERS & MAILERS
144 Cherry Valley Ave (11552-1213)
PHONE..................516 485-1600
Joseph Grzymalski, *President*
Patricia Grzymalski, *Vice Pres*
▲ **EMP:** 14
SQ FT: 10,000
SALES (est): 1.1MM **Privately Held**
SIC: 2752 7331 Commercial printing, lithographic; mailing service

(G-16885)
GENESIS ONE UNLIMITED
Also Called: Eb Automation Industries
600 Pinebrook Ave (11552-4225)
PHONE..................516 208-5863
Earl Birkett, *Principal*
EMP: 6
SALES: 250K **Privately Held**
SIC: 2759 3497 Imprinting; gold foil or leaf

(G-16886)
INDEPENDENT HOME PRODUCTS LLC
59 Hempstead Gardens Dr (11552-2641)
PHONE..................718 541-1256
Abbie Spetner, *Principal*
Yale Lipschik, *CFO*
▲ **EMP:** 20
SALES (est): 3.1MM **Privately Held**
SIC: 3088 3431 Hot tubs, plastic or fiberglass; bathtubs: enameled iron, cast iron or pressed metal

(G-16887)
INTERNTONAL CONSMR CONNECTIONS
Also Called: Wilson Picture Frames
5 Terminal Rd Unit A (11552-1151)
PHONE..................516 481-3438
Fax: 516 538-1938
Mark Sternberg, *President*
Alan Kohn, *Shareholder*
EMP: 12
SQ FT: 5,000
SALES: 750K **Privately Held**
SIC: 2499 7699 Picture & mirror frames, wood; picture framing, custom

(G-16888)
J GIMBEL INC
275 Hempstead Tpke Ste A (11552-1540)
PHONE..................718 296-5200
Fax: 718 296-6188
Jackie Sherman, *President*
Leonard Gimbel, *Vice Pres*
Lorie Gimbel, *Treasurer*
EMP: 20
SQ FT: 17,000
SALES (est): 2.5MM **Privately Held**
WEB: www.rollershades.com
SIC: 2591 Blinds vertical; window shades

(G-16889)
KONRAD PROSTHETICS & ORTHOTICS (PA)
596 Jennings Ave (11552-3706)
PHONE..................516 485-9164
Fax: 516 485-9170
Kurt Konrad, *President*
Elsbeth Konrad, *Corp Secy*
EMP: 6
SQ FT: 200
SALES (est): 733K **Privately Held**
SIC: 3842 7352 5999 Surgical appliances & supplies; invalid supplies rental; artificial limbs

(G-16890)
LANCO MANUFACTURING CO
384 Hempstead Tpke (11552-1304)
PHONE..................516 292-8953
Joseph Lancer, *Partner*
Irwin Lamcer, *Partner*
Irwin Lancer, *Partner*
EMP: 5
SQ FT: 10,000
SALES (est): 39.3K **Privately Held**
SIC: 3561 Pumps & pumping equipment

(G-16891)
MAGIC TECH CO LTD
401 Hempstead Tpke (11552-1311)
PHONE..................516 539-7944
EMP: 5
SALES (est): 440K **Privately Held**
SIC: 3699 5065 Mfg And Dist Karoke Machines

(G-16892)
MULTITONE FINISHING CO INC
56 Hempstead Gardens Dr (11552-2642)
PHONE..................516 485-1043
Fax: 516 485-1043
Edward Mc Carthy, *President*
Harvey Pollack, *Vice Pres*
EMP: 8 **EST:** 1963
SQ FT: 4,700
SALES (est): 660K **Privately Held**
SIC: 3471 Finishing, metals or formed products

(G-16893)
MUTUAL ENGRAVING COMPANY INC
497 Hempstead Ave (11552-2738)
P.O. Box 129 (11552-0129)
PHONE..................516 489-0534
Fax: 516 486-6400
Salvatore Forelli, *President*
Robert Forelli, *Vice Pres*
Emma Cooper, *Project Mgr*
John Battaglia, *Mfg Staff*
Lou Ewanitsko, *Treasurer*
EMP: 65 **EST:** 1939
SQ FT: 15,000
SALES (est): 7.5MM **Privately Held**
WEB: www.mutualengraving.com
SIC: 2754 2796 2791 2752 Stationery: gravure printing; platemaking services; typesetting; commercial printing, lithographic

(G-16894)
PROFESSIONAL REMODELERS INC
340 Hempstead Ave Unit A (11552-2061)
PHONE..................516 565-9300
Thomas Stallone, *President*
Marlyn Prousard, *Manager*
EMP: 5
SALES (est): 486.2K **Privately Held**
SIC: 1389 Construction, repair & dismantling services

(G-16895)
STONE EXPO & CABINETRY LLC
7 Terminal Rd (11552-1105)
PHONE..................516 292-2988
Annie Liu, *Manager*
▲ **EMP:** 16
SALES (est): 2MM **Privately Held**
SIC: 2434 2542 Wood kitchen cabinets; counters or counter display cases: except wood

(G-16896)
US PUMP CORP
707 Woodfield Rd (11552-3826)
PHONE..................516 303-7799
Nissim Isaacson, *Ch of Bd*
▲ **EMP:** 5
SALES (est): 727.2K **Privately Held**
SIC: 1381 1241 Drilling water intake wells; redrilling oil & gas wells; mining services: lignite

West Henrietta
Monroe County

(G-16897)
ALL AMERICAN PRECISION TL MOLD
Also Called: All American Mold
1325 John St (14586-9121)
PHONE..................585 436-3080
Fax: 585 436-8183
Mike Veltri, *President*
EMP: 12
SQ FT: 17,000
SALES (est): 1.4MM **Privately Held**
WEB: www.all-americanmold.com
SIC: 3089 3544 Plastic processing; industrial molds

(G-16898)
ALSTOM SIGNALING INC
1025 John St Ste 100h (14586-9781)
PHONE..................800 717-4477
Nicolas Jacqmin, *Vice Pres*
Seby Kottackal, *Engineer*
Richard Basehore, *Manager*
Antonio Garcia, *Technology*
EMP: 4 **EST:** 1990
SALES (est): 1MM **Privately Held**
SIC: 3669 Transportation signaling devices

(G-16899)
ALSTOM TRANSPORTATION INC
1025 John St Ste 100h (14586-9781)
PHONE..................800 717-4477
Gabriel Colceag, *COO*
EMP: 34
SALES (corp-wide): 54.7MM **Privately Held**
SIC: 3743 8711 7629 Railroad equipment; engineering services; electrical repair shops
HQ: Alstom Transportation Inc.
641 Lexington Ave Fl 28
New York NY 10022
212 692-5353

(G-16900)
AMERICAN FILTRATION TECH INC
100 Thruway Park Dr (14586-9798)
PHONE..................585 359-4130
Fax: 585 359-4782
Richard Felber, *President*
Amy Colf, *Admin Mgr*
EMP: 13
SQ FT: 36,000
SALES (est): 3.3MM **Privately Held**
SIC: 3569 3564 Filters; blowers & fans

(G-16901)
APOLLO OPTICAL SYSTEMS INC
925 John St (14586-9780)
PHONE..................585 272-6170
G Michael Morris, *CEO*
Daniel McGarry, *President*
Claude Tribastone, *President*
Gwen Murphy, *QC Mgr*
Richard Young, *Engineer*
EMP: 38
SALES (est): 8.2MM **Privately Held**
WEB: www.apolloptical.com
SIC: 3827 Optical instruments & lenses

(G-16902)
APPAIRENT TECHNOLOGIES INC (PA)
150 Lucius Gordon Dr (14586-9687)
PHONE..................585 214-2460
Fax: 585 214-2461
Chris O'Donnell, *CEO*
Jim Allen, *President*
Rick Alvin, *Vice Pres*
EMP: 5
SQ FT: 2,500
SALES (est): 1.2MM **Privately Held**
WEB: www.appairent.com
SIC: 3663 Radio broadcasting & communications equipment

(G-16903)
B C MANUFACTURING INC
100 Thruway Park Dr (14586-9798)
PHONE..................585 482-1080
Fax: 585 482-2658
Bob Collins, *President*
EMP: 5
SQ FT: 5,500
SALES (est): 800.5K **Privately Held**
SIC: 3599 Machine shop, jobbing & repair

(G-16904)
BRANDYS MOLD AND TOOL CTR LTD (PA)
10 Riverton Way (14586-9754)
PHONE..................585 334-8333
Fax: 585 334-2005
Michaela Perkins, *President*

West Henrietta - Monroe County (G-16905)

Dan Morse, *General Mgr*
Franz Brandstetter, *Vice Pres*
EMP: 15
SALES (est): 1.5MM **Privately Held**
SIC: 3089 Plastic processing

(G-16905)
BRINKMAN PRECISION INC
Also Called: B P I
100 Park Centre Dr (14586-9688)
PHONE.................................585 429-5001
Andrew J Laniak, *CEO*
Robert J Brinkman, *Ch of Bd*
Kevin Orlop, *Prdtn Mgr*
Matt Staffieri, *Production*
Bob Coffey, *QC Mgr*
EMP: 85
SALES (est): 18.3MM
SALES (corp-wide): 112.8MM **Privately Held**
WEB: www.brinkmanprecision.com
SIC: 3324 5047 Aerospace investment castings, ferrous; medical equipment & supplies
PA: Brinkman International Group, Inc.
　　167 Ames St
　　Rochester NY 14611
　　585 429-5000

(G-16906)
COHBER PRESS INC (PA)
Also Called: Kodak Gallery - Cohber
1000 John St (14586-9757)
P.O. Box 93100, Rochester (14692-7300)
PHONE.................................585 475-9100
Fax: 585 475-9406
Eric C Webber, *Ch of Bd*
Howard Buzz, *Chairman*
Dan Mahany, *COO*
Chris Bowen, *Vice Pres*
Chris Beahon, *Manager*
EMP: 90 **EST:** 1925
SQ FT: 49,000
SALES (est): 15.8MM **Privately Held**
WEB: www.cohber.com
SIC: 2752 2791 2789 Commercial printing, offset; photo-offset printing; typesetting; bookbinding & related work

(G-16907)
COOPERVISION INC
180 Thruway Park Dr (14586-9798)
PHONE.................................585 385-6810
Michelle McDonagh, *Director*
EMP: 660
SALES (corp-wide): 1.9B **Publicly Held**
SIC: 3851 Contact lenses
HQ: Coopervision, Inc.
　　209 High Point Dr
　　Victor NY 14564
　　585 385-6810

(G-16908)
DELPHI AUTOMOTIVE SYSTEMS LLC
5500 W Henrietta Rd (14586-9701)
PHONE.................................585 359-6000
Fax: 585 239-6116
Bruce Gardephe, *Engineer*
Amanda Reid, *Engineer*
Richard B Roe, *Engineer*
Randy Welch, *Engineer*
Walter Cossa, *Project Engr*
EMP: 209 **Privately Held**
WEB: www.delphiauto.com
SIC: 3714 Motor vehicle parts & accessories
HQ: Delphi Automotive Systems, Llc
　　5725 Delphi Dr
　　Troy MI 48098

(G-16909)
DELPHI AUTOMOTIVE SYSTEMS LLC
5500 W Henrietta Rd (14586-9701)
PHONE.................................585 359-6000
Jim Zizleman, *Manager*
EMP: 600 **Privately Held**
WEB: www.delphiauto.com
SIC: 3714 8731 3694 3564 Motor vehicle parts & accessories; commercial physical research; engine electrical equipment; blowers & fans
HQ: Delphi Automotive Systems, Llc
　　5725 Delphi Dr
　　Troy MI 48098

(G-16910)
DELPHI AUTOMOTIVE SYSTEMS LLC
Also Called: Delphi Powertrain Systems
5500 W Henrietta Rd (14586-9701)
PHONE.................................585 359-6000
Walter Piock, *Branch Mgr*
EMP: 38 **Privately Held**
SIC: 3714 Motor vehicle parts & accessories
HQ: Delphi Automotive Systems, Llc
　　5725 Delphi Dr
　　Troy MI 48098

(G-16911)
FORTEQ NORTH AMERICA INC
150 Park Centre Dr (14586-9688)
PHONE.................................585 427-9410
Martin Van Manen, *CEO*
Rune Bakke, *Principal*
Joseph Buonocure, *Principal*
Willaim Banks, *Vice Pres*
Joerge Hotz, *Plant Mgr*
▲ **EMP:** 70
SQ FT: 29,000
SALES (est): 25.2MM **Privately Held**
SIC: 3089 Plastic containers, except foam
PA: Transmission Technology Holding Ag
　　C/O Bar & Karrer
　　Zug ZG
　　582 615-900

(G-16912)
GENESEE METAL STAMPINGS INC
975 John St (14586-9780)
PHONE.................................585 475-0450
Fax: 585 475-0469
Gerard Caschette, *Principal*
Duanise Allen, *Human Res Mgr*
John Cook, *Manager*
EMP: 5
SALES (est): 574.8K **Privately Held**
SIC: 3469 Stamping metal for the trade

(G-16913)
GEOSPATIAL SYSTEMS INC (DH)
150 Lucius Gordon Dr # 211 (14586-9687)
PHONE.................................585 427-8310
Maxime Elbaz, *President*
William Kent PHD, *Vice Pres*
Steven Randy Olson, *Vice Pres*
Matt Kremens, *Engineer*
Robert Delach, *CFO*
EMP: 11
SQ FT: 3,000
SALES (est): 1.3MM
SALES (corp-wide): 2.1B **Publicly Held**
SIC: 3861 Aerial cameras
HQ: Teledyne Optech Incorporated
　　300 Interchange Way
　　Vaughan ON L4K 5
　　905 660-0808

(G-16914)
HAMMER PACKAGING CORP (PA)
200 Lucius Gordon Dr (14586-9685)
P.O. Box 22678, Rochester (14692-2678)
PHONE.................................585 424-3880
James E Hammer, *President*
Jason Hammer, *Vice Pres*
Marty Karpie, *Vice Pres*
Louis Lovoli, *Vice Pres*
Tom Mason, *Vice Pres*
▲ **EMP:** 255 **EST:** 1912
SQ FT: 92,000
SALES: 119.2MM **Privately Held**
WEB: www.hammerpackaging.com
SIC: 2759 Labels & seals: printing

(G-16915)
KATIKATI INC
150 Lucius Gordon Dr (14586-9687)
PHONE.................................585 678-1764
Prathap James Ambaichelvan, *CEO*
Sanjay Hiranandani, *COO*
Allyson Hiranandani, *Vice Pres*
EMP: 5
SALES (est): 276.1K **Privately Held**
SIC: 3714 5013 8733 Motor vehicle electrical equipment; testing equipment, electrical: automotive; research institute

(G-16916)
MICROGEN SYSTEMS INC
150 Lucius Gordon Dr # 117 (14586-9687)
PHONE.................................585 214-2426
Robert Andosca, *CEO*
Evan Grundman, *Electrical Engi*
Michael Perrotta, *CFO*
EMP: 8
SQ FT: 3,000
SALES (est): 689.7K **Privately Held**
SIC: 3676 Electronic resistors

(G-16917)
MOFFETT TURF EQUIPMENT INC
33 Thruway Park Dr (14586-9795)
PHONE.................................585 334-0100
Fax: 585 334-6332
Thomas Houseknecht, *President*
Ben Mancuso, *Vice Pres*
Patty Nicosia, *Controller*
EMP: 35 **EST:** 2010
SQ FT: 45,000
SALES: 3MM **Privately Held**
SIC: 3523 Turf equipment, commercial

(G-16918)
ORAFOL AMERICAS INC
200 Park Centre Dr (14586-9674)
PHONE.................................585 272-0290
Fax: 585 272-0313
Keith Steadman, *Engng Exec*
Bryan K Parks, *Branch Mgr*
Dave Jacob, *Manager*
EMP: 11
SALES (corp-wide): 533.7MM **Privately Held**
SIC: 3827 5048 Optical instruments & lenses; optometric equipment & supplies
HQ: Orafol Americas Inc.
　　1100 Oracal Pkwy
　　Black Creek GA 31308
　　912 851-5000

(G-16919)
OUTDOOR GROUP LLC
1325 John St (14586-9121)
PHONE.................................585 201-5358
Greg Steil,
EMP: 150 **EST:** 2012
SALES (est): 17MM **Privately Held**
SIC: 3949 Archery equipment, general

(G-16920)
OVITZ CORPORATION
150 Lucius Gordon Dr # 123 (14586-9687)
PHONE.................................585 474-4695
Joseph Rosenshein, *Principal*
Joung Yoon Kim, *Principal*
Walter Rusnak, *Principal*
EMP: 9
SQ FT: 1,000
SALES (est): 529.8K **Privately Held**
SIC: 3841 Diagnostic apparatus, medical

(G-16921)
PERFECT FORM MANUFACTURING LLC
1325 John St (14586-9121)
PHONE.................................585 500-5923
Marcia Koch, *General Mgr*
Greg Steil,
Dylan Bates,
Peter Crawford,
Matthew Kruger,
EMP: 5
SQ FT: 3,200
SALES (est): 76.9K **Privately Held**
SIC: 3949 Bows, archery

(G-16922)
PHARMADVA LLC
150 Lucius Gordon Dr # 211 (14586-9687)
PHONE.................................585 469-1410
Joshua Eddy, *Finance Mgr*
Jonathan Sacks, *Mng Member*
Duane Girdner,
EMP: 6
SQ FT: 6,400
SALES: 80K **Privately Held**
SIC: 3845 Electromedical equipment

(G-16923)
POLYSHOT CORPORATION
75 Lucius Gordon Dr (14586-9682)
PHONE.................................585 292-5010
Fax: 585 292-5015
Douglas C Hepler, *President*
▲ **EMP:** 20
SQ FT: 13,000
SALES (est): 4.8MM **Privately Held**
WEB: www.polyshot.com
SIC: 3442 Metal doors, sash & trim; molding, trim & stripping

(G-16924)
ROCHESTER PRECISION OPTICS LLC
Also Called: R P O
850 John St (14586-9748)
PHONE.................................585 292-5450
William Hurley, *CEO*
Richard Kellogg, *Facilities Mgr*
Robert Benson, *Engineer*
Rick Berg, *Engineer*
Gregory Schenker, *Engineer*
◆ **EMP:** 190
SQ FT: 104,500
SALES (est): 56.8MM **Privately Held**
WEB: www.rpoptics.com
SIC: 3827 Lenses, optical: all types except ophthalmic; lens mounts; lens grinding equipment, except ophthalmic; optical elements & assemblies, except ophthalmic

(G-16925)
SEMANS ENTERPRISES INC
Also Called: New Cov Manufacturing
25 Hendrix Rd Ste E (14586-9205)
PHONE.................................585 444-0097
Fax: 585 328-4332
William A Semans II, *Ch of Bd*
Carol Maue- Semans, *Vice Pres*
EMP: 19
SQ FT: 10,000
SALES: 1.8MM **Privately Held**
SIC: 3449 Miscellaneous metalwork

(G-16926)
SIMPORE INC
150 Lucius Gordon Dr # 121 (14586-9687)
PHONE.................................585 748-5980
Richard D Richmond, *Ch of Bd*
Thomas Gaborski, *President*
Christopher Striemer, *Vice Pres*
James Roussie, *VP Opers*
Nick Cobb, *Sales Mgr*
EMP: 7
SQ FT: 400
SALES (est): 520K **Privately Held**
WEB: www.simpore.com
SIC: 3821 Laboratory equipment: fume hoods, distillation racks, etc.

(G-16927)
SWAGELOK WESTERN NY
10 Thruway Park Dr (14586-9702)
PHONE.................................585 359-8470
EMP: 5
SALES (est): 569.2K **Privately Held**
SIC: 3823 Mfg Process Control Instruments

(G-16928)
VUZIX CORPORATION (PA)
25 Hendrix Rd Ste A (14586-9205)
PHONE.................................585 359-5900
Fax: 585 359-4172
Paul J Travers, *President*
Paul Boris, *COO*
Lance Anderson, *Vice Pres*
Grant Russell, *CFO*
EMP: 24 **EST:** 1997
SQ FT: 29,000
SALES: 2.1MM **Publicly Held**
WEB: www.icuiti.com
SIC: 3577 Computer peripheral equipment

(G-16929)
VWR EDUCATION LLC
Ward's Natural Science
5100 W Henrietta Rd (14586-9729)
PHONE.................................585 359-2502
Michael Harvey, *Maint Spvr*
Susan Bernholdt, *Human Res Dir*
Janice Gaub, *Marketing Staff*
Kathy Smith, *Programmer Anys*
Cindy Kent, *Executive*

GEOGRAPHIC SECTION

West Nyack - Rockland County (G-16954)

EMP: 250
SALES (corp-wide): 4.5B **Publicly Held**
SIC: 2741 3821 5049 5192 Miscellaneous publishing; laboratory apparatus & furniture; scientific & engineering equipment & supplies; books, periodicals & newspapers
HQ: Vwr Education, Llc
777 E Park Dr
Tonawanda NY 14150
800 242-2042

(G-16930)
WAVODYNE THERAPEUTICS INC
150 Lucius Gordon Dr (14586-9687)
PHONE..................................954 632-6630
James New, *CEO*
EMP: 2 EST: 2015
SQ FT: 200
SALES: 500MM **Privately Held**
SIC: 2834 Druggists' preparations (pharmaceuticals)

West Hurley
Ulster County

(G-16931)
ANATOLI INC
43 Basin Rd Ste 11 (12491-5201)
PHONE..................................845 334-9000
Fax: 845 334-9099
Kostas Michalopoulos, *President*
Joan Ramos, *Admin Sec*
EMP: 16
SQ FT: 4,300
SALES (est): 1.4MM **Privately Held**
SIC: 3911 3961 5094 Jewelry, precious metal; costume jewelry; jewelry

West Islip
Suffolk County

(G-16932)
ACT COMMUNICATIONS GROUP INC
170 Higbie Ln (11795-3238)
PHONE..................................631 669-2403
Fax: 631 669-7768
Richard Carpenter, *President*
Robert Carpenter, *Vice Pres*
Larry Boyd, *Manager*
Angie Carpenter, *Director*
EMP: 18
SQ FT: 1,000
SALES (est): 1.5MM **Privately Held**
WEB: www.actcommgroup.com
SIC: 2791 2752 7311 Typesetting; commercial printing, offset; advertising agencies

(G-16933)
ACTION BULLET RESISTANT
263 Union Blvd (11795-3007)
PHONE..................................631 422-0888
Leonard J Simonetti, *President*
Jeff Farinacci, *Project Mgr*
Brian Sweeney, *Controller*
Edward Simonetti, *Sales Mgr*
Trish Simonetti, *Manager*
EMP: 12
SQ FT: 14,000
SALES (est): 2.3MM **Privately Held**
WEB: www.actionbullet.com
SIC: 3442 Window & door frames

(G-16934)
JEM TOOL & DIE CORP
81 Paris Ct (11795-2815)
PHONE..................................631 539-8734
Fax: 516 249-8370
Roy Stevens, *President*
Bill Jimenez, *Vice Pres*
Sylvia Goodwin, *Bookkeeper*
EMP: 10 EST: 1961
SQ FT: 8,000
SALES (est): 1.2MM **Privately Held**
SIC: 3545 Machine tool attachments & accessories

(G-16935)
SAL MA INSTRUMENT CORP
10 Clearwater Ln (11795-5036)
PHONE..................................631 242-2227
Alfred Mahany, *President*
EMP: 9 EST: 1963
SQ FT: 7,500
SALES (est): 1.2MM **Privately Held**
SIC: 3599 Machine shop, jobbing & repair

(G-16936)
SECUREVUE INC
28 Trues Dr (11795-5139)
PHONE..................................631 587-5850
Donald Softness, *President*
EMP: 5
SQ FT: 1,000
SALES: 500K **Privately Held**
WEB: www.securevue.net
SIC: 3699 Security devices

(G-16937)
SPC MARKETING COMPANY
Also Called: Meat Industry Newsletter
191 Norma Ave (11795-1510)
P.O. Box 221, Brightwaters (11718-0221)
PHONE..................................631 661-2727
Stephen R Flanagan, *Owner*
EMP: 5
SQ FT: 1,200
SALES (est): 437K **Privately Held**
SIC: 2721 Periodicals: publishing only

(G-16938)
V A P TOOL & DYE
436 W 4th St (11795-2414)
PHONE..................................631 587-5262
Victor Pons, *Owner*
EMP: 7
SQ FT: 4,700
SALES (est): 400K **Privately Held**
SIC: 3599 Machine shop, jobbing & repair

(G-16939)
W & W MANUFACTURING CO
239 Higbie Ln (11795-2825)
P.O. Box 817, Deer Park (11729-0981)
PHONE..................................516 942-0011
Jeffrey Weitzman, *President*
Ronie Rosenbaum, *Vice Pres*
Saundrice Lucas, *Administration*
▲ EMP: 15
SALES (est): 2.2MM **Privately Held**
WEB: www.w-manufacturing.com
SIC: 3691 3825 3663 Storage batteries; instruments to measure electricity; radio & TV communications equipment

West Nyack
Rockland County

(G-16940)
AMP-LINE CORP
3 Amethyst Ct (10994-1142)
PHONE..................................845 623-3288
Guosen Luo, *President*
EMP: 10
SALES (est): 1.3MM **Privately Held**
SIC: 3699 Pulse amplifiers

(G-16941)
ANGEL MEDIA AND PUBLISHING
Also Called: Rockland Review Publishing
26 Snake Hill Rd (10994-1625)
PHONE..................................845 727-4949
Fax: 845 727-4944
Joseph Miele, *President*
Joseph Neile, *Publisher*
Arnold Heydt, *Vice Pres*
Mary Cortes, *Manager*
EMP: 6
SALES (est): 391.6K **Privately Held**
WEB: www.rocklandreviewnews.com
SIC: 2711 Newspapers

(G-16942)
BEL-BEE PRODUCTS INCORPORATED
100 Snake Hill Rd Ste 1 (10994-1627)
PHONE..................................845 353-0300
Vincent Belmont, *Ch of Bd*
Joanne Belmont, *Controller*
Herbert Giller, *Manager*
EMP: 15
SQ FT: 25,000
SALES (est): 3.4MM **Privately Held**
WEB: www.bel-bee.com
SIC: 3469 Metal stampings

(G-16943)
BILLY BEEZ USA LLC
1282 Palisades Center Dr (10994-6202)
PHONE..................................845 915-4709
EMP: 7
SALES (corp-wide): 14.2MM **Privately Held**
SIC: 3949 5137 7999 Playground equipment; women's & children's dresses, suits, skirts & blouses; amusement ride
PA: Billy Beez Usa, Llc
3 W 35th St Fl 3
New York NY 10001
646 606-2249

(G-16944)
BYLADA FOODS LLC
250 W Nyack Rd Ste 110 (10994-1745)
PHONE..................................845 623-1300
Meade Bradshaw, *Branch Mgr*
EMP: 53
SALES (corp-wide): 8.5MM **Privately Held**
SIC: 2099 Food preparations
PA: Bylada Foods Llc
140 W Commercial Ave
Moonachie NJ 07074
201 933-7474

(G-16945)
CROTON WATCH CO INC
250 W Nyack Rd Ste 114 (10994-1745)
PHONE..................................800 443-7639
David Mermelstein, *Ch of Bd*
Avrami Mermelstein, *COO*
Lynn Friedman, *Controller*
Karene Lynen, *Cust Svc Dir*
▲ EMP: 26
SQ FT: 18,000
SALES (est): 4.8MM **Privately Held**
WEB: www.crotonwatch.com
SIC: 3873 Watches & parts, except crystals & jewels

(G-16946)
GANNETT STLLITE INFO NTWRK LLC
1 Crosfield Ave (10994-2222)
PHONE..................................845 578-2300
Tony Davenport, *Branch Mgr*
EMP: 30
SALES (corp-wide): 3B **Publicly Held**
WEB: www.usatoday.com
SIC: 2711 2752 Newspapers: publishing only, not printed on site; commercial printing, lithographic
HQ: Gannett Satellite Information Network, Llc
7950 Jones Branch Dr
Mc Lean VA 22102
703 854-6000

(G-16947)
GENERAL BEARING CORPORATION (DH)
44 High St (10994-2702)
PHONE..................................845 358-6000
Fax: 845 358-7414
David L Gussack, *CEO*
Thomas J Uhlig, *President*
Joseph Hoo, *Vice Pres*
Corby W Self, *Vice Pres*
Jeffrey Williams, *Vice Pres*
▲ EMP: 120 EST: 1958
SQ FT: 190,000
SALES (est): 134.9MM
SALES (corp-wide): 546.3MM **Privately Held**
WEB: www.generalbearing.com
SIC: 3562 Ball & roller bearings; ball bearings & parts; roller bearings & parts
HQ: Skf Usa Inc.
890 Forty Foot Rd
Lansdale PA 19446
267 436-6000

(G-16948)
INTERCOS AMERICA INC
120 Brookhill Dr (10994-2127)
PHONE..................................845 732-3910
EMP: 6 EST: 2016
SALES (est): 119.8K **Privately Held**
SIC: 2844 Toilet preparations

(G-16949)
MAINLY MONOGRAMS INC
Also Called: Mercury Apparel
260 W Nyack Rd Ste 1 (10994-1750)
PHONE..................................845 624-4923
Dan Alexander Sr, *CEO*
Dan Alexander Jr, *CFO*
Zaharo Ula Alexander, *Treasurer*
Judy Creek, *Office Mgr*
EMP: 45
SQ FT: 19,000
SALES (est): 5.1MM **Privately Held**
SIC: 2395 7336 5611 5621 Embroidery products, except schiffli machine; silk screen design; clothing, sportswear, men's & boys'; women's sportswear; gifts & novelties

(G-16950)
NICE-PAK PRODUCTS INC
100 Brookhill Dr (10994-2133)
PHONE..................................845 353-6090
Jennifer Thriston, *Manager*
EMP: 25
SALES (corp-wide): 416.3MM **Privately Held**
SIC: 2621 Towels, tissues & napkins: paper & stock; sanitary tissue paper
PA: Nice-Pak Products, Inc.
2 Nice Pak Park
Orangeburg NY 10962
845 365-2772

(G-16951)
PEARL RIVER PASTRIES LLC
Also Called: Pearl River Pastry Chocolates
389 W Nyack Rd (10994-1723)
PHONE..................................845 735-5100
Steve Pierson, *VP Sales*
Renae Goyette, *Branch Mgr*
Joseph Koffman, *Mng Member*
John Slootmaker, *Manager*
Martin Koffman,
EMP: 50
SQ FT: 10,000
SALES: 7MM **Privately Held**
SIC: 2053 5441 Pastries (danish): frozen; candy, nut & confectionery stores

(G-16952)
PEARSON EDUCATION INC
59 Brookhill Dr (10994-2122)
PHONE..................................201 236-7000
Michael Schuering, *Exec VP*
Cheryl Gayser, *Human Res Mgr*
EMP: 14
SALES (corp-wide): 5.6B **Privately Held**
WEB: www.phgenit.com
SIC: 2721 2731 Periodicals; book publishing
HQ: Pearson Education, Inc.
221 River St
Hoboken NJ 07030
201 236-7000

(G-16953)
PICCINI MNM INC
35 Highland Ave (10994-1719)
PHONE..................................845 741-6770
Richard Piccininni, *President*
EMP: 7
SALES: 700K **Privately Held**
SIC: 2499 Decorative wood & woodwork

(G-16954)
PLASTIC-CRAFT PRODUCTS CORP
744 W Nyack Rd (10994-1998)
P.O. Box K (10994-0713)
PHONE..................................845 358-3010
Fax: 845 358-3007
Young Nguyen, *General Mgr*
Mark Brecher, *Chairman*
Nancy Brecher, *Treasurer*
Marge Garrison, *Financial Exec*
Jerry Green, *Office Mgr*
EMP: 28
SQ FT: 30,000
SALES (est): 7.3MM **Privately Held**
SIC: 3089 5162 Plastic processing; plastics materials & basic shapes

(PA)=Parent Co (HQ)=Headquarters (DH)=Div Headquarters
○ = New Business established in last 2 years

West Nyack - Rockland County (G-16955)

(G-16955)
REFLECTIVE SHOPPER USA LLC
251 W Nyack Rd Ste C (10994-1724)
PHONE 855 735-3222
Michael Reisbeum, *Director*
EMP: 2 **EST:** 2016
SALES: 2MM **Privately Held**
SIC: 2393 Canvas bags

(G-16956)
STEVEN MADDEN LTD
1661 Palisades Center Dr (10994-6206)
PHONE 845 348-7026
Steve Madden, *Branch Mgr*
EMP: 75
SALES (corp-wide): 1.4B **Publicly Held**
SIC: 3143 Men's footwear, except athletic
PA: Steven Madden, Ltd.
    5216 Barnett Ave
    Long Island City NY 11104
    718 446-1800

(G-16957)
TILCON NEW YORK INC (DH)
Also Called: Totowa Asphalt
162 Old Mill Rd (10994-1406)
PHONE 845 358-4500
Fax: 845 480-3128
Christopher J Madden, *Ch of Bd*
John Cooney Jr, *President*
Sean Osullivan, *Vice Pres*
Dan Batelli, *Transptn Dir*
Jeff Russell, *Plant Mgr*
▲ **EMP:** 270 **EST:** 1964
SALES (est): 430.6MM
SALES (corp-wide): 28.6B **Privately Held**
WEB: www.tilconny.com
SIC: 1429 Trap rock, crushed & broken-quarrying; dolomitic marble, crushed & broken-quarrying
HQ: Tilcon Inc.
    301 Hartford Ave
    Newington CT 06111
    860 223-3651

(G-16958)
TILCON NEW YORK INC
1 Crusher Rd (10994-1601)
PHONE 845 358-3100
Bernardo Culnes, *Systems Staff*
John Deangelis, *Maintence Staff*
EMP: 65
SALES (corp-wide): 28.6B **Privately Held**
WEB: www.tilconny.com
SIC: 1429 1442 1423 Trap rock, crushed & broken-quarrying; dolomitic marble, crushed & broken-quarrying; construction sand & gravel; crushed & broken granite
HQ: Tilcon New York Inc.
    162 Old Mill Rd
    West Nyack NY 10994
    845 358-4500

West Point
Orange County

(G-16959)
PENN ENTERPRISES INC
845 Washington Rd (10996-1111)
PHONE 845 446-0765
Fax: 845 446-4130
Joseph Fotovich, *Principal*
Russell Williams, *Project Mgr*
EMP: 13
SALES (corp-wide): 9.3MM **Privately Held**
WEB: www.pennenterprises.com
SIC: 3633 Household laundry equipment
PA: Penn Enterprises, Inc
    5260 S Stonehaven Dr
    Springfield MO 65809
    417 379-5889

West Sand Lake
Rensselaer County

(G-16960)
BONDED CONCRETE INC
Rr 43 (12196)
PHONE 518 674-2854
Tom Coemente, *President*
EMP: 10
SALES (corp-wide): 10.8MM **Privately Held**
WEB: www.bondedconcrete.com
SIC: 3273 Ready-mixed concrete
PA: Bonded Concrete, Inc.
    303 Watervliet Shaker Rd
    Watervliet NY 12189
    518 273-5800

(G-16961)
TROY SAND & GRAVEL CO INC
Rr 43 (12196)
P.O. Box 489 (12196-0489)
PHONE 518 674-2854
Jude Clemente, *President*
EMP: 15
SALES (corp-wide): 24.2MM **Privately Held**
SIC: 1442 5032 Construction sand & gravel; stone, crushed or broken
PA: Troy Sand & Gravel Co., Inc.
    34 Grange Rd
    West Sand Lake NY 12196
    518 203-5115

West Sayville
Suffolk County

(G-16962)
ACCUCUT INC
120 Easy St (11796-1238)
PHONE 631 567-2868
Dan Carbone, *CEO*
Joanne Caruso, *Administration*
EMP: 5
SALES: 370K **Privately Held**
SIC: 3441 Fabricated structural metal

(G-16963)
DOR-A-MAR CANVAS PRODUCTS CO
182 Cherry Ave (11796-1200)
PHONE 631 750-9202
Fax: 631 750-9203
Thomas Degirolamo, *President*
Nancy Dolan, *Office Mgr*
Kenneth Degirolamo, *Manager*
EMP: 18 **EST:** 1959
SQ FT: 6,000
SALES: 1.5MM **Privately Held**
WEB: www.doramar.com
SIC: 2394 Canvas & related products

(G-16964)
FIRE ISLAND SEA CLAM CO INC
132 Atlantic Ave (11796-1904)
P.O. Box 2124, Montauk (11954-0905)
PHONE 631 589-2199
Fax: 631 589-0515
John Kingston, *President*
Jean Kingston, *Admin Sec*
EMP: 3 **EST:** 1977
SQ FT: 3,500
SALES: 10MM **Privately Held**
WEB: www.fireislandassn.org
SIC: 2431 5812 Moldings, wood: unfinished & prefinished; seafood restaurants

(G-16965)
KUSSMAUL ELECTRONICS CO INC
170 Cherry Ave (11796-1200)
P.O. Box 147, Lynnfield MA (01940-0147)
PHONE 631 218-0298
Fax: 631 244-9009
Thomas H Nugent, *Ch of Bd*
Marilyn Kussmaul, *Vice Pres*
Ernest Kussmaul, *Engineer*
Phil Sgroi, *Engineer*
Colin Chambless, *VP Sales*
◆ **EMP:** 50
SQ FT: 30,000
SALES (est): 11.6MM
SALES (corp-wide): 5.6MM **Privately Held**
WEB: www.maul.com
SIC: 3629 3625 Battery chargers, rectifying or nonrotating; control equipment, electric
HQ: Mission Critical Electronics, Llc
    2200 Ross Ave Ste 4050
    Dallas TX 75201

(G-16966)
PECK & HALE LLC
180 Division Ave (11796-1303)
PHONE 631 589-2510
Fax: 631 589-2925
John Szeglin, *President*
Dan Becker, *General Mgr*
Jose Diaz-Bujan, *Opers Mgr*
Jose Diaz Bujan, *Opers Staff*
David Mazzara, *Purch Agent*
▲ **EMP:** 40 **EST:** 1946
SQ FT: 27,000
SALES (est): 8.8MM **Privately Held**
WEB: www.peckhale.com
SIC: 3743 3462 3496 Railroad equipment; iron & steel forgings; miscellaneous fabricated wire products

West Seneca
Erie County

(G-16967)
ABI PACKAGING INC
1703 Union Rd (14224-2060)
PHONE 716 677-2900
Roger Severson, *CEO*
Barb Thurber, *Manager*
EMP: 20
SALES (est): 1.6MM **Privately Held**
SIC: 3086 Plastics foam products

(G-16968)
BIG DATA BIZVIZ LLC
1075 East And West Rd (14224-3669)
PHONE 716 803-2367
Avin Jain, *CEO*
Rajesh Thanki, *CEO*
EMP: 2
SALES (est): 1.5MM **Privately Held**
SIC: 7372 Business oriented computer software

(G-16969)
BUFFALO HEARG & SPEECH
1026 Union Rd (14224-3445)
PHONE 716 558-1105
Joe Cozzo, *CEO*
Amy Hensley, *Manager*
EMP: 45
SALES (corp-wide): 345.9K **Privately Held**
SIC: 3842 Hearing aids
PA: Buffalo Hearing And Speech Center Foundation, Inc.
    50 E North St
    Buffalo NY 14203
    716 885-8318

(G-16970)
CONSUMERS BEVERAGES INC
1375 Union Rd (14224-2936)
PHONE 716 675-4934
Fax: 716 675-4934
Tony Kiminski, *Manager*
Kevin Frankey, *Manager*
EMP: 8
SALES (corp-wide): 21.6MM **Privately Held**
WEB: www.consumerbeverages.com
SIC: 2086 Bottled & canned soft drinks
PA: Consumers Beverages, Inc.
    2230 S Park Ave
    Buffalo NY
    716 826-9200

(G-16971)
EBENEZER RAILCAR SERVICES INC
1005 Indian Church Rd (14224-1305)
P.O. Box 363, Buffalo (14224-0363)
PHONE 716 674-5650
Fax: 716 674-8703
Jeffrey F Schmarje, *President*
David P Egner, *Vice Pres*
Bob Wingels, *Vice Pres*
Robert Wingels, *Vice Pres*
Janet Jemiolo, *Accounts Mgr*
EMP: 50 **EST:** 1981
SQ FT: 30,000
SALES (est): 16.6MM
SALES (corp-wide): 35.1MM **Privately Held**
WEB: www.ersindustries.com
SIC: 3743 4789 Railroad equipment; railroad car repair
PA: Ers Industries, Inc.
    1005 Indian Church Rd
    West Seneca NY 14224
    716 675-2040

(G-16972)
ELITE MEDICAL SUPPLY OF NY
1900 Ridge Rd (14224-3332)
PHONE 716 712-0881
Fax: 716 712-0882
Elwira Kulawik, *Principal*
EMP: 6
SALES (est): 550K **Privately Held**
SIC: 3841 Medical instruments & equipment, blood & bone work

(G-16973)
FIVE STAR INDUSTRIES INC
114 Willowdale Dr (14224-3571)
PHONE 716 674-2589
Fax: 716 897-5107
Greg Vastola, *President*
Joel Long, *Vice Pres*
EMP: 27
SQ FT: 10,000
SALES (est): 4.4MM **Privately Held**
SIC: 3444 3599 Sheet metalwork; machine shop, jobbing & repair

(G-16974)
GEMCOR AUTOMATION LLC
100 Gemcor Dr (14224-2055)
PHONE 716 674-9300
Fax: 716 674-3171
William Mangus, *CEO*
Tony Goddard, *COO*
Gary Szymkowiak, *Opers Staff*
Mark Alessi, *Electrical Engi*
Wayne Piacente, *CFO*
EMP: 87
SQ FT: 90,000
SALES (est): 30.8MM
SALES (corp-wide): 200MM **Privately Held**
SIC: 3542 Spinning, spline rolling & winding machines
HQ: Ascent Aerospace, Llc
    1395 S Lyon St
    Santa Ana CA 92705
    949 455-0665

(G-16975)
GORDEN AUTOMOTIVE EQUIPMENT
60 N America Dr (14224-2225)
PHONE 716 674-2700
Richard Deney, *President*
Thomas Gormley, *Exec VP*
Herman Deney, *Vice Pres*
Michael Russo, *Treasurer*
Joel Deney, *Manager*
EMP: 10
SALES (est): 978K **Privately Held**
SIC: 3599 Machine shop, jobbing & repair

(G-16976)
GRIFFIN AUTOMATION INC
240 Westminster Rd (14224-1930)
P.O. Box 183, Buffalo (14224-0183)
PHONE 716 674-2300
Fax: 716 674-2309
Jerald Bidlack, *COO*
John Shephard, *COO*
Charles Peskir, *Purch Mgr*
John Shepphard, *Accounting Mgr*
John Shepherd, *Finance*
EMP: 25
SQ FT: 40,000
SALES: 2.5MM **Privately Held**
WEB: www.griffinautomation.com
SIC: 3569 Assembly machines, non-metalworking

GEOGRAPHIC SECTION
Westbury - Nassau County (G-17002)

(G-16977)
INTERNATIONAL CONTROL PRODUCTS
Also Called: ICP
1700 Union Rd Ste 2 (14224-2052)
PHONE......................716 558-4400
Fax: 716 558-0118
Stephen Gill, *President*
Kevin Gill, *Vice Pres*
Tracey Pacanowski, *Admin Sec*
EMP: 10
SQ FT: 5,000
SALES: 1.6MM **Privately Held**
WEB: www.icproducts.net
SIC: 3621 Electric motor & generator auxiliary parts

(G-16978)
KATHERINE BLIZNIAK (PA)
525 Bullis Rd (14224-2511)
PHONE......................716 674-8545
Katherine Blizniak, *President*
EMP: 6
SALES (est): 619.1K **Privately Held**
SIC: 3732 5091 Boat building & repairing; boat accessories & parts

(G-16979)
KEMPER SYSTEM AMERICA INC (DH)
1200 N America Dr (14224-5303)
PHONE......................716 558-2971
Richard Doornink, *Managing Dir*
Jim Horsley, *Opers Mgr*
Christian Schaefer, *CFO*
Joe Hoekzema, *Regl Sales Mgr*
Katherine Lehman, *Mktg Coord*
▲ **EMP:** 25
SQ FT: 45,000
SALES (est): 12.6MM
SALES (corp-wide): 273.4MM **Privately Held**
WEB: www.kempersystem.net
SIC: 2899 Chemical preparations
HQ: Kemper System Gmbh & Co. Kg
    Hollandische Str. 32-36
    Vellmar 34246
    561 829-50

(G-16980)
MAYER BROS APPLE PRODUCTS INC (PA)
3300 Transit Rd (14224-2525)
PHONE......................716 668-1787
John A Mayer, *Ch of Bd*
James Kalec, *Sales Mgr*
Samantha Burris, *Manager*
Linda Tryka, *Executive*
▲ **EMP:** 95 **EST:** 1852
SQ FT: 2,800
SALES (est): 30.1MM **Privately Held**
WEB: www.mayerbros.com
SIC: 2033 2086 5499 5963 Fruit juices: fresh; pasteurized & mineral waters, bottled & canned; juices, fruit or vegetable; bottled water delivery

(G-16981)
SALLY BEAUTY SUPPLY LLC
310 Main St (14224-2819)
PHONE......................716 831-3286
Barbara Miller, *Manager*
EMP: 5
SALES (corp-wide): 3.9B **Publicly Held**
WEB: www.sallybeauty.com
SIC: 2844 Toilet preparations
HQ: Sally Beauty Supply Llc
    3001 Colorado Blvd
    Denton TX 76210
    940 898-7500

(G-16982)
SE-MAR ELECTRIC CO INC
101 South Ave (14224-2090)
PHONE......................716 674-7404
Fax: 716 674-3878
Robert Haungs, *President*
John Simson, *Principal*
Stephen Graham, *Mfg Staff*
Nancy J Haungs, *Treasurer*
▲ **EMP:** 20
SQ FT: 30,000
SALES: 4.9MM **Privately Held**
SIC: 3613 5571 Control panels, electric; motorcycles

(G-16983)
SENECA WEST PRINTING INC
860 Center Rd (14224-2207)
PHONE......................716 675-8010
Fax: 716 675-4637
Charles Pohlman, *President*
Charles Pohlman Jr, *Vice Pres*
Karen Pohlman, *Office Mgr*
EMP: 6 **EST:** 1965
SQ FT: 4,000
SALES (est): 781.5K **Privately Held**
SIC: 2752 2759 Lithographing on metal; letterpress printing

(G-16984)
X PRESS SIGNS INC
1780 Union Rd Ste 106 (14224-2026)
PHONE......................716 892-3000
Richard A Johnson Jr, *President*
Darin Spalti, *Vice Pres*
EMP: 6
SALES (est): 550.4K **Privately Held**
SIC: 3993 Signs & advertising specialties

(G-16985)
YOST NEON DISPLAYS INC
20 Ransier Dr (14224-2230)
PHONE......................716 674-6780
Michael Yost, *President*
Deborah Yost, *Vice Pres*
EMP: 5
SALES (est): 475.4K **Privately Held**
WEB: www.yostneon.com
SIC: 3993 1751 Neon signs; cabinet building & installation

West Winfield
Herkimer County

(G-16986)
CHRISTIAN FABRICATION LLC
122 South St (13491-2827)
PHONE......................315 822-0135
Jamie Christian, *Mng Member*
Jeffery Maine, *Officer*
EMP: 3
SQ FT: 1,296
SALES: 1.5MM **Privately Held**
SIC: 3441 7353 Fabricated structural metal; heavy construction equipment rental

(G-16987)
PRECISIONMATICS CO INC
Also Called: Helmer Avenue
1 Helmer Ave (13491)
P.O. Box 250 (13491-0250)
PHONE......................315 822-6324
Fax: 315 822-6944
Laslo Pustay, *Ch of Bd*
Steve Pustay, *Opers Staff*
Judy Williams, *QC Mgr*
John Macintosh, *Engineer*
Peter McClave, *Engineer*
EMP: 50
SQ FT: 22,000
SALES (est): 9.1MM **Privately Held**
WEB: www.precisionmatics.com
SIC: 3599 Machine shop, jobbing & repair; custom machinery

Westbury
Nassau County

(G-16988)
ACCURATE WELDING SERVICE INC
Also Called: Accurate Welding Svce
615 Main St (11590-4903)
PHONE......................516 333-1730
Fax: 516 333-1773
Joseph Titone, *President*
Charles Titone Jr, *Vice Pres*
EMP: 5
SQ FT: 5,800
SALES: 300K **Privately Held**
SIC: 3599 7692 3446 Machine shop, jobbing & repair; welding repair; architectural metalwork

(G-16989)
ADVANCED FROZEN FOODS INC
28 Urban Ave (11590-4822)
P.O. Box 887 (11590-0887)
PHONE......................516 333-6344
Roy Tuccillo, *President*
▲ **EMP:** 50
SALES (est): 9.3MM **Privately Held**
SIC: 2015 Poultry slaughtering & processing

(G-16990)
ADVANCED SURFACE FINISHING
111 Magnolia Ave (11590-4719)
PHONE......................516 876-9710
Fax: 516 334-6039
Peter Tobias, *President*
Barbara Maini, *Office Mgr*
EMP: 25
SQ FT: 15,000
SALES: 1.8MM **Privately Held**
WEB: www.advancedsurfacefinishing.com
SIC: 3479 Painting, coating & hot dipping

(G-16991)
AIRNET COMMUNICATIONS CORP
Also Called: Airnet North Division
609 Cantiague Rock Rd # 5 (11590-1721)
PHONE......................516 338-0008
Louis Pryce, *Manager*
EMP: 15 **Privately Held**
WEB: www.airnetcom.com
SIC: 3663 Radio & TV communications equipment
HQ: Airnet Communications Corporation
    295 North Dr Ste G
    Melbourne FL

(G-16992)
ALL TYPE SCREW MACHINE PDTS
Also Called: Skelton Screw Products Co
100 New York Ave (11590-4909)
PHONE......................516 334-5100
Fax: 516 997-6732
Eileen Sinn, *President*
EMP: 6
SQ FT: 5,000
SALES: 300K **Privately Held**
SIC: 3451 Screw machine products

(G-16993)
AMERICAN LINEAR MANUFACTURERS (PA)
629 Main St (11590-4923)
PHONE......................516 333-1351
Frank Tabone, *President*
EMP: 10
SQ FT: 2,000
SALES: 4.3MM **Privately Held**
SIC: 3545 3599 Machine tool accessories; custom machinery

(G-16994)
AMERICAN OFFICE SUPPLY INC
400 Post Ave Ste 105 (11590-2226)
PHONE......................516 294-9444
Fax: 516 248-3585
Joseph Caldwell, *President*
Josheph Caldwell, *President*
EMP: 11
SALES (est): 1.6MM **Privately Held**
WEB: www.aoslink.com
SIC: 2759 5943 Commercial printing; stationery stores

(G-16995)
AN EXCELSIOR ELEVATOR CORP
640 Main St Unit 2 (11590-4937)
PHONE......................516 408-3070
Fax: 516 479-1800
Eric Petzold, *CEO*
Nancy Snyder, *Manager*
EMP: 16
SALES (est): 3.4MM **Privately Held**
SIC: 3534 5084 7699 Elevators & equipment; elevators; elevators: inspection, service & repair

(G-16996)
ARKWIN INDUSTRIES INC (HQ)
686 Main St (11590-5093)
PHONE......................516 333-2640
Fax: 516 333-4187
William Maglio, *Ch of Bd*
Daniel Berlin, *President*
Laurie Pickering, *General Mgr*
Richard Vonsalzen, *General Mgr*
Frank Robilotto, *Chairman*
EMP: 242 **EST:** 1951
SQ FT: 110,000
SALES (est): 71.2MM
SALES (corp-wide): 3.1B **Publicly Held**
WEB: www.arkwin.com
SIC: 3728 Aircraft parts & equipment
PA: Transdigm Group Incorporated
    1301 E 9th St Ste 3000
    Cleveland OH 44114
    216 706-2960

(G-16997)
ATLAS GRAPHICS INC
567 Main St (11590-4811)
PHONE......................516 997-5527
Fax: 516 408-3000
Joy Newell, *President*
EMP: 5 **EST:** 1947
SQ FT: 3,000
SALES: 300K **Privately Held**
WEB: www.atlasgraphics.com
SIC: 2796 Photoengraving plates, linecuts or halftones

(G-16998)
AVANEL INDUSTRIES INC
121 Hopper St (11590-4803)
PHONE......................516 333-0990
Fax: 516 334-2666
Ingo Kurth, *President*
Chris Kurth, *Vice Pres*
EMP: 12
SQ FT: 8,500
SALES: 1.5MM **Privately Held**
WEB: www.avanelindustries.com
SIC: 3825 5049 Test equipment for electronic & electric measurement; scientific & engineering equipment & supplies

(G-16999)
BIORECLAMATIONIVT LLC (PA)
Also Called: Bioivt
123 Frost St Ste 115 (11590-5034)
PHONE......................516 483-1196
Kenneth Gatz,
EMP: 55
SALES (est): 21.4MM **Privately Held**
SIC: 2836 Biological products, except diagnostic; veterinary biological products

(G-17000)
CAB-NETWORK INC
Also Called: Four Quarter
1500 Shames Dr Unit B (11590-1772)
PHONE......................516 334-8666
Fax: 516 334-8988
Martin Chin, *President*
Patrick Chin, *Treasurer*
EMP: 6
SQ FT: 11,000
SALES: 975K **Privately Held**
SIC: 2511 Kitchen & dining room furniture

(G-17001)
CARTER PRECISION METALS LLC
99 Urban Ave (11590-4800)
PHONE......................516 333-1917
Frank Carter, *Managing Dir*
EMP: 9
SALES (est): 490.1K **Privately Held**
WEB: www.emtmfg.com
SIC: 3599 3365 Machine & other job shop work; aluminum foundries

(G-17002)
CENTRAL ISLAND JUICE CORP
128 Magnolia Ave (11590-4720)
P.O. Box 498, West Hempstead (11552-0498)
PHONE......................516 338-8301
Jules Saunder, *President*
Robert Ciolino, *Vice Pres*
Nancy Decrescenzo, *Manager*
EMP: 10
SQ FT: 21,000

Westbury - Nassau County (G-17003)

GEOGRAPHIC SECTION

SALES (est): 1.4MM **Privately Held**
SIC: 2033 Fruit juices: fresh

(G-17003)
COMPUTER INSTRUMENTS CORP
963a Brush Hollow Rd (11590-1710)
PHONE..................516 876-8400
Fax: 516 876-9153
Elsa Markovits Wilen, *President*
Don Wilen, *Vice Pres*
EMP: 40 **EST:** 1950
SQ FT: 20,000
SALES (est): 6.2MM **Privately Held**
WEB: www.computerinstruments.com
SIC: 3812 3823 3824 3829 Search & navigation equipment; industrial flow & liquid measuring instruments; fluid meters & counting devices; integrating & totalizing meters for gas & liquids; measuring & controlling devices; aircraft & motor vehicle measurement equipment

(G-17004)
DEPENDABLE ACME THREADED PDTS
167 School St (11590-3371)
PHONE..................516 338-4700
Fax: 516 997-5464
Annette Farragher, *President*
Magdalene Vogric, *Corp Secy*
EMP: 6 **EST:** 1958
SQ FT: 3,000
SALES: 500K **Privately Held**
WEB: www.dependableacme.com
SIC: 3452 Nuts, metal

(G-17005)
DIONICS-USA INC
96b Urban Ave (11590-4823)
PHONE..................516 997-7474
Bernard Kravitz, *President*
Kenneth Davis, *Director*
EMP: 7
SALES (est): 939.9K **Privately Held**
SIC: 3674 Semiconductors & related devices; integrated circuits, semiconductor networks, etc.; hybrid integrated circuits; photovoltaic devices, solid state

(G-17006)
E B B GRAPHICS INC
Also Called: Sir Speedy
75 State St (11590-5004)
PHONE..................516 750-5510
Jack Bloom, *President*
James Cirillo, *General Mgr*
Brandon Bloom, *Principal*
Adrienne Bloom, *Vice Pres*
EMP: 10
SQ FT: 1,000
SALES (est): 1.3MM **Privately Held**
WEB: www.sirspeedyny.net
SIC: 2791 2789 2752 Typesetting; bookbinding & related work; commercial printing, lithographic; commercial printing, offset

(G-17007)
EAST HILLS INSTRUMENT INC
60 Shames Dr (11590-1767)
PHONE..................516 621-8686
Cary Ratner, *CEO*
EMP: 19
SQ FT: 10,000
SALES (est): 4.2MM **Privately Held**
SIC: 3821 3823 3824 3825 Laboratory measuring apparatus; industrial instrmnts msrmnt display/control process variable; fluid meters & counting devices; instruments to measure electricity; analytical instruments; measuring & controlling devices

(G-17008)
EI ELECTRONICS INC
Also Called: Electro Industries
1800 Shames Dr (11590-1730)
PHONE..................516 334-0870
Fax: 516 338-4741
Erran Kagan, *Ch of Bd*
James Kearney, *Design Engr*
Tom David, *Sales Mgr*
Sean Bell, *Regl Sales Mgr*
Joanne San Roque, *Sales Engr*
EMP: 11

SALES (est): 1.4MM **Privately Held**
SIC: 3825 Meters: electric, pocket, portable, panelboard, etc.

(G-17009)
EMITLED INC
Also Called: Led Next
2300 Shames Dr (11590-1748)
PHONE..................516 531-3533
Asi Levy, *President*
EMP: 5
SALES (est): 649.3K **Privately Held**
SIC: 3641 Electric light bulbs, complete

(G-17010)
EXECUTIVE BUSINESS MEDIA INC
Also Called: EBM
825 Old Country Rd (11590-5589)
PHONE..................516 334-3030
Fax: 516 334-3059
Helen Scheller, *Chairman*
Fred Schane, *Vice Pres*
Katherine Youssis, *Accountant*
Steven Maiselson, *Financial Exec*
Dick Moran, *Sales Mgr*
EMP: 50
SQ FT: 4,100
SALES (est): 28.9MM **Privately Held**
WEB: www.ebmpubs.com
SIC: 2721 Magazines: publishing only, not printed on site

(G-17011)
FABRIC QUILTERS UNLIMITED INC
1400 Shames Dr (11590-1780)
PHONE..................516 333-2866
Fax: 516 333-4016
John Brunning, *President*
Karen Brunning, *Marketing Staff*
EMP: 25 **EST:** 1959
SQ FT: 7,500
SALES (est): 1.7MM **Privately Held**
SIC: 2392 2391 2591 Bedspreads & bed sets: made from purchased materials; comforters & quilts: made from purchased materials; draperies, plastic & textile: from purchased materials; window blinds; window shades

(G-17012)
FEINSTEIN IRON WORKS INC
990 Brush Hollow Rd (11590-1783)
PHONE..................516 997-8300
Fax: 718 335-3243
Daniel Feinstein, *CEO*
Howard Feinstein, *President*
Murray Gold, *Vice Pres*
Iris Echevarria, *Administration*
EMP: 32 **EST:** 1931
SQ FT: 45,000
SALES (est): 8.4MM **Privately Held**
WEB: www.feinsteinironworks.com
SIC: 3441 Fabricated structural metal

(G-17013)
FOUR K MACHINE SHOP INC
54 Brooklyn Ave (11590-4902)
PHONE..................516 997-0752
Fax: 516 997-2547
Aaron Feder, *President*
Steven Braverman, *Corp Secy*
Joe Roysman, *Vice Pres*
EMP: 6
SQ FT: 5,000
SALES (est): 700K **Privately Held**
SIC: 3599 Machine shop, jobbing & repair

(G-17014)
G & G C MACHINE & TOOL CO INC
18 Sylvester St (11590-4911)
PHONE..................516 873-0999
Fax: 516 873-0986
George Christoforou, *President*
Georgia Christoforou, *Vice Pres*
Anthony Marino, *Manager*
EMP: 7
SQ FT: 8,200
SALES (est): 1MM **Privately Held**
SIC: 3599 Machine & other job shop work

(G-17015)
G A RICHARDS & CO INC
18 Sylvester St (11590-4791)
PHONE..................516 334-5412
Fax: 516 334-6730
Benjamin Jankowski, *President*
Edward Kaider, *Vice Pres*
Paul Meeter, *Buyer*
Tony Miliusis, *Engineer*
Barbara Fisherman, *Office Mgr*
EMP: 12
SQ FT: 5,500
SALES (est): 2.1MM **Privately Held**
SIC: 3469 Machine parts, stamped or pressed metal

(G-17016)
G FRIED CARPERT SERVICE
Also Called: G Fried Carpet and Design Ctr
800 Old Country Rd (11590-5419)
PHONE..................516 333-3900
Wendy Fried, *President*
Phillip Ferrall, *Vice Pres*
EMP: 20
SALES (est): 1.4MM **Privately Held**
SIC: 2392 Linings, carpet: textile, except felt

(G-17017)
GARY ROTH & ASSOCIATES LTD
1400 Old Country Rd # 305 (11590-5119)
PHONE..................516 333-1000
Gary Roth, *Partner*
EMP: 30
SALES (est): 4MM **Privately Held**
SIC: 3578 8742 Billing machines; management consulting services

(G-17018)
GENERAL CRYOGENIC TECH LLC
400 Shames Dr (11590-1753)
PHONE..................516 334-8200
J Hanny Ruddy,
Ralph Cohan,
Peter Dahal,
EMP: 10
SALES (est): 1.6MM **Privately Held**
SIC: 3559 Cryogenic machinery, industrial

(G-17019)
H FREUND WOODWORKING CO INC
589 Main St (11590-4900)
PHONE..................516 334-3774
Fax: 516 334-2179
Frank Freund, *President*
Hubert Freund Jr, *Vice Pres*
EMP: 15 **EST:** 1962
SQ FT: 13,000
SALES: 1.2MM **Privately Held**
SIC: 2521 Wood office furniture

(G-17020)
HALCYON BUSINESS PUBLICATIONS
Also Called: Area Development Magazine
400 Post Ave Ste 304 (11590-2226)
PHONE..................800 735-2732
Fax: 516 338-0100
Dennis Shea, *President*
Dennis J Shea, *President*
Richard Bodo, *Vice Pres*
Talea Gormican, *Production*
Jacqueline Mauro, *Controller*
EMP: 16
SQ FT: 3,700
SALES (est): 2.4MM **Privately Held**
WEB: www.locationusa.com
SIC: 2721 Magazines: publishing only, not printed on site

(G-17021)
HARPER PRODUCTS LTD
Also Called: Pencoa
117 State St (11590-5022)
PHONE..................516 997-2330
Fax: 516 333-3947
Robert Perlmutter, *CEO*
Rick Perlmutter, *President*
Karen Miller, *Vice Pres*
Helen Perlmutter, *Vice Pres*
Karen Perlmutter, *Vice Pres*
▲ **EMP:** 106
SQ FT: 30,000

SALES (est): 13.4MM **Privately Held**
SIC: 3951 Pens & mechanical pencils

(G-17022)
IMPERIAL INSTRUMENT CORP
Also Called: Imperial Instrmnt & Mach
18 Sylvester St (11590-4911)
PHONE..................516 739-6644
Andre Cassata, *President*
EMP: 7 **EST:** 1956
SQ FT: 5,000
SALES (est): 400K **Privately Held**
SIC: 3599 Machine shop, jobbing & repair

(G-17023)
IMPRESS GRAPHIC TECHNOLOGIES
141 Linden Ave (11590-3227)
P.O. Box 13187, Hauppauge (11788-0577)
PHONE..................516 781-0845
Darlene Bifone, *President*
John P Bifone, *Vice Pres*
▲ **EMP:** 12
SQ FT: 7,500
SALES (est): 1.4MM **Privately Held**
SIC: 2759 Commercial printing

(G-17024)
J B TOOL & DIE CO INC
629 Main St (11590-4923)
PHONE..................516 333-1480
Fax: 516 333-1729
Frank Tabone, *President*
Joseph Tabone, *Vice Pres*
EMP: 28 **EST:** 1946
SQ FT: 14,000
SALES (est): 2MM **Privately Held**
WEB: www.jbtool-die.com
SIC: 3599 3544 Machine shop, jobbing & repair; special dies, tools, jigs & fixtures

(G-17025)
JOHN HASSALL LLC (HQ)
609 Cantiague Rock Rd # 1 (11590-1721)
PHONE..................516 334-6200
Fax: 516 222-1911
Monty Gillespie, *President*
Gina Hicks, *Purch Agent*
Danielle Martin, *Purch Agent*
Mike Genitempo, *Engineer*
Jim Spagnuolo, *Engineer*
▲ **EMP:** 83
SQ FT: 65,000
SALES (est): 18.9MM
SALES (corp-wide): 140.2MM **Privately Held**
SIC: 3452 3399 Rivets, metal; metal fasteners
PA: Novaria Group, L.L.C.
6300 Ridglea Pl Ste 800
Fort Worth TX 76116
817 381-3810

(G-17026)
JOHN HASSALL LLC
Also Called: Sky Aerospace Products
609 Cantiague Rock Rd # 1 (11590-1721)
PHONE..................323 869-0150
Monty Gillespie, *President*
Jack Wilson, *VP Opers*
Song Kim, *Engineer*
Michelle Allen, *Controller*
Lorraine Faber, *Human Res Mgr*
▼ **EMP:** 75
SQ FT: 17,000
SALES (est): 6.4MM
SALES (corp-wide): 140.2MM **Privately Held**
WEB: www.skymfg.net
SIC: 3452 Bolts, nuts, rivets & washers
HQ: John Hassall, Llc
609 Cantiague Rock Rd # 1
Westbury NY 11590
516 334-6200

(G-17027)
JUDITH LEWIS PRINTER INC
1915 Ladenburg Dr (11590-5917)
PHONE..................516 997-7777
Judith Lewis, *President*
EMP: 6
SQ FT: 2,000
SALES (est): 460K **Privately Held**
SIC: 2752 2759 Commercial printing, offset; letterpress printing

▲ = Import ▼ = Export
◆ = Import/Export

GEOGRAPHIC SECTION
Westbury - Nassau County (G-17054)

(G-17028)
KAS DIRECT LLC
Also Called: Babyganics
1600 Stewart Ave Ste 411 (11590-6654)
PHONE..................516 934-0541
Kevin Schwartz, *CEO*
Mark Ellis, *CFO*
EMP: 50 **EST:** 2008
SQ FT: 15,000
SALES (est): 14.6MM
SALES (corp-wide): 4.1B **Privately Held**
SIC: 2676 Infant & baby paper products
PA: S. C. Johnson & Son, Inc.
    1525 Howe St
    Racine WI 53403
    262 260-2000

(G-17029)
KEMP METAL PRODUCTS INC
2300 Shames Dr (11590-1748)
PHONE..................516 997-8860
Fax: 516 334-7188
Mark Raskin, *President*
Richard Raskin, *Corp Secy*
Scott Raskin, *Director*
EMP: 30 **EST:** 1946
SQ FT: 10,000
SALES (est): 9.7MM **Privately Held**
WEB: www.kempmetalproducts.com
SIC: 3915 Jewelry parts, unassembled

(G-17030)
KENWIN SALES CORP
Also Called: Levitt Industrial Textile
1100 Shames Dr (11590-1765)
P.O. Box 7150, Hicksville (11802-7150)
PHONE..................516 933-7553
Beth Foley, *CEO*
Andrew Kanter, *President*
EMP: 8
SQ FT: 2,000
SALES (est): 1MM **Privately Held**
WEB: www.levittextiles.com
SIC: 3965 Fasteners

(G-17031)
KPP LTD
Also Called: Admor Blinds & Window Fashion
81 Urban Ave (11590-4821)
PHONE..................516 338-5201
Fax: 516 338-4256
Michael Parker, *President*
Dan Kossman, *Vice Pres*
Rita Parker, *Treasurer*
EMP: 7
SQ FT: 1,700
SALES (est): 650K **Privately Held**
WEB: www.admorblinds.com
SIC: 2591 7641 Blinds vertical; reupholstery & furniture repair

(G-17032)
LIBERTY BRASS TURNING CO INC
1200 Shames Dr Unit C (11590-1766)
PHONE..................718 784-2911
Fax: 718 784-2038
David Zuckerwise, *CEO*
Peter Zuckerwise, *President*
Marshall Johnson, *Safety Mgr*
Barry Bogel, *CFO*
▲ **EMP:** 45 **EST:** 1919
SQ FT: 20,000
SALES (est): 12.9MM **Privately Held**
WEB: www.libertybrass.com
SIC: 3451 3429 3432 Screw machine products; manufactured hardware (general); plumbing fixture fittings & trim

(G-17033)
LONG ISLAND COMPOST CORP
100 Urban Ave (11590-4823)
PHONE..................516 334-6600
Fax: 516 289-1077
Charles Vigliotti, *CEO*
Ed Warner, *Plant Mgr*
Arnold Vigliotti, *Shareholder*
Dominic Vigliotti, *Shareholder*
EMP: 120
SALES (est): 29.3MM **Privately Held**
WEB: www.licompost.com
SIC: 2875 Compost

(G-17034)
LOTUS APPAREL DESIGNS INC
661 Oakwood Ct (11590-5926)
PHONE..................646 236-9363
Fang Mercedes, *President*
Rey Mercedez, *Owner*
▲ **EMP:** 2
SALES: 1.3MM **Privately Held**
SIC: 2339 7389 Service apparel, washable: women's;

(G-17035)
LOVE UNLIMITED NY INC
762 Summa Ave (11590-5011)
PHONE..................718 359-8500
Tom Terrino, *CEO*
Allison Bizinsky, *Manager*
EMP: 45 **EST:** 1953
SQ FT: 25,000
SALES (est): 7.7MM **Privately Held**
WEB: www.mbslove.com
SIC: 2759 2752 Decals: printing; commercial printing, lithographic

(G-17036)
MATCH EYEWEAR LLC
1600 Shames Dr (11590-1761)
PHONE..................516 877-0170
Fax: 516 877-0160
Helen Junda, *VP Finance*
Jonathan Pratt,
Ethan Goodman,
▲ **EMP:** 35
SQ FT: 17,000
SALES (est): 4MM **Privately Held**
WEB: www.floateyewear.com
SIC: 3229 3827 5995 Optical glass; optical instruments & lenses; optical goods stores

(G-17037)
MATERIAL MEASURING CORPORATION
121 Hopper St (11590-4803)
PHONE..................516 334-6167
Fax: 516 334-2667
Ingo O Kurth, *President*
EMP: 5
SALES: 340K **Privately Held**
SIC: 3821 Laboratory equipment: fume hoods, distillation racks, etc.

(G-17038)
METPAR CORP
95 State St (11590-5006)
P.O. Box 1873 (11590-9065)
PHONE..................516 333-2600
Fax: 516 333-2618
Ronald S Mondolino, *President*
Jimmy Fallarino, *Mfg Mgr*
Vincent Salierno, *Site Mgr*
Howard Young, *Purch Mgr*
Dave Vera, *Purchasing*
▲ **EMP:** 80 **EST:** 1952
SQ FT: 65,000
SALES (est): 24.2MM **Privately Held**
WEB: www.metpar.com
SIC: 3431 3088 Metal sanitary ware; toilet fixtures, plastic

(G-17039)
MILLER & WEBER INC
507 Davie St (11590-5955)
PHONE..................718 821-7110
Fax: 718 821-1673
Deanne Miller, *President*
▲ **EMP:** 22 **EST:** 1941
SQ FT: 5,000
SALES (est): 3.5MM **Privately Held**
WEB: www.millerweber.com
SIC: 3829 8734 3823 Measuring & controlling devices; thermometers, liquid-in-glass & bimetal type; hydrometers, except industrial process type; testing laboratories; industrial instrmnts msrmnt display/control process variable

(G-17040)
MINERALBIOUS CORP
Also Called: Dr Mineral
28 Northcote Rd (11590-1504)
PHONE..................516 498-9715
Dong Young Kim, *CEO*
▲ **EMP:** 12
SALES (est): 877.8K **Privately Held**
SIC: 3295 Minerals, ground or treated

(G-17041)
MONTERO INTERNATIONAL INC
149 Sullivan Ln Unit 1 (11590-3387)
PHONE..................212 695-1787
Raymond Hagigi, *President*
▲ **EMP:** 6
SQ FT: 7,500
SALES (est): 682.1K **Privately Held**
SIC: 2329 2325 Shirt & slack suits: men's, youths' & boys'; men's & boys' dress slacks & shorts

(G-17042)
NEW YORK READY MIX INC
Also Called: Commercial Concrete
120 Rushmore St (11590-4816)
PHONE..................516 338-6969
Rick Cerrone, *President*
Ron Notaroantonio, *Vice Pres*
EMP: 5
SQ FT: 4,000
SALES (est): 615.7K **Privately Held**
SIC: 3271 Blocks, concrete or cinder: standard

(G-17043)
P & L DEVELOPMENT LLC
200 Hicks St (11590-3323)
PHONE..................516 986-1700
Mitchell Singer, *Branch Mgr*
EMP: 88
SALES (corp-wide): 303.5MM **Privately Held**
SIC: 2834 Pharmaceutical preparations
PA: P & L Development, Llc
    200 Hicks St
    Westbury NY 11590
    516 986-1700

(G-17044)
P & L DEVELOPMENT LLC
Also Called: Pl Developments New York
275 Grand Blvd Unit 1 (11590-3570)
PHONE..................516 986-1700
EMP: 88
SALES (corp-wide): 303.5MM **Privately Held**
SIC: 2834 Pharmaceutical preparations
PA: P & L Development, Llc
    200 Hicks St
    Westbury NY 11590
    516 986-1700

(G-17045)
P & L DEVELOPMENT LLC (PA)
Also Called: Pl Developments
200 Hicks St (11590-3323)
PHONE..................516 986-1700
Mitchell Singer, *Ch of Bd*
William Kent, *President*
Evan Singer, *President*
John Francis, *Senior VP*
Dana S Toops, *Senior VP*
◆ **EMP:** 58
SALES (est): 303.5MM **Privately Held**
WEB: www.pldevelopments.com
SIC: 2834 Pharmaceutical preparations

(G-17046)
PARFUSE CORP
65 Kinkel St (11590-4914)
P.O. Box 50a (11568-0050)
PHONE..................516 997-1795
Fax: 516 997-5047
Angelina J Paris, *President*
Amy Kuna, *Corp Secy*
Donald A Paris, *Vice Pres*
EMP: 35
SQ FT: 10,000
SALES (est): 4MM **Privately Held**
SIC: 7692 3398 3341 Brazing; metal heat treating; secondary nonferrous metals

(G-17047)
PNI CAPITAL PARTNERS
1400 Old Country Rd # 103 (11590-5119)
PHONE..................516 466-7120
Michael Packman, *Ch of Bd*
EMP: 7
SALES (est): 698.6K **Privately Held**
SIC: 3452 Pins

(G-17048)
POWER SCRUB IT INC
Also Called: Alltec Products
75 Urban Ave (11590-4829)
PHONE..................516 997-2500
Louis Mangione, *President*
EMP: 13
SALES (est): 2MM **Privately Held**
SIC: 3589 High pressure cleaning equipment

(G-17049)
PRECISION MECHANISMS CORP
50 Bond St (11590-5002)
PHONE..................516 333-5955
Fax: 516 333-5956
Daniel Z Petrasek, *President*
Emilia Petrasek, *Vice Pres*
Lou Libassi, *Opers Staff*
David Jones, *Manager*
Bob Lacock, *Manager*
EMP: 30 **EST:** 1957
SQ FT: 5,000
SALES (est): 6.3MM **Privately Held**
WEB: www.precisionmechanisms.com
SIC: 3566 3625 3593 3545 Speed changers, drives & gears; relays & industrial controls; fluid power cylinders & actuators; machine tool accessories

(G-17050)
PRINCE OF THE SEA LTD
28 Urban Ave (11590-4822)
P.O. Box 887 (11590-0887)
PHONE..................516 333-6344
Roy Tuccillo, *President*
EMP: 33
SQ FT: 11,000
SALES (est): 2.9MM **Privately Held**
SIC: 2092 Fish, fresh: prepared; fish, frozen: prepared

(G-17051)
PROCOMPONENTS INC (PA)
Also Called: P C I Manufacturing Div
900 Merchants Concourse (11590-5142)
PHONE..................516 683-0909
Fax: 516 683-1919
Barry Reed Lubman, *President*
Alan Lubman, *Corp Secy*
Mitchel Laurence, *Vice Pres*
Mitchel Lubman, *Vice Pres*
EMP: 25 **Privately Held**
SIC: 3672 3674 8711 Printed circuit boards; semiconductors & related devices; consulting engineer

(G-17052)
R C HENDERSON STAIR BUILDERS
100 Summa Ave (11590-5000)
PHONE..................516 876-9898
Fax: 516 876-9899
Richard Henderson, *President*
Jason Henderson, *Vice Pres*
Julie Henderson, *Treasurer*
EMP: 10
SQ FT: 8,000
SALES: 1MM **Privately Held**
SIC: 2431 Staircases, stairs & railings; stair railings, wood

(G-17053)
S & B MACHINE WORKS INC
111 New York Ave (11590-4924)
PHONE..................516 997-2666
Eileen Sinn, *CEO*
Frederick Sinn Jr, *President*
Doris Reeder, *Manager*
EMP: 23
SQ FT: 10,000
SALES (est): 5MM **Privately Held**
WEB: www.sbmachineworks.com
SIC: 3444 3599 Sheet metalwork; machine shop, jobbing & repair

(G-17054)
SENTINEL PRINTING INC
Also Called: Sir Speedy
75 State St (11590-5004)
PHONE..................516 334-7400
Fax: 516 921-5070
Steve Ross, *President*
EMP: 5
SQ FT: 2,200

Westbury - Nassau County (G-17055)

SALES (est): 500K Privately Held
SIC: 2759 2791 2789 2752 Envelopes: printing; stationery: printing; business forms: printing; typesetting; bookbinding & related work; commercial printing, lithographic

(G-17055)
SPECTRONICS CORPORATION
956 Brush Hollow Rd (11590-1714)
PHONE.....................516 333-4840
Fax: 516 333-4859
William B Cooper, Ch of Bd
Jonathan D Cooper, President
Richard Cooper, Vice Pres
John Duerr, Vice Pres
Robert Reynolds, Prdtn Mgr
▲ EMP: 190 EST: 1950
SQ FT: 98,000
SALES (est): 58.8MM Privately Held
WEB: www.spectroline.com
SIC: 3646 3544 Fluorescent lighting fixtures, commercial; special dies, tools, jigs & fixtures

(G-17056)
STRATHMORE DIRECTORIES LTD
Also Called: Strathmore Publications
26 Bond St (11590-5002)
PHONE.....................516 997-2525
Fax: 516 997-8639
Jack Pizzo, President
Karla Osuna, Chief
EMP: 25
SALES (est): 2.6MM Privately Held
WEB: www.strathmore-ltd.com
SIC: 2721 2741 Trade journals: publishing & printing; miscellaneous publishing

(G-17057)
TAPEMAKER SALES CO INC
48 Urban Ave (11590-4822)
PHONE.....................516 333-0592
Fax: 516 333-0643
Arthur Brandwein, President
Helena Brandwein, Corp Secy
Mordy Brandwein, Vice Pres
Alexander Melamed, Manager
EMP: 8
SQ FT: 11,100
SALES (est): 560K Privately Held
SIC: 2759 Labels & seals: printing

(G-17058)
TAYLOR COMMUNICATIONS INC
1600 Stewart Ave Ste 301 (11590-6611)
PHONE.....................718 352-0220
Chris Petro, Branch Mgr
EMP: 10
SALES (corp-wide): 4.3B Privately Held
WEB: www.stdreg.com
SIC: 2761 Manifold business forms
HQ: Taylor Communications, Inc.
4205 S 96th St
Omaha NE 68127
402 898-6200

(G-17059)
TEE PEE AUTO SALES CORP
Also Called: Tri-State Towing Equipment NY
52 Swan St (11590)
PHONE.....................516 338-9333
Tom Decillis, President
Peter Pizzo, Vice Pres
Tracy Decillis, Office Mgr
EMP: 10
SALES (est): 1.1MM Privately Held
SIC: 3711 Truck & tractor truck assembly

(G-17060)
TEMPO INDUSTRIES INC
90 Hopper St (11590-4802)
PHONE.....................516 334-6900
Stuart Braunstein, President
Jade Beetle, Principal
▲ EMP: 1
SALES: 1MM Privately Held
SIC: 3993 7389 Advertising novelties; telephone services

(G-17061)
TISHCON CORP (PA)
30 New York Ave (11590-4907)
P.O. Box 331 (11590-0300)
PHONE.....................516 333-3056
Fax: 516 997-1052
Raj K Chopra, Ch of Bd
Vipin Patel, President
Kamal Chopra, Senior VP
Tina Bartley, Manager
▲ EMP: 125 EST: 1977
SALES (est): 59MM Privately Held
WEB: www.qgel.com
SIC: 2834 Vitamin preparations; pills, pharmaceutical

(G-17062)
TISHCON CORP
Also Called: Geotec
30 New York Ave (11590-4907)
P.O. Box 331 (11590-0300)
PHONE.....................516 333-3056
Raj Chopra, Manager
EMP: 150
SALES (corp-wide): 59MM Privately Held
WEB: www.qgel.com
SIC: 2834 Pharmaceutical preparations
PA: Tishcon Corp.
30 New York Ave
Westbury NY 11590
516 333-3056

(G-17063)
TISHCON CORP
41 New York Ave (11590-4908)
PHONE.....................516 333-3050
Raj Chopra, Branch Mgr
EMP: 150
SALES (corp-wide): 59MM Privately Held
SIC: 2834 Pharmaceutical preparations
PA: Tishcon Corp.
30 New York Ave
Westbury NY 11590
516 333-3056

(G-17064)
TISHCON CORP
36 New York Ave (11590-4907)
PHONE.....................516 333-3050
Hemant Pandit, Safety Mgr
EMP: 150
SALES (corp-wide): 59MM Privately Held
WEB: www.qgel.com
SIC: 2834 Vitamin preparations; pills, pharmaceutical
PA: Tishcon Corp.
30 New York Ave
Westbury NY 11590
516 333-3056

(G-17065)
TRIUM STRS-LG ISLD LLC
717 Main St (11590-5021)
PHONE.....................516 997-5757
Fanis Estevez, Production
Jolis Rodriguez, Manager
William Gross, Director
Leonard Gross,
EMP: 99
SALES (est): 19.4MM Publicly Held
SIC: 3721 Aircraft
PA: Triumph Group, Inc.
899 Cassatt Rd Ste 210
Berwyn PA 19312

(G-17066)
TRIUMPH GROUP INC
Also Called: Triumph Structures-Long Island
717 Main St (11590-5021)
PHONE.....................516 997-5757
EMP: 62
SALES (corp-wide): 3.8B Publicly Held
SIC: 3724 Mfg Aircraft Engines/Parts
PA: Triumph Group, Inc.
899 Cassatt Rd Ste 210
Berwyn PA 19312
610 251-1000

(G-17067)
TWIN COUNTY RECYCLING CORP (PA)
113 Magnolia Ave (11590-4719)
PHONE.....................516 827-6900
Fax: 516 827-5906
Carlos Lizza, President
Frank Lizza Jr, Controller
EMP: 13
SQ FT: 2,000
SALES (est): 1.2MM Privately Held
WEB: www.twincountyunitedway.com
SIC: 2951 4953 5032 Asphalt paving mixtures & blocks; recycling, waste materials; aggregate

(G-17068)
UTILITY MANUFACTURING CO INC
700 Main St (11590-5020)
PHONE.....................516 997-6300
Fax: 516 997-6345
Wilbur Kranz, CEO
Audie Kranz, President
John Heenan, Plant Mgr
Mark Sophie, Accountant
Caroline Costas, Executive
EMP: 30
SQ FT: 44,000
SALES (est): 7MM Privately Held
WEB: www.utilitychemicals.com
SIC: 2899 2891 Chemical preparations; adhesives & sealants

(G-17069)
VALPLAST INTERNATIONAL CORP
200 Shames Dr (11590-1784)
PHONE.....................516 442-3923
Peter S Nagy, President
Shabab Rahman, Business Mgr
Peter Nagy, Vice Pres
Daniel Irazary, Manager
Victor Sala, Manager
▲ EMP: 11
SQ FT: 10,500
SALES: 2.5MM Privately Held
WEB: www.valplast.com
SIC: 3559 3843 Plastics working machinery; dental equipment & supplies

(G-17070)
VESCOM STRUCTURAL SYSTEMS INC
Also Called: Tms Development
100 Shames Dr Unit 1 (11590-1741)
PHONE.....................516 876-8100
Joel Person, President
EMP: 10
SALES (est): 53.3K Privately Held
WEB: www.vescomstructures.com
SIC: 3299 Floor composition, magnesite

Westerlo
Albany County

(G-17071)
HANNAY REELS INC
553 State Route 143 (12193-2618)
PHONE.....................518 797-3791
Fax: 518 797-3259
Eric A Hannay, CEO
Roger A Hannay, Ch of Bd
Marcia Casullo, General Mgr
Dennis Fancher, COO
Elaine Hannay Gruener, Vice Pres
◆ EMP: 147 EST: 1933
SQ FT: 205,000
SALES: 55.9MM Privately Held
WEB: www.hannay.com
SIC: 3569 3499 Firehose equipment: driers, rack & reels; reels, cable: metal

Westernville
Oneida County

(G-17072)
G J OLNEY INC
9057 Dopp Hill Rd (13486-7700)
PHONE.....................315 827-4208
G Joseph Olney, President
David Olney, Vice Pres
EMP: 20 EST: 1917
SQ FT: 4,000
SALES (est): 4.1MM Privately Held
SIC: 3556 Food products machinery

Westfield
Chautauqua County

(G-17073)
20 BLISS ST INC
61 E Main St (14787-1305)
PHONE.....................716 326-2790
Ralph Wilson, President
Janice Wilson, Vice Pres
EMP: 5
SALES (est): 200K Privately Held
SIC: 1321 Natural gasoline production

(G-17074)
A TRUSTED NAME INC
35 Franklin St (14787-1039)
PHONE.....................716 326-7400
Jeff Gerdy, President
EMP: 12
SQ FT: 4,000
SALES (est): 810K Privately Held
WEB: www.atrustedname.com
SIC: 2395 5199 5941 Decorative & novelty stitching, for the trade; advertising specialties; sporting goods & bicycle shops

(G-17075)
BETTER BAKED FOODS INC
25 Jefferson St (14787-1010)
P.O. Box D (14787)
PHONE.....................716 326-4651
Fax: 716 326-4693
Rodney Bloomquist, Plant Mgr
Greg Leone, Facilities Mgr
Gregory Leone, Manager
Bob Brown, Maintence Staff
EMP: 100
SQ FT: 66,400
SALES (corp-wide): 148.9MM Privately Held
WEB: www.betterbaked.com
SIC: 2051 Bread, cake & related products
HQ: Better Baked Foods, Inc.
56 Smedley St
North East PA 16428
814 725-8778

(G-17076)
CROWN HILL STONE INC
59 Franklin St (14787-1037)
P.O. Box 76, Stow (14785-0076)
PHONE.....................716 326-4601
Fax: 716 326-4600
Geoffrey Turner, President
Jeannette Turner, Corp Secy
Sue Zanghi, Sales Mgr
Donna Arnold, Manager
EMP: 32
SQ FT: 1,296
SALES (est): 3.3MM Privately Held
SIC: 3272 3281 Building stone, artificial: concrete; fireplace & chimney material: concrete; cut stone & stone products

(G-17077)
NATIONAL GRAPE COOP ASSN INC (PA)
80 State St (14787)
PHONE.....................716 326-5200
Fax: 716 326-5111
Randolph Graham, President
Joseph C Falcone, Vice Pres
Harold Smith, Vice Pres
Timothy A Buss, CPA
Linda G Greenberg, Manager
◆ EMP: 20
SQ FT: 50,000
SALES: 608.4MM Privately Held
SIC: 2033 2037 Fruit juices: packaged in cans, jars, etc.; fruit juices: concentrated, hot pack; tomato juice: packaged in cans, jars, etc.; jams, jellies & preserves: packaged in cans, jars, etc.; frozen fruits & vegetables; fruit juices, frozen; fruit juice concentrates, frozen

(G-17078)
QUALITY GUIDES
Also Called: Westfield Publication
39 E Main St (14787-1303)
P.O. Box 38 (14787-0038)
PHONE.....................716 326-3163

Ogden Newspapers, *Owner*
Melissa Bramer, *Exec Dir*
Maureen Delbalso, *Executive*
EMP: 7
SALES (est): 292K **Privately Held**
SIC: 2711 Newspapers

(G-17079)
RENOLD HOLDINGS INC (DH)
Also Called: Renold Ajax
100 Bourne St (14787-9706)
PHONE.................................716 326-3121
Mike Conley, *President*
Carl Cain, *Design Engr*
Wincent Woodeard, *Controller*
▲ **EMP:** 2
SQ FT: 100,000
SALES (est): 34.6MM
SALES (corp-wide): 228.6MM **Privately Held**
WEB: www.renoldajax.com
SIC: 3568 5085 Power transmission equipment; couplings, shaft: rigid, flexible, universal joint, etc.; power transmission equipment & apparatus
HQ: Renold International Holdings Limited
Renold House
Manchester M22 5
161 498-4500

(G-17080)
RENOLD INC
100 Bourne St (14787-9706)
P.O. Box A (14787)
PHONE.................................716 326-3121
Fax: 716 326-6121
Mike Conley, *Ch of Bd*
Malcolm Graham, *Exec VP*
Ian Butterworth, *Mfg Dir*
Susan Miller, *Mfg Dir*
Robert Macko, *Purchasing*
▲ **EMP:** 100 **EST:** 1920
SQ FT: 100,000
SALES (est): 26.5MM
SALES (corp-wide): 228.6MM **Privately Held**
WEB: www.renoldajax.com
SIC: 3568 3535 3566 Power transmission equipment; couplings, shaft: rigid, flexible, universal joint, etc.; conveyors & conveying equipment; belt conveyor systems, general industrial use; speed changers, drives & gears
HQ: Renold Holdings Inc.
100 Bourne St
Westfield NY 14787
716 326-3121

(G-17081)
WAFFENBAUCH USA
165 Academy St (14787-1308)
PHONE.................................716 326-4508
Sam Villafrank, *CEO*
EMP: 48
SALES: 250K **Privately Held**
SIC: 1382 Oil & gas exploration services

(G-17082)
WELCH FOODS INC A COOPERATIVE
2 S Portage St (14787-1492)
PHONE.................................716 326-5252
David Moore, *General Mgr*
Robert W McMillin, *Principal*
Tim S Hilaire, *Vice Pres*
Vivian Tseng, *Vice Pres*
Thomas M Curtin, *Manager*
EMP: 175
SALES (corp-wide): 608.4MM **Privately Held**
WEB: www.welchs.com
SIC: 2033 Fruit juices: packaged in cans, jars, etc.
HQ: Welch Foods Inc., A Cooperative
300 Baker Ave Ste 101
Concord MA 01742
978 371-1000

(G-17083)
WELCH FOODS INC A COOPERATIVE
100 N Portage St (14787-1092)
PHONE.................................716 326-3131
Fax: 716 326-5491
Wilson Haller, *Branch Mgr*
EMP: 26

SALES (corp-wide): 608.4MM **Privately Held**
WEB: www.welchs.com
SIC: 2033 Canned fruits & specialties
HQ: Welch Foods Inc., A Cooperative
300 Baker Ave Ste 101
Concord MA 01742
978 371-1000

(G-17084)
WINE GROUP INC
Also Called: Mogen David Winegroup
85 Bourne St (14787-9706)
PHONE.................................716 326-3151
Fax: 716 326-4442
Eugene Schwartz, *Vice Pres*
Jean Schwartz, *Manager*
EMP: 60
SQ FT: 83,120
SALES (corp-wide): 131.8MM **Privately Held**
SIC: 2084 Wines
HQ: The Wine Group Inc
17000 E State Highway 120
Ripon CA 95366
209 599-4111

Westhampton
Suffolk County

(G-17085)
DAVE SANDEL CRANES INC
56 S Country Rd (11977-1314)
PHONE.................................631 325-5588
David Sandel, *President*
EMP: 7
SALES: 1MM **Privately Held**
SIC: 3531 Cranes

(G-17086)
HAMPTON SAND CORP
1 High St (11977)
P.O. Box 601, Speonk (11972-0601)
PHONE.................................631 325-5533
Barbara Dawson, *President*
Stan Warshaw, *Manager*
EMP: 8
SQ FT: 1,000
SALES (est): 1.2MM **Privately Held**
SIC: 1442 5261 5032 4953 Sand mining; gravel mining; top soil; brick, stone & related material; recycling, waste materials

Westhampton Beach
Suffolk County

(G-17087)
FRAME WORKS AMERICA INC
Also Called: Spectaculars
146 Mill Rd (11978-2345)
PHONE.................................631 288-1300
William Vetri, *President*
EMP: 40
SQ FT: 1,500
SALES: 3MM **Privately Held**
SIC: 3851 Eyeglasses, lenses & frames

(G-17088)
MICHAEL K LENNON INC
Also Called: Pine Barrens Printing
851 Riverhead Rd (11978-1210)
P.O. Box 704, Westhampton (11977-0704)
PHONE.................................631 288-5200
Fax: 631 288-1036
Michael K Lennon, *President*
Tom Lennon, *CFO*
EMP: 30
SQ FT: 11,000
SALES (est): 4.9MM **Privately Held**
WEB: www.pinebarrensprinting.com
SIC: 2752 Commercial printing, lithographic

(G-17089)
SHUGAR PUBLISHING
Also Called: Qsr Medical Communications
99b Main St (11978-2607)
PHONE.................................631 288-4404
Fax: 631 288-4435
Vivian Mahl, *President*
C S Pithumoni, *Editor*

Dorine Kitay, *Manager*
EMP: 8
SQ FT: 250
SALES: 1.5MM **Privately Held**
WEB: www.practicalgastro.com
SIC: 2721 Periodicals: publishing only

(G-17090)
SOUTHAMPTON TOWN NEWSPAPERS
Also Called: Western Edition
12 Mitchell Rd (11978-2609)
P.O. Box 1071 (11978-7071)
PHONE.................................631 288-1100
Cailin Brophy, *Editor*
Magaret Halsey, *Treasurer*
Frank Costanca, *Manager*
EMP: 10
SALES (corp-wide): 3.9MM **Privately Held**
WEB: www.southamptonpress.com
SIC: 2711 Newspapers
PA: Southampton Town Newspapers Inc
135 Windmill Ln
Southampton NY 11968
631 283-4100

Westmoreland
Oneida County

(G-17091)
MOHAWK METAL MFG & SLS
4901 State Route 233 (13490-1309)
PHONE.................................315 853-7663
William F Schrock, *President*
EMP: 5
SQ FT: 20,000
SALES (est): 2.5MM **Privately Held**
SIC: 2421 Building & structural materials, wood

(G-17092)
PERSONAL GRAPHICS CORPORATION
5123 State Route 233 (13490-1311)
PHONE.................................315 853-3421
Fax: 315 853-2696
Paul Hillman, *President*
EMP: 7
SQ FT: 7,000
SALES (est): 380K **Privately Held**
SIC: 2759 Screen printing

(G-17093)
RISING STARS SOCCER CLUB CNY
4980 State Route 233 (13490-1308)
P.O. Box 423, Rome (13442-0423)
PHONE.................................315 381-3096
Frank Conestabile, *Owner*
EMP: 10
SALES (est): 494.4K **Privately Held**
SIC: 3949 Sporting & athletic goods

(G-17094)
SHAFER & SONS
Also Called: Storage Sheds
4932 State Route 233 (13490-1308)
PHONE.................................315 853-5285
John H Shafer, *Partner*
Jason Shafer, *Partner*
Joe Shafer, *Partner*
Kathleen Shafer, *Partner*
EMP: 5
SQ FT: 8,000
SALES (est): 709.8K **Privately Held**
WEB: www.ssheds.com
SIC: 2452 5039 Prefabricated buildings, wood; prefabricated buildings

(G-17095)
SIERSON CRANE & WELDING INC
4822 State Route 233 (13490-1306)
PHONE.................................315 723-6914
Mitchell R Sierson, *President*
EMP: 6
SALES (est): 837.1K **Privately Held**
SIC: 3531 Cranes

Westport
Essex County

(G-17096)
CHAMPLAIN VALLEY MIL CORP INC
6679 Main St (12993)
PHONE.................................518 962-4711
Fax: 518 962-8799
Samuel M Sherman, *President*
Derinda Sherman, *Vice Pres*
Ayra Pettit, *Admin Sec*
EMP: 9
SQ FT: 9,500
SALES (est): 1.5MM **Privately Held**
SIC: 2041 Flour & other grain mill products

Westtown
Orange County

(G-17097)
FROST PUBLICATIONS INC
55 Laurel Hill Dr (10998-3921)
P.O. Box 178 (10998-0178)
PHONE.................................845 726-3232
Don Frost, *Owner*
EMP: 5
SALES (est): 417.9K **Privately Held**
SIC: 2721 1521 Periodicals: publishing & printing; single-family housing construction

(G-17098)
GARRISON WOODWORKING INC
226 Hoslers Rd (10998-3527)
P.O. Box 916, Port Jervis (12771-0916)
PHONE.................................845 726-3525
James W Boyd, *President*
Charles O'Neill, *Treasurer*
EMP: 10
SQ FT: 2,400
SALES (est): 845.1K **Privately Held**
SIC: 2434 2431 Wood kitchen cabinets; millwork

(G-17099)
GRANT-NOREN
83 Ridge Rd (10998-2602)
PHONE.................................845 726-4281
Daniel Grant, *Partner*
Ingela Noren, *Partner*
EMP: 5
SALES: 180K **Privately Held**
SIC: 2499 Picture & mirror frames, wood

White Plains
Westchester County

(G-17100)
A & C/FURIA ELECTRIC MOTORS
75 Lafayette Ave (10603-1613)
PHONE.................................914 949-0585
Fax: 914 949-8034
Andrew Cerone, *President*
EMP: 11
SQ FT: 5,000
SALES (est): 1.9MM **Privately Held**
SIC: 7694 7699 5999 5251 Electric motor repair; pumps & pumping equipment repair; compressor repair; motors, electric; pumps & pumping equipment; fans, electric

(G-17101)
ACRS INC
1311 Mmroneck Ave Ste 260 (10605)
PHONE.................................914 288-8100
Kenneth F Bernstein, *Ch of Bd*
EMP: 11
SALES (est): 796.4K **Privately Held**
SIC: 1231 Anthracite mining

White Plains - Westchester County (G-17102)

(G-17102)
ALAMAR PRINTING INC
Also Called: PIP Printing
190 E Post Rd Frnt 1 (10601-4918)
PHONE..................914 993-9007
Fax: 914 993-0029
Mary Jane Goldman, *President*
Scott Annicelli, *CFO*
EMP: 10
SQ FT: 6,500
SALES (est): 1.7MM Privately Held
SIC: 2752 2754 Commercial printing, offset; business form & card printing, gravure; promotional printing, gravure; stationery & invitation printing, gravure

(G-17103)
ALCONOX INC
30 Glenn St Ste 309 (10603-3252)
PHONE..................914 948-4040
Fax: 914 948-4088
Rhoda Schemin, *President*
Elliot Lebowitz, *COO*
Jill Zisnan, *Vice Pres*
Andrew Jacobson, *Engineer*
Stacy Silverstein, *Marketing Mgr*
EMP: 6 **EST:** 1946
SQ FT: 4,000
SALES (est): 1.5MM Privately Held
WEB: www.alconox.com
SIC: 2841 Detergents, synthetic organic or inorganic alkaline

(G-17104)
AMENDOLA MBL & STONE CTR INC
560 Tarrytown Rd (10607-1316)
PHONE..................914 997-7968
Fax: 914 946-3128
Sergio Amendola, *President*
Joseph Amendola, *Vice Pres*
Shauna Dibuono, *Sales Staff*
Maria Amendola, *Admin Sec*
▲ **EMP:** 62
SQ FT: 3,500
SALES (est): 7.3MM Privately Held
SIC: 3281 2493 5999 5211 Granite, cut & shaped; marbleboard (stone face hard board); stones, crystalline: rough; tile, ceramic

(G-17105)
AMERICAN INTL MEDIA LLC
Also Called: Rugby Magazine
11 Martine Ave Ste 870 (10606-4025)
PHONE..................845 359-4225
Ajon Prusmack, *Principal*
Morrin Burnett, *Controller*
EMP: 10
SQ FT: 3,000
SALES (est): 890K Privately Held
SIC: 2721 Magazines: publishing & printing

(G-17106)
APPLE PRESS
23 Harrison Blvd (10604-1901)
PHONE..................914 723-6660
Jody Majthenyi, *Owner*
EMP: 7
SQ FT: 4,800
SALES (est): 559.3K Privately Held
SIC: 2752 7334 Commercial printing, offset; photocopying & duplicating services

(G-17107)
ARTYARNS
70 Westmoreland Ave (10606-2315)
PHONE..................914 428-0333
Fax: 914 220-0152
Elliot Schreier, *President*
Iris Schreier, *Vice Pres*
EMP: 8
SALES (est): 904.4K Privately Held
WEB: www.artyarns.com
SIC: 2269 Dyeing: raw stock yarn & narrow fabrics

(G-17108)
BAIRNCO CORPORATION (DH)
1133 Westchester Ave N-222 (10603-3516)
PHONE..................914 461-1300
Glen M Kassan, *Ch of Bd*
John J Quicke, *President*
Ken Bayne, *CFO*
Lawrence C Maingot, *CFO*
Michele Giglietta, *Manager*

◆ **EMP:** 20
SQ FT: 11,000
SALES (est): 75.8MM
SALES (corp-wide): 1.1B Publicly Held
WEB: www.bairnco.com
SIC: 2821 3556 Plastics materials & resins; meat, poultry & seafood processing machinery; slicers, commercial, food

(G-17109)
BAKER PRODUCTS INC
5 Oakley Rd (10606-3701)
PHONE..................212 459-2323
Jeff Brown, *President*
▲ **EMP:** 6
SQ FT: 1,500
SALES (est): 1.2MM Privately Held
SIC: 3111 3172 Case leather; cosmetic bags

(G-17110)
BALLANTRAE LITHOGRAPHERS INC
96 Wayside Dr (10607-2726)
PHONE..................914 592-3275
Fax: 914 347-7573
Steve Quagliano, *President*
Ralph Bocchimuzzo, *Vice Pres*
Rocco Quagliano, *Treasurer*
EMP: 6
SQ FT: 5,000
SALES (est): 610K Privately Held
SIC: 2752 Commercial printing, lithographic; commercial printing, offset

(G-17111)
BEACON PRESS INC
32 Cushman Rd (10606-3706)
PHONE..................212 691-5050
Kenneth B Weiner, *President*
EMP: 4 **EST:** 1913
SQ FT: 3,000
SALES: 2MM Privately Held
WEB: www.beaconpress.com
SIC: 2752 Commercial printing, offset

(G-17112)
BENFIELD CONTROL SYSTEMS INC
25 Lafayette Ave (10603-1613)
PHONE..................914 948-6660
Fax: 914 948-5145
Daniel J McLaughlin, *President*
Dominic Devito, *Managing Dir*
Roy C Kohli, *Chairman*
Miguel Guerrero, *Project Engr*
William Roloff, *CFO*
EMP: 10
SALES (est): 5.4MM
SALES (corp-wide): 240MM Privately Held
WEB: www.benfieldcontrolsystems.com
SIC: 3613 8711 Control panels, electric; engineering services
PA: H.H. Benfield Electric Supply Company, Inc.
25 Lafayette Ave
White Plains NY 10603
914 948-6660

(G-17113)
BOTTLING GROUP LLC
Also Called: Pepsi Beverages Company
1111 Westchester Ave (10604-3525)
PHONE..................800 789-2626
James B Lindsey Jr, *President*
Graig Reese, *General Mgr*
Marjorie Lindsey, *Corp Secy*
Dick Graeber, *Vice Pres*
Joe Fonseca, *Plant Mgr*
EMP: 400 **EST:** 1932
SQ FT: 1,000,000
SALES: 102.9MM
SALES (corp-wide): 62.8B Publicly Held
SIC: 2086 Carbonated beverages, nonalcoholic: bottled & canned; soft drinks: packaged in cans, bottles, etc.
HQ: Pepsi-Cola Bottling Group
1111 Westchester Ave
White Plains NY 10604
914 767-6000

(G-17114)
BOTTLING GROUP LLC (HQ)
Also Called: Pepsi Beverages Company
1111 Westchester Ave (10604-3525)
PHONE..................914 767-6000
Albert P Carey, *CEO*
Zein Abdalla, *President*
Crystal Kennedy, *Info Tech Mgr*
Joanna Sweet, *Administration*
Patricia Hanley, *Legal Staff*
◆ **EMP:** 8
SALES (est): 8.8B
SALES (corp-wide): 62.8B Publicly Held
WEB: www.bottlinggroup.com
SIC: 2086 Bottled & canned soft drinks; carbonated soft drinks, bottled & canned; carbonated beverages, nonalcoholic: bottled & canned
PA: Pepsico, Inc.
700 Anderson Hill Rd
Purchase NY 10577
914 253-2000

(G-17115)
BRISTOL/WHITE PLAINS
305 North St (10605-2208)
PHONE..................914 681-1800
EMP: 7
SALES (est): 1.1MM Privately Held
SIC: 2621 Bristols

(G-17116)
BUNGE LIMITED FINANCE CORP
50 Main St (10606-1901)
PHONE..................914 684-2800
Adam Johnson, *General Mgr*
Brian Zachman, *Principal*
Josh Bergman, *Project Mgr*
Ian Messmore, *Project Mgr*
Vicente Neto, *Project Mgr*
EMP: 121
SALES (est): 44.4MM Privately Held
SIC: 2079 Edible fats & oils
PA: Bunge Limited
C/O Conyers, Dill & Pearman
Hamilton

(G-17117)
BYRAM CONCRETE & SUPPLY LLC
145 Virginia Rd (10603-2232)
PHONE..................914 682-4477
Fax: 914 682-4486
John R Percham, *Principal*
Charlie Smallen, *Accounts Mgr*
EMP: 11
SALES (est): 1.2MM Privately Held
SIC: 3273 Ready-mixed concrete

(G-17118)
C P CHEMICAL CO INC
25 Home St (10606-2306)
PHONE..................914 428-2517
Fax: 914 428-2517
Walter Hasselman Jr, *President*
Kim Couch, *Office Mgr*
EMP: 5
SQ FT: 20,000
SALES: 900K Privately Held
WEB: www.tripolymer.com
SIC: 3086 2899 2873 Insulation or cushioning material, foamed plastic; foam charge mixtures; fertilizers: natural (organic), except compost

(G-17119)
CAMEO PROCESS CORP
15 Stewart Pl Apt 7g (10603-3808)
PHONE..................914 948-0082
Fax: 914 948-0083
Edwin Goldstein, *President*
S G Goldstein, *Treasurer*
EMP: 2
SALES: 6MM Privately Held
SIC: 2671 Resinous impregnated paper for packaging

(G-17120)
CARBONFREE CHEMICALS SPE I LLC
1 N Lexington Ave (10601-1712)
PHONE..................914 421-4900
Nadeem S Nisar, *President*
Nadeem Nisar, *Managing Dir*
Heather Taormina, *Admin Asst*

EMP: 40
SALES (est): 1.4MM Privately Held
SIC: 3624 Carbon & graphite products

(G-17121)
CLASSIC COLLECTIONS FINE ART
20 Haarlem Ave Ste 408 (10603-2233)
PHONE..................914 591-4500
Larry Tolchin, *President*
EMP: 6
SQ FT: 5,000
SALES (est): 596K Privately Held
SIC: 2741 Art copy: publishing only, not printed on site

(G-17122)
CN GROUP INCORPORATED
76 Mamaroneck Ave (10601-4217)
PHONE..................914 358-5690
Jerry Duenas, *President*
EMP: 910
SALES (est): 43.7MM Privately Held
SIC: 3089 3841 2821 Automotive parts, plastic; surgical & medical instruments; plastics materials & resins

(G-17123)
COMBE INCORPORATED (PA)
1101 Westchester Ave (10604-3503)
PHONE..................914 694-5454
Fax: 914 694-1926
Richard G Powers, *President*
Christopher B Combe, *Principal*
Paolo Buonomo, *Area Mgr*
Jerome S Darby, *Senior VP*
Dominic P Demain, *Senior VP*
▼ **EMP:** 240 **EST:** 1949
SQ FT: 68,000
SALES (est): 166MM Privately Held
WEB: www.combe.com
SIC: 2841 2834 Soap & other detergents; soap: granulated, liquid, cake, flaked or chip; pharmaceutical preparations

(G-17124)
COPY STOP INC
Also Called: L K Printing
50 Main St Ste 32 (10606-1920)
PHONE..................914 428-5188
Fax: 914 428-8907
Richard Koh, *President*
Josh Green, *Manager*
EMP: 5
SQ FT: 800
SALES (est): 790.2K Privately Held
SIC: 2752 Commercial printing, lithographic

(G-17125)
DANNON COMPANY INC (HQ)
Also Called: Dannonewave
100 Hillside Ave Fl 3 (10603-2863)
P.O. Box 5004 (10602-5004)
PHONE..................914 872-8400
Gustavo Valle, *CEO*
Geno Finan, *General Mgr*
Steve Holmes, *General Mgr*
Didier Menu, *General Mgr*
Federico Muyshondt, *General Mgr*
▲ **EMP:** 6
SQ FT: 35,000
SALES (est): 894.6MM
SALES (corp-wide): 685.2MM Privately Held
WEB: www.dannon.com
SIC: 2026 Yogurt
PA: Danone
17 Boulevard Haussmann
Paris 75009
149 485-000

(G-17126)
DANONE NUTRICIA EARLY
100 Hillside Ave (10603-2861)
PHONE..................914 872-8556
Luciana Nunez, *General Mgr*
EMP: 20
SQ FT: 30,000
SALES (est): 1.5MM Privately Held
SIC: 2023 Canned baby formula

GEOGRAPHIC SECTION

White Plains - Westchester County (G-17152)

(G-17127)
DAVID YURMAN ENTERPRISES LLC
125 Westchester Ave # 1060 (10601-4546)
PHONE..................914 539-4444
David Yurman, *CEO*
Liz Candela, *Sales Associate*
Jason Drucker, *Executive*
EMP: 9
SALES (corp-wide): 276.9MM **Privately Held**
SIC: 3911 Jewelry, precious metal
PA: David Yurman Enterprises Llc
24 Vestry St
New York NY 10013
212 896-1550

(G-17128)
DEBT RESOLVE INC
1133 Westchester Ave S-223 (10604-3545)
PHONE..................914 949-5500
Bruce E Bellmare, *CEO*
William M Mooney Jr, *Ch of Bd*
Rene A Samson, *Vice Pres*
EMP: 2
SALES (est): 4.4MM **Privately Held**
WEB: www.debtresolve.com
SIC: 7372 7322 Prepackaged software; business oriented computer software; collection agency, except real estate

(G-17129)
EFFICIENCY PRINTING CO INC
126 S Lexington Ave (10605-2510)
P.O. Box 157, Valhalla (10595-0157)
PHONE..................914 949-8611
Fax: 914 949-8516
EMP: 13 **EST:** 1944
SQ FT: 5,000
SALES (est): 1.4MM **Privately Held**
SIC: 2752 2759 Commercial Printer

(G-17130)
ELECTRO PLATING SERVICE INC
127 Oakley Ave (10601-3903)
PHONE..................914 948-3777
Fax: 914 948-1627
Julian Galperin, *President*
EMP: 12 **EST:** 1930
SQ FT: 27,000
SALES (est): 353.8K **Privately Held**
WEB: www.smithwarren.com
SIC: 3471 Electroplating of metals or formed products

(G-17131)
ESCHOLAR LLC
222 Bloomingdale Rd # 107 (10605-1517)
PHONE..................914 989-2900
Shawn Bay, *CEO*
Wolf Boehme, *President*
Sue Holden, *Vice Pres*
Cristy Heffernan, *Office Mgr*
Juan Guerrero, *Manager*
EMP: 11
SQ FT: 2,500
SALES (est): 2.5MM **Privately Held**
WEB: www.escholar.com
SIC: 3695 5045 Computer software tape & disks: blank, rigid & floppy; computer software

(G-17132)
ETHIS COMMUNICATIONS INC
44 Church St Ste 200 (10601-1919)
PHONE..................212 791-1440
Fax: 212 791-4980
David Kellner, *Owner*
Mike Smolinsky, *Editor*
Adam Gundaker, *Vice Pres*
Lindsay Hermanson, *Prdtn Mgr*
Deborahanne Sandke, *Art Dir*
EMP: 7
SALES (est): 900K **Privately Held**
SIC: 2741 Miscellaneous publishing

(G-17133)
EXCELL PRINT & PROMOTIONS INC
50 Main St Ste 100 (10606-1901)
PHONE..................914 437-8668
David Quas, *President*
EMP: 8
SALES (est): 586.6K **Privately Held**
SIC: 2759 7389 Promotional printing;

(G-17134)
F-O-R SOFTWARE LLC (PA)
Also Called: Two-Four Software
10 Bank St Ste 880 (10606-1933)
PHONE..................914 220-8800
Chris Davis, *Managing Dir*
David Accolla, *Director*
John Feeney, *Director*
Kevin Ouderkirk,
Brian McLaughlin, *Analyst*
EMP: 21
SQ FT: 2,100
SALES (est): 3MM **Privately Held**
WEB: www.twofour.com
SIC: 7372 Prepackaged software

(G-17135)
FARMERS HUB LLC (HQ)
Also Called: House of Serengeti
8 Francine Ct (10607-1201)
PHONE..................914 380-2945
Oseovbie Imoukhuede, *Mng Member*
EMP: 6
SALES (est): 227.3K **Privately Held**
SIC: 2099 Tea blending
PA: Heureka Llc
8 Francine Ct
White Plains NY 10607
914 380-2945

(G-17136)
FORDHAM MARBLE CO INC
45 Crane Ave (10603-3702)
PHONE..................914 682-6699
Mario Serdo, *President*
EMP: 15
SALES (est): 1.2MM **Privately Held**
SIC: 3272 3281 Art marble, concrete; cut stone & stone products

(G-17137)
GARRETT J CRONIN
Also Called: Minute Man Printing Company
1 Stuart Way (10607-1805)
PHONE..................914 761-9299
Garrett J Cronin, *Principal*
EMP: 5
SALES (est): 171.7K **Privately Held**
SIC: 2759 7389 Commercial printing;

(G-17138)
GAS RECOVERY SYSTEMS LLC (HQ)
Also Called: Gas Recovery Systems Illinois
1 N Lexington Ave Ste 620 (10601-1721)
PHONE..................914 421-4903
Thomas Gesicki, *President*
Anthony Albao, *Vice Pres*
Peter Anderson, *Controller*
Carlo Fidani, *Director*
EMP: 12
SQ FT: 2,500
SALES (est): 33.7MM
SALES (corp-wide): 158.2MM **Privately Held**
SIC: 1389 Removal of condensate gasoline from field (gathering) lines
PA: Fortistar Llc
1 N Lexington Ave Ste 620
White Plains NY 10601
914 421-4900

(G-17139)
GEMINI MANUFACTURING LLC
Also Called: Jet Line
56 Lafayette Ave Ste 380 (10603-1684)
P.O. Box 869, Mahopac (10541-0869)
PHONE..................914 375-0855
Jon Granek, *Regl Sales Mgr*
Eric Levin, *Mng Member*
▲ **EMP:** 160
SQ FT: 100,000
SALES (est): 15.8MM **Privately Held**
WEB: www.jetlinepromo.com
SIC: 2754 Promotional printing, gravure

(G-17140)
GREAT BRANDS OF EUROPE INC
Also Called: Lu Biscuits
100 Hillside Ave Fl 3 (10603-2862)
PHONE..................914 872-8804
David McLean, *Business Mgr*
Joe Porter, *Business Mgr*
Regi Sanders, *Business Mgr*
Elio Pacheco, *Vice Pres*
Tony Cicio, *Vice Pres*
▲ **EMP:** 6
SALES (est): 400K **Privately Held**
WEB: www.danone.com
SIC: 2052 Cookies & crackers

(G-17141)
GREENKISSNY INC
75 S Broadway (10601-4413)
PHONE..................914 304-4323
Ann Anderson, *CEO*
EMP: 6
SALES (est): 150.9K **Privately Held**
SIC: 2834 Pharmaceutical preparations

(G-17142)
GROWTH PRODUCTS LTD
80 Lafayette Ave (10603-1603)
PHONE..................914 428-1316
Clare Reinbergen, *Ch of Bd*
Joanne Elaslaoui, *Human Res Mgr*
Jason Gray, *Sales Mgr*
Melissa Mancini, *Admin Asst*
▼ **EMP:** 50
SALES (est): 10.8MM **Privately Held**
SIC: 2873 Nitrogenous fertilizers

(G-17143)
HAIGHTS CROSS OPERATING CO (HQ)
10 New King St Ste 102 (10604-1208)
PHONE..................914 289-9400
Peter J Quandt, *Ch of Bd*
Linda Koons, *Exec VP*
Kevin M Mc Alley, *Exec VP*
Mark Kurtz, *Vice Pres*
Paul J Crecca, *CFO*
EMP: 22
SALES (est): 76.4MM
SALES (corp-wide): 96.4MM **Privately Held**
SIC: 2731 Book publishing
PA: Haights Cross Communications, Inc.
136 Madison Ave Fl 8
New York NY 10016
212 209-0500

(G-17144)
HANDCRAFT CABINETRY INC
230 Ferris Ave Ste 1 (10603-3461)
PHONE..................914 681-9437
Michael Ford, *President*
EMP: 9
SQ FT: 4,000
SALES (est): 1.2MM **Privately Held**
WEB: www.handcraftcabinetry.com
SIC: 2517 Home entertainment unit cabinets, wood

(G-17145)
HANDY & HARMAN (DH)
1133 Westchester Ave N-222 (10604-3571)
PHONE..................914 461-1300
Jeffrey A Svoboda, *President*
Paul E Dixon, *Senior VP*
James McCabe, *Senior VP*
Paul W Bucha, *Vice Pres*
Robert A Davidow, *Vice Pres*
◆ **EMP:** 20
SQ FT: 17,000
SALES (est): 344.7MM
SALES (corp-wide): 1.1B **Publicly Held**
SIC: 3356 3399 3341 3317 Precious metals; gold & gold alloy: rolling, drawing or extruding; silver & silver alloy: rolling, drawing or extruding; gold & gold alloy bars, sheets, strip, etc.; powder, metal; flakes, metal; silver powder; secondary precious metals; gold smelting & refining (secondary); silver smelting & refining (secondary); steel pipe & tubes; tubing, mechanical or hypodermic sizes: cold drawn stainless; wire products, ferrous/iron: made in wiredrawing plants; cable, steel: insulated or armored

(G-17146)
HANDY & HARMAN GROUP LTD (DH)
1133 Westchester Ave N-222 (10604-3571)
PHONE..................914 461-1300
Warren G Lichtenstein, *Chairman*
James F McCabe, *CFO*
EMP: 17
SALES: 559.4MM
SALES (corp-wide): 1.1B **Publicly Held**
SIC: 3462 Turbine engine forgings, ferrous

(G-17147)
HOGIL PHARMACEUTICAL CORP
237 Mmaroneck Ave Ste 207 (10605)
PHONE..................914 681-1800
David Trager, *President*
Howard Wendy, *Chairman*
Suzanne Sabatino, *COO*
Joann Hyppelite, *Manager*
▲ **EMP:** 10
SQ FT: 3,500
SALES (est): 2.1MM **Privately Held**
WEB: www.hogil.com
SIC: 2834 3841 5047 5122 Pharmaceutical preparations; surgical & medical instruments; medical & hospital equipment; drugs, proprietaries & sundries

(G-17148)
HORNELL BREWING CO INC
222 Bloomingdale Rd Ste 4 (10605-1513)
PHONE..................914 597-7911
John M Ferolito, *President*
EMP: 5
SALES (est): 279.6K **Privately Held**
SIC: 2082 Malt beverages

(G-17149)
HTF COMPONENTS INC
134 Bowbell Rd (10607-1141)
PHONE..................914 703-6795
Fred Silva, *President*
Michael C Silva, *Vice Pres*
Tracy Silva, *Manager*
EMP: 9
SQ FT: 1,545
SALES (est): 1.5MM **Privately Held**
WEB: www.htfcomponents.com
SIC: 3699 5065 Electrical equipment & supplies; electronic parts & equipment

(G-17150)
INTERSTATE THERMOGRAPHERS CORP
70 Westmoreland Ave (10606-2315)
PHONE..................914 948-1745
Fax: 914 948-0577
Juan Carlos Cardoso, *President*
Claudio Cardoso, *Vice Pres*
Ella Bradshaw, *Office Mgr*
EMP: 4
SALES (est): 1MM **Privately Held**
SIC: 2759 2752 Thermography; commercial printing, offset

(G-17151)
ITT AEROSPACE CONTROLS LLC
4 W Red Oak Ln (10604-3603)
PHONE..................914 641-2000
Marcy Barberio, *Marketing Mgr*
Menotti Lombardi, *Mng Member*
Ken I Bianchi, *Program Mgr*
Max Baigent, *Manager*
Ed Kupp, *Manager*
EMP: 6
SALES (est): 1MM **Privately Held**
SIC: 3625 Motor controls & accessories

(G-17152)
ITT INC (PA)
1133 Westchester Ave N-100 (10604-3543)
PHONE..................914 641-2000
Frank T Macinnis, *Ch of Bd*
Denise L Ramos, *President*
Farrokh Batliwala, *President*
David J Malinas, *President*
Luca Savi, *COO*
EMP: 15 **EST:** 1920
SALES: 2.4B **Publicly Held**
SIC: 3594 3625 3823 3812 Fluid power pumps & motors; control equipment, electric; fluidic devices, circuits & systems for process control; radar systems & equipment

White Plains - Westchester County (G-17153) GEOGRAPHIC SECTION

(G-17153)
ITT INDUSTRIES HOLDINGS INC (DH)
1133 Westchester Ave N-100 (10604-3543)
PHONE.....................914 641-2000
Mary Beth Gustafsson, *President*
Steve Giuliano, *Senior VP*
Daryl Bowker, *Vice Pres*
Michael Savinelli, *Vice Pres*
Thomas Scalera, *CFO*
EMP: 8 EST: 2004
SALES (est): 1.9MM
SALES (corp-wide): 2.4B **Publicly Held**
SIC: 2611 4731 Pulp mills; freight consolidation
HQ: International Standard Electric Corporation
1105 N Market St Ste 1217
Wilmington DE 19801
302 427-3769

(G-17154)
ITT LLC (HQ)
1133 Westchester Ave N-100 (10604-3543)
PHONE.....................914 641-2000
Fax: 914 616-2950
Denise L Ramos, *President*
Farrokh Batliwala, *President*
Aris C Chicles, *President*
Luca Savi, *President*
Neil W Yeargin, *President*
◆ **EMP:** 450 EST: 1920
SALES: 2.4B
SALES (corp-wide): 2.4B **Publicly Held**
WEB: www.ittind.com
SIC: 3594 3625 3823 3812 Fluid power pumps & motors; control equipment, electric; fluidic devices, circuits & systems for process control; radar systems & equipment
PA: Itt Inc.
1133 Westchester Ave N-100
White Plains NY 10604
914 641-2000

(G-17155)
JOURNAL NEWS
1133 Westchester Ave N-110 (10604-3511)
PHONE.....................914 694-5000
EMP: 6
SALES (est): 180.7K **Privately Held**
SIC: 2711 Newspapers-Publishing/Printing

(G-17156)
KINRO MANUFACTURING INC (DH)
200 Mmaroneck Ave Ste 301 (10601)
PHONE.....................817 483-7791
Jason Lippert, *President*
Scott Mereness, *Vice Pres*
Gary McPhail, *CFO*
▲ **EMP:** 1 EST: 1997
SALES (est): 141.6MM
SALES (corp-wide): 1.6B **Publicly Held**
SIC: 3442 Metal doors, sash & trim
HQ: Kinro Manufacturing, Inc.
3501 County Road 6 E
Elkhart IN 46514
574 535-1125

(G-17157)
L K PRINTING CORP
Also Called: Royal Press
50 Main St Ste 32 (10606-1920)
PHONE.....................914 761-1944
Richard Koh, *President*
Josh Greene, *Vice Pres*
Josh Green, *Manager*
EMP: 6 EST: 1961
SQ FT: 1,200
SALES: 700K **Privately Held**
SIC: 2752 Commercial printing, offset

(G-17158)
L S Z INC
Also Called: Alconox
30 Glenn St Ste 309 (10603-3252)
PHONE.....................914 948-4040
Elliot Lebowitz, *CEO*
EMP: 8
SALES (est): 680.9K **Privately Held**
WEB: www.ledizolv.com
SIC: 2841 Detergents, synthetic organic or inorganic alkaline

(G-17159)
LIFE PILL LABORATORIES LLC
50 Main St Ste 100 (10606-1901)
PHONE.....................914 682-2146
Alfred Sparman,
Lena Wills, *Admin Sec*
EMP: 6
SALES (est): 267.4K **Privately Held**
SIC: 2834 Pharmaceutical preparations

(G-17160)
LSIL & CO INC
Also Called: Lori Silverman Shoes
2 Greene Ln (10605-5111)
PHONE.....................914 761-0998
Lori Silverman, *President*
EMP: 7
SALES (est): 467.6K **Privately Held**
SIC: 3144 5661 Boots, canvas or leather: women's; women's shoes

(G-17161)
LYDIA H SOIFER & ASSOC INC
Also Called: Soifer Center, The
1025 Westchester Ave (10604-3508)
PHONE.....................914 683-5401
Fax: 914 683-5431
Lydia H Soifer, *President*
Lydia Sorfer, *President*
Susanne McIntyre, *Psychologist*
Allison Sidel, *Psychologist*
Heather Ironside M S, *Director*
EMP: 10
SALES (est): 1MM **Privately Held**
SIC: 3841 Diagnostic apparatus, medical

(G-17162)
MAIO FUEL COMPANY LP
46 Fairview Ave (10603-3403)
PHONE.....................914 683-1154
Mario Cafagno, *Principal*
EMP: 5 EST: 2011
SALES (est): 252.2K **Privately Held**
SIC: 2869 Fuels

(G-17163)
MEASUREMENT INCORPORATED
7-11 S Broadway Ste 402 (10601-3546)
PHONE.....................914 682-1969
Sara Silver, *Research*
EMP: 19
SALES (corp-wide): 83MM **Privately Held**
SIC: 2759 Commercial printing
PA: Measurement Incorporated
423 Morris St
Durham NC 27701
919 683-2413

(G-17164)
META-THERM CORP
Also Called: Bio-Nutritional Products
70 W Red Oak Ln (10604-3602)
PHONE.....................914 697-4840
Murray Flashner, *President*
▲ **EMP:** 15
SQ FT: 15,000
SALES: 4MM **Privately Held**
SIC: 2099 Food preparations

(G-17165)
MICROSOFT CORPORATION
125 Westchester Ave (10601-4522)
PHONE.....................914 323-2150
EMP: 599
SALES (corp-wide): 89.9B **Publicly Held**
SIC: 7372 Prepackaged software
PA: Microsoft Corporation
1 Microsoft Way
Redmond WA 98052
425 882-8080

(G-17166)
NATIONAL HEALTH PROM ASSOC
711 Westchester Ave # 301 (10604-3539)
PHONE.....................914 421-2525
Fax: 914 683-6998
Gilbert J Botvin, *President*
Richard Zwierko, *Vice Pres*
Thomas Papini, *Controller*
Monica Mitchell, *Accounting Mgr*
Stephanie Phillips, *Director*
EMP: 22

SQ FT: 120,000
SALES (est): 1.9MM **Privately Held**
SIC: 2741 Miscellaneous publishing

(G-17167)
NESTLE USA INC
1311 Mmroneck Ave Ste 350 (10605)
PHONE.....................914 272-4021
David Rosenbluth, *Principal*
EMP: 139
SALES (corp-wide): 88.4B **Publicly Held**
SIC: 2023 Evaporated milk
HQ: Nestle Usa, Inc.
800 N Brand Blvd
Glendale CA 91203
818 549-6000

(G-17168)
NEW ENGLAND RECLAMATION INC
20 Haarlem Ave (10603-2223)
PHONE.....................914 949-2000
Janet Peckham, *Ch of Bd*
John Peckhan, *President*
James V De Forest, *Exec VP*
Thomas Vitti, *Treasurer*
EMP: 15
SALES (est): 1.4MM
SALES (corp-wide): 200.6MM **Privately Held**
WEB: www.peckham.com
SIC: 3399 Metal powders, pastes & flakes
PA: Peckham Industries, Inc.
20 Haarlem Ave Ste 200
White Plains NY 10603
914 949-2000

(G-17169)
NU2 SYSTEMS LLC
155 Lafayette Ave (10603-1602)
PHONE.....................914 719-7272
Isac Tabib,
Mehdi Daryadel,
Elias Wexler,
EMP: 10
SQ FT: 15,000
SALES (est): 419K **Privately Held**
SIC: 3669 Intercommunication systems, electric

(G-17170)
OSAKA GAS ENERGY AMERICA CORP
1 N Lexington Ave Ste 504 (10601-1724)
PHONE.....................914 253-5500
Shojiro Oka, *Principal*
Tatsuro Tsukamoto, *Business Mgr*
John Drake, *Vice Pres*
Bette Jacques, *Human Res Dir*
Hiroyuki Harada, *Deputy Dir*
▲ **EMP:** 15
SALES (est): 701.4K
SALES (corp-wide): 10.4B **Privately Held**
SIC: 2911 Gases & liquefied petroleum gases
PA: Osaka Gas Co., Ltd.
4-1-2, Hiranomachi, Chuo-Ku
Osaka OSK 541-0
662 054-537

(G-17171)
PARAMOUNT CORD & BRACKETS
6 Tournament Dr (10605-5121)
PHONE.....................212 325-9100
Fax: 718 325-9814
Gary Rosenkranz, *President*
EMP: 8
SQ FT: 8,000
SALES (est): 640K **Privately Held**
WEB: www.pccords.com
SIC: 2211 Corduroys, cotton; basket weave fabrics, cotton

(G-17172)
PATTERSON BLACKTOP CORP (HQ)
20 Haarlem Ave (10603-2223)
PHONE.....................914 949-2000
John Peckham, *President*
Janet G Peckham, *President*
John R Peckham, *President*
James V De Forest, *Exec VP*
Thomas Vitti, *Treasurer*
EMP: 30

SALES (est): 2.8MM
SALES (corp-wide): 200.6MM **Privately Held**
SIC: 2951 Asphalt paving mixtures & blocks
PA: Peckham Industries, Inc.
20 Haarlem Ave Ste 200
White Plains NY 10603
914 949-2000

(G-17173)
PATTERSON MATERIALS CORP (HQ)
20 Haarlem Ave (10603-2223)
PHONE.....................914 949-2000
Janet G Peckham, *Co-President*
John R Peckham, *Co-President*
James V De Forest, *Exec VP*
EMP: 17
SQ FT: 15,000
SALES (est): 2.8MM
SALES (corp-wide): 200.6MM **Privately Held**
SIC: 2951 Asphalt paving mixtures & blocks
PA: Peckham Industries, Inc.
20 Haarlem Ave Ste 200
White Plains NY 10603
914 949-2000

(G-17174)
PEARSON LONGMAN LLC (DH)
10 Bank St Ste 1030 (10606-1952)
PHONE.....................212 641-2400
Jeff Taylor, *President*
Roger A Brown, *Vice Pres*
John Stallon, *Vice Pres*
Thomas Wharton, *Vice Pres*
Herbert Yeates, *Treasurer*
EMP: 40
SALES (est): 124.4MM
SALES (corp-wide): 5.6B **Privately Held**
SIC: 2731 2711 Books: publishing & printing; newspapers, publishing & printing
HQ: Pearson Inc.
1330 Hudson St
New York NY 10013
212 641-2400

(G-17175)
PECKHAM INDUSTRIES INC (PA)
20 Haarlem Ave Ste 200 (10603-2223)
PHONE.....................914 949-2000
Fax: 914 949-2075
John R Peckham, *President*
Gary W Metcalf, *Vice Pres*
Joseph Wildermuth, *Vice Pres*
Darryl Crespino, *Plant Mgr*
Jennifer Sablich, *Project Mgr*
▲ **EMP:** 30 EST: 1924
SQ FT: 15,000
SALES (est): 200.6MM **Privately Held**
WEB: www.peckham.com
SIC: 2951 Concrete, asphaltic (not from refineries)

(G-17176)
PECKHAM MATERIALS CORP (HQ)
20 Haarlem Ave Ste 200 (10603-2223)
PHONE.....................914 686-2045
John R Peckham, *President*
Gary Metcalf, *Vice Pres*
Peter Simoneau, *Vice Pres*
John Giorgianne, *Plant Mgr*
Matt Rice, *Plant Mgr*
EMP: 100
SQ FT: 5,000
SALES (est): 24.5MM
SALES (corp-wide): 200.6MM **Privately Held**
SIC: 2951 1611 5032 Asphalt & asphaltic paving mixtures (not from refineries); concrete, asphaltic (not from refineries); highway & street paving contractor; paving mixtures
PA: Peckham Industries, Inc.
20 Haarlem Ave Ste 200
White Plains NY 10603
914 949-2000

GEOGRAPHIC SECTION

White Plains - Westchester County (G-17200)

(G-17177)
PENTON BUSINESS MEDIA INC
Fleet Owner Magazine
707 Westchester Ave # 101 (10604-3102)
PHONE..................................914 949-8500
Paul Kisseberth, *Branch Mgr*
EMP: 14
SALES (corp-wide): 501.3K **Privately Held**
SIC: 2731 Book publishing
HQ: Penton Business Media, Inc.
1166 Avenue Of The Americ
New York NY 10036
212 204-4200

(G-17178)
PEPSI-COLA BOTTLING GROUP (DH)
Also Called: Pepsico
1111 Westchester Ave (10604-4000)
PHONE..................................914 767-6000
Sean Bishop, *President*
Jenny Nelson, *General Mgr*
Mike Satterfield, *District Mgr*
Dick W Boyce, *Senior VP*
Jeff Campbell, *Senior VP*
◆ **EMP:** 2
SALES (est): 189.6MM
SALES (corp-wide): 62.8B **Publicly Held**
SIC: 2086 Carbonated soft drinks, bottled & canned
HQ: Pepsi-Cola Metropolitan Bottling Company, Inc.
1111 Westchester Ave
White Plains NY 10604
914 767-6000

(G-17179)
PEPSI-COLA METRO BTLG CO INC (HQ)
Also Called: Pepsico
1111 Westchester Ave (10604-4000)
PHONE..................................914 767-6000
Fax: 914 767-1075
Philip A Marineau, *President*
Christine Oconnell, *Publisher*
Robert Carl Biggart, *Chairman*
Lenny Sorbara, *Business Mgr*
Dick W Boyce, *Senior VP*
◆ **EMP:** 5
SQ FT: 100,000
SALES (est): 24.6B
SALES (corp-wide): 62.8B **Publicly Held**
WEB: www.joy-of-cola.com
SIC: 2086 2087 Carbonated soft drinks, bottled & canned; syrups, drink
PA: Pepsico, Inc.
700 Anderson Hill Rd
Purchase NY 10577
914 253-2000

(G-17180)
PEPSI-COLA OPERATING COMPANY (HQ)
1111 Westchester Ave (10604-4000)
PHONE..................................914 767-6000
John Kayhill, *President*
Steve Schuckenbrock, *CIO*
Vicky Kurak, *Analyst*
EMP: 43
SALES (est): 23.7MM
SALES (corp-wide): 62.8B **Publicly Held**
SIC: 2086 Bottled & canned soft drinks
PA: Pepsico, Inc.
700 Anderson Hill Rd
Purchase NY 10577
914 253-2000

(G-17181)
PEPSICO INC
1111 Westchester Ave (10604-4000)
PHONE..................................914 253-2000
EMP: 309
SALES (corp-wide): 62.8B **Publicly Held**
SIC: 2096 Potato chips & similar snacks
PA: Pepsico, Inc.
700 Anderson Hill Rd
Purchase NY 10577
914 253-2000

(G-17182)
PEPSICO INC
150 Airport Rd Hngr V (10604-1219)
PHONE..................................914 253-3474
Archie Walker, *Branch Mgr*

Robert A Baldwin, *Manager*
EMP: 28
SALES (corp-wide): 62.8B **Publicly Held**
WEB: www.pepsico.com
SIC: 2086 Carbonated soft drinks, bottled & canned
PA: Pepsico, Inc.
700 Anderson Hill Rd
Purchase NY 10577
914 253-2000

(G-17183)
PEPSICO INC
1111 Westchester Ave (10604-4000)
PHONE..................................914 767-6976
Jim Dohr, *Principal*
Neal Bronzo, *Vice Pres*
EMP: 58
SALES (corp-wide): 62.8B **Publicly Held**
SIC: 2096 Potato chips & similar snacks
PA: Pepsico, Inc.
700 Anderson Hill Rd
Purchase NY 10577
914 253-2000

(G-17184)
PEPSICO WORLD TRADING CO INC
1111 Westchester Ave (10604-4000)
PHONE..................................914 767-6000
Chris Adamski, *President*
EMP: 8
SALES (est): 389.1K
SALES (corp-wide): 62.8B **Publicly Held**
SIC: 2086 Carbonated soft drinks, bottled & canned
PA: Pepsico, Inc.
700 Anderson Hill Rd
Purchase NY 10577
914 253-2000

(G-17185)
PETER PAUPER PRESS INC
202 Mmaroneck Ave Ste 400 (10601)
PHONE..................................914 681-0144
Fax: 914 681-0389
Laurence Beilenson, *President*
Evelyn Beilenson, *Principal*
Nick Beilenson, *Principal*
Virginia Reynolds, *Prdtn Mgr*
Claudine Gandolfi, *Sales Mgr*
▲ **EMP:** 25 **EST:** 1982
SQ FT: 4,004
SALES (est): 3.2MM **Privately Held**
WEB: www.peterpauper.com
SIC: 2731 Books: publishing only

(G-17186)
PFIZER INC
4 Martine Ave (10606-4016)
PHONE..................................914 437-5868
EMP: 146
SALES (corp-wide): 49.6B **Publicly Held**
SIC: 2834 Mfg Pharmaceutical Medicinal Preparations
PA: Pfizer Inc.
235 E 42nd St
New York NY 10017
212 733-2323

(G-17187)
PLASTICYCLE CORPORATION (PA)
245 Main St Ste 430 (10601-2425)
PHONE..................................914 997-8862
Fax: 914 997-6884
Anthony R Corso, *Ch of Bd*
Anthony Corso, *Vice Pres*
Tony Corso, *Human Res Mgr*
Mike Tukav, *Manager*
EMP: 40
SQ FT: 40,000
SALES (est): 6.5MM **Privately Held**
SIC: 3089 Plastic processing

(G-17188)
PREMIER WOODCRAFT LTD
277 Martine Ave 214 (10601-3401)
PHONE..................................610 383-6724
Joseph J Arena, *President*
Eric Svalgard, *Vice Pres*
Greg Nelms, *Controller*
Anna Arena, *Admin Sec*
EMP: 40
SQ FT: 30,000

SALES (est): 3.7MM **Privately Held**
SIC: 2511 2522 2521 2434 Wood household furniture; office furniture, except wood; wood office furniture; wood kitchen cabinets

(G-17189)
READENT INC
Also Called: Jazzles
445 Hamilton Ave Ste 1102 (10601-1832)
PHONE..................................212 710-3004
Andrew Squire, *CEO*
Len Smith, *Manager*
◆ **EMP:** 11
SQ FT: 2,500
SALES (est): 492.2K **Privately Held**
SIC: 3999 3944 Education aids, devices & supplies; games, toys & children's vehicles

(G-17190)
REEBOK INTERNATIONAL LTD
125 Westchester Ave (10601-4522)
PHONE..................................914 948-3719
EMP: 205
SALES (corp-wide): 20.4B **Privately Held**
SIC: 3149 Children's footwear, except athletic
HQ: Reebok International Ltd.
1895 J W Foster Blvd
Canton MA 02021
781 401-5000

(G-17191)
S & H UNIFORM CORP
1 Aqueduct Rd (10606-1003)
PHONE..................................914 937-6800
Rhoda Ross, *CEO*
Glen Ross, *President*
Dan Berkowitz, *Manager*
Bobbie Marko, *Manager*
Kevin Ross, *Executive*
▼ **EMP:** 65
SQ FT: 50,000
SALES (est): 11.4MM **Privately Held**
WEB: www.sandhuniforms.com
SIC: 2326 7389 Men's & boys' work clothing; telemarketing services

(G-17192)
S D WARREN COMPANY
925 Westchester Ave # 115 (10604-3507)
PHONE..................................914 696-5544
Katherine Haynes, *Regl Sales Mgr*
Brent Demichael, *Branch Mgr*
EMP: 60
SALES (corp-wide): 0 **Privately Held**
SIC: 2679 Paper products, converted
HQ: S. D. Warren Company
255 State St Fl 4
Boston MA 02109
617 423-7300

(G-17193)
SABRA DIPPING COMPANY LLC (DH)
777 Westchester Ave Fl 3 (10604-3520)
PHONE..................................914 372-3900
Fax: 718 204-0417
Shali Shalit-Shoval, *CEO*
Frank Armetta, *COO*
John Boes, *Exec VP*
Luciano Lopez-May, *Exec VP*
Doug Pearson, *Vice Pres*
▲ **EMP:** 75
SALES (est): 272MM **Privately Held**
SIC: 2035 Spreads, sandwich: salad dressing base
HQ: Strauss Group Ltd
49 Hasivim
Petah Tikva 49595
367 521-11

(G-17194)
SAFE FLIGHT INSTRUMENT CORP
20 New King St (10604-1204)
PHONE..................................914 220-1125
Fax: 914 946-7882
Randall Greene, *President*
Bob Teter, *Vice Pres*
Joe Wilson, *Vice Pres*
Joseph Tiseo, *Project Dir*
Dick Smith, *Plant Mgr*
▲ **EMP:** 150 **EST:** 1946
SQ FT: 42,600

SALES (est): 35.3MM **Privately Held**
WEB: www.safeflight.com
SIC: 3812 7699 Aircraft flight instruments; aircraft control systems, electronic; aircraft flight instrument repair

(G-17195)
SOFTLINK INTERNATIONAL
297 Knollwood Rd Ste 301 (10607-1849)
PHONE..................................914 574-8197
Prakash S Kamat, *CEO*
Sunil Nikhar, *President*
Praveen Lobo, *Vice Pres*
Prashant Chougule, *Manager*
EMP: 45
SQ FT: 1,200
SALES: 872.9K **Privately Held**
WEB: www.softlinkinternational.com
SIC: 7372 Prepackaged software

(G-17196)
STARFIRE HOLDING CORPORATION (PA)
445 Hamilton Ave Ste 1210 (10601-1833)
PHONE..................................914 614-7000
Carl Celian Icahn, *Ch of Bd*
Keith Cozza, *Vice Pres*
EMP: 50
SALES (est): 1B **Privately Held**
SIC: 3743 4741 4789 Freight cars & equipment; rental of railroad cars; railroad car repair

(G-17197)
STARFUELS INC (HQ)
50 Main St (10606-1901)
PHONE..................................914 289-4800
Robert Ryneveld, *Managing Dir*
EMP: 3 **EST:** 2012
SALES: 21.5MM
SALES (corp-wide): 1MM **Privately Held**
SIC: 3339 2911 1241 Precious metals; oils, fuel; coal mining services
PA: Starcommodities, Inc.
285 Grand Ave Bldg 3
Englewood NJ 07631
201 685-0400

(G-17198)
STEEL EXCEL INC (HQ)
1133 Westchester Ave N-222 (10604-3571)
PHONE..................................914 461-1300
Jack L Howard, *CEO*
Douglas Woodworth, *CFO*
▲ **EMP:** 6
SALES: 132.6MM
SALES (corp-wide): 1.1B **Publicly Held**
WEB: www.adaptec.com
SIC: 1389 7032 Oil & gas wells: building, repairing & dismantling; sporting & recreational camps
PA: Steel Partners Holdings L.P.
590 Madison Ave Rm 3202
New York NY 10022
212 520-2300

(G-17199)
STUDIO FUN INTERNATIONAL INC
44 S Broadway Fl 7 (10604-4417)
PHONE..................................914 238-1000
Fax: 914 238-7653
Harold Clark, *President*
William Magill, *Vice Pres*
Rosanne McManus, *Vice Pres*
Clifford Dupree, *Admin Sec*
Rosana Sbaragil, *Admin Asst*
▲ **EMP:** 30
SALES (est): 8.2MM
SALES (corp-wide): 1.3B **Privately Held**
WEB: www.rd.com
SIC: 2731 Book publishing
HQ: Trusted Media Brands, Inc.
750 3rd Ave Fl 3
New York NY 10017
914 238-1000

(G-17200)
SYMBIO TECHNOLOGIES LLC
333 Mamaroneck Ave (10605-1440)
PHONE..................................914 576-1205
Boyoung Kwon, *Opers Mgr*
Diane Romm, *Marketing Staff*
Lew Tischler, *Manager*
Gideon Romm, *CTO*
Roger Del Russo,

White Plains - Westchester County (G-17201)

EMP: 7
SALES (est): 1.1MM Privately Held
WEB: www.symbio-technologies.com
SIC: 3575 Computer terminals

(G-17201)
TALBOTS INC
125 Westchester Ave # 2460 (10601-4541)
PHONE..................................914 328-1034
Fax: 914 644-8270
Hana Haughton, *Manager*
Sharon See, *Manager*
EMP: 7
SALES (corp-wide): 1.3B Privately Held
SIC: 3961 Costume jewelry
HQ: The Talbots Inc
1 Talbots Dr Ste 1
Hingham MA 02043
781 749-7600

(G-17202)
TELEMERGENCY LTD
3 Quincy Ln (10605-5431)
PHONE..................................914 629-4222
Elliot I Baum, *President*
▲ **EMP:** 5
SQ FT: 1,400
SALES (est): 530K Privately Held
WEB: www.telemergency300.com
SIC: 3669 Emergency alarms

(G-17203)
TENSA SOFTWARE
66 Greenvale Cir (10607-1602)
PHONE..................................914 686-5376
Dilib Kha, *Owner*
EMP: 10
SALES (est): 600K Privately Held
SIC: 7372 Prepackaged software

(G-17204)
TRUSTED MEDIA BRANDS INC
44 S Broadway Fl 7 (10601-4417)
PHONE..................................914 244-5244
Bill Jankowski, *Info Tech Dir*
EMP: 11
SALES (corp-wide): 1.3B Privately Held
SIC: 2721 2731 5961 2741 Magazines: publishing only, not printed on site; books: publishing only; books, mail order (except book clubs); record &/or tape (music or video) club, mail order; miscellaneous publishing
HQ: Trusted Media Brands, Inc.
750 3rd Ave Fl 3
New York NY 10017
914 238-1000

(G-17205)
VALVOLINE INC
374 Central Ave (10606-1210)
PHONE..................................914 684-0170
Pat Demosthene, *Branch Mgr*
EMP: 7
SALES (corp-wide): 1.9B Publicly Held
SIC: 2992 Oils & greases, blending & compounding
PA: Valvoline Inc.
100 Valvoline Way
Lexington KY 40509
800 832-6825

(G-17206)
VDO LAB INC
400 Tarrytown Rd (10607-1314)
PHONE..................................914 949-1741
Fax: 914 949-5743
Hussein Jaffer, *President*
Mustafe Hirji, *Vice Pres*
Ahled Hirji, *Admin Sec*
EMP: 5
SQ FT: 2,110
SALES (est): 559.2K Privately Held
SIC: 3695 Video recording tape, blank

(G-17207)
VERONA PHARMA INC ✪
50 Main St Ste 1000 (10606-1900)
PHONE..................................914 797-5007
Jan-Anders Karlsson, *CEO*
Kenneth Newman, *Vice Pres*
EMP: 11 **EST:** 2017
SALES (est): 531K Privately Held
SIC: 2834 Pharmaceutical preparations

(G-17208)
VIBRA TECH INDUSTRIES INC
126 Oakley Ave (10601-3904)
PHONE..................................914 946-1916
Kenneth Strati, *President*
Cheryl Sieland, *Office Mgr*
EMP: 11 **EST:** 1962
SQ FT: 12,000
SALES (est): 730K Privately Held
SIC: 3471 Finishing, metals or formed products

(G-17209)
WATKINS WELDING AND MCH SP INC
87 Westmoreland Ave (10606-2316)
PHONE..................................914 949-6168
Fax: 914 949-8165
Charles G Watkins, *President*
Inge Watkins, *Treasurer*
EMP: 7
SQ FT: 1,850
SALES (est): 300K Privately Held
SIC: 7692 3599 Welding repair; machine shop, jobbing & repair

(G-17210)
WAYNE PRINTING INC
Also Called: Wayne Printing & Lithographic
70 W Red Oak Ln Fl 4 (10604-3602)
PHONE..................................914 761-2400
Fax: 914 761-2710
Jeffrey Wayne, *President*
EMP: 10 **EST:** 1946
SQ FT: 1,000
SALES (est): 1.5MM Privately Held
WEB: www.wayneprinting.com
SIC: 2752 Commercial printing, offset

(G-17211)
WESTCHESTER LAW JOURNAL INC
Also Called: Wlj Printers
199 Main St Ste 301 (10601-3206)
PHONE..................................914 948-0715
Fax: 914 948-3014
Lyle Salmon, *President*
▲ **EMP:** 5
SQ FT: 1,350
SALES (est): 580K Privately Held
WEB: www.westchesterlawjournal.com
SIC: 2721 7389 Trade journals: publishing only, not printed on site; legal & tax services

(G-17212)
WESTCHESTER MAILING SERVICE
Also Called: Westmail Press
39 Westmoreland Ave Fl 2 (10606-1937)
PHONE..................................914 948-1116
Fax: 914 948-9317
George Lusk, *President*
EMP: 30
SQ FT: 15,000
SALES (est): 2.9MM Privately Held
SIC: 2752 7331 2791 2789 Commercial printing, offset; mailing service; typesetting; bookbinding & related work

(G-17213)
WESTCHESTER WINE WAREHOUSE LLC
53 Tarrytown Rd Ste 1 (10607-1655)
PHONE..................................914 824-1400
Fax: 914 824-1401
Ben Khurana,
Rude Seleimi,
EMP: 15
SALES (est): 2.4MM Privately Held
WEB: www.westchesterwine.com
SIC: 2084 2389 Wines; cummerbunds

(G-17214)
WESTFAIR COMMUNICATIONS INC
Also Called: Westchester County Bus Jurnl
3 Westchester Park Dr G7 (10604-3420)
PHONE..................................914 694-3600
Fax: 914 694-3699
Dolores Delbello, *CEO*
Konstantine Wells, *Accounts Exec*
Marcia Pflug, *Sales Staff*
Susan Barbash, *Manager*
Hans Maru, *CIO*
EMP: 35
SALES (est): 2.3MM Privately Held
SIC: 2711 2721 Newspapers: publishing only, not printed on site; periodicals

(G-17215)
WRKBOOK LLC ✪
19 Brookdale Ave (10603-3201)
PHONE..................................914 355-1293
William De Andrade, *CEO*
Eric Wiener, *CTO*
EMP: 10 **EST:** 2017
SALES (est): 50K Privately Held
SIC: 7372 7389 Prepackaged software;

(G-17216)
XEROX CORPORATION
8 Hangar Rd (10604-1310)
PHONE..................................914 397-1319
Paul Yuhasz, *Manager*
Brien Zimmermann, *Manager*
EMP: 23
SALES (corp-wide): 10.7B Publicly Held
WEB: www.xerox.com
SIC: 3861 Photographic equipment & supplies
PA: Xerox Corporation
201 Merritt 7
Norwalk CT 06851
203 968-3000

Whitehall
Washington County

(G-17217)
ADIRONDACK NATURAL STONE LLC
8986 State Route 4 (12887-1800)
P.O. Box 225 (12887-0225)
PHONE..................................518 499-0602
Fax: 518 499-0602
Andre Hagadorn, *Owner*
Greg Cummings, *Sales Staff*
Karen Doran, *Sales Staff*
◆ **EMP:** 35
SALES (est): 9MM Privately Held
WEB: www.adirondacknaturalstone.com
SIC: 1411 Granite, dimension-quarrying

(G-17218)
MAPLEWOOD ICE CO INC
9785 State Route 4 (12887-2317)
P.O. Box 62 (12887-0062)
PHONE..................................518 499-2345
Fax: 518 499-2347
David O Wood, *President*
Donna Wood, *Corp Secy*
Douglas Wood, *Vice Pres*
Thomas Pomaineille, *Safety Dir*
EMP: 30
SQ FT: 6,000
SALES (est): 5.9MM Privately Held
SIC: 2097 5078 Manufactured ice; refrigeration equipment & supplies

(G-17219)
VERMONT STRUCTURAL SLATE CO
Buckley Rd (12887)
PHONE..................................518 499-1912
Robert Tucker, *Manager*
EMP: 12
SALES (corp-wide): 10.3MM Privately Held
WEB: www.vermontstructuralslate.com
SIC: 3281 Cut stone & stone products
PA: Vermont Structural Slate Co Inc
3 Prospect St
Fair Haven VT 05743
802 265-4933

Whitesboro
Oneida County

(G-17220)
COLLEGE CALENDAR COMPANY
148 Clinton St (13492-2501)
PHONE..................................315 768-8242
Carter Reul, *Owner*
Steve Tibits, *Manager*
EMP: 10
SALES (est): 850K Privately Held
SIC: 2721 Periodicals

(G-17221)
EVERSAN INC
34 Main St Ste 3 (13492-1039)
PHONE..................................315 736-3967
Fax: 315 736-4058
Mustafa Evke, *CEO*
Allan R Roberts, *Vice Pres*
Nick Wilson, *Sales Dir*
Michele Moran, *Director*
▲ **EMP:** 14
SALES (est): 2.6MM Privately Held
WEB: www.eversan.com
SIC: 3625 3674 3993 Timing devices, electronic; microprocessors; scoreboards, electric

(G-17222)
QUALITY COMPONENTS FRAMING SYS
44 Mohawk St Bldg 10 (13492-1232)
PHONE..................................315 768-1167
Fax: 315 768-3056
Daniel R Webb, *President*
EMP: 13
SQ FT: 30,000
SALES (est): 1.6MM Privately Held
WEB: www.qcwallpanels.com
SIC: 3253 Clay wall & floor tile

(G-17223)
S R SLOAN INC (PA)
8111 Halsey Rd (13492-3707)
P.O. Box 560, New Hartford (13413-0560)
PHONE..................................315 736-7730
Fax: 315 732-5315
Sheldon R Sloan, *CEO*
Stephen R Sloan, *President*
Will Compton, *Opers Mgr*
Melissa Cummings, *CFO*
Richard Stokes, *Manager*
EMP: 77 **EST:** 1960
SQ FT: 60,000
SALES (est): 16.9MM Privately Held
WEB: www.srsloan.com
SIC: 2431 2439 Staircases & stairs, wood; trusses, wooden roof

(G-17224)
TELECOMMUNICATION CONCEPTS
Also Called: T C I
329 Oriskany Blvd (13492-1424)
PHONE..................................315 736-8523
Don Ryan, *President*
EMP: 5
SALES (est): 787.4K Privately Held
WEB: www.telecommunicationconcepts.com
SIC: 3661 1731 Telephones & telephone apparatus; telephone & telephone equipment installation

(G-17225)
TURBINE ENGINE COMP UTICA
8273 Halsey Rd (13492-3803)
PHONE..................................315 768-8070
Fax: 315 768-8014
Rob Cohen, *President*
Derek Hallmark, *General Mgr*
Mike Finley, *Plant Mgr*
Brian Spychalski, *Opers Mgr*
Mike Findlay, *Facilities Mgr*
EMP: 1300
SQ FT: 250,000
SALES (est): 212.8MM Privately Held
SIC: 3724 3511 3429 3842 Aircraft engines & engine parts; turbines & turbine generator sets & parts; clamps, couplings, nozzles & other metal hose fittings; surgical appliances & supplies; guided missile & space vehicle parts & auxiliary equipment
PA: U C A Holdings, Inc.
1 W Pack Sq Ste 305
Asheville NC 28801

▲ = Import ▼ = Export
◆ = Import/Export

GEOGRAPHIC SECTION

Williamson - Wayne County (G-17251)

(G-17226)
WHITESBORO SPRING & ALIGNMENT (PA)
Also Called: Whitesboro Spring Svce
247 Oriskany Blvd (13492-1596)
PHONE.................................315 736-4441
Fax: 315 736-4459
Stewart Wattenbe Jr, *President*
Melanie Wattenbe, *CFO*
EMP: 11
SQ FT: 2,500
SALES (est): 1MM **Privately Held**
SIC: 3493 7539 7538 Leaf springs: automobile, locomotive, etc.; brake repair, automotive; general automotive repair shops

Whitestone
Queens County

(G-17227)
ANTICO CASALE USA LLC
1244 Clintonville St 2c (11357-1849)
PHONE.................................914 760-1100
Gerard Ambrosio, *Managing Dir*
Gaetano De Luca,
Fiori Franzese,
Gianluca Nastro,
▲ **EMP:** 4
SQ FT: 800
SALES: 2.6MM **Privately Held**
SIC: 2032 Italian foods: packaged in cans, jars, etc.

(G-17228)
APHRODITIES
2007 Francis Lewis Blvd (11357-3930)
PHONE.................................718 224-1774
John Milonas, *Owner*
EMP: 8
SALES (est): 774.8K **Privately Held**
SIC: 2051 5812 Bread, cake & related products; coffee shop; cafe

(G-17229)
ATLAS FENCE & RAILING CO INC
Also Called: Atlas Fence Co
15149 7th Ave (11357-1236)
PHONE.................................718 767-2200
Toll Free:..866 -
Tom Pappas, *President*
Mike Pigone, *Controller*
Josephine USS, *Office Mgr*
EMP: 20
SQ FT: 12,000
SALES (est): 4.1MM **Privately Held**
SIC: 3446 2499 3089 Fences, gates, posts & flagpoles; fences or posts, ornamental iron or steel; fencing, docks & other outdoor wood structural products; fences, gates & accessories: plastic

(G-17230)
BA SPORTS NUTRITION LLC
Also Called: Bodyarmor
1720 Whitestone Expy # 101 (11357-3000)
PHONE.................................718 357-7402
Phil Chao, *Opers Staff*
Thomas Hadley, *CFO*
Mike Repole, *Mng Member*
Lance Collins, *Mng Member*
Carole Oziel, *Manager*
EMP: 106
SALES: 125MM **Privately Held**
SIC: 2086 Fruit drinks (less than 100% juice): packaged in cans, etc.

(G-17231)
BERARDI BAKERY INC
15045 12th Rd (11357-1809)
PHONE.................................718 746-9529
Vito Berardi, *President*
EMP: 7
SQ FT: 2,800
SALES (est): 490K **Privately Held**
SIC: 2051 Bakery: wholesale or wholesale/retail combined

(G-17232)
CARAVELLA FOOD CORP
16611 Cryders Ln (11357-2832)
PHONE.................................646 552-0455
Tatiana Odato, *President*

Danny Odato, *Vice Pres*
◆ **EMP:** 12
SQ FT: 3,500
SALES (est): 590.1K **Privately Held**
SIC: 3556 Oilseed crushing & extracting machinery

(G-17233)
CREATIVE WINDOW FASHIONS INC
315 Cresthaven Ln (11357-1148)
PHONE.................................718 746-5817
Steven Lepow, *President*
Meri Gregurovic, *Corp Secy*
EMP: 100
SQ FT: 120,000
SALES (est): 7.5MM **Privately Held**
WEB: www.creativewindowfashions.net
SIC: 2258 Curtains & curtain fabrics, lace

(G-17234)
CROWN AIRCRAFT LIGHTING INC
1021 Clintonville St # 4 (11357-1845)
P.O. Box 570432 (11357-0432)
PHONE.................................718 767-3410
Fax: 718 352-2305
Michelle Virgilio, *President*
Linda Virgilio, *Vice Pres*
EMP: 9
SQ FT: 4,000
SALES (est): 900.7K **Privately Held**
SIC: 3728 Aircraft parts & equipment

(G-17235)
FRENZ GROUP LLC
14932 3rd Ave (11357-1139)
PHONE.................................212 465-0908
Chariklia Varellas, *Mng Member*
Tracy Latteri, *Manager*
▲ **EMP:** 5
SQ FT: 1,300
SALES (est): 676.3K **Privately Held**
WEB: www.frenzgroup.com
SIC: 3171 Handbags, women's

(G-17236)
HARRIS CORPORATION
1902 Whitestone Expy # 204 (11357-3059)
PHONE.................................718 767-1100
Dominic Catinella, *Manager*
EMP: 18
SALES (corp-wide): 5.9B **Publicly Held**
SIC: 3663 5065 Radio & TV communications equipment; telephone equipment
PA: Harris Corporation
    1025 W Nasa Blvd
    Melbourne FL 32919
    321 727-9100

(G-17237)
HENGYUAN COPPER USA INC
14107 20th Ave Ste 506 (11357-3045)
PHONE.................................718 357-6666
Zhifu Yan, *President*
EMP: 8
SALES (est): 747.1K **Privately Held**
SIC: 3331 Refined primary copper products
PA: Shandong Hengyuan Copper Industry Co., Ltd.
    Shuixidong, East Fifth Road, North Of Huaihe Rd., Dongying Distr
    Dongying
    546 810-9555

(G-17238)
HUDSON EASTERN INDUSTRIES INC
1118 143rd Pl (11357-2355)
P.O. Box 570085 (11357-0085)
PHONE.................................917 295-5818
Theresa Marino, *Principal*
EMP: 5
SALES (est): 202.7K **Privately Held**
SIC: 3999 Manufacturing industries

(G-17239)
JENMAR DOOR & GLASS INC
15038 12th Ave (11357-1808)
PHONE.................................718 767-7900
Millie Risi, *CEO*
Alan Risi, *Principal*
EMP: 5 EST: 2015
SQ FT: 12,000

SALES (est): 267.5K **Privately Held**
SIC: 3442 Metal doors

(G-17240)
LIF INDUSTRIES INC
Also Called: LI Fireproof Door
1105 Clintonville St (11357-1813)
P.O. Box 570171 (11357-0171)
PHONE.................................718 767-8800
Fax: 718 746-6065
Nick Parise, *Branch Mgr*
Joanna Maj, *Admin Asst*
EMP: 50
SQ FT: 23,136
SALES (corp-wide): 22.9MM **Privately Held**
SIC: 3442 3429 7699 5211 Fire doors, metal; manufactured hardware (general); door & window repair; door & window products; door frames, all materials
PA: Lif Industries, Inc.
    5 Harbor Park Dr Ste 1
    Port Washington NY 11050
    516 390-6800

(G-17241)
NEW YORK DIGITAL PRINT CENTER
15050 14th Rd Ste 1 (11357-2607)
PHONE.................................718 767-1953
Fax: 718 353-7103
Joann Derasmo, *President*
EMP: 6
SALES (est): 610K **Privately Held**
SIC: 2752 Commercial printing, lithographic

(G-17242)
PEPPERMINTS SALON INC
15722 Powells Cove Blvd (11357-1332)
PHONE.................................718 357-6304
Evangelia Parlionas, *President*
Felicia Diaram, *Manager*
Margarita Parlionas, *Admin Sec*
EMP: 10
SALES (est): 1.1MM **Privately Held**
SIC: 2844 Cosmetic preparations

(G-17243)
SECURITY DEFENSE SYSTEM
15038 12th Ave (11357-1808)
PHONE.................................718 769-7900
Millie Risi, *President*
Alan Risi, *Consultant*
EMP: 8
SQ FT: 8,000
SALES: 11.5MM **Privately Held**
SIC: 3699 7382 Security devices; protective devices, security

(G-17244)
TOCARE LLC
Also Called: Whitestone Pharmacy
15043b 14th Ave Fl 1 (11357-1864)
PHONE.................................718 767-0618
Roberto Viola,
Nella Viola,
EMP: 9
SALES (est): 1MM **Privately Held**
SIC: 2834 5122 Pharmaceutical preparations; pharmaceuticals

(G-17245)
TRIBCO LLC
Also Called: Queens Tribune
15050 14th Rd Ste 2 (11357-2607)
PHONE.................................718 357-7400
Fax: 212 357-9417
Laura Chamberlin, *General Mgr*
Bruce Adler, *Editor*
Joshua Dake, *Prdtn Mgr*
Paul Mastronardi, *CFO*
Bob Borkenstein, *Controller*
EMP: 44
SQ FT: 2,000
SALES (est): 3.2MM **Privately Held**
WEB: www.queenstribune.com
SIC: 2711 Newspapers: publishing only, not printed on site

(G-17246)
TRIBOROUGH ELECTRIC
15044 11th Ave (11357-1806)
PHONE.................................718 321-2144
Peter Gargiulo, *Principal*
Lisa Narson, *Office Mgr*

EMP: 7
SALES (est): 1MM **Privately Held**
SIC: 3699 Electrical equipment & supplies

(G-17247)
WORLD JOURNAL LLC (HQ)
14107 20th Ave Fl 2 (11357-6093)
PHONE.................................718 746-8889
Fax: 718 746-6445
Jacob MA, *Ch of Bd*
Pily Wang, *Vice Ch Bd*
Joseph Hsu, *Editor*
LI Yu, *Editor*
Abby Mui, *Accounting Mgr*
▲ **EMP:** 150
SQ FT: 50,000
SALES (est): 54.9MM **Privately Held**
WEB: www.wjnews.net
SIC: 2711 Newspapers: publishing only, not printed on site
PA: Cooper Investors Inc.
    14107 20th Ave Ste 602
    Flushing NY 11357
    718 767-8895

Whitney Point
Broome County

(G-17248)
ADVANCED GRAPHICS COMPANY
2607 Main St (13862-2223)
P.O. Box 311 (13862-0311)
PHONE.................................607 692-7875
Rosemarie Fralick, *Owner*
▼ **EMP:** 10 EST: 1957
SQ FT: 5,000
SALES (est): 901.2K **Privately Held**
SIC: 2672 3479 2759 Labels (unprinted), gummed: made from purchased materials; name plates: engraved, etched, etc.; screen printing

(G-17249)
POINT CANVAS COMPANY INC
5952 State Route 26 (13862-1211)
PHONE.................................607 692-4381
Lori Warfield, *President*
Sharon Dahulich, *Vice Pres*
Wayne Dahulich, *Treasurer*
Danny Warfield, *Admin Sec*
EMP: 5
SALES (est): 75K **Privately Held**
SIC: 2394 2395 5199 Canvas & related products; embroidery & art needlework; canvas products

Wht Sphr Spgs
Sullivan County

(G-17250)
KLEIN & SONS LOGGING INC
3114 State Route 52 (12787-5802)
PHONE.................................845 292-6682
Fax: 845 292-5849
Ronald Klein, *President*
Dale Klein, *Admin Sec*
EMP: 18
SQ FT: 3,900
SALES (est): 2.3MM **Privately Held**
SIC: 2411 Logging camps & contractors

Williamson
Wayne County

(G-17251)
DR PEPPER SNAPPLE GROUP INC
Also Called: Mott's
4363 State Route 104 (14589-9332)
PHONE.................................315 589-4911
John Adam, *Facilities Dir*
Stephen Taylor, *Opers Mgr*
Frederick M Dale, *Opers Staff*
Stephen Brisson, *Production*
Jeffrey N Glahn, *Chief Engr*
EMP: 250 **Publicly Held**
WEB: www.maunalai.com

Williamson - Wayne County (G-17252)

SIC: 2086 2087 2084 Soft drinks: packaged in cans, bottles, etc.; flavoring extracts & syrups; wines, brandy & brandy spirits
PA: Dr Pepper Snapple Group, Inc.
5301 Legacy Dr
Plano TX 75024

(G-17252)
FINGER LAKES TRELLIS SUPPLY
4041a Railroad Ave (14589-9391)
PHONE............................315 904-4007
Todd Smith, *Owner*
Susana Catlin, *Principal*
▲ EMP: 5
SALES (est): 722.6K **Privately Held**
SIC: 2431 5211 Trellises, wood; doors, storm: wood or metal

(G-17253)
LAGONER FARMS INC
6954 Tuckahoe Rd (14589-9590)
PHONE............................315 589-4899
Mark Lagoner, *President*
Dianna Lagoner, *Admin Sec*
EMP: 52
SQ FT: 8,000
SALES: 1.5MM **Privately Held**
SIC: 2033 0191 Fruits: packaged in cans, jars, etc.; general farms, primarily crop

(G-17254)
SALMON CREK CABINETRY INC
6687 Salmon Creek Rd (14589-9557)
PHONE............................315 589-5419
Charles Ciurca, *President*
EMP: 21
SALES (est): 1.5MM **Privately Held**
SIC: 2434 Wood kitchen cabinets

(G-17255)
THATCHER COMPANY NEW YORK INC
4135 Rte 104 (14589)
P.O. Box 118 (14589-0118)
PHONE............................315 589-9330
Fax: 315 589-9835
Craig N Thatcher, *President*
Chris Pavlick, *General Mgr*
J Christopher Pavlick, *Vice Pres*
Gavin Lapray, *Credit Mgr*
Gail Peacock, *Credit Mgr*
▲ EMP: 45
SALES (est): 15.7MM
SALES (corp-wide): 111.2MM **Privately Held**
SIC: 2819 5169 Industrial inorganic chemicals; chemicals & allied products
PA: Thatcher Group, Inc
1905 W Fortune Rd
Salt Lake City UT 84104
801 972-4587

(G-17256)
TRIHEX MANUFACTURING INC
6708 Pound Rd (14589-9751)
PHONE............................315 589-9331
Fax: 315 589-2024
Roger Lester, *President*
Dina Lester, *Manager*
EMP: 6 EST: 1979
SQ FT: 12,000
SALES: 600K **Privately Held**
SIC: 3451 3452 Screw machine products; bolts, nuts, rivets & washers

Williamstown
Oswego County

(G-17257)
C G & SON MACHINING INC
87 Nichols Rd (13493-2415)
PHONE............................315 964-2430
Brian Gardner, *CEO*
EMP: 5
SALES: 703.6K **Privately Held**
SIC: 7692 Welding repair

Williamsville
Erie County

(G-17258)
17 BAKERS LLC
8 Los Robles St (14221-6719)
PHONE............................844 687-6836
Anthony Habib, *CEO*
Anthony Habibm, *CEO*
Ashley Battaglia, *Principal*
EMP: 10 EST: 2015
SALES (est): 342.9K **Privately Held**
SIC: 2052 Bakery products, dry

(G-17259)
ALETHEAS CHOCOLATES INC (PA)
8301 Main St (14221-6139)
PHONE............................716 633-8620
Gust E Tassy, *President*
Dean Tassy, *Vice Pres*
Nick Malgieri, *Accounting Mgr*
EMP: 21
SQ FT: 10,000
SALES (est): 2.1MM **Privately Held**
WEB: www.aletheas.com
SIC: 2066 Chocolate

(G-17260)
ALEXANDRIA PROFESSIONAL LLC
5500 Main St Ste 103 (14221-6737)
PHONE............................716 242-8514
Lina Kennedy, *Branch Mgr*
EMP: 9
SALES (corp-wide): 389.8K **Privately Held**
SIC: 2844 Toilet preparations
PA: 938023 Ontario Inc
149 King St
Port Colborne ON L3K 4
289 478-1040

(G-17261)
ASHTON-POTTER USA LTD
Also Called: Hig Capital
10 Curtwright Dr (14221-7072)
PHONE............................716 633-2000
Fax: 716 633-2525
Miles S Nadal, *Ch of Bd*
Barry Switzer, *President*
Joe Sheeran, *Senior VP*
Kelly Smith, *Senior VP*
Bob Morreale, *Vice Pres*
▲ EMP: 170
SQ FT: 104,000
SALES (est): 26.9MM **Privately Held**
WEB: www.ashtonpotter.com
SIC: 2754 2759 Trading stamps: gravure printing; trading stamps: printing
HQ: H.I.G. Capital, L.L.C.
1450 Brickell Ave Fl 31
Miami FL 33131
305 379-2322

(G-17262)
AT&T CORP
8200 Transit Rd Ste 200 (14221-2820)
PHONE............................716 639-0673
EMP: 6
SALES (corp-wide): 163.7B **Publicly Held**
WEB: www.att.com
SIC: 3663 Mobile communication equipment
HQ: At&T Corp.
1 At&T Way
Bedminster NJ 07921
800 403-3302

(G-17263)
BEE PUBLICATIONS INC
Also Called: Amherst Bee
5564 Main St (14221-5410)
PHONE............................716 632-4700
Fax: 716 633-8601
Trey Measer, *President*
George J Measer III, *President*
Michael Measer, *Vice Pres*
Cynthia Guszik, *Sales Mgr*
Al Pitzonka, *Accounts Exec*
EMP: 55
SQ FT: 3,000
SALES: 3.1MM **Privately Held**
WEB: www.beenews.com
SIC: 2711 Newspapers: publishing only, not printed on site

(G-17264)
BROETJE AUTOMATION-USA INC
165 Lawrence Bell Dr # 116 (14221-7900)
PHONE............................716 204-8640
Ken Benczkowski, *President*
Jeremy Harris, *General Mgr*
Laura Ballard, *Manager*
Brian Orourke, *Manager*
EMP: 120
SQ FT: 200,000
SALES (est): 25.7MM
SALES (corp-wide): 9.1MM **Privately Held**
SIC: 3365 Aerospace castings, aluminum
HQ: Broetje-Automation Gmbh
Am Autobahnkreuz 14
Rastede 26180
440 296-60

(G-17265)
CABOODLE PRINTING INC
1975 Wehrle Dr Ste 120 (14221-7022)
PHONE............................716 693-6000
John Doyle, *President*
Gary Wodarczak, *Vice Pres*
Jack Jaeger, *Accounts Mgr*
Alexander Pawlicki, *Creative Dir*
EMP: 6
SALES (est): 985.9K **Privately Held**
WEB: www.caboodleprinting.com
SIC: 2752 Commercial printing, lithographic

(G-17266)
CANADA GOOSE US INC (DH)
300 International Dr (14221-5781)
PHONE............................888 276-6297
Dani Reiss, *President*
EMP: 7
SALES (est): 1.5MM
SALES (corp-wide): 15.1B **Privately Held**
SIC: 2339 2337 Women's & misses' outerwear; women's & misses' suits & coats
HQ: Canada Goose Holdings Inc
250 Bowie Ave
Toronto ON M6E 4
888 668-0625

(G-17267)
CLOUD TORONTO INC
1967 Wehrle Dr Ste 1 (14221-8452)
PHONE............................408 569-4542
Adam Noop, *Owner*
EMP: 10
SALES: 2.5MM **Privately Held**
SIC: 3679 Electronic circuits

(G-17268)
DAWN FOOD PRODUCTS INC
160 Lawrence Bell Dr # 120 (14221-7897)
PHONE............................716 830-8214
EMP: 107
SALES (corp-wide): 1.8B **Privately Held**
SIC: 2045 Doughnut mixes, prepared: from purchased flour
HQ: Dawn Food Products, Inc.
3333 Sargent Rd
Jackson MI 49201

(G-17269)
ELASTOMERS INC
2095 Wehrle Dr (14221-7097)
PHONE............................716 633-4883
Fax: 716 633-4461
Robert J Kunkel Sr, *President*
Robert J Kunkel Jr, *Vice Pres*
EMP: 8
SQ FT: 12,250
SALES: 700K **Privately Held**
SIC: 2821 Elastomers, nonvulcanizable (plastics)

(G-17270)
ENGINEERED PLASTICS INC
300 International Dr # 100 (14221-5783)
PHONE............................800 682-2525
Ken Szekely, *President*
Ken Lawrence, *Vice Pres*
▲ EMP: 20
SQ FT: 2,000
SALES (est): 3.8MM **Privately Held**
SIC: 3996 Tile, floor: supported plastic

(G-17271)
FRITO-LAY NORTH AMERICA INC
25 Curtwright Dr (14221-7073)
PHONE............................716 631-2360
Kert King, *General Mgr*
Matthew Miller, *Opers Mgr*
Jeff Quinn, *Safety Mgr*
David Bogart, *Director*
EMP: 80
SALES (est): 62.8B **Publicly Held**
WEB: www.fritolay.com
SIC: 2096 Corn chips & other corn-based snacks
HQ: Frito-Lay North America, Inc.
7701 Legacy Dr
Plano TX 75024

(G-17272)
GOODWILL INDS WSTN NY INC
4311 Transit Rd (14221-7231)
PHONE............................716 633-3305
Tammy Smith, *General Mgr*
EMP: 17
SALES (corp-wide): 8.3MM **Privately Held**
SIC: 3999 Barber & beauty shop equipment
PA: Goodwill Industries Of Western New York, Inc.
1119 William St
Buffalo NY 14206
716 854-3494

(G-17273)
LEGAL SERVICING LLC
2801 Wehrle Dr Ste 5 (14221-7381)
PHONE............................716 565-9300
EMP: 6
SALES (est): 584.3K **Privately Held**
SIC: 1389 Roustabout service

(G-17274)
ORTHO DENT LABORATORY INC
6325 Sheridan Dr (14221-4848)
PHONE............................716 839-1900
James Wright, *President*
Michael Wright, *Manager*
EMP: 14
SQ FT: 1,000
SALES (est): 1.1MM **Privately Held**
WEB: www.wlof.net
SIC: 3843 Orthodontic appliances

(G-17275)
ORTHO-CLINICAL DIAGNOSTICS INC
15 Limestone Dr (14221-7051)
PHONE............................716 631-1281
Sue Riester, *Branch Mgr*
EMP: 37
SQ FT: 5,600
SALES (corp-wide): 916.5MM **Privately Held**
WEB: www.orthoclinical.com
SIC: 2835 Blood derivative diagnostic agents
PA: Ortho-Clinical Diagnostics, Inc.
1001 Us Highway 202
Raritan NJ 08869
908 218-8000

(G-17276)
PATUGA LLC
7954 Transit Rd 316 (14221-4117)
PHONE............................716 204-7220
Joseph Pandolfino,
EMP: 5 EST: 2015
SALES (est): 270.4K **Privately Held**
SIC: 3911 7389 Jewelry, precious metal;

(G-17277)
SCHMITT SALES INC
Also Called: Robo Self Serve
5095 Main St (14221-5203)
PHONE............................716 632-8595
Joe Betts, *Manager*
EMP: 8
SQ FT: 2,347
SALES (corp-wide): 99.9MM **Privately Held**
WEB: www.schmittsales.com
SIC: 1389 Gas field services

PA: Schmitt Sales, Inc.
2101 Saint Ritas Ln
Buffalo NY 14221
716 639-1500

(G-17278)
SENECA RESOURCES CORPORATION
165 Lawrence Bell Dr (14221-7900)
PHONE.................................716 630-6750
Fax: 716 630-6777
Scott Brown, *Principal*
Jonathan Wilkins, *Manager*
EMP: 18
SALES (corp-wide): 1.7B **Publicly Held**
WEB: www.srcx.com
SIC: 1382 Oil & gas exploration services
HQ: Seneca Resources Corporation
1201 Louisiana St Ste 400
Houston TX 77002
713 654-2600

(G-17279)
SOLMAC INC
1975 Wehrle Dr Ste 130 (14221-7022)
PHONE.................................716 630-7061
Borris Soldo, *President*
John Barrett, *General Mgr*
EMP: 9
SALES (est): 1.7MM **Privately Held**
SIC: 3599 Machine shop, jobbing & repair

(G-17280)
SRC LIQUIDATION COMPANY
435 Lawrence Bell Dr # 4 (14221-8440)
PHONE.................................716 631-3900
EMP: 5 **Publicly Held**
SIC: 2754 Printing
PA: Src Liquidation Company
600 Albany St
Dayton OH 45417
937 221-1000

(G-17281)
SUCCESSWARE INC
8860 Main St 102 (14221-7640)
PHONE.................................716 565-2338
Fax: 716 565-2328
Phil Di RE, *President*
Roy Powell, *Treasurer*
Timothy McGuire, *Sales Dir*
Gerri Di RE, *Admin Asst*
EMP: 15
SQ FT: 1,600
SALES (est): 926.1K
SALES (corp-wide): 33.3B **Privately Held**
WEB: www.successware21.com
SIC: 7372 Prepackaged software
HQ: Clockwork Home Services, Inc.
12 Greenway Plz Ste 250
Houston TX 77046
941 366-9692

(G-17282)
TEALEAFS
5416 Main St (14221-5362)
PHONE.................................716 688-8022
Sydney Hoffman, *Owner*
EMP: 5
SALES (est): 397.4K **Privately Held**
SIC: 2087 Beverage bases

(G-17283)
TOWN OF AMHERST
Also Called: Park's Department
450 Maple Rd (14221-3162)
PHONE.................................716 631-7113
Fax: 716 631-7240
Dan Raily, *Manager*
EMP: 40
SQ FT: 15,600 **Privately Held**
WEB: www.apdny.org
SIC: 2531 9111 Picnic tables or benches, park; mayors' offices
PA: Town Of Amherst
5583 Main St Ste 1
Williamsville NY 14221
716 631-7082

(G-17284)
WEST SENECA BEE INC
5564 Main St (14221-5410)
PHONE.................................716 632-4700
EMP: 60
SQ FT: 4,500

SALES (est): 1.5MM **Privately Held**
SIC: 2711 Newspapers-Publishing/Printing

Williston Park
Nassau County

(G-17285)
GREENWAY CABINETRY INC
485 Willis Ave (11596-1725)
PHONE.................................516 877-0009
Frank Tommasini, *President*
David Kolodny, *Office Mgr*
EMP: 10
SALES (est): 630K **Privately Held**
SIC: 2434 Wood kitchen cabinets

(G-17286)
SCHARF AND BREIT INC
2 Hillside Ave Ste F (11596-2335)
PHONE.................................516 282-0287
Christopher Aives, *President*
K Rasmussen, *Assistant VP*
EMP: 50
SQ FT: 22,000
SALES (est): 3.5MM **Privately Held**
SIC: 2329 Sweaters & sweater jackets: men's & boys'

(G-17287)
T RS GREAT AMERICAN REST
17 Hillside Ave (11596-2303)
PHONE.................................516 294-1680
Fax: 516 294-1885
Patrick Miele, *President*
EMP: 10
SALES (est): 917.4K **Privately Held**
SIC: 2035 Seasonings & sauces, except tomato & dry

Willsboro
Essex County

(G-17288)
COMMONWEALTH HOME FASHION INC
31 Station Rd (12996)
P.O. Box 339 (12996-0339)
PHONE.................................514 384-8290
Fax: 518 963-8146
Harvey Levenson, *President*
Bill Clay, *Plant Mgr*
Susan Trombly, *Administration*
▲ **EMP:** 90
SQ FT: 151,000
SALES (est): 10.4MM
SALES (corp-wide): 12.5MM **Privately Held**
WEB: www.comhomfash.com
SIC: 2259 Curtains & bedding, knit
PA: Decors De Maison Commonwealth Inc
8800 Boul Pie-Ix
Montreal QC
514 384-8290

(G-17289)
GENERAL COMPOSITES INC
39 Myers Way (12996-4539)
PHONE.................................518 963-7333
Joseph M Callahan Jr, *CEO*
Jeffrey G Allott, *Ch of Bd*
Daniel Albert, *Controller*
Allison Whalen, *Office Mgr*
Ed Marvin, *Manager*
▲ **EMP:** 41
SQ FT: 40,000
SALES (est): 7.7MM **Privately Held**
WEB: www.generalcomposites.com
SIC: 3089 8711 Synthetic resin finished products; consulting engineer

Wilmington
Essex County

(G-17290)
ADIRONDACK CHOCOLATE CO LTD (PA)
Also Called: Candy Man
5680 Ny State Rte 86 (12997)
PHONE.................................518 946-7270
Joe Dougherty, *President*
EMP: 10 **EST:** 1962
SQ FT: 800
SALES (est): 1MM **Privately Held**
WEB: www.candymanonline.com
SIC: 2066 5441 Chocolate candy, solid; candy

Wilson
Niagara County

(G-17291)
LYNX PRODUCT GROUP LLC
650 Lake St (14172-9600)
PHONE.................................716 751-3100
Fax: 716 751-3101
Dawn Coe, *Purchasing*
Renee Moshier, *Office Mgr*
Stu Monteith, *Manager*
Donald Basil,
David T Beckinghausen,
EMP: 38
SQ FT: 28,000
SALES (est): 9.2MM **Privately Held**
WEB: www.lynxpg.com
SIC: 3582 Washing machines, laundry; commercial, incl. coin-operated

(G-17292)
VALAIR INC
87 Harbor St (14172-9749)
P.O. Box 27 (14172-0027)
PHONE.................................716 751-9480
Fax: 716 751-9491
Donald E Sinclair Jr, *Ch of Bd*
John Sinclair, *President*
Linda J Sinclair, *Corp Secy*
Pete Lepsch, *Director*
EMP: 12
SQ FT: 4,000
SALES (est): 1.7MM **Privately Held**
SIC: 3599 Machine shop, jobbing & repair

(G-17293)
WOODCOCK BROTHERS BREWING COMP
638 Lake St (14172-9600)
P.O. Box 66 (14172-0066)
PHONE.................................716 333-4000
Fax: 716 333-4002
Tim Woodcock, *President*
EMP: 9
SALES (est): 959.8K **Privately Held**
SIC: 2082 Malt beverages

Windsor
Broome County

(G-17294)
DEVONIAN STONE NEW YORK INC
463 Atwell Hill Rd (13865-3623)
PHONE.................................607 655-2600
Fax: 607 655-2623
Robert Bellospirito, *President*
Tim Hertzog, *Controller*
Peggy Rosenphal, *Sales Executive*
▲ **EMP:** 28
SQ FT: 7,000
SALES (est): 2.1MM **Privately Held**
WEB: www.devonianstone.com
SIC: 3281 1459 Cut stone & stone products; stoneware clay mining

(G-17295)
WINDSOR UNITED INDUSTRIES LLC
10 Park St (13865)
PHONE.................................607 655-3300
Dennis Garges,
EMP: 40
SALES (est): 3.4MM **Privately Held**
SIC: 2499 Decorative wood & woodwork

Wingdale
Dutchess County

(G-17296)
HUNT COUNTRY FURNITURE INC (PA)
19 Dog Tail Corners Rd (12594-1218)
P.O. Box 680 (12594-0680)
PHONE.................................845 832-6601
Todd Gazzoli, *General Mgr*
Randy Williams, *Chairman*
▲ **EMP:** 80
SQ FT: 60,000
SALES (est): 8.7MM **Privately Held**
WEB: www.huntcountryfurniture.com
SIC: 2511 2599 Chairs, household, except upholstered: wood; restaurant furniture, wood or metal

(G-17297)
WESTCHESTER MODULAR HOMES INC
30 Reagans Mill Rd (12594-1101)
PHONE.................................845 832-9400
Fax: 845 832-6698
Charles W Hatcher, *President*
John Colucci, *Vice Pres*
Jim Woodside, *Sales Staff*
Grover Greiner, *Manager*
EMP: 125
SQ FT: 104,000
SALES (est): 20.9MM **Privately Held**
WEB: www.westchestermodular.com
SIC: 2452 Modular homes, prefabricated, wood

Wolcott
Wayne County

(G-17298)
CAHOON FARMS INC
10951 Lummisville Rd (14590-9549)
P.O. Box 190 (14590-0190)
PHONE.................................315 594-8081
Fax: 315 594-1678
Donald D Cahoon Jr, *President*
Renee Lanclos, *General Mgr*
William Cahoon, *Vice Pres*
Dave Green, *Opers Staff*
Sheila Rigerman, *QC Mgr*
EMP: 35
SQ FT: 44,000
SALES (est): 10.2MM **Privately Held**
SIC: 2033 0723 2037 0175 Fruit juices: fresh; fruit (fresh) packing services; frozen fruits & vegetables; deciduous tree fruits

(G-17299)
CARBALLO CONTRACT MACHINING
Also Called: C C M
6205 Lake Ave (14590-1040)
PHONE.................................315 594-2511
Jeannie Brockmyer, *Owner*
Bryan Brockmyre, *Manager*
EMP: 5
SQ FT: 3,000
SALES (est): 360K **Privately Held**
WEB: www.ccmprecision.biz
SIC: 3599 Machine & other job shop work

(G-17300)
EAGLE WELDING MACHINE
13458 Ridge Rd (14590-9602)
PHONE.................................315 594-1845
Gary Buckalew, *Principal*
EMP: 9
SALES: 1MM **Privately Held**
SIC: 7692 Welding repair

Wolcott - Wayne County (G-17301)

(G-17301)
MARSHALL INGREDIENTS LLC
5786 Limekiln Rd (14590-9354)
PHONE..................800 796-9353
EMP: 6
SALES (corp-wide): 787.7K Privately Held
SIC: 2034 Fruits, dried or dehydrated, except freeze-dried
PA: Marshall Ingredients Llc
5740 Limekiln Rd
Wolcott NY

(G-17302)
WAYUGA COMMUNITY NEWSPAPERS
Also Called: Waguya News
12039 E Main St (14590-1021)
PHONE..................315 594-2506
Chuck Palermo, Manager
EMP: 6
SQ FT: 5,004
SALES (corp-wide): 2.5MM Privately Held
WEB: www.wayuga.com
SIC: 2711 4225 Newspapers, publishing & printing; general warehousing
PA: Wayuga Community Newspapers Inc
6784 Main St
Red Creek NY 13143
315 754-6229

Woodbury
Nassau County

(G-17303)
ARIZONA BEVERAGE COMPANY LLC (HQ)
Also Called: Arizona Beverages USA
60 Crossways Park Dr W # 400 (11797-2018)
PHONE..................516 812-0300
Jim Dar, Vice Pres
Rick Adonailo, CFO
Ali Carbone, Marketing Staff
Mark Striegel, Marketing Staff
Anthony Galeno, Office Mgr
▼ EMP: 3
SALES (est): 2.4MM
SALES (corp-wide): 74.6MM Privately Held
SIC: 2086 Iced tea & fruit drinks, bottled & canned
PA: Hornell Brewing Co., Inc.
60 Crossways Park Dr W # 400
Woodbury NY 11797
516 812-0300

(G-17304)
CLEVER DEVICES LTD (PA)
300 Crossways Park Dr (11797-2035)
PHONE..................516 433-6100
Frank Ingrassia, CEO
Andrew Stanton, COO
Buddy Coleman, Exec VP
Steve Bennett, Senior VP
Dean Soucy, Senior VP
EMP: 43
SQ FT: 10,000
SALES (est): 18.6MM Privately Held
WEB: www.cleverdevices.net
SIC: 3679 3663 Recording & playback apparatus, including phonograph; radio & TV communications equipment

(G-17305)
COMPOSITECH LTD
4 Fairbanks Blvd (11797-2604)
PHONE..................516 835-1458
Jonas Medney, Ch of Bd
Christopher F Johnson, President
Richard Depoto, Vice Pres
Ralph W Segalowitz, Vice Pres
Samuel S Gross, Treasurer
EMP: 110
SQ FT: 33,000
SALES (est): 11.5MM Privately Held
WEB: www.compositech.com
SIC: 3674 6794 Semiconductors & related devices; patent owners & lessors

(G-17306)
CRAZY COWBOY BREWING CO LLC
60 Crossways Park Dr W # 400 (11797-2018)
PHONE..................516 812-0576
David Menashi, CEO
EMP: 25
SALES (est): 809.2K Privately Held
SIC: 2082 Malt beverage products

(G-17307)
E & W MANUFACTURING CO INC
15 Pine Dr (11797-1509)
PHONE..................516 367-8571
Elliot Wald, President
EMP: 21
SQ FT: 15,000
SALES (est): 1.7MM Privately Held
SIC: 3991 Paint brushes

(G-17308)
F & V DISTRIBUTION COMPANY LLC
1 Arizona Plz (11797-1125)
PHONE..................516 812-0393
Don Vultaggio, Principal
EMP: 5 Privately Held
SIC: 2086 Iced tea & fruit drinks, bottled & canned
PA: F & V Distribution Company, Llc
60 Crossways Park Dr W # 400
Woodbury NY 11797

(G-17309)
GEM MINE CORP
84 Cypress Dr (11797-1523)
PHONE..................516 367-1075
Fax: 212 391-5645
Camillo Pizzo, President
Bob D'Ambrosio, Finance
EMP: 7
SALES (est): 644.8K Privately Held
SIC: 3911 Jewelry, precious metal

(G-17310)
GLOBAL VIDEO LLC (HQ)
Also Called: Guidance Channel
1000 Woodbury Rd Ste 1 (11797-2530)
PHONE..................516 222-2600
David Rust, President
EMP: 60
SALES (est): 20.8MM
SALES (corp-wide): 1.1B Publicly Held
WEB: www.sunburstvm.com
SIC: 2741 5961 5092 6719 Catalogs: publishing & printing; book club, mail order; educational toys; investment holding companies, except banks
PA: School Specialty, Inc.
W6316 Design Dr
Greenville WI 54942
920 734-5712

(G-17311)
HOWARD CHARLES INC
180 Froehlich Farm Blvd (11797-2923)
P.O. Box 544, Mahopac (10541-0544)
PHONE..................917 902-6934
Charles Breslin, Principal
EMP: 7
SALES (est): 743.3K Privately Held
SIC: 3089 Plastic kitchenware, tableware & houseware

(G-17312)
LENCORE ACOUSTICS CORP (PA)
1 Crossways Park Dr W (11797-2014)
PHONE..................516 682-9292
Fax: 516 682-4785
Jack D Leonard, Ch of Bd
Tim Deblaey, Vice Pres
Jonathan Leonard, Vice Pres
Alison Friedson, Purch Mgr
Patricia Camastra, Purch Agent
EMP: 10
SQ FT: 2,200
SALES (est): 5.6MM Privately Held
WEB: www.lencore.com
SIC: 3446 Partitions & supports/studs, including accoustical systems; acoustical suspension systems, metal

(G-17313)
LI SCRIPT LLC
333 Crossways Park Dr (11797-2066)
PHONE..................631 321-3850
Fax: 631 321-3859
Michael Shamalov, Owner
EMP: 30
SALES (est): 6.7MM Privately Held
SIC: 2752 Commercial printing, lithographic

(G-17314)
MANHATTAN MILLING & DRYING CO
78 Pond Rd (11797-1616)
PHONE..................516 496-1041
John Mc Auley, President
Robert Mc Auley, Treasurer
EMP: 20
SQ FT: 37,500
SALES (est): 1.2MM Privately Held
SIC: 2099 Spices, including grinding

(G-17315)
PHOTO INDUSTRY INC
Also Called: Pemystifying Diital
7600 Jericho Tpke Ste 301 (11797-1705)
PHONE..................516 364-0016
Fax: 516 364-0140
Allan Lavine, President
Jerry Grossman, Vice Pres
EMP: 10
SQ FT: 1,200
SALES (est): 980K Privately Held
SIC: 2721 Magazines: publishing only, not printed on site

(G-17316)
PROVIDENT FUEL INC
4 Stillwell Ln (11797-1104)
PHONE..................516 224-4427
Douglas Robalino, Principal
EMP: 9
SALES (est): 1.2MM Privately Held
SIC: 2869 Fuels

(G-17317)
RAYTECH CORPORATION (HQ)
97 Froehlich Farm Blvd (11797-2903)
PHONE..................718 259-7388
Larry W Singleton, President
Howard Mandell, CFO
Alfred Klee, Internal Med
EMP: 9
SQ FT: 7,000
SALES (est): 109.1MM
SALES (corp-wide): 123.9MM Privately Held
WEB: www.raytech.com
SIC: 3499 Friction material, made from powdered metal
PA: Raytech Corp Asbestos Personal Injury Settlement Trust
190 Willis Ave
Mineola NY 11501
516 747-0300

(G-17318)
RESEARCH FRONTIERS INC (PA)
240 Crossways Park Dr (11797-2033)
PHONE..................516 364-1902
Fax: 516 364-3798
Joseph M Harary, President
Michael R Lapointe, Vice Pres
Steven M Slovak, Vice Pres
Seth L Van Voorhees, CFO
EMP: 11 EST: 1930
SQ FT: 9,500
SALES: 1.2MM Publicly Held
WEB: www.refr-spd.com
SIC: 3829 Measuring & controlling devices

(G-17319)
ROYAL PAINT ROLLER CORP
Also Called: Royal Paint Roller Mfg
1 Harvard Dr (11797-3302)
PHONE..................516 367-4370
Randy Boritz, President
Gloria Boritz, Admin Sec
EMP: 25 EST: 1968
SQ FT: 23,000
SALES (est): 2MM Privately Held
SIC: 3991 Paint rollers

(G-17320)
SORFIN YOSHIMURA LTD
100 Crossways Park Dr # 215 (11797-2012)
PHONE..................516 802-4600
Scott Fink, President
Manny Prieto, Vice Pres
◆ EMP: 7
SALES (est): 167.9K Privately Held
SIC: 3825 Battery testers, electrical

(G-17321)
VEECO INSTRUMENTS INC
100 Sunnyside Blvd Ste B (11797-2925)
PHONE..................516 677-0200
Fax: 516 349-9079
Edward Braun, President
Keith Johnson, President
Alan Kass, Business Mgr
Robert Oates, Exec VP
Bill Miller, Senior VP
EMP: 230
SALES (corp-wide): 332.4MM Publicly Held
WEB: www.veeco.com
SIC: 3826 3823 Analytical instruments; industrial instrmnts msrmnt display/control process variable
PA: Veeco Instruments Inc.
1 Terminal Dr
Plainview NY 11803
516 677-0200

(G-17322)
WIN-HOLT EQUIPMENT CORP (PA)
Also Called: Win-Holt Equipment Group
20 Crossways Park Dr N # 205 (11797-2007)
PHONE..................516 222-0335
Fax: 516 222-0538
Jonathan J Holtz, CEO
Dominick Scarfogliero, President
Jason Womack, President
Courtney Guerrero, General Mgr
Jose Ponce, COO
▲ EMP: 45
SQ FT: 10,000
SALES (est): 83.7MM Privately Held
WEB: www.winholt.com
SIC: 2099 Food preparations

(G-17323)
WOODBURY SYSTEMS GROUP INC
30 Glenn Dr (11797-2104)
P.O. Box 346, Plainview (11803-0346)
PHONE..................516 364-2653
William L Fitzgerald, President
Deirdre Volpe, Vice Pres
EMP: 6
SALES: 792.5K Privately Held
WEB: www.woodsysgrp.com
SIC: 7372 Prepackaged software

Woodhaven
Queens County

(G-17324)
JO-VIN DECORATORS INC
9423 Jamaica Ave (11421-2287)
PHONE..................718 441-9350
Fax: 718 441-1447
Vincent Pappalando, Ch of Bd
Annamarie Silbersweig, Manager
Leo Pappalardo, Admin Sec
EMP: 40 EST: 1956
SQ FT: 20,000
SALES (est): 4.7MM Privately Held
WEB: www.jo-vin.com
SIC: 2391 2299 2392 2394 Curtains & draperies; tops & top processing, man-made or other fiber; bedspreads & bed sets: made from purchased materials; shades, canvas: made from purchased materials

(G-17325)
LATINO SHOW MAGAZINE INC
8025 88th Rd (11421-2423)
PHONE..................718 709-1151
Cesar Florez, Publisher
EMP: 5

GEOGRAPHIC SECTION

Woodside - Queens County (G-17352)

SALES (est): 216.8K Privately Held
SIC: 2721 Magazines: publishing & printing

(G-17326)
STEINDL CAST STONE CO INC
9107 76th St (11421-2817)
PHONE..................718 296-8530
John Steindl Jr, *President*
James Steindl, *Vice Pres*
EMP: 6 EST: 1928
SQ FT: 2,800
SALES: 500K Privately Held
WEB: www.steindlcaststone.com
SIC: 3272 Cast stone, concrete

Woodhull
Steuben County

(G-17327)
OWLETTS SAW MILLS
4214 Cook Rd (14898-9630)
PHONE..................607 525-6340
Walt Owlett, *Owner*
EMP: 5
SALES (est): 269.8K Privately Held
SIC: 2421 Sawmills & planing mills, general

Woodmere
Nassau County

(G-17328)
ALLIED PHARMACY PRODUCTS INC
544 Green Pl (11598-1923)
PHONE..................516 374-8862
Stuart Meadow, *Principal*
Donna Meadow, *VP Opers*
EMP: 5
SALES (est): 569.2K Privately Held
SIC: 2834 5047 Pharmaceutical preparations; medical & hospital equipment

(G-17329)
BENISHTY BROTHERS CORP
233 Mosher Ave (11598-1655)
PHONE..................646 339-9991
EMP: 5
SALES (est): 311.3K Privately Held
SIC: 3524 Lawn & garden mowers & accessories

(G-17330)
CINDERELLAS SWEETS LTD
Also Called: Shabtai Gourmet
874 Lakeside Dr (11598-1916)
PHONE..................516 374-7976
Cynthia Itzkowitz, *President*
Andrew Itzkowitz, *Vice Pres*
Sid Itzkowitz, *Prdtn Mgr*
EMP: 27
SALES (est): 1.3MM Privately Held
SIC: 2051 Bakery: wholesale or wholesale/retail combined

(G-17331)
GLASGOW PRODUCTS INC
886 Lakeside Dr (11598-1916)
PHONE..................516 374-5937
Fax: 516 561-8891
Paul J Glasgow, *President*
Dorothy Glasgow, *Treasurer*
EMP: 25
SQ FT: 3,000
SALES (est): 3.4MM Privately Held
WEB: www.glasgowproducts.com
SIC: 3535 8711 Conveyors & conveying equipment; consulting engineer

(G-17332)
SPANCRAFT LTD
920 Railroad Ave (11598-1697)
PHONE..................516 295-0055
Fax: 516 569-3333
Philip A Engel, *President*
Steven Engel, *Vice Pres*
◆ EMP: 10

SALES (est): 1.1MM Privately Held
WEB: www.spancraft.com
SIC: 2519 Household furniture, except wood or metal: upholstered

Woodridge
Sullivan County

(G-17333)
PROFESSIONAL CAB DETAILING CO
Also Called: Procab
Navograrsky Rd (12789)
P.O. Box 727 (12789-0727)
PHONE..................845 436-7282
Keith Bahr-Tioson, *Owner*
EMP: 10
SQ FT: 15,000
SALES (est): 600K Privately Held
WEB: www.procab.com
SIC: 2511 2431 Kitchen & dining room furniture; millwork

Woodside
Queens County

(G-17334)
A SUNSHINE GLASS & ALUMINUM
2901 Brooklyn Queens Expy (11377-1242)
PHONE..................718 932-8080
Fax: 718 932-6028
Scong Lee, *Principal*
Chris Lee, *Manager*
Justin Lee, *Manager*
Julie Kim, *Admin Sec*
▲ EMP: 20
SALES (est): 1.5MM Privately Held
SIC: 3211 5023 Flat glass; glassware

(G-17335)
AIREACTOR INC
6110 Laurel Hill Blvd (11377-5864)
PHONE..................718 326-2433
Fax: 718 326-7179
Ralph Landano, *President*
Paul Pizem, *Manager*
▲ EMP: 12 EST: 1926
SQ FT: 8,000
SALES (est): 2.4MM Privately Held
WEB: www.aireactor.com
SIC: 2842 7699 Specialty cleaning, polishes & sanitation goods; specialty cleaning preparations; deodorants, nonpersonal; miscellaneous building item repair services

(G-17336)
BALDWIN RIBBON & STAMPING CORP
3956 63rd St (11377-3649)
PHONE..................718 335-6700
Fax: 718 478-3449
Ronald Steinberg, *President*
EMP: 15 EST: 1946
SQ FT: 5,000
SALES (est): 2MM Privately Held
SIC: 2399 Emblems, badges & insignia; military insignia

(G-17337)
BIELECKY BROS INC (PA)
5022 72nd St (11377-6084)
PHONE..................718 424-4764
Edwood Bielecky, *President*
Ray Hassan, *Controller*
Anthony Malkun, *Sales Staff*
Peter Bielecky, *Admin Sec*
EMP: 22
SQ FT: 24,000
SALES: 3.3MM Privately Held
WEB: www.bieleckybrothers.com
SIC: 2519 Rattan furniture: padded or plain; wicker & rattan furniture

(G-17338)
C & T TOOL & INSTRUMENT CO
Also Called: C&T Tool & Instrmnt
4125 58th St (11377-4748)
PHONE..................718 429-1253

Constantine Tsamis, *Chairman*
EMP: 24
SQ FT: 1,690
SALES (est): 2.2MM Privately Held
SIC: 3599 3542 3444 3441 Machine shop, jobbing & repair; machine tools, metal forming type; sheet metalwork; fabricated structural metal

(G-17339)
C L PRECISION MACHINE & TL CO
5015 70th St (11377-6020)
PHONE..................718 651-8475
Fax: 718 651-8475
George Lolis, *President*
EMP: 5 EST: 1967
SQ FT: 1,200
SALES: 250K Privately Held
SIC: 3599 Machine shop, jobbing & repair

(G-17340)
CAR-GO INDUSTRIES INC (PA)
5007 49th St (11377-7335)
PHONE..................718 472-1443
Drori Benman, *President*
EMP: 8
SQ FT: 5,000
SALES (est): 9.3MM Privately Held
SIC: 3714 Motor vehicle parts & accessories

(G-17341)
CODY PRINTING CORP
3728 56th St (11377-2438)
PHONE..................718 651-8854
Kyu Hwang, *CEO*
Kyung Shin, *President*
EMP: 9
SQ FT: 3,000
SALES (est): 990K Privately Held
WEB: www.codyprinting.com
SIC: 2752 Commercial printing, lithographic

(G-17342)
DAMIANOU SPORTSWEAR INC
6001 31st Ave Ste 2 (11377-1205)
PHONE..................718 204-5600
Fax: 718 204-5081
Paul Damianou, *President*
Pat Damianou, *Corp Secy*
Elenitsa Damianou, *Vice Pres*
DOE Chand, *Controller*
EMP: 62
SQ FT: 24,000
SALES (est): 5.5MM Privately Held
SIC: 2335 Women's, juniors' & misses' dresses

(G-17343)
DOMOTECK INTERIORS INC
2430 Brooklyn Queens Expy # 1 (11377-7825)
PHONE..................718 433-4300
Fax: 718 433-4301
Raja Mustafa, *President*
Konstantinos Mabrikos, *Vice Pres*
Angela Mathews, *Manager*
EMP: 5
SQ FT: 5,000
SALES: 500K Privately Held
SIC: 1411 Limestone & marble dimension stone; argillite, dimension-quarrying

(G-17344)
ECUADOR NEWS INC
6403 Roosevelt Ave Fl 2 (11377-3643)
PHONE..................718 205-7014
Fax: 718 205-2250
Edgar Arboleda, *President*
Marcelo Arboleda, *Exec Dir*
EMP: 15
SALES (est): 570K Privately Held
WEB: www.ecuadornews.net
SIC: 2711 Newspapers

(G-17345)
FIRECOM INC (PA)
Also Called: Bio Service
3927 59th St (11377-3435)
PHONE..................718 899-6100
Paul Mendez, *Ch of Bd*
Howard Kogan, *COO*
Howard L Kogen, *COO*
Antoine J Sayour, *Senior VP*

Dale Fergus, *Vice Pres*
EMP: 130 EST: 1978
SQ FT: 16,000
SALES (est): 53.7MM Privately Held
SIC: 3669 1799 Fire detection systems, electric; fire escape installation

(G-17346)
FIRST LINE PRINTING INC
3728 56th St (11377-2438)
PHONE..................718 606-0860
Sergio Torres, *President*
EMP: 10
SQ FT: 10,000
SALES (est): 2.5MM Privately Held
SIC: 2752 Commercial printing, lithographic

(G-17347)
FURNITURE DSIGN BY KNOSSOS INC
2430 Bklyn Qns Expy Ste 3 (11377-7825)
PHONE..................718 729-0404
Steve Tepelidis, *Ch of Bd*
George Despo, *President*
Satyabrata Chowdhury, *Bookkeeper*
EMP: 24
SQ FT: 23,185
SALES: 2.5MM Privately Held
SIC: 2499 Decorative wood & woodwork

(G-17348)
GENESIS ELECTRICAL MOTORS
Also Called: Genesis Electl Motor
6010 32nd Ave (11377-2019)
PHONE..................718 274-7030
Hercules Minnelli, *President*
Beatrice Minnelli, *Corp Secy*
EMP: 5
SQ FT: 4,000
SALES (est): 864.9K Privately Held
SIC: 7694 Electric motor repair

(G-17349)
GLOBE ELECTRONIC HARDWARE INC
3424 56th St (11377-2122)
P.O. Box 770727 (11377-0727)
PHONE..................718 457-0303
Caroline Dennehy, *President*
Paul Murphy, *COO*
M Dennehy, *Vice Pres*
Patrick M Dennehy, *Vice Pres*
EMP: 14 EST: 1976
SQ FT: 8,800
SALES (est): 930K Privately Held
WEB: www.globelectronics.com
SIC: 3451 5072 Screw machine products; hardware

(G-17350)
INTERNATIONAL CREATIVE MET INC
Also Called: I C M
3728 61st St (11377-2538)
P.O. Box 770661 (11377-0661)
PHONE..................718 424-8179
Setrak Onnik Agonian, *President*
▼ EMP: 14
SQ FT: 8,000
SALES (est): 1.2MM Privately Held
WEB: www.icmetal.com
SIC: 3446 3599 Architectural metalwork; machine shop, jobbing & repair

(G-17351)
KETCHAM PUMP CO INC
3420 64th St (11377-2398)
PHONE..................718 457-0800
Fax: 718 672-1408
Stuart Hruska, *President*
B Tonry, *Manager*
EMP: 15 EST: 1903
SQ FT: 10,000
SALES (est): 3.5MM Privately Held
SIC: 3561 Pumps & pumping equipment

(G-17352)
KOKOROKO CORPORATION
Also Called: Kokoroko Bakery
4755 47th St (11377-6546)
PHONE..................718 433-4321
Ivonne D Penaherrera, *President*
EMP: 8

Woodside - Queens County

SALES (est): 631.8K **Privately Held**
SIC: 2051 Bakery: wholesale or wholesale/retail combined

(G-17353)
MC COY TOPS AND INTERIORS INC
Also Called: Mc Coy Tops and Covers
6914 49th Ave (11377-6002)
PHONE.................................718 458-5800
John Proimos, *President*
EMP: 8
SQ FT: 6,000
SALES (est): 740K **Privately Held**
SIC: 2399 2394 Seat covers, automobile; convertible tops, canvas or boat: from purchased materials

(G-17354)
METALOCKE INDUSTRIES INC
3202 57th St (11377-1919)
PHONE.................................718 267-9200
Fax: 718 267-9300
Tom Sadi, *President*
Tanveer Sadiq, *Vice Pres*
Ramona Sadig, *Asst Office Mgr*
EMP: 6 **EST:** 1936
SQ FT: 10,000
SALES (est): 630K **Privately Held**
SIC: 2431 Doors & door parts & trim, wood

(G-17355)
METRO MACHINING & FABRICATING
3234 61st St (11377-2030)
PHONE.................................718 545-0104
Nicholas Dorazio, *President*
EMP: 7
SALES (est): 570K **Privately Held**
SIC: 3599 Machine shop, jobbing & repair

(G-17356)
MULTI TECH ELECTRIC
2526 50th St (11377-7823)
PHONE.................................718 606-2695
Mario Torres, *Vice Pres*
Laurie Torres, *Administration*
EMP: 10
SALES (est): 921.7K **Privately Held**
SIC: 3699 Electrical equipment & supplies

(G-17357)
NATIONAL ELEV CAB & DOOR CORP
Also Called: Necd
5315 37th Ave (11377-2474)
PHONE.................................718 478-5900
Fax: 718 478-0087
Harold Friedman, *CEO*
John Ferella, *President*
Jeffrey Friedman, *Exec VP*
George Karazim, *Plant Mgr*
Man Au-Yeung, *Engineer*
▲ **EMP:** 50 **EST:** 1930
SQ FT: 30,000
SALES (est): 16.8MM **Privately Held**
WEB: www.necd.com
SIC: 3534 Elevators & equipment

(G-17358)
NORTH AMERICAN MBL SYSTEMS INC
3354 62nd St (11377-2236)
PHONE.................................718 898-8700
Thomas Crowley, *President*
Connor Crowley, *Owner*
EMP: 33
SALES (est): 5.9MM **Privately Held**
SIC: 3663 Radio broadcasting & communications equipment

(G-17359)
NYC TRADE PRINTERS CORP
3245 62nd St (11377-2031)
PHONE.................................718 606-0610
Ely Toledo, *President*
Felix Toledo, *Manager*
EMP: 12
SQ FT: 5,000
SALES (est): 1.6MM **Privately Held**
SIC: 2711 Commercial printing & newspaper publishing combined

(G-17360)
ORTHOPEDIC TREATMENT FACILITY
4906 Queens Blvd (11377-4462)
PHONE.................................718 898-7326
Gary Marano, *President*
Anthony Marano, *Vice Pres*
EMP: 8
SQ FT: 2,800
SALES (est): 700K **Privately Held**
SIC: 3842 Limbs, artificial; braces, orthopedic

(G-17361)
PACEMAKER PACKAGING CORP
7200 51st Rd (11377-7631)
PHONE.................................718 458-1188
Fax: 718 429-2907
Emil Romotzki, *President*
Michele Romotzki, *Manager*
Helga Romotzki, *Admin Sec*
EMP: 10 **EST:** 1964
SQ FT: 7,000
SALES (est): 1.8MM **Privately Held**
SIC: 3565 Packaging machinery

(G-17362)
PFEIL & HOLING INC
5815 Northern Blvd (11377-2297)
PHONE.................................718 545-4600
Sy Stricker, *President*
David Gordils, *General Mgr*
Margo Stricker, *Corp Secy*
◆ **EMP:** 75 **EST:** 1923
SQ FT: 50,000
SALES (est): 13.3MM **Privately Held**
WEB: www.cakedeco.com
SIC: 2064 5046 5999 Cake ornaments, confectionery; bakery equipment & supplies; cake decorating supplies

(G-17363)
PIEMONTE HOME MADE RAVIOLI CO (PA)
Also Called: Piemonte Company
3436 65th St (11377-2329)
PHONE.................................718 429-1972
Fax: 718 429-6076
Mario Bertorelli, *President*
Flavio Bertorelli, *Vice Pres*
▲ **EMP:** 16 **EST:** 1945
SQ FT: 14,000
SALES (est): 1.6MM **Privately Held**
WEB: www.piemonteravioli.com
SIC: 2098 5812 Macaroni products (e.g. alphabets, rings & shells), dry; noodles (e.g. egg, plain & water), dry; spaghetti, dry; eating places

(G-17364)
PLAYBILL INCORPORATED
3715 61st St (11377-2593)
PHONE.................................718 335-4033
Lewis Cole, *Finance Other*
Laura Goldman, *Manager*
EMP: 20
SALES (corp-wide): 21.6MM **Privately Held**
SIC: 2789 Bookbinding & repairing: trade, edition, library, etc.
PA: Playbill Incorporated
729 7th Ave Fl 4
New York NY 10019
212 557-5757

(G-17365)
RE 99 CENTS INC
4905 Roosevelt Ave (11377-4457)
PHONE.................................718 639-2325
EMP: 6 **EST:** 2009
SALES (est): 492.6K **Privately Held**
SIC: 3643 Mfg Conductive Wiring Devices

(G-17366)
RED WHITE & BLUE ENTPS CORP
3443 56th St (11377-2121)
PHONE.................................718 565-8080
Vasilios Katranis, *President*
EMP: 5
SALES (est): 634.2K **Privately Held**
SIC: 2521 5712 2541 2434 Wood office filing cabinets & bookcases; customized furniture & cabinets; table or counter tops, plastic laminated; wood kitchen cabinets

(G-17367)
ROBERT-MASTERS CORP
3217 61st St (11377-2029)
PHONE.................................718 545-1030
Roberto C Orellana, *President*
▲ **EMP:** 7
SQ FT: 10,000
SALES (est): 1MM **Privately Held**
SIC: 3442 Rolling doors for industrial buildings or warehouses, metal

(G-17368)
SAFEWORKS LLC
Also Called: Spider
3030 60th St Ste 1 (11377-1234)
PHONE.................................800 696-5577
Fax: 718 326-9835
Valerie Pierce, *Owner*
David Herdrich, *Manager*
EMP: 18
SALES (corp-wide): 2B **Privately Held**
WEB: www.safeworks.com
SIC: 3446 7629 7353 Scaffolds, mobile or stationary: metal; electrical equipment repair, high voltage; heavy construction equipment rental
HQ: Safeworks, Llc
365 Upland Dr
Tukwila WA 98188
206 575-6445

(G-17369)
SPAETH DESIGN INC
6006 37th Ave (11377-2541)
PHONE.................................718 606-9685
Sandra L Spaeth, *President*
David Spaeth, *Chairman*
Dorothy Spaeth, *Corp Secy*
Tim Scalia, *Controller*
Andrea Bradin, *Manager*
▲ **EMP:** 35 **EST:** 1945
SQ FT: 27,000
SALES (est): 7.6MM **Privately Held**
WEB: www.spaethdesign.com
SIC: 2653 Display items, corrugated: made from purchased materials

(G-17370)
SPECTRUM ON BROADWAY
6106 34th Ave (11377-2228)
PHONE.................................718 932-5388
Fax: 718 932-0150
Harvey Brooks, *President*
Michael Gyscek, *Vice Pres*
Joseph Morra, *Vice Pres*
EMP: 12
SALES (est): 1.9MM **Privately Held**
WEB: www.spectrumsignsinc.com
SIC: 3993 Signs & advertising specialties

(G-17371)
SPECTRUM SIGNS INC
6106 34th Ave (11377-2228)
PHONE.................................631 756-1010
Harvey Brooks, *President*
Michael Gyscek, *Vice Pres*
Joseph Morra, *Vice Pres*
Joseph Dimaggio, *VP Human Res*
EMP: 45
SQ FT: 20,000
SALES (est): 5.7MM **Privately Held**
SIC: 3993 Electric signs; signs, not made in custom sign painting shops

(G-17372)
STAINLESS METALS INC
6001 31st Ave Ste 1 (11377-1205)
PHONE.................................718 784-1454
Fred Meier, *President*
Dan Meier, *Vice Pres*
EMP: 11 **EST:** 1927
SQ FT: 14,000
SALES (est): 1.4MM **Privately Held**
WEB: www.stainlessmetals.com
SIC: 3443 3431 Tanks, standard or custom fabricated: metal plate; sinks: enameled iron, cast iron or pressed metal

(G-17373)
SUPER-TEK PRODUCTS INC
2544 Borough Pl (11377-7815)
PHONE.................................718 278-7900
Fax: 718 204-6013
Dianne Herbert, *General Mgr*
Harry Paullison, *General Mgr*
John Garuti Jr, *Chairman*
Luis Aguirre, *Business Mgr*
Harry Paulson, *Vice Pres*
▲ **EMP:** 45 **EST:** 1959
SQ FT: 45,000
SALES (est): 14.4MM **Privately Held**
WEB: www.super-tek.com
SIC: 2891 Adhesives & sealants; epoxy adhesives; adhesives, plastic

(G-17374)
SYNERGX SYSTEMS INC (HQ)
3927 59th St (11377-3435)
PHONE.................................516 433-4700
Paul Mendez, *President*
Denise Hajek, *Purch Agent*
John A Poserina, *CFO*
Chris Anzalone, *Sales Mgr*
Vincent Milanesi, *Sales Mgr*
EMP: 89
SQ FT: 16,400
SALES (est): 18.8MM
SALES (corp-wide): 53.7MM **Privately Held**
WEB: www.synergxsystems.com
SIC: 3669 7382 Emergency alarms; fire alarm apparatus, electric; fire detection systems, electric; transportation signaling devices; security systems services; burglar alarm maintenance & monitoring
PA: Firecom, Inc.
3927 59th St
Woodside NY 11377
718 899-6100

(G-17375)
UTLEYS INCORPORATED
3123 61st St (11377-1222)
PHONE.................................718 956-1661
Fax: 718 956-4414
George Utley III, *President*
John Utley, *Vice Pres*
Jane DOE, *Admin Asst*
EMP: 45
SQ FT: 6,500
SALES: 7MM **Privately Held**
WEB: www.utleys.com
SIC: 3565 Packaging machinery

(G-17376)
VERNON PLATING WORKS INC
3318 57th St (11377-2298)
PHONE.................................718 639-1124
Fax: 718 639-1124
Kenneth Abrahami, *CEO*
Alan Hyman, *President*
EMP: 15
SQ FT: 20,000
SALES (est): 1.2MM **Privately Held**
SIC: 3471 Electroplating of metals or formed products

Woodstock
Ulster County

(G-17377)
BIG INDIE - BEAUTIFUL BOY LLC (PA) ✪
41 Plochmann Ln (12498-1615)
PHONE.................................917 464-5599
Karl Hartman, *Executive*
Declan Baldwin,
EMP: 5 **EST:** 2017
SQ FT: 300
SALES (est): 733K **Privately Held**
SIC: 3861 Motion picture film

(G-17378)
CUSTOM PATCHES INC
1760 Glasco Tpke (12498-2120)
P.O. Box 22, Mount Marion (12456-0022)
PHONE.................................845 679-6320
Sophia Preza, *President*
Kari Gilbert, *Manager*
EMP: 35
SALES: 500K **Privately Held**
SIC: 2395 Pleating & stitching

(G-17379)
INNOVATIVE PDTS OF AMER INC
Also Called: I P A
234 Tinker St (12498-1126)
PHONE.................................845 679-4500
Peter Vinci, *President*

GEOGRAPHIC SECTION

Yaphank - Suffolk County (G-17403)

Vince Mow, *President*
Shauna Perry, *Sls & Mktg Exec*
Jennifer Vinci, *Treasurer*
Razzaq Vinci, *Technician*
▲ **EMP:** 32
SQ FT: 18,000
SALES: 9.6MM **Privately Held**
WEB: www.ipatools.com
SIC: 3569 Lubrication equipment, industrial

(G-17380)
MARSHA FLEISHER
Also Called: Loominus Handwoven
18 Tinker St (12498-1233)
PHONE..................................845 679-6500
Marsha Fleisher, *Owner*
Andrea Rose, *General Mgr*
EMP: 10
SALES (est): 786.4K **Privately Held**
SIC: 2282 5632 2211 Weaving yarn: throwing & twisting; women's accessory & specialty stores; broadwoven fabric mills, cotton

(G-17381)
ROTRON INCORPORATED (HQ)
Also Called: Ametek Rotron
55 Hasbrouck Ln (12498-1894)
PHONE..................................845 679-2401
Fax: 845 679-1870
Robert J Vogel, *President*
Michael Denicola, *Vice Pres*
Kenneth Berryann, *Mfg Staff*
Steve Johnson, *Purchasing*
Matthew Clark, *Engineer*
▲ **EMP:** 300
SQ FT: 110,000
SALES (est): 225.1MM
SALES (corp-wide): 3.8B **Publicly Held**
WEB: www.rotronmilaero.com
SIC: 3564 Blowers & fans
PA: Ametek, Inc.
  1100 Cassatt Rd
  Berwyn PA 19312
  610 647-2121

(G-17382)
ROTRON INCORPORATED
Also Called: Ametek Rotron
9 Hasbrouck Ln (12498)
PHONE..................................845 679-2401
Charles Lohwasser, *Principal*
EMP: 44
SALES (corp-wide): 3.8B **Publicly Held**
SIC: 3564 Blowers & fans
HQ: Rotron Incorporated
  55 Hasbrouck Ln
  Woodstock NY 12498
  845 679-2401

Woodville
Jefferson County

(G-17383)
RURAL HILL SAND AND GRAV CORP
10262 County Route 79 (13650-2028)
P.O. Box 128, Belleville (13611-0128)
PHONE..................................315 846-5212
Fax: 315 846-5033
David Staie, *President*
EMP: 12 **EST:** 1956
SQ FT: 1,000
SALES (est): 1.7MM **Privately Held**
SIC: 1442 3273 Construction sand mining; gravel mining; ready-mixed concrete

Wyandanch
Suffolk County

(G-17384)
A & D ENTRANCES LLC
105 Wyandanch Ave (11798-4441)
Rural Route 213-37 39th Ave, Bayside (11361)
PHONE..................................718 989-2441
David L Viteri, *President*
Kimberly Viteri, *Vice Pres*
Kimberly Matos, *Manager*
◆ **EMP:** 15

SALES (est): 3.9MM **Privately Held**
SIC: 3534 Elevators & equipment

(G-17385)
ACCRA SHEETMETAL LLC
1359 Straight Path (11798-4336)
P.O. Box 1219 (11798-0219)
PHONE..................................631 920-2087
Orlando Stokes,
EMP: 7
SQ FT: 4,000
SALES: 500K **Privately Held**
SIC: 3444 Sheet metalwork

(G-17386)
ADVANCE GRAFIX EQUIPMENT INC
150 Wyandanch Ave (11798-4436)
PHONE..................................917 202-4593
Bally Mohan, *President*
EMP: 4
SALES: 1.2MM **Privately Held**
SIC: 3555 Printing presses

(G-17387)
CANNOLI FACTORY INC
75 Wyandanch Ave (11798-4441)
PHONE..................................631 643-2700
Fax: 631 643-2777
Michael Zucaro, *President*
▲ **EMP:** 50
SQ FT: 30,000
SALES (est): 9.5MM **Privately Held**
SIC: 2051 5149 Pastries, e.g. danish: except frozen; bakery products

(G-17388)
COBBLESTONE BAKERY CORP
39 Wyandanch Ave (11798-4441)
PHONE..................................631 491-3777
Frank Laferlita, *CEO*
Michael Laferlita, *Admin Sec*
EMP: 40
SQ FT: 20,000
SALES (est): 797.2K **Privately Held**
SIC: 2053 Pies, bakery: frozen

(G-17389)
CORINTHIAN CAST STONE INC
115 Wyandanch Ave (11798-4441)
PHONE..................................631 920-2340
Jason Hirschhorn, *Ch of Bd*
Jason Duran, *Controller*
John Foy, *Marketing Staff*
▲ **EMP:** 47 **EST:** 1998
SQ FT: 20,000
SALES (est): 15.4MM **Privately Held**
WEB: www.corinthiancaststone.com
SIC: 3272 Stone, cast concrete

(G-17390)
ENTERPRISE CONTAINER LLC
44 Island Container Plz (11798-2200)
PHONE..................................631 253-4400
Edward Berkowitz, *Branch Mgr*
EMP: 20
SALES (corp-wide): 2.3MM **Privately Held**
SIC: 2653 Corrugated boxes, partitions, display items, sheets & pad; boxes, corrugated: made from purchased materials; pads, solid fiber: made from purchased materials
PA: Enterprise Container Llc
  575 N Midland Ave
  Saddle Brook NJ 07663
  201 797-7200

(G-17391)
ISLAND CONTAINER CORP
44 Island Container Plz (11798-2229)
PHONE..................................631 253-4400
Fax: 631 253-4410
Edward Berkowitz, *Ch of Bd*
Rochelle Berkowitz, *Corp Secy*
Gary Berkowitz, *Vice Pres*
Robert Jeffreys, *Vice Pres*
Richard Erario, *Safety Mgr*
EMP: 100 **EST:** 1956
SQ FT: 108,000
SALES (est): 26.4MM **Privately Held**
WEB: www.islandcontainer.com
SIC: 2653 Boxes, corrugated: made from purchased materials

(G-17392)
T G M PRODUCTS INC
90 Wyandanch Ave Unit E (11798-4458)
PHONE..................................631 491-0515
Thomas G Miller, *President*
EMP: 6
SALES (est): 610K **Privately Held**
SIC: 3841 Surgical instruments & apparatus

(G-17393)
WELD-BUILT BODY CO INC
276 Long Island Ave (11798-3199)
PHONE..................................631 643-9700
Fax: 631 491-4728
Joseph Milan, *President*
Diana Nelson, *Vice Pres*
Harry Brown, *Director*
EMP: 30 **EST:** 1949
SQ FT: 55,000
SALES (est): 2.1MM **Privately Held**
WEB: www.weldbuilt.com
SIC: 3713 Truck bodies (motor vehicles); car carrier bodies

Wynantskill
Rensselaer County

(G-17394)
CASCADES NEW YORK INC
148 Hudson River Rd (12198)
PHONE..................................518 238-1900
Amrio Plourde, *Principal*
EMP: 175
SALES (corp-wide): 2.9B **Privately Held**
SIC: 2679 Pressed fiber & molded pulp products except food products
HQ: Cascades New York Inc.
  1845 Emerson St
  Rochester NY 14606
  585 527-8110

Wyoming
Wyoming County

(G-17395)
AKA ENTERPRISES
164 Main St (14591-9703)
P.O. Box 58 (14591-0058)
PHONE..................................716 474-4579
Andy Kreutter, *Owner*
EMP: 20
SALES: 4MM **Privately Held**
SIC: 2434 Wood kitchen cabinets

(G-17396)
MARKIN TUBING LP (PA)
1 Markin Ln (14591)
P.O. Box 242 (14591-0242)
PHONE..................................585 495-6211
Maurice J Cunniffe, *Partner*
Allen I Skott, *Partner*
William Carter, *Partner*
John W Dyke, *Partner*
Brigitte Pennell, *Opers Mgr*
▲ **EMP:** 89
SQ FT: 250,000
SALES (est): 19.9MM **Privately Held**
SIC: 3317 Tubes, wrought: welded or lock joint

(G-17397)
MARKIN TUBING INC
Pearl Creek Rd (14591)
PHONE..................................585 495-6211
Fax: 585 495-6482
Barton P Dambra, *President*
Maurice Cunnife, *Chairman*
Arthur A Smith, *Vice Pres*
Gus Bertrand, *Opers Staff*
Matt Mess, *Opers Staff*
EMP: 150
SALES (est): 20.7MM **Privately Held**
WEB: www.markintubing.com
SIC: 3317 3312 Tubes, wrought: welded or lock joint; structural shapes & pilings, steel

(G-17398)
TEXAS BRINE COMPANY LLC
Also Called: Plant Office
1346 Saltvale Rd (14591-9511)
PHONE..................................585 495-6228
Ted Grabowski, *President*
Sandra Wilkinson, *Office Mgr*
Matt Slezak, *Manager*
EMP: 8
SALES (corp-wide): 305.1MM **Privately Held**
SIC: 2819 Brine
HQ: Texas Brine Company, Llc
  4800 San Felipe St
  Houston TX 77056
  713 877-2700

(G-17399)
TMP TECHNOLOGIES INC
Also Called: Advanced Rubber Products
6110 Lamb Rd (14591-9754)
PHONE..................................585 495-6231
Fax: 585 495-6526
Holly Mitchell, *General Mgr*
Eric Snyder, *Prdtn Mgr*
Susan Lee, *Purch Agent*
Robert Flowers, *Manager*
Sally Scully, *Receptionist*
EMP: 60
SALES (corp-wide): 19.7MM **Privately Held**
WEB: www.tmptech.com
SIC: 3069 Medical & laboratory rubber sundries & related products
PA: Tmp Technologies, Inc.
  1200 Northland Ave
  Buffalo NY 14215
  716 895-6100

Yaphank
Suffolk County

(G-17400)
AARCO PRODUCTS INC
21 Old Dock Rd (11980-9734)
PHONE..................................631 924-5461
Fax: 631 924-5843
George M Demartino, *Ch of Bd*
Theresa Ben AVI, *Accounts Mgr*
Deanna Freeman, *Admin Asst*
David Ciancio, *Administration*
Scott Schillinger, *Administration*
▲ **EMP:** 15 **EST:** 1975
SQ FT: 10,000
SALES (est): 3.9MM **Privately Held**
WEB: www.aarcoproducts.com
SIC: 2493 2542 Bulletin boards, wood; office & store showcases & display fixtures

(G-17401)
ALTERNATIVE SERVICE INC
111 Old Dock Rd (11980-9613)
PHONE..................................631 345-9500
Russell Drake, *President*
John Cochrane, *Vice Pres*
▲ **EMP:** 15
SQ FT: 15,000
SALES (est): 1.4MM **Privately Held**
SIC: 3444 5084 7699 3541 Sheet metalwork; industrial machine parts; industrial machinery & equipment repair; machine tools, metal cutting type

(G-17402)
AMERICAN ELECTRONIC PRODUCTS
Also Called: A E P
86 Horseblock Rd Unit F (11980-9743)
PHONE..................................631 924-1299
Fax: 631 924-5910
Robert Gazza, *President*
Warren Azzinaro, *Vice Pres*
EMP: 15
SQ FT: 6,000
SALES (est): 2.2MM **Privately Held**
SIC: 2899 Ink or writing fluids

(G-17403)
CABLES UNLIMITED INC
3 Old Dock Rd (11980-9702)
PHONE..................................631 563-6363
Darren Clark, *President*
Scott Johnson, *Manager*

EMP: 40
SQ FT: 12,000
SALES: 7.5MM
SALES (corp-wide): 30.2MM **Publicly Held**
WEB: www.cables-unlimited.com
SIC: 3679 5063 Harness assemblies for electronic use: wire or cable; electronic wire & cable
PA: Rf Industries, Ltd.
7610 Miramar Rd Ste 6000
San Diego CA 92126
858 549-6340

(G-17404)
CHIPLOGIC INC
14a Old Dock Rd (11980-9701)
PHONE................................631 617-6317
Harry Perry, *President*
Carmen Ramos, *QC Mgr*
Mamie Perweiler, *Manager*
EMP: 10
SQ FT: 3,500
SALES (est): 1.5MM **Privately Held**
SIC: 3679 Electronic circuits

(G-17405)
COSA XENTAUR CORPORATION (PA)
84 Horseblock Rd Unit G (11980-9742)
PHONE................................631 345-3434
Fax: 631 924-7337
Christoph Mueller, *CEO*
W Craig Allshouse, *President*
Kortney Cocchiaro, *Export Mgr*
Michael Schlitz, *Mfg Staff*
Sharon Cannarella, *Purch Agent*
◆ EMP: 30 EST: 1969
SQ FT: 4,500
SALES (est): 12.5MM **Privately Held**
WEB: www.cosa-instrument.com
SIC: 3823 Computer interface equipment for industrial process control

(G-17406)
EMS DEVELOPMENT CORPORATION (DH)
Also Called: Ultra Electronics, Ems
95 Horseblock Rd Unit 2 (11980-2301)
PHONE................................631 924-4736
Fax: 631 345-6216
Peter A Crawford, *President*
Charles Coakley, *Plant Mgr*
Carol Haunstein, *QC Mgr*
Chris Geraghty, *Engineer*
Mike Ravel, *Engineer*
▲ EMP: 60 EST: 1972
SQ FT: 60,000
SALES (est): 22.1MM
SALES (corp-wide): 967.3MM **Privately Held**
WEB: www.ultra-ems.com
SIC: 3825 3613 3677 3621 Instruments to measure electricity; time switches, electrical switchgear apparatus; switchgear & switchgear accessories; electronic coils, transformers & other inductors; electric motor & generator parts; rectifiers (electrical apparatus)
HQ: Ultra Electronics Defense Inc.
4101 Smith School Rd
Austin TX 78744
512 327-6795

(G-17407)
EMS DEVELOPMENT CORPORATION
95 Horseblock Rd Unit 2a (11980-2301)
PHONE................................631 345-6200
Peter Crawford, *President*
EMP: 90
SALES (corp-wide): 967.3MM **Privately Held**
SIC: 3675 3677 3577 3612 Electronic capacitors; electronic coils, transformers & other inductors; computer peripheral equipment; power & distribution transformers
HQ: Ems Development Corporation
95 Horseblock Rd Unit 2
Yaphank NY 11980
631 924-4736

(G-17408)
EMTRON HYBRIDS INC
86 Horseblock Rd Unit G (11980-9743)
PHONE................................631 924-9668
Fax: 631 924-0637
Damian Emery, *President*
EMP: 20
SQ FT: 6,000
SALES (est): 2.8MM **Privately Held**
WEB: www.emtronhybrids.com
SIC: 3674 2396 Hybrid integrated circuits; automotive & apparel trimmings

(G-17409)
FRAMERICA CORPORATION
2 Todd Ct (11980-2101)
P.O. Box 699 (11980-0699)
PHONE................................631 650-1000
Eugene Eichner, *President*
Gordon Van Vechten, *Corp Secy*
Michael Filan, *Controller*
Catherine Michael, *Credit Mgr*
Todd Hranicka, *VP Sales*
◆ EMP: 100
SQ FT: 100,000
SALES (est): 32.9MM **Privately Held**
WEB: www.framerica.com
SIC: 2499 5023 Picture frame molding, finished; frames & framing, picture & mirror

(G-17410)
H B MILLWORK INC
9 Old Dock Rd (11980-9702)
PHONE................................631 924-4195
Fax: 631 924-1421
Timothy Hollowell, *Principal*
EMP: 6
SALES (corp-wide): 1.9MM **Privately Held**
WEB: www.hbmillwork.com
SIC: 2431 Millwork
PA: H B Millwork Inc
500 Long Island Ave
Medford NY 11763
631 289-8086

(G-17411)
L D FLECKEN INC
11 Old Dock Rd Unit 11 (11980-9622)
PHONE................................631 777-4881
Leo D Flecken, *President*
Debbie Siderine, *Office Mgr*
EMP: 13
SQ FT: 8,000
SALES (est): 1.5MM **Privately Held**
WEB: www.ldflecken.com
SIC: 3499 Metal household articles

(G-17412)
LYNTRONICS INC
7 Old Dock Rd Unit 1 (11980-9637)
PHONE................................631 205-1061
Fax: 631 205-1072
Anthony Vigliotti, *President*
EMP: 20
SQ FT: 12,000
SALES (est): 2.5MM **Privately Held**
SIC: 3679 5063 Harness assemblies for electronic use: wire or cable; batteries, dry cell

(G-17413)
MAHARAM FABRIC CORPORATION
74 Horseblock Rd (11980-9757)
PHONE................................631 582-3434
EMP: 6
SALES (corp-wide): 2.2B **Publicly Held**
WEB: www.maharam.com
SIC: 2221 Automotive fabrics, manmade fiber
HQ: Maharam Fabric Corporation
74 Horseblock Rd
Yaphank NY 11980
631 582-3434

(G-17414)
NANOPROBES INC
95 Horseblock Rd Unit 1 (11980-2301)
PHONE................................631 205-9490
Fax: 631 205-9493
James Hainfeld, *President*
Wenqiu Liu, *General Mgr*
Fred Furuya, *Vice Pres*
Cat Hainfeld, *Mktg Dir*
Victoria Kowalski, *Admin Asst*
EMP: 14
SALES: 250K **Privately Held**
WEB: www.nanoprobes.com
SIC: 2836 Biological products, except diagnostic

(G-17415)
RUGA GRINDING & MFG CORP
84 Horseblock Rd Unit A (11980-9742)
PHONE................................631 924-5067
Fax: 631 924-3091
Harry Gaenzle, *President*
Ronnie Ganzle, *Treasurer*
Joie Cascillo, *Admin Sec*
EMP: 8
SQ FT: 5,000
SALES (est): 881.1K **Privately Held**
SIC: 3599 Machine shop, jobbing & repair

(G-17416)
SCOTTS COMPANY LLC
Also Called: Vigliotti's Great Garden
445 Horseblock Rd (11980-9629)
PHONE................................631 289-7444
Fax: 631 289-1077
Charles Vigliotti, *President*
Richard Schwerer, *Manager*
Michelle Bunch, *Manager*
EMP: 20
SALES (corp-wide): 2.8B **Publicly Held**
WEB: www.licompost.com
SIC: 2875 5261 5083 2421 Compost; fertilizer; landscaping equipment; sawmills & planing mills, general
HQ: The Scotts Company Llc
14111 Scottslawn Rd
Marysville OH 43040
937 644-3729

(G-17417)
SEARLES GRAPHICS INC (PA)
56 Old Dock Rd (11980-9701)
PHONE................................631 345-2202
Fax: 631 345-0975
Kenneth Searles, *President*
Christine Searles, *Vice Pres*
Richard Searles, *Vice Pres*
Gary Lorandini, *Prdtn Mgr*
Leigh Searles, *Treasurer*
EMP: 35
SALES (est): 4.5MM **Privately Held**
WEB: www.searlesgraphics.com
SIC: 2752 Commercial printing, offset

(G-17418)
SHAD INDUSTRIES INC
7 Old Dock Rd Unit 1 (11980-9637)
PHONE................................631 504-6028
Lenore A Veltry, *President*
EMP: 5
SALES (est): 457.1K **Privately Held**
SIC: 3692 Primary batteries, dry & wet

(G-17419)
SOKOLIN LLC (PA)
Also Called: Sokolin Wine
445 Sills Rd Unit K (11980)
PHONE................................631 537-4434
Fax: 631 537-4435
Marc Abbaticchio, *President*
BJ Calloway, *Senior VP*
Matt Nowakowski, *Vice Pres*
Daron Watson, *Sales Staff*
David Smydo, *Mng Member*
EMP: 26 EST: 1934
SQ FT: 15,000
SALES (est): 2.2MM **Privately Held**
SIC: 2084 Wines

(G-17420)
SWITCHES AND SENSORS INC
86 Horseblock Rd Unit J (11980-9743)
PHONE................................631 924-2167
Joe Calvitto, *President*
Rudolph Baldeo, *Engineer*
EMP: 10
SQ FT: 6,200
SALES (est): 1.5MM **Privately Held**
SIC: 3625 Switches, electronic applications

(G-17421)
TRIBOLOGY INC
Also Called: Tech Lube
35 Old Dock Rd (11980-9702)
PHONE................................631 345-3000
Fax: 631 345-3001
William Krause, *President*
Bruce Stebbins, *President*
Lee Day, *Sales Mgr*
Paul Anderson, *Mktg Dir*
Lori Nardello, *Director*
▲ EMP: 25
SQ FT: 21,000
SALES (est): 5.9MM **Privately Held**
WEB: www.techlube.com
SIC: 2992 2842 Lubricating oils & greases; specialty cleaning, polishes & sanitation goods

(G-17422)
TURBO PLASTICS CORP INC
18 Old Dock Rd 20 (11980-9701)
PHONE................................631 345-9768
Arthur Anderson, *President*
EMP: 15
SALES: 1.1MM **Privately Held**
SIC: 3089 Injection molding of plastics

(G-17423)
TWIN PANE INSULATED GL CO INC
86 Horseblock Rd Unit D (11980-9743)
P.O. Box 279 (11980-0279)
PHONE................................631 924-1060
Fax: 631 924-1096
William F Willett, *President*
Rachel Willett, *Treasurer*
Marjorie Mayor, *Officer*
EMP: 15
SQ FT: 11,000
SALES (est): 3.1MM **Privately Held**
SIC: 3211 5039 Construction glass; glass construction materials

(G-17424)
W J ALBRO MACHINE WORKS INC
Also Called: Albro Gear & Instrument
86 Horseblock Rd Unit L (11980-9743)
PHONE................................631 345-0657
Fax: 631 345-0663
Kevin Albro, *President*
William Albro, *Vice Pres*
William Ambro Jr, *Treasurer*
EMP: 9
SQ FT: 2,000
SALES: 775K **Privately Held**
SIC: 3599 3728 3621 3566 Custom machinery; gears, aircraft power transmission; aircraft propellers & associated equipment; motors & generators; speed changers, drives & gears; iron & steel forgings

(G-17425)
XENTAUR CORPORATION
84 Horseblock Rd Unit G (11980-9742)
PHONE................................631 345-3434
Fax: 631 345-5349
Christopher Mueller, *CEO*
Craig Allshouse, *President*
Laura Patanella, *Buyer*
Lewis Ayres, *Engineer*
Brian Flanagan, *Engineer*
EMP: 23
SALES (est): 5.7MM **Privately Held**
WEB: www.xentaur.com
SIC: 3823 Industrial instrmnts msrmnt display/control process variable

Yonkers
Westchester County

(G-17426)
ALETEIA USA INC
86 Main St Ste 303 (10701-8805)
PHONE................................914 502-1855
Axel D'Epinay, *CFO*
EMP: 5
SQ FT: 900
SALES (est): 143.5K **Privately Held**
SIC: 2741

(G-17427)
ALLCOM ELECTRIC CORP
104 Crescent Pl (10704-2519)
PHONE................................914 803-0433
Anna Protosanousis, *Principal*

GEOGRAPHIC SECTION

Yonkers - Westchester County (G-17453)

EMP: 7 **EST:** 2009
SALES: 1MM **Privately Held**
SIC: 3699 Electrical equipment & supplies

(G-17428)
ALPHA-EN CORPORATION
28 Wells Ave Ste 2 (10701-7045)
PHONE..................914 418-2000
Jerry I Feldman, *Ch of Bd*
Steven M Payne, *President*
George McKeegan, *Exec VP*
Emilie Bodoin, *Director*
EMP: 15 **EST:** 1997
SQ FT: 4,000
SALES (est): 2.5MM **Privately Held**
SIC: 2819 6794 Lithium compounds, inorganic; patent buying, licensing, leasing

(G-17429)
ALTMAN STAGE LIGHTING CO INC
Also Called: Altman Lighting
57 Alexander St (10701-2714)
PHONE..................914 476-7987
Fax: 914 966-1980
Robert Altman, *Ch of Bd*
Dwarak Parvatum, *COO*
Susan Fry, *Exec VP*
Randall Altman, *Vice Pres*
Derek Lubsen, *Vice Pres*
▲ **EMP:** 125 **EST:** 1953
SQ FT: 75,000
SALES (est): 44.7MM **Privately Held**
WEB: www.altmanlighting.com
SIC: 3648 3646 Stage lighting equipment; commercial indusl & institutional electric lighting fixtures

(G-17430)
AMERICAN CANVAS BINDERS CORP
430 Nepperhan Ave (10701-6601)
PHONE..................914 969-0300
Richard Maslowski, *President*
EMP: 6
SQ FT: 10,000
SALES (est): 412K **Privately Held**
SIC: 2241 Narrow fabric mills

(G-17431)
APF MANAGEMENT COMPANY LLC
60 Fullerton Ave (10704-1097)
PHONE..................914 665-5400
EMP: 110
SALES (est): 8.8MM **Privately Held**
SIC: 3231 Framed mirrors

(G-17432)
APF MANUFACTURING COMPANY LLC (PA)
Also Called: Apf Munn Master Frame Makers
60 Fullerton Ave (10704-1097)
PHONE..................914 963-6300
Oudit Harbhajan,
EMP: 30 **EST:** 2014
SQ FT: 52,000
SALES (est): 2MM **Privately Held**
SIC: 2499 3231 Picture & mirror frames, wood; framed mirrors

(G-17433)
ASR GROUP INTERNATIONAL INC (HQ)
1 Federal St (10705-1079)
P.O. Box 509 (10702-0509)
PHONE..................914 963-2400
Antonio Contreras Jr, *Co-President*
Antonio L Contreras Jr, *Co-President*
Luis Fernandez, *Co-President*
Gregory A Maitner, *Vice Pres*
Armando A Tabernilla, *Vice Pres*
◆ **EMP:** 250
SQ FT: 385,000
SALES (est): 95.1MM
SALES (corp-wide): 287.4MM **Privately Held**
WEB: www.tasrc.com
SIC: 2062 5149 Cane sugar refining; granulated cane sugar from purchased raw sugar or syrup; sugar, honey, molasses & syrups

PA: American Sugar Refining, Inc.
1 N Clematis St Ste 200
West Palm Beach FL 33401
561 366-5100

(G-17434)
BARRON METAL PRODUCTS INC
286 Nepperhan Ave (10701-3403)
PHONE..................914 965-1232
Richard Cleary, *President*
Robert Cleary, *Vice Pres*
EMP: 20
SQ FT: 15,000
SALES (est): 1.9MM **Privately Held**
SIC: 3544 3469 Special dies & tools; metal stampings

(G-17435)
BARTIZAN DATA SYSTEMS LLC
217 Riverdale Ave (10705-1131)
PHONE..................914 965-7977
Joanna Stasuk, *Mktg Dir*
Lewis C Hoff,
Elizabeth Mazei,
EMP: 25
SQ FT: 43,000
SALES (est): 1.5MM **Privately Held**
WEB: www.bartizan.com
SIC: 3555 Printing trades machinery; engraving machinery & equipment, except plates

(G-17436)
BELMAY HOLDING CORPORATION
Also Called: Scent 2 Market
1 Odell Plz Ste 123 (10701-6800)
PHONE..................914 376-1515
Fax: 914 376-1784
Theodore Kesten, *CEO*
Tim Fawcett, *Managing Dir*
Greg Banwer, *Vice Pres*
Eileen Hedrick, *Vice Pres*
Brent Pope, *Vice Pres*
▲ **EMP:** 25 **EST:** 1967
SQ FT: 26,000
SALES (est): 9.5MM **Privately Held**
WEB: www.belmay.com
SIC: 2844 Hair preparations, including shampoos

(G-17437)
BIOINS INC
1767 Central Park Ave # 258 (10710-2828)
PHONE..................646 398-3718
EMP: 10
SALES (est): 1.5MM **Privately Held**
SIC: 3821 Laboratory apparatus & furniture

(G-17438)
BRUCCI LTD
861 Nepperhan Ave (10703-2013)
PHONE..................914 965-0707
Fax: 914 965-1965
Murray Bober, *Ch of Bd*
Howard Marcus, *Vice Pres*
Allan Shapiro, *Treasurer*
EMP: 25
SQ FT: 10,800
SALES (est): 3.8MM **Privately Held**
SIC: 2844 5399 Cosmetic preparations; warehouse club stores

(G-17439)
CAROLINAS DESSERTS INC
1562 Central Park Ave (10710-6001)
PHONE..................914 779-4000
EMP: 8
SALES (est): 587.4K **Privately Held**
SIC: 2051 Bakery: wholesale or wholesale/retail combined

(G-17440)
CAROLYN RAY INC
578 Nepperhan Ave Ste C10 (10701-6670)
PHONE..................914 476-0619
Fax: 914 476-0677
Carolyn Ray, *President*
EMP: 6
SALES (est): 695.9K **Privately Held**
WEB: www.carolynray.com
SIC: 2261 Finishing plants, cotton

(G-17441)
CASA NUEVA CUSTOM FURNISHING
510 Nepperhan Ave (10701-6602)
PHONE..................914 476-2272
Fax: 914 476-0560
Antonio Figueroa, *President*
EMP: 7
SQ FT: 12,500
SALES (est): 1.2MM **Privately Held**
SIC: 3553 Furniture makers' machinery, woodworking

(G-17442)
CDNV WOOD CARVING FRAMES INC (PA)
498 Nepperhan Ave (10701-6604)
PHONE..................914 375-3447
Fax: 914 375-3726
Cristobal S Venegas, *President*
David Venegas, *Vice Pres*
▲ **EMP:** 18
SALES (est): 1.3MM **Privately Held**
WEB: www.cdnv.com
SIC: 2499 Picture & mirror frames, wood

(G-17443)
CEP TECHNOLOGIES CORPORATION (PA)
763 Saw Mill River Rd (10710-4001)
PHONE..................914 968-4100
Fax: 914 968-4151
Kenneth W Kaufman, *President*
Francine Kaufman, *Vice Pres*
Michael Wagner, *Vice Pres*
John Rossi, *Opers Mgr*
Peter Dubno, *Engineer*
▲ **EMP:** 40 **EST:** 1960
SQ FT: 22,000
SALES (est): 7.5MM **Privately Held**
SIC: 3469 Metal stampings

(G-17444)
CLOVER WIRE FORMING CO INC
1021 Saw Mill River Rd (10710-3292)
PHONE..................914 375-0400
Fax: 914 375-0406
George Margareten, *President*
▲ **EMP:** 30 **EST:** 1957
SQ FT: 35,000
SALES (est): 6.4MM **Privately Held**
WEB: www.cloverwire.com
SIC: 3496 3316 Miscellaneous fabricated wire products; cold finishing of steel shapes

(G-17445)
CONSUMER REPORTS INC (PA)
Also Called: Consumers Union
101 Truman Ave (10703-1044)
PHONE..................914 378-2000
Fax: 914 378-2904
Walter D Bristol, *Ch of Bd*
James Guest, *President*
Marta Tellado, *President*
Steve Findlay, *Managing Dir*
Jeff Bartlett, *Editor*
EMP: 400 **EST:** 1936
SQ FT: 180,000
SALES: 263MM **Privately Held**
SIC: 2741 2721 7389 Miscellaneous publishing; magazines: publishing only, not printed on site; fund raising organizations

(G-17446)
COSTELLO BROS PETROLEUM CORP (PA)
990 Mclean Ave Ste 3 (10704-4180)
PHONE..................914 237-3189
Fax: 914 237-1806
Frank Costello, *President*
Kristopher Costello, *Vice Pres*
EMP: 6
SQ FT: 1,200
SALES (est): 737.7K **Privately Held**
SIC: 2999 5983 Fuel briquettes & waxes; fuel oil dealers

(G-17447)
CREATIVE CABINETRY CORPORATION
42 Morsemere Pl (10701-1511)
PHONE..................914 963-6061
Karl Melnychuk, *President*

Francis Melnychuk, *Admin Sec*
EMP: 5
SQ FT: 6,000
SALES: 400K **Privately Held**
SIC: 2522 2521 Cabinets, office: except wood; cabinets, office: wood

(G-17448)
CREATIVE SOLUTIONS GROUP INC (PA)
Also Called: Diam International
555 Tuckahoe Rd (10710-5709)
PHONE..................914 771-4200
Edward Winder, *CEO*
Williaml Ecker, *Ch of Bd*
Jorg Niederhufner, *Opers Staff*
Lori Dvizac, *Purch Mgr*
▲ **EMP:** 500
SALES (est): 84.5MM **Privately Held**
WEB: www.diam-int.com
SIC: 3993 Displays & cutouts, window & lobby

(G-17449)
DALEE BOOKBINDING CO INC
Also Called: Creations In Canvas
129 Clinton Pl (10701-4719)
PHONE..................914 965-1660
Fax: 914 965-1802
David Hutter, *President*
Danae Carter, *Manager*
EMP: 16 **EST:** 1965
SQ FT: 12,000
SALES (est): 1MM **Privately Held**
WEB: www.daleebook.com
SIC: 2789 2782 Bookbinding & related work; blankbooks

(G-17450)
DAYLEEN INTIMATES INC
Also Called: Dominique Intimate Apparel
540 Nepperhan Ave (10701-6630)
PHONE..................914 969-5900
Mike Chernoff, *President*
▲ **EMP:** 24
SQ FT: 20,000
SALES (est): 6MM **Privately Held**
SIC: 2341 4225 Women's & children's undergarments; general warehousing & storage

(G-17451)
DIMAIO MILLWORK CORPORATION
12 Bright Pl (10705-1342)
PHONE..................914 476-1937
Ralph Dimaio Jr, *President*
Sal Fino, *Project Mgr*
Dom Capogna, *Prdtn Mgr*
Rosemary Perrone, *Bookkeeper*
EMP: 35
SQ FT: 20,000
SALES (est): 6.4MM **Privately Held**
WEB: www.dimaiomillwork.com
SIC: 2521 Wood office furniture

(G-17452)
DOLLAR POPULAR INC
473 S Broadway (10705-3249)
P.O. Box 312150, Jamaica (11431-2150)
PHONE..................914 375-0361
Muhammad Irfan, *Ch of Bd*
EMP: 9
SALES (est): 713.4K **Privately Held**
SIC: 3643 Outlets, electric: convenience

(G-17453)
DOMINO FOODS INC
Also Called: Domino Sugar
1 Federal St (10705-1079)
PHONE..................800 729-4840
Fax: 914 486-4486
Gregory H Smith, *Senior VP*
Laura Harkins, *Vice Pres*
Maria Machita, *Vice Pres*
Shane Deal, *Plant Mgr*
Stacey Shaefer, *Project Engr*
EMP: 12
SALES (corp-wide): 287.4MM **Privately Held**
SIC: 2062 Granulated cane sugar from purchased raw sugar or syrup
HQ: Domino Foods Inc
99 Wood Ave S Ste 901
Iselin NJ 08830
732 590-1173

Yonkers - Westchester County (G-17454)   **GEOGRAPHIC SECTION**

(G-17454)
ECKER WINDOW CORP
1 Odell Plz (10701-1402)
PHONE 914 776-0000
Fax: 914 776-0030
Robert Ecker, *CEO*
Jim De Koch, *Vice Pres*
Howard Ecker, *Vice Pres*
Bryce Evadne, *Manager*
Ebrahim Miandoabi, *Manager*
EMP: 100
SQ FT: 5,000
SALES (est): 22.3MM **Privately Held**
SIC: 2431 1751 Windows & window parts & trim, wood; window & door installation & erection

(G-17455)
ECONOCRAFT WORLDWIDE MFG INC
56 Worth St Frnt Unit (10701-5508)
PHONE 914 966-2280
Fax: 718 585-0788
Shlomo Malki, *President*
Eran Malki, *Vice Pres*
Amir Malki, *Admin Sec*
▼ **EMP:** 5
SQ FT: 27,000
SALES (est): 907.3K **Privately Held**
WEB: www.econocraft.com
SIC: 3589 Car washing machinery

(G-17456)
ELECTRONIC DEVICES INC (HQ)
Also Called: E D I
21 Gray Oaks Ave (10710-3205)
PHONE 914 965-4400
Fax: 914 965-5531
Jimmy Huang, *President*
Zhi Huang, *Exec VP*
Donald Bedell, *Vice Pres*
Steven Huang, *Vice Pres*
Henry Kolokowsky, *Vice Pres*
▲ **EMP:** 30
SQ FT: 45,000
SALES (est): 1.2MM **Privately Held**
WEB: www.edidiodes.com
SIC: 3674 5065 Rectifiers, solid state; diodes, solid state (germanium, silicon, etc.); solid state electronic devices; electronic parts & equipment
PA: North Technology Inc
    161 Tices Ln
    East Brunswick NJ 08816
    732 390-2828

(G-17457)
EMPIRE OPEN MRI
1915 Central Park Ave # 25 (10710-2949)
PHONE 914 961-1777
Michael Singer, *Owner*
EMP: 6
SALES (est): 485K **Privately Held**
SIC: 3845 Ultrasonic scanning devices, medical

(G-17458)
FABRIC CONCEPTS FOR INDUSTRY
Also Called: Awning Man, The
354 Ashburton Ave (10701-6014)
PHONE 914 375-2565
Fax: 914 375-1459
Daniel Burke, *President*
EMP: 17
SALES (est): 1.5MM **Privately Held**
SIC: 2394 Awnings, fabric: made from purchased materials

(G-17459)
FITZGERALD PUBLISHING CO INC
Also Called: Golden Legacy Ilstrd Histry
1853 Central Park Ave # 8 (10710-2948)
PHONE 914 793-5016
Bertram Fitzgerald, *President*
Jeanette Fitzgerald, *Vice Pres*
EMP: 5
SALES: 300K **Privately Held**
SIC: 2741 Miscellaneous publishing

(G-17460)
FLEETCOM INC
1081 Yonkers Ave (10704-3123)
PHONE 914 776-5582
Mike Rosenzweig, *President*
Joe Gomez, *Manager*
EMP: 15 **EST:** 1984
SALES (est): 1MM **Privately Held**
SIC: 3663 Radio broadcasting & communications equipment

(G-17461)
FOWLER ROUTE CO INC
25 Sunnyside Dr (10705-1763)
PHONE 917 653-4640
EMP: 17
SALES (corp-wide): 5.9MM **Privately Held**
SIC: 3582 Commercial laundry equipment
PA: Fowler Route Co., Inc.
    565 Rahway Ave
    Union NJ 07083
    908 686-3400

(G-17462)
GANNETT STLLITE INFO NTWRK INC
Also Called: Herald Statesman
1 Odell Plz (10701-1402)
PHONE 914 965-5000
Fax: 914 694-5382
John Gambrill, *Branch Mgr*
EMP: 50
SALES (corp-wide): 3B **Publicly Held**
WEB: www.usatoday.com
SIC: 2711 Newspapers: publishing only, not printed on site
HQ: Gannett Satellite Information Network, Llc
    7950 Jones Branch Dr
    Mc Lean VA 22102
    703 854-6000

(G-17463)
GLOBAL LIGHTING INC
201 Saw Mill River Rd 3 (10701-5711)
PHONE 914 591-4095
Nadeem Razi, *CEO*
EMP: 7 **EST:** 2003
SALES (est): 206.8K **Privately Held**
SIC: 3646 5063 Chandeliers, commercial; lighting fixtures

(G-17464)
GOLDEN RENEWABLE ENERGY LLC
700 Nepperhan Ave (10703-2312)
PHONE 914 920-9800
Franklin Canosa, *CFO*
Christina Vlassis, *Human Res Mgr*
Nicholas Canosa,
Jason Provost,
EMP: 5
SALES (est): 950K **Privately Held**
SIC: 2869 Fuels

(G-17465)
GOTHAM PEN CO INC
Also Called: Gotham Pen and Pencil
1 Roundtop Rd (10710-2327)
PHONE 212 675-7904
Fax: 718 294-6699
Marshall Futterman, *President*
▲ **EMP:** 22 **EST:** 1955
SQ FT: 15,000
SALES (est): 2.5MM **Privately Held**
SIC: 3951 3952 2796 Ball point pens & parts; pencils & pencil parts, mechanical; markers, soft tip (felt, fabric, plastic, etc.); pencils & leads, including artists'; engraving on copper, steel, wood or rubber: printing plates

(G-17466)
GRAPHITE METALLIZING CORP (PA)
Also Called: Graphalloy
1050 Nepperhan Ave (10703-1432)
PHONE 914 968-8400
Fax: 914 968-8468
Eben T Walker, *Ch of Bd*
Viridiana Bermejo, *Business Mgr*
Giovanni Loconte, *Plant Mgr*
Michael Haynes, *Mfg Spvr*
Akram Marjieh, *Project Engr*
◆ **EMP:** 94 **EST:** 1913
SQ FT: 95,000
SALES (est): 64.2MM **Privately Held**
WEB: www.graphalloy.com
SIC: 3624 Carbon & graphite products; brushes & brush stock contacts, electric

(G-17467)
GREYSTON BAKERY INC
104 Alexander St (10701-2535)
PHONE 914 375-1510
Fax: 914 375-1514
Michael Brady, *Ch of Bd*
Julius Walls, *President*
Joan Cotter, *Vice Pres*
Rodney Johnson, *Prdtn Mgr*
Joseph Mancini, *Opers Staff*
◆ **EMP:** 130
SQ FT: 10,000
SALES (est): 1.5MM
SALES (corp-wide): 1.8MM **Privately Held**
WEB: www.greystonbakery.com
SIC: 2051 Cakes, pies & pastries
PA: Greyston Foundation Inc.
    21 Park Ave
    Yonkers NY 10703
    914 376-3900

(G-17468)
HANA SHEET METAL INC
9 Celli Pl 11 (10701-4805)
P.O. Box 156, Atlantic Beach (11509-0156)
PHONE 914 377-0773
Awni A Hana, *Ch of Bd*
EMP: 8
SALES (est): 1.2MM **Privately Held**
SIC: 3444 Sheet metalwork

(G-17469)
HEMISPHERE NOVELTIES INC
167 Saw Mill River Rd 3c (10701-6621)
P.O. Box 1240 (10703-8240)
PHONE 914 378-4100
Fax: 914 378-4091
Max Wolfeld, *President*
Jeffrey Wolfeld, *Corp Secy*
◆ **EMP:** 25
SQ FT: 12,000
SALES (est): 3.6MM **Privately Held**
WEB: www.hemispherenovelties.com
SIC: 3172 3965 5091 5131 Personal leather goods; fasteners, buttons, needles & pins; fishing tackle; buttons; belt & buckle assembly kits

(G-17470)
HIGHER POWER INDUSTRIES INC
11 Sunny Slope Ter (10703-1714)
PHONE 914 709-9800
Anna Dibello Battista, *President*
Warren J Azzara Jr, *Principal*
EMP: 9
SALES (est): 571.4K **Privately Held**
SIC: 3312 3743 Locomotive wheels, rolled; industrial locomotives & parts; railroad locomotives & parts, electric or non-electric; tenders, locomotive

(G-17471)
HORNE ORGANIZATION INC (PA)
15 Arthur Pl (10701-1702)
PHONE 914 572-1330
Leon H Horne Jr, *President*
Jackie Arce, *Office Mgr*
EMP: 10
SQ FT: 1,500
SALES (est): 2.6MM **Privately Held**
SIC: 2752 7336 Commercial printing, lithographic; graphic arts & related design

(G-17472)
HUDSON SCENIC STUDIO INC (PA)
130 Fernbrook St (10705-1764)
PHONE 914 375-0900
Fax: 914 378-9134
Neil Mazzella, *CEO*
John C Boyd, *Vice Pres*
Joanne Veneziano, *Administration*
▲ **EMP:** 113
SQ FT: 56,000
SALES (est): 19MM **Privately Held**
WEB: www.hudsonscenic.com
SIC: 3999 Theatrical scenery

(G-17473)
ITR INDUSTRIES INC (PA)
441 Saw Mill River Rd (10701-4913)
PHONE 914 964-7063
Mario F Rolla, *Ch of Bd*
Adrienne Rola, *President*
Peter M Rolla, *President*
▲ **EMP:** 21
SALES (est): 195.7MM **Privately Held**
SIC: 3431 3429 3446 3088 Shower stalls, metal; manufactured hardware (general); architectural metalwork; shower stalls, fiberglass & plastic

(G-17474)
J KENDALL LLC
Also Called: J K Fertility
71 Belvedere Dr (10705-2813)
PHONE 646 739-4956
Fax: 718 634-0348
Julius K Smalls, *CEO*
EMP: 5
SALES (est): 370K **Privately Held**
SIC: 2759 Screen printing

(G-17475)
JENRAY PRODUCTS INC
252 Lake Ave Fl 2a (10701-5706)
PHONE 914 375-5596
Fax: 914 375-2096
Raymond D'Urso, *President*
▲ **EMP:** 26 **EST:** 1999
SQ FT: 22,000
SALES (est): 3.3MM **Privately Held**
SIC: 3999 Sprays, artificial & preserved

(G-17476)
KAWASAKI RAIL CAR INC (DH)
29 Wells Ave Bldg 4 (10701-8815)
PHONE 914 376-4700
Fax: 914 376-4779
Hiroji Iwasaki, *CEO*
Yuichi Yamamoto, *President*
Steven Vangellow, *General Mgr*
Yoshinori Kanehana, *Exec VP*
Mike Doyle, *Plant Mgr*
▲ **EMP:** 196
SQ FT: 28,000
SALES (est): 79.9MM
SALES (corp-wide): 13.3B **Privately Held**
SIC: 3743 Railroad equipment, except locomotives; railway motor cars; train cars & equipment, freight or passenger
HQ: Kawasaki Motors Manufacturing Corp., U.S.A.
    6600 Nw 27th St
    Lincoln NE 68524
    402 476-6600

(G-17477)
KIMBER MFG
1120 Saw Mill River Rd (10710-3229)
PHONE 914 721-8417
Leslie P Edelman, *President*
EMP: 7
SALES (est): 174K **Privately Held**
SIC: 3599 Industrial machinery

(G-17478)
KIMBER MFG INC
16 Harrison Ave (10705-2606)
PHONE 914 965-0753
Leslie Edelman, *Owner*
EMP: 5
SALES (corp-wide): 92.3MM **Privately Held**
SIC: 3599 Machine shop, jobbing & repair
PA: Kimber Mfg., Inc.
    1 Lawton St
    Yonkers NY 10705
    914 964-0771

(G-17479)
KIMBER MFG INC (PA)
1 Lawton St (10705-2617)
PHONE 914 964-0771
Fax: 914 964-8605
Leslie Edelmen, *Ch of Bd*
Abdool Jamal, *Managing Dir*
Ralph Karanian, *COO*
Doron Segal, *Vice Pres*
Robert Nemergut, *Mfg Dir*
▲ **EMP:** 220
SQ FT: 50,000

GEOGRAPHIC SECTION

Yonkers - Westchester County (G-17507)

SALES (est): 92.3MM **Privately Held**
WEB: www.kimbermfg.com
SIC: 3599 Machine shop, jobbing & repair

(G-17480)
LIGHTING BY DOM YONKERS INC
Also Called: Sparkle Light Manufacturing
253 S Broadway (10705-1351)
PHONE 914 968-8700
Fax: 914 968-8716
Dominick Di Gennaro Jr, *President*
Dominick Di Di Gennaro, *Personnel Exec*
EMP: 5 **EST:** 1979
SQ FT: 5,000
SALES (est): 640K **Privately Held**
SIC: 3646 Commercial indusl & institutional electric lighting fixtures

(G-17481)
M SANTOLIQUIDO CORP
Also Called: San Signs & Awnings
925 Saw Mill River Rd (10710-3238)
PHONE 914 375-6674
Fax: 914 375-6689
Michael Santoliquido, *President*
Lucille Santoliquido, *Vice Pres*
Lucille Liquido, *Director*
EMP: 11 **EST:** 1995
SQ FT: 10,000
SALES (est): 1.1MM **Privately Held**
WEB: www.sansigns.com
SIC: 3993 Signs & advertising specialties

(G-17482)
MAGNIFICAT INC
86 Main St Ste 303 (10701-8805)
P.O. Box 822 (10702-0822)
PHONE 914 502-1820
Gerber Contreras, *Opers Mgr*
Francois Piebo, *Accountant*
Claire Gilligan, *Assoc Editor*
Axel Depinay, *Info Tech Mgr*
Fleurus Mame,
▲ **EMP:** 18
SALES (est): 2.5MM
SALES (corp-wide): 1.6K **Privately Held**
SIC: 2721 Periodicals
PA: Magnificat Films
    10 Rue De Penthievre
    Paris

(G-17483)
MARBLE WORKS INC
660 Saw Mill River Rd (10710-4009)
PHONE 914 376-3653
Fax: 914 376-6938
Sabo Barmaksiz, *President*
Aldo Turelli, *General Mgr*
Rumeldo Turollis, *Manager*
▲ **EMP:** 30
SALES (est): 3.4MM **Privately Held**
SIC: 3281 Granite, cut & shaped; marble, building: cut & shaped

(G-17484)
MARPLEX FURNITURE CORPORATION
167 Saw Mill Rver Rd Fl 1 (10701)
PHONE 914 969-7755
Fax: 914 969-1200
Peter Bizzarro, *President*
EMP: 5
SQ FT: 13,000
SALES (est): 481.1K **Privately Held**
SIC: 2541 Display fixtures, wood

(G-17485)
MICROMOLD PRODUCTS INC
7 Odell Plz 133 (10701-1407)
PHONE 914 969-2850
Fax: 914 969-2736
Arthur Lukach, *Ch of Bd*
Justin Lukach, *President*
Frank Pino, *Human Resources*
Tricia Lombardo, *Sales Staff*
Monique Nunn, *Sales Staff*
EMP: 25 **EST:** 1954
SQ FT: 13,000
SALES (est): 5.3MM **Privately Held**
WEB: www.micromold.com
SIC: 3089 3494 3053 3084 Plastic containers, except foam; valves & pipe fittings; gaskets, packing & sealing devices; plastics pipe; steel pipe & tubes; fabricated pipe & fittings

(G-17486)
MIRROR-TECH MANUFACTURING CO
286 Nepperhan Ave (10701-3403)
PHONE 914 965-1232
Richard Cleary, *President*
EMP: 16 **EST:** 1961
SQ FT: 7,000
SALES: 750K **Privately Held**
SIC: 3231 Mirrored glass; mirrors, truck & automobile: made from purchased glass

(G-17487)
NASH ELECTRIC SERVICES INC
3 Glover Ave (10704-4203)
PHONE 914 226-8375
EMP: 10
SALES (corp-wide): 191.9K **Privately Held**
SIC: 3699 Electrical equipment & supplies
PA: Nash Electric Services Inc.
    4360 Bullard Ave
    Bronx NY 10466
    646 447-7495

(G-17488)
OCTOPUS ADVANCED SYSTEMS INC
27 Covington Rd (10710-3515)
PHONE 914 771-6110
Nikolai Prokhorenkov, *Ch of Bd*
EMP: 1
SALES: 2MM **Privately Held**
SIC: 3669 Emergency alarms

(G-17489)
ON LINE POWER TECHNOLOGIES
113 Sunnyside Dr (10705-2830)
PHONE 914 968-4440
Linda Hack, *President*
Bruce Hack, *Vice Pres*
EMP: 2
SALES (est): 10MM **Privately Held**
SIC: 3568 5063 7389 Power transmission equipment; electrical apparatus & equipment;

(G-17490)
ORZA BAKERY INC
261 New Main St Ste 263 (10701-4103)
PHONE 914 965-5736
Fax: 914 965-2017
Vital Tovar, *President*
Ubaldo Tovar, *Vice Pres*
EMP: 17
SQ FT: 8,000
SALES (est): 3MM **Privately Held**
SIC: 2051 Breads, rolls & buns

(G-17491)
OTIS ELEVATOR COMPANY
1 Odell Plz Ste 120 (10701-1415)
PHONE 914 375-7800
Fax: 914 375-7830
Marc Zolle, *Manager*
EMP: 12
SALES (corp-wide): 57.2B **Publicly Held**
WEB: www.otis.com
SIC: 3534 Elevators & equipment
HQ: Otis Elevator Company
    1 Carrier Pl
    Farmington CT 06032
    860 674-3000

(G-17492)
OUREM IRON WORKS INC
498 Nepperhan Ave Ste 5 (10701-6604)
PHONE 914 476-4856
Arthur Viera, *President*
Yvette Matos, *Office Mgr*
Marco Vivanco, *Manager*
EMP: 12 **EST:** 1977
SQ FT: 25,000
SALES (est): 2.6MM **Privately Held**
SIC: 3446 1799 Fences or posts, ornamental iron or steel; fence construction

(G-17493)
P PASCAL INC
Also Called: P Pascal Coffee Roasters
960 Nepperhan Ave (10703-1726)
P.O. Box 347 (10703-0347)
PHONE 914 969-7933
Fax: 914 969-8248

Dean Pialtos, *President*
James Ranni, *Corp Secy*
Barbara Pialtos, *Vice Pres*
Charles Pialtos, *Vice Pres*
Olla Naber, *Admin Sec*
EMP: 27
SQ FT: 15,000
SALES (est): 4MM **Privately Held**
SIC: 2095 Roasted coffee

(G-17494)
PANE DORO
166 Ludlow St (10701-1036)
PHONE 914 964-0043
Roger Nehme, *Owner*
EMP: 15
SALES (est): 1.1MM **Privately Held**
SIC: 2051 Cakes, bakery: except frozen

(G-17495)
PENNYSAVER GROUP INC
80 Alexander St (10701-2715)
PHONE 914 966-1400
Fax: 914 966-1486
Ed Levitt, *Manager*
Charol Russo, *Manager*
EMP: 10
SALES (corp-wide): 7.8MM **Privately Held**
WEB: www.nysaver.com
SIC: 2711 Newspapers, publishing & printing
PA: Pennysaver Group Inc.
    510 Fifth Ave
    Pelham NY
    914 592-5222

(G-17496)
PIETRO DEMARCO IMPORTERS INC
1185 Saw Mill River Rd # 4 (10710-3241)
PHONE 914 969-3201
Pietro Demarco, *President*
Anthony Demarco, *Vice Pres*
▲ **EMP:** 10
SALES (est): 1.2MM **Privately Held**
SIC: 2079 Olive oil

(G-17497)
POMPIAN MANUFACTURING CO INC
280 Nepperhan Ave (10701-3403)
PHONE 914 476-7076
Fax: 914 476-7095
EMP: 8
SQ FT: 10,000
SALES: 900K **Privately Held**
SIC: 3645 5063 Mfg & Whol Electrical Equipment & Electronic Ballast

(G-17498)
PREPAC DESIGNS INC
25 Abner Pl (10704-3015)
PHONE 914 524-7800
Manuel Mendez, *President*
Maggie Cott, *Vice Pres*
Patti Miranda, *Credit Mgr*
Ilene Greenberg, *Sales Staff*
Yesenia Morales, *Sales Staff*
▲ **EMP:** 4
SQ FT: 1,500
SALES: 2.5MM **Privately Held**
WEB: www.designerschoiceline.com
SIC: 3161 Luggage

(G-17499)
RECREATIONAL EQUIPMENT INC
49 Fitzgerald St (10710-7508)
PHONE 914 410-9500
EMP: 6
SALES (corp-wide): 2.5B **Privately Held**
SIC: 3949 Camping equipment & supplies
PA: Recreational Equipment, Inc.
    6750 S 228th St
    Kent WA 98032
    253 395-3780

(G-17500)
ROBERT VIGGIANI
Also Called: Irv & Vic Sportswear Co
37 Vredenburgh Ave Ste B (10704-2150)
PHONE 914 423-4046
Fax: 914 423-4047
Robert Viggiani, *Owner*

EMP: 5
SQ FT: 975
SALES (est): 510.6K **Privately Held**
SIC: 2329 5699 Riding clothes:, men's, youths' & boys'; riding apparel

(G-17501)
RUMSEY CORP
Also Called: B2b Cleaning Services
15 Rumsey Rd (10705-1623)
PHONE 914 751-3640
Anna Negron, *President*
EMP: 6
SALES (est): 300K **Privately Held**
SIC: 3672 7349 Printed circuit boards; building & office cleaning services; office cleaning or charring; cleaning service, industrial or commercial; window cleaning

(G-17502)
SKIL-CARE CORPORATION
29 Wells Ave Bldg 4 (10701-8815)
PHONE 914 963-2040
Fax: 914 963-2567
Martin Prenskean, *Ch of Bd*
Arnold Silverman, *President*
Stephen Wareen, *Vice Pres*
Stephen Warhaftig, *Vice Pres*
▲ **EMP:** 125 **EST:** 1978
SQ FT: 55,000
SALES (est): 17.7MM **Privately Held**
WEB: www.skilcare.com
SIC: 3842 2392 2241 Wheelchairs; household furnishings; narrow fabric mills

(G-17503)
STANSON AUTOMATED LLC
145 Saw Mill River Rd # 2 (10701-6615)
PHONE 866 505-7826
Stewart Iskowitz, *Mng Member*
Joel Iskowitz, *Mng Member*
EMP: 10
SALES (est): 910K **Privately Held**
SIC: 3578 Automatic teller machines (ATM)

(G-17504)
STAR DESK PAD CO INC
60 Mclean Ave (10705-2317)
PHONE 914 963-9400
Fax: 914 963-2580
Sidney Newman, *President*
▲ **EMP:** 45 **EST:** 1946
SQ FT: 60,000
SALES: 2.4MM **Privately Held**
WEB: www.stardesk.com
SIC: 3199 3999 Desk sets, leather; desk pads, except paper

(G-17505)
SWAROVSKI NORTH AMERICA LTD
6080 Mall Walk (10704-1223)
PHONE 914 423-4132
EMP: 7
SALES (corp-wide): 3.7B **Privately Held**
SIC: 3961 Costume jewelry
HQ: Swarovski North America Limited
    1 Kenney Dr
    Cranston RI 02920
    401 463-6400

(G-17506)
T C DUNHAM PAINT COMPANY INC
581 Saw Mill River Rd (10701-4924)
PHONE 914 969-4202
Fax: 914 969-3990
Isaac Schwartz, *Ch of Bd*
Eoy Fisch, *Vice Pres*
Eli Fish, *Manager*
Dunham Yossy, *Manager*
EMP: 25
SQ FT: 5,000
SALES: 12MM **Privately Held**
WEB: www.dunhampaint.com
SIC: 2851 Paints & allied products

(G-17507)
TODD SYSTEMS INC
50 Ash St (10701-3900)
PHONE 914 963-3400
Kenneth Todd, *President*
K H Todd, *Chairman*
Ruthann Todd, *Vice Pres*
▲ **EMP:** 60 **EST:** 1964
SQ FT: 25,000

(PA)=Parent Co (HQ)=Headquarters (DH)=Div Headquarters
✪ = New Business established in last 2 years

Yonkers - Westchester County (G-17508)

SALES (est): 9.4MM **Privately Held**
WEB: www.toddsystems.com
SIC: **3677** Electronic transformers

(G-17508)
TOPPS-ALL PRODUCTS OF YONKERS
148 Ludlow St Ste 2 (10705-7014)
PHONE..........................914 968-4226
Fax: 914 968-9883
Edward J Bolwell Jr, *President*
EMP: 15 EST: 1939
SALES: 2.5MM **Privately Held**
SIC: **2842** Cleaning or polishing preparations; automobile polish

(G-17509)
TOY ADMIRATION CO INC
60 Mclean Ave (10705-2317)
PHONE..........................914 963-9400
Fax: 914 963-2580
Sidney Newman, *President*
Alice Newman, *Treasurer*
EMP: 30 EST: 1945
SQ FT: 60,000
SALES: 2MM **Privately Held**
SIC: **3942** 5945 Dolls, except stuffed toy animals; hobby, toy & game shops

(G-17510)
TWO RIVERS COMPUTING INC
976 Mclean Ave (10704-4105)
P.O. Box 498 (10702-0498)
PHONE..........................914 968-9239
Gus Horowitz, *President*
Suzanne Haig, *Vice Pres*
EMP: 6
SALES (est): 398.1K **Privately Held**
SIC: **7372** Prepackaged software

(G-17511)
VALENTI NECKWEAR CO INC
540 Nepperhan Ave Ste 564 (10701-6611)
PHONE..........................914 969-0700
Albert Valentine, *President*
EMP: 8
SALES: 250K **Privately Held**
WEB: www.valentineckwear.com
SIC: **2323** 2339 Men's & boys' neckwear; neckwear & ties: women's, misses' & juniors'

(G-17512)
VALEO
4 Executive Plz Ste 114 (10701-6803)
PHONE..........................800 634-2704
Brian Anderson, *President*
Alexandre Depraete, *Project Mgr*
Cheryl Cash, *Prdtn Mgr*
Leon Lane, *Opers Spvr*
Rusty Bailiff, *Opers Staff*
EMP: 9
SALES (est): 610K **Privately Held**
SIC: **2399** 5091 5099 Glove mending on factory basis; fitness equipment & supplies; safety equipment & supplies

(G-17513)
VINYLINE WINDOW AND DOOR INC
636 Saw Mill River Rd (10710-4009)
PHONE..........................914 476-3500
Fax: 914 476-3506
Carmen Cangialosi, *President*
Henry Nagani, *Owner*
Robert Gramagila, *Vice Pres*
EMP: 10
SQ FT: 10,000
SALES: 600K **Privately Held**
SIC: **3089** Windows, plastic

(G-17514)
WHEEL & TIRE DEPOT EX CORP
584 Yonkers Ave (10704-2637)
PHONE..........................914 375-2100
Jose Calderon, *Manager*
EMP: 8
SALES (est): 1.3MM **Privately Held**
SIC: **3312** Wheels

(G-17515)
WHITNEY BOIN STUDIO INC
42 Warburton Ave Ste 1 (10701-2786)
PHONE..........................914 377-4385
Whitney Boin, *President*

Theresa Boin, *Vice Pres*
Olympia Meccia, *Opers Mgr*
EMP: 6
SALES (est): 820.9K **Privately Held**
WEB: www.whitneyboinstudio.com
SIC: **3911** Jewelry apparel

(G-17516)
WINESOFT INTERNATIONAL CORP
503 S Broadway Ste 220 (10705-6202)
PHONE..........................914 400-6247
Marco Vicens, *Manager*
EMP: 6
SALES (est): 242.4K **Privately Held**
WEB: www.winesoftusa.com
SIC: **7372** Application computer software

(G-17517)
YEWTREE MILLWORKS CORP
372 Ashburton Ave (10701-6015)
PHONE..........................914 320-5851
Keith Murphy, *President*
EMP: 5
SALES (est): 266.2K **Privately Held**
SIC: **2851** Paints & allied products

(G-17518)
YONKERS CABINETS INC
1179 Yonkers Ave (10704-3210)
PHONE..........................914 668-2133
Wai Hing Yip, *Owner*
EMP: 8
SALES (est): 839K **Privately Held**
SIC: **2434** Wood kitchen cabinets

(G-17519)
YONKERS TIME PUBLISHING CO
Also Called: Martinelli Publications
40 Larkin Plz (10701-2748)
PHONE..........................914 965-4000
Fax: 914 965-4026
Franchesca Martinelli, *Owner*
EMP: 15 EST: 1934
SQ FT: 6,000
SALES (est): 520K **Privately Held**
WEB: www.martinellipublications.com
SIC: **2711** Newspapers: publishing only, not printed on site

(G-17520)
YONKERS WHL BEER DISTRS INC
424 Riverdale Ave (10705-2908)
PHONE..........................914 963-8600
Fax: 914 963-7739
Richard McDine, *Owner*
EMP: 5
SALES (est): 347.5K **Privately Held**
SIC: **2082** Beer (alcoholic beverage)

York
Livingston County

(G-17521)
DAVIS TRAILER WORLD LLC
Also Called: Davis Trlr World & Cntry Mall
1640 Main St (14592)
P.O. Box 260 (14592-0260)
PHONE..........................585 538-6640
Marsha Kingdon, *Bookkeeper*
Dean Davis,
Susan Davis,
EMP: 10 EST: 1987
SALES: 3MM **Privately Held**
WEB: www.davistrailerworld.com
SIC: **3715** Truck trailers

Yorktown Heights
Westchester County

(G-17522)
ADVANCED TCHNCAL SOLUTIONS INC
Also Called: Ats
2986 Navajo Rd Ste 100 (10598-1834)
P.O. Box 28 (10598-0028)
PHONE..........................914 214-8230
Joe Yaniv, *President*
David Wright, *VP Opers*

▲ EMP: 10
SQ FT: 2,000
SALES: 5MM **Privately Held**
SIC: **3569** 5049 Lubrication equipment, industrial; engineers' equipment & supplies

(G-17523)
BULLETIN BOARDS & DIRCTRY PDTS
2986 Navajo Rd Ste 1 (10598-1800)
PHONE..........................914 248-8008
Fax: 914 248-5150
Charles Kranz, *President*
Jerry Martin, *Vice Pres*
Esther Glickman, *Admin Sec*
EMP: 15 EST: 1921
SQ FT: 40,000
SALES (est): 1.6MM **Privately Held**
SIC: **2493** Bulletin boards, wood; bulletin boards, cork

(G-17524)
BUSINESS MANAGEMENT SYSTEMS
Also Called: Fisau
2404 Loring Pl (10598-3721)
PHONE..........................914 245-8558
Zak Kogan, *CEO*
Leonid Kogan, *President*
Mark Milyavsky, *Vice Pres*
Scott Oldham, *Director*
EMP: 11
SALES (est): 1.4MM **Privately Held**
WEB: www.fisau.com
SIC: **7372** Prepackaged software

(G-17525)
CHASE MEDIA GROUP
1520 Front St (10598-4638)
PHONE..........................914 962-3871
Bruce Apar, *Publisher*
Al Mack, *Production*
David Cohen, *Controller*
Cynthia Cusumano, *Human Resources*
Donald Hosmer, *Accounts Exec*
EMP: 15
SALES (est): 738.8K **Privately Held**
SIC: **2711** Newspapers: publishing only, not printed on site

(G-17526)
CROWN DELTA CORPORATION
1550 Front St (10598-4638)
PHONE..........................914 245-8910
Fax: 914 245-8912
Anthony Konopka, *CEO*
Richard Bartkus, *Vice Pres*
Mark Konopka, *Opers Mgr*
Kevin Konopka, *Opers Staff*
Anthony J Konopka, *CFO*
▲ EMP: 35
SQ FT: 30,000
SALES (est): 9.6MM **Privately Held**
WEB: www.crowndelta.com
SIC: **2869** Silicones

(G-17527)
GAME SPORTSWEAR LTD (PA)
1401 Front St (10598-4639)
PHONE..........................914 962-1701
Fax: 914 892-2411
Enrico Genovese, *President*
Leslie Tandler, *Vice Pres*
Andrea Cancellieri, *VP Sls/Mktg*
Gina M Furano, *Treasurer*
Jennifer Lopez, *Sales Staff*
▲ EMP: 25
SQ FT: 76,000
SALES (est): 18.2MM **Privately Held**
SIC: **2253** 2339 Knit outerwear mills; women's & misses' outerwear

(G-17528)
MAKARENKO STUDIOS INC
2984 Saddle Ridge Dr (10598-2327)
PHONE..........................914 968-7673
Boris Makarenko, *President*
Sviatoslaw Makarenko, *Treasurer*
EMP: 5 EST: 1976
SALES (est): 290K **Privately Held**
SIC: **3231** 1542 Stained glass: made from purchased glass; religious building construction

(G-17529)
MEGA GRAPHICS INC
1725 Front St Ste 1 (10598-4651)
PHONE..........................914 962-1402
Robert Pierro, *Principal*
EMP: 5
SALES (est): 418.2K **Privately Held**
SIC: **2759** Commercial printing

(G-17530)
NORTHERN TIER PUBLISHING CORP
Also Called: North County News
1520 Front St (10598-4638)
PHONE..........................914 962-4748
Fax: 914 962-6763
John Chase, *President*
Jean Secor, *Vice Pres*
Rick Pezzullo, *Advt Staff*
Carla Chase, *Admin Sec*
EMP: 11
SQ FT: 2,000
SALES (est): 710.7K **Privately Held**
SIC: **2711** Newspapers: publishing only, not printed on site

(G-17531)
PARACE BIONICS LLC
276 Landmark Ct (10598-4131)
PHONE..........................877 727-2231
Vandette Carter, *CEO*
EMP: 5
SALES (est): 343.4K **Privately Held**
SIC: **3841** Surgical & medical instruments

(G-17532)
PIC NIC LLC
123 Holmes Ct (10598-2820)
PHONE..........................914 245-6500
Rick Rezzenico, *Partner*
EMP: 8
SALES (est): 893.8K **Privately Held**
SIC: **3556** Ice cream manufacturing machinery

(G-17533)
Q OMNI INC
1994 Commerce St (10598-4412)
PHONE..........................914 962-2726
Kwan Lee, *Owner*
EMP: 6
SALES (est): 542.4K **Privately Held**
SIC: **3582** Drycleaning equipment & machinery, commercial

(G-17534)
RICHARD ANTHONY CORP
Also Called: Richard Anthony Custom Mllwk
1500 Front St Ste 12 (10598-4648)
P.O. Box 240 (10598-0240)
PHONE..........................914 922-7141
Richard Scavelli, *CEO*
Angela Desiena, *Vice Pres*
EMP: 28
SALES (est): 2.8MM **Privately Held**
SIC: **2431** Millwork

(G-17535)
SHOP SMART CENTRAL INC
Also Called: Chase Press
1520 Front St (10598-4638)
PHONE..........................914 962-3871
Carla Chase, *President*
Rose Mary, *Human Res Mgr*
Al Mack, *Supervisor*
EMP: 7
SALES (est): 599.5K **Privately Held**
SIC: **2741** Business service newsletters: publishing & printing

(G-17536)
SIGNS INK LTD
3255 Crompond Rd (10598-3605)
PHONE..........................914 739-9059
Fax: 914 739-9728
Dick Hederson, *President*
Matthew Beachak, *Vice Pres*
Timothy Beachak, *Sales Staff*
Steve Chester, *Sales Staff*
Dustin Miller, *Graphic Designe*
EMP: 10
SQ FT: 1,000
SALES (est): 1.5MM **Privately Held**
SIC: **3993** Signs & advertising specialties

GEOGRAPHIC SECTION

(G-17537)
WOODTRONICS INC
1661 Front St Ste 3 (10598-4650)
PHONE.................................914 962-5205
Fax: 914 962-6114
Jan Efraimsen, *President*
EMP: 5
SQ FT: 4,500
SALES (est): 510K **Privately Held**
SIC: 2499 Decorative wood & woodwork

(G-17538)
YORKTOWN PRINTING CORP
1520 Front St (10598-4697)
PHONE.................................914 962-2526
Fax: 914 962-4820
John W Chase, *President*
Laura Lampel, *Admin Mgr*
EMP: 150
SQ FT: 80,000
SALES (est): 17.7MM **Privately Held**
WEB: www.yzipmail.com
SIC: 2752 Commercial printing, lithographic

Yorkville
Oneida County

(G-17539)
HUBBELL GALVANIZING INC
5124 Commercial Dr (13495-1109)
P.O. Box 37, New York Mills (13417-0037)
PHONE.................................315 736-8311
Daniel Merritt Hubbell, *President*
EMP: 7
SALES (est): 112.7K **Privately Held**
SIC: 3479 Coating, rust preventive; coating electrodes

(G-17540)
O W HUBBELL & SONS INC
Also Called: Hubbell Galvanising
5124 Commercial Dr (13495-1109)
P.O. Box 37, New York Mills (13417-0037)
PHONE.................................315 736-8311
Fax: 315 736-0381
Allen W Hubbell, *Ch of Bd*
Jock Hubbell, *President*
Vinnie Pham, *Accountant*
James Delude, *Human Resources*
Emmite White, *Human Resources*
▲ **EMP:** 35 **EST:** 1925
SQ FT: 8,000
SALES (est): 5.1MM
SALES (corp-wide): 6.1MM **Privately Held**
WEB: www.hubbellgalvanizing.com
SIC: 3479 Galvanizing of iron, steel or end-formed products
PA: W Hubbell & Sons Inc
  5124 Commercial Dr
  Yorkville NY 13495
  315 736-8311

(G-17541)
ORISKANY MANUFACTURING LLC
2 Wurz Ave (13495-1118)
PHONE.................................315 732-4962
Michael Fitzgerald, *CEO*
EMP: 14 **EST:** 2009
SALES (est): 2.6MM **Privately Held**
SIC: 3999 Manufacturing industries

(G-17542)
ORISKANY MFG TECH LLC
Also Called: Omt
2 Wurz Ave (13495-1118)
PHONE.................................315 732-4962
Fax: 315 732-6165
Stephen Palmieri, *Production*
Mike Reile, *Production*
Thomas Dutcher, *Purch Mgr*
James Caraco, *Engineer*
Debbie Ashe, *Manager*
▲ **EMP:** 30
SQ FT: 30,000
SALES (est): 7.4MM **Privately Held**
WEB: www.oriskanymfg.com
SIC: 3441 3317 Fabricated structural metal; welded pipe & tubes

(G-17543)
OTIS ELEVATOR COMPANY
5172 Commercial Dr (13495-1110)
PHONE.................................315 736-0167
Fax: 315 736-1580
Kerry Greer, *Sales/Mktg Mgr*
EMP: 12
SALES (corp-wide): 57.2B **Publicly Held**
WEB: www.otis.com
SIC: 3534 7699 Elevators & equipment; elevators: inspection, service & repair
HQ: Otis Elevator Company
  1 Carrier Pl
  Farmington CT 06032
  860 674-3000

(G-17544)
VICKS LITHOGRAPH & PRTG CORP (PA)
5166 Commercial Dr (13495-1173)
P.O. Box 270 (13495-0270)
PHONE.................................315 272-2401
Fax: 315 736-1901
Dwight E Vicks III, *Ch of Bd*
Dwight E Vicks III, *Ch of Bd*
Frances Driscoll, *General Mgr*
Dwight E Vicks Jr, *Chairman*
Leo McStoy, *Controller*
EMP: 110
SQ FT: 130,000
SALES (est): 22MM **Privately Held**
SIC: 2732 2789 2752 Books: printing only; bookbinding & related work; commercial printing, lithographic

(G-17545)
VICKS LITHOGRAPH & PRTG CORP
5210 Commercial Dr (13495-1111)
P.O. Box 270 (13495-0270)
PHONE.................................315 736-9344
Frank Driscoll, *Manager*
EMP: 130
SALES (corp-wide): 22MM **Privately Held**
SIC: 2732 2752 Book printing; commercial printing, lithographic
PA: Vicks Lithograph & Printing Corp.
  5166 Commercial Dr
  Yorkville NY 13495
  315 272-2401

(G-17546)
W HUBBELL & SONS INC (PA)
5124 Commercial Dr (13495-1109)
P.O. Box 37, New York Mills (13417-0037)
PHONE.................................315 736-8311
Allen W Hubbell, *Principal*
Allen W Hubbel, *Principal*
Steve Mulvihill, *Principal*
EMP: 6
SQ FT: 8,000
SALES (est): 6.1MM **Privately Held**
SIC: 3479 Galvanizing of iron, steel or end-formed products

(G-17547)
WAYNES WELDING INC
66 Calder Ave (13495-1601)
PHONE.................................315 768-6146
Fax: 315 768-2785
Wayne A Ramsey, *President*
Keith Ives, *Sales Staff*
Joyce Smith, *Manager*
EMP: 20
SQ FT: 9,000
SALES (est): 2.9MM **Privately Held**
SIC: 7692 3599 Welding repair; machine shop, jobbing & repair

Youngstown
Niagara County

(G-17548)
KINETIC FUEL TECHNOLOGY INC
Also Called: Kinetic Laboratories
1205 Balmer Rd (14174-9773)
PHONE.................................716 745-1461
Fax: 716 745-1468
Timothy M Booth, *Ch of Bd*
Eric Fragale, *President*
EMP: 5
SQ FT: 4,500
SALES: 1.2MM **Privately Held**
SIC: 2911 Fuel additives

SIC INDEX

Standard Industrial Classification Alphabetical Index

SIC NO	PRODUCT

A

3291 Abrasive Prdts
2891 Adhesives & Sealants
3563 Air & Gas Compressors
3585 Air Conditioning & Heating Eqpt
3721 Aircraft
3724 Aircraft Engines & Engine Parts
3728 Aircraft Parts & Eqpt, NEC
2812 Alkalies & Chlorine
3363 Aluminum Die Castings
3354 Aluminum Extruded Prdts
3365 Aluminum Foundries
3355 Aluminum Rolling & Drawing, NEC
3353 Aluminum Sheet, Plate & Foil
3483 Ammunition, Large
3826 Analytical Instruments
2077 Animal, Marine Fats & Oils
1231 Anthracite Mining
2389 Apparel & Accessories, NEC
2387 Apparel Belts
3446 Architectural & Ornamental Metal Work
7694 Armature Rewinding Shops
3292 Asbestos products
2952 Asphalt Felts & Coatings
3822 Automatic Temperature Controls
3581 Automatic Vending Machines
3465 Automotive Stampings
2396 Automotive Trimmings, Apparel Findings, Related Prdts

B

2673 Bags: Plastics, Laminated & Coated
2674 Bags: Uncoated Paper & Multiwall
3562 Ball & Roller Bearings
2836 Biological Prdts, Exc Diagnostic Substances
2782 Blankbooks & Looseleaf Binders
3312 Blast Furnaces, Coke Ovens, Steel & Rolling Mills
3564 Blowers & Fans
3732 Boat Building & Repairing
3452 Bolts, Nuts, Screws, Rivets & Washers
2732 Book Printing, Not Publishing
2789 Bookbinding
2731 Books: Publishing & Printing
3131 Boot & Shoe Cut Stock & Findings
2342 Brassieres, Girdles & Garments
2051 Bread, Bakery Prdts Exc Cookies & Crackers
3251 Brick & Structural Clay Tile
3991 Brooms & Brushes
3995 Burial Caskets
2021 Butter

C

3578 Calculating & Accounting Eqpt
2064 Candy & Confectionery Prdts
2033 Canned Fruits, Vegetables & Preserves
2032 Canned Specialties
2394 Canvas Prdts
3624 Carbon & Graphite Prdts
3955 Carbon Paper & Inked Ribbons
3592 Carburetors, Pistons, Rings & Valves
2273 Carpets & Rugs
2823 Cellulosic Man-Made Fibers
3241 Cement, Hydraulic
3253 Ceramic Tile
2043 Cereal Breakfast Foods
2022 Cheese
1479 Chemical & Fertilizer Mining
2899 Chemical Preparations, NEC
2067 Chewing Gum
2361 Children's & Infants' Dresses & Blouses
3261 China Plumbing Fixtures & Fittings
3262 China, Table & Kitchen Articles
2066 Chocolate & Cocoa Prdts
2111 Cigarettes
2121 Cigars
2257 Circular Knit Fabric Mills
3255 Clay Refractories
1459 Clay, Ceramic & Refractory Minerals, NEC
1241 Coal Mining Svcs
3479 Coating & Engraving, NEC
2095 Coffee
3316 Cold Rolled Steel Sheet, Strip & Bars
3582 Commercial Laundry, Dry Clean & Pressing Mchs
2759 Commercial Printing
2754 Commercial Printing: Gravure
2752 Commercial Printing: Lithographic
3646 Commercial, Indl & Institutional Lighting Fixtures

3669 Communications Eqpt, NEC
3577 Computer Peripheral Eqpt, NEC
3572 Computer Storage Devices
3575 Computer Terminals
3271 Concrete Block & Brick
3272 Concrete Prdts
3531 Construction Machinery & Eqpt
1442 Construction Sand & Gravel
2679 Converted Paper Prdts, NEC
3535 Conveyors & Eqpt
2052 Cookies & Crackers
3366 Copper Foundries
1021 Copper Ores
2298 Cordage & Twine
2653 Corrugated & Solid Fiber Boxes
3961 Costume Jewelry & Novelties
2261 Cotton Fabric Finishers
2211 Cotton, Woven Fabric
2074 Cottonseed Oil Mills
3466 Crowns & Closures
1311 Crude Petroleum & Natural Gas
1423 Crushed & Broken Granite
1422 Crushed & Broken Limestone
1429 Crushed & Broken Stone, NEC
3643 Current-Carrying Wiring Devices
2391 Curtains & Draperies
3087 Custom Compounding Of Purchased Plastic Resins
3281 Cut Stone Prdts
3421 Cutlery
2865 Cyclic-Crudes, Intermediates, Dyes & Org Pigments

D

3843 Dental Eqpt & Splys
2835 Diagnostic Substances
2675 Die-Cut Paper & Board
3544 Dies, Tools, Jigs, Fixtures & Indl Molds
1411 Dimension Stone
2047 Dog & Cat Food
3942 Dolls & Stuffed Toys
2591 Drapery Hardware, Window Blinds & Shades
2381 Dress & Work Gloves
2034 Dried Fruits, Vegetables & Soup
1381 Drilling Oil & Gas Wells

E

3263 Earthenware, Whiteware, Table & Kitchen Articles
3634 Electric Household Appliances
3641 Electric Lamps
3694 Electrical Eqpt For Internal Combustion Engines
3629 Electrical Indl Apparatus, NEC
3699 Electrical Machinery, Eqpt & Splys, NEC
3845 Electromedical & Electrotherapeutic Apparatus
3313 Electrometallurgical Prdts
3675 Electronic Capacitors
3677 Electronic Coils & Transformers
3679 Electronic Components, NEC
3571 Electronic Computers
3678 Electronic Connectors
3676 Electronic Resistors
3471 Electroplating, Plating, Polishing, Anodizing & Coloring
3534 Elevators & Moving Stairways
3431 Enameled Iron & Metal Sanitary Ware
2677 Envelopes
2892 Explosives

F

2241 Fabric Mills, Cotton, Wool, Silk & Man-Made
3499 Fabricated Metal Prdts, NEC
3498 Fabricated Pipe & Pipe Fittings
3443 Fabricated Plate Work
3069 Fabricated Rubber Prdts, NEC
3441 Fabricated Structural Steel
2399 Fabricated Textile Prdts, NEC
2295 Fabrics Coated Not Rubberized
2297 Fabrics, Nonwoven
3523 Farm Machinery & Eqpt
3965 Fasteners, Buttons, Needles & Pins
2875 Fertilizers, Mixing Only
2655 Fiber Cans, Tubes & Drums
2091 Fish & Seafoods, Canned & Cured
2092 Fish & Seafoods, Fresh & Frozen
3211 Flat Glass
2087 Flavoring Extracts & Syrups
2045 Flour, Blended & Prepared
2041 Flour, Grain Milling
3824 Fluid Meters & Counters

3593 Fluid Power Cylinders & Actuators
3594 Fluid Power Pumps & Motors
3492 Fluid Power Valves & Hose Fittings
2657 Folding Paperboard Boxes
3556 Food Prdts Machinery
2099 Food Preparations, NEC
3149 Footwear, NEC
2053 Frozen Bakery Prdts
2037 Frozen Fruits, Juices & Vegetables
2038 Frozen Specialties
2371 Fur Goods
2599 Furniture & Fixtures, NEC

G

3944 Games, Toys & Children's Vehicles
3524 Garden, Lawn Tractors & Eqpt
3053 Gaskets, Packing & Sealing Devices
2369 Girls' & Infants' Outerwear, NEC
3221 Glass Containers
3231 Glass Prdts Made Of Purchased Glass
1041 Gold Ores
3321 Gray Iron Foundries
2771 Greeting Card Publishing
3769 Guided Missile/Space Vehicle Parts & Eqpt, NEC
3761 Guided Missiles & Space Vehicles
2861 Gum & Wood Chemicals
3275 Gypsum Prdts

H

3423 Hand & Edge Tools
3425 Hand Saws & Saw Blades
3171 Handbags & Purses
3429 Hardware, NEC
2426 Hardwood Dimension & Flooring Mills
2435 Hardwood Veneer & Plywood
2353 Hats, Caps & Millinery
3433 Heating Eqpt
3536 Hoists, Cranes & Monorails
2252 Hosiery, Except Women's
2251 Hosiery, Women's Full & Knee Length
2392 House furnishings: Textile
3142 House Slippers
3639 Household Appliances, NEC
3651 Household Audio & Video Eqpt
3631 Household Cooking Eqpt
2519 Household Furniture, NEC
3633 Household Laundry Eqpt
3632 Household Refrigerators & Freezers
3635 Household Vacuum Cleaners

I

2097 Ice
2024 Ice Cream
2819 Indl Inorganic Chemicals, NEC
3823 Indl Instruments For Meas, Display & Control
3569 Indl Machinery & Eqpt, NEC
3567 Indl Process Furnaces & Ovens
3537 Indl Trucks, Tractors, Trailers & Stackers
2813 Industrial Gases
2869 Industrial Organic Chemicals, NEC
3543 Industrial Patterns
1446 Industrial Sand
3491 Industrial Valves
2816 Inorganic Pigments
3825 Instrs For Measuring & Testing Electricity
3519 Internal Combustion Engines, NEC
3462 Iron & Steel Forgings
1011 Iron Ores

J

3915 Jewelers Findings & Lapidary Work
3911 Jewelry: Precious Metal

K

2253 Knit Outerwear Mills
2254 Knit Underwear Mills
2259 Knitting Mills, NEC

L

3821 Laboratory Apparatus & Furniture
2258 Lace & Warp Knit Fabric Mills
3952 Lead Pencils, Crayons & Artist's Mtrls
2386 Leather & Sheep Lined Clothing
3151 Leather Gloves & Mittens
3199 Leather Goods, NEC
3111 Leather Tanning & Finishing
3648 Lighting Eqpt, NEC

SIC INDEX

SIC NO	PRODUCT
3274	Lime
3996	Linoleum & Hard Surface Floor Coverings, NEC
2085	Liquors, Distilled, Rectified & Blended
2411	Logging
2992	Lubricating Oils & Greases
3161	Luggage

M

SIC NO	PRODUCT
2098	Macaroni, Spaghetti & Noodles
3545	Machine Tool Access
3541	Machine Tools: Cutting
3542	Machine Tools: Forming
3599	Machinery & Eqpt, Indl & Commercial, NEC
3322	Malleable Iron Foundries
2083	Malt
2082	Malt Beverages
2761	Manifold Business Forms
3999	Manufacturing Industries, NEC
3953	Marking Devices
2515	Mattresses & Bedsprings
3829	Measuring & Controlling Devices, NEC
3586	Measuring & Dispensing Pumps
2011	Meat Packing Plants
3568	Mechanical Power Transmission Eqpt, NEC
2833	Medicinal Chemicals & Botanical Prdts
2329	Men's & Boys' Clothing, NEC
2323	Men's & Boys' Neckwear
2325	Men's & Boys' Separate Trousers & Casual Slacks
2321	Men's & Boys' Shirts
2311	Men's & Boys' Suits, Coats & Overcoats
2322	Men's & Boys' Underwear & Nightwear
2326	Men's & Boys' Work Clothing
3143	Men's Footwear, Exc Athletic
3412	Metal Barrels, Drums, Kegs & Pails
3411	Metal Cans
3442	Metal Doors, Sash, Frames, Molding & Trim
3497	Metal Foil & Leaf
3398	Metal Heat Treating
2514	Metal Household Furniture
1081	Metal Mining Svcs
1099	Metal Ores, NEC
3469	Metal Stampings, NEC
3549	Metalworking Machinery, NEC
2026	Milk
2023	Milk, Condensed & Evaporated
2431	Millwork
3296	Mineral Wool
3295	Minerals & Earths: Ground Or Treated
3532	Mining Machinery & Eqpt
3496	Misc Fabricated Wire Prdts
2741	Misc Publishing
3449	Misc Structural Metal Work
1499	Miscellaneous Nonmetallic Mining
2451	Mobile Homes
3061	Molded, Extruded & Lathe-Cut Rubber Mechanical Goods
3716	Motor Homes
3714	Motor Vehicle Parts & Access
3711	Motor Vehicles & Car Bodies
3751	Motorcycles, Bicycles & Parts
3621	Motors & Generators
3931	Musical Instruments

N

SIC NO	PRODUCT
1321	Natural Gas Liquids
2711	Newspapers: Publishing & Printing
2873	Nitrogenous Fertilizers
3297	Nonclay Refractories
3644	Noncurrent-Carrying Wiring Devices
3364	Nonferrous Die Castings, Exc Aluminum
3463	Nonferrous Forgings
3369	Nonferrous Foundries: Castings, NEC
3357	Nonferrous Wire Drawing
3299	Nonmetallic Mineral Prdts, NEC
1481	Nonmetallic Minerals Svcs, Except Fuels

O

SIC NO	PRODUCT
2522	Office Furniture, Except Wood
3579	Office Machines, NEC
1382	Oil & Gas Field Exploration Svcs
1389	Oil & Gas Field Svcs, NEC
3533	Oil Field Machinery & Eqpt
3851	Ophthalmic Goods
3827	Optical Instruments
3489	Ordnance & Access, NEC
3842	Orthopedic, Prosthetic & Surgical Appliances/Splys

P

SIC NO	PRODUCT
3565	Packaging Machinery
2851	Paints, Varnishes, Lacquers, Enamels
2671	Paper Coating & Laminating for Packaging
2672	Paper Coating & Laminating, Exc for Packaging
3554	Paper Inds Machinery
2621	Paper Mills
2631	Paperboard Mills
2542	Partitions & Fixtures, Except Wood
2951	Paving Mixtures & Blocks
3951	Pens & Mechanical Pencils
2844	Perfumes, Cosmetics & Toilet Preparations
2721	Periodicals: Publishing & Printing
3172	Personal Leather Goods
2879	Pesticides & Agricultural Chemicals, NEC
2911	Petroleum Refining
2834	Pharmaceuticals
3652	Phonograph Records & Magnetic Tape
2874	Phosphatic Fertilizers
3861	Photographic Eqpt & Splys
2035	Pickled Fruits, Vegetables, Sauces & Dressings
3085	Plastic Bottles
3086	Plastic Foam Prdts
3083	Plastic Laminated Plate & Sheet
3084	Plastic Pipe
3088	Plastic Plumbing Fixtures
3089	Plastic Prdts
3082	Plastic Unsupported Profile Shapes
3081	Plastic Unsupported Sheet & Film
2821	Plastics, Mtrls & Nonvulcanizable Elastomers
2796	Platemaking & Related Svcs
2395	Pleating & Stitching For The Trade
3432	Plumbing Fixture Fittings & Trim, Brass
3264	Porcelain Electrical Splys
2096	Potato Chips & Similar Prdts
3269	Pottery Prdts, NEC
2015	Poultry Slaughtering, Dressing & Processing
3546	Power Hand Tools
3612	Power, Distribution & Specialty Transformers
3448	Prefabricated Metal Buildings & Cmpnts
2452	Prefabricated Wood Buildings & Cmpnts
7372	Prepackaged Software
2048	Prepared Feeds For Animals & Fowls
3229	Pressed & Blown Glassware, NEC
3692	Primary Batteries: Dry & Wet
3399	Primary Metal Prdts, NEC
3339	Primary Nonferrous Metals, NEC
3334	Primary Production Of Aluminum
3331	Primary Smelting & Refining Of Copper
3672	Printed Circuit Boards
2893	Printing Ink
3555	Printing Trades Machinery & Eqpt
2999	Products Of Petroleum & Coal, NEC
2531	Public Building & Related Furniture
2611	Pulp Mills
3561	Pumps & Pumping Eqpt

R

SIC NO	PRODUCT
3663	Radio & T V Communications, Systs & Eqpt, Broadcast/Studio
3671	Radio & T V Receiving Electron Tubes
3743	Railroad Eqpt
3273	Ready-Mixed Concrete
2493	Reconstituted Wood Prdts
3695	Recording Media
3625	Relays & Indl Controls
3645	Residential Lighting Fixtures
2044	Rice Milling
2384	Robes & Dressing Gowns
3547	Rolling Mill Machinery & Eqpt
3351	Rolling, Drawing & Extruding Of Copper
3356	Rolling, Drawing-Extruding Of Nonferrous Metals
3021	Rubber & Plastic Footwear
3052	Rubber & Plastic Hose & Belting

S

SIC NO	PRODUCT
2068	Salted & Roasted Nuts & Seeds
2656	Sanitary Food Containers
2676	Sanitary Paper Prdts
2013	Sausages & Meat Prdts
2421	Saw & Planing Mills
3596	Scales & Balances, Exc Laboratory
2397	Schiffli Machine Embroideries
3451	Screw Machine Prdts
3812	Search, Detection, Navigation & Guidance Systs & Instrs
3341	Secondary Smelting & Refining Of Nonferrous Metals
3674	Semiconductors
3589	Service Ind Machines, NEC
2652	Set-Up Paperboard Boxes
3444	Sheet Metal Work
3731	Shipbuilding & Repairing
2079	Shortening, Oils & Margarine
3993	Signs & Advertising Displays
2262	Silk & Man-Made Fabric Finishers
2221	Silk & Man-Made Fiber
1044	Silver Ores
3914	Silverware, Plated & Stainless Steel Ware
3484	Small Arms
3482	Small Arms Ammunition
2841	Soap & Detergents
2086	Soft Drinks
2436	Softwood Veneer & Plywood
2842	Spec Cleaning, Polishing & Sanitation Preparations
3559	Special Ind Machinery, NEC
2429	Special Prdt Sawmills, NEC
3566	Speed Changers, Drives & Gears
3949	Sporting & Athletic Goods, NEC
2678	Stationery Prdts
3511	Steam, Gas & Hydraulic Turbines & Engines
3325	Steel Foundries, NEC
3324	Steel Investment Foundries
3317	Steel Pipe & Tubes
3493	Steel Springs, Except Wire
3315	Steel Wire Drawing & Nails & Spikes
3691	Storage Batteries
3259	Structural Clay Prdts, NEC
2439	Structural Wood Members, NEC
2063	Sugar, Beet
2061	Sugar, Cane
2062	Sugar, Cane Refining
2843	Surface Active & Finishing Agents, Sulfonated Oils
3841	Surgical & Medical Instrs & Apparatus
3613	Switchgear & Switchboard Apparatus
2824	Synthetic Organic Fibers, Exc Cellulosic
2822	Synthetic Rubber (Vulcanizable Elastomers)

T

SIC NO	PRODUCT
3795	Tanks & Tank Components
3661	Telephone & Telegraph Apparatus
2393	Textile Bags
2269	Textile Finishers, NEC
2299	Textile Goods, NEC
3552	Textile Machinery
2284	Thread Mills
2296	Tire Cord & Fabric
3011	Tires & Inner Tubes
2141	Tobacco Stemming & Redrying
2131	Tobacco, Chewing & Snuff
3799	Transportation Eqpt, NEC
3792	Travel Trailers & Campers
3713	Truck & Bus Bodies
3715	Truck Trailers
2791	Typesetting

U

SIC NO	PRODUCT
1094	Uranium, Radium & Vanadium Ores

V

SIC NO	PRODUCT
3494	Valves & Pipe Fittings, NEC
2076	Vegetable Oil Mills
3647	Vehicular Lighting Eqpt

W

SIC NO	PRODUCT
3873	Watch & Clock Devices & Parts
2385	Waterproof Outerwear
3548	Welding Apparatus
7692	Welding Repair
2046	Wet Corn Milling
2084	Wine & Brandy
3495	Wire Springs
2331	Women's & Misses' Blouses
2335	Women's & Misses' Dresses
2339	Women's & Misses' Outerwear, NEC
2337	Women's & Misses' Suits, Coats & Skirts
3144	Women's Footwear, Exc Athletic
2341	Women's, Misses' & Children's Underwear & Nightwear
2441	Wood Boxes
2449	Wood Containers, NEC
2511	Wood Household Furniture
2512	Wood Household Furniture, Upholstered
2434	Wood Kitchen Cabinets
2521	Wood Office Furniture
2448	Wood Pallets & Skids
2499	Wood Prdts, NEC
2491	Wood Preserving
2517	Wood T V, Radio, Phono & Sewing Cabinets
2541	Wood, Office & Store Fixtures
3553	Woodworking Machinery
2231	Wool, Woven Fabric

X

SIC NO	PRODUCT
3844	X-ray Apparatus & Tubes

Y

SIC NO	PRODUCT
2281	Yarn Spinning Mills
2282	Yarn Texturizing, Throwing, Twisting & Winding Mills

SIC INDEX

Standard Industrial Classification Numerical Index

SIC NO	PRODUCT

10 METAL MINING
1011 Iron Ores
1021 Copper Ores
1041 Gold Ores
1044 Silver Ores
1081 Metal Mining Svcs
1094 Uranium, Radium & Vanadium Ores
1099 Metal Ores, NEC

12 COAL MINING
1231 Anthracite Mining
1241 Coal Mining Svcs

13 OIL AND GAS EXTRACTION
1311 Crude Petroleum & Natural Gas
1321 Natural Gas Liquids
1381 Drilling Oil & Gas Wells
1382 Oil & Gas Field Exploration Svcs
1389 Oil & Gas Field Svcs, NEC

14 MINING AND QUARRYING OF NONMETALLIC MINERALS, EXCEPT FUELS
1411 Dimension Stone
1422 Crushed & Broken Limestone
1423 Crushed & Broken Granite
1429 Crushed & Broken Stone, NEC
1442 Construction Sand & Gravel
1446 Industrial Sand
1459 Clay, Ceramic & Refractory Minerals, NEC
1479 Chemical & Fertilizer Mining
1481 Nonmetallic Minerals Svcs, Except Fuels
1499 Miscellaneous Nonmetallic Mining

20 FOOD AND KINDRED PRODUCTS
2011 Meat Packing Plants
2013 Sausages & Meat Prdts
2015 Poultry Slaughtering, Dressing & Processing
2021 Butter
2022 Cheese
2023 Milk, Condensed & Evaporated
2024 Ice Cream
2026 Milk
2032 Canned Specialties
2033 Canned Fruits, Vegetables & Preserves
2034 Dried Fruits, Vegetables & Soup
2035 Pickled Fruits, Vegetables, Sauces & Dressings
2037 Frozen Fruits, Juices & Vegetables
2038 Frozen Specialties
2041 Flour, Grain Milling
2043 Cereal Breakfast Foods
2044 Rice Milling
2045 Flour, Blended & Prepared
2046 Wet Corn Milling
2047 Dog & Cat Food
2048 Prepared Feeds For Animals & Fowls
2051 Bread, Bakery Prdts Exc Cookies & Crackers
2052 Cookies & Crackers
2053 Frozen Bakery Prdts
2061 Sugar, Cane
2062 Sugar, Cane Refining
2063 Sugar, Beet
2064 Candy & Confectionery Prdts
2066 Chocolate & Cocoa Prdts
2067 Chewing Gum
2068 Salted & Roasted Nuts & Seeds
2074 Cottonseed Oil Mills
2076 Vegetable Oil Mills
2077 Animal, Marine Fats & Oils
2079 Shortening, Oils & Margarine
2082 Malt Beverages
2083 Malt
2084 Wine & Brandy
2085 Liquors, Distilled, Rectified & Blended
2086 Soft Drinks
2087 Flavoring Extracts & Syrups
2091 Fish & Seafoods, Canned & Cured
2092 Fish & Seafoods, Fresh & Frozen
2095 Coffee
2096 Potato Chips & Similar Prdts
2097 Ice
2098 Macaroni, Spaghetti & Noodles
2099 Food Preparations, NEC

21 TOBACCO PRODUCTS
2111 Cigarettes
2121 Cigars
2131 Tobacco, Chewing & Snuff
2141 Tobacco Stemming & Redrying

22 TEXTILE MILL PRODUCTS
2211 Cotton, Woven Fabric
2221 Silk & Man-Made Fiber
2231 Wool, Woven Fabric
2241 Fabric Mills, Cotton, Wool, Silk & Man-Made
2251 Hosiery, Women's Full & Knee Length
2252 Hosiery, Except Women's
2253 Knit Outerwear Mills
2254 Knit Underwear Mills
2257 Circular Knit Fabric Mills
2258 Lace & Warp Knit Fabric Mills
2259 Knitting Mills, NEC
2261 Cotton Fabric Finishers
2262 Silk & Man-Made Fabric Finishers
2269 Textile Finishers, NEC
2273 Carpets & Rugs
2281 Yarn Spinning Mills
2282 Yarn Texturizing, Throwing, Twisting & Winding Mills
2284 Thread Mills
2295 Fabrics Coated Not Rubberized
2296 Tire Cord & Fabric
2297 Fabrics, Nonwoven
2298 Cordage & Twine
2299 Textile Goods, NEC

23 APPAREL AND OTHER FINISHED PRODUCTS MADE FROM FABRICS AND SIMILAR MATERIAL
2311 Men's & Boys' Suits, Coats & Overcoats
2321 Men's & Boys' Shirts
2322 Men's & Boys' Underwear & Nightwear
2323 Men's & Boys' Neckwear
2325 Men's & Boys' Separate Trousers & Casual Slacks
2326 Men's & Boys' Work Clothing
2329 Men's & Boys' Clothing, NEC
2331 Women's & Misses' Blouses
2335 Women's & Misses' Dresses
2337 Women's & Misses' Suits, Coats & Skirts
2339 Women's & Misses' Outerwear, NEC
2341 Women's, Misses' & Children's Underwear & Nightwear
2342 Brassieres, Girdles & Garments
2353 Hats, Caps & Millinery
2361 Children's & Infants' Dresses & Blouses
2369 Girls' & Infants' Outerwear, NEC
2371 Fur Goods
2381 Dress & Work Gloves
2384 Robes & Dressing Gowns
2385 Waterproof Outerwear
2386 Leather & Sheep Lined Clothing
2387 Apparel Belts
2389 Apparel & Accessories, NEC
2391 Curtains & Draperies
2392 House furnishings: Textile
2393 Textile Bags
2394 Canvas Prdts
2395 Pleating & Stitching For The Trade
2396 Automotive Trimmings, Apparel Findings, Related Prdts
2397 Schiffli Machine Embroideries
2399 Fabricated Textile Prdts, NEC

24 LUMBER AND WOOD PRODUCTS, EXCEPT FURNITURE
2411 Logging
2421 Saw & Planing Mills
2426 Hardwood Dimension & Flooring Mills
2429 Special Prdt Sawmills, NEC
2431 Millwork
2434 Wood Kitchen Cabinets
2435 Hardwood Veneer & Plywood
2436 Softwood Veneer & Plywood
2439 Structural Wood Members, NEC
2441 Wood Boxes
2448 Wood Pallets & Skids
2449 Wood Containers, NEC
2451 Mobile Homes
2452 Prefabricated Wood Buildings & Cmpnts
2491 Wood Preserving
2493 Reconstituted Wood Prdts
2499 Wood Prdts, NEC

25 FURNITURE AND FIXTURES
2511 Wood Household Furniture
2512 Wood Household Furniture, Upholstered
2514 Metal Household Furniture
2515 Mattresses & Bedsprings
2517 Wood T V, Radio, Phono & Sewing Cabinets
2519 Household Furniture, NEC
2521 Wood Office Furniture
2522 Office Furniture, Except Wood
2531 Public Building & Related Furniture
2541 Wood, Office & Store Fixtures
2542 Partitions & Fixtures, Except Wood
2591 Drapery Hardware, Window Blinds & Shades
2599 Furniture & Fixtures, NEC

26 PAPER AND ALLIED PRODUCTS
2611 Pulp Mills
2621 Paper Mills
2631 Paperboard Mills
2652 Set-Up Paperboard Boxes
2653 Corrugated & Solid Fiber Boxes
2655 Fiber Cans, Tubes & Drums
2656 Sanitary Food Containers
2657 Folding Paperboard Boxes
2671 Paper Coating & Laminating for Packaging
2672 Paper Coating & Laminating, Exc for Packaging
2673 Bags: Plastics, Laminated & Coated
2674 Bags: Uncoated Paper & Multiwall
2675 Die-Cut Paper & Board
2676 Sanitary Paper Prdts
2677 Envelopes
2678 Stationery Prdts
2679 Converted Paper Prdts, NEC

27 PRINTING, PUBLISHING, AND ALLIED INDUSTRIES
2711 Newspapers: Publishing & Printing
2721 Periodicals: Publishing & Printing
2731 Books: Publishing & Printing
2732 Book Printing, Not Publishing
2741 Misc Publishing
2752 Commercial Printing: Lithographic
2754 Commercial Printing: Gravure
2759 Commercial Printing
2761 Manifold Business Forms
2771 Greeting Card Publishing
2782 Blankbooks & Looseleaf Binders
2789 Bookbinding
2791 Typesetting
2796 Platemaking & Related Svcs

28 CHEMICALS AND ALLIED PRODUCTS
2812 Alkalies & Chlorine
2813 Industrial Gases
2816 Inorganic Pigments
2819 Indl Inorganic Chemicals, NEC
2821 Plastics, Mtrls & Nonvulcanizable Elastomers
2822 Synthetic Rubber (Vulcanizable Elastomers)
2823 Cellulosic Man-Made Fibers
2824 Synthetic Organic Fibers, Exc Cellulosic
2833 Medicinal Chemicals & Botanical Prdts
2834 Pharmaceuticals
2835 Diagnostic Substances
2836 Biological Prdts, Exc Diagnostic Substances
2841 Soap & Detergents
2842 Spec Cleaning, Polishing & Sanitation Preparations
2843 Surface Active & Finishing Agents, Sulfonated Oils
2844 Perfumes, Cosmetics & Toilet Preparations
2851 Paints, Varnishes, Lacquers, Enamels
2861 Gum & Wood Chemicals
2865 Cyclic-Crudes, Intermediates, Dyes & Org Pigments
2869 Industrial Organic Chemicals, NEC
2873 Nitrogenous Fertilizers
2874 Phosphatic Fertilizers
2875 Fertilizers, Mixing Only
2879 Pesticides & Agricultural Chemicals, NEC
2891 Adhesives & Sealants
2892 Explosives
2893 Printing Ink
2899 Chemical Preparations, NEC

29 PETROLEUM REFINING AND RELATED INDUSTRIES
2911 Petroleum Refining
2951 Paving Mixtures & Blocks
2952 Asphalt Felts & Coatings
2992 Lubricating Oils & Greases
2999 Products Of Petroleum & Coal, NEC

30 RUBBER AND MISCELLANEOUS PLASTICS PRODUCTS
3011 Tires & Inner Tubes
3021 Rubber & Plastic Footwear
3052 Rubber & Plastic Hose & Belting
3053 Gaskets, Packing & Sealing Devices
3061 Molded, Extruded & Lathe-Cut Rubber Mechanical Goods
3069 Fabricated Rubber Prdts, NEC
3081 Plastic Unsupported Sheet & Film
3082 Plastic Unsupported Profile Shapes

SIC INDEX

SIC NO	PRODUCT
3083	Plastic Laminated Plate & Sheet
3084	Plastic Pipe
3085	Plastic Bottles
3086	Plastic Foam Prdts
3087	Custom Compounding Of Purchased Plastic Resins
3088	Plastic Plumbing Fixtures
3089	Plastic Prdts

31 LEATHER AND LEATHER PRODUCTS

- 3111 Leather Tanning & Finishing
- 3131 Boot & Shoe Cut Stock & Findings
- 3142 House Slippers
- 3143 Men's Footwear, Exc Athletic
- 3144 Women's Footwear, Exc Athletic
- 3149 Footwear, NEC
- 3151 Leather Gloves & Mittens
- 3161 Luggage
- 3171 Handbags & Purses
- 3172 Personal Leather Goods
- 3199 Leather Goods, NEC

32 STONE, CLAY, GLASS, AND CONCRETE PRODUCTS

- 3211 Flat Glass
- 3221 Glass Containers
- 3229 Pressed & Blown Glassware, NEC
- 3231 Glass Prdts Made Of Purchased Glass
- 3241 Cement, Hydraulic
- 3251 Brick & Structural Clay Tile
- 3253 Ceramic Tile
- 3255 Clay Refractories
- 3259 Structural Clay Prdts, NEC
- 3261 China Plumbing Fixtures & Fittings
- 3262 China, Table & Kitchen Articles
- 3263 Earthenware, Whiteware, Table & Kitchen Articles
- 3264 Porcelain Electrical Splys
- 3269 Pottery Prdts, NEC
- 3271 Concrete Block & Brick
- 3272 Concrete Prdts
- 3273 Ready-Mixed Concrete
- 3274 Lime
- 3275 Gypsum Prdts
- 3281 Cut Stone Prdts
- 3291 Abrasive Prdts
- 3292 Asbestos products
- 3295 Minerals & Earths: Ground Or Treated
- 3296 Mineral Wool
- 3297 Nonclay Refractories
- 3299 Nonmetallic Mineral Prdts, NEC

33 PRIMARY METAL INDUSTRIES

- 3312 Blast Furnaces, Coke Ovens, Steel & Rolling Mills
- 3313 Electrometallurgical Prdts
- 3315 Steel Wire Drawing & Nails & Spikes
- 3316 Cold Rolled Steel Sheet, Strip & Bars
- 3317 Steel Pipe & Tubes
- 3321 Gray Iron Foundries
- 3322 Malleable Iron Foundries
- 3324 Steel Investment Foundries
- 3325 Steel Foundries, NEC
- 3331 Primary Smelting & Refining Of Copper
- 3334 Primary Production Of Aluminum
- 3339 Primary Nonferrous Metals, NEC
- 3341 Secondary Smelting & Refining Of Nonferrous Metals
- 3351 Rolling, Drawing & Extruding Of Copper
- 3353 Aluminum Sheet, Plate & Foil
- 3354 Aluminum Extruded Prdts
- 3355 Aluminum Rolling & Drawing, NEC
- 3356 Rolling, Drawing-Extruding Of Nonferrous Metals
- 3357 Nonferrous Wire Drawing
- 3363 Aluminum Die Castings
- 3364 Nonferrous Die Castings, Exc Aluminum
- 3365 Aluminum Foundries
- 3366 Copper Foundries
- 3369 Nonferrous Foundries: Castings, NEC
- 3398 Metal Heat Treating
- 3399 Primary Metal Prdts, NEC

34 FABRICATED METAL PRODUCTS, EXCEPT MACHINERY AND TRANSPORTATION EQUIPMENT

- 3411 Metal Cans
- 3412 Metal Barrels, Drums, Kegs & Pails
- 3421 Cutlery
- 3423 Hand & Edge Tools
- 3425 Hand Saws & Saw Blades
- 3429 Hardware, NEC
- 3431 Enameled Iron & Metal Sanitary Ware
- 3432 Plumbing Fixture Fittings & Trim, Brass
- 3433 Heating Eqpt
- 3441 Fabricated Structural Steel
- 3442 Metal Doors, Sash, Frames, Molding & Trim
- 3443 Fabricated Plate Work
- 3444 Sheet Metal Work
- 3446 Architectural & Ornamental Metal Work
- 3448 Prefabricated Metal Buildings & Cmpnts
- 3449 Misc Structural Metal Work
- 3451 Screw Machine Prdts
- 3452 Bolts, Nuts, Screws, Rivets & Washers
- 3462 Iron & Steel Forgings
- 3463 Nonferrous Forgings
- 3465 Automotive Stampings
- 3466 Crowns & Closures
- 3469 Metal Stampings, NEC
- 3471 Electroplating, Plating, Polishing, Anodizing & Coloring
- 3479 Coating & Engraving, NEC
- 3482 Small Arms Ammunition
- 3483 Ammunition, Large
- 3484 Small Arms
- 3489 Ordnance & Access, NEC
- 3491 Industrial Valves
- 3492 Fluid Power Valves & Hose Fittings
- 3493 Steel Springs, Except Wire
- 3494 Valves & Pipe Fittings, NEC
- 3495 Wire Springs
- 3496 Misc Fabricated Wire Prdts
- 3497 Metal Foil & Leaf
- 3498 Fabricated Pipe & Pipe Fittings
- 3499 Fabricated Metal Prdts, NEC

35 INDUSTRIAL AND COMMERCIAL MACHINERY AND COMPUTER EQUIPMENT

- 3511 Steam, Gas & Hydraulic Turbines & Engines
- 3519 Internal Combustion Engines, NEC
- 3523 Farm Machinery & Eqpt
- 3524 Garden, Lawn Tractors & Eqpt
- 3531 Construction Machinery & Eqpt
- 3532 Mining Machinery & Eqpt
- 3533 Oil Field Machinery & Eqpt
- 3534 Elevators & Moving Stairways
- 3535 Conveyors & Eqpt
- 3536 Hoists, Cranes & Monorails
- 3537 Indl Trucks, Tractors, Trailers & Stackers
- 3541 Machine Tools: Cutting
- 3542 Machine Tools: Forming
- 3543 Industrial Patterns
- 3544 Dies, Tools, Jigs, Fixtures & Indl Molds
- 3545 Machine Tool Access
- 3546 Power Hand Tools
- 3547 Rolling Mill Machinery & Eqpt
- 3548 Welding Apparatus
- 3549 Metalworking Machinery, NEC
- 3552 Textile Machinery
- 3553 Woodworking Machinery
- 3554 Paper Inds Machinery
- 3555 Printing Trades Machinery & Eqpt
- 3556 Food Prdts Machinery
- 3559 Special Ind Machinery, NEC
- 3561 Pumps & Pumping Eqpt
- 3562 Ball & Roller Bearings
- 3563 Air & Gas Compressors
- 3564 Blowers & Fans
- 3565 Packaging Machinery
- 3566 Speed Changers, Drives & Gears
- 3567 Indl Process Furnaces & Ovens
- 3568 Mechanical Power Transmission Eqpt, NEC
- 3569 Indl Machinery & Eqpt, NEC
- 3571 Electronic Computers
- 3572 Computer Storage Devices
- 3575 Computer Terminals
- 3577 Computer Peripheral Eqpt, NEC
- 3578 Calculating & Accounting Eqpt
- 3579 Office Machines, NEC
- 3581 Automatic Vending Machines
- 3582 Commercial Laundry, Dry Clean & Pressing Mchs
- 3585 Air Conditioning & Heating Eqpt
- 3586 Measuring & Dispensing Pumps
- 3589 Service Ind Machines, NEC
- 3592 Carburetors, Pistons, Rings & Valves
- 3593 Fluid Power Cylinders & Actuators
- 3594 Fluid Power Pumps & Motors
- 3596 Scales & Balances, Exc Laboratory
- 3599 Machinery & Eqpt, Indl & Commercial, NEC

36 ELECTRONIC AND OTHER ELECTRICAL EQUIPMENT AND COMPONENTS, EXCEPT COMPUTER

- 3612 Power, Distribution & Specialty Transformers
- 3613 Switchgear & Switchboard Apparatus
- 3621 Motors & Generators
- 3624 Carbon & Graphite Prdts
- 3625 Relays & Indl Controls
- 3629 Electrical Indl Apparatus, NEC
- 3631 Household Cooking Eqpt
- 3632 Household Refrigerators & Freezers
- 3633 Household Laundry Eqpt
- 3634 Electric Household Appliances
- 3635 Household Vacuum Cleaners
- 3639 Household Appliances, NEC
- 3641 Electric Lamps
- 3643 Current-Carrying Wiring Devices
- 3644 Noncurrent-Carrying Wiring Devices
- 3645 Residential Lighting Fixtures
- 3646 Commercial, Indl & Institutional Lighting Fixtures
- 3647 Vehicular Lighting Eqpt
- 3648 Lighting Eqpt, NEC
- 3651 Household Audio & Video Eqpt
- 3652 Phonograph Records & Magnetic Tape
- 3661 Telephone & Telegraph Apparatus
- 3663 Radio & T V Communications, Systs & Eqpt, Broadcast/Studio
- 3669 Communications Eqpt, NEC
- 3671 Radio & T V Receiving Electron Tubes
- 3672 Printed Circuit Boards
- 3674 Semiconductors
- 3675 Electronic Capacitors
- 3676 Electronic Resistors
- 3677 Electronic Coils & Transformers
- 3678 Electronic Connectors
- 3679 Electronic Components, NEC
- 3691 Storage Batteries
- 3692 Primary Batteries: Dry & Wet
- 3694 Electrical Eqpt For Internal Combustion Engines
- 3695 Recording Media
- 3699 Electrical Machinery, Eqpt & Splys, NEC

37 TRANSPORTATION EQUIPMENT

- 3711 Motor Vehicles & Car Bodies
- 3713 Truck & Bus Bodies
- 3714 Motor Vehicle Parts & Access
- 3715 Truck Trailers
- 3716 Motor Homes
- 3721 Aircraft
- 3724 Aircraft Engines & Engine Parts
- 3728 Aircraft Parts & Eqpt, NEC
- 3731 Shipbuilding & Repairing
- 3732 Boat Building & Repairing
- 3743 Railroad Eqpt
- 3751 Motorcycles, Bicycles & Parts
- 3761 Guided Missiles & Space Vehicles
- 3769 Guided Missile/Space Vehicle Parts & Eqpt, NEC
- 3792 Travel Trailers & Campers
- 3795 Tanks & Tank Components
- 3799 Transportation Eqpt, NEC

38 MEASURING, ANALYZING AND CONTROLLING INSTRUMENTS; PHOTOGRAPHIC, MEDICAL AN

- 3812 Search, Detection, Navigation & Guidance Systs & Instrs
- 3821 Laboratory Apparatus & Furniture
- 3822 Automatic Temperature Controls
- 3823 Indl Instruments For Meas, Display & Control
- 3824 Fluid Meters & Counters
- 3825 Instrs For Measuring & Testing Electricity
- 3826 Analytical Instruments
- 3827 Optical Instruments
- 3829 Measuring & Controlling Devices, NEC
- 3841 Surgical & Medical Instrs & Apparatus
- 3842 Orthopedic, Prosthetic & Surgical Appliances/Splys
- 3843 Dental Eqpt & Splys
- 3844 X-ray Apparatus & Tubes
- 3845 Electromedical & Electrotherapeutic Apparatus
- 3851 Ophthalmic Goods
- 3861 Photographic Eqpt & Splys
- 3873 Watch & Clock Devices & Parts

39 MISCELLANEOUS MANUFACTURING INDUSTRIES

- 3911 Jewelry: Precious Metal
- 3914 Silverware, Plated & Stainless Steel Ware
- 3915 Jewelers Findings & Lapidary Work
- 3931 Musical Instruments
- 3942 Dolls & Stuffed Toys
- 3944 Games, Toys & Children's Vehicles
- 3949 Sporting & Athletic Goods, NEC
- 3951 Pens & Mechanical Pencils
- 3952 Lead Pencils, Crayons & Artist's Mtrls
- 3953 Marking Devices
- 3955 Carbon Paper & Inked Ribbons
- 3961 Costume Jewelry & Novelties
- 3965 Fasteners, Buttons, Needles & Pins
- 3991 Brooms & Brushes
- 3993 Signs & Advertising Displays
- 3995 Burial Caskets
- 3996 Linoleum & Hard Surface Floor Coverings, NEC
- 3999 Manufacturing Industries, NEC

73 BUSINESS SERVICES

- 7372 Prepackaged Software

76 MISCELLANEOUS REPAIR SERVICES

- 7692 Welding Repair
- 7694 Armature Rewinding Shops

SIC SECTION

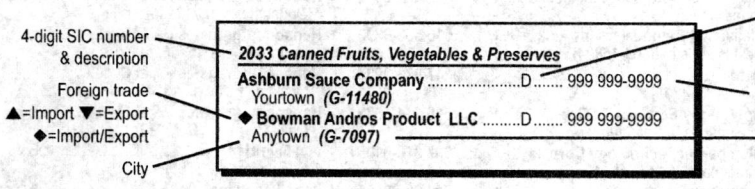

- See footnotes for symbols and codes identification.
- The SIC codes in this section are from the latest Standard Industrial Classification manual published by the U.S. Government's Office of Management and Budget. For more information regarding SICs, see the Explanatory Notes.
- Companies may be listed under multiple classifications.

10 METAL MINING

1011 Iron Ores
Essar Steel Minnesota LLC .... G 212 292-2600
 New York (G-10115)

1021 Copper Ores
Global Gold Corporation .... F 914 925-0020
 Rye (G-15084)

1041 Gold Ores
Andes Gold Corporation .... D 212 541-2495
 New York (G-9200)
▲ Capital Gold Corporation .... G 212 668-0842
 New York (G-9575)
Fuda Group (usa) Corporation .... G 646 751-7488
 New York (G-10268)
Global Gold Corporation .... F 914 925-0020
 Rye (G-15084)
Gncc Capital Inc .... G 702 951-9793
 New York (G-10367)

1044 Silver Ores
Global Gold Corporation .... F 914 925-0020
 Rye (G-15084)
▲ Rochester Silver Works LLC .... E 585 477-9501
 Rochester (G-14670)

1081 Metal Mining Svcs
◆ Coremet Trading Inc .... G 212 964-3600
 New York (G-9784)

1094 Uranium, Radium & Vanadium Ores
Global Gold Corporation .... F 914 925-0020
 Rye (G-15084)

1099 Metal Ores, NEC
Alcoa USA Corp .... F 212 518-5400
 New York (G-9127)
American Douglas Metals Inc .... F 716 856-3170
 Buffalo (G-2824)

12 COAL MINING

1231 Anthracite Mining
Acrs Inc .... F 914 288-8100
 White Plains (G-17101)

1241 Coal Mining Svcs
Desku Group Inc .... G 646 436-1464
 Brooklyn (G-1857)
Dowa International Corp .... F 212 697-3217
 New York (G-9968)
Lessoilcom .... G 516 319-5052
 Franklin Square (G-5374)
Randgold Resources Ltd .... G 212 815-2129
 New York (G-11827)
Starfuels Inc .... G 914 289-4800
 White Plains (G-17197)
Trimet Coal LLC .... E 718 951-3654
 Brooklyn (G-2699)
▲ US Pump Corp .... G 516 303-7799
 West Hempstead (G-16896)

13 OIL AND GAS EXTRACTION

1311 Crude Petroleum & Natural Gas
Chanse Petroleum Corporation .... G 212 682-3789
 New York (G-9629)
China N E Petro Holdings Ltd .... A 212 307-3568
 New York (G-9650)
County Energy Corp .... G 718 626-7000
 Brooklyn (G-1807)
Dlh Energy Service LLC .... G 716 410-0028
 Lakewood (G-7315)
Flownet LLC .... G 716 685-4036
 Lancaster (G-7340)
Green Buffalo Fuel LLC .... F 716 768-0600
 Tonawanda (G-16185)
▲ Hess Corporation .... B 212 997-8500
 New York (G-10507)
Hess Energy Exploration Ltd .... G 732 750-6500
 New York (G-10508)
Hess Explrtion Prod Hldngs Ltd .... G 732 750-6000
 New York (G-10509)
Hess Pipeline Corporation .... C 212 997-8500
 New York (G-10511)
Hess Tioga Gas Plant LLC .... C 212 997-8500
 New York (G-10512)
Ipp Energy LLC .... G 607 773-3307
 Binghamton (G-923)
Kimmeridge Energy MGT Co LLC .... F 646 517-7252
 New York (G-10887)
Lukoil Americas Corporation .... C 212 421-4141
 New York (G-11090)
MRC Global (us) Inc .... F 607 739-8575
 Horseheads (G-6613)
Repsol Oil & Gas Usa LLC .... F 607 562-4000
 Horseheads (G-6618)
Reserve Gas Company Inc .... G 716 937-9484
 Alden (G-185)
Resource PTRlm&ptrochmcl Intl .... E 212 537-3856
 New York (G-11874)
Rocket Tech Fuel Corp .... F 516 810-8947
 Bay Shore (G-732)
Speedway LLC .... F 631 738-2536
 Lake Grove (G-7291)
Stedman Energy Inc .... G 716 789-3018
 Mayville (G-8250)

1321 Natural Gas Liquids
20 Bliss St Inc .... G 716 326-2790
 Westfield (G-17073)
Blue Rhino Global Sourcing Inc .... E 516 752-0670
 Melville (G-8329)
Center State Propane LLC .... G 315 841-4044
 Waterville (G-16700)
Green Buffalo Fuel LLC .... F 716 768-0600
 Tonawanda (G-16185)
Nfe Management LLC .... F 212 798-6100
 New York (G-11442)
Paraco Gas Corporation .... G 845 279-8414
 Brewster (G-1223)
Paraco Gas Corporation .... E 800 647-4427
 Rye Brook (G-15099)
Western Oil and Gas JV Inc .... G 914 967-4758
 Rye (G-15095)

1381 Drilling Oil & Gas Wells
Alden Aurora Gas Company Inc .... G 716 937-9484
 Alden (G-177)
Barber & Deline Enrgy Svcs LLC .... F 315 696-8961
 Tully (G-16298)

Barber & Deline LLC .... F 607 749-2619
 Tully (G-16299)
Copper Ridge Oil Inc .... G 716 372-4021
 Jamestown (G-7019)
Geotechnical Drilling Inc .... D 516 616-6055
 Mineola (G-8546)
Lenape Energy Inc .... G 585 344-1200
 Alexander (G-190)
Lukoil North America LLC .... E 212 421-4141
 New York (G-11091)
Schneider Amalco Inc .... F 917 470-9674
 New York (G-12009)
Steel Partners Holdings LP .... E 212 520-2300
 New York (G-12212)
Turner Undgrd Instilations Inc .... F 585 739-0238
 Henrietta (G-6323)
U S Energy Development Corp .... D 716 636-0401
 Getzville (G-5617)
▲ US Pump Corp .... G 516 303-7799
 West Hempstead (G-16896)
Western Oil and Gas JV Inc .... G 914 967-4758
 Rye (G-15095)

1382 Oil & Gas Field Exploration Svcs
Able Environmental Services .... G 631 567-6585
 Bohemia (G-998)
Aegis Oil Limited Ventures LLC .... F 646 233-4900
 New York (G-9099)
America Capital Energy Corp .... G 212 983-8316
 New York (G-9161)
▲ Aquifer Drilling & Testing Inc .... C 516 616-6026
 Mineola (G-8528)
▲ Aterra Exploration LLC .... E 212 315-0030
 New York (G-9300)
Bistate Oil Management Corp .... F 212 935-4110
 New York (G-9456)
FT Seismic Support Inc .... G 607 527-8595
 Campbell (G-3357)
Hess Energy Exploration Ltd .... G 732 750-6500
 New York (G-10508)
Hess Explrtion Prod Hldngs Ltd .... G 732 750-6000
 New York (G-10509)
JP Oil Group Inc .... G 607 563-1360
 Sidney (G-15462)
KKR Ntral Rsources Fund I-A LP .... G 212 750-8300
 New York (G-10895)
Lenape Energy Inc .... G 585 344-1200
 Alexander (G-190)
Lenape Resources Inc .... F 585 344-1200
 Alexander (G-191)
Madoff Energy III LLC .... G 212 744-1918
 New York (G-11122)
Mep Alaska LLC .... G 646 535-9005
 Brooklyn (G-2302)
Native Amercn Enrgy Group Inc .... G 718 408-2323
 Forest Hills (G-5332)
Norse Energy Corp USA .... G 716 568-2048
 Buffalo (G-3117)
Occidental Energy Mktg Inc .... G 212 632-4950
 New York (G-11507)
Range Rsurces - Appalachia LLC .... G 716 753-3385
 Mayville (G-8249)
Sanguine Gas Exploration LLC .... G 212 582-8555
 New York (G-11986)
Schlumberger Technology Corp .... C 607 378-0105
 Horseheads (G-6621)
Seneca Resources Corporation .... F 716 630-6750
 Williamsville (G-17278)
Smith International Inc .... D 212 350-9400
 New York (G-12133)

13 OIL AND GAS EXTRACTION

Somerset Production Co LLC .... G 716 932-6480
Buffalo *(G-3217)*
▲ Springfield Oil Services Inc .... F 914 315-6812
Harrison *(G-6009)*
Springfield Oil Services Inc .... G 516 482-5995
Great Neck *(G-5857)*
U S Energy Development Corp .... D 716 636-0401
Getzville *(G-5617)*
Unco United Oil Holdings LLC .... F 212 481-1003
New York *(G-12466)*
Waffenbauch USA .... E 716 326-4508
Westfield *(G-17081)*
Warren Energy Services LLC .... F 212 697-9660
New York *(G-12619)*
Wellspring Omni Holdings Corp .... A 212 318-9800
New York *(G-12638)*

1389 Oil & Gas Field Svcs, NEC

A & Mt Realty Group LLC .... F 718 974-5871
Brooklyn *(G-1527)*
◆ Acu Rite Companies Inc .... G 716 661-1700
Jamestown *(G-7004)*
Ah Elctronic Test Eqp Repr Ctr .... F 631 234-8979
Central Islip *(G-3509)*
Alba Fuel Corp .... G 718 931-1700
Bronx *(G-1267)*
Alice Perkins .... G 716 378-5100
Salamanca *(G-15125)*
Arm Construction Company Inc .... G 646 235-6520
East Elmhurst *(G-4410)*
Babula Construction Inc .... G 716 681-0886
Lancaster *(G-7329)*
Barber & Deline Enrgy Svcs LLC .... F 315 696-8961
Tully *(G-16298)*
Bass Oil & Chemical Llc .... F 718 628-4444
Brooklyn *(G-1667)*
Bluebar Oil Co Inc .... F 315 245-4328
Blossvale *(G-991)*
Case Brothers Inc .... G 716 925-7172
Limestone *(G-7472)*
Cotton Well Drilling Co Inc .... G 716 672-2788
Sheridan *(G-15422)*
Darrell Mitchell .... G 646 659-7075
Arverne *(G-422)*
Dimension Development Corp .... G 718 361-8825
Long Island City *(G-7745)*
Empire State Pipeline .... G 585 321-1560
Rush *(G-15071)*
Essar Americas .... G 212 292-2600
New York *(G-10114)*
Fame Construction Inc .... E 718 626-1000
Astoria *(G-440)*
Five Star Field Services .... G 347 446-6816
Long Beach *(G-7671)*
Fuel Energy Services USA Ltd .... E 607 846-2650
Horseheads *(G-6607)*
Gas Field Specialists Inc .... D 716 378-6422
Horseheads *(G-6608)*
Gas Recovery Systems LLC .... F 914 421-4903
White Plains *(G-17138)*
Gotham Energy 360 LLC .... F 917 338-1023
New York *(G-10380)*
Grit Energy Services Inc .... G 212 701-4500
New York *(G-10409)*
I & S of NY Inc .... F 716 373-7001
Allegany *(G-204)*
Iron Eagle Group Inc .... G 888 481-4445
New York *(G-10704)*
Jay Little Oil Well Servi .... G 716 925-8905
Limestone *(G-7473)*
Jemcap Servicing LLC .... G 212 213-9353
New York *(G-10758)*
Legal Servicing LLC .... G 716 565-9300
Williamsville *(G-17273)*
Lenape Energy Inc .... G 585 344-1200
Alexander *(G-190)*
Marcellus Energy Services LLC .... E 607 236-0038
Candor *(G-3404)*
Mep Alaska LLC .... G 646 535-9005
Brooklyn *(G-2302)*
Metro Group Inc .... D 718 392-3616
Long Island City *(G-7841)*
Northeastern Air Quality Inc .... F 518 857-3641
Albany *(G-111)*
Occhioerosso John .... F 718 541-7025
Staten Island *(G-15738)*
P & C Gas Measurements Service .... F 716 257-3412
Cattaraugus *(G-3466)*
Petro Inc .... G 516 686-1717
Plainview *(G-13657)*

Petro Inc .... G 516 686-1900
Hicksville *(G-6412)*
Prefab Construction Inc .... F 631 821-9613
Sound Beach *(G-15535)*
Professional Remodelers Inc .... G 516 565-9300
West Hempstead *(G-16894)*
Rpc Inc .... E 347 873-3935
Elmont *(G-4738)*
Sabre Energy Services LLC .... F 518 514-1572
Slingerlands *(G-15500)*
Schlumberger Technology Corp .... C 607 378-0105
Horseheads *(G-6621)*
Schmitt Sales Inc .... G 716 632-8595
Williamsville *(G-17277)*
Schneider Amalco Inc .... F 917 470-9674
New York *(G-12009)*
Smith International Inc .... D 212 350-9400
New York *(G-12133)*
Sovereign Servicing System LLC .... F 914 779-1400
Bronxville *(G-1503)*
Speedway LLC .... F 718 815-6897
Staten Island *(G-15759)*
▲ Steel Excel Inc .... G 914 461-1300
White Plains *(G-17198)*
Superior Energy Services Inc .... G 716 483-0100
Jamestown *(G-7067)*
T A S Sales Service LLC .... G 518 234-4919
Cobleskill *(G-3764)*
Terra Enrgy Resource Tech Inc .... F 212 286-9197
New York *(G-12323)*
U S Energy Development Corp .... D 716 636-0401
Getzville *(G-5617)*
Wellspring Omni Holdings Corp .... A 212 318-9800
New York *(G-12638)*

14 MINING AND QUARRYING OF NONMETALLIC MINERALS, EXCEPT FUELS

1411 Dimension Stone

◆ Adirondack Natural Stone LLC .... E 518 499-0602
Whitehall *(G-17217)*
Alice Perkins .... G 716 378-5100
Salamanca *(G-15125)*
Cold Spring Granite Company .... E 518 647-8191
Au Sable Forks *(G-474)*
Dominic De Nigris Inc .... E 718 597-4460
Bronx *(G-1319)*
Domoteck Interiors Inc .... E 718 433-4300
Woodside *(G-17343)*
Finger Lakes Stone Co Inc .... F 607 273-4646
Ithaca *(G-6878)*
Hadeka Stone Corp .... E 518 282-9605
Hampton *(G-5981)*
Hillburn Granite Company Inc .... G 845 357-8900
Hillburn *(G-6441)*
▲ Hilltop Slate Inc .... E 518 642-1453
Middle Granville *(G-8432)*
Imerys Usa Inc .... F 315 287-0780
Gouverneur *(G-5761)*
▲ Minerals Technologies Inc .... E 212 878-1800
New York *(G-11302)*
▲ New York Quarries Inc .... F 518 756-3138
Alcove *(G-175)*
Suffolk Granite Manufacturing .... E 631 226-4774
Lindenhurst *(G-7509)*
Vermont Multicolor Slate .... G 518 642-2400
Middle Granville *(G-8435)*

1422 Crushed & Broken Limestone

Barrett Paving Materials Inc .... F 315 737-9471
Clayville *(G-3712)*
Cobleskill Stone Products Inc .... F 518 299-3066
Prattsville *(G-13961)*
Cobleskill Stone Products Inc .... F 518 295-7121
Schoharie *(G-15338)*
Cobleskill Stone Products Inc .... F 518 234-0221
Cobleskill *(G-3760)*
Cobleskill Stone Products Inc .... F 607 637-4271
Hancock *(G-5984)*
Dolomite Products Company Inc .... F 315 524-1998
Rochester *(G-14337)*
Hanson Aggregates PA Inc .... E 315 858-1100
Jordanville *(G-7160)*
Hanson Aggregates PA Inc .... F 518 568-2444
Saint Johnsville *(G-15120)*
Hanson Aggregates PA LLC .... E 315 469-5501
Jamesville *(G-7083)*

Hanson Aggregates PA LLC .... E 315 685-3321
Skaneateles *(G-15485)*
Hanson Aggregates PA LLC .... F 315 393-3743
Ogdensburg *(G-13136)*
Hanson Aggregates PA LLC .... E 585 624-1220
Honeoye Falls *(G-6558)*
Hanson Aggregates PA LLC .... F 315 821-7222
Oriskany Falls *(G-13342)*
Hanson Aggregates PA LLC .... E 315 789-6202
Oaks Corners *(G-13089)*
Jml Quarries Inc .... E 845 932-8206
Cochecton *(G-3766)*
John Vespa Inc .... F 315 788-6330
Watertown *(G-16678)*
Lafarge North America Inc .... F 716 876-8788
Tonawanda *(G-16195)*
Lilac Quarries LLC .... G 607 867-4016
Mount Upton *(G-8700)*
Patterson Materials Corp .... E 845 832-6000
New Windsor *(G-8993)*
Schaefer Entps of Deposit .... E 607 467-4990
Deposit *(G-4303)*
Shelby Crushed Stone Inc .... E 585 798-4501
Medina *(G-8314)*
◆ Specialty Minerals Inc .... E 212 878-1800
New York *(G-12178)*
Upstone Materials Inc .... E 518 891-0236
Saranac Lake *(G-15167)*

1423 Crushed & Broken Granite

MCM Natural Stone Inc .... F 585 586-6510
Rochester *(G-14523)*
Suffolk Granite Manufacturing .... E 631 226-4774
Lindenhurst *(G-7509)*
Tilcon New York Inc .... D 845 358-3100
West Nyack *(G-16958)*

1429 Crushed & Broken Stone, NEC

Barrett Paving Materials Inc .... F 315 737-9471
Clayville *(G-3712)*
Cayuga Crushed Stone Inc .... E 607 533-4273
Lansing *(G-7373)*
County Line Stone Co Inc .... E 716 542-5435
Akron *(G-18)*
Dolomite Products Company Inc .... E 585 586-2568
Penfield *(G-13522)*
Hanson Aggregates PA LLC .... F 315 393-3743
Ogdensburg *(G-13136)*
Hanson Aggregates PA LLC .... F 315 821-7222
Oriskany Falls *(G-13342)*
Labrador Stone Inc .... G 570 465-2120
Binghamton *(G-928)*
Masten Enterprises LLC .... C 845 932-8206
Cochecton *(G-3767)*
Peckham Materials Corp .... E 518 747-3353
Hudson Falls *(G-6680)*
Rock Iroquois Products Inc .... E 585 637-6834
Brockport *(G-1247)*
Shelby Crushed Stone Inc .... E 585 798-4501
Medina *(G-8314)*
Sparclean MBL Refinishing Inc .... G 718 445-2351
Ridgewood *(G-14137)*
▲ Tilcon New York Inc .... B 845 358-4500
West Nyack *(G-16957)*
Tilcon New York Inc .... E 845 778-5591
Walden *(G-16557)*
Tilcon New York Inc .... D 845 480-3249
Flushing *(G-5306)*
Tilcon New York Inc .... D 845 615-0216
Goshen *(G-5754)*
Tilcon New York Inc .... D 845 457-3158
Montgomery *(G-8639)*
Tilcon New York Inc .... D 845 358-3100
West Nyack *(G-16958)*
Upstone Materials Inc .... D 518 561-5321
Plattsburgh *(G-13735)*

1442 Construction Sand & Gravel

110 Sand Company .... E 631 694-2822
Melville *(G-8319)*
110 Sand Company .... F 631 694-2822
West Babylon *(G-16786)*
A Colarusso and Son Inc .... E 518 828-3218
Hudson *(G-6631)*
Barrett Paving Materials Inc .... G 607 723-5367
Binghamton *(G-887)*
Belangers Gravel & Stone Inc .... G 585 728-3906
Wayland *(G-16733)*
Bonsal American Inc .... E 631 208-8073
Calverton *(G-3314)*

SIC SECTION

20 FOOD AND KINDRED PRODUCTS

Buffalo Crushed Stone Inc .... F 716 566-9636
Franklinville (G-5378)
Buffalo Crushed Stone Inc .... G 607 587-8102
Alfred Station (G-199)
Callanan Industries Inc .... E 845 331-6868
Kingston (G-7211)
Central Dover Development .... G 917 709-3266
Dover Plains (G-4338)
Chenango Asphalt Products .... F 607 334-3117
Norwich (G-13038)
Country Side Sand & Gravel .... G 716 988-3271
Collins (G-3840)
Country Side Sand & Gravel .... F 716 988-3271
South Dayton (G-15541)
Dalrymple Grav & Contg Co Inc ...... F 607 739-0391
Pine City (G-13577)
Dalrymple Grav & Contg Co Inc ...... E 607 529-3235
Chemung (G-3621)
Dalrymple Holding Corp .... G 607 737-6200
Pine City (G-13578)
Dicks Concrete Co Inc .... E 845 374-5966
New Hampton (G-8844)
Diehl Development Inc .... G 585 494-2920
Bergen (G-843)
E F Lippert Co Inc .... F 716 373-1100
Allegany (G-202)
E Tetz & Sons Inc .... D 845 692-4486
Middletown (G-8470)
Eagle Harbor Sand & Gravel Inc ..... G 585 798-4501
Albion (G-167)
East Coast Mines Ltd .... E 631 653-5445
East Quogue (G-4469)
Elam Sand & Gravel Corp .... G 585 657-8000
Bloomfield (G-981)
Frew Run Gravel Products Inc .... G 716 569-4712
Frewsburg (G-5464)
Genoa Sand & Gravel Lnsg .... G 607 533-4551
Freeville (G-5448)
Greenebuild LLC .... F 917 562-0556
Brooklyn (G-2054)
H L Robinson Sand & Gravel .... F 607 659-5153
Candor (G-3403)
Hampton Sand Corp .... G 631 325-5533
Westhampton (G-17086)
Hanson Aggregates East LLC .... G 315 536-9391
Penn Yan (G-13536)
Hanson Aggregates East LLC .... E 315 548-2911
Phelps (G-13556)
Hanson Aggregates PA Inc .... E 315 858-1100
Jordanville (G-7160)
Hanson Aggregates PA Inc .... F 518 568-2444
Saint Johnsville (G-15120)
Hanson Aggregates PA LLC .... E 585 624-1220
Honeoye Falls (G-6558)
Hanson Aggregates PA LLC .... E 315 469-5501
Jamesville (G-7083)
Hanson Aggregates PA LLC .... E 315 685-3321
Skaneateles (G-15485)
Hanson Aggregates PA LLC .... E 315 782-2300
Watertown (G-16674)
Hanson Aggregates PA LLC .... F 315 821-7222
Oriskany Falls (G-13342)
Hanson Aggregates PA LLC .... E 315 789-6202
Oaks Corners (G-13089)
Hanson Aggregates PA LLC .... E 585 624-3800
Honeoye Falls (G-6557)
Hanson Aggregates PA LLC .... E 585 436-3250
Rochester (G-14440)
IA Construction Corporation .... G 716 933-8787
Portville (G-13893)
John Vespa Inc .... F 315 788-6330
Watertown (G-16678)
Johnson S Sand Gravel Inc .... G 315 771-1450
La Fargeville (G-7263)
Knight Sttlement Sand Grav LLC .... E 607 776-2048
Bath (G-659)
Lafarge North America Inc .... E 716 651-9235
Lancaster (G-7346)
Lafarge North America Inc .... E 518 756-5000
Ravena (G-14036)
Lazarek Inc .... G 315 343-1242
Oswego (G-13359)
Little Valley Sand & Gravel .... G 716 938-6676
Little Valley (G-7534)
McEwan Trucking & Grav Produc ... G 716 609-1828
East Concord (G-4407)
Milestone Construction Corp .... G 718 459-8500
Rego Park (G-14048)
Mitchell Stone Products LLC .... G 518 359-7029
Tupper Lake (G-16301)

▲ New York Sand & Stone LLC .... G 718 596-2897
Maspeth (G-8188)
Northeast Solite Corporation .... E 845 246-2177
Mount Marion (G-8694)
Palumbo Sand & Gravel Company ... E 845 832-3356
Dover Plains (G-4341)
R G King General Construction .... G 315 583-3560
Adams Center (G-4)
R J Valente Gravel Inc .... E 518 279-1001
Cropseyville (G-4085)
Rd2 Construction & Dem LLC .... F 718 980-1650
Staten Island (G-15750)
Republic Construction Co Inc .... G 914 235-3654
New Rochelle (G-8969)
Robinson Concrete Inc .... E 315 253-6666
Auburn (G-513)
Rock Mountain Farms Inc .... G 845 647-9084
Ellenville (G-4652)
Ruby Engineering LLC .... G 646 391-4600
Brooklyn (G-2536)
Rural Hill Sand and Grav Corp .... F 315 846-5212
Woodville (G-17383)
Rush Gravel Corp .... G 585 533-1740
Honeoye Falls (G-6563)
Sagaponack Sand & Gravel Corp ... E 631 537-2424
Bridgehampton (G-1233)
Seneca Stone Corporation .... G 607 737-6200
Pine City (G-13579)
Seven Springs Gravel Pdts LLC ..... G 585 343-4336
Batavia (G-647)
Shelby Crushed Stone Inc .... F 585 798-4501
Medina (G-8314)
Smith Sand & Gravel Inc .... G 315 673-4124
Marcellus (G-8120)
Sparrow Mining Co .... G 718 519-6600
Bronx (G-1458)
Speyside Holdings LLC .... E 845 928-2221
Highland Mills (G-6440)
Syracusa Sand and Gravel Inc .... F 585 924-7146
Victor (G-16529)
Syracuse Sand & Gravel LLC .... G 315 548-8207
Fulton (G-5489)
Tilcon New York Inc .... E 845 942-0602
Tomkins Cove (G-16153)
Tilcon New York Inc .... G 845 358-3100
West Nyack (G-16958)
Titus Mountain Sand & Grav LLC ... G 518 483-3740
Malone (G-8049)
Tri City Highway Products Inc .... F 607 722-2967
Binghamton (G-951)
Tri-City Highway Products Inc .... F 518 294-9964
Richmondville (G-14102)
Troy Sand & Gravel Co Inc .... F 518 674-2854
West Sand Lake (G-16961)
United Materials LLC .... G 716 662-0564
Orchard Park (G-13326)
US Allegro Inc .... E 347 408-6601
Maspeth (G-8204)

1446 Industrial Sand

◆ American Minerals Inc .... F 646 747-4222
New York (G-9176)
New Jersey Pulverizing Co Inc .... E 516 921-9595
Syosset (G-15852)
Precision Elctro Mnrl Pmco Inc .... E 716 284-2484
Niagara Falls (G-12881)
St Silicones Inc .... G 518 664-0745
Mechanicville (G-8262)

1459 Clay, Ceramic & Refractory Minerals, NEC

▲ Applied Minerals Inc .... E 212 226-4265
Brooklyn (G-1620)
Callahan & Nannini Quarry Inc .... G 845 496-4323
Salisbury Mills (G-15139)
▲ Devonian Stone New York Inc ..... F 607 655-2600
Windsor (G-17294)
Grosso Materials Inc .... F 845 361-5211
Montgomery (G-8631)

1479 Chemical & Fertilizer Mining

▲ American Rock Salt Company LLC .. E 585 991-6878
Retsof (G-14064)
Morton Salt Inc .... F 585 493-2511
Silver Springs (G-15472)
Steel City Salt LLC .... G 716 532-0000
Collins (G-3843)

1481 Nonmetallic Minerals Svcs, Except Fuels

▲ Crystal Ceres Industries Inc .... D 716 283-0445
Niagara Falls (G-12830)
Resource Capital Funds LP .... G 631 692-9111
Huntington (G-6713)

1499 Miscellaneous Nonmetallic Mining

Avs Gem Stone Corp .... G 212 944-6380
New York (G-9334)
◆ Barton Mines Company LLC .... C 518 798-5462
Glens Falls (G-5688)
▲ Capital Gold Corporation .... G 212 668-0842
New York (G-9575)
Didco Inc .... F 212 997-5022
Rego Park (G-14044)
▲ Double Star USA Inc .... G 212 929-2210
Brooklyn (G-1876)
▲ Dynamic Design Group Inc .... G 212 840-9400
New York (G-9999)
Gemfields USA Incorporated .... G 212 398-5400
New York (G-10311)
Hargrave Development .... F 716 877-7880
Kenmore (G-7175)
Herkimer Diamond Mines Inc .... E 315 891-7355
Herkimer (G-6327)
Kotel Importers Inc .... F 212 245-6200
New York (G-10919)
Ray Griffiths Inc .... G 212 689-7209
New York (G-11831)
Romance & Co Inc .... G 212 382-0337
New York (G-11932)
Signature Diamond Entps LLC .... E 212 869-5115
New York (G-12093)

20 FOOD AND KINDRED PRODUCTS

2011 Meat Packing Plants

A To Z Kosher Meat Products Co ... E 718 384-7400
Brooklyn (G-1535)
Adirondack Meat Company Inc ...... F 518 585-2333
Ticonderoga (G-16146)
Bliss-Poston The Second Wind ...... G 212 481-1055
New York (G-9467)
◆ Caribbean Foods Delight Inc .... D 845 398-3000
Tappan (G-16103)
Chefs Delight Packing Co .... F 718 388-8581
Brooklyn (G-1776)
▲ Cni Meat & Produce Inc .... G 516 599-5929
Valley Stream (G-16430)
▼ Crescent Duck Farm Inc .... E 631 722-8700
Aquebogue (G-384)
Delft Blue LLC .... C 315 768-7100
New York Mills (G-12740)
▲ Domestic Casing Co .... G 718 522-1902
Brooklyn (G-1873)
◆ DRG New York Holdings Corp .... D 914 668-9000
Mount Vernon (G-8723)
Fairbank Reconstruction Corp .... D 800 628-3276
Ashville (G-426)
Frank Wardynski & Sons Inc .... E 716 854-6083
Buffalo (G-2970)
◆ Globex Kosher Foods Inc .... E 718 630-5555
Brooklyn (G-2030)
Gold Medal Packing Inc .... G 315 337-1911
Oriskany (G-13334)
Hilltown Pork Inc .... F 518 781-4050
Canaan (G-3359)
Huda Kawshai LLC .... G 929 255-7009
Jamaica (G-6956)
Ives Farm Market .... G 315 592-4880
Fulton (G-5477)
Joel Kiryas Meat Market Corp .... F 845 782-9194
Monroe (G-8593)
Kamerys Wholesale Meats Inc .... G 716 372-6756
Olean (G-13170)
Martin D Whitbeck .... G 607 746-7642
Delhi (G-4265)
Old World Provisions Inc .... D 518 465-7307
Troy (G-16268)
Orleans Custom Packing Inc .... G 585 314-8227
Holley (G-6516)
▼ Robert & William Inc .... G 631 727-5780
Riverhead (G-14167)
▲ Sahlen Packing Company Inc ..... G 716 852-8677
Buffalo (G-3204)
Sam A Lupo & Sons Inc .... G 800 388-5352
Endicott (G-4833)

Employee Codes: A=Over 500 employees, B=251-500
C=101-250, D=51-100, E=20-50, F=10-19, G=5-9

2018 Harris
New York Manufacturers Directory

707

20 FOOD AND KINDRED PRODUCTS SIC SECTION

Side Hill Farmers Coop Inc ....G.... 315 447-4693
Canastota *(G-3399)*
The Smoke House of Catskills ....G.... 845 246-8767
Saugerties *(G-15226)*
Tri-Town Packing Corp ....F.... 315 389-5101
Brasher Falls *(G-1171)*
USA Halal Foods Inc ....G.... 718 291-9111
Long Island City *(G-7939)*
We Work ....G.... 877 673-6628
New York *(G-12628)*

2013 Sausages & Meat Prdts

Adirondack Meat Company Inc ....F.... 518 585-2333
Ticonderoga *(G-16146)*
▲ **Alle Processing Corp** ....C.... 718 894-2000
Maspeth *(G-8143)*
Alps Provision Co Inc ....E.... 718 721-4477
Astoria *(G-430)*
Arnolds Meat Food Products ....E.... 718 384-8071
Brooklyn *(G-1631)*
Atlantic Pork & Provisions Inc ....E.... 718 272-9550
Jamaica *(G-6930)*
Bianca Burgers LLC ....F.... 516 764-9591
Rockville Centre *(G-14816)*
Big Johns Adirondack Inc ....G.... 518 587-3680
Saratoga Springs *(G-15173)*
Birds Eye Holdings Inc ....A.... 585 383-1850
Rochester *(G-14250)*
Brooklyn Bangers LLC ....F.... 718 875-3535
Brooklyn *(G-1719)*
Brooklyn Casing Co Inc ....G.... 718 522-0866
Brooklyn *(G-1721)*
Buffalo Provisions Co Inc ....F.... 718 292-4300
Elmhurst *(G-4671)*
Camellia General Provision Co ....E.... 716 893-5352
Buffalo *(G-2887)*
◆ **Caribbean Foods Delight Inc** ....D.... 845 398-3000
Tappan *(G-16103)*
▲ **Cibao Meat Products Inc** ....D.... 718 993-5072
Bronx *(G-1299)*
▲ **Cni Meat & Produce Inc** ....G.... 516 599-5929
Valley Stream *(G-16430)*
De Ans Pork Products Inc ....E.... 718 788-2464
Brooklyn *(G-1845)*
Dinos Sausage & Meat Co Inc ....F.... 315 732-2661
Utica *(G-16348)*
▲ **Domestic Casing Co** ....G.... 718 522-1902
Brooklyn *(G-1873)*
Elmgang Enterprises I Inc ....F.... 212 868-4142
New York *(G-10065)*
Fairbank Reconstruction Corp ....D.... 800 628-3276
Ashville *(G-426)*
Frank Wardynski & Sons Inc ....E.... 716 854-6083
Buffalo *(G-2970)*
Freirich Julian Co Inc ....E.... 718 361-9111
Long Island City *(G-7775)*
▲ **Hansel n Gretel Brand Inc** ....C.... 718 326-0041
Glendale *(G-5671)*
Hanzlian Sausage Incorporated ....G.... 716 891-5247
Cheektowaga *(G-3603)*
Hilltown Pork Inc ....E.... 518 781-4050
Canaan *(G-3359)*
Holy Cow Kosher LLC ....G.... 347 788-8620
Spring Valley *(G-15611)*
Jacks Gourmet LLC ....F.... 718 954-4681
Brooklyn *(G-2128)*
Lancaster Quality Pork Inc ....F.... 718 439-8822
Brooklyn *(G-2194)*
Marathon Enterprises Inc ....D.... 718 665-2560
Bronx *(G-1389)*
Milan Provision Co Inc ....E.... 718 899-7678
Corona *(G-4026)*
Mineo & Sapio Meats Inc ....G.... 716 884-2398
Buffalo *(G-3087)*
Mr Pierogi LLC ....F.... 718 499-7821
Brooklyn *(G-2345)*
▲ **Niagara Tying Service Inc** ....E.... 716 825-0066
Buffalo *(G-3114)*
Original Crunch Roll Fctry LLC ....G.... 716 402-5030
Amherst *(G-258)*
Patla Enterprises Inc ....G.... 315 790-0143
Sherrill *(G-15429)*
Picone Meat Specialties Ltd ....G.... 914 381-3002
Mamaroneck *(G-8075)*
Pork King Sausage Inc ....E.... 718 542-2810
Bronx *(G-1432)*
▲ **Prime Food Processing Corp** ....D.... 718 963-2323
Brooklyn *(G-2455)*
Provisionaire & Co LLC ....E.... 646 681-8600
Brooklyn *(G-2473)*

▲ **Rapa Independent North America** ....G.... 518 561-0513
Plattsburgh *(G-13723)*
Reliable Brothers Inc ....E.... 518 273-6732
Green Island *(G-5879)*
Rosina Food Products Inc ....C.... 716 668-0123
Buffalo *(G-3193)*
Rosina Holding Inc ....G.... 716 668-0123
Buffalo *(G-3194)*
Salarinos Italian Foods Inc ....F.... 315 697-9766
Canastota *(G-3398)*
Schaller Manufacturing Corp ....D.... 718 721-5480
New York *(G-12004)*
Schonwetter Enterprises Inc ....E.... 518 237-0171
Cohoes *(G-3782)*
Schrader Meat Market ....F.... 607 869-6328
Romulus *(G-14870)*
▲ **Sun Ming Jan Inc** ....F.... 718 418-8221
Brooklyn *(G-2641)*
▲ **Syracuse Casing Co Inc** ....F.... 315 475-0309
Syracuse *(G-16073)*
Tower Isles Frozen Foods Ltd ....D.... 718 495-2626
Brooklyn *(G-2690)*
Tyson Deli Inc ....B.... 716 826-6400
Buffalo *(G-3255)*
White Eagle Packing Co Inc ....F.... 518 374-4366
Schenectady *(G-15335)*
Zweigles Inc ....D.... 585 546-1740
Rochester *(G-14806)*

2015 Poultry Slaughtering, Dressing & Processing

▲ **Advanced Frozen Foods Inc** ....E.... 516 333-6344
Westbury *(G-16989)*
▲ **Alle Processing Corp** ....C.... 718 894-2000
Maspeth *(G-8143)*
Campanellis Poultry Farm Inc ....G.... 845 482-2222
Bethel *(G-859)*
▼ **Crescent Duck Farm Inc** ....E.... 631 722-8700
Aquebogue *(G-384)*
Egg Low Farms Inc ....F.... 607 674-4653
Sherburne *(G-15413)*
Goya Foods Inc ....D.... 716 549-0076
Angola *(G-380)*
▲ **Hansel n Gretel Brand Inc** ....C.... 718 326-0041
Glendale *(G-5671)*
Hlw Acres LLC ....G.... 585 591-0795
Attica *(G-472)*
◆ **Hoskie Co Inc** ....D.... 718 628-8672
Brooklyn *(G-2084)*
Hudson Valley Foie Gras LLC ....F.... 845 292-2500
Ferndale *(G-5179)*
JW Consulting Inc ....G.... 845 325-7070
Monroe *(G-8594)*
▲ **K&Ns Foods Usa LLC** ....E.... 315 598-8080
Fulton *(G-5479)*
MB Food Processing Inc ....B.... 845 436-5001
South Fallsburg *(G-15543)*
Murray Bresky Consultants Ltd ....B.... 845 436-5001
South Fallsburg *(G-15544)*
Ready Egg Farms Inc ....G.... 607 674-4653
Sherburne *(G-15416)*
Sing Ah Poultry ....G.... 718 625-7253
Brooklyn *(G-2591)*
Vineland Kosher Poultry Inc ....F.... 718 921-1347
Brooklyn *(G-2746)*
Wendels Poultry Farm ....G.... 716 592-2299
East Concord *(G-4408)*

2021 Butter

Canalside Creamery Inc ....G.... 716 695-2876
North Tonawanda *(G-12983)*
◆ **O-At-Ka Milk Products Coop Inc** ....B.... 585 343-0536
Batavia *(G-645)*
Pure Ghee Inc ....G.... 718 224-7399
Flushing *(G-5292)*

2022 Cheese

Agri-Mark Inc ....D.... 518 497-6644
Chateaugay *(G-3584)*
Artisanal Brands Inc ....E.... 914 441-3591
Bronxville *(G-1499)*
Castelli America LLC ....D.... 716 782-2101
Ashville *(G-423)*
Cemac Foods Corp ....F.... 914 835-0526
Harrison *(G-5999)*
Cheese Experts USA Ltd Lblty ....G.... 908 275-3889
Staten Island *(G-15678)*
Crosswinds Farm & Creamery ....G.... 607 327-0363
Ovid *(G-13370)*

East Hill Creamery LLC ....G.... 585 237-3622
Perry *(G-13546)*
Emkay Trading Corp ....G.... 914 592-9000
Elmsford *(G-4757)*
Emkay Trading Corp ....E.... 585 492-3800
Arcade *(G-392)*
Empire Cheese Inc ....C.... 585 968-1552
Cuba *(G-4095)*
▲ **Euphrates Inc** ....D.... 518 762-3488
Johnstown *(G-7142)*
F Cappiello Dairy Pdts Inc ....E.... 518 374-5064
Schenectady *(G-15281)*
Fly Creek Cder Mill Orchrd Inc ....G.... 607 547-9692
Fly Creek *(G-5319)*
Four Fat Fowl Inc ....G.... 518 733-5230
Stephentown *(G-15779)*
Friendship Dairies LLC ....C.... 585 973-3031
Friendship *(G-5466)*
◆ **Gharana Industries LLC** ....G.... 315 651-4004
Waterloo *(G-16649)*
Great Lakes Cheese NY Inc ....D.... 315 232-4511
Adams *(G-3)*
▲ **Habco Corp** ....E.... 631 789-1400
Amityville *(G-290)*
HP Hood LLC ....D.... 607 295-8134
Arkport *(G-408)*
HP Hood LLC ....D.... 315 829-3339
Vernon *(G-16458)*
▲ **Hudson Valley Creamery LLC** ....F.... 518 851-2570
Hudson *(G-6648)*
Instantwhip of Buffalo Inc ....E.... 716 892-7031
Buffalo *(G-3027)*
Kraft Heinz Foods Company ....B.... 315 376-6575
Lowville *(G-7965)*
Kraft Heinz Foods Company ....B.... 607 527-4584
Campbell *(G-3358)*
Kraft Heinz Foods Company ....C.... 607 865-7131
Walton *(G-16569)*
Kutters Cheese Factory Inc ....E.... 585 599-3693
Corfu *(G-3978)*
Lactalis American Group Inc ....D.... 716 827-2622
Buffalo *(G-3059)*
◆ **Lactalis American Group Inc** ....B.... 716 823-6262
Buffalo *(G-3060)*
Leprino Foods Company ....C.... 570 888-9658
Waverly *(G-16729)*
Lumazu LLC ....G.... 518 623-3372
Warrensburg *(G-16600)*
Lumazu LLC ....F.... 518 623-3372
Warrensburg *(G-16601)*
Mondelez Global LLC ....G.... 845 567-4701
Newburgh *(G-12790)*
▼ **Mongiello Sales Inc** ....E.... 845 436-4200
Hurleyville *(G-6769)*
Mongiellos Itln Cheese Spc LLC ....C.... 845 436-4200
Hurleyville *(G-6770)*
Mozzarella Fresca Incorporated ....G.... 559 752-4823
Buffalo *(G-3096)*
▲ **Noga Dairies Inc** ....F.... 516 293-5448
Farmingdale *(G-5076)*
Original Hrkmer Cnty Chese Inc ....D.... 315 895-7428
Ilion *(G-6782)*
Pecoraro Dairy Products Inc ....G.... 718 388-2379
Brooklyn *(G-2424)*
Rainbeau Ridge Farm ....G.... 914 234-2197
Bedford Hills *(G-803)*
Red Creek Cold Storage LLC ....G.... 315 576-2069
Red Creek *(G-14038)*
Sandvoss Farms LLC ....G.... 585 297-7044
East Bethany *(G-4406)*
Sargento Foods Inc ....C.... 920 893-8484
New York *(G-11992)*
Sorrento Lactalis Inc ....G.... 716 823-6262
Buffalo *(G-3221)*
▲ **Taam Tov Foods Inc** ....G.... 718 788-8880
Brooklyn *(G-2662)*
◆ **World Cheese Co Inc** ....F.... 718 965-1700
Brooklyn *(G-2780)*

2023 Milk, Condensed & Evaporated

Alpina Foods Inc ....F.... 855 886-1914
Batavia *(G-622)*
Baby Central LLC ....G.... 718 372-2229
Brooklyn *(G-1660)*
Century Tom Inc ....G.... 347 654-3179
Flushing *(G-5237)*
Dairy Farmers America Inc ....C.... 585 409-2200
Batavia *(G-632)*
Danone Nutricia Early ....E.... 914 872-8556
White Plains *(G-17126)*

SIC SECTION
20 FOOD AND KINDRED PRODUCTS

Dynatabs LLC .... F 718 376-6084
Brooklyn (G-1889)
El-Gen LLC .... G....... 631 218-3400
Bohemia (G-1060)
Friendship Dairies LLC .... C 585 973-3031
Friendship (G-5466)
Frieslndcmpina Ingrdnts N Amer .... E 607 746-0196
Delhi (G-4264)
▼ GNI Commerce Inc .... G....... 347 275-1155
Brooklyn (G-2034)
◆ Hain Celestial Group Inc .... C 516 587-5000
New Hyde Park (G-8882)
Infant Formula Laboratory Svc .... F 718 257-3000
Brooklyn (G-2103)
◆ Kerry Bfnctnal Ingredients Inc .... D 607 334-1700
Norwich (G-13048)
Makers Nutrition LLC .... E 631 456-5397
Hauppauge (G-6151)
◆ Nationwide Dairy Inc .... G....... 347 689-8148
Brooklyn (G-2359)
Nestle Usa Inc .... C 914 272-4021
White Plains (G-17167)
◆ O-At-Ka Milk Products Coop Inc .... B 585 343-0536
Batavia (G-645)
Physiologics LLC .... F 800 765-6775
Ronkonkoma (G-14993)
◆ Rich Products Corporation .... A 716 878-8000
Buffalo (G-3185)
Solivaira Specialties Inc .... D 716 693-4009
North Tonawanda (G-13014)
▼ Sugar Foods Corporation .... E 212 753-6900
New York (G-12249)
Upstate Niagara Coop Inc .... C 716 892-2121
Buffalo (G-3264)
Vitakem Nutraceutical Inc .... C 631 956-8343
Smithtown (G-15524)
Vitamin Power Incororated .... G....... 631 676-5790
Hauppauge (G-6253)

2024 Ice Cream

▲ Allied Food Products Inc .... F 718 230-4227
Brooklyn (G-1588)
Berrywild .... G....... 212 686-5848
New York (G-9415)
Bleecker Pastry Tartufo Inc .... G....... 718 937-9830
Long Island City (G-7720)
Blue Marble Ice Cream .... F 718 858-5551
Brooklyn (G-1700)
Blue Pig Ice Cream Factory .... G....... 914 271-3850
Croton On Hudson (G-4088)
Byrne Dairy Inc .... E 315 475-2111
Syracuse (G-15898)
Byrne Dairy Inc .... B 315 475-2121
La Fayette (G-7267)
Carols Polar Parlor .... G....... 315 468-3404
Syracuse (G-15904)
Chobani Idaho LLC .... G....... 208 432-2248
Norwich (G-13043)
Clinton Creamery Inc .... F 917 324-9699
Laurelton (G-7412)
▲ Crepini LLC .... E 347 422-0829
Brooklyn (G-1816)
▼ Crowley Foods Inc .... E 800 637-0019
Binghamton (G-900)
Delicioso Coco Helado Inc .... F 718 292-1930
Bronx (G-1317)
Df Mavens Inc .... E 347 813-4705
Astoria (G-434)
Elegant Desserts By Metro Inc .... F 718 388-1323
Brooklyn (G-1914)
Ffc Holding Corp Subsidiaries .... F 716 366-5400
Dunkirk (G-4366)
▼ Fieldbrook Foods Corporation .... C 716 366-5400
Dunkirk (G-4367)
Four Brothers Italian Bakery .... G....... 914 741-5434
Hawthorne (G-6269)
Fresh Ice Cream Company LLC .... F 347 603-6021
Brooklyn (G-2006)
G Pesso & Sons Inc .... G....... 718 224-9130
Bayside (G-766)
GM Ice Cream Inc .... G....... 646 236-7383
Queens Village (G-13993)
▲ Grom Columbus LLC .... G....... 212 974-3444
New York (G-10412)
HP Hood LLC .... D 315 829-3339
Vernon (G-16458)
HP Hood LLC .... A 607 772-6580
Binghamton (G-916)
Ice Cream Man Inc .... E 518 692-8382
Greenwich (G-5909)
JMS Ices Inc .... F 718 448-0853
Staten Island (G-15714)
Jones Humdinger .... F 607 771-6501
Binghamton (G-927)
Kozy Shack Enterprises LLC .... C 516 870-3000
Hicksville (G-6388)
La Cremeria .... G....... 212 226-6758
New York (G-10945)
▲ LArte Del Gelato Gruppo Inc .... F 718 383-6600
Long Island City (G-7815)
Lickity Splits .... G....... 585 345-6091
Batavia (G-642)
Lumazu LLC .... G....... 518 623-3372
Warrensburg (G-16600)
Lumazu LLC .... F 518 623-3372
Warrensburg (G-16601)
Macadoodles .... G....... 607 652-9019
Stamford (G-15645)
▲ Macedonia Ltd .... F 718 462-3596
Brooklyn (G-2253)
Main Street Sweets .... F 914 332-5757
Tarrytown (G-16117)
Mamas .... G....... 518 399-2828
Burnt Hills (G-3293)
Marina Ice Cream .... G....... 718 235-3000
Brooklyn (G-2271)
Marvel Dairy Whip Inc .... G....... 516 889-4232
Lido Beach (G-7463)
Moonlight Creamery .... G....... 585 223-0880
Fairport (G-4870)
MSQ Corporation .... G....... 718 465-0900
Queens Village (G-13998)
My Most Favorite Food .... G....... 212 580-5130
New York (G-11353)
Ninas Custard .... E 716 636-0345
Getzville (G-5613)
Nutrifast LLC .... F 347 671-3181
New York (G-11490)
NY Froyo LLC .... G....... 516 312-4588
Deer Park (G-4208)
▲ Olympic Ice Cream Co Inc .... E 718 849-6200
Richmond Hill (G-14089)
Olympic Ice Cream Co Inc .... E 718 849-6200
Jamaica (G-6974)
Original Fowlers Choclat Inc .... G....... 716 668-2113
Cheektowaga (G-3612)
Paleteria Fernandez Inc .... E 914 315-1598
Mamaroneck (G-8074)
▲ Perrys Ice Cream Company Inc .... B 716 542-5492
Akron (G-24)
Phyljohn Distributors Inc .... F 518 459-2775
Albany (G-120)
Piazzas Ice Cream Ice Hse Inc .... F 718 818-8811
Staten Island (G-15742)
◆ Pop Bar LLC .... G....... 212 255-4874
New York (G-11705)
Primo Frozen Desserts Inc .... G....... 718 252-2312
Brooklyn (G-2456)
Pulmuone Foods Usa Inc .... E 845 365-3300
Tappan (G-16106)
Purity Ice Cream Co Inc .... F 607 272-1545
Ithaca (G-6908)
Quaker Bonnet Inc .... G....... 716 885-7208
Buffalo (G-3172)
▼ Quality Dairy Farms Inc .... E 315 942-2611
Boonville (G-1166)
Scoops R US Incorporated .... G....... 212 730-7959
New York (G-12024)
Smartys Corner .... G....... 607 239-5276
Endicott (G-4834)
▲ Spatula LLC .... F 917 582-8684
New York (G-12176)
Stewarts Processing Corp .... D 518 581-1200
Ballston Spa (G-609)
▲ Sweet Melodys LLC .... E 716 580-3227
East Amherst (G-4389)
Swirl Bliss LLC .... G....... 516 867-9475
North Baldwin (G-12927)
Tia Lattrell .... G....... 845 373-9494
Amenia (G-220)
▲ TLC-Lc Inc .... E 212 756-8900
New York (G-12375)
Twisters .... G....... 585 346-3730
Livonia (G-7592)
Unilever United States Inc .... F 212 546-0200
New York (G-12474)
Unilever United States Inc .... C 212 546-0200
New York (G-12475)
Van Alphen & Doran Corp .... G....... 518 782-9242
Schenectady (G-15332)
▲ Van Leeuwen Artisan Ice Cream .... G....... 718 701-1630
Brooklyn (G-2736)
Victory Garden .... G....... 212 206-7273
New York (G-12564)
Washburns Dairy Inc .... E 518 725-0629
Gloversville (G-5743)
Wicked Spoon Inc .... F 646 335-2890
New York (G-12657)
Yog N Go Inc .... G....... 585 319-8110
East Rochester (G-4486)
Zings Company LLC .... G....... 631 454-0339
Farmingdale (G-5154)

2026 Milk

Bliss Foods Inc .... G....... 212 732-8888
New York (G-9465)
Bliss Foods Inc .... F 212 732-8888
New York (G-9466)
Byrne Dairy Inc .... B 315 475-2121
La Fayette (G-7267)
▲ Chobani LLC .... C 607 337-1246
Norwich (G-13042)
Chobani LLC .... G....... 607 847-6181
New Berlin (G-8826)
▼ Crowley Foods Inc .... E 800 637-0019
Binghamton (G-900)
▲ Currant Company LLC .... G....... 845 266-8999
Staatsburg (G-15637)
Dairy Farmers America Inc .... E 816 801-6440
East Syracuse (G-4535)
▲ Dannon Company Inc .... G....... 914 872-8400
White Plains (G-17125)
Dean Foods Company .... D 315 452-5001
East Syracuse (G-4538)
Dwyer Farm LLC .... G....... 914 456-2742
Walden (G-16552)
Elmhurst Dairy Inc .... C 718 526-3442
Jamaica (G-6946)
Emkay Trading Corp .... E 585 492-3800
Arcade (G-392)
▲ Fage USA Dairy Industry Inc .... B 518 762-5912
Johnstown (G-7143)
◆ Fage USA Holdings .... G....... 518 762-5912
Johnstown (G-7144)
Finger Lakes Cheese Trail .... F 607 857-5726
Odessa (G-13129)
Garelick Farms LLC .... C 518 283-0820
East Greenbush (G-4422)
▼ Hanan Products Company Inc .... E 516 938-1000
Hicksville (G-6382)
HP Hood LLC .... D 607 295-8134
Arkport (G-408)
HP Hood LLC .... C 315 363-3870
Oneida (G-13179)
HP Hood LLC .... B 315 658-2132
La Fargeville (G-7262)
HP Hood LLC .... B 518 218-9097
Albany (G-88)
HP Hood LLC .... D 315 829-3339
Vernon (G-16458)
HP Hood LLC .... A 607 772-6580
Binghamton (G-916)
Instantwhip of Buffalo Inc .... E 716 892-7031
Buffalo (G-3027)
Kesso Foods Inc .... G....... 718 777-5303
East Elmhurst (G-4415)
▲ Kong Kee Food Corp .... E 718 937-2746
Long Island City (G-7809)
Kraft Heinz Foods Company .... C 607 865-7131
Walton (G-16569)
Kraft Heinz Foods Company .... B 607 527-4584
Campbell (G-3358)
Maple Hill Creamery LLC .... E 518 758-7777
Stuyvesant (G-15804)
Maple Hill Creamery LLC .... G....... 518 758-7777
Kinderhook (G-7197)
Midland Farms Inc .... D 518 436-7038
Menands (G-8408)
Mountain Side Farms Inc .... E 718 526-3442
Jamaica (G-6971)
Mualema LLC .... G....... 609 820-6098
New York (G-11344)
▲ Noga Dairies Inc .... F 516 293-5448
Farmingdale (G-5076)
◆ O-At-Ka Milk Products Coop Inc .... B 585 343-0536
Batavia (G-645)
P & F Bakers Inc .... G....... 516 931-6821
Hicksville (G-6407)
Purity Ice Cream Co Inc .... F 607 272-1545
Ithaca (G-6908)

SIC

Employee Codes: A=Over 500 employees, B=251-500
C=101-250, D=51-100, E=20-50, F=10-19, G=5-9
2018 Harris
New York Manufacturers Directory
709

20 FOOD AND KINDRED PRODUCTS SIC SECTION

Saputo Dairy Foods Usa LLC ......D 607 746-2141
Delhi *(G-4267)*

Steuben Foods Incorporated ......C 716 655-4000
Elma *(G-4669)*

Steuben Foods Incorporated ......F 718 291-3333
Jamaica *(G-6989)*

Stewarts Processing Corp ......D 518 581-1200
Ballston Spa *(G-609)*

Twist It Top It ......F 718 793-8947
Forest Hills *(G-5336)*

Upstate Niagara Coop Inc ......A 716 892-3156
Buffalo *(G-3263)*

Upstate Niagara Coop Inc ......C 585 458-1880
Rochester *(G-14775)*

Upstate Niagara Coop Inc ......E 716 484-7178
Jamestown *(G-7073)*

Upstate Niagara Coop Inc ......D 315 389-5111
North Lawrence *(G-12951)*

Upstate Niagara Coop Inc ......C 716 892-2121
Buffalo *(G-3264)*

Whitney Foods Inc ......F 718 291-3333
Jamaica *(G-7000)*

Yo Fresh Inc ......E 845 634-1616
New City *(G-8841)*

Yo Fresh Inc ......E 518 982-0659
Clifton Park *(G-3738)*

2032 Canned Specialties

▲ A & G Food Distributors LLC ......G 917 939-3457
Bayside *(G-757)*

▲ Antico Casale Usa LLC ......G 914 760-1100
Whitestone *(G-17227)*

◆ Beech-Nut Nutrition Company ......B 518 839-0300
Amsterdam *(G-336)*

Borgattis Ravioli Egg Noodles ......G 718 367-3799
Bronx *(G-1286)*

Delicious Foods Inc ......F 718 446-9352
Corona *(G-4019)*

◆ Eve Sales Corp ......F 718 589-6800
Bronx *(G-1331)*

▲ Global Food Source & Co Inc ......G 914 320-9615
Tuckahoe *(G-16294)*

Goya Foods Inc ......D 716 549-0076
Angola *(G-380)*

Grandma Browns Beans Inc ......F 315 963-7221
Mexico *(G-8430)*

◆ Iberia Foods Corp ......D 718 272-8900
Brooklyn *(G-2092)*

Indira Foods Inc ......F 718 343-1500
Floral Park *(G-5215)*

Kawasho Foods USA Inc ......F 212 841-7400
New York *(G-10859)*

Marketplace Slutions Group LLC ......E 631 868-0111
Holbrook *(G-6490)*

Morris Kitchen Inc ......F 646 413-5186
Brooklyn *(G-2339)*

Phillip Juan ......G 800 834-4543
Staten Island *(G-15740)*

◆ Sahadi Fine Foods Inc ......E 718 369-0100
Brooklyn *(G-2554)*

Sangster Foods Inc ......F 212 993-9129
Brooklyn *(G-2556)*

Steuben Foods Incorporated ......F 718 291-3333
Jamaica *(G-6989)*

2033 Canned Fruits, Vegetables & Preserves

Amiram Dror Inc ......F 212 979-9505
Brooklyn *(G-1609)*

Andros Bowman Products LLC ......G 540 217-4100
Lyndonville *(G-7994)*

◆ Apple & Eve LLC ......D 516 621-1122
Port Washington *(G-13822)*

Beths Farm Kitchen ......G 518 799-3414
Stuyvesant Falls *(G-15805)*

Birds Eye Holdings Inc ......A 585 383-1850
Rochester *(G-14250)*

◆ Brooklyn Btlg Milton NY Inc ......C 845 795-2171
Milton *(G-8516)*

Cahoon Farms Inc ......E 315 594-8081
Wolcott *(G-17298)*

Central Island Juice Corp ......F 516 338-8301
Westbury *(G-17002)*

Cheribundi Inc ......E 800 699-0460
Geneva *(G-5585)*

◆ Cliffstar LLC ......A 716 366-6100
Dunkirk *(G-4361)*

Club 1100 ......G 585 235-3478
Rochester *(G-14301)*

Dells Cherries LLC ......E 718 624-4380
Brooklyn *(G-1850)*

Dells Cherries LLC ......E 718 624-4380
Brooklyn *(G-1851)*

Eleanors Best ......F 845 809-5621
Garrison *(G-5569)*

Fly Creek Cder Mill Orchrd Inc ......G 607 547-9692
Fly Creek *(G-5319)*

Fresh Fanatic Inc ......G 516 521-6574
Brooklyn *(G-2005)*

▼ Fruitcrown Products Corp ......E 631 694-5800
Farmingdale *(G-5003)*

◆ Giovanni Food Co Inc ......D 315 457-2373
Baldwinsville *(G-569)*

Glk Foods LLC ......E 585 289-4414
Shortsville *(G-15456)*

◆ Global Natural Foods Inc ......E 845 439-3292
Livingston Manor *(G-7589)*

Goya Foods Inc ......D 716 549-0076
Angola *(G-380)*

Green Valley Foods LLC ......G 315 926-4280
Marion *(G-8124)*

Hc Brill Co Inc ......G 716 685-4000
Lancaster *(G-7343)*

Jets Lefrois Corp ......G 585 637-5003
Brockport *(G-1245)*

Kaltech Food Packaging Inc ......E 845 856-1210
Port Jervis *(G-13810)*

Kensington & Sons LLC ......E 646 430-8298
New York *(G-10875)*

▲ L and S Packing Co ......D 631 845-1717
Farmingdale *(G-5037)*

Lagoner Farms Inc ......D 315 589-4899
Williamson *(G-17253)*

◆ Lidestri Foods Inc ......B 585 377-7700
Fairport *(G-4867)*

Life Juice Brands LLC ......G 585 944-7982
Pittsford *(G-13595)*

Lollipop Tree Inc ......E 845 471-8733
Auburn *(G-504)*

▲ Mayer Bros Apple Products Inc ......D 716 668-1787
West Seneca *(G-16980)*

Mizkan America Inc ......D 585 765-9171
Lyndonville *(G-7995)*

Morris Kitchen Inc ......F 646 413-5186
Brooklyn *(G-2339)*

◆ Motts LLP ......C 972 673-8088
Elmsford *(G-4775)*

◆ National Grape Coop Assn Inc ......E 716 326-5200
Westfield *(G-17077)*

New York Pasta Authority Inc ......F 347 787-2130
Brooklyn *(G-2374)*

▼ Old Dutch Mustard Co Inc ......G 516 466-0522
Great Neck *(G-5843)*

Private Lbel Fods Rchester Inc ......E 585 254-9205
Rochester *(G-14625)*

Sarabeths Kitchen LLC ......G 718 589-2900
Bronx *(G-1447)*

▲ Sbk Preserves Inc ......E 800 773-7378
Bronx *(G-1448)*

◆ Seneca Foods Corporation ......E 315 926-8100
Marion *(G-8129)*

Seneca Foods Corporation ......C 315 781-8733
Geneva *(G-5597)*

Seneca Foods Corporation ......F 315 926-4277
Marion *(G-8131)*

Seneca Foods Corporation ......E 585 658-2211
Leicester *(G-7444)*

▲ Sneaky Chef Foods LLC ......F 914 301-3277
Tarrytown *(G-16131)*

Spf Holdings II LLC ......G 212 750-8300
New York *(G-12185)*

US Juice Partners LLC ......G 516 621-1122
Port Washington *(G-13888)*

◆ Victoria Fine Foods LLC ......D 718 649-1635
Brooklyn *(G-2742)*

Vincents Food Corp ......F 516 481-3544
Carle Place *(G-3425)*

Welch Foods Inc A Cooperative ......C 716 326-5252
Westfield *(G-17082)*

Welch Foods Inc A Cooperative ......E 716 326-3131
Westfield *(G-17083)*

Wolfgang B Gourmet Foods Inc ......F 518 719-1727
Catskill *(G-3463)*

2034 Dried Fruits, Vegetables & Soup

▲ Allied Food Products Inc ......F 718 230-4227
Brooklyn *(G-1588)*

◆ Associated Brands Inc ......B 585 798-3475
New York *(G-9291)*

Goya Foods Inc ......D 716 549-0076
Angola *(G-380)*

◆ Hain Celestial Group Inc ......C 516 587-5000
New Hyde Park *(G-8882)*

Interntional Gourmet Soups Inc ......E 212 768-7687
Staten Island *(G-15709)*

Marshall Ingredients LLC ......G 800 796-9353
Wolcott *(G-17301)*

▲ Peeled Inc ......F 212 706-2001
Brooklyn *(G-2425)*

◆ Settons Intl Foods Inc ......E 631 543-8090
Commack *(G-3868)*

Shoreline Fruit LLC ......D 585 765-2639
Lyndonville *(G-7996)*

▲ Wm E Martin and Sons Co Inc ......E 516 605-2444
Roslyn *(G-15048)*

2035 Pickled Fruits, Vegetables, Sauces & Dressings

Allen Pickle Works Inc ......F 516 676-0640
Glen Cove *(G-5622)*

American Specialty Mfg Co ......F 585 544-5600
Rochester *(G-14215)*

Baldwin Richardson Foods Co ......C 315 986-2727
Macedon *(G-8010)*

Batampte Pickle Products Inc ......D 718 251-2100
Brooklyn *(G-1669)*

Birds Eye Holdings Inc ......A 585 383-1850
Rochester *(G-14250)*

Bushwick Kitchen LLC ......G 917 297-1045
Brooklyn *(G-1741)*

▲ Classic Cooking LLC ......D 718 439-0200
Jamaica *(G-6941)*

Elwood International Inc ......F 631 842-6600
Copiague *(G-3925)*

French Associates Inc ......F 718 387-9880
Fresh Meadows *(G-5454)*

Glk Foods LLC ......E 585 289-4414
Shortsville *(G-15456)*

▲ Gold Pure Food Products Co Inc ......D 516 483-5600
Hempstead *(G-6296)*

Goya Foods Inc ......D 716 549-0076
Angola *(G-380)*

Gravymaster Inc ......E 203 453-1893
Canajoharie *(G-3360)*

Heintz & Weber Co Inc ......G 716 852-7171
Buffalo *(G-3010)*

Instantwhip of Buffalo Inc ......E 716 892-7031
Buffalo *(G-3027)*

Jets Lefrois Corp ......G 585 637-5003
Brockport *(G-1245)*

Kensington & Sons LLC ......E 646 430-8298
New York *(G-10875)*

▲ L and S Packing Co ......D 631 845-1717
Farmingdale *(G-5037)*

Lollipop Tree Inc ......E 845 471-8733
Auburn *(G-504)*

Lucinas Gourmet Food Inc ......G 646 835-9784
Long Island City *(G-7823)*

▲ Mandarin Soy Sauce Inc ......E 845 343-1505
Middletown *(G-8483)*

◆ Materne North America Corp ......B 212 675-7881
New York *(G-11202)*

▲ Metzger Speciality Brands ......G 212 957-0055
New York *(G-11271)*

Mizkan America Inc ......F 585 798-5720
Medina *(G-8311)*

Mizkan America Inc ......D 585 765-9171
Lyndonville *(G-7995)*

▲ Moldova Pickles & Salads Inc ......G 718 284-2220
Brooklyn *(G-2334)*

▼ Old Dutch Mustard Co Inc ......G 516 466-0522
Great Neck *(G-5843)*

▲ Rob Salamida Company Inc ......F 607 729-4868
Johnson City *(G-7136)*

▲ Sabra Dipping Company LLC ......D 914 372-3900
White Plains *(G-17193)*

Sassy Sauce Inc ......G 585 621-1050
Rochester *(G-14690)*

Sum Sum LLC ......G 516 812-3959
Oceanside *(G-13121)*

T RS Great American Rest ......F 516 294-1680
Williston Park *(G-17287)*

▲ Twin Marquis Inc ......D 718 386-6868
Brooklyn *(G-2710)*

Unilever United States Inc ......F 212 546-0200
New York *(G-12474)*

Unilever United States Inc ......C 212 546-0200
New York *(G-12475)*

United Farm Processing Corp ......C 718 933-6060
Bronx *(G-1484)*

United Pickle Products Corp .... E 718 933-6060
  Bronx (G-1485)
◆ Victoria Fine Foods LLC .... D 718 649-1635
  Brooklyn (G-2742)
◆ Wanjashan International LLC .... F 845 343-1505
  Middletown (G-8505)
Whalens Horseradish Products .... G 518 587-6404
  Galway (G-5498)

2037 Frozen Fruits, Juices & Vegetables

Atlantic Farm & Food Inc .... F 718 441-3152
  Richmond Hill (G-14079)
Birds Eye Foods Inc .... G 716 988-3218
  South Dayton (G-15539)
Blend Smoothie Bar .... G 845 568-7366
  New Windsor (G-8979)
Cahoon Farms Inc .... E 315 594-8081
  Wolcott (G-17298)
Cheribundi Inc .... E 800 699-0460
  Geneva (G-5585)
▲ Classic Cooking LLC .... D 718 439-0200
  Jamaica (G-6941)
Copra .... G 917 224-1727
  New York (G-9780)
▲ Dynamic Health Labs Inc .... E 718 858-0100
  Brooklyn (G-1887)
Fly Creek Cder Mill Orchrd Inc .... G 607 547-9692
  Fly Creek (G-5319)
◆ Global Natural Foods Inc .... E 845 439-3292
  Livingston Manor (G-7589)
H&F Products Inc .... G 845 651-6100
  Monroe (G-8591)
Hain Blueprint Inc .... E 212 414-5741
  New Hyde Park (G-8881)
▲ Metzger Speciality Brands .... G 212 957-0055
  New York (G-11271)
◆ National Grape Coop Assn Inc .... E 716 326-5200
  Westfield (G-17077)
◆ Pepsico Inc .... A 914 253-2000
  Purchase (G-13981)
▲ Prime Food Processing Corp .... D 718 963-2323
  Brooklyn (G-2455)
Pura Fruta LLC .... F 415 279-5727
  Long Island City (G-7880)
Purely Maple Inc .... F 646 524-7135
  New York (G-11776)
◆ Seneca Foods Corporation .... E 315 926-8100
  Marion (G-8129)
T & Smoothie Inc .... G 631 804-6653
  Patchogue (G-13461)
Tami Great Food Corp .... G 845 352-7901
  Monsey (G-8619)
Zoe Sakoutis LLC .... E 212 414-5741
  New York (G-12736)

2038 Frozen Specialties

▲ Alle Processing Corp .... C 718 894-2000
  Maspeth (G-8143)
▲ America NY RI Wang Fd Group Co ..... E 718 628-8999
  Maspeth (G-8145)
▲ Classic Cooking LLC .... D 718 439-0200
  Jamaica (G-6941)
Codinos Limited Inc .... E 518 372-3308
  Schenectady (G-15272)
D R M Management Inc .... E 716 668-0333
  Depew (G-4278)
Delicious Foods Inc .... F 718 446-9352
  Corona (G-4019)
Dufour Pastry Kitchens Inc .... E 718 402-8800
  Bronx (G-1322)
▲ Dvash Foods Inc .... F 845 578-1959
  Monsey (G-8607)
F & R Enterprises Inc .... G 315 841-8189
  Waterville (G-16701)
Finger Food Products Inc .... E 716 297-4888
  Sanborn (G-15146)
▲ Freeze-Dry Foods Inc .... E 585 589-6399
  Albion (G-168)
Hong Hop Co Inc .... E 212 962-1735
  New York (G-10546)
▲ Julians Recipe LLC .... G 888 640-8880
  Brooklyn (G-2158)
Juno Chefs .... D 845 294-5400
  Goshen (G-5750)
Kraft Heinz Foods Company .... B 585 226-4400
  Avon (G-537)
Les Chateaux De France Inc .... E 516 239-6795
  Inwood (G-6800)
▲ Milmar Food Group II LLC .... C 845 294-5400
  Goshen (G-5752)

Salarinos Italian Foods Inc .... F 315 697-9766
  Canastota (G-3398)
▲ Seviroli Foods Inc .... C 516 222-6220
  Garden City (G-5546)
Tami Great Food Corp .... G 845 352-7901
  Monsey (G-8619)
▲ Tuv Taam Corp .... E 718 855-2207
  Brooklyn (G-2708)
Unilever United States Inc .... F 212 546-0200
  New York (G-12474)
Unilever United States Inc .... C 212 546-0200
  New York (G-12475)

2041 Flour, Grain Milling

ADM Milling Co .... D 716 849-7333
  Buffalo (G-2814)
Archer-Daniels-Midland Company .... E 518 828-4691
  Hudson (G-6634)
Archer-Daniels-Midland Company .... D 518 828-4691
  Hudson (G-6635)
Ardent Mills LLC .... E 518 447-1700
  Albany (G-46)
◆ Birkett Mills .... G 315 536-3311
  Penn Yan (G-13529)
Birkett Mills .... E 315 536-4112
  Penn Yan (G-13530)
Cargill Incorporated .... G 716 665-6570
  Kennedy (G-7182)
Champlain Valley Mil Corp Inc .... G 518 962-4711
  Westport (G-17096)
Cochecton Mills Inc .... G 845 932-8282
  Cochecton (G-3765)
Frozen Pastry Products Corp .... E 845 364-9833
  Spring Valley (G-15608)
General Mills Inc .... E 716 856-6060
  Buffalo (G-2984)
Losurdo Foods Inc .... E 518 842-1500
  Amsterdam (G-355)
Ohio Baking Company Inc .... E 315 724-2033
  Utica (G-16378)
◆ Sheppard Grain Enterprises LLC .... E 315 548-9271
  Phelps (G-13560)

2043 Cereal Breakfast Foods

◆ Associated Brands Inc .... B 585 798-3475
  New York (G-9291)
Chia Usa LLC .... F 212 226-7512
  New York (G-9643)
Gabila Food Products Inc .... E 631 789-2220
  Copiague (G-3928)
General Mills Inc .... D 716 856-6060
  Buffalo (G-2985)
Group International LLC .... G 718 475-8805
  Flushing (G-5253)
Kellogg Company .... E 315 452-0310
  North Syracuse (G-12968)
Kellogg Company .... A 845 365-5284
  Orangeburg (G-13255)
Kraft Heinz Foods Company .... A 914 335-2500
  Tarrytown (G-16116)
◆ Pepsico Inc .... A 914 253-2000
  Purchase (G-13981)
Sangster Foods Inc .... F 212 993-9129
  Brooklyn (G-2556)
Sanzdranz LLC .... G 518 894-8625
  Delmar (G-4271)
Sanzdranz LLC .... G 518 894-8625
  Schenectady (G-15316)

2044 Rice Milling

▼ Gassho Body & Mind Inc .... G 518 695-9991
  Schuylerville (G-15341)
▲ Real Co Inc .... G 347 433-8549
  Valley Cottage (G-16412)

2045 Flour, Blended & Prepared

Aryzta LLC .... D 310 417-4700
  Rochester (G-14232)
▲ Bektrom Foods Inc .... G 516 802-3800
  Syosset (G-15835)
Cohens Bakery Inc .... E 716 892-8149
  Buffalo (G-2899)
Dawn Food Products Inc .... C 716 830-8214
  Williamsville (G-17268)
Elis Bread (eli Zabar) Inc .... F 212 772-2011
  New York (G-10058)
Lollipop Tree Inc .... G 845 471-8733
  Auburn (G-504)

New Hope Mills Inc .... F 315 252-2676
  Auburn (G-507)
Tosca Brick Oven Pizza Real .... G 718 430-0026
  Bronx (G-1471)

2046 Wet Corn Milling

Anthony Gigi Inc .... G 860 984-1943
  Shirley (G-15435)
Archer-Daniels-Midland Company .... E 585 346-2311
  Lakeville (G-7305)
Machoonjdgroup .... G 856 345-4689
  Medford (G-8287)
▲ Sweetwater Energy Inc .... G 585 647-5760
  Rochester (G-14732)

2047 Dog & Cat Food

◆ Colgate-Palmolive Company .... A 212 310-2000
  New York (G-9726)
Dog Good Products LLC .... G 212 789-7000
  New York (G-9947)
Hills Pet Products Inc .... G 212 310-2000
  New York (G-10522)
Hound & Gatos Pet Foods Corp .... G 212 618-1917
  New York (G-10560)
Nestle Purina Petcare Company .... B 716 366-8080
  Dunkirk (G-4369)
◆ Pet Proteins LLC .... G 888 293-1029
  New York (G-11649)
Robert Abady Dog Food Co Ltd .... F 845 473-1900
  Poughkeepsie (G-13946)
Scooby Rendering & Inc .... G 315 793-1014
  Utica (G-16382)

2048 Prepared Feeds For Animals & Fowls

Archer-Daniels-Midland Company .... D 716 849-7333
  Buffalo (G-2838)
Bailey Boonville Mills Inc .... G 315 942-2131
  Boonville (G-1159)
Baker Commodities Inc .... E 585 482-1880
  Rochester (G-14239)
Cargill Incorporated .... E 315 622-3533
  Liverpool (G-7538)
Central Garden & Pet Company .... G 631 451-8021
  Selden (G-15370)
Central Garden & Pet Company .... G 212 877-1270
  New York (G-9616)
Cochecton Mills Inc .... G 845 932-8282
  Cochecton (G-3765)
Commodity Resource Corporation .... F 585 538-9500
  Caledonia (G-3305)
Gramco Inc .... G 716 592-2845
  Springville (G-15632)
Grandma Maes Cntry Nturals LLC .... G 212 348-8171
  New York (G-10391)
Heath Manufacturing Company .... G 800 444-3140
  Batavia (G-639)
J & M Feed Corporation .... G 631 281-2152
  Shirley (G-15444)
Kent Nutrition Group Inc .... F 315 788-0032
  Watertown (G-16680)
Lowville Farmers Coop Inc .... E 315 376-6587
  Lowville (G-7966)
Narrowsburg Feed & Grain Co .... F 845 252-3936
  Narrowsburg (G-8814)
Nutra-Vet Research Corp .... F 845 473-1900
  Poughkeepsie (G-13941)
Pace Manufacturing Company .... G 607 936-0431
  Painted Post (G-13418)
Pine Tree Farms Inc .... F 607 532-4312
  Interlaken (G-6788)
Scotts Feed Inc .... E 518 483-3110
  Malone (G-8046)
Southern States Coop Inc .... F 315 438-4500
  East Syracuse (G-4580)
Veterinary Biochemical Ltd .... G 845 473-1900
  Poughkeepsie (G-13955)
Wagners LLC .... G 516 933-6580
  Jericho (G-7121)

2051 Bread, Bakery Prdts Exc Cookies & Crackers

3 Bears Gluten Free Bakery .... F 315 323-0277
  Potsdam (G-13894)
3rd Avenue Doughnut Inc .... F 718 748-3294
  Brooklyn (G-1515)
40 Street Baking Inc .... G 212 683-4700
  Brooklyn (G-1517)
527 Franco Bakery Corporation .... G 718 993-4200
  Bronx (G-1250)

20 FOOD AND KINDRED PRODUCTS SIC SECTION

999 Bagels Inc ....G....... 718 915-0742
Brooklyn *(G-1523)*

A & M Appel Distributing Inc ....G....... 516 735-1172
Massapequa *(G-8206)*

A Angonoa Inc ....D....... 718 762-4466
College Point *(G-3798)*

A T A Bagel Shoppe Inc ....G....... 718 352-4948
Bayside *(G-759)*

Above The Rest Baking Corp ....D....... 718 313-9222
Bronx *(G-1258)*

Addeo Bakers Inc ....F....... 718 367-8316
Bronx *(G-1264)*

Aladdin Bakers Inc ....C....... 718 499-1818
Brooklyn *(G-1573)*

Alicias Bakery Inc ....G....... 914 235-4689
New Rochelle *(G-8930)*

Allies GF Goodies LLC ....F....... 516 216-1719
Hicksville *(G-6345)*

▲ Alrajs Inc ....E....... 631 225-0300
Lindenhurst *(G-7474)*

Always Baked Fresh ....G....... 631 648-0811
Holbrook *(G-6459)*

American Vintage Wine Biscuit ....G....... 718 361-1003
Long Island City *(G-7690)*

Amincor Inc ....C....... 347 821-3452
New York *(G-9186)*

Amiram Dror Inc ....F....... 212 979-9505
Brooklyn *(G-1609)*

▲ Amy Scherber Inc ....F....... 212 462-4338
New York *(G-9193)*

Andrew Sapienza Bakery Inc ....E....... 516 437-1715
Elmont *(G-4728)*

Aphrodities ....G....... 718 224-1774
Whitestone *(G-17228)*

Aryzta LLC ....C....... 585 235-8160
Rochester *(G-14233)*

Aryzta LLC ....D....... 310 417-4700
Rochester *(G-14232)*

B & D Enterprises of Utica ....D....... 315 735-3311
New Hartford *(G-8846)*

B Cake NY LLC ....G....... 347 787-7199
Brooklyn *(G-1658)*

Bagel Club Inc ....F....... 718 423-6106
Bayside *(G-762)*

Bagel Grove Inc ....E....... 315 724-8015
Utica *(G-16332)*

Bagel Land ....E....... 585 442-3080
Rochester *(G-14237)*

Bagel Lites LLC ....G....... 855 813-7888
Long Island City *(G-7711)*

Bagelovers Inc ....F....... 607 844-3683
Dryden *(G-4345)*

▼ Bagels By Bell Ltd ....E....... 718 272-2780
Oceanside *(G-13093)*

Baked Cupcakery ....G....... 716 773-2050
Grand Island *(G-5766)*

Bakery & Coffee Shop ....G....... 315 287-1829
Gouverneur *(G-5757)*

Berardi Bakery Inc ....G....... 718 746-9529
Whitestone *(G-17231)*

Better Baked Foods Inc ....D....... 716 326-4651
Westfield *(G-17075)*

Bien Cuit LLC ....E....... 718 852-0200
Brooklyn *(G-1692)*

Bimbo Bakeries ....G....... 631 274-4906
Deer Park *(G-4132)*

Bimbo Bakeries ....F....... 518 463-2221
Albany *(G-53)*

Bimbo Bakeries Usa Inc ....G....... 716 692-9140
Tonawanda *(G-16166)*

Bimbo Bakeries Usa Inc ....G....... 718 601-1561
Bronx *(G-1283)*

Bimbo Bakeries Usa Inc ....G....... 718 545-0291
Long Island City *(G-7716)*

Bimbo Bakeries Usa Inc ....E....... 516 877-2850
Mineola *(G-8531)*

Bimbo Bakeries Usa Inc ....C....... 716 372-8444
Olean *(G-13156)*

Bimbo Bakeries Usa Inc ....F....... 516 887-1024
Lynbrook *(G-7975)*

Bimbo Bakeries Usa Inc ....F....... 315 379-9069
Canton *(G-3406)*

Bimbo Bakeries Usa Inc ....C....... 718 463-6300
Maspeth *(G-8151)*

Bimbo Bakeries Usa Inc ....F....... 518 489-4053
Albany *(G-54)*

Bimbo Bakeries Usa Inc ....E....... 203 531-2311
Bay Shore *(G-675)*

Bimbo Bakeries Usa Inc ....D....... 315 253-9782
Auburn *(G-483)*

Bimbo Bakeries Usa Inc ....F....... 716 706-0450
Lancaster *(G-7330)*

Bimbo Bakeries Usa Inc ....F....... 315 785-7060
Watertown *(G-16659)*

Bimbo Bakeries Usa Inc ....D....... 845 568-0943
Newburgh *(G-12773)*

Bimbo Bakeries Usa Inc ....E....... 800 856-8544
Vestal *(G-16463)*

Bimbo Bakeries Usa Inc ....C....... 315 782-4189
Watertown *(G-16660)*

Bimbo Bakeries Usa Inc ....F....... 845 294-5282
Goshen *(G-5746)*

▲ Bimbo Foods Bakeries Inc ....C....... 631 273-6000
Bay Shore *(G-676)*

Blackbirds Brooklyn LLC ....E....... 917 362-4080
Brooklyn *(G-1699)*

Blondie S Bakeshop Inc ....G....... 631 424-4545
Centerport *(G-3500)*

Bread Factory LLC ....E....... 914 637-8150
New Rochelle *(G-8934)*

Bread Market Cafe ....G....... 212 768-9292
New York *(G-9509)*

Brighton Bakery ....G....... 315 475-2948
Syracuse *(G-15894)*

Brooklyn Sweet Spot Inc ....G....... 718 522-2577
Brooklyn *(G-1734)*

Butter Cooky Bakery ....G....... 516 354-3831
Floral Park *(G-5204)*

▲ Cannoli Factory Inc ....E....... 631 643-2700
Wyandanch *(G-17387)*

Caputo Bakery Inc ....G....... 718 875-6871
Brooklyn *(G-1758)*

Carmine Street Bagels Inc ....F....... 212 691-3041
Staten Island *(G-15676)*

Carolinas Desserts Inc ....G....... 914 779-4000
Yonkers *(G-17439)*

Carter Street Bakery Inc ....G....... 585 749-7104
Rochester *(G-14280)*

Chambord LLC ....E....... 718 859-1110
Brooklyn *(G-1772)*

Charlotte Neuville Design LLC ....G....... 646 530-4570
Brooklyn *(G-1775)*

Chocnyc LLC ....G....... 917 804-4848
New York *(G-9656)*

Cinderellas Sweets Ltd ....E....... 516 374-7976
Woodmere *(G-17330)*

Circle 5 Deli Corp ....G....... 718 525-5687
Jamaica *(G-6938)*

City Bakery Inc ....E....... 212 366-1414
New York *(G-9681)*

Coccadotts Inc ....F....... 518 438-4937
Albany *(G-70)*

Cohens Bakery Inc ....E....... 716 892-8149
Buffalo *(G-2899)*

Commitment 2000 Inc ....E....... 716 439-1206
Buffalo *(G-2903)*

Cookie Connection Inc ....G....... 315 422-2253
Syracuse *(G-15925)*

Costanzos Bakery Inc ....C....... 716 656-9093
Buffalo *(G-2911)*

Creative Relations LLC ....G....... 212 462-4392
New York *(G-9809)*

Cupcake Contessas Corporation ....G....... 516 307-1222
North Bellmore *(G-12935)*

Cuzins Duzin Corp ....G....... 347 724-6200
Kew Gardens *(G-7189)*

D-Lite Donuts ....G....... 718 626-5953
Astoria *(G-433)*

Daly Meghan ....F....... 347 699-3259
Brooklyn *(G-1837)*

Damascus Bakery Inc ....C....... 718 855-1456
Brooklyn *(G-1838)*

Delicias Andinas Food Corp ....E....... 718 416-2922
Flushing *(G-5244)*

Dipaolo Baking Co Inc ....D....... 585 303-5013
Rochester *(G-14331)*

Duane Park Patisserie Inc ....F....... 212 274-8447
New York *(G-9985)*

Eileens Special Cheesecake ....G....... 212 966-5585
New York *(G-10044)*

Enterprise Bagels Inc ....F....... 845 896-3823
Fishkill *(G-5190)*

Ericeira Inc ....G....... 516 294-4034
Mineola *(G-8543)*

Famous Doughnuts Inc ....G....... 716 834-6356
Buffalo *(G-2958)*

Fayda Manufacturing Corp ....F....... 718 456-9331
Brooklyn *(G-1965)*

FB Sale LLC ....G....... 315 986-9999
Macedon *(G-8017)*

Felix Roma & Sons Inc ....D....... 607 748-3336
Endicott *(G-4816)*

▲ Ferrara Bakery & Cafe Inc ....D....... 212 226-6150
New York *(G-10206)*

Flour Power Bakery Cafe ....G....... 917 747-6895
Livingston Manor *(G-7588)*

Food Gems Ltd ....E....... 718 296-7788
Ozone Park *(G-13405)*

Fotis Oneonta Italian Bakery ....G....... 607 432-3871
Oneonta *(G-13209)*

Fratellis LLC ....E....... 607 722-5663
Binghamton *(G-910)*

Fritters & Buns Inc ....G....... 845 227-6609
Hopewell Junction *(G-6576)*

Fung Wong Bakery Inc ....E....... 212 267-4037
New York *(G-10272)*

Gabila & Sons Mfg Inc ....E....... 631 789-2220
Copiague *(G-3927)*

Geddes Bakery Co Inc ....E....... 315 437-8084
North Syracuse *(G-12962)*

Gennaris Itln French Bky Inc ....G....... 516 997-8968
Carle Place *(G-3415)*

George Retzos ....G....... 315 422-2913
Syracuse *(G-15973)*

Giovanni Bakery Corp ....F....... 212 695-4296
New York *(G-10341)*

Glenn Wayne Wholesale Bky Inc ....D....... 631 289-9200
Bohemia *(G-1069)*

▼ Gluten Free Bake Shop Inc ....E....... 845 782-5307
Mountainville *(G-8793)*

Golden Glow Cookie Co Inc ....E....... 718 379-6223
Bronx *(G-1347)*

Good Bread Bakery ....F....... 914 939-3900
Port Chester *(G-13775)*

Gourmet Toast Corp ....G....... 718 852-4536
Brooklyn *(G-2045)*

Great American Dessert Co LLC ....D....... 718 894-3494
Maspeth *(G-8173)*

Greenvale Bagel Inc ....E....... 516 221-8221
Wantagh *(G-16578)*

◆ Greyston Bakery Inc ....C....... 914 375-1510
Yonkers *(G-17467)*

Grimaldis Home Bread Inc ....D....... 718 497-1425
Ridgewood *(G-14121)*

H & S Edible Products Corp ....E....... 914 413-3489
Mount Vernon *(G-8733)*

H H B Bakery of Little Neck ....G....... 718 631-7004
Flushing *(G-5254)*

Hagadah Passover Bakery ....G....... 718 638-1589
Brooklyn *(G-2061)*

Hahns Old Fashioned Cake Co ....F....... 631 249-3456
Farmingdale *(G-5012)*

Hana Pastries Inc ....G....... 718 369-7593
Brooklyn *(G-2064)*

Harrison Bakery West ....E....... 315 422-1468
Syracuse *(G-15977)*

▲ Heidelberg Group Inc ....E....... 315 866-0999
Herkimer *(G-6326)*

Herris Gourmet Inc ....G....... 917 578-2308
Brooklyn *(G-2076)*

Hum Limited Liability Corp ....G....... 631 525-2174
Nesconset *(G-8822)*

Jarets Stuffed Cupcakes ....G....... 607 658-9096
Endicott *(G-4820)*

Jerrys Bagels ....G....... 516 791-0063
Valley Stream *(G-16437)*

Jim Romas Bakery Inc ....E....... 607 748-7425
Endicott *(G-4823)*

▲ JJ Cassone Bakery Inc ....B....... 914 939-1568
Port Chester *(G-13777)*

Jonathan Lord Corp ....F....... 631 563-4445
Bohemia *(G-1081)*

Juniors Cheesecake Inc ....G....... 212 302-2000
Brooklyn *(G-2160)*

King Cracker Corp ....F....... 516 539-9251
Hempstead *(G-6301)*

Kokoroko Corporation ....G....... 718 433-4321
Woodside *(G-17352)*

Kossars Bialys LLC ....G....... 212 473-4810
New York *(G-10917)*

Kossars On Grand LLC ....F....... 212 473-4810
New York *(G-10918)*

L American Ltd ....F....... 716 372-9480
Olean *(G-13171)*

La Calenita Bakery & Cafeteria ....G....... 718 205-8273
Elmhurst *(G-4677)*

La Prima Bakery Inc ....F....... 718 584-4442
Bronx *(G-1381)*

Ladybird Bakery Inc ....G....... 718 499-8108
Brooklyn *(G-2189)*

SIC SECTION
20 FOOD AND KINDRED PRODUCTS

Larosa Cupcakes .... G 347 866-3920
Staten Island *(G-15719)*

Libbys Bakery Cafe LLC .... G 603 918-8825
Ticonderoga *(G-16149)*

Lillys Homestyle Bakeshop Inc .... D 718 491-2904
Brooklyn *(G-2225)*

Ljmm Inc .... E 845 454-5876
Poughkeepsie *(G-13932)*

M & M Bagel Corp .... F 516 295-1222
Cedarhurst *(G-3484)*

Mac Crete Corporation .... F 718 932-1803
Long Island City *(G-7827)*

Made Close LLC .... G 917 837-1357
Brooklyn *(G-2255)*

Magnolia Operating LLC .... E 212 265-2777
New York *(G-11135)*

Make My Cake II Inc .... G 212 234-2344
New York *(G-11141)*

Maplehurst Bakeries LLC .... B 315 735-5000
Frankfort *(G-5364)*

Maxwell Bakery Inc .... E 718 498-2200
Brooklyn *(G-2289)*

McKee Foods Corporation .... A 631 979-9364
Hauppauge *(G-6154)*

Mds Hot Bagels Deli Inc .... G 718 438-5650
Brooklyn *(G-2293)*

Megamatt Inc .... F 516 536-3541
Rockville Centre *(G-14823)*

Melita Corp .... C 718 392-7280
Astoria *(G-447)*

Millers Bulk Food and Bakery .... G 585 798-9700
Medina *(G-8310)*

Miss Grimble Associates Inc .... F 718 665-2253
Bronx *(G-1402)*

Modern Itln Bky of W Babylon .... C 631 589-7300
Oakdale *(G-13077)*

Mollys Cupcakes New York .... G 212 255-5441
New York *(G-11320)*

Mother Mousse Ltd .... G 718 983-8366
Staten Island *(G-15730)*

New Hope Mills Mfg Inc .... E 315 252-2676
Auburn *(G-508)*

New Mount Pleasant Bakery .... E 518 374-7577
Schenectady *(G-15307)*

New Star Bakery .... E 718 961-8868
Flushing *(G-5278)*

Nibble Inc Baking Co .... G 518 334-3950
Troy *(G-16266)*

Niebylski Bakery Inc .... G 718 721-5152
Astoria *(G-449)*

▼ Nightingale Food Entps Inc .... G 347 577-1630
New York *(G-11448)*

Nildas Desserts Limited .... F 845 454-5876
Poughkeepsie *(G-13940)*

Ohio Baking Company Inc .... E 315 724-2033
Utica *(G-16378)*

▲ Old Poland Foods LLC .... F 718 486-7700
Brooklyn *(G-2400)*

Operative Cake Corp .... E 718 278-5600
Bronx *(G-1418)*

Orza Bakery Inc .... F 914 965-5736
Yonkers *(G-17490)*

Ossining Bakery Lmp Inc .... G 914 941-2654
Ossining *(G-13348)*

OWayne Enterprises Inc .... E 718 326-2200
Maspeth *(G-8192)*

Oz Baking Company Ltd .... G 516 466-5114
Great Neck *(G-5845)*

▲ Palagonia Bakery Co Inc .... D 718 272-5400
Brooklyn *(G-2415)*

Pane DOro .... F 914 964-0043
Yonkers *(G-17494)*

Parkway Bread Distributors Inc .... G 845 362-1221
Pomona *(G-13760)*

Peking Food LLC .... E 718 628-8080
Brooklyn *(G-2426)*

Perrottas Bakery Inc .... G 518 283-4711
Troy *(G-16270)*

Pesces Bakery Inc .... G 845 246-4730
Saugerties *(G-15220)*

Placid Baker .... G 518 326-2657
Troy *(G-16273)*

Presser Kosher Baking Corp .... E 718 375-5088
Brooklyn *(G-2453)*

Quaker Bonnet Inc .... G 716 885-7208
Buffalo *(G-3172)*

R & H Baking Co Inc .... E 718 852-1768
Brooklyn *(G-2489)*

Rambachs International Bakery .... F 518 563-1721
Plattsburgh *(G-13722)*

Rays Italian Bakery Inc .... F 516 825-9170
Valley Stream *(G-16447)*

▲ Rays Restaurant & Bakery Inc .... G 718 441-7707
Jamaica *(G-6982)*

Reisman Bros Bakery Inc .... F 718 331-1975
Brooklyn *(G-2507)*

Richard Engdal Baking Corp .... F 914 777-9600
Mamaroneck *(G-8077)*

Rm Bakery LLC .... E 718 472-3036
Maspeth *(G-8198)*

Rock Hill Bakehouse Ltd .... E 518 743-1627
Gansevoort *(G-5503)*

Rockland Bakery Inc .... D 845 623-5800
Nanuet *(G-8807)*

Roma Bakery Inc .... F 516 825-9170
Valley Stream *(G-16449)*

Roslyn Bread Company Inc .... E 516 625-1470
Roslyn Heights *(G-15056)*

Royal Caribbean Jamaican Bky .... E 914 668-6868
Mount Vernon *(G-8774)*

◆ Royal Sweet Bakery Inc .... F 718 567-7770
Brooklyn *(G-2534)*

Ruthys Cheesecake Rugelach Bky .... F 212 463-8800
New York *(G-11956)*

Saint Honore Pastry Shop Inc .... G 516 767-2555
Port Washington *(G-13878)*

Sandford Blvd Donuts Inc .... G 914 663-7708
Mount Vernon *(G-8776)*

Sapienza Pastry Inc .... E 516 352-5232
Elmont *(G-4739)*

▲ Satispie LLC .... E 716 982-4600
Rochester *(G-14691)*

Scaife Enterprises Inc .... F 585 454-5231
Rochester *(G-14693)*

Settepani Inc .... E 718 349-6524
Brooklyn *(G-2571)*

Slims Bagels Unlimited Inc .... E 718 229-1140
Oakland Gardens *(G-13086)*

Smith Street Bread Co LLC .... F 718 797-9712
Brooklyn *(G-2601)*

Soutine Inc .... G 212 496-1450
New York *(G-12170)*

Stebe Shcjhjff .... F 839 383-9833
Poughkeepsie *(G-13952)*

Sugarbear Cupcakes .... G 917 698-9005
Jamaica *(G-6990)*

▲ Sullivan St Bky - Hlls Kit Inc .... E 212 265-5580
New York *(G-12250)*

Sunrise Baking Co LLC .... C 718 499-0800
Brooklyn *(G-2643)*

T&B Bakery Corp .... G 646 642-4300
Maspeth *(G-8202)*

Tarrytown Bakery Inc .... F 914 631-0209
Tarrytown *(G-16133)*

Tates Wholesale LLC .... C 631 780-6511
East Moriches *(G-4451)*

Tilaros Bakery Inc .... G 716 488-3209
Jamestown *(G-7070)*

Triboro Bagel Co Inc .... E 718 359-9245
Flushing *(G-5308)*

Two Sisters Kiev Bakery Inc .... G 718 769-2626
Brooklyn *(G-2711)*

Two Sisters Kiev Bakery Inc .... F 718 627-5438
Brooklyn *(G-2712)*

Uncle Wallys LLC .... E 631 205-0455
Shirley *(G-15453)*

Valencia Bakery Inc .... E 718 991-6400
Bronx *(G-1486)*

Village Lantern Baking Corp .... G 631 225-1690
Lindenhurst *(G-7517)*

Vito & Sons Bakery .... F 201 617-8501
Brooklyn *(G-2752)*

Waldorf Bakers Inc .... F 718 665-2253
Bronx *(G-1492)*

▲ Wenner Bread Products Inc .... B 800 869-6262
Bayport *(G-756)*

Zaro Bake Shop Inc .... C 718 993-7327
Bronx *(G-1498)*

Zuckerbakers Inc .... F 516 785-6900
Wantagh *(G-16585)*

2052 Cookies & Crackers

17 Bakers LLC .... F 844 687-6836
Williamsville *(G-17258)*

212kiddish Inc .... G 718 705-7227
Brooklyn *(G-1512)*

AAA Noodle Products Mfg .... G 212 431-4090
New York *(G-9045)*

▲ Alrajs Inc .... E 631 225-0300
Lindenhurst *(G-7474)*

▲ Aron Streit Inc .... E 212 475-7000
Orangeburg *(G-13241)*

Aryzta LLC .... C 585 235-8160
Rochester *(G-14233)*

Butterwood Desserts Inc .... E 716 652-0131
West Falls *(G-16876)*

Chipita America Inc .... E 845 292-2540
Ferndale *(G-5176)*

City Baking LLC .... G 718 392-8514
Long Island City *(G-7726)*

Cone Buddy System Inc .... F 585 427-9940
Rochester *(G-14306)*

Cookie Factory LLC .... E 518 268-1060
Troy *(G-16254)*

▲ Cookies United LLC .... C 631 581-4000
Islip *(G-6846)*

Cooking With Chef Michelle LLC .... G 516 662-2324
Calverton *(G-3317)*

▼ Creative Food Ingredients Inc .... C 585 237-2213
Perry *(G-13545)*

D F Stauffer Biscuit Co Inc .... E 585 968-2700
Cuba *(G-4094)*

Danny Macaroons Inc .... G 260 622-8463
New York *(G-9860)*

Decorated Cookie Company LLC .... E 315 487-2111
Syracuse *(G-15943)*

▲ Elenis Nyc Inc .... E 718 361-8136
Long Island City *(G-7758)*

Falcones Cookie Land Ltd .... G 718 236-4200
Brooklyn *(G-1960)*

Golden Glow Cookie Co Inc .... E 718 379-6223
Bronx *(G-1347)*

▲ Great Brands of Europe Inc .... G 914 872-8804
White Plains *(G-17140)*

Jonathan Lord Corp .... F 631 563-4445
Bohemia *(G-1081)*

▲ Kaltec Food Packaging Inc .... E 845 856-9888
Port Jervis *(G-13809)*

Keebler Company .... F 585 948-8010
Oakfield *(G-13084)*

Keebler Company .... E 631 234-3700
Hauppauge *(G-6128)*

Keebler Company .... E 845 365-5200
Orangeburg *(G-13254)*

▼ La Vita Health Foods Ltd .... G 845 368-4101
Suffern *(G-15815)*

Ladybird Bakery Inc .... G 718 499-8108
Brooklyn *(G-2189)*

▲ Larte Del Gelato Inc .... G 212 366-0570
New York *(G-10966)*

Linden Cookies Inc .... E 845 268-5050
Congers *(G-3884)*

Lloyd Price Icon Food Brands .... F 914 764-8624
Pound Ridge *(G-13960)*

McDuffies of Scotland Inc .... E 716 759-8510
Clarence *(G-3691)*

My Most Favorite Food .... G 212 580-5130
New York *(G-11353)*

New Mount Pleasant Bakery .... E 518 374-7577
Schenectady *(G-15307)*

One Girl Cookies Ltd .... F 212 675-4996
Brooklyn *(G-2403)*

Pdi Cone Co Inc .... D 716 825-8750
Buffalo *(G-3139)*

◆ Pepsico Inc .... A 914 253-2000
Purchase *(G-13981)*

Quaker Bonnet Inc .... G 716 885-7208
Buffalo *(G-3172)*

Sapienza Pastry Inc .... E 516 352-5232
Elmont *(G-4739)*

Treehouse Private Brands Inc .... C 716 693-4715
Tonawanda *(G-16228)*

United Baking Co Inc .... F 631 413-5116
Central Islip *(G-3540)*

United Baking Co Inc .... G 631 205-0455
Shirley *(G-15454)*

Wonton Food Inc .... E 718 784-8178
Long Island City *(G-7955)*

▲ Wonton Food Inc .... C 718 628-6868
Brooklyn *(G-2778)*

Zaro Bake Shop Inc .... C 718 993-7327
Bronx *(G-1498)*

2053 Frozen Bakery Prdts

Bello LLC .... C 516 623-8800
Freeport *(G-5399)*

Brooklyn Baby Cakes Inc .... G 917 334-2518
Brooklyn *(G-1718)*

Butterwood Desserts Inc .... E 716 652-0131
West Falls *(G-16876)*

S I C

Employee Codes: A=Over 500 employees, B=251-500
C=101-250, D=51-100, E=20-50, F=10-19, G=5-9

20 FOOD AND KINDRED PRODUCTS SIC SECTION

▲ Circle Peak Capital MGT LLC E 646 230-8812
New York *(G-9673)*

Cobblestone Bakery Corp E 631 491-3777
Wyandanch *(G-17388)*

Culinary Arts Specialties Inc D 716 656-8943
Cheektowaga *(G-3594)*

Deiorio Foods Inc E 315 732-7612
Utica *(G-16345)*

Dufour Pastry Kitchens Inc E 718 402-8800
Bronx *(G-1322)*

Fratellis LLC E 607 722-5663
Binghamton *(G-910)*

Kates Kakes G 518 466-8671
Schenectady *(G-15299)*

Ko Fro Foods Inc E 718 972-6480
Brooklyn *(G-2177)*

▲ LArte Del Gelato Gruppo Inc F 718 383-6600
Long Island City *(G-7815)*

Liddabit Sweets G 917 912-1370
Brooklyn *(G-2218)*

Maplehurst Bakeries LLC B 315 735-5000
Frankfort *(G-5364)*

Micosta Enterprises Inc G 518 822-9708
Hudson *(G-6657)*

Pearl River Pastries LLC E 845 735-5100
West Nyack *(G-16951)*

◆ Rich Holdings Inc D 716 878-8000
Buffalo *(G-3184)*

◆ Rich Products Corporation A 716 878-8000
Buffalo *(G-3185)*

▼ Saj of Freeport Corp C 516 623-8800
Freeport *(G-5435)*

▲ Wenner Bread Products Inc B 800 869-6262
Bayport *(G-756)*

2061 Sugar, Cane

▲ Supreme Chocolatier LLC E 718 761-9600
Staten Island *(G-15767)*

2062 Sugar, Cane Refining

◆ Asr Group International Inc C 914 963-2400
Yonkers *(G-17433)*

Cane Sugar LLC G 212 329-2695
New York *(G-9567)*

Domino Foods Inc F 800 729-4840
Yonkers *(G-17453)*

▲ Sweeteners Plus Inc D 585 728-3770
Lakeville *(G-7309)*

2063 Sugar, Beet

Beets Love Production LLC E 585 270-2471
Rochester *(G-14245)*

2064 Candy & Confectionery Prdts

5th Avenue Chocolatiere Ltd F 516 561-1570
Valley Stream *(G-16423)*

▲ 5th Avenue Chocolatiere Ltd G 212 935-5454
Freeport *(G-5388)*

Aigner Chocolates Inc G 718 544-1850
Forest Hills *(G-5325)*

▲ Alrajs Inc E 631 225-0300
Lindenhurst *(G-7474)*

Amiram Dror Inc F 212 979-9505
Brooklyn *(G-1609)*

C Howard Company Inc G 631 286-7940
Bellport *(G-822)*

▼ Calico Cottage Inc E 631 841-2100
Amityville *(G-277)*

▲ Chocolat Moderne LLC G 212 229-4797
New York *(G-9657)*

Chocolate Pizza Company Inc F 315 673-4098
Marcellus *(G-8118)*

Chocolations LLC G 914 777-3600
Mamaroneck *(G-8060)*

▲ Chocomaker Inc G 716 877-3146
Buffalo *(G-2893)*

Custom Candy Concepts Inc G 516 824-3228
Inwood *(G-6793)*

Demets Candy Company LLC G 607 562-8600
Horseheads *(G-6602)*

Dilese International Inc F 716 855-3500
Buffalo *(G-2931)*

Dylans Candy Bar Inc F 646 735-0078
New York *(G-9998)*

Eatingevolved LLC F 631 675-2440
Setauket *(G-15400)*

▲ Fairbanks Mfg LLC C 845 341-0002
Middletown *(G-8474)*

Fine and Raw Chocolate G 718 366-3633
Brooklyn *(G-1975)*

Gertrude Hawk Chocolates Inc E
Watertown *(G-16673)*

Glennys Inc G 516 377-1400
Brooklyn *(G-2027)*

▲ Godiva Chocolatier Inc E 212 984-5900
New York *(G-10368)*

Gravymaster Inc E 203 453-1893
Canajoharie *(G-3360)*

Handsome Dans LLC G 917 965-2499
New York *(G-10449)*

Hedonist Artisan Chocolates F 585 461-2815
Rochester *(G-14452)*

Hercules Candy Co F 315 463-4339
East Syracuse *(G-4551)*

Hudson Valley Chocolatier Inc F 845 831-8240
Beacon *(G-781)*

▼ In Room Plus Inc E 716 838-9433
Buffalo *(G-3023)*

Jo-Mart Candies Corp F 718 375-1277
Brooklyn *(G-2142)*

Joseph Shalhoub & Son Inc F 718 871-6300
Brooklyn *(G-2149)*

▲ Joyva Corp D 718 497-0170
Brooklyn *(G-2153)*

Keep Healthy Inc F 631 651-9090
Northport *(G-13031)*

Lady-N-Th-wndow Chocolates Inc F 631 549-1059
Huntington *(G-6702)*

◆ Lanco Corporation C 631 231-2300
Ronkonkoma *(G-14957)*

Little Bird Chocolates Inc G 646 620-6395
Massapequa *(G-8211)*

Momn Pops Inc E 845 567-0640
Cornwall *(G-4009)*

▲ Mrchocolatecom LLC F 718 875-9772
Brooklyn *(G-2347)*

▲ N Make Mold Inc E 716 877-3146
Buffalo *(G-3101)*

▼ Naples Vly Mrgers Acqstons LLC G 585 490-1339
Naples *(G-8813)*

Noras Candy Shop F 315 337-4530
Rome *(G-14853)*

Nycjbs LLC F 212 533-1888
New York *(G-11496)*

OH How Cute Inc G 347 838-6031
Staten Island *(G-15739)*

Papa Bubble G 212 966-2599
New York *(G-11575)*

◆ Pfeil & Holing Inc D 718 545-4600
Woodside *(G-17362)*

Premium Sweets USA Inc G 718 739-6000
Jamaica *(G-6978)*

▲ Rajbhog Foods Inc E 718 358-5105
Flushing *(G-5294)*

▲ Richardson Brands Company C 800 839-8938
Canajoharie *(G-3361)*

Robert Pikcilingis F 518 355-1860
Altamont *(G-215)*

Roger L Urban Inc E 716 693-5391
North Tonawanda *(G-13010)*

Salty Road Inc G 347 673-3925
Brooklyn *(G-2555)*

◆ Satin Fine Foods Inc D 845 469-1034
Chester *(G-3642)*

▲ Scaccianoce Inc F 718 991-4462
Bronx *(G-1449)*

Seaward Candies G 585 638-6761
Holley *(G-6518)*

◆ Settons Intl Foods Inc E 631 543-8090
Commack *(G-3868)*

▲ Simply Natural Foods LLC E 631 543-9600
Commack *(G-3869)*

Steve & Andys Organics Inc G 718 499-7933
Brooklyn *(G-2629)*

Stones Homemade Candies Inc G 315 343-8401
Oswego *(G-13367)*

◆ Sweetworks Inc C 716 634-4545
Buffalo *(G-3230)*

◆ Tomric Systems Inc G 716 854-6050
Buffalo *(G-3247)*

Valenti Distributing G 716 824-2304
Blasdell *(G-962)*

▲ Vidal Candies USA Inc G 609 781-8169
New York *(G-12565)*

◆ Vigneri Chocolate Inc G 585 254-6160
Rochester *(G-14782)*

Wellspring Corp G 212 529-5454
New York *(G-12637)*

Worlds Finest Chocolate Inc C 718 332-2442
Brooklyn *(G-2782)*

2066 Chocolate & Cocoa Prdts

▲ 5th Avenue Chocolatiere Ltd G 212 935-5454
Freeport *(G-5388)*

5th Avenue Chocolatiere Ltd F 516 561-1570
Valley Stream *(G-16423)*

Adirondack Chocolate Co Ltd F 518 946-7270
Wilmington *(G-17290)*

Aigner Chocolates Inc G 718 544-1850
Forest Hills *(G-5325)*

Aletheas Chocolates Inc E 716 633-8620
Williamsville *(G-17259)*

Amiram Dror Inc F 212 979-9505
Brooklyn *(G-1609)*

◆ Associated Brands Inc B 585 798-3475
New York *(G-9291)*

Big Heart Pet Brands E 716 891-6566
Buffalo *(G-2864)*

▲ Cemoi Inc G 212 583-4920
New York *(G-9611)*

Chocolate By Design Inc G 631 737-0082
Bohemia *(G-1029)*

Chocolate Pizza Company Inc F 315 673-4098
Marcellus *(G-8118)*

Commodore Chocolatier USA Inc F 845 561-3960
Newburgh *(G-12774)*

Ctac Holdings LLC E 212 924-2280
Brooklyn *(G-1822)*

Dilese International Inc F 716 855-3500
Buffalo *(G-2931)*

Dolce Vite International LLC G 713 962-5767
Brooklyn *(G-1871)*

Doma Marketing Inc G 516 684-1111
Port Washington *(G-13833)*

Eating Evolved Inc G 516 510-2601
East Setauket *(G-4499)*

Emvi Inc G 518 883-5111
Broadalbin *(G-1240)*

Encore Chocolates Inc G 585 266-2970
Rochester *(G-14370)*

▲ Ernex Corporation Inc E 718 951-2251
Brooklyn *(G-1938)*

Fox 416 Corp E 718 385-4600
Brooklyn *(G-2001)*

Gnosis Chocolate Inc G 646 688-5549
Long Island City *(G-7780)*

▲ Godiva Chocolatier Inc E 212 984-5900
New York *(G-10368)*

Godiva Chocolatier Inc E 718 271-3603
Elmhurst *(G-4675)*

Godiva Chocolatier Inc E 718 677-1452
Brooklyn *(G-2036)*

Godiva Chocolatier Inc G 212 809-8990
New York *(G-10369)*

Greenwood Winery LLC E 315 432-8132
East Syracuse *(G-4547)*

Hershey Kiss 203 Inc G 516 503-3740
Wantagh *(G-16579)*

▲ Jacques Torres Chocolate LLC E 212 414-2462
New York *(G-10733)*

Jo-Mart Candies Corp F 718 375-1277
Brooklyn *(G-2142)*

▲ Joyva Corp D 718 497-0170
Brooklyn *(G-2153)*

Lady-N-Th-wndow Chocolates Inc F 631 549-1059
Huntington *(G-6702)*

◆ Lanco Corporation C 631 231-2300
Ronkonkoma *(G-14957)*

▲ Landies Candies Co Inc F 716 834-8212
Buffalo *(G-3062)*

▲ Le Chocolat LLC G 845 352-8301
Monsey *(G-8608)*

▲ Le Chocolate of Rockland LLC E 845 533-4125
Suffern *(G-15816)*

▲ Madelaine Chocolate Novlt Inc D 718 945-1500
Rockaway Beach *(G-14810)*

Madisons Delight LLC F 718 720-8900
Staten Island *(G-15724)*

Mast Brothers Inc E 718 388-2625
Brooklyn *(G-2283)*

▲ Max Brenner Union Square LLC G 646 467-8803
New York *(G-11210)*

Mbny LLC F 646 467-8810
New York *(G-11216)*

Micosta Enterprises Inc G 518 822-9708
Hudson *(G-6657)*

Momn Pops Inc E 845 567-0640
Cornwall *(G-4009)*

20 FOOD AND KINDRED PRODUCTS

Nibmor Project LLC .... F 718 374-5091
  Great Neck (G-5840)
Noras Candy Shop .... F 315 337-4530
  Rome (G-14853)
Parkside Candy Co Inc .... F 716 833-7540
  Buffalo (G-3137)
▲ Reserve Confections Inc .... F 845 371-7744
  Spring Valley (G-15622)
Rip Van Wafels Inc .... E 415 529-5403
  Brooklyn (G-2516)
Robert Pikcilingis .... F 518 355-1860
  Altamont (G-215)
Roger L Urban Inc .... E 716 693-5391
  North Tonawanda (G-13010)
◆ Settons Intl Foods Inc .... E 631 543-8090
  Commack (G-3868)
▲ Simply Natural Foods LLC .... E 631 543-9600
  Commack (G-3869)
▲ Superior Confections Inc .... D 718 698-3300
  Staten Island (G-15766)
▲ Sweetriot Inc .... G 212 431-7468
  New York (G-12277)
◆ Sweetworks Inc .... C 716 634-4545
  Buffalo (G-3230)
The Chocolate Shop .... G 716 882-5055
  Buffalo (G-3241)
Yes Were Nuts Ltd .... G 516 374-1940
  Hewlett (G-6341)

2067 Chewing Gum

▲ Ford Gum & Machine Company Inc .D 716 542-4561
  Akron (G-19)
Simply Gum Inc .... E 917 721-8032
  New York (G-12106)
◆ Sweetworks Inc .... C 716 634-4545
  Buffalo (G-3230)

2068 Salted & Roasted Nuts & Seeds

▲ American Almond Pdts Co Inc .... D 718 875-8310
  Brooklyn (G-1597)
Our Daily Eats LLC .... F 518 810-8412
  Albany (G-114)
◆ Peeled Inc .... F 212 706-2001
  Brooklyn (G-2425)
◆ Sahadi Fine Foods Inc .... E 718 369-0100
  Brooklyn (G-2554)
◆ Scaccianoce Inc .... F 718 991-4462
  Bronx (G-1449)
◆ Settons Intl Foods Inc .... E 631 543-8090
  Commack (G-3868)
▼ Sugar Foods Corporation .... E 212 753-6900
  New York (G-12249)
Whitsons Food Svc Bronx Corp .... B 631 424-2700
  Islandia (G-6843)

2074 Cottonseed Oil Mills

▲ Perimondo LLC .... G 212 749-0721
  New York (G-11637)

2076 Vegetable Oil Mills

▲ Jax Coco USA LLC .... G 347 688-8198
  New York (G-10744)

2077 Animal, Marine Fats & Oils

Baker Commodities Inc .... E 585 482-1880
  Rochester (G-14239)

2079 Shortening, Oils & Margarine

▲ Bonelli Foods LLC .... G 212 346-0942
  New York (G-9486)
Bunge Limited Finance Corp .... C 914 684-2800
  White Plains (G-17116)
C B S Food Products Corp .... F 718 452-2500
  Brooklyn (G-1745)
Consumer Flavoring Extract Co .... F 718 435-0201
  Brooklyn (G-1797)
F Olivers LLC .... G 585 244-2585
  Rochester (G-14389)
▲ Healthy Brand Oil Corp .... E 718 937-0806
  Long Island City (G-7786)
◆ Kerry Bfnctnal Ingredients Inc .... D 607 334-1700
  Norwich (G-13048)
L LLC .... E 716 885-3918
  Buffalo (G-3057)
▲ Pietro Demarco Importers Inc .... F 914 969-3201
  Yonkers (G-17496)
Pinos Press Inc .... G 315 935-0110
  Syracuse (G-16034)

2082 Malt Beverages

Anheuser-Busch LLC .... C 315 638-0365
  Baldwinsville (G-566)
Anheuser-Busch LLC .... C 212 573-8800
  New York (G-9209)
Anheuser-Busch Companies LLC .... C 718 589-2610
  Bronx (G-1275)
Anheuser-Busch Inbev Fin Inc .... F 212 573-8800
  New York (G-9210)
Barrier Brewing Company LLC .... G 516 316-4429
  Long Beach (G-7668)
Black River Brewing Co Inc .... G 315 755-2739
  Watertown (G-16661)
Brazen Street LLC .... G 516 305-7951
  Brooklyn (G-1712)
▲ Brewery Ommegang Ltd .... E 607 286-4144
  Cooperstown (G-3909)
▲ Castle Brands Inc .... D 646 356-0200
  New York (G-9596)
Constellation Brands Inc .... D 585 678-7100
  Victor (G-16493)
Coopers Cave Ale Co S-Corp .... F 518 792-0007
  Glens Falls (G-5692)
Cooperstown Brewing Co LLC .... G 607 286-9330
  Oneonta (G-13204)
Crazy Cowboy Brewing Co LLC .... E 516 812-0576
  Woodbury (G-17306)
Custom Brewcrafters Inc .... F 585 624-4386
  Honeoye Falls (G-6554)
Decrescente Distributing Co .... D 518 664-9866
  Mechanicville (G-8257)
Duvel Mortgage USA Inc .... G 607 267-6121
  Cooperstown (G-3911)
Empire Brewing Company Inc .... D 315 925-8308
  Syracuse (G-15956)
Equilibrium Brewery LLC .... G 201 245-0292
  Middletown (G-8473)
Five Burroughs Brewing Co .... G 718 355-8575
  Brooklyn (G-1981)
Gilded Otter Brewing Co .... D 845 256-1700
  New Paltz (G-8919)
▲ High Falls Brewing Company LLC .... C 585 546-1030
  Rochester (G-14454)
High Falls Operating Co LLC .... A 585 546-1030
  Rochester (G-14455)
Hoptron Brewtique .... G 631 438-0296
  Patchogue (G-13448)
Hornell Brewing Co Inc .... G 914 597-7911
  White Plains (G-17148)
Horns & Halos Cft Brewing LLC .... E 585 507-7248
  Caledonia (G-3308)
Hyde Park Brewing Co Inc .... E 845 229-8277
  Hyde Park (G-6773)
Independent Brewers Untd Corp .... G 585 263-9308
  Rochester (G-14468)
Indian Ladder Farmstead Brewer .... G 518 577-1484
  Altamont (G-210)
Ithaca Beer Company Inc .... E 607 272-1305
  Ithaca (G-6888)
Keegan Ales LLC .... F 845 331-2739
  Kingston (G-7221)
Keuka Brewing Co LLC .... G 607 868-4648
  Hammondsport (G-5979)
▲ Labatt USA LLC .... D 716 604-1050
  Buffalo (G-3058)
Long Ireland Brewing LLC .... E 631 403-4303
  Riverhead (G-14160)
▲ Mad Scntsts Brwing Prtners LLC .... F 347 766-2739
  Brooklyn (G-2254)
▲ Marnier-Lapostolle Inc .... D 212 207-4350
  New York (G-11187)
▲ Middle Ages Brewing Company .... G 315 476-4250
  Syracuse (G-16008)
Millercoors LLC .... E 585 385-0670
  Pittsford (G-13598)
Montauk Brewing Company Inc .... F 631 668-8471
  Montauk (G-8624)
Newburgh Brewing Company LLC .... G 845 569-2337
  Newburgh (G-12791)
▼ North American Breweries Inc .... F 585 546-1030
  Rochester (G-14559)
North Amrcn Brwries Hldngs LLC .... E 585 546-1030
  Rochester (G-14562)
Olde Saratoga Brewing .... F 518 581-0492
  Saratoga Springs (G-15195)
Other Half Brewing Co .... G 347 987-3527
  Brooklyn (G-2411)
Remarkable Liquids LLC .... D 518 861-5351
  Altamont (G-214)

Rising Sons 6 Brewing Coinc .... G 607 368-4836
  Corning (G-3999)
▲ Vanberg & Dewulf Co Inc .... G 607 547-8184
  Cooperstown (G-3912)
Vernon Wine & Liquor Inc .... G 718 784-5096
  Long Island City (G-7943)
Wagner Vineyards & Brewing Co .... E 607 582-6574
  Lodi (G-7666)
Woodcock Brothers Brewing Comp .... G 716 333-4000
  Wilson (G-17293)
Yonkers Whl Beer Distrs Inc .... E 914 963-8600
  Yonkers (G-17520)

2083 Malt

▲ Great Western Malting Co .... G 800 496-7732
  Champlain (G-3569)
Queen City Malting LLC .... G 716 481-1313
  Buffalo (G-3175)

2084 Wine & Brandy

Allied Wine Corp .... F 845 796-4160
  South Fallsburg (G-15542)
Americana Vineyards & Winery .... F 607 387-6801
  Interlaken (G-6785)
Anyelas Vineyards LLC .... F 315 685-3797
  Skaneateles (G-15476)
Arrowhead Spring Vineyards LLC .... G 716 434-8030
  Lockport (G-7598)
Atwater Estate Vineyards LLC .... E 607 546-8463
  Burdett (G-3290)
Austin Nichols & Co Inc .... F 519 561-5225
  New York (G-9319)
Bibo International LLC .... F 617 304-2242
  New York (G-9436)
Billsboro Winery .... G 315 789-9538
  Geneva (G-5582)
Brooklyn Winery LLC .... F 347 763-1506
  Brooklyn (G-1736)
▲ Brotherhood Americas .... E 845 496-3661
  Washingtonville (G-16621)
Casa Larga Vineyards .... F 585 223-4210
  Fairport (G-4855)
Casa Larga Vineyards .... G 585 223-4210
  Fairport (G-4856)
Cascade Mountain Winery & Rest .... F 845 373-9021
  Amenia (G-218)
▲ Cava Spiliadis USA .... E 212 247-8214
  New York (G-9605)
Chautauqua Wine Company Inc .... G 716 934-9463
  Silver Creek (G-15469)
City Winery Napa LLC .... F 212 633-4399
  New York (G-9685)
Clinton Vineyards Inc .... G 845 266-5372
  Clinton Corners (G-3748)
Cobblestone Frm Winery Vinyrd .... F 315 549-1004
  Romulus (G-14669)
Constellation Brands Inc .... D 585 678-7100
  Victor (G-16493)
Constellation Brands Inc .... E 585 393-4880
  Canandaigua (G-3368)
Constellation Brands Smo LLC .... G 585 396-7161
  New York (G-9768)
Constellation Brands US Oprs .... A 585 396-7600
  Canandaigua (G-3369)
▲ Constellation Brands US Oprs .... B 585 396-7600
  Canandaigua (G-3370)
Coyote Moon LLC .... F 315 686-5600
  Clayton (G-3711)
▼ Cruzin Management Inc .... E 212 641-8700
  New York (G-9818)
◆ Davos Brands LLC .... F 212 779-1911
  New York (G-9887)
Deer Run Enterprises Inc .... F 585 346-0850
  Geneseo (G-5580)
Di Borghese Castello LLC .... F 631 734-5111
  Cutchogue (G-4097)
▲ Dorset Farms Inc .... F 631 734-6010
  Peconic (G-13494)
Dr Pepper Snapple Group Inc .... C 315 589-4911
  Williamson (G-17251)
▲ Dreyfus Ashby Inc .... F 212 818-0770
  New York (G-9980)
Duck Walk Vinyards .... F 631 726-7555
  Water Mill (G-16627)
▲ Dutch Spirits LLC .... F 518 398-1022
  Pine Plains (G-13582)
Dutchess Wines LLC .... F 845 876-1319
  Rhinebeck (G-14068)
▲ Eagle Crest Vineyard LLC .... G 585 346-5760
  Conesus (G-3874)

Employee Codes: A=Over 500 employees, B=251-500
C=101-250, D=51-100, E=20-50, F=10-19, G=5-9

20 FOOD AND KINDRED PRODUCTS

East Branch Winery Inc .... G 607 292-3999
  Dundee (G-4351)
▲ East End Vineyards LLC .... G 718 468-0500
  Queens Village (G-13992)
Edrington Group Usa LLC .... E 212 352-6000
  New York (G-10036)
Fly Creek Cder Mill Orchrd Inc .... G 607 547-9692
  Fly Creek (G-5319)
Fox Run Vineyards Inc .... F 315 536-4616
  Penn Yan (G-13535)
Frank Wines Inc .... G 646 765-6637
  New York (G-10252)
Freedom Run Winery Inc .... G 716 433-4132
  Lockport (G-7616)
▲ Gabriella Importers Inc .... G 212 579-3945
  Bohemia (G-1066)
Gabriella Importers Inc .... F 212 579-3945
  New York (G-10286)
Glenora Wine Cellars Inc .... E 607 243-9500
  Dundee (G-4353)
Grapes & Grains .... G 518 283-9463
  Rensselaer (G-14057)
Greenwood Winery LLC .... E 315 432-8132
  East Syracuse (G-4547)
Hazlitts 1852 Vineyards Inc .... E 607 546-9463
  Hector (G-6282)
▲ Hermann J Wiemer Vineyard .... G 607 243-7971
  Dundee (G-4354)
Heron Hill Vineyards Inc .... E 607 868-4241
  Hammondsport (G-5978)
Hickory Road Land Co LLC .... G 607 243-9114
  Dundee (G-4355)
Hoffman & Hoffman .... G 315 536-4773
  Penn Yan (G-13537)
Hosmer Inc .... F 888 467-9463
  Ovid (G-13371)
Hunt Country Vineyards .... E 315 595-2812
  Branchport (G-1169)
▲ J Petrocelli Wine Cellars LLC .... E 631 765-1100
  Peconic (G-13495)
Joseph Zakon Winery Ltd .... G 718 604-1430
  Brooklyn (G-2150)
▲ Konstantin D FRAnk& Sons Vini ..... E 607 868-4884
  Hammondsport (G-5980)
L & D Acquisition LLC .... F 585 531-9000
  Naples (G-8811)
Lafayette Chateau .... G 607 546-2062
  Hector (G-6283)
▲ Lakewood Vineyards Inc .... F 607 535-9252
  Watkins Glen (G-16720)
Lamoreaux Landing WI .... D 607 582-6162
  Lodi (G-7665)
Lieb Cellars LLC .... E 631 298-1942
  Mattituck (G-8239)
Lockhouse Distillery .... G 716 768-4898
  Buffalo (G-3068)
Lucas Vineyards & Winery .... F 607 532-4825
  Interlaken (G-6787)
Malina Management Company Inc ...... E 607 535-9614
  Montour Falls (G-8649)
Merritt Estate Winery Inc .... F 716 965-4800
  Forestville (G-5341)
▲ Millbrook Winery Inc .... F 845 677-8383
  Millbrook (G-8513)
▲ Montezuma Winery LLC .... G 315 568-8190
  Seneca Falls (G-15389)
Negys New Land Vinyrd Winery .... G 315 585-4432
  Geneva (G-5595)
▲ North House Vineyards Inc .... G 631 779-2817
  Jamesport (G-7002)
Olde Chtqua Vneyards Ltd Lblty .... F 716 792-2749
  Portland (G-13891)
▲ Paumanok Vineyards Ltd .... E 631 722-8800
  Aquebogue (G-385)
Pellegrini Vineyards LLC .... G 631 734-4111
  Cutchogue (G-4098)
Pindar Vineyards LLC .... E 631 734-6200
  Peconic (G-13496)
Prejean Winery Inc .... F 315 536-7524
  Penn Yan (G-13539)
▲ Premium Wine Group LLC .... E 631 298-1900
  Mattituck (G-8241)
Pugliese Vineyards Inc .... G 631 734-4057
  Cutchogue (G-4099)
Quinn and Co of NY Ltd .... D 212 868-1900
  New York (G-11800)
Red Newt Cellars Inc .... F 607 546-4100
  Hector (G-6284)
Red Tail Ridge Inc .... G 315 536-4580
  Penn Yan (G-13540)

Rock Stream Vineyards .... G 607 243-8322
  Rock Stream (G-14808)
Royal Wine Corporation .... F 845 236-4000
  Marlboro (G-8136)
Sheldrake Point Vineyard LLC .... F 607 532-8967
  Ovid (G-13373)
▲ Shinn Winery LLC .... G 631 804-0367
  Mattituck (G-8242)
SMK Wines & Liquors LLC .... G 212 685-7651
  New York (G-12134)
Sokolin LLC .... E 631 537-4434
  Yaphank (G-17419)
▲ Solstars Inc .... G 212 605-0430
  New York (G-12151)
Spanish Artisan Wine Group LLC .... G 914 414-6982
  Patterson (G-13468)
Standing Stone Vineyards .... G 607 582-6051
  Hector (G-6285)
Swedish Hill Vineyard Inc .... G 607 403-0029
  Romulus (G-14872)
Thirsty Owl Wine Company .... G 607 869-5805
  Ovid (G-13374)
Thousand Islands Winery LLC .... E 315 482-9306
  Alexandria Bay (G-195)
Tickle Hill Winery .... G 607 546-7740
  Hector (G-6286)
Trader Joes Company .... E 212 529-6326
  New York (G-12409)
Vedell North Fork LLC .... G 631 323-3526
  Cutchogue (G-4100)
▲ Vindagra USA Incorporated .... G 516 605-1960
  Melville (G-8392)
Wagner Vineyards & Brewing Co .... E 607 582-6574
  Lodi (G-7666)
Westchester Wine Warehouse LLC ..... F 914 824-1400
  White Plains (G-17213)
Wine Group Inc .... D 716 326-3151
  Westfield (G-17084)
Wine Market .... G 516 328-8800
  New Hyde Park (G-8917)
Wine Services Inc .... G 631 722-3800
  Riverhead (G-14174)
▲ Wolffer Estate Vineyard Inc .... E 631 537-5106
  Sagaponack (G-15109)
Woodbury Vineyards Inc .... G 716 679-9463
  Fredonia (G-5386)

2085 Liquors, Distilled, Rectified & Blended

Austin Nichols & Co Inc .... F 519 561-5225
  New York (G-9319)
▲ Braided Oak Spirits LLC .... F 845 381-1525
  Middletown (G-8463)
▲ Castle Brands Inc .... D 646 356-0200
  New York (G-9596)
Constellation Brands Inc .... D 585 678-7100
  Victor (G-69)
▼ Cruzin Management Inc .... E 212 641-8700
  New York (G-9818)
▲ Dutch Spirits LLC .... F 518 398-1022
  Pine Plains (G-13582)
Evolution Spirits Inc .... G 917 543-7880
  New York (G-10149)
Finger Lakes Distilling .... F 607 546-5510
  Burdett (G-3291)
Honeoye Falls Distillery LLC .... F 201 780-4618
  Honeoye Falls (G-6559)
Iron Smoke Whiskey LLC .... E 585 388-7584
  Fairport (G-4863)
▲ Leblon Holdings LLC .... E 212 741-2675
  New York (G-10988)
▲ Leblon LLC .... F 954 649-0148
  New York (G-10989)
▲ Leblon LLC .... E 786 281-5672
  New York (G-10990)
Long Island Spirits Inc .... F 631 630-9322
  Calverton (G-3320)
Madison County Distillery LLC .... G 315 391-6070
  Cazenovia (G-3474)
▲ Marnier-Lapostolle Inc .... D 212 207-4350
  New York (G-11187)
◆ Pernod Ricard Usa LLC .... E 212 372-5400
  New York (G-11640)
Prohibition Distillery LLC .... G 917 685-8989
  Roscoe (G-15034)
◆ Russian Standard Vodka USA Inc ... G 212 679-1894
  New York (G-11955)
▲ Sovereign Brands LLC .... E 212 343-8366
  New York (G-12171)
▲ Tuthilltown Spirits LLC .... F 845 255-1527
  Gardiner (G-5564)

2086 Soft Drinks

3v Company Inc .... E 718 858-7333
  Brooklyn (G-1516)
A Health Obsession LLC .... E 347 850-4587
  Brooklyn (G-1534)
American Bottling Company .... F 516 714-0002
  Ronkonkoma (G-14894)
Ariesun Inc .... E 866 274-3049
  Mount Vernon (G-8708)
▼ Arizona Beverage Company LLC .... G 516 812-0300
  Woodbury (G-17303)
Austin Nichols & Co Inc .... F 519 561-5225
  New York (G-9319)
Ba Sports Nutrition LLC .... C 718 357-7402
  Whitestone (G-17230)
Beverage Works Incorporated .... G 718 834-0500
  Brooklyn (G-1689)
Beverage Works Nj Inc .... F 631 293-3501
  Farmingdale (G-4961)
Beverage Works Ny Inc .... E 718 812-2034
  Brooklyn (G-1690)
▲ Blue Star Beverages Corp .... G 718 381-3535
  Brooklyn (G-1703)
Borabora Fruit Juices Inc .... G 845 795-1027
  Highland (G-6430)
Bottling Group LLC .... E 315 788-6751
  Watertown (G-16662)
Bottling Group LLC .... B 800 789-2626
  White Plains (G-17113)
◆ Bottling Group LLC .... G 914 767-6000
  White Plains (G-17114)
▲ Boylan Bottling Co Inc .... E 800 289-7978
  New York (G-9499)
▲ Brands Within Reach LLC .... F 847 720-9090
  Mamaroneck (G-8057)
Brave Chefs Incorporated .... G 347 956-5905
  Little Neck (G-7530)
◆ Brooklyn Btlg Milton NY Inc .... C 845 795-2171
  Milton (G-8516)
▲ Cell-Nique Corporation .... G 888 417-9343
  Castleton On Hudson (G-3446)
Cheribundi Inc .... E 800 699-0460
  Geneva (G-5585)
Chohehco LLC .... E 315 420-4624
  Skaneateles (G-15478)
◆ Cliffstar LLC .... A 716 366-6100
  Dunkirk (G-4361)
Clintons Ditch Coop Co Inc .... C 315 699-2695
  Cicero (G-3672)
Coca-Cola Bottling Co of NY .... F 518 459-2010
  Albany (G-69)
Coca-Cola Bottling Company .... E 518 483-0422
  Malone (G-8039)
▲ Coca-Cola Btlg Co Buffalo Inc .... C 716 874-4610
  Tonawanda (G-16175)
Coca-Cola Btlg Co of NY Inc .... F 845 562-3037
  New Windsor (G-8982)
Coca-Cola Btlg Co of NY Inc .... E 718 326-3331
  Maspeth (G-8153)
Coca-Cola Btlg Co of NY Inc .... F 914 592-4574
  Elmsford (G-4750)
Coca-Cola Btlg Co of NY Inc .... F 718 416-7575
  Maspeth (G-8154)
Coca-Cola Btlg Co of NY Inc .... F 315 457-9221
  Syracuse (G-15919)
Coca-Cola Btlg Co of NY Inc .... F 631 434-3535
  Hauppauge (G-6068)
Coca-Cola Btlg Co of NY Inc .... F 718 420-6800
  Staten Island (G-15679)
Coca-Cola Btlg Co of NY Inc .... F 914 789-1580
  Elmsford (G-4751)
Coca-Cola Refreshments USA Inc ...... F 718 401-5200
  Bronx (G-1302)
Coca-Cola Refreshments USA Inc ...... E 315 785-8907
  Watertown (G-16667)
Coca-Cola Refreshments USA Inc ...... E 914 592-0806
  Hawthorne (G-6268)
Consumers Beverages Inc .... E 716 837-3087
  Buffalo (G-2907)
Consumers Beverages Inc .... G 716 675-4934
  West Seneca (G-16970)
Cornell Beverages Inc .... F 718 381-3000
  Brooklyn (G-1803)
Crystal Rock LLC .... E 716 626-7460
  Buffalo (G-2914)
Dirty Lemon Beverages LLC .... G 877 897-7784
  New York (G-9935)
Doheny Nice and Easy .... G 518 793-1733
  Glens Falls (G-5693)

SIC SECTION

20 FOOD AND KINDRED PRODUCTS

Dr Pepper Snapple Group Inc .... C 315 589-4911
  Williamson (G-17251)
Dr Pepper Snapple Group Inc .... D 914 846-2300
  Elmsford (G-4756)
Dr Pepper Snapple Group Inc .... G 718 246-6200
  Brooklyn (G-1879)
East Coast Cultures LLC .... F 917 261-3010
  Kingston (G-7217)
▼ Energy Brands Inc .... D 212 545-6000
  New York (G-10089)
F & V Distribution Company LLC .... G 516 812-0393
  Woodbury (G-17308)
Fancy Flamingo LLC .... G 516 209-7306
  New York (G-10187)
Gangi Distributors Inc .... F 718 442-5745
  Staten Island (G-15697)
General Cinema Bevs of Ohio .... A 914 767-6000
  Somers (G-15531)
Global Brands Inc .... G 845 358-1212
  Nyack (G-13068)
▲ Goodo Beverage Company .... F 718 328-6400
  Bronx (G-1348)
Grayhawk Leasing LLC .... G 914 767-6000
  Somers (G-15532)
Green Zone Food Service Inc .... G 917 709-1728
  Corona (G-4020)
◆ Hain Celestial Group Inc .... C 516 587-5000
  New Hyde Park (G-8882)
Heart of Tea .... F 917 725-3164
  New York (G-10494)
Hmo Beverage Corp .... G 917 371-6100
  Brooklyn (G-2078)
Hydrive Energy .... G 914 925-9100
  Rye (G-15086)
Johnnie Ryan Co Inc .... F 716 282-1606
  Niagara Falls (G-12856)
Juices Enterprises Inc .... G 718 953-1860
  Brooklyn (G-2157)
Just Beverages LLC .... F 480 388-1133
  Glens Falls (G-5699)
Kraft Heinz Foods Company .... A 914 335-2500
  Tarrytown (G-16116)
La Cola 1 Inc .... G 917 509-6669
  New York (G-10944)
Let Water Be Water LLC .... E 212 627-2630
  New York (G-11012)
Linda Wine & Spirit .... G 718 703-5707
  Brooklyn (G-2228)
▲ Liquid Management Partners LLC ... F 516 775-5050
  New Hyde Park (G-8892)
Load/N/Go Beverage Corp .... F 585 218-4019
  Rochester (G-14502)
Long Island Brand Bevs LLC .... D 855 542-2832
  Long Island City (G-7822)
Long Island Iced Tea Corp .... E 855 542-2832
  Farmingdale (G-5045)
Manhattan Special Bottling .... F 718 388-4144
  Brooklyn (G-2262)
▲ Mayer Bros Apple Products Inc .... D 716 668-1787
  West Seneca (G-16980)
Meadowbrook Distributing Corp .... D 516 226-9000
  Garden City (G-5532)
Mnm Service Distributors Inc .... G 914 337-5268
  Bronxville (G-1501)
Monfefo LLC .... G 347 779-2600
  Brooklyn (G-2336)
N Y Winstons Inc .... D 212 665-3166
  New York (G-11361)
Nantucket Allserve Inc .... D 914 612-4000
  Elmsford (G-4778)
New York Bottling Co Inc .... F 718 963-3232
  Bronx (G-1410)
▲ New York Spring Water Inc .... E 212 777-4649
  New York (G-11427)
Nexbev Industries LLC .... F 917 626-5255
  Pearl River (G-13486)
▲ Nirvana Inc .... G 315 942-4900
  Forestport (G-5338)
Pepsi Beverages Co .... G 518 782-2150
  Latham (G-7402)
Pepsi Bottling Ventures LLC .... D 631 772-6144
  Patchogue (G-13457)
Pepsi Bottling Ventures LLC .... E 631 226-9000
  Amityville (G-321)
Pepsi Btlg Group Globl Fin LLC .... G 914 767-6000
  Somers (G-15533)
Pepsi-Cola Bottling Co NY Inc .... B 718 649-2465
  College Point (G-3826)
Pepsi-Cola Bottling Co NY Inc .... B 914 699-2600
  Mount Vernon (G-8760)

Pepsi-Cola Bottling Co NY Inc .... G 718 786-8550
  Maspeth (G-8195)
Pepsi-Cola Bottling Co NY Inc .... D 718 892-1570
  Bronx (G-1425)
◆ Pepsi-Cola Bottling Group .... G 914 767-6000
  White Plains (G-17178)
◆ Pepsi-Cola Metro Btlg Co Inc .... G 914 767-6000
  White Plains (G-17179)
Pepsi-Cola Metro Btlg Co Inc .... E 914 253-2000
  Purchase (G-13979)
Pepsi-Cola Metro Btlg Co Inc .... D 607 795-1399
  Horseheads (G-6615)
Pepsi-Cola Newburgh Btlg Inc .... C 845 562-5400
  Newburgh (G-12797)
Pepsi-Cola Operating Company .... E 914 767-6000
  White Plains (G-17180)
Pepsi-Cola Sales and Dist Inc .... G 914 253-2000
  Purchase (G-13980)
Pepsico .... F 419 252-0247
  Hawthorne (G-6276)
▲ Pepsico .... E 914 801-1500
  Valhalla (G-16395)
Pepsico Inc .... B 914 742-4500
  Valhalla (G-16396)
Pepsico Inc .... A 914 253-2000
  Purchase (G-13982)
Pepsico Inc .... E 914 253-3474
  White Plains (G-17182)
Pepsico Inc .... E 914 253-2713
  Purchase (G-13983)
◆ Pepsico Inc .... A 914 253-2000
  Purchase (G-13981)
Pepsico Capital Resources Inc .... G 914 253-2000
  Purchase (G-13984)
Pepsico Sales Inc .... G 914 253-2000
  Purchase (G-13985)
Pepsico World Trading Co Inc .... G 914 767-6000
  White Plains (G-17184)
Purely Maple LLC .... F 203 997-9309
  New York (G-11777)
▲ Quench It Inc .... E 845 462-5400
  Poughkeepsie (G-13945)
Rochester Coca Cola Bottling .... D 607 739-5678
  Horseheads (G-6620)
Rochester Coca Cola Bottling .... D 585 546-3900
  Rochester (G-14660)
Saratoga Spring Water Company .... E 518 584-6363
  Saratoga Springs (G-15202)
Save More Beverage Corp .... G 518 371-2520
  Halfmoon (G-5938)
▲ Scotia Beverages Inc .... A 518 370-3621
  Schenectady (G-15318)
Shopping Center Wine & Liquor .... G 914 528-1600
  Mohegan Lake (G-8579)
Snapp Too Enterprise .... G 718 224-5252
  Flushing (G-5299)
Snapple Beverage Corp (del) .... D 914 612-4000
  Rye Brook (G-15101)
Stewarts Processing Corp .... G 518 581-1200
  Ballston Spa (G-609)
Street King LLC .... G 212 400-2200
  New York (G-12235)
Superleaf LLC .... G 888 887-4318
  Brooklyn (G-2650)
Switch Beverage Company LLC .... F 203 202-7383
  Port Washington (G-13885)
Treo Brands LLC .... G 914 341-1850
  Harrison (G-6011)
Unilever United States Inc .... F 212 546-0200
  New York (G-12474)
Unilever United States Inc .... C 212 546-0200
  New York (G-12475)
▲ Water Resources Group LLC .... G 631 824-9088
  Cold Spring Harbor (G-3796)

2087 Flavoring Extracts & Syrups

3v Company Inc .... E 718 858-7333
  Brooklyn (G-1516)
Agua Enerviva LLC .... F 516 597-5440
  Bethpage (G-863)
▲ American Almond Pdts Co Inc .... D 718 875-8310
  Brooklyn (G-1597)
American Juice Company LLC .... G 347 620-0252
  New York (G-9173)
Baldwin Richardson Foods Co .... C 315 986-2727
  Macedon (G-8010)
Better Fresh Corp .... G 718 628-3682
  Brooklyn (G-1688)
▲ Boylan Bottling Co Inc .... E 800 289-7978
  New York (G-9499)

▲ Buffalo Blends Inc .... E 716 825-4422
  Buffalo (G-2871)
◆ Citrus and Allied Essences Ltd .... E 516 354-1200
  Floral Park (G-5207)
Constellation Brands Inc .... D 585 678-7100
  Victor (G-16493)
Consumer Flavoring Extract Co .... F 718 435-0201
  Brooklyn (G-1797)
Craftmaster Flavor Technology .... F 631 789-8607
  Amityville (G-282)
Danisco US Inc .... D 585 277-4300
  Rochester (G-14322)
▲ Delbia Do Company Inc .... G 718 585-2226
  Bronx (G-1315)
Delbia Do Company Inc .... F 718 585-2226
  Bronx (G-1316)
Dr Pepper Snapple Group Inc .... C 315 589-4911
  Williamson (G-17251)
DSM Nutritional Products LLC .... C 518 372-5155
  Schenectady (G-15276)
DSM Nutritional Products LLC .... C 518 372-5155
  Glenville (G-5716)
▼ Flavormatic Industries Inc .... E 845 297-9100
  Wappingers Falls (G-16587)
Fox 416 Corp .... E 718 385-4600
  Brooklyn (G-2001)
Hispanica Intl Dights Amer Inc .... F 866 928-5070
  New York (G-10529)
◆ Interntnal Flvors Frgrnces Inc .... C 212 765-5500
  New York (G-10681)
Mapleland Farms LLC .... G 518 854-7669
  Salem (G-15138)
◆ Motts LLP .... C 972 673-8088
  Elmsford (G-4775)
Mr Smoothie .... G 845 296-1686
  Poughkeepsie (G-13938)
Natural Organics Labroratories .... B 631 957-5600
  Amityville (G-314)
◆ Pepsi-Cola Metro Btlg Co Inc .... G 914 767-6000
  White Plains (G-17179)
◆ Pepsico Inc .... A 914 253-2000
  Purchase (G-13981)
▼ Roar Beverages LLC .... E 631 683-5565
  Huntington (G-6715)
◆ Star Kay White Inc .... D 845 268-2600
  Congers (G-3885)
Synergy Flavors NY Company LLC ...... G 585 232-6648
  Rochester (G-14735)
Tealeafs .... G 716 688-8022
  Williamsville (G-17282)
Torre Products Co Inc .... E 212 925-8989
  New York (G-12396)
◆ Virginia Dare Extract Co Inc .... C 718 788-6320
  Brooklyn (G-2747)
Wynn Starr Flavors Inc .... E 845 584-3080
  Congers (G-3888)

2091 Fish & Seafoods, Canned & Cured

◆ Acme Smoked Fish Corp .... D 954 942-5598
  Brooklyn (G-1556)
▲ Banner Smoked Fish Inc .... D 718 449-1992
  Brooklyn (G-1663)
Blue Ocean Food Trading LLC .... G 718 689-4291
  Brooklyn (G-1701)
◆ Catsmo LLC .... G 845 895-2296
  Wallkill (G-16562)
Deelka Vision Corp .... E 718 937-4121
  Sunnyside (G-15827)
Harbors Maine Lobster LLC .... E 516 775-2400
  New Hyde Park (G-8884)
▲ Premium Ocean LLC .... F 917 231-1061
  Bronx (G-1434)
Samaki Inc .... G 845 858-1012
  Port Jervis (G-13815)
Sangster Foods Inc .... E 212 993-9129
  Brooklyn (G-2556)

2092 Fish & Seafoods, Fresh & Frozen

6th Ave Gourmet Inc .... G 845 782-9067
  Monroe (G-8582)
Fish To Dish Inc .... F 718 972-7600
  Brooklyn (G-1979)
▲ Foo Yuan Food Products Co Inc ..... G 212 925-2840
  Long Island City (G-7773)
Montauk Inlet Seafood Inc .... G 631 668-3419
  Montauk (G-8625)
Oceans Cuisine Ltd .... F 631 209-9200
  Ridge (G-14105)
Prince of The Sea Ltd .... E 516 333-6344
  Westbury (G-17050)

20 FOOD AND KINDRED PRODUCTS SIC SECTION

◆ **Rich Products Corporation** A 716 878-8000
Buffalo *(G-3185)*

▲ **Shine Foods USA Inc** G 516 784-9674
Glen Oaks *(G-5655)*

2095 Coffee

Altaro Corp F 855 674-2455
Tarrytown *(G-16109)*

▲ **Bh Coffee Company LLC** D 914 377-2500
Elmsford *(G-4745)*

Birch Guys LLC G 917 763-0751
Long Island City *(G-7717)*

BK Associates Intl Inc F 607 432-1499
Oneonta *(G-13196)*

Brooklyn Roasting Works LLC G 718 855-1000
Brooklyn *(G-1731)*

Cafe Kubal F 315 278-2812
Syracuse *(G-15901)*

Caranda Emporium LLC F 212 866-7100
New York *(G-9577)*

◆ **Coffee Holding Co Inc** D 718 832-0800
Staten Island *(G-15680)*

Death Wish Coffee Company LLC F 518 400-1050
Round Lake *(G-15061)*

▲ **Eldorado Coffee Roasters Ltd** D 718 418-4100
Maspeth *(G-8167)*

Elite Roasters Inc F 716 626-0307
East Amherst *(G-4386)*

▲ **Empire Coffee Company Inc** E 914 934-1100
Port Chester *(G-13773)*

Fal Coffee Inc F 718 305-4255
Brooklyn *(G-1959)*

Gillies Coffee Company E 718 499-7766
Brooklyn *(G-2024)*

Gorilla Coffee Inc G 917 297-8947
Brooklyn *(G-2041)*

Gorilla Coffee Inc G 718 230-3244
Brooklyn *(G-2042)*

Irving Farm Coffee Co Inc G 212 206-0707
New York *(G-10706)*

John A Vassilaros & Son Inc E 718 886-4140
Flushing *(G-5264)*

Joseph H Navaie F 607 936-9030
Corning *(G-3995)*

Kraft Heinz Foods Company A 914 335-2500
Tarrytown *(G-16116)*

Maidstone Coffee Co E 585 272-1040
Rochester *(G-14512)*

Monkey Joe Roasting Company G 845 331-4598
Kingston *(G-7231)*

New York Gourmet Coffee Inc G 631 254-0076
Bay Shore *(G-719)*

▲ **Orens Daily Roast Inc** G 212 348-5400
New York *(G-11538)*

P Pascal Inc E 914 969-7933
Yonkers *(G-17493)*

▲ **Paul De Lima Company Inc** D 315 457-3725
Liverpool *(G-7566)*

Paul De Lima Company Inc E 315 457-3725
Cicero *(G-3678)*

▲ **Paul Delima Coffee Company** G 315 457-3725
Cicero *(G-3679)*

Peaks Coffee Company G 315 565-1900
Cazenovia *(G-3477)*

▲ **Regal Trading Inc** E 914 694-6100
Purchase *(G-13986)*

▲ **S J McCullagh Inc** E 716 856-3473
Buffalo *(G-3201)*

Sangster Foods Inc F 212 993-9129
Brooklyn *(G-2556)*

Star Mountain JFK Inc G 718 553-6787
Jamaica *(G-6988)*

Vega Coffee Inc G 415 881-7969
New York *(G-12538)*

Where Is Utica Cof Rasting Inc F 315 269-8898
Utica *(G-16389)*

▲ **White Coffee Corp** D 718 204-7900
Astoria *(G-461)*

2096 Potato Chips & Similar Prdts

Birds Eye Holdings Inc A 585 383-1850
Rochester *(G-14250)*

BSD Top Direct Inc G 646 468-0156
West Babylon *(G-16802)*

▲ **Emmi USA Inc** F 845 268-9990
Orangeburg *(G-13247)*

Frito-Lay North America Inc D 716 631-2360
Williamsville *(G-17271)*

Frito-Lay North America Inc E 585 343-5456
Batavia *(G-635)*

Frito-Lay North America Inc D 607 775-7000
Binghamton *(G-911)*

Glennys Inc G 516 377-1400
Brooklyn *(G-2027)*

◆ **Hain Celestial Group Inc** C 516 587-5000
New Hyde Park *(G-8882)*

◆ **Ideal Snacks Corporation** C 845 292-7000
Liberty *(G-7459)*

◆ **Pepsico Inc** A 914 253-2000
Purchase *(G-13981)*

Pepsico Inc B 914 253-2000
White Plains *(G-17181)*

Pepsico Inc D 914 767-6976
White Plains *(G-17183)*

Proformance Foods Inc G 703 869-3413
Brooklyn *(G-2469)*

Pupellos Organic Chips Inc F 718 710-9154
Oakdale *(G-13079)*

Robs Really Good LLC F 516 671-4411
Sea Cliff *(G-15364)*

Saratoga Chips LLC G 877 901-6950
Saratoga Springs *(G-15201)*

Switch Beverage Company LLC F 203 202-7383
Port Washington *(G-13885)*

Terrells Potato Chip Co Inc D 315 437-2786
Syracuse *(G-16081)*

▲ **TLC-Lc Inc** E 212 756-8900
New York *(G-12375)*

Tortilleria Chinantla Inc G 718 302-0101
Brooklyn *(G-2687)*

2097 Ice

Adirondack Ice & Air Inc F 518 483-4340
Malone *(G-8036)*

Annies Ice G 585 593-5605
Wellsville *(G-16774)*

Arctic Glacier Minnesota Inc E 585 388-0080
Fairport *(G-4849)*

Arctic Glacier Newburgh Inc G 718 456-2013
Brooklyn *(G-1625)*

Arctic Glacier Newburgh Inc F 845 561-0549
Newburgh *(G-12771)*

Arctic Glacier PA Inc E 610 494-8200
Fairport *(G-4850)*

Arctic Glacier Texas Inc E 215 283-0326
Fairport *(G-4851)*

Arctic Glacier USA E 215 283-0326
Fairport *(G-4852)*

Clayville Ice Co Inc G 315 839-5405
Clayville *(G-3713)*

Henry Newman LLC F 607 273-8512
Ithaca *(G-6883)*

Huntington Ice & Cube Corp F 718 456-2013
Brooklyn *(G-2087)*

Ice Cube Inc G 613 254-0071
Deer Park *(G-4174)*

◆ **Mamitas Ices Ltd** F 718 738-3238
Ozone Park *(G-13409)*

Maplewood Ice Co Inc E 518 499-2345
Whitehall *(G-17218)*

South Shore Ice Co Inc F 516 379-2056
Roosevelt *(G-15032)*

2098 Macaroni, Spaghetti & Noodles

AAA Noodle Products Mfg G 212 431-4090
New York *(G-9045)*

Bedessee Imports Ltd E 718 272-1300
Brooklyn *(G-1674)*

Borgattis Ravioli Egg Noodles G 718 367-3799
Bronx *(G-1286)*

Canton Noodle Corporation G 212 226-3276
New York *(G-9570)*

Cassinelli Food Products Inc G 718 274-4881
Long Island City *(G-7724)*

Dairy Maid Raviolo Mfg F 718 449-2620
Brooklyn *(G-1836)*

Deer Park Macaroni Co Inc G 631 667-4600
Deer Park *(G-4150)*

Deer Park Macaroni Co Inc F 631 667-4600
Deer Park *(G-4151)*

Hong Hop Co Inc E 212 962-1735
New York *(G-10546)*

Momofuku 171 First Avenue LLC D 212 777-7773
New York *(G-11322)*

Nodus Noodle Corporation G 718 309-3725
Sunnyside *(G-15829)*

Noodle Education Inc E 646 289-7800
New York *(G-11469)*

▲ **Piemonte Home Made Ravioli Co** F 718 429-1972
Woodside *(G-17363)*

Piemonte Home Made Ravioli Co G 212 226-0475
New York *(G-11680)*

Queen Ann Macaroni Mfg Co Inc G 718 256-1061
Brooklyn *(G-2485)*

Raffettos Corp E 212 777-1261
New York *(G-11813)*

Ravioli Store Inc G 718 729-9300
Long Island City *(G-7888)*

▲ **Twin Marquis Inc** D 718 386-6868
Brooklyn *(G-2710)*

Wing Heung Noodle Inc F 212 966-7496
New York *(G-12670)*

Wing Kei Noodle Inc F 212 226-1644
New York *(G-12671)*

Wonton Food Inc F 212 677-8865
New York *(G-12682)*

Yum Yum Noodle Bar G 845 679-7992
Kingston *(G-7253)*

2099 Food Preparations, NEC

212kiddish Inc G 718 705-7227
Brooklyn *(G-1512)*

3v Company Inc E 718 858-7333
Brooklyn *(G-1516)*

ABC Peanut Butter LLC B 212 661-6886
New York *(G-9048)*

Ahhmigo LLC F 212 315-1818
New York *(G-9111)*

▲ **Amalfi Ingredients LLC** G 631 392-1526
Deer Park *(G-4118)*

▲ **American Almond Pdts Co Inc** D 718 875-8310
Brooklyn *(G-1597)*

Andros Bowman Products LLC G 540 217-4100
Lyndonville *(G-7994)*

Armour Bearer Group Inc G 646 812-4487
Arverne *(G-421)*

Aromasong Usa Inc F 718 838-9669
Brooklyn *(G-1632)*

Aryzta LLC D 310 417-4700
Rochester *(G-14232)*

◆ **Associated Brands Inc** B 585 798-3475
New York *(G-9291)*

Bainbridge & Knight LLC E 212 986-5100
New York *(G-9360)*

Baldwin Richardson Foods Co C 315 986-2727
Macedon *(G-8010)*

▲ **Barilla America Ny Inc** C 585 226-5600
Avon *(G-536)*

Beak & Skiff Cider Mill Inc G 315 677-5105
La Fayette *(G-7265)*

▲ **Bektrom Foods Inc** G 516 802-3800
Syosset *(G-15835)*

Bel Americas Inc G 646 454-8220
New York *(G-9396)*

Blue Tortilla LLC G 631 451-0100
Selden *(G-15369)*

▲ **Bombay Kitchen Foods Inc** F 516 767-7401
Port Washington *(G-13825)*

Brightline Ventures I LLC E 212 626-6829
New York *(G-9513)*

Broome County E 607 785-9567
Endicott *(G-4805)*

Buna Besta Tortillas G 347 987-3995
Brooklyn *(G-1739)*

Butterwood Desserts Inc E 716 652-0131
West Falls *(G-16876)*

Bylada Foods LLC D 845 623-1300
West Nyack *(G-16944)*

Capitol City Specialties Co G 518 486-8935
Albany *(G-59)*

▲ **Casablanca Foods LLC** G 212 317-1111
New York *(G-9593)*

◆ **Castella Imports Inc** C 631 231-5500
Hauppauge *(G-6060)*

Chan & Chan (usa) Corp G 718 388-9633
Brooklyn *(G-1773)*

Chan Kee Dried Bean Curd Inc G 718 622-0820
Brooklyn *(G-1774)*

▲ **Chemicolloid Laboratories Inc** F 516 747-2666
New Hyde Park *(G-8866)*

Child Nutrition Prog Dept Ed D 212 371-1000
New York *(G-9644)*

▲ **China Huaren Organic Pdts Inc** G 212 232-0120
New York *(G-9647)*

Chopt Creative Salad Co LLC F 646 233-2923
New York *(G-9658)*

Conagra Brands Inc F 212 461-2410
New York *(G-9753)*

Cookiebaker LLC G 716 878-8000
Buffalo *(G-2909)*

D R M Management Inc .... E 716 668-0333
Depew *(G-4278)*
Deedee Desserts LLC .... G 716 627-2330
Lake View *(G-7303)*
Diva Farms Ltd .... G 315 735-4397
Utica *(G-16349)*
▲ **Dundee Foods LLC** .... F 585 377-7700
Fairport *(G-4860)*
Event Services Corporation .... G 315 488-9357
Solvay *(G-15530)*
▲ **Extreme Spices Inc** .... G 917 496-4081
Maspeth *(G-8168)*
Fanshawe Foods LLC .... F 212 757-3130
New York *(G-10188)*
▲ **Far Eastern Coconut Company** .... F 631 851-8800
Central Islip *(G-3522)*
Farmers Hub LLC .... G 914 380-2945
White Plains *(G-17135)*
Fleischmanns Vinegar Co Inc .... E 315 587-4414
North Rose *(G-12952)*
Flik International/Compass .... E 212 450-4750
New York *(G-10232)*
Fresh Tortillas Si Inc .... G 718 979-6666
Staten Island *(G-15696)*
Frito-Lay North America Inc .... D 607 775-7000
Binghamton *(G-911)*
Gillies Coffee Company .... E 718 499-7766
Brooklyn *(G-2024)*
▼ **Glenn Foods Inc** .... F 516 377-1400
Freeport *(G-5413)*
▲ **Gold Pure Food Products Co Inc** .... D 516 483-5600
Hempstead *(G-6296)*
Golden Taste Inc .... E 845 356-4133
Spring Valley *(G-15609)*
▲ **Gourmet Boutique LLC** .... C 718 977-1200
Jamaica *(G-6952)*
Gourmet Crafts Inc .... F 718 372-0505
Brooklyn *(G-2044)*
▲ **Gourmet Guru Inc** .... E 718 842-2828
Bronx *(G-1349)*
Gourmet Toast Corp .... G 718 852-4536
Brooklyn *(G-2045)*
Gravymaster Inc .... E 203 453-1893
Canajoharie *(G-3360)*
Great Eastern Pasta Works LLC .... E 631 956-0889
West Babylon *(G-16820)*
H & S Edible Products Corp .... E 914 413-3489
Mount Vernon *(G-8733)*
Hong Hop Co Inc .... E 212 962-1735
New York *(G-10546)*
HP Hood LLC .... D 607 295-8134
Arkport *(G-408)*
Instantwhip of Buffalo Inc .... E 716 892-7031
Buffalo *(G-3027)*
▲ **Johns Ravioli Company Inc** .... F 914 576-7030
New Rochelle *(G-8960)*
▲ **Joyva Corp** .... D 718 497-0170
Brooklyn *(G-2153)*
Kale Factory Inc .... G 917 363-6361
Brooklyn *(G-2166)*
◆ **Kerry Bfnctnal Ingredients Inc** .... D 607 334-1700
Norwich *(G-13048)*
Kerry Inc .... G 845 584-3081
Congers *(G-3883)*
◆ **Kozy Shack Enterprises LLC** .... C 516 870-3000
Hicksville *(G-6387)*
Kozy Shack Enterprises LLC .... C 516 870-3000
Hicksville *(G-6388)*
Kraft Heinz Foods Company .... A 914 335-2500
Tarrytown *(G-16116)*
Kraft Heinz Foods Company .... B 585 226-4400
Avon *(G-537)*
La Escondida Inc .... G 845 562-1387
Newburgh *(G-12786)*
▲ **La Flor Products Company Inc** .... E 631 851-9601
Hauppauge *(G-6136)*
Labella Pasta Inc .... G 845 331-9130
Kingston *(G-7224)*
Lakeside Cider Mill Farm Inc .... G 518 399-8359
Ballston Lake *(G-581)*
▲ **Lams Foods Inc** .... F 718 217-0476
Queens Village *(G-13997)*
Land OLakes Inc .... G 516 681-2980
Hicksville *(G-6390)*
▲ **Larte Del Gelato Inc** .... G 212 366-0570
New York *(G-10966)*
Lollipop Tree Inc .... E 845 471-8733
Auburn *(G-504)*
Lugo Nutrition Inc .... G 302 573-2503
Nyack *(G-13069)*

M & M Food Products Inc .... F 718 821-1970
Brooklyn *(G-2246)*
Maizteca Foods Inc .... E 718 641-3933
South Richmond Hill *(G-15558)*
Mandalay Food Products Inc .... G 718 230-3370
Brooklyn *(G-2259)*
Manhattan Milling & Drying Co .... E 516 496-1041
Woodbury *(G-17314)*
▲ **Maramont Corporation** .... B 718 439-8900
Brooklyn *(G-2266)*
▲ **Martens Country Kit Pdts LLC** .... F 315 776-8821
Port Byron *(G-13762)*
▲ **Mediterrean Dyro Company** .... E 718 786-4888
Long Island City *(G-7839)*
Merb LLC .... F 631 393-3621
Farmingdale *(G-5057)*
▲ **Meta-Therm Corp** .... F 914 697-4840
White Plains *(G-17164)*
Mighty Quinns Barbeque LLC .... C 973 777-8340
New York *(G-11287)*
Milnot Holding Corporation .... G 518 839-0300
Amsterdam *(G-358)*
Mizkan America Inc .... F 585 798-5720
Medina *(G-8311)*
Mizkan America Inc .... D 585 765-9171
Lyndonville *(G-7995)*
Mizkan Americas Inc .... F 315 483-6944
Sodus *(G-15525)*
Moira New Hope Food Pantry .... E 518 529-6524
Moira *(G-8581)*
Momentive Performance Mtls Inc .... D 914 784-4807
Tarrytown *(G-16121)*
Mondelez Global LLC .... G 585 345-3300
Batavia *(G-643)*
Morris Kitchen Inc .... F 646 413-5186
Brooklyn *(G-2339)*
Mullers Cider House LLC .... G 585 287-5875
Rochester *(G-14544)*
▲ **Natural Lab Inc** .... G 718 321-8848
Flushing *(G-5277)*
Naturally Free Food Inc .... G 631 361-9710
Smithtown *(G-15515)*
Nestle Healthcare Ntrtn Inc .... G 516 249-5085
Farmingdale *(G-5074)*
New York Ravioli Pasta Co Inc .... E 516 270-2852
New Hyde Park *(G-8897)*
Nine Pin Ciderworks LLC .... F 518 449-9999
Albany *(G-109)*
Noaspence Inc .... G 516 433-7848
Hicksville *(G-6401)*
North Shore Farms Two Ltd .... G 516 280-6880
Mineola *(G-8560)*
▼ **Old Dutch Mustard Co Inc** .... G 516 466-0522
Great Neck *(G-5843)*
Omg Desserts Inc .... F 585 698-1561
Rochester *(G-14569)*
▲ **Once Again Nut Butter Collectv** .... D 585 468-2535
Nunda *(G-13059)*
Original Hrkmer Cnty Chese Inc .... D 315 895-7428
Ilion *(G-6782)*
P-Hgh 2 Co Inc .... G 954 534-6058
Buffalo *(G-3131)*
▲ **Parnasa International Inc** .... G 516 394-0400
Valley Stream *(G-16442)*
Peaceful Valley Maple Farm .... G 518 762-0491
Johnstown *(G-7150)*
▲ **Peanut Butter & Co Inc** .... E 212 757-3130
New York *(G-11604)*
Pelican Bay Ltd .... F 718 729-9300
Long Island City *(G-7869)*
Pellicano Specialty Foods Inc .... F 716 822-2366
Buffalo *(G-3140)*
Pennant Ingredients Inc .... D 585 235-8160
Rochester *(G-14595)*
Ponti Rossi Inc .... G 347 506-9616
Brooklyn *(G-2441)*
Purespice LLC .... G 617 549-8400
Hopewell Junction *(G-6584)*
Radicle Farm LLC .... G 315 226-3294
New York *(G-11812)*
▲ **Raw Indulgence Ltd** .... F 866 498-4671
Hawthorne *(G-6278)*
Rawpothecary Inc .... G 917 783-7770
Brooklyn *(G-2498)*
▲ **Real Co Inc** .... G 347 433-8549
Valley Cottage *(G-16412)*
▲ **Redland Foods Corp** .... F 716 288-9061
Cheektowaga *(G-3616)*
◆ **Rich Products Corporation** .... A 716 878-8000
Buffalo *(G-3185)*

▲ **Rob Salamida Company Inc** .... F 607 729-4868
Johnson City *(G-7136)*
Sabra Dipping Company LLC .... F 516 249-0151
Farmingdale *(G-5117)*
Salvador Colletti Blank .... G 718 217-6725
Douglaston *(G-4334)*
Sapienza Pastry Inc .... E 516 352-5232
Elmont *(G-4739)*
Schutt Cider Mill .... F 585 872-2924
Webster *(G-16760)*
▲ **Seasons Soyfood Inc** .... G 718 797-9896
Brooklyn *(G-2567)*
◆ **Settons Intl Foods Inc** .... E 631 543-8090
Commack *(G-3868)*
Sfoglini LLC .... F 646 872-1035
Brooklyn *(G-2572)*
▲ **Sneaky Chef Foods LLC** .... F 914 301-3277
Tarrytown *(G-16131)*
Solata Foods LLC .... E 845 245-4812
Newburgh *(G-12803)*
▲ **SOS Chefs of New York Inc** .... G 212 505-5813
New York *(G-12164)*
Spf Holdings II LLC .... G 212 750-8300
New York *(G-12185)*
▲ **Steinway Pasta & Gelati Inc** .... F 718 246-5414
Brooklyn *(G-2628)*
▼ **Sugar Foods Corporation** .... E 212 753-6900
New York *(G-12249)*
Sugar Shack Desert Company Inc .... G 518 523-7540
Lake Placid *(G-7300)*
Tea Life LLC .... G 516 365-7711
Manhasset *(G-8100)*
Terrace Management Inc .... E 914 737-0400
Cortlandt Manor *(G-4080)*
Tortilla Heaven Inc .... E 845 339-1550
Kingston *(G-7245)*
▲ **Tuv Taam Corp** .... E 718 855-2207
Brooklyn *(G-2708)*
▲ **Twin Marquis Inc** .... D 718 386-6868
Brooklyn *(G-2710)*
▲ **U S Sugar Co Inc** .... E 716 828-1170
Buffalo *(G-3256)*
UFS Industries Inc .... D 718 822-1100
Mount Vernon *(G-8790)*
Ultra Thin Ready To Bake Pizza .... E 516 679-6655
Deer Park *(G-4243)*
◆ **Victoria Fine Foods LLC** .... D 718 649-1635
Brooklyn *(G-2742)*
Vinegar Hill Asset LLC .... G 718 469-0342
Brooklyn *(G-2745)*
▲ **VIP Foods Inc** .... E 718 821-5330
Ridgewood *(G-14143)*
Whitsons Food Svc Bronx Corp .... B 631 424-2700
Islandia *(G-6843)*
▲ **Win-Holt Equipment Corp** .... E 516 222-0335
Woodbury *(G-17322)*
▲ **Wm E Martin and Sons Co Inc** .... E 516 605-2444
Roslyn *(G-15048)*
▲ **Wonder Natural Foods Corp** .... G 631 726-4433
Water Mill *(G-16629)*
Wonton Food Inc .... E 718 784-8178
Long Island City *(G-7955)*
▲ **Wonton Food Inc** .... C 718 628-6868
Brooklyn *(G-2778)*
Wonton Food Inc .... F 212 677-8865
New York *(G-12682)*

21 TOBACCO PRODUCTS

2111 Cigarettes

East End .... F 716 532-2622
Collins *(G-3841)*
Epuffer Inc .... G 718 374-6030
Brooklyn *(G-1935)*
Jacobs Tobacco Company .... E 518 358-4948
Hogansburg *(G-6453)*
◆ **Philip Morris Intl Inc** .... D 917 663-2000
New York *(G-11666)*
PMI Global Services Inc .... E 917 663-2000
New York *(G-11701)*
R J Reynolds Tobacco Company .... C 716 871-1553
Tonawanda *(G-16214)*
Schweitzer-Mauduit Intl Inc .... C 518 329-4222
Ancram *(G-375)*
▲ **Seneca Manufacturing Company** .... G 716 945-4400
Salamanca *(G-15133)*
Seneca Nation Enterprise .... F 716 934-7430
Irving *(G-6807)*
Vector Group Ltd .... B 212 409-2800
New York *(G-12536)*

Employee Codes: A=Over 500 employees, B=251-500
C=101-250, D=51-100, E=20-50, F=10-19, G=5-9

2018 Harris
New York Manufacturers Directory

719

21 TOBACCO PRODUCTS

2121 Cigars

American Cigar ....G....... 718 969-0008
  Fresh Meadows *(G-5451)*
Davidoff Gneva Madison Ave Inc ....G....... 212 751-9060
  New York *(G-9884)*
Mafco Consolidated Group Inc ....F....... 212 572-8600
  New York *(G-11123)*
Martinez Hand Made Cigars ....G....... 212 239-4049
  New York *(G-11192)*

2131 Tobacco, Chewing & Snuff

Elab Smokers Boutique ....G....... 585 865-4513
  Rochester *(G-14362)*
Mafco Consolidated Group Inc ....F....... 212 572-8600
  New York *(G-11123)*
National Tobacco Company LP ....F....... 212 253-8185
  New York *(G-11376)*

2141 Tobacco Stemming & Redrying

Schweitzer-Mauduit Intl Inc ....C....... 518 329-4222
  Ancram *(G-375)*

22 TEXTILE MILL PRODUCTS

2211 Cotton, Woven Fabric

1510 Associates LLC ....G....... 212 828-8720
  New York *(G-9006)*
A and J Apparel Corp ....G....... 212 398-8899
  New York *(G-9030)*
A3 Apparel LLC 888 403-9669
  New York *(G-9043)*
Accolade USA Inc ....C....... 866 423-5071
  Cheektowaga *(G-3590)*
Advanced Fashions Technology ....G....... 212 221-0606
  New York *(G-9092)*
Alliance Exports LLC ....G....... 347 208-3547
  New York *(G-9138)*
▲ Ann Gish Inc ....G....... 212 969-9200
  New York *(G-9213)*
▲ Apollo Apparel Group LLC ....F....... 212 398-6585
  New York *(G-9226)*
▲ AV Denim Inc ....E....... 212 764-6668
  New York *(G-9322)*
Avitto Leather Goods Inc ....G....... 212 219-7501
  New York *(G-9332)*
▲ Axis Na LLC ....G....... 212 840-4005
  New York *(G-9337)*
Bandier Corp ....G....... 212 242-5400
  New York *(G-9366)*
◆ Basileus Company LLC ....F....... 315 963-3516
  Manlius *(G-8101)*
▲ Benartex Inc ....E....... 212 840-3250
  New York *(G-9404)*
▲ Beyond Loom Inc ....G....... 212 575-3100
  New York *(G-9429)*
Bill Blass Group LLC ....G....... 212 689-8957
  New York *(G-9448)*
Blu Sand LLC ....G....... 212 564-1147
  New York *(G-9470)*
Brooklyn Denim Co ....F....... 718 782-2600
  Brooklyn *(G-1724)*
▲ Brunschwig & Fils LLC ....F....... 800 538-1880
  Bethpage *(G-864)*
◆ Cai Inc ....E....... 212 819-0008
  New York *(G-9547)*
Charming Fashion Inc ....G....... 212 730-2872
  New York *(G-9635)*
Creation Baumann USA Inc ....E....... 516 764-7431
  Rockville Centre *(G-14818)*
Cy Fashion Corp ....G....... 212 730-8600
  New York *(G-9832)*
Designway Ltd ....G....... 212 254-2220
  New York *(G-9911)*
▲ Equipment Apparel LLC ....D....... 212 502-1890
  New York *(G-10105)*
Fab Industries Corp ....E....... 516 498-3200
  Great Neck *(G-5824)*
▲ French Accnt Rugs & Tapestries ......G....... 212 686-6097
  New York *(G-10256)*
Geordie Magee Uphl & Canvas ....G....... 315 676-7679
  Brewerton *(G-1200)*
◆ Gerli & Co Inc ....E....... 212 213-1919
  New York *(G-10329)*
Gotham T-Shirt Corp ....G....... 516 676-0900
  Sea Cliff *(G-15363)*
▲ Gw Acquisition LLC ....E....... 212 736-4848
  New York *(G-10430)*
Haleys Comet Seafood Corp ....E....... 212 571-1828
  New York *(G-10441)*

Hanesbrands Inc ....G....... 212 576-9300
  New York *(G-10452)*
▲ Harley Robert D Company Ltd ....G....... 212 947-1872
  New York *(G-10458)*
▲ Horizon Apparel Mfg Inc ....G....... 516 361-4878
  Atlantic Beach *(G-468)*
Internationl Studios Inc ....G....... 212 819-1616
  New York *(G-10680)*
Joy of Learning 718 443-6463
  Brooklyn *(G-2151)*
▲ Jrg Apparel Group Company Ltd .....E....... 212 997-0900
  New York *(G-10812)*
Knightly Endeavors ....F....... 845 340-0949
  Kingston *(G-7223)*
▲ La Lame Inc ....F....... 212 921-9770
  New York *(G-10947)*
◆ Lydall Performance Mtl Inc ....C....... 518 273-6320
  Green Island *(G-5877)*
▲ Magic Brands International LLC ....F....... 212 563-4999
  New York *(G-11130)*
Marsha Fleisher ....F....... 845 679-6500
  Woodstock *(G-17380)*
▼ Mason Contract Products LLC ....E....... 516 328-6900
  New Hyde Park *(G-8894)*
Meder Textile Co Inc ....E....... 516 883-0409
  Port Washington *(G-13861)*
Medline Industries Inc ....B....... 845 344-3301
  Middletown *(G-8484)*
Mgk Group Inc ....E....... 212 989-2732
  New York *(G-11273)*
Michael Stuart Inc ....E....... 718 821-0704
  Brooklyn *(G-2314)*
N Y Contract Seating Inc ....G....... 718 417-9298
  Maspeth *(G-8183)*
Navas Designs Inc ....E....... 818 988-9050
  New York *(G-11382)*
▲ Neilson International Inc ....G....... 631 454-0400
  Farmingdale *(G-5073)*
Nochairs Inc ....G....... 917 748-8731
  New York *(G-11465)*
◆ Northpoint Trading Inc ....F....... 212 481-8001
  New York *(G-11478)*
▲ Northwest Textile Holding Inc ....D....... 516 484-6996
  Roslyn *(G-15046)*
◆ Ortex Home Textile Inc ....G....... 718 241-7298
  Brooklyn *(G-2407)*
Pacific City International ....F....... 646 309-1250
  New York *(G-11566)*
Paramount Cord & Brackets ....G....... 212 325-9100
  White Plains *(G-17171)*
Perfect Print Inc ....E....... 718 832-5280
  Brooklyn *(G-2430)*
▲ Phoenix Usa LLC ....G....... 646 351-6598
  New York *(G-11671)*
Premium 5 Kids LLC ....F....... 212 563-4999
  New York *(G-11721)*
▲ Refuel Inc ....G....... 917 645-2974
  New York *(G-11850)*
▲ Renaissnce Crpt Tapestries Inc ....F....... 212 696-0080
  New York *(G-11863)*
▲ Richloom Home Fashions Corp ....F....... 212 685-5400
  New York *(G-11896)*
▲ Scalamandre Wallpaper Inc ....B....... 631 467-8800
  Hauppauge *(G-6210)*
Schneider Mills Inc ....C....... 828 632-0801
  New York *(G-12013)*
SD Eagle Global Inc ....E....... 516 822-1778
  Jericho *(G-7118)*
Shahin Designs Inc ....G....... 212 737-7225
  New York *(G-12060)*
Shindo Usa Inc ....G....... 212 868-9311
  New York *(G-12074)*
▲ Sita Finishing Inc ....F....... 718 417-5295
  Brooklyn *(G-2594)*
Sky Laundromat Inc ....E....... 718 639-7070
  Jamaica *(G-6986)*
Ssjjj Manufacturing LLC ....E....... 516 498-3200
  Great Neck *(G-5858)*
Star Draperies Inc ....F....... 631 756-7121
  Farmingdale *(G-5125)*
Success Apparel LLC ....G....... 212 502-1890
  New York *(G-12248)*
▲ Taikoh USA Inc ....F....... 646 556-6652
  New York *(G-12296)*
▲ US Design Group Ltd ....F....... 212 354-4070
  New York *(G-12505)*
Versailles Drapery Upholstery ....F....... 212 533-2059
  Long Island City *(G-7944)*
Wallace Home Design Ctr ....G....... 631 765-3890
  Southold *(G-15585)*

◆ Westpoint Home LLC ....A....... 212 930-2074
  New York *(G-12643)*
Westpoint International Inc ....F....... 212 930-2044
  New York *(G-12644)*
▲ Xing Lin USA Intl Corp ....G....... 212 947-4846
  New York *(G-12703)*

2221 Silk & Man-Made Fiber

A B C Elastic Corp ....G....... 718 388-2953
  Brooklyn *(G-1530)*
Albany International Corp ....C....... 518 445-2200
  Rensselaer *(G-14053)*
Apex Texicon Inc ....E....... 516 239-4400
  New York *(G-9223)*
Art People Inc ....G....... 212 431-4865
  New York *(G-9263)*
▲ Beyond Loom Inc ....G....... 212 575-3100
  New York *(G-9429)*
▲ Concepts Nyc Inc ....E....... 212 244-1033
  New York *(G-9754)*
Creation Baumann USA Inc ....E....... 516 764-7431
  Rockville Centre *(G-14818)*
Eastern Silk Mills Inc ....E....... 212 730-1300
  New York *(G-10017)*
Ess Bee Industries Inc ....E....... 718 894-5202
  Brooklyn *(G-1942)*
◆ Fabric Resources Intl Ltd ....F....... 516 829-4550
  Great Neck *(G-5825)*
◆ Fiber Glass Industries Inc ....D....... 518 842-4000
  Amsterdam *(G-345)*
Fiber Glass Industries Inc ....D....... 518 843-3533
  Amsterdam *(G-346)*
Fibrix LLC ....E....... 716 683-4100
  Depew *(G-4281)*
▲ Frp Apparel Group LLC ....G....... 212 695-8000
  New York *(G-10263)*
◆ Gerli & Co Inc ....E....... 212 213-1919
  New York *(G-10329)*
Greenbuds LLC ....G....... 718 483-9212
  Brooklyn *(G-2053)*
Himatsingka America Inc ....E....... 212 252-0802
  New York *(G-10524)*
▲ Himatsingka Holdings NA Inc ....E....... 212 545-8929
  New York *(G-10525)*
Intertex USA Inc ....F....... 212 279-3601
  New York *(G-10683)*
◆ Ivi Services Inc ....D....... 607 729-5111
  Binghamton *(G-924)*
▲ Jag Manufacturing Inc ....E....... 518 762-9558
  Johnstown *(G-7147)*
Jakob Schlaepfer Inc ....G....... 212 221-2323
  New York *(G-10736)*
JM Manufacturer Inc ....G....... 212 869-0626
  New York *(G-10781)*
Judscott Handprints Ltd ....F....... 914 347-5515
  Elmsford *(G-4768)*
Kragel Co Inc ....G....... 716 648-1344
  Hamburg *(G-5955)*
▲ La Lame Inc ....G....... 212 921-9770
  New York *(G-10947)*
▼ Laregence Inc ....E....... 212 736-2548
  New York *(G-10964)*
Maharam Fabric Corporation ....G....... 631 582-3434
  Yaphank *(G-17413)*
Marly Home Industries USA Inc ....G....... 718 388-3030
  Brooklyn *(G-2276)*
Mgk Group Inc ....E....... 212 989-2732
  New York *(G-11273)*
National Contract Industries ....G....... 212 249-0045
  New York *(G-11370)*
▲ New York Poplin LLC ....G....... 718 768-3296
  Brooklyn *(G-2375)*
▲ Newtex Industries Inc ....E....... 585 924-9135
  Victor *(G-16517)*
Pierce Arrow Drapery Mfg ....G....... 716 876-3023
  Buffalo *(G-3148)*
▲ Polytex Inc ....D....... 716 549-5100
  Angola *(G-381)*
▲ Richloom Home Fashions Corp ....F....... 212 685-5400
  New York *(G-11896)*
▲ Scalamandre Silks Inc ....D....... 212 980-3888
  New York *(G-12002)*
▲ Scalamandre Wallpaper Inc ....B....... 631 467-8800
  Hauppauge *(G-6210)*
Schneider Mills Inc ....C....... 828 632-0801
  New York *(G-12013)*
◆ Simplicity Creative Group Inc ....A....... 212 686-7676
  New York *(G-12105)*
Stark Scalamandre Fabric LLC ....D....... 212 376-2900
  New York *(G-12210)*

SIC SECTION
22 TEXTILE MILL PRODUCTS

Stern & Stern Industries Inc .... D 607 324-4485
  Hornell *(G-6594)*
Superior Fiber Mills Inc .... E 718 782-7500
  Brooklyn *(G-2649)*
Tli Import Inc .... G 917 578-4568
  Brooklyn *(G-2681)*
Toltec Fabrics Inc .... C 212 706-9310
  New York *(G-12378)*
Toray Industries Inc .... G 212 697-8150
  New York *(G-12394)*
◆ Unique Quality Fabrics Inc .... G 845 343-3070
  Middletown *(G-8503)*
▲ US Home Textiles Group LLC .... G 212 768-3030
  New York *(G-12508)*
◆ Westpoint Home LLC .... A 212 930-2074
  New York *(G-12643)*
White Plains Drapery Uphl Inc .... E 914 381-0908
  Mamaroneck *(G-8083)*
▲ Zorlu USA Inc .... F 212 689-4622
  New York *(G-12739)*

2231 Wool, Woven Fabric

▲ Acker & LI Mills Corporation .... G 212 307-7247
  New York *(G-9065)*
▲ Alicia Adams Alpaca Inc .... G 845 868-3366
  Millbrook *(G-8510)*
▲ Beyond Loom Inc .... G 212 575-3100
  New York *(G-9429)*
◆ Citisource Industries Inc .... E 212 683-1033
  New York *(G-9678)*
Equissentials LLC .... F 607 432-2856
  Oneonta *(G-13208)*
◆ Fabric Resources Intl Ltd .... F 516 829-4550
  Great Neck *(G-5825)*
▲ Hawkins Fabrics Inc .... E 518 773-9550
  Gloversville *(G-5729)*
▲ Interaxissourcingcom Inc .... E 212 905-6001
  New York *(G-10666)*
▲ Light House Hill Marketing .... F 212 354-1338
  New York *(G-11024)*
▲ Loomstate LLC .... G 212 219-2300
  New York *(G-11060)*
▲ Matt Textile Inc .... G 212 967-6010
  New York *(G-11205)*
Nazim Izzak Inc .... G 212 920-5546
  Long Island City *(G-7852)*
▲ Oakhurst Partners LLC .... G 212 502-3220
  New York *(G-11505)*
▲ Pinder International Inc .... G 631 273-0324
  Hauppauge *(G-6190)*
▲ Scalamandre Wallpaper Inc .... B 631 467-8800
  Hauppauge *(G-6210)*
◆ Warren Corporation .... C 917 379-3434
  New York *(G-12618)*
Woolmark Americas Inc .... G 347 767-3160
  New York *(G-12685)*
▲ Yarnz International Inc .... G 212 868-5883
  New York *(G-12711)*

2241 Fabric Mills, Cotton, Wool, Silk & Man-Made

Albany International Corp .... C 518 445-2200
  Rensselaer *(G-14053)*
Ambind Corp .... G 716 836-4365
  Buffalo *(G-2822)*
American Canvas Binders Corp .... G 914 969-0300
  Yonkers *(G-17430)*
▲ American Trim Mfg Inc .... E 518 239-8151
  Durham *(G-4379)*
▲ Bardwil Industries Inc .... E 212 944-1870
  New York *(G-9369)*
Breton Industries Inc .... D 518 842-3030
  Amsterdam *(G-337)*
Champion Zipper Corp .... G 212 239-0414
  New York *(G-9627)*
▲ Colonial Tag & Label Co Inc .... F 516 482-0508
  Great Neck *(G-5816)*
▲ Danray Textiles Corp .... F 212 354-5213
  New York *(G-9862)*
Depot Label Company Inc .... G 631 467-2952
  Patchogue *(G-13443)*
Eiseman-Ludmar Co Inc .... F 516 932-6990
  Hicksville *(G-6372)*
▲ Essential Ribbons Inc .... G 212 967-4173
  New York *(G-10118)*
▲ Fashion Ribbon Co Inc .... E 718 482-6108
  Long Island City *(G-7767)*
H Group Inc .... F 212 719-5500
  New York *(G-10434)*
Imperial-Harvard Label Co .... F 212 736-8420
  New York *(G-10620)*
Itc Mfg Group Inc .... G 212 684-3696
  New York *(G-10711)*
▲ J & M Textile Co Inc .... F 212 268-8000
  New York *(G-10715)*
Jakob Schlaepfer Inc .... G 212 221-2323
  New York *(G-10736)*
▲ La Lame Inc .... G 212 921-9770
  New York *(G-10947)*
Label Source Inc .... G 212 244-1403
  New York *(G-10948)*
▲ Labels Inter-Global Inc .... F 212 398-0006
  New York *(G-10949)*
Labeltex Mills Inc .... G 212 279-6165
  New York *(G-10950)*
Marketing Action Xecutives Inc .... G 212 971-9155
  New York *(G-11183)*
▲ Mergence Studios Ltd .... F 212 288-5616
  Hauppauge *(G-6159)*
New Classic Trade Inc .... G 347 822-9052
  Jamaica *(G-6972)*
New York Binding Co Inc .... G 718 729-2454
  Long Island City *(G-7857)*
▲ Newtex Industries Inc .... E 585 924-9135
  Victor *(G-16517)*
▲ R-Pac International Corp .... G 212 465-1818
  New York *(G-11810)*
▲ Scalamandre Silks Inc .... D 212 980-3888
  New York *(G-12002)*
▲ Schoen Trimming & Cord Co Inc .... F 212 255-3949
  New York *(G-12014)*
◆ Simplicity Creative Group Inc .... A 212 686-7676
  New York *(G-12105)*
▲ Skil-Care Corporation .... C 914 963-2040
  Yonkers *(G-17502)*
▲ Sml USA Inc .... E 212 736-8800
  New York *(G-12135)*
Solstiss Inc .... G 212 719-9194
  New York *(G-12152)*
▲ Sturges Manufacturing Co Inc .... D 315 732-6159
  Utica *(G-16384)*
Tamber Knits Inc .... E 212 730-1121
  New York *(G-12298)*
Triangle Label Tag Inc .... G 718 875-3030
  Brooklyn *(G-2697)*
Valley Industrial Products Inc .... E 631 385-9300
  Huntington *(G-6727)*

2251 Hosiery, Women's Full & Knee Length

Brach Knitting Mills Inc .... F 845 651-4450
  Florida *(G-5217)*
▲ Classic Hosiery Inc .... G 845 342-6661
  Middletown *(G-8465)*
Ellis Products Corp .... G 516 791-3732
  Valley Stream *(G-16431)*
▲ Fine Sheer Industries Inc .... F 212 594-4224
  New York *(G-10216)*
◆ Gina Group LLC .... E 212 947-2445
  New York *(G-10339)*
▼ Hot Sox Company Incorporated ...... E 212 957-2000
  New York *(G-10557)*

2252 Hosiery, Except Women's

▲ Ace Drop Cloth Canvas Pdts Inc .... E 718 731-1550
  Bronx *(G-1261)*
▲ Ashko Group LLC .... F 212 594-6050
  New York *(G-9283)*
Customize Elite Socks LLC .... G 212 533-8551
  New York *(G-9829)*
Etc Hosiery & Underwear Ltd .... G 212 947-5151
  New York *(G-10130)*
▲ Fine Sheer Industries Inc .... F 212 594-4224
  New York *(G-10216)*
Galiva Inc .... G 903 600-5755
  Brooklyn *(G-2013)*
Gbg Socks LLC .... E 646 839-7000
  New York *(G-10300)*
◆ Gina Group LLC .... E 212 947-2445
  New York *(G-10339)*
▲ Haddad Hosiery LLC .... G 212 251-0022
  New York *(G-10438)*
▲ High Point Design LLC .... F 212 354-2400
  New York *(G-10517)*
▼ Hot Sox Company Incorporated ...... E 212 957-2000
  New York *(G-10557)*
La Strada Dance Footwear Inc .... G 631 242-1401
  Deer Park *(G-4187)*
▲ Leadertex Intl Inc .... E 212 563-2242
  New York *(G-10983)*
▲ Look By M Inc .... G 212 213-4019
  New York *(G-11057)*
Lr Acquisition LLC .... F 212 301-8765
  New York *(G-11083)*
New Hampton Creations Inc .... G 212 244-7474
  New York *(G-11410)*
◆ Palmbay Ltd .... G 718 424-3388
  Flushing *(G-5285)*
Richard Edelson .... G 914 428-7573
  Hartsdale *(G-6018)*
Socks and More of NY Inc .... G 718 769-1785
  Brooklyn *(G-2603)*
Spartan Brands Inc .... F 212 340-0320
  New York *(G-12175)*
Sticky Socks LLC .... G 212 541-5927
  New York *(G-12228)*
Strassburg Medical LLC .... G 716 433-9368
  North Tonawanda *(G-13016)*
United Retail II .... E 212 966-9692
  New York *(G-12485)*
▲ You and ME Legwear LLC .... F 212 279-9292
  New York *(G-12718)*
Z Best Printing Inc .... F 631 595-1400
  Deer Park *(G-4255)*

2253 Knit Outerwear Mills

▲ 180s LLC .... E 410 534-6320
  New York *(G-9007)*
79 Metro Ltd .... G 212 944-4030
  New York *(G-9025)*
A & B Finishing Inc .... E 718 522-4702
  Brooklyn *(G-1524)*
Accurate Knitting Corp .... G 646 552-2216
  Brooklyn *(G-1550)*
Alpha Knitting Mills Inc .... E 718 628-6300
  Brooklyn *(G-1591)*
American T Shirts Inc .... G 212 563-7125
  New York *(G-9180)*
Andrea Strongwater .... G 212 873-0905
  New York *(G-9202)*
▲ Asian Global Trading Corp .... F 718 786-0998
  Long Island City *(G-7704)*
▲ B & B Sweater Mills Inc .... E 718 456-8693
  Brooklyn *(G-1656)*
Beachbuttons LLC .... G 917 306-9369
  New York *(G-9387)*
▲ Betsy & Adam Ltd .... E 212 302-3750
  New York *(G-9425)*
▲ Binghamton Knitting Co Inc .... E 607 722-6941
  Binghamton *(G-889)*
Blueberry Knitting Inc .... G 718 599-6520
  Brooklyn *(G-1704)*
Central Mills Inc .... G 212 221-0748
  New York *(G-9617)*
▲ Charter Ventures LLC .... F 212 868-0222
  New York *(G-9636)*
▲ Domani Fashions Corp .... G 718 797-0505
  Brooklyn *(G-1872)*
▲ Dressy Tessy Inc .... G 212 869-0750
  New York *(G-9978)*
E I Du Pont De Nemours & Co .... E 716 876-4420
  Buffalo *(G-2938)*
Elegant Headwear Co Inc .... G 212 695-8520
  New York *(G-10051)*
▲ Emerald Holdings Inc .... G 718 797-4404
  Brooklyn *(G-1921)*
Endres Knitwear Co Inc .... G 718 933-8687
  Bronx *(G-1330)*
Fashion Avenue Knits Inc .... F 718 456-9000
  New York *(G-10196)*
Fast-Trac Entertainment Ltd .... G 888 758-8886
  New York *(G-10199)*
▲ Freedom Rains Inc .... G 646 710-4512
  New York *(G-10255)*
Gabani Inc .... G 631 283-4930
  Southampton *(G-15567)*
▲ GAME Sportswear Ltd .... E 914 962-1701
  Yorktown Heights *(G-17527)*
▲ Gce International Inc .... D 212 704-4800
  New York *(G-10304)*
▲ Gildan Apparel USA Inc .... D 212 476-0341
  New York *(G-10336)*
▲ Golden Leaves Knitwear Inc .... E 718 875-8235
  Brooklyn *(G-2038)*
Grand Processing Inc .... E 718 388-0600
  Brooklyn *(G-2049)*
Great Adirondack Yarn Company .... F 518 843-3381
  Amsterdam *(G-349)*
▲ Hamil America Inc .... F 212 244-2645
  New York *(G-10444)*

22 TEXTILE MILL PRODUCTS — SIC SECTION

Hanesbrands Inc .... F 646 472-4117
New York (G-10451)
Hania By Anya Cole LLC .... G 212 302-3550
New York (G-10453)
▲ Hertling Trousers Inc .... E 718 784-6100
Brooklyn (G-2077)
IaMmaliamills LLC .... G 805 845-2137
Brooklyn (G-2091)
Imperial Sweater Mills Inc .... G 718 871-4414
Brooklyn (G-2098)
J & E Talit Inc .... G 718 850-1333
Richmond Hill (G-14088)
Jeric Knit Wear .... G 631 979-8827
Smithtown (G-15513)
Jfs Inc .... F 646 264-1200
New York (G-10769)
▲ Jj Basics LLC .... E 212 768-4779
New York (G-10778)
▲ Julia Knit Inc .... G 718 848-1900
Ozone Park (G-13407)
K & S Childrens Wear Inc .... E 718 624-0006
Brooklyn (G-2162)
▲ Kc Collections LLC .... G 212 302-4412
New York (G-10865)
KD Dids Inc .... G 718 402-2012
Bronx (G-1373)
Keryakos Inc .... E 518 344-7092
Schenectady (G-15300)
Knit Illustrated Inc .... E 212 268-9054
New York (G-10900)
Knit Resource Center Ltd .... E 212 221-1990
New York (G-10901)
Lids Corporation .... G 518 459-7060
Albany (G-98)
▲ Lloyds Fashions Inc .... D 631 435-3353
Brentwood (G-1187)
Lynch Knitting Mills Inc .... E 718 821-3436
Brooklyn (G-2243)
▲ M A M Knitting Mills Corp .... E 800 570-0093
Brooklyn (G-2248)
▲ M B M Manufacturing Inc .... F 718 769-4148
Brooklyn (G-2250)
Machinit Inc .... G 631 454-9297
Farmingdale (G-5048)
Mann Consultants LLC .... E 914 763-0512
Waccabuc (G-16541)
Manrico Usa Inc .... G 212 794-4200
New York (G-11163)
Marble Knits Inc .... E 718 237-7990
Brooklyn (G-2267)
Mars Fashions Inc .... E 718 402-2200
Bronx (G-1391)
Matchables Inc .... F 718 389-9318
Brooklyn (G-2285)
Mdj Sales Associates Inc .... G 914 420-5897
Mamaroneck (G-8072)
Metro Knitting Corp .... E 718 894-0765
Middle Village (G-8449)
Mongru Neckwear Inc .... E 718 706-0406
Long Island City (G-7847)
Native Textiles Inc .... G 212 951-5100
New York (G-11377)
New York Sweater Company Inc .... E 845 629-9533
New York (G-11428)
North Star Knitting Mills Inc .... G 718 894-4848
Glendale (G-5675)
NY Denim Inc .... F 212 764-6668
New York (G-11492)
Phillips-Van Heusen Europe .... F 212 381-3500
New York (G-11668)
Premier Knits Ltd .... F 718 323-8264
Ozone Park (G-13410)
▲ Pvh Corp .... D 212 381-3500
New York (G-11780)
Rags Knitwear Ltd .... F 718 782-8417
Brooklyn (G-2492)
◆ Ralph Lauren Corporation .... B 212 318-7000
New York (G-11819)
S & T Knitting Co Inc .... E 607 722-7558
Conklin (G-3900)
S & V Knits Inc .... E 631 752-1595
Farmingdale (G-5116)
S & W Knitting Mills Inc .... E 718 237-2416
Brooklyn (G-2545)
Sage Knitwear Inc .... G 718 628-7902
West Babylon (G-16856)
Sares International Inc .... G 718 366-8412
Brooklyn (G-2557)
Sarug Inc .... D 718 339-2791
Brooklyn (G-2558)

Sarug Inc .... G 718 381-7300
Ridgewood (G-14135)
▲ Summit Apparel Inc .... E 631 213-8299
Hauppauge (G-6226)
Sweater Brand Inc .... E 718 797-0505
Brooklyn (G-2655)
▲ T & R Knitting Mills Inc .... E 718 497-4017
Glendale (G-5681)
T & R Knitting Mills Inc .... G 212 840-8665
New York (G-12287)
Tomas Maier .... E 212 988-8686
New York (G-12384)
▲ United Knitwear International .... G 212 354-2920
New York (G-12484)
Unlimited Jeans Co Inc .... F 212 661-6355
New York (G-12493)
Warm .... E 212 925-1200
New York (G-12613)
Warnaco Inc .... F 718 722-3000
Brooklyn (G-2760)
Winter Water Factory .... G 646 387-3247
Brooklyn (G-2777)
WR Design Corp .... E 212 354-9000
New York (G-12695)

2254 Knit Underwear Mills

▲ Balanced Tech Corp .... E 212 768-8330
New York (G-9362)
In Toon Amkor Fashions Inc .... E 718 937-4546
Long Island City (G-7793)
Jockey International Inc .... E 212 840-4900
New York (G-10785)
Jockey International Inc .... E 518 761-0965
Lake George (G-7286)
▲ Komar Kids LLC .... F 212 725-1500
New York (G-10911)
Maidenform LLC .... E 201 436-9200
New York (G-11137)
Native Textiles Inc .... G 212 951-5100
New York (G-11377)
Spartan Brands Inc .... F 212 340-0320
New York (G-12175)

2257 Circular Knit Fabric Mills

A-One Moving & Storage Inc .... E 718 266-6002
Brooklyn (G-1542)
Apex Aridyne Corp .... G 516 239-4400
Inwood (G-6789)
Apex Texicon Inc .... E 516 239-4400
New York (G-9223)
Cap USA Jerseyman Harlem Inc .... G 212 222-7942
New York (G-9572)
Gehring Tricot Corporation .... C 315 429-8551
Dolgeville (G-4329)
Hill Knitting Mills Inc .... F 718 846-5000
Richmond Hill (G-14087)
Lemral Knitwear Inc .... D 718 210-0175
Brooklyn (G-2211)
▲ Lifestyle Design Usa Ltd .... G 212 279-9400
New York (G-11021)
S & W Knitting Mills Inc .... E 718 237-2416
Brooklyn (G-2545)

2258 Lace & Warp Knit Fabric Mills

Apex Aridyne Corp .... G 516 239-4400
Inwood (G-6789)
Apex Texicon Inc .... E 516 239-4400
New York (G-9223)
▲ Binghamton Knitting Co Inc .... E 607 722-6941
Binghamton (G-889)
Creative Window Fashions Inc .... D 718 746-5817
Whitestone (G-17233)
Eagle Lace Dyeing Corp .... F 212 947-2712
New York (G-10010)
Fab Industries Corp .... E 516 498-3200
Great Neck (G-5824)
▲ Gehring Tricot Corporation .... D 315 429-8551
Garden City (G-5520)
Gehring Tricot Corporation .... C 315 429-8551
Dolgeville (G-4329)
George Knitting Mills Corp .... G 212 242-3300
New York (G-10326)
Helmont Mills Inc .... G 518 568-7913
Saint Johnsville (G-15121)
Hosel & Ackerson Inc .... G 212 575-1490
New York (G-10552)
Hudson Fabrics LLC .... F 518 671-6100
Hudson (G-6647)
▲ Ipm US Inc .... G 212 481-7967
New York (G-10696)

▲ Klauber Brothers Inc .... D 212 686-2531
New York (G-10897)
Litchfield Fabrics of NC .... G 518 773-9500
Gloversville (G-5732)
Mary Bright Inc .... G 212 677-1970
New York (G-11195)
Mohawk Fabric Company Inc .... F 518 842-3090
Amsterdam (G-359)
Orbit Industries LLC .... G 914 244-1500
Mount Kisco (G-8681)
Solstiss Inc .... G 212 719-9194
New York (G-12152)
Somerset Dyeing & Finishing .... E 518 773-7383
Gloversville (G-5736)
▲ Somerset Industries Inc .... E 518 773-7383
Gloversville (G-5737)
Ssjjj Manufacturing LLC .... G 516 498-3200
Great Neck (G-5858)
Sunwin Global Industry Inc .... G 646 370-6196
New York (G-12261)
Super-Trim Inc .... E 212 255-2370
New York (G-12263)
▲ Veratex Inc .... F 212 683-9300
New York (G-12544)

2259 Knitting Mills, NEC

▲ Bank-Miller Co Inc .... E 914 227-9357
Pelham (G-13514)
▲ Commonwealth Home Fashion Inc .... D 514 384-8290
Willsboro (G-17288)
▲ Hawkins Fabrics Inc .... E 518 773-9550
Gloversville (G-5729)
Maidenform LLC .... F 201 436-9200
New York (G-11137)
Nochairs Inc .... G 917 748-8731
New York (G-11465)
Sextet Fabrics Inc .... F 516 593-0608
East Rockaway (G-4491)

2261 Cotton Fabric Finishers

All About Art Inc .... F 718 321-0755
Flushing (G-5232)
B & K Dye Cutting Inc .... G 718 497-5216
Brooklyn (G-1657)
Basiloff LLC .... G 646 671-0353
New York (G-9381)
Carolyn Ray Inc .... G 914 476-0619
Yonkers (G-17440)
Central Textiles Inc .... F 212 213-8740
New York (G-9618)
D & R Silk Screening Ltd .... F 631 234-7464
Central Islip (G-3520)
Dyenamix Inc .... G 212 941-6642
New York (G-9997)
Dynamic Screenprinting .... G 518 487-4256
Albany (G-74)
Judscott Handprints Ltd .... G 914 347-5515
Elmsford (G-4768)
Lee Dyeing Company NC Inc .... F 518 736-5232
Johnstown (G-7149)
Loremanss Embroidery Engrav .... F 518 834-9205
Keeseville (G-7168)
Marcel Finishing Corp .... E 718 381-2889
Plainview (G-13645)
Mountain T-Shirts Inc .... G 518 943-4533
Catskill (G-3460)
Printery .... G 315 253-7403
Auburn (G-511)
Prismatic Dyeing & Finshg Inc .... D 845 561-1800
Newburgh (G-12798)
Reynolds Drapery Service Inc .... F 315 845-8632
Newport (G-12816)
▲ Santee Print Works .... F 212 997-1570
New York (G-11988)
Sciane Enterprises Inc .... G 845 452-2400
Poughkeepsie (G-13949)
Steve Poli Sales .... G 315 487-0394
Camillus (G-3352)
Tramwell Inc .... G 315 789-2762
Geneva (G-5599)
Ward Sales Co Inc .... G 315 476-5276
Syracuse (G-16093)
Z Best Printing Inc .... F 631 595-1400
Deer Park (G-4255)

2262 Silk & Man-Made Fabric Finishers

American Spray-On Corp .... E 212 929-2100
New York (G-9179)
▲ Ann Gish Inc .... G 212 969-9200
New York (G-9213)

22 TEXTILE MILL PRODUCTS

▲ Beckmann Converting Inc .... E 518 842-0073
  Amsterdam *(G-335)*
Central Textiles Inc .... F 212 213-8740
  New York *(G-9618)*
Dyenamix Inc .... G 212 941-6642
  New York *(G-9997)*
Eastern Silk Mills Inc .... G 212 730-1300
  New York *(G-10017)*
Efs Designs .... G 718 852-9511
  Brooklyn *(G-1908)*
◆ Fabric Resources Intl Ltd .... F 516 829-4550
  Great Neck *(G-5825)*
▲ Gehring Tricot Corporation .... D 315 429-8551
  Garden City *(G-5520)*
Intertex USA Inc .... F 212 279-3601
  New York *(G-10683)*
Judscott Handprints Ltd .... F 914 347-5515
  Elmsford *(G-4768)*
Knucklehead Embroidery Inc .... G 607 797-2725
  Johnson City *(G-7129)*
Marcel Finishing Corp .... E 718 381-2889
  Plainview *(G-13645)*
▲ Mv Corp Inc .... C 631 273-8020
  Bay Shore *(G-717)*
Prismatic Dyeing & Finshg Inc .... D 845 561-1800
  Newburgh *(G-12798)*
▲ Raxon Fabrics Corp .... F 212 532-6816
  New York *(G-11830)*
Rescuestuff Inc .... E 718 318-7570
  Peekskill *(G-13505)*
Screen Gems Inc .... G 845 561-0036
  New Windsor *(G-8999)*
Toltec Fabrics Inc .... C 212 706-9310
  New York *(G-12378)*
Valley Stream Sporting Gds Inc .... E 516 593-7800
  Lynbrook *(G-7992)*

2269 Textile Finishers, NEC

Albany Engnered Composites Inc ...... F 518 445-2200
  Albany *(G-36)*
American Country Quilts & Lin .... G 631 283-5466
  Southampton *(G-15562)*
Artyarns .... G 914 428-0333
  White Plains *(G-17107)*
Ben-Sak Textile Inc .... E 212 279-5122
  New York *(G-9403)*
▲ China Ting Fashion Group (usa) ...... G 212 716-1600
  New York *(G-9653)*
▲ Duck River Textiles Inc .... G 212 679-2980
  New York *(G-9987)*
Flexene Corp .... E 631 491-0580
  West Babylon *(G-16818)*
Hosel & Ackerson Inc .... G 212 575-1490
  New York *(G-10552)*
▲ Majestic Rayon Corporation .... E 212 929-6443
  New York *(G-11140)*
Marcel Finishing Corp .... E 718 381-2889
  Plainview *(G-13645)*
National Spinning Co Inc .... E 212 382-6400
  New York *(G-11374)*
Newcastle Fabrics Corp .... G 718 388-6600
  Brooklyn *(G-2378)*
◆ Paxar Corporation .... E 845 398-3229
  Orangeburg *(G-13260)*
Prismatic Dyeing & Finshg Inc .... D 845 561-1800
  Newburgh *(G-12798)*
Skin Prints Inc .... G 845 920-8756
  Pearl River *(G-13490)*
▲ Sml USA Inc .... E 212 736-8800
  New York *(G-12135)*

2273 Carpets & Rugs

Aladdin Manufacturing Corp .... E 212 561-8715
  New York *(G-9121)*
Auto-Mat Company Inc .... E 516 938-7373
  Hicksville *(G-6349)*
Bloomsburg Carpet Inds Inc .... E 212 688-7447
  New York *(G-9468)*
▲ Carpet Fabrications Intl .... E 914 381-6060
  Mamaroneck *(G-8058)*
Edward Fields Incorporated .... F 212 310-0400
  New York *(G-10038)*
▲ Elizabeth Eakins Inc .... F 212 628-1950
  New York *(G-10062)*
Eskayel Inc .... G 347 703-8084
  Brooklyn *(G-1940)*
▲ Excellent Art Mfg Corp .... F 718 388-7075
  Inwood *(G-6795)*
Interfaceflor LLC .... E 212 686-8284
  New York *(G-10670)*

Jbl Trading LLC .... G 347 394-5592
  New York *(G-10749)*
Kalati Company Inc .... G 516 423-9132
  Great Neck *(G-5834)*
Lanes Flr Cvrngs Intriors Inc .... E 212 532-5200
  New York *(G-10962)*
▲ Loom Concepts LLC .... G 212 813-9586
  New York *(G-11059)*
▲ Lorena Canals USA Inc .... G 844 567-3622
  Hastings On Hudson *(G-6025)*
Mannington Mills Inc .... G 212 251-0290
  New York *(G-11161)*
▲ Mark Nelson Designs LLC .... F 646 422-7020
  New York *(G-11179)*
Mgk Group Inc .... E 212 989-2732
  New York *(G-11273)*
Michaelian & Kohlberg Inc .... G 212 431-9009
  New York *(G-11278)*
North Sunshine LLC .... F 307 027-1634
  Valley Cottage *(G-16410)*
◆ Northpoint Trading Inc .... F 212 481-8001
  New York *(G-11478)*
Odegard Inc .... F 212 545-0069
  Long Island City *(G-7860)*
Pawling Corporation .... D 845 373-9300
  Wassaic *(G-16622)*
Quality Carpet One Floor & HM .... G 718 941-4200
  Brooklyn *(G-2478)*
▲ Renaissnce Crpt Tapestries Inc .... F 212 696-0080
  New York *(G-11863)*
Rosecore Division .... F 516 504-4530
  Great Neck *(G-5852)*
Safavieh Inc .... A 516 945-1900
  Port Washington *(G-13877)*
▲ Scalamandre Silks Inc .... D 212 980-3888
  New York *(G-12002)*
Shaw Contract Flrg Svcs Inc .... G 212 953-7429
  New York *(G-12067)*
Shyam Ahuja Limited .... G 212 644-5910
  New York *(G-12080)*
▲ Sunrise Tile Inc .... G 718 939-0538
  Flushing *(G-5303)*
Tandus Centiva Inc .... C 212 206-7170
  New York *(G-12302)*
Tdg Operations LLC .... G 212 779-4300
  New York *(G-12309)*
Tiger 21 LLC .... G 212 360-1700
  New York *(G-12356)*
▲ Tsar USA LLC .... F 646 415-7968
  New York *(G-12438)*
Wells Rugs Inc .... G 516 676-2056
  Glen Cove *(G-5644)*

2281 Yarn Spinning Mills

Advanced Yarn Technologies Inc .... E 518 239-6600
  Durham *(G-4378)*
▲ Colortex Inc .... G 212 564-2000
  New York *(G-9734)*
Great Adirondack Yarn Company .... F 518 843-3381
  Amsterdam *(G-349)*
▲ Missiontex Inc .... G 718 532-9053
  Brooklyn *(G-2327)*
National Spinning Co Inc .... E 212 382-6400
  New York *(G-11374)*
Printz and Patternz LLC .... G 518 944-6020
  Schenectady *(G-15311)*
▼ United Thread Mills Corp .... G 516 536-3900
  Oceanside *(G-13124)*

2282 Yarn Texturizing, Throwing, Twisting & Winding Mills

Janes Designer Yrn Pttrns Inc .... G 347 260-3071
  New York *(G-10740)*
▲ La Lame Inc .... E 212 921-9770
  New York *(G-10947)*
▲ Majestic Rayon Corporation .... E 212 929-6443
  New York *(G-11140)*
Marsha Fleisher .... F 845 679-6500
  Woodstock *(G-17380)*

2284 Thread Mills

Albany International Corp .... C 607 749-7226
  Homer *(G-6543)*
American Quality Embroidery .... G 631 467-3200
  Ronkonkoma *(G-14895)*
One In A Million Inc .... G 516 829-1111
  Valley Stream *(G-16441)*
▼ United Thread Mills Corp .... G 516 536-3900
  Oceanside *(G-13124)*

2295 Fabrics Coated Not Rubberized

▲ A-One Laminating Corp .... G 718 266-6002
  Brooklyn *(G-1541)*
A-One Moving & Storage Inc .... E 718 266-6002
  Brooklyn *(G-1542)*
Architectural Fiberglass Corp .... E 631 842-4772
  Copiague *(G-3918)*
▲ Beckmann Converting Inc .... E 518 842-0073
  Amsterdam *(G-335)*
Breton Industries Inc .... D 518 842-3030
  Amsterdam *(G-337)*
▲ Chemprene Inc .... C 845 831-2800
  Beacon *(G-777)*
▲ Chemprene Holding Inc .... C 845 831-2800
  Beacon *(G-778)*
Co2 Textiles LLC .... G 212 269-2222
  New York *(G-9707)*
▲ Comfort Care Textiles Inc .... E 631 543-0531
  Commack *(G-3854)*
▲ Eurotex Inc .... F 716 205-8861
  Niagara Falls *(G-12837)*
◆ Fabric Resources Intl Ltd .... F 516 829-4550
  Great Neck *(G-5825)*
◆ GE Polymershapes .... F 516 433-4092
  Hicksville *(G-6376)*
GM Insulation Corp .... F 516 354-6000
  Elmont *(G-4732)*
▲ Imperial Laminators Co Inc .... F 718 272-9500
  Brooklyn *(G-2096)*
Kiltronx Enviro Systems LLC .... E 917 971-7177
  Hauppauge *(G-6129)*
New York Cutting & Gumming Co ...... E 212 563-4146
  Middletown *(G-8489)*
▲ Newtex Industries Inc .... E 585 924-9135
  Victor *(G-16517)*
▼ Perry Plastics Inc .... E 718 747-5600
  Flushing *(G-5288)*
Piedmont Plastics Inc .... E 518 724-0563
  Albany *(G-121)*
Precision Custom Coatings LLC .... C 212 868-5770
  New York *(G-11717)*
▲ Tonoga Inc .... C 518 658-3202
  Petersburg *(G-13551)*
▲ Tpi Industries LLC .... E 845 692-2820
  Middletown *(G-8500)*

2296 Tire Cord & Fabric

Albany International Corp .... C 518 445-2230
  Menands *(G-8397)*
DC Fabrication & Welding Inc .... G 845 295-0215
  Ferndale *(G-5177)*
Designatronics Incorporated .... B 516 328-3300
  Hicksville *(G-6367)*
Haines Equipment Inc .... E 607 566-8531
  Avoca *(G-534)*
York Industries Inc .... E 516 746-3736
  Garden City Park *(G-5559)*

2297 Fabrics, Nonwoven

Albany International Corp .... C 518 445-2200
  Rensselaer *(G-14053)*
◆ Fabrication Enterprises Inc .... E 914 591-9300
  Elmsford *(G-4761)*
▲ Imperial Laminators Co Inc .... F 718 272-9500
  Brooklyn *(G-2096)*
▲ Legendary Auto Interiors Ltd .... E 315 331-1212
  Newark *(G-12754)*
Mgk Group Inc .... E 212 989-2732
  New York *(G-11273)*
◆ Saint-Gobain Adfors Amer Inc .... D 716 775-3900
  Grand Island *(G-5783)*
Saint-Gobain Adfors Amer Inc .... D 585 589-4401
  Albion *(G-173)*

2298 Cordage & Twine

▲ A & A Line & Wire Corp .... F 718 456-2657
  Maspeth *(G-8139)*
Albany International Corp .... C 607 749-7226
  Homer *(G-6543)*
All-Lifts Incorporated .... E 518 465-3461
  Albany *(G-42)*
Cables and Chips Inc .... E 212 619-3132
  New York *(G-9544)*
▲ Continental Cordage Corp .... D 315 655-9800
  Cazenovia *(G-3470)*
Cortland Company Inc .... C 607 753-8276
  Cortland *(G-4040)*
◆ Fiber Instrument Sales Inc .... E 315 736-2206
  Oriskany *(G-13333)*

Employee Codes: A=Over 500 employees, B=251-500
C=101-250, D=51-100, E=20-50, F=10-19, G=5-9

Fiberone LLC ... F ... 315 434-8877
East Syracuse *(G-4543)*

▲ Gladding Braided Products LLC ... E ... 315 653-7211
South Otselic *(G-15555)*

Sampo Inc ... E ... 315 896-2606
Barneveld *(G-617)*

◆ Simplicity Creative Group Inc ... A ... 212 686-7676
New York *(G-12105)*

T M International LLC ... G ... 718 842-0949
Bronx *(G-1469)*

Triad Network Technologies ... E ... 585 924-8505
Victor *(G-16533)*

2299 Textile Goods, NEC

A Thousand Cranes Inc ... F ... 212 724-9596
New York *(G-9039)*

▲ Ace Drop Cloth Canvas Pdts Inc ... E ... 718 731-1550
Bronx *(G-1261)*

Alok Inc ... G ... 212 643-4360
New York *(G-9148)*

American Home Mfg LLC ... G ... 212 643-0680
New York *(G-9169)*

▲ Arabella Textiles LLC ... G ... 212 679-0611
New York *(G-9240)*

Architectural Textiles USA Inc ... E ... 212 213-6972
New York *(G-9246)*

◆ Benson Mills Inc ... E ... 718 236-6743
Brooklyn *(G-1682)*

Blc Textiles Inc ... E ... 844 500-7900
Mineola *(G-8532)*

Buperiod PBC ... G ... 917 406-9804
Brooklyn *(G-1740)*

◆ Copen United LLC ... G ... 212 819-0008
New York *(G-9778)*

Courtaulds Textiles Ltd ... F ... 212 946-8000
New York *(G-9797)*

◆ David King Linen Inc ... F ... 718 241-7298
New York *(G-9876)*

Dean Trading Corp ... F ... 718 485-0600
Brooklyn *(G-1846)*

Eskayel Inc ... G ... 347 703-8084
Brooklyn *(G-1940)*

Federal Prison Industries ... D ... 518 897-4000
Ray Brook *(G-14037)*

▲ Feldman Company Inc ... F ... 212 966-1303
New York *(G-10203)*

Fibrix LLC ... E ... 716 683-4100
Depew *(G-4281)*

Fil Doux Inc ... F ... 212 202-1459
Brooklyn *(G-1973)*

▲ Ghani Textiles Inc ... G ... 718 859-4561
Brooklyn *(G-2023)*

▲ Global Resources Sg Inc ... F ... 212 686-1411
New York *(G-10362)*

Ino-Tex LLC ... G ... 212 400-2205
New York *(G-10647)*

◆ Ivi Services Inc ... D ... 607 729-5111
Binghamton *(G-924)*

▲ James Thompson & Company Inc ... G ... 212 686-4242
New York *(G-10738)*

Jo-Vin Decorators Inc ... E ... 718 441-9350
Woodhaven *(G-17324)*

Jonice Industires ... G ... 516 640-4283
Hempstead *(G-6300)*

▲ K F I Inc ... G ... 516 546-2904
Roosevelt *(G-15030)*

▲ La Lame Inc ... G ... 212 921-9770
New York *(G-10947)*

▲ Lintex Linens Inc ... B ... 212 679-8046
New York *(G-11032)*

▲ Lr Paris LLC ... G ... 703 652-1132
New York *(G-11084)*

▲ Manrico Usa Inc ... G ... 212 794-4200
New York *(G-11164)*

▲ Navy Plum LLC ... G ... 845 641-7441
Monsey *(G-8611)*

Novita Fabrics Furnishing Corp ... F ... 516 299-4500
Glen Cove *(G-5636)*

Return Textiles LLC ... G ... 646 408-0108
New York *(G-11877)*

Rovel Manufacturing Co Inc ... G ... 516 365-2752
Roslyn *(G-15047)*

S Hellerman Inc ... F ... 718 622-2995
Brooklyn *(G-2549)*

◆ Sabbsons International Inc ... F ... 718 360-1947
Brooklyn *(G-2551)*

▲ Sam Salem & Son LLC ... F ... 212 695-6020
New York *(G-11979)*

▼ Shannon Entps Wstn NY Inc ... D ... 716 693-7954
North Tonawanda *(G-13011)*

▲ Simple Elegance New York Inc ... F ... 718 360-1947
Brooklyn *(G-2589)*

Sivko Furs Inc ... G ... 607 698-4827
Canisteo *(G-3405)*

Solivaira Specialties Inc ... D ... 716 693-4009
North Tonawanda *(G-13014)*

◆ Solvaira Specialties Inc ... C ... 716 693-4040
North Tonawanda *(G-13015)*

◆ Soundcoat Company Inc ... D ... 631 242-2200
Deer Park *(G-4236)*

Southern Adrndck Fbr Prdcrs CP ... G ... 518 692-2700
Greenwich *(G-5913)*

Superior Fiber Mills Inc ... E ... 718 782-7500
Brooklyn *(G-2649)*

Thistle Hill Weavers ... G ... 518 284-2729
Cherry Valley *(G-3624)*

▼ TRM Linen Inc ... G ... 718 686-6075
Brooklyn *(G-2702)*

Vincent Manufacturing Co Inc ... F ... 315 823-0280
Little Falls *(G-7528)*

▲ Yankee Corp ... F ... 718 589-1377
Bronx *(G-1496)*

23 APPAREL AND OTHER FINISHED PRODUCTS MADE FROM FABRICS AND SIMILAR MATERIAL

2311 Men's & Boys' Suits, Coats & Overcoats

▲ Adrian Jules Ltd ... D ... 585 342-5886
Rochester *(G-14190)*

▲ Advance Apparel Intl Inc ... G ... 212 944-0984
New York *(G-9083)*

Allytex LLC ... G ... 518 376-7539
Ballston Spa *(G-590)*

◆ Amerimade Coat Inc ... G ... 212 216-0925
New York *(G-9184)*

Bestec Concept Inc ... G ... 718 937-5848
Long Island City *(G-7715)*

Bindle and Keep ... G ... 917 740-5002
Brooklyn *(G-1698)*

▲ Blueduck Trading Ltd ... G ... 212 268-3122
New York *(G-9475)*

▲ Canali USA Inc ... E ... 212 767-0205
New York *(G-9562)*

▲ Check Group LLC ... D ... 212 221-4700
New York *(G-9637)*

▲ Christian Casey LLC ... E ... 212 500-2200
New York *(G-9660)*

Christian Casey LLC ... E ... 212 500-2200
New York *(G-9661)*

▲ Concorde Apparel Company LLC ... G ... 212 307-7848
New York *(G-9756)*

Crisada Inc ... G ... 718 729-9730
Long Island City *(G-7735)*

Donna Karan Company LLC ... C ... 212 789-1500
New York *(G-9952)*

▲ Donna Karan Company LLC ... B ... 212 789-1500
New York *(G-9953)*

Elite Uniforms Ltd ... G ... 516 487-5481
Great Neck *(G-5821)*

▲ Excelled Sheepskin & Lea Coat ... F ... 212 594-5843
New York *(G-10157)*

▲ G-III Apparel Group Ltd ... B ... 212 403-0500
New York *(G-10282)*

Giliberto Designs Inc ... E ... 212 695-0216
New York *(G-10337)*

▲ Great 4 Image Inc ... E ... 518 424-2058
Rensselaer *(G-14058)*

▲ Hana Sportswear Inc ... E ... 315 639-6332
Dexter *(G-4308)*

Hickey Freeman Tailored CL Inc ... B ... 585 467-7240
Rochester *(G-14453)*

◆ Hugo Boss Usa Inc ... D ... 212 940-0600
New York *(G-10574)*

J & X Production Inc ... F ... 718 200-1228
New York *(G-10716)*

John Kochis Custom Designs ... G ... 212 244-6046
New York *(G-10788)*

▲ Kozinn+sons Merchant Tailors ... E ... 212 643-1916
New York *(G-10921)*

▲ L F Fashion Orient Intl Co Ltd ... G ... 917 667-3398
New York *(G-10939)*

▲ M Hidary & Co Inc ... D ... 212 736-6540
New York *(G-11102)*

▲ Manchu New York Inc ... G ... 212 921-5050
New York *(G-11150)*

▲ Martin Greenfield Clothiers ... C ... 718 497-5480
Brooklyn *(G-2279)*

Med-Eng LLC ... E ... 315 713-0103
Ogdensburg *(G-13140)*

▲ Michael Andrews LLC ... F ... 212 677-1755
New York *(G-11275)*

▲ Mv Corp Inc ... C ... 631 273-8020
Bay Shore *(G-717)*

▲ Occunomix International LLC ... E ... 631 741-1940
Port Jeff STA *(G-13792)*

Opposuits USA Inc ... E ... 917 438-8878
New York *(G-11530)*

Otex Protective Inc ... G ... 585 232-7160
Rochester *(G-14580)*

Pat & Rose Dress Inc ... D ... 212 279-1357
New York *(G-11593)*

Primo Coat Corp ... E ... 718 349-2070
Long Island City *(G-7877)*

Proper Cloth LLC ... G ... 646 964-4221
New York *(G-11758)*

Public School ... G ... 212 302-1108
New York *(G-11768)*

◆ Ralph Lauren Corporation ... B ... 212 318-7000
New York *(G-11819)*

▲ Roth Clothing Co Inc ... G ... 718 384-4927
Brooklyn *(G-2528)*

Royal Clothing Corp ... G ... 718 436-5841
Brooklyn *(G-2530)*

▲ Shane Tex Inc ... F ... 516 486-7522
Hempstead *(G-6309)*

Strong Group Inc ... G ... 516 766-6300
Oceanside *(G-13119)*

Therese The Childrens Collectn ... G ... 518 346-2315
Schenectady *(G-15328)*

Tom James Company ... F ... 212 581-6968
New York *(G-12381)*

Tom James Company ... F ... 212 593-0204
New York *(G-12382)*

Uniforms By Park Coats Inc ... E ... 718 499-1182
Brooklyn *(G-2717)*

▲ Urban Textiles Inc ... F ... 212 777-1900
New York *(G-12501)*

Vf Imagewear Inc ... E ... 718 352-2363
Bayside *(G-772)*

Vinci Enterprise Corp ... F ... 212 768-7888
New York *(G-12570)*

Woodmere Fabrics Inc ... G ... 212 695-0144
New York *(G-12684)*

▲ Wp Lavori USA Inc ... G ... 212 244-6074
New York *(G-12694)*

▲ Xmh-Hfi Inc ... A ... 585 467-7240
Rochester *(G-14801)*

Yong Ji Productions Inc ... E ... 917 559-4616
Corona *(G-4032)*

2321 Men's & Boys' Shirts

Americo Group Inc ... E ... 212 563-2700
New York *(G-9181)*

▲ Americo Group Inc ... E ... 212 563-2700
New York *(G-9182)*

▲ Andy & Evan Industries Inc ... G ... 212 967-7908
New York *(G-9204)*

Arthur Gluck Shirtmakers Inc ... F ... 212 755-8165
Brooklyn *(G-1638)*

▲ August Silk Inc ... E ... 212 643-2400
New York *(G-9315)*

August Silk Inc ... G ... 212 643-2400
New York *(G-9316)*

▲ Ben Wachter Associates Inc ... G ... 212 736-4064
New York *(G-9401)*

◆ Bowe Industries Inc ... D ... 718 441-6464
Glendale *(G-5661)*

Bowe Industries Inc ... D ... 718 441-6464
Glendale *(G-5662)*

▲ Check Group LLC ... D ... 212 221-4700
New York *(G-9637)*

▲ Christian Casey LLC ... E ... 212 500-2200
New York *(G-9660)*

Christian Casey LLC ... E ... 212 500-2200
New York *(G-9661)*

Colony Holdings Intl LLC ... F ... 212 868-2800
New York *(G-9730)*

Cyberlimit Inc ... F ... 212 840-9597
New York *(G-9833)*

◆ Donna Karan International Inc ... F ... 212 789-1500
New York *(G-9954)*

Donna Karan International Inc ... G ... 212 768-5800
New York *(G-9955)*

Ferris USA LLC ... G ... 617 895-8102
New York *(G-10207)*

◆ Garan Incorporated ... C ... 212 563-1292
New York *(G-10294)*

SIC SECTION 23 APPAREL AND OTHER FINISHED PRODUCTS MADE FROM FABRICS AND SIMILAR MATERIAL

▼ **Garan Manufacturing Corp**..............G....... 212 563-2000
New York *(G-10295)*
Gbg National Brands Group LLC..........G....... 646 839-7000
New York *(G-10299)*
Gce International Inc..........................D....... 773 263-1210
New York *(G-10306)*
◆ **Great Universal Corp**........................F....... 917 302-0065
New York *(G-10400)*
Groupe 16sur20 LLC..............................F....... 212 625-1620
New York *(G-10415)*
▲ **Haddad Bros Inc**..................................F....... 212 563-2117
New York *(G-10437)*
Ibrands International LLC....................F....... 212 354-1330
New York *(G-10593)*
Interbrand LLC..G....... 212 840-9595
New York *(G-10667)*
Jacks and Jokers 52 LLC........................G....... 917 740-2595
New York *(G-10727)*
Jordache Enterprises Inc........................D....... 212 944-1330
New York *(G-10799)*
▲ **Jordache Enterprises Inc**......................C....... 212 643-8400
New York *(G-10800)*
Just Brass Inc..G....... 212 724-5447
New York *(G-10826)*
▲ **Kt Group Inc**..G....... 212 760-2500
New York *(G-10931)*
Lt2 LLC...E....... 212 684-1510
New York *(G-11086)*
▲ **M S B International Ltd**........................F....... 212 302-5551
New York *(G-11105)*
▲ **Mega Sourcing Inc**..................................G....... 646 682-0304
Merrick *(G-8424)*
Miltons of New York Inc..........................G....... 212 997-3359
New York *(G-11298)*
▲ **Mulitex Usa Inc**......................................G....... 212 398-0440
New York *(G-11346)*
▲ **Nat Nast Company Inc**............................G....... 212 575-1186
New York *(G-11365)*
Oxford Industries Inc................................F....... 212 840-2288
New York *(G-11554)*
Perry Ellis International Inc....................F....... 212 536-5400
New York *(G-11641)*
Perry Ellis International Inc....................G....... 212 536-5499
New York *(G-11642)*
◆ **Perry Ellis Menswear LLC**........................C....... 212 221-7500
New York *(G-11643)*
Phillips-Van Heusen Europe......................F....... 212 381-3500
New York *(G-11668)*
▲ **Pvh Corp**..D....... 212 381-3500
New York *(G-11780)*
Pvh Corp...G....... 845 561-0233
New Windsor *(G-8995)*
Pvh Corp...G....... 631 254-8200
Deer Park *(G-4220)*
Pvh Corp...G....... 212 719-2600
New York *(G-11783)*
Ralph Lauren Corporation........................G....... 212 421-1570
New York *(G-11820)*
◆ **Ralph Lauren Corporation**......................B....... 212 318-7000
New York *(G-11819)*
▲ **Roffe Accessories Inc**..............................F....... 212 213-1440
New York *(G-11924)*
Saad Collection Inc....................................G....... 212 937-0341
New York *(G-11966)*
▲ **Schwartz Textile Converting Co**..............E....... 718 499-8243
Brooklyn *(G-2562)*
Sifonya Inc...G....... 212 620-4512
New York *(G-12087)*
▲ **Sue & Sam Co Inc**......................................E....... 718 436-1672
Brooklyn *(G-2640)*
◆ **Warnaco Inc**..B....... 212 287-8000
New York *(G-12615)*
Warnaco Inc...F....... 718 722-3000
Brooklyn *(G-2760)*
Whittall & Shon..G....... 212 594-2626
New York *(G-12656)*
Yale Trouser Corporation..........................F....... 516 255-0700
Oceanside *(G-13128)*

2322 Men's & Boys' Underwear & Nightwear

▲ **Apparel Partnership Group LLC**..............G....... 212 302-7722
New York *(G-9230)*
Becks Classic Mfg Inc..................................D....... 631 435-3800
Brentwood *(G-1175)*
▲ **Candlesticks Inc**..F....... 212 947-8900
New York *(G-9566)*
▲ **Check Group LLC**......................................D....... 212 221-4700
New York *(G-9637)*
▲ **Christian Casey LLC**..................................E....... 212 500-2200
New York *(G-9660)*
Christian Casey LLC....................................E....... 212 500-2200
New York *(G-9661)*
▲ **Comme-Ci Comme-CA AP Group**..........E....... 631 300-1035
Hauppauge *(G-6070)*
▲ **Revolutionwear Inc**....................................G....... 617 669-9191
New York *(G-11881)*
▲ **Sleepwear Holdings Inc**............................C....... 516 466-4738
New York *(G-12126)*
▲ **Solo Licensing Corp**..................................G....... 212 244-5505
New York *(G-12150)*
▲ **Tommy John Inc**..E....... 800 708-3490
New York *(G-12387)*
◆ **Twist Intimate Group LLC**........................G....... 212 695-5990
New York *(G-12451)*
◆ **Warnaco Group Inc**....................................E....... 212 287-8000
New York *(G-12614)*
◆ **Warnaco Inc**..B....... 212 287-8000
New York *(G-12615)*
Warnaco Inc...F....... 718 722-3000
Brooklyn *(G-2760)*
▲ **Waterbury Garment LLC**............................E....... 212 725-1500
New York *(G-12625)*
▲ **Wickers Sportswear Inc**............................G....... 631 543-1700
Commack *(G-3872)*

2323 Men's & Boys' Neckwear

Countess Mara Inc..G....... 212 768-7300
New York *(G-9795)*
Emunas Sales Inc..F....... 718 621-3138
Brooklyn *(G-1928)*
Fogel Neckwear Corp....................................D....... 212 686-7673
New York *(G-10236)*
J M C Bow Co Inc..F....... 718 686-8110
Brooklyn *(G-2124)*
JS Blank & Co Inc..E....... 212 689-4835
New York *(G-10813)*
Mallory & Church LLC..................................G....... 212 868-7888
New York *(G-11146)*
▲ **MANE Enterprises Inc**................................D....... 718 472-4955
Long Island City *(G-7830)*
Mongru Neckwear Inc....................................E....... 718 706-0406
Long Island City *(G-7847)*
◆ **Perry Ellis Menswear LLC**..........................C....... 212 221-7500
New York *(G-11643)*
◆ **Ralph Lauren Corporation**..........................B....... 212 318-7000
New York *(G-11819)*
Randa Accessories Lea Gds LLC..................D....... 212 354-5100
New York *(G-11825)*
▲ **Roffe Accessories Inc**..................................F....... 212 213-1440
New York *(G-11924)*
▲ **S Broome and Co Inc**..................................D....... 718 663-6800
Long Island City *(G-7899)*
▲ **Selini Neckwear Inc**....................................G....... 212 268-5488
New York *(G-12044)*
▲ **Tie King Inc**..E....... 718 768-8484
Brooklyn *(G-2679)*
Tie King Inc..G....... 212 714-9611
New York *(G-12355)*
Tie View Neckwear Co Inc..............................G....... 718 853-4156
Brooklyn *(G-2680)*
Valenti Neckwear Co Inc................................G....... 914 969-0700
Yonkers *(G-17511)*
W B Bow Tie Corp..F....... 212 683-6130
New York *(G-12601)*
◆ **Warnaco Inc**..B....... 212 287-8000
New York *(G-12615)*
Wetherall Contracting NY Inc........................G....... 718 894-7011
Middle Village *(G-8451)*

2325 Men's & Boys' Separate Trousers & Casual Slacks

▲ **Adrian Jules Ltd**..D....... 585 342-5886
Rochester *(G-14190)*
Bruno & Canio Ltd..E....... 845 624-3060
Nanuet *(G-8799)*
▲ **Check Group LLC**..D....... 212 221-4700
New York *(G-9637)*
▲ **Christian Casey LLC**......................................E....... 212 500-2200
New York *(G-9660)*
Christian Casey LLC..E....... 212 500-2200
New York *(G-9661)*
Donna Karan Company LLC............................C....... 212 789-1500
New York *(G-9952)*
▲ **Donna Karan Company LLC**........................B....... 212 789-1500
New York *(G-9953)*
◆ **Donna Karan International Inc**....................F....... 212 789-1500
New York *(G-9954)*
Donna Karan International Inc......................G....... 212 768-5800
New York *(G-9955)*
Gbg Denim Usa LLC..F....... 646 839-7000
New York *(G-10298)*
Groupe 16sur20 LLC..F....... 212 625-1620
New York *(G-10415)*
Guess Inc..E....... 845 928-3930
Central Valley *(G-3552)*
Guess Inc..E....... 315 539-5634
Waterloo *(G-16650)*
Guess Inc..E....... 212 286-9856
New York *(G-10422)*
Guess Inc..E....... 716 298-3561
Niagara Falls *(G-12849)*
▲ **Hertling Trousers Inc**......................................E....... 718 784-6100
Brooklyn *(G-2077)*
Hot Kiss Inc..G....... 212 730-0404
New York *(G-10555)*
◆ **Hugo Boss Usa Inc**..D....... 212 940-0600
New York *(G-10574)*
▲ **Int Trading USA LLC**......................................C....... 212 760-2338
New York *(G-10657)*
Jordache Enterprises Inc..................................D....... 212 944-1330
New York *(G-10799)*
▲ **Jordache Enterprises Inc**................................C....... 212 643-8400
New York *(G-10800)*
Kalikow Brothers LP..E....... 212 643-0315
New York *(G-10840)*
Kaltex America Inc..F....... 212 971-0575
New York *(G-10842)*
Leng Universal Inc..F....... 212 398-6800
New York *(G-11000)*
Levi Strauss & Co..F....... 212 944-8555
New York *(G-11013)*
Levi Strauss & Co..F....... 917 213-6263
Flushing *(G-5272)*
Lucky Brand Dungarees LLC............................E....... 631 350-7358
Huntington Station *(G-6752)*
▲ **M Hidary & Co Inc**..D....... 212 736-6540
New York *(G-11102)*
▲ **M S B International Ltd**..................................F....... 212 302-5551
New York *(G-11105)*
▲ **Martin Greenfield Clothiers**..........................C....... 718 497-5480
Brooklyn *(G-2279)*
Messex Group Inc..G....... 646 229-2582
New York *(G-11266)*
Miltons of New York Inc....................................G....... 212 997-3359
New York *(G-11298)*
▲ **Montero International Inc**..............................G....... 212 695-1787
Westbury *(G-17041)*
▲ **Mulitex Usa Inc**..G....... 212 398-0440
New York *(G-11346)*
▲ **One Jeanswear Group Inc**................................B....... 212 835-3500
New York *(G-11520)*
◆ **Passport Brands Inc**..E....... 646 459-2625
New York *(G-11592)*
Pat & Rose Dress Inc..D....... 212 279-1357
New York *(G-11593)*
Perry Ellis International Inc..............................F....... 212 536-5400
New York *(G-11641)*
◆ **Perry Ellis Menswear LLC**................................C....... 212 221-7500
New York *(G-11643)*
Primo Coat Corp..E....... 718 349-2070
Long Island City *(G-7877)*
◆ **Ralph Lauren Corporation**................................B....... 212 318-7000
New York *(G-11819)*
◆ **Ryba General Merchandise Inc**........................G....... 718 522-2028
Brooklyn *(G-2539)*
Sean John Clothing Inc..E....... 212 500-2200
New York *(G-12029)*
Sean John Clothing Inc..E....... 212 500-2200
New York *(G-12030)*
▲ **Xmh-Hfi Inc**..A....... 585 467-7240
Rochester *(G-14801)*
Yale Trouser Corporation....................................F....... 516 255-0700
Oceanside *(G-13128)*

2326 Men's & Boys' Work Clothing

5 Star Apparel LLC..G....... 212 563-1233
New York *(G-9022)*
▲ **Ace Drop Cloth Canvas Pdts Inc**......................E....... 718 731-1550
Bronx *(G-1261)*
▲ **Adar Medical Uniform LLC**..............................F....... 718 935-1197
Brooklyn *(G-1559)*
AKOS Group Ltd..E....... 212 683-4747
New York *(G-9119)*
American Apparel Ltd..G....... 516 504-4559
Great Neck *(G-5805)*
Badgley Mischka Licensing LLC..........................E....... 212 921-1585
New York *(G-9354)*
Beardslee Realty..G....... 516 747-5557
Mineola *(G-8530)*

SIC

Employee Codes: A=Over 500 employees, B=251-500
C=101-250, D=51-100, E=20-50, F=10-19, G=5-9
2018 Harris
New York Manufacturers Directory
725

23 APPAREL AND OTHER FINISHED PRODUCTS MADE FROM FABRICS AND SIMILAR MATERIAL SIC SECTION

▲ Bespoke Apparel Inc ..... G 212 382-0330
New York (G-9419)
▲ Best Medical Wear Ltd ..... G 718 858-5544
Brooklyn (G-1686)
Bestec Concept Inc ..... G 718 937-5848
Long Island City (G-7715)
▲ Billion Tower Intl LLC ..... F 212 220-0608
New York (G-9449)
Broadway Knitting Mills Inc ..... G 716 692-4421
North Tonawanda (G-12979)
Classic Designer Workshop Inc ..... G 212 730-8480
New York (G-9690)
▲ Courage Clothing Co Inc ..... F 212 354-5690
New York (G-9796)
Dalcom USA Ltd ..... F 516 466-7733
Great Neck (G-5819)
David Christy ..... G 607 863-4610
Cincinnatus (G-3681)
Doral Apparel Group Inc ..... G 917 208-5652
New York (G-9959)
▲ Du Monde Trading Inc ..... E 212 944-1306
New York (G-9984)
▲ E J Manufacturing Inc ..... G 516 313-9380
Merrick (G-8417)
▲ Eighteen Liana Trading Inc ..... E 718 369-4247
New York (G-10043)
Enzo Manzoni LLC ..... G 212 464-7000
Brooklyn (G-1932)
Far East Industries Inc ..... G 718 687-2482
New Hyde Park (G-8878)
Ferris USA LLC ..... G 617 895-8102
New York (G-10207)
◆ HC Contracting Inc ..... D 212 643-9292
New York (G-10477)
Hillary Merchant Inc ..... G 646 575-9242
New York (G-10521)
Intrigue Concepts Inc ..... G 800 424-8170
Roosevelt (G-15029)
Joseph Abboud Manufacturing ..... G 212 586-9140
New York (G-10803)
Kollage Work Too Ltd ..... G 212 695-1821
New York (G-10910)
Kse Sportsman Media Inc ..... D 212 852-6600
New York (G-10929)
Lady Brass Co Inc ..... G 516 887-8040
Hewlett (G-6332)
Medline Industries Inc ..... B 845 344-3301
Middletown (G-8484)
▲ Mesh LLC ..... E 646 839-7000
New York (G-11263)
New York Hospital Disposable ..... E 718 384-1620
Brooklyn (G-2373)
Norcorp Inc ..... E 914 666-1310
Mount Kisco (G-8680)
▲ Occunomix International LLC ..... E 631 741-1940
Port Jeff STA (G-13792)
▲ Penfli Industries Inc ..... F 212 947-6080
Great Neck (G-5848)
Rag & Bone Industries LLC ..... E 212 249-3331
New York (G-11814)
▲ Rag & Bone Industries LLC ..... D 212 278-8214
New York (G-11815)
Richard Manufacturing Co Inc ..... G 718 254-0958
Brooklyn (G-2513)
▲ Ruleville Manufacturing Co Inc ..... G 212 695-1620
New York (G-11953)
▼ S & H Uniform Corp ..... D 914 937-6800
White Plains (G-17191)
Sarar Usa Inc ..... G 845 928-8874
Central Valley (G-3554)
Stealth Inc ..... F 718 252-7900
Brooklyn (G-2623)
▲ Untuckit LLC ..... C 201 214-9054
New York (G-12494)
▲ Ventura Enterprise Co Inc ..... E 212 391-0170
New York (G-12541)
Vf Imagewear Inc ..... E 718 352-2363
Bayside (G-772)

2329 Men's & Boys' Clothing, NEC

Adpro Sports LLC ..... D 716 854-5116
Buffalo (G-2815)
▲ Alexander Wang Incorporated ..... D 212 532-3103
New York (G-9133)
All Net Ltd ..... F 516 504-4559
Great Neck (G-5803)
▲ Alleson of Rochester Inc ..... D 800 641-0041
Rochester (G-14202)
▲ Alpha 6 Distributions LLC ..... F 516 801-8290
Locust Valley (G-7659)
▲ American Challenge Enterprises ..... G 631 595-7171
New Hyde Park (G-8860)
Apogee Retail NY ..... G 516 731-1727
Levittown (G-7445)
Bandit International Ltd ..... F 718 402-2100
Bronx (G-1279)
▲ Beluga Inc ..... E 212 594-5511
New York (G-9400)
◆ Benetton Trading Usa Inc ..... G 212 593-0290
New York (G-9406)
Bernette Apparel LLC ..... F 212 279-5526
New York (G-9413)
Bert Wassererman ..... G 212 759-5210
New York (G-9416)
▲ Big Idea Brands LLC ..... F 212 938-0270
New York (G-9444)
Bilco Industries Inc ..... F 917 783-5008
New York (G-9447)
Billion Tower USA LLC ..... G 212 220-0608
New York (G-9450)
Brigantine Inc ..... G 212 354-8550
New York (G-9511)
Broadway Knitting Mills Inc ..... G 716 692-4421
North Tonawanda (G-12979)
▲ Broken Threads Inc ..... G 212 730-4351
New York (G-9519)
▲ Brunschwig & Fils LLC ..... F 800 538-1880
Bethpage (G-864)
By Robert James ..... G 212 253-2121
New York (G-9538)
Caps Teamwear Inc ..... G 585 663-1750
Rochester (G-14277)
Caroda Inc ..... E 212 630-9986
New York (G-9583)
Central Mills Inc ..... C 212 221-0748
New York (G-9617)
City Jeans Inc ..... G 718 239-5353
Bronx (G-1301)
Clique Apparel Inc ..... G 516 375-7969
Valley Stream (G-16429)
Columbia Sportswear Company ..... C 631 274-6091
Deer Park (G-4141)
▲ Comme-Ci Comme-CA AP Group ..... E 631 300-1035
Hauppauge (G-6070)
Continental Knitting Mills ..... G 631 242-5330
Deer Park (G-4142)
▲ Cotton Emporium Inc ..... G 718 894-3365
Glendale (G-5665)
▲ Cougar Sport Inc ..... E 212 947-3054
New York (G-9792)
Craftatlantic LLC ..... F 646 726-4205
New York (G-9804)
▲ David Peyser Sportswear Inc ..... B 631 231-7788
Bay Shore (G-689)
David Peyser Sportswear Inc ..... E 212 695-7716
New York (G-9877)
▲ Eb Couture Ltd ..... E 212 912-0190
New York (G-10023)
▲ Endurance LLC ..... E 212 719-2500
New York (G-10086)
Eon Collections ..... E 212 695-1263
New York (G-10101)
◆ Eternal Fortune Fashion LLC ..... F 212 965-5322
New York (G-10131)
Ferris USA LLC ..... G 617 895-8102
New York (G-10207)
Feyem USA Inc ..... G 845 363-6253
Brewster (G-1216)
▲ G-III Apparel Group Ltd ..... B 212 403-0500
New York (G-10282)
Gametime Sportswear Plus LLC ..... G 315 724-5893
Utica (G-16358)
◆ General Sportwear Company Inc ..... G 212 764-5820
New York (G-10317)
Groupe 16sur20 LLC ..... F 212 625-1620
New York (G-10415)
Haculla Nyc Inc ..... F 718 886-3163
Fresh Meadows (G-5455)
Hansae Co Ltd ..... G 212 354-6690
New York (G-10455)
▼ Herman Kay Company Ltd ..... C 212 239-2025
New York (G-10505)
◆ Hf Mfg Corp ..... G 212 594-9142
New York (G-10513)
Hockey Facility ..... G 518 452-7396
Albany (G-86)
House Pearl Fashions (us) Ltd ..... F 212 840-3183
New York (G-10564)
▲ I Spiewak & Sons Inc ..... E 212 695-1620
New York (G-10588)
Ifg Corp ..... C 212 629-9600
New York (G-10605)
Ifg Corp ..... G 212 239-8615
New York (G-10606)
Jacob Hidary Foundation Inc ..... F 212 736-6540
New York (G-10731)
John Varvatos Company ..... E 212 812-8000
New York (G-10793)
Joseph (uk) Inc ..... G 212 570-0077
New York (G-10802)
Just Bottoms & Tops Inc ..... F 212 564-3202
New York (G-10825)
Kicks Closet Sportswear Inc ..... G 347 577-0857
Bronx (G-1376)
▲ Kidz World Inc ..... F 212 563-4949
New York (G-10883)
▲ King Sales Inc ..... F 718 301-9862
Brooklyn (G-2172)
▲ Komar Luxury Brands ..... G 646 472-0060
New York (G-10913)
▲ Lakeview Sportswear Corp ..... G 800 965-6550
Brooklyn (G-2192)
Linder New York LLC ..... F 646 678-5819
New York (G-11029)
▲ London Paris Ltd ..... G 718 564-4793
Brooklyn (G-2237)
Luxe Imagine Consulting LLC ..... G 212 273-9770
New York (G-11095)
▲ M A M Knitting Mills Corp ..... E 800 570-0093
Brooklyn (G-2248)
▲ M Hidary & Co Inc ..... D 212 736-6540
New York (G-11102)
Maiyet Inc ..... G 212 343-9999
New York (G-11139)
Mann Consultants LLC ..... E 914 763-0512
Waccabuc (G-16541)
Mayberry Shoe Company Inc ..... G 315 692-4086
Manlius (G-8107)
▲ Mee Accessories LLC ..... C 917 262-1000
New York (G-11244)
▲ Miss Group ..... G 212 391-2535
New York (G-11307)
▲ Montero International Inc ..... G 212 695-1787
Westbury (G-17041)
▲ Nautica International Inc ..... D 212 541-5757
New York (G-11381)
▲ Nepenthes America Inc ..... G 212 343-4262
New York (G-11389)
▲ Nevaeh Jeans Company ..... G 845 641-4255
New York (G-11400)
Nine West Holdings Inc ..... G 212 575-2571
New York (G-11455)
▲ North American Mills Inc ..... F 212 695-6146
New York (G-11473)
▲ Nyc Idol Apparel Inc ..... G 212 997-9797
New York (G-11494)
On The Double Inc ..... G 518 431-3571
Germantown (G-5603)
▲ One Step Up Ltd ..... D 212 398-1110
New York (G-11521)
Oxford Industries Inc ..... E 212 247-7712
New York (G-11553)
P & I Sportswear Inc ..... G 718 934-4587
New York (G-11559)
Piaget ..... F 212 355-6444
New York (G-11675)
Prestige Global NY Sls Corp ..... G 212 776-4322
New York (G-11726)
Pride & Joys Inc ..... F 212 594-9820
New York (G-11729)
Ps38 LLC ..... F 212 819-1123
New York (G-11763)
▲ Pti-Pacific Inc ..... G 212 414-8495
New York (G-11765)
Pvh Corp ..... G 212 381-3800
New York (G-11781)
R J Liebe Athletic Company ..... D 585 237-6111
Perry (G-13548)
◆ Ralph Lauren Corporation ..... B 212 318-7000
New York (G-11819)
▲ Ramsbury Property Us Inc ..... F 212 223-6250
New York (G-11823)
Robert Viggiani ..... G 914 423-4046
Yonkers (G-17500)
Rp55 Inc ..... G 212 840-4035
New York (G-11947)
▲ Ruleville Manufacturing Co Inc ..... G 212 695-1620
New York (G-11953)
▲ S & S Fashions Inc ..... G 718 328-0001
Bronx (G-1442)

SIC SECTION 23 APPAREL AND OTHER FINISHED PRODUCTS MADE FROM FABRICS AND SIMILAR MATERIAL

S & W Knitting Mills Inc	E	718 237-2416	Brooklyn *(G-2545)*
Sanctuary Brands LLC	G	212 704-4014	New York *(G-11982)*
Sandy Dalal Ltd	G	212 532-5822	New York *(G-11985)*
▼ **Sb Corporation**	G	212 822-3166	New York *(G-11999)*
Scharf and Breit Inc	E	516 282-0287	Williston Park *(G-17286)*
▲ **Schwartz Textile Converting Co**	E	718 499-8243	Brooklyn *(G-2562)*
▲ **Sister Sister Inc**	G	212 629-9600	New York *(G-12110)*
Sport Athleisure Ltd	F	212 868-6505	New York *(G-12189)*
▲ **Standard Manufacturing Co Inc**	D	518 235-2200	Troy *(G-16280)*
▲ **Sterling Possessions Ltd**	G	212 594-0418	New York *(G-12221)*
Swimwear Anywhere Inc	E	845 858-4141	Port Jervis *(G-13817)*
Tamka Sport LLC	G	718 224-7820	Douglaston *(G-4337)*
Tbhl International LLC	F	212 799-2007	New York *(G-12307)*
◆ **Tibana Finishing Inc**	E	718 417-5375	Ridgewood *(G-14140)*
▲ **Tillsonburg Company USA Inc**	E	267 994-8096	New York *(G-12360)*
Under Armour Inc	E	518 761-6787	Lake George *(G-7289)*
▲ **Uniqlo USA LLC**	F	877 486-4756	New York *(G-12479)*
Valley Stream Sporting Gds Inc	E	516 593-7800	Lynbrook *(G-7992)*
▲ **Versailles Industries LLC**	G	212 792-9615	New York *(G-12549)*
Vf Outdoor Inc	E	718 698-6215	Staten Island *(G-15775)*
Vf Outdoor LLC	E	845 928-4900	Central Valley *(G-3556)*
◆ **Warnaco Group Inc**	E	212 287-8000	New York *(G-12614)*
◆ **Warnaco Inc**	B	212 287-8000	New York *(G-12615)*
Warnaco Inc	F	718 722-3000	Brooklyn *(G-2760)*
Warrior Sports Inc	G	315 536-0937	Penn Yan *(G-13544)*

2331 Women's & Misses' Blouses

18 Rocks LLC	E	631 465-9990	Melville *(G-8320)*
79 Metro Ltd	G	212 944-4030	New York *(G-9025)*
▲ **Accessries Direct Intl USA Inc**	F	646 448-8200	New York *(G-9060)*
Agi Brooks Production Co Inc	F	212 268-1533	New York *(G-9107)*
▲ **Alexander Wang Incorporated**	D	212 532-3103	New York *(G-9133)*
▲ **Alfred Dunner Inc**	D	212 478-4300	New York *(G-9134)*
Amerex Corporation	G	212 221-3151	New York *(G-9160)*
▲ **Anna Sui Corp**	E	212 768-1951	New York *(G-9214)*
Apparel Group Ltd	E	212 328-1200	New York *(G-9229)*
▲ **August Silk Inc**	E	212 643-2400	New York *(G-9315)*
August Silk Inc	G	212 643-2400	New York *(G-9316)*
▲ **Ben Wachter Associates Inc**	G	212 736-4064	New York *(G-9401)*
▲ **Bernard Chaus Inc**	D	212 354-1280	New York *(G-9411)*
Bernard Chaus Inc	C	646 562-4700	New York *(G-9412)*
◆ **Bowe Industries Inc**	D	718 441-6464	Glendale *(G-5661)*
Brach Knitting Mills Inc	F	845 651-4450	Florida *(G-5217)*
Brooke Leigh Ltd	F	212 736-9098	New York *(G-9520)*
▲ **Courage Clothing Co Inc**	F	212 354-5690	New York *(G-9796)*
Cyberlimit Inc	F	212 840-9597	New York *(G-9833)*
▲ **Cynthia Rowley Inc**	F	212 242-3803	New York *(G-9835)*
Donna Karan Company LLC	C	212 789-1500	New York *(G-9952)*
▲ **Donna Karan Company LLC**	B	212 789-1500	New York *(G-9953)*
◆ **Donna Karan International Inc**	F	212 789-1500	New York *(G-9954)*
Donna Karan International Inc	G	212 768-5800	New York *(G-9955)*
Elie Tahari Ltd	G	212 398-2622	New York *(G-10054)*
Elie Tahari Ltd	D	212 763-2000	New York *(G-10056)*
Embassy Apparel Inc	F	212 768-8330	New York *(G-10071)*
◆ **Fetherston Design Group LLC**	E	212 643-7537	New York *(G-10208)*
Feyem USA Inc	G	845 363-6253	Brewster *(G-1216)*
Fourtys Ny Inc	F	212 382-0301	New York *(G-10243)*
Fuller Sportswear Co Inc	G	516 773-3353	Great Neck *(G-5830)*
Gabrielle Andra	G	212 366-9624	New York *(G-10287)*
◆ **Garan Incorporated**	C	212 563-1292	New York *(G-10294)*
▼ **Garan Manufacturing Corp**	G	212 563-2000	New York *(G-10295)*
▲ **Gce International Inc**	D	212 704-4800	New York *(G-10304)*
Geoffrey Beene Inc	E	212 371-5570	New York *(G-10323)*
▲ **Gildan Apparel USA Inc**	D	212 476-0341	New York *(G-10336)*
Glamourpuss Nyc LLC	G	212 722-1370	New York *(G-10346)*
▲ **Golden Horse Enterprise NY Inc**	G	212 594-3339	New York *(G-10373)*
Grey State Apparel LLC	E	212 255-4216	New York *(G-10403)*
Hansae Co Ltd	G	212 354-6690	New York *(G-10455)*
▲ **Ind Rev LLC**	F	212 221-4700	New York *(G-10628)*
▲ **International Direct Group Inc**	E	212 921-9036	New York *(G-10676)*
▲ **Jeanjer LLC**	A	212 944-1330	New York *(G-10756)*
Jordache Enterprises Inc	D	212 944-1330	New York *(G-10799)*
▲ **Jordache Enterprises Inc**	C	212 643-8400	New York *(G-10800)*
◆ **Kate Spade & Company**	B	212 354-4900	New York *(G-10854)*
▼ **Krasner Group Inc**	G	212 268-4100	New York *(G-10925)*
Ksk International Inc	E	212 354-7770	New York *(G-10930)*
◆ **Land n Sea Inc**	D	212 703-2980	New York *(G-10959)*
Lea & Viola Inc	G	646 918-6866	New York *(G-10981)*
▲ **Liberty Apparel Company Inc**	E	718 625-4000	New York *(G-11017)*
Lt2 LLC	E	212 684-1510	New York *(G-11086)*
▲ **M S B International Ltd**	F	212 302-5551	New York *(G-11105)*
▲ **Maggy London International Ltd**	D	212 944-7199	New York *(G-11129)*
▲ **Mega Sourcing Inc**	G	646 682-0304	Merrick *(G-8424)*
Melwood Partners Inc	G	516 307-8030	Garden City *(G-5533)*
▲ **Mulitex Usa Inc**	G	212 398-0440	New York *(G-11346)*
▲ **Necessary Objects Ltd**	E	212 334-9888	Long Island City *(G-7854)*
▲ **Nyc Knitwear Inc**	E	212 840-1313	New York *(G-11495)*
Orchard Apparel Group Ltd	G	212 268-8701	New York *(G-11535)*
Orchid Manufacturing Co Inc	F	212 840-5700	New York *(G-11536)*
Paddy Lee Fashions Inc	F	718 786-6020	Long Island City *(G-7865)*
Pat & Rose Dress Inc	D	212 279-1357	New York *(G-11593)*
▲ **Permit Fashion Group Inc**	G	212 912-0988	New York *(G-11639)*
Phillips-Van Heusen Europe	F	212 381-3500	New York *(G-11668)*
Plugg LLC	F	212 840-6655	New York *(G-11700)*
▲ **Pvh Corp**	D	212 381-3500	New York *(G-11780)*
Pvh Corp	G	212 719-2600	New York *(G-11783)*
▲ **Ramy Brook LLC**	E	212 744-2789	New York *(G-11824)*
▲ **Raven New York LLC**	G	212 584-9690	New York *(G-11829)*
▲ **Rhoda Lee Inc**	D	212 840-5700	New York *(G-11886)*
▲ **Rio Apparel USA Inc**	G	212 869-9150	New York *(G-11898)*
Robert Danes Danes Inc	G	212 226-1351	New York *(G-11910)*
▲ **S & S Manufacturing Co Inc**	D	212 444-6000	New York *(G-11961)*
Saad Collection Inc	G	212 937-0341	New York *(G-11966)*
Soho Apparel Ltd	G	212 840-1109	New York *(G-12146)*
Spencer AB Inc	G	646 831-3728	New York *(G-12184)*
Stitch & Couture Inc	E	212 947-9204	New York *(G-12229)*
▲ **Style Partners Inc**	F	212 904-1499	New York *(G-12245)*
Sweet Apparel Inc	G	212 221-3321	New York *(G-12275)*
T Rj Shirts Inc	G	347 642-3071	East Elmhurst *(G-4418)*
Tahari ASL LLC	B	212 763-2800	New York *(G-12295)*
◆ **Tibana Finishing Inc**	E	718 417-5375	Ridgewood *(G-14140)*
▲ **Triumph Apparel Corporation**	E	212 302-2606	New York *(G-12429)*
Turn On Products Inc	F	212 764-4545	New York *(G-12447)*
▲ **Turn On Products Inc**	D	212 764-2121	New York *(G-12446)*
Ursula of Switzerland Inc	E	518 237-2580	Waterford *(G-16645)*
Vanity Room Inc	F	212 921-7154	New York *(G-12526)*
▲ **Ventura Enterprise Co Inc**	E	212 391-0170	New York *(G-12541)*
Westside Clothing Co Inc	G	212 273-9898	New York *(G-12646)*
Yeohlee Inc	F	212 631-8099	New York *(G-12712)*

2335 Women's & Misses' Dresses

18 Rocks LLC	E	631 465-9990	Melville *(G-8320)*
◆ **A & M Rosenthal Entps Inc**	E	646 638-9600	New York *(G-9028)*
Agi Brooks Production Co Inc	F	212 268-1533	New York *(G-9107)*
Allison Che Fashion Inc	F	212 391-1433	New York *(G-9141)*
Alvina Vlenta Couture Collectn	F	212 921-7058	New York *(G-9156)*
Alvina Vlenta Couture Collectn	G	212 921-7058	New York *(G-9157)*
▲ **Amj DOT LLC**	G	718 775-3288	Brooklyn *(G-1610)*
Amsale Aberra LLC	E	212 695-5936	New York *(G-9191)*
Anna B Inc	G	516 680-6609	Syosset *(G-15834)*
▲ **Anna Sui Corp**	E	212 768-1951	New York *(G-9214)*
Arcangel Inc	G	347 771-0789	New York *(G-9244)*
▲ **Arteast LLC**	G	212 965-8787	New York *(G-9267)*
▲ **August Silk Inc**	E	212 643-2400	New York *(G-9315)*
August Silk Inc	G	212 643-2400	New York *(G-9316)*
B S J Limited	E	212 764-4600	New York *(G-9344)*
▲ **B S J Limited**	G	212 221-8403	New York *(G-9345)*

S I C

Employee Codes: A=Over 500 employees, B=251-500
C=101-250, D=51-100, E=20-50, F=10-19, G=5-9

2018 Harris
New York Manufacturers Directory

727

23 APPAREL AND OTHER FINISHED PRODUCTS MADE FROM FABRICS AND SIMILAR MATERIAL SIC SECTION

Bari-Jay Fashions Inc..........E 212 921-1551
New York *(G-9373)*
▲ **Bernard Chaus Inc**..........D 212 354-1280
New York *(G-9411)*
Birnbaum & Bullock Ltd..........G 212 242-2914
New York *(G-9455)*
▲ **Bms Designs Inc**..........E 718 828-5792
Bronx *(G-1284)*
Brides Inc..........G 718 435-6092
Brooklyn *(G-1713)*
▲ **Cachet Industries Inc**..........E 212 944-2188
New York *(G-9546)*
Carol Peretz..........F 516 248-6300
Mineola *(G-8534)*
▲ **China Ting Fashion Group (usa)**..........G 212 716-1600
New York *(G-9653)*
Christian Siriano Holdings LLC..........G 212 695-5494
New York *(G-9663)*
▲ **Christos Inc**..........E 212 921-0025
New York *(G-9666)*
▲ **Couture Inc**..........G 212 921-1166
New York *(G-9798)*
Crisada Inc..........G 718 729-9730
Long Island City *(G-7735)*
▲ **Csco LLC**..........E 212 221-5100
New York *(G-9819)*
CTS LLC..........G 212 278-0058
New York *(G-9820)*
▲ **Cynthia Rowley Inc**..........F 212 242-3803
New York *(G-9835)*
D J Night Ltd..........E 212 302-9050
New York *(G-9839)*
Dalma Dress Mfg Co Inc..........E 212 391-8296
Greenvale *(G-5898)*
Damianou Sportswear Inc..........D 718 204-5600
Woodside *(G-17342)*
▲ **Dave & Johnny Ltd**..........E 212 302-9050
New York *(G-9871)*
Diamond Bridal Collection Ltd..........E 212 302-0210
New York *(G-9923)*
Donna Karan Company LLC..........C 212 789-1500
New York *(G-9952)*
Donna Karan Company LLC..........C 716 297-0752
Niagara Falls *(G-12833)*
▲ **Donna Karan Company LLC**..........B 212 789-1500
New York *(G-9953)*
◆ **Donna Karan International Inc**..........F 212 789-1500
New York *(G-9954)*
Donna Karan International Inc..........G 212 768-5800
New York *(G-9955)*
Elana Laderos Ltd..........F 212 764-0840
New York *(G-10047)*
Elizabeth Fillmore LLC..........G 212 647-0863
New York *(G-10063)*
Everlasting Memories..........G 716 833-1111
Blasdell *(G-956)*
▲ **Faviana International Inc**..........E 212 594-4422
New York *(G-10200)*
Four Seasons Fashion Mfg Inc..........E 212 947-6820
New York *(G-10242)*
G-III Apparel Group Ltd..........E 212 403-0500
New York *(G-10283)*
Geoffrey Beene Inc..........E 212 371-5570
New York *(G-10323)*
Haddad Bros Inc..........E 718 377-5505
Brooklyn *(G-2060)*
▲ **Halmode Apparel Inc**..........A 212 819-9114
New York *(G-10442)*
Haute By Blair Stanley LLC..........G 212 557-7868
New York *(G-10472)*
▲ **I S C A Corp**..........F 212 719-5123
New York *(G-10587)*
▲ **Icer Scrubs LLC**..........F 212 221-4700
New York *(G-10597)*
Infinity Sourcing Services LLC..........G 212 868-2900
New York *(G-10636)*
J R Nites..........G 212 354-9670
New York *(G-10723)*
Jaclyn Inc..........F 212 736-5657
New York *(G-10729)*
▲ **Jiranimo Industries Ltd**..........F 212 921-5106
New York *(G-10776)*
▼ **Jlm Couture Inc**..........D 212 921-7058
New York *(G-10780)*
▲ **Jon Teri Sports Inc**..........E 212 398-0657
New York *(G-10796)*
▲ **Jovani Fashion Ltd**..........E 212 279-0222
New York *(G-10810)*
▲ **Judys Group Inc**..........E 212 921-0515
New York *(G-10815)*
▲ **Jump Design Group Inc**..........C 212 869-3300
New York *(G-10820)*
◆ **Kasper Group LLC**..........C 212 354-4311
New York *(G-10853)*
▲ **Kelly Grace Corp**..........D 212 704-9603
New York *(G-10870)*
▼ **Krasner Group Inc**..........G 212 268-4100
New York *(G-10925)*
▲ **L F Fashion Orient Intl Co Ltd**..........G 917 667-3398
New York *(G-10939)*
▲ **Lily & Taylor Inc**..........F 212 564-5459
New York *(G-11028)*
◆ **Lm Mignon LLC**..........F 212 730-9221
New York *(G-11044)*
Lmr Group Inc..........G 212 730-9221
New York *(G-11045)*
▲ **Lou Sally Fashions Corp**..........E 212 354-9670
New York *(G-11075)*
Lou Sally Fashions Corp..........E 212 354-1283
New York *(G-11076)*
Lovely Bride LLC..........G 212 924-2050
New York *(G-11082)*
▲ **McCall Pattern Company**..........C 212 465-6800
New York *(G-11219)*
Melwood Partners Inc..........G 516 307-8030
Garden City *(G-5533)*
▲ **Millennium Productions Inc**..........F 212 944-6203
New York *(G-11293)*
◆ **Milliore Fashion Inc**..........G 212 302-0001
New York *(G-11296)*
▲ **Necessary Objects Ltd**..........E 212 334-9888
Long Island City *(G-7854)*
▲ **Paris Wedding Center Corp**..........F 347 368-4085
Flushing *(G-5286)*
Paris Wedding Center Corp..........E 212 267-8088
New York *(G-11586)*
Parsley Apparel Corp..........E 631 981-7181
Ronkonkoma *(G-14989)*
Pat & Rose Dress Inc..........D 212 279-1357
New York *(G-11593)*
Patra Ltd..........F 212 764-6575
New York *(G-11595)*
Patra Ltd..........F 212 764-6575
New York *(G-11596)*
▲ **Patra Ltd**..........E 212 764-6575
New York *(G-11597)*
Paula Varsalona Ltd..........F 212 570-9100
New York *(G-11601)*
▲ **Phoebe Company LLC**..........D 212 302-5556
New York *(G-11669)*
PJ Designs Inc..........E 212 355-3100
New York *(G-11691)*
Plugg LLC..........F 212 840-6655
New York *(G-11700)*
Post Modern Productions Inc..........G 212 719-3916
New York *(G-11711)*
▲ **Product Development Intl LLC**..........G 212 279-6170
New York *(G-11748)*
▲ **Pronovias USA Inc**..........E 212 897-6393
New York *(G-11755)*
Quality Patterns Inc..........D 212 704-0355
New York *(G-11794)*
▲ **R & M Richards Inc**..........D 212 921-8820
New York *(G-11808)*
Ralph Lauren Corporation..........F 212 221-7751
New York *(G-11822)*
▲ **Raven New York LLC**..........G 212 584-9690
New York *(G-11829)*
Rogan LLC..........G 212 680-1407
New York *(G-11925)*
▲ **Rogan LLC**..........E 646 496-9339
New York *(G-11926)*
◆ **Ronni Nicole Group LLC**..........E 212 764-1000
New York *(G-11933)*
Sg Nyc LLC..........E 310 210-1837
New York *(G-12053)*
▲ **Shane Tex Inc**..........F 516 486-7522
Hempstead *(G-6309)*
Skinz Inc..........E 516 593-3139
Lynbrook *(G-7988)*
Spencer AB Inc..........G 646 831-3728
New York *(G-12184)*
▲ **SSG Fashions Ltd**..........G 212 221-0933
New York *(G-12203)*
Stitch & Couture Inc..........E 212 947-9204
New York *(G-12229)*
Studio Krp LLC..........F 310 589-5777
New York *(G-12242)*
▲ **Style Partners Inc**..........F 212 904-1499
New York *(G-12245)*
Tabrisse Collections Inc..........F 212 921-1014
New York *(G-12293)*
Tahari ASL LLC..........B 212 763-2800
New York *(G-12295)*
Texport Fabrics Corp..........F 212 226-6066
New York *(G-12326)*
Therese The Childrens Collectn..........G 518 346-2315
Schenectady *(G-15328)*
▲ **Thread LLC**..........G 212 414-8844
New York *(G-12351)*
Tom & Linda Platt Inc..........F 212 221-7208
New York *(G-12379)*
Turn On Products Inc..........F 212 764-4545
New York *(G-12447)*
Ursula of Switzerland Inc..........E 518 237-2580
Waterford *(G-16645)*
Vanity Room Inc..........F 212 921-7154
New York *(G-12526)*
▲ **Vera Wang Group LLC**..........C 212 575-6400
New York *(G-12542)*
▲ **Wear Abouts Apparel Inc**..........F 212 827-0888
New York *(G-12630)*
▲ **Worth Collection Ltd**..........E 212 268-0312
New York *(G-12691)*
Yeohlee Inc..........F 212 631-8099
New York *(G-12712)*

2337 Women's & Misses' Suits, Coats & Skirts

2h International Corp..........G 347 623-9380
Forest Hills *(G-5324)*
79 Metro Ltd..........G 212 944-4030
New York *(G-9025)*
▲ **Adar Medical Uniform LLC**..........F 718 935-1197
Brooklyn *(G-1559)*
Adrienne Landau Designs Inc..........F 212 695-8362
New York *(G-9080)*
▲ **Age Manufacturers Inc**..........D 718 927-0048
Brooklyn *(G-1569)*
Agi Brooks Production Co Inc..........F 212 268-1533
New York *(G-9107)*
▲ **Alfred Dunner Inc**..........D 212 478-4300
New York *(G-9134)*
▲ **Alicia Adams Alpaca Inc**..........G 845 868-3366
Millbrook *(G-8510)*
◆ **Amerimade Coat Inc**..........G 212 216-0925
New York *(G-9184)*
▲ **Anna Sui Corp**..........E 212 768-1951
New York *(G-9214)*
Bestec Concept Inc..........G 718 937-5848
Long Island City *(G-7715)*
Bindle and Keep..........G 917 740-5002
Brooklyn *(G-1698)*
▲ **Blatt Searle & Company Ltd**..........E 212 730-7717
Long Island City *(G-7719)*
Brooke Leigh Ltd..........F 212 736-9098
New York *(G-9520)*
Bruno & Canio Ltd..........E 845 624-3060
Nanuet *(G-8799)*
Canada Goose Us Inc..........G 888 276-6297
Williamsville *(G-17266)*
▼ **Carolina Herrera Ltd**..........E 212 944-5757
New York *(G-9588)*
▲ **Countess Corporation**..........G 212 869-7070
New York *(G-9794)*
Donna Karan Company LLC..........F 212 372-6500
New York *(G-9951)*
Donna Karan Company LLC..........C 212 789-1500
New York *(G-9952)*
▲ **Donna Karan Company LLC**..........B 212 789-1500
New York *(G-9953)*
◆ **Donna Karan International Inc**..........F 212 789-1500
New York *(G-9954)*
Donna Karan International Inc..........G 212 768-5800
New York *(G-9955)*
Elie Tahari Ltd..........D 212 398-2622
New York *(G-10055)*
Elie Tahari Ltd..........D 631 329-8883
East Hampton *(G-4430)*
Elie Tahari Ltd..........D 973 671-6300
New York *(G-10057)*
Elie Tahari Ltd..........D 212 763-2000
New York *(G-10056)*
Elie Tahari Ltd..........G 212 398-2622
New York *(G-10054)*
▲ **Excelled Sheepskin & Lea Coat**..........F 212 594-5843
New York *(G-10157)*
Four Seasons Fashion Mfg Inc..........E 212 947-6820
New York *(G-10242)*

23 APPAREL AND OTHER FINISHED PRODUCTS MADE FROM FABRICS AND SIMILAR MATERIAL

▲ G-III Apparel Group Ltd .... B 212 403-0500
  New York *(G-10282)*
G-III Leather Fashions Inc .... E 212 403-0500
  New York *(G-10284)*
G18 Corporation .... G 212 869-0010
  New York *(G-10285)*
Geoffrey Beene Inc .... E 212 371-5570
  New York *(G-10323)*
▲ Global Gold Inc .... E 212 239-4657
  New York *(G-10359)*
◆ Hampshire Sub II Inc .... D 631 321-0923
  New York *(G-10446)*
▲ Harrison Sportswear Inc .... F 212 391-1051
  New York *(G-10463)*
▼ Herman Kay Company Ltd .... C 212 239-2025
  New York *(G-10505)*
◆ Hugo Boss Usa Inc .... D 212 940-0600
  New York *(G-10574)*
◆ J Percy For Mrvin Rchards Ltd .... E 212 944-5300
  New York *(G-10721)*
▲ Jeanjer LLC .... A 212 944-1330
  New York *(G-10756)*
▲ Jon Teri Sports Inc .... E 212 398-0657
  New York *(G-10796)*
▲ Judys Group Inc .... E 212 921-0515
  New York *(G-10815)*
Julia Jordan Corporation .... F 646 214-3090
  New York *(G-10817)*
Kayo of California .... G 212 354-6336
  New York *(G-10862)*
▲ Kozinn+sons Merchant Tailors .... E 212 643-1916
  New York *(G-10921)*
Lady Brass Co Inc .... G 516 887-8040
  Hewlett *(G-6332)*
▲ Levy Group Inc .... C 212 398-0707
  New York *(G-11014)*
▲ Lf Outerwear LLC .... D 212 239-2025
  New York *(G-11015)*
▲ Lily & Taylor Inc .... F 212 564-5459
  New York *(G-11028)*
Linrich Designs Inc .... G 212 382-2257
  New York *(G-11031)*
▲ Maggy Boutique Ltd .... E 212 997-5222
  New York *(G-11128)*
▲ Marlou Garments Inc .... F 516 739-7100
  New Hyde Park *(G-8893)*
Miny Group Inc .... G 212 925-6722
  New York *(G-11305)*
Mp Studio Inc .... G 212 302-5666
  New York *(G-11336)*
Nine West Holdings Inc .... C 212 642-3860
  New York *(G-11458)*
▲ Nyc Idol Apparel Inc .... G 212 997-9797
  New York *(G-11494)*
Opposuits USA Inc .... E 917 438-8878
  New York *(G-11530)*
Pat & Rose Dress Inc .... G 212 279-1357
  New York *(G-11593)*
▲ Permit Fashion Group Inc .... G 212 912-0988
  New York *(G-11639)*
Primo Coat Corp .... E 718 349-2070
  Long Island City *(G-7877)*
Public School .... G 212 302-1108
  New York *(G-11768)*
▲ R & M Richards Inc .... D 212 921-8820
  New York *(G-11808)*
▲ Rhoda Lee Inc .... D 212 840-5700
  New York *(G-11886)*
▲ Shane Tex Inc .... F 516 486-7522
  Hempstead *(G-6309)*
Spc Global LLC .... G 646 723-3238
  New York *(G-12177)*
▲ Standard Manufacturing Co Inc .... D 518 235-2200
  Troy *(G-16280)*
▲ Style Partners Inc .... F 212 904-1499
  New York *(G-12245)*
Tenby LLC .... C 646 863-5890
  New York *(G-12322)*
Terrapin Station Ltd .... F 716 874-6677
  Buffalo *(G-3240)*
Theory LLC .... D 212 762-2300
  New York *(G-12334)*
Theory LLC .... G 212 879-0265
  New York *(G-12335)*
Theory LLC .... G 631 204-0231
  Southampton *(G-15577)*
▲ Tiger Fashion Inc .... E 212 244-1175
  New York *(G-12357)*
▲ Tiger J LLC .... E 212 465-9300
  New York *(G-12358)*

Travis Ayers Inc .... E 212 921-5165
  New York *(G-12416)*
Turn On Products Inc .... F 212 764-4545
  New York *(G-12447)*
Uniforms By Park Coats Inc .... E 718 499-1182
  Brooklyn *(G-2717)*
▲ Uniqlo USA LLC .... G 877 486-4756
  New York *(G-12479)*
Ursula of Switzerland Inc .... E 518 237-2580
  Waterford *(G-16645)*
View Collections Inc .... F 212 944-4030
  New York *(G-12566)*
Yeohlee Inc .... F 212 631-8099
  New York *(G-12712)*
Zaralo LLC .... G 212 764-4590
  New York *(G-12724)*

2339 Women's & Misses' Outerwear, NEC

1 Atelier LLC .... G 917 916-2968
  New York *(G-9004)*
▲ 31 Phillip Lim LLC .... E 212 354-6540
  New York *(G-9018)*
525 America LLC .... G 212 921-5688
  New York *(G-9023)*
◆ 5th & Ocean Clothing Inc .... C 716 604-9000
  Buffalo *(G-2804)*
▲ 6th Avenue Showcase Inc .... G 212 382-0400
  New York *(G-9024)*
A & B Finishing Inc .... E 718 522-4702
  Brooklyn *(G-1524)*
◆ A H Schreiber Co Inc .... D 212 594-7234
  New York *(G-9036)*
▲ Accessory Street LLC .... E 212 686-8990
  New York *(G-9059)*
▲ Accessries Direct Intl USA Inc .... F 646 448-8200
  New York *(G-9060)*
Adpro Sports LLC .... D 716 854-5116
  Buffalo *(G-2815)*
Aerobic Wear Inc .... G 631 673-1830
  Huntington Station *(G-6730)*
▲ Age Manufacturers Inc .... D 718 927-0048
  Brooklyn *(G-1569)*
AKOS Group Ltd .... E 212 683-4747
  New York *(G-9119)*
▲ Alfred Dunner Inc .... D 212 478-4300
  New York *(G-9134)*
▲ Alleson of Rochester Inc .... E 800 641-0041
  Rochester *(G-14202)*
Ally Nyc Corp .... G 212 447-7277
  New York *(G-9145)*
▲ Alpha 6 Distributions LLC .... F 516 801-8290
  Locust Valley *(G-7659)*
▲ Amber Bever Inc .... G 212 391-4911
  Brooklyn *(G-1594)*
American Apparel Trading Corp .... G 212 764-5990
  New York *(G-9163)*
▲ American Challenge Enterprises .... G 631 595-7171
  New Hyde Park *(G-8860)*
▲ Angel-Made In Heaven Inc .... G 212 869-5678
  New York *(G-9206)*
Angel-Made In Heaven Inc .... G 718 832-4778
  Brooklyn *(G-1611)*
▲ Anna Sui Corp .... E 212 768-1951
  New York *(G-9214)*
▲ Argee America Inc .... G 212 768-9840
  New York *(G-9250)*
Aura International Mfg Inc .... G 212 719-1418
  New York *(G-9317)*
▲ Avalin LLC .... F 212 842-2286
  New York *(G-9325)*
AZ Yashir Bapaz Inc .... G 212 947-7357
  New York *(G-9338)*
▲ B Tween LLC .... F 212 819-9040
  New York *(G-9347)*
Bag Bazaar Ltd .... E 212 689-3508
  New York *(G-9357)*
▲ Bagznyc Corp .... F 212 643-8202
  New York *(G-9358)*
Bam Sales LLC .... G 212 781-3000
  New York *(G-9364)*
Bandier Corp .... G 212 242-5400
  New York *(G-9366)*
Bandit International Ltd .... F 718 402-2100
  Bronx *(G-1279)*
Bands N Bows .... G 718 984-4316
  Staten Island *(G-15663)*
▲ Bank-Miller Co Inc .... E 914 227-9357
  Pelham *(G-13514)*
▲ Bernard Chaus Inc .... D 212 354-1280
  New York *(G-9411)*

Bernard Chaus Inc .... C 646 562-4700
  New York *(G-9412)*
Bestec Concept Inc .... G 718 937-5848
  Long Island City *(G-7715)*
▲ Bh Brand Inc .... E 212 239-1635
  New York *(G-9433)*
Big Bang Clothing Inc .... G 212 221-0379
  New York *(G-9442)*
Bilco Industries Inc .... F 917 783-5008
  New York *(G-9447)*
Blue Cast Denim Co Inc .... E 212 719-1182
  Huntington *(G-6689)*
▲ Blueduck Trading Ltd .... G 212 268-3122
  New York *(G-9475)*
Botkier Ny LLC .... G 212 343-2782
  New York *(G-9493)*
Brigantine Inc .... G 212 354-8550
  New York *(G-9511)*
Brooke Leigh Ltd .... G 212 736-9098
  New York *(G-9520)*
C & C Athletic Inc .... G 845 713-4670
  Walden *(G-16550)*
▲ Cai Design Inc .... G 212 401-9973
  New York *(G-9548)*
Canada Goose Inc .... G 888 276-6297
  New York *(G-9561)*
Canada Goose Us Inc .... G 888 276-6297
  Williamsville *(G-17266)*
▲ Candlesticks Inc .... E 212 947-8900
  New York *(G-9566)*
▲ Carolina Amato Inc .... E 212 768-9095
  New York *(G-9587)*
▼ Carolina Herrera Ltd .... E 212 944-5757
  New York *(G-9588)*
Casuals Etc Inc .... D 212 838-1319
  New York *(G-9598)*
◆ Cathy Daniels Ltd .... E 212 354-8000
  New York *(G-9604)*
◆ Central Apparel Group Ltd .... E 212 868-6505
  New York *(G-9614)*
Central Mills Inc .... E 212 221-0748
  New York *(G-9642)*
▲ China Ting Fashion Group (usa) .... G 212 716-1600
  New York *(G-9653)*
▲ Chloe International Inc .... E 212 730-6661
  New York *(G-9655)*
▲ Christina Sales Inc .... F 212 391-0710
  New York *(G-9664)*
▲ City Sites Sportswear Inc .... E 718 375-2990
  Brooklyn *(G-1784)*
▲ Collection Xiix Ltd .... C 212 686-8990
  New York *(G-9729)*
▲ Comint Apparel Group LLC .... E 212 947-7474
  New York *(G-9743)*
▲ Comme-Ci Comme-CA AP Group .... E 631 300-1035
  Hauppauge *(G-6070)*
Consolidated Fashion Corp .... G 212 719-3000
  New York *(G-9766)*
Continental Knitting Mills .... G 631 242-5330
  Deer Park *(G-4142)*
▲ Cynthia Rowley Inc .... F 212 242-3803
  New York *(G-9835)*
▲ Daily Wear Sportswear Corp .... G 718 972-0533
  Brooklyn *(G-1835)*
Dalma Dress Mfg Co Inc .... E 212 391-8296
  Greenvale *(G-5898)*
Dana Michele LLC .... G 917 757-7777
  New York *(G-9853)*
▲ Dani II Inc .... F 212 869-5999
  New York *(G-9857)*
Danice Stores Inc .... F 212 665-0389
  New York *(G-9858)*
▲ Design For All LLC .... E 212 523-0021
  New York *(G-9905)*
▲ DFA New York LLC .... E 212 523-0021
  New York *(G-9919)*
Dianos Kathryn Designs .... G 212 267-1584
  New York *(G-9927)*
▲ Donna Karan Company LLC .... G 212 789-1500
  New York *(G-9952)*
▲ Donna Karan Company LLC .... B 212 789-1500
  New York *(G-9953)*
◆ Donna Karan International Inc .... F 212 789-1500
  New York *(G-9954)*
Donna Karan International Inc .... G 212 768-5800
  New York *(G-9955)*
Doral Apparel Group Inc .... G 917 208-5652
  New York *(G-9959)*
▲ Double Take Fashions Inc .... G 718 832-9000
  New York *(G-9962)*

Employee Codes: A=Over 500 employees, B=251-500
C=101-250, D=51-100, E=20-50, F=10-19, G=5-9

23 APPAREL AND OTHER FINISHED PRODUCTS MADE FROM FABRICS AND SIMILAR MATERIAL

▼ Dr Jayscom .... G 888 437-5297
New York *(G-9973)*
▲ Drew Philips Corp .... G 212 354-0095
New York *(G-9979)*
▲ Du Monde Trading Inc .... E 212 944-1306
New York *(G-9984)*
▲ Eileen Fisher Inc .... C 914 591-5700
Irvington *(G-6810)*
El-La Design Inc .... G 212 382-1080
New York *(G-10046)*
Elie Tahari Ltd .... G 212 398-2622
New York *(G-10054)*
Elie Tahari Ltd .... D 212 398-2622
New York *(G-10055)*
◆ Elizabeth Gillett Ltd .... G 212 629-7993
New York *(G-10064)*
Elizabeth Wilson .... G 516 486-2157
Uniondale *(G-16314)*
▲ Emerald Holdings Inc .... G 718 797-4404
Brooklyn *(G-1921)*
Emerson & Oliver LLC .... G 585 775-9929
Rochester *(G-14365)*
▲ F & J Designs Inc .... G 212 302-8755
New York *(G-10167)*
▲ Fad Inc .... E 631 385-2460
Huntington *(G-6694)*
Falls Manufacturing Inc .... G 518 672-7189
Philmont *(G-13565)*
Fashion Ave Sweater Knits LLC .... D 212 302-8282
New York *(G-10195)*
▲ Feldman Manufacturing Corp .... D 718 433-1700
Long Island City *(G-7768)*
First Love Fashions LLC .... F 212 256-1089
New York *(G-10221)*
Four Dee Inc .... D 718 615-1695
Brooklyn *(G-1999)*
Four Seasons Fashion Mfg Inc ..... E 212 947-6820
New York *(G-10242)*
▲ French Atmosphere Inc .... F 516 371-9100
New York *(G-10257)*
Fusion Pro Performance Ltd .... F 917 833-0761
New York *(G-10274)*
▲ G-III Apparel Group Ltd .... B 212 403-0500
New York *(G-10282)*
G-III Leather Fashions Inc .... E 212 403-0500
New York *(G-10284)*
▲ GAME Sportswear Ltd .... E 914 962-1701
Yorktown Heights *(G-17527)*
◆ Garan Incorporated .... C 212 563-1292
New York *(G-10294)*
▼ Garan Manufacturing Corp .... G 212 563-2000
New York *(G-10295)*
Gbg Denim Usa LLC .... F 646 839-7000
New York *(G-10298)*
Gbg West LLC .... C 646 839-7000
New York *(G-10303)*
Geoffrey Beene Inc .... E 212 371-5570
New York *(G-10323)*
▲ Gfb Fashions Ltd .... F 212 239-9230
New York *(G-10331)*
Giulietta LLC .... G 212 334-1859
Brooklyn *(G-2025)*
▲ GMC Mercantile Corp .... F 212 498-9488
New York *(G-10366)*
▲ Golden Leaves Knitwear Inc ...... E 718 875-8235
Brooklyn *(G-2038)*
▲ Great Wall Corp .... C 212 704-4372
Long Island City *(G-7783)*
▲ Halmode Apparel Inc .... A 212 819-9114
New York *(G-10442)*
◆ Hampshire Sub II Inc .... D 631 321-0923
New York *(G-10446)*
▲ Hana Sportswear Inc .... E 315 639-6332
Dexter *(G-4308)*
▲ HB Athletic Inc .... F 914 560-8422
New Rochelle *(G-8955)*
◆ HC Contracting Inc .... D 212 643-9292
New York *(G-10477)*
Hearts of Palm LLC .... E 212 944-6660
New York *(G-10495)*
Hearts of Palm LLC .... D 212 944-6660
New York *(G-10496)*
▼ Herman Kay Company Ltd .... C 212 239-2025
New York *(G-10505)*
Hoehn Inc .... F 518 463-8900
Albany *(G-87)*
▲ Hot Line Industries Inc .... F 516 764-0400
Plainview *(G-13634)*
▲ Hot Shot Hk LLC .... E 212 921-1111
New York *(G-10556)*

House Pearl Fashions (us) Ltd ...... F 212 840-3183
New York *(G-10564)*
▲ I ABC Corporation .... E 315 639-3100
Dexter *(G-4309)*
Idra Alta Moda LLC .... F 914 644-8202
New York *(G-10604)*
Ifg Corp .... C 212 629-9600
New York *(G-10605)*
▲ Ikeddi Enterprises Inc .... F 212 302-7644
New York *(G-10611)*
Ikeddi Enterprises Inc .... G 212 302-7644
New York *(G-10612)*
In Moda com Inc .... E 718 788-4466
New York *(G-10623)*
▲ Int Trading USA LLC .... C 212 760-2338
New York *(G-10657)*
▲ Intriguing Threads Apparel Inc .. F 212 768-8733
New York *(G-10689)*
Isabel Toledo Enterprises Inc .... F 212 685-0948
New York *(G-10707)*
J & E Talit Inc .... G 718 850-1333
Richmond Hill *(G-14088)*
◆ J Percy For Mrvin Rchards Ltd .. E 212 944-5300
New York *(G-10721)*
Jaxis Inc .... F 212 302-7611
Brooklyn *(G-2134)*
Jaya Apparel Group LLC .... F 212 764-4980
New York *(G-10746)*
▲ Jeanjer LLC .... A 212 944-1330
New York *(G-10756)*
▲ JEnvie Sport Inc .... F 212 967-2322
New York *(G-10760)*
Jesse Joeckel .... G 631 668-2772
Montauk *(G-8623)*
◆ Joe Benbasset Inc .... F 212 268-4920
New York *(G-10786)*
Jomat New York Inc .... F 718 369-7641
Brooklyn *(G-2145)*
▲ Jonathan Michael Coat Corp .... G 212 239-9230
New York *(G-10798)*
▲ Jonden Manufacturing Co Inc .. F 516 442-4895
Oceanside *(G-13103)*
Jordache Enterprises Inc .... D 212 944-1330
New York *(G-10799)*
▲ Jordache Enterprises Inc .... E 212 643-8400
New York *(G-10800)*
Joseph Abboud Manufacturing ..... G 212 586-9140
New York *(G-10803)*
▲ Jsc Designs Inc .... E 212 302-1001
New York *(G-10814)*
▲ Judys Group Inc .... E 212 921-0515
New York *(G-10815)*
Just Bottoms & Tops Inc .... F 212 564-3202
New York *(G-10825)*
▼ K T P Design Co Inc .... F 212 481-6613
New York *(G-10833)*
Kaltex America Inc .... F 212 971-0575
New York *(G-10842)*
Karen Kane Inc .... F 212 827-0980
New York *(G-10847)*
Kasper Group LLC .... F 212 354-4311
New York *(G-10852)*
▲ Katz Martell Fashion Trdg Intl ... F 212 840-0070
New York *(G-10857)*
Kayo of California .... F 212 354-6336
New York *(G-10862)*
Kicks Closet Sportswear Inc .... F 347 577-0857
Bronx *(G-1376)*
Koral Industries .... F 212 719-0392
New York *(G-10914)*
▲ Krasner Group Inc .... G 212 268-4100
New York *(G-10925)*
Ksk International Inc .... G 212 354-7770
New York *(G-10930)*
▲ Lahoya Enterprise Inc .... E 718 886-8799
College Point *(G-3818)*
▲ Lai Apparel Design Inc .... F 212 382-1075
New York *(G-10954)*
◆ Land n Sea Inc .... F 212 703-2980
New York *(G-10959)*
Lea Apparel Inc .... F 718 418-2800
Glendale *(G-5672)*
Leesa Designs Ltd .... G 631 261-3991
Centerport *(G-3503)*
◆ Leggiadro International Inc .... E 212 997-8766
New York *(G-10996)*
Lemral Knitwear Inc .... F 718 210-0175
Brooklyn *(G-2211)*
Leng Universal Inc .... F 212 398-6800
New York *(G-11000)*

▲ Leslie Stuart Co Inc .... F 212 629-4551
New York *(G-11011)*
Lgb Inc .... E 212 278-8280
New York *(G-11016)*
▲ Liberty Apparel Company Inc ... E 718 625-4000
New York *(G-11017)*
Life Style Design Group .... E 212 391-8666
New York *(G-11020)*
▲ Light Inc .... G 212 629-3255
New York *(G-11025)*
▲ Lily & Taylor Inc .... F 212 564-5459
New York *(G-11028)*
Linrich Designs Inc .... G 212 382-2257
New York *(G-11031)*
▲ Liquid Knits Inc .... F 718 706-6600
Long Island City *(G-7819)*
▲ Lotus Apparel Designs Inc .... G 646 236-9363
Westbury *(G-17034)*
Luxe Imagine Consulting LLC ...... G 212 273-9770
New York *(G-11095)*
▲ M A M Knitting Mills Corp .... E 800 570-0093
Brooklyn *(G-2248)*
▲ Mag Brands LLC .... D 212 629-9600
New York *(G-11124)*
▲ Maggy Boutique Ltd .... E 212 997-5222
New York *(G-11128)*
Maiyet Inc .... G 212 343-9999
New York *(G-11139)*
Malia Mills Inc .... G 212 354-4200
Brooklyn *(G-2258)*
▲ Manchu New York Inc .... G 212 921-5050
New York *(G-11150)*
▲ Manchu Times Fashion Inc ...... G 212 921-5050
New York *(G-11151)*
▲ Mango Usa Inc .... E 718 998-6050
Brooklyn *(G-2260)*
Marcasiano Inc .... G 212 614-9412
New York *(G-11168)*
▲ Marconi Intl USA Co Ltd .... E 212 391-2626
New York *(G-11170)*
Marina Holding Corp .... F 718 646-9283
Brooklyn *(G-2270)*
Mars Fashions Inc .... E 718 402-2200
Bronx *(G-1391)*
Max Leon Inc .... F 845 928-8201
Central Valley *(G-3553)*
Mayberry Shoe Company Inc .... G 315 692-4086
Manlius *(G-8107)*
▲ Medi-Tech International Corp ... E 800 333-0109
Brooklyn *(G-2295)*
▲ Meryl Diamond Ltd .... D 212 730-0333
New York *(G-11262)*
Meskita Lifestyle Brands LLC .... E 212 695-5054
New York *(G-11264)*
Michael Feldman Inc .... D 718 433-1700
Long Island City *(G-7842)*
Miguelina Inc .... F 212 925-0320
New York *(G-11288)*
◆ Mikael Aghal LLC .... F 212 596-4010
New York *(G-11289)*
▲ Millennium Productions Inc ...... F 212 944-6203
New York *(G-11293)*
Miltons of New York Inc .... G 212 997-3359
New York *(G-11298)*
MISS Sportswear Inc .... F 212 391-2535
Brooklyn *(G-2324)*
▲ MISS Sportswear Inc .... G 212 391-2535
Brooklyn *(G-2325)*
MISS Sportswear Inc .... F 718 369-6012
Brooklyn *(G-2326)*
▲ Moes Wear Apparel Inc .... F 718 940-1597
Brooklyn *(G-2333)*
Morelle Products Ltd .... F 212 391-8070
New York *(G-11329)*
▲ Mv Corp Inc .... C 631 273-8020
Bay Shore *(G-717)*
▲ Mystic Inc .... B 212 239-2025
New York *(G-11358)*
▲ Necessary Objects Ltd .... E 212 334-9888
Long Island City *(G-7854)*
▲ New Concepts of New York LLC .. E 212 695-4999
Brooklyn *(G-2368)*
▲ New York Accessory Group Inc .. E ... 212 532-7911
New York *(G-11416)*
Nine West Holdings Inc .... G 212 642-3860
New York *(G-11453)*
Nine West Holdings Inc .... G 212 221-6376
New York *(G-11454)*
Nine West Holdings Inc .... E 212 822-1300
New York *(G-11456)*

23 APPAREL AND OTHER FINISHED PRODUCTS MADE FROM FABRICS AND SIMILAR MATERIAL

Nine West Holdings Inc ....E....... 215 785-4000
  New York *(G-11457)*
Nine West Holdings Inc ....E....... 212 575-2571
  New York *(G-11455)*
Nine West Holdings Inc ....E....... 212 642-3860
  New York *(G-11459)*
Nlhe LLC ....E....... 212 594-0012
  New York *(G-11460)*
▲ Noah Enterprises Ltd ....G....... 212 736-2888
  New York *(G-11464)*
▲ Ocean Waves Swim LLC ....G....... 212 967-4481
  New York *(G-11508)*
▲ ODY Accessories Inc ....E....... 212 239-0580
  New York *(G-11510)*
On The Double Inc ....G....... 518 431-3571
  Germantown *(G-5603)*
▲ One Jeanswear Group Inc ....B....... 212 835-3500
  New York *(G-11520)*
▲ One Step Up Ltd ....D....... 212 398-1110
  New York *(G-11521)*
Only Hearts Ltd ....E....... 718 783-3218
  New York *(G-11523)*
▲ Outerstuff LLC ....E....... 212 594-9700
  New York *(G-11548)*
P & I Sportswear Inc ....G....... 718 934-4587
  New York *(G-11559)*
Pacific Alliance Usa Inc ....G....... 336 500-8184
  New York *(G-11564)*
▲ Pacific Alliance Usa Inc ....E....... 646 839-7000
  New York *(G-11565)*
Paddy Lee Fashions Inc ....F....... 718 786-6020
  Long Island City *(G-7865)*
Park Avenue Sportswear Ltd ....F....... 718 369-0520
  Brooklyn *(G-2422)*
◆ Passport Brands Inc ....E....... 646 459-2625
  New York *(G-11592)*
Pat & Rose Dress Inc ....D....... 212 279-1357
  New York *(G-11593)*
▲ Penfli Industries Inc ....F....... 212 947-6080
  Great Neck *(G-5848)*
▲ Permit Fashion Group Inc ....G....... 212 912-0988
  New York *(G-11639)*
Petrunia LLC ....G....... 607 277-1930
  Ithaca *(G-6905)*
Plugg LLC ....E....... 212 840-6655
  New York *(G-11700)*
▲ Popnyc 1 LLC ....G....... 646 684-4600
  New York *(G-11706)*
Pride & Joys Inc ....F....... 212 594-9820
  New York *(G-11729)*
Primo Coat Corp ....E....... 718 349-2070
  Long Island City *(G-7877)*
▲ Pti-Pacific Inc ....G....... 212 414-8495
  New York *(G-11765)*
Pvh Corp ....D....... 212 502-6300
  New York *(G-11782)*
Pvh Corp ....G....... 212 381-3800
  New York *(G-11781)*
RAK Finishing Corp ....E....... 718 416-4242
  Howard Beach *(G-6626)*
Ralph Lauren Corporation ....G....... 917 934-4200
  New York *(G-11821)*
▲ Ramsbury Property Us Inc ....F....... 212 223-6250
  New York *(G-11823)*
▲ RD Intrntnl Style ....G....... 212 382-2360
  New York *(G-11836)*
Rene Portier Inc ....G....... 718 853-7896
  Brooklyn *(G-2511)*
▲ Republic Clothing Corporation ....E....... 212 719-3000
  New York *(G-11868)*
Republic Clothing Group Inc ....C....... 212 719-3000
  New York *(G-11869)*
▲ Rhoda Lee Inc ....D....... 212 840-5700
  New York *(G-11886)*
▲ Richard Leeds Intl Inc ....E....... 212 532-4546
  New York *(G-11888)*
Richard Manufacturing Co Inc ....G....... 718 254-0958
  Brooklyn *(G-2513)*
▲ Ritchie Corp ....E....... 212 768-0083
  New York *(G-11902)*
Robespierre Inc ....G....... 212 764-8810
  New York *(G-11913)*
▲ Robespierre Inc ....C....... 212 594-0012
  New York *(G-11914)*
Rogers Group Inc ....E....... 212 643-9292
  New York *(G-11928)*
▲ Rvc Enterprises LLC ....E....... 212 391-4600
  New York *(G-11957)*
▲ S & S Manufacturing Co Inc ....D....... 212 444-6000
  New York *(G-11961)*

S & V Knits Inc ....E....... 631 752-1595
  Farmingdale *(G-5116)*
S & W Knitting Mills Inc ....E....... 718 237-2416
  Brooklyn *(G-2545)*
▲ S Broome and Co Inc ....D....... 718 663-6800
  Long Island City *(G-7899)*
▲ S2 Sportswear Inc ....F....... 347 335-0713
  Brooklyn *(G-2550)*
Salisbury Sportswear Inc ....G....... 516 221-9519
  Bellmore *(G-817)*
▲ Sam Hee International Inc ....G....... 212 594-7815
  New York *(G-11978)*
▲ Sarina Accessories LLC ....F....... 212 239-8106
  New York *(G-11993)*
▲ Sea Waves Inc ....G....... 516 766-4201
  Oceanside *(G-13118)*
Senneth LLC ....G....... 347 232-3170
  Monsey *(G-8617)*
▲ Sensational Collection Inc ....G....... 212 840-7388
  New York *(G-12047)*
Sentimental Inc ....G....... 212 221-0282
  New York *(G-12049)*
Shirl-Lynn of New York ....G....... 315 363-5898
  Oneida *(G-13189)*
▲ Smooth Industries Incorporated ..E....... 212 869-1080
  New York *(G-12138)*
Snowman ....G....... 212 239-8818
  New York *(G-12142)*
Spectrum Apparel Inc ....G....... 212 239-2025
  New York *(G-12181)*
Sport Athleisure Ltd ....F....... 212 868-6505
  New York *(G-12191)*
▲ SRP Apparel Group Inc ....G....... 212 764-4810
  New York *(G-12201)*
Ssa Trading Ltd ....F....... 646 465-9500
  New York *(G-12202)*
▲ SSG Fashions Ltd ....G....... 212 221-0933
  New York *(G-12203)*
St John ....G....... 718 720-8367
  Staten Island *(G-15760)*
St John ....G....... 718 771-4541
  Brooklyn *(G-2616)*
▲ Standard Manufacturing Co Inc ...D....... 518 235-2200
  Troy *(G-16280)*
Steilmann European Selections ....D....... 914 997-0015
  Port Chester *(G-13783)*
▲ Sterling Possessions Ltd ....G....... 212 594-0418
  New York *(G-12221)*
Stony Apparel Corp ....G....... 212 391-0022
  New York *(G-12232)*
▲ Street Beat Sportswear Inc ....F....... 718 302-1500
  Brooklyn *(G-2632)*
▲ Sunynams Fashions Ltd ....G....... 212 268-5200
  New York *(G-12262)*
▲ Survival Inc ....G....... 631 385-5060
  Centerport *(G-3506)*
Swatfame Inc ....G....... 212 944-8022
  New York *(G-12273)*
◆ Swimwear Anywhere Inc ....D....... 631 420-1400
  Farmingdale *(G-5131)*
Swimwear Anywhere Inc ....E....... 845 858-4141
  Port Jervis *(G-13817)*
Tahari ASL LLC ....B....... 212 763-2800
  New York *(G-12295)*
▲ Tailored Sportsman LLC ....F....... 646 366-8733
  New York *(G-12297)*
Tamka Sport LLC ....G....... 718 224-7820
  Douglaston *(G-4337)*
Tbhl International LLC ....F....... 212 799-2007
  New York *(G-12307)*
Texwood Inc (u S A) ....G....... 212 262-8383
  New York *(G-12327)*
▲ THE Design Group Inc ....F....... 212 681-1548
  New York *(G-12330)*
▲ Tiger J LLC ....E....... 212 465-9300
  New York *(G-12358)*
▲ Tillsonburg Company USA Inc ....G....... 267 994-8096
  New York *(G-12360)*
Toni Industries Inc ....F....... 212 921-0700
  Great Neck *(G-5864)*
▲ TR Designs Inc ....E....... 212 398-9300
  New York *(G-12408)*
▲ Turn On Products Inc ....D....... 212 764-2121
  New York *(G-12446)*
Turn On Products Inc ....F....... 212 764-4545
  New York *(G-12447)*
▲ Untuckit LLC ....C....... 201 214-9054
  New York *(G-12494)*
▲ Urban Apparel Group Inc ....E....... 212 947-7009
  New York *(G-12498)*

▲ Uspa Accessories LLC ....C....... 212 868-2590
  New York *(G-12513)*
Valenti Neckwear Co Inc ....G....... 914 969-0700
  Yonkers *(G-17511)*
▲ Venus Manufacturing Co Inc ......D....... 315 639-3100
  Dexter *(G-4310)*
Vf Imagewear Inc ....E....... 718 352-2363
  Bayside *(G-772)*
Vf Outdoor Inc ....E....... 845 928-4900
  Central Valley *(G-3556)*
Vf Sportswear Inc ....E....... 212 541-5757
  New York *(G-12557)*
◆ Warnaco Group Inc ....E....... 212 287-8000
  New York *(G-12614)*
Warrior Sports Inc ....G....... 315 536-0937
  Penn Yan *(G-13544)*
▲ West Pacific Enterprises Corp ....G....... 212 564-6800
  New York *(G-12641)*
▲ White Gate Holdings Inc ....G....... 212 564-3266
  New York *(G-12652)*
Yigal-Azrouel Inc ....E....... 212 302-1194
  New York *(G-12713)*
▲ Z-Ply Corp ....E....... 212 398-7011
  New York *(G-12721)*
▼ Zar Group LLC ....G....... 212 944-2510
  New York *(G-12723)*
◆ Zg Apparel Group LLC ....E....... 212 944-2510
  New York *(G-12730)*
Zia Power Inc ....E....... 845 661-8388
  New York *(G-12731)*
▲ Zoomers Inc ....E....... 718 369-2656
  Brooklyn *(G-2796)*

2341 Women's, Misses' & Children's Underwear & Nightwear

Allure Fashions Inc ....G....... 516 829-2470
  Great Neck *(G-5804)*
▲ Ann Gish Inc ....G....... 212 969-9200
  New York *(G-9213)*
▲ Apparel Partnership Group LLC ..G....... 212 302-7722
  New York *(G-9230)*
▲ Ariela and Associates Intl LLC ....E....... 212 683-4131
  New York *(G-9252)*
Becks Classic Mfg Inc ....E....... 631 435-3800
  Brentwood *(G-1175)*
Beverly Creations Inc ....F....... 800 439-6855
  New York *(G-9428)*
▲ Candlesticks Inc ....E....... 212 947-8900
  New York *(G-9566)*
Classic Designer Workshop Inc ....G....... 212 730-8480
  New York *(G-9690)*
▲ Comme-Ci Comme-CA AP Group ..E....... 631 300-1035
  Hauppauge *(G-6070)*
▲ Dayleen Intimates Inc ....G....... 914 969-5900
  Yonkers *(G-17450)*
Enticing Lingerie Inc ....E....... 718 998-8625
  Brooklyn *(G-1931)*
Faye Bernard Loungewear ....G....... 718 951-7245
  Brooklyn *(G-1966)*
▲ Handcraft Manufacturing Corp ....E....... 212 251-0022
  New York *(G-10448)*
▲ Intimateco LLC ....G....... 212 239-4411
  New York *(G-10686)*
▲ Kokin Inc ....E....... 212 643-8225
  New York *(G-10908)*
▲ Komar Layering LLC ....E....... 212 725-1500
  New York *(G-10912)*
▲ Komar Luxury Brands ....G....... 646 472-0060
  New York *(G-10913)*
Lady Ester Lingerie Corp ....E....... 212 689-1729
  New York *(G-10951)*
Loungehouse LLC ....E....... 646 524-2965
  New York *(G-11080)*
▲ Luxerdame Co Inc ....E....... 718 752-9800
  Long Island City *(G-7825)*
Mrt Textile Inc ....G....... 800 674-1073
  New York *(G-11341)*
Natori Company Incorporated ....G....... 212 532-7796
  New York *(G-11379)*
▲ Natori Company Incorporated ....D....... 212 532-7796
  New York *(G-11378)*
Only Hearts Ltd ....E....... 718 783-3218
  New York *(G-11523)*
▲ Richard Leeds Intl Inc ....E....... 212 532-4546
  New York *(G-11888)*
▲ Sleepwear Holdings Inc ....C....... 516 466-4738
  New York *(G-12126)*
▲ Solo Licensing Corp ....G....... 212 244-5505
  New York *(G-12150)*

Employee Codes: A=Over 500 employees, B=251-500
C=101-250, D=51-100, E=20-50, F=10-19, G=5-9

23 APPAREL AND OTHER FINISHED PRODUCTS MADE FROM FABRICS AND SIMILAR MATERIAL — SIC SECTION

Vanity Fair Brands LP ....C....... 212 548-1548
  New York (G-12525)
Wacoal International Corp ....D....... 212 532-6100
  New York (G-12605)
◆ Warnaco Group Inc ....E....... 212 287-8000
  New York (G-12614)
◆ Warnaco Inc ....B....... 212 287-8000
  New York (G-12615)
Warnaco Inc ....F....... 718 722-3000
  Brooklyn (G-2760)
▲ Waterbury Garment LLC ....E....... 212 725-1500
  New York (G-12625)
▲ Wickers Sportswear Inc ....G....... 631 543-1700
  Commack (G-3872)

2342 Brassieres, Girdles & Garments

Burlen Corp ....F....... 212 684-0052
  New York (G-9532)
▲ Cupid Foundations Inc ....D....... 212 686-6224
  New York (G-9824)
Deunall Corporation ....C....... 516 667-8875
  Levittown (G-7449)
E P Sewing Pleating Inc ....E....... 212 967-2575
  New York (G-10003)
East Coast Molders Inc ....C....... 516 240-6000
  Oceanside (G-13098)
Edith Lances Corp ....E....... 212 683-1990
  New York (G-10034)
Enticing Lingerie Inc ....E....... 718 998-8625
  Brooklyn (G-1931)
Higgins Supply Company Inc ....D....... 607 836-6474
  Mc Graw (G-8253)
Luxerdame Co Inc ....E....... 718 752-9800
  Long Island City (G-7825)
▲ New York Elegance Entps Inc ....F....... 212 685-3088
  New York (G-11420)
▲ Prime Garments Inc ....F....... 212 354-7294
  New York (G-11731)
▼ Rago Foundations LLC ....D....... 718 728-8436
  Astoria (G-453)
Sensual Inc ....E....... 212 869-1450
  New York (G-12048)
▲ Valmont Inc ....F....... 212 685-1653
  New York (G-12519)
Wacoal America Inc ....C....... 718 794-1032
  Bronx (G-1491)
Wacoal America Inc ....E....... 212 743-9600
  New York (G-12604)
◆ Warnaco Group Inc ....E....... 212 287-8000
  New York (G-12614)
◆ Warnaco Inc ....B....... 212 287-8000
  New York (G-12615)
Warnaco Inc ....F....... 718 722-3000
  Brooklyn (G-2760)

2353 Hats, Caps & Millinery

▲ A-1 Skull Cap Corp ....E....... 718 633-9333
  Brooklyn (G-1540)
Albrizio Inc ....G....... 212 719-5290
  Brooklyn (G-1576)
Athletic Cap Co Inc ....E....... 718 398-1300
  Staten Island (G-15661)
Bonk Sam Unforms Civilian Cap ....E....... 718 585-0665
  Bronx (G-1285)
▲ Cookies Inc ....A....... 646 452-5552
  New York (G-9776)
Dorel Hat Co ....E....... 845 831-5231
  Beacon (G-779)
▲ Flexfit Llc ....D....... 516 932-8800
  Hicksville (G-6373)
Gce International Inc ....F....... 212 868-0500
  New York (G-10305)
Genesco Inc ....G....... 585 227-3080
  Rochester (G-14414)
Hankin Brothers Cap Co ....F....... 716 892-8840
  Buffalo (G-3004)
◆ Hat Attack Inc ....E....... 718 994-1000
  Bronx (G-1353)
Kays Caps Inc ....G....... 518 273-6079
  Troy (G-16242)
▲ Kim Eugenia Inc ....G....... 212 674-1345
  New York (G-10884)
▲ Kingform Cap Company Inc ....D....... 516 822-2501
  Hicksville (G-6386)
▲ Kokin Inc ....E....... 212 643-8225
  New York (G-10908)
▲ Kraft Hat Manufacturers Inc ....D....... 845 735-6200
  Pearl River (G-13484)
▲ Lenore Marshall Inc ....G....... 212 947-5945
  New York (G-11002)
Lids Corporation ....E....... 718 338-7790
  Brooklyn (G-2219)
▲ Lloyds Fashions Inc ....D....... 631 435-3353
  Brentwood (G-1187)
Makins Hats Ltd ....G....... 212 594-6666
  New York (G-11143)
Matthews Hats ....G....... 718 859-4683
  Brooklyn (G-2288)
Mega Power Sports Corporation ....G....... 212 627-3380
  New York (G-11246)
New ERA Cap Co Inc ....B....... 716 604-9000
  Buffalo (G-3106)
◆ New ERA Cap Co Inc ....G....... 716 604-9000
  Buffalo (G-3107)
New ERA Cap Co Inc ....F....... 716 549-0445
  Derby (G-4307)
Paletot Ltd ....E....... 212 268-3774
  New York (G-11569)
Room At The Top Inc ....F....... 718 257-0766
  Brooklyn (G-2526)
Tanen Cap Co ....F....... 212 254-7100
  Brooklyn (G-2667)
Therese The Childrens Collectn ....G....... 518 346-2315
  Schenectady (G-15328)
Whittall & Shon ....G....... 212 594-2626
  New York (G-12656)

2361 Children's & Infants' Dresses & Blouses

▲ Andy & Evan Industries Inc ....G....... 212 967-7908
  New York (G-9204)
▲ Bonpoint Inc ....E....... 212 246-3291
  New York (G-9488)
◆ Bowe Industries Inc ....D....... 718 441-6464
  Glendale (G-5661)
▲ Brooke Maya Inc ....E....... 212 279-2340
  New York (G-9521)
Carters Inc ....G....... 585 387-9043
  Rochester (G-14281)
Carters Inc ....G....... 315 637-3128
  Fayetteville (G-5171)
Carters Inc ....G....... 718 980-1759
  Staten Island (G-15677)
Carters Inc ....G....... 631 549-6781
  Huntington Station (G-6737)
▲ Cheri Mon Baby LLC ....G....... 212 354-5511
  New York (G-9640)
▲ Consolidated Childrens AP Inc ....G....... 212 239-8615
  New York (G-9764)
Cream Bebe ....F....... 917 578-2088
  Brooklyn (G-1811)
E-Play Brands LLC ....G....... 212 563-2646
  New York (G-10007)
◆ Garan Incorporated ....C....... 212 563-1292
  New York (G-10294)
▼ Garan Manufacturing Corp ....G....... 212 563-2000
  New York (G-10295)
Gce International Inc ....F....... 212 868-0500
  New York (G-10305)
◆ General Sportwear Company Inc ....G....... 212 764-5820
  New York (G-10317)
▲ Gerson & Gerson Inc ....D....... 212 244-6775
  New York (G-10330)
▲ Grand Knitting Mills Inc ....E....... 631 226-5000
  Amityville (G-289)
▲ Great Universal Corp ....F....... 917 302-0065
  New York (G-10400)
▲ Gw Acquisition LLC ....E....... 212 736-4848
  New York (G-10430)
Haddad Bros Inc ....E....... 718 377-5505
  Brooklyn (G-2060)
▲ Haddad Bros Inc ....F....... 212 563-2117
  New York (G-10437)
Hard Ten Clothing Inc ....F....... 212 302-1321
  New York (G-10457)
◆ JM Originals Inc ....C....... 845 647-3003
  Ellenville (G-4648)
Jordache Enterprises Inc ....D....... 212 944-1330
  New York (G-10799)
▲ Jordache Enterprises Inc ....C....... 212 643-8400
  New York (G-10800)
▲ Land n Sea Inc ....D....... 212 703-2980
  New York (G-10959)
▲ Manchu New York Inc ....F....... 212 921-5050
  New York (G-11150)
Michael Stuart Inc ....E....... 718 821-0704
  Brooklyn (G-2314)
Rosenau Beck Inc ....F....... 212 279-6202
  New York (G-11938)
▲ S & C Bridals LLC ....F....... 212 789-7000
  New York (G-11960)
▲ Silly Phillie Creations Inc ....E....... 718 492-6300
  Brooklyn (G-2583)
◆ Skip Hop Inc ....E....... 646 902-9874
  New York (G-12118)
Skip Hop Holdings Inc ....G....... 212 868-9850
  New York (G-12119)
Sports Products America LLC ....E....... 212 594-5511
  New York (G-12192)
▲ Star Childrens Dress Co Inc ....D....... 212 279-1524
  New York (G-12208)
▲ Sue & Sam Co Inc ....E....... 718 436-1672
  Brooklyn (G-2640)
Thats My Girl Inc ....G....... 212 695-0020
  Brooklyn (G-2675)
ZIC Sportswear Inc ....E....... 718 361-9022
  Long Island City (G-7962)
▲ Zinnias Inc ....F....... 718 746-8551
  Bellerose (G-808)

2369 Girls' & Infants' Outerwear, NEC

Aerobic Wear Inc ....G....... 631 673-1830
  Huntington Station (G-6730)
◆ Amerimade Coat Inc ....E....... 212 216-0925
  New York (G-9184)
Baby Uv/Kids Uv Inc ....F....... 917 301-9020
  Stony Brook (G-15787)
▲ Babyfair Inc ....E....... 212 736-7989
  New York (G-9352)
▲ Best Brands Consumer Pdts Inc ....G....... 212 684-7456
  New York (G-9420)
▲ Candlesticks Inc ....F....... 212 947-8900
  New York (G-9566)
Detour Apparel Inc ....G....... 212 221-3265
  New York (G-9914)
▲ Devil Dog Manufacturing Co Inc ....G....... 845 647-4411
  Ellenville (G-4647)
▲ Domani Fashions Corp ....G....... 718 797-0505
  Brooklyn (G-1872)
E-Play Brands LLC ....G....... 212 563-2646
  New York (G-10007)
▲ Fine Sheer Industries Inc ....F....... 212 594-4224
  New York (G-10216)
▲ Franco Apparel Group Inc ....D....... 212 967-7272
  New York (G-10249)
◆ Garan Incorporated ....C....... 212 563-1292
  New York (G-10294)
▼ Garan Manufacturing Corp ....G....... 212 563-2000
  New York (G-10295)
◆ General Sportwear Company Inc ....G....... 212 764-5820
  New York (G-10317)
◆ Gerson & Gerson Inc ....D....... 212 244-6775
  New York (G-10330)
▲ Gw Acquisition LLC ....E....... 212 736-4848
  New York (G-10430)
Haddad Bros Inc ....E....... 718 377-5505
  Brooklyn (G-2060)
▲ Ideal Creations Inc ....E....... 212 563-5928
  New York (G-10600)
▲ In Mocean Group LLC ....D....... 212 944-0317
  New York (G-10622)
▲ Isfel Co Inc ....G....... 212 736-6216
  New York (G-10708)
▲ Jeanjer LLC ....A....... 212 944-1330
  New York (G-10756)
Jgx LLC ....G....... 212 575-1244
  New York (G-10770)
◆ JM Originals Inc ....C....... 845 647-3003
  Ellenville (G-4648)
Jomat New York Inc ....E....... 718 369-7641
  Brooklyn (G-2145)
Jordache Enterprises Inc ....D....... 212 944-1330
  New York (G-10799)
▲ Jordache Enterprises Inc ....C....... 212 643-8400
  New York (G-10800)
K & S Childrens Wear Inc ....E....... 718 624-0006
  Brooklyn (G-2162)
Kahn-Lucas-Lancaster Inc ....D....... 212 239-2407
  New York (G-10837)
◆ Land n Sea Inc ....D....... 212 703-2980
  New York (G-10959)
Leng Universal Inc ....F....... 212 398-6800
  New York (G-11000)
▲ Liberty Apparel Company Inc ....E....... 718 625-4000
  New York (G-11017)
◆ Lollytogs Ltd ....D....... 212 502-6000
  New York (G-11053)
▲ M Hidary & Co Inc ....D....... 212 736-6540
  New York (G-11102)
Michael Stuart Inc ....E....... 718 821-0704
  Brooklyn (G-2314)

SIC SECTION
23 APPAREL AND OTHER FINISHED PRODUCTS MADE FROM FABRICS AND SIMILAR MATERIAL

Miltons of New York Inc G 212 997-3359
New York *(G-11298)*

▲ Outerstuff LLC E 212 594-9700
New York *(G-11548)*

◆ Oxygen Inc G 516 433-1144
Hicksville *(G-6405)*

Pink Crush LLC G 718 788-6978
New York *(G-11686)*

▲ Pti-Pacific Inc G 212 414-8495
New York *(G-11765)*

Rogers Group Inc E 212 643-9292
New York *(G-11928)*

▼ S Rothschild & Co Inc C 212 354-8550
New York *(G-11964)*

Sch Dpx Corporation G 917 405-5377
New York *(G-12003)*

▲ Silly Phillie Creations Inc E 718 492-6300
Brooklyn *(G-2583)*

▲ Sister Sister Inc G 212 629-9600
New York *(G-12110)*

Sleepy Head Inc F 718 237-9655
Brooklyn *(G-2597)*

Swatfame Inc G 212 944-8022
New York *(G-12273)*

Therese The Childrens Collectn G 518 346-2315
Schenectady *(G-15328)*

◆ Warnaco Group Inc E 212 287-8000
New York *(G-12614)*

▲ Waterbury Garment LLC E 212 725-1500
New York *(G-12625)*

Yigal-Azrouel Inc E 212 302-1194
New York *(G-12713)*

▲ Z-Ply Corp E 212 398-7011
New York *(G-12721)*

ZIC Sportswear Inc E 718 361-9022
Long Island City *(G-7962)*

▲ Zinnias Inc F 718 746-8551
Bellerose *(G-808)*

2371 Fur Goods

▲ Anage Inc F 212 944-6533
New York *(G-9195)*

Anastasia Furs International G 212 868-9241
New York *(G-9198)*

Arbeit Bros Inc G 212 736-9761
New York *(G-9241)*

▲ Avante G 516 782-4888
Great Neck *(G-5810)*

B Smith Furs Inc F 212 967-5290
New York *(G-9346)*

▲ Best Brands Consumer Pdts Inc G 212 684-7456
New York *(G-9420)*

▲ Blum & Fink Inc F 212 695-2606
New York *(G-9477)*

▲ CPT Usa LLC E 212 575-1616
New York *(G-9801)*

▲ Dennis Basso Couture Inc F 212 794-4500
New York *(G-9899)*

Fox Unlimited Inc G 212 736-3071
New York *(G-10245)*

Georgy Creative Fashions Inc G 212 279-4885
New York *(G-10328)*

◆ J Percy For Mrvin Rchards Ltd E 212 944-5300
New York *(G-10721)*

Jerry Sorbara Furs Inc F 212 594-3897
New York *(G-10761)*

◆ Kaitery Furs Ltd G 718 204-1396
Long Island City *(G-7805)*

Miller & Berkowitz Ltd F 212 244-5459
New York *(G-11294)*

Mink Mart Inc G 212 868-2785
New York *(G-11304)*

Moschos Furs Inc G 212 244-0255
New York *(G-11333)*

N Pologeorgis Furs Inc F 212 563-2250
New York *(G-11359)*

Samuel Schulman Furs Inc E 212 736-5550
New York *(G-11981)*

Sekas International Ltd F 212 629-6095
New York *(G-12040)*

▲ Stallion Inc E 718 706-0111
Long Island City *(G-7910)*

Stefan Furs Inc G 212 594-2788
New York *(G-12214)*

Steves Original Furs Inc E 212 967-8007
New York *(G-12227)*

Superior Furs Inc F 516 365-4123
Manhasset *(G-8099)*

Tom Moriber Furs Inc F 212 244-2180
New York *(G-12383)*

USA Furs By George Inc G 212 643-1415
New York *(G-12511)*

Xanadu G 212 465-0580
New York *(G-12700)*

2381 Dress & Work Gloves

Falls Manufacturing Inc G 518 672-7189
Philmont *(G-13565)*

◆ Fownes Brothers & Co Inc E 212 683-0150
New York *(G-10244)*

Fownes Brothers & Co Inc E 518 752-4411
Gloversville *(G-5726)*

Gce International Inc F 212 868-0500
New York *(G-10305)*

▲ Manzella Knitting G 716 825-0808
Orchard Park *(G-13306)*

2384 Robes & Dressing Gowns

Jisan Trading Corporation E 212 244-1269
New York *(G-10777)*

▲ Komar Luxury Brands G 646 472-0060
New York *(G-10913)*

Lady Ester Lingerie Corp E 212 689-1729
New York *(G-10951)*

Mata Fashions LLC G 917 716-7894
New York *(G-11199)*

▲ Natori Company Incorporated D 212 532-7796
New York *(G-11378)*

◆ Palmbay Ltd G 718 424-3388
Flushing *(G-5285)*

▲ Richard Leeds Intl Inc E 212 532-4546
New York *(G-11888)*

Sketch Studio Trading Inc G 212 244-2875
New York *(G-12114)*

2385 Waterproof Outerwear

A W R Group Inc F 718 729-0412
Long Island City *(G-7676)*

▲ Essex Manufacturing Inc D 212 239-0080
New York *(G-10119)*

Float Tech Inc G 518 266-0964
Troy *(G-16257)*

▲ Hercules Group Inc E 212 813-8000
Port Washington *(G-13842)*

▲ Levy Group Inc C 212 398-0707
New York *(G-11014)*

▲ Mycra Pac Designer Wear Inc G 925 631-6878
New York *(G-11355)*

▲ Top Fortune Usa Ltd G 516 608-2694
Lynbrook *(G-7991)*

2386 Leather & Sheep Lined Clothing

▲ Andrew M Schwartz LLC G 212 391-7070
New York *(G-9203)*

Avanti U S A Ltd F 716 695-5800
Tonawanda *(G-16162)*

Cockpit Usa Inc F 212 575-1616
New York *(G-9719)*

▲ Cockpit Usa Inc F 212 575-1616
New York *(G-9720)*

Cockpit Usa Inc F 908 558-9704
New York *(G-9721)*

▲ Dada Group US Inc G 631 888-0818
Bayside *(G-764)*

▲ Excelled Sheepskin & Lea Coat F 212 594-5843
New York *(G-10157)*

▲ G-III Apparel Group Ltd B 212 403-0500
New York *(G-10282)*

G-III Leather Fashions Inc E 212 403-0500
New York *(G-10284)*

Georgy Creative Fashions Inc G 212 279-4885
New York *(G-10328)*

▼ Gloria Apparel Inc F 212 947-0869
New York *(G-10364)*

▲ J Lowy Co G 718 338-7324
Brooklyn *(G-2123)*

◆ J Percy For Mrvin Rchards Ltd E 212 944-5300
New York *(G-10721)*

Lost Worlds Inc G 212 923-3423
New York *(G-11073)*

Louis Schwartz G 845 356-6624
Spring Valley *(G-15615)*

Studio One Leather Design Inc F 212 760-1701
New York *(G-12243)*

▲ US Authentic LLC G 914 767-0295
Katonah *(G-7163)*

2387 Apparel Belts

Barrera Jose & Maria Co Ltd E 212 239-1994
New York *(G-9376)*

◆ Coach Inc B 212 594-1850
New York *(G-9714)*

▲ Coach Stores Inc A 212 643-9727
New York *(G-9717)*

▲ Courtlandt Boot Jack Co Inc E 718 445-6200
Flushing *(G-5242)*

▲ Daniel M Friedman & Assoc Inc E 212 695-5545
New York *(G-9859)*

Dynasty Belts Inc E 516 625-6280
New Hyde Park *(G-8873)*

Gbg USA Inc D 646 839-7083
New York *(G-10301)*

Gbg USA Inc E 212 615-3400
New York *(G-10302)*

Nassau Suffolk Brd of Womens E 631 666-8835
Bay Shore *(G-718)*

▲ New Classic Inc F 718 609-1100
Long Island City *(G-7855)*

P M Belts Usa Inc E 800 762-3580
Brooklyn *(G-2413)*

◆ Perry Ellis Menswear LLC C 212 221-7500
New York *(G-11643)*

Queue Solutions LLC F 631 750-6440
Bohemia *(G-1121)*

Randa Accessories Lea Gds LLC D 212 354-5100
New York *(G-11825)*

Sandy Duftler Designs Ltd F 516 379-3084
North Baldwin *(G-12925)*

Sh Leather Novelty Company G 718 387-7742
Brooklyn *(G-2574)*

▲ Trafalgar Company LLC G 212 768-8800
New York *(G-12411)*

Universal Elliot Corp G 212 736-8877
New York *(G-12491)*

Walco Leather Co Inc E 212 243-2244
Bedford *(G-795)*

Xinya International Trading Co G 212 216-9681
New York *(G-12704)*

2389 Apparel & Accessories, NEC

▲ A Lunt Design Inc F 716 662-0781
Orchard Park *(G-13272)*

▲ Accessries Direct Intl USA Inc F 646 448-8200
New York *(G-9060)*

▲ Adf Accessories Inc G 516 450-5755
Lynbrook *(G-7971)*

▲ Apollo Apparel Group LLC F 212 398-6585
New York *(G-9226)*

Barbara Matera Ltd D 212 475-5006
New York *(G-9367)*

▲ Bh Brand Inc E 212 239-1635
New York *(G-9433)*

Brooklyn Denim Co F 718 782-2600
Brooklyn *(G-1724)*

▲ Carter Enterprises LLC E 718 853-5052
Brooklyn *(G-1762)*

▲ Cortland Industries Inc F 212 575-2710
New York *(G-9788)*

Costume Armour Inc F 845 534-9120
Cornwall *(G-4008)*

▲ Costume Culture By Franco LLC G 718 821-7100
Glendale *(G-5664)*

Craft Clerical Clothes Inc G 212 764-6122
New York *(G-9803)*

Creative Costume Co G 212 564-5552
Liverpool *(G-7542)*

▲ Crosswinds Sourcing LLC G 646 438-6904
New York *(G-9814)*

Cygnet Studio Inc F 646 450-4550
New York *(G-9834)*

D-C Theatricks G 716 847-0180
Buffalo *(G-2919)*

Danny R Couture Corp G 212 594-1095
New York *(G-9861)*

David & Young Co Inc G 212 594-6034
New York *(G-9873)*

Davis G 716 833-4678
Buffalo *(G-2922)*

▲ Dreamwave LLC E 212 594-4250
New York *(G-9976)*

▲ Dvf Studio LLC D 212 741-6607
New York *(G-9993)*

Dvf Studio LLC G 646 576-8009
New York *(G-9994)*

▲ Eb Couture Ltd E 212 912-0190
New York *(G-10023)*

Employee Codes: A=Over 500 employees, B=251-500
C=101-250, D=51-100, E=20-50, F=10-19, G=5-9
2018 Harris
New York Manufacturers Directory
733

Eric Winterling Inc ....E.... 212 629-7686
New York *(G-10108)*
▼ **Euroco Costumes Inc** ....G.... 212 629-9665
New York *(G-10139)*
Foot Locker Retail Inc ....F.... 516 827-5306
Hicksville *(G-6374)*
▲ **Gce International Inc** ....D.... 212 704-4800
New York *(G-10304)*
▲ **HB Athletic Inc** ....F.... 914 560-8422
New Rochelle *(G-8955)*
Hoehn Inc ....F.... 518 463-8900
Albany *(G-87)*
▲ **Hpk Industries LLC** ....F.... 315 724-0196
Utica *(G-16362)*
Hudson Dying & Finishing LLC ....E.... 518 752-4389
Gloversville *(G-5731)*
Intercotton Company Inc ....G.... 212 265-3809
New York *(G-10669)*
Izquierdo Studios Ltd ....F.... 212 807-9757
New York *(G-10712)*
J & C Finishing ....E.... 718 456-1087
Ridgewood *(G-14123)*
J M C Bow Co Inc ....F.... 718 686-8110
Brooklyn *(G-2124)*
Jersey Express Inc ....F.... 716 834-6151
Buffalo *(G-3035)*
▲ **Jimeale Incorporated** ....G.... 917 686-5383
New York *(G-10774)*
▲ **JM Studio Inc** ....F.... 646 546-5514
New York *(G-10782)*
Jmk Enterprises LLC ....G.... 845 634-8100
New City *(G-8833)*
John Kristiansen New York Inc ....F.... 212 388-1097
New York *(G-10789)*
Jolibe Atelier LLC ....F.... 347 882-6617
New York *(G-10795)*
Jonathan Meizler LLC ....G.... 212 213-2977
New York *(G-10797)*
▲ **Joseph Industries Inc** ....G.... 212 764-0010
New York *(G-10804)*
▲ **Kidz Concepts LLC** ....D.... 212 398-1110
New York *(G-10882)*
Kiton Building Corp ....E.... 212 486-3224
New York *(G-10893)*
Koon Enterprises LLC ....G.... 718 886-3163
Fresh Meadows *(G-5456)*
Kww Productions Corp ....F.... 212 398-8181
New York *(G-10935)*
▲ **Lakeland Industries Inc** ....C.... 631 981-9700
Ronkonkoma *(G-14956)*
▲ **Lakeview Innovations Inc** ....F.... 212 502-6702
New York *(G-10956)*
Linder New York LLC ....F.... 646 678-5819
New York *(G-11029)*
▲ **Lr Paris LLC** ....G.... 703 652-1132
New York *(G-11084)*
M2 Fashion Group Holdings Inc ....G.... 917 208-2948
New York *(G-11108)*
▲ **Meryl Diamond Ltd** ....D.... 212 730-0333
New York *(G-11262)*
Moresca Clothing and Costume ....F.... 845 331-6012
Ulster Park *(G-16309)*
My Hanky Inc ....F.... 646 321-0869
Brooklyn *(G-2350)*
▲ **New York Accessory Group Inc** ....E.... 212 532-7911
New York *(G-11416)*
New York Hospital Disposable ....E.... 718 384-1620
Brooklyn *(G-2373)*
▲ **New York Popular Inc** ....D.... 718 499-2020
Brooklyn *(G-2376)*
Nmny Group LLC ....E.... 212 944-6500
New York *(G-11462)*
NY 1 Art Gallery Inc ....G.... 917 698-0626
New Hyde Park *(G-8898)*
▲ **NY Orthopedic Usa Inc** ....D.... 718 852-5330
Brooklyn *(G-2393)*
Parsons-Meares Ltd ....D.... 212 242-3378
Long Island City *(G-7866)*
Patient-Wear LLC ....G.... 914 740-7770
Bronx *(G-1423)*
◆ **Perry Ellis Menswear LLC** ....C.... 212 221-7500
New York *(G-11643)*
▲ **Ppr Direct Marketing LLC** ....G.... 718 965-8600
Brooklyn *(G-2447)*
▲ **Prolink Industries Inc** ....F.... 212 354-5690
New York *(G-11752)*
RA Newhouse Inc ....D.... 516 248-6670
Mineola *(G-8565)*
▲ **Rainforest Apparel LLC** ....G.... 212 840-0880
New York *(G-11817)*
Randa Accessories Lea Gds LLC ....D.... 212 354-5100
New York *(G-11825)*
Ribz LLC ....G.... 212 764-9595
New York *(G-11887)*
▲ **Rjm2 Ltd** ....G.... 212 944-1660
New York *(G-11906)*
Robert Miller Associates LLC ....F.... 718 392-1640
Long Island City *(G-7892)*
▲ **Rose Solomon Co** ....E.... 718 855-1788
Brooklyn *(G-2527)*
▲ **Rosetti Handbags and ACC** ....E.... 212 273-3765
New York *(G-11939)*
▲ **Roth Clothing Co Inc** ....G.... 718 384-4927
Brooklyn *(G-2528)*
◆ **Rubies Costume Company Inc** ....B.... 718 846-1008
Richmond Hill *(G-14093)*
Rubies Costume Company Inc ....D.... 631 777-3300
Bay Shore *(G-736)*
Rubies Costume Company Inc ....C.... 718 441-0834
Richmond Hill *(G-14094)*
Rubies Costume Company Inc ....C.... 631 951-3688
Bay Shore *(G-737)*
Rubies Costume Company Inc ....E.... 516 326-1500
Melville *(G-8382)*
Rubies Costume Company Inc ....C.... 718 846-1008
Richmond Hill *(G-14095)*
Rubies Masquerade Company LLC ....G.... 718 846-1008
Richmond Hill *(G-14096)*
▲ **S & B Fashion Inc** ....G.... 718 482-1386
Long Island City *(G-7898)*
Schneeman Studio Limited ....G.... 212 244-3330
New York *(G-12008)*
▲ **Shamron Mills Ltd** ....G.... 212 354-0430
New York *(G-12062)*
South Central Boyz ....G.... 718 496-7270
Brooklyn *(G-2611)*
▲ **Swank Inc** ....B.... 212 867-2600
New York *(G-12270)*
▲ **Timeless Fashions LLC** ....G.... 212 730-9328
New York *(G-12370)*
Tr Apparel LLC ....E.... 310 595-4337
New York *(G-12406)*
Tr Apparel LLC ....G.... 646 358-3888
New York *(G-12407)*
▲ **Trafalgar Company LLC** ....G.... 212 768-8800
New York *(G-12411)*
Trash and Vaudeville Inc ....G.... 212 777-1727
New York *(G-12415)*
Twcc Product and Sales ....E.... 212 614-9364
New York *(G-12450)*
▲ **Ufo Contemporary Inc** ....F.... 212 226-5400
New York *(G-12461)*
Unified Inc led ....F.... 646 370-4650
New York *(G-12470)*
Warner ....G.... 716 446-0663
Buffalo *(G-3274)*
Westchester Wine Warehouse LLC ....F.... 914 824-1400
White Plains *(G-17213)*
Zam Barrett Dialogue Inc ....G.... 646 649-0140
Brooklyn *(G-2793)*

2391 Curtains & Draperies

Abalene Decorating Services ....E.... 718 782-2000
New York *(G-9046)*
Anthony Lawrence of New York ....E.... 212 206-8820
Long Island City *(G-7694)*
Associated Drapery & Equipment ....F.... 516 671-5245
Monroe *(G-8583)*
◆ **Baby Signature Inc** ....G.... 212 686-1700
New York *(G-9351)*
◆ **Belle Maison USA Ltd** ....E.... 718 805-0200
Richmond Hill *(G-14081)*
Bettertex Inc ....F.... 212 431-3373
New York *(G-9426)*
◆ **Bramson House Inc** ....C.... 516 764-5006
Freeport *(G-5400)*
C & G of Kingston Inc ....D.... 845 331-0148
Kingston *(G-7209)*
Cabriole Designs Inc ....G.... 212 593-4528
New York *(G-9545)*
◆ **County Draperies Inc** ....E.... 845 342-9009
Middletown *(G-8467)*
Deangelis Ltd ....E.... 212 348-8225
Glen Head *(G-5645)*
▼ **Decorative Novelty Co Inc** ....F.... 718 965-8600
Brooklyn *(G-1848)*
Delta Upholsterers Inc ....E.... 212 489-3308
New York *(G-9896)*
Drapery Industries Inc ....F.... 585 232-2992
Rochester *(G-14338)*
Fabric Quilters Unlimited Inc ....E.... 516 333-2866
Westbury *(G-17011)*
Henry B Urban Inc ....E.... 212 489-3308
New York *(G-10500)*
▲ **J Edlin Interiors Ltd** ....F.... 212 243-2111
New York *(G-10718)*
Jo-Vin Decorators Inc ....E.... 718 441-9350
Woodhaven *(G-17324)*
Laminated Window Products Inc ....F.... 631 242-6883
Bay Shore *(G-708)*
▼ **Laregence Inc** ....E.... 212 736-2548
New York *(G-10964)*
◆ **Louis Hornick & Co Inc** ....G.... 212 679-2448
New York *(G-11077)*
Majestic Curtains LLC ....G.... 718 898-0774
Elmhurst *(G-4678)*
▼ **Mason Contract Products LLC** ....D.... 516 328-6900
New Hyde Park *(G-8894)*
McCarroll Uphl Designs LLC ....G.... 518 828-0500
Hudson *(G-6655)*
▲ **Mistdoda Inc** ....E.... 919 735-7111
New York *(G-11309)*
▲ **Mutual Sales Corp** ....E.... 718 361-8373
Long Island City *(G-7848)*
Northast Coml Win Trtments Inc ....D.... 845 331-0148
Kingston *(G-7232)*
◆ **Revman International Inc** ....E.... 212 894-3100
New York *(G-11880)*
Reynolds Drapery Service Inc ....F.... 315 845-8632
Newport *(G-12816)*
▲ **Richloom Fabrics Corp** ....F.... 212 685-5400
New York *(G-11894)*
▲ **Richloom Fabrics Group Inc** ....F.... 212 685-5400
New York *(G-11895)*
▲ **Richloom Home Fashions Corp** ....F.... 212 685-5400
New York *(G-11896)*
▲ **Royal Home Fashions Inc** ....G.... 212 689-7222
New York *(G-11942)*
Seaway Mats Inc ....G.... 518 483-2560
Malone *(G-8047)*
Showeray Co ....D.... 718 965-3633
Brooklyn *(G-2578)*
Shyam Ahuja Limited ....G.... 212 644-5910
New York *(G-12080)*
Terbo Ltd ....G.... 718 847-2860
Richmond Hill *(G-14099)*
Wayne Decorators Inc ....G.... 718 529-4200
Jamaica *(G-6999)*
Wcd Window Coverings Inc ....E.... 845 336-4511
Lake Katrine *(G-7295)*
White Plains Drapery Uphl Inc ....E.... 914 381-0908
Mamaroneck *(G-8083)*
White Workroom Inc ....G.... 212 941-5910
New York *(G-12654)*

2392 House furnishings: Textile

AEP Environmental LLC ....F.... 716 446-0739
Buffalo *(G-2818)*
▲ **Alen Sands York Associates Ltd** ....F.... 212 563-6305
New York *(G-9130)*
Alexandra Ferguson LLC ....G.... 718 788-7768
Brooklyn *(G-1580)*
▲ **Anhui Skyworth LLC** ....D.... 917 940-6903
Hempstead *(G-6288)*
▲ **Ann Gish Inc** ....G.... 212 969-9200
New York *(G-9213)*
Apex Real Holdings Inc ....G.... 877 725-2150
Brooklyn *(G-1616)*
▲ **Area Inc** ....G.... 212 924-7084
New York *(G-9249)*
▲ **Arlee Home Fashions Inc** ....D.... 212 689-0020
New York *(G-9253)*
▲ **August Silk Inc** ....E.... 212 643-2400
New York *(G-9315)*
August Silk Inc ....G.... 212 643-2400
New York *(G-9316)*
◆ **Baby Signature Inc** ....G.... 212 686-1700
New York *(G-9351)*
▲ **Bardwil Industries Inc** ....E.... 212 944-1870
New York *(G-9369)*
◆ **Belle Maison USA Ltd** ....E.... 718 805-0200
Richmond Hill *(G-14081)*
Benson Sales Co Inc ....F.... 718 236-6743
Brooklyn *(G-1683)*
◆ **Bramson House Inc** ....C.... 516 764-5006
Freeport *(G-5400)*
▲ **Broder Mfg Inc** ....G.... 718 366-1667
Brooklyn *(G-1717)*
C & G of Kingston Inc ....D.... 845 331-0148
Kingston *(G-7209)*

SIC SECTION 23 APPAREL AND OTHER FINISHED PRODUCTS MADE FROM FABRICS AND SIMILAR MATERIAL

▲ **Caddy Concepts Inc** ....F 516 570-6279
Great Neck *(G-5812)*
▲ **Catalina Products Corp** ....E 718 336-8288
Brooklyn *(G-1766)*
▲ **Cathay Home Inc** ....E 212 213-0988
New York *(G-9602)*
▲ **Continental Quilting Co Inc** ....E 718 499-9100
New Hyde Park *(G-8869)*
◆ **County Draperies Inc** ....E 845 342-9009
Middletown *(G-8467)*
▼ **Cpac Inc** ....E 585 382-3223
Leicester *(G-7442)*
▲ **Creative Home Furnishings** ....G 631 582-8000
Central Islip *(G-3517)*
Creative Scents USA Inc ....G 718 522-5901
Brooklyn *(G-1814)*
▲ **Dico Products Corporation** ....F 315 797-0470
Utica *(G-16346)*
Elegant Linen Inc ....G 718 492-0297
Brooklyn *(G-1915)*
▲ **Elegant Linen Inc** ....E 718 871-3535
Brooklyn *(G-1916)*
Ess Bee Industries Inc ....E 718 894-5202
Brooklyn *(G-1942)*
▲ **Excellent Art Mfg Corp** ....F 718 388-7075
Inwood *(G-6795)*
EY Industries Inc ....F 718 624-9122
Brooklyn *(G-1952)*
Fabric Quilters Unlimited Inc ....E 516 333-2866
Westbury *(G-17011)*
Franks Cushions Inc ....F 718 848-1216
Maspeth *(G-8172)*
G Fried Carpet Service ....E 516 333-3900
Westbury *(G-17016)*
▲ **Geneva Home Fashion LLC** ....F 212 213-8323
New York *(G-10319)*
▲ **Handy Laundry Products Corp** ....G 800 263-5973
Airmont *(G-13)*
Henry B Urban Inc ....E 212 489-3308
New York *(G-10500)*
▲ **Himatsingka America Inc** ....E 212 545-8929
New York *(G-10523)*
Hollander HM Fshons Hldngs LLC ....F 212 575-0400
New York *(G-10541)*
Hollander Sleep Products LLC ....D 212 575-0400
New York *(G-10542)*
Home Fashions Intl LLC ....E 212 689-3579
New York *(G-10544)*
Home Fashions Intl LLC ....F 212 684-0091
New York *(G-10545)*
◆ **Indigo Home Inc** ....G 212 684-4146
New York *(G-10632)*
▲ **Ingenious Designs LLC** ....C 631 254-3376
Ronkonkoma *(G-14941)*
Jdt International LLC ....G 212 400-7570
New York *(G-10753)*
Jo-Vin Decorators Inc ....E 718 441-9350
Woodhaven *(G-17324)*
▲ **Josie Accessories Inc** ....D 212 889-6376
New York *(G-10807)*
▲ **Kaltex North America Inc** ....F 212 894-3200
New York *(G-10843)*
▲ **Kartell Us Inc** ....G 212 966-6665
New York *(G-10848)*
▲ **Kim Seybert Inc** ....F 212 564-7850
New York *(G-10885)*
◆ **Madison Industries Inc** ....F 212 679-5110
New York *(G-11121)*
McCarroll Uphl Designs LLC ....G 518 828-0500
Hudson *(G-6655)*
Medline Industries Inc ....B 845 344-3301
Middletown *(G-8484)*
Mgk Group Inc ....E 212 989-2732
New York *(G-11273)*
Michael Stuart Inc ....E 718 821-0704
Brooklyn *(G-2314)*
MMS H& F Inc ....G 718 785-6663
Jamaica *(G-6969)*
▲ **National Wire & Metal Tech Inc** ....E 716 661-9180
Jamestown *(G-7054)*
▲ **Nationwide Tarps Incorporated** ....D 518 843-1545
Amsterdam *(G-362)*
Nbets Corporation ....G 516 785-1259
Wantagh *(G-16582)*
◆ **Northpoint Trading Inc** ....F 212 481-8001
New York *(G-11478)*
Paramount Textiles Inc ....F 212 966-1040
New York *(G-11583)*
▲ **Perfex Corporation** ....F 315 826-3600
Poland *(G-13757)*
Performance Sourcing Group Inc ....E 914 636-2100
Scarsdale *(G-15251)*
▲ **Place Vendome Holding Co Inc** ....C 212 696-0765
New York *(G-11693)*
Premier Skirting Products Inc ....F 516 239-6581
Lawrence *(G-7422)*
Prime Feather Industries Ltd ....F 718 326-8701
Suffern *(G-15818)*
▲ **Q Squared Design LLC** ....E 212 686-8860
New York *(G-11788)*
▲ **R & M Industries Inc** ....F 212 366-6414
New York *(G-11807)*
Repellem Consumer Pdts Corp ....F 631 273-3992
Bohemia *(G-1122)*
◆ **Revman International Inc** ....E 212 894-3100
New York *(G-11880)*
▲ **Richloom Corp** ....F 212 685-5400
New York *(G-11893)*
▲ **Richloom Fabrics Corp** ....F 212 685-5400
New York *(G-11894)*
▲ **Richloom Fabrics Group Inc** ....F 212 685-5400
New York *(G-11895)*
▲ **Royal Copenhagen Inc** ....F 845 454-4442
Poughkeepsie *(G-13947)*
▲ **Royal Home Fashions Inc** ....G 212 689-7222
New York *(G-11942)*
Showeray Co ....D 718 965-3633
Brooklyn *(G-2578)*
▲ **Silly Phillie Creations Inc** ....E 718 492-6300
Brooklyn *(G-2583)*
▲ **Skil-Care Corporation** ....C 914 963-2040
Yonkers *(G-17502)*
Sleepable Sofas Ltd ....D 973 546-4502
New York *(G-12125)*
▲ **Sleeping Partners Intl Inc** ....F 212 254-1515
Brooklyn *(G-2596)*
▲ **Soft-Tex International Inc** ....D 800 366-2324
Waterford *(G-16642)*
◆ **Sunham Home Fashions LLC** ....D 212 695-1218
New York *(G-12258)*
Superior Decorators Inc ....F 718 381-4793
Glendale *(G-5680)*
Sure Fit Inc ....E 212 395-9340
New York *(G-12266)*
Tablecloths For Granted Ltd ....F 518 370-5481
Schenectady *(G-15326)*
Terbo Ltd ....G 718 847-2860
Richmond Hill *(G-14099)*
▲ **Thor Marketing Corp** ....G 201 247-7103
Valley Cottage *(G-16419)*
▲ **University Table Cloth Company** ....F 845 371-3876
Spring Valley *(G-15627)*
Wayne Decorators Inc ....G 718 529-4200
Jamaica *(G-6999)*
William Harvey Studio Inc ....G 718 599-4343
Brooklyn *(G-2769)*

2393 Textile Bags

▲ **Ace Drop Cloth Canvas Pdts Inc** ....E 718 731-1550
Bronx *(G-1261)*
Advanced Medical Mfg Corp ....E 845 369-7535
Suffern *(G-15806)*
▲ **Aka Sport Inc** ....F 631 858-9888
Dix Hills *(G-4312)*
Carry Hot Inc ....F 212 279-7535
New York *(G-9590)*
Clear Edge Crosible Inc ....D 315 685-3466
Skaneateles Falls *(G-15489)*
GPM Associates LLC ....G 585 359-1770
Rush *(G-15074)*
GPM Associates LLC ....E 585 335-3940
Dansville *(G-4103)*
▲ **H G Maybeck Co Inc** ....E 718 297-4410
Jamaica *(G-6954)*
▲ **Health Matters America Inc** ....F 716 235-8772
Buffalo *(G-3009)*
◆ **Ivi Services Inc** ....D 607 729-5111
Binghamton *(G-924)*
▲ **Jag Manufacturing Inc** ....E 518 762-9558
Johnstown *(G-7147)*
Jakes Sneakers Inc ....G 718 233-1132
Brooklyn *(G-2133)*
Johnson Outdoors Inc ....C 607 779-2200
Binghamton *(G-926)*
Kragel Co Inc ....G 716 648-1344
Hamburg *(G-5955)*
▲ **Kush Oasis Enterprises LLC** ....G 516 513-1316
Syosset *(G-15847)*
Mgk Group Inc ....E 212 989-2732
New York *(G-11273)*
Paulpac LLC ....G 631 283-7610
Southampton *(G-15572)*
Redco Foods Inc ....D 315 823-1300
Little Falls *(G-7525)*
Reflective Shopper Usa LLC ....G 855 735-3222
West Nyack *(G-16955)*
▼ **Select Fabricators Inc** ....F 585 393-0650
Canandaigua *(G-3387)*
Wayne Decorators Inc ....G 718 529-4200
Jamaica *(G-6999)*

2394 Canvas Prdts

125-127 Main Street Corp ....F 631 477-1500
Greenport *(G-5894)*
Abble Awning Co Inc ....G 516 822-1200
Bethpage *(G-861)*
▲ **Ace Canvas & Tent Corp** ....F 631 648-0614
Ronkonkoma *(G-14876)*
▲ **Ace Drop Cloth Canvas Pdts Inc** ....E 718 731-1550
Bronx *(G-1261)*
Acme Awning Co Inc ....F 718 409-1881
Bronx *(G-1263)*
▼ **Air Structures Amercn Tech Inc** ....E 914 937-4500
Port Chester *(G-13765)*
Allen Boat Co Inc ....G 716 842-0800
Buffalo *(G-2819)*
Anchor Canvas LLC ....G 631 265-5602
Smithtown *(G-15505)*
Automtive Uphl Cnvertible Tops ....G 914 961-4242
Tuckahoe *(G-16293)*
Awning Mart Inc ....G 315 699-5928
Cicero *(G-3671)*
Awnings Plus Inc ....F 716 693-3690
Tonawanda *(G-16163)*
Breton Industries Inc ....D 518 842-3030
Amsterdam *(G-337)*
Broadway Neon Sign Corp ....F 908 241-4177
Ronkonkoma *(G-14910)*
Brock Awnings Ltd ....F 631 765-5200
Hampton Bays *(G-5982)*
C E King & Sons Inc ....G 631 324-4944
East Hampton *(G-4426)*
Canvas Products Company Inc ....F 516 742-1058
Mineola *(G-8533)*
Capitol Awning Co Inc ....F 212 505-1717
Jamaica *(G-6936)*
Classic Awnings Inc ....F 716 649-0390
Hamburg *(G-5943)*
▲ **Covergrip Corporation** ....G 855 268-3747
Bohemia *(G-1037)*
▲ **Custom Canvas Manufacturing Co** ....E 716 852-6372
Buffalo *(G-2917)*
▲ **Custom European Imports Inc** ....E 845 357-5718
Sloatsburg *(G-15502)*
▲ **Dhs Systems LLC** ....F 845 359-6066
Orangeburg *(G-13246)*
Di Sanos Creative Canvas Inc ....G 315 894-3137
Frankfort *(G-5360)*
Dor-A-Mar Canvas Products Co ....F 631 750-9202
West Sayville *(G-16963)*
Doyle-Hild Sailmakers ....G 718 885-2255
Bronx *(G-1320)*
◆ **Durasol Systems Inc** ....D 845 610-1100
Chester *(G-3632)*
Fabric Concepts For Industry ....F 914 375-2565
Yonkers *(G-17458)*
▲ **Jag Manufacturing Inc** ....E 518 762-9558
Johnstown *(G-7147)*
Jamestown Awning Inc ....G 716 483-1435
Jamestown *(G-7038)*
Jo-Vin Decorators Inc ....E 718 441-9350
Woodhaven *(G-17324)*
Johnson Outdoors Inc ....C 607 779-2200
Binghamton *(G-926)*
Kingston Building Products LLC ....G 914 665-0707
Mount Vernon *(G-8744)*
Kohler Awning Inc ....E 716 685-3333
Buffalo *(G-3054)*
Kragel Co Inc ....G 716 648-1344
Hamburg *(G-5955)*
Kraus & Sons Inc ....F 212 620-0408
New York *(G-10926)*
Laminated Window Products Inc ....F 631 242-6883
Bay Shore *(G-708)*
Lanza Corp ....G 914 937-6360
Port Chester *(G-13778)*
▲ **Leiter Sukkahs Inc** ....G 718 436-0303
Brooklyn *(G-2210)*
M & M Canvas & Awnings Inc ....G 631 424-5370
Islandia *(G-6838)*

S I C

Employee Codes: A=Over 500 employees, B=251-500
C=101-250, D=51-100, E=20-50, F=10-19, G=5-9

2018 Harris
New York Manufacturers Directory

735

Mauceri Sign Inc ....F 718 656-7700
Jamaica *(G-6965)*
Mc Coy Tops and Interiors Inc ....G 718 458-5800
Woodside *(G-17353)*
▼ **Melbourne C Fisher Yacht Sails** ....G 631 673-5055
Huntington Station *(G-6753)*
▼ **Meyco Products Inc** ....E 631 421-9800
Melville *(G-8366)*
▲ **Nationwide Tarps Incorporated** ....D 518 843-1545
Amsterdam *(G-362)*
Northern Awning & Sign Company ....G 315 782-8515
Watertown *(G-16690)*
Perma Tech Inc ....E 716 854-0707
Buffalo *(G-3145)*
Point Canvas Company Inc ....G 607 692-4381
Whitney Point *(G-17249)*
Quantum Sails Rochester LLC ....G 585 342-5200
Rochester *(G-14640)*
Sausbiers Awning Shop Inc ....G 518 828-3748
Hudson *(G-6664)*
▼ **Select Fabricators Inc** ....F 585 393-0650
Canandaigua *(G-3387)*
Service Canvas Co Inc ....F 716 853-0558
Buffalo *(G-3211)*
Steinway Awning II LLC ....G 718 729-2965
Astoria *(G-458)*
TG Peppe Inc ....G 516 239-7852
Lawrence *(G-7426)*
Toptec Products LLC ....F 631 421-9800
Melville *(G-8391)*
Ulmer Sales LLC ....F 718 885-1700
Bronx *(G-1483)*
Utility Canvas Inc ....G 845 255-9290
Gardiner *(G-5565)*
Vinyl Works Inc ....E 518 786-1200
Latham *(G-7410)*
▲ **Y & A Trading Inc** ....F 718 436-6333
Brooklyn *(G-2785)*

2395 Pleating & Stitching For The Trade

A Garys Treasures ....F 518 383-1171
Clifton Park *(G-3719)*
A Trusted Name Inc ....F 716 326-7400
Westfield *(G-17074)*
▲ **Active World Solutions Inc** ....G 718 922-9404
Brooklyn *(G-1558)*
Aditiany Inc ....G 212 997-8440
New York *(G-9076)*
All About Art Inc ....F 718 321-0755
Flushing *(G-5232)*
All American Awards Inc ....F 631 567-2025
Bohemia *(G-1007)*
American Country Quilts & Lin ....G 631 283-5466
Southampton *(G-15562)*
American Quality Embroidery ....G 631 467-3200
Ronkonkoma *(G-14895)*
Arena Graphics Inc ....G 516 767-5108
Port Washington *(G-13823)*
Athletic Cap Co Inc ....E 718 398-1300
Staten Island *(G-15661)*
Clinton Clrs & EMB Shoppe Inc ....G 315 853-8421
Clinton *(G-3743)*
Clpa Embroidery ....G 516 409-0002
Bellmore *(G-812)*
Control Research Inc ....G 631 225-1111
Amityville *(G-281)*
Custom Patches Inc ....E 845 679-6320
Woodstock *(G-17378)*
Design Archives Inc ....G 212 768-0617
New York *(G-9904)*
Dirt T Shirts Inc ....E 845 336-4230
Kingston *(G-7216)*
▲ **Eagle Regalia Co Inc** ....F 845 425-2245
Spring Valley *(G-15604)*
East Coast Embroidery Ltd ....G 631 254-3878
Deer Park *(G-4155)*
Eiseman-Ludmar Co Inc ....F 516 932-6990
Hicksville *(G-6372)*
Expressions Punching & Digitiz ....G 718 291-1177
Jamaica *(G-6947)*
F X Graphix Inc ....G 716 871-1511
Buffalo *(G-2957)*
Glenda Inc ....G 718 442-8981
Staten Island *(G-15699)*
▲ **Holland & Sherry Inc** ....E 212 542-8410
New York *(G-10540)*
Hosel & Ackerson Inc ....G 212 575-1490
New York *(G-10552)*
Human Technologies Corporation ....F 315 735-3532
Utica *(G-16364)*

Instant Monogramming Inc ....G 585 654-5550
Rochester *(G-14471)*
▲ **Jomar Industries Inc** ....E 845 357-5773
Airmont *(G-14)*
Kabrics ....G 607 962-6344
Corning *(G-3996)*
Karishma Fashions Inc ....G 718 565-5404
Jackson Heights *(G-6923)*
Kevin J Kassman ....G 585 529-4245
Rochester *(G-14491)*
Knucklehead Embroidery Inc ....G 607 797-2725
Johnson City *(G-7129)*
Loremanss Embroidery Engrav ....F 518 834-9205
Keeseville *(G-7168)*
Mainly Monograms Inc ....E 845 624-4923
West Nyack *(G-16949)*
Milaaya Inc ....G 212 764-6386
New York *(G-11291)*
Monte Goldman Embroidery Co ....F 212 874-5397
New York *(G-11327)*
Mrinalini Inc ....G 646 510-2747
New York *(G-11339)*
Northeast Stitches & Ink Inc ....E 518 798-5549
South Glens Falls *(G-15551)*
▲ **NY Embroidery Inc** ....E 516 822-6456
Hicksville *(G-6403)*
On The Job Embroidery & AP ....G 914 381-3556
Mamaroneck *(G-8073)*
Pass Em-Entries Inc ....F 718 392-0100
Long Island City *(G-7867)*
Penn & Fletcher Inc ....F 212 239-6868
Long Island City *(G-7870)*
Pink Inc ....E 212 352-8282
New York *(G-11685)*
Planet Embroidery ....F 718 381-4827
Ridgewood *(G-14130)*
Point Canvas Company Inc ....G 607 692-4381
Whitney Point *(G-17249)*
Quist Industries Ltd ....F 718 243-2800
Brooklyn *(G-2487)*
Rescuestuff Inc ....G 718 318-7570
Peekskill *(G-13505)*
River Rat Design ....F 315 393-4770
Ogdensburg *(G-13142)*
Ross L Sports Screening Inc ....F 716 824-5350
Buffalo *(G-3195)*
Round Top Knit & Screening ....G 518 622-3600
Round Top *(G-15064)*
Royal Tees Inc ....G 845 357-9448
Suffern *(G-15820)*
Sand Hill Industries Inc ....G 518 885-7991
Ballston Spa *(G-607)*
Sciane Enterprises Inc ....G 845 452-2400
Poughkeepsie *(G-13949)*
Screen Gems Inc ....G 845 561-0036
New Windsor *(G-8999)*
Screen The World Inc ....F 631 475-0023
Holtsville *(G-6534)*
Shykat Promotions ....G 866 574-2757
Forestville *(G-5343)*
Stanley Pleating Stitching Co ....E 718 392-2417
Long Island City *(G-7914)*
Stephen M Kiernan ....E 716 836-6300
Buffalo *(G-3224)*
Stucki Embroidery Works Inc ....F 845 657-2308
Boiceville *(G-1155)*
Stylist Pleating Corp ....F 718 384-8181
Brooklyn *(G-2639)*
Todd Walbridge ....G 585 254-3018
Rochester *(G-14755)*
U All Inc ....E 518 438-2558
Albany *(G-144)*
▲ **U S Embroidery Inc** ....F 718 585-9662
Bronx *(G-1482)*
Uniform Namemakers Inc ....F 716 626-5474
Buffalo *(G-3259)*
Verdonette Inc ....G 212 719-2003
New York *(G-12545)*
Vogue Too Plting Stitching EMB ....F 212 354-1022
New York *(G-12591)*
Voyager Emblems Inc ....C 416 255-3421
Buffalo *(G-3271)*
Wicked Smart LLC ....F 518 459-2855
Watervliet *(G-16717)*

2396 Automotive Trimmings, Apparel Findings, Related Prdts

Acorn Products Corp ....F 315 894-4868
Ilion *(G-6778)*

Albert Siy ....G 718 359-0389
Flushing *(G-5231)*
American Spray-On Corp ....E 212 929-2100
New York *(G-9179)*
▲ **Amoseastern Apparel Inc** ....F 212 921-1859
New York *(G-9189)*
Angel Textiles Inc ....G 212 532-0900
New York *(G-9205)*
▲ **Apple Imprints Apparel Inc** ....E 716 893-1130
Buffalo *(G-2836)*
▲ **Apsco Sports Enterprises Inc** ....D 718 965-9500
Brooklyn *(G-1622)*
Aro-Graph Corporation ....G 315 463-8693
Syracuse *(G-15877)*
Art Flag Company Inc ....F 212 334-1890
New York *(G-9259)*
▲ **Artistic Ribbon Novelty Co Inc** ....E 212 255-4224
New York *(G-9271)*
Athletic Cap Co Inc ....E 718 398-1300
Staten Island *(G-15661)*
Barnaby Prints Inc ....F 845 477-2501
Greenwood Lake *(G-5917)*
Bondy Printing Corp ....G 631 242-1510
Bay Shore *(G-677)*
Bpe Studio Inc ....G 212 868-9896
New York *(G-9500)*
C H Thompson Company Inc ....D 607 724-1094
Binghamton *(G-897)*
◆ **Cai Inc** ....E 212 819-0008
New York *(G-9547)*
Casual Friday Inc ....F 585 544-9470
Rochester *(G-14282)*
Coe Displays Inc ....G 718 937-5658
Long Island City *(G-7730)*
Cooper & Clement Inc ....E 315 454-8135
Syracuse *(G-15926)*
Creative Images & Applique ....D 718 821-8700
Maspeth *(G-8157)*
D & R Silk Screening Ltd ....F 631 234-7464
Central Islip *(G-3520)*
Decal Makers Inc ....E 516 221-7200
Bellmore *(G-813)*
Dirt T Shirts Inc ....E 845 336-4230
Kingston *(G-7216)*
Eagle Finishing ....E 718 497-7875
Brooklyn *(G-1897)*
Eagle Lace Dyeing Corp ....F 212 947-2712
New York *(G-10010)*
▲ **Empire Bias Binding Co Inc** ....F 718 545-0300
Long Island City *(G-7759)*
Emtron Hybrids Inc ....E 631 924-9668
Yaphank *(G-17408)*
Flp Group LLC ....F 315 252-7583
Auburn *(G-495)*
▲ **Freeport Screen & Stamping** ....E 516 379-0330
Freeport *(G-5412)*
Galli Shirts and Sports AP ....G 845 226-7305
Stormville *(G-15801)*
Hollywood Advertising Banners ....E 631 842-3000
Copiague *(G-3932)*
Human Technologies Corporation ....F 315 735-3532
Utica *(G-16364)*
Ihd Motorsports LLC ....F 979 690-1669
Binghamton *(G-920)*
Irene Cerone ....G 315 668-2899
Brewerton *(G-1201)*
J M L Productions Inc ....D 718 643-1674
Brooklyn *(G-2125)*
Jack J Florio Jr ....G 716 434-9123
Lockport *(G-7625)*
Kenmar Shirts Inc ....E 718 824-3880
Bronx *(G-1375)*
Kevin J Kassman ....G 585 529-4245
Rochester *(G-14491)*
L I C Screen Printing Inc ....E 516 546-7289
Merrick *(G-8421)*
▲ **Legendary Auto Interiors Ltd** ....E 315 331-1212
Newark *(G-12754)*
Lending Trimming Co Inc ....D 212 242-7502
New York *(G-10999)*
Loremanss Embroidery Engrav ....F 518 834-9205
Keeseville *(G-7168)*
Mart-Tex Athletics Inc ....E 631 454-9583
Farmingdale *(G-5052)*
Mas Cutting Inc ....G 212 869-0826
New York *(G-11196)*
Master Craft Finishers Inc ....E 631 586-0540
Deer Park *(G-4195)*
Master Image Printing Inc ....G 914 347-4400
Elmsford *(G-4772)*

Mountain T-Shirts Inc ....G....... 518 943-4533
Catskill (G-3460)
New York Binding Co Inc ....E....... 718 729-2454
Long Island City (G-7857)
Northeast Stitches & Ink Inc ....E....... 518 798-5549
South Glens Falls (G-15551)
▲ Pangea Brands LLC ....G....... 617 638-0001
New York (G-11573)
Pangea Brands LLC ....G....... 617 638-0001
New York (G-11574)
Park Avenue Imprints LLC ....G....... 716 822-5737
Buffalo (G-3136)
Patrick Rohan ....G....... 718 781-2573
Monticello (G-8646)
Paula Varsalona Ltd ....F....... 212 570-9100
New York (G-11601)
▲ Perfect Shoulder Company Inc ....E....... 914 699-8100
Mount Vernon (G-8761)
▲ Phoenix Ribbon Co Inc ....G....... 212 239-0155
New York (G-11670)
Polkadot Usa Inc ....G....... 914 835-3697
Mamaroneck (G-8076)
Printz and Patternz LLC ....G....... 518 944-6020
Schenectady (G-15311)
Rainbow Lettering ....G....... 607 732-5751
Elmira (G-4713)
Randy Sixberry ....G....... 315 265-6211
Potsdam (G-13901)
Round Top Knit & Screening ....G....... 518 622-3600
Round Top (G-15064)
Sellco Industries Inc ....E....... 607 756-7594
Cortland (G-4068)
◆ Simplicity Creative Group Inc ....A....... 212 686-7676
New York (G-12105)
Solidus Industries Inc ....D....... 607 749-4540
Homer (G-6550)
Special Tees ....E....... 718 980-0987
Staten Island (G-15758)
Starline Usa Inc ....C....... 716 773-0100
Grand Island (G-5785)
Todd Walbridge ....G....... 585 254-3018
Rochester (G-14755)
U All Inc ....E....... 518 438-2558
Albany (G-144)
Viewsport International Inc ....G....... 585 259-1562
Penfield (G-13528)
Wicked Smart LLC ....F....... 518 459-2855
Watervliet (G-16717)
Zan Optics Products Inc ....E....... 718 435-0533
Brooklyn (G-2794)

2397 Schiffli Machine Embroideries

American Images Inc ....F....... 716 825-8888
Buffalo (G-2825)
Rmb Embroidery Service ....G....... 585 271-5560
Rochester (G-14652)

2399 Fabricated Textile Prdts, NEC

AAa Amercn Flag Dctg Co Inc ....G....... 212 279-3524
New York (G-9044)
Ace Banner & Flag Company ....F....... 212 620-9111
New York (G-9062)
▲ American Leather Specialties ....D....... 800 556-6488
Brooklyn (G-1601)
American Puff Corp ....D....... 516 379-1300
Freeport (G-5396)
Arista Flag Corporation ....F....... 845 246-7700
Saugerties (G-15209)
Art Flag Company Inc ....F....... 212 334-1890
New York (G-9259)
Automtive Uphl Cnvertible Tops ....G....... 914 961-4242
Tuckahoe (G-16293)
Baldwin Ribbon & Stamping Corp ....F....... 718 335-6700
Woodside (G-17336)
Becks Classic Mfg Inc ....D....... 631 435-3800
Brentwood (G-1175)
▲ Big Apple Sign Corp ....E....... 212 629-3650
New York (G-9441)
Big Apple Sign Corp ....E....... 631 342-0303
Islandia (G-6826)
Breton Industries Inc ....D....... 518 842-3030
Amsterdam (G-337)
▲ Caldeira USA Inc ....G....... 212 532-2292
New York (G-9550)
City Signs Inc ....G....... 718 375-5933
Brooklyn (G-1783)
Davis Restraint Systems Inc ....F....... 631 563-1500
Bohemia (G-1047)
Dkm Sales LLC ....E....... 716 893-7777
Buffalo (G-2932)
Dream Green Productions ....G....... 917 267-8920
Warwick (G-16611)
▲ Eagle Regalia Co Inc ....F....... 845 425-2245
Spring Valley (G-15604)
Hampton Transport Inc ....F....... 631 716-4445
Coram (G-3966)
▲ HMS Productions Inc ....D....... 212 719-9190
New York (G-10535)
Hollywood Banners Inc ....E....... 631 842-3000
Copiague (G-3933)
Jeans Inc ....G....... 646 223-1122
New York (G-10757)
K Pat Incorporated ....G....... 212 688-5728
New York (G-10830)
▲ Kamali Group Inc ....G....... 516 627-4000
Great Neck (G-5836)
Koring Bros Inc ....G....... 888 233-1292
New Rochelle (G-8961)
Kraus & Sons Inc ....F....... 212 620-0408
New York (G-10926)
Mama Luca Production Inc ....G....... 212 582-9700
New York (G-11148)
Mc Coy Tops and Interiors Inc ....G....... 718 458-5800
Woodside (G-17353)
▲ National Flag & Display Co Inc ....E....... 212 228-6600
New York (G-11371)
National Parachute Industries ....E....... 908 782-1646
Palenville (G-13423)
Osprey Boat ....G....... 631 331-4153
Mount Sinai (G-8698)
▲ Paragon Corporation ....F....... 516 484-6090
Port Washington (G-13872)
▲ Penthouse Manufacturing Co Inc ....B....... 516 379-1300
Freeport (G-5429)
▲ Radio Circle Realty Inc ....E....... 914 241-8742
Mount Kisco (G-8685)
Regal Emblem Co Inc ....F....... 212 925-8833
New York (G-11851)
Saratoga Horseworks Ltd ....E....... 518 843-6756
Amsterdam (G-368)
Sellco Industries Inc ....E....... 607 756-7594
Cortland (G-4068)
▲ Skd Tactical Inc ....G....... 845 897-2889
Highland Falls (G-6437)
Stonegate Stables ....G....... 518 746-7133
Fort Edward (G-5355)
▲ Triple E Manufacturing ....F....... 716 761-6996
Sherman (G-15425)
Valeo ....G....... 800 634-2704
Yonkers (G-17512)
Yoland Corporation ....E....... 718 499-4803
Brooklyn (G-2789)

24 LUMBER AND WOOD PRODUCTS, EXCEPT FURNITURE

2411 Logging

3b Timber Company Inc ....F....... 315 942-6580
Boonville (G-1158)
Attica Package Company Inc ....F....... 585 591-0510
Attica (G-471)
▼ B & B Forest Products Ltd ....F....... 518 622-0811
Cairo (G-3296)
Baker Logging & Firewood ....G....... 585 374-5733
Naples (G-8810)
Central Timber Co Inc ....G....... 518 638-6338
Granville (G-5789)
Chad Pierson ....G....... 518 251-0186
Bakers Mills (G-556)
Chip It All Ltd ....G....... 631 473-2040
Port Jefferson (G-13797)
Clearlake Land Co Inc ....F....... 315 848-2427
Star Lake (G-15648)
Couture Logging Inc ....G....... 607 753-6445
Cortland (G-4046)
Couture Timber Harvesting ....G....... 607 836-4719
Mc Graw (G-8252)
Dan Beers ....G....... 607 316-8895
Earlville (G-4384)
Daniel & Lois Lyndaker Logging ....G....... 315 346-6527
Castorland (G-3451)
Davis Logging & Lumber ....G....... 315 245-1040
Camden (G-3342)
Decker Forest Products Inc ....G....... 607 563-2345
Sidney (G-15460)
Donald Snyder Jr ....F....... 315 265-4485
Potsdam (G-13896)
Ed Beach Forest Management ....G....... 607 538-1745
Bloomville (G-988)
Finger Lakes Timber Co Inc ....G....... 585 346-2990
Livonia (G-7591)
Garland Logging LLC ....G....... 518 483-1170
Malone (G-8041)
George Chilson Logging ....G....... 607 732-1558
Elmira (G-4699)
GL & RL Logging Inc ....F....... 518 883-3936
Broadalbin (G-1241)
Got Wood LLC ....G....... 315 440-8857
Cleveland (G-3718)
Guldenschuh Logging & Lbr LLC ....G....... 585 538-4750
Caledonia (G-3307)
Harris Logging Inc ....E....... 518 792-1083
Queensbury (G-14011)
Homer Logging Contractor ....G....... 607 753-8553
Homer (G-6548)
J & S Logging Inc ....E....... 315 262-2112
South Colton (G-15537)
Kapstone Container Corporation ....D....... 518 842-2450
Amsterdam (G-352)
Kevin Regan Logging Ltd ....G....... 315 245-3890
Camden (G-3345)
Klein & Sons Logging Inc ....F....... 845 292-6682
Wht Sphr Spgs (G-17250)
Lizotte Logging Inc ....F....... 518 359-2200
Tupper Lake (G-16300)
Lyndaker Timber Harvesting LLC ....F....... 315 346-1328
Castorland (G-3452)
Matteson Logging Inc ....G....... 585 593-3037
Wellsville (G-16780)
Mountain Forest Products Inc ....G....... 518 597-3674
Crown Point (G-4093)
Murray Logging LLC ....G....... 518 834-7372
Keeseville (G-7169)
Northern Timber Harvesting LLC ....F....... 585 233-7330
Alfred Station (G-200)
Oak Valley Logging Inc ....G....... 518 622-8249
Cairo (G-3301)
Paul J Mitchell Logging Inc ....E....... 518 359-7029
Tupper Lake (G-16302)
Peters LLC ....G....... 607 637-5470
Hancock (G-5988)
Richard Bauer Logging ....G....... 585 343-4149
Alexander (G-193)
Richards Logging LLC ....F....... 518 359-2775
Tupper Lake (G-16303)
Robert W Butts Logging Co ....G....... 518 643-2897
Peru (G-13550)
Robert W Still ....F....... 315 942-5594
Ava (G-529)
Russell Bass ....F....... 607 637-5253
Hancock (G-5989)
Schaefer Logging Inc ....F....... 607 467-4990
Deposit (G-4304)
Seaway Timber Harvesting Inc ....D....... 315 769-5970
Massena (G-8231)
Smoothbore International Inc ....G....... 315 754-8124
Red Creek (G-14039)
Snyder Logging ....F....... 315 265-1462
Potsdam (G-13902)
Tim Cretin Logging & Sawmill ....F....... 315 946-4476
Lyons (G-8003)
Timothy L Simpson ....G....... 518 234-1401
Sharon Springs (G-15407)
Tonche Timber LLC ....G....... 845 389-3489
Amsterdam (G-370)
Van Cpeters Logging Inc ....G....... 607 637-3574
Hancock (G-5990)
Wadsworth Logging Inc ....F....... 518 863-6870
Gloversville (G-5742)
William Ward Logging ....F....... 518 946-7826
Jay (G-7089)

2421 Saw & Planing Mills

A D Bowman & Son Lumber Co ....E....... 607 692-2595
Castle Creek (G-3445)
Adams Lumber Co Inc ....F....... 716 358-2815
Cattaraugus (G-3464)
Amish Structure ....G....... 607 257-1070
Dryden (G-4344)
Angelica Forest Products Inc ....G....... 585 466-3205
Angelica (G-376)
Axtell Bradtke Lumber Co ....G....... 607 265-3850
Masonville (G-8137)
B & B Lumber Company Inc ....D....... 866 282-0582
Jamesville (G-7077)
B & J Lumber Co Inc ....G....... 518 677-3845
Cambridge (G-3332)
Baillie Lumber Co LP ....E....... 315 942-5284
Boonville (G-1160)

S I C

Employee Codes: A=Over 500 employees, B=251-500
C=101-250, D=51-100, E=20-50, F=10-19, G=5-9
2018 Harris
New York Manufacturers Directory
737

Bissel-Babcock Millwork Inc ....F 716 761-6976
Sherman *(G-15423)*

Bono Sawdust Supply Co Inc ....G 718 446-1374
Corona *(G-4014)*

Brookside Lumber Inc ....F 315 497-0937
Moravia *(G-8656)*

Capital Sawmill Service ....G 518 479-0729
Nassau *(G-8816)*

Carlson Wood Products Inc ....G 716 287-2923
Sinclairville *(G-15473)*

Casters Custom Sawing ....G 315 387-5104
Sandy Creek *(G-15159)*

Clements Burrville Sawmill ....G 315 782-4549
Watertown *(G-16666)*

Cote Hardwood Products Inc ....F 607 898-5737
Locke *(G-7595)*

Crawford Furniture Mfg Corp ....C 716 483-2102
Jamestown *(G-7020)*

▲ Curran Renewable Energy LLC ....E 315 769-2000
Massena *(G-8225)*

Dansville Logging & Lumber ....E 585 335-5879
Dansville *(G-4102)*

Dlr Enterprises LLC ....G 315 813-2911
Sherrill *(G-15427)*

Donver Incorporated ....F 716 945-1910
Kill Buck *(G-7195)*

Embassy Millwork Inc ....F 518 839-0965
Amsterdam *(G-344)*

Farney Lumber Corporation ....F 315 346-6013
Lowville *(G-7964)*

▼ Garden State Shavings Inc ....F 845 544-2835
Warwick *(G-16612)*

◆ GM Palmer Inc ....F 585 492-2990
Arcade *(G-393)*

Great Jones Lumber Corp ....F 212 254-5560
New York *(G-10398)*

Greater Niagara Bldg Ctr Inc ....F 716 299-0543
Niagara Falls *(G-12846)*

Greene Lumber Co LP ....E 607 278-6101
Davenport *(G-4105)*

Gutchess Freedom Inc ....D 716 492-2824
Freedom *(G-5387)*

◆ Gutchess Lumber Co Inc ....C 607 753-3393
Cortland *(G-4052)*

Hawkeye Forest Products LP ....F 608 534-6156
Hamburg *(G-5951)*

Hennig Custom Woodwork Corp ....G 516 536-3460
Oceanside *(G-13101)*

◆ J & J Log & Lumber Corp ....D 845 832-6535
Dover Plains *(G-4339)*

J A Yansick Lumber Co Inc ....E 585 492-4312
Arcade *(G-395)*

L J Valente Inc ....G 518 674-3750
Averill Park *(G-533)*

Lyons & Sullivan Inc ....G 518 584-1523
Saratoga Springs *(G-15192)*

Machina Deus Lex Inc ....G 917 577-0972
Jamaica *(G-6962)*

Mallery Lumber LLC ....G 607 637-2236
Hancock *(G-5987)*

McDonough Hardwoods Ltd ....E 315 829-3449
Vernon Center *(G-16460)*

Meltz Lumber Co of Mellenville ....E 518 672-7021
Hudson *(G-6656)*

Mettowee Lumber & Plastics Co ....C 518 642-1100
Granville *(G-5793)*

Mohawk Metal Mfg & Sls ....G 315 853-7663
Westmoreland *(G-17091)*

One Tree Dist ....G 315 701-2924
Syracuse *(G-16024)*

Owletts Saw Mills ....G 607 525-6340
Woodhull *(G-17327)*

▼ PA Pellets LLC ....F 814 848-9970
Pittsford *(G-13600)*

Pallets Inc ....E 518 747-4177
Fort Edward *(G-5351)*

PDJ Inc ....E 315 655-8824
Cazenovia *(G-3476)*

Petteys Lumber ....G 518 792-5943
Fort Ann *(G-5344)*

Piccini Industries Ltd ....E 845 365-0614
Orangeburg *(G-13262)*

Potter Lumber Co Inc ....E 716 373-1260
Allegany *(G-205)*

Rudy Stempel & Family Sawmill ....G 518 872-0431
East Berne *(G-4405)*

Russell Bass ....F 607 637-5253
Hancock *(G-5989)*

S Donadic Woodworking Inc ....D 718 361-9888
Sunnyside *(G-15830)*

▼ Salamanca Lumber Company Inc ....E 716 945-4810
Salamanca *(G-15131)*

Saw Mill Pediatrics Pllc ....G 914 449-6064
Pleasantville *(G-13750)*

Scotts Company LLC ....E 631 289-7444
Yaphank *(G-17416)*

Simplicity Bandsaw Inc ....G 716 557-8805
Hinsdale *(G-6450)*

Spiegel Woodworks Inc ....F 845 336-8090
Kingston *(G-7239)*

St Lawrence Lumber Inc ....G 315 649-2990
Three Mile Bay *(G-16145)*

Swanson Lumber ....G 716 499-1726
Gerry *(G-5605)*

▲ Tri-State Brick & Stone NY Inc ....D 212 366-0300
New York *(G-12423)*

Tupper Lake Hardwoods Inc ....E 518 359-8248
Tupper Lake *(G-16305)*

Upstate Increte Incorporated ....G 585 254-2010
Rochester *(G-14774)*

Urrey Lumber ....G 518 827-4851
Middleburgh *(G-8453)*

▼ Wagner Millwork Inc ....D 607 687-5362
Owego *(G-13386)*

Weather Tight Exteriors ....G 631 375-5108
Ridge *(G-14108)*

Wolski Wood Works Inc ....G 718 577-9816
Flushing *(G-5313)*

Wyde Lumber ....F 845 513-5571
Monticello *(G-8647)*

2426 Hardwood Dimension & Flooring Mills

A D Bowman & Son Lumber Co ....E 607 692-2595
Castle Creek *(G-3445)*

▲ Artistic Frame Corp ....C 212 289-2100
New York *(G-9270)*

B & B Lumber Company Inc ....D 866 282-0582
Jamesville *(G-7077)*

Carlson Wood Products Inc ....G 716 287-2923
Sinclairville *(G-15473)*

Cassadaga Designs Inc ....G 716 595-3030
Cassadaga *(G-3442)*

Clements Burrville Sawmill ....G 315 782-4549
Watertown *(G-16666)*

Custom Woodwork Ltd ....F 631 727-5260
Riverhead *(G-14151)*

Designer Hardwood Flrg CNY Inc ....F 315 207-0044
Oswego *(G-13354)*

Donver Incorporated ....F 716 945-1910
Kill Buck *(G-7195)*

Empire Exhibits & Displays Inc ....F 518 266-9362
Mechanicville *(G-8258)*

Fibron Products Inc ....E 716 886-2378
Buffalo *(G-2961)*

▼ Fitzpatrick and Weller Inc ....D 716 699-2393
Ellicottville *(G-4655)*

Fountain Tile Outlet Inc ....G 718 927-4555
Brooklyn *(G-1998)*

Guldenschuh Logging & Lbr LLC ....G 585 538-4750
Caledonia *(G-3307)*

◆ Gutchess Lumber Co Inc ....C 607 753-3393
Cortland *(G-4052)*

H B Millwork Inc ....F 631 289-8086
Medford *(G-8277)*

Horizon Floors I LLC ....G 212 509-9686
New York *(G-10549)*

◆ J & J Log & Lumber Corp ....D 845 832-6535
Dover Plains *(G-4339)*

J A Yansick Lumber Co Inc ....E 585 492-4312
Arcade *(G-395)*

Jim Quinn ....F 518 356-0398
Schenectady *(G-15297)*

▲ Legno Veneto USA ....G 716 651-9169
Depew *(G-4285)*

Madison & Dunn ....G 585 563-7760
Rochester *(G-14509)*

Mason Carvings Inc ....G 716 484-7884
Jamestown *(G-7050)*

Mm of East Aurora LLC ....F 716 651-9663
Buffalo *(G-3089)*

◆ MP Caroll Inc ....F 716 683-8520
Cheektowaga *(G-3607)*

Mullican Flooring LP ....E 716 537-2642
Holland *(G-6509)*

North Hudson Woodcraft Corp ....E 315 429-3105
Dolgeville *(G-4330)*

▼ Norton-Smith Hardwoods Inc ....G 716 945-0346
Salamanca *(G-15130)*

Petteys Lumber ....G 518 792-5943
Fort Ann *(G-5344)*

Potter Lumber Co Inc ....E 716 373-1260
Allegany *(G-205)*

▼ Potter Lumber Co LLC ....D 814 438-7888
Hamburg *(G-5960)*

Premier Hardwood Products Inc ....E 315 492-1786
Jamesville *(G-7084)*

Randolph Dimension Corporation ....F 716 358-6901
Randolph *(G-14030)*

Revival Industries Inc ....F 315 868-1085
Ilion *(G-6784)*

S Donadic Woodworking Inc ....D 718 361-9888
Sunnyside *(G-15830)*

Sirianni Hardwoods Inc ....E 607 962-4688
Painted Post *(G-13420)*

▲ Tectonic Flooring USA LLC ....G 212 686-2700
New York *(G-12316)*

Tupper Lake Hardwoods Inc ....E 518 359-8248
Tupper Lake *(G-16305)*

Vitobob Furniture Inc ....G 516 676-1696
Long Island City *(G-7945)*

◆ Wagner Hardwoods LLC ....E 607 594-3321
Cayuta *(G-3467)*

Wagner Hardwoods LLC ....C 607 594-3321
Cayuta *(G-3468)*

▼ Wagner Millwork Inc ....D 607 687-5362
Owego *(G-13386)*

Wood Floor Expo Inc ....G 212 472-0671
New York *(G-12683)*

Wrights Hardwoods Inc ....E 716 595-2345
Cassadaga *(G-3443)*

2429 Special Prdt Sawmills, NEC

RWS Manufacturing Inc ....G 518 361-1657
Queensbury *(G-14022)*

2431 Millwork

A Losee & Sons ....G 516 676-3060
Glen Cove *(G-5621)*

A W Hamel Stair Mfg Inc ....F 518 346-3031
Schenectady *(G-15256)*

Ace Fire Door Corp ....E 718 901-0001
Bronx *(G-1262)*

Adams Interior Fabrications ....F 631 249-8282
Massapequa *(G-8207)*

Adirondack Stairs Inc ....F 845 246-2525
Saugerties *(G-15207)*

▲ Adriatic Wood Products Inc ....E 718 922-4621
Brooklyn *(G-1562)*

American Wood Column Corp ....G 718 782-3163
Brooklyn *(G-1608)*

Amstutze Woodworking ....G 518 946-8206
Upper Jay *(G-16327)*

Apollo Windows & Doors Inc ....F 718 386-3326
Brooklyn *(G-1617)*

Architctral Mllwk Installation ....E 631 499-0755
East Northport *(G-4453)*

Artistic Ironworks Inc ....G 631 665-4285
Bay Shore *(G-671)*

Atlantic Stairs Corp ....G 718 417-8818
Brooklyn *(G-1649)*

▲ Attica Millwork Inc ....F 585 591-2333
Attica *(G-470)*

Auburn Custom Millwork Inc ....G 315 253-3843
Auburn *(G-477)*

Bator Bintor Inc ....F 347 546-6503
Brooklyn *(G-1670)*

▲ Bauerschmidt & Sons Inc ....D 718 528-3500
Jamaica *(G-6934)*

Beaver Creek Industries Inc ....G 607 545-6382
Canaseraga *(G-3391)*

Bennett Stair Company Inc ....G 518 384-1554
Ballston Lake *(G-579)*

Bloch Industries LLC ....D 585 334-9600
Rochester *(G-14253)*

Blooming Grove Stair Co ....F 845 783-4245
Monroe *(G-8585)*

Blooming Grove Stair Co ....G 845 791-4016
Monticello *(G-8642)*

BNC Innovative Woodworking ....F 718 277-2800
Brooklyn *(G-1705)*

Braga Woodworks ....G 845 342-4636
Middletown *(G-8462)*

Brauen Constrution ....G 585 492-0042
Arcade *(G-390)*

Broadway Neon Sign Corp ....F 908 241-4177
Ronkonkoma *(G-14910)*

▲ Burt Millwork Corporation ....E 718 257-4601
Albertson *(G-156)*

Capital District Stairs Inc ....G 518 383-2449
Halfmoon *(G-5931)*

Capital Kit Cab & Door Mfrs ... G ... 718 886-0303
College Point *(G-3805)*
Carob Industries Inc ... F ... 631 225-0900
Lindenhurst *(G-7481)*
◆ **Case Group LLC** ... E ... 518 720-3100
Green Island *(G-5872)*
Chautauqua Woods Corp ... E ... 716 366-3808
Dunkirk *(G-4360)*
Christiana Millwork Inc ... E ... 315 492-9099
Jamesville *(G-7079)*
▲ **City Store Gates Mfg Corp** ... E ... 718 939-9700
College Point *(G-3806)*
Clearwood Custom Carpentry and ... E ... 315 432-8422
East Syracuse *(G-4533)*
Columbus Woodworking Inc ... G ... 607 674-4546
Sherburne *(G-15412)*
Concepts In Wood of CNY ... E ... 315 463-8084
Syracuse *(G-15923)*
Cousins Furniture & Hm Imprvs ... E ... 631 254-3752
Deer Park *(G-4143)*
Craftsmen Woodworkers Ltd ... E ... 718 326-3350
Maspeth *(G-8156)*
Creative Laminates Inc ... F ... 315 463-7580
Syracuse *(G-15931)*
Crown Mill Work Corp ... G ... 845 371-2200
Monsey *(G-8605)*
Crown Woodworking Corp ... G ... 718 974-6415
Brooklyn *(G-1819)*
Cuccio-Zanetti Inc ... G ... 518 587-1363
Middle Grove *(G-8437)*
▲ **Custom Door & Mirror Inc** ... E ... 631 414-7725
Farmingdale *(G-4980)*
Custom Stair & Millwork Co ... G ... 315 839-5793
Sauquoit *(G-15228)*
Custom Wood Inc ... G ... 718 927-4700
Brooklyn *(G-1828)*
D K P Wood Railings & Stairs ... F ... 631 665-8656
Bay Shore *(G-688)*
D R Cornue Woodworks ... G ... 315 655-9463
Cazenovia *(G-3471)*
▲ **DAngelo Home Collections Inc** ... G ... 917 267-8920
Warwick *(G-16609)*
Dbs Interiors Corp ... F ... 631 491-3013
West Babylon *(G-16813)*
DC Contracting & Building Corp ... F ... 631 385-1117
Huntington Station *(G-6740)*
Deer Pk Stair Bldg Mllwk Inc ... E ... 631 363-5000
Blue Point *(G-993)*
Deerfield Millwork Inc ... F ... 631 726-9663
Water Mill *(G-16626)*
▲ **Dorm Company Corporation** ... G ... 502 551-6195
Cheektowaga *(G-3596)*
Duncan & Son Carpentry Inc ... E ... 914 664-4311
Mount Vernon *(G-8724)*
Dune Woodworking ... G ... 631 996-2482
Riverhead *(G-14152)*
Ecker Window Corp ... D ... 914 776-0000
Yonkers *(G-17454)*
Ed Negron Fine Woodworking ... G ... 718 246-1016
Brooklyn *(G-1904)*
Efj Inc ... D ... 518 234-4799
Cobleskill *(G-3762)*
EM Pfaff & Son Inc ... F ... 607 739-3691
Horseheads *(G-6604)*
Empire Building Products Inc ... G ... 518 695-6094
Schuylerville *(G-15340)*
▲ **Fancy Windows & Doors Mfg Corp** ... G ... 718 366-7800
Brooklyn *(G-1961)*
▲ **Finger Lakes Trellis Supply** ... G ... 315 904-4007
Williamson *(G-17252)*
Fire Island Sea Clam Co Inc ... G ... 631 589-2199
West Sayville *(G-16964)*
Five Star Millwork LLC ... F ... 845 920-0247
Pearl River *(G-13478)*
Fontrick Door Inc ... E ... 585 345-6032
Batavia *(G-634)*
Funda-Mantels LLC ... G ... 631 924-1404
Mastic *(G-8235)*
G & G Window Repair Inc ... F ... 585 334-3370
Rush *(G-15073)*
Garrison Woodworking Inc ... F ... 845 726-3525
Westtown *(G-17098)*
Grace Ryan & Magnus Mllwk LLC ... D ... 914 665-0902
Mount Vernon *(G-8731)*
◆ **Griffon Corporation** ... E ... 212 957-5000
New York *(G-10405)*
▲ **Gw Manufacturing** ... E ... 718 386-8078
Ridgewood *(G-14122)*
H B Millwork Inc ... F ... 631 289-8086
Medford *(G-8277)*
H B Millwork Inc ... G ... 631 924-4195
Yaphank *(G-17410)*
Highland Organization Corp ... E ... 631 991-3240
Deer Park *(G-4172)*
Hulley Holding Company Inc ... F ... 716 332-3982
Kenmore *(G-7178)*
I Meglio Corp ... E ... 631 617-6900
Brentwood *(G-1181)*
▲ **Ideal Wood Products Inc** ... E ... 315 823-1124
Little Falls *(G-7522)*
Ignelzi Interiors Inc ... E ... 718 464-0279
Queens Village *(G-13995)*
Inform Studio Inc ... F ... 718 401-6149
Bronx *(G-1364)*
Island Stairs Corp ... G ... 347 645-0560
Staten Island *(G-15710)*
Island Street Lumber Co Inc ... G ... 716 692-4127
North Tonawanda *(G-12996)*
J Percoco Industries Inc ... G ... 631 312-4572
Bohemia *(G-1075)*
◆ **J Zeluck Inc** ... E ... 718 251-8060
Brooklyn *(G-2127)*
Jacobs Woodworking LLC ... G ... 315 427-8999
Syracuse *(G-15984)*
Jays Furniture Products Inc ... E ... 716 876-8854
Buffalo *(G-3031)*
JEm Wdwkg & Cabinets Inc ... F ... 518 828-5361
Hudson *(G-6650)*
John Langenbacher Co Inc ... E ... 718 328-0141
Bronx *(G-1371)*
KB Millwork Inc ... G ... 516 280-2183
Levittown *(G-7451)*
Kelly Window Systems Inc ... E ... 631 420-8500
Farmingdale *(G-5033)*
Kng Construction Co Inc ... F ... 212 595-1451
Warwick *(G-16615)*
Krefab Corporation ... F ... 631 842-5151
Huntington *(G-6701)*
Living Doors Inc ... F ... 631 924-5393
Medford *(G-8285)*
M & D Millwork LLC ... F ... 631 789-1439
Amityville *(G-307)*
Mack Wood Working ... G ... 845 657-6625
Shokan *(G-15455)*
Marretti USA Inc ... G ... 212 255-5565
New York *(G-11188)*
Mason Woodworks LLC ... G ... 917 363-7052
Brooklyn *(G-2281)*
Medina Millworks LLC ... G ... 585 798-2969
Medina *(G-8309)*
Mestel Brothers Stairs & Rails ... C ... 516 496-4127
Syosset *(G-15848)*
Metalocke Industries Inc ... G ... 718 267-9200
Woodside *(G-17354)*
Metropolitan Fine Mllwk Corp ... F ... 914 669-4900
North Salem *(G-12955)*
Michael Bernstein Design Assoc ... E ... 718 456-9277
Brooklyn *(G-2313)*
Michbi Doors Inc ... D ... 631 231-9050
Brentwood *(G-1189)*
Midwood Signs & Design Inc ... G ... 718 499-9041
Brooklyn *(G-2316)*
Millco Woodworking LLC ... F ... 585 526-6844
Hall *(G-5940)*
▲ **Miller Blaker Inc** ... D ... 718 665-3930
Bronx *(G-1401)*
Millwright Wdwrk Installetion ... E ... 631 587-2635
West Babylon *(G-16842)*
Mind Designs Inc ... G ... 631 563-3644
Farmingville *(G-5168)*
Monroe Stair Products Inc ... E ... 845 783-4245
Monroe *(G-8598)*
Monroe Stair Products Inc ... G ... 845 791-4016
Monticello *(G-8644)*
Ne & Ws Inc ... G ... 718 326-4699
Maspeth *(G-8185)*
▲ **Nordic Interior Inc** ... C ... 718 456-7000
College Point *(G-3824)*
North Fork Wood Works Inc ... G ... 631 255-4028
Mattituck *(G-8240)*
Northern Forest Pdts Co Inc ... G ... 315 942-6955
Boonville *(G-1164)*
Old World Mouldings Inc ... G ... 631 563-8660
Bohemia *(G-1109)*
Overhead Door Corporation ... D ... 518 828-7652
Hudson *(G-6659)*
P H Custom Woodworking Corp ... E ... 917 801-1444
Bronx *(G-1419)*
Paul David Enterprises Inc ... G ... 646 667-5530
New York *(G-11599)*
Pella Corporation ... B ... 607 223-2023
Johnson City *(G-7131)*
Pella Corporation ... B ... 607 231-8550
Johnson City *(G-7132)*
Pella Corporation ... B ... 607 238-2812
Johnson City *(G-7133)*
Pella Corporation ... B ... 516 385-3622
Albertson *(G-161)*
Pella Corporation ... B ... 607 238-2812
Johnson City *(G-7134)*
Pella Corporation ... B ... 516 385-3622
Albertson *(G-162)*
Pella Corporation ... B ... 607 231-8550
Johnson City *(G-7135)*
Pella Corporation ... C ... 631 208-0710
Calverton *(G-3322)*
Peter Productions Devivi Inc ... F ... 315 568-8484
Waterloo *(G-16653)*
▲ **Pgs Millwork Inc** ... D ... 212 244-6610
New York *(G-11663)*
Piccini Industries Ltd ... E ... 845 365-0614
Orangeburg *(G-13262)*
Professional Cab Detailing Co ... F ... 845 436-7282
Woodridge *(G-17333)*
Props Displays & Interiors ... F ... 212 620-3840
New York *(G-11759)*
Quaker Millwork & Lumber Inc ... E ... 716 662-3388
Orchard Park *(G-13318)*
▲ **Quality Millwork Corp** ... E ... 718 892-2250
Bronx *(G-1437)*
Quality Stair Builders Inc ... F ... 631 694-0711
Farmingdale *(G-5103)*
R C Henderson Stair Builders ... F ... 516 876-9898
Westbury *(G-17052)*
Randolph Dimension Corporation ... F ... 716 358-6901
Randolph *(G-14030)*
RB Woodcraft Inc ... E ... 315 474-2429
Syracuse *(G-16043)*
Red Tail Moulding & Mllwk LLC ... G ... 516 852-4613
Center Moriches *(G-3493)*
Richard Anthony Corp ... E ... 914 922-7141
Yorktown Heights *(G-17534)*
Rj Millworkers Inc ... E ... 607 433-0525
Oneonta *(G-13215)*
Rochester Colonial Mfg Corp ... D ... 585 254-8191
Rochester *(G-14661)*
Rochester Lumber Company ... E ... 585 924-7171
Farmington *(G-5164)*
Rockaway Stairs Ltd ... G ... 718 945-0047
Far Rockaway *(G-4931)*
Roode Hoek & Co Inc ... F ... 718 522-5921
Brooklyn *(G-2525)*
Royal Windows Mfg Corp ... E ... 631 435-8888
Bay Shore *(G-735)*
Royalton Millwork & Design ... G ... 716 439-4092
Lockport *(G-7643)*
Russin Lumber Corp ... F ... 845 457-4000
Newburgh *(G-12801)*
S Donadic Woodworking Inc ... D ... 718 361-9888
Sunnyside *(G-15830)*
S R Sloan Inc ... D ... 315 736-7730
Whitesboro *(G-17223)*
▲ **Scanga Woodworking Corp** ... E ... 845 265-9115
Cold Spring *(G-3791)*
Second Generation Wood Stairs ... F ... 718 370-0085
Staten Island *(G-15757)*
Select Interior Door Ltd ... E ... 585 535-9900
North Java *(G-12950)*
Shawmut Woodworking & Sup Inc ... G ... 212 920-8900
New York *(G-12068)*
Specialty Services ... G ... 585 728-5650
Wayland *(G-16735)*
Spiegel Woodworks Inc ... F ... 845 336-8090
Kingston *(G-7239)*
Stairworld Inc ... G ... 718 441-9722
Richmond Hill *(G-14097)*
Stated Island Stair Inc ... G ... 718 317-9276
Staten Island *(G-15761)*
Staten Island Stair Inc ... G ... 718 317-9276
Staten Island *(G-15763)*
Stealth Archtctral Windows Inc ... F ... 718 821-6666
Brooklyn *(G-2622)*
Syracuse Industrial Sls Co Ltd ... F ... 315 478-5751
Syracuse *(G-16077)*
TDS Woodworking Inc ... F ... 718 442-5298
Staten Island *(G-15768)*
Three R Enterprises Inc ... E ... 585 254-5050
Rochester *(G-14752)*
Tiedemann Waldemar Inc ... F ... 716 875-5665
Buffalo *(G-3244)*

Employee Codes: A=Over 500 employees, B=251-500
C=101-250, D=51-100, E=20-50, F=10-19, G=5-9
2018 Harris
New York Manufacturers Directory
739

24 LUMBER AND WOOD PRODUCTS, EXCEPT FURNITURE

Unadilla Silo Company Inc ....D....... 607 369-9341
  Sidney (G-15466)
Unicenter Millwork Inc ....G....... 716 741-8201
  Clarence Center (G-3707)
United Rockland Holding Co Inc ....E....... 845 357-1900
  Suffern (G-15822)
Universal Custom Millwork Inc ....D....... 518 330-6622
  Amsterdam (G-372)
▲ Upstate Door Inc ....D....... 585 786-3880
  Warsaw (G-16607)
Urban Woodworks Ltd ....G....... 718 827-1570
  Brooklyn (G-2730)
Vander Heyden Woodworking ....G....... 212 242-0525
  New York (G-12523)
▼ Wagner Millwork Inc ....D....... 607 687-5362
  Owego (G-13386)
Window Technologies LLC ....G....... 402 464-0202
  New York (G-12668)
Wolfe Lumber Mill Inc ....G....... 716 772-7750
  Gasport (G-5575)
Wood Innovations of Suffolk ....G....... 631 698-2345
  Medford (G-8297)
Wood Talk ....G....... 631 940-3085
  Bay Shore (G-748)
Xylon Industries Inc ....G....... 631 293-4717
  Farmingdale (G-5153)
Yesteryears Vintage Doors LLC ....G....... 315 324-5250
  Hammond (G-5974)
Zanzano Woodworking Inc ....F....... 914 725-6025
  Scarsdale (G-15255)
Zeller Woodworks LLC ....F....... 585 254-7607
  Rochester (G-14803)

2434 Wood Kitchen Cabinets

Able Kitchen ....F....... 877 268-1264
  Cedarhurst (G-3482)
Acme Kitchenettes Corp ....E....... 518 828-4191
  Hudson (G-6632)
Aka Enterprises ....E....... 716 474-4579
  Wyoming (G-17395)
▲ Aki Cabinets Inc ....E....... 718 721-2541
  Astoria (G-429)
Amoroso Wood Products Co Inc ......G....... 631 249-4998
  Melville (G-8327)
Andike Millwork Inc ....G....... 718 894-1796
  Maspeth (G-8146)
▲ Artone LLC ....D....... 716 664-2232
  Jamestown (G-7008)
Atlantic States Distributing ....G....... 518 427-6364
  Menands (G-8400)
Auburn-Watson Corp ....F....... 716 876-8000
  Depew (G-4272)
▲ Bauerschmidt & Sons Inc ....D....... 718 528-3500
  Jamaica (G-6934)
Bloch Industries LLC ....D....... 585 334-9600
  Rochester (G-14253)
Cabinet Shapes Corp ....F....... 718 784-6255
  Long Island City (G-7722)
Cabinetry By Tbr Inc ....G....... 516 365-8500
  Manhasset (G-8088)
Cabinets By Stanley Inc ....G....... 718 222-5861
  Brooklyn (G-1749)
Cambridge Kitchens Mfg Inc ....F....... 516 935-5100
  Hicksville (G-6353)
Candlelight Cabinetry Inc ....C....... 716 434-2114
  Lockport (G-7603)
Capital Kit Cab & Door Mfrs ....G....... 718 886-0303
  College Point (G-3805)
Carefree Kitchens Inc ....G....... 631 567-2120
  Holbrook (G-6464)
Carlos & Alex Atelier Inc ....E....... 718 441-8911
  Richmond Hill (G-14083)
Casa Collection Inc ....G....... 718 694-0272
  Brooklyn (G-1764)
▲ Catskill Craftsmen Inc ....D....... 607 652-7321
  Stamford (G-15644)
Central Kitchen Corp ....F....... 631 283-1029
  Southampton (G-15564)
Chicone Builders LLC ....G....... 607 535-6540
  Montour Falls (G-8648)
Classic Cabinets ....F....... 845 357-4331
  Suffern (G-15809)
Clearwood Custom Carpentry and ...G....... 315 432-8422
  East Syracuse (G-4533)
Columbia Cabinets LLC ....G....... 212 972-7550
  Mount Kisco (G-8665)
Columbia Cabinets LLC ....F....... 518 283-1700
  Saratoga Springs (G-15178)
Commercial Millworks Inc ....G....... 315 475-7479
  Syracuse (G-15921)

Cosmopolitan Cabinet Company ....G....... 631 467-4960
  Ronkonkoma (G-14918)
▼ Craft Custom Woodwork Co Inc ...F....... 718 821-2162
  Maspeth (G-8155)
Creative Cabinet Corp America ....E....... 631 751-5768
  Stony Brook (G-15790)
Custom CAS Inc ....F....... 718 726-3575
  Long Island City (G-7736)
Custom Woodcraft LLC ....G....... 315 843-4234
  Munnsville (G-8796)
D & M Custom Cabinets Inc ....F....... 516 678-2818
  Oceanside (G-13095)
Dak Mica and Wood Products ....G....... 631 467-0749
  Ronkonkoma (G-14920)
Dbs Interiors Corp ....F....... 631 491-3013
  West Babylon (G-16813)
Deakon Homes and Interiors ....F....... 518 271-0342
  Troy (G-16255)
Di Fiore and Sons Custom Wdwkg ..G....... 718 278-1663
  Long Island City (G-7744)
EC Wood & Company Inc ....F....... 718 388-2287
  Deer Park (G-4157)
EM Pfaff & Son Inc ....F....... 607 739-3691
  Horseheads (G-6604)
Enterprise Wood Products Inc ....F....... 718 853-9243
  Brooklyn (G-1930)
Fantasy Home Improvement Corp ...F....... 718 277-4021
  Brooklyn (G-1962)
Fina Cabinet Corp ....F....... 718 409-2900
  Mount Vernon (G-8726)
Fra-Rik Formica Fabg Co Inc ....F....... 718 597-3335
  Bronx (G-1339)
Garrison Woodworking Inc ....F....... 845 726-3525
  Westtown (G-17098)
▲ Glissade New York LLC ....F....... 631 756-4800
  Farmingdale (G-5007)
Greenway Cabinetry Inc ....F....... 516 877-0009
  Williston Park (G-17285)
Hearth Cabinets and More Ltd ....G....... 315 641-1197
  Liverpool (G-7545)
Hendrickson Custom Cabinetry ....F....... 718 401-0137
  Bronx (G-1358)
Hollywood Cabinets Co ....F....... 516 354-0857
  Elmont (G-4733)
Home Ideal Inc ....F....... 718 762-8998
  Flushing (G-5259)
Ignelzi Interiors Inc ....F....... 718 464-0279
  Queens Village (G-13995)
J Percoco Industries Inc ....F....... 631 312-4572
  Bohemia (G-1075)
Jordache Woodworking Corp ....F....... 718 349-3373
  Brooklyn (G-2146)
K-Binet Inc ....G....... 845 348-1149
  Blauvelt (G-966)
▲ Kalnitz Kitchens Inc ....G....... 716 684-1700
  Buffalo (G-3043)
▲ Kw Distributors Group Inc ....F....... 718 843-3500
  Ozone Park (G-13408)
Longo Commercial Cabinets Inc .....F....... 631 225-4290
  Lindenhurst (G-7491)
Lyn Jo Kitchens Inc ....F....... 718 336-6060
  Brooklyn (G-2242)
▲ Material Process Systems Inc ....F....... 718 302-3081
  Brooklyn (G-2286)
Matteo & Antonio Bartolotta ....F....... 315 252-2220
  Auburn (G-506)
McGraw Wood Products LLC ....F....... 607 836-6465
  Mc Graw (G-8254)
Mega Cabinets Inc ....F....... 631 789-4112
  Amityville (G-311)
Methods Tooling & Mfg Inc ....F....... 845 246-7100
  Mount Marion (G-8693)
▲ Metro Kitchens Corp ....F....... 718 434-1166
  Brooklyn (G-2310)
Michael Bernstein Design Assoc ....E....... 718 456-9277
  Brooklyn (G-2313)
Michael P Mmarr ....F....... 315 623-9380
  Constantia (G-3907)
Millco Woodworking LLC ....F....... 585 526-6844
  Hall (G-5940)
Modern Cabinet Company Inc ....E....... 845 473-4900
  Poughkeepsie (G-13936)
▲ N Y Elli Design Corp ....F....... 718 228-0014
  Maspeth (G-8184)
Nagad Cabinets Inc ....G....... 718 382-7200
  Brooklyn (G-2353)
Neo Cabinetry LLC ....F....... 718 403-0456
  Brooklyn (G-2364)
▲ New York Vanity and Mfg Co ....E....... 718 417-1010
  Freeport (G-5425)

NY Cabinet Factory Inc ....F....... 718 256-6541
  Brooklyn (G-2392)
▲ Pgs Millwork Inc ....D....... 212 244-6610
  New York (G-11663)
Piccini Industries Ltd ....E....... 845 365-0614
  Orangeburg (G-13262)
Precision Dental Cabinets Inc ....F....... 631 543-3870
  Smithtown (G-15518)
Premier Woodcraft Ltd ....E....... 610 383-6624
  White Plains (G-17188)
Premium Woodworking LLC ....G....... 631 485-3133
  West Babylon (G-16849)
R & M Thermofoil Doors Inc ....G....... 718 206-4991
  Jamaica (G-6980)
Ralph Payne ....F....... 718 222-4200
  Brooklyn (G-2496)
Red White & Blue Entps Corp ....G....... 718 565-8080
  Woodside (G-17366)
Ribble Lumber Inc ....G....... 315 536-6221
  Penn Yan (G-13541)
Royal Custom Cabinets ....G....... 315 376-6042
  Lowville (G-7970)
S & V Custom Furniture Mfg ....F....... 516 746-8299
  Mineola (G-8569)
S Donadic Woodworking Inc ....D....... 718 361-9888
  Sunnyside (G-15830)
▲ Salko Kitchens Inc ....F....... 845 565-4420
  New Windsor (G-8998)
Salmon Creek Cabinetry Inc ....E....... 315 589-5419
  Williamson (G-17254)
Serway Bros Inc ....E....... 315 337-0601
  Rome (G-14864)
Sherry-Mica Products Inc ....G....... 631 471-7513
  Ronkonkoma (G-15009)
Silva Cabinetry Inc ....F....... 914 737-7697
  Buchanan (G-2801)
Skyline Custom Cabinetry Inc ....G....... 631 393-2983
  Farmingdale (G-5120)
▲ Stone Expo & Cabinetry LLC ....F....... 516 292-2988
  West Hempstead (G-16895)
Tristate Contract Sales LLC ....G....... 845 782-2614
  Chester (G-3648)
Upstate Cabinet Co Inc ....F....... 585 429-5090
  Rochester (G-14773)
Viola Cabinet Corporation ....G....... 716 284-6327
  Niagara Falls (G-12905)
▲ W Designe Inc ....E....... 914 736-1058
  Peekskill (G-13509)
White House Cabinet Shop LLC ......G....... 607 674-9358
  Sherburne (G-15421)
William Brooks Woodworking ....F....... 718 495-9767
  Brooklyn (G-2768)
▲ Win Wood Cabinetry Inc ....G....... 516 304-2216
  Greenvale (G-5901)
Wood Etc Inc ....F....... 315 484-9663
  Syracuse (G-16099)
Yonkers Cabinets Inc ....F....... 914 668-2133
  Yonkers (G-17518)
Your Furniture Designers Inc ....G....... 845 947-3046
  West Haverstraw (G-16879)
Your Way Custom Cabinets Inc ....G....... 914 371-1870
  Mount Vernon (G-8792)

2435 Hardwood Veneer & Plywood

Geonex International Corp ....F....... 212 473-4555
  New York (G-10324)
Kings Quartet Corp ....G....... 845 986-9090
  Warwick (G-16614)
Northeast Panel & Truss LLC ....E....... 845 339-3656
  Kingston (G-7234)
Sure-Lock Industries LLC ....F....... 315 207-0044
  Oswego (G-13368)
▲ Veneer One Inc ....E....... 516 536-6480
  Oceanside (G-13125)

2436 Softwood Veneer & Plywood

H B Millwork Inc ....F....... 631 289-8086
  Medford (G-8277)

2439 Structural Wood Members, NEC

Architctral Mllwk Installation ....E....... 631 499-0755
  East Northport (G-4453)
Empire Building Products Inc ....G....... 518 695-6094
  Schuylerville (G-15340)
Faulkner Truss Company Inc ....G....... 315 536-8894
  Dresden (G-4343)
Harvest Homes Inc ....E....... 518 895-2341
  Delanson (G-4259)
New England Barns Inc ....E....... 631 445-1461
  Southold (G-15584)

24 LUMBER AND WOOD PRODUCTS, EXCEPT FURNITURE

Niagara Truss & Pallet LLC ....F 716 433-5400
  Lockport (G-7637)
Northeast Panel & Truss LLC ....E 845 339-3656
  Kingston (G-7234)
P & R Truss Co ....E 716 496-5484
  Chaffee (G-3563)
Pdj Components Inc ....E 845 469-9191
  Chester (G-3638)
Proof Industries Inc ....G 631 694-7663
  Farmingdale (G-5100)
Railtech Composites Inc ....F 518 324-6190
  Plattsburgh (G-13721)
Rochester Lumber Company ....E 585 924-7171
  Farmington (G-5164)
S R Sloan Inc ....D 315 736-7730
  Whitesboro (G-17223)
Steele Truss Company Inc ....E 518 562-4663
  Plattsburgh (G-13727)
Stephenson Lumber Company Inc ....E 518 548-7521
  Speculator (G-15587)
Structural Wood Corporation ....E 315 388-4442
  Waddington (G-16542)
Timber Frames Inc ....G 585 374-6405
  Canandaigua (G-3388)
Ufp New York LLC ....E 716 496-5484
  Chaffee (G-3564)
Ufp New York LLC ....E 518 828-2888
  Hudson (G-6668)
Ufp New York LLC ....E 315 253-2758
  Auburn (G-524)
Ufp New York LLC ....E 607 563-1556
  Sidney (G-15465)
Unadilla Silo Company Inc ....D 607 369-9341
  Sidney (G-15466)

2441 Wood Boxes

Abbot & Abbot Box Corp ....F 888 930-5972
  Long Island City (G-7678)
Bragley Mfg Co Inc ....E 718 622-7469
  Brooklyn (G-1711)
Bristol Boarding Inc ....G 585 271-7860
  Rochester (G-14265)
Falvo Manufacturing Co Inc ....F 315 738-7682
  Utica (G-16353)
Great Lakes Specialites ....E 716 672-4622
  Fredonia (G-5383)
M &L Industry of NY Inc ....E 845 827-6255
  Highland Mills (G-6439)
McGraw Wood Products LLC ....E 607 836-6465
  Mc Graw (G-8254)
McIntosh Box & Pallet Co Inc ....F 315 789-8750
  Geneva (G-5594)
McIntosh Box & Pallet Co Inc ....D 315 675-8511
  Bernhards Bay (G-857)
McIntosh Box & Pallet Co Inc ....E 315 446-9350
  Rome (G-14848)
Norjac Boxes Inc ....E 631 842-1300
  Copiague (G-3940)
Philpac Corporation ....E 716 875-8005
  Buffalo (G-3147)
Quality Woodworking Corp ....F 718 875-3437
  Brooklyn (G-2483)
Reuter Pallet Pkg Sys Inc ....G 845 457-9937
  Montgomery (G-8638)
Technical Packaging Inc ....F 516 223-2300
  Baldwin (G-561)

2448 Wood Pallets & Skids

219 South West ....G 315 474-2065
  Syracuse (G-15864)
A D Bowman & Son Lumber Co ....E 607 692-2595
  Castle Creek (G-3445)
Abbot & Abbot Box Corp ....F 888 930-5972
  Long Island City (G-7678)
▲ Airline Container Services ....G 516 371-4125
  Lido Beach (G-7461)
B & B Lumber Company Inc ....D 866 282-0582
  Jamesville (G-7077)
B&B Albany Pallet Company LLC ....E 315 492-1786
  Jamesville (G-7078)
Berry Industrial Group Inc ....E 845 353-8338
  Nyack (G-13062)
Best Pallet & Crate LLC ....E 518 438-2945
  Albany (G-52)
Chemung Cnty Chpter Nysarc Inc ....C 607 734-6151
  Elmira (G-4688)
Clements Burrville Sawmill ....E 315 782-4549
  Watertown (G-16666)
▼ Concord Express Cargo Inc ....G 718 276-7200
  Jamaica (G-6942)

Crawford Furniture Mfg Corp ....C 716 483-2102
  Jamestown (G-7020)
Custom Shipping Products Inc ....F 716 355-4437
  Clymer (G-3758)
D & F Pallet Inc ....F 716 672-2984
  Fredonia (G-5381)
Dimensional Mills Inc ....G 518 746-1047
  Hudson Falls (G-6671)
Dwa Pallet Inc ....G 518 746-1047
  Hudson Falls (G-6672)
Essex Box & Pallet Co Inc ....E 518 834-7279
  Keeseville (G-7166)
Four-Way Pallet Corp ....E 631 351-3401
  Huntington Station (G-6744)
G & H Wood Products LLC ....F 716 372-5510
  Olean (G-13169)
Great Lakes Specialites ....E 716 672-4622
  Fredonia (G-5383)
Just Wood Pallets Inc ....G 718 644-7013
  New Windsor (G-8986)
Lindley Wood Works Inc ....F 607 523-7786
  Lindley (G-7519)
McIntosh Box & Pallet Co Inc ....D 315 675-8511
  Bernhards Bay (G-857)
McIntosh Box & Pallet Co Inc ....F 315 789-8750
  Geneva (G-5594)
McIntosh Box & Pallet Co Inc ....E 315 446-9350
  Rome (G-14848)
Nefab Packaging North East LLC ....E 518 346-9105
  Scotia (G-15351)
Neville Mfg Svc & Dist Inc ....F 716 834-3038
  Cheektowaga (G-3610)
North Shore Pallet Inc ....E 631 673-4700
  Huntington Station (G-6756)
Northeast Pallet & Cont Co Inc ....F 518 271-0535
  Troy (G-16267)
Ongweoweh Corp ....D 607 266-7070
  Ithaca (G-6903)
Orleans Pallet Company Inc ....E 585 589-0781
  Albion (G-170)
Pallet Division Inc ....G 585 328-3780
  Rochester (G-14589)
Pallet Services Inc ....E 585 647-4020
  Rochester (G-14590)
Pallets Inc ....E 518 747-4177
  Fort Edward (G-5351)
Pallets R US Inc ....E 631 758-2360
  Bellport (G-834)
Paul Bunyan Products Inc ....E 315 696-6164
  Cortland (G-4062)
Peco Pallet Inc ....E 914 376-5444
  Irvington (G-6816)
Peter C Herman Inc ....E 315 926-4100
  Marion (G-8128)
Pooran Pallet Inc ....E 718 938-7970
  Bronx (G-1431)
Reuter Pallet Pkg Sys Inc ....G 845 457-9937
  Montgomery (G-8638)
Sanjay Pallets Inc ....E 347 590-2485
  Bronx (G-1446)
▼ Sg Blocks Inc ....G 615 585-2639
  Brooklyn (G-2573)
Steven Coffey Pallet S Inc ....E 585 261-6783
  Rochester (G-14728)
Vansantis Development Inc ....E 315 461-0113
  Liverpool (G-7581)
Wolfe Lumber Mill Inc ....G 716 772-7750
  Gasport (G-5575)

2449 Wood Containers, NEC

Abbot & Abbot Box Corp ....F 888 930-5972
  Long Island City (G-7678)
David Isseks & Sons Inc ....F 212 966-8694
  New York (G-9875)
Essex Box & Pallet Co Inc ....E 518 834-7279
  Keeseville (G-7166)
Great Lakes Specialites ....E 716 672-4622
  Fredonia (G-5383)
Hood Industries Inc ....F 716 836-0301
  Buffalo (G-3014)
J & M Packaging Inc ....F 631 608-3069
  Hauppauge (G-6124)
Northeast Pallet & Cont Co Inc ....F 518 271-0535
  Troy (G-16267)
Pluribus Products Inc ....E 718 852-1614
  Bayville (G-775)
R D A Container Corporation ....E 585 247-2323
  Gates (G-5578)
Rosenwach Tank Co Inc ....E 212 972-4411
  Astoria (G-454)

Wolfe Lumber Mill Inc ....G 716 772-7750
  Gasport (G-5575)

2451 Mobile Homes

All Star Carts & Vehicles Inc ....D 631 666-5581
  Bay Shore (G-667)
Champion Home Builders Inc ....C 315 841-4122
  Sangerfield (G-15160)
Leatherstocking Mobile Home PA ....G 315 839-5691
  Sauquoit (G-15229)

2452 Prefabricated Wood Buildings & Cmpnts

Alta Industries Ltd ....F 845 586-3336
  Halcottsville (G-5927)
Best Mdlr HMS Afrbe P Q& S In ....F 631 204-0049
  Southampton (G-15563)
Bill Lake Homes Construction ....D 518 673-2424
  Sprakers (G-15601)
Cort Contracting ....F 845 758-1190
  Red Hook (G-14041)
Duro-Shed Inc ....E 585 344-0800
  Buffalo (G-2936)
Eastern Exterior Wall ....E 631 589-3880
  Bohemia (G-1057)
Energy Panel Structures Inc ....G 315 923-7777
  Clyde (G-3750)
Energy Panel Structures Inc ....G 585 343-1777
  Clyde (G-3751)
Energy Panel Structures Inc ....G 518 355-6708
  Schenectady (G-15278)
Harvest Homes Inc ....E 518 895-2341
  Delanson (G-4259)
Historcal Soc of Mddltown Walk ....G 845 342-0941
  Middletown (G-8478)
Jabo Agricultural Inc ....G 631 475-1800
  Patchogue (G-13450)
Lapp Management Corp ....F 607 243-5141
  Himrod (G-6448)
Northern Design & Bldg Assoc ....E 518 747-2200
  Queensbury (G-14019)
Roscoe Brothers Inc ....F 607 844-3750
  Dryden (G-4347)
Shafer & Sons ....E 315 853-5285
  Westmoreland (G-17094)
▲ Shelter Enterprises Inc ....D 518 237-4100
  Cohoes (G-3783)
Walpole Woodworkers Inc ....G 631 726-2859
  Water Mill (G-16628)
Westchester Modular Homes Inc ....C 845 832-9400
  Wingdale (G-17297)
Whitley East LLC ....D 718 403-0050
  Brooklyn (G-2764)
Wood Tex Products LLC ....G 607 243-5141
  Himrod (G-6449)

2491 Wood Preserving

Bestway Enterprises Inc ....E 607 753-8261
  Cortland (G-4034)
Bestway of New York Inc ....G 607 753-8261
  Cortland (G-4035)
▲ Colorspec Coatings Intl Inc ....F 631 472-8251
  Holbrook (G-6468)
Donver Incorporated ....F 716 945-1910
  Kill Buck (G-7195)
Genesee Reserve Buffalo LLC ....E 716 824-3116
  Buffalo (G-2988)
Northeast Treaters Inc ....E 518 945-2660
  Athens (G-463)
Northeast Treaters NY LLC ....E 518 945-2660
  Athens (G-464)
◆ Osmose Holdings Inc ....A 716 882-5905
  Depew (G-4291)
Wego International Floors LLC ....F 516 487-3510
  Great Neck (G-5868)

2493 Reconstituted Wood Prdts

▲ Aarco Products Inc ....F 631 924-5461
  Yaphank (G-17400)
▲ Amendola MBL & Stone Ctr Inc ......D 914 997-7968
  White Plains (G-17104)
Bedford Wdwrk Instllations Inc ....G 914 764-9434
  Bedford (G-791)
Bulletin Boards & Dirctry Pdts ....F 914 248-8008
  Yorktown Heights (G-17523)
▲ Continental Buchanan LLC ....F 703 480-3800
  Buchanan (G-2799)
Hi-Temp Fabrication Inc ....F 716 852-5655
  Buffalo (G-3012)

Employee Codes: A=Over 500 employees, B=251-500
C=101-250, D=51-100, E=20-50, F=10-19, G=5-9

24 LUMBER AND WOOD PRODUCTS, EXCEPT FURNITURE

Niagara Fiberboard Inc ....E 716 434-8881
  Lockport (G-7635)
Northeastern Products Corp ....E 518 623-3161
  Warrensburg (G-16602)
Zircar Refr Composites Inc ....F 845 651-2200
  Florida (G-5224)

2499 Wood Prdts, NEC

A Van Hoek Woodworking Limited ....G 718 599-4388
  Brooklyn (G-1536)
◆ Aakron Rule Corp ....C 716 542-5483
  Akron (G-17)
▲ Abbott Industries Inc ....E 718 291-0800
  Jamaica (G-6926)
AC Moore Incorporated ....G 516 796-5831
  Bethpage (G-862)
Aces Over Eights Inc ....G 585 292-9690
  Rochester (G-14184)
Adams Interior Fabrications ....F 631 249-8282
  Massapequa (G-8207)
Aid Wood Working ....F 631 244-7768
  Bohemia (G-1006)
▲ Amci Ltd ....D 718 937-5858
  Long Island City (G-7689)
American Casino Equipment Mfg ....F 631 242-2440
  Deer Park (G-4119)
American Woods & Veneers Works ....E 718 937-2195
  Long Island City (G-7692)
Andike Millwork Inc ....G 718 894-1796
  Maspeth (G-8146)
Apf Manufacturing Company LLC ......F 914 963-6300
  Yonkers (G-17432)
Architectural Dctg Co LLC ....E 845 483-1340
  Poughkeepsie (G-13906)
Architectural Enhancements Inc ....F 845 343-9663
  Middletown (G-8460)
Art Essentials of New York ....G 845 368-1100
  Airmont (G-11)
Atelier Viollet Corp ....G 718 782-1727
  Brooklyn (G-1646)
Atlas Fence & Railing Co Inc ....E 718 767-2200
  Whitestone (G-17229)
Babcock Co Inc ....E 607 776-3341
  Bath (G-653)
◆ Betterbee Inc ....F 518 314-0575
  Greenwich (G-5905)
▲ Brooks Woodworking Inc ....F 914 666-2029
  Mount Kisco (G-8664)
Budd Woodwork Inc ....F 718 389-1110
  Brooklyn (G-1738)
Cabinet Shapes Corp ....F 718 784-6255
  Long Island City (G-7722)
▲ Catskill Craftsmen Inc ....D 607 652-7321
  Stamford (G-15644)
▲ Cdnv Wood Carving Frames Inc .....F 914 375-3447
  Yonkers (G-17442)
▲ Cffco USA Inc ....G 718 747-1118
  Jericho (G-7095)
▼ Cfp Purchasing Inc ....G 705 806-0383
  Flushing (G-5238)
▲ Channel Manufacturing Inc ....E 516 944-6271
  Port Washington (G-13827)
Charles Freihofer Baking Co ....G 518 463-2221
  Albany (G-62)
Cherry Creek Woodcraft Inc ....E 716 988-3211
  South Dayton (G-15540)
▲ Cowee Forest Products Inc ....E 518 658-2233
  Berlin (G-854)
Craz Woodworking Assoc Inc ....F 631 205-1890
  Bellport (G-823)
Daniel Demarco and Assoc Inc ....E 631 598-7000
  Amityville (G-283)
Designs By Robert Scott Inc ....E 718 609-2535
  Brooklyn (G-1856)
Di Fiore and Sons Custom Wdwkg .....G 718 278-1663
  Long Island City (G-7744)
Di Vico Craft Products Ltd ....G 845 265-9390
  Cold Spring (G-3787)
Digital Fabrication Wkshp Inc ....G 518 249-6500
  Hudson (G-6641)
Drummond Framing Inc ....F 212 647-1701
  New York (G-9983)
Ed Negron Fine Woodworking ....G 718 246-1016
  Brooklyn (G-1904)
Elephants Custom Furniture Inc ....D 917 509-3581
  Brooklyn (G-1918)
◆ Enchante Accessories Inc ....C 212 689-6008
  New York (G-10080)
Encore Retail Systems Inc ....F 718 385-3443
  Mamaroneck (G-8066)

Essex Box & Pallet Co Inc ....E 518 834-7279
  Keeseville (G-7166)
▲ FG Galassi Moulding Co Inc ....E 845 258-2100
  Goshen (G-5749)
Fibron Products Inc ....E 716 886-2378
  Buffalo (G-2961)
Frame Shoppe & Art Gallery ....E 516 365-6014
  Manhasset (G-8093)
◆ Framerica Corporation ....F 631 650-1000
  Yaphank (G-17409)
▲ Fred M Lawrence Co Inc ....E 718 786-7227
  Bay Shore (G-699)
Furniture Dsgn By Knossos Inc ....G 718 729-0404
  Woodside (G-17347)
Galas Framing Services ....F 718 706-0007
  Long Island City (G-7776)
General Art Company Inc ....E 212 255-1298
  New York (G-10315)
◆ Globus Cork Inc ....G 347 963-4059
  Bronx (G-1346)
Grant-Noren ....G 845 726-4281
  Westtown (G-17099)
Graphics Slution Providers Inc ....G 845 677-5088
  Lagrangeville (G-7278)
Green Renewable Inc ....E 518 658-2233
  Berlin (G-855)
Grohe America Inc ....G 212 206-8820
  New York (G-10410)
Hennig Custom Woodwork Corp ....G 516 536-3460
  Oceanside (G-13101)
House of Heydenryk Jr Inc ....F 212 206-9611
  New York (G-10561)
Hubray Inc ....F 800 645-2855
  North Baldwin (G-12924)
▲ Imperial Frames & Albums LLC ....G 718 832-9793
  Brooklyn (G-2095)
Innova Interiors Inc ....E 718 401-2122
  Bronx (G-1365)
Interntonal Consmr Connections ....F 516 481-3438
  West Hempstead (G-16887)
Interstate Wood Products Inc ....E 631 842-4488
  Amityville (G-296)
James King Woodworking Inc ....E 518 761-6091
  Queensbury (G-14013)
Jeffrey John ....G 631 842-2850
  Amityville (G-299)
Jordache Woodworking Corp ....F 718 349-3373
  Brooklyn (G-2146)
Julius Lowy Frame Restoring Co ....E 212 861-8585
  New York (G-10819)
K & B Woodworking Inc ....G 518 634-7253
  Cairo (G-3300)
Lanwood Industries Inc ....E 718 786-3000
  Bay Shore (G-709)
Lanza Corp ....G 914 937-6360
  Port Chester (G-13778)
◆ Lco Destiny LLC ....G 315 782-3302
  Watertown (G-16684)
Long Lumber and Supply Corp ....G 518 439-1661
  Slingerlands (G-15499)
M & R Woodworking & Finishing ....G 718 486-5480
  Brooklyn (G-2247)
▲ M A Moslow & Bros Inc ....E 716 896-2950
  Buffalo (G-3070)
McGraw Wood Products LLC ....E 607 836-6465
  Mc Graw (G-8254)
McIntosh Box & Pallet Co Inc ....E 315 446-9350
  Rome (G-14848)
Meadowwood NY LLC ....G 212 729-5400
  New York (G-11230)
Meeco Sullivan LLC ....G 800 232-3625
  Warwick (G-16617)
◆ N Sketch Build Inc ....G 800 975-0597
  Fishkill (G-5195)
▲ North American Enclosures Inc .....E 631 234-9500
  Central Islip (G-3534)
Northast Ctr For Bekeeping LLC ....F 800 632-3379
  Greenwich (G-5910)
Northern Forest Pdts Co Inc ....G 315 942-6955
  Boonville (G-1164)
P B & H Moulding Corporation ....E 315 455-1756
  Fayetteville (G-5174)
Paramount Graphix ....G 845 367-5003
  Port Jervis (G-13813)
Pdj Components Inc ....E 845 469-9191
  Chester (G-3638)
Pella Corporation ....C 631 208-0710
  Calverton (G-3322)
▲ Pgs Millwork Inc ....D 212 244-6610
  New York (G-11663)

Piccini Mnm Inc ....G 845 741-6770
  West Nyack (G-16953)
Picture Perfect Framing ....G 718 851-1884
  Brooklyn (G-2432)
Premium Mulch & Materials Inc ....F 631 320-3666
  Coram (G-3972)
Prime Wood Products ....G 518 792-1407
  Queensbury (G-14021)
▲ Putnam Rolling Ladder Co Inc ....C 212 226-5147
  New York (G-11779)
Putnam Rolling Ladder Co Inc ....F 718 381-8219
  Brooklyn (G-2476)
Quattro Frameworks Inc ....F 718 361-2620
  Long Island City (G-7885)
Quebracho Inc ....F 718 326-3605
  Brooklyn (G-2484)
▲ R P M Industries Inc ....E 315 255-1105
  Auburn (G-512)
Regence Picture Frames Inc ....F 718 779-0888
  Lynbrook (G-7985)
Revival Industries Inc ....F 315 868-1085
  Ilion (G-6784)
Richard Rothbard Inc ....G 845 355-2300
  Slate Hill (G-15496)
Rose Fence Inc ....F 516 223-0777
  Baldwin (G-560)
Ryers Creek Corp ....E 607 523-6617
  Corning (G-4000)
Sky Frame & Art Inc ....E 212 925-7856
  New York (G-12120)
▲ Structural Industries Inc ....C 631 471-5200
  Bohemia (G-1134)
Superior Wood Turnings ....F 716 483-1254
  Jamestown (G-7069)
Swiss Madison LLC ....F 434 623-4766
  Brooklyn (G-2656)
T Eason Land Surveyor ....G 631 474-2200
  Port Jeff STA (G-13795)
Thomas Matthews Wdwkg Ltd ....F 631 287-3657
  Southampton (G-15578)
Thomas Matthews Wdwkg Ltd ....G 631 287-2023
  Southampton (G-15579)
Ultimate Styles of America ....F 631 254-0219
  Bay Shore (G-746)
▲ Unisource Food Eqp Systems Inc ..G 516 681-0537
  Holbrook (G-6506)
Walpole Woodworkers Inc ....G 631 726-2859
  Water Mill (G-16628)
Wholesale Mulch & Sawdust Inc ....F 607 687-2637
  Owego (G-13387)
Windsor United Industries LLC ....E 607 655-3300
  Windsor (G-17295)
Wood Innovations of Suffolk ....G 631 698-2345
  Medford (G-8297)
Woodmotif ....F 516 564-8325
  Hempstead (G-6312)
Woodtronics Inc ....G 914 962-5205
  Yorktown Heights (G-17537)
▲ York Ladder Inc ....G 718 784-6666
  Long Island City (G-7959)

25 FURNITURE AND FIXTURES

2511 Wood Household Furniture

A & S Woodworking Inc ....G 518 821-0832
  Hudson (G-6630)
A-1 Manhattan Custom Furn Inc ....G 212 750-9800
  Island Park (G-6817)
American Epoxy and Metal Inc ....G 718 828-7828
  Scarsdale (G-15245)
Anthony Lawrence of New York ....E 212 206-8820
  Long Island City (G-7694)
Arthur Brown W Mfg Co ....E 631 243-5594
  Deer Park (G-4126)
▲ Arthur Lauer Inc ....E 845 255-7871
  Gardiner (G-5560)
Artisan Woodworking Ltd ....G 516 486-0818
  West Hempstead (G-16880)
Atelier Viollet Corp ....G 718 782-1727
  Brooklyn (G-1646)
Bel Art International ....E 718 402-2100
  Bronx (G-1281)
▲ Benchmark Furniture Mfg ....D 718 257-4707
  Brooklyn (G-1679)
Black River Woodworking LLC ....G 315 376-8405
  Castorland (G-3450)
Brueton Industries Inc ....D 516 379-3400
  Freeport (G-5401)
▲ Bush Industries Inc ....C 716 665-2000
  Jamestown (G-7013)

Cab-Network Inc....G....516 334-8666
Westbury (G-17000)
Carlos & Alex Atelier Inc....E....718 441-8911
Richmond Hill (G-14083)
Carver Creek Enterprises Inc....G....585 657-7511
Bloomfield (G-977)
Cassadaga Designs Inc....G....716 595-3030
Cassadaga (G-3442)
▲ Catskill Craftsmen Inc....D....607 652-7321
Stamford (G-15644)
▲ Charles H Beckley Inc....F....718 665-2218
Bronx (G-1297)
Comerford Hennessy At Home Inc....G....631 537-6200
Bridgehampton (G-1231)
▲ Community Products LLC....C....845 658-8799
Rifton (G-14144)
Concepts In Wood of CNY....E....315 463-8084
Syracuse (G-15923)
Conesus Lake Association Inc....E....585 346-6864
Lakeville (G-7306)
Cousins Furniture & Hm Imprvs....E....631 254-3752
Deer Park (G-4143)
Crawford Furniture Mfg Corp....C....716 483-2102
Jamestown (G-7020)
Custom Display Manufacture....G....516 783-6491
North Bellmore (G-12936)
Custom Woodcraft LLC....F....315 843-4234
Munnsville (G-8796)
▲ D & W Design Inc....E....845 343-3366
Middletown (G-8468)
David Sutherland Showrooms - N....G....212 871-9717
New York (G-9879)
Dbs Interiors Corp....F....631 491-3013
West Babylon (G-16813)
Dcl Furniture Manufacturing....E....516 248-2683
Mineola (G-8538)
Deakon Homes and Interiors....F....518 271-0342
Troy (G-16255)
Designs By Robert Scott Inc....E....718 609-2535
Brooklyn (G-1856)
Dessin/Fournir Inc....F....212 758-0844
New York (G-9912)
▲ Dinette Depot Ltd....D....516 515-9623
Brooklyn (G-1865)
Ducduc LLC....F....212 226-1868
New York (G-9986)
▲ Dune Inc....G....212 925-6171
New York (G-9989)
East End Country Kitchens Inc....F....631 727-2258
Calverton (G-3318)
▲ Eclectic Cntract Furn Inds Inc....F....212 967-5504
New York (G-10029)
El Greco Woodworking Inc....E....716 483-0315
Jamestown (G-7025)
Emilia Interiors Inc....F....718 629-4202
Brooklyn (G-1923)
▲ Ercole Nyc Inc....F....212 675-2218
Brooklyn (G-1937)
Eugenia Selective Living Inc....F....631 277-1461
Islip (G-6847)
Eurocraft Custom Furniture....G....718 956-0600
Long Island City (G-7761)
Falcon Chair and Table Inc....E....716 664-7136
Falconer (G-4904)
▲ Feinkind Inc....G....800 289-6136
Irvington (G-6811)
Fenix Furniture Co....E....631 273-3500
Bay Shore (G-698)
▲ Fiber-Seal of New York Inc....G....212 888-5580
New York (G-10209)
Final Dimension Inc....G....718 786-0100
Maspeth (G-8171)
Fine Arts Furniture Inc....G....212 744-9139
Long Island City (G-7769)
▲ Forecast Consoles Inc....E....631 253-9000
Hauppauge (G-6102)
Franz Fischer Inc....F....718 821-1300
Brooklyn (G-2003)
Fred Schulz Inc....G....845 724-3409
Poughquag (G-13957)
French & Itln Furn Craftsmen....G....718 599-5000
Brooklyn (G-2004)
Furniture Doctor Inc....G....585 657-6941
Bloomfield (G-982)
Glendale Architectural WD Pdts....E....718 326-2700
Glendale (G-5669)
◆ Hard Manufacturing Co Inc....D....716 893-1800
Buffalo (G-3005)
▲ Harden Furniture LLC....C....315 675-3600
Mc Connellsville (G-8251)

Hayman-Chaffey Designs Inc....F....212 889-7771
New York (G-10473)
Henry B Urban Inc....E....212 489-3308
New York (G-10500)
▲ Hunt Country Furniture Inc....D....845 832-6601
Wingdale (G-17296)
Icon Design LLC....E....585 768-6040
Le Roy (G-7434)
Innovant Inc....G....212 929-4883
New York (G-10645)
▲ Inova LLC....E....866 528-2804
Altamont (G-211)
Inter Craft Custom Furniture....G....718 278-2573
Astoria (G-443)
J Percoco Industries Inc....G....631 312-4572
Bohemia (G-1075)
K & B Woodworking Inc....G....518 634-7253
Cairo (G-3300)
Kazac Inc....G....631 249-7299
Farmingdale (G-5031)
Kittinger Company Inc....E....716 876-1000
Buffalo (G-3050)
Knoll Inc....D....212 343-4124
New York (G-10902)
▲ L& JG Stickley Incorporated....A....315 682-5500
Manlius (G-8106)
Lanoves Inc....G....718 384-1880
Brooklyn (G-2195)
Lemode Concepts Inc....G....631 841-0796
Amityville (G-305)
Little Wolf Cabinet Shop Inc....E....212 734-1116
New York (G-11039)
Long Lumber and Supply Corp....F....518 439-1661
Slingerlands (G-15499)
▲ M & C Furniture....G....718 422-2136
Brooklyn (G-2244)
M T D Corporation....F....631 491-3905
West Babylon (G-16837)
Machias Furniture Factory Inc....G....716 353-8687
Machias (G-8023)
◆ Mackenzie-Childs LLC....C....315 364-6118
Aurora (G-528)
Manchester Wood Inc....C....518 642-9518
Granville (G-5792)
McGraw Wood Products LLC....E....607 836-6465
Mc Graw (G-8254)
Mica International Ltd....F....516 378-3400
Freeport (G-5423)
New Day Woodwork Inc....E....718 275-1721
Glendale (G-5674)
Nicholas Dfine Furn Decorators....F....914 245-8982
Bronx (G-1413)
▲ Patrick Mackin Custom Furn....G....718 237-2592
Brooklyn (G-2423)
Piccini Industries Ltd....E....845 365-0614
Orangeburg (G-13262)
▼ Pillow Perfections Ltd Inc....G....718 383-2259
Brooklyn (G-2434)
Premier Woodcraft Ltd....E....610 383-6624
White Plains (G-17188)
◆ Premiere Living Products LLC....F....631 873-4337
Dix Hills (G-4318)
Professional Cab Detailing Co....F....845 436-7282
Woodridge (G-17333)
Raff Enterprises....G....518 218-7883
Albany (G-127)
Recycled Brooklyn Group LLC....F....917 902-0662
Brooklyn (G-2504)
▼ Reis D Furniture Mfg....E....516 248-5676
Mineola (G-8567)
◆ Renco Group Inc....G....212 541-6000
New York (G-11864)
Sitecraft Inc....G....718 729-4900
Astoria (G-456)
Stillwater Wood & Iron....G....518 664-4501
Stillwater (G-15783)
▲ Sundown Ski & Sport Shop Inc....E....631 737-8600
Lake Grove (G-7292)
▲ Triple J Bedding LLC....G....718 643-8005
Brooklyn (G-2701)
Universal Designs Inc....G....718 721-1111
Long Island City (G-7938)
Wallace Home Design Ctr....G....631 765-3890
Southold (G-15585)
Walpole Woodworkers Inc....G....631 726-2859
Water Mill (G-16628)
Walter P Sauer LLC....E....718 937-0600
Brooklyn (G-2759)
William Somerville Maintenance....D....212 534-4600
New York (G-12663)

Woodmotif Inc....F....516 564-8325
Hempstead (G-6312)
◆ World Trading Center Inc....G....631 273-3330
Hauppauge (G-6260)
Your Furniture Designers Inc....G....845 947-3046
West Haverstraw (G-16879)

2512 Wood Household Furniture, Upholstered

▲ Arthur Lauer Inc....E....845 255-7871
Gardiner (G-5560)
▲ Artone LLC....D....716 664-2232
Jamestown (G-7008)
August Studios....G....718 706-6487
Long Island City (G-7709)
▲ Avanti Furniture Corp....F....516 293-8220
Farmingdale (G-4957)
▲ Classic Sofa Ltd....D....212 620-0485
New York (G-9692)
Deangelis Ltd....E....212 348-8225
Glen Head (G-5645)
Delta Upholsterers Inc....E....212 489-3308
New York (G-9896)
Doreen Interiors Ltd....E....212 255-9008
New Hyde Park (G-8872)
Elan Upholstery Inc....F....631 563-0650
Bohemia (G-1061)
Falvo Manufacturing Co Inc....F....315 738-7682
Utica (G-16353)
▲ Fiber-Seal of New York Inc....G....212 888-5580
New York (G-10209)
Furniture By Craftmaster Ltd....G....631 750-0658
Bohemia (G-1065)
H & H Furniture Co....G....718 850-5252
Jamaica (G-6953)
Hallagan Manufacturing Co Inc....D....315 331-4640
Newark (G-12751)
▲ Harden Furniture LLC....C....315 675-3600
Mc Connellsville (G-8251)
Henry B Urban Inc....E....212 489-3308
New York (G-10500)
Jackson Dakota Inc....F....718 786-8600
Long Island City (G-7797)
▲ Jackson Dakota Inc....G....212 838-9444
New York (G-10728)
Jays Furniture Products Inc....E....716 876-8854
Buffalo (G-3031)
Kittinger Company Inc....E....716 876-1000
Buffalo (G-3050)
◆ Mackenzie-Childs LLC....C....315 364-6118
Aurora (G-528)
Matteo & Antonio Bartolotta....F....315 252-2220
Auburn (G-506)
Mazza Classics Incorporated....G....631 390-9060
Farmingdale (G-5055)
McCarroll Uphl Designs LLC....G....518 828-0500
Hudson (G-6655)
Mitchell Gold Co....D....516 627-3525
Manhasset (G-8096)
Nicholas Dfine Furn Decorators....F....914 245-8982
Bronx (G-1413)
Pheonix Custom Furniture Ltd....E....212 727-2648
Long Island City (G-7872)
◆ Princeton Upholstery Co Inc....D....845 343-2196
Middletown (G-8493)
Rob Herschenfeld Design Inc....F....718 456-6801
Brooklyn (G-2520)
Simon S Decorating Inc....G....718 339-2931
Brooklyn (G-2588)
▲ Slava Industries Incorporated....G....718 499-4850
Brooklyn (G-2595)
Sleepable Sofas Ltd....D....973 546-4502
New York (G-12125)
▲ Smith & Watson....E....212 686-6444
New York (G-12132)
Sofa Doctor Inc....G....718 292-6300
Bronx (G-1456)
Two Worlds Arts Ltd....G....212 929-2210
Brooklyn (G-2713)
Versailles Drapery Upholstery....F....212 533-2059
Long Island City (G-7944)
Walco Leather Co Inc....E....212 243-2244
Bedford (G-795)
Wallace Home Design Ctr....G....631 765-3890
Southold (G-15585)
Yepes Fine Furniture....E....718 383-0221
Brooklyn (G-2787)

S I C

25 FURNITURE AND FIXTURES

2514 Metal Household Furniture

▲ American Best Cabinets Inc .... E 845 369-6666
Suffern *(G-15807)*
Brueton Industries Inc .... D 516 379-3400
Freeport *(G-5401)*
◆ Charles P Rogers Brass Beds .... F 212 675-4400
New York *(G-9633)*
▲ CIDC Corp .... F 718 342-5820
Brooklyn *(G-1779)*
▲ D & W Design Inc .... E 845 343-3366
Middletown *(G-8468)*
◆ Embassy Dinettes Inc .... G 631 253-2292
Deer Park *(G-4160)*
F&M Ornamental Designs LLC .... G 212 353-2600
New York *(G-10170)*
▲ F&M Ornamental Designs LLC .... F 908 241-7776
New York *(G-10171)*
Furniture Doctor Inc .... G 585 657-6941
Bloomfield *(G-982)*
▲ Glissade New York LLC .... G 631 756-4800
Farmingdale *(G-5007)*
◆ Hard Manufacturing Co Inc .... D 716 893-1800
Buffalo *(G-3005)*
▲ Hellas Stone Inc .... G 718 545-4716
Astoria *(G-442)*
La Forge Francaise Ltd Inc .... G 631 591-0572
Riverhead *(G-14158)*
▲ Majestic Home Imprvs Distr .... G 718 853-5079
Brooklyn *(G-2256)*
Manhattan Cabinets Inc .... G 212 548-2436
New York *(G-11152)*
Meeker Sales Corp .... G 718 384-5400
Brooklyn *(G-2297)*
Methods Tooling & Mfg Inc .... E 845 246-7100
Mount Marion *(G-8693)*
▲ NK Medical Products Inc .... G 716 759-7200
Amherst *(G-252)*
▲ Novum Medical Products Inc .... F 716 759-7200
Amherst *(G-253)*
Precision Orna Ir Works Inc .... G 718 379-5200
Bronx *(G-1433)*
◆ Renco Group Inc .... G 212 541-6000
New York *(G-11864)*
Royal Metal Products Inc .... E 518 966-4442
Surprise *(G-15832)*
▲ Slava Industries Incorporated .... G 718 499-4850
Brooklyn *(G-2595)*
Steelcraft Manufacturing Co .... F 718 277-2404
Brooklyn *(G-2624)*

2515 Mattresses & Bedsprings

▲ Brook North Farms Inc .... F 315 834-9390
Auburn *(G-486)*
Casper Science LLC .... G 212 633-4309
New York *(G-9594)*
▲ Charles H Beckley Inc .... F 718 665-2218
Bronx *(G-1297)*
▲ Comfort Bedding Inc .... E 718 485-7662
Brooklyn *(G-1793)*
Dixie Foam Ltd .... G 212 645-8999
Brooklyn *(G-1868)*
Duxiana Dux Bed .... G 212 755-2600
New York *(G-9992)*
E & G Bedding Corp .... E 718 369-1092
Brooklyn *(G-1890)*
◆ Hard Manufacturing Co Inc .... D 716 893-1800
Buffalo *(G-3005)*
▼ Ideal Manufacturing Inc .... E 585 872-7190
East Rochester *(G-4481)*
Jamestown Mattress Co .... E 716 665-2247
Jamestown *(G-7043)*
KKR Millennium GP LLC .... A 212 750-8300
New York *(G-10894)*
◆ M R C Industries Inc .... C 516 328-6900
Port Washington *(G-13860)*
Metro Mattress Corp .... E 716 205-2300
Niagara Falls *(G-12864)*
Natural Dreams LLC .... G 718 760-4202
Corona *(G-4027)*
▲ Otis Bedding Mfg Co Inc .... E 716 825-2599
Buffalo *(G-3127)*
◆ Quality Foam Inc .... F 718 381-3644
Brooklyn *(G-2479)*
Rollers Inc .... G 716 837-0700
Buffalo *(G-3192)*
▲ Royal Bedding Co Buffalo Inc .... E 716 895-1414
Buffalo *(G-3197)*
Sealy Mattress Co Albany Inc .... B 518 880-1600
Troy *(G-16244)*

Sleep Improvement Center Inc .... F 516 536-5799
Rockville Centre *(G-14827)*
Sleepable Sofas Ltd .... D 973 546-4502
New York *(G-12125)*
▲ Steinbock-Braff Inc .... F 718 972-6500
Brooklyn *(G-2627)*
▲ VSM Investors LLC .... F 212 351-1600
New York *(G-12597)*
Zzz Mattress Manufacturing .... F 718 454-1468
Saint Albans *(G-15112)*

2517 Wood T V, Radio, Phono & Sewing Cabinets

Cleary Custom Cabinets Inc .... F 516 939-2475
Hicksville *(G-6357)*
Dbs Interiors Corp .... F 631 491-3013
West Babylon *(G-16813)*
Handcraft Cabinetry Inc .... G 914 681-9437
White Plains *(G-17144)*
Loffreno Cstm Interiors Contg .... E 718 981-0319
Staten Island *(G-15721)*
Time Base Corporation .... E 631 293-4068
Edgewood *(G-4630)*
▲ W Designe Inc .... F 914 736-1058
Peekskill *(G-13509)*

2519 Household Furniture, NEC

3phase Industries LLC .... G 347 763-2942
Brooklyn *(G-1514)*
▲ Albert Menin Interiors Ltd .... F 212 876-3041
Bronx *(G-1268)*
Anandamali Inc .... F 212 343-8964
New York *(G-9197)*
Bielecky Bros Inc .... F 718 424-4764
Woodside *(G-17337)*
▲ Comely International Trdg Inc .... G 212 683-1240
New York *(G-9742)*
Culin/Colella Inc .... G 914 698-7727
Mamaroneck *(G-8063)*
Dbs Interiors Corp .... F 631 491-3013
West Babylon *(G-16813)*
Eugenia Selective Living Inc .... F 631 277-1461
Islip *(G-6847)*
Harome Designs LLC .... G 631 864-1900
Commack *(G-3860)*
▲ Holland & Sherry Inc .... E 212 542-8410
New York *(G-10540)*
▲ L & JG Stickley Incorporated .... A 315 682-5500
Manlius *(G-8106)*
Matthew Shively LLC .... G 914 937-3531
Port Chester *(G-13779)*
Mbh Furniture Innovations Inc .... G 845 354-8202
Spring Valley *(G-15617)*
▲ Olollo Inc .... G 877 701-0110
Brooklyn *(G-2402)*
Ready To Assemble Company Inc .... E 516 825-4397
Valley Stream *(G-16448)*
Rent-A-Center Inc .... G 718 322-2400
Jamaica *(G-6984)*
Safcore LLC .... G 917 627-5263
Brooklyn *(G-2552)*
◆ Spancraft Ltd .... F 516 295-0055
Woodmere *(G-17332)*
▲ Vondom LLC .... G 212 207-3252
New York *(G-12595)*

2521 Wood Office Furniture

▲ A G Master Crafts Ltd .... F 516 745-6262
Garden City *(G-5506)*
▲ Artistic Products LLC .... E 631 435-0200
Hauppauge *(G-6045)*
▲ Artone LLC .... D 716 664-2232
Jamestown *(G-7008)*
B D B Typewriter Supply Works .... E 718 232-4800
Brooklyn *(G-1659)*
▲ Bauerschmidt & Sons Inc .... D 718 528-3500
Jamaica *(G-6934)*
Bloch Industries LLC .... D 585 334-9600
Rochester *(G-14253)*
Brueton Industries Inc .... D 516 379-3400
Freeport *(G-5401)*
▲ Bush Industries Inc .... C 716 665-2000
Jamestown *(G-7013)*
▼ Ccn International Inc .... D 315 789-4400
Geneva *(G-5584)*
Centre Interiors Wdwkg Co Inc .... E 718 323-1343
Ozone Park *(G-13402)*
Chicone Builders LLC .... F 607 535-6540
Montour Falls *(G-8648)*

Commercial Display Design LLC .... F 607 336-7353
Norwich *(G-13044)*
Concepts In Wood of CNY .... E 315 463-8084
Syracuse *(G-15923)*
▼ Craft Custom Woodwork Co Inc .... F 718 821-2162
Maspeth *(G-8155)*
Creative Cabinetry Corporation .... G 914 963-6061
Yonkers *(G-17447)*
Culin/Colella Inc .... G 914 698-7727
Mamaroneck *(G-8063)*
DAF Office Networks Inc .... G 315 699-7070
Cicero *(G-3673)*
Dates Weiser Furniture Corp .... D 716 891-1700
Buffalo *(G-2921)*
Davinci Designs Inc .... F 631 595-1095
Deer Park *(G-4148)*
Dcl Furniture Manufacturing .... E 516 248-2683
Mineola *(G-8538)*
Deakon Homes and Interiors .... F 518 271-0342
Troy *(G-16255)*
Designs By Robert Scott Inc .... E 718 609-2535
Brooklyn *(G-1856)*
Dimaio Millwork Corporation .... E 914 476-1937
Yonkers *(G-17451)*
Divine Art Furniture Inc .... G 718 834-0111
Brooklyn *(G-1867)*
▲ E-Systems Group LLC .... E 607 775-1100
Conklin *(G-3893)*
Eugenia Selective Living Inc .... F 631 277-1461
Islip *(G-6847)*
Exhibit Corporation America .... E 718 937-2600
Long Island City *(G-7763)*
F E Hale Mfg Co .... D 315 894-5490
Frankfort *(G-5361)*
Fina Cabinet Corp .... G 718 409-2900
Mount Vernon *(G-8726)*
▲ Forecast Consoles Inc .... E 631 253-9000
Hauppauge *(G-6102)*
Furniture By Craftmaster Ltd .... G 631 750-0658
Bohemia *(G-1065)*
Glendale Architectural WD Pdts .... E 718 326-2700
Glendale *(G-5669)*
▲ Gunlocke Company LLC .... C 585 728-5111
Wayland *(G-16734)*
H Freund Woodworking Co Inc .... F 516 334-3774
Westbury *(G-17019)*
▲ Harden Furniture LLC .... C 315 675-3600
Mc Connellsville *(G-8251)*
Heartwood Specialties Inc .... E 607 654-0102
Hammondsport *(G-5977)*
Hni Corporation .... C 212 683-2232
New York *(G-10536)*
▲ Humanscale Corporation .... B 212 725-4749
New York *(G-10578)*
▲ Innovant Inc .... C 631 348-1900
Islandia *(G-6834)*
Innovant Inc .... D 212 929-4883
New York *(G-10644)*
Interior Solutions of Wny LLC .... G 716 332-0372
Buffalo *(G-3028)*
Kazac Inc .... G 631 249-7299
Farmingdale *(G-5031)*
Kittinger Company Inc .... E 716 876-1000
Buffalo *(G-3050)*
Knoll Inc .... D 716 891-1700
Buffalo *(G-3051)*
Knoll Inc .... D 212 343-4124
New York *(G-10902)*
Krefab Corporation .... F 631 842-5151
Huntington *(G-6701)*
▲ Lake Country Woodworkers Ltd .... E 585 374-6353
Naples *(G-8812)*
Loffreno Cstm Interiors Contg .... E 718 981-0319
Staten Island *(G-15721)*
Longo Commercial Cabinets Inc .... E 631 225-4290
Lindenhurst *(G-7491)*
M T D Corporation .... F 631 491-3905
West Babylon *(G-16837)*
Materials Design Workshop .... F 718 893-1954
Bronx *(G-1393)*
Matteo & Antonio Bartolotta .... F 315 252-2220
Auburn *(G-506)*
▲ Miller Blaker Inc .... D 718 665-3930
Bronx *(G-1401)*
Millers Millworks Inc .... E 585 494-1420
Bergen *(G-8812)*
▲ N Y Elli Design Corp .... F 718 228-0014
Maspeth *(G-8184)*
New Dimensions Office Group .... D 718 387-0995
Brooklyn *(G-2370)*

25 FURNITURE AND FIXTURES

Nicholas Dfine Furn Decorators .... F 914 245-8982
  Bronx *(G-1413)*
Omega Furniture Manufacturing .... F 315 463-7428
  Syracuse *(G-16023)*
Pheonix Custom Furniture Ltd .... E 212 727-2648
  Long Island City *(G-7872)*
Piccini Industries Ltd .... E 845 365-0614
  Orangeburg *(G-13262)*
▲ Poppin Inc .... D 212 391-7200
  New York *(G-11707)*
Premier Woodcraft Ltd .... E 610 383-6624
  White Plains *(G-17188)*
▲ Prince Seating Corp .... E 718 363-2300
  Brooklyn *(G-2458)*
◆ Princeton Upholstery Co Inc .... D 845 343-2196
  Middletown *(G-8493)*
Red White & Blue Entps Corp .... G 718 565-8080
  Woodside *(G-17366)*
Riverfront Costume Design .... G 716 693-2501
  North Tonawanda *(G-13008)*
Saraval Industries .... G 516 768-9033
  Nyack *(G-13070)*
Stylecraft Interiors Inc .... F 516 487-2133
  Great Neck *(G-5862)*
▲ Technology Desking Inc .... E 212 257-6998
  New York *(G-12315)*
Three R Enterprises Inc .... E 585 254-5050
  Rochester *(G-14752)*
Universal Designs Inc .... G 718 721-1111
  Long Island City *(G-7938)*
▲ Upstate Office Liquidators Inc .... F 607 722-9234
  Johnson City *(G-7137)*
Wood Etc Inc .... F 315 484-9663
  Syracuse *(G-16099)*
Woodmotif Inc .... F 516 564-8325
  Hempstead *(G-6312)*
Your Furniture Designers Inc .... G 845 947-3046
  West Haverstraw *(G-16879)*
Zographos Designs Ltd .... G 212 545-0227
  New York *(G-12737)*

2522 Office Furniture, Except Wood

3phase Industries LLC .... G 347 763-2942
  Brooklyn *(G-1514)*
Able Steel Equipment Co Inc .... F 718 361-9240
  Long Island City *(G-7679)*
Afco Systems Inc .... C 631 249-9441
  Farmingdale *(G-4938)*
Allcraft Fabricators Inc .... D 631 951-4100
  Hauppauge *(G-6034)*
Aronowitz Metal Works .... G 845 356-1660
  Monsey *(G-8603)*
▲ Artone LLC .... D 716 664-2232
  Jamestown *(G-7008)*
Aztec Industries Inc .... G 631 585-1331
  Ronkonkoma *(G-14903)*
Brueton Industries Inc .... G 516 379-3400
  Freeport *(G-5401)*
Creative Cabinetry Corporation .... G 914 963-6061
  Yonkers *(G-17447)*
▲ Davies Office Refurbishing Inc .... C 518 426-7188
  Albany *(G-72)*
Davinci Designs Inc .... F 631 595-1095
  Deer Park *(G-4148)*
Dcl Furniture Manufacturing .... E 516 248-2683
  Mineola *(G-8538)*
Deakon Homes and Interiors .... F 518 271-0342
  Troy *(G-16255)*
▲ E-Systems Group LLC .... F 607 775-1100
  Conklin *(G-3893)*
Eugenia Selective Living Inc .... F 631 277-1461
  Islip *(G-6847)*
Exhibit Corporation America .... E 718 937-2600
  Long Island City *(G-7763)*
Falvo Manufacturing Co Inc .... F 315 738-7682
  Utica *(G-16353)*
▲ Forecast Consoles Inc .... G 631 253-9000
  Hauppauge *(G-6102)*
FX INC .... F 212 244-2240
  New York *(G-10277)*
◆ Hergo Ergonomic Support .... E 718 894-0639
  Maspeth *(G-8175)*
Hudson Valley Office Furn Inc .... G 845 565-6673
  Newburgh *(G-12784)*
Inscape Inc .... E 716 665-6210
  Falconer *(G-4910)*
Integrated Tech Support Svcs .... G 718 454-2497
  Saint Albans *(G-15111)*
Keilhauer .... F 646 742-0192
  New York *(G-10869)*

Kimball Office Inc .... E 212 753-6161
  New York *(G-10886)*
Knoll Inc .... D 212 343-4124
  New York *(G-10902)*
Larson Metal Manufacturing Co .... G 716 665-6807
  Jamestown *(G-7049)*
▲ Lucia Group Inc .... G 631 392-4900
  Deer Park *(G-4192)*
Modern Metal Fabricators Inc .... G 518 966-4142
  Hannacroix *(G-5991)*
▲ Natural Stone & Cabinet Inc .... G 718 388-2988
  Brooklyn *(G-2360)*
New Dimensions Office Group .... D 718 387-0995
  Brooklyn *(G-2370)*
Piccini Industries Ltd .... E 845 365-0614
  Orangeburg *(G-13262)*
▲ Poppin Inc .... D 212 391-7200
  New York *(G-11707)*
Premier Woodcraft Ltd .... E 610 383-6624
  White Plains *(G-17188)*
▲ Prince Seating Corp .... E 718 363-2300
  Brooklyn *(G-2458)*
Riverfront Costume Design .... G 716 693-2501
  North Tonawanda *(G-13008)*
Roberts Office Furn Cncpts Inc .... E 315 451-9185
  Liverpool *(G-7572)*
Royal Metal Products Inc .... G 518 966-4442
  Surprise *(G-15832)*
Saturn Sales Inc .... G 519 658-5125
  Niagara Falls *(G-12892)*
▼ Schwab Corp .... E 585 381-4900
  Rochester *(G-14696)*
Seating Inc .... E 800 468-2475
  Nunda *(G-13060)*
▼ Ulrich Planfiling Eqp Corp .... E 716 763-1815
  Lakewood *(G-7319)*
◆ Vitra Inc .... F 212 463-5700
  New York *(G-12585)*
Workplace Interiors LLC .... F 585 425-7420
  Fairport *(G-4894)*
Zographos Designs Ltd .... G 212 545-0227
  New York *(G-12737)*

2531 Public Building & Related Furniture

Able Steel Equipment Co Inc .... F 718 361-9240
  Long Island City *(G-7679)*
American Bptst Chrches Mtro NY .... G 212 870-3195
  New York *(G-9164)*
Artistry in Wood of Syracuse .... F 315 431-4022
  East Syracuse *(G-4523)*
▲ Artone LLC .... D 716 664-2232
  Jamestown *(G-7008)*
B/E Aerospace Inc .... E 631 563-6400
  Bohemia *(G-1018)*
B/E Aerospace Inc .... C 631 589-0877
  Bohemia *(G-1019)*
Chair Factory .... E 718 363-2383
  Brooklyn *(G-1771)*
E & D Specialty Stands Inc .... E 716 337-0161
  North Collins *(G-12944)*
East/West Industries Inc .... E 631 981-5900
  Ronkonkoma *(G-14924)*
▲ Forecast Consoles Inc .... G 631 253-9000
  Hauppauge *(G-6102)*
Hartford Hwy Dept .... G 315 724-0654
  New Hartford *(G-8851)*
▲ Inova LLC .... E 866 528-2804
  Altamont *(G-211)*
Jays Furniture Products Inc .... F 716 876-8854
  Buffalo *(G-3031)*
Jcdecaux Mallscape LLC .... E 646 834-1200
  New York *(G-10751)*
Johnson Controls Inc .... D 518 884-8313
  Ballston Spa *(G-598)*
Johnson Controls Inc .... G 518 694-4822
  Albany *(G-92)*
Johnson Controls Inc .... E 585 671-1930
  Webster *(G-16750)*
Johnson Controls Inc .... C 585 724-2232
  Rochester *(G-14485)*
Keck Group Inc .... F 845 988-5757
  Warwick *(G-16613)*
▲ Maximum Security Products Corp .... E 518 233-1800
  Waterford *(G-16634)*
Maxsecure Systems Inc .... G 800 657-4336
  Buffalo *(G-3080)*
▲ N Y Elli Design Corp .... E 718 228-0014
  Maspeth *(G-8184)*
Pluribus Products Inc .... E 718 852-1614
  Bayville *(G-775)*

Readyjet Technical Svcs Inc .... F 518 705-4019
  Johnstown *(G-7154)*
Rosenwach Tank Co Inc .... E 212 972-4411
  Astoria *(G-454)*
Seating Inc .... E 800 468-2475
  Nunda *(G-13060)*
▲ Steeldeck Ny Inc .... F 718 599-3700
  Brooklyn *(G-2625)*
▼ Stidd Systems Inc .... E 631 477-2400
  Greenport *(G-5895)*
▲ Studio 21 LA Inc .... E 718 965-6579
  Brooklyn *(G-2634)*
◆ Testori Interiors Inc .... F 518 298-4400
  Champlain *(G-3574)*
Town of Amherst .... E 716 631-7113
  Williamsville *(G-17283)*
Tymor Park .... G 845 724-5691
  Lagrangeville *(G-7285)*
▲ Unifor Inc .... F 212 673-3434
  New York *(G-12472)*

2541 Wood, Office & Store Fixtures

16 Tons Inc .... E 718 418-8446
  Brooklyn *(G-1511)*
Abaco Steel Products Inc .... G 631 589-1800
  Bohemia *(G-997)*
▲ Abbott Industries Inc .... E 718 291-0800
  Jamaica *(G-6926)*
All Merchandise Display Corp .... G 718 257-2221
  Highland Mills *(G-6438)*
Allegany Laminating and Supply .... G 716 372-2424
  Allegany *(G-201)*
Alrod Associates Inc .... G 631 981-2193
  Ronkonkoma *(G-14892)*
Arcy Plastic Laminates Inc .... E 518 235-0753
  Albany *(G-45)*
▲ Array Marketing Group Inc .... E 212 750-3367
  New York *(G-9257)*
▲ Artone LLC .... D 716 664-2232
  Jamestown *(G-7008)*
Auburn Custom Millwork Inc .... G 315 253-3843
  Auburn *(G-477)*
▲ Auratic Inc .... E 914 413-8154
  New York *(G-9318)*
Bator Bintor Inc .... F 347 546-6503
  Brooklyn *(G-1670)*
▲ Bauerschmidt & Sons Inc .... D 718 528-3500
  Jamaica *(G-6934)*
Bloch Industries LLC .... D 585 334-9600
  Rochester *(G-14253)*
Champion Millwork Inc .... E 315 463-0711
  Syracuse *(G-15911)*
CNA Specialties Inc .... G 631 567-7929
  Sayville *(G-15235)*
Contempra Design Inc .... G 718 984-8586
  Staten Island *(G-15681)*
Countertops & Cabinets Inc .... G 315 433-1038
  Syracuse *(G-15930)*
Creative Counter Tops Inc .... G 845 471-6480
  Poughkeepsie *(G-13913)*
Custom Countertops Inc .... G 716 685-2871
  Depew *(G-4277)*
Custom Design Kitchens Inc .... G 518 355-4446
  Duanesburg *(G-4350)*
Custom Wood Inc .... G 718 927-4700
  Brooklyn *(G-1828)*
▲ David Flatt Furniture Ltd .... F 718 937-7944
  Long Island City *(G-7739)*
Dbs Interiors Corp .... F 631 491-3013
  West Babylon *(G-16813)*
Deakon Homes and Interiors .... F 518 271-0342
  Troy *(G-16255)*
Delocon Wholesale Inc .... F 716 592-2711
  Springville *(G-15630)*
E F Thresh Inc .... G 315 437-7301
  East Syracuse *(G-4539)*
Empire Archtctural Systems Inc .... E 518 773-5109
  Johnstown *(G-7141)*
Empire Fabricators Inc .... G 585 235-3050
  Rochester *(G-14366)*
Encore Retail Systems Inc .... F 718 385-3443
  Mamaroneck *(G-8066)*
Falvo Manufacturing Co Inc .... F 315 738-7682
  Utica *(G-16353)*
Farrington Packaging Corp .... E 315 733-4600
  Utica *(G-16353)*
Fina Cabinet Corp .... G 718 409-2900
  Mount Vernon *(G-8726)*
Fleetwood Cabinet Co Inc .... G 516 379-2139
  Brooklyn *(G-1986)*

25 FURNITURE AND FIXTURES

▲ Forecast Consoles Inc ....E 631 253-9000
  Hauppauge *(G-6102)*
Frank J Martello ....G 585 235-2780
  Rochester *(G-14403)*
Gaughan Construction Corp ....G 718 850-9577
  Richmond Hill *(G-14086)*
▲ Gotham City Industries Inc ....E 914 713-0979
  Scarsdale *(G-15247)*
Greenleaf Cabinet Makers LLC ......F 315 432-4600
  Syracuse *(G-15974)*
▲ Hamlet Products Inc ....F 914 665-0307
  Mount Vernon *(G-8734)*
Heartwood Specialties Inc ....G 607 654-0102
  Hammondsport *(G-5977)*
Home Ideal Inc ....G 718 762-8998
  Flushing *(G-5259)*
▲ Home4u Inc ....G 347 262-7214
  Brooklyn *(G-2082)*
Hunter Metal Industries Inc ....D 631 475-5900
  East Patchogue *(G-4467)*
▲ Icestone LLC ....E 718 624-4900
  Brooklyn *(G-2093)*
▲ Industrial Support Inc ....D 716 662-2954
  Buffalo *(G-3024)*
Integrated Wood Components Inc ..E 607 467-1739
  Deposit *(G-4301)*
Inter State Laminates Inc ....G 518 283-8355
  Poestenkill *(G-13754)*
J M P Display Fixture Co Inc ....G 718 649-0333
  Brooklyn *(G-2126)*
Johnny Mica Inc ....G 631 225-5213
  Lindenhurst *(G-7488)*
Joseph Fedele ....G 718 448-3658
  Staten Island *(G-15716)*
▲ Karp Associates Inc ....D 631 768-8300
  Melville *(G-8362)*
Kitchen Specialty Craftsmen ....G 607 739-0833
  Elmira *(G-4707)*
Koeppels Kustom Kitchens Inc .....G 518 489-0092
  Albany *(G-96)*
L & J Interiors Inc ....G 631 218-0838
  Bohemia *(G-1084)*
▲ Leo D Bernstein & Sons Inc ......E 212 337-9578
  New York *(G-11003)*
Lif Distributing Inc ....F 631 630-6900
  Islandia *(G-6837)*
▲ Lifestyle-Trimco ....E 718 257-9101
  Brooklyn *(G-2220)*
Longo Commercial Cabinets Inc ....E 631 225-4290
  Lindenhurst *(G-7491)*
▲ Madjek Inc ....D 631 842-4475
  Amityville *(G-308)*
▲ Marietta Corporation ....B 607 753-6746
  Cortland *(G-4057)*
Marplex Furniture Corporation .....G 914 969-7755
  Yonkers *(G-17484)*
Metropolitan Granite & MBL Inc ....G 585 342-7020
  Rochester *(G-14526)*
Michael P Mmarr ....G 315 623-9380
  Constantia *(G-3907)*
▲ New Business Solutions Inc .....E 631 789-1500
  Amityville *(G-315)*
New Dimensions Office Group ......D 718 387-0995
  Brooklyn *(G-2370)*
Nlr Counter Tops LLC ....G 347 295-0410
  New York *(G-11461)*
P & B Woodworking Inc ....F 845 744-2508
  Pine Bush *(G-13576)*
Pine Hill Fabricators ....G 716 823-2474
  Buffalo *(G-3150)*
Precision Built Tops LLC ....G 607 336-5417
  Norwich *(G-13053)*
▲ Premier Woodworking Inc ....E 631 236-4100
  Hauppauge *(G-6197)*
R H Guest Incorporated ....G 718 675-7600
  Brooklyn *(G-2490)*
Rasjada Enterprises Ltd ....F 631 242-1055
  Bay Shore *(G-728)*
Red White & Blue Entps Corp ....G 718 565-8080
  Woodside *(G-17366)*
Ridge Cabinet & Showcase Inc .....E 585 663-0560
  Rochester *(G-14649)*
Rochester Countertop Inc ....F 585 338-2260
  Rochester *(G-14662)*
Serway Bros Inc ....E 315 337-0601
  Rome *(G-14864)*
Sharonana Enterprises Inc ....E 631 875-5619
  Coram *(G-3973)*
Solid Surfaces Inc ....D 585 292-5340
  Rochester *(G-14716)*

▲ Space-Craft Worldwide Inc ....E 631 603-3000
  Edgewood *(G-4625)*
Specialty Services ....G 585 728-5650
  Wayland *(G-16735)*
Steelcraft Manufacturing Co ....F 718 277-2404
  Brooklyn *(G-2624)*
▲ Steeldeck Ny Inc ....F 718 599-3700
  Brooklyn *(G-2625)*
Stein Industries Inc ....F 631 789-2222
  Amityville *(G-325)*
Stereo Advantage Inc ....F 716 656-7161
  Cheektowaga *(G-3617)*
Telesca-Heyman Inc ....G 212 534-3442
  New York *(G-12319)*
Three R Enterprises Inc ....E 585 254-5050
  Rochester *(G-14752)*
Total Display Solutions Inc ....F 607 724-9999
  Binghamton *(G-950)*
Triad Counter Corp ....E 631 750-0615
  Bohemia *(G-1143)*
Unico Inc ....F 845 562-9255
  Newburgh *(G-12806)*
Universal Designs Inc ....G 718 721-1111
  Long Island City *(G-7938)*
Vitarose Corp of America ....G 718 951-9700
  Brooklyn *(G-2751)*
Wilbedone Inc ....E 607 756-8813
  Cortland *(G-4071)*
Wilsonart Intl Holdings LLC ....F 516 935-6980
  Bethpage *(G-878)*
Wineracksscom Inc ....E 845 658-7181
  Tillson *(G-16152)*
Wolak Inc ....G 315 839-5366
  Clayville *(G-3717)*

2542 Partitions & Fixtures, Except Wood

260 Oak Street Inc ....G 877 852-4676
  Buffalo *(G-2802)*
▲ Aarco Products Inc ....F 631 924-5461
  Yaphank *(G-17400)*
Abaco Steel Products Inc ....G 631 589-1800
  Bohemia *(G-997)*
▲ Abbott Industries Inc ....F 718 291-0800
  Jamaica *(G-6926)*
Able Steel Equipment Co Inc ....F 718 361-9240
  Long Island City *(G-7679)*
Air Crafters Inc ....C 631 471-7788
  Ronkonkoma *(G-14883)*
▲ All American Metal Corporation ..G 516 223-1760
  Freeport *(G-5392)*
All American Metal Corporation ....G 516 623-0222
  Freeport *(G-5393)*
All Racks Industries Inc ....E 212 244-1069
  New York *(G-9135)*
Alrod Associates Inc ....F 631 981-2193
  Ronkonkoma *(G-14892)*
American Standard Mfg Inc ....E 518 868-2512
  Central Bridge *(G-3507)*
ASAP Rack Rental Inc ....G 718 499-4495
  Brooklyn *(G-1640)*
▲ Avf Inc ....F 951 360-7111
  Buffalo *(G-2849)*
Bobrick Washroom Equipment Inc .G 518 877-7444
  Clifton Park *(G-3723)*
▲ Bridge Metal Industries LLC ......C 914 663-9200
  Mount Vernon *(G-8712)*
Clark Specialty Co Inc ....E 607 776-3193
  Bath *(G-655)*
◆ Core Group Displays Inc ....E 845 876-5109
  Rhinebeck *(G-14067)*
Custom Fixtures Inc ....G 718 965-1141
  Brooklyn *(G-1825)*
Dakota Systems Mfg Corp ....G 631 249-5811
  Farmingdale *(G-4983)*
Data Control Inc ....G 585 265-2980
  Ontario *(G-13221)*
Dejah Associates Inc ....E 631 265-2185
  Bay Shore *(G-692)*
Display Components Mfg Inc ....E 631 420-0600
  West Babylon *(G-16814)*
▲ Display Technologies LLC ....D 718 321-3100
  New Hyde Park *(G-8871)*
▲ E-Systems Group LLC ....F 607 775-1100
  Conklin *(G-3893)*
Eazy Movements ....G 716 837-2083
  Buffalo *(G-2945)*
Evans & Paul LLC ....F 516 576-0800
  Plainview *(G-13629)*
Exclusive Designs ....F 516 378-5258
  Freeport *(G-5407)*

◆ Fixtures 2000 Inc ....B 631 236-4100
  Hauppauge *(G-6100)*
Four S Showcase Manufacturing ..G 718 649-4900
  Brooklyn *(G-2000)*
Frazier Industrial Company ....D 315 539-9256
  Waterloo *(G-16648)*
◆ Gaylord Bros Inc ....D 315 457-5070
  North Syracuse *(G-12961)*
▲ Gerald Frd Packg Display LLC ...F 716 692-2705
  Tonawanda *(G-16182)*
Glaro Inc ....D 631 234-1717
  Hauppauge *(G-6108)*
▲ Glasbau Hahn America LLC ....G 845 566-3331
  Newburgh *(G-12780)*
◆ Global Steel Products Corp ....C 631 586-3455
  Deer Park *(G-4169)*
▲ Hamlet Products Inc ....F 914 665-0307
  Mount Vernon *(G-8734)*
Hawver Display Inc ....E 585 544-2290
  Rochester *(G-14449)*
◆ Hergo Ergonomic Support ....E 718 894-0639
  Maspeth *(G-8175)*
Hunter Metal Industries Inc ....D 631 475-5900
  East Patchogue *(G-4467)*
◆ Inscape (new York) Inc ....D 716 665-6210
  Falconer *(G-4909)*
Inscape Inc ....E 716 665-6210
  Falconer *(G-4910)*
Jack Luckner Steel Shelving Co ...G 718 363-0500
  Maspeth *(G-8178)*
Joldeson One Aerospace Inds ......D 718 848-7396
  Ozone Park *(G-13406)*
▲ Knickerbocker Partition Corp .....E 516 546-0550
  Freeport *(G-5418)*
▲ La Mar Lighting Co Inc ....D 631 777-7700
  Farmingdale *(G-5039)*
Ledan Inc ....E 631 239-1226
  Northport *(G-13032)*
▲ Lifestyle-Trimco ....E 718 257-9101
  Brooklyn *(G-2220)*
Locker Masters Inc ....F 518 288-3203
  Granville *(G-5790)*
▲ Lucia Group Inc ....E 631 392-4900
  Deer Park *(G-4192)*
Manhattan Display Inc ....G 718 392-1365
  Long Island City *(G-7832)*
▲ Mass Mdsg Self Selection Eqp ..E 631 234-3300
  Bohemia *(G-1097)*
▲ Maximum Security Products Corp .E 518 233-1800
  Waterford *(G-16634)*
Mechtronics Corporation ....E 845 831-9300
  Beacon *(G-783)*
Mega Vision Inc ....G 718 228-1065
  Brooklyn *(G-2298)*
▲ Millennium Stl Rack Rntals Inc ..G 718 965-4736
  Brooklyn *(G-2320)*
▲ Milton Merl & Associates Inc .....E 212 634-9292
  New York *(G-11297)*
▲ Mobile Media Inc ....G 845 744-8080
  Pine Bush *(G-13575)*
Modern Craft Bar Rest Equip ....G 631 226-5647
  Lindenhurst *(G-7496)*
Modu-Craft Inc ....G 716 694-0709
  Tonawanda *(G-16200)*
Nationwide Exhibitor Svcs Inc ....F 631 467-2034
  Central Islip *(G-3532)*
▲ New Business Solutions Inc ......E 631 789-1500
  Amityville *(G-315)*
▲ Parabit Systems Inc ....E 516 378-4800
  Roosevelt *(G-15031)*
R H Guest Incorporated ....G 718 675-7600
  Brooklyn *(G-2490)*
S & K Counter Tops Inc ....G 716 662-7986
  Orchard Park *(G-13321)*
Steven Kraus Associates Inc ....G 631 923-2033
  Huntington *(G-6721)*
▲ Stone Expo & Cabinetry LLC .....F 516 292-2988
  West Hempstead *(G-16895)*
▲ Sturdy Store Displays Inc ....E 718 389-9919
  Brooklyn *(G-2638)*
Ted-Steel Industries Ltd ....G 212 279-3878
  New York *(G-12317)*
Traco Manufacturing Inc ....E 585 343-2434
  Batavia *(G-651)*
Tri-Boro Shlving Prtition Corp ....F 718 782-8527
  Ridgewood *(G-14142)*
Trylon Wire & Metal Works Inc ......E 718 542-4472
  Bronx *(G-1480)*
Visual Millwork & Fix Mfg Inc ....D 718 267-7800
  Deer Park *(G-4250)*

Yaloz Mould & Die Co Inc E 718 389-1131
Brooklyn *(G-2786)*
Your Furniture Designers Inc G 845 947-3046
West Haverstraw *(G-16879)*

2591 Drapery Hardware, Window Blinds & Shades

Abalene Decorating Services E 718 782-2000
New York *(G-9046)*
Blinds To Go (us) Inc E 718 477-9523
Staten Island *(G-15668)*
▲ **Blindtek Designer Systems Inc** F 914 347-7100
Elmsford *(G-4746)*
◆ **Comfortex Corporation** C 518 273-3333
Watervliet *(G-16707)*
D & D Window Tech Inc G 212 308-2822
New York *(G-9838)*
Designers Touch Inc G 718 641-3718
Long Beach *(G-7669)*
Drapery Industries Inc F 585 232-2992
Rochester *(G-14338)*
▲ **Evolve Guest Controls LLC** F 855 750-9090
Port Washington *(G-13836)*
Fabric Quilters Unlimited Inc E 516 333-2866
Westbury *(G-17011)*
▲ **Hunter Douglas Inc** D 845 664-7000
Pearl River *(G-13482)*
Hunter Douglas Inc C 212 588-0564
New York *(G-10580)*
Instant Verticals Inc F 631 501-0001
Farmingdale *(G-5019)*
J Gimbel Inc E 718 296-5200
West Hempstead *(G-16888)*
KPP Ltd G 516 338-5201
Westbury *(G-17031)*
▲ **Levolor Window Furnishings Inc** B 845 664-7000
Pearl River *(G-13485)*
▼ **Manhattan Shade & Glass Co Inc** D 212 288-5616
New York *(G-11157)*
McCarroll Uphl Designs LLC G 518 828-0500
Hudson *(G-6655)*
◆ **Mechoshade Systems Inc** C 718 729-2020
Long Island City *(G-7838)*
Nu Ways Inc G 585 254-7510
Rochester *(G-14567)*
◆ **P E Guerin** D 212 243-5270
New York *(G-11561)*
Pj Decorators Inc E 516 735-9693
East Meadow *(G-4447)*
Solar Screen Co Inc G 718 592-8222
Corona *(G-4030)*
Tentina Window Fashions Inc C 631 957-9585
Lindenhurst *(G-7513)*
TLC Vision (usa) Corporation G 914 395-3949
Hartsdale *(G-6021)*
Vertical Research Partners LLC F 212 257-6499
New York *(G-12554)*
Wcd Window Coverings Inc E 845 336-4511
Lake Katrine *(G-7295)*
▲ **Windowcraft Inc** F 516 294-3580
Garden City Park *(G-5557)*
Windowtex Inc F 877 294-3580
Garden City Park *(G-5558)*

2599 Furniture & Fixtures, NEC

▼ **A-Plus Restaurant Equipment** G 718 522-2656
Brooklyn *(G-1543)*
▲ **Adirondack Scenic Inc** D 518 638-8000
Argyle *(G-407)*
▲ **AFC Industries Inc** D 718 747-0237
College Point *(G-3802)*
All Star Carts & Vehicles Inc D 631 666-5581
Bay Shore *(G-667)*
▲ **Arper USA Inc** G 212 647-8900
New York *(G-9256)*
Artistry In Wood of Syracuse F 315 431-4022
East Syracuse *(G-4523)*
Brandt Equipment LLC G 718 994-0800
Bronx *(G-1287)*
Bullock Boys LLC F 518 783-6161
Latham *(G-7383)*
Carts Mobile Food Eqp Corp E 718 788-5540
Brooklyn *(G-1763)*
Creative Stone & Cabinets G 631 772-6548
Selden *(G-15371)*
Dellet Industries Inc F 718 965-0101
Brooklyn *(G-1849)*
Dine Rite Seating Products Inc E 631 226-8899
Lindenhurst *(G-7485)*
Durall Dolly LLC F 802 728-7122
Brooklyn *(G-1884)*
Evans & Paul LLC E 516 576-0800
Plainview *(G-13629)*
Excel Commercial Seating E 828 428-8338
West Babylon *(G-16816)*
Futon City Discounters Inc F 315 437-1328
Syracuse *(G-15965)*
G Z G Rest & Kit Met Works F 718 788-8621
Brooklyn *(G-2012)*
Halfway House LLC G 518 873-2198
Elizabethtown *(G-4642)*
◆ **Hard Manufacturing Co Inc** D 716 893-1800
Buffalo *(G-3005)*
▲ **Hunt Country Furniture Inc** D 845 832-6601
Wingdale *(G-17296)*
Ideoli Group Inc F 212 705-8769
Port Washington *(G-13845)*
Inova LLC F 518 861-3400
Altamont *(G-212)*
▲ **Inova LLC** E 866 528-2804
Altamont *(G-211)*
Interiors-Pft Inc E 212 244-9600
Long Island City *(G-7795)*
J P Installations Warehouse F 914 576-3188
New Rochelle *(G-8959)*
Kedco Inc F 516 454-7800
Farmingdale *(G-5032)*
Kinfolk Studios Inc E 347 799-2946
Brooklyn *(G-2170)*
Kinplex Corp E 631 242-4800
Edgewood *(G-4618)*
L & D Manufacturing Corp G 718 665-5226
Bronx *(G-1379)*
Lafayette Pub Inc E 212 925-4242
New York *(G-10952)*
▲ **Lb Furniture Industries LLC** C 518 828-1501
Hudson *(G-6654)*
▲ **Maxsun Corporation** F 718 418-6800
Maspeth *(G-8182)*
Modern Craft Bar Rest Equip G 631 226-5647
Lindenhurst *(G-7496)*
Modu-Craft Inc G 716 694-0709
North Tonawanda *(G-13000)*
Modu-Craft Inc G 716 694-0709
Tonawanda *(G-16200)*
Monroe Table Company Inc F 716 945-7700
Salamanca *(G-15129)*
▲ **N3a Corporation** D 516 284-6799
Inwood *(G-6802)*
▲ **NK Medical Products Inc** G 716 759-7200
Amherst *(G-252)*
▲ **Novum Medical Products Inc** F 716 759-7200
Amherst *(G-253)*
▼ **Porta Decor** G 516 826-6900
Hicksville *(G-6415)*
R V H Estates Inc G 914 664-9888
Mount Vernon *(G-8771)*
▲ **Ramler International Ltd** E 516 353-3106
Syosset *(G-15857)*
Restaurant 570 8th Avenue LLC F 646 722-8191
New York *(G-11875)*
Rollhaus Seating Products Inc F 718 729-9111
Long Island City *(G-7893)*
Sandys Deli Inc G 518 297-6951
Rouses Point *(G-15068)*
Smart Space Products LLC G 877 777-2441
New York *(G-12130)*
▼ **Starliner Shipping & Travel** G 718 385-1515
Brooklyn *(G-2621)*
T O Gronlund Company Inc F 212 679-3535
New York *(G-12291)*
T-Company LLC G 646 290-6365
Smithtown *(G-15522)*
Tao Group LLC G 646 625-4818
New York *(G-12303)*
Thornwood Products Ltd E 914 769-9161
Thornwood *(G-16144)*
Timeless Decor LLC C 315 782-5759
Watertown *(G-16697)*
▲ **VSM Investors LLC** G 212 351-1600
New York *(G-12597)*
Wood Etc Inc F 315 484-9663
Syracuse *(G-16099)*

26 PAPER AND ALLIED PRODUCTS

2611 Pulp Mills

Advanced Recovery & Recycl LLC F 315 450-3301
Baldwinsville *(G-565)*
Andritz Inc E 518 745-2988
Glens Falls *(G-5686)*
APC Paper Company Inc D 315 384-4225
Norfolk *(G-12914)*
▲ **Cenibra Inc** G 212 818-8242
New York *(G-9612)*
Central Nat Pulp & Ppr Sls Inc A 914 696-9000
Purchase *(G-13971)*
Fcr LLC G 845 926-1071
Beacon *(G-780)*
Georgia-Pacific Corrugared LLC D 585 343-3800
Batavia *(G-637)*
Hamlin Bottle & Can Return Inc G 585 259-1301
Brockport *(G-1244)*
Harvest Technologies Inc G 518 899-7124
Ballston Spa *(G-597)*
International Paper Company C 607 775-1550
Conklin *(G-3894)*
▲ **ITT Engineered Valves LLC** E 662 257-6982
Seneca Falls *(G-15384)*
ITT Industries Holdings Inc G 914 641-2000
White Plains *(G-17153)*
Norton Pulpstones Incorporated G 716 433-9400
Lockport *(G-7638)*
Parsons & Whittemore Inc E 914 937-9009
Port Chester *(G-13780)*
Parsons Whittemore Entps Corp E 914 937-9009
Port Chester *(G-13781)*
R D S Mountain View Trucking G 315 823-4265
Little Falls *(G-7524)*
◆ **Repapers Corporation** F 305 691-1635
Hicksville *(G-6416)*
Sierra Processing LLC F 518 433-0020
Schenectady *(G-15320)*
Suffolk Indus Recovery Corp D 631 732-6403
Coram *(G-3974)*

2621 Paper Mills

▲ **A-One Laminating Corp** G 718 266-6002
Brooklyn *(G-1541)*
Albany International Corp C 518 445-2230
Menands *(G-8397)*
▲ **Ampac Paper LLC** B 845 778-5511
Walden *(G-16549)*
Andex Corp E 585 328-3790
Rochester *(G-14220)*
APC Paper Company Inc D 315 384-4225
Norfolk *(G-12914)*
Atlas Recycling LLC G 212 925-3280
New York *(G-9309)*
▼ **Automation Papers Inc** G 315 432-0565
Syracuse *(G-15882)*
▲ **Bigrow Paper Mfg Corp** F 718 624-4439
Brooklyn *(G-1694)*
Bristol Core Inc F 585 919-0302
Canandaigua *(G-3365)*
Bristol/White Plains G 914 681-1800
White Plains *(G-17115)*
BSD Aluminum Foil LLC E 347 689-3875
Brooklyn *(G-1737)*
Burrows Paper Corporation D 315 823-2300
Little Falls *(G-7520)*
Burrows Paper Corporation D 315 823-2300
Little Falls *(G-7521)*
▲ **Carta Usa LLC** E 585 436-3012
Rochester *(G-14279)*
▲ **Cascades Tssue Group-Sales Inc** E 819 363-5100
Waterford *(G-16631)*
Chem-Puter Friendly Inc E 631 331-2259
Mount Sinai *(G-8696)*
Citigroup Inc D 212 816-6000
New York *(G-9677)*
Clearwater Paper Corporation D 315 287-1200
Gouverneur *(G-5759)*
▲ **Cottrell Paper Company Inc** E 518 885-1702
Rock City Falls *(G-14807)*
◆ **Crosstex International Inc** D 631 582-6777
Hauppauge *(G-6079)*
Datagraphic Business Systems G 516 485-9069
Brentwood *(G-1177)*
Donne Dieu G 212 226-0573
Brooklyn *(G-1874)*
Dunmore Corporation D 845 279-5061
Brewster *(G-1214)*
Dunn Paper - Natural Dam Inc D 315 287-1200
Gouverneur *(G-5760)*
Euro Fine Paper Inc G 516 238-5253
Garden City *(G-5516)*
Fibercel Packaging LLC E 716 933-8703
Portville *(G-13892)*

▲ Flower Cy Tissue Mills Co Inc ....E 585 458-9200
Rochester (G-14398)
◆ Freeport Paper Industries Inc ....D 631 851-1555
Central Islip (G-3523)
▲ Galison Publishing LLC ....E 212 354-8840
New York (G-10288)
Georgia-Pacific LLC ....A 518 561-3500
Plattsburgh (G-13692)
▼ Gooding Co Inc ....E 716 434-5501
Lockport (G-7622)
Gratitude & Company Inc ....G 607 277-3188
Ithaca (G-6881)
Hollingsworth & Vose Company ....C 518 695-8000
Greenwich (G-5908)
Huhtamaki Inc ....A 315 593-5311
Fulton (G-5475)
International Paper Company ....A 518 585-6761
Ticonderoga (G-16148)
International Paper Company ....C 845 986-6409
Tuxedo Park (G-16307)
International Paper Company ....C 607 775-1550
Conklin (G-3894)
International Paper Company ....C 315 797-5120
Utica (G-16369)
▲ Irving Consumer Products Inc ....B 518 747-4151
Fort Edward (G-5350)
Kapstone Container Corporation ....D 518 842-2450
Amsterdam (G-352)
▲ Knowlton Technologies LLC ....C 315 782-0600
Watertown (G-16683)
◆ Lenaro Paper Co Inc ....F 631 439-8800
Central Islip (G-3529)
Lion Die-Cutting Co Inc ....E 718 383-8841
Brooklyn (G-2231)
Minimill Technologies Inc ....F 315 692-4557
Syracuse (G-16011)
Mohawk Fine Papers Inc ....E 518 237-1741
Cohoes (G-3776)
▲ Mohawk Fine Papers Inc ....B 518 237-1740
Cohoes (G-3775)
Morcon Inc ....C 518 677-8511
Cambridge (G-3337)
National Paper Converting Inc ....G 607 687-6049
Owego (G-13381)
Neenah Northeast LLC ....D 315 782-5800
Brownville (G-2798)
◆ Nice-Pak Products Inc ....B 845 365-2772
Orangeburg (G-13258)
Nice-Pak Products Inc ....E 845 353-6090
West Nyack (G-16950)
North End Paper Co Inc ....G 315 593-8100
Fulton (G-5485)
▼ Omniafiltra LLC ....E 315 346-7300
Beaver Falls (G-790)
Pactiv LLC ....G 585 394-1525
Canandaigua (G-3380)
Palisades Paper Inc ....G 845 354-0333
Spring Valley (G-15619)
▲ Paper Solutions Inc ....F 718 499-4226
Brooklyn (G-2418)
◆ Plastirun Corporation ....E 631 273-2626
Brentwood (G-1190)
◆ Potsdam Specialty Paper Inc ....D 315 265-4000
Potsdam (G-13899)
▲ Precare Corp ....G 631 667-1055
Hauppauge (G-6195)
▲ Precision Charts Inc ....E 631 244-8295
Bohemia (G-1116)
◆ Professional Disposables Inc ....A 845 365-1700
Orangeburg (G-13266)
Refill Services LLC ....G 607 369-5864
Sidney (G-15463)
Sabin Robbins Paper Company ....E 513 874-5270
New York (G-11967)
Sca Tissue North America LLC ....E 518 692-8434
Greenwich (G-5912)
Sca Tissue North America LLC ....C 518 583-2785
Saratoga Springs (G-15203)
▲ Scalamandre Wallpaper Inc ....B 631 467-8800
Hauppauge (G-6210)
Schweitzer-Mauduit Intl Inc ....C 518 329-4222
Ancram (G-375)
Stephen Singer Pattern Co Inc ....F 212 947-2902
New York (G-12220)
Summit Fincl Disclosure LLC ....E 212 913-0510
New York (G-12255)
▲ T & L Trading Co ....G 718 782-5550
Brooklyn (G-2658)
Tag Envelope Co Inc ....E 718 389-6844
College Point (G-3835)
Twin Rivers Paper Company LLC ....E 315 348-8491
Lyons Falls (G-8005)
Twin Rivers Paper Company LLC ....C 315 823-2300
Little Falls (G-7527)
United Data Forms Inc ....F 631 218-0104
Bohemia (G-1148)
Verso Corporation ....B 212 599-2700
New York (G-12550)
Verso Paper Management LP ....A 781 320-8660
New York (G-12551)
Verso Paper Management LP ....G 212 599-2700
New York (G-12552)

2631 Paperboard Mills

Alpine Paper Box Co Inc ....E 718 345-4040
Brooklyn (G-1592)
▲ American Wire Tie Inc ....E 716 337-2412
North Collins (G-12942)
Base Container Inc ....F 718 636-2004
Brooklyn (G-1666)
▲ Burt Rigid Box Inc ....F 607 433-2510
Oneonta (G-13199)
Carthage Specialty Pprbd Inc ....D 315 493-2120
Carthage (G-3437)
Cascades New York Inc ....C 716 285-3681
Niagara Falls (G-12824)
▼ Continental Kraft Corp ....G 516 681-9090
Jericho (G-7097)
Di Domenico Packaging Co Inc ....G 718 727-5454
Staten Island (G-15685)
Enterprise Folding Box Co Inc ....E 716 876-6421
Buffalo (G-2955)
Farrington Packaging Corp ....E 315 733-4600
Utica (G-16354)
▲ Greenpac Mill LLC ....C 716 299-0560
Niagara Falls (G-12848)
Interface Performance Mtls Inc ....D 518 686-3400
Hoosick Falls (G-6567)
International Paper Company ....C 607 775-1550
Conklin (G-3894)
Kapstone Container Corporation ....D 518 842-2450
Amsterdam (G-352)
M&F Stringing LLC ....E 914 664-1600
Mount Vernon (G-8749)
Ms Paper Products Co Inc ....G 718 624-0248
Brooklyn (G-2348)
Neenah Northeast LLC ....D 315 782-5800
Brownville (G-2798)
Niagara Fiberboard Inc ....E 716 434-8881
Lockport (G-7635)
Pactiv LLC ....E 585 248-1213
Pittsford (G-13601)
Paper Box Corp ....D 212 226-7490
New York (G-11576)
Pdf Seal Incorporated ....E 631 595-7035
Deer Park (G-4212)
Pkg Group ....G 212 965-0112
New York (G-11692)
Prestige Box Corporation ....E 516 773-3115
Great Neck (G-5850)
Professional Packg Svcs Inc ....E 518 677-5100
Eagle Bridge (G-4381)
Small Packages Inc ....G 845 255-7710
New Paltz (G-8923)
▲ Tin Box Company of America Inc ....E 631 845-1600
Farmingdale (G-5142)
▲ Westrock - Solvay Llc ....C 315 484-9050
Syracuse (G-16095)
Westrock CP LLC ....D 315 484-9050
Syracuse (G-16096)
Westrock Mwv LLC ....C 212 688-5000
New York (G-12645)

2652 Set-Up Paperboard Boxes

A Fleisig Paper Box Corp ....F 212 226-7490
New York (G-9033)
American Package Company Inc ....E 718 389-4444
Brooklyn (G-1603)
▲ Brick & Ballerstein Inc ....D 718 497-1400
Ridgewood (G-14116)
Burt Rigid Box Inc ....D 607 433-2510
Oneonta (G-13198)
Cascades New York Inc ....D 718 340-2100
Maspeth (G-8152)
Clarke-Boxit Corporation ....G 716 487-1950
Jamestown (G-7015)
Drescher Paper Box Inc ....F 716 854-0288
Buffalo (G-2934)
Earlville Paper Box Co Inc ....E 315 691-2131
Earlville (G-4385)
▲ F M Howell & Company ....D 607 734-6291
Elmira (G-4697)
Fairview Paper Box Corp ....E 585 786-5230
Warsaw (G-16604)
Friedel Paper Box & Converting ....G 315 437-3325
Baldwinsville (G-568)
Jordon Box Company Inc ....E 315 422-3419
Syracuse (G-15989)
Ketchum Manufacturing Co Inc ....F 518 696-3331
Lake Luzerne (G-7296)
Lionel Habas Associates Inc ....F 212 860-8454
New York (G-11033)
Parlor City Paper Box Co Inc ....D 607 772-0600
Binghamton (G-937)
▲ Paul T Freund Corporation ....D 315 597-4873
Palmyra (G-13438)
Prestige Box Corporation ....E 516 773-3115
Great Neck (G-5850)
Propak Inc ....G 518 677-5100
Eagle Bridge (G-4382)
▲ Pure Trade Us Inc ....E 212 256-1600
New York (G-11774)
▲ Seneca FLS Spc & Logistics Co ....D 315 568-4139
Seneca Falls (G-15393)

2653 Corrugated & Solid Fiber Boxes

Action Rack Display Mfg ....F 718 257-7111
Brooklyn (G-1557)
Ares Printing and Packg Corp ....C 718 858-8760
Brooklyn (G-1627)
▼ Arma Container Corp ....E 631 254-1200
Deer Park (G-4125)
Bellotti Packaging Inc ....F 315 433-0131
East Syracuse (G-4527)
Brand Box USA LLC ....G 607 584-7682
Binghamton (G-894)
Buckeye Corrugated Inc ....D 585 924-1600
Victor (G-16489)
Burt Rigid Box Inc ....D 607 433-2510
Oneonta (G-13198)
Calpac Incorporated ....F 631 789-0502
Amityville (G-278)
Cascades New York Inc ....C 518 346-6151
Schenectady (G-15268)
Cattaraugus Containers Inc ....E 716 676-2000
Franklinville (G-5379)
▲ Color Carton Corp ....D 718 665-0840
Bronx (G-1303)
Displays & Beyond Inc ....F 718 805-7786
Glendale (G-5666)
Dory Enterprises Inc ....F 607 565-7079
Waverly (G-16726)
Enterprise Container LLC ....E 631 253-4400
Wyandanch (G-17390)
Fennell Industries LLC ....E 607 733-6693
Elmira (G-4698)
Fiber USA Corp ....G 718 888-1512
Flushing (G-5249)
Gavin Mfg Corp ....E 631 467-0040
Farmingdale (G-5005)
▲ General Die and Die Cutng Inc ....D 516 665-3584
Roosevelt (G-15028)
◆ General Fibre Products Corp ....D 516 358-7500
New Hyde Park (G-8880)
Georgia-Pacific LLC ....C 518 346-6151
Schenectady (G-15290)
Inner-Pak Container Inc ....F 631 289-9700
Patchogue (G-13449)
International Paper Company ....C 585 663-1000
Rochester (G-14473)
International Paper Company ....F 716 852-2144
Buffalo (G-3029)
International Paper Company ....D 518 372-6461
Glenville (G-5717)
International Paper Company ....C 607 775-1550
Conklin (G-3894)
Island Container Corp ....D 631 253-4400
Wyandanch (G-17391)
J & M Packaging Inc ....F 631 608-3069
Hauppauge (G-6124)
Jamestown Cont of Rochester ....D 585 254-9190
Rochester (G-14481)
▼ Jamestown Container Corp ....C 716 665-4623
Falconer (G-4912)
Kapstone Container Corporation ....D 518 842-2450
Amsterdam (G-352)
Key Container Corp ....G 631 582-3847
East Islip (G-4437)
Lakeside Container Corp ....F 518 561-6150
Plattsburgh (G-13701)

Land Packaging Corp .... F 914 472-5976
Scarsdale *(G-15249)*
▲ Lee Philips Packaging Inc .... F 631 580-3306
Ronkonkoma *(G-14959)*
M C Packaging Corporation .... E 631 643-3763
Babylon *(G-547)*
Mazel Supply .... G 212 947-2213
Brooklyn *(G-2290)*
Mechtronics Corporation .... E 845 831-9300
Beacon *(G-783)*
▲ Mkt329 Inc .... F 631 249-5500
Farmingdale *(G-5068)*
▲ Mp Displays LLC .... G 845 268-4113
Valley Cottage *(G-16409)*
▲ Niagara Sheets LLC .... D 716 692-1129
North Tonawanda *(G-13001)*
Norampac New England Inc .... C 860 923-9563
Schenectady *(G-15308)*
Norampac New York City Inc .... C 718 340-2100
Maspeth *(G-8189)*
Packaging Corporation America .... C 315 457-6780
Liverpool *(G-7564)*
Packaging Corporation America .... F 315 785-9083
Watertown *(G-16692)*
Pactiv LLC .... C 315 457-6780
Liverpool *(G-7565)*
Pactiv LLC .... E 585 248-1213
Pittsford *(G-13601)*
Parlor City Paper Box Co Inc .... D 607 772-0600
Binghamton *(G-937)*
Philpac Corporation .... E 716 875-8005
Buffalo *(G-3147)*
President Cont Group II LLC .... B 845 516-1600
Middletown *(G-8492)*
Prestige Box Corporation .... E 516 773-3115
Great Neck *(G-5850)*
Professional Packg Svcs Inc .... E 518 677-5100
Eagle Bridge *(G-4381)*
R D A Container Corporation .... E 585 247-2323
Gates *(G-5578)*
▲ Seneca FLS Spc & Logistics Co .... D 315 568-4139
Seneca Falls *(G-15393)*
▲ Spaeth Design Inc .... E 718 606-9685
Woodside *(G-17369)*
▲ Specialized Packg Group Inc .... G 315 638-4355
Baldwinsville *(G-574)*
Specialized Packg Radisson LLC .... C 315 638-4355
Baldwinsville *(G-575)*
Star Corrugated Box Co Inc .... G 718 386-3200
Flushing *(G-5301)*
Syracuse Corrugated Box Corp .... F 315 437-9901
East Syracuse *(G-4582)*
Technical Library Service Inc .... F 212 219-0770
Brooklyn *(G-2670)*
Technical Packaging Inc .... F 516 223-2300
Baldwin *(G-561)*
Track 7 Inc .... G 845 544-1810
Warwick *(G-16618)*
Valentine Packaging Corp .... F 718 418-6000
Maspeth *(G-8205)*
Westrock - Southern Cont LLC .... C 315 487-6111
Camillus *(G-3355)*
Westrock Cp LLC .... C 770 448-2193
New Hartford *(G-8858)*
Westrock CP LLC .... C 716 694-1000
North Tonawanda *(G-13023)*
Westrock CP LLC .... C 716 692-6510
North Tonawanda *(G-13024)*
Westrock Rkt Company .... C 330 296-5155
Deer Park *(G-4251)*
Westrock Rkt Company .... C 770 448-2193
Camillus *(G-3356)*

2655 Fiber Cans, Tubes & Drums

Acran Spill Containment Inc .... G 631 841-2300
Amityville *(G-274)*
American Intrmdal Cont Mfg LLC .... G 631 774-6790
Hauppauge *(G-6041)*
Caraustar Industries Inc .... G 716 874-0393
Buffalo *(G-2888)*
Carthage Fibre Drum Inc .... F 315 493-2730
Carthage *(G-3436)*
Consolidated Container Co LLC .... C 585 262-6470
Rochester *(G-14309)*
▲ Custom Manufacturing Inc .... G 607 569-2738
Hammondsport *(G-5976)*
▲ Diemolding Corporation .... G 315 363-4710
Wampsville *(G-16574)*
Greif Inc .... D 716 836-4200
Tonawanda *(G-16186)*
Industrial Paper Tube Inc .... F 718 893-5000
Bronx *(G-1363)*
Kuraray America Inc .... F 212 986-2230
New York *(G-10932)*
Philpac Corporation .... E 716 875-8005
Buffalo *(G-3147)*
▲ Skydyne Company .... D 845 858-6400
Port Jervis *(G-13816)*
Syraco Products Inc .... F 315 476-5306
Syracuse *(G-16072)*

2656 Sanitary Food Containers

Amscan Inc .... F 845 469-9116
Chester *(G-3626)*
Amscan Inc .... D 845 782-0490
Harriman *(G-5993)*
Apexx Omni-Graphics Inc .... D 718 326-3330
Maspeth *(G-8147)*
Consolidated Container Co LLC .... C 585 262-6470
Rochester *(G-14309)*
Hadp LLC .... F 518 831-6824
Scotia *(G-15348)*
International Paper Company .... C 607 775-1550
Conklin *(G-3894)*
▲ Last Straw Inc .... E 516 371-2727
Lawrence *(G-7418)*
Pactiv LLC .... C 518 562-6101
Plattsburgh *(G-13712)*
◆ Plastirun Corporation .... E 631 273-2626
Brentwood *(G-1190)*
▲ Sqp Inc .... C 518 831-6800
Schenectady *(G-15322)*

2657 Folding Paperboard Boxes

Abbot & Abbot Box Corp .... F 888 930-5972
Long Island City *(G-7678)*
Alpha Packaging Industries Inc .... E 718 267-4115
Long Island City *(G-7687)*
▲ Arkay Packaging Corporation .... E 631 273-2000
Hauppauge *(G-6043)*
Burt Rigid Box Inc .... D 607 433-2510
Oneonta *(G-13198)*
Cattaraugus Containers Inc .... E 716 676-2000
Franklinville *(G-5379)*
Climax Packaging Inc .... C 315 376-8000
Lowville *(G-7963)*
▲ Color Carton Corp .... D 718 665-0840
Bronx *(G-1303)*
Designers Folding Box Corp .... E 716 853-5141
Buffalo *(G-2929)*
Diamond Packaging Holdings LLC .... G 585 334-8030
Rochester *(G-14327)*
Disc Graphics Inc .... C 631 300-1129
Hauppauge *(G-6085)*
▲ Disc Graphics Inc .... C 631 234-1400
Hauppauge *(G-6086)*
▲ F M Howell & Company .... D 607 734-6291
Elmira *(G-4697)*
Flower City Printing Inc .... C 585 663-9000
Rochester *(G-14396)*
Gavin Mfg Corp .... E 631 467-0040
Farmingdale *(G-5005)*
◆ Gaylord Bros Inc .... D 315 457-5070
North Syracuse *(G-12961)*
▲ HSM Packaging Corporation .... D 315 476-7996
Liverpool *(G-7546)*
▲ Knoll Printing & Packaging Inc .... E 516 621-0100
Syosset *(G-15846)*
M C Packaging Corporation .... E 631 643-3763
Babylon *(G-547)*
◆ Mod-Pac Corp .... C 716 898-8480
Buffalo *(G-3091)*
Multi Packg Solutions Intl Ltd .... F 646 885-0005
New York *(G-11348)*
▲ Novel Box Company Ltd .... E 718 965-2222
Brooklyn *(G-2388)*
Pactiv LLC .... C 518 562-6101
Plattsburgh *(G-13712)*
Paper Box Corp .... D 212 226-7490
New York *(G-11576)*
Premier Packaging Corporation .... E 585 924-8460
Victor *(G-16520)*
Prestige Box Corporation .... E 516 773-3115
Great Neck *(G-5850)*
▲ Specialized Packg Group Inc .... G 315 638-4355
Baldwinsville *(G-574)*
Specialized Packg Radisson LLC .... C 315 638-4355
Baldwinsville *(G-575)*
▲ Standard Group .... E 718 335-5500
Great Neck *(G-5859)*
▲ Standard Group LLC .... C 718 507-6430
Great Neck *(G-5860)*
Viking Industries Inc .... D 845 883-6325
New Paltz *(G-8927)*
Visitainer Corp .... E 718 636-0300
Brooklyn *(G-2749)*

2671 Paper Coating & Laminating for Packaging

▲ Allen-Bailey Tag & Label Inc .... D 585 538-2324
Caledonia *(G-3303)*
▲ Allied Converters Inc .... E 914 235-1585
New Rochelle *(G-8931)*
American Packaging Corporation .... G 585 254-2002
Rochester *(G-14213)*
▲ American Packaging Corporation .... C 585 254-9500
Rochester *(G-14214)*
Anasia Inc .... G 718 588-1407
Bronx *(G-1274)*
Apexx Omni-Graphics Inc .... D 718 326-3330
Maspeth *(G-8147)*
Ares Box LLC .... D 718 858-8760
Brooklyn *(G-1626)*
Arm Global Solutions Inc .... G 844 276-4525
Rochester *(G-14226)*
Bemis Company Inc .... C 631 794-2900
Edgewood *(G-4608)*
Berry Plastics Corporation .... B 315 986-6270
Macedon *(G-8013)*
Cameo Process Corp .... G 914 948-0082
White Plains *(G-17119)*
CCL Label Inc .... C 716 852-2155
Buffalo *(G-2889)*
Classic Labels Inc .... E 631 467-2300
Patchogue *(G-13442)*
Colad Group LLC .... D 716 961-1776
Buffalo *(G-2900)*
Cove Point Holdings LLC .... F 212 599-3388
New York *(G-9800)*
Craft Packaging Inc .... G 718 633-4045
Brooklyn *(G-1810)*
De Luxe Packaging Corp .... E 416 754-4633
Saugerties *(G-15212)*
Depot Label Company Inc .... G 631 467-2952
Patchogue *(G-13443)*
Ecoplast & Packaging LLC .... G 718 996-0800
Brooklyn *(G-1902)*
▲ F M Howell & Company .... D 607 734-6291
Elmira *(G-4697)*
▲ Folene Packaging LLC .... G 917 626-6740
Brooklyn *(G-1992)*
◆ General Fibre Products Corp .... D 516 358-7500
New Hyde Park *(G-8880)*
General Trade Mark La .... E 718 979-7261
Staten Island *(G-15698)*
Idesco Corp .... F 212 889-2530
New York *(G-10602)*
International Paper Company .... C 585 663-1000
Rochester *(G-14473)*
▲ K Sidrane Inc .... E 631 393-6974
Farmingdale *(G-5028)*
▲ Kal Pac Corp .... F 845 457-7013
Montgomery *(G-8633)*
Mason Transparent Package Inc .... E 718 792-6000
Bronx *(G-1392)*
Multi Packaging Solutions Inc .... C 516 488-2000
Hicksville *(G-6400)*
◆ Multi Packaging Solutions Inc .... E 646 885-0005
New York *(G-11347)*
Nameplate Mfrs of Amer .... E 631 752-0055
Farmingdale *(G-5070)*
Nova Packaging Ltd Inc .... E 914 232-8406
Katonah *(G-7161)*
▲ Packstar Group Inc .... D 716 853-1688
Buffalo *(G-3133)*
▲ Pactech Packaging LLC .... D 585 458-8008
Rochester *(G-14587)*
Pactiv LLC .... C 518 562-6101
Plattsburgh *(G-13712)*
Paperworks Industries Inc .... F 913 621-0922
Baldwinsville *(G-572)*
Patco Tapes Inc .... G 718 497-1527
Maspeth *(G-8194)*
Penta-Tech Coated Products LLC .... F 315 986-4098
Macedon *(G-8019)*
Pliant LLC .... B 315 986-6286
Macedon *(G-8020)*
Pregis LLC .... D 518 743-3100
Glens Falls *(G-5712)*

Employee Codes: A=Over 500 employees, B=251-500
C=101-250, D=51-100, E=20-50, F=10-19, G=5-9
2018 Harris
New York Manufacturers Directory
749

- ◆ **Print Pack Inc** C 404 460-7000 Farmingdale *(G-5098)*
- ▲ **Printex Packaging Corporation** D 631 234-4300 Islandia *(G-6840)*
- ▲ **Quality Circle Products Inc** D 914 736-6600 Montrose *(G-8653)*
- ▲ **RMS Packaging Inc** F 914 205-2070 Peekskill *(G-13506)*
- ▼ **Rynone Packaging Corp** G 607 565-8173 Waverly *(G-16731)*
- **Saint-Gobain Prfmce Plas Corp** C 518 642-2200 Granville *(G-5796)*
- ▲ **Shaant Industries Inc** E 716 366-3654 Dunkirk *(G-4374)*
- **Smart USA Inc** E 718 416-4400 Glendale *(G-5679)*
- ▲ **Time Release Sciences Inc** E 716 823-4580 Buffalo *(G-3245)*
- ◆ **Transcntinental Ultra Flex Inc** B 718 272-9100 Brooklyn *(G-2693)*
- ▲ **Tri-Plex Packaging Corporation** E 212 481-6070 New York *(G-12422)*
- ▲ **Universal Packg Systems Inc** A 631 543-2277 Hauppauge *(G-6245)*
- **Valley Industrial Products Inc** E 631 385-9300 Huntington *(G-6727)*
- **W E W Container Corporation** E 718 827-8150 Brooklyn *(G-2757)*
- **Westrock Mwv LLC** C 212 688-5000 New York *(G-12645)*

2672 Paper Coating & Laminating, Exc for Packaging

- ▲ **A-One Laminating Corp** G 718 266-6002 Brooklyn *(G-1541)*
- **Adflex Corporation** E 585 454-2950 Rochester *(G-14189)*
- ▼ **Advanced Graphics Company** F 607 692-7875 Whitney Point *(G-17248)*
- **Albany International Corp** D 518 447-6400 Menands *(G-8398)*
- ▲ **Allen-Bailey Tag & Label Inc** D 585 538-2324 Caledonia *(G-3303)*
- **Avery Dennison Corporation** C 845 680-3873 Orangeburg *(G-13242)*
- **Avery Dennison Corporation** C 626 304-2000 New York *(G-9329)*
- **Berry Specialty Tapes LLC** C 631 727-6000 Riverhead *(G-14150)*
- **C & R De Santis Inc** E 718 447-5076 Staten Island *(G-15673)*
- **CCL Label Inc** C 716 852-2155 Buffalo *(G-2889)*
- **Classic Labels Inc** E 631 467-2300 Patchogue *(G-13442)*
- **Cove Point Holdings LLC** F 212 599-3388 New York *(G-9800)*
- **Cytec Industries Inc** D 716 372-9650 Olean *(G-13162)*
- **D W S Associates Inc** E 631 667-6666 Deer Park *(G-4147)*
- **Dunmore Corporation** D 845 279-5061 Brewster *(G-1214)*
- **Eis Inc** D 585 426-5330 Rochester *(G-14361)*
- **Felix Schoeller North Amer Inc** D 315 298-8425 Pulaski *(G-13962)*
- **Greenbush Tape & Label Inc** E 518 465-2389 Albany *(G-83)*
- **Itac Label & Tag Corp** G 718 625-2148 Brooklyn *(G-2117)*
- ▲ **K Sidrane Inc** E 631 393-6974 Farmingdale *(G-5028)*
- ▲ **Kleen Stik Industries Inc** F 718 984-5031 Staten Island *(G-15718)*
- **Label Gallery Inc** E 607 334-3244 Norwich *(G-13049)*
- **Label Makers Inc** E 631 319-6329 Bohemia *(G-1085)*
- **Liberty Label Mfg Inc** F 631 737-2365 Holbrook *(G-6486)*
- ◆ **Merco Hackensack Inc** G 845 357-3699 Hillburn *(G-6442)*
- **Micro Essential Laboratory** E 718 338-3618 Brooklyn *(G-2315)*
- **Miken Companies Inc** D 716 668-6311 Buffalo *(G-3085)*
- ▲ **Mohawk Fine Papers Inc** B 518 237-1740 Cohoes *(G-3775)*
- **Neenah Northeast LLC** C 315 376-3571 Lowville *(G-7968)*
- **New York Cutting & Gumming Co** E 212 563-4146 Middletown *(G-8489)*
- **Oaklee International Inc** D 631 436-7900 Ronkonkoma *(G-14983)*
- ▲ **Overnight Labels Inc** E 631 242-4240 Deer Park *(G-4210)*
- ▲ **P C I Paper Conversions Inc** C 315 437-1641 Syracuse *(G-16027)*
- ▲ **Paris Art Label Co Inc** D 631 467-2300 Patchogue *(G-13455)*
- **Patco Tapes Inc** G 718 497-1527 Maspeth *(G-8194)*
- **Princeton Label & Packaging** E 609 490-0800 Patchogue *(G-13458)*
- ▲ **Rochester 100 Inc** C 585 475-0200 Rochester *(G-14655)*
- ▲ **S & S Prtg Die-Cutting Co Inc** F 718 388-8990 Brooklyn *(G-2543)*
- **Stoney Croft Converters Inc** F 718 608-9800 Staten Island *(G-15764)*
- **Syracuse Label Co Inc** D 315 422-1037 Syracuse *(G-16078)*
- **T L F Graphics Inc** D 585 272-5500 Rochester *(G-14740)*
- ◆ **Tape-It Inc** E 631 243-4100 Bay Shore *(G-743)*
- ▲ **Tri Star Label Inc** G 914 237-4800 Mount Vernon *(G-8786)*
- ▲ **Tri-Flex Label Corp** E 631 293-0411 Farmingdale *(G-5143)*
- **Triangle Label Tag Inc** G 718 875-3030 Brooklyn *(G-2697)*
- **Valley Industrial Products Inc** E 631 385-9300 Huntington *(G-6727)*

2673 Bags: Plastics, Laminated & Coated

- **Adart Polyethylene Bag Mfg** G 516 932-1001 Plainview *(G-13606)*
- ▲ **Aladdin Packaging LLC** D 631 273-4747 Hauppauge *(G-6033)*
- **Alco Plastics Inc** E 716 683-3020 Lancaster *(G-7325)*
- ▲ **Allied Converters Inc** E 914 235-1585 New Rochelle *(G-8931)*
- ▲ **Amby International Inc** G 718 645-0964 Brooklyn *(G-1595)*
- **American Packaging Corporation** G 585 254-2002 Rochester *(G-14213)*
- ▲ **American Packaging Corporation** C 585 254-9500 Rochester *(G-14214)*
- ▲ **API Industries Inc** B 845 365-2200 Orangeburg *(G-13239)*
- **API Industries Inc** C 845 365-2200 Orangeburg *(G-13240)*
- ▲ **Bag Arts The Art Packaging LLC** G 212 684-7020 New York *(G-9356)*
- **Baggu** G 347 457-5266 Brooklyn *(G-1662)*
- ▲ **Bags Unlimited Inc** E 585 436-6282 Rochester *(G-14238)*
- **Berry Global Inc** C 315 986-2161 Macedon *(G-8011)*
- ▲ **Bison Bag Co Inc** D 716 434-4380 Lockport *(G-7600)*
- **Capitol Poly Corp** E 718 855-6000 Brooklyn *(G-1757)*
- **Clear View Bag Company Inc** C 518 458-7153 Albany *(G-64)*
- **Colden Closet LLC** G 716 713-6125 East Aurora *(G-4393)*
- **Connover Packaging Inc** G 585 377-2510 East Rochester *(G-4475)*
- **Courier Packaging Inc** E 718 349-2390 Brooklyn *(G-1808)*
- **Craft Pak Inc** G 718 257-2700 Staten Island *(G-15683)*
- **Ecoplast & Packaging LLC** G 718 996-0800 Brooklyn *(G-1902)*
- **Edco Supply Corporation** D 718 788-8108 Brooklyn *(G-1905)*
- **Excellent Poly Inc** F 718 768-6555 Brooklyn *(G-1948)*
- **Filmpak Extrusion LLC** D 631 293-6767 Melville *(G-8348)*
- ▲ **Fortune Poly Products Inc** F 718 361-0767 Jamaica *(G-6948)*
- ▼ **Franklin Poly Film Inc** E 718 492-3523 Brooklyn *(G-2002)*
- **Garb-O-Liner Inc** G 914 235-1585 New Rochelle *(G-8949)*
- **Golden Group International Ltd** G 845 440-1025 Patterson *(G-13464)*
- ▲ **H G Maybeck Co Inc** E 718 297-4410 Jamaica *(G-6954)*
- ◆ **Ivi Services Inc** D 607 729-5111 Binghamton *(G-924)*
- **Jad Corp of America** E 718 762-8900 College Point *(G-3816)*
- ▲ **Jay Bags Inc** G 845 459-6500 Spring Valley *(G-15612)*
- ▲ **JM Murray Center Inc** C 607 756-9913 Cortland *(G-4055)*
- **JM Murray Center Inc** C 607 756-0246 Cortland *(G-4056)*
- ▲ **Josh Packaging Inc** E 631 822-1660 Hauppauge *(G-6127)*
- **Kemco Sales LLC** F 203 762-1902 East Rochester *(G-4482)*
- ▲ **Maco Bag Corporation** C 315 226-1000 Newark *(G-12755)*
- ◆ **Magcrest Packaging Inc** G 845 425-0451 Monsey *(G-8609)*
- **Manhattan Poly Bag Corporation** E 917 689-7549 Brooklyn *(G-2261)*
- **Mason Transparent Package Inc** E 718 792-6000 Bronx *(G-1392)*
- **Metpak Inc** G 917 309-0196 Brooklyn *(G-2309)*
- ▲ **Metropolitan Packg Mfg Corp** E 718 383-2700 Brooklyn *(G-2312)*
- **Milla Global Inc** G 516 488-3601 Brooklyn *(G-2319)*
- **Mint-X Products Corporation** F 877 646-8224 College Point *(G-3822)*
- **Modern Plastic Bags Mfg Inc** G 718 237-2985 Brooklyn *(G-2332)*
- ▲ **Nap Industries Inc** D 718 625-4948 Brooklyn *(G-2355)*
- ▲ **New York Packaging Corp** D 516 746-0600 New Hyde Park *(G-8896)*
- ▲ **New York Packaging II LLC** C 516 746-0600 Garden City *(G-5536)*
- ▲ **Noteworthy Industries Inc** C 518 842-2662 Amsterdam *(G-365)*
- **Nova Packaging Ltd Inc** E 914 232-8406 Katonah *(G-7161)*
- ▲ **Pacific Poly Product Corp** F 718 786-7129 Long Island City *(G-7864)*
- ▲ **Pack America Corp** G 212 508-6666 New York *(G-11568)*
- **Pactiv LLC** C 585 394-5125 Canandaigua *(G-3381)*
- **Pactiv LLC** C 518 793-2524 Glens Falls *(G-5710)*
- **Paradise Plastics LLC** E 718 788-3733 Brooklyn *(G-2419)*
- ▲ **Paramount Equipment Inc** E 631 981-4422 Ronkonkoma *(G-14988)*
- ▲ **Poly Craft Industries Corp** E 631 630-6731 Hauppauge *(G-6193)*
- ◆ **Poly-Pak Industries Inc** B 631 293-6767 Melville *(G-8377)*
- **Polyseal Packaging Corp** E 718 792-5530 Bronx *(G-1429)*
- ▲ **Primo Plastics Inc** E 718 349-1000 Brooklyn *(G-2457)*
- ▲ **Protective Lining Corp** D 718 854-3838 Brooklyn *(G-2472)*
- **Rainbow Poly Bag Co Inc** E 718 386-3500 Brooklyn *(G-2495)*
- ▲ **Rege Inc** F 845 565-7772 New Windsor *(G-8996)*
- **Repellem Consumer Pdts Corp** F 631 273-3992 Bohemia *(G-1122)*
- ▲ **Rtr Bag & Co Ltd** G 212 620-0011 New York *(G-11950)*
- **Salerno Packaging Inc** F 518 563-3636 Plattsburgh *(G-13724)*
- ▼ **Select Fabricators Inc** F 585 393-0650 Canandaigua *(G-3387)*
- **Star Poly Bag Inc** F 718 384-3130 Brooklyn *(G-2620)*
- **Supreme Poly Plastics Inc** E 718 456-9300 Brooklyn *(G-2652)*
- ▲ **T M I Plastics Industries Inc** F 718 383-0363 Brooklyn *(G-2659)*
- ▲ **Tai Seng** G 718 399-6311 Brooklyn *(G-2665)*

SIC SECTION
26 PAPER AND ALLIED PRODUCTS

Technipoly Manufacturing Inc ....E 718 383-0363
Brooklyn *(G-2671)*
▲ Trinity Packaging Corporation..........F 914 273-4111
Armonk *(G-419)*
Trinity Packaging Corporation..............E 716 668-3111
Buffalo *(G-3251)*
United Plastics Inc ....G 718 389-2255
Brooklyn *(G-2721)*
W E W Container Corporation ....E 718 827-8150
Brooklyn *(G-2757)*
▲ Wally Packaging Inc...........................G 718 377-5323
Brooklyn *(G-2758)*

2674 Bags: Uncoated Paper & Multiwall

333 J & M Food Corp ....F 718 381-1493
Ridgewood *(G-14109)*
▲ American Packaging Corporation ......C 585 254-9500
Rochester *(G-14214)*
▲ Ampac Paper LLC ....B 845 778-5511
Walden *(G-16549)*
APC Paper Company Inc........................D 315 384-4225
Norfolk *(G-12914)*
▲ Bag Arts The Art Packaging LLC.......G 212 684-7020
New York *(G-9356)*
▲ Custom Eco Friendly LLC ....G 347 227-0229
Roslyn *(G-15042)*
Kapstone Container Corporation ....D 518 842-2450
Amsterdam *(G-352)*
Lin Jin Feng..G 718 232-3039
Brooklyn *(G-2226)*
Polyseal Packaging Corp ....E 718 792-5530
Bronx *(G-1429)*
▲ R P Fedder Corp..................................E 585 288-1600
Rochester *(G-14643)*
▲ Rtr Bag & Co Ltd ....G 212 620-0011
New York *(G-11950)*
◆ Shalam Imports Inc ....F 718 686-6271
Brooklyn *(G-2576)*

2675 Die-Cut Paper & Board

Able National Corp................................E 718 386-8801
Brooklyn *(G-1549)*
All Out Die Cutting Inc..........................E 718 346-6666
Brooklyn *(G-1586)*
Allied Sample Card Co Inc ....E 718 238-0523
Brooklyn *(G-1589)*
American Dsplay Die Ctters Inc.............E 212 645-1274
New York *(G-9166)*
Art Industries of New York ....E 212 633-9200
New York *(G-9260)*
▲ Borden & Riley Paper Co Inc ....E 718 454-9494
Hollis *(G-6520)*
Dia ....G 212 675-4097
New York *(G-9920)*
▲ General Die and Die Cutng Inc ....D 516 665-3584
Roosevelt *(G-15028)*
◆ General Fibre Products Corp ....D 516 358-7500
New Hyde Park *(G-8880)*
Glens Falls Business Forms Inc............F 518 798-6643
Queensbury *(G-14009)*
Hubray Inc ....F 800 645-2855
North Baldwin *(G-12924)*
▼ Kleer-Fax Inc ....D 631 225-1100
Amityville *(G-303)*
Leather Indexes Corp ....D 516 827-1900
Hicksville *(G-6391)*
Lion Die-Cutting Co Inc ....E 718 383-8841
Brooklyn *(G-2231)*
Manufacturers Indexing Pdts.................G 631 271-0956
Halesite *(G-5928)*
Mid Island Die Cutting Corp...................C 631 293-0180
Farmingdale *(G-5062)*
Miken Companies Inc ....D 716 668-6311
Buffalo *(G-3085)*
New Horizon Graphics Inc ....E 631 231-8055
Hauppauge *(G-6173)*
New York Cutting & Gumming Co ....E 212 563-4146
Middletown *(G-8489)*
Norampac New York City Inc ....C 718 340-2100
Maspeth *(G-8189)*
▲ Orange Die Cutting Corp....................C 845 562-0900
Newburgh *(G-12794)*
▲ Paperworld Inc ....E 516 221-2702
Bellmore *(G-815)*
Precision Diecutting Inc.........................G 315 776-8465
Port Byron *(G-13764)*
Premier Packaging Corporation ....E 585 924-8460
Victor *(G-16520)*
▲ S & S Prtg Die-Cutting Co Inc ....F 718 388-8990
Brooklyn *(G-2543)*

Spectrum Prtg Lithography Inc ....F 212 255-3131
New York *(G-12182)*
Ums Manufacturing LLC ....F 518 562-2410
Plattsburgh *(G-13734)*
▲ Welsh Gold Stampers Inc..................E 718 984-5031
Staten Island *(G-15776)*

2676 Sanitary Paper Prdts

Alyk Inc ....F 917 968-2552
New York *(G-9158)*
Attends Healthcare Inc ....A 212 338-5100
New York *(G-9311)*
Becks Classic Mfg Inc ....D 631 435-3800
Brentwood *(G-1175)*
◆ Bentley Manufacturing Inc ....G 212 714-1800
New York *(G-9408)*
Cascades Tssue Group-Sales Inc ....D 518 238-1900
Waterford *(G-16630)*
▲ Cellu Tissue - Long Island LLC.........C 631 232-2626
Central Islip *(G-3514)*
Corman USA Inc....................................G 718 727-7455
Staten Island *(G-15682)*
◆ Crosstex International Inc ....D 631 582-6777
Hauppauge *(G-6079)*
Deluxe Packaging Corp.........................F 845 246-6090
Saugerties *(G-15213)*
First Quality Hygienic Inc.......................G 516 829-3030
Great Neck *(G-5827)*
◆ First Quality Products Inc.................F 516 829-4949
Great Neck *(G-5828)*
▲ Florelle Tissue Corporation ....E 647 997-7405
Brownville *(G-2797)*
Georgia-Pacific LLC...............................A 518 561-3500
Plattsburgh *(G-13692)*
HFC Prestige Intl US LLC ....A 212 389-7800
New York *(G-10514)*
Kas Direct LLC ....E 516 934-0541
Westbury *(G-17028)*
L VII Resilient LLC ....F 631 987-5819
Medford *(G-8284)*
▲ Maxim Hygiene Products Inc ....F 516 621-3323
Mineola *(G-8556)*
Monthly Gift Inc.....................................G 888 444-9661
New York *(G-11328)*
▲ Mr Disposable Inc ....F 718 388-8574
Brooklyn *(G-2344)*
▲ N3a Corporation................................D 516 284-6799
Inwood *(G-6802)*
◆ Nice-Pak Products Inc ....B 845 365-2772
Orangeburg *(G-13258)*
Nuk USA LLC...G 914 366-2820
Tarrytown *(G-16123)*
Nutek Disposables Inc...........................G 516 829-3030
Great Neck *(G-5841)*
Precare Corp ....G 631 524-5171
Hauppauge *(G-6194)*
▲ Precare Corp ....G 631 667-1055
Hauppauge *(G-6195)*
Procter & Gamble Company ....C 646 885-4201
New York *(G-11747)*
◆ Professional Disposables Inc ....A 845 365-1700
Orangeburg *(G-13266)*
◆ Rochester Midland Corporation........C 585 336-2200
Rochester *(G-14665)*
▲ Select Products Holdings LLC ....E 855 777-3532
Huntington *(G-6720)*
◆ Skip Hop Inc......................................E 646 902-9874
New York *(G-12118)*
Skip Hop Holdings Inc...........................G 212 868-9850
New York *(G-12119)*
▲ Sqp Inc ....C 518 831-6800
Schenectady *(G-15322)*
▲ US Alliance Paper Inc ....C 631 254-3030
Edgewood *(G-4632)*
Waymor1 Inc..E 518 677-8511
Cambridge *(G-3339)*

2677 Envelopes

Apec Paper Industries Ltd ....G 212 730-0088
New York *(G-9222)*
Buffalo Envelope Inc ....F 716 686-0100
Depew *(G-4274)*
▲ Cambridge-Pacific Inc ....E 518 677-5988
Cambridge *(G-3333)*
Cenveo Inc...D 716 662-2800
Orchard Park *(G-13283)*
Conformer Products Inc.........................F 516 504-6300
Great Neck *(G-5817)*
CPW Direct Mail Group LLC..................E 631 588-6565
Farmingdale *(G-4975)*

East Cast Envlope Graphics LLC ....E 718 326-2424
Maspeth *(G-8165)*
Jacmax Industries LLC..........................G 718 439-3743
Brooklyn *(G-2129)*
▼ Kleer-Fax Inc ....D 631 225-1100
Amityville *(G-303)*
Mercury Envelope Co Inc......................D 516 678-6744
Rockville Centre *(G-14824)*
Old Ue LLC ....B 718 707-0700
Long Island City *(G-7861)*
◆ Poly-Pak Industries Inc ....B 631 293-6767
Melville *(G-8377)*
Premier Packaging Corporation ....E 585 924-8460
Victor *(G-16520)*
▲ Rochester 100 Inc ....C 585 475-0200
Rochester *(G-14655)*
Westrock Mwv LLC................................C 212 688-5000
New York *(G-12645)*
X-L Envelope and Printing Inc...............F 716 852-2135
Buffalo *(G-3284)*

2678 Stationery Prdts

Allen William & Company Inc ....C 212 675-6461
Glendale *(G-5659)*
▲ Anne Taintor Inc................................G 718 483-9312
Brooklyn *(G-1613)*
Bak USA Technologies Corp..................E 716 248-2704
Buffalo *(G-2852)*
▲ Cos TEC Manufacturing Corp...........G 631 589-7170
Bohemia *(G-1035)*
Duck Flats Pharma.................................G 315 689-3407
Elbridge *(G-4638)*
▲ Dynamic Intl Mfrs & Distrs Inc ....F 347 993-1914
Suffern *(G-15810)*
▲ General Diaries Corporation.............F 516 371-2244
Inwood *(G-6797)*
▲ Innovative Designs LLC ....E 212 695-0892
New York *(G-10646)*
▲ International Design Assoc Ltd ....G 212 687-0333
New York *(G-10675)*
▼ Kleer-Fax Inc ....D 631 225-1100
Amityville *(G-303)*
Leather Indexes Corp ....D 516 827-1900
Hicksville *(G-6391)*
▲ P C I Paper Conversions Inc ....C 315 437-1641
Syracuse *(G-16027)*
Paper Magic Group Inc..........................B 631 521-3682
New York *(G-11577)*
▲ Princton Archtctural Press LLC.........F 518 671-6100
Hudson *(G-6662)*
▲ USA Custom Pad Corp ....E 607 563-9550
Sidney *(G-15467)*
Westrock Mwv LLC ....C 212 688-5000
New York *(G-12645)*

2679 Converted Paper Prdts, NEC

Accent Label & Tag Co Inc.....................G 631 244-7066
Ronkonkoma *(G-14875)*
Adelphi Paper Hangings ....G 518 284-9066
Sharon Springs *(G-15404)*
▲ Aigner Label Holder Corp..................F 845 562-4510
New Windsor *(G-8976)*
▲ Allen-Bailey Tag & Label Inc ....D 585 538-2324
Caledonia *(G-3303)*
▲ Allied Converters Inc ....E 914 235-1585
New Rochelle *(G-8931)*
Aniiwe Inc..G 347 683-1891
Brooklyn *(G-1612)*
Apexx Omni-Graphics Inc......................D 718 326-3330
Maspeth *(G-8147)*
▼ Auto Data Systems Inc ....E 631 667-2382
Deer Park *(G-4128)*
▲ Avco Industries Inc ....F 631 851-1555
Central Islip *(G-3511)*
Beetins Wholesale Inc...........................F 718 524-0899
Staten Island *(G-15665)*
Best Time Processor LLC ....G 917 455-4126
Richmond Hill *(G-14082)*
Bigname Commerce LLC ....D 631 693-1070
Amityville *(G-276)*
Cascades New York Inc.........................C 518 238-1900
Wynantskill *(G-17394)*
▲ CCT (us) Inc.......................................F 716 297-7509
Niagara Falls *(G-12825)*
▲ Deltacraft Paper Company LLC ....C 716 856-5135
Buffalo *(G-2925)*
Depot Label Company Inc.....................G 631 467-2952
Patchogue *(G-13443)*
Eagles Nest Holdings LLC ....E 513 874-5270
New York *(G-10011)*

Employee Codes: A=Over 500 employees, B=251-500
C=101-250, D=51-100, E=20-50, F=10-19, G=5-9
2018 Harris
New York Manufacturers Directory
751

S
I
C

26 PAPER AND ALLIED PRODUCTS

Emergent Power Inc ....G..... 201 441-3590
  Latham (G-7389)
Eskayel Inc ....G..... 347 703-8084
  Brooklyn (G-1940)
▲ Felix Schoeller North Amer Inc........C..... 315 298-5133
  Pulaski (G-13963)
Flavor Paper Ltd ....F..... 718 422-0230
  Brooklyn (G-1985)
▲ Gardei Industries LLC ....F..... 716 693-7100
  North Tonawanda (G-12991)
Gavin Mfg Corp ....E..... 631 467-0040
  Farmingdale (G-5005)
◆ Gaylord Bros Inc ....D..... 315 457-5070
  North Syracuse (G-12961)
◆ General Fibre Products Corp ....D..... 516 358-7500
  New Hyde Park (G-8880)
Gerald McGlone ....G..... 518 482-2613
  Colonie (G-3846)
◆ Global Tissue Group Inc ....E..... 631 924-3019
  Medford (G-8276)
▼ Gooding Co Inc ....E..... 716 434-5501
  Lockport (G-7622)
▲ Graphic Cntrls Acqisition Corp ....B..... 716 853-7500
  Buffalo (G-2994)
Graphic Controls Holdings Inc ....F..... 716 853-7500
  Buffalo (G-2995)
Greenfiber Albany Inc ....D..... 518 842-1470
  Gloversville (G-5727)
Howard J Moore Company Inc ....E..... 631 351-8467
  Plainview (G-13635)
Interface Performance Mtls ....F..... 315 346-3100
  Beaver Falls (G-789)
▲ Interntnal Bus Cmmncations Inc ....E..... 516 352-4505
  New Hyde Park (G-8887)
Jerry Tomaselli ....F..... 718 965-1400
  Brooklyn (G-2136)
▲ K Sidrane Inc ....E..... 631 393-6974
  Farmingdale (G-5028)
▲ Katz Group Americas Inc ....E..... 716 995-3059
  Sanborn (G-15149)
Larkin Anya Ltd ....G..... 718 361-1827
  Long Island City (G-7814)
▲ Lulu DK LLC ....G..... 212 223-4234
  New York (G-11092)
▲ M C Packaging Corporation ....E..... 631 694-3012
  Farmingdale (G-5047)
M C Packaging Corporation ....E..... 631 643-3763
  Babylon (G-547)
▲ Marketing Group International ....G..... 631 754-8095
  Northport (G-13034)
Master Image Printing Inc ....G..... 914 347-4400
  Elmsford (G-4772)
Mid-York Press Inc ....D..... 607 674-4491
  Sherburne (G-15415)
Millcraft Paper Company ....E..... 716 856-5135
  Buffalo (G-3086)
National Advertising & Prtg ....G..... 212 629-7650
  New York (G-11369)
Northeastern Paper Corp ....G..... 631 659-3634
  Huntington (G-6705)
▲ Noteworthy Industries Inc ....C..... 518 842-2662
  Amsterdam (G-365)
▲ P C I Paper Conversions Inc ....E..... 315 437-1641
  Syracuse (G-16027)
P C I Paper Conversions Inc ....F..... 315 437-1641
  Syracuse (G-16030)
▲ Pack America Corp ....G..... 212 508-6666
  New York (G-11568)
▲ Paperworld Inc ....E..... 516 221-2702
  Bellmore (G-815)
▲ Paradigm Mktg Consortium Inc ....E..... 516 677-6012
  Syosset (G-15855)
▲ Plug Power Inc ....B..... 518 782-7700
  Latham (G-7404)
Precision Label Corporation ....F..... 631 270-4490
  Farmingdale (G-5097)
Quadra Flex Corp ....G..... 607 758-7066
  Cortland (G-4065)
▲ Quality Circle Products Inc ....G..... 914 736-6600
  Montrose (G-8653)
RB Converting Inc ....G..... 607 777-1325
  Binghamton (G-940)
S D Warren Company ....D..... 914 696-5544
  White Plains (G-17192)
▲ Shell Containers Inc (ny) ....E..... 516 352-4505
  New Hyde Park (G-8906)
▲ Sml USA Inc ....E..... 212 736-8800
  New York (G-12135)
▲ Specialty Quality Packg LLC ....D..... 914 580-3200
  Scotia (G-15354)

Stanley Paper Co Inc ....F..... 518 489-1131
  Albany (G-136)
Stickershopcom Inc ....G..... 631 563-4323
  Bayport (G-755)
Stoney Croft Converters Inc ....F..... 718 608-9800
  Staten Island (G-15764)
Sunnyside Decorative Prints Co ....G..... 516 671-1935
  Glen Cove (G-5643)
Tag Envelope Co Inc ....E..... 718 389-6844
  College Point (G-3835)
▲ Tri-Flex Label Corp ....E..... 631 293-0411
  Farmingdale (G-5143)
▲ Trinity Packaging Corporation ....F..... 914 273-4111
  Armonk (G-419)
▼ VIP Paper Trading Inc ....E..... 212 382-4642
  New York (G-12573)
Waymor1 Inc ....F..... 518 677-8511
  Cambridge (G-3339)
Web-Tech Packaging Inc ....F..... 716 684-4520
  Lancaster (G-7372)
Winghing 8 Ltd ....G..... 718 439-0021
  Brooklyn (G-2776)

27 PRINTING, PUBLISHING, AND ALLIED INDUSTRIES

2711 Newspapers: Publishing & Printing

21st Century Fox America Inc ....G..... 845 735-1116
  Pearl River (G-13476)
50+ Lifestyle ....G..... 631 286-0058
  Bellport (G-819)
◆ A C J Communications Inc ....F..... 631 587-5612
  Babylon (G-541)
A Zimmer Ltd ....D..... 315 422-7011
  Syracuse (G-15866)
Adirondack Publishing Co Inc ....E..... 518 891-2600
  Saranac Lake (G-15162)
Advance Magazine Pubis Inc ....E..... 212 450-7000
  New York (G-9088)
▲ Advance Publications Inc ....D..... 718 981-1234
  Staten Island (G-15653)
Advertiser Publications Inc ....F..... 845 783-1111
  Chester (G-3625)
▲ Afro Times Newspaper ....F..... 718 636-9500
  Brooklyn (G-1568)
After 50 Inc ....G..... 716 832-9300
  Lancaster (G-7323)
Albany Catholic Press Assoc ....E..... 518 453-6688
  Albany (G-35)
Albany Student Press Inc ....E..... 518 442-5665
  Albany (G-41)
Albion-Holley Pennysaver Inc ....E..... 585 589-5641
  Albion (G-164)
Algemeiner Journal Inc ....F..... 718 771-0400
  Brooklyn (G-1582)
All Island Media Inc ....C..... 631 698-8400
  Edgewood (G-4606)
All Island Media Inc ....F..... 516 942-8400
  Hicksville (G-6343)
Alm Media LLC ....B..... 212 457-9400
  New York (G-9146)
Alm Media Holdings Inc ....B..... 212 457-9400
  New York (G-9147)
American City Bus Journals Inc ....E..... 716 541-1654
  Buffalo (G-2823)
American Media Inc ....D..... 212 545-4800
  New York (G-9174)
American Media Inc ....D..... 212 545-4800
  New York (G-9175)
American Sports Media ....G..... 585 924-4250
  Victor (G-16484)
American Sports Media LLC ....G..... 585 377-9636
  Rochester (G-14216)
Amnews Corporation ....E..... 212 932-7400
  New York (G-9187)
Amnewyork ....D..... 212 239-5555
  New York (G-9188)
Angel Media and Publishing ....G..... 845 727-4949
  West Nyack (G-16941)
Angola Pennysaver Inc ....F..... 716 549-1164
  Angola (G-379)
AR Publishing Company Inc ....F..... 212 482-0303
  New York (G-9239)
Architects Newspaper LLC ....F..... 212 966-0630
  New York (G-9245)
Artvoice ....F..... 716 881-6604
  Buffalo (G-2839)
Asahi Shimbun America Inc ....D..... 212 398-0257
  New York (G-9278)

Aspect Printing Inc ....E..... 347 789-4284
  Brooklyn (G-1642)
Auburn Publishing Co ....D..... 315 253-5311
  Auburn (G-479)
Bangla Patrika Inc ....G..... 718 482-9923
  Long Island City (G-7712)
Bee Publications Inc ....D..... 716 632-4700
  Williamsville (G-17263)
Belsito Communications Inc ....E..... 845 534-9700
  New Windsor (G-8978)
▼ Best Line Inc ....G..... 917 670-6210
  Staten Island (G-15666)
Beth Kobliner Company LLC ....G..... 212 501-8407
  New York (G-9423)
Bleezarde Publishing Inc ....F..... 518 756-2030
  Ravena (G-14033)
Blue and White Publishing Inc ....F..... 215 431-3339
  New York (G-9471)
Boonville Herald Inc ....G..... 315 942-4449
  Boonville (G-1161)
Bornomala USA Inc ....G..... 347 753-2355
  Jackson Heights (G-6921)
Bradford Publications Inc ....C..... 716 373-2500
  Olean (G-13157)
Brasilans Press Pblcations Inc ....E..... 212 764-6161
  New York (G-9507)
Brooklyn Journal Publications ....E..... 718 422-7400
  Brooklyn (G-1728)
Brooklyn Rail Inc ....F..... 718 349-8427
  Brooklyn (G-1729)
Buffalo Law Journal ....G..... 716 541-1600
  Buffalo (G-2875)
▲ Buffalo News Inc ....A..... 716 849-4401
  Buffalo (G-2879)
Buffalo Standard Printing Corp ....F..... 716 835-9454
  Buffalo (G-2882)
Bureau of National Affairs Inc ....E..... 212 687-4530
  New York (G-9531)
Business First of New York ....E..... 716 854-5822
  Buffalo (G-2884)
Business First of New York ....E..... 518 640-6800
  Latham (G-7384)
Business Journals ....F..... 212 790-5100
  New York (G-9535)
Camden News Inc ....G..... 315 245-1849
  Camden (G-3340)
Canandaigua Msgnr Incorporated ....D..... 585 394-0770
  Canandaigua (G-3366)
Canarsie Courier Inc ....F..... 718 257-0600
  Brooklyn (G-1754)
Capital Region Wkly Newspapers ....E..... 518 877-7160
  Albany (G-58)
Catskill Delaware Publications ....F..... 845 887-5200
  Callicoon (G-3312)
Catskill Mountain Publishing ....F..... 845 586-2601
  Arkville (G-409)
Cdc Publishing LLC ....E..... 215 579-1695
  Morrisville (G-8661)
Chase Media Group ....F..... 914 962-3871
  Yorktown Heights (G-17525)
Chester West County Press ....G..... 914 684-0006
  Mount Vernon (G-8716)
China Daily Distribution Corp ....E..... 212 537-8888
  New York (G-9646)
China Newsweek Corporation ....F..... 212 481-2510
  New York (G-9651)
▲ Chinese Medical Report Inc ....G..... 718 359-5676
  Flushing (G-5239)
Christian Press Inc ....G..... 718 886-4400
  Flushing (G-5240)
Chronicle ....G..... 347 969-7281
  Bronx (G-1298)
Chronicle Express ....F..... 315 536-4422
  Penn Yan (G-13531)
Citizen Publishing Corp ....F..... 845 627-1414
  Nanuet (G-8800)
City Newspaper ....G..... 585 244-3329
  Rochester (G-14297)
Clarion Publications Inc ....F..... 585 243-3530
  Geneseo (G-5579)
CNY Business Review Inc ....F..... 315 472-3104
  Syracuse (G-15917)
Colors Fashion Inc ....F..... 212 629-0401
  New York (G-9733)
Columbia Daily Spectator ....E..... 212 854-9550
  New York (G-9735)
Community Media Group LLC ....F..... 518 439-4949
  Delmar (G-4269)
Community Media LLC ....E..... 212 229-1890
  New York (G-9749)

Community News Group LLC ...C ... 718 260-2500
Brooklyn *(G-1795)*
Community Newspaper Group LLC ...F ... 607 432-1000
Oneonta *(G-13203)*
Community Newspaper Group LLC ...E ... 518 565-4114
Plattsburgh *(G-13688)*
Community Newsppr Holdings Inc ...E ... 585 798-1400
Medina *(G-8302)*
Community Newsppr Holdings Inc ...D ... 716 693-1000
Niagara Falls *(G-12827)*
Community Newsppr Holdings Inc ...D ... 716 282-2311
Niagara Falls *(G-12828)*
Community Newsppr Holdings Inc ...E ... 716 439-9222
Lockport *(G-7605)*
Copia Interactive LLC ...F ... 212 481-0520
New York *(G-9779)*
Cortland Standard Printing Co ...D ... 607 756-5665
Cortland *(G-4045)*
Country Folks ...G ... 585 343-9721
Batavia *(G-631)*
Courier-Life Inc ...C ... 718 260-2500
Brooklyn *(G-1809)*
CT Publications Co ...G ... 718 592-2196
Corona *(G-4018)*
Daily Cornell Sun ...E ... 607 273-0746
Ithaca *(G-6873)*
Daily Freeman ...F ... 845 331-5000
Kingston *(G-7215)*
Daily Gazette Company ...B ... 518 374-4141
Schenectady *(G-15274)*
Daily Gazette Company ...C ... 518 395-3060
Schenectady *(G-15275)*
Daily Mail & Greene Cnty News ...F ... 518 943-2100
Catskill *(G-3455)*
▲ **Daily News LP** ...A ... 212 210-2100
New York *(G-9845)*
Daily Orange Corporation ...E ... 315 443-2314
Syracuse *(G-15940)*
Daily Racing Form LLC ...F ... 212 514-2180
New York *(G-9847)*
Daily Record ...F ... 585 232-2035
Rochester *(G-14320)*
Daily World Press Inc ...F ... 212 922-9201
New York *(G-9848)*
Dale Press Inc ...E ... 718 543-6200
Bronx *(G-1313)*
Danet Inc ...F ... 718 266-4444
Brooklyn *(G-1839)*
Dans Paper Inc ...D ... 631 537-0500
Southampton *(G-15565)*
Das Yidishe Licht Inc ...G ... 718 387-3166
Brooklyn *(G-1841)*
Dbg Media ...G ... 718 599-6828
Brooklyn *(G-1844)*
Delaware County Times Inc ...G ... 607 746-2176
Delhi *(G-4262)*
Denton Publications Inc ...D ... 518 873-6368
Elizabethtown *(G-4640)*
Denton Publications Inc ...E ... 518 561-9680
Plattsburgh *(G-13689)*
Der Blatt Inc ...F ... 845 783-1148
Monroe *(G-8588)*
Der Yid Inc ...E ... 718 797-3900
Brooklyn *(G-1855)*
Digital One USA Inc ...F ... 718 396-4890
Flushing *(G-5245)*
Division Street News Corp ...F ... 518 234-2515
Cobleskill *(G-3761)*
▲ **Document Journal Inc** ...G ... 646 586-3099
New York *(G-9946)*
DOT Publishing ...F ... 315 593-2510
Fulton *(G-5470)*
▲ **Dow Jones & Company Inc** ...B ... 609 627-2999
New York *(G-9965)*
Dow Jones & Company Inc ...E ... 212 597-5983
New York *(G-9966)*
Dray Enterprises Inc ...F ... 585 768-2201
Le Roy *(G-7431)*
E W Smith Publishing Co ...F ... 845 562-1218
New Windsor *(G-8983)*
Eagle Media Partners LP ...E ... 315 434-8889
Syracuse *(G-15949)*
East Hampton Ind News Inc ...E ... 631 324-2500
East Hampton *(G-4428)*
East Hampton Star Inc ...E ... 631 324-0002
East Hampton *(G-4429)*
Ecclesiastical Communications ...F ... 212 688-2399
New York *(G-10027)*
Economist Newspaper NA Inc ...E ... 212 554-0676
New York *(G-10033)*

Ecuador News Inc ...F ... 718 205-7014
Woodside *(G-17344)*
El Aguila ...G ... 212 410-2450
New York *(G-10045)*
El Diario LLC ...C ... 212 807-4600
Brooklyn *(G-1910)*
Empire Publishing Inc ...F ... 516 829-4000
Far Rockaway *(G-4928)*
Empire State Weeklies Inc ...E ... 585 671-1533
Webster *(G-16747)*
Epoch Times International Inc ...G ... 212 239-2808
New York *(G-10102)*
Event Journal Inc ...G ... 516 470-1811
Bethpage *(G-866)*
Evercore Partners Svcs E LLC ...A ... 212 857-3100
New York *(G-10144)*
Exhibits & More ...G ... 585 924-4040
Victor *(G-16500)*
Expositor Newspapers Inc ...G ... 585 427-2468
Rochester *(G-14387)*
▲ **Fairchild Publications Inc** ...A ... 212 630-4000
New York *(G-10181)*
Finger Lakes Media Inc ...F ... 607 243-7600
Dundee *(G-4352)*
Finger Lakes Printing Co Inc ...E ... 315 789-3333
Geneva *(G-5588)*
Fire Island Tide Publication ...F ... 631 567-7470
Sayville *(G-15239)*
Firefighters Journal ...E ... 718 391-0283
Long Island City *(G-7770)*
First Choice News Inc ...G ... 212 477-2044
New York *(G-10218)*
Five Islands Publishing Inc ...F ... 631 583-5345
Bronx *(G-1335)*
Four Directions Inc ...E ... 315 829-8388
Vernon *(G-16457)*
▲ **Francepress LLC** ...G ... 646 202-9828
New York *(G-10247)*
Fredonia Pennysaver Inc ...G ... 716 679-1509
Fredonia *(G-5382)*
Freetime Magazine Inc ...G ... 585 473-2266
Rochester *(G-14404)*
French Morning LLC ...G ... 646 290-7463
New York *(G-10258)*
▲ **FT Publications Inc** ...D ... 212 641-6500
New York *(G-10266)*
FT Publications Inc ...E ... 212 641-2420
New York *(G-10267)*
Fulton Newspapers Inc ...E ... 315 598-6397
Fulton *(G-5471)*
Gallagher Printing Inc ...E ... 716 873-2434
Buffalo *(G-2977)*
Gannett Co Inc ...E ... 516 484-7510
Port Washington *(G-13840)*
Gannett Co Inc ...D ... 585 232-7100
Rochester *(G-14408)*
Gannett Co Inc ...G ... 585 924-3406
Farmington *(G-5160)*
Gannett Co Inc ...E ... 914 278-9315
New Rochelle *(G-8948)*
Gannett Co Inc ...D ... 607 798-1234
Vestal *(G-16470)*
Gannett Co Inc ...G ... 585 346-4150
Lakeville *(G-7307)*
Gannett Stllite Info Ntwrk Inc ...E ... 914 965-5000
Yonkers *(G-17462)*
Gannett Stllite Info Ntwrk Inc ...D ... 585 798-1400
Medina *(G-8305)*
Gannett Stllite Info Ntwrk Inc ...F ... 914 381-3400
Mamaroneck *(G-8068)*
Gannett Stllite Info Ntwrk LLC ...E ... 845 578-2300
West Nyack *(G-16946)*
Gannett Stllite Info Ntwrk LLC ...C ... 845 454-2000
Poughkeepsie *(G-13920)*
▲ **Gatehouse Media LLC** ...C ... 585 598-0030
Pittsford *(G-13589)*
Gatehouse Media LLC ...E ... 315 792-5000
Utica *(G-16359)*
Gatehouse Media LLC ...G ... 607 776-2121
Bath *(G-656)*
Gatehouse Media LLC ...F ... 315 866-2220
Herkimer *(G-6325)*
Gatehouse Media LLC ...D ... 607 936-4651
Corning *(G-3993)*
Gatehouse Media LLC ...D ... 585 394-0770
Canandaigua *(G-3376)*
Gatehouse Media LLC ...C ... 607 324-1425
Hornell *(G-6590)*
Gatehouse Media MO Holdings ...G ... 530 846-3661
Pittsford *(G-13590)*

Gatehuse Media PA Holdings Inc ...E ... 585 598-0030
Pittsford *(G-13591)*
Gateway Newspapers Inc ...G ... 845 628-8400
Mahopac *(G-8026)*
General Media Strategies Inc ...G ... 212 586-4141
New York *(G-10316)*
Gleaner Company Ltd ...G ... 718 657-0788
Jamaica *(G-6951)*
Glens Falls Newspapers Inc ...G ... 518 792-3131
Glens Falls *(G-5696)*
Good Health Healthcare Newsppr ...F ... 585 421-8109
Victor *(G-16503)*
Great North Road Media Inc ...F ... 646 619-1355
New York *(G-10399)*
Guidance Group Inc ...F ... 631 756-4618
Melville *(G-8354)*
▲ **Hagedorn Communications Inc** ...D ... 914 636-7400
New Rochelle *(G-8951)*
Haitian Times Inc ...G ... 718 230-8700
New Rochelle *(G-8952)*
Hamodia Corp ...F ... 718 853-9094
Brooklyn *(G-2063)*
Hearst Business Media Corp ...F ... 631 650-4441
Great River *(G-5870)*
▲ **Hearst Communications Inc** ...A ... 415 777-7825
New York *(G-10480)*
▲ **Hearst Corporation** ...A ... 212 649-2000
New York *(G-10482)*
Hearst Corporation ...A ... 518 454-5694
Albany *(G-85)*
Hearst Corporation ...E ... 212 649-2275
New York *(G-10491)*
Herald Press Inc ...G ... 718 784-5255
Long Island City *(G-7787)*
Herald Publishing Company LLC ...G ... 315 470-2022
New York *(G-10503)*
High Ridge News LLC ...G ... 718 548-7412
Bronx *(G-1359)*
Highline Media LLC ...C ... 859 692-2100
New York *(G-10520)*
Holdens Screen Supply Corp ...G ... 212 627-2727
New York *(G-10539)*
Home Reporter Inc ...E ... 718 238-6600
Brooklyn *(G-2081)*
Hudson News Inc ...G ... 212 971-6800
New York *(G-10570)*
Hudson Valley Black Press ...G ... 845 562-1313
Newburgh *(G-12783)*
Huersch Marketing Group LLC ...F ... 518 874-1045
Green Island *(G-5875)*
IMG The Daily ...G ... 212 541-5640
New York *(G-10618)*
▲ **Impremedia LLC** ...D ... 212 807-4785
Brooklyn *(G-2099)*
India Abroad Publications Inc ...D ... 212 929-1727
New York *(G-10631)*
Investment News ...E ... 212 210-0100
New York *(G-10692)*
Investors Business Daily Inc ...F ... 212 626-7676
New York *(G-10693)*
Irish Echo Newspaper Corp ...F ... 212 482-4818
New York *(G-10702)*
Irish Tribune Inc ...F ... 212 684-3366
New York *(G-10703)*
Ithaca Journal News Co Inc ...E ... 607 272-2321
Ithaca *(G-6889)*
Jewish Journal ...G ... 718 630-9350
Brooklyn *(G-2139)*
Jewish Press Inc ...C ... 718 330-1100
Brooklyn *(G-2140)*
Jewish Week Inc ...E ... 212 921-7822
New York *(G-10766)*
Jobs Weekly Inc ...F ... 716 648-5627
Hamburg *(G-5952)*
John Lor Publishing Ltd ...E ... 631 475-1000
Patchogue *(G-13451)*
Johnson Acquisition Corp ...F ... 518 828-1616
Hudson *(G-6652)*
Johnson Newspaper Corporation ...E ... 518 483-4700
Malone *(G-8042)*
Journal News ...G ... 914 694-5000
White Plains *(G-17155)*
Journal Register Company ...D ... 518 584-4242
Saratoga Springs *(G-15191)*
Journal Register Company ...E ... 212 257-7212
New York *(G-10809)*
Kch Publications Inc ...E ... 516 671-2360
Glen Cove *(G-5632)*
▲ **Korea Central Daily News Inc** ...D ... 718 361-7700
Long Island City *(G-7810)*

Employee Codes: A=Over 500 employees, B=251-500
C=101-250, D=51-100, E=20-50, F=10-19, G=5-9
2018 Harris
New York Manufacturers Directory
753

27 PRINTING, PUBLISHING, AND ALLIED INDUSTRIES SIC SECTION

▲ **Korea Times New York Inc** D 718 784-4526
Long Island City *(G-7811)*

Korea Times New York Inc G 718 729-5555
Long Island City *(G-7812)*

Korea Times New York Inc G 718 961-7979
Flushing *(G-5269)*

L & M Publications Inc E 516 378-3133
Garden City *(G-5525)*

Lantern Hall LLC G 718 381-2122
Brooklyn *(G-2196)*

▲ **Lebhar-Friedman Inc** E 212 756-5000
New York *(G-10986)*

Lebhar-Friedman Inc C 212 756-5000
New York *(G-10987)*

Lee Enterprises Incorporated C 518 792-3131
Glens Falls *(G-5702)*

Lee Newspapers Inc F 518 673-3237
Palatine Bridge *(G-13421)*

Lee Publications Inc D 518 673-3237
Palatine Bridge *(G-13422)*

LI Community Newspapers Inc G 516 747-8282
Mineola *(G-8553)*

Litmor Publishing Corp F 516 931-0012
Garden City *(G-5527)*

Livingston County News G 585 243-1234
Geneseo *(G-5581)*

Lmg National Publishing Inc E 585 598-6874
Fairport *(G-4868)*

Local Media Group Inc B 845 341-1100
Middletown *(G-8480)*

Local Media Group Inc E 845 341-1100
Middletown *(G-8481)*

Local Media Group Inc D 845 341-1100
Middletown *(G-8482)*

Local Media Group Inc F 845 794-3712
Monticello *(G-8643)*

Local Media Group Inc F 845 340-4910
Kingston *(G-7226)*

Long Island Business News E 631 737-1700
Ronkonkoma *(G-14961)*

Long Island Catholic Newspaper E 516 594-1212
Rockville Centre *(G-14822)*

Long Island Cmnty Nwsppers Inc D 516 482-4490
Mineola *(G-8555)*

Long Island Cmnty Nwsppers Inc F 631 427-7000
Huntington *(G-6703)*

Long Islander Newspapers LLC G 631 427-7000
Huntington *(G-6704)*

Louis Vuitton North Amer Inc G 212 644-2574
New York *(G-11079)*

Lowville Newspaper Corporation G 315 376-3525
Lowville *(G-7967)*

Made Fresh Daily G 212 285-2253
New York *(G-11119)*

Main Street Connect LLC F 203 803-4110
Armonk *(G-415)*

Malone Newspapers Corp E 518 483-2000
Malone *(G-8045)*

Manchester Newspaper Inc E 518 642-1234
Granville *(G-5791)*

Manhattan Media LLC E 212 268-8600
New York *(G-11154)*

Manhattan Times Inc F 212 569-5800
New York *(G-11158)*

Mark I Publications Inc E 718 205-8000
Glendale *(G-5673)*

Market Place Publications E 516 997-7909
Carle Place *(G-3421)*

Markets Media LLC G 646 442-4646
New York *(G-11185)*

Massapequa Post E 516 798-5100
Massapequa Park *(G-8221)*

Melmont Fine Pringng/Graphics G 516 939-2253
Bethpage *(G-872)*

Merchandiser Inc G 315 462-6411
Clifton Springs *(G-3739)*

Mexico Independent Inc E 315 963-3763
Watertown *(G-16687)*

Miami Media LLC F 212 268-8600
New York *(G-11274)*

Mid-York Press Inc D 607 674-4491
Sherburne *(G-15415)*

Ming Pao (new York) Inc E 718 786-2888
Long Island City *(G-7843)*

Ming Pao (new York) Inc F 212 334-2220
New York *(G-11303)*

Ming Pao (new York) Inc D 718 786-2888
Long Island City *(G-7844)*

Minority Reporter Inc G 585 225-3628
Rochester *(G-14535)*

Moneypaper Inc F 914 925-0022
Rye *(G-15090)*

Moneysaver Advertising Inc F 585 593-1275
Olean *(G-13172)*

Mortgage Press Ltd E 516 409-1400
Wantagh *(G-16581)*

Nassau County Publications G 516 481-5400
Hempstead *(G-6306)*

▲ **National Herald Inc** E 718 784-5255
Long Island City *(G-7851)*

Neighbor Newspapers G 631 226-2636
Farmingdale *(G-5072)*

Neighbor To Neighbor News Inc G 585 492-2525
Arcade *(G-397)*

New Berlin Gazette E 607 847-6131
Norwich *(G-13050)*

New Living Inc G 631 751-8819
Patchogue *(G-13454)*

New Media Investment Group Inc B 212 479-3160
New York *(G-11412)*

New Ski Inc E 607 277-7000
Ithaca *(G-6902)*

New York Cvl Srvc Emplys Pblsh F 212 962-2690
New York *(G-11418)*

New York Daily Challenge Inc E 718 636-9500
Brooklyn *(G-2372)*

New York Daily News G 212 248-2100
New York *(G-11419)*

▲ **New York IL Bo Inc** F 718 961-1538
Flushing *(G-5279)*

New York Press Inc E 212 268-8600
New York *(G-11425)*

▲ **New York Times Company** B 212 556-1234
New York *(G-11429)*

New York Times Company F 718 281-7000
Flushing *(G-5280)*

New York Times Company F 212 556-4300
New York *(G-11430)*

New York University E 212 998-4300
New York *(G-11431)*

New York1 News Operations F 212 379-3311
New York *(G-11432)*

News Communications Inc F 212 689-2500
New York *(G-11434)*

News Corporation C 212 416-3400
New York *(G-11435)*

News India Usa LLC G 212 675-7515
New York *(G-11436)*

News India USA Inc F 212 675-7515
New York *(G-11437)*

News of The Highlands Inc F 845 534-7771
Cornwall *(G-4011)*

News Report Inc E 718 851-6607
Brooklyn *(G-2379)*

Newsday LLC B 631 843-4050
Melville *(G-8370)*

Newsday LLC C 631 843-3135
Melville *(G-8371)*

Newspaper Delivery Solutions G 718 370-1111
Staten Island *(G-15731)*

Newspaper Publisher LLC F 607 775-0472
Conklin *(G-3896)*

Newspaper Times Union F 518 454-5676
Albany *(G-108)*

Newsweek LLC G 646 867-7100
New York *(G-11439)*

Nick Lugo Inc F 212 348-2100
New York *(G-11445)*

Nikkei America Inc E 212 261-6200
New York *(G-11450)*

Nordic Press Inc G 212 686-3356
New York *(G-11470)*

North Country This Week G 315 265-1000
Potsdam *(G-13898)*

Northern NY Newspapers Corp C 315 782-1000
Watertown *(G-16691)*

Northern Tier Publishing Corp F 914 962-4748
Yorktown Heights *(G-17530)*

▲ **Noticia Hispanoamericana Inc** E 516 223-5678
Baldwin *(G-559)*

Novoye Rsskoye Slovo Pubg Corp D 646 460-4566
Brooklyn *(G-2389)*

Nyc Community Media LLC F 212 229-1890
Brooklyn *(G-2395)*

Nyc Trade Printers Corp F 718 606-0610
Woodside *(G-17359)*

Nyp Holdings Inc D 718 260-2500
Brooklyn *(G-2396)*

▲ **Nyp Holdings Inc** A 212 997-9272
New York *(G-11500)*

Nyt Capital LLC F 212 556-1234
New York *(G-11503)*

Oak Lone Publishing Co Inc E 518 792-1126
Glens Falls *(G-5708)*

Observer G 347 915-5638
Brooklyn *(G-2397)*

Observer Daily Sunday Newsppr D 716 366-3000
Dunkirk *(G-4370)*

Ogden Newspapers Inc C 716 487-1111
Jamestown *(G-7055)*

Oneida Publications Inc E 315 363-5100
Oneida *(G-13185)*

Ottaway Newspapers Inc F 845 343-2181
Middletown *(G-8490)*

Outlook Newspaper E 845 356-6261
Suffern *(G-15817)*

Owego Pennysaver Press Inc F 607 687-2434
Owego *(G-13383)*

Page Front Group Inc G 716 823-8222
Lackawanna *(G-7272)*

Panagraphics Inc G 716 312-8088
Orchard Park *(G-13312)*

Patchogue Advance Inc E 631 475-1000
Patchogue *(G-13456)*

▲ **Peace Times Weekly Inc** G 718 762-6500
Flushing *(G-5287)*

▼ **Pearson Inc** D 212 641-2400
New York *(G-11610)*

Pearson Longman LLC E 212 641-2400
White Plains *(G-17174)*

Pennysaver Group Inc F 914 966-1400
Yonkers *(G-17495)*

Post Journal F 716 487-1111
Jamestown *(G-7056)*

Prometheus International Inc F 718 472-0700
Long Island City *(G-7878)*

Prospect News F 212 374-2800
New York *(G-11760)*

Publishing Group America Inc F 646 658-0550
New York *(G-11769)*

Putnam Cnty News Recorder LLC F 845 265-2468
Cold Spring *(G-3789)*

Quality Guides G 716 326-3163
Westfield *(G-17078)*

R W Publications Div of Wtrhs E 716 714-5620
Elma *(G-4666)*

R W Publications Div of Wtrhs E 716 714-5620
Elma *(G-4667)*

Realtimetraderscom E 716 632-6600
Buffalo *(G-3181)*

Record G 518 270-1200
Saratoga Springs *(G-15199)*

Record Advertiser E 716 693-1000
North Tonawanda *(G-13006)*

Record Review LLC F 914 244-0533
Katonah *(G-7162)*

Rheinwald Printing Co Inc F 585 637-5100
Brockport *(G-1246)*

Richner Communications Inc C 516 569-4000
Garden City *(G-5543)*

Richner Communications Inc G 516 569-4000
Lawrence *(G-7424)*

Ridgewood Times Prtg & Pubg E 718 821-7500
Ridgewood *(G-14134)*

Right World View E 914 406-2994
Purchase *(G-13987)*

Rizzoli Intl Publications Inc F 212 308-2000
New York *(G-11905)*

Rochester Business Journal E 585 546-8303
Rochester *(G-14658)*

Rochester Catholic Press F 585 529-9530
Rochester *(G-14659)*

Rochester Democrat & Chronicle E 585 232-7100
Rochester *(G-14663)*

Rocket Communications Inc F 716 873-2594
Buffalo *(G-3190)*

Royal News Corp F 212 564-8972
New York *(G-11944)*

Ruby Newco LLC G 212 852-7000
New York *(G-11951)*

Russkaya Reklama Inc E 718 769-3000
Brooklyn *(G-2538)*

S G New York LLC F 631 698-8400
Edgewood *(G-4623)*

S G New York LLC E 631 665-4000
Bohemia *(G-1124)*

S I Communications Inc F 914 725-2500
Scarsdale *(G-15253)*

Sag Harbor Express G 631 725-1700
Sag Harbor *(G-15106)*

Salamanca Press Penny Saver E 716 945-1500
Salamanca *(G-15132)*
Sample News Group LLC D 315 343-3800
Oswego *(G-13365)*
Satellite Network Inc F 718 336-2698
Brooklyn *(G-2560)*
Sb New York Inc D 212 457-7790
New York *(G-12000)*
Schneps Publications Inc E 718 224-5863
Bayside *(G-769)*
Seabay Media Holdings LLC G 212 457-7790
New York *(G-12028)*
Second Amendment Foundation G 716 885-6408
Buffalo *(G-3209)*
Seneca County Area Shopper G 607 532-4333
Ovid *(G-13372)*
Seneca Media Inc D 607 324-1425
Hornell *(G-6593)*
Seneca Media Inc F 585 593-5300
Wellsville *(G-16784)*
Service Advertising Group Inc F 718 361-6161
Long Island City *(G-7904)*
◆ **Shelter Island Reporter Inc** G 631 749-1000
Shelter Island *(G-15410)*
Sing Tao Newspapers NY Ltd F 212 431-9030
Brooklyn *(G-2592)*
Sing Tao Newspapers NY Ltd E 718 821-0123
Brooklyn *(G-2593)*
▲ **Sing Tao Newspapers NY Ltd** E 212 699-3800
New York *(G-12107)*
SM News Plus Incorporated G 212 888-0153
New York *(G-12128)*
Smithtown News Inc E 631 265-2100
Smithtown *(G-15521)*
Southampton Town Newspapers E 631 283-4100
Southampton *(G-15576)*
Southampton Town Newspapers F 631 288-1100
Westhampton Beach *(G-17090)*
Spartacist Publishing Co E 212 732-7860
New York *(G-12173)*
Spartan Publishing Inc F 716 664-7373
Jamestown *(G-7061)*
Sports Pblications Prod NY LLC D 212 366-7700
New York *(G-12191)*
Sports Reporter Inc G 212 737-2750
New York *(G-12193)*
Spring Publishing Corporation G 718 782-0881
Brooklyn *(G-2614)*
Ssrja LLC F 718 725-7020
Jamaica *(G-6987)*
▲ **St Lawrence County Newspapers** D 315 393-1003
Ogdensburg *(G-13143)*
Star Community Publishing C 631 843-4050
Melville *(G-8384)*
Star Sports Corp E 516 773-4075
Great Neck *(G-5861)*
Star-Gazette Fund Inc C 607 734-5151
Elmira *(G-4715)*
Steffen Publishing Inc D 315 865-4100
Holland Patent *(G-6514)*
Stratconglobal Inc G 212 989-2355
New York *(G-12234)*
Straus Communications F 845 782-4000
Chester *(G-3643)*
Straus Newspapers Inc E 845 782-4000
Chester *(G-3644)*
Stuart Communications Inc F 845 252-7414
Narrowsburg *(G-8815)*
Sun-Times Media Group Inc E 716 945-1644
Salamanca *(G-15136)*
Syracuse Catholic Press Assn G 315 422-8153
Syracuse *(G-16074)*
Tablet Publishing Company Inc E 718 965-7333
Brooklyn *(G-2664)*
Tefft Publishers Inc G 518 692-9290
Greenwich *(G-5914)*
Tegna Inc C 716 849-2222
Buffalo *(G-3238)*
Tenney Media Group D 315 853-5569
Clinton *(G-3747)*
The Earth Times Foundation G 718 297-0488
Brooklyn *(G-2676)*
The Sandhar Corp G 718 523-0819
Jamaica *(G-6994)*
Thestreet Inc D 212 321-5000
New York *(G-12337)*
Thousand Islands Printing Co G 315 482-2581
Alexandria Bay *(G-194)*
Times Beacon Record Newspapers F 631 331-1154
East Setauket *(G-4513)*
Times Review Newspaper Corp E 631 354-8031
Mattituck *(G-8243)*
Tioga County Courier G 607 687-0108
Owego *(G-13385)*
Tompkins Weekly Inc G 607 539-7100
Ithaca *(G-6913)*
Tri-Town News Inc E 607 561-3515
Sidney *(G-15464)*
Tri-Village Publishers Inc D 518 843-1100
Amsterdam *(G-371)*
Tribco LLC E 718 357-7400
Whitestone *(G-17245)*
Tribune Entertainment Co Del E 203 866-2204
New York *(G-12425)*
Tricycle Foundation Inc G 800 873-9871
New York *(G-12426)*
Trilake Three Press Corp G 518 359-2462
Tupper Lake *(G-16304)*
Tryp Times Square G 212 246-8800
New York *(G-12437)*
Ubm Inc A 212 600-3000
New York *(G-12458)*
Ubm LLC F 516 562-5000
New York *(G-12459)*
Ubm LLC D 516 562-7800
New Hyde Park *(G-8912)*
Ulster County Press Office G 845 687-4480
High Falls *(G-6429)*
Ulster Publishing Co Inc E 845 334-8205
Kingston *(G-7247)*
Ulster Publishing Co Inc F 845 255-7005
New Paltz *(G-8926)*
Unified Media Inc F 917 595-2710
New York *(G-12471)*
Urdu Times G 718 297-8700
Jamaica *(G-6997)*
US Hispanic Media Inc G 212 885-8000
Brooklyn *(G-2732)*
USA Today International Corp G 703 854-3400
New York *(G-12512)*
Vnovom Svete G 212 302-9480
New York *(G-12588)*
Vpj Publication Inc E 718 845-3221
Howard Beach *(G-6628)*
W H White Publications Inc G 914 725-2500
Dobbs Ferry *(G-4328)*
W M T Publications Inc F 585 244-3329
Rochester *(G-14783)*
Wallkill Lodge No 627 F&Am F 845 778-7148
Walden *(G-16558)*
Wallkill Valley Publications E 845 561-0170
Newburgh *(G-12810)*
Wappingers Falls Shopper Inc E 845 297-3723
Wappingers Falls *(G-16598)*
Wave Publishing Co Inc F 718 634-4000
Rockaway Beach *(G-14811)*
Wayuga Community Newspapers E 315 754-6229
Red Creek *(G-14040)*
Wayuga Community Newspapers G 315 594-2506
Wolcott *(G-17302)*
Webster Ontrio Wlwrth Pnnysver F 585 265-3620
Webster *(G-16767)*
Weekly Ajkal F 718 565-2100
Jackson Heights *(G-6925)*
Weekly Business News Corp G 212 689-5888
New York *(G-12631)*
Weisbeck Publishing Printing G 716 937-9226
Alden *(G-189)*
West Publishing Corporation E 212 922-1920
New York *(G-12642)*
West Seneca Bee Inc D 716 632-4700
Williamsville *(G-17284)*
Westbury Times D 516 747-8282
Mineola *(G-8572)*
Westfair Communications Inc E 914 694-3600
White Plains *(G-17214)*
Westside News Inc F 585 352-3411
Spencerport *(G-15598)*
William B Collins Company D 518 773-8272
Gloversville *(G-5744)*
William Boyd Printing Co Inc C 518 339-5832
Latham *(G-7411)*
William J Kline & Son Inc D 518 843-1100
Amsterdam *(G-374)*
Williamsburg Bulletin G 718 387-0123
Brooklyn *(G-2771)*
Wolfe Publications Inc C 585 394-0770
Canandaigua *(G-3389)*
World Journal LLC G 212 879-3933
New York *(G-12690)*
▲ **World Journal LLC** C 718 746-8889
Whitestone *(G-17247)*
World Journal LLC E 718 445-2277
Flushing *(G-5314)*
World Journal LLC F 718 871-5000
Brooklyn *(G-2781)*
▲ **Yated Neeman Inc** F 845 369-1600
Monsey *(G-8621)*
Yoga In Daily Life - NY Inc G 718 539-8548
College Point *(G-3837)*
Yonkers Time Publishing Co F 914 965-4000
Yonkers *(G-17519)*
Zenith Color Comm Group Inc E 212 989-4400
Long Island City *(G-7961)*

2721 Periodicals: Publishing & Printing

21st Century Fox America Inc D 212 447-4600
New York *(G-9014)*
21st Century Fox America Inc D 212 852-7000
New York *(G-9013)*
▲ **2600 Enterprises Inc** F 631 474-2677
Saint James *(G-15113)*
A Guideposts Church Corp C 212 251-8100
New York *(G-9035)*
Abp International Inc E 212 490-3999
New York *(G-9051)*
Academy of Political Science G 212 870-2500
New York *(G-9055)*
Access Intelligence LLC A 212 204-4269
New York *(G-9057)*
Adirondack Life Inc F 518 946-2191
Jay *(G-7088)*
▲ **Advance Magazine Publs Inc** A 212 286-2860
New York *(G-9085)*
Advance Magazine Publs Inc D 212 790-4422
New York *(G-9086)*
Advance Magazine Publs Inc D 212 286-2860
New York *(G-9087)*
Advance Magazine Publs Inc C 212 450-7000
New York *(G-9088)*
Advance Magazine Publs Inc D 212 697-0126
New York *(G-9089)*
▲ **Advance Publications Inc** D 718 981-1234
Staten Island *(G-15653)*
Advanced Research Media Inc F 631 751-9696
Setauket *(G-15398)*
Adventure Publishing Group E 212 575-4510
New York *(G-9097)*
Aeon America Inc G 914 584-0275
New York *(G-9100)*
▲ **Alcoholics Anonymous Grapevine** F 212 870-3400
New York *(G-9128)*
Alm Media LLC B 212 457-9400
New York *(G-9146)*
Alm Media Holdings Inc B 212 457-9400
New York *(G-9147)*
▲ **Alpha Media Group Inc** B 212 302-2626
New York *(G-9150)*
America Press Inc E 212 581-4640
New York *(G-9162)*
American Graphic Design Awards G 212 696-4380
New York *(G-9167)*
▲ **American Inst Chem Engineers** D 646 495-1355
New York *(G-9170)*
American Institute Physics Inc C 516 576-2410
Melville *(G-8326)*
American Intl Media LLC F 845 359-4225
White Plains *(G-17105)*
American Jewish Committee G 212 891-1400
New York *(G-9171)*
American Jewish Congress Inc E 212 879-4500
New York *(G-9172)*
American Physical Society D 631 591-4025
Ridge *(G-14104)*
American Towman Network Inc F 845 986-4546
Warwick *(G-16608)*
Analysts In Media (aim) Inc E 212 488-1777
New York *(G-9196)*
Animal Fair Media Inc F 212 629-0392
New York *(G-9212)*
Annointed Buty Ministries LLC G 646 867-3796
Brooklyn *(G-1614)*
Archaelogy Magazine E 718 472-3050
Long Island City *(G-7699)*
Archie Comic Publications Inc D 914 381-5155
Pelham *(G-13513)*
Art & Understanding Inc G 518 426-9010
Albany *(G-47)*
Artifex Press LLC F 212 414-1482
New York *(G-9269)*

S I C

Employee Codes: A=Over 500 employees, B=251-500
C=101-250, D=51-100, E=20-50, F=10-19, G=5-9
2018 Harris
New York Manufacturers Directory
755

27 PRINTING, PUBLISHING, AND ALLIED INDUSTRIES SIC SECTION

▲ **Artnews Ltd** .... F 212 398-1690
New York *(G-9274)*
Aspen Publishers Inc .... A 212 771-0600
New York *(G-9288)*
Aspire One Communications LLC .... F 201 281-2998
Cornwall *(G-4007)*
Association For Cmpt McHy Inc .... D 212 869-7440
New York *(G-9292)*
Athlon Spt Communications Inc .... E 212 478-1910
New York *(G-9302)*
Atlantic Monthly Group Inc .... E 202 266-7000
New York *(G-9303)*
Backstage LLC .... E 212 493-4243
Brooklyn *(G-1661)*
▲ **Bazaar** .... G 212 903-5497
New York *(G-9385)*
Beauty Fashion Inc .... E 212 840-8800
New York *(G-9389)*
Bedford Freeman & Worth .... C 212 576-9400
New York *(G-9391)*
Bedford Communications Inc .... E 212 807-8220
New York *(G-9393)*
Beer Marketers Insights Inc .... G 845 507-0040
Suffern *(G-15808)*
Bellerophon Publications Inc .... E 212 627-9977
New York *(G-9399)*
▲ **Berger & Wild LLC** .... G 646 415-8459
New York *(G-9410)*
Bernhard Arnold & Company Inc .... G 212 907-1500
New York *(G-9414)*
▲ **Bertelsmann Inc** .... E 212 782-1000
New York *(G-9417)*
Bertelsmann Pubg Group Inc .... A 212 782-1000
New York *(G-9418)*
▲ **Beverage Media Group Inc** .... F 212 571-3232
New York *(G-9427)*
Binah Magazines Corp .... G 718 305-5200
Brooklyn *(G-1697)*
BJ Magazines Inc .... G 212 367-9705
New York *(G-9458)*
Blackbook Media Corp .... E 212 334-1800
New York *(G-9461)*
Blue Horizon Media Inc .... F 212 661-7878
New York *(G-9472)*
Bnei Aram Soba Inc .... F 718 645-4460
Brooklyn *(G-1706)*
Boardman Simons Publishing .... E 212 620-7200
New York *(G-9482)*
Bondi Digital Publishing LLC .... G 212 405-1655
New York *(G-9485)*
Boy Scouts of America .... G 212 532-0985
New York *(G-9498)*
Brant Art Publications Inc .... E 212 941-2800
New York *(G-9505)*
▲ **Brant Publications Inc** .... E 212 941-2800
New York *(G-9506)*
Brownstone Publishers Inc .... E 212 473-8200
New York *(G-9525)*
Buffalo Spree Publishing Inc .... G 585 413-0040
Rochester *(G-14266)*
Buffalo Spree Publishing Inc .... E 716 783-9119
Buffalo *(G-2881)*
Bullett Media LLC .... F 212 242-2123
New York *(G-9530)*
Bust Inc .... G 212 675-1707
Brooklyn *(G-1743)*
Bz Media LLC .... F 631 421-4158
Melville *(G-8330)*
C Q Communications Inc .... E 516 681-2922
Hicksville *(G-6352)*
Cambridge University Press .... D 212 337-5000
New York *(G-9558)*
Canopy Canopy Canopy Inc .... G 347 529-5182
New York *(G-9568)*
Capco Marketing .... F 315 699-1687
Baldwinsville *(G-567)*
Capital Reg Wkly Newsppr Group .... F 518 674-2841
Averill Park *(G-531)*
Carol Group Ltd .... G 212 505-2030
New York *(G-9586)*
Cdc Publishing LLC .... E 215 579-1695
Morrisville *(G-8661)*
▼ **Centennial Media LLC** .... F 646 527-7320
New York *(G-9613)*
Center For Inquiry Inc .... F 716 636-4869
Amherst *(G-233)*
Cfo Publishing LLC .... C 212 459-3004
New York *(G-9623)*
Choice Magazine Listening Inc .... G 516 883-8280
Port Washington *(G-13828)*
City and State Ny LLC .... E 212 268-0442
New York *(G-9680)*
City Real Estate Book Inc .... G 516 593-2949
Valley Stream *(G-16428)*
Civil Svc Rtred Employees Assn .... F 718 937-0290
Long Island City *(G-7727)*
Clarion Publications Inc .... F 585 243-3530
Geneseo *(G-5579)*
▲ **Clp Pb LLC** .... E 212 340-8100
New York *(G-9704)*
▲ **CMX Media LLC** .... E 917 793-5831
New York *(G-9706)*
CNY Business Review Inc .... F 315 472-3104
Syracuse *(G-15917)*
Coda Media Inc .... G 917 478-2565
New York *(G-9722)*
College Calendar Company .... F 315 768-8242
Whitesboro *(G-17220)*
Commentary Inc .... F 212 891-1400
New York *(G-9744)*
Commonweal Foundation Inc .... F 212 662-4200
New York *(G-9747)*
Complex Media Inc .... E 917 793-5831
New York *(G-9752)*
Conde Nast .... E 212 630-3642
New York *(G-9757)*
Conde Nast International Inc .... D 212 286-2860
New York *(G-9758)*
Conference Board Inc .... C 212 759-0900
New York *(G-9760)*
Congress For Jewish Culture .... G 212 505-8040
New York *(G-9761)*
Consumer Reports Inc .... B 914 378-2000
Yonkers *(G-17445)*
Continuity Publishing Inc .... F 212 869-4170
New York *(G-9771)*
Convenience Store News .... G 214 217-7800
New York *(G-9774)*
Cornell University .... E 607 254-2473
Ithaca *(G-6872)*
Crain Communications Inc .... C 212 210-0100
New York *(G-9805)*
Crains New York Business .... E 212 210-0250
New York *(G-9806)*
Creative Magazine Inc .... G 516 378-0800
Merrick *(G-8415)*
Credit Union Journal Inc .... G 212 803-8200
New York *(G-9811)*
▲ **Daily Beast Company LLC** .... E 212 445-4600
New York *(G-9844)*
Data Key Communication LLC .... F 315 445-2347
Fayetteville *(G-5172)*
▲ **Davis Ziff Publishing Inc** .... D 212 503-3500
New York *(G-9885)*
Davler Media Group LLC .... E 212 315-0800
New York *(G-9886)*
Delaware County Times Inc .... G 607 746-2176
Delhi *(G-4262)*
Demos Medical Publishing LLC .... F 516 889-1791
New York *(G-9897)*
Dennis Publishing Inc .... D 646 717-9500
New York *(G-9900)*
Denton Publications Inc .... E 518 561-9680
Plattsburgh *(G-13689)*
▲ **Departures Magazine** .... E 212 382-5600
New York *(G-9902)*
Direct Mktg Edctl Fndation Inc .... G 212 790-1512
New York *(G-9933)*
Discover Media LLC .... E 212 624-4800
New York *(G-9937)*
Dissent Magazine .... F 212 316-3120
New York *(G-9939)*
Distinction Magazine Inc .... E 631 843-3522
Melville *(G-8341)*
Dj Publishing Inc .... E 516 767-2500
Port Washington *(G-13832)*
Doctorow Communications Inc .... F 845 708-5166
New City *(G-8830)*
Dotto Wagner .... G 315 342-8020
Oswego *(G-13355)*
▲ **Dow Jones & Company Inc** .... B 609 627-2999
New York *(G-9965)*
Dow Jones & Company Inc .... E 212 597-5983
New York *(G-9966)*
Dow Jones Aer Company Inc .... A 212 416-2000
New York *(G-9967)*
Downtown Media Group LLC .... F 646 723-4510
New York *(G-9970)*
E W Williams Publications .... G 212 661-1516
New York *(G-10005)*
Earl G Graves Pubg Co Inc .... D 212 242-8000
New York *(G-10012)*
Ebner Publishing International .... G 646 742-0740
New York *(G-10025)*
Economist Intelligence Unit NA .... D 212 554-0600
New York *(G-10031)*
▲ **Economist Newspaper Group Inc** .... C 212 541-0500
New York *(G-10032)*
Eidosmedia Inc .... E 646 795-2100
New York *(G-10042)*
Elite Traveler LLC .... F 646 430-7900
New York *(G-10061)*
Elmont North Little League .... G 516 775-8210
Elmont *(G-4731)*
Envy Publishing Group Inc .... G 212 253-9874
New York *(G-10100)*
Equal Opprtnity Pblcations Inc .... F 631 421-9421
Melville *(G-8344)*
▲ **Essence Communications Inc** .... C 212 522-1212
New York *(G-10116)*
Essential Publications US LLC .... G 646 707-0898
New York *(G-10117)*
Et Publishing Intl LLC .... F 212 838-7220
New York *(G-10129)*
Excelsior Publications .... G 607 746-7600
Delhi *(G-4263)*
Executive Business Media Inc .... E 516 334-3030
Westbury *(G-17010)*
▲ **Faces Magazine Inc** .... F 201 843-4004
Poughkeepsie *(G-13918)*
Fahy-Williams Publishing Inc .... F 315 781-6820
Geneva *(G-5587)*
▲ **Fairchild Publications Inc** .... A 212 630-4000
New York *(G-10181)*
Fairchild Publishing LLC .... G 212 286-3897
New York *(G-10182)*
Family Publishing Group Inc .... E 914 381-7474
Mamaroneck *(G-8067)*
Fashion Calendar International .... G 212 289-0420
New York *(G-10197)*
Forum Publishing Co .... G 631 754-5000
Centerport *(G-3501)*
Francis Emory Fitch Inc .... E 212 619-3800
New York *(G-10248)*
Fridge Magazine Inc .... G 212 997-7673
New York *(G-10260)*
Frontiers Unlimited Inc .... G 631 283-4663
Southampton *(G-15566)*
Frost Publications Inc .... G 845 726-3232
Westtown *(G-17097)*
▲ **Frozen Food Digest Inc** .... G 212 557-8600
New York *(G-10262)*
Fun Media Inc .... E 646 472-0135
New York *(G-10271)*
Genomeweb LLC .... F 212 651-5636
New York *(G-10322)*
Getting The Word Out Inc .... G 518 891-9352
Saranac Lake *(G-15165)*
Glamour Magazine .... G 212 286-2860
New York *(G-10345)*
Global Entity Media Inc .... G 631 580-7772
Ronkonkoma *(G-14934)*
Global Finance Magazine .... G 212 524-3223
New York *(G-10355)*
Global Finance Media Inc .... F 212 447-7900
New York *(G-10356)*
▲ **Golfing Magazine** .... G 516 822-5446
Hicksville *(G-6380)*
Good Times Magazine .... G 516 280-2100
Carle Place *(G-3416)*
Government Data Publication .... E 347 789-8719
Brooklyn *(G-2046)*
Grants Financial Publishing .... F 212 809-7994
New York *(G-10393)*
▲ **Graphis Inc** .... F 212 532-9387
New York *(G-10396)*
Green Apple Courage Inc .... G 716 614-4673
Buffalo *(G-2999)*
Gruner + Jahr Prtg & Pubg Co .... C 212 463-1000
New York *(G-10418)*
◆ **Gruner + Jahr USA Group Inc** .... B 866 323-9336
New York *(G-10419)*
Guernica .... F 914 414-7318
Brooklyn *(G-2056)*
Guilford Publications Inc .... D 212 431-9800
New York *(G-10425)*
H F W Communications Inc .... F 315 703-7979
East Syracuse *(G-4548)*
H W Wilson Company Inc .... B 718 588-8635
Bronx *(G-1352)*

SIC SECTION

27 PRINTING, PUBLISHING, AND ALLIED INDUSTRIES

Halcyon Business Publications	F	800 735-2732	Westbury *(G-17020)*
Hammer Communications Inc	F	631 261-5806	Northport *(G-13030)*
Hamptons Magazine	E	631 283-7125	Southampton *(G-15568)*
Hamptons Media LLC	G	631 283-6900	Southampton *(G-15569)*
Harpers Magazine Foundation	E	212 420-5720	New York *(G-10462)*
Hart Energy Publishing Lllp	G	212 621-4621	New York *(G-10467)*
Hatherleigh Company Ltd	G	607 538-1092	Hobart *(G-6451)*
Haymarket Group Ltd	F	212 239-0855	New York *(G-10474)*
▲ Haymarket Media Inc	C	646 638-6000	New York *(G-10475)*
Healthy Way of Life Magazine	G	718 616-1681	Brooklyn *(G-2069)*
Hearst Bus Communications Inc	G	212 649-2000	New York *(G-10478)*
Hearst Business Media	D	516 227-1300	Uniondale *(G-16318)*
Hearst Business Media Corp	G	631 650-6151	Great River *(G-5869)*
Hearst Business Media Corp	F	631 650-4441	Great River *(G-5870)*
Hearst Business Publishing Inc	F	212 969-7500	New York *(G-10479)*
▲ Hearst Corporation	A	212 649-2000	New York *(G-10482)*
Hearst Corporation	E	212 649-3100	New York *(G-10483)*
Hearst Corporation	E	212 903-5366	New York *(G-10484)*
Hearst Corporation	D	516 382-4580	New York *(G-10486)*
Hearst Corporation	A	518 454-5694	Albany *(G-85)*
Hearst Corporation	D	212 649-4271	New York *(G-10488)*
Hearst Corporation	D	212 204-4300	New York *(G-10489)*
Hearst Corporation	D	212 903-5000	New York *(G-10490)*
Hearst Corporation	E	212 649-2275	New York *(G-10491)*
▲ Hearst Holdings Inc	F	212 649-2000	New York *(G-10493)*
Hello and Hola Media Inc	E	212 807-4795	Brooklyn *(G-2071)*
Herman Hall Communications	F	718 941-1879	Brooklyn *(G-2075)*
Highline Media LLC	C	859 692-2100	New York *(G-10520)*
▲ Historic TW Inc	E	212 484-8000	New York *(G-10530)*
Holmes Group The Inc	G	212 333-2300	New York *(G-10543)*
Homesell Inc	F	718 514-0346	Staten Island *(G-15705)*
Hotelinteractive Inc	F	631 424-7755	Smithtown *(G-15510)*
Human Life Foundation Inc	G	212 685-5210	New York *(G-10576)*
▲ Humana Press Inc	E	212 460-1500	New York *(G-10577)*
I On Youth	G	716 832-6509	Buffalo *(G-3019)*
Icarus Enterprises Inc	G	917 969-4461	New York *(G-10596)*
Icd Publications Inc	E	631 246-9300	Islandia *(G-6833)*
Imek Media LLC	E	212 422-9000	New York *(G-10616)*
Impact Journals LLC	G	800 922-0957	Orchard Park *(G-13298)*
Impressions Inc	G	212 594-5954	New York *(G-10621)*
Index Magazine	G	212 243-1428	New York *(G-10630)*
Infinitlink Corporation	G	934 777-0180	West Babylon *(G-16822)*
Ink Publishing Corporation	G	347 294-1220	Brooklyn *(G-2104)*
Institute of Electrical and El	E	212 705-8900	New York *(G-10655)*
Institutional Invester	G	212 224-3300	New York *(G-10656)*
Intellignc The Ftr Cmptng Nwsl	F	212 222-1123	New York *(G-10662)*
Intellitravel Media Inc	G	646 695-6700	New York *(G-10663)*
Intercultural Alliance Artists	G	917 406-1202	Flushing *(G-5261)*
Interhellenic Publishing Inc	G	212 967-5016	New York *(G-10671)*
International Center For Postg	G	607 257-5860	Ithaca *(G-6886)*
International Data Group Inc	E	212 331-7883	New York *(G-10674)*
Interntnl Publcatns Media Grup	G	917 604-9602	New York *(G-10682)*
Interview Inc	E	212 941-2900	New York *(G-10684)*
Irish America Inc	E	212 725-2993	New York *(G-10701)*
Japan America Learning Ctr Inc	F	914 723-7600	Scarsdale *(G-15248)*
Jerome Levy Forecasting Center	G	914 244-8617	Mount Kisco *(G-8673)*
▲ Jobson Medical Information LLC	C	212 274-7000	New York *(G-10784)*
JSD Communications Inc	F	914 588-1841	Bedford *(G-792)*
Kbs Communications LLC	F	212 765-7124	New York *(G-10864)*
Keller International Pubg LLC	E	516 829-9210	Port Washington *(G-13853)*
▼ L F International Inc	D	212 756-5000	New York *(G-10940)*
L I F Publishing Corp	E	631 345-5200	Shirley *(G-15445)*
L Magazine LLC	F	212 807-1254	Brooklyn *(G-2186)*
Lagardere North America Inc	E	212 477-7373	New York *(G-10953)*
▲ Latina Media Ventures LLC	E	212 642-0200	New York *(G-10970)*
Latino Show Magazine Inc	G	718 709-1151	Woodhaven *(G-17325)*
Laurtom Inc	E	914 273-2233	Mount Kisco *(G-8677)*
Leadership Directories Inc	E	212 627-4140	New York *(G-10982)*
▲ Lebhar-Friedman Inc	E	212 756-5000	New York *(G-10986)*
Lebhar-Friedman Inc	C	212 756-5000	New York *(G-10987)*
Livid Magazine	F	929 340-7123	Brooklyn *(G-2234)*
Locations Magazine	G	212 288-4745	New York *(G-11047)*
▲ Lockwood Trade Journal Co Inc	E	212 391-2060	Long Island City *(G-7821)*
Long Island Catholic Newspaper	E	516 594-1212	Rockville Centre *(G-14822)*
Ltb Media (usa) Inc	D	212 447-9555	Southampton *(G-15570)*
Lucky Magazine	F	212 286-6220	New York *(G-11087)*
Luminary Publishing Inc	F	845 334-8600	Kingston *(G-7228)*
Luria Communications Inc	G	631 329-4922	East Hampton *(G-4433)*
M Shanken Communications Inc	C	212 684-4224	New York *(G-11106)*
▲ Macfadden Cmmnctions Group LLC	C	212 979-4800	New York *(G-11111)*
Macmillan Holdings LLC	F	212 576-9428	New York *(G-11114)*
Mag Inc	E	607 257-6970	Ithaca *(G-6894)*
Magazine I Spectrum E	E	212 419-7555	New York *(G-11125)*
▲ Magnificat Inc	F	914 502-1820	Yonkers *(G-17482)*
Manhattan Media LLC	E	212 268-8600	New York *(G-11154)*
Mann Publications Inc	E	212 840-6266	New York *(G-11159)*
Mansueto Ventures LLC	C	212 389-5300	New York *(G-11166)*
▲ Marie Claire USA	D	212 841-8493	New York *(G-11173)*
Maritime Activity Reports	E	212 477-6700	New York *(G-11176)*
▲ Mark Levine	F	212 677-4457	New York *(G-11178)*
▲ Martha Stewart Living	C	212 827-8000	New York *(G-11189)*
▲ Martha Stewart Living Omni LLC	B	212 827-8000	New York *(G-11190)*
Martinelli Holdings LLC	E	302 504-1361	Rye *(G-15088)*
▲ Marvel Entertainment LLC	C	212 576-4000	New York *(G-11193)*
Mary Ann Liebert Inc	D	914 740-2100	New Rochelle *(G-8962)*
Mass Appeal Magazine	G	718 858-0979	Brooklyn *(G-2282)*
Mathisen Ventures Inc	G	212 986-1025	New York *(G-11203)*
McCarthy LLC	F	646 862-5354	New York *(G-11220)*
McMahon Group LLC	D	212 957-5300	New York *(G-11227)*
Med Reviews LLC	E	212 239-5860	New York *(G-11232)*
Media Press Corp	E	212 791-6347	New York *(G-11234)*
Medikidz Usa Inc	G	646 895-9319	New York *(G-11242)*
Meredith Corporation	C	212 557-6600	New York *(G-11254)*
Meredith Corporation	F	212 499-2000	New York *(G-11255)*
Meredith Corporation	D	515 284-2157	New York *(G-11256)*
Mergent Inc	B	212 413-7700	New York *(G-11257)*
Metrosource Publishing Inc	F	212 691-5127	New York *(G-11269)*
Miami Media LLC	F	212 268-8600	New York *(G-11274)*
Mishpacha Magazine Inc	G	718 686-9339	Brooklyn *(G-2323)*
Modern Farmer Media Inc	F	518 828-7447	Hudson *(G-6658)*
Music & Sound Retailer Inc	E	516 767-2500	Port Washington *(G-13866)*
Nation Company LP	E	212 209-5400	New York *(G-11367)*
Nation Magazine	E	212 209-5400	New York *(G-11368)*
National Marketing Services	F	516 942-9595	Roslyn Heights *(G-15055)*
National Review Inc	E	212 679-7330	New York *(G-11373)*
▼ Nature America Inc	B	212 726-9200	New York *(G-11380)*
▲ NBM Publishing Inc	G	212 643-5407	New York *(G-11384)*
NCM Publishers Inc	G	212 691-9100	New York *(G-11385)*
Nervecom Inc	F	212 625-9914	New York *(G-11390)*
New Art Publications Inc	F	718 636-9100	Brooklyn *(G-2367)*
New Hope Media LLC	G	646 366-0830	New York *(G-11411)*
New York Media LLC	C	212 508-0700	New York *(G-11423)*
Newsgraphics of Delmar Inc	E	518 439-5363	Delmar *(G-4270)*
Next Step Publishing Inc	F	585 742-1260	Victor *(G-16518)*
Niche Media Holdings LLc	E	702 990-2500	New York *(G-11443)*
Nickelodeon Magazines Inc	G	212 541-1949	New York *(G-11446)*
Njf Publishing Corp	G	631 345-5200	Shirley *(G-15450)*
▲ Northeast Group	D	518 563-8214	Plattsburgh *(G-13709)*
Northeast Prtg & Dist Co Inc	G	514 577-3545	Plattsburgh *(G-13710)*
Northside Media Group LLC	F	917 318-6513	Brooklyn *(G-2385)*
Northside Media Group LLC	E	917 318-6513	Brooklyn *(G-2386)*
Nova Science Publishers Inc	F	631 231-7269	Hauppauge *(G-6175)*
Nsgv Inc	E	212 367-3167	New York *(G-11483)*
Nsgv Inc	E	212 367-3100	New York *(G-11484)*
Nyemac Inc	G	631 668-1303	Montauk *(G-8626)*

SIC

Employee Codes: A=Over 500 employees, B=251-500
C=101-250, D=51-100, E=20-50, F=10-19, G=5-9

2018 Harris
New York Manufacturers Directory

757

27 PRINTING, PUBLISHING, AND ALLIED INDUSTRIES SIC SECTION

Nylon LLc...E... 212 226-6454
New York *(G-11497)*
Nylon Media Inc...F... 212 226-6454
New York *(G-11498)*
Nyrev Inc...E... 212 757-8070
New York *(G-11501)*
Odyssey Mag Pubg Group Inc...E... 212 545-4800
New York *(G-11511)*
Optionline LLC...E... 516 218-3225
Garden City *(G-5538)*
Paper Publishing Company Inc...E... 212 226-4405
New York *(G-11578)*
Parade Publications Inc...E... 212 450-7000
New York *(G-11581)*
Parents Guide Network Corp...E... 212 213-8840
New York *(G-11584)*
Pati Inc...F... 718 244-6788
Jamaica *(G-6976)*
Pearson Education Inc...F... 201 236-7000
West Nyack *(G-16952)*
▲ Penhouse Media Group Inc...C... 212 702-6000
New York *(G-11625)*
Pensions & Investments...E... 212 210-0763
New York *(G-11626)*
▲ Penton Media Inc...B... 212 204-4200
New York *(G-11627)*
Penton Media Inc...G... 212 204-4200
New York *(G-11628)*
Periodical Services Co Inc...F... 518 822-9300
Hudson *(G-6660)*
Photo Industry Inc...F... 516 364-0016
Woodbury *(G-17315)*
Playbill Incorporated...E... 212 557-5757
New York *(G-11695)*
Pointwise Information Service...F... 315 457-4111
Liverpool *(G-7568)*
Preparatory Magazine Group...D... 718 761-4800
Staten Island *(G-15745)*
Prescribing Reference Inc...D... 646 638-6000
New York *(G-11723)*
Professnal Spt Pblications Inc...C... 212 697-1460
New York *(G-11749)*
Professnal Spt Pblications Inc...D... 516 327-9500
Elmont *(G-4737)*
Psychonomic Society Inc...E... 512 381-1494
New York *(G-11764)*
Public Relations Soc Amer Inc...E... 212 460-1400
New York *(G-11767)*
Pwxyz LLC...G... 212 377-5500
New York *(G-11785)*
Q Communications Inc...G... 212 594-6520
New York *(G-11786)*
Quest Media Llc...F... 646 840-3404
New York *(G-11798)*
Ragozin Data...E... 212 674-3123
Long Island City *(G-7886)*
Ralph Martinelli...E... 914 345-3055
Elmsford *(G-4783)*
Ramholtz Publishing Inc...D... 718 761-4800
Staten Island *(G-15749)*
Rd Publications Inc...C... 914 238-1000
Pleasantville *(G-13748)*
Rda Holding Co...F... 914 238-1000
New York *(G-11837)*
Readers Digest Assn Incthe...F... 414 423-0100
New York *(G-11839)*
Real Est Book of Long Island...F... 516 364-5000
Syosset *(G-15858)*
Real Estate Media Inc...E... 212 929-6976
New York *(G-11841)*
Redbook Magazine...F... 212 649-3331
New York *(G-11845)*
◆ Relx Inc...E... 212 309-8100
New York *(G-11858)*
Relx Inc...E... 212 463-6644
New York *(G-11859)*
Relx Inc...B... 212 633-3900
New York *(G-11860)*
Res Media Group Inc...F... 212 320-3750
New York *(G-11870)*
Rfp LLC...E... 212 838-7733
New York *(G-11883)*
Risk Society Management Pubg...E... 212 286-9364
New York *(G-11901)*
Rnd Enterprises Inc...G... 212 627-0165
New York *(G-11907)*
Rodale Inc...B... 212 697-2040
New York *(G-11921)*
Rolling Stone Magazine...G... 212 484-1616
New York *(G-11930)*
Romantic Times Inc...F... 718 237-1097
Brooklyn *(G-2524)*
Ross Communications Associates...F... 631 393-5089
Melville *(G-8381)*
Rough Draft Publishing LLC...F... 212 741-4773
New York *(G-11940)*
Rsl Media LLC...G... 212 307-6760
New York *(G-11949)*
Ruby Newco LLC...G... 212 852-7000
New York *(G-11951)*
Rye Record...G... 914 713-3213
Rye *(G-15093)*
Sandow Media LLC...F... 646 805-0200
New York *(G-11984)*
Saveur Magazine...E... 212 219-7400
New York *(G-11997)*
▲ Scholastic Corporation...G... 212 343-6100
New York *(G-12015)*
◆ Scholastic Inc...A... 800 724-6527
New York *(G-12016)*
▲ Securities Data Publishing Inc...G... 212 631-1411
New York *(G-12033)*
Security Letter...G... 212 348-1553
New York *(G-12034)*
Shoreline Publishing Inc...G... 914 738-7869
Pelham *(G-13519)*
Shugar Publishing...G... 631 288-4404
Westhampton Beach *(G-17089)*
Simmons-Boardman Pubg Corp...G... 212 620-7200
New York *(G-12101)*
Small Business Advisors Inc...F... 516 374-1387
Atlantic Beach *(G-469)*
Smart & Strong LLC...E... 212 938-2051
New York *(G-12129)*
Smooth Magazine...F... 212 925-1150
New York *(G-12139)*
Society For The Study...G... 212 822-8806
New York *(G-12144)*
Sound Communications Inc...E... 516 767-2500
Port Washington *(G-13884)*
▲ Source Media LLC...C... 212 803-8200
New York *(G-12168)*
Spc Marketing Company...G... 631 661-2727
West Islip *(G-16937)*
Spin Magazine Media...G... 212 231-7400
New York *(G-12187)*
▲ Sports Illustrated For Kids...E... 212 522-1212
New York *(G-12190)*
Spotlight Publications LLC...G... 914 345-9473
Elmsford *(G-4794)*
Springer Adis Us LLC...F... 212 460-1500
New York *(G-12195)*
Springer Healthcare LLC...E... 212 460-1500
New York *(G-12197)*
Springer Publishing Co LLC...E... 212 431-4370
New York *(G-12198)*
◆ Springer Scnce + Bus Media LLC...D... 781 871-6600
New York *(G-12199)*
Standard Analytics Io Inc...G... 917 882-5422
New York *(G-12205)*
Staten Island Parent Magazine...G... 718 761-4800
Staten Island *(G-15762)*
Steffen Publishing Inc...D... 315 865-4100
Holland Patent *(G-6514)*
Strathmore Directories Ltd...E... 516 997-2525
Westbury *(G-17056)*
Stuff Magazine...G... 212 302-2626
New York *(G-12244)*
Suburban Publishing Inc...F... 845 463-0542
Fishkill *(G-5196)*
Suffolk Community Council Inc...G... 631 434-9277
Deer Park *(G-4238)*
Summit Professional Networks...D... 212 557-7480
New York *(G-12256)*
Surface Magazine...E... 646 805-0200
New York *(G-12268)*
Sussex Publishers LLC...E... 212 260-7210
New York *(G-12269)*
Swaps Monitor Publications Inc...F... 212 742-8550
New York *(G-12271)*
Swift Fulfillment Services...G... 516 593-1198
Lynbrook *(G-7990)*
T V Trade Media Inc...F... 212 288-3933
New York *(G-12292)*
Testa Communications Inc...E... 516 767-2500
Port Washington *(G-13886)*
The PRS Group Inc...F... 315 431-0511
East Syracuse *(G-4583)*
Thestreet Inc...D... 212 321-5000
New York *(G-12337)*
Thomas International Pubg Co...F... 212 613-3441
New York *(G-12341)*
Thomas Publishing Company LLC...G... 212 695-0500
New York *(G-12344)*
Thomas Publishing Company LLC...G... 212 695-0500
New York *(G-12345)*
Thomas Publishing Company LLC...B... 212 695-0500
New York *(G-12342)*
Time Inc...E... 212 522-1212
New York *(G-12362)*
◆ Time Inc...A... 212 522-1212
New York *(G-12363)*
Time Inc...E... 212 522-0361
New York *(G-12364)*
▲ Time Inc Affluent Media Group...B... 212 382-5600
New York *(G-12365)*
Time Inc Affluent Media Group...G... 212 382-5600
New York *(G-12366)*
▲ Time Out New York Partners LP...D... 646 432-3000
New York *(G-12367)*
Time Warner Companies Inc...D... 212 484-8000
New York *(G-12369)*
TMC Usa LLC...G... 518 587-8920
Saratoga Springs *(G-15205)*
Towse Publishing Co...F... 914 235-3095
New Rochelle *(G-8971)*
Trader Interntnal Publications...G... 914 631-6856
Sleepy Hollow *(G-15497)*
Trans-High Corporation...E... 212 387-0500
New York *(G-12412)*
◆ Trusted Media Brands Inc...A... 914 238-1000
New York *(G-12435)*
Trusted Media Brands Inc...F... 646 293-6025
New York *(G-12436)*
Trusted Media Brands Inc...F... 914 244-5244
White Plains *(G-17204)*
TV Guide Magazine LLC...G... 800 866-1400
New York *(G-12448)*
▲ TV Guide Magazine Group Inc...D... 212 852-7500
New York *(G-12449)*
▲ U S Japan Publication NY Inc...G... 212 252-8833
New York *(G-12457)*
Ubm Inc...A... 212 600-3000
New York *(G-12458)*
Ubm LLC...D... 516 562-7800
New Hyde Park *(G-8912)*
Ubm LLC...F... 516 562-5000
New York *(G-12459)*
Ulster Publishing Co Inc...E... 845 334-8205
Kingston *(G-7247)*
Universal Cmmncations of Miami...C... 212 986-5100
New York *(G-12489)*
Uptown Media Group LLC...E... 212 360-5073
New York *(G-12496)*
Urban Racercom...G... 718 279-2202
Bayside *(G-771)*
Urbandaddy Inc...F... 212 929-7905
New York *(G-12502)*
US China Magazine...E... 212 663-4333
New York *(G-12504)*
US Frontline News Inc...E... 212 922-9090
New York *(G-12507)*
▲ US News & World Report Inc...C... 212 716-6800
New York *(G-12509)*
US Weekly LLC...D... 212 484-1616
New York *(G-12510)*
Valassis Communications Inc...G... 585 627-4138
Rochester *(G-14778)*
Valiant Entertainment LLC...E... 212 972-0361
New York *(G-12518)*
Value Line Inc...D... 212 907-1500
New York *(G-12520)*
Value Line Publishing LLC...C... 201 842-8054
New York *(G-12521)*
◆ Vanity Fair...F... 212 286-6052
New York *(G-12524)*
Vending Times Inc...F... 516 442-1850
Rockville Centre *(G-14831)*
Veranda Publications Inc...G... 212 903-5206
New York *(G-12543)*
Vibe Media Group LLC...D... 212 448-7300
New York *(G-12561)*
Vickers Stock Research Corp...E... 212 425-7500
New York *(G-12562)*
▲ Visionaire Publishing LLC...E... 646 434-6091
New York *(G-12581)*
Vogue Magazine...D... 212 286-2860
New York *(G-12590)*
Wall Street Reporter Magazine...D... 212 363-2600
New York *(G-12609)*

SIC SECTION
27 PRINTING, PUBLISHING, AND ALLIED INDUSTRIES

Wallkill Valley Publications .... E 845 561-0170
  Newburgh *(G-12810)*
Watch Journal LLC .... G 212 229-1500
  New York *(G-12621)*
Weider Publications LLC .... C 212 545-4800
  New York *(G-12632)*
Welcome Magazine Inc .... F 716 839-3121
  Amherst *(G-272)*
▲ Wenner Media LLC .... B 212 484-1616
  New York *(G-12639)*
▲ Westchester Law Journal Inc .... G 914 948-0715
  White Plains *(G-17211)*
Western New York Family Mag .... G 716 836-3486
  Buffalo *(G-3279)*
Westfair Communications Inc .... E 914 694-3600
  White Plains *(G-17214)*
Wine & Spirits Magazine Inc .... G 212 695-4660
  New York *(G-12669)*
Winsight LLC .... G 646 708-7309
  New York *(G-12674)*
Womens E News Inc .... G 212 244-1720
  New York *(G-12681)*
Working Mother Media Inc .... D 212 351-6400
  New York *(G-12686)*
World Business Media LLC .... F 212 344-0759
  Massapequa Park *(G-8224)*
World Guide Publishing .... E 800 331-7840
  New York *(G-12689)*
Wsn Inc .... G 212 924-7620
  New York *(G-12696)*
Yale Robbins Inc .... D 212 683-5700
  New York *(G-12709)*

2731 Books: Publishing & Printing

450 Ridge St Inc .... G 716 754-2789
  Lewiston *(G-7453)*
▲ Abbeville Press Inc .... E 212 366-5585
  New York *(G-9047)*
Adir Publishing Co .... F 718 633-9437
  Brooklyn *(G-1561)*
▲ Advance Publications Inc .... D 718 981-1234
  Staten Island *(G-15653)*
Ai Entertainment Holdings LLC .... F 212 247-6400
  New York *(G-9113)*
Aip Publishing LLC .... C 516 576-2200
  Melville *(G-8323)*
▲ Alba House Publishers .... F 718 698-2759
  Staten Island *(G-15654)*
Alfred Publishing Co Inc .... D 315 736-1572
  Oriskany *(G-13328)*
▲ Allworth Communications Inc .... F 212 777-8395
  New York *(G-9144)*
Alm Media LLC .... B 212 457-9400
  New York *(G-9146)*
Alm Media Holdings Inc .... B 212 457-9400
  New York *(G-9147)*
Amereon Ltd 631 298-5100
  Mattituck *(G-8238)*
▲ American Inst Chem Engineers .... D 646 495-1355
  New York *(G-9170)*
American Institute Physics Inc .... C 516 576-2410
  Melville *(G-8326)*
Amherst Media Inc .... F 716 874-4450
  Buffalo *(G-2827)*
▼ Amsco School Publications Inc .... D 212 886-6500
  New York *(G-9192)*
Annuals Publishing Co Inc .... F 212 505-0950
  New York *(G-9215)*
▲ Anthroposophic Press Inc .... G 518 851-2054
  Clifton Park *(G-3721)*
Apollo Investment Fund VII LP .... G 212 515-3200
  New York *(G-9227)*
Arbor Books Inc .... E 201 236-9990
  New York *(G-9242)*
Aspen Publishers Inc .... A 212 771-0600
  New York *(G-9288)*
▲ Assouline Publishing Inc .... F 212 989-6769
  New York *(G-9293)*
▲ Ateres Publishing & Bk Bindery .... F 718 935-9355
  Brooklyn *(G-1647)*
Atlas & Company LLC .... E 212 234-3100
  New York *(G-9306)*
◆ Barrons Educational Series Inc .... G 631 434-3311
  Hauppauge *(G-6051)*
Bear Port Publishing Company .... F 877 337-8577
  New York *(G-9388)*
Beauty Fashion Inc .... E 212 840-8800
  New York *(G-9389)*
Bedford Freeman & Worth .... C 212 576-9400
  New York *(G-9391)*

Bedford Freeman & Worth .... D 212 375-7000
  New York *(G-9392)*
Bedrock Communications .... G 212 532-4150
  New York *(G-9394)*
▲ Benchmark Education Co LLC .... D 914 637-7200
  New Rochelle *(G-8933)*
▲ Bertelsmann Inc .... E 212 782-1000
  New York *(G-9417)*
Bertelsmann Pubg Group Inc .... A 212 782-1000
  New York *(G-9418)*
▲ Bicker Inc .... F 212 688-0085
  New York *(G-9437)*
▲ Bloomsbury Publishing Inc .... D 212 419-5300
  New York *(G-9469)*
Bmg Rights Management (us) LLC .... E 212 561-3000
  New York *(G-9480)*
Boardman Simons Publishing .... E 212 620-7200
  New York *(G-9482)*
▲ Bobley-Harmann Corporation .... G 516 433-3800
  Ronkonkoma *(G-14908)*
▲ Bonnier Publishing Usa Inc .... E 212 321-0237
  New York *(G-9487)*
Booklinks Publishing Svcs LLC .... F 718 852-2116
  Brooklyn *(G-1708)*
Booklyn Artists Alliance .... G 718 383-9621
  Brooklyn *(G-1709)*
Boydell & Brewer Inc .... F 585 275-0419
  Rochester *(G-14261)*
▲ Bright Kids Nyc Inc .... E 917 539-4575
  New York *(G-9512)*
British American Publishing .... E 518 786-6000
  Latham *(G-7382)*
Brown Publishing Network Inc .... G 212 682-3330
  New York *(G-9523)*
▼ Burns Archive Photographic Dis .... G 212 889-1938
  New York *(G-9533)*
Byliner Inc .... E 415 680-3608
  New York *(G-9541)*
Callaway Arts & Entrmt Inc .... F 646 465-4667
  New York *(G-9553)*
Cambridge University Press .... D 212 337-5000
  New York *(G-9558)*
Campus Course Paks Inc .... G 516 877-3967
  Garden City *(G-5512)*
Canopy Books LLC .... G 516 354-4888
  Massapequa *(G-8208)*
Castle Connolly Medical Ltd .... E 212 367-8400
  New York *(G-9597)*
CB Publishing LLC .... G 516 354-4888
  Floral Park *(G-5206)*
CCC Publications Inc .... G 718 306-1008
  Brooklyn *(G-1767)*
▲ Central Cnfrnce of Amrcn Rbbis .... F 212 972-3636
  New York *(G-9615)*
Chain Store Age Magazine .... G 212 756-5000
  New York *(G-9625)*
Christian Book Publishing .... E 646 559-2533
  New York *(G-9659)*
▼ Church Publishing Incorporated .... G 212 592-1800
  New York *(G-9667)*
Cinderella Press Ltd .... E 212 431-3130
  New York *(G-9669)*
▲ Clarkson N Potter Inc .... F 212 782-9000
  New York *(G-9689)*
Codesters Inc .... G 646 232-1025
  New York *(G-9723)*
▲ Columbia University Press .... E 212 459-0600
  New York *(G-9738)*
Columbia University Press .... E 212 459-0600
  New York *(G-9739)*
Columbia University Press .... E 212 459-0600
  New York *(G-9740)*
Conde Nast .... E 212 630-3642
  New York *(G-9757)*
Confrtrnity of Prescious Blood .... G 718 436-1120
  Brooklyn *(G-1796)*
Congress For Jewish Culture .... F 212 505-8040
  New York *(G-9761)*
Continuum Intl Pubg Group Inc .... F 646 649-4215
  New York *(G-9773)*
Cornell University .... D 607 277-2338
  Ithaca *(G-6871)*
Crabtree Publishing Inc .... F 212 496-5040
  New York *(G-9802)*
Curriculum Associates LLC .... F 978 313-1355
  Brooklyn *(G-1824)*
D C I Technical Inc .... F 516 355-0464
  Franklin Square *(G-5372)*
Daheshist Publishing Co Ltd .... F 212 581-8360
  New York *(G-9843)*

▲ Davis Ziff Publishing Inc .... D 212 503-3500
  New York *(G-9885)*
Definition Press Inc .... F 212 777-4490
  New York *(G-9891)*
Delaney Books Inc .... F 516 921-8888
  Syosset *(G-15840)*
Demos Medical Publishing LLC .... F 516 889-1791
  New York *(G-9897)*
Divine Phoenix LLC .... A 585 737-1482
  Skaneateles *(G-15480)*
▲ Dorling Kindersley Publishing .... D 212 213-4800
  New York *(G-9961)*
Dreams To Print 718 483-8020
  Brooklyn *(G-1881)*
E W Williams Publications .... E 212 661-1516
  New York *(G-10005)*
Eagle Art Publishing Inc .... E 212 685-7411
  New York *(G-10009)*
Edwin Mellen Press Inc .... E 716 754-2796
  Lewiston *(G-7455)*
▲ Egmont US Inc .... G 212 685-0102
  New York *(G-10041)*
Eleanor Ettinger Inc .... E 212 925-7474
  New York *(G-10048)*
▲ Entertainment Weekly Inc .... C 212 522-5600
  New York *(G-10097)*
F P H Communications .... G 212 528-1728
  New York *(G-10169)*
Faces Magazine Inc .... D 845 454-7420
  Poughkeepsie *(G-13919)*
▲ Facts On File Inc .... D 212 967-8800
  New York *(G-10179)*
▲ Fairchild Publications Inc .... A 212 630-4000
  New York *(G-10181)*
Family Publishing Group Inc .... E 914 381-7474
  Mamaroneck *(G-8067)*
▲ Farrar Straus and Giroux LLC .... D 212 741-6900
  New York *(G-10192)*
Feminist Press Inc .... G 212 817-7915
  New York *(G-10205)*
Folio Graphics Co Inc .... F 718 763-2076
  Brooklyn *(G-1993)*
▲ Foxhill Press Inc .... E 212 995-9620
  New York *(G-10246)*
Frank Merriwell Inc .... F 516 921-8888
  Syosset *(G-15843)*
Franklin Report LLC .... G 212 639-9100
  New York *(G-10253)*
Future Us Inc .... D 844 779-2822
  New York *(G-10276)*
Ggp Publishing Inc .... F 914 834-8896
  Harrison *(G-6004)*
▲ Gildan Media Corp .... F 718 459-6299
  Flushing *(G-5251)*
Government Data Publication 347 789-8719
  Brooklyn *(G-2046)*
Gq Magazine .... G 212 286-2860
  New York *(G-10385)*
Grand Central Publishing .... C 212 364-1200
  New York *(G-10388)*
▲ Graphis Inc .... F 212 532-9387
  New York *(G-10396)*
Grey House Publishing Inc .... E 845 483-3535
  Poughkeepsie *(G-13924)*
Grey House Publishing Inc .... E 518 789-8700
  Amenia *(G-219)*
Grolier International Inc .... G 212 343-6100
  New York *(G-10411)*
Guilford Publications Inc .... D 212 431-9800
  New York *(G-10425)*
Guilford Publications Inc .... G 800 365-7006
  New York *(G-10426)*
H W Wilson Company Inc .... B 718 588-8635
  Bronx *(G-1352)*
◆ Hachette Book Group Inc .... B 800 759-0190
  New York *(G-10436)*
▲ Haights Cross Cmmnications Inc .... E 212 209-0500
  New York *(G-10439)*
Haights Cross Operating Co .... E 914 289-9400
  White Plains *(G-17143)*
▲ Harpercollins Publishers LLC .... A 212 207-7000
  New York *(G-10460)*
Harpercollins Publishers LLC .... E 212 553-4200
  New York *(G-10461)*
▲ Harry N Abrams Incorporated .... D 212 206-7715
  New York *(G-10464)*
Harvard University Press .... D 212 337-0280
  New York *(G-10470)*
Hearst Business Media Corp .... F 631 650-4441
  Great River *(G-5870)*

Employee Codes: A=Over 500 employees, B=251-500
C=101-250, D=51-100, E=20-50, F=10-19, G=5-9

27 PRINTING, PUBLISHING, AND ALLIED INDUSTRIES

▲ Hearst Corporation .... A 212 649-2000
  New York *(G-10482)*
Hearst Corporation .... E 212 649-2275
  New York *(G-10491)*
▲ Helvetica Press Incorporated ... G 212 737-1857
  New York *(G-10499)*
▲ Henry Holt and Company LLC ... D 646 307-5095
  New York *(G-10502)*
Highline Media LLC .... C 859 692-2100
  New York *(G-10520)*
▲ Hippocrene Books Inc .... G 212 685-4371
  New York *(G-10527)*
Houghton Mifflin Harcourt Pubg ... E 212 420-5800
  New York *(G-10558)*
Houghton Mifflin Harcourt Pubg ... C 914 747-2709
  Thornwood *(G-16143)*
▲ Hudson Park Press Inc .... G 212 929-8898
  New York *(G-10571)*
▲ Humana Press Inc .... E 212 460-1500
  New York *(G-10577)*
Iat Interactive LLC .... E 914 273-2233
  Mount Kisco *(G-8670)*
Infobase Publishing Company .... G 212 967-8800
  New York *(G-10637)*
Infopro Digital Inc .... C 212 457-9400
  New York *(G-10638)*
Interntnl Publcatns Media Grup ... G 917 604-9602
  New York *(G-10682)*
Ir Media Group (usa) Inc .... E 212 425-9649
  New York *(G-10697)*
James Morgan Publishing .... G 212 655-5470
  New York *(G-10737)*
Jim Henson Company Inc .... E 212 794-2400
  New York *(G-10772)*
John Wiley & Sons Inc .... D 845 457-6250
  Montgomery *(G-8632)*
▲ Jonathan David Publishers Inc ... F 718 456-8611
  Middle Village *(G-8446)*
▲ Judaica Press Inc .... G 718 972-6202
  Brooklyn *(G-2155)*
▲ Juris Publishing Inc .... F 631 351-5430
  Huntington *(G-6700)*
▲ K T A V Publishing House Inc ... F 201 963-9524
  Brooklyn *(G-2165)*
Kensington Publishing Corp .... D 212 407-1500
  New York *(G-10876)*
▲ Klutz .... E 650 687-2600
  New York *(G-10898)*
Kobalt Music Pubg Amer Inc ...... D 212 247-6204
  New York *(G-10903)*
▲ Kodansha USA Inc .... G 917 322-6200
  New York *(G-10906)*
Kwesi Legesse LLC .... G 347 581-9872
  Brooklyn *(G-2182)*
▲ Le Book Publishing Inc .... G 212 334-5252
  New York *(G-10977)*
Learningexpress LLC .... E 646 274-6454
  New York *(G-10984)*
▲ Lee & Low Books Incorporated ... F 212 779-4400
  New York *(G-10992)*
Legal Strategies Inc .... G 516 377-3940
  Merrick *(G-8423)*
Lexis Publishing .... C 518 487-3000
  Menands *(G-8405)*
▼ Library Tales Publishing Inc ... G 347 394-2629
  New York *(G-11018)*
Lippincott Massie McQuilkin L ... F 212 352-2055
  New York *(G-11034)*
▲ Literary Classics of US .... F 212 308-3360
  New York *(G-11036)*
Liveright Publishing Corp .... G 212 354-5500
  New York *(G-11042)*
Living Well Innovations Inc .... G 646 517-3200
  Hauppauge *(G-6138)*
Looseleaf Law Publications Inc ... F 718 359-5559
  Flushing *(G-5275)*
M&M Printing Inc .... G 516 796-3020
  Carle Place *(G-3420)*
Macmillan College Pubg Co Inc ... F 212 702-2000
  New York *(G-11113)*
▲ Macmillan Publishers Inc .... A 646 307-5151
  New York *(G-11115)*
▲ Macmillan Publishing Group LLC ... B 212 674-5151
  New York *(G-11116)*
▲ Malhame Publs & Importers Inc ... E 631 694-8600
  Bohemia *(G-1096)*
▲ Marshall Cavendish Corp .... E 914 332-8888
  Tarrytown *(G-16118)*
▲ Martha Stewart Living .... C 212 827-8000
  New York *(G-11189)*

Mary Ann Liebert Inc .... D 914 740-2100
  New Rochelle *(G-8962)*
Mathisen Ventures Inc .... G 212 986-1025
  New York *(G-11203)*
▲ McBooks Press Inc .... G 607 272-2114
  Ithaca *(G-6895)*
McGraw-Hill Education Inc .... E 646 766-2000
  New York *(G-11222)*
McGraw-Hill Glbl Edctn Hldngs ... D 646 766-2000
  New York *(G-11223)*
McGraw-Hill School Education H ... B 646 766-2000
  New York *(G-11224)*
McGraw-Hill School Educatn LLC ... A 646 766-2060
  New York *(G-11225)*
Mediaplanet Publishing Hse Inc ... E 646 922-1400
  New York *(G-11237)*
Medikidz Usa Inc .... G 646 895-9319
  New York *(G-11242)*
Meegenius Inc .... G 212 283-7285
  New York *(G-11245)*
▲ Melcher Media Inc .... F 212 727-2322
  New York *(G-11249)*
Meredith Corporation .... G 515 284-2157
  New York *(G-11256)*
Merkos Llnyonei Chinuch Inc ... E 718 778-0226
  Brooklyn *(G-2305)*
▲ Mesorah Publications Ltd ..... G 718 921-9000
  Brooklyn *(G-2307)*
Metro Creative Graphics Inc .... G 212 947-5100
  New York *(G-11268)*
Micro Publishing Inc .... G 212 533-9180
  New York *(G-11280)*
Modern Language Assn Amer Inc ... C 646 576-5000
  New York *(G-11315)*
▲ Monacelli Press LLC .... G 212 229-9925
  New York *(G-11323)*
▲ Mondo Publishing Inc .... E 212 268-3560
  New York *(G-11324)*
▲ Moznaim Publishing Co Inc ... G 718 853-0525
  Brooklyn *(G-2342)*
▲ Mud Puddle Books Inc .... G 212 647-9168
  New York *(G-11345)*
◆ Multi Packaging Solutions Inc ... G 646 885-0005
  New York *(G-11347)*
N A R Associates Inc .... G 845 557-8713
  Barryville *(G-620)*
National Learning Corp .... F 516 921-8888
  Syosset *(G-15850)*
Nationwide Custom Services ... G 845 365-0414
  Tappan *(G-16105)*
Natural E Creative LLC .... F 516 488-1143
  New Hyde Park *(G-8895)*
▲ NBM Publishing Inc .... G 212 643-5407
  New York *(G-11384)*
New City Press Inc .... G 845 229-0335
  Hyde Park *(G-6774)*
New Directions Publishing .... G 212 255-0230
  New York *(G-11405)*
New Press .... E 212 629-8802
  New York *(G-11413)*
New York Legal Publishing ...... G 518 459-1100
  Menands *(G-8409)*
New York Qrtrly Foundation Inc ... F 917 843-8825
  Brooklyn *(G-2377)*
Newkirk Products Inc .... C 518 862-3200
  Albany *(G-107)*
News Corporation .... C 212 416-3400
  New York *(G-11435)*
News India USA Inc .... F 212 675-7515
  New York *(G-11437)*
North Shore Home Improver .... F 631 474-2824
  Port Jeff STA *(G-13790)*
▲ North-South Books Inc .... E 212 706-4545
  New York *(G-11476)*
Nova Science Publishers Inc ... F 631 231-7269
  Hauppauge *(G-6175)*
Other Press LLC .... G 212 414-0054
  New York *(G-11546)*
Oxford Book Company Inc ...... C 212 227-2120
  New York *(G-11551)*
◆ Oxford University Press LLC ... B 212 726-6000
  New York *(G-11555)*
Oxford University Press LLC ... G 212 726-6000
  New York *(G-11556)*
Ozmodyl Ltd .... G 212 226-0622
  New York *(G-11558)*
P J D Publications Ltd .... G 516 626-0650
  New Hyde Park *(G-8901)*
Pace Walkers of America Inc .... F 631 444-2147
  Port Jefferson *(G-13800)*

▲ Palgrave Macmillan Ltd .... G 646 307-5028
  New York *(G-11570)*
▲ Papercutz Inc .... G 646 559-4681
  New York *(G-11579)*
▲ Parachute Publishing LLC ..... E 212 337-6743
  New York *(G-11580)*
Pearson Education Inc .... E 845 340-8700
  Kingston *(G-7235)*
Pearson Education Inc .... F 212 782-3337
  New York *(G-11607)*
Pearson Education Inc .... E 212 366-2000
  New York *(G-11608)*
Pearson Education Inc .... F 201 236-7000
  West Nyack *(G-16952)*
▲ Pearson Education Holdings Inc ... A 201 236-6716
  New York *(G-11609)*
▼ Pearson Inc .... D 212 641-2400
  New York *(G-11610)*
Pearson Longman LLC .... C 917 981-2200
  New York *(G-11611)*
Pearson Longman LLC .... E 212 641-2400
  White Plains *(G-17174)*
Pegasus Books NY Ltd .... G 646 343-9509
  New York *(G-11618)*
Penguin Random House LLC ... E 212 782-1000
  New York *(G-11621)*
Penguin Random House LLC ... B 212 782-9000
  New York *(G-11622)*
Penguin Random House LLC ... A 212 572-6162
  New York *(G-11623)*
Penguin Random House LLC ... A 212 782-9000
  New York *(G-11624)*
Penguin Random House LLC ... C 212 366-2377
  Albany *(G-117)*
Penton Business Media Inc ..... F 914 949-8500
  White Plains *(G-17177)*
Peri-Facts Academy .... G 585 275-6037
  Rochester *(G-14597)*
Perseus Fisher Books LLC ...... D 212 340-8100
  New York *(G-11645)*
Peter Lang Publishing Inc .... F 212 647-7700
  New York *(G-11651)*
▲ Peter Mayer Publishers Inc ... F 212 673-2210
  New York *(G-11652)*
▲ Peter Pauper Press Inc .... E 914 681-0144
  White Plains *(G-17185)*
Petersons Nelnet LLC .... C 609 896-1800
  Albany *(G-118)*
▲ Phaidon Press Inc .... E 212 652-5400
  New York *(G-11664)*
▲ Philipp Feldheim Inc .... G 845 356-2282
  Nanuet *(G-8806)*
Picador USA .... E 646 307-5629
  New York *(G-11678)*
Poetry Mailing List Marsh Hawk ... G 516 766-1891
  Oceanside *(G-13112)*
Poets House Inc .... F 212 431-7920
  New York *(G-11702)*
▲ Powerhouse Cultural Entrmt Inc ... F 212 604-9074
  Brooklyn *(G-2444)*
Preserving Chrstn Publications ... G 315 942-6617
  Boonville *(G-1165)*
▲ Prestel Publishing LLC .... F 212 995-2720
  New York *(G-11725)*
▲ Princeton Archtctural Press LLC ... F 518 671-6100
  Hudson *(G-6662)*
Pro Publica Inc .... D 212 514-5250
  New York *(G-11746)*
▲ Profits Direct Inc .... G 631 851-4083
  Ronkonkoma *(G-14996)*
Project Energy Savers LLC ...... F 718 596-4231
  Brooklyn *(G-2470)*
▲ Prometheus Books Inc .... F 716 691-2158
  Amherst *(G-259)*
PSR Press Ltd .... F 716 754-2266
  Lewiston *(G-7457)*
Pwxyz LLC .... G 212 377-7500
  New York *(G-11785)*
▲ Quarto Group Inc .... E 212 779-0700
  New York *(G-11796)*
Rapid Intellect Group Inc .... F 518 929-3210
  Chatham *(G-3587)*
Rda Holding Co .... F 914 238-1000
  New York *(G-11837)*
Readers Dgest Yung Fmilies Inc ... E 914 238-1000
  Pleasantville *(G-13749)*
Reading Room Inc .... G 212 463-1029
  New York *(G-11840)*
Relx Inc .... C 607 772-2600
  Conklin *(G-3899)*

◆ Relx Inc ... E ... 212 309-8100 New York (G-11858)
Repertoire International De Ll ... E ... 212 817-1990 New York (G-11867)
Research Centre of Kabbalah ... G ... 718 805-0380 Richmond Hill (G-14091)
▲ Richard C Owen Publishers Inc ... F ... 914 232-3903 Somers (G-15534)
◆ Rizzoli Intl Publications Inc ... E ... 212 387-3400 New York (G-11903)
Rizzoli Intl Publications Inc ... F ... 212 387-3572 New York (G-11904)
▲ Rosen Publishing Group Inc ... C ... 212 777-3017 New York (G-11937)
▲ Ryland Peters & Small Inc ... G ... 646 791-5410 New York (G-11959)
S P Books Inc ... G ... 212 431-5011 New York (G-11963)
Samuel French Inc ... E ... 212 206-8990 New York (G-11980)
▲ Scholastic Corporation ... G ... 212 343-6100 New York (G-12015)
◆ Scholastic Inc ... A ... 800 724-6527 New York (G-12016)
Scholastic Inc ... E ... 212 343-6100 New York (G-12017)
Scholium International Inc ... G ... 516 883-8032 Port Washington (G-13880)
Second Chance Press Inc ... G ... 631 725-1101 Sag Harbor (G-15108)
▲ Seven Stories Press Inc ... G ... 212 226-8760 New York (G-12052)
▲ Sheridan House Inc ... G ... 914 725-5431 Scarsdale (G-15254)
Simmons-Boardman Pubg Corp ... G ... 212 620-7200 New York (G-12101)
Simon & Schuster Inc ... D ... 212 698-7000 New York (G-12102)
Simon Schuster Digital Sls Inc ... D ... 212 698-4391 New York (G-12104)
Six Boro Publishing ... G ... 347 589-6756 New York (G-12112)
▲ Skyhorse Publishing Inc ... E ... 212 643-6816 New York (G-12121)
Social Register Association ... F ... 646 612-7314 New York (G-12143)
Soho Press Inc ... G ... 212 260-1900 New York (G-12147)
Spartacist Publishing Co ... E ... 212 732-7860 New York (G-12173)
Springer Adis Us LLC ... F ... 212 460-1500 New York (G-12195)
Springer Customer Svc Ctr LLC ... B ... 212 460-1500 New York (G-12196)
Springer Publishing Co LLC ... E ... 212 431-4370 New York (G-12198)
◆ Springer Scnce + Bus Media LLC ... D ... 781 871-6600 New York (G-12199)
▲ Square One Publishers Inc ... F ... 516 535-2010 Garden City Park (G-5555)
Stanley M Indig ... G ... 718 692-0648 Brooklyn (G-2618)
Station Hill of Barrytown ... G ... 845 758-5293 Barrytown (G-619)
Steffen Publishing Inc ... D ... 315 865-4100 Holland Patent (G-6514)
STf Services Inc ... E ... 315 463-8506 East Syracuse (G-4581)
Stonesong Press LLC ... G ... 212 929-4600 New York (G-12231)
Storybooks Forever ... F ... 716 822-7845 Buffalo (G-3226)
▲ Studio Fun International Inc ... E ... 914 238-1000 White Plains (G-17199)
Suny At Binghamton ... D ... 607 777-2316 Binghamton (G-946)
Sweet Mouth Inc ... E ... 800 433-7758 New York (G-12276)
▲ Syracuse University Press Inc ... E ... 315 443-5534 Syracuse (G-16080)
T G S Inc ... G ... 516 629-6905 Locust Valley (G-7664)
Targum Press USA Inc ... G ... 248 355-2266 Brooklyn (G-2668)
Teachers College Columbia Univ ... E ... 212 678-3929 New York (G-12312)
Thornwillow Press Ltd ... G ... 212 980-0738 New York (G-12350)
Time Home Entertainment Inc ... E ... 212 522-1212 New York (G-12361)
Time Inc ... E ... 212 522-1212 New York (G-12362)
Tom Doherty Associates Inc ... E ... 212 388-0100 New York (G-12380)
◆ Trusted Media Brands Inc ... A ... 914 238-1000 New York (G-12435)
Trusted Media Brands Inc ... F ... 646 293-6025 New York (G-12436)
Trusted Media Brands Inc ... F ... 914 244-5244 White Plains (G-17204)
▲ Unisystems Inc ... E ... 212 826-0850 New York (G-12482)
▲ United Synggue Cnsrvtive Jdism ... E ... 212 533-7800 New York (G-12487)
▲ Vaad LHafotzas Sichoes ... F ... 718 778-5436 Brooklyn (G-2733)
▲ Vandam Inc ... F ... 212 929-0416 New York (G-12522)
▲ Vantage Press Inc ... E ... 212 736-1767 New York (G-12527)
Vaultcom Inc ... E ... 212 366-4212 New York (G-12535)
Verso Inc ... G ... 718 246-8160 Brooklyn (G-2740)
▲ W W Norton & Company Inc ... C ... 212 354-5500 New York (G-12602)
W W Norton & Company Inc ... G ... 212 354-5500 New York (G-12603)
▲ Waldman Publishing Corporation ... F ... 212 730-9590 New York (G-12607)
Warodean Corporation ... G ... 718 359-5559 Flushing (G-5312)
◆ William H Sadlier Inc ... C ... 212 233-3646 New York (G-12661)
William S Hein & Co Inc ... D ... 716 882-2600 Getzville (G-5619)
William S Hein & Co Inc ... D ... 716 882-2600 Buffalo (G-3282)
Windows Media Publishing LLC ... E ... 917 732-7892 Brooklyn (G-2775)
Wolters Kluwer US Inc ... F ... 212 894-8920 New York (G-12680)
Wolters Kluwer US Inc ... E ... 631 517-8060 Babylon (G-552)
Woodward/White Inc ... F ... 718 509-6082 Brooklyn (G-2779)
Wordwise Inc ... G ... 914 232-5366 Katonah (G-7164)
◆ Workman Publishing Co Inc ... C ... 212 254-5900 New York (G-12687)
Workman Publishing Co Inc ... C ... 212 254-5900 New York (G-12688)
Worth Publishers Inc ... C ... 212 475-6000 New York (G-12692)
▲ YS Publishing Co Inc ... G ... 212 682-9360 New York (G-12719)
Zinepak LLC ... F ... 212 706-8621 New York (G-12732)
Zola Books Inc ... G ... 917 822-4950 New York (G-12738)

2732 Book Printing, Not Publishing

450 Ridge St Inc ... G ... 716 754-2789 Lewiston (G-7453)
B-Squared Inc ... E ... 212 777-2044 New York (G-9349)
Bedford Freeman & Worth ... C ... 212 576-9400 New York (G-9391)
Bmg Printing and Promotion LLC ... G ... 631 231-9200 Bohemia (G-1022)
Book1one LLC ... G ... 585 458-2101 Rochester (G-14260)
Bridge Enterprises Inc ... G ... 718 625-6622 Brooklyn (G-1714)
Cct Inc ... G ... 212 532-3355 New York (G-9606)
Centrisource Inc ... G ... 716 871-1105 Tonawanda (G-16173)
E Graphics Corporation ... G ... 718 486-9767 Brooklyn (G-1893)
Electronic Printing Inc ... G ... 631 218-2200 Hauppauge (G-6094)
▲ Experiment LLC ... G ... 212 889-1659 New York (G-10161)
Flare Multicopy Corp ... E ... 718 258-8860 Brooklyn (G-1983)
▲ Hamilton Printing Company Inc ... C ... 518 732-2161 Troy (G-16260)
▲ Hudson Valley Paper Works Inc ... F ... 845 569-8883 Newburgh (G-12785)
In-House Inc ... F ... 718 445-9007 College Point (G-3812)
▲ Kravitz Design Inc ... G ... 212 625-1644 New York (G-10928)
▲ Literary Classics of US ... F ... 212 308-3360 New York (G-11036)
▲ Logical Operations Inc ... C ... 585 350-7000 Rochester (G-14503)
▲ North Country Books Inc ... G ... 315 735-4877 Utica (G-16376)
Printing Factory LLC ... F ... 718 451-0500 Brooklyn (G-2462)
Promotional Sales Books LLC ... G ... 212 675-0364 New York (G-11753)
Royal Fireworks Printing Co ... F ... 845 726-3333 Unionville (G-16326)
Steffen Publishing Inc ... D ... 315 865-4100 Holland Patent (G-6514)
▼ Sterling Pierce Company Inc ... E ... 516 593-1170 East Rockaway (G-4492)
Stop Entertainment Inc ... F ... 212 242-7867 Monroe (G-8599)
▲ Syracuse Cultural Workers Prj ... F ... 315 474-1132 Syracuse (G-16076)
The Nugent Organization Inc ... F ... 212 645-6600 Oceanside (G-13123)
Tobay Printing Co Inc ... E ... 631 842-3300 Copiague (G-3957)
◆ Twp America Inc ... G ... 212 274-8090 New York (G-12453)
Vicks Lithograph & Prtg Corp ... C ... 315 272-2401 Yorkville (G-17544)
Vicks Lithograph & Prtg Corp ... C ... 315 736-9344 Yorkville (G-17545)
Willis Mc Donald Co Inc ... F ... 212 366-1526 New York (G-12665)
Worzalla Publishing Company ... C ... 212 967-7909 New York (G-12693)

2741 Misc Publishing

▲ 212 Media LLC ... E ... 212 710-3092 New York (G-9012)
Abkco Music & Records Inc ... D ... 212 399-0300 New York (G-9050)
ABRA Media Inc ... G ... 518 398-1010 Pine Plains (G-13581)
Absolute Color Corporation ... G ... 212 868-0404 New York (G-9054)
Adcomm Graphics Inc ... E ... 212 645-1298 West Babylon (G-16790)
Add Associates Inc ... G ... 315 449-3474 Cicero (G-3670)
Adirondack Pennysaver Inc ... E ... 518 563-0100 Plattsburgh (G-13678)
Affluent Design Inc ... F ... 631 655-2556 Mastic Beach (G-8236)
Ai Media Group Inc ... F ... 212 660-2400 New York (G-9114)
Albany Student Press Inc ... E ... 518 442-5665 Albany (G-41)
Albion-Holley Pennysaver Inc ... E ... 585 589-5641 Albion (G-164)
Aleteia Usa Inc ... G ... 914 502-1855 Yonkers (G-17426)
▼ Alfred Mainzer Inc ... E ... 718 392-4200 Long Island City (G-7683)
All Times Publishing LLC ... E ... 315 422-7011 Syracuse (G-15868)
Alley Music Corp ... E ... 212 779-7977 New York (G-9137)
Alm Media LLC ... B ... 212 457-9400 New York (G-9146)
Alm Media Holdings Inc ... B ... 212 457-9400 New York (G-9147)
American Hsptals Patient Guide ... F ... 518 346-1099 Schenectady (G-15259)
American Media Inc ... D ... 212 545-4800 New York (G-9174)
American Media Inc ... C ... 212 545-4800 New York (G-9175)
Amy Pak Publishing Inc ... G ... 585 964-8188 Holley (G-6515)
An Group Inc ... G ... 631 549-4090 Melville (G-8328)
Anglo II Ltd ... G ... 212 563-4980 New York (G-9208)
Answer Printing Inc ... F ... 212 922-2922 New York (G-9216)
AR Media Inc ... E ... 212 352-0731 New York (G-9238)

S I C

Employee Codes: A=Over 500 employees, B=251-500 C=101-250, D=51-100, E=20-50, F=10-19, G=5-9
2018 Harris New York Manufacturers Directory
761

27 PRINTING, PUBLISHING, AND ALLIED INDUSTRIES SIC SECTION

Art Asiapacific Publishing LLC	G	212 255-6003	New York *(G-9258)*
Aspen Publishers Inc	A	212 771-0600	New York *(G-9288)*
Associated Publishing Company	E	325 676-4032	Buffalo *(G-2840)*
Atlas Music Publishing LLC	G	646 502-5170	New York *(G-9307)*
Atypon Systems Inc	F	212 524-7060	New York *(G-9313)*
Auto Market Publications Inc	G	631 667-0500	Deer Park *(G-4129)*
Avalon Copy Centers Amer Inc	D	315 471-3333	Syracuse *(G-15883)*
Avalon Copy Centers Amer Inc	E	716 995-7777	Buffalo *(G-2847)*
Award Publishing Limited	G	212 246-0405	New York *(G-9335)*
Badoud Communications Inc	C	315 472-7821	Syracuse *(G-15886)*
Bdg Media Inc	E	917 951-9768	New York *(G-9386)*
▲ Black Book Photography Inc	F	212 979-6700	New York *(G-9460)*
Blood Moon Productions Ltd	G	718 556-9410	Staten Island *(G-15669)*
▲ Boosey & Hawkes Inc	E	212 358-5300	New York *(G-9490)*
Bourne Music Publishers	F	212 391-4300	New York *(G-9496)*
Bright Line Eting Slutions LLC	E	585 245-2956	Pittsford *(G-13585)*
Brownstone Publishers Inc	E	212 473-8200	New York *(G-9525)*
Bucksense Inc	E	877 710-2825	New York *(G-9527)*
Bulkley Dunton	E	212 863-1800	New York *(G-9528)*
Burdick Publications Inc	G	315 685-9500	Skaneateles *(G-15477)*
Business Directory Inc	F	718 486-8099	Brooklyn *(G-1742)*
Byliner Inc	E	415 680-3608	New York *(G-9541)*
◆ Bys Publishing LLC	G	315 655-9431	Cazenovia *(G-3469)*
▲ C F Peters Corp	E	718 416-7800	Glendale *(G-5663)*
Cambridge Info Group Inc	F	301 961-6700	New York *(G-9557)*
Cambridge Whos Who Pubg Inc	E	516 833-8440	Uniondale *(G-16312)*
Carbert Music Inc	E	212 725-9277	New York *(G-9579)*
Carl Fischer LLC	E	212 777-0900	New York *(G-9580)*
Castle Connolly Medical Ltd	E	212 367-8400	New York *(G-9597)*
Catholic News Publishing Co	F	914 632-7771	Mamaroneck *(G-8059)*
Cayuga Press Cortland Inc	E	888 229-8421	Liverpool *(G-7540)*
Ceo Cast Inc	F	212 732-4300	New York *(G-9621)*
Charing Cross Music Inc	G	212 541-7571	New York *(G-9630)*
Cherry Lane Magazine LLC	D	212 561-3000	New York *(G-9641)*
China Press	G	212 683-8282	New York *(G-9652)*
▼ Christopher Anthony Pubg Co	F	516 826-9205	Wantagh *(G-16577)*
Church Bulletin Inc	F	631 249-4994	West Babylon *(G-16809)*
City of New York	E	718 965-8787	Brooklyn *(G-1781)*
▲ City Post Express Inc	G	718 995-8690	Jamaica *(G-6940)*
Classic Collections Fine Art	G	914 591-4500	White Plains *(G-17121)*
Classpass Inc	E	888 493-5953	New York *(G-9693)*
Clearstep Technologies LLC	G	315 952-3628	Camillus *(G-3350)*
Coastal Publications Inc	F	631 725-1700	Sag Harbor *(G-15104)*
Color Unlimited Inc	G	212 802-7547	New York *(G-9731)*
Communications & Energy Corp	F	315 446-5723	Syracuse *(G-15922)*
Community Cpons Frnchising Inc	E	516 277-1968	Glen Cove *(G-5625)*
Community Newsppr Holdings Inc	D	716 282-2311	Niagara Falls *(G-12828)*
Complete Publishing Solutions	G	212 242-7321	New York *(G-9751)*
Comps Inc	F	516 676-0400	Glen Cove *(G-5626)*
Consumer Reports Inc	B	914 378-2000	Yonkers *(G-17445)*
Couture Press	F	310 734-4831	New York *(G-9799)*
Custom Publishing Group Ltd	G	212 840-8800	New York *(G-9827)*
D C I Technical Inc	F	516 355-0464	Franklin Square *(G-5372)*
▼ Daily Racing Form Inc	C	212 366-7600	New York *(G-9846)*
Dailycandy Inc	E	646 230-8719	New York *(G-9849)*
Dapper Dads Inc	G	917 903-8045	Brooklyn *(G-1840)*
Dayton T Brown Inc	B	631 589-6300	Bohemia *(G-1048)*
Desi Talk LLC	F	212 675-7515	New York *(G-9903)*
Dezawy LLC	G	917 436-8820	New York *(G-9918)*
▲ DK Publishing	F	212 366-2000	New York *(G-9942)*
Dlc Comprehensive Medical PC	F	718 857-1200	Brooklyn *(G-1869)*
Dohnsco Inc	G	516 773-4800	Manhasset *(G-8092)*
Downtown Music LLC	G	212 625-2980	New York *(G-9971)*
Draper Associates Incorporated	F	212 255-2727	New York *(G-9975)*
Dryve LLC	G	646 279-3648	Bronx *(G-1321)*
Dwell Life Inc	E	212 382-2010	New York *(G-9995)*
East Meet East Inc	G	646 481-0033	New York *(G-10015)*
Easy Book Publishing Inc	G	518 459-6281	Albany *(G-75)*
Economy 24/7 Inc	E	917 403-8876	Brooklyn *(G-1901)*
Elite Daily Inc	B	212 402-9097	New York *(G-10059)*
◆ Elsevier Inc	B	212 633-3773	New York *(G-10067)*
Energy Intelligence Group Inc	E	212 532-1112	New York *(G-10090)*
Enhance A Colour Corp	E	212 490-3620	New York *(G-10093)*
Enjoy City North Inc	D	607 584-5061	Binghamton *(G-908)*
Entrainant Inc	G	212 946-4724	New York *(G-10098)*
Epost International Inc	G	212 352-9390	New York *(G-10103)*
Equityarcade LLC	G	678 232-1301	Brooklyn *(G-1936)*
Ethis Communications Inc	G	212 791-1440	White Plains *(G-17132)*
Euphorbia Productions Ltd	G	212 533-1700	New York *(G-10136)*
▲ Experiment Publishing LLC	G	212 889-1273	New York *(G-10162)*
F+w Media Inc	G	212 447-1400	New York *(G-10172)*
Family Publications Ltd	F	212 947-2177	New York *(G-10186)*
Fantasy Sports Media Group Inc	E	416 917-6002	New York *(G-10190)*
▲ Fashiondex Inc	G	914 271-6121	New York *(G-10198)*
Federated Media Publishing LLC	G	917 677-7976	New York *(G-10202)*
Fidazzel Inc	G	917 557-3860	Bronx *(G-1333)*
Finger Lakes Massage Group	F	607 272-9024	Ithaca *(G-6877)*
First Games Publr Netwrk Inc	D	212 983-0501	New York *(G-10219)*
Fischler Hockey Service	F	212 749-4152	New York *(G-10225)*
Fitzgerald Publishing Co Inc	G	914 793-5016	Yonkers *(G-17459)*
▲ Foundation Center Inc	C	212 620-4230	New York *(G-10241)*
Franklin-Douglas Inc	F	516 883-0121	Port Washington *(G-13838)*
Fredonia Pennysaver Inc	G	716 679-1509	Fredonia *(G-5382)*
Freeville Publishing Co Inc	F	607 844-9119	Freeville *(G-5447)*
Froebe Group LLC	G	646 649-2150	New York *(G-10261)*
▲ G Schirmer Inc	G	212 254-2100	New York *(G-10280)*
G Schirmer Inc	E	845 469-4699	Chester *(G-3634)*
Gametime Media Inc	G	212 860-2090	New York *(G-10293)*
Gannett Co Inc	D	607 352-2702	Johnson City *(G-7124)*
Gds Publishing Inc	F	212 796-2000	New York *(G-10307)*
Gen Publishing Inc	D	914 834-3880	New Rochelle *(G-8950)*
Genius Media Group Inc	F	509 670-7502	Brooklyn *(G-2020)*
Glassview LLC	E	646 844-4922	New York *(G-10350)*
Global Grind Digital	E	212 840-9399	New York *(G-10360)*
Global Video LLC	D	516 222-2600	Woodbury *(G-17310)*
Golden Eagle Marketing LLC	G	212 726-1242	New York *(G-10372)*
Golf Directories USA Inc	G	516 365-5351	Manhasset *(G-8094)*
Gooding & Associates Inc	F	631 749-3313	Shelter Island *(G-15409)*
Government Data Publication	E	347 789-8719	Brooklyn *(G-2046)*
Grant Hamilton	F	716 652-0320	East Aurora *(G-4396)*
Greater Rchster Advertiser Inc	E	585 385-1974	East Rochester *(G-4479)*
Grey House Publishing Inc	E	518 789-8700	Amenia *(G-219)*
Grey House Publishing Inc	E	845 483-3535	Poughkeepsie *(G-13924)*
Gruner & Jahr USA	F	212 782-7870	New York *(G-10417)*
Guest Informat LLC	F	212 557-3010	New York *(G-10423)*
Guilford Publications Inc	D	212 431-9800	New York *(G-10425)*
Guilford Publications Inc	G	800 365-7006	New York *(G-10426)*
Hampton Press Incorporated	G	646 638-3800	New York *(G-10447)*
Harborside Press	G	631 470-4967	Huntington *(G-6695)*
Harpercollins	G	212 207-7000	New York *(G-10459)*
Hart Energy Publishing Lllp	G	212 621-4621	New York *(G-10467)*
Hearst Business Media	D	516 227-1300	Uniondale *(G-16318)*
Hearst Communications Inc	C	212 649-2000	New York *(G-10481)*
Hearst Corporation	E	212 830-2980	New York *(G-10487)*
Hearst Digital Studios Inc	E	212 969-7552	New York *(G-10492)*
Helium Media Inc	G	917 596-4081	New York *(G-10498)*
Herff Jones LLC	E	607 936-2366	Corning *(G-3994)*
Hibert Publishing LLC	G	914 381-7474	Rye *(G-15085)*
◆ Hibu Inc	C	516 730-1900	East Meadow *(G-4445)*
Highline Media LLC	C	859 692-2100	New York *(G-10520)*
▲ Historic TW Inc	E	212 484-8000	New York *(G-10530)*
History Publishing Company LLC	G	845 398-8161	Palisades *(G-13426)*
Hola Publishing Co	G	718 424-3129	Long Island City *(G-7790)*
Home Service Publications	G	914 238-1000	Pleasantville *(G-13746)*
▲ Humana Press Inc	E	212 460-1500	New York *(G-10577)*

SIC SECTION
27 PRINTING, PUBLISHING, AND ALLIED INDUSTRIES

Humor Rainbow Incorporated ......E 646 402-9113
New York *(G-10579)*
Ibt Media Inc ......E 646 867-7100
New York *(G-10594)*
Infinitlink Corporation ......G 934 777-0180
West Babylon *(G-16822)*
Infoservices International ......F 631 549-1805
Cold Spring Harbor *(G-3794)*
Integrated Copyright Group ......E 615 329-3999
New York *(G-10658)*
Intuition Publishing Limited ......G 212 838-7115
New York *(G-10691)*
Israeli Yellow Pages ......E 718 520-1000
Kew Gardens *(G-7191)*
Jewish Heritage For Blind ......G 718 338-4999
Brooklyn *(G-2138)*
▲ **Jobson Medical Information LLC** ......C 212 274-7000
New York *(G-10784)*
▲ **John Szoke Graphics Inc** ......G 212 219-8300
New York *(G-10792)*
Johnny Bienstock Music ......E 212 779-7977
New York *(G-10794)*
Kalel Partners LLC ......F 347 561-7804
Flushing *(G-5265)*
Kendor Music Inc ......F 716 492-1254
Delevan *(G-4261)*
Kjckd Inc ......G 518 435-9696
Latham *(G-7395)*
Korangy Publishing Inc ......D 212 260-1332
New York *(G-10915)*
▲ **Korean Yellow Pages** ......F 718 461-0073
Flushing *(G-5270)*
Kraus Organization Limited ......G 212 686-5411
New York *(G-10927)*
Kyra Communications Corp ......F 516 783-6244
Seaford *(G-15366)*
L & L Trucking Inc ......E 315 339-2550
Rome *(G-14846)*
Lagunatic Music & Filmworks ......F 212 353-9600
Brooklyn *(G-2191)*
Language and Graphics Inc ......G 212 315-5266
New York *(G-10963)*
Largo Music Inc ......G 212 756-5080
New York *(G-10965)*
Leadership Directories Inc ......E 212 627-4140
New York *(G-10982)*
Ledes Group Inc ......F 212 840-8800
New York *(G-10991)*
Lefrak Entertainment Co Ltd ......G 212 586-3600
New York *(G-10995)*
Lightbulb Press Inc ......E 212 485-8800
New York *(G-11026)*
Lino Press Inc ......E 718 665-2625
Bronx *(G-1387)*
Llcs Publishing Corp ......F 718 569-2703
Brooklyn *(G-2235)*
London Theater News Ltd ......F 212 517-8608
New York *(G-11054)*
Long Islands Best Inc ......G 855 542-3785
Bohemia *(G-1090)*
Lucky Peach LLC ......G 212 228-0031
New York *(G-11088)*
Ludlow Music Inc ......F 212 594-9795
New York *(G-11089)*
Luminary Publishing Inc ......F 845 334-8600
Kingston *(G-7228)*
Mac Innes Enterprises Inc ......E 325 676-4032
Buffalo *(G-3072)*
Macmillan Academic Pubg Inc ......F 212 226-1476
New York *(G-11112)*
Mailers-Pblsher Wlfare Tr Fund ......G 212 869-5986
New York *(G-11138)*
▲ **Mapeasy Inc** ......F 631 537-6213
Wainscott *(G-16548)*
Marketresearchcom Inc ......F 212 807-2600
New York *(G-11184)*
Mary Ann Liebert Inc ......D 914 740-2100
New Rochelle *(G-8962)*
Mathisen Ventures Inc ......G 212 986-1025
New York *(G-11203)*
Maximillion Communications LLC ......D 212 564-3945
New York *(G-11212)*
▲ **Media Transcripts Inc** ......E 212 362-1481
New York *(G-11235)*
Media Trust LLC ......G 212 802-1162
New York *(G-11236)*
Medical Daily Inc ......E 646 867-7100
New York *(G-11239)*
Medical Information Systems ......G 516 621-7200
Port Washington *(G-13863)*

Mens Journal LLC ......A 212 484-1616
New York *(G-11251)*
▲ **Menucha Publishers Inc** ......F 718 232-0856
Brooklyn *(G-2301)*
Merchant Publishing Inc ......F 212 691-6666
New York *(G-11253)*
Merrill Corporation Inc ......D 212 620-5600
New York *(G-11260)*
Metro Group Inc ......G 716 434-4055
Lockport *(G-7630)*
Mexico Independent Inc ......E 315 963-3763
Watertown *(G-16687)*
Michael Karp Music Inc ......G 212 840-3285
New York *(G-11277)*
Millennium Medical Publishing ......F 212 995-2211
New York *(G-11292)*
Mindbodygreen LLC ......E 347 529-6952
Brooklyn *(G-2321)*
Minyanville Media Inc ......E 212 991-6200
New York *(G-11306)*
Mom Dad Publishing Inc ......E 646 476-9170
New York *(G-11321)*
Morey Publishing ......E 516 284-3300
Farmingdale *(G-5069)*
Mortgage Press Ltd ......E 516 409-1400
Wantagh *(G-16581)*
Mosby Holdings Corp ......G 212 309-8100
New York *(G-11332)*
▲ **Mpl Communications Inc** ......G 212 246-5881
New York *(G-11338)*
Mt Morris Shopper Inc ......G 585 658-3520
Mount Morris *(G-8695)*
Mtm Publishing Inc ......G 212 242-6930
New York *(G-11343)*
Multi-Health Systems Inc ......D 800 456-3003
Cheektowaga *(G-3608)*
▲ **Music Sales Corporation** ......G 212 254-2100
New York *(G-11350)*
My Publisher Inc ......G 212 935-5215
New York *(G-11354)*
Narratively Inc ......E 203 536-0332
Brooklyn *(G-2356)*
National Health Prom Assoc ......E 914 421-2525
White Plains *(G-17166)*
National Rding Styles Inst Inc ......F 516 921-5500
Syosset *(G-15851)*
Network Journal Inc ......G 212 962-3791
New York *(G-11397)*
New York Legal Publishing ......G 518 459-1100
Menands *(G-8409)*
Nimbletv Inc ......F 646 502-7010
New York *(G-11451)*
O Val Nick Music Co Inc ......G 212 873-2179
New York *(G-11504)*
Oakwood Publishing Co ......G 516 482-7720
Great Neck *(G-5842)*
One Story Inc ......G 917 816-3659
Brooklyn *(G-2404)*
Open-Xchange Inc ......F 914 332-5720
Tarrytown *(G-16124)*
Openroad Integrated Media Inc ......E 212 691-0900
New York *(G-11527)*
▲ **Osprey Publishing Inc** ......G 212 419-5300
New York *(G-11545)*
Outlook Newspaper ......E 845 356-6261
Suffern *(G-15817)*
Outreach Publishing Corp ......G 718 773-0525
Brooklyn *(G-2412)*
Pace Editions Inc ......E 212 421-3237
New York *(G-11562)*
Pace Editions Inc ......G 212 675-7431
New York *(G-11563)*
Panoply Media LLC ......E 646 382-5423
Brooklyn *(G-2416)*
Paragon Publishing Inc ......G 718 302-2093
Brooklyn *(G-2420)*
▲ **Peer International Corp** ......E 212 265-3910
New York *(G-11613)*
Peermusic III Ltd ......F 212 265-3910
New York *(G-11615)*
Peermusic Ltd ......F 212 265-3910
New York *(G-11616)*
▲ **Per Annum Inc** ......E 212 647-8700
New York *(G-11630)*
Petersons Nelnet LLC ......C 609 896-1800
Albany *(G-118)*
Playlife LLC ......G 646 207-9082
New York *(G-11696)*
Portfolio Media Inc ......C 646 783-7100
New York *(G-11708)*

Press Express ......G 914 592-3790
Elmsford *(G-4781)*
Primary Wave Publishing LLC ......G 212 661-6990
New York *(G-11730)*
Princess Music Publishing Co ......E 212 586-0240
New York *(G-11734)*
Professnal Spt Pblications Inc ......F 516 327-9500
Elmont *(G-4736)*
Publishers Clearing House LLC ......E 516 249-4063
Melville *(G-8379)*
Quality Patterns Inc ......D 212 704-0355
New York *(G-11794)*
Qworldstar Inc ......G 212 768-4500
New York *(G-11805)*
R W Publications Div of Wtrhs ......E 716 714-5620
Elma *(G-4666)*
Rda Holding Co ......F 914 238-1000
New York *(G-11837)*
Redspring Communications Inc ......E 518 587-0547
Saratoga Springs *(G-15200)*
Refinery 29 Inc ......D 212 966-3112
New York *(G-11849)*
Regan Arts LLC ......F 646 488-6610
New York *(G-11853)*
▲ **Reliable Press II Inc** ......F 718 840-5812
Brooklyn *(G-2508)*
Renegade Nation Online LLC ......G 212 868-9000
New York *(G-11866)*
Repertoire International De Ll ......E 212 817-1990
New York *(G-11867)*
Reservoir Media Management Inc ......F 212 675-0541
New York *(G-11871)*
Rheinwald Printing Co Inc ......F 585 637-5100
Brockport *(G-1246)*
Riot New Media Group Inc ......G 604 700-4896
Brooklyn *(G-2515)*
Rockefeller University ......G 212 327-8568
New York *(G-11918)*
Rolling Stone Magazine ......G 212 484-1616
New York *(G-11930)*
Rosemont Press Incorporated ......G 212 239-4770
Deer Park *(G-4226)*
▲ **Rough Guides US Ltd** ......D 212 414-3635
New York *(G-11941)*
Royalty Network Inc ......G 212 967-4300
New York *(G-11946)*
Rsl Media LLC ......G 212 307-6760
New York *(G-11949)*
S G New York LLC ......E 631 665-4000
Bohemia *(G-1124)*
Sacks and Company New York ......G 212 741-1000
New York *(G-11969)*
Sag Harbor Express ......G 631 725-1700
Sag Harbor *(G-15106)*
Sagelife Parenting LLC ......G 315 299-5713
Syracuse *(G-16052)*
Salamanca Press Penny Saver ......E 716 945-1500
Salamanca *(G-15132)*
◆ **Scepter Publishers Inc** ......G 212 354-0670
New Rochelle *(G-8970)*
Scholastic Inc ......D 212 343-7100
New York *(G-12018)*
Screen Gems-EMI Music Inc ......D 212 786-8000
New York *(G-12026)*
Seabay Media Holdings LLC ......G 212 457-7790
New York *(G-12028)*
Selby Marketing Associates Inc ......F 585 377-0750
Fairport *(G-4882)*
Select Information Exchange ......F 212 496-6435
New York *(G-12042)*
Sentinel Printing Services Inc ......D 845 562-1218
New Windsor *(G-9000)*
Sephardic Yellow Pages ......E 718 998-0299
Brooklyn *(G-2569)*
Service Advertising Group Inc ......F 718 361-6161
Long Island City *(G-7904)*
Service Education Incorporated ......G 585 264-9240
Victor *(G-16526)*
▲ **Shapiro Bernstein & Co Inc** ......F 212 588-0878
New York *(G-12065)*
Sharedbook Inc ......E 646 442-8840
New York *(G-12066)*
Shop Smart Central Inc ......G 914 962-3871
Yorktown Heights *(G-17535)*
▲ **Sing Tao Newspapers NY Ltd** ......E 212 699-3800
New York *(G-12107)*
Skylark Publications Ltd ......G 607 535-9866
Watkins Glen *(G-16721)*
Slosson Edctl Publications Inc ......F 716 652-0930
East Aurora *(G-4403)*

SIC

Employee Codes: A=Over 500 employees, B=251-500
C=101-250, D=51-100, E=20-50, F=10-19, G=5-9
2018 Harris
New York Manufacturers Directory
763

Sneaker News Inc ....G....347 687-1588
New York *(G-12140)*
Social Science Electronic Pubg ....F....585 442-8170
Rochester *(G-14714)*
Soho Editions Inc ....E....914 591-5100
Mohegan Lake *(G-8580)*
◆ Sony Music Holdings Inc ....A....212 833-8000
New York *(G-12162)*
▲ Sony/Atv Music Publishing LLC ....E....212 833-7730
New York *(G-12163)*
Southampton Town Newspapers ....E....631 283-4100
Southampton *(G-15576)*
Space 150 ....C....612 332-6458
Brooklyn *(G-2612)*
Spirit Music Group Inc ....E....212 533-7672
New York *(G-12188)*
Standard Analytics Io Inc ....G....917 882-5422
New York *(G-12205)*
Statebook LLC ....G....845 383-1991
Kingston *(G-7240)*
Stephen Singer Pattern Co Inc ....F....212 947-2902
New York *(G-12220)*
STf Services Inc ....E....315 463-8506
East Syracuse *(G-4581)*
Straight Arrow Publishing Co ....C....212 484-1616
New York *(G-12233)*
Strathmore Directories Ltd ....E....516 997-2525
Westbury *(G-17056)*
Student Lifeline Inc ....E....516 327-0800
Franklin Square *(G-5377)*
Summit Communications ....G....914 273-5504
Armonk *(G-417)*
Super Express USA Pubg Corp ....F....212 227-5800
Richmond Hill *(G-14098)*
Supermedia LLC ....D....212 513-9700
New York *(G-12265)*
Tablet Publishing Company Inc ....E....718 965-7333
Brooklyn *(G-2664)*
Taylor & Francis Group LLC ....C....212 216-7800
New York *(G-12306)*
▲ Te Neues Publishing Company ....F....212 627-9090
New York *(G-12310)*
Tenney Media Group ....D....315 853-5569
Clinton *(G-3747)*
Thehuffingtonpostcom Inc ....E....212 245-7844
New York *(G-12332)*
Theskimm Inc ....F....212 228-4628
New York *(G-12336)*
Thomas Publishing Company LLC ....B....212 695-0500
New York *(G-12342)*
Thomas Publishing Company LLC ....D....212 695-0500
New York *(G-12343)*
Thomson Reuters Corporation ....F....212 393-9461
New York *(G-12348)*
▲ Thomson Reuters Corporation ....A....646 223-4000
New York *(G-12349)*
Time Warner Companies Inc ....D....212 484-8000
New York *(G-12369)*
Total Webcasting Inc ....G....845 883-0909
New Paltz *(G-8924)*
Trader Interntnal Publications ....G....914 631-6856
Sleepy Hollow *(G-15497)*
Trading Edge Ltd ....G....347 699-7079
Ridgewood *(G-14141)*
Treiman Publications Corp ....G....607 657-8473
Berkshire *(G-853)*
Tribune Entertainment Co Del ....E....203 866-2204
New York *(G-12425)*
Tribune Media Services Inc ....B....518 792-9914
Queensbury *(G-14026)*
▲ Triumph Learning LLC ....E....212 652-0200
New York *(G-12430)*
◆ Trusted Media Brands Inc ....A....914 238-1000
New York *(G-12435)*
Trusted Media Brands Inc ....F....914 244-5244
White Plains *(G-17204)*
Turbo Express Inc ....G....718 723-3686
Jamaica *(G-6996)*
Two Palms Press Inc ....F....212 965-8598
New York *(G-12452)*
Ubm Inc ....A....212 600-3000
New York *(G-12458)*
Ucc Guide Inc ....F....518 434-0909
Albany *(G-145)*
Underline Communications LLC ....F....212 994-4340
New York *(G-12467)*
▲ Universal Edition Inc ....D....917 213-2177
New York *(G-12490)*
Urban Mapping Inc ....F....415 946-8170
New York *(G-12500)*
▲ USA Custom Pad Corp ....E....607 563-9550
Sidney *(G-15467)*
Value Line Inc ....D....212 907-1500
New York *(G-12520)*
▲ Vandam Inc ....F....212 929-0416
New York *(G-12522)*
Vending Times Inc ....F....516 442-1850
Rockville Centre *(G-14831)*
Vendome Group LLC ....D....646 795-3899
New York *(G-12540)*
Viamedia Corporation ....G....718 485-7792
Brooklyn *(G-2741)*
Vidbolt Inc ....G....716 560-8944
Buffalo *(G-3268)*
Viewfinder Inc ....G....212 831-0939
New York *(G-12567)*
Vincys Printing Ltd ....F....518 355-4363
Schenectady *(G-15333)*
Vinous Group LLC ....G....917 275-5184
New York *(G-12571)*
Visant Secondary Holdings Corp ....E....914 595-8200
Armonk *(G-420)*
VWR Education LLC ....C....585 359-2502
West Henrietta *(G-16929)*
Want-Ad Digest Inc ....F....518 279-1181
Troy *(G-16287)*
▼ Warner Music Inc ....D....212 275-2000
New York *(G-12617)*
Watchanish LLC ....F....917 558-0404
New York *(G-12622)*
Wayuga Community Newspapers ....E....315 754-6229
Red Creek *(G-14040)*
Welcome Rain Publishers LLC ....G....212 686-1909
New York *(G-12634)*
Wmg Acquisition Corp ....F....212 275-2000
New York *(G-12676)*
Wmg Holding Company Inc ....A....212 275-2000
New York *(G-12677)*
▲ Won & Lee Inc ....E....516 222-0712
Garden City *(G-5552)*
Yam TV LLC ....G....917 932-5418
New York *(G-12710)*
Yellow Pages Inc ....G....845 639-6060
New City *(G-8840)*
Zazoom LLC ....F....212 321-2100
New York *(G-12726)*

2752 Commercial Printing: Lithographic

12pt Printing LLC ....G....718 376-2120
Brooklyn *(G-1510)*
2 1 2 Postcards Inc ....E....212 767-8227
New York *(G-9008)*
2 X 4 Inc ....E....212 647-1170
New York *(G-9009)*
21st Century Fox America Inc ....D....212 852-7000
New York *(G-9013)*
3g Graphics LLC ....G....716 634-2585
Amherst *(G-221)*
450 Ridge St Inc ....G....716 754-2789
Lewiston *(G-7453)*
514 Adams Corporation ....G....516 352-6948
Franklin Square *(G-5369)*
518 Prints LLC ....G....518 674-5346
Averill Park *(G-530)*
6727 11th Ave Corp ....F....718 837-8787
Brooklyn *(G-1520)*
A & D Offset Printers Ltd ....G....516 746-2476
Mineola *(G-8520)*
A & M Litho Inc ....E....516 342-9727
Bethpage *(G-860)*
A C Envelope Inc ....G....516 420-0646
Farmingdale *(G-4933)*
▲ A Esteban & Company Inc ....E....212 989-7000
New York *(G-9031)*
A Esteban & Company Inc ....E....212 714-2227
New York *(G-9032)*
A I P Printing & Stationers ....G....631 929-5529
Wading River *(G-16543)*
A Q P Inc ....G....585 256-1690
Rochester *(G-14175)*
ABC Check Printing Corp ....F....718 855-4702
Brooklyn *(G-1546)*
Academy Printing Services Inc ....G....631 765-3346
Southold *(G-15581)*
Accuprint ....G....518 456-2431
Albany *(G-31)*
Ace Printing & Publishing Inc ....F....718 939-0040
Flushing *(G-5229)*
Act Communications Group Inc ....F....631 669-2403
West Islip *(G-16932)*
Ad Vantage Press ....G....212 941-8355
New York *(G-9069)*
Adirondack Publishing Co Inc ....E....518 891-2600
Saranac Lake *(G-15162)*
Ads-N-Color Inc ....E....718 797-0900
Brooklyn *(G-1563)*
▲ Advance Publications Inc ....D....718 981-1234
Staten Island *(G-15653)*
Advanced Business Group Inc ....F....212 398-1010
New York *(G-9090)*
Advanced Digital Printing LLC ....E....718 649-1500
New York *(G-9091)*
Advantage Press Inc ....F....518 584-3405
Saratoga Springs *(G-15170)*
Advantage Printing Inc ....F....718 820-0688
Kew Gardens *(G-7187)*
▲ Advantage Quick Print Inc ....G....212 989-5644
New York *(G-9095)*
Advertising Lithographers ....F....212 966-7771
New York *(G-9098)*
Agrecolor Inc ....F....516 741-8700
Mineola *(G-8525)*
Ahw Printing Corp ....F....516 536-3600
Oceanside *(G-13091)*
Alamar Printing Inc ....F....914 993-9007
White Plains *(G-17102)*
Albany Letter Shop Inc ....G....518 434-1172
Albany *(G-37)*
Albert Siy ....G....718 359-0389
Flushing *(G-5231)*
Aldine Inc (ny) ....D....212 226-2870
New York *(G-9129)*
Alexander Polakovich ....G....718 229-6200
Bayside *(G-761)*
All Color Business Spc Ltd ....G....516 420-0649
Deer Park *(G-4115)*
All Color Offset Printers Inc ....G....516 420-0649
Farmingdale *(G-4943)*
All Time Products Inc ....G....718 464-1400
Queens Village *(G-13990)*
Allen William & Company Inc ....C....212 675-6461
Glendale *(G-5659)*
Allied Reproductions Inc ....E....212 255-2472
New York *(G-9140)*
Allstatebannerscom Corporation ....G....718 300-1256
Long Island City *(G-7685)*
Alpha Printing Corp ....F....315 454-5507
Syracuse *(G-15872)*
Alpina Color Graphics Inc ....G....212 285-2700
New York *(G-9151)*
Alpina Copyworld Inc ....F....212 683-3511
New York *(G-9152)*
Alpine Business Group Inc ....G....212 989-4198
New York *(G-9153)*
Amax Printing Inc ....F....718 384-8600
Maspeth *(G-8144)*
American Business Forms Inc ....E....716 836-5111
Amherst *(G-226)*
American Icon Industries Inc ....G....845 561-1299
Newburgh *(G-12770)*
American Print Solutions Inc ....E....718 246-7800
Brooklyn *(G-1604)*
Amsterdam Printing & Litho Inc ....F....518 792-6501
Queensbury *(G-14002)*
Amsterdam Printing & Litho Inc ....F....518 842-6000
Amsterdam *(G-333)*
Amsterdam Printing & Litho Inc ....E....518 842-6000
Amsterdam *(G-334)*
▲ Anne Taintor Inc ....G....718 483-9312
Brooklyn *(G-1613)*
Answer Printing Inc ....F....212 922-2922
New York *(G-9216)*
Apple Press ....G....914 723-6660
White Plains *(G-17106)*
Arcade Inc ....A....212 541-2600
New York *(G-9243)*
Ares Printing and Packg Corp ....C....718 858-8760
Brooklyn *(G-1627)*
Argo Envelope Corp ....D....718 729-2700
Long Island City *(G-7700)*
Argo Lithographers Inc ....E....718 729-2700
Long Island City *(G-7702)*
Arista Innovations Inc ....E....516 746-2262
Mineola *(G-8529)*
Arnold Printing Corp ....F....607 272-7800
Ithaca *(G-6859)*
Arnold Taylor Printing Inc ....G....516 781-0564
Bellmore *(G-809)*
Aro-Graph Corporation ....G....315 463-8693
Syracuse *(G-15877)*

27 PRINTING, PUBLISHING, AND ALLIED INDUSTRIES

Art Digital Technologies LLC ....F 646 649-4820
  Brooklyn (G-1636)
Art Scroll Printing Corp ....F 212 929-2413
  New York (G-9265)
Artina Group Inc ....E 914 592-1850
  Elmsford (G-4743)
Artscroll Printing Corp ....E 212 929-2413
  New York (G-9275)
Asn Inc ....E 718 894-0800
  Maspeth (G-8149)
Atlantic Color Corp ....E 631 345-3800
  Shirley (G-15436)
Atlas Print Solutions Inc ....F 212 949-8775
  New York (G-9308)
Avm Printing Inc ....F 631 351-1331
  Hauppauge (G-6049)
▲ Avon Reproductions Inc ....E 631 273-2400
  Hauppauge (G-6050)
B & P Jays Inc ....G 716 668-8408
  Buffalo (G-2851)
B D B Typewriter Supply Works ....E 718 232-4800
  Brooklyn (G-1659)
Badoud Communications Inc ....C 315 472-7821
  Syracuse (G-15886)
Bajan Group Inc ....E 518 464-2884
  Latham (G-7381)
Ballantrae Lithographers Inc ....G 914 592-3275
  White Plains (G-17110)
Barone Offset Printing Corp ....F 212 989-5500
  Mohegan Lake (G-8577)
Bartolomeo Publishing Inc ....F 631 420-4949
  West Babylon (G-16799)
Batavia Press LLC ....G 585 343-4429
  Batavia (G-625)
Bates Jackson Engraving Co Inc ....E 716 854-3000
  Buffalo (G-2855)
Baum Christine and John Corp ....G 585 621-8910
  Rochester (G-14241)
Beacon Press Inc ....G 212 691-5050
  White Plains (G-17111)
Beastons Budget Printing ....G 585 244-2721
  Rochester (G-14244)
Beehive Press Inc ....G 718 654-1200
  Bronx (G-1280)
Bel Aire Offset Corp ....G 718 539-8333
  College Point (G-3804)
▲ Benchemark Printing Inc ....D 518 393-1361
  Schenectady (G-15262)
Benchmark Graphics Ltd ....F 212 683-1711
  New York (G-9405)
Benjamin Printing Inc ....F 315 788-7922
  Adams (G-2)
Bennett Multimedia Inc ....F 718 629-1454
  Brooklyn (G-1680)
Bennett Printing Corporation ....F 718 629-1454
  Brooklyn (G-1681)
Bernard Hall ....G 585 425-3340
  Fairport (G-4853)
Bevilacque Group LLC ....F 212 414-8858
  Port Washington (G-13824)
▲ Beyer Graphics Inc ....D 631 543-3900
  Commack (G-3850)
Billing Coding and Prtg Inc ....G 718 827-9409
  Brooklyn (G-1696)
Bishop Print Shop Inc ....G 607 965-8155
  Edmeston (G-4635)
Bittner Company LLC ....F 585 214-1790
  Rochester (G-14251)
Bk Printing Inc ....G 315 565-5396
  East Syracuse (G-4528)
Bluesoho ....F 646 805-2583
  New York (G-9476)
Bmg Printing and Promotion LLC ....G 631 231-9200
  Bohemia (G-1022)
Boka Printing Inc ....G 607 725-3235
  Binghamton (G-893)
Boncraft Inc ....D 716 662-9720
  Tonawanda (G-16167)
Bondy Printing Corp ....G 631 242-1510
  Bay Shore (G-677)
Boulevard Printing ....G 716 837-3800
  Tonawanda (G-16168)
Boxcar Press Incorporated ....E 315 473-0930
  Syracuse (G-15893)
BP Beyond Printing Inc ....G 516 328-2700
  Hempstead (G-6290)
▼ BP Digital Imaging LLC ....G 607 753-0022
  Cortland (G-4038)
Brennans Quick Print Inc ....G 518 793-4999
  Glens Falls (G-5689)

Bridge Printing Inc ....G 212 243-5390
  Long Island City (G-7721)
Brodock Press Inc ....D 315 735-9577
  Utica (G-16333)
Brooklyn Circus ....F 718 858-0919
  Brooklyn (G-1722)
Brooks Litho Digital Group Inc ....G 631 789-4500
  Deer Park (G-4136)
Brown Printers of Troy Inc ....F 518 235-4080
  Troy (G-16250)
Brown Printing Company ....E 212 782-7800
  New York (G-9522)
Brownstone Capitl Partners LLC ....G 212 889-0069
  New York (G-9524)
Business Card Express Inc ....E 631 669-3400
  West Babylon (G-16804)
C & R De Santis Inc ....E 718 447-5076
  Staten Island (G-15673)
C K Printing ....G 718 965-0388
  Brooklyn (G-1746)
C To C Design & Print Inc ....F 631 885-4020
  Ronkonkoma (G-14911)
Caboodle Printing Inc ....G 716 693-6000
  Williamsville (G-17265)
Cadmus Journal Services Inc ....D 607 762-5365
  Conklin (G-3890)
Canaan Printing Inc ....F 718 729-3100
  Bayside (G-763)
Canandaigua Msgnr Incorporated ....D 585 394-0770
  Canandaigua (G-3366)
Canastota Publishing Co Inc ....G 315 697-9010
  Canastota (G-3394)
Candid Litho Printing Ltd ....D 212 431-3800
  Farmingdale (G-4965)
Canfield & Tack Inc ....D 585 235-7710
  Rochester (G-14275)
Canyon Publishing Inc ....F 212 334-0227
  New York (G-9571)
Capital Dst Print & Imaging ....G 518 456-6773
  Schenectady (G-15265)
Carges Entps of Canandaigua ....G 585 394-2600
  Canandaigua (G-3367)
Carlara Group Ltd ....G 914 769-2020
  Pleasantville (G-13744)
Carnels Printing Inc ....G 516 883-3355
  Port Washington (G-13826)
Carr Communications Group LLC ....F 607 748-0481
  Vestal (G-16466)
Castlereagh Printcraft Inc ....D 516 623-1728
  Freeport (G-5402)
Cathedral Corporation ....C 315 338-0021
  Rome (G-14837)
Catskill Delaware Publications ....F 845 887-5200
  Callicoon (G-3312)
Cayuga Press Cortland Inc ....E 888 229-8421
  Liverpool (G-7540)
▲ Cazar Printing & Advertising ....G 718 446-4606
  Corona (G-4015)
Cds Productions Inc ....F 518 385-8255
  Schenectady (G-15269)
Cedar West Inc ....G 631 467-1444
  Ronkonkoma (G-14915)
Chakra Communications Inc ....E 607 748-7491
  Endicott (G-4806)
Chakra Communications Inc ....E 716 505-7300
  Lancaster (G-7333)
Challenge Graphics Svcs Inc ....E 631 586-0171
  Deer Park (G-4138)
Chan Luu LLC ....G 212 398-3163
  New York (G-9628)
Chenango Union Printing Inc ....G 607 334-2112
  Norwich (G-13040)
Cherry Lane Lithographing Corp ....E 516 293-9294
  Plainview (G-13617)
▲ China Imprint LLC ....G 585 563-3391
  Rochester (G-14295)
Chromagraphics Press Inc ....G 631 367-6160
  Melville (G-8332)
Cilyox Inc ....F 716 853-3809
  Buffalo (G-2894)
Circle Press Inc ....D 212 924-4277
  New York (G-9674)
Clarsons Corp ....F 585 235-8775
  Rochester (G-14299)
Classic Color Graphics Inc ....G 516 822-9090
  Hicksville (G-6354)
Classic Color Graphics Inc ....G 516 822-9090
  Hicksville (G-6355)
Cloud Printing ....G 212 775-0888
  New York (G-9701)

Cody Printing Corp ....G 718 651-8854
  Woodside (G-17341)
Coe Displays Inc ....G 718 937-5658
  Long Island City (G-7730)
Cohber Press Inc ....D 585 475-9100
  West Henrietta (G-16906)
Colad Group LLC ....D 716 961-1776
  Buffalo (G-2900)
Color Card LLC ....F 631 232-1300
  Central Islip (G-3516)
▲ Color Carton Corp ....D 718 665-0840
  Bronx (G-9523)
Color-Aid Corporation ....G 212 673-5500
  Hudson Falls (G-6670)
Colorfast ....F 212 929-2440
  New York (G-9732)
Colorfully Yours Inc ....F 631 242-8600
  Bay Shore (G-685)
Combine Graphics Corp ....G 212 695-4044
  Forest Hills (G-5328)
Commerce Offset Ltd ....G 914 769-6671
  Thornwood (G-16141)
Commercial Press Inc ....G 315 274-0028
  Canton (G-3407)
Commercial Print & Imaging ....E 716 597-0100
  Buffalo (G-2902)
Community Media LLC ....E 212 229-1890
  New York (G-9749)
Community Newspaper Group LLC ....F 607 432-1000
  Oneonta (G-13203)
Compass Printing Plus ....F 518 891-7050
  Saranac Lake (G-15163)
Compass Printing Plus ....G 518 523-3308
  Saranac Lake (G-15164)
Complemar Print LLC ....F 716 875-7238
  Buffalo (G-2904)
Composite Forms Inc ....F 914 937-1808
  Port Chester (G-13768)
Compucolor Associates Inc ....E 516 358-0000
  New Hyde Park (G-8868)
▲ Concept Printing Inc ....G 845 353-4040
  Nyack (G-13064)
Conkur Printing Co Inc ....E 212 541-5980
  New York (G-9762)
Consolidated Color Press Inc ....F 212 929-8197
  New York (G-9765)
Constas Printing Corporation ....G 315 474-2176
  Syracuse (G-15924)
Copy Stop Inc ....G 914 428-5188
  White Plains (G-17124)
Coral Color Process Ltd ....E 631 543-5200
  Commack (G-3855)
▲ Coral Graphic Services Inc ....C 516 576-2100
  Hicksville (G-6359)
Coral Graphic Services Inc ....C 516 576-2100
  Hicksville (G-6360)
Cosmos Communications Inc ....C 718 482-1800
  Long Island City (G-7734)
Coughlin Printing Group ....G 315 788-8560
  Watertown (G-16668)
Courier Printing Corp ....G 607 467-2191
  Deposit (G-4300)
Craig Envelope Corp ....E 718 786-4277
  Hicksville (G-6361)
Crawford Print Shop Inc ....G 607 359-4970
  Addison (G-5)
Create-A-Card Inc ....G 631 584-2273
  Saint James (G-15114)
Creative Forms Inc ....G 212 431-7540
  New York (G-9807)
Creative Printing Corp ....G 212 226-3870
  New York (G-9808)
Cronin Enterprises Inc ....G 914 345-9600
  Elmsford (G-4754)
D G M Graphics Inc ....F 516 223-2220
  Merrick (G-8416)
Daily Record ....F 585 232-2035
  Rochester (G-14320)
Dan Trent Company Inc ....G 716 822-1422
  Buffalo (G-2920)
Dark Star Lithograph Corp ....G 845 634-3780
  New City (G-8829)
Datorib Inc ....G 631 698-6222
  Selden (G-15372)
David Helsing ....G 607 796-2681
  Horseheads (G-6601)
Dawn Paper Co Inc ....F 516 596-9110
  East Rockaway (G-4489)
Dealer-Presscom Inc ....G 631 589-0434
  Bohemia (G-1049)

Employee Codes: A=Over 500 employees, B=251-500
C=101-250, D=51-100, E=20-50, F=10-19, G=5-9

27 PRINTING, PUBLISHING, AND ALLIED INDUSTRIES SIC SECTION

Deanco Digital Printing LLC F 212 371-2025
Sunnyside *(G-15826)*
Decal Makers Inc E 516 221-7200
Bellmore *(G-813)*
Decal Techniques Inc G 631 491-1800
Bay Shore *(G-690)*
Dejay Litho Inc F 631 319-6916
Bohemia *(G-1050)*
Dell Communications Inc G 212 989-3434
New York *(G-9895)*
Delta Press Inc E 212 989-3445
High Falls *(G-6427)*
Denton Advertising Inc F 631 586-4333
Bohemia *(G-1052)*
Denton Publications Inc D 518 873-6368
Elizabethtown *(G-4640)*
Dependable Lithographers Inc F 718 472-4200
Long Island City *(G-7741)*
▲ **Design Distributors Inc** D 631 242-2000
Deer Park *(G-4152)*
Design Lithographers Inc F 212 645-8900
New York *(G-9906)*
Designlogocom Inc G 212 564-0200
New York *(G-9909)*
Dick Bailey Service Inc F 718 522-4363
Brooklyn *(G-1861)*
Digital Color Concepts Inc E 212 989-4888
New York *(G-9928)*
Digital Imaging Tech LLC G 518 885-4400
Ballston Spa *(G-592)*
Digital United Color Prtg Inc G 845 986-9846
Warwick *(G-16610)*
Dispatch Graphics Inc F 212 307-5943
New York *(G-9938)*
Distinctive Printing Inc G 212 727-3000
New York *(G-9940)*
Diversified Envelope Ltd F 585 615-4697
Rochester *(G-14333)*
Division Street News Corp F 518 234-2515
Cobleskill *(G-3761)*
Doco Quick Print Inc G 315 782-6623
Watertown *(G-16671)*
Donmar Printing Co F 516 280-2239
Mineola *(G-8539)*
▲ **Donnelley Financial LLC** B 212 425-0298
New York *(G-9957)*
Dovelin Printing Company Inc F 718 302-3951
Brooklyn *(G-1877)*
Dowd - Witbeck Printing Corp F 518 274-2421
Troy *(G-16256)*
DP Murphy Co Inc D 631 673-9400
Deer Park *(G-4154)*
Dual Print & Mail LLC D 716 775-8001
Grand Island *(G-5768)*
Dual Print & Mail LLC D 716 684-3825
Cheektowaga *(G-3597)*
Dupli Graphics Corporation C 315 234-7286
Syracuse *(G-15945)*
Dupli Graphics Corporation G 315 422-4732
Syracuse *(G-15946)*
Dyenamix Inc G 212 941-6642
New York *(G-9997)*
E B B Graphics Inc F 516 750-5510
Westbury *(G-17006)*
E L Smith Printing Co Inc E 201 373-0111
New City *(G-8831)*
E W Smith Publishing Co F 845 562-1218
New Windsor *(G-8983)*
Eagle Graphics Inc G 585 244-5006
Rochester *(G-14343)*
East Coast Thermographers Inc E 718 321-3211
College Point *(G-3807)*
East Ridge Quick Print F 585 266-4911
Rochester *(G-14344)*
Eastern Hills Printing G 716 741-3300
Clarence *(G-3687)*
Eastside Printers F 315 437-6515
East Syracuse *(G-4540)*
Eastwood Litho Inc E 315 437-2626
Syracuse *(G-15950)*
Echo Appellate Press Inc G 516 432-3601
Long Beach *(G-7670)*
Edgian Press Inc G 516 931-2114
Hicksville *(G-6371)*
Edwards Graphic Co Inc G 718 548-6858
Bronx *(G-1329)*
Efficiency Printing Co Inc F 914 949-8611
White Plains *(G-17129)*
Eleanor Ettinger Inc E 212 925-7474
New York *(G-10048)*
Elmat Quality Printing Ltd F 516 569-5722
Cedarhurst *(G-3483)*
Empire Press Co G 718 756-9500
Brooklyn *(G-1926)*
Engrav-O-Type Press Inc F 585 262-7590
Rochester *(G-14372)*
Entermarket G 914 437-7268
Mount Kisco *(G-8669)*
Enterprise Press Inc C 212 741-2111
New York *(G-10096)*
Evolution Impressions Inc D 585 473-6600
Rochester *(G-14382)*
Excel Graphics Services Inc F 212 929-2183
New York *(G-10155)*
Excelsior Graphics Inc G 212 730-6200
New York *(G-10158)*
Execuprint Inc G 585 288-5570
Rochester *(G-14385)*
Executive Prtg & Direct Mail G 914 592-3200
Elmsford *(G-4760)*
F & B Photo Offset Co Inc G 516 431-5433
Island Park *(G-6819)*
F & D Services Inc F 718 984-1635
Staten Island *(G-15693)*
F & T Graphics Inc F 631 643-1000
Hauppauge *(G-6097)*
F J Remey Co Inc E 516 741-5112
Mineola *(G-8544)*
F5 Networks Inc G 888 882-7535
New York *(G-10175)*
Falconer Printing & Design Inc F 716 665-2121
Falconer *(G-4906)*
Fambus Inc G 607 785-3700
Endicott *(G-4815)*
Farthing Press Inc G 716 852-4674
Buffalo *(G-2959)*
Fasprint G 518 483-4631
Malone *(G-8040)*
Federal Envelope Inc F 212 243-8380
New York *(G-10201)*
Final Touch Printing Inc F 845 352-2677
Spring Valley *(G-15607)*
Finer Touch Printing Corp F 516 944-8000
Port Washington *(G-13837)*
First Displays Inc F 347 642-5972
Long Island City *(G-7771)*
First Line Printing Inc F 718 606-0860
Woodside *(G-17346)*
Fitch Graphics Ltd E 212 619-3800
New York *(G-10228)*
▲ **Five Star Prtg & Mailing Svcs** F 212 929-0300
New York *(G-10229)*
Flare Multicopy Corp E 718 258-8860
Brooklyn *(G-1983)*
Flower City Printing Inc G 585 512-1235
Rochester *(G-14397)*
Flower City Printing Inc C 585 663-9000
Rochester *(G-14396)*
Flp Group LLC F 315 252-7583
Auburn *(G-495)*
▲ **Flynns Inc** E 212 339-8700
New York *(G-10234)*
Fort Orange Press Inc E 518 489-3233
Albany *(G-81)*
Forward Enterprises Inc F 585 235-7670
Rochester *(G-14401)*
Francis Emory Fitch Inc E 212 619-3800
New York *(G-10248)*
Frederick Coon Inc E 716 683-6812
Elma *(G-4661)*
Freeville Publishing Co Inc F 607 844-9119
Freeville *(G-5447)*
Fulton Newspapers Inc E 315 598-6397
Fulton *(G-5471)*
G & P Printing Inc G 212 274-8092
New York *(G-10278)*
G W Canfield & Son Inc G 315 735-5522
Utica *(G-16357)*
Gallagher Printing Inc E 716 873-2434
Buffalo *(G-2977)*
▲ **Gallant Graphics Ltd** E 845 868-1166
Stanfordville *(G-15647)*
Gannett Stllite Info Ntwrk LLC E 845 578-2300
West Nyack *(G-16946)*
▲ **Garden City Printers & Mailers** F 516 485-1600
West Hempstead *(G-16884)*
Gatehouse Media LLC D 585 394-0770
Canandaigua *(G-3376)*
Gateway Prtg & Graphics Inc E 716 823-3873
Hamburg *(G-5949)*
Gazette Press Inc E 914 963-8300
Rye *(G-15082)*
Gbv Promotions Inc F 631 231-7300
Bay Shore *(G-700)*
Gem Reproduction Services Corp G 845 298-0172
Wappingers Falls *(G-16590)*
Gemson Graphics Inc G 516 873-8400
Albertson *(G-158)*
General Business Supply Inc D 518 720-3939
Watervliet *(G-16709)*
Geneva Printing Company Inc G 315 789-8191
Geneva *(G-5591)*
Genie Instant Printing Co Inc F 212 575-8258
New York *(G-10321)*
Glens Falls Printing LLC F 518 793-0555
Glens Falls *(G-5697)*
Global Graphics Inc F 718 939-4967
Flushing *(G-5252)*
Gmp LLC D 914 939-0571
Port Chester *(G-13774)*
Gn Printing E 718 784-1713
Long Island City *(G-7779)*
Golos Printing Inc G 607 732-1896
Elmira Heights *(G-4723)*
▼ **Gooding Co Inc** E 716 434-5501
Lockport *(G-7622)*
Gotham Ink Corp G 516 677-1969
Syosset *(G-15845)*
Government Data Publication E 347 789-8719
Brooklyn *(G-2046)*
GPM Associates LLC E 585 335-3940
Dansville *(G-4103)*
Grand Meridian Printing Inc E 718 937-3888
Long Island City *(G-7781)*
Grand Prix Litho Inc E 631 242-4182
Holbrook *(G-6478)*
▲ **Graphic Cntrls Acqisition Corp** B 716 853-7500
Buffalo *(G-2994)*
Graphic Controls Holdings Inc F 716 853-7500
Buffalo *(G-2995)*
Graphic Fabrications Inc G 516 763-3222
Rockville Centre *(G-14819)*
Graphicomm Inc G 716 283-0830
Niagara Falls *(G-12845)*
Graphics of Utica G 315 797-4868
Remsen *(G-14052)*
Graphics Plus Printing Inc E 607 299-0500
Cortland *(G-4051)*
Great Eastern Color Lith D 845 454-7420
Poughkeepsie *(G-13923)*
Green Girl Prtg & Msgnr Inc G 212 575-0357
New York *(G-10401)*
Greenwood Graphics Inc F 516 822-4856
Hicksville *(G-6381)*
Grover Cleveland Press Inc F 716 564-2222
Amherst *(G-243)*
Guaranteed Printing Svc Co Inc E 212 929-2410
Long Island City *(G-7784)*
H T L & S Ltd F 718 435-4474
Brooklyn *(G-2059)*
H&E Service Corp D 646 472-1936
Garden City *(G-5522)*
Haig Press Inc E 631 582-5800
Hauppauge *(G-6111)*
Hamptons Magazine E 631 283-7125
Southampton *(G-15568)*
Harmon and Castella Printing F 845 471-9163
Poughkeepsie *(G-13925)*
Hearst Corporation A 518 454-5694
Albany *(G-85)*
Hempstead Sentinel Inc F 516 486-5000
Hempstead *(G-6297)*
Heritage Printing Center G 518 563-8240
Plattsburgh *(G-13695)*
HI Speed Envelope Co Inc F 718 617-1600
Mount Vernon *(G-8735)*
Hill Crest Press G 518 943-0671
Catskill *(G-3457)*
Hillside Printing Inc F 718 658-6719
Jamaica *(G-6955)*
Hks Printing Company Inc F 212 675-2529
New York *(G-10533)*
▲ **Hooek Produktion Inc** G 212 367-9111
New York *(G-10547)*
Horne Organization Inc F 914 572-1330
Yonkers *(G-17471)*
Hospitality Graphics Inc G 212 643-6700
New York *(G-10553)*
Huckleberry Inc G 631 630-5450
Hauppauge *(G-6119)*

27 PRINTING, PUBLISHING, AND ALLIED INDUSTRIES

Company	Code	Phone
Hudson Envelope Corporation, New York (G-10569)	E	212 473-6666
▲ Hudson Park Press Inc, New York (G-10571)	G	212 929-8898
Hudson Printing Co Inc, New York (G-10572)	E	718 937-8600
Hugh F McPherson Inc, Cheektowaga (G-3604)	G	716 668-6107
Hunt Graphics Inc, Coram (G-3967)	G	631 751-5349
I 2 Print Inc, Long Island City (G-7791)	F	718 937-8800
Impala Press Ltd, Ronkonkoma (G-14940)	G	631 588-4262
In-House Inc, College Point (G-3812)	F	718 445-9007
In-Step Marketing Inc, New York (G-10624)	F	212 797-3450
Ink Well, Brooklyn (G-2105)	G	718 253-9736
Ink-It Printing Inc, College Point (G-3813)	G	718 229-5590
Instant Again LLC, Rochester (G-14470)	E	585 436-8003
Instant Stream Inc, New York (G-10654)	E	917 438-7182
International Newsppr Prtg Co, Glen Head (G-5649)	E	516 626-6095
Interstate Litho Corp, Brentwood (G-1182)	D	631 232-6025
Interstate Thermographers Corp, White Plains (G-17150)	G	914 948-1745
Iron Horse Graphics Ltd, Bridgehampton (G-1232)	G	631 537-3400
Iver Printing Inc, New Hyde Park (G-8888)	G	718 275-2070
J & J Printing Inc, Syracuse (G-15983)	G	315 458-7411
J A T Printing Inc, Huntington (G-6699)	G	631 427-1155
J F B & Sons Lithographers, Lake Ronkonkoma (G-7302)	D	631 467-1444
J P Printing Inc, Farmingdale (G-5023)	G	516 293-6110
J V Haring & Son, Staten Island (G-15713)	F	718 720-1947
Jack J Florio Jr, Lockport (G-7625)	G	716 434-9123
Jacobs Press Inc, Auburn (G-501)	F	315 252-4861
Jam Printing Publishing Inc, Elmsford (G-4766)	G	914 345-8400
James Conolly Printing Co, Rochester (G-14480)	E	585 426-4150
Jane Lewis, Binghamton (G-925)	G	607 722-0584
Japan Printing & Graphics Inc, New York (G-10741)	G	212 406-2905
JDS Graphics Inc, New York (G-10752)	F	973 330-3300
Jfb Print Solutions Inc, Lido Beach (G-7462)	G	631 694-8300
Johnnys Ideal Printing Co, Hudson (G-6651)	G	518 828-6666
Jon Lyn Ink Inc, Merrick (G-8420)	G	516 546-2312
◆ Joseph Paul, Brooklyn (G-2148)	G	718 693-4269
Judith Lewis Printer Inc, Westbury (G-17027)	G	516 997-7777
Jurist Company Inc, Long Island City (G-7801)	G	212 243-8008
Just Press Print LLC, Rochester (G-14488)	G	585 783-1300
Kader Lithograph Company Inc, Long Island City (G-7804)	C	917 664-4380
Kaleidoscope Imaging Inc, New York (G-10838)	E	212 631-9947
Karr Graphics Corp, Long Island City (G-7806)	E	212 645-6000
Kas-Ray Industries Inc, New York (G-10849)	F	212 620-3144
Kaufman Brothers Printing, New York (G-10858)	G	212 563-1854
Kaymil Printing Company Inc, New York (G-10861)	G	212 594-3718
Keeners East End Litho Inc, East Hampton (G-4432)	G	631 324-8565
Keller Bros & Miller Inc, Buffalo (G-3045)	G	716 854-2374
Kent Associates Inc, New York (G-10877)	G	212 675-0722
Kenyon Press Inc, Sherburne (G-15414)	G	607 674-9066
Key Brand Entertainment Inc, New York (G-10879)	C	212 966-5400
Kim Jae Printing Co Inc, Roslyn Heights (G-15053)	G	212 691-6289
Kinaneco Inc, Syracuse (G-15994)	E	315 468-6201
King Lithographers Inc, Mount Vernon (G-8743)	E	914 667-4200
Kingsbury Printing Co Inc, Queensbury (G-14015)	G	518 747-6606
Kjckd Inc, Latham (G-7395)	G	518 435-9696
▲ Kling Magnetics Inc, Chatham (G-3586)	E	518 392-4000
Knickerbocker Graphics Svcs, New York (G-10899)	F	212 244-7485
Kolcorp Industries Ltd, New York (G-10909)	F	212 354-0400
◆ Kwik Ticket Inc, Brooklyn (G-2183)	G	718 421-3800
L & K Graphics Inc, Deer Park (G-4185)	G	631 667-2269
L I F Publishing Corp, Shirley (G-15445)	G	631 345-5200
L K Printing Corp, White Plains (G-17157)	G	914 761-1944
L M N Printing Company Inc, Valley Stream (G-16438)	E	516 285-8526
Label Gallery Inc, Norwich (G-13049)	G	607 334-3244
Lake Placid Advertisers Wkshp, Lake Placid (G-7299)	E	518 523-3359
Laser Printer Checks Corp, Monroe (G-8595)	G	845 782-5837
Laumont Labs Inc, New York (G-10972)	E	212 664-0595
Leader Printing Inc, Merrick (G-8422)	F	516 546-1544
Lee Printing Inc, Brooklyn (G-2206)	G	718 237-1651
Lehmann Printing Company Inc, New York (G-10997)	G	212 929-2395
Leigh Scott Enterprises Inc, Bellerose (G-806)	G	718 343-5440
Lennons Litho Inc, Herkimer (G-6329)	F	315 866-3156
Levon Graphics Corp, Farmingdale (G-5043)	D	631 753-2022
LI Script LLC, Woodbury (G-17313)	G	631 321-3850
Liberty Label Mfg Inc, Holbrook (G-6486)	F	631 737-2365
Litho Dynamics Inc, Hawthorne (G-6273)	G	914 769-1759
Lithomatic Business Forms Inc, New York (G-11037)	G	212 255-6700
Litmor Publishing Corp, Garden City (G-5527)	F	516 931-0012
Lmg National Publishing Inc, Fairport (G-4868)	E	585 598-6874
Logo Print Company, Hornell (G-6592)	G	607 324-5403
Loudon Ltd, East Northport (G-4460)	G	631 757-4447
Louis Heindl & Son Inc, Rochester (G-14504)	E	585 454-5080
Love Unlimited NY Inc, Westbury (G-17035)	E	718 359-8500
Loy L Press Inc, Buffalo (G-3069)	G	716 634-5966
Lynmar Printing Corp, Amityville (G-306)	G	631 957-8500
▲ M L Design Inc, New York (G-11104)	G	212 233-0213
M T M Printing Co Inc, College Point (G-3820)	F	718 353-3297
M3 Graphic Group Ltd, New York (G-11109)	G	212 366-0863
Madison Printing Corp, Ithaca (G-6893)	G	607 273-3535
Magazines & Brochures Inc, Buffalo (G-3074)	G	716 875-9699
Mahin Impressions Inc, Riverhead (G-14163)	G	212 871-9777
Malone Industrial Press Inc, Malone (G-8044)	G	518 483-5880
Manifestation-Glow Press Inc, Fresh Meadows (G-5458)	G	718 380-5259
Mansfield Press Inc, New York (G-11165)	F	212 265-5411
Marcal Printing Inc, Hicksville (G-6393)	G	516 942-9500
Marcy Printing Inc, Brooklyn (G-2269)	G	718 935-9100
Mark T Westinghouse, Catskill (G-3459)	E	518 678-3262
Marketshare LLC, Brentwood (G-1188)	G	631 273-0598
Marks Corpex Banknote Co, Bay Shore (G-713)	G	631 968-0277
Marlow Printing Co Inc, Brooklyn (G-2275)	E	718 625-4948
▼ Marsid Group Ltd, Carle Place (G-3422)	G	516 334-1603
Mason & Gore Inc, Rye (G-15089)	E	914 921-1025
Master Image Printing Inc, Elmsford (G-4772)	G	914 347-4400
Mc Squared Nyc Inc, New York (G-11217)	F	212 947-2260
McG Graphics Inc, Dix Hills (G-4317)	G	631 499-0730
Mdi Holdings LLC, New York (G-11228)	A	212 559-1127
Mdr Printing Corp, Manhasset (G-8095)	G	516 627-3221
▲ Medallion Associates Inc, New York (G-11233)	E	212 929-9130
▲ Mercury Print Productions Inc, Rochester (G-14525)	C	585 458-7900
Merrill New York Company Inc, New York (G-11261)	C	212 229-6500
Messenger Press, Ballston Spa (G-603)	G	518 885-9231
Michael K Lennon Inc, Westhampton Beach (G-17088)	E	631 288-5200
Mickelberry Communications Inc, New York (G-11279)	G	212 832-0303
Microera Printers Inc, Rochester (G-14530)	E	585 783-1300
Mid Atlantic Graphics Corp, Shirley (G-15448)	E	631 345-3800
Mid-York Press Inc, Sherburne (G-15415)	D	607 674-4491
Middletown Press, Middletown (G-8485)	G	845 343-1895
Midgley Printing Corp, Syracuse (G-16009)	G	315 475-1864
Midstate Printing Corp, Liverpool (G-7560)	E	315 475-4101
Mikam Graphics LLC, New York (G-11290)	D	212 684-9393
Miken Companies Inc, Buffalo (G-3085)	D	716 668-6311
Miller Enterprises CNY Inc, Manlius (G-8108)	C	315 682-4999
Miller Printing & Litho Inc, Amsterdam (G-357)	G	518 842-0001
▲ Mines Press Inc, Cortlandt Manor (G-4078)	C	914 788-1800
Minuteman Press Inc, Nanuet (G-8805)	G	845 623-2277
Minuteman Press Intl Inc, Jamaica (G-6968)	G	718 343-5440
Mitchell Prtg & Mailing Inc, Oswego (G-13360)	F	315 343-3531
MJB Printing Corp, Islip (G-6850)	G	631 581-0177
Mod-Pac Corp, Buffalo (G-3092)	D	716 447-9013
Monarch Graphics Inc, Central Islip (G-3531)	F	631 232-1300
Moneast Inc, Wappingers Falls (G-16595)	G	845 298-8898
Monte Press Inc, Bronx (G-1406)	G	718 325-4999
Mooney-Keehley Inc, Rochester (G-14541)	G	585 271-1573
Moore Printing Company Inc, Canandaigua (G-3378)	G	585 394-1533
Multimedia Services Inc, Corning (G-3997)	E	607 936-3186
Multiple Imprssons of Rchester, Rochester (G-14545)	G	585 546-1160
Mutual Engraving Company Inc, West Hempstead (G-16893)	D	516 489-0534

Employee Codes: A=Over 500 employees, B=251-500, C=101-250, D=51-100, E=20-50, F=10-19, G=5-9

27 PRINTING, PUBLISHING, AND ALLIED INDUSTRIES

Company	Code	Phone
Nameplate Mfrs of Amer, Farmingdale (G-5070)	E	631 752-0055
Nash Printing Inc, Plainview (G-13651)	F	516 935-4567
National Reproductions Inc, New York (G-11372)	E	212 619-3800
NCR Corporation, Ithaca (G-6901)	C	607 273-5310
Nesher Printing Inc, New York (G-11393)	G	212 760-2521
New Goldstar 1 Printing Corp, New York (G-11409)	G	212 343-3909
New Horizon Graphics Inc, Hauppauge (G-6173)	E	631 231-8055
New York Digital Print Center, Whitestone (G-17241)	G	718 767-1953
New York Press & Graphics Inc, Albany (G-106)	F	518 489-7089
New York Typing & Printing Co, Forest Hills (G-5334)	G	718 268-7900
Newburgh Envelope Corp, Newburgh (G-12792)	G	845 566-4211
Newport Graphics Inc, New York (G-11433)	E	212 924-2600
Newsgraphics of Delmar Inc, Delmar (G-4270)	E	518 439-5363
North Delaware Printing Inc, Tonawanda (G-16206)	G	716 692-0576
Northeast Commercial Prtg Inc, Albany (G-110)	G	518 459-5047
▲ Northeast Prtg & Dist Co Inc, Plattsburgh (G-13711)	E	518 563-8214
Northern NY Newspapers Corp, Watertown (G-16691)	C	315 782-1000
Observer Daily Sunday Newsppr, Dunkirk (G-4370)	D	716 366-3000
Office Grabs NY Inc, Brooklyn (G-2398)	E	212 444-1331
▼ Official Offset Corporation, Amityville (G-316)	E	631 957-8500
Old Ue LLC, Long Island City (G-7861)	B	718 707-0700
Olympic Press Inc, New York (G-11516)	F	212 242-4934
Orbis Brynmore Lithographics, New York (G-11533)	G	212 987-2100
Orffeo Printing & Imaging Inc, Lancaster (G-7352)	G	716 681-5757
▲ Orlandi Inc, Farmingdale (G-5081)	D	631 756-0110
Orlandi Inc, Farmingdale (G-5082)	E	631 756-0110
Ozipko Enterprises Inc, Rochester (G-14581)	G	585 424-6740
P & W Press Inc, New York (G-11560)	E	646 486-3417
P D R Inc, Plainview (G-13655)	G	516 829-5300
Pace Editions Inc, New York (G-11563)	F	212 675-7431
Paladino Prtg & Graphics Inc, Flushing (G-5284)	G	718 279-6000
Pama Enterprises Inc, Great Neck (G-5846)	G	516 504-6300
▲ Panther Graphics Inc, Rochester (G-14591)	E	585 546-7163
▲ Paper House Productions Inc, Saugerties (G-15219)	E	845 246-7261
Parkside Printing Co Inc, Jericho (G-7112)	F	516 933-5423
Parrinello Printing Inc, Buffalo (G-3138)	F	716 633-7780
Patrick Ryans Modern Press, Albany (G-115)	F	518 434-2921
▲ Paul Michael Group Inc, Ronkonkoma (G-14990)	G	631 585-5700
◆ Paxar Corporation, Orangeburg (G-13260)	E	845 398-3229
Paya Printing of NY Inc, Albertson (G-160)	G	516 625-8346
Peachtree Enterprises Inc, Long Island City (G-7868)	E	212 989-3445
Perception Imaging Inc, Holbrook (G-6495)	F	631 676-5262
Perfect Forms and Systems Inc, Smithtown (G-15517)	F	631 462-1100
Persch Service Print Inc, Dunkirk (G-4371)	G	716 366-2677
Petcap Press Corporation, Long Island City (G-7871)	F	718 609-0910
Petit Printing Corp, Getzville (G-5615)	G	716 871-9490
Phillip Tissicher, Brooklyn (G-2431)	F	718 282-3310
Phoenix Graphics Inc, Rochester (G-14601)	E	585 232-4040
Photo Agents Ltd, Huntington (G-6709)	G	631 421-0258
Pic A Poc Enterprises Inc, Ronkonkoma (G-14994)	G	631 981-2094
Pine Bush Printing Co Inc, Albany (G-122)	G	518 456-2431
Pioneer Printers Inc, North Tonawanda (G-13004)	F	716 693-7100
Platinum Printing & Graphics, Farmingdale (G-5092)	G	631 249-3325
Play-It Productions Inc, Port Washington (G-13873)	G	212 695-6530
Pollack Graphics Inc, New York (G-11703)	G	212 727-8400
Pop Printing Incorporated, Brooklyn (G-2442)	F	212 808-7800
Positive Print Litho Offset, New York (G-11710)	G	212 431-4850
Post Road, New York (G-11712)	F	203 545-2122
Pre Cycled Inc, Brewster (G-1225)	G	845 278-7611
Precision Envelope Co Inc, Farmingdale (G-5096)	G	631 694-3990
Preebro Printing, Brooklyn (G-2451)	G	718 633-7300
Press of Fremont Payne Inc, New York (G-11724)	G	212 966-6570
Presstek Printing LLC, Rochester (G-14621)	F	585 467-8140
Presstek Printing LLC, Rochester (G-14622)	F	585 266-2770
Prestige Envelope & Lithograph, Merrick (G-8426)	F	631 521-7043
Prestone Press LLC, Long Island City (G-7875)	C	347 468-7900
Pricet Printing, Cazenovia (G-3478)	G	315 655-0369
Print & Graphics Group, Clifton Park (G-3730)	G	518 371-4649
▲ Print Better Inc, Ridgewood (G-14131)	G	347 348-1841
Print By Premier LLC, New York (G-11736)	G	212 947-1365
Print Center Inc, Cold Spring Harbor (G-3795)	G	718 643-9559
Print Cottage LLC, Massapequa Park (G-8222)	F	516 369-1749
Print It Here, Massapequa (G-8213)	G	516 308-7785
Print It Inc, Monsey (G-8613)	G	845 371-2227
Print Management Group Inc, New York (G-11738)	G	212 213-1555
Print Market Inc, Deer Park (G-4218)	G	631 940-8181
▲ Print Media Inc, New York (G-11739)	D	212 563-4040
Print On Demand Initiative Inc, Rochester (G-14623)	F	585 239-6044
Print Seforim Bzul Inc, Brooklyn (G-2461)	G	718 679-1011
Print Shop, Horseheads (G-6617)	G	607 734-4937
Print Solutions Plus Inc, Liverpool (G-7571)	G	315 234-3801
Printcorp Inc, Ronkonkoma (G-14995)	F	631 696-0641
Printech Business Systems Inc, New York (G-11740)	F	212 290-2542
Printers 3 Inc, Hauppauge (G-6198)	G	631 351-1331
Printing Prep Inc, Buffalo (G-3163)	G	716 852-5071
Printing Resources Inc, Albany (G-124)	E	518 482-2470
Printing Sales Group Limited, Brooklyn (G-2464)	F	718 258-8860
Printing Spectrum Inc, East Setauket (G-4509)	F	631 689-1010
Printing X Press Ions, Dix Hills (G-4319)	G	631 242-1992
Printinghouse Press Ltd, New York (G-11742)	G	212 719-0990
Printroc Inc, Rochester (G-14624)	F	585 461-2556
Printutopia, Brooklyn (G-2466)	F	718 788-1545
Printz and Patternz LLC, Schenectady (G-15311)	G	518 944-6020
Pro Printing, Lynbrook (G-7983)	G	516 561-9700
Professional Solutions Print, Hauppauge (G-6200)	G	631 231-9300
Profile Printing & Graphics, Hauppauge (G-6201)	G	631 273-2727
Progressive Color Graphics, Great Neck (G-5851)	E	212 292-8787
Progressive Graphics & Prtg, Newark (G-12762)	G	315 331-3635
Prompt Printing Inc, Farmingdale (G-5099)	G	631 454-6524
Pronto Printer, Cortlandt Manor (G-4079)	G	914 737-0800
Psychonomic Society Inc, New York (G-11764)	E	512 381-1494
Quad/Graphics Inc, Long Island City (G-7881)	E	718 706-7600
Quad/Graphics Inc, Saratoga Springs (G-15198)	A	518 581-4000
Quad/Graphics Inc, New York (G-11791)	A	212 206-5535
Quad/Graphics Inc, New York (G-11792)	A	212 741-1001
Quadrangle Quickprints Ltd, Melville (G-8380)	G	631 694-4464
Quality Graphics Tri State, Pearl River (G-13489)	G	845 735-2523
Quantum Color Inc, Niagara Falls (G-12883)	E	716 283-8700
Quicker Printer Inc, Elmira (G-4712)	G	607 734-8622
Quickprint, Canandaigua (G-3386)	F	585 394-2600
R & J Graphics Inc, Farmingdale (G-5105)	F	631 293-6611
R & L Press Inc, Staten Island (G-15747)	G	718 447-8557
R & L Press of SI Inc, Staten Island (G-15748)	G	718 667-3258
R D Printing Associates Inc, Farmingdale (G-5106)	F	631 390-5964
▲ R Hochman Papers Incorporated, Brooklyn (G-2491)	F	516 466-6414
Raith America Inc, Troy (G-16274)	E	518 874-3000
Rapid Print and Marketing Inc, Victor (G-16523)	F	585 924-1520
Rapid Rays Printing & Copying, Buffalo (G-3179)	G	716 852-0550
Rapid Reproductions LLC, Oxford (G-13389)	G	607 843-2221
Rapid Service Engraving Co, Buffalo (G-3180)	G	716 896-4555
Rasco Graphics Inc, New York (G-11828)	G	212 206-0447
RBHM Incorporated, Brooklyn (G-2500)	F	609 259-4900
Ready Check Glo Inc, East Northport (G-4463)	G	516 547-1849
Redi Records Payroll, Brooklyn (G-2505)	F	718 854-6990
Reflex Offset Inc, Deer Park (G-4224)	G	516 746-4142
Register Graphics Inc, Randolph (G-14031)	E	716 358-2921
REM Printing Inc, Albany (G-130)	G	518 438-7338
Remsen Graphics Corp, Brooklyn (G-2510)	G	718 643-7500
Resonant Legal Media LLC, New York (G-11872)	E	212 687-7100
Resonant Legal Media LLC, New York (G-11873)	D	800 781-3591
Rgm Signs Inc, Staten Island (G-15754)	G	718 442-0598
Rheinwald Printing Co Inc, Brockport (G-1246)	F	585 637-5100
Richard Ruffner, Central Islip (G-3536)	F	631 234-4600
RIT Printing Corp, Bay Shore (G-731)	F	631 586-6220
Rmd Holding Inc, Mahopac (G-8031)	G	845 628-0030

Rmf Print Management Group..............F 716 683-4351
Depew (G-4297)
Robert Portegello Graphics..................G....... 718 241-8118
Brooklyn (G-2521)
Robert Tabatznik Assoc Inc..................F 845 336-4555
Kingston (G-7237)
Rosemont Press Incorporated..............E 212 239-4770
New York (G-11935)
Rosen Mandell & Immerman Inc...........E 212 691-2277
New York (G-11936)
Royal Tees Inc..G....... 845 357-9448
Suffern (G-15820)
Rv Printing..G....... 631 567-8658
Holbrook (G-6498)
Ry-Gan Printing Inc ....G....... 585 482-7770
Rochester (G-14684)
Ryan Printing Inc ....E 845 535-3235
Blauvelt (G-969)
Sammba Printing Inc..............................G....... 516 944-4449
Port Washington (G-13879)
Sample News Group LLC.......................D....... 315 343-3800
Oswego (G-13365)
Sand Hill Industries Inc.........................G....... 518 885-7991
Ballston Spa (G-607)
▲ Sanford Printing Inc...........................G....... 718 461-1202
Flushing (G-5298)
Scotti Graphics Inc................................E 212 367-9602
Long Island City (G-7901)
Scriven Duplicating Service..................G....... 518 233-8180
Troy (G-16277)
SDS Business Cards Inc.......................F 516 747-3131
Syosset (G-15860)
Seaboard Graphic Services LLC..........E 315 652-4200
Liverpool (G-7574)
Searles Graphics Inc ....E 631 345-2202
Yaphank (G-17417)
Security Offset Services Inc.................G....... 631 944-6031
Huntington (G-6719)
Seifert Graphics Inc...............................F 315 736-2744
Oriskany (G-13337)
Select-A-Form Inc..................................D....... 631 981-3076
Holbrook (G-6499)
Seneca West Printing Inc......................G....... 716 675-8010
West Seneca (G-16983)
Sentinel Printing Inc..............................G....... 516 334-7400
Westbury (G-17054)
Shield Press Inc......................................G....... 212 431-7489
New York (G-12071)
Shipman Printing Inds Inc.....................E 716 504-7700
Niagara Falls (G-12893)
Shipman Printing Inds Inc.....................G....... 716 504-7700
Sanborn (G-15155)
Shipmtes/Printmates Holdg Corp..........D....... 518 370-1158
Scotia (G-15353)
Shoreline Publishing Inc........................G....... 914 738-7869
Pelham (G-13519)
Sign World Inc...E 212 619-9000
Brooklyn (G-2581)
Sizzal LLC..E 212 354-6123
Long Island City (G-7907)
Sloane Design Inc...................................G....... 212 539-0184
Brooklyn (G-2599)
Source Envelope Inc...............................G....... 866 284-0707
Farmingdale (G-5122)
Source One Promotional Product.........G....... 516 208-6996
Merrick (G-8428)
South Bridge Press Inc...........................G....... 212 233-4047
New York (G-12169)
Spectrum Prtg Lithography Inc.............F 212 255-3131
New York (G-12182)
Speedcard Inc ....G....... 631 472-1904
Holbrook (G-6501)
Speedway Press Inc................................G....... 315 343-3531
Oswego (G-13366)
Sputnick 84 LLC......................................G....... 844 667-7468
New York (G-12200)
St Gerard Enterprises Inc.......................F 631 473-2003
Port Jeff STA (G-13793)
St James Printing Inc..............................G....... 631 981-2095
Ronkonkoma (G-15012)
▲ St Lawrence County Newspapers....D....... 315 393-1003
Ogdensburg (G-13143)
St Vincent Press Inc................................F 585 325-5320
Rochester (G-14723)
▲ Standwill Packaging Inc.....................E 631 752-1236
Farmingdale (G-5124)
Star Press Pearl River Inc......................G....... 845 268-2294
Valley Cottage (G-16415)
▲ Star Quality Printing Inc....................F 631 273-1900
Hauppauge (G-6224)

Steffen Publishing Inc............................D....... 315 865-4100
Holland Patent (G-6514)
Sterling North America Inc....................E 631 243-6933
Hauppauge (G-6225)
▼ Sterling Pierce Company Inc............E 516 593-1170
East Rockaway (G-4492)
Sterling United Inc.................................G....... 716 835-9290
Amherst (G-262)
Steval Graphics Concepts Inc...............F 516 576-0220
Plainview (G-13663)
Stevens Bandes Graphics Corp............F 212 675-1128
New York (G-12226)
Stevenson Printing Co Inc.....................G....... 516 676-1233
Glen Cove (G-5642)
Stony Brook University..........................E 631 632-6434
Stony Brook (G-15793)
Stony Point Graphics Ltd.......................G....... 845 786-3322
Stony Point (G-15799)
Stubbs Printing Inc.................................G....... 315 769-8641
Massena (G-8232)
Studley Printing & Publishing................F 518 563-1414
Plattsburgh (G-13730)
Stylistic Press Inc...................................F 212 675-0797
New York (G-12247)
Suffolk Copy Center Inc.........................G....... 631 665-0570
Bay Shore (G-740)
Summit MSP LLC....................................G....... 716 433-1014
Lockport (G-7646)
Summit Print & Mail LLC........................G....... 716 433-1014
Lockport (G-7647)
Sun Printing Incorporated......................E 607 337-3034
Norwich (G-13055)
Superior Print On Demand.....................G....... 607 240-5231
Vestal (G-16478)
Syracuse Computer Forms Inc..............E 315 478-0108
Syracuse (G-16075)
Sz - Design & Print Inc...........................F 845 352-0395
Monsey (G-8618)
T C Peters Printing Co Inc.....................G....... 315 724-4149
Utica (G-16385)
Taylor..G....... 518 954-2832
Amsterdam (G-369)
Technipoly Manufacturing Inc...............E 718 383-0363
Brooklyn (G-2671)
▲ Tele-Pak Inc...E 845 426-2300
Monsey (G-8620)
Teller Printing Corp.................................G....... 718 486-3662
Brooklyn (G-2674)
The Kingsbury Printing Co Inc...............G....... 518 747-6606
Hudson Falls (G-6681)
The Nugent Organization Inc.................F 212 645-6600
Oceanside (G-13123)
Thomas Group Inc...................................F 212 947-6400
New York (G-12340)
Three Star Offset Printing.......................F 516 867-8223
Freeport (G-5442)
Tobay Printing Co Inc.............................E 631 842-3300
Copiague (G-3957)
Tom & Jerry Printcraft Forms.................E 914 777-7468
Mamaroneck (G-8081)
Top Copi Reproductions Inc...................F 212 571-4141
New York (G-12389)
▲ Toppan Printing Co Amer Inc............E 212 596-7747
New York (G-12391)
Torsaf Printers Inc...................................G....... 516 569-5577
Hewlett (G-6337)
Total Concept Graphic Inc......................G....... 212 229-2626
New York (G-12399)
Tovie Asarese Royal Prtg Co.................G....... 716 885-7692
Buffalo (G-3249)
Trade Mark Graphics Inc.........................G....... 718 306-0001
Brooklyn (G-2692)
Transaction Printer Group......................G....... 607 274-2500
Ithaca (G-6915)
◆ Transcntinental Ultra Flex Inc...........B....... 718 272-9100
Brooklyn (G-2693)
Transcontinental Printing GP.................G....... 716 626-3078
Amherst (G-267)
Tremont Offset Inc...................................G....... 718 892-7333
Bronx (G-1472)
Tri Kolor Printing & Sty...........................F 315 474-6753
Syracuse (G-16085)
Tri-Lon Clor Lithographers Ltd...............E 212 255-6140
New York (G-12421)
Tri-Star Offset Corp.................................E 718 894-5555
Maspeth (G-8203)
Tri-Town News Inc...................................E 607 561-3515
Sidney (G-15464)
Triad Printing Inc.....................................G....... 845 343-2722
Middletown (G-8501)

Tripi Engraving Co Inc............................E 718 383-6500
Brooklyn (G-2700)
Tropp Printing Corp.................................G....... 212 233-4519
New York (G-12431)
Troy Sign & Printing ....G....... 718 994-4482
Bronx (G-1478)
Tucker Printers Inc..................................D....... 585 359-3030
Henrietta (G-6322)
▲ Twenty-First Century Press Inc........F 716 837-0800
Buffalo (G-3254)
Twin Counties Pro Printers Inc..............F 518 828-3278
Hudson (G-6667)
Unicom Graphic Communications........G....... 212 221-2456
New York (G-12469)
Upstate Printing Inc.................................F 315 475-6140
Syracuse (G-16088)
V & J Graphics Inc...................................G....... 315 363-1933
Oneida (G-13191)
V C N Group Ltd Inc.................................G....... 516 223-4812
North Baldwin (G-12928)
Valentine Printing Corp...........................G....... 718 444-4400
Brooklyn (G-2734)
Vanguard Graphics LLC..........................C....... 607 272-1212
Ithaca (G-6916)
▲ Variable Graphics LLC........................G....... 212 691-2323
New York (G-12528)
Vectra Inc..G....... 718 361-1000
Long Island City (G-7940)
Veterans Offset Printing Inc...................G....... 585 288-2900
Rochester (G-14781)
Viatech Pubg Solutions Inc.....................E 631 968-8500
Bay Shore (G-747)
Vic-Gina Printing Company Inc..............G....... 914 636-0200
New Rochelle (G-8973)
Vicks Lithograph & Prtg Corp.................C....... 315 736-9344
Yorkville (G-17545)
Vicks Lithograph & Prtg Corp.................C....... 315 272-2401
Yorkville (G-17544)
Vincys Printing Ltd..................................F 518 355-4363
Schenectady (G-15333)
VIP Printing..G....... 718 641-9361
Howard Beach (G-6627)
▲ Virgil Mountain Inc..............................G....... 212 378-0007
New York (G-12574)
Vivona Business Printers Inc..................G....... 516 496-3453
Syosset (G-15862)
Wall Street Business Pdts Inc.................E 212 563-4014
New York (G-12608)
Wallkill Valley Publications.....................E 845 561-0170
Newburgh (G-12810)
Walnut Printing Inc...................................G....... 718 707-0100
Long Island City (G-7947)
Wappingers Falls Shopper Inc...............E 845 297-3723
Wappingers Falls (G-16598)
Warren Printing Inc..................................F 212 627-5000
Long Island City (G-7948)
Wayne Printing Inc...................................F 914 761-2400
White Plains (G-17210)
Webb-Mason Inc.......................................E 716 276-8792
Buffalo (G-3276)
Webster Printing Corporation.................F 585 671-1533
Webster (G-16768)
Weeks & Reichel Printing Inc.................G....... 631 589-1443
Sayville (G-15244)
Weicro Graphics Inc................................E 631 253-3360
West Babylon (G-16872)
Westchester Mailing Service..................E 914 948-1116
White Plains (G-17212)
Westmore Litho Corp..............................G....... 718 361-9403
Long Island City (G-7950)
Westypo Printers Inc...............................G....... 914 737-7394
Peekskill (G-13512)
William Boyd Printing Co Inc..................C....... 518 339-5832
Latham (G-7411)
William Charles Prtg Co Inc...................E 516 349-0900
Plainview (G-13674)
William J Kline & Son Inc........................D....... 518 843-1100
Amsterdam (G-374)
William J Ryan..G....... 585 392-6200
Hilton (G-6447)
Wilson Press LLC.....................................E 315 568-9693
Seneca Falls (G-15395)
Winner Press Inc......................................E 718 937-7715
Long Island City (G-7953)
Winson Surnamer Inc..............................G....... 718 729-8787
Long Island City (G-7954)
▲ Won & Lee Inc......................................E 516 222-0712
Garden City (G-5552)
Woodbury Printing Plus + Inc.................G....... 845 928-6610
Central Valley (G-3557)

S
I
C

Employee Codes: A=Over 500 employees, B=251-500
C=101-250, D=51-100, E=20-50, F=10-19, G=5-9
2018 Harris
New York Manufacturers Directory
769

Worldwide Ticket Craft ....D.... 516 538-6200
Merrick (G-8429)
Wynco Press One Inc ....G.... 516 354-6145
Glen Oaks (G-5656)
X Myles Mar Inc ....E.... 212 683-2015
New York (G-12699)
X-L Envelope and Printing Inc ....F.... 716 852-2135
Buffalo (G-3284)
Yorktown Printing Corp ....C.... 914 962-2526
Yorktown Heights (G-17538)
Zacmel Graphics LLC ....G.... 631 944-6031
Deer Park (G-4256)
Zenger Group Inc ....E.... 716 871-1058
Tonawanda (G-16238)
Zenger Partners LLC ....E.... 716 876-2284
Kenmore (G-7181)

2754 Commercial Printing: Gravure

Adflex Corporation ....E.... 585 454-2950
Rochester (G-14189)
Advanced Printing New York Inc ....G.... 212 840-8108
New York (G-9093)
Alamar Printing Inc ....F.... 914 993-9007
White Plains (G-17102)
Alfa Card Inc ....G.... 718 326-7107
Glendale (G-5658)
▲ American Packaging Corporation ....C.... 585 254-9500
Rochester (G-14214)
American Print Solutions Inc ....G.... 718 208-2309
Brooklyn (G-1605)
▲ Ashton-Potter USA Ltd ....C.... 716 633-2000
Williamsville (G-17261)
Benton Announcements Inc ....F.... 716 836-4100
Buffalo (G-2861)
C C Industries Inc ....F.... 518 581-7633
Saratoga Springs (G-15174)
Clarion Publications Inc ....F.... 585 243-3530
Geneseo (G-5579)
▲ Clintrak Clinical Labeling S ....D.... 888 479-3900
Bohemia (G-1031)
Color Industries LLC ....G.... 718 392-8301
Long Island City (G-7731)
Copy Corner Inc ....G.... 718 388-4545
Brooklyn (G-1802)
Dijifi LLC ....F.... 646 519-2447
Brooklyn (G-1864)
Ecoplast & Packaging LLC ....G.... 718 996-0800
Brooklyn (G-1902)
▲ Gemini Manufacturing LLC ....C.... 914 375-0855
White Plains (G-17139)
◆ Gruner + Jahr USA Group Inc ....B.... 866 323-9336
New York (G-10419)
Image Sales & Marketing Inc ....G.... 516 238-7023
Massapequa Park (G-8219)
Jack J Florio Jr ....G.... 716 434-9123
Lockport (G-7625)
Janco Press Inc ....F.... 631 563-3003
Bohemia (G-1077)
Karr Graphics Corp ....E.... 212 645-6000
Long Island City (G-7806)
Kinaneco Inc ....E.... 315 468-6201
Syracuse (G-15994)
Krepe Kraft Inc ....B.... 716 826-7086
Buffalo (G-3055)
Lane Park Graphics Inc ....G.... 914 273-5898
Patterson (G-13466)
Leonardo Printing Corp ....G.... 914 664-7890
Mount Vernon (G-8746)
Liberty Label Mfg Inc ....F.... 631 737-2365
Holbrook (G-6486)
Mastro Graphic Arts Inc ....E.... 585 436-7570
Rochester (G-14520)
McG Graphics Inc ....G.... 631 499-0730
Dix Hills (G-4317)
Mod-Pac Corp ....D.... 716 447-9013
Buffalo (G-3092)
Mrs John L Strong & Co LLC ....F.... 212 838-3775
New York (G-11340)
Mutual Engraving Company Inc ....D.... 516 489-0534
West Hempstead (G-16893)
▲ Niagara Label Company Inc ....F.... 716 542-3000
Akron (G-22)
Paya Printing of NY Inc ....G.... 516 625-8346
Albertson (G-160)
Sommer and Sons Printing Inc ....F.... 716 822-4311
Buffalo (G-3218)
SRC Liquidation Company ....G.... 716 631-3900
Williamsville (G-17280)
▲ Tele-Pak Inc ....E.... 845 426-2300
Monsey (G-8620)
Trust of Colum Unive In The Ci ....F.... 212 854-2793
New York (G-12434)

2759 Commercial Printing

2 1 2 Postcards Inc ....E.... 212 767-8227
New York (G-9008)
4 Over 4com Inc ....G.... 718 932-2700
Astoria (G-428)
461 New Lots Avenue LLC ....G.... 347 303-9305
Brooklyn (G-1518)
5 Stars Printing Corp ....F.... 718 461-4612
Flushing (G-5227)
6727 11th Ave Corp ....F.... 718 837-8787
Brooklyn (G-1520)
A & A Graphics Inc II ....G.... 516 735-0078
Seaford (G-15365)
A C Envelope Inc ....G.... 516 420-0646
Farmingdale (G-4933)
▲ A Graphic Printing Inc ....G.... 212 233-9696
New York (G-9034)
A M & J Digital ....G.... 518 434-2579
Menands (G-8395)
A Tradition of Excellence Inc ....G.... 845 638-4595
New City (G-8828)
A&P Master Images LLC ....F.... 315 793-1934
Utica (G-16328)
◆ Abigal Press Inc ....D.... 718 641-5350
Ozone Park (G-13401)
Academy Printing Services Inc ....G.... 631 765-3346
Southold (G-15581)
Accel Printing & Graphics ....G.... 914 241-3369
Mount Kisco (G-8663)
Acme Screenprinting LLC ....G.... 716 565-1052
Buffalo (G-2812)
Actioncraft Products Inc ....G.... 516 883-6423
Port Washington (G-13818)
▲ Active World Solutions Inc ....G.... 718 922-9404
Brooklyn (G-1558)
Ad Publications Inc ....F.... 585 248-2888
Pittsford (G-13584)
Adco Innvtive Prmtnal Pdts Inc ....G.... 716 805-1076
Buffalo (G-2813)
Adflex Corporation ....E.... 585 454-2950
Rochester (G-14189)
Adirondack Pennysaver Inc ....E.... 518 563-0100
Plattsburgh (G-13678)
Advance Finance Group LLC ....D.... 212 630-5900
New York (G-9084)
▼ Advanced Graphics Company ....F.... 607 692-7875
Whitney Point (G-17248)
Albert Siy ....G.... 718 359-0389
Flushing (G-5231)
Aldine Inc (ny) ....D.... 212 226-2870
New York (G-9129)
Alicia F Herdlein ....G.... 585 344-4411
Batavia (G-621)
▲ Allsafe Technologies Inc ....D.... 716 691-0400
Amherst (G-225)
Alpina Copyworld Inc ....F.... 212 683-3511
New York (G-9152)
Alpine Business Group Inc ....G.... 212 989-4198
New York (G-9153)
▲ Alvin J Bart & Sons Inc ....C.... 718 417-1300
Glendale (G-5660)
Always Printing ....G.... 914 481-5209
Port Chester (G-13767)
AMA Precision Screening Inc ....F.... 585 293-0820
Churchville (G-3663)
Amax Printing Inc ....F.... 718 384-8600
Maspeth (G-8144)
◆ American Casting and Mfg Corp ....D.... 800 342-0333
Plainview (G-13611)
American Office Supply Inc ....F.... 516 294-9444
Westbury (G-16994)
Amerikom Group Inc ....D.... 212 675-1329
New York (G-9183)
Amsterdam Printing & Litho Inc ....F.... 518 792-6501
Queensbury (G-14003)
Ansun Graphics Inc ....F.... 315 437-6869
Syracuse (G-15874)
Apple Enterprises Inc ....E.... 718 361-2200
Long Island City (G-7695)
April Printing Co Inc ....F.... 212 685-7455
New York (G-9235)
Arca Ink LLC ....G.... 518 798-0100
South Glens Falls (G-15546)
Arena Graphics Inc ....G.... 516 767-5108
Port Washington (G-13823)
Argo Envelope Corp ....D.... 718 729-2700
Long Island City (G-7700)
Argo Lithographers Inc ....E.... 718 729-2700
Long Island City (G-7702)
Arista Innovations Inc ....E.... 516 746-2262
Mineola (G-8529)
▲ Artistic Typography Corp ....G.... 212 463-8880
New York (G-9272)
Artistics Printing Corp ....G.... 516 561-2121
Franklin Square (G-5370)
Artscroll Printing Corp ....E.... 212 929-2413
New York (G-9275)
▲ Ashton-Potter USA Ltd ....C.... 716 633-2000
Williamsville (G-17261)
Asn Inc ....E.... 718 894-0800
Maspeth (G-8149)
Aspect Printing Inc ....E.... 347 789-4284
Brooklyn (G-1642)
Astro Label & Tag Ltd ....G.... 718 435-4474
Brooklyn (G-1643)
▲ Bags Unlimited Inc ....E.... 585 436-6282
Rochester (G-14238)
Balajee Enterprises Inc ....G.... 212 629-6150
New York (G-9361)
Barnaby Prints Inc ....F.... 845 477-2501
Greenwood Lake (G-5917)
Bartolomeo Publishing Inc ....G.... 631 420-4949
West Babylon (G-16799)
Batavia Legal Printing Inc ....G.... 585 768-2100
Le Roy (G-7428)
Batavia Press LLC ....E.... 585 343-4429
Batavia (G-625)
Bates Jackson Engraving Co Inc ....E.... 716 854-3000
Buffalo (G-2855)
Bco Industries Western NY Inc ....E.... 716 877-2800
Tonawanda (G-16165)
BDR Creative Concepts Inc ....F.... 516 942-7768
Farmingdale (G-4959)
Bedford Freeman & Worth ....C.... 212 576-9400
New York (G-9391)
Beebie Printing & Art Agcy Inc ....G.... 518 725-4528
Gloversville (G-5723)
Beis Moshiach Inc ....E.... 718 778-8000
Brooklyn (G-1676)
▲ Benchemark Printing Inc ....D.... 518 393-1361
Schenectady (G-15262)
Berkshire Business Forms Inc ....F.... 518 828-2600
Hudson (G-6639)
Bestype Digital Imaging LLC ....F.... 212 966-6886
New York (G-9421)
Bfc Print Network Inc ....G.... 716 838-4532
Amherst (G-230)
Bidpress LLC ....G.... 267 973-8876
New York (G-9438)
▲ Big Apple Sign Corp ....E.... 212 629-3650
New York (G-9441)
Bizbash Media Inc ....E.... 646 638-3600
New York (G-9457)
▲ Bobley-Harmann Corporation ....G.... 516 433-3800
Ronkonkoma (G-14908)
Body Builders Inc ....G.... 718 492-7997
Brooklyn (G-1707)
Bondy Printing Corp ....G.... 631 242-1510
Bay Shore (G-677)
BP Beyond Printing Inc ....G.... 516 328-2700
Hempstead (G-6290)
Bradley Marketing Group Inc ....G.... 212 967-6100
New York (G-9501)
Bridge Fulfillment Inc ....G.... 718 625-6622
Brooklyn (G-1715)
Brodock Press Inc ....D.... 315 735-9577
Utica (G-16333)
Brooks Litho Digital Group Inc ....G.... 631 789-4500
Deer Park (G-4136)
Buffalo Newspress Inc ....C.... 716 852-1600
Buffalo (G-2880)
Burr & Son Inc ....G.... 315 446-1550
Syracuse (G-15896)
Business Card Express Inc ....E.... 631 669-3400
West Babylon (G-16804)
C & C Athletic Inc ....G.... 845 713-4670
Walden (G-16550)
C F Print Ltd Inc ....F.... 631 567-2110
Deer Park (G-4137)
Cama Graphics Inc ....F.... 718 707-9747
Long Island City (G-7723)
Candid Worldwide LLC ....G.... 212 799-5300
Farmingdale (G-4966)
Carib Prints Ltd ....F.... 646 210-2863
Bronx (G-1290)
▲ Casual Home Worldwide Inc ....G.... 631 789-2999
Amityville (G-279)

27 PRINTING, PUBLISHING, AND ALLIED INDUSTRIES

▲ Century Direct LLC .... C 212 763-0600
  Islandia (G-6827)
Chakra Communications Inc .... E 607 748-7491
  Endicott (G-4806)
Check-O-Matic Inc .... G 845 781-7675
  Monroe (G-8587)
Chenango Union Printing Inc .... G 607 334-2112
  Norwich (G-13040)
Christian Bus Endeavors Inc .... F 315 788-8560
  Watertown (G-16665)
Chroma Communications Inc .... G 631 289-8871
  Medford (G-8271)
CHv Printed Company .... F 516 997-1101
  East Meadow (G-4439)
Citiforms Inc .... E 212 334-9671
  New York (G-9676)
Classic Album .... E 718 388-2818
  Brooklyn (G-1785)
Classic Labels Inc .... E 631 467-2300
  Patchogue (G-13442)
Clear Channel Outdoor Inc .... F 212 812-0000
  New York (G-9696)
Colad Group LLC .... D 716 961-1776
  Buffalo (G-2900)
Colonial Label Systems Inc .... E 631 254-0111
  Bay Shore (G-683)
▲ Colonial Tag & Label Co Inc .... F 516 482-0508
  Great Neck (G-5816)
Color Card LLC .... F 631 232-1300
  Central Islip (G-3516)
Comgraph Sales Service .... G 716 601-7243
  Elma (G-4660)
Commercial Press Inc .... G 315 274-0028
  Canton (G-3407)
Control Research Inc .... G 631 225-1111
  Amityville (G-281)
Cooper & Clement Inc .... E 315 454-8135
  Syracuse (G-15926)
Copy Room Inc .... F 212 371-8600
  New York (G-9781)
Copy X/Press Ltd .... D 631 585-2200
  Ronkonkoma (G-14916)
CPW Direct Mail Group LLC .... G 631 588-6565
  Farmingdale (G-4975)
Craig Envelope Corp .... E 718 786-4277
  Hicksville (G-6361)
Create-A-Card Inc .... G 631 584-2273
  Saint James (G-15114)
Crisray Printing Corp .... E 631 293-3770
  Farmingdale (G-4976)
Curtis Prtg Co The Del Press .... G 518 477-4820
  East Greenbush (G-4421)
Custom 101 Prints Inc .... F 718 708-4425
  Bronx (G-1309)
Custom Prtrs Guilderland Inc .... F 518 456-2811
  Guilderland (G-5924)
Custom Sportswear Corp .... G 914 666-9200
  Bedford Hills (G-797)
D B F Associates .... G 718 328-0005
  Bronx (G-1310)
D G M Graphics Inc .... F 516 223-2220
  Merrick (G-8416)
D3 Repro Group .... G 347 507-1075
  Long Island City (G-7738)
DArcy Printing and Lithog .... E 212 924-1554
  New York (G-9863)
Dash Printing Inc .... G 212 643-8534
  New York (G-9866)
Data Flow Inc .... G 631 436-9200
  Medford (G-8273)
▲ Data Palette Info Svcs LLC .... D 718 433-1060
  Port Washington (G-13830)
Delft Printing Inc .... G 716 683-1100
  Lancaster (G-7335)
Dental Tribune America LLC .... F 212 244-7181
  New York (G-9901)
▲ Design Distributors Inc .... D 631 242-2000
  Deer Park (G-4152)
DEW Graphics Inc .... E 212 727-4820
  New York (G-9917)
Diamond Inscription Tech .... F 646 366-7944
  New York (G-9926)
Digital Brewery LLC .... G 646 665-2106
  Astoria (G-435)
Digital Evolution Inc .... E 212 732-2722
  New York (G-9929)
Direct Print Inc .... F 212 987-6003
  New York (G-9934)
Dit Prints Incorporated .... G 518 885-4400
  Ballston Spa (G-593)

Diversified Envelope Ltd .... F 585 615-4697
  Rochester (G-14333)
Division Den-Bar Enterprises .... G 914 381-2220
  Mamaroneck (G-8065)
Dkm Sales LLC .... E 716 893-7777
  Buffalo (G-2932)
Doctor Print Inc .... E 631 873-4560
  Hauppauge (G-6088)
Donald Bruhnke .... F 212 600-1260
  New York (G-9949)
Doremus FP LLC .... E 212 366-3800
  New York (G-9960)
▲ Drns Corp .... F 718 369-4530
  Brooklyn (G-1883)
Dupli Graphics Corporation .... C 315 234-7286
  Syracuse (G-15945)
Dupli Graphics Corporation .... G 315 422-4732
  Syracuse (G-15946)
Dutchess Plumbing & Heating .... G 845 889-8255
  Staatsburg (G-15638)
Dynamic Packaging Inc .... F 718 388-0800
  Brooklyn (G-1888)
E&I Printing .... F 212 206-0506
  New York (G-10006)
Eagle Envelope Company Inc .... G 607 387-3195
  Syracuse (G-15948)
East Coast Thermographers Inc .... E 718 321-3211
  College Point (G-3807)
Eastwood Litho Inc .... G 315 437-2626
  Syracuse (G-15950)
Edgian Press Inc .... G 516 931-2114
  Hicksville (G-6371)
Efficiency Printing Co Inc .... G 914 949-8611
  White Plains (G-17129)
Efs Designs .... G 718 852-9511
  Brooklyn (G-1908)
Ehs Group LLC .... G 914 937-6162
  Port Chester (G-13772)
Elm Graphics Inc .... G 315 737-5984
  New Hartford (G-8848)
Empire Business Forms Inc .... F 845 471-5666
  Poughkeepsie (G-13917)
Endeavor Printing LLC .... G 718 570-2720
  Long Island City (G-7760)
Enterprise Press Inc .... C 212 741-2111
  New York (G-10096)
Evenhouse Printing .... G 716 649-2666
  Hamburg (G-2959)
Evergreen Corp Central NY .... F 315 454-4175
  Syracuse (G-15959)
Excell Print & Promotions Inc .... G 914 437-8668
  White Plains (G-17133)
Excellent Printing Inc .... G 718 384-7272
  Brooklyn (G-1949)
Excelsus Solutions LLC .... E 585 533-0003
  Rochester (G-14384)
Exotic Print and Paper Inc .... F 212 807-0465
  New York (G-10160)
▲ Expedi-Printing Inc .... C 516 513-0919
  Great Neck (G-5822)
Eye Graphics & Printing Inc .... G 718 488-0606
  Brooklyn (G-1953)
F & B Photo Offset Co Inc .... G 516 431-5433
  Island Park (G-6819)
F A Printing .... G 212 974-5982
  New York (G-10168)
Fairmount Press .... G 212 255-2300
  New York (G-10183)
Falconer Printing & Design Inc ..... F 716 665-2121
  Falconer (G-4906)
Farthing Press Inc .... G 716 852-4674
  Buffalo (G-2959)
Federal Envelope Inc .... F 212 243-8380
  New York (G-10201)
Fedex Office & Print Svcs Inc .... G 718 982-5223
  Staten Island (G-15694)
Fineline Thermographers Inc .... G 718 643-1100
  Brooklyn (G-1976)
First2print Inc .... E 212 868-6886
  New York (G-10222)
▲ Flexo Transparent LLC .... C 716 825-7710
  Buffalo (G-2966)
Flp Group LLC .... F 315 252-7583
  Auburn (G-495)
Force Digital Media Inc .... G 631 243-0243
  Deer Park (G-4165)
Forward Enterprises Inc .... F 585 235-7670
  Rochester (G-14401)
Franklin Packaging Inc .... G 631 582-8900
  Northport (G-13029)

Fred Weidner & Son Printers .... G 212 964-8676
  New York (G-10254)
Frederick Coon Inc .... E 716 683-6812
  Elma (G-4661)
▲ Freeport Screen & Stamping ..... E 516 379-0330
  Freeport (G-5412)
Freeville Publishing Co Inc .... F 607 844-9119
  Freeville (G-5447)
Fresh Prints LLC .... E 917 826-2752
  New York (G-10259)
Fulcrum Promotions & Prtg LLC ... G 203 909-6362
  New York (G-10269)
G&J Graphics Inc .... G 718 409-9874
  Bronx (G-1342)
▲ Gallant Graphics Ltd .... G 845 868-1166
  Stanfordville (G-15647)
Garrett J Cronin .... G 914 761-9299
  White Plains (G-17137)
Gary Stock Corporation .... G 914 276-2700
  Croton Falls (G-4087)
▲ Gatehouse Media LLC .... C 585 598-0030
  Pittsford (G-13589)
Gazette Press Inc .... E 914 963-8300
  Rye (G-15082)
GE Healthcare Fincl Svcs Inc .... G 212 713-2000
  New York (G-10308)
Gem Reproduction Services Corp G 845 298-0172
  Wappingers Falls (G-16590)
Gem West Inc .... G 631 567-4228
  Patchogue (G-13445)
Gemson Graphics Inc .... E 516 873-8400
  Albertson (G-158)
General Business Supply Inc .... D 518 720-3939
  Watervliet (G-16709)
General Trade Mark La .... E 718 979-7261
  Staten Island (G-15698)
Genesis One Unlimited .... G 516 208-5863
  West Hempstead (G-16885)
Genie Instant Printing Co Inc .... F 212 575-8258
  New York (G-10321)
Golos Printing Inc .... G 607 732-1896
  Elmira Heights (G-4723)
Grado Group Inc .... G 718 556-4200
  Staten Island (G-15701)
Grand Meridian Printing Inc .... E 718 937-3888
  Long Island City (G-7781)
Graph-Tex Inc .... F 607 756-7791
  Cortland (G-4049)
Graph-Tex Inc .... G 607 756-1875
  Cortland (G-4050)
Graphic Lab Inc .... E 212 682-1815
  New York (G-10394)
Graphic Printing .... G 718 701-4433
  Bronx (G-1350)
Graphics 247 Corp .... G 718 729-2470
  Long Island City (G-7782)
Graphics For Industry Inc .... F 212 889-6202
  New York (G-10395)
Graphics Plus Printing Inc .... E 607 299-0500
  Cortland (G-4051)
Greenbush Tape & Label Inc .... E 518 465-2389
  Albany (G-83)
Grover Cleveland Press Inc .... F 716 564-2222
  Amherst (G-243)
Gruber Display Co Inc .... G 718 882-8220
  Bronx (G-1351)
H T L & S Ltd .... F 718 435-4474
  Brooklyn (G-2059)
Haig Press Inc .... E 631 582-5800
  Hauppauge (G-6111)
▲ Hammer Packaging Corp .... B 585 424-3880
  West Henrietta (G-16914)
Handone Studios Inc .... G 585 421-8175
  Fairport (G-4862)
Harmon and Castella Printing .... F 845 471-9163
  Poughkeepsie (G-13925)
Hart Reproduction Services .... G 212 704-0556
  New York (G-10468)
Hearst Corporation .... B 212 767-5800
  New York (G-10485)
Herrmann Group LLC .... G 716 876-9798
  Kenmore (G-7176)
HI Speed Envelope Co Inc .... F 718 617-1600
  Mount Vernon (G-8735)
Hi-Tech Packg World-Wide LLC .... G 845 947-1912
  New Windsor (G-8985)
Hill Crest Press .... G 518 943-0671
  Catskill (G-3457)
Horace J Metz .... G 716 873-9103
  Kenmore (G-7177)

Employee Codes: A=Over 500 employees, B=251-500
C=101-250, D=51-100, E=20-50, F=10-19, G=5-9

27 PRINTING, PUBLISHING, AND ALLIED INDUSTRIES

Company	Code	Phone
Hospitality Inc, New York (G-10554)	E	212 268-1930
Hudson Envelope Corporation, New York (G-10569)	E	212 473-6666
Human Technologies Corporation, Utica (G-16364)	F	315 735-3532
▲ I N K T Inc, New York (G-10586)	F	212 957-2700
Idc Printing & Sty Co Inc, Lynbrook (G-7979)	G	516 599-0400
Image Typography Inc, Holbrook (G-6479)	G	631 218-6932
▲ Impress Graphic Technologies, Westbury (G-17023)	F	516 781-0845
Impressive Imprints, North Tonawanda (G-12994)	F	716 692-0905
Incodema3d LLC, Freeville (G-5449)	E	607 269-4390
Industrial Test Eqp Co Inc, Port Washington (G-13846)	E	516 883-6423
Info Label Inc, Halfmoon (G-5933)	F	518 664-0791
Integrated Graphics Inc, New York (G-10659)	E	212 592-5600
Interstate Thermographers Corp, White Plains (G-17150)	G	914 948-1745
Iron Horse Graphics Ltd, Bridgehampton (G-1232)	G	631 537-3400
Island Silkscreen Inc, East Northport (G-4458)	G	631 757-4567
Issacs Yisroel, Brooklyn (G-2115)	G	718 851-7430
Itc Mfg Group Inc, New York (G-10711)	F	212 684-3696
J Kendall LLC, Yonkers (G-17474)	G	646 739-4956
J M L Productions Inc, Brooklyn (G-2125)	D	718 643-1674
J N White Associates Inc, Perry (G-13547)	D	585 237-5191
J T Printing 21, Staten Island (G-15712)	G	718 484-3939
Jack J Florio Jr, Lockport (G-7625)	G	716 434-9123
Janco Press Inc, Bohemia (G-1077)	F	631 563-3003
Japan Printing & Graphics Inc, New York (G-10741)	G	212 406-2905
Joed Press, New York (G-10787)	G	212 243-3620
John Auguliaro Printing Co, Brooklyn (G-2144)	G	718 382-5283
Johnnys Ideal Printing Co, Hudson (G-6651)	G	518 828-6666
▲ Jomar Industries Inc, Airmont (G-14)	E	845 357-5773
Jomart Associates Inc, Islandia (G-6836)	E	212 627-2153
Jon Lyn Ink Inc, Merrick (G-8420)	G	516 546-2312
Judith Lewis Printer Inc, Westbury (G-17027)	G	516 997-7777
K & B Stamping Co Inc, Mount Vernon (G-8741)	G	914 664-8555
Kallen Corp, New York (G-10841)	G	212 242-1470
Karr Graphics Corp, Long Island City (G-7806)	E	212 645-6000
▲ Kates Paperie Ltd, New York (G-10855)	G	212 966-3904
Kaufman Brothers Printing, New York (G-10858)	G	212 563-1854
Kaymil Printing Company Inc, New York (G-10861)	G	212 594-3718
▲ Kenan International Trading, Corona (G-4023)	G	718 672-4922
Kenmar Shirts Inc, Bronx (G-1375)	E	718 824-3880
Key Computer Svcs of Chelsea, New York (G-10880)	D	212 206-8060
Kim Jae Printing Co Inc, Roslyn Heights (G-15053)	G	212 691-6289
Kinaneco Inc, Syracuse (G-15994)	G	315 468-6201
Knucklehead Embroidery Inc, Johnson City (G-7129)	G	607 797-2725
Kroger Packaging Inc, Farmingdale (G-5036)	G	631 249-6690
Kurrier Inc, Brooklyn (G-2180)	G	718 389-3018
L & M Uniserv Corp, Brooklyn (G-2185)	G	718 854-3700
L I C Screen Printing Inc, Merrick (G-8421)	G	516 546-7289
▲ Labels Inter-Global Inc, New York (G-10949)	F	212 398-0006
Lake Placid Advertisers Wkshp, Lake Placid (G-7299)	E	518 523-3359
Landlord Guard Inc, New York (G-10960)	F	212 695-6505
Lauricella Press Inc, Brentwood (G-1186)	E	516 931-5906
Lennons Litho Inc, Herkimer (G-6329)	G	315 866-3156
Leo Paper Inc, New York (G-11005)	G	917 305-0708
Levon Graphics Corp, Farmingdale (G-5043)	D	631 753-2022
Lifeforms Printing, Depew (G-4287)	G	716 685-4500
Linco Printing Inc, Long Island City (G-7817)	E	718 937-5141
Linda Campbell, Bronx (G-1386)	G	718 994-4026
Linden Forms & Systems Inc, Brooklyn (G-2229)	E	212 219-1100
Lion In The Sun Park Slope Ltd, Brooklyn (G-2232)	G	718 369-4006
Logomax Inc, Farmingdale (G-5044)	G	631 420-0484
Loremanss Embroidery Engrav, Keeseville (G-7168)	F	518 834-9205
Louis Heindl & Son Inc, Rochester (G-14504)	G	585 454-5080
Love Unlimited NY Inc, Westbury (G-17035)	G	718 359-8500
Loy L Press Inc, Buffalo (G-3069)	G	716 634-5966
M C Packaging Corporation, Babylon (G-547)	E	631 643-3763
M T M Printing Co Inc, College Point (G-3820)	G	718 353-3297
Magazines & Brochures Inc, Buffalo (G-3074)	G	716 875-9699
Makerbot Industries LLC, New York (G-11142)	E	347 457-5758
Malone Industrial Press Inc, Malone (G-8044)	E	518 483-5880
Mark T Westinghouse, Catskill (G-3459)	G	518 678-3262
Marlow Printing Co Inc, Brooklyn (G-2275)	E	718 625-4948
Mason Transparent Package Inc, Bronx (G-1392)	E	718 792-6000
Maspeth Press Inc, Maspeth (G-8180)	G	718 429-2363
Master Image Printing Inc, Elmsford (G-4772)	G	914 347-4400
◆ Mastercraft Decorators Inc, Fairport (G-4869)	E	585 223-5150
Mastro Graphic Arts Inc, Rochester (G-14520)	E	585 436-7570
Matt Industries Inc, Syracuse (G-16005)	C	315 472-1316
Matthew-Lee Corporation, Lindenhurst (G-7494)	F	631 226-0100
McAuliffe Paper Inc, Liverpool (G-7558)	G	315 453-2222
Measurement Incorporated, White Plains (G-17163)	F	914 682-1969
▲ Medallion Associates Inc, New York (G-11233)	E	212 929-9130
Media Signs LLC, Brooklyn (G-2296)	G	718 252-7575
Mega Graphics Inc, Yorktown Heights (G-17529)	G	914 962-1402
▲ Menu Solutions Inc, Bronx (G-1394)	G	718 575-5160
Merchandiser Inc, Clifton Springs (G-3739)	G	315 462-6411
Merlin Printing Inc, Amityville (G-312)	G	631 842-6666
Merrill Communications LLC, New York (G-11258)	E	212 620-5600
Merrill Corporation, New York (G-11259)	D	917 934-7300
Merrill New York Company Inc, New York (G-11261)	C	212 229-6500
Metro Creative Graphics Inc, New York (G-11268)	E	212 947-5100
Middletown Press, Middletown (G-8485)	G	845 343-1895
Midgley Printing Corp, Syracuse (G-16009)	G	315 475-1864
Miken Companies Inc, Buffalo (G-3085)	D	716 668-6311
Mimeocom Inc, New York (G-11299)	B	212 847-3000
▲ Mines Press Inc, Cortlandt Manor (G-4078)	C	914 788-1800
Mini Graphics Inc, Hauppauge (G-6165)	D	516 223-6464
Mixture Screen Printing, Newburgh (G-12788)	G	845 561-2857
Modern Decal Co, Liverpool (G-7561)	G	315 622-2778
Moore Printing Company Inc, Canandaigua (G-3378)	G	585 394-1533
Mpe Graphics Inc, Bohemia (G-1101)	F	631 582-8900
◆ Multi Packaging Solutions Inc, New York (G-11347)	E	646 885-0005
▲ Mv Corp Inc, Bay Shore (G-717)	C	631 273-8020
Nathan Printing Express Inc, Scarsdale (G-15250)	G	914 472-0914
New Art Signs Co Inc, Glen Head (G-5651)	G	718 443-0900
New Buffalo Shirt Factory Inc, Buffalo (G-3105)	G	716 436-5839
▲ New Deal Printing Corp, New York (G-11404)	G	718 729-5800
New York Christan Times Inc, Brooklyn (G-2371)	G	718 638-6397
New York Legal Publishing, Menands (G-8409)	G	518 459-1100
New York Sample Card Co Inc, New York (G-11426)	E	212 242-1242
Newport Business Solutions Inc, Bohemia (G-1105)	F	631 319-6129
▲ Niagara Label Company Inc, Akron (G-22)	F	716 542-3000
Niagara Sample Book Co Inc, Niagara Falls (G-12867)	F	716 284-6151
Noble Checks Inc, Brooklyn (G-2383)	G	212 537-6241
Nomad Editions LLC, Bronxville (G-1502)	F	212 918-0992
North American DF Inc, Staten Island (G-15732)	G	718 698-2500
North American Graphics Inc, New York (G-11472)	F	212 725-2200
North Six Inc, New York (G-11475)	F	212 463-7227
Northwind Graphics, Ballston Spa (G-605)	G	518 899-9651
Nys Nyu-Cntr Intl Cooperation, New York (G-11502)	E	212 998-3680
One In A Million Inc, Valley Stream (G-16441)	G	516 829-1111
Ontario Label Graphics Inc, Lockport (G-7639)	F	716 434-8505
Origin Press Inc, Mineola (G-8563)	G	516 746-2262
P & W Press Inc, New York (G-11560)	E	646 486-3417
Pace Editions Inc, New York (G-11563)	G	212 675-7431
Paratore Signs Inc, Syracuse (G-16031)	G	315 455-5551
Patrick Rohan, Monticello (G-8646)	G	718 781-2573
Patrick Ryans Modern Press, Albany (G-115)	F	518 434-2921
Paulin Investment Company, Amityville (G-320)	E	631 957-8500
PBR Graphics Inc, Albany (G-116)	G	518 458-2909
PDM Studios Inc, Tonawanda (G-16210)	G	716 694-8337
PDQ Shipping Services, New Paltz (G-8922)	G	845 255-5500
Penny Lane Printing Inc, Avon (G-539)	D	585 226-8111
Personal Graphics Corporation, Westmoreland (G-17092)	G	315 853-3421
Peter Papastrat, Binghamton (G-938)	G	607 723-8112
Photo Agents Ltd, Huntington (G-6709)	G	631 421-0258

Pierrepont Visual Graphics....G....585 305-9672
Rochester *(G-14604)*
▲ Poly-Flex Corp....F....631 586-9500
Edgewood *(G-4620)*
Pony Farm Press & Graphics....G....607 432-9020
Oneonta *(G-13214)*
Precision Envelope Co Inc....G....631 694-3990
Farmingdale *(G-5096)*
Precision Label Corporation....F....631 270-4490
Farmingdale *(G-5097)*
Premier Ink Systems Inc....E....845 782-5802
Harriman *(G-5995)*
Presstek Printing LLC....F....585 266-2770
Rochester *(G-14622)*
Print City Corp....F....212 487-9778
New York *(G-11737)*
▲ Print House Inc....D....718 443-7500
Brooklyn *(G-2459)*
Print Mall....G....718 437-7700
Brooklyn *(G-2460)*
◆ Print Pack Inc....C....404 460-7000
Farmingdale *(G-5098)*
Print Shoppe....G....315 792-9585
Utica *(G-16380)*
Printech Business Systems Inc....F....212 290-2542
New York *(G-11740)*
Printed Image....G....716 821-1880
Buffalo *(G-3162)*
Printery....G....516 922-3250
Oyster Bay *(G-13399)*
Printfacility Inc....G....212 349-4009
New York *(G-11741)*
Printing Max New York Inc....G....718 692-1400
Brooklyn *(G-2463)*
Printing Prmtnal Solutions LLC....F....315 474-1110
Syracuse *(G-16035)*
Printing Resources Inc....E....518 482-2470
Albany *(G-124)*
Printout Copy Corp....E....718 855-4040
Brooklyn *(G-2465)*
Printworks Printing & Design....G....315 433-8587
Syracuse *(G-16036)*
Priority Printing Entps Inc....F....646 285-0684
New York *(G-11743)*
Proof 7 Ltd....F....212 680-1843
New York *(G-11757)*
▲ Publimax Printing Corp....G....718 366-7133
Ridgewood *(G-14133)*
Quadra Flex Corp....G....607 758-7066
Cortland *(G-4065)*
Quality Graphics West Seneca....G....716 668-4528
Cheektowaga *(G-3615)*
Quality Impressions Inc....G....646 613-0002
New York *(G-11793)*
Quality Offset LLC....G....347 342-4660
Long Island City *(G-7884)*
Quist Industries Ltd....F....718 243-2800
Brooklyn *(G-2487)*
R & M Graphics of New York....F....212 929-0294
New York *(G-11806)*
R R Donnelley & Sons Company....F....716 763-2613
Lakewood *(G-7317)*
R R Donnelley & Sons Company....D....518 438-9722
Albany *(G-126)*
Rainbow Lettering....G....607 732-5751
Elmira *(G-4713)*
RBHM Incorporated....F....609 259-4900
Brooklyn *(G-2500)*
Regal Screen Printing Intl....G....845 356-8181
Spring Valley *(G-15621)*
Republican Registrar Inc....G....315 497-1551
Moravia *(G-8658)*
Rfn Inc....F....516 764-5100
Bay Shore *(G-729)*
Richard Ruffner....F....631 234-4600
Central Islip *(G-3536)*
Richs Sttches EMB Screenprint....G....845 621-2175
Mahopac *(G-8030)*
▲ Rike Enterprises Inc....F....631 277-8338
Islip *(G-6851)*
RIT Printing Corp....F....631 586-6220
Bay Shore *(G-731)*
Rose Graphics LLC....F....516 547-6142
West Babylon *(G-16854)*
Round Top Knit & Screening....G....518 622-3600
Round Top *(G-15064)*
Royal Tees Inc....G....845 357-9448
Suffern *(G-15820)*
RR Donnelley & Sons Company....G....646 755-8125
New York *(G-11948)*
S & S Graphics Inc....F....914 668-4230
Mount Vernon *(G-8775)*
▲ S & S Prtg Die-Cutting Co Inc....F....718 388-8990
Brooklyn *(G-2543)*
S L C Industries Incorporated....F....607 775-2299
Binghamton *(G-943)*
Salamanca Press Penny Saver....E....716 945-1500
Salamanca *(G-15132)*
Sammba Printing Inc....G....516 944-4449
Port Washington *(G-13879)*
Sand Hill Industries Inc....G....518 885-7991
Ballston Spa *(G-607)*
Scan-A-Chrome Color Inc....G....631 532-6146
Copiague *(G-3948)*
Scancorp Inc....F....315 454-5596
Syracuse *(G-16054)*
Scotti Graphics Inc....E....212 367-9602
Long Island City *(G-7901)*
Screen The World Inc....F....631 475-0023
Holtsville *(G-6534)*
SDS Business Cards Inc....F....516 747-3131
Syosset *(G-15860)*
Select-A-Form Inc....D....631 981-3076
Holbrook *(G-6499)*
Seneca West Printing Inc....G....716 675-8010
West Seneca *(G-16983)*
Sentinel Printing Inc....G....516 334-7400
Westbury *(G-17054)*
Sephardic Yellow Pages....E....718 998-0299
Brooklyn *(G-2569)*
Seri Systems Inc....E....585 272-5515
Rochester *(G-14703)*
Shapeways Inc....D....914 356-5816
New York *(G-12064)*
Sharp Printing Inc....G....716 731-3994
Sanborn *(G-15154)*
Shipman Printing Inds Inc....E....716 504-7700
Niagara Falls *(G-12893)*
Shore Line Monogramming Inc....F....914 698-8000
Mamaroneck *(G-8080)*
Short Run Forms Inc....D....631 567-7171
Bohemia *(G-1130)*
Shykat Promotions....G....866 574-2757
Forestville *(G-5343)*
Sign Shop Inc....G....631 226-4145
Copiague *(G-3951)*
Silk Screen Art Inc....F....518 762-8423
Johnstown *(G-7155)*
Silver Griffin Inc....F....518 272-7771
Troy *(G-16279)*
◆ Sino Printing Inc....F....212 334-6896
New York *(G-12109)*
Soho Letterpress Inc....F....718 788-2518
Brooklyn *(G-2604)*
Solarz Bros Printing Corp....G....718 383-1330
Brooklyn *(G-2608)*
Source Envelope Inc....G....866 284-0707
Farmingdale *(G-5122)*
Spaulding Law Printing Inc....G....315 422-4805
Syracuse *(G-16065)*
Spectrum Prtg Lithography Inc....F....212 255-3131
New York *(G-12182)*
Speedy Enterprise of USA Corp....G....718 463-3000
Flushing *(G-5300)*
Spst Inc....G....607 798-6952
Vestal *(G-16477)*
St James Printing Inc....G....631 981-2095
Ronkonkoma *(G-15012)*
▲ Standwill Packaging Inc....E....631 752-1236
Farmingdale *(G-5124)*
Star Press Pearl River Inc....G....845 268-2294
Valley Cottage *(G-16415)*
Starcraft Press Inc....G....718 383-6700
Long Island City *(G-7915)*
Starfire Printing Inc....G....631 736-1495
Holtsville *(G-6535)*
Stellar Printing Inc....D....718 361-1600
Long Island City *(G-7918)*
Stickershopcom Inc....G....631 563-4323
Bayport *(G-755)*
Stony Point Graphics Ltd....G....845 786-3322
Stony Point *(G-15799)*
Stromberg Brand Corporation....F....914 739-7410
Valley Cottage *(G-16417)*
Structured 3d Inc....G....346 704-2614
Amityville *(G-326)*
Superior Print On Demand....G....607 240-5231
Vestal *(G-16478)*
Swift Multigraphics LLC....G....585 442-8000
Rochester *(G-14733)*
Syracuse Label Co Inc....D....315 422-1037
Syracuse *(G-16078)*
▲ Syracuse Letter Company Inc....F....315 476-8328
Bridgeport *(G-1236)*
T L F Graphics Inc....D....585 272-5500
Rochester *(G-14740)*
T S O General Corp....E....631 952-5320
Brentwood *(G-1193)*
T&K Printing Inc....F....718 439-9454
Brooklyn *(G-2661)*
T-Base Communications USA Inc....E....315 713-0013
Ogdensburg *(G-13144)*
Table Tops Paper Corp....G....718 831-6440
Brooklyn *(G-2663)*
▲ Tape Printers Inc....F....631 249-5585
Farmingdale *(G-5135)*
Tapemaker Sales Co Inc....G....516 333-0592
Westbury *(G-17057)*
Tapemaker Supply Company LLC....G....914 693-3407
Hartsdale *(G-6020)*
Tara Rific Screen Printing Inc....G....718 583-6864
Bronx *(G-1470)*
Tc Transcontinental USA Inc....G....818 993-4767
New York *(G-12308)*
Tcmf Inc....D....607 724-1094
Binghamton *(G-948)*
▲ Tele-Pak Inc....E....845 426-2300
Monsey *(G-8620)*
The Gramecy Group....G....518 348-1325
Clifton Park *(G-3736)*
Thomson Press (india) Limited....G....646 318-0369
Long Island City *(G-7929)*
Todd Walbridge....G....585 254-3018
Rochester *(G-14755)*
Top Copi Reproductions Inc....F....212 571-4141
New York *(G-12389)*
Toppan Vintage Inc....D....212 596-7747
New York *(G-12392)*
Toprint Ltd....G....718 439-0469
Brooklyn *(G-2686)*
Total Solution Graphics Inc....G....718 706-1540
Long Island City *(G-7930)*
Tovie Asarese Royal Prtg Co....G....716 885-7692
Buffalo *(G-3249)*
◆ Transcntinental Ultra Flex Inc....B....718 272-9100
Brooklyn *(G-2693)*
Tri Kolor Printing & Sty....F....315 474-6753
Syracuse *(G-16085)*
Tri-Lon Clor Lithographers Ltd....E....212 255-6140
New York *(G-12421)*
Triangle Label Tag Inc....G....718 875-3030
Brooklyn *(G-2697)*
Tripi Engraving Co Inc....E....718 383-6500
Brooklyn *(G-2700)*
U All Inc....E....518 438-2558
Albany *(G-144)*
United Print Group Inc....F....718 392-4242
Long Island City *(G-7936)*
▲ Universal Screening Associates....F....718 232-2744
Brooklyn *(G-2728)*
Unlimited Ink Inc....E....631 582-0696
Hauppauge *(G-6246)*
▲ USA Custom Pad Corp....E....607 563-9550
Sidney *(G-15467)*
Varick Street Litho Inc....G....646 843-0800
New York *(G-12529)*
Venus Printing Company....F....212 967-8900
Hewlett *(G-6339)*
Veterans Offset Printing Inc....G....585 288-2900
Rochester *(G-14781)*
Vez Inc....G....718 273-7002
Staten Island *(G-15774)*
Viking Athletics Ltd....E....631 957-8000
Lindenhurst *(G-7515)*
Voss Signs LLC....E....315 682-6418
Manlius *(G-8109)*
W N Vanalstine & Sons Inc....D....518 237-1436
Cohoes *(G-3786)*
Webster Printing Corporation....F....585 671-1533
Webster *(G-16768)*
Weeks & Reichel Printing Inc....G....631 589-1443
Sayville *(G-15244)*
Weicro Graphics Inc....E....631 253-3360
West Babylon *(G-16872)*
▲ Welsh Gold Stampers Inc....E....718 984-5031
Staten Island *(G-15776)*
Were Forms Inc....G....585 482-4400
Rochester *(G-14789)*
Westypo Printers Inc....G....914 737-7394
Peekskill *(G-13512)*

Employee Codes: A=Over 500 employees, B=251-500
C=101-250, D=51-100, E=20-50, F=10-19, G=5-9
2018 Harris
New York Manufacturers Directory
773

Wheeler/Rinstar Ltd ....F 212 244-1130
New York (G-12649)
Willco Fine Art Ltd ....F 718 935-9567
New York (G-12659)
William Charles Prtg Co Inc ....E 516 349-0900
Plainview (G-13674)
William J Ryan ....G 585 392-6200
Hilton (G-6447)
Willis Mc Donald Co Inc ....F 212 366-1526
New York (G-12665)
Wilson Press LLC ....E 315 568-9693
Seneca Falls (G-15395)
▲ Won & Lee Inc ....E 516 222-0712
Garden City (G-5552)
Worldwide Ticket Craft ....D 516 538-6200
Merrick (G-8429)
X Myles Mar Inc ....E 212 683-2015
New York (G-12699)
X Press Screen Printing ....G 716 679-7788
Dunkirk (G-4377)
Xl Graphics Inc ....G 212 929-8700
New York (G-12705)
Xpress Printing Inc ....G 516 605-1000
Plainview (G-13675)
▲ Zacks Enterprises Inc ....E 800 366-4924
Orangeburg (G-13270)
Zan Optics Products Inc ....E 718 435-0533
Brooklyn (G-2794)

2761 Manifold Business Forms

▲ Abra-Ka-Data Systems Ltd ....E 631 667-5550
Deer Park (G-4111)
Amsterdam Printing & Litho Inc ....F 518 842-6000
Amsterdam (G-333)
Amsterdam Printing & Litho Inc ....E 518 842-6000
Amsterdam (G-334)
Bmg Printing and Promotion LLC ....G 631 231-9200
Bohemia (G-1022)
Boces Business Office ....F 607 763-3300
Binghamton (G-892)
Five Boro Holding LLC ....F 718 431-9500
Brooklyn (G-1980)
Gateway Prtg & Graphics Inc ....E 716 823-3873
Hamburg (G-5949)
Idc Printing & Sty Co Inc ....G 516 599-0400
Lynbrook (G-7979)
Linden Forms & Systems Inc ....E 212 219-1100
Brooklyn (G-2229)
Maggio Data Forms Printing Ltd ....C 631 348-0343
Hauppauge (G-6150)
Marcy Business Forms Inc ....G 718 935-9100
Brooklyn (G-2268)
◆ Multi Packaging Solutions Inc ....E 646 885-0005
New York (G-11347)
P P I Business Forms Inc ....G 716 825-1241
Buffalo (G-3129)
Resonant Legal Media LLC ....D 800 781-3591
New York (G-11873)
Richard Ruffner ....F 631 234-4600
Central Islip (G-3536)
▲ Rmf Printing Technologies Inc ....E 716 683-7500
Lancaster (G-7364)
RR Donnelley & Sons Company ....D 716 773-0647
Grand Island (G-5781)
RR Donnelley & Sons Company ....D 716 773-0300
Grand Island (G-5782)
Select-A-Form Inc ....D 631 981-3076
Holbrook (G-6499)
▲ Specialized Printed Forms Inc ....E 585 538-2381
Caledonia (G-3310)
Syracuse Computer Forms Inc ....E 315 478-0108
Syracuse (G-16075)
Taylor Communications Inc ....F 937 221-1303
Melville (G-8388)
Taylor Communications Inc ....F 718 352-0220
Westbury (G-17058)
Williamson Law Book Co ....F 585 924-3400
Victor (G-16537)

2771 Greeting Card Publishing

1/2 Off Cards Wantagh Inc ....G 516 809-9832
Wantagh (G-16576)
▲ Anne Taintor Inc ....G 718 483-9312
Brooklyn (G-1613)
Avanti Press Inc ....E 212 414-1025
New York (G-9326)
Massimo Friedman Inc ....E 716 836-0408
Buffalo (G-3078)
▲ Paper House Productions Inc ....E 845 246-7261
Saugerties (G-15219)
Paper Magic Group Inc ....B 631 521-3682
New York (G-11577)
▲ Quotable Cards Inc ....G 212 420-7552
New York (G-11802)
Schurman Fine Papers ....C 212 206-0067
New York (G-12020)

2782 Blankbooks & Looseleaf Binders

ABC Check Printing Corp ....F 718 855-4702
Brooklyn (G-1546)
Acco Brands USA LLC ....C 847 541-9500
Ogdensburg (G-13130)
▲ Albumx Corp ....D 914 939-6878
Port Chester (G-13766)
▲ Art Leather Mfg Co Inc ....A 516 867-4716
Oyster Bay (G-13392)
Brewer-Cantelmo Co Inc ....E 212 244-4600
New York (G-9510)
Brookvale Records Inc ....F 631 587-7722
West Babylon (G-16801)
Classic Album ....E 718 388-2818
Brooklyn (G-1785)
▲ Classic Album LLC ....D 718 388-2818
Brooklyn (G-1786)
Colad Group LLC ....D 716 961-1776
Buffalo (G-2900)
Consolidated Loose Leaf Inc ....E 212 924-5800
New York (G-9767)
Dalee Bookbinding Co Inc ....F 914 965-1660
Yonkers (G-17449)
▲ Datamax International Inc ....E 212 693-0933
New York (G-9870)
Deluxe Corporation ....B 845 362-4054
Spring Valley (G-15603)
Dorose Novelty Co Inc ....F 718 451-3088
East Elmhurst (G-4413)
Federal Sample Card Corp ....D 718 458-1344
Elmhurst (G-4673)
Foster - Gordon Manufacturing ....G 631 589-6776
Bohemia (G-1064)
▲ General Diaries Corporation ....F 516 371-2244
Inwood (G-6797)
GPM Associates LLC ....E 585 335-3940
Dansville (G-4103)
◆ Graphic Image Incorporated ....C 631 249-9600
Melville (G-8353)
King Album Inc ....E 631 253-9500
West Babylon (G-16833)
Lanwood Industries Inc ....E 718 786-3000
Bay Shore (G-709)
Leather Craftsmen Inc ....C 631 752-9000
Farmingdale (G-5041)
Leather Craftsmen Inc ....E 714 429-9763
Farmingdale (G-5042)
Leather Indexes Corp ....D 516 827-1900
Hicksville (G-6391)
Motema Music LLC ....G 212 860-6969
New York (G-11335)
▲ Mypublisher Inc ....F 914 773-4312
Elmsford (G-4776)
New York Sample Card Co Inc ....E 212 242-1242
New York (G-11426)
Niagara Sample Book Co Inc ....F 716 284-6151
Niagara Falls (G-12867)
▲ Quo Vadis Editions Inc ....E 716 648-2602
Hamburg (G-5963)
▲ Quotable Cards Inc ....G 212 420-7552
New York (G-11802)
Renegade Nation Ltd ....F 212 868-9000
New York (G-11865)
▲ Roger Michael Press Inc ....F 732 752-0800
Brooklyn (G-2523)
Sellco Industries Inc ....E 607 756-7594
Cortland (G-4068)
Simon & Simon LLC ....G 202 419-0490
New York (G-12103)
Tm Music Inc ....F 212 471-4000
New York (G-12376)
Tommy Boy Entertainment LLC ....F 212 388-8300
New York (G-12386)
Wmg Acquisition Corp ....F 212 275-2000
New York (G-12676)
Wood Designs Deluxe Corp ....G 917 414-4640
Island Park (G-6823)

2789 Bookbinding

514 Adams Corporation ....G 516 352-6948
Franklin Square (G-5369)
A-1 Products Inc ....G 718 789-1818
Brooklyn (G-1539)
A-Quick Bindery LLC ....G 631 491-1110
West Babylon (G-16788)
Agrecolor Inc ....F 516 741-8700
Mineola (G-8525)
Argo Lithographers Inc ....E 718 729-2700
Long Island City (G-7702)
Arista Innovations Inc ....E 516 746-2262
Mineola (G-8529)
▲ Ateres Publishing & Bk Bindery ....F 718 935-9355
Brooklyn (G-1647)
Baum Christine and John Corp ....G 585 621-8910
Rochester (G-14241)
Beastons Budget Printing ....G 585 244-2721
Rochester (G-14244)
▲ Benchemark Printing Inc ....D 518 393-1361
Schenectady (G-15262)
Bernard Hall ....G 585 425-3340
Fairport (G-4853)
▲ Beyer Graphics Inc ....D 631 543-3900
Commack (G-3850)
Bg Bindery Inc ....G 631 767-4242
Maspeth (G-8150)
Boncraft Inc ....D 716 662-9720
Tonawanda (G-16167)
Bondy Printing Corp ....G 631 242-1510
Bay Shore (G-677)
Brodock Press Inc ....D 315 735-9577
Utica (G-16333)
Brooks Litho Digital Group Inc ....G 631 789-4500
Deer Park (G-4136)
C & C Bindery Co Inc ....E 631 752-7078
Farmingdale (G-4963)
Carlara Group Ltd ....G 914 769-2020
Pleasantville (G-13744)
Carnels Printing Inc ....G 516 883-3355
Port Washington (G-13826)
Castlereagh Printcraft Inc ....D 516 623-1728
Freeport (G-5402)
Chakra Communications Inc ....E 607 748-7491
Endicott (G-4806)
Challenge Graphics Svcs Inc ....E 631 586-0171
Deer Park (G-4138)
Classic Album ....E 718 388-2818
Brooklyn (G-1785)
Cohber Press Inc ....D 585 475-9100
West Henrietta (G-16906)
Copy Corner Inc ....G 718 388-4545
Brooklyn (G-1802)
Copy Room Inc ....F 212 371-8600
New York (G-9781)
Cosmos Communications Inc ....C 718 482-1800
Long Island City (G-7734)
D G M Graphics Inc ....F 516 223-2220
Merrick (G-8416)
Dalee Bookbinding Co Inc ....F 914 965-1660
Yonkers (G-17449)
David Helsing ....G 607 796-2681
Horseheads (G-6601)
Dependable Lithographers Inc ....F 718 472-4200
Long Island City (G-7741)
Dispatch Graphics Inc ....F 212 307-5943
New York (G-9938)
Division Den-Bar Enterprises ....G 914 381-2220
Mamaroneck (G-8065)
Dowd - Witbeck Printing Corp ....F 518 274-2421
Troy (G-16256)
DP Murphy Co Inc ....D 631 673-9400
Deer Park (G-4154)
E B B Graphics Inc ....F 516 750-5510
Westbury (G-17006)
E L Smith Printing Co Inc ....E 201 373-0111
New City (G-8831)
Eastside Printers ....F 315 437-6515
East Syracuse (G-4540)
Eastwood Litho Inc ....E 315 437-2626
Syracuse (G-15950)
Erhard & Gilcher Inc ....E 315 474-1072
Syracuse (G-15958)
Flare Multicopy Corp ....E 718 258-8860
Brooklyn (G-1983)
Flp Group LLC ....F 315 252-7583
Auburn (G-495)
Foster - Gordon Manufacturing ....G 631 589-6776
Bohemia (G-1064)
Fulton Newspapers Inc ....E 315 598-6397
Fulton (G-5471)
Gateway Prtg & Graphics Inc ....E 716 823-3873
Hamburg (G-5949)
Gazette Press Inc ....E 914 963-8300
Rye (G-15082)

27 PRINTING, PUBLISHING, AND ALLIED INDUSTRIES

Gild-Rite Inc .....G..... 631 752-9000
 Farmingdale (G-5006)
Gold Pride Press Inc .....E..... 585 224-8800
 Rochester (G-14431)
Graphicomm .....G..... 716 283-0830
 Niagara Falls (G-12845)
Haig Press Inc .....E..... 631 582-5800
 Hauppauge (G-6111)
▲ Hamilton Printing Company Inc .....C..... 518 732-2161
 Troy (G-16260)
Hudson Printing Co Inc .....E..... 718 937-8600
 New York (G-10572)
In-House Inc .....F..... 718 445-9007
 College Point (G-3812)
Interstate Litho Corp .....D..... 631 232-6025
 Brentwood (G-1182)
▲ J Mackenzie Ltd .....E..... 585 321-1770
 Rochester (G-14477)
Jack J Florio Jr .....G..... 716 434-9123
 Lockport (G-7625)
James Conolly Printing Co .....E..... 585 426-4150
 Rochester (G-14480)
Jane Lewis .....G..... 607 722-0584
 Binghamton (G-925)
Johnnys Ideal Printing Co .....E..... 518 828-6666
 Hudson (G-6651)
Jon Lyn Ink Inc .....G..... 516 546-2312
 Merrick (G-8420)
Kader Lithograph Company Inc .....C..... 917 664-4380
 Long Island City (G-7804)
Kaufman Brothers Printing .....G..... 212 563-1854
 New York (G-10858)
King Lithographers Inc .....E..... 914 667-4200
 Mount Vernon (G-8743)
Louis Heindl & Son Inc .....G..... 585 454-5080
 Rochester (G-14504)
Loy L Press Inc .....G..... 716 634-5966
 Buffalo (G-3069)
▲ Melcher Media Inc .....F..... 212 727-2322
 New York (G-11249)
▲ Mercury Print Productions Inc .....C..... 585 458-7900
 Rochester (G-14525)
Mid Island Group .....E..... 631 293-0180
 Farmingdale (G-5063)
Mid-Island Bindery Inc .....E..... 631 293-0180
 Farmingdale (G-5064)
Midgley Printing Corp .....G..... 315 475-1864
 Syracuse (G-16009)
▲ Mines Press Inc .....C..... 914 788-1800
 Cortlandt Manor (G-4078)
Moneast Inc .....G..... 845 298-8898
 Wappingers Falls (G-16595)
Multiple Imprssons of Rchester .....G..... 585 546-1160
 Rochester (G-14545)
Mutual Library Bindery Inc .....E..... 315 455-6638
 East Syracuse (G-4565)
Newport Graphics Inc .....E..... 212 924-2600
 New York (G-11433)
On The Spot Binding Inc .....E..... 718 497-2200
 Ridgewood (G-14129)
Ozipko Enterprises Inc .....G..... 585 424-6740
 Rochester (G-14581)
Piroke Trade Inc .....G..... 646 515-1537
 Brooklyn (G-2436)
Playbill Incorporated .....E..... 718 335-4033
 Woodside (G-17364)
Prestige Envelope & Lithograph .....F..... 631 521-7043
 Merrick (G-8426)
Printech Business Systems Inc .....F..... 212 290-2542
 New York (G-11740)
Printing Resources Inc .....E..... 518 482-2470
 Albany (G-124)
Pro Printing .....G..... 516 561-9700
 Lynbrook (G-7983)
Progressive Graphics & Prtg .....G..... 315 331-3635
 Newark (G-12762)
Prompt Bindery Co Inc .....F..... 212 675-5181
 New York (G-11754)
Psychonomic Society Inc .....G..... 512 381-1494
 New York (G-11764)
Quad/Graphics Inc .....A..... 518 581-4000
 Saratoga Springs (G-15198)
Quality Bindery Service Inc .....E..... 716 883-5185
 Buffalo (G-3173)
Reynolds Book Bindery LLC .....F..... 607 772-8937
 Binghamton (G-941)
Richard Ruffner .....F..... 631 234-4600
 Central Islip (G-3536)
Riverside Mfg Acquisition LLC .....C..... 585 458-2090
 Rochester (G-14650)

Rmd Holding Inc .....G..... 845 628-0030
 Mahopac (G-8031)
▲ Roger Michael Press Inc .....F..... 732 752-0800
 Brooklyn (G-2523)
Rosemont Press Incorporated .....E..... 212 239-4770
 New York (G-11935)
Rosen Mandell & Immerman Inc .....E..... 212 691-2277
 New York (G-11936)
Sentinel Printing Inc .....G..... 516 334-7400
 Westbury (G-17054)
Shipman Printing Inds Inc .....E..... 716 504-7700
 Niagara Falls (G-12893)
Spectrum Prtg Lithography Inc .....F..... 212 255-3131
 New York (G-12182)
▼ Sterling Pierce Company Inc .....E..... 516 593-1170
 East Rockaway (G-4492)
Thomas Group Inc .....F..... 212 947-6400
 New York (G-12340)
Tobay Printing Co Inc .....E..... 631 842-3300
 Copiague (G-3957)
Tom & Jerry Printcraft Forms .....E..... 914 777-7468
 Mamaroneck (G-8081)
Tri-Lon Clor Lithographers Ltd .....E..... 212 255-6140
 New York (G-12421)
▲ Twenty-First Century Press Inc .....F..... 716 837-0800
 Buffalo (G-3254)
Vicks Lithograph & Prtg Corp .....C..... 315 272-2401
 Yorkville (G-17544)
Vin-Clair Inc .....E..... 845 429-4998
 West Haverstraw (G-16878)
Webster Printing Corporation .....F..... 585 671-1533
 Webster (G-16768)
▲ Welsh Gold Stampers Inc .....E..... 718 984-5031
 Staten Island (G-15776)
Westchester Mailing Service .....E..... 914 948-1116
 White Plains (G-17212)
Whitford Development Inc .....F..... 631 471-7711
 Port Jefferson (G-13802)
William Charles Prtg Co Inc .....F..... 516 349-0900
 Plainview (G-13674)
Wilson Press LLC .....E..... 315 568-9693
 Seneca Falls (G-15395)
▲ Won & Lee Inc .....E..... 516 222-0712
 Garden City (G-5552)
Wynco Press One Inc .....G..... 516 354-6145
 Glen Oaks (G-5656)
X Myles Mar Inc .....E..... 212 683-2015
 New York (G-12699)
Zan Optics Products Inc .....F..... 718 435-0533
 Brooklyn (G-2794)
Zenger Partners LLC .....E..... 716 876-2284
 Kenmore (G-7181)

2791 Typesetting

514 Adams Corporation .....G..... 516 352-6948
 Franklin Square (G-5369)
Act Communications Group Inc .....F..... 631 669-2403
 West Islip (G-16932)
▲ Advance Publications Inc .....D..... 718 981-1234
 Staten Island (G-15653)
Agrecolor Inc .....F..... 516 741-8700
 Mineola (G-8525)
Alabaster Group Inc .....G..... 516 867-8223
 Freeport (G-5391)
Albion-Holley Pennysaver Inc .....E..... 585 589-5641
 Albion (G-164)
Arista Innovations Inc .....E..... 516 746-2262
 Mineola (G-8529)
▲ Art Resources Transfer Inc .....G..... 212 255-2919
 New York (G-9264)
▲ Artistic Typography Corp .....G..... 212 463-8880
 New York (G-9272)
Artscroll Printing Corp .....E..... 212 929-2413
 New York (G-9275)
Bates Jackson Engraving Co Inc .....E..... 716 854-3000
 Buffalo (G-2855)
Baum Christine and John Corp .....G..... 585 621-8910
 Rochester (G-14241)
Bco Industries Western NY Inc .....E..... 716 877-2800
 Tonawanda (G-16165)
Beastons Budget Printing .....G..... 585 244-2721
 Rochester (G-14244)
Beehive Press Inc .....G..... 718 654-1200
 Bronx (G-1280)
▲ Benchmark Printing Inc .....D..... 518 393-1361
 Schenectady (G-15262)
Bernard Hall .....G..... 585 425-3340
 Fairport (G-4853)
▲ Beyer Graphics Inc .....D..... 631 543-3900
 Commack (G-3850)

Boncraft Inc .....D..... 716 662-9720
 Tonawanda (G-16167)
Bondy Printing Corp .....G..... 631 242-1510
 Bay Shore (G-677)
Brodock Press Inc .....D..... 315 735-9577
 Utica (G-16333)
Brooks Litho Digital Group Inc .....G..... 631 789-4500
 Deer Park (G-4136)
Bytheway Publishing Services .....F..... 607 334-8365
 Norwich (G-13037)
Carlara Group Ltd .....G..... 914 769-2020
 Pleasantville (G-13744)
Carnels Printing Inc .....G..... 516 883-3355
 Port Washington (G-13826)
Castleagh Printcraft Inc .....D..... 516 623-1728
 Freeport (G-5402)
Cds Productions Inc .....F..... 518 385-8255
 Schenectady (G-15269)
Chakra Communications Inc .....E..... 716 505-7300
 Lancaster (G-7333)
Chakra Communications Inc .....E..... 607 748-7491
 Endicott (G-4806)
Challenge Graphics Svcs Inc .....E..... 631 586-0171
 Deer Park (G-4138)
Clarsons Corp .....F..... 585 235-8775
 Rochester (G-14299)
Cohber Press Inc .....D..... 585 475-9100
 West Henrietta (G-16906)
Consolidated Color Press Inc .....F..... 212 929-8197
 New York (G-9765)
Cortland Standard Printing Co .....D..... 607 756-5665
 Cortland (G-4045)
Cosmos Communications Inc .....C..... 718 482-1800
 Long Island City (G-7734)
Csw Inc .....F..... 585 247-4010
 Rochester (G-14315)
D G M Graphics Inc .....F..... 516 223-2220
 Merrick (G-8416)
Desktop Publishing Concepts .....F..... 631 752-1934
 Farmingdale (G-4985)
Digital Color Concepts Inc .....E..... 212 989-4888
 New York (G-9928)
Digital Page LLC .....F..... 518 446-9129
 Albany (G-73)
Dispatch Graphics Inc .....E..... 212 307-5943
 New York (G-9938)
Dowd - Witbeck Printing Corp .....F..... 518 274-2421
 Troy (G-16256)
DP Murphy Co Inc .....G..... 631 673-9400
 Deer Park (G-4154)
Draper Associates Incorporated .....F..... 212 255-2727
 New York (G-9975)
E B B Graphics Inc .....F..... 516 750-5510
 Westbury (G-17006)
Eastwood Litho Inc .....E..... 315 437-2626
 Syracuse (G-15950)
Empire Press Co .....G..... 718 756-9500
 Brooklyn (G-1926)
Falconer Printing & Design Inc .....F..... 716 665-2121
 Falconer (G-4906)
Flare Multicopy Corp .....E..... 718 258-8860
 Brooklyn (G-1983)
Flp Group LLC .....F..... 315 252-7583
 Auburn (G-495)
Fort Orange Press Inc .....E..... 518 489-3233
 Albany (G-81)
Fulton Newspapers Inc .....E..... 315 598-6397
 Fulton (G-5471)
▲ Gallant Graphics Ltd .....E..... 845 868-1166
 Stanfordville (G-15647)
Gateway Prtg & Graphics Inc .....E..... 716 823-3873
 Hamburg (G-5949)
Gazette Press Inc .....E..... 914 963-8300
 Rye (G-15082)
▲ Gg Design and Printing .....G..... 718 321-3220
 New York (G-10332)
Graphic Fabrications Inc .....E..... 516 763-3222
 Rockville Centre (G-14819)
Graphicomm Inc .....G..... 716 283-0830
 Niagara Falls (G-12845)
Grid Typographic Services Inc .....F..... 212 627-0303
 New York (G-10404)
Hamptons Magazine .....F..... 631 283-7125
 Southampton (G-15568)
Hks Printing Company Inc .....F..... 212 675-2529
 New York (G-10533)
Hugh F McPherson Inc .....G..... 716 668-6107
 Cheektowaga (G-3604)
In-House Inc .....F..... 718 445-9007
 College Point (G-3812)

Employee Codes: A=Over 500 employees, B=251-500
C=101-250, D=51-100, E=20-50, F=10-19, G=5-9

Interstate Litho Corp....D....631 232-6025
Brentwood (G-1182)
Jack J Florio Jr....G....716 434-9123
Lockport (G-7625)
James Conolly Printing Co....E....585 426-4150
Rochester (G-14480)
Jane Lewis....G....607 722-0584
Binghamton (G-925)
Johnnys Ideal Printing Co....G....518 828-6666
Hudson (G-6651)
Jon Lyn Ink Inc....G....516 546-2312
Merrick (G-8420)
L M N Printing Company Inc....E....516 285-8526
Valley Stream (G-16438)
Lake Placid Advertisers Wkshp....E....518 523-3359
Lake Placid (G-7299)
Leigh Scott Enterprises Inc....G....718 343-5440
Bellerose (G-806)
Litmor Publishing Corp....F....516 931-0012
Garden City (G-5527)
Loudon Ltd....G....631 757-4447
East Northport (G-4460)
Louis Heindl & Son Inc....G....585 454-5080
Rochester (G-14504)
Loy L Press Inc....G....716 634-5966
Buffalo (G-3069)
▲ Medallion Associates Inc....E....212 929-9130
New York (G-11233)
▲ Mercury Print Productions Inc....C....585 458-7900
Rochester (G-14525)
Midgley Printing Corp....G....315 475-1864
Syracuse (G-16009)
▲ Mines Press Inc....C....914 788-1800
Cortlandt Manor (G-4078)
Moneast Inc....G....845 298-8898
Wappingers Falls (G-16595)
Multiple Imprssons of Rchester....G....585 546-1160
Rochester (G-14545)
Mutual Engraving Company Inc....D....516 489-0534
West Hempstead (G-16893)
News India USA Inc....F....212 675-7515
New York (G-11437)
Newspaper Publisher LLC....F....607 775-0472
Conklin (G-3896)
▼ Official Offset Corporation....E....631 957-8500
Amityville (G-316)
Ozipko Enterprises Inc....G....585 424-6740
Rochester (G-14581)
P D R Inc....G....516 829-5300
Plainview (G-13655)
Panagraphics Inc....G....716 312-8088
Orchard Park (G-13312)
Patrick Ryans Modern Press....F....518 434-2921
Albany (G-115)
Presstek Printing LLC....F....585 467-8140
Rochester (G-14621)
Prestige Envelope & Lithograph....F....631 521-7043
Merrick (G-8426)
Printery....G....516 922-3250
Oyster Bay (G-13399)
Printing Resources Inc....E....518 482-2470
Albany (G-124)
Pro Printing....G....516 561-9700
Lynbrook (G-7983)
Progressive Graphics & Prtg....G....315 331-3635
Newark (G-12762)
Publishing Synthesis Ltd....G....212 219-0135
New York (G-11770)
Quad/Graphics Inc....A....518 581-4000
Saratoga Springs (G-15198)
Quicker Printer Inc....G....607 734-8622
Elmira (G-4712)
Rmd Holding Inc....G....845 628-0030
Mahopac (G-8031)
Rubber Stamps Inc....E....212 675-1180
Mineola (G-8568)
Scotti Graphics Inc....E....212 367-9602
Long Island City (G-7901)
Sentinel Printing Inc....G....516 334-7400
Westbury (G-17054)
Stone Crest Industries Inc....G....607 652-2665
Stamford (G-15646)
Syracuse Computer Forms Inc....E....315 478-0108
Syracuse (G-16075)
Thomas Group Inc....F....212 947-6400
New York (G-12340)
Times Review Newspaper Corp....E....631 354-8031
Mattituck (G-8243)
Tobay Printing Co Inc....E....631 842-3300
Copiague (G-3957)
Tom & Jerry Printcraft Forms....E....914 777-7468
Mamaroneck (G-8081)
Torsaf Printers Inc....G....516 569-5577
Hewlett (G-6337)
Tri Kolor Printing & Sty....F....315 474-6753
Syracuse (G-16085)
Tri-Lon Clor Lithographers Ltd....E....212 255-6140
New York (G-12421)
Tripi Engraving Co Inc....E....718 383-6500
Brooklyn (G-2700)
Voss Signs LLC....E....315 682-6418
Manlius (G-8109)
Wallkill Valley Publications....E....845 561-0170
Newburgh (G-12810)
Webster Printing Corporation....F....585 671-1533
Webster (G-16768)
Westchester Mailing Service....E....914 948-1116
White Plains (G-17212)
Wilson Press LLC....E....315 568-9693
Seneca Falls (G-15395)
Woodbury Printing Plus + Inc....G....845 928-6610
Central Valley (G-3557)
Worldwide Ticket Craft....D....516 538-6200
Merrick (G-8429)
Wynco Press One Inc....G....516 354-6145
Glen Oaks (G-5656)
X Myles Mar Inc....E....212 683-2015
New York (G-12699)
Zenger Partners LLC....E....716 876-2284
Kenmore (G-7181)

2796 Platemaking & Related Svcs

Absolute Color Corporation....G....212 868-0404
New York (G-9054)
Adflex Corporation....E....585 454-2950
Rochester (G-14189)
Aldine Inc (ny)....D....212 226-2870
New York (G-9129)
Allstate Sign & Plaque Corp....F....631 242-2828
Deer Park (G-4117)
Atlas Graphics Inc....G....516 997-5527
Westbury (G-16997)
Chakra Communications Inc....E....716 505-7300
Lancaster (G-7333)
Charles Henricks Inc....F....212 243-5800
New York (G-9632)
Circle Press Inc....D....212 924-4277
New York (G-9674)
Csw Inc....F....585 247-4010
Rochester (G-14315)
▲ Custom House Engravers Inc....G....631 567-3004
Bohemia (G-1042)
D & A Offset Services Inc....F....212 924-0612
New York (G-9837)
David Fehlman....G....315 455-8888
Syracuse (G-15942)
Dowd - Witbeck Printing Corp....F....518 274-2421
Troy (G-16256)
Eastern Color Stripping Inc....F....631 563-3700
Bohemia (G-1056)
▲ Gallant Graphics Ltd....E....845 868-1166
Stanfordville (G-15647)
Gazette Press Inc....E....914 963-8300
Rye (G-15082)
▲ Gotham Pen Co Inc....E....212 675-7904
Yonkers (G-17465)
Karr Graphics Corp....E....212 645-6000
Long Island City (G-7806)
Koehlr-Gibson Mkg Graphics Inc....E....716 838-5960
Buffalo (G-3053)
Lane Park Litho Plate....E....212 255-9100
New York (G-10961)
Lazer Incorporated....E....336 744-8047
Rochester (G-14497)
Leo P Callahan Inc....F....607 797-7314
Binghamton (G-929)
Lgn Materials & Solutions....F....888 414-0005
Mount Vernon (G-8747)
Micro Publishing Inc....G....212 533-9180
New York (G-11280)
Miroddi Imaging Inc....G....516 624-6898
Oyster Bay (G-13398)
Mutual Engraving Company Inc....D....516 489-0534
West Hempstead (G-16893)
P & H Thermotech Inc....G....585 624-1310
Lima (G-7469)
Rapid Service Engraving Co....G....716 896-4555
Buffalo (G-3180)
▲ Rigidized Metals Corporation....E....716 849-4703
Buffalo (G-3186)
Rotation Dynamics Corporation....E....585 352-9023
Spencerport (G-15597)
Syracuse Computer Forms Inc....E....315 478-0108
Syracuse (G-16075)
Tobay Printing Co Inc....E....631 842-3300
Copiague (G-3957)
Torch Graphics Inc....E....212 679-4334
New York (G-12395)
Tripi Engraving Co Inc....E....718 383-6500
Brooklyn (G-2700)
▲ Welsh Gold Stampers Inc....E....718 984-5031
Staten Island (G-15776)
Wilcro Inc....G....716 632-4204
Buffalo (G-3280)

28 CHEMICALS AND ALLIED PRODUCTS

2812 Alkalies & Chlorine

Chemours Company Fc LLC....E....716 278-5100
Niagara Falls (G-12826)
Church & Dwight Co Inc....F....518 887-5109
Schenectady (G-15270)
Indian Springs Mfg Co Inc....F....315 635-6101
Baldwinsville (G-570)
Occidental Chemical Corp....E....716 278-7795
Niagara Falls (G-12873)
Occidental Chemical Corp....E....716 773-8100
Grand Island (G-5780)
Occidental Chemical Corp....C....716 278-7794
Niagara Falls (G-12874)
Olin Chlor Alkali Logistics....C....716 278-6411
Niagara Falls (G-12875)

2813 Industrial Gases

Air Products and Chemicals Inc....D....518 463-4273
Glenmont (G-5682)
Airgas Inc....E....585 436-7780
Rochester (G-14197)
Airgas Inc....F....518 690-0068
Albany (G-33)
Airgas Usa LLC....F....585 436-7781
Rochester (G-14198)
Airgas USA LLC....E....315 433-1295
Syracuse (G-15867)
Fountainhead Group Inc....C....708 598-7100
New York Mills (G-12743)
Linde Gas North America LLC....E....518 713-2015
Cohoes (G-3773)
Linde Gas North America LLC....F....315 431-4081
Syracuse (G-15999)
Linde LLC....E....716 847-0748
Buffalo (G-3065)
Linde LLC....D....518 439-8187
Feura Bush (G-5180)
Linde Merchant Production Inc....G....315 593-1360
Fulton (G-5483)
Matheson Tri-Gas Inc....G....518 203-5003
Cohoes (G-3774)
Matheson Tri-Gas Inc....F....518 439-0362
Feura Bush (G-5181)
Neon....F....212 727-5628
New York (G-11388)
▼ Oxair Ltd....G....716 298-8288
Niagara Falls (G-12876)
Praxair Inc....E....845 267-2337
Valley Cottage (G-16411)
Praxair Inc....E....716 649-1600
Hamburg (G-5961)
Praxair Inc....E....518 482-4360
Albany (G-123)
Praxair Inc....E....716 286-4600
Niagara Falls (G-12879)
Praxair Inc....C....845 359-4200
Orangeburg (G-13263)
Praxair Inc....E....716 879-4000
Tonawanda (G-16213)
Praxair Distribution Inc....G....315 457-5821
Liverpool (G-7569)
Praxair Distribution Inc....F....315 735-6153
Marcy (G-8122)

2816 Inorganic Pigments

▲ Applied Minerals Inc....E....212 226-4265
Brooklyn (G-1620)
BASF Beauty Care Solutions LLC....G....631 689-0200
Stony Brook (G-15788)
BASF Corporation....B....914 737-2554
Peekskill (G-13497)

SIC SECTION

28 CHEMICALS AND ALLIED PRODUCTS

▲ **Heany Industries Inc**........D....... 585 889-2700
Scottsville *(G-15358)*

2819 Indl Inorganic Chemicals, NEC

2 Elements Real Est LLC........G....... 315 635-4662
Baldwinsville *(G-563)*
Aithaca Chemical Corp........F....... 516 229-2330
Uniondale *(G-16311)*
Akzo Nobel Chemicals LLC........C....... 914 674-5008
Dobbs Ferry *(G-4324)*
Alpha-En Corporation........F....... 914 418-2000
Yonkers *(G-17428)*
Ames Goldsmith Corp........F....... 518 792-7435
Glens Falls *(G-5685)*
Anchor Commerce Trading Corp........G....... 516 881-3485
Atlantic Beach *(G-467)*
Arkema Inc........C....... 585 243-6359
Piffard *(G-13573)*
Auterra Inc........G....... 518 382-9600
Schenectady *(G-15260)*
BASF Corporation........G....... 973 245-6000
Tarrytown *(G-16112)*
BASF Corporation........B....... 914 788-1627
Peekskill *(G-13498)*
BASF Corporation........B....... 212 450-8280
New York *(G-9379)*
BASF Corporation........C....... 631 689-0200
East Setauket *(G-4497)*
BASF Corporation........B....... 914 785-2000
Tarrytown *(G-16111)*
Benzsay & Harrison Inc........G....... 518 895-2311
Delanson *(G-4257)*
◆ **Buffalo Tungsten Inc**........D....... 716 759-6353
Depew *(G-4276)*
Byk USA Inc........E....... 845 469-5800
Chester *(G-3629)*
Calgon Carbon Corporation........G....... 716 531-9113
North Tonawanda *(G-12982)*
Carbide-Usa LLC........G....... 607 331-9353
Elmira *(G-4687)*
Carbon Activated Corporation........G....... 716 662-2005
Orchard Park *(G-13281)*
▼ **Cerion Energy Inc**........E....... 585 271-5630
Rochester *(G-14289)*
Cerion LLC........F....... 585 271-5630
Rochester *(G-14290)*
Chemours Company Fc LLC........E....... 716 278-5100
Niagara Falls *(G-12826)*
Chemtrade Chemicals US LLC........E....... 315 430-7650
Syracuse *(G-15912)*
Chemtrade Chemicals US LLC........G....... 315 478-2323
Syracuse *(G-15913)*
Danisco US Inc........D....... 585 277-4300
Rochester *(G-14322)*
▲ **Dynasty Chemical Corp**........E....... 518 463-1146
Menands *(G-8402)*
E I Du Pont De Nemours & Co........E....... 585 339-4200
Rochester *(G-14342)*
Emco Chemical (usa) Corp........E....... 718 797-3652
Brooklyn *(G-1920)*
◆ **Esm Group Inc**........F....... 716 446-8914
Amherst *(G-239)*
Esm Special Metals & Tech Inc........E....... 716 446-8914
Amherst *(G-241)*
Ferro Corporation........E....... 585 586-8770
East Rochester *(G-4477)*
Ferro Corporation........C....... 315 536-3357
Penn Yan *(G-13532)*
Ferro Electronics Materials........C....... 716 278-9400
Niagara Falls *(G-12841)*
FMC Corporation........E....... 716 735-3761
Middleport *(G-8455)*
▲ **Germanium Corp America Inc**........F....... 315 853-4900
Clinton *(G-3744)*
Hampshire Chemical Corp........D....... 315 539-9221
Waterloo *(G-16651)*
Incitec Pivot Limited........G....... 212 238-3010
New York *(G-10625)*
▲ **Innovative Municipal Pdts US**........E....... 800 387-5777
Glenmont *(G-5684)*
Interstate Chemical Co Inc........F....... 585 344-2822
Batavia *(G-641)*
Isonics Corporation........G....... 212 356-7400
New York *(G-10710)*
◆ **Kowa American Corporation**........E....... 212 303-7800
New York *(G-10920)*
Lakeshore Carbide Inc........G....... 716 462-4349
Lake View *(G-7304)*
Lawn Elements Inc........F....... 631 656-9711
Holbrook *(G-6485)*

▼ **Meliorum Technologies Inc**........G....... 585 313-0616
Rochester *(G-14524)*
▲ **Minerals Technologies Inc**........E....... 212 878-1800
New York *(G-11302)*
Moog Inc........D....... 716 731-6300
Niagara Falls *(G-12865)*
Multisorb Tech Intl LLC........G....... 716 824-8900
Buffalo *(G-3099)*
Multisorb Technologies Inc........G....... 716 668-4191
Cheektowaga *(G-3609)*
Multisorb Technologies Inc........E....... 716 656-1402
Buffalo *(G-3100)*
Next Potential LLC........G....... 401 742-5190
New York *(G-11441)*
▲ **Niagara Refining LLC**........E....... 716 706-1400
Depew *(G-4289)*
◆ **North American Hoganas Inc**........E....... 716 285-3451
Niagara Falls *(G-12869)*
Poly Scientific R&D Corp........E....... 631 586-0400
Bay Shore *(G-721)*
▲ **Polyset Company Inc**........E....... 518 664-6000
Mechanicville *(G-8260)*
Praxair Inc........F....... 716 879-2000
Tonawanda *(G-16212)*
Precision Elctro Mnrl Pmco Inc........E....... 716 284-2484
Niagara Falls *(G-12881)*
PVS Chemical Solutions Inc........D....... 716 825-5762
Buffalo *(G-3168)*
PVS Technologies Inc........E....... 716 825-5762
Buffalo *(G-3169)*
S E A Supplies Ltd........F....... 516 694-6677
Plainview *(G-13661)*
Sabre Energy Services LLC........F....... 518 514-1572
Slingerlands *(G-15500)*
Scientific Polymer Products........G....... 585 265-0413
Ontario *(G-13236)*
Signa Chemistry Inc........F....... 212 933-4101
New York *(G-12092)*
Somerville Acquisitions Co Inc........F....... 845 856-5261
Huguenot *(G-6682)*
Somerville Tech Group Inc........D....... 908 782-9500
Huguenot *(G-6683)*
Specialty Minerals Inc........G....... 518 585-7982
Ticonderoga *(G-16150)*
◆ **Specialty Minerals Inc**........E....... 212 878-1800
New York *(G-12178)*
◆ **Summit Research Labs Inc**........C....... 845 856-5261
Huguenot *(G-6684)*
▼ **Tangram Company LLC**........E....... 631 758-0460
Holtsville *(G-6538)*
Texas Brine Company LLC........G....... 585 495-6228
Wyoming *(G-17398)*
▲ **Thatcher Company New York Inc**........E....... 315 589-9330
Williamson *(G-17255)*
Tibro Water Technologies Ltd........F....... 647 426-3415
Sherrill *(G-15432)*
Transport National Dev Inc........E....... 716 662-0270
Orchard Park *(G-13325)*
UOP LLC........E....... 716 879-7600
Tonawanda *(G-16232)*
US Peroxide........G....... 716 775-5585
Grand Island *(G-5788)*
▲ **Van De Mark Chemical Co Inc**........D....... 716 433-6764
Lockport *(G-7655)*
◆ **Vanchlor Company Inc**........F....... 716 434-2624
Lockport *(G-7656)*
Vanchlor Company Inc........F....... 716 434-2624
Lockport *(G-7657)*
▲ **VWR Chemicals LLC**........E....... 518 297-4444
Rouses Point *(G-15069)*
◆ **Washington Mills Elec Mnrls**........D....... 716 278-6600
Niagara Falls *(G-12907)*

2821 Plastics, Mtrls & Nonvulcanizable Elastomers

▲ **Adam Scott Designs Inc**........E....... 212 420-8866
New York *(G-9071)*
◆ **American Acrylic Corporation**........E....... 631 422-2200
West Babylon *(G-16795)*
American Epoxy and Metal Inc........G....... 718 828-7828
Scarsdale *(G-15245)*
◆ **APS American Polymers Svcs Inc**........G....... 212 362-7711
New York *(G-9236)*
▼ **Ashley Resin Corp**........G....... 718 851-8111
Brooklyn *(G-1641)*
▲ **Astro Chemical Company Inc**........E....... 518 399-5338
Ballston Lake *(G-578)*
Atc Plastics LLC........E....... 212 375-2515
New York *(G-9297)*

◆ **Bairnco Corporation**........E....... 914 461-1300
White Plains *(G-17108)*
◆ **Bamberger Polymers Intl Corp**........F....... 516 622-3600
Jericho *(G-7094)*
▲ **Barrett Bronze Inc**........E....... 914 699-6060
Mount Vernon *(G-8710)*
Bso Energy Corp........F....... 212 520-1827
New York *(G-9526)*
Ccmi Inc........G....... 315 781-3270
Geneva *(G-5583)*
Clarence Resins and Chemicals........G....... 716 406-9804
Clarence Center *(G-3699)*
CN Group Incorporated........A....... 914 358-5690
White Plains *(G-17122)*
▲ **Coda Resources Ltd**........D....... 718 649-1666
Brooklyn *(G-1789)*
Craftech........D....... 518 828-5011
Chatham *(G-3585)*
Creations In Lucite Inc........G....... 718 871-2000
Brooklyn *(G-1812)*
Cytec Industries Inc........D....... 716 372-9650
Olean *(G-13162)*
▼ **Cytec Olean Inc**........D....... 716 372-9650
Olean *(G-13163)*
De Originals Ltd........G....... 516 474-6544
Old Westbury *(G-13153)*
▲ **Dewitt Plastics Inc**........F....... 315 255-1209
Auburn *(G-491)*
Dice America Inc........G....... 585 869-6200
Victor *(G-16497)*
Durez Corporation........F....... 716 286-0100
Niagara Falls *(G-12834)*
E I Du Pont De Nemours & Co........E....... 716 876-4420
Buffalo *(G-2938)*
Elastomers Inc........G....... 716 633-4883
Williamsville *(G-17269)*
Empire Plastics Inc........E....... 607 754-9132
Endwell *(G-4840)*
Endurart Inc........E....... 212 473-7000
New York *(G-10087)*
Everfab Inc........D....... 716 655-1550
East Aurora *(G-4395)*
Exxonmobil Chemical Company........C....... 315 966-1000
Macedon *(G-8016)*
▲ **Fougera Pharmaceuticals Inc**........C....... 631 454-7677
Melville *(G-8350)*
◆ **GE Plastics**........G....... 518 475-5011
Selkirk *(G-15377)*
▲ **General Vy-Coat LLC**........E....... 718 266-6002
Brooklyn *(G-2019)*
George M Dujack........G....... 518 279-1303
Troy *(G-16258)*
Global Plastics LP........F....... 800 417-4605
New York *(G-10361)*
Hanet Plastics Usa Inc........G....... 518 324-5850
Plattsburgh *(G-13694)*
Hexion Inc........E....... 518 792-8040
South Glens Falls *(G-15548)*
Hutchinson Industries Inc........E....... 716 852-1435
Buffalo *(G-3016)*
Imperial Polymers Inc........G....... 718 387-4741
Brooklyn *(G-2097)*
International Casein Corp Cal........G....... 516 466-4363
Great Neck *(G-5832)*
▲ **John C Dolph Company Inc**........E....... 732 329-2333
Schenectady *(G-15298)*
▲ **Jrlon Inc**........D....... 315 597-4067
Palmyra *(G-13434)*
◆ **Kent Chemical Corporation**........E....... 212 521-1700
New York *(G-10878)*
Macneil Polymers Inc........F....... 716 681-7755
Buffalo *(G-3073)*
Majestic Mold & Tool Inc........F....... 315 695-2079
Phoenix *(G-13569)*
Manufacturers Indexing Pdts........G....... 631 271-0956
Halesite *(G-5928)*
Maviano Corp........G....... 845 494-2598
Monsey *(G-8610)*
▲ **MB Plastics Inc**........F....... 718 523-1180
Greenlawn *(G-5892)*
▼ **Meliorum Technologies Inc**........G....... 585 313-0616
Rochester *(G-14524)*
◆ **Mitsui Chemicals America Inc**........E....... 914 253-0777
Rye Brook *(G-15098)*
Momentive Performance Mtls Inc........D....... 914 784-4807
Tarrytown *(G-16121)*
▲ **Nationwide Tarps Incorporated**........D....... 518 843-1545
Amsterdam *(G-362)*
Newmat Northeast Corp........F....... 631 253-9277
West Babylon *(G-16846)*

Employee Codes: A=Over 500 employees, B=251-500
C=101-250, D=51-100, E=20-50, F=10-19, G=5-9

2018 Harris
New York Manufacturers Directory

777

S
I
C

Parker-Hannifin Corporation....E....315 926-4211
Marion *(G-8127)*
▼ Pawling Corporation....C....845 855-1000
Pawling *(G-13474)*
Perfect Poly Inc....E....631 265-0539
Nesconset *(G-8825)*
Plaslok Corp....E....716 681-7755
Buffalo *(G-3151)*
Plexi Craft Quality Products....F....212 924-3244
New York *(G-11699)*
Polycast Industries Inc....G....631 595-2530
Bay Shore *(G-722)*
▲ Queen City Manufacturing Inc....G....716 877-1102
Buffalo *(G-3176)*
Rodgard Corporation....E....716 852-1435
Buffalo *(G-3191)*
Sabic Innovative Plas US LLC....B....518 475-5011
Selkirk *(G-15380)*
▲ Saga International Recycl LLC....G....718 621-5900
Brooklyn *(G-2553)*
Saint-Gobain Prfmce Plas Corp....C....518 686-7301
Hoosick Falls *(G-6572)*
Saint-Gobain Prfmce Plas Corp....C....518 642-2200
Granville *(G-5796)*
▲ SC Medical Overseas Inc....G....516 935-8500
Jericho *(G-7117)*
Solid Surfaces Inc....D....585 292-5340
Rochester *(G-14716)*
Telechemische Inc....G....845 561-3237
Newburgh *(G-12805)*
▼ Terphane Holdings LLC....G....585 657-5800
Bloomfield *(G-984)*
◆ Terphane Inc....D....585 657-5800
Bloomfield *(G-985)*
▼ Tmp Technologies Inc....D....716 895-6100
Buffalo *(G-3246)*
◆ Toray Holding (usa) Inc....E....212 697-8150
New York *(G-12393)*
Toray Industries Inc....G....212 697-8150
New York *(G-12394)*
▲ Transpo Industries Inc....E....914 636-1000
New Rochelle *(G-8972)*
Tri-Seal Holdings Inc....D....845 353-3300
Blauvelt *(G-972)*
Unico Inc....F....845 562-9255
Newburgh *(G-12806)*
Wilsonart Intl Holdings LLC....E....516 935-6980
Bethpage *(G-878)*
WR Smith & Sons Inc....G....845 620-9400
Nanuet *(G-8809)*

2822 Synthetic Rubber (Vulcanizable Elastomers)

Canton Bio-Medical Inc....E....518 283-5963
Poestenkill *(G-13752)*
David Fehlman....G....315 455-8888
Syracuse *(G-15942)*
▲ Depco Inc....F....631 582-1995
Hauppauge *(G-6083)*
▲ Dynax Corporation....G....914 764-0202
Pound Ridge *(G-13959)*
▲ Hilord Chemical Corporation....E....631 234-7373
Hauppauge *(G-6117)*
▲ Integrated Liner Tech Inc....E....518 621-7422
Rensselaer *(G-14059)*
Release Coatings New York Inc....G....585 593-2335
Wellsville *(G-16782)*
Silicone Products & Technology....C....716 684-1155
Lancaster *(G-7368)*
▲ Specialty Silicone Pdts Inc....E....518 885-8826
Ballston Spa *(G-608)*
Vasquez Tito....F....212 944-0441
New York *(G-12533)*

2823 Cellulosic Man-Made Fibers

3M Company....B....716 876-1596
Tonawanda *(G-16154)*
◆ Cortland Cable Company Inc....E....607 753-8276
Cortland *(G-4039)*
Cytec Industries Inc....D....716 372-9650
Olean *(G-13162)*
E I Du Pont De Nemours & Co....E....716 876-4420
Buffalo *(G-2938)*
International Fiber Corp....F....716 693-4040
North Tonawanda *(G-12995)*
Solivaira Specialties Inc....D....716 693-4009
North Tonawanda *(G-13014)*
◆ Solvaira Specialties Inc....C....716 693-4040
North Tonawanda *(G-13015)*

2824 Synthetic Organic Fibers, Exc Cellulosic

Dal-Tile Corporation....G....718 894-9574
Maspeth *(G-8159)*
▲ Dynax Corporation....G....914 764-0202
Pound Ridge *(G-13959)*
Fibrix LLC....E....716 683-4100
Depew *(G-4281)*
Marly Home Industries USA Inc....G....718 388-3030
Brooklyn *(G-2276)*
Solid Surface Acrylics LLC....F....716 743-1870
North Tonawanda *(G-13013)*
Solutia Business Entps Inc....F....314 674-1000
New York *(G-12154)*
◆ Stein Fibers Ltd....F....518 489-5700
Albany *(G-137)*
Vybion Inc....F....607 266-0860
Ithaca *(G-6918)*

2833 Medicinal Chemicals & Botanical Prdts

Abh Natures Products Inc....E....631 249-5783
Edgewood *(G-4602)*
Accredo Health Incorporated....G....718 353-3012
Flushing *(G-5228)*
▼ Ajes Pharmaceuticals LLC....E....631 608-1728
Copiague *(G-3917)*
Albany Molecular Research Inc....F....518 433-7700
Rensselaer *(G-14054)*
Albany Molecular Research Inc....F....518 512-2000
Rensselaer *(G-14055)*
Alo Acquisition LLC....G....518 464-0279
Albany *(G-43)*
Asept Pak Inc....E....518 651-2026
Malone *(G-8038)*
◆ Bio-Botanica Inc....D....631 231-0987
Hauppauge *(G-6053)*
Biotemper....G....516 302-7985
Carle Place *(G-3413)*
Collaborative Laboratories....D....631 689-0200
East Setauket *(G-4498)*
Cosmic Enterprise....G....718 342-6257
Brooklyn *(G-1806)*
G C Hanford Manufacturing Co....C....315 476-7418
Syracuse *(G-15967)*
GE Healthcare Inc....F....516 626-2799
Port Washington *(G-13841)*
▲ Gemini Pharmaceuticals Inc....C....631 543-3334
Commack *(G-3859)*
Good Earth Inc....G....716 684-8111
Lancaster *(G-7341)*
Healthee Endeavors Inc....G....718 653-5499
Bronx *(G-1355)*
Healthy N Fit Intl Inc....F....914 271-6040
Croton On Hudson *(G-4090)*
Immudyne Inc....F....914 244-1777
Mount Kisco *(G-8671)*
Kannalife Sciences Inc....G....516 669-3219
Lloyd Harbor *(G-7594)*
Lee Yuen Fung Trading Co Inc....F....212 594-9595
New York *(G-10994)*
▲ Mercer Milling Co....E....315 701-1334
Liverpool *(G-7559)*
▲ Natural Organics Inc....C....631 293-0030
Melville *(G-8368)*
Natures Bounty Co....F....631 200-2000
Bayport *(G-753)*
Natures Bounty Co....F....631 244-2065
Ronkonkoma *(G-14976)*
Natures Bounty Co....F....518 452-5813
Albany *(G-105)*
Natures Bounty Co....D....631 244-2021
Ronkonkoma *(G-14977)*
◆ Natures Bounty Co....A....631 200-2000
Ronkonkoma *(G-14978)*
Natures Bounty Co....D....631 200-7338
Ronkonkoma *(G-14979)*
Natures Bounty Co....F....631 588-3492
Holbrook *(G-6493)*
◆ Nbty Manufacturing LLC....E....631 567-9500
Ronkonkoma *(G-14980)*
Nutra Solutions USA Inc....E....631 392-1900
Deer Park *(G-4207)*
Nutraqueen LLC....F....347 368-6568
New York *(G-11489)*
Nutrascience Labs Inc....E....631 247-0660
Farmingdale *(G-5078)*
Only Natural Inc....F....516 897-7001
Oceanside *(G-13110)*
◆ Pfizer Inc....A....212 733-2323
New York *(G-11657)*
Pfizer Overseas LLC....G....212 733-2323
New York *(G-11662)*
Princeton Sciences....G....845 368-1214
Airmont *(G-16)*
Proper Chemical Ltd....G....631 420-8000
Farmingdale *(G-5101)*
Regeneron Pharmaceuticals Inc....E....518 488-6000
Rensselaer *(G-14061)*
Setauket Manufacturing Co....G....631 231-7272
Ronkonkoma *(G-15008)*
Stauber California Inc....F....845 651-4443
Florida *(G-5222)*
▲ Ucb Pharma Inc....B....919 767-2555
Rochester *(G-14765)*
Vitalize Labs LLC....G....212 966-6130
New York *(G-12584)*
Vitamix Laboratories Inc....E....631 465-9245
Commack *(G-3871)*
Wacf Enterprise Inc....E....631 745-5841
Northport *(G-13035)*
▲ Wellquest International Inc....G....212 689-9094
New York *(G-12636)*

2834 Pharmaceuticals

3v Company Inc....E....718 858-7333
Brooklyn *(G-1516)*
5th Avenue Pharmacy Inc....G....718 439-8585
Brooklyn *(G-1519)*
872 Hunts Point Pharmacy Inc....G....718 991-3519
Bronx *(G-1251)*
888 Pharmacy Inc....F....718 871-8833
Brooklyn *(G-1522)*
A & Z Pharmaceutical Inc....D....631 952-3802
Hauppauge *(G-6026)*
◆ A & Z Pharmaceutical Inc....C....631 952-3800
Hauppauge *(G-6027)*
Abh Pharma Inc....D....631 392-4692
Edgewood *(G-4603)*
Abraxis Bioscience LLC....G....716 773-0800
Grand Island *(G-5764)*
▲ Acorda Therapeutics Inc....C....914 347-4300
Ardsley *(G-402)*
▲ Actavis Laboratories Ny Inc....D....631 693-8000
Copiague *(G-3915)*
Actinium Pharmaceuticals Inc....E....646 677-3870
New York *(G-9067)*
Advance Pharmaceutical Inc....E....631 981-4600
Holtsville *(G-6525)*
▲ Affymax Inc....G....650 812-8700
New York *(G-9104)*
Aiping Pharmaceutical Inc....G....631 952-3802
Hauppauge *(G-6031)*
Akari Therapeutics PLC....G....646 350-0702
New York *(G-9117)*
▲ Alfred Khalily Inc....F....516 504-0059
Great Neck *(G-5802)*
Allied Pharmacy Products Inc....G....516 374-8862
Woodmere *(G-17328)*
▲ Altaire Pharmaceuticals Inc....C....631 722-5988
Aquebogue *(G-383)*
American Bio Medica Corp....D....518 758-8158
Kinderhook *(G-7196)*
American Hormones Inc....F....845 471-7272
Poughkeepsie *(G-13904)*
American Regent Inc....B....631 924-4000
Shirley *(G-15434)*
Amneal Pharmaceuticals LLC....E....908 231-1911
Brookhaven *(G-1504)*
Amneal Pharmaceuticals LLC....E....631 952-0214
Brookhaven *(G-1505)*
▲ Amneal Pharmaceuticals LLC....E....908 947-3120
Brookhaven *(G-1506)*
Anacor Pharmaceuticals Inc....C....212 733-2323
New York *(G-9194)*
Angiogenex Inc....G....347 468-6799
New York *(G-9207)*
Anima Mundi Herbals LLC....G....415 279-5727
Long Island City *(G-7693)*
Anterios Inc....G....212 303-1683
New York *(G-9217)*
Apothecus Pharmaceutical Corp....F....516 624-8200
Oyster Bay *(G-13391)*
Ark Sciences Inc....G....646 943-1520
Islandia *(G-6825)*
Asence Inc....E....347 335-2606
New York *(G-9280)*
Athenex Inc....C....716 427-2950
Buffalo *(G-2842)*
Athenex Inc....D....716 427-2950
Buffalo *(G-2843)*

SIC SECTION

28 CHEMICALS AND ALLIED PRODUCTS

Athenex Pharma Solutions LLC ....G....... 877 463-7823
Clarence *(G-3684)*
Atlantic Essential Pdts Inc ....D....... 631 434-8333
Hauppauge *(G-6046)*
Auven Therapeutics MGT LP ....F....... 212 616-4000
New York *(G-9321)*
Auxilium Pharmaceuticals Inc ....F....... 484 321-2022
Rye *(G-15080)*
Avenue Therapeutics Inc ....G....... 781 652-4500
New York *(G-9328)*
Axim Biotechnologies Inc ....F....... 212 751-0001
New York *(G-9336)*
Azurrx Biopharma Inc ....F....... 646 699-7855
Brooklyn *(G-1655)*
▲ **Barc Usa Inc** ....E....... 516 719-1052
New Hyde Park *(G-8863)*
BASF Corporation ....B....... 914 785-2000
Tarrytown *(G-16111)*
Bausch & Lomb Holdings Inc ....G....... 585 338-6000
New York *(G-9384)*
◆ **Bausch & Lomb Incorporated** ....B....... 585 338-6000
Rochester *(G-14242)*
Baxter International Inc ....G....... 845 457-9370
Montgomery *(G-8627)*
Beyondspring Inc ....E....... 646 305-6387
New York *(G-9431)*
Beyondspring Phrmceuticals Inc ....F....... 646 305-6387
New York *(G-9432)*
Bi Nutraceuticals Inc ....D....... 631 232-1105
Central Islip *(G-3513)*
Bicon Pharmaceutical Inc ....F....... 631 593-4199
Deer Park *(G-4131)*
◆ **Bio-Botanica Inc** ....D....... 631 231-0987
Hauppauge *(G-6053)*
Biomed Pharmaceuticals Inc ....G....... 914 592-0525
Hawthorne *(G-6267)*
▲ **Biospecifics Technologies Corp** ....G....... 516 593-7000
Lynbrook *(G-7976)*
Bli International Inc ....C....... 631 940-9000
Deer Park *(G-4133)*
Bristol-Myers Squibb Company ....A....... 212 546-4000
New York *(G-9516)*
Bristol-Myers Squibb Company ....E....... 315 432-2000
East Syracuse *(G-4529)*
Bristol-Myers Squibb Company ....C....... 516 832-2191
Garden City *(G-5511)*
Bronson Nutritionals LLC ....E....... 631 750-0000
Hauppauge *(G-6057)*
Campbell Alliance Group Inc ....E....... 212 377-2740
New York *(G-9560)*
Cancer Targeting Systems ....G....... 212 965-4534
New York *(G-9564)*
Cellvation Inc ....G....... 212 554-4520
New York *(G-9608)*
Central Islip Pharmacy Inc ....G....... 631 234-6039
Central Islip *(G-3515)*
Century Grand Inc ....F....... 212 925-3838
New York *(G-9620)*
Cerovene Inc ....F....... 845 359-1101
Orangeburg *(G-13243)*
Cerovene Inc ....F....... 845 267-2055
Valley Cottage *(G-16403)*
Chartwell Pharma Nda B2 Holdin ....G....... 845 268-5000
Congers *(G-3879)*
Chartwell Pharmaceuticals LLC ....D....... 845 268-5000
Congers *(G-3880)*
Cleveland Biolabs Inc ....E....... 716 849-6810
Buffalo *(G-2896)*
Cognigen Corporation ....D....... 716 633-3463
Buffalo *(G-2898)*
▼ **Combe Incorporated** ....C....... 914 694-5454
White Plains *(G-17123)*
Container Tstg Solutions LLC ....F....... 716 487-3300
Jamestown *(G-7018)*
Container Tstg Solutions LLC ....F....... 716 487-3300
Sinclairville *(G-15474)*
Contract Pharmacal Corp ....E....... 631 231-4610
Hauppauge *(G-6073)*
Contract Pharmacal Corp ....C....... 631 231-4610
Hauppauge *(G-6074)*
Contract Pharmacal Corp ....E....... 631 231-4610
Hauppauge *(G-6075)*
Contract Pharmacal Corp ....D....... 631 231-4610
Hauppauge *(G-6076)*
Contract Pharmacal Corp ....C....... 631 231-4610
Hauppauge *(G-6077)*
Contract Pharmacal Corp ....F....... 631 231-4610
Hauppauge *(G-6078)*
Contract Phrmctcals Ltd Nagara ....C....... 716 887-3400
Buffalo *(G-2908)*
Cortice Biosciences Inc ....F....... 646 747-9090
New York *(G-9787)*
▲ **CRS Nuclear Services LLC** ....F....... 716 810-0688
Cheektowaga *(G-3593)*
▲ **Danbury Pharma LLC** ....E....... 631 393-6333
Farmingdale *(G-4984)*
Delcath Systems Inc ....E....... 212 489-2100
New York *(G-9893)*
Dr Reddys Laboratories NY Inc ....E....... 518 827-7702
Middleburgh *(G-8452)*
Drt Laboratories LLC ....G....... 845 547-2034
Airmont *(G-12)*
DSM Nutritional Products LLC ....C....... 518 372-5155
Schenectady *(G-15276)*
DSM Nutritional Products LLC ....C....... 518 372-5155
Glenville *(G-5716)*
Durata Therapeutics Inc ....G....... 646 871-6400
New York *(G-9991)*
Easton Pharmaceuticals Inc ....G....... 347 284-0192
Lewiston *(G-7454)*
Eckerson Drugs Inc ....F....... 845 352-1800
Spring Valley *(G-15605)*
▼ **Edlaw Pharmaceuticals Inc** ....E....... 631 454-6888
Farmingdale *(G-4994)*
Eli Lilly and Company ....F....... 516 622-2244
New Hyde Park *(G-8876)*
▲ **Encysive Pharmaceuticals Inc** ....E....... 212 733-2323
New York *(G-10082)*
Enumeral Biomedical Corp ....G....... 347 227-4787
New York *(G-10099)*
Enzo Life Sciences Inc ....E....... 631 694-7070
Farmingdale *(G-4997)*
◆ **Enzo Life Sciences Intl Inc** ....E....... 610 941-0430
Farmingdale *(G-4998)*
Eon Labs Inc ....F....... 516 478-9700
New Hyde Park *(G-8877)*
▲ **Epic Pharma LLC** ....C....... 718 276-8600
Laurelton *(G-7413)*
Erika T Schwartz MD PC ....G....... 212 873-3420
New York *(G-10110)*
▲ **FB Laboratories Inc** ....E....... 631 750-0000
Hauppauge *(G-6098)*
Flushing Pharmacy Inc ....C....... 718 260-8999
Brooklyn *(G-1989)*
▲ **Forest Laboratories LLC** ....C....... 212 421-7850
New York *(G-10237)*
Forest Laboratories LLC ....D....... 212 421-7850
Hauppauge *(G-6103)*
Forest Laboratories LLC ....C....... 631 858-6010
Commack *(G-3857)*
Fortress Biotech Inc ....F....... 781 652-4500
New York *(G-10239)*
▲ **Fougera Pharmaceuticals Inc** ....C....... 631 454-7677
Melville *(G-8350)*
Fougera Pharmaceuticals Inc ....C....... 631 454-7677
Hicksville *(G-6375)*
Freeda Vitamins Inc ....E....... 718 433-4337
Long Island City *(G-7774)*
Fresenius Kabi Usa LLC ....B....... 716 773-0053
Grand Island *(G-5771)*
Fresenius Kabi USA LLC ....E....... 716 773-0800
Grand Island *(G-5772)*
▲ **Futurebiotics LLC** ....E....... 631 273-6300
Hauppauge *(G-6105)*
G C Hanford Manufacturing Co ....C....... 315 476-7418
Syracuse *(G-15967)*
▼ **Gamma Enterprises LLC** ....E....... 631 755-1080
West Babylon *(G-16819)*
▲ **Generics Bidco I LLC** ....G....... 256 859-4011
Chestnut Ridge *(G-3651)*
▲ **Geritrex LLC** ....E....... 914 668-4003
Mount Vernon *(G-8727)*
Geritrex Holdings Inc ....G....... 914 668-4003
Mount Vernon *(G-8728)*
Glaxosmithkline LLC ....E....... 845 341-7590
Montgomery *(G-8630)*
Glaxosmithkline LLC ....E....... 845 797-3259
Wappingers Falls *(G-16591)*
Glaxosmithkline LLC ....E....... 585 738-9025
Rochester *(G-14427)*
Glaxosmithkline LLC ....E....... 716 913-5679
Buffalo *(G-2990)*
Glaxosmithkline LLC ....D....... 518 239-6901
East Durham *(G-4409)*
Glaxosmithkline LLC ....E....... 518 852-9637
Mechanicville *(G-8259)*
Global Alliance For Tb ....E....... 212 227-7540
New York *(G-10351)*
Glycobia Inc ....G....... 607 339-0051
Ithaca *(G-6880)*
Greenkissny Inc ....G....... 914 304-4323
White Plains *(G-17141)*
Greentree Pharmacy Inc ....F....... 718 768-2700
Brooklyn *(G-2055)*
Guosa Life Sciences Inc ....F....... 718 813-7806
North Baldwin *(G-12923)*
▲ **H W Naylor Co Inc** ....F....... 607 263-5145
Morris *(G-8660)*
Healthone Pharmacy Inc ....F....... 718 495-9015
Brooklyn *(G-2068)*
HHS Pharmaceuticals Inc ....F....... 347 674-1670
New York *(G-10516)*
▲ **Hi-Tech Pharmacal Co Inc** ....C....... 631 789-8228
Amityville *(G-293)*
▲ **Hogil Pharmaceutical Corp** ....F....... 914 681-1800
White Plains *(G-17147)*
Holistic Blends Inc ....G....... 315 468-4300
Syracuse *(G-15979)*
Hospira Inc ....C....... 716 684-9400
Buffalo *(G-3015)*
Ibio Inc ....E....... 302 355-0650
New York *(G-10591)*
◆ **Ima Life North America Inc** ....C....... 716 695-6354
Tonawanda *(G-16191)*
Innogenix Inc ....F....... 631 450-4704
Amityville *(G-295)*
Innovative Labs LLC ....D....... 631 231-5522
Hauppauge *(G-6121)*
Inolife Technologies Inc ....G....... 212 348-5600
New York *(G-10648)*
▼ **Intellicell Biosciences Inc** ....G....... 646 576-8700
New York *(G-10660)*
Intercept Pharmaceuticals Inc ....D....... 646 747-1000
New York *(G-10668)*
International Life Science ....G....... 631 549-0471
Huntington *(G-6698)*
▲ **Intra-Cellular Therapies Inc** ....E....... 212 923-3344
New York *(G-10687)*
Intstrux LLC ....E....... 646 688-2782
New York *(G-10690)*
Invagen Pharmaceuticals Inc ....C....... 631 949-6367
Central Islip *(G-3525)*
▲ **Invagen Pharmaceuticals Inc** ....B....... 631 231-3233
Hauppauge *(G-6123)*
Ip Med Inc ....G....... 516 766-3800
Oceanside *(G-13102)*
Izun Pharmaceuticals Corp ....F....... 212 618-6357
New York *(G-10713)*
Jerome Stvens Phrmcuticals Inc ....F....... 631 567-1113
Bohemia *(G-1078)*
▲ **JRS Pharma LP** ....E....... 845 878-8300
Patterson *(G-13465)*
▲ **Kabco Pharmaceuticals Inc** ....G....... 631 842-3600
Amityville *(G-300)*
Kadmon Corporation LLC ....F....... 212 308-6000
New York *(G-10835)*
Kadmon Holdings Inc ....D....... 212 308-6000
New York *(G-10836)*
Kannalife Sciences Inc ....G....... 516 669-3219
Lloyd Harbor *(G-7594)*
Kbl Healthcare LP ....G....... 212 319-5555
New York *(G-10863)*
◆ **Kent Chemical Corporation** ....E....... 212 521-1700
New York *(G-10878)*
Kingston Pharma LLC ....G....... 315 705-4019
Massena *(G-8228)*
▲ **Klg Usa LLC** ....A....... 845 856-5311
Port Jervis *(G-13811)*
Life Pill Laboratories LLC ....G....... 914 682-2146
White Plains *(G-17159)*
▲ **Liptis Pharmaceuticals USA Inc** ....A....... 845 627-0260
Spring Valley *(G-15614)*
LNK International Inc ....D....... 631 435-3500
Hauppauge *(G-6139)*
LNK International Inc ....D....... 631 435-3500
Hauppauge *(G-6140)*
LNK International Inc ....D....... 631 435-3500
Hauppauge *(G-6141)*
LNK International Inc ....D....... 631 543-3787
Hauppauge *(G-6142)*
LNK International Inc ....D....... 631 435-3500
Hauppauge *(G-6143)*
LNK International Inc ....D....... 631 231-3415
Hauppauge *(G-6144)*
LNK International Inc ....D....... 631 231-4020
Hauppauge *(G-6145)*
▲ **Lotta Luv Beauty LLC** ....F....... 646 786-2847
New York *(G-11074)*
▲ **Luitpold Pharmaceuticals Inc** ....B....... 631 924-4000
Shirley *(G-15446)*

SIC

Employee Codes: A=Over 500 employees, B=251-500
C=101-250, D=51-100, E=20-50, F=10-19, G=5-9

2018 Harris
New York Manufacturers Directory

779

28 CHEMICALS AND ALLIED PRODUCTS — SIC SECTION

Macrochem Corporation ....G...... 212 514-8094
New York (G-11117)

Mallinckrodt LLC ....A...... 607 538-9124
Hobart (G-6452)

▲ Marco Hi-Tech JV LLC ....G...... 212 798-8100
New York (G-11169)

▲ Marietta Corporation ....B...... 607 753-6746
Cortland (G-4057)

Marken LLP ....G...... 631 396-7454
Farmingdale (G-5050)

Maxus Pharmaceuticals Inc ....F...... 631 249-0003
Farmingdale (G-5054)

Medek Laboratories Inc ....E...... 845 943-4988
Monroe (G-8597)

▲ Medtech Products Inc ....F...... 914 524-6810
Tarrytown (G-16119)

◆ Mentholatum Company ....E...... 716 677-2500
Orchard Park (G-13309)

▲ Mercer Milling Co ....E...... 315 701-1434
Liverpool (G-7559)

Mesoblast Inc ....G...... 212 880-2060
New York (G-11265)

Mskcc Rmipc ....F...... 212 639-6212
New York (G-11342)

Mustang Bio Inc ....G...... 781 652-4500
New York (G-11351)

Nanorx Inc ....G...... 914 671-0224
Chappaqua (G-3581)

Natural Organics Laboratories ....B...... 631 957-5600
Amityville (G-314)

Natures Bounty (ny) Inc ....F...... 631 567-9500
Bohemia (G-1103)

▲ Natures Bounty (ny) Inc ....A...... 631 580-6137
Ronkonkoma (G-14975)

▲ Natures Value Inc ....C...... 631 846-2500
Coram (G-3969)

ND Labs Inc ....F...... 516 612-4900
Lynbrook (G-7982)

Neurotrope Inc ....G...... 973 242-0005
New York (G-11399)

Noho Health Inc ....E...... 877 227-3631
New York (G-11467)

▲ Norwich Pharmaceuticals Inc ...B...... 607 335-3000
Norwich (G-13052)

Nostrand Pharmacy LLC ....G...... 718 282-2956
Brooklyn (G-2387)

Novartis Corporation ....E...... 914 592-7476
Tarrytown (G-16122)

Novartis Corporation ....D...... 718 276-8600
Laurelton (G-7414)

Novartis Pharmaceuticals Corp ...G...... 718 276-8600
Laurelton (G-7415)

Noven Pharmaceuticals Inc ....E...... 212 682-4420
New York (G-11481)

Nutra-Scientifics LLC ....G...... 917 238-8510
Pomona (G-13759)

Nutraceutical Wellness LLC ....G...... 888 454-3320
New York (G-11488)

Nutrascience Labs Inc ....E...... 631 247-0660
Farmingdale (G-5078)

NV Prrcone MD Cosmeceuticals ...G...... 212 734-2537
New York (G-11491)

NY Phrmacy Compounding Ctr Inc ...G...... 201 403-5151
Astoria (G-450)

Ohr Pharmaceutical Inc ....F...... 212 682-8452
New York (G-11512)

Oligomerix Inc ....G...... 914 997-8877
New York (G-11514)

Ony Biotech Inc ....E...... 716 636-9096
Amherst (G-257)

Ony Inc Baird Researchpark ....E...... 716 636-9096
Buffalo (G-3124)

Ophthotech Corporation ....C...... 212 845-8200
New York (G-11529)

Organic Frog Inc ....G...... 516 897-0369
Hauppauge (G-6182)

OSI Pharmaceuticals LLC ....D...... 631 847-0175
Farmingdale (G-5083)

▼ OSI Pharmaceuticals LLC ....G...... 631 962-2000
Farmingdale (G-5084)

Ovid Therapeutics Inc ....E...... 646 661-7661
New York (G-11550)

P & L Development LLC ....D...... 516 986-1700
Westbury (G-17043)

P & L Development LLC ....F...... 516 986-1700
Westbury (G-17044)

◆ P & L Development LLC ....D...... 516 986-1700
Westbury (G-17045)

Pace Up Pharmaceuticals LLC .....F...... 631 450-4495
Lindenhurst (G-7502)

◆ Pall Corporation ....A...... 516 484-5400
Port Washington (G-13870)

▲ Par Pharmaceutical Inc ....A...... 845 573-5500
Chestnut Ridge (G-3653)

Par Phrmceutical Companies Inc ...E...... 845 573-5500
Chestnut Ridge (G-3654)

Par Sterile Products LLC ....A...... 845 573-5500
Chestnut Ridge (G-3655)

Pdk Labs Inc ....G...... 631 273-2630
Hauppauge (G-6184)

Perrigo Company ....E...... 718 960-9900
Bronx (G-1426)

Perrigo New York Inc ....F...... 718 901-2800
Bronx (G-1427)

▲ Perrigo New York Inc ....B...... 718 960-9900
Bronx (G-1428)

Petnet Solutions Inc ....G...... 865 218-2000
New York (G-11654)

▲ Pfizer HCP Corporation ....G...... 212 733-2323
New York (G-11656)

◆ Pfizer Inc ....A...... 212 733-2323
New York (G-11657)

Pfizer Inc ....B...... 518 297-6611
Rouses Point (G-15066)

Pfizer Inc ....C...... 914 437-5868
White Plains (G-17186)

Pfizer Inc ....C...... 937 746-3603
New York (G-11658)

Pfizer Inc ....D...... 212 733-6276
New York (G-11659)

Pfizer Inc ....C...... 804 257-2000
New York (G-11660)

Pfizer Inc ....C...... 212 733-2323
New York (G-11661)

Pfizer Overseas LLC ....G...... 212 733-2323
New York (G-11662)

▲ Pharbest Pharmaceuticals Inc ....E...... 631 249-5130
Farmingdale (G-5087)

▲ Pharmaceutic Labs LLC ....G...... 518 608-1060
Albany (G-119)

Pharmalife Inc ....G...... 631 249-4040
Farmingdale (G-5088)

▲ Pharmavantage LLC ....G...... 631 321-8171
Babylon (G-549)

Phoenix Laboratories Inc ....C...... 516 822-1230
Farmingdale (G-5089)

▲ Photomedex Inc ....E...... 888 966-1010
Orangeburg (G-13261)

Pine Pharmaceuticals LLC ....G...... 716 248-1025
Tonawanda (G-16211)

Polygen Pharmaceuticals Inc ......E...... 631 392-4044
Edgewood (G-4621)

Precision Pharma Services Inc ...C...... 631 752-7314
Melville (G-8378)

Premium Processing Corp ....D...... 631 232-1105
Babylon (G-551)

◆ Prestige Brands Intl LLC ....F...... 914 524-6810
Tarrytown (G-16126)

▲ Prime Pack LLC ....F...... 732 253-7734
New York (G-11732)

Progenics Pharmaceuticals Inc ..D...... 646 975-2500
New York (G-11750)

Purine Pharma LLC ....E...... 315 705-4030
Mount Vernon (G-8768)

Purinepharma LLC ....G...... 732 485-1400
Massena (G-8230)

▲ Purity Products Inc ....D...... 516 767-1967
Plainview (G-13659)

Quality Nature Inc ....G...... 718 484-4666
Brooklyn (G-2480)

Quogue Capital LLC ....G...... 212 554-4475
New York (G-11801)

Quva Pharma Inc ....G...... 973 224-7795
New York (G-11804)

R J S Direct Marketing Inc ....F...... 631 667-5768
Deer Park (G-4222)

Randob Labs Ltd ....G...... 845 534-2197
Cornwall (G-4012)

▲ Regeneron Pharmaceuticals Inc ...B...... 914 847-7000
Tarrytown (G-16128)

Regenron Hlthcare Slutions Inc ...A...... 914 847-7000
Tarrytown (G-16129)

Relmada Therapeutics Inc ....F...... 646 677-3853
New York (G-11857)

Retrophin LLC ....G...... 646 564-3680
New York (G-11876)

Rij Pharmaceutical Corporation ...E...... 845 692-5799
Middletown (G-8494)

Rls Holdings Inc ....G...... 716 418-7274
Clarence (G-3697)

◆ Rohto USA Inc ....G...... 716 677-2500
Orchard Park (G-13320)

Ropack USA Inc ....F...... 631 482-7777
Commack (G-3866)

S1 Biopharma Inc ....G...... 201 839-0941
New York (G-11965)

▲ Safetec of America Inc ....D...... 716 895-1822
Buffalo (G-3202)

Salutem Group LLC ....G...... 347 620-2640
New York (G-11977)

Saptalis Pharmaceuticals LLC .....F...... 631 231-2751
Hauppauge (G-6209)

Satnam Distributors LLC ....G...... 516 802-0600
Jericho (G-7116)

Scarguard Labs LLC ....F...... 516 482-8050
Great Neck (G-5856)

Sciarra Laboratories Inc ....G...... 516 933-7853
Hicksville (G-6420)

▲ Sciegen Pharmaceuticals Inc ....G...... 631 434-2723
Hauppauge (G-6211)

Scienta Pharmaceuticals LLC ......G...... 845 589-0774
Valley Cottage (G-16414)

Seidlin Consulting ....G...... 212 496-2043
New York (G-12039)

Shennong Pharmaceuticals Inc ...E...... 347 422-2200
New York (G-12070)

Shrineeta Pharmacy ....G...... 212 234-7959
New York (G-12078)

Shrineeta Pharmacy Inc ....G...... 212 234-7959
New York (G-12079)

Siga Technologies Inc ....E...... 212 672-9100
New York (G-12088)

▲ Silarx Pharmaceuticals Inc ....D...... 845 352-4020
Carmel (G-3433)

Silver Oak Pharmacy Inc ....G...... 718 922-3400
Brooklyn (G-2584)

Sincerus LLC ....G...... 800 419-2804
Brooklyn (G-2590)

Skills Alliance Inc ....G...... 646 492-5300
New York (G-12115)

Skincare Products Inc ....G...... 917 837-5255
New York (G-12117)

Slv Labs LLC ....G...... 631 901-1170
Hauppauge (G-6217)

Stemline Therapeutics Inc ....E...... 646 502-2311
New York (G-12216)

Steri-Pharma LLC ....E...... 315 473-7180
Syracuse (G-16069)

Sterrx LLC ....E...... 518 324-7879
Plattsburgh (G-13728)

Sterrx LLC ....F...... 518 324-7879
Plattsburgh (G-13729)

Strategic Pharma Services Inc ...F...... 631 231-5424
Brentwood (G-1192)

Strativa Pharmaceuticals ....F...... 201 802-4000
Spring Valley (G-15623)

Sunquest Pharmaceuticals Inc ...F...... 855 478-6779
Hicksville (G-6424)

Synergy Pharmaceuticals Inc .....F...... 212 297-0020
New York (G-12284)

Syntho Pharmaceuticals Inc ....G...... 631 755-9898
Farmingdale (G-5132)

▲ Tg Therapeutics Inc ....D...... 212 554-4484
New York (G-12328)

▲ Time-Cap Laboratories Inc ....C...... 631 753-9090
Farmingdale (G-5141)

▲ Tishcon Corp ....C...... 516 333-3056
Westbury (G-17061)

Tishcon Corp ....C...... 516 333-3050
Westbury (G-17062)

Tishcon Corp ....C...... 516 333-3050
Westbury (G-17063)

Tishcon Corp ....C...... 516 333-3050
Westbury (G-17064)

▼ Tmp Technologies Inc ....D...... 716 895-6100
Buffalo (G-3246)

Tocare LLC ....G...... 718 767-0618
Whitestone (G-17244)

Tongli Pharmaceuticals USA Inc ...E...... 212 842-8837
Flushing (G-5307)

Tonix Phrmceuticals Holdg Corp ...E...... 212 980-9155
New York (G-12388)

▲ Topiderm Inc ....C...... 631 226-7979
Amityville (G-330)

▲ Topix Pharmaceuticals Inc ....B...... 631 226-7979
Amityville (G-331)

Transparency Life Sciences LLC ...F...... 862 252-1216
New York (G-12414)

Triceutical Inc ....F...... 631 249-0003
Bronx (G-1475)

Tyme Technologies Inc.....................G...... 646 205-1603
  New York *(G-12456)*
▲ Ucb Pharma Inc..............................B...... 919 767-2555
  Rochester *(G-14765)*
▼ Unipharm Inc..................................E...... 212 564-3634
  New York *(G-12478)*
United-Guardian Inc..........................E...... 631 273-0900
  Hauppauge *(G-6244)*
▲ Unither Manufacturing LLC..............C...... 585 475-9000
  Rochester *(G-14769)*
▲ Velocity Pharma LLC......................G...... 516 312-7585
  Farmingdale *(G-5147)*
▼ Venus Pharmaceuticals Intl Inc.......F...... 631 249-4140
  Hauppauge *(G-6248)*
Verona Pharma Inc............................F...... 914 797-5007
  White Plains *(G-17207)*
Very Best Irtj.......................................F...... 914 271-6585
  Croton On Hudson *(G-4092)*
Vida-Blend LLC..................................E...... 518 627-4138
  Amsterdam *(G-373)*
Viropro Inc...G...... 650 300-5190
  New York *(G-12576)*
▲ Vita-Nat Inc......................................G...... 631 293-6000
  Farmingdale *(G-5148)*
Vitalis LLC..G...... 646 831-7338
  New York *(G-12583)*
▲ Vitane Pharmaceuticals Inc............E...... 845 267-6700
  Congers *(G-3887)*
Vvs International Inc..........................G...... 212 302-5410
  New York *(G-12599)*
Wavodyne Therapeutics Inc..............G...... 954 632-6630
  West Henrietta *(G-16930)*
Wellmill LLC.......................................F...... 631 465-9245
  Farmingdale *(G-5152)*
Wyeth Holdings LLC..........................D...... 845 602-5000
  Pearl River *(G-13493)*
◆ Wyeth LLC..A...... 973 660-5000
  New York *(G-12697)*
X-Gen Pharmaceuticals Inc...............G...... 607 562-2700
  Big Flats *(G-880)*
X-Gen Pharmaceuticals Inc...............E...... 631 261-8188
  Elmira *(G-4720)*
X-Gen Pharmaceuticals Inc...............E...... 607 562-2700
  Horseheads *(G-6624)*
Xstelos Holdings Inc..........................G...... 212 729-4962
  New York *(G-12707)*
Ys Marketing Inc................................E...... 718 778-6080
  Brooklyn *(G-2791)*
Zenith Solutions.................................G...... 718 575-8570
  Flushing *(G-5316)*
Zeo Health Ltd...................................F...... 845 353-5185
  Valley Cottage *(G-16421)*
Zinerva Pharmaceuticals LLC............G...... 630 729-4184
  Clarence Center *(G-3708)*
▲ Zitomer...G...... 212 737-5560
  New York *(G-12734)*

2835 Diagnostic Substances

Bella International Inc........................E...... 716 484-0102
  Jamestown *(G-7009)*
Biochemical Diagnostics Inc..............E...... 631 595-9200
  Edgewood *(G-4609)*
▲ Biopool Us Inc..................................E...... 716 483-3851
  Jamestown *(G-7010)*
▲ Chembio Diagnostic Systems Inc....C...... 631 924-1135
  Medford *(G-8269)*
▲ Chembio Diagnostics Inc.................C...... 631 924-1135
  Medford *(G-8270)*
▲ Clark Laboratories Inc.....................F...... 716 483-3851
  Jamestown *(G-7014)*
Danisco US Inc...................................D...... 585 256-5200
  Rochester *(G-14321)*
Darmiyan LLC.....................................G...... 917 689-0389
  New York *(G-9864)*
◆ E-Z-Em Inc.......................................E...... 609 524-2864
  Melville *(G-8343)*
Eagle International LLC......................E...... 917 282-2536
  Nanuet *(G-8802)*
Enzo Life Sciences Inc......................E...... 631 694-7070
  Farmingdale *(G-4997)*
Gotham Veterinary Center PC...........E...... 212 222-1900
  New York *(G-10381)*
Immco Diagnostics Inc......................D...... 716 691-6911
  Buffalo *(G-3022)*
Inolife Technologies Inc....................G...... 212 348-5600
  New York *(G-10648)*
Ithaca Pregancy Center.....................G...... 607 753-3909
  Cortland *(G-4053)*
Kannalife Sciences Inc......................G...... 516 669-3219
  Lloyd Harbor *(G-7594)*

Ken-Ton Open Mri PC........................G...... 716 876-7000
  Kenmore *(G-7179)*
Lesanne Life Sciences LLC..............G...... 914 234-0860
  Bedford *(G-793)*
Lifelink Monitoring Corp....................F...... 845 336-2098
  Bearsville *(G-787)*
Lifescan Inc..B...... 516 557-2693
  Wantagh *(G-16580)*
Northeast Doulas...............................G...... 845 621-0654
  Mahopac *(G-8029)*
Ortho-Clinical Diagnostics Inc..........E...... 716 631-1281
  Williamsville *(G-17275)*
Ortho-Clinical Diagnostics Inc..........E...... 585 453-3000
  Rochester *(G-14577)*
Siemens Hlthcare Dgnostics Inc......E...... 914 631-0475
  Tarrytown *(G-16130)*
Ufc Biotechnology..............................G...... 716 777-3776
  Amherst *(G-269)*
▲ US Diagnostics Inc...........................E...... 866 216-5308
  New York *(G-12506)*
◆ Welch Allyn Inc.................................A...... 315 685-4100
  Skaneateles Falls *(G-15494)*
Working Family Solutions Inc..........G...... 845 802-6182
  Saugerties *(G-15227)*

2836 Biological Prdts, Exc Diagnostic Substances

▲ Acorda Therapeutics Inc..................C...... 914 347-4300
  Ardsley *(G-402)*
Advance Biofactures Corp.................E...... 516 593-7000
  Lynbrook *(G-7972)*
◆ AG Biotech Inc..................................G...... 585 346-0020
  Livonia *(G-7590)*
▲ Akshar Extracts Inc..........................E...... 631 588-9727
  Ronkonkoma *(G-14885)*
Albany Molecular Research Inc........G...... 518 512-2234
  Albany *(G-38)*
▲ Albany Molecular Research Inc........B...... 518 512-2000
  Albany *(G-39)*
Angus Chemical Company.................E...... 716 283-1434
  Niagara Falls *(G-12819)*
AV Therapeutics Inc...........................E...... 917 497-5523
  New York *(G-9323)*
Bioreclamationivt LLC........................G...... 516 483-1196
  Westbury *(G-16999)*
C T M Industries Ltd..........................E...... 718 479-3300
  Jamaica *(G-6935)*
Coral Blood Service...........................F...... 800 483-4888
  Elmsford *(G-4752)*
Cypress Bioscience Inc.....................F...... 858 452-2323
  New York *(G-9836)*
D C I Plasma Center Inc....................G...... 914 241-1646
  Mount Kisco *(G-8667)*
Debmar-Mercury..................................E...... 212 669-5025
  New York *(G-9890)*
▲ Ecological Laboratories Inc.............D...... 516 823-3441
  Lynbrook *(G-7978)*
Instrumentation Laboratory Co.........C...... 845 680-0028
  Orangeburg *(G-13253)*
International Aids Vaccine Ini...........C...... 212 847-1111
  New York *(G-10672)*
International Aids Vaccine Ini...........F...... 646 381-8066
  Brooklyn *(G-2109)*
Ip Med Inc..G...... 516 766-3800
  Oceanside *(G-13102)*
Kadmon Holdings Inc........................D...... 212 308-6000
  New York *(G-10836)*
Lake Immunogenics Inc....................E...... 585 265-1973
  Ontario *(G-13227)*
Life Technologies Corporation..........D...... 716 774-6700
  Grand Island *(G-5775)*
Man of World......................................G...... 212 915-0017
  New York *(G-11149)*
Nanoprobes Inc..................................F...... 631 205-9490
  Yaphank *(G-17414)*
Nelco Laboratories Inc.....................E...... 631 242-0082
  Deer Park *(G-4202)*
Nxxi Inc..G...... 914 701-4500
  Purchase *(G-13978)*
Oligomerix Inc....................................G...... 914 997-8877
  New York *(G-11514)*
Omrix Biopharmaceuticals Inc..........E...... 908 218-0707
  New York *(G-11517)*
Rentschler Biotechnologie GMBH.....E...... 631 656-7137
  Hauppauge *(G-6203)*
Roar Biomedical Inc...........................G...... 631 591-2749
  Calverton *(G-3325)*
Siga Technologies Inc.......................E...... 212 672-9100
  New York *(G-12088)*

Stemcultures LLC..............................G...... 518 621-0848
  Rensselaer *(G-14062)*
Synergy Pharmaceuticals Inc...........G...... 212 227-8611
  New York *(G-12283)*
Vyera Pharmaceuticals LLC.............E...... 646 356-5577
  New York *(G-12600)*
Wyeth Holdings LLC..........................D...... 845 602-5000
  Pearl River *(G-13493)*
◆ Wyeth LLC..A...... 973 660-5000
  New York *(G-12697)*
▼ Zeptometrix Corporation..................D...... 716 882-0920
  Buffalo *(G-3288)*

2841 Soap & Detergents

Alabu Inc..G...... 518 665-0411
  Mechanicville *(G-8255)*
Alconox Inc..G...... 914 948-4040
  White Plains *(G-17103)*
Aura Detergent LLC..........................F...... 718 824-2162
  Bronx *(G-1277)*
▼ Baums Castorine Company Inc.......G...... 315 336-8154
  Rome *(G-14834)*
Bfma Holding Corporation.................F...... 607 753-6746
  Cortland *(G-4036)*
Chemite Inc..G...... 607 529-3218
  Waverly *(G-16725)*
Cleanse TEC.......................................E...... 718 346-9111
  Brooklyn *(G-1787)*
◆ Colgate-Palmolive Company.............A...... 212 310-2000
  New York *(G-9726)*
Colgate-Palmolive Nj Inc...................E...... 212 310-2000
  New York *(G-9728)*
▼ Combe Incorporated..........................C...... 914 694-5454
  White Plains *(G-17123)*
Cosco Enterprises Inc......................G...... 718 383-4488
  Ridgewood *(G-14117)*
▼ Cpac Inc...E...... 585 382-3223
  Leicester *(G-7442)*
◆ Crosstex International Inc................D...... 631 582-6777
  Hauppauge *(G-6079)*
Dr Jacobs Naturals LLC....................E...... 718 265-1522
  Brooklyn *(G-1878)*
Ecolab Inc..F...... 716 683-6298
  Cheektowaga *(G-3598)*
Emulso Corp.......................................G...... 716 854-2889
  Tonawanda *(G-16178)*
Enviro Service & Supply Corp..........F...... 347 838-6500
  Staten Island *(G-15692)*
Gfl USA Inc..G...... 917 297-8701
  Brooklyn *(G-2022)*
Glissen Chemical Co Inc...................E...... 718 436-4200
  Brooklyn *(G-2029)*
Greenmaker Industries LLC..............F...... 866 684-7800
  Farmingdale *(G-5009)*
▲ H & H Laboratories Inc....................F...... 718 624-8041
  Brooklyn *(G-2057)*
H & H Laboratories Inc.....................F...... 718 624-8041
  Brooklyn *(G-2058)*
HFC Prestige Intl US LLC.................A...... 212 389-7800
  New York *(G-10514)*
◆ King Research Inc............................E...... 718 788-0122
  Brooklyn *(G-2171)*
L S Z Inc..G...... 914 948-4040
  White Plains *(G-17158)*
Marietta Corporation..........................B...... 607 753-0982
  Cortland *(G-4058)*
Maybelline Inc....................................A...... 212 885-1310
  New York *(G-11214)*
▲ Medtech Products Inc.......................F...... 914 524-6810
  Tarrytown *(G-16119)*
▲ Monroe Fluid Technology Inc..........E...... 585 392-3434
  Hilton *(G-6444)*
Mooseberry Soap Co LLC.................G...... 315 332-8913
  Newark *(G-12758)*
Natures Warehouse............................F...... 800 215-4372
  Philadelphia *(G-13564)*
Pro-Line Solutions Inc......................G...... 914 664-0002
  Mount Vernon *(G-8765)*
▲ Robert Racine...................................E...... 518 677-0224
  Cambridge *(G-3338)*
Ronbar Laboratories Inc...................F...... 718 937-6755
  Long Island City *(G-7894)*
S & S Soap Co Inc.............................E...... 718 585-2900
  Bronx *(G-1443)*
Sabon Management LLC...................F...... 212 982-0968
  New York *(G-11968)*
Schneider M Soap & Chemical Co..G...... 718 389-1000
  Ridgewood *(G-14136)*
Sunfeather Natural Soap Co Inc.......G...... 315 265-1776
  Potsdam *(G-13903)*

28 CHEMICALS AND ALLIED PRODUCTS

▲ T S Pink Corp .... F 607 432-1100
  Oneonta (G-13216)
Unilever United States Inc .... F 212 546-0200
  New York (G-12474)
Unilever United States Inc .... C 212 546-0200
  New York (G-12475)

2842 Spec Cleaning, Polishing & Sanitation Preparations

Adirondack Waste MGT Inc .... G 518 585-2224
  Ticonderoga (G-16147)
▲ Aireactor Inc .... F 718 326-2433
  Woodside (G-17335)
American Wax Company Inc .... E 718 392-8080
  Long Island City (G-7691)
Arrow Chemical Corp .... F 516 377-7770
  Freeport (G-5398)
▲ Bennett Manufacturing Co Inc .... C 716 937-9161
  Alden (G-178)
Bono Sawdust Supply Co Inc .... G 718 446-1374
  Corona (G-4014)
Caltex International Ltd .... E 315 425-1040
  Syracuse (G-15902)
◆ Car-Freshner Corporation .... C 315 788-6250
  Watertown (G-16663)
Car-Freshner Corporation .... D 315 788-6250
  Watertown (G-16664)
Castoleum Corporation .... F 914 664-5877
  Mount Vernon (G-8715)
Chem-Puter Friendly Inc .... E 631 331-2259
  Mount Sinai (G-8696)
▲ Chemclean Corporation .... F 718 525-4500
  Jamaica (G-6937)
City of New York .... C 718 236-2693
  Brooklyn (G-1782)
Clean All of Syracuse LLC .... G 315 472-9189
  Syracuse (G-15916)
Cleanse TEC .... E 718 346-9111
  Brooklyn (G-1787)
◆ Colgate-Palmolive Company .... A 212 310-2000
  New York (G-9726)
Collinite Corporation .... G 315 732-2282
  Utica (G-16336)
Comfort Wax Incorporated .... F 718 204-7028
  Astoria (G-431)
Connie French Cleaners Inc .... E 516 487-1343
  Great Neck (G-5818)
Connies Laundry .... G 716 822-2800
  Buffalo (G-2906)
Conrad Blasius Equipment Co .... G 516 753-1200
  Plainview (G-13620)
County Waste Management Inc .... G 914 592-5007
  Harrison (G-6002)
▼ Cpac Inc .... E 585 382-3223
  Leicester (G-7442)
▲ Crescent Marketing Inc .... C 716 337-0145
  North Collins (G-12943)
◆ Crosstex International Inc .... D 631 582-6777
  Hauppauge (G-6079)
Emulso Corp .... G 716 854-2889
  Tonawanda (G-16178)
Enviro Service & Supply Corp .... F 347 838-6500
  Staten Island (G-15692)
FBC Chemical Corporation .... G 716 681-1581
  Lancaster (G-7339)
Finger Lakes Chemicals Inc .... E 585 454-4760
  Rochester (G-14392)
Four Sasons Multi-Services Inc .... G 347 843-6262
  Bronx (G-1338)
George Basch Co Inc .... F 516 378-8100
  North Bellmore (G-12937)
▲ Gliptone Manufacturing Inc .... F 631 285-7250
  Ronkonkoma (G-14933)
Greenmaker Industries LLC .... F 866 684-7800
  Farmingdale (G-5009)
Griffin Chemical Company LLC .... G 716 693-2465
  North Tonawanda (G-12993)
Grillbot LLC .... G 646 258-5639
  New York (G-10406)
HFC Prestige Intl US LLC .... A 212 389-7800
  New York (G-10514)
James Richard Specialty Chem .... G 914 478-7500
  Hastings On Hudson (G-6024)
◆ King Research Inc .... E 718 788-0122
  Brooklyn (G-2171)
▲ Laundress Inc .... F 212 209-0074
  New York (G-10973)
Lb Laundry Inc .... G 347 399-8030
  Flushing (G-5271)

Mdi Holdings LLC .... A 212 559-1127
  New York (G-11228)
◆ Micro Powders Inc .... E 914 332-6400
  Tarrytown (G-16120)
Mirandy Products Ltd .... E 516 489-6800
  South Hempstead (G-15554)
Noble Pine Products Co Inc .... F 914 664-5877
  Mount Vernon (G-8756)
Nuvite Chemical Compounds Corp ..... F 718 383-8351
  Brooklyn (G-2391)
Olin Chlor Alkali Logistics .... C 716 278-6411
  Niagara Falls (G-12875)
P S M Group Inc .... E 716 532-6686
  Forestville (G-5342)
Premier Brands of America Inc .... E 718 325-3000
  Mount Vernon (G-8764)
▲ Premier Brands of America Inc .... C 914 667-6200
  Mount Vernon (G-8763)
▲ Progressive Products LLC .... E 914 417-6022
  Rye Brook (G-15100)
◆ Rochester Midland Corporation .... C 585 336-2200
  Rochester (G-14665)
Royce Associates A Ltd Partnr .... G 516 367-6298
  Jericho (G-7115)
▲ Safetec of America Inc .... D 716 895-1822
  Buffalo (G-3202)
Scully Sanitation .... G 315 899-8996
  West Edmeston (G-16875)
Sensor & Decontamination Inc .... F 301 526-8389
  Binghamton (G-944)
Simply Amazing Enterprises Inc .... G 631 503-6452
  Melville (G-8383)
Solvents Company Inc .... G 631 595-9300
  Kingston (G-7238)
Spic and Span Company .... F 914 524-6823
  Tarrytown (G-16132)
Spongebath LLC .... G 917 475-1347
  Astoria (G-457)
Spray Nine Corporation .... D 800 477-7299
  Johnstown (G-7157)
◆ Strahl & Pitsch Inc .... E 631 669-0175
  West Babylon (G-16865)
◆ Synco Chemical Corporation .... E 631 567-5300
  Bohemia (G-1137)
Tjb Sunshine Enterprises .... F 518 384-6483
  Ballston Lake (G-587)
Topps-All Products of Yonkers .... F 914 968-4226
  Yonkers (G-17508)
▲ Tribology Inc .... E 631 345-3000
  Yaphank (G-17421)
TWI-Laq Industries Inc .... E 718 638-5860
  Bronx (G-1481)
U S Plychmical Overseas Corp .... E 845 356-5530
  Chestnut Ridge (G-3657)
◆ US Nonwovens Corp .... A 631 952-0100
  Brentwood (G-1196)
US Polychemical Holding Corp .... E 845 356-5530
  Spring Valley (G-15628)
▲ Walter G Legge Company Inc .... G 914 737-5040
  Peekskill (G-13510)
Wedding Gown Preservation Co .... D 607 748-7999
  Endicott (G-4839)

2843 Surface Active & Finishing Agents, Sulfonated Oils

▲ Androme Leather Inc .... F 518 773-7945
  Gloversville (G-5721)
BASF Corporation .... B 914 785-2000
  Tarrytown (G-16111)
Bigsky Technologies LLC .... G 585 218-9499
  Rochester (G-14249)
Comander Terminals LLC .... E 516 922-7600
  Oyster Bay (G-13394)
Halmark Architectural Finshg .... E 718 272-1831
  Brooklyn (G-2062)
Momentive Performance Mtls Inc ...... D 914 784-4807
  Tarrytown (G-16121)
Suit-Kote Corporation .... F 716 683-8850
  Buffalo (G-3227)

2844 Perfumes, Cosmetics & Toilet Preparations

▲ 3lab Inc .... F 201 567-9100
  New York (G-9020)
Abbe Laboratories Inc .... F 631 756-2223
  Farmingdale (G-4936)
AEP Environmental LLC .... F 716 446-0739
  Buffalo (G-2818)

Alan F Bourguet .... F 516 883-4315
  Port Washington (G-13820)
◆ Albion Cosmetics Inc .... G 212 869-1052
  New York (G-9125)
Alexandria Professional LLC .... G 716 242-8514
  Williamsville (G-17260)
◆ All Cultures Inc .... E 631 293-3143
  Greenlawn (G-5890)
▲ Allan John Company .... F 212 940-2210
  New York (G-9136)
Angel Tips Nail Salon .... G 718 225-8300
  Little Neck (G-7529)
Antimony New York LLC .... G 917 232-1836
  New York (G-9219)
▲ Ardex Cosmetics of America .... E 518 283-6700
  Troy (G-16248)
Aromasong Usa Inc .... F 718 838-9669
  Brooklyn (G-1632)
Art of Shaving - Fl LLC .... G 212 362-1493
  New York (G-9262)
Bare Escentuals Inc .... G 646 537-0070
  New York (G-9371)
▲ Becca Inc .... F 646 568-6250
  New York (G-9390)
Bellarno International Ltd .... G 212 302-4107
  New York (G-9397)
▲ Belmay Holding Corporation .... E 914 376-1515
  Yonkers (G-17436)
◆ Bio-Botanica Inc .... E 631 231-0987
  Hauppauge (G-6053)
▲ Bobbi Brown Prof Cosmt Inc .... E 646 613-6500
  New York (G-9483)
▲ Borghese Inc .... E 212 659-5318
  New York (G-9491)
British Science Corporation .... G 212 980-8700
  Staten Island (G-15672)
Brucci Ltd .... E 914 965-0707
  Yonkers (G-17438)
Butterfly Beauty LLC .... G 646 604-4289
  New York (G-9536)
▲ Bycmac Corp .... E 845 255-0884
  Gardiner (G-5561)
▲ California Fragrance Company .... E 631 424-4023
  Huntington Station (G-6736)
Cassini Parfums Ltd .... G 212 753-7540
  New York (G-9595)
▲ China Huaren Organic Pdts Inc .... G 212 232-0120
  New York (G-9647)
◆ Christian Dior Perfumes LLC .... E 212 931-2200
  New York (G-9662)
Clark Botanicals Inc .... F 914 826-4319
  Bronxville (G-1500)
▲ Clinique Laboratories LLC .... E 212 572-4200
  New York (G-9698)
Clinique Services Inc .... E 212 572-4200
  New York (G-9699)
Colgat-Plmolive Centl Amer Inc .... G 212 310-2000
  New York (G-9725)
◆ Colgate-Palmolive Company .... A 212 310-2000
  New York (G-9726)
Colgate-Palmolive Company .... B 718 506-3961
  Queens Village (G-13991)
Colgate-Palmolive Globl Trdg .... G 212 310-2000
  New York (G-9727)
Collaborative Laboratories .... D 631 689-0200
  East Setauket (G-4498)
Common Sense Natural Soap .... E 518 677-0224
  Cambridge (G-3334)
Conopco Inc .... E 585 647-8322
  Rochester (G-14308)
Coty Inc .... C 212 389-7000
  New York (G-9789)
◆ Coty Inc .... D 212 389-7000
  New York (G-9790)
◆ Coty US LLC .... C 212 389-7000
  New York (G-9791)
Coty US LLC .... B 212 389-7000
  Uniondale (G-16313)
▼ Cpac Inc .... E 585 382-3223
  Leicester (G-7442)
Delbia Do Company Inc .... F 718 585-2226
  Bronx (G-1316)
▲ Delbia Do Company Inc .... F 718 585-2226
  Bronx (G-1315)
▲ Dermatech Labs Inc .... F 631 225-1700
  Lindenhurst (G-7484)
Distribio USA LLC .... G 212 989-6077
  New York (G-9941)
Drt Laboratories LLC .... G 845 547-2034
  Airmont (G-12)

SIC SECTION
28 CHEMICALS AND ALLIED PRODUCTS

Editions De Prfums Madison LLC ....F 646 666-0527
New York (G-10035)
◆ EL Erman International Ltd..........G....... 212 444-9440
Brooklyn (G-1911)
Elias Fragrances Inc ....F 718 693-6400
Rye Brook (G-15096)
▲ Elite Parfums Ltd ....D....... 212 983-2640
New York (G-10060)
◆ Essie Cosmetics Ltd ....D....... 212 818-1500
New York (G-10120)
Estee Lauder Companies Inc..........A....... 917 606-3240
New York (G-10121)
Estee Lauder Companies Inc..........G....... 212 756-4800
New York (G-10122)
Estee Lauder Companies Inc..........A....... 212 572-4200
New York (G-10123)
◆ Estee Lauder Companies Inc ....A....... 212 572-4200
New York (G-10124)
Estee Lauder Companies Inc..........A....... 646 602-7590
New York (G-10125)
▲ Estee Lauder Inc ....A....... 212 572-4200
New York (G-10126)
Estee Lauder Inc ....D....... 631 531-1000
Melville (G-8345)
Estee Lauder Inc ....C....... 631 454-7000
Melville (G-8346)
Estee Lauder Inc ....D....... 212 756-4800
New York (G-10127)
▲ Estee Lauder International Inc..........G....... 212 572-4200
New York (G-10128)
◆ Eternal Love Parfums Corp ....G....... 516 921-6100
Syosset (G-15841)
Ex-It Medical Devices Inc ....G....... 212 653-0637
New York (G-10153)
▲ F L Demeter Inc ....E....... 516 487-5187
Great Neck (G-5823)
▼ Flavormatic Industries Inc ....E....... 845 297-9100
Wappingers Falls (G-16587)
FMC International Ltd..........G....... 914 935-0918
Purchase (G-13972)
▲ Forsythe Cosmetic Group Ltd ....D....... 516 239-4200
Freeport (G-5411)
▲ Four Paws Products Ltd..........D....... 631 436-7421
Ronkonkoma (G-14931)
▲ Fragrance Acquisitions LLC ....D....... 845 534-9172
Newburgh (G-12776)
Fragrance Outlet Inc..........F 845 928-1408
Central Valley (G-3551)
▲ Fsr Beauty Ltd..........G....... 212 447-0036
New York (G-10265)
Fusion Brands America Inc ....E....... 212 269-1387
New York (G-10273)
▼ Gassho Body & Mind Inc..........G....... 518 695-9991
Schuylerville (G-15341)
Gfl USA Inc ....G....... 917 297-8701
Brooklyn (G-2022)
Glacee Skincare LLC ....G....... 212 690-7632
New York (G-10344)
Good Home Co Inc..........G....... 212 352-1509
New York (G-10377)
▲ Gurwitch Products LLC..........D....... 281 275-7000
New York (G-10429)
▲ H & H Laboratories Inc ....F 718 624-8041
Brooklyn (G-2057)
H & H Laboratories Inc ....G....... 718 624-8041
Brooklyn (G-2058)
◆ Hain Celestial Group Inc..........C....... 516 587-5000
New Hyde Park (G-8882)
Hair Ventures LLC..........F 718 664-7689
Irvington (G-6813)
HFC Prestige Intl US LLC ....A....... 212 389-7800
New York (G-10514)
Hogan Flavors & Fragrances ....E....... 212 598-4310
New York (G-10537)
▲ Inter Parfums Inc..........D....... 212 983-2640
New York (G-10664)
Intercos America Inc..........G....... 845 732-3910
West Nyack (G-16948)
◆ Interntnal Flvors Frgrnces Inc..........C....... 212 765-5500
New York (G-10681)
▲ Jackel Inc..........D....... 908 359-2039
New York (G-10726)
◆ Jean Philippe Fragrances LLC..........D....... 212 983-2640
New York (G-10755)
▲ JP Filling Inc..........D....... 845 534-4793
Mountainville (G-8794)
Judith N Graham Inc..........G....... 914 921-5446
Rye (G-15087)
June Jacobs Labs LLC..........D....... 212 471-4830
New York (G-10823)

Kantian Skincare LLC..........G....... 631 780-4711
Smithtown (G-15514)
Kind Group LLC ....G....... 212 645-0800
New York (G-10888)
◆ King Research Inc..........E....... 718 788-0122
Brooklyn (G-2171)
▲ Klg Usa LLC..........A....... 845 856-5311
Port Jervis (G-13811)
▲ Lady Burd Exclusive Cosmt Inc ....C....... 631 454-0444
Farmingdale (G-5040)
Laurice El Badry Rahme Ltd..........G....... 212 633-1641
New York (G-10974)
▲ Le Labo Holding LLC..........E....... 844 316-9319
New York (G-10978)
Le Labo Holding LLC..........E....... 646 719-1740
Brooklyn (G-2202)
Lechler Laboratories Inc..........E....... 845 426-6800
Spring Valley (G-15613)
Liddell Corporation..........F 716 297-8557
Niagara Falls (G-12859)
LOreal Usa Inc..........B....... 212 818-1500
New York (G-11064)
LOreal Usa Inc..........B....... 917 606-9554
New York (G-11065)
LOreal Usa Inc..........E....... 212 389-4201
New York (G-11066)
LOreal Usa Inc..........G....... 212 984-4704
New York (G-11067)
LOreal Usa Inc..........B....... 646 658-5477
New York (G-11068)
▲ LOreal USA Products Inc ....G....... 212 818-1500
New York (G-11069)
Lornamead Inc ....D....... 716 874-7190
Tonawanda (G-16196)
◆ Lornamead Inc..........D....... 716 874-7190
New York (G-11072)
Malin + Goetz Inc ....F 212 244-7771
New York (G-11145)
◆ Mana Products Inc ....B....... 718 361-2550
Long Island City (G-7828)
Mana Products Inc..........B....... 718 361-5204
Long Island City (G-7829)
▲ Marietta Corporation..........B....... 607 753-6746
Cortland (G-4057)
Marvellissima Intl Ltd ....G....... 212 682-7306
New York (G-11194)
Maybelline Inc..........A....... 212 885-1310
New York (G-11214)
▲ Mehron Inc..........E....... 845 426-1700
Chestnut Ridge (G-3652)
◆ Mentholatum Company..........E....... 716 677-2500
Orchard Park (G-13309)
▲ MZB Accessories LLC..........D....... 718 472-7500
Long Island City (G-7849)
Nature Only Inc ....G....... 917 922-6539
Forest Hills (G-5333)
Naturpathica Holistic Hlth Inc..........D....... 631 329-8792
East Hampton (G-4434)
New Avon LLC..........F 716 572-4842
Buffalo (G-3104)
New Avon LLC..........A....... 212 282-8500
New York (G-11403)
▲ Newburgh Distribution Corp..........G....... 845 561-6330
New Windsor (G-8991)
Oasis Cosmetic Labs Inc ....F 631 758-0038
Holtsville (G-6531)
Olan Laboratories Inc..........G....... 631 582-2082
Hauppauge (G-6177)
◆ P S Pibbs Inc..........D....... 718 445-8046
Flushing (G-5283)
▲ Paula Dorf Cosmetics Inc..........E....... 212 582-0073
New York (G-11600)
Pdk Labs Inc..........D....... 631 273-2630
Hauppauge (G-6184)
Peppermints Salon Inc ....F 718 357-6304
Whitestone (G-17242)
▼ Perfume Americana Inc ....G....... 212 683-8029
New York (G-11634)
▼ Perfume Amrcana Whlesalers Inc ....F 212 683-8029
New York (G-11635)
▲ Perfumers Workshop Intl Ltd..........G....... 212 644-8950
New York (G-11636)
▲ Peter Thomas Roth Labs LLC..........E....... 212 581-5800
New York (G-11653)
Plastic & Reconstructive Svcs ....G....... 914 584-5605
Mount Kisco (G-8683)
Precision Cosmetics Mfg Co ....G....... 914 667-1200
Mount Vernon (G-8762)
Procter & Gamble Company..........C....... 646 885-4201
New York (G-11747)

Professional Buty Holdings Inc..........F 631 787-8576
Hauppauge (G-6199)
▲ Puig Usa Inc ....F 212 271-5940
New York (G-11771)
Pureology Research LLC ....F 212 984-4360
New York (G-11778)
Quality King Distributors Inc ....C....... 631 439-2027
Ronkonkoma (G-14998)
Quip Nyc Inc..........G....... 703 615-1076
Brooklyn (G-2486)
Redken 5th Avenue Nyc LLC ....G....... 212 984-5113
New York (G-11846)
▲ Revlon Inc..........B....... 212 527-4000
New York (G-11878)
▲ Revlon Consumer Products Corp ....B....... 212 527-4000
New York (G-11879)
▲ Robell Research Inc..........G....... 212 755-6577
New York (G-11909)
▲ Robert Racine..........E....... 518 677-0224
Cambridge (G-3338)
Sally Beauty Supply LLC..........G....... 716 831-3286
West Seneca (G-16981)
Salonclick LLC ....F 718 643-6793
New York (G-11976)
Scent-A-Vision Inc ....E....... 631 424-4905
Huntington Station (G-6759)
Scientific Solutions Globl LLC ....F 516 543-3376
Carle Place (G-3423)
Selective Beauty Corporation..........F 585 336-7600
New York (G-12043)
◆ Shiseido Americas Corporation..........G....... 212 805-2300
New York (G-12077)
▼ Skin Atelier Inc ....F 845 294-1202
Goshen (G-5753)
Skin Nutrition Intl Inc..........E....... 212 231-8355
New York (G-12116)
Sml Acquisition LLC ....C....... 914 592-3130
Elmsford (G-4793)
▼ Soft Sheen Products Inc ....G....... 212 818-1500
New York (G-12145)
▲ Solabia USA Inc..........G....... 212 847-2397
New York (G-12148)
St Tropez Inc..........G....... 800 366-6383
New York (G-12204)
Stamapro Inc ....G....... 888 623-5003
Carle Place (G-3424)
▲ Sundial Brands LLC..........C....... 631 842-8800
Amityville (G-327)
Sundial Group LLC ....E....... 631 842-8800
Amityville (G-329)
Symrise Inc..........E....... 845 469-7675
Chester (G-3645)
Temptu Inc..........G....... 718 937-9503
Long Island City (G-7926)
▲ Thompson Ferrier LLC ....G....... 212 244-2212
New York (G-12347)
▲ Tomia Beauty Brands LLC ....G....... 917 301-0125
New York (G-12385)
▲ Topiderm Inc..........C....... 631 226-7979
Amityville (G-330)
Tula Life LLC ....G....... 201 895-3309
New York (G-12443)
Unilever United States Inc..........F 212 546-0200
New York (G-12474)
Unilever United States Inc..........C....... 212 546-0200
New York (G-12475)
United-Guardian Inc..........E....... 631 273-0900
Hauppauge (G-6244)
▲ Universal Packg Systems Inc ....A....... 631 543-2277
Hauppauge (G-6245)
▼ Value Fragrances Inc..........G....... 845 294-5726
Goshen (G-5756)
▲ Verla International Ltd ....B....... 845 561-2440
New Windsor (G-9003)
▲ Victoria Albi Intl Inc..........F 212 689-2600
New York (G-12563)
Xania Labs Inc..........G....... 718 361-2550
Long Island City (G-7957)
▲ Yoyo Lip Gloss Inc ....F 718 357-6304
Astoria (G-462)
▲ Zela International Co ....E....... 518 436-1833
Albany (G-154)
Zotos International Inc ....B....... 315 781-3207
Geneva (G-5601)

2851 Paints, Varnishes, Lacquers, Enamels

A & B Color Corp (del)..........G....... 718 441-5482
Kew Gardens (G-7186)
Absolute Coatings Inc ....E....... 914 636-0700
New Rochelle (G-8929)

S I C

Employee Codes: A=Over 500 employees, B=251-500
C=101-250, D=51-100, E=20-50, F=10-19, G=5-9
2018 Harris
New York Manufacturers Directory
783

28 CHEMICALS AND ALLIED PRODUCTS

Akzo Nobel Coatings Inc .... E 610 603-7589
 Long Island City (G-7682)
▲ Angiotech Biocoatings Corp .... E 585 321-1130
 Henrietta (G-6315)
Anthony River Inc .... F 315 475-1315
 Syracuse (G-15875)
Atc Plastics LLC .... E 212 375-2515
 New York (G-9297)
Atlas Coatings Group Corp .... D 718 469-8787
 Brooklyn (G-1650)
B & F Architectural Support Gr .... E 212 279-6488
 New York (G-9340)
Barson Composites Corporation .... E 516 752-7882
 Old Bethpage (G-13147)
Benjamin Moore & Co .... E 518 736-1723
 Johnstown (G-7139)
Cytec Industries Inc .... D 716 372-9650
 Olean (G-13162)
Delta Polymers Inc .... G 631 254-6240
 Bay Shore (G-693)
Designer Epoxy Finishes Inc .... G 646 943-6044
 Melville (G-8340)
▲ Emco Finishing Products Inc .... E 716 483-1176
 Jamestown (G-7027)
◆ Enecon Corporation .... D 516 349-0022
 Medford (G-8274)
Eric S Turner & Company Inc .... F 914 235-7114
 New Rochelle (G-8943)
▲ Excel Paint Applicators Inc .... G 347 221-1968
 Inwood (G-6794)
Farrow and Ball Inc .... F 212 752-5544
 New York (G-10193)
Fayette Street Coatings Inc .... G 315 488-5401
 Syracuse (G-15962)
Fayette Street Coatings Inc .... F 315 488-5401
 Liverpool (G-7544)
▲ Fougera Pharmaceuticals Inc .... C 631 454-7677
 Melville (G-8350)
G & M Dege Inc .... F 631 475-1450
 East Patchogue (G-4466)
Gabriela Systems Ltd .... G 631 225-7952
 Lindenhurst (G-7487)
Garco Manufacturing Corp Inc .... F 718 287-3330
 Brooklyn (G-2014)
General Coatings Tech Inc .... F 718 821-1232
 Ridgewood (G-14120)
▲ General Vy-Coat LLC .... E 718 266-6002
 Brooklyn (G-2019)
▲ Heany Industries Inc .... D 585 889-2700
 Scottsville (G-15358)
Industrial Finishing Products .... F 718 342-4871
 Brooklyn (G-2102)
Inglis Co Inc .... G 315 475-1315
 Syracuse (G-15982)
Inhance Technologies LLC .... E 716 825-9031
 Buffalo (G-3026)
Insulating Coatings Corp .... F 607 723-1727
 Binghamton (G-922)
▲ John C Dolph Company Inc .... E 732 329-2333
 Schenectady (G-15298)
▲ Jrlon Inc .... D 315 597-4067
 Palmyra (G-13434)
Liberty Panel Center Inc .... F 718 647-2763
 Brooklyn (G-2217)
Masterdisk Corporation .... F 212 541-5022
 Elmsford (G-4773)
▲ Mercury Paint Corporation .... D 718 469-8787
 Brooklyn (G-2303)
Musicskins LLC .... F 646 827-4271
 Brooklyn (G-2349)
Nautical Marine Paint Corp .... E 718 462-7000
 Brooklyn (G-2361)
Nochem Paint Stripping Inc .... G 631 563-2750
 Blue Point (G-994)
▲ Nortek Powder Coating LLC .... F 315 337-2339
 Rome (G-14854)
◆ Paint Over Rust Products Inc .... E 914 636-0700
 New Rochelle (G-8964)
▲ Peter Kwasny Inc .... G 727 641-1462
 Hauppauge (G-6187)
Rapid Removal LLC .... F 716 665-4663
 Falconer (G-4917)
Reddi Car Corp .... G 631 589-3141
 Sayville (G-15243)
Regent Paints Inc .... G 917 966-4011
 Glendale (G-5676)
Robert Greenburg .... G 845 586-2226
 Margaretville (G-8123)
Royce Associates A Ltd Partnr .... G 516 367-6298
 Jericho (G-7115)

Si Group Inc .... C 518 347-4200
 Rotterdam Junction (G-15060)
◆ Si Group Inc .... C 518 347-4200
 Schenectady (G-15319)
▲ Sml Brothers Holding Corp .... D 718 402-2000
 Bronx (G-1455)
Starlite Pnt & Varnish Co Inc .... G 718 292-6420
 Bronx (G-1462)
T C Dunham Paint Company Inc .... G 914 969-4202
 Yonkers (G-17506)
▼ T J Ronan Paint Corp .... F 718 292-1100
 Bronx (G-1468)
◆ Talyarps Corporation .... D 914 699-3030
 Pelham (G-13520)
Talyarps Corporation .... G 914 699-3030
 Mount Vernon (G-8781)
▼ Uc Coatings Corporation .... E 716 833-9366
 Buffalo (G-3257)
Yewtree Millworks Corp .... G 914 320-5851
 Yonkers (G-17517)

2861 Gum & Wood Chemicals

▲ Metro Products & Services LLC .... F 866 846-8486
 Brooklyn (G-2311)
Ocip Holding LLC .... G 646 589-6180
 New York (G-11509)
Prismatic Dyeing & Finshg Inc .... D 845 561-1800
 Newburgh (G-12798)
▼ Tioga Hardwoods Inc .... F 607 657-8686
 Berkshire (G-852)
Westrock Mwv LLC .... C 212 688-5000
 New York (G-12645)

2865 Cyclic-Crudes, Intermediates, Dyes & Org Pigments

Chemours Company Fc LLC .... E 716 278-5100
 Niagara Falls (G-12826)
▲ Crowley Tar Products Co Inc .... C 212 682-1200
 New York (G-9815)
Deep Dyeing Inc .... F 718 418-7187
 Manhasset (G-8091)
Durez Corporation .... F 716 286-0100
 Niagara Falls (G-12834)
East Cast Clor Compounding Inc .... G 631 491-9000
 West Babylon (G-16815)
F M Group Inc .... F 845 589-0102
 Congers (G-3881)
▲ Jos H Lowenstein and Sons Inc .... D 718 218-8013
 Brooklyn (G-2147)
▲ LTS (chemical) Inc .... F 845 494-2940
 Orangeburg (G-13256)
Magic Tank LLC .... G 877 646-2442
 New York (G-11133)
◆ Micro Powders Inc .... E 914 332-6400
 Tarrytown (G-16120)
◆ Mitsui Chemicals America Inc .... E 914 253-0777
 Rye Brook (G-15098)
Premier Brands of America Inc .... F 718 325-3000
 Mount Vernon (G-8764)
Rand Machine Products Inc .... F 716 985-4681
 Sinclairville (G-15475)
◆ Si Group Inc .... C 518 347-4200
 Schenectady (G-15319)
Si Group Inc .... C 518 347-4200
 Rotterdam Junction (G-15059)
▲ Sml Brothers Holding Corp .... D 718 402-2000
 Bronx (G-1455)

2869 Industrial Organic Chemicals, NEC

A and L Home Fuel LLC .... G 607 638-1994
 Schenevus (G-15336)
Akzo Nobel Chemicals LLC .... G 716 778-8554
 Burt (G-3294)
Akzo Nobel Functional Chem LLC ..... D 845 276-8200
 Brewster (G-1205)
Akzo Nobel Inc .... G 914 674-5181
 Dobbs Ferry (G-4325)
Ames Goldsmith Corp .... F 518 792-7435
 Glens Falls (G-5685)
Arcadia Chem Preservative LLC .... G 516 466-5258
 Great Neck (G-5806)
Arkema Inc .... G 585 243-6359
 Piffard (G-13573)
Avstar Fuel Systems Inc .... G 315 255-1955
 Auburn (G-482)
◆ Balchem Corporation .... B 845 326-5600
 New Hampton (G-8842)
Bamboo Global Industries .... G 973 943-1878
 New York (G-9365)

BASF Corporation .... B 518 465-6534
 Rensselaer (G-14056)
BASF Corporation .... B 914 785-2000
 Tarrytown (G-16111)
Brockyn Corporation .... F 631 244-2770
 Bohemia (G-1023)
Buell Fuel LLC .... F 315 841-3000
 Deansboro (G-4109)
Caltex International Ltd .... G 315 425-1040
 Syracuse (G-15902)
CAM Fuel Inc .... G 718 246-4306
 Brooklyn (G-1752)
Castle Fuels Corporation .... G 914 381-6600
 Harrison (G-5998)
Centar Fuel Co Inc .... G 516 538-2424
 West Hempstead (G-16882)
China Ruitai Intl Holdings Ltd .... G 718 740-2278
 Hollis (G-6521)
Classic Flavors Fragrances Inc .... G 212 777-0004
 New York (G-9691)
Collaborative Laboratories .... D 631 689-0200
 East Setauket (G-4498)
Comax Aromatics Corporation .... G 631 249-0505
 Melville (G-8334)
◆ Comax Manufacturing Corp .... D 631 249-0505
 Melville (G-8335)
Comboland Packing Corp .... D 718 858-4200
 Brooklyn (G-1792)
Consolidated Edison Co NY Inc .... F 914 933-2936
 Rye (G-15081)
Crabtree & Evelyn Ltd .... G 845 928-4831
 Central Valley (G-3548)
Craftmaster Flavor Technology .... F 631 789-8607
 Amityville (G-282)
▲ Crown Delta Corporation .... E 914 245-8910
 Yorktown Heights (G-17526)
◆ Cumberland Packing Corp .... B 718 858-4200
 Brooklyn (G-1823)
D-Best Equipment Corp .... E 516 358-0965
 West Hempstead (G-16883)
Dancker Sellew & Douglas Inc .... G 908 231-1600
 East Syracuse (G-4536)
Danisco US Inc .... D 585 256-5200
 Rochester (G-14321)
Degennaro Fuel Service LLC .... G 518 239-6350
 Medusa (G-8318)
Dib Managmnt Inc .... F 718 439-8190
 Brooklyn (G-1860)
Eastman Chemical Company .... D 585 722-2905
 Rochester (G-14346)
Economy Energy LLC .... G 845 222-3384
 Peekskill (G-13500)
Enviro Service & Supply Corp .... F 347 838-6500
 Staten Island (G-15692)
Evonik Corporation .... G 518 233-7090
 Waterford (G-16632)
Fire Island Fuel .... G 631 772-1482
 Shirley (G-15441)
Flavors Holdings Inc .... G 212 572-8677
 New York (G-10231)
FMC Corporation .... C 716 879-0400
 Tonawanda (G-16181)
Friendly Fuel Incorporated .... G 518 581-7036
 Saratoga Springs (G-15182)
Friendly Star Fuel Inc .... G 718 369-8801
 Brooklyn (G-2007)
Fuel Energy Services USA Ltd .... E 607 846-2650
 Horseheads (G-6607)
Fuel Soul .... G 516 379-0810
 Merrick (G-8419)
Fuel Tank Envmtl Svcs Corp .... G 631 374-9083
 Centerport (G-3502)
Full Motion Beverage Inc .... G 631 585-1100
 Plainview (G-13632)
Givaudan Fragrances Corp .... C 212 649-8800
 New York (G-10342)
Golden Renewable Energy LLC .... G 914 920-9800
 Yonkers (G-17464)
Hampshire Chemical Corp .... D 315 539-9221
 Waterloo (G-16651)
Henpecked Husband Farms Corp ...... G 631 728-2800
 Speonk (G-15599)
Hexion Inc .... E 518 792-8040
 South Glens Falls (G-15548)
Highrange Fuels Inc .... G 914 930-8300
 Cortlandt Manor (G-4076)
Hudson Technologies Company .... E 845 735-6000
 Pearl River (G-13481)
Hunts Point Clean Energy LLC .... G 203 451-5143
 Pearl River (G-13483)

28 CHEMICALS AND ALLIED PRODUCTS

▼ International Mtls & Sups Inc .... G 518 834-9899
  Keeseville *(G-7167)*
◆ Interntnal Flvors Frgrnces Inc .... C 212 765-5500
  New York *(G-10681)*
▲ Islechem LLC .... E 716 773-8401
  Grand Island *(G-5774)*
J&R Fuel of LI Inc .... G 631 234-1959
  Central Islip *(G-3528)*
Jmg Fuel Inc .... G 631 579-4319
  Ronkonkoma *(G-14948)*
▲ Jos H Lowenstein and Sons Inc .... D 718 218-8013
  Brooklyn *(G-2147)*
JRs Fuels Inc .... G 518 622-9939
  Cairo *(G-3299)*
◆ Kent Chemical Corporation .... E 212 521-1700
  New York *(G-10878)*
Kore Infrastructure LLC .... G 646 532-9060
  Glen Cove *(G-5633)*
Leroux Fuels .... F 518 563-3653
  Plattsburgh *(G-13702)*
Liberty Food and Fuel .... G 315 299-4039
  Syracuse *(G-15997)*
Lift Safe - Fuel Safe Inc .... F 315 423-7702
  Syracuse *(G-15998)*
Lo-Co Fuel Corp .... G 631 929-5086
  Wading River *(G-16544)*
Logo .... G 212 846-2568
  New York *(G-11050)*
Mafco Consolidated Group Inc .... F 212 572-8600
  New York *(G-11123)*
Maio Fuel Company LP .... G 914 683-1154
  White Plains *(G-17162)*
▲ Marval Industries Inc .... D 914 381-2400
  Mamaroneck *(G-8071)*
MNS Fuel Corp .... F 516 735-3835
  Ronkonkoma *(G-14971)*
Molecular Glasses Inc .... G 585 210-2861
  Rochester *(G-14539)*
Momentive Performance Mtls .... A 614 986-2495
  Waterford *(G-16637)*
◆ Momentive Performance Mtls Inc .... E 518 237-3330
  Waterford *(G-16638)*
Momentive Prfmce Mtls Holdings .... A 518 533-4600
  Albany *(G-102)*
Morgan Fuel & Heating Co Inc .... E 845 856-7831
  Port Jervis *(G-13812)*
Morgan Fuel & Heating Co Inc .... E 845 246-4931
  Saugerties *(G-15217)*
Morgan Fuel & Heating Co Inc .... E 845 626-7766
  Kerhonkson *(G-7185)*
Mpm Holdings Inc .... G 518 237-3330
  Waterford *(G-16639)*
Mpm Intermediate Holdings Inc .... G 518 237-3330
  Waterford *(G-16640)*
Mpm Silicones LLC .... A 518 233-3330
  Waterford *(G-16641)*
Mt Fuel Corp .... G 631 445-2047
  Setauket *(G-15403)*
N & L Fuel Corp .... G 718 863-3538
  Bronx *(G-1407)*
Nagle Fuel Corporation .... G 212 304-4618
  New York *(G-11362)*
North East Fuel Group Inc .... G 718 984-6774
  Staten Island *(G-15735)*
Northeastern Fuel Corp .... G 917 560-6241
  Staten Island *(G-15736)*
Oak-Bark Corporation .... G 518 372-5691
  Scotia *(G-15352)*
Patdan Fuel Corporation .... G 718 326-3668
  Middle Village *(G-8450)*
Poly Scientific R&D Corp .... E 631 586-0400
  Bay Shore *(G-721)*
Polymer Slutions Group Fin LLC .... G 212 771-1717
  New York *(G-11704)*
Provident Fuel Inc .... G 516 224-4427
  Woodbury *(G-17316)*
Quality Fuel 1 Corporation .... G 631 392-4090
  North Babylon *(G-12920)*
RE Fuel .... G 631 909-3316
  Moriches *(G-8659)*
Remsen Fuel Inc .... G 718 984-9551
  Staten Island *(G-15752)*
▲ Rose Solomon Co .... E 718 855-1788
  Brooklyn *(G-2527)*
Royce Associates A Ltd Partnr .... G 516 367-6298
  Jericho *(G-7115)*
S&B Alternative Fuels Inc .... G 631 585-6637
  Lake Grove *(G-7290)*
Smith & Sons Fuels Inc .... G 518 661-6112
  Mayfield *(G-8245)*

Solvents Company Inc .... F 631 595-9300
  Kingston *(G-7238)*
Southbay Fuel Injectors .... G 516 442-4707
  Rockville Centre *(G-14829)*
▲ Specialty Silicone Pdts Inc .... E 518 885-8826
  Ballston Spa *(G-608)*
▼ Sugar Foods Corporation .... E 212 753-6900
  New York *(G-12249)*
Sundial Fragrances & Flavors .... G 631 842-8800
  Amityville *(G-328)*
Symrise Inc .... E 646 459-5000
  New York *(G-12280)*
Symrise Inc .... E 845 469-7675
  Chester *(G-3645)*
Telechemische Inc .... E 845 561-3237
  Newburgh *(G-12805)*
▲ Twin Lake Chemical Inc .... F 716 433-3824
  Lockport *(G-7653)*
Unified Solutions For Clg Inc .... E 718 782-8800
  Brooklyn *(G-2716)*
▲ United Biochemicals LLC .... E 716 731-5161
  Sanborn *(G-15156)*
Value Fragrances & Flavors Inc .... F 845 294-5726
  Goshen *(G-5755)*
Wecare Organics LLC .... E 315 689-1937
  Jordan *(G-7159)*
Western New York Energy LLC .... E 585 798-9693
  Medina *(G-8317)*
Yankee Fuel Inc .... G 631 880-8810
  West Babylon *(G-16873)*
York Fuel Incorporated .... G 718 951-0202
  Brooklyn *(G-2790)*
Zymtrnix Catalytic Systems Inc .... G 918 694-8206
  Ithaca *(G-6920)*

2873 Nitrogenous Fertilizers

Agrium Advanced Tech US Inc .... F 631 286-0598
  Bohemia *(G-1005)*
C P Chemical Co Inc .... E 914 428-2517
  White Plains *(G-17118)*
▼ Growth Products Ltd .... E 914 428-1316
  White Plains *(G-17142)*
Ocip Holding LLC .... G 646 589-6180
  New York *(G-11509)*
Rt Solutions LLC .... G 585 245-3456
  Rochester *(G-14683)*
Scotts Company LLC .... G 631 478-6843
  Hauppauge *(G-6212)*

2874 Phosphatic Fertilizers

International Ord Tech Inc .... D 716 664-1100
  Jamestown *(G-7036)*
Mdi Holdings LLC .... A 212 559-1127
  New York *(G-11228)*
Occidental Chemical Corp .... G 716 694-3827
  North Tonawanda *(G-13002)*
Occidental Chemical Corp .... C 716 278-7794
  Niagara Falls *(G-12874)*

2875 Fertilizers, Mixing Only

Carolina Eastern-Vail Inc .... E 518 854-9785
  Salem *(G-15137)*
Commodity Resource Corporation .... F 585 538-9500
  Caledonia *(G-3305)*
Growmark Fs LLC .... F 585 538-2186
  Caledonia *(G-3306)*
Long Island Compost Corp .... C 516 334-6600
  Westbury *(G-17033)*
Scotts Company LLC .... E 631 289-7444
  Yaphank *(G-17416)*

2879 Pesticides & Agricultural Chemicals, NEC

Agrochem Inc .... E 518 226-4850
  Saratoga Springs *(G-15171)*
BASF Corporation .... B 914 785-2000
  Tarrytown *(G-16111)*
▲ Bioworks Inc .... G 585 924-4362
  Victor *(G-16487)*
E I Du Pont De Nemours & Co .... C 718 761-0043
  Staten Island *(G-15688)*
FMC Corporation .... E 716 735-3761
  Middleport *(G-8455)*
G & S Farm & Home Inc .... G 716 542-9922
  Akron *(G-20)*
Island Marketing Corp .... G 516 739-0500
  Mineola *(G-8549)*
Noble Pine Products Co Inc .... F 914 664-5877
  Mount Vernon *(G-8756)*

2891 Adhesives & Sealants

Able National Corp .... E 718 386-8801
  Brooklyn *(G-1549)*
Adirondack Spclty Adhsives Inc .... F 518 869-5736
  Albany *(G-32)*
Advanced Polymer Solutions LLC .... G 516 621-5800
  Port Washington *(G-13819)*
All Out Die Cutting Inc .... E 718 346-6666
  Brooklyn *(G-1586)*
▲ Angiotech Biocoatings Corp .... E 585 321-1130
  Henrietta *(G-6315)*
▲ Aremco Products Inc .... F 845 268-0039
  Valley Cottage *(G-16402)*
◆ Beacon Adhesives Inc .... E 914 699-3400
  Mount Vernon *(G-8711)*
Best Adhesives Company Inc .... E 718 417-3800
  Ridgewood *(G-14115)*
Classic Labels Inc .... E 631 467-2300
  Patchogue *(G-13442)*
▲ Continental Buchanan LLC .... D 703 480-3800
  Buchanan *(G-2799)*
▲ Deal International Inc .... E 585 288-4444
  Rochester *(G-14325)*
Hexion Inc .... E 518 792-8040
  South Glens Falls *(G-15548)*
Hudson Industries Corporation .... E 518 762-4638
  Johnstown *(G-7146)*
J M Canty Inc .... E 716 625-4227
  Lockport *(G-7624)*
Legacy USA LLC .... E 888 383-3330
  Bronx *(G-1383)*
Northern Adhesives Inc .... E 718 388-5834
  Brooklyn *(G-2384)*
P C I Paper Conversions Inc .... D 315 703-8300
  Syracuse *(G-16028)*
P C I Paper Conversions Inc .... E 315 634-3317
  Syracuse *(G-16029)*
Polycast Industries Inc .... G 631 595-2530
  Bay Shore *(G-722)*
▲ Polyset Company Inc .... E 518 664-6000
  Mechanicville *(G-8260)*
PPG Architectural Finishes Inc .... E 585 271-1363
  Rochester *(G-14610)*
R-Co Products Corporation .... F 800 854-7657
  Lakewood *(G-7318)*
Ran Mar Enterprises Ltd .... F 631 666-4754
  Bay Shore *(G-727)*
Royal Adhesives & Sealants LLC .... F 315 451-1755
  Syracuse *(G-16049)*
▲ Saint Gobain Grains & Powders .... A 716 731-8200
  Niagara Falls *(G-12888)*
Saint-Gobain Prfmce Plas Corp .... C 518 642-2200
  Granville *(G-5796)*
Sg-TEC LLC .... E 631 750-6161
  Bohemia *(G-1128)*
Solenis LLC .... E 315 461-4730
  Liverpool *(G-7575)*
▲ Super-Tek Products Inc .... E 718 278-7900
  Woodside *(G-17373)*
Utility Manufacturing Co Inc .... E 516 997-6300
  Westbury *(G-17068)*
Walsh & Hughes Inc .... G 631 427-5904
  Huntington Station *(G-6766)*
Wild Works Incorporated .... G 716 891-4197
  Albany *(G-151)*

2892 Explosives

Dyno Nobel Inc .... D 845 338-2144
  Ulster Park *(G-16308)*
Maxam North America Inc .... G 313 322-8651
  Ogdensburg *(G-13139)*

2893 Printing Ink

Atlas Coatings Corp .... D 718 402-2000
  Bronx *(G-1276)*
Bishop Print Shop Inc .... G 607 965-8155
  Edmeston *(G-4635)*
▲ Calchem Corporation .... E 631 423-5696
  Ronkonkoma *(G-14912)*
Flint Group Incorporated .... E 585 458-1223
  Rochester *(G-14395)*
Gotham Ink & Color Co Inc .... E 845 947-4000
  Stony Point *(G-15795)*
▲ Image Specialists Inc .... F 631 475-0867
  Saint James *(G-15116)*
Inglis Co Inc .... G 315 475-1315
  Syracuse *(G-15982)*
Intrinsiq Materials Inc .... E 585 301-4432
  Rochester *(G-14475)*

Employee Codes: A=Over 500 employees, B=251-500
C=101-250, D=51-100, E=20-50, F=10-19, G=5-9

◆ Micro Powders Inc ... E ... 914 332-6400
Tarrytown *(G-16120)*
Millennium Rmnfctred Toner Inc ... F ... 718 585-9887
Bronx *(G-1400)*
Mitsubishi Chemical Amer Inc ... E ... 212 223-3043
New York *(G-11310)*
▲ Specialty Ink Co Inc ... F ... 631 586-3666
Blue Point *(G-995)*
▼ Standard Screen Supply Corp ... F ... 212 627-2727
New York *(G-12206)*
Superior Printing Ink Co Inc ... G ... 716 685-6763
Cheektowaga *(G-3618)*
Wikoff Color Corporation ... F ... 585 458-0653
Rochester *(G-14791)*

2899 Chemical Preparations, NEC

Aiping Pharmaceutical Inc ... G ... 631 952-3802
Hauppauge *(G-6031)*
Akzo Nobel Chemicals LLC ... G ... 716 778-8554
Burt *(G-3294)*
Akzo Nobel Chemicals LLC ... C ... 914 674-5008
Dobbs Ferry *(G-4324)*
▲ Alonzo Fire Works Display Inc ... G ... 518 664-9994
Mechanicville *(G-8256)*
American Electronic Products ... F ... 631 924-1299
Yaphank *(G-17402)*
Anabec Inc ... G ... 716 759-1674
Clarence *(G-3683)*
▲ Aufhauser Corporation ... F ... 516 694-8696
Plainview *(G-13614)*
◆ Balchem Corporation ... B ... 845 326-5600
New Hampton *(G-8842)*
Barson Composites Corporation ... E ... 516 752-7882
Old Bethpage *(G-13147)*
BASF Corporation ... B ... 914 785-2000
Tarrytown *(G-16111)*
Bass Oil Company Inc ... E ... 718 628-4444
Brooklyn *(G-1668)*
▼ Bcp Ingredients Inc ... D ... 845 326-5600
New Hampton *(G-8843)*
Beyond Beauty Basics LLC ... F ... 516 731-7100
Levittown *(G-7447)*
▲ Bonide Products Inc ... C ... 315 736-8231
Oriskany *(G-13329)*
◆ C & A Service Inc ... G ... 516 354-1200
Floral Park *(G-5205)*
C P Chemical Co Inc ... G ... 914 428-2517
White Plains *(G-17118)*
Calfonex Company ... F ... 845 778-2212
Walden *(G-16551)*
Cargill Incorporated ... D ... 607 535-6300
Watkins Glen *(G-16719)*
Carpet Beaters LLC ... G ... 877 375-9336
Rosedale *(G-15036)*
Chromananotech LLC ... G ... 607 239-9626
Vestal *(G-16467)*
◆ Citrus and Allied Essences Ltd ... E ... 516 354-1200
Floral Park *(G-5207)*
Classic Flavors Fragrances Inc ... G ... 212 777-0004
New York *(G-9691)*
Crystal Fusion Tech Inc ... F ... 631 253-9800
Lindenhurst *(G-7482)*
Cytec Industries Inc ... D ... 716 372-9650
Olean *(G-13162)*
Danisco US Inc ... D ... 585 256-5200
Rochester *(G-14321)*
E I Du Pont De Nemours & Co ... E ... 585 339-4200
Rochester *(G-14342)*
▲ Ecological Laboratories Inc ... D ... 516 823-3441
Lynbrook *(G-7978)*
Engineering Maint Pdts Inc ... F ... 516 624-9774
Oyster Bay *(G-13395)*
Evans Chemetics LP ... D ... 315 539-9221
Waterloo *(G-16646)*
F M Group Inc ... F ... 845 589-0102
Congers *(G-3881)*
Fantasy Fireworks Display ... G ... 518 664-1809
Stillwater *(G-15781)*
◆ Fireworks By Grucci Inc ... E ... 631 286-0088
Bellport *(G-826)*
▼ Fitzsimmons Systems Inc ... F ... 315 214-7010
Cazenovia *(G-3472)*
▼ Flame Control Coatings LLC ... E ... 716 282-1399
Niagara Falls *(G-12842)*
Foseco Inc ... F ... 914 345-4760
Tarrytown *(G-16115)*
Fppf Chemical Co Inc ... G ... 716 856-9607
Buffalo *(G-2969)*
▲ Geliko LLC ... E ... 212 876-5620
New York *(G-10309)*
Gordon Fire Equipment LLC ... G ... 845 691-5700
Highland *(G-6431)*
▲ Greenfield Manufacturing Inc ... F ... 518 581-2368
Saratoga Springs *(G-15185)*
Halfmoon Town Water Department ... G ... 518 233-7489
Waterford *(G-16633)*
Hampshire Chemical Corp ... D ... 315 539-9221
Waterloo *(G-16651)*
Hanson Aggregates PA LLC ... F ... 585 436-3250
Rochester *(G-14440)*
Healthcare Consulting Svcs Inc ... F ... 860 740-8660
West Babylon *(G-16821)*
Heterochemical Corporation ... F ... 516 561-8225
Valley Stream *(G-16435)*
HHS Pharmaceuticals Inc ... F ... 347 674-1670
New York *(G-10516)*
Horizon Power Source LLC ... E ... 877 240-0580
Glen Cove *(G-5631)*
▼ I A S National Inc ... E ... 631 423-6900
Huntington Station *(G-6748)*
Icynene US Acquisition Corp ... G ... 800 758-7325
Buffalo *(G-3020)*
Indium Corporation of America ... E ... 315 793-8200
Utica *(G-16366)*
Instrumentation Laboratory Co ... C ... 845 680-0028
Orangeburg *(G-13253)*
International Fire-Shield Inc ... F ... 315 255-1006
Auburn *(G-499)*
◆ Island Pyrochemical Inds Corp ... F ... 516 746-2100
Mineola *(G-8551)*
Johnson Manufacturing Company ... F ... 716 881-3030
Buffalo *(G-3038)*
▲ Kemper System America Inc ... E ... 716 558-2971
West Seneca *(G-16979)*
◆ Kent Chemical Corporation ... E ... 212 521-1700
New York *(G-10878)*
Luxfer Magtech Inc ... D ... 631 727-8600
Riverhead *(G-14162)*
Mdi Holdings LLC ... A ... 212 559-1127
New York *(G-11228)*
◆ Micro Powders Inc ... E ... 914 332-6400
Tarrytown *(G-16120)*
Momentive Performance ... G ... 281 325-3536
Waterford *(G-16636)*
Momentive Performance Mtls Inc ... D ... 914 784-4807
Tarrytown *(G-16121)*
▲ Monroe Fluid Technology Inc ... E ... 585 392-3434
Hilton *(G-6444)*
Nalco Company LLC ... E ... 518 796-1985
Saratoga Springs *(G-15193)*
Natures Warehouse ... F ... 800 215-4372
Philadelphia *(G-13564)*
New Fine Chemicals Inc ... G ... 631 321-8151
Lindenhurst *(G-7498)*
Octagon Process LLC ... G ... 845 680-8800
Orangeburg *(G-13259)*
▲ Penetron International Ltd ... F ... 631 941-9700
East Setauket *(G-4507)*
Pure Kemika LLC ... G ... 718 745-2200
Flushing *(G-5293)*
PVS Chemical Solutions Inc ... D ... 716 825-5762
Buffalo *(G-3168)*
▼ Pyrotechnique By Grucci Inc ... E ... 540 639-8800
Bellport *(G-837)*
▲ Real Co Inc ... G ... 347 433-8549
Valley Cottage *(G-16412)*
Reddi Car Corp ... G ... 631 589-3141
Sayville *(G-15243)*
Reliance Fluid Tech LLC ... E ... 716 332-0988
Niagara Falls *(G-12885)*
◆ Rochester Midland Corporation ... C ... 585 336-2200
Rochester *(G-14665)*
Roto Salt Company Inc ... E ... 315 536-3742
Penn Yan *(G-13542)*
Royce Associates A Ltd Partnr ... G ... 516 367-6298
Jericho *(G-7115)*
Safeguard Inc ... F ... 631 929-3273
Wading River *(G-16545)*
Solvents Company Inc ... F ... 631 595-9300
Kingston *(G-7238)*
▲ Specialty Ink Co Inc ... F ... 631 586-3666
Blue Point *(G-995)*
◆ Specialty Minerals Inc ... E ... 212 878-1800
New York *(G-12178)*
▼ Supresta US LLC ... E ... 914 674-9434
Ardsley *(G-405)*
▲ Tam Ceramics LLC ... D ... 716 278-9480
Niagara Falls *(G-12898)*
▼ Tangram Company LLC ... E ... 631 758-0460
Holtsville *(G-6538)*
Technic Inc ... F ... 516 349-0700
Plainview *(G-13665)*
▲ Topaz Industries Inc ... F ... 631 207-0700
Holtsville *(G-6540)*
Torre Products Co Inc ... G ... 212 925-8989
New York *(G-12396)*
US Salt LLC ... D ... 607 535-2721
Watkins Glen *(G-16723)*
Utility Manufacturing Co Inc ... E ... 516 997-6300
Westbury *(G-17068)*
Venue Graphics Supply Inc ... F ... 718 361-1690
Long Island City *(G-7942)*
Water Wise of America Inc ... G ... 585 232-1210
Rochester *(G-14784)*
Water Wise of America Inc ... G ... 585 232-1210
Rochester *(G-14785)*
▼ Watson Bowman Acme Corp ... D ... 716 691-8162
Amherst *(G-271)*
Wyeth Holdings LLC ... D ... 845 602-5000
Pearl River *(G-13493)*
Yiwen Usa Inc ... F ... 212 370-0828
New York *(G-12715)*
▲ Young Explosives Corp ... D ... 585 394-1783
Canandaigua *(G-3390)*
Yr Blanc & Co LLC ... G ... 716 800-3999
Buffalo *(G-3287)*
▲ Zircar Ceramics Inc ... E ... 845 651-6600
Florida *(G-5223)*

29 PETROLEUM REFINING AND RELATED INDUSTRIES

2911 Petroleum Refining

209 Discount Oil ... E ... 845 386-2090
Middletown *(G-8458)*
Algafuel America ... G ... 516 295-2257
Hewlett *(G-6331)*
◆ C & A Service Inc ... G ... 516 354-1200
Floral Park *(G-5205)*
California Petro Trnspt Corp ... G ... 212 302-5151
New York *(G-9551)*
◆ Citrus and Allied Essences Ltd ... E ... 516 354-1200
Floral Park *(G-5207)*
E and V Energy Corporation ... F ... 315 786-2067
Watertown *(G-16672)*
▲ E-Zoil Products Inc ... E ... 716 213-0103
Tonawanda *(G-16177)*
Enertech Labs Inc ... G ... 716 332-9074
Buffalo *(G-2952)*
Ergun Inc ... G ... 631 721-0049
Roslyn Heights *(G-15050)*
Fppf Chemical Co Inc ... G ... 716 856-9607
Buffalo *(G-2969)*
Fuel Energy Services USA Ltd ... E ... 607 846-2650
Horseheads *(G-6607)*
Global Earth Energy ... G ... 716 332-7150
Buffalo *(G-2991)*
Green Global Energy Inc ... G ... 716 501-9770
Niagara Falls *(G-12847)*
Heat USA II LLC ... F ... 212 254-4328
College Point *(G-3811)*
Heat USA II LLC ... E ... 212 564-4328
New York *(G-10497)*
▲ Hess Corporation ... B ... 212 997-8500
New York *(G-10507)*
Hess Oil Virgin Island Corp ... A ... 212 997-8500
New York *(G-10510)*
Hess Pipeline Corporation ... C ... 212 997-8500
New York *(G-10511)*
Hudson Energy Services LLC ... G ... 630 300-0013
Suffern *(G-15813)*
Hygrade Fuel Inc ... G ... 516 741-0723
Mineola *(G-8547)*
▲ Industrial Raw Materials LLC ... F ... 212 688-8080
Plainview *(G-13636)*
◆ Kent Chemical Corporation ... E ... 212 521-1700
New York *(G-10878)*
Kinetic Fuel Technology Inc ... G ... 716 745-1461
Youngstown *(G-17548)*
Koch Supply & Trading LP ... G ... 212 319-4895
New York *(G-10905)*
▲ Koster Keunen Waxes Ltd ... F ... 631 589-0400
Sayville *(G-15241)*
Northern Biodiesel Inc ... G ... 585 545-4534
Ontario *(G-13228)*
Oil Solutions Intl Inc ... G ... 631 608-8889
Amityville *(G-318)*
▲ Osaka Gas Energy America Corp ... F ... 914 253-5500
White Plains *(G-17170)*

Performance Diesel Service LLC.........F 315 854-5269
Plattsburgh *(G-13714)*
Petre Alii Petroleum.........G....... 315 785-1037
Watertown *(G-16693)*
R H Crown Co Inc.........E 518 762-4589
Johnstown *(G-7153)*
Regulus Energy LLC.........F 716 200-7417
Tonawanda *(G-16215)*
Ringhoff Fuel Inc.........G....... 631 878-0663
East Moriches *(G-4450)*
Solvents Company Inc.........F 631 595-9300
Kingston *(G-7238)*
Starfuels Inc.........G....... 914 289-4800
White Plains *(G-17197)*
Suit-Kote Corporation.........D....... 585 268-7127
Belmont *(G-841)*
▲ **Summit Lubricants Inc**.........E 585 815-0798
Batavia *(G-649)*
Tri-State Biodiesel LLC.........D....... 718 860-6600
Bronx *(G-1474)*
Tricon Des LLC.........G....... 619 227-0778
Bronx *(G-1476)*

2951 Paving Mixtures & Blocks

A Colarusso and Son Inc.........E 518 828-3218
Hudson *(G-6631)*
Albany Asp & Aggregates Corp.........E 518 436-8916
Albany *(G-34)*
All Phases Asp & Ldscpg Dsgn.........F 631 588-1372
Ronkonkoma *(G-14889)*
Alliance Paving Materials Inc.........G....... 315 337-0795
Rome *(G-14832)*
Amfar Asphalt Corp.........G....... 631 269-9660
Kings Park *(G-7199)*
Atlas Bituminous Co Inc.........F 315 457-2394
Syracuse *(G-15880)*
Barrett Paving Materials Inc.........E 315 353-6611
Norwood *(G-13058)*
Barrett Paving Materials Inc.........F 315 737-9471
Clayville *(G-3712)*
Barrett Paving Materials Inc.........G....... 607 723-5367
Binghamton *(G-887)*
Barrett Paving Materials Inc.........F 315 788-2037
Watertown *(G-16658)*
Bross Quality Paving.........G....... 845 532-7116
Ellenville *(G-4646)*
C & C Ready-Mix Corporation.........E 607 797-5108
Vestal *(G-16465)*
C & C Ready-Mix Corporation.........F 607 687-1690
Owego *(G-13376)*
Callanan Industries Inc.........E 845 457-3158
Montgomery *(G-8628)*
▲ **Callanan Industries Inc**.........C....... 518 374-2222
Albany *(G-57)*
Callanan Industries Inc.........E 845 331-6868
Kingston *(G-7211)*
Canal Asphalt Inc.........F 914 667-8500
Mount Vernon *(G-8714)*
Cobleskill Stone Products Inc.........F 607 432-8321
Oneonta *(G-13202)*
Cobleskill Stone Products Inc.........F 607 637-4271
Hancock *(G-5984)*
Cofire Paving Corporation.........E 718 463-1403
Flushing *(G-5241)*
Cold Mix Manufacturing Corp.........F 718 463-1444
Mount Vernon *(G-8718)*
Cosmicoat of Wny Inc.........G....... 716 772-2644
Gasport *(G-5571)*
Deans Paving Inc.........G....... 315 736-7601
Marcy *(G-8121)*
Doctor Pavers.........G....... 516 342-6016
Bethpage *(G-865)*
Dolomite Products Company Inc.........E 315 524-1998
Rochester *(G-14337)*
Dolomite Products Company Inc.........F 607 324-3636
Hornell *(G-6587)*
Dolomite Products Company Inc.........E 585 586-2568
Penfield *(G-13522)*
Dolomite Products Company Inc.........F 585 768-7295
Le Roy *(G-7430)*
Dolomite Products Company Inc.........F 585 352-0460
Spencerport *(G-15593)*
G&G Sealcoating and Paving Inc.........E 585 787-1500
Ontario *(G-13224)*
Gernatt Asphalt Products Inc.........E 716 532-3371
Collins *(G-3842)*
Gernatt Asphalt Products Inc.........G 716 496-5111
Springville *(G-15631)*
Grace Associates Inc.........G....... 718 767-9000
Harrison *(G-6005)*
Graymont Materials Inc.........E 518 561-5200
Plattsburgh *(G-13693)*
Hanson Aggregates East LLC.........E 585 343-1787
Stafford *(G-15641)*
Hanson Aggregates PA LLC.........E 585 624-3800
Honeoye Falls *(G-6557)*
Iroquois Rock Products Inc.........F 585 381-7010
Rochester *(G-14476)*
J Pahura Contractors.........G....... 585 589-5793
Albion *(G-169)*
Jamestown Macadam Inc.........F 716 664-5108
Jamestown *(G-7042)*
Jet-Black Sealers Inc.........G....... 716 891-4197
Buffalo *(G-3036)*
John T Montecalvo Inc.........G....... 631 325-1492
Speonk *(G-15600)*
Kal-Harbour Inc.........F 518 266-0690
Albany *(G-93)*
King Road Materials Inc.........E 518 381-9995
Albany *(G-94)*
King Road Materials Inc.........F 518 382-5354
Schenectady *(G-15301)*
Kings Park Asphalt Corporation.........G....... 631 269-9774
Hauppauge *(G-6130)*
Lafarge North America Inc.........E 518 756-5000
Ravena *(G-14036)*
Monticello Black Top Corp.........G....... 845 434-7280
Thompsonville *(G-16138)*
Morlyn Asphalt Corp.........G....... 845 888-2695
Cochecton *(G-3768)*
Narde Paving Company Inc.........E 607 737-7177
Elmira *(G-4710)*
▲ **Nicolia Concrete Products Inc**.........D....... 631 669-0700
Lindenhurst *(G-7500)*
Northeastern Sealcoat Inc.........F 585 544-4372
Rochester *(G-14563)*
Northern Bituminous Mix Inc.........G....... 315 598-2141
Fulton *(G-5486)*
▲ **Package Pavement Company Inc**.........D....... 845 221-2224
Stormville *(G-15802)*
Pallette Stone Corporation.........E 518 584-2421
Gansevoort *(G-5501)*
Parks Paving & Sealing Inc.........F 315 737-5761
Sauquoit *(G-15230)*
Patterson Blacktop Corp.........E 914 949-2000
White Plains *(G-17172)*
Patterson Materials Corp.........F 914 949-2000
White Plains *(G-17173)*
Pavco Asphalt Inc.........E 631 289-3223
Holtsville *(G-6532)*
▲ **Peckham Industries Inc**.........E 914 949-2000
White Plains *(G-17175)*
Peckham Industries Inc.........F 518 943-0155
Catskill *(G-3461)*
Peckham Industries Inc.........F 518 893-2176
Greenfield Center *(G-5889)*
Peckham Industries Inc.........G....... 518 945-1120
Athens *(G-465)*
Peckham Materials Corp.........G....... 845 562-5370
Newburgh *(G-12796)*
Peckham Materials Corp.........D....... 914 686-2045
White Plains *(G-17176)*
Peckham Materials Corp.........E 518 945-1120
Athens *(G-466)*
Peckham Materials Corp.........F 518 494-2313
Chestertown *(G-3650)*
Peckham Materials Corp.........E 518 747-3353
Hudson Falls *(G-6680)*
Posillico Materials LLC.........F 631 249-1872
Farmingdale *(G-5094)*
Prima Asphalt and Concrete.........F 631 289-3223
Holtsville *(G-6533)*
PSI Transit Mix Corp.........G....... 631 382-7930
Smithtown *(G-15519)*
R Schleider Contracting Corp.........G....... 631 269-4249
Kings Park *(G-7204)*
Rason Asphalt Inc.........G....... 631 293-6210
Farmingdale *(G-5107)*
Rason Asphalt Inc.........G....... 516 239-7880
Lawrence *(G-7423)*
Rason Asphalt Inc.........G....... 516 671-1500
Glen Cove *(G-5639)*
Rochester Asphalt Materials.........G....... 585 381-7010
Rochester *(G-14656)*
Rochester Seal Pro LLC.........G....... 585 594-3818
Rochester *(G-14669)*
Seabreeze Pavement of Ny LLC.........G....... 585 338-2333
Rochester *(G-14699)*
Sheldon Slate Products Co Inc.........E 518 642-1280
Middle Granville *(G-8434)*
◆ **Suit-Kote Corporation**.........C....... 607 753-1100
Cortland *(G-4069)*
Suit-Kote Corporation.........F 315 735-8501
Oriskany *(G-13338)*
Suit-Kote Corporation.........E 585 473-6321
Rochester *(G-14730)*
Suit-Kote Corporation.........E 607 535-2743
Watkins Glen *(G-16722)*
Suit-Kote Corporation.........E 716 664-3750
Jamestown *(G-7065)*
Swift River Associates Inc.........G....... 716 875-0902
Tonawanda *(G-16225)*
Thalle Industries Inc.........E 914 762-3415
Briarcliff Manor *(G-1229)*
Tri City Highway Products Inc.........E 607 722-2967
Binghamton *(G-951)*
Tri-City Highway Products Inc.........E 518 294-9964
Richmondville *(G-14102)*
Twin County Recycling Corp.........F 516 827-6900
Westbury *(G-17067)*
Ultimate Pavers Corp.........E 917 417-2652
Staten Island *(G-15772)*
▲ **Unilock New York Inc**.........G....... 845 278-6700
Brewster *(G-1227)*
Universal Ready Mix Inc.........G....... 516 746-4535
New Hyde Park *(G-8915)*
Upstone Materials Inc.........G....... 518 873-2275
Lewis *(G-7452)*
Upstone Materials Inc.........D....... 518 561-5321
Plattsburgh *(G-13735)*
Vestal Asphalt Inc.........F 607 785-3393
Vestal *(G-16480)*
Zielinskis Asphalt Inc.........F 315 306-4057
Oriskany Falls *(G-13343)*

2952 Asphalt Felts & Coatings

▲ **Aremco Products Inc**.........F 845 268-0039
Valley Cottage *(G-16402)*
Barrett Paving Materials Inc.........E 315 353-6611
Norwood *(G-13058)*
Callanan Industries Inc.........E 845 457-3158
Montgomery *(G-8628)*
Johns Manville Corporation.........E 518 565-3000
Plattsburgh *(G-13699)*
K-D Stone Inc.........F 518 642-2082
Middle Granville *(G-8433)*
◆ **Marathon Roofing Products Inc**.........F 716 685-3340
Orchard Park *(G-13307)*
Northeastern Sealcoat Inc.........F 585 544-4372
Rochester *(G-14563)*
Peckham Materials Corp.........E 518 747-3353
Hudson Falls *(G-6680)*
▲ **Polyset Company Inc**.........E 518 664-6000
Mechanicville *(G-8260)*
Savage & Son Installations LLC.........E 585 342-7533
Rochester *(G-14692)*
Sheldon Slate Products Co Inc.........E 518 642-1280
Middle Granville *(G-8434)*
Spray-Tech Finishing Inc.........F 716 664-6317
Jamestown *(G-7062)*
Suit-Kote Corporation.........E 607 535-2743
Watkins Glen *(G-16722)*
Texture Plus Inc.........E 631 218-9200
Bohemia *(G-1140)*
Tntpaving.........G....... 607 372-4911
Endicott *(G-4836)*

2992 Lubricating Oils & Greases

▲ **Battenfeld Grease Oil Corp NY**.........E 716 695-2100
North Tonawanda *(G-12978)*
▼ **Battenfeld-American Inc**.........E 716 822-8410
Buffalo *(G-2856)*
▼ **Baums Castorine Company Inc**.........G....... 315 336-8154
Rome *(G-14834)*
Beka World LP.........G....... 905 821-1050
Buffalo *(G-2858)*
Bestline International RES Inc.........G....... 518 631-2177
Schenectady *(G-15263)*
▲ **Black Bear Company Inc**.........E 718 784-7330
Long Island City *(G-7718)*
▲ **Blaser Production Inc**.........F 845 294-3200
Goshen *(G-5747)*
◆ **Blaser Swisslube Holding Corp**.........F 845 294-3200
Goshen *(G-5748)*
Castoleum Corporation.........F 914 664-5877
Mount Vernon *(G-8715)*
◆ **Chemlube International LLC**.........F 914 381-5800
Harrison *(G-6000)*
◆ **Chemlube Marketing Inc**.........F 914 381-5800
Harrison *(G-6001)*

SIC

Employee Codes: A=Over 500 employees, B=251-500
C=101-250, D=51-100, E=20-50, F=10-19, G=5-9
2018 Harris
New York Manufacturers Directory
787

29 PETROLEUM REFINING AND RELATED INDUSTRIES

◆ Finish Line Technologies Inc ....E 631 666-7300
  Hauppauge (G-6099)
Industrial Oil Tank Service ....F 315 736-6080
  Oriskany (G-13335)
▲ Inland Vacuum Industries Inc ....F 585 293-3330
  Churchville (G-3667)
▲ Interdynamics ....F 914 241-1423
  Mount Kisco (G-8672)
▲ Loobrica International Corp ....G 347 997-0296
  Staten Island (G-15722)
Mdi Holdings LLC ....A 212 559-1127
  New York (G-11228)
▲ Monroe Fluid Technology Inc ....E 585 392-3434
  Hilton (G-6444)
Noco Incorporated ....G 716 833-6626
  Tonawanda (G-16205)
Oil and Lubricant Depot LLC ....G 718 258-9220
  Amityville (G-317)
▲ Ore-Lube Corporation ....F 631 205-0030
  Bellport (G-833)
Polycast Industries Inc ....G 631 595-2530
  Bay Shore (G-722)
Safety-Kleen Systems Inc ....F 716 855-2212
  Buffalo (G-3203)
▲ Specialty Silicone Pdts Inc ....E 518 885-8826
  Ballston Spa (G-608)
Tallmans Express Lube ....G 315 266-1033
  New Hartford (G-8857)
▲ Tribology Inc ....E 631 345-3000
  Yaphank (G-17421)
Valvoline Inc ....G 914 684-0170
  White Plains (G-17205)

2999 Products Of Petroleum & Coal, NEC

▼ Cooks Intl Ltd Lblty Co ....G 212 741-4407
  New York (G-9777)
Costello Bros Petroleum Corp ....F 914 237-3189
  Yonkers (G-17446)
Hh Liquidating Corp ....A 646 282-2500
  New York (G-10515)
Industrial Raw Materials LLC ....G 212 688-8080
  New York (G-10634)
▲ Premier Ingridients Inc ....F 516 641-6763
  Great Neck (G-5849)

30 RUBBER AND MISCELLANEOUS PLASTICS PRODUCTS

3011 Tires & Inner Tubes

East Coast Intl Tire Inc ....F 718 386-9088
  Maspeth (G-8166)
▼ Handy & Harman Ltd ....A 212 520-2300
  New York (G-10450)
McCarthy Tire Svc Co NY Inc ....F 518 449-5185
  Menands (G-8407)
New York CT Loc246 Seiu Wel BF ....G 212 233-0616
  New York (G-11417)
Roli Retreads Inc ....E 631 694-7670
  Farmingdale (G-5112)
Sph Group Holdings LLC ....F 212 520-2300
  New York (G-12186)
◆ Sumitomo Rubber Usa LLC ....A 716 879-8200
  Tonawanda (G-16223)

3021 Rubber & Plastic Footwear

▲ Anthony L & S LLC ....G 212 386-7245
  New York (G-9218)
Crocs Inc ....F 845 928-3002
  Central Valley (G-3549)
▲ Detny Footwear Inc ....G 212 423-1040
  New York (G-9913)
Homegrown For Good LLC ....F 857 540-6361
  New Rochelle (G-8957)
Inkkas LLC ....G 646 845-9803
  New York (G-10643)
Little Eric Shoes On Madison ....G 212 717-1513
  New York (G-11038)
▲ Mango Usa Inc ....E 718 998-6050
  Brooklyn (G-2260)
Nike Inc ....E 212 226-5433
  New York (G-11449)
Nike Inc ....E 631 242-3014
  Deer Park (G-4205)
Nike Inc ....E 631 960-0184
  Islip Terrace (G-6855)
Nike Inc ....G 716 298-5615
  Niagara Falls (G-12868)
▲ Pro Line Manufacturing Co LLC ....E 973 692-9696
  New York (G-11745)

Skechers USA Inc ....F 718 585-3024
  Bronx (G-1454)
Soludos LLC ....F 212 219-1101
  New York (G-12153)
▲ Timing Group LLC ....F 646 878-2600
  New York (G-12372)
Vans Inc ....F 631 724-1011
  Lake Grove (G-7293)
Vans Inc ....F 718 349-2311
  Brooklyn (G-2737)
Wallico Shoes Corp ....G 212 826-7171
  New York (G-12611)

3052 Rubber & Plastic Hose & Belting

▲ Anchor Tech Products Corp ....E 914 592-0240
  Elmsford (G-4742)
Cataract Hose Co ....G 914 941-9019
  Ossining (G-13345)
Deer Park Driveshaft & Hose ....G 631 667-4091
  Deer Park (G-4149)
▲ Flex Enterprises Inc ....E 585 742-1000
  Victor (G-16501)
Habasit America Inc ....D 716 824-8484
  Buffalo (G-3001)
▲ Hitachi Cable America Inc ....F 914 694-9200
  Purchase (G-13973)
Honeywell International Inc ....G 518 270-0200
  Troy (G-16241)
Index Incorporated ....F 440 632-5400
  Bronx (G-1362)
Jain Irrigation Inc ....D 315 755-4400
  Watertown (G-16676)
Jed Lights Inc ....F 516 812-5001
  Deer Park (G-4180)
◆ Mason Industries Inc ....B 631 348-0282
  Hauppauge (G-6152)
▲ Mercer Rubber Co ....F 631 348-0282
  Hauppauge (G-6158)
Moreland Hose & Belting Corp ....G 631 563-7071
  Oakdale (G-13078)
◆ Peraflex Hose Inc ....F 716 876-8806
  Buffalo (G-3143)
▲ Sampla Belting North Amer LLC ......E 716 667-7450
  Lackawanna (G-7275)
Standard Motor Products Inc ....B 718 392-0200
  Long Island City (G-7912)
▲ Superflex Ltd ....F 718 768-1400
  Brooklyn (G-2646)
TI Group Auto Systems LLC ....G 315 568-7042
  Seneca Falls (G-15394)
Troy Belting and Supply Co ....D 518 272-4920
  Watervliet (G-16715)
Van Slyke Belting LLC ....G 518 283-5479
  Poestenkill (G-13756)
▲ WF Lake Corp ....F 518 798-9934
  Queensbury (G-14027)

3053 Gaskets, Packing & Sealing Devices

A L Sealing ....G 315 699-6900
  Chittenango (G-3659)
▲ Allstate Gasket & Packing Inc ....F 631 254-4050
  Deer Park (G-4116)
American Sealing Technology ....F 631 254-0019
  Deer Park (G-4121)
Apex Packing & Rubber Co Inc ....F 631 420-8150
  Farmingdale (G-4951)
Apple Rubber Products Inc ....C 716 684-7649
  Lancaster (G-7328)
▲ Bag Arts Ltd ....F 212 684-7020
  New York (G-9355)
Boonville Manufacturing Corp ....G 315 942-4368
  Boonville (G-1162)
Commercial Gaskets New York ....F 212 244-8130
  New York (G-9745)
▲ Everlast Seals and Supply LLC ....F 718 388-7373
  Brooklyn (G-1946)
▲ Frank Lowe Rbr & Gasket Co Inc ....E 631 777-2707
  Shirley (G-15442)
Gaddis Industrial Equipment ....F 516 759-3100
  Glen Cove (G-5629)
Garlock Sealing Tech LLC ....A 315 597-4811
  Palmyra (G-13432)
GM Components Holdings LLC ....G 716 439-2402
  Lockport (G-7621)
Hollingsworth & Vose Company ....C 518 695-8000
  Greenwich (G-5908)
Interface Performance Mtls Inc ....G 315 592-8100
  Fulton (G-5476)
Interface Performance Mtls Inc ....D 518 684-3400
  Hoosick Falls (G-6567)

Jed Lights Inc ....F 516 812-5001
  Deer Park (G-4180)
John Crane Inc ....D 315 593-6237
  Fulton (G-5478)
▲ Make-Waves Instrument Corp ....E 716 681-7524
  Buffalo (G-3076)
Micromold Products Inc ....E 914 969-2850
  Yonkers (G-17485)
◆ Noroc Enterprises Inc ....E 718 585-3230
  Bronx (G-1414)
▲ Prince Rubber & Plas Co Inc ....E 225 272-1653
  Buffalo (G-3161)
Quick Cut Gasket & Rubber ....F 716 684-8628
  Lancaster (G-7361)
▲ S A S Industries Inc ....F 631 727-1441
  Manorville (G-8112)
Schlegel Electronic Mtls Inc ....F 585 295-2030
  Rochester (G-14694)
▲ Schlegel Systems Inc ....E 585 427-7200
  Rochester (G-14695)
Seal & Design Inc ....E 315 432-8021
  Syracuse (G-16058)
Sealcraft Industries Inc ....F 718 517-2000
  Brooklyn (G-2566)
SKF USA Inc ....D 716 661-2600
  Jamestown (G-7060)
Technical Packaging Inc ....F 516 223-2300
  Baldwin (G-561)
Temper Corporation ....E 518 853-3467
  Fonda (G-5322)
Thermal Foams/Syracuse Inc ....E 315 699-8734
  Cicero (G-3680)
Unique Packaging Corporation ....G 514 341-5872
  Champlain (G-3576)
USA Sealing Inc ....E 716 288-9952
  Cheektowaga (G-3620)
Web Seal Inc ....E 585 546-1320
  Rochester (G-14786)
▲ Xto Incorporated ....D 315 451-7807
  Liverpool (G-7585)

3061 Molded, Extruded & Lathe-Cut Rubber Mechanical Goods

Apple Rubber Products Inc ....C 716 684-7649
  Lancaster (G-7328)
Bridgestone APM Company ....D 419 423-9552
  Sanborn (G-15141)
▲ Camso Manufacturing Usa Ltd ....D 518 561-7528
  Plattsburgh (G-13685)
Delford Industries Inc ....D 845 342-3901
  Middletown (G-8469)
Finzer Holding LLC ....E 315 597-1147
  Palmyra (G-13431)
Mechanical Rubber Pdts Co Inc ....F 845 986-2271
  Warwick (G-16616)
▲ Moldtech Inc ....E 716 685-3344
  Lancaster (G-7351)
Ms Spares LLC ....G 607 223-3024
  Clay (G-3709)
▼ Pawling Corporation ....C 845 855-1000
  Pawling (G-13474)
Pawling Corporation ....D 845 373-9300
  Wassaic (G-16622)
Pawling Engineered Pdts Inc ....C 845 855-1000
  Pawling (G-13475)
Pilot Products Inc ....F 718 728-2141
  Long Island City (G-7873)
Precision Extrusion Inc ....E 518 792-1199
  Glens Falls (G-5711)
R & A Industrial Products ....G 716 823-4300
  Buffalo (G-3177)
The Centro Company Inc ....G 914 533-2200
  South Salem (G-15561)
▲ Triangle Rubber Co Inc ....E 631 589-9400
  Bohemia (G-1144)

3069 Fabricated Rubber Prdts, NEC

▲ Adam Scott Designs Inc ....E 212 420-8866
  New York (G-9071)
Advanced Back Technologies ....G 631 231-0076
  Hauppauge (G-6029)
▲ Apple Rubber Products Inc ....E 716 684-6560
  Lancaster (G-7327)
Apple Rubber Products Inc ....C 716 684-7649
  Lancaster (G-7328)
Buffalo Lining & Fabricating ....G 716 883-6500
  Buffalo (G-2876)
▼ Cementex Latex Corp ....F 212 741-1770
  New York (G-9609)

30 RUBBER AND MISCELLANEOUS PLASTICS PRODUCTS

Certified Health Products Inc..............E....... 718 339-7498
Brooklyn *(G-1770)*
▲ Chamberlin Rubber Company Inc.........E....... 585 427-7780
Rochester *(G-14291)*
▲ Chemprene Inc..............................C....... 845 831-2800
Beacon *(G-777)*
▲ Chemprene Holding Inc....................C....... 845 831-2800
Beacon *(G-778)*
Continental Latex Corp......................F....... 718 783-7883
Brooklyn *(G-1798)*
Enbi Indiana Inc.............................E....... 585 647-1627
Rochester *(G-14369)*
Enviroform Recycled Pdts Inc................G....... 315 789-1810
Geneva *(G-5586)*
Finzer Holding LLC..........................G....... 315 597-1147
Palmyra *(G-13431)*
Foam Products Inc..........................E....... 718 292-4830
Bronx *(G-1337)*
▲ Geri-Gentle Corporation....................G....... 917 804-7807
Brooklyn *(G-2021)*
◆ Great American Industries Inc...............G....... 607 729-9331
Vestal *(G-16472)*
▲ Hampton Art LLC...........................E....... 631 924-1335
Medford *(G-8278)*
Hti Recycling LLC...........................E....... 716 433-9294
Lockport *(G-7623)*
Idg LLC.....................................E....... 315 797-1000
Utica *(G-16365)*
Impladent Ltd...............................G....... 718 465-1810
Jamaica *(G-6957)*
Inflation Systems Inc........................E....... 914 381-8070
Mamaroneck *(G-8069)*
Jamestown Scientific Inds LLC...............F....... 716 665-3224
Jamestown *(G-7045)*
Kelson Products Inc........................G....... 716 825-2585
Orchard Park *(G-13302)*
Life Medical Technologies LLC...............F....... 845 894-2121
Hopewell Junction *(G-6582)*
◆ Magic Touch Icewares Intl..................G....... 212 794-2852
New York *(G-11134)*
▲ Mam USA Corporation......................F....... 914 269-2500
Purchase *(G-13977)*
◆ Mason Industries Inc.......................B....... 631 348-0282
Hauppauge *(G-6152)*
▲ Mercer Rubber Co..........................C....... 631 348-0282
Hauppauge *(G-6158)*
Mhxco Foam Company LLC..................F....... 518 843-8400
Amsterdam *(G-356)*
▲ Moldtech Inc................................E....... 716 685-3344
Lancaster *(G-7351)*
Newyork Pedorthic Associates...............G....... 718 236-7700
Brooklyn *(G-2380)*
▲ Package Print Technologies.................E....... 716 871-9905
Buffalo *(G-3132)*
Par-Foam Products Inc.....................C....... 716 855-2066
Buffalo *(G-3135)*
▼ Pawling Corporation........................C....... 845 855-1000
Pawling *(G-13474)*
▲ Power Up Manufacturing Inc................E....... 716 876-4890
Buffalo *(G-3156)*
▲ Prince Rubber & Plas Co Inc................E....... 225 272-1653
Buffalo *(G-3161)*
Remedies Surgical Supplies..................G....... 718 599-5301
Brooklyn *(G-2509)*
Rotation Dynamics Corporation..............E....... 585 352-9023
Spencerport *(G-15597)*
Rubber Stamps Inc..........................E....... 212 675-1180
Mineola *(G-8568)*
▼ Rubberform Recycled Pdts LLC..............F....... 716 478-0404
Lockport *(G-7644)*
▲ Schlegel Systems Inc.......................C....... 585 427-7200
Rochester *(G-14695)*
SD Christie Associates Inc..................G....... 914 734-1800
Peekskill *(G-13507)*
Seaway Mats Inc............................G....... 518 483-2560
Malone *(G-8047)*
Short Jj Associates Inc......................F....... 315 986-3511
Macedon *(G-8021)*
▲ Tire Conversion Tech Inc...................E....... 518 372-1600
Latham *(G-7406)*
▼ Tmp Technologies Inc......................D....... 716 895-6100
Buffalo *(G-3246)*
Tmp Technologies Inc......................D....... 585 495-6231
Wyoming *(G-17399)*
▼ Traffic Logix Corporation...................G....... 866 915-6449
Spring Valley *(G-15624)*
▲ Triangle Rubber Co Inc.....................E....... 631 589-9400
Bohemia *(G-1144)*
▲ Turner Bellows Inc..........................E....... 585 235-4456
Rochester *(G-14763)*

Vehicle Manufacturers Inc...................E....... 631 851-1700
Hauppauge *(G-6247)*
Wall Protection Products LLC................E....... 877 943-6826
Wassaic *(G-16624)*
Zylon Corporation............................F....... 845 425-9469
Monsey *(G-8622)*

3081 Plastic Unsupported Sheet & Film

▲ Ace Canvas & Tent Corp...................F....... 631 648-0614
Ronkonkoma *(G-14876)*
◆ American Acrylic Corporation...............E....... 631 422-2200
West Babylon *(G-16795)*
▲ API Industries Inc...........................B....... 845 365-2200
Orangeburg *(G-13239)*
API Industries Inc...........................C....... 845 365-2200
Orangeburg *(G-13240)*
▲ Astra Products Inc..........................G....... 631 464-4747
Copiague *(G-3921)*
Berry Global Inc.............................C....... 315 986-2161
Macedon *(G-8011)*
Berry Plastics Corporation...................B....... 315 986-6270
Macedon *(G-8013)*
Bfgg Investors Group LLC...................E....... 585 424-3456
Rochester *(G-14248)*
Clear View Bag Company Inc...............C....... 518 458-7153
Albany *(G-64)*
▲ Comco Plastics Inc.........................E....... 718 849-9000
Huntington Station *(G-6738)*
D Bag Lady Inc..............................G....... 585 425-8095
Fairport *(G-4858)*
Dunmore Corporation.......................D....... 845 279-5061
Brewster *(G-1214)*
Ecoplast & Packaging LLC..................E....... 718 996-0800
Brooklyn *(G-1902)*
Edco Supply Corporation...................D....... 718 788-8108
Brooklyn *(G-1905)*
Excellent Poly Inc...........................E....... 718 768-6555
Brooklyn *(G-1948)*
Farber Plastics Inc..........................E....... 516 378-4860
Freeport *(G-5408)*
Farber Trucking Corp.......................E....... 516 378-4860
Freeport *(G-5409)*
▲ Favorite Plastic Corp.......................C....... 718 253-7000
Brooklyn *(G-1964)*
▼ Franklin Poly Film Inc......................E....... 718 492-3523
Brooklyn *(G-2002)*
Great Lakes Plastics Co Inc.................E....... 716 896-3100
Buffalo *(G-2997)*
Integument Technologies Inc................F....... 716 873-1199
Tonawanda *(G-16193)*
◆ Island Pyrochemical Inds Corp.............F....... 516 746-2100
Mineola *(G-8551)*
▲ Kent Chemical Corporation.................E....... 212 521-1700
New York *(G-10878)*
Kings Film & Sheet Inc.....................E....... 718 624-7510
Brooklyn *(G-2174)*
Knf Clean Room Products Corp.............E....... 631 588-6100
Ronkonkoma *(G-14951)*
▲ Knoll Printing & Packaging Inc..............E....... 516 621-0100
Syosset *(G-15846)*
Latham International Inc....................F....... 518 346-5292
Schenectady *(G-15302)*
▲ Latham International Inc....................E....... 518 783-7776
Latham *(G-7396)*
▲ Maco Bag Corporation......................C....... 315 226-1000
Newark *(G-12755)*
Msi Inc.......................................F....... 845 639-6683
New City *(G-8834)*
▲ Nationwide Tarps Incorporated.............D....... 518 843-1545
Amsterdam *(G-362)*
Nova Packaging Ltd Inc....................E....... 914 232-8406
Katonah *(G-7161)*
Nuhart & Co Inc............................D....... 718 383-8484
Brooklyn *(G-2390)*
Oaklee International Inc.....................D....... 631 436-7900
Ronkonkoma *(G-14983)*
Orafol Americas Inc........................E....... 585 272-0309
Henrietta *(G-6321)*
Pace Polyethylene Mfg Co Inc..............E....... 914 381-3000
Harrison *(G-6007)*
Pacific Designs Intl Inc......................G....... 718 364-2867
Bronx *(G-1420)*
▲ Plascal Corp.................................E....... 516 249-2200
Farmingdale *(G-5091)*
Pliant LLC...................................B....... 315 986-6286
Macedon *(G-8020)*
Pocono Pool Products-North...............E....... 518 283-1023
Rensselaer *(G-14060)*
▲ Potential Poly Bag Inc......................G....... 718 258-0800
Brooklyn *(G-2443)*

▲ Precision Packaging Pdts Inc...............C....... 585 638-8200
Holley *(G-6517)*
R & F Boards & Dividers Inc.................G....... 718 331-1529
Brooklyn *(G-2488)*
Rainbow Poly Bag Co Inc...................E....... 718 386-3500
Brooklyn *(G-2495)*
Robeco/Ascot Products Inc.................G....... 516 248-1521
Garden City *(G-5544)*
▲ Royal Plastics Corp.........................E....... 718 647-7500
Brooklyn *(G-2533)*
Sand Hill Industries Inc......................E....... 518 885-7991
Ballston Spa *(G-607)*
▲ Scapa North America......................E....... 315 413-1111
Liverpool *(G-7573)*
Sentinel Products Corp......................F....... 518 568-7036
Saint Johnsville *(G-15124)*
▲ Shaant Industries Inc.......................E....... 716 366-3654
Dunkirk *(G-4374)*
◆ Swimline Corp..............................E....... 631 254-2155
Edgewood *(G-4626)*
▲ Top Quality Products Inc...................G....... 212 213-1988
New York *(G-12390)*
Toray Industries Inc.........................G....... 212 697-8150
New York *(G-12394)*
Tri-Seal Holdings Inc........................D....... 845 353-3300
Blauvelt *(G-972)*
Trinity Packaging Corporation...............E....... 716 668-3111
Buffalo *(G-3251)*
▲ Turner Bellows Inc..........................E....... 585 235-4456
Rochester *(G-14763)*
Vinyl Materials Inc..........................E....... 631 586-9444
Deer Park *(G-4249)*

3082 Plastic Unsupported Profile Shapes

Chelsea Plastics Inc........................F....... 212 924-4530
New York *(G-9630)*
▲ Comco Plastics Inc.........................E....... 718 849-9000
Huntington Station *(G-6738)*
▲ Finger Lakes Extrusion Corp...............E....... 585 905-0632
Canandaigua *(G-3375)*
▼ Franklin Poly Film Inc......................E....... 718 492-3523
Brooklyn *(G-2002)*
Great Lakes Plastics Co Inc.................E....... 716 896-3100
Buffalo *(G-2997)*
Hancor Inc..................................D....... 607 565-3033
Waverly *(G-16728)*
Howard J Moore Company Inc.............E....... 631 351-8467
Plainview *(G-13635)*
◆ Mitsui Chemicals America Inc.............E....... 914 253-0777
Rye Brook *(G-15098)*
▲ Ontario Plastics Inc........................E....... 585 663-2644
Rochester *(G-14572)*

3083 Plastic Laminated Plate & Sheet

▼ ADC Acquisition Company.................E....... 518 377-6471
Niskayuna *(G-12910)*
Advanced Assembly Services Inc...........G....... 716 217-8144
Angola *(G-378)*
Advanced Structures Corp..................F....... 631 667-5000
Deer Park *(G-4113)*
Allred & Associates Inc.....................E....... 315 252-2559
Elbridge *(G-4637)*
◆ American Acrylic Corporation...............E....... 631 422-2200
West Babylon *(G-16795)*
Anthony River Inc..........................F....... 315 475-1315
Syracuse *(G-15875)*
Architctral Dsgn Elements LLC..............G....... 718 218-7800
Brooklyn *(G-1623)*
▲ Blue Sky Plastic Production................F....... 718 366-3966
Brooklyn *(G-1702)*
▲ Clear Cast Technologies Inc...............E....... 914 945-0848
Ossining *(G-13346)*
Displays By Rioux Inc......................G....... 315 458-3639
North Syracuse *(G-12958)*
▲ Favorite Plastic Corp.......................C....... 718 253-7000
Brooklyn *(G-1964)*
◆ Griffon Corporation.........................E....... 212 957-5000
New York *(G-10405)*
▲ Inland Paper Products Corp................E....... 718 827-8150
Brooklyn *(G-2106)*
Inter State Laminates Inc...................E....... 518 283-8355
Poestenkill *(G-13754)*
Iridium Industries Inc.......................E....... 516 504-9700
Great Neck *(G-5833)*
Jaguar Industries Inc.......................F....... 845 947-1800
Haverstraw *(G-6261)*
Jay Moulding Corporation..................E....... 518 237-4200
Cohoes *(G-3772)*
▲ Nalge Nunc International Corp............A....... 585 498-2661
Rochester *(G-14547)*

Employee Codes: A=Over 500 employees, B=251-500
C=101-250, D=51-100, E=20-50, F=10-19, G=5-9

Norton Performance Plas Corp ... G ... 518 642-2200
Granville (G-5795)

On Time Plastics Inc ... G ... 516 442-4280
Freeport (G-5426)

Solid Surface Acrylics Inc ... F ... 716 743-1870
North Tonawanda (G-13012)

Strux Corp ... E ... 516 768-3969
Lindenhurst (G-7508)

Synthetic Textiles Inc ... G ... 716 842-2598
Buffalo (G-3231)

▲ Unico Special Products Inc ... E ... 845 562-9255
Newburgh (G-12807)

3084 Plastic Pipe

▲ Advanced Distribution System ... D ... 845 848-2357
Palisades (G-13425)

▲ BMC LLC ... E ... 716 681-7755
Buffalo (G-2866)

Hancor Inc ... D ... 607 565-3033
Waverly (G-16728)

Micromold Products Inc ... E ... 914 969-2850
Yonkers (G-17485)

◆ National Pipe & Plastics Inc ... C ... 607 729-9381
Vestal (G-16474)

North American Pipe Corp ... F ... 516 338-2863
Jericho (G-7111)

▲ Prince Rubber & Plas Co Inc ... E ... 225 272-1653
Buffalo (G-3161)

3085 Plastic Bottles

▲ Alphamed Bottles Inc ... F ... 631 275-5042
Hauppauge (G-6036)

▼ Capitol Plastic Products Inc ... C ... 518 627-0051
Amsterdam (G-339)

◆ Chapin International Inc ... C ... 585 343-3140
Batavia (G-628)

◆ Chapin Manufacturing Inc ... C ... 585 343-3140
Batavia (G-629)

Cortland Plastics Intl LLC ... E ... 607 662-0120
Cortland (G-4043)

David Johnson ... F ... 315 493-4735
Carthage (G-3441)

Intrapac International Corp ... C ... 518 561-2030
Plattsburgh (G-13697)

Kybod Group LLC ... G ... 408 306-1657
New York (G-10936)

▲ Nalge Nunc International Corp ... A ... 585 498-2661
Rochester (G-14547)

Pvc Container Corporation ... C ... 518 672-7721
Philmont (G-13566)

Samco Scientific Corporation ... C ... 800 522-3359
Rochester (G-14687)

▲ Schless Bottles Inc ... F ... 718 236-2790
Brooklyn (G-2561)

▲ Vista Packaging Inc ... E ... 718 854-9200
Brooklyn (G-2750)

Weber Intl Packg Co LLC ... D ... 518 561-8282
Plattsburgh (G-13738)

3086 Plastic Foam Prdts

24 Seven Enterprises Inc ... G ... 845 563-9033
New Windsor (G-8974)

ABI Packaging Inc ... E ... 716 677-2900
West Seneca (G-16967)

Arm Rochester Inc ... F ... 585 354-5077
Rochester (G-14227)

Barclay Brown Corp ... F ... 718 376-7166
Brooklyn (G-1665)

Berry Plastics Corporation ... B ... 315 986-6270
Macedon (G-8013)

▲ Burnett Process Inc ... G ... 585 254-8080
Rochester (G-14269)

C P Chemical Co Inc ... G ... 914 428-2517
White Plains (G-17118)

Calpac Incorporated ... F ... 631 789-0502
Amityville (G-278)

Carlisle Construction Mtls LLC ... D ... 386 753-0786
Montgomery (G-8629)

▲ Cellect LLC ... C ... 508 744-6906
Saint Johnsville (G-15118)

▲ Cellect Plastics LLC ... D ... 518 568-7036
Saint Johnsville (G-15119)

Chesu Inc ... F ... 239 564-2803
East Hampton (G-4427)

China Xd Plastics Company Ltd ... G ... 212 747-1118
New York (G-9654)

◆ Chocolate Delivery Systems Inc ... D ... 716 854-6050
Buffalo (G-2892)

Dura Foam Inc ... E ... 718 894-2488
Maspeth (G-8163)

Fedex Ground Package Sys Inc ... G ... 800 463-3339
Plattsburgh (G-13691)

First Qlty Packg Solutions LLC ... F ... 516 829-3030
Great Neck (G-5826)

Foam Products Inc ... E ... 718 292-4830
Bronx (G-1337)

▲ General Vy-Coat LLC ... E ... 718 266-6002
Brooklyn (G-2019)

◆ Great American Industries Inc ... G ... 607 729-9331
Vestal (G-16472)

Hopp Companies Inc ... F ... 516 358-4170
New Hyde Park (G-8886)

▲ Interntnal Bus Cmmncations Inc ... E ... 516 352-4505
New Hyde Park (G-8887)

J & M Packaging Inc ... F ... 631 608-3069
Hauppauge (G-6124)

▼ Jamestown Container Corp ... C ... 716 665-4623
Falconer (G-4912)

Jem Container Corp ... F ... 800 521-0145
Plainview (G-13640)

▲ Knoll Printing & Packaging Inc ... E ... 516 621-0100
Syosset (G-15846)

▲ Lamar Plastics Packaging Ltd ... D ... 516 378-2500
Freeport (G-5419)

◆ Latham International Inc ... G ... 518 783-7776
Latham (G-7396)

Latham Pool Products Inc ... E ... 260 432-8731
Latham (G-7398)

Lewis & Myers Inc ... G ... 585 494-1410
Bergen (G-847)

New York State Foam Enrgy LLC ... G ... 845 534-4656
Cornwall (G-4010)

Par-Foam Products Inc ... C ... 716 855-2066
Buffalo (G-3135)

Philpac Corporation ... E ... 716 875-8005
Buffalo (G-3147)

Pliant LLC ... B ... 315 986-6286
Macedon (G-8020)

▲ Printex Packaging Corporation ... D ... 631 234-4300
Islandia (G-6840)

Professional Packg Svcs Inc ... E ... 518 677-5100
Eagle Bridge (G-4381)

R D A Container Corporation ... E ... 585 247-2323
Gates (G-5578)

Rimco Plastics Corp ... E ... 607 739-3864
Horseheads (G-6619)

Saint-Gobain Prfmce Plas Corp ... C ... 518 642-2200
Granville (G-5796)

▲ Shell Containers Inc (ny) ... E ... 516 352-4505
New Hyde Park (G-8906)

▲ Shelter Enterprises Inc ... D ... 518 237-4100
Cohoes (G-3783)

▲ Skd Distribution Corp ... E ... 718 525-6000
Jericho (G-7120)

Snow Craft Co Inc ... E ... 516 739-1399
New Hyde Park (G-8907)

◆ Soundcoat Company Inc ... D ... 631 242-2200
Deer Park (G-4236)

Stephen Gould Corporation ... F ... 212 497-8180
New York (G-12219)

Strux Corp ... E ... 516 768-3969
Lindenhurst (G-7508)

Technical Packaging Inc ... F ... 516 223-2300
Baldwin (G-561)

▲ Thermal Foams/Syracuse Inc ... G ... 716 874-6474
Buffalo (G-3242)

▼ Tmp Technologies Inc ... D ... 716 895-6100
Buffalo (G-3246)

TSS Foam Industries Corp ... F ... 585 538-2321
Caledonia (G-3311)

◆ W Stuart Smith Inc ... E ... 585 742-3310
Victor (G-16535)

Walnut Packaging Inc ... E ... 631 293-3836
Farmingdale (G-5150)

3087 Custom Compounding Of Purchased Plastic Resins

Advance Chemicals Usa Inc ... G ... 718 633-1030
Brooklyn (G-1564)

◆ Ampacet Corporation ... A ... 914 631-6600
Tarrytown (G-16110)

Atc Plastics LLC ... E ... 212 375-2515
New York (G-9297)

Cryovac Inc ... C ... 585 436-3211
Rochester (G-14313)

Lahr Recycling & Resins Inc ... F ... 585 425-8608
Fairport (G-4866)

▲ Marval Industries Inc ... D ... 914 381-2400
Mamaroneck (G-8071)

▲ Polyset Company Inc ... E ... 518 664-6000
Mechanicville (G-8260)

◆ Si Group Inc ... C ... 518 347-4200
Schenectady (G-15319)

◆ Solepoxy Inc ... D ... 716 372-6300
Olean (G-13175)

3088 Plastic Plumbing Fixtures

Allegany Laminating and Supply ... G ... 716 372-2424
Allegany (G-201)

An-Cor Industrial Plastics Inc ... D ... 716 695-3141
North Tonawanda (G-12972)

▼ Bow Industrial Corporation ... D ... 518 561-0190
Champlain (G-3566)

D & M Enterprises Incorporated ... G ... 914 937-6430
Port Chester (G-13769)

Gms Hicks Street Corporation ... E ... 718 858-1010
Brooklyn (G-2033)

▲ Independent Home Products LLC ... E ... 718 541-1256
West Hempstead (G-16886)

▲ ITR Industries Inc ... E ... 914 964-7063
Yonkers (G-17473)

▲ Metpar Corp ... D ... 516 333-2600
Westbury (G-17038)

On Point Reps Inc ... G ... 518 258-2268
Montgomery (G-8635)

▲ Quality Enclosures Inc ... E ... 631 234-0115
Central Islip (G-3535)

3089 Plastic Prdts

▲ 311 Industries Corp ... G ... 607 846-4520
Endicott (G-4802)

3M Company ... B ... 716 876-1596
Tonawanda (G-16154)

A & G Heat Sealing ... G ... 631 724-7764
Smithtown (G-15503)

▲ A R Arena Products Inc ... E ... 585 277-1680
Rochester (G-14176)

A R V Precision Mfg Inc ... G ... 631 293-9643
Farmingdale (G-4934)

A-1 Products Inc ... G ... 718 789-1818
Brooklyn (G-1539)

▲ Abbott Industries Inc ... E ... 718 291-0800
Jamaica (G-6926)

▲ Abr Molding Andy LLC ... F ... 212 576-1821
Ridgewood (G-14111)

Ace Molding & Tool Inc ... G ... 631 567-2355
Bohemia (G-1002)

Acme Awning Co Inc ... F ... 718 409-1881
Bronx (G-1263)

◆ Adirondack Plas & Recycl Inc ... E ... 518 746-9212
Argyle (G-406)

Albany International Corp ... C ... 607 749-7226
Homer (G-6543)

◆ Albea Cosmetics America Inc ... E ... 212 371-5100
New York (G-9124)

▲ Albest Metal Stamping Corp ... D ... 718 388-6000
Brooklyn (G-1575)

All American Precision Tl Mold ... F ... 585 436-3080
West Henrietta (G-16897)

▲ Allen Field Co Inc ... F ... 631 665-2782
Brightwaters (G-1237)

▲ Alliance Precision Plas Corp ... C ... 585 426-5310
Rochester (G-14204)

Alliance Precision Plas Corp ... E ... 585 426-5310
Rochester (G-14205)

▲ Allsafe Technologies Inc ... D ... 716 691-0400
Amherst (G-225)

Alpha Incorporated ... G ... 718 765-1614
Brooklyn (G-1590)

Aluminum Injection Mold Co LLC ... G ... 585 502-6087
Le Roy (G-7427)

Amadeo Serrano ... G ... 516 608-8359
Freeport (G-5395)

Amcor Rigid Plastics Usa LLC ... E ... 716 366-2440
Dunkirk (G-4356)

◆ American Casting and Mfg Corp ... D ... 800 342-0333
Plainview (G-13611)

American Casting and Mfg Corp ... G ... 516 349-7010
Plainview (G-13612)

▲ American Intl Trimming ... G ... 718 369-9643
Brooklyn (G-1600)

American Package Company Inc ... E ... 718 389-4444
Brooklyn (G-1603)

American Spacer Technologies ... G ... 518 828-1339
Hudson (G-6633)

American Visuals Inc ... G ... 631 694-6104
Farmingdale (G-4949)

An-Cor Industrial Plastics Inc ... D ... 716 695-3141
North Tonawanda (G-12972)

30 RUBBER AND MISCELLANEOUS PLASTICS PRODUCTS

▲ Anka Tool & Die Inc ....E 845 268-4116
   Congers *(G-3875)*
▲ Anna Young Assoc Ltd ....C 516 546-4400
   Freeport *(G-5397)*
Apexx Omni-Graphics Inc 718 326-3330
   Maspeth *(G-8147)*
Aquarium Pump & Piping Systems ....F 631 567-5555
   Sayville *(G-15232)*
▼ Armstrong Mold Corporation .....E 315 437-1517
   East Syracuse *(G-4521)*
Armstrong Mold Corporation ....D 315 437-1517
   East Syracuse *(G-4522)*
Associated Materials LLC ....F 631 467-4535
   Ronkonkoma *(G-14901)*
Atlas Fence & Railing Co Inc ....E 718 767-2200
   Whitestone *(G-17229)*
▲ Autronic Plastics Inc ....D 516 333-7577
   Central Islip *(G-3510)*
Avanti U S A Ltd ....F 716 695-5800
   Tonawanda *(G-16162)*
Aztec Tool Co Inc ....E 631 243-1144
   Edgewood *(G-4607)*
▲ Baird Mold Making Inc ....G 631 667-0322
   Bay Shore *(G-673)*
◆ Baralan Usa Inc ....E 718 849-5768
   Richmond Hill *(G-14080)*
Barton Tool Inc ....G 716 665-2801
   Falconer *(G-4899)*
Benners Gardens LLC ....F 518 828-1055
   Hudson *(G-6638)*
Berry Global Inc ....C 315 986-2161
   Macedon *(G-8011)*
Berry Global Inc ....C 315 484-0397
   Solvay *(G-15528)*
Berry Global Group Inc ....F 315 986-6270
   Macedon *(G-8012)*
Berry Plastics Group Inc ....G 716 366-2112
   Dunkirk *(G-4357)*
▲ Billie-Ann Plastics Pkg Corp .....E 718 497-3409
   Brooklyn *(G-1695)*
▼ Bo-Mer Plastics LLC ....E 315 252-7216
   Auburn *(G-485)*
Bragley Mfg Co Inc ....E 718 622-7469
   Brooklyn *(G-1711)*
Brandys Mold and Tool Ctr Ltd .....F 585 334-8333
   West Henrietta *(G-16904)*
Bst United Corp ....F 631 777-2110
   Farmingdale *(G-4962)*
Buffalo Polymer Processors Inc ...E 716 537-3153
   Holland *(G-6507)*
Burnham Polymeric Inc ....G 518 792-3040
   Fort Edward *(G-5348)*
Buttons & Trimcom Inc ....F 212 868-1971
   New York *(G-9537)*
C & M Products Inc ....G 315 471-3303
   Syracuse *(G-15899)*
▲ Cambridge Security Seals LLC ..E 845 520-4111
   Pomona *(G-13758)*
Capco Wai Shing LLC ....G 212 268-1976
   New York *(G-9573)*
Capitol Cups Inc ....E 518 627-0051
   Amsterdam *(G-338)*
Captive Plastics LLC ....D 716 366-2112
   Dunkirk *(G-4358)*
Carolina Precision Plas LLC ....D 631 981-0743
   Ronkonkoma *(G-14914)*
Cast-All Corporation ....E 516 741-4025
   Mineola *(G-8535)*
Cast-All Corporation ....E 516 741-4025
   Mineola *(G-8536)*
Castino Corporation ....G 845 229-0341
   Hyde Park *(G-6772)*
Cdj Stamping Inc ....G 585 224-8120
   Rochester *(G-14283)*
▼ Cementex Latex Corp ....F 212 741-1770
   New York *(G-9609)*
Centro Inc ....B 212 791-9450
   New York *(G-9619)*
▲ Century Mold Company Inc ......D 585 352-8600
   Rochester *(G-14287)*
▲ Century Mold Mexico LLC ....G 585 352-8600
   Rochester *(G-14288)*
Certainteed Corporation ....B 716 827-7560
   Buffalo *(G-2891)*
▲ Champlain Plastics Inc ....D 518 297-3700
   Rouses Point *(G-15065)*
◆ Chem-Tainer Industries Inc ....E 631 422-8300
   West Babylon *(G-16808)*
Chem-Tek Systems Inc ....F 631 253-3010
   Bay Shore *(G-681)*

Chenango Valley Tech Inc ....E 607 674-4115
   Sherburne *(G-15411)*
◆ Chocolate Delivery Systems Inc ....D 716 854-6050
   Buffalo *(G-2892)*
Christi Plastics Inc ....G 585 436-8510
   Rochester *(G-14296)*
Cjk Manufacturing LLC ....F 585 663-6370
   Rochester *(G-14298)*
Clifford H Jones Inc ....G 716 693-2444
   Tonawanda *(G-16174)*
CN Group Incorporated ....A 914 358-5690
   White Plains *(G-17132)*
▲ Colonie Plastics Corp ....C 631 434-6969
   Bay Shore *(G-684)*
Color Craft Finishing Corp ....F 631 563-3230
   Bohemia *(G-1034)*
▲ Commodore Machine Co Inc .....F 585 657-6916
   Bloomfield *(G-978)*
▲ Commodore Plastics LLC ....F 585 657-7777
   Bloomfield *(G-979)*
◆ Confer Plastics Inc ....C 800 635-3213
   North Tonawanda *(G-12985)*
Consolidated Container Co LLC ..F 585 343-9351
   Batavia *(G-630)*
Continental Latex Corp ....F 718 783-7883
   Brooklyn *(G-1798)*
CPI of Falconer Inc ....E 716 664-4444
   Falconer *(G-4901)*
Craftech ....D 518 828-5011
   Chatham *(G-3585)*
Craftech Industries Inc ....D 518 828-5001
   Hudson *(G-6640)*
Cs Manufacturing Limited ....E 607 587-8154
   Alfred *(G-196)*
▲ CSP Technologies Inc ....E 518 627-0051
   Amsterdam *(G-342)*
CT Industrial Supply Co Inc ....F 718 417-3226
   Brooklyn *(G-1821)*
▲ Cubbies Unlimited Corporation ...F 631 586-8572
   Deer Park *(G-4146)*
▲ Currier Plastics Inc ....D 315 255-1779
   Auburn *(G-489)*
▲ Custom Door & Mirror Inc ....E 631 414-7725
   Farmingdale *(G-4980)*
▲ Custom House Engravers Inc ...F 631 567-3004
   Bohemia *(G-1042)*
Custom Lucite Creations Inc ....F 718 871-2000
   Brooklyn *(G-1827)*
▲ Cy Plastics Works Inc ....F 585 229-2555
   Honeoye *(G-6551)*
Dacobe Enterprises LLC ....F 315 368-0093
   Utica *(G-16343)*
Dawnex Industries Inc ....F 718 384-0199
   Brooklyn *(G-1843)*
Di Domenico Packaging Co Inc ...F 718 727-5454
   Staten Island *(G-15685)*
Diamond Packaging Holdings LLC ....G 585 334-8030
   Rochester *(G-14327)*
▲ Digitac Inc ....F 732 215-4020
   Brooklyn *(G-1863)*
Discover Casting Inc ....F 212 302-5060
   New York *(G-9936)*
Displays By Rioux Inc ....E 315 458-3639
   North Syracuse *(G-12958)*
Dortronics Systems Inc ....F 631 725-0505
   Sag Harbor *(G-15105)*
Dutchland Plastics LLC ....C 315 280-0247
   Sherrill *(G-15428)*
◆ E & T Plastic Mfg Co Inc ....F 718 729-6226
   Long Island City *(G-7751)*
▲ E-Z Ware Dishes Inc ....G 718 376-3244
   Brooklyn *(G-1896)*
East Cast Clor Compounding Inc ...G 631 491-9000
   West Babylon *(G-16815)*
East Pattern & Model Corp ....E 585 461-3240
   Fairport *(G-4861)*
Eastern Enterprise Corp ....F 718 727-8600
   Staten Island *(G-15690)*
Eastern Industrial Steel Corp ....G 845 639-9749
   New City *(G-8832)*
▲ Eck Plastic Arts Inc ....E 607 722-3227
   Binghamton *(G-905)*
Egli Machine Company Inc ....E 607 563-3663
   Sidney *(G-15461)*
▲ Elara Fdsrvice Disposables LLC ...G 877 893-3244
   Jericho *(G-7100)*
Em-Kay Molds Inc ....F 716 895-6180
   Buffalo *(G-2949)*
▲ Engineered Composites Inc ....E 716 362-0295
   Buffalo *(G-2953)*

Engineered Molding Tech LLC .....F 518 482-2004
   Albany *(G-78)*
▲ Epp Team Inc ....D 585 454-4995
   Rochester *(G-14375)*
Ernie Green Industries Inc ....D 585 295-8951
   Rochester *(G-14377)*
Ernie Green Industries Inc ....C 585 647-2300
   Rochester *(G-14378)*
Ernie Green Industries Inc ....D 585 647-2300
   Rochester *(G-14379)*
▲ Etna Products Co Inc ....F 212 989-7591
   New York *(G-10132)*
▲ Eugene G Danner Mfg Inc ....E 631 234-5261
   Central Islip *(G-3521)*
Euro Woodworking Inc ....G 718 246-9172
   Brooklyn *(G-1944)*
▲ Europrojects Intl Inc ....G 917 262-0795
   New York *(G-10140)*
Everblock Systems LLC ....G 844 422-5625
   New York *(G-10143)*
▲ Extreme Molding LLC ....E 518 326-9319
   Watervliet *(G-16708)*
Faro Industries Inc ....F 585 647-6000
   Rochester *(G-14390)*
Fbm Galaxy Inc ....F 315 463-5144
   East Syracuse *(G-4542)*
Fei Products LLC ....E 716 693-6230
   North Tonawanda *(G-12990)*
▲ Felchar Manufacturing Corp ......A 607 723-3106
   Binghamton *(G-909)*
Fiber Laminations Limited ....F 716 692-1825
   Tonawanda *(G-16180)*
▲ Fibre Materials Corp ....E 516 349-1660
   Plainview *(G-13631)*
▲ Finger Lakes Extrusion Corp .....E 585 905-0632
   Canandaigua *(G-3375)*
Form A Rockland Plastics Inc ......G 315 848-3300
   Cranberry Lake *(G-4083)*
Form-Tec Inc ....E 516 867-0200
   Freeport *(G-5410)*
Formatix Corp ....F 631 467-3399
   Ronkonkoma *(G-14930)*
Formed Plastics Inc ....D 516 334-2300
   Carle Place *(G-3414)*
▲ Forteq North America Inc ....D 585 427-9410
   West Henrietta *(G-16911)*
Frisch Plastics Corp ....E 973 685-5936
   Hartsdale *(G-6017)*
G and G Service ....G 518 785-9247
   Latham *(G-7390)*
G N R Plastics Inc ....G 631 724-8758
   Smithtown *(G-15509)*
▲ Gagne Associates Inc ....E 800 800-5954
   Johnson City *(G-7123)*
Galt Industries Inc ....E 212 758-0770
   New York *(G-10290)*
◆ Gary Plastic Packaging Corp .....B 718 893-2200
   Bronx *(G-1343)*
Gen-West Associates LLC ....G 315 255-1779
   Auburn *(G-496)*
▲ General Composites Inc ....E 518 963-7333
   Willsboro *(G-17289)*
▲ Genesee Precision Inc ....E 585 344-0385
   Batavia *(G-636)*
Genpak LLC ....C 845 343-7971
   Middletown *(G-8476)*
◆ Germanow-Simon Corporation ...E 585 232-1440
   Rochester *(G-14420)*
Gifford Group Inc ....F 212 569-8500
   New York *(G-10334)*
Global Marine Power Inc ....F 631 208-2933
   Calverton *(G-3319)*
Global Security Tech LLC ....F 917 838-4507
   New York *(G-10363)*
GPM Associates LLC ....E 585 335-3940
   Dansville *(G-4103)*
▲ Great Pacific Entps US Inc ....E 518 761-2593
   Glens Falls *(G-5698)*
GSE Composites Inc ....F 631 389-1300
   Hauppauge *(G-6110)*
H & H Hulls Inc ....G 518 828-1339
   Hudson *(G-6646)*
H Risch Inc ....D 585 442-0110
   Rochester *(G-14435)*
Hall Construction Pdts & Svcs .....G 518 747-7047
   Hudson Falls *(G-6678)*
▲ Hamlet Products Inc ....F 914 665-0307
   Mount Vernon *(G-8734)*
▲ Hansa Plastics Inc ....F 631 269-9050
   Kings Park *(G-7201)*

Employee Codes: A=Over 500 employees, B=251-500
C=101-250, D=51-100, E=20-50, F=10-19, G=5-9

30 RUBBER AND MISCELLANEOUS PLASTICS PRODUCTS

Company	Code	Phone
Harbec Inc — Ontario (G-13225)	D	585 265-0010
Hart To Hart Industries Inc — Chaffee (G-3562)	G	716 492-2709
Highland Injection Molding — Salamanca (G-15127)	D	716 945-2424
Hlp Klearfold Packaging Pdts — New York (G-10534)	F	718 554-3271
Hornet Group Inc — Port Jervis (G-13808)		845 858-6400
Howard Charles Inc — Woodbury (G-17311)	G	917 902-6934
Iadc Inc — Staten Island (G-15707)	F	718 238-0623
Ilion Plastics Inc — Ilion (G-6780)	F	315 894-4868
Illinois Tool Works Inc — Millerton (G-8514)	D	860 435-2574
Imco Inc — Spencerport (G-15594)	E	585 352-7810
Imperial Polymers Inc — Brooklyn (G-2097)	G	718 387-4741
Industrial Paper Tube Inc — Bronx (G-1363)	F	718 893-5000
▲ Ingenious Designs LLC — Ronkonkoma (G-14941)	C	631 254-3376
Inhance Technologies LLC — Buffalo (G-3026)	E	716 825-9031
▼ Innovative Plastics Corp — Orangeburg (G-13252)	C	845 359-7500
Inteva Products LLC — New York (G-10685)	B	248 655-8886
Iridium Industries Inc — Great Neck (G-5833)	E	516 504-9700
▲ ISO Plastics Corp — Mount Vernon (G-8739)	D	914 663-8300
J M R Plastics Corporation — Middle Village (G-8445)	G	718 898-9825
J T Systematic — Endwell (G-4841)	G	607 754-0929
Jamestown Plastics Inc — Brocton (G-1249)	E	716 792-4144
Joe Pietryka Incorporated — Pawling (G-13473)		845 855-1201
Johnson Manufacturing Co — Bayport (G-752)	G	631 472-1184
JSM Vinyl Products Inc — New Hyde Park (G-8890)	F	516 775-4520
▲ K & H Industries Inc — Hamburg (G-5953)	F	716 312-0088
K & H Industries Inc — Hamburg (G-5954)	E	716 312-0088
K & H Precision Products Inc — Honeoye Falls (G-6560)	E	585 624-4894
K2 Plastics Inc — Bergen (G-846)	G	585 494-2727
▲ Kasson & Keller Inc — Fonda (G-5320)	A	518 853-3421
Kc Tag Co — Amsterdam (G-353)	G	518 842-6666
▲ Kelta Inc — Edgewood (G-4616)	E	631 789-5000
Kenney Manufacturing Displays — Brentwood (G-1185)	F	631 231-5563
Kernow North America — Pittsford (G-13594)	F	585 586-3590
▼ Kleer-Fax Inc — Amityville (G-303)	D	631 225-1100
▲ Kling Magnetics Inc — Chatham (G-3586)	E	518 392-4000
◆ Kobe Steel USA Holdings Inc — New York (G-10904)	G	212 751-9400
▲ Koonichi Inc — Fresh Meadows (G-5457)	G	718 886-8338
L I C Screen Printing Inc — Merrick (G-8421)	E	516 546-7289
L K Manufacturing Corp — West Babylon (G-16834)	E	631 243-6910
Leidel Corporation — Bohemia (G-1088)	E	631 244-0900
▲ M & M Molding Corp — Central Islip (G-3530)	C	631 582-1900
M I T Poly-Cart Corp — New York (G-11103)	G	212 724-7290
▲ Macauto Usa Inc — Rochester (G-14506)	E	585 342-2060
▲ Major-IPC Inc — Liberty (G-7460)	G	845 292-2200
Markwik Corp — Hicksville (G-6396)	F	516 470-1990
▲ Marval Industries Inc — Mamaroneck (G-8071)	D	914 381-2400
Master Molding Inc — Farmingdale (G-5053)	F	631 694-1444
Md4 Holdings Inc — East Syracuse (G-4563)	F	315 434-1869
Mechanical Rubber Pdts Co Inc — Warwick (G-16616)	F	845 986-2271
Memory Protection Devices Inc — Farmingdale (G-5056)	F	631 249-0001
▲ Mercury Plastics Corp — Brooklyn (G-2304)	E	718 498-5400
▲ Metal Cladding Inc — Lockport (G-7629)	F	716 434-5513
Metropltan Data Sltons MGT Inc — Farmingdale (G-5060)	F	516 586-5520
Mettowee Lumber & Plastics Co — Granville (G-5793)	C	518 642-1100
Micromold Products Inc — Yonkers (G-17485)	E	914 969-2850
Midbury Industries Inc — Freeport (G-5424)	F	516 868-0600
Miller Technology Inc — Farmingdale (G-5065)	F	631 694-2224
Milne Mfg Inc — Gasport (G-5574)	F	716 772-2536
Minico Industries Inc — Bay Shore (G-716)	G	631 595-1455
▲ Mirage Moulding Mfg Inc — Farmingdale (G-5066)	F	631 843-6168
▲ Mold-A-Matic Corporation — Oneonta (G-13211)	E	607 433-2121
▲ Monarch Plastics Inc — Frewsburg (G-5465)	E	716 569-2175
▲ Msi-Molding Solutions Inc — Rome (G-14850)	F	315 736-2412
◆ Multi Packaging Solutions Inc — New York (G-11347)		646 885-0005
▲ Mystic Apparel LLC — New York (G-11357)	E	212 279-2466
▲ Nalge Nunc International Corp — Rochester (G-14547)	A	585 498-2661
Natech Plastics Inc — Ronkonkoma (G-14974)	F	631 580-3506
New York Cutting & Gumming Co — Middletown (G-8489)	E	212 563-4146
New York Manufactured Products — Rochester (G-14552)	F	585 254-9353
Niagara Fiberglass Inc — Buffalo (G-3109)	F	716 822-3921
◆ Nordon Inc — Rochester (G-14558)	D	585 546-6200
▲ Northeast Windows Usa Inc — Merrick (G-8425)	E	516 378-6577
Norwesco Inc — Owego (G-13382)	F	607 687-8081
▲ Novel Box Company Ltd — Brooklyn (G-2388)	E	718 965-2222
▲ Novelty Crystal Corp — Long Island City (G-7858)	E	718 458-6700
◆ Ocala Group LLC — New Hyde Park (G-8899)	F	516 233-2750
▲ Oneida Molded Plastics LLC — Oneida (G-13183)	C	315 363-7980
Oneida Molded Plastics LLC — Oneida (G-13184)	D	315 363-7990
Oneonta Fence — Oneonta (G-13212)		607 433-6707
▲ Ontario Plastics Inc — Rochester (G-14572)	E	585 663-2644
P M Plastics Inc — Orchard Park (G-13311)	E	716 662-1255
P V C Molding Technologies — Newark (G-12761)	F	315 331-1212
Pace Window and Door Corp — Victor (G-16519)	F	585 924-8350
Pactiv Corporation — Glens Falls (G-5709)	C	518 743-3100
Pactiv LLC — Canandaigua (G-3382)	G	847 482-2000
Pactiv LLC — Plattsburgh (G-13713)	C	518 562-6120
Pactiv LLC — Canandaigua (G-3383)	C	585 393-3229
Pactiv LLC — Canandaigua (G-3384)	A	585 393-3149
Pactiv LLC — Canandaigua (G-3381)	C	585 394-5125
Pactiv LLC — Glens Falls (G-5710)	F	518 793-2524
Patmian LLC — New York (G-11594)	B	212 758-0770
▼ Pawling Corporation — Pawling (G-13474)	C	845 855-1000
Pawling Engineered Pdts Inc — Pawling (G-13475)	C	845 855-1000
Peconic Plastics Inc — Quogue (G-14028)	F	631 653-3676
▲ Peek A Boo USA Inc — New York (G-11612)	E	201 533-8700
▲ Pelican Products Co Inc — Bronx (G-1424)	E	718 860-3220
Peninsula Plastics Ltd — Buffalo (G-3141)	D	716 854-3050
Performance Advantage Co Inc — Lancaster (G-7357)	F	716 683-7413
Perma Tech Inc — Buffalo (G-3145)	E	716 854-0707
Philcom Ltd — Buffalo (G-3146)	G	716 875-8005
Phoenix Services Group LLC — Hudson (G-6661)	E	518 828-6611
Pii Holdings Inc — Buffalo (G-3149)	G	716 876-9951
Piper Plastics Corp — Copiague (G-3942)	E	631 842-6889
Plascoline Inc — New York (G-11694)	F	917 410-5754
Plastic Solutions Inc — Bayport (G-754)	E	631 234-9013
Plastic Sys/Gr Bflo Inc — Buffalo (G-3152)	G	716 835-7555
Plastic Works — New Rochelle (G-8965)	E	914 576-2050
Plastic-Craft Products Corp — West Nyack (G-16954)	E	845 358-3010
Plasticware LLC — Monsey (G-8612)	F	845 267-0790
Plasticycle Corporation — White Plains (G-17187)	E	914 997-6882
Pleasure Chest Sales Ltd — New York (G-11697)	F	212 242-4185
◆ PMI Industries LLC — Rochester (G-14605)	E	585 464-8050
Polymer Conversions Inc — Orchard Park (G-13315)	D	716 662-8550
Polymer Engineered Pdts Inc — Rochester (G-14607)	D	585 426-1811
▲ Powertex Inc — Rouses Point (G-15067)	E	518 297-4000
▲ Ppr Direct Inc — Brooklyn (G-2446)	F	718 965-8600
▲ Precision Techniques Inc — Stony Point (G-15798)	D	718 991-1440
Prestige Hangers Str Fixs Corp — Brooklyn (G-2454)	G	718 522-6777
Primoplast Inc — Bohemia (G-1117)	F	631 750-0680
▲ Prince Rubber & Plas Co Inc — Buffalo (G-3161)	E	225 272-1653
▲ Printex Packaging Corporation — Islandia (G-6840)	D	631 234-4300
◆ Protective Industries Inc — Buffalo (G-3165)	C	716 876-9951
Protective Industries Inc — Buffalo (G-3166)	C	716 876-9855
Pulse Plastics Products Inc — Bronx (G-1435)	E	718 328-5224
Pvc Container Corporation — Philmont (G-13566)	C	518 672-7721
Pylantis New York LLC — Groton (G-5923)	G	310 429-5911
▲ Q Squared Design LLC — New York (G-11788)	E	212 686-8860
Quality Lineals Usa Inc — Merrick (G-8427)	G	516 378-6577
Quoin LLC — Rye (G-15092)	A	914 967-9400
▲ R P M Industries Inc — Auburn (G-512)	E	315 255-1105
▲ Rainbow Plastics Inc — Brooklyn (G-2494)	F	718 218-7288
Richlar Industries Inc — East Syracuse (G-4574)	F	315 463-5144
Rimco Plastics Corp — Horseheads (G-6619)	E	607 739-3864
Robinson Knife — Buffalo (G-3189)	F	716 685-6300
Rochling Advent Tool & Mold LP — Rochester (G-14677)	D	585 254-2000

SIC SECTION
31 LEATHER AND LEATHER PRODUCTS

▲ Roth Global Plastics Inc .... E 315 475-0100
  Syracuse (G-16048)
◆ Royal Industries Inc .... E 718 369-3046
  Brooklyn (G-2531)
Royce Associates A Ltd Partnr 516 367-6298
  Jericho (G-7115)
▲ Rui Xing International Trdg Co .... G 516 298-2667
  Hicksville (G-6417)
Russell Plastics Tech Co Inc .... C 631 963-8602
  Lindenhurst (G-7504)
Rynone Manufacturing Corp .... F 607 565-8187
  Waverly (G-16730)
Sabic Innovative Plastics .... E 713 448-7474
  East Greenbush (G-4424)
Saint-Gobain Prfmce Plas Corp .... E 518 283-5963
  Poestenkill (G-13755)
SAV Thermo Inc .... F 631 249-9444
  West Babylon (G-16857)
▲ Schlegel Systems Inc .... C 585 427-7200
  Rochester (G-14695)
Seal Reinforced Fiberglass Inc .... E 631 842-2230
  Copiague (G-3949)
Seal Reinforced Fiberglass Inc .... E 631 842-2230
  Copiague (G-3950)
Seaway Mats Inc .... G 518 483-2560
  Malone (G-8047)
Shamrock Plastic Corporation 585 328-6040
  Rochester (G-14704)
Shamrock Plastics & Tool Inc 585 328-6040
  Rochester (G-14705)
Sigma Worldwide LLC .... G 646 217-0629
  New York (G-12089)
Silgan Plastics LLC .... C 315 536-5690
  Penn Yan (G-13543)
Silvatrim Corp .... C 212 675-0933
  New York (G-12097)
▲ Skd Distribution Corp .... E 718 525-6000
  Jericho (G-7120)
▲ Sonoco-Crellin Intl Inc .... B 518 392-2000
  Chatham (G-3588)
▲ Southern Tier Plastics Inc .... D 607 723-2601
  Binghamton (G-945)
Space Age Plstic Fbrcators Inc .... F 718 324-4062
  Bronx (G-1457)
Space Sign 718 961-1112
  College Point (G-3834)
Staroba Plastics Inc .... C 716 537-3153
  Holland (G-6511)
▲ Sterling Molded Products Inc .... E 845 344-4546
  Middletown (G-8498)
Streamline Plastics Co Inc .... E 718 401-4000
  Bronx (G-1464)
▲ Structural Industries Inc .... C 631 471-5200
  Bohemia (G-1134)
Stuart Mold & Manufacturing .... F 716 488-9765
  Falconer (G-4921)
◆ Summit Manufacturing LLC .... G 631 952-1570
  Bay Shore (G-741)
▲ Supreme Poultry Inc .... E 718 472-0300
  Long Island City (G-7924)
▲ Surprise Plastics Inc .... C 718 492-6355
  Brooklyn (G-2654)
Sweet Tooth Enterprises LLC .... E 631 752-2888
  West Babylon (G-16867)
Syntec Technologies Inc 585 768-2513
  Rochester (G-14736)
▲ Syracuse Plastics LLC .... C 315 637-9881
  Liverpool (G-7578)
T A Tool & Molding Inc .... F 631 293-0172
  Farmingdale (G-5133)
Termatec Molding Inc .... F 315 483-4150
  Sodus (G-15527)
◆ Tessy Plastics Corp .... B 315 689-3924
  Skaneateles (G-15488)
Tessy Plastics Corp .... A 315 689-3924
  Elbridge (G-4639)
Teva Womens Health Inc .... F 716 693-6230
  North Tonawanda (G-13020)
▲ Thermold Corporation .... C 315 697-3924
  Canastota (G-3400)
Think Green Junk Removal Inc .... G 845 297-7771
  Wappingers Falls (G-16597)
▲ Tii Technologies Inc .... E 516 364-9300
  Edgewood (G-4629)
Tint World .... G 631 458-1999
  Medford (G-8295)
Titherington Design & Mfg .... F 518 324-2205
  Plattsburgh (G-13733)
▲ Toolroom Express Inc .... D 607 723-5373
  Conklin (G-3902)

▲ Toray Industries Inc .... G 212 697-8150
  New York (G-12394)
▲ Transpo Industries Inc .... E 914 636-1000
  New Rochelle (G-8972)
Tri-State Window Factory Corp .... D 631 667-8600
  Deer Park (G-4242)
Trimac Molding Services 607 967-2900
  Bainbridge (G-554)
Tulip Molded Plastics Corp .... G 716 282-1261
  Niagara Falls (G-12902)
Tully Products Inc .... G 716 773-3166
  Grand Island (G-5787)
Turbo Plastics Corp Inc .... F 631 345-9768
  Yaphank (G-17422)
▲ TVI Imports LLC .... G 631 793-3077
  Massapequa Park (G-8223)
Unifab Inc .... G 585 235-1760
  Rochester (G-14768)
Unifuse LLC .... F 845 889-4000
  Staatsburg (G-15639)
United Plastics Inc .... G 718 389-2255
  Brooklyn (G-2721)
▲ Universal Strapping Inc .... G 845 268-2500
  Valley Cottage (G-16420)
Usheco Inc .... F 845 658-9200
  Kingston (G-7250)
▲ Van Blarcom Closures Inc .... C 718 855-3810
  Brooklyn (G-2735)
◆ Viele Manufacturing Corp .... B 718 893-2200
  Bronx (G-1490)
Villeroy & Boch Usa Inc .... G 212 213-8149
  New York (G-12569)
Vinyl Materials Inc .... G 631 586-9444
  Deer Park (G-4249)
Vinyline Window and Door Inc .... F 914 476-3500
  Yonkers (G-17513)
Visitainer Corp .... E 718 636-0300
  Brooklyn (G-2749)
Vitarose Corp of America .... G 718 951-9700
  Brooklyn (G-2751)
◆ W Kintz Plastics Inc .... C 518 296-8513
  Howes Cave (G-6629)
Waddington North America Inc .... F 585 638-8200
  Holley (G-6519)
Weather Products Corporation 315 474-8593
  Syracuse (G-16094)
Window Tech Systems Inc .... E 518 899-9000
  Ballston Spa (G-610)
Zan Optics Products Inc .... E 718 435-0533
  Brooklyn (G-2794)
Zone Fabricators Inc .... F 718 272-0200
  Ozone Park (G-13414)

31 LEATHER AND LEATHER PRODUCTS

3111 Leather Tanning & Finishing

A-1 Products Inc .... G 718 789-1818
  Brooklyn (G-1539)
▲ Adam Scott Designs Inc .... E 212 420-8866
  New York (G-9071)
▲ Androme Leather Inc .... F 518 773-7945
  Gloversville (G-5721)
Ariel Tian LLC .... G 212 457-1266
  Forest Hills (G-5327)
▲ Arrow Leather Finishing Inc .... E 518 762-3121
  Johnstown (G-7138)
▲ Aston Leather Inc .... E 212 481-2760
  New York (G-9294)
Automotive Leather Group LLC .... F 516 627-4000
  Great Neck (G-5809)
▲ Baker Products Inc .... E 212 459-2323
  White Plains (G-17109)
▲ Colonial Tanning Corporation .... G 518 725-7171
  Gloversville (G-5724)
▲ Corium Corporation .... F 914 381-0100
  Mamaroneck (G-8062)
▲ Edsim Leather Co Inc .... E 212 695-8500
  New York (G-10037)
Givi Inc .... F 212 586-5029
  New York (G-10343)
Graphic Image Associates LLC .... D 631 249-9600
  Melville (G-8352)
◆ Graphic Image Incorporated .... C 631 249-9600
  Melville (G-8353)
Hastings Hide Inc 516 295-2400
  Inwood (G-6798)
◆ Hat Attack Inc .... E 718 994-1000
  Bronx (G-1353)

Hohenforst Splitting Co Inc .... G 518 725-0012
  Gloversville (G-5730)
John Gailer Inc .... E 212 243-5662
  Long Island City (G-7799)
Justin Gregory Inc .... G 631 249-5187
  Deer Park (G-4182)
Kamali Automotive Group Inc .... F 516 627-4000
  Great Neck (G-5835)
▲ Kamali Group Inc .... G 516 627-4000
  Great Neck (G-5836)
▲ Legendary Auto Interiors Ltd .... E 315 331-1212
  Newark (G-12754)
Mohawk River Leather Works .... F 518 853-3900
  Fultonville (G-5494)
◆ Myers Group LLC .... G 973 761-6414
  New York (G-11356)
▲ Pacific Worldwide Inc .... F 212 502-3360
  New York (G-11567)
▲ Pan American Leathers Inc .... G 978 741-4150
  New York (G-11572)
▲ Pearl Leather Finishers Inc .... D 518 762-4543
  Johnstown (G-7151)
▲ Pearl Leather Group LLC .... F 516 627-4047
  Great Neck (G-5847)
▲ Rainbow Leather Inc .... F 718 939-8762
  College Point (G-3829)
Shadal LLC .... E 212 319-5946
  New York (G-12057)
▲ Simco Leather Corporation .... E 518 762-7100
  Johnstown (G-7156)
▲ Street Smart Designs Inc .... G 646 865-0056
  New York (G-12236)
System of AME Binding .... F 631 390-8560
  Central Islip (G-3539)
Tandy Leather Factory Inc .... G 845 480-3588
  Nyack (G-13071)
▲ Trebbianno LLC .... E 212 868-2770
  New York (G-12418)
Vic Demayos Inc .... G 845 626-4343
  Accord (G-1)
Walco Leather Co Inc .... E 212 243-2244
  Bedford (G-795)
◆ Wood & Hyde Leather Co Inc .... E 518 725-7105
  Gloversville (G-5745)

3131 Boot & Shoe Cut Stock & Findings

▲ Age Manufacturers Inc .... D 718 927-0048
  Brooklyn (G-1569)
Counter Evolution .... G 212 647-7505
  New York (G-9793)
Custom Countertops Inc .... G 716 646-1579
  Orchard Park (G-13291)
Custom Countertops Inc .... G 716 685-2871
  Depew (G-4277)
Custom Design Kitchens Inc .... F 518 355-4446
  Duanesburg (G-4350)
▲ Golden Pacific Lxj Inc .... G 267 975-6537
  New York (G-10375)
MBA Orthotics Inc .... G 631 392-4755
  Bay Shore (G-714)
▲ Premier Brands of America Inc .... C 914 667-6200
  Mount Vernon (G-8763)
Priscilla Quart Co Firts .... G 516 365-2755
  Manhasset (G-8098)
▲ Randall Loeffler Inc .... E 212 226-8787
  New York (G-11826)
Tread Quarters .... G 800 876-6676
  Rochester (G-14758)
Upper Ninty LLC .... G 646 863-3105
  New York (G-12495)
Wash Quarters LLC .... G 989 802-2017
  Wallkill (G-16567)

3142 House Slippers

RG Barry Corporation .... F 212 244-3145
  New York (G-11884)

3143 Men's Footwear, Exc Athletic

Air Skate & Air Jump Corp .... G 212 967-1201
  New York (G-9116)
Air Skate & Air Jump Corp .... F 212 967-1201
  Brooklyn (G-1571)
▲ Bm America LLC .... E 201 438-7733
  New York (G-9478)
◆ Coach Inc .... B 212 594-1850
  New York (G-9714)
▲ Detny Footwear Inc .... G 212 423-1040
  New York (G-9913)
▲ GH Bass & Co .... E 646 768-4600
  New York (G-10333)

31 LEATHER AND LEATHER PRODUCTS

◆ Jerry Miller Molded Shoes Inc .... F 716 881-3920
  Buffalo (G-3034)
Kcp Holdco Inc .... F 212 265-1500
  New York (G-10866)
Kcp Operating Company LLC .... D 212 265-1500
  New York (G-10867)
Kenneth Cole Productions LP .... E 212 265-1500
  New York (G-10872)
▲ Kenneth Cole Productions Inc .... B 212 265-1500
  New York (G-10873)
Lake View Manufacturing LLC .... F 315 364-7892
  King Ferry (G-7198)
▲ Neumann Jutta New York Inc .... F 212 982-7048
  New York (G-11398)
Nicholas Kirkwood LLC .... G 646 559-5239
  New York (G-11444)
▲ Pedifix Inc .... E 845 277-2850
  Brewster (G-1224)
Phillips-Van Heusen Europe .... F 212 381-3500
  New York (G-11668)
▲ Pvh Corp .... D 212 381-3500
  New York (G-11780)
Rockport Company LLC .... D 631 243-0418
  Deer Park (G-4225)
Rockport Company LLC .... G 718 271-3627
  Elmhurst (G-4680)
Steven Madden Ltd .... D 845 348-7026
  West Nyack (G-16956)
Steven Madden Ltd .... E 212 736-3283
  New York (G-12224)
◆ Steven Madden Ltd .... B 718 446-1800
  Long Island City (G-7919)
T O Dey Service Corp .... F 212 683-6300
  New York (G-12290)
▲ Tic TAC Toes Mfg Corp .... D 518 773-8187
  Gloversville (G-5741)
Tru Mold Shoes Inc .... E 716 881-4484
  Buffalo (G-3253)

3144 Women's Footwear, Exc Athletic

Adl Design Inc .... G 516 949-6658
  Huntington (G-6685)
Akh Group LLC .... G 646 320-8720
  New York (G-9118)
◆ Alpargatas Usa Inc .... E 646 277-7171
  New York (G-9149)
Attitudes Footwear Inc .... G 212 754-9113
  New York (G-9312)
◆ Coach Inc .... B 212 594-1850
  New York (G-9714)
▲ Detny Footwear Inc .... G 212 423-1040
  New York (G-9913)
▲ Everlast Worldwide Inc .... E 212 239-0990
  New York (G-10147)
▲ GH Bass & Co .... E 646 768-4600
  New York (G-10333)
◆ Jerry Miller Molded Shoes Inc .... F 716 881-3920
  Buffalo (G-3034)
Kcp Operating Company LLC .... D 212 265-1500
  New York (G-10867)
▲ Kenneth Cole Productions Inc .... B 212 265-1500
  New York (G-10873)
Lake View Manufacturing LLC .... F 315 364-7892
  King Ferry (G-7198)
Lsil & Co Inc .... G 914 761-0998
  White Plains (G-17160)
▲ Mango Usa Inc .... E 718 998-6050
  Brooklyn (G-2260)
▲ Neumann Jutta New York Inc .... F 212 982-7048
  New York (G-11398)
Nicholas Kirkwood LLC .... G 646 559-5239
  New York (G-11444)
▲ Nine West Footwear Corporation .... B 800 999-1877
  New York (G-11452)
▲ Pedifix Inc .... E 845 277-2850
  Brewster (G-1224)
S & W Ladies Wear .... G 718 431-2800
  Brooklyn (G-2546)
Steven Madden Ltd .... D 212 695-5545
  New York (G-12225)
◆ Steven Madden Ltd .... B 718 446-1800
  Long Island City (G-7919)
T O Dey Service Corp .... F 212 683-6300
  New York (G-12290)
▲ Tic TAC Toes Mfg Corp .... D 518 773-8187
  Gloversville (G-5741)
Tru Mold Shoes Inc .... E 716 881-4484
  Buffalo (G-3253)

3149 Footwear, NEC

Custom Sports Lab Inc .... G 212 832-1648
  New York (G-9828)
▲ Everlast Worldwide Inc .... E 212 239-0990
  New York (G-10147)
▲ GH Bass & Co .... E 646 768-4600
  New York (G-10333)
Kicks Closet Sportswear Inc .... G 347 577-0857
  Bronx (G-1376)
La Strada Dance Footwear Inc 631 242-1401
  Deer Park (G-4187)
▲ Mango Usa Inc .... E 718 998-6050
  Brooklyn (G-2260)
Mayberry Shoe Company Inc .... G 315 692-4086
  Manlius (G-8107)
McM Products USA Inc .... E 646 756-4090
  New York (G-11226)
Reebok International Ltd .... E 212 221-6375
  New York (G-11847)
Reebok International Ltd .... C 914 948-3719
  White Plains (G-17190)
Reebok International Ltd .... E 718 370-0471
  Staten Island (G-15751)
◆ Steven Madden Ltd .... B 718 446-1800
  Long Island City (G-7919)
▲ Vsg International LLC .... G 718 300-8171
  Brooklyn (G-2756)

3151 Leather Gloves & Mittens

American Target Marketing Inc .... E 518 725-4369
  Gloversville (G-5720)
▲ Fieldtex Products Inc .... C 585 427-2940
  Rochester (G-14391)
◆ Fownes Brothers & Co Inc .... E 212 683-0150
  New York (G-10244)
Fownes Brothers & Co Inc 518 752-4411
  Gloversville (G-5726)
Protech (llc) .... E 518 725-7785
  Gloversville (G-5734)
Samco LLC .... E 518 725-4705
  Gloversville (G-5735)
USA Sewing Inc 315 792-8017
  Utica (G-16386)
▲ Worldwide Protective Pdts LLC .... C 877 678-4568
  Hamburg (G-5969)

3161 Luggage

▲ 212 Biz LLC .... G 212 391-4444
  New York (G-9010)
▲ Adam Scott Designs Inc 212 420-8866
  New York (G-9071)
▲ Aka Sport Inc .... F 631 858-9888
  Dix Hills (G-4312)
Atlantic Specialty Co Inc .... E 845 356-2502
  Monsey (G-8604)
Barclay Brown Corp .... F 718 376-7166
  Brooklyn (G-1665)
Bragley Mfg Co Inc 718 622-7469
  Brooklyn (G-1711)
Calvin Klein Inc .... E 212 292-9000
  New York (G-9556)
▲ Carry-All Canvas Bag Co Inc .... G 718 375-4230
  Brooklyn (G-1761)
▲ Coach Stores Inc .... A 212 643-9727
  New York (G-9717)
Deluxe Travel Store Inc 718 435-8111
  Brooklyn (G-1853)
▲ Dlx Industries Inc .... D 718 272-9420
  Brooklyn (G-1870)
Donna Morgan LLC .... E 212 575-2550
  New York (G-9956)
Ead Cases .... F 845 343-2111
  Middletown (G-8471)
Fibre Case & Novelty Co Inc 212 254-6060
  New York (G-10210)
▲ Fieldtex Products Inc 585 427-2940
  Rochester (G-14391)
◆ Fish & Crown Ltd .... D 212 707-9603
  New York (G-10226)
▲ Golden Bridge Group Inc 718 335-8882
  Elmhurst (G-4676)
Goyard Inc 212 813-0005
  New York (G-10383)
Goyard Miami LLC 212 813-0005
  New York (G-10384)
Hornet Group Inc 845 858-6400
  Port Jervis (G-13808)
Junk In My Trunk Inc 631 420-5865
  Farmingdale (G-5027)
▲ Lo & Sons Inc .... F 917 775-4025
  Brooklyn (G-2236)
▲ Merzon Leather Co Inc .... C 718 782-6260
  Brooklyn (G-2306)
▲ Prepac Designs Inc .... G 914 524-7800
  Yonkers (G-17498)
Progressive Fibre Products Co .... E 212 566-2720
  New York (G-11751)
Randa Accessories Lea Gds LLC .... D 212 354-5100
  New York (G-11825)
Rhino Trunk & Case Inc .... F 585 244-4553
  Rochester (G-14647)
▲ Roadie Products Inc .... E 631 567-8588
  Holbrook (G-6497)
▼ Rose Trunk Mfg Co Inc .... F 516 766-6686
  Oceanside (G-13115)
◆ Royal Industries Inc .... E 718 369-3046
  Brooklyn (G-2531)
Sigma Worldwide LLC .... G 646 217-0629
  New York (G-12089)
▲ Three Point Ventures LLC .... F 585 697-3444
  Rochester (G-14751)
▲ Trafalgar Company LLC .... G 212 768-8800
  New York (G-12411)
▲ Trunk & Trolley LLC .... G 212 947-9001
  New York (G-12433)
Tumi Inc .... C 212 447-8747
  New York (G-12444)
Tumi Inc 212 742-8020
  New York (G-12445)
Xstatic Pro Inc .... F 718 237-2299
  Brooklyn (G-2784)

3171 Handbags & Purses

▲ Affordable Luxury Group Inc .... G 631 523-9266
  New York (G-9103)
▲ Ahq LLC 212 328-1560
  New York (G-9112)
Akh Group LLC .... G 646 320-8720
  New York (G-9118)
Atalla Handbags Inc .... G 718 965-5500
  Brooklyn (G-1645)
▲ Bagznyc Corp .... F 212 643-8202
  New York (G-9358)
▲ Baikal Inc .... D 212 239-4650
  New York (G-9359)
Coach Inc .... G 212 615-2082
  New York (G-9708)
Coach Inc .... F 212 581-4115
  New York (G-9709)
Coach Inc .... F 718 760-0624
  Elmhurst (G-4672)
Coach Inc .... F 585 425-7720
  Victor (G-16492)
Coach Inc .... E 212 245-4148
  New York (G-9710)
Coach Inc .... E 212 473-6925
  New York (G-9711)
Coach Inc .... F 212 754-0041
  New York (G-9712)
Coach Inc .... F 212 675-6403
  New York (G-9713)
◆ Coach Inc .... B 212 594-1850
  New York (G-9714)
Coach Inc .... G 518 456-5657
  Albany (G-68)
Coach Leatherware Intl 212 594-1850
  New York (G-9715)
▲ Coach Services Inc .... G 212 594-1850
  New York (G-9716)
▲ Coach Stores Inc .... A 212 643-9727
  New York (G-9717)
Dani Accessories Inc .... E 631 692-4505
  Cold Spring Harbor (G-3793)
Deux Lux Inc .... G 212 620-0801
  New York (G-9915)
▲ Essex Manufacturing Inc .... D 212 239-0080
  New York (G-10119)
Formart Corp .... F 212 819-1819
  New York (G-10238)
▲ Frenz Group LLC .... G 212 465-0908
  Whitestone (G-17235)
Kcp Holdco Inc .... F 212 265-1500
  New York (G-10866)
▲ Kenneth Cole Productions Inc .... B 212 265-1500
  New York (G-10873)
McM Products USA Inc .... E 646 756-4090
  New York (G-11226)
▲ Nine West Footwear Corporation .... B 800 999-1877
  New York (G-11452)

▲ Pure Trade Us Inc ......E 212 256-1600
New York (G-11774)
Quilted Koala Ltd ......F 800 223-5678
New York (G-11799)
◆ Renco Group Inc ......G 212 541-6000
New York (G-11864)
▲ Roadie Products Inc ......E 631 567-8588
Holbrook (G-6497)
▲ Rodem Incorporated ......F 212 779-7122
New York (G-11922)

3172 Personal Leather Goods

▲ Ada Gems Corp ......G 212 719-0100
New York (G-9070)
American Puff Corp ......D 516 379-1300
Freeport (G-5396)
▲ Art Leather Mfg Co Inc ......A 516 867-4716
Oyster Bay (G-13392)
Astucci US Ltd ......F 718 752-9700
Long Island City (G-7706)
▲ Astucci US Ltd ......G 212 725-3171
New York (G-9295)
Atlantic Specialty Co Inc ......E 845 356-2502
Monsey (G-8604)
▲ Baker Products Inc ......G 212 459-2323
White Plains (G-17109)
▲ Bauble Bar Inc ......D 646 664-4803
New York (G-9383)
◆ Coach Inc ......B 212 594-1850
New York (G-9714)
▲ Coach Stores Inc ......A 212 643-9727
New York (G-9717)
▲ Datamax International Inc ......E 212 693-0933
New York (G-9870)
Elco Manufacturing Co Inc ......F 516 767-3577
Port Washington (G-13835)
▲ Excelled Sheepskin & Lea Coat ......F 212 594-5843
New York (G-10157)
Fahrenheit NY Inc ......G 212 354-6554
New York (G-10180)
Form A Rockland Plastics Inc ......G 315 848-3300
Cranberry Lake (G-4083)
Grownbeans Inc ......G 212 989-3486
New York (G-10416)
▲ Helgen Industries Inc ......C 631 841-6300
Amityville (G-292)
◆ Hemisphere Novelties Inc ......E 914 378-4100
Yonkers (G-17469)
House of Portfolios Co Inc ......G 212 206-7323
New York (G-10562)
House of Portfolios Co Inc ......F 212 206-7323
New York (G-10563)
International Time Products ......G 516 931-0005
Jericho (G-7105)
Just Brass Inc ......G 212 724-5447
New York (G-10826)
K Displays ......F 718 854-6045
Brooklyn (G-2163)
L Y Z Creations Ltd Inc ......E 718 768-2977
Brooklyn (G-2187)
Leather Artisan ......G 518 359-3102
Childwold (G-3658)
◆ Leather Impact Inc ......G 212 382-2788
New York (G-10985)
▲ M G New York Inc ......F 212 371-5566
New York (G-11099)
▲ Merzon Leather Co Inc ......C 718 782-6260
Brooklyn (G-2306)
▲ Montana Global LLC ......G 212 213-1572
Jamaica (G-6970)
▲ Neumann Jutta New York Inc ......F 212 982-7048
New York (G-11398)
▲ Penthouse Manufacturing Co Inc ......B 516 379-1300
Freeport (G-5429)
Randa Accessories Lea Gds LLC ......D 212 354-5100
New York (G-11825)
Roma Industries LLC ......G 212 268-0723
New York (G-11931)
Slim Line Case Co Inc ......F 585 546-3639
Rochester (G-14713)
▲ Trafalgar Company LLC ......G 212 768-8800
New York (G-12411)
Unique Packaging Corporation ......G 514 341-5872
Champlain (G-3576)
Walco Leather Co Inc ......E 212 243-2244
Bedford (G-795)

3199 Leather Goods, NEC

Adirondack Leather Pdts Inc ......F 607 547-5798
Fly Creek (G-5317)
Art Craft Leather Goods Inc ......F 718 257-7401
Brooklyn (G-1635)
▲ Art Leather Mfg Co Inc ......A 516 867-4716
Oyster Bay (G-13392)
▲ Courtlandt Boot Jack Co Inc ......E 718 445-6200
Flushing (G-5242)
Deluxe Travel Store Inc ......G 718 435-8111
Brooklyn (G-1853)
Dog Good Products LLC ......G 212 789-7000
New York (G-9947)
▲ Dvf Studio LLC ......D 212 741-6607
New York (G-9993)
Dvf Studio LLC ......G 646 576-8009
New York (G-9994)
East West Global Sourcing Inc ......G 917 887-2286
Brooklyn (G-1898)
Equicenter Inc ......E 585 742-2522
Honeoye Falls (G-6555)
Fahrenheit NY Inc ......G 212 354-6554
New York (G-10180)
▼ Finger Lakes Lea Crafters LLC ......F 315 252-4107
Auburn (G-493)
▲ Fiorentina LLC ......G 516 208-5448
Merrick (G-8418)
▲ Helgen Industries Inc ......C 631 841-6300
Amityville (G-292)
▲ Import-Export Corporation ......F 718 707-0880
Long Island City (G-7792)
Kamali Leather Corp ......G 518 762-2522
Johnstown (G-7148)
Leather Outlet ......G 518 668-0328
Lake George (G-7287)
Max 200 Performance Dog Eqp ......E 315 776-9588
Port Byron (G-13763)
McM Products USA Inc ......E 646 756-4090
New York (G-11226)
▲ Perrone Leather LLC ......D 518 853-4300
Fultonville (G-5496)
▲ Sampla Belting North Amer LLC ......E 716 667-7450
Lackawanna (G-7275)
▲ Star Desk Pad Co Inc ......E 914 963-9400
Yonkers (G-17504)
◆ Tucano Usa Inc ......G 212 966-9211
New York (G-12441)
◆ Unique Overseas Inc ......G 516 466-9792
Great Neck (G-5865)
Walco Leather Co Inc ......E 212 243-2244
Bedford (G-795)

32 STONE, CLAY, GLASS, AND CONCRETE PRODUCTS

3211 Flat Glass

▲ A Sunshine Glass & Aluminum ......E 718 932-8080
Woodside (G-17334)
Corning Incorporated ......E 607 974-8496
Corning (G-3988)
Corning Incorporated ......D 315 379-3200
Canton (G-3408)
Corning Incorporated ......G 607 974-6729
Painted Post (G-13417)
▲ Europrojects Intl Inc ......G 917 262-0795
New York (G-10140)
Express Building Supply Inc ......E 516 608-0379
Oceanside (G-13099)
Glass Apps LLC ......F 310 987-1536
New York (G-10347)
▲ Global Glass Corp ......G 516 681-2309
Hicksville (G-6378)
Guardian Industries LLC ......B 315 787-7000
Geneva (G-5592)
▲ Hecht & Sohn Glass Co Inc ......G 718 782-8295
Brooklyn (G-2070)
▲ Lafayette Mirror & Glass Co ......G 718 768-0660
New Hyde Park (G-8891)
▲ Lazer Marble & Granite Corp ......G 718 859-9644
Brooklyn (G-2198)
▼ Manhattan Shade & Glass Co Inc ......D 212 288-5616
New York (G-11157)
◆ Munn Works LLC ......E 914 665-6100
Mount Vernon (G-8755)
Pilkington North America Inc ......C 315 438-3341
Syracuse (G-16033)
RG Glass Creations Inc ......E 212 675-0030
New York (G-11885)
Saxon Glass Technologies Inc ......F 607 587-9630
Alfred (G-197)
▲ Schott Corporation ......D 914 831-2200
Elmsford (G-4786)
Schott Gemtron Corporation ......C 423 337-3522
Elmsford (G-4787)
Schott Government Services LLC ......G 703 418-1409
Elmsford (G-4788)
▲ Schott Solar Pv Inc ......G 888 457-6527
Elmsford (G-4790)
South Seneca Vinyl LLC ......G 315 585-6050
Romulus (G-14871)
▼ Stefan Sydor Optics Inc ......E 585 271-7300
Rochester (G-14726)
Strong Tempering GL Indust LLC ......F 718 765-0007
Brooklyn (G-2633)
▲ Tempco Glass Fabrication LLC ......G 718 461-6888
Flushing (G-5305)
Tower Insulating Glass LLC ......E 516 887-3300
North Bellmore (G-12939)
Twin Pane Insulated GL Co Inc ......F 631 924-1060
Yaphank (G-17423)
Window-Fix Inc ......E 718 854-3475
Brooklyn (G-2773)
▲ Zered Inc ......F 718 353-7464
College Point (G-3838)

3221 Glass Containers

Anchor Glass Container Corp ......B 607 737-1933
Elmira Heights (G-4721)
◆ Baralan Usa Inc ......E 718 849-5768
Richmond Hill (G-14080)
Certainteed Corporation ......C 716 823-3684
Lackawanna (G-7269)
▲ Glopak USA Corp ......E 347 869-9252
College Point (G-3809)
Glopak USA Corp ......D 516 433-3214
Hicksville (G-6379)
Intrapac International Corp ......C 518 561-2030
Plattsburgh (G-13697)
◆ Lidestri Foods Inc ......B 585 377-7700
Fairport (G-4867)
▲ Liquor Bottle Packg Intl Inc ......G 212 922-2813
New York (G-11035)
Owens-Brockway Glass Cont Inc ......C 315 258-3211
Auburn (G-510)
Pennsauken Packing Company LLC ......G 585 377-7700
Fairport (G-4875)
▲ Rocco Bormioli Glass Co Inc ......E 212 719-0606
New York (G-11917)
▲ Saint Gobain Grains & Powders ......A 716 731-8200
Niagara Falls (G-12888)
▲ Schott Corporation ......D 914 831-2200
Elmsford (G-4786)
▲ SGD North America ......E 212 753-4200
New York (G-12054)
SGD Pharma Packaging Inc ......G 212 223-7100
New York (G-12055)
Velvet Healing By Alma Corp ......G 347 271-4220
Bronx (G-1488)

3229 Pressed & Blown Glassware, NEC

Architectural Glass Inc ......F 845 831-3116
Beacon (G-776)
▲ Art and Cook Inc ......F 718 567-7778
Brooklyn (G-1633)
▼ Bedford Downing Glass ......G 718 418-6409
Brooklyn (G-1675)
Biolitec Inc ......E 413 525-0600
New York (G-9454)
▲ Bronx Wstchester Tempering Inc ......E 914 663-9400
Mount Vernon (G-8713)
Co-Optics America Lab Inc ......E 607 432-0557
Oneonta (G-13201)
Complete Fiber Solutions Inc ......G 718 828-8900
Bronx (G-1305)
◆ Corning Incorporated ......A 607 974-9000
Corning (G-3983)
Corning Incorporated ......D 607 974-9000
Corning (G-3984)
Corning Incorporated ......E 607 974-1274
Painted Post (G-13416)
Corning Incorporated ......E 607 974-9000
Corning (G-3985)
Corning Incorporated ......D 315 379-3200
Canton (G-3408)
Corning Incorporated ......E 607 433-3100
Oneonta (G-13205)
Corning Incorporated ......E 607 248-1200
Corning (G-3986)
Corning Incorporated ......G 607 974-4488
Corning (G-3987)
Corning Incorporated ......G 607 974-6729
Painted Post (G-13417)

SIC

Employee Codes: A=Over 500 employees, B=251-500
C=101-250, D=51-100, E=20-50, F=10-19, G=5-9
2018 Harris
New York Manufacturers Directory
795

▼ **Corning International Corp** .... G 607 974-9000
Corning *(G-3989)*
Corning Specialty Mtls Inc .... G 607 974-9000
Corning *(G-3991)*
Corning Tropel Corporation .... C 585 377-3200
Fairport *(G-4857)*
◆ **Corning Vitro Corporation** .... A 607 974-8605
Corning *(G-3992)*
▲ **Daylight Technology USA Inc** .... G 973 255-8100
Maspeth *(G-8160)*
▲ **Depp Glass Inc** .... F 718 784-8500
Long Island City *(G-7742)*
▲ **Eye Deal Eyewear Inc** .... G 716 297-1500
Niagara Falls *(G-12838)*
Formcraft Display Products .... G 914 632-1410
New Rochelle *(G-8945)*
◆ **Germanow-Simon Corporation** .... E 585 232-1440
Rochester *(G-14420)*
▲ **Gillinder Brothers Inc** .... D 845 856-5375
Port Jervis *(G-13807)*
Glasteel Parts & Services Inc .... E 585 235-1010
Rochester *(G-14426)*
▲ **Gray Glass Inc** .... E 718 217-2943
Queens Village *(G-13994)*
Ion Optics Inc .... F 518 339-6853
Albany *(G-89)*
▲ **Jay Strongwater Holdings LLC** .... A 646 657-0558
New York *(G-10745)*
▲ **Jinglebell Inc** .... G 914 219-5395
Armonk *(G-414)*
◆ **King Research Inc** .... E 718 788-0122
Brooklyn *(G-2171)*
▲ **Led Lumina USA LLC** .... G 631 750-4433
Bohemia *(G-1086)*
◆ **Lighting Holdings Intl LLC** .... A 845 306-1850
Purchase *(G-13976)*
Mata Ig .... G 212 979-7921
New York *(G-11200)*
▲ **Match Eyewear LLC** .... E 516 877-0170
Westbury *(G-17036)*
▼ **Navitar Inc** .... D 585 359-4000
Rochester *(G-14550)*
New York Enrgy Synthetics Inc .... G 212 634-4787
New York *(G-11421)*
Owens Corning Sales LLC .... B 518 475-3600
Feura Bush *(G-5182)*
▲ **Pasabahce USA** .... G 212 683-1600
New York *(G-11591)*
Photonic Controls LLC .... F 607 562-4585
Horseheads *(G-6616)*
Saint-Gobain Prfmce Plas Corp .... C 518 686-7301
Hoosick Falls *(G-6571)*
Schott Corporation .... D 315 255-2791
Auburn *(G-514)*
▲ **Schott Corporation** .... D 914 831-2200
Elmsford *(G-4786)*
▲ **Scientifics Direct Inc** .... F 716 773-7500
Tonawanda *(G-16220)*
▲ **Semrok Inc** .... D 585 594-7050
Rochester *(G-14702)*
▲ **Sleepy Hollow Chimney Sup Ltd** .... F 631 231-2333
Brentwood *(G-1191)*
Somers Stain Glass Inc .... F 631 586-7772
Deer Park *(G-4235)*
▼ **Stefan Sydor Optics Inc** .... E 585 271-7300
Rochester *(G-14726)*
◆ **Volpi Manufacturing USA Co Inc** .... E 315 255-1737
Auburn *(G-525)*

3231 Glass Prdts Made Of Purchased Glass

▲ **Ad Notam LLC** .... F 631 951-2020
Hauppauge *(G-6028)*
Adirondack Stained Glass Works .... G 518 725-0387
Gloversville *(G-5719)*
Apf Management Company LLC .... C 914 665-5400
Yonkers *(G-17431)*
Apf Manufacturing Company LLC .... E 914 963-6300
Yonkers *(G-17432)*
Batavia Precision Glass LLC .... G 585 343-6050
Buffalo *(G-2854)*
Benson Industries Inc .... F 212 779-3230
New York *(G-9407)*
C B Management Services Inc .... F 845 735-2300
Pearl River *(G-13477)*
▲ **Campus Crafts Inc** .... G 585 328-6780
Rochester *(G-14274)*
▲ **Carvart Glass Inc** .... F 212 675-0030
New York *(G-9591)*
Chapman Stained Glass Studio .... G 518 449-5552
Albany *(G-61)*
Community Glass Inc .... G 607 737-8860
Elmira *(G-4689)*
▲ **Depp Glass Inc** .... F 718 784-8500
Long Island City *(G-7742)*
▲ **Dundy Glass & Mirror Corp** .... E 718 723-5800
Springfield Gardens *(G-15629)*
Dunlea Whl GL & Mirror Inc .... G 914 664-5277
Mount Vernon *(G-8725)*
Executive Mirror Doors Inc .... G 631 234-1090
Ronkonkoma *(G-14928)*
Exquisite Glass & Stone Inc .... G 718 937-9266
Astoria *(G-439)*
Flickinger Glassworks Inc .... G 718 875-1531
Brooklyn *(G-1987)*
G & M Clearview Inc .... G 845 781-4877
Monroe *(G-8590)*
▲ **Glassfab Inc** .... E 585 262-4000
Rochester *(G-14425)*
▲ **Global Glass Corp** .... G 516 681-2309
Hicksville *(G-6378)*
▲ **Gmd Industries Inc** .... G 718 445-8779
College Point *(G-3810)*
Granville Glass & Granite .... G 518 812-0492
Hudson Falls *(G-6676)*
▲ **Gray Glass Inc** .... E 718 217-2943
Queens Village *(G-13994)*
▲ **Hecht & Sohn Glass Co Inc** .... G 718 782-8295
Brooklyn *(G-2070)*
Immco Diagnostics Inc .... D 716 691-6911
Buffalo *(G-3022)*
▲ **Jimmy Crystal New York Co Ltd** .... E 212 594-0858
New York *(G-10775)*
▲ **Jinglebell Inc** .... G 914 219-5395
Armonk *(G-414)*
▲ **Kasson & Keller Inc** .... A 518 853-3421
Fonda *(G-5320)*
▲ **Lafayette Mirror & Glass Co** .... G 718 768-0660
New Hyde Park *(G-8891)*
Lalique North America Inc .... E 212 355-6550
New York *(G-10958)*
Makarenko Studios Inc .... G 914 968-7673
Yorktown Heights *(G-17528)*
Michbi Doors Inc .... D 631 231-9050
Brentwood *(G-1189)*
Mirror-Tech Manufacturing Co .... F 914 965-1232
Yonkers *(G-17486)*
Mri Northtowns Group PC .... F 716 836-4646
Buffalo *(G-3097)*
◆ **Munn Works LLC** .... E 914 665-6100
Mount Vernon *(G-8755)*
Oldcastle Building Envelope .... G 212 957-5400
New York *(G-11513)*
Oldcastle Buildingenvelope Inc .... C 631 234-2200
Hauppauge *(G-6178)*
Oneida International Inc .... G 315 361-3000
Oneida *(G-13182)*
Oneida Silversmiths Inc .... G 315 361-3000
Oneida *(G-13186)*
Our Terms Fabricators Inc .... E 631 752-1517
West Babylon *(G-16847)*
Pal Manufacturing Corp .... E 516 937-1990
Hicksville *(G-6409)*
Potters Industries LLC .... E 315 265-4920
Potsdam *(G-13900)*
Prisma Glass & Mirror Inc .... G 718 366-7191
Ridgewood *(G-14132)*
▲ **Quality Enclosures Inc** .... E 631 234-0115
Central Islip *(G-3535)*
Rauch Industries Inc .... E 704 867-5333
Tarrytown *(G-16127)*
Rn Furniture Corp .... G 347 960-9622
Richmond Hill *(G-14092)*
Rochester Colonial Mfg Corp .... D 585 254-8191
Rochester *(G-14661)*
◆ **Rochester Insulated Glass Inc** .... D 585 289-3611
Manchester *(G-8085)*
Rohlfs Stined Leaded GL Studio .... E 914 699-4848
Mount Vernon *(G-8773)*
◆ **Rosco Inc** .... C 718 526-2601
Jamaica *(G-6985)*
Royal Metal Products Inc .... E 518 966-4442
Surprise *(G-15832)*
Safelite Glass Corp .... G 716 685-1358
Depew *(G-4298)*
Select Interior Door Ltd .... E 585 535-9900
North Java *(G-12950)*
Somers Stain Glass Inc .... F 631 586-7772
Deer Park *(G-4235)*
▲ **Stark Aquarium Products Co Inc** .... E 718 445-5357
Flushing *(G-5302)*
Sunburst Studios Inc .... G 718 768-6360
Brooklyn *(G-2642)*
▲ **Swift Glass Co Inc** .... D 607 733-7166
Elmira Heights *(G-4727)*
▲ **Taylor Made Group LLC** .... E 518 725-0681
Gloversville *(G-5739)*
▲ **Taylor Products Inc** .... G 518 773-9312
Gloversville *(G-5740)*
TEC Glass & Inst LLC .... G 315 926-7639
Marion *(G-8132)*
Timeless Decor LLC .... C 315 782-5759
Watertown *(G-16697)*
Unico Inc .... F 845 562-9255
Newburgh *(G-12806)*
Upstate Insulated Glass Inc .... G 315 475-4960
Central Square *(G-3546)*
Vitarose Corp of America .... G 718 951-9700
Brooklyn *(G-2751)*
Vitrix Inc .... G 607 936-8707
Corning *(G-4005)*

3241 Cement, Hydraulic

Ciment St-Laurent Inc .... C 518 943-4040
Catskill *(G-3454)*
Euro Gear (usa) Inc .... G 518 578-1775
Plattsburgh *(G-13690)*
Hanson Aggregates New York LLC .... F 716 665-4620
Jamesville *(G-7081)*
Lafarge Building Materials Inc .... F 518 756-5000
Ravena *(G-14035)*
Lafarge North America Inc .... E 716 651-9235
Lancaster *(G-7346)*
Lafarge North America Inc .... G 716 854-5791
Buffalo *(G-3061)*
Lafarge North America Inc .... E 716 772-2621
Lockport *(G-7626)*
Lafarge North America Inc .... D 914 930-3027
Buchanan *(G-2800)*
Lafarge North America Inc .... E 518 756-5000
Ravena *(G-14036)*
▲ **Lehigh Cement Company** .... C 518 792-1137
Glens Falls *(G-5703)*
Pallette Stone Corporation .... E 518 584-2421
Gansevoort *(G-5501)*
Upstone Materials Inc .... G 518 873-2275
Lewis *(G-7452)*

3251 Brick & Structural Clay Tile

Certified Flameproofing Corp .... G 631 265-4824
Smithtown *(G-15506)*
Everblock Systems LLC .... G 844 422-5625
New York *(G-10143)*
◆ **Noroc Enterprises Inc** .... C 718 585-3230
Bronx *(G-1414)*
Semco Ceramics Inc .... G 315 782-3000
Watertown *(G-16694)*
▲ **Stone and Bath Gallery** .... G 718 438-4500
Brooklyn *(G-2631)*

3253 Ceramic Tile

▲ **Aremco Products Inc** .... F 845 268-0039
Valley Cottage *(G-16402)*
Artsaics Studios Inc .... G 631 254-2558
Deer Park *(G-4127)*
Dal-Tile Corporation .... G 914 835-1801
Harrison *(G-6003)*
▲ **Ercole Nyc Inc** .... F 212 675-2218
Brooklyn *(G-1937)*
▲ **Hastings Tile & Bath Inc** .... F 516 379-3500
Ronkonkoma *(G-14939)*
▲ **Lazer Marble & Granite Corp** .... G 718 859-9644
Brooklyn *(G-2198)*
NY Tilemakers .... G 989 278-8453
Brooklyn *(G-2394)*
Quality Components Framing Sys .... F 315 768-1167
Whitesboro *(G-17222)*
Quemere International LLC .... G 914 934-8366
Port Chester *(G-13782)*
Semco Ceramics Inc .... G 315 782-3000
Watertown *(G-16694)*
Tile Shop Inc .... G 585 424-2180
Rochester *(G-14754)*

3255 Clay Refractories

Filtros Ltd .... E 585 586-8770
East Rochester *(G-4478)*
▼ **Hoffmans Trade Group LLC** .... G 518 250-5556
Troy *(G-16261)*

32 STONE, CLAY, GLASS, AND CONCRETE PRODUCTS

◆ Saint-Gobain Strl Ceramics ....A 716 278-6233
   Niagara Falls (G-12891)
Upstate Refractory Svcs Inc ....E 315 331-2955
   Newark (G-12767)

3259 Structural Clay Prdts, NEC

▲ American Chimney Supplies Inc ....G 631 434-2020
   Hauppauge (G-6039)
Bistrian Cement Corporation ....F 631 324-1123
   East Hampton (G-4425)
▲ Boston Valley Pottery Inc ....D 716 649-7490
   Orchard Park (G-13277)
Chimney Doctors Americas Corp ....G 631 868-3586
   Bayport (G-751)
Jq Woodworking Inc ....G 516 766-3424
   Oceanside (G-13104)
Lenon Models Inc ....G 212 229-1581
   New York (G-11001)

3261 China Plumbing Fixtures & Fittings

▼ AMG Global LLC ....G 212 602-1818
   New York (G-9185)
▲ Gamma Products Inc ....D 845 562-3332
   New Windsor (G-8984)
▲ Kraus USA Inc ....F 800 775-0703
   Port Washington (G-13856)
▲ Larcent Enterprises Inc ....E 845 562-3332
   New Windsor (G-8987)
▲ Stone and Bath Gallery ....G 718 438-4500
   Brooklyn (G-2631)

3262 China, Table & Kitchen Articles

Carmona Nyc LLC ....G 718 227-6662
   Rego Park (G-14043)
Jill Fagin Enterprises Inc ....G 212 674-9383
   New York (G-10771)
▲ Korin Japanese Trading Corp ....E 212 587-7021
   New York (G-10916)
Oneida International Inc ....G 315 361-3000
   Oneida (G-13182)
Oneida Silversmiths Inc ....G 315 361-3000
   Oneida (G-13186)
Swissmar Inc ....G 905 764-1121
   Niagara Falls (G-12896)

3263 Earthenware, Whiteware, Table & Kitchen Articles

Ceramica Varm ....G 914 381-6215
   New Rochelle (G-8937)
▲ Green Wave International Inc ....G 718 499-3371
   Brooklyn (G-2052)
▲ Jill Fenichell Inc ....G 718 237-2490
   Brooklyn (G-2141)
▲ Korin Japanese Trading Corp ....E 212 587-7021
   New York (G-10916)
Lifestyle International LLC ....G 917 757-0067
   New York (G-11022)
Lifetime Stainless Steel Corp ....G 585 924-9393
   Victor (G-16512)
◆ Mackenzie-Childs LLC ....C 315 364-6118
   Aurora (G-528)
Williams-Sonoma Stores Inc ....F 212 633-2203
   New York (G-12664)

3264 Porcelain Electrical Splys

▲ Arnold Magnetic Tech Corp ....C 585 385-9010
   Rochester (G-14228)
▲ Cetek Inc ....E 845 452-3510
   Poughkeepsie (G-13911)
Corning Incorporated ....E 607 974-1274
   Painted Post (G-13416)
Eneflux Armtek Magnetics Inc ....G 516 576-3434
   Medford (G-8275)
Ferro Electronics Materials ....C 716 278-9400
   Niagara Falls (G-12841)
◆ Ferro Electronics Materials ....G 315 536-3357
   Penn Yan (G-13533)
Ferro Electronics Materials ....C 315 536-3357
   Penn Yan (G-13534)
Filtros Ltd ....E 585 586-8770
   East Rochester (G-4478)
▲ Hitachi Metals America Ltd ....E 914 694-9200
   Purchase (G-13975)
◆ Hoosier Magnetics Inc ....E 315 323-5832
   Ogdensburg (G-13137)
▲ Lapp Insulators LLC ....C 585 768-6221
   Le Roy (G-7436)

▲ Victor Insulators Inc ....C 585 924-2127
   Victor (G-16534)

3269 Pottery Prdts, NEC

American Country Quilts & Lin ....G 631 283-5466
   Southampton (G-15562)
▲ Saint Gobain Grains & Powders ....A 716 731-8200
   Niagara Falls (G-12888)
▲ Saint-Gbain Advnced Crmics LLC ...C 716 278-6066
   Niagara Falls (G-12889)
Schiller Stores Inc ....G 845 928-4316
   Central Valley (G-3555)

3271 Concrete Block & Brick

Ace Cntracting Consulting Corp ....G 631 567-4752
   Bohemia (G-1001)
All American Concrete Corp ....G 718 497-3301
   Brooklyn (G-1583)
All County Block & Supply Corp ....G 631 589-3675
   Bohemia (G-1008)
Arnan Development Corp ....D 607 432-8391
   Oneonta (G-13194)
Barrasso & Sons Trucking Inc ....E 631 581-0360
   Islip Terrace (G-6854)
Brickit ....G 631 727-8977
   Hauppauge (G-6056)
Chenango Concrete Corp ....F 607 334-2545
   Norwich (G-13039)
Chimney Doctors Americas Corp ....G 631 868-3586
   Bayport (G-751)
Colonie Block and Supply Co ....G 518 869-8411
   Colonie (G-3845)
Cossitt Concrete Products Inc ....F 315 824-2700
   Hamilton (G-5970)
▲ Cranesville Block Co Inc ....E 518 684-6154
   Amsterdam (G-341)
Cranesville Block Co Inc ....E 315 773-2296
   Felts Mills (G-5175)
Creative Yard Designs Inc ....G 315 706-6143
   Manlius (G-8103)
Crest Haven Precast Inc ....E 518 483-4750
   Burke (G-3292)
Dicks Concrete Co Inc ....E 845 374-5966
   New Hampton (G-8844)
Duke Concrete Products Inc ....E 518 793-7743
   Queensbury (G-14008)
Edgewood Industries Inc ....G 516 227-2447
   Garden City (G-5514)
Everblock Systems LLC ....G 844 422-5625
   New York (G-10143)
Felicetti Concrete Products ....G 716 284-5740
   Niagara Falls (G-12839)
▼ Fort Miller Service Corp ....E 518 695-5000
   Greenwich (G-5907)
▼ Get Real Surfaces Inc ....F 845 337-4483
   Poughkeepsie (G-13921)
Gone South Concrete Block Inc ....E 315 598-2141
   Fulton (G-5473)
Grace Associates Inc ....G 718 767-9000
   Harrison (G-6005)
Grandview Block & Supply Co ....E 518 346-7981
   Schenectady (G-15292)
Great American Awning & Patio ....F 518 899-2300
   Ballston Spa (G-596)
Hanson Aggregates New York LLC ...G 607 276-5881
   Almond (G-206)
▲ Imperia Masonry Supply Corp ......G 914 738-0900
   Pelham (G-13517)
Jenna Concrete Corporation ....E 718 842-5250
   Bronx (G-1369)
Jenna Harlem River Inc ....G 718 842-5997
   Bronx (G-1370)
Lafarge North America Inc ....E 518 756-5000
   Ravena (G-14036)
Lage Industries Corporation ....F 718 342-3400
   Brooklyn (G-2190)
Modern Block LLC ....G 315 923-7443
   Clyde (G-3754)
Montfort Brothers Inc ....E 845 896-6694
   Fishkill (G-5194)
Morningstar Concrete Products ....F 716 693-4020
   Tonawanda (G-16201)
New York Ready Mix Inc ....G 516 338-6969
   Westbury (G-17042)
▲ Nicolia Concrete Products Inc ......D 631 669-0700
   Lindenhurst (G-7500)
Northeast Mesa Inc ....G 845 878-9344
   Carmel (G-3430)
Palumbo Block Co Inc ....E 845 832-6100
   Dover Plains (G-4340)

Phelps Cement Products Inc ....E 315 548-9415
   Phelps (G-13558)
Radiation Shielding Systems ....F 888 631-2278
   Suffern (G-15819)
Riefler Concrete Products LLC ....C 716 649-3260
   Hamburg (G-5964)
Smithtown Concrete Products ....G 631 265-1815
   Saint James (G-15117)
Suffolk Cement Products Inc ....E 631 727-2317
   Calverton (G-3328)
Superior Block Corp ....F 718 421-0900
   Brooklyn (G-2647)
Taylor Concrete Products Inc ....E 315 788-2191
   Watertown (G-16696)
Troys Landscape Supply Co Inc ....F 518 785-1526
   Cohoes (G-3784)
Unilock Ltd ....E 716 822-6074
   Buffalo (G-3260)
▲ Unilock New York Inc ....G 845 278-6700
   Brewster (G-1227)

3272 Concrete Prdts

A & R Concrete Products LLC ....E 845 562-0640
   New Windsor (G-8975)
Access Products Inc ....G 800 679-4022
   Buffalo (G-2809)
Accurate Precast ....F 718 345-2910
   Brooklyn (G-1551)
▲ Afco Precast Sales Corp ....D 631 924-7114
   Middle Island (G-8438)
▲ Alp Stone Inc ....F 718 706-6166
   Long Island City (G-7686)
Alpine Building Supply Inc ....G 718 456-2522
   Ridgewood (G-14112)
▲ American Chimney Supplies Inc ...G 631 434-2020
   Hauppauge (G-6039)
Arnan Development Corp ....D 607 432-8391
   Oneonta (G-13194)
Baliva Concrete Products Inc ....E 585 328-8442
   Rochester (G-14240)
Barrett Paving Materials Inc ....G 315 737-9471
   Clayville (G-3712)
Beck Vault Company ....G 315 337-7590
   Rome (G-14835)
Binghamton Burial Vault Co Inc ....F 607 722-4931
   Binghamton (G-888)
Binghamton Precast & Sup Corp ....E 607 722-0334
   Binghamton (G-890)
Bistrian Cement Corporation ....F 631 324-1123
   East Hampton (G-4425)
Buffalo Crushed Stone Inc ....E 716 826-7310
   Buffalo (G-2872)
Callanan Industries Inc ....G 315 697-9569
   Canastota (G-3393)
▲ Callanan Industries Inc ....E 518 374-2222
   Albany (G-57)
Callanan Industries Inc ....G 845 331-6868
   Kingston (G-7211)
Callanan Industries Inc ....E 518 785-5666
   Latham (G-7385)
▲ Castek Inc ....G 914 636-1000
   New Rochelle (G-8936)
▲ Chim-Cap Corp ....E 800 262-9622
   Farmingdale (G-4968)
Chimney Doctors Americas Corp ....G 631 868-3586
   Bayport (G-751)
City Mason Corp ....F 718 658-3796
   Jamaica (G-6939)
▲ Coastal Pipeline Products Corp ....E 631 369-4000
   Calverton (G-3316)
▲ Copeland Coating Company Inc ...F 518 766-2932
   Nassau (G-8817)
Coral Cast LLC ....G 516 349-1300
   Plainview (G-13622)
▲ Corinthian Cast Stone Inc ....G 631 920-2340
   Wyandanch (G-17389)
Cossitt Concrete Products Inc ....F 315 824-2700
   Hamilton (G-5970)
Crown Hill Stone Inc ....E 716 326-4601
   Westfield (G-17076)
David Kucera Inc ....E 845 255-1044
   Gardiner (G-5562)
Diamond Precast Products Inc ....F 631 874-3777
   Center Moriches (G-3489)
Dillner Precast Inc ....G 631 421-9130
   Lloyd Harbor (G-7593)
Dillner Precast Inc ....G 631 421-9130
   Huntington Station (G-6741)
Doric Vault of Wny Inc ....F 716 828-1776
   Buffalo (G-2933)

Employee Codes: A=Over 500 employees, B=251-500
C=101-250, D=51-100, E=20-50, F=10-19, G=5-9

Duke Company .... G 607 347-4455
Ithaca *(G-6874)*
Duranm Inc .... G 914 774-3367
Cortlandt Manor *(G-4073)*
▲ **Dynasty Metal Works Inc** .... G 631 284-3719
Riverhead *(G-14153)*
East Main Associates .... D 585 624-1990
Lima *(G-7466)*
Eastern Granite Inc .... G 718 356-9139
Staten Island *(G-15691)*
▲ **Eaton Brothers Corp** .... G 716 649-8250
Hamburg *(G-5945)*
Elderlee Incorporated .... C 315 789-6670
Oaks Corners *(G-13088)*
Express Concrete Inc .... G 631 273-4224
Brentwood *(G-1180)*
Fordham Marble Co Inc .... F 914 682-6699
White Plains *(G-17136)*
Foro Marble Co Inc .... E 718 852-2322
Brooklyn *(G-1995)*
▲ **Fort Miller Group Inc** .... B 518 695-5000
Greenwich *(G-5906)*
▼ **Fort Miller Service Corp** .... F 518 695-5000
Greenwich *(G-5907)*
Galle & Zinter Inc .... G 716 833-4212
Buffalo *(G-2978)*
Gamble & Gamble Inc .... G 716 731-3239
Sanborn *(G-15147)*
Geotech Associates Ltd .... G 631 286-0251
Brookhaven *(G-1507)*
▼ **Get Real Surfaces Inc** .... F 845 337-4483
Poughkeepsie *(G-13921)*
Glens Falls Ready Mix Inc .... F 518 793-1695
Queensbury *(G-14010)*
Glenwood Cast Stone Inc .... G 718 859-6500
Brooklyn *(G-2028)*
Grace Associates Inc .... G 718 767-9000
Harrison *(G-6005)*
Great ATL Pr-Cast Con Statuary .... G 718 948-5677
Staten Island *(G-15703)*
Guardian Concrete Inc .... F 518 372-0080
Schenectady *(G-15294)*
H F Cary & Sons .... G 607 598-2563
Lockwood *(G-7658)*
Hanson Aggregates East LLC .... G 716 372-1574
Allegany *(G-203)*
Healthy Basement Systems LLC .... F 516 650-9046
Medford *(G-8280)*
▲ **Heidenhain International Inc** .... C 716 661-1700
Jamestown *(G-7033)*
Ideal Burial Vault Company .... G 585 599-2242
Corfu *(G-3977)*
Island Ready Mix Inc .... E 631 874-3777
Center Moriches *(G-3492)*
Jab Concrete Supply Corp .... E 718 842-5250
Bronx *(G-1367)*
Jefferson Concrete Corp .... D 315 788-4171
Watertown *(G-16677)*
Jenna Concrete Corporation .... E 718 842-5250
Bronx *(G-1369)*
Jenna Harlem River Inc .... G 718 842-5997
Bronx *(G-1370)*
John E Potente & Sons Inc .... G 516 935-8585
Hicksville *(G-6385)*
▲ **Key Cast Stone Company Inc** .... E 631 789-2145
Amityville *(G-302)*
Lafarge North America Inc .... E 518 756-5000
Ravena *(G-14036)*
Lakelands Concrete Pdts Inc .... E 585 624-1990
Lima *(G-7467)*
Lhv Precast Inc .... E 845 336-8880
Kingston *(G-7225)*
Long Island Geotech .... G 631 473-1044
Port Jefferson *(G-13798)*
Long Island Green Guys .... G 631 664-4306
Riverhead *(G-14161)*
Long Island Precast Inc .... E 631 286-0240
Brookhaven *(G-1508)*
M K Ulrich Construction Inc .... F 716 893-5777
Buffalo *(G-3071)*
Meditub Incorporated .... F 866 633-4882
Lawrence *(G-7420)*
Mid-Hudson Concrete Pdts Inc .... G 845 265-3141
Cold Spring *(G-3788)*
Milano Granite and Marble Corp .... F 718 477-7200
Staten Island *(G-15727)*
▲ **Nicolia Concrete Products Inc** .... D 631 669-0700
Lindenhurst *(G-7500)*
Northeast Concrete Pdts Inc .... F 518 563-0700
Plattsburgh *(G-13708)*
▲ **NY Tempering LLC** .... G 718 326-8989
Maspeth *(G-8190)*
Oldcastle Precast Inc .... F 518 767-2116
South Bethlehem *(G-15536)*
Oldcastle Precast Inc .... E 518 767-2112
Selkirk *(G-15378)*
Oneida Sales & Service Inc .... F 716 270-0433
Lackawanna *(G-7271)*
P J R Industries Inc .... E 716 825-9300
Buffalo *(G-3128)*
Pelkowski Precast Corp .... F 631 269-5727
Kings Park *(G-7203)*
Preload Concrete Structures .... E 631 231-8100
Hauppauge *(G-6196)*
Presbrey-Leland Inc .... G 914 949-2264
Valhalla *(G-16397)*
Quikrete Companies Inc .... E 716 213-2027
Lackawanna *(G-7273)*
Rain Catchers Seamless Gutters .... G 516 520-1956
Bethpage *(G-877)*
Riefler Concrete Products LLC .... C 716 649-3260
Hamburg *(G-5964)*
Robert M Vault .... G 315 243-1447
Bridgeport *(G-1235)*
Robinson Concrete Inc .... E 315 253-6666
Auburn *(G-513)*
Roman Stone Construction Co .... E 631 667-0566
Bay Shore *(G-733)*
▲ **Royal Marble & Granite Inc** .... G 516 536-5900
Oceanside *(G-13116)*
St Raymond Monument Co .... G 718 824-3600
Bronx *(G-1460)*
Stag Brothers Cast Stone Co .... G 718 629-0975
Brooklyn *(G-2617)*
Steindl Cast Stone Co Inc .... G 718 296-8530
Woodhaven *(G-17326)*
Suffolk Cement Precast Inc .... G 631 727-4432
Calverton *(G-3327)*
▲ **Suhor Industries Inc** .... F 585 377-5100
Fairport *(G-4890)*
Suhor Industries Inc .... G 716 483-6818
Jamestown *(G-7064)*
Sunnycrest Inc .... E 315 252-7214
Auburn *(G-518)*
Superior Aggragates Supply LLC .... E 516 333-2923
Lindenhurst *(G-7511)*
Superior Walls Upstate NY Inc .... D 585 624-9390
Lima *(G-7471)*
Superior Wlls of Hdson Vly Inc .... E 845 485-4033
Poughkeepsie *(G-13953)*
Taylor Concrete Products Inc .... E 315 788-2191
Watertown *(G-16696)*
Towne House Restorations Inc .... G 718 497-9200
Long Island City *(G-7932)*
▲ **Transpo Industries Inc** .... E 914 636-1000
New Rochelle *(G-8972)*
▲ **Unilock New York Inc** .... G 845 278-6700
Brewster *(G-1227)*
Universal Step Inc .... G 315 437-7611
East Syracuse *(G-4589)*
Upstone Materials Inc .... G 518 483-2671
Malone *(G-8050)*
Upstone Materials Inc .... G 518 873-2275
Lewis *(G-7452)*
▲ **Walter G Legge Company Inc** .... G 914 737-5040
Peekskill *(G-13510)*
Wel Made Enterprises Inc .... F 631 752-1238
Farmingdale *(G-5151)*
Woodards Concrete Products Inc .... E 845 361-3471
Bullville *(G-3289)*
▲ **Woodside Granite Industries** .... G 585 589-6500
Albion *(G-174)*

3273 Ready-Mixed Concrete

A-1 Transitmix Inc .... F 718 292-3200
Bronx *(G-1256)*
Advanced Ready Mix Corp .... F 718 497-5020
Brooklyn *(G-1565)*
All American Transit Mix Corp .... G 718 417-3654
Brooklyn *(G-1584)*
Atlas Concrete Batching Corp .... D 718 523-3000
Jamaica *(G-6931)*
Atlas Transit Mix Corp .... C 718 523-3000
Jamaica *(G-6932)*
Barney & Dickenson Inc .... E 607 729-1536
Vestal *(G-16462)*
Barrett Paving Materials Inc .... F 315 788-2037
Watertown *(G-16658)*
Best Concrete Mix Corp .... E 718 463-5500
Flushing *(G-5236)*
Bonded Concrete Inc .... E 518 273-5800
Watervliet *(G-16704)*
Bonded Concrete Inc .... F 518 674-2854
West Sand Lake *(G-16960)*
▲ **Brewster Transit Mix Corp** .... E 845 279-3738
Brewster *(G-1210)*
Brewster Transit Mix Corp .... E 845 279-3738
Brewster *(G-1211)*
Byram Concrete & Supply LLC .... F 914 682-4477
White Plains *(G-17117)*
C & C Ready-Mix Corporation .... E 607 797-5108
Vestal *(G-16465)*
C & C Ready-Mix Corporation .... F 607 687-1690
Owego *(G-13376)*
Capital Concrete Inc .... G 716 648-8001
Hamburg *(G-5942)*
Casa Redimix Concrete Corp .... F 718 589-1555
Bronx *(G-1291)*
Ccz Ready Mix Concrete Corp .... G 516 579-7352
Levittown *(G-7448)*
Cemex Cement Inc .... D 212 317-6000
New York *(G-9610)*
Century Ready Mix Inc .... G 631 888-2200
West Babylon *(G-16806)*
Champion Materials Inc .... G 315 493-2654
Carthage *(G-3439)*
Champion Materials Inc .... E 315 493-2654
Carthage *(G-3440)*
Chenango Concrete Corp .... F 518 294-9964
Richmondville *(G-14101)*
Clark Concrete Co Inc .... G 315 478-4101
Syracuse *(G-15915)*
Classic Concrete Corp .... F 516 822-1800
Hicksville *(G-6356)*
Clemente Latham Concrete Corp .... D 518 374-2222
Schenectady *(G-15271)*
Cobleskill Red E Mix & Supply .... F 518 234-2015
Amsterdam *(G-340)*
Corona Ready Mix Inc .... F 718 271-5940
Corona *(G-4017)*
Cortland Ready Mix Inc .... F 607 753-3063
Cortland *(G-4044)*
Cossitt Concrete Products Inc .... F 315 824-2700
Hamilton *(G-5970)*
Costanza Ready Mix Inc .... G 516 783-4444
North Bellmore *(G-12934)*
Cranesville Block Co Inc .... E 315 732-2135
Utica *(G-16340)*
Cranesville Block Co Inc .... F 845 292-1585
Liberty *(G-7458)*
Cranesville Block Co Inc .... E 845 896-5687
Fishkill *(G-5189)*
Cranesville Block Co Inc .... E 845 331-1775
Kingston *(G-7214)*
Cranesville Block Co Inc .... G 315 384-4000
Norfolk *(G-12915)*
▲ **Cranesville Block Co Inc** .... E 518 684-6154
Amsterdam *(G-341)*
Cranesville Block Co Inc .... E 315 773-2296
Felts Mills *(G-5175)*
Custom Mix Inc .... G 516 797-7090
Massapequa Park *(G-8218)*
Dalrymple Grav & Contg Co Inc .... F 607 739-0391
Pine City *(G-13577)*
Dalrymple Holding Corp .... E 607 737-6200
Pine City *(G-13578)*
Deer Park Sand & Gravel Corp .... E 631 586-2323
Bay Shore *(G-691)*
Dicks Concrete Co Inc .... E 845 374-5966
New Hampton *(G-8844)*
Dunkirk Construction Products .... G 716 366-5220
Dunkirk *(G-4362)*
E Tetz & Sons Inc .... D 845 692-4486
Middletown *(G-8470)*
East Coast Spring Mix Inc .... G 845 355-1215
New Hampton *(G-8845)*
Electric City Concrete Co Inc .... E 518 887-5560
Amsterdam *(G-343)*
Empire Transit Mix Inc .... E 718 384-3000
Brooklyn *(G-1927)*
F H Stickles & Son Inc .... F 518 851-9048
Livingston *(G-7587)*
Ferrara Bros LLC .... E 718 939-3030
Flushing *(G-5248)*
Fulmont Ready-Mix Company Inc .... E 518 887-5560
Amsterdam *(G-347)*
G & J Rdymx & Masnry Sup Inc .... F 718 454-0800
Hollis *(G-6523)*
Glens Falls Ready Mix Inc .... G 518 793-1695
Amsterdam *(G-348)*

32 STONE, CLAY, GLASS, AND CONCRETE PRODUCTS

Glens Falls Ready Mix Inc ....F 518 793-1695
  Queensbury *(G-14010)*
Grandview Concrete Corp ....E 518 346-7981
  Schenectady *(G-15293)*
Greco Bros Rdymx Con Co Inc ....G 718 855-6271
  Brooklyn *(G-2050)*
Haley Concrete Inc ....F 716 492-0849
  Delevan *(G-4260)*
Hanson Aggregates East LLC ....F 585 798-0762
  Medina *(G-8307)*
Hanson Aggregates East LLC ....F 716 372-1574
  Falconer *(G-4907)*
Hanson Aggregates East LLC ....E 315 548-2911
  Phelps *(G-13556)*
Hanson Aggregates New York LLC .....F 716 665-4620
  Jamestown *(G-7032)*
Hanson Aggregates New York LLC .....F 585 638-5841
  Pavilion *(G-13472)*
Hanson Aggregates New York LLC .....C 315 469-5501
  Jamesville *(G-7082)*
Inwood Material ....F 516 371-1842
  Inwood *(G-6799)*
Iroquois Rock Products Inc ....F 585 381-7010
  Rochester *(G-14476)*
Island Ready Mix Inc ....E 631 874-3777
  Center Moriches *(G-3492)*
James Town Macadam Inc ....D 716 665-4504
  Falconer *(G-4911)*
Jenna Concrete Corporation ....E 718 842-5250
  Bronx *(G-1369)*
Jenna Harlem River Inc ....G 718 842-5997
  Bronx *(G-1370)*
Jet Redi Mix Concrete Inc ....F 631 580-3640
  Ronkonkoma *(G-14947)*
King Road Materials Inc ....F 518 382-5354
  Albany *(G-95)*
Kings Park Ready Mix Corp ....F 631 269-4330
  Kings Park *(G-7202)*
Lafarge North America Inc ....F 518 756-5000
  Ravena *(G-14036)*
Lazarek Inc ....G 315 343-1242
  Oswego *(G-13359)*
Lehigh Cement Company ....E 518 943-5940
  Catskill *(G-3458)*
Lewbro Ready Mix Inc ....G 315 497-0498
  Groton *(G-5921)*
Manitou Concrete ....F 585 424-6040
  Rochester *(G-14513)*
Manzione Ready Mix Corp ....G 718 628-3837
  Brooklyn *(G-2265)*
Mastro Concrete Inc ....G 718 528-6788
  Rosedale *(G-15038)*
Mix N Mac LLC ....G 845 381-5536
  Middletown *(G-8486)*
N Y Western Concrete Corp ....G 585 343-6850
  Batavia *(G-644)*
New Atlantic Ready Mix Corp ....G 718 812-0739
  Hollis *(G-6524)*
Nex-Gen Ready Mix Corp ....G 347 231-0073
  Bronx *(G-1412)*
Nicolia Ready Mix Inc ....E 631 669-7000
  Lindenhurst *(G-7501)*
Northern Ready-Mix Inc ....E 315 598-2141
  Fulton *(G-5487)*
Oldcastle Precast Inc ....F 518 767-2116
  South Bethlehem *(G-15536)*
Oneida Sales & Service Inc ....F 716 270-0433
  Lackawanna *(G-7271)*
Otsego Ready Mix Inc ....F 607 432-3400
  Oneonta *(G-13213)*
Precision Ready Mix Inc ....G 718 658-5600
  Jamaica *(G-6977)*
Presti Ready Mix Concrete Inc ....G 516 378-6006
  Freeport *(G-5430)*
Quality Ready Mix Inc ....F 516 437-0100
  New Hyde Park *(G-8903)*
Queens Ready Mix Inc ....G 718 526-4919
  Jamaica *(G-6979)*
Quikrete Companies Inc ....E 315 673-2020
  Marcellus *(G-8119)*
Residential Fences Corp ....F 631 205-9758
  Ridge *(G-14107)*
Richmond Ready Mix Corp ....F 917 731-8400
  Staten Island *(G-15755)*
Riefler Concrete Products LLC ....C 716 649-3262
  Hamburg *(G-5964)*
Robinson Concrete Inc ....F 315 253-6666
  Auburn *(G-513)*
Robinson Concrete Inc ....F 315 492-6200
  Jamesville *(G-7085)*

Robinson Concrete Inc ....F 315 676-4662
  Brewerton *(G-1202)*
Rochester Asphalt Materials ....D 585 924-7360
  Farmington *(G-5163)*
Rochester Asphalt Materials ....G 585 381-7010
  Rochester *(G-14656)*
Rural Hill Sand and Grav Corp ....F 315 846-5212
  Woodville *(G-17383)*
Russian Mix Inc ....G 347 385-7198
  Brooklyn *(G-2537)*
Saunders Concrete Co Inc ....F 607 756-7905
  Cortland *(G-4067)*
Scara-Mix Inc ....F 718 442-7357
  Staten Island *(G-15756)*
Seville Central Mix Corp ....D 516 868-3000
  Freeport *(G-5438)*
Seville Central Mix Corp ....G 516 293-6190
  Old Bethpage *(G-13151)*
Seville Central Mix Corp ....G 516 239-8333
  Lawrence *(G-7425)*
South Shore Ready Mix Inc ....G 516 872-3049
  Valley Stream *(G-16451)*
Star Ready Mix East Inc ....F 631 289-8787
  East Hampton *(G-4436)*
Star Ready Mix Inc ....F 631 289-8787
  Medford *(G-8294)*
Stephen Miller Gen Contrs Inc ....E 518 661-5601
  Gloversville *(G-5738)*
Suffolk Cement Products Inc ....F 631 727-2317
  Calverton *(G-3328)*
Sullivan Concrete Inc ....F 845 888-2235
  Cochecton *(G-3769)*
T Mix Inc ....G 646 379-6814
  Brooklyn *(G-2660)*
TEC - Crete Transit Mix Corp ....E 718 657-6880
  Ridgewood *(G-14139)*
Thousand Island Ready Mix Con ....G 315 686-3203
  La Fargeville *(G-7264)*
Torrington Industries Inc ....G 315 676-4662
  Central Square *(G-3545)*
United Materials LLC ....D 716 683-1432
  North Tonawanda *(G-13022)*
United Materials LLC ....E 716 731-2332
  Sanborn *(G-15157)*
United Materials LLC ....G 716 662-0564
  Orchard Park *(G-13326)*
United Transit Mix Inc ....F 718 416-3400
  Brooklyn *(G-2723)*
Upstone Materials Inc ....F 315 265-8036
  Plattsburgh *(G-13736)*
Upstone Materials Inc ....G 315 764-0251
  Massena *(G-8233)*
Upstone Materials Inc ....G 518 873-2275
  Lewis *(G-7452)*
Upstone Materials Inc ....D 518 561-5321
  Plattsburgh *(G-13735)*
US Concrete Inc ....E 718 853-4644
  Roslyn Heights *(G-15058)*
US Concrete Inc ....E 718 438-6800
  Brooklyn *(G-2731)*
W F Saunders & Sons Inc ....G 315 469-3217
  Nedrow *(G-8819)*
Watertown Concrete Inc ....F 315 788-1040
  Watertown *(G-16698)*

3274 Lime

Lime Energy Co ....G 704 892-4442
  Buffalo *(G-3064)*
Masick Soil Conservation Co ....F 518 827-5354
  Schoharie *(G-15339)*
▲ Minerals Technologies Inc ....E 212 878-1800
  New York *(G-11302)*

3275 Gypsum Prdts

▲ Continental Buchanan LLC ....D 703 480-3800
  Buchanan *(G-2799)*
East Pattern & Model Corp ....E 585 461-3240
  Fairport *(G-4861)*
Empire Gypsum Pdts & Sup Corp .....G 914 592-8141
  Elmsford *(G-4758)*
Lafarge North America Inc ....D 914 930-3027
  Buchanan *(G-2800)*
United States Gypsum Company ....C 585 948-5221
  Oakfield *(G-13085)*

3281 Cut Stone Prdts

Adirondack Precision Cut Stone ....F 518 681-3060
  Queensbury *(G-14001)*
Alart Inc ....G 212 840-1508
  New York *(G-9122)*

▲ Amendola MBL & Stone Ctr Inc .....D 914 997-7968
  White Plains *(G-17104)*
American Bluestone LLC ....F 607 369-2235
  Sidney *(G-15457)*
Aurora Stone Group LLC ....F 315 471-6869
  East Syracuse *(G-4525)*
▲ Barra & Trumbore Inc ....G 845 626-5442
  Kerhonkson *(G-7183)*
Busch Products Inc ....G 315 474-8422
  Syracuse *(G-15897)*
Callanan Industries Inc ....G 845 331-6868
  Kingston *(G-7211)*
Capital Stone LLC ....F 518 382-7588
  Schenectady *(G-15266)*
Capital Stone Saratoga LLC ....G 518 226-8677
  Saratoga Springs *(G-15175)*
Crown Hill Stone Inc ....F 716 326-4601
  Westfield *(G-17076)*
Dalrymple Holding Corp ....F 607 737-6200
  Pine City *(G-13578)*
Denton Stoneworks Inc ....F 516 746-1500
  Garden City Park *(G-5553)*
▲ Devonian Stone New York Inc ......F 607 655-2600
  Windsor *(G-17294)*
Dicamillo Marble and Granite ....E 845 878-0078
  Patterson *(G-13462)*
◆ Domenick Denigris Inc ....F 718 823-2264
  Bronx *(G-1318)*
Dominic De Nigris Inc ....F 718 597-4460
  Bronx *(G-1319)*
▲ European Marble Works Co Inc ....F 718 387-9778
  Garden City *(G-5517)*
◆ Evergreen Slate Company Inc ....D 518 642-2530
  Middle Granville *(G-8431)*
First Presbyterian Church ....G 315 252-3861
  Auburn *(G-494)*
Fordham Marble Co Inc ....G 914 682-6699
  White Plains *(G-17136)*
Geneva Granite Co Inc ....F 315 789-8142
  Geneva *(G-5590)*
▲ Glen Plaza Marble & Gran Inc ......G 516 671-1100
  Glen Cove *(G-5630)*
▲ Granite & Marble Works Inc ....F 518 584-2800
  Gansevoort *(G-5500)*
Granite Tops Inc ....E 914 699-2909
  Mount Vernon *(G-8732)*
▲ Granite Works LLC ....G 607 565-7012
  Waverly *(G-16727)*
Graymont Materials Inc ....F 518 561-5200
  Plattsburgh *(G-13693)*
Hanson Aggregates East LLC ....F 315 493-3721
  Great Bend *(G-5798)*
Hanson Aggregates PA LLC ....G 315 789-6202
  Oaks Corners *(G-13089)*
House of Stone Inc ....G 845 782-7271
  Monroe *(G-8592)*
▲ Icestone LLC ....E 718 624-4900
  Brooklyn *(G-2093)*
▲ International Stone Accessrs ....G 718 522-5399
  Brooklyn *(G-2110)*
Iroquois Rock Products Inc ....F 585 381-7010
  Rochester *(G-14476)*
▲ Italian Marble & Granite Inc ....F 716 741-1800
  Clarence Center *(G-3702)*
Jamestown Kitchen & Bath Inc ....G 716 665-2299
  Jamestown *(G-7041)*
▲ Lace Marble & Granite Inc ....G 347 425-1645
  Brooklyn *(G-2188)*
Marble Doctors LLC ....E 203 628-8339
  New York *(G-11167)*
▲ Marble Works Inc ....G 914 376-3653
  Yonkers *(G-17483)*
Masonville Stone Incorporated ....G 607 265-3597
  Masonville *(G-8138)*
MCM Natural Stone Inc ....F 585 586-6510
  Rochester *(G-14523)*
▲ Minerals Technologies Inc ....E 212 878-1800
  New York *(G-11302)*
Monroe Industries Inc ....G 585 226-8230
  Avon *(G-538)*
▲ New York Marble and Stone Corp ..F 718 729-7272
  Maspeth *(G-8187)*
▲ New York Quarries Inc ....G 518 756-3138
  Alcove *(G-175)*
North American Slate Inc ....G 518 642-1702
  Granville *(G-5794)*
North American Stone Inc ....G 585 266-4020
  Rochester *(G-14561)*
North Shore Monuments Inc ....G 516 759-2156
  Glen Head *(G-5653)*

32 STONE, CLAY, GLASS, AND CONCRETE PRODUCTS

Northeast Solite Corporation .... E 845 246-2177
  Mount Marion (G-8694)
Pallette Stone Corporation .... E 518 584-2421
  Gansevoort (G-5501)
PR & Stone & Tile Inc .... G 718 383-1115
  Brooklyn (G-2448)
Premier Group NY .... F 212 229-1200
  New York (G-11720)
Puccio Design International .... F 516 248-6426
  Garden City (G-5542)
Rivera .... G 718 458-1488
  Flushing (G-5295)
Roto Salt Company Inc .... E 315 536-3742
  Penn Yan (G-13542)
▲ Royal Marble & Granite Inc .... G 516 536-5900
  Oceanside (G-13116)
Salsburg Dimensional Stone .... E 631 653-6790
  Brookhaven (G-1509)
Sanford Stone LLC .... E 607 467-1313
  Deposit (G-4302)
Seneca Stone Corporation .... F 315 549-8253
  Fayette (G-5170)
Seneca Stone Corporation .... E 607 737-6200
  Pine City (G-13579)
Sheldon Slate Products Co Inc .... E 518 642-1280
  Middle Granville (G-8434)
Stone & Terrazzo World Inc .... G 718 361-6899
  Long Island City (G-7920)
Suffolk Granite Manufacturing .... E 631 226-4774
  Lindenhurst (G-7509)
Thalle Industries Inc .... E 914 762-3415
  Briarcliff Manor (G-1229)
▲ Unilock New York Inc .... G 845 278-6700
  Brewster (G-1227)
▲ Unique MBL Gran Orgnztion Corp ...G 718 482-0440
  Long Island City (G-7935)
Vermont Natural Stoneworks .... E 518 642-2460
  Middle Granville (G-8436)
Vermont Structural Slate Co .... F 518 499-1912
  Whitehall (G-17219)
W F Saunders & Sons Inc .... F 315 469-3217
  Nedrow (G-8819)
White Plains Marble Inc .... E 914 347-6000
  Elmsford (G-4801)

3291 Abrasive Prdts

09 Flshy Bll/Dsert Sunrise LLC .... G 518 583-6638
  Saratoga Springs (G-15168)
American Douglas Metals Inc .... F 716 856-3170
  Buffalo (G-2824)
▲ Barker Brothers Incorporated .... D 718 456-6400
  Ridgewood (G-14114)
◆ Barton Mines Company LLC .... C 518 798-5462
  Glens Falls (G-5688)
Bedrock Landscaping Mtls Corp .... G 631 587-4950
  Babylon (G-543)
▲ Buffalo Abrasives Inc .... E 716 693-3856
  North Tonawanda (G-12980)
Charles A Hones Inc .... G 607 273-5720
  Ithaca (G-6870)
Conrad Blasius Equipment Co .... G 516 753-1200
  Plainview (G-13620)
◆ Datum Alloys Inc .... G 607 239-6274
  Endicott (G-4808)
▲ Dedeco International Sales Inc .... E 845 887-4840
  Long Eddy (G-7674)
▲ Dico Products Corporation .... F 315 797-0470
  Utica (G-16346)
◆ Dimanco Inc .... G 315 797-0470
  Utica (G-16347)
◆ Divine Brothers Company .... C 315 797-0470
  Utica (G-16350)
▼ EAC Holdings of NY Corp .... E 716 822-2500
  Buffalo (G-2939)
◆ Electro Abrasives LLC .... E 716 822-2500
  Buffalo (G-2947)
Global Abrasive Products Inc .... E 716 438-0047
  Lockport (G-7617)
▲ Imerys Fsed Mnrl Ngara FLS Inc ...E 716 286-1250
  Niagara Falls (G-12852)
Jta USA Inc .... G 718 722-0902
  Brooklyn (G-2154)
Malyn Industrial Ceramics Inc .... G 716 741-1510
  Clarence Center (G-3705)
Meloon Foundries LLC .... E 315 454-3231
  Syracuse (G-16006)
▲ Pellets LLC .... G 716 693-1750
  North Tonawanda (G-13003)
▲ Precision Abrasives Corp .... E 716 826-5833
  Orchard Park (G-13316)

Precision Elctro Mnrl Pmco Inc .... E 716 284-2484
  Niagara Falls (G-12881)
Raulli and Sons Inc .... E 315 479-2515
  Syracuse (G-16042)
Saint-Gbain Advnced Crmics LLC .... E 716 691-2000
  Amherst (G-260)
Saint-Gobain Abrasives Inc .... B 518 266-2200
  Watervliet (G-16712)
▲ Select-Tech Inc .... G 845 895-8111
  Wallkill (G-16566)
Smm - North America Trade Corp .... G 212 604-0710
  New York (G-12136)
Sunbelt Industries Inc .... F 315 823-2947
  Little Falls (G-7526)
▲ Uneeda Enterprizes Inc .... C 800 431-2494
  Spring Valley (G-15626)
Warren Cutlery Corp .... F 845 876-3444
  Rhinebeck (G-14072)
◆ Washington Mills Elec Mnrls .... D 716 278-6600
  Niagara Falls (G-12907)
▲ Washington Mills Tonawanda Inc ...E 716 693-4550
  Tonawanda (G-16234)

3292 Asbestos products

Andujar Asbestos and Lead .... G 716 228-6757
  Buffalo (G-2830)
Regional MGT & Consulting Inc .... F 718 599-3718
  Brooklyn (G-2506)
Shenfield Studio LLC .... F 315 436-8869
  Syracuse (G-16063)

3295 Minerals & Earths: Ground Or Treated

A&B Conservation LLC .... G 845 282-7272
  Monsey (G-8601)
Allied Aero Services Inc .... G 631 277-9368
  Brentwood (G-1172)
DSM Nutritional Products LLC .... C 518 372-5155
  Schenectady (G-15276)
DSM Nutritional Products LLC .... E 518 372-5155
  Glenville (G-5716)
▲ Mineralbious Corp .... G 516 498-9715
  Westbury (G-17040)
▲ Minerals Technologies Inc .... E 212 878-1800
  New York (G-11302)
Norlite LLC .... B 518 235-0030
  Cohoes (G-3778)
Northeast Solite Corporation .... E 845 246-2646
  Saugerties (G-15218)
Northeast Solite Corporation .... E 845 246-2177
  Mount Marion (G-8694)
▲ Opta Minerals .... F 905 689-7361
  Buffalo (G-3125)
Oro Avanti Inc .... G 516 487-5185
  Great Neck (G-5844)
Skyline Inc .... G 631 403-4131
  East Setauket (G-4511)

3296 Mineral Wool

▲ Burnett Process Inc .... G 585 254-8080
  Rochester (G-14269)
Elliot Industries Inc .... G 716 287-3100
  Ellington (G-4658)
Fbm Galaxy Inc .... G 315 463-5144
  East Syracuse (G-4542)
Lencore Acoustics Corp .... F 315 384-9114
  Norfolk (G-12916)
Mecho Systems .... F 718 729-8373
  Long Island City (G-7837)
Owens Corning Sales LLC .... B 518 475-3600
  Feura Bush (G-5182)
Primary Plastics Inc .... F 607 785-4865
  Endwell (G-4843)
Richlar Industries Inc .... F 315 463-5144
  East Syracuse (G-4574)
◆ Soundcoat Company Inc .... D 631 242-2200
  Deer Park (G-4236)
▲ Ssf Production LLC .... F 518 324-3407
  Plattsburgh (G-13726)
Unifrax Corporation .... E 716 278-3800
  Niagara Falls (G-12903)
Unifrax I LLC .... C 716 696-3000
  Tonawanda (G-16230)

3297 Nonclay Refractories

▲ Ask Chemicals Hi-Tech LLC .... D 607 587-9146
  Alfred Station (G-198)
▲ Blasch Precision Ceramics Inc .... D 518 436-1263
  Menands (G-8401)

Capitol Restoration Corp .... G 516 783-1425
  North Bellmore (G-12932)
▲ Ceramaterials LLC .... G 518 701-6722
  Port Jervis (G-13803)
Filtros Ltd .... E 585 586-8770
  East Rochester (G-4478)
Global Alumina Corporation .... G 212 351-0000
  New York (G-10352)
Global Alumina Services Co .... E 212 309-8060
  New York (G-10353)
Hanyan & Higgins Company Inc .... G 315 769-8838
  Massena (G-8227)
Lucideon .... F 518 382-0082
  Schenectady (G-15303)
◆ Monofrax LLC .... C 716 483-7200
  Falconer (G-4915)
▼ Rembar Company LLC .... F 914 693-2620
  Dobbs Ferry (G-4326)
Roccera LLC .... F 585 426-0887
  Rochester (G-14654)
Saint-Gobain Dynamics Inc .... F 716 278-6007
  Niagara Falls (G-12890)
▲ Silicon Carbide Products Inc .... E 607 562-8599
  Horseheads (G-6622)
Surmet Ceramics Corporation .... F 716 875-4091
  Buffalo (G-3229)
Unifrax I LLC .... C 716 696-3000
  Tonawanda (G-16230)
▲ Zircar Refr Composites Inc .... G 845 651-4481
  Florida (G-5225)
▲ Zircar Zirconia Inc .... E 845 651-3040
  Florida (G-5226)

3299 Nonmetallic Mineral Prdts, NEC

American Crmic Process RES LLC .... G 315 828-6268
  Phelps (G-13552)
American Wood Column Corp .... G 718 782-3163
  Brooklyn (G-1608)
Argosy Composite Advanced Mate ...F 212 268-0003
  New York (G-9251)
B & R Promotional Products .... G 212 563-0040
  New York (G-9341)
▲ Barrett Bronze Inc .... E 914 699-6060
  Mount Vernon (G-8710)
Beyond Design Inc .... G 607 865-7487
  Walton (G-16568)
Brooklyn Remembers Inc .... F 718 491-1705
  Brooklyn (G-1730)
▲ Cetek Inc .... E 845 452-3510
  Poughkeepsie (G-13911)
▲ Design Research Ltd .... C 212 228-7675
  New York (G-9907)
Dream Statuary Inc .... G 718 647-2024
  Brooklyn (G-1880)
Elliot Gantz & Company Inc .... E 631 249-0680
  Farmingdale (G-4996)
Enrg Inc .... F 716 873-2939
  Buffalo (G-2954)
Essex Works Ltd .... G 718 495-4575
  Brooklyn (G-1943)
Everblock Systems LLC .... G 844 422-5625
  New York (G-10143)
▲ Foster Reeve & Associates Inc .... G 718 609-0090
  Brooklyn (G-1997)
Fra-Rik Formica Fabg Co Inc .... G 718 597-3335
  Bronx (G-1339)
Halo Associates .... G 212 691-9549
  New York (G-10443)
▲ Heany Industries Inc .... D 585 889-2700
  Scottsville (G-15358)
Jonas Louis Paul Studios Inc .... G 518 851-2211
  Hudson (G-6653)
Kodiak Studios Inc .... G 718 769-5399
  Brooklyn (G-2178)
▲ Reliance Mica Co Inc .... G 718 788-0282
  Rockaway Park (G-14815)
▲ S & J Trading Inc .... G 718 347-1323
  Floral Park (G-5216)
▲ Starfire Systems Inc .... F 518 899-9336
  Schenectady (G-15323)
Studio Associates of New York .... G 212 268-1163
  New York (G-12241)
▲ Ufx Holding I Corporation .... G 212 644-5900
  New York (G-12462)
Ufx Holding II Corporation .... G 212 644-5900
  New York (G-12463)
Unifrax Holding Co .... G 212 644-5900
  New York (G-12473)
▲ Unifrax I LLC .... C 716 768-6500
  Tonawanda (G-16231)

Unifrax I LLC ... C ... 716 696-3000
Tonawanda *(G-16230)*
Vescom Structural Systems Inc ... F ... 516 876-8100
Westbury *(G-17070)*

33 PRIMARY METAL INDUSTRIES

3312 Blast Furnaces, Coke Ovens, Steel & Rolling Mills

A-1 Iron Works Inc ... G ... 718 927-4766
Brooklyn *(G-1538)*
Albaluz Films LLC ... G ... 347 613-2321
New York *(G-9123)*
▲ Allvac ... F ... 716 433-4411
Lockport *(G-7597)*
▲ American Chimney Supplies Inc ... G ... 631 434-2020
Hauppauge *(G-6039)*
Artistic Ironworks Inc ... G ... 631 665-4285
Bay Shore *(G-671)*
B H M Metal Products Co ... G ... 845 292-5297
Kauneonga Lake *(G-7165)*
Baker Tool & Die ... G ... 716 694-2025
North Tonawanda *(G-12976)*
Baker Tool & Die & Die ... G ... 716 694-2025
North Tonawanda *(G-12977)*
Belmet Products Inc ... E ... 718 542-8220
Bronx *(G-1282)*
Bonura and Sons Iron Works ... F ... 718 381-4100
Franklin Square *(G-5371)*
Bryant Manufacturing Wny Inc ... G ... 716 894-8282
Buffalo *(G-2869)*
China Industrial Steel Inc ... G ... 646 328-1502
New York *(G-9648)*
Coventry Manufacturing Co Inc ... E ... 914 668-2212
Mount Vernon *(G-8719)*
◆ Crucible Industries LLC ... B ... 800 365-1180
Syracuse *(G-15933)*
Cs Manufacturing Limited ... E ... 607 587-8154
Alfred *(G-196)*
DAgostino Iron Works Inc ... G ... 585 235-8850
Rochester *(G-14319)*
Dakota Systems Mfg Corp ... G ... 631 249-5811
Farmingdale *(G-4983)*
David Fehlman ... G ... 315 455-8888
Syracuse *(G-15942)*
◆ Dunkirk Specialty Steel LLC ... C ... 716 366-1000
Dunkirk *(G-4364)*
Elderlee Incorporated ... C ... 315 789-6670
Oaks Corners *(G-13088)*
Fuller Tool Incorporated ... F ... 315 891-3183
Newport *(G-12814)*
Hallock Fabricating Corp ... G ... 631 727-2441
Riverhead *(G-14156)*
▼ Handy & Harman Ltd ... A ... 212 520-2300
New York *(G-10450)*
Higher Power Industries Inc ... G ... 914 709-9800
Yonkers *(G-17470)*
Hitachi Metals America Ltd ... E ... 914 694-9200
Purchase *(G-13974)*
Hmi Metal Powders ... C ... 315 839-5421
Clayville *(G-3714)*
▲ Homogeneous Metals Inc ... D ... 315 839-5421
Clayville *(G-3715)*
Image Iron Works Inc ... G ... 718 592-8276
Corona *(G-4021)*
◆ Jaquith Industries Inc ... E ... 315 478-5700
Syracuse *(G-15985)*
Jfe Engineering Corporation ... F ... 212 310-9320
New York *(G-10767)*
Jfe Steel America Inc ... G ... 212 310-9320
New York *(G-10768)*
▲ Juniper Elbow Co Inc ... C ... 718 326-2546
Middle Village *(G-8447)*
Kenbenco Inc ... F ... 845 246-3066
Saugerties *(G-15215)*
Lino International Inc ... G ... 516 482-7100
Great Neck *(G-5838)*
▲ Mardek LLC ... G ... 585 735-9333
Pittsford *(G-13597)*
Markin Tubing LP ... F ... 585 495-6211
Buffalo *(G-3077)*
Markin Tubing Inc ... C ... 585 495-6211
Wyoming *(G-17397)*
Matrix Steel Company Inc ... G ... 718 381-6800
Brooklyn *(G-2287)*
N C Iron Works Inc ... G ... 718 633-4660
Brooklyn *(G-2352)*
◆ Niagara Specialty Metals Inc ... E ... 716 542-5552
Akron *(G-23)*
Nitro Wheels Inc ... F ... 716 337-0709
North Collins *(G-12946)*
▲ Nucor Steel Auburn Inc ... B ... 315 253-4561
Auburn *(G-509)*
Pecker Iron Works LLC ... G ... 914 665-0100
Mount Kisco *(G-8682)*
Qsf Inc ... G ... 585 247-6200
Gates *(G-5577)*
Quality Stainless Steel NY Inc ... F ... 718 748-1785
Brooklyn *(G-2481)*
R D Specialties Inc ... F ... 585 265-0220
Webster *(G-16756)*
Recon Construction Corp ... E ... 718 939-1305
Little Neck *(G-7532)*
◆ Renco Group Inc ... G ... 212 541-6000
New York *(G-11864)*
Republic Steel Inc ... B ... 716 827-2800
Blasdell *(G-958)*
Rochester Structural LLC ... E ... 585 436-1250
Rochester *(G-14674)*
Safespan Platform Systems Inc ... E ... 716 694-1100
Tonawanda *(G-16217)*
Samuel Son & Co Inc ... G ... 716 856-6500
Blasdell *(G-959)*
Sims Group USA Holdings Corp ... D ... 718 786-6031
Long Island City *(G-7906)*
Sph Group Holdings LLC ... F ... 212 520-2300
New York *(G-12186)*
Spin-Rite Corporation ... F ... 585 266-5200
Rochester *(G-14720)*
Tdy Industries LLC ... E ... 716 433-4411
Lockport *(G-7648)*
Tl Group Auto Systems LLC ... G ... 315 568-7042
Seneca Falls *(G-15394)*
▲ Tonawanda Coke Corporation ... D ... 716 876-6222
Tonawanda *(G-16226)*
Tri Valley Iron Inc ... F ... 845 365-1013
Palisades *(G-13428)*
Universal Stainless & Alloy ... D ... 716 366-1000
Dunkirk *(G-4376)*
Vell Company Inc ... G ... 845 365-1013
Palisades *(G-13429)*
◆ Viraj - USA Inc ... G ... 516 280-8380
Garden City *(G-5549)*
Wheel & Tire Depot Ex Corp ... G ... 914 375-2100
Yonkers *(G-17514)*

3313 Electrometallurgical Prdts

◆ CCA Holding Inc ... C ... 716 446-8800
Amherst *(G-232)*
Globe Metallurgical Inc ... D ... 716 804-0862
Niagara Falls *(G-12844)*
▲ Golden Egret LLC ... G ... 516 922-2839
East Norwich *(G-4465)*
◆ Medima LLC ... C ... 716 741-0400
Clarence *(G-3693)*
Real Industry Inc ... F ... 805 435-1255
New York *(G-11842)*
Thyssenkrupp Materials NA Inc ... F ... 212 972-8800
New York *(G-12354)*

3315 Steel Wire Drawing & Nails & Spikes

A&B Iron Works Inc ... G ... 347 466-3193
Brooklyn *(G-1537)*
▲ Able Industries Inc ... F ... 914 739-5685
Cortlandt Manor *(G-4072)*
▲ Aerospace Wire & Cable Inc ... E ... 718 358-2345
College Point *(G-3801)*
Alexscoe LLC ... E ... 315 463-9207
East Syracuse *(G-4517)*
▲ American Wire Tie Inc ... E ... 716 337-2412
North Collins *(G-12942)*
▲ Aruvil International Inc ... E ... 212 447-5020
New York *(G-9277)*
Bekaert Corporation ... E ... 716 830-1321
Amherst *(G-229)*
▲ Braun Horticulture Inc ... G ... 716 282-6101
Niagara Falls *(G-12821)*
CFS Enterprises Inc ... E ... 718 585-0500
Bronx *(G-1295)*
▲ Cobra Manufacturing Corp ... G ... 845 514-2505
Lake Katrine *(G-7294)*
▲ Continental Cordage Corp ... D ... 315 655-9800
Cazenovia *(G-3470)*
▲ Dragon Trading Inc ... G ... 212 717-1496
New York *(G-9974)*
▲ Dsr International Corp ... G ... 631 427-2600
Great Neck *(G-5820)*
EB Acquisitions LLC ... D ... 212 355-3310
New York *(G-10022)*
Forsyth Industries Inc ... E ... 716 652-1070
Buffalo *(G-2968)*
◆ Handy & Harman ... E ... 914 461-1300
White Plains *(G-17145)*
Hanes Supply Inc ... E ... 518 438-0139
Albany *(G-84)*
Hitachi Metals America Ltd ... E ... 914 694-9200
Purchase *(G-13974)*
▲ Hohmann & Barnard Inc ... E ... 631 234-0600
Hauppauge *(G-6118)*
▲ Island Industries Corp ... G ... 631 451-8825
Coram *(G-3968)*
▲ Lee Spring Company LLC ... C ... 718 362-5183
Brooklyn *(G-2207)*
Liberty Fabrication Inc ... G ... 718 495-5735
Brooklyn *(G-2216)*
Master-Halco Inc ... F ... 631 585-8150
Ronkonkoma *(G-14966)*
Northeast Wire and Cable Co ... G ... 716 297-8483
Niagara Falls *(G-12870)*
▲ Nupro Technologies LLC ... F ... 412 422-5922
Canandaigua *(G-3379)*
▲ Nyi Building Products Inc ... F ... 518 458-7500
Clifton Park *(G-3729)*
Omega Wire Inc ... D ... 315 689-7115
Jordan *(G-7158)*
Oneonta Fence ... G ... 607 433-6707
Oneonta *(G-13212)*
▲ Owl Wire & Cable LLC ... C ... 315 697-2011
Canastota *(G-3396)*
▲ Qmc Technologies Inc ... F ... 716 681-0810
Depew *(G-4295)*
▲ Rolling Gate Supply Corp ... G ... 718 366-5258
Glendale *(G-5677)*
Rose Fence Inc ... F ... 516 223-0777
Baldwin *(G-560)*
▲ Sigmund Cohn Corp ... D ... 914 664-5300
Mount Vernon *(G-8780)*
Spectrum Cable Corporation ... G ... 585 235-7714
Rochester *(G-14719)*
▲ Styles Manufacturing Corp ... G ... 516 763-5303
Oceanside *(G-13120)*
▲ Tappan Wire & Cable Inc ... C ... 845 353-9000
Blauvelt *(G-971)*
Technical Wldg Fabricators LLC ... F ... 518 463-2229
Albany *(G-140)*
Web Associates Inc ... G ... 716 883-3377
Buffalo *(G-3275)*

3316 Cold Rolled Steel Sheet, Strip & Bars

Aero-Data Metal Crafters Inc ... C ... 631 471-7733
Ronkonkoma *(G-14882)*
▲ Clover Wire Forming Co Inc ... E ... 914 375-0400
Yonkers *(G-17444)*
◆ Gibraltar Industries Inc ... D ... 716 826-6500
Buffalo *(G-2989)*
Hitachi Metals America Ltd ... E ... 914 694-9200
Purchase *(G-13974)*
Niagara Lasalle Corporation ... D ... 716 827-7010
Buffalo *(G-3111)*
Northeast Cnstr Inds Inc ... F ... 845 565-1000
Montgomery *(G-8634)*
◆ Renco Group Inc ... G ... 212 541-6000
New York *(G-11864)*
Rough Brothers Holding Co ... G ... 716 826-6500
Buffalo *(G-3196)*
Worthington Industries Inc ... D ... 315 336-5500
Rome *(G-14868)*

3317 Steel Pipe & Tubes

Coventry Manufacturing Co Inc ... E ... 914 668-2212
Mount Vernon *(G-8719)*
◆ Handy & Harman ... E ... 914 461-1300
White Plains *(G-17145)*
Liberty Pipe Incorporated ... G ... 516 747-2472
Mineola *(G-8554)*
▲ Markin Tubing LP ... D ... 585 495-6211
Wyoming *(G-17396)*
Markin Tubing LP ... F ... 585 495-6211
Buffalo *(G-3077)*
Markin Tubing Inc ... C ... 585 495-6211
Wyoming *(G-17397)*
McHone Industries Inc ... D ... 716 945-3380
Salamanca *(G-15128)*
Micromold Products Inc ... E ... 914 969-2850
Yonkers *(G-17485)*
Ocean Steel Corporation ... E ... 607 584-7500
Conklin *(G-3897)*
▲ Oriskany Mfg Tech LLC ... E ... 315 732-4962
Yorkville *(G-17542)*

SIC

33 PRIMARY METAL INDUSTRIES

Stony Brook Mfg Co Inc .... E 631 369-9530
Calverton *(G-3326)*
▲ Super Steelworks Corporation .... G 718 386-4770
Deer Park *(G-4239)*
Thyssenkrupp Materials NA Inc .... G 585 279-0000
Rochester *(G-14753)*
TI Group Auto Systems LLC .... G 315 568-7042
Seneca Falls *(G-15394)*
▼ Tricon Piping Systems Inc .... F 315 655-4178
Canastota *(G-3401)*
▲ Welded Tube Usa Inc .... D 716 828-1111
Lackawanna *(G-7276)*

3321 Gray Iron Foundries

Acme Nipple Mfg Co Inc .... G 716 873-7491
Buffalo *(G-2811)*
Auburn Foundry Inc .... F 315 253-4441
Auburn *(G-478)*
Cpp - Guaymas .... C 315 687-0014
Chittenango *(G-3661)*
▲ Dragon Trading Inc .... G 212 717-1496
New York *(G-9974)*
En Tech Corp .... F 845 398-0776
Tappan *(G-16104)*
Field Wares LLC .... G 508 380-6545
High Falls *(G-6428)*
▲ Hitachi Metals America Ltd .... G 914 694-9200
Purchase *(G-13975)*
Jamestown Iron Works Inc .... F 716 665-2818
Falconer *(G-4913)*
Matrix Steel Company Inc .... G 718 381-6800
Brooklyn *(G-2287)*
McWane Inc .... B 607 734-2211
Elmira *(G-4708)*
▲ Noresco Industrial Group Inc .... G 516 759-3355
Glen Cove *(G-5635)*
Oneida Foundries Inc .... E 315 363-4570
Oneida *(G-13181)*
Penner Elbow Company Inc .... F 718 526-9000
Elmhurst *(G-4679)*
S M S C Inc .... G 315 942-4394
Boonville *(G-1167)*
▲ Staub Usa Inc .... G 914 747-0300
Pleasantville *(G-13751)*

3322 Malleable Iron Foundries

Eastern Company .... D 315 468-6251
Solvay *(G-15529)*
Emcom Industries Inc .... G 716 852-3711
Buffalo *(G-2950)*
▲ Noresco Industrial Group Inc .... E 516 759-3355
Glen Cove *(G-5635)*
◆ Plattco Corporation .... E 518 563-4640
Plattsburgh *(G-13715)*

3324 Steel Investment Foundries

Brinkman Precision Inc .... D 585 429-5001
West Henrietta *(G-16905)*
Consoldted Precision Pdts Corp .... B 315 687-0014
Chittenango *(G-3660)*
▲ Cpp-Syracuse Inc .... E 315 687-0014
Chittenango *(G-3662)*
Cs Manufacturing Limited .... E 607 587-8154
Alfred *(G-196)*
Jbf Stainless LLC .... E 315 569-2800
Frankfort *(G-5363)*
Quality Castings Inc .... E 732 409-3203
Long Island City *(G-7883)*
Worldwide Resources Inc .... F 718 760-5000
Brooklyn *(G-2783)*

3325 Steel Foundries, NEC

A & V Castings Inc .... G 212 997-0042
New York *(G-9029)*
Amt Incorporated .... E 518 284-2910
Sharon Springs *(G-15405)*
Brinkman Intl Group Inc .... G 585 429-5000
Rochester *(G-14263)*
C J Winter Machine Tech .... E 585 429-5000
Rochester *(G-14271)*
Eastern Industrial Steel Corp .... G 845 639-9749
New City *(G-8832)*
Frazer & Jones Co .... D 315 468-6251
Syracuse *(G-15964)*
▲ Pcore Electric Company Inc .... D 585 768-1200
Le Roy *(G-7440)*
Steel Craft Rolling Door .... F 631 608-8662
Copiague *(G-3952)*

3331 Primary Smelting & Refining Of Copper

Hengyuan Copper USA Inc .... G 718 357-6666
Whitestone *(G-17237)*
Sherburne Metal Sales Inc .... F 607 674-4441
Sherburne *(G-15417)*
◆ Tecnofil Chenango SAC .... E 607 674-4441
Sherburne *(G-15420)*

3334 Primary Production Of Aluminum

Alcoa USA Corp .... F 212 518-5400
New York *(G-9127)*
Greene Brass & Alum Fndry LLC .... G 607 656-4204
Bloomville *(G-990)*

3339 Primary Nonferrous Metals, NEC

▲ AAA Catalytic Recycling Inc .... F 631 920-7944
Farmingdale *(G-4935)*
American Material Processing .... F 315 695-6204
Phoenix *(G-13568)*
Ames Goldsmith Corp .... E 518 792-7435
Glens Falls *(G-5685)*
Billanti Casting Co Inc .... E 516 775-4800
New Hyde Park *(G-8864)*
Doral Refining Corp .... E 516 223-3684
Freeport *(G-5405)*
Eco-Bat America LLC .... C 845 692-4414
Middletown *(G-8472)*
Electro Alloy Recovery Inc .... G 631 879-7530
Bohemia *(G-1062)*
Euro Pacific Precious Metals .... E 212 481-0310
New York *(G-10138)*
General Refining & Smelting .... G 516 538-4747
Hempstead *(G-6294)*
General Refining Corporation .... G 516 538-4747
Hempstead *(G-6295)*
▲ Germanium Corp America Inc .... G 315 732-3744
Utica *(G-16360)*
Globe Metallurgical Inc .... D 716 804-0862
Niagara Falls *(G-12844)*
Goldmark Products Inc .... E 631 777-3343
Farmingdale *(G-5008)*
▼ Handy & Harman Ltd .... A 212 520-2300
New York *(G-10450)*
Hh Liquidating Corp .... A 646 282-2500
New York *(G-10515)*
Marina Jewelry Co Inc .... G 212 354-5027
New York *(G-11175)*
▲ Materion Advanced Materials ..... C 800 327-1355
Buffalo *(G-3079)*
Materion Advanced Materials .... G 800 327-1355
Brewster *(G-1220)*
◆ Medima LLC .... G 716 741-0400
Clarence *(G-3693)*
Rochester Silver Works LLC .... G 585 743-1610
Rochester *(G-14671)*
RS Precision Industries Inc .... E 631 420-0424
Farmingdale *(G-5115)*
S & W Metal Trading Corp .... G 212 719-5070
Brooklyn *(G-2547)*
Sabin Metal Corporation .... C 585 538-2194
Scottsville *(G-15361)*
▲ Saes Smart Materials Inc .... G 315 266-2026
New Hartford *(G-8855)*
▲ Sigmund Cohn Corp .... D 914 664-5300
Mount Vernon *(G-8780)*
Sph Group Holdings LLC .... G 212 520-2300
New York *(G-12186)*
Starfuels Inc .... G 914 289-4800
White Plains *(G-17197)*
Tdy Industries LLC .... E 716 433-4411
Lockport *(G-7648)*
▲ Umicore Technical Materials .... C 518 792-7700
Glens Falls *(G-5713)*
Umicore USA Inc .... G 919 874-7171
Glens Falls *(G-5714)*
Wallace Refiners Inc .... E 212 391-2649
New York *(G-12610)*
Zerovalent Nanometals Inc .... G 585 298-8592
Rochester *(G-14804)*

3341 Secondary Smelting & Refining Of Nonferrous Metals

Advanced Precision Technology ...... F 845 279-3540
Brewster *(G-1204)*
Amt Incorporated .... E 518 284-2910
Sharon Springs *(G-15405)*
Ben Weitsman of Albany LLC .... E 518 462-4444
Albany *(G-50)*
Cora Materials Corp .... F 516 488-6300
New Hyde Park *(G-8870)*
Eco-Bat America LLC .... C 845 692-4414
Middletown *(G-8472)*
Encore Refining and Recycling .... G 631 319-1910
Holbrook *(G-6474)*
General Refining & Smelting .... G 516 538-4747
Hempstead *(G-6294)*
▲ Germanium Corp America Inc .... G 315 853-4900
Clinton *(G-3744)*
◆ Handy & Harman .... E 914 461-1300
White Plains *(G-17145)*
Island Recycling Corp .... G 631 234-6688
Central Islip *(G-3526)*
Karbra Company .... C 212 736-9300
New York *(G-10846)*
▲ Metalico Aluminum Recovery Inc ..E 315 463-9500
Syracuse *(G-16007)*
Parfuse Corp .... E 516 997-1795
Westbury *(G-17046)*
Pluribus Products Inc .... E 718 852-1614
Bayville *(G-775)*
Real Industry Inc .... F 805 435-1255
New York *(G-11842)*
S & W Metal Trading Corp .... G 212 719-5070
Brooklyn *(G-2547)*
▲ Sabin Metal Corporation .... F 631 329-1695
East Hampton *(G-4435)*
Sabin Metal Corporation .... C 585 538-2194
Scottsville *(G-15361)*
Scepter Inc .... E 315 568-4225
Seneca Falls *(G-15390)*
Sims Group USA Holdings Corp ..... D 718 786-6031
Long Island City *(G-7906)*
Special Metals Corporation .... D 716 366-5663
Dunkirk *(G-4375)*

3351 Rolling, Drawing & Extruding Of Copper

Aurubis Buffalo Inc .... F 716 879-6700
Buffalo *(G-2844)*
▲ Aurubis Buffalo Inc .... B 716 879-6700
Buffalo *(G-2845)*
Camden Wire Co Inc .... A 315 245-3800
Camden *(G-3341)*
▲ Continental Cordage Corp .... D 315 655-9800
Cazenovia *(G-3470)*
International Wire Group .... F 315 245-3800
Camden *(G-3343)*
◆ Milward Alloys Inc .... E 716 434-5536
Lockport *(G-7631)*
Omega Wire Inc .... D 315 689-7115
Jordan *(G-7158)*
▲ Omega Wire Inc .... B 315 245-3800
Camden *(G-3346)*
▲ Owi Corporation .... G 315 245-4305
Camden *(G-3347)*
Performance Wire & Cable Inc .... F 315 245-2594
Camden *(G-3348)*
Sherburne Metal Sales Inc .... F 607 674-4441
Sherburne *(G-15417)*

3353 Aluminum Sheet, Plate & Foil

Alcoa Fastening Systems .... E 585 368-5049
Rochester *(G-14200)*
Alcoa USA Corp .... F 212 518-5400
New York *(G-9127)*
◆ Alufoil Products Co Inc .... F 631 231-4141
Hauppauge *(G-6037)*
American Douglas Metals Inc .... F 716 856-3170
Buffalo *(G-2824)*
◆ Arconic Inc .... D 212 836-2758
New York *(G-9248)*
BSD Aluminum Foil LLC .... E 347 689-3875
Brooklyn *(G-1737)*
Hadco Metal Trading Co LLC .... G 631 270-9724
Melville *(G-8355)*
Novelis Corporation .... B 315 342-1036
Oswego *(G-13362)*
Novelis Corporation .... B 315 349-0121
Oswego *(G-13363)*
▲ USA Foil Inc .... E 631 234-5252
Brentwood *(G-1197)*

3354 Aluminum Extruded Prdts

◆ A-Fab Initiatives Inc .... G 716 877-5257
Buffalo *(G-2807)*
Alumi-Tech LLC .... G 585 663-7010
Penfield *(G-13521)*
Amt Incorporated .... E 518 284-2910
Sharon Springs *(G-15405)*

◆ **Arconic Inc** D 212 836-2758 — New York *(G-9248)*
Constellium E 212 675-5087 — New York *(G-9769)*
▼ **Flagpoles Incorporated** D 631 751-5500 — East Setauket *(G-4501)*
▲ **Itts Industrial Inc** G 718 605-6934 — Staten Island *(G-15711)*
▼ **J Sussman Inc** E 718 297-0228 — Jamaica *(G-6958)*
Jem Threading Specialties Inc G 718 665-3341 — Bronx *(G-1368)*
▲ **Keymark Corporation** A 518 853-3421 — Fonda *(G-5321)*
▲ **Minitec Framing Systems LLC** F 585 924-4690 — Victor *(G-16515)*
North American Pipe Corp F 516 338-2863 — Jericho *(G-7111)*
▼ **North Coast Outfitters Ltd** E 631 727-5580 — Riverhead *(G-14164)*
Pioneer Window Holdings Inc E 518 762-5526 — Johnstown *(G-7152)*
Super Sweep Inc F 631 223-8205 — Huntington Station *(G-6761)*
Swiss Tool Corporation E 631 842-7766 — Copiague *(G-3954)*

3355 Aluminum Rolling & Drawing, NEC

◆ **Arconic Inc** D 212 836-2758 — New York *(G-9248)*
Irtronics Instruments Inc F 914 693-6291 — Ardsley *(G-404)*
Mitsubishi Chemical Amer Inc E 212 223-3043 — New York *(G-11310)*
▲ **N A Alumil Corporation** G 718 355-9393 — Long Island City *(G-7850)*
▲ **Novelis Inc** E 315 349-0121 — Oswego *(G-13364)*
▲ **Sl Partners Inc** G 516 433-1415 — Hicksville *(G-6421)*

3356 Rolling, Drawing-Extruding Of Nonferrous Metals

▲ **Aufhauser Corporation** F 516 694-8696 — Plainview *(G-13614)*
Aufhauser Manufacturing Corp E 516 694-8696 — Plainview *(G-13615)*
Braze Alloy Inc G 718 815-5757 — Staten Island *(G-15671)*
▲ **Cathay Resources Inc** G 516 922-2839 — East Norwich *(G-4464)*
▲ **Continental Cordage Corp** D 315 655-9800 — Cazenovia *(G-3470)*
▲ **Cpp-Syracuse Inc** E 315 687-0014 — Chittenango *(G-3662)*
Eco-Bat America LLC C 845 692-4414 — Middletown *(G-8472)*
◆ **Handy & Harman** E 914 461-1300 — White Plains *(G-17145)*
Hh Liquidating Corp A 646 282-2500 — New York *(G-10515)*
▲ **Indium Corporation of America** E 800 446-3486 — Clinton *(G-3745)*
Indium Corporation of America E 315 793-8200 — Utica *(G-16366)*
Indium Corporation of America E 315 381-2330 — Utica *(G-16367)*
Jewelers Solder Supply Inc F 718 637-1256 — Brooklyn *(G-2137)*
▲ **Medi-Ray Inc** D 877 898-3003 — Tuckahoe *(G-16295)*
▲ **Nationwide Precision Pdts Corp** B 585 272-7100 — Rochester *(G-14549)*
Nickel City Studios Photo Jour G 716 200-0956 — Buffalo *(G-3115)*
Nickel Group LLC G 212 706-7906 — Rockaway Park *(G-14814)*
NY Titanium Inc G 718 227-4244 — Staten Island *(G-15737)*
RB Diamond Inc G 212 398-4560 — New York *(G-11835)*
▲ **Selectrode Industries Inc** G 631 547-5470 — Huntington Station *(G-6760)*
▲ **Sigmund Cohn Corp** D 914 664-5300 — Mount Vernon *(G-8780)*
▲ **Special Metals Corporation** D 315 798-2900 — New Hartford *(G-8856)*
T L Diamond & Company Inc G 212 249-6660 — New York *(G-12288)*
Titanium Dem Remediation Group F 716 433-4100 — Lockport *(G-7650)*
▲ **Vestal Electronic Devices LLC** F 607 773-8461 — Endicott *(G-4838)*

3357 Nonferrous Wire Drawing

Cable Your World Inc G 631 509-1180 — Port Jeff STA *(G-13787)*
Caldwell Bennett Inc E 315 337-8540 — Oriskany *(G-13330)*
Camden Wire Co Inc A 315 245-3800 — Camden *(G-3341)*
Colonial Wire & Cable Co Inc D 631 234-8500 — Hauppauge *(G-6069)*
Complete Fiber Solutions Inc G 718 828-8900 — Bronx *(G-1305)*
▲ **Continental Cordage Corp** D 315 655-9800 — Cazenovia *(G-3470)*
▲ **Convergent Cnnctivity Tech Inc** G 845 651-5250 — Florida *(G-5218)*
Corning Cable Systems Cr Un G 607 974-9000 — Corning *(G-3982)*
Corning Incorporated G 646 521-9600 — New York *(G-9786)*
Corning Incorporated G 607 974-6729 — Painted Post *(G-13417)*
◆ **Corning Incorporated** A 607 974-9000 — Corning *(G-3983)*
Corning Incorporated E 607 248-1200 — Corning *(G-3986)*
Corning Optcal Cmmncations LLC F 607 974-7543 — Corning *(G-3990)*
Corning Specialty Mtls Inc G 607 974-9000 — Corning *(G-3991)*
◆ **Cortland Cable Company Inc** E 607 753-8276 — Cortland *(G-4039)*
County WD Applnc & TV Srvc of F 585 328-7417 — Rochester *(G-14311)*
▲ **Fiberdyne Labs Inc** D 315 895-8470 — Frankfort *(G-5362)*
Hyperline Systems Inc G 613 736-8500 — Brooklyn *(G-2090)*
▲ **International Wire Group Inc** B 315 245-2000 — Camden *(G-3344)*
Jaguar Industries Inc F 845 947-1800 — Haverstraw *(G-6261)*
▲ **Kris-Tech Wire Company Inc** E 315 339-5268 — Rome *(G-14845)*
◆ **Leviton Manufacturing Co Inc** B 631 812-6000 — Melville *(G-8363)*
▲ **Monroe Cable Company Inc** C 845 692-2800 — Middletown *(G-8487)*
▲ **Rdi Inc** F 914 773-1000 — Mount Kisco *(G-8686)*
Rockland Insulated Wire Cable G 845 429-3103 — Haverstraw *(G-6263)*
Siemens Corporation F 202 434-7800 — New York *(G-12084)*
Siemens USA Holdings Inc B 212 258-4000 — New York *(G-12086)*
Sinclair Technologies Inc E 716 874-3682 — Hamburg *(G-5966)*
Steelflex Electro Corp D 516 226-4466 — Lindenhurst *(G-7506)*
▲ **Tappan Wire & Cable Inc** C 845 353-9000 — Blauvelt *(G-971)*
TLC-The Light Connection Inc D 315 736-7384 — Oriskany *(G-13341)*
▲ **United Wire Technologies Inc** F 315 623-7203 — Constantia *(G-3908)*
Universal Builders Supply Inc F 845 758-8801 — Red Hook *(G-14042)*
▲ **Whirlwind Music Distrs Inc** D 800 733-9473 — Rochester *(G-14790)*

3363 Aluminum Die Castings

▲ **Albest Metal Stamping Corp** D 718 388-6000 — Brooklyn *(G-1575)*
Crown Die Casting Corp E 914 667-5400 — Mount Vernon *(G-8720)*
Greene Brass & Alum Fndry LLC G 607 656-4204 — Bloomville *(G-990)*
▲ **Greenfield Industries Inc** D 516 623-9230 — Freeport *(G-5415)*
ITT Corporation D 315 568-2811 — Seneca Falls *(G-15383)*
ITT LLC D 914 641-2000 — Seneca Falls *(G-15387)*
▼ **Jamestown Bronze Works Inc** G 716 665-2302 — Jamestown *(G-7039)*
Louis Iannettoni D 315 454-3231 — Syracuse *(G-16002)*
▲ **Pinnacle Manufacturing Co Inc** E 585 343-5664 — Batavia *(G-646)*
Tpi Arcade Inc D 585 492-0122 — Arcade *(G-400)*

3364 Nonferrous Die Castings, Exc Aluminum

▲ **Albest Metal Stamping Corp** D 718 388-6000 — Brooklyn *(G-1575)*
◆ **American Casting and Mfg Corp** D 800 342-0333 — Plainview *(G-13611)*
American Casting and Mfg Corp G 516 349-7010 — Plainview *(G-13612)*
Cast-All Corporation E 516 741-4025 — Mineola *(G-8536)*
Cast-All Corporation E 516 741-4025 — Mineola *(G-8535)*
Crown Die Casting Corp E 914 667-5400 — Mount Vernon *(G-8720)*
Crown Novelty Works Inc G 631 253-0949 — Melville *(G-8338)*
Greenfield Die Casting Corp E 516 623-9230 — Freeport *(G-5414)*
Mar-A-Thon Filters Inc G 631 957-4774 — Lindenhurst *(G-7492)*
▲ **Pinnacle Manufacturing Co Inc** E 585 343-5664 — Batavia *(G-646)*
Thomas Foundry LLC G 315 361-9048 — Oneida *(G-13190)*

3365 Aluminum Foundries

Airflex Industrial Inc E 631 752-1234 — Farmingdale *(G-4940)*
American Blade Mfg LLC F 607 432-4518 — Oneonta *(G-13193)*
American Blade Mfg LLC G 607 656-4204 — Greene *(G-5880)*
Amt Incorporated E 518 284-2910 — Sharon Springs *(G-15405)*
▼ **Armstrong Mold Corporation** E 315 437-1517 — East Syracuse *(G-4521)*
Armstrong Mold Corporation D 315 437-1517 — East Syracuse *(G-4522)*
◆ **August Thomsen Corp** E 516 676-7100 — Glen Cove *(G-5623)*
▼ **Auto-Mate Technologies LLC** F 631 727-8886 — Riverhead *(G-14149)*
Broetje Automation-Usa Inc C 716 204-8640 — Williamsville *(G-17264)*
Carter Precision Metals LLC G 516 333-1917 — Westbury *(G-17001)*
Consoldted Precision Pdts Corp B 315 687-0014 — Chittenango *(G-3660)*
Corbett Stves Pttern Works Inc E 585 546-7109 — Rochester *(G-14310)*
Crown Die Casting Corp E 914 667-5400 — Mount Vernon *(G-8720)*
E M T Manufacturing Inc F 516 333-1917 — East Meadow *(G-4442)*
East Pattern & Model Corp E 585 461-3240 — Fairport *(G-4861)*
Eastern Castings Co F 518 677-5610 — Cambridge *(G-3335)*
Eastern Strategic Materials E 212 332-1619 — New York *(G-10018)*
▲ **Hitachi Metals America Ltd** E 914 694-9200 — Purchase *(G-13975)*
J & J Bronze & Aluminum Cast E 718 383-2111 — Brooklyn *(G-2120)*
Massena Metals Inc F 315 769-3846 — Massena *(G-8229)*
Meloon Foundries LLC E 315 454-3231 — Syracuse *(G-16006)*
Micro Instrument Corp D 585 458-3150 — Rochester *(G-14528)*
◆ **Milward Alloys Inc** E 716 434-5536 — Lockport *(G-7631)*
Mpi Consulting Incorporated G 631 253-2377 — West Babylon *(G-16844)*
Pyrotek Incorporated D 607 756-3050 — Cortland *(G-4064)*
Smart USA Inc E 718 416-4400 — Glendale *(G-5679)*
Taylor Metalworks Inc C 716 662-3113 — Orchard Park *(G-13323)*
WGB Industries Inc F 716 693-5527 — Tonawanda *(G-16235)*

Employee Codes: A=Over 500 employees, B=251-500
C=101-250, D=51-100, E=20-50, F=10-19, G=5-9

2018 Harris
New York Manufacturers Directory

803

33 PRIMARY METAL INDUSTRIES

Wolff & Dungey Inc .... E 315 475-2105
  Syracuse *(G-16098)*

3366 Copper Foundries

American Blade Mfg LLC .... G 607 656-4204
  Greene *(G-5880)*
American Blade Mfg LLC .... F 607 432-4518
  Oneonta *(G-13193)*
Amt Incorporated .... E 518 284-2910
  Sharon Springs *(G-15405)*
Argos Inc .... E 845 528-0576
  Putnam Valley *(G-13989)*
Art Bedi-Makky Foundry Corp .... G 718 383-4191
  Brooklyn *(G-1634)*
David Fehlman .... G 315 455-8888
  Syracuse *(G-15942)*
Discover Casting Inc .... F 212 302-5060
  New York *(G-9936)*
▲ Eastern Frging Corp .... F 516 747-6640
  New Hyde Park *(G-8874)*
Excalbur Brnze Sculpture Fndry ...... E 718 366-3444
  Brooklyn *(G-1947)*
J & J Bronze & Aluminum Cast .... E 718 383-2111
  Brooklyn *(G-2120)*
Meloon Foundries LLC .... E 315 454-3231
  Syracuse *(G-16006)*
▲ Modern Art Foundry Inc .... E 718 728-2030
  Astoria *(G-448)*
Omega Wire Inc .... E 315 337-4300
  Rome *(G-14856)*
Omega Wire Inc .... D 315 689-7115
  Jordan *(G-7158)*
▲ Rodeo of NY Inc .... E 212 730-0744
  New York *(G-11923)*

3369 Nonferrous Foundries: Castings, NEC

Allstar Casting Corporation .... E 212 563-0909
  New York *(G-9142)*
Argos Inc .... E 845 528-0576
  Putnam Valley *(G-13989)*
Buffalo Metal Casting Co Inc .... E 716 874-6211
  Buffalo *(G-2877)*
▲ Cardona Industries USA Ltd .... G 516 466-5200
  Great Neck *(G-5813)*
Carrera Casting Corp .... C 212 382-3296
  New York *(G-9589)*
Cast-All Corporation .... E 516 741-4025
  Mineola *(G-8535)*
City Casting Corp .... G 212 938-0511
  New York *(G-9682)*
Controlled Castings Corp .... E 516 349-1718
  Plainview *(G-13621)*
▲ Cpp-Syracuse Inc .... E 315 687-0014
  Chittenango *(G-3662)*
Crown Die Casting Corp .... E 914 667-5400
  Mount Vernon *(G-8720)*
General Motors LLC .... B 315 764-2000
  Massena *(G-8226)*
Globalfoundries US Inc .... C 518 305-9013
  Malta *(G-8051)*
Globalfoundries US Inc .... F 408 462-3900
  Ballston Spa *(G-595)*
Greenfield Die Casting Corp .... E 516 623-9230
  Freeport *(G-5414)*
J & J Bronze & Aluminum Cast .... E 718 383-2111
  Brooklyn *(G-2120)*
▼ Jamestown Bronze Works Inc .... G 716 665-2302
  Jamestown *(G-7039)*
K & H Precision Products Inc .... E 585 624-4894
  Honeoye Falls *(G-6560)*
Karbra Company .... C 212 736-9300
  New York *(G-10846)*
Kelly Foundry & Machine Co .... E 315 732-8313
  Utica *(G-16370)*
Lamothermic Corp .... D 845 278-6118
  Brewster *(G-1219)*
▲ Medi-Ray Inc .... D 877 898-3003
  Tuckahoe *(G-16295)*
Miller Technology Inc .... G 631 694-2224
  Farmingdale *(G-5065)*
◆ Plattco Corporation .... E 518 563-4640
  Plattsburgh *(G-13715)*
▲ Polich Tallix Inc .... D 845 567-9464
  Walden *(G-16554)*
Quality Castings Inc .... E 732 409-3203
  Long Island City *(G-7883)*
Summit Aerospace Inc .... G 718 433-1326
  Long Island City *(G-7922)*
Wemco Casting LLC .... D 631 563-8050
  Bohemia *(G-1153)*

▲ Zierick Manufacturing Corp .... D 800 882-8020
  Mount Kisco *(G-8690)*

3398 Metal Heat Treating

A1 International Heat Treating .... G 718 863-5552
  Bronx *(G-1257)*
Aterian Investment Partners LP ..... E 212 547-2806
  New York *(G-9299)*
B & W Heat Treating Company ...... E 716 876-8184
  Tonawanda *(G-16164)*
Bodycote Syracuse Heat Treatin .... E 315 451-0000
  Syracuse *(G-15891)*
Bodycote Thermal Proc Inc .... E 585 436-7876
  Rochester *(G-14258)*
Bsv Metal Finishers Inc .... E 585 349-7072
  Spencerport *(G-15591)*
Buffalo Armory LLC .... E 716 935-6346
  Buffalo *(G-2870)*
Burke Frging Heat Treating Inc ...... E 585 235-6060
  Rochester *(G-14268)*
Burton Industries Inc .... E 631 643-6660
  West Babylon *(G-16803)*
Captech Industries LLC .... D 347 374-1182
  Rome *(G-14836)*
Cpp - Steel Treaters .... E 315 736-3081
  Oriskany *(G-13331)*
Elmira Heat Treating Inc .... E 607 734-1577
  Elmira *(G-4695)*
Expedient Heat Treating Corp .... E 716 433-1177
  North Tonawanda *(G-12988)*
◆ Gibraltar Industries Inc .... D 716 826-6500
  Buffalo *(G-2989)*
▲ Graywood Companies Inc .... E 585 254-7000
  Rochester *(G-14433)*
Great Lakes Metal Treating .... F 716 694-1240
  Tonawanda *(G-16184)*
Hercules Heat Treating Corp .... E 718 625-1266
  Brooklyn *(G-2073)*
Hi-Temp Brazing Inc .... E 631 491-4917
  Deer Park *(G-4170)*
International Ord Tech Inc .... D 716 664-1100
  Jamestown *(G-7036)*
Jasco Heat Treating Inc .... E 585 388-0071
  Fairport *(G-4865)*
Metal Improvement Company LLC . D 607 533-7000
  Lansing *(G-7374)*
Milgo Industrial Inc .... D 718 388-6476
  Brooklyn *(G-2317)*
Milgo Industrial Inc .... E 718 387-0406
  Brooklyn *(G-2318)*
Modern Heat Trting Forging Inc ..... F 716 884-2176
  Buffalo *(G-3093)*
Parfuse Corp .... E 516 997-1795
  Westbury *(G-17046)*
Rochester Steel Treating Works ..... F 585 546-3348
  Rochester *(G-14673)*
Rough Brothers Holding Co .... G 716 826-6500
  Buffalo *(G-3196)*

3399 Primary Metal Prdts, NEC

Advantech Industries Inc .... C 585 247-0701
  Rochester *(G-14196)*
Ames Advanced Materials Corp ..... D 518 792-5808
  South Glens Falls *(G-15545)*
Ames Goldsmith Corp .... F 518 792-7435
  Glens Falls *(G-5685)*
Bridge Components Inc .... G 716 731-1184
  Sanborn *(G-15140)*
◆ Buffalo Tungsten Inc .... F 716 759-6353
  Depew *(G-4276)*
Cintube Ltd .... F 518 324-3333
  Plattsburgh *(G-13687)*
▲ Cws Powder Coatings Company LP G ... 845 398-2911
  Blauvelt *(G-964)*
▲ Handy & Harman .... E 914 461-1300
  White Plains *(G-17145)*
Hje Company Inc .... G 518 792-8733
  Queensbury *(G-14012)*
▼ HK Metal Trading Ltd .... G 212 868-3333
  New York *(G-10532)*
▲ Imerys Steelcasting Usa Inc ...... D 716 278-1634
  Niagara Falls *(G-12853)*
◆ John Hassall LLC .... E 516 334-6200
  Westbury *(G-17025)*
New England Reclamation Inc .... F 914 949-2000
  White Plains *(G-17168)*
Oerlikon Metco (us) Inc .... G 716 270-2228
  Amherst *(G-256)*
Pmb Precision Products Inc .... E 631 491-6753
  North Babylon *(G-12919)*

Reed Systems Ltd .... F 845 647-3660
  Ellenville *(G-4651)*
▼ Rembar Company LLC .... E 914 693-2620
  Dobbs Ferry *(G-4326)*
Specialty Fabricators .... F 631 256-6982
  Oakdale *(G-13080)*
Tam Ceramics Group of Ny LLC ... D 716 278-9400
  Niagara Falls *(G-12897)*
◆ Universal Metals Inc .... G 516 829-0896
  Great Neck *(G-5866)*
Ys Metal .... G 518 512-5275
  Albany *(G-153)*

34 FABRICATED METAL PRODUCTS, EXCEPT MACHINERY AND TRANSPORTATION EQUIPMENT

3411 Metal Cans

Anheuser-Busch Companies LLC .. G 718 589-2610
  Bronx *(G-1275)*
Ardagh Metal Packaging USA Inc . C 607 584-3300
  Conklin *(G-3889)*
Ball Metal Beverage Cont Corp ..... C 845 692-3800
  Middletown *(G-8461)*
Ball Metal Beverage Cont Corp ..... C 518 587-6030
  Saratoga Springs *(G-15172)*
Brakewell Stl Fabricators Inc .... E 845 469-9131
  Chester *(G-3628)*
Cmc-Kuhnke Inc .... F 518 694-3310
  Albany *(G-65)*
Erie Engineered Products Inc .... E 716 206-0204
  Lancaster *(G-7338)*
Hornet Group Inc .... D 845 858-6400
  Port Jervis *(G-13808)*
J C Industries Inc .... E 631 420-1920
  West Babylon *(G-16826)*
Marley Spoon Inc .... C 646 934-6970
  New York *(G-11186)*
Metal Container Corporation .... C 845 567-1500
  New Windsor *(G-8989)*
◆ Reynolds Metals Company LLC . G 212 518-5400
  New York *(G-11882)*
Seneca Foods Corporation .... D 315 926-0531
  Marion *(G-8130)*
Silgan Containers Mfg Corp .... C 315 946-4826
  Lyons *(G-8002)*
Tio Foods LLC .... F 305 672-6645
  New York *(G-12373)*

3412 Metal Barrels, Drums, Kegs & Pails

Abbot & Abbot Box Corp .... F 888 930-5972
  Long Island City *(G-7678)*
Erie Engineered Products Inc .... E 716 206-0204
  Lancaster *(G-7338)*
Hornet Group Inc .... D 845 858-6400
  Port Jervis *(G-13808)*
▲ Medi-Ray Inc .... D 877 898-3003
  Tuckahoe *(G-16295)*
Mobile Mini Inc .... F 315 732-4555
  Utica *(G-16373)*
Westrock - Southern Cont LLC ..... C 315 487-6111
  Camillus *(G-3355)*
Westrock CP LLC .... C 716 694-1000
  North Tonawanda *(G-13023)*

3421 Cutlery

Advanced Machine Design Co Inc . E 716 826-2000
  Buffalo *(G-2817)*
Art of Shaving - Fl LLC .... G 212 823-9410
  New York *(G-9261)*
BSD Aluminum Foil LLC .... E 347 689-3875
  Brooklyn *(G-1737)*
▲ Cutco Cutlery Corporation .... B 716 372-3111
  Olean *(G-13161)*
Gibar Inc .... C 315 452-5656
  Cicero *(G-3675)*
▲ Great American Tool Co Inc ...... G 716 646-5700
  Hamburg *(G-5950)*
HFC Prestige Intl US LLC .... A 212 389-7800
  New York *(G-10514)*
Inquiring Minds Inc .... F 845 246-5775
  Saugerties *(G-15214)*
John A Eberly Inc .... G 315 449-3034
  Syracuse *(G-15986)*
▲ Klein Cutlery LLC .... D 585 928-2500
  Bolivar *(G-1156)*
▲ Korin Japanese Trading Corp ... E 212 587-7021
  New York *(G-10916)*

34 FABRICATED METAL PRODUCTS, EXCEPT MACHINERY AND TRANSPORTATION EQUIPMENT

◆ Lifetime Brands Inc .... B 516 683-6000
   Garden City *(G-5526)*
Mpdraw LLC .... E 212 228-8383
   New York *(G-11337)*
Niabraze LLC .... F 716 447-1082
   Tonawanda *(G-16203)*
▲ Novelty Crystal Corp .... E 718 458-6700
   Long Island City *(G-7858)*
Oneida International Inc .... G 315 361-3000
   Oneida *(G-13182)*
Oneida Silversmiths Inc .... G 315 361-3000
   Oneida *(G-13186)*
▲ Ontario Knife Company .... D 716 676-5527
   Franklinville *(G-5380)*
Palladia Inc .... G 212 206-3669
   New York *(G-11571)*
Ratan Ronkonkoma .... G 631 588-6800
   Ronkonkoma *(G-15001)*
▲ Revlon Consumer Products Corp .. B 212 527-4000
   New York *(G-11879)*
▲ Schilling Forge Inc .... E 315 454-4421
   Syracuse *(G-16055)*
Schrader Meat Market .... F 607 869-6328
   Romulus *(G-14870)*
Servotronics Inc .... C 716 655-5990
   Elma *(G-4668)*
Sherrill Manufacturing Inc .... C 315 280-0727
   Sherrill *(G-15430)*
Starfire Swords Ltd Inc .... E 607 589-7244
   Spencer *(G-15588)*
▲ Treyco Products Corp .... G 716 693-6525
   Tonawanda *(G-16229)*
▲ Utica Cutlery Company .... D 315 733-4663
   Utica *(G-16387)*
Warren Cutlery Corp .... F 845 876-3444
   Rhinebeck *(G-14072)*
Woods Knife Corporation .... E 516 798-4972
   Massapequa *(G-8217)*

3423 Hand & Edge Tools

Allway Tools Inc .... D 718 792-3636
   Bronx *(G-1270)*
Ames Companies Inc .... E 607 739-4544
   Pine Valley *(G-13583)*
Ames Companies Inc .... D 607 369-9595
   Unadilla *(G-16310)*
Best Way Tools By Anderson Inc ... G 631 586-4702
   Deer Park *(G-4130)*
Boucheron Joaillerie USA Inc .... E 212 715-7330
   New York *(G-9494)*
Circo File Corp .... G 516 922-1848
   Oyster Bay *(G-13393)*
Classic Tool Design Inc .... E 845 562-8700
   New Windsor *(G-8981)*
Clopay Ames True Tmper Hldng ..... F 516 938-5544
   Jericho *(G-7096)*
Coastel Cable Tools Inc .... G 315 471-5361
   Syracuse *(G-15918)*
▲ Dead Ringer LLC .... G 585 355-4685
   Rochester *(G-14324)*
▲ Design Source By Lg Inc .... E 212 274-0022
   New York *(G-9908)*
▲ Dresser-Argus Inc .... G 718 643-1540
   Brooklyn *(G-1882)*
Edward C Lyons Company Inc .... G 718 515-5361
   Bronx *(G-1327)*
Edward C Muller Corp .... F 718 881-7270
   Bronx *(G-1328)*
Empire Devleopment .... G 716 789-2097
   Mayville *(G-8246)*
Gei International Inc .... F 315 463-9261
   East Syracuse *(G-4546)*
Huron TI Cutter Grinding Inc .... E 631 420-7000
   Farmingdale *(G-5015)*
▲ Hydramec Inc .... E 585 593-5190
   Scio *(G-15342)*
◆ Ivy Classic Industries Inc .... E 914 632-8200
   New Rochelle *(G-8958)*
▲ Lancaster Knives Inc .... E 716 683-5050
   Lancaster *(G-7347)*
Metro City Group Inc .... G 516 781-2500
   Bellmore *(G-814)*
Nyc District Council Ubcja .... G 212 366-7500
   New York *(G-11493)*
Robinson Tools LLC .... G 585 586-5432
   Penfield *(G-13526)*
Royal Molds Inc .... F 718 382-7686
   Brooklyn *(G-2532)*
▲ Schilling Forge Inc .... E 315 454-4421
   Syracuse *(G-16055)*

▲ Snyder Manufacturing Inc .... E 716 945-0354
   Salamanca *(G-15134)*
◆ Swimline International Corp ...... C 631 254-2155
   Edgewood *(G-4627)*
The Swatch Group U S Inc .... G 212 297-9192
   New York *(G-12331)*
▲ U S Air Tool Co Inc .... F 631 471-3300
   Ronkonkoma *(G-15017)*
Wall Tool & Tape Corp .... E 718 641-6813
   Ozone Park *(G-13412)*
Winters Railroad Service Inc .... G 716 337-2668
   North Collins *(G-12948)*
Woods Knife Corporation .... E 516 798-4972
   Massapequa *(G-8217)*
York Industries Inc .... E 516 746-3736
   Garden City Park *(G-5559)*

3425 Hand Saws & Saw Blades

Allway Tools Inc .... D 718 792-3636
   Bronx *(G-1270)*
◆ Amana Tool Corp .... D 631 752-1300
   Farmingdale *(G-4947)*
▲ Diamond Saw Works Inc .... E 716 496-7417
   Chaffee *(G-3560)*
Dinosaw Inc .... E 518 828-9942
   Hudson *(G-6642)*
Niabraze LLC .... F 716 447-1082
   Tonawanda *(G-16203)*
Quality Saw & Knife Inc .... F 631 491-4747
   West Babylon *(G-16850)*
▼ Suffolk McHy & Pwr Tl Corp ...... G 631 289-7153
   Patchogue *(G-13460)*

3429 Hardware, NEC

A & L Doors & Hardware LLC .... F 718 585-8400
   Bronx *(G-1252)*
Advantage Wholesale Supply LLC .. D 718 284-5346
   Brooklyn *(G-1566)*
American Casting and Mfg Corp .... G 516 349-7010
   Plainview *(G-13612)*
Amertac Holdings Inc .... G 610 336-1330
   Monsey *(G-8602)*
Barry Industries Inc .... E 212 242-5200
   New York *(G-9377)*
Bfg Marine Inc .... F 631 586-5500
   Bay Shore *(G-674)*
Boa Security Technologies Corp .... E 516 576-0295
   Huntington *(G-6690)*
Boehm Surgical Instrument .... F 585 436-6584
   Rochester *(G-14259)*
▲ Cant Live Without It LLC .... D 844 517-9355
   New York *(G-9569)*
Cast-All Corporation .... E 516 741-4025
   Mineola *(G-8535)*
▲ City Store Gates Mfg Corp .... E 718 939-9700
   College Point *(G-3806)*
▲ Classic Brass Inc .... D 716 763-1400
   Lakewood *(G-7312)*
▲ Crest Lock Co Inc .... E 718 345-9898
   Brooklyn *(G-1817)*
D Best Service Co Inc .... G 718 972-6133
   Brooklyn *(G-1829)*
Daniel Demarco and Assoc Inc ...... G 631 598-7000
   Amityville *(G-283)*
▼ Darman Manufacturing Coinc .... F 315 724-9632
   Utica *(G-16344)*
▲ Decorative Hardeware .... G 914 238-5251
   Chappaqua *(G-3579)*
▲ Delta Lock Company LLC .... F 631 238-7035
   Bohemia *(G-1051)*
Designatronics Incorporated .... B 516 328-3300
   Hicksville *(G-6367)*
▲ Dico Products Corporation .... F 315 797-0470
   Utica *(G-16346)*
Dortronics Systems Inc .... E 631 725-0505
   Sag Harbor *(G-15105)*
Dover Marine Mfg & Sup Co Inc .... G 631 667-4300
   Deer Park *(G-4153)*
▲ Dreamseats LLC .... F 631 656-1066
   Commack *(G-3856)*
Eazy Locks LLC .... G 718 327-7770
   Far Rockaway *(G-4927)*
▲ ER Butler & Co Inc .... E 212 925-3565
   New York *(G-10107)*
Excelco Developments Inc .... E 716 934-2651
   Silver Creek *(G-15470)*
Fastener Dimensions Inc .... F 718 847-6321
   Ozone Park *(G-13404)*
Fuccillo Ford Nelliston Inc .... G 518 993-5555
   Nelliston *(G-8820)*

G Marks Hdwr Liquidating Corp ..... D 631 225-5400
   Amityville *(G-287)*
▲ H A Guden Company Inc .... E 631 737-2900
   Ronkonkoma *(G-14937)*
Industrial Electronic Hardware .... D 718 492-4440
   Brooklyn *(G-2101)*
Ingham Industries Inc .... G 631 242-2493
   Holbrook *(G-6480)*
International Key Supply LLC .... F 631 983-6096
   Farmingdale *(G-5020)*
▲ ITR Industries Inc .... E 914 964-7063
   Yonkers *(G-17473)*
◆ Jaquith Industries Inc .... E 315 478-5700
   Syracuse *(G-15985)*
Kelley Bros Hardware Corp .... G 315 852-3302
   De Ruyter *(G-4106)*
▲ Kenstan Lock & Hardware Co Inc .. E 631 423-1977
   Plainview *(G-13642)*
▲ Key High Vacuum Products Inc .. C 516 584-5959
   Nesconset *(G-8823)*
▲ Kilian Manufacturing Corp .... D 315 432-0700
   Syracuse *(G-15993)*
Kyntec Corporation .... G 716 810-6956
   Buffalo *(G-3056)*
▲ Legendary Auto Interiors Ltd .... E 315 331-1212
   Newark *(G-12754)*
▲ Liberty Brass Turning Co Inc .... E 718 784-2911
   Westbury *(G-17032)*
Lif Industries Inc .... F 718 767-8800
   Whitestone *(G-17240)*
Lightron Corporation .... G 516 938-5544
   Jericho *(G-7107)*
Magellan Aerospace Processing .... G 631 694-1818
   West Babylon *(G-16838)*
▲ Magnetic Aids Inc .... G 845 863-1400
   Newburgh *(G-12787)*
Morgik Metal Designs .... F 212 463-0304
   New York *(G-11330)*
Mpi Consulting Incorporated .... F 631 253-2377
   West Babylon *(G-16843)*
◆ Nanz Custom Hardware Inc ...... E 212 367-7000
   New York *(G-11364)*
Nanz Custom Hardware Inc .... E 212 367-7000
   Deer Park *(G-4200)*
◆ Napco Security Tech Inc .... A 631 842-9400
   Amityville *(G-313)*
▲ Nielsen Hardware Corporation .. E 607 821-1475
   Binghamton *(G-936)*
◆ Northknight Logistics Inc .... F 716 283-3090
   Niagara Falls *(G-12871)*
▲ Orbital Holdings Inc .... E 951 360-7100
   Buffalo *(G-3126)*
▲ P & F Industries Inc .... E 631 694-9800
   Melville *(G-8375)*
◆ P E Guerin .... E 212 243-5270
   New York *(G-11561)*
Pk30 System LLC .... F 212 473-8050
   Stone Ridge *(G-15786)*
▲ Progressive Hardware Co Inc ... G 631 445-1826
   East Northport *(G-4462)*
Real Design Inc .... F 315 429-3071
   Dolgeville *(G-4332)*
▲ RKI Building Spc Co Inc .... G 718 728-7788
   College Point *(G-3830)*
Rollson Inc .... G 631 423-9578
   Huntington *(G-6717)*
◆ Rosco Inc .... C 718 526-2601
   Jamaica *(G-6985)*
Safe Skies LLC .... G 888 632-5027
   New York *(G-11970)*
▼ Samscreen Inc .... F 607 722-3979
   Conklin *(G-3901)*
Southco Inc .... B 585 624-2545
   Honeoye Falls *(G-6564)*
Syraco Products Inc .... F 315 476-5306
   Syracuse *(G-16072)*
▼ Tattersall Industries LLC .... E 518 381-4270
   Schenectady *(G-15327)*
▲ Taylor Made Group LLC .... E 518 725-0681
   Gloversville *(G-5739)*
Tools & Stamping Corp .... G 718 392-4040
   Brooklyn *(G-2683)*
Trico Manufacturing Corp .... G 718 349-6565
   Brooklyn *(G-2698)*
Turbine Engine Comp Utica .... A 315 768-8070
   Whitesboro *(G-17225)*
▲ United Metal Industries Inc ...... G 516 354-6800
   New Hyde Park *(G-8913)*
▲ Water Street Brass Corporation .. E 716 763-0059
   Lakewood *(G-7320)*

▲ **Weber-Knapp Company**...C... 716 484-9135
Jamestown *(G-7075)*
William H Jackson Company...G... 718 784-4482
Long Island City *(G-7952)*
▲ **Wolo Mfg Corp**...E... 631 242-0333
Deer Park *(G-4253)*
Yaloz Mould & Die Co Inc...E... 718 389-1131
Brooklyn *(G-2786)*
York Industries Inc...E... 516 746-3736
Garden City Park *(G-5559)*

3431 Enameled Iron & Metal Sanitary Ware

◆ **Advance Tabco Inc**...D... 631 242-8270
Edgewood *(G-4605)*
CNA Specialties Inc...G... 631 567-7929
Sayville *(G-15235)*
▲ **Independent Home Products LLC**...E... 718 541-1256
West Hempstead *(G-16886)*
▲ **ITR Industries Inc**...E... 914 964-7063
Yonkers *(G-17473)*
Kenbenco Inc...F... 845 246-3066
Saugerties *(G-15215)*
Ketcham Medicine Cabinets...E... 631 615-6151
Ronkonkoma *(G-14950)*
▲ **Kraus USA Inc**...F... 800 775-0703
Port Washington *(G-13856)*
▲ **Metpar Corp**...D... 516 333-2600
Westbury *(G-17038)*
Porcelain Refinishing Corp...F... 516 352-4841
Flushing *(G-5290)*
▲ **Sola Home Expo Inc**...G... 718 646-3383
Brooklyn *(G-2605)*
Stainless Metals Inc...F... 718 784-1454
Woodside *(G-17372)*
Unico Inc...F... 845 562-9255
Newburgh *(G-12806)*
Vanity Fair Bathmart Inc...F... 718 584-6700
Bronx *(G-1487)*
▲ **Watermark Designs Holdings Ltd**...D... 718 257-2800
Brooklyn *(G-2761)*

3432 Plumbing Fixture Fittings & Trim, Brass

A B S Brass Products Inc...F... 718 497-2115
Brooklyn *(G-1531)*
Acme Parts Inc...E... 718 649-1750
Brooklyn *(G-1555)*
Artys Sprnklr Svc Instllation...F... 516 538-4371
East Meadow *(G-4438)*
Corona Plumbing & Htg Sup Inc...G... 718 424-4133
Corona *(G-4016)*
Coronet Parts Mfg Co Inc...E... 718 649-1750
Brooklyn *(G-1804)*
Coronet Parts Mfg Co Inc...E... 718 649-1750
Brooklyn *(G-1805)*
▲ **ER Butler & Co Inc**...E... 212 925-3565
New York *(G-10107)*
Ferguson...G... 718 937-9500
Maspeth *(G-8170)*
G Sicuranza Ltd...G... 516 759-0259
Glen Cove *(G-5628)*
Giagni Enterprises LLC...G... 914 699-6500
Mount Vernon *(G-8729)*
Giagni International Corp...G... 914 699-6500
Mount Vernon *(G-8730)*
Hanco Metal Products Inc...F... 212 787-5992
Brooklyn *(G-2065)*
Holyoke Fittings Inc...F... 718 649-0710
Brooklyn *(G-2080)*
▲ **I W Industries Inc**...C... 631 293-9494
Melville *(G-8359)*
▲ **Jacknob International Ltd**...D... 631 546-6560
Hauppauge *(G-6126)*
L A S Replacement Parts Inc...F... 718 583-4700
Bronx *(G-1380)*
▲ **Liberty Brass Turning Co Inc**...E... 718 784-2911
Westbury *(G-17032)*
Malyn Industrial Ceramics Inc...G... 716 741-1510
Clarence Center *(G-3705)*
Mark Posner...G... 718 258-6241
Brooklyn *(G-2273)*
Martin Brass Works Inc...G... 718 523-3146
Jamaica *(G-6964)*
◆ **P E Guerin**...D... 212 243-5270
New York *(G-11561)*
Roccera LLC...F... 585 426-0887
Rochester *(G-14654)*
Toto USA Inc...G... 917 237-0665
New York *(G-12401)*
Toto USA Inc...G... 770 282-8686
New York *(G-12402)*
▲ **Watermark Designs Holdings Ltd**...D... 718 257-2800
Brooklyn *(G-2761)*

3433 Heating Eqpt

A Nuclimate Qulty Systems Inc...F... 315 431-0226
Syracuse *(G-15865)*
American Comfort Direct LLC...E... 201 364-8309
New York *(G-9165)*
Atlantis Energy Systems Inc...G... 916 438-2930
Poughkeepsie *(G-13908)*
Atlantis Solar Inc...F... 916 226-9183
Potsdam *(G-13895)*
Best Boilers Inc...F... 718 372-4210
Brooklyn *(G-1685)*
Biotech Energy Inc...G... 800 340-1387
Plattsburgh *(G-13682)*
Carrier Corporation...B... 315 432-6000
Syracuse *(G-15907)*
▲ **Chentronics Corporation**...E... 607 334-5531
Norwich *(G-13041)*
▲ **CIDC Corp**...F... 718 342-5820
Brooklyn *(G-1779)*
◆ **Dyson-Kissner-Moran Corp**...E... 212 661-4600
Poughkeepsie *(G-13915)*
Economy Pump & Motor Repair...G... 718 433-2600
Astoria *(G-436)*
◆ **ECR International Inc**...D... 315 797-1310
Utica *(G-16351)*
ECR International Inc...C... 716 366-5500
Dunkirk *(G-4365)*
▲ **Embassy Industries Inc**...C... 631 435-0209
Hauppauge *(G-6095)*
Empire Industrial Burner Svc...F... 631 242-4619
Deer Park *(G-4161)*
Fedders Islandaire Inc...D... 631 471-2900
East Setauket *(G-4500)*
Fisonic Corp...G... 212 732-3777
Long Island City *(G-7772)*
▲ **Fisonic Corp**...F... 716 763-0295
New York *(G-10227)*
◆ **Flynn Burner Corporation**...E... 914 636-1320
New Rochelle *(G-8944)*
Frederick Cowan & Company Inc...F... 631 369-0360
Riverhead *(G-14155)*
▲ **Fulton Heating Solutions Inc**...D... 315 298-5121
Pulaski *(G-13966)*
▼ **Fulton Volcanic Inc**...D... 315 298-5121
Pulaski *(G-13967)*
▲ **Hawkencatskills LLC**...G... 518 966-8900
Greenville *(G-5903)*
I-Evolve Techonology Services...F... 801 566-5268
Amherst *(G-244)*
▲ **Integrated Solar Tech LLC**...G... 914 249-9364
Port Chester *(G-13776)*
▲ **Juniper Elbow Co Inc**...C... 718 326-2546
Middle Village *(G-8447)*
Jus-Sar Fuel Inc...G... 845 791-8900
Harris *(G-5997)*
Marathon Heater Co Inc...G... 607 657-8113
Richford *(G-14076)*
◆ **Mx Solar USA LLC**...C... 732 356-7300
New York *(G-11352)*
Nanopv Corporation...C... 609 851-3666
Liverpool *(G-7562)*
New Energy Systems Group...C... 917 573-0302
New York *(G-11406)*
▲ **North Pk Innovations Group Inc**...G... 716 699-2031
Ellicottville *(G-4657)*
O C P Inc...E... 516 679-2000
Farmingdale *(G-5079)*
▲ **Omega Heater Company Inc**...D... 631 588-8820
Ronkonkoma *(G-14984)*
▲ **Original Convector Specialist**...G... 718 342-5820
Brooklyn *(G-2406)*
▲ **Prism Solar Technologies Inc**...E... 845 883-4200
Highland *(G-6434)*
◆ **RE Hansen Industries Inc**...C... 631 471-2900
East Setauket *(G-4510)*
Real Goods Solar Inc...C... 845 708-0800
New City *(G-8837)*
▲ **Roberts-Gordon LLC**...D... 716 852-4400
Buffalo *(G-3188)*
Rockmills Steel Products Corp...F... 718 366-8300
Maspeth *(G-8199)*
▲ **Slant/Fin Corporation**...B... 516 484-2600
Greenvale *(G-5899)*
Solar Energy Systems LLC...F... 718 389-1545
Brooklyn *(G-2606)*
Unilux Advanced Mfg LLC...E... 518 344-7490
Schenectady *(G-15331)*
Vincent Genovese...G... 631 281-8170
Mastic Beach *(G-8237)*

3441 Fabricated Structural Steel

760 NI Holdings...E... 716 821-1391
Buffalo *(G-2805)*
▲ **A & T Iron Works Inc**...E... 914 632-8992
New Rochelle *(G-8928)*
◆ **A-Fab Initiatives Inc**...G... 716 877-5257
Buffalo *(G-2807)*
▲ **A/C Design & Fabrication Corp**...G... 718 227-8100
Staten Island *(G-15652)*
AAA Welding and Fabrication of...G... 585 254-2830
Rochester *(G-14177)*
Abalon Precision Mfg Corp...F... 914 665-7700
Mount Vernon *(G-8702)*
Abalon Precision Mfg Corp...F... 718 589-5682
Mount Vernon *(G-8703)*
▲ **Acadia Stairs**...G... 845 765-8600
Fishkill *(G-5187)*
Accucut Inc...G... 631 567-2868
West Sayville *(G-16962)*
Achilles Construction Co Inc...G... 718 389-4717
Mount Vernon *(G-8705)*
Ackroyd Metal Fabricators Inc...F... 518 434-1281
Menands *(G-8396)*
Adsco Manufacturing Corp...D... 716 827-5450
Buffalo *(G-2816)*
Advanced Thermal Systems Inc...E... 716 681-1800
Lancaster *(G-7322)*
Advantage Machining Inc...F... 716 731-6418
Niagara Falls *(G-12818)*
Aero-Data Metal Crafters Inc...C... 631 471-7733
Ronkonkoma *(G-14882)*
Airflex Corp...D... 631 752-1219
Farmingdale *(G-4939)*
Aldo Frustacci Iron Works Inc...F... 718 768-0707
Brooklyn *(G-1577)*
All-City Metal Inc...E... 718 937-3975
Maspeth *(G-8142)*
Alp Steel Corp...E... 716 854-3030
Buffalo *(G-2821)*
American Aerogel Corporation...E... 585 328-2140
Rochester *(G-14211)*
Apollo Steel Corporation...F... 716 283-8758
Niagara Falls *(G-12820)*
Asp Industries Inc...E... 585 254-9130
Rochester *(G-14235)*
Atlantis Equipment Corporation...F... 518 733-5910
Stephentown *(G-15778)*
B H M Metal Products Co...G... 845 292-5297
Kauneonga Lake *(G-7165)*
B P Nash Co Inc...F... 315 445-1310
East Syracuse *(G-4526)*
▲ **Barber Welding Inc**...E... 315 834-6645
Weedsport *(G-16772)*
Barker Steel LLC...E... 518 465-6221
Albany *(G-49)*
Barry Steel Fabrication Inc...E... 716 433-2144
Lockport *(G-7599)*
Bear Metal Works Inc...F... 716 824-4350
Buffalo *(G-2857)*
▲ **Bennett Manufacturing Co Inc**...C... 716 937-9161
Alden *(G-178)*
Bereza Iron Works Inc...F... 585 254-6311
Rochester *(G-14246)*
Blackstone Advanced Tech LLC...C... 716 665-5410
Jamestown *(G-7011)*
Bms Manufacturing Co Inc...E... 607 535-2426
Watkins Glen *(G-16718)*
Bob Murphy Inc...F... 607 729-3553
Vestal *(G-16464)*
Bombardier Transportation...D... 607 324-0216
Hornell *(G-6586)*
Bombardier Trnsp Holdings USA...D... 607 776-4791
Bath *(G-654)*
Bristol Metals Inc...F... 585 657-7665
Bloomfield *(G-976)*
Burnt Hills Fabricators Inc...F... 518 885-1115
Ballston Spa *(G-591)*
C & C Custom Metal Fabricators...G... 631 235-9646
Hauppauge *(G-6059)*
C & C Metal Fabrications Inc...F... 315 598-7607
Fulton *(G-5467)*
C & T Tool & Instrument Co...E... 718 429-1253
Woodside *(G-17338)*
Cameron Bridge Works LLC...E... 607 734-9456
Elmira *(G-4685)*
▲ **Cameron Mfg & Design Inc**...C... 607 739-3606
Horseheads *(G-6599)*

Carpenter Industries Inc ....F 315 463-4284
Syracuse *(G-15905)*
Castle Harvester Co Inc ....G....... 585 526-5884
Seneca Castle *(G-15381)*
CBM Fabrications Inc ....E 518 399-8023
Ballston Lake *(G-580)*
Chautauqua Machine Spc LLC ....F 716 782-3276
Ashville *(G-424)*
Christian Fabrication LLC ....G....... 315 822-0135
West Winfield *(G-16986)*
Cives Corporation ....C 315 287-2200
Gouverneur *(G-5758)*
Cobbe Industries Inc ....E 716 287-2661
Gerry *(G-5604)*
Cobra Operating Industries LLC ....G....... 607 639-1700
Afton *(G-9)*
Coco Architectureal Grilles ....G....... 631 482-9449
Farmingdale *(G-4970)*
Columbia Metal Fabricators ....G....... 631 476-7527
Port Jeff STA *(G-13788)*
Computerized Metal Bending Ser ....F....... 631 249-1177
West Babylon *(G-16810)*
Cottonwood Metals Inc ....E 646 807-8674
Bohemia *(G-1036)*
County Fabricators ....F 914 741-0219
Pleasantville *(G-13745)*
Cyncal Steel Fabricators Inc ....F 631 254-5600
Bay Shore *(G-687)*
D N Gannon Fabricating Inc ....G....... 315 463-7466
Syracuse *(G-15939)*
Dennies Manufacturing Inc ....E 585 393-4646
Canandaigua *(G-3371)*
Diversified Manufacturing Inc ....F 716 681-7670
Lancaster *(G-7336)*
Donald Stefan ....G 716 492-1110
Chaffee *(G-3561)*
▲ **Dynasty Metal Works Inc** ....G....... 631 284-3719
Riverhead *(G-14153)*
E B Atlas Steel Corp ....F 716 876-0900
Buffalo *(G-2937)*
Eastern Manufacturing Inc ....F 716 741-4572
Clarence Center *(G-3700)*
Eastern Welding Inc ....G....... 631 727-0306
Riverhead *(G-14154)*
Elevator Accessories Mfg ....F 914 739-7004
Peekskill *(G-13501)*
Elmira Metal Works Inc ....G....... 607 734-9813
Elmira *(G-4696)*
Empire Industrial Systems Corp ....F 631 242-4619
Bay Shore *(G-697)*
Empire Metal Fabricators Inc ....G....... 585 288-2140
Rochester *(G-14367)*
Eps Iron Works Inc ....G....... 516 294-5840
Mineola *(G-8542)*
Erie Engineered Products Inc ....E 716 206-0204
Lancaster *(G-7338)*
Everfab Inc ....D....... 716 655-1550
East Aurora *(G-4395)*
Excel Industries Inc ....E 716 542-5468
Clarence *(G-3689)*
Farmingdale Iron Works Inc ....G....... 631 249-5995
Farmingdale *(G-5000)*
Feinstein Iron Works Inc ....E 516 997-8300
Westbury *(G-17012)*
Fence Plaza Corp ....G....... 718 469-2200
Brooklyn *(G-1970)*
Five Corners Repair Inc ....F 585 322-7369
Bliss *(G-974)*
▼ **Flagpoles Incorporated** ....D....... 631 751-5500
East Setauket *(G-4501)*
▲ **Fort Miller Group Inc** ....B 518 695-5000
Greenwich *(G-5906)*
Frazier Industrial Company ....D....... 315 539-9256
Waterloo *(G-16648)*
Fred A Nudd Corporation ....E 315 524-2531
Ontario *(G-13223)*
Gasport Welding & Fabg Inc ....F 716 772-7205
Gasport *(G-5572)*
George Industries LLC ....C 607 748-3371
Endicott *(G-4818)*
◆ **Gibraltar Industries Inc** ....D....... 716 826-6500
Buffalo *(G-2989)*
Glenridge Fabricators Inc ....F 718 456-2297
Glendale *(G-5670)*
Hallock Fabricating Corp ....G....... 631 727-2441
Riverhead *(G-14156)*
Hansen Steel ....E 585 398-2020
Farmington *(G-5161)*
Homer Iron Works LLC ....G....... 607 749-3963
Homer *(G-6547)*
Hudson Steel Fabricators ....E 585 454-3923
Rochester *(G-14460)*
Industrial Fabricating Corp ....E 315 437-3353
East Syracuse *(G-4553)*
▲ **Industrial Support Inc** ....D....... 716 662-2954
Buffalo *(G-3024)*
◆ **Inscape (new York) Inc** ....D....... 716 665-6210
Falconer *(G-4909)*
International Metals Trdg LLC ....G....... 866 923-0182
Melville *(G-8361)*
Irony Limited Inc ....G....... 631 329-4065
East Hampton *(G-4431)*
Irv Schroder & Sons Inc ....E 518 828-0194
Stottville *(G-15803)*
Irving Woodlands LLC ....E 607 723-4862
Conklin *(G-3895)*
J F M Sheet Metal Inc ....G....... 631 737-8494
Ronkonkoma *(G-14944)*
J M Haley Corp ....C 631 845-5200
Farmingdale *(G-5021)*
Jaab Precision Inc ....G....... 631 218-3725
Ronkonkoma *(G-14946)*
James Woerner Inc ....G....... 631 454-9330
Farmingdale *(G-5024)*
Jbs LLC ....E 518 346-0001
Scotia *(G-15350)*
Jentsch & Co Inc ....G 716 852-4111
Buffalo *(G-3033)*
Joy Edward Company ....E 315 474-3360
East Syracuse *(G-4561)*
Jpw Structural Contracting Inc ....E 315 432-1111
Syracuse *(G-15990)*
K & E Fabricating Company Inc ....F 716 829-1829
Buffalo *(G-3040)*
Kal Manufacturing Corporation ....E 585 265-4310
Webster *(G-16751)*
KDO Industries Inc ....G....... 631 608-4612
Amityville *(G-301)*
King Steel Iron Work Corp ....F 718 384-7500
Brooklyn *(G-2173)*
Kleinfelder John ....G....... 716 753-3163
Mayville *(G-8247)*
Knj Fabricators LLC ....F 347 234-6985
Bronx *(G-1378)*
Koenig Iron Works Inc ....E 718 433-0900
Long Island City *(G-7808)*
Kryten Iron Works Inc ....G....... 914 345-0990
Hawthorne *(G-6272)*
Kuno Steel Products Corp ....F 516 938-8500
Hicksville *(G-6389)*
Leading Edge Fabrication ....G....... 631 274-9797
Deer Park *(G-4188)*
Leray Homes Inc ....G....... 315 788-6087
Watertown *(G-16685)*
Lindenhurst Fabricators Inc ....G....... 631 226-3737
Lindenhurst *(G-7489)*
Linita Design & Mfg Corp ....E 716 566-7753
Lackawanna *(G-7270)*
▲ **M & L Steel & Ornamental Iron** ....F 718 816-8660
Staten Island *(G-15723)*
▲ **Mageba USA LLC** ....E 212 317-1991
New York *(G-11126)*
▲ **Major-IPC Inc** ....G....... 845 292-2200
Liberty *(G-7460)*
▲ **Marex Aquisition Corp** ....C 585 458-3940
Rochester *(G-14518)*
▲ **Marovato Industries Inc** ....F 718 389-0800
Brooklyn *(G-2277)*
◆ **Mason Industries Inc** ....B 631 348-0282
Hauppauge *(G-6152)*
Maspeth Steel Fabricators Inc ....G....... 718 361-9192
Long Island City *(G-7834)*
Maspeth Welding Inc ....E 718 497-5430
Maspeth *(G-8181)*
Metal Concepts ....G....... 845 592-1863
Beacon *(G-784)*
Metal Crafts Inc ....G....... 718 443-3333
Brooklyn *(G-2308)*
Metal Fab LLC ....G....... 607 775-3200
Binghamton *(G-932)*
Metal Works of NY Inc ....G....... 718 525-9440
Jamaica *(G-6966)*
Miller Metal Fabricating Inc ....G....... 585 359-3400
Rochester *(G-14534)*
Miscellnous Ir Fabricators Inc ....E 518 355-1822
Schenectady *(G-15306)*
Mobile Mini Inc ....F 315 732-4555
Utica *(G-16373)*
▼ **Monarch Metal Fabrication Inc** ....G....... 631 563-8967
Bohemia *(G-1100)*
Mount Vernon Iron Works Inc ....G....... 914 668-7064
Mount Vernon *(G-8754)*
Nathan Steel Corp ....F 315 797-1335
Utica *(G-16375)*
Nb Elctrcal Enclsures Mfrs Inc ....G....... 718 272-8792
Brooklyn *(G-2362)*
Nci Group Inc ....D....... 315 339-1245
Rome *(G-14852)*
New Vision Industries Inc ....F 607 687-7700
Endicott *(G-4827)*
New York Manufactured Products ....F 585 254-9353
Rochester *(G-14552)*
North E Rggers Erectors NY Inc ....E 518 842-6377
Amsterdam *(G-363)*
▲ **North Eastern Fabricators Inc** ....E 718 542-0450
New York *(G-11474)*
Northeast Fabricators LLC ....D....... 607 865-4031
Walton *(G-16570)*
Oehlers Wldg & Fabrication Inc ....F 716 821-1800
Buffalo *(G-3120)*
Orange County Ironworks LLC ....E 845 769-3000
Montgomery *(G-8636)*
▲ **Oriskany Mfg Tech LLC** ....E 315 732-4962
Yorkville *(G-17542)*
P K G Equipment Incorporated ....E 585 436-4650
Rochester *(G-14585)*
Patsy Strocchia & Sons Iron Wo ....F 516 625-8800
Albertson *(G-159)*
Pcx Aerostructures LLC ....E 631 249-7901
Ronkonkoma *(G-14991)*
Pcx Aerostructures LLC ....E 631 467-2632
Farmingdale *(G-5085)*
Peralta Metal Works Inc ....G....... 718 649-8661
Brooklyn *(G-2429)*
Perma Tech Inc ....E 716 854-0707
Buffalo *(G-3145)*
▲ **Pierce Industries LLC** ....E 585 458-0888
Rochester *(G-14603)*
Pirod Inc ....E 631 231-7660
Hauppauge *(G-6191)*
Port Authority of NY & NJ ....D....... 718 390-2534
Staten Island *(G-15744)*
Portfab LLC ....E 718 542-3600
Amityville *(G-322)*
Precision Metals Corp ....E 631 586-5032
Bay Shore *(G-723)*
Precision Polish LLC ....E 315 894-3792
Frankfort *(G-5366)*
Prime Materials Recovery Inc ....G....... 315 697-5251
Canastota *(G-3397)*
▲ **Productand Design Inc** ....F 718 858-2440
Brooklyn *(G-2467)*
R & J Sheet Metal Distrs Inc ....G....... 518 433-1525
Albany *(G-125)*
R&S Steel LLC ....E 315 281-0123
Rome *(G-14859)*
Raulli and Sons Inc ....D....... 315 479-6693
Syracuse *(G-16040)*
REO Welding Inc ....F 518 238-1022
Cohoes *(G-3780)*
▲ **Risa Management Corp** ....E 718 361-2606
Maspeth *(G-8197)*
Riverside Iron LLC ....F 315 535-4864
Gouverneur *(G-5762)*
RJ Precision LLC ....G....... 585 768-8030
Stafford *(G-15642)*
▲ **Robert E Derecktor Inc** ....D....... 914 698-0962
Mamaroneck *(G-8078)*
Romar Contracting Inc ....G....... 845 778-2737
Walden *(G-16555)*
Roth Design & Consulting Inc ....E 718 209-0193
Brooklyn *(G-2529)*
Rothe Welding Inc ....G....... 845 246-3051
Saugerties *(G-15222)*
Rough Brothers Holding Co ....G....... 716 826-6500
Buffalo *(G-3196)*
Rs Automation ....F 585 589-0199
Albion *(G-172)*
▲ **Rus Industries Inc** ....E 716 284-7828
Niagara Falls *(G-12887)*
Schenectady Steel Co Inc ....E 518 355-3220
Schenectady *(G-15317)*
Schneider Brothers Corporation ....E 315 458-8369
Syracuse *(G-16056)*
Schuler-Subra Inc ....G....... 716 893-3100
Buffalo *(G-3206)*
▲ **Seibel Modern Mfg & Wldg Corp** ....D....... 716 683-1536
Lancaster *(G-7367)*
Sentry Metal Blast Inc ....E 716 285-5241
Lockport *(G-7645)*

SIC

Employee Codes: A=Over 500 employees, B=251-500
C=101-250, D=51-100, E=20-50, F=10-19, G=5-9
2018 Harris
New York Manufacturers Directory
807

34 FABRICATED METAL PRODUCTS, EXCEPT MACHINERY AND TRANSPORTATION EQUIPMENT SIC SECTION

Silverstone Shtmtl Fbrications..............G....... 718 422-0380
Brooklyn *(G-2586)*
Specialty Steel Fabg Corp......................F....... 718 893-6326
Bronx *(G-1459)*
Specialty Wldg & Fabg NY Inc...............D....... 315 426-1807
Syracuse *(G-16066)*
Standard Steel Fabricators....................F....... 518 765-4820
Voorheesville *(G-16540)*
Steel Tech SA LLC.................................G....... 845 786-3691
Thiells *(G-16137)*
▲ Stone Bridge Iron and Stl Inc............D....... 518 695-3752
Gansevoort *(G-5504)*
▼ Stone Well Bodies & Mch Inc............E....... 315 497-3512
Genoa *(G-5602)*
STS Steel Inc..D....... 518 370-2693
Schenectady *(G-15324)*
Supreme Steel Inc..................................F....... 631 884-1320
Lindenhurst *(G-7512)*
Team Fabrication Inc..............................G....... 716 655-4038
West Falls *(G-16877)*
Titan Steel Corp.....................................F....... 315 656-7046
Kirkville *(G-7256)*
Torino Indus Fabrication Inc..................G....... 631 509-1640
Bellport *(G-839)*
Triboro Iron Works Inc...........................G....... 718 361-9600
Long Island City *(G-7934)*
Triton Builders Inc.................................E....... 631 841-2534
Amityville *(G-332)*
Tropical Driftwood Originals.................G....... 516 623-0980
Roosevelt *(G-15033)*
Tymetal Corp...E....... 518 692-9930
Greenwich *(G-5915)*
Ulster Precision Inc...............................E....... 845 338-0995
Kingston *(G-7246)*
United Iron Inc.......................................E....... 914 667-5700
Mount Vernon *(G-8791)*
United Structure Solution Inc................F....... 347 227-7526
New York *(G-12486)*
Universal Metal Works LLC....................F....... 315 598-7607
Fulton *(G-5490)*
▲ Vance Metal Fabricators Inc.............D....... 315 789-5626
Geneva *(G-5600)*
Vulcan Iron Works Inc...........................G....... 631 395-6846
Manorville *(G-8114)*
Vulcraft of New York Inc........................C....... 607 529-9000
Chemung *(G-3622)*
Ward Steel Company Inc........................E....... 315 451-4566
Liverpool *(G-7582)*
▼ Watson Bowman Acme Corp...............D....... 716 691-8162
Amherst *(G-271)*
Welding Metallurgy Inc..........................E....... 631 253-0500
Hauppauge *(G-6256)*
Whitacre Engineering Company.............G....... 315 622-1075
Liverpool *(G-7584)*
Wilston Enterprises Inc..........................F....... 716 483-1411
Jamestown *(G-7076)*
Winters Railroad Service Inc..................G....... 716 337-2668
North Collins *(G-12948)*

3442 Metal Doors, Sash, Frames, Molding & Trim

A & L Doors & Hardware LLC................F....... 718 585-8400
Bronx *(G-1252)*
▲ A & S Window Associates Inc...........E....... 718 275-7900
Glendale *(G-5657)*
A G M Deco Inc......................................F....... 718 624-6200
Brooklyn *(G-1532)*
▲ A G M Deco Inc..................................F....... 718 624-6200
Brooklyn *(G-1533)*
Accurate Metal Weather Strip................G....... 914 668-6042
Mount Vernon *(G-8704)*
Ace Fire Door Corp.................................E....... 718 901-0001
Bronx *(G-1262)*
▲ Acme Architectural Pdts Inc.............D....... 718 384-7800
Brooklyn *(G-1554)*
Action Bullet Resistant...........................F....... 631 422-0888
West Islip *(G-16933)*
Advanced Door Solutions Inc.................G....... 631 773-6100
Holbrook *(G-6457)*
Air Tite Manufacturing Inc.....................C....... 516 897-0295
Long Beach *(G-7667)*
All United Window Corp.........................E....... 718 624-0490
Brooklyn *(G-1587)*
Alpine Overhead Doors Inc....................E....... 631 456-7800
East Setauket *(G-4494)*
Altype Fire Door Corp............................G....... 718 292-3500
Bronx *(G-1272)*
▲ Alumil Fabrication Inc........................F....... 845 469-2874
Newburgh *(G-12769)*
Amarr Company......................................F....... 585 426-8290
Rochester *(G-14210)*
American Rolling Door Ltd.....................G....... 718 273-0485
Staten Island *(G-15658)*
American Steel Gate Corp......................G....... 718 291-4050
Jamaica *(G-6928)*
Assa Abloy Entrance Systems US..........E....... 315 492-6600
East Syracuse *(G-4524)*
▲ Bison Steel Incorporated...................G....... 716 683-0900
Depew *(G-4273)*
Brooklyn Store Front Co Inc...................G....... 718 384-4372
Brooklyn *(G-1733)*
▲ Champion Aluminum Corp.................C....... 631 656-3424
Hauppauge *(G-6062)*
Corkhill Manufacturing Co Inc...............G....... 718 528-7413
Jamaica *(G-6943)*
D D & L Inc..F....... 607 729-9131
Binghamton *(G-902)*
Dawson Metal Company Inc...................C....... 716 664-3811
Jamestown *(G-7022)*
▲ Dayton Industries Inc.........................E....... 718 542-8144
Bronx *(G-1314)*
Deronde Doors and Frames Inc.............F....... 716 895-8888
Buffalo *(G-2927)*
Dural Door Company Inc........................F....... 718 729-1333
Long Island City *(G-7749)*
Eastern Storefronts & Mtls Inc..............F....... 631 471-7065
Ronkonkoma *(G-14925)*
◆ Ellison Bronze Inc...............................D....... 716 665-6522
Falconer *(G-4902)*
Empire Archtctural Systems Inc..............E....... 518 773-5109
Johnstown *(G-7141)*
Excel Aluminum Products Inc.................G....... 315 471-0925
Syracuse *(G-15960)*
▲ F A Alpine Windows Mfg....................F....... 845 469-5700
Chester *(G-3633)*
Five Boro Doors Mouldings Inc..............G....... 718 865-9371
Oceanside *(G-13100)*
Gamma North Corporation......................E....... 716 902-5100
Alden *(G-181)*
General Fire-Proof Door Corp.................E....... 718 893-5500
Bronx *(G-1344)*
◆ Global Steel Products Corp................C....... 631 586-3455
Deer Park *(G-4169)*
◆ Great American Industries Inc...........G....... 607 729-9331
Vestal *(G-16472)*
◆ Griffon Corporation.............................E....... 212 957-5000
New York *(G-10405)*
Grover Aluminum Products Inc...............E....... 631 475-3500
Patchogue *(G-13446)*
Gscp Emax Acquisition LLC....................G....... 212 902-1000
New York *(G-10421)*
▲ Hopes Windows Inc............................C....... 716 665-5124
Jamestown *(G-7034)*
I Fix Screen..G....... 631 421-1938
Centereach *(G-3497)*
◆ Inscape (new York) Inc.......................D....... 716 665-6210
Falconer *(G-4909)*
Inter-Fence Co Inc...................................E....... 718 939-9700
College Point *(G-3814)*
Interntional Fireprof Door Inc................F....... 718 783-1310
Brooklyn *(G-2111)*
▲ Interstate Window Corporation.........D....... 631 231-0800
Brentwood *(G-1183)*
▼ J Sussman Inc......................................E....... 718 297-0228
Jamaica *(G-6958)*
▲ Jaidan Industries Inc...........................F....... 516 944-3650
Port Washington *(G-13849)*
Jenmar Door & Glass Inc........................G....... 718 767-7900
Whitestone *(G-17239)*
▲ Karey Kassl Corp.................................E....... 516 349-8484
Plainview *(G-13641)*
▲ Karp Associates Inc.............................D....... 631 768-8300
Melville *(G-8362)*
▲ Kasson & Keller Inc.............................A....... 518 853-3421
Fonda *(G-5320)*
Kelly Window Systems Inc......................E....... 631 420-8500
Farmingdale *(G-5033)*
▲ Kinro Manufacturing Inc.....................G....... 817 483-7791
White Plains *(G-17156)*
L & L Overhead Garage Doors................G....... 718 721-2518
Long Island City *(G-7813)*
Lif Industries Inc.....................................D....... 516 390-6800
Port Washington *(G-13858)*
Lif Industries Inc.....................................E....... 718 767-8800
Whitestone *(G-17240)*
▼ M & D Installers Inc.............................D....... 718 782-6978
Brooklyn *(G-2245)*
Markar Architectural Products................G....... 716 685-4104
Lancaster *(G-7350)*
Master Window & Door Corp..................F....... 718 782-5407
Brooklyn *(G-2284)*
▲ McKeon Rolling Stl Door Co Inc........E....... 631 803-3000
Bellport *(G-830)*
Mercury Lock and Door Service.............E....... 718 542-7048
Bronx *(G-1395)*
Metalline Fire Door Co Inc......................E....... 718 583-2320
Bronx *(G-1396)*
Michbi Doors Inc.....................................D....... 631 231-9050
Brentwood *(G-1189)*
Milanese Commercial Door LLC.............F....... 518 658-0398
Berlin *(G-856)*
Milgo Industrial Inc.................................D....... 718 388-6476
Brooklyn *(G-2317)*
Milgo Industrial Inc.................................G....... 718 387-0406
Brooklyn *(G-2318)*
New Bgnnngs Win Door Dstrs LLC.......F....... 845 214-0698
Poughkeepsie *(G-13939)*
Norandex Inc Vestal................................G....... 607 786-0778
Vestal *(G-16475)*
▼ North American Door Corp................F....... 518 566-0161
Plattsburgh *(G-13707)*
◆ Optimum Window Mfg Corp..............E....... 845 647-1900
Ellenville *(G-4650)*
Overhead Door Corporation....................D....... 518 828-7652
Hudson *(G-6659)*
Pal Manufacturing Corp..........................E....... 516 937-1990
Hicksville *(G-6409)*
Pioneer Window Holdings Inc................F....... 516 822-7000
Hicksville *(G-6414)*
Pioneer Window Holdings Inc................E....... 518 762-5526
Johnstown *(G-7152)*
Pk30 System LLC....................................F....... 212 473-8050
Stone Ridge *(G-15786)*
▲ Polyshot Corporation..........................E....... 585 292-5010
West Henrietta *(G-16923)*
▲ Presray Corporation...........................E....... 845 373-9300
Wassaic *(G-16623)*
Raydoor Inc...G....... 212 421-0641
New York *(G-11833)*
Renewal By Andersen LLC.....................E....... 631 843-1716
Farmingdale *(G-5108)*
▲ Robert-Masters Corp.........................G....... 718 545-1030
Woodside *(G-17367)*
Rochester Colonial Mfg Corp.................D....... 585 254-8191
Rochester *(G-14661)*
Rochester Lumber Company..................E....... 585 924-7171
Farmington *(G-5164)*
Rohlfs Stined Leaded GL Studio.............E....... 914 699-4848
Mount Vernon *(G-8773)*
Roly Door Sales Inc.................................G....... 716 877-1515
Hamburg *(G-5965)*
▼ Schwab Corp.......................................E....... 585 381-4900
Rochester *(G-14696)*
Shade & Shutter Systems of NY............G....... 631 208-0275
Southampton *(G-15575)*
Slanto Manufacturing Inc.......................E....... 516 759-5721
Glen Cove *(G-5641)*
Statewide Fireproof Door Co..................F....... 845 268-6043
Valley Cottage *(G-16416)*
Steelmasters Inc......................................E....... 718 498-2854
Brooklyn *(G-2626)*
Sunrise Door Solutions...........................G....... 631 464-4139
Copiague *(G-3953)*
Superior Stl Door Trim Co Inc.................F....... 716 665-3256
Jamestown *(G-7068)*
Supreme Fire-Proof Door Co Inc............F....... 718 665-4224
Bronx *(G-1466)*
Texas Home Security Inc.........................E....... 516 747-2100
New Hyde Park *(G-8910)*
Thermal Tech Doors Inc..........................E....... 516 745-0100
Garden City *(G-5548)*
Thompson Overhead Door Co Inc..........F....... 718 788-2470
Brooklyn *(G-2678)*
United Steel Products Inc......................D....... 914 968-7782
Flushing *(G-5311)*
▲ United Steel Products Inc..................D....... 718 478-5330
Corona *(G-4031)*
Universal Fire Proof Door.......................E....... 718 455-8442
Brooklyn *(G-2726)*
Vr Containment LLC................................G....... 917 972-3441
Fresh Meadows *(G-5461)*
Window Rama Enterprises Inc...............G....... 631 462-9054
Commack *(G-3873)*
Window Tech Systems Inc......................E....... 518 899-9000
Ballston Spa *(G-610)*
Windowman Inc (usa).............................G....... 718 246-2626
Brooklyn *(G-2774)*

3443 Fabricated Plate Work

828 Express Inc ....G 917 577-9019
Staten Island *(G-15649)*
▲ A K Allen Co Inc ....C 516 747-5450
Mineola *(G-8522)*
A L Eastmond & Sons Inc ....D 718 378-3000
Bronx *(G-1254)*
▲ Aavid Niagara LLC ....E 716 297-0652
Niagara Falls *(G-12817)*
▲ Acro Industries Inc ....C 585 254-3661
Rochester *(G-14186)*
▲ Aerco International Inc ....C 845 580-8000
Blauvelt *(G-963)*
Aero-Data Metal Crafters Inc ....C 631 471-7733
Ronkonkoma *(G-14882)*
All-State Diversified Pdts Inc ....E 315 472-4728
Syracuse *(G-15869)*
Alliance Innovative Mfg Inc ....E 716 822-1626
Lackawanna *(G-7268)*
▲ Allstate Gasket & Packing Inc ....F 631 254-4050
Deer Park *(G-4116)*
American Boiler Tank Wldg Inc ....E 518 463-5012
Albany *(G-44)*
◆ American Precision Inds Inc ....C 716 691-9100
Amherst *(G-227)*
Ametek Inc ....C 516 832-7710
Garden City *(G-5508)*
▼ Amherst Stnless Fbrication LLC ....E 716 691-7012
Amherst *(G-228)*
◆ API Heat Transf Thermasys Corp ....A 716 684-6700
Buffalo *(G-2834)*
API Heat Transfer Company ....G 716 684-6700
Buffalo *(G-2835)*
API Heat Transfer Inc ....C 585 496-5755
Arcade *(G-387)*
Arvos Inc ....B 585 593-2700
Wellsville *(G-16775)*
Atlantic Industrial Tech Inc ....E 631 234-3131
Shirley *(G-15437)*
Aurora Indus Machining Inc ....E 716 826-7911
Orchard Park *(G-13275)*
Bellmore Steel Products Corp ....F 516 785-9667
Bellmore *(G-811)*
Bigbee Steel and Tank Company ....E 518 273-0801
Watervliet *(G-16703)*
Blackstone Advanced Tech LLC ....C 716 665-5410
Jamestown *(G-7011)*
Bos-Hatten Inc ....F 716 662-7030
Orchard Park *(G-13276)*
Breton Industries Inc ....D 518 842-3030
Amsterdam *(G-337)*
Bridgehampton Steel & Wldg Inc ....F 631 537-2486
Bridgehampton *(G-1230)*
Bruce Pierce ....G 716 731-9310
Sanborn *(G-15142)*
▼ Buflovak LLC ....E 716 895-2100
Buffalo *(G-2883)*
Byelocorp Scientific Inc ....E 212 785-2580
New York *(G-9539)*
C & F Fabricators & Erectors ....G 607 432-3520
Colliersville *(G-3839)*
Cardinal Tank Corp ....E 718 625-4350
Brooklyn *(G-1759)*
▲ Charles Ross & Son Company ....D 631 234-0500
Hauppauge *(G-6064)*
▲ Cigar Box Studios Inc ....F 845 236-9283
Marlboro *(G-8135)*
CMS Heat Transfer Division Inc ....E 631 968-0084
Bohemia *(G-1033)*
Contech Engnered Solutions LLC ....F 716 870-9091
Orchard Park *(G-13288)*
▼ Costanzos Welding Inc ....E 716 282-0845
Niagara Falls *(G-12829)*
Crown Tank Company LLC ....G 855 276-9682
Horseheads *(G-6600)*
Cyclotherm of Watertown Inc ....E 315 782-1100
Watertown *(G-16670)*
David Isseks & Sons Inc ....E 212 966-8694
New York *(G-9875)*
Direkt Force LLC ....E 716 652-3022
East Aurora *(G-4394)*
Doyle & Roth Mfg Co Inc ....F 212 269-7840
New York *(G-9972)*
◆ ECR International Inc ....D 315 797-1310
Utica *(G-16351)*
ECR International Inc ....C 716 366-5500
Dunkirk *(G-4365)*
Empire Industrial Systems Corp ....F 631 242-4619
Bay Shore *(G-697)*
Endicott Precision Inc ....C 607 754-7076
Endicott *(G-4811)*
Energy Nuclear Operations ....E 315 342-0055
Oswego *(G-13356)*
Erie Engineered Products Inc ....E 716 206-0204
Lancaster *(G-7338)*
Exergy LLC ....E 516 832-9300
Garden City *(G-5518)*
Expert Industries Inc ....E 718 434-6060
Brooklyn *(G-1951)*
Feldmeier Equipment Inc ....D 315 823-2000
Syracuse *(G-15963)*
Fluid Handling LLC ....C 716 897-2800
Cheektowaga *(G-3599)*
Fross Industries Inc ....E 716 297-0652
Niagara Falls *(G-12843)*
Fuel Efficiency LLC ....G 315 923-2511
Clyde *(G-3752)*
▲ Fulton Boiler Works Inc ....D 315 298-5121
Pulaski *(G-13964)*
Fulton Boiler Works Inc ....C 315 298-5121
Pulaski *(G-13965)*
Gasport Welding & Fabg Inc ....F 716 772-7205
Gasport *(G-5572)*
General Electric Company ....G 585 593-2700
Wellsville *(G-16778)*
General Oil Equipment Co Inc ....E 716 691-7012
Amherst *(G-242)*
Glenridge Fabricators Inc ....F 718 456-2297
Glendale *(G-5670)*
◆ Global Steel Products Corp ....C 631 586-3455
Deer Park *(G-4169)*
◆ Graham Corporation ....B 585 343-2216
Batavia *(G-638)*
Hyperbaric Technologies Inc ....G 518 842-3030
Amsterdam *(G-350)*
Industrial Fabricating Corp ....E 315 437-8234
East Syracuse *(G-4554)*
Inex Inc ....G 716 537-2270
Holland *(G-6508)*
J & T Metal Products Co Inc ....E 631 226-7400
West Babylon *(G-16825)*
J M Canty Inc ....E 716 625-4227
Lockport *(G-7624)*
J W Stevens Co Inc ....G 315 472-6311
East Syracuse *(G-4559)*
◆ Jaquith Industries Inc ....E 315 478-5700
Syracuse *(G-15985)*
Jbren Corp ....F 716 332-5928
Buffalo *(G-3032)*
John R Robinson Inc ....E 718 786-6088
Long Island City *(G-7800)*
Joshua Liner Gallery LLC ....F 212 244-7415
New York *(G-10806)*
K Industries Inc ....G 631 897-2125
Bellport *(G-828)*
Kintex Inc ....D 716 297-0652
Niagara Falls *(G-12857)*
Lane Enterprises Inc ....F 607 776-3366
Bath *(G-660)*
▲ Lifetime Chimney Supply LLC ....G 516 576-8144
Plainview *(G-13643)*
Manhattan Cooling Towers Inc ....F 212 279-1045
Long Island City *(G-7831)*
▲ Marex Aquisition Corp ....C 585 458-3940
Rochester *(G-14518)*
Marine Boiler & Welding Inc ....F 718 378-1900
Bronx *(G-1390)*
Methods Tooling & Mfg Inc ....E 845 246-7100
Mount Marion *(G-8693)*
Metrofab Pipe Incorporated ....F 516 349-7373
Plainview *(G-13647)*
Miller Metal Fabricating Inc ....G 585 359-3400
Rochester *(G-14534)*
Mitsubishi Chemical Amer Inc ....E 212 223-3043
New York *(G-11310)*
Modutank Inc ....F 718 392-1112
Long Island City *(G-7846)*
Mono-Systems Inc ....E 716 821-1344
Buffalo *(G-3094)*
▲ Motivair Corporation ....E 716 691-9222
Amherst *(G-250)*
Mount Kisco Transfer Stn Inc ....G 914 666-6350
Mount Kisco *(G-8678)*
Nitram Energy Inc ....E 716 662-6540
Orchard Park *(G-13310)*
North American Svcs Group LLC ....F 518 885-1820
Ballston Spa *(G-604)*
Perforated Screen Surfaces ....E 866 866-8690
Conklin *(G-3898)*
▲ Pfaudler US Inc ....C 585 235-1000
Rochester *(G-14599)*
Roemac Industrial Sales Inc ....G 716 692-7332
North Tonawanda *(G-13009)*
Rosenwach Tank Co Inc ....E 212 972-4411
Astoria *(G-454)*
Ross Metal Fabricators Inc ....E 631 586-7000
Deer Park *(G-4227)*
Saraga Industries Corp ....G 631 842-4049
Amityville *(G-324)*
Sargent Manufacturing Inc ....G 212 722-7000
New York *(G-11991)*
Schwabel Fabricating Co Inc ....E 716 876-2086
Tonawanda *(G-16219)*
▲ Seibel Modern Mfg & Wldg Corp ....D 716 683-1536
Lancaster *(G-7367)*
▲ Slant/Fin Corporation ....B 516 484-2600
Greenvale *(G-5899)*
Slantco Manufacturing Inc ....G 516 484-2600
Greenvale *(G-5900)*
SPX Corporation ....B 585 436-5550
Rochester *(G-14721)*
Stainless Metals Inc ....F 718 784-1454
Woodside *(G-17372)*
▲ Stavo Industries Inc ....F 845 331-4552
Kingston *(G-7241)*
Steelways Inc ....E 845 562-0860
Newburgh *(G-12804)*
Stutzman Management Corp ....F 800 735-2013
Lancaster *(G-7369)*
Supreme Boilers Inc ....G 718 342-2220
Brooklyn *(G-2651)*
Taylor Tank Company Inc ....E 718 434-1300
Brooklyn *(G-2669)*
Themis Chimney Inc ....F 718 937-4716
Brooklyn *(G-2677)*
Thermotech Corp ....G 716 823-3311
Buffalo *(G-3243)*
Troy Boiler Works Inc ....E 518 274-2650
Troy *(G-16282)*
United Wind Inc ....F 800 268-9896
Brooklyn *(G-2724)*
◆ Vship Co ....F 718 706-8566
Astoria *(G-459)*
Water Cooling Corp ....G 718 723-6500
Rosedale *(G-15039)*
Wayne Integrated Tech Corp ....E 631 242-0213
Edgewood *(G-4633)*
West Metal Works Inc ....E 716 895-4900
Buffalo *(G-3278)*
Wsf Industries Inc ....E 716 692-4930
Tonawanda *(G-16237)*
▲ Yula Corporation ....E 718 991-0900
Bronx *(G-1497)*
Zone Fabricators Inc ....F 718 272-0200
Ozone Park *(G-13414)*

3444 Sheet Metal Work

303 Contracting Inc ....E 716 896-2122
Orchard Park *(G-13271)*
A & L Shtmtl Fabrications Corp ....E 718 842-1600
Bronx *(G-1253)*
Aabco Sheet Metal Co Inc ....D 718 821-1166
Ridgewood *(G-14110)*
Abdo Shtmtl & Fabrication Inc ....G 315 894-4664
Frankfort *(G-5358)*
Aberdeen Blower & Shtmtl Works ....G 631 661-6100
West Babylon *(G-16789)*
Accra Sheetmetal LLC ....G 631 920-2087
Wyandanch *(G-17385)*
Accurate Specialty Metal Fabri ....E 718 418-6895
Middle Village *(G-8442)*
▲ Acme Architectural Pdts Inc ....D 718 384-7800
Brooklyn *(G-1554)*
▲ Acro Industries Inc ....C 585 254-3661
Rochester *(G-14186)*
Acro-Fab Ltd ....E 315 564-6688
Hannibal *(G-5992)*
Advanced Precision Technology ....F 845 279-3540
Brewster *(G-1204)*
Advantech Industries Inc ....C 585 247-0701
Rochester *(G-14196)*
Aero Trades Mfg Corp ....E 516 746-3360
Mineola *(G-8523)*
Aero-Data Metal Crafters Inc ....C 631 471-7733
Ronkonkoma *(G-14882)*
Aeroduct Inc ....E 516 248-9550
Mineola *(G-8524)*
Afco Systems Inc ....C 631 249-9441
Farmingdale *(G-4938)*

Employee Codes: A=Over 500 employees, B=251-500
C=101-250, D=51-100, E=20-50, F=10-19, G=5-9
2018 Harris
New York Manufacturers Directory
809

34 FABRICATED METAL PRODUCTS, EXCEPT MACHINERY AND TRANSPORTATION EQUIPMENT

Air Louver & Damper Inc .... E 718 392-3232
  Maspeth *(G-8141)*
Air Louver & Damper Inc .... F 718 392-3232
  Long Island City *(G-7681)*
Aj Genco Mch Sp McHy Rdout Svc ...... F 716 664-4925
  Falconer *(G-4896)*
Aldo Frustacci Iron Works Inc .... F 718 768-0707
  Brooklyn *(G-1577)*
Aleta Industries Inc .... F 718 349-0040
  Brooklyn *(G-1579)*
Alfred B Parella .... G 518 872-1238
  Altamont *(G-208)*
Alkemy Machine LLC .... E 585 436-8730
  Rochester *(G-14201)*
All Around Spiral Inc .... G 631 588-0220
  Ronkonkoma *(G-14887)*
All Island Blower & Shtmtl .... F 631 567-7070
  Bohemia *(G-1009)*
All Star Carts & Vehicles Inc .... D 631 666-5581
  Bay Shore *(G-667)*
▲ Allen Machine Products Inc .... E 631 630-8800
  Hauppauge *(G-6035)*
Alliance Welding & Steel Fabg .... F 516 775-7600
  Floral Park *(G-5199)*
Allure Metal Works Inc .... F 631 588-0220
  Ronkonkoma *(G-14891)*
Alnik Service Corporation .... G 516 873-7300
  New Hyde Park *(G-8859)*
Alpine Machine Inc .... F 607 272-1344
  Ithaca *(G-6858)*
▲ Alternative Service Inc .... F 631 345-9500
  Yaphank *(G-17401)*
Amsco Inc .... F 716 823-4213
  Buffalo *(G-2829)*
Apparatus Mfg Inc .... G 845 471-5116
  Poughkeepsie *(G-13905)*
▲ Arcadia Mfg Group Inc .... E 518 434-6213
  Green Island *(G-5871)*
Arcadia Mfg Group Inc .... G 518 434-6213
  Menands *(G-8399)*
Architctral Shetmetal Pdts Inc .... G 518 381-6144
  Scotia *(G-15345)*
Arlan Damper Corporation .... E 631 589-7431
  Bohemia *(G-1015)*
Art Precision Metal Products .... F 631 842-8889
  Copiague *(G-3920)*
▲ Ascension Industries Inc .... D 716 693-9381
  North Tonawanda *(G-12974)*
Asm USA Inc .... F 212 925-2906
  New York *(G-9287)*
Asp Industries Inc .... E 585 254-9130
  Rochester *(G-14235)*
Atlantis Equipment Corporation .... F 518 733-5910
  Stephentown *(G-15778)*
Auburn Tank & Manufacturing Co ..... F 315 255-2788
  Auburn *(G-480)*
▲ Austin Mohawk and Company LLC .E 315 793-3000
  Utica *(G-16331)*
Auto Body Services LLC .... F 631 431-4640
  Lindenhurst *(G-7477)*
Avalanche Fabrication Inc .... F 585 545-4000
  Ontario *(G-13218)*
◆ B & B Sheet Metal Inc .... F 718 433-2501
  Long Island City *(G-7710)*
B & H Precision Fabricators .... F 631 563-9620
  Bohemia *(G-1017)*
B & R Sheet .... G 718 558-5544
  Jamaica *(G-6933)*
Banner Metalcraft Inc .... D 631 563-7303
  Ronkonkoma *(G-14906)*
Bargold Storage Systems LLC .... E 718 247-7000
  Long Island City *(G-7713)*
Batavia Enclosures Inc .... F 585 344-1797
  Arcade *(G-388)*
Berjen Metal Industries Ltd .... G 631 673-7979
  Huntington *(G-6688)*
Best Tinsmith Supply Inc .... G 518 863-2541
  Northville *(G-13036)*
Blackstone Advanced Tech LLC .... C 716 665-5410
  Jamestown *(G-7011)*
Boss Precision Ltd .... D 585 352-7070
  Spencerport *(G-15590)*
Broadway Neon Sign Corp .... F 908 241-4177
  Ronkonkoma *(G-14910)*
Brothers Roofing Supplies Co .... E 718 779-0280
  East Elmhurst *(G-4411)*
C & T Tool & Instrument Co .... E 718 429-1253
  Woodside *(G-17338)*
C J & C Sheet Metal Corp .... F 631 376-9425
  West Babylon *(G-16805)*

▲ Cannon Industries Inc .... D 585 254-8080
  Rochester *(G-14276)*
CBM Fabrications Inc 518 399-8023
  Ballston Lake *(G-580)*
Center Sheet Metal Inc .... C 718 378-4476
  Bronx *(G-1293)*
▲ Cetek Inc 845 452-3510
  Poughkeepsie *(G-13911)*
Chamtek Mfg Inc 585 328-4900
  Rochester *(G-14293)*
Cherry Holding Ltd .... G 516 679-3748
  North Bellmore *(G-12933)*
Choppy V M & Sons LLC .... E 518 266-1444
  Troy *(G-16253)*
Citros Building Materials Co .... E 718 779-0727
  East Elmhurst *(G-4412)*
City Cooling Enterprises Inc .... G 718 331-7400
  Brooklyn *(G-1780)*
Clark Specialty Co Inc .... E 607 776-3193
  Bath *(G-655)*
Construction Parts Whse Inc .... G 315 445-1310
  East Syracuse *(G-4534)*
CPI Industries Inc .... D 631 909-3434
  Manorville *(G-8111)*
Craft-Tech Mfg Corp .... G 631 563-4949
  Bohemia *(G-1038)*
Crown Die Casting Corp 914 667-5400
  Mount Vernon *(G-8720)*
Custom Sheet Metal Corp .... G 315 463-9105
  Syracuse *(G-15936)*
Cutting Edge Metal Works .... E 631 981-8333
  Holtsville *(G-6528)*
Cw Metals Inc 917 416-7906
  Long Island City *(G-7737)*
D & G Sheet Metal Co Inc .... F 718 326-9111
  Maspeth *(G-8158)*
D and D Sheet Metal Corp 718 465-7585
  Jamaica *(G-6945)*
Dart Awning Inc .... F 718 945-4224
  Freeport *(G-5404)*
Dawson Metal Company Inc .... C 716 664-3811
  Jamestown *(G-7022)*
Dayton T Brown Inc .... B 631 589-6300
  Bohemia *(G-1048)*
Delta Sheet Metal Corp .... C 718 429-5805
  Long Island City *(G-7740)*
Dimar Manufacturing Corp 716 759-0351
  Clarence *(G-3685)*
▲ Dj Acquisition Management Corp ..D 585 265-3000
  Ontario *(G-13222)*
Doortec Archtctural Met GL LLC .... E 718 567-2730
  Brooklyn *(G-1875)*
DOT Tool Co Inc 607 724-7001
  Binghamton *(G-904)*
Dundas-Jafine Inc 716 681-9690
  Alden *(G-180)*
Dynasty Stainless Steel & Meta .... E 718 205-6623
  Maspeth *(G-8164)*
E G M Restaurant Equipment Mfg .... B 718 782-9800
  Brooklyn *(G-1892)*
Elderlee Incorporated .... C 315 789-6670
  Oaks Corners *(G-13088)*
Elevator Accessories Mfg .... E 914 739-7004
  Peekskill *(G-13501)*
Elmsford Sheet Metal Works Inc 914 739-6300
  Cortlandt Manor *(G-4074)*
Empire Air Specialties Inc 518 689-4440
  Albany *(G-77)*
Empire Ventilation Eqp Co Inc .... F 718 728-2143
  Florida *(G-5219)*
Endicott Precision Inc 607 754-7076
  Endicott *(G-4811)*
Engineering Mfg Tech LLC 607 754-7111
  Endicott *(G-4813)*
Expert Industries Inc 718 434-6060
  Brooklyn *(G-1951)*
F M L Industries Inc 607 749-7273
  Homer *(G-6545)*
Federal Sheet Metal Works Inc .... F 315 735-4730
  Utica *(G-16355)*
Five Star Awnings Inc .... F 718 860-6070
  Ridgewood *(G-14119)*
Five Star Industries Inc 716 674-2589
  West Seneca *(G-16973)*
Franchet Metal Craft Inc 718 658-6400
  Jamaica *(G-6949)*
Fred A Nudd Corporation 315 524-2531
  Ontario *(G-13223)*
Genesee Building Products LLC 585 548-2726
  Stafford *(G-15640)*

GM Sheet Metal Inc .... F 718 349-2830
  Brooklyn *(G-2032)*
Goergen-Mackwirth Co Inc .... E 716 874-4800
  Buffalo *(G-2993)*
Golden Group International Ltd .... G 845 440-1025
  Patterson *(G-13464)*
Gottlieb Schwartz Family .... E 718 761-2010
  Staten Island *(G-15700)*
Greene Technologies Inc .... D 607 656-4166
  Greene *(G-5884)*
Gt Innovations LLC .... G 585 739-7659
  Bergen *(G-844)*
H & M Leasing Corp .... G 631 225-5246
  Copiague *(G-3930)*
Hana Sheet Metal Inc 914 377-0773
  Yonkers *(G-17468)*
Hansen Steel .... E 585 398-2020
  Farmington *(G-5161)*
Harbor Elc Fabrication Tls Inc .... E 914 636-4400
  New Rochelle *(G-8954)*
Hart To Hart Industries Inc .... G 716 492-2709
  Chaffee *(G-3562)*
Hatfield Metal Fab Inc 845 454-9078
  Poughkeepsie *(G-13926)*
◆ Hergo Ergonomic Support 718 894-0639
  Maspeth *(G-8175)*
Hermann Gerdens Inc .... G 631 841-3132
  Copiague *(G-3931)*
Hi-Tech Industries NY Inc .... E 607 217-7361
  Johnson City *(G-7125)*
Hrd Metal Products Inc .... G 631 243-6700
  Deer Park *(G-4173)*
▲ Hunter Douglas Inc .... D 845 664-7000
  Pearl River *(G-13482)*
I Rauchs Sons Inc 718 507-8844
  East Elmhurst *(G-4414)*
IEC Electronics Corp .... C 585 647-1760
  Rochester *(G-14464)*
Illinois Tool Works Inc .... E 607 770-4945
  Binghamton *(G-921)*
Imperial Damper & Louver Co .... E 718 731-3800
  Bronx *(G-1361)*
▼ Incodema Inc 607 277-7070
  Ithaca *(G-6884)*
Industrial Fabricating Corp .... E 315 437-3353
  East Syracuse *(G-4553)*
Intellimetal Inc .... D 585 424-3260
  Rochester *(G-14472)*
Interior Metals .... E 718 439-7324
  Brooklyn *(G-2108)*
Jamestown Advanced Pdts Corp ...... E 716 483-3406
  Jamestown *(G-7037)*
◆ Jaquith Industries Inc 315 478-5700
  Syracuse *(G-15985)*
Jar Metals Inc .... F 845 425-8901
  Nanuet *(G-8804)*
Joe P Industries Inc .... F 631 293-7889
  Farmingdale *(G-5026)*
▲ Juniper Elbow Co Inc .... C 718 326-2546
  Middle Village *(G-8447)*
K Barthelmes Mfg Co Inc .... F 585 328-8140
  Rochester *(G-14489)*
Kal Manufacturing Corporation .... E 585 265-4310
  Webster *(G-16751)*
Karo Sheet Metal Inc 718 542-8420
  Brooklyn *(G-2168)*
Kassis Superior Sign Co Inc .... F 315 463-7446
  Syracuse *(G-15992)*
Ke Durasol Awnings Inc 845 610-1100
  Chester *(G-3636)*
▲ Kenan International Trading .... G 718 672-4922
  Corona *(G-4023)*
Ksm Group Ltd 716 751-6006
  Newfane *(G-12811)*
▲ Lambro Industries Inc .... D 631 842-8088
  Amityville *(G-304)*
Lane Enterprises Inc .... E 518 885-4385
  Ballston Spa *(G-599)*
Leader Sheet Metal Inc .... F 347 271-4961
  Bronx *(G-1382)*
Liffey Sheet Metal Corp .... F 347 381-1134
  Long Island City *(G-7816)*
Lotus Awnings Enterprises Inc .... G 718 965-4824
  Brooklyn *(G-2240)*
M&G Duravent Inc .... E 518 463-7284
  Albany *(G-99)*
Maloya Laser Inc .... E 631 543-2327
  Commack *(G-3863)*
Manufacturing Resources Inc .... E 631 481-0041
  Rochester *(G-14514)*

34 FABRICATED METAL PRODUCTS, EXCEPT MACHINERY AND TRANSPORTATION EQUIPMENT

▲ Marex Aquisition Corp ....C....... 585 458-3940
  Rochester (G-14518)
Mariah Metal Products Inc ....G....... 516 938-9783
  Hicksville (G-6394)
Mason Scott Industries LLC ....F....... 516 349-1800
  Roslyn Heights (G-15054)
▲ McAlpin Industries ....C....... 585 266-3060
  Rochester (G-14521)
McHone Industries Inc ....D....... 716 945-3380
  Salamanca (G-15128)
MD International Industries ....E....... 631 254-3100
  Deer Park (G-4197)
Mega Vision Inc ....E....... 718 228-1065
  Brooklyn (G-2298)
Merz Metal & Machine Corp ....E....... 716 893-7786
  Buffalo (G-3083)
Metal Solutions Inc ....E....... 315 732-6271
  Utica (G-16371)
Metal Tek Products ....G....... 516 586-4514
  Plainview (G-13646)
Metalsmith Inc ....G....... 631 467-1500
  Holbrook (G-6492)
Methods Tooling & Mfg Inc ....E....... 845 246-7100
  Mount Marion (G-8693)
Metro Duct Systems Inc ....F....... 718 278-4294
  Long Island City (G-7840)
Middleby Corporation ....E....... 631 226-6688
  Lindenhurst (G-7495)
Mitsubishi Chemical Amer Inc ....E....... 212 223-3043
  New York (G-11310)
▼ Monarch Metal Fabrication Inc .....G....... 631 563-8967
  Bohemia (G-1100)
Ms Spares LLC ....G....... 607 223-3024
  Clay (G-3709)
N & L Instruments Inc ....F....... 631 471-4000
  Ronkonkoma (G-14973)
Nci Group Inc ....D....... 315 339-1245
  Rome (G-14852)
Nelson Air Device Corporation ....C....... 718 729-3801
  Maspeth (G-8186)
▼ North Coast Outfitters Ltd ....E....... 631 727-5580
  Riverhead (G-14164)
Northeast Fabricators LLC ....D....... 607 865-4031
  Walton (G-16570)
Northern Awning & Sign Company ...G....... 315 782-8515
  Watertown (G-16690)
Olympic Manufacturing Inc ....E....... 631 231-8900
  Hauppauge (G-6179)
Omc Inc ....C....... 718 731-5001
  Bronx (G-1417)
P R B Metal Products Inc ....F....... 631 467-1800
  Ronkonkoma (G-14986)
Pal Aluminum Inc ....G....... 516 937-1990
  Hicksville (G-6408)
Pal Aluminum Inc ....G....... 718 262-0091
  Jamaica (G-6975)
Pathfinder Industries Inc ....E....... 315 593-2483
  Fulton (G-5488)
PDQ Manufacturing Co Inc ....D....... 845 889-3123
  Rhinebeck (G-14069)
Penasack Machine Company Inc ....E....... 585 589-7044
  Albion (G-171)
Penner Elbow Company Inc ....F....... 718 526-9000
  Elmhurst (G-4679)
Pirnat Precise Metals Inc ....G....... 631 293-9169
  Farmingdale (G-5090)
Plattsburgh Sheet Metal Inc ....G....... 518 561-4930
  Plattsburgh (G-13716)
Precision Fabrication LLC ....G....... 585 591-3449
  Attica (G-473)
Precision Metals Corp ....E....... 631 586-5032
  Bay Shore (G-723)
Precision Mtal Fabricators Inc ....F....... 718 832-9805
  Brooklyn (G-2449)
Precision Systems Mfg Inc ....E....... 315 451-3480
  Liverpool (G-7570)
Product Integration & Mfg Inc ....E....... 585 436-6260
  Rochester (G-14628)
Prokosch and Sonn Sheet Metal ....E....... 845 562-4211
  Newburgh (G-12799)
Protofast Holding Corp ....G....... 631 753-2549
  Copiague (G-3944)
R D R Industries Inc ....F....... 315 866-5020
  Mohawk (G-8576)
Radiation Shielding Systems ....F....... 888 631-2278
  Suffern (G-15819)
Rami Sheet Metal Inc ....G....... 845 426-2948
  Spring Valley (G-15620)
Rand Products Manufacturing Co ...G....... 518 374-9871
  Schenectady (G-15312)

Rayco Manufacturing Co Inc ....F....... 516 431-2006
  Jamaica (G-6981)
Read Manufacturing Company Inc ...E....... 631 567-4487
  Holbrook (G-6496)
Reynolds Manufacturing Inc ....F....... 607 562-8936
  Big Flats (G-879)
▲ Rigidized Metals Corporation ....E....... 716 849-4703
  Buffalo (G-3186)
▲ Robert E Derecktor Inc ....D....... 914 698-0962
  Mamaroneck (G-8078)
Rochester Colonial Mfg Corp ....D....... 585 254-8191
  Rochester (G-14661)
Rollson Inc ....E....... 631 423-9578
  Huntington (G-6717)
Royal Metal Products Inc ....E....... 518 966-4442
  Surprise (G-15832)
S & B Machine Works Inc ....E....... 516 997-2666
  Westbury (G-17053)
S & J Sheet Metal Supply ....G....... 718 384-0800
  Brooklyn (G-2540)
S & T Machine Inc ....F....... 718 272-2484
  Brooklyn (G-2544)
Savaco Inc ....E....... 716 751-9455
  Newfane (G-12812)
Service Mfg Group Inc ....E....... 716 893-1482
  Buffalo (G-3213)
Service Mfg Group Inc ....F....... 716 893-1482
  Buffalo (G-3212)
Shanghai Stove Inc ....F....... 718 599-4583
  Brooklyn (G-2577)
Simmons Fabricating Svc Inc ....G....... 845 635-3755
  Pleasant Valley (G-13743)
Solidus Industries Inc ....D....... 607 749-4540
  Homer (G-6550)
Space Sign ....F....... 718 961-1112
  College Point (G-3834)
▲ Spence Engineering Company Inc ...C....... 845 778-5566
  Walden (G-16556)
Standard Industrial Works Inc ....F....... 631 888-0130
  Bay Shore (G-739)
Steel Sales Inc ....E....... 607 674-6363
  Sherburne (G-15419)
Steel Work Inc ....E....... 585 232-1555
  Rochester (G-14725)
Steelcraft Manufacturing Co ....F....... 718 277-2404
  Brooklyn (G-2624)
Sterling Industries Inc ....E....... 631 753-3070
  Farmingdale (G-5128)
▲ Studco Building Systems US LLC ...E....... 585 545-3000
  Webster (G-16762)
Superior Elec Enclosure Inc ....G....... 718 797-9090
  Brooklyn (G-2648)
Superior Exteriors of Buffalo ....F....... 716 873-1000
  East Amherst (G-4388)
T Lemme Mechanical Inc ....E....... 518 436-4136
  Menands (G-8411)
Tatra Mfg Corporation ....F....... 631 691-1184
  Copiague (G-3955)
▲ TCS Industries Inc ....D....... 585 426-1160
  Rochester (G-14742)
Technimetal Precision Inds ....E....... 631 231-8900
  Hauppauge (G-6234)
Themis Chimney Inc ....F....... 718 937-4716
  Brooklyn (G-2677)
Tri-Metal Industries Inc ....E....... 716 691-3323
  Amherst (G-268)
Tri-State Metals LLC ....F....... 914 347-8157
  Elmsford (G-4796)
▲ Tri-Technologies Inc ....E....... 914 699-2001
  Mount Vernon (G-8787)
▲ Trident Precision Mfg Inc ....D....... 585 265-2010
  Webster (G-16764)
Tripar Manufacturing Co Inc ....G....... 631 563-0855
  Bohemia (G-1145)
Truform Manufacturing Corp ....D....... 585 458-1090
  Rochester (G-14762)
Trylon Wire & Metal Works Inc ....E....... 718 542-4472
  Bronx (G-1480)
Ucr Steel Group LLC ....F....... 718 764-3414
  Uniondale (G-16324)
Ucr Steel Group LLC ....F....... 718 764-3414
  Ronkonkoma (G-15018)
Ulster Precision Inc ....E....... 845 338-0995
  Kingston (G-7246)
▼ Ultimate Prcision Met Pdts Inc .....C....... 631 249-9441
  Farmingdale (G-5146)
Unadilla Silo Company Inc ....D....... 607 369-9341
  Sidney (G-15466)
United Sheet Metal Corp ....E....... 718 482-1197
  Long Island City (G-7937)

Universal Precision Corp ....E....... 585 321-9760
  Rochester (G-14771)
Universal Shielding Corp ....E....... 631 667-7900
  Deer Park (G-4244)
▲ Vance Metal Fabricators Inc ....D....... 315 789-5626
  Geneva (G-5600)
Vin Mar Precision Metal Inc ....F....... 631 563-6608
  Copiague (G-3960)
Vitarose Corp of America ....G....... 718 951-9700
  Brooklyn (G-2751)
◆ Voss Manufacturing Inc ....D....... 716 731-5062
  Sanborn (G-15158)
▲ Wainland Inc ....E....... 718 626-2233
  Astoria (G-460)
Wayne Integrated Tech Corp ....E....... 631 242-0213
  Edgewood (G-4633)
Wenig Corporation ....E....... 718 542-3600
  Bronx (G-1494)
Wg Sheet Metal Corp ....G....... 718 235-3093
  Brooklyn (G-2763)
William Kanes Mfg Corp ....G....... 718 346-1515
  Brooklyn (G-2770)
▲ Zahk Sales Inc ....G....... 631 348-9300
  Islandia (G-6844)

3446 Architectural & Ornamental Metal Work

786 Iron Works Corp ....G....... 718 418-4808
  Brooklyn (G-1521)
▲ A & T Iron Works Inc ....E....... 914 632-8992
  New Rochelle (G-8928)
A1 Ornamental Iron Works Inc ....G....... 718 265-3055
  Brooklyn (G-1544)
Aca Quality Building Pdts LLC ....E....... 718 991-2423
  Bronx (G-1260)
Accurate Welding Service Inc ....G....... 516 333-1730
  Westbury (G-16988)
▲ Acme Architectural Pdts Inc ....D....... 718 384-7800
  Brooklyn (G-1554)
Aero-Data Metal Crafters Inc ....C....... 631 471-7733
  Ronkonkoma (G-14882)
Airflex Industrial Inc ....E....... 631 752-1234
  Farmingdale (G-4940)
Airflex Industrial Inc ....D....... 631 752-1234
  Farmingdale (G-4941)
Aldo Frustacci Iron Works Inc ....F....... 718 768-0707
  Brooklyn (G-1577)
Aldos Iron Works Inc ....G....... 718 834-0408
  Brooklyn (G-1578)
All American Metal Corporation ......E....... 516 623-0222
  Freeport (G-5393)
All American Stairs & Railing ....F....... 718 441-8400
  Richmond Hill (G-14078)
All Metal Specialties Inc ....E....... 716 664-6009
  Jamestown (G-7005)
▲ Allied Bronze Corp (del Corp) ......E....... 646 421-6400
  New York (G-9139)
Alpha Iron Works LLC ....F....... 585 424-7260
  Rochester (G-14208)
▲ Arcadia Mfg Group Inc ....E....... 518 434-6213
  Green Island (G-5871)
Arcadia Mfg Group Inc ....E....... 518 434-6213
  Menands (G-8399)
Armento Incorporated ....G....... 716 875-2423
  Kenmore (G-7173)
Artistic Ironworks Inc ....G....... 631 665-4285
  Bay Shore (G-671)
Atlas Fence & Railing Co Inc ....E....... 718 767-2200
  Whitestone (G-17229)
Babylon Iron Works Inc ....F....... 631 643-3311
  West Babylon (G-16798)
Bobrick Washroom Equipment Inc ...D....... 518 877-7444
  Clifton Park (G-3723)
Bracci Ironworks Inc ....F....... 718 629-2374
  Brooklyn (G-1710)
C & F Iron Works Inc ....F....... 914 592-2450
  Elmsford (G-4747)
C & F Steel Corp ....F....... 914 592-3928
  Elmsford (G-4748)
Cabezon Design Group Inc ....F....... 718 488-9868
  Brooklyn (G-1748)
Caliper Architecture PC ....E....... 718 302-2427
  Brooklyn (G-1750)
Caliperstudio Co ....E....... 718 302-2427
  Brooklyn (G-1751)
▲ City Store Gates Mfg Corp ....E....... 718 939-9700
  College Point (G-3806)
Creative Metal Fabricators ....G....... 631 567-2266
  Bohemia (G-1039)
Custom Design Metals Inc ....G....... 631 563-2444
  Bohemia (G-1041)

Employee Codes: A=Over 500 employees, B=251-500
C=101-250, D=51-100, E=20-50, F=10-19, G=5-9

34 FABRICATED METAL PRODUCTS, EXCEPT MACHINERY AND TRANSPORTATION EQUIPMENT

D V S Iron & Aluminum Works .... G 718 768-7961
  Brooklyn *(G-1832)*
Duke of Iron Inc .... G 631 543-3600
  Smithtown *(G-15508)*
E & J Iron Works Inc .... E 718 665-6040
  Bronx *(G-1324)*
E F Iron Works & Construction .... G 631 242-4766
  Bay Shore *(G-696)*
▲ E S P Metal Crafts Inc .... G 718 381-2443
  Brooklyn *(G-1894)*
Ej Group Inc .... G 315 699-2601
  Cicero *(G-3674)*
Elevator Accessories Mfg .... F 914 739-7004
  Peekskill *(G-13501)*
Fence Plaza Corp .... G 718 469-2200
  Brooklyn *(G-1970)*
Fjs Industries Inc .... F 917 428-3797
  Brooklyn *(G-1982)*
▼ Flagpoles Incorporated .... D 631 751-5500
  East Setauket *(G-4501)*
Flushing Iron Weld Inc .... E 718 359-2208
  Flushing *(G-5250)*
Forest Iron Works Inc .... E 516 671-4229
  Locust Valley *(G-7661)*
G C D M Ironworks Inc .... E 914 347-2058
  Elmsford *(G-4762)*
▲ Giumenta Corp .... E 718 832-1200
  Brooklyn *(G-2026)*
◆ Global Steel Products Corp .... C 631 586-3455
  Deer Park *(G-4169)*
Grillmaster Inc .... E 718 272-9191
  Howard Beach *(G-6625)*
Hi-Tech Metals Inc .... E 718 894-1212
  Maspeth *(G-8176)*
Imperial Damper & Louver Co .... E 718 731-3800
  Bronx *(G-1361)*
Inter-Fence Co Inc .... E 718 939-9700
  College Point *(G-3814)*
▼ International Creative Met Inc .... F 718 424-8179
  Woodside *(G-17350)*
Iron Art Inc .... G 914 592-7977
  Elmsford *(G-4765)*
Iron Worker .... F 516 338-2756
  Smithtown *(G-15512)*
Irony Limited Inc .... G 631 329-4065
  East Hampton *(G-4431)*
▲ ITR Industries Inc .... E 914 964-7063
  Yonkers *(G-17473)*
Jamaica Iron Works Inc .... F 718 657-4849
  Jamaica *(G-6959)*
Jamestown Fab Stl & Sup Inc .... G 716 665-2227
  Jamestown *(G-7040)*
▲ Jaxson Rollforming Inc .... E 631 842-7775
  Amityville *(G-298)*
Jerry Cardullo Iron Works Inc .... F 631 242-8881
  Bay Shore *(G-707)*
▲ Jonathan Metal & Glass Ltd .... D 718 846-8000
  Jamaica *(G-6960)*
Kammetal Inc .... F 718 722-9991
  Brooklyn *(G-2167)*
Kenal Services Corp .... G 315 788-9226
  Watertown *(G-16679)*
Kendi Iron Works Inc .... G 718 821-2722
  Brooklyn *(G-2169)*
▼ Keuka Studios Inc .... G 585 624-5960
  Rush *(G-15076)*
Kleinfelder John .... G 716 753-3163
  Mayville *(G-8247)*
Kms Contracting Inc .... F 718 495-6500
  Brooklyn *(G-2175)*
Koenig Iron Works Inc .... E 718 433-0900
  Long Island City *(G-7808)*
Kryten Iron Works Inc .... G 914 345-0990
  Hawthorne *(G-6272)*
Lencore Acoustics Corp .... F 516 682-9292
  Woodbury *(G-17312)*
Lopopolo Iron Works Inc .... G 718 339-0572
  Brooklyn *(G-2239)*
M B C Metal Inc .... F 718 384-6713
  Brooklyn *(G-2249)*
Martin Chafkin .... G 718 383-1155
  Brooklyn *(G-2278)*
Martin Orna Ir Works II Inc .... G 516 354-3923
  Elmont *(G-4734)*
▲ Material Process Systems Inc .... F 718 302-3081
  Brooklyn *(G-2286)*
▲ Maximum Security Products Corp .... E 518 233-1800
  Waterford *(G-16634)*
McAllisters Precision Wldg Inc .... F 518 221-3455
  Menands *(G-8406)*

▲ Melto Metal Products Co Inc .... E 516 546-8866
  Freeport *(G-5422)*
Mestel Brothers Stairs & Rails .... C 516 496-4127
  Syosset *(G-15848)*
Metalworks Inc .... E 718 319-0011
  Bronx *(G-1397)*
▼ Metro Door Inc .... D 800 669-3667
  Islandia *(G-6839)*
Milgo Industrial Inc .... E 718 388-6476
  Brooklyn *(G-2317)*
Milgo Industrial Inc .... E 718 387-0406
  Brooklyn *(G-2318)*
▲ Mison Concepts Inc .... E 516 933-8000
  Hicksville *(G-6398)*
▲ Modern Art Foundry Inc .... E 718 728-2030
  Astoria *(G-448)*
Moon Gates Company .... E 718 426-0023
  East Elmhurst *(G-4417)*
Morgik Metal Designs .... E 212 463-0304
  New York *(G-11330)*
Moro Corporation .... E 607 724-4241
  Binghamton *(G-933)*
New Dimensions Office Group .... D 718 387-0995
  Brooklyn *(G-2370)*
New England Tool Co Ltd .... E 845 651-7550
  Florida *(G-5221)*
▲ Old Dutchmans Wrough Iron Inc .... E 716 688-2034
  Getzville *(G-5614)*
Oldcastle Precast Inc .... E 518 767-2116
  South Bethlehem *(G-15536)*
Ornametal Inc .... E 845 562-5151
  Newburgh *(G-12795)*
Ourem Iron Works Inc .... E 914 476-4856
  Yonkers *(G-17492)*
▲ Paley Studios Ltd .... F 585 232-5260
  Rochester *(G-14588)*
▲ Paragon Aquatics .... E 845 452-5500
  Lagrangeville *(G-7282)*
Pawling Corporation .... D 845 373-9300
  Wassaic *(G-16622)*
Peconic Ironworks Ltd .... F 631 204-0323
  Southampton *(G-15573)*
Phoenix Metal Designs Inc .... E 516 597-4100
  Hicksville *(G-6413)*
Pk30 System LLC .... E 212 473-8050
  Stone Ridge *(G-15786)*
◆ Pole-Tech Co Inc .... E 631 689-5525
  East Setauket *(G-4508)*
Railings By New Star Brass .... E 516 358-1153
  Brooklyn *(G-2493)*
Raulli and Sons Inc .... F 315 474-1370
  Syracuse *(G-16041)*
Raulli and Sons Inc .... D 315 479-6693
  Syracuse *(G-16040)*
Raulli Iron Works Inc .... E 315 337-8070
  Rome *(G-14860)*
Riverside Iron LLC .... E 315 535-4864
  Gouverneur *(G-5762)*
Rollson Inc .... F 631 423-9578
  Huntington *(G-6717)*
Royal Metal Products Inc .... E 518 966-4442
  Surprise *(G-15832)*
▲ S A Baxter LLC .... G 845 469-7995
  Chester *(G-3641)*
S R S Inc .... E 732 548-6630
  Maspeth *(G-8200)*
▲ Safespan Platform Systems Inc .... D 716 694-3332
  Tonawanda *(G-16218)*
Safeworks LLC .... G 800 696-5577
  Woodside *(G-17368)*
▲ Shanker Industries Inc .... E 631 940-9889
  Deer Park *(G-4233)*
Stain Rail Systems Inc .... F 732 548-6630
  Maspeth *(G-8201)*
Steel Sales Inc .... E 607 674-6363
  Sherburne *(G-15419)*
Steel Work Inc .... E 585 232-1555
  Rochester *(G-14725)*
Steps Plus Inc .... G 315 432-0885
  Syracuse *(G-16068)*
Studio 40 Inc .... E 212 420-8631
  Brooklyn *(G-2635)*
Studio Dellarte .... E 718 599-3715
  Brooklyn *(G-2636)*
Superior Metal & Woodwork Inc .... E 631 465-9004
  Farmingdale *(G-5129)*
Tee Pee Fence and Railing .... E 718 658-8323
  Jamaica *(G-6993)*
▲ Tensator Inc .... D 631 666-0300
  Bay Shore *(G-744)*

Tonys Ornamental Ir Works Inc .... E 315 337-3730
  Rome *(G-14866)*
Tri State Shearing Bending Inc .... F 718 485-2200
  Brooklyn *(G-2695)*
Triple H Construction Inc .... E 516 280-8252
  East Meadow *(G-4448)*
Tropical Driftwood Originals .... G 516 623-0980
  Roosevelt *(G-15033)*
Tymetal Corp .... E 518 692-9930
  Greenwich *(G-5915)*
United Iron Inc .... E 914 667-5700
  Mount Vernon *(G-8791)*
United Steel Products Inc .... D 914 968-7782
  Flushing *(G-5311)*
Universal Steel Fabricators .... F 718 342-0782
  Brooklyn *(G-2729)*
Village Wrought Iron Inc .... F 315 683-5589
  Fabius *(G-4848)*
Vr Containment LLC .... G 917 972-3441
  Fresh Meadows *(G-5461)*
Waverly Iron Corp .... E 631 732-2800
  Medford *(G-8296)*
West End Iron Works Inc .... G 518 456-1105
  Albany *(G-150)*
Z-Studios Dsign Fbrication LLC .... G 347 512-4210
  Brooklyn *(G-2792)*

3448 Prefabricated Metal Buildings & Cmpnts

All American Building .... G 607 797-7123
  Binghamton *(G-882)*
▲ Austin Mohawk and Company LLC .... E 315 793-3000
  Utica *(G-16331)*
▲ Birdair Inc .... D 716 633-9500
  Amherst *(G-231)*
Deraffele Mfg Co Inc .... E 914 636-6850
  New Rochelle *(G-8939)*
Energy Panel Structures Inc .... G 315 923-7777
  Clyde *(G-3750)*
Energy Panel Structures Inc .... G 585 343-1777
  Clyde *(G-3751)*
Energy Panel Structures Inc .... E 518 355-6708
  Schenectady *(G-15278)*
▲ Fillmore Greenhouses Inc .... E 585 567-2678
  Portageville *(G-13890)*
▲ Framing Technology Inc .... E 585 464-8470
  Rochester *(G-14402)*
▲ Guardian Booth LLC .... F 844 992-6684
  Spring Valley *(G-15610)*
Landmark Group Inc .... E 845 358-0350
  Valley Cottage *(G-16406)*
Latium USA Trading LLC .... D 631 563-4000
  Holbrook *(G-6484)*
Man Products Inc .... E 631 789-6500
  Farmingdale *(G-5049)*
Metadure Defense & SEC LLC .... F 631 249-2141
  Farmingdale *(G-5058)*
▼ Metallic Ladder Mfg Corp .... F 716 358-6201
  Randolph *(G-14029)*
Metals Building Products .... E 844 638-2527
  Holbrook *(G-6491)*
Mobile Mini Inc .... F 315 732-4555
  Utica *(G-16373)*
Mobile Mini Inc .... E 631 543-4900
  Commack *(G-3864)*
Morton Buildings Inc .... E 585 786-8191
  Warsaw *(G-16605)*
Nci Group Inc .... D 315 339-1245
  Rome *(G-14852)*
Overhead Door Corporation .... D 518 828-7652
  Hudson *(G-6659)*
Precision Fabrication LLC .... G 585 591-3449
  Attica *(G-473)*
Qub9 Inc .... G 585 484-1808
  Rochester *(G-14641)*
Sunbilt Solar Pdts By Sussman .... D 718 297-0228
  Jamaica *(G-6991)*
T Shore Products Ltd .... E 315 252-9174
  Auburn *(G-519)*
Universal Shielding Corp .... E 631 667-7900
  Deer Park *(G-4244)*
Veerhouse Voda Haiti LLC .... E 917 353-5944
  New York *(G-12537)*
Walpole Woodworkers Inc .... G 631 726-2859
  Water Mill *(G-16628)*

3449 Misc Structural Metal Work

A&B McKeon Glass Inc .... G 718 525-2152
  Staten Island *(G-15651)*

SIC SECTION 34 FABRICATED METAL PRODUCTS, EXCEPT MACHINERY AND TRANSPORTATION EQUIPMENT

▲ **Abasco Inc** ....E 716 649-4790
Hamburg *(G-5941)*
Accurate Metal Weather Strip ....G 914 668-6042
Mount Vernon *(G-8704)*
Agl Industries Inc ....E 718 326-7597
Maspeth *(G-8140)*
▲ **AM Architectural Metal & Glass** ....E 845 942-8848
Garnerville *(G-5567)*
Arista Steel Designs Corp ....G 718 965-7077
Brooklyn *(G-1629)*
▲ **Baco Enterprises Inc** ....D 718 589-6225
Bronx *(G-1278)*
Barker Steel LLC ....E 518 465-6221
Albany *(G-49)*
City Evolutionary ....G 718 861-7585
Bronx *(G-1300)*
Coral Management Corp ....G 718 893-9286
Bronx *(G-1306)*
▲ **Designs By Novello Inc** ....G 914 934-7711
Port Chester *(G-13770)*
▲ **Dimension Fabricators Inc** ....E 518 374-1936
Scotia *(G-15346)*
Empire Metal Finishing Inc ....E 718 545-6700
Astoria *(G-438)*
Fala Technologies Inc ....E 845 336-4000
Kingston *(G-7218)*
Ferro Fabricators Inc ....F 718 703-0007
Brooklyn *(G-1971)*
GCM Metal Industries Inc ....F 718 386-4059
Brooklyn *(G-2016)*
Genesee Metal Products Inc ....E 585 968-6000
Wellsville *(G-16779)*
Halmark Architectural Finshg ....E 718 272-1831
Brooklyn *(G-2062)*
Harbor Wldg & Fabrication Corp ....F 631 667-1880
Bay Shore *(G-702)*
Hornet Group Inc ....D 845 858-6400
Port Jervis *(G-13808)*
◆ **Inscape (new York) Inc** ....D 716 665-6210
Falconer *(G-4909)*
Integrity Tool Incorporated ....F 315 524-4409
Ontario *(G-13226)*
Janed Enterprises ....F 631 694-4494
Farmingdale *(G-5025)*
Klein Reinforcing Services Inc ....F 585 352-9433
Spencerport *(G-15595)*
Kraman Iron Works Inc ....F 212 460-8400
New York *(G-10924)*
▲ **Lakeside Capital Corporation** ....E 716 664-2555
Jamestown *(G-7048)*
Lane Enterprises Inc ....E 518 885-4385
Ballston Spa *(G-599)*
▲ **Longstem Organizers Inc** ....G 914 777-2174
Jefferson Valley *(G-7091)*
▲ **Metal Products Intl LLC** ....G 716 215-1930
Niagara Falls *(G-12863)*
Metalsigma Usa Inc ....G 212 731-4346
New York *(G-11267)*
New York Steel Services Co ....G 718 291-7770
Jamaica *(G-6973)*
Northern Metalworks Corp ....G 646 523-1689
Selden *(G-15374)*
Orange County Ironworks LLC ....E 845 769-3000
Montgomery *(G-8636)*
▲ **Orbital Holdings Inc** ....E 951 360-7100
Buffalo *(G-3126)*
▲ **Paragon Aquatics** ....E 845 452-5500
Lagrangeville *(G-7282)*
Pierce Steel Fabricators ....F 716 372-7652
Olean *(G-13174)*
Ppi Corp ....E 585 880-7277
Rochester *(G-14611)*
▲ **Risa Management Corp** ....E 718 361-2606
Maspeth *(G-8197)*
Riverside Iron LLC ....F 315 535-4864
Gouverneur *(G-5762)*
▲ **Rolite Mfg Inc** ....E 716 683-0259
Lancaster *(G-7365)*
▲ **Rollform of Jamestown Inc** ....F 716 665-5310
Jamestown *(G-7058)*
Semans Enterprises Inc ....F 585 444-0097
West Henrietta *(G-16925)*
Signature Metal MBL Maint LLC ....D 718 292-8280
Bronx *(G-1453)*
Sims Steel Corporation ....E 631 587-8670
Lindenhurst *(G-7505)*
Sinn-Tech Industries Inc ....G 631 643-1171
West Babylon *(G-16859)*
▲ **Siw Inc** ....F 631 888-0130
Bay Shore *(G-738)*
Steel Sales Inc ....E 607 674-6363
Sherburne *(G-15419)*
Tebbens Steel LLC ....F 631 208-8330
Calverton *(G-3329)*
Tonys Ornamental Ir Works Inc ....E 315 337-3730
Rome *(G-14866)*
Torino Industrial Inc ....F 631 509-1640
Bellport *(G-840)*
United Iron Inc ....E 914 667-5700
Mount Vernon *(G-8791)*
West Metal Works Inc ....E 716 895-4900
Buffalo *(G-3278)*
Wide Flange Inc ....F 718 492-8705
Brooklyn *(G-2765)*

3451 Screw Machine Prdts

Acme Precision Screw Pdts Inc ....F 585 328-2028
Rochester *(G-14185)*
Albert Gates Inc ....D 585 594-9401
North Chili *(G-12940)*
All Type Screw Machine Pdts ....G 516 334-5100
Westbury *(G-16992)*
▲ **Anderson Precision Inc** ....D 716 484-1148
Jamestown *(G-7007)*
Andros Manufacturing Corp ....F 585 663-5700
Rochester *(G-14221)*
Brinkman Intl Group Inc ....G 585 429-5000
Rochester *(G-14263)*
Broda Machine Co Inc ....F 716 297-3221
Niagara Falls *(G-12822)*
C R C Manufacturing Inc ....F 585 254-8820
Rochester *(G-14272)*
C&C Automatics Inc ....E 315 331-1436
Newark *(G-12750)*
Century Metal Parts Corp ....E 631 667-0800
Bay Shore *(G-680)*
Craftech Industries Inc ....D 518 828-5001
Hudson *(G-6640)*
Curtis Screw Co Inc ....E 716 898-7800
Buffalo *(G-2916)*
Elmira Grinding Works Inc ....F 607 734-1579
Wellsburg *(G-16773)*
Emory Machine & Tool Co Inc ....E 585 436-9610
Farmington *(G-5159)*
Five Star Tool Co Inc ....E 585 328-9580
Rochester *(G-14394)*
Globe Electronic Hardware Inc ....F 718 457-0303
Woodside *(G-17349)*
Gsp Components Inc ....D 585 436-3377
Rochester *(G-14434)*
Hanco Metal Products Inc ....F 212 787-5992
Brooklyn *(G-2065)*
▲ **I W Industries Inc** ....C 631 293-9494
Melville *(G-8359)*
J & J Swiss Precision Inc ....E 631 243-5584
Deer Park *(G-4176)*
Kaddis Manufacturing Corp ....G 585 624-3070
Honeoye Falls *(G-6561)*
Kathleen B Mead ....G 585 247-0146
Webster *(G-16752)*
Ktd Screw Machine Inc ....G 631 243-6861
Deer Park *(G-4184)*
Lexington Machining LLC ....D 585 235-0880
Rochester *(G-14499)*
Lexington Machining LLC ....C 585 235-0880
Rochester *(G-14500)*
▲ **Liberty Brass Turning Co Inc** ....E 718 784-2911
Westbury *(G-17032)*
M Manastrip-M Corporation ....G 518 664-2089
Clifton Park *(G-3726)*
Manacraft Precision Inc ....F 914 654-0967
Pelham *(G-13518)*
Manth-Brownell Inc ....C 315 687-7263
Kirkville *(G-7254)*
Marmach Machine Inc ....G 585 768-8800
Le Roy *(G-7438)*
Micro Threaded Products Inc ....G 585 288-0080
Rochester *(G-14529)*
Miggins Screw Products Inc ....G 845 279-2307
Brewster *(G-1222)*
Muller Tool Inc ....E 716 895-3658
Buffalo *(G-3098)*
Multimatic Products Inc ....D 800 767-7633
Ronkonkoma *(G-14972)*
▲ **Murphy Manufacturing Co Inc** ....G 585 223-0100
Fairport *(G-4871)*
Norwood Screw Machine Parts ....F 516 481-6644
Mineola *(G-8562)*
▲ **Precision Machine Tech LLC** ....D 585 467-1840
Rochester *(G-14617)*
R P M Machine Co ....G 585 671-3744
Webster *(G-16757)*
Ranney Precision ....F 716 731-6418
Niagara Falls *(G-12884)*
Selflock Screw Products Co Inc ....E 315 541-4464
Syracuse *(G-16060)*
▲ **Supply Technologies (ny)** ....F 212 966-3310
Albany *(G-139)*
Supreme Screw Products Inc ....D 718 293-6600
Plainview *(G-13664)*
T & L Automatics Inc ....C 585 647-3717
Rochester *(G-14739)*
TAC Screw Products Inc ....F 585 663-5840
Rochester *(G-14741)*
Taylor Metalworks Inc ....C 716 662-3113
Orchard Park *(G-13323)*
Teale Machine Company Inc ....D 585 244-6700
Rochester *(G-14744)*
▲ **Thuro Metal Products Inc** ....E 631 435-0444
Brentwood *(G-1194)*
▲ **Tri-Technologies Inc** ....E 914 699-2001
Mount Vernon *(G-8787)*
Trihex Manufacturing Inc ....G 315 589-9331
Williamson *(G-17256)*
Triple Point Manufacturing ....G 631 218-4988
Bohemia *(G-1146)*
Umbro Machine & Tool Co Inc ....F 845 876-4669
Rhinebeck *(G-14071)*
Vanguard Metals Inc ....F 631 234-6500
Central Islip *(G-3541)*
Verns Machine Co Inc ....E 315 926-4223
Marion *(G-8133)*

3452 Bolts, Nuts, Screws, Rivets & Washers

▲ **American Pride Fasteners LLC** ....E 631 940-8292
Bay Shore *(G-669)*
Anthony Manno & Co Inc ....G 631 445-1834
Deer Park *(G-4123)*
▲ **Baco Enterprises Inc** ....D 718 589-6225
Bronx *(G-1278)*
Buckley Qc Fasteners Inc ....E 716 662-1490
Orchard Park *(G-13278)*
Craftech Industries Inc ....D 518 828-5001
Hudson *(G-6640)*
Dependable Acme Threaded Pdts ....G 516 338-4700
Westbury *(G-17004)*
Fastener Dimensions Inc ....E 718 847-6321
Ozone Park *(G-13404)*
Huck International Inc ....C 845 331-7300
Kingston *(G-7220)*
J T D Stamping Co Inc ....E 631 643-4144
West Babylon *(G-16827)*
Jem Threading Specialties Inc ....G 718 665-3341
Bronx *(G-1368)*
Jin Pin Market Inc ....G 718 898-0788
Jackson Heights *(G-6922)*
John F Rafter Inc ....G 716 992-3425
Eden *(G-4600)*
▲ **John Hassall LLC** ....D 516 334-6200
Westbury *(G-17025)*
▼ **John Hassall LLC** ....D 323 869-0150
Westbury *(G-17026)*
Kinemotive Corporation ....E 631 249-6440
Farmingdale *(G-5035)*
LD McCauley LLC ....C 716 662-6744
Orchard Park *(G-13305)*
◆ **Marksmen Manufacturing Corp** ....E 800 305-6942
Deer Park *(G-4194)*
Pin Pharma Inc ....G 212 543-2583
New York *(G-11683)*
Pins N Needles ....G 212 535-6222
New York *(G-11687)*
Pni Capital Partners ....G 516 466-7120
Westbury *(G-17047)*
Radax Industries Inc ....E 585 265-2055
Webster *(G-16758)*
Rochester Stampings Inc ....F 585 467-5241
Rochester *(G-14672)*
Schaefer Machine Co Inc ....E 516 248-6880
Mineola *(G-8570)*
▲ **Sesco Industries Inc** ....F 718 939-5137
College Point *(G-3832)*
Simon Defense Inc ....G 516 217-6000
Middle Island *(G-8441)*
Socket Products Mfg Corp ....G 631 232-9870
Islandia *(G-6841)*
Southco Inc ....B 585 624-2545
Honeoye Falls *(G-6564)*
Superior Washer & Gasket Corp ....D 631 273-8282
Hauppauge *(G-6227)*

S I C

Employee Codes: A=Over 500 employees, B=251-500
C=101-250, D=51-100, E=20-50, F=10-19, G=5-9

2018 Harris
New York Manufacturers Directory

813

34 FABRICATED METAL PRODUCTS, EXCEPT MACHINERY AND TRANSPORTATION EQUIPMENT

▲ Supply Technologies (ny) ....F 212 966-3310
   Albany *(G-139)*
▲ Tamperproof Screw Company Inc ...F 516 931-1616
   Hicksville *(G-6425)*
Teka Precision Inc ....G 845 753-1900
   Nyack *(G-13072)*
Treo Industries Inc ....G 631 737-4022
   Bohemia *(G-1142)*
Trihex Manufacturing Inc ....G 315 589-9331
   Williamson *(G-17256)*
▲ Zierick Manufacturing Corp ....D 800 882-8020
   Mount Kisco *(G-8690)*

3462 Iron & Steel Forgings

Alry Tool and Die Co Inc ....E 716 693-2419
   Tonawanda *(G-16159)*
▲ Ball Chain Mfg Co Inc ....D 914 664-7500
   Mount Vernon *(G-8709)*
▲ Biltron Automotive Products ....E 631 928-8613
   Port Jeff STA *(G-13786)*
Borgwarner Ithaca LLC ....B 607 257-6700
   Ithaca *(G-6864)*
▲ Borgwarner Morse TEC LLC ....C 607 257-6700
   Ithaca *(G-6866)*
Burke Frging Heat Treating Inc .....E 585 235-6060
   Rochester *(G-14268)*
Columbus McKinnon Corporation ...D 716 689-5400
   Getzville *(G-5610)*
▲ Crown Industrial ....G 607 745-8709
   Cortland *(G-4047)*
Delaware Valley Forge Inc ....E 716 447-9140
   Buffalo *(G-2924)*
▲ Designatronics Incorporated ....G 516 328-3300
   Hicksville *(G-6366)*
▲ Dragon Trading Inc ....G 212 717-1496
   New York *(G-9974)*
▲ Firth Rixson Inc ....D 585 328-1383
   Rochester *(G-14393)*
Gear Motions Incorporated ....E 716 885-1080
   Buffalo *(G-2982)*
Gear Motions Incorporated ....E 315 488-0100
   Syracuse *(G-15970)*
General Motors LLC ....A 716 879-5000
   Buffalo *(G-2986)*
Great Lakes Gear Co Inc ....G 716 694-0715
   Tonawanda *(G-16183)*
Handy & Harman Group Ltd ....E 914 461-1300
   White Plains *(G-17146)*
▲ Hohmann & Barnard Inc ....E 631 234-0600
   Hauppauge *(G-6118)*
Hohmann & Barnard Inc ....E 518 357-9757
   Schenectady *(G-15295)*
▲ Jrlon Inc ....D 315 597-4067
   Palmyra *(G-13434)*
Kurz and Zobel Inc ....G 585 254-9060
   Rochester *(G-14494)*
Mattessich Iron LLC ....G 315 409-8496
   Memphis *(G-8394)*
Metrofab Pipe Incorporated ....F 516 349-7373
   Plainview *(G-13647)*
▲ Peck & Hale LLC ....E 631 589-2510
   West Sayville *(G-16966)*
Perfect Gear & Instrument ....F 516 328-3330
   New Hyde Park *(G-8902)*
Perfect Gear & Instrument ....E 516 873-6122
   Garden City Park *(G-5554)*
Pro-Gear Co Inc ....G 716 684-3811
   Buffalo *(G-3164)*
Riley Gear Corporation ....E 716 694-0900
   North Tonawanda *(G-13007)*
S R & R Industries Inc ....G 845 692-8329
   Middletown *(G-8496)*
▲ Schilling Forge Inc ....E 315 454-4421
   Syracuse *(G-16055)*
▲ Secs Inc ....E 914 667-5600
   Mount Vernon *(G-8777)*
Secs Inc ....E 914 667-5600
   Mount Vernon *(G-8778)*
Special Metals Corporation ....D 716 366-5663
   Dunkirk *(G-4375)*
Stoffel Polygon Systems Inc ....F 914 961-2000
   Tuckahoe *(G-16296)*
Superior Motion Controls Inc ....E 516 420-2921
   Farmingdale *(G-5130)*
Superite Gear Instr of Hppauge ....G 631 234-0100
   Hauppauge *(G-6228)*
Trojan Steel ....E 518 686-7426
   Hoosick Falls *(G-6573)*
Upstate Piping Products Inc ....G 518 238-3457
   Waterford *(G-16644)*

Viking Iron Works Inc ....F 845 471-5010
   Poughkeepsie *(G-13956)*
▲ Vulcan Steam Forging Co ....E 716 875-3680
   Buffalo *(G-3272)*
W J Albro Machine Works Inc ....G 631 345-0657
   Yaphank *(G-17424)*
York Industries Inc ....E 516 746-3736
   Garden City Park *(G-5559)*

3463 Nonferrous Forgings

◆ Arconic Inc ....D 212 836-2758
   New York *(G-9248)*
▲ Hammond & Irving Inc ....G 315 253-6265
   Auburn *(G-498)*
▲ Nak International Corp ....D 516 997-4212
   Jericho *(G-7109)*
Penn State Metal Fabri ....G 718 786-8814
   Brooklyn *(G-2428)*
Special Metals Corporation ....D 716 366-5663
   Dunkirk *(G-4375)*

3465 Automotive Stampings

Albert Kemperle Inc ....E 718 629-1084
   Brooklyn *(G-1574)*
Automotive LLC ....F 248 728-8642
   Batavia *(G-624)*
Ford Motor Company ....B 716 821-4000
   Buffalo *(G-2967)*
Kustom Korner ....F 716 646-0173
   Hamburg *(G-5956)*
M & W Aluminum Products Inc ......F 315 414-0005
   Syracuse *(G-16003)*
P R B Metal Products Inc ....E 631 467-1800
   Ronkonkoma *(G-14986)*
▲ Racing Industries Inc ....E 631 905-0100
   Calverton *(G-3324)*
Sage Parts Plus ....E 718 651-1898
   Flushing *(G-5297)*
Thyssenkrupp Materials NA Inc .....D 585 279-0000
   Rochester *(G-14753)*
Utica Metal Products Inc ....D 315 732-6163
   Utica *(G-16388)*

3466 Crowns & Closures

Protocase Incorporated ....C 866 849-3911
   Lewiston *(G-7456)*
Reynolds Packaging McHy Inc ....D 716 358-6451
   Falconer *(G-4918)*
▲ Van Blarcom Closures Inc ....C 718 855-3810
   Brooklyn *(G-2735)*

3469 Metal Stampings, NEC

4m Precision Industries Inc ....E 315 252-8415
   Auburn *(G-475)*
▲ A-1 Stamping & Spinning Corp .....F 718 388-2626
   Rockaway Park *(G-14812)*
Able National Corp ....E 718 386-8801
   Brooklyn *(G-1549)*
Acme Architectural Products ....B 718 360-0700
   Brooklyn *(G-1553)*
Acme Kitchenettes Corp ....E 518 828-4191
   Hudson *(G-6632)*
▲ Acro Industries Inc ....C 585 254-3661
   Rochester *(G-14186)*
Action Machined Products Inc ....F 631 842-2333
   Copiague *(G-3916)*
Advanced Structures Corp ....F 631 667-5000
   Deer Park *(G-4113)*
Afco Systems Inc ....C 631 249-9441
   Farmingdale *(G-4938)*
▲ Ajl Manufacturing Inc ....C 585 254-1128
   Rochester *(G-14199)*
▲ Albest Metal Stamping Corp ....E 718 388-6000
   Brooklyn *(G-1575)*
All Out Die Cutting Inc ....F 718 346-6666
   Brooklyn *(G-1586)*
▲ Allen Machine Products Inc ....E 631 630-8800
   Hauppauge *(G-6035)*
▲ Allied Metal Spinning Corp ....D 718 893-3300
   Bronx *(G-1269)*
Alton Manufacturing Inc ....E 585 458-2600
   Rochester *(G-14209)*
American Metal Spinning Pdts ......G 631 454-6276
   West Babylon *(G-16796)*
American Mtal Stmping Spinning ..F 718 384-1500
   Brooklyn *(G-1602)*
Arnell Inc ....C 516 486-7098
   Hempstead *(G-6289)*

Arro Manufacturing LLC ....F 716 763-6203
   Lakewood *(G-7310)*
▼ Arro Tool & Die Inc ....F 716 763-6203
   Lakewood *(G-7311)*
Art Precision Metal Products ....F 631 842-8889
   Copiague *(G-3920)*
B & R Tool Inc ....G 718 948-2729
   Staten Island *(G-15662)*
B H M Metal Products Co ....G 845 292-5297
   Kauneonga Lake *(G-7165)*
Bailey Manufacturing Co LLC ....E 716 965-2731
   Forestville *(G-5340)*
Barnes Group Inc ....G 315 457-9200
   Syracuse *(G-15887)*
Barron Metal Products Inc ....E 914 965-1232
   Yonkers *(G-17434)*
Bel-Bee Products Incorporated ......F 845 353-0300
   West Nyack *(G-16942)*
Belmet Products Inc ....E 718 542-8220
   Bronx *(G-1282)*
Belrix Industries Inc ....G 716 821-5964
   Buffalo *(G-2859)*
Bowen Products Corporation ....G 315 498-4481
   Nedrow *(G-8818)*
▲ Brach Machine Inc ....F 585 343-9134
   Batavia *(G-627)*
Bridgeport Metalcraft Inc ....G 315 623-9597
   Constantia *(G-3906)*
Bryant Machine Co Inc ....F 716 894-8282
   Buffalo *(G-2868)*
C & H Precision Tools Inc ....E 631 758-3806
   Holtsville *(G-6527)*
▲ Cameo Metal Products Inc ....E 718 788-1106
   Brooklyn *(G-1753)*
▲ Cannon Industries Inc ....D 585 254-8080
   Rochester *(G-14276)*
▲ Cep Technologies Corporation ......E 914 968-4100
   Yonkers *(G-17443)*
Cgs Fabrication LLC ....E 585 347-6127
   Webster *(G-16740)*
▲ Chamart Exclusives Inc ....G 914 345-3870
   Elmsford *(G-4749)*
Charles A Rogers Entps Inc ....E 585 924-6400
   Victor *(G-16490)*
Check-Mate Industries Inc ....E 631 491-1777
   West Babylon *(G-16807)*
Chivvis Enterprises Inc ....F 631 842-9055
   Copiague *(G-3923)*
Cnc Manufacturing Corp ....E 718 728-6800
   Long Island City *(G-7729)*
Cobbe Industries Inc ....E 716 287-2661
   Gerry *(G-5604)*
▲ Coda Resources Ltd ....D 718 649-1666
   Brooklyn *(G-1789)*
Colonial Precision Machinery ....G 631 249-0738
   Farmingdale *(G-4971)*
Compac Development Corporation ..D 631 881-4903
   Hauppauge *(G-6072)*
Compar Manufacturing Corp ....E 212 304-2777
   New York *(G-9750)*
Corbett Stves Pttern Works Inc .....E 585 546-7109
   Rochester *(G-14310)*
◆ Corning Vitro Corporation ....A 607 974-8605
   Corning *(G-3992)*
◆ Creative Design and Mch Inc ....E 845 778-9001
   Rock Tavern *(G-14809)*
Crosby Company ....E 716 852-3522
   Buffalo *(G-2913)*
Custom Metal Incorporated ....F 631 643-4075
   West Babylon *(G-16812)*
D-K Manufacturing Corp ....E 315 592-4327
   Fulton *(G-5469)*
▲ Dayton Industries Inc ....E 718 542-8144
   Bronx *(G-1314)*
Dayton Rogers New York LLC ....D 585 349-4040
   Rochester *(G-14323)*
Die-Matic Products LLC ....E 516 433-7900
   Plainview *(G-13627)*
▲ Dunkirk Metal Products Wny LLC ..E 716 366-2555
   Dunkirk *(G-4363)*
Electric Motors and Pumps Inc ......G 718 935-9118
   Brooklyn *(G-1912)*
Endicott Precision Inc ....C 607 754-7076
   Endicott *(G-4811)*
Engineering Mfg Tech LLC ....D 607 754-7111
   Endicott *(G-4813)*
Erdle Perforating Holdings Inc ......D 585 247-4700
   Rochester *(G-14376)*
Fabrication Specialties Corp ....G 631 242-0326
   Deer Park *(G-4163)*

SIC SECTION 34 FABRICATED METAL PRODUCTS, EXCEPT MACHINERY AND TRANSPORTATION EQUIPMENT

Falso Industries Inc .... E 315 463-0266
Syracuse *(G-15961)*
▲ **Feldware Inc** .... E 718 372-0486
Brooklyn *(G-1969)*
Forkey Construction & Fabg Inc .... E 607 849-4879
Cortland *(G-4048)*
Forsyth Industries Inc .... E 716 652-1070
Buffalo *(G-2968)*
▲ **Freeport Screen & Stamping** .... E 516 379-0330
Freeport *(G-5412)*
G A Richards & Co Inc .... F 516 334-5412
Westbury *(G-17015)*
▲ **Gasser & Sons Inc** .... C 631 543-6600
Commack *(G-3858)*
Gay Sheet Metal Dies Inc .... G 716 877-0208
Buffalo *(G-2981)*
Gem Metal Spinning & Stamping .... G 718 729-7014
Long Island City *(G-7778)*
Genesee Metal Stampings Inc .... G 585 475-0450
West Henrietta *(G-16912)*
German Machine & Assembly Inc .... E 585 546-4200
Rochester *(G-14419)*
◆ **Gleason Works** .... A 585 473-1000
Rochester *(G-14429)*
Great Lakes Pressed Steel Corp .... E 716 885-4037
Buffalo *(G-2998)*
Greene Technologies Inc .... D 607 656-4166
Greene *(G-5884)*
Hy-Grade Metal Products Corp .... G 315 475-4221
Syracuse *(G-15980)*
▲ **Hyman Podrusnick Co Inc** .... G 718 853-4502
Brooklyn *(G-2089)*
International Ord Tech Inc .... D 716 664-1100
Jamestown *(G-7036)*
J P Machine Products Inc .... F 631 249-9229
Farmingdale *(G-5022)*
Johnson & Hoffman LLC .... D 516 742-3333
Carle Place *(G-3418)*
K Tooling LLC .... F 607 637-3781
Hancock *(G-5986)*
▲ **Kerns Manufacturing Corp** .... C 718 784-4044
Long Island City *(G-7807)*
▼ **Koch Metal Spinning Co Inc** .... D 716 835-3631
Buffalo *(G-3052)*
▲ **Korin Japanese Trading Corp** .... E 212 587-7021
New York *(G-10916)*
Lamparts Co Inc .... F 914 723-8986
Mount Vernon *(G-8745)*
▲ **Lancaster Knives Inc** .... E 716 683-5050
Lancaster *(G-7347)*
▲ **Lb Furniture Industries LLC** .... C 518 828-1501
Hudson *(G-6654)*
Long Island Metalform Inc .... F 631 242-9088
Deer Park *(G-4191)*
M F Manufacturing Enterprises .... G 516 822-5135
Hicksville *(G-6392)*
Maehr Industries Inc .... G 631 924-1661
Bellport *(G-829)*
▲ **Magic Novelty Co Inc** .... E 212 304-2777
New York *(G-11131)*
Mantel & Mantel Stamping Corp .... G 631 467-1916
Ronkonkoma *(G-14964)*
▲ **Marex Aquisition Corp** .... C 585 458-3940
Rochester *(G-14518)*
Matov Industries Inc .... E 718 392-5060
Long Island City *(G-7836)*
McHone Industries Inc .... D 716 945-3380
Salamanca *(G-15128)*
Mega Tool & Mfg Corp .... E 607 734-8398
Elmira *(G-4709)*
Nash Metalware Co Inc .... F 315 339-5794
Rome *(G-14851)*
National Computer & Electronic .... G 631 242-7222
Deer Park *(G-4201)*
National Die & Button Mould Co .... E 201 939-7800
Brooklyn *(G-2357)*
▲ **National Wire & Metal Tech Inc** .... E 716 661-9180
Jamestown *(G-7054)*
▲ **Novel Box Company Ltd** .... E 718 965-2222
Brooklyn *(G-2388)*
▲ **OEM Solutions Inc** .... G 716 864-9324
Clarence *(G-3694)*
▲ **Oxo International Inc** .... C 212 242-3333
New York *(G-11557)*
P R B Metal Products Inc .... F 631 467-1800
Ronkonkoma *(G-14986)*
▲ **P&G Metal Components Corp** .... D 716 896-7900
Buffalo *(G-3130)*
Pall Corporation .... A 607 753-6041
Cortland *(G-4059)*
Pervi Precision Company Inc .... G 631 589-5557
Bohemia *(G-1113)*
Precision Photo-Fab Inc .... D 716 821-9393
Buffalo *(G-3158)*
Precision Tl Die & Stamping Co .... F 516 561-0041
Valley Stream *(G-16444)*
Premier Metals Group .... E 585 436-4020
Rochester *(G-14619)*
▲ **Progressus Company Inc** .... F 516 255-0245
Rockville Centre *(G-14825)*
Pronto Tool & Die Co Inc .... E 631 981-8920
Ronkonkoma *(G-14997)*
Quality Metal Stamping LLC .... G 516 255-9000
Rockville Centre *(G-14826)*
▲ **R G Flair Co Inc** .... E 631 586-7311
Bay Shore *(G-726)*
Rayco Manufacturing Co Inc .... F 516 431-2006
Jamaica *(G-6981)*
Reynolds Manufacturing Inc .... F 607 562-8936
Big Flats *(G-879)*
Richter Metalcraft Corporation .... E 845 895-2025
Wallkill *(G-16565)*
▲ **Rigidized Metals Corporation** .... E 716 849-4703
Buffalo *(G-3186)*
Rochester Stampings Inc .... F 585 467-5241
Rochester *(G-14672)*
▲ **Rolite Mfg Inc** .... E 716 683-0259
Lancaster *(G-7365)*
Russco Metal Spinning Co Inc .... F 516 872-6055
Oceanside *(G-13117)*
▲ **S & S Prtg Die-Cutting Co Inc** .... F 718 388-8990
Brooklyn *(G-2543)*
S D Z Metal Spinning Stamping .... F 718 778-3600
Brooklyn *(G-2548)*
Schiller Stores Inc .... G 631 208-9400
Riverhead *(G-14168)*
Seneca Ceramics Corp .... G 315 781-0100
Phelps *(G-13559)*
Sharon Manufacturing Co Inc .... G 631 242-8870
Deer Park *(G-4234)*
Sharon Metal Stamping Corp .... G 718 828-4510
Bronx *(G-1450)*
Simplex Manufacturing Co Inc .... F 315 252-7524
Auburn *(G-516)*
Smithers Tools & Mch Pdts Inc .... D 845 876-3063
Rhinebeck *(G-14070)*
Solidus Industries Inc .... D 607 749-4540
Homer *(G-6550)*
Square Stamping Mfg Corp .... E 315 896-2641
Barneveld *(G-618)*
▼ **Stampcrete International Ltd** .... E 315 451-2837
Liverpool *(G-7577)*
▲ **Stamped Fittings Inc** .... E 607 733-9988
Elmira Heights *(G-4726)*
▲ **Stever-Locke Industries Inc** .... G 585 624-3450
Honeoye Falls *(G-6565)*
Surving Studios .... F 845 355-1430
Middletown *(G-8499)*
Tooling Enterprises Inc .... F 716 842-0445
Buffalo *(G-3248)*
Tools & Stamping Corp .... G 718 392-4040
Brooklyn *(G-2683)*
Toronto Metal Spinning and Ltg .... E 905 793-1174
Niagara Falls *(G-12900)*
▲ **Tri-Technologies Inc** .... E 914 699-2001
Mount Vernon *(G-8787)*
▲ **Trident Precision Mfg Inc** .... D 585 265-2010
Webster *(G-16764)*
TRW Automotive Inc .... B 315 255-3311
Auburn *(G-522)*
TRW Automotive US LLC .... C 315 255-3311
Auburn *(G-523)*
▲ **Twinco Mfg Co Inc** .... E 631 231-0022
Hauppauge *(G-6243)*
▼ **Ultimate Prcision Met Pdts Inc** .... C 631 249-9441
Farmingdale *(G-5146)*
Universal Shielding Corp .... E 631 667-7900
Deer Park *(G-4244)*
Van Reenen Tool & Die Inc .... F 585 288-6000
Rochester *(G-14779)*
Vanity Fair Bathmart Inc .... F 718 584-6700
Bronx *(G-1487)*
Volkert Precision Tech Inc .... E 718 464-9500
Queens Village *(G-13999)*
Vosky Precision Machining Corp .... F 631 737-3200
Ronkonkoma *(G-15024)*
W & H Stampings Inc .... E 631 234-6161
Hauppauge *(G-6254)*
Web Associates Inc .... G 716 883-3377
Buffalo *(G-3275)*
Wessie Machine Inc .... G 315 926-4060
Marion *(G-8134)*
Wilmax Usa LLC .... F 917 388-2790
New York *(G-12666)*
WR Smith & Sons Inc .... G 845 620-9400
Nanuet *(G-8809)*
Zeta Machine Corp .... G 631 471-8832
Ronkonkoma *(G-15026)*

3471 Electroplating, Plating, Polishing, Anodizing & Coloring

21st Century Finishes Inc .... F 516 221-7000
North Bellmore *(G-12931)*
Abetter Processing Corp .... F 718 252-2223
Brooklyn *(G-1547)*
Able Anodizing Corp .... F 718 252-0660
Brooklyn *(G-1548)*
ABS Metal Corp .... G 646 302-9018
Hewlett *(G-6330)*
Aircraft Finishing Corp .... F 631 422-5000
West Babylon *(G-16792)*
Airmarine Electroplating Corp .... G 516 623-4406
Freeport *(G-5390)*
Anthony River Inc .... F 315 475-1315
Syracuse *(G-15875)*
Astro Electroplating Inc .... E 631 968-0656
Bay Shore *(G-672)*
B & W Heat Treating Company .... G 716 876-8184
Tonawanda *(G-16164)*
Barnes Metal Finishing Inc .... F 585 798-4817
Medina *(G-8298)*
▲ **Berkman Bros Inc** .... E 718 782-1827
Brooklyn *(G-1684)*
Bfg Manufacturing Services Inc .... E 716 362-0888
Buffalo *(G-2863)*
Buffalo Metal Finishing Co .... G 716 883-2751
Buffalo *(G-2878)*
C H Thompson Company Inc .... D 607 724-1094
Binghamton *(G-897)*
Carpenter Industries Inc .... F 315 463-4284
Syracuse *(G-15905)*
Coating Technology Inc .... E 585 546-7170
Rochester *(G-14303)*
Control Electropolishing Corp .... F 718 858-6634
Brooklyn *(G-1799)*
D & I Finishing Inc .... G 631 471-3034
Bohemia *(G-1044)*
D & W Enterprises LLC .... F 585 590-6727
Medina *(G-8303)*
Dan Kane Plating Co Inc .... F 212 675-4947
New York *(G-9852)*
Dura Spec Inc .... F 718 526-3053
North Baldwin *(G-12921)*
Eastside Oxide Co .... E 607 734-1253
Elmira *(G-4693)*
Electro Plating Service Inc .... F 914 948-3777
White Plains *(G-17130)*
Empire Metal Finishing Inc .... E 718 545-6700
Astoria *(G-438)*
▼ **Epner Technology Incorporated** .... E 718 782-5948
Brooklyn *(G-1933)*
Epner Technology Incorporated .... E 718 782-8722
Brooklyn *(G-1934)*
Eric S Turner & Company Inc .... F 914 235-7114
New Rochelle *(G-8943)*
▲ **Ever-Nu-Metal Products Inc** .... F 646 423-5833
Brooklyn *(G-1945)*
F & H Metal Finishing Co Inc .... F 585 798-2151
Medina *(G-8304)*
Fallon Inc .... E 718 326-7226
Maspeth *(G-8169)*
Finest Cc Corp .... G 917 574-4525
Bronx *(G-1334)*
First Impressions Finishing .... G 631 467-2244
Ronkonkoma *(G-14929)*
Frontier Plating .... G 716 896-2811
Buffalo *(G-2974)*
G J C Ltd Inc .... E 607 770-4500
Binghamton *(G-912)*
Galmer Ltd .... G 718 392-4609
Long Island City *(G-7777)*
General Galvanizing Sup Co Inc .... E 718 589-4300
Bronx *(G-1345)*
General Plating LLC .... E 585 423-0830
Rochester *(G-14412)*
Genesee Vly Met Finshg Co Inc .... G 585 232-4412
Rochester *(G-14416)*
Greene Technologies Inc .... D 607 656-4166
Greene *(G-5884)*

S I C

Employee Codes: A=Over 500 employees, B=251-500
C=101-250, D=51-100, E=20-50, F=10-19, G=5-9

2018 Harris
New York Manufacturers Directory

815

34 FABRICATED METAL PRODUCTS, EXCEPT MACHINERY AND TRANSPORTATION EQUIPMENT

Company	Code	Phone
Halmark Architectural Finshg Brooklyn (G-2062)	E	718 272-1831
Hartchrom Inc Watervliet (G-16710)	F	518 880-0411
Harvard Maintenance Inc New York (G-10469)	A	212 682-2617
▲ I W Industries Inc Melville (G-8359)	C	631 293-9494
▲ Jay Strongwater Holdings LLC New York (G-10745)	A	646 657-0558
John Larocca & Son Inc Huntington Station (G-6750)	G	631 423-5256
Kent Electro-Plating Corp Dix Hills (G-4315)	F	718 358-9599
Key Tech Finishing Buffalo (G-3046)	E	716 832-1232
▲ Keymark Corporation Fonda (G-5321)	A	518 853-3421
Keystone Corporation Buffalo (G-3048)	E	716 832-1232
L W S Inc Ronkonkoma (G-14953)	F	631 580-0472
Maracle Industrial Finshg Co Rochester (G-14516)	E	585 387-9077
Master Craft Finishers Inc Deer Park (G-4195)	E	631 586-0540
McAlpin Industries Inc Rochester (G-14522)	E	585 544-5335
Metal Man Restoration Mount Vernon (G-8750)	F	914 662-4218
Multitone Finishing Co Inc West Hempstead (G-16892)	G	516 485-1043
▲ Nas CP Corp College Point (G-3823)	E	718 961-6757
Nassau Chromium Plating Co Inc Mineola (G-8559)	E	516 746-6666
North East Finishing Co Inc Copiague (G-3941)	F	631 789-8000
Oerlikon Blzers Cating USA Inc Buffalo (G-3121)	E	716 564-8557
P3 Technologies Rochester (G-14586)	G	585 730-7340
Paradigm Group LLC Bronx (G-1421)	G	718 860-1538
Praxair Surface Tech Inc Orangeburg (G-13264)	C	845 398-8322
▲ Precious Plate Inc Niagara Falls (G-12880)	D	716 283-0690
Products Superb Inc Clyde (G-3756)	G	315 923-7057
Psb Ltd Rochester (G-14630)	F	585 654-7078
Rainbow Powder Coating Corp Deer Park (G-4223)	G	631 586-4019
Rayco of Schenectady Inc Amsterdam (G-367)	F	518 212-5113
Reynolds Tech Fabricators Inc East Syracuse (G-4573)	E	315 437-0532
Rochester Overnight Pltg LLC Rochester (G-14667)	D	585 328-4590
Saccomize Inc Bronx (G-1445)	G	818 287-3000
Sandys Bumper Mart Inc Syracuse (G-16053)	G	315 472-8149
Sas Maintenance Services Inc Brooklyn (G-2559)	F	718 837-2124
Sherrill Manufacturing Inc Sherrill (G-15430)	C	315 280-0727
Silverman & Gorf Inc Brooklyn (G-2585)	F	718 625-1309
Surface Finish Technology Elmira (G-4716)	E	607 732-2909
T & M Plating Inc New York (G-12286)	E	212 967-1110
Tcmf Inc Binghamton (G-948)	D	607 724-1094
Thomas Foundry LLC Oneida (G-13190)	G	315 361-9048
Tripp Plating Works Inc Buffalo (G-3252)	F	716 894-2424
Tronic Plating Co Inc Farmingdale (G-5145)	F	516 293-7883
Tropical Driftwood Originals Roosevelt (G-15033)	G	516 623-0980
Tru-Tone Metal Products Inc Brooklyn (G-2705)	E	718 386-5960
US Electroplating Corp West Babylon (G-16869)	G	631 293-1998
Utica Metal Products Inc Utica (G-16388)	D	315 732-6163
Vernon Plating Works Inc Woodside (G-17376)	F	718 639-1124
Vibra Tech Industries Inc White Plains (G-17208)	F	914 946-1916
▲ Victoria Plating Co Inc Bronx (G-1489)	D	718 589-1550
West Falls Machine Co Inc East Aurora (G-4404)	F	716 655-0440
Wilco Finishing Corp Brooklyn (G-2767)	E	718 417-6405

3479 Coating & Engraving, NEC

Company	Code	Phone
Accurate Pnt Powdr Coating Inc Rochester (G-14182)	F	585 235-1650
Advanced Coating Service LLC Rochester (G-14192)	G	585 247-3970
Advanced Coating Techniques Babylon (G-542)	E	631 643-4555
▼ Advanced Graphics Company Whitney Point (G-17248)	F	607 692-7875
Advanced Surface Finishing Westbury (G-16990)	E	516 876-9710
Aircraft Finishing Corp West Babylon (G-16792)	F	631 422-5000
All Spec Finishing Inc Binghamton (G-883)	E	607 770-9174
▲ Angiotech Biocoatings Corp Henrietta (G-6315)	F	585 321-1130
Applause Coating LLC Brentwood (G-1173)	F	631 231-5223
Ascribe Inc Rochester (G-14234)	E	585 413-0298
Ashburns Inc New York (G-9281)	G	212 227-5692
Barson Composites Corporation Old Bethpage (G-13147)	E	516 752-7882
▲ Berkman Bros Inc Brooklyn (G-1684)	E	718 782-1827
Buffalo Finishing Works Inc Buffalo (G-2873)	G	716 893-5266
Buffalo Metal Finishing Co Buffalo (G-2878)	G	716 883-2751
C & M Products Inc Syracuse (G-15899)	G	315 471-3303
C H Thompson Company Inc Binghamton (G-897)	D	607 724-1094
Chepaume Industries LLC Vernon (G-16456)	G	315 829-6400
Chromalloy Gas Turbine LLC Middletown (G-8464)	E	845 692-8912
Clad Metal Specialties Inc Bay Shore (G-682)	F	631 666-7750
Cnv Architectural Coatings Inc Brooklyn (G-1788)	F	718 418-9584
Color Craft Finishing Corp Bohemia (G-1034)	F	631 563-3230
Color ME Mine Rochester (G-14304)	F	585 383-8420
▲ Custom House Engravers Inc Bohemia (G-1042)	F	631 567-3004
Custom Laser Inc Lockport (G-7606)	E	716 434-8600
D & I Finishing Inc Bohemia (G-1044)	F	631 471-3034
Deloka LLC Lyons (G-7999)	G	315 946-6910
Duzmor Painting Inc Le Roy (G-7432)	G	585 768-4760
Dynocoat Inc Holbrook (G-6472)	F	631 244-9344
Eastern Silver of Boro Park Brooklyn (G-1900)	G	718 854-5600
▲ Electronic Coating Tech Inc Cohoes (G-3771)	F	518 688-2048
Elegance Coating Ltd Champlain (G-3568)	E	386 668-8379
Everlasting Images Endicott (G-4814)	F	607 785-8743
F & H Metal Finishing Co Inc Medina (G-8304)	F	585 798-2151
▲ Fougera Pharmaceuticals Inc Melville (G-8350)	C	631 454-7677
▲ Frontier Ht-Dip Glvanizing Inc Buffalo (G-2972)	F	716 875-2091
Future Spray Finishing Co Deer Park (G-4168)	G	631 242-6252
Greene Technologies Inc Greene (G-5884)	D	607 656-4166
Harold Wood Co Inc Buffalo (G-3007)	F	716 873-1535
Hatfield Metal Fab Inc Poughkeepsie (G-13926)	E	845 454-9078
▲ Heany Industries Inc Scottsville (G-15358)	D	585 889-2700
▲ Hilord Chemical Corporation Hauppauge (G-6117)	E	631 234-7373
Hitemco Medical Applications Old Bethpage (G-13149)	C	516 752-7882
Hubbell Galvanizing Inc Yorkville (G-17539)	G	315 736-8311
Hudson Valley Coatings LLC Congers (G-3882)	G	845 398-1778
Industrial Paint Services Corp Owego (G-13377)	F	607 687-0107
▼ Jamestown Bronze Works Inc Jamestown (G-7039)	G	716 665-2302
▲ Jrlon Inc Palmyra (G-13434)	D	315 597-4067
▲ Keymark Corporation Fonda (G-5321)	A	518 853-3421
Kwong CHI Metal Fabrication Brooklyn (G-2184)	G	718 369-6429
▲ Lodolce Machine Co Inc Saugerties (G-15216)	E	845 246-7017
Mac Artspray Finishing Corp Brooklyn (G-2252)	F	718 649-3800
Master Craft Finishers Inc Deer Park (G-4195)	E	631 586-0540
McHugh Painting Co Inc Clarence (G-3692)	F	716 741-8077
▲ Metal Cladding Inc Lockport (G-7629)	D	716 434-5513
Modern Coating and Research Palmyra (G-13437)	E	315 597-3517
◆ Momentive Performance Mtls Inc Waterford (G-16638)	E	518 237-3330
Momentive Prfmce Mtls Holdings Albany (G-102)	A	518 533-4600
Monroe County Auto Svcs Inc Rochester (G-14540)	E	585 764-3741
Mpm Holdings Inc Waterford (G-16639)	G	518 237-3330
Mpm Intermediate Holdings Inc Waterford (G-16640)	E	518 237-3330
Nameplate Mfrs of Amer Farmingville (G-5070)	E	631 752-0055
NC Industries Inc Buffalo (G-3103)	F	248 528-5200
Newchem Inc Newark (G-12759)	E	315 331-7680
▲ O W Hubbell & Sons Inc Yorkville (G-17540)	E	315 736-8311
Oerlikon Blzers Cating USA Inc Amherst (G-254)	E	716 270-2228
Oerlikon Blzers Cating USA Inc Amherst (G-255)	E	716 270-2228
Oerlikon Blzers Cating USA Inc Buffalo (G-3121)	E	716 564-8557
Paradigm Group LLC Bronx (G-1421)	G	718 860-1538
Piper Plastics Corp Copiague (G-3942)	E	631 842-6889
Precision Design Systems Inc Rochester (G-14614)	E	585 426-4500
Precision Laser Technology LLC Rochester (G-14616)	F	585 458-6208
Pro-Teck Coating Inc Holland (G-6510)	F	716 537-2619
▲ Qualicoat Inc Churchville (G-3669)	F	585 293-2650
R S T Cable and Tape Inc Ronkonkoma (G-15000)	G	631 981-0096
Rayana Designs Inc Long Island City (G-7889)	F	718 786-2040
Read Manufacturing Company Inc Holbrook (G-6496)	E	631 567-4487
Rims Like New Inc Middletown (G-8495)	F	845 537-0396
Sentry Metal Blast Inc Lockport (G-7645)	F	716 285-5241
Sequa Corporation Orangeburg (G-13269)	E	201 343-1122
Solidus Industries Inc Homer (G-6550)	D	607 749-4540
Specialty Bldg Solutions Inc West Babylon (G-16863)	G	631 393-6918
Steel Partners Holdings LP New York (G-12212)	E	212 520-2300
Stuart-Dean Co Inc Long Island City (G-7921)	F	718 472-1326

SIC SECTION   34 FABRICATED METAL PRODUCTS, EXCEPT MACHINERY AND TRANSPORTATION EQUIPMENT

▲ Superior Metals & Processing ....G...... 718 545-7500
  Long Island City *(G-7923)*
Swain Technology Inc ....F...... 585 889-2786
  Scottsville *(G-15362)*
Tailored Coatings Inc ....G...... 716 893-4869
  Buffalo *(G-3234)*
The Gramecy Group ....G...... 518 348-1325
  Clifton Park *(G-3736)*
Tj Powder Coaters LLC ....G...... 607 724-4779
  Binghamton *(G-949)*
Trojan Metal Fabrication Inc ....E...... 631 968-5040
  Bay Shore *(G-745)*
▲ Turbine Arfoil Cating Repr LLC ....C...... 845 692-8912
  Middletown *(G-8502)*
W Hubbell & Sons Inc ....G...... 315 736-8311
  Yorkville *(G-17546)*
W W Custom Clad Inc ....D...... 518 673-3322
  Canajoharie *(G-3362)*

3482 Small Arms Ammunition

Benjamin Sheridan Corporation ....G...... 585 657-6161
  Bloomfield *(G-975)*
CIC International Ltd ....D...... 212 213-0089
  Brooklyn *(G-1778)*
▲ Crosman Corporation ....E...... 585 657-6161
  Bloomfield *(G-980)*
Crosman Corporation ....E...... 585 398-3920
  Farmington *(G-5157)*

3483 Ammunition, Large

CIC International Ltd ....D...... 212 213-0089
  Brooklyn *(G-1778)*
Circor Aerospace Inc ....D...... 631 737-1900
  Hauppauge *(G-6065)*

3484 Small Arms

Benjamin Sheridan Corporation ....G...... 585 657-6161
  Bloomfield *(G-975)*
▲ Crosman Corporation ....E...... 585 657-6161
  Bloomfield *(G-980)*
Crosman Corporation ....E...... 585 398-3920
  Farmington *(G-5157)*
Dan Wesson Corp ....F...... 607 336-1174
  Norwich *(G-13045)*
Hart Rifle Barrel Inc ....G...... 315 677-9841
  Syracuse *(G-15978)*
Kyntec Corporation ....G...... 716 810-6956
  Buffalo *(G-3056)*
Magpump LLC ....G...... 585 444-9812
  Henrietta *(G-6320)*
Oriskany Arms Inc ....F...... 315 737-2196
  Oriskany *(G-13336)*
▼ Redding-Hunter Inc ....E...... 607 753-3331
  Cortland *(G-4066)*
Remington Arms Company LLC ....A...... 315 895-3482
  Ilion *(G-6783)*
Sycamore Hill Designs Inc ....G...... 585 820-7322
  Victor *(G-16528)*
▲ Tri-Technologies Inc ....E...... 914 699-2001
  Mount Vernon *(G-8787)*

3489 Ordnance & Access, NEC

CIC International Ltd ....D...... 212 213-0089
  Brooklyn *(G-1778)*
Dyno Nobel Inc ....D...... 845 338-2144
  Ulster Park *(G-16308)*
◆ Island Ordnance Systems LLC ....F...... 516 746-2100
  Mineola *(G-8550)*
▲ Magellan Aerospace NY Inc ....C...... 718 699-4000
  Corona *(G-4025)*
▼ Mil-Spec Industries Corp ....G...... 516 625-5787
  Glen Cove *(G-5634)*

3491 Industrial Valves

ADC Industries Inc ....E...... 516 596-1304
  Valley Stream *(G-16424)*
▲ Air System Products Inc ....F...... 716 683-0435
  Lancaster *(G-7324)*
Byelocorp Scientific Inc ....E...... 212 785-2580
  New York *(G-9539)*
Caithness Equities Corporation ....E...... 212 599-2112
  New York *(G-9549)*
◆ Curtiss-Wright Flow Ctrl Corp ....C...... 631 293-3800
  Farmingdale *(G-4978)*
Curtiss-Wright Flow Ctrl Corp ....C...... 631 293-3800
  Farmingdale *(G-4979)*
Digital Home Creations Inc ....G...... 585 576-7070
  Webster *(G-16745)*

Doyle & Roth Mfg Co Inc ....F...... 212 269-7840
  New York *(G-9972)*
Dresser-Rand Company ....A...... 585 596-3100
  Wellsville *(G-16777)*
◆ Flomatic Corporation ....E...... 518 761-9797
  Glens Falls *(G-5695)*
▲ Flow-Safe Inc ....E...... 716 662-2585
  Orchard Park *(G-13293)*
ITT LLC ....C...... 315 568-4733
  Seneca Falls *(G-15386)*
J H Buscher Inc ....G...... 716 667-2003
  Orchard Park *(G-13300)*
▲ John N Fehlinger Co Inc ....F...... 212 233-5656
  New York *(G-10791)*
McWane Inc ....B...... 607 734-2211
  Elmira *(G-4708)*
▲ Murphy Manufacturing Co Inc ....G...... 585 223-0100
  Fairport *(G-4871)*
◆ Plattco Corporation ....E...... 518 563-4640
  Plattsburgh *(G-13715)*
▲ Precision Valve & Automtn Inc ......C...... 518 371-2684
  Cohoes *(G-3779)*
▲ Spence Engineering Company Inc ...C...... 845 778-5566
  Walden *(G-16556)*
Syraco Products Inc ....E...... 315 476-5306
  Syracuse *(G-16072)*
▲ Total Energy Fabrication Corp ....G...... 580 363-1500
  North Salem *(G-12956)*
▲ Town Food Service Eqp Co Inc ......F...... 718 388-5650
  Brooklyn *(G-2691)*
Trac Regulators Inc ....E...... 914 699-9352
  Mount Vernon *(G-8785)*
Tyco Simplexgrinnell ....E...... 315 437-9664
  East Syracuse *(G-4586)*
◆ William E Williams Valve Corp ....E...... 718 392-1660
  Long Island City *(G-7951)*

3492 Fluid Power Valves & Hose Fittings

▲ A K Allen Co Inc ....C...... 516 747-5450
  Mineola *(G-8522)*
Aalborg Instrs & Contrls Inc ....D...... 845 398-3160
  Orangeburg *(G-13238)*
▲ Aerco International Inc ....C...... 845 580-8000
  Blauvelt *(G-963)*
▲ BW Elliott Mfg Co LLC ....B...... 607 772-0404
  Binghamton *(G-896)*
Direkt Force LLC ....E...... 716 652-3022
  East Aurora *(G-4394)*
Dmic Inc ....F...... 716 743-4360
  North Tonawanda *(G-12987)*
Dsti Inc ....G...... 716 557-2362
  Olean *(G-13165)*
Dynamic Sealing Tech Inc ....G...... 716 376-0708
  Olean *(G-13166)*
◆ Eastport Operating Partners LP ......E...... 212 387-8791
  New York *(G-10020)*
▲ Key High Vacuum Products Inc .....E...... 631 584-5959
  Nesconset *(G-8823)*
Kinemotive Corporation ....G...... 631 249-6440
  Farmingdale *(G-5035)*
▲ KSA Manufacturing LLC ....F...... 315 488-0809
  Camillus *(G-3351)*
Lourdes Industries Inc ....D...... 631 234-6600
  Hauppauge *(G-6146)*
Moog Inc ....B...... 716 687-4954
  East Aurora *(G-4400)*
◆ Moog Inc ....A...... 716 652-2000
  Elma *(G-4664)*
Own Instrument Inc ....E...... 914 668-6546
  Mount Vernon *(G-8758)*
▲ Power Drives Inc ....D...... 716 822-3600
  Buffalo *(G-3155)*
Servotronics Inc ....C...... 716 655-5990
  Elma *(G-4668)*
▲ Steel & Obrien Mfg Inc ....D...... 585 492-5800
  Arcade *(G-399)*
Tactair Fluid Controls Inc ....C...... 315 451-3928
  Liverpool *(G-7579)*
Upstate Tube Inc ....G...... 315 488-5636
  Camillus *(G-3354)*
Young & Franklin Inc ....D...... 315 457-3110
  Liverpool *(G-7586)*

3493 Steel Springs, Except Wire

Angelica Spring Company Inc ....F...... 585 466-7892
  Angelica *(G-377)*
Chet Kruszkas Service Inc ....F...... 716 662-7450
  Orchard Park *(G-13284)*
Isolation Dynamics Corp ....E...... 631 491-5670
  West Babylon *(G-16823)*

▲ Lee Spring Company LLC ....C...... 718 362-5183
  Brooklyn *(G-2207)*
▲ Midstate Spring Inc ....E...... 315 437-2623
  Syracuse *(G-16010)*
▲ Newport Magnetics Inc ....G...... 315 845-8878
  Newport *(G-12815)*
▲ Red Onyx Industrial Pdts LLC ....E...... 516 459-6035
  Huntington *(G-6712)*
Temper Corporation ....E...... 518 853-3467
  Fonda *(G-5322)*
Whitesboro Spring & Alignment ....F...... 315 736-4441
  Whitesboro *(G-17226)*
Whiting Door Mfg Corp ....D...... 716 542-3070
  Akron *(G-28)*

3494 Valves & Pipe Fittings, NEC

▲ A K Allen Co Inc ....C...... 516 747-5450
  Mineola *(G-8522)*
Aalborg Instrs & Contrls Inc ....D...... 845 398-3160
  Orangeburg *(G-13238)*
Advanced Thermal Systems Inc ....E...... 716 681-1800
  Lancaster *(G-7322)*
▲ Anderson Precision Inc ....G...... 716 484-1148
  Jamestown *(G-7007)*
◆ Curtiss-Wright Flow Ctrl Corp ....C...... 631 293-3800
  Farmingdale *(G-4978)*
▼ Delaware Mfg Inds Corp ....G...... 716 743-4360
  North Tonawanda *(G-12986)*
▼ Devin Mfg Inc ....F...... 585 496-5770
  Arcade *(G-391)*
◆ Flomatic Corporation ....E...... 518 761-9797
  Glens Falls *(G-5695)*
Ford Regulator Valve Corp ....G...... 718 497-3255
  Brooklyn *(G-1994)*
Goodman Main Stopper Mfg Co ....F...... 718 875-5140
  Brooklyn *(G-2040)*
J H Robotics Inc ....E...... 607 729-3758
  Johnson City *(G-7127)*
▲ Key High Vacuum Products Inc .....E...... 631 584-5959
  Nesconset *(G-8823)*
Kingston Hoops Summer ....G...... 845 401-6830
  Kingston *(G-7222)*
Lance Valves ....F...... 716 681-5825
  Lancaster *(G-7348)*
Legacy Valve LLC ....F...... 914 403-5075
  Valhalla *(G-16394)*
Lemode Plumbing & Heating ....E...... 718 545-3336
  Astoria *(G-445)*
M Manastrip-M Corporation ....G...... 518 664-2089
  Clifton Park *(G-3726)*
▲ Make-Waves Instrument Corp ....E...... 716 681-7524
  Buffalo *(G-3076)*
Martin Brass Works Inc ....F...... 718 523-3146
  Jamaica *(G-6964)*
Micromold Products Inc ....E...... 914 969-2850
  Yonkers *(G-17485)*
Rand Machine Products Inc ....D...... 716 665-5217
  Falconer *(G-4916)*
Ross Valve Mfg ....G...... 518 274-0961
  Troy *(G-16275)*
Sigmamotor Inc ....E...... 716 735-3115
  Middleport *(G-8457)*
Smiths Gas Service Inc ....E...... 518 438-0400
  Albany *(G-134)*
▲ Spence Engineering Company Inc ...C...... 845 778-5566
  Walden *(G-16556)*
▲ Steel & Obrien Mfg Inc ....D...... 585 492-5800
  Arcade *(G-399)*
Sure Flow Equipment Inc ....E...... 800 263-8251
  Tonawanda *(G-16224)*
▲ Total Piping Solutions Inc ....F...... 716 372-0160
  Olean *(G-13176)*
▲ United Pipe Nipple Co Inc ....F...... 516 295-2468
  Hewlett *(G-6338)*
Venco Sales Inc ....E...... 631 754-0782
  Huntington *(G-6729)*
◆ William E Williams Valve Corp ....E...... 718 392-1660
  Long Island City *(G-7951)*

3495 Wire Springs

Ajax Wire Specialty Co Inc ....F...... 516 935-2333
  Hicksville *(G-6342)*
Barnes Group Inc ....G...... 315 457-9200
  Syracuse *(G-15887)*
Commerce Spring Corp ....F...... 631 293-4844
  Farmingdale *(G-4844)*
Commercial Communications LLC ....G...... 845 343-9078
  Middletown *(G-8466)*
Fennell Spring Company LLC ....D...... 607 739-3541
  Horseheads *(G-6606)*

Employee Codes: A=Over 500 employees, B=251-500
C=101-250, D=51-100, E=20-50, F=10-19, G=5-9

34 FABRICATED METAL PRODUCTS, EXCEPT MACHINERY AND TRANSPORTATION EQUIPMENT

Kinemotive Corporation .... E 631 249-6440
  Farmingdale *(G-5035)*
▲ Lee Spring Company LLC .... C 718 362-5183
  Brooklyn *(G-2207)*
Lee Spring LLC .... E 718 236-2222
  Brooklyn *(G-2208)*
▲ Midstate Spring Inc .... E 315 437-2623
  Syracuse *(G-16010)*
▼ Pullman Mfg Corporation .... G 585 334-1350
  Rochester *(G-14631)*
Teka Precision Inc .... G 845 753-1900
  Nyack *(G-13072)*
◆ The Caldwell Manufacturing Co .. D 585 352-3790
  Rochester *(G-14748)*
The Caldwell Manufacturing Co ..... E 585 352-2803
  Victor *(G-16532)*
Unimex Corporation .... D 212 755-8800
  New York *(G-12477)*
Unimex Corporation .... E 718 236-2222
  Brooklyn *(G-2719)*

3496 Misc Fabricated Wire Prdts

369 River Road Inc .... E 716 694-5001
  North Tonawanda *(G-12970)*
▲ Abbott Industries Inc .... E 718 291-0800
  Jamaica *(G-6926)*
▲ Aeroflex Incorporated .... B 516 694-6700
  Plainview *(G-13608)*
▲ Albest Metal Stamping Corp .... D 718 388-6000
  Brooklyn *(G-1575)*
All-Lifts Incorporated .... E 518 465-3461
  Albany *(G-42)*
▲ American Intl Trimming .... G 718 369-9643
  Brooklyn *(G-1600)*
▲ American Wire Tie Inc .... E 716 337-2412
  North Collins *(G-12942)*
Angelica Spring Company Inc .... F 585 466-7892
  Angelica *(G-377)*
Bayshore Wire Products Corp .... F 631 451-8825
  Coram *(G-3964)*
▲ Better Wire Products Inc .... E 716 883-3377
  Buffalo *(G-2862)*
▲ Brook North Farms Inc .... E 315 834-9390
  Auburn *(G-486)*
▲ Cable Management Solutions Inc ... E 631 674-0004
  Bay Shore *(G-678)*
▲ Chemprene Inc .... C 845 831-2800
  Beacon *(G-777)*
▲ Chemprene Holding Inc .... C 845 831-2800
  Beacon *(G-778)*
▲ Clover Wire Forming Co Inc .... E 914 375-0400
  Yonkers *(G-17444)*
▼ Cobra Systems Inc .... F 845 338-6675
  Bloomington *(G-987)*
◆ Columbus McKinnon Corporation .. C 716 689-5400
  Getzville *(G-5607)*
Columbus McKinnon Corporation ... E 716 689-5400
  Getzville *(G-5608)*
Columbus McKinnon Corporation ... E 716 689-5400
  Getzville *(G-5609)*
Compar Manufacturing Corp .... E 212 304-2777
  New York *(G-9750)*
▲ Continental Cordage Corp .... D 315 655-9800
  Cazenovia *(G-3470)*
◆ Cortland Cable Company Inc ...... E 607 753-8276
  Cortland *(G-4039)*
▲ Cuba Specialty Mfg Co Inc .... F 585 567-4176
  Fillmore *(G-5183)*
Cuddeback Machining Inc .... C 585 392-5889
  Hilton *(G-6443)*
▲ Dico Products Corporation .... F 315 797-0470
  Utica *(G-16346)*
Engineering Mfg Tech LLC .... D 607 754-7111
  Endicott *(G-4813)*
Flanagans Creative Disp Inc .... E 845 858-2542
  Port Jervis *(G-13806)*
Flatcut LLC .... G 212 542-5732
  Brooklyn *(G-1984)*
▲ G Bopp USA Inc .... E 845 296-1065
  Wappingers Falls *(G-16589)*
Habasit America Inc .... D 716 824-8484
  Buffalo *(G-3001)*
Hitachi Metals America Ltd .... E 914 694-9200
  Purchase *(G-13974)*
▲ Hohmann & Barnard Inc .... E 631 234-0600
  Hauppauge *(G-6118)*
Hohmann & Barnard Inc .... E 518 357-9757
  Schenectady *(G-15295)*
Interstate Wood Products Inc .... E 631 842-4488
  Amityville *(G-296)*

J Davis Manufacturing Co Inc .... E 315 337-7574
  Rome *(G-14844)*
Joldeson One Aerospace Inds .... D 718 848-7396
  Ozone Park *(G-13406)*
Kehr-Buffalo Wire Frame Co Inc .... E 716 897-2288
  Buffalo *(G-3044)*
▲ Lubow Machine Corp .... F 631 226-1700
  Copiague *(G-3936)*
Lyn Jo Enterprises Ltd .... E 716 753-2776
  Mayville *(G-8248)*
▲ Magic Novelty Co Inc .... E 212 304-2777
  New York *(G-11131)*
▲ Nexans Energy USA Inc .... C 845 469-2141
  Chester *(G-3637)*
Nyc Fireplaces & Kitchens .... E 718 326-4328
  Maspeth *(G-8191)*
Oneida Sales & Service Inc .... E 716 822-8205
  Buffalo *(G-3123)*
▲ Peck & Hale LLC .... E 631 589-2510
  West Sayville *(G-16966)*
Quality Industrial Services .... F 716 667-7703
  Orchard Park *(G-13319)*
Reelcology Inc .... F 845 258-1880
  Pine Island *(G-13580)*
◆ Renco Group Inc .... G 212 541-6000
  New York *(G-11864)*
▲ Rose Fence Inc .... E 516 223-0777
  Freeport *(G-5434)*
Rose Fence Inc .... E 516 790-2308
  Halesite *(G-5929)*
Rose Fence Inc .... E 516 223-0777
  Baldwin *(G-560)*
SCI Bore Inc .... G 212 674-7128
  New York *(G-12021)*
▲ Selectrode Industries Inc .... G 631 547-5470
  Huntington Station *(G-6760)*
▲ Sigmund Cohn Corp .... D 914 664-5300
  Mount Vernon *(G-8780)*
Sinclair International Company ...... E 518 798-2361
  Queensbury *(G-14025)*
Star Wire Mesh Fabricators .... E 212 831-4133
  New York *(G-12209)*
Sunward Electronics Inc .... F 518 687-0030
  Troy *(G-16281)*
Teka Precision Inc .... G 845 753-1900
  Nyack *(G-13072)*
Trylon Wire & Metal Works Inc .... E 718 542-4472
  Bronx *(G-1480)*
Ultra Clarity Corp .... E 719 470-1010
  Spring Valley *(G-15625)*
Utility Engineering Co .... E 845 735-8900
  Pearl River *(G-13492)*
▲ Weico Wire & Cable Inc .... E 631 254-2970
  Edgewood *(G-4634)*

3497 Metal Foil & Leaf

◆ Alufoil Products Co Inc .... F 631 231-4141
  Hauppauge *(G-6037)*
American Packaging Corporation ... E 585 254-2002
  Rochester *(G-14213)*
▲ American Packaging Corporation .. C 585 254-9500
  Rochester *(G-14214)*
De Luxe Packaging Corp .... E 416 754-4633
  Saugerties *(G-15212)*
Genesis One Unlimited .... G 516 208-5863
  West Hempstead *(G-16885)*
Oak-Mitsui Inc .... D 518 686-8060
  Hoosick Falls *(G-6569)*
▲ Oak-Mitsui Technologies LLC ..... E 518 686-4961
  Hoosick Falls *(G-6570)*
Pactiv LLC .... E 518 793-2524
  Glens Falls *(G-5710)*
Quick Roll Leaf Mfg Co Inc .... E 845 457-1500
  Montgomery *(G-8637)*
Steel Partners Holdings LP .... E 212 520-2300
  New York *(G-12212)*
Thermal Process Cnstr Co .... E 631 293-6400
  Farmingdale *(G-5139)*
Tri-State Food Jobbers Inc .... G 718 921-1211
  Brooklyn *(G-2696)*

3498 Fabricated Pipe & Pipe Fittings

Accord Pipe Fabricators Inc .... E 718 657-3900
  Jamaica *(G-6927)*
Advanced Thermal Systems Inc .... E 716 681-1800
  Lancaster *(G-7322)*
Albany Nipple and Pipe Mfg .... E 518 270-2162
  Troy *(G-16239)*
▲ Arcadia Mfg Group Inc .... E 518 434-6213
  Green Island *(G-5871)*

Arcadia Mfg Group Inc .... G 518 434-6213
  Menands *(G-8399)*
▲ Cobey Inc .... C 716 362-9550
  Buffalo *(G-2897)*
Coventry Manufacturing Co Inc ..... E 914 668-2212
  Mount Vernon *(G-8719)*
D & G Welding Inc .... G 716 873-3088
  Buffalo *(G-2918)*
Daikin Applied Americas Inc .... D 315 253-2771
  Auburn *(G-490)*
Falcon Perspectives Inc .... E 718 706-9168
  Long Island City *(G-7766)*
Flatcut LLC .... G 212 542-5732
  Brooklyn *(G-1984)*
H & H Metal Specialty Inc .... E 716 665-2110
  Jamestown *(G-7031)*
J D Steward Inc .... G 718 358-0169
  Flushing *(G-5263)*
James Woerner Inc .... G 631 454-9330
  Farmingdale *(G-5024)*
▲ Juniper Elbow Co Inc .... E 718 326-2546
  Middle Village *(G-8447)*
▲ Juniper Industries Florida Inc ..... E 718 326-2546
  Middle Village *(G-8448)*
▲ Leo International Inc .... E 718 290-8005
  Brooklyn *(G-2214)*
◆ Leroy Plastics Inc .... D 585 768-8158
  Le Roy *(G-7437)*
Long Island Pipe Supply Inc .... G 718 456-7877
  Flushing *(G-5274)*
Long Island Pipe Supply Inc .... G 518 270-2159
  Troy *(G-16243)*
Long Island Pipe Supply Inc .... E 516 222-8008
  Garden City *(G-5529)*
M Manastrip-M Corporation .... G 518 664-2089
  Clifton Park *(G-3726)*
Met Weld International LLC .... D 518 765-2318
  Altamont *(G-213)*
Micromold Products Inc .... E 914 969-2850
  Yonkers *(G-17485)*
Ram Fabricating LLC .... E 315 437-6654
  Syracuse *(G-16039)*
Rochester Tube Fabricators .... F 585 254-0290
  Rochester *(G-14676)*
▲ Spinco Metal Products Inc .... D 315 331-6285
  Newark *(G-12764)*
Star Tubing Corp .... G 716 483-1703
  Jamestown *(G-7063)*
Tag Flange & Machining Inc .... E 516 536-1300
  Oceanside *(G-13122)*
Truly Tubular Fitting Corp .... F 914 664-8686
  Mount Vernon *(G-8788)*
Tube Fabrication Company Inc ...... F 716 673-1871
  Fredonia *(G-5384)*
Wedco Fabrications Inc .... G 718 852-6330
  College Point *(G-3836)*

3499 Fabricated Metal Prdts, NEC

901 D LLC .... E 845 369-1111
  Airmont *(G-10)*
A D Mfg Corp .... F 516 352-6161
  Floral Park *(G-5197)*
▲ Access Display Group Inc .... E 516 678-7772
  Freeport *(G-5389)*
Albany Mtal Fbrcation Holdings ..... G 518 463-5161
  Albany *(G-40)*
Alpine Paper Box Co Inc .... E 718 345-4040
  Brooklyn *(G-1592)*
American Standard Mfg Inc .... E 518 868-2512
  Central Bridge *(G-3507)*
Aquarium Pump & Piping Systems .. F 631 567-5555
  Sayville *(G-15232)*
▲ Arnold Magnetic Tech Corp .... C 585 385-9010
  Rochester *(G-14228)*
Atech-Seh Metal Fabricator .... E 716 895-8888
  Buffalo *(G-2841)*
Backyard Fence Inc .... F 518 452-9496
  Albany *(G-48)*
Brakewell Stl Fabricators Inc .... E 845 469-9131
  Chester *(G-3628)*
Bristol Gift Co Inc .... F 845 496-2821
  Washingtonville *(G-16620)*
Brooklyn Cstm Met Fbrction Inc ..... E 718 499-1573
  Brooklyn *(G-1723)*
Brzozka Industries Inc .... F 631 588-8164
  Holbrook *(G-6462)*
Buttons & Trimcom Inc .... F 212 868-1971
  New York *(G-9537)*
C & M Products Inc .... G 315 471-3303
  Syracuse *(G-15899)*

35 INDUSTRIAL AND COMMERCIAL MACHINERY AND COMPUTER EQUIPMENT

▲ Carpentier Industries LLC ....F 585 385-5550
East Rochester (G-4474)
◆ Chapin International Inc ....C 585 343-3140
Batavia (G-628)
◆ Chapin Manufacturing Inc ....C 585 343-3140
Batavia (G-629)
Clad Industries LLC ....G 585 413-4359
Macedon (G-8014)
▲ Classic Medallics Inc ....E 718 392-5410
Mount Vernon (G-8717)
Cleveland Polymer Tech LLC ....G 518 326-9146
Watervliet (G-16706)
Consolidated Barricades Inc ....G 518 922-7944
Fultonville (G-5492)
Criterion Bell & Specialty ....E 718 788-2600
Brooklyn (G-1818)
Crystallizations Systems Inc ....F 631 467-0090
Holbrook (G-6469)
Custom Frame & Molding Co ....F 631 491-9091
West Babylon (G-16811)
Di Highway Sign Structure Corp .....E 315 736-8312
New York Mills (G-12741)
Dimar Manufacturing Corp ....C 716 759-0351
Clarence (G-3685)
Dobrin Industries Inc ....G 800 353-2229
Lockport (G-7609)
Dz9 Power LLC ....G 877 533-5530
Olean (G-13167)
Elias Artmetal Inc ....F 516 873-7501
Mineola (G-8540)
Empire Metal Finishing Inc ....E 718 545-6700
Astoria (G-438)
▲ Fabritex Inc ....F 706 376-6584
New York (G-10177)
Factory East ....E 718 280-1558
Brooklyn (G-1957)
Finger Lakes Conveyors Inc ....G 315 539-9246
Waterloo (G-16647)
Frame Shoppe & Art Gallery ....G 516 365-6014
Manhasset (G-8093)
Galmer Ltd ....G 718 392-4609
Long Island City (G-7777)
◆ Gardall Safe Corporation ....E 315 432-9115
Syracuse (G-15968)
▲ Garment Care Systems LLC ....G 518 674-1826
Averill Park (G-532)
Gcm Steel Products Inc ....F 718 386-3346
Brooklyn (G-2017)
◆ Gibraltar Industries Inc ....D 716 826-6500
Buffalo (G-2989)
◆ Hannay Reels Inc ....C 518 797-3791
Westerlo (G-17071)
Hatfield Metal Fab Inc ....E 845 454-9078
Poughkeepsie (G-13926)
▲ Icestone LLC ....E 718 624-4900
Brooklyn (G-2093)
Inpro Corporation ....G 716 332-4699
Tonawanda (G-16192)
◆ Inter Pacific Consulting Corp ......G 718 460-2787
Flushing (G-5260)
James D Rubino Inc ....E 631 244-8730
Bohemia (G-1076)
▲ Jay Strongwater Holdings LLC ..A 646 657-0558
New York (G-10745)
JE Monahan Fabrications LLC ....F 518 761-0414
Queensbury (G-14014)
▼ Jordan Panel Systems Corp ....E 631 754-4900
East Northport (G-4459)
▲ Kefa Industries Group Inc ....G 718 568-9297
Rego Park (G-14046)
Kwong CHI Metal Fabrication ....G 718 369-6429
Brooklyn (G-2184)
L D Flecken Inc ....F 631 777-4881
Yaphank (G-17411)
▲ Lr Paris LLC ....G 703 652-1132
New York (G-11084)
Machinery Mountings Inc ....F 631 851-0480
Hauppauge (G-6149)
Magnaworks Technology Inc ....G 631 218-3431
Bohemia (G-1095)
▲ Magnetic Aids Inc ....G 845 863-1400
Newburgh (G-12787)
▲ Materion Brewster LLC ....D 845 279-0900
Brewster (G-1221)
▲ Maximum Security Products Corp .E 518 233-1800
Waterford (G-16634)
McD Metals LLC ....F 518 456-9694
Albany (G-100)
▼ Metallic Ladder Mfg Corp ....F 716 358-6201
Randolph (G-14029)

MMC Magnetics Corp ....F 631 435-9888
Hauppauge (G-6167)
National Maint Contg Corp ....D 716 285-1583
Niagara Falls (G-12866)
New Dimension Awards Inc ....G 718 236-8200
Brooklyn (G-2369)
New York Manufactured Products ...F 585 254-9353
Rochester (G-14552)
Noll Reynolds Met Fabrication ....G 315 422-3333
Syracuse (G-16019)
▲ Nrd LLC ....E 716 773-7634
Grand Island (G-5779)
PBL Industries Corp ....F 631 979-4266
Smithtown (G-15516)
Peak Motion Inc ....G 716 534-4925
Clarence (G-3695)
▲ Peelle Company ....G 631 231-6000
Hauppauge (G-6185)
Picture Perfect Framing ....G 718 851-1884
Brooklyn (G-2432)
▲ Polich Tallix Inc ....D 845 567-9464
Walden (G-16554)
▲ Polymag Inc ....E 631 286-4111
Bellport (G-836)
▲ Precision Magnetics LLC ....E 585 385-9010
Rochester (G-14618)
Precision Spclty Fbrctions LLC ......F 716 824-2108
Buffalo (G-3159)
Protocase Incorporated ....G 866 849-3911
Lewiston (G-7456)
Range Repair Warehouse ....G 585 235-0980
Penfield (G-13525)
Raytech Corp Asbestos Personal ...F 516 747-0300
Mineola (G-8566)
Raytech Corporation ....G 718 259-7388
Woodbury (G-17317)
Reelcology Inc ....E 845 258-1880
Pine Island (G-13580)
Romac Electronics Inc ....F 516 349-7900
Plainview (G-13660)
Rough Brothers Holding Co ....G 716 826-6500
Buffalo (G-3196)
▲ Rush Gold Manufacturing Ltd .....D 516 781-3155
Bellmore (G-816)
▲ Saratoga Trunk and Furniture .....F 518 463-3252
Albany (G-131)
▼ Schwab Corp ....E 585 381-4900
Rochester (G-14696)
Secureit Tactical Inc ....F 800 651-8835
Syracuse (G-16059)
◆ Seetin Design Group Inc ....F 718 486-5610
Brooklyn (G-2568)
◆ Sono-Tek Corporation ....D 845 795-2020
Milton (G-8518)
Split Rock Trading Co Inc ....G 631 929-3261
Wading River (G-16546)
▲ Structural Industries Inc ....C 631 471-5200
Bohemia (G-1134)
▲ Stylebuilt Accessories Inc ....F 917 439-0578
East Rockaway (G-4493)
▲ Technomag Inc ....G 631 246-6142
East Setauket (G-4512)
Thyssenkrupp Materials NA Inc ......F 212 972-8800
New York (G-12354)
Total Metal Resource ....F 718 384-7818
Brooklyn (G-2688)
Trine Rolled Moulding Corp ....F 718 828-5200
Bronx (G-1477)
◆ Truebite Inc ....E 607 785-7664
Vestal (G-16479)
Ulster County Iron Works LLC ....G 845 255-0003
New Paltz (G-8925)
Win-Holt Equipment Corp ....C 516 222-0433
Garden City (G-5551)
▼ Wtbi Inc ....G 631 547-1993
Huntington Station (G-6767)

35 INDUSTRIAL AND COMMERCIAL MACHINERY AND COMPUTER EQUIPMENT

3511 Steam, Gas & Hydraulic Turbines & Engines

Atlantic Projects Company Inc ....F 518 878-2065
Clifton Park (G-3722)
Awr Energy Inc ....F 585 469-7750
Plattsburgh (G-13680)

Beowawe Binary LLC ....E 646 829-3900
New York (G-9409)
▲ Cooper Turbocompressor Inc .....B 716 896-6600
Buffalo (G-2910)
▲ Corfu Machine Inc ....E 585 418-4083
Corfu (G-3975)
Dresser-Rand Company ....A 585 596-3100
Wellsville (G-16777)
Dresser-Rand Group Inc ....D 716 375-3000
Olean (G-13164)
Frontier Hydraulics Corp ....F 716 694-2070
Buffalo (G-2973)
▲ Gas Turbine Controls Corp ....E 914 693-0830
Hawthorne (G-6270)
GE Global Research ....E 518 387-5000
Niskayuna (G-12911)
GE Transportation Eng Systems .....G 518 258-9276
Schenectady (G-15282)
General Electric Company ....B 518 385-2211
Schenectady (G-15284)
General Electric Company ....B 203 373-2756
Schenectady (G-15285)
General Electric Company ....B 518 385-3716
Schenectady (G-15286)
General Electric Company ....B 518 385-2211
Schenectady (G-15287)
General Electric Company ....B 518 387-5000
Schenectady (G-15288)
General Electric Company ....B 518 385-3439
Schenectady (G-15289)
General Electric Company ....A 518 385-4022
Schenectady (G-15283)
General Electric Company ....B 518 385-7620
Niskayuna (G-12912)
▲ Hdm Hydraulics LLC ....D 716 694-8004
Tonawanda (G-16187)
Ingersoll-Rand Company ....E 716 896-6600
Buffalo (G-3025)
▲ Mannesmann Corporation ....D 212 258-4000
New York (G-11160)
Mission Critical Energy Inc ....G 716 276-8465
Getzville (G-5612)
Omega Industries & Development ..E 516 349-8010
Plainview (G-13654)
◆ Prime Turbine Parts LLC ....E 518 306-7306
Saratoga Springs (G-15197)
Siemens Government Tech Inc ....B 585 593-1234
Wellsville (G-16785)
Signa Chemistry Inc ....F 212 933-4101
New York (G-12092)
▲ Stork H & E Turbo Blading Inc ...C 607 277-4968
Ithaca (G-6911)
Tgp Flying Cloud Holdings LLC ......E 646 829-3900
New York (G-12329)
Turbine Engine Comp Utica ....A 315 768-8070
Whitesboro (G-17225)
Turbo Machined Products LLC ....E 315 895-3010
Frankfort (G-5368)
Tuthill Corporation ....B 631 727-1097
Riverhead (G-14172)
Weaver Wind Energy LLC ....G 607 379-9463
Freeville (G-5450)
Wind Products Inc ....G 212 292-3135
Brooklyn (G-2772)
Worldwide Gas Turbine Pdts Inc ....G 518 877-7200
Clifton Park (G-3737)

3519 Internal Combustion Engines, NEC

AB Engine ....E 518 557-3510
Latham (G-7377)
Briggs & Stratton Corporation ....F 315 495-0100
Sherrill (G-15426)
Briggs & Stratton Corporation ....C 315 495-0100
Munnsville (G-8795)
Cummins - Allison Corp ....D 718 263-2482
Kew Gardens (G-7188)
◆ Cummins Inc ....D 716 456-2676
Lakewood (G-7313)
Cummins Inc ....A 716 456-2111
Lakewood (G-7314)
Cummins Inc ....B 812 377-5000
Jamestown (G-7021)
Cummins Inc ....B 718 892-2400
Bronx (G-1308)
Cummins Northeast LLC ....E 315 437-2296
Syracuse (G-15935)
D & W Diesel Inc ....F 518 437-1300
Latham (G-7387)
Jack W Miller ....G 585 538-2399
Scottsville (G-15359)

Employee Codes: A=Over 500 employees, B=251-500
C=101-250, D=51-100, E=20-50, F=10-19, G=5-9

▲ **Mannesmann Corporation** ....D 212 258-4000
New York *(G-11160)*
Omega Industries & Development ....E 516 349-8010
Plainview *(G-13654)*
Perkins International Inc ....G 309 675-1000
Buffalo *(G-3144)*
Washer Solutions Inc ....F 585 742-6388
Victor *(G-16536)*

3523 Farm Machinery & Eqpt

Bdp Industries Inc ....E 518 695-6851
Greenwich *(G-5904)*
▲ **Bean King International LLC** ....F 845 268-3135
Congers *(G-3877)*
◆ **Chapin Manufacturing Inc** ....C 585 343-3140
Batavia *(G-629)*
Don Beck Inc ....G 585 493-3040
Castile *(G-3444)*
Eastern Welding Inc ....G 631 727-0306
Riverhead *(G-14154)*
◆ **Fountainhead Group Inc** ....C 315 736-0037
New York Mills *(G-12742)*
Good Earth Organics Corp ....E 716 684-8111
Lancaster *(G-7342)*
Haines Equipment Inc ....E 607 566-8531
Avoca *(G-534)*
House of The Foaming Case Inc ....G 718 454-0101
Saint Albans *(G-15110)*
Jain Irrigation Inc ....D 315 755-4400
Watertown *(G-16676)*
Landpro Equipment LLC ....B 716 665-3110
Falconer *(G-4914)*
Moffett Turf Equipment Inc ....E 585 334-0100
West Henrietta *(G-16917)*
▲ **Oxbo International Corporation** ....D 585 548-2665
Byron *(G-3295)*
P & D Equipment Sales LLC ....G 585 343-2394
Alexander *(G-192)*
Plant-Tech2o Inc ....G 516 483-7845
Hempstead *(G-6307)*
Renaldos Sales and Service Ctr ....G 716 337-3760
North Collins *(G-12947)*
Richard Stewart ....G 518 632-5363
Hartford *(G-6015)*
Road Cases USA Inc ....E 631 563-0633
Bohemia *(G-1123)*
Vansridge Dairy LLC ....E 315 364-8569
Scipio Center *(G-15344)*
Westmoor Ltd ....F 315 363-1500
Sherrill *(G-15433)*
Zappala Farms AG Systems Inc ....E 315 626-6293
Cato *(G-3453)*

3524 Garden, Lawn Tractors & Eqpt

Benishty Brothers Corp ....G 646 339-9991
Woodmere *(G-17329)*
Briggs & Stratton Corporation ....C 315 495-0100
Munnsville *(G-8795)*
Capital E Financial Group ....F 212 319-6550
New York *(G-9574)*
Cazenovia Equipment Co Inc ....G 315 736-0898
Clinton *(G-3742)*
◆ **Chapin International Inc** ....C 585 343-3140
Batavia *(G-628)*
◆ **Chapin Manufacturing Inc** ....C 585 343-3140
Batavia *(G-629)*
Clopay Ames True Tmper Hldng ....F 516 938-5544
Jericho *(G-7096)*
▲ **Eaton Brothers Corp** ....G 716 649-8250
Hamburg *(G-5945)*
Fradan Manufacturing Corp ....F 914 632-3653
New Rochelle *(G-8947)*
◆ **Kadco Usa Inc** ....G 518 661-6068
Mayfield *(G-8244)*
Real Bark Mulch LLC ....G 518 747-3650
Fort Edward *(G-5353)*
Rhett M Clark Inc ....G 585 538-9570
Caledonia *(G-3309)*
Saxby Implement Corp ....F 585 624-2938
Mendon *(G-8414)*

3531 Construction Machinery & Eqpt

▲ **AAAA York Inc** ....F 718 784-6666
Long Island City *(G-7677)*
Air-Flo Mfg Co Inc ....D 607 733-8284
Elmira *(G-4684)*
Anderson Equipment Company ....D 716 877-1992
Tonawanda *(G-16160)*
Applied Technology Mfg Corp ....E 607 687-2200
Owego *(G-13375)*
▲ **BW Elliott Mfg Co LLC** ....B 607 772-0404
Binghamton *(G-896)*
▲ **C J Logging Equipment Inc** ....E 315 942-5431
Boonville *(G-1163)*
Capitol Eq 2 LLC ....G 518 886-8341
Saratoga Springs *(G-15176)*
CCS Machinery Inc ....F 631 968-0900
Bay Shore *(G-679)*
Ceno Technologies Inc ....G 716 885-5050
Buffalo *(G-2890)*
Cimline Inc ....G 518 880-4073
Albany *(G-63)*
Cives Corporation ....D 315 543-2321
Harrisville *(G-6014)*
Cooper Industries LLC ....E 315 477-7000
Syracuse *(G-15928)*
Crane Equipment & Service Inc ....G 716 689-5400
Amherst *(G-236)*
Dave Sandel Cranes Inc ....G 631 325-5588
Westhampton *(G-17085)*
Diamond Coring & Cutting Inc ....G 718 381-4545
Maspeth *(G-8161)*
◆ **Dover Global Holdings Inc** ....F 212 922-1640
New York *(G-9964)*
Drillco National Group Inc ....E 718 726-9801
Long Island City *(G-7747)*
ET Oakes Corporation ....E 631 232-0002
Hauppauge *(G-6096)*
Gei International Inc ....F 315 463-9261
East Syracuse *(G-4546)*
Got Wood LLC ....G 315 440-8857
Cleveland *(G-3718)*
Hansteel (usa) Inc ....G 212 226-0105
New York *(G-10456)*
Highway Garage ....G 518 568-2837
Saint Johnsville *(G-15122)*
Industrial Handling Svcs Inc ....G 518 399-0488
Alplaus *(G-207)*
Kinedyne Inc ....F 716 667-6833
Orchard Park *(G-13303)*
▲ **Kinshofer Usa Inc** ....E 716 731-4333
Sanborn *(G-15150)*
Kyntec Corporation ....G 716 810-6956
Buffalo *(G-3056)*
Line Ward Corporation ....G 716 675-7373
Buffalo *(G-3066)*
Lomin Construction Company ....G 516 759-5734
Glen Head *(G-5650)*
▲ **Mettle Concept Inc** ....G 888 501-0680
New York *(G-11270)*
▲ **Midland Machinery Co Inc** ....D 716 692-1200
Tonawanda *(G-16199)*
Minimax Concrete Corp ....G 716 444-8908
Grand Island *(G-5777)*
▲ **Munson Machinery Company Inc** ....E 315 797-0090
Utica *(G-16374)*
New Eagle Silo Corp ....G 585 492-1300
Arcade *(G-398)*
Oneida Sales & Service Inc ....E 716 822-8205
Buffalo *(G-3123)*
Oneida Sales & Service Inc ....F 716 270-0433
Lackawanna *(G-7271)*
▲ **Oswald Manufacturing Co Inc** ....E 516 883-8850
Port Washington *(G-13867)*
◆ **Ozteck Industries Inc** ....E 516 883-8857
Port Washington *(G-13868)*
Park Ave Bldg & Roofg Sups LLC ....E 718 403-0100
Brooklyn *(G-2421)*
Patterson Blacktop Corp ....G 845 628-3425
Carmel *(G-3431)*
Pauls Rods & Restos Inc ....G 631 665-7637
Deer Park *(G-4211)*
Peckham Materials Corp ....E 518 747-3353
Hudson Falls *(G-6680)*
Penn Can Equipment Corporation ....G 315 378-0337
Lyons *(G-8001)*
Penn State Metal Fabri ....G 718 786-8814
Brooklyn *(G-2428)*
Pier-Tech Inc ....E 516 442-5420
Oceanside *(G-13111)*
▲ **Precision Product Inc** ....G 718 852-7127
Brooklyn *(G-2450)*
Presti Ready Mix Concrete Inc ....G 516 378-6006
Freeport *(G-5430)*
Primoplast Inc ....F 631 750-0680
Bohemia *(G-1117)*
Pro-Tech Wldg Fabrication Inc ....E 585 436-9855
Rochester *(G-14626)*
▲ **Professional Pavers Corp** ....E 718 784-7853
Rego Park *(G-14050)*
Railworks Transit Systems Inc ....E 212 502-7900
New York *(G-11816)*
Rapistak Corporation ....G 716 822-2804
Blasdell *(G-957)*
Rochester Asphalt Materials ....G 315 524-4619
Walworth *(G-16572)*
S R & R Industries Inc ....G 845 692-8329
Middletown *(G-8496)*
▲ **Schutte-Buffalo Hammermill LLC** ....E 716 855-1202
Buffalo *(G-3207)*
Seville Central Mix Corp ....D 516 293-6190
Old Bethpage *(G-13151)*
Sierson Crane & Welding Inc ....G 315 723-6914
Westmoreland *(G-17095)*
T S P Corp ....F 585 768-6769
Le Roy *(G-7441)*
Technopaving New York Inc ....G 631 351-6472
Huntington Station *(G-6763)*
Town of Ohio ....E 315 392-2055
Forestport *(G-5339)*
Vanhouten Motorsports ....G 315 387-6312
Lacona *(G-7277)*
X-Treme Ready Mix Inc ....G 718 739-3384
Jamaica *(G-7001)*
Ziegler Truck & Diesl Repr Inc ....G 315 782-7278
Watertown *(G-16699)*

3532 Mining Machinery & Eqpt

American Material Processing ....F 315 318-0017
Phoenix *(G-13567)*
▲ **Drillco Equipment Co Inc** ....E 718 777-5986
Long Island City *(G-7746)*
Flatcut LLC ....G 212 542-5732
Brooklyn *(G-1984)*
Lawson M Whiting Inc ....G 315 986-3064
Macedon *(G-8018)*
▲ **Munson Machinery Company Inc** ....E 315 797-0090
Utica *(G-16374)*
Universal Metal Fabricators ....F 845 331-8248
Kingston *(G-7248)*

3533 Oil Field Machinery & Eqpt

Anchor Commerce Trading Corp ....G 516 881-3485
Atlantic Beach *(G-467)*
Basin Holdings US LLC ....E 212 695-7376
New York *(G-9382)*
◆ **Blue Tee Corp** ....A 212 598-0880
New York *(G-9473)*
◆ **Derrick Corporation** ....C 716 683-9010
Buffalo *(G-2928)*
Derrick Corporation ....C 716 685-4892
Cheektowaga *(G-3595)*
▼ **Desmi-Afti Inc** ....E 716 662-0632
Orchard Park *(G-13292)*
Schlumberger Technology Corp ....C 607 378-0105
Horseheads *(G-6621)*
Smith International Inc ....F 585 265-2330
Ontario *(G-13237)*

3534 Elevators & Moving Stairways

◆ **A & D Entrances LLC** ....F 718 989-2441
Wyandanch *(G-17384)*
Access Elevator & Lift Inc ....G 716 483-3696
Jamestown *(G-7003)*
◆ **Allround Logistics Inc** ....G 718 544-8945
Forest Hills *(G-5326)*
An Excelsior Elevator Corp ....F 516 408-3070
Westbury *(G-16995)*
Ankom Development LLC ....G 315 986-1937
Macedon *(G-8007)*
Automated Elevator Systems ....E 845 595-1063
Greenwood Lake *(G-5916)*
Bhi Elevator Cabs Inc ....F 516 431-5665
Island Park *(G-6818)*
Big Apple Elevtr Srv & Consult ....G 212 279-0700
New York *(G-9440)*
CEC Elevator Cab Corp ....D 718 328-3632
Bronx *(G-1292)*
◆ **Dover Global Holdings Inc** ....F 212 922-1640
New York *(G-9964)*
Dural Door Company Inc ....F 718 729-1333
Long Island City *(G-7749)*
E Z Entry Doors Inc ....F 716 434-3440
Lockport *(G-7611)*
Eag Electric Inc ....G 201 376-5103
Staten Island *(G-15689)*
▲ **Eazylift Albany LLC** ....G 518 452-6929
Latham *(G-7388)*
Elevator Accessories Mfg ....F 914 739-7004
Peekskill *(G-13501)*

35 INDUSTRIAL AND COMMERCIAL MACHINERY AND COMPUTER EQUIPMENT

Elevator Ventures Corporation ....D 212 375-1900
  Ozone Park *(G-13403)*
Herbert Wolf Corp ....G 212 242-0300
  New York *(G-10504)*
Interface Products Co Inc ....G 631 242-4605
  Bay Shore *(G-705)*
Island Custom Stairs Inc ....G 631 205-5335
  Medford *(G-8282)*
Keystone Iron & Wire Works Inc ....G 844 258-7986
  East Rockaway *(G-4490)*
Kinglift Elevator Inc ....G 917 923-3517
  New York *(G-10892)*
▲ Monitor Elevator Products LLC ....D 631 543-4334
  Hauppauge *(G-6169)*
▲ National Elev Cab & Door Corp ......E 718 478-5900
  Woodside *(G-17357)*
Northern Lifts Elevator Co LLC ....G 518 644-2831
  Bolton Landing *(G-1157)*
Otis Elevator Company ....F 315 736-0167
  Yorkville *(G-17543)*
Otis Elevator Company ....E 917 339-9600
  New York *(G-11547)*
Otis Elevator Company ....F 914 375-7800
  Yonkers *(G-17491)*
Otis Elevator Company ....E 518 426-4006
  Albany *(G-113)*
Palmer Industries Inc ....G 607 754-8741
  Endicott *(G-4829)*
Rokon Tech LLC ....G 718 429-0729
  Elmhurst *(G-4681)*
S & H Enterprises Inc ....G 888 323-8755
  Queensbury *(G-14023)*
Schindler Elevator Corporation ....C 212 708-1000
  New York *(G-12005)*
Schindler Elevator Corporation ....C 718 417-3131
  Glendale *(G-5678)*
Schindler Elevator Corporation ....D 516 860-1321
  Hicksville *(G-6419)*
Schindler Elevator Corporation ....E 800 225-3123
  New York *(G-12006)*
▲ Sgl Services Corp ....E 718 630-0392
  New York *(G-12056)*
Thyssenkrupp Elevator Corp ....D 212 268-2020
  New York *(G-12353)*
Velis Associates Inc ....G 631 225-4220
  Lindenhurst *(G-7514)*

3535 Conveyors & Eqpt

4695 Main Street Snyder Inc ....G 716 833-3270
  Buffalo *(G-2803)*
American Material Processing ....F 315 318-0017
  Phoenix *(G-13567)*
▲ Chemprene Inc ....C 845 831-2800
  Beacon *(G-777)*
▲ Chemprene Holding Inc ....C 845 831-2800
  Beacon *(G-778)*
◆ Columbus McKinnon Corporation ...C 716 689-5400
  Getzville *(G-5607)*
Columbus McKinnon Corporation ....C 716 689-5400
  Getzville *(G-5608)*
Columbus McKinnon Corporation ....C 716 689-5400
  Getzville *(G-5609)*
▲ Dairy Conveyor Corp ....G 845 278-7878
  Brewster *(G-1212)*
▼ Desmi-Afti Inc ....E 716 662-0632
  Orchard Park *(G-13292)*
General Splice Corporation ....G 914 271-5131
  Croton On Hudson *(G-4089)*
Glasgow Products Inc ....E 516 374-5937
  Woodmere *(G-17331)*
▲ Greenbelt Industries Inc ....E 800 668-1114
  Buffalo *(G-3000)*
Haines Equipment Inc ....E 607 566-8531
  Avoca *(G-534)*
Hohl Machine & Conveyor Co Inc ......E 716 882-7210
  Buffalo *(G-3013)*
▼ I J White Corporation ....D 631 293-3788
  Farmingdale *(G-5016)*
International Robotics Inc ....F 914 630-1060
  Larchmont *(G-7375)*
▲ J D Handling Systems Inc ....F 518 828-9676
  Ghent *(G-5620)*
Joldeson One Aerospace Inds ....D 718 848-7396
  Ozone Park *(G-13406)*
Northeast Conveyors Inc ....E 585 768-8912
  Lima *(G-7468)*
Noto Industrial Corp ....G 631 736-7600
  Coram *(G-3971)*
Raymond Corporation ....E 315 643-5000
  East Syracuse *(G-4572)*

◆ Raymond Corporation ....A 800 235-7200
  Greene *(G-5887)*
Re-Al Industrial Corp ....G 716 542-4556
  Akron *(G-25)*
▲ Renold Inc ....D 716 326-3121
  Westfield *(G-17080)*
▲ Rlp Holdings Inc ....G 716 852-0832
  Buffalo *(G-3187)*
Rota Pack Inc ....F 631 274-1037
  Farmingdale *(G-5113)*
Shako Inc ....G 315 437-1294
  East Syracuse *(G-4577)*
Speedways Conveyors Inc ....E 716 893-2222
  Buffalo *(G-3223)*
Troy Belting and Supply Co ....D 518 272-4920
  Watervliet *(G-16715)*
United Rbotic Integrations LLC ....G 716 683-8334
  Alden *(G-188)*
▲ Ward Industrial Equipment Inc ......G 716 856-6966
  Buffalo *(G-3273)*

3536 Hoists, Cranes & Monorails

American Material Processing ....F 315 695-6204
  Phoenix *(G-13568)*
Columbus McKinnon Corporation ....D 716 689-5400
  Amherst *(G-235)*
◆ Columbus McKinnon Corporation ...C 716 689-5400
  Getzville *(G-5607)*
Columbus McKinnon Corporation ....C 716 689-5400
  Getzville *(G-5608)*
Columbus McKinnon Corporation ....C 716 689-5400
  Getzville *(G-5609)*
Debrucque Cleveland Tramrail S ....G 315 697-5160
  Canastota *(G-3395)*
Dun-Rite Spclized Carriers LLC ....F 718 991-1100
  Bronx *(G-1323)*
▲ Gorbel Inc ....C 585 924-6262
  Fishers *(G-5186)*
Gorbel Inc ....F 800 821-0086
  Victor *(G-16504)*
Kleinfelder John ....G 716 753-3163
  Mayville *(G-8247)*
Konecranes Inc ....F 585 359-4450
  Henrietta *(G-6318)*
▲ Mannesmann Corporation ....D 212 258-4000
  New York *(G-11160)*
Marros Equipment & Trucks ....F 315 539-8702
  Waterloo *(G-16652)*
▲ Mohawk Resources Ltd ....D 518 842-1431
  Amsterdam *(G-360)*
▲ Reimann & Georger Corporation ...E 716 895-1156
  Buffalo *(G-3182)*
T Shore Products Ltd ....G 315 252-9174
  Auburn *(G-519)*
Thego Corporation ....G 631 776-2472
  Bellport *(G-838)*
◆ US Hoists Corp ....G 631 472-3030
  Calverton *(G-3330)*

3537 Indl Trucks, Tractors, Trailers & Stackers

Arlington Equipment Corp ....G 518 798-5867
  Queensbury *(G-14006)*
Arpac LLC ....F 315 471-5103
  Syracuse *(G-15878)*
Artcraft Building Services ....G 845 895-3893
  Wallkill *(G-16561)*
ASAP Rack Rental Inc ....G 718 499-4495
  Brooklyn *(G-1640)*
Atlantic Engineer Products LLC ....E 518 822-1800
  Hudson *(G-6636)*
B & J Delivers Inc ....G 631 524-5550
  Brentwood *(G-1174)*
▲ Channel Manufacturing Inc ....E 516 944-6271
  Port Washington *(G-13827)*
◆ Columbus McKinnon Corporation ...C 716 689-5400
  Getzville *(G-5607)*
Columbus McKinnon Corporation ....C 716 689-5400
  Getzville *(G-5608)*
Columbus McKinnon Corporation ....C 716 689-5400
  Getzville *(G-5609)*
▲ Continental Lift Truck Inc ....F 718 738-4738
  South Ozone Park *(G-15556)*
Crown Equipment Corporation ....D 516 822-5100
  Hicksville *(G-6363)*
▼ Devin Mfg Inc ....F 585 496-5770
  Arcade *(G-391)*
DI Manufacturing Inc ....E 315 432-8977
  North Syracuse *(G-12959)*

◆ Ducon Technologies Inc ....F 631 694-1700
  New York *(G-9988)*
Ducon Technologies Inc ....E 631 420-4900
  Farmingdale *(G-4988)*
E-One Inc ....D 716 646-6790
  Hamburg *(G-5944)*
Elramida Holdings Inc ....E 646 280-0503
  Brooklyn *(G-1919)*
Jasper Transport LLC ....E 315 729-5760
  Penn Yan *(G-13538)*
◆ Koke Inc ....E 800 535-5303
  Queensbury *(G-14016)*
Meteor Express Inc ....F 718 551-9177
  Jamaica *(G-6967)*
Mettler-Toledo Inc ....E 607 257-6000
  Ithaca *(G-6896)*
Mil & Mir Steel Products Co ....G 718 328-7596
  Bronx *(G-1399)*
Palpross Incorporated ....F 845 469-2188
  Selkirk *(G-15379)*
Pb08 Inc ....G 347 866-7353
  Hicksville *(G-6410)*
◆ Raymond Consolidated Corp ....C 800 235-7200
  Greene *(G-5886)*
◆ Raymond Corporation ....A 800 235-7200
  Greene *(G-5887)*
Raymond Corporation ....C 607 656-2311
  East Syracuse *(G-4570)*
Raymond Corporation ....B 315 463-5000
  East Syracuse *(G-4571)*
Raymond Corporation ....E 315 643-5000
  East Syracuse *(G-4572)*
Raymond Sales Corporation ....G 607 656-2311
  Greene *(G-5888)*
Sherco Services LLC ....C 516 676-3028
  Glen Cove *(G-5640)*
Speedways Conveyors Inc ....E 716 893-2222
  Buffalo *(G-3223)*
Stanley Industrial Eqp LLC ....G 315 656-8733
  Kirkville *(G-7255)*
Ward Lafrance Truck Corp ....F 518 893-1865
  Saratoga Springs *(G-15206)*
Win-Holt Equipment Corp ....C 516 222-0433
  Garden City *(G-5551)*

3541 Machine Tools: Cutting

Abtex Corporation ....E 315 536-7403
  Dresden *(G-4342)*
Adria Machine & Tool Inc ....E 585 889-3360
  Scottsville *(G-15355)*
Advanced Machine Design Co Inc ....E 716 826-2000
  Buffalo *(G-2817)*
Aip Mc Holdings LLC ....A 212 627-2360
  New York *(G-9115)*
Alpine Machine Inc ....F 607 272-1344
  Ithaca *(G-6858)*
▲ Alternative Service Inc ....F 631 345-9500
  Yaphank *(G-17401)*
Alton Manufacturing Inc ....D 585 458-2600
  Rochester *(G-14209)*
▲ Ascension Industries Inc ....D 716 693-9381
  North Tonawanda *(G-12974)*
Aztec Mfg of Rochester ....G 585 352-8152
  Spencerport *(G-15589)*
▲ Baldwin Machine Works Inc ....E 631 842-9110
  Copiague *(G-3922)*
▲ Brinkman Products Inc ....B 585 235-4545
  Rochester *(G-14264)*
Bystronic Inc ....G 631 231-3677
  Hauppauge *(G-6058)*
Coastel Cable Tools Inc ....E 315 471-5361
  Syracuse *(G-15918)*
Connex Grinding & Machining ....G 315 946-4340
  Lyons *(G-7998)*
Crowley Fabg Machining Co Inc ....F 607 484-0299
  Endicott *(G-4807)*
Dinosaw Inc ....E 518 828-9942
  Hudson *(G-6642)*
East Coast Tool & Mfg ....G 716 826-5183
  Buffalo *(G-2941)*
Elmira Grinding Works Inc ....F 607 734-1579
  Wellsburg *(G-16773)*
Five Star Tool Co Inc ....E 585 328-9580
  Rochester *(G-14394)*
Gb Aero Engine LLC ....B 914 925-9600
  Rye *(G-15083)*
Genco John ....G 716 483-5446
  Jamestown *(G-7028)*
◆ Gleason Corporation ....E 585 473-1000
  Rochester *(G-14428)*

Employee Codes: A=Over 500 employees, B=251-500
C=101-250, D=51-100, E=20-50, F=10-19, G=5-9

◆ Gleason Works ....A 585 473-1000
Rochester (G-14429)
▲ Graywood Companies Inc ....E 585 254-7000
Rochester (G-14433)
H S Assembly Inc ....G 585 266-4287
Rochester (G-14436)
Halpern Tool Corp ....G 914 633-0038
New Rochelle (G-8953)
▲ Hardinge Inc ....B 607 734-2281
Elmira (G-4701)
Hartchrom Inc ....F 518 880-0411
Watervliet (G-16710)
High Speed Hammer Company Inc ....F 585 266-4287
Rochester (G-14456)
IPC/Razor LLC ....D 212 551-4500
New York (G-10695)
Ish Precision Machine Corp ....F 718 436-8858
Brooklyn (G-2114)
J Vogler Enterprise LLC ....F 585 247-1625
Rochester (G-14478)
Jalex Industries Ltd ....F 631 491-5072
West Babylon (G-16828)
Johnson Mch & Fibr Pdts Co Inc ....F 716 665-2003
Jamestown (G-7047)
◆ Kps Capital Partners LP ....E 212 338-5100
New York (G-10922)
Kyocera Precision Tools Inc ....F 607 687-0012
Owego (G-13378)
▲ Lancaster Knives Inc ....E 716 683-5050
Lancaster (G-7347)
Lk Industries Inc ....G 716 941-9202
Glenwood (G-5718)
▲ Lubow Machine Corp ....F 631 226-1700
Copiague (G-3936)
▲ Montrose Equipment Sales Inc ....F 718 388-7446
Brooklyn (G-2337)
Mortech Industries Inc ....G 845 628-6138
Mahopac (G-8028)
Multimatic Products Inc ....D 800 767-7633
Ronkonkoma (G-14972)
▲ Munson Machinery Company Inc ....E 315 797-0090
Utica (G-16374)
Myles Tool Company Inc ....E 716 731-1300
Sanborn (G-15151)
Nifty Bar Grinding & Cutting ....E 585 381-0450
Penfield (G-13524)
▼ Omega Consolidated Corporation ....E 585 392-9262
Hilton (G-6445)
▲ Omega Tool Measuring Mchs Inc ....E 585 598-7800
Fairport (G-4872)
P & R Industries Inc ....E 585 266-6725
Rochester (G-14583)
Ppi Corp ....E 585 880-7277
Rochester (G-14611)
▲ Precise Tool & Mfg Inc ....D 585 247-0700
Rochester (G-14613)
Producto Corporation ....C 716 484-7131
Jamestown (G-7057)
R Steiner Technologies Inc ....E 585 425-5912
Fairport (G-4881)
Rapid Precision Machining Inc ....D 585 467-0780
Rochester (G-14645)
▲ Rush Machinery Inc ....G 585 554-3070
Rushville (G-15078)
▲ S & S Machinery Corp ....E 718 492-7400
Brooklyn (G-2541)
S & S Machinery Corp ....E 718 492-7400
Brooklyn (G-2542)
Selflock Screw Products Co Inc ....E 315 541-4464
Syracuse (G-16060)
Seneca Falls Capital Inc ....G 315 568-5804
Seneca Falls (G-15391)
Seneca Falls Machine Tool Co ....D 315 568-5804
Seneca Falls (G-15392)
▲ Simmons Machine Tool Corp ....C 518 462-5431
Menands (G-8410)
▼ Stephen Bader Company Inc ....F 518 753-4456
Valley Falls (G-16422)
Swiss Specialties Inc ....F 631 567-8800
Wading River (G-16547)
Teka Precision Inc ....G 845 753-1900
Nyack (G-13072)
Transport National Dev Inc ....E 716 662-0270
Orchard Park (G-13324)
Truemade Products Inc ....G 631 981-4755
Ronkonkoma (G-15016)
Verns Machine Co Inc ....E 315 926-4223
Marion (G-8133)
Welch Machine Inc ....G 585 647-3578
Rochester (G-14787)
▼ World LLC ....F 631 940-9121
Deer Park (G-4254)
Zwack Incorporated ....E 518 733-5135
Stephentown (G-15780)
Zyp Precision LLC ....G 315 539-3667
Waterloo (G-16654)

3542 Machine Tools: Forming

Adaptive Mfg Tech Inc ....E 631 580-5400
Ronkonkoma (G-14878)
Advanced Machine Design Co Inc ....E 716 826-2000
Buffalo (G-2817)
Advantage Metalwork Finshg LLC ....D 585 454-0160
Rochester (G-14195)
American Racing Headers Inc ....E 631 608-1427
Deer Park (G-4120)
Arconic Inc ....G 716 358-6451
Falconer (G-4898)
Austin Industries Inc ....G 585 589-1353
Albion (G-165)
Bars Precision Inc ....F 585 742-6380
Mendon (G-8412)
Bdp Industries Inc ....E 518 695-6851
Greenwich (G-5904)
Brinkman Intl Group Inc ....G 585 429-5000
Rochester (G-14263)
Buffalo Machine Tls of Niagara ....F 716 201-1310
Lockport (G-7602)
C & T Tool & Instrument Co ....E 718 429-1253
Woodside (G-17338)
C J Winter Machine Tech ....E 585 429-5000
Rochester (G-14271)
Commodore Manufacutring Corp ....E 718 788-2600
Brooklyn (G-1794)
◆ Dover Global Holdings Inc ....F 212 922-1640
New York (G-9964)
▼ Ecko Fin & Tooling Inc ....F 716 487-0200
Jamestown (G-7024)
Gemcor Automation LLC ....D 716 674-9300
West Seneca (G-16974)
▲ Gh Induction Atmospheres LLC ....E 585 368-2120
Rochester (G-14423)
High Speed Hammer Company Inc ....F 585 266-4287
Rochester (G-14456)
▲ Hydramec Inc ....E 585 593-5190
Scio (G-15342)
◆ Kobe Steel USA Holdings Inc ....G 212 751-9400
New York (G-10904)
Lourdes Systems Inc ....F 631 234-7077
Hauppauge (G-6147)
▲ Lubow Machine Corp ....F 631 226-1700
Copiague (G-3936)
Manhasset Tool & Die Co Inc ....F 716 684-6066
Lancaster (G-7349)
Miller Mechanical Services Inc ....E 518 792-0430
Glens Falls (G-5705)
▼ Mpi Incorporated ....D 845 471-7630
Poughkeepsie (G-13937)
Precision Eforming LLC ....F 607 753-7730
Cortland (G-4063)
Prim Hall Enterprises Inc ....F 518 561-7408
Plattsburgh (G-13719)
Producto Corporation ....C 716 484-7131
Jamestown (G-7057)
Raloid Tool Co Inc ....F 518 664-4261
Mechanicville (G-8261)
Schaefer Machine Co Inc ....E 516 248-6880
Mineola (G-8570)
Servotec Usa LLC ....G 518 671-6120
Hudson (G-6665)
▼ Smart High Voltage Solutions ....F 631 563-6724
Bohemia (G-1132)
Special Metals Corporation ....D 716 366-5663
Dunkirk (G-4375)
▲ Standard Paper Box Machine Co ....E 718 328-3300
Bronx (G-1461)
◆ Strippit Inc ....C 716 542-5500
Akron (G-26)
Taumel Metalforming Corp ....G 845 878-3100
Patterson (G-13469)
▲ Trueforge Global McHy Corp ....G 516 825-7040
Rockville Centre (G-14830)
▲ U S Air Tool Co Inc ....F 631 471-3300
Ronkonkoma (G-15017)
Uhmac Inc ....F 716 537-2343
Holland (G-6512)
Vader Systems LLC ....F 716 688-1600
Getzville (G-5618)
▼ Win Set Technologies LLC ....F 631 234-7077
Centereach (G-3499)

3543 Industrial Patterns

A & T Tooling LLC ....G 716 601-7299
Lancaster (G-7321)
▼ Armstrong Mold Corporation ....E 315 437-1517
East Syracuse (G-4521)
Armstrong Mold Corporation ....D 315 437-1517
East Syracuse (G-4522)
Bianca Group Ltd ....G 212 768-3011
New York (G-9435)
City Pattern Shop Inc ....F 315 463-5239
Syracuse (G-15914)
G Haynes Holdings Inc ....G 607 538-1160
Bloomville (G-989)
IBlt Inc ....E 212 768-0292
New York (G-10592)
K & H Precision Products Inc ....E 585 624-4894
Honeoye Falls (G-6560)
Studio One Leather Design Inc ....F 212 760-1701
New York (G-12243)
W N R Pattern & Tool Inc ....G 716 681-9334
Lancaster (G-7371)
Wolff & Dungey Inc ....E 315 475-2105
Syracuse (G-16098)
Woodward Industries Inc ....F 716 692-2242
Tonawanda (G-16236)

3544 Dies, Tools, Jigs, Fixtures & Indl Molds

A & D Tool Inc ....G 631 243-4339
Dix Hills (G-4311)
Aaron Tool & Mold Inc ....G 585 426-5100
Rochester (G-14178)
▲ Accede Mold & Tool Co Inc ....D 585 254-6490
Rochester (G-14180)
Accurate Tool & Die LLC ....F 585 254-2830
Rochester (G-14183)
Ace Specialty Co Inc ....G 716 874-3670
Tonawanda (G-16156)
All American Precision Tl Mold ....F 585 436-3080
West Henrietta (G-16897)
All Out Die Cutting Inc ....E 718 346-6666
Brooklyn (G-1586)
▲ Alliance Precision Plas Corp ....C 585 426-5310
Rochester (G-14204)
Alliance Precision Plas Corp ....E 585 426-5310
Rochester (G-14205)
Allmetal Chocolate Mold Co Inc ....F 631 752-2888
West Babylon (G-16793)
▲ Allstate Tool and Die Inc ....D 585 426-0400
Rochester (G-14206)
Alry Tool and Die Co Inc ....E 716 693-2419
Tonawanda (G-16159)
Alton Manufacturing Inc ....D 585 458-2600
Rochester (G-14209)
▲ Amada Tool America Inc ....D 585 344-3900
Batavia (G-623)
American Dies Inc ....F 718 387-1900
Brooklyn (G-1599)
American Dsplay Die Ctters Inc ....E 212 645-1274
New York (G-9166)
American Orthotic Lab Co Inc ....G 718 961-6487
College Point (G-3803)
Amsco Inc ....F 716 823-4213
Buffalo (G-2829)
▲ Anka Tool & Die Inc ....E 845 268-4116
Congers (G-3875)
Arnell Inc ....G 516 486-7098
Hempstead (G-6289)
Arro Manufacturing LLC ....F 716 763-6203
Lakewood (G-7310)
▼ Arro Tool & Die Inc ....F 716 763-6203
Lakewood (G-7311)
Art Precision Metal Products ....F 631 842-8889
Copiague (G-3920)
Artisan Management Group Inc ....G 716 569-4094
Frewsburg (G-5462)
▲ Ascension Industries Inc ....D 716 693-9381
North Tonawanda (G-12974)
Barron Metal Products Inc ....E 914 965-1232
Yonkers (G-17434)
Bennett Die & Tool Inc ....E 607 739-5629
Horseheads (G-6598)
Bennett Die & Tool Inc ....F 607 273-2836
Ithaca (G-6860)
Blue Chip Mold Inc ....F 585 647-1790
Rochester (G-14254)
Brayley Tool & Machine Inc ....G 585 342-7190
Rochester (G-14262)
Brighton Tool & Die Designers ....F 716 876-0879
Tonawanda (G-16169)

SIC SECTION
35 INDUSTRIAL AND COMMERCIAL MACHINERY AND COMPUTER EQUIPMENT

Carbaugh Tool Company Inc ....E 607 739-3293
Elmira (G-4686)
▲ Century Mold Company Inc ....D 585 352-8600
Rochester (G-14287)
Chamtek Mfg Inc ....E 585 328-4900
Rochester (G-14293)
Charles A Rogers Entps Inc ....E 585 924-6400
Victor (G-16490)
Chenango Valley Tech Inc ....E 607 674-4115
Sherburne (G-15411)
Clifford H Jones Inc ....F 716 693-2444
Tonawanda (G-16174)
Coil Stamping Inc ....F 631 588-3040
Holbrook (G-6467)
Columbia Dentoform Corporation ....E 718 482-1569
Long Island City (G-7732)
Cosmo Electronic Machine Corp ....E 631 249-2535
Farmingdale (G-4973)
Cuddeback Machining Inc ....G 585 392-5889
Hilton (G-6443)
Custom Molding Solutions Inc ....E 585 293-1702
Churchville (G-3665)
▲ Cy Plastics Works Inc ....E 585 229-2555
Honeoye (G-6551)
▲ D Maldari & Sons Inc ....E 718 499-3555
Brooklyn (G-1830)
Dewes Gumbs Die Co Inc ....G 718 784-9755
Long Island City (G-7743)
▲ Diemax of Rochester Inc ....G 585 288-3912
Rochester (G-14328)
Diemolding Corporation ....F 315 363-4710
Wampsville (G-16575)
Dixon Tool and Manufacturing ....F 585 235-1352
Rochester (G-14334)
DOT Tool Co Inc ....G 607 724-7001
Binghamton (G-904)
Dynamic Dies Inc ....F 585 247-4010
Rochester (G-14341)
East Pattern & Model Corp ....E 585 461-3240
Fairport (G-4861)
▲ Eberhardt Enterprises Inc ....F 585 458-7681
Rochester (G-14360)
▼ Eden Tool & Die Inc ....G 716 992-4240
Eden (G-4599)
Egli Machine Company Inc ....E 607 563-3663
Sidney (G-15461)
Electro Form Corp ....F 607 722-6404
Binghamton (G-906)
Electronic Die Corp ....F 718 455-3200
Brooklyn (G-1913)
Enhanced Tool Inc ....E 716 691-5200
Amherst (G-238)
Etna Tool & Die Corporation ....F 212 475-4350
New York (G-10133)
Everfab Inc ....D 716 655-1550
East Aurora (G-4395)
Evergreen Corp Central NY ....F 315 454-4175
Syracuse (G-15959)
Fuller Tool Incorporated ....F 315 891-3183
Newport (G-12814)
G N R Plastics Inc ....G 631 724-8758
Smithtown (G-15509)
Gatti Tool & Mold Inc ....F 585 328-1350
Rochester (G-14409)
Gay Sheet Metal Dies Inc ....G 716 877-0208
Buffalo (G-2981)
▲ General Die and Die Cutng Inc ....D 516 665-3584
Roosevelt (G-15028)
▲ Genesee Precision Inc ....E 585 344-0385
Batavia (G-636)
▲ Globmarble LLC ....G 347 717-4088
Brooklyn (G-2031)
▲ Graywood Companies Inc ....E 585 254-7000
Rochester (G-14433)
Great Lakes Pressed Steel Corp ....E 716 885-4037
Buffalo (G-2998)
Handy Tool & Mfg Co Inc ....E 718 478-9203
Brooklyn (G-2067)
HNST Mold Inspections LLC ....G 845 215-9258
Nanuet (G-8803)
Hy-Tech Mold Inc ....F 585 247-2450
Rochester (G-14461)
▲ Hytech Tool & Die Inc ....G 716 488-2796
Jamestown (G-7035)
▲ Industrial Tool & Die Co Inc ....F 518 273-7383
Troy (G-16262)
Intek Precision ....G 585 293-0853
Churchville (G-3668)
Inter Molds Inc ....G 631 667-8580
Bay Shore (G-704)

Intri-Cut Inc ....F 716 691-5200
Amherst (G-246)
J B Tool & Die Co Inc ....E 516 333-1480
Westbury (G-17024)
J T Systematic ....G 607 754-0929
Endwell (G-4841)
James B Crowell & Sons Inc ....G 845 895-3464
Wallkill (G-16564)
James Wire Die Co ....G 315 894-3233
Ilion (G-6781)
K & H Precision Products Inc ....E 585 624-4894
Honeoye Falls (G-6560)
K D M Die Company Inc ....F 716 828-9000
Buffalo (G-3041)
Keyes Machine Works Inc ....G 585 426-5059
Gates (G-5576)
Knise & Krick Inc ....E 315 422-3516
Syracuse (G-15995)
▲ Light Waves Concept Inc ....F 212 677-6400
Brooklyn (G-2223)
Long Island Tool & Die Inc ....G 631 225-0600
Copiague (G-3935)
M J M Tooling Corp ....G 718 292-3590
Bronx (G-1388)
Machine Tool Specialty ....G 315 699-5287
Cicero (G-3677)
Machinecraft Inc ....E 585 436-1070
Rochester (G-14507)
Magnus Precision Mfg Inc ....D 315 548-8032
Phelps (G-13557)
Manhasset Tool & Die Co Inc ....F 716 684-6066
Lancaster (G-7349)
▲ Mannesmann Corporation ....D 212 258-4000
New York (G-11160)
Mantel & Mantel Stamping Corp ....G 631 467-1916
Ronkonkoma (G-14964)
Manufacturers Tool & Die Co ....G 585 352-1080
Spencerport (G-15596)
May Tool & Die Inc ....G 716 695-1033
Tonawanda (G-16198)
Mega Tool & Mfg Corp ....E 607 734-8398
Elmira (G-4709)
Micro Instrument Corp ....D 585 458-3150
Rochester (G-14528)
Micron Inds Rochester Inc ....G 585 247-6130
Rochester (G-14533)
Mold-Rite Plastics LLC ....G 518 561-1812
Plattsburgh (G-13704)
Moldcraft Inc ....E 716 684-1126
Depew (G-4288)
Ms Machining Inc ....G 607 723-1105
Binghamton (G-934)
Multifold Die Ctng Finshg Corp ....G 631 232-1235
Hauppauge (G-6170)
Mustang-Major Tool & Die Co ....G 716 992-9200
Eden (G-4601)
▲ Nas CP Corp ....E 718 961-6757
College Point (G-3823)
National Steel Rule Die Inc ....F 718 402-1396
Bronx (G-1409)
Niagara Fiberglass Inc ....E 716 822-3921
Buffalo (G-3109)
Niagara Punch & Die Corp ....G 716 896-7619
Buffalo (G-3112)
▼ Nicoform Inc ....E 585 454-5530
Rochester (G-14557)
Nijon Tool Co Inc ....F 631 242-3434
Deer Park (G-4204)
◆ Nordon Inc ....D 585 546-6200
Rochester (G-14558)
Northern Design Inc ....G 716 652-7071
East Aurora (G-4402)
P & H Machine Shop Inc ....G 585 247-5500
Rochester (G-14582)
P & R Industries Inc ....E 585 266-6725
Rochester (G-14583)
P & R Industries Inc ....F 585 544-1811
Rochester (G-14584)
P Tool & Die Co Inc ....E 585 889-1340
North Chili (G-12941)
▲ P&G Metal Components Corp ....D 716 896-7900
Buffalo (G-3130)
Pacific Die Cast Inc ....F 845 778-6374
Walden (G-16553)
Palma Tool & Die Company Inc ....E 716 681-4685
Lancaster (G-7353)
Paragon Steel Rule Dies Inc ....F 585 254-3395
Rochester (G-14592)
Patmian LLC ....B 212 758-0770
New York (G-11594)

Peak Motion Inc ....G 716 534-4925
Clarence (G-3695)
Phelinger Tool & Die Corp ....G 716 685-1780
Alden (G-184)
Pivot Punch Corporation ....D 716 625-8000
Lockport (G-7640)
Plastic Solutions Inc ....E 631 234-9013
Bayport (G-754)
◆ PMI Industries LLC ....E 585 464-8050
Rochester (G-14605)
Ppi Corp ....E 585 880-7277
Rochester (G-14611)
Precise Punch Corporation ....F 716 625-8000
Lockport (G-7641)
▲ Precision Grinding & Mfg Corp ....C 585 458-4300
Rochester (G-14615)
Precision Machining and Mfg ....G 845 647-5380
Wawarsing (G-16732)
Precision Systems Mfg Inc ....E 315 451-3480
Liverpool (G-7570)
Precision Tl Die & Stamping Co ....F 516 561-0041
Valley Stream (G-16444)
Prime Tool & Die LLC ....G 607 334-5435
Norwich (G-13054)
Producto Corporation ....C 716 484-7131
Jamestown (G-7057)
Pronto Tool & Die Co Inc ....E 631 981-8920
Ronkonkoma (G-14997)
Prototype Manufacturing Corp ....F 716 695-1700
North Tonawanda (G-13005)
Quality Lineals Usa Inc ....E 516 378-6577
Freeport (G-5432)
Raloid Tool Co Inc ....F 518 664-4261
Mechanicville (G-8261)
Ram Precision Tool Inc ....G 716 759-8722
Lancaster (G-7362)
Rand Machine Products Inc ....D 716 665-5217
Falconer (G-4916)
Rand Machine Products Inc ....G 716 985-4681
Sinclairville (G-15475)
Rid Lom Precision Mfg ....E 585 594-8600
Rochester (G-14648)
Rochester Stampings Inc ....F 585 467-5241
Rochester (G-14672)
Rochester Tool and Mold Inc ....F 585 464-9336
Rochester (G-14675)
Rochling Advent Tool & Mold LP ....D 585 254-2000
Rochester (G-14677)
▲ Romold Inc ....F 585 529-4440
Rochester (G-14679)
Rossi Tool & Dies Inc ....G 845 267-8246
Valley Cottage (G-16413)
Royal Molds Inc ....F 718 382-7686
Brooklyn (G-2532)
S B Whistler & Sons Inc ....E 585 798-3000
Medina (G-8313)
Saturn Industries Inc ....E 518 828-9956
Hudson (G-6663)
Sb Molds LLC ....D 845 352-3700
Monsey (G-8616)
Sharon Metal Stamping Corp ....G 718 828-4510
Bronx (G-1450)
Silicone Products & Technology ....C 716 684-1155
Lancaster (G-7368)
▲ Spectronics Corporation ....C 516 333-4840
Westbury (G-17055)
Stamp Rite Tool & Die Inc ....G 718 752-0334
Long Island City (G-7911)
Star Mold Co Inc ....G 631 694-2283
Farmingdale (G-5126)
◆ Strippit Inc ....C 716 542-5500
Akron (G-26)
Stuart Tool & Die Inc ....E 716 488-1975
Falconer (G-4922)
Synergy Tooling Systems Inc ....E 716 834-4457
Amherst (G-264)
Syntec Technologies Inc ....F 585 464-9336
Rochester (G-14737)
T A Tool & Molding Inc ....F 631 293-0172
Farmingdale (G-5133)
Thayer Tool & Die Inc ....F 716 782-4841
Ashville (G-427)
Tips & Dies Inc ....F 315 337-4161
Rome (G-14865)
Tooling Enterprises Inc ....F 716 842-0445
Buffalo (G-3248)
Tools & Stamping Corp ....G 718 392-4040
Brooklyn (G-2683)
Trimaster/Htech Holding LLC ....G 212 257-6772
New York (G-12427)

SIC

Employee Codes: A=Over 500 employees, B=251-500
C=101-250, D=51-100, E=20-50, F=10-19, G=5-9
2018 Harris
New York Manufacturers Directory
823

Trinity Tools Inc....E....716 694-1111
North Tonawanda (G-13021)
Turning Point Tool LLC....G....585 288-7380
Rochester (G-14764)
▼ Ultimate Prcision Met Pdts Inc....C....631 249-9441
Farmingdale (G-5146)
Universal Tooling Corporation....F....716 985-4691
Gerry (G-5606)
Van Reenen Tool & Die Inc....F....585 288-6000
Rochester (G-14779)
▲ Van Thomas Inc....E....585 426-1414
Rochester (G-14780)
W N R Pattern & Tool Inc....G....716 681-9334
Lancaster (G-7371)
Xli Corporation....D....585 436-2250
Rochester (G-14800)
Z Works Inc....G....631 750-0612
Bohemia (G-1154)

3545 Machine Tool Access

Advance D Tech Inc....F....845 534-8248
Cornwall (G-4006)
Ale-Techniques Inc....F....845 687-7200
High Falls (G-6426)
Ameri-Cut Tool Grinding Inc....G....716 692-3900
North Tonawanda (G-12971)
American Linear Manufacturers....F....516 333-1351
Westbury (G-16993)
Atwood Tool & Machine Inc....E....607 648-6543
Chenango Bridge (G-3623)
B & B Precision Mfg Inc....E....585 226-6226
Avon (G-535)
▲ Baldwin Machine Works Inc....G....631 842-9110
Copiague (G-3922)
Bdp Industries Inc....E....518 695-6851
Greenwich (G-5904)
Bnm Product Service....G....631 750-1586
Holbrook (G-6460)
Boro Park Cutting Tool Corp....E....718 720-0610
Staten Island (G-15670)
Brinkman Intl Group Inc....G....585 429-5000
Rochester (G-14263)
C J Winter Machine Tech....E....585 429-5000
Rochester (G-14271)
▲ Champion Cutting Tool Corp....E....516 536-8200
Rockville Centre (G-14817)
Circo File Corp....G....516 922-1848
Oyster Bay (G-13393)
▲ Curran Manufacturing Corp....E....631 273-1010
Hauppauge (G-6081)
Curran Manufacturing Corp....E....631 273-1010
Hauppauge (G-6082)
Custom Service Solutions Inc....G....585 637-3760
Brockport (G-1242)
▲ Designatronics Incorporated....G....516 328-3300
Hicksville (G-6366)
Dinosaw Inc....E....518 828-9942
Hudson (G-6642)
Dock Hardware Incorporated....F....585 266-7920
Rochester (G-14335)
Dorsey Metrology Intl Inc....E....845 229-2929
Poughkeepsie (G-13914)
▲ Drill America Inc....G....516 764-5700
Oceanside (G-13097)
Dura-Mill Inc....E....518 899-2255
Ballston Spa (G-594)
East Side Machine Inc....E....585 265-4560
Webster (G-16746)
Egli Machine Company Inc....E....607 563-3663
Sidney (G-15461)
Everfab Inc....D....716 655-1550
East Aurora (G-4395)
▲ F W Roberts Mfg Co Inc....F....716 434-3555
Lockport (G-7614)
Flashflo Manufacturing Inc....F....716 826-9500
Buffalo (G-2962)
▲ Flexbar Machine Corporation....E....631 582-8440
Islandia (G-6831)
Fred M Velepec Co Inc....E....718 821-6636
Glendale (G-5668)
Fronhofer Tool Company Inc....E....518 692-2496
Cossayuna (G-4081)
▲ Gardei Industries LLC....F....716 693-7100
North Tonawanda (G-12991)
Genesee Manufacturing Co Inc....G....585 266-3201
Rochester (G-14415)
Genius Tools Americas Corp....F....716 662-6872
Orchard Park (G-13295)
◆ Germanow-Simon Corporation....E....585 232-1440
Rochester (G-14420)

▲ Graywood Companies Inc....E....585 254-7000
Rochester (G-14433)
▲ Griffin Manufacturing Company....E....585 265-1991
Webster (G-16748)
▲ Hardinge Inc....B....607 734-2281
Elmira (G-4701)
▲ Heidenhain International Inc....C....716 661-1700
Jamestown (G-7033)
Hubbard Tool and Die Corp....E....315 337-7840
Rome (G-14843)
Huron Tl Cutter Grinding Inc....E....631 420-7000
Farmingdale (G-5015)
▼ Innex Industries Inc....E....585 247-3575
Rochester (G-14469)
Innovative Automation Inc....F....631 439-3300
Farmingdale (G-5018)
J H Robotics Inc....E....607 729-3758
Johnson City (G-7127)
JD Tool Inc....G....607 786-3129
Endicott (G-4822)
Jem Tool & Die Corp....F....631 539-8734
West Islip (G-16934)
JW Burg Machine & Tool Inc....G....716 434-0015
Clarence Center (G-3704)
◆ Kps Capital Partners LP....E....212 338-5100
New York (G-10922)
▲ Lancaster Knives Inc....E....716 683-5050
Lancaster (G-7347)
Linde LLC....D....716 773-7552
Grand Island (G-5776)
Lovejoy Chaplet Corporation....E....518 686-5232
Hoosick Falls (G-6568)
▲ M & S Precision Machine Co LLC....F....518 747-1193
Queensbury (G-14017)
Macinnes Tool Corporation....E....585 467-1920
Rochester (G-14508)
▲ Make-Waves Instrument Corp....E....716 681-7524
Buffalo (G-3076)
Mausner Equipment Co Inc....C....631 689-7358
Setauket (G-15402)
Melland Gear Instr of Huppauge....E....631 234-0100
Hauppauge (G-6156)
Methods Tooling & Mfg Inc....E....845 246-7100
Mount Marion (G-8693)
◆ Mibro Group....D....716 631-5713
Buffalo (G-3084)
Michael Fiore Ltd....G....516 561-8238
Valley Stream (G-16440)
◆ Micro Centric Corporation....E....800 573-1139
Plainview (G-13649)
Miller Metal Fabricating Inc....G....585 359-3400
Rochester (G-14534)
Morgood Tools Inc....D....585 436-8828
Rochester (G-14542)
Myles Tool Company Inc....E....716 731-1300
Sanborn (G-15151)
NC Industries Inc....F....248 528-5200
Buffalo (G-3103)
New Market Products Co Inc....F....607 292-6226
Wayne (G-16736)
Northeastern Water Jet Inc....F....518 843-4988
Amsterdam (G-364)
Northfeld Precision Instr Corp....E....516 431-1112
Island Park (G-6822)
Novatech Inc....E....716 892-6682
Cheektowaga (G-3611)
▲ Omega Tool Measuring Mchs Inc....E....585 598-7800
Fairport (G-4872)
▲ Park Enterprises Rochester Inc....C....585 546-4200
Rochester (G-14593)
▲ Ppi Corp....D....585 243-0300
Rochester (G-14612)
▲ Precision Grinding & Mfg Corp....C....585 458-4300
Rochester (G-14615)
Precision Mechanisms Corp....E....516 333-5955
Westbury (G-17049)
▲ Production Metal Cutting Inc....F....585 458-7136
Rochester (G-14629)
Ptc Precision LLC....E....607 748-8294
Endwell (G-4845)
Robert J Faraone....G....585 232-7160
Rochester (G-14653)
Rochling Advent Tool & Mold LP....D....585 254-2000
Rochester (G-14677)
Ross JC Inc....G....716 439-1161
Lockport (G-7642)
Rota File Corporation....E....516 496-7200
Syosset (G-15859)
S & R Tool Inc....G....585 346-2029
Lakeville (G-7308)

▲ S & S Machinery Corp....E....718 492-7400
Brooklyn (G-2541)
S S Precision Gear & Instr....G....718 457-7474
Corona (G-4029)
Safina Center....G....808 888-9440
Stony Brook (G-15792)
◆ Schenck Corporation....D....631 242-4010
Deer Park (G-4229)
◆ Schenck Trebel Corp....D....631 242-4397
Deer Park (G-4230)
Scomac Inc....F....585 494-2200
Bergen (G-851)
Seneca Falls Machine Tool Co....D....315 568-5804
Seneca Falls (G-15392)
Sinn- Tech Industries Inc....F....631 643-1171
West Babylon (G-16858)
Socket Products Mfg Corp....G....631 232-9870
Islandia (G-6841)
Steiner Technologies Inc....F....585 425-5910
Fairport (G-4887)
Streamline Precision Inc....G....585 421-9050
Fairport (G-4888)
Streamline Precision Inc....G....585 421-9050
Fairport (G-4889)
◆ Strippit Inc....C....716 542-5500
Akron (G-26)
▲ Thuro Metal Products Inc....E....631 435-0444
Brentwood (G-1194)
Townline Machine Co Inc....F....315 462-3413
Clifton Springs (G-3741)
Transport National Dev Inc....E....716 662-0270
Orchard Park (G-13325)
▲ Trident Precision Mfg Inc....D....585 265-2010
Webster (G-16764)
Trimaster/Htech Holding LLC....G....212 257-6772
New York (G-12427)
Trinity Tools Inc....E....716 694-1111
North Tonawanda (G-13021)
▲ Truebite Inc....F....607 786-3184
Endicott (G-4837)
Universal Tooling Corporation....F....716 985-4691
Gerry (G-5606)
Vandilay Industries Inc....E....631 226-3064
West Babylon (G-16870)
Velmex Inc....E....585 657-6151
Bloomfield (G-986)
▲ Willemin Macodel Incorporated....F....914 345-3504
Hawthorne (G-6281)
Xactra Technologies Inc....D....585 426-2030
Rochester (G-14795)

3546 Power Hand Tools

Allied Motion Technologies Inc....C....315 782-5910
Watertown (G-16656)
▲ Awt Supply Corp....G....516 437-9105
Elmont (G-4730)
Black & Decker (us) Inc....B....914 235-6300
Brewster (G-1209)
Black & Decker (us) Inc....G....716 884-6220
Buffalo (G-2865)
Black & Decker (us) Inc....G....631 952-2008
Hauppauge (G-6054)
Dean Manufacturing Inc....F....607 770-1300
Vestal (G-16468)
▲ Dynabrade Inc....C....716 631-0100
Clarence (G-3686)
▲ Great American Tool Co Inc....G....716 646-5700
Hamburg (G-5950)
Huck International Inc....C....845 331-7300
Kingston (G-7220)
◆ Ivy Classic Industries Inc....E....914 632-8200
New Rochelle (G-8958)
Kelley Farm & Garden Inc....E....518 234-2332
Cobleskill (G-3763)
▲ Meritool LLC....F....716 699-6005
Ellicottville (G-4656)
New York Industrial Works Inc....G....718 292-0615
Bronx (G-1411)
◆ P & F Industries Inc....E....631 694-9800
Melville (G-8375)
◆ Rbhammers Corp....F....845 353-5042
Blauvelt (G-968)
▲ Reimann & Georger Corporation....E....716 895-1156
Buffalo (G-3182)
▲ Stature Electric Inc....B....315 782-5910
Watertown (G-16695)
▼ Thomas C Wilson LLC....E....718 729-3360
Long Island City (G-7928)

35 INDUSTRIAL AND COMMERCIAL MACHINERY AND COMPUTER EQUIPMENT

3547 Rolling Mill Machinery & Eqpt

- Anthony Manufacturing Inc ..... G 631 957-9424
  Lindenhurst *(G-7476)*
- ◆ Ivy Classic Industries Inc ..... E 914 632-8200
  New Rochelle *(G-8958)*
- Johnston Dandy Company ..... G 315 455-5773
  Syracuse *(G-15988)*
- ▲ Mannesmann Corporation ..... D 212 258-4000
  New York *(G-11160)*
- Polymag Tek Inc ..... F 585 235-8390
  Rochester *(G-14606)*

3548 Welding Apparatus

- Apogee Translite Inc ..... E 631 254-6975
  Deer Park *(G-4124)*
- ▲ Lubow Machine Corp ..... F 631 226-1700
  Copiague *(G-3936)*
- McAllisters Precision Wldg Inc ..... F 518 221-3455
  Menands *(G-8406)*
- Riverview Industries Inc ..... G 845 265-5284
  Cold Spring *(G-3790)*
- ▲ Vante Inc ..... F 716 778-7691
  Newfane *(G-12813)*

3549 Metalworking Machinery, NEC

- Advanced Machine Design Co Inc ..... E 716 826-2000
  Buffalo *(G-2817)*
- ▲ Alliance Automation Systems ..... C 585 426-2700
  Rochester *(G-14203)*
- ▲ Autostat Corporation ..... F 516 379-9447
  Roosevelt *(G-15027)*
- ▲ Bartell Machinery Systems LLC ..... C 315 336-7600
  Rome *(G-14833)*
- Carpenter Manufacturing Co ..... E 315 682-9176
  Manlius *(G-8102)*
- Charles A Rogers Entps Inc ..... E 585 924-6400
  Victor *(G-16490)*
- Duall Finishing Inc ..... G 716 827-1707
  Buffalo *(G-2935)*
- ▲ Esm II Inc ..... E 716 446-8888
  Amherst *(G-240)*
- ▲ Expert Metal Slitters Corp ..... G 718 361-2735
  Long Island City *(G-7765)*
- ▲ Hardinge Inc ..... B 607 734-2281
  Elmira *(G-4701)*
- Hje Company Inc ..... E 518 792-8733
  Queensbury *(G-14012)*
- ▲ Hover-Davis Inc ..... C 585 352-9590
  Rochester *(G-14459)*
- Manufacturing Resources Inc ..... E 631 481-0041
  Rochester *(G-14514)*
- ▲ MGS Manufacturing Inc ..... E 315 337-3350
  Rome *(G-14849)*
- ▲ Mold-A-Matic Corporation ..... E 607 433-2121
  Oneonta *(G-13211)*
- Mono-Systems Inc ..... E 716 821-1344
  Buffalo *(G-3094)*
- Mtwli Precision Corp ..... E 631 244-3767
  Bohemia *(G-1102)*
- ▲ Munson Machinery Company Inc ..... E 315 797-0090
  Utica *(G-16374)*
- Pems Tool & Machine Inc ..... E 315 823-3595
  Little Falls *(G-7523)*
- Precision Systems Mfg Inc ..... E 315 451-3480
  Liverpool *(G-7570)*
- ▲ Reelex Packaging Solutions Inc ..... E 845 878-7878
  Patterson *(G-13467)*
- Riverside Machinery Company ..... E 718 492-7400
  Brooklyn *(G-2519)*
- ▲ S & S Machinery Corp ..... E 718 492-7400
  Brooklyn *(G-2541)*
- S & S Machinery Corp ..... E 718 492-7400
  Brooklyn *(G-2542)*
- Serge Duct Designs Inc ..... E 718 783-7799
  Brooklyn *(G-2570)*
- ◆ Strippit Inc ..... C 716 542-5500
  Akron *(G-26)*
- ◆ Tessy Plastics Corp ..... B 315 689-3924
  Skaneateles *(G-15488)*
- Unidex Corporation Western NY ..... F 585 786-3170
  Warsaw *(G-16606)*
- Vader Systems LLC ..... F 716 688-1600
  Getzville *(G-5618)*
- ▲ Van Blarcom Closures Inc ..... C 718 855-3810
  Brooklyn *(G-2735)*
- ◆ Voss Manufacturing Inc ..... D 716 731-5062
  Sanborn *(G-15158)*
- ▲ Xto Incorporated ..... D 315 451-7807
  Liverpool *(G-7585)*

3552 Textile Machinery

- Aglika Trade LLC ..... F 727 424-1944
  Middle Village *(G-8443)*
- Angel Textiles Inc ..... G 212 532-0900
  New York *(G-9205)*
- Big Apple Sign Corp ..... E 631 342-0303
  Islandia *(G-6826)*
- Chroma Logic ..... G 716 736-2458
  Ripley *(G-14147)*
- Corbertex LLC ..... E 212 971-0008
  New York *(G-9783)*
- ◆ Eastman Machine Company ..... C 716 856-2200
  Buffalo *(G-2943)*
- EMC Fintech ..... F 716 488-9071
  Falconer *(G-4903)*
- Herr Manufacturing Co Inc ..... E 716 754-4341
  Tonawanda *(G-16190)*
- Herrmann Group LLC ..... G 716 876-9798
  Kenmore *(G-7176)*
- Mjk Cutting Inc ..... F 718 384-7613
  Brooklyn *(G-2328)*
- Mohawk Valley Knt McHy Co Inc ..... F 315 736-3038
  New York Mills *(G-12745)*
- Rfb Associates Inc ..... E 518 271-0551
  Fort Edward *(G-5354)*
- Schwabel Fabricating Co Inc ..... E 716 876-2086
  Tonawanda *(G-16219)*
- Screen Team Inc ..... F 718 786-2424
  Long Island City *(G-7902)*
- Simtec Industries Corporation ..... G 631 293-0080
  Farmingdale *(G-5119)*
- Thread Check Inc ..... D 631 231-1515
  Hauppauge *(G-6238)*

3553 Woodworking Machinery

- Cannonsville Lumber Inc ..... G 607 467-3380
  Deposit *(G-4299)*
- Casa Nueva Custom Furnishing ..... G 914 476-2272
  Yonkers *(G-17441)*
- ◆ Cem Machine Inc ..... E 315 493-4258
  Carthage *(G-3438)*
- Corbett Stves Pttern Works Inc ..... E 585 546-7109
  Rochester *(G-14310)*
- Downtown Interiors Inc ..... F 212 337-0230
  New York *(G-9969)*
- ▲ Hardinge Inc ..... B 607 734-2281
  Elmira *(G-4701)*
- Hat Factory Furniture Co ..... G 914 788-6288
  Peekskill *(G-13503)*
- ◆ James L Taylor Mfg Co ..... E 845 452-3780
  Poughkeepsie *(G-13929)*
- James L Taylor Mfg Co ..... E 845 452-3780
  Poughkeepsie *(G-13930)*
- ◆ Merritt Machinery LLC ..... E 716 434-5558
  Lockport *(G-7628)*
- ◆ Oneida Air Systems Inc ..... E 315 476-5151
  Syracuse *(G-16025)*
- Paratus Industries Inc ..... E 716 826-2000
  Orchard Park *(G-13313)*
- Phoenix Wood Wrights Ltd ..... F 631 727-9691
  Riverhead *(G-14165)*
- US Sander LLC ..... G 518 875-9157
  Esperance *(G-4846)*

3554 Paper Inds Machinery

- Automecha International Ltd ..... E 607 843-2235
  Oxford *(G-13388)*
- Cyclotherm of Watertown Inc ..... E 315 782-1100
  Watertown *(G-16670)*
- ▲ F W Roberts Mfg Co Inc ..... F 716 434-3555
  Lockport *(G-7614)*
- Fbm Galaxy Inc ..... E 315 463-5144
  East Syracuse *(G-4542)*
- Friedel Paper Box & Converting ..... G 315 437-3325
  Baldwinsville *(G-568)*
- GL&v USA Inc ..... E 518 747-2444
  Hudson Falls *(G-6674)*
- ▲ GL&v USA Inc ..... E 518 747-2444
  Hudson Falls *(G-6675)*
- Haanen Packard Machinery Inc ..... E 518 747-2330
  Hudson Falls *(G-6677)*
- Interntnal Strpping Diecutting ..... G 718 383-7720
  Brooklyn *(G-2112)*
- Jacob Inc ..... E 646 450-3067
  Brooklyn *(G-2130)*
- Johnston Dandy Company ..... G 315 455-5773
  Syracuse *(G-15988)*
- Kadant Inc ..... F 518 793-8801
  Glens Falls *(G-5700)*

Lake Image Systems Inc ..... F 585 321-3630
  Henrietta *(G-6319)*
- Richlar Industries Inc ..... F 315 463-5144
  East Syracuse *(G-4574)*
- Rsb Associates Inc ..... F 518 281-5067
  Altamont *(G-216)*
- Sinclair International Company ..... E 518 798-2361
  Queensbury *(G-14025)*
- ▲ Sonicor Inc ..... F 631 920-6555
  West Babylon *(G-16861)*
- ▲ Standard Paper Box Machine Co ..... E 718 328-3300
  Bronx *(G-1461)*
- Verso Corporation ..... B 212 599-2700
  New York *(G-12550)*

3555 Printing Trades Machinery & Eqpt

- A C Envelope Inc ..... E 516 420-0646
  Farmingdale *(G-4933)*
- A-Mark Machinery Corp ..... F 631 643-6300
  West Babylon *(G-16787)*
- Advance Grafix Equipment Inc ..... G 917 202-4593
  Wyandanch *(G-17386)*
- Anand Printing Machinery Inc ..... G 631 667-3079
  Deer Park *(G-4122)*
- Apexx Omni-Graphics Inc ..... D 718 326-3330
  Maspeth *(G-8147)*
- ▲ Awt Supply Corp ..... E 516 437-9105
  Elmont *(G-4730)*
- Bartizan Data Systems LLC ..... E 914 965-7977
  Yonkers *(G-17435)*
- ▲ Bmp America Inc ..... E 585 798-0950
  Medina *(G-8300)*
- C M E Corp ..... E 315 451-7101
  Syracuse *(G-15900)*
- Castleragh Printcraft Inc ..... D 516 623-1728
  Freeport *(G-5402)*
- Copy4les Inc ..... F 212 487-9778
  New York *(G-9782)*
- Csw Inc ..... F 585 247-4010
  Rochester *(G-14315)*
- Daige Products Inc ..... F 516 621-2100
  Albertson *(G-157)*
- Davis International Inc ..... E 585 421-8175
  Fairport *(G-4859)*
- Exacta LLC ..... G 716 406-2303
  Clarence Center *(G-3701)*
- ◆ Halm Industries Co Inc ..... D 516 676-6700
  Glen Head *(G-5646)*
- Halm Instrument Co Inc ..... D 516 676-6700
  Glen Head *(G-5647)*
- ◆ Hodgins Engraving Co Inc ..... D 585 343-4444
  Batavia *(G-640)*
- ▲ Impressions International Inc ..... G 585 442-5240
  Rochester *(G-14467)*
- Innotech Graphic Eqp Corp ..... G 845 268-6900
  Valley Cottage *(G-16405)*
- ◆ International Imaging Mtls Inc ..... A 716 691-6333
  Amherst *(G-245)*
- ▲ Lexar Global LLC ..... E 845 352-9700
  Valley Cottage *(G-16407)*
- ▲ Mekatronics Incorporated ..... E 516 883-6805
  Port Washington *(G-13865)*
- ◆ Micro Powders Inc ..... E 914 332-6400
  Tarrytown *(G-16120)*
- Mount Vernon Machine Inc ..... E 845 268-9400
  Valley Cottage *(G-16408)*
- Newport Business Solutions Inc ..... F 631 319-6129
  Bohemia *(G-1105)*
- ▲ Package Print Technologies ..... E 716 871-9905
  Buffalo *(G-3132)*
- ◆ Paxar Corporation ..... E 845 398-3229
  Orangeburg *(G-13260)*
- Perretta Graphics Corp ..... E 845 473-0550
  Poughkeepsie *(G-13943)*
- Prim Hall Enterprises Inc ..... F 518 561-7408
  Plattsburgh *(G-13719)*
- Rollers Inc ..... E 716 837-0700
  Buffalo *(G-3192)*
- Rubber Stamps Inc ..... E 212 675-1180
  Mineola *(G-8568)*
- Southern Graphic Systems LLC ..... E 315 695-7079
  Phoenix *(G-13571)*
- Speclfty Bus Mchs Holdings LLC ..... E 212 587-9600
  New York *(G-12180)*
- Sterling Toggle Inc ..... E 631 491-0500
  West Babylon *(G-16864)*
- ▲ Super Web Inc ..... E 631 643-9100
  West Babylon *(G-16866)*
- Total Offset Inc ..... F 212 966-4482
  New York *(G-12400)*

Employee Codes: A=Over 500 employees, B=251-500
C=101-250, D=51-100, E=20-50, F=10-19, G=5-9

35 INDUSTRIAL AND COMMERCIAL MACHINERY AND COMPUTER EQUIPMENT — SIC SECTION

Universal Metal Fabricators ....F...... 845 331-8248
  Kingston (G-7248)
◆ Vits International Inc ....E...... 845 353-5000
  Blauvelt (G-973)
Voodoo Manufacturing Inc ....G...... 646 893-8366
  Brooklyn (G-2755)
Woerner Industries Inc ....E...... 585 436-1934
  Rochester (G-14793)

3556 Food Prdts Machinery

◆ Ag-Pak Inc ....F...... 716 772-2651
  Gasport (G-5570)
◆ Bairnco Corporation ....E...... 914 461-1300
  White Plains (G-17108)
Bakers Pride Oven Co Inc ....C...... 914 576-0200
  New Rochelle (G-8932)
Bari Engineering Corp ....E...... 212 966-2080
  New York (G-9372)
Blue Toad Hard Cider ....E...... 585 424-5508
  Rochester (G-14255)
Bonduelle USA Inc ....E...... 585 948-5252
  Oakfield (G-13083)
▲ Brooklyn Brew Shop LLC ....F...... 718 874-0119
  Brooklyn (G-1720)
▼ Buflovak LLC ....E...... 716 895-2100
  Buffalo (G-2883)
C-Flex Bearing Co Inc ....F...... 315 895-7454
  Frankfort (G-5359)
◆ Caravella Food Corp ....F...... 646 552-0455
  Whitestone (G-17232)
Carts Mobile Food Eqp Corp ....E...... 718 788-5540
  Brooklyn (G-1763)
▲ Chemicolloid Laboratories Inc ....F...... 516 747-2666
  New Hyde Park (G-8866)
Chester-Jensen Company ....E...... 610 876-6276
  Cattaraugus (G-3465)
Delaval Inc ....F...... 585 599-4696
  Corfu (G-3976)
Delsur Parts ....G...... 631 630-1606
  Brentwood (G-1178)
Desu Machinery Corporation ....D...... 716 681-5798
  Depew (G-4279)
▲ Elmar Industries Inc ....F...... 716 681-5650
  Depew (G-4280)
Esquire Mechanical Corp ....G...... 718 625-4006
  Brooklyn (G-1941)
ET Oakes Corporation ....E...... 631 232-0002
  Hauppauge (G-6096)
Expert Industries Inc ....E...... 718 434-6060
  Brooklyn (G-1951)
Fresh Harvest Incorporated ....G...... 845 296-1024
  Wappingers Falls (G-16588)
G J Olney Inc ....E...... 315 827-4208
  Westernville (G-17072)
Goodnature Products Inc ....F...... 716 855-3325
  Orchard Park (G-13296)
Haines Equipment Inc ....E...... 607 566-8531
  Avoca (G-534)
Home Maide Inc ....F...... 845 837-1700
  Harriman (G-5994)
▼ I J White Corporation ....D...... 631 293-3788
  Farmingdale (G-5016)
Juice Press LLC ....E...... 212 777-0034
  New York (G-10816)
Kedco Inc ....F...... 516 454-7800
  Farmingdale (G-5032)
Kinplex Corp ....E...... 631 242-4800
  Edgewood (G-4618)
Los Olivos Ltd ....E...... 631 773-6439
  Farmingdale (G-5046)
◆ Ludwig Holdings Corp ....D...... 845 340-9727
  Kingston (G-7227)
Lyophilization Systems Inc ....E...... 845 338-0456
  New Paltz (G-8921)
M & E Mfg Co Inc ....D...... 845 331-7890
  Kingston (G-7229)
Mary F Morse ....E...... 315 866-2741
  Mohawk (G-8575)
Mohawk Valley Manufacturing ....G...... 315 797-0851
  Frankfort (G-5365)
◆ National Equipment Corporation ..F...... 718 585-0200
  Harrison (G-6006)
National Equipment Corporation ....E...... 718 585-0200
  Bronx (G-1408)
▲ Olmstead Products Corp ....F...... 516 681-3700
  Hicksville (G-6404)
P & M LLC ....E...... 631 842-2200
  Amityville (G-319)
Pic Nic LLC ....G...... 914 245-6500
  Yorktown Heights (G-17532)

◆ Purvi Enterprises Incorporated ....G...... 347 808-9448
  Maspeth (G-8196)
Sidco Food Distribution Corp ....F...... 718 733-3939
  Bronx (G-1451)
▲ Simply Natural Foods LLC ....E...... 631 543-9600
  Commack (G-3869)
Singlecut Beersmiths LLC ....F...... 718 606-0788
  Astoria (G-455)
▲ SPX Flow Tech Systems Inc ......D...... 716 692-3000
  Getzville (G-5616)
▼ Unisource Food Eqp Systems Inc..G...... 516 681-0537
  Holbrook (G-6506)
US Beverage Net Inc ....E...... 315 579-2025
  Syracuse (G-16089)
▲ Vr Food Equipment Inc ....E...... 315 531-8133
  Farmington (G-5166)
Wilder Manufacturing Co Inc ....D...... 516 222-0433
  Garden City (G-5550)
Win-Holt Equipment Corp ....C...... 516 222-0433
  Garden City (G-5551)
Wired Coffee and Bagel Inc ....F...... 518 506-3194
  Malta (G-8054)
Zaro Bake Shop Inc ....D...... 212 292-0175
  New York (G-12725)

3559 Special Ind Machinery, NEC

Accurate McHning Incorporation ....F...... 315 689-1428
  Elbridge (G-4636)
▲ Addex Inc ....G...... 781 344-5800
  Newark (G-12749)
◆ Adirondack Plas & Recycl Inc ....E...... 518 746-9212
  Argyle (G-406)
▼ Andela Tool & Machine Inc ....G...... 315 858-0055
  Richfield Springs (G-14074)
▲ Arbe Machinery Inc ....F...... 631 756-2477
  Farmingdale (G-4953)
▲ Aremco Products Inc ....F...... 845 268-0039
  Valley Cottage (G-16402)
Automotion Parking Systems LLC ..G...... 516 565-5600
  West Hempstead (G-16881)
B&K Precision Corporation ....F...... 631 369-2665
  Manorville (G-8110)
Ben Weitsman of Albany LLC ....F...... 518 462-4444
  Albany (G-50)
Blue Star Products Inc ....F...... 631 952-3204
  Hauppauge (G-6055)
Byfusion Inc ....F...... 347 563-5286
  Brooklyn (G-1744)
▲ Cameo Metal Products Inc ....E...... 718 788-1106
  Brooklyn (G-1753)
◆ Caswell Inc ....F...... 315 946-1213
  Lyons (G-7997)
CBA Group LLC ....A...... 607 779-7522
  Conklin (G-3891)
◆ Century-Tech Inc ....G...... 516 493-9800
  Hempstead (G-6292)
▲ Charles Ross & Son Company ....F...... 631 234-0500
  Hauppauge (G-6064)
Cleaning Tech Group LLC ....F...... 716 665-2340
  Jamestown (G-7016)
Crumbrubber Technology Inc ....F...... 718 468-3988
  Hollis (G-6522)
▲ Cryomech Inc ....F...... 315 455-2555
  Syracuse (G-15934)
Curtin-Hebert Co Inc ....F...... 518 725-7157
  Gloversville (G-5725)
Cvd Equipment Corporation ....F...... 845 246-3631
  Saugerties (G-15211)
▲ Cvd Equipment Corporation ....C...... 631 981-7081
  Central Islip (G-3518)
Cvd Equipment Corporation ....F...... 631 582-4365
  Central Islip (G-3519)
▲ Designatronics Incorporated ......E...... 516 328-3300
  Hicksville (G-6366)
Digital Matrix Corp ....E...... 516 481-7990
  Farmingdale (G-4987)
Eastend Enforcement Products ......F...... 631 878-8424
  Center Moriches (G-3490)
Eltee Tool & Die Co ....F...... 607 748-4301
  Endicott (G-4809)
Emhart Glass Manufacturing Inc ....C...... 607 734-3671
  Horseheads (G-6605)
Force Dynamics Inc ....F...... 607 546-5023
  Trumansburg (G-16291)
General Cryogenic Tech LLC ....F...... 516 334-8200
  Westbury (G-17018)
George Ponte Inc ....F...... 914 243-4202
  Jefferson Valley (G-7090)
◆ Germanow-Simon Corporation ....E...... 585 232-1440
  Rochester (G-14420)

▲ Glass Star America Inc ....F...... 631 291-9432
  Center Moriches (G-3491)
Globalfoundries US Inc ....F...... 512 457-3900
  Hopewell Junction (G-6578)
Gordon S Anderson Mfg Co ....G...... 845 677-3304
  Millbrook (G-8511)
Haanen Packard Machinery Inc ......E...... 518 747-2330
  Hudson Falls (G-6677)
Herbert Jaffe Inc ....G...... 718 392-1956
  Long Island City (G-7788)
▲ High Frequency Tech Co Inc ......F...... 631 242-3020
  Deer Park (G-4171)
▲ Hitachi Metals America Ltd ....E...... 914 694-9200
  Purchase (G-13975)
Illinois Tool Works Inc ....C...... 716 681-8222
  Lancaster (G-7344)
▲ Innovation Associates Inc ....C...... 607 798-9376
  Johnson City (G-7126)
▼ Innovation In Motion Inc ....G...... 407 878-7561
  Long Beach (G-7672)
Innovative Cleaning Solutions ....G...... 716 731-4408
  Sanborn (G-15148)
James Morris ....E...... 315 824-8519
  Hamilton (G-5971)
Kabar Manufacturing Corp ....E...... 631 694-1036
  Farmingdale (G-5030)
▲ Kabar Manufacturing Corp ....E...... 631 694-6857
  Farmingdale (G-5029)
Lam Research Corporation ....E...... 845 896-0606
  Fishkill (G-5192)
▲ Maharlika Holdings LLC ....F...... 631 319-6203
  Ronkonkoma (G-14963)
▲ Materials Recovery Company ......F...... 518 274-3681
  Troy (G-16264)
Michael Benalt Inc ....E...... 845 628-1008
  Mahopac (G-8027)
▲ Munson Machinery Company Inc ..E...... 315 797-0090
  Utica (G-16374)
◆ National Equipment Corporation ..F...... 718 585-0200
  Harrison (G-6006)
National Equipment Corporation ....E...... 718 585-0200
  Bronx (G-1408)
Northeast Data ....G...... 845 331-5554
  Kingston (G-7233)
▲ Northrock Industries Inc ....E...... 631 924-6130
  Bohemia (G-1107)
Nycon Diamond & Tools Corp ....G...... 855 937-6922
  Bohemia (G-1108)
◆ Optipro Systems LLC ....D...... 585 265-0160
  Ontario (G-13230)
P K G Equipment Incorporated ......E...... 585 436-4650
  Rochester (G-14585)
▲ Park Assist LLC ....D...... 646 666-7525
  New York (G-11587)
Pearl Technologies Inc ....E...... 315 365-2632
  Savannah (G-15231)
◆ Pfaudler Inc ....B...... 585 464-5663
  Rochester (G-14598)
▲ Precision Process Inc ....D...... 716 731-1587
  Niagara Falls (G-12882)
◆ Qes Solutions Inc ....D...... 585 783-1455
  Rochester (G-14634)
▲ Quality Strapping Inc ....G...... 718 418-1111
  Brooklyn (G-2482)
▼ Queenaire Technologies Inc ....G...... 315 393-5454
  Ogdensburg (G-13141)
R & B Machinery Corp ....G...... 716 894-3332
  Buffalo (G-3178)
Reefer Tek Llc ....G...... 347 590-1067
  Bronx (G-1439)
Reynolds Tech Fabricators Inc ....E...... 315 437-0532
  East Syracuse (G-4573)
Rfb Associates Inc ....E...... 518 271-0551
  Fort Edward (G-5354)
Riverview Associates Inc ....F...... 585 235-5980
  Rochester (G-14651)
Shred Center ....G...... 716 664-3052
  Jamestown (G-7059)
Sj Associates Inc ....E...... 516 942-3232
  Jericho (G-7119)
▲ Sonicor Inc ....F...... 631 920-6555
  West Babylon (G-16861)
Spectrum Catalysts Inc ....G...... 631 560-3683
  Central Islip (G-3537)
Stainless Design Concepts Ltd ......E...... 845 246-3631
  Saugerties (G-15224)
Surepure Inc ....G...... 917 368-8480
  New York (G-12267)
T-Rex Supply Corporation ....G...... 516 308-0505
  Hempstead (G-6310)

Technic Inc ... F ... 516 349-0700
Plainview (G-13665)
Tokyo Electron America Inc ... G ... 518 289-3100
Malta (G-8053)
Tompkins Metal Finishing Inc ... D ... 585 344-2600
Batavia (G-650)
Tompkins Srm LLC ... G ... 315 422-8763
Syracuse (G-16083)
Ui Acquisition Holding Co ... G ... 607 779-7522
Conklin (G-3903)
Ui Holding Company ... G ... 607 779-7522
Conklin (G-3904)
▲ Ultrepet LLC ... D ... 781 275-6400
Albany (G-146)
◆ Universal Instruments Corp ... C ... 800 842-9732
Conklin (G-3905)
Universal Thin Film Lab Corp ... G ... 845 562-0601
Newburgh (G-12808)
▲ Valplast International Corp ... F ... 516 442-3923
Westbury (G-17069)
▲ Veeco Instruments Inc ... B ... 516 677-0200
Plainview (G-13671)
West Metal Works Inc ... E ... 716 895-4900
Buffalo (G-3278)
Wilt Industries Inc ... G ... 518 548-4961
Lake Pleasant (G-7301)

3561 Pumps & Pumping Eqpt

Air Flow Pump Corp ... G ... 718 241-2800
Brooklyn (G-1570)
▲ Air Techniques Inc ... B ... 516 433-7676
Melville (G-8324)
▲ American Ship Repairs Company ... F ... 718 435-5570
Brooklyn (G-1607)
◆ Armstrong Pumps Inc ... D ... 716 693-8813
North Tonawanda (G-12973)
▲ Buffalo Pumps Inc ... C ... 716 693-1850
North Tonawanda (G-12981)
Century-Tech Inc ... F ... 718 326-9400
Hempstead (G-6291)
Curaegis Technologies Inc ... E ... 585 254-1100
Rochester (G-14316)
Daikin Applied Americas Inc ... D ... 315 253-2771
Auburn (G-490)
▲ Federal Pump Corporation ... E ... 718 451-2000
Brooklyn (G-1967)
Fisonic Corp ... G ... 212 732-3777
Long Island City (G-7772)
▲ Fisonic Corp ... F ... 716 763-0295
New York (G-10227)
Flow Control LLC ... C ... 914 323-5700
Rye Brook (G-15097)
▲ Fluid Handling LLC ... G ... 716 897-2800
Cheektowaga (G-3600)
▲ Gardner Dnver Oberdorfer Pumps ... E ... 315 437-0361
Syracuse (G-15969)
Geopump Inc ... G ... 585 798-6666
Medina (G-8306)
Goulds Pumps Incorporated ... B ... 315 258-4949
Auburn (G-497)
◆ Goulds Pumps LLC ... A ... 315 568-2811
Seneca Falls (G-15382)
ITT Corporation ... D ... 315 568-2811
Seneca Falls (G-15383)
ITT Goulds Pumps Inc ... A ... 914 641-2129
Seneca Falls (G-15385)
▲ ITT Water Technology Inc ... B ... 315 568-2811
Seneca Falls (G-15388)
▲ John N Fehlinger Co Inc ... F ... 212 233-5656
New York (G-10791)
Ketcham Pump Co Inc ... F ... 718 457-0800
Woodside (G-17351)
Lanco Manufacturing Co ... G ... 516 292-8953
West Hempstead (G-16890)
◆ Liberty Pumps Inc ... C ... 800 543-2550
Bergen (G-848)
Linde LLC ... D ... 716 773-7552
Grand Island (G-5776)
▲ Mannesmann Corporation ... D ... 212 258-4000
New York (G-11160)
McWane Inc ... B ... 607 734-2211
Elmira (G-4708)
Oberdorfer Pumps Inc ... E ... 315 437-0361
Syracuse (G-16021)
▲ Oyster Bay Pump Works Inc ... F ... 516 933-4500
Hicksville (G-6406)
Pentair Water Pool and Spa Inc ... E ... 845 452-5500
Lagrangeville (G-7283)
◆ Pulsafeeder Inc ... C ... 585 292-8000
Rochester (G-14632)
▲ Sihi Pumps Inc ... E ... 716 773-6450
Grand Island (G-5784)
▲ Stavo Industries Inc ... F ... 845 331-4552
Kingston (G-7241)
Trench & Marine Pump Co Inc ... E ... 212 423-9098
Bronx (G-1473)
◆ Voss Usa Inc ... C ... 212 995-2255
New York (G-12596)
◆ Wastecorp Pumps LLC ... F ... 888 829-2783
New York (G-12620)
Water Cooling Corp ... G ... 718 723-6500
Rosedale (G-15039)
Westmoor Ltd ... F ... 315 363-1500
Sherrill (G-15433)
Xylem Inc ... F ... 716 862-4123
Seneca Falls (G-15396)
Xylem Inc ... C ... 315 258-4949
Auburn (G-527)
Xylem Inc ... D ... 315 239-2499
Seneca Falls (G-15397)
Xylem Inc ... B ... 914 323-5700
Rye Brook (G-15102)

3562 Ball & Roller Bearings

A Hyatt Ball Co Ltd ... G ... 518 747-0272
Fort Edward (G-5347)
American Refuse Supply Inc ... G ... 718 893-8157
Bronx (G-1273)
David Fehlman ... G ... 315 455-8888
Syracuse (G-15942)
◆ Dimanco Inc ... G ... 315 797-0470
Utica (G-16347)
▲ General Bearing Corporation ... C ... 845 358-6000
West Nyack (G-16947)
▲ Kilian Manufacturing Corp ... D ... 315 432-0700
Syracuse (G-15993)
Lemoyne Machine Products Corp ... G ... 315 454-0708
Syracuse (G-15996)
▲ Mageba USA LLC ... E ... 212 317-1991
New York (G-11126)
▲ Nes Bearing Company Inc ... E ... 716 372-6532
Olean (G-13173)
Raydon Precision Bearing Co ... G ... 516 887-2582
Lynbrook (G-7984)
S/N Precision Enterprises Inc ... E ... 518 283-8002
Troy (G-16276)
▼ Sandle Custom Bearing Corp ... G ... 585 593-7000
Wellsville (G-16783)
▲ Schatz Bearing Corporation ... D ... 845 452-6000
Poughkeepsie (G-13948)
SKF USA Inc ... D ... 716 661-2869
Falconer (G-4919)
SKF USA Inc ... D ... 716 661-2600
Jamestown (G-7060)
SKF USA Inc ... D ... 716 661-2600
Falconer (G-4920)
Workshop Art Fabrication ... F ... 845 331-0385
Kingston (G-7252)

3563 Air & Gas Compressors

▲ Adams Sfc Inc ... E ... 716 877-2608
Tonawanda (G-16157)
▲ Air Techniques Inc ... B ... 516 433-7676
Melville (G-8324)
◆ Atlas Copco Comptec LLC ... B ... 518 765-3344
Voorheesville (G-16538)
Auburn Vacuum Forming Co Inc ... F ... 315 253-2440
Auburn (G-481)
Auto Body Services LLC ... F ... 631 431-4640
Lindenhurst (G-7477)
Bedford Precision Parts Corp ... E ... 914 241-2211
Bedford Hills (G-796)
Buffalo Compressed Air Inc ... G ... 716 783-8673
Cheektowaga (G-3591)
◆ Chapin International Inc ... C ... 585 343-3140
Batavia (G-628)
◆ Chapin Manufacturing Inc ... C ... 585 343-3140
Batavia (G-629)
Comairco Equipment Inc ... G ... 716 656-0211
Cheektowaga (G-3592)
▲ Cooper Turbocompressor Inc ... B ... 716 896-6600
Buffalo (G-2910)
▲ Crosman Corporation ... E ... 585 657-6161
Bloomfield (G-980)
Crosman Corporation ... E ... 585 398-3920
Farmington (G-5157)
▲ Cyclone Air Power Inc ... G ... 718 447-3038
Staten Island (G-15684)
Dresser-Rand Group Inc ... D ... 716 375-3000
Olean (G-13164)
▲ Eastern Air Products LLC ... F ... 716 391-1866
Lancaster (G-7337)
▲ Edwards Vacuum LLC ... D ... 800 848-9800
Sanborn (G-15145)
◆ Fountainhead Group Inc ... C ... 315 736-0037
New York Mills (G-12742)
Fountainhead Group Inc ... C ... 708 598-7100
New York Mills (G-12743)
Gas Tchnlogy Enrgy Cncepts LLC ... G ... 716 831-9695
Buffalo (G-2980)
GM Components Holdings LLC ... B ... 716 439-2463
Lockport (G-7619)
GM Components Holdings LLC ... B ... 716 439-2011
Lockport (G-7620)
◆ Graham Corporation ... B ... 585 343-2216
Batavia (G-638)
Idex Corporation ... G ... 585 292-8121
Rochester (G-14463)
Kinequip Inc ... F ... 716 694-5000
Buffalo (G-3049)
Mahle Indstrbeteiligungen GMBH ... D ... 716 319-6700
Amherst (G-248)
▲ Precision Plus Vacuum Parts ... D ... 716 297-2039
Sanborn (G-15152)
Screw Compressor Tech Inc ... F ... 716 827-6600
Buffalo (G-3208)
Spfm Corp ... G ... 718 788-6800
Brooklyn (G-2613)
Turbopro Inc ... G ... 716 681-8651
Alden (G-187)
Vac Air Service Inc ... F ... 716 665-2206
Jamestown (G-7074)

3564 Blowers & Fans

Acme Engineering Products Inc ... E ... 518 236-5659
Mooers (G-8654)
Aeromed Inc ... G ... 518 843-9144
Utica (G-16330)
Air Crafters Inc ... C ... 631 471-7788
Ronkonkoma (G-14883)
Air Engineering Filters Inc ... G ... 914 238-5945
Chappaqua (G-3578)
Air Export Mechanical ... G ... 917 709-5310
Flushing (G-5230)
Air Wave Air Conditioning Co ... E ... 212 545-1122
Bronx (G-1266)
▲ Airgle Corporation ... E ... 866 501-7750
Ronkonkoma (G-14884)
American Filtration Tech Inc ... F ... 585 359-4130
West Henrietta (G-16900)
Ametek Technical & Indus Pdts ... E ... 845 246-3401
Saugerties (G-15208)
Apgn Inc ... E ... 518 324-4150
Plattsburgh (G-13679)
Applied Safety LLC ... G ... 718 608-6292
Long Island City (G-7697)
◆ Austin Air Systems Limited ... D ... 716 856-3700
Buffalo (G-2846)
◆ Automotive Filters Mfg Inc ... F ... 631 435-1010
Bohemia (G-1016)
Beecher Emssn Sltn Tchnlgs LLC ... F ... 607 796-0149
Horseheads (G-6596)
Beltran Associates Inc ... E ... 718 252-2996
Brooklyn (G-1677)
▲ Beltran Technologies Inc ... E ... 718 338-3311
Brooklyn (G-1678)
Buffalo Bioblower Tech LLC ... G ... 716 625-8618
Lockport (G-7601)
▲ Buffalo Filter LLC ... D ... 716 835-7000
Lancaster (G-7331)
Camfil USA Inc ... G ... 518 456-6085
Syracuse (G-15903)
▲ Canarm Ltd ... G ... 800 267-4427
Ogdensburg (G-13134)
Clean Gas Systems Inc ... E ... 631 467-1600
Hauppauge (G-6066)
Daikin Applied Americas Inc ... D ... 315 253-2771
Auburn (G-490)
Delphi Automotive Systems LLC ... A ... 585 359-6000
West Henrietta (G-16909)
Ducon Technologies Inc ... E ... 631 420-4900
Farmingdale (G-4988)
◆ Ducon Technologies Inc ... F ... 631 694-1700
New York (G-9988)
Dundas-Jafine Inc ... E ... 716 681-9690
Alden (G-180)
Filta Clean Co Inc ... E ... 718 495-3800
Brooklyn (G-1974)
Filtros Ltd ... E ... 585 586-8770
East Rochester (G-4478)

S
I
C

Employee Codes: A=Over 500 employees, B=251-500
C=101-250, D=51-100, E=20-50, F=10-19, G=5-9
2018 Harris
New York Manufacturers Directory
827

35 INDUSTRIAL AND COMMERCIAL MACHINERY AND COMPUTER EQUIPMENT

SIC SECTION

▲ Healthway Home Products Inc ....E 315 298-2904
  Pulaski *(G-13968)*
Healthway Products Company ....E 315 207-1410
  Oswego *(G-13357)*
◆ Hilliard Corporation ....B 607 733-7121
  Elmira *(G-4703)*
Hilliard Corporation ....F 607 733-7121
  Elmira *(G-4704)*
◆ Howden North America Inc ....D 803 741-2700
  Depew *(G-4283)*
Howden North America Inc ....D 716 817-6900
  Depew *(G-4284)*
Isolation Systems Inc ....F 716 694-6390
  North Tonawanda *(G-12997)*
JT Systems Inc ....F 315 622-1980
  Liverpool *(G-7552)*
▲ Low-Cost Mfg Co Inc ....E 516 627-3282
  Carle Place *(G-3419)*
Moffitt Fan Corporation ....G 585 768-7010
  Le Roy *(G-7439)*
Nexstar Holding Corp ....E 716 929-9000
  Amherst *(G-251)*
▼ North American Filter Corp ....D 800 265-8943
  Newark *(G-12760)*
◆ Northland Filter Intl LLC ....E 315 207-1410
  Oswego *(G-13361)*
Oestreich Metal Works Inc ....G 315 463-4268
  Syracuse *(G-16022)*
◆ Oneida Air Systems Inc ....E 315 476-5151
  Syracuse *(G-16025)*
Parker-Hannifin Corporation ....D 248 628-6017
  Lancaster *(G-7355)*
Phytofilter Technologies Inc ....E 518 507-6399
  Saratoga Springs *(G-15196)*
Pliotron Company America LLC ....G 716 298-4457
  Niagara Falls *(G-12878)*
▲ R P Fedder Corp ....E 585 288-1600
  Rochester *(G-14643)*
Rapid Fan & Blower Inc ....F 718 786-2060
  Long Island City *(G-7887)*
Roome Technologies Inc ....G 585 229-4437
  Honeoye *(G-6552)*
▲ Rotron Incorporated ....B 845 679-2401
  Woodstock *(G-17381)*
Rotron Incorporated ....E 845 679-2401
  Woodstock *(G-17382)*
Sbb Inc ....G 315 422-2376
  East Syracuse *(G-4576)*
◆ Standard Motor Products Inc ....B 718 392-0200
  Long Island City *(G-7912)*
Sullivan Bazinet Bongio Inc ....E 315 437-6500
  Syracuse *(G-16070)*
Veteran Air LLC ....E 315 720-1101
  Syracuse *(G-16092)*

3565 Packaging Machinery

A & G Heat Sealing ....G 631 724-7764
  Smithtown *(G-15503)*
All Packaging McHy & Sups Corp ....F 631 588-7310
  Ronkonkoma *(G-14888)*
Automecha International Ltd ....E 607 843-2235
  Oxford *(G-13388)*
Brooks Bottling Co LLC ....F 607 432-1782
  Oneonta *(G-13197)*
Desu Machinery Corporation ....D 716 681-5798
  Depew *(G-4279)*
◆ Dover Global Holdings Inc ....F 212 922-1640
  New York *(G-9964)*
Filling Equipment Co Inc ....F 718 445-2111
  College Point *(G-3808)*
Fourteen Arnold Ave Corp ....F 315 272-1700
  Utica *(G-16356)*
Haines Equipment Inc ....E 607 566-8531
  Avoca *(G-534)*
Hypres Inc ....E 914 592-1190
  Elmsford *(G-4764)*
K C Technical Services Inc ....G 315 589-7170
  Bohemia *(G-1082)*
▲ Kabar Manufacturing Corp ....E 631 694-6857
  Farmingdale *(G-5029)*
◆ Kaps-All Packaging Systems ....D 631 574-8778
  Riverhead *(G-14157)*
Millwood Inc ....F 518 233-1475
  Waterford *(G-16635)*
▲ Modern Packaging Inc ....D 631 595-2437
  Deer Park *(G-4199)*
National Equipment Corporation ....E 718 585-0200
  Bronx *(G-1408)*
Niagara Scientific Inc ....D 315 437-0821
  East Syracuse *(G-4566)*

▲ Orics Industries Inc ....E 718 461-8613
  Farmingdale *(G-5080)*
Overhead Door Corporation ....D 518 828-7652
  Hudson *(G-6659)*
Pacemaker Packaging Corp ....F 718 458-1188
  Woodside *(G-17361)*
◆ Packaging Dynamics Ltd ....E 631 563-4499
  Bohemia *(G-1110)*
Reynolds Packaging McHy Inc ....E 716 358-6451
  Falconer *(G-4918)*
Rfb Associates Inc ....F 518 271-0551
  Fort Edward *(G-5354)*
Rota Pack Inc ....F 631 274-1037
  Farmingdale *(G-5113)*
Save O Seal Corporation Inc ....G 914 592-3031
  Elmsford *(G-4785)*
Sharon Manufacturing Co Inc ....G 631 242-8870
  Deer Park *(G-4234)*
Softpack International Inc ....G 631 544-7014
  Kings Park *(G-7205)*
▲ Turbofil Packaging Mchs LLC ....F 914 239-3878
  Mount Vernon *(G-8789)*
▲ Universal Packg Systems Inc ....A 631 543-2277
  Hauppauge *(G-6245)*
Utleys Incorporated ....E 718 956-1661
  Woodside *(G-17375)*
▲ Vetroelite Inc ....G 925 724-7900
  New York *(G-12555)*
Volckening Inc ....F 718 748-0294
  Brooklyn *(G-2754)*

3566 Speed Changers, Drives & Gears

American Torque Inc ....F 718 526-2433
  Jamaica *(G-6929)*
▲ Biltron Automotive Products ....E 631 928-8613
  Port Jeff STA *(G-13786)*
▲ Buffalo Gear Inc ....E 716 731-2100
  Sanborn *(G-15143)*
Buffalo Power Elec Ctr De ....E 716 651-1600
  Depew *(G-4275)*
Designatronics Incorporated ....B 516 328-3300
  Hicksville *(G-6367)*
◆ Gleason Works ....A 585 473-1000
  Rochester *(G-14429)*
Harmonic Drive LLC ....G 631 231-6630
  Hauppauge *(G-6112)*
▲ Interparts International Inc ....E 516 576-2000
  Plainview *(G-13639)*
▲ John G Rubino Inc ....E 315 253-7396
  Auburn *(G-502)*
▲ Jrlon Inc ....D 315 597-4067
  Palmyra *(G-13434)*
Khk Usa Inc ....G 516 248-3850
  Mineola *(G-8552)*
Magna Products Corp ....E 585 647-2280
  Rochester *(G-14510)*
McGuigan Inc ....E 631 750-6222
  Bohemia *(G-1098)*
Niagara Gear Corporation ....E 716 874-3131
  Buffalo *(G-3110)*
Nidec Indus Automtn USA LLC ....E 716 774-1193
  Grand Island *(G-5778)*
▲ Nuttall Gear L L C ....E 716 298-4100
  Niagara Falls *(G-12872)*
Oliver Gear Inc ....E 716 885-1080
  Buffalo *(G-3122)*
◆ Ondrivesus Corp ....E 516 771-6777
  Freeport *(G-5427)*
Peerless-Winsmith Inc ....C 716 592-9311
  Springville *(G-15634)*
Perfection Gear Inc ....C 716 592-9310
  Springville *(G-15635)*
Precipart Corporation ....E 631 694-3100
  Farmingdale *(G-5095)*
Precision Mechanisms Corp ....E 516 333-5955
  Westbury *(G-17049)*
▲ Renold Inc ....D 716 326-3121
  Westfield *(G-17080)*
Rochester Gear Inc ....E 585 254-5442
  Rochester *(G-14664)*
W J Albro Machine Works Inc ....G 631 345-0657
  Yaphank *(G-17424)*

3567 Indl Process Furnaces & Ovens

▲ Ambrell Corporation ....F 585 889-0236
  Scottsville *(G-15356)*
▼ Buflovak LLC ....E 716 895-2100
  Buffalo *(G-2883)*
▼ Cooks Intl Ltd Lblty Co ....G 212 741-4407
  New York *(G-9777)*

Cosmos Electronic Machine Corp ....E 631 249-2535
  Farmingdale *(G-4974)*
Cvd Equipment Corporation ....F 631 582-4365
  Central Islip *(G-3519)*
Easco Boiler Corp ....E 718 378-3000
  Bronx *(G-1326)*
▲ Embassy Industries Inc ....C 631 435-0209
  Hauppauge *(G-6095)*
▼ Fulton Volcanic Inc ....G 315 298-5121
  Pulaski *(G-13967)*
◆ Harper International Corp ....D 716 276-9900
  Buffalo *(G-3008)*
▲ Hpi Co Inc ....G 718 851-2753
  Brooklyn *(G-2085)*
Igniter Systems Inc ....E 716 542-5511
  Akron *(G-21)*
J H Buhrmaster Company Inc ....E 518 843-1700
  Amsterdam *(G-351)*
Linde LLC ....E 716 773-7552
  Grand Island *(G-5776)*
Parker-Hannifin Corporation ....D 716 685-4040
  Lancaster *(G-7356)*
Radiant Pro Ltd ....E 516 763-5678
  Oceanside *(G-13114)*
Thermal Process Cnstr Co ....E 631 293-6400
  Farmingdale *(G-5139)*
Ultraflex Power Technologies ....G 631 467-6814
  Ronkonkoma *(G-15019)*
Vent-A-Kiln Corporation ....E 716 876-2023
  Buffalo *(G-3266)*
Vincent Genovese ....G 631 281-8170
  Mastic Beach *(G-8237)*

3568 Mechanical Power Transmission Eqpt, NEC

Advanced Thermal Systems Inc ....E 716 681-1800
  Lancaster *(G-7322)*
Babbitt Bearings Incorporated ....D 315 479-6603
  Syracuse *(G-15885)*
▲ Borgwarner Morse TEC LLC ....C 607 257-6700
  Ithaca *(G-6866)*
▲ BW Elliott Mfg Co LLC ....E 607 772-0404
  Binghamton *(G-896)*
C-Flex Bearing Co Inc ....F 315 895-7454
  Frankfort *(G-5359)*
Champlain Hudson Power Ex Inc ....E 518 465-0710
  Albany *(G-60)*
▲ Cierra Industries Inc ....F 315 252-6630
  Auburn *(G-487)*
◆ Cobham Management Services Inc ..A 716 662-0006
  Orchard Park *(G-13287)*
Designatronics Incorporated ....F 516 328-3300
  Hicksville *(G-6369)*
Designatronics Incorporated ....B 516 328-3300
  Hicksville *(G-6367)*
Eaw Electronic Systems Inc ....G 845 471-5290
  Poughkeepsie *(G-13916)*
▲ Fait Usa Inc ....E 215 674-5310
  New York *(G-10184)*
◆ Howden North America Inc ....D 803 741-2700
  Depew *(G-4283)*
Hudson Power Transmission Co ....G 718 622-3869
  Brooklyn *(G-2086)*
Huron TI Cutter Grinding Inc ....E 631 420-7000
  Farmingdale *(G-5015)*
Kaddis Manufacturing Corp ....G 585 624-3070
  Honeoye Falls *(G-6561)*
Kinemotive Corporation ....E 631 249-6440
  Farmingdale *(G-5035)*
Liston Manufacturing Inc ....E 716 695-2111
  North Tonawanda *(G-12999)*
Ls Power Equity Partners LP ....G 212 615-3456
  New York *(G-11085)*
Machine Components Corp ....E 516 694-7222
  Plainview *(G-13644)*
◆ Magtrol Inc ....E 716 668-5555
  Buffalo *(G-3075)*
Metallized Carbon Corporation ....C 914 941-3738
  Ossining *(G-13347)*
On Line Power Technologies ....G 914 968-4440
  Yonkers *(G-17489)*
▲ Package One Inc ....E 518 344-5425
  Schenectady *(G-15310)*
▲ Renold Holdings Inc ....G 716 326-3121
  Westfield *(G-17079)*
▲ Renold Inc ....D 716 326-3121
  Westfield *(G-17080)*
▲ Sepac Inc ....E 607 732-2030
  Elmira *(G-4714)*

▼ **Watson Bowman Acme Corp** ....D 716 691-8162
Amherst *(G-271)*

York Industries Inc ....E 516 746-3736
Garden City Park *(G-5559)*

3569 Indl Machinery & Eqpt, NEC

▲ **Adams Sfc Inc** ....E 716 877-2608
Tonawanda *(G-16157)*

▲ **Advanced Tchncal Solutions Inc** ....F 914 214-8230
Yorktown Heights *(G-17522)*

Airsep Corporation ....D 716 691-0202
Amherst *(G-222)*

▲ **Alliance Automation Systems** ....C 585 426-2700
Rochester *(G-14203)*

Allied Inspection Services LLC ....F 716 489-3199
Falconer *(G-4897)*

▲ **American Felt & Filter Co Inc** ....D 845 561-3560
New Windsor *(G-8977)*

American Filtration Tech Inc ....F 585 359-4130
West Henrietta *(G-16900)*

American Material Processing ....F 315 318-0017
Phoenix *(G-13567)*

▲ **Audubon Machinery Corporation** ....D 716 564-5165
North Tonawanda *(G-12975)*

Automated Cells & Eqp Inc ....E 607 936-1341
Painted Post *(G-13415)*

Better Power Inc ....G 585 475-1321
Rochester *(G-14247)*

Bowen Products Corporation ....G 315 498-4481
Nedrow *(G-8818)*

▲ **Bullex Inc** ....F 518 689-2023
Albany *(G-55)*

Burnett Process Inc ....E 585 277-1623
Rochester *(G-14270)*

Chart Industries Inc ....E 716 691-0202
Amherst *(G-234)*

Cleaning Tech Group LLC ....E 716 665-2340
Jamestown *(G-7016)*

Crandall Filling Machinery Inc ....G 716 897-3486
Buffalo *(G-2912)*

◆ **Cross Filtration Ltd Lblty Co** ....G 315 412-1539
Moravia *(G-8657)*

▲ **Distech Systems Inc** ....G 585 254-7020
Rochester *(G-14332)*

Dragow Inc ....E 585 786-3603
Gainesville *(G-5497)*

Dynamasters Inc ....G 585 458-9970
Rochester *(G-14340)*

Eastern Precision Mfg ....G 845 358-1951
Nyack *(G-13066)*

▲ **Filter Tech Inc** ....D 315 682-8815
Manlius *(G-8104)*

▲ **Finesse Creations Inc** ....F 718 692-2100
Brooklyn *(G-1977)*

Firematic Supply Co Inc ....E 631 924-3181
East Yaphank *(G-4593)*

First Due Fire Equipment Inc ....F 845 222-1329
Garnerville *(G-5568)*

Foseco Inc ....F 914 345-4760
Tarrytown *(G-16115)*

◆ **Fountainhead Group Inc** ....C 315 736-0037
New York Mills *(G-12742)*

Gem Fabrication of NC ....G 704 278-6713
Garden City *(G-5521)*

Graver Technologies LLC ....E 585 624-1330
Honeoye Falls *(G-6556)*

Griffin Automation Inc ....E 716 674-2300
West Seneca *(G-16976)*

◆ **Guyson Corporation of USa** ....E 518 587-7894
Saratoga Springs *(G-15186)*

◆ **Hannay Reels Inc** ....C 518 797-3791
Westerlo *(G-17071)*

◆ **Hilliard Corporation** ....B 607 733-7121
Elmira *(G-4703)*

Hilliard Corporation ....F 607 733-7121
Elmira *(G-4704)*

Honeybee Robotics Ltd ....E 212 966-0661
Brooklyn *(G-2083)*

▲ **Hubco Inc** ....G 716 683-5940
Alden *(G-182)*

▲ **Innovative Pdts of Amer Inc** ....E 845 679-4500
Woodstock *(G-17379)*

Island Automated Gate Co LLC ....G 631 425-0196
Huntington Station *(G-6749)*

J H Robotics Inc ....E 607 729-3758
Johnson City *(G-7127)*

Javlyn Process Systems LLC ....E 585 424-5580
Rochester *(G-14482)*

Kyntec Corporation ....G 716 810-6956
Buffalo *(G-3056)*

Lifc Corp ....G 516 426-5737
Port Washington *(G-13859)*

Long Island Pipe Supply Inc ....E 516 222-8008
Garden City *(G-5528)*

▲ **Lubow Machine Corp** ....F 631 226-1700
Copiague *(G-3936)*

Lydall Performance Mtls Inc ....F 518 273-6320
Green Island *(G-5878)*

Machine Tool Repair & Sales ....G 631 580-2550
Holbrook *(G-6489)*

Markpericom ....G 516 208-6824
Oceanside *(G-13109)*

McHone Industries Inc ....D 716 945-3380
Salamanca *(G-15128)*

Mep Alaska LLC ....G 646 535-9005
Brooklyn *(G-2302)*

New Vision Industries Inc ....F 607 687-7700
Endicott *(G-4827)*

▼ **North American Filter Corp** ....D 800 265-8943
Newark *(G-12760)*

◆ **Pall Corporation** ....A 516 484-5400
Port Washington *(G-13870)*

Pall Corporation ....A 607 753-6041
Cortland *(G-4059)*

Parker-Hannifin Corporation ....D 248 628-6017
Lancaster *(G-7355)*

Peerless Mfg Co ....E 716 539-7400
Orchard Park *(G-13314)*

Peregrine Industries Inc ....G 631 838-2870
New York *(G-11632)*

Pyrotek Incorporated ....E 716 731-3221
Sanborn *(G-15153)*

Quality Manufacturing Sys LLC ....G 716 763-0988
Lakewood *(G-7316)*

◆ **Reliable Autmtc Sprnklr Co Inc** ....B 800 431-1588
Elmsford *(G-4784)*

Rfb Associates Inc ....F 518 271-0551
Fort Edward *(G-5354)*

▲ **SC Supply Chain Management LLC** ....G 212 344-3322
New York *(G-12001)*

Sentry Automatic Sprinkler ....F 631 723-3095
Riverhead *(G-14169)*

Service Filtration Corp ....E 716 877-2608
Tonawanda *(G-16221)*

Sidco Filter Corporation ....E 585 289-3100
Manchester *(G-8086)*

Sinclair International Company ....E 518 798-2361
Queensbury *(G-14025)*

▲ **Sonicor Inc** ....F 631 920-6555
West Babylon *(G-16861)*

▲ **Stavo Industries Inc** ....F 845 331-4552
Kingston *(G-7241)*

Stavo Industries Inc ....E 845 331-5389
Kingston *(G-7242)*

▲ **Sussman-Automatic Corporation** ....D 347 609-7652
Long Island City *(G-7925)*

▲ **Taylor Devices Inc** ....C 716 694-0800
North Tonawanda *(G-13019)*

▲ **Trident Precision Mfg Inc** ....D 585 265-2010
Webster *(G-16764)*

Tyco Simplexgrinnell ....E 315 437-9664
East Syracuse *(G-4586)*

Tyco Simplexgrinnell ....E 716 483-0079
Jamestown *(G-7072)*

Tyco Simplexgrinnell ....D 315 337-6333
Taberg *(G-16100)*

Uipath ....C 844 432-0455
New York *(G-12464)*

Universal Metal Fabricators ....F 845 331-8248
Kingston *(G-7248)*

Veeco Process Equipment Inc ....C 516 677-0200
Plainview *(G-13672)*

William R Shoemaker Inc ....G 716 649-0511
Hamburg *(G-5968)*

3571 Electronic Computers

▲ **Alliance Magnetic LLC** ....G 914 944-1690
Ossining *(G-13344)*

Apple Bank For Savings ....G 718 486-7294
Brooklyn *(G-1618)*

Apple Commuter Inc ....G 917 299-0066
New Hyde Park *(G-8861)*

Apple Healing & Relaxation ....G 718 278-1089
Long Island City *(G-7696)*

Apple Med Urgent Care PC ....G 914 523-5965
Mount Vernon *(G-8707)*

▲ **Argon Corp** ....F 516 487-5314
Great Neck *(G-5807)*

Arnouse Digital Devices Corp ....D 516 673-4444
New Hyde Park *(G-8862)*

B-Reel Films Inc ....E 917 388-3836
New York *(G-9348)*

▲ **Binghamton Simulator Co Inc** ....E 607 321-2980
Binghamton *(G-891)*

▲ **Columbia Telecom Group** ....G 631 501-5000
New York *(G-9737)*

Computer Conversions Corp ....E 631 261-3300
East Northport *(G-4454)*

Critical Link LLC ....E 315 425-4045
Syracuse *(G-15932)*

Data-Pac Mailing Systems Corp ....F 585 671-0210
Webster *(G-16744)*

Datacom Systems Inc ....E 315 463-9541
East Syracuse *(G-4537)*

Dees Audio & Vision ....G 585 719-9256
Rochester *(G-14326)*

▲ **Digicom International Inc** ....F 631 249-8999
Farmingdale *(G-4986)*

▲ **Dynamic Decisions Inc** ....F 908 755-5000
Fresh Meadows *(G-5453)*

▲ **E-Systems Group LLC** ....E 607 775-1100
Conklin *(G-3893)*

Ebc Technologies LLC ....D 631 729-8182
Hauppauge *(G-6091)*

Electronic Systems Inc ....G 631 589-4389
Holbrook *(G-6473)*

▲ **Elo Touch Solutions Inc** ....E 585 427-2802
Rochester *(G-14364)*

Envent Systems Inc ....G 646 294-6980
Pelham *(G-13516)*

Facsimile Cmmncations Inds Inc ....D 212 741-6400
New York *(G-10178)*

▲ **Flash Ventures Inc** ....F 212 255-7070
New York *(G-10230)*

G S Communications USA Inc ....E 718 389-7371
Brooklyn *(G-2011)*

Go Go Apple Inc ....G 646 264-8909
Elmhurst *(G-4674)*

Group Enterainment LLC ....G 212 868-5233
New York *(G-10414)*

H&L Computers Inc ....E 516 873-8088
Flushing *(G-5255)*

▲ **Hand Held Products Inc** ....B 315 554-6000
Skaneateles Falls *(G-15490)*

Hi-Tech Advanced Solutions Inc ....F 718 926-3488
Forest Hills *(G-5330)*

Human Electronics Inc ....G 315 724-9850
Utica *(G-16363)*

IBM World Trade Corporation ....G 914 765-1900
Armonk *(G-411)*

International Bus Mchs Corp ....A 607 754-9558
Endicott *(G-4819)*

Irpenscom ....G 585 507-7997
Penfield *(G-13523)*

J & N Computer Services Inc ....F 585 388-8780
Fairport *(G-4864)*

▲ **Kemp Technologies Inc** ....E 631 345-5292
New York *(G-10871)*

Lockheed Martin Corporation ....C 516 228-2000
Uniondale *(G-16320)*

M&C Associates LLC ....E 631 467-8760
Hauppauge *(G-6148)*

Medsim-Eagle Simulation Inc ....F 607 658-9354
Endicott *(G-4824)*

N & G of America Inc ....F 516 428-3414
Plainview *(G-13650)*

N & L Instruments Inc ....F 631 471-4000
Ronkonkoma *(G-14973)*

NCR Corporation ....C 516 876-7200
Jericho *(G-7110)*

Northpoint Digital LLC ....G 212 819-1700
New York *(G-11477)*

One Technologies LLC ....G 718 509-0704
Brooklyn *(G-2405)*

Oracle America Inc ....D 518 427-9353
Albany *(G-112)*

Oracle America Inc ....D 585 317-4648
Fairport *(G-4873)*

Photon Vision Systems Inc ....F 607 749-2689
Homer *(G-6549)*

Policy ADM Solutions Inc ....E 914 332-4320
Tarrytown *(G-16125)*

Qualtronic Devices Inc ....F 631 360-0859
Smithtown *(G-15520)*

Revivn Inc ....F 347 762-8193
Brooklyn *(G-2512)*

Revonate Manufacturing LLC ....E 315 433-1160
Syracuse *(G-16045)*

Stargate Computer Corp ....G 516 474-4799
Port Jeff STA *(G-13794)*

S
I
C

Employee Codes: A=Over 500 employees, B=251-500
C=101-250, D=51-100, E=20-50, F=10-19, G=5-9
2018 Harris
New York Manufacturers Directory
829

▲ Telxon Corporation ....E.... 631 738-2400
Holtsville (G-6539)
Todd Enterprises Inc ....D.... 516 773-8087
Great Neck (G-5863)
▲ Toshiba Amer Info Systems Inc ....B.... 949 583-3000
New York (G-12397)
◆ Toshiba America Inc ....E.... 212 596-0600
New York (G-12398)
Transland Sourcing LLC ....G.... 718 596-5704
Brooklyn (G-2694)
Wantagh Computer Center ....F.... 516 826-2189
Wantagh (G-16584)
Wilcro Inc ....G.... 716 632-4204
Buffalo (G-3280)
Yellow E House Inc ....G.... 718 888-2000
Flushing (G-5315)

3572 Computer Storage Devices

Datalink Computer Products ....F.... 914 666-2358
Mount Kisco (G-8668)
Emcs LLC ....G.... 716 523-2002
Hamburg (G-5947)
Formats Unlimited Inc ....F.... 631 249-9200
Deer Park (G-4166)
Garland Technology LLC ....F.... 716 242-8500
Buffalo (G-2979)
Gim Electronics Corp ....F.... 516 942-3382
Hicksville (G-6377)
Globalfoundries US Inc ....C.... 518 305-9013
Malta (G-8051)
Matrox Graphics Inc ....G.... 518 561-4417
Plattsburgh (G-13703)
Quantum Asset Recovery ....G.... 716 393-2712
Buffalo (G-3174)
Quantum Knowledge LLC ....G.... 631 727-6111
Riverhead (G-14166)
Quantum Logic Corp ....G.... 516 746-1380
New Hyde Park (G-8904)
Quantum Mechanics Ny LLC ....G.... 917 519-7077
Huntington (G-6711)
Sale 121 Corp ....D.... 240 855-8988
New York (G-11972)
◆ Sony Corporation of America ....C.... 212 833-8000
New York (G-12157)
◆ Technologies Application LLC ....F.... 607 275-0345
Cortland (G-4070)
Todd Enterprises Inc ....D.... 516 773-8087
Great Neck (G-5863)
▲ Toshiba Amer Info Systems Inc ....B.... 949 583-3000
New York (G-12397)
William S Hein & Co Inc ....D.... 716 882-2600
Getzville (G-5619)

3575 Computer Terminals

901 D LLC ....E.... 845 369-1111
Airmont (G-10)
AG Neovo Professional Inc ....F.... 212 647-9080
New York (G-9106)
Cine Design Group LLC ....G.... 646 747-0734
New York (G-9670)
▲ Clayton Dubilier & Rice Fun ....E.... 212 407-5200
New York (G-9695)
Igt Global Solutions Corp ....D.... 518 382-2900
Schenectady (G-15296)
Integra Microsystem 1988 Inc ....G.... 718 609-6099
Brooklyn (G-2107)
International Bus Mchs Corp ....A.... 845 433-1234
Poughkeepsie (G-13927)
Nu - Communitek LLC ....F.... 516 433-3553
Hicksville (G-6402)
Orbit International Corp ....C.... 631 435-8300
Hauppauge (G-6180)
PC Solutions & Consulting ....G.... 607 735-0466
Elmira (G-4711)
Shadowtv Inc ....G.... 212 445-2540
New York (G-12058)
Symbio Technologies LLC ....G.... 914 576-1205
White Plains (G-17200)
▲ Touchstone Technology Inc ....F.... 585 458-2690
Rochester (G-14756)
Ultra-Scan Corporation ....F.... 716 832-6269
Amherst (G-270)
Wey Inc ....G.... 212 532-3299
New York (G-12648)

3577 Computer Peripheral Eqpt, NEC

A I T Computers Inc ....G.... 518 266-9010
Troy (G-16245)
Aalborg Instrs & Contrls Inc ....D.... 845 398-3160
Orangeburg (G-13238)
Advanced Barcode Tech Inc ....F.... 516 570-8100
Great Neck (G-5799)
Aero-Vision Technologies Inc ....G.... 631 643-8349
Melville (G-8322)
Aeroflex Plainview Inc ....C.... 631 231-9100
Hauppauge (G-6030)
▲ Andrea Electronics Corporation ....G.... 631 719-1800
Bohemia (G-1012)
Annese & Associates Inc ....G.... 716 972-0076
Buffalo (G-2831)
▲ Anorad Corporation ....C.... 631 380-2100
East Setauket (G-4495)
Aruba Networks Inc ....G.... 732 343-1305
New York (G-9276)
Atlaz International Ltd ....F.... 516 239-1854
Lawrence (G-7416)
▲ Aventura Technologies Inc ....E.... 631 300-4000
Commack (G-3848)
B V M Associates ....G.... 631 254-6220
Shirley (G-15438)
▲ Binghamton Simulator Co Inc ....E.... 607 321-2980
Binghamton (G-891)
Blue Skies ....G.... 631 392-1140
Deer Park (G-4134)
Broadnet Technologies Inc ....F.... 315 443-3694
Syracuse (G-15895)
Cal Blen Electronic Industries ....F.... 631 242-6243
Huntington (G-6691)
Capture Globa Integ Solut Inc ....G.... 718 352-0579
Bayside Hills (G-773)
Chem-Puter Friendly Inc ....E.... 631 331-2259
Mount Sinai (G-8696)
Chemung Cnty Chpter Nysarc Inc ....C.... 607 734-6151
Elmira (G-4688)
Cisco Systems Inc ....C.... 212 714-4000
New York (G-9675)
▲ Clayton Dubilier & Rice Fun ....E.... 212 407-5200
New York (G-9695)
CNy Business Solutions ....G.... 315 733-5031
Utica (G-16335)
Control Logic Corporation ....G.... 607 965-6423
West Burlington (G-16874)
CPW Direct Mail Group LLC ....E.... 631 588-6565
Farmingdale (G-4975)
▲ Data Device Corporation ....B.... 631 567-5600
Bohemia (G-1045)
Datatran Labs Inc ....G.... 845 856-4313
Port Jervis (G-13805)
▲ Dia-Nielsen USA Incorporated ....G.... 856 642-9700
Buffalo (G-2930)
▲ Digiorange Inc ....G.... 718 787-1500
Brooklyn (G-1862)
▲ Dynamic Decisions Inc ....F.... 908 755-5000
Fresh Meadows (G-5453)
◆ Eastman Kodak Company ....B.... 585 724-4000
Rochester (G-14348)
Ems Development Corporation ....D.... 631 345-6200
Yaphank (G-17407)
Future Star Digatech ....F.... 718 666-0350
Brooklyn (G-2009)
◆ Gasoft Equipment Inc ....F.... 845 863-1010
Newburgh (G-12777)
Glowa Manufacturing Inc ....E.... 607 770-0811
Binghamton (G-913)
Gunther Partners LLC ....G.... 212 521-2930
New York (G-10428)
▲ Hand Held Products Inc ....B.... 315 554-6000
Skaneateles Falls (G-15490)
Hand Held Products Inc ....G.... 315 554-6000
Skaneateles Falls (G-15491)
▲ Hauppauge Computer Works Inc ....E.... 631 434-1600
Hauppauge (G-6113)
▲ Hauppauge Digital Inc ....E.... 631 434-1600
Hauppauge (G-6114)
◆ Hergo Ergonomic Support ....E.... 718 894-0639
Maspeth (G-8175)
Hf Technologies LLC ....E.... 585 254-5030
Hamlin (G-5973)
▲ Hitachi Metals America Ltd ....E.... 914 694-9200
Purchase (G-13975)
HP Inc ....D.... 212 835-1640
New York (G-10566)
▲ Humanscale Corporation ....B.... 212 725-4749
New York (G-10578)
IBM World Trade Corporation ....G.... 914 765-1900
Armonk (G-411)
Innovative Systems of New York ....G.... 516 541-7410
Massapequa Park (G-8220)
Inpora Technologies LLC ....D.... 646 838-2474
New York (G-10650)
Iweb Design Inc ....F.... 805 243-8305
Bronx (G-1366)
Jadak LLC ....F.... 315 701-0678
North Syracuse (G-12966)
Jadak Technologies Inc ....D.... 315 701-0678
North Syracuse (G-12967)
▲ Kantek Inc ....E.... 516 594-4600
Oceanside (G-13105)
Lockheed Martin ....E.... 315 456-3333
Syracuse (G-16000)
Lsc Peripherals Incorporated ....G.... 631 244-0707
Bohemia (G-1092)
Luminescent Systems Inc ....B.... 716 655-0800
East Aurora (G-4398)
Macrolink Inc ....E.... 631 924-8200
Medford (G-8288)
Maia Systems LLC ....G.... 718 206-0100
Jamaica (G-6963)
Marco Manufacturing Inc ....E.... 845 485-1571
Poughkeepsie (G-13934)
Mdi Holdings LLC ....A.... 212 559-1127
New York (G-11228)
Medsim-Eagle Simulation Inc ....F.... 607 658-9354
Endicott (G-4824)
Mg Imaging ....G.... 212 704-4073
New York (G-11272)
Mirion Technologies Ist Corp ....D.... 607 562-4300
Horseheads (G-6612)
▲ Mp Displays LLC ....G.... 845 268-4113
Valley Cottage (G-16409)
NCR Corporation ....C.... 607 273-5310
Ithaca (G-6901)
▲ Norazza Inc ....G.... 716 706-1160
Buffalo (G-3116)
O Rama Light Inc ....E.... 518 539-9000
South Glens Falls (G-15552)
Orbit International Corp ....C.... 631 435-8300
Hauppauge (G-6180)
P C Rfrs Radiology ....G.... 212 586-5700
Long Island City (G-7862)
◆ Paxar Corporation ....E.... 845 398-3229
Orangeburg (G-13260)
Pda Panache Corp ....G.... 631 776-0523
Bohemia (G-1112)
Peoples Choice M R I ....F.... 716 681-7377
Buffalo (G-3142)
Perceptive Pixel Inc ....E.... 701 367-5845
New York (G-11631)
Performance Technologies Inc ....E.... 585 256-0200
Rochester (G-14596)
Phoenix Venture Fund LLC ....E.... 212 759-1909
New York (G-11672)
▲ QED Technologies Intl Inc ....E.... 585 256-6540
Rochester (G-14633)
▲ Rdi Inc ....F.... 914 773-1000
Mount Kisco (G-8686)
Reliable Elec Mt Vernon Inc ....E.... 914 668-4440
Mount Vernon (G-8772)
Rodale Wireless Inc ....E.... 631 231-0044
Hauppauge (G-6205)
Ruhle Companies Inc ....E.... 914 287-4000
Valhalla (G-16398)
S G I ....G.... 917 386-0385
New York (G-11962)
Scroll Media Inc ....G.... 617 395-8904
New York (G-12027)
Secuprint Inc ....G.... 585 341-3100
Rochester (G-14700)
Sequential Electronics Systems ....E.... 914 592-1345
Elmsford (G-4791)
▲ Sima Technologies LLC ....G.... 412 828-9130
Hauppauge (G-6215)
◆ Sony Corporation of America ....C.... 212 833-8000
New York (G-12157)
▲ Symbol Technologies LLC ....A.... 631 737-6851
Holtsville (G-6536)
Symbol Technologies LLC ....F.... 631 738-2400
Bohemia (G-1136)
Symbol Technologies LLC ....G.... 631 738-3346
Holtsville (G-6537)
Symbol Technologies LLC ....F.... 631 218-3907
Holbrook (G-6504)
Synaptics Incorporated ....F.... 585 899-4300
Rochester (G-14734)
T&K Printing Inc ....F.... 718 439-9454
Brooklyn (G-2661)
▲ Technomag Inc ....G.... 631 246-6142
East Setauket (G-4512)
Todd Enterprises Inc ....D.... 516 773-8087
Great Neck (G-5863)

Torrent Ems LLC ....F 716 312-4099
Lockport (G-7651)
▲ Toshiba Amer Info Systems Inc ....B 949 583-3000
New York (G-12397)
Transact Technologies Inc ....D 607 257-8901
Ithaca (G-6914)
Vader Systems LLC ....F 716 688-1600
Getzville (G-5618)
▲ Vishay Thin Film LLC ....C 716 283-4025
Niagara Falls (G-12906)
Vuzix Corporation ....E 585 359-5900
West Henrietta (G-16928)
Wantagh Computer Center ....F 516 826-2189
Wantagh (G-16584)
▼ Watson Productions LLC ....F 516 334-9766
Hauppauge (G-6255)
Welch Allyn Inc ....A 315 685-4100
Skaneateles Falls (G-15493)
Wilson & Wilson Group ....G 212 729-4736
Forest Hills (G-5337)
X Brand Editions ....G 718 482-7646
Long Island City (G-7956)
Xerox Corporation ....D 516 677-1500
Melville (G-8393)
Xerox Corporation ....E 585 423-3538
Rochester (G-14798)
Xerox Corporation ....C 585 427-4500
Rochester (G-14797)
▲ Z-Axis Inc ....D 315 548-5000
Phelps (G-13563)
Zebra Technologies Entp Corp ....E 800 722-6234
Holtsville (G-6542)

3578 Calculating & Accounting Eqpt

Gary Roth & Associates Ltd ....E 516 333-1000
Westbury (G-17017)
▲ Hand Held Products Inc ....B 315 554-6000
Skaneateles Falls (G-15490)
Hopp Companies Inc ....F 516 358-4170
New Hyde Park (G-8886)
International Mdse Svcs Inc ....G 914 699-4000
Mount Vernon (G-8738)
Jpmorgan Chase Bank Nat Assn ....G 718 944-7964
Bronx (G-1372)
Jpmorgan Chase Bank Nat Assn ....G 718 767-3592
College Point (G-3817)
Jpmorgan Chase Bank Nat Assn ....G 718 668-0346
Staten Island (G-15717)
K&G of Syracuse Inc ....G 315 446-1921
Syracuse (G-15991)
Kenney Manufacturing Displays ....F 631 231-5563
Brentwood (G-1185)
◆ Logic Controls Inc ....E 516 248-0400
Bethpage (G-870)
Merchant Service Pymnt Access ....G 212 561-5516
Uniondale (G-16321)
Mid Enterprise Inc ....G 631 924-3933
Middle Island (G-8440)
▲ Parabit Systems Inc ....E 516 378-4800
Roosevelt (G-15031)
Powa Technologies Inc ....E 347 344-7848
New York (G-11713)
Sharenet Inc ....G 315 477-1100
Syracuse (G-16062)
Stanson Automated LLC ....F 866 505-7826
Yonkers (G-17503)

3579 Office Machines, NEC

Action Technologies Inc ....G 718 278-1000
Long Island City (G-7680)
Automecha International Ltd ....E 607 843-2235
Oxford (G-13388)
Central Time Clock Inc ....F 718 784-4900
Long Island City (G-7725)
Cummins - Allison Corp ....D 718 263-2482
Kew Gardens (G-7188)
Dominion Voting Systems Inc ....F 404 955-9799
Jamestown (G-7023)
▲ Magnetic Technologies Corp ....D 585 385-9010
Rochester (G-14511)
National Time Recording Eqp Co ....F 212 227-3310
New York (G-11375)
Neopost USA Inc ....E 631 435-9100
Hauppauge (G-6172)
Pitney Bowes Inc ....E 212 564-7548
New York (G-11688)
Pitney Bowes Inc ....E 203 356-5000
New York (G-11689)
Pitney Bowes Inc ....C 518 283-0345
Troy (G-16271)
Pitney Bowes Inc ....E 516 822-0900
Jericho (G-7113)
▲ Staplex Company Inc ....E 718 768-3333
Brooklyn (G-2619)
Widmer Time Recorder Company ....F 212 227-0405
New York (G-12658)

3581 Automatic Vending Machines

American Lckr SEC Systems Inc ....E 716 699-2773
Ellicottville (G-4654)
Cubic Trnsp Systems Inc ....F 212 255-1810
New York (G-9821)
Global Payment Tech Inc ....F 516 887-0700
Valley Stream (G-16434)
▲ Global Payment Tech Inc ....E 631 563-2500
Bohemia (G-1070)
Vengo Inc ....G 866 526-7054
Long Island City (G-7941)

3582 Commercial Laundry, Dry Clean & Pressing Mchs

Fowler Route Co Inc ....F 917 653-4640
Yonkers (G-17461)
▲ G A Braun Inc ....D 315 475-3123
North Syracuse (G-12960)
G A Braun Inc ....E 315 475-3123
Syracuse (G-15966)
Lb Laundry Inc ....G 347 399-8030
Flushing (G-5271)
Lynx Product Group LLC ....E 716 751-3100
Wilson (G-17291)
▼ Maxi Companies Inc ....G 315 446-1002
De Witt (G-4108)
Pressure Washing Services Inc ....G 607 286-7458
Milford (G-8509)
Q Omni Inc ....G 914 962-2726
Yorktown Heights (G-17533)
Thermopatch Corporation ....D 315 446-8110
Syracuse (G-16082)

3585 Air Conditioning & Heating Eqpt

A Nuclimate Qulty Systems Inc ....F 315 431-0226
Syracuse (G-15865)
A&S Refrigeration Equipment ....G 718 993-6030
Bronx (G-1255)
AC Air Cooling Co Inc ....F 718 933-1011
Bronx (G-1259)
Advance Energy Tech Inc ....E 518 371-2140
Halfmoon (G-5930)
Alfa Laval Kathabar Inc ....G 716 875-2000
Tonawanda (G-16158)
▲ Alstrom Corporation ....E 718 824-4901
Bronx (G-1271)
American Refrigeration Inc ....G 212 699-4000
New York (G-9178)
▲ Atmost Refrigeration Co Inc ....G 518 828-2180
Hudson (G-6637)
Balticare Inc ....F 646 380-9470
New York (G-9363)
Besicorp Ltd ....F 845 336-7700
Kingston (G-7208)
Bombardier Trnsp Holdings USA ....D 607 776-4791
Bath (G-654)
Carrier Corporation ....E 315 432-6000
Syracuse (G-15906)
Carrier Corporation ....B 315 463-5744
East Syracuse (G-4530)
Carrier Corporation ....A 315 432-6000
Syracuse (G-15908)
Carrier Corporation ....B 315 432-6000
East Syracuse (G-4531)
Carrier Corporation ....B 315 432-3844
East Syracuse (G-4532)
Carrier Corporation ....B 315 432-6000
Syracuse (G-15907)
Chart Inc ....F 518 272-3565
Troy (G-16252)
Chudnow Manufacturing Co Inc ....E 516 593-4222
Oceanside (G-13094)
Cleanroom Systems Inc ....E 315 452-7400
North Syracuse (G-12957)
Colburns AC Rfrgn ....F 716 569-3695
Frewsburg (G-5463)
▲ Cold Point Corporation ....E 315 339-2331
Rome (G-14838)
▲ Columbia Pool Accessories Inc ....G 718 993-0389
Bronx (G-1304)
Daikin Applied Americas Inc ....D 315 253-2771
Auburn (G-490)
Dundas-Jafine Inc ....E 716 681-9690
Alden (G-180)
▲ Duro Dyne Corporation ....C 631 249-9000
Farmingdale (G-4989)
◆ Duro Dyne Machinery Corp ....E 631 249-9000
Bay Shore (G-694)
▲ Duro Dyne National Corp ....C 631 249-9000
Bay Shore (G-695)
Economy Pump & Motor Repair ....G 718 433-2600
Astoria (G-436)
Elima-Draft Incorporated ....G 631 375-2830
Setauket (G-15401)
EMC Fintech ....F 716 488-9071
Falconer (G-4903)
Empire Air Systems LLC ....F 718 377-1549
Brooklyn (G-1924)
▲ Enviromaster International LLC ....D 315 336-3716
Rome (G-14839)
Environmental Temp Systems LLC ....G 516 640-5818
Mineola (G-8541)
Fedders Islandaire Inc ....D 631 471-2900
East Setauket (G-4500)
Foster Refrigerators Entp ....F 518 671-6036
Hudson (G-6644)
Fts Systems Inc ....D 845 687-5300
Stone Ridge (G-15785)
GM Components Holdings LLC ....B 716 439-2463
Lockport (G-7619)
GM Components Holdings LLC ....B 716 439-2011
Lockport (G-7620)
◆ Graham Corporation ....B 585 343-2216
Batavia (G-638)
Grillmaster Inc ....E 718 272-9191
Howard Beach (G-6625)
Healthway Products Company ....E 315 207-1410
Oswego (G-13357)
▲ Heaven Fresh USA Inc ....G 800 642-0367
Niagara Falls (G-12850)
▲ Hoshizaki Nrtheastern Dist Ctr ....G 516 605-1411
Plainview (G-13633)
▲ Hydro-Air Components Inc ....C 716 827-6510
Buffalo (G-3018)
▲ Ice Air LLC ....E 914 668-4700
Mount Vernon (G-8737)
JE Miller Inc ....F 315 437-6811
East Syracuse (G-4560)
John F Krell Jr ....G 315 492-3201
Syracuse (G-15987)
Kedco Inc ....F 516 454-7800
Farmingdale (G-5032)
Keeler Services ....G 607 776-5757
Bath (G-658)
▲ Klearbar Inc ....G 516 684-9892
Port Washington (G-13855)
Layton Manufacturing Corp ....E 718 498-6000
Brooklyn (G-2197)
Lightron Corporation ....G 516 938-5544
Jericho (G-7107)
M M Tool and Manufacturing ....G 845 691-4140
Highland (G-6432)
Manning Lewis Div Rubicon Inds ....E 908 687-2400
Brooklyn (G-2263)
Marathon Heater Co Inc ....G 607 657-8113
Richford (G-14076)
▼ Mgr Equipment Corp ....E 516 239-3030
Inwood (G-6801)
◆ Millrock Technology Inc ....E 845 339-5700
Kingston (G-7230)
Mohawk Cabinet Company Inc ....F 518 725-0645
Gloversville (G-5733)
▲ Motivair Corporation ....E 716 691-9222
Amherst (G-250)
MSP Technologycom LLC ....G 631 424-7542
Centerport (G-3505)
▼ Nationwide Coils Inc ....G 914 277-7396
Mount Kisco (G-8679)
▼ Niagara Blower Company ....C 800 426-5169
Tonawanda (G-16204)
▲ Niagara Dispensing Tech Inc ....F 716 636-9827
Buffalo (G-3108)
Northern Air Systems Inc ....E 585 594-5050
Rochester (G-14564)
Opticool Solutions LLC ....F 585 347-6127
Webster (G-16753)
Parker-Hannifin Corporation ....D 716 685-4040
Lancaster (G-7356)
◆ Pfannenberg Inc ....D 716 685-6866
Lancaster (G-7358)
Pfannenberg Manufacturing LLC ....D 716 685-6866
Lancaster (G-7359)

SIC

Employee Codes: A=Over 500 employees, B=251-500
C=101-250, D=51-100, E=20-50, F=10-19, G=5-9
2018 Harris
New York Manufacturers Directory
831

Pro Metal of NY Corp G 516 285-0440
Valley Stream *(G-16445)*
◆ **RE Hansen Industries Inc** C 631 471-2900
East Setauket *(G-4510)*
Roemac Industrial Sales Inc G 716 692-7332
North Tonawanda *(G-13009)*
▲ **Rubicon Industries Corp** E 718 434-4700
Brooklyn *(G-2535)*
S & V Restaurant Eqp Mfrs Inc E 718 220-1140
Bronx *(G-1444)*
Siemens Industry Inc E 716 568-0983
Buffalo *(G-3214)*
Solitec Incorporated F 315 298-4213
Pulaski *(G-13969)*
Split Systems Corp G 516 223-5511
North Baldwin *(G-12926)*
◆ **Standard Motor Products Inc** B 718 392-0200
Long Island City *(G-7912)*
▼ **Storflex Holdings Inc** C 607 962-2137
Corning *(G-4003)*
Supermarket Equipment Depo Inc G 718 665-6200
Bronx *(G-1465)*
Thomson Industries Inc F 716 691-9100
Amherst *(G-266)*
Trane US Inc D 718 721-8844
Long Island City *(G-7933)*
Trane US Inc G 914 593-0303
Elmsford *(G-4795)*
Trane US Inc E 315 234-1500
East Syracuse *(G-4585)*
Trane US Inc E 518 785-1315
Latham *(G-7407)*
Trane US Inc E 585 256-2500
Rochester *(G-14757)*
Trane US Inc E 716 626-1260
Buffalo *(G-3250)*
Trane US Inc E 631 952-9477
Plainview *(G-13666)*
Transcolux Corp G 315 768-1500
New York Mills *(G-12747)*
▲ **Transit Air Inc** E 607 324-0216
Hornell *(G-6595)*
▲ **Universal Coolers Inc** G 718 788-8621
Brooklyn *(G-2725)*
Universal Parent and Youth F 917 754-2426
Brooklyn *(G-2727)*
York International Corporation D 718 389-4152
Long Island City *(G-7958)*

3586 Measuring & Dispensing Pumps

Aptargroup Inc C 845 639-3700
Congers *(G-3876)*
▲ **Charles Ross & Son Company** D 631 234-0500
Hauppauge *(G-6064)*
Economy Pump & Motor Repair G 718 433-2600
Astoria *(G-436)*
◆ **Pulsafeeder Inc** C 585 292-8000
Rochester *(G-14632)*
Schlumberger Technology Corp C 607 378-0105
Horseheads *(G-6621)*
▲ **Valois of America Inc** C 845 639-3700
Congers *(G-3886)*

3589 Service Ind Machines, NEC

240 Michigan Street Inc F 716 434-6010
Lockport *(G-7596)*
Abe Pool Service G 845 473-7730
Hyde Park *(G-6771)*
Advance Food Service Co Inc C 631 242-4800
Edgewood *(G-4604)*
◆ **Advance Tabco Inc** D 631 242-8270
Edgewood *(G-4605)*
▲ **Airgle Corporation** E 866 501-7750
Ronkonkoma *(G-14884)*
American Comfort Direct LLC E 201 364-8309
New York *(G-9165)*
Arista Coffee Inc G 347 531-0813
Maspeth *(G-8148)*
▲ **Arpa USA** G 212 965-4099
New York *(G-9255)*
◆ **Atlantic Ultraviolet Corp** E 631 234-3275
Hauppauge *(G-6047)*
▲ **Attias Oven Corp** G 718 499-0145
Brooklyn *(G-1651)*
Bakers Pride Oven Co Inc C 914 576-0200
New Rochelle *(G-8932)*
◆ **Blue Tee Corp** A 212 598-0880
New York *(G-9473)*
Business Advisory Services G 718 337-3740
Far Rockaway *(G-4926)*
Carts Mobile Food Eqp Corp E 718 788-5540
Brooklyn *(G-1763)*
Chester Shred-It/West E 914 407-2502
Valhalla *(G-16391)*
City of Kingston F 845 331-2490
Kingston *(G-7213)*
City of Olean G 716 376-5694
Olean *(G-13158)*
City of Oneonta G 607 433-3470
Oneonta *(G-13200)*
Clearcove Systems Inc F 585 734-3012
Victor *(G-16491)*
Custom Klean Corp F 315 865-8101
Holland Patent *(G-6513)*
Dyna-Vac Equipment Inc F 315 865-8084
Stittville *(G-15784)*
▼ **Econocraft Worldwide Mfg Inc** G 914 966-2280
Yonkers *(G-17455)*
Empire Division Inc D 315 476-6273
Syracuse *(G-15957)*
▲ **Environment-One Corporation** C 518 346-6161
Schenectady *(G-15279)*
Ewt Holdings III Corp F 212 644-5900
New York *(G-10151)*
Ferguson Enterprises Inc E 800 437-1146
New Hyde Park *(G-8879)*
H2o Solutions Inc F 518 527-0915
Stillwater *(G-15782)*
Heliojet Cleaning Tech Inc F 585 768-8710
Le Roy *(G-7433)*
Hercules International Inc E 631 423-6900
Huntington Station *(G-6746)*
Hobart Corporation E 585 427-9000
Rochester *(G-14458)*
Hudson Xinde Energy Inc G 212 220-7112
New York *(G-10573)*
▼ **I A S National Inc** E 631 423-6900
Huntington Station *(G-6748)*
IMC Teddy Food Service E 631 789-8881
Amityville *(G-294)*
▲ **Integrated Water Management** G 607 844-4276
Dryden *(G-4346)*
▲ **Key High Vacuum Products Inc** E 631 584-5959
Nesconset *(G-8823)*
▲ **Kinplex Corp** E 631 242-4800
Edgewood *(G-4617)*
Kinplex Corp E 631 242-4800
Edgewood *(G-4618)*
Klee Corp G 585 272-0320
Rochester *(G-14492)*
▲ **Korin Japanese Trading Corp** E 212 587-7021
New York *(G-10916)*
Liquid Industries Inc G 716 628-2999
Niagara Falls *(G-12860)*
Menpin Supply Corp F 718 415-4168
Brooklyn *(G-2300)*
Metro Group Inc D 718 392-3616
Long Island City *(G-7841)*
Metro Lube G 718 947-1167
Rego Park *(G-14047)*
National Vac Envmtl Svcs Corp E 518 743-0563
Glens Falls *(G-5706)*
Neptune Soft Water Inc F 315 446-5151
Syracuse *(G-16017)*
New Windsor Waste Water Plant F 845 561-2550
New Windsor *(G-8990)*
Northeast Water Systems LLC G 585 943-9225
Kendall *(G-7172)*
Orege North America Inc G 770 862-9388
New York *(G-11537)*
Ossining Village of Inc G 914 202-9668
Ossining *(G-13349)*
Oxford Cleaners G 212 734-0006
New York *(G-11552)*
▲ **Oyster Bay Pump Works Inc** F 516 933-4500
Hicksville *(G-6406)*
Pathfinder 103 Inc G 315 363-4260
Oneida *(G-13187)*
Pentair Water Pool and Spa Inc E 845 452-5500
Lagrangeville *(G-7283)*
▲ **Pleatco LLC** D 516 609-0200
Glen Cove *(G-5637)*
Power Scrub It Inc F 516 997-2500
Westbury *(G-17048)*
Pure Planet Waters LLC F 718 676-7900
Brooklyn *(G-2475)*
R C Kolstad Water Corp G 585 216-2230
Ontario *(G-13232)*
▲ **R-S Restaurant Eqp Mfg Corp** F 212 925-0335
New York *(G-11811)*
Richard R Cain Inc F 845 229-7410
Hyde Park *(G-6775)*
Roger & Sons Inc G 212 226-4734
New York *(G-11927)*
Royal Prestige Lasting Co F 516 280-5148
Hempstead *(G-6308)*
Strategies North America Inc G 716 945-6053
Salamanca *(G-15135)*
▲ **Toga Manufacturing Inc** G 631 242-4800
Edgewood *(G-4631)*
Water Energy Systems LLC G 844 822-7665
New York *(G-12624)*
▲ **Water Technologies Inc** G 315 986-0000
Macedon *(G-8022)*
Water Treatment Services Inc G 914 241-2261
Bedford Hills *(G-804)*
Wetlook Detailing Inc G 212 390-8877
Brooklyn *(G-2762)*
Wilder Manufacturing Co Inc D 516 222-0433
Garden City *(G-5550)*
Yr Blanc & Co LLC G 716 800-3999
Buffalo *(G-3287)*

3592 Carburetors, Pistons, Rings & Valves

▲ **Fcmp Inc** F 716 692-4623
Tonawanda *(G-16179)*
Valvetech Inc E 315 548-4551
Phelps *(G-13562)*

3593 Fluid Power Cylinders & Actuators

▲ **A K Allen Co Inc** C 516 747-5450
Mineola *(G-8522)*
Actuant Corporation E 607 753-8276
Cortland *(G-4033)*
Allenair Corporation D 516 747-5450
Mineola *(G-8527)*
▲ **Ameritool Mfg Inc** E 315 668-2172
Central Square *(G-3543)*
Direkt Force LLC E 716 652-3022
East Aurora *(G-4394)*
◆ **Eastport Operating Partners LP** G 212 387-8791
New York *(G-10020)*
Hydra Technology Corp G 716 896-8316
Buffalo *(G-3017)*
▲ **ITT Enidine Inc** B 716 662-1900
Orchard Park *(G-13299)*
Precision Mechanisms Corp E 516 333-5955
Westbury *(G-17049)*
Skytravel (usa) LLC F 518 888-2610
Schenectady *(G-15321)*
Springville Mfg Co Inc E 716 592-4957
Springville *(G-15636)*
Starcyl USA Corp F 877 782-7295
Champlain *(G-3573)*
Tactair Fluid Controls Inc C 315 451-3928
Liverpool *(G-7579)*
Triumph Actuation Systems LLC D 516 378-0162
Freeport *(G-5443)*
Young & Franklin Inc D 315 457-3110
Liverpool *(G-7586)*

3594 Fluid Power Pumps & Motors

Atlantic Industrial Tech Inc E 631 234-3131
Shirley *(G-15437)*
Huck International Inc C 845 331-7300
Kingston *(G-7220)*
Hydroacoustics Inc F 585 359-1000
Henrietta *(G-6317)*
ITT Corporation D 315 568-2811
Seneca Falls *(G-15383)*
ITT Inc F 914 641-2000
White Plains *(G-17152)*
◆ **ITT LLC** B 914 641-2000
White Plains *(G-17154)*
Parker-Hannifin Corporation C 716 686-6400
Lancaster *(G-7354)*
Parker-Hannifin Corporation C 585 425-7000
Fairport *(G-4874)*
Trench & Marine Pump Co Inc E 212 423-9098
Bronx *(G-1473)*
Triumph Actuation Systems LLC D 516 378-0162
Freeport *(G-5443)*

3596 Scales & Balances, Exc Laboratory

A & K Equipment Incorporated G 705 428-3573
Watertown *(G-16655)*
▲ **Circuits & Systems Inc** E 516 593-4301
East Rockaway *(G-4488)*

SIC SECTION
35 INDUSTRIAL AND COMMERCIAL MACHINERY AND COMPUTER EQUIPMENT

◆ Itin Scale Co Inc .... E 718 336-5900
Brooklyn *(G-2118)*
Measupro Inc .... F 845 425-8777
Spring Valley *(G-15618)*
Mettler-Toledo Inc .... C 607 257-6000
Ithaca *(G-6896)*
S R Instruments Inc .... E 716 693-5977
Tonawanda *(G-16216)*
Scale-Tronix Inc .... F 914 948-8117
Skaneateles *(G-15487)*
Weighing & Systems Tech Inc ...... G 518 274-2797
Troy *(G-16288)*

3599 Machinery & Eqpt, Indl & Commercial, NEC

A & G Precision Corp .... F 631 957-5613
Amityville *(G-273)*
A & L Machine Company Inc .... G 631 463-3111
Islandia *(G-6824)*
A and K Machine and Welding ..... G 631 231-2552
Bay Shore *(G-663)*
A P Manufacturing .... G 909 228-3049
Bohemia *(G-996)*
A R V Precision Mfg Inc .... G 631 293-9643
Farmingdale *(G-4934)*
A-Line Technologies Inc .... F 607 772-2439
Binghamton *(G-881)*
Abk Enterprises Inc .... G 631 348-0555
Central Islip *(G-3508)*
Absolute Manufacturing Inc .... G 631 563-7466
Bohemia *(G-999)*
Acad Design Corp .... G 585 254-6960
Rochester *(G-14179)*
▲ Accede Mold & Tool Co Inc ..... D 585 254-6490
Rochester *(G-14180)*
▲ Accurate Industrial Machining .. E 631 242-0566
Holbrook *(G-6456)*
Accurate Welding Service Inc ...... G 516 333-1730
Westbury *(G-16988)*
Acme Industries of W Babylon ..... F 631 737-5231
Ronkonkoma *(G-14877)*
▲ Acro Industries Inc .... C 585 254-3661
Rochester *(G-14186)*
Acro-Fab Ltd .... E 315 564-6688
Hannibal *(G-5992)*
Active Manufacturing Inc .... F 607 775-3162
Kirkwood *(G-7257)*
Adaptive Mfg Tech Inc .... E 631 580-5400
Ronkonkoma *(G-14878)*
Addison Precision Mfg Corp .... D 585 254-1386
Rochester *(G-14188)*
Advan-Tech Manufacturing Inc .... E 716 667-1500
Orchard Park *(G-13274)*
Advance Precision Industries .... G 631 491-0910
West Babylon *(G-16791)*
Advanced Aerospace Machining ... G 631 694-7745
Farmingdale *(G-4937)*
Advanced Machine Inc .... F 585 423-8255
Rochester *(G-14194)*
Advanced Mfg Techniques .... G 518 877-8560
Clifton Park *(G-3720)*
Aero Specialties Manufacturing .... G 631 242-7200
Deer Park *(G-4114)*
AG Tech Welding Corp .... G 845 398-0005
Tappan *(G-16102)*
Aj Genco Mch Sp McHy Rdout Svc .. F 716 664-4925
Falconer *(G-4896)*
Akraturn Mfg Inc .... D 607 775-2802
Kirkwood *(G-7258)*
Aljo Precision Products Inc .... E 516 420-4419
Old Bethpage *(G-13145)*
Alkemy Machine LLC .... G 585 436-8730
Rochester *(G-14201)*
Allen Tool Phoenix Inc .... E 315 463-7533
East Syracuse *(G-4518)*
Allied Industrial Products Co .... G 716 664-3893
Jamestown *(G-7006)*
▲ Aloi Solutions LLC .... E 585 292-0920
Rochester *(G-14207)*
▲ Alpha Fasteners Corp .... G 516 867-6188
Freeport *(G-5394)*
Alpha Manufacturing Corp .... F 631 249-3700
Farmingdale *(G-4946)*
Alpine Machine Inc .... F 607 272-1344
Ithaca *(G-6858)*
Altamont Spray Welding Inc .... G 518 861-8870
Altamont *(G-209)*
Amacon Corporation .... F 631 293-1888
West Babylon *(G-16794)*

American Linear Manufacturers .... F 516 333-1351
Westbury *(G-16993)*
▲ American Wire Tie Inc .... E 716 337-2412
North Collins *(G-12942)*
Ancon Gear & Instrument Corp .... F 631 694-5255
Amityville *(G-275)*
▲ Antab Mch Sprfinishing Lab Inc ... G 585 865-8290
Rochester *(G-14223)*
Applied Technology Mfg Corp ...... E 607 687-2200
Owego *(G-13375)*
◆ Arbe Machinery Inc .... F 631 756-2477
Farmingdale *(G-4953)*
Archimedes Products Inc .... G 631 589-1215
Bohemia *(G-1014)*
Architectural Coatings Inc .... F 718 418-9584
Brooklyn *(G-1624)*
Argencord Machine Corp Inc .... G 631 842-8990
Copiague *(G-3919)*
Argo General Machine Work Inc .. G 718 392-4605
Long Island City *(G-7701)*
Armstrong Mold Corporation .... D 315 437-1517
East Syracuse *(G-4522)*
Arrow Grinding Inc .... G 716 693-3333
Tonawanda *(G-16161)*
Art Precision Metal Products .... F 631 842-8889
Copiague *(G-3920)*
Artisan Machining Inc .... G 631 589-1416
Ronkonkoma *(G-14900)*
Artisan Management Group Inc ... G 716 569-4094
Frewsburg *(G-5462)*
Astra Tool & Instr Mfg Corp .... E 914 747-3863
Hawthorne *(G-6266)*
Atlantis Equipment Corporation ... F 518 733-5910
Stephentown *(G-15778)*
Auburn Bearing & Mfg Inc .... G 315 986-7600
Macedon *(G-8009)*
AW Mack Manufacturing Co Inc .. F 845 452-4050
Poughkeepsie *(G-13909)*
B & R Industries Inc .... F 631 736-2275
Medford *(G-8267)*
B C Manufacturing Inc .... G 585 482-1080
West Henrietta *(G-16903)*
Babbitt Bearings Inc .... D 315 479-6603
Syracuse *(G-15884)*
Babbitt Bearings Incorporated ..... D 315 479-6603
Syracuse *(G-15885)*
Badge Machine Products Inc .... E 585 394-0330
Canandaigua *(G-3364)*
Barton Tool Inc .... G 716 665-2801
Falconer *(G-4899)*
Bay Horse Innovations Nyinc ...... G 607 898-3337
Groton *(G-5918)*
BEAM Manufacturing Corp .... F 631 253-2724
West Babylon *(G-16800)*
Belden Manufacturing Inc .... E 607 238-0998
Kirkwood *(G-7259)*
Bill Shea Enterprises Inc .... G 585 343-2284
Batavia *(G-626)*
Birch Machine & Tool Inc .... F 716 735-9802
Middleport *(G-8454)*
Blading Services Unlimited LLC .. F 315 875-5313
Canastota *(G-3392)*
Blair Cnstr Fabrication Sp .... G 315 253-2321
Auburn *(G-484)*
Bliss Machine Inc .... F 585 492-5128
Arcade *(G-389)*
Blue Manufacturing Co Inc .... G 607 796-2463
Millport *(G-8515)*
Bms Manufacturing Co Inc .... G 607 535-2426
Watkins Glen *(G-16718)*
Breed Enterprises Inc .... G 585 388-0126
Fairport *(G-4854)*
Broadalbin Manufacturing Corp ... E 518 883-5313
Broadalbin *(G-1239)*
Bruce Pierce .... G 716 731-9310
Sanborn *(G-15142)*
Bryant Machine & Development ... F 716 894-8282
Buffalo *(G-2867)*
Buxton Machine and Tool Co Inc .. F 716 876-2312
Buffalo *(G-2885)*
C & H Machining Inc .... F 631 582-6737
Bohemia *(G-1026)*
C & T Tool & Instrument Co .... F 718 429-1253
Woodside *(G-17338)*
C L Precision Machine & TI Co ... G 718 651-8475
Woodside *(G-17339)*
C R C Manufacturing Inc .... F 585 254-8820
Rochester *(G-14272)*
▲ Calvary Design Team Inc .... C 585 347-6127
Webster *(G-16738)*

Canfield Machine & Tool LLC ...... E 315 593-8062
Fulton *(G-5468)*
▲ Capy Machine Shop Inc .... E 631 694-6916
Melville *(G-8331)*
Carballo Contract Machining .... G 315 594-2511
Wolcott *(G-17299)*
Carbaugh Tool Company Inc .... E 607 739-3293
Elmira *(G-4686)*
Cardish Machine Works Inc .... G 518 273-2329
Watervliet *(G-16705)*
Carter Precision Metals LLC .... G 516 333-1917
Westbury *(G-17001)*
Casey Machine Co Inc .... D 716 651-0150
Lancaster *(G-7332)*
Catapult .... G 323 839-6204
New York *(G-9600)*
Cayuga Tool and Die Inc .... G 607 533-7400
Groton *(G-5920)*
CBM Fabrications Inc .... E 518 399-8023
Ballston Lake *(G-580)*
Cda Machine Inc .... G 585 671-5959
Webster *(G-16739)*
Cdl Manufacturing Inc .... G 585 589-2533
Albion *(G-166)*
Certified Fabrications Inc .... F 716 731-8123
Sanborn *(G-15144)*
Certified Prcsion McHining Inc ... G 631 244-3671
Bohemia *(G-1028)*
▲ Cetek Inc .... G 845 452-3510
Poughkeepsie *(G-13911)*
Charl Industries Inc .... E 631 234-0100
Hauppauge *(G-6063)*
Charles V Weber Machine Shop ... G 518 272-8033
Troy *(G-16251)*
Chart Inc .... F 518 272-3565
Troy *(G-16252)*
Chautqua Prcsion Machining Inc .. F 716 763-3752
Ashville *(G-425)*
◆ Chocovision Corporation .... G 845 473-4970
Poughkeepsie *(G-13912)*
▼ City Gear Inc .... G 914 450-4746
Irvington *(G-6809)*
Cjn Machinery Corp .... G 631 244-8030
Holbrook *(G-6465)*
Classic Auto Crafts Inc .... G 518 966-8003
Greenville *(G-5902)*
Conesus Lake Association Inc .... E 585 346-6864
Lakeville *(G-7306)*
Conrad Blasius Equipment Co ..... G 516 753-1200
Plainview *(G-13620)*
Converter Design Inc .... G 518 745-7138
Glens Falls *(G-5691)*
Corbett Stves Pttern Works Inc ... E 585 546-7109
Rochester *(G-14310)*
Cortland Machine and Tool Co .... G 607 756-5852
Cortland *(G-4042)*
Courser Inc .... G 607 739-3861
Elmira *(G-4690)*
Craftsman Manufacturing Co In ... G 585 426-5780
Rochester *(G-14312)*
▼ Cubitek Inc .... F 631 665-6900
Brentwood *(G-1176)*
▲ Cyclone Air Power Inc .... G 718 447-3038
Staten Island *(G-15684)*
D J Crowell Co Inc .... G 716 684-3343
Alden *(G-179)*
D K Machine Inc .... F 518 747-0626
Fort Edward *(G-5349)*
D-K Manufacturing Corp .... G 315 592-4327
Fulton *(G-5469)*
Darco Manufacturing Inc .... E 315 432-8905
Syracuse *(G-15941)*
Daves Precision Machine Shop ... F 845 626-7263
Kerhonkson *(G-7184)*
David Fehlman .... G 315 455-8888
Syracuse *(G-15942)*
Deck Bros Inc .... G 716 852-0262
Buffalo *(G-2923)*
Delaney Machine Products Ltd ... G 631 225-1032
Lindenhurst *(G-7483)*
Dennies Manufacturing Inc .... E 585 393-4646
Canandaigua *(G-3371)*
Denny Machine Co Inc .... D 716 873-6865
Buffalo *(G-2926)*
Dependable Tool & Die Co Inc ... G 315 453-5696
Syracuse *(G-15944)*
Dern Moore Machine Company Inc .. G 716 433-6243
Lockport *(G-7608)*
Derosa Fabrications Inc .... E 631 563-0640
Bohemia *(G-1053)*

Employee Codes: A=Over 500 employees, B=251-500
C=101-250, D=51-100, E=20-50, F=10-19, G=5-9

▼ **Devin Mfg Inc** .... F 585 496-5770
Arcade *(G-391)*

Dewey Machine & Tool Inc .... G 607 749-3930
Homer *(G-6544)*

DMD Machining Technology Inc .... G 585 659-8180
Kendall *(G-7171)*

Dormitory Authority - State NY .... G 631 434-1487
Brentwood *(G-1179)*

Dougs Machine Shop Inc .... G 585 905-0004
Canandaigua *(G-3372)*

Duetto Integrated Systems Inc .... F 631 851-0102
Islandia *(G-6830)*

Dyna-Tech Quality Inc .... G 585 458-9970
Rochester *(G-14339)*

Dynak Inc .... F 585 271-2255
Churchville *(G-3666)*

E & R Machine Inc .... E 716 434-6639
Lockport *(G-7610)*

E B Industries LLC .... E 631 293-8565
Farmingdale *(G-4990)*

E B Trottnow Machine Spc .... F 716 694-0600
Eden *(G-4598)*

E J Willis Company Inc .... F 315 891-7602
Middleville *(G-8508)*

E M T Manufacturing Inc .... F 516 333-1917
East Meadow *(G-4442)*

▲ **Eagle Bridge Machine & Tl Inc** .... E 518 686-4541
Eagle Bridge *(G-4380)*

Eagle Instruments Inc .... G 914 939-6843
Port Chester *(G-13771)*

Eastern Machine and Electric .... G 716 284-8271
Niagara Falls *(G-12835)*

Eastern Precision Machining .... G 631 286-4758
Bellport *(G-824)*

Edr Industries Inc .... F 516 868-1928
Freeport *(G-5406)*

▲ **Edsal Machine Products Inc** .... F 718 439-9163
Brooklyn *(G-1907)*

▲ **Edwin J McKenica & Sons Inc** .... F 716 823-4646
Buffalo *(G-2946)*

Efficient Automated Mch Corp .... F 718 937-9393
Long Island City *(G-7756)*

Ehrlich Enterprises Inc .... F 631 956-0690
Hauppauge *(G-6092)*

▲ **Elg Utica Alloys Inc** .... E 315 733-0475
Herkimer *(G-6324)*

Elg Utica Alloys Holdings Inc .... G 315 733-0475
Utica *(G-16352)*

Elite Machine Inc .... G 585 289-4733
Manchester *(G-8084)*

Elite Precise Manufacturer LLC .... G 518 993-3040
Fort Plain *(G-5356)*

Emcom Industries Inc .... G 716 852-3711
Buffalo *(G-2950)*

Emory Machine & Tool Co Inc .... E 585 436-9610
Farmington *(G-5159)*

Empire Plastics Inc .... E 607 754-9132
Endwell *(G-4840)*

Empro Niagara Inc .... G 716 433-2769
Lockport *(G-7612)*

Endicott Precision Inc .... C 607 754-7076
Endicott *(G-4811)*

Engineering Mfg Tech LLC .... D 607 754-7111
Endicott *(G-4813)*

Estebania Enterprises Inc .... G 585 529-9330
Rochester *(G-14380)*

ET Oakes Corporation .... E 631 232-0002
Hauppauge *(G-6096)*

ET Precision Optics Inc .... D 585 254-2560
Rochester *(G-14381)*

Etna Tool & Die Corporation .... F 212 475-4350
New York *(G-10133)*

Euro Gear (usa) Inc .... G 518 578-1775
Plattsburgh *(G-13690)*

Everfab Inc .... D 716 655-1550
East Aurora *(G-4395)*

Exact Machining & Mfg .... G 585 334-7090
Rochester *(G-14383)*

Excel Industries Inc .... E 716 542-5468
Clarence *(G-3689)*

Exigo Precision Inc .... G 585 254-5818
Rochester *(G-14386)*

Expert Machine Services Inc .... G 718 786-1200
Long Island City *(G-7764)*

F M L Industries Inc .... G 607 749-7273
Homer *(G-6545)*

▲ **Fairview Fitting & Mfg Inc** .... D 716 614-0320
North Tonawanda *(G-12989)*

Farrant Screw Machine Products .... G 585 457-3213
Java Village *(G-7087)*

Felton Machine Co Inc .... E 716 215-9001
Niagara Falls *(G-12840)*

Fenbar Prcision Machinists Inc .... F 914 769-5506
Thornwood *(G-16142)*

Fermer Precision Inc .... D 315 822-6371
Ilion *(G-6779)*

Ferraro Manufacturing Company .... G 631 752-1509
Farmingdale *(G-5001)*

Ferro Machine Co Inc .... G 845 398-3641
Orangeburg *(G-13250)*

▲ **Finesse Creations Inc** .... F 718 692-2100
Brooklyn *(G-1977)*

Five Star Industries Inc .... E 716 674-2589
West Seneca *(G-16973)*

▲ **Flex-Hose Company Inc** .... E 315 437-1903
East Syracuse *(G-4544)*

Forbes Precision Inc .... F 585 865-7069
Rochester *(G-14400)*

Four K Machine Shop Inc .... G 516 997-0752
Westbury *(G-17013)*

Frederick Machine Repair Inc .... G 716 332-0104
Buffalo *(G-2971)*

Fross Industries Inc .... E 716 297-0652
Niagara Falls *(G-12843)*

Fulton Tool Co Inc .... E 315 598-2900
Fulton *(G-5472)*

Fultonville Machine & Tool Co .... F 518 853-4441
Fultonville *(G-5493)*

Future Screw Machine Pdts Inc .... F 631 765-1610
Southold *(G-15582)*

G & G C Machine & Tool Co Inc .... G 516 873-0999
Westbury *(G-17014)*

Gamma Instrument Co Inc .... G 516 486-5526
Hempstead *(G-6293)*

Gefa Instrument Corp .... F 516 420-4419
Old Bethpage *(G-13148)*

Gem Manufacturing Inc .... G 585 235-1670
Rochester *(G-14411)*

Genco John .... G 716 483-5446
Jamestown *(G-7028)*

General Cutting Inc .... F 631 580-5011
Ronkonkoma *(G-14932)*

Genesis Machining Corp .... F 516 377-1197
North Baldwin *(G-12922)*

Gentner Precision Components .... G 315 597-5734
Palmyra *(G-13433)*

Giuliante Machine Tool Inc .... E 914 835-0008
Peekskill *(G-13502)*

Gli-Dex Sales Corp .... E 716 692-6501
North Tonawanda *(G-12992)*

Globe Grinding Corp .... F 631 694-1970
Copiague *(G-3929)*

Gmr Manufacturing Inc .... G 631 582-2600
Central Islip *(G-3524)*

Gorden Automotive Equipment .... F 716 674-2700
West Seneca *(G-16975)*

Gpp Post-Closing Inc .... E 585 334-4640
Rush *(G-15075)*

▲ **Greno Industries Inc** .... G 518 393-4195
Scotia *(G-15347)*

Grind .... G 646 558-3250
New York *(G-10407)*

Gullo Machine & Tool Inc .... F 585 657-7318
Bloomfield *(G-983)*

H & H Technologies Inc .... E 631 567-3526
Ronkonkoma *(G-14936)*

H C Young Tool & Machine Co .... G 315 463-0663
Syracuse *(G-15975)*

H F Brown Machine Co Inc .... F 315 732-6129
Utica *(G-16361)*

H T Specialty Inc .... F 585 458-4060
Rochester *(G-14437)*

Hagner Industries Inc .... G 716 873-5720
Buffalo *(G-3003)*

Hallock Fabricating Corp .... G 631 727-2441
Riverhead *(G-14156)*

Hartman Enterprises Inc .... D 315 363-7300
Oneida *(G-13178)*

Harwitt Industries Inc .... F 516 623-9787
Freeport *(G-5416)*

Haskell Machine & Tool Inc .... F 607 749-2421
Homer *(G-6546)*

▲ **Hebeler LLC** .... C 716 873-9300
Tonawanda *(G-16188)*

Hebeler Process Solutions LLC .... E 716 873-9300
Tonawanda *(G-16189)*

Herbert Wolf Corp .... G 212 242-0300
New York *(G-10504)*

Herkimer Tool & Machining Corp .... F 315 866-2110
Herkimer *(G-6328)*

Hes Inc .... G 607 359-2974
Addison *(G-7)*

Hi-Tech Cnc Machining Corp .... G 914 668-5090
Mount Vernon *(G-8736)*

Hi-Tech Industries NY Inc .... E 607 217-7361
Johnson City *(G-7125)*

Hoercher Industries Inc .... G 585 398-2982
East Rochester *(G-4480)*

Hohl Machine & Conveyor Co Inc .... E 716 882-7210
Buffalo *(G-3013)*

▲ **HSM Machine Works Inc** .... E 631 924-6600
Medford *(G-8281)*

Hubbard Tool and Die Corp .... E 315 337-7840
Rome *(G-14843)*

Hunter Machine Inc .... E 585 924-7480
Victor *(G-16505)*

Hw Specialties Co Inc .... F 631 589-0745
Bohemia *(G-1071)*

Hypur Precision Machining Inc .... F 631 584-8498
East Setauket *(G-4503)*

I D Machine Inc .... G 607 796-2549
Elmira *(G-4705)*

Imperial Instrument Corp .... G 516 739-6644
Westbury *(G-17022)*

Indian Springs Mfg Co Inc .... F 315 635-6101
Baldwinsville *(G-570)*

Industrial Precision Pdts Inc .... E 315 343-4421
Oswego *(G-13358)*

Industrial Services of Wny .... G 716 799-7788
Niagara Falls *(G-12854)*

Ingleside Machine Co Inc .... D 585 924-3046
Farmington *(G-5162)*

Interactive Instruments Inc .... G 518 347-0955
Scotia *(G-15349)*

International Climbing Mchs .... G 607 288-4001
Ithaca *(G-6887)*

▼ **International Creative Met Inc** .... F 718 424-8179
Woodside *(G-17350)*

▲ **International Tool & Mch Inc** .... F 585 654-6955
Rochester *(G-14474)*

Ironshore Holdings Inc .... F 315 457-1052
Liverpool *(G-7550)*

Island Instrument Corp .... G 631 243-0550
Deer Park *(G-4175)*

Island Machine Inc .... G 518 562-1232
Plattsburgh *(G-13698)*

▲ **ISO Plastics Corp** .... D 914 663-8300
Mount Vernon *(G-8739)*

J & G Machine & Tool Co Inc .... F 315 310-7130
Marion *(G-8126)*

J & J Swiss Precision Inc .... E 631 243-5584
Deer Park *(G-4176)*

J & J Tl Die Mfg & Stampg Corp .... G 845 228-0242
Carmel *(G-3428)*

J & L Precision Co Inc .... G 585 768-6388
Le Roy *(G-7435)*

J B Tool & Die Co Inc .... E 516 333-1480
Westbury *(G-17024)*

J D Cousins Inc .... E 716 824-1098
Buffalo *(G-3030)*

J F Machining Company Inc .... F 716 791-3910
Ransomville *(G-14032)*

J R S Precision Machining .... G 631 737-1330
Ronkonkoma *(G-14945)*

J Soehner Corporation .... F 516 599-2534
Rockville Centre *(G-14821)*

J T Systematic .... G 607 754-0929
Endwell *(G-4841)*

Jack Merkel Inc .... G 631 234-2600
Hauppauge *(G-6125)*

Jacobi Tool & Die Mfg Inc .... G 631 736-5394
Medford *(G-8283)*

▲ **Jam Industries Inc** .... E 585 458-9830
Rochester *(G-14479)*

Jamar Precision Products Co .... F 631 254-0234
Deer Park *(G-4177)*

Jamestown Iron Works Inc .... F 716 665-2818
Falconer *(G-4913)*

Javcon Machine Inc .... G 631 586-1890
Deer Park *(G-4179)*

Javin Machine Corp .... F 631 643-3322
West Babylon *(G-16829)*

Jet Sew Corporation .... F 315 896-2683
Barneveld *(G-613)*

Jewelers Machinist Co Inc .... G 631 661-5020
Babylon *(G-546)*

JF Machine Shop Inc .... F 631 491-7273
West Babylon *(G-16830)*

John J Mazur Inc .... F 631 242-4554
Deer Park *(G-4181)*

SIC SECTION
35 INDUSTRIAL AND COMMERCIAL MACHINERY AND COMPUTER EQUIPMENT

Johnnys Machine Shop.........G....... 631 338-9733
West Babylon *(G-16831)*
Johnson Mch & Fibr Pdts Co Inc.........F....... 716 665-2003
Jamestown *(G-7047)*
Johnston Precision Inc.........G....... 315 253-4181
Auburn *(G-503)*
Jolin Machining Corp.........F....... 631 589-1305
Bohemia *(G-1080)*
Jordan Machine Inc.........G....... 585 647-3585
Rochester *(G-14486)*
Just In Time Cnc Machining.........F....... 585 335-2010
Dansville *(G-4104)*
▲ **K & H Industries Inc**.........F....... 716 312-0088
Hamburg *(G-5953)*
K & H Precision Products Inc.........E....... 585 624-4894
Honeoye Falls *(G-6560)*
K D M Die Company Inc.........F....... 716 828-9000
Buffalo *(G-3041)*
K Hein Machines Inc.........G....... 607 748-1546
Vestal *(G-16473)*
Kal Manufacturing Corporation.........E....... 585 265-4310
Webster *(G-16751)*
▲ **Keller Technology Corporation**.........C....... 716 693-3840
Tonawanda *(G-16194)*
Kenwell Corporation.........D....... 315 592-4263
Fulton *(G-5480)*
Keyes Machine Works Inc.........G....... 585 426-5059
Gates *(G-5576)*
Kimber Mfg.........G....... 914 721-8417
Yonkers *(G-17477)*
Kimber Mfg Inc.........G....... 914 965-0753
Yonkers *(G-17478)*
▲ **Kimber Mfg Inc**.........C....... 914 964-0771
Yonkers *(G-17479)*
Kimber Mfg Inc.........D....... 406 758-2222
Elmsford *(G-4769)*
Kinemotive Corporation.........E....... 631 249-6440
Farmingdale *(G-5035)*
▲ **KMA Corporation**.........G....... 518 743-1330
Glens Falls *(G-5701)*
Konar Precision Mfg Inc.........G....... 631 242-4466
Deer Park *(G-4183)*
Kondor Technologies Inc.........F....... 631 471-8832
Ronkonkoma *(G-14952)*
Kramartron Precision Inc.........G....... 845 368-3668
Tallman *(G-16101)*
Kronenberger Mfg Corp.........E....... 585 385-2340
East Rochester *(G-4483)*
Krug Precision Inc.........G....... 516 944-9350
Port Washington *(G-13857)*
Kurtz Truck Equipment Inc.........F....... 607 849-3468
Marathon *(G-8115)*
Kurz and Zobel Inc.........G....... 585 254-9060
Rochester *(G-14494)*
Kz Precision Inc.........F....... 716 683-3202
Lancaster *(G-7345)*
L & S Metals Inc.........E....... 716 692-6865
North Tonawanda *(G-12998)*
L P R Precision Parts & Tls Co.........F....... 631 293-7334
Farmingdale *(G-5038)*
Labco of Palmyra Inc.........F....... 315 597-5202
Palmyra *(G-13436)*
▲ **Lagasse Works Inc**.........G....... 315 946-9202
Lyons *(G-8000)*
Lagoe-Oswego Corp.........E....... 315 343-3160
Rochester *(G-14495)*
Lakeside Industries Inc.........F....... 716 386-3031
Bemus Point *(G-842)*
Lakeside Precision Inc.........E....... 716 366-5030
Dunkirk *(G-4368)*
Laser & Electron Beam Inc.........G....... 603 626-6080
New York *(G-10967)*
Lasticks Aerospace Inc.........F....... 631 242-8484
Bay Shore *(G-710)*
Leetech Manufacturing Inc.........G....... 631 563-1442
Bohemia *(G-1087)*
Lewis Machine Co Inc.........G....... 718 625-0799
Brooklyn *(G-2215)*
Liberty Machine & Tool.........G....... 315 699-3242
Cicero *(G-3676)*
▲ **Linda Tool & Die Corporation**.........E....... 718 522-2066
Brooklyn *(G-2227)*
▲ **Lodolce Machine Co Inc**.........E....... 845 246-7017
Saugerties *(G-15216)*
Loughlin Manufacturing Corp.........F....... 631 585-4422
Bohemia *(G-1091)*
▲ **Lwa Works Inc**.........G....... 518 271-8360
Watervliet *(G-16711)*
▲ **M & S Precision Machine Co LLC**.........F....... 518 747-1193
Queensbury *(G-14017)*
Macro Tool & Machine Company.........G....... 845 223-3824
Lagrangeville *(G-7280)*
Maehr Industries Inc.........G....... 631 924-1661
Bellport *(G-829)*
▲ **Magellan Aerospace Bethel Inc**.........C....... 203 798-9373
Corona *(G-4024)*
Magellan Aerospace NY Inc.........C....... 631 589-2440
Bohemia *(G-1094)*
Malisa Branko Inc.........F....... 631 225-9741
Copiague *(G-3937)*
Manth Mfg Inc.........E....... 716 693-6525
Tonawanda *(G-16197)*
Manuf Appld Renova Sys.........G....... 518 654-9084
Corinth *(G-3981)*
Mar-A-Thon Filters Inc.........G....... 631 957-4774
Lindenhurst *(G-7492)*
Mardon Tool & Die Co Inc.........F....... 585 254-4545
Rochester *(G-14517)*
◆ **Marksmen Manufacturing Corp**.........E....... 800 305-6942
Deer Park *(G-4194)*
Massapqua Prcsion McHining Ltd.........G....... 631 789-1485
Amityville *(G-310)*
▲ **Master Machine Incorporated**.........F....... 716 487-2555
Jamestown *(G-7051)*
Matic Industries Inc.........G....... 718 886-5470
College Point *(G-3821)*
Matrix Machining Corp.........G....... 631 643-6690
West Babylon *(G-16839)*
Mayfair Machine Company Inc.........G....... 631 981-6644
Ronkonkoma *(G-14967)*
Mc Ivor Manufacturing Inc.........G....... 716 825-1808
Buffalo *(G-3081)*
McGuigan Inc.........E....... 631 750-6222
Bohemia *(G-1098)*
Meade Machine Co Inc.........G....... 315 923-1703
Clyde *(G-3753)*
Medco Machine LLC.........G....... 315 986-2109
Walworth *(G-16571)*
Mega Tool & Mfg Corp.........E....... 607 734-8398
Elmira *(G-4709)*
Meridian Manufacturing Inc.........G....... 518 885-0450
Ballston Spa *(G-602)*
Metal Parts Manufacturing Inc.........G....... 315 831-2530
Barneveld *(G-614)*
Metro Machining & Fabricating.........G....... 718 545-0104
Woodside *(G-17355)*
Micro Instrument Corp.........D....... 585 458-3150
Rochester *(G-14528)*
Micro-Tech Machine Inc.........E....... 315 331-6671
Newark *(G-12757)*
Miles Machine Inc.........G....... 716 484-6026
Jamestown *(G-7053)*
Milex Precision Inc.........F....... 631 595-2393
Bay Shore *(G-715)*
Miller Technology Inc.........G....... 631 694-2224
Farmingdale *(G-5065)*
Minutemen Precsn McHning Tool.........E....... 631 467-4900
Ronkonkoma *(G-14970)*
Mitchell Machine Tool LLC.........G....... 585 254-7520
Rochester *(G-14536)*
▲ **Modern Packaging Inc**.........D....... 631 595-2437
Deer Park *(G-4199)*
Modern-TEC Manufacturing Inc.........G....... 716 625-8700
Lockport *(G-7632)*
Morco Products Corp.........F....... 718 853-4005
Brooklyn *(G-2338)*
Morris Machining Service Inc.........G....... 585 527-8100
Rochester *(G-14543)*
Mount Vernon Machine Inc.........E....... 845 268-9400
Valley Cottage *(G-16408)*
Ms Machining Inc.........G....... 607 723-1105
Binghamton *(G-934)*
Ms Spares LLC.........G....... 607 223-3024
Clay *(G-3709)*
Muller Tool Inc.........E....... 716 895-3658
Buffalo *(G-3098)*
Nassau Tool Works Inc.........E....... 631 328-7031
West Babylon *(G-16845)*
Neptune Machine Inc.........E....... 718 852-4100
Brooklyn *(G-2365)*
NET & Die Inc.........E....... 315 592-4311
Fulton *(G-5484)*
New Age Precision Tech Inc.........E....... 631 471-4000
Ronkonkoma *(G-14981)*
New York State Tool Co Inc.........F....... 315 737-8985
Chadwicks *(G-3558)*
Niagara Precision Inc.........E....... 716 439-0956
Lockport *(G-7636)*
▼ **Nicoform Inc**.........E....... 585 454-5530
Rochester *(G-14557)*
Nitro Manufacturing LLC.........G....... 716 646-9900
North Collins *(G-12945)*
North-East Machine Inc.........G....... 518 746-1837
Hudson Falls *(G-6679)*
Northeast Hardware Specialties.........F....... 516 487-6868
Mineola *(G-8561)*
Northern Machining Inc.........F....... 315 384-3189
Norfolk *(G-12917)*
Northern Tier Cnc Inc.........G....... 518 236-4702
Mooers Forks *(G-8655)*
O & S Machine & Tool Co Inc.........G....... 716 941-5542
Colden *(G-3797)*
Olmstead Machine Inc.........F....... 315 587-9864
North Rose *(G-12954)*
Optics Technology Inc.........G....... 585 586-0950
Pittsford *(G-13599)*
Orchard Hill Mch & Tl Co Inc.........G....... 315 245-0015
Blossvale *(G-992)*
▲ **P & F Industries of NY Corp**.........G....... 718 894-3501
Maspeth *(G-8193)*
P T E Inc.........F....... 516 775-3839
Floral Park *(G-5213)*
◆ **Pall Corporation**.........A....... 516 484-5400
Port Washington *(G-13870)*
Pall Corporation.........A....... 607 753-6041
Cortland *(G-4059)*
Parker Machine Company Inc.........F....... 518 747-0675
Fort Edward *(G-5352)*
Peko Precision Products Inc.........F....... 585 301-1386
Rochester *(G-14594)*
Pems Tool & Machine Inc.........E....... 315 823-3595
Little Falls *(G-7523)*
Performance Mfg Inc.........F....... 716 735-3500
Middleport *(G-8456)*
Pervi Precision Company Inc.........G....... 631 589-5557
Bohemia *(G-1113)*
Phoenix Mch Pdts of Hauppauge.........G....... 631 234-0100
Hauppauge *(G-6189)*
Pol-Tek Industries Ltd.........F....... 716 823-1502
Buffalo *(G-3154)*
Port Everglades Machine Works.........F....... 516 367-2280
Plainview *(G-13658)*
Port Jervis Machine Corp.........G....... 845 856-6210
Port Jervis *(G-13814)*
▼ **Posimech Inc**.........E....... 631 924-5959
Medford *(G-8292)*
Ppi Corp.........E....... 585 880-7277
Rochester *(G-14611)*
Pre-Tech Plastics Inc.........E....... 518 942-5950
Mineville *(G-8574)*
Precision Arms Inc.........G....... 845 225-1130
Carmel *(G-3432)*
Precision Disc Grinding Corp.........F....... 516 747-5450
Mineola *(G-8564)*
Precision Metals Corp.........E....... 631 586-5032
Bay Shore *(G-723)*
Precision Systems Mfg Inc.........E....... 315 451-3480
Liverpool *(G-7570)*
Precision Tool and Mfg.........E....... 518 678-3130
Palenville *(G-13424)*
Precisionmatics Co Inc.........E....... 315 822-6324
West Winfield *(G-16987)*
Premier Machining Tech Inc.........G....... 716 608-1311
Buffalo *(G-3160)*
Production Milling Company.........G....... 914 666-0792
Bedford Hills *(G-802)*
Progressive Mch & Design LLC.........C....... 585 924-5250
Victor *(G-16521)*
Progressive Tool Company Inc.........E....... 607 748-8294
Endwell *(G-4844)*
Pronto Tool & Die Co Inc.........E....... 631 981-8920
Ronkonkoma *(G-14997)*
Proto Machine Inc.........F....... 631 392-1159
Bay Shore *(G-725)*
Prz Technologies Inc.........F....... 716 683-1300
Lancaster *(G-7360)*
Qta Machining Inc.........F....... 716 862-8108
Buffalo *(G-3171)*
Qualified Manufacturing Corp.........F....... 631 249-4440
Farmingdale *(G-5102)*
Quality Machining Service Inc.........G....... 315 736-5774
New York Mills *(G-12746)*
Qualtech Tool & Machine Inc.........F....... 585 223-9227
Fairport *(G-4880)*
R & S Machine Center Inc.........F....... 518 563-4016
Plattsburgh *(G-13720)*
R E F Precision Products.........F....... 631 242-4471
Deer Park *(G-4221)*
Rand Machine Products Inc.........D....... 716 665-5217
Falconer *(G-4916)*

S
I
C

Employee Codes: A=Over 500 employees, B=251-500
C=101-250, D=51-100, E=20-50, F=10-19, G=5-9
2018 Harris
New York Manufacturers Directory
835

35 INDUSTRIAL AND COMMERCIAL MACHINERY AND COMPUTER EQUIPMENT

▼ Redding-Hunter Inc .... E 607 753-3331
Cortland *(G-4066)*
Reliance Machining Inc .... E 718 784-0314
Long Island City *(G-7890)*
Ren Tool & Manufacturing Co .... F 518 377-2123
Schenectady *(G-15314)*
RGH Associates Inc .... F 631 643-1111
West Babylon *(G-16852)*
▲ Richard Manno & Company Inc .... D 631 643-2200
West Babylon *(G-16853)*
Richards Machine Tool Co Inc .... E 716 683-3380
Lancaster *(G-7363)*
Rick-Mic Industries Inc .... G 631 563-8389
Ronkonkoma *(G-15003)*
Rinaldi Precision Machine .... F 631 242-4141
Bay Shore *(G-730)*
Ripley Machine & Tool Co Inc .... F 716 736-3205
Ripley *(G-14148)*
Riverside Machinery Company .... G 718 492-7400
Brooklyn *(G-2518)*
Rjs Machine Works Inc .... G 716 826-1778
Lackawanna *(G-7274)*
Rmw Filtration Products Co LLC .... G 631 226-9412
Copiague *(G-3947)*
Roboshop Inc .... G 315 437-6454
Syracuse *(G-16046)*
Roccera LLC .... F 585 426-0887
Rochester *(G-14654)*
Rochester Atomated Systems Inc .... E 585 594-3222
Rochester *(G-14657)*
Rochester Tool and Mold Inc .... F 585 464-9336
Rochester *(G-14675)*
Roger Latari .... G 631 580-2422
Ronkonkoma *(G-15004)*
Rona Precision Inc .... G 631 737-4034
Ronkonkoma *(G-15005)*
Rossi Tool & Dies Inc .... G 845 267-8246
Valley Cottage *(G-16413)*
Rozal Industries Inc .... E 631 420-4277
Farmingdale *(G-5114)*
Rt Machined Specialties .... G 716 731-2055
Niagara Falls *(G-12886)*
RTD Manufacturing Inc .... G 315 337-3151
Rome *(G-14863)*
Ruga Grinding & Mfg Corp .... G 631 924-5067
Yaphank *(G-17415)*
S & B Machine Works Inc .... E 516 997-2666
Westbury *(G-17053)*
S & H Machine Company Inc .... G 716 834-1194
Buffalo *(G-3199)*
S R & R Industries Inc .... G 845 692-8329
Middletown *(G-8496)*
Sal MA Instrument Corp .... G 631 242-2227
West Islip *(G-16935)*
Saturn Industries Inc .... E 518 828-9956
Hudson *(G-6663)*
Schwabel Fabricating Co Inc .... E 716 876-2086
Tonawanda *(G-16219)*
▲ Scientific Tool Co Inc .... F 315 431-4243
Syracuse *(G-16057)*
SDJ Machine Shop Inc .... F 585 458-1236
Rochester *(G-14698)*
Seanair Machine Co Inc .... F 631 694-2820
Farmingdale *(G-5118)*
Secondary Services Inc .... F 716 896-4000
Buffalo *(G-3210)*
Seeley Machine Inc .... E 518 798-9510
Queensbury *(G-14024)*
Semi-Linear Inc .... G 212 243-2108
New York *(G-12045)*
▲ Service Machine & Tool Company ..... E 607 732-0413
Elmira Heights *(G-4725)*
Shar-Mar Machine Company .... G 631 567-8040
Bohemia *(G-1129)*
Sick Inc .... E 585 347-2000
Webster *(G-16761)*
Sigma Manufacturing Inds Inc .... F 718 842-9180
Bronx *(G-1452)*
Sigmamotor Inc .... E 716 735-3115
Middleport *(G-8457)*
Smidgens Inc .... G 585 624-1486
Lima *(G-7470)*
Smith Metal Works Newark Inc .... E 315 331-1651
Newark *(G-12763)*
Smith Tool & Die Inc .... G 607 674-4165
Sherburne *(G-15418)*
Smithers Tools & Mch Pdts Inc .... D 845 876-3063
Rhinebeck *(G-14070)*
Snyder Industries Inc .... D 716 694-1240
Tonawanda *(G-16222)*

Solmac Inc .... G 716 630-7061
Williamsville *(G-17279)*
▲ Sotek Inc .... D 716 821-5961
Blasdell *(G-960)*
Source Technologies .... F 718 708-0305
Brooklyn *(G-2610)*
Spartan Precision Machining .... E 516 546-5171
West Babylon *(G-16862)*
Springville Mfg Co Inc .... E 716 592-4957
Springville *(G-15636)*
Stanfordville Mch & Mfg Co Inc .... D 845 868-2266
Poughkeepsie *(G-13951)*
Staub Machine Company Inc .... E 716 649-4211
Hamburg *(G-5967)*
Stony Manufacturing Inc .... G 716 652-6730
Elma *(G-4670)*
▲ Strecks Inc .... E 518 273-4410
Watervliet *(G-16714)*
Strong Forge & Fabrication .... E 585 343-5251
Batavia *(G-648)*
Summit Instrument Corp .... G 516 433-0140
Hicksville *(G-6423)*
▲ Superior Technology Inc .... F 585 352-6556
Rochester *(G-14731)*
Superior Welding .... G 631 676-2751
Holbrook *(G-6503)*
▲ Supply Technologies (ny) .... F 212 966-3310
Albany *(G-139)*
Swissway Inc .... G 631 351-5350
Huntington Station *(G-6762)*
▲ Sylhan LLC .... E 631 243-6600
Edgewood *(G-4628)*
Syntec Technologies Inc .... F 585 464-9336
Rochester *(G-14737)*
T M Machine Inc .... G 716 822-0817
Buffalo *(G-3233)*
T R P Machine Inc .... F 631 567-9620
Bohemia *(G-1138)*
Tangent Machine & Tool Corp .... F 631 249-3088
Farmingdale *(G-5134)*
Tarsia Technical Industries .... E 631 231-8322
Hauppauge *(G-6230)*
Taylor Precision Machining .... F 607 535-3101
Montour Falls *(G-8651)*
Tchnologies N MRC Ameerica LLC ...... G 716 822-4300
Buffalo *(G-3235)*
Ted Westbrook .... G 716 625-4443
Lockport *(G-7649)*
Temrick Inc .... F 631 567-8860
Bohemia *(G-1139)*
Tennyson Machine Co Inc .... G 914 668-5468
Mount Vernon *(G-8783)*
Theodosiou Inc .... F 718 728-6800
Long Island City *(G-7927)*
TI Group Auto Systems LLC .... G 315 568-7042
Seneca Falls *(G-15394)*
Ticonderoga Mch & Wldg Corp .... G 518 585-7444
Ticonderoga *(G-16151)*
Tioga Tool Inc .... F 607 785-6005
Endicott *(G-4835)*
Tobeyco Manufacturing Co Inc .... F 607 962-2446
Corning *(G-4004)*
▲ Toolroom Express Inc .... D 607 723-5373
Conklin *(G-3902)*
Towpath Machine Corp .... G 315 252-0112
Auburn *(G-521)*
Trebor Instrument Corp .... G 631 423-7026
Dix Hills *(G-4322)*
Triangle Grinding Machine Corp .... G 631 643-3636
West Babylon *(G-16868)*
Tricon Machine LLC .... G 585 671-0679
Webster *(G-16763)*
Tripar Manufacturing Co Inc .... G 631 563-0855
Bohemia *(G-1145)*
Triple Point Manufacturing .... E 631 218-4988
Bohemia *(G-1146)*
Triplett Machine Inc .... D 315 548-3198
Phelps *(G-13561)*
Triplex Industries Inc .... F 585 621-6920
Rochester *(G-14759)*
Truarc Fabrication .... G 518 691-0430
Gansevoort *(G-5505)*
▲ Twinco Mfg Co Inc .... E 631 231-0022
Hauppauge *(G-6243)*
Two Bills Machine & Tool Co .... F 516 437-2585
Floral Park *(G-5214)*
U-Cut Enterprises Inc .... G 315 492-9316
Jamesville *(G-7086)*
Ultra Tool and Manufacturing .... F 585 467-3700
Rochester *(G-14766)*

United Machining Inc .... G 631 589-6751
Bohemia *(G-1149)*
Universal Metal Fabricators .... F 845 331-8248
Kingston *(G-7248)*
▲ Upturn Industries Inc .... E 607 967-2923
Bainbridge *(G-555)*
Ushers Machine and Tool Co Inc .... F 518 877-5501
Round Lake *(G-15062)*
V A P Tool & Dye .... G 631 587-5262
West Islip *(G-16938)*
V Lake Industries Inc .... G 716 885-9141
Buffalo *(G-3265)*
Vader Systems LLC .... F 716 688-1600
Getzville *(G-5618)*
Valair Inc .... E 716 751-9480
Wilson *(G-17292)*
Van Laeken Richard .... E 315 331-0289
Newark *(G-12768)*
Van Reenen Tool & Die Inc .... F 585 288-6000
Rochester *(G-14779)*
▲ Van Thomas Inc .... E 585 426-1414
Rochester *(G-14780)*
Vanguard Metals Inc .... F 631 234-6500
Central Islip *(G-3541)*
Verns Machine Co Inc .... E 315 926-4223
Marion *(G-8133)*
Victoria Precision Inc .... G 845 473-9309
Hyde Park *(G-6777)*
Village Decoration Ltd .... E 315 437-2522
East Syracuse *(G-4591)*
Visimetrics Corporation .... G 716 871-7070
Buffalo *(G-3270)*
Vosky Precision Machining Corp .... F 631 737-3200
Ronkonkoma *(G-15024)*
◆ Voss Manufacturing Inc .... D 716 731-5062
Sanborn *(G-15158)*
Vytek Inc .... F 631 750-1770
Bohemia *(G-1152)*
W H Jones & Son Inc .... F 716 875-8233
Kenmore *(G-7180)*
W J Albro Machine Works Inc .... G 631 345-0657
Yaphank *(G-17424)*
Walsh & Sons Machine Inc .... G 845 526-0301
Mahopac *(G-8035)*
Washburn Manufacturing Tech .... G 607 387-3991
Trumansburg *(G-16292)*
Watkins Welding and Mch Sp Inc .... G 914 949-6168
White Plains *(G-17209)*
Wayne Integrated Tech Corp .... E 631 242-0213
Edgewood *(G-4633)*
Waynes Welding Inc .... E 315 768-6146
Yorkville *(G-17547)*
Weaver Machine & Tool Co Inc .... F 315 253-4422
Auburn *(G-526)*
Weiss Industries Inc .... E 518 784-9643
Valatie *(G-16390)*
◆ Wendt Corporation .... D 716 391-1200
Buffalo *(G-3277)*
West Falls Machine Co Inc .... F 716 655-0440
East Aurora *(G-4404)*
▲ Westchstr Crnkshft Grndng .... G 718 651-3900
East Elmhurst *(G-4419)*
Wiggby Precision Machine Corp .... E 718 439-6900
Brooklyn *(G-2766)*
Willard Machine .... F 716 885-1630
Buffalo *(G-3281)*
William Kanes Mfg Corp .... G 718 346-1515
Brooklyn *(G-2770)*
William Moon Iron Works Inc .... F 518 943-3861
Catskill *(G-3462)*
Williams Tool Inc .... E 315 737-7226
Chadwicks *(G-3559)*
Winn Manufacturing Inc .... E 518 642-3515
Granville *(G-5797)*
Woods Machine and Tool LLC .... F 607 699-3253
Nichols *(G-12909)*
Wordingham Machine Co Inc .... E 585 924-2294
Rochester *(G-14794)*
Wrightcut EDM & Machine Inc .... G 607 733-5018
Elmira *(G-4719)*
Zip Products Inc .... F 585 482-0044
Rochester *(G-14805)*

36 ELECTRONIC AND OTHER ELECTRICAL EQUIPMENT AND COMPONENTS, EXCEPT COMPUTER

3612 Power, Distribution & Specialty Transformers

Allanson Inc..........G....... 631 293-3880
Farmingdale *(G-4944)*
Arstan Products International..........F....... 516 433-1313
Hicksville *(G-6348)*
Berkshire Transformer..........G....... 631 467-5328
Central Islip *(G-3512)*
Buffalo Power Elec Ctr De..........E....... 716 651-1600
Depew *(G-4275)*
Caddell Burns Manufacturing Co..........E....... 631 757-1772
Northport *(G-13026)*
Cooper Power Systems LLC..........B....... 716 375-7100
Olean *(G-13160)*
Current Controls Inc..........C....... 585 593-1544
Wellsville *(G-16776)*
Dyco Electronics Inc..........D....... 607 324-2030
Hornell *(G-6588)*
Electron Coil Inc..........D....... 607 336-7414
Norwich *(G-13046)*
Ems Development Corporation..........D....... 631 345-6200
Yaphank *(G-17407)*
Exxelia-Raf Tabtronics LLC..........E....... 585 243-4331
Piffard *(G-13574)*
Frederick Cowan & Company Inc..........F....... 631 369-0360
Riverhead *(G-14155)*
General Electric Company..........A....... 518 385-4022
Schenectady *(G-15283)*
General Electric Company..........E....... 518 385-7620
Niskayuna *(G-12912)*
Hale Electrical Dist Svcs Inc..........G....... 716 818-7595
Wales Center *(G-16560)*
K Road Power Management LLC..........F....... 212 351-0535
New York *(G-10832)*
Kepco Inc..........E....... 718 461-7000
Flushing *(G-5266)*
Kepco Inc..........D....... 718 461-7000
Flushing *(G-5267)*
Kepco Inc..........E....... 718 461-7000
Flushing *(G-5268)*
Marvel Equipment Corp Inc..........G....... 718 383-6597
Brooklyn *(G-2280)*
Mitchell Electronics Corp..........E....... 914 699-3800
Mount Vernon *(G-8753)*
▲ **Niagara Transformer Corp**..........D....... 716 896-6500
Buffalo *(G-3113)*
▲ **Piller Power Systems Inc**..........E....... 845 695-6658
Middletown *(G-8491)*
Precision Electronics Inc..........F....... 631 842-4900
Copiague *(G-3943)*
Ram Transformer Technologies..........F....... 914 632-3988
New Rochelle *(G-8967)*
Reenergy Black River LLC..........E....... 315 773-2314
Fort Drum *(G-5346)*
Sag Harbor Industries Inc..........E....... 631 725-0440
Sag Harbor *(G-15107)*
Schneider Electric It Corp..........F....... 646 335-0216
New York *(G-12011)*
Schneider Electric Usa Inc..........F....... 585 377-1313
Penfield *(G-13527)*
Siemens Corporation..........F....... 202 434-7800
New York *(G-12084)*
Siemens USA Holdings Inc..........B....... 212 258-4000
New York *(G-12086)*
▲ **Spellman High Vltage Elec Corp**..........B....... 631 630-3000
Hauppauge *(G-6222)*
▲ **Spence Engineering Company Inc**..........C....... 845 778-5566
Walden *(G-16556)*
Sunward Electronics Inc..........F....... 518 687-0030
Troy *(G-16281)*
▲ **Switching Power Inc**..........D....... 631 981-7231
Ronkonkoma *(G-15013)*
Telephone Sales & Service Co..........E....... 212 233-8505
New York *(G-12318)*
Transistor Devices Inc..........E....... 631 471-7492
Ronkonkoma *(G-15015)*
Veeco Instruments Inc..........C....... 516 349-8300
Plainview *(G-13670)*

3613 Switchgear & Switchboard Apparatus

▲ **Abasco Inc**..........E....... 716 649-4790
Hamburg *(G-5941)*
All City Switchboard Corp..........E....... 718 956-7244
Long Island City *(G-7684)*
Allied Circuits LLC..........E....... 716 551-0285
Buffalo *(G-2820)*
Atlas Switch Co Inc..........E....... 516 222-6280
Garden City *(G-5509)*
Avanti Control Systems Inc..........G....... 518 921-4368
Gloversville *(G-5722)*
Benfield Control Systems Inc..........F....... 914 948-6660
White Plains *(G-17112)*
Boulay Fabrication Inc..........F....... 315 677-5247
La Fayette *(G-7266)*
C A M Graphics Co Inc..........E....... 631 842-3400
Farmingdale *(G-4964)*
Claddagh Electronics Ltd..........E....... 718 784-0571
Long Island City *(G-7728)*
Cooper Industries LLC..........E....... 315 477-7000
Syracuse *(G-15928)*
Cooper Power Systems LLC..........B....... 716 375-7100
Olean *(G-13160)*
Custom Controls..........G....... 315 253-4785
Scipio Center *(G-15343)*
Electric Swtchbard Sltions LLC..........G....... 718 643-1105
New Hyde Park *(G-8875)*
Electrotech Service Eqp Corp..........E....... 718 626-7700
Astoria *(G-437)*
▲ **Ems Development Corporation**..........D....... 631 924-4736
Yaphank *(G-17406)*
Inertia Switch Inc..........E....... 845 359-8300
Orangeburg *(G-13251)*
Junior Achievement of Eastrn NY..........G....... 518 783-4336
Latham *(G-7393)*
◆ **Leviton Manufacturing Co Inc**..........B....... 631 812-6000
Melville *(G-8363)*
Link Control Systems Inc..........F....... 631 471-3950
Ronkonkoma *(G-14960)*
▲ **Marquardt Switches Inc**..........C....... 315 655-8050
Cazenovia *(G-3475)*
Micro Instrument Corp..........D....... 585 458-3150
Rochester *(G-14528)*
Odyssey Controls Inc..........G....... 585 548-9800
Bergen *(G-850)*
Pacs Switchgear LLC..........G....... 516 465-7100
Bethpage *(G-876)*
Product Station Inc..........F....... 516 942-4220
Jericho *(G-7114)*
Real Industry Inc..........F....... 805 435-1255
New York *(G-11842)*
Schneider Electric Usa Inc..........C....... 646 335-0220
New York *(G-12012)*
▲ **Se-Mar Electric Co Inc**..........E....... 716 674-7404
West Seneca *(G-16982)*
Select Controls Inc..........E....... 631 567-9010
Bohemia *(G-1127)*
Sinclair Technologies Inc..........E....... 716 874-3682
Hamburg *(G-5966)*
Smith Control Systems Inc..........F....... 518 828-7646
Hudson *(G-6666)*
Soc America Inc..........F....... 631 472-6666
Ronkonkoma *(G-15010)*
▲ **Switching Power Inc**..........D....... 631 981-7231
Ronkonkoma *(G-15013)*
Trac Regulators Inc..........E....... 914 699-9352
Mount Vernon *(G-8785)*
▲ **Transit Air Inc**..........E....... 607 324-0216
Hornell *(G-6595)*

3621 Motors & Generators

▲ **Aeroflex Incorporated**..........B....... 516 694-6700
Plainview *(G-13608)*
Aeroflex Plainview Inc..........B....... 516 694-6700
Plainview *(G-13609)*
Aeroflex Plainview Inc..........C....... 631 231-9100
Hauppauge *(G-6030)*
▲ **Allied Motion Technologies Inc**..........C....... 716 242-8634
Amherst *(G-224)*
Allied Motion Technologies Inc..........C....... 315 782-5910
Watertown *(G-16656)*
◆ **American Precision Inds Inc**..........C....... 716 691-9100
Amherst *(G-227)*
Ametek Inc..........G....... 631 467-8400
Ronkonkoma *(G-14896)*
Ametek Inc..........D....... 607 763-4700
Binghamton *(G-885)*
Ametek Inc..........D....... 585 263-7700
Rochester *(G-14218)*
Apogee Power Usa Inc..........F....... 202 746-2890
Hartsdale *(G-6016)*
▲ **Applied Power Systems Inc**..........E....... 516 935-2230
Hicksville *(G-6346)*
▲ **ARC Systems Inc**..........E....... 631 582-8020
Hauppauge *(G-6042)*
▲ **Automation Source Technologies**..........F....... 631 643-1678
West Babylon *(G-16797)*
Cellgen Inc..........G....... 516 889-9300
Freeport *(G-5403)*
Chart Inc..........F....... 518 272-3565
Troy *(G-16252)*
Chemark International USA Inc..........G....... 631 593-4566
Deer Park *(G-4140)*
Con Rel Auto Electric Inc..........E....... 518 356-1646
Schenectady *(G-15273)*
Cummins Inc..........B....... 812 377-5000
Jamestown *(G-7021)*
▲ **Current Applications Inc**..........E....... 315 788-4689
Watertown *(G-16669)*
▲ **D & D Motor Systems Inc**..........E....... 315 701-0861
Syracuse *(G-15938)*
Designatronics Incorporated..........B....... 516 328-3300
Hicksville *(G-6367)*
EDP Renewables North Amer LLC..........G....... 518 426-1650
Albany *(G-76)*
Electron Coil Inc..........D....... 607 336-7414
Norwich *(G-13046)*
Elton El Mantle Inc..........G....... 315 432-9067
Syracuse *(G-15955)*
Emes Motor Inc..........G....... 718 387-2445
Brooklyn *(G-1922)*
Empire Division Inc..........D....... 315 476-6273
Syracuse *(G-15957)*
▲ **Ems Development Corporation**..........D....... 631 924-4736
Yaphank *(G-17406)*
Ener-G Cogen LLC..........G....... 718 551-7170
New York *(G-10088)*
Ener-G-Rotors Inc..........G....... 518 372-2608
Schenectady *(G-15277)*
▲ **Eni Technology Inc**..........B....... 585 427-8300
Rochester *(G-14374)*
▲ **Faradyne Motors LLC**..........F....... 315 331-5985
Palmyra *(G-13430)*
▲ **Felchar Manufacturing Corp**..........A....... 607 723-3106
Binghamton *(G-909)*
Franklin Electric Co Inc..........A....... 718 244-7744
Jamaica *(G-6950)*
▼ **Gaffney Kroese Supply Corp**..........F....... 516 228-5091
Garden City *(G-5519)*
General Electric Company..........B....... 518 385-2211
Schenectady *(G-15287)*
Generation Power LLC..........G....... 315 234-2451
Syracuse *(G-15972)*
▲ **Getec Inc**..........F....... 845 292-0800
Ferndale *(G-5178)*
Got Power Inc..........G....... 631 767-9493
Ronkonkoma *(G-14935)*
Hes Inc..........G....... 607 359-2974
Addison *(G-7)*
▲ **IEC Holden Corporation**..........F....... 518 213-3991
Plattsburgh *(G-13696)*
Independent Field Svc LLC..........G....... 315 559-9243
Syracuse *(G-15981)*
Industrial Test Eqp Co Inc..........E....... 516 883-6423
Port Washington *(G-13846)*
Intelligen Power Systems LLC..........G....... 212 750-0373
Old Bethpage *(G-13150)*
International Control Products..........F....... 716 558-4400
West Seneca *(G-16977)*
Island Components Group Inc..........F....... 631 563-4224
Holbrook *(G-6482)*
▲ **John G Rubino Inc**..........E....... 315 253-7396
Auburn *(G-502)*
K Road Moapa Solar LLC..........F....... 212 351-0535
New York *(G-10831)*
Kaddis Manufacturing Corp..........G....... 585 624-3070
Honeoye Falls *(G-6561)*
Lcdrives Corp..........F....... 860 712-8926
Potsdam *(G-13897)*
Magna Products Corp..........E....... 585 647-2280
Rochester *(G-14510)*
▲ **Makerbot Industries LLC**..........C....... 347 334-6800
Brooklyn *(G-2257)*
▲ **Matrix Railway Corp**..........G....... 631 643-1483
West Babylon *(G-16840)*
Mks Medical Electronics..........C....... 585 292-7400
Rochester *(G-14538)*
▲ **Modular Devices Inc**..........D....... 631 345-3100
Shirley *(G-15449)*
▲ **Moley Magnetics Inc**..........G....... 716 434-4023
Lockport *(G-7633)*
Nidec Motor Corporation..........F....... 315 434-9303
East Syracuse *(G-4567)*

▲ Power and Composite Tech LLC ....D 518 843-6825
Amsterdam *(G-366)*

Power Gneration Indus Engs Inc ....F 315 633-9389
Bridgeport *(G-1234)*

Powercomplete LLC ....G 212 228-4129
New York *(G-11714)*

Premco Inc ....F 914 636-7095
New Rochelle *(G-8966)*

Princetel Inc ....F 914 579-2410
Hawthorne *(G-6277)*

Protective Power Systms & Cntr ....F 845 773-9016
Poughkeepsie *(G-13944)*

R M S Motor Corporation ....F 607 723-2323
Binghamton *(G-939)*

Ruhle Companies Inc ....E 914 287-4000
Valhalla *(G-16398)*

Sag Harbor Industries Inc ....E 631 725-0440
Sag Harbor *(G-15107)*

▲ Sima Technologies LLC ....G 412 828-9130
Hauppauge *(G-6215)*

▲ Sopark Corp ....C 716 822-0434
Buffalo *(G-3219)*

▲ Stature Electric Inc ....B 315 782-5910
Watertown *(G-16695)*

Supergen Products LLC ....G 315 573-7887
Newark *(G-12765)*

▲ Taro Manufacturing Company Inc ....F 315 252-9430
Auburn *(G-520)*

Troy Belting and Supply Co ....D 518 272-4920
Watervliet *(G-16715)*

▲ Vdc Electronics Inc ....F 631 683-5850
Huntington *(G-6728)*

W J Albro Machine Works Inc ....G 631 345-0657
Yaphank *(G-17424)*

▲ Wind Solutions LLC ....G 518 813-8029
Esperance *(G-4847)*

3624 Carbon & Graphite Prdts

▲ Carbon Graphite Materials Inc ....G 716 792-7979
Brocton *(G-1248)*

Carbonfree Chemicals Spe I LLC ....E 914 421-4900
White Plains *(G-17120)*

▲ Ceramaterials LLC ....G 518 701-6722
Port Jervis *(G-13803)*

Go Blue Technologies Ltd ....G 631 404-6285
North Babylon *(G-12918)*

◆ Graphite Metallizing Corp ....D 914 968-8400
Yonkers *(G-17466)*

Hh Liquidating Corp ....A 646 282-2500
New York *(G-10515)*

J V Precision Inc ....G 518 851-3200
Hudson *(G-6649)*

▲ Kureha Advanced Materials Inc ....F 724 295-3352
New York *(G-10933)*

▲ Lifestyle Design Usa Ltd ....G 212 279-9400
New York *(G-11021)*

Metal Coated Fibers Inc ....E 518 280-8514
Schenectady *(G-15304)*

Metallized Carbon Corporation ....C 914 941-3738
Ossining *(G-13347)*

▲ Mwi Inc ....D 585 424-4200
Rochester *(G-14546)*

Pyrotek Incorporated ....E 716 731-3221
Sanborn *(G-15153)*

Saturn Industries Inc ....E 518 828-9956
Hudson *(G-6663)*

3625 Relays & Indl Controls

Addex Inc ....G 315 331-7700
Newark *(G-12748)*

Adeptronics Incorporated ....G 631 667-0659
Bay Shore *(G-665)*

Afi Cybernetics Corporation ....E 607 732-3244
Elmira *(G-4682)*

Air Crafters Inc ....C 631 471-7788
Ronkonkoma *(G-14883)*

◆ Altronix Corp ....D 718 567-8181
Brooklyn *(G-1593)*

◆ American Precision Inds Inc ....C 716 691-9100
Amherst *(G-227)*

▲ Anderson Instrument Co Inc ....D 518 922-5315
Fultonville *(G-5491)*

Bakery Innovative Tech Corp ....F 631 758-3081
Patchogue *(G-13440)*

Bemco of Western Ny Inc ....G 716 823-8400
Buffalo *(G-2860)*

Bomac Inc ....F 315 433-9181
Syracuse *(G-15892)*

▲ Burgess-Manning Inc ....D 716 662-6540
Orchard Park *(G-13280)*

▲ C D A Inc ....G 631 473-1595
Nesconset *(G-8821)*

Calia Technical Inc ....G 718 447-3928
Staten Island *(G-15675)*

Con Rel Auto Electric Inc ....E 518 356-1646
Schenectady *(G-15273)*

◆ Conic Systems Inc ....F 845 856-4053
Port Jervis *(G-13804)*

Continental Instruments LLC ....E 631 842-9400
Amityville *(G-280)*

▲ Cox & Company Inc ....C 212 366-0200
Plainview *(G-13623)*

Datatran Labs Inc ....G 845 856-4313
Port Jervis *(G-13805)*

Designatronics Incorporated ....B 516 328-3300
Hicksville *(G-6367)*

▲ Designatronics Incorporated ....G 516 328-3300
Hicksville *(G-6366)*

Deutsch Relays ....F 631 342-1700
Hauppauge *(G-6084)*

▲ Digital Instruments Inc ....F 716 874-5848
Tonawanda *(G-16176)*

Dortronics Systems Inc ....E 631 725-0505
Sag Harbor *(G-15105)*

▲ Dri Relays Inc ....D 631 342-1700
Hauppauge *(G-6089)*

◆ Dyson-Kissner-Moran Corp ....E 212 661-4600
Poughkeepsie *(G-13915)*

Eaton Corporation ....C 212 319-2100
New York *(G-10021)*

Eaton Corporation ....C 585 394-1780
Canandaigua *(G-3373)*

Eaton Corporation ....C 516 353-3017
East Meadow *(G-4443)*

Eaton Corporation ....G 716 691-0008
Buffalo *(G-2944)*

Eaton Hydraulics LLC ....G 716 375-7132
Olean *(G-13168)*

Eatons Crouse Hinds Business ....F 315 477-7000
Syracuse *(G-15953)*

Edo LLC ....C 631 630-4000
Amityville *(G-286)*

Electro-Kinetics Inc ....F 845 887-4930
Callicoon *(G-3313)*

Electronic Machine Parts LLC ....F 631 434-3700
Hauppauge *(G-6093)*

▲ Elevator Systems Inc ....E 516 239-4044
Garden City *(G-5515)*

Enetics Inc ....G 585 924-5010
Victor *(G-16499)*

Entertron Industries Inc ....E 716 772-7216
Lockport *(G-7613)*

▲ Eversan Inc ....F 315 736-3967
Whitesboro *(G-17221)*

Exfo Burleigh Pdts Group Inc ....D 585 301-1530
Canandaigua *(G-3374)*

Fics Inc ....E 607 359-4474
Addison *(G-6)*

▲ Fortitude Industries ....D 607 324-1500
Hornell *(G-6589)*

G C Controls Inc ....E 607 656-4117
Greene *(G-5883)*

Gemtrol Inc ....G 716 894-0716
Buffalo *(G-2983)*

General Control Systems Inc ....E 518 270-8045
Green Island *(G-5873)*

General Oil Equipment Co Inc ....E 716 691-7012
Amherst *(G-242)*

Goddard Design Co ....G 718 599-0170
Brooklyn *(G-2035)*

▲ Hasco Componets ....E 516 328-9292
New Hyde Park *(G-8885)*

▲ I D E Processes Corporation ....F 718 544-1177
Kew Gardens *(G-7190)*

I E D Corp ....F 631 348-0424
Islandia *(G-6832)*

▲ ICM Controls Corp ....F 315 233-5266
North Syracuse *(G-12964)*

Industrial Indxing Systems Inc ....E 585 924-9181
Victor *(G-16506)*

Inertia Switch Inc ....E 845 359-8300
Orangeburg *(G-13251)*

▲ Infitec Inc ....D 315 433-1150
East Syracuse *(G-4557)*

▲ Interntnal Cntrls Msrmnts Corp ....C 315 233-5266
North Syracuse *(G-12965)*

ITT Aerospace Controls LLC ....G 914 641-2000
White Plains *(G-17151)*

ITT Corporation ....E 585 269-7109
Hemlock *(G-6287)*

ITT Corporation ....D 315 568-2811
Seneca Falls *(G-15383)*

ITT Inc ....F 914 641-2000
White Plains *(G-17152)*

ITT LLC ....D 315 258-4904
Auburn *(G-500)*

ITT LLC ....D 914 641-2000
Seneca Falls *(G-15387)*

◆ ITT LLC ....B 914 641-2000
White Plains *(G-17154)*

JE Miller Inc ....F 315 437-6811
East Syracuse *(G-4560)*

Kaman Automation Inc ....D 585 254-8840
Rochester *(G-14490)*

◆ Kearney-National Inc ....F 212 661-4600
New York *(G-10868)*

◆ Kussmaul Electronics Co Inc ....E 631 218-0298
West Sayville *(G-16965)*

L-3 Cmmnctons Ntronix Holdings ....D 212 697-1111
New York *(G-10942)*

Linde LLC ....D 716 773-7552
Grand Island *(G-5776)*

Logitek Inc ....D 631 567-1100
Bohemia *(G-1089)*

Machine Components Corp ....E 516 694-7222
Plainview *(G-13644)*

Magnus Precision Mfg Inc ....D 315 548-8032
Phelps *(G-13557)*

◆ Magtrol Inc ....E 716 668-5555
Buffalo *(G-3075)*

▲ Makerbot Industries LLC ....C 347 334-6800
Brooklyn *(G-2257)*

▲ Marine & Indus Hydraulics Inc ....F 914 698-2036
Mamaroneck *(G-8070)*

▲ Marquardt Switches Inc ....C 315 655-8050
Cazenovia *(G-3475)*

◆ Mason Industries Inc ....B 631 348-0282
Hauppauge *(G-6152)*

Mason Industries Inc ....G 631 348-0282
Hauppauge *(G-6153)*

Micromod Automation Inc ....E 585 321-9200
Rochester *(G-14531)*

▼ Micropen Technologies Corp ....D 585 624-2610
Honeoye Falls *(G-6562)*

Moog Inc ....C 716 805-8100
East Aurora *(G-4401)*

◆ Moog Inc ....A 716 652-2000
Elma *(G-4664)*

▲ Morris Products Inc ....F 518 743-0523
Queensbury *(G-14018)*

N E Controls LLC ....F 315 626-2480
Syracuse *(G-16016)*

▲ Nas-Tra Automotive Inds Inc ....C 631 225-1225
Lindenhurst *(G-7497)*

National Time Recording Eqp Co ....F 212 227-3310
New York *(G-11375)*

Nitram Energy Inc ....E 716 662-6540
Orchard Park *(G-13310)*

North Point Technologies ....E 607 238-1114
Johnson City *(G-7130)*

North Point Technology LLC ....F 866 885-3377
Endicott *(G-4828)*

Nsi Industries LLC ....C 800 841-2505
Mount Vernon *(G-8757)*

▲ Omntec Mfg Inc ....E 631 981-2001
Ronkonkoma *(G-14985)*

Panelogic Inc ....E 607 962-6319
Corning *(G-3998)*

Peerless Instrument Co Inc ....C 631 396-6500
Farmingdale *(G-5086)*

Peraton Inc ....E 315 838-7000
Rome *(G-14857)*

Powr-UPS Corp ....E 631 345-5700
Shirley *(G-15451)*

Precision Electronics Inc ....F 631 842-4900
Copiague *(G-3943)*

Precision Mechanisms Corp ....E 516 333-5955
Westbury *(G-17049)*

◆ Pulsafeeder Inc ....C 585 292-8000
Rochester *(G-14632)*

Rasp Incorporated ....E 518 747-8020
Gansevoort *(G-5502)*

▲ Rochester Industrial Ctrl Inc ....D 315 524-4555
Ontario *(G-13234)*

Rockwell Automation Inc ....E 585 487-2700
Pittsford *(G-13602)*

Rotork Controls Inc ....F 585 328-1550
Rochester *(G-14680)*

▲ Rotork Controls Inc ....C 585 328-1550
Rochester *(G-14681)*

36 ELECTRONIC AND OTHER ELECTRICAL EQUIPMENT AND COMPONENTS, EXCEPT COMPUTER

Ruhle Companies Inc ....E 914 287-4000
  Valhalla *(G-16398)*
◆ Schmersal Inc ....E 914 347-4775
  Hawthorne *(G-6279)*
Select Controls Inc ....E 631 567-9010
  Bohemia *(G-1127)*
Sequential Electronics Systems ....E 914 592-1345
  Elmsford *(G-4791)*
Service Mfg Group Inc ....F 716 893-1482
  Buffalo *(G-3212)*
▲ Soft-Noze Usa Inc ....G 315 732-2726
  Frankfort *(G-5367)*
◆ Soundcoat Company Inc ....D 631 242-2200
  Deer Park *(G-4236)*
Ssac Inc 800 843-8848
  Baldwinsville *(G-576)*
▲ Stetron International Inc ....F 716 854-3443
  Buffalo *(G-3225)*
Switches and Sensors Inc ....F 631 924-2167
  Yaphank *(G-17420)*
Teale Machine Company Inc ....D 585 244-6700
  Rochester *(G-14744)*
Techniflo Corporation ....G 716 741-3500
  Clarence Center *(G-3706)*
▲ Teknic Inc ....G 585 784-7454
  Victor *(G-16530)*
▲ Tork Inc ....D 914 664-3542
  Mount Vernon *(G-8784)*
Transistor Devices Inc ....E 631 471-7492
  Ronkonkoma *(G-15015)*
Trident Valve Actuator Co ....F 914 698-2650
  Mamaroneck *(G-8082)*
◆ Unimar Inc ....F 315 699-4400
  Syracuse *(G-16087)*
US Drives Inc ....D 716 731-1606
  Niagara Falls *(G-12904)*
Vibration & Noise Engrg Corp ....G 716 827-4959
  Orchard Park *(G-13327)*
▲ Vibration Eliminator Co Inc ....E 631 841-4000
  Copiague *(G-3959)*
Weldcomputer Corporation ....F 518 283-2897
  Troy *(G-16289)*
Young & Franklin Inc ....D 315 457-3110
  Liverpool *(G-7586)*
Zeppelin Electric Company Inc ....G 631 928-9467
  East Setauket *(G-4516)*

3629 Electrical Indl Apparatus, NEC

▲ Alliance Control Systems Inc ....G 845 279-4430
  Brewster *(G-1206)*
American Fuel Cell LLC ....G 585 474-3993
  Rochester *(G-14212)*
Applied Energy Solutions LLC ....E 585 538-3270
  Caledonia *(G-3304)*
▲ Applied Power Systems Inc ....E 516 935-2230
  Hicksville *(G-6346)*
C & M Circuits Inc ....E 631 589-0208
  Bohemia *(G-1027)*
Calibration Technologies Inc ....G 631 676-6133
  Centereach *(G-3495)*
Cellular Empire Inc ....D 800 778-3513
  Brooklyn *(G-1768)*
China Lithium Technologies ....G 212 391-2688
  New York *(G-9649)*
▲ Curtis Instruments Inc ....C 914 666-2971
  Mount Kisco *(G-8666)*
Curtis/Palmer Hydroelectric LP ....G 518 654-6297
  Corinth *(G-3979)*
Cygnus Automation Inc ....E 631 981-0909
  Bohemia *(G-1043)*
Donald R Husband Inc ....G 607 770-1990
  Johnson City *(G-7122)*
Eluminocity US Inc ....G 651 528-1165
  New York *(G-10068)*
▲ Ems Development Corporation ....D 631 924-4736
  Yaphank *(G-17406)*
Ems Technologies Inc ....E 607 723-3676
  Binghamton *(G-907)*
Endicott Research Group Inc ....D 607 754-9187
  Endicott *(G-4812)*
Energy Harvesters LLC ....G 617 325-9852
  Rochester *(G-14371)*
◆ G B International Trdg Co Ltd ....E 607 785-0938
  Endicott *(G-4817)*
General Electric Company ....E 518 459-4110
  Albany *(G-82)*
General Electric Company ....B 518 746-5750
  Hudson Falls *(G-6673)*
GM Components Holdings LLC ....B 716 439-2463
  Lockport *(G-7619)*

GM Components Holdings LLC ....B 716 439-2011
  Lockport *(G-7620)*
GW Lisk Company Inc ....E 315 548-2165
  Phelps *(G-13555)*
Key Signals ....G 631 433-2962
  East Moriches *(G-4449)*
◆ Kussmaul Electronics Co Inc ....E 631 218-0298
  West Sayville *(G-16965)*
▲ Nrd LLC ....E 716 773-7634
  Grand Island *(G-5779)*
Solid Sealing Technology Inc ....E 518 266-6019
  Watervliet *(G-16713)*
▲ Tonoga Inc ....C 518 658-3202
  Petersburg *(G-13551)*
Viking Technologies Ltd ....E 631 957-8000
  Lindenhurst *(G-7516)*
◆ Walter R Tucker Entps Ltd ....F 607 467-2866
  Deposit *(G-4305)*

3631 Household Cooking Eqpt

Applince Installation Svc Corp ....E 716 884-7425
  Buffalo *(G-2837)*
Bakers Pride Oven Co Inc ....C 914 576-0200
  New Rochelle *(G-8932)*
▲ Korin Japanese Trading Corp ....E 212 587-7021
  New York *(G-10916)*
▲ Oxo International Inc ....C 212 242-3333
  New York *(G-11557)*
◆ Toshiba America Inc ....E 212 596-0600
  New York *(G-12398)*

3632 Household Refrigerators & Freezers

Acme Kitchenettes Corp ....E 518 828-4191
  Hudson *(G-6632)*
Ae Fund Inc 315 698-7650
  Brewerton *(G-1199)*
Dover Corporation ....G 212 922-1640
  New York *(G-9963)*
◆ Felix Storch Inc ....C 718 893-3900
  Bronx *(G-1332)*
General Electric Company ....A 518 385-4022
  Schenectady *(G-15283)*
Robin Industries Ltd ....F 718 218-9616
  Brooklyn *(G-2522)*
Sure-Kol Refrigerator Co Inc ....F 718 625-0601
  Brooklyn *(G-2653)*

3633 Household Laundry Eqpt

AES Electronics Inc ....G 212 371-8120
  New York *(G-9101)*
Coinmach Service Corp ....A 516 349-8555
  Plainview *(G-13618)*
CSC Serviceworks Inc ....D 516 349-8555
  Plainview *(G-13624)*
CSC Serviceworks Holdings ....E 516 349-8555
  Plainview *(G-13625)*
Penn Enterprises Inc ....F 845 446-0765
  West Point *(G-16959)*
Pluslux LLC 516 371-4400
  Inwood *(G-6805)*
Spin Holdco Inc ....G 516 349-8555
  Plainview *(G-13662)*

3634 Electric Household Appliances

A & M LLC ....G 212 354-1341
  New York *(G-9027)*
▲ Abbott Industries Inc ....E 718 291-0800
  Jamaica *(G-6926)*
▲ Advanced Response Corporation ...G 212 459-0887
  New York *(G-9094)*
Algonquin Power ....G 315 393-5595
  Ogdensburg *(G-13131)*
American Comfort Direct LLC ....E 201 364-8309
  New York *(G-9165)*
Dampits International Inc ....G 212 581-3047
  New York *(G-9851)*
▼ Fulton Volcanic Inc ....G 315 298-5121
  Pulaski *(G-13967)*
General Electric Company ....G 315 554-2000
  Skaneateles *(G-15482)*
Goodnature Products Inc ....F 716 855-3325
  Orchard Park *(G-13296)*
▲ Harrys Inc ....D 888 212-6855
  New York *(G-10466)*
▲ Heaven Fresh USA Inc 800 642-0367
  Niagara Falls *(G-12850)*
Hrg Group Inc ....E 212 906-8555
  New York *(G-10567)*

▲ Peek A Boo USA Inc ....G 201 533-8700
  New York *(G-11612)*
▲ Quality Life Inc ....F 718 939-5787
  College Point *(G-3828)*
Quip Nyc Inc ....G 703 615-1076
  Brooklyn *(G-2486)*
Remedies Surgical Supplies ....G 718 599-5301
  Brooklyn *(G-2509)*
Schlesinger Siemans Elec LLC ....F 718 386-6230
  New York *(G-12007)*
Sundance Industries Inc ....G 845 795-5809
  Milton *(G-8519)*
▲ Tactica International Inc ....F 212 575-0500
  New York *(G-12294)*
▲ Uniware Houseware Corp ....E 631 242-7400
  Brentwood *(G-1195)*
US Health Equipment Company ....E 845 658-7576
  Kingston *(G-7249)*
Valad Electric Heating Corp ....F 888 509-4927
  Montgomery *(G-8640)*
Valid Electric Corp ....E 914 631-9436
  Montgomery *(G-8641)*
Vincent Genovese ....G 631 281-8170
  Mastic Beach *(G-8237)*
◆ World Trading Center Inc ....G 631 273-3330
  Hauppauge *(G-6260)*

3635 Household Vacuum Cleaners

American Comfort Direct LLC ....E 201 364-8309
  New York *(G-9165)*
D & C Cleaning Inc ....F 631 789-5659
  Copiague *(G-3924)*
▲ Global Resources Sg Inc ....F 212 686-1411
  New York *(G-10362)*
▲ Nationwide Sales and Service ....F 631 491-6625
  Farmingdale *(G-5071)*
Tri County Custom Vacuum ....G 845 774-7595
  Monroe *(G-8600)*

3639 Household Appliances, NEC

A Gatty Products Inc ....G 914 592-3903
  Elmsford *(G-4741)*
▼ Ajmadison Corp ....D 718 532-1800
  Brooklyn *(G-1572)*
Barrage ....E 212 586-9390
  New York *(G-9375)*
Design Solutions LI Inc ....G 631 656-8700
  Saint James *(G-15115)*
Hobart Corporation ....F 631 864-3440
  Commack *(G-3861)*
Jado Sewing Machines Inc ....E 718 784-2314
  Long Island City *(G-7798)*
Marine Park Appliances LLC ....F 718 513-1808
  Brooklyn *(G-2272)*
Platinum Carting Corp 631 649-4322
  Bay Shore *(G-720)*

3641 Electric Lamps

◆ Atlantic Ultraviolet Corp ....E 631 234-3275
  Hauppauge *(G-6047)*
Boehm Surgical Instrument ....F 585 436-6584
  Rochester *(G-14259)*
Emitled Inc ....G 516 531-3533
  Westbury *(G-17009)*
▲ Foscarini Inc ....G 212 257-4412
  New York *(G-10240)*
General Electric Company ....A 518 385-4022
  Schenectady *(G-15283)*
Goldstar Lighting LLC ....F 646 543-6811
  New York *(G-10376)*
▲ K & H Industries Inc ....F 716 312-0088
  Hamburg *(G-5953)*
K & H Industries Inc ....F 716 312-0088
  Hamburg *(G-5954)*
▲ Kreon Inc ....G 516 470-9522
  Bethpage *(G-869)*
▲ La Mar Lighting Co Inc ....D 631 777-7700
  Farmingdale *(G-5039)*
▲ Led Waves Inc ....F 347 416-6182
  Brooklyn *(G-2205)*
◆ Lighting Holdings Intl LLC ....A 845 306-1850
  Purchase *(G-13976)*
▲ Lowel-Light Manufacturing Inc ....E 718 921-0600
  Brooklyn *(G-2241)*
Lumia Energy Solutions LLC ....G 516 478-5795
  Jericho *(G-7108)*
▲ Make-Waves Instrument Corp ....E 716 681-7524
  Buffalo *(G-3076)*
Oledworks LLC ....E 585 287-6802
  Rochester *(G-14568)*

Employee Codes: A=Over 500 employees, B=251-500
C=101-250, D=51-100, E=20-50, F=10-19, G=5-9

Philips Elec N Amer Corp ....C 607 776-3692
Bath (G-661)
Preston Glass Industries Inc ....E 718 997-8888
Forest Hills (G-5335)
▲ Ric-Lo Productions Ltd ....E 845 469-2285
Chester (G-3640)
▲ Saratoga Lighting Holdings LLC ....G 212 906-7800
New York (G-11990)
◆ Satco Products Inc ....D 631 243-2022
Edgewood (G-4624)
Siemens Corporation ....F 202 434-7800
New York (G-12084)
Siemens USA Holdings Inc ....B 212 258-4000
New York (G-12086)
Welch Allyn Inc ....A 315 685-4347
Skaneateles Falls (G-15495)
▲ Westron Corporation ....E 516 678-2300
Oceanside (G-13127)

3643 Current-Carrying Wiring Devices

99cent World and Variety Corp ....G 212 740-0010
New York (G-9026)
Alstom Signaling Inc ....E 585 274-8700
Schenectady (G-15258)
Andros Manufacturing Corp ....F 585 663-5700
Rochester (G-14221)
Another 99 Cent Paradise ....G 718 786-4578
Sunnyside (G-15825)
Atc Plastics LLC ....E 212 375-2515
New York (G-9297)
Automatic Connector Inc ....F 631 543-5000
Hauppauge (G-6048)
Bassin Technical Sales Co ....E 914 698-9358
Mamaroneck (G-8056)
Belden Inc ....B 607 796-5600
Horseheads (G-6597)
Bronx New Way Corp ....G 347 431-1385
Bronx (G-1288)
C A M Graphics Co Inc ....E 631 842-3400
Farmingdale (G-4964)
Charlton Precision Pdts Inc ....G 845 338-2351
Kingston (G-7212)
Command Components Corporation ....G 631 666-4411
Bay Shore (G-686)
Cooper Power Systems LLC ....B 716 375-7100
Olean (G-13160)
▲ Cox & Company Inc ....C 212 366-0200
Plainview (G-13623)
Crown Die Casting Corp ....E 914 667-5400
Mount Vernon (G-8720)
▲ Delfingen Us-New York Inc ....E 716 215-0300
Niagara Falls (G-12832)
Delta Metal Products Co Inc ....E 718 855-4200
Brooklyn (G-1852)
Dollar Popular Inc ....G 914 375-0361
Yonkers (G-17452)
EB Acquisitions LLC ....D 212 355-3310
New York (G-10022)
Exxelia-Raf Tabtronics LLC ....E 585 243-4331
Piffard (G-13574)
◆ Fiber Instrument Sales Inc ....C 315 736-2206
Oriskany (G-13333)
Heary Bros Lghtning Protection ....E 716 941-6141
Springville (G-15633)
Inertia Switch Inc ....E 845 359-8300
Orangeburg (G-13251)
International Key Supply LLC ....F 631 983-6096
Farmingdale (G-5020)
Jaguar Industries Inc ....F 845 947-1800
Haverstraw (G-6261)
Joldeson One Aerospace Inds ....D 718 848-7396
Ozone Park (G-13406)
▲ K & H Industries Inc ....F 716 312-0088
Hamburg (G-5953)
▲ Kelta Inc ....E 631 789-5000
Edgewood (G-4616)
L3 Technologies Inc ....A 631 436-7400
Hauppauge (G-6133)
◆ Leviton Manufacturing Co Inc ....B 631 812-6000
Melville (G-8363)
◆ Lighting Holdings Intl LLC ....A 845 306-1850
Purchase (G-13976)
Lite Brite Manufacturing Inc ....F 718 855-9797
Brooklyn (G-2233)
Lourdes Industries Inc ....D 631 234-6600
Hauppauge (G-6146)
▲ MD Electronics Corporation ....D 716 488-0300
Jamestown (G-7052)
▲ Micro Contacts Inc ....E 516 433-4830
Hicksville (G-6397)
Mini-Circuits Fort Wayne LLC ....B 718 934-4500
Brooklyn (G-2322)
▲ Monarch Electric Products Inc ....G 718 583-7996
Bronx (G-1405)
Mono-Systems Inc ....E 716 821-1344
Buffalo (G-3094)
▲ NEa Manufacturing Corp ....E 516 371-4200
Inwood (G-6803)
Orbit International Corp ....C 631 435-8300
Hauppauge (G-6180)
◆ Pass & Seymour Inc ....B 315 468-6211
Syracuse (G-16032)
Pei/Genesis Inc ....G 631 256-1747
Farmingville (G-5169)
RE 99 Cents Inc ....G 718 639-2325
Woodside (G-17365)
Reynolds Packaging McHy Inc ....D 716 358-6451
Falconer (G-4918)
Rodale Wireless Inc ....E 631 231-0044
Hauppauge (G-6205)
▲ Russell Industries Inc ....F 516 536-5000
Lynbrook (G-7986)
Saturn Industries Inc ....E 518 828-9956
Hudson (G-6663)
▼ Sector Microwave Inds Inc ....D 631 242-2245
Deer Park (G-4232)
Sinclair Technologies Inc ....E 716 874-3682
Hamburg (G-5966)
▲ SL Industries Inc ....D 212 520-2300
New York (G-12124)
▲ Stever-Locke Industries Inc ....G 585 624-3450
Honeoye Falls (G-6565)
▲ Superpower Inc ....E 518 346-1414
Schenectady (G-15325)
▲ Switching Power Inc ....D 631 981-7231
Ronkonkoma (G-15013)
Swivelier Company Inc ....D 845 353-1455
Blauvelt (G-970)
▲ Tappan Wire & Cable Inc ....C 845 353-9000
Blauvelt (G-971)
▲ Tii Technologies Inc ....E 516 364-9300
Edgewood (G-4629)
Utility Systems Tech Inc ....F 518 326-4142
Watervliet (G-16716)
▲ Whirlwind Music Distrs Inc ....D 800 733-9473
Rochester (G-14790)
▲ Zierick Manufacturing Corp ....D 800 882-8020
Mount Kisco (G-8690)

3644 Noncurrent-Carrying Wiring Devices

Alumiseal Corp ....E 518 329-2820
Copake Falls (G-3914)
Cables and Chips Inc ....E 212 619-3132
New York (G-9544)
Chase Corporation ....F 631 827-0476
Northport (G-13027)
Complete SEC & Contrls Inc ....F 631 421-7200
Huntington Station (G-6739)
Delta Metal Products Co Inc ....E 718 855-4200
Brooklyn (G-1852)
▲ Gerome Technologies Inc ....D 518 463-1324
Menands (G-8404)
Heat and Frost Inslatrs & Asbs ....G 718 784-3456
Astoria (G-441)
Highland Valley Supply Inc ....F 845 849-2863
Wappingers Falls (G-16592)
▲ J H C Fabrications Inc ....E 718 649-0065
Brooklyn (G-2121)
Jpmorgan Chase Bank Nat Assn ....F 845 298-2461
Wappingers Falls (G-16594)
▲ Lapp Insulators LLC ....C 585 768-6221
Le Roy (G-7436)
Pole Position Raceway ....G 716 683-7223
Cheektowaga (G-3613)
▲ Producto Electric Corp ....E 845 359-4900
Orangeburg (G-13265)
▲ Quadristi LLC ....F 585 279-3318
Rochester (G-14635)
Speedzone Inc ....G 631 750-1973
Oakdale (G-13081)
▲ Superflex Ltd ....E 718 768-1400
Brooklyn (G-2646)
▲ Varflex Corporation ....C 315 336-4400
Rome (G-14867)
▲ Veja Electronics Inc ....D 631 321-6086
Deer Park (G-4247)
▲ Volt Tek Inc ....F 585 377-2050
Fairport (G-4893)
▲ Von Roll Usa Inc ....C 518 344-7100
Schenectady (G-15334)
▲ Zierick Manufacturing Corp ....D 800 882-8020
Mount Kisco (G-8690)

3645 Residential Lighting Fixtures

▲ A-1 Stamping & Spinning Corp ....F 718 388-2626
Rockaway Park (G-14812)
◆ Adesso Inc ....E 212 736-4440
New York (G-9074)
▲ Aesthonics Inc ....D 646 723-2463
Brooklyn (G-1567)
Artemis Studios Inc ....D 718 788-6022
Brooklyn (G-1637)
▲ Canarm Ltd ....G 800 267-4427
Ogdensburg (G-13134)
Cooper Lighting LLC ....E 315 579-2873
Syracuse (G-15929)
▲ Cooper Lighting LLC ....C 516 470-1000
Hicksville (G-6358)
Crownlite Mfg Corp ....E 631 589-9100
Bohemia (G-1040)
Custom Lampshades Inc ....F 718 254-0500
Brooklyn (G-1826)
▲ David Weeks Studio ....F 212 966-3433
New York (G-9880)
Decor By Dene Inc ....F 718 376-5566
Brooklyn (G-1847)
▲ Dreyfus Ashby Inc ....E 212 818-0770
New York (G-9980)
Eaton Corporation ....E 315 579-2872
Syracuse (G-15951)
▲ ER Butler & Co Inc ....E 212 925-3565
New York (G-10107)
Excalbur Brnze Sculpture Fndry ....E 718 366-3444
Brooklyn (G-1947)
◆ Hudson Valley Lighting Inc ....D 845 561-0300
Wappingers Falls (G-16593)
▲ Jamaica Lamp Corp ....E 718 776-5039
Queens Village (G-13996)
Jimco Lamp & Manufacturing Co ....G 631 218-2152
Islip (G-6848)
Judis Lampshades Inc ....G 917 561-3921
Brooklyn (G-2156)
Lasvit Inc ....G 212 219-3043
New York (G-10968)
▲ Lexstar Inc ....E 845 947-1415
Haverstraw (G-6262)
▲ Litelab Corp ....C 716 856-4300
Buffalo (G-3067)
Lyric Lighting Ltd Inc ....G 718 497-0109
Ridgewood (G-14127)
Matov Industries Inc ....E 718 392-5060
Long Island City (G-7836)
▲ Modulightor Inc ....F 212 371-0336
New York (G-11318)
New Generation Lighting Inc ....F 212 966-0328
New York (G-11408)
Nulux Inc ....E 718 383-1112
Ridgewood (G-14128)
Philips Elec N Amer Corp ....C 607 776-3692
Bath (G-661)
Pompian Manufacturing Co Inc ....G 914 476-7076
Yonkers (G-17497)
▲ Preciseled Inc ....F 516 418-5337
Valley Stream (G-16443)
▲ Prestigeline Inc ....D 631 273-3636
Bay Shore (G-724)
▲ Quality HM Brands Holdings LLC ....A 718 292-2024
Bronx (G-1436)
Quoizel Inc ....E 631 436-4402
Hauppauge (G-6202)
Rapid-Lite Fixture Corporation ....F 347 599-2600
Brooklyn (G-2497)
Remains Lighting ....E 212 675-8051
New York (G-11861)
Sandy Littman Inc ....G 845 562-1112
Newburgh (G-12802)
▲ Saratoga Lighting Holdings LLC ....G 212 906-7800
New York (G-11990)
◆ Satco Products Inc ....D 631 243-2022
Edgewood (G-4624)
Savwatt Usa Inc ....G 646 478-2676
New York (G-11998)
▲ Solarwaterway Inc ....E 888 998-5337
Brooklyn (G-2607)
◆ Swarovski Lighting Ltd ....B 518 563-7500
Plattsburgh (G-13731)
Swarovski Lighting Ltd ....B 518 324-6378
Plattsburgh (G-13732)
Swivelier Company Inc ....D 845 353-1455
Blauvelt (G-970)

SIC SECTION — 36 ELECTRONIC AND OTHER ELECTRICAL EQUIPMENT AND COMPONENTS, EXCEPT COMPUTER

Tarsier Ltd — C — 212 401-6181
New York *(G-12305)*
Tudor Electrical Supply Co Inc — G — 212 867-7550
New York *(G-12442)*
Ulster Precision Inc — E — 845 338-0995
Kingston *(G-7246)*
▲ Vaughan Designs Inc — G — 212 319-7070
New York *(G-12534)*
▲ Vision Quest Lighting Inc — E — 631 737-4800
Ronkonkoma *(G-15022)*
Vonn LLC — F — 888 604-8666
Long Island City *(G-7946)*
▲ Wainland Inc — E — 718 626-2233
Astoria *(G-460)*

3646 Commercial, Indl & Institutional Lighting Fixtures

A & L Lighting Ltd — F — 718 821-1188
Medford *(G-8264)*
▲ A-1 Stamping & Spinning Corp — F — 718 388-2626
Rockaway Park *(G-14812)*
AEP Environmental LLC — F — 716 446-0739
Buffalo *(G-2818)*
▲ Aesthonics Inc — D — 646 723-2463
Brooklyn *(G-1567)*
Al Energy Solutions Led Llc — E — 646 380-6670
New York *(G-9120)*
▲ Altman Stage Lighting Co Inc — C — 914 476-7987
Yonkers *(G-17429)*
▲ American Scientific Ltg Corp — E — 718 369-1100
Brooklyn *(G-1606)*
Apogee Translite Inc — E — 631 254-6975
Deer Park *(G-4124)*
Apparatus LLC — E — 646 527-9732
New York *(G-9228)*
Aquarii Inc — G — 315 672-8807
Camillus *(G-3349)*
Aristocrat Lighting Inc — F — 718 522-0003
Brooklyn *(G-1630)*
▲ Arlee Lighting Corp — G — 516 595-8558
Inwood *(G-6790)*
Awaken Led Company — F — 802 338-5971
Champlain *(G-3565)*
Big Shine Worldwide Inc — G — 845 444-5255
Newburgh *(G-12772)*
▲ Canarm Ltd — G — 800 267-4427
Ogdensburg *(G-13134)*
Cooper Industries LLC — E — 315 477-7000
Syracuse *(G-15928)*
▲ Cooper Lighting LLC — C — 516 470-1000
Hicksville *(G-6358)*
Crownlite Mfg Corp — E — 631 589-9100
Bohemia *(G-1040)*
▲ DAc Lighting Inc — E — 914 698-5959
Mamaroneck *(G-8064)*
▲ Dreyfus Ashby Inc — E — 212 818-0770
New York *(G-9980)*
E-Ffinergy Group LLC — G — 845 547-2424
Suffern *(G-15811)*
Ecs Global — F — 718 855-5888
Brooklyn *(G-1903)*
▲ Edison Price Lighting Inc — C — 718 685-0700
Long Island City *(G-7752)*
Edison Price Lighting Inc — D — 718 685-0700
Long Island City *(G-7753)*
Electric Lighting Agencies — E — 212 645-4580
New York *(G-10049)*
▲ Elegance Lighting Ltd — F — 631 509-0640
Centereach *(G-3496)*
Global Lighting Inc — G — 914 591-4095
Yonkers *(G-17463)*
Green Beam Led Inc — G — 718 439-6262
Brooklyn *(G-2051)*
▲ Green Energy Concepts Inc — G — 845 238-2574
Chester *(G-3635)*
◆ Hudson Valley Lighting Inc — D — 845 561-0300
Wappingers Falls *(G-16593)*
Ideoli Group Inc — F — 212 705-8769
Port Washington *(G-13845)*
▲ Jesco Lighting Inc — E — 718 366-3211
Port Washington *(G-13850)*
▲ Jesco Lighting Group LLC — D — 718 366-3211
Port Washington *(G-13851)*
▲ La Mar Lighting Co Inc — D — 631 777-7700
Farmingdale *(G-5039)*
LDI Lighting Inc — G — 718 384-4490
Brooklyn *(G-2199)*
LDI Lighting Inc — G — 718 384-4490
Brooklyn *(G-2200)*
▲ Legion Lighting Co Inc — E — 718 498-1770
Brooklyn *(G-2209)*
▲ Light Waves Concept Inc — F — 212 677-6400
Brooklyn *(G-2223)*
Lighting By Dom Yonkers Inc — G — 914 968-8700
Yonkers *(G-17480)*
▲ Lighting Services Inc — D — 845 942-2800
Stony Point *(G-15797)*
▲ Linear Lighting Corporation — C — 718 361-7552
Long Island City *(G-7818)*
Lite Brite Manufacturing Inc — F — 718 855-9797
Brooklyn *(G-2233)*
▲ Lite-Makers Inc — E — 718 739-9300
Jamaica *(G-6961)*
Litelab Corp — G — 718 361-6829
Long Island City *(G-7820)*
▲ Litelab Corp — C — 716 856-4300
Buffalo *(G-3067)*
▲ LSI Lightron Inc — A — 845 562-5500
New Windsor *(G-8988)*
▲ Lukas Lighting Inc — E — 800 841-4011
Long Island City *(G-7824)*
Luminatta Inc — G — 914 664-3600
Mount Vernon *(G-8748)*
Luminescent Systems Inc — B — 716 655-0800
East Aurora *(G-4398)*
▲ Luxo Corporation — F — 914 345-0067
Elmsford *(G-4770)*
▲ Magniflood Inc — E — 631 226-1000
Amityville *(G-309)*
Matov Industries Inc — E — 718 392-5060
Long Island City *(G-7836)*
▲ Modulightor Inc — F — 212 371-0336
New York *(G-11318)*
▲ North American Mfg Entps Inc — E — 718 524-4370
Staten Island *(G-15733)*
North American Mfg Entps Inc — F — 718 524-4370
Staten Island *(G-15734)*
Nulux Inc — E — 718 383-1112
Ridgewood *(G-14128)*
Oledworks LLC — E — 585 287-6802
Rochester *(G-14568)*
Philips Lighting N Amer Corp — C — 646 265-7170
New York *(G-11667)*
▲ Preciseled Inc — F — 516 418-5337
Valley Stream *(G-16443)*
Primelite Manufacturing Corp — G — 516 868-4411
Freeport *(G-5431)*
Rapid-Lite Fixture Corporation — F — 347 599-2600
Brooklyn *(G-2497)*
Remains Lighting — E — 212 675-8051
New York *(G-11861)*
S E A Supplies Ltd — F — 516 694-6677
Plainview *(G-13661)*
Sandy Littman Inc — G — 845 562-1112
Newburgh *(G-12802)*
▲ Saratoga Lighting Holdings LLC — G — 212 906-7800
New York *(G-11990)*
▲ Savenergy Inc — G — 516 239-1958
Garden City *(G-5545)*
Savwatt Usa Inc — G — 646 478-2676
New York *(G-11998)*
▲ Selux Corporation — C — 845 691-7723
Highland *(G-6435)*
Solarpath Inc — G — 201 490-4499
New York *(G-12149)*
▲ Solarwaterway Inc — E — 888 998-5337
Brooklyn *(G-2607)*
▲ Sonneman-A Way of Light — G — 845 926-5469
Wappingers Falls *(G-16596)*
▲ Spectronics Corporation — C — 516 333-4840
Westbury *(G-17055)*
Swivelier Company Inc — D — 845 353-1455
Blauvelt *(G-970)*
Twinkle Lighting Inc — G — 718 225-0939
Flushing *(G-5309)*
Versaponents Inc — F — 631 242-3387
Deer Park *(G-4248)*
▲ Vision Quest Lighting Inc — E — 631 737-4800
Ronkonkoma *(G-15022)*
Vital Vio Inc — F — 914 245-6048
Troy *(G-16286)*
Vonn LLC — F — 888 604-8666
Long Island City *(G-7946)*
Xeleum Lighting LLC — F — 954 617-8170
Mount Kisco *(G-8689)*
▲ Zumtobel Lighting Inc — C — 845 691-6262
Highland *(G-6436)*

3647 Vehicular Lighting Eqpt

Aerospace Lighting Corporation — D — 631 563-6400
Bohemia *(G-1004)*
▲ Astronics Corporation — C — 716 805-1599
East Aurora *(G-4391)*
B/E Aerospace Inc — E — 631 563-6400
Bohemia *(G-1018)*
Copy Cat — G — 718 934-2192
Brooklyn *(G-1801)*
Licenders — G — 212 759-5200
New York *(G-11019)*
Luminescent Systems Inc — B — 716 655-0800
East Aurora *(G-4398)*
▼ Mobile Fleet Inc — G — 631 206-2920
Hauppauge *(G-6168)*
Power and Cnstr Group Inc — E — 585 889-6020
Scottsville *(G-15360)*
Truck-Lite Co LLC — E — 716 665-2614
Falconer *(G-4923)*
◆ Truck-Lite Co LLC — C — 716 665-6214
Falconer *(G-4924)*
▲ Wolo Mfg Corp — E — 631 242-0333
Deer Park *(G-4253)*

3648 Lighting Eqpt, NEC

Al Energy Solutions Led Llc — E — 646 380-6670
New York *(G-9120)*
▲ Altman Stage Lighting Co Inc — C — 914 476-7987
Yonkers *(G-17429)*
Broadway National Group LLC — D — 800 797-4467
Ronkonkoma *(G-14909)*
▲ CEIT Corp — F — 518 825-0649
Plattsburgh *(G-13686)*
▲ Coldstream Group Inc — F — 914 698-5959
Mamaroneck *(G-8061)*
Cooper Industries LLC — E — 315 477-7000
Syracuse *(G-15928)*
◆ Creative Stage Lighting Co Inc — E — 518 251-3302
North Creek *(G-12949)*
Edison Power & Light Co Inc — F — 718 522-0002
Brooklyn *(G-1906)*
Eluminocity US Inc — G — 651 528-1165
New York *(G-10068)*
▲ Enchante Lites LLC — G — 212 602-1818
New York *(G-10081)*
▲ Expo Furniture Designs Inc — F — 516 674-1420
Glen Cove *(G-5627)*
▲ Fabbian USA Corp — G — 973 882-3824
New York *(G-10176)*
General Led Corp — G — 516 280-2854
Mineola *(G-8545)*
Goddard Design Co — G — 718 599-0170
Brooklyn *(G-2035)*
Gordon S Anderson Mfg Co — G — 845 677-3304
Millbrook *(G-8511)*
Gti Graphic Technology Inc — E — 845 562-7066
Newburgh *(G-12781)*
▲ HB Architectural Lighting Inc — E — 347 851-4123
Bronx *(G-1354)*
Illumination Technologies Inc — F — 315 463-4673
East Syracuse *(G-4552)*
Island Lite Louvers Inc — E — 631 608-4250
Amityville *(G-297)*
J M Canty Inc — E — 716 625-4227
Lockport *(G-7624)*
◆ Jaquith Industries Inc — E — 315 478-5700
Syracuse *(G-15985)*
Jed Lights Inc — F — 516 812-5001
Deer Park *(G-4180)*
Jt Roselle Lighting & Sup Inc — F — 914 666-3700
Mount Kisco *(G-8674)*
▲ Julian A McDermott Corporation — E — 718 456-3606
Ridgewood *(G-14124)*
▲ La Mar Lighting Co Inc — D — 631 777-7700
Farmingdale *(G-5039)*
Lamparts Co Inc — F — 914 723-8986
Mount Vernon *(G-8745)*
Lbg Acquisition LLC — E — 212 226-1276
New York *(G-10976)*
Light Blue USA LLC — G — 718 475-2515
Brooklyn *(G-2221)*
Lighting Collaborative Inc — G — 212 253-7220
Brooklyn *(G-2224)*
Lighting N Beyond LLC — G — 718 669-9142
Blauvelt *(G-967)*
Lighting Sculptures Inc — F — 631 242-3387
Deer Park *(G-4190)*
Lindsey Adelman — E — 718 623-3013
Brooklyn *(G-2230)*

Employee Codes: A=Over 500 employees, B=251-500
C=101-250, D=51-100, E=20-50, F=10-19, G=5-9

2018 Harris
New York Manufacturers Directory

841

SIC

Luminescent Systems Inc ....B 716 655-0800
East Aurora *(G-4398)*

Medtek Lighting Corporation ....G 518 745-7264
Glens Falls *(G-5704)*

Methods Tooling & Mfg Inc ....E 845 246-7100
Mount Marion *(G-8693)*

Mjk Enterprises LLC ....G 917 653-9042
Brooklyn *(G-2329)*

Northern Air Technology Inc ....G 585 594-5050
Rochester *(G-14565)*

◆ Olive Led Lighting Inc ....G 718 746-0830
College Point *(G-3825)*

Outdoor Lightning Perspectives ....G 631 266-6200
Huntington *(G-6707)*

Power and Cnstr Group Inc ....E 585 889-6020
Scottsville *(G-15360)*

Projector Lamp Services LLC ....F 631 244-0051
Bohemia *(G-1119)*

Psg Innovations Inc ....F 917 299-8986
Valley Stream *(G-16446)*

▲ Ric-Lo Productions Ltd ....E 845 469-2285
Chester *(G-3640)*

Rodac USA Corp ....E 716 741-3931
Clarence *(G-3698)*

▲ Saratoga Lighting Holdings LLC ....G 212 906-7800
New York *(G-11990)*

Secret Celebrity Licensing LLC ....G 212 812-9277
New York *(G-12031)*

Sensio America ....F 877 501-5337
Clifton Park *(G-3732)*

Serway Bros Inc ....E 315 337-0601
Rome *(G-14864)*

Shakuff LLC ....G 212 675-0383
Brooklyn *(G-2575)*

Siemens Electro Industrial Sa ....A 212 258-4000
New York *(G-12085)*

▲ Sir Industries Inc ....G 631 234-2444
Hauppauge *(G-6216)*

◆ Star Headlight Lantern Co Inc ....C 585 226-9500
Avon *(G-540)*

Strider Global LLC ....G 212 726-1302
New York *(G-12238)*

Tarsier Ltd ....C 212 401-6181
New York *(G-12305)*

▲ Tecnolux Incorporated ....G 718 369-3900
Brooklyn *(G-2672)*

▲ Times Square Stage Ltg Co Inc ....E 845 947-3034
Stony Point *(G-15800)*

Truck-Lite Co LLC ....E 716 665-2614
Falconer *(G-4923)*

▲ USA Illumination Inc ....E 845 565-8500
New Windsor *(G-9002)*

Vertex Innovative Solutions In ....F 315 437-6711
Syracuse *(G-16091)*

Vincent Conigliaro ....F 845 340-0489
Kingston *(G-7251)*

▲ Visual Effects Inc ....F 718 324-0011
Jamaica *(G-6998)*

Vivid Rgb Lighting LLC ....G 718 635-0817
Peekskill *(G-13508)*

3651 Household Audio & Video Eqpt

A and K Global Inc ....D 718 412-1876
Bayside *(G-758)*

▲ Accent Speaker Technology Ltd ....G 631 738-2540
Holbrook *(G-6455)*

▲ Aguilar Amplification LLC ....F 212 431-9109
New York *(G-9110)*

All In Audio Inc ....F 718 506-0948
Brooklyn *(G-1585)*

Amplitech Group Inc ....G 631 521-7831
Bohemia *(G-1011)*

▲ Andrea Electronics Corporation ....G 631 719-1800
Bohemia *(G-1012)*

▲ Ashly Audio Inc ....E 585 872-0010
Webster *(G-16737)*

▲ Audio Technology New York Inc ....F 718 369-7528
Brooklyn *(G-1654)*

Audio Video Invasion Inc ....F 516 345-2636
Plainview *(G-13613)*

▼ Audiosavings Inc ....F 888 445-1555
Inwood *(G-6791)*

Avcom of Virginia Inc ....D 585 924-4560
Victor *(G-16485)*

AVI-Spl Employee ....B 212 840-4801
New York *(G-9330)*

B & H Electronics Corp ....E 845 782-5000
Monroe *(G-8584)*

▲ B & K Components Ltd ....D 323 776-4277
Buffalo *(G-2850)*

▲ Bayit Home Automation Corp ....E 973 988-2638
Brooklyn *(G-1671)*

Broadcast Manager Inc ....G 212 509-1200
New York *(G-9517)*

Citation Manufacturing Co Inc ....G 845 425-6868
Spring Valley *(G-15602)*

▲ Communication Power Corp ....E 631 434-7306
Hauppauge *(G-6071)*

Convergent Audio Tech Inc ....G 585 359-2700
Rush *(G-15070)*

Covington Sound ....G 646 256-7486
Bronx *(G-1307)*

Data Interchange Systems Inc ....G 914 277-7775
Purdys *(G-13988)*

▲ Digitac Inc ....F 732 215-4020
Brooklyn *(G-1863)*

Digital Home Creations Inc ....G 585 576-7070
Webster *(G-16745)*

G E Inspection Technologies LP ....C 315 554-2000
Skaneateles *(G-15481)*

General Electric Company ....G 315 554-2000
Skaneateles *(G-15482)*

Gilmores Sound Advice Inc ....F 212 265-4445
New York *(G-10338)*

◆ Globa Phoni Compu Techn Solut ....E 607 257-7279
Ithaca *(G-6879)*

▲ Global Market Development Inc ....E 631 667-1002
Edgewood *(G-4613)*

Granada Electronics Inc ....G 718 387-1157
Brooklyn *(G-2048)*

Hope International Productions ....F 212 247-3188
New York *(G-10548)*

Ilab America Inc ....G 631 615-5053
Selden *(G-15373)*

Interaction Insight Corp ....G 800 285-2950
New York *(G-10665)*

▲ Jwin Electronics Corp ....D 516 626-7188
Port Washington *(G-13852)*

▲ Key Digital Systems Inc ....E 914 667-9700
Mount Vernon *(G-8742)*

L A R Electronics Corp ....G 716 285-0555
Niagara Falls *(G-12858)*

L3 Technologies Inc ....A 631 436-7400
Hauppauge *(G-6133)*

Laird Telemedia ....C 845 339-9555
Mount Marion *(G-8692)*

Lamm Industries Inc ....G 718 368-0181
Brooklyn *(G-2193)*

Masterdisk Corporation ....F 212 541-5022
Elmsford *(G-4773)*

▼ Navitar Inc ....D 585 359-4000
Rochester *(G-14550)*

▲ NEa Manufacturing Corp ....E 516 371-4200
Inwood *(G-6803)*

▲ New Audio LLC ....E 212 213-6060
New York *(G-11402)*

New Wop Records ....G 631 617-9732
Deer Park *(G-4203)*

Nykon Inc ....G 315 483-0504
Sodus *(G-15526)*

Professional Technology Inc ....G 315 337-4156
Rome *(G-14858)*

Pure Acoustics Inc ....G 718 788-4411
Brooklyn *(G-2474)*

Request Inc ....E 518 899-1254
Halfmoon *(G-5936)*

Request Serious Play LLC ....G 518 899-1254
Halfmoon *(G-5937)*

◆ Samson Technologies Corp ....D 631 784-2200
Hicksville *(G-6418)*

◆ Scy Manufacturing Inc ....G 516 986-3083
Inwood *(G-6806)*

Shyk International Corp ....G 212 663-3302
New York *(G-12081)*

▲ Sima Technologies LLC ....G 412 828-9130
Hauppauge *(G-6215)*

Sing Trix ....F 212 352-1500
New York *(G-12108)*

◆ Sony Corporation of America ....C 212 833-8000
New York *(G-12157)*

▲ Sound Video Systems Wny LLC ....F 716 684-8200
Buffalo *(G-3222)*

Speaqua Corp ....E 858 334-9042
Deer Park *(G-4237)*

Theodore A Rapp Associates ....G 845 469-2100
Chester *(G-3647)*

Tkm Technologies Inc ....G 631 474-4700
Port Jeff STA *(G-13796)*

◆ Toshiba America Inc ....E 212 596-0600
New York *(G-12398)*

Touchtunes Music Corporation ....D 847 419-3300
New York *(G-12403)*

Tunecore Inc ....E 646 651-1060
Brooklyn *(G-2706)*

Video Technology Services Inc ....F 516 937-9700
Syosset *(G-15861)*

Vincent Conigliaro ....F 845 340-0489
Kingston *(G-7251)*

Vtb Holdings Inc ....G 914 345-2255
Valhalla *(G-16399)*

▲ Whirlwind Music Distrs Inc ....D 800 733-9473
Rochester *(G-14790)*

▲ Wyrestorm Technologies LLC ....F 518 289-1293
Round Lake *(G-15063)*

▲ Yorkville Sound Inc ....G 716 297-2920
Niagara Falls *(G-12908)*

3652 Phonograph Records & Magnetic Tape

▲ A To Z Media Inc ....F 212 260-0237
New York *(G-9040)*

Abkco Music & Records Inc ....D 212 399-0300
New York *(G-9050)*

Atlantic Recording Corp ....B 212 707-2000
New York *(G-9304)*

▲ Bertelsmann Inc ....E 212 782-1000
New York *(G-9417)*

Bridge Records Inc ....G 914 654-9270
New Rochelle *(G-8935)*

C & C Duplicators Inc ....E 631 244-0800
Bohemia *(G-1025)*

Chesky Records Inc ....F 212 586-7799
New York *(G-9642)*

Columbia Records Inc ....F 212 833-8000
New York *(G-9736)*

Cult Records LLC ....G 718 395-2077
New York *(G-9822)*

▲ Dorling Kindersley Publishing ....D 212 213-4800
New York *(G-9961)*

Eks Manufacturing Inc ....F 917 217-0784
Brooklyn *(G-1909)*

Emusiccom Inc ....E 212 201-9240
New York *(G-10079)*

Europadisk LLC ....E 718 407-7300
Long Island City *(G-7762)*

▲ Extreme Group Holdings LLC ....F 212 833-8000
New York *(G-10164)*

High Quality Video Inc ....F 212 686-9534
New York *(G-10518)*

His Productions USA Inc ....G 212 594-3737
New York *(G-10528)*

▲ Historic TW Inc ....E 212 484-8000
New York *(G-10530)*

Hope International Productions ....F 212 247-3188
New York *(G-10548)*

Imago Recording Company ....G 212 751-3033
New York *(G-10615)*

John Marshall Sound Inc ....G 212 265-6066
New York *(G-10790)*

Lefrak Entertainment Co Ltd ....G 212 586-3600
New York *(G-10995)*

Masterdisk Corporation ....F 212 541-5022
Elmsford *(G-4773)*

Media Technologies Ltd ....F 631 467-7900
Eastport *(G-4596)*

Mmo Music Group Inc ....G 914 592-1188
Elmsford *(G-4774)*

Optic Solution LLC ....F 518 293-4034
Saranac *(G-15161)*

Peer-Southern Productions Inc ....E 212 265-3910
New York *(G-11614)*

Pete Levin Music Inc ....G 845 247-9211
Saugerties *(G-15221)*

Pivot Records LLC ....F 718 417-1213
Brooklyn *(G-2437)*

▲ Recorded Anthlogy of Amrcn Mus ....F 212 290-1695
Brooklyn *(G-2503)*

Roadrunner Records Inc ....E 212 274-7500
New York *(G-11908)*

Side Hustle Music Group LLC ....F 800 219-4003
New York *(G-12082)*

▲ Sony Broadband Entertainment ....F 212 833-6800
New York *(G-12156)*

◆ Sony Corporation of America ....C 212 833-8000
New York *(G-12157)*

▲ Sony Music Entertainment ....A 212 833-8500
New York *(G-12159)*

Sony Music Entertainment Inc ....A 212 833-8000
New York *(G-12160)*

Sony Music Entertainment Inc ....E 212 833-5057
New York *(G-12161)*

SIC SECTION
36 ELECTRONIC AND OTHER ELECTRICAL EQUIPMENT AND COMPONENTS, EXCEPT COMPUTER

◆ **Sony Music Holdings Inc** ....A....... 212 833-8000
New York *(G-12162)*

Sterling Sound Inc ....E....... 212 604-9433
New York *(G-12222)*

Taste and See Entrmt Inc ....G....... 516 285-3010
Valley Stream *(G-16452)*

Time Warner Companies Inc ....D....... 212 484-8000
New York *(G-12369)*

Universal Music Group Inc ....F....... 212 333-8237
New York *(G-12492)*

Vaire LLC ....G....... 631 271-4933
Huntington Station *(G-6765)*

Warner Music Group Corp ....B....... 212 275-2000
New York *(G-12616)*

▼ **Warner Music Inc** ....D....... 212 275-2000
New York *(G-12617)*

Wea International Inc ....D....... 212 275-1300
New York *(G-12629)*

Wmg Holding Company Inc ....A....... 212 275-2000
New York *(G-12677)*

3661 Telephone & Telegraph Apparatus

5yz Logistics LLC ....A....... 516 813-9500
Plainview *(G-13605)*

ABS Talkx Inc ....G....... 631 254-9100
Bay Shore *(G-664)*

Access 24 ....G....... 845 358-5397
Valley Cottage *(G-16400)*

◆ **Afh Industries Incorporated** ....F....... 646 351-1700
New York *(G-9105)*

▼ **Aines Manufacturing Corp** ....E....... 631 471-3900
Islip *(G-6845)*

Alcatel-Lucent USA Inc ....D....... 516 349-4900
Plainview *(G-13610)*

Alternative Technology Corp ....G....... 914 478-5900
Hastings On Hudson *(G-6022)*

▲ **Astrocom Electronics Inc** ....D....... 607 432-1930
Oneonta *(G-13195)*

▲ **Audio-Sears Corp** ....D....... 607 652-7305
Stamford *(G-15643)*

Avaya Services Inc ....G....... 866 462-8292
New York *(G-9327)*

Call Forwarding Technologies ....G....... 516 621-3600
Greenvale *(G-5897)*

▲ **Clayton Dubilier & Rice Fun** ....E....... 212 407-5200
New York *(G-9695)*

▲ **Columbia Telecom Group** ....G....... 631 501-5000
New York *(G-9737)*

Corning Incorporated ....E....... 607 248-1200
Corning *(G-3986)*

Corning Incorporated ....G....... 607 974-6729
Painted Post *(G-13417)*

◆ **Corning Incorporated** ....A....... 607 974-9000
Corning *(G-3983)*

Eagle Telephonics Inc ....F....... 631 471-3600
Bohemia *(G-1055)*

▲ **ESi Cases & Accessories Inc** ....E....... 212 883-8838
New York *(G-10113)*

◆ **Fiber Instrument Sales Inc** ....C....... 315 736-2206
Oriskany *(G-13333)*

▲ **Fiberall Corp** ....E....... 516 371-5200
Inwood *(G-6796)*

▲ **Fiberwave Corporation** ....C....... 718 802-9011
Brooklyn *(G-1972)*

▲ **Forerunner Technologies Inc** ....E....... 631 337-2100
Bohemia *(G-1063)*

Fujitsu Ntwrk Cmmnications Inc ....F....... 845 731-2000
Pearl River *(G-13479)*

Harris Corporation ....E....... 585 244-5830
Rochester *(G-14446)*

▲ **I D Tel Corp** ....F....... 718 876-6000
Staten Island *(G-15706)*

Interdgital Communications LLC ....C....... 631 622-4000
Melville *(G-8360)*

▲ **Kelta Inc** ....E....... 631 789-5000
Edgewood *(G-4616)*

Kent Optronics Inc ....F....... 845 897-0138
Hopewell Junction *(G-6581)*

L3 Technologies Inc ....A....... 631 436-7400
Hauppauge *(G-6133)*

Maia Systems LLC ....G....... 718 206-0100
Jamaica *(G-6963)*

▲ **Parabit Systems Inc** ....E....... 516 378-4800
Roosevelt *(G-15031)*

Performance Technologies Inc ....E....... 585 256-0200
Rochester *(G-14596)*

▲ **Powermate Cellular** ....G....... 718 833-9400
Brooklyn *(G-2445)*

Prager Metis Cpas LLC ....F....... 212 972-7555
New York *(G-11715)*

Quality One Wireless LLC ....C....... 631 233-3337
Ronkonkoma *(G-14999)*

R I R Communications Systems ....G....... 718 706-9957
Mount Vernon *(G-8769)*

R I R Communications Systems ....E....... 718 706-9957
Mount Vernon *(G-8770)*

▲ **Redcom Laboratories Inc** ....C....... 585 924-6567
Victor *(G-16524)*

▲ **Rus Industries Inc** ....E....... 716 284-7828
Niagara Falls *(G-12887)*

◆ **Sandstone Technologies Corp** ....G....... 585 785-5537
Rochester *(G-14688)*

Sandstone Technologies Corp ....G....... 585 785-5537
Rochester *(G-14689)*

Shoretel Inc ....G....... 877 654-3573
Rochester *(G-14706)*

Siemens Corporation ....F....... 202 434-7800
New York *(G-12084)*

Siemens Industry Inc ....G....... 607 936-9512
Corning *(G-4002)*

Siemens USA Holdings Inc ....B....... 212 258-4000
New York *(G-12086)*

▼ **Simrex Corporation** ....G....... 716 206-0174
Buffalo *(G-3215)*

▼ **Splice Technologies Inc** ....G....... 631 924-8108
Manorville *(G-8113)*

Telecommunication Concepts ....G....... 315 736-8523
Whitesboro *(G-17224)*

Telephonics Corporation ....D....... 631 755-7659
Farmingdale *(G-5136)*

▲ **Telephonics Corporation** ....A....... 631 755-7000
Farmingdale *(G-5137)*

Terahertz Technologies Inc ....G....... 315 736-3642
Oriskany *(G-13340)*

▲ **Tii Technologies Inc** ....E....... 516 364-9300
Edgewood *(G-4629)*

▲ **Toshiba Amer Info Systems Inc** ....B....... 949 583-3000
New York *(G-12397)*

◆ **Toshiba America Inc** ....E....... 212 596-0600
New York *(G-12398)*

3663 Radio & T V Communications, Systs & Eqpt, Broadcast/Studio

2p Agency Usa Inc ....G....... 212 203-5586
Brooklyn *(G-1513)*

Actv Inc (del Corp) ....D....... 212 995-9500
New York *(G-9068)*

Advanced Comm Solutions ....G....... 914 693-5076
Ardsley *(G-403)*

AG Adriano Goldschmied Inc ....G....... 845 928-8616
Central Valley *(G-3547)*

Airnet Communications Corp ....F....... 516 338-0008
Westbury *(G-16991)*

Ametek CTS Us Inc ....E....... 631 467-8400
Ronkonkoma *(G-14897)*

Amplitech Inc ....G....... 631 521-7738
Bohemia *(G-1010)*

Amplitech Group Inc ....G....... 631 521-7831
Bohemia *(G-1011)*

▲ **Andrea Electronics Corporation** ....G....... 631 719-1800
Bohemia *(G-1012)*

▲ **Apex Airtronics Inc** ....E....... 718 485-8560
Brooklyn *(G-1615)*

Appairent Technologies Inc ....G....... 585 214-2460
West Henrietta *(G-16902)*

Arcom Automatics LLC ....G....... 315 422-1230
Syracuse *(G-15876)*

▲ **Armstrong Transmitter Corp** ....F....... 315 673-1269
Marcellus *(G-8117)*

▲ **Arrow-Communication Labs Inc** ....B....... 315 422-1230
Syracuse *(G-15879)*

▲ **Ashly Audio Inc** ....E....... 585 872-0010
Webster *(G-16737)*

AT&T Corp ....G....... 716 639-0673
Williamsville *(G-17262)*

AVI-Spl Employee ....B....... 212 840-4801
New York *(G-9330)*

B & H Electronics Corp ....E....... 845 782-5000
Monroe *(G-8584)*

Basil S Kadhim ....G....... 888 520-5192
New York *(G-9380)*

Bayside Beepers & Cellular ....G....... 718 343-3888
Glen Oaks *(G-5654)*

Belden Inc ....B....... 607 796-5600
Horseheads *(G-6597)*

Benchmark Media Systems Inc ....F....... 315 437-6300
Syracuse *(G-15888)*

Bet Networks Incorporated ....E....... 212 846-8111
New York *(G-9422)*

Big Fish Entertainment LLC ....C....... 646 797-4955
New York *(G-9443)*

Bullitt Mobile LLC ....D....... 631 424-1749
Bohemia *(G-1024)*

Century Metal Parts Corp ....E....... 631 667-0800
Bay Shore *(G-680)*

Chyronhego Corporation ....D....... 631 845-2000
Melville *(G-8333)*

▼ **CJ Component Products LLC** ....G....... 631 567-3733
Oakdale *(G-13074)*

Clever Devices Ltd ....E....... 516 433-6100
Woodbury *(G-17304)*

Click It Inc ....D....... 631 686-2900
Hauppauge *(G-6067)*

▲ **Cmb Wireless Group LLC** ....B....... 631 750-4700
Bohemia *(G-1032)*

Cntry Cross Communications LLC ....F....... 386 758-9696
Jamestown *(G-7017)*

▲ **Columbia Telecom Group** ....G....... 631 501-5000
New York *(G-9737)*

▲ **Communication Power Corp** ....E....... 631 434-7306
Hauppauge *(G-6071)*

▲ **Comtech PST Corp** ....C....... 631 777-8900
Melville *(G-8336)*

◆ **Comtech Telecom Corp** ....C....... 631 962-7000
Melville *(G-8337)*

▲ **Eagle Comtronics Inc** ....C....... 315 451-3313
Liverpool *(G-7543)*

◆ **Edo LLC** ....G....... 631 630-4000
Amityville *(G-284)*

Edo LLC ....A....... 631 630-4200
Amityville *(G-285)*

Eeg Enterprises Inc ....F....... 516 293-7472
Farmingdale *(G-4995)*

▼ **Electro-Metrics Corporation** ....E....... 518 762-2600
Johnstown *(G-7140)*

Elite Cellular Accessories Inc ....E....... 877 390-2502
Deer Park *(G-4158)*

▲ **Eni Mks Products Group** ....F....... 585 427-8300
Rochester *(G-14373)*

▲ **Eni Technology Inc** ....B....... 585 427-8300
Rochester *(G-14374)*

Evado Filip ....F....... 917 774-8666
New York *(G-10142)*

Fei-Zyfer Inc ....G....... 714 933-4045
Uniondale *(G-16316)*

Fleetcom Inc ....F....... 914 776-5582
Yonkers *(G-17460)*

Flycell Inc ....D....... 212 400-1212
New York *(G-10233)*

Fujitsu Ntwrk Cmmnications Inc ....F....... 845 731-2000
Pearl River *(G-13479)*

◆ **GE Mds LLC** ....C....... 585 242-9600
Rochester *(G-14410)*

Geosync Microwave Inc ....G....... 631 760-5567
Hauppauge *(G-6107)*

◆ **Globecomm Systems Inc** ....C....... 631 231-9800
Hauppauge *(G-6109)*

◆ **Griffon Corporation** ....E....... 212 957-5000
New York *(G-10405)*

Gurley Precision Instrs Inc ....C....... 518 272-6300
Troy *(G-16259)*

Hamtronics Inc ....G....... 585 392-9430
Rochester *(G-14438)*

▲ **Hand Held Products Inc** ....B....... 315 554-6000
Skaneateles Falls *(G-15490)*

Harris Corporation ....A....... 585 244-5830
Rochester *(G-14441)*

Harris Corporation ....B....... 585 244-5830
Rochester *(G-14447)*

Harris Corporation ....F....... 718 767-1100
Whitestone *(G-17236)*

Harris Corporation ....B....... 585 244-5830
Rochester *(G-14448)*

Hopewell Precision Inc ....E....... 845 221-2737
Hopewell Junction *(G-6579)*

Icell Inc ....C....... 516 590-0007
Hempstead *(G-6298)*

▲ **Icon Enterprises Intl Inc** ....E....... 718 752-9764
Mohegan Lake *(G-8578)*

◆ **Igo Inc** ....E....... 408 596-0061
New York *(G-10608)*

Iheartcommunications Inc ....C....... 585 454-4884
Rochester *(G-14465)*

Iheartcommunications Inc ....E....... 212 603-4660
New York *(G-10609)*

Imagine Communications Corp ....F....... 212 303-4200
New York *(G-10614)*

Imobile of Ny LLC ....G....... 212 505-3355
New York *(G-10619)*

S I C

Employee Codes: A=Over 500 employees, B=251-500
C=101-250, D=51-100, E=20-50, F=10-19, G=5-9

2018 Harris
New York Manufacturers Directory

843

36 ELECTRONIC AND OTHER ELECTRICAL EQUIPMENT AND COMPONENTS, EXCEPT COMPUTER SIC SECTION

▼ **Innovation In Motion Inc**.....G..... 407 878-7561
Long Beach *(G-7672)*
Intelibs Inc.....G..... 877 213-2640
Stony Brook *(G-15791)*
It Commodity Sourcing Inc.....G..... 718 677-1577
Brooklyn *(G-2116)*
▲ **John Mezzalingua Assoc LLC**.....C..... 315 431-7100
Liverpool *(G-7551)*
▲ **L-3 Cmmnctons Fgn Holdings Inc**.....E..... 212 697-1111
New York *(G-10941)*
L3 Technologies Inc.....B..... 631 231-1700
Hauppauge *(G-6132)*
L3 Technologies Inc.....A..... 631 436-7400
Hauppauge *(G-6133)*
L3 Technologies Inc.....D..... 607 721-5465
Kirkwood *(G-7261)*
L3 Technologies Inc.....D..... 631 231-1700
Hauppauge *(G-6134)*
L3 Technologies Inc.....D..... 631 436-7400
Hauppauge *(G-6135)*
▲ **L3 Technologies Inc**.....B..... 212 697-1111
New York *(G-10943)*
Listec Video Corp.....G..... 631 273-3029
Hauppauge *(G-6137)*
Loral Space & Commnctns Holdng.....E..... 212 697-1105
New York *(G-11061)*
Loral Space Communications Inc.....B..... 212 697-1105
New York *(G-11062)*
Loral Spacecom Corporation.....E..... 212 697-1105
New York *(G-11063)*
▲ **M&S Accessory Network Corp**.....F..... 347 492-7790
New York *(G-11107)*
▲ **Magnet-Ndctive Systems Ltd USA**.....E..... 585 924-4000
Victor *(G-16514)*
▲ **Maritime Broadband Inc**.....E..... 347 404-6041
Long Island City *(G-7833)*
Mark Peri International.....F..... 516 208-6824
Oceanside *(G-13108)*
Millennium Antenna Corp.....F..... 315 798-9374
Utica *(G-16372)*
Mini-Circuits Fort Wayne LLC.....B..... 718 934-4500
Brooklyn *(G-2322)*
Mirion Tech Imaging LLC.....E..... 607 562-4300
Horseheads *(G-6611)*
Mks Medical Electronics.....C..... 585 292-7400
Rochester *(G-14538)*
Motorola Solutions Inc.....C..... 518 348-0833
Halfmoon *(G-5934)*
Motorola Solutions Inc.....C..... 718 330-2163
Brooklyn *(G-2341)*
Motorola Solutions Inc.....C..... 518 869-9517
Albany *(G-103)*
Movin On Sounds and SEC Inc.....E..... 516 489-2350
Franklin Square *(G-5375)*
▼ **Navitar Inc**.....D..... 585 359-4000
Rochester *(G-14550)*
NBC Universal LLC.....E..... 718 482-8310
Long Island City *(G-7853)*
North American MBL Systems Inc.....E..... 718 898-8700
Woodside *(G-17358)*
Nycom Business Solutions Inc.....G..... 516 345-6000
Franklin Square *(G-5376)*
Orbcomm Inc.....F..... 703 433-6396
Utica *(G-16379)*
Parrys Incorporated.....F..... 315 824-0002
Hamilton *(G-5972)*
Persistent Systems LLC.....E..... 212 561-5895
New York *(G-11646)*
▲ **Prime View USA Inc**.....G..... 212 730-4905
New York *(G-11733)*
Quanta Electronics Inc.....F..... 631 961-9953
Centereach *(G-3498)*
▲ **Quintel Usa Inc**.....E..... 585 420-8364
Rochester *(G-14642)*
Rehabilitation International.....G..... 212 420-1500
Jamaica *(G-6983)*
Rodale Wireless Inc.....E..... 631 231-0044
Hauppauge *(G-6205)*
Ruhle Companies Inc.....E..... 914 287-4000
Valhalla *(G-16398)*
Sartek Industries Inc.....G..... 631 473-3555
Port Jefferson *(G-13801)*
Sdr Technology Inc.....G..... 716 583-1249
Alden *(G-186)*
▲ **Sentry Technology Corporation**.....F..... 800 645-4224
Ronkonkoma *(G-15007)*
Sequential Electronics Systems.....E..... 914 592-1345
Elmsford *(G-4791)*
Shoretel Inc.....G..... 877 654-3573
Rochester *(G-14706)*
Silicon Imaging Inc.....G..... 518 374-3367
Niskayuna *(G-12913)*
Sinclair Technologies Inc.....E..... 716 874-3682
Hamburg *(G-5966)*
Specialty Microwave Corp.....F..... 631 737-2175
Ronkonkoma *(G-15011)*
Spectracom Corporation.....E..... 585 321-5800
Rochester *(G-14718)*
Srtech Industry Corp.....E..... 718 496-7001
Oakland Gardens *(G-13087)*
STI-Co Industries Inc.....E..... 716 662-2680
Orchard Park *(G-13322)*
▲ **Telephonics Corporation**.....A..... 631 755-7000
Farmingdale *(G-5137)*
▲ **Telxon Corporation**.....E..... 631 738-2400
Holtsville *(G-6539)*
Times Square Studios Ltd.....C..... 212 930-7720
New York *(G-12371)*
Toura LLC.....F..... 646 652-8668
Brooklyn *(G-2689)*
United Satcom Inc.....G..... 718 359-4100
Flushing *(G-5310)*
▲ **Vicon Industries Inc**.....C..... 631 952-2288
Hauppauge *(G-6250)*
Village Video Productions Inc.....G..... 631 752-9311
West Babylon *(G-16871)*
Vuum LLC.....G..... 212 868-3459
New York *(G-12598)*
▲ **W & W Manufacturing Co**.....F..... 516 942-0011
West Islip *(G-16939)*
▲ **Whirlwind Music Distrs Inc**.....D..... 800 733-9473
Rochester *(G-14790)*
Wireless Communications Inc.....G..... 845 353-5921
Nyack *(G-13073)*
Zetek Corporation.....F..... 212 668-1485
New York *(G-12729)*

3669 Communications Eqpt, NEC

All Metro Emrgncy Response Sys.....G..... 516 750-9100
Lynbrook *(G-7973)*
All Products Designs.....G..... 631 748-6901
Smithtown *(G-15504)*
Alstom Signaling Inc.....G..... 800 717-4477
West Henrietta *(G-16898)*
▲ **Alstom Signaling Inc**.....B..... 585 783-2000
Schenectady *(G-15257)*
Alstom Signaling Inc.....E..... 585 274-8700
Schenectady *(G-15258)*
Andrea Systems LLC.....E..... 631 390-3140
Farmingdale *(G-4950)*
Apex Signal Corporation.....D..... 631 567-1100
Bohemia *(G-1013)*
Apple Core Electronics Inc.....F..... 718 628-4068
Brooklyn *(G-1619)*
AVI-Spl Employee.....B..... 212 840-4801
New York *(G-9330)*
BNo Intl Trdg Co Inc.....G..... 716 487-1900
Jamestown *(G-7012)*
Capstream Technologies LLC.....G..... 716 945-7100
Salamanca *(G-15126)*
Comet Flasher Inc.....G..... 716 821-9595
Buffalo *(G-2901)*
Cq Traffic Control Devices LLC.....G..... 518 767-0057
Selkirk *(G-15376)*
Curbell Medical Products Inc.....F..... 716 667-2520
Orchard Park *(G-13289)*
▲ **Curbell Medical Products Inc**.....C..... 716 667-2520
Orchard Park *(G-13290)*
Datasonic Inc.....G..... 516 248-7330
East Meadow *(G-4441)*
Detector Pro.....G..... 845 635-3488
Pleasant Valley *(G-13742)*
Fire Apparatus Service Tech.....G..... 716 753-3538
Sherman *(G-15424)*
Firecom Inc.....C..... 718 899-6100
Woodside *(G-17345)*
Firetronics Inc.....G..... 516 997-5151
Jericho *(G-7102)*
Frequency Electronics Inc.....B..... 516 794-4500
Uniondale *(G-16317)*
Fuel Watchman Sales & Service.....F..... 718 665-6100
Bronx *(G-1340)*
▲ **General Traffic Equipment Corp**.....F..... 845 569-9000
Newburgh *(G-12779)*
Goddard Design Co.....G..... 718 599-0170
Brooklyn *(G-2035)*
Harris Corporation.....A..... 413 263-6200
Rochester *(G-14444)*
Intelligent Traffic Systems.....G..... 631 567-5994
Bohemia *(G-1074)*
▲ **Intercall Systems Inc**.....E..... 516 294-4524
Mineola *(G-8548)*
Kentronics Inc.....G..... 631 567-5994
Bohemia *(G-1083)*
▲ **L-3 Cmmnctons Fgn Holdings Inc**.....E..... 212 697-1111
New York *(G-10941)*
▲ **L3 Technologies Inc**.....B..... 212 697-1111
New York *(G-10943)*
Lifewatch Inc.....F..... 800 716-1433
Hewlett *(G-6333)*
Light Phone Inc.....G..... 415 595-0044
Brooklyn *(G-2222)*
Lik LLC.....F..... 516 848-5135
Northport *(G-13033)*
▲ **McDowell Research Co Inc**.....D..... 315 332-7100
Newark *(G-12756)*
◆ **Napco Security Tech Inc**.....A..... 631 842-9400
Amityville *(G-313)*
North Hills Signal Proc Corp.....F..... 516 682-7740
Syosset *(G-15854)*
▲ **Nrd LLC**.....E..... 716 773-7634
Grand Island *(G-5779)*
Nu2 Systems LLC.....F..... 914 719-7272
White Plains *(G-17169)*
Octopus Advanced Systems Inc.....G..... 914 771-6110
Yonkers *(G-17488)*
Personal Alarm SEC Systems.....F..... 212 448-1944
New York *(G-11647)*
Power Line Constructors Inc.....E..... 315 853-6183
Clinton *(G-3746)*
Response Care Inc.....G..... 585 671-4144
Webster *(G-16759)*
▼ **Roanwell Corporation**.....E..... 718 401-0288
Bronx *(G-1440)*
Sentry Devices Corp.....G..... 631 491-3191
Dix Hills *(G-4321)*
Simplexgrinnell LP.....D..... 585 288-6200
Rochester *(G-14711)*
Simplexgrinnell LP.....E..... 518 952-6040
Clifton Park *(G-3734)*
Simplexgrinnell LP.....G..... 845 774-4120
Harriman *(G-5996)*
Simplexgrinnell LP.....E..... 315 437-4660
East Syracuse *(G-4578)*
Simplexgrinnell LP.....F..... 607 338-5100
East Syracuse *(G-4579)*
▼ **Simrex Corporation**.....G..... 716 206-0174
Buffalo *(G-3215)*
◆ **Star Headlight Lantern Co Inc**.....C..... 585 226-9500
Avon *(G-540)*
Synergx Systems Inc.....D..... 516 433-4700
Woodside *(G-17374)*
Telebyte Inc.....E..... 631 423-3232
Hauppauge *(G-6236)*
▲ **Telemergency Ltd**.....G..... 914 629-4222
White Plains *(G-17202)*
▲ **Telephonics Corporation**.....A..... 631 755-7000
Farmingdale *(G-5137)*
Telephonics Corporation.....F..... 631 755-7000
Huntington *(G-6723)*
Telesite USA Inc.....F..... 631 952-2288
Hauppauge *(G-6237)*
Toweriq Inc.....F..... 844 626-7638
Long Island City *(G-7931)*
Traffic Lane Closures LLC.....G..... 845 228-6100
Brewster *(G-1226)*
▲ **Twinco Mfg Co Inc**.....E..... 631 231-0022
Hauppauge *(G-6243)*
▲ **TX Rx Systems Inc**.....C..... 716 549-4700
Angola *(G-382)*
Unitone Communication Systems.....G..... 212 777-9090
New York *(G-12488)*
UTC Fire SEC Americas Corp Inc.....D..... 518 456-0444
Albany *(G-148)*
▲ **Vicon Industries Inc**.....C..... 631 952-2288
Hauppauge *(G-6250)*
◆ **Visiontron Corp**.....E..... 631 582-8600
Hauppauge *(G-6252)*
▲ **Werma (usa) Inc**.....G..... 315 414-0200
East Syracuse *(G-4592)*
Zetek Corporation.....F..... 212 668-1485
New York *(G-12729)*

3671 Radio & T V Receiving Electron Tubes

▲ **E-Beam Services Inc**.....G..... 516 622-1422
Hicksville *(G-6370)*
Harris Corporation.....E..... 585 244-5830
Rochester *(G-14446)*
▲ **New Sensor Corporation**.....D..... 718 937-8300
Long Island City *(G-7856)*

SIC SECTION   36 ELECTRONIC AND OTHER ELECTRICAL EQUIPMENT AND COMPONENTS, EXCEPT COMPUTER

Passur Aerospace Inc ....G...... 631 589-6800
  Bohemia *(G-1111)*
▲ Thomas Electronics Inc..............C...... 315 923-2051
  Clyde *(G-3757)*
Y & Z Precision Inc ....F...... 516 349-8243
  Plainview *(G-13676)*

3672 Printed Circuit Boards

◆ A A Technology Inc ....D...... 631 913-0400
  Ronkonkoma *(G-14873)*
▲ Advance Circuit Technology Inc......E...... 585 328-2000
  Rochester *(G-14191)*
▲ Advance Micro Power Corp ....F...... 631 471-6157
  Ronkonkoma *(G-14879)*
Advanced Digital Info Corp ....E...... 607 266-4000
  Ithaca *(G-6856)*
Advanced Manufacturing Svc Inc ......E...... 631 676-5210
  Ronkonkoma *(G-14880)*
American Quality Technology ....F...... 607 777-9488
  Binghamton *(G-884)*
◆ American Tchncal Ceramics Corp ....B...... 631 622-4700
  Huntington Station *(G-6732)*
▲ Ansen Corporation ....G...... 315 393-3573
  Ogdensburg *(G-13132)*
Ansen Corporation ....C...... 315 393-3573
  Ogdensburg *(G-13133)*
Bryit Group LLC ....F...... 631 563-6603
  Holbrook *(G-6461)*
Bsu Inc ....E...... 607 272-8100
  Ithaca *(G-6867)*
Buffalo Circuits Inc ....G...... 716 662-2113
  Orchard Park *(G-13279)*
▲ C & D Assembly Inc ....E...... 607 898-4275
  Groton *(G-5919)*
C A M Graphics Co Inc ....E...... 631 842-3400
  Farmingdale *(G-4964)*
Chautauqua Circuits Inc ....G...... 716 366-5771
  Dunkirk *(G-4359)*
Coast To Coast Circuits Inc ....E...... 585 254-2980
  Rochester *(G-14302)*
Cygnus Automation Inc ....E...... 631 981-0909
  Bohemia *(G-1043)*
Della Systems Inc ....F...... 631 580-0010
  Ronkonkoma *(G-14921)*
Entertron Industries Inc ....E...... 716 772-7216
  Lockport *(G-7613)*
Falconer Electronics Inc ....D...... 716 665-4176
  Falconer *(G-4905)*
Geometric Circuits Inc ....D...... 631 249-0230
  Holbrook *(G-6477)*
Hazlow Electronics Inc ....E...... 585 325-5323
  Rochester *(G-14450)*
I 3 Manufacturing Services Inc ....G...... 607 238-7077
  Binghamton *(G-917)*
I3 Electronics Inc ....C...... 607 238-7077
  Binghamton *(G-919)*
▲ IEC Electronics Corp ....A...... 315 331-7742
  Newark *(G-12752)*
IEC Electronics Wire Cable Inc ....D...... 585 924-9010
  Newark *(G-12753)*
Irtronics Instruments Inc ....F...... 914 693-6291
  Ardsley *(G-404)*
▲ Isine Inc ....G...... 631 913-4400
  Ronkonkoma *(G-14942)*
Jabil Circuit Inc ....B...... 845 471-9237
  Poughkeepsie *(G-13928)*
Kendall Circuits Inc ....E...... 631 473-3636
  Mount Sinai *(G-8697)*
Mpl Inc ....E...... 607 266-0480
  Ithaca *(G-6899)*
Nationwide Circuits Inc ....E...... 585 328-0791
  Rochester *(G-14548)*
▲ NEa Manufacturing Corp ....E...... 516 371-4200
  Inwood *(G-6803)*
▼ Oakdale Industrial Elec Corp ....F...... 631 737-4090
  Ronkonkoma *(G-14982)*
Ormec Systems Corp ....E...... 585 385-3520
  Rochester *(G-14573)*
▲ Park Electrochemical Corp ....C...... 631 465-3600
  Melville *(G-8376)*
Performance Technologies Inc ....E...... 585 256-0200
  Rochester *(G-14596)*
Procomponents Inc ....E...... 516 683-0909
  Westbury *(G-17051)*
Rce Manufacturing LLC ....G...... 631 856-9005
  Commack *(G-3865)*
▲ Rochester Industrial Ctrl Inc ....D...... 315 524-4555
  Ontario *(G-13234)*
Rumsey Corp ....G...... 914 751-3640
  Yonkers *(G-17501)*

S K Circuits Inc ....F...... 703 376-8718
  Oneida *(G-13188)*
Sag Harbor Industries Inc ....E...... 631 725-0440
  Sag Harbor *(G-15107)*
Sanmina Corporation ....B...... 607 689-5000
  Owego *(G-13384)*
▲ Sopark Corp ....C...... 716 822-0434
  Buffalo *(G-3219)*
▲ Stetron International Inc ....F...... 716 854-3443
  Buffalo *(G-3225)*
▲ Stever-Locke Industries Inc ....G...... 585 624-3450
  Honeoye Falls *(G-6565)*
Surf-Tech Manufacturing Corp ....F...... 631 589-1194
  Bohemia *(G-1135)*
TCS Electronics Inc ....E...... 585 337-4301
  Farmington *(G-5165)*
Transistor Devices Inc ....E...... 631 471-7492
  Ronkonkoma *(G-15015)*
Windsor Technology LLC ....E...... 585 461-2500
  Rochester *(G-14792)*

3674 Semiconductors

Able Electronics Inc ....F...... 631 924-5386
  Bellport *(G-820)*
Accumetrics Inc ....F...... 716 684-0002
  Latham *(G-7378)*
Accumetrics Associates Inc ....F...... 518 393-2200
  Latham *(G-7379)*
▲ Acolyte Technologies Corp ....F...... 212 629-3239
  New York *(G-9066)*
Advis Inc ....G...... 585 568-0100
  Caledonia *(G-3302)*
▼ Aeroflex Holding Corp ....B...... 516 694-6700
  Plainview *(G-13607)*
▲ Aeroflex Incorporated ....B...... 516 694-6700
  Plainview *(G-13608)*
Aeroflex Plainview Inc ....B...... 516 694-6700
  Plainview *(G-13609)*
Aeroflex Plainview Inc ....C...... 631 231-9100
  Hauppauge *(G-6030)*
Akoustis Inc ....E...... 585 919-3073
  Canandaigua *(G-3363)*
Aljo-Gefa Precision Mfg LLC ....G...... 516 420-4419
  Old Bethpage *(G-13146)*
American Fuel Cell LLC ....G...... 585 474-3993
  Rochester *(G-14212)*
▲ Artemis Inc ....G...... 631 232-2424
  Hauppauge *(G-6044)*
▲ Atlantis Energy Systems Inc ....F...... 845 486-4052
  Poughkeepsie *(G-13907)*
Atlantis Energy Systems Inc ....G...... 916 438-2930
  Poughkeepsie *(G-13908)*
Autodyne Manufacturing Co Inc ....F...... 631 957-5858
  Lindenhurst *(G-7478)*
Automated Control Logic Inc ....F...... 914 769-8880
  Thornwood *(G-16139)*
Beech Grove Technology Inc ....G...... 845 223-6844
  Hopewell Junction *(G-6574)*
Besicorp Ltd ....F...... 845 336-7700
  Kingston *(G-7208)*
Bga Technology LLC ....F...... 631 750-4600
  Bohemia *(G-1021)*
Bharat Electronics Limited ....G...... 516 248-4021
  Garden City *(G-5510)*
CAM Touchview Products Inc ....F...... 631 842-3400
  Sag Harbor *(G-15103)*
▲ Central Semiconductor Corp ....D...... 631 435-1110
  Hauppauge *(G-6061)*
Ceres Technologies Inc ....D...... 845 247-4701
  Saugerties *(G-15210)*
Cold Springs R & D Inc ....F...... 315 413-1237
  Syracuse *(G-15920)*
Compositech Ltd ....E...... 516 835-1458
  Woodbury *(G-17305)*
Convergent Med MGT Svcs LLC ....G...... 718 921-6159
  Brooklyn *(G-1800)*
Cooper Power Systems LLC ....B...... 716 375-7100
  Olean *(G-13160)*
Corning Incorporated ....E...... 607 248-1200
  Corning *(G-3986)*
◆ Corning Incorporated ....A...... 607 974-9000
  Corning *(G-3983)*
Corning Incorporated ....G...... 607 974-6729
  Painted Post *(G-13417)*
Corning Specialty Mtls Inc ....G...... 607 974-9000
  Corning *(G-3991)*
Crystalonics Inc ....F...... 631 981-6140
  Ronkonkoma *(G-14919)*
Curtiss-Wright Controls ....F...... 631 756-4740
  Farmingdale *(G-4977)*

Cypress Semiconductor Corp ....F...... 631 261-1358
  Northport *(G-13028)*
▲ Data Device Corporation ....B...... 631 567-5600
  Bohemia *(G-1045)*
▲ Data Display USA Inc ....G...... 631 218-2130
  Holbrook *(G-6471)*
Dionics-Usa Inc ....G...... 516 997-7474
  Westbury *(G-17005)*
DJS Nyc Inc ....G...... 845 445-8618
  Monsey *(G-8606)*
Dynamic Photography Inc ....G...... 516 381-2951
  Roslyn *(G-15043)*
▲ Electronic Devices Inc ....E...... 914 965-4400
  Yonkers *(G-17456)*
Elite Semi Conductor Products ....G...... 631 884-8400
  Lindenhurst *(G-7486)*
Ely Beach Solar LLC ....G...... 718 796-9400
  New York *(G-10069)*
Emagin Corporation ....D...... 845 838-7900
  Hopewell Junction *(G-6575)*
Emtron Hybrids Inc ....E...... 631 924-9668
  Yaphank *(G-17408)*
▲ Endicott Interconnect Tech Inc .....A...... 866 820-4820
  Endicott *(G-4810)*
Enrg Inc ....F...... 716 873-2939
  Buffalo *(G-2954)*
▲ Eversan Inc ....F...... 315 736-3967
  Whitesboro *(G-17221)*
General Microwave Corporation ....F...... 516 802-0900
  Syosset *(G-15844)*
General Semiconductor Inc ....G...... 631 300-3818
  Hauppauge *(G-6106)*
Globalfoundries US 2 LLC ....C...... 512 457-3900
  Hopewell Junction *(G-6577)*
Globalfoundries US Inc ....C...... 512 457-3900
  Hopewell Junction *(G-6578)*
Globalfoundries US Inc ....C...... 408 462-3900
  Ballston Spa *(G-595)*
Gs Direct LLC ....E...... 212 902-1000
  New York *(G-10420)*
Gurley Precision Instrs Inc ....C...... 518 272-6300
  Troy *(G-16259)*
H K Technologies Inc ....G...... 212 779-0100
  New York *(G-10435)*
Hi-Tron Semiconductor Corp ....F...... 631 231-1500
  Hauppauge *(G-6116)*
▲ Hipotronics Inc ....C...... 845 279-8091
  Brewster *(G-1217)*
▲ Hisun Optoelectronics Co Ltd ......F...... 718 886-6966
  Flushing *(G-5258)*
I E D Corp ....F...... 631 348-0424
  Islandia *(G-6832)*
▲ Ic Technologies LLC ....G...... 212 966-7895
  New York *(G-10595)*
Idalia Solar Technologies LLC ....G...... 212 792-3913
  New York *(G-10598)*
Ilc Holdings Inc ....G...... 631 567-5600
  Bohemia *(G-1072)*
▲ Ilc Industries LLC ....G...... 631 567-5600
  Bohemia *(G-1073)*
▲ Intech 21 Inc ....G...... 516 626-7221
  Port Washington *(G-13847)*
INTEL Corporation ....D...... 408 765-8080
  Getzville *(G-5611)*
International Bus Mchs Corp ....B...... 212 324-5000
  New York *(G-10673)*
International Bus Mchs Corp ....C...... 800 426-4968
  Hopewell Junction *(G-6580)*
Intex Company Inc ....D...... 516 223-0200
  Freeport *(G-5417)*
▲ Isine Inc ....G...... 631 913-4400
  Ronkonkoma *(G-14942)*
Isonics Corporation ....G...... 212 356-7400
  New York *(G-10710)*
J H Rhodes Company Inc ....F...... 315 829-3600
  Vernon *(G-16459)*
▲ Lakestar Semi Inc ....F...... 212 974-6254
  New York *(G-10955)*
Lasermax Inc ....E...... 585 272-5420
  Rochester *(G-14496)*
◆ Leviton Manufacturing Co Inc ....B...... 631 812-6000
  Melville *(G-8363)*
Light Blue USA LLC ....G...... 718 475-2515
  Brooklyn *(G-2221)*
Lightspin Technologies Inc ....G...... 301 656-7600
  Endwell *(G-4842)*
Logitek Inc ....D...... 631 567-1100
  Bohemia *(G-1089)*
LSI Computer Systems ....E...... 631 271-0400
  Melville *(G-8364)*

Employee Codes: A=Over 500 employees, B=251-500
C=101-250, D=51-100, E=20-50, F=10-19, G=5-9

36 ELECTRONIC AND OTHER ELECTRICAL EQUIPMENT AND COMPONENTS, EXCEPT COMPUTER

M C Products ....E 631 471-4070
  Holbrook *(G-6488)*
Marcon Services ....G 516 223-8019
  Freeport *(G-5421)*
▲ Marktech International Corp ....E 518 956-2980
  Latham *(G-7401)*
▲ Materion Brewster LLC ....D 845 279-0900
  Brewster *(G-1221)*
▼ McG Electronics Inc ....E 631 586-5125
  Deer Park *(G-4196)*
Micro Contract Manufacturing ....D 631 738-7874
  Medford *(G-8289)*
▲ Micro Semicdtr Researches LLC ....G 646 863-6070
  New York *(G-11281)*
Microchip Technology Inc ....G 631 233-3280
  Hauppauge *(G-6162)*
Microchip Technology Inc ....C 607 785-5992
  Endicott *(G-4825)*
Micromem Technologies ....F 212 672-1806
  New York *(G-11282)*
Mini-Circuits Fort Wayne LLC ....B 718 934-4500
  Brooklyn *(G-2322)*
MMC Magnetics Corp ....F 631 435-9888
  Hauppauge *(G-6167)*
Monolithic Coatings Inc ....G 914 621-2765
  Sharon Springs *(G-15406)*
Nanomas Technologies Inc ....F 607 821-4208
  Endicott *(G-4826)*
▲ Nationwide Tarps Incorporated ....D 518 843-1545
  Amsterdam *(G-362)*
▼ Navitar Inc ....D 585 359-4000
  Rochester *(G-14550)*
Nsi Industries LLC ....C 800 841-2505
  Mount Vernon *(G-8757)*
Oledworks LLC ....E 585 287-6802
  Rochester *(G-14568)*
On Semiconductor Corporation ....G 585 784-5770
  Rochester *(G-14571)*
▲ Onyx Solar Group LLC ....G 917 951-9732
  New York *(G-11525)*
Orbit International Corp ....C 631 435-8300
  Hauppauge *(G-6180)*
Panasonic Corp North America ....D 888 765-2489
  Buffalo *(G-3134)*
▲ Park Electrochemical Corp ....C 631 465-3600
  Melville *(G-8376)*
▲ Passive-Plus Inc ....F 631 425-0938
  Huntington *(G-6708)*
◆ Philips Medical Systems Mr ....B 518 782-1122
  Latham *(G-7403)*
Piezo Electronics Research ....F 845 735-9349
  Pearl River *(G-13487)*
Plures Technologies Inc ....G 585 905-0554
  Canandaigua *(G-3385)*
Procomponents Inc ....E 516 683-0909
  Westbury *(G-17051)*
Pvi Solar Inc ....G 212 280-2100
  New York *(G-11784)*
Renewable Energy Inc ....G 718 690-2691
  Little Neck *(G-7533)*
Riverhawk Company LP ....E 315 624-7171
  New Hartford *(G-8854)*
▲ RSM Electron Power Inc ....D 631 586-7600
  Deer Park *(G-4228)*
RSM Electron Power Inc ....D 631 586-7600
  Hauppauge *(G-6207)*
Ruhle Companies Inc ....E 914 287-4000
  Valhalla *(G-16398)*
S3j Electronics LLC ....E 716 206-1309
  Lancaster *(G-7366)*
Schott Corporation ....D 315 255-2791
  Auburn *(G-514)*
Schott Lithotec USA Corp ....D 845 463-5300
  Elmsford *(G-4789)*
▲ Schott Solar Pv Inc ....G 888 457-6527
  Elmsford *(G-4790)*
Semitronics Corp ....E 516 223-0200
  Freeport *(G-5437)*
Sendyne Corp ....G 212 966-0663
  New York *(G-12046)*
Senera Co Inc ....F 516 639-3774
  Valley Stream *(G-16450)*
Silicon Pulsed Power LLC ....G 610 407-4700
  Clifton Park *(G-3733)*
Sinclair Technologies Inc ....E 716 874-3682
  Hamburg *(G-5966)*
▲ Solar Thin Films Inc ....F 516 341-7787
  Uniondale *(G-16322)*
Solid Cell Inc ....G 585 426-5000
  Rochester *(G-14715)*

Sonotec US Inc ....C 631 415-4758
  Islandia *(G-6842)*
▲ Spectron Glass & Electronics ....F 631 582-5600
  Hauppauge *(G-6218)*
▲ Standard Microsystems Corp ....D 631 435-6000
  Hauppauge *(G-6223)*
▲ Stetron International Inc ....F 716 854-3443
  Buffalo *(G-3225)*
▲ Sumitomo Elc USA Holdings Inc ....E 212 490-6610
  New York *(G-12254)*
▼ Super Conductor Materials Inc ....F 845 368-0240
  Suffern *(G-15821)*
Swissbit Na Inc ....G 914 935-1400
  Port Chester *(G-13784)*
Symwave Inc ....E 949 542-4400
  Hauppauge *(G-6229)*
Tarsier Ltd ....C 212 401-6181
  New York *(G-12305)*
▲ Tel Technology Center Amer LLC ...E 512 424-4200
  Albany *(G-141)*
Telephonics Corporation ....E 631 549-6000
  Huntington *(G-6722)*
Telephonics Tlsi Corp ....E 631 470-8854
  Huntington *(G-6725)*
Thales Laser SA ....D 585 223-2370
  Fairport *(G-4891)*
Thermo Cidtec Inc ....G 315 451-9410
  Liverpool *(G-7580)*
Thermoaura Inc ....F 518 813-4997
  Albany *(G-142)*
Tlsi Incorporated ....D 631 470-8880
  Huntington *(G-6726)*
▲ Tork Inc ....D 914 664-3542
  Mount Vernon *(G-8784)*
◆ Truebite Inc ....F 607 785-7664
  Vestal *(G-16479)*
University At Albany ....D 518 437-8686
  Albany *(G-147)*
Veriled Inc ....G 877 521-5520
  New York *(G-12546)*
Vgg Holding LLC ....G 212 415-6700
  New York *(G-12558)*
Viking Technologies Ltd ....E 631 957-8000
  Lindenhurst *(G-7516)*
Vistec Lithography Inc ....F 518 874-3184
  Troy *(G-16284)*
Warner Energy LLC ....G 315 457-3828
  Liverpool *(G-7583)*
Washington Foundries Inc ....G 516 374-8447
  Hewlett *(G-6340)*
Widetronix Inc ....D 607 330-4752
  Ithaca *(G-6919)*
▲ Yingli Green Enrgy Amricas Inc .....E 888 686-8820
  New York *(G-12714)*
▲ Zastech Inc ....E 516 496-4777
  Syosset *(G-15863)*

3675 Electronic Capacitors

◆ American Tchncal Ceramics Corp ...B 631 622-4700
  Huntington Station *(G-6732)*
▲ American Techical Ceramics ....E 631 622-4758
  Huntington Station *(G-6733)*
American Technical Ceramics ....D 631 622-4700
  Huntington Station *(G-6734)*
AVX Corporation ....D 716 372-6611
  Olean *(G-13155)*
▲ Custom Electronics Inc ....D 607 432-3880
  Oneonta *(G-13207)*
Electron Coil Inc ....D 607 336-7414
  Norwich *(G-13046)*
Ems Development Corporation ....D 631 345-6200
  Yaphank *(G-17407)*
▲ Hipotronics Inc ....C 845 279-8091
  Brewster *(G-1217)*
Integer Holdings Corporation ....E 716 937-5100
  Alden *(G-183)*
Kemet Properties LLC ....E 718 654-8079
  Bronx *(G-1374)*
▲ Knowles Cazenovia Inc ....C 315 655-8710
  Cazenovia *(G-3473)*
▲ MTK Electronics Inc ....E 631 924-7666
  Medford *(G-8290)*
▲ Passive-Plus Inc ....F 631 425-0938
  Huntington *(G-6708)*
▲ Roberts-Gordon LLC ....D 716 852-4400
  Buffalo *(G-3188)*
▲ Stk Electronics Inc ....E 315 655-8476
  Cazenovia *(G-3479)*
Strux Corp ....E 516 768-3969
  Lindenhurst *(G-7508)*

▲ Tronser Inc ....G 315 655-9528
  Cazenovia *(G-3480)*
Viking Technologies Ltd ....E 631 957-8000
  Lindenhurst *(G-7516)*
▲ Virtue Paintball LLC ....G 631 617-5560
  Hauppauge *(G-6251)*
Voltronics LLC ....E 410 749-2424
  Cazenovia *(G-3481)*

3676 Electronic Resistors

Dahua Electronics Corporation ....E 718 886-2188
  Flushing *(G-5243)*
Hvr Advnced Pwr Components Inc ....F 716 693-4700
  Cheektowaga *(G-3605)*
▲ Kionix Inc ....C 607 257-1080
  Ithaca *(G-6891)*
Microgen Systems Inc ....G 585 214-2426
  West Henrietta *(G-16916)*
▼ Micropen Technologies Corp ....D 585 624-2610
  Honeoye Falls *(G-6562)*
▲ Passive-Plus Inc ....F 631 425-0938
  Huntington *(G-6708)*
▲ Stetron International Inc ....F 716 854-3443
  Buffalo *(G-3225)*
▲ Virtue Paintball LLC ....G 631 617-5560
  Hauppauge *(G-6251)*
Vishay Americas Inc ....C 315 938-7575
  Henderson *(G-6313)*
▲ Vishay Thin Film LLC ....C 716 283-4025
  Niagara Falls *(G-12906)*

3677 Electronic Coils & Transformers

▲ Aeroflex Incorporated ....B 516 694-6700
  Plainview *(G-13608)*
▲ All Shore Industries Inc ....F 718 720-0018
  Staten Island *(G-15655)*
▲ Allen Avionics Inc ....E 516 248-8080
  Mineola *(G-8526)*
◆ American Precision Inds Inc ....C 716 691-9100
  Amherst *(G-227)*
American Precision Inds Inc ....D 716 652-3600
  East Aurora *(G-4390)*
American Precision Inds Inc ....D 585 496-5755
  Arcade *(G-386)*
American Trans-Coil Corp ....F 516 922-9640
  Oyster Bay *(G-13390)*
▲ Applied Power Systems Inc ....E 516 935-2230
  Hicksville *(G-6346)*
Atlantic Transformer Inc ....F 716 795-3258
  Barker *(G-611)*
▲ Bel Transformer Inc ....D 516 239-5777
  Inwood *(G-6792)*
Beta Transformer Tech Corp ....E 631 244-7393
  Bohemia *(G-1020)*
▲ Bright Way Supply Inc ....F 718 833-2882
  Brooklyn *(G-1716)*
Caddell Burns Manufacturing Co ....E 631 757-1772
  Northport *(G-13026)*
▲ Data Device Corporation ....B 631 567-5600
  Bohemia *(G-1045)*
Electron Coil Inc ....D 607 336-7414
  Norwich *(G-13046)*
Ems Development Corporation ....E 631 345-6200
  Yaphank *(G-17407)*
▲ Ems Development Corporation .....D 631 924-4736
  Yaphank *(G-17406)*
▲ Eni Technology Inc ....B 585 427-8300
  Rochester *(G-14374)*
Es Beta Inc ....E 631 582-6740
  Ronkonkoma *(G-14927)*
▲ Esc Control Electronics LLC ....E 631 467-5328
  Sayville *(G-15236)*
Exxelia-Raf Tabtronics LLC ....F 585 243-4331
  Piffard *(G-13574)*
▲ Fil-Coil (fc) Corp ....E 631 467-5328
  Sayville *(G-15237)*
Fil-Coil International LLC ....F 631 467-5328
  Sayville *(G-15238)*
Frequency Selective Networks ....F 718 424-7500
  Valley Stream *(G-16433)*
Fuse Electronics Inc ....G 607 352-3222
  Kirkwood *(G-7260)*
Gowanda - Bti LLC ....D 716 492-4081
  Arcade *(G-394)*
▲ Hammond Manufacturing Co Inc ..F 716 630-7030
  Cheektowaga *(G-3602)*
▲ Hipotronics Inc ....C 845 279-8091
  Brewster *(G-1217)*
Island Audio Engineering ....G 631 543-2372
  Commack *(G-3862)*

SIC SECTION — 36 ELECTRONIC AND OTHER ELECTRICAL EQUIPMENT AND COMPONENTS, EXCEPT COMPUTER

Company	Code	Phone
M F L B Inc — Bay Shore (G-712)	F	631 254-8300
Microwave Filter Company Inc — East Syracuse (G-4564)	E	315 438-4700
Mini-Circuits Fort Wayne LLC — Brooklyn (G-2322)	B	718 934-4500
▲ Misonix Inc — Farmingdale (G-5067)	D	631 694-9555
Mitchell Electronics Corp — Mount Vernon (G-8753)	E	914 699-3800
Mohawk Electro Techniques Inc — Barneveld (G-615)	D	315 896-2661
▲ MTK Electronics Inc — Medford (G-8290)	E	631 924-7666
▲ NEa Manufacturing Corp — Inwood (G-6803)	E	516 371-4200
New York Fan Coil LLC — Coram (G-3970)	G	646 580-1344
Precision Electronics Inc — Copiague (G-3943)	F	631 842-4900
Prms Inc — Shirley (G-15452)	G	631 851-7945
▲ Rdi Inc — Mount Kisco (G-8686)	F	914 773-1000
Sag Harbor Industries Inc — Sag Harbor (G-15107)	E	631 725-0440
Service Filtration Corp — Tonawanda (G-16221)	E	716 877-2608
Tdk-Lambda Americas Inc — Hauppauge (G-6231)	F	631 967-3000
▲ Todd Systems Inc — Yonkers (G-17507)	D	914 963-3400
Tte Filters LLC — Gowanda (G-5763)	G	716 532-2234
Urban Technologies Inc — Fredonia (G-5385)	G	716 672-2709

3678 Electronic Connectors

Company	Code	Phone
Accessories For Electronics — South Hempstead (G-15553)	E	631 847-0158
Amphenol Corporation — Sidney (G-15458)	B	607 563-5364
Amphenol Corporation — Sidney (G-15459)	A	607 563-5011
Automatic Connector Inc — Hauppauge (G-6048)	F	631 543-5000
Belden Inc — Horseheads (G-6597)	B	607 796-5600
▲ Casa Innovations Inc — Brooklyn (G-1765)	G	718 965-6600
▲ EBY Electro Inc — Plainview (G-13628)	E	516 576-7777
▲ Executive Machines Inc — Brooklyn (G-1950)	E	718 965-6600
▲ Felchar Manufacturing Corp — Binghamton (G-909)	A	607 723-3106
I Trade Technology Ltd — Suffern (G-15814)	G	615 348-7233
Ieh Corporation — Brooklyn (G-2094)	C	718 492-4440
▲ Keystone Electronics Corp — Astoria (G-444)	C	718 956-8900
Kirtas Inc — Victor (G-16510)	E	585 924-5999
▼ Kirtas Inc — Victor (G-16511)	E	585 924-2420
◆ Leviton Manufacturing Co Inc — Melville (G-8363)	B	631 812-6000
◆ Mason Industries Inc — Hauppauge (G-6152)	B	631 348-0282
▲ Mill-Max Mfg Corp — Oyster Bay (G-13397)	C	516 922-6000
Mini-Circuits Fort Wayne LLC — Brooklyn (G-2322)	B	718 934-4500
▲ NEa Manufacturing Corp — Inwood (G-6803)	E	516 371-4200
▲ Power Connector Inc — Bohemia (G-1114)	E	631 563-7878
◆ Ppc Broadband Inc — East Syracuse (G-4569)	B	315 431-7200
Princetel Inc — Hawthorne (G-6277)	F	914 579-2410
▲ Rdi Inc — Mount Kisco (G-8686)	F	914 773-1000
Resonance Technologies Inc — Ronkonkoma (G-15002)	E	631 237-4901
Sitewatch Technology LLC — East Quogue (G-4471)	G	207 778-3246
Supplynet Inc — Valley Cottage (G-16418)	G	800 826-0279
Sureseal Corporation — Norwich (G-13056)	G	607 336-6676
▲ Taro Manufacturing Company Inc — Auburn (G-520)	F	315 252-9430
▲ Universal Remote Control Inc — Harrison (G-6012)	D	914 630-4343
▲ Virtue Paintball LLC — Hauppauge (G-6251)	G	631 617-5560
▲ Whirlwind Music Distrs Inc — Rochester (G-14790)	D	800 733-9473

3679 Electronic Components, NEC

Company	Code	Phone
3835 Lebron Rest Eqp & Sup Inc — New York (G-9019)	E	212 942-8258
901 D LLC — Airmont (G-10)	E	845 369-1111
▲ A K Allen Co Inc — Mineola (G-8522)	E	516 747-5450
A R V Precision Mfg Inc — Farmingdale (G-4934)	G	631 293-9643
AAR Allen Services Inc — Garden City (G-5507)	E	516 222-9000
Accessories For Electronics — South Hempstead (G-15553)	E	631 847-0158
▲ Advance Circuit Technology Inc — Rochester (G-14191)	E	585 328-2000
▲ Advanced Interconnect Mfg Inc — Victor (G-16483)	D	585 742-2220
Aeroflex Plainview Inc — Plainview (G-13609)	B	516 694-6700
Aeroflex Plainview Inc — Hauppauge (G-6030)	C	631 231-9100
▲ Albatros North America Inc — Ballston Spa (G-589)	E	518 381-7100
▲ All Shore Industries Inc — Staten Island (G-15655)	F	718 720-0018
▲ Allen Avionics Inc — Mineola (G-8526)	E	516 248-8080
Alloy Machine & Tool Co Inc — Lynbrook (G-7974)	G	516 593-3445
Altec Datacom LLC — Bay Shore (G-668)	G	631 242-2417
American Aerospace Contrls Inc — Farmingdale (G-4948)	E	631 694-5100
American Quality Technology — Binghamton (G-884)	F	607 777-9488
▲ Amphenol Intrconnect Pdts Corp — Endicott (G-4803)	G	607 754-4444
Ampro International Inc — Brewster (G-1207)	E	845 278-4910
Amron Electronics Inc — Ronkonkoma (G-14898)	E	631 737-1234
▲ Anaren Inc — East Syracuse (G-4519)	A	315 432-8909
Antenna & Radome Res Assoc — Bay Shore (G-670)	E	631 231-8400
▲ Apollo Display Tech Corp — Ronkonkoma (G-14899)	E	631 580-4360
Applied Concepts Inc — Tully (G-16297)	E	315 696-6676
▲ Applied Power Systems Inc — Hicksville (G-6346)	E	516 935-2230
▲ Apx Technologies Inc — Hicksville (G-6347)	E	516 433-1313
▲ Arnold-Davis LLC — Binghamton (G-886)	C	607 772-1201
Arstan Products International — Hicksville (G-6348)	F	516 433-1313
B H M Metal Products Co — Kauneonga Lake (G-7165)	G	845 292-5297
B3cg Interconnect Usa Inc — Plattsburgh (G-13681)	F	450 491-4040
Badger Technologies Inc — Farmington (G-5155)	E	585 869-7101
▲ Badger Technologies Inc — Farmington (G-5156)	D	585 869-7101
BC Systems Inc — Setauket (G-15399)	E	631 751-9370
Becker Electronics Inc — Ronkonkoma (G-14907)	D	631 619-9100
▲ Behlman Electronics Inc — Hauppauge (G-6052)	E	631 435-0410
Berkshire Transformer — Central Islip (G-3512)	E	631 467-5328
Bryit Group LLC — Holbrook (G-6461)	F	631 563-6603
Bud Barger Assoc Inc — Farmingville (G-5167)	G	631 696-6703
C A M Graphics Co Inc — Farmingdale (G-4964)	E	631 842-3400
Cables Unlimited Inc — Yaphank (G-17403)	E	631 563-6363
▲ Canfield Electronics Inc — Lindenhurst (G-7480)	F	631 585-4100
Centroid Inc — Plainview (G-13616)	E	516 349-0070
Chiplogic Inc — Yaphank (G-17404)	F	631 617-6317
Clever Devices Ltd — Woodbury (G-17304)	E	516 433-6100
Cloud Toronto Inc — Williamsville (G-17267)	F	408 569-4542
Cobham Holdings (us) Inc — Orchard Park (G-13285)	A	716 662-0006
Cobham Holdings Inc — Orchard Park (G-13286)	A	716 662-0006
Communications & Energy Corp — Syracuse (G-15922)	F	315 446-5723
▲ Condor Electronics Corp — Rochester (G-14305)	E	585 235-1500
Crystal Is Inc — Troy (G-16240)	E	518 271-7375
D & S Supplies Inc — Astoria (G-432)	E	718 721-5256
Dimension Technologies Inc — Rochester (G-14330)	E	585 436-3530
Dortronics Systems Inc — Sag Harbor (G-15105)	E	631 725-0505
Dynamic Hybirds Inc — Syracuse (G-15947)	D	315 426-8110
▲ Eastland Electronics Co Inc — Ronkonkoma (G-14926)	G	631 580-3800
◆ Edo LLC — Amityville (G-284)	B	631 630-4000
▼ Electronics & Innovation Ltd — Rochester (G-14363)	F	585 214-0598
Engagement Technology LLC — Elmsford (G-4759)	F	914 591-7600
▲ Eni Technology Inc — Rochester (G-14374)	B	585 427-8300
▲ Esc Control Electronics LLC — Sayville (G-15236)	E	631 467-5328
Espey Mfg & Electronics Corp — Saratoga Springs (G-15180)	C	518 584-4100
▲ Fair-Rite Products Corp — Wallkill (G-16563)	C	845 895-2055
Fei Communications Inc — Uniondale (G-16315)	E	516 794-4500
Felluss Recording — New York (G-10204)	F	212 727-8055
Fine Sounds Group Inc — New York (G-10217)	F	212 364-0219
Frequency Electronics Inc — Uniondale (G-16317)	B	516 794-4500
General Microwave Corporation — Syosset (G-15844)	F	516 802-0900
Gotenna Inc — Brooklyn (G-2043)	F	415 894-2616
▲ Grado Laboratories Inc — Brooklyn (G-2047)	F	718 435-5340
▲ Haynes Roberts Inc — New York (G-10476)	F	212 989-1901
Hazlow Electronics Inc — Rochester (G-14450)	E	585 325-5323
▲ Hipotronics Inc — Brewster (G-1217)	C	845 279-8091
Hypres Inc — Elmsford (G-4764)	E	914 592-1190
I3 Assembly LLC — Binghamton (G-918)	D	607 238-7077
▲ IEC Electronics Corp — Newark (G-12752)	A	315 331-7742
Imrex LLC — Oyster Bay (G-13396)	B	516 479-3675
Innovative Power Products Inc — Holbrook (G-6481)	E	631 563-0088
Island Circuits International — College Point (G-3815)	G	516 625-5555
Island Research and Dev Corp — Ronkonkoma (G-14943)	F	631 471-7100
Jaguar Industries Inc — Haverstraw (G-6261)	F	845 947-1800
▲ Jenlor Ltd — Fayetteville (G-5173)	F	315 637-9080
▲ Jet Components Inc — Islandia (G-6835)	F	631 436-7300
◆ Kearney-National Inc — New York (G-10868)	F	212 661-4600
▲ Keltron Electronics (de Corp) — Ronkonkoma (G-14949)	F	631 567-6300

Employee Codes: A=Over 500 employees, B=251-500, C=101-250, D=51-100, E=20-50, F=10-19, G=5-9

36 ELECTRONIC AND OTHER ELECTRICAL EQUIPMENT AND COMPONENTS, EXCEPT COMPUTER SIC SECTION

▲ L-3 Cmmnctons Fgn Holdings Inc....E....... 212 697-1111
New York (G-10941)
L3 Technologies Inc....E....... 631 289-0363
Patchogue (G-13453)
▲ L3 Technologies Inc....B....... 212 697-1111
New York (G-10943)
Lexan Industries Inc....F....... 631 434-7586
Bay Shore (G-711)
Lighthouse Components....E....... 917 993-6820
New York (G-11027)
Logitek Inc....D....... 631 567-1100
Bohemia (G-1089)
Lyntronics Inc....E....... 631 205-1061
Yaphank (G-17412)
M W Microwave Corp....F....... 516 295-1814
Lawrence (G-7419)
Marcon Electronic Systems LLC....G....... 516 633-6396
Freeport (G-5420)
Mechanical Pwr Conversion LLC....F....... 607 766-9620
Binghamton (G-930)
▲ Mekatronics Incorporated....E....... 516 883-6805
Port Washington (G-13865)
Meridian Technologies Inc....E....... 516 285-1000
Elmont (G-4735)
▲ Merit Electronic Design Co Inc....C....... 631 667-9699
Edgewood (G-4619)
Mezmeriz Inc....G....... 607 216-8140
Ithaca (G-6897)
Microwave Circuit Tech Inc....E....... 631 845-1041
Farmingdale (G-5061)
Microwave Filter Company Inc....E....... 315 438-4700
East Syracuse (G-4564)
▲ Mid Hdson Wkshp For The Dsbled....E....... 845 471-3820
Poughkeepsie (G-13935)
Mini-Circuits Fort Wayne LLC....B....... 718 934-4500
Brooklyn (G-2322)
Mirion Technologies Ist Corp....D....... 607 562-4300
Horseheads (G-6612)
MLS Sales....G....... 516 681-2736
Bethpage (G-873)
◆ Momentive Performance Mtls Inc....E....... 518 237-3330
Waterford (G-16638)
Mpm Holdings Inc....G....... 518 237-3330
Waterford (G-16639)
Mpm Intermediate Holdings Inc....G....... 518 237-3330
Waterford (G-16640)
▲ NEa Manufacturing Corp....E....... 516 371-4200
Inwood (G-6803)
Nelson Holdings Ltd....G....... 607 772-1794
Binghamton (G-935)
New York Digital Corporation....F....... 631 630-9798
Huntington Station (G-6755)
▲ North Hills Signal Proc Corp....G....... 516 682-7700
Syosset (G-15853)
▼ Oakdale Industrial Elec Corp....F....... 631 737-4090
Ronkonkoma (G-14982)
Opus Technology Corporation....F....... 631 271-1883
Melville (G-8374)
Orbit International Corp....C....... 631 435-8300
Hauppauge (G-6180)
Orbit International Corp....D....... 631 435-8300
Hauppauge (G-6181)
Orthogonal....G....... 585 254-2775
Rochester (G-14578)
Paal Technologies Inc....G....... 631 319-6262
Ronkonkoma (G-14987)
▲ Passive-Plus Inc....F....... 631 425-0938
Huntington (G-6708)
Pcb Group Inc....E....... 716 684-0001
Depew (G-4292)
Pcb Piezotronics Inc....B....... 716 684-0003
Depew (G-4294)
◆ Philips Medical Systems Mr....B....... 518 782-1122
Latham (G-7403)
Phoenix Cables Corporation....C....... 845 691-6253
Highland (G-6433)
Photonamics Inc....F....... 585 426-3774
Rochester (G-14602)
Plura Broadcast Inc....G....... 516 997-5675
Massapequa (G-8212)
Polycast Industries Inc....G....... 631 595-2530
Bay Shore (G-722)
▲ Precision Assembly Tech Inc....E....... 631 699-9400
Bohemia (G-1115)
Premier Systems LLC....G....... 631 587-9700
Babylon (G-550)
Prime Electronic Components....F....... 631 254-0101
Deer Park (G-4217)
Pvi Solar Inc....G....... 212 280-2100
New York (G-11784)
▲ Quality Contract Assemblies....F....... 585 663-9030
Rochester (G-14636)
R L C Electronics Inc....D....... 914 241-1334
Mount Kisco (G-8684)
▲ Rdi Inc....F....... 914 773-1000
Mount Kisco (G-8686)
Rem-Tronics Inc....D....... 716 934-2697
Dunkirk (G-4372)
Rochester Industrial Ctrl Inc....D....... 315 524-4555
Ontario (G-13235)
▲ Rochester Industrial Ctrl Inc....D....... 315 524-4555
Ontario (G-13234)
Ruhle Companies Inc....E....... 914 287-4000
Valhalla (G-16398)
▲ Russell Industries Inc....F....... 516 536-5000
Lynbrook (G-7986)
Safe Circuits Inc....G....... 631 586-3682
Dix Hills (G-4320)
Sayeda Manufacturing Corp....F....... 631 345-2525
Medford (G-8293)
SC Textiles Inc....G....... 631 944-6262
Huntington (G-6718)
▲ Scientific Components Corp....B....... 718 934-4500
Brooklyn (G-2563)
Scientific Components Corp....B....... 718 368-2060
Brooklyn (G-2564)
Secs Inc....E....... 914 667-5600
Mount Vernon (G-8778)
▲ Sendec Corp....C....... 585 425-3390
Fairport (G-4883)
Sendec Corp....E....... 585 425-5965
Fairport (G-4884)
▲ SL Industries Inc....D....... 212 520-2300
New York (G-12124)
Sln Group Inc....G....... 718 677-5969
Brooklyn (G-2598)
Sonaer Inc....G....... 631 756-4780
West Babylon (G-16860)
▲ Sopark Corp....C....... 716 822-0434
Buffalo (G-3219)
Space Coast Semiconductor Inc....F....... 631 414-7131
Farmingdale (G-5123)
▲ Spectron Glass & Electronics....F....... 631 582-5600
Hauppauge (G-6218)
Spectron Systems Technology....F....... 631 582-5600
Hauppauge (G-6219)
Spectrum Microwave Inc....E....... 315 253-6241
Auburn (G-517)
▲ Stetron International Inc....F....... 716 854-3443
Buffalo (G-3225)
Sturges Elec Pdts Co Inc....E....... 607 844-8604
Dryden (G-4348)
Superior Motion Controls Inc....E....... 516 420-2921
Farmingdale (G-5130)
▲ Surmotech LLC....D....... 585 742-1220
Victor (G-16527)
T-S-K Electronics Inc....G....... 716 693-3916
North Tonawanda (G-13017)
TCS Electronics Inc....E....... 585 337-4301
Farmington (G-5165)
◆ Tdk USA Corporation....D....... 516 535-2600
Uniondale (G-16323)
Te Connectivity Corporation....E....... 585 785-2500
Rochester (G-14743)
Telephonics Corporation....E....... 631 549-6000
Huntington (G-6722)
▲ Telephonics Corporation....A....... 631 755-7000
Farmingdale (G-5137)
Three Five III-V Materials Inc....F....... 212 213-8290
New York (G-12352)
Tlsi Incorporated....D....... 631 470-8880
Huntington (G-6726)
Tony Baird Electronics Inc....G....... 315 422-4430
Syracuse (G-16084)
Torotron Corporation....G....... 718 428-6992
Fresh Meadows (G-5460)
▲ Trading Services International....F....... 212 501-0142
New York (G-12410)
▲ Ultralife Corporation....A....... 315 332-7100
Newark (G-12766)
Ultravolt Inc....D....... 631 471-4444
Ronkonkoma (G-15020)
Unison Industries LLC....B....... 607 335-5000
Norwich (G-13057)
▲ Vestal Electronic Devices LLC....F....... 607 773-8461
Endicott (G-4838)
Voices For All LLC....G....... 518 261-1664
Mechanicville (G-8263)
W D Technology Inc....G....... 914 779-8738
Eastchester (G-4595)
▲ Walter G Legge Company Inc....G....... 914 737-5040
Peekskill (G-13510)
Werlatone Inc....E....... 845 278-2220
Patterson (G-13470)
Xedit Corp....G....... 718 380-1592
Queens Village (G-14000)

3691 Storage Batteries

Amco Intl Mfg & Design Inc....E....... 718 388-8668
Brooklyn (G-1596)
Battery Energy Storage Systems....G....... 518 256-7029
Troy (G-16249)
Battery Research and Tstg Inc....F....... 315 342-2373
Oswego (G-13353)
▲ Battsco LLC....G....... 516 586-6544
Hicksville (G-6351)
Bren-Trnics Batteries Intl Inc....G....... 631 499-5155
Commack (G-3851)
Bren-Trnics Batteries Intl LLC....E....... 631 499-5155
Commack (G-3852)
◆ Bren-Tronics Inc....C....... 631 499-5155
Commack (G-3853)
Cellec Technologies Inc....G....... 585 454-9166
Rochester (G-14286)
China Lithium Technologies....G....... 212 391-2688
New York (G-9649)
El-Don Battery Post Inc....G....... 716 627-3697
Hamburg (G-5946)
Exide Technologies....G....... 585 344-0656
Batavia (G-633)
Hrg Group Inc....E....... 212 906-8555
New York (G-10567)
Johnson Controls Inc....C....... 585 724-2232
Rochester (G-14485)
New Energy Systems Group....C....... 917 573-0302
New York (G-11406)
Synergy Digital....F....... 718 643-2742
Brooklyn (G-2657)
▲ Ultralife Corporation....A....... 315 332-7100
Newark (G-12766)
▲ W & W Manufacturing Co....F....... 516 942-0011
West Islip (G-16939)

3692 Primary Batteries: Dry & Wet

◆ Bren-Tronics Inc....C....... 631 499-5155
Commack (G-3853)
▲ Electrochem Solutions Inc....D....... 716 759-5800
Clarence (G-3688)
▲ Empire Scientific....G....... 630 510-8636
Deer Park (G-4162)
Shad Industries Inc....G....... 631 504-6028
Yaphank (G-17418)
▲ TAe Trans Atlantic Elec Inc....E....... 631 595-9206
Deer Park (G-4240)

3694 Electrical Eqpt For Internal Combustion Engines

▲ ARC Systems Inc....E....... 631 582-8020
Hauppauge (G-6042)
▲ Autel US Inc....G....... 631 923-2620
Farmingdale (G-4956)
Con Rel Auto Electric Inc....E....... 518 356-1646
Schenectady (G-15273)
Cummins Inc....B....... 812 377-5000
Jamestown (G-7021)
Delphi Automotive Systems LLC....A....... 585 359-6000
West Henrietta (G-16909)
Eastern Unit Exch Rmnfacturing....F....... 718 739-7113
Floral Park (G-5210)
Eluminocity US Inc....G....... 651 528-1165
New York (G-10068)
Ev-Box North America Inc....G....... 646 930-6305
New York (G-10141)
International Key Supply LLC....F....... 631 983-6096
Farmingdale (G-5020)
▲ Karlyn Industries Inc....F....... 845 351-2249
Southfields (G-15580)
◆ Kearney-National Inc....F....... 212 661-4600
New York (G-10868)
◆ Leviton Manufacturing Co Inc....B....... 631 812-6000
Melville (G-8363)
▲ Magnum Shielding Corporation....E....... 585 381-9957
Pittsford (G-13596)
Martinez Specialties Inc....G....... 607 898-3053
Groton (G-5922)
▲ Nas-Tra Automotive Inds Inc....C....... 631 225-1225
Lindenhurst (G-7497)
▲ Sopark Corp....C....... 716 822-0434
Buffalo (G-3219)

36 ELECTRONIC AND OTHER ELECTRICAL EQUIPMENT AND COMPONENTS, EXCEPT COMPUTER

◆ Standard Motor Products Inc .... B 718 392-0200
  Long Island City *(G-7912)*
▲ Taro Manufacturing Company Inc .... F 315 252-9430
  Auburn *(G-520)*
▲ Zenith Autoparts Corp .... E 845 344-1382
  Middletown *(G-8507)*
▲ Zierick Manufacturing Corp .... D 800 882-8020
  Mount Kisco *(G-8690)*

3695 Recording Media

Aarfid LLC .... G 716 992-3999
  Eden *(G-4597)*
BMA Media Services Inc .... E 585 385-2060
  Rochester *(G-14256)*
Connectiva Systems Inc .... F 646 722-8741
  New York *(G-9763)*
Continuity Software Inc .... E 646 216-8628
  New York *(G-9772)*
Dm2 Media LLC .... E 646 419-4357
  New York *(G-9943)*
Escholar LLC .... F 914 989-2900
  White Plains *(G-17131)*
Infinite Software Solutions .... F 718 982-1315
  Staten Island *(G-15708)*
John J Richardson .... F 516 538-6339
  Lawrence *(G-7417)*
▲ L & M Optical Disc LLC .... D 718 649-3500
  New York *(G-10938)*
Longtail Studios Inc .... E 646 443-8146
  New York *(G-11056)*
Medicine Rules Inc .... G 631 334-5395
  East Setauket *(G-4504)*
Multi-Health Systems Inc .... D 800 456-3003
  Cheektowaga *(G-3608)*
Next Big Sound Inc .... G 646 657-9837
  New York *(G-11440)*
Orpheo USA Corp .... G 212 464-8255
  New York *(G-11540)*
Phreesia New York .... B 888 654-7473
  New York *(G-11673)*
▲ Professional Tape Corporation .... G 516 656-5519
  Glen Cove *(G-5638)*
◆ Sony Corporation of America .... E 212 833-8000
  New York *(G-12157)*
Sony Dadc US Inc .... B 212 833-8800
  New York *(G-12158)*
▲ Stamper Technology Inc .... G 585 247-8370
  Rochester *(G-14724)*
VDO Lab Inc .... G 914 949-1741
  White Plains *(G-17206)*
West African Movies .... G 718 731-2190
  Bronx *(G-1495)*

3699 Electrical Machinery, Eqpt & Splys, NEC

303 Contracting Inc .... E 716 896-2122
  Orchard Park *(G-13271)*
331 Holding Inc .... E 585 924-1740
  Victor *(G-16482)*
3krf LLC .... G 516 208-6824
  Oceanside *(G-13090)*
A & S Electric .... G 212 228-2030
  Brooklyn *(G-1528)*
Aabacs Group Inc .... F 718 961-3577
  College Point *(G-3799)*
Advance Energy Systems NY LLC .... G 315 735-5125
  Utica *(G-16329)*
Advanced Mfg Techniques .... G 518 877-8560
  Clifton Park *(G-3720)*
Advanced Photonics Inc .... F 631 471-3693
  Ronkonkoma *(G-14881)*
▲ Albatros North America Inc .... E 518 381-7100
  Ballston Spa *(G-589)*
Alexy Associates Inc .... E 845 482-3000
  Bethel *(G-858)*
▲ All Shore Industries Inc .... F 718 720-0018
  Staten Island *(G-15655)*
Allcom Electric Corp .... G 914 803-0433
  Yonkers *(G-17427)*
Altaquip LLC .... G 631 580-4740
  Ronkonkoma *(G-14893)*
◆ Altronix Corp .... D 718 567-8181
  Brooklyn *(G-1593)*
American Avionic Tech Corp .... G 631 924-8200
  Medford *(G-8266)*
Amertac Holdings Inc .... G 610 336-1400
  Monsey *(G-8602)*
Ameta International Co Ltd .... G 416 992-8036
  Buffalo *(G-2826)*
Ametek Inc .... D 585 263-7700
  Rochester *(G-14218)*

AMP-Line Corp .... F 845 623-3288
  West Nyack *(G-16940)*
Analog Digital Technology LLC .... G 585 698-1845
  Rochester *(G-14219)*
Assa Abloy Entrance Systems US .... E 315 492-6600
  East Syracuse *(G-4524)*
▲ Atlantic Electronic Tech LLC .... G 800 296-2177
  Brooklyn *(G-1648)*
Atlas Switch Co Inc .... E 516 222-6280
  Garden City *(G-5509)*
Audible Difference Inc .... E 212 662-4848
  Brooklyn *(G-1652)*
Audible Difference Inc .... E 212 662-4848
  Brooklyn *(G-1653)*
Avalonics Inc .... E 516 238-7074
  Levittown *(G-7446)*
B & H Electronics Corp .... E 845 782-5000
  Monroe *(G-8584)*
Bare Beauty Laser Hair Removal .... G 718 278-2273
  New York *(G-9370)*
▲ BDB Technologies LLC .... G 800 921-4270
  New York *(G-1672)*
▲ Binghamton Simulator Co Inc .... E 607 321-2980
  Binghamton *(G-891)*
Bombardier Trnsp Holdings USA .... D 607 776-4791
  Bath *(G-654)*
Branson Ultrasonics Corp .... E 585 624-8000
  Honeoye Falls *(G-6553)*
◆ Bren-Tronics Inc .... C 631 499-5155
  Commack *(G-3853)*
BSC Associates LLC .... F 607 321-2980
  Binghamton *(G-895)*
▲ Buffalo Filter LLC .... D 716 835-7000
  Lancaster *(G-7331)*
C & G Video Systems Inc .... G 315 452-1490
  Liverpool *(G-7536)*
Canary Connect Inc .... C 212 390-8576
  New York *(G-9563)*
▲ Castle Power Solutions LLC .... G 518 743-1000
  South Glens Falls *(G-15547)*
Cathay Global Co Inc .... G 718 229-0920
  Bayside Hills *(G-774)*
Century Systems Ltd .... G 718 543-5991
  Bronx *(G-1294)*
Ces Industries Inc .... E 631 782-7088
  Islandia *(G-6828)*
Comsec Ventures International .... E 518 523-1600
  Lake Placid *(G-7297)*
▲ Cooper Crouse-Hinds LLC .... B 866 764-5454
  Syracuse *(G-15927)*
Cooper Industries LLC .... E 315 477-7000
  Syracuse *(G-15928)*
Cooper Power Systems LLC .... B 716 375-7100
  Olean *(G-13160)*
Cooperfriedman Elc Sup Co Inc .... G 718 269-4906
  Long Island City *(G-7733)*
▲ Crysta-Lyn Chemical Company .... G 607 296-4721
  Binghamton *(G-901)*
Custom Sound and Video .... E 585 424-5000
  Rochester *(G-14317)*
CVI Laser LLC .... D 585 244-7220
  Rochester *(G-14318)*
Da Electric .... E 347 270-3422
  Bronx *(G-1312)*
Dahill Distributors Inc .... G 347 371-9453
  Brooklyn *(G-1834)*
Denmar Electric .... F 845 624-4430
  Nanuet *(G-8801)*
Detekion Security Systems Inc .... F 607 729-7179
  Vestal *(G-16469)*
Dorsey Metrology Intl Inc .... E 845 229-2929
  Poughkeepsie *(G-13914)*
◆ Dyson-Kissner-Moran Corp .... E 212 661-4600
  Poughkeepsie *(G-13915)*
East Side Development Corp .... G 585 242-9219
  Rochester *(G-14345)*
Eastco Manufacturing Corp .... F 914 738-5667
  Pelham *(G-13515)*
Eaton Crouse-Hinds .... C 315 477-7000
  Syracuse *(G-15952)*
Edo LLC .... A 631 630-4200
  Amityville *(G-285)*
Emco Electric Services LLC .... G 212 420-9766
  New York *(G-10073)*
▲ Emcom Inc .... D 315 255-5300
  Auburn *(G-492)*
Empire Plastics Inc .... E 607 754-9132
  Endwell *(G-4840)*
▲ Euchner USA Inc .... G 315 701-0315
  East Syracuse *(G-4541)*

▲ Evergreen High Voltage LLC .... G 281 814-9973
  Lake Placid *(G-7298)*
Exfo Burleigh Pdts Group Inc .... D 585 301-1530
  Canandaigua *(G-3374)*
Eyelock Corporation .... G 855 393-5625
  New York *(G-10165)*
Eyelock LLC .... G 855 393-5625
  New York *(G-10166)*
EZ Lift Operator Corp .... G 845 356-1676
  Spring Valley *(G-15606)*
Fairview Bell and Intercom .... G 718 627-8621
  Brooklyn *(G-1958)*
◆ Fiber Instrument Sales Inc .... C 315 736-2206
  Oriskany *(G-13333)*
Fire Fox Security Corp .... G 917 981-9280
  Brooklyn *(G-1978)*
Flanagan Electric Corp .... G 631 567-2976
  Holbrook *(G-6476)*
Forte Network .... G 631 390-9050
  East Northport *(G-4457)*
Full Circle Studios LLC .... G 716 875-7740
  Buffalo *(G-2975)*
FWC Networks Inc .... F 718 408-1558
  Brooklyn *(G-2010)*
G X Electric Corporation .... E 212 921-0400
  New York *(G-10281)*
Gb Group Inc .... E 212 594-3748
  New York *(G-10297)*
General Electric Company .... G 315 554-2000
  Skaneateles *(G-15482)*
▲ Gerome Technologies Inc .... D 518 463-1324
  Menands *(G-8404)*
Green Island Power Authority .... E 518 273-0661
  Green Island *(G-5874)*
Gsa Upstate NY .... G 631 244-5744
  Oakdale *(G-13076)*
Guardian Systems Tech Inc .... F 716 481-5597
  East Aurora *(G-4397)*
▲ Hampton Technologies LLC .... E 631 924-1335
  Medford *(G-8279)*
◆ Hawk-I Security Inc .... G 631 656-1056
  Hauppauge *(G-6115)*
◆ Hergo Ergonomic Support .... E 718 894-0639
  Maspeth *(G-8175)*
Highlander Realty Inc .... E 914 235-8073
  New Rochelle *(G-8956)*
Home Depot USA Inc .... C 845 561-6540
  Newburgh *(G-12782)*
Htf Components Inc .... G 914 703-6795
  White Plains *(G-17149)*
▲ Iba Industrial Inc .... E 631 254-6800
  Edgewood *(G-4614)*
Iconix Inc .... F 516 513-1420
  Hauppauge *(G-6120)*
Ingham Industries Inc .... F 631 242-2493
  Holbrook *(G-6480)*
Innovative Video Tech Inc .... F 631 388-5700
  Hauppauge *(G-6122)*
Intellicheck Mobilisa Inc .... E 516 992-1900
  Jericho *(G-7104)*
Intelligent Ctrl Systems LLC .... G 516 340-1011
  Huntington *(G-6697)*
▲ Isolation Technology Inc .... G 631 253-3314
  West Babylon *(G-16824)*
Issco Corporation .... F 212 732-8748
  Garden City *(G-5524)*
◆ Itin Scale Co Inc .... E 718 336-5900
  Brooklyn *(G-2118)*
J H M Engineering .... E 718 871-1810
  Brooklyn *(G-2122)*
▲ Kinetic Marketing Inc .... E 212 620-0600
  New York *(G-10790)*
Knf Clean Room Products Corp .... E 631 588-7000
  Ronkonkoma *(G-14951)*
▲ Koregon Enterprises Inc .... G 450 218-6836
  Champlain *(G-3571)*
Kyle R Lawrence Electric Inc .... G 315 502-4181
  Palmyra *(G-13435)*
L-3 Cmmnctns Ntronix Holdings .... D 212 697-1111
  New York *(G-10942)*
L3 Technologies Inc .... D 607 721-5465
  Kirkwood *(G-7261)*
Lasermax Inc .... D 585 272-5420
  Rochester *(G-14496)*
Lucas Electric .... G 516 809-8619
  Seaford *(G-15367)*
Lyn Jo Enterprises Ltd .... G 716 753-2776
  Mayville *(G-8248)*
Madison Electric .... F 718 358-4121
  Cambria Heights *(G-3331)*

Employee Codes: A=Over 500 employees, B=251-500
C=101-250, D=51-100, E=20-50, F=10-19, G=5-9

Magic Tech Co Ltd .... G 516 539-7944
West Hempstead *(G-16891)*
Manhattan Scientifics Inc .... F 212 541-2405
New York *(G-11156)*
Manhole Brrier SEC Systems Inc .... E 516 741-1032
Kew Gardens *(G-7194)*
Manor Electric Supply Corp .... F 718 648-8003
Brooklyn *(G-2264)*
Manufacturing Solutions Inc .... E 585 235-3320
Rochester *(G-14515)*
Marzullo Electric LLC .... G 315 455-1050
Syracuse *(G-16004)*
Mitsubishi Elc Pwr Pdts Inc .... G 516 962-2813
Melville *(G-8367)*
Mkj Communications Corp .... F 212 206-0072
New York *(G-11312)*
Multi Tech Electric .... F 718 606-2695
Woodside *(G-17356)*
◆ Napco Security Tech Inc .... A 631 842-9400
Amityville *(G-313)*
Nash Electric Services Inc .... F 914 226-8375
Yonkers *(G-17487)*
National Security Systems Inc .... E 516 627-2222
Manhasset *(G-8097)*
▼ Navitar Inc .... D 585 359-4000
Rochester *(G-14550)*
Nbn Technologies LLC .... G 585 355-5556
Rochester *(G-14551)*
▲ Ncc Ny LLC .... E 718 943-7000
Brooklyn *(G-2363)*
News/Sprts Microwave Rentl Inc .... E 619 670-0572
New York *(G-11438)*
Nk Electric LLC .... G 914 271-0222
Croton On Hudson *(G-4091)*
Northrop Grumman Intl Trdg Inc .... G 716 626-7233
Buffalo *(G-3118)*
▲ OEM Solutions Inc .... G 716 864-9324
Clarence *(G-3694)*
Optimum Applied Systems Inc .... F 845 471-3333
Poughkeepsie *(G-13942)*
▲ Parabit Systems Inc .... E 516 378-4800
Roosevelt *(G-15031)*
▲ Photomedex Inc .... E 888 966-1010
Orangeburg *(G-13261)*
▲ Piller Power Systems Inc .... E 845 695-6658
Middletown *(G-8491)*
Pinpoint Systems Intl Inc .... D 631 775-2100
Bellport *(G-835)*
▲ Promptus Electronic Hdwr Inc .... E 914 699-4700
Mount Vernon *(G-8767)*
▲ Protex International Corp .... D 631 563-4250
Bohemia *(G-1120)*
Rbw Studio LLC .... E 212 388-1621
Brooklyn *(G-2501)*
Rockwell Collins Simulation .... D 607 352-1298
Binghamton *(G-942)*
Rodale Wireless Inc .... E 631 231-0044
Hauppauge *(G-6205)*
▲ Ross Electronics Ltd .... E 718 569-6643
Haverstraw *(G-6264)*
Schuler-Haas Electric Corp .... G 607 936-3514
Painted Post *(G-13419)*
▲ Scorpion Security Products Inc .... G 607 724-9999
Vestal *(G-16476)*
Securevue Inc .... G 631 587-5850
West Islip *(G-16936)*
Security Defense System .... G 718 769-7900
Whitestone *(G-17243)*
▲ Security Dynamics Inc .... F 631 392-1701
Bohemia *(G-1126)*
Sensor Films Incorporated .... E 585 738-3500
Victor *(G-16525)*
Shield Security Doors Ltd .... G 202 468-3308
New York *(G-12072)*
▲ Sima Technologies LLC .... G 412 828-9130
Hauppauge *(G-6215)*
Simulaids Inc .... D 845 679-2475
Saugerties *(G-15223)*
Skae Power Solutions LLC .... E 845 365-9103
Palisades *(G-13427)*
Smithers Tools & Mch Pdts Inc .... D 845 876-3063
Rhinebeck *(G-14070)*
▲ Sonicor Inc .... F 631 920-6555
West Babylon *(G-16861)*
▲ Spirent Inc .... G 631 208-0680
Riverhead *(G-14170)*
Striano Electric Co Inc .... E 516 408-4969
Garden City Park *(G-5556)*
Sunwire Electric Corp .... G 718 456-7500
Brooklyn *(G-2644)*
T Jn Electric .... F 917 560-0981
Mahopac *(G-8033)*
T Jn Electric Inc .... G 845 628-6970
Mahopac *(G-8034)*
Tectran Inc .... G 800 776-5549
Cheektowaga *(G-3619)*
Teledyne Optech Inc .... F 585 427-8310
Rochester *(G-14747)*
Telephonics Corporation .... D 631 755-7000
Farmingdale *(G-5138)*
Telephonics Corporation .... D 631 470-8800
Huntington *(G-6724)*
Tory Electric .... G 914 292-5036
Bedford *(G-794)*
Triborough Electric .... G 718 321-2144
Whitestone *(G-17246)*
▲ Trident Precision Mfg Inc .... D 585 265-2010
Webster *(G-16764)*
Triton Infosys Inc .... E 877 308-2388
New York *(G-12428)*
U E Systems Incorporated .... E 914 592-1220
Elmsford *(G-4797)*
▲ Uncharted Play Inc .... E 646 675-7783
New York *(G-12465)*
United Technologies Corp .... B 866 788-5095
Pittsford *(G-13603)*
Uptek Solutions Corp .... F 631 256-5565
Bohemia *(G-1150)*
▲ V E Power Door Co Inc .... E 631 231-4500
Brentwood *(G-1198)*
▲ Videotec Security Inc .... G 518 825-0020
Plattsburgh *(G-13737)*
Werner Brothers Electric Inc .... G 518 377-3056
Rexford *(G-14066)*
Windowman Inc (usa) .... G 718 246-2626
Brooklyn *(G-2774)*
◆ World Trading Center Inc .... G 631 273-3330
Hauppauge *(G-6260)*
▲ Z-Axis Inc .... D 315 548-5000
Phelps *(G-13563)*
Zappone Chrysler Jeep Ddge Inc .... F 518 982-0610
Halfmoon *(G-5939)*

37 TRANSPORTATION EQUIPMENT

3711 Motor Vehicles & Car Bodies

AB Fire Inc .... G 917 416-6444
Brooklyn *(G-1545)*
Air Flow Manufacturing .... F 607 733-8284
Elmira *(G-4683)*
Antiques & Collectible Autos .... G 716 825-3990
Buffalo *(G-2832)*
Antonicelli Vito Race Car .... G 716 684-2205
Buffalo *(G-2833)*
Armor Dynamics Inc .... F 845 658-9200
Kingston *(G-7207)*
▲ Auto Sport Designs Inc .... F 631 425-1555
Huntington Station *(G-6735)*
Brothers-In-Lawn Property .... G 716 279-6191
Tonawanda *(G-16170)*
Cabot Coach Builders Inc .... G 516 625-4000
Roslyn Heights *(G-15049)*
CIC International Ltd .... D 212 213-0089
Brooklyn *(G-1778)*
Conti Auto Body Corp .... G 516 921-6435
Syosset *(G-15837)*
▲ Daimler Buses North Amer Inc .... A 315 768-8101
Oriskany *(G-13332)*
Dejana Trck Utility Eqp Co LLC .... C 631 544-9000
Kings Park *(G-7200)*
Dejana Trck Utility Eqp Co LLC .... E 631 549-0944
Huntington *(G-6693)*
Empire Coachworks Intl LLC .... D 732 257-7981
Suffern *(G-15812)*
Fiberglass Replacement Parts .... F 716 893-6471
Buffalo *(G-2960)*
◆ Global Fire Corporation .... E 888 320-1799
New York *(G-10357)*
JP Bus & Truck Repair Ltd .... F 914 592-2872
Elmsford *(G-4767)*
▲ Jtekt Torsen North America .... F 585 464-5000
Rochester *(G-14487)*
Leonard Bus Sales Inc .... G 607 467-3100
Rome *(G-14847)*
Madrid Fire District .... G 315 322-4346
Madrid *(G-8024)*
Marcovicci-Wenz Engineering .... G 631 467-9040
Ronkonkoma *(G-14965)*
◆ Medical Coaches Incorporated .... E 607 432-1333
Oneonta *(G-13210)*
Pcb Coach Builders Corp .... G 718 897-7606
Rego Park *(G-14049)*
▲ Prevost Car US Inc .... C 518 957-2052
Plattsburgh *(G-13717)*
▲ Ranger Design Us Inc .... E 800 565-5321
Ontario *(G-13233)*
Roberts Nichols Fire Apparatus .... G 518 431-1945
Cohoes *(G-3781)*
Sabre Enterprises Inc .... G 315 430-3127
Syracuse *(G-16051)*
Scehenvus Fire Dist .... D 607 638-9017
Schenevus *(G-15337)*
Smart Systems Inc .... E 607 776-5380
Bath *(G-662)*
Tee Pee Auto Sales Corp .... F 516 338-9333
Westbury *(G-17059)*
Tesla Motors Inc .... A 212 206-1204
New York *(G-12325)*
Transprttion Collaborative Inc .... E 845 988-2333
Warwick *(G-16619)*
Troyer Inc .... F 585 352-5590
Rochester *(G-14760)*
Wendys Auto Express Inc .... G 845 624-6100
Nanuet *(G-8808)*

3713 Truck & Bus Bodies

Able Weldbuilt Industries Inc .... F 631 643-9700
Deer Park *(G-4110)*
▲ Brunner International Inc .... C 585 798-6000
Medina *(G-8301)*
◆ Concrete Mixer Supplycom Inc .... G 716 375-5565
Olean *(G-13159)*
Conti Auto Body Corp .... G 516 921-6435
Syosset *(G-15837)*
▲ Daimler Buses North Amer Inc .... A 315 768-8101
Oriskany *(G-13332)*
Demartini Oil Equipment Svc .... G 518 463-5752
Glenmont *(G-5683)*
Donver Incorporated .... F 716 945-1910
Kill Buck *(G-7195)*
Eastern Welding Inc .... G 631 727-0306
Riverhead *(G-14154)*
Ekostinger Inc .... F 585 739-0450
East Rochester *(G-4476)*
Fiberglass Replacement Parts .... F 716 893-6471
Buffalo *(G-2960)*
General Welding & Fabg Inc .... G 585 697-7660
Rochester *(G-14413)*
Jeffersonville Volunteer .... E 845 482-3110
Jeffersonville *(G-7093)*
Kurtz Truck Equipment Inc .... F 607 849-3468
Marathon *(G-8115)*
Marros Equipment & Trucks .... F 315 539-8702
Waterloo *(G-16652)*
Premium Bldg Components Inc .... E 518 885-0194
Ballston Spa *(G-606)*
Renaldos Sales and Service Ctr .... G 716 337-3760
North Collins *(G-12947)*
Rexford Services Inc .... G 716 366-6671
Dunkirk *(G-4373)*
▲ Tectran Mfg Inc .... D 800 776-5549
Buffalo *(G-3237)*
Unicell Body Company Inc .... E 716 853-8628
Buffalo *(G-3258)*
Unicell Body Company Inc .... F 716 853-8628
Schenectady *(G-15330)*
Unicell Body Company Inc .... F 585 424-2660
Rochester *(G-14767)*
USA Body Inc .... G 315 852-6123
De Ruyter *(G-4107)*
Weld-Built Body Co Inc .... E 631 643-9700
Wyandanch *(G-17393)*

3714 Motor Vehicle Parts & Access

4bumpers Llc .... F 212 721-9600
New York *(G-9021)*
A-Line Technologies Inc .... F 607 772-2439
Binghamton *(G-881)*
◆ Actasys Inc .... G 617 834-0666
Watervliet *(G-16702)*
Agri Services Co .... G 716 937-6618
Alden *(G-176)*
Allomatic Products Company .... G 516 775-0330
Floral Park *(G-5200)*
▲ Alloy Metal Products LLC .... F 315 676-2405
Central Square *(G-3542)*
American Auto ACC Incrporation .... E 718 886-6600
Flushing *(G-5233)*
American Refuse Supply Inc .... G 718 893-8157
Bronx *(G-1273)*

Anchor Commerce Trading Corp ... G ... 516 881-3485
Atlantic Beach *(G-467)*
◆ API Heat Transf Thermasys Corp ... A ... 716 684-6700
Buffalo *(G-2834)*
Apsis USA Inc ... F ... 631 421-6800
Farmingdale *(G-4952)*
▲ ARC Remanufacturing Inc ... D ... 718 728-0701
Long Island City *(G-7698)*
Auburn Bearing & Mfg Inc ... G ... 315 986-7600
Macedon *(G-8009)*
Automotive Accessories Group ... B ... 212 736-8100
New York *(G-9320)*
◆ Automotive Filters Mfg Inc ... F ... 631 435-1010
Bohemia *(G-1016)*
Axle Express ... E ... 518 347-2220
Schenectady *(G-15261)*
▲ Axle Teknology LLC ... G ... 631 423-3044
Huntington *(G-6687)*
Bam Enterprises Inc ... G ... 716 773-7634
Grand Island *(G-5767)*
Banner Transmission & Eng Co ... F ... 516 221-9459
Bellmore *(G-810)*
Bigbee Steel and Tank Company ... E ... 518 273-0801
Watervliet *(G-16703)*
▲ Biltron Automotive Products ... E ... 631 928-8613
Port Jeff STA *(G-13786)*
Borgwarner Inc ... E ... 607 257-1800
Ithaca *(G-6863)*
Borgwarner Morse TEC Inc ... D ... 607 266-5111
Ithaca *(G-6865)*
▲ Borgwarner Morse TEC LLC ... C ... 607 257-6700
Ithaca *(G-6866)*
Borgwarner Morse TEC LLC ... D ... 607 257-6700
Cortland *(G-4037)*
Car-Go Industries Inc ... G ... 718 472-1443
Woodside *(G-17340)*
Classic & Performance Spc ... E ... 716 759-1800
Lancaster *(G-7334)*
▲ CRS Remanufacturing Co Inc ... F ... 718 739-1720
Jamaica *(G-6944)*
Cubic Trnsp Systems Inc ... F ... 212 255-1810
New York *(G-9821)*
Cummins Inc ... A ... 716 456-2111
Lakewood *(G-7314)*
Cummins Inc ... B ... 812 377-5000
Jamestown *(G-7021)*
Curtis L Maclean L C ... B ... 716 898-7800
Buffalo *(G-2915)*
▲ Custom Sitecom LLC ... F ... 631 420-4238
Farmingdale *(G-4981)*
Deer Park Driveshaft & Hose ... G ... 631 667-4091
Deer Park *(G-4149)*
Delphi Automotive LLP ... G ... 716 438-4886
Amherst *(G-237)*
Delphi Automotive Systems LLC ... C ... 585 359-6000
West Henrietta *(G-16908)*
Delphi Automotive Systems LLC ... A ... 585 359-6000
West Henrietta *(G-16909)*
Delphi Automotive Systems LLC ... E ... 585 359-6000
West Henrietta *(G-16910)*
Delphi Thermal Systems ... F ... 716 439-2454
Lockport *(G-7607)*
Dennys Drive Shaft Service ... G ... 716 875-6640
Kenmore *(G-7174)*
Dmic Inc ... F ... 716 743-4360
North Tonawanda *(G-12987)*
Drive Shaft Shop Inc ... F ... 631 348-1818
Hauppauge *(G-6090)*
Electron Top Mfg Co Inc ... E ... 718 846-7400
Richmond Hill *(G-14084)*
Electronic Machine Parts LLC ... F ... 631 434-3700
Hauppauge *(G-6093)*
Enplas America Inc ... G ... 646 892-7811
New York *(G-10095)*
Exten II LLC ... F ... 716 895-2214
Buffalo *(G-2956)*
▲ Extreme Auto Accessories Corp ... F ... 718 978-6722
South Ozone Park *(G-15557)*
Factory Wheel Warehouse Inc ... G ... 516 605-2131
Plainview *(G-13630)*
▲ Fast By Gast Inc ... G ... 716 773-1536
Grand Island *(G-5770)*
▲ Fcmp Inc ... F ... 716 692-4623
Tonawanda *(G-16179)*
General Motors LLC ... B ... 315 764-2000
Massena *(G-8226)*
◆ Gleason Works ... A ... 585 473-1000
Rochester *(G-14429)*
GM Components Holdings LLC ... C ... 716 439-2237
Lockport *(G-7618)*
GM Components Holdings LLC ... B ... 585 647-7000
Rochester *(G-14430)*
GM Components Holdings LLC ... B ... 716 439-2463
Lockport *(G-7619)*
GM Components Holdings LLC ... B ... 716 439-2011
Lockport *(G-7620)*
▲ Interparts International Inc ... E ... 516 576-2000
Plainview *(G-13639)*
▲ ITT Enidine Inc ... B ... 716 662-1900
Orchard Park *(G-13299)*
Johnson Controls Inc ... C ... 585 724-2232
Rochester *(G-14485)*
Jt Precision Inc ... E ... 716 795-3860
Barker *(G-612)*
▲ Jtekt Torsen North America ... F ... 585 464-5000
Rochester *(G-14487)*
K M Drive Line Inc ... G ... 718 599-0628
Brooklyn *(G-2164)*
▲ Karlyn Industries Inc ... F ... 845 351-2249
Southfields *(G-15580)*
Katikati Inc ... G ... 585 678-1764
West Henrietta *(G-16915)*
◆ Kearney-National Inc ... F ... 212 661-4600
New York *(G-10868)*
▲ Kerns Manufacturing Corp ... C ... 718 784-4044
Long Island City *(G-7807)*
Kurtz Truck Equipment Inc ... F ... 607 849-3468
Marathon *(G-8115)*
▲ Lee World Industries LLC ... C ... 212 265-8866
New York *(G-10993)*
▲ Lemans Corporation ... G ... 518 885-7500
Ballston Spa *(G-600)*
M2 Race Systems Inc ... G ... 607 882-9078
Ithaca *(G-6892)*
◆ Magtrol Inc ... E ... 716 668-5555
Buffalo *(G-3075)*
Mahle Behr USA Inc ... B ... 716 439-2011
Lockport *(G-7627)*
Mahle Industries Incorporated ... F ... 248 735-3623
Amherst *(G-249)*
Marcovicci-Wenz Engineering ... G ... 631 467-9040
Ronkonkoma *(G-14965)*
▲ Motor Components LLC ... D ... 607 737-8011
Elmira Heights *(G-4724)*
▲ Nas-Tra Automotive Inds Inc ... C ... 631 225-1225
Lindenhurst *(G-7497)*
Nassau Auto Remanufacturer ... G ... 516 485-4500
Hempstead *(G-6305)*
▼ Norcatec LLC ... E ... 516 222-7070
Garden City *(G-5537)*
Northeastern Transparts Inc ... F ... 716 833-0792
Hamburg *(G-5958)*
Omega Industries & Development ... E ... 516 349-8010
Plainview *(G-13654)*
◆ P & F Industries Inc ... E ... 631 694-9800
Melville *(G-8375)*
◆ Pall Corporation ... A ... 516 484-5400
Port Washington *(G-13870)*
Pall Corporation ... A ... 607 753-6041
Cortland *(G-4059)*
Par-Foam Products Inc ... C ... 716 855-2066
Buffalo *(G-3135)*
Parker-Hannifin Corporation ... D ... 248 628-6017
Lancaster *(G-7355)*
Performance Designed By Peters ... F ... 585 223-9062
Fairport *(G-4876)*
Phillip J Ortiz Manufacturing ... G ... 845 226-7030
Hopewell Junction *(G-6583)*
▲ Powerflow Inc ... D ... 716 892-1014
Buffalo *(G-3157)*
Pro Torque ... E ... 631 218-8700
Bohemia *(G-1118)*
Pro-Value Distribution Inc ... G ... 585 783-1461
Rochester *(G-14627)*
◆ Rosco Inc ... C ... 718 526-2601
Jamaica *(G-6985)*
▲ Rpb Distributors LLC ... G ... 914 244-3600
Mount Kisco *(G-8687)*
Secor Marketing Group Inc ... G ... 914 381-3600
Mamaroneck *(G-8079)*
Smith Metal Works Newark Inc ... E ... 315 331-1651
Newark *(G-12763)*
▲ Specialty Silicone Pdts Inc ... E ... 518 885-8826
Ballston Spa *(G-608)*
◆ Standard Motor Products Inc ... B ... 718 392-0200
Long Island City *(G-7912)*
Steering Columns Galore Inc ... G ... 845 278-5762
Mahopac *(G-8032)*
Temper Corporation ... G ... 518 853-3467
Fonda *(G-5323)*
Terrys Transmission ... G ... 315 458-4333
North Syracuse *(G-12969)*
Tesla Motors Inc ... A ... 212 206-1204
New York *(G-12325)*
TI Group Auto Systems LLC ... G ... 315 568-7042
Seneca Falls *(G-15394)*
▲ Titanx Engine Cooling Inc ... B ... 716 665-7129
Jamestown *(G-7071)*
Transcedar Industries Ltd ... G ... 716 731-6442
Niagara Falls *(G-12901)*
Troyer Inc ... F ... 585 352-5590
Rochester *(G-14760)*
TRW Automotive Inc ... B ... 315 255-3311
Auburn *(G-522)*
Vehicle Safety Dept ... F ... 315 458-6683
Syracuse *(G-16090)*
▼ Whiting Door Mfg Corp ... B ... 716 542-5427
Akron *(G-27)*
▲ Wolo Mfg Corp ... E ... 631 242-0333
Deer Park *(G-4253)*
Yomiuri International Inc ... G ... 212 752-2196
New York *(G-12716)*
Zwack Incorporated ... E ... 518 733-5135
Stephentown *(G-15780)*

3715 Truck Trailers

◆ Blue Tee Corp ... A ... 212 598-0880
New York *(G-9473)*
Cross Country Mfg Inc ... F ... 607 656-4103
Greene *(G-5881)*
Cross Country Mfg Inc ... F ... 607 656-4103
Greene *(G-5882)*
Davis Trailer World LLC ... F ... 585 538-6640
York *(G-17521)*
Full Service Auto Body Inc ... F ... 718 831-9300
Floral Park *(G-5211)*
G L 7 Sales Plus Ltd ... G ... 631 696-8290
Coram *(G-3965)*
General Welding & Fabg Inc ... G ... 716 652-0033
Elma *(G-4662)*
Seneca Truck & Trailer Inc ... G ... 315 781-1100
Geneva *(G-5598)*
▼ Stone Well Bodies & Mch Inc ... E ... 315 497-3512
Genoa *(G-5602)*

3716 Motor Homes

Authority Transportation Inc ... F ... 888 933-1268
Dix Hills *(G-4314)*

3721 Aircraft

Alliant Tchsystems Oprtons LLC ... E ... 631 737-6100
Ronkonkoma *(G-14890)*
Altius Aviation LLC ... G ... 315 455-7555
Syracuse *(G-15873)*
▲ Ascent Aerospace Holdings LLC ... G ... 212 916-8142
New York *(G-9279)*
Atk Gasl Inc ... F ... 631 737-6100
Ronkonkoma *(G-14902)*
Barclay Tagg Racing ... E ... 631 404-8269
Floral Park *(G-5203)*
Boeing Company ... A ... 201 259-9400
New York *(G-9484)*
◆ Calspan Corporation ... C ... 716 631-6955
Buffalo *(G-2886)*
Calspan Corporation ... F ... 716 236-1040
Niagara Falls *(G-12823)*
CIC International Ltd ... D ... 212 213-0089
Brooklyn *(G-1778)*
Drone Usa Inc ... E ... 212 220-8795
New York *(G-9981)*
Grumman Field Support Services ... D ... 516 575-0574
Bethpage *(G-867)*
▲ Joka Industries Inc ... E ... 631 589-0444
Bohemia *(G-1079)*
Lesly Enterprise & Associates ... G ... 631 988-1301
Deer Park *(G-4189)*
Lockheed Martin Corporation ... E ... 716 297-1000
Niagara Falls *(G-12861)*
Lockheed Martin Corporation ... G ... 212 953-1510
New York *(G-11048)*
Lockheed Martin Corporation ... E ... 315 456-1548
Liverpool *(G-7553)*
Lockheed Martin Corporation ... D ... 315 793-5800
New Hartford *(G-8852)*
Luminati Aerospace LLC ... F ... 631 574-2616
Calverton *(G-3321)*
M & H Research and Dev Corp ... G ... 607 734-2346
Beaver Dams *(G-788)*
Moog Inc ... B ... 716 687-4954
East Aurora *(G-4400)*

Employee Codes: A=Over 500 employees, B=251-500
C=101-250, D=51-100, E=20-50, F=10-19, G=5-9
2018 Harris
New York Manufacturers Directory
851

Northrop Grumman Systems Corp ....A.... 516 575-0574
Bethpage *(G-875)*

Northrop Grumman Systems Corp ....D.... 716 626-4600
Buffalo *(G-3119)*

Northrop Grumman Systems Corp ....G.... 631 423-1014
Huntington *(G-6706)*

Pro Drones Usa LLC ....F.... 718 530-3558
New York *(G-11744)*

Sikorsky Aircraft Corporation ....D.... 585 424-1990
Rochester *(G-14710)*

Tech Park Food Services LLC ....G.... 585 295-1250
Rochester *(G-14745)*

Trium Strs-Lg Isld LLC ....D.... 516 997-5757
Westbury *(G-17065)*

3724 Aircraft Engines & Engine Parts

Advanced Atomization Tech LLC ....B.... 315 923-2341
Clyde *(G-3749)*

▲ ARC Systems Inc ....E.... 631 582-8020
Hauppauge *(G-6042)*

B H Aircraft Company Inc ....D.... 631 580-9747
Ronkonkoma *(G-14905)*

Chromalloy American LLC ....E.... 845 230-7355
Orangeburg *(G-13244)*

Chromalloy Gas Turbine LLC ....C.... 845 359-2462
Orangeburg *(G-13245)*

Chromalloy Gas Turbine LLC ....E.... 845 692-8912
Middletown *(G-8464)*

Colonial Group LLC ....E.... 516 349-8010
Plainview *(G-13619)*

▲ Davis Aircraft Products Co Inc ....C.... 631 563-1500
Bohemia *(G-1046)*

▲ Dyna-Empire Inc ....C.... 516 222-2700
Garden City *(G-5513)*

Gb Aero Engine LLC ....B.... 914 925-9600
Rye *(G-15083)*

General Electric Company ....A.... 518 385-4022
Schenectady *(G-15283)*

General Electric Company ....E.... 518 385-7620
Niskayuna *(G-12912)*

Honeywell International Inc ....A.... 315 554-6643
Skaneateles Falls *(G-15492)*

Honeywell International Inc ....A.... 845 342-4400
Middletown *(G-8479)*

Honeywell International Inc ....A.... 212 964-5111
Melville *(G-8357)*

Howe Machine & Tool Corp ....F.... 516 931-5687
Bethpage *(G-868)*

▲ ITT Enidine Inc ....B.... 716 662-1900
Orchard Park *(G-13299)*

▲ Kerns Manufacturing Corp ....C.... 718 784-4044
Long Island City *(G-7807)*

Lourdes Industries Inc ....D.... 631 234-6600
Hauppauge *(G-6146)*

▲ Magellan Aerospace Bethel Inc ....C.... 203 798-9373
Corona *(G-4024)*

Magellan Aerospace Processing ....G.... 631 694-1818
West Babylon *(G-16838)*

McGuigan Inc ....E.... 631 750-6222
Bohemia *(G-1098)*

Nell-Joy Industries Inc ....E.... 631 842-8989
Copiague *(G-3939)*

Omega Industries & Development ....E.... 516 349-8010
Plainview *(G-13654)*

SOS International LLC ....B.... 212 742-2410
New York *(G-12165)*

SOS International LLC ....C.... 212 742-2410
New York *(G-12166)*

▲ Therm Incorporated ....C.... 607 272-8500
Ithaca *(G-6912)*

Triumph Actuation Systems LLC ....D.... 516 378-0162
Freeport *(G-5443)*

Triumph Group Inc ....D.... 516 997-5757
Westbury *(G-17066)*

Turbine Engine Comp Utica ....A.... 315 768-8070
Whitesboro *(G-17225)*

United Technologies Corp ....G.... 315 432-7849
East Syracuse *(G-4588)*

3728 Aircraft Parts & Eqpt, NEC

Aero Trades Mfg Corp ....E.... 516 746-3360
Mineola *(G-8523)*

Air Industries Group ....D.... 631 881-4920
Hauppauge *(G-6032)*

▲ Air Industries Machining Corp ....C.... 631 968-5000
Bay Shore *(G-666)*

▲ Alcoa Fastening Systems ....C.... 845 334-7203
Kingston *(G-7206)*

Alken Industries Inc ....D.... 631 467-2000
Ronkonkoma *(G-14886)*

Alro Machine Tool & Die Co Inc ....F.... 631 226-5020
Lindenhurst *(G-7475)*

Arkwin Industries Inc ....C.... 516 333-2640
Westbury *(G-16996)*

Armacel Armor Corporation ....E.... 805 384-1144
New York *(G-9254)*

▲ Astronics Corporation ....C.... 716 805-1599
East Aurora *(G-4391)*

Ausco Inc ....D.... 516 944-9882
Farmingdale *(G-4955)*

B & B Precision Components Inc ....G.... 631 273-3321
Ronkonkoma *(G-14904)*

B/E Aerospace Inc ....E.... 631 563-6400
Bohemia *(G-1018)*

Bar Fields Inc ....F.... 347 587-7795
Brooklyn *(G-1664)*

▲ Blair Industries Inc ....E.... 631 924-6600
Medford *(G-8268)*

Canfield Aerospace & Mar Inc ....E.... 631 648-1050
Ronkonkoma *(G-14913)*

Caravan International Corp ....G.... 212 223-7190
New York *(G-9578)*

Carleton Technologies Inc ....B.... 716 662-0006
Orchard Park *(G-13282)*

Circor Aerospace Inc ....D.... 631 737-1900
Hauppauge *(G-6065)*

▲ Cox & Company Inc ....C.... 212 366-0200
Plainview *(G-13623)*

CPI Aerostructures Inc ....B.... 631 586-5200
Edgewood *(G-4610)*

Crown Aircraft Lighting Inc ....G.... 718 767-3410
Whitestone *(G-17234)*

▲ Davis Aircraft Products Co Inc ....C.... 631 563-1500
Bohemia *(G-1046)*

Design/Ol Inc ....F.... 631 474-5536
Port Jeff STA *(G-13789)*

▲ Dresser-Argus Inc ....G.... 718 643-1540
Brooklyn *(G-1882)*

Ducommun Aerostructures NY Inc ....B.... 518 731-2791
Coxsackie *(G-4082)*

▲ Dyna-Empire Inc ....C.... 516 222-2700
Garden City *(G-5513)*

East/West Industries Inc ....E.... 631 981-5900
Ronkonkoma *(G-14924)*

Eastern Precision Machining ....G.... 631 286-4758
Bellport *(G-824)*

◆ Edo LLC ....G.... 631 630-4000
Amityville *(G-284)*

Engineered Metal Products Inc ....G.... 631 842-3780
Copiague *(G-3926)*

Enlighten Air Inc ....G.... 917 656-1248
New York *(G-10094)*

Ensil Technical Services Inc ....E.... 716 282-1020
Niagara Falls *(G-12836)*

Excelco Developments Inc ....E.... 716 934-2651
Silver Creek *(G-15470)*

Excelco/Newbrook Inc ....D.... 716 934-2644
Silver Creek *(G-15471)*

Fluid Mechanisms Hauppauge Inc ....E.... 631 234-0100
Hauppauge *(G-6101)*

GE Aviation Systems LLC ....C.... 631 467-5500
Bohemia *(G-1067)*

▲ GKN Aerospace Monitor Inc ....B.... 562 619-8558
Amityville *(G-288)*

◆ Gleason Works ....A.... 585 473-1000
Rochester *(G-14429)*

▲ Gny Equipment LLC ....F.... 631 667-1010
Bay Shore *(G-701)*

Goodrich Corporation ....C.... 315 838-1200
Rome *(G-14840)*

Handy Tool & Mfg Co Inc ....E.... 718 478-9203
Brooklyn *(G-2067)*

Hicksville Machine Works Corp ....F.... 516 931-1524
Hicksville *(G-6383)*

Honeywell International Inc ....B.... 516 577-2000
Melville *(G-8358)*

▲ HSM Machine Works Inc ....E.... 631 924-6600
Medford *(G-8281)*

Jac Usa Inc ....G.... 212 841-7430
New York *(G-10725)*

Jamco Aerospace Inc ....E.... 631 586-7900
Deer Park *(G-4178)*

◆ Jaquith Industries Inc ....E.... 315 478-5700
Syracuse *(G-15985)*

Joldeson One Aerospace Inds ....D.... 718 848-7396
Ozone Park *(G-13406)*

Jrsmm LLC ....G.... 607 331-1549
Elmira *(G-4706)*

Lai International Inc ....D.... 763 780-0060
Green Island *(G-5876)*

Loar Group Inc ....C.... 212 210-9348
New York *(G-11046)*

▲ Magellan Aerospace Bethel Inc ....C.... 203 798-9373
Corona *(G-4024)*

▲ Magellan Aerospace NY Inc ....C.... 718 699-4000
Corona *(G-4025)*

Magellan Aerospace NY Inc ....C.... 631 589-2440
Bohemia *(G-1094)*

MD International Industries ....E.... 631 254-3100
Deer Park *(G-4197)*

Metadure Parts & Sales Inc ....F.... 631 249-2141
Farmingdale *(G-5059)*

◆ Metal Dynamics Intl Corp ....G.... 631 231-1153
Hauppauge *(G-6160)*

Milex Precision Inc ....F.... 631 595-2393
Bay Shore *(G-715)*

Min-Max Machine Ltd ....F.... 631 585-4378
Ronkonkoma *(G-14969)*

Minutemen Precsn McHning Tool ....E.... 631 467-4900
Ronkonkoma *(G-14970)*

◆ Moog Inc ....A.... 716 652-2000
Elma *(G-4664)*

Nassau Tool Works Inc ....E.... 631 328-7031
West Babylon *(G-16845)*

Norsk Titanium US Inc ....G.... 949 735-9463
Plattsburgh *(G-13706)*

Omega Industries & Development ....E.... 516 349-8010
Plainview *(G-13654)*

Parker-Hannifin Corporation ....C.... 631 231-3737
Clyde *(G-3755)*

▼ Posimech Inc ....E.... 631 924-5959
Medford *(G-8292)*

Precision Cnc ....G.... 631 847-3999
Deer Park *(G-4216)*

▲ Precision Gear Incorporated ....C.... 718 321-7200
College Point *(G-3827)*

Reese Manufacturing Inc ....G.... 631 842-3780
Copiague *(G-3946)*

Ripi Precision Co Inc ....F.... 631 694-2453
Farmingdale *(G-5110)*

S & L Aerospace Metals LLC ....D.... 718 326-1821
Flushing *(G-5296)*

Santa Fe Manufacturing Corp ....G.... 631 234-0100
Hauppauge *(G-6208)*

Servotronics Inc ....C.... 716 655-5990
Elma *(G-4668)*

▲ Styles Aviation Inc ....G.... 845 677-8185
Lagrangeville *(G-7284)*

▼ Sumner Industries Inc ....F.... 631 666-7290
Bay Shore *(G-742)*

Superior Motion Controls Inc ....E.... 516 420-2921
Farmingdale *(G-5130)*

Tangent Machine & Tool Corp ....E.... 631 249-3088
Farmingdale *(G-5134)*

Tdl Manufacturing Inc ....F.... 215 538-8820
Hauppauge *(G-6232)*

Tek Precision Co Ltd ....E.... 631 242-0330
Deer Park *(G-4241)*

Tens Machine Company Inc ....E.... 631 981-3321
Holbrook *(G-6505)*

TPC Inc ....G.... 315 438-8605
East Syracuse *(G-4584)*

Triumph Actuation Systems LLC ....D.... 516 378-0162
Freeport *(G-5443)*

Usairports Services Inc ....E.... 585 527-6835
Rochester *(G-14776)*

Vosky Precision Machining Corp ....F.... 631 737-3200
Ronkonkoma *(G-15024)*

W J Albro Machine Works Inc ....G.... 631 345-0657
Yaphank *(G-17424)*

Wilco Industries Inc ....G.... 631 676-2593
Ronkonkoma *(G-15025)*

Young & Franklin Inc ....D.... 315 457-3110
Liverpool *(G-7586)*

3731 Shipbuilding & Repairing

Alpha Marine Repair ....E.... 718 816-7150
Staten Island *(G-15657)*

Caddell Dry Dock & Repr Co Inc ....C.... 718 442-2112
Staten Island *(G-15674)*

Cgsi Group LLC ....F.... 516 986-5503
Bronx *(G-1296)*

Clark Rigging & Rental Corp ....F.... 585 265-2910
Webster *(G-16741)*

▲ Dragon Trading Inc ....G.... 212 717-1496
New York *(G-9974)*

Excelco Developments Inc ....E.... 716 934-2651
Silver Creek *(G-15470)*

Excelco/Newbrook Inc ....D.... 716 934-2644
Silver Creek *(G-15471)*

SIC SECTION
37 TRANSPORTATION EQUIPMENT

George G Sharp Inc ....E 212 732-2800
New York (G-10325)
Highland Museum & Lighthouse ....F 508 487-1121
Cairo (G-3298)
Huntington Ingalls Inc ....E 518 884-3834
Saratoga Springs (G-15188)
▲ May Ship Repair Contg Corp ....E 718 442-9700
Staten Island (G-15726)
McQuilling Partners Inc ....E 516 227-5718
Garden City (G-5531)
▼ Metalcraft Marine Us Inc ....F 315 501-4015
Cape Vincent (G-3410)
▲ Moran Shipyard Corporation ....C 718 981-5600
Staten Island (G-15728)
Moran Towing Corporation ....G 718 981-5600
Staten Island (G-15729)
Port Everglades Machine Works ....F 516 367-2280
Plainview (G-13658)
▲ Reynolds Shipyard Corporation ....F 718 981-2800
Staten Island (G-15753)
▲ Robert E Derecktor Inc ....D 914 698-0962
Mamaroneck (G-8078)
Scarano Boat Building Inc ....E 518 463-3401
Albany (G-132)
Steelways Inc ....E 845 562-0860
Newburgh (G-12804)
United Ship Repair Inc ....F 718 237-2800
Brooklyn (G-2722)
Viking Mar Wldg Ship Repr LLC ....F 718 758-4116
Brooklyn (G-2744)
Weldrite Closures Inc ....E 585 429-8790
Rochester (G-14788)

3732 Boat Building & Repairing

Allen Boat Co Inc ....G 716 842-0800
Buffalo (G-2819)
▼ American Metalcraft Marine ....G 315 686-9891
Clayton (G-3710)
▲ AVS Laminates Inc ....E 631 286-2136
Bellport (G-821)
Cayuga Wooden Boatworks Inc ....E 315 253-7447
Ithaca (G-6868)
Coecles Hbr Marina & Boat Yard ....F 631 749-0856
Shelter Island (G-15408)
Eastern Welding Inc ....G 631 727-0306
Riverhead (G-14154)
Fantasy Glass Compan ....G 845 786-5818
Stony Point (G-15794)
Gar Wood Custom Boats ....G 518 494-2966
Brant Lake (G-1170)
Global Marine Power Inc ....E 631 208-2933
Calverton (G-3319)
▲ Hacker Boat Company Inc ....E 518 543-6731
Silver Bay (G-15468)
Hampton Shipyards Inc ....F 631 653-6777
East Quogue (G-4470)
▲ Jag Manufacturing Inc ....E 518 762-9558
Johnstown (G-7147)
Katherine Blizniak ....G 716 674-8545
West Seneca (G-16978)
▼ Marathon Boat Group Inc ....F 607 849-3211
Marathon (G-8116)
▲ May Ship Repair Contg Corp ....E 718 442-9700
Staten Island (G-15726)
▼ Metalcraft Marine Us Inc ....F 315 501-4015
Cape Vincent (G-3410)
Mokai Manufacturing Inc ....G 845 566-8287
Newburgh (G-12789)
▲ Robert E Derecktor Inc ....D 914 698-0962
Mamaroneck (G-8078)
Rocking The Boat Inc ....F 718 466-5799
Bronx (G-1441)
Scarano Boatbuilding Inc ....E 518 463-3401
Albany (G-133)
Superboats Inc ....G 631 226-1761
Lindenhurst (G-7510)
Tumblehome Boatshop ....G 518 623-5050
Warrensburg (G-16603)
Wooden Boatworks ....G 631 477-6507
Greenport (G-5896)

3743 Railroad Eqpt

Acf Industries Holding LLC ....G 212 702-4363
New York (G-9064)
Alstom Signaling Inc ....E 585 274-8700
Schenectady (G-15258)
Alstom Transportation Inc ....E 212 692-5353
New York (G-9155)
Alstom Transportation Inc ....E 800 717-4477
West Henrietta (G-16899)
American Motive Power Inc ....E 585 335-3132
Dansville (G-4101)
▲ Bombardier Mass Transit Corp ....B 518 566-0150
Plattsburgh (G-13683)
Bombardier Transportation ....D 607 324-0216
Hornell (G-6586)
CAF Usa Inc ....D 607 737-3004
Elmira Heights (G-4722)
▲ Cox & Company Inc ....C 212 366-0200
Plainview (G-13623)
▲ Eagle Bridge Machine & Tl Inc ....E 518 686-4541
Eagle Bridge (G-4380)
Ebenezer Railcar Services Inc ....E 716 674-5650
West Seneca (G-16971)
General Electric Company ....E 845 567-7410
Newburgh (G-12778)
▲ Gray Manufacturing Inds LLC ....F 607 281-1325
Hornell (G-6591)
Highcrest Investors LLC ....D 212 702-4323
New York (G-10519)
Higher Power Industries Inc ....G 914 709-9800
Yonkers (G-17470)
Horne Products Inc ....G 631 293-0773
Farmingdale (G-5014)
Hudson Machine Works Inc ....C 845 279-1413
Brewster (G-1218)
▲ Kawasaki Rail Car Inc ....C 914 376-4700
Yonkers (G-17476)
Knorr Brake Company LLC ....G 518 561-1387
Plattsburgh (G-13700)
▲ Knorr Brake Holding Corp ....G 315 786-5356
Watertown (G-16681)
▲ Knorr Brake Truck Systems Co ....B 315 786-5200
Watertown (G-16682)
▲ Koshii Maxelum America Inc ....E 845 471-0500
Poughkeepsie (G-13931)
▲ New York Air Brake LLC ....C 315 786-5219
Watertown (G-16688)
Niagara Cooler Inc ....G 716 434-1235
Lockport (G-7634)
▲ Peck & Hale LLC ....E 631 589-2510
West Sayville (G-16966)
Rand Machine Products Inc ....D 716 665-5217
Falconer (G-4916)
Seisenbacher Inc ....F 585 730-4960
Rochester (G-14701)
▲ Semec Corp ....F 518 825-0160
Plattsburgh (G-13725)
Starfire Holding Corporation ....E 914 614-7000
White Plains (G-17196)
▲ Strato Transit Components LLC ....G 518 686-4541
Eagle Bridge (G-4383)
Transco Railway Products Inc ....E 716 824-1219
Blasdell (G-961)
▲ Twinco Mfg Co Inc ....E 631 231-0022
Hauppauge (G-6243)
Westcode Incorporated ....E 607 766-9881
Binghamton (G-953)
Westinghouse A Brake Tech Corp ....D 518 561-0044
Plattsburgh (G-13739)
Westinghouse A Brake Tech Corp ....F 914 347-8650
Elmsford (G-4800)

3751 Motorcycles, Bicycles & Parts

Bignay Inc ....G 786 346-1673
New York (G-9446)
▲ East Coast Cycle LLC ....G 631 780-5360
Farmingdale (G-4992)
▲ Evelo Inc ....G 917 251-8743
Rockaway Park (G-14813)
Golub Corporation ....D 518 943-3903
Catskill (G-3456)
Golub Corporation ....D 518 899-6063
Malta (G-8052)
Golub Corporation ....D 315 363-0679
Oneida (G-13177)
Golub Corporation ....D 607 336-2588
Norwich (G-13047)
Golub Corporation ....D 518 583-3697
Saratoga Springs (G-15183)
Golub Corporation ....D 518 822-0076
Hudson (G-6645)
Golub Corporation ....D 607 235-7240
Binghamton (G-914)
Golub Corporation ....D 845 344-0327
Middletown (G-8477)
Great American Bicycle LLC ....E 518 584-8100
Saratoga Springs (G-15184)
Ihd Motorsports LLC ....F 979 690-1669
Binghamton (G-920)
Indian Larry Legacy ....G 718 609-9184
Brooklyn (G-2100)
Orange County Choppers Inc ....G 845 522-5200
Newburgh (G-12793)
Palmer Industries Inc ....G 607 754-1954
Endicott (G-4831)
◆ Piaggio Group Americas Inc ....E 212 380-4400
New York (G-11676)
Pidyon Controls Inc ....G 212 683-9523
New York (G-11679)
Price Chopper Operating Co ....F 518 562-3565
Plattsburgh (G-13718)
Price Chopper Operating Co ....G 518 456-5115
Guilderland (G-5925)
Robs Cycle Supply ....G 315 292-6878
Syracuse (G-16047)
▲ Social Bicycles Inc ....E 917 746-7624
Brooklyn (G-2602)
Sumax Cycle Products Inc ....F 315 768-1058
Oriskany (G-13339)
Super Price Chopper Inc ....F 716 893-3323
Buffalo (G-3228)
▲ Worksman Trading Corp ....E 718 322-2000
Ozone Park (G-13413)
Ying Ke Youth Age Group Inc ....F 929 402-8458
Dix Hills (G-4323)

3761 Guided Missiles & Space Vehicles

Edo LLC ....A 631 630-4200
Amityville (G-285)
Lockheed Martin Corporation ....A 315 456-0123
Liverpool (G-7554)
Lockheed Martin Corporation ....A 607 751-2000
Owego (G-13379)
Lockheed Martin Corporation ....D 607 751-7434
Owego (G-13380)
Lockheed Martin Overseas LLC ....D 301 897-6923
Liverpool (G-7557)

3769 Guided Missile/Space Vehicle Parts & Eqpt, NEC

Gb Aero Engine LLC ....B 914 925-9600
Rye (G-15083)
▲ GKN Aerospace Monitor Inc ....B 562 619-8558
Amityville (G-288)
▲ L-3 Cmmnctons Fgn Holdings Inc ....E 212 697-1111
New York (G-10941)
L3 Technologies Inc ....A 631 436-7400
Hauppauge (G-6133)
▲ L3 Technologies Inc ....B 212 697-1111
New York (G-10943)
Lockheed Martin Corporation ....E 716 297-1000
Niagara Falls (G-12861)
▲ Magellan Aerospace NY Inc ....C 718 699-4000
Corona (G-4025)
◆ Moog Inc ....A 716 652-2000
Elma (G-4664)
Saturn Industries Inc ....E 518 828-9956
Hudson (G-6663)
Servotronics Inc ....C 716 655-5990
Elma (G-4668)
SKF USA Inc ....D 716 661-2869
Falconer (G-4919)
SKF USA Inc ....D 716 661-2600
Falconer (G-4920)
Turbine Engine Comp Utica ....A 315 768-8070
Whitesboro (G-17225)
Unison Industries LLC ....B 607 335-5000
Norwich (G-13057)

3792 Travel Trailers & Campers

All Star Carts & Vehicles Inc ....D 631 666-5581
Bay Shore (G-667)

3795 Tanks & Tank Components

Federal Prison Industries ....C 845 386-6819
Otisville (G-13369)
Lourdes Industries Inc ....D 631 234-6600
Hauppauge (G-6146)
◆ Tecmotiv (usa) Inc ....E 905 669-5911
Niagara Falls (G-12899)

3799 Transportation Eqpt, NEC

Adirondack Power Sports ....G 518 481-6269
Malone (G-8037)
Bombardier Trnsp Holdings USA ....D 607 776-4791
Bath (G-654)
Bullet Industries Inc ....G 585 352-0836
Spencerport (G-15592)

S I C

Employee Codes: A=Over 500 employees, B=251-500
C=101-250, D=51-100, E=20-50, F=10-19, G=5-9
2018 Harris
New York Manufacturers Directory
853

37 TRANSPORTATION EQUIPMENT

Clopay Ames True Tmper Hldng ....F 516 938-5544
  Jericho (G-7096)
▲ Club Protector Inc ....G 716 652-4787
  Elma (G-4659)
Kens Service & Sales Inc ....F 716 683-1155
  Elma (G-4663)
Mdek Inc ....G 347 569-7318
  Brooklyn (G-2292)
Performance Custom Trailer ....G 518 504-4021
  Lake George (G-7288)
Rolling Star Manufacturing Inc ....E 315 896-4767
  Barneveld (G-616)
Tectran Inc ....G 800 776-5549
  Cheektowaga (G-3619)
Truck-Lite Sub Inc ....G 800 888-7095
  Falconer (G-4925)
Truxton Corp ....G 718 842-6000
  Bronx (G-1479)

38 MEASURING, ANALYZING AND CONTROLLING INSTRUMENTS; PHOTOGRAPHIC, MEDICAL AN

3812 Search, Detection, Navigation & Guidance Systs & Instrs

901 D LLC ....E 845 369-1111
  Airmont (G-10)
Accipiter Radar Corporation ....G 716 508-4432
  Orchard Park (G-13273)
Accutrak Inc ....F 212 925-5330
  New York (G-9061)
▲ Aeroflex Incorporated ....B 516 694-6700
  Plainview (G-13608)
Ametek Inc ....D 585 263-7700
  Rochester (G-14218)
Amherst Systems Inc ....C 716 631-0610
  Buffalo (G-2828)
▲ Artemis Inc ....G 631 232-2424
  Hauppauge (G-6044)
Atair Aerospace Inc ....F 718 923-1709
  Brooklyn (G-1644)
▲ Aventura Technologies Inc ....E 631 300-4000
  Commack (G-3848)
B & Z Technologies LLC ....G 631 675-9666
  East Setauket (G-4496)
▲ Bae Systems Controls Inc ....A 607 770-2000
  Endicott (G-4804)
C Speed LLC ....E 315 453-1043
  Liverpool (G-7537)
C-Flex Bearing Co Inc ....F 315 895-7454
  Frankfort (G-5359)
CIC International Ltd ....D 212 213-0089
  Brooklyn (G-1778)
▲ Clayton Dubilier & Rice Fun ....E 212 407-5200
  New York (G-9695)
Cobham Holdings (us) Inc ....A 716 662-0006
  Orchard Park (G-13285)
Cobham Holdings Inc ....E 716 662-0006
  Orchard Park (G-13286)
Computer Instruments Corp ....E 516 876-8400
  Westbury (G-17003)
▲ Cox & Company Inc ....C 212 366-0200
  Plainview (G-13623)
▲ Dyna-Empire Inc ....C 516 222-2700
  Garden City (G-5513)
Eastern Strategic Materials ....E 212 332-1619
  New York (G-10018)
◆ Edo LLC ....G 631 630-4000
  Amityville (G-284)
Edo LLC ....A 631 630-4200
  Amityville (G-285)
Emergency Beacon Corp ....F 914 576-2700
  New Rochelle (G-8941)
Excelsior Mlt-Cltural Inst Inc ....F 706 627-4285
  Flushing (G-5247)
Facilamatic Instrument Corp ....F 516 825-6300
  Valley Stream (G-16432)
Flightline Electronics Inc ....D 585 742-5340
  Victor (G-16502)
Frequency Electronics Inc ....E 516 794-4500
  Uniondale (G-16317)
Gryphon Sensors LLC ....F 315 452-8882
  North Syracuse (G-12963)
Harris Corporation ....A 585 269-6600
  Rochester (G-14442)
Harris Corporation ....B 585 269-5001
  Rochester (G-14443)

Harris Corporation ....C 585 269-5000
  Rochester (G-14445)
Harris Corporation ....C 703 668-6239
  Rome (G-14841)
▲ Ihi Inc ....E 212 599-8100
  New York (G-10610)
Inertia Switch Inc ....E 845 359-8300
  Orangeburg (G-13251)
▲ Inficon Inc ....C 315 434-1149
  East Syracuse (G-4555)
Infrared Components Corp ....E 315 732-1544
  Utica (G-16368)
ITT Corporation ....D 315 568-2811
  Seneca Falls (G-15383)
ITT Inc ....F 914 641-2000
  White Plains (G-17152)
◆ ITT LLC ....B 914 641-2000
  White Plains (G-17154)
ITT LLC ....D 914 641-2000
  Seneca Falls (G-15387)
Joldeson One Aerospace Inds ....D 718 848-7396
  Ozone Park (G-13406)
▲ Kerns Manufacturing Corp ....E 718 784-4044
  Long Island City (G-7807)
▲ Kwadair LLC ....G 646 824-2511
  Brooklyn (G-2181)
▲ L-3 Cmmnctns Fgn Holdings Inc ......E 212 697-1111
  New York (G-10941)
▲ L3 Technologies Inc ....E 212 697-1111
  New York (G-10943)
Laufer Wind Group LLC ....F 212 792-3912
  New York (G-10971)
Lockheed Martin Corporation ....A 607 751-2000
  Owego (G-13379)
Lockheed Martin Corporation ....D 607 751-7434
  Owego (G-13380)
Lockheed Martin Corporation ....E 315 456-6604
  Syracuse (G-16001)
Lockheed Martin Corporation ....E 212 697-1105
  New York (G-11049)
Lockheed Martin Corporation ....E 716 297-1000
  Niagara Falls (G-12861)
Lockheed Martin Corporation ....E 315 456-0123
  Liverpool (G-7554)
Lockheed Martin Global Inc ....E 315 456-2982
  Liverpool (G-7555)
Lockheed Martin Overseas ....E 315 456-0123
  Liverpool (G-7556)
Logitek Inc ....D 631 567-1100
  Bohemia (G-1089)
▲ Magellan Aerospace NY Inc ....C 718 699-4000
  Corona (G-4025)
Metro Dynmc Scntific Instr Lab ....E 631 842-4300
  West Babylon (G-16841)
Mirion Technologies Ist Corp ....D 607 562-4300
  Horseheads (G-6612)
Mod-A-Can Inc ....E 516 931-8545
  Hicksville (G-6399)
◆ Moog Inc ....A 716 652-2000
  Elma (G-4664)
Moog Inc ....E 716 687-4778
  Elma (G-4665)
▲ Moor Electronics Inc ....G 716 821-5304
  Buffalo (G-3095)
New York Nautical Inc ....E 212 962-4522
  New York (G-11424)
No Longer Empty Inc ....G 202 413-4262
  New York (G-11463)
Northrop Grumman Corporation ....A 703 280-2900
  Bethpage (G-874)
Norwich Aero Products Inc ....D 607 336-7636
  Norwich (G-13051)
Optic Solution LLC ....F 518 293-4034
  Saranac (G-15161)
Orthstar Enterprises Inc ....D 607 562-2100
  Horseheads (G-6614)
Penetradar Corporation ....F 716 731-2629
  Niagara Falls (G-12877)
Rodale Wireless Inc ....E 631 231-0044
  Hauppauge (G-6205)
Saab Defense and SEC USA LLC ....F 315 445-5009
  East Syracuse (G-4575)
▲ Safe Flight Instrument Corp ....E 914 220-1125
  White Plains (G-17194)
▼ Select Fabricators Inc ....F 585 393-0650
  Canandaigua (G-3387)
Sensormatic Electronics LLC ....F 845 365-3125
  Orangeburg (G-13268)
▲ Sentry Technology Corporation ....E 631 739-2000
  Ronkonkoma (G-15006)

▲ Sentry Technology Corporation ....F 800 645-4224
  Ronkonkoma (G-15007)
Srctec LLC ....C 315 452-8700
  Syracuse (G-16067)
Systems Drs C3 Inc ....B 716 631-6200
  Buffalo (G-3232)
▲ Telephonics Corporation ....A 631 755-7000
  Farmingdale (G-5137)
▼ Traffic Logix Corporation ....G 866 915-6449
  Spring Valley (G-15624)
Transistor Devices Inc ....E 631 471-7492
  Ronkonkoma (G-15015)
Tusk Manufacturing Inc ....E 631 567-3349
  Bohemia (G-1147)
U E Systems Incorporated ....E 914 592-1220
  Elmsford (G-4797)
U S Tech Corporation ....F 315 437-7207
  East Syracuse (G-4587)
UNI Source Technology ....F 514 748-8888
  Champlain (G-3575)
Vacuum Instrument Corporation ....D 631 737-0900
  Ronkonkoma (G-15021)
Virtualapt Corp ....G 917 293-3173
  Brooklyn (G-2748)
◆ VJ Technologies Inc ....E 631 589-8800
  Bohemia (G-1151)
Woodbine Products Inc ....E 631 586-3770
  Hauppauge (G-6259)
▼ Worldwide Arntcal Cmpnents Inc ....F 631 842-3780
  Copiague (G-3962)
Worldwide Arntcal Cmpnents Inc ....G 631 842-3780
  Copiague (G-3963)

3821 Laboratory Apparatus & Furniture

Adirondack Machine Corporation ....G 518 792-2258
  Hudson Falls (G-6669)
▲ Air Techniques Inc ....B 516 433-7676
  Melville (G-8324)
Anaren Microwave Inc ....G 315 432-8909
  East Syracuse (G-4520)
Ankom Technology Corp ....E 315 986-8090
  Macedon (G-8008)
Biodesign Inc of New York ....F 845 454-6610
  Carmel (G-3426)
Bioins Inc ....F 646 398-3718
  Yonkers (G-17437)
Biospherix Ltd ....E 315 387-3414
  Parish (G-13439)
Crystal Linton Technologies ....F 585 444-8784
  Rochester (G-14314)
▲ Dynamica Inc ....G 212 818-1900
  New York (G-10000)
East Hills Instrument Inc ....F 516 621-8686
  Westbury (G-17007)
Fts Systems Inc ....D 845 687-5300
  Stone Ridge (G-15785)
◆ Fungilab Inc ....G 631 750-6361
  Hauppauge (G-6104)
Healthalliance Hospital ....G 845 338-2500
  Kingston (G-7219)
▲ Hyman Podrusnick Co Inc ....G 718 853-4502
  Brooklyn (G-2089)
Instrumentation Laboratory Co ....C 845 680-0028
  Orangeburg (G-13253)
▲ Integrated Liner Tech Inc ....E 518 621-7422
  Rensselaer (G-14059)
Integrted Work Envronments LLC ......G 716 725-5088
  East Amherst (G-4387)
◆ Itin Scale Co Inc ....E 718 336-5900
  Brooklyn (G-2118)
▲ J H C Fabrications Inc ....E 718 649-0065
  Brooklyn (G-2121)
▲ Jamestown Metal Products LLC ......C 716 665-5313
  Jamestown (G-7044)
Lab Crafters Inc ....E 631 471-7755
  Ronkonkoma (G-14954)
Lomir Inc ....F 518 483-7697
  Malone (G-8043)
Maripharm Laboratories ....F 716 984-6520
  Niagara Falls (G-12862)
Material Measuring Corporation ....G 516 334-6167
  Westbury (G-17037)
Modu-Craft Inc ....F 716 694-0709
  Tonawanda (G-16200)
Modu-Craft Inc ....G 716 694-0709
  North Tonawanda (G-13000)
▲ Nalge Nunc International Corp ....A 585 498-2661
  Rochester (G-14547)
Newport Corporation ....E 585 248-4246
  Rochester (G-14555)

Next Advance Inc F 518 674-3510
Troy *(G-16265)*
Radon Testing Corp of America F 914 345-3380
Elmsford *(G-4782)*
S P Industries Inc D 845 255-5000
Gardiner *(G-5563)*
▲ Scientific Industries Inc E 631 567-4700
Bohemia *(G-1125)*
Simpore Inc G 585 748-5980
West Henrietta *(G-16926)*
SPS Medical Supply Corp F 585 968-2377
Cuba *(G-4096)*
▲ Staplex Company Inc E 718 768-3333
Brooklyn *(G-2619)*
Steriliz LLC G 585 415-5411
Rochester *(G-14727)*
Theta Industries Inc F 516 883-4088
Port Washington *(G-13887)*
▲ Vistalab Technologies Inc E 914 244-6226
Brewster *(G-1228)*
Vivus Technologies LLC G 585 798-6658
Medina *(G-8316)*
VWR Education LLC C 585 359-2502
West Henrietta *(G-16929)*

3822 Automatic Temperature Controls

▲ A K Allen Co Inc C 516 747-5450
Mineola *(G-8522)*
Advantex Solutions Inc G 718 278-2290
Bellerose *(G-805)*
Air Louver & Damper Inc E 718 392-3232
Maspeth *(G-8141)*
Air Louver & Damper Inc F 718 392-3232
Long Island City *(G-7681)*
Airflex Industrial Inc E 631 752-1234
Farmingdale *(G-4940)*
▲ Anderson Instrument Co Inc D 518 922-5315
Fultonville *(G-5491)*
Automated Bldg MGT Systems Inc E 516 216-5603
Floral Park *(G-5202)*
Automated Building Controls G 914 381-2860
Mamaroneck *(G-8055)*
Bilbee Controls Inc F 518 622-3033
Cairo *(G-3297)*
▲ Biorem Environmental Inc E 585 924-2220
Victor *(G-16486)*
▲ Bitzer Scroll Inc D 315 463-2101
Syracuse *(G-15890)*
Black River Generations LLC E 315 773-2314
Fort Drum *(G-5345)*
Building Management Assoc Inc E 718 542-4779
Bronx *(G-1289)*
Care Enterprises Inc G 631 472-8155
Bayport *(G-749)*
Carrier Corporation B 315 432-6000
Syracuse *(G-15907)*
Cascade Technical Services LLC F 516 596-6300
Lynbrook *(G-7977)*
Cascade Technical Services LLC G 518 355-2201
Schenectady *(G-15267)*
Clean Room Depot Inc F 631 589-3033
Holbrook *(G-6466)*
▲ Cox & Company Inc C 212 366-0200
Plainview *(G-13623)*
Daikin Applied Americas Inc D 315 253-2771
Auburn *(G-490)*
Day Automation Systems Inc D 585 924-4630
Victor *(G-16496)*
E Global Solutions Inc G 516 767-5138
Port Washington *(G-13834)*
East Hudson Watershed Corp G 845 319-6349
Patterson *(G-13463)*
Eastern Strategic Materials E 212 332-1619
New York *(G-10018)*
▲ Evolve Guest Controls LLC F 855 750-9090
Port Washington *(G-13836)*
Fedders Islandaire Inc D 631 471-2900
East Setauket *(G-4500)*
Fuel Watchman Sales & Service F 718 665-6100
Bronx *(G-1340)*
Grillmaster Inc E 718 272-9191
Howard Beach *(G-6625)*
Heating & Burner Supply Inc G 718 665-0006
Bronx *(G-1357)*
Henderson Products Inc E 315 785-0994
Watertown *(G-16675)*
▲ Infitec Inc D 315 433-1150
East Syracuse *(G-4557)*
Intellidyne LLC F 516 676-0777
Plainview *(G-13637)*
Intrepid Control Service Inc G 718 886-8771
Flushing *(G-5262)*
Irtronics Instruments Inc F 914 693-6291
Ardsley *(G-404)*
Johnson Controls Inc E 585 924-9346
Victor *(G-16508)*
Johnson Controls Inc E 914 593-5200
Hawthorne *(G-6271)*
Johnson Controls Inc E 716 688-7340
Buffalo *(G-3037)*
Johnson Controls Inc C 585 724-2232
Rochester *(G-14485)*
Leo Schultz G 716 969-0945
Cheektowaga *(G-3606)*
Logical Control Solutions Inc F 585 424-5340
Victor *(G-16513)*
Long Island Analytical Labs F 631 472-3400
Holbrook *(G-6487)*
Microb Phase Services F 518 877-8948
Clifton Park *(G-3728)*
Pii Holdings Inc G 716 876-9951
Buffalo *(G-3149)*
Protective Industries Inc D 716 876-9951
Buffalo *(G-3167)*
◆ Protective Industries Inc C 716 876-9951
Buffalo *(G-3165)*
◆ Pulsafeeder Inc C 585 292-8000
Rochester *(G-14632)*
◆ RE Hansen Industries Inc C 631 471-2900
East Setauket *(G-4510)*
Reuse Action Incorporated G 716 949-0900
Buffalo *(G-3183)*
Siemens Industry Inc D 716 568-0983
Amherst *(G-261)*
Siemens Industry Inc E 585 797-2300
Rochester *(G-14707)*
▲ Svyz Trading Corp G 718 220-1140
Bronx *(G-1467)*
T S B A Group Inc E 718 565-6000
Sunnyside *(G-15831)*
▲ Transit Air Inc E 607 324-0216
Hornell *(G-6595)*
Unisend LLC G 585 414-9575
Webster *(G-16765)*
Use Acquisition LLC F 516 812-6800
New Hyde Park *(G-8916)*
Virtual Super LLC G 212 685-6400
New York *(G-12578)*
Zebra Environmental Corp F 516 596-6300
Lynbrook *(G-7993)*

3823 Indl Instruments For Meas, Display & Control

A C T Associates F 716 759-8348
Clarence *(G-3682)*
Aalborg Instrs & Contrls Inc D 845 398-3160
Orangeburg *(G-13238)*
Ametek Inc D 585 263-7700
Rochester *(G-14218)*
Anchor Commerce Trading Corp G 516 881-3485
Atlantic Beach *(G-467)*
▲ Anderson Instrument Co Inc D 518 922-5315
Fultonville *(G-5491)*
▲ Applied Power Systems Inc E 516 935-2230
Hicksville *(G-6346)*
Aspex Incorporated E 212 966-0410
New York *(G-9290)*
ATI Trading Inc F 718 888-7918
Flushing *(G-5235)*
Aureonic G 518 791-9331
Gansevoort *(G-5499)*
B Live LLC G 212 489-0721
New York *(G-9343)*
Bae Systems Info & Elec Sys G 631 912-1525
Greenlawn *(G-5891)*
Beauty America LLC E 917 744-1430
Great Neck *(G-5811)*
◆ Blue Tee Corp A 212 598-0880
New York *(G-9473)*
Cal Blen Electronic Industries F 631 242-6243
Huntington *(G-6691)*
▲ Calibrated Instruments Inc F 914 741-5700
Manhasset *(G-8089)*
Cemtrex Inc C 631 756-9116
Farmingdale *(G-4967)*
Ceres Technologies Inc D 845 247-4701
Saugerties *(G-15210)*
▲ Classic Automation LLC E 585 241-6010
Webster *(G-16742)*
Computer Instruments Corp E 516 876-8400
Westbury *(G-17003)*
Conax Technologies LLC C 716 684-4500
Buffalo *(G-2905)*
◆ Cosa Xentaur Corporation E 631 345-3434
Yaphank *(G-17405)*
Danaher Corporation C 516 443-9432
New York *(G-9854)*
◆ Dau Thrmal Slutions N Amer Inc E 585 678-9025
Macedon *(G-8015)*
◆ Defelsko Corporation D 315 393-4450
Ogdensburg *(G-13135)*
Digital Analysis Corporation F 315 685-0760
Skaneateles *(G-15479)*
Digitronik Dev Labs Inc F 585 360-0043
Rochester *(G-14329)*
Display Logic USA Inc G 631 406-1922
Hauppauge *(G-6087)*
▲ Dyna-Empire Inc C 516 222-2700
Garden City *(G-5513)*
East Hills Instrument Inc F 516 621-8686
Westbury *(G-17007)*
Electrcal Instrumentation Ctrl F 518 861-5789
Delanson *(G-4258)*
Electronic Machine Parts LLC F 631 434-3700
Hauppauge *(G-6093)*
Emerson Electric Co E 212 244-2490
New York *(G-10074)*
Enerac Inc F 516 997-1554
Holbrook *(G-6475)*
Ewt Holdings III Corp F 212 644-5900
New York *(G-10151)*
Fts Systems Inc D 845 687-5300
Stone Ridge *(G-15785)*
Gizmo Products Inc G 585 301-0970
Rochester *(G-14424)*
Gurley Precision Instrs Inc C 518 272-6300
Troy *(G-16259)*
Hades Manufacturing Corp F 631 249-4244
Farmingdale *(G-5011)*
Harris Corporation C 703 668-6239
Rome *(G-14841)*
▲ Heidenhain International Inc C 716 661-1700
Jamestown *(G-7033)*
Herman H Sticht Company Inc G 718 852-7602
Brooklyn *(G-2074)*
◆ Hilliard Corporation B 607 733-7121
Elmira *(G-4703)*
Hilliard Corporation F 607 733-7121
Elmira *(G-4704)*
Industrial Machine Repair G 607 272-0717
Ithaca *(G-6885)*
▲ Inficon Inc C 315 434-1149
East Syracuse *(G-4555)*
Inficon Holding AG G 315 434-1100
East Syracuse *(G-4556)*
▲ Integrated Control Corp E 631 673-5100
Huntington *(G-6696)*
ITT Corporation D 315 568-2811
Seneca Falls *(G-15383)*
ITT Inc F 914 641-2000
White Plains *(G-17152)*
ITT LLC D 914 641-2000
Seneca Falls *(G-15387)*
◆ ITT LLC B 914 641-2000
White Plains *(G-17154)*
▲ Kessler Thermometer Corp G 631 841-5500
West Babylon *(G-16832)*
▲ Koehler Instrument Company Inc D 631 589-3800
Holtsville *(G-6529)*
Macrolink Inc E 631 924-8200
Medford *(G-8288)*
◆ Magtrol Inc E 716 668-5555
Buffalo *(G-3075)*
Malcon Inc F 914 666-7146
Bedford Hills *(G-801)*
Mark - 10 Corporation E 631 842-9200
Copiague *(G-3938)*
Mausner Equipment Co Inc C 631 689-7358
Setauket *(G-15402)*
Medsafe Systems Inc G 516 883-8222
Port Washington *(G-13864)*
Micromod Automtn & Contrls Inc F 585 321-9209
Rochester *(G-14532)*
▲ Miller & Weber Inc E 718 821-7110
Westbury *(G-17039)*
Mks Instruments Inc E 585 292-7472
Rochester *(G-14537)*
New Scale Technologies Inc E 585 924-4450
Victor *(G-16516)*

S I C

Employee Codes: A=Over 500 employees, B=251-500
C=101-250, D=51-100, E=20-50, F=10-19, G=5-9
2018 Harris
New York Manufacturers Directory
855

Nidec Indus Automtn USA LLC ....E 716 774-1193
Grand Island *(G-5778)*
Norwich Aero Products Inc ....D 607 336-7636
Norwich *(G-13051)*
Nutec Components Inc ....F 631 242-1224
Deer Park *(G-4206)*
Oden Machinery Inc ....E 716 874-3000
Tonawanda *(G-16207)*
Ormec Systems Corp ....E 585 385-3520
Rochester *(G-14573)*
Orthstar Enterprises Inc ....D 607 562-2100
Horseheads *(G-6614)*
Partlow Corporation ....C 518 922-5315
Fultonville *(G-5495)*
Pcb Group Inc ....E 716 684-0001
Depew *(G-4292)*
▲ Pneumercator Company Inc ....E 631 293-8450
Hauppauge *(G-6192)*
Poseidon Systems LLC ....F 585 239-6025
Rochester *(G-14608)*
◆ Pulsafeeder Inc ....C 585 292-8000
Rochester *(G-14632)*
R K B Opto-Electronics Inc ....F 315 455-6636
Syracuse *(G-16038)*
Riverhawk Company LP ....E 315 624-7171
New Hartford *(G-8854)*
Robat Inc ....G 518 812-6244
Clifton Park *(G-3731)*
Roessel & Co Inc ....G 585 458-5560
Rochester *(G-14678)*
▲ Rotronic Instrument Corp ....F 631 348-6844
Hauppauge *(G-6206)*
Rwb Controls Inc ....G 716 897-4341
Buffalo *(G-3198)*
Schneider Elc Systems USA Inc ....F 214 527-3099
New York *(G-12010)*
Select Controls Inc ....E 631 567-9010
Bohemia *(G-1127)*
Sequential Electronics Systems ....E 914 592-1345
Elmsford *(G-4791)*
Siemens Industry Inc ....C 631 218-1000
Bohemia *(G-1131)*
Sixnet LLC ....D 518 877-5173
Ballston Lake *(G-585)*
▲ Sixnet Holdings LLC ....G 518 877-5173
Ballston Lake *(G-586)*
Solar Metrology LLC ....G 845 247-4701
Holbrook *(G-6500)*
Springfield Control Systems ....G 718 631-0870
Douglaston *(G-4336)*
Swagelok Western NY ....G 585 359-8470
West Henrietta *(G-16927)*
Taber Acquisition Corp ....D 716 694-4000
North Tonawanda *(G-13018)*
Tel-Tru Inc ....D 585 295-0225
Rochester *(G-14746)*
Telog Instruments Inc ....E 585 742-3000
Victor *(G-16531)*
Thread Check Inc ....D 631 231-1515
Hauppauge *(G-6238)*
▼ Transtech Systems Inc ....E 518 370-5558
Latham *(G-7408)*
Vacuum Instrument Corporation ....D 631 737-0900
Ronkonkoma *(G-15021)*
Veeco Instruments Inc ....C 516 677-0200
Woodbury *(G-17321)*
Vertiv Services Inc ....G 516 349-8500
Plainview *(G-13673)*
Vetra Systems Corporation ....G 631 434-3185
Hauppauge *(G-6249)*
Viatran Corporation ....E 716 564-7813
Tonawanda *(G-16233)*
Vibro-Laser Instrs Corp LLC ....G 518 874-2700
Glens Falls *(G-5715)*
▲ Weiss Instruments Inc ....D 631 207-1200
Holtsville *(G-6541)*
▲ Winters Instruments Inc ....E 281 880-8607
Buffalo *(G-3283)*
Xentaur Corporation ....E 631 345-3434
Yaphank *(G-17425)*

3824 Fluid Meters & Counters

Aalborg Instrs & Contrls Inc ....D 845 398-3160
Orangeburg *(G-13238)*
Cmp Advnced Mech Sltons NY LLC ....G 607 352-1712
Binghamton *(G-898)*
Computer Instruments Corp ....E 516 876-8400
Westbury *(G-17003)*
▲ Curtis Instruments Inc ....C 914 666-2971
Mount Kisco *(G-8666)*
▲ Designatronics Incorporated ....G 516 328-3300
Hicksville *(G-6366)*
Designatronics Incorporated ....E 516 328-3970
Hicksville *(G-6368)*
East Hills Instrument Inc ....F 516 621-8686
Westbury *(G-17007)*
Encore Electronics Inc ....E 518 584-5354
Saratoga Springs *(G-15179)*
▲ Environment-One Corporation ....C 518 346-6161
Schenectady *(G-15279)*
Flexim Americas Corporation ....F 631 492-2300
Edgewood *(G-4612)*
G & O Equipment Corp ....G 718 218-7844
Bronx *(G-1341)*
Gurley Precision Instrs Inc ....C 518 272-6300
Troy *(G-16259)*
Heat-Timer Corporation ....E 212 481-2020
Bronx *(G-1356)*
K-Technologies Inc ....E 716 828-4444
Buffalo *(G-3042)*
Melland Gear Instr of Huppauge ....E 631 234-0100
Hauppauge *(G-6156)*
Schlumberger Technology Corp ....C 607 378-0105
Horseheads *(G-6621)*
Siemens Industry Inc ....C 631 231-3600
Hauppauge *(G-6213)*
SPX Flow Us LLC ....G 585 436-5550
Rochester *(G-14722)*
Turbo Machined Products LLC ....E 315 895-3010
Frankfort *(G-5368)*
Vantage Mfg & Assembly LLC ....E 845 471-5290
Poughkeepsie *(G-13954)*
Vepo Solutions LLC ....G 914 384-2121
Cross River *(G-4086)*
▲ Walter R Tucker Entps Ltd ....E 607 467-2866
Deposit *(G-4305)*

3825 Instrs For Measuring & Testing Electricity

Agilent Technologies Inc ....A 877 424-4536
New York *(G-9108)*
Ah Elctronic Test Eqp Repr Ctr ....F 631 234-8979
Central Islip *(G-3509)*
Allied Motion Systems Corp ....F 716 691-5868
Amherst *(G-223)*
▲ Allied Motion Technologies Inc ....C 716 242-8634
Amherst *(G-224)*
American Quality Technology ....F 607 777-9488
Binghamton *(G-884)*
Ametek Inc ....D 585 263-7700
Rochester *(G-14218)*
Anmar Acquisition LLC ....G 585 352-7777
Rochester *(G-14222)*
Apogee Power Usa Inc ....F 202 746-2890
Hartsdale *(G-6016)*
Aurora Technical Services Ltd ....G 716 652-1463
East Aurora *(G-4392)*
Automated Control Logic Inc ....F 914 769-8880
Thornwood *(G-16139)*
Automation Correct LLC ....G 315 299-3589
Syracuse *(G-15881)*
Avanel Industries Inc ....F 516 333-0990
Westbury *(G-16998)*
Avcom of Virginia Inc ....D 585 924-4560
Victor *(G-16485)*
C Speed LLC ....E 315 453-1043
Liverpool *(G-7537)*
C-Flex Bearing Co Inc ....F 315 895-7454
Frankfort *(G-5359)*
Calmetrics Inc ....G 631 580-2522
Holbrook *(G-6463)*
▲ Cetek Inc ....E 845 452-3510
Poughkeepsie *(G-13911)*
Cgw Corp ....G 631 472-6600
Bayport *(G-750)*
Clarke Hess Communication RES ....G 631 698-3350
Medford *(G-8272)*
▲ Clayton Dubilier & Rice Fun ....E 212 407-5200
New York *(G-9695)*
▲ Comtech PST Corp ....C 631 777-8900
Melville *(G-8336)*
▲ Curtis Instruments Inc ....C 914 666-2971
Mount Kisco *(G-8666)*
East Hills Instrument Inc ....F 516 621-8686
Westbury *(G-17007)*
Edo LLC ....F 631 218-1413
Bohemia *(G-1058)*
Edo LLC ....A 631 630-4200
Amityville *(G-285)*
El Electronics Inc ....F 516 334-0870
Westbury *(G-17008)*
▲ Ems Development Corporation ....D 631 924-4736
Yaphank *(G-17406)*
Enertiv Inc ....G 646 350-3525
New York *(G-10091)*
Epoch Microelectronics Inc ....G 914 332-8570
Valhalla *(G-16393)*
Everest Bbn Inc ....F 212 268-7979
New York *(G-10145)*
▲ Evergreen High Voltage LLC ....G 281 814-9973
Lake Placid *(G-7298)*
Fluid Metering Inc ....E 516 922-6050
Syosset *(G-15842)*
Frequency Electronics Inc ....B 516 794-4500
Uniondale *(G-16317)*
Gcns Technology Group Inc ....G 347 713-8160
Brooklyn *(G-2018)*
General Microwave Corporation ....F 516 802-0900
Syosset *(G-15844)*
Hamilton Marketing Corporation ....G 585 395-0678
Brockport *(G-1243)*
Herman H Sticht Company Inc ....G 718 852-7602
Brooklyn *(G-2074)*
▲ Hipotronics Inc ....C 845 279-8091
Brewster *(G-1217)*
▲ Iet Labs Inc ....F 516 334-5959
Roslyn Heights *(G-15052)*
International Insurance Soc ....G 212 815-9291
New York *(G-10678)*
◆ Interntnal Elctronic Mchs Corp ....E 518 268-1636
Troy *(G-16263)*
John Ramsey Elec Svcs LLC ....G 585 298-9596
Victor *(G-16507)*
Jre Test LLC ....G 585 298-9736
Victor *(G-16509)*
Larry Kings Corporation ....G 718 481-8741
Rosedale *(G-15037)*
Lexan Industries Inc ....F 631 434-7586
Bay Shore *(G-711)*
Linde LLC ....D 716 773-7552
Grand Island *(G-5776)*
Logitek Inc ....D 631 567-1100
Bohemia *(G-1089)*
▼ Ludl Electronic Products Ltd ....E 914 769-6111
Hawthorne *(G-6274)*
▲ Macrodyne Inc ....F 518 383-3800
Clifton Park *(G-3727)*
▲ Magnetic Analysis Corporation ....D 914 530-2000
Elmsford *(G-4771)*
◆ Magtrol Inc ....E 716 668-5555
Buffalo *(G-3075)*
▲ Make-Waves Instrument Corp ....E 716 681-7524
Buffalo *(G-3076)*
Millivac Instruments Inc ....G 518 355-8300
Schenectady *(G-15305)*
▲ Nas CP Corp ....E 718 961-6757
College Point *(G-3823)*
New York Enrgy Synthetics Inc ....G 212 634-4787
New York *(G-11421)*
North Atlantic Industries Inc ....C 631 567-1100
Bohemia *(G-1106)*
Northeast Metrology Corp ....F 716 827-3770
Depew *(G-4290)*
Omni-ID Usa Inc ....E 585 697-9913
Rochester *(G-14570)*
Optimized Devices Inc ....F 914 769-6100
Pleasantville *(G-13747)*
Peerless Instrument Co Inc ....C 631 396-6500
Farmingdale *(G-5086)*
Performance Systems Contg Inc ....E 607 277-6240
Ithaca *(G-6904)*
Photonix Technologies Inc ....F 607 786-4600
Endicott *(G-4832)*
Practical Instrument Elec Inc ....F 585 872-9350
Webster *(G-16755)*
Pragmatics Technology Inc ....G 845 795-5071
Milton *(G-8517)*
Precision Filters Inc ....E 607 277-3550
Ithaca *(G-6907)*
Primesouth Inc ....F 585 567-4191
Fillmore *(G-5184)*
◆ Pulsafeeder Inc ....C 585 292-8000
Rochester *(G-14632)*
Pulsar Technology Systems Inc ....G 718 361-9292
Long Island City *(G-7879)*
▲ Quadlogic Controls Corporation ....D 212 930-9300
Long Island City *(G-7882)*
▲ Qualitrol Company LLC ....C 586 643-3717
Fairport *(G-4879)*

38 MEASURING, ANALYZING AND CONTROLLING INSTRUMENTS; PHOTOGRAPHIC, MEDICAL AN

R K B Opto-Electronics Inc .... F 315 455-6636
  Syracuse *(G-16038)*
Ramsey Electronics LLC .... E 585 924-4560
  Victor *(G-16522)*
Rodale Wireless Inc .... E 631 231-0044
  Hauppauge *(G-6205)*
S R Instruments Inc .... E 716 693-5977
  Tonawanda *(G-16216)*
Schlumberger Technology Corp ..... C 607 378-0105
  Horseheads *(G-6621)*
Scientific Components Corp .... E 631 243-4901
  Deer Park *(G-4231)*
Scj Associates Inc .... E 585 359-0600
  Rochester *(G-14697)*
◆ Sorfin Yoshimura Ltd .... E 516 802-4600
  Woodbury *(G-17320)*
T & C Power Conversion Inc .... F 585 482-5551
  Rochester *(G-14738)*
▲ Teledyne Lecroy Inc .... C 845 425-2000
  Chestnut Ridge *(G-3656)*
Trek Inc .... F 716 438-7555
  Lockport *(G-7652)*
◆ Urban Green Energy Inc .... E 917 720-5681
  New York *(G-12499)*
▲ Vermed Inc .... D 800 669-6905
  Buffalo *(G-3267)*
Viatran Corporation .... E 716 564-7813
  Tonawanda *(G-16233)*
▲ W & W Manufacturing Co .... F 516 942-0011
  West Islip *(G-16939)*
W D Technology Inc .... G 914 779-8738
  Eastchester *(G-4595)*
▲ Walter R Tucker Entps Ltd .... E 607 467-2866
  Deposit *(G-4305)*
Xelic Incorporated .... F 585 415-2764
  Pittsford *(G-13604)*
▲ Zumbach Electronics Corp .... D 914 241-7080
  Mount Kisco *(G-8691)*

3826 Analytical Instruments

A S A Precision Co Inc .... G 845 482-4870
  Jeffersonville *(G-7092)*
Advanced Mtl Analytics LLC .... G 321 684-0528
  Vestal *(G-16461)*
Advion Inc .... E 607 266-9162
  Ithaca *(G-6857)*
Applied Biophysics Inc .... G 518 880-6860
  Troy *(G-16246)*
Applied Image Inc .... E 585 482-0300
  Rochester *(G-14225)*
Bristol Instruments Inc .... E 585 924-2620
  Victor *(G-16488)*
Brookhaven Instruments Corp .... E 631 758-3200
  Holtsville *(G-6526)*
Caltex International Ltd .... E 315 425-1040
  Syracuse *(G-15902)*
Cambridge Manufacturing LLC .... G 516 326-1350
  New Hyde Park *(G-8865)*
▲ Carl Zeiss Inc .... C 914 747-1800
  Thornwood *(G-16140)*
Ceres Technologies Inc .... D 845 247-4701
  Saugerties *(G-15210)*
Chromosense LLC .... E 347 770-5421
  Brooklyn *(G-1777)*
Corning Incorporated .... E 607 974-6729
  Painted Post *(G-13417)*
CTB Enterprise LLC .... E 631 563-0088
  Holbrook *(G-6470)*
East Coast Envmtl Group Inc .... G 516 352-1946
  Farmingdale *(G-4993)*
East Hills Instrument Inc .... F 516 621-8686
  Westbury *(G-17007)*
EMD Millipore Corporation .... G 845 621-6560
  Mahopac *(G-8025)*
Ewt Holdings III Corp .... F 212 644-5900
  New York *(G-10151)*
Exfo Burleigh Pdts Group Inc .... D 585 301-1530
  Canandaigua *(G-3374)*
Finger Lakes Radiology LLC .... G 315 787-5399
  Geneva *(G-5589)*
Gemprint Corporation .... E 212 997-0007
  New York *(G-10313)*
General Microwave Corporation ..... F 516 802-0900
  Syosset *(G-15844)*
High Voltage Inc .... E 518 329-3275
  Copake *(G-3913)*
Islandia Mri Associates PC .... F 631 234-2828
  Central Islip *(G-3527)*
Micro Photo Acoustics Inc .... G 631 750-6035
  Ronkonkoma *(G-14968)*

▲ MMC Enterprises Corp .... G 800 435-1088
  Hauppauge *(G-6166)*
▼ Multiwire Laboratories Ltd .... G 607 257-3378
  Ithaca *(G-6900)*
Nanotronics Imaging Inc .... E 212 401-6209
  Brooklyn *(G-2354)*
▲ Nexgen Enviro Systems Inc .... G 631 226-2930
  Lindenhurst *(G-7499)*
Niagara Scientific Inc .... D 315 437-0821
  East Syracuse *(G-4566)*
Novartis Pharmaceuticals Corp ...... G 888 669-6682
  New York *(G-11480)*
Phymetrix Inc .... G 631 627-3950
  Medford *(G-8291)*
Porous Materials Inc .... E 607 257-5544
  Ithaca *(G-6906)*
▲ Qioptiq Inc .... E 585 223-2370
  Fairport *(G-4878)*
Rheonix Inc .... D 607 257-1242
  Ithaca *(G-6909)*
Smartpill Corporation .... E 716 882-0701
  Buffalo *(G-3216)*
Spectra Vista Corporation .... G 845 471-7007
  Poughkeepsie *(G-13950)*
Thermo Fisher Scientific Inc .... G 716 774-6700
  Grand Island *(G-5786)*
Thermo Fisher Scientific Inc .... B 585 458-8008
  Rochester *(G-14749)*
Thermo Fisher Scientific Inc .... A 585 899-7610
  Rochester *(G-14750)*
Tokyo Electron America Inc .... G 518 292-4200
  Albany *(G-143)*
Uptek Solutions Corp .... F 631 256-5565
  Bohemia *(G-1150)*
Veeco Instruments Inc .... C 516 677-0200
  Woodbury *(G-17321)*

3827 Optical Instruments

21st Century Optics Inc .... E 347 527-1079
  Long Island City *(G-7675)*
▲ Advanced Glass Industries Inc ... D 585 458-8040
  Rochester *(G-14193)*
▲ Aeroflex Incorporated .... B 516 694-6700
  Plainview *(G-13608)*
Aeroflex Plainview Inc .... B 516 694-6700
  Plainview *(G-13609)*
▲ Anorad Corporation .... C 631 380-2100
  East Setauket *(G-4495)*
Apollo Optical Systems Inc .... E 585 272-6170
  West Henrietta *(G-16901)*
◆ Applied Coatings Holding Corp ... G 585 482-0300
  Rochester *(G-14224)*
Applied Image Inc .... E 585 482-0300
  Rochester *(G-14225)*
Ariel Optics Inc .... G 585 265-4820
  Ontario *(G-13217)*
▼ Binoptics LLC .... F 607 257-3200
  Ithaca *(G-6862)*
Caliber Imging Diagnostics Inc .... E 585 239-9800
  Rochester *(G-14273)*
▲ Carl Zeiss Inc .... C 914 747-1800
  Thornwood *(G-16140)*
CK Coatings .... G 585 502-0425
  Le Roy *(G-7429)*
Claude Tribastone Inc .... G 585 265-3776
  Ontario *(G-13219)*
Corning Tropel Corporation .... C 585 377-3200
  Fairport *(G-4857)*
CVI Laser LLC .... D 585 244-7220
  Rochester *(G-14318)*
▲ Digitac Inc .... F 732 215-4020
  Brooklyn *(G-1863)*
Dorsey Metrology Intl Inc .... G 845 229-2929
  Poughkeepsie *(G-13914)*
▲ Dynamic Laboratories Inc .... E 631 231-7474
  Ronkonkoma *(G-14923)*
Eele Laboratories LLC .... F 631 244-0051
  Bohemia *(G-1059)*
Enplas America Inc .... G 646 892-7811
  New York *(G-10095)*
Evergreen Bleachers Inc .... G 518 654-9084
  Corinth *(G-3980)*
Exfo Burleigh Pdts Group Inc .... D 585 301-1530
  Canandaigua *(G-3374)*
▲ Genesis Vision Inc .... E 585 254-0193
  Rochester *(G-14418)*
Gradient Lens Corporation .... E 585 235-2620
  Rochester *(G-14432)*
Gurley Precision Instrs Inc .... C 518 272-6300
  Troy *(G-16259)*

Halo Optical Products Inc .... D 518 773-4256
  Gloversville *(G-5728)*
◆ Hart Specialties Inc .... D 631 226-5600
  Amityville *(G-291)*
Hudson Mirror LLC .... E 914 930-8906
  Peekskill *(G-13504)*
▲ Isp Optics Corporation .... D 914 591-3070
  Irvington *(G-6814)*
▲ Jml Optical Industries LLC .... E 585 248-8900
  Rochester *(G-14484)*
Keon Optics Inc .... F 845 429-7103
  Stony Point *(G-15796)*
Kevin Freeman .... E 631 447-5321
  Patchogue *(G-13452)*
Leica Microsystems Inc .... G 716 686-3000
  Depew *(G-4286)*
Lens Triptar Co Inc .... F 585 473-4470
  Rochester *(G-14498)*
▼ Lumetrics Inc .... E 585 214-2455
  Rochester *(G-14505)*
Machida Incorporated .... G 845 365-0600
  Orangeburg *(G-13257)*
▲ Match Eyewear LLC .... E 516 877-0170
  Westbury *(G-17036)*
▲ Meopta USA Inc .... G 631 436-5900
  Hauppauge *(G-6157)*
Metavac LLC .... E 631 207-2344
  Holtsville *(G-6530)*
Micatu Inc .... G 888 705-8836
  Horseheads *(G-6610)*
▼ Navitar Inc .... D 585 359-4000
  Rochester *(G-14550)*
▲ Newport Rochester Inc .... E 585 262-1325
  Rochester *(G-14556)*
◆ Nikon Instruments Inc .... D 631 547-4200
  Melville *(G-8372)*
▲ North American Enclosures Inc .. E 631 234-9500
  Central Islip *(G-3534)*
Novanta Inc .... G 818 341-5151
  Syracuse *(G-16020)*
◆ Optics Plus Inc .... G 716 744-2636
  Tonawanda *(G-16208)*
Optics Technology Inc .... G 585 586-0950
  Pittsford *(G-13599)*
Optimax Systems Inc .... C 585 265-1020
  Ontario *(G-13229)*
◆ Optipro Systems LLC .... D 585 265-0160
  Ontario *(G-13230)*
Orafol Americas Inc .... F 585 272-0290
  West Henrietta *(G-16918)*
Photon Gear Inc .... F 585 265-3360
  Ontario *(G-13231)*
Planar Optics Inc .... G 585 671-0100
  Webster *(G-16754)*
Plx Inc .... G 631 586-4190
  Deer Park *(G-4214)*
▲ Qioptiq Inc .... E 585 223-2370
  Fairport *(G-4878)*
▲ Quality Vision Intl Inc .... D 585 544-0400
  Rochester *(G-14637)*
▲ Quality Vision Services Inc .... D 585 544-0450
  Rochester *(G-14638)*
Rochester Photonics Corp .... D 585 387-0674
  Rochester *(G-14668)*
◆ Rochester Precision Optics LLC .. C 585 292-5450
  West Henrietta *(G-16924)*
RPC Photonics Inc .... F 585 272-2840
  Rochester *(G-14682)*
Santa Fe Manufacturing Corp .... G 631 234-0100
  Hauppauge *(G-6208)*
Schott Corporation .... D 315 255-2791
  Auburn *(G-514)*
Spectral Systems LLC .... E 845 896-2200
  Hopewell Junction *(G-6585)*
Spectrum Thin Films Inc .... E 631 901-1010
  Hauppauge *(G-6221)*
▼ Stefan Sydor Optics Inc .... E 585 271-7300
  Rochester *(G-14726)*
Steven John Opticians .... G 718 543-3336
  Bronx *(G-1463)*
Surgical Design Corp .... F 914 273-2445
  Armonk *(G-418)*
Synergy Intrntnal Optrnics LLC .... E 631 277-0500
  Ronkonkoma *(G-15014)*
▲ Tele-Vue Optics Inc .... E 845 469-4551
  Chester *(G-3646)*
Unimed Optical .... G 718 384-3600
  Brooklyn *(G-2718)*
US Optical LLC .... E 315 463-4800
  East Syracuse *(G-4590)*

Employee Codes: A=Over 500 employees, B=251-500
C=101-250, D=51-100, E=20-50, F=10-19, G=5-9

2018 Harris
New York Manufacturers Directory

38 MEASURING, ANALYZING AND CONTROLLING INSTRUMENTS; PHOTOGRAPHIC, MEDICAL AN

Va Inc .... E 585 385-5930
Rochester *(G-14777)*

Victory Vision Care Inc .... G 718 622-2020
Brooklyn *(G-2743)*

Videk Inc .... E 585 377-0377
Fairport *(G-4892)*

◆ Welch Allyn Inc .... A 315 685-4100
Skaneateles Falls *(G-15494)*

Westchester Technologies Inc ..... E 914 736-1034
Peekskill *(G-13511)*

3829 Measuring & Controlling Devices, NEC

Accuvein Inc .... D 816 997-9400
Medford *(G-8265)*

Andor Design Corp .... G 516 364-1619
Syosset *(G-15833)*

Aspex Incorporated .... E 212 966-0410
New York *(G-9290)*

Aurora Technical Services Ltd ..... G 716 652-1463
East Aurora *(G-4392)*

Biodesign Inc of New York .... F 845 454-6610
Carmel *(G-3426)*

▲ Carl Zeiss Inc .... C 914 747-1800
Thornwood *(G-16140)*

Circor Aerospace Inc .... D 631 737-1900
Hauppauge *(G-6065)*

Climatronics Corp .... F 541 471-7111
Bohemia *(G-1030)*

Computer Instruments Corp .... E 516 876-8400
Westbury *(G-17003)*

Cosense Inc .... E 516 364-9161
Syosset *(G-15838)*

Cubic Trnsp Systems Inc .... F 212 255-1810
New York *(G-9821)*

Dayton T Brown Inc .... B 631 589-6300
Bohemia *(G-1048)*

◆ Defelsko Corporation .... D 315 393-4450
Ogdensburg *(G-13135)*

Dispersion Technology Inc .... G 914 241-4777
Bedford Hills *(G-799)*

Dylix Corporation .... E 719 773-2985
Grand Island *(G-5769)*

▲ Dyna-Empire Inc .... C 516 222-2700
Garden City *(G-5513)*

▲ Dynamic Systems Inc .... E 518 283-5350
Poestenkill *(G-13753)*

East Hills Instrument Inc .... F 516 621-8686
Westbury *(G-17007)*

Eastern Niagra Radiology .... E 716 882-6544
Buffalo *(G-2942)*

Electrical Controls Link .... E 585 924-7010
Victor *(G-16498)*

Electro-Optical Products Corp ..... G 718 456-6000
Ridgewood *(G-14118)*

Elsag North America LLC .... G 877 773-5724
Brewster *(G-1215)*

Enerac Inc .... F 516 997-1554
Holbrook *(G-6475)*

Erbessd Reliability LLC .... E 518 874-2700
Glens Falls *(G-5694)*

▲ Fougera Pharmaceuticals Inc .. C 631 454-7677
Melville *(G-8350)*

Freeman Technology Inc .... E 732 829-8345
Bayside *(G-765)*

G E Inspection Technologies LP ... C 315 554-2000
Skaneateles *(G-15481)*

Gei International Inc .... F 315 463-9261
East Syracuse *(G-4546)*

◆ Germanow-Simon Corporation ... E 585 232-1440
Rochester *(G-14420)*

◆ Gleason Corporation .... A 585 473-1000
Rochester *(G-14428)*

◆ Gleason Works .... A 585 473-1000
Rochester *(G-14429)*

Gurley Precision Instrs Inc .... C 518 272-6300
Troy *(G-16259)*

H D M Labs Inc .... G 516 431-8357
Island Park *(G-6820)*

Hci Engineering .... G 315 336-3450
Rome *(G-14842)*

▲ Helmel Engineering Pdts Inc .... E 716 297-8644
Niagara Falls *(G-12851)*

Herman H Sticht Company Inc ... G 718 852-7602
Brooklyn *(G-2074)*

▲ Highway Toll ADM LLC .... F 516 684-9584
Roslyn Heights *(G-15051)*

▲ Hipotronics Inc .... E 845 279-8091
Brewster *(G-1217)*

Imaginant Inc .... E 585 264-0480
Pittsford *(G-13592)*

Industrial Test Eqp Co Inc .... E 516 883-6423
Port Washington *(G-13846)*

◆ Itin Scale Co Inc .... E 718 336-5900
Brooklyn *(G-2118)*

James A Staley Co Inc .... F 845 878-3344
Carmel *(G-3429)*

Kem Medical Products Corp .... E 631 454-6565
Farmingdale *(G-5034)*

Kinemotive Corporation .... E 631 249-6440
Farmingdale *(G-5035)*

Kld Labs Inc .... E 631 549-4222
Hauppauge *(G-6131)*

L N D Incorporated .... E 516 678-6141
Oceanside *(G-13106)*

Liberty Controls Inc .... E 718 461-0600
College Point *(G-3819)*

Machine Technology Inc .... G 845 454-4030
Poughkeepsie *(G-13933)*

▲ Magnetic Analysis Corporation ... E 914 530-2000
Elmsford *(G-4771)*

▲ Magtrol Inc .... E 716 668-5555
Buffalo *(G-3075)*

▲ Make-Waves Instrument Corp ... E 716 681-7524
Buffalo *(G-3076)*

▲ Mason Industries Inc .... B 631 348-0282
Hauppauge *(G-6152)*

Mechanical Technology Inc .... E 518 218-2550
Albany *(G-101)*

▲ Miller & Weber Inc .... E 718 821-7110
Westbury *(G-17039)*

Mirion Tech Conax Nuclear Inc ... E 716 681-1973
Buffalo *(G-3088)*

Mirion Technologies Ist Corp .... D 607 562-4300
Horseheads *(G-6612)*

Mobius Labs Inc .... E 518 961-2600
Rexford *(G-14065)*

MTI Instruments Inc .... F 518 218-2550
Albany *(G-104)*

MTS Systems Corporation .... E 518 899-2140
Ballston Lake *(G-583)*

Nis Manufacturing Inc .... G 518 456-2566
Cohoes *(G-3777)*

Norwich Aero Products Inc .... D 607 336-7636
Norwich *(G-13051)*

Nuclear Diagnostic Pdts NY Inc ... G 516 575-4201
Plainview *(G-13653)*

Orolia Usa Inc .... E 585 321-5800
Rochester *(G-14574)*

▲ Oyster Bay Pump Works Inc ... F 516 933-4500
Hicksville *(G-6406)*

Parker-Hannifin Corporation .... B 631 231-3737
Hauppauge *(G-6183)*

Pcb Piezotronics Inc .... E 716 684-0001
Depew *(G-4293)*

Peerless Instrument Co Inc .... C 631 396-6500
Farmingdale *(G-5086)*

▲ Peyser Instrument Corporation ... E 631 841-3600
West Babylon *(G-16848)*

Poseidon Systems LLC .... F 585 239-6025
Rochester *(G-14608)*

Precision Design Systems Inc .... E 585 426-4500
Rochester *(G-14614)*

Qhi Group Incorporated .... G 646 512-5727
New York *(G-11789)*

Research Frontiers Inc .... F 516 364-1902
Woodbury *(G-17318)*

Riverhawk Company LP .... E 315 624-7171
New Hartford *(G-8854)*

RJ Harvey Instrument Corp .... E 845 359-3943
Tappan *(G-16107)*

S P Industries Inc .... D 845 255-5000
Gardiner *(G-5563)*

▲ Schenck Corporation .... E 631 242-4010
Deer Park *(G-4229)*

▲ Schenck Trebel Corp .... E 631 242-4397
Deer Park *(G-4230)*

▲ Schott Corporation .... E 914 831-2200
Elmsford *(G-4786)*

SKF USA Inc .... E 716 661-2600
Jamestown *(G-7060)*

▲ Teledyne Lecroy Inc .... C 845 425-2000
Chestnut Ridge *(G-3656)*

Telog Instruments Inc .... E 585 742-3000
Victor *(G-16531)*

Titan Controls Inc .... F 516 358-2407
New York *(G-12374)*

U E Systems Incorporated .... E 914 592-1220
Elmsford *(G-4797)*

Vacuum Instrument Corporation ... D 631 737-0900
Ronkonkoma *(G-15021)*

Vector Magnetics LLC .... E 607 273-8351
Ithaca *(G-6917)*

Videk Inc .... E 585 377-0377
Fairport *(G-4892)*

◆ VJ Technologies Inc .... E 631 589-8800
Bohemia *(G-1151)*

Voice Analysis Clinic .... G 212 245-3803
New York *(G-12592)*

▲ Weiss Instruments Inc .... D 631 207-1200
Holtsville *(G-6541)*

Xeku Corporation .... F 607 761-1447
Vestal *(G-16481)*

York Industries Inc .... E 516 746-3736
Garden City Park *(G-5559)*

Zomega Terahertz Corporation ... F 585 347-4337
Webster *(G-16771)*

3841 Surgical & Medical Instrs & Apparatus

Abyrx Inc .... F 914 357-2600
Irvington *(G-6808)*

Accumed Corp .... G 716 853-1800
Buffalo *(G-2810)*

Advanced Placement LLC .... G 949 281-9086
Holbrook *(G-6458)*

Advantage Plus Diagnostics Inc ... G 631 393-5044
Melville *(G-8321)*

Aerolase Corporation .... D 914 345-8300
Tarrytown *(G-16108)*

Ala Scientific Instruments Inc ..... E 631 393-6401
Farmingdale *(G-4942)*

AM Bickford Inc .... F 716 652-1590
Wales Center *(G-16559)*

American Bio Medica Corp .... E 518 758-8158
Kinderhook *(G-7196)*

◆ American Diagnostic Corp ...... D 631 273-6155
Hauppauge *(G-6040)*

▲ American Healthcare Supply Inc ... F 212 674-3636
New York *(G-9168)*

Angiodynamics Inc .... B 518 975-1400
Queensbury *(G-14004)*

Angiodynamics Inc .... B 518 792-4112
Glens Falls *(G-5687)*

Angiodynamics Inc .... B 518 742-4430
Queensbury *(G-14005)*

Angiodynamics Inc .... B 518 795-1400
Latham *(G-7380)*

Argon Medical Devices Inc .... G 585 321-1130
Henrietta *(G-6316)*

Astra Tool & Instr Mfg Corp .... E 914 747-3863
Hawthorne *(G-6266)*

Avery Biomedical Devices Inc .... F 631 864-1600
Commack *(G-3849)*

◆ Bausch & Lomb Incorporated ... B 585 338-6000
Rochester *(G-14242)*

Baxter Healthcare Corporation ... B 800 356-3454
Medina *(G-8299)*

Beacon Spch Lnge Pthlgy Phys ... F 516 626-1635
Roslyn *(G-15040)*

Becton Dickinson and Company ... B 845 353-3371
Nyack *(G-13061)*

Biochemical Diagnostics Inc .... E 631 595-9200
Edgewood *(G-4609)*

▲ Biodex Medical Systems Inc ... C 631 924-9000
Shirley *(G-15439)*

Biodex Medical Systems Inc ...... E 631 924-3146
Shirley *(G-15440)*

Bioresearch Inc .... E 212 734-5315
Pound Ridge *(G-13958)*

Boehm Surgical Instrument .... F 585 436-6584
Rochester *(G-14259)*

Bovie Medical Corporation .... C 914 468-4009
Purchase *(G-13970)*

▲ Buffalo Filter LLC .... D 716 835-7000
Lancaster *(G-7331)*

▲ Buxton Medical Equipment Corp ... E 631 957-4500
Lindenhurst *(G-7479)*

C R Bard Inc .... B 518 793-2531
Queensbury *(G-14007)*

C R Bard Inc .... A 518 793-2531
Glens Falls *(G-5690)*

Caliber Imging Diagnostics Inc ... E 585 239-9800
Rochester *(G-14273)*

Clerio Vision Inc .... E 617 216-7881
Rochester *(G-14300)*

CN Group Incorporated .... A 914 358-5690
White Plains *(G-17122)*

Cognitiveflow Sensor Tech .... G 631 513-9369
Stony Brook *(G-15789)*

◆ Conmed Corporation .... B 315 797-8375
Utica *(G-16339)*

38 MEASURING, ANALYZING AND CONTROLLING INSTRUMENTS; PHOTOGRAPHIC, MEDICAL AN

Conmed Corporation .... D 315 797-8375
  Utica (G-16338)
Corning Tropel Corporation .... C 585 377-3200
  Fairport (G-4857)
Cynosure Inc .... G 516 594-3333
  Hicksville (G-6365)
Daxor Corporation .... E 212 244-0555
  New York (G-9888)
Delcath Systems Inc .... E 212 489-2100
  New York (G-9893)
Derm/Buro Inc .... G 516 694-8300
  Plainview (G-13626)
▲ Designs For Vision Inc .... E 631 585-3300
  Ronkonkoma (G-14922)
◆ E-Z-Em Inc .... E 609 524-2864
  Melville (G-8343)
▲ East Coast Orthoic & Pros Cor ...... D 516 248-5566
  Deer Park (G-4156)
Elite Medical Supply of NY .... G 716 712-0881
  West Seneca (G-16972)
▲ Elliquence LLC .... F 516 277-9000
  Baldwin (G-557)
Endovor Inc .... G 214 679-7385
  New York (G-10084)
Endovor LLC .... G 214 679-7385
  New York (G-10085)
▲ Esc Control Electronics LLC .... E 631 467-5328
  Sayville (G-15236)
Extek Inc .... E 585 533-1672
  Rush (G-15072)
Eyeglass Service Industries .... G 914 666-3150
  Bedford Hills (G-800)
◆ Fabrication Enterprises Inc .... E 914 591-9300
  Elmsford (G-4761)
▲ Flexbar Machine Corporation .... E 631 582-8440
  Islandia (G-6831)
Fluorologic Inc .... G 585 248-2796
  Pittsford (G-13588)
Ftt Medical Inc .... G 585 444-0980
  Rochester (G-14406)
◆ Future Diagnostics LLC .... E 347 434-6700
  Brooklyn (G-2008)
▲ Gaymar Industries Inc .... B 800 828-7341
  Orchard Park (G-13294)
▲ Getinge Usa Inc .... C 800 475-9040
  Rochester (G-14422)
Gradian Health Systems Inc .... G 212 537-0340
  New York (G-10386)
Hanger Inc .... E 516 678-3650
  Rockville Centre (G-14820)
▲ Harmac Medical Products Inc .... C 716 897-4500
  Buffalo (G-3006)
▲ Hogil Pharmaceutical Corp .... F 914 681-1800
  White Plains (G-17147)
Huron TI Cutter Grinding Inc .... E 631 420-7000
  Farmingdale (G-5015)
Hurryworks LLC .... D 516 998-4600
  Port Washington (G-13843)
Incredible Scents Inc .... G 516 656-3300
  Glen Head (G-5648)
Integer Holdings Corporation .... D 716 759-5200
  Clarence (G-3690)
Intersurgical Incorporated .... F 315 451-2900
  East Syracuse (G-4558)
Ip Med Inc .... G 516 766-3800
  Oceanside (G-13102)
J H M Engineering .... E 718 871-1810
  Brooklyn (G-2122)
Jaracz Jr Joseph Paul .... F 716 533-1377
  Orchard Park (G-13301)
Ken-Ton Open Mri PC .... G 716 876-7000
  Kenmore (G-7179)
Lake Region Medical Inc .... C 716 662-5025
  Orchard Park (G-13304)
Liberty Install Inc .... F 631 651-5655
  Centerport (G-3504)
Lydia H Soifer & Assoc Inc .... F 914 683-5401
  White Plains (G-17161)
Manhattan Eastside Dev Corp .... F 212 305-3275
  New York (G-11153)
Mdi East Inc .... E 518 747-8730
  South Glens Falls (G-15549)
◆ Medical Depot Inc .... B 516 998-4600
  Port Washington (G-13862)
Medical Technology Products .... G 631 285-6640
  Greenlawn (G-5893)
Medipoint Inc .... F 516 294-8820
  Mineola (G-8557)
Medline Industries Inc .... B 845 344-3301
  Middletown (G-8484)

Medsource Technologies LLC .... D 716 662-5025
  Orchard Park (G-13308)
Memory Md Inc .... G 917 318-0215
  New York (G-11250)
Mick Radio Nuclear Instrument ...... F 718 597-3999
  Mount Vernon (G-8752)
▲ Misonix Inc .... D 631 694-9555
  Farmingdale (G-5067)
Modular Medical Corp .... E 718 829-2626
  Bronx (G-1403)
▲ Monaghan Medical Corporation ..... D 518 561-7330
  Plattsburgh (G-13705)
◆ Moog Inc .... A 716 652-2000
  Elma (G-4664)
N Y B P Inc .... G 585 624-2541
  Mendon (G-8413)
Nano Vibronix Inc .... G 516 374-8330
  Cedarhurst (G-3486)
Nanobionovum LLC .... G 518 581-1171
  Saratoga Springs (G-15194)
▲ Nasco Enterprises Inc .... G 516 921-9696
  Syosset (G-15849)
Nasiff Associates Inc .... G 315 676-2346
  Central Square (G-3544)
▲ Navilyst Medical Inc .... A 800 833-9973
  Glens Falls (G-5707)
Njr Medical Devices .... E 440 258-8204
  Cedarhurst (G-3487)
▲ Novamed-Usa Inc .... G 914 789-2100
  Elmsford (G-4779)
◆ Ocala Group LLC .... F 516 233-2750
  New Hyde Park (G-8899)
Omnicare Anesthesia PC .... G 718 433-0044
  Astoria (G-451)
▲ Orics Industries Inc .... E 718 461-8613
  Farmingdale (G-5080)
Ortho Medical Products .... F 212 879-3700
  New York (G-11541)
Ortho-Clinical Diagnostics Inc .... G 585 453-4771
  Rochester (G-14575)
Ortho-Clinical Diagnostics Inc .... F 585 453-5200
  Rochester (G-14576)
Orthocon Inc .... E 914 357-2600
  Irvington (G-6815)
Ovitz Corporation .... G 585 474-4695
  West Henrietta (G-16920)
▲ P Ryton Corp .... F 718 937-7052
  Long Island City (G-7863)
Pall Corporation .... A 607 753-6041
  Cortland (G-4059)
◆ Pall Corporation .... A 516 484-5400
  Port Washington (G-13870)
Parace Bionics LLC .... G 877 727-2231
  Yorktown Heights (G-17531)
Parkchester Dps LLC .... C 718 823-4411
  Bronx (G-1422)
Pavmed Inc .... G 212 401-1951
  New York (G-11603)
Peter Digioia .... G 516 644-5517
  Plainview (G-13656)
▼ Pharma-Smart International Inc ...... E 585 427-0730
  Rochester (G-14600)
Praxis Powder Technology Inc .... E 518 812-0112
  Queensbury (G-14020)
Precimed Inc .... E 716 759-5600
  Clarence (G-3696)
▲ Proactive Medical Products LLC ..... G 845 205-6004
  Mount Vernon (G-8766)
Professional Medical Devices .... F 914 835-0614
  Harrison (G-6008)
Progressive Orthotics Ltd .... G 631 732-5556
  Selden (G-15375)
Rdd Pharma Inc .... G 302 319-9970
  New York (G-11838)
▲ Reichert Inc .... C 716 686-4500
  Depew (G-4296)
▲ Repro Med Systems Inc .... G 845 469-2042
  Chester (G-3639)
Responselink Inc .... G 518 424-7776
  Latham (G-7405)
RJ Harvey Instrument Corp .... F 845 359-3943
  Tappan (G-16107)
Robert Bosch LLC .... E 315 733-3312
  Utica (G-16381)
▲ Schilling Forge Inc .... E 315 454-4421
  Syracuse (G-16055)
Seedlngs Lf Scnce Ventures LLC .... G 917 913-8511
  New York (G-12036)
Seneca TEC Inc .... G 585 381-2645
  Fairport (G-4885)

▼ Sigma Intl Gen Med Apprtus LLC ... B 585 798-3901
  Medina (G-8315)
Simulaids Inc .... D 845 679-2475
  Saugerties (G-15223)
Skyler Brand Ventures LLC .... G 646 979-5904
  New York (G-12122)
Solid-Look Corporation .... G 917 683-1780
  Douglaston (G-4335)
Sonomed Inc .... E 516 354-0900
  New Hyde Park (G-8908)
St Silicones Corporation .... F 518 406-3208
  Clifton Park (G-3735)
Stj Enterprises .... D 516 612-0110
  Cedarhurst (G-3488)
Surgical Design Corp .... F 914 273-2445
  Armonk (G-418)
T G M Products Inc .... G 631 491-0515
  Wyandanch (G-17392)
Tril Inc .... G 631 645-7989
  Copiague (G-3958)
▲ Vante Inc .... F 716 778-7691
  Newfane (G-12813)
▲ Vasomedical Inc .... B 516 997-4600
  Plainview (G-13668)
Vasomedical Solutions Inc .... D 516 997-4600
  Plainview (G-13669)
Viterion Corporation .... G 914 333-6033
  Elmsford (G-4799)
Vizio Medical Devices LLC .... G 646 845-7382
  New York (G-12587)
▲ W A Baum Co Inc .... G 631 226-3940
  Copiague (G-3961)
Welch Allyn Inc .... A 315 685-4100
  Skaneateles Falls (G-15493)
◆ Welch Allyn Inc .... A 315 685-4100
  Skaneateles Falls (G-15494)
Welch Allyn Inc .... A 315 685-4347
  Skaneateles Falls (G-15495)
Wyeth Holdings LLC .... D 845 602-5000
  Pearl River (G-13493)

3842 Orthopedic, Prosthetic & Surgical Appliances/Splys

▲ 54321 Us Inc .... F 716 695-0258
  Tonawanda (G-16155)
Aaaaar Orthopedics Inc .... G 845 278-4938
  Brewster (G-1203)
▲ Advanced Enterprises Inc .... F 845 342-1009
  Middletown (G-8459)
Advanced Prosthetics Orthotics ...... F 516 365-7225
  Manhasset (G-8087)
Advantage Orthotics Inc .... G 631 368-1754
  East Northport (G-4452)
Aero Healthcare (us) LLC .... G 855 225-2376
  Valley Cottage (G-16401)
Agnovos Healthcare LLC .... G 646 502-5860
  New York (G-9109)
Apollo Orthotics Corp .... G 516 333-3223
  Carle Place (G-3411)
Aramsco Inc .... F 718 361-7540
  Ridgewood (G-14113)
Argon Medical Devices Inc .... G 585 321-1130
  Henrietta (G-6316)
Arimed Orthotics Prosthetics P ...... F 718 875-8754
  Brooklyn (G-1628)
Arimed Orthotics Prosthetics P ...... F 718 979-6155
  Staten Island (G-15660)
Avanti U S A Ltd .... F 716 695-5800
  Tonawanda (G-16162)
Backtech Inc .... G 973 279-0838
  New York (G-9353)
Benway-Haworth-Lwlr-Iacosta He .... F 518 432-4070
  Albany (G-51)
Bio-Chem Barrier Systems LLC ...... G 631 261-2682
  Northport (G-13025)
▲ Biodex Medical Systems Inc .... C 631 924-9000
  Shirley (G-15439)
Biodex Medical Systems Inc .... E 631 924-3146
  Shirley (G-15440)
Bionic Eye Technologies Inc .... G 845 505-5254
  Fishkill (G-5188)
Brannock Device Co Inc .... E 315 475-9862
  Liverpool (G-7535)
Buffalo Hearg & Speech .... E 716 558-1105
  West Seneca (G-16969)
Byer California .... G 212 944-8989
  New York (G-9540)
Church Communities NY Inc .... E 518 589-5103
  Elka Park (G-4643)

Employee Codes: A=Over 500 employees, B=251-500
C=101-250, D=51-100, E=20-50, F=10-19, G=5-9

38 MEASURING, ANALYZING AND CONTROLLING INSTRUMENTS; PHOTOGRAPHIC, MEDICAL AN SIC SECTION

Church Communities NY Inc ....E 518 589-5103
Elka Park *(G-4644)*

▲ **Cirrus Healthcare Products LLC** ....E 631 692-7600
Cold Spring Harbor *(G-3792)*

Cityscape Ob/Gyn PLLC ....F 212 683-3595
New York *(G-9686)*

Columbia Dentoform Corporation ....E 718 482-1569
Long Island City *(G-7732)*

▲ **Community Products LLC** ....C 845 658-8799
Rifton *(G-14144)*

Community Products LLC ....E 845 658-7720
Chester *(G-3630)*

Community Products LLC ....E 845 572-3433
Chester *(G-3631)*

Community Products LLC ....E 518 589-5103
Elka Park *(G-4645)*

Complete Orthopedic Svcs Inc ....E 516 357-9113
East Meadow *(G-4440)*

Cranial Technologies Inc ....F 914 472-0975
Scarsdale *(G-15246)*

Creative Orthotics & Prosthet ....F 607 734-7215
Elmira *(G-4691)*

Creative Orthotics Prosthetics ....G 607 771-4672
Binghamton *(G-899)*

Creative Orthotics Prosthetics ....G 607 431-2526
Oneonta *(G-13206)*

Crosley Medical Products Inc ....F 631 595-2547
Deer Park *(G-4144)*

Custom Sports Lab Inc ....G 212 832-1648
New York *(G-9828)*

▲ **Cy Plastics Works Inc** ....E 585 229-2555
Honeoye *(G-6551)*

Depuy Synthes Inc ....C 607 271-2500
Horseheads *(G-6603)*

Derm/Buro Inc ....G 516 694-8300
Plainview *(G-13626)*

East Cast Orthtics Prosthetics ....F 716 856-5192
Buffalo *(G-2940)*

East Coast Orthoic & Pros Cor ....F 212 923-2161
New York *(G-10014)*

Eis Inc ....D 585 426-5330
Rochester *(G-14361)*

Elwood Specialty Products Inc ....F 716 877-6622
Buffalo *(G-2948)*

Eschen Prosthetic & Orthotic L ....E 212 606-1262
New York *(G-10111)*

◆ **Euromed Inc** ....D 845 359-4039
Orangeburg *(G-13249)*

Family Hearing Center ....G 845 897-3059
Fishkill *(G-5191)*

Far Rockaway Drugs Inc ....F 718 471-2500
Far Rockaway *(G-4929)*

Fiber Foot Appliances Inc ....F 631 465-9199
Farmingdale *(G-5002)*

Flexible Lifeline Systems Inc ....E 716 896-4949
Buffalo *(G-2964)*

Flo-Tech Orthotic & Prosthetic ....G 607 387-3070
Trumansburg *(G-16290)*

Future Mobility Products Inc ....E 716 783-9130
Buffalo *(G-2976)*

Gadabout USA Wheelchairs Inc ....F 585 338-2110
Rochester *(G-14407)*

▲ **Getinge Sourcing LLC** ....C 585 475-1400
Rochester *(G-14421)*

▲ **Getinge Usa Inc** ....C 800 475-9040
Rochester *(G-14422)*

Gfh Orthotic & Prosthetic Labs ....G 631 467-3725
Bohemia *(G-1068)*

Go Blue Technologies Ltd ....G 631 404-6285
North Babylon *(G-12918)*

Goldberg Prosthetic & Orthotic ....F 631 689-6606
East Setauket *(G-4502)*

Grand Slam Holdings LLC ....E 212 583-5000
New York *(G-10389)*

Great Lakes Orthopedic Labs ....G 716 878-7307
Buffalo *(G-2996)*

Green Prosthetics & Orthotics ....G 716 484-1088
Jamestown *(G-7030)*

▲ **Hal-Hen Company Inc** ....E 516 294-3200
New Hyde Park *(G-8883)*

▲ **Hand Care Inc** ....G 516 747-5649
Roslyn *(G-15044)*

Hanger Inc ....G 718 575-5504
Forest Hills *(G-5329)*

Hanger Prsthetcs & Ortho Inc ....F 607 277-6620
Ithaca *(G-6882)*

Hanger Prsthetcs & Ortho Inc ....G 607 776-8013
Bath *(G-657)*

Hanger Prsthetcs & Ortho Inc ....G 607 771-4672
Binghamton *(G-915)*

Hanger Prsthetcs & Ortho Inc ....G 315 472-5200
Syracuse *(G-15976)*

Hanger Prsthetcs & Ortho Inc ....G 585 292-9510
Rochester *(G-14439)*

Hanger Prsthetcs & Ortho Inc ....D 607 795-1220
Elmira *(G-4700)*

Hanger Prsthetcs & Ortho Inc ....G 315 789-4810
Geneva *(G-5593)*

▲ **Harvy Surgical Supply Corp** ....E 718 939-1122
Flushing *(G-5257)*

Hearing Spech Ctr of Rochester ....E 585 286-9373
Webster *(G-16749)*

Hersco-Orthotic Labs Corp ....E 718 391-0416
Long Island City *(G-7789)*

Higgins Supply Company Inc ....D 607 836-6474
Mc Graw *(G-8253)*

Howmedica Osteonics Corp ....G 518 783-1880
Latham *(G-7391)*

Hygrade ....G 718 488-9000
Brooklyn *(G-2088)*

Instrumentation Laboratory Co ....C 845 680-0028
Orangeburg *(G-13253)*

Integer Holdings Corporation ....D 716 759-5200
Clarence *(G-3690)*

J P R Pharmacy Inc ....F 718 327-0600
Far Rockaway *(G-4930)*

J-K Prosthetics & Orthotics ....E 914 699-2077
Mount Vernon *(G-8740)*

Kem Medical Products Corp ....G 631 454-6565
Farmingdale *(G-5034)*

Klemmt Orthotics & Prosthetics ....G 607 770-4400
Johnson City *(G-7128)*

Konrad Prosthetics & Orthotics ....G 516 485-9164
West Hempstead *(G-16889)*

▲ **Lakeland Industries Inc** ....C 631 981-9700
Ronkonkoma *(G-14956)*

Langer Biomechanics Inc ....D 800 645-5520
Ronkonkoma *(G-14958)*

Latorre Orthopedic Laboratory ....F 518 786-8655
Latham *(G-7400)*

Lehneis Orthotics Prosthetic ....G 631 369-3115
Riverhead *(G-14159)*

Lorelei Orthotics Prosthetics ....G 212 727-2011
New York *(G-11070)*

M H Mandelbaum Orthotic ....F 631 473-8668
Port Jefferson *(G-13799)*

Mayflower Splint Co ....E 631 549-5131
Dix Hills *(G-4316)*

▲ **Medi-Ray Inc** ....D 877 898-3003
Tuckahoe *(G-16295)*

▲ **Medi-Tech International Corp** ....E 800 333-0109
Brooklyn *(G-2295)*

Medical Acoustics LLC ....F 716 218-7353
Buffalo *(G-3082)*

Medical Action Industries Inc ....C 631 231-4600
Hauppauge *(G-6155)*

Medline Industries Inc ....B 845 344-3301
Middletown *(G-8484)*

Monaghan Medical Corporation ....G 315 472-2136
Syracuse *(G-16013)*

National Prosthetic Orthot ....G 718 767-8400
Bayside *(G-768)*

New Dynamics Corporation ....E 845 692-0022
Middletown *(G-8488)*

New England Orthotic & Prost ....G 212 682-9313
New York *(G-11407)*

New York Rhbilitative Svcs LLC ....F 516 239-0990
Lawrence *(G-7421)*

Nortech Laboratories Inc ....F 631 501-1452
Farmingdale *(G-5077)*

North Shore Orthtics Prsthtics ....G 631 928-3040
Port Jeff STA *(G-13791)*

Northwell Health Inc ....B 888 387-5811
New York *(G-11479)*

▲ **Nova Health Systems Inc** ....G 315 798-9018
Utica *(G-16377)*

Nucare Pharmacy Inc ....F 212 426-9300
New York *(G-11485)*

Nucare Pharmacy West LLC ....F 212 462-2525
New York *(G-11486)*

▲ **NY Orthopedic Usa Inc** ....D 718 852-5330
Brooklyn *(G-2393)*

▲ **Occunomix International LLC** ....E 631 741-1940
Port Jeff STA *(G-13792)*

Orcam Inc ....F 800 713-3741
New York *(G-11534)*

Ortho Medical Products ....F 212 879-3700
New York *(G-11541)*

Ortho Rite Inc ....E 914 235-9100
New Rochelle *(G-8963)*

Orthocraft Inc ....G 718 951-1700
Brooklyn *(G-2408)*

Orthopedic Arts Laboratory Inc ....G 718 858-2400
Brooklyn *(G-2409)*

Orthopedic Treatment Facility ....G 718 898-7326
Woodside *(G-17360)*

Orthotics & Prosthetics Dept ....F 585 341-9299
Rochester *(G-14579)*

Overhead Door Corporation ....D 518 828-7652
Hudson *(G-6659)*

▲ **Pall Biomedical Inc** ....C 516 484-3600
Port Washington *(G-13869)*

Pall Corporation ....A 607 753-6041
Cortland *(G-4059)*

Pall Corporation ....A 607 753-6041
Cortland *(G-4060)*

Pall Corporation ....A 516 484-2818
Port Washington *(G-13871)*

Pall Corporation ....A 607 753-6041
Cortland *(G-4061)*

Palmer Industries Inc ....G 607 754-8741
Endicott *(G-4829)*

▲ **Palmer Industries Inc** ....E 607 754-2957
Endicott *(G-4830)*

Palmer Industries Inc ....G 607 754-1954
Endicott *(G-4831)*

Paradigm Spine LLC ....E 888 273-9897
New York *(G-11582)*

▲ **Premier Brands of America Inc** ....C 914 667-6200
Mount Vernon *(G-8763)*

▲ **Proficient Surgical Eqp Inc** ....G 516 487-1175
Port Washington *(G-13874)*

▲ **Profoot Inc** ....E 718 965-8600
Brooklyn *(G-2468)*

Progressive Orthotics Ltd ....G 631 732-5556
Selden *(G-15375)*

Progressive Orthotics Ltd ....F 631 447-3860
East Patchogue *(G-4468)*

Prosthetic Rehabilitation Ctr ....G 845 565-8255
Newburgh *(G-12800)*

Prosthetics By Nelson Inc ....F 716 894-6666
Cheektowaga *(G-3614)*

Prosthodontic & Implant Den ....G 212 319-6363
New York *(G-11762)*

Rehablitation Tech of Syracuse ....G 315 426-9920
Syracuse *(G-16044)*

◆ **Robert Busse & Co Inc** ....B 631 435-4711
Hauppauge *(G-6204)*

Robert Cohen ....G 718 789-0996
Ozone Park *(G-13411)*

Rochester Orthopedic Labs ....G 585 272-1060
Rochester *(G-14666)*

▲ **Roner Inc** ....G 718 392-6020
Long Island City *(G-7895)*

Roner Inc ....C 718 392-6020
Long Island City *(G-7896)*

Sampsons Prsthtic Orthotic Lab ....E 518 374-6011
Schenectady *(G-15315)*

Schuster & Richard Labortories ....G 718 358-8607
College Point *(G-3831)*

Scientific Plastics Inc ....F 212 967-1199
New York *(G-12022)*

◆ **Silipos Holding LLC** ....E 716 283-0700
Niagara Falls *(G-12894)*

▲ **Skil-Care Corporation** ....C 914 963-2040
Yonkers *(G-17502)*

Sontek Industries Inc ....G 781 749-3055
New York *(G-12155)*

◆ **SPS Medical Supply Corp** ....D 585 359-0130
Rush *(G-15077)*

SPS Medical Supply Corp ....F 585 968-2377
Cuba *(G-4096)*

Stafford Labs Orthotics/Prosth ....F 845 692-5227
Middletown *(G-8497)*

Steriliz LLC ....G 585 415-5411
Rochester *(G-14727)*

Steris Corporation ....G 877 887-1788
Melville *(G-8385)*

Stj Orthotic Services Inc ....F 631 956-0181
Lindenhurst *(G-7507)*

Syracuse Prosthetic Center Inc ....G 315 476-9697
Syracuse *(G-16079)*

▲ **Tape Systems Inc** ....F 914 668-3700
Mount Vernon *(G-8782)*

▲ **TDS Fitness Equipment** ....E 607 733-6789
Elmira *(G-4717)*

Todt Hill Audiological Svcs ....G 718 816-1952
Staten Island *(G-15771)*

Tonawanda Limb & Brace Inc ....G 716 695-1131
Tonawanda *(G-16227)*

SIC SECTION 38 MEASURING, ANALYZING AND CONTROLLING INSTRUMENTS; PHOTOGRAPHIC, MEDICAL AN

Tumble Forms Inc ....E 315 429-3101
Dolgeville *(G-4333)*
Turbine Engine Comp Utica ....A 315 768-8070
Whitesboro *(G-17225)*
Ultrapedics Ltd ....G 718 748-4806
Brooklyn *(G-2715)*
Upstate Medical Solutions Inc ....G 716 799-3782
Buffalo *(G-3262)*
Vcp Mobility Inc ....B 718 356-7827
Staten Island *(G-15773)*
Venture Respiratory Inc ....F 718 437-3633
Brooklyn *(G-2739)*
▲ **VSM Investors LLC** ....G 212 351-1600
New York *(G-12597)*
▲ **Widex Usa Inc** ....D 718 360-1000
Hauppauge *(G-6257)*
William H Shapiro ....G 212 263-7037
New York *(G-12662)*
Womens Health Care PC ....G 718 850-0009
Richmond Hill *(G-14100)*
Wyeth Holdings LLC ....D 845 602-5000
Pearl River *(G-13493)*
Xylon Industries Inc ....G 631 293-4717
Farmingdale *(G-5153)*

3843 Dental Eqpt & Splys

A D K Dental Lab ....G 518 563-6093
Plattsburgh *(G-13677)*
A-Implant Dental Lab Corp ....G 212 582-4720
New York *(G-9041)*
▲ **Air Techniques Inc** ....B 516 433-7676
Melville *(G-8324)*
Art Dental Laboratory Inc ....G 516 437-1882
Floral Park *(G-5201)*
Avalonbay Communities Inc ....E 516 484-7766
Glen Cove *(G-5624)*
Boehm Surgical Instrument ....F 585 436-6584
Rochester *(G-14259)*
Brandt Equipment LLC ....G 718 994-0800
Bronx *(G-1287)*
▲ **Buffalo Dental Mfg Co Inc** ....E 516 496-7200
Syosset *(G-15836)*
Cettel Studio of New York Inc ....G 518 494-3622
Chestertown *(G-3649)*
◆ **Cmp Industries LLC** ....E 518 434-3147
Albany *(G-66)*
Cmp Industries LLC ....G 518 434-3147
Albany *(G-67)*
Columbia Dentoform Corporation ....E 718 482-1569
Long Island City *(G-7732)*
▲ **Corning Rubber Company Inc** ....F 631 738-0041
Ronkonkoma *(G-14917)*
Cpac Equipment Inc ....F 585 382-3223
Leicester *(G-7443)*
◆ **Crosstex International Inc** ....D 631 582-6777
Hauppauge *(G-6079)*
Crosstex International Inc ....F 631 582-6777
Hauppauge *(G-6080)*
Cynosure Inc ....G 516 594-3333
Hicksville *(G-6365)*
Darby Dental Supply ....G 516 688-6421
Jericho *(G-7099)*
▲ **Dedeco International Sales Inc** ....E 845 887-4840
Long Eddy *(G-7674)*
▲ **Dentek Oral Care Inc** ....D 865 983-1300
Tarrytown *(G-16114)*
Gallery 57 Dental ....E 212 246-8700
New York *(G-10289)*
Gan Kavod Inc ....G 315 797-3114
New Hartford *(G-8850)*
Glaxosmithkline LLC ....D 518 239-6901
East Durham *(G-4409)*
Grasers Dental Ceramics ....G 716 649-5100
Orchard Park *(G-13297)*
Henry Schein Inc ....E 315 431-0340
East Syracuse *(G-4550)*
Henry Schein Fincl Svcs LLC ....G 631 843-5500
Melville *(G-8356)*
Impladent Ltd ....G 718 465-1810
Jamaica *(G-6957)*
J H M Engineering ....E 718 871-1810
Brooklyn *(G-2122)*
Jeffrey D Menoff ....G 716 665-1468
Jamestown *(G-7046)*
▲ **JM Murray Center Inc** ....C 607 756-9913
Cortland *(G-4055)*
JM Murray Center Inc ....C 607 756-0246
Cortland *(G-4056)*
Kay See Dental Mfg Co ....F 816 842-2817
New York *(G-10860)*
Lelab Dental Laboratory Inc ....G 516 561-5050
Valley Stream *(G-16439)*
Light Dental Labs Inc ....G 516 785-7730
Massapequa *(G-8210)*
◆ **Lornamead Inc** ....D 716 874-7190
New York *(G-11072)*
Lucas Dental Equipment Co Inc ....F 631 244-2807
Bohemia *(G-1093)*
Luitpold Pharmaceuticals Inc ....E 631 924-4000
Shirley *(G-15447)*
Marotta Dental Studio Inc ....E 631 249-7520
Farmingdale *(G-5051)*
Martins Dental Studio ....G 315 788-0800
Watertown *(G-16686)*
Mini-Max Dntl Repr Eqpmnts Inc ....G 631 242-0322
Deer Park *(G-4198)*
Nu Life Restorations of L I ....D 516 489-5200
Old Westbury *(G-13154)*
Oramaax Dental Products Inc ....F 516 771-8514
Freeport *(G-5428)*
Ortho Dent Laboratory Inc ....F 716 839-1900
Williamsville *(G-17274)*
Precision Dental Cabinets Inc ....F 631 543-3870
Smithtown *(G-15518)*
Precision Dental Ceramics of B ....F 716 681-4133
Bowmansville *(G-1168)*
Professional Manufacturers ....F 631 586-2440
Deer Park *(G-4219)*
Sabra Dental Products ....G 914 945-0836
Ossining *(G-13352)*
Safe-Dent Enterprises LLC ....G 845 362-0141
Monsey *(G-8615)*
▲ **Schilling Forge Inc** ....E 315 454-4421
Syracuse *(G-16055)*
Sentage Corporation ....E 914 664-2200
Mount Vernon *(G-8779)*
Smile Specialists ....G 877 337-6135
New York *(G-12131)*
Stylecraft Interiors Inc ....F 516 487-2133
Great Neck *(G-5862)*
Temrex Corporation ....E 516 868-6221
Freeport *(G-5441)*
Tiger Supply Inc ....G 631 293-2700
Farmingdale *(G-5140)*
Total Dntl Implant Sltions LLC ....G 212 877-3777
Valley Stream *(G-16453)*
▲ **Valplast International Corp** ....F 516 442-3923
Westbury *(G-17069)*
Vincent Martino Dental Lab ....F 716 674-7800
Buffalo *(G-3269)*
Yes Dental Laboratory Inc ....E 914 333-7550
Tarrytown *(G-16135)*

3844 X-ray Apparatus & Tubes

▲ **Air Techniques Inc** ....B 516 433-7676
Melville *(G-8324)*
American Access Care LLC ....F 631 582-9729
Hauppauge *(G-6038)*
▲ **Biodex Medical Systems Inc** ....C 631 924-9000
Shirley *(G-15439)*
▲ **Community Products LLC** ....C 845 658-8799
Rifton *(G-14144)*
Dra Imaging PC ....E 845 296-1057
Wappingers Falls *(G-16586)*
▲ **Flow X Ray Corporation** ....D 631 242-9729
Deer Park *(G-4164)*
Genesis Digital Imaging Inc ....G 310 305-7358
Rochester *(G-14417)*
Mitegen LLC ....G 607 266-8877
Ithaca *(G-6898)*
▼ **Multiwire Laboratories Ltd** ....G 607 257-3378
Ithaca *(G-6900)*
New York Imaging Service Inc ....F 716 834-8022
Tonawanda *(G-16202)*
Phantom Laboratory Inc ....F 518 692-1190
Greenwich *(G-5911)*
Photo Medic Equipment Inc ....D 631 242-6600
Deer Park *(G-4213)*
▲ **Quantum Medical Imaging LLC** ....D 631 567-5800
Rochester *(G-14639)*
R M F Health Management L L C ....E 718 854-5400
Wantagh *(G-16583)*
▼ **RC Imaging Inc** ....G 585 392-4336
Hilton *(G-6446)*
Siemens Corporation ....F 202 434-7800
New York *(G-12084)*
Siemens USA Holdings Inc ....B 212 258-4000
New York *(G-12086)*
Surescan Corporation ....E 607 321-0042
Binghamton *(G-947)*
◆ **VJ Technologies Inc** ....E 631 589-8800
Bohemia *(G-1151)*
◆ **Wolf X-Ray Corporation** ....D 631 242-9729
Deer Park *(G-4252)*

3845 Electromedical & Electrotherapeutic Apparatus

Advd Heart Phys & Surgs ....F 212 434-3000
New York *(G-9096)*
Argon Medical Devices Inc ....G 585 321-1130
Henrietta *(G-6316)*
▲ **Biofeedback Instrument Corp** ....G 212 222-5665
New York *(G-9453)*
▲ **Buffalo Filter LLC** ....D 716 835-7000
Lancaster *(G-7331)*
C R Bard Inc ....A 518 793-2531
Glens Falls *(G-5690)*
Caliber Imging Diagnostics Inc ....E 585 239-9800
Rochester *(G-14273)*
Cardiac Life Products Inc ....G 585 267-7775
East Rochester *(G-4473)*
City Sports Imaging Inc ....E 212 481-3600
New York *(G-9684)*
Complex Biosystems Inc ....G 315 464-8007
Liverpool *(G-7541)*
Conmed Andover Medical Inc ....F 315 797-8375
Utica *(G-16337)*
Conmed Corporation ....D 315 797-8375
Utica *(G-16338)*
◆ **Conmed Corporation** ....B 315 797-8375
Utica *(G-16339)*
Ddc Technologies Inc ....G 516 594-1533
Oceanside *(G-13096)*
Elizabeth Wood ....G 315 492-5470
Syracuse *(G-15954)*
Empire Open Mri ....G 914 961-1777
Yonkers *(G-17457)*
Equivital Inc ....E 646 513-4169
New York *(G-10106)*
Excel Technology Inc ....F 212 355-3400
New York *(G-10156)*
Fonar Corporation ....C 631 694-2929
Melville *(G-8349)*
Forest Medical LLC ....G 315 434-9000
East Syracuse *(G-4545)*
Gary Gelbfish MD ....G 718 258-3004
Brooklyn *(G-2015)*
Global Instrumentation LLC ....F 315 682-0272
Manlius *(G-8105)*
Gravity East Village Inc ....G 212 388-9788
New York *(G-10397)*
Health Care Originals Inc ....G 585 471-8215
Rochester *(G-14451)*
Imacor Inc ....E 516 393-0970
Garden City *(G-5523)*
▲ **Infimed Inc** ....D 315 453-4545
Liverpool *(G-7547)*
Infimed Inc ....G 585 383-1710
Pittsford *(G-13593)*
Integrated Medical Devices ....G 315 457-4200
Liverpool *(G-7549)*
J H M Engineering ....E 718 871-1810
Brooklyn *(G-2122)*
Jadak LLC ....F 315 701-0678
North Syracuse *(G-12966)*
Jaracz Jr Joseph Paul ....G 716 533-1377
Orchard Park *(G-13301)*
Jarvik Heart Inc ....E 212 397-3911
New York *(G-10742)*
Juvly Aesthetics Inc ....D 614 686-3627
New York *(G-10829)*
Kal Manufacturing Corporation ....E 585 265-4310
Webster *(G-16751)*
Laser and Varicose Vein Trtmnt ....G 718 667-1777
Staten Island *(G-15720)*
Med Services Inc ....D 631 218-6450
Bohemia *(G-1099)*
▲ **Misonix Inc** ....D 631 694-9555
Farmingdale *(G-5067)*
Nanovibronix Inc ....F 914 233-3004
Elmsford *(G-4777)*
Natus Medical Incorporated ....G 631 457-4430
Hauppauge *(G-6171)*
Netech Corporation ....F 631 531-0100
Farmingdale *(G-5075)*
New Primecare ....G 516 822-4031
Hewlett *(G-6334)*
New York Laser & Aestheticks ....G 516 627-7777
Roslyn *(G-15045)*

S I C

Employee Codes: A=Over 500 employees, B=251-500
C=101-250, D=51-100, E=20-50, F=10-19, G=5-9

New York Marine Elec Inc.....G..... 631 734-6050
Hampton Bays *(G-5983)*
Nirx Medical Technologies LLC.....F..... 516 676-6479
Glen Head *(G-5652)*
▲ **Novamed-Usa Inc**.....E..... 914 789-2100
Elmsford *(G-4779)*
Ocean Cardiac Monitoring.....G..... 631 777-3700
Deer Park *(G-4209)*
Pharmadva LLC.....G..... 585 469-1410
West Henrietta *(G-16922)*
◆ **Philips Medical Systems Mr**.....B..... 518 782-1122
Latham *(G-7403)*
▲ **Photomedex Inc**.....E..... 888 966-1010
Orangeburg *(G-13261)*
▲ **Photonics Industries Intl Inc**.....D..... 631 218-2240
Ronkonkoma *(G-14992)*
Quadrant Biosciences Inc.....F..... 315 614-2325
Syracuse *(G-16037)*
▲ **Radiancy Inc**.....F..... 845 398-1647
Orangeburg *(G-13267)*
Ray Medica Inc.....E..... 952 885-0500
New York *(G-11832)*
▲ **Sonicor Inc**.....F..... 631 920-6555
West Babylon *(G-16861)*
Sonomed Inc.....E..... 516 354-0900
New Hyde Park *(G-8908)*
▲ **Soterix Medical Inc**.....F..... 888 990-8327
New York *(G-12167)*
Stand Up Mri of Lynbrook PC.....G..... 516 256-1558
Lynbrook *(G-7989)*
Stj Enterprises.....D..... 516 612-0110
Cedarhurst *(G-3488)*
Sun Scientific Inc.....G..... 914 479-5108
Dobbs Ferry *(G-4327)*
Teledyne Optech Inc.....F..... 585 427-8310
Rochester *(G-14747)*
Ultradian Diagnostics LLC.....G..... 518 618-0046
Rensselaer *(G-14063)*
University of Rochester.....B..... 585 275-3483
Rochester *(G-14772)*
▲ **Vasomedical Inc**.....B..... 516 997-4600
Plainview *(G-13668)*
▲ **Vermed Inc**.....D..... 800 669-6905
Buffalo *(G-3267)*
Visiplex Instruments Corp.....D..... 845 365-0190
Elmsford *(G-4798)*
▲ **Z-Axis Inc**.....D..... 315 548-5000
Phelps *(G-13563)*

3851 Ophthalmic Goods

21st Century Optics Inc.....E..... 347 527-1079
Long Island City *(G-7675)*
Accu Coat Inc.....G..... 585 288-2330
Rochester *(G-14181)*
Acuity Polymers Inc.....G..... 585 458-8409
Rochester *(G-14187)*
Alden Optical Laboratory Inc.....F..... 716 937-9181
Lancaster *(G-7326)*
Art-Craft Optical Company Inc.....E..... 585 546-6640
Rochester *(G-14231)*
Bausch & Lomb Holdings Inc.....G..... 585 338-6000
New York *(G-9384)*
◆ **Bausch & Lomb Incorporated**.....B..... 585 338-6000
Rochester *(G-14242)*
Bausch & Lomb Incorporated.....B..... 585 338-6000
Rochester *(G-14243)*
Co-Optics America Lab Inc.....E..... 607 432-0557
Oneonta *(G-13201)*
Colors In Optics Ltd.....D..... 718 845-0300
New Hyde Park *(G-8867)*
Coopervision Inc.....A..... 585 385-6810
West Henrietta *(G-16907)*
Coopervision Inc.....A..... 585 889-3301
Scottsville *(G-15357)*
▲ **Coopervision Inc**.....C..... 585 385-6810
Victor *(G-16494)*
▲ **Coopervision Inc**.....D..... 585 385-6810
Victor *(G-16495)*
▲ **Corinne McCormack Inc**.....F..... 212 868-7919
New York *(G-9785)*
Corneal Design Corporation.....F..... 301 670-7076
Lima *(G-7465)*
▲ **Designs For Vision Inc**.....C..... 631 585-3300
Ronkonkoma *(G-14922)*
Doug Lambertson Od.....G..... 718 698-9300
Staten Island *(G-15687)*
Edroy Products Co Inc.....G..... 845 358-6600
Nyack *(G-13067)*
Empire Optical Inc.....F..... 585 454-4470
Rochester *(G-14368)*

Equicheck LLC.....G..... 631 987-6356
Patchogue *(G-13444)*
▲ **Esc Control Electronics LLC**.....E..... 631 467-5328
Sayville *(G-15236)*
Essilor Laboratories Amer Inc.....E..... 845 365-6700
Orangeburg *(G-13248)*
▲ **Eye Deal Eyewear Inc**.....G..... 716 297-1500
Niagara Falls *(G-12838)*
▲ **Eyeworks Inc**.....G..... 585 454-4470
Rochester *(G-14388)*
Frame Works America Inc.....E..... 631 288-1300
Westhampton Beach *(G-17087)*
Glasses USA LLC.....F..... 212 784-6094
New York *(G-10349)*
Hirsch Optical Corp.....D..... 516 752-2211
Farmingdale *(G-5013)*
▲ **His Vision Inc**.....E..... 585 254-0022
Rochester *(G-14457)*
Humanware USA Inc.....E..... 800 722-3393
Champlain *(G-3570)*
J I Intrntnal Contact Lens Lab.....G..... 718 997-1212
Rego Park *(G-14045)*
Kathmando Valley Preservation.....F..... 212 727-0074
New York *(G-10856)*
Lens Lab.....G..... 718 379-2020
Bronx *(G-1385)*
Lens Lab Express.....G..... 718 921-5488
Brooklyn *(G-2212)*
Lens Lab Express of Graham Ave.....G..... 718 486-0117
Brooklyn *(G-2213)*
Lens Lab Express Southern Blvd.....G..... 718 626-5184
Astoria *(G-446)*
M Factory USA Inc.....G..... 917 410-7878
Brooklyn *(G-2251)*
Mager & Gougelman Inc.....G..... 212 661-3939
New York *(G-11127)*
Mager & Gougelman Inc.....G..... 212 661-3939
Hempstead *(G-6302)*
Mager & Gougelman Inc.....G..... 516 489-0202
Hempstead *(G-6303)*
Mark F Rosenhaft N A O.....G..... 516 374-1010
Cedarhurst *(G-3485)*
Modo Retail LLC.....E..... 212 965-4900
New York *(G-11316)*
▲ **Moscot Wholesale Corp**.....G..... 212 647-1550
New York *(G-11334)*
North Bronx Retinal & Ophthlmi.....G..... 347 535-4932
Bronx *(G-1415)*
Oakley Inc.....D..... 212 575-0960
New York *(G-11506)*
Optika Eyes Ltd.....G..... 631 567-8852
Sayville *(G-15242)*
▲ **Optisource International Inc**.....E..... 631 924-8360
Bellport *(G-832)*
Optogenics of Syracuse Inc.....D..... 315 446-3000
Syracuse *(G-16026)*
▲ **Parker Warby Retail Inc**.....E..... 646 517-5223
New York *(G-11589)*
Spectacle Optical Inc.....G..... 646 706-1015
Rego Park *(G-14051)*
Strauss Eye Prosthetics Inc.....G..... 585 424-1350
Rochester *(G-14729)*
Surgical Design Corp.....F..... 914 273-2445
Armonk *(G-418)*
▲ **Tri-Supreme Optical LLC**.....D..... 631 249-2020
Farmingdale *(G-5144)*
Winchester Optical Company.....E..... 607 734-4251
Elmira *(G-4718)*
Wyeth Holdings LLC.....D..... 845 602-5000
Pearl River *(G-13493)*
Xinya International Trading Co.....G..... 212 216-9681
New York *(G-12704)*
▲ **Zyloware Corporation**.....D..... 914 708-1200
Port Chester *(G-13785)*

3861 Photographic Eqpt & Splys

▲ **Air Techniques Inc**.....B..... 516 433-7676
Melville *(G-8324)*
▲ **All-Pro Imaging Corp**.....E..... 516 433-7676
Melville *(G-8325)*
Apexx Omni-Graphics Inc.....D..... 718 326-3330
Maspeth *(G-8147)*
Astrodyne Inc.....G..... 516 536-5755
Oceanside *(G-13092)*
AVI-Spl Employee.....B..... 212 840-4801
New York *(G-9330)*
Avid Technology Inc.....E..... 212 983-2424
New York *(G-9331)*
▲ **Bescor Video Accessories Ltd**.....F..... 631 420-1717
Farmingdale *(G-4960)*

Big Indie - Beautiful Boy LLC.....G..... 917 464-5599
Woodstock *(G-17377)*
▲ **Cannon Industries Inc**.....D..... 585 254-8080
Rochester *(G-14276)*
Carestream Health Inc.....B..... 585 627-1800
Rochester *(G-14278)*
◆ **Champion Photochemistry Inc**.....D..... 585 760-6444
Rochester *(G-14292)*
Chemung Cnty Chpter Nysarc Inc.....C..... 607 734-6151
Elmira *(G-4688)*
▲ **Columbia Telecom Group**.....G..... 631 501-5000
New York *(G-9737)*
▼ **Cpac Inc**.....E..... 585 382-3223
Leicester *(G-7442)*
Creatron Services Inc.....E..... 516 437-5119
Floral Park *(G-5208)*
Critical Imaging LLC.....E..... 315 732-5020
Utica *(G-16341)*
▲ **Dnp Electronics America LLC**.....D..... 212 503-1060
New York *(G-9944)*
Dolby Laboratories Inc.....F..... 212 767-1700
New York *(G-9948)*
Eastchester Photo Services.....G..... 914 961-6596
Eastchester *(G-4594)*
Eastman Kodak Company.....D..... 585 722-2187
Rochester *(G-14347)*
◆ **Eastman Kodak Company**.....B..... 585 724-4000
Rochester *(G-14348)*
Eastman Kodak Company.....D..... 585 724-5600
Rochester *(G-14349)*
Eastman Kodak Company.....D..... 585 722-9695
Pittsford *(G-13587)*
Eastman Kodak Company.....D..... 585 726-6261
Rochester *(G-14350)*
Eastman Kodak Company.....D..... 585 724-4000
Rochester *(G-14351)*
Eastman Kodak Company.....F..... 800 698-3324
Rochester *(G-14352)*
Eastman Kodak Company.....D..... 585 722-4385
Rochester *(G-14353)*
Eastman Kodak Company.....D..... 585 588-5598
Rochester *(G-14354)*
Eastman Kodak Company.....C..... 585 726-7000
Rochester *(G-14355)*
Eastman Kodak Company.....G..... 585 722-4007
Rochester *(G-14356)*
Eastman Kodak Company.....D..... 585 588-3896
Rochester *(G-14357)*
Eastman Kodak Company.....E..... 585 724-4000
Rochester *(G-14358)*
Eastman Park Micrographics Inc.....E..... 866 934-4376
Rochester *(G-14359)*
Ebsco Industries Inc.....G..... 585 398-2000
Farmington *(G-5158)*
Efam Enterprises LLC.....E..... 718 204-1760
Long Island City *(G-7754)*
Emda Inc.....F..... 631 243-6363
Edgewood *(G-4611)*
Facsimile Cmmncations Inds Inc.....D..... 212 741-6400
New York *(G-10178)*
Fanvision Entertainment LLC.....G..... 917 297-7428
New York *(G-10191)*
Fluxdata Incorporated.....G..... 800 425-0176
Rochester *(G-14399)*
▲ **Focus Camera Inc**.....C..... 718 437-8800
Brooklyn *(G-1990)*
Garys Loft.....G..... 212 244-0970
New York *(G-10296)*
Geospatial Systems Inc.....F..... 585 427-8310
West Henrietta *(G-16913)*
Gpc International Inc.....G..... 631 752-9600
Melville *(G-8351)*
Henrys Deals Inc.....E..... 347 821-4685
Brooklyn *(G-2072)*
▲ **Hilord Chemical Corporation**.....E..... 631 234-7373
Hauppauge *(G-6117)*
Jack L Popkin & Co Inc.....G..... 718 361-6700
Kew Gardens *(G-7192)*
Just Lamps of New York Inc.....F..... 716 626-2240
Buffalo *(G-3039)*
Kelmar Systems Inc.....F..... 631 421-1230
Huntington Station *(G-6751)*
◆ **Kodak Alaris Inc**.....B..... 585 290-2891
Rochester *(G-14493)*
Kogeto Inc.....G..... 646 490-8169
New York *(G-10907)*
▲ **Konica Mnolta Sups Mfg USA Inc**.....D..... 845 294-8400
Goshen *(G-5751)*
Kyle Editing LLC.....G..... 212 675-3464
New York *(G-10937)*

Labgrafix Printing Inc ....G 516 280-8300
Lynbrook *(G-7980)*
Lake Image Systems Inc ....F 585 321-3630
Henrietta *(G-6319)*
▲ **Lanel Inc** ....F 516 437-5119
Floral Park *(G-5212)*
Lasertech Crtridge RE-Builders ....G 518 373-1246
Clifton Park *(G-3725)*
▲ **Lowel-Light Manufacturing Inc** ....E 718 921-0600
Brooklyn *(G-2241)*
▲ **Mekatronics Incorporated** ....E 516 883-6805
Port Washington *(G-13865)*
Mirion Technologies Ist Corp ....D 607 562-4300
Horseheads *(G-6612)*
▲ **Norazza Inc** ....G 716 706-1160
Buffalo *(G-3116)*
◆ **Printer Components Inc** ....G 585 924-5190
Fairport *(G-4877)*
Qls Solutions Group Inc ....E 716 852-2203
Buffalo *(G-3170)*
▲ **Rear View Safety Inc** ....E 855 815-3842
Brooklyn *(G-2502)*
Rockland Colloid Corp ....G 845 359-5559
Piermont *(G-13572)*
Seneca TEC Inc ....G 585 381-2645
Fairport *(G-4885)*
Shelley Promotions Inc ....G 212 924-4987
New York *(G-12069)*
▲ **Sima Technologies LLC** ....G 412 828-9130
Hauppauge *(G-6215)*
Stallion Technologies Inc ....G 315 622-1176
Liverpool *(G-7576)*
Thermo Cidtec Inc ....E 315 451-9410
Liverpool *(G-7580)*
Tiffen Company LLC ....G 631 273-2500
Hauppauge *(G-6239)*
▲ **Tiffen Company LLC** ....D 631 273-2500
Hauppauge *(G-6240)*
Toner-N-More Inc ....G 718 232-6200
Brooklyn *(G-2682)*
Truesense Imaging Inc ....C 585 784-5500
Rochester *(G-14761)*
▲ **Turner Bellows Inc** ....E 585 235-4456
Rochester *(G-14763)*
Va Inc ....E 585 385-5930
Rochester *(G-14777)*
▲ **Vishay Thin Film LLC** ....C 716 283-4025
Niagara Falls *(G-12906)*
Watec America Corporation ....E 702 434-6111
Middletown *(G-8506)*
Xerox Corporation ....F 585 423-4711
Rochester *(G-14796)*
Xerox Corporation ....A 585 422-4564
Webster *(G-16769)*
Xerox Corporation ....B 212 716-4000
New York *(G-12701)*
Xerox Corporation ....E 914 397-1319
White Plains *(G-17216)*
Xerox Corporation ....D 585 425-6100
Fairport *(G-4895)*
Xerox Corporation ....D 212 330-1386
New York *(G-12702)*
Xerox Corporation ....E 845 918-3147
Suffern *(G-15823)*
Xerox Corporation ....E 518 434-6543
Albany *(G-152)*
Xerox Corporation ....C 585 427-4500
Rochester *(G-14797)*
Xerox Corporation ....D 585 423-5090
Webster *(G-16770)*
Xerox Corporation ....C 585 264-5584
Rochester *(G-14799)*
Xerox Corporation ....D 716 831-3300
Buffalo *(G-3285)*

3873 Watch & Clock Devices & Parts

▲ **American Time Mfg Ltd** ....F 585 266-5120
Rochester *(G-14217)*
▲ **Croton Watch Co Inc** ....E 800 443-7639
West Nyack *(G-16945)*
▲ **E Gluck Corporation** ....C 718 784-0700
Little Neck *(G-7531)*
▲ **Ewatchfactory Corp** ....G 212 564-8318
New York *(G-10150)*
▼ **First Sbf Holding Inc** ....F 845 425-9882
Valley Cottage *(G-16404)*
▲ **Game Time LLC** ....F 914 557-9662
New York *(G-10291)*
▲ **Geneva Watch Company Inc** ....E 212 221-1177
New York *(G-10320)*
H Best Ltd ....F 212 354-2400
New York *(G-10432)*
Hammerman Bros Inc ....G 212 956-2800
New York *(G-10445)*
Justa Company ....G 718 932-6139
Long Island City *(G-7802)*
Life Watch Technology Inc ....D 917 669-2428
Flushing *(G-5273)*
Marco Moore Inc ....D 212 575-2090
Great Neck *(G-5839)*
National Time Recording Eqp Co ....F 212 227-3310
New York *(G-11375)*
Olympic Jewelry Inc ....G 212 768-7004
New York *(G-11515)*
◆ **Pavana USA Inc** ....G 646 833-8811
New York *(G-11602)*
◆ **Pedre Corp** ....E 212 868-2935
Hicksville *(G-6411)*
▲ **Precision International Co Inc** ....G 212 268-9090
New York *(G-11719)*
Richemont North America Inc ....G 212 891-2440
New York *(G-11889)*
▲ **Sarina Accessories LLC** ....F 212 239-8106
New York *(G-11993)*
▲ **Stuhrling Original LLC** ....G 718 840-5760
Brooklyn *(G-2637)*
▲ **TWI Watches LLC** ....E 718 663-3969
Brooklyn *(G-2709)*
▲ **Visage Swiss Watch LLC** ....G 212 594-7991
New York *(G-12580)*
▲ **Watchcraft Inc** ....G 347 531-0382
Long Island City *(G-7949)*

39 MISCELLANEOUS MANUFACTURING INDUSTRIES

3911 Jewelry: Precious Metal

A & V Castings Inc ....G 212 997-0042
New York *(G-9029)*
A Jaffe Inc ....C 212 843-7464
New York *(G-9038)*
Aaron Group LLC ....D 718 392-5454
Mount Vernon *(G-8701)*
Abraham Jwly Designers & Mfrs ....F 212 944-1149
New York *(G-9052)*
Abrimian Bros Corp ....F 212 382-1106
New York *(G-9053)*
Adamor Inc ....G 212 688-8885
New York *(G-9072)*
AF Design Inc ....G 347 548-5273
New York *(G-9102)*
Alart Inc ....G 212 840-1508
New York *(G-9122)*
◆ **Albea Cosmetics America Inc** ....E 212 371-5100
New York *(G-9124)*
Alchemy Simya Inc ....E 646 230-1122
New York *(G-9126)*
Alex Sepkus Inc ....F 212 391-8466
New York *(G-9131)*
Alexander Primak Jewelry Inc ....D 212 398-0287
New York *(G-9132)*
▲ **Alfred Butler Inc** ....F 516 829-7460
Great Neck *(G-5801)*
All The Rage Inc ....G 516 605-2001
Hicksville *(G-6344)*
▲ **Almond Jewelers Inc** ....F 516 933-6000
Port Washington *(G-13821)*
▲ **Alpine Creations Ltd** ....G 212 308-9353
New York *(G-9154)*
Ambras Fine Jewelry Inc ....E 718 784-5252
Long Island City *(G-7688)*
American Craft Jewelers Inc ....G 718 972-0945
Brooklyn *(G-1598)*
American Originals Corporation ....G 212 836-4155
New York *(G-9177)*
Anatoli Inc ....F 845 334-9000
West Hurley *(G-16931)*
Ancient Modern Art LLC ....F 212 302-0080
New York *(G-9199)*
▲ **Anima Group LLC** ....G 917 913-2053
New York *(G-9211)*
Apicella Jewelers Inc ....E 212 840-2024
New York *(G-9224)*
▲ **AR & AR Jewelry Inc** ....E 212 764-7916
New York *(G-9237)*
Arringement International Inc ....G 347 323-7974
Flushing *(G-5234)*
Art-TEC Jewelry Designs Ltd ....E 212 719-2941
New York *(G-9266)*
▲ **Asher Jewelry Company Inc** ....D 212 302-6233
Great Neck *(G-5808)*
▲ **Ashi Diamonds LLC** ....E 212 319-8291
New York *(G-9282)*
Ateret LLC ....G 212 819-0777
New York *(G-9298)*
Atlantic Precious Metal Cast ....G 718 937-7100
Long Island City *(G-7708)*
Atr Jewelry Inc ....F 212 819-0075
New York *(G-9310)*
B K Jewelry Contractor Inc ....E 212 398-9093
New York *(G-9342)*
Barber Brothers Jewelry Mfg ....F 212 819-0666
New York *(G-9368)*
Baroka Creations Inc ....G 212 768-0527
New York *(G-9374)*
Bartholomew Mazza Ltd Inc ....E 212 935-4530
New York *(G-9378)*
Bellataire Diamonds Inc ....F 212 687-8881
New York *(G-9398)*
Benlee Enterprises LLC ....F 212 730-7330
Long Island City *(G-7714)*
▲ **BH Multi Com Corp** ....E 212 944-0020
New York *(G-9434)*
Bielka Inc ....G 212 980-6841
New York *(G-9439)*
Billanti Casting Co Inc ....E 516 775-4800
New Hyde Park *(G-8864)*
BJG Services LLC ....E 516 592-5692
New York *(G-9459)*
Bourghol Brothers Inc ....G 845 268-9752
Congers *(G-3878)*
Bral Nader Fine Jewelry Inc ....G 800 493-1222
New York *(G-9503)*
▲ **Brannkey Inc** ....D 212 371-1515
New York *(G-9504)*
Brilliant Jewelers/Mjj Inc ....C 212 353-2326
New York *(G-9514)*
Bristol Seamless Ring Corp ....F 212 874-2645
New York *(G-9515)*
Burke & Bannayan ....G 585 723-1010
Rochester *(G-14267)*
Carlo Monte Designs Inc ....G 212 935-5611
New York *(G-9581)*
Carol Dauplaise Ltd ....E 212 997-5290
New York *(G-9584)*
Carr Manufacturing Jewelers ....G 518 783-6093
Latham *(G-7386)*
Carvin French Jewelers Inc ....E 212 755-6474
New York *(G-9592)*
Chaindom Enterprises Inc ....G 212 719-4778
New York *(G-9626)*
Chameleon Gems Inc ....F 516 829-3333
Great Neck *(G-5814)*
Charis & Mae Inc ....G 212 641-0816
New York *(G-9631)*
Charles Perrella Inc ....E 845 348-4777
Nyack *(G-13063)*
▲ **Charles Vaillant Inc** ....G 212 752-4832
New York *(G-9634)*
▲ **Christopher Designs Inc** ....E 212 382-1013
New York *(G-9665)*
▲ **Cigar Oasis Inc** ....G 516 520-5258
Farmingdale *(G-4969)*
▲ **CJ Jewelry Inc** ....F 212 719-2464
New York *(G-9687)*
▲ **Clyde Duneier Inc** ....D 212 398-1122
New York *(G-9705)*
Concord Jewelry Mfg Co LLC ....E 212 719-4030
New York *(G-9755)*
▲ **Creative Gold LLC** ....E 718 686-2225
Brooklyn *(G-1813)*
Crescent Wedding Rings Inc ....G 212 869-8296
New York *(G-9813)*
Crown Jewelers Intl Inc ....G 212 420-7800
New York *(G-9816)*
▲ **Csi International Inc** ....E 800 441-2895
Niagara Falls *(G-12831)*
D Oro Onofrio Inc ....G 718 491-2961
Brooklyn *(G-1831)*
Dasan Inc ....E 212 244-5410
New York *(G-9865)*
David Friedman Chain Co Inc ....F 212 684-1760
New York *(G-9874)*
David Howell Product Design ....E 914 666-4080
Bedford Hills *(G-798)*
▲ **David S Diamonds Inc** ....F 212 921-8029
New York *(G-9878)*
David Weisz & Sons Inc ....G 212 840-4747
New York *(G-9881)*

SIC

Employee Codes: A=Over 500 employees, B=251-500
C=101-250, D=51-100, E=20-50, F=10-19, G=5-9

2018 Harris
New York Manufacturers Directory

863

David Yurman Enterprises LLC G 914 539-4444
White Plains *(G-17127)*

◆ **David Yurman Enterprises LLC** B 212 896-1550
New York *(G-9882)*

David Yurman Enterprises LLC G 516 627-1700
Manhasset *(G-8090)*

David Yurman Enterprises LLC G 845 928-8660
Central Valley *(G-3550)*

David Yurman Retail LLC G 877 226-1400
New York *(G-9883)*

Diamond Distributors Inc G 212 921-9188
New York *(G-9925)*

Diana Kane Incorporated G 718 638-6520
Brooklyn *(G-1858)*

Dimoda Designs Inc E 212 355-8166
New York *(G-9932)*

Donna Distefano Ltd G 212 594-3757
New York *(G-9950)*

Doris Panos Designs Ltd G 631 245-0580
Melville *(G-8342)*

▲ **Duran Jewelry Inc** G 212 431-1959
New York *(G-9990)*

Dweck Industries Inc G 718 615-1695
Brooklyn *(G-1885)*

E Chabot Ltd E 212 575-1026
Brooklyn *(G-1891)*

◆ **E M G Creations Inc** F 212 643-0960
New York *(G-10002)*

▲ **Eagle Regalia Co Inc** F 845 425-2245
Spring Valley *(G-15604)*

Earring King Jewelry Mfg Inc G 718 544-7947
New York *(G-10013)*

Eastern Jewelry Mfg Co Inc E 212 840-0001
New York *(G-10016)*

Echo Group Inc F 917 608-7440
New York *(G-10028)*

Eclipse Collection Jewelers F 212 764-6883
New York *(G-10030)*

Ed Levin Inc E 518 677-8595
Cambridge *(G-3336)*

Efron Designs Ltd G 718 482-8440
Long Island City *(G-7757)*

Elegant Jewelers Mfg Co Inc F 212 869-4951
New York *(G-10052)*

▼ **Ema Jewelry Inc** D 212 575-8989
New York *(G-10070)*

Emsaru USA Corp G 212 459-9355
New York *(G-10076)*

Eshel Jewelry Mfg Co Inc F 212 588-8800
New York *(G-10112)*

Eternal Line G 845 856-1999
Sparrow Bush *(G-15586)*

Euro Bands Inc F 212 719-9777
New York *(G-10137)*

F M Abdulky Inc F 607 272-7373
Ithaca *(G-6875)*

F M Abdulky Inc G 607 272-7373
Ithaca *(G-6876)*

Fam Creations E 212 869-4833
New York *(G-10185)*

Fantasia Jewelry Inc E 212 921-9590
New York *(G-10189)*

Feldman Jewelry Creations Inc G 718 438-8895
Brooklyn *(G-1968)*

First Image Design Corp E 212 221-8282
New York *(G-10220)*

Five Star Creations Inc E 845 783-1187
Monroe *(G-8589)*

Frank Blancato Inc F 212 768-1495
New York *(G-10251)*

Gem Mine Corp G 516 367-1075
Woodbury *(G-17309)*

Gem-Bar Setting Inc G 212 869-9238
New York *(G-10310)*

Gemoro Inc G 212 768-8844
New York *(G-10312)*

Gemveto Jewelry Company Inc E 212 755-2522
New York *(G-10314)*

George Lederman Inc G 212 753-4556
New York *(G-10327)*

Giovane Ltd E 212 332-7373
New York *(G-10340)*

Global Gem Corporation G 212 350-9936
New York *(G-10358)*

Gold & Diamonds Wholesale Outl G 718 438-7888
Brooklyn *(G-2037)*

Goldarama Company Inc G 212 730-7299
New York *(G-10370)*

Golden Integrity Inc E 212 764-6753
New York *(G-10374)*

Goldmark Products Inc E 631 777-3343
Farmingdale *(G-5008)*

Gorga Fehren Fine Jewelry LLC G 646 861-3595
New York *(G-10379)*

Gottlieb & Sons Inc E 212 575-1907
New York *(G-10382)*

▲ **Gramercy Jewelry Mfg Corp** E 212 268-0461
New York *(G-10387)*

Grandeur Creations Inc G 212 643-1277
New York *(G-10390)*

▲ **Guild Diamond Products Inc** F 212 871-0007
New York *(G-10424)*

Gumuchian Fils Ltd F 212 593-3118
New York *(G-10427)*

H & T Goldman Corporation G 800 822-0272
New York *(G-10431)*

H C Kionka & Co Inc F 212 227-3155
New York *(G-10433)*

Hammerman Bros Inc G 212 956-2800
New York *(G-10445)*

Hanna Altinis Co Inc E 718 706-1134
Long Island City *(G-7785)*

▲ **Hansa Usa LLC** E 646 412-6407
New York *(G-10454)*

▲ **Harry Winston Inc** C 212 399-1000
New York *(G-10465)*

▲ **Haskell Jewels Ltd** E 212 764-3332
New York *(G-10471)*

Henry Design Studios Inc G 516 801-2760
Locust Valley *(G-7662)*

Henry Dunay Designs Inc E 212 768-9700
New York *(G-10501)*

▲ **Hjn Inc** F 212 398-9564
New York *(G-10531)*

Horo Creations LLC G 212 719-4818
New York *(G-10551)*

Houles USA Inc G 212 935-3900
New York *(G-10559)*

Hw Holdings Inc G 212 399-1000
New York *(G-10581)*

Hy Gold Jewelers Inc G 212 744-3202
New York *(G-10582)*

Ilico Jewelry Inc G 516 482-0201
Great Neck *(G-5831)*

Imena Jewelry Manufacturer Inc F 212 827-0073
New York *(G-10617)*

Incon Gems Inc F 212 221-8560
New York *(G-10626)*

▲ **Indonesian Imports Inc** E 888 800-5899
New York *(G-10633)*

▲ **Innovative Jewelry Inc** G 718 408-8950
Bay Shore *(G-703)*

Inori Jewels F 347 703-5078
New York *(G-10649)*

Intentions Jewelry LLC G 845 226-4650
Lagrangeville *(G-7279)*

Iradj Moini Couture Ltd F 212 594-9242
New York *(G-10698)*

Iridesse Inc F 212 230-6000
New York *(G-10700)*

Iriniri Designs Ltd F 845 469-7934
Sugar Loaf *(G-15824)*

J H Jewelry Co Inc F 212 239-1330
New York *(G-10719)*

J J Creations Inc E 718 392-2828
Long Island City *(G-7796)*

J R Gold Designs Ltd F 212 922-9292
New York *(G-10722)*

▲ **Jacmel Jewelry Inc** C 718 349-4300
New York *(G-10730)*

Jacobs & Cohen Inc E 212 714-2702
New York *(G-10732)*

▲ **Jacoby Enterprises LLC** G 718 435-0289
Brooklyn *(G-2132)*

Jaguar Casting Co Inc E 212 869-0197
New York *(G-10734)*

Jaguar Jewelry Casting NY Inc G 212 768-4848
New York *(G-10735)*

▲ **Jane Bohan Inc** G 212 529-6090
New York *(G-10739)*

Jasani Designs Usa Inc G 212 257-6465
New York *(G-10743)*

▲ **Jay Strongwater Holdings LLC** A 646 657-0558
New York *(G-10745)*

Jay-Aimee Designs Inc C 718 609-0333
Hicksville *(G-6384)*

Jayden Star LLC E 212 686-0400
New York *(G-10747)*

▲ **JC Crystal Inc** E 212 594-0858
New York *(G-10750)*

Jean & Alex Jewelry Mfg & Cons F 212 935-7621
New York *(G-10754)*

Jeff Cooper Inc F 516 333-8200
Carle Place *(G-3417)*

Jewelmak Inc E 212 398-2999
New York *(G-10762)*

Jewelry Arts Manufacturing E 212 382-3583
New York *(G-10763)*

Jewels By Star Ltd E 212 308-3490
New York *(G-10764)*

Jeweltex Mfg Corp F 212 921-8188
New York *(G-10765)*

▲ **Jimmy Crystal New York Co Ltd** E 212 594-0858
New York *(G-10775)*

▲ **JK Jewelry Inc** D 585 292-0770
Rochester *(G-14483)*

JK Manufacturing Inc G 212 683-3535
Locust Valley *(G-7663)*

Joan Boyce Ltd G 212 867-7474
New York *(G-10783)*

Jordan Scott Designs Ltd E 212 947-4250
New York *(G-10801)*

▲ **Jotaly Inc** A 212 886-6000
New York *(G-10808)*

Julius Cohen Jewelers Inc G 212 371-3050
Brooklyn *(G-2159)*

▲ **Justin Ashley Designs Inc** G 718 707-0200
Long Island City *(G-7803)*

▲ **Justperfectmsp Ltd** E 877 201-0005
New York *(G-10827)*

▲ **Justyna Kaminska NY Inc** G 917 423-5527
New York *(G-10828)*

▲ **Kaprielian Enterprises Inc** D 212 645-6623
New York *(G-10845)*

Karbra Company C 212 736-9300
New York *(G-10846)*

Keith Lewis Studio Inc G 845 339-5629
Rifton *(G-14146)*

▼ **Krasner Group Inc** G 212 268-4100
New York *(G-10925)*

Kurt Gaum Inc F 212 719-2836
New York *(G-10934)*

▲ **La Fina Design Inc** G 212 689-6725
New York *(G-10946)*

▲ **Lali Jewelry Inc** G 212 944-2277
New York *(G-10957)*

▲ **Le Hook Rouge LLC** G 212 947-6272
Brooklyn *(G-2201)*

Le Paveh Ltd F 212 736-6110
New York *(G-10979)*

Le Roi Inc F 315 342-3681
Fulton *(G-5482)*

▲ **Le Vian Corp** D 516 466-7200
Great Neck *(G-5837)*

Le Vian Corp E 516 466-7200
New York *(G-10980)*

Leo Ingwer Inc E 212 719-1342
New York *(G-11004)*

Leo Schachter & Co Inc D 212 688-2000
New York *(G-11006)*

Les Ateliers Tamalet E 929 325-7976
New York *(G-11008)*

Leser Enterprises Ltd F 212 644-8921
New York *(G-11009)*

Lindsay-Hoenig Ltd G 212 575-9711
New York *(G-11030)*

▲ **Lokai Holdings LLC** F 646 979-3474
New York *(G-11052)*

Loremi Jewelry Inc E 212 840-3429
New York *(G-11071)*

Louis Tamis & Sons Inc E 212 684-1760
New York *(G-11078)*

Love Bright Jewelry Inc E 516 620-2509
Oceanside *(G-13107)*

M & S Quality Co Ltd F 212 302-8757
New York *(G-11097)*

M A R A Metals Ltd G 718 786-7868
Long Island City *(G-7826)*

M H Manufacturing Incorporated G 212 461-6900
New York *(G-11100)*

M Heskia Company Inc G 212 768-1845
New York *(G-11101)*

Magnum Creation Inc F 212 642-0993
New York *(G-11136)*

Manny Grunberg Inc E 212 302-6173
New York *(G-11162)*

Marco Moore Inc D 212 575-2090
Great Neck *(G-5839)*

Marina Jewelry Co Inc G 212 354-5027
New York *(G-11175)*

39 MISCELLANEOUS MANUFACTURING INDUSTRIES

Company	Code	Phone
Mark King Jewelry Inc — New York (G-11177)	G	212 921-0746
Mark Robinson Inc — New York (G-11180)	G	212 223-3515
Markowitz Jewelry Co Inc — Monroe (G-8596)	E	845 774-1175
Marlborough Jewels Inc — Brooklyn (G-2274)	G	718 768-2000
▲ Martin Flyer Incorporated — New York (G-11191)	E	212 840-8899
Master Craft Jewelry Co Inc — Lynbrook (G-7981)	D	516 599-1012
Masterpiece Color LLC — New York (G-11197)	G	917 279-6056
Mavito Fine Jewelry Ltd Inc — New York (G-11209)	F	212 398-9384
Maxine Denker Inc — Staten Island (G-15725)	G	212 689-1440
▲ MB Plastics Inc — Greenlawn (G-5892)	F	718 523-1180
ME & Ro Inc — New York (G-11229)	G	212 431-8744
▲ Mellem Corporation — Binghamton (G-931)	F	607 723-0001
◆ Mer Gems Corp — New York (G-11252)	G	212 714-9129
▲ Mgd Brands Inc — Plainview (G-13648)	E	516 545-0150
Michael Anthony Jewelers LLC — Mount Vernon (G-8751)	C	914 699-0000
Michael Bondanza Inc — New York (G-11276)	E	212 869-0043
Midura Jewels Inc — New York (G-11286)	G	213 265-8090
Milla Global Inc — Brooklyn (G-2319)	G	516 488-3601
Mimi So International LLC — New York (G-11300)	E	212 300-8600
Min Ho Designs Inc — New York (G-11301)	G	212 838-3667
▲ MJM Jewelry Corp — New York (G-11311)	E	212 354-5014
MJM Jewelry Corp — Brooklyn (G-2330)	D	718 596-1600
Monelle Jewelry — New York (G-11325)	G	212 977-9535
Mwsi Inc — Hawthorne (G-6275)	D	914 347-4200
▲ N Y Bijoux Corp — New York (G-11360)	G	212 244-9585
Neil Savalia Inc — New York (G-11386)	F	212 869-0123
▲ Nicolo Raineri — New York (G-11447)	G	212 925-6128
North American Mint Inc — Rochester (G-14560)	G	585 654-8500
NP Roniet Creations Inc — New York (G-11482)	G	212 302-1847
O C Tanner Company — Rye (G-15091)	G	914 921-2025
Oscar Heyman & Bros Inc — New York (G-11543)	E	212 593-0400
Osnat Gad Inc — New York (G-11544)	G	212 957-0535
Overnight Mountings Inc — New Hyde Park (G-8900)	D	516 865-3000
▲ Paragon Corporation — Port Washington (G-13872)	F	516 484-6090
Park West Jewelery Inc — New York (G-11588)	G	646 329-6145
Patuga LLC — Williamsville (G-17276)	G	716 204-7220
Pearl Erwin Inc — New York (G-11605)	E	212 889-7410
Pesselnik & Cohen Inc — New York (G-11648)	G	212 925-0287
Peter Atman Inc — New York (G-11650)	F	212 644-8882
PHC Restoration Holdings LLC — New York (G-11665)	F	212 643-0517
▲ Photograve Corporation — Staten Island (G-15741)	E	718 667-4825
▲ Pink Box Accessories LLC — Brooklyn (G-2435)	G	716 777-4477
Pronto Jewelry Inc — New York (G-11756)	E	212 719-9455
Punch Fashions LLC — New York (G-11773)	G	646 519-7333
◆ Q Ed Creations — New York (G-11787)	G	212 391-1155
R & R Grosbard Inc — New York (G-11809)	E	212 575-0077
R Klein Jewelry Co Inc — Massapequa (G-8214)	D	516 482-3260
R M Reynolds — Geneva (G-5596)	G	315 789-7365
Rand & Paseka Mfg Co Inc — Freeport (G-5433)	C	516 867-1500
▲ Regal Jewelry Inc — New York (G-11852)	E	212 382-1695
Reinhold Brothers Inc — New York (G-11854)	E	212 867-8310
Renaissance Bijou Ltd — New York (G-11862)	G	212 869-1969
Richards & West Inc — East Rochester (G-4485)	D	585 461-4088
Richline Group Inc — New York (G-11890)	E	212 643-2908
Richline Group Inc — New York (G-11891)	C	212 764-8454
Richline Group Inc — New York (G-11892)	C	914 699-0000
▲ Riva Jewelry Manufacturing Inc — Brooklyn (G-2517)	C	718 361-3100
Robert Bartholomew Ltd — Port Washington (G-13876)	E	516 767-2970
◆ Roberto Coin Inc — New York (G-11912)	F	212 486-4545
Robin Stanley Inc — New York (G-11915)	G	212 871-0007
▲ Royal Jewelry Mfg Inc — Great Neck (G-5853)	E	212 302-2500
Royal Miracle Corp — New York (G-11943)	G	212 921-5797
Rubinstein Jewelry Mfg Co — Long Island City (G-7897)	F	718 784-8650
Rudolf Friedman Inc — New York (G-11952)	E	212 869-5070
Rumson Acquisition LLC — New York (G-11954)	F	718 349-4300
▲ Ryan Gems Inc — New York (G-11958)	E	212 697-0149
▲ S & M Ring Corp — Hewlett (G-6336)	E	212 382-0900
▲ S Kashi & Sons Inc — Great Neck (G-5854)	F	212 869-9393
S Scharf Inc — Massapequa (G-8215)	F	516 541-9552
▲ Samuel B Collection Inc — Great Neck (G-5855)	E	516 466-1826
Sanoy Inc — New York (G-11987)	E	212 695-6384
Sarkisians Jewelry Co — New York (G-11994)	G	212 869-1060
Satco Castings Service Inc — New Hyde Park (G-8905)	E	516 354-1500
Satellite Incorporated — New York (G-11996)	G	212 221-6687
Scott Kay Inc — New York (G-12025)	C	201 287-0100
▲ Select Jewelry Inc — Long Island City (G-7903)	D	718 784-3626
▲ Shah Diamonds Inc — New York (G-12059)	F	212 888-9393
Shanu Gems Inc — New York (G-12063)	F	212 921-4470
Sharodine Inc — Port Washington (G-13883)	G	516 767-3548
Shining Creations Inc — New City (G-8838)	G	845 358-4911
▲ Shiro Limited — New York (G-12076)	G	212 780-0007
Simco Manufacturing Jewelers — New York (G-12098)	F	212 575-8390
Simka Diamond Corp — New York (G-12100)	F	212 921-4420
Somerset Manufacturers Inc — Roslyn Heights (G-15057)	E	516 626-3832
▲ Spark Creations Inc — New York (G-12172)	F	212 575-8385
Standard Wedding Band Co — Garden City (G-5547)	G	516 294-0954
Stanley Creations Inc — Long Island City (G-7913)	C	718 361-6100
Stanmark Jewelry Inc — New York (G-12207)	G	212 730-2557
◆ Sterling Possessions Ltd — New York (G-12221)	F	212 594-0418
Stone House Associates Inc — New York (G-12230)	G	212 221-7447
Sulphur Creations Inc — New York (G-12251)	G	212 719-2223
Sumer Gold Ltd — New York (G-12253)	G	212 354-8677
Suna Bros Inc — New York (G-12257)	E	212 869-5670
Sunrise Jewelers of NY Inc — Massapequa (G-8216)	G	516 541-1302
Tambetti Inc — New York (G-12299)	G	212 751-9584
Tamsen Z LLC — New York (G-12300)	G	212 292-6412
Tanagro Jewelry Corp — New York (G-12301)	G	212 753-2817
Technical Service Industries — Jamaica (G-6992)	E	212 719-9800
Teena Creations Inc — Freeport (G-5440)	C	516 867-1500
▲ Temple St Clair LLC — New York (G-12321)	E	212 219-8664
Thomas Sasson Co Inc — New York (G-12346)	G	212 697-4998
Tiga Holdings Inc — Beacon (G-786)	G	845 838-3000
▲ Trianon Collection Inc — New York (G-12424)	G	212 921-9450
▲ Ultra Fine Jewelry Mfg — Plainview (G-13667)	G	516 349-2848
▲ UNI Jewelry Inc — New York (G-12468)	G	212 398-1818
▲ Unimax Supply Co Inc — New York (G-12476)	G	212 925-1051
Unique Designs Inc — New York (G-12480)	F	212 575-7701
United Brothers Jewelry Inc — New York (G-12483)	E	212 921-2558
Valentin & Kalich Jwly Mfg Ltd — New York (G-12516)	E	212 575-9044
Valentine Jewelry Mfg Co Inc — New York (G-12517)	E	212 382-0606
▲ Variety Gem Co Inc — Great Neck (G-5867)	F	212 921-1820
▲ Verragio Ltd — New York (G-12547)	E	212 868-8181
Viktor Gold Enterprise Corp — New York (G-12568)	G	212 768-8885
Von Musulin Patricia — New York (G-12593)	G	212 206-8345
W & B Mazza & Sons Inc — North Baldwin (G-12930)	G	516 379-4130
Walter Edbril Inc — New York (G-12612)	E	212 532-3253
Weisco Inc — New York (G-12633)	F	212 575-8989
Whitney Boin Studio Inc — Yonkers (G-17515)	G	914 377-4385
William Goldberg Diamond Corp — New York (G-12660)	E	212 980-4343
Xomox Jewelry Inc — New York (G-12706)	G	212 944-8428
▲ Yofah Religious Articles Inc — Brooklyn (G-2788)	E	718 435-3288
Yurman Retail Inc — New York (G-12720)	G	888 398-7626
Zeeba Jewelry Mfg Inc — New York (G-12728)	G	212 997-1009
Zelman & Friedman Jwly Mfg Co — Long Island City (G-7960)	E	718 349-3400

3914 Silverware, Plated & Stainless Steel Ware

Company	Code	Phone
All American Awards Inc — Bohemia (G-1007)	F	631 567-2025
Atlantic Trophy Co Inc — New York (G-9305)	G	212 684-6020
▲ Csi International Inc — Niagara Falls (G-12831)	E	800 441-2895
▲ D W Haber & Son Inc — Bronx (G-1311)	E	718 993-6405
Denvin Inc — Brooklyn (G-1854)	E	718 232-3389
▲ Dwm International Inc — Long Island City (G-7750)	F	646 290-7448
Endurart Inc — New York (G-10087)	E	212 473-7000
Oneida International Inc — Oneida (G-13182)	G	315 361-3000
Oneida Silversmiths Inc — Oneida (G-13186)	G	315 361-3000

Employee Codes: A=Over 500 employees, B=251-500
C=101-250, D=51-100, E=20-50, F=10-19, G=5-9

▼ **Quest Bead & Cast Inc** ....G.... 212 354-1737
New York *(G-11797)*

R Goldsmith ....F.... 718 239-1396
Bronx *(G-1438)*

Sherrill Manufacturing Inc ....C.... 315 280-0727
Sherrill *(G-15430)*

Silver City Group Inc ....G.... 315 363-0344
Sherrill *(G-15431)*

▲ **Studio Silversmiths Inc** ....E.... 718 418-6785
Ridgewood *(G-14138)*

Swed Masters Workshop LLC ....F.... 212 644-8822
New York *(G-12274)*

▲ **Utica Cutlery Company** ....D.... 315 733-4663
Utica *(G-16387)*

Valerie Bohigian ....G.... 914 631-8866
Sleepy Hollow *(G-15498)*

3915 Jewelers Findings & Lapidary Work

A J C Jewelry Contracting Inc ....G.... 212 594-3703
New York *(G-9037)*

A J M Enterprises ....F.... 716 626-7294
Buffalo *(G-2806)*

Ace Diamond Corp ....G.... 212 730-8231
New York *(G-9063)*

Alex and Ani LLC ....G.... 914 481-1506
Rye *(G-15079)*

Allstar Casting Corporation ....E.... 212 563-0909
New York *(G-9142)*

Ampex Casting Corporation ....F.... 212 719-1318
New York *(G-9190)*

Antwerp Diamond Distributors ....F.... 212 319-3300
New York *(G-9220)*

Antwerp Sales Intl Inc ....F.... 212 354-6515
New York *(G-9221)*

Asa Manufacturing Inc ....E.... 718 853-3033
Brooklyn *(G-1639)*

Asco Castings Inc ....G.... 212 719-9800
Long Island City *(G-7703)*

Asur Jewelry Inc ....G.... 718 472-1687
Long Island City *(G-7707)*

Baroka Creations Inc ....G.... 212 768-0527
New York *(G-9374)*

Boucheron Joaillerie USA Inc ....G.... 212 715-7330
New York *(G-9494)*

Carrera Casting Corp ....C.... 212 382-3296
New York *(G-9589)*

▲ **Christopher Designs Inc** ....E.... 212 382-1013
New York *(G-9665)*

Classic Creations Inc ....G.... 516 498-1991
Great Neck *(G-5815)*

▲ **Creative Tools & Supply Inc** ....G.... 212 279-7077
New York *(G-9810)*

D M J Casting Inc ....G.... 212 719-1951
New York *(G-9840)*

D R S Watch Materials ....E.... 212 819-0470
New York *(G-9841)*

Danhier Co LLC ....F.... 212 563-7683
New York *(G-9856)*

Dialase Inc ....G.... 212 575-8833
New York *(G-9921)*

Diamex Inc ....G.... 212 575-8145
New York *(G-9922)*

Diamond Boutique ....G.... 516 444-3373
Port Washington *(G-13831)*

Diamond Constellation Corp ....G.... 212 819-0324
New York *(G-9924)*

Dresdiam Inc ....E.... 212 819-2217
New York *(G-9977)*

Dweck Industries Inc ....E.... 718 615-1695
Brooklyn *(G-1886)*

▲ **E Schreiber Inc** ....E.... 212 382-0280
New York *(G-10004)*

Engelack Gem Corporation ....G.... 212 719-3094
New York *(G-10092)*

Fine Cut Diamonds Corporation ....G.... 212 575-8780
New York *(G-10215)*

Fischer Diamonds Inc ....F.... 212 869-1990
New York *(G-10223)*

▲ **Fischler Diamonds Inc** ....G.... 212 921-8196
New York *(G-10224)*

Frank Billanti Casting Co Inc ....F.... 212 221-0440
New York *(G-10250)*

Gemini Manufactures ....F.... 716 633-0306
Cheektowaga *(G-3601)*

Goldmark Inc ....E.... 718 438-0295
Brooklyn *(G-2039)*

▲ **Guild Diamond Products Inc** ....F.... 212 871-0007
New York *(G-10424)*

Hershel Horowitz Corp ....G.... 212 719-1710
New York *(G-10506)*

Ideal Brilliant Co Inc ....F.... 212 840-2044
New York *(G-10599)*

Igc New York Inc ....G.... 212 764-0949
New York *(G-10607)*

J A G Diamond Manufacturers ....G.... 212 575-0660
New York *(G-10717)*

J Klagsbrun Inc ....G.... 212 712-9388
New York *(G-10720)*

Jaguar Casting Co Inc ....E.... 212 869-0197
New York *(G-10734)*

Jewelry Arts Manufacturing ....E.... 212 382-3583
New York *(G-10763)*

Jim Wachtler Inc ....G.... 212 755-4367
New York *(G-10773)*

▲ **Julius Klein Group** ....E.... 212 719-1811
New York *(G-10818)*

Kaleko Bros ....G.... 212 819-0100
New York *(G-10839)*

▲ **Kaprielian Enterprises Inc** ....D.... 212 645-6623
New York *(G-10845)*

Karbra Company ....C.... 212 736-9300
New York *(G-10846)*

Kemp Metal Products Inc ....E.... 516 997-8860
Westbury *(G-17029)*

▲ **Lazare Kaplan Intl Inc** ....D.... 212 972-9700
New York *(G-10975)*

Leo Schachter Diamonds LLC ....D.... 212 688-2000
New York *(G-11007)*

Loremi Jewelry Inc ....E.... 212 840-3429
New York *(G-11071)*

▲ **Magic Novelty Co Inc** ....E.... 212 304-2777
New York *(G-11131)*

Mavito Fine Jewelry Ltd Inc ....F.... 212 398-9384
New York *(G-11209)*

Max Kahan Inc ....F.... 212 575-4646
New York *(G-11211)*

ME & Ro Inc ....G.... 212 431-8744
New York *(G-11229)*

Miller & Veit Inc ....F.... 212 247-2275
New York *(G-11295)*

Nathan Berrie & Sons Inc ....G.... 516 432-8500
Island Park *(G-6821)*

New York Findings Corp ....F.... 212 925-5745
New York *(G-11422)*

Nyman Jewelry Inc ....G.... 212 944-1976
New York *(G-11499)*

▲ **Perma Glow Ltd Inc** ....F.... 212 575-9677
New York *(G-11638)*

Precision Diamond Cutters Inc ....G.... 212 719-4438
New York *(G-11718)*

▲ **R G Flair Co Inc** ....E.... 631 586-7311
Bay Shore *(G-726)*

Renco Manufacturing Inc ....E.... 718 392-8877
Long Island City *(G-7891)*

Satco Castings Service Inc ....E.... 516 354-1500
New Hyde Park *(G-8905)*

▲ **Shah Diamonds Inc** ....F.... 212 888-9393
New York *(G-12059)*

Stephen J Lipkins Inc ....G.... 631 249-8866
Farmingdale *(G-5127)*

Steven Galapo Diamonds LLC ....G.... 212 221-3000
New York *(G-12223)*

Sunshine Diamond Cutter Inc ....G.... 212 221-1028
New York *(G-12260)*

T M W Diamonds Mfg Co ....G.... 212 869-8444
New York *(G-12289)*

▲ **Touch Adjust Clip Co Inc** ....G.... 631 589-3077
Bohemia *(G-1141)*

▲ **Townley Inc** ....E.... 212 779-0544
New York *(G-12404)*

United Gemdiam Inc ....E.... 718 851-5083
Brooklyn *(G-2720)*

Via America Fine Jewelry Inc ....G.... 212 302-1218
New York *(G-12560)*

Waldman Alexander M Diamond Co ....E.... 212 921-8098
New York *(G-12606)*

William Goldberg Diamond Corp ....E.... 212 980-4343
New York *(G-12660)*

Windiam Usa Inc ....G.... 212 542-0949
New York *(G-12667)*

◆ **Zak Jewelry Tools Inc** ....F.... 212 768-8122
New York *(G-12722)*

Zirconia Creations Intl ....G.... 212 239-3730
New York *(G-12733)*

3931 Musical Instruments

Albert Augustine Ltd ....D.... 718 913-9635
Mount Vernon *(G-8706)*

Barbera Transduser Systems ....F.... 718 816-3025
Staten Island *(G-15664)*

DAddario & Company Inc ....D.... 631 439-3300
Melville *(G-8339)*

DAddario & Company Inc ....E.... 718 599-6660
Brooklyn *(G-1833)*

◆ **DAddario & Company Inc** ....A.... 631 439-3300
Farmingdale *(G-4982)*

▲ **DAndrea Inc** ....E.... 516 496-2200
Syosset *(G-15839)*

▲ **DAngelico Guitars of America** ....G.... 732 380-0995
New York *(G-9855)*

▲ **Dimarzio Inc** ....E.... 718 442-6655
Staten Island *(G-15686)*

▲ **E & O Mari Inc** ....D.... 845 562-4400
Newburgh *(G-12775)*

Elsener Organ Works Inc ....G.... 631 254-2744
Deer Park *(G-4159)*

▲ **Evans Manufacturing LLC** ....D.... 631 439-3300
Farmingdale *(G-4999)*

Fodera Guitars Inc ....F.... 718 832-3455
Brooklyn *(G-1991)*

Gluck Orgelbau Inc ....G.... 212 233-2684
New York *(G-10365)*

Guitar Specialist Inc ....G.... 914 533-5589
South Salem *(G-15559)*

▲ **Hipshot Products Inc** ....F.... 607 532-9404
Interlaken *(G-6786)*

J D Calato Manufacturing Co ....E.... 716 285-3546
Niagara Falls *(G-12855)*

Jason Ladanye Guitar Piano & H ....E.... 518 527-3973
Albany *(G-91)*

Kerner and Merchant ....G.... 315 463-8023
East Syracuse *(G-4562)*

▲ **Leonard Carlson** ....G.... 518 477-4710
East Greenbush *(G-4423)*

▲ **Luthier Musical Corp** ....G.... 212 397-6038
New York *(G-11094)*

▲ **Mari Strings Inc** ....F.... 212 799-6781
New York *(G-11172)*

Muzet Inc ....F.... 315 452-0050
Syracuse *(G-16015)*

Nathan Love LLC ....F.... 212 925-7111
New York *(G-11366)*

▲ **New Sensor Corporation** ....D.... 718 937-8300
Long Island City *(G-7856)*

Rico International ....G.... 818 767-7711
Farmingdale *(G-5109)*

Roli USA Inc ....F.... 412 600-4840
New York *(G-11929)*

▲ **Sadowsky Guitars Ltd** ....F.... 718 433-1990
Long Island City *(G-7900)*

◆ **Samson Technologies Corp** ....D.... 631 784-2200
Hicksville *(G-6418)*

Siegfrieds Call Inc ....G.... 845 765-2275
Beacon *(G-785)*

Sound Source Inc ....G.... 585 271-5370
Rochester *(G-14717)*

▲ **Steinway Inc** ....A.... 718 721-2600
Long Island City *(G-7916)*

◆ **Steinway and Sons** ....C.... 718 721-2600
Long Island City *(G-7917)*

◆ **Steinway Musical Instrs Inc** ....E.... 781 894-9770
New York *(G-12215)*

▲ **Stuart Spector Designs Ltd** ....G.... 845 246-6124
Saugerties *(G-15225)*

3942 Dolls & Stuffed Toys

◆ **ADC Dolls Inc** ....C.... 212 244-4500
New York *(G-9073)*

Beila Group Inc ....F.... 212 260-1948
New York *(G-9395)*

▲ **Best Toy Manufacturing Ltd** ....F.... 718 855-9040
Brooklyn *(G-1687)*

◆ **Commonwealth Toy Novelty Inc** ....E.... 212 242-4070
New York *(G-9748)*

Community Products LLC ....E.... 518 589-5103
Elka Park *(G-4645)*

Cosmetics Plus Ltd ....G.... 516 768-7250
Amagansett *(G-217)*

Dana Michele LLC ....G.... 917 757-7777
New York *(G-9853)*

Fierce Fun Toys LLC ....G.... 646 322-7172
New York *(G-10213)*

▲ **Goldberger Company LLC** ....F.... 212 924-1194
New York *(G-10371)*

Jim Henson Company Inc ....E.... 212 794-2400
New York *(G-10772)*

▲ **Jupiter Creations Inc** ....G.... 917 493-9393
New York *(G-10824)*

▲ **Lovee Doll & Toy Co Inc** ....G.... 212 242-1545
New York *(G-11081)*

Madame Alexander Doll Co LLC ....D 212 244-4500
New York (G-11118)
Mattel Inc ....F 716 714-8514
East Aurora (G-4399)
Minted Green Inc ....G 845 458-1845
Airmont (G-15)
North American Bear Co Inc ....F 212 388-0700
New York (G-11471)
◆ Skip Hop Inc ....E 646 902-9874
New York (G-12118)
Skip Hop Holdings Inc ....G 212 868-9850
New York (G-12119)
▲ Tonner Doll Company Inc ....E 845 339-9537
Kingston (G-7244)
Toy Admiration Co Inc ....E 914 963-9400
Yonkers (G-17509)
Ward Sales Co Inc ....G 315 476-5276
Syracuse (G-16093)
▲ Well-Made Toy Mfg Corporation ....E 718 381-4225
Port Washington (G-13889)

3944 Games, Toys & Children's Vehicles

212 Db Corp ....E 212 652-5600
New York (G-9011)
▲ ATI Model Products Inc ....E 631 694-7022
Farmingdale (G-4954)
▲ Babysafe Usa LLC ....G 877 367-4141
Afton (G-8)
◆ Barron Games Intl Co LLC ....F 716 630-0054
Buffalo (G-2853)
▲ Buffalo Games Inc ....D 716 827-8393
Buffalo (G-2874)
▲ C T A Digital Inc ....E 845 513-0433
Monroe (G-8586)
Church Communities NY Inc ....E 518 589-5103
Elka Park (G-4643)
Church Communities NY Inc ....E 518 589-5103
Elka Park (G-4644)
Compoz A Puzzle Inc ....G 516 883-2311
Port Washington (G-13829)
▲ Dakott LLC ....G 888 805-6795
New York (G-9850)
Dana Michele LLC ....G 917 757-7777
New York (G-9853)
▲ Design Works Craft Inc ....G 631 244-5749
Bohemia (G-1054)
Drescher Paper Box Inc ....F 716 854-0288
Buffalo (G-2934)
▲ E C C Corp ....G 518 873-6494
Elizabethtown (G-4641)
Ellis Products Corp ....G 516 791-3732
Valley Stream (G-16431)
Famous Box Scooter Co ....G 631 943-2013
West Babylon (G-16817)
Gargraves Trackage Corporation ....G 315 483-6577
North Rose (G-12953)
▲ Haba USA ....G 800 468-6873
Skaneateles (G-15483)
▲ Habermaass Corporation ....F 315 685-8919
Skaneateles (G-15484)
▲ Innovative Designs LLC ....E 212 695-0892
New York (G-10646)
Jim Henson Company Inc ....E 212 794-2400
New York (G-10772)
Joel Zelcer ....F 917 525-6790
Brooklyn (G-2143)
▲ Jupiter Creations Inc ....G 917 493-9393
New York (G-10824)
▲ Kidtellect Inc ....G 617 803-1456
New York (G-10881)
Kidz Toyz Inc ....G 914 261-4453
Mount Kisco (G-8675)
▲ Kling Magnetics Inc ....E 518 392-4000
Chatham (G-3586)
Littlebits Electronics Inc ....D 917 464-4577
New York (G-11040)
▲ Marvel Entertainment LLC ....C 212 576-4000
New York (G-11193)
▲ Master Art Corp ....G 845 362-6430
Spring Valley (G-15616)
Master Juvenile Products Inc ....F 845 647-8400
Ellenville (G-4649)
Mattel Inc ....F 716 714-8514
East Aurora (G-4399)
▲ Mechanical Displays Inc ....G 718 258-5588
Brooklyn (G-2294)
▲ Ogosport LLC ....G 718 554-0777
Brooklyn (G-2399)
Pidyon Controls Inc ....G 212 683-9523
New York (G-11679)
Pride Lines Ltd ....G 631 225-0033
Lindenhurst (G-7503)
R F Giardina Co ....F 516 922-1364
Oyster Bay (G-13400)
◆ Readent Inc ....F 212 710-3004
White Plains (G-17189)
Sandbox Brands Inc ....G 212 647-8877
New York (G-11983)
Spectrum Crafts Inc ....E 631 244-5749
Bohemia (G-1133)
Toymax Inc ....G 212 633-6611
New York (G-12405)
Tucker Jones House Inc ....E 631 642-9092
East Setauket (G-4514)
Vogel Applied Technologies ....G 212 677-3136
New York (G-12589)
Way Out Toys Inc ....G 212 689-9094
New York (G-12627)
Whats Next Manufacturing Inc ....E 585 492-1014
Arcade (G-401)
Wobbleworks Inc ....F 718 618-9904
New York (G-12678)

3949 Sporting & Athletic Goods, NEC

A Hyatt Ball Co Ltd ....G 518 747-0272
Fort Edward (G-5347)
Absolute Fitness US Corp ....D 732 979-8582
Bayside (G-760)
Adirondack Outdoor Center LLC ....G 315 369-2300
Old Forge (G-13152)
Adpro Sports LLC ....D 716 854-5116
Buffalo (G-2815)
Alternatives For Children ....E 631 271-0777
Dix Hills (G-4313)
▲ Apparel Production Inc ....E 212 278-8362
New York (G-9231)
▲ Asia Connection LLC ....F 212 369-4644
New York (G-9285)
▲ Athalon Sportgear Inc ....G 212 268-8070
New York (G-9301)
Azibi Ltd ....F 212 869-6550
New York (G-9339)
Bears Management Group Inc ....G 585 624-5694
Lima (G-7464)
Billy Beez Usa LLC ....G 315 741-5099
Syracuse (G-15889)
Billy Beez Usa LLC ....F 646 606-2249
New York (G-9451)
Billy Beez Usa LLC ....G 845 915-4709
West Nyack (G-16943)
▼ Blades ....F 212 477-1059
New York (G-9462)
Bob Perani Sport Shops Inc ....G 585 427-2930
Rochester (G-14257)
Bruynswick Sales Inc ....F 845 789-2049
New Paltz (G-8918)
Buffalo Sports Inc ....G 716 826-7700
Blasdell (G-955)
Bungers Surf Shop ....G 631 244-3646
Sayville (G-15234)
Burnt Mill Smithing ....G 585 293-2380
Churchville (G-3664)
Burton Corporation ....D 802 862-4500
Champlain (G-3567)
Car Doctor Motor Sports LLC ....G 631 537-1548
Water Mill (G-16625)
Cascade Helmets Holdings Inc ....G 315 453-3073
Liverpool (G-7539)
▲ Chapman Skateboard Co Inc ....G 631 321-4773
Deer Park (G-4139)
Charm Mfg Co Inc ....E 607 565-8161
Waverly (G-16724)
City Sports Inc ....G 212 730-2009
New York (G-9683)
Cooperstown Bat Co Inc ....F 607 547-2415
Fly Creek (G-5318)
Cooperstown Bat Co Inc ....G 607 547-2415
Cooperstown (G-3910)
▲ Copper John Corporation ....F 315 258-9269
Auburn (G-488)
Cortland Line Mfg LLC ....E 607 756-2851
Cortland (G-4041)
▲ Cy Plastics Works Inc ....E 585 229-2555
Honeoye (G-6551)
D Squared Technologies Inc ....G 516 932-7319
Jericho (G-7098)
▼ Devin Mfg Inc ....F 585 496-5770
Arcade (G-391)
◆ Eastern Jungle Gym Inc ....E 845 878-9800
Carmel (G-3427)
Elmira Country Club Inc ....G 607 734-6251
Elmira (G-4694)
▲ Everlast Sports Mfg Corp ....E 212 239-0990
New York (G-10146)
▲ Everlast Worldwide Inc ....E 212 239-0990
New York (G-10147)
▲ Excellent Art Mfg Corp ....F 718 388-7075
Inwood (G-6795)
Fishing Valley LLC ....G 716 523-6158
Lockport (G-7615)
Florida North Inc ....F 518 868-2888
Sloansville (G-15501)
Fly-Tyers Carry-All LLC ....G 607 821-1460
Charlotteville (G-3583)
◆ Fownes Brothers & Co Inc ....E 212 683-0150
New York (G-10244)
Fownes Brothers & Co Inc ....E 518 752-4411
Gloversville (G-5726)
Good Show Sportwear Inc ....F 212 334-8751
New York (G-10378)
Grace Wheeler ....G 716 664-6501
Jamestown (G-7029)
Grand Slam Safety LLC ....G 315 766-7008
Croghan (G-4084)
▼ Gym Store Inc ....G 718 366-7804
Maspeth (G-8174)
▲ Hana Sportswear Inc ....E 315 639-6332
Dexter (G-4308)
Hart Sports Inc ....G 631 385-1805
Huntington Station (G-6745)
Heads & Tails Lure Co ....G 607 739-7900
Horseheads (G-6609)
Hector Pt Sr Rehab Svc Pllc ....G 518 371-5554
Clifton Park (G-3724)
Herrmann Group LLC ....G 716 876-9798
Kenmore (G-7176)
Hinspergers Poly Industries ....E 585 798-6625
Medina (G-8308)
Hootz Family Bowling Inc ....F 518 756-4668
Ravena (G-14034)
▲ Hypoxico Inc ....G 212 972-1009
New York (G-10584)
▲ Imagination Playground LLC ....G 212 463-0334
New York (G-10613)
◆ Imperial Pools Inc ....C 518 786-1200
Latham (G-7392)
▲ International Leisure Pdts Inc ....E 631 254-2155
Edgewood (G-4615)
▲ J R Products Inc ....G 716 633-7565
Clarence Center (G-3703)
▲ Jag Manufacturing Inc ....E 518 762-9558
Johnstown (G-7147)
Joe Moro ....G 607 272-0591
Ithaca (G-6890)
Johnson Outdoors Inc ....C 607 779-2200
Binghamton (G-926)
Kohlberg Sports Group Inc ....G 914 241-7430
Mount Kisco (G-8676)
◆ Latham Pool Products Inc ....C 518 951-1000
Latham (G-7397)
▲ Mac Swed Inc ....F 212 684-7730
New York (G-11110)
Makiplastic ....G 716 772-2222
Gasport (G-5573)
Mattel Inc ....F 716 714-8514
East Aurora (G-4399)
▲ Maverik Lacrosse LLC ....A 516 213-3050
New York (G-11208)
Michael Britt Inc ....G 516 248-2010
Mineola (G-8558)
Morris Golf Ventures ....E 631 283-0559
Southampton (G-15571)
▲ Nalge Nunc International Corp ....A 585 498-2661
Rochester (G-14547)
▼ North Coast Outfitters Ltd ....E 631 727-5580
Riverhead (G-14164)
Northern King Lures Inc ....G 585 865-3373
Rochester (G-14566)
▲ Olympia Sports Company Inc ....F 914 347-4737
Elmsford (G-4780)
▲ Otis Products Inc ....C 315 348-4300
Lyons Falls (G-8004)
Outdoor Group LLC ....C 585 201-5358
West Henrietta (G-16919)
Paddock Chevrolet Golf Dome ....E 716 504-4059
Tonawanda (G-16209)
▲ Peloton Interactive Inc ....E 866 650-1996
New York (G-11620)
Perfect Form Manufacturing LLC ....G 585 500-5923
West Henrietta (G-16921)

S I C

Employee Codes: A=Over 500 employees, B=251-500
C=101-250, D=51-100, E=20-50, F=10-19, G=5-9
2018 Harris
New York Manufacturers Directory
867

39 MISCELLANEOUS MANUFACTURING INDUSTRIES

▲ Performance Lacrosse Group Inc .....G....... 315 453-3073
  Liverpool *(G-7567)*
▲ Physicalmind Institute .....F....... 212 343-2150
  New York *(G-11674)*
Pilgrim Surf & Supply .....G....... 718 218-7456
  Brooklyn *(G-2433)*
PNC Sports .....G....... 516 665-2244
  Deer Park *(G-4215)*
Pocono Pool Products-North .....E....... 518 283-1023
  Rensselaer *(G-14060)*
Polytech Pool Mfg Inc .....F....... 718 492-8991
  Brooklyn *(G-2440)*
PRC Liquidating Company .....E....... 212 823-9626
  New York *(G-11716)*
Pro Hitter Corp .....F....... 845 358-8670
  New City *(G-8836)*
Promats Athletics LLC .....E....... 607 746-8911
  Delhi *(G-4266)*
▲ Quaker Boy Inc .....E....... 716 662-3979
  Orchard Park *(G-13317)*
Qubicaamf Worldwide LLC .....C....... 315 376-6541
  Lowville *(G-7969)*
Radar Sports LLC .....G....... 516 678-1919
  Oceanside *(G-13113)*
Rawlings Sporting Goods Co Inc .....D....... 315 429-8511
  Dolgeville *(G-4331)*
Recreational Equipment Inc .....G....... 914 410-9500
  Yonkers *(G-17499)*
Rising Stars Soccer Club CNY .....F....... 315 381-3096
  Westmoreland *(G-17093)*
◆ Rome Specialty Company Inc .....E....... 315 337-8200
  Rome *(G-14862)*
Roscoe Little Store Inc .....G....... 607 498-5553
  Roscoe *(G-15035)*
Rottkamp Tennis Inc .....E....... 631 421-0040
  Huntington Station *(G-6757)*
Sampo Inc .....E....... 315 896-2606
  Barneveld *(G-617)*
Sea Isle Custom Rod Builders .....G....... 516 868-8855
  Freeport *(G-5436)*
Seaway Mats Inc .....E....... 518 483-2560
  Malone *(G-8047)*
Shehawken Archery Co Inc .....F....... 607 967-8333
  Bainbridge *(G-553)*
Sportsfield Specialties Inc .....E....... 607 746-8911
  Delhi *(G-4268)*
Stephenson Custom Case Company .....E....... 905 542-8762
  Niagara Falls *(G-12895)*
Sunny Scuba Inc .....G....... 212 333-4915
  New York *(G-12259)*
◆ Swimline Corp .....E....... 631 254-2155
  Edgewood *(G-4626)*
▲ TDS Fitness Equipment .....E....... 607 733-6789
  Elmira *(G-4717)*
Tosch Products Ltd .....G....... 315 672-3040
  Camillus *(G-3353)*
▲ Vertical Lax Inc .....G....... 518 669-3699
  Albany *(G-149)*
Viking Athletics Ltd .....E....... 631 957-8000
  Lindenhurst *(G-7515)*
Warrior Sports Inc .....G....... 315 536-0937
  Penn Yan *(G-13544)*
Watson Adventures LLC .....G....... 212 564-8293
  New York *(G-12626)*
▲ Wilbar International Inc .....D....... 631 951-9800
  Hauppauge *(G-6258)*

3951 Pens & Mechanical Pencils

▲ A & L Pen Manufacturing Corp .....D....... 718 499-8966
  Brooklyn *(G-1526)*
◆ Aakron Rule Corp .....C....... 716 542-5483
  Akron *(G-17)*
Effanjay Pens Inc .....E....... 212 316-9565
  Long Island City *(G-7755)*
▲ Gotham Pen Co Inc .....E....... 212 675-7904
  Yonkers *(G-17465)*
▲ Harper Products Ltd .....C....... 516 997-2330
  Westbury *(G-17021)*
Henry Morgan .....F....... 718 317-5013
  Staten Island *(G-15704)*
▲ Mark Dri Products Inc .....G....... 516 484-6200
  Bethpage *(G-871)*
▲ Mercury Pen Company Inc .....G....... 518 899-9653
  Ballston Lake *(G-582)*
▲ Pelican Products Co Inc .....G....... 718 860-3220
  Bronx *(G-1424)*
▲ STS Refill America LLC .....G....... 516 934-8008
  Hicksville *(G-6422)*

3952 Lead Pencils, Crayons & Artist's Mtrls

◆ Aakron Rule Corp .....C....... 716 542-5483
  Akron *(G-17)*
Clapper Hollow Designs Inc .....E....... 518 234-9561
  Cobleskill *(G-3759)*
Effanjay Pens Inc .....E....... 212 316-9565
  Long Island City *(G-7755)*
Frames Plus Inc .....F....... 518 462-1842
  Menands *(G-8403)*
◆ Golden Artist Colors Inc .....C....... 607 847-6154
  New Berlin *(G-8827)*
▲ Gotham Pen Co Inc .....E....... 212 675-7904
  Yonkers *(G-17465)*
Handmade Frames Inc .....F....... 718 782-8364
  Brooklyn *(G-2066)*
Lopez Restorations Inc .....F....... 718 383-1555
  Brooklyn *(G-2238)*
◆ Micro Powders Inc .....E....... 914 332-6400
  Tarrytown *(G-16120)*
North America Pastel Artists .....G....... 718 463-4701
  Flushing *(G-5281)*
▲ R & F Handmade Paints Inc .....F....... 845 331-3112
  Kingston *(G-7236)*
▲ Simon Liu Inc .....F....... 718 567-2011
  Brooklyn *(G-2587)*
▲ Sml Brothers Holding Corp .....F....... 718 402-2000
  Bronx *(G-1455)*
▲ Spaulding & Rogers Mfg Inc .....D....... 518 768-2070
  Voorheesville *(G-16539)*
Timeless Decor LLC .....C....... 315 782-5759
  Watertown *(G-16697)*
Utrecht Manufacturing Corp .....G....... 212 675-8699
  New York *(G-12515)*

3953 Marking Devices

A & M Steel Stamps Inc .....G....... 516 741-6223
  Mineola *(G-8521)*
Bianca Group Ltd .....E....... 212 768-3011
  New York *(G-9435)*
C M E Corp .....F....... 315 451-7101
  Syracuse *(G-15900)*
▲ Cannizzaro Seal & Engraving Co .....E....... 718 513-6125
  Brooklyn *(G-1756)*
▼ Crafters Workshop Inc .....G....... 914 345-2838
  Elmsford *(G-4753)*
Dab-O-Matic Corp .....G....... 914 699-7070
  Mount Vernon *(G-8722)*
East Coast Thermographers Inc .....E....... 718 321-3211
  College Point *(G-3807)*
Effanjay Pens Inc .....E....... 212 316-9565
  Long Island City *(G-7755)*
▲ Hampton Art LLC .....F....... 631 924-1335
  Medford *(G-8278)*
▲ Heidenhain International Inc .....C....... 716 661-1700
  Jamestown *(G-7033)*
◆ Hodgins Engraving Co Inc .....D....... 585 343-4444
  Batavia *(G-640)*
I & I Systems .....F....... 845 753-9126
  Tuxedo Park *(G-16306)*
Joseph Treu Successors Inc .....G....... 212 691-7026
  New York *(G-10805)*
Kelly Foundry & Machine Co .....E....... 315 732-8313
  Utica *(G-16370)*
Koehlr-Gibson Mkg Graphics Inc .....E....... 716 838-5960
  Buffalo *(G-3053)*
Krengel Manufacturing Co Inc .....F....... 212 227-1901
  Fulton *(G-5481)*
Long Island Stamp & Seal Co .....F....... 718 628-8550
  Ridgewood *(G-14126)*
Michael Todd Stevens .....G....... 585 436-9957
  Rochester *(G-14527)*
Name Base Inc .....G....... 212 545-1400
  New York *(G-11363)*
New York Marking Devices Corp .....G....... 585 454-5188
  Rochester *(G-14554)*
New York Marking Devices Corp .....G....... 315 463-8641
  Syracuse *(G-16018)*
Rubber Stamp X Press .....F....... 631 423-1322
  Huntington Station *(G-6758)*
Rubber Stamps Inc .....E....... 212 675-1180
  Mineola *(G-8568)*
Sales Tax Asset Rceivable Corp .....E....... 212 788-5874
  New York *(G-11974)*
◆ Specialty Ink Co Inc .....F....... 631 586-3666
  Blue Point *(G-995)*
▼ Tech Products Inc .....E....... 718 442-4900
  Staten Island *(G-15770)*
Thermopatch Corporation .....D....... 315 446-8110
  Syracuse *(G-16082)*

UI Corp .....G....... 201 203-4453
  Bayside *(G-770)*
Ulano Product Inc .....C....... 718 622-5200
  Brooklyn *(G-2714)*
▲ United Silicone Inc .....D....... 716 681-8222
  Lancaster *(G-7370)*
United Sttes Brnze Sign of Fla .....E....... 516 352-5155
  New Hyde Park *(G-8914)*
Ward Sales Co Inc .....G....... 315 476-5276
  Syracuse *(G-16093)*

3955 Carbon Paper & Inked Ribbons

Guttz Corporation of America .....F....... 914 591-9600
  Irvington *(G-6812)*
Hf Technologies LLC .....E....... 585 254-5030
  Hamlin *(G-5973)*
◆ International Imaging Mtls Inc .....A....... 716 691-6333
  Amherst *(G-245)*
Northeast Toner Inc .....G....... 518 899-5545
  Ballston Lake *(G-584)*
◆ Printer Components Inc .....G....... 585 924-5190
  Fairport *(G-4877)*
Qls Solutions Group Inc .....F....... 716 852-2203
  Buffalo *(G-3170)*
Smartoners Inc .....G....... 718 975-0197
  Brooklyn *(G-2600)*
▲ Summit Technologies LLC .....E....... 631 590-1040
  Holbrook *(G-6502)*

3961 Costume Jewelry & Novelties

Accessory Plays LLC .....E....... 212 564-7301
  New York *(G-9058)*
▲ Alexis Bittar LLC .....C....... 718 422-7580
  Brooklyn *(G-1581)*
◆ Allure Jewelry and ACC LLC .....E....... 646 226-8057
  New York *(G-9143)*
Anatoli .....F....... 845 334-9000
  West Hurley *(G-16931)*
Aniiwe Inc .....G....... 347 683-1891
  Brooklyn *(G-1612)*
Barrera Jose & Maria Co Ltd .....E....... 212 239-1994
  New York *(G-9376)*
▼ Ben-Amun Co Inc .....E....... 212 944-6480
  New York *(G-9402)*
Beth Ward Studios LLC .....F....... 646 922-7575
  New York *(G-9424)*
Bnns Co Inc .....E....... 212 302-1844
  New York *(G-9481)*
Carol For Eva Graham Inc .....F....... 212 889-8686
  New York *(G-9585)*
Carvin French Jewelers Inc .....E....... 212 755-6474
  New York *(G-9592)*
Catherine Stein Designs Inc .....E....... 212 840-1188
  New York *(G-9603)*
Ciner Manufacturing Co Inc .....E....... 212 947-3770
  New York *(G-9672)*
▲ Columbus Trading Corp .....F....... 212 564-1780
  New York *(G-9741)*
Custom Pins Inc .....G....... 914 690-9378
  Elmsford *(G-4755)*
Dabby-Reid Ltd .....F....... 212 356-0040
  New York *(G-9842)*
Designs On Fifth Ltd .....G....... 212 921-4162
  New York *(G-9910)*
▼ Ema Jewelry Inc .....D....... 212 575-8989
  New York *(G-10070)*
Erickson Beamon Ltd .....F....... 212 643-4810
  New York *(G-10109)*
▲ Eu Design LLC .....E....... 212 420-7788
  New York *(G-10135)*
Fantasia Jewelry Inc .....E....... 212 921-9590
  New York *(G-10189)*
Fashion Accents LLC .....F....... 401 331-6626
  New York *(G-10194)*
Five Star Creations Inc .....E....... 845 783-1187
  Monroe *(G-8589)*
Formart Corp .....F....... 212 819-1819
  New York *(G-10238)*
Greenbeads Llc .....G....... 212 327-2765
  New York *(G-10402)*
Grinnell Designs Ltd .....E....... 212 391-5277
  New York *(G-10408)*
Holbrooke Inc .....E....... 646 397-4674
  New York *(G-10538)*
▲ Horly Novelty Co Inc .....G....... 212 226-4800
  New York *(G-10550)*
▲ I Love Accessories Inc .....G....... 212 239-1875
  New York *(G-10585)*
▲ International Inspirations Ltd .....E....... 212 465-8500
  New York *(G-10677)*

39 MISCELLANEOUS MANUFACTURING INDUSTRIES

▲ J & H Creations Inc .... E 212 465-0962
  New York *(G-10714)*
J J Creations Inc .... E 718 392-2828
  Long Island City *(G-7796)*
Jay Turoff .... F 718 856-7300
  Brooklyn *(G-2135)*
Jaymar Jewelry Co Inc .... G 212 564-4788
  New York *(G-10748)*
Jewelry Arts Manufacturing .... E 212 382-3583
  New York *(G-10763)*
Jill Fagin Enterprises Inc .... G 212 674-9383
  New York *(G-10771)*
Jj Fantasia Inc .... G 212 868-1198
  New York *(G-10779)*
▲ K2 International Corp .... G 212 947-1734
  New York *(G-10834)*
Kenneth J Lane Inc .... F 212 868-1780
  New York *(G-10874)*
Krainz Creations Inc .... E 212 583-1555
  New York *(G-10923)*
Leonore Doskow Inc .... E 914 737-1335
  Cortlandt Manor *(G-4077)*
▲ Lesilu Productions Inc .... E 212 947-6419
  New York *(G-11010)*
▲ Magic Novelty Co Inc .... E 212 304-2777
  New York *(G-11131)*
Marlborough Jewels Inc .... G 718 768-2000
  Brooklyn *(G-2274)*
Masterpiece Diamonds LLC .... F 212 986-1515
  New York *(G-11198)*
▲ Mataci Inc .... E 212 502-1899
  New York *(G-11201)*
Maurice Max Inc .... E 212 334-6573
  New York *(G-11206)*
Mwsi Inc .... D 914 347-4200
  Hawthorne *(G-6275)*
▲ Nes Jewelry Inc .... D 212 502-0025
  New York *(G-11392)*
Noir Jewelry LLC .... G 212 465-8500
  New York *(G-11468)*
Orion Fashions Holdings LLC .... E 212 764-3332
  New York *(G-11539)*
Pearl Erwin Inc .... E 212 889-7410
  New York *(G-11605)*
Pearl Erwin Inc .... E 212 883-0650
  New York *(G-11606)*
Pepe Creations Inc .... F 212 391-1514
  New York *(G-11629)*
Pincharming Inc .... E 516 663-5115
  Garden City *(G-5539)*
Reino Manufacturing Co Inc .... F 914 636-8990
  New Rochelle *(G-8968)*
▲ Rush Gold Manufacturing Ltd ..... D 516 781-3155
  Bellmore *(G-816)*
▲ Salmco Jewelry Corp .... F 212 695-8792
  New York *(G-11975)*
Sanoy Inc .... E 212 695-6384
  New York *(G-11987)*
▲ Sarina Accessories LLC .... F 212 239-8106
  New York *(G-11993)*
Shira Accessories Ltd .... F 212 594-4455
  New York *(G-12075)*
Steezys LLC .... G 646 276-5333
  New York *(G-12213)*
▲ Stephan & Company ACC Ltd .... E 212 481-3888
  New York *(G-12218)*
Swarovski North America Ltd .... G 914 423-4132
  Yonkers *(G-17505)*
Swarovski North America Ltd .... G 212 695-1502
  New York *(G-12272)*
Talbots Inc .... G 914 328-1034
  White Plains *(G-17201)*
▲ Toho Shoji (new York) Inc .... F 212 868-7466
  New York *(G-12377)*
Top Shelf Jewelry Inc .... F 845 647-4661
  Ellenville *(G-4653)*
▲ Tycoon International Inc .... G 212 563-7107
  New York *(G-12454)*
▲ Vetta Jewelry Inc .... E 212 564-8250
  New York *(G-12556)*
▲ Vitafede .... G 213 488-0136
  New York *(G-12582)*
Von Musulin Patricia .... G 212 206-8345
  New York *(G-12593)*
Yacoubian Jewelers Inc .... E 212 302-6729
  New York *(G-12708)*
Ziva Gem LLC .... F 646 416-5828
  New York *(G-12735)*

3965 Fasteners, Buttons, Needles & Pins

▲ American Pride Fasteners LLC ... E 631 940-8292
  Bay Shore *(G-669)*
Buttons & Trimcom Inc .... F 212 868-1971
  New York *(G-9537)*
Champion Zipper Corp .... G 212 239-0414
  New York *(G-9627)*
▲ Clo-Shure Intl Inc .... G 212 268-5029
  New York *(G-9700)*
Columbia Button Nailhead Corp .... F 718 386-3414
  Brooklyn *(G-1791)*
Connection Mold Inc .... G 585 458-6463
  Rochester *(G-14307)*
CPI of Falconer Inc .... E 716 664-4444
  Falconer *(G-4901)*
Cw Fasteners & Zippers Corp .... F 212 594-3203
  New York *(G-9831)*
▲ E-Won Industrial Co Inc .... E 212 750-9610
  New York *(G-10008)*
▲ Empire State Metal Pdts Inc ...... E 718 847-1617
  Richmond Hill *(G-14085)*
◆ Emsig Manufacturing Corp .... F 718 784-7717
  New York *(G-10077)*
Emsig Manufacturing Corp .... E 518 828-7301
  Hudson *(G-6643)*
Emsig Manufacturing Corp .... E 718 784-7717
  New York *(G-10078)*
▲ Eu Design LLC .... G 212 420-7788
  New York *(G-10135)*
▲ Fasteners Depot LLC .... F 718 622-4222
  Brooklyn *(G-1963)*
Hardware Specialty Co Inc .... F 315 434-9093
  East Syracuse *(G-4549)*
◆ Hemisphere Novelties Inc .... E 914 378-4100
  Yonkers *(G-17469)*
Itc Mfg Group Inc .... F 212 684-3696
  New York *(G-10711)*
Jem Threading Specialties Inc ...... G 718 665-3341
  Bronx *(G-1368)*
▲ Joyce Trimming Inc .... G 212 719-3110
  New York *(G-10811)*
Kane-M Inc .... G 973 777-2797
  New York *(G-10844)*
Karp Overseas Corporation .... E 718 784-2105
  Maspeth *(G-8179)*
Kenwin Sales Corp .... G 516 933-7553
  Westbury *(G-17030)*
Kraus & Sons Inc .... F 212 620-0408
  New York *(G-10926)*
M H Stryke Co Inc .... F 631 242-2660
  Deer Park *(G-4193)*
Maxine Denker Inc .... G 212 689-1440
  Staten Island *(G-15725)*
▲ Mona Slide Fasteners Inc .... E 718 325-7700
  Bronx *(G-1404)*
National Die & Button Mould Co ... E 201 939-7800
  Brooklyn *(G-2357)*
Rings Wire Inc .... F 212 741-9779
  New York *(G-11897)*
▲ Riri USA Inc .... G 212 268-3866
  New York *(G-11899)*
Shimada Shoji (hk) Limited .... G 212 268-0465
  New York *(G-12073)*
Tamber Knits Inc .... E 212 730-1121
  New York *(G-12298)*

3991 Brooms & Brushes

◆ 131-11 Atlantic RE Inc .... D 718 441-7700
  Richmond Hill *(G-14077)*
Abtex Corporation .... E 315 536-7403
  Dresden *(G-4342)*
Braun Bros Brushes Inc .... E 631 667-2179
  Valley Stream *(G-16427)*
▲ Braun Industries Inc .... E 516 741-6000
  Albertson *(G-155)*
▲ Brushtech (disc) Inc .... E 518 563-8420
  Plattsburgh *(G-13684)*
◆ Colgate-Palmolive Company .... A 212 310-2000
  New York *(G-9726)*
▼ Cpac Inc .... E 585 382-3223
  Leicester *(G-7442)*
▲ Culicover & Shapiro Inc .... G 516 597-4888
  Hicksville *(G-6364)*
E & W Manufacturing Co Inc .... E 516 367-8571
  Woodbury *(G-17307)*
▲ FM Brush Co Inc .... F 718 821-5939
  Glendale *(G-5667)*
▲ Full Circle Home LLC .... G 212 432-0001
  New York *(G-10270)*
K & R Allied Inc .... F 718 625-6610
  Brooklyn *(G-2161)*
▲ Kirschner Brush LLC .... E 718 292-1809
  Bronx *(G-1377)*
▲ Linzer Products Corp .... C 631 253-3333
  West Babylon *(G-16836)*
Marketshare LLC .... G 631 273-0598
  Brentwood *(G-1188)*
Pan American Roller Inc .... G 914 762-8700
  Ossining *(G-13350)*
▲ Perfex Corporation .... E 315 826-3600
  Poland *(G-13757)*
Premier Paint Roller Co LLC .... F 718 441-7700
  Richmond Hill *(G-14090)*
Rossiter & Schmitt Co Inc .... G 516 937-3610
  Bay Shore *(G-734)*
Royal Paint Roller Corp .... E 516 367-4370
  Woodbury *(G-17319)*
Teka Fine Line Brushes Inc .... F 718 692-2928
  Brooklyn *(G-2673)*
▲ Violife LLC .... G 914 207-1820
  New York *(G-12572)*
Volckening Inc .... E 718 748-0294
  Brooklyn *(G-2754)*
▲ Walter R Tucker Entps Ltd .... E 607 467-2866
  Deposit *(G-4305)*
Young & Swartz Inc .... F 716 852-2171
  Buffalo *(G-3286)*

3993 Signs & Advertising Displays

A 3-D Signs & Awnings Inc .... G 718 252-7575
  Brooklyn *(G-1529)*
A B C Mc Cleary Sign Co Inc .... F 315 493-3550
  Carthage *(G-3435)*
A M S Sign Designs .... G 631 467-7722
  Centereach *(G-3494)*
◆ Aakron Rule Corp .... C 716 542-5483
  Akron *(G-17)*
ABC Windows and Signs Corp ..... F 718 353-6210
  College Point *(G-3800)*
Accurate Signs & Awnings Inc .... F 718 788-0302
  Brooklyn *(G-1552)*
Acme Signs of Baldwinsville .... G 315 638-4865
  Baldwinsville *(G-564)*
Ad Makers Long Island Inc .... F 631 595-9100
  Deer Park *(G-4112)*
Adirondack Sign Perfect Inc .... G 518 409-7446
  Saratoga Springs *(G-15169)*
Adstream America LLC .... F 212 804-8498
  New York *(G-9081)*
All Signs .... G 973 736-2113
  Staten Island *(G-15656)*
Alley Cat Signs Inc .... F 631 924-7446
  Middle Island *(G-8439)*
Allied Decorations Co Inc .... F 315 637-0273
  Syracuse *(G-15870)*
Allstate Sign & Plaque Corp .... F 631 242-2828
  Deer Park *(G-4117)*
American Car Signs Inc .... E 518 227-1173
  Duanesburg *(G-4349)*
American Visuals Inc .... E 631 694-6104
  Farmingdale *(G-4949)*
Amsterdam Printing & Litho Inc ... F 518 842-6000
  Amsterdam *(G-333)*
Amsterdam Printing & Litho Inc ... E 518 842-6000
  Amsterdam *(G-334)*
Architectural Sign Group Inc .... G 516 326-1800
  Elmont *(G-4729)*
Art Parts Signs Inc .... G 585 381-2134
  East Rochester *(G-4472)*
Artkraft Strauss LLC .... E 212 265-5155
  New York *(G-9273)*
Artscroll Printing Corp .... E 212 929-2413
  New York *(G-9275)*
Asi Sign Systems Inc .... G 646 742-1320
  New York *(G-9284)*
Asi Sign Systems Inc .... G 716 775-0104
  Grand Island *(G-5765)*
Atomic Signworks .... G 315 779-7446
  Watertown *(G-16657)*
▲ Azar International Inc .... E 845 624-8808
  Nanuet *(G-8797)*
Bedford Precision Parts Corp ...... E 914 241-2211
  Bedford Hills *(G-796)*
Big Apple Sign Corp .... F 631 342-0303
  Islandia *(G-6826)*
▲ Big Apple Sign Corp .... E 212 629-3650
  New York *(G-9441)*
Bmg Printing and Promotion LLC .. G 631 231-9200
  Bohemia *(G-1022)*

Employee Codes: A=Over 500 employees, B=251-500
C=101-250, D=51-100, E=20-50, F=10-19, G=5-9

Broadway National Group LLC D 800 797-4467
Ronkonkoma ***(G-14909)***
Broadway Neon Sign Corp F 908 241-4177
Ronkonkoma ***(G-14910)***
Brooklyn Signs LLC G 718 252-7575
Brooklyn ***(G-1732)***
Buckeye Corrugated Inc D 585 924-1600
Victor ***(G-16489)***
Bulow & Associates Inc G 716 838-0298
Tonawanda ***(G-16171)***
Cab Signs Inc E 718 479-2424
Brooklyn ***(G-1747)***
Central Rede Sign Co Inc G 716 213-0797
Tonawanda ***(G-16172)***
▲ Chameleon Color Cards Ltd D 716 625-9452
Lockport ***(G-7604)***
Chautauqua Sign Co Inc G 716 665-2222
Falconer ***(G-4900)***
Checklist Boards Corporation G 585 586-0152
Rochester ***(G-14294)***
City Signs Inc G 718 375-5933
Brooklyn ***(G-1783)***
Climax Packaging Inc C 315 376-8000
Lowville ***(G-7963)***
Clinton Signs Inc G 585 482-1620
Webster ***(G-16743)***
Coe Displays Inc G 718 937-5658
Long Island City ***(G-7730)***
Colad Group LLC D 716 961-1776
Buffalo ***(G-2900)***
Colonial Redi Record Corp E 718 972-7433
Brooklyn ***(G-1790)***
Community Products LLC E 845 658-8351
Rifton ***(G-14145)***
▲ Creative Solutions Group Inc B 914 771-4200
Yonkers ***(G-17448)***
▲ Crown Sign Systems Inc F 914 375-2118
Mount Vernon ***(G-8721)***
Custom Display Manufacture G 516 783-6491
North Bellmore ***(G-12936)***
Decal Makers Inc E 516 221-7200
Bellmore ***(G-813)***
Decree Signs & Graphics Inc F 973 278-3603
Floral Park ***(G-5209)***
Design A Sign of Putnam Inc G 845 279-5328
Brewster ***(G-1213)***
Designplex LLC G 845 358-6647
Nyack ***(G-13065)***
Display Marketing Group Inc E 631 348-4450
Islandia ***(G-6829)***
Display Presentations Ltd D 631 951-4050
Brooklyn ***(G-1866)***
▲ Display Producers Inc C 718 904-1200
New Rochelle ***(G-8940)***
Displays & Beyond Inc F 718 805-7786
Glendale ***(G-5666)***
Dkm Sales LLC E 716 893-7777
Buffalo ***(G-2932)***
▲ DSI Group Inc C 800 553-2202
Maspeth ***(G-8162)***
Dura Engraving Corporation E 718 706-6400
Long Island City ***(G-7748)***
East End Sign Design Inc G 631 399-2574
Mastic ***(G-8234)***
Eastern Concepts Ltd F 718 472-3377
Sunnyside ***(G-15828)***
▼ Eastern Metal of Elmira Inc D 607 734-2295
Elmira ***(G-4692)***
▼ Edge Display Group Entp Inc F 631 498-1373
Bellport ***(G-825)***
Elderlee Incorporated C 315 789-6670
Oaks Corners ***(G-13088)***
▲ Eversan Inc F 315 736-3967
Whitesboro ***(G-17221)***
Executive Sign Corp G 212 397-4050
Cornwall On Hudson ***(G-4013)***
Executive Sign Corporation G 212 397-4050
New York ***(G-10159)***
Exhibit Corporation America E 718 937-2600
Long Island City ***(G-7763)***
▲ Faster-Form Corp D 800 327-3676
New Hartford ***(G-8849)***
Fastsigns F 518 456-7446
Albany ***(G-79)***
Flado Enterprises Inc G 716 668-6400
Depew ***(G-4282)***
▲ Flair Display Inc D 718 324-9330
Bronx ***(G-1336)***
Fletcher Enterprises Inc G 716 837-7446
Buffalo ***(G-2963)***
Flexlume Sign Corporation G 716 884-2020
Buffalo ***(G-2965)***
Forrest Engraving Co Inc F 845 228-0200
New Rochelle ***(G-8946)***
Fortune Sign G 646 383-8682
Brooklyn ***(G-1996)***
▼ Fossil Industries Inc E 631 254-9200
Deer Park ***(G-4167)***
Frank Torrone & Sons Inc F 718 273-7600
Staten Island ***(G-15695)***
G I Certified Inc G 212 397-1945
New York ***(G-10279)***
Gloede Neon Signs Ltd Inc F 845 471-4366
Poughkeepsie ***(G-13922)***
Graphic Signs & Awnings Ltd G 718 227-6000
Staten Island ***(G-15702)***
Graphitek Inc F 518 686-5966
Hoosick Falls ***(G-6566)***
Greyline Signs Inc G 716 947-4526
Derby ***(G-4306)***
Hadley Exhibits Inc D 716 874-3666
Buffalo ***(G-3002)***
Hanson Sign Screen Prcess Corp E 716 661-3900
Falconer ***(G-4908)***
Hermosa Corp E 315 768-4320
New York Mills ***(G-12744)***
HI Tech Signs of NY Inc G 516 794-7880
East Meadow ***(G-4444)***
Hollywood Signs Inc G 917 577-7333
Brooklyn ***(G-2079)***
◆ ID Signsystems Inc E 585 266-5750
Rochester ***(G-14462)***
Ideal Signs Inc G 718 292-9196
Bronx ***(G-1360)***
Image360 G 585 272-1234
Rochester ***(G-14466)***
Impressive Imprints Inc G 631 293-6161
Farmingdale ***(G-5017)***
▲ International Patterns Inc D 631 952-2000
Plainview ***(G-13638)***
Island Nameplate Inc G 845 651-4005
Florida ***(G-5220)***
▲ Jaf Converters Inc E 631 842-3131
Copiague ***(G-3934)***
Jal Signs Inc F 516 536-7280
Baldwin ***(G-558)***
Jax Signs and Neon Inc G 607 727-3420
Endicott ***(G-4821)***
Jay Turoff F 718 856-7300
Brooklyn ***(G-2135)***
Jem Sign Corp G 516 867-4466
Hempstead ***(G-6299)***
▲ Jomar Industries Inc E 845 357-5773
Airmont ***(G-14)***
Joseph Struhl Co Inc F 516 741-3660
New Hyde Park ***(G-8889)***
JP Signs G 518 569-3907
Chazy ***(G-3589)***
K & B Stamping Co Inc G 914 664-8555
Mount Vernon ***(G-8741)***
Keep America Beautiful Inc G 518 842-4388
Amsterdam ***(G-354)***
▲ Kenan International Trading G 718 672-4922
Corona ***(G-4023)***
King Displays Inc F 212 629-8455
New York ***(G-10891)***
▲ Kling Magnetics Inc E 518 392-4000
Chatham ***(G-3586)***
KP Industries Inc F 516 679-3161
North Bellmore ***(G-12938)***
Kraus & Sons Inc F 212 620-0408
New York ***(G-10926)***
L I C Screen Printing Inc E 516 546-7289
Merrick ***(G-8421)***
L Miller Design Inc G 631 242-1163
Deer Park ***(G-4186)***
L S Sign Co Inc F 718 469-8600
Ridgewood ***(G-14125)***
L Y Z Creations Ltd Inc E 718 768-2977
Brooklyn ***(G-2187)***
▲ Lamar Plastics Packaging Ltd D 516 378-2500
Freeport ***(G-5419)***
◆ Lanco Corporation C 631 231-2300
Ronkonkoma ***(G-14957)***
Lanza Corp G 914 937-6360
Port Chester ***(G-13778)***
▼ Letterama Inc G 516 349-0800
West Babylon ***(G-16835)***
Liberty Awnings & Signs Inc G 347 203-1470
East Elmhurst ***(G-4416)***
▲ Lifestyle-Trimco E 718 257-9101
Brooklyn ***(G-2220)***
Linear Signs Inc F 631 532-5330
Lindenhurst ***(G-7490)***
M Santoliquido Corp F 914 375-6674
Yonkers ***(G-17481)***
Manhattan Neon Sign Corp F 212 714-0430
New York ***(G-11155)***
Marigold Signs Inc F 516 433-7446
Hicksville ***(G-6395)***
Mastercraft Manufacturing Co G 718 729-5620
Long Island City ***(G-7835)***
Mauceri Sign Inc F 718 656-7700
Jamaica ***(G-6965)***
▲ Maxworld Inc G 212 242-7588
New York ***(G-11213)***
Mds USA Inc E 718 358-5588
Flushing ***(G-5276)***
▲ Mechtronics Corporation C 845 231-1400
Beacon ***(G-782)***
Mechtronics Corporation E 845 831-9300
Beacon ***(G-783)***
Mekanism Inc E 212 226-2772
New York ***(G-11248)***
Metropolitan Sign & Riggin G 718 231-0010
Bronx ***(G-1398)***
Metropolitan Signs Inc G 315 638-1448
Baldwinsville ***(G-571)***
Midwood Signs & Design Inc G 718 499-9041
Brooklyn ***(G-2316)***
▲ Millennium Signs & Display Inc E 516 292-8000
Hempstead ***(G-6304)***
Miller Mohr Display Inc G 631 941-2769
East Setauket ***(G-4505)***
Mixture Screen Printing G 845 561-2857
Newburgh ***(G-12788)***
Modern Decal Co G 315 622-2778
Liverpool ***(G-7561)***
Modulex New York Inc G 646 742-1320
New York ***(G-11317)***
Mohawk Sign Systems Inc E 518 842-5303
Amsterdam ***(G-361)***
Monasani Signs Inc G 631 266-2635
East Northport ***(G-4461)***
Morris Brothers Sign Svc Inc G 212 675-9130
New York ***(G-11331)***
Motion Message Inc F 631 924-9500
Bellport ***(G-831)***
Movinads & Signs LLC G 518 378-3000
Halfmoon ***(G-5935)***
Mr Sign Usa Inc F 718 218-3321
Brooklyn ***(G-2346)***
▼ Mystic Display Co Inc G 718 485-2651
Brooklyn ***(G-2351)***
Nameplate Mfrs of Amer E 631 752-0055
Farmingdale ***(G-5070)***
Nas Quick Sign Inc G 716 876-7599
Buffalo ***(G-3102)***
National Advertising & Prtg G 212 629-7650
New York ***(G-11369)***
National Prfmce Solutions Inc D 718 833-4767
Brooklyn ***(G-2358)***
Nationwide Exhibitor Svcs Inc F 631 467-2034
Central Islip ***(G-3532)***
New Art Signs Co Inc G 718 443-0900
Glen Head ***(G-5651)***
▲ New Dimensions Research Corp C 631 694-1356
Melville ***(G-8369)***
New Kit On The Block G 631 757-5655
Bohemia ***(G-1104)***
New Style Signs Limited Inc F 212 242-7848
New York ***(G-11414)***
▲ Newline Products Inc C 972 881-3318
New Windsor ***(G-8992)***
Noel Assoc G 516 371-5420
Inwood ***(G-6804)***
Norampac New York City Inc C 718 340-2100
Maspeth ***(G-8189)***
North Shore Neon Sign Co Inc E 718 937-4848
Flushing ***(G-5282)***
Northeast Promotional Group In G 518 793-1024
South Glens Falls ***(G-15550)***
Northeastern Sign Corp G 315 265-6657
South Colton ***(G-15538)***
Northern Awning & Sign Company G 315 782-8515
Watertown ***(G-16690)***
▲ Nysco Products LLC D 718 792-9000
Bronx ***(G-1416)***
Olson Sign Company Inc G 518 370-2118
Schenectady ***(G-15309)***

39 MISCELLANEOUS MANUFACTURING INDUSTRIES

On The Mark Digital Printing & ....G....... 716 823-3373
  Hamburg *(G-5959)*
▲ Orlandi Inc ....D....... 631 756-0110
  Farmingdale *(G-5081)*
Orlandi Inc ....E....... 631 756-0110
  Farmingdale *(G-5082)*
Pama Enterprises Inc ....G....... 516 504-6300
  Great Neck *(G-5846)*
Penn Signs Inc ....E....... 718 797-1112
  Brooklyn *(G-2427)*
Pereira & ODell LLC ....E....... 212 897-1000
  New York *(G-11633)*
Plasti-Vue Corp ....G....... 718 463-2300
  Flushing *(G-5289)*
▲ Platinum Sales Promotion Inc ....G....... 718 361-0200
  Long Island City *(G-7874)*
Polyplastic Forms Inc ....E....... 631 249-5011
  Farmingdale *(G-5093)*
Poncio Signs ....G....... 718 543-4851
  Bronx *(G-1430)*
Precision Signscom Inc ....D....... 631 842-5060
  Amityville *(G-323)*
Premier Sign Systems LLC ....E....... 585 235-0390
  Rochester *(G-14620)*
▲ Promotional Development Inc ....D....... 718 485-8550
  Brooklyn *(G-2471)*
Props Displays & Interiors ....F....... 212 620-3840
  New York *(G-11759)*
Pyx Inc ....G....... 718 469-4253
  Brooklyn *(G-2477)*
Qcr Express Corp ....G....... 888 924-5888
  Astoria *(G-452)*
Quick Sign F X ....F....... 516 249-6531
  Farmingdale *(G-5104)*
Quorum Group LLC ....D....... 585 798-8888
  Medina *(G-8312)*
R & J Displays Inc ....E....... 631 491-3500
  West Babylon *(G-16851)*
Rapp Signs Inc ....F....... 607 656-8167
  Greene *(G-5885)*
Ray Sign Inc ....F....... 518 377-1471
  Schenectady *(G-15313)*
Resonant Legal Media LLC ....G....... 800 781-3591
  New York *(G-11873)*
Rgm Signs Inc ....G....... 718 442-0598
  Staten Island *(G-15754)*
Riverwood Signs By Dandev Desi ....G....... 845 229-0282
  Hyde Park *(G-6776)*
Rocket Fuel Inc ....F....... 212 594-8888
  New York *(G-11919)*
Rome Sign & Display Co ....G....... 315 336-0550
  Rome *(G-14861)*
▲ Royal Promotion Group Inc ....F....... 212 246-3780
  New York *(G-11945)*
Rpf Associates Inc ....G....... 631 462-7446
  Commack *(G-3867)*
▲ Rsquared Ny Inc ....D....... 631 521-8700
  Edgewood *(G-4622)*
Santoro Signs Inc ....G....... 716 895-8875
  Buffalo *(G-3205)*
Saxton Corporation ....E....... 518 732-7705
  Castleton On Hudson *(G-3449)*
Sellco Industries Inc ....E....... 607 756-7594
  Cortland *(G-4068)*
Seneca Signs LLC ....G....... 315 446-9420
  Syracuse *(G-16061)*
Sign & Signs ....G....... 718 941-6200
  Brooklyn *(G-2579)*
Sign A Rama Inc ....F....... 631 952-3324
  Hauppauge *(G-6214)*
Sign A Rama of Syracuse ....G....... 315 446-9420
  Syracuse *(G-16064)*
Sign Center Inc ....F....... 212 967-2113
  New York *(G-12090)*
Sign City of New York Inc ....G....... 718 661-1118
  College Point *(G-3833)*
Sign Company ....G....... 212 967-2113
  New York *(G-12091)*
▲ Sign Design Group New York Inc ....F....... 718 392-0779
  Long Island City *(G-7905)*
Sign Group Inc ....E....... 718 438-7103
  Brooklyn *(G-2580)*
Sign Guys LLC ....G....... 315 253-4276
  Auburn *(G-515)*
Sign Here Enterprises LLC ....G....... 914 328-3111
  Hartsdale *(G-6019)*
Sign Impressions Inc ....G....... 585 723-0420
  Rochester *(G-14708)*
Sign Language Inc ....G....... 585 237-2620
  Perry *(G-13549)*

Sign Studio Inc ....F....... 518 266-0877
  Troy *(G-16278)*
Sign Works Incorporated ....E....... 914 592-0700
  Elmsford *(G-4792)*
Sign World Inc ....E....... 212 619-9000
  Brooklyn *(G-2581)*
Signature Industries Inc ....F....... 516 679-5177
  Freeport *(G-5439)*
Signature Name Plate Co Inc ....G....... 585 321-9960
  Rochester *(G-14709)*
Signexpo Enterprises Inc ....F....... 212 925-8585
  Jamaica *(G-12095)*
▲ Signs & Decal Corp ....F....... 718 486-6400
  Brooklyn *(G-2582)*
Signs Inc ....G....... 518 483-4759
  Malone *(G-8048)*
Signs Ink Ltd ....F....... 914 739-9059
  Yorktown Heights *(G-17536)*
Signs of Success Ltd ....F....... 516 295-6000
  Lynbrook *(G-7987)*
Smith Graphics Inc ....G....... 631 420-4180
  Farmingdale *(G-5121)*
Snyders Neon Displays Inc ....G....... 518 857-4100
  Colonie *(G-3847)*
Space Sign ....F....... 718 961-1112
  College Point *(G-3834)*
Spanjer Corp ....F....... 347 448-8033
  Long Island City *(G-7909)*
Specialty Signs Co Inc ....F....... 212 243-8521
  New York *(G-12179)*
Spectrum On Broadway ....F....... 718 932-5388
  Woodside *(G-17370)*
Spectrum Signs Inc ....E....... 631 756-1010
  Woodside *(G-17371)*
Speedy Sign A Rama USA Inc ....G....... 516 783-1075
  Bellmore *(G-818)*
Starlite Media LLC ....G....... 212 909-7700
  New York *(G-12211)*
Steel-Brite Ltd ....F....... 631 589-4044
  Oakdale *(G-13082)*
Stepping Stones One Day Signs ....G....... 518 237-5774
  Waterford *(G-16643)*
Stickershopcom Inc ....F....... 631 563-4323
  Bayport *(G-755)*
Strategic Signage Sourcing LLC ....F....... 518 450-1093
  Saratoga Springs *(G-15204)*
Suma Industries Inc ....G....... 646 436-5202
  New York *(G-12252)*
Super Neon Light Co Inc ....G....... 718 236-5667
  Brooklyn *(G-2645)*
T J Signs Unlimited LLC ....E....... 631 273-4800
  Islip *(G-6852)*
▼ Tech Products Inc ....F....... 718 442-4900
  Staten Island *(G-15770)*
▲ Tempo Industries Inc ....G....... 516 334-6900
  Westbury *(G-17060)*
Three Gems Inc ....G....... 516 248-0388
  New Hyde Park *(G-8911)*
Timely Signs Inc ....G....... 516 285-5339
  Elmont *(G-4740)*
Timely Signs of Kingston Inc ....F....... 845 331-8710
  Kingston *(G-7243)*
Tj Signs Unlimited LLC ....E....... 631 273-4800
  Islip *(G-6853)*
Todd Walbridge ....G....... 585 254-3018
  Rochester *(G-14755)*
Trans-Lux Corporation ....D....... 800 243-5544
  New York *(G-12413)*
Tru-Art Sign Co Inc ....F....... 718 658-5068
  Jamaica *(G-6995)*
Turoff Tower Graphics Inc ....F....... 718 856-7300
  Brooklyn *(G-2707)*
Ulrich Sign Co Inc ....F....... 716 434-0167
  Lockport *(G-7654)*
Ultimate Signs & Designs Inc ....E....... 516 481-0800
  Hempstead *(G-30)*
Unique Display Mfg Corp ....G....... 516 546-3800
  Freeport *(G-5444)*
United Print Group Inc ....F....... 718 392-4242
  Long Island City *(G-7936)*
United Sttes Brnze Sign of Fla ....E....... 516 352-5155
  New Hyde Park *(G-8914)*
Universal 3d Innovation Inc ....F....... 516 837-9423
  Valley Stream *(G-16454)*
Universal Signs and Svc Inc ....E....... 631 446-1121
  Deer Park *(G-4245)*
USA Signs of America Inc ....D....... 631 254-2900
  Deer Park *(G-4246)*
Valle Signs and Awnings ....F....... 516 408-3440
  Uniondale *(G-16325)*

Valley Creek Side Inc ....G....... 315 839-5526
  Clayville *(G-3716)*
Vez Inc ....G....... 718 273-7002
  Staten Island *(G-15774)*
Viana Signs Corp ....F....... 516 887-2000
  Oceanside *(G-13126)*
Victory Signs Inc ....G....... 315 762-0220
  Canastota *(G-3402)*
▲ Visual Citi Inc ....C....... 631 482-3030
  Lindenhurst *(G-7518)*
▲ Visual Effects Inc ....F....... 718 324-0011
  Jamaica *(G-6998)*
Visual ID Source Inc ....F....... 516 307-9759
  Mineola *(G-8571)*
Visual Impact Graphics Inc ....G....... 585 548-7118
  Batavia *(G-652)*
Vital Signs & Graphics Co Inc ....G....... 518 237-8372
  Cohoes *(G-3785)*
▲ Von Pok & Chang New York Inc ....G....... 212 599-0556
  New York *(G-12594)*
Voss Signs LLC ....E....... 315 682-6418
  Manlius *(G-8109)*
Wedel Sign Company Inc ....G....... 631 727-4577
  Riverhead *(G-14173)*
Westchester Signs Inc ....G....... 914 666-7446
  Mount Kisco *(G-8688)*
Whispr Group Inc ....F....... 212 924-3979
  New York *(G-12651)*
Wizard Equipment Inc ....G....... 315 414-9999
  Syracuse *(G-16097)*
▲ WI Concepts & Production Inc ....G....... 516 538-5300
  Freeport *(G-5445)*
Woodbury Printing Plus + Inc ....G....... 845 928-6610
  Central Valley *(G-3557)*
X Press Signs Inc ....G....... 716 892-3000
  West Seneca *(G-16984)*
Yellowpagecitycom ....F....... 585 410-6688
  Rochester *(G-14802)*
▲ Yong Xin Kitchen Supplies Inc ....F....... 212 995-8908
  New York *(G-12717)*
Yost Neon Displays Inc ....G....... 716 674-6780
  West Seneca *(G-16985)*
Z-Car-D Corp ....E....... 631 424-2077
  Huntington Station *(G-6768)*

3995 Burial Caskets

Milso Industries Inc ....F....... 631 234-1133
  Hauppauge *(G-6164)*
North Hudson Woodcraft Corp ....E....... 315 429-3105
  Dolgeville *(G-4330)*

3996 Linoleum & Hard Surface Floor Coverings, NEC

East To West Architectral Pdts ......G....... 631 433-9690
  East Northport *(G-4455)*
▲ Engineered Plastics Inc ....E....... 800 682-2525
  Williamsville *(G-17270)*
Heritage Contract Flooring LLC .....E....... 716 853-1555
  Buffalo *(G-3011)*
Signature Systems Group LLC ......F....... 800 569-2751
  New York *(G-12094)*

3999 Manufacturing Industries, NEC

141 Industries LLC ....F....... 978 273-8831
  New York *(G-9005)*
A & L Asset Management Ltd ....C....... 718 566-1500
  Brooklyn *(G-1525)*
A & W Metal Works Inc ....F....... 845 352-2346
  Garnerville *(G-5566)*
A&M Model Makers LLC ....G....... 626 813-9661
  Macedon *(G-8006)*
Accenta Incorporated ....G....... 716 565-6262
  Buffalo *(G-2808)*
Accessible Bath Tech LLC ....F....... 518 937-1518
  Albany *(G-30)*
Accurate Pnt Powdr Coating Inc ....F....... 585 235-1650
  Rochester *(G-14182)*
Active Manufacturing Inc ....F....... 607 775-3162
  Kirkwood *(G-7257)*
Adel Rootstein (usa) Inc ....E....... 718 499-5650
  Brooklyn *(G-1560)*
Adults and Children With Learn .....E....... 516 593-8230
  East Rockaway *(G-4487)*
AFP Manufacturing Corp ....F....... 516 466-6464
  Great Neck *(G-5800)*
▲ Age Manufacturers Inc ....D....... 718 927-0048
  Brooklyn *(G-1569)*
Air Flow Manufacturing ....F....... 607 733-8284
  Elmira *(G-4683)*

▲ **Aloi Solutions LLC** ....E 585 292-0920
Rochester *(G-14207)*
▲ **American Culture Hair Inc** ....E 631 242-3142
Huntington Station *(G-6731)*
▲ **Arcadia Mfg Group Inc** ....E 518 434-6213
Green Island *(G-5871)*
Arcadia Mfg Group Inc ....G 518 434-6213
Menands *(G-8399)*
Arnprior Rpid Mfg Slutions Inc ....C 585 617-6301
Rochester *(G-14229)*
Arnprior Rpid Mfg Slutions Inc ....G 585 617-6301
Rochester *(G-14230)*
Artemis Studios Inc ....D 718 788-6022
Brooklyn *(G-1637)*
Ascribe Inc ....E 585 413-0298
Rochester *(G-14234)*
◆ **Astron Candle Manufacturing Co** ....G 718 728-3330
Long Island City *(G-7705)*
Atlas Metal Industries Inc ....G 607 776-2048
Hammondsport *(G-5975)*
▲ **Avanti Advanced Mfg Corp** ....G 716 541-8945
Buffalo *(G-2848)*
B & R Promotional Products ....G 212 563-0040
New York *(G-9341)*
B F G Elcpltg and Mfg Co ....E 716 362-0888
Blasdell *(G-954)*
Balance Enterprises Inc ....G 516 822-3183
Hicksville *(G-6350)*
Baldwin Ribbon & Stamping Corp ....F 718 335-6700
Woodside *(G-17336)*
Beast Vapes Nyc ....G 718 714-8139
Brooklyn *(G-1673)*
Bee Green Industries Inc ....G 516 334-3525
Carle Place *(G-3412)*
Best Priced Products Inc ....G 914 345-3800
Elmsford *(G-4744)*
◆ **Betterbee Inc** ....F 518 314-0575
Greenwich *(G-5905)*
Beyond Vape ....G 917 909-1113
Brooklyn *(G-1691)*
Biocontinuum Group Inc ....G 212 406-1060
New York *(G-9452)*
Blackbox Biometrics Inc ....E 585 329-3399
Rochester *(G-14252)*
Blanche P Field LLC ....E 212 355-6616
New York *(G-9463)*
▲ **Blandi Products LLC** ....F 908 377-2885
New York *(G-9464)*
▲ **Boom LLC** ....E 646 218-0752
New York *(G-9489)*
Bridge City Vape Co LLC ....G 845 625-7962
Poughkeepsie *(G-13910)*
Brooklyn Industries LLC ....G 718 788-5250
Brooklyn *(G-1725)*
Brooklyn Industries LLC ....F 718 486-6464
Brooklyn *(G-1726)*
Brooklyn Industries LLC ....F 718 789-2764
Brooklyn *(G-1727)*
Brooklyn Vape ....G 917 336-7363
Brooklyn *(G-1735)*
Bullex Inc ....E 518 689-2023
Albany *(G-56)*
Callanan Industries Inc ....G 518 382-5354
Schenectady *(G-15264)*
▲ **Candle In The Window Inc** ....F 718 852-5743
Brooklyn *(G-1755)*
Candles By Foster ....G 914 739-9226
Peekskill *(G-13499)*
▲ **Cathedral Candle Co** ....D 315 422-9119
Syracuse *(G-15909)*
▲ **Center Line Studios Inc** ....F 845 534-7143
New Windsor *(G-8980)*
Chan & Chan (usa) Corp ....G 718 388-9633
Brooklyn *(G-1773)*
◆ **Christian Dior Perfumes LLC** ....C 212 931-2200
New York *(G-9662)*
Clara Papa ....G 315 733-2660
Utica *(G-16334)*
Columbia Dentoform Corporation ....E 718 482-1569
Long Island City *(G-7732)*
Commercial Fabrics Inc ....F 716 694-0641
North Tonawanda *(G-12984)*
Copesetic Inc ....F 315 684-7780
Morrisville *(G-8662)*
Cortlandt Smoke and Vape ....G 914 930-7592
Montrose *(G-8652)*
Costume Armour Inc ....F 845 534-9120
Cornwall *(G-4008)*
Creative Models & Prototypes ....G 516 433-6828
Hicksville *(G-6362)*
Creative Vape ....G 347 927-0982
Brooklyn *(G-1815)*
Criterion Bell & Specialty ....E 718 788-2600
Brooklyn *(G-1818)*
◆ **Crusader Candle Co Inc** ....E 718 625-0005
Brooklyn *(G-1820)*
D & M Enterprises Incorporated ....G 914 937-6430
Port Chester *(G-13769)*
▲ **De Meo Brothers Inc** ....G 212 268-1400
New York *(G-9889)*
Deva Concepts LLC ....E 212 343-0344
New York *(G-9916)*
Diane Studios Inc ....D 718 788-6007
Brooklyn *(G-1859)*
Dj Pirrone Industries Inc ....G 518 864-5496
Pattersonville *(G-13471)*
Dolmen ....F 912 596-1537
Conklin *(G-3892)*
Donorwall Inc ....F 212 766-9670
New York *(G-9958)*
Dragon Vapes Nyc ....G 718 801-7855
Flushing *(G-5246)*
E-Z Global Wholesale Inc ....G 888 769-7888
Brooklyn *(G-1895)*
▲ **Eagle Regalia Co Inc** ....F 845 425-2245
Spring Valley *(G-15604)*
East Penn Manufacturing Co ....G 631 321-7161
Babylon *(G-544)*
▲ **Eastern Feather & Down Corp** ....G 718 387-4100
Brooklyn *(G-1899)*
EDM Mfg ....G 631 669-1966
Babylon *(G-545)*
Empire City Vape LLC ....G 718 676-6166
Brooklyn *(G-1925)*
◆ **Eser Realty Corp** ....E 718 383-0565
Brooklyn *(G-1939)*
Essex Industries ....G 518 942-6671
Mineville *(G-8573)*
▲ **Essex Manufacturing Inc** ....D 212 239-0080
New York *(G-10119)*
Eton Institute ....F 855 334-3688
New York *(G-10134)*
▼ **Falk Industries Inc** ....F 518 725-2777
Johnstown *(G-7145)*
▲ **Faster-Form Corp** ....D 800 327-3676
New Hartford *(G-8849)*
Federal Sample Card Corp ....D 718 458-1344
Elmhurst *(G-4673)*
Feraco Industries ....G 631 547-8120
Huntington Station *(G-6742)*
Fingerprint America Inc ....G 518 435-1609
Albany *(G-80)*
◆ **Fish & Crown Ltd** ....D 212 707-9603
New York *(G-10226)*
Five Star Creations Inc ....E 845 783-1187
Monroe *(G-8589)*
▲ **Four Paws Products Ltd** ....D 631 436-7421
Ronkonkoma *(G-14931)*
Freedom Mfg LLC ....F 518 584-0441
Saratoga Springs *(G-15181)*
Fun Industries of NY ....F 631 845-3805
Farmingdale *(G-5004)*
▲ **Genesis Mannequins USA II Inc** ....G 212 505-6600
New York *(G-10318)*
Givi Inc ....F 212 586-5029
New York *(G-10343)*
Goldmont Enterprises Inc ....F 212 947-3633
Middle Village *(G-8444)*
Goodwill Inds of Greater NY ....C 914 621-0781
Baldwin Place *(G-562)*
Goodwill Inds Wstn NY Inc ....F 716 633-3305
Williamsville *(G-17272)*
Gottavape ....G 518 945-8273
Schenectady *(G-15291)*
Grand Island Animal Hospital ....E 716 773-7645
Grand Island *(G-5773)*
▲ **Gustbuster Ltd** ....G 631 391-9000
Farmingdale *(G-5010)*
Hair Color Research Group Inc ....E 718 445-6026
Flushing *(G-5256)*
Handmade Frames Inc ....F 718 782-8364
Brooklyn *(G-2066)*
High Times Vape ....G 631 569-5322
Patchogue *(G-13447)*
◆ **Hoskie Co Inc** ....D 718 628-8672
Brooklyn *(G-2084)*
Hrg Group Inc ....E 212 906-8555
New York *(G-10567)*
Hs Homeworx LLC ....G 646 870-0406
New York *(G-10568)*
Hudson Eastern Industries Inc ....G 917 295-5818
Whitestone *(G-17238)*
▲ **Hudson Scenic Studio Inc** ....C 914 375-0900
Yonkers *(G-17472)*
▼ **Identfication Data Imaging LLC** ....G 516 484-6500
Port Washington *(G-13844)*
Image Tech ....F 716 635-0167
Buffalo *(G-3021)*
Innovative Industries LLC ....G 718 784-7300
Long Island City *(G-7794)*
▲ **International Design Assoc Ltd** ....G 212 687-0333
New York *(G-10675)*
Iquit Cig LLC ....G 718 475-1422
Brooklyn *(G-2113)*
Islip Miniture Golf ....G 631 940-8900
Bay Shore *(G-706)*
◆ **Ivy Enterprises Inc** ....B 516 621-9779
Port Washington *(G-13848)*
◆ **J & A Usa Inc** ....G 631 243-3336
Brentwood *(G-1184)*
J & R Unique Giftware ....E 718 821-0398
Maspeth *(G-8177)*
J T Systematic ....G 607 754-0929
Endwell *(G-4841)*
Jacobs Juice Corp ....G 646 255-2860
Brooklyn *(G-2131)*
Jags Manufacturing Network Inc ....G 631 750-6367
Holbrook *(G-6483)*
▲ **Jamaica Lamp Corp** ....E 718 776-5039
Queens Village *(G-13996)*
Jason & Jean Products Inc ....F 718 271-8300
Corona *(G-4022)*
▲ **Jenalex Creative Marketing Inc** ....G 212 935-2266
New York *(G-10759)*
▲ **Jenray Products Inc** ....E 914 375-5596
Yonkers *(G-17475)*
JG Innovative Industries Inc ....G 718 784-7300
Kew Gardens *(G-7193)*
Jimco Lamp & Manufacturing Co ....G 631 218-2152
Islip *(G-6848)*
John Gailer Inc ....E 212 243-5662
Long Island City *(G-7799)*
John Prior ....G 516 520-9801
East Meadow *(G-4446)*
Joya LLC ....F 718 852-6979
Brooklyn *(G-2152)*
Jpm Fine Woodworking LLC ....G 516 236-7605
Jericho *(G-7106)*
Just Right Carbines LLC ....G 585 261-5331
Canandaigua *(G-3377)*
Kafko (us) Corp ....G 877 721-7665
Latham *(G-7394)*
Kelly Foundry & Machine Co ....E 315 732-8313
Utica *(G-16370)*
Ketchum Manufacturing Co Inc ....F 518 696-3331
Lake Luzerne *(G-7296)*
Kevco Industries ....G 845 255-7407
New Paltz *(G-8920)*
King Displays Inc ....F 212 629-8455
New York *(G-10891)*
▲ **Kittywalk Systems Inc** ....G 516 627-8418
Port Washington *(G-13854)*
▲ **Kkw Corp** ....E 631 589-5454
Sayville *(G-15240)*
▲ **Lab-Aids Inc** ....E 631 737-1133
Ronkonkoma *(G-14955)*
Learnimation ....G 917 868-7261
Brooklyn *(G-2203)*
Lemetric Hair Centers Inc ....F 212 986-5620
New York *(G-10998)*
Lemon Brothers Foundation Inc ....F 347 920-2749
Bronx *(G-1384)*
▲ **Leo D Bernstein & Sons Inc** ....E 212 337-9578
New York *(G-11003)*
Liberty Displays Inc ....E 716 743-1757
Amherst *(G-247)*
▲ **Lifestyle-Trimco** ....E 718 257-9101
Brooklyn *(G-2220)*
Lois Kitchen LLC ....G 216 308-9335
New York *(G-11051)*
Lux Mundi Corp ....G 631 244-4596
Ronkonkoma *(G-14962)*
M & S Schmalberg Inc ....F 212 244-2090
New York *(G-11098)*
M and J Hair Center Inc ....F 516 872-1010
Garden City *(G-5530)*
Mack Studios Displays Inc ....E 315 252-7542
Auburn *(G-505)*
Malouf Colette Inc ....F 212 941-9588
New York *(G-11147)*

73 BUSINESS SERVICES

Marilyn Model Management Inc ....F 646 556-7587
New York *(G-11174)*
Martec Industries ....F 585 458-3940
Rochester *(G-14519)*
Martin Chafkin ....G 718 383-1155
Brooklyn *(G-2278)*
▲ McGaw Group LLC ....F 212 876-8822
New York *(G-11221)*
▲ Meisel-Peskin Co Inc ....D 718 497-1840
Brooklyn *(G-2299)*
▲ Mgd Brands Inc ....E 516 545-0150
Plainview *(G-13648)*
Miss Jessies LLC ....G 718 643-9016
New York *(G-11308)*
Mission Crane Service Inc ....D 718 937-3333
Long Island City *(G-7845)*
▲ Mitco Manufacturing ....G 800 338-8908
Garden City *(G-5535)*
Mitten Manufacturing Inc ....G 315 437-7564
Syracuse *(G-16012)*
Molly Vapes Inc ....G 718 743-0120
Brooklyn *(G-2335)*
▲ Moti Inc ....F 718 436-4280
Brooklyn *(G-2340)*
Mr Vape Guru ....G 845 796-2274
Monticello *(G-8645)*
▲ Muench-Kreuzer Candle Company ..D 315 471-4515
Syracuse *(G-16014)*
My Industries Inc ....G 845 638-2257
New City *(G-8835)*
Nationwide Exhibitor Svcs Inc ....F 631 467-2034
Central Islip *(G-3532)*
Nitro Manufacturing LLC ....F 716 646-9900
Hamburg *(G-5957)*
Northast Ctr For Bekeeping LLC ....F 800 632-3379
Greenwich *(G-5910)*
◆ Northern Lights Entps Inc ....C 585 593-1200
Wellsville *(G-16781)*
Northern New York Rural ....G 518 891-9460
Saranac Lake *(G-15166)*
Nsj Group Ltd ....F 631 893-9300
Babylon *(G-548)*
Nubian Heritage ....G 631 265-3551
Hauppauge *(G-6176)*
O Brien Gere Mfg Inc ....G 315 437-6100
Liverpool *(G-7563)*
Ogd V-Hvac Inc ....E 315 858-1002
Van Hornesville *(G-16455)*
▲ Ohserase Manufacturing LLC ....E 518 358-9309
Akwesasne *(G-29)*
▲ Ohserase Manufacturing LLC ....E 518 358-9309
Hogansburg *(G-6454)*
▲ Old Williamsburgh Candle Corp ....C 718 566-1500
Brooklyn *(G-2401)*
Oledworks LLC ....E 585 287-6802
Rochester *(G-14568)*
Omicron Technologies Inc ....E 631 434-7697
Holbrook *(G-6494)*
Oriskany Manufacturing LLC ....G 315 732-4962
Yorkville *(G-17541)*
▲ Orlandi Inc ....D 631 756-0110
Farmingdale *(G-5081)*
Orlandi Inc ....E 631 756-0110
Farmingdale *(G-5082)*
Oso Industries Inc ....G 917 709-2050
Brooklyn *(G-2410)*
◆ Our Own Candle Company Inc ....F 716 769-5000
Findley Lake *(G-5185)*
◆ P S Pibbs Inc ....G 718 445-8046
Flushing *(G-5283)*
Paperworks Industries Inc ....F 913 621-0922
Baldwinsville *(G-572)*
▲ Patience Brewster Inc ....F 315 685-8336
Skaneateles *(G-15486)*
PCI Industries Corp ....E 914 662-2700
Mount Vernon *(G-8759)*
Performance Precision Mfg LLC ....G 518 993-3033
Fort Plain *(G-5357)*
Petland Discounts Inc ....G 516 821-3194
Hewlett *(G-6335)*
▲ Pets n People Inc ....G 631 232-1200
Hauppauge *(G-6188)*
Premium Assure Inc ....G 605 252-9999
Brooklyn *(G-2452)*
▲ Production Resource Group LLC ....D 877 774-7088
Armonk *(G-416)*
Production Resource Group LLC ....E 845 567-5700
New Windsor *(G-8994)*
▲ Promotional Development Inc ....D 718 485-8550
Brooklyn *(G-2471)*

Props Displays & Interiors ....F 212 620-3840
New York *(G-11759)*
Pyrotek Incorporated ....F 716 731-3221
Sanborn *(G-15153)*
Qps Die Cutters Finishers Corp ....E 718 966-1811
Staten Island *(G-15746)*
Qualbuys LLC ....G 855 884-3274
Syosset *(G-15856)*
Quality Candle Mfg Co Inc ....F 631 842-8475
Copiague *(G-3945)*
Quest Manufacturing Inc ....F 716 312-8000
Hamburg *(G-5962)*
▲ R V Dow Enterprises Inc ....F 585 454-5862
Rochester *(G-14644)*
Ray Gold Shade Inc ....F 718 377-8892
Brooklyn *(G-2499)*
◆ Readent Inc ....F 212 710-3004
White Plains *(G-17189)*
Remus Industries ....G 914 906-1544
Ossining *(G-13351)*
Rockwell Video Solutions LLC ....F 631 745-0582
Southampton *(G-15574)*
Rutcarele Inc ....G 347 830-5353
Corona *(G-4028)*
Ryers Creek Corp ....E 607 523-6617
Corning *(G-4000)*
S & H Enterprises Inc ....F 888 323-8755
Queensbury *(G-14023)*
S B Manufacturing LLC ....F 845 352-3700
Monsey *(G-8614)*
▲ S M Frank & Company Inc ....G 914 739-3100
New Windsor *(G-8997)*
Saakshi Inc ....G 315 475-3988
Syracuse *(G-16050)*
Sector4vapes ....G 607 377-2224
Corning *(G-4001)*
▲ Select Industries New York Inc ....F 800 723-5333
New York *(G-12041)*
Shake-N-Go Fashion Inc ....E 516 944-7777
Port Washington *(G-13881)*
◆ Shake-N-Go Fashion Inc ....E 516 944-7777
Port Washington *(G-13882)*
Shyam Ahuja Limited ....G 212 644-5910
New York *(G-12080)*
▲ Siegel & Stockman Inc ....G 212 633-1508
New York *(G-12083)*
▲ Simcha Candle Co Inc ....G 845 783-0406
New Windsor *(G-9001)*
Smoke N Vape ....E 212 390-1654
New York *(G-12137)*
▲ Soggy Doggy Productions LLC ....F 877 504-4811
Larchmont *(G-7376)*
Sonaal Industries Inc ....G 718 383-3860
Brooklyn *(G-2609)*
◆ Spartan Brands Inc ....F 212 340-0320
New York *(G-12174)*
Spectrum Brands Inc ....B 631 232-1200
Hauppauge *(G-6220)*
▲ Star Desk Pad Co Inc ....E 914 963-9400
Yonkers *(G-17504)*
▲ Steeldeck Ny Inc ....F 718 599-3700
Brooklyn *(G-2625)*
Stiegelbauer Associates Inc ....F 718 624-0835
Brooklyn *(G-2630)*
▼ Strategic Mktg Promotions Inc ....F 845 623-7777
Pearl River *(G-13491)*
Swift Multigraphics LLC ....G 585 442-8000
Rochester *(G-14733)*
▲ Tactica International Inc ....F 212 575-0500
New York *(G-12294)*
Teachspin Inc ....F 716 725-6116
Buffalo *(G-3236)*
Techgrass ....F 646 719-2000
New York *(G-12314)*
▲ Tent and Table Com LLC ....F 716 570-0258
Buffalo *(G-3239)*
▲ Thompson Ferrier LLC ....F 212 244-2212
New York *(G-12347)*
Tii Industries Inc ....F 631 789-5000
Copiague *(G-3956)*
Tiki Industries Inc ....G 516 779-3629
Riverhead *(G-14171)*
Time2vape LLC ....F 718 335-0401
Jackson Heights *(G-6924)*
▲ Topoo Industries Incorporated ....G 718 331-3755
Brooklyn *(G-2685)*
Trendsformers Ltd Liability Co ....F 888 700-2423
New York *(G-12419)*
▼ Tri-Force Sales LLC ....E 732 261-5507
New York *(G-12420)*

▲ Tri-Plex Packaging Corporation ....E 212 481-6070
New York *(G-12422)*
Trove Inc ....F 212 268-2046
Brooklyn *(G-2703)*
▲ TV Guilfoil & Associates Inc ....G 315 453-0920
Syracuse *(G-16086)*
▲ Unique Petz LLC ....F 212 714-1800
New York *(G-12481)*
▲ Unistel LLC ....D 585 341-4600
Webster *(G-16766)*
Unither Manufacturing LLC ....F 585 274-5430
Rochester *(G-14770)*
Unlimited Industries Inc ....G 631 666-9483
Brightwaters *(G-1238)*
Uptown Nails LLC ....C 800 748-1881
New York *(G-12497)*
Vape Flavorium ....G 607 346-7276
Horseheads *(G-6623)*
Vape Paradise Inc ....G 845 467-4517
Middletown *(G-8504)*
Vape4style Inc ....G 718 395-0406
Brooklyn *(G-2738)*
▲ Water Splash Inc ....G 800 936-3430
Champlain *(G-3577)*
▲ Welsh Gold Stampers Inc ....E 718 984-5031
Staten Island *(G-15776)*
Woodfalls Industries ....F 518 236-7201
Plattsburgh *(G-13740)*
Z Vape Station/Atlantic Smoke ....G 516 442-0548
Freeport *(G-5446)*
Zebrowski Industries Inc ....G 716 532-3911
Collins *(G-3844)*
▲ Zip-Jack Industries Ltd ....E 914 592-2000
Tarrytown *(G-16136)*
Zmz Mfg Inc ....G 518 234-4336
Warnerville *(G-16599)*

73 BUSINESS SERVICES

7372 Prepackaged Software

2k Inc ....G 646 536-3007
New York *(G-9015)*
30dc Inc ....G 212 962-4400
New York *(G-9016)*
30dc Inc ....F 212 962-4400
New York *(G-9017)*
A K A Computer Consulting Inc ....G 718 351-5200
Staten Island *(G-15650)*
A2ia Corp ....F 917 237-0390
New York *(G-9042)*
Aarfid LLC ....G 716 992-3999
Eden *(G-4597)*
Abel Noser Solutions LLC ....E 646 432-4000
New York *(G-9049)*
Accela Inc ....F 631 563-5005
Ronkonkoma *(G-14874)*
Accelify Solutions LLC ....E 888 922-2354
New York *(G-9056)*
Adgorithmics LLC ....G 646 277-8728
New York *(G-9075)*
Adl Data Systems Inc ....E 914 591-1800
Hawthorne *(G-6265)*
Adobe Systems Inc ....E 212 471-0904
New York *(G-9077)*
Adobe Systems Incorporated ....C 212 592-1400
New York *(G-9078)*
Adobe Systems Incorporated ....E 212 471-0904
New York *(G-9079)*
Adtech Us Inc ....C 212 402-4840
New York *(G-9082)*
Advanced Cmpt Sftwr Consulting ....G 718 300-3577
Bronx *(G-1265)*
Advanced Comfort Systems Inc ....F 518 884-8444
Ballston Spa *(G-588)*
Advanced Cyber Security Corp ....E 866 417-9155
Bohemia *(G-1003)*
Agrinetix Cmpt Systems LLC ....F 877 978-5477
Henrietta *(G-6314)*
Amcom Software Inc ....F 212 951-7600
New York *(G-9159)*
Andigo New Media Inc ....G 212 727-8445
New York *(G-9201)*
Ansa Systems of USA Inc ....G 718 835-3743
Valley Stream *(G-16425)*
Apogy LLC ....E 866 766-1723
New York *(G-9225)*
Appfigures Inc ....F 212 343-7900
New York *(G-9232)*
Application Security Inc ....D 212 912-4100
New York *(G-9233)*

Employee Codes: A=Over 500 employees, B=251-500
C=101-250, D=51-100, E=20-50, F=10-19, G=5-9

73 BUSINESS SERVICES SIC SECTION

Company	Loc	Phone
Appliedea Inc — New York (G-9234)	G	212 920-6822
Apprenda Inc — Troy (G-16247)	D	518 383-2130
Appsbidder Inc — Brooklyn (G-1621)	G	917 880-4269
APS Enterprise Software Inc — Huntington (G-6686)	E	631 784-7720
Archive360 Inc — New York (G-9247)	E	212 731-2438
Articulate Global Inc — New York (G-9268)	C	800 861-4880
Arumai Technologies Inc — Armonk (G-410)	F	914 217-0038
Asite LLC — New York (G-9286)	D	203 545-3089
Aspen Research Group Ltd — New York (G-9289)	F	212 425-9588
AT&T Corp — New York (G-9296)	F	212 317-7048
Augury Inc — New York (G-9314)	F	347 699-5011
Automated & MGT Solutions LLC — East Greenbush (G-4420)	G	518 283-5352
Automated Office Systems Inc — Valley Stream (G-16426)	F	516 396-5555
Avalanche Studios New York Inc — New York (G-9324)	D	212 993-6447
Avocode Inc — New York (G-9333)	F	646 934-8410
Aycan Medical Systems LLC — Rochester (G-14236)	F	585 271-3078
B601 V2 Inc — New York (G-9350)	G	646 391-6431
Base Systems Inc — Brewster (G-1208)	G	845 278-1991
Beyondly Inc — New York (G-9430)	F	646 658-3665
Big Data Bizviz LLC — West Seneca (G-16968)	G	716 803-2367
Big White Wall Holding Inc — New York (G-9445)	F	917 281-2649
Bigwood Systems Inc — Ithaca (G-6861)	G	607 257-0915
Billing Blocks Inc — Staten Island (G-15667)	F	718 442-5006
Blue Wolf Group LLC — New York (G-9474)	D	866 455-9653
BMC Software Inc — New York (G-9479)	E	212 402-1500
Botify Corporation — New York (G-9492)	F	617 576-2005
Boundless Spatial Inc — New York (G-9495)	E	646 831-5531
Boxbee Inc — New York (G-9497)	G	646 612-7839
Brainpop LLC — New York (G-9502)	E	212 574-6017
Brainworks Software Dev Corp — Sayville (G-15233)	G	631 563-5000
Braze — New York (G-9508)	E	504 327-7269
Brigadoon Software Inc — Nanuet (G-8798)	G	845 624-0909
Broadway Technology LLC — New York (G-9518)	E	646 912-6450
Bull Street LLC — New York (G-9529)	G	212 495-9855
Buncee LLC — Calverton (G-3315)	F	631 591-1390
Business Integrity Inc — New York (G-9534)	G	718 238-2008
Business Management Systems — Yorktown Heights (G-17524)	F	914 245-8558
Byte Consulting Inc — New York (G-9542)	G	646 500-8606
C S I G Inc — Kingston (G-7210)	G	845 383-3800
Ca Inc — New York (G-9543)	A	800 225-5224
California US Holdings Inc — New York (G-9552)	A	212 726-6500
Callaway Digital Arts Inc — New York (G-9554)	E	212 675-3050
Callidus Software Inc — New York (G-9555)	F	212 554-7300
Caminus Corporation — New York (G-9559)	D	212 515-3600
Candex Solutions Inc — New York (G-9565)	G	215 650-3214
Capital Programs Inc — New York (G-9576)	G	212 842-4640
Careconnector — Brooklyn (G-1760)	G	919 360-2987
Carnival Inc — New York (G-9582)	G	415 781-9815
Catalyst Group Inc — New York (G-9599)	G	212 243-7777
Catch Ventures Inc — New York (G-9601)	F	347 620-4351
Catholic News Publishing Co — Mamaroneck (G-8059)	F	914 632-7771
Cavalry Solutions — Syracuse (G-15910)	G	315 422-1699
Cbord Group Inc — Ithaca (G-6869)	C	607 257-2410
Cdml Computer Services Ltd — Fresh Meadows (G-5452)	G	718 428-9063
Cegid Corporation — New York (G-9607)	G	212 757-9038
Ceipal LLC — Rochester (G-14284)	G	585 351-2934
Ceipal LLC — Rochester (G-14285)	G	585 584-1316
Celonis Inc — Brooklyn (G-1769)	G	941 615-9670
Ceros Inc — New York (G-9622)	E	347 744-9250
Cgi Technologies Solutions Inc — New York (G-9624)	F	212 682-7411
Checkm8 Inc — New York (G-9638)	G	212 268-0048
Chequedcom Inc — Saratoga Springs (G-15177)	G	888 412-0699
Childrens Progress Inc — New York (G-9645)	E	212 730-0905
Cinch Technologies Inc — New York (G-9668)	G	212 266-0022
Cinedigm Software — New York (G-9671)	G	212 206-9001
Citixsys Technologies Inc — New York (G-9679)	G	212 745-1365
Clarityad Inc — New York (G-9688)	G	646 397-4198
Classroom Inc — New York (G-9694)	G	212 545-8400
▲ Clayton Dubilier & Rice Fun — New York (G-9695)	E	212 407-5200
Clearview Social Inc — Buffalo (G-2895)	G	801 414-7675
Clever Goats Media LLC — New York (G-9697)	G	917 512-0340
Cloud Rock Group LLC — Roslyn (G-15041)	G	516 967-6023
Cloudparc Inc — New York (G-9702)	G	954 665-5962
Cloudsense Inc — New York (G-9703)	G	917 880-6195
Coalition On Positive Health — New York (G-9718)	F	212 633-2500
Cognotion Inc — New York (G-9724)	G	347 692-0640
Comet Informatics LLC — Pittsford (G-13586)	G	585 385-2310
Commercehub Inc — Albany (G-71)	G	518 810-0700
Commify Technology — New York (G-9746)	F	917 603-1822
Comprehensive Dental Tech — Hancock (G-5985)	G	607 467-4456
Condeco Software Inc — New York (G-9759)	G	917 677-7600
Construction Technology Inc — Valhalla (G-16392)	G	914 747-8900
Contactive Inc — New York (G-9770)	E	646 476-9059
Conversant LLC — New York (G-9775)	G	212 471-9570
Coocoo SMS Inc — Huntington (G-6692)	F	646 459-4260
Creditiq Inc — New York (G-9812)	F	888 988-4223
Cross Border Transactions LLC — Tarrytown (G-16113)	G	646 767-7342
Crunched Inc — New York (G-9817)	G	415 484-9909
CTI Software Inc — Deer Park (G-4145)	G	631 253-3550
Cuffs Planning & Models Ltd — New Rochelle (G-8938)	G	914 632-1883
Cultureiq Inc — New York (G-9823)	G	212 755-8633
Curaegis Technologies Inc — Rochester (G-14316)	E	585 254-1100
Cureatr Inc — New York (G-9825)	E	212 203-3927
Curemdcom Inc — New York (G-9826)	A	212 509-6200
Customshow Inc — New York (G-9830)	G	800 255-5303
Cyandia Inc — Syracuse (G-15937)	F	315 679-4268
Cybersports Inc — Utica (G-16342)	G	315 737-7150
Dartcom Incorporated — New Hartford (G-8847)	G	315 790-5456
Dashlane Inc — New York (G-9867)	E	212 596-7510
Data Implementation Inc — New York (G-9868)	G	212 979-2015
Datadog Inc — New York (G-9869)	E	866 329-4466
Davel Systems Inc — Brooklyn (G-1842)	G	718 382-6024
Dbase LLC — Binghamton (G-903)	G	607 729-0234
Debt Resolve Inc — White Plains (G-17128)	G	914 949-5500
Defran Systems Inc — New York (G-9892)	E	212 727-8342
Delivery Systems Inc — New York (G-9894)	F	212 221-7007
Deniz Information Systems — New York (G-9898)	G	212 750-5199
Digital Associates LLC — Smithtown (G-15507)	G	631 983-6075
Digital Brewery LLC — Astoria (G-435)	G	646 665-2106
Diligent Board Member Svcs LLC — New York (G-9930)	E	212 741-8181
Diligent Corporation — New York (G-9931)	B	212 741-8181
Do It Different Inc — New York (G-9945)	G	917 842-0230
Document Strategies LLC — Rochester (G-14336)	F	585 506-9000
Dow Jones & Company Inc — New York (G-9966)	E	212 597-5983
Dropcar Inc — New York (G-9982)	G	646 342-1595
Dwnld Inc — New York (G-9996)	E	484 483-6572
Dynamo Development Inc — New York (G-10001)	G	212 385-1552
E H Hurwitz & Associates — Bronx (G-1325)	G	718 884-3766
Eastnets Americas Corp — New York (G-10019)	F	212 631-0666
Ebeling Associates Inc — Halfmoon (G-5932)	F	518 688-8700
EBM Care Inc — New York (G-10024)	G	212 500-5000
Eccella Corporation — New York (G-10026)	G	855 879-3223
Efront Financial Solutions Inc — New York (G-10039)	E	212 220-0660
Eft Analytics Inc — New York (G-10040)	G	212 290-2300
Electronic Arts Inc — New York (G-10050)	G	212 672-0722
Elepath Inc — Brooklyn (G-1917)	G	347 417-4975
Elevondata Labs Inc — New York (G-10053)	G	470 222-5438
Elodina Inc — New York (G-10066)	G	646 402-5202
Emblaze Systems Inc — New York (G-10072)	C	212 371-1100
Empire Innovation Group LLC — Buffalo (G-2951)	F	716 852-5000
Empowrx LLC — New York (G-10075)	G	212 755-3577
Endava Inc — New York (G-10083)	G	212 920-7240
Enterprise Network NY Inc — Brooklyn (G-1929)	F	516 263-0641
Enterprise Tech Group Inc — New Rochelle (G-8942)	F	914 588-0327
Epicor Software Corporation — Schenectady (G-15280)	E	805 496-6789

SIC SECTION

73 BUSINESS SERVICES

Company	Code	Phone
Equilend Holdings LLC — New York (G-10104)	E	212 901-2200
Ert Software Inc — Blauvelt (G-965)	G	845 358-5721
Evidon Inc — New York (G-10148)	D	917 262-2530
Ex El Enterprises Ltd — New York (G-10152)	F	212 489-4500
Exact Solutions Inc — New York (G-10154)	F	212 707-8627
Exchange My Mail Inc — Jericho (G-7101)	F	516 605-1835
Express Checkout LLC — New York (G-10163)	G	646 512-2068
EZ Newsletter LLC — Brooklyn (G-1954)	F	412 943-7777
EZ Systems US Inc — Brooklyn (G-1955)	C	212 634-6899
F R A M Technologies Inc — Brooklyn (G-1956)	G	718 338-6230
F-O-R Software LLC — New York (G-10173)	F	212 231-9506
F-O-R Software LLC — White Plains (G-17134)	E	914 220-8800
F-O-R Software LLC — New York (G-10174)	G	212 724-3920
▲ Facts On File Inc — New York (G-10179)	D	212 967-8800
Falconstor Software Inc — Melville (G-8347)	C	631 777-5188
Fastnet Software Intl Inc — East Northport (G-4456)	F	888 740-7790
Femtech Women Powered Software — Franklin Square (G-5373)	D	516 328-2631
Fidelus Technologies LLC — New York (G-10211)	D	212 616-7800
Fidesa US Corporation — New York (G-10212)	B	212 269-9000
Filestream Inc — Locust Valley (G-7660)	F	516 759-4100
Findmine Inc — New York (G-10214)	F	925 787-6181
Flextrade Systems Inc — Great Neck (G-5829)	C	516 627-8993
Flogic Inc — Hastings On Hudson (G-6023)	F	914 478-1352
Fog Creek Software Inc — New York (G-10235)	G	866 364-2733
Formats Unlimited Inc — Deer Park (G-4166)	F	631 249-9200
Frazer Computing Inc — Canton (G-3409)	G	315 379-3500
▼ Freshop Inc — Rochester (G-14405)	E	585 738-6035
Fruit St Hlth Pub Benefit Corp — New York (G-10264)	G	347 960-6400
Fuel Data Systems Inc — Middletown (G-8475)	G	800 447-7870
Fusion Telecom Intl Inc — New York (G-10275)	C	212 201-2400
Galaxy Software LLC — Oakdale (G-13075)	G	631 244-8405
Games For Change Inc — New York (G-10292)	G	212 242-4922
Geoweb3d Inc — Vestal (G-16471)	F	607 323-1114
Gifts Software Inc — New York (G-10335)	E	904 438-6000
Glassbox US Inc — New York (G-10348)	D	917 378-2933
Glitnir Ticketing Inc — Levittown (G-7450)	G	516 390-5168
Global Applctions Solution LLC — New York (G-10354)	G	212 741-9595
Globalquest Solutions Inc — Buffalo (G-2992)	F	716 601-3524
Grantoo LLC — New York (G-10392)	G	646 356-0460
Group Commerce Inc — New York (G-10413)	F	646 346-0598
Hailo Network Usa Inc — New York (G-10440)	G	646 561-8552
Happy Software Inc — Saratoga Springs (G-15187)	E	518 584-4668
Health Care Compliance — Jericho (G-7103)	F	516 478-4100
Heartland Commerce Inc — Pearl River (G-13480)	E	845 920-0800
Heineck Associates Inc — Bellport (G-827)	F	631 207-2347
High Performance Sftwr USA Inc — Valley Stream (G-16436)	E	866 616-4958
Hinge Inc — New York (G-10526)	F	502 445-3111
Hovee Inc — New York (G-10565)	F	646 249-6200
Hudson Software Corporation — Elmsford (G-4763)	E	914 773-0400
Human Condition Safety Inc — New York (G-10575)	F	646 867-0644
Huntington Services Inc — Massapequa (G-8209)	G	516 795-8500
Hyperlaw Inc — New York (G-10583)	F	212 873-6982
IAC Search LLC — New York (G-10589)	E	212 314-7300
Iac/Interactivecorp — New York (G-10590)	A	212 314-7300
Identifycom Inc — New York (G-10601)	G	212 235-0000
Idoc Software Inc — New York (G-10603)	G	516 680-9090
Igambit Inc — Smithtown (G-15511)	E	631 670-6777
Incentivate Health LLC — Saratoga Springs (G-15189)	G	518 469-8491
Incycle Software Corp — New York (G-10627)	G	212 626-2608
Indegy Inc — New York (G-10629)	E	866 801-5394
Infinity Augmented Reality Inc — New York (G-10635)	G	917 677-2084
Info Quick Solutions — Liverpool (G-7548)	E	315 463-1400
Infobase Publishing Company — New York (G-10637)	F	212 967-8800
Infor Global Solutions Inc — New York (G-10639)	D	646 336-1700
Informa Solutions Inc — New York (G-10640)	F	516 543-3733
Informatica LLC — New York (G-10641)	F	212 845-7650
Informerly Inc — New York (G-10642)	G	646 238-7137
Innovation MGT Group Inc — Shirley (G-15443)	F	800 889-0987
Inprotopia Corporation — New York (G-10651)	F	917 338-7501
Insight Unlimited Inc — Chappaqua (G-3580)	G	914 861-2090
Insight Venture Partners IV — New York (G-10652)	C	212 230-9200
Inspired Entertainment Inc — New York (G-10653)	F	646 565-3861
Instrumental Software Tech — Saratoga Springs (G-15190)	F	518 602-0001
INTEL Corporation — Getzville (G-5611)	D	408 765-8080
Intelligize Incorporated — New York (G-10661)	F	571 612-8580
International Bus Mchs Corp — Armonk (G-412)	E	914 345-5219
International Bus Mchs Corp — Armonk (G-413)	E	914 499-2000
International MGT Netwrk — New York (G-10679)	F	646 401-0032
Internodal International Inc — Southold (G-15583)	E	631 765-0037
Intralinks Holdings Inc — New York (G-10688)	F	212 543-7700
Invision Inc — New York (G-10694)	G	212 557-5554
Ipsidy Inc — Long Beach (G-7673)	D	407 951-8640
Irene Goodman Literary Agency — New York (G-10699)	G	212 604-0330
Irv Inc — New York (G-10705)	E	212 334-4507
Isimulate LLC — Albany (G-90)	G	877 947-2831
Isisnet LLC — New York (G-10709)	G	212 239-1205
Ivalua Inc — Brooklyn (G-2119)	F	650 930-9710
J9 Technologies Inc — New York (G-10724)	E	412 586-5038
Joseph A Filippazzo Software — Staten Island (G-15715)	G	718 987-1626
Jpm and Associates — Uniondale (G-16319)	F	516 483-4699
Jump Ramp Games Inc — New York (G-10821)	E	212 500-1456
Jumprope Inc — New York (G-10822)	G	347 927-5867
Kaseya US Sales LLC — New York (G-10850)	D	415 694-5700
Kasisto Inc — New York (G-10851)	E	917 734-4750
Kastor Consulting Inc — Bayside (G-767)	E	718 224-9109
Key Computer Svcs of Chelsea — New York (G-10880)	D	212 206-8060
Keynote Systems Corporation — Buffalo (G-3047)	G	716 564-1332
Kindling Inc — New York (G-10889)	F	212 400-6296
Klara Technologies Inc — New York (G-10896)	F	844 215-5272
Knight Life Entertainment — Brooklyn (G-2176)	G	646 733-8911
Kronos Incorporated — Albany (G-97)	E	518 459-5545
Latchable Inc — New York (G-10969)	E	646 833-0604
Latham Software Sciences Inc — Latham (G-7399)	F	518 785-1100
Laurus Development Inc — Buffalo (G-3063)	F	716 823-1202
Learningateway LLC — Brooklyn (G-2204)	G	212 920-7969
Liftforward Inc — New York (G-11023)	F	917 693-4993
Lincdoc LLC — East Rochester (G-4484)	G	585 563-1669
Live Vote II Inc — New York (G-11041)	G	646 343-9053
Livetiles Corp — New York (G-11043)	F	917 472-7887
Lmt Technology Solutions — Rochester (G-14501)	F	585 784-7470
Lookbooks Media Inc — New York (G-11058)	F	646 737-3360
Lovingly LLC — Fishkill (G-5193)	E	845 977-0775
Loyaltyplant Inc — Forest Hills (G-5331)	F	551 221-2701
Luluvise Inc — New York (G-11093)	E	914 309-7812
Lynx Analytics Inc — New York (G-11096)	G	475 227-7347
Madhat Inc — New York (G-11120)	G	518 947-0732
Magic Numbers Inc — New York (G-11132)	G	646 839-8578
Magsoft Corporation — Ballston Spa (G-601)	E	518 877-8390
Maler Technologies Inc — New York (G-11144)	G	212 391-2070
Marcus Goldman Inc — New York (G-11171)	F	212 431-0707
Market Factory Inc — New York (G-11181)	F	212 625-9988
Market Logic Software Inc — New York (G-11182)	F	646 405-1041
Matrixcare Inc — New York (G-11204)	F	518 583-6400
Maven Marketing LLC — New York (G-11207)	F	615 510-3248
Maz Digital Inc — New York (G-11215)	E	646 692-9799
McAfee LLC — New York (G-11218)	F	646 728-1440
Mdamerica Wellness Inc — Melville (G-8365)	F	631 396-0991
Mdcare911 LLC — Brooklyn (G-2291)	F	917 640-4869
Mealplan Corp — New York (G-11231)	G	909 706-8398
Mediapost Communications LLC — New York (G-11238)	E	212 204-2000
Medical Transcription Billing — New York (G-11240)	A	631 863-1198
Medidata Solutions Inc — New York (G-11241)	B	212 918-1800
Medius Software Inc — New York (G-11243)	F	877 295-0058
Meethappy Inc — Seaford (G-15368)	F	917 903-0591
Mej Beats LLC — New York (G-11247)	G	516 707-6655

Employee Codes: A=Over 500 employees, B=251-500
C=101-250, D=51-100, E=20-50, F=10-19, G=5-9

73 BUSINESS SERVICES — SIC SECTION

Company	Code	Phone
Meta Pharmacy Systems Inc — Garden City (G-5534)	E	516 488-6189
Micro Systems Specialists Inc — Millbrook (G-8512)	G	845 677-6150
Microcad Trning Consulting Inc — Lagrangeville (G-7281)	G	617 923-0500
Microcad Trning Consulting Inc — Hauppauge (G-6161)	G	631 291-9484
Microsoft Corporation — White Plains (G-17165)	A	914 323-2150
Microsoft Corporation — Huntington Station (G-6754)	G	631 760-2340
Microsoft Corporation — New York (G-11283)	F	212 245-2100
Microsoft Corporation — Hauppauge (G-6163)	D	516 380-1531
Microstrategy Incorporated — New York (G-11284)	F	888 537-8135
Midas Mdici Group Holdings Inc — New York (G-11285)	G	212 792-0920
Mml Software Ltd — East Setauket (G-4506)	E	631 941-1313
Mnn Holding Company LLC — Brooklyn (G-2331)	F	404 558-5251
Mobile Data Systems Inc — Nesconset (G-8824)	G	631 360-3400
Mobile Hatch Inc — New York (G-11313)	G	212 314-7300
Mobileapp Systems LLC — Buffalo (G-3090)	G	716 667-2780
Mobo Systems Inc — New York (G-11314)	D	212 260-0895
Molabs Inc — New York (G-11319)	G	310 721-6828
Mongodb Inc — New York (G-11326)	A	646 727-4092
Mpr Magazine App Inc — Brooklyn (G-2343)	E	718 403-0303
Multimedia Plus Inc — New York (G-11349)	F	212 982-3229
Nastel Technologies Inc — Plainview (G-13652)	C	631 761-9100
Navatar Group Inc — New York (G-11383)	E	212 863-9655
Nemaris Inc — New York (G-11387)	E	646 794-8648
Nervve Technologies Inc — New York (G-11391)	E	716 800-2250
Netegrity Inc — Central Islip (G-3533)	C	631 342-6000
Netologic Inc — New York (G-11394)	E	212 269-3796
Netsuite Inc — New York (G-11395)	G	646 652-5700
Network Infrstructure Tech Inc — New York (G-11396)	G	212 404-7340
Neverware Inc — New York (G-11401)	F	516 302-3223
New Triad For Collaborative — New York (G-11415)	E	212 873-9610
Nift Group Inc — Brooklyn (G-2381)	G	504 505-1144
Nikish Software Corp — Hauppauge (G-6174)	G	631 754-1618
Nitel Inc — Brooklyn (G-2382)	G	347 731-1558
Noetic Partners Inc — New York (G-11466)	F	212 836-4351
Northrop Grumman Systems Corp — Rome (G-14855)	E	315 336-0500
Numerix LLC — New York (G-11487)	D	212 302-2220
Olympic Software & Consulting — Melville (G-8373)	G	631 351-0655
Omx (us) Inc — New York (G-11518)	A	646 428-2800
On Demand Books LLC — New York (G-11519)	G	212 966-2222
One-Blue LLC — New York (G-11522)	G	212 223-4380
Ontra Presentations LLC — New York (G-11524)	G	212 213-1315
Openfin Inc — New York (G-11526)	G	917 450-8822
Operative Media Inc — New York (G-11528)	C	212 994-8930
Oracle Corporation — New York (G-11531)	C	212 508-7700
Orangenius Inc — New York (G-11532)	F	631 742-0648
Orthstar Enterprises Inc — Horseheads (G-6614)	D	607 562-2100
Os33 Inc — New York (G-11542)	G	708 336-3466
Overture Media Inc — New York (G-11549)	G	917 446-7455
P8h Inc — Brooklyn (G-2414)	E	212 343-1142
Pap Chat Inc — Brooklyn (G-2417)	G	516 350-1888
Par Technology Corporation — New Hartford (G-8853)	D	315 738-0600
Pareteum Corporation — New York (G-11585)	D	212 984-1096
Parlor Labs Inc — New York (G-11590)	G	866 801-7323
Patient Portal Tech Inc — Baldwinsville (G-573)	F	315 638-2030
Patron Technology Inc — New York (G-11598)	G	212 271-4328
Pb Mapinfo Corporation — Troy (G-16269)	A	518 285-6000
Peer Software Incorporated — Hauppauge (G-6186)	G	631 979-1770
Pefin Technologies LLC — New York (G-11617)	G	917 715-3720
Pegasystems Inc — New York (G-11619)	E	212 626-6550
Perry Street Software Inc — New York (G-11644)	G	415 935-1429
Pexip Inc — New York (G-11655)	E	703 338-3544
Piano Software Inc — New York (G-11677)	D	646 350-1999
Pilot Inc — New York (G-11681)	E	212 951-1133
Pilot Inc — New York (G-11682)	E	212 951-1133
Pingmd Inc — New York (G-11684)	G	212 632-2665
Pitney Bowes Software Inc — Troy (G-16272)	F	518 272-0014
Piwik Pro LLC — New York (G-11690)	G	888 444-0049
Plain Digital Inc — Scarsdale (G-15252)	G	914 310-0280
Platform Experts Inc — Brooklyn (G-2438)	G	646 843-7100
Playfitness Corp — Staten Island (G-15743)	G	917 497-5443
Playground NY Inc — Brooklyn (G-2439)	F	505 920-7236
Plectica LLC — New York (G-11698)	G	917 304-7052
Pointman LLC — Buffalo (G-3153)	F	716 842-1439
Poly Software International — Pearl River (G-13488)	G	845 735-9301
Portable Tech Solutions LLC — Calverton (G-3323)	F	631 727-8084
Portware LLC — New York (G-11709)	D	212 425-5233
Powa Technologies Inc — New York (G-11713)	E	347 344-7848
Practicepro Software Systems — Garden City (G-5540)	G	516 222-0010
Preplay Inc — New York (G-11722)	F	917 297-7428
Pretlist — New York (G-11727)	G	646 368-1849
Pricing Engine Inc — New York (G-11728)	F	917 549-3289
Prime Research Solutions LLC — Flushing (G-5291)	G	917 836-7941
Principia Partners LLC — New York (G-11735)	D	212 480-2270
Professional Access LLC — Chappaqua (G-3582)	G	212 432-2844
Proginet Corporation — Garden City (G-5541)	E	516 535-3600
Prospector Network — New York (G-11761)	E	212 601-2781
Pts Financial Technology LLC — New York (G-11766)	E	844 825-7634
Pulse Insights LLC — New York (G-11772)	G	888 718-6860
Pupa Tek Inc — Huntington (G-6710)	G	631 664-7817
Purebase Networks Inc — New York (G-11775)	G	646 670-8964
Qlogix Entertainment LLC — New York (G-11790)	G	215 459-6315
Quality and Asrn Tech Corp — Ridge (G-14106)	G	646 450-6762
Quartet Financial Systems Inc — New York (G-11795)	F	845 358-6071
Quovo Inc — New York (G-11803)	E	646 216-9437
Radnor-Wallace — Port Washington (G-13875)	G	516 767-2131
Raleigh and Drake Pbc — New York (G-11818)	F	212 625-8212
Rational Retention LLC — Albany (G-128)	E	518 489-3000
Rational Retention LLC — Albany (G-129)	E	518 489-3000
Razorfish LLC — New York (G-11834)	F	212 798-6600
Reality Analytics Inc — New York (G-11843)	G	347 363-2200
Reason Software Company Inc — New York (G-11844)	F	646 664-1038
Red Oak Software Inc — Rochester (G-14646)	G	585 454-3170
Reentry Games Inc — New York (G-11848)	G	646 421-0080
Relavis Corporation — New York (G-11855)	E	212 995-2900
Reliant Security — New York (G-11856)	E	917 338-2200
Revivn Inc — Brooklyn (G-2512)	F	347 762-8193
Ringlead Inc — Huntington (G-6714)	F	310 906-0545
Rision Inc — New York (G-11900)	G	212 987-2628
Ritnoa Inc — Bellerose (G-807)	E	212 660-2148
Robert Ehrlich — New York (G-11911)	G	516 353-4617
Robly Digital Marketing LLC — New York (G-11916)	E	917 238-0730
Robocom Us LLC — Farmingdale (G-5111)	F	631 861-2045
Robot Fruit Inc — Huntington (G-6716)	G	631 423-7250
Rockport Pa LLC — New York (G-11920)	F	212 482-8580
Roomactually LLC — New York (G-11934)	G	646 388-1922
RPS Holdings Inc — Ithaca (G-6910)	E	607 257-7778
Ryba Software Inc — Fresh Meadows (G-5459)	G	718 264-9352
S C T — Rochester (G-14685)	F	585 467-7740
Safe Passage International Inc — Rochester (G-14686)	F	585 292-4910
Sakonnet Technology LLC — New York (G-11971)	E	212 849-9267
Salentica Systems Inc — New York (G-11973)	E	212 672-1777
San Jae Educational Resou — Pomona (G-13761)	G	845 364-5458
Sapphire Systems Inc — New York (G-11989)	G	212 905-0100
Sas Institute Inc — New York (G-11995)	F	212 757-3826
▲ Scholastic Corporation — New York (G-12015)	G	212 343-6100
◆ Scholastic Inc — New York (G-12016)	A	800 724-6527
Schoolnet Inc — New York (G-12019)	C	646 496-9000
Sciterra LLC — New York (G-12023)	G	646 883-3724
Sculptgraphicz Inc — Brooklyn (G-2565)	G	646 837-7302
Secured Services Inc — New York (G-12032)	G	866 419-3900
Seed Media Group LLC — New York (G-12035)	E	646 502-7050
Sefaira Inc — New York (G-12037)	E	855 733-2472
Segovia Technology Co — New York (G-12038)	F	212 868-4412
Serendipity Consulting Corp — South Salem (G-15560)	F	914 763-8251
Serraview America Inc — New York (G-12050)	D	800 903-3716

76 MISCELLANEOUS REPAIR SERVICES

Company	Code	Phone
Servicenow Inc, New York (G-12051)	F	914 318-1168
Shake Inc, New York (G-12061)	F	650 544-5479
Shiprite Software Inc, Utica (G-16383)	G	315 733-6191
Shoretel Inc, Rochester (G-14706)	G	877 654-3573
Shritec Consultants Inc, Albertson (G-163)	G	516 621-7072
Siemens Product Life Mgmt Sftw, Fairport (G-4886)	E	585 389-8699
Signpost Inc, New York (G-12096)	C	877 334-2837
Similarweb Inc, New York (G-12099)	F	347 685-5422
Sitecompli LLC, New York (G-12111)	E	800 564-1152
Sixteen Markets Inc, New York (G-12113)	F	347 759-1024
Skillsoft Corporation, Rochester (G-14712)	G	585 240-7500
Skystem LLC, New York (G-12123)	G	877 778-3320
Slidebean Incorporated, New York (G-12127)	F	866 365-0588
Slyde Inc, Long Island City (G-7908)	F	917 331-2114
Smn Medical PC, Rye (G-15094)	F	844 362-2428
Sneakers Software Inc, New York (G-12141)	E	800 877-9221
▲ Social Bicycles Inc, Brooklyn (G-2602)	E	917 746-7624
Softlink International, White Plains (G-17195)	E	914 574-8197
Software & General Services Co, Walworth (G-16573)	G	315 986-4184
Solve Advisors Inc, Rockville Centre (G-14828)	G	646 699-5041
Somml Health LLC, Albany (G-135)	G	518 880-2170
Soroc Technology Corp, Buffalo (G-3220)	G	716 849-5913
Special Circle Inc, New Hyde Park (G-8909)	F	516 595-9988
Spektrix Inc, New York (G-12183)	G	646 741-5110
Spring Inc, New York (G-12194)	G	646 732-0323
Squond Inc, Brooklyn (G-2615)	E	718 778-6630
SS&c Financial Services LLC, Harrison (G-6010)	C	914 670-3600
Stensul Inc, New York (G-12217)	E	212 380-8620
Stop N Shop LLC, Albany (G-138)	G	518 512-9657
Strada Soft Inc, Staten Island (G-15765)	G	718 556-6940
Striata Inc, New York (G-12237)	D	212 918-4677
Structured Retail Products, New York (G-12239)	G	212 224-3692
Structuredweb Inc, New York (G-12240)	E	201 325-3110
Styleclick Inc, New York (G-12246)	D	212 329-0300
Successware Inc, Williamsville (G-17281)	F	716 565-2338
Suite Solutions Inc, Amherst (G-263)	E	716 929-3050
Super Company Inc, Syracuse (G-16071)	G	315 569-5153
Super Software, New City (G-8839)	G	845 735-0000
Superchat LLC, New York (G-12264)	G	212 352-8581
Sutton Place Software Inc, Melville (G-8386)	G	631 421-1737
Symantec Corporation, New York (G-12278)	D	646 487-6000
Symphony Talent LLC, New York (G-12279)	D	212 999-9000
Synced Inc, New York (G-12281)	G	917 565-5591
Synco Technologies Inc, New York (G-12282)	G	212 255-2031
Synergy Resources Inc, Central Islip (G-3538)	E	631 665-2050
Syntel Inc, (G-12285)	F	212 785-9810
Syrasoft LLC, Baldwinsville (G-577)	G	315 708-0341
Systems Trading Inc, Melville (G-8387)	F	718 261-8900
Tabi Inc, Flushing (G-5304)	G	347 701-1051
Talaera, Brooklyn (G-2666)		206 229-0631
Tap2play LLC, New York (G-12304)	G	914 960-6232
Targetprocess Inc, Amherst (G-265)	F	877 718-2617
Teachergaming LLC, New York (G-12311)	F	866 644-9323
Teachley LLC, (G-12313)	G	347 552-1272
Team Builders Inc, Staten Island (G-15769)	F	718 979-1005
Tech Software LLC, Melville (G-8389)	G	516 986-3050
Tel Tech International, Melville (G-8390)	E	516 393-5174
Telmar Information Services, New York (G-12320)		212 725-3000
Tensa Software, White Plains (G-17203)	F	914 686-5376
Tequipment Inc, Huntington Station (G-6764)	D	516 922-3508
Terranua US Corp, New York (G-12324)	F	212 852-9028
Theirapp LLC, New York (G-12333)	E	212 896-1255
Thing Daemon Inc, New York (G-12338)	F	917 746-9895
Thinktrek Inc, New York (G-12339)	F	212 884-8399
▲ Thomson Reuters Corporation, New York (G-12349)	A	646 223-4000
Tika Mobile Inc, New York (G-12359)	G	646 650-5545
Time To Know Inc, New York (G-12368)	F	212 230-1210
Tootter Inc, Brooklyn (G-2684)	E	212 204-7937
Tpa Computer Corp, Carmel (G-3434)	F	877 866-6044
Trac Medical Solutions Inc, Schenectady (G-15329)	G	518 346-7799
Tradepaq Corporation, Tarrytown (G-16134)	F	914 332-9174
Tradewins Publishing Corp, Smithtown (G-15523)	G	631 361-6916
Transportgistics Inc, Mount Sinai (G-8699)	F	631 567-4100
Treauu Inc, New York (G-12417)	G	703 731-0196
Trovvit Inc, Brooklyn (G-2704)	F	718 908-5376
True Erp New York, Hauppauge (G-6241)	E	631 582-7210
Trueex LLC, New York (G-12432)	E	646 786-8526
Tss-Transport Snltn Sstms, New York (G-12439)	G	917 267-8534
Ttg LLC, New York (G-12440)	G	917 777-0959
Tunaverse Media Inc, Hauppauge (G-6242)	G	631 778-8350
Two Rivers Computing Inc, Yonkers (G-17510)	G	914 968-9239
Tyme Global Technologies LLC, New York (G-12455)	E	212 796-1950
U X World Inc, Hawthorne (G-6280)	G	914 375-6167
Udisense Inc, New York (G-12460)	G	858 442-9875
UI Information & Insights Inc, Latham (G-7409)	E	518 640-9200
Upstate Records Management LLC, Keeseville (G-7170)	G	518 834-1144
Urthworx Inc, New York (G-12503)		646 373-7535
Usq Group LLC, New York (G-12514)	G	212 777-7751
Value Spring Technology Inc, Harrison (G-6013)	F	917 705-4658
Varnish Software Inc, New York (G-12530)	G	201 857-2832
Varonis Systems Inc, New York (G-12531)	A	877 292-8767
Varsity Monitor LLC, New York (G-12532)	G	212 691-6292
Vehicle Tracking Solutions LLC, Commack (G-3870)	E	631 586-7400
Velocity Outsourcing LLC, New York (G-12539)	E	212 891-4043
Verris Inc, New York (G-12548)		201 565-1648
Vertana Group LLC, New York (G-12553)	G	646 430-8226
Vhx Corporation, New York (G-12559)	F	347 689-1446
Vicarious Visions Inc, Troy (G-16283)	D	518 283-4090
Viridis Learning Inc, New York (G-12575)	G	347 420-9181
Virtual Frameworks Inc, New York (G-12577)	F	646 690-8207
Virtusphere Inc, Binghamton (G-952)	F	607 760-2207
Virtuvent Inc, New York (G-12579)	G	646 845-0387
Visible Systems Corporation, Oneida (G-13192)	E	508 628-1510
Visual Listing Systems Inc, East Setauket (G-4515)	G	631 689-7222
Vita Rara Inc, Troy (G-16285)	G	518 369-7356
Vizbee Inc, New York (G-12586)	G	650 787-1424
Vline Inc, Brooklyn (G-2753)	G	512 222-5464
Vormittag Associates Inc, Ronkonkoma (G-15023)	G	800 824-7776
Vortex Ventures Inc, North Baldwin (G-12929)	G	516 946-8345
Wagner Technical Services Inc, Newburgh (G-12809)	F	845 566-4018
Watchitoo Inc, New York (G-12623)	G	212 354-5888
Water Oracle, Rhinebeck (G-14073)		845 876-8327
West Internet Trading Company, New York (G-12640)	G	415 484-5848
Wetpaintcom Inc, New York (G-12647)	E	206 859-6300
Whentech LLC, New York (G-12650)	F	212 571-0042
White Label Partners LLC, New York (G-12653)	G	917 445-6650
Whiteboard Ventures Inc, New York (G-12655)	F	855 972-6346
Winesoft International Corp, Yonkers (G-17516)	G	914 400-6247
Wink Inc, New York (G-12672)	E	212 389-1382
Wink Labs Inc, New York (G-12673)	E	916 717-0437
Wizq Inc, New York (G-12675)	F	586 381-9048
Wochit Inc, New York (G-12679)	G	212 979-8343
Woodbury Systems Group Inc, Woodbury (G-17323)	G	516 364-2653
Wrkbook LLC, White Plains (G-17215)	F	914 355-1293
X Function Inc, New York (G-12698)	E	212 231-0092
Xborder Entertainment LLC, Plattsburgh (G-13741)	G	518 726-7036
Ypis of Staten Island Inc, Staten Island (G-15777)	G	718 815-4557
Zedge Inc, New York (G-12727)	D	330 577-3424
Zipari Inc, Brooklyn (G-2795)	E	855 558-7884

76 MISCELLANEOUS REPAIR SERVICES

7692 Welding Repair

Company	Code	Phone
303 Contracting Inc, Orchard Park (G-13271)	E	716 896-2122
A & J Machine & Welding Inc, Farmingdale (G-4932)	F	631 845-7586
AAA Welding and Fabrication of, Rochester (G-14177)	G	585 254-2830

Employee Codes: A=Over 500 employees, B=251-500
C=101-250, D=51-100, E=20-50, F=10-19, G=5-9

76 MISCELLANEOUS REPAIR SERVICES

Company	Code	Phone
Accurate Welding Service Inc	G	516 333-1730
Westbury (G-16988)		
Acro-Fab Ltd	E	315 564-6688
Hannibal (G-5992)		
Airweld Inc	G	631 924-6366
Ridge (G-14103)		
Aj Genco Mch Sp McHy Rdout Svc	F	716 664-4925
Falconer (G-4896)		
Allen Tool Phoenix Inc	G	315 463-7533
East Syracuse (G-4518)		
Alliance Services Corp	F	516 775-7600
Floral Park (G-5198)		
Alliance Welding & Steel Fabg	F	516 775-7600
Floral Park (G-5199)		
Alloy Metal Works Inc	G	631 694-8163
Farmingdale (G-4945)		
Alpine Machine Inc	F	607 272-1344
Ithaca (G-6858)		
ARC TEC Wldg & Fabrication Inc	G	718 982-9274
Staten Island (G-15659)		
Atlantis Equipment Corporation	F	518 733-5910
Stephentown (G-15778)		
▲ Barber Welding Inc	E	315 834-6645
Weedsport (G-16772)		
Benemy Welding & Fabrication	G	315 548-8500
Phelps (G-13553)		
Big Apple Welding Supply	G	718 439-3959
Brooklyn (G-1693)		
Bms Manufacturing Co Inc	E	607 535-2426
Watkins Glen (G-16718)		
Bracci Ironworks Inc	F	718 629-2374
Brooklyn (G-1710)		
Brenseke George Wldg Ir Works	G	631 271-4870
Deer Park (G-4135)		
Broadalbin Manufacturing Corp	E	518 883-5313
Broadalbin (G-1239)		
Bruce Pierce	G	716 731-9310
Sanborn (G-15142)		
C G & Son Machining Inc	F	315 964-2430
Williamstown (G-17257)		
CBM Fabrications Inc	E	518 399-8023
Ballston Lake (G-580)		
Certified Fabrications Inc	F	716 731-8123
Sanborn (G-15144)		
Chautauqua Machine Spc LLC	F	716 782-3276
Ashville (G-424)		
Competicion Mower Repair	G	516 280-6584
Mineola (G-8537)		
Cs Automation Inc	F	315 524-5123
Ontario (G-13220)		
Custom Laser Inc	E	716 434-8600
Lockport (G-7606)		
D & G Welding Inc	G	716 873-3088
Buffalo (G-2918)		
Deck Bros Inc	E	716 852-0262
Buffalo (G-2923)		
Dennies Manufacturing Inc	E	585 393-4646
Canandaigua (G-3371)		
Donald Stefan	G	716 492-1110
Chaffee (G-3561)		
Dorgan Welding Service	G	315 462-9030
Phelps (G-13554)		
E B Industries LLC	E	631 293-8565
Farmingdale (G-4991)		
Eagle Welding Machine	G	315 594-1845
Wolcott (G-17300)		
Etna Tool & Die Corporation	F	212 475-4350
New York (G-10133)		
Excelco/Newbrook Inc	D	716 934-2644
Silver Creek (G-15471)		
F M L Industries Inc	G	607 749-7273
Homer (G-6545)		
Flushing Boiler & Welding Co	G	718 463-1266
Brooklyn (G-1988)		
Formac Welding Inc	G	631 421-5525
Huntington Station (G-6743)		
Fuller Fabrications	G	315 469-7415
Jamesville (G-7080)		
G & C Welding Co Inc	G	516 883-3228
Port Washington (G-13839)		
Gasport Welding & Fabg Inc	F	716 772-7205
Gasport (G-5572)		
Gc Mobile Services Inc	G	914 736-9730
Cortlandt Manor (G-4075)		
Genco John	G	716 483-5446
Jamestown (G-7028)		
General Welding & Fabg Inc	G	716 652-0033
Elma (G-4662)		
General Welding & Fabg Inc	G	716 681-8200
Buffalo (G-2987)		
Guthrie Heli-ARC Inc	G	585 548-5053
Bergen (G-845)		
Hadfield Inc	F	631 981-4314
Ronkonkoma (G-14938)		
Hadleys Fab-Weld Inc	G	315 926-5101
Marion (G-8125)		
Hansen Steel	E	585 398-2020
Farmington (G-5161)		
Hartman Enterprises Inc	D	315 363-7300
Oneida (G-13178)		
Haskell Machine & Tool Inc	F	607 749-2421
Homer (G-6546)		
Haun Welding Supply Inc	G	607 846-2289
Elmira (G-4702)		
Haun Welding Supply Inc	G	315 592-5012
Fulton (G-5474)		
Homer Iron Works LLC	G	607 749-3963
Homer (G-6547)		
Huntington Welding & Iron	G	631 423-3331
Huntington Station (G-6747)		
In Northeast Precision Welding	G	518 441-2260
Castleton On Hudson (G-3447)		
Ingleside Machine Co Inc	D	585 924-3046
Farmington (G-5162)		
Jacksons Welding LLC	G	607 756-2725
Cortland (G-4054)		
▼ Kon Tat Group Corporation	G	718 207-5022
Brooklyn (G-2179)		
L & S Metals Inc	E	716 692-6865
North Tonawanda (G-12998)		
▲ Lagasse Works Inc	G	315 946-9202
Lyons (G-8000)		
Lagoe-Oswego Corp	G	315 343-3160
Rochester (G-14495)		
Linita Design & Mfg Corp	E	716 566-7753
Lackawanna (G-7270)		
M and M Industrial Welding	G	631 451-6044
Medford (G-8286)		
M M Welding	G	315 363-3980
Oneida (G-13180)		
Maple Grove Corp	E	585 492-5286
Arcade (G-396)		
Maria Dionisio Welding Inc	G	631 956-0815
Lindenhurst (G-7493)		
Maspeth Welding Inc	E	718 497-5430
Maspeth (G-8181)		
Meades Welding and Fabricating	G	631 581-1555
Islip (G-6849)		
Mega Tool & Mfg Corp	F	607 734-8398
Elmira (G-4709)		
Miller Metal Fabricating Inc	G	585 359-3400
Rochester (G-14534)		
▲ Modern Mechanical Fab Inc	G	518 298-5177
Champlain (G-3572)		
Mooradian Hydraulics & Eqp Co	F	518 766-3866
Castleton On Hudson (G-3448)		
Ms Spares LLC	G	607 223-3024
Clay (G-3709)		
New Age Ironworks Inc	F	718 277-1895
Brooklyn (G-2366)		
New York Manufacturing Corp	G	585 254-9353
Rochester (G-14553)		
North Country Welding Inc	G	315 788-9718
Watertown (G-16689)		
NY Iron Inc	F	718 302-9000
Long Island City (G-7859)		
Parfuse Corp	E	516 997-1795
Westbury (G-17046)		
Phillip J Ortiz Manufacturing	G	845 226-7030
Hopewell Junction (G-6583)		
Phoenix Welding & Fabg Inc	G	315 695-2223
Phoenix (G-13570)		
Pro-Tech Wldg Fabrication Inc	E	585 436-9855
Rochester (G-14626)		
Qsf Inc	G	585 247-6200
Gates (G-5577)		
Quality Industrial Services	F	716 667-7703
Orchard Park (G-13319)		
Reliable Welding & Fabrication	G	631 758-2637
Patchogue (G-13459)		
REO Welding Inc	F	518 238-1022
Cohoes (G-3780)		
Rini Tank & Truck Service	F	718 384-6606
Brooklyn (G-2514)		
Rj Welding & Fabricating Inc	G	315 523-1288
Clifton Springs (G-3740)		
Robert M Brown	F	607 426-6250
Montour Falls (G-8650)		
Rothe Welding Inc	G	845 246-3051
Saugerties (G-15222)		
S & D Welding Corp	G	631 454-0383
West Babylon (G-16855)		
S J B Fabrication	F	716 895-0281
Buffalo (G-3200)		
Smithers Tools & Mch Pdts Inc	D	845 876-3063
Rhinebeck (G-14070)		
▲ Strecks Inc	E	518 273-4410
Watervliet (G-16714)		
Tangent Machine & Tool Corp	E	631 249-3088
Farmingdale (G-5134)		
▲ Technapulse LLC	F	631 234-8700
Hauppauge (G-6233)		
▲ Tek Weld	F	631 694-5503
Hauppauge (G-6235)		
Tracey Welding Co Inc	G	518 756-6309
Coeymans (G-3770)		
W R P Welding Ltd	G	631 249-8859
Farmingdale (G-5149)		
Walters & Walters Inc	G	347 202-8535
Bronx (G-1493)		
Watkins Welding and Mch Sp Inc	G	914 949-6168
White Plains (G-17209)		
Waynes Welding Inc	E	315 768-6146
Yorkville (G-17547)		
Welding and Brazing Svcs Inc	G	607 397-1009
Richfield Springs (G-14075)		
Welding Chapter of New York	G	212 481-1496
New York (G-12635)		
West Metal Works Inc	E	716 895-4900
Buffalo (G-3278)		

7694 Armature Rewinding Shops

Company	Code	Phone
A & C/Furia Electric Motors	F	914 949-0585
White Plains (G-17100)		
Aai Acquisition LLC	D	800 333-0519
Auburn (G-476)		
Accurate Marine Specialties	G	631 589-5502
Bohemia (G-1000)		
Alpha DC Motors Inc	F	315 432-9039
Syracuse (G-15871)		
B & R Electric Motor Inc	G	631 752-7533
Farmingdale (G-4958)		
B J S Electric	G	845 774-8166
Chester (G-3627)		
Bayshore Electric Motors	G	631 475-1397
Patchogue (G-13441)		
Daves Electric Motors & Pumps	G	212 982-2930
New York (G-9872)		
Electric Motor Specialty Inc	G	716 487-1458
Jamestown (G-7026)		
Ener-G-Rotors Inc	E	518 372-2608
Schenectady (G-15277)		
General Electric Company	E	315 456-3304
Syracuse (G-15971)		
General Electric Company	E	518 459-4110
Albany (G-82)		
Genesis Electrical Motors	G	718 274-7030
Woodside (G-17348)		
Lawtons Electric Motor Service	G	315 393-2728
Ogdensburg (G-13138)		
Longo New York Inc	F	212 929-7128
New York (G-11055)		
Northeastern Electric Motors	G	518 793-5939
Hadley (G-5926)		
Power-Flo Technologies Inc	D	315 399-5801
East Syracuse (G-4568)		
Power-Flo Technologies Inc	E	585 426-4607
Rochester (G-14609)		
Premco Inc	F	914 636-7095
New Rochelle (G-8966)		
Prime Electric Motors Inc	G	718 784-1124
Long Island City (G-7876)		
RC Entps Bus & Trck Inc	G	518 568-5753
Saint Johnsville (G-15123)		
Sunset Ridge Holdings Inc	G	716 487-1458
Jamestown (G-7066)		
Troy Belting and Supply Co	D	518 272-4920
Watervliet (G-16715)		
United Richter Electrical Mtrs	F	716 855-1945
Buffalo (G-3261)		

ALPHABETIC SECTION

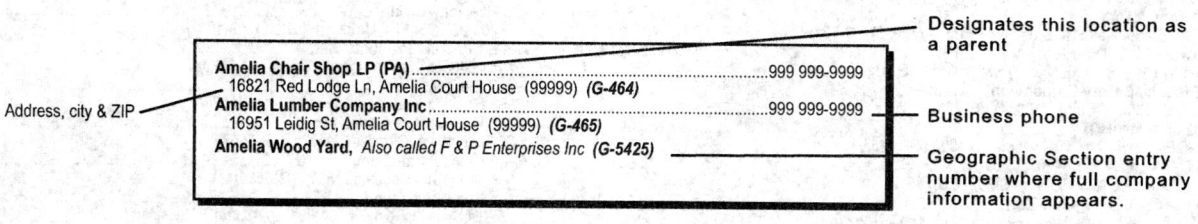

See footnotes for symbols and codes identification.
* Companies listed alphabetically.
* Complete physical or mailing address.

09 Flshy Bll/Dsert Sunrise LLC 518 583-6638
  2 Smith Bridge Rd Saratoga Springs (12866) *(G-15168)*
1 Atelier LLC 917 916-2968
  347 W 36th St New York (10018) *(G-9004)*
1/2 Off Cards Wantagh Inc 516 809-9832
  1162 Wantagh Ave Wantagh (11793) *(G-16576)*
110 Sand Company (PA) 631 694-2822
  136 Spagnoli Rd Melville (11747) *(G-8319)*
110 Sand Company 631 694-2822
  170 Cabot St West Babylon (11704) *(G-16786)*
116 26 Street, Brooklyn *Also called Angel-Made In Heaven Inc (G-1611)*
125-127 Main Street Corp 631 477-1500
  125 Main St 127 Greenport (11944) *(G-5894)*
12pt Printing LLC 718 376-2120
  2053 E 1st St Brooklyn (11223) *(G-1510)*
131-11 Atlantic RE Inc 718 441-7700
  13111 Atlantic Ave Ste 1 Richmond Hill (11418) *(G-14077)*
141 Industries LLC 978 273-8831
  300 E 5th St Apt 11 New York (10003) *(G-9005)*
1510 Associates LLC 212 828-8720
  1500 Lexington Ave New York (10029) *(G-9006)*
16 Tons Inc 718 418-8446
  27 Knickerbocker Ave Brooklyn (11237) *(G-1511)*
17 Bakers LLC 844 687-6836
  8 Los Robles St Williamsville (14221) *(G-17258)*
18 Rocks LLC 631 465-9990
  102 Marcus Dr Melville (11747) *(G-8320)*
180s LLC (HQ) 410 534-6320
  1 Liberty Plz Rm 3500 New York (10006) *(G-9007)*
1884 Collection, New York *Also called Anima Group LLC (G-9211)*
1gpn, New York *Also called First Games Publr Netwrk Inc (G-10219)*
1st Responder Newspaper, New Windsor *Also called Belsito Communications Inc (G-8978)*
2 1 2 Postcards Inc 212 767-8227
  121 Varick St Frnt B New York (10013) *(G-9008)*
2 Elements Real Est LLC 315 635-4662
  33 Water St Baldwinsville (13027) *(G-563)*
2 X 4 Inc 212 647-1170
  180 Varick St Rm 1610 New York (10014) *(G-9009)*
20 Bliss St Inc 716 326-2790
  61 E Main St Westfield (14787) *(G-17073)*
209 Discount Oil 845 386-2090
  10 Sands Station Rd Middletown (10940) *(G-8458)*
212 Biz LLC (PA) 212 391-4444
  525 Fashion Ave Rm 2301 New York (10018) *(G-9010)*
212 Db Corp 212 652-5600
  30 W 22nd St Fl 6 New York (10010) *(G-9011)*
212 Media LLC 212 710-3092
  460 Park Ave S Fl 4 New York (10016) *(G-9012)*
212kiddish Inc 718 705-7227
  168 Spencer St Brooklyn (11205) *(G-1512)*
219 South West 315 474-2065
  219 S West St Syracuse (13202) *(G-15864)*
21st Century Finishes Inc 516 221-7000
  1895 Newbridge Rd North Bellmore (11710) *(G-12931)*
21st Century Fox America Inc (HQ) 212 852-7000
  1211 Ave Of The Americas New York (10036) *(G-9013)*
21st Century Fox America Inc 212 447-4600
  200 Madison Ave Fl 8 New York (10016) *(G-9014)*
21st Century Fox America Inc 845 735-1116
  1 Blue Hill Plz Ste 1525 Pearl River (10965) *(G-13476)*
21st Century Optics Inc (HQ) 347 527-1079
  4700 33rd St Fl 1r Long Island City (11101) *(G-7675)*
24 Seven Enterprises Inc 845 563-9033
  1073 State Route 94 Ste 9 New Windsor (12553) *(G-8974)*
24-Hour Heating & Cooling Svc, New York Mills *Also called Transcolux Corp (G-12747)*
240 Michigan Street Inc 716 434-6010
  240 Michigan St Lockport (14094) *(G-7596)*
260 Oak Street Inc 877 852-4676
  260 Oak St Buffalo (14203) *(G-2802)*

2600 Enterprises Inc 631 474-2677
  2 Flowerfield Ste 30 Saint James (11780) *(G-15113)*
2fish 5loaves Comminty Pantry, Arverne *Also called Armour Bearer Group Inc (G-421)*
2h International Corp 347 623-9380
  6766 108th St Apt D1 Forest Hills (11375) *(G-5324)*
2k Inc 646 536-3007
  622 Broadway Fl 6 New York (10012) *(G-9015)*
2p Agency Usa Inc 212 203-5586
  1674 E 22nd St Apt 3a Brooklyn (11229) *(G-1513)*
3 Bears Gluten Free Bakery 315 323-0277
  51 Market St Potsdam (13676) *(G-13894)*
30 Degrees Weatherproof, New York *Also called David Peyser Sportswear Inc (G-9877)*
303 Contracting Inc (HQ) 716 896-2122
  5486 Powers Rd Orchard Park (14127) *(G-13271)*
30dc Inc (PA) 212 962-4400
  80 Broad St Fl 5 New York (10004) *(G-9016)*
30dc Inc 212 962-4400
  80 Broad St Fl 5 New York (10004) *(G-9017)*
31 Phillip Lim LLC (PA) 212 354-6540
  304 Hudson St Fl 8 New York (10013) *(G-9018)*
311 Industries Corp 607 846-4520
  434 Airport Rd Endicott (13760) *(G-4802)*
3239603400 La Head Quarters, New York *Also called Peer International Corp (G-11613)*
331 Holding Inc 585 924-1740
  100 Rawson Rd Ste 205 Victor (14564) *(G-16482)*
333 J & M Food Corp 718 381-1493
  333 Seneca Ave Ridgewood (11385) *(G-14109)*
369 River Road Inc 716 694-5001
  369 River Rd North Tonawanda (14120) *(G-12970)*
3835 Lebron Rest Eqp & Sup Inc 212 942-8258
  3835 9th Ave New York (10034) *(G-9019)*
39th Street Music-Div, New York *Also called Michael Karp Music Inc (G-11277)*
3b Timber Company Inc 315 942-6580
  8745 Industrial Dr Boonville (13309) *(G-1158)*
3doodler, New York *Also called Wobbleworks Inc (G-12678)*
3g Graphics LLC 716 634-2585
  7138 Transit Rd Amherst (14221) *(G-221)*
3krf LLC 516 208-6824
  3516 Hargale Rd Oceanside (11572) *(G-13090)*
3lab Inc 201 567-9100
  525 7th Ave Rm 2300 New York (10018) *(G-9020)*
3M Company 716 876-1596
  305 Sawyer Ave Tonawanda (14150) *(G-16154)*
3phase Industries LLC 347 763-2942
  481 Van Buren St Unit 9a Brooklyn (11221) *(G-1514)*
3rd Avenue Doughnut Inc 718 748-3294
  7111 3rd Ave Brooklyn (11209) *(G-1515)*
3v Company Inc 718 858-7333
  110 Bridge St Ste 3 Brooklyn (11201) *(G-1516)*
4 Over 4com Inc 718 932-2700
  1941 46th St Astoria (11105) *(G-428)*
40 Street Baking Inc 212 683-4700
  8617 17th Ave Brooklyn (11214) *(G-1517)*
450 Ridge St Inc 716 754-2789
  450 Ridge St Lewiston (14092) *(G-7453)*
461 New Lots Avenue LLC 347 303-9305
  461 New Lots Ave Brooklyn (11207) *(G-1518)*
4695 Main Street Snyder Inc 716 833-3270
  358 Walton Dr Buffalo (14226) *(G-2803)*
4bumpers Llc 212 721-9600
  285 New Wstmnster End Ave New York (10023) *(G-9021)*
4m Precision Industries Inc 315 252-8415
  4000 Technology Park Blvd Auburn (13021) *(G-475)*
5 Star Apparel LLC 212 563-1233
  31 W 34th St Fl 3 New York (10001) *(G-9022)*
5 Stars Printing Corp 718 461-4612
  13330 32nd Ave Flushing (11354) *(G-5227)*
50+ Lifestyle 631 286-0058
  146 S Country Rd Ste 4 Bellport (11713) *(G-819)*

514 Adams Corporation....516 352-6948
781 Hempstead Tpke Franklin Square (11010) ***(G-5369)***
518 Prints LLC....518 674-5346
1548 Burden Lake Rd Ste 4 Averill Park (12018) ***(G-530)***
525 America LLC (PA)....212 921-5688
525 7th Ave Rm 1000 New York (10018) ***(G-9023)***
527 Franco Bakery Corporation....718 993-4200
527 E 138th St Bronx (10454) ***(G-1250)***
54321 Us Inc (HQ)....716 695-0258
295 Fire Tower Dr Tonawanda (14150) ***(G-16155)***
5th & Ocean Clothing Inc....716 604-9000
160 Delaware Ave Buffalo (14202) ***(G-2804)***
5th Avenue Chocolatiere Ltd....516 561-1570
396 Rockaway Ave Valley Stream (11581) ***(G-16423)***
5th Avenue Chocolatiere Ltd (PA)....212 935-5454
114 Church St Freeport (11520) ***(G-5388)***
5th Avenue Pharmacy Inc....718 439-8585
4818 5th Ave Ste 1 Brooklyn (11220) ***(G-1519)***
5yz Logistics LLC....516 813-9500
206 Terminal Dr Plainview (11803) ***(G-13605)***
6727 11th Ave Corp....718 837-8787
6727 11th Ave Brooklyn (11219) ***(G-1520)***
6th Ave Gourmet Inc....845 782-9067
51 Forest Rd Unit 116 Monroe (10950) ***(G-8582)***
6th Avenue Showcase Inc....212 382-0400
241 W 37th St Frnt 2 New York (10018) ***(G-9024)***
760 NI Holdings....716 821-1391
760 Northland Ave Buffalo (14211) ***(G-2805)***
786 Iron Works Corp....718 418-4808
50 Morgan Ave Brooklyn (11237) ***(G-1521)***
79 Metro Ltd (PA)....212 944-4030
265 W 37th St Rm 205 New York (10018) ***(G-9025)***
828 Express Inc....917 577-9019
619 Elbe Ave Staten Island (10304) ***(G-15649)***
872 Hunts Point Pharmacy Inc....718 991-3519
872 Hunts Point Ave Bronx (10474) ***(G-1251)***
888 Pharmacy Inc....718 871-8833
4821 8th Ave Brooklyn (11220) ***(G-1522)***
901 D LLC....845 369-1111
360 Route 59 Ste 3 Airmont (10952) ***(G-10)***
999 Bagels Inc....718 915-0742
1410 86th St Brooklyn (11228) ***(G-1523)***
99cent World and Variety Corp....212 740-0010
4242 Broadway New York (10033) ***(G-9026)***
A & A Graphics Inc II....516 735-0078
615 Arlington Dr Seaford (11783) ***(G-15365)***
A & A Line & Wire Corp....718 456-2657
5118 Grand Ave Ste 10 Maspeth (11378) ***(G-8139)***
A & B Color Corp (del) (PA)....718 441-5482
8204 Lefferts Blvd # 356 Kew Gardens (11415) ***(G-7186)***
A & B Finishing Inc....718 522-4702
401 Park Ave Brooklyn (11205) ***(G-1524)***
A & C/Furia Electric Motors....914 949-0585
75 Lafayette Ave White Plains (10603) ***(G-17100)***
A & D Entrances LLC....718 989-2441
105 Wyandanch Ave Wyandanch (11798) ***(G-17384)***
A & D Offset Printers Ltd....516 746-2476
146 2nd St Apt 3 Mineola (11501) ***(G-8520)***
A & D Tool Inc....631 243-4339
30 Pashen Pl Dix Hills (11746) ***(G-4311)***
A & F Trucking & Excavating, Salamanca *Also called Alice Perkins* ***(G-15125)***
A & G Food Distributors LLC....917 939-3457
21610 47th Ave Apt 3b Bayside (11361) ***(G-757)***
A & G Heat Sealing....631 724-7764
1 Albatross Ln Smithtown (11787) ***(G-15503)***
A & G Precision Corp....631 957-5613
680 Albany Ave Amityville (11701) ***(G-273)***
A & J Machine & Welding Inc....631 845-7586
6040 New Hwy Farmingdale (11735) ***(G-4932)***
A & J Washroom Accessories, New Windsor *Also called Gamma Products Inc* ***(G-8984)***
A & K Equipment Incorporated....705 428-3573
407 Sherman St Watertown (13601) ***(G-16655)***
A & L Asset Management Ltd....718 566-1500
143 Alabama Ave Brooklyn (11207) ***(G-1525)***
A & L Doors & Hardware LLC....718 585-8400
375 E 163rd St Frnt 2 Bronx (10451) ***(G-1252)***
A & L Lighting Ltd....718 821-1188
15 Commercial Blvd Medford (11763) ***(G-8264)***
A & L Machine Company Inc....631 463-3111
200 Blydenburg Rd Ste 9 Islandia (11749) ***(G-6824)***
A & L Pen Manufacturing Corp....718 499-8966
145 12th St Brooklyn (11215) ***(G-1526)***
A & L Shtmtl Fabrications Corp....718 842-1600
1243 Oakpoint Ave Bronx (10474) ***(G-1253)***
A & M LLC....212 354-1341
29 W 46th St New York (10036) ***(G-9027)***
A & M Appel Distributing Inc....516 735-1172
500 N Atlanta Ave Massapequa (11758) ***(G-8206)***
A & M Home Improvement, Maspeth *Also called Andike Millwork Inc* ***(G-8146)***
A & M Litho Inc....516 342-9727
4 Hunt Pl Bethpage (11714) ***(G-860)***
A & M Rosenthal Entps Inc....646 638-9600
8 W 38th St Fl 4 New York (10018) ***(G-9028)***
A & M Steel Stamps Inc....516 741-6223
55 Windsor Ave Mineola (11501) ***(G-8521)***
A & Mt Realty Group LLC....718 974-5871
1979 Pacific St Fl 1 Brooklyn (11233) ***(G-1527)***
A & R Concrete Products LLC....845 562-0640
7 Ruscitti Rd New Windsor (12553) ***(G-8975)***
A & S Electric....212 228-2030
952 Flushing Ave Brooklyn (11206) ***(G-1528)***
A & S Window Associates Inc....718 275-7900
8819 76th Ave Glendale (11385) ***(G-5657)***
A & S Woodworking Inc....518 821-0832
9 Partition St Hudson (12534) ***(G-6630)***
A & T Iron Works Inc....914 632-8992
25 Cliff St New Rochelle (10801) ***(G-8928)***
A & T Tooling LLC....716 601-7299
91 Beach Ave Lancaster (14086) ***(G-7321)***
A & U America's Aids Magazine, Albany *Also called Art & Understanding Inc* ***(G-47)***
A & V Castings Inc....212 997-0042
257 W 39th St Fl 16w New York (10018) ***(G-9029)***
A & W Metal Works Inc....845 352-2346
55 W Railroad Ave 5 Garnerville (10923) ***(G-5566)***
A & Z Pharmaceutical Inc....631 952-3802
350 Wireless Blvd Ste 200 Hauppauge (11788) ***(G-6026)***
A & Z Pharmaceutical Inc (PA)....631 952-3800
180 Oser Ave Hauppauge (11788) ***(G-6027)***
A 3-D Signs & Awnings Inc....718 252-7575
6404 14th Ave Brooklyn (11219) ***(G-1529)***
A A C, Farmingdale *Also called American Aerospace Contrls Inc* ***(G-4948)***
A A P C O Screen Prntng/Sprtwr, Binghamton *Also called Peter Papastrat* ***(G-938)***
A A Technology Inc....631 913-0400
101 Trade Zone Dr Ronkonkoma (11779) ***(G-14873)***
A and J Apparel Corp....212 398-8899
209 W 38th St Rm 1207 New York (10018) ***(G-9030)***
A and K Global Inc....718 412-1876
3312 208th St Bayside (11361) ***(G-758)***
A and K Machine and Welding....631 231-2552
20 Drexel Dr Bay Shore (11706) ***(G-663)***
A and L Home Fuel LLC....607 638-1994
601 Smokey Ave Schenevus (12155) ***(G-15336)***
A Angonoa Inc (PA)....718 762-4466
11505 15th Ave College Point (11356) ***(G-3798)***
A B C Elastic Corp....718 388-2953
889 Metropolitan Ave Brooklyn (11211) ***(G-1530)***
A B C Mc Cleary Sign Co Inc....315 493-3550
40230 State Route 3 Carthage (13619) ***(G-3435)***
A B S Brass Products Inc....718 497-2115
185 Moore St Brooklyn (11206) ***(G-1531)***
A C Envelope Inc....516 420-0646
51 Heisser Ln Ste B Farmingdale (11735) ***(G-4933)***
A C J Communications Inc....631 587-5612
65 Deer Park Ave Ste 2 Babylon (11702) ***(G-541)***
A C T Associates....716 759-8348
10100 Main St Clarence (14031) ***(G-3682)***
A Colarusso and Son Inc (PA)....518 828-3218
91 Newman Rd Hudson (12534) ***(G-6631)***
A D Bowman & Son Lumber Co....607 692-2595
1737 Us Highway 11 Castle Creek (13744) ***(G-3445)***
A D C, Hauppauge *Also called American Diagnostic Corp* ***(G-6040)***
A D K Dental Lab....518 563-6093
87 Hammond Ln Plattsburgh (12901) ***(G-13677)***
A D M, North Tonawanda *Also called Riverfront Costume Design* ***(G-13008)***
A D Mfg Corp....516 352-6161
24844 Jericho Tpke Floral Park (11001) ***(G-5197)***
A D T, Mineola *Also called Aquifer Drilling & Testing Inc* ***(G-8528)***
A Division A & Liquid Systems, North Tonawanda *Also called Buffalo Pumps Inc* ***(G-12981)***
A E P, Yaphank *Also called American Electronic Products* ***(G-17402)***
A Esteban & Company Inc (PA)....212 989-7000
132 W 36th St Rm 1000 New York (10018) ***(G-9031)***
A Esteban & Company Inc....212 714-2227
132 W 36th St Rm 1000 New York (10018) ***(G-9032)***
A Fleisig Paper Box Corp....212 226-7490
1751 2nd Ave Apt 10a New York (10128) ***(G-9033)***
A G I, Rochester *Also called Advanced Glass Industries Inc* ***(G-14193)***
A G M Deco Inc....718 624-6200
305 Wallabout St 307 Brooklyn (11206) ***(G-1532)***
A G M Deco Inc (PA)....718 624-6200
741 Myrtle Ave Brooklyn (11205) ***(G-1533)***
A G Master Crafts Ltd....516 745-6262
5 South St Ste A Garden City (11530) ***(G-5506)***
A Garys Treasures....518 383-1171
629 Plank Rd Clifton Park (12065) ***(G-3719)***
A Gatty Products Inc....914 592-3903
1 Warehouse Ln Elmsford (10523) ***(G-4741)***
A Gatty Svce, Elmsford *Also called A Gatty Products Inc* ***(G-4741)***
A Graphic Printing Inc....212 233-9696
49 Market St Frnt 2 New York (10002) ***(G-9034)***
A Guideposts Church Corp....212 251-8100
16 E 34th St Fl 21 New York (10016) ***(G-9035)***
A H Schreiber Co Inc (PA)....212 594-7234
460 W 34th St Fl 10 New York (10001) ***(G-9036)***
A Health Obsession LLC....347 850-4587
2184 Mcdonald Ave Brooklyn (11223) ***(G-1534)***

ALPHABETIC SECTION

Abalene Decorating Services

A Hyatt Ball Co Ltd 518 747-0272
School St Fort Edward (12828) ***(G-5347)***

A I M, Victor *Also called Advanced Interconnect Mfg Inc* ***(G-16483)***

A I P Printing & Stationers 631 929-5529
6198 N Country Rd Wading River (11792) ***(G-16543)***

A I T Computers Inc 518 266-9010
157 Hoosick St Troy (12180) ***(G-16245)***

A J C Jewelry Contracting Inc 212 594-3703
247 W 30th St Fl 3 New York (10001) ***(G-9037)***

A J Congress, New York *Also called American Jewish Congress Inc* ***(G-9172)***

A J Gnco Mch Shp/Mchnery Rdout, Falconer *Also called Aj Genco Mch Sp McHy Rdout Svc* ***(G-4896)***

A J Hollander Enterprises, Inwood *Also called Hastings Hide Inc* ***(G-6798)***

A J M Enterprises 716 626-7294
348 Cayuga Rd Buffalo (14225) ***(G-2806)***

A Jaffe Inc 212 843-7464
592 5th Ave Fl 3 New York (10036) ***(G-9038)***

A K A Computer Consulting Inc 718 351-5200
1412 Richmond Rd Staten Island (10304) ***(G-15650)***

A K Allen Co Inc 516 747-5450
255 E 2nd St Mineola (11501) ***(G-8522)***

A L Eastmond & Sons Inc (PA) 718 378-3000
1175 Leggett Ave Bronx (10474) ***(G-1254)***

A L Sealing 315 699-6900
2280 Osborne Rd Chittenango (13037) ***(G-3659)***

A Losee & Sons 516 676-3060
68 Landing Rd Glen Cove (11542) ***(G-5621)***

A Lunt Design Inc 716 662-0781
5755 Big Tree Rd Orchard Park (14127) ***(G-13272)***

A M & J Digital 518 434-2579
800 N Pearl St Ste 5 Menands (12204) ***(G-8395)***

A M F/Coughlin Printing, Watertown *Also called Coughlin Printing Group* ***(G-16668)***

A M I, New York *Also called Weider Publications LLC* ***(G-12632)***

A M S Sign Designs 631 467-7722
2360 Middle Country Rd Centereach (11720) ***(G-3494)***

A Nuclimate Qulty Systems Inc 315 431-0226
1 General Motors Dr Ste 5 Syracuse (13206) ***(G-15865)***

A P Manufacturing 909 228-3049
21 Floyds Run Bohemia (11716) ***(G-996)***

A P S, Hicksville *Also called Applied Power Systems Inc* ***(G-6346)***

A Petteys Lumber, Fort Ann *Also called Petteys Lumber* ***(G-5344)***

A Q P Inc 585 256-1690
2975 Brighton Henrietta T Rochester (14623) ***(G-14175)***

A R Arena Products Inc 585 277-1680
2101 Mount Read Blvd Rochester (14615) ***(G-14176)***

A R V Precision Mfg Inc 631 293-9643
60 Baiting Place Rd Ste B Farmingdale (11735) ***(G-4934)***

A S A Precision Co Inc 845 482-4870
295 Jffersonville N Br Rd Jeffersonville (12748) ***(G-7092)***

A S L, Brooklyn *Also called American Scientific Ltg Corp* ***(G-1606)***

A S P, Albany *Also called Albany Student Press Inc* ***(G-41)***

A Strongwater Designs, New York *Also called Andrea Strongwater* ***(G-9202)***

A Sunshine Glass & Aluminum 718 932-8080
2901 Brooklyn Queens Expy Woodside (11377) ***(G-17334)***

A T A Bagel Shoppe Inc 718 352-4948
20814 Cross Island Pkwy Bayside (11360) ***(G-759)***

A T C, Oyster Bay *Also called American Trans-Coil Corp* ***(G-13390)***

A T M, Hornell *Also called Fortitude Industries* ***(G-6589)***

A Thousand Cranes Inc 212 724-9596
208 W 79th St Apt 2 New York (10024) ***(G-9039)***

A To Z Kosher Meat Products Co 718 384-7400
123 Borinquen Pl Brooklyn (11211) ***(G-1535)***

A To Z Media Inc (PA) 212 260-0237
243 W 30th St Fl 6 New York (10001) ***(G-9040)***

A Tradition of Excellence Inc 845 638-4595
85b Maple Ave New City (10956) ***(G-8828)***

A Trusted Name Inc 716 326-7400
35 Franklin St Westfield (14787) ***(G-17074)***

A V T, New York *Also called AV Therapeutics Inc* ***(G-9323)***

A Van Hoek Woodworking Limited 718 599-4388
71 Montrose Ave Brooklyn (11206) ***(G-1536)***

A W Hamel Stair Mfg Inc 518 346-3031
3111 Amsterdam Rd Schenectady (12302) ***(G-15256)***

A W R Group Inc 718 729-0412
3715 Hunters Point Ave Long Island City (11101) ***(G-7676)***

A W S, Port Chester *Also called D & M Enterprises Incorporated* ***(G-13769)***

A Yashir Bapa, New York *Also called AZ Yashir Bapaz Inc* ***(G-9338)***

A Zimmer Ltd 315 422-7011
W Tenesee St Syracuse (13204) ***(G-15866)***

A&B Conservation LLC 845 282-7272
12 Maple Leaf Rd Monsey (10952) ***(G-8601)***

A&B Iron Works Inc 347 466-3193
137 Conover St Brooklyn (11231) ***(G-1537)***

A&B McKeon Glass Inc 718 525-2152
69 Roff St Staten Island (10304) ***(G-15651)***

A&M Model Makers LLC 626 813-9661
1675 Wayneport Rd Ste 1 Macedon (14502) ***(G-8006)***

A&P Master Images LLC 315 793-1934
205 Water St Utica (13502) ***(G-16328)***

A&S Refrigeration Equipment 718 993-6030
557 Longfellow Ave Bronx (10474) ***(G-1255)***

A-1 Iron Works Inc 718 927-4766
2413 Atlantic Ave Brooklyn (11233) ***(G-1538)***

A-1 Manhattan Custom Furn Inc 212 750-9800
4315 Austin Blvd Island Park (11558) ***(G-6817)***

A-1 Products Inc 718 789-1818
165 Classon Ave Brooklyn (11205) ***(G-1539)***

A-1 Skull Cap Corp 718 633-9333
1212 36th St Brooklyn (11218) ***(G-1540)***

A-1 Stamping & Spinning Corp 718 388-2626
225 Beach 143rd St Rockaway Park (11694) ***(G-14812)***

A-1 Transitmix Inc 718 292-3200
431 E 165th St Frnt 1 Bronx (10456) ***(G-1256)***

A-Fab Initiatives Inc 716 877-5257
99 Bud Mil Dr Buffalo (14206) ***(G-2807)***

A-Implant Dental Lab Corp 212 582-4720
10 Park Ave New York (10016) ***(G-9041)***

A-Line Technologies Inc 607 772-2439
197 Corporate Dr Binghamton (13904) ***(G-881)***

A-Mark Machinery Corp 631 643-6300
101 Lamar St West Babylon (11704) ***(G-16787)***

A-One Laminating Corp 718 266-6002
1636 Coney Island Ave 2b Brooklyn (11230) ***(G-1541)***

A-One Moving & Storage Inc 718 266-6002
1725 Avenue M Brooklyn (11230) ***(G-1542)***

A-Plus Restaurant Equipment 718 522-2656
623 Sackett St Brooklyn (11217) ***(G-1543)***

A-Quick Bindery LLC 631 491-1110
30 Gleam St Unit C West Babylon (11704) ***(G-16788)***

A-R Payne Cabinet Comp, Brooklyn *Also called Ralph Payne* ***(G-2496)***

A. Lange & Sohne Corporate, New York *Also called Richemont North America Inc* ***(G-11889)***

A.L. Blades, Hornell *Also called Dolomite Products Company Inc* ***(G-6587)***

A.S.I. Fancies Ltd, New York *Also called Antwerp Sales Intl Inc* ***(G-9221)***

A/C Design & Fabrication Corp 718 227-8100
638 Sharrotts Rd Staten Island (10309) ***(G-15652)***

A1 International Heat Treating 718 863-5552
905 Brush Ave Bronx (10465) ***(G-1257)***

A1 Ornamental Iron Works Inc 718 265-3055
61 Jefferson St Brooklyn (11206) ***(G-1544)***

A1 Skullcaps, Brooklyn *Also called A-1 Skull Cap Corp* ***(G-1540)***

A2ia Corp 917 237-0390
24 W 40th St Fl 3 New York (10018) ***(G-9042)***

A3 Apparel LLC 888 403-9669
1407 Broadway Rm 716a New York (10018) ***(G-9043)***

AAa Amercn Flag Dctg Co Inc 212 279-3524
36 W 37th St Rm 409 New York (10018) ***(G-9044)***

AAA Catalytic Recycling Inc 631 920-7944
345 Eastern Pkwy Farmingdale (11735) ***(G-4935)***

AAA Noodle Products Mfg 212 431-4090
102 Bowery New York (10013) ***(G-9045)***

AAA Welding and Fabrication of 585 254-2830
1085 Lyell Ave Rochester (14606) ***(G-14177)***

AAAA York Inc 718 784-6666
3720 12th St Long Island City (11101) ***(G-7677)***

Aaaaaa Creative Designs, New York *Also called Paper Box Corp* ***(G-11576)***

Aaaaar Orthopedics Inc 845 278-4938
141 Main St Brewster (10509) ***(G-1203)***

Aabacs Group Inc 718 961-3577
1509 132nd St College Point (11356) ***(G-3799)***

Aabco Sheet Metal Co Inc (PA) 718 821-1166
47 40 Metropolitan Ave Ridgewood (11385) ***(G-14110)***

Aai Acquisition LLC 800 333-0519
70 Wright Cir Auburn (13021) ***(G-476)***

Aai Manufacturing Div, Bronx *Also called Sharon Metal Stamping Corp* ***(G-1450)***

Aakron Rule Corp (PA) 716 542-5483
8 Indianola Ave Akron (14001) ***(G-17)***

Aalborg Instrs & Contrls Inc 845 398-3160
20 Corporate Dr Orangeburg (10962) ***(G-13238)***

Aand D Maintenance, Bridgehampton *Also called Bridgehampton Steel & Wldg Inc* ***(G-1230)***

AAR Allen Services Inc 516 222-9000
747 Zeckendorf Blvd Garden City (11530) ***(G-5507)***

Aarco Products Inc 631 924-5461
21 Old Dock Rd Yaphank (11980) ***(G-17400)***

Aarfid LLC (PA) 716 992-3999
3780 Yochum Rd Eden (14057) ***(G-4597)***

Aaron Group LLC 718 392-5454
115 S Macquesten Pkwy Mount Vernon (10550) ***(G-8701)***

Aaron Tool & Mold Inc 585 426-5100
620 Trolley Blvd Rochester (14606) ***(G-14178)***

Aatc, Medford *Also called American Avionic Tech Corp* ***(G-8266)***

Aatech, Clyde *Also called Advanced Atomization Tech LLC* ***(G-3749)***

Aavid Niagara LLC (HQ) 716 297-0652
3315 Haseley Dr Niagara Falls (14304) ***(G-12817)***

AB Engine 518 557-3510
4a Northway Ln Latham (12110) ***(G-7377)***

AB Fire Inc 917 416-6444
1554 61st St Brooklyn (11219) ***(G-1545)***

Abaco Steel Products Inc 631 589-1800
1560 Locust Ave Bohemia (11716) ***(G-997)***

Abalene Decorating Services 718 782-2000
315 W 39th St Rm 611 New York (10018) ***(G-9046)***

ALPHABETIC

Abalon Precision Mfg Corp (PA) 914 665-7700
717 S 3rd Ave Mount Vernon (10550) ***(G-8702)***

Abalon Precision Mfg Corp 718 589-5682
717 S 3rd Ave Mount Vernon (10550) ***(G-8703)***

Abasco Inc 716 649-4790
5225 Southwestern Blvd Hamburg (14075) ***(G-5941)***

Abbe Laboratories Inc 631 756-2223
1095 Broadhollow Rd Ste E Farmingdale (11735) ***(G-4936)***

Abbeville Press Inc 212 366-5585
116 W 23rd St Fl 5 New York (10011) ***(G-9047)***

Abbeville Publishing Group, New York *Also called Abbeville Press Inc* ***(G-9047)***

Abble Awning Co Inc 516 822-1200
313 Broadway Ste 315 Bethpage (11714) ***(G-861)***

Abbot & Abbot Box Corp 888 930-5972
3711 10th St Long Island City (11101) ***(G-7678)***

Abbot & Abbot Packing Service, Long Island City *Also called Abbot & Abbot Box Corp* ***(G-7678)***

Abbot Flag Co Div, Spring Valley *Also called Eagle Regalia Co Inc* ***(G-15604)***

Abbott Industries Inc (PA) 718 291-0800
9525 149th St Jamaica (11435) ***(G-6926)***

ABC Casting, Jamaica *Also called Technical Service Industries* ***(G-6992)***

ABC Check Printing Corp 718 855-4702
544 Park Ave Ste 308 Brooklyn (11205) ***(G-1546)***

ABC Peanut Butter LLC 212 661-6886
295 Madison Ave Ste 1618 New York (10017) ***(G-9048)***

ABC Showerdoors, Brooklyn *Also called All United Window Corp* ***(G-1587)***

ABC Television Network, New York *Also called Times Square Studios Ltd* ***(G-12371)***

ABC Windows and Signs Corp 718 353-6210
12606 18th Ave College Point (11356) ***(G-3800)***

Abco Printing Company, Brooklyn *Also called RBHM Incorporated* ***(G-2500)***

Abdo Shtmtl & Fabrication Inc 315 894-4664
4293 Acme Rd Frankfort (13340) ***(G-5358)***

Abe Pool Service 845 473-7730
793 Violet Ave Hyde Park (12538) ***(G-6771)***

Abel Noser Solutions LLC 646 432-4000
1 Battery Park Plz # 601 New York (10004) ***(G-9049)***

Abercrombie & Fitch, Brooklyn *Also called Apsco Sports Enterprises Inc* ***(G-1622)***

Aberdeen Blower & Shtmtl Works 631 661-6100
401 Columbus Ave West Babylon (11704) ***(G-16789)***

Abetter Processing Corp 718 252-2223
984 E 35th St Brooklyn (11210) ***(G-1547)***

ABG Accessories, New York *Also called Elegant Headwear Co Inc* ***(G-10051)***

Abh Natures Products Inc 631 249-5783
131 Heartland Blvd Edgewood (11717) ***(G-4602)***

Abh Pharma Inc 631 392-4692
131 Heartland Blvd Edgewood (11717) ***(G-4603)***

ABI Packaging Inc 716 677-2900
1703 Union Rd West Seneca (14224) ***(G-16967)***

Abigal Press Inc 718 641-5350
9735 133rd Ave Ozone Park (11417) ***(G-13401)***

Abk Enterprises Inc 631 348-0555
403 E Suffolk Ave Central Islip (11749) ***(G-3508)***

Abkco Music & Records Inc (PA) 212 399-0300
85 5th Ave Fl 11 New York (10003) ***(G-9050)***

Able Anodizing Corp 718 252-0660
1767 Bay Ridge Ave Brooklyn (11204) ***(G-1548)***

Able Electronics Inc 631 924-5386
18 Sawgrass Dr Bellport (11713) ***(G-820)***

Able Environmental Services 631 567-6585
1599 Ocean Ave Bohemia (11716) ***(G-998)***

Able Industries Inc 914 739-5685
18 Brook Ln Cortlandt Manor (10567) ***(G-4072)***

Able Kitchen 877 268-1264
540 Willow Ave Unit B Cedarhurst (11516) ***(G-3482)***

Able Kitchen Supplies, Cedarhurst *Also called Able Kitchen* ***(G-3482)***

Able National Corp 718 386-8801
49 Wyckoff Ave Brooklyn (11237) ***(G-1549)***

Able Printing, West Babylon *Also called Weicro Graphics Inc* ***(G-16872)***

Able Steel Equipment Co Inc 718 361-9240
5002 23rd St Long Island City (11101) ***(G-7679)***

Able Weldbuilt Industries Inc 631 643-9700
1050 Grand Blvd Deer Park (11729) ***(G-4110)***

Able Wire Co, Cortlandt Manor *Also called Able Industries Inc* ***(G-4072)***

Above The Rest Baking Corp 718 313-9222
531-533 Bryant Ave Bronx (10474) ***(G-1258)***

Abp International Inc 212 490-3999
1466 Broadway Ste 910 New York (10036) ***(G-9051)***

Abr Molding Andy LLC 212 576-1821
1624 Centre St Ridgewood (11385) ***(G-14111)***

ABRA Media Inc 518 398-1010
2773 W Church St Pine Plains (12567) ***(G-13581)***

Abra-Ka-Data Systems Ltd 631 667-5550
39 W Jefryn Blvd Ste 1 Deer Park (11729) ***(G-4111)***

Abraham Jwly Designers & Mfrs 212 944-1149
37 W 47th St Ste 202 New York (10036) ***(G-9052)***

Abraxis Bioscience LLC 716 773-0800
3159 Staley Rd Grand Island (14072) ***(G-5764)***

Abrimian Bros Corp 212 382-1106
48 W 48th St Ste 805 New York (10036) ***(G-9053)***

ABS Metal Corp 646 302-9018
58 Holly Rd Hewlett (11557) ***(G-6330)***

ABS Talkx Inc 631 254-9100
34 Cleveland Ave Bay Shore (11706) ***(G-664)***

Absolute Business Products, Port Washington *Also called Jaidan Industries Inc* ***(G-13849)***

Absolute Coatings Inc 914 636-0700
38 Portman Rd New Rochelle (10801) ***(G-8929)***

Absolute Color Corporation 212 868-0404
109 W 27th St Frnt 2 New York (10001) ***(G-9054)***

Absolute Engineering Company, Bohemia *Also called Absolute Manufacturing Inc* ***(G-999)***

Absolute Fitness US Corp 732 979-8582
21337 39th Ave Ste 322 Bayside (11361) ***(G-760)***

Absolute Manufacturing Inc 631 563-7466
210 Knickerbocker Ave Bohemia (11716) ***(G-999)***

ABT, Great Neck *Also called Advanced Barcode Tech Inc* ***(G-5799)***

Abtex Corporation 315 536-7403
89 Main St Dresden (14441) ***(G-4342)***

Abyrx Inc 914 357-2600
1 Bridge St Ste 121 Irvington (10533) ***(G-6808)***

AC Air Cooling Co Inc 718 933-1011
1637 Stillwell Ave Bronx (10461) ***(G-1259)***

AC Air Cooling Company, Bronx *Also called Air Wave Air Conditioning Co* ***(G-1266)***

AC DC Power Systems & Contrls, Poughkeepsie *Also called Protective Power Systms & Cntr* ***(G-13944)***

AC Moore Incorporated 516 796-5831
3988 Hempstead Tpke Bethpage (11714) ***(G-862)***

Aca Quality Building Pdts LLC 718 991-2423
1322 Garrison Ave Bronx (10474) ***(G-1260)***

Acad Design Corp 585 254-6960
975 Mount Read Blvd Rochester (14606) ***(G-14179)***

Academy of Political Science 212 870-2500
475 Riverside Dr Ste 1274 New York (10115) ***(G-9055)***

Academy Printing Services Inc 631 765-3346
42 Hortons Ln Southold (11971) ***(G-15581)***

Acadia Stairs 845 765-8600
73 Route 9 Ste 3 Fishkill (12524) ***(G-5187)***

Accede Mold & Tool Co Inc 585 254-6490
1125 Lexington Ave Rochester (14606) ***(G-14180)***

Accel Printing & Graphics 914 241-3369
128 Radio Circle Dr Ste 2 Mount Kisco (10549) ***(G-8663)***

Accela Inc 631 563-5005
100 Comac St Ste 2 Ronkonkoma (11779) ***(G-14874)***

Accelify Solutions LLC 888 922-2354
16 W 36th St Rm 902 New York (10018) ***(G-9056)***

Accent Label & Tag Co Inc (PA) 631 244-7066
348 Woodlawn Ave Ronkonkoma (11779) ***(G-14875)***

Accent Printing &GRaphics, Wayland *Also called Specialty Services* ***(G-16735)***

Accent Speaker Technology Ltd 631 738-2540
1511 Lincoln Ave Holbrook (11741) ***(G-6455)***

Accenta Incorporated 716 565-6262
150 Lawrence Bell Dr # 108 Buffalo (14221) ***(G-2808)***

Accesory Headquarters, New York *Also called Ahq LLC* ***(G-9112)***

Access 24 845 358-5397
570 Kings Hwy Fl 4 Valley Cottage (10989) ***(G-16400)***

Access Display Group Inc 516 678-7772
151 S Main St Freeport (11520) ***(G-5389)***

Access Elevator & Lift Inc (PA) 716 483-3696
1209 E 2nd St Jamestown (14701) ***(G-7003)***

Access Intelligence LLC 212 204-4269
249 W 17th St New York (10011) ***(G-9057)***

Access Products Inc 800 679-4022
241 Main St Ste 100 Buffalo (14203) ***(G-2809)***

Accessible Bath Tech LLC 518 937-1518
6 Albright Ave Albany (12203) ***(G-30)***

Accessories For Electronics 631 847-0158
620 Mead Ter South Hempstead (11550) ***(G-15553)***

Accessory Plays LLC 212 564-7301
29 W 36th St New York (10018) ***(G-9058)***

Accessory Street LLC 212 686-8990
1370 Broadway New York (10018) ***(G-9059)***

Accessries Direct Intl USA Inc 646 448-8200
1450 Broadway Fl 22 New York (10018) ***(G-9060)***

Accipiter Radar Corporation 716 508-4432
40 Centre Dr Ste 3 Orchard Park (14127) ***(G-13273)***

Acco Brands USA LLC 847 541-9500
941 Acco Way Ogdensburg (13669) ***(G-13130)***

Acco North America, Ogdensburg *Also called Acco Brands USA LLC* ***(G-13130)***

Accolade USA Inc 866 423-5071
60 Industrial Pkwy # 397 Cheektowaga (14227) ***(G-3590)***

Accord Pipe Fabricators Inc 718 657-3900
9226 180th St Jamaica (11433) ***(G-6927)***

Accounts Payable Department, Ronkonkoma *Also called Natures Bounty Co* ***(G-14976)***

Accra Sheetmetal LLC 631 920-2087
1359 Straight Path Wyandanch (11798) ***(G-17385)***

Accredo Health Incorporated 718 353-3012
14330 38th Ave Apt 1f Flushing (11354) ***(G-5228)***

Accu Coat Inc 585 288-2330
111 Humboldt St Ste 8 Rochester (14609) ***(G-14181)***

Accucut Inc 631 567-2868
120 Easy St West Sayville (11796) ***(G-16962)***

Accumed Corp 716 853-1800
2564 Walden Ave Ste 101 Buffalo (14225) ***(G-2810)***

Accumetrics Inc 716 684-0002
6 British American Blvd # 100 Latham (12110) ***(G-7378)***

Accumetrics Associates Inc 518 393-2200
6 British American Blvd # 100 Latham (12110) ***(G-7379)***
Accuprint (PA) 518 456-2431
2005 Western Ave Ste 1 Albany (12203) ***(G-31)***
Accurate Industrial Machining 631 242-0566
1711 Church St Holbrook (11741) ***(G-6456)***
Accurate Knitting Corp 646 552-2216
1478 E 26th St Brooklyn (11210) ***(G-1550)***
Accurate Marine Specialties 631 589-5502
2200 Artic Ave Bohemia (11716) ***(G-1000)***
Accurate McHning Incorporation 315 689-1428
251 State Route 5 Elbridge (13060) ***(G-4636)***
Accurate Metal Weather Strip 914 668-6042
725 S Fulton Ave Mount Vernon (10550) ***(G-8704)***
Accurate Pnt Powdr Coating Inc 585 235-1650
606 Hague St Rochester (14606) ***(G-14182)***
Accurate Precast 718 345-2910
1957 Pitkin Ave Brooklyn (11207) ***(G-1551)***
Accurate Signs & Awnings Inc 718 788-0302
247 Prospect Ave Ste 2 Brooklyn (11215) ***(G-1552)***
Accurate Specialty Metal Fabri 718 418-6895
6420 Admiral Ave Middle Village (11379) ***(G-8442)***
Accurate Tool & Die LLC 585 254-2830
1085 Lyell Ave Rochester (14606) ***(G-14183)***
Accurate Welding Service Inc 516 333-1730
615 Main St Westbury (11590) ***(G-16988)***
Accurate Welding Svce, Westbury *Also called Accurate Welding Service Inc* ***(G-16988)***
Accusonic Voice Systems, Edgewood *Also called Global Market Development Inc* ***(G-4613)***
Accutrak Inc 212 925-5330
432 Washington St Ste 113 New York (10013) ***(G-9061)***
Accuvein Inc (PA) 816 997-9400
3243 Route 112 Ste 2 Medford (11763) ***(G-8265)***
Ace, Brooklyn *Also called Montrose Equipment Sales Inc* ***(G-2337)***
Ace Banner & Flag Company 212 620-9111
107 W 27th St New York (10001) ***(G-9062)***
Ace Banner Flag & Graphics, New York *Also called Ace Banner & Flag Company* ***(G-9062)***
Ace Canvas & Tent Corp 631 648-0614
155 Raynor Ave Ronkonkoma (11779) ***(G-14876)***
Ace Cntracting Consulting Corp 631 567-4752
515 Johnson Ave Bohemia (11716) ***(G-1001)***
Ace Diamond Corp 212 730-8231
30 W 47th St Ste 808r New York (10036) ***(G-9063)***
Ace Drop Cloth Canvas Pdts Inc 718 731-1550
4216 Park Ave Bronx (10457) ***(G-1261)***
Ace Drop Cloth Co, Bronx *Also called Ace Drop Cloth Canvas Pdts Inc* ***(G-1261)***
Ace Fire Door Corp 718 901-0001
4000 Park Ave Bronx (10457) ***(G-1262)***
Ace Manufacturing, Rochester *Also called Jam Industries Inc* ***(G-14479)***
Ace Molding & Tool Inc 631 567-2355
51 Floyds Run Bohemia (11716) ***(G-1002)***
Ace Printing & Publishing Inc 718 939-0040
14951 Roosevelt Ave Flushing (11354) ***(G-5229)***
Ace Printing Co, Flushing *Also called Ace Printing & Publishing Inc* ***(G-5229)***
Ace Specialty Co Inc 716 874-3670
695 Ensminger Rd Tonawanda (14150) ***(G-16156)***
Acec, New York *Also called America Capital Energy Corp* ***(G-9161)***
Acem, Deer Park *Also called American Casino Equipment Mfg* ***(G-4119)***
Aces Over Eights Inc 585 292-9690
1100 Jefferson Rd Ste 22 Rochester (14623) ***(G-14184)***
Acf Industries Holding LLC (HQ) 212 702-4363
767 5th Ave New York (10153) ***(G-9064)***
Achilles Construction Co Inc 718 389-4717
373 Hayward Ave Mount Vernon (10552) ***(G-8705)***
Acj Communications, Massapequa Park *Also called Massapequa Post* ***(G-8221)***
Acker & Ll Mills Corporation 212 307-7247
44 W 62nd St Apt 3b New York (10023) ***(G-9065)***
Ackroyd Metal Fabricators Inc 518 434-1281
966 Broadway Ste 2 Menands (12204) ***(G-8396)***
Acl, Thornwood *Also called Automated Control Logic Inc* ***(G-16139)***
Acm, New York *Also called Association For Cmpt McHy Inc* ***(G-9292)***
Acme Architectural Products 718 360-0700
513 Porter Ave Brooklyn (11222) ***(G-1553)***
Acme Architectural Pdts Inc (PA) 718 384-7800
251 Lombardy St Brooklyn (11222) ***(G-1554)***
Acme Architectural Walls, Brooklyn *Also called Acme Architectural Pdts Inc* ***(G-1554)***
Acme Awning Co Inc 718 409-1881
435 Van Nest Ave Bronx (10460) ***(G-1263)***
Acme Engineering Products Inc 518 236-5659
2330 State Route 11 Mooers (12958) ***(G-8654)***
Acme Industries of W Babylon 631 737-5231
125 Gary Way Ste 2 Ronkonkoma (11779) ***(G-14877)***
Acme Kitchenettes Corp 518 828-4191
4269 Us Route 9 Hudson (12534) ***(G-6632)***
Acme Marine, Calverton *Also called US Hoists Corp* ***(G-3330)***
Acme Marine Hoist, Bellport *Also called Thego Corporation* ***(G-838)***
Acme Nipple Mfg Co Inc 716 873-7491
1930 Elmwood Ave Buffalo (14207) ***(G-2811)***
Acme Office Group, Brooklyn *Also called New Dimensions Office Group* ***(G-2370)***
Acme Parts Inc 718 649-1750
901 Elton St Brooklyn (11208) ***(G-1555)***
Acme Precision Screw Pdts Inc 585 328-2028
623 Glide St Rochester (14606) ***(G-14185)***
Acme Screenprinting LLC 716 565-1052
247 Cayuga Rd Ste 25e Buffalo (14225) ***(G-2812)***
Acme Signs of Baldwinsville 315 638-4865
3 Marble St Baldwinsville (13027) ***(G-564)***
Acme Smoked Fish Corp (PA) 954 942-5598
30 Gem St 56 Brooklyn (11222) ***(G-1556)***
Acolyte Technologies Corp 212 629-3239
44 E 32nd St Rm 901 New York (10016) ***(G-9066)***
Acorda Therapeutics Inc (PA) 914 347-4300
420 Saw Mill River Rd Ardsley (10502) ***(G-402)***
Acorn, New York *Also called Music Sales Corporation* ***(G-11350)***
Acorn Products Corp 315 894-4868
27 Pleasant Ave Ilion (13357) ***(G-6778)***
Acran Spill Containment Inc (PA) 631 841-2300
599 Albany Ave Amityville (11701) ***(G-274)***
Acro Industries Inc 585 254-3661
554 Colfax St Rochester (14606) ***(G-14186)***
Acro-Fab Ltd 315 564-6688
55 Rochester St Hannibal (13074) ***(G-5992)***
Acrolite, Elbridge *Also called Accurate McHning Incorporation* ***(G-4636)***
Acrs Inc 914 288-8100
1311 Mmroneck Ave Ste 260 White Plains (10605) ***(G-17101)***
ACS, Ballston Spa *Also called Advanced Comfort Systems Inc* ***(G-588)***
Act Communications Group Inc 631 669-2403
170 Higbie Ln West Islip (11795) ***(G-16932)***
Actasys Inc 617 834-0666
805 25th St Watervliet (12189) ***(G-16702)***
Actavis Laboratories Ny Inc 631 693-8000
33 Ralph Ave Copiague (11726) ***(G-3915)***
Actinium Pharmaceuticals Inc 646 677-3870
275 Madison Ave Ste 702 New York (10016) ***(G-9067)***
Action Bullet Resistant 631 422-0888
263 Union Blvd West Islip (11795) ***(G-16933)***
Action Machined Products Inc 631 842-2333
1355 Bangor St Copiague (11726) ***(G-3916)***
Action Rack Display Mfg 718 257-7111
980 Alabama Ave Brooklyn (11207) ***(G-1557)***
Action Technologies Inc 718 278-1000
3809 33rd St Apt 1 Long Island City (11101) ***(G-7680)***
Actioncraft Products Inc 516 883-6423
2 Manhasset Ave Port Washington (11050) ***(G-13818)***
Active Business Systems, Long Island City *Also called Action Technologies Inc* ***(G-7680)***
Active Manufacturing Inc 607 775-3162
32 Laughlin Rd Kirkwood (13795) ***(G-7257)***
Active Process Supply, New York *Also called Standard Screen Supply Corp* ***(G-12206)***
Active World Solutions Inc 718 922-9404
609 Fountain Ave Brooklyn (11208) ***(G-1558)***
Actuant Corporation 607 753-8276
44 River St Cortland (13045) ***(G-4033)***
Actv Inc (del Corp) (HQ) 212 995-9500
233 Park Ave S Fl 10 New York (10003) ***(G-9068)***
Acu Rite Companies Inc 716 661-1700
1 Precision Way Jamestown (14701) ***(G-7004)***
Acuity Polymers Inc 585 458-8409
1667 Lake Ave Ste 303 Rochester (14615) ***(G-14187)***
Ad Makers Long Island Inc 631 595-9100
60 E Jefryn Blvd Ste 3 Deer Park (11729) ***(G-4112)***
Ad Notam LLC 631 951-2020
135 Ricefield Ln Hauppauge (11788) ***(G-6028)***
Ad Publications Inc 585 248-2888
8 Greenwood Park Pittsford (14534) ***(G-13584)***
Ad Vantage Press 212 941-8355
481 Washington St Fl 7 New York (10013) ***(G-9069)***
Ada Gems Corp 212 719-0100
10 W 47th St Ste 707 New York (10036) ***(G-9070)***
Adam Scott Designs Inc 212 420-8866
118 E 25th St Fl 11 New York (10010) ***(G-9071)***
Adamor Inc 212 688-8885
17 E 48th St Rm 901 New York (10017) ***(G-9072)***
Adams Interior Fabrications 631 249-8282
8 Iroquois Pl Massapequa (11758) ***(G-8207)***
Adams Lumber Co Inc 716 358-2815
6052 Adams Rd Cattaraugus (14719) ***(G-3464)***
Adams Press, Franklin Square *Also called 514 Adams Corporation* ***(G-5369)***
Adams Ridge, Lancaster *Also called Markar Architectural Products* ***(G-7350)***
Adams Sfc Inc (HQ) 716 877-2608
225 E Park Dr Tonawanda (14150) ***(G-16157)***
Adaptive Mfg Tech Inc 631 580-5400
181 Remington Blvd Ronkonkoma (11779) ***(G-14878)***
Adar Medical Uniform LLC 718 935-1197
307 Richardson St Brooklyn (11222) ***(G-1559)***
Adart Poly Bag Mfg, Plainview *Also called Adart Polyethylene Bag Mfg* ***(G-13606)***
Adart Polyethylene Bag Mfg 516 932-1001
1 W Ames Ct Ste 201 Plainview (11803) ***(G-13606)***
ADC Acquisition Company 518 377-6471
2 Commerce Park Rd Niskayuna (12309) ***(G-12910)***
ADC Dolls Inc 212 244-4500
112 W 34th St Ste 1207 New York (10120) ***(G-9073)***
ADC Industries Inc (PA) 516 596-1304
181a E Jamaica Ave Valley Stream (11580) ***(G-16424)***

ALPHABETIC

(PA)=Parent Co (HQ)=Headquarters (DH)=Div Headquarters
2018 Harris
New York Manufacturers Directory
883

Adco Innvtive Prmtnal Pdts Inc — 716 805-1076
300 Delaware Ave Ste 202 Buffalo (14202) *(G-2813)*
Adcomm Graphics Inc — 212 645-1298
21 Lamar St West Babylon (11704) *(G-16790)*
Add Associates Inc — 315 449-3474
6333 Daedalus Rd Cicero (13039) *(G-3670)*
Addeo Bakers Inc — 718 367-8316
2372 Hughes Ave Bronx (10458) *(G-1264)*
Addex Inc — 315 331-7700
251 Murray St Newark (14513) *(G-12748)*
Addex Inc (PA) — 781 344-5800
251 Murray St Newark (14513) *(G-12749)*
Addison Precision Mfg Corp — 585 254-1386
500 Avis St Rochester (14615) *(G-14188)*
Additude Magazine, New York Also called New Hope Media LLC *(G-11411)*
Adel Rootstein (usa) Inc — 718 499-5650
145 18th St Brooklyn (11215) *(G-1560)*
Adelphi Paper Hangings — 518 284-9066
102 Main St Sharon Springs (13459) *(G-15404)*
Adeptronics Incorporated — 631 667-0659
281 Skip Ln Ste C Bay Shore (11706) *(G-665)*
Adesso Inc (PA) — 212 736-4440
360 W 31st St Rm 909 New York (10001) *(G-9074)*
Adf Accessories Inc — 516 450-5755
381 Sunrise Hwy Unit 5r Lynbrook (11563) *(G-7971)*
Adflex Corporation — 585 454-2950
300 Ormond St Rochester (14605) *(G-14189)*
Adgorithmics LLC (PA) — 646 277-8728
260 Madison Ave Fl 8 New York (10016) *(G-9075)*
ADI, Brooklyn Also called Audible Difference Inc *(G-1652)*
Adir Publishing Co — 718 633-9437
1212 36th St Brooklyn (11218) *(G-1561)*
Adirondack Beverage Co Inc, Schenectady Also called Scotia Beverages Inc *(G-15318)*
Adirondack Chocolate Co Ltd (PA) — 518 946-7270
5680 Ny State Rte 86 Wilmington (12997) *(G-17290)*
Adirondack Daily Enterprise, Saranac Lake Also called Adirondack Publishing Co Inc *(G-15162)*
ADIRONDACK EXPLORER, Saranac Lake Also called Getting The Word Out Inc *(G-15165)*
Adirondack Home News, Holland Patent Also called Steffen Publishing Inc *(G-6514)*
Adirondack Ice & Air Inc — 518 483-4340
26 Railroad St Malone (12953) *(G-8036)*
Adirondack Leather Pdts Inc — 607 547-5798
196 Cemetery Rd Fly Creek (13337) *(G-5317)*
Adirondack Life Inc (PA) — 518 946-2191
Rr 9 Box North Jay (12941) *(G-7088)*
Adirondack Life Magazine, Jay Also called Adirondack Life Inc *(G-7088)*
Adirondack Machine Corporation — 518 792-2258
84 Boulevard St Hudson Falls (12839) *(G-6669)*
Adirondack Meat Company Inc — 518 585-2333
30 Commerce Dr Ticonderoga (12883) *(G-16146)*
Adirondack Natural Stone LLC — 518 499-0602
8986 State Route 4 Whitehall (12887) *(G-17217)*
Adirondack Outdoor Center LLC (PA) — 315 369-2300
2839 State Route 28 Old Forge (13420) *(G-13152)*
Adirondack Pennysaver Inc — 518 563-0100
177 Margaret St Plattsburgh (12901) *(G-13678)*
Adirondack Plas & Recycl Inc (PA) — 518 746-9212
453 County Route 45 Argyle (12809) *(G-406)*
Adirondack Power Sports — 518 481-6269
5378 State Route 37 Malone (12953) *(G-8037)*
Adirondack Precision Cut Stone (PA) — 518 681-3060
536 Queensbury Ave Queensbury (12804) *(G-14001)*
Adirondack Publishing Co Inc (HQ) — 518 891-2600
54 Broadway Saranac Lake (12983) *(G-15162)*
Adirondack Sanitary Service, Ticonderoga Also called Adirondack Waste MGT Inc *(G-16147)*
Adirondack Scenic Inc — 518 638-8000
439 County Route 45 Ste 1 Argyle (12809) *(G-407)*
Adirondack Sign Perfect Inc — 518 409-7446
72 Ballston Ave Saratoga Springs (12866) *(G-15169)*
Adirondack Splcty Adhsives Inc — 518 869-5736
4258 Albany St Albany (12205) *(G-32)*
Adirondack Stained Glass Works — 518 725-0387
29 W Fulton St Ste 6 Gloversville (12078) *(G-5719)*
Adirondack Stairs Inc — 845 246-2525
990 Kings Hwy Saugerties (12477) *(G-15207)*
Adirondack Studios, Argyle Also called Adirondack Scenic Inc *(G-407)*
Adirondack Waste MGT Inc — 518 585-2224
963 New York State 9n Ticonderoga (12883) *(G-16147)*
Adirondack-Aire, Rome Also called Cold Point Corporation *(G-14838)*
Adirondex, Malone Also called Adirondack Ice & Air Inc *(G-8036)*
Aditiany Inc — 212 997-8440
37 W 39th St Rm 1100 New York (10018) *(G-9076)*
Adjmi Apparel Group, New York Also called Beluga Inc *(G-9400)*
Adjustable Shelving, Melville Also called Karp Associates Inc *(G-8362)*
Adl Data Systems Inc — 914 591-1800
9 Skyline Dr Ste 4 Hawthorne (10532) *(G-6265)*
Adl Design Inc — 516 949-6658
4 W Mall Dr Huntington (11743) *(G-6685)*
ADM, Buffalo Also called Archer-Daniels-Midland Company *(G-2838)*
ADM, Hudson Also called Archer-Daniels-Midland Company *(G-6635)*
ADM, Lakeville Also called Archer-Daniels-Midland Company *(G-7305)*
ADM Milling Co — 716 849-7333
250 Ganson St Buffalo (14203) *(G-2814)*
Admor Blinds & Window Fashion, Westbury Also called KPP Ltd *(G-17031)*
Adobe Systems Inc — 212 471-0904
1540 Broadway Fl 17 New York (10036) *(G-9077)*
Adobe Systems Incorporated — 212 592-1400
100 5th Ave Fl 5 New York (10011) *(G-9078)*
Adobe Systems Incorporated — 212 471-0904
8 W 40th St Fl 8 New York (10018) *(G-9079)*
Adotta America, New York Also called Europrojects Intl Inc *(G-10140)*
Adpro Sports LLC — 716 854-5116
55 Amherst Villa Rd Buffalo (14225) *(G-2815)*
Adrean Printing, New Rochelle Also called Vic-Gina Printing Company Inc *(G-8973)*
Adria Machine & Tool Inc — 585 889-3360
966 North Rd Scottsville (14546) *(G-15355)*
Adrian Jules Ltd — 585 342-5886
1392 E Ridge Rd Rochester (14621) *(G-14190)*
Adrian-Jules Custom Tailor, Rochester Also called Adrian Jules Ltd *(G-14190)*
Adriatic Wood Products Inc — 718 922-4621
1994 Industrial Park Rd Brooklyn (11207) *(G-1562)*
Adrienne Landau Designs Inc — 212 695-8362
519 8th Ave Fl 21 New York (10018) *(G-9080)*
Ads-N-Color Inc — 718 797-0900
20 Jay St Ste 530 Brooklyn (11201) *(G-1563)*
Adsco Manufacturing Corp — 716 827-5450
4979 Lake Ave Buffalo (14219) *(G-2816)*
Adstream America LLC (HQ) — 212 804-8498
345 7th Ave Fl 6 New York (10001) *(G-9081)*
Adtech, Rochester Also called Analog Digital Technology LLC *(G-14219)*
Adtech Us Inc — 212 402-4840
770 Broadway Fl 4 New York (10003) *(G-9082)*
Adults and Children With Learn — 516 593-8230
22 Alice Ct East Rockaway (11518) *(G-4487)*
Advan-Tech Manufacturing Inc — 716 667-1500
3645 California Rd Orchard Park (14127) *(G-13274)*
Advance Apparel Intl Inc — 212 944-0984
265 W 37th St Rm 906 New York (10018) *(G-9083)*
Advance Biofactures Corp — 516 593-7000
35 Wilbur St Lynbrook (11563) *(G-7972)*
Advance Chemicals Usa Inc — 718 633-1030
1230 57th St Brooklyn (11219) *(G-1564)*
Advance Circuit Technology Inc — 585 328-2000
19 Jetview Dr Rochester (14624) *(G-14191)*
Advance Construction Group, New York Also called B & F Architectural Support Gr *(G-9340)*
Advance D Tech Inc — 845 534-8248
2 Mill St Stop 19 Cornwall (12518) *(G-4006)*
Advance Energy Systems NY LLC — 315 735-5125
17 Tilton Rd Utica (13501) *(G-16329)*
Advance Energy Tech Inc — 518 371-2140
1 Solar Dr Halfmoon (12065) *(G-5930)*
Advance Finance Group LLC — 212 630-5900
101 Park Ave Frnt New York (10178) *(G-9084)*
Advance Food Service Co Inc — 631 242-4800
200 Heartland Blvd Edgewood (11717) *(G-4604)*
Advance Grafix Equipment Inc — 917 202-4593
150 Wyandanch Ave Wyandanch (11798) *(G-17386)*
ADVANCE MAGAZINE PUBLISHERS, INC., New York Also called Advance Magazine Publs Inc *(G-9087)*
Advance Magazine Publs Inc (HQ) — 212 286-2860
1 World Trade Ctr Fl 43 New York (10007) *(G-9085)*
Advance Magazine Publs Inc — 212 790-4422
1166 Ave Of The Amrcs 14 New York (10036) *(G-9086)*
Advance Magazine Publs Inc — 212 286-2860
1166 Ave Of The Amrcs 1 New York (10036) *(G-9087)*
Advance Magazine Publs Inc — 212 450-7000
711 3rd Ave Rm 700 New York (10017) *(G-9088)*
Advance Magazine Publs Inc — 212 697-0126
750 3rd Ave Frnt G New York (10017) *(G-9089)*
Advance Micro Power Corp — 631 471-6157
2190 Smithtown Ave Ronkonkoma (11779) *(G-14879)*
Advance Pharmaceutical Inc (PA) — 631 981-4600
895 Waverly Ave Holtsville (11742) *(G-6525)*
Advance Precision Industries — 631 491-0910
9 Mahan St Unit A West Babylon (11704) *(G-16791)*
Advance Pressure Products, Ithaca Also called Porous Materials Inc *(G-6906)*
Advance Publications Inc (PA) — 718 981-1234
950 W Fingerboard Rd Staten Island (10305) *(G-15653)*
Advance Tabco Inc (HQ) — 631 242-8270
200 Heartland Blvd Edgewood (11717) *(G-4605)*
Advanced Aerospace Machining — 631 694-7745
154 Rome St Farmingdale (11735) *(G-4937)*
Advanced Assembly Services Inc — 716 217-8144
35 S Main St Angola (14006) *(G-378)*
Advanced Atomization Tech LLC — 315 923-2341
124 Columbia St Clyde (14433) *(G-3749)*
Advanced Back Technologies — 631 231-0076
89 Ste F Cabot Ct Hauppauge (11788) *(G-6029)*
Advanced Barcode Tech Inc — 516 570-8100
175 E Shore Rd Ste 228 Great Neck (11023) *(G-5799)*
Advanced Business Group Inc — 212 398-1010
266 W 37th St Fl 15 New York (10018) *(G-9090)*

Advanced Cmpt Sftwr Consulting 718 300-3577
2236 Pearsall Ave Bronx (10469) ***(G-1265)***
Advanced Coating Service LLC 585 247-3970
15 Hytec Cir Rochester (14606) ***(G-14192)***
Advanced Coating Techniques 631 643-4555
313 Wyandanch Ave Babylon (11704) ***(G-542)***
Advanced Coating Technologies, Amherst *Also called Bekaert Corporation* ***(G-229)***
Advanced Comfort Systems Inc 518 884-8444
12b Commerce Dr Ballston Spa (12020) ***(G-588)***
Advanced Comm Solutions 914 693-5076
38 Ridge Rd Ardsley (10502) ***(G-403)***
Advanced Cyber Security Corp 866 417-9155
3880 Veterans Memorial Hw Bohemia (11716) ***(G-1003)***
Advanced Digital Info Corp 607 266-4000
10 Brown Rd Ithaca (14850) ***(G-6856)***
Advanced Digital Printing LLC 718 649-1500
65 W 36th St Fl 11 New York (10018) ***(G-9091)***
Advanced Distribution System 845 848-2357
275 Oak Tree Rd Palisades (10964) ***(G-13425)***
Advanced Door Solutions Inc 631 773-6100
1363 Lincoln Ave Ste 7 Holbrook (11741) ***(G-6457)***
Advanced Doors, Holbrook *Also called Advanced Door Solutions Inc* ***(G-6457)***
Advanced Enterprises Inc 845 342-1009
366 Highland Ave Ext Middletown (10940) ***(G-8459)***
Advanced Fashions Technology 212 221-0606
110 W 40th St Rm 1100 New York (10018) ***(G-9092)***
Advanced Foam Products Div, Buffalo *Also called Tmp Technologies Inc* ***(G-3246)***
Advanced Frozen Foods Inc 516 333-6344
28 Urban Ave Westbury (11590) ***(G-16989)***
Advanced Glass Industries Inc 585 458-8040
1335 Emerson St Rochester (14606) ***(G-14193)***
Advanced Graphics Company 607 692-7875
2607 Main St Whitney Point (13862) ***(G-17248)***
Advanced Interconnect Mfg Inc (HQ) 585 742-2220
780 Canning Pkwy Victor (14564) ***(G-16483)***
Advanced Machine Design Co Inc 716 826-2000
45 Roberts Ave Buffalo (14206) ***(G-2817)***
Advanced Machine Inc 585 423-8255
439 Central Ave Ste 108 Rochester (14605) ***(G-14194)***
Advanced Manufacturing Svc Inc 631 676-5210
100 13th Ave Ste 2 Ronkonkoma (11779) ***(G-14880)***
Advanced Medical Mfg Corp 845 369-7535
7-11 Suffern Pl Ste 2 Suffern (10901) ***(G-15806)***
Advanced Mfg Techniques 518 877-8560
453 Kinns Rd Clifton Park (12065) ***(G-3720)***
Advanced Mtl Analytics LLC 321 684-0528
85 Murray Hl Rd Ste 2115 Vestal (13850) ***(G-16461)***
Advanced Photonics Inc 631 471-3693
151 Trade Zone Dr Ronkonkoma (11779) ***(G-14881)***
Advanced Placement LLC 949 281-9086
60 Lorraine Ct Holbrook (11741) ***(G-6458)***
Advanced Polymer Solutions LLC 516 621-5800
99 Seaview Blvd Ste 1a Port Washington (11050) ***(G-13819)***
Advanced Polymers Intl, Syracuse *Also called Royal Adhesives & Sealants LLC* ***(G-16049)***
Advanced Precision Technology 845 279-3540
577 N Main St Ste 7 Brewster (10509) ***(G-1204)***
Advanced Printing New York Inc 212 840-8108
263 W 38th St New York (10018) ***(G-9093)***
Advanced Prosthetics Orthotics 516 365-7225
50 Maple Pl Manhasset (11030) ***(G-8087)***
Advanced Quickprinting, Rochester *Also called A Q P Inc* ***(G-14175)***
Advanced Ready Mix Corp 718 497-5020
239 Ingraham St Brooklyn (11237) ***(G-1565)***
Advanced Recovery & Recycl LLC 315 450-3301
3475 Linda Ln Baldwinsville (13027) ***(G-565)***
Advanced Research Media Inc 631 751-9696
60 Route 25a Ste 1 Setauket (11733) ***(G-15398)***
Advanced Response Corporation 212 459-0887
345 W 58th St Apt 11a New York (10019) ***(G-9094)***
Advanced Rubber Products, Wyoming *Also called Tmp Technologies Inc* ***(G-17399)***
Advanced Structures Corp (PA) 631 667-5000
235 W Industry Ct Deer Park (11729) ***(G-4113)***
Advanced Surface Finishing 516 876-9710
111 Magnolia Ave Westbury (11590) ***(G-16990)***
Advanced Tchncal Solutions Inc 914 214-8230
2986 Navajo Rd Ste 100 Yorktown Heights (10598) ***(G-17522)***
Advanced Technology Division, Plainview *Also called Technic Inc* ***(G-13665)***
Advanced Thermal Systems Inc 716 681-1800
15 Enterprise Dr Lancaster (14086) ***(G-7322)***
Advanced Yarn Technologies Inc 518 239-6600
4750 State Hwy 145 Durham (12422) ***(G-4378)***
Advantage Machining Inc 716 731-6418
6421 Wendt Dr Niagara Falls (14304) ***(G-12818)***
Advantage Metalwork Finshg LLC 585 454-0160
1000 University Ave # 700 Rochester (14607) ***(G-14195)***
Advantage Orthotics Inc 631 368-1754
337 Larkfield Rd East Northport (11731) ***(G-4452)***
Advantage Plus Diagnostics Inc 631 393-5044
200 Broadhollow Rd Melville (11747) ***(G-8321)***
Advantage Press Inc 518 584-3405
74 Warren St Saratoga Springs (12866) ***(G-15170)***
Advantage Printing Inc 718 820-0688
12034 Queens Blvd Ste 310 Kew Gardens (11415) ***(G-7187)***
Advantage Quick Print Inc 212 989-5644
30 E 33rd St Frnt B New York (10016) ***(G-9095)***
Advantage Wholesale Supply LLC 718 284-5346
172 Empire Blvd Brooklyn Brooklyn (11225) ***(G-1566)***
Advantage Wood Shop, Cheektowaga *Also called Stereo Advantage Inc* ***(G-3617)***
Advantech Industries Inc 585 247-0701
3850 Buffalo Rd Rochester (14624) ***(G-14196)***
Advantex Solutions Inc 718 278-2290
24845 Jericho Tpke Bellerose (11426) ***(G-805)***
Advd Heart Phys & Surgs 212 434-3000
130 E 77th St Fl 4 New York (10075) ***(G-9096)***
Adventure Publishing Group 212 575-4510
307 7th Ave Rm 1601 New York (10001) ***(G-9097)***
Advertiser, Albany *Also called Capital Region Wkly Newspapers* ***(G-58)***
Advertiser Publications Inc 845 783-1111
148 State Route 17m Chester (10918) ***(G-3625)***
Advertiser, The, Averill Park *Also called Capital Reg Wkly Newsppr Group* ***(G-531)***
Advertising Lithographers 212 966-7771
121 Varick St Fl 9 New York (10013) ***(G-9098)***
Advion Inc (PA) 607 266-9162
10 Brown Rd Ste 101 Ithaca (14850) ***(G-6857)***
Advis Inc 585 568-0100
2218 River Rd Caledonia (14423) ***(G-3302)***
Ae Fund Inc 315 698-7650
5860 Mckinley Rd Brewerton (13029) ***(G-1199)***
Aegis Oil Limited Ventures LLC 646 233-4900
14 Wall St Fl 20 New York (10005) ***(G-9099)***
Aeon America Inc 914 584-0275
80 5th Ave Ste 1805 New York (10011) ***(G-9100)***
AEP Environmental LLC 716 446-0739
2495 Main St Ste 230 Buffalo (14214) ***(G-2818)***
Aerco International Inc (HQ) 845 580-8000
100 Oritani Dr Blauvelt (10913) ***(G-963)***
Aero Brand Inks, Blue Point *Also called Specialty Ink Co Inc* ***(G-995)***
Aero Healthcare (us) LLC 855 225-2376
616 Corporate Way Ste 6 Valley Cottage (10989) ***(G-16401)***
Aero Specialties Manufacturing 631 242-7200
20 Burt Dr Deer Park (11729) ***(G-4114)***
Aero Trades Mfg Corp 516 746-3360
65 Jericho Tpke Mineola (11501) ***(G-8523)***
Aero-Data Metal Crafters Inc 631 471-7733
2085 5th Ave Ronkonkoma (11779) ***(G-14882)***
Aero-Vision Technologies Inc (PA) 631 643-8349
7 Round Tree Dr Melville (11747) ***(G-8322)***
Aerobic Wear Inc 631 673-1830
16 Depot Rd Huntington Station (11746) ***(G-6730)***
Aeroduct Inc 516 248-9550
134 Herricks Rd Mineola (11501) ***(G-8524)***
Aeroflex Holding Corp 516 694-6700
35 S Service Rd Plainview (11803) ***(G-13607)***
Aeroflex Incorporated (HQ) 516 694-6700
35 S Service Rd Plainview (11803) ***(G-13608)***
Aeroflex Plainview Inc (HQ) 516 694-6700
35 S Service Rd Plainview (11803) ***(G-13609)***
Aeroflex Plainview Inc 631 231-9100
350 Kennedy Dr Hauppauge (11788) ***(G-6030)***
Aerolase Corporation 914 345-8300
777 Old Saw Mill River Rd # 2 Tarrytown (10591) ***(G-16108)***
Aeromed Inc 518 843-9144
1821 Broad St Ste 1 Utica (13501) ***(G-16330)***
Aerospace Lighting Corporation (HQ) 631 563-6400
355 Knickerbocker Ave Bohemia (11716) ***(G-1004)***
Aerospace Wire & Cable Inc 718 358-2345
12909 18th Ave College Point (11356) ***(G-3801)***
AES Electronics Inc 212 371-8120
135 E 54th St Apt 10j New York (10022) ***(G-9101)***
Aesthonics Inc 646 723-2463
21 Belvidere St Fl 3 Brooklyn (11206) ***(G-1567)***
AF Design Inc 347 548-5273
1239 Broadway Ste 310 New York (10001) ***(G-9102)***
Afab Initiative, Buffalo *Also called American Douglas Metals Inc* ***(G-2824)***
AFC Industries Inc 718 747-0237
1316 133rd Pl Ste 1 College Point (11356) ***(G-3802)***
Afco Modular Enclosure Systems, Farmingdale *Also called Afco Systems Inc* ***(G-4938)***
Afco Precast Sales Corp 631 924-7114
114 Rocky Point Rd Middle Island (11953) ***(G-8438)***
Afco Systems Inc 631 249-9441
200 Finn Ct Ste 1 Farmingdale (11735) ***(G-4938)***
Afe, South Hempstead *Also called Accessories For Electronics* ***(G-15553)***
Aferge Mds, Rochester *Also called GE Mds LLC* ***(G-14410)***
Affco, New Windsor *Also called American Felt & Filter Co Inc* ***(G-8977)***
Affiliated Services Group, Huntington *Also called SC Textiles Inc* ***(G-6718)***
Affluent Design Inc 631 655-2556
48 Biltmore Dr Mastic Beach (11951) ***(G-8236)***
Affordable Luxury Group Inc 631 523-9266
10 W 33rd St Rm 615 New York (10001) ***(G-9103)***
Affymax Inc 650 812-8700
630 5th Ave Ste 2260 New York (10111) ***(G-9104)***
Afh Industries Incorporated 646 351-1700
110 W 34th St Fl 7 New York (10001) ***(G-9105)***

ALPHABETIC

(PA)=Parent Co (HQ)=Headquarters (DH)=Div Headquarters
2018 Harris
New York Manufacturers Directory
885

Afi Cybernetics Corporation....607 732-3244
713 Batavia St Elmira (14904) **(G-4682)**
AFP Industries, Lancaster *Also called Air System Products Inc* **(G-7324)**
AFP Manufacturing Corp....516 466-6464
9 Park Pl Great Neck (11021) **(G-5800)**
African American Observer, New York *Also called General Media Strategies Inc* **(G-10316)**
Afro Times Newspaper....718 636-9500
1195 Atlantic Ave Brooklyn (11216) **(G-1568)**
After 50 Inc....716 832-9300
5 W Main St Rear Lancaster (14086) **(G-7323)**
AG Adriano Goldschmied Inc....845 928-8616
216 Red Apple Ct Central Valley (10917) **(G-3547)**
AG Biotech Inc....585 346-0020
3578 Shoreline Dr Livonia (14487) **(G-7590)**
AG Kids, New York *Also called Premium 5 Kids LLC* **(G-11721)**
AG Neovo Professional Inc....212 647-9080
156 5th Ave Ste 434 New York (10010) **(G-9106)**
AG Tech Welding Corp....845 398-0005
238 Oak Tree Rd Tappan (10983) **(G-16102)**
Ag-Pak Inc....716 772-2651
8416 Telegraph Rd Gasport (14067) **(G-5570)**
Age Manufacturers Inc....718 927-0048
10624 Avenue D Brooklyn (11236) **(G-1569)**
Age Timberline Mamba, Farmingdale *Also called Amana Tool Corp* **(G-4947)**
Agi Brooks Production Co Inc (PA)....212 268-1533
7 E 14th St Apt 615 New York (10003) **(G-9107)**
Agilent Technologies Inc....877 424-4536
399 Park Ave New York (10022) **(G-9108)**
Agl Industries Inc....718 326-7597
5912 57th St Maspeth (11378) **(G-8140)**
Aglika Trade LLC....727 424-1944
5905 74th St Middle Village (11379) **(G-8443)**
Agn Professional, New York *Also called AG Neovo Professional Inc* **(G-9106)**
Agnovos Healthcare LLC....646 502-5860
140 Broadway Fl 46 New York (10005) **(G-9109)**
Agrecolor Inc (PA)....516 741-8700
400 Sagamore Ave Mineola (11501) **(G-8525)**
Agri Services Co....716 937-6618
13899 North Rd Alden (14004) **(G-176)**
Agri-Mark Inc....518 497-6644
39 Mccadam Ln Chateaugay (12920) **(G-3584)**
Agrinetix Cmpt Systems LLC....877 978-5477
370 Summit Point Dr 1a Henrietta (14467) **(G-6314)**
Agrinetix, LLC, Henrietta *Also called Agrinetix Cmpt Systems LLC* **(G-6314)**
Agrium Advanced Tech US Inc....631 286-0598
165 Orville Dr Bohemia (11716) **(G-1005)**
Agrochem Inc....518 226-4850
26 Freedom Way Saratoga Springs Saratoga Springs (12866) **(G-15171)**
Agua Enerviva LLC....516 597-5440
15 Grumman Rd W Ste 1300 Bethpage (11714) **(G-863)**
Aguilar Amplification LLC....212 431-9109
599 Broadway Fl 7 New York (10012) **(G-9110)**
Agway, Akron *Also called G & S Farm & Home Inc* **(G-20)**
Agway, Cobleskill *Also called Kelley Farm & Garden Inc* **(G-3763)**
Ah Elctronic Test Eqp Repr Ctr....631 234-8979
7 Olive St Central Islip (11722) **(G-3509)**
Ahhmigo LLC....212 315-1818
120 Cent Park S Rm 7c New York (10019) **(G-9111)**
Ahlstrom Kamyr, Glens Falls *Also called Andritz Inc* **(G-5686)**
Ahq LLC....212 328-1560
10 W 33rd St Rm 306 New York (10001) **(G-9112)**
Ahw Printing Corp....516 536-3600
2920 Long Beach Rd Oceanside (11572) **(G-13091)**
Ai Entertainment Holdings LLC (HQ)....212 247-6400
730 5th Ave Fl 20 New York (10019) **(G-9113)**
Ai Media Group Inc....212 660-2400
1359 Broadway Fl 5 New York (10018) **(G-9114)**
AICHE, New York *Also called American Inst Chem Engineers* **(G-9170)**
Aicm, Hauppauge *Also called American Intrmdal Cont Mfg LLC* **(G-6041)**
Aid Wood Working....631 244-7768
1555 Ocean Ave Ste C Bohemia (11716) **(G-1006)**
Aigner Chocolates Inc (PA)....718 544-1850
10302 Metropolitan Ave Forest Hills (11375) **(G-5325)**
Aigner Index,, New Windsor *Also called Aigner Label Holder Corp* **(G-8976)**
Aigner Label Holder Corp....845 562-4510
218 Mac Arthur Ave New Windsor (12553) **(G-8976)**
Aimee Kestenberg, New York *Also called Affordable Luxury Group Inc* **(G-9103)**
Aines Manufacturing Corp....631 471-3900
96 E Bayberry Rd Islip (11751) **(G-6845)**
Aip Aerospace, New York *Also called Ascent Aerospace Holdings LLC* **(G-9279)**
Aip Mc Holdings LLC....212 627-2360
330 Madison Ave Fl 28 New York (10017) **(G-9115)**
Aip Publishing LLC....516 576-2200
1305 Walt Whitman Rd # 300 Melville (11747) **(G-8323)**
Aiping Pharmaceutical Inc....631 952-3802
350w Wireless Blvd Hauppauge (11788) **(G-6031)**
Air Conditioning, Bronx *Also called AC Air Cooling Co Inc* **(G-1259)**
Air Crafters Inc....631 471-7788
2085 5th Ave Ronkonkoma (11779) **(G-14883)**
Air Engineering Filters Inc....914 238-5945
17 Memorial Dr Chappaqua (10514) **(G-3578)**
Air Export Mechanical....917 709-5310
4108 Parsons Blvd Apt 4r Flushing (11355) **(G-5230)**
Air Flow Manufacturing....607 733-8284
365 Upper Oakwood Ave Elmira (14903) **(G-4683)**
Air Flow Pump Corp....718 241-2800
8412 Foster Ave Brooklyn (11236) **(G-1570)**
Air Flow Pump Supply, Brooklyn *Also called Air Flow Pump Corp* **(G-1570)**
Air Industries Group (PA)....631 881-4920
3609 Motor Pkwy Ste 100 Hauppauge (11788) **(G-6032)**
Air Industries Machining Corp....631 968-5000
1460 5th Ave Bay Shore (11706) **(G-666)**
Air Louver & Damper Inc....718 392-3232
5670 58th Pl Maspeth (11378) **(G-8141)**
Air Louver & Damper Inc (PA)....718 392-3232
2121 44th Rd Long Island City (11101) **(G-7681)**
Air Preheater, Wellsville *Also called Arvos Inc* **(G-16775)**
Air Products and Chemicals Inc....518 463-4273
461 River Rd Glenmont (12077) **(G-5682)**
Air Skate & Air Jump Corp....212 967-1201
1385 Broadway New York (10018) **(G-9116)**
Air Skate & Air Jump Corp (PA)....212 967-1201
2208 E 5th St Brooklyn (11223) **(G-1571)**
Air Structures Amercn Tech Inc....914 937-4500
211 S Ridge St Ste 3 Port Chester (10573) **(G-13765)**
Air System Products Inc....716 683-0435
51 Beach Ave Lancaster (14086) **(G-7324)**
Air Techniques Inc (HQ)....516 433-7676
1295 Walt Whitman Rd Melville (11747) **(G-8324)**
Air Tite Manufacturing Inc....516 897-0295
724 Park Pl Ste B Long Beach (11561) **(G-7667)**
Air Wave Air Conditioning Co....212 545-1122
1637 Stillwell Ave Bronx (10461) **(G-1266)**
Air-Flo Mfg Co Inc....607 733-8284
365 Upper Oakwood Ave Elmira (14903) **(G-4684)**
Air-O-Tronics, Cazenovia *Also called Stk Electronics Inc* **(G-3479)**
Aircraft Finishing Corp (PA)....631 422-5000
100 Field St Unit A West Babylon (11704) **(G-16792)**
Aireactor Inc....718 326-2433
6110 Laurel Hill Blvd Woodside (11377) **(G-17335)**
Airflex Corp....631 752-1219
965 Conklin St Farmingdale (11735) **(G-4939)**
Airflex Industrial Inc (PA)....631 752-1234
965 Conklin St Farmingdale (11735) **(G-4940)**
Airflex Industrial Inc....631 752-1234
937 Conklin St Farmingdale (11735) **(G-4941)**
Airgas Inc....585 436-7780
77 Deep Rock Rd Rochester (14624) **(G-14197)**
Airgas Inc....518 690-0068
84 Karner Rd Albany (12205) **(G-33)**
Airgas Usa LLC....585 436-7781
77 Deep Rock Rd Rochester (14624) **(G-14198)**
Airgas USA LLC....315 433-1295
121 Boxwood Ln Syracuse (13206) **(G-15867)**
Airgle Corporation....866 501-7750
711 Koehler Ave Ste 3 Ronkonkoma (11779) **(G-14884)**
Airline Container Services....516 371-4125
354 Harbor Dr Lido Beach (11561) **(G-7461)**
Airline Container Svces, Lido Beach *Also called Airline Container Services* **(G-7461)**
Airmarine Electroplating Corp....516 623-4406
388 Woodcleft Ave Freeport (11520) **(G-5390)**
Airnet Communications Corp....516 338-0008
609 Cantiague Rock Rd # 5 Westbury (11590) **(G-16991)**
Airnet North Division, Westbury *Also called Airnet Communications Corp* **(G-16991)**
Airport Press, The, Jamaica *Also called Pati Inc* **(G-6976)**
Airport Printing & Stationers, Wading River *Also called A I P Printing & Stationers* **(G-16543)**
Airsep, Amherst *Also called Chart Industries Inc* **(G-234)**
Airsep Corporation....716 691-0202
260 Creekside Dr Ste 100 Amherst (14228) **(G-222)**
Airtech Lab, Brooklyn *Also called Dib Managmnt Inc* **(G-1860)**
Airweld Inc....631 924-6366
1740 Middle Country Rd Ridge (11961) **(G-14103)**
Aithaca Chemical Corp....516 229-2330
50 Charles Lindbergh Blvd # 400 Uniondale (11553) **(G-16311)**
Aj Genco Mch Sp McHy Rdout Svc....716 664-4925
235 Carter St Falconer (14733) **(G-4896)**
Ajax Wire Specialty Co Inc....516 935-2333
119 Bloomingdale Rd Hicksville (11801) **(G-6342)**
Ajes Pharmaceuticals LLC....631 608-1728
11a Lincoln St Copiague (11726) **(G-3917)**
Ajl Manufacturing Inc....585 254-1128
100 Holleder Pkwy Rochester (14615) **(G-14199)**
Ajmadison Corp....718 532-1800
3605 13th Ave Brooklyn (11218) **(G-1572)**
Aka Enterprises....716 474-4579
164 Main St Wyoming (14591) **(G-17395)**
Aka Sport Inc....631 858-9888
16 Princeton Dr Dix Hills (11746) **(G-4312)**
Akari Therapeutics PLC....646 350-0702
24 W 40th St Fl 8 New York (10018) **(G-9117)**

ALPHABETIC SECTION

Akh Group LLC 646 320-8720
  601 W 26th St Rm M228 New York (10001) *(G-9118)*
Akhon Samoy Weekly, Flushing Also called Digital One USA Inc *(G-5245)*
Aki Cabinets Inc 718 721-2541
  2636 2nd St Astoria (11102) *(G-429)*
AKOS Group Ltd 212 683-4747
  315 5th Ave Fl 11 New York (10016) *(G-9119)*
Akoustis Inc 585 919-3073
  5450 Campus Dr Canandaigua (14424) *(G-3363)*
Akraturn Mfg Inc 607 775-2802
  1743 Us Route 11 Kirkwood (13795) *(G-7258)*
Akribos Watches, Brooklyn Also called TWI Watches LLC *(G-2709)*
Akron-Corfu Pennysaver, Elma Also called R W Publications Div of Wtrhs *(G-4666)*
Akshar Extracts Inc 631 588-9727
  59 Remington Blvd Ronkonkoma (11779) *(G-14885)*
Akzo Nobel Central Research, Dobbs Ferry Also called Akzo Nobel Chemicals LLC *(G-4324)*
Akzo Nobel Chemicals LLC 914 674-5008
  7 Livingstone Ave Dobbs Ferry (10522) *(G-4324)*
Akzo Nobel Chemicals LLC 716 778-8554
  2153 Lockport Olcott Rd Burt (14028) *(G-3294)*
Akzo Nobel Coatings Inc 610 603-7589
  4602 21st St Long Island City (11101) *(G-7682)*
Akzo Nobel Functional Chem LLC 845 276-8200
  281 Fields Ln Brewster (10509) *(G-1205)*
Akzo Nobel Inc 914 674-5181
  7 Livingstone Ave Dobbs Ferry (10522) *(G-4325)*
Al Cohens Famous Rye Bread Bky, Buffalo Also called Cohens Bakery Inc *(G-2899)*
Al Energy Solutions Led Llc 646 380-6670
  1140 Ave Of The Americas New York (10036) *(G-9120)*
Ala Scientific Instruments Inc 631 393-6401
  60 Marine St Ste 1 Farmingdale (11735) *(G-4942)*
Alabaster Group Inc 516 867-8223
  188 N Main St Freeport (11520) *(G-5391)*
Alabu Inc 518 665-0411
  30 Graves Rd Mechanicville (12118) *(G-8255)*
Alabu Skin Care, Mechanicville Also called Alabu Inc *(G-8255)*
Aladdin Bakers Inc (PA) 718 499-1818
  240 25th St Brooklyn (11232) *(G-1573)*
Aladdin Manufacturing Corp 212 561-8715
  295 5th Ave Ste 1412 New York (10016) *(G-9121)*
Aladdin Packaging LLC 631 273-4747
  115 Engineers Rd Ste 100 Hauppauge (11788) *(G-6033)*
Alamar Printing Inc 914 993-9007
  190 E Post Rd Frnt 1 White Plains (10601) *(G-17102)*
Alan F Bourguet 516 883-4315
  63 Essex Ct Port Washington (11050) *(G-13820)*
Alart Inc 212 840-1508
  578 5th Ave Unit 33 New York (10036) *(G-9122)*
Alba Fuel Corp 718 931-1700
  2135 Wllmsbrdge Rd Fl 2 Bronx (10461) *(G-1267)*
Alba House Publishers 718 698-2759
  2187 Victory Blvd Staten Island (10314) *(G-15654)*
Albaluz Films LLC 347 613-2321
  954 Lexington Ave New York (10021) *(G-9123)*
Albany Asp & Aggregates Corp 518 436-8916
  101 Dunham Dr Albany (12202) *(G-34)*
Albany Catholic Press Assoc 518 453-6688
  40 N Main Ave Ste 2 Albany (12203) *(G-35)*
Albany Engnered Composites Inc 518 445-2200
  455 Patroon Creek Blvd Albany (12206) *(G-36)*
Albany International Corp 518 445-2230
  1373 Broadway Menands (12204) *(G-8397)*
Albany International Corp 607 749-7226
  156 S Main St Homer (13077) *(G-6543)*
Albany International Corp 518 447-6400
  1373 Broadway Menands (12204) *(G-8398)*
Albany International Corp 518 445-2200
  253 Troy Rd Rensselaer (12144) *(G-14053)*
Albany Letter Shop Inc 518 434-1172
  16 Van Zandt St Ste 20 Albany (12207) *(G-37)*
Albany Molecular Research Inc 518 512-2234
  21 Corporate Cir Albany (12203) *(G-38)*
Albany Molecular Research Inc 518 433-7700
  81 Columbia Tpke Rensselaer (12144) *(G-14054)*
Albany Molecular Research Inc (HQ) 518 512-2000
  26 Corporate Cir Albany (12203) *(G-39)*
Albany Molecular Research Inc 518 512-2000
  33 Riverside Ave Rensselaer (12144) *(G-14055)*
Albany Mtal Fbrcation Holdings 518 463-5161
  67 Henry Johnson Blvd Albany (12210) *(G-40)*
Albany Nipple and Pipe Mfg 518 270-2162
  60 Cohoes Ave Ste 100a Troy (12183) *(G-16239)*
Albany Student Press Inc 518 442-5665
  1400 Washington Ave Cc329 Albany (12222) *(G-41)*
Albatros North America Inc 518 381-7100
  6 Mccrea Hill Rd Ballston Spa (12020) *(G-589)*
Albea Cosmetics America Inc (HQ) 212 371-5100
  595 Madison Ave Fl 10 New York (10022) *(G-9124)*
Albert Augustine Ltd 718 913-9635
  161 S Macquesten Pkwy Mount Vernon (10550) *(G-8706)*
Albert Gates Inc 585 594-9401
  3434 Union St North Chili (14514) *(G-12940)*

Albert Kemperle Inc 718 629-1084
  890 E 51st St Brooklyn (11203) *(G-1574)*
Albert Menin Interiors Ltd 212 876-3041
  2417 3rd Ave Fl 3 Bronx (10451) *(G-1268)*
Albert Siy 718 359-0389
  13508 Booth Memorial Ave Flushing (11355) *(G-5231)*
Albest Metal Stamping Corp 718 388-6000
  1 Kent Ave Brooklyn (11249) *(G-1575)*
Albion Cosmetics Inc 212 869-1052
  110 E 42nd St Rm 1506 New York (10017) *(G-9125)*
Albion-Holley Pennysaver Inc 585 589-5641
  170 N Main St Albion (14411) *(G-164)*
Albrizio Couture, Brooklyn Also called Albrizio Inc *(G-1576)*
Albrizio Inc 212 719-5290
  257 Varet St Ste Mgmt Brooklyn (11206) *(G-1576)*
Albro Gear & Instrument, Yaphank Also called W J Albro Machine Works Inc *(G-17424)*
Albumx Corp 914 939-6878
  21 Grace Church St Port Chester (10573) *(G-13766)*
Alcatel-Lucent USA Inc 516 349-4900
  1 Fairchild Ct Ste 340 Plainview (11803) *(G-13610)*
Alchemy Simya Inc 646 230-1122
  161 Avnue Of The Americas New York (10013) *(G-9126)*
Alco Plastics Inc 716 683-3020
  35 Ward Rd Lancaster (14086) *(G-7325)*
Alco Products Div, Orchard Park Also called Nitram Energy Inc *(G-13310)*
Alco Products USA, Orchard Park Also called Peerless Mfg Co *(G-13314)*
Alcoa, Falconer Also called Arconic Inc *(G-4898)*
Alcoa Fastening Systems 585 368-5049
  181 Mckee Rd Rochester (14611) *(G-14200)*
Alcoa Fastening Systems 845 334-7203
  1 Corporate Dr Kingston (12401) *(G-7206)*
Alcoa USA Corp (HQ) 212 518-5400
  390 Park Ave New York (10022) *(G-9127)*
Alcoholics Anonymous Grapevine (PA) 212 870-3400
  475 Riverside Dr Ste 1264 New York (10115) *(G-9128)*
Alconox, White Plains Also called L S Z Inc *(G-17158)*
Alconox Inc 914 948-4040
  30 Glenn St Ste 309 White Plains (10603) *(G-17103)*
Alden Advertiser, Alden Also called Weisbeck Publishing Printing *(G-189)*
Alden Aurora Gas Company Inc 716 937-9484
  13441 Railroad St Alden (14004) *(G-177)*
Alden Optical Laboratory Inc 716 937-9181
  6 Lancaster Pkwy Lancaster (14086) *(G-7326)*
Aldine Inc (ny) 212 226-2870
  150 Varick St Fl 5 New York (10013) *(G-9129)*
Aldo Frustacci Iron Works Inc 718 768-0707
  165 27th St Brooklyn (11232) *(G-1577)*
Aldos Iron Works Inc 718 834-0408
  75 Van Brunt St Brooklyn (11231) *(G-1578)*
Ale-Techniques Inc 845 687-7200
  2452b Lucas Tpke High Falls (12440) *(G-6426)*
Alen Sands York Associates Ltd 212 563-6305
  236 W 26th St Rm 801 New York (10001) *(G-9130)*
Aleta Industries Inc 718 349-0040
  40 Ash St Brooklyn (11222) *(G-1579)*
Aleteia Usa Inc 914 502-1855
  86 Main St Ste 303 Yonkers (10701) *(G-17426)*
Aletheas Chocolates Inc (PA) 716 633-8620
  8301 Main St Williamsville (14221) *(G-17259)*
Alex and Ani LLC 914 481-1506
  52 Purchase St Rye (10580) *(G-15079)*
Alex Sepkus Inc 212 391-8466
  42 W 48th St Ste 501 New York (10036) *(G-9131)*
Alexander Polakovich 718 229-6200
  4235 Bell Blvd Bayside (11361) *(G-761)*
Alexander Primak Jewelry Inc 212 398-0287
  529 5th Ave Fl 15 New York (10017) *(G-9132)*
Alexander Wang Incorporated (PA) 212 532-3103
  386 Broadway Fl 3 New York (10013) *(G-9133)*
Alexandra Ferguson LLC 718 788-7768
  67 35th St Unit 1 Brooklyn (11232) *(G-1580)*
Alexander Furs, New York Also called Samuel Schulman Furs Inc *(G-11981)*
Alexandria Professional LLC 716 242-8514
  5500 Main St Ste 103 Williamsville (14221) *(G-17260)*
Alexandros, New York Also called Anastasia Furs International *(G-9198)*
Alexis Bittar LLC (PA) 718 422-7580
  45 Main St Ste 725 Brooklyn (11201) *(G-1581)*
Alexscoe LLC 315 463-9207
  6852 Manlius Center Rd East Syracuse (13057) *(G-4517)*
Alexy Associates Inc 845 482-3000
  86 Jim Stephenson Rd Bethel (12720) *(G-858)*
Alfa Card Inc 718 326-7107
  7915 Cooper Ave Glendale (11385) *(G-5658)*
Alfa Chem, Great Neck Also called Alfred Khalily Inc *(G-5802)*
Alfa Laval Kathabar Inc 716 875-2000
  91 Sawyer Ave Tonawanda (14150) *(G-16158)*
Alfred B Parella 518 872-1238
  20 Reservoir Rd Altamont (12009) *(G-208)*
Alfred Butler Inc 516 829-7460
  107 Grace Ave Great Neck (11021) *(G-5801)*
Alfred Dunner Inc (PA) 212 478-4300
  1333 Broadway Fl 12 New York (10018) *(G-9134)*

(PA)=Parent Co (HQ)=Headquarters (DH)=Div Headquarters

Alfred Khalily Inc 516 504-0059
2 Harbor Way Great Neck (11024) ***(G-5802)***
Alfred Mainzer Inc (PA) 718 392-4200
2708 40th Ave Long Island City (11101) ***(G-7683)***
Alfred Music, Oriskany *Also called Alfred Publishing Co Inc* ***(G-13328)***
Alfred Publishing Co Inc 315 736-1572
123 Dry Rd Oriskany (13424) ***(G-13328)***
Algafuel America 516 295-2257
289 Meadowview Ave Hewlett (11557) ***(G-6331)***
Algemeiner Journal Inc 718 771-0400
508 Montgomery St Brooklyn (11225) ***(G-1582)***
Algonquin Books Chapel Hl Div, New York *Also called Workman Publishing Co Inc* ***(G-12687)***
Algonquin Power 315 393-5595
19 Mill St Ogdensburg (13669) ***(G-13131)***
Ali & Kris, New York *Also called Brooke Leigh Ltd* ***(G-9520)***
Ali Ro, New York *Also called Donna Morgan LLC* ***(G-9956)***
Alice & Trixie, New York *Also called Millennium Productions Inc* ***(G-11293)***
Alice Perkins 716 378-5100
148 Washington St Salamanca (14779) ***(G-15125)***
Alicia Adams Alpaca Inc 845 868-3366
3262 Franklin Ave Millbrook (12545) ***(G-8510)***
Alicia F Herdlein 585 344-4411
5450 E Main Street Rd Batavia (14020) ***(G-621)***
Alicias Bakery Inc 914 235-4689
498 Main St Ste A New Rochelle (10801) ***(G-8930)***
Alison Wine & Vineyard, Rhinebeck *Also called Dutchess Wines LLC* ***(G-14068)***
Aljo Precision Products Inc 516 420-4419
205 Bethpge Sweet Holw Old Bethpage (11804) ***(G-13145)***
Aljo-Gefa Precision Mfg LLC 516 420-4419
205 Bethpage Sweet Holw Old Bethpage (11804) ***(G-13146)***
Alkemy Machine LLC 585 436-8730
1600 Lexington Ave 103c Rochester (14606) ***(G-14201)***
Alken Industries Inc 631 467-2000
2175 5th Ave Ronkonkoma (11779) ***(G-14886)***
All About Art Inc 718 321-0755
4128 Murray St Flushing (11355) ***(G-5232)***
All American Awards Inc 631 567-2025
331 Knickerbocker Ave Bohemia (11716) ***(G-1007)***
All American Building 607 797-7123
109 Crestmont Rd Binghamton (13905) ***(G-882)***
All American Concrete Corp 718 497-3301
239 Ingraham St Brooklyn (11237) ***(G-1583)***
All American Metal Corporation (PA) 516 223-1760
200 Buffalo Ave Freeport (11520) ***(G-5392)***
All American Metal Corporation 516 623-0222
200 Buffalo Ave Freeport (11520) ***(G-5393)***
All American Mold, West Henrietta *Also called All American Precision Tl Mold* ***(G-16897)***
All American Precision Tl Mold 585 436-3080
1325 John St West Henrietta (14586) ***(G-16897)***
All American Stairs & Railing 718 441-8400
13023 91st Ave Richmond Hill (11418) ***(G-14078)***
All American Transit Mix Corp 718 417-3654
46 Knickerbocker Ave Brooklyn (11237) ***(G-1584)***
All American Uniform, Bohemia *Also called All American Awards Inc* ***(G-1007)***
All Around Spiral Inc 631 588-0220
10 Fleetwood Ct Ronkonkoma (11779) ***(G-14887)***
All Cast Foundry, Brooklyn *Also called J & J Bronze & Aluminum Cast* ***(G-2120)***
All City Switchboard Corp 718 956-7244
3541 11th St Long Island City (11106) ***(G-7684)***
All Color Business Spc Ltd 516 420-0649
305 Suburban Ave Deer Park (11729) ***(G-4115)***
All Color Business Specialties, Farmingdale *Also called All Color Offset Printers Inc* ***(G-4943)***
All Color Offset Printers Inc 516 420-0649
51 Henry St Ste A Farmingdale (11735) ***(G-4943)***
All County Block & Supply Corp 631 589-3675
899 Lincoln Ave Bohemia (11716) ***(G-1008)***
All Craft Jewelry Supply, New York *Also called Creative Tools & Supply Inc* ***(G-9810)***
All Cultures Inc 631 293-3143
12 Gates St Greenlawn (11740) ***(G-5890)***
All Gone Restoration, Staten Island *Also called Occhioerosso John* ***(G-15738)***
All In Audio Inc 718 506-0948
5314 16th Ave Ste 83 Brooklyn (11204) ***(G-1585)***
All Island Blower & Shtmtl 631 567-7070
1585 Smithtown Ave Unit C Bohemia (11716) ***(G-1009)***
All Island Media Inc (PA) 631 698-8400
1 Rodeo Dr Edgewood (11717) ***(G-4606)***
All Island Media Inc 516 942-8400
325 Duffy Ave Unit 2 Hicksville (11801) ***(G-6343)***
All Merchandise Display Corp 718 257-2221
4 Pheasant Run Highland Mills (10930) ***(G-6438)***
All Metal Specialties Inc 716 664-6009
300 Livingston Ave Jamestown (14701) ***(G-7005)***
All Metro Emrgncy Response Sys 516 750-9100
50 Broadway Lynbrook (11563) ***(G-7973)***
All Net Ltd 516 504-4559
15 Cuttermill Rd Ste 145 Great Neck (11021) ***(G-5803)***
All Out Die Cutting Inc 718 346-6666
49 Wyckoff Ave Ste 1 Brooklyn (11237) ***(G-1586)***
All Packaging McHy & Sups Corp 631 588-7310
90 13th Ave Unit 11 Ronkonkoma (11779) ***(G-14888)***
All Phases Asp & Ldscpg Dsgn 631 588-1372
60 18th Ave Ronkonkoma (11779) ***(G-14889)***
All Products Designs 631 748-6901
227a Route 111 Smithtown (11787) ***(G-15504)***
All Racks Industries Inc 212 244-1069
361 W 36th St Frnt A New York (10018) ***(G-9135)***
All Shore Industries Inc 718 720-0018
1 Edgewater St Ste 215 Staten Island (10305) ***(G-15655)***
All Signs 973 736-2113
63 Bridgetown St Staten Island (10314) ***(G-15656)***
All Spec Finishing Inc 607 770-9174
219 Clinton St Binghamton (13905) ***(G-883)***
All Star Carts & Vehicles Inc 631 666-5581
1565 5th Industrial Ct B Bay Shore (11706) ***(G-667)***
All Star Fabricators, Thornwood *Also called Thornwood Products Ltd* ***(G-16144)***
All The Rage Inc 516 605-2001
147 W Cherry St Unit 1 Hicksville (11801) ***(G-6344)***
All Time Products Inc 718 464-1400
21167 Jamaica Ave Queens Village (11428) ***(G-13990)***
All Times Publishing LLC 315 422-7011
1415 W Genesee St Syracuse (13204) ***(G-15868)***
All Type Screw Machine Pdts 516 334-5100
100 New York Ave Westbury (11590) ***(G-16992)***
All United Window Corp 718 624-0490
85 Classon Ave 97 Brooklyn (11205) ***(G-1587)***
All Weather Outerwear, Brooklyn *Also called Lakeview Sportswear Corp* ***(G-2192)***
All-City Metal Inc 718 937-3975
5435 46th St Maspeth (11378) ***(G-8142)***
All-Lifts Incorporated 518 465-3461
27-39 Thatcher St Albany (12207) ***(G-42)***
All-Pro Imaging Corp 516 433-7676
1295 Walt Whitman Rd Melville (11747) ***(G-8325)***
All-State Diversified Pdts Inc 315 472-4728
8 Dwight Park Dr Syracuse (13209) ***(G-15869)***
All-Tech, Brooklyn *Also called Integra Microsystem 1988 Inc* ***(G-2107)***
Allan John Company 212 940-2210
611 5th Ave Fl 7 New York (10022) ***(G-9136)***
Allanson Inc (HQ) 631 293-3880
99 Adams Blvd Farmingdale (11735) ***(G-4944)***
Allcom Electric Corp 914 803-0433
104 Crescent Pl Yonkers (10704) ***(G-17427)***
Allcraft Fabricators Inc 631 951-4100
150 Wireless Blvd Hauppauge (11788) ***(G-6034)***
Alle Processing Corp 718 894-2000
5620 59th St Maspeth (11378) ***(G-8143)***
Allegany Laminating and Supply 716 372-2424
158 W Main St Allegany (14706) ***(G-201)***
Allegiant Health, Deer Park *Also called Bli International Inc* ***(G-4133)***
Allegra Print & Imaging, Schenectady *Also called Capital Dst Print & Imaging* ***(G-15265)***
Allegra Printing, Buffalo *Also called Loy L Press Inc* ***(G-3069)***
Allen Air, Mineola *Also called A K Allen Co Inc* ***(G-8522)***
Allen Avionics Inc 516 248-8080
255 E 2nd St Mineola (11501) ***(G-8526)***
Allen Boat Co Inc 716 842-0800
370 Babcock St Rear Buffalo (14206) ***(G-2819)***
Allen Field Co Inc 631 665-2782
256 Orinoco Dr Ste A Brightwaters (11718) ***(G-1237)***
Allen Machine Products Inc 631 630-8800
120 Ricefield Ln Ste 100 Hauppauge (11788) ***(G-6035)***
Allen Pickle Works Inc 516 676-0640
36 Garvies Point Rd Glen Cove (11542) ***(G-5622)***
Allen Tool Phoenix Inc 315 463-7533
6821 Ellicott Dr East Syracuse (13057) ***(G-4518)***
Allen William & Company Inc 212 675-6461
7119 80th St Ste 8315 Glendale (11385) ***(G-5659)***
Allen-Bailey Tag & Label Inc (PA) 585 538-2324
3177 Lehigh St Caledonia (14423) ***(G-3303)***
Allenair Corporation 516 747-5450
255 E 2nd St Mineola (11501) ***(G-8527)***
Alleson Athletic, Rochester *Also called Alleson of Rochester Inc* ***(G-14202)***
Alleson of Rochester Inc (PA) 800 641-0041
2921 Brighton Henrietta Rochester (14623) ***(G-14202)***
Alley Cat Signs Inc 631 924-7446
506 Middle Country Rd Middle Island (11953) ***(G-8439)***
Alley Music Corp 212 779-7977
126 E 38th St New York (10016) ***(G-9137)***
Alliance Automation Systems 585 426-2700
400 Trabold Rd Rochester (14624) ***(G-14203)***
Alliance Control Systems Inc 845 279-4430
577 N Main St Ste 9 Brewster (10509) ***(G-1206)***
Alliance Exports LLC 347 208-3547
22 E 127th St Apt 1 New York (10035) ***(G-9138)***
Alliance Innovative Mfg Inc 716 822-1626
1 Alliance Dr Lackawanna (14218) ***(G-7268)***
Alliance Magnetic LLC 914 944-1690
100 Executive Blvd # 202 Ossining (10562) ***(G-13344)***
Alliance Paving Materials Inc 315 337-0795
846 Lawrence St Rome (13440) ***(G-14832)***
Alliance Precision Plas Corp (PA) 585 426-5310
1220 Lee Rd Rochester (14606) ***(G-14204)***

Alliance Precision Plas Corp..........585 426-5310
105 Elmore Dr Rochester (14606) ***(G-14205)***
Alliance Services Corp..........516 775-7600
23 Van Siclen Ave Floral Park (11001) ***(G-5198)***
Alliance Welding & Steel Fabg..........516 775-7600
15 Van Siclen Ave Floral Park (11001) ***(G-5199)***
Alliant Tchsystems Oprtons LLC..........631 737-6100
77 Raynor Ave Ronkonkoma (11779) ***(G-14890)***
Allied, Buffalo *Also called Mibro Group* ***(G-3084)***
Allied Aero Services Inc..........631 277-9368
506 Grand Blvd Brentwood (11717) ***(G-1172)***
Allied Bronze Corp (del Corp)..........646 421-6400
32 Avenue Of The Americas New York (10013) ***(G-9139)***
Allied Circuits LLC..........716 551-0285
22 James E Casey Dr Buffalo (14206) ***(G-2820)***
Allied Converters Inc..........914 235-1585
64 Drake Ave New Rochelle (10805) ***(G-8931)***
Allied Decorations Co Inc..........315 637-0273
720 Erie Blvd W Syracuse (13204) ***(G-15870)***
Allied Food Products Inc..........718 230-4227
251 Saint Marks Ave Brooklyn (11238) ***(G-1588)***
Allied Industrial Products Co..........716 664-3893
880 E 2nd St Jamestown (14701) ***(G-7006)***
Allied Industries, Jamestown *Also called Allied Industrial Products Co* ***(G-7006)***
Allied Inspection Services LLC..........716 489-3199
4 Carter St Falconer (14733) ***(G-4897)***
Allied K & R Broom & Brush Co, Brooklyn *Also called K & R Allied Inc* ***(G-2161)***
Allied Metal Spinning Corp..........718 893-3300
1290 Viele Ave Bronx (10474) ***(G-1269)***
Allied Motion Systems Corp (HQ)..........716 691-5868
495 Commerce Dr Ste 3 Amherst (14228) ***(G-223)***
Allied Motion Technologies Inc (PA)..........716 242-8634
495 Commerce Dr Ste 3 Amherst (14228) ***(G-224)***
Allied Motion Technologies Inc..........315 782-5910
22543 Fisher Rd Watertown (13601) ***(G-16656)***
Allied Orthopedics, Ozone Park *Also called Robert Cohen* ***(G-13411)***
Allied Pharmacy Products Inc..........516 374-8862
544 Green Pl Woodmere (11598) ***(G-17328)***
Allied Products, New York *Also called Biofeedback Instrument Corp* ***(G-9453)***
Allied Reproductions Inc..........212 255-2472
121 Varick St Fl 9 New York (10013) ***(G-9140)***
Allied Sample Card Co Inc..........718 238-0523
140 58th St Ste 7a Brooklyn (11220) ***(G-1589)***
Allied Sign Co, Syracuse *Also called Allied Decorations Co Inc* ***(G-15870)***
Allied Wine Corp..........845 796-4160
121 Main St South Fallsburg (12779) ***(G-15542)***
Allies GF Goodies LLC..........516 216-1719
1b W Village Grn Hicksville (11801) ***(G-6345)***
Allison Che Fashion Inc (PA)..........212 391-1433
1400 Broadway Lbby 5 New York (10018) ***(G-9141)***
Allmetal Chocolate Mold Co Inc..........631 752-2888
135 Dale St West Babylon (11704) ***(G-16793)***
Allomatic Products Company..........516 775-0330
102 Jericho Tpke Ste 104 Floral Park (11001) ***(G-5200)***
Alloy Machine & Tool Co Inc..........516 593-3445
169 Vincent Ave Lynbrook (11563) ***(G-7974)***
Alloy Metal Products LLC..........315 676-2405
193 Us Route 11 Central Square (13036) ***(G-3542)***
Alloy Metal Works Inc..........631 694-8163
146 Verdi St Farmingdale (11735) ***(G-4945)***
Allred & Associates Inc..........315 252-2559
321 Rte 5 W Elbridge (13060) ***(G-4637)***
Allround Logistics Inc (PA)..........718 544-8945
7240 Ingram St Forest Hills (11375) ***(G-5326)***
Allround Maritime Services, Forest Hills *Also called Allround Logistics Inc* ***(G-5326)***
Allsafe Technologies Inc..........716 691-0400
290 Creekside Dr Amherst (14228) ***(G-225)***
Allstar Casting Corporation..........212 563-0909
240 W 37th St Frnt 7 New York (10018) ***(G-9142)***
Allstate Banners, Long Island City *Also called Allstatebannerscom Corporation* ***(G-7685)***
Allstate Gasket & Packing Inc..........631 254-4050
31 Prospect Pl Deer Park (11729) ***(G-4116)***
Allstate Sign & Plaque Corp..........631 242-2828
70 Burt Dr Deer Park (11729) ***(G-4117)***
Allstate Tool and Die Inc..........585 426-0400
15 Coldwater Cres Rochester (14624) ***(G-14206)***
Allstatebannerscom Corporation..........718 300-1256
3511 9th St Long Island City (11106) ***(G-7685)***
Allstateelectronics, Brooklyn *Also called Henrys Deals Inc* ***(G-2072)***
Allsupermarkets, Ridgewood *Also called 333 J & M Food Corp* ***(G-14109)***
Alltec Products, Westbury *Also called Power Scrub It Inc* ***(G-17048)***
Alltek Labeling Systems, Staten Island *Also called Stoney Croft Converters Inc* ***(G-15764)***
Allure Fashions Inc..........516 829-2470
8 Barstow Rd Apt 2e Great Neck (11021) ***(G-5804)***
Allure Jewelry and ACC LLC (PA)..........646 226-8057
15 W 36th St Fl 12 New York (10018) ***(G-9143)***
Allure Metal Works Inc..........631 588-0220
71 Hoffman Ln Ronkonkoma (11749) ***(G-14891)***
Allvac..........716 433-4411
695 Ohio St Lockport (14094) ***(G-7597)***
Allway Tools Inc..........718 792-3636
1255 Seabury Ave Bronx (10462) ***(G-1270)***
Allworth Communications Inc..........212 777-8395
10 E 23rd St Ste 510 New York (10010) ***(G-9144)***
Allworth Press, New York *Also called Allworth Communications Inc* ***(G-9144)***
Ally Nyc Corp..........212 447-7277
230 W 39th St Rm 525 New York (10018) ***(G-9145)***
Allytex LLC..........518 376-7539
540 Acland Blvd Ballston Spa (12020) ***(G-590)***
Alm Media LLC (HQ)..........212 457-9400
120 Broadway Fl 5 New York (10271) ***(G-9146)***
Alm Media Holdings Inc (PA)..........212 457-9400
120 Broadway Fl 5 New York (10271) ***(G-9147)***
Almond Group, Port Washington *Also called Almond Jewelers Inc* ***(G-13821)***
Almond Jewelers Inc..........516 933-6000
16 S Maryland Ave Port Washington (11050) ***(G-13821)***
Almost Famous Clothing, New York *Also called Turn On Products Inc* ***(G-12446)***
Alnik Service Corporation..........516 873-7300
20 Tulip Pl New Hyde Park (11040) ***(G-8859)***
Alo Acquisition LLC (HQ)..........518 464-0279
26 Corporate Cir Albany (12203) ***(G-43)***
Aloi Materials Handling, Rochester *Also called Aloi Solutions LLC* ***(G-14207)***
Aloi Solutions LLC (PA)..........585 292-0920
140 Commerce Dr Rochester (14623) ***(G-14207)***
Alok Inc..........212 643-4360
7 W 34th St Ste 79105 New York (10001) ***(G-9148)***
Alonzo Fire Works Display Inc (PA)..........518 664-9994
12 County Route 75 Mechanicville (12118) ***(G-8256)***
Alp Steel Corp..........716 854-3030
650 Exchange St Buffalo (14210) ***(G-2821)***
Alp Stone Inc..........718 706-6166
2520 50th Ave Fl 2 Long Island City (11101) ***(G-7686)***
Alpargatas Usa Inc..........646 277-7171
33 E 33rd St Rm 501 New York (10016) ***(G-9149)***
Alpha 6 Distributions LLC..........516 801-8290
11 Oyster Bay Rd Locust Valley (11560) ***(G-7659)***
Alpha Boats Unlimited, Weedsport *Also called Barber Welding Inc* ***(G-16772)***
Alpha DC Motors Inc..........315 432-9039
5949 E Molloy Rd Syracuse (13211) ***(G-15871)***
Alpha Fasteners Corp..........516 867-6188
154 E Merrick Rd Freeport (11520) ***(G-5394)***
Alpha Incorporated..........718 765-1614
265 80th St Brooklyn (11209) ***(G-1590)***
Alpha Iron Works LLC..........585 424-7260
65 Goodway Dr S Rochester (14623) ***(G-14208)***
Alpha Knitting Mills Inc..........718 628-6300
41 Varick Ave Ste Mgmt Brooklyn (11237) ***(G-1591)***
Alpha Manufacturing Corp..........631 249-3700
152 Verdi St Farmingdale (11735) ***(G-4946)***
Alpha Marine Repair..........718 816-7150
88 Coursen Pl Staten Island (10304) ***(G-15657)***
Alpha Media Group Inc (PA)..........212 302-2626
415 Madison Ave Fl 4 New York (10017) ***(G-9150)***
Alpha Packaging Industries Inc..........718 267-4115
2004 33rd St Long Island City (11105) ***(G-7687)***
Alpha Printing Corp..........315 454-5507
131 Falso Dr Syracuse (13211) ***(G-15872)***
Alpha-En Corporation..........914 418-2000
28 Wells Ave Ste 2 Yonkers (10701) ***(G-17428)***
AlphaGraphics, Rochester *Also called Bittner Company LLC* ***(G-14251)***
Alphamed Bottles Inc..........631 275-5042
360 Oser Ave Hauppauge (11788) ***(G-6036)***
Alpina Color Graphics Inc..........212 285-2700
27 Cliff St Rm 502 New York (10038) ***(G-9151)***
Alpina Copyworld Inc (PA)..........212 683-3511
134 E 28th St New York (10016) ***(G-9152)***
Alpina Digital, New York *Also called Alpina Copyworld Inc* ***(G-9152)***
Alpina Foods Inc..........855 886-1914
5011 Agpark Dr W Batavia (14020) ***(G-622)***
Alpine Building Supply Inc..........718 456-2522
4626 Metropolitan Ave Ridgewood (11385) ***(G-14112)***
Alpine Business Group Inc (PA)..........212 989-4198
30 E 33rd St Frnt B New York (10016) ***(G-9153)***
Alpine Creations Ltd..........212 308-9353
17 E 48th St Fl 6 New York (10017) ***(G-9154)***
Alpine Creative Group, New York *Also called Alpine Business Group Inc* ***(G-9153)***
Alpine Machine Inc..........607 272-1344
1616 Trumansburg Rd Ithaca (14850) ***(G-6858)***
Alpine Overhead Doors Inc..........631 456-7800
8 Hulse Rd Ste 1 East Setauket (11733) ***(G-4494)***
Alpine Paper Box Co Inc..........718 345-4040
2246 Fulton St Brooklyn (11233) ***(G-1592)***
Alps Provision Co Inc..........718 721-4477
2270 45th St Astoria (11105) ***(G-430)***
Alps Sweet Shop, Beacon *Also called Hudson Valley Chocolatier Inc* ***(G-781)***
Alrajs Inc (PA)..........631 225-0300
146 Albany Ave Lindenhurst (11757) ***(G-7474)***
Alro Machine Tool & Die Co Inc..........631 226-5020
585 W Hoffman Ave Lindenhurst (11757) ***(G-7475)***
Alrod Associates Inc..........631 981-2193
710 Union Pkwy Ste 9 Ronkonkoma (11779) ***(G-14892)***

ALPHABETIC

Alry Tool and Die Co Inc.................716 693-2419
  386 Fillmore Ave Tonawanda (14150) *(G-16159)*
Alside Supply Center, Ronkonkoma Also called Associated Materials LLC *(G-14901)*
Alstom Signaling Inc...................800 717-4477
  1025 John St Ste 100h West Henrietta (14586) *(G-16898)*
Alstom Signaling Inc (HQ)...............585 783-2000
  1 River Rd Schenectady (12345) *(G-15257)*
Alstom Signaling Inc...................585 274-8700
  1 River Rd Schenectady (12345) *(G-15258)*
Alstom Transportation Inc (HQ)...........212 692-5353
  641 Lexington Ave Fl 28 New York (10022) *(G-9155)*
Alstom Transportation Inc................800 717-4477
  1025 John St Ste 100h West Henrietta (14586) *(G-16899)*
Alstrom Corporation....................718 824-4901
  1408 Seabury Ave Bronx (10461) *(G-1271)*
Alstrom Trnspt Info Solutions, Schenectady Also called Alstom Signaling Inc *(G-15257)*
Alta Industries Ltd.....................845 586-3336
  46966 State Hwy 30 Halcottsville (12438) *(G-5927)*
Alta Log Homes, Halcottsville Also called Alta Industries Ltd *(G-5927)*
Altaire Pharmaceuticals Inc..............631 722-5988
  311 West Ln Aquebogue (11931) *(G-383)*
Altamont Spray Welding Inc..............518 861-8870
  133 Lewis Rd Altamont (12009) *(G-209)*
Altaquip LLC..........................631 580-4740
  200 13th Ave Unit 6 Ronkonkoma (11779) *(G-14893)*
Altaro Corp...........................855 674-2455
  520 White Plains Rd Tarrytown (10591) *(G-16109)*
Altec Datacom LLC....................631 242-2417
  70 Corbin Ave Ste I Bay Shore (11706) *(G-668)*
Alternative Service Inc..................631 345-9500
  111 Old Dock Rd Yaphank (11980) *(G-17401)*
Alternative Technology Corp.............914 478-5900
  1 North St Ste 1 Hastings On Hudson (10706) *(G-6022)*
Alternatives For Children.................631 271-0777
  600 S Service Rd Dix Hills (11746) *(G-4313)*
Altius Aviation LLC....................315 455-7555
  113 Tuskegee Rd Ste 2 Syracuse (13211) *(G-15873)*
Altman Lighting, Yonkers Also called Altman Stage Lighting Co Inc *(G-17429)*
Altman Stage Lighting Co Inc............914 476-7987
  57 Alexander St Yonkers (10701) *(G-17429)*
Alton Manufacturing Inc.................585 458-2600
  825 Lee Rd Rochester (14606) *(G-14209)*
Altro Business Forms Div, New York Also called New Deal Printing Corp *(G-11404)*
Altronix Corp..........................718 567-8181
  140 58th St Bldg A3w Brooklyn (11220) *(G-1593)*
Altum Press, Long Island City Also called Cama Graphics Inc *(G-7723)*
Altype Fire Door Corp...................718 292-3500
  886 E 149th St Bronx (10455) *(G-1272)*
Aluf Plastics Division, Orangeburg Also called API Industries Inc *(G-13239)*
Alufoil Products Co Inc.................631 231-4141
  135 Oser Ave Ste 3 Hauppauge (11788) *(G-6037)*
Alumi-Tech LLC.......................585 663-7010
  1640 Harris Rd Penfield (14526) *(G-13521)*
Alumidock, Randolph Also called Metallic Ladder Mfg Corp *(G-14029)*
Alumil Fabrication Inc...................845 469-2874
  1900 Corporate Blvd Newburgh (12550) *(G-12769)*
Aluminum Injection Mold Co LLC..........585 502-6087
  8741 Lake Street Rd Ste 4 Le Roy (14482) *(G-7427)*
Alumiseal Corp........................518 329-2820
  118 N Mountain Rd Copake Falls (12517) *(G-3914)*
Alvin J Bart, Glendale Also called Allen William & Company Inc *(G-5659)*
Alvin J Bart & Sons Inc..................718 417-1300
  7119 80th St Ste 8315 Glendale (11385) *(G-5660)*
Alvina Vlenta Couture Collectn............212 921-7058
  525 Fashion Ave Rm 1703 New York (10018) *(G-9156)*
Alvina Vlenta Couture Collectn............212 921-7058
  225 W 37th St New York (10018) *(G-9157)*
Always Baked Fresh...................631 648-0811
  331 Dante Ct Ste F Holbrook (11741) *(G-6459)*
Always Printing........................914 481-5209
  149 Highland St Port Chester (10573) *(G-13767)*
Alyk Inc..............................917 968-2552
  440 Park Ave S Fl 14 New York (10016) *(G-9158)*
AM Architectural Metal & Glass...........845 942-8848
  5 Bridge St Garnerville (10923) *(G-5567)*
AM Bickford Inc.......................716 652-1590
  12318 Big Tree Rd Wales Center (14169) *(G-16559)*
AM Display, Highland Mills Also called All Merchandise Display Corp *(G-6438)*
Am-Best Emblems, Boiceville Also called Stucki Embroidery Works Inc *(G-1155)*
Am-Pol Eagle, Buffalo Also called Buffalo Standard Printing Corp *(G-2882)*
AMA Precision Screening Inc.............585 293-0820
  456 Sanford Rd N Churchville (14428) *(G-3663)*
Amacon Corporation....................631 293-1888
  49 Alder St Unit A West Babylon (11704) *(G-16794)*
Amada Tool America Inc.................585 344-3900
  4 Treadeasy Ave Ste A Batavia (14020) *(G-623)*
Amadeo Serrano.......................516 608-8359
  36 Frankel Ave Freeport (11520) *(G-5395)*
Amalfi Ingredients LLC..................631 392-1526
  94 E Jefryn Blvd Ste H Deer Park (11729) *(G-4118)*
Amana Tool Corp......................631 752-1300
  120 Carolyn Blvd Farmingdale (11735) *(G-4947)*
Amarr Company.......................585 426-8290
  550 Mile Crssing Blvd 1 Rochester (14624) *(G-14210)*
Amarr Garage Doors, Rochester Also called Amarr Company *(G-14210)*
Amax Industrial Products, Bohemia Also called Brockyn Corporation *(G-1023)*
Amax Printing Inc......................718 384-8600
  6417 Grand Ave Maspeth (11378) *(G-8144)*
Amazing Meals, Maspeth Also called Alle Processing Corp *(G-8143)*
Amber Bever Inc.......................212 391-4911
  8604 Avenue M 1 Brooklyn (11236) *(G-1594)*
Ambind Corp..........................716 836-4365
  Cheektowaga Buffalo (14225) *(G-2822)*
Ambras Fine Jewelry Inc.................718 784-5252
  3100 47th Ave Unit 3 Long Island City (11101) *(G-7688)*
Ambras Fjc, Long Island City Also called Ambras Fine Jewelry Inc *(G-7688)*
Ambrell Corporation (HQ)................585 889-0236
  39 Main St Scottsville (14546) *(G-15356)*
Amby International Inc...................718 645-0964
  1460 E 12th St Brooklyn (11230) *(G-1595)*
Amci Ltd..............................718 937-5858
  3302 48th Ave Long Island City (11101) *(G-7689)*
Amco Intl Mfg & Design Inc...............718 388-8668
  10 Conselyea St Brooklyn (11211) *(G-1596)*
Amcom Software Inc....................212 951-7600
  256 W 38th St Fl 8 New York (10018) *(G-9159)*
Amcor Rigid Plastics Usa LLC.............716 366-2440
  1 Cliffstar Ave Dunkirk (14048) *(G-4356)*
Amendola MBL & Stone Ctr Inc............914 997-7968
  560 Tarrytown Rd White Plains (10607) *(G-17104)*
Amereon Ltd..........................631 298-5100
  800 Wickham Ave Mattituck (11952) *(G-8238)*
Amerex Corporation....................212 221-3151
  512 7th Ave Fl 9 New York (10018) *(G-9160)*
Ameri Serv South, Jamestown Also called Vac Air Service Inc *(G-7074)*
Ameri-Cut Tool Grinding Inc..............716 692-3900
  1020 Oliver St North Tonawanda (14120) *(G-12971)*
America Capital Energy Corp.............212 983-8316
  405 Lexington Ave Fl 65 New York (10174) *(G-9161)*
America NY RI Wang Fd Group Co.........718 628-8999
  5885 58th Ave Maspeth (11378) *(G-8145)*
America Press Inc (PA)...................212 581-4640
  106 W 56th St New York (10019) *(G-9162)*
American Access Care LLC...............631 582-9729
  32 Central Ave Hauppauge (11788) *(G-6038)*
American Acrylic Corporation.............631 422-2200
  400 Sheffield Ave West Babylon (11704) *(G-16795)*
American Aerogel Corporation............585 328-2140
  460 Buffalo Rd Ste 200a Rochester (14611) *(G-14211)*
American Aerospace Contrls Inc...........631 694-5100
  570 Smith St Farmingdale (11735) *(G-4948)*
American Almond Pdts Co Inc (PA)........718 875-8310
  103 Walworth St Brooklyn (11205) *(G-1597)*
American Apparel Ltd...................516 504-4559
  15 Cuttermill Rd Ste 145 Great Neck (11021) *(G-5805)*
American Apparel Trading Corp (PA)......212 764-5990
  209 W 38th St Rm 1004 New York (10018) *(G-9163)*
American Attitude, New York Also called Kww Productions Corp *(G-10935)*
American Auto ACC Incrporation (PA)......718 886-6600
  3506 Leavitt St Apt Cfc Flushing (11354) *(G-5233)*
American Avionic Tech Corp..............631 924-8200
  25 Industrial Blvd Medford (11763) *(G-8266)*
American Best Cabinets Inc...............845 369-6666
  397 Spook Rock Rd Suffern (10901) *(G-15807)*
American Bio Medica Corp (PA)...........518 758-8158
  122 Smith Rd Kinderhook (12106) *(G-7196)*
American Blade Mfg LLC (PA).............607 432-4518
  138 Roundhouse Rd Oneonta (13820) *(G-13193)*
American Blade Mfg LLC.................607 656-4204
  47 Birdsall St Greene (13778) *(G-5880)*
American Bluestone LLC.................607 369-2235
  760 Quarry Rd Sidney (13838) *(G-15457)*
American Boiler Tank Wldg Inc............518 463-5012
  53 Pleasant St Albany (12207) *(G-44)*
American Bottling Company..............516 714-0002
  2004 Orville Dr N Ronkonkoma (11779) *(G-14894)*
American Bptst Chrches Mtro NY..........212 870-3195
  527 W 22nd St New York (10011) *(G-9164)*
American Business Forms Inc.............716 836-5111
  3840 E Robinson Rd # 249 Amherst (14228) *(G-226)*
American Canvas Binders Corp............914 969-0300
  430 Nepperhan Ave Yonkers (10701) *(G-17430)*
American Car Signs Inc..................518 227-1173
  1483 W Duane Lake Rd Duanesburg (12056) *(G-4349)*
American Casino Equipment Mfg...........631 242-2440
  45 W Jefryn Blvd Ste 107 Deer Park (11729) *(G-4119)*
American Casting and Mfg Corp (PA)......800 342-0333
  51 Commercial St Plainview (11803) *(G-13611)*
American Casting and Mfg Corp...........516 349-7010
  65 S Terminal Dr Plainview (11803) *(G-13612)*
American Challenge Enterprises...........631 595-7171
  1804 Plaza Ave Ste 6 New Hyde Park (11040) *(G-8860)*

American Chimney Supplies Inc.....631 434-2020
129 Oser Ave Ste B Hauppauge (11788) *(G-6039)*
American Cigar.....718 969-0008
6940 Fresh Meadow Ln Fresh Meadows (11365) *(G-5451)*
American City Bus Journals Inc.....716 541-1654
465 Main St Ste 100 Buffalo (14203) *(G-2823)*
American Cleaning Solutions, Long Island City *Also called American Wax Company Inc* *(G-7691)*
American Comfort Direct LLC.....201 364-8309
708 3rd Ave Fl 6 New York (10017) *(G-9165)*
American Country Quilts & Lin.....631 283-5466
134 Mariner Dr Unit C Southampton (11968) *(G-15562)*
American Craft Jewelers Inc (PA).....718 972-0945
3611 14th Ave Ste 522 Brooklyn (11218) *(G-1598)*
American Crmic Process RES LLC.....315 828-6268
835 Mcivor Rd Phelps (14532) *(G-13552)*
American Culture, Greenlawn *Also called All Cultures Inc* *(G-5890)*
American Culture Hair Inc.....631 242-3142
159 E 2nd St Huntington Station (11746) *(G-6731)*
American Diagnostic Corp.....631 273-6155
55 Commerce Dr Hauppauge (11788) *(G-6040)*
American Dies Inc.....718 387-1900
37 Provost St Brooklyn (11222) *(G-1599)*
American Douglas Metals Inc.....716 856-3170
99 Bud Mil Dr Buffalo (14206) *(G-2824)*
American Dsplay Die Ctters Inc.....212 645-1274
121 Varick St Rm 301 New York (10013) *(G-9166)*
American Electronic Products.....631 924-1299
86 Horseblock Rd Unit F Yaphank (11980) *(G-17402)*
American Epoxy and Metal Inc.....718 828-7828
83 Cushman Rd Scarsdale (10583) *(G-15245)*
American Express Publishing, New York *Also called Time Inc Affluent Media Group* *(G-12365)*
American Felt & Filter Co Inc.....845 561-3560
361 Walsh Ave New Windsor (12553) *(G-8977)*
American Filtration Tech Inc.....585 359-4130
100 Thruway Park Dr West Henrietta (14586) *(G-16900)*
American Fuel Cell LLC.....585 474-3993
1200 Ridgeway Ave Ste 123 Rochester (14615) *(G-14212)*
American Glass Light, Newburgh *Also called Sandy Littman Inc* *(G-12802)*
American Graphic Design Awards.....212 696-4380
89 5th Ave Ste 901 New York (10003) *(G-9167)*
American Healthcare Supply Inc.....212 674-3636
304 Park Ave S New York (10010) *(G-9168)*
American Heritage Magazine, New York *Also called Nsgv Inc* *(G-11484)*
American Home Mfg LLC (HQ).....212 643-0680
302 5th Ave New York (10001) *(G-9169)*
American Hormones Inc.....845 471-7272
69 W Cedar St Ste 2 Poughkeepsie (12601) *(G-13904)*
American Hose & Hydralics, Bronx *Also called American Refuse Supply Inc* *(G-1273)*
American Hsptals Patient Guide.....518 346-1099
1890 Maxon Rd Ext Schenectady (12308) *(G-15259)*
American Icon Industries Inc.....845 561-1299
392 N Montgomery St Ste 2 Newburgh (12550) *(G-12770)*
American Images Inc.....716 825-8888
25 Imson St Buffalo (14210) *(G-2825)*
American Inst Chem Engineers (PA).....646 495-1355
120 Wall St Fl 23 New York (10005) *(G-9170)*
American Institute Physics Inc.....516 576-2410
Hntngton Qad Ste 1n1-2 Melville (11747) *(G-8326)*
American Intl Media LLC.....845 359-4225
11 Martine Ave Ste 870 White Plains (10606) *(G-17105)*
American Intl Trimming.....718 369-9643
80 39th St Brooklyn (11232) *(G-1600)*
American Intrmdal Cont Mfg LLC.....631 774-6790
150 Motor Pkwy Ste 401 Hauppauge (11788) *(G-6041)*
American Jewish Committee.....212 891-1400
561 Fashion Ave Fl 16 New York (10018) *(G-9171)*
American Jewish Congress Inc (PA).....212 879-4500
825 3rd Ave Fl 181800 New York (10022) *(G-9172)*
American Juice Company LLC.....347 620-0252
224 W 35th St Fl 11 New York (10001) *(G-9173)*
American Lckr SEC Systems Inc.....716 699-2773
12 Martha St Ellicottville (14731) *(G-4654)*
American Leather Specialties.....800 556-6488
87 34th St Unit 1 Brooklyn (11232) *(G-1601)*
American Linear Manufacturers (PA).....516 333-1351
629 Main St Westbury (11590) *(G-16993)*
American Marking Systems, Fulton *Also called Krengel Manufacturing Co Inc* *(G-5481)*
American Material Processing.....315 318-0017
126 Bankrupt Rd Phoenix (13135) *(G-13567)*
American Material Processing.....315 695-6204
126 Bankrupt Rd Phoenix (13135) *(G-13568)*
American Media Inc.....212 545-4800
4 New York Plz Fl 2 New York (10004) *(G-9174)*
American Media Inc (PA).....212 545-4800
4 New York Plz Fl 2 New York (10004) *(G-9175)*
American Metal, Rome *Also called Nash Metalware Co Inc* *(G-14851)*
American Metal Spinning Pdts.....631 454-6276
21 Eads St West Babylon (11704) *(G-16796)*
American Metalcraft Marine.....315 686-9891
690 Riverside Dr Clayton (13624) *(G-3710)*
American Minerals Inc (HQ).....646 747-4222
21 W 46th St Fl 14 New York (10036) *(G-9176)*
American Motive Power Inc.....585 335-3132
9431 Foster Wheeler Rd Dansville (14437) *(G-4101)*
American Mtal Stmping Spinning.....718 384-1500
1 Nassau Ave Brooklyn (11222) *(G-1602)*
American Office Supply Inc.....516 294-9444
400 Post Ave Ste 105 Westbury (11590) *(G-16994)*
American Originals Corporation.....212 836-4155
1156 Avenue Of The Americ New York (10036) *(G-9177)*
American Orthotic Lab Co Inc.....718 961-6487
924 118th St College Point (11356) *(G-3803)*
American Package Company Inc.....718 389-4444
226 Franklin St Brooklyn (11222) *(G-1603)*
American Packaging Corporation.....585 254-2002
1555 Lyell Ave Rochester (14606) *(G-14213)*
American Packaging Corporation (PA).....585 254-9500
777 Driving Park Ave Rochester (14613) *(G-14214)*
American Physical Society.....631 591-4025
1 Research Rd Ridge (11961) *(G-14104)*
American Precision Inds Inc (HQ).....716 691-9100
45 Hazelwood Dr Amherst (14228) *(G-227)*
American Precision Inds Inc.....716 652-3600
270 Quaker Rd East Aurora (14052) *(G-4390)*
American Precision Inds Inc.....585 496-5755
95 North St Arcade (14009) *(G-386)*
American Pride Fasteners LLC.....631 940-8292
195 S Fehr Way Bay Shore (11706) *(G-669)*
American Print Solutions Inc.....718 246-7800
561 President St Brooklyn (11215) *(G-1604)*
American Print Solutions Inc (PA).....718 208-2309
2233 Nostrand Ave Ste 7 Brooklyn (11210) *(G-1605)*
American Printing & Envelope, New York *Also called Apec Paper Industries Ltd* *(G-9222)*
American Printing and Off Sups, Kingston *Also called Robert Tabatznik Assoc Inc* *(G-7237)*
American Printing Eqp & Sup, Elmont *Also called Awt Supply Corp* *(G-4730)*
American Products, Rochester *Also called American Time Mfg Ltd* *(G-14217)*
American Profile Magazine, New York *Also called Publishing Group America Inc* *(G-11769)*
American Puff Corp.....516 379-1300
225 Buffalo Ave Freeport (11520) *(G-5396)*
American Quality Embroidery (PA).....631 467-3200
740 Koehler Ave Ronkonkoma (11779) *(G-14895)*
American Quality Technology.....607 777-9488
6 Emma St Binghamton (13905) *(G-884)*
American Racing Headers Inc.....631 608-1427
880 Grand Blvd Deer Park (11729) *(G-4120)*
American Refrigeration Inc (HQ).....212 699-4000
142 W 57th St Fl 17 New York (10019) *(G-9178)*
American Refuse Supply Inc.....718 893-8157
521 Longfellow Ave Bronx (10474) *(G-1273)*
American Regent Inc.....631 924-4000
5 Ramsey Rd Shirley (11967) *(G-15434)*
American Regent Laboratories, Shirley *Also called American Regent Inc* *(G-15434)*
American Rock Salt Company LLC (PA).....585 991-6878
3846 Retsof Rd Retsof (14539) *(G-14064)*
American Rolling Door Ltd.....718 273-0485
40 Dolson Pl Staten Island (10303) *(G-15658)*
American Scientific Ltg Corp.....718 369-1100
25 12th St Ste 4 Brooklyn (11215) *(G-1606)*
American Sealing Technology.....631 254-0019
31 Prospect Pl Deer Park (11729) *(G-4121)*
American Ship Repairs Company.....718 435-5570
1011 38th St 13 Brooklyn (11219) *(G-1607)*
American Signcrafters, Islip *Also called Tj Signs Unlimited LLC* *(G-6853)*
American Signcrafters, Islip *Also called T J Signs Unlimited LLC* *(G-6852)*
American Silk Mills, New York *Also called Gerli & Co Inc* *(G-10329)*
American Spacer Technologies.....518 828-1339
35 Industrial Tract Anx Hudson (12534) *(G-6633)*
American Specialty Mfg Co.....585 544-5600
272 Hudson Ave Rochester (14605) *(G-14215)*
American Sports Media.....585 924-4250
106 Cobblestone Court Dr # 323 Victor (14564) *(G-16484)*
American Sports Media LLC (PA).....585 377-9636
2604 Elmwood Ave Ste 343 Rochester (14618) *(G-14216)*
American Spray-On Corp.....212 929-2100
22 W 21st St Fl 2 New York (10010) *(G-9179)*
American Standard Mfg Inc.....518 868-2512
106 Industrial Park Ln Central Bridge (12035) *(G-3507)*
American Steel Gate Corp.....718 291-4050
10510 150th St Jamaica (11435) *(G-6928)*
American T Shirts Inc.....212 563-7125
225 W 39th St Fl 6 New York (10018) *(G-9180)*
American Target Marketing Inc.....518 725-4369
11 Cayadutta St Gloversville (12078) *(G-5720)*
American Tchncal Ceramics Corp (HQ).....631 622-4700
1 Norden Ln Huntington Station (11746) *(G-6732)*
American Techical Ceramics.....631 622-4758
11 Stepar Pl Huntington Station (11746) *(G-6733)*
American Technical Ceramics.....631 622-4700
17 Stepar Pl Huntington Station (11746) *(G-6734)*
American Time Mfg Ltd.....585 266-5120
1600 N Clinton Ave Ste 1 Rochester (14621) *(G-14217)*

ALPHABETIC

American Torque Inc 718 526-2433
10522 150th St Jamaica (11435) *(G-6929)*
American Towman Expeditions, Warwick Also called American Towman Network Inc *(G-16608)*
American Towman Network Inc 845 986-4546
7 West St Warwick (10990) *(G-16608)*
American Trans-Coil Corp 516 922-9640
69 Hamilton Ave Ste 3 Oyster Bay (11771) *(G-13390)*
American Trim Mfg Inc 518 239-8151
4750 State Hwy 145 Durham (12422) *(G-4379)*
American Turf Monthly, Great Neck Also called Star Sports Corp *(G-5861)*
American Vintage Wine Biscuit 718 361-1003
4003 27th St Long Island City (11101) *(G-7690)*
American Visual Display, Farmingdale Also called American Visuals Inc *(G-4949)*
American Visuals Inc 631 694-6104
90 Gazza Blvd Farmingdale (11735) *(G-4949)*
American Wax Company Inc 718 392-8080
3930 Review Ave Long Island City (11101) *(G-7691)*
American Wire Tie Inc (PA) 716 337-2412
2073 Franklin St North Collins (14111) *(G-12942)*
American Wood Column Corp 718 782-3163
913 Grand St Brooklyn (11211) *(G-1608)*
American Woods & Veneers Works 718 937-2195
4735 27th St Long Island City (11101) *(G-7692)*
Americana Vineyards & Winery 607 387-6801
4367 E Covert Rd Interlaken (14847) *(G-6785)*
Americo Group Inc 212 563-2700
498 7th Ave Fl 8 New York (10018) *(G-9181)*
Americo Group Inc (PA) 212 563-2700
1411 Broadway Fl 2 New York (10018) *(G-9182)*
Amerikom Group Inc 212 675-1329
247 W 30th St Rm 6w New York (10001) *(G-9183)*
Amerimade Coat Inc 212 216-0925
463 Fashion Ave Rm 802 New York (10018) *(G-9184)*
Ameritool Mfg Inc 315 668-2172
64 Corporate Park Dr Central Square (13036) *(G-3543)*
Amertac Holdings Inc (PA) 610 336-1330
25 Robert Pitt Dr Monsey (10952) *(G-8602)*
Ames Advanced Materials Corp (HQ) 518 792-5808
50 Harrison Ave South Glens Falls (12803) *(G-15545)*
Ames Companies Inc 607 739-4544
114 Smith Rd Pine Valley (14872) *(G-13583)*
Ames Companies Inc 607 369-9595
196 Clifton St Unadilla (13849) *(G-16310)*
Ames Goldsmith Corp 518 792-7435
21 Rogers St Glens Falls (12801) *(G-5685)*
Ameta International Co Ltd 416 992-8036
2221 Kenmore Ave Ste 108 Buffalo (14207) *(G-2826)*
Ametal International, Brooklyn Also called Kon Tat Group Corporation *(G-2179)*
Ametek Inc 631 467-8400
903 S 2nd St Ronkonkoma (11779) *(G-14896)*
Ametek Inc 516 832-7710
300 Endo Blvd Garden City (11530) *(G-5508)*
Ametek Inc 607 763-4700
33 Lewis Rd Ste 6 Binghamton (13905) *(G-885)*
Ametek CTS Us Inc 631 467-8400
903 S 2nd St Ronkonkoma (11779) *(G-14897)*
Ametek Inc 585 263-7700
255 Union St N Rochester (14605) *(G-14218)*
Ametek Power Instruments, Rochester Also called Ametek Inc *(G-14218)*
Ametek Rotron, Woodstock Also called Rotron Incorporated *(G-17381)*
Ametek Rotron, Woodstock Also called Rotron Incorporated *(G-17382)*
Ametek Technical & Indus Pdts 845 246-3401
75 North St Saugerties (12477) *(G-15208)*
Amfar Asphalt Inc 631 269-6660
137 Old Northport Rd Kings Park (11754) *(G-7199)*
AMG Global, New York Also called Enchante Lites LLC *(G-10081)*
AMG Global LLC (HQ) 212 602-1818
15 W 34th St Fl 8 New York (10001) *(G-9185)*
AMG Global NY & Enchante ACC, New York Also called AMG Global LLC *(G-9185)*
Amherst Bee, Williamsville Also called Bee Publications Inc *(G-17263)*
Amherst Media Inc 716 874-4450
175 Rano St Ste 200 Buffalo (14207) *(G-2827)*
Amherst Stnless Fbrication LLC 716 691-7012
60 John Glenn Dr Amherst (14228) *(G-228)*
Amherst Systems Inc (HQ) 716 631-0610
1740 Wehrle Dr Buffalo (14221) *(G-2828)*
AMI, New York Also called American Media Inc *(G-9174)*
AMI Brands, Mamaroneck Also called Brands Within Reach LLC *(G-8057)*
Amica Magazine, New York Also called Rizzoli Intl Publications Inc *(G-11905)*
Amincor Inc 347 821-3452
1350 Ave Of Amrcas Fl 24 New York (10019) *(G-9186)*
Amiram Dror Inc (PA) 212 979-9505
226 India St Brooklyn (11222) *(G-1609)*
Amish Structure 607 257-1070
32 North St Dryden (13053) *(G-4344)*
Amj DOT LLC 718 775-3288
1726 E 7th St Brooklyn (11223) *(G-1610)*
Amneal Pharmaceuticals LLC 908 231-1911
50 Horseblock Rd Brookhaven (11719) *(G-1504)*

Amneal Pharmaceuticals LLC 631 952-0214
50 Horseblock Rd Brookhaven (11719) *(G-1505)*
Amneal Pharmaceuticals LLC (HQ) 908 947-3120
50 Horseblock Rd Brookhaven (11719) *(G-1506)*
Amnews Corporation 212 932-7400
2340 Frdrick Duglass Blvd New York (10027) *(G-9187)*
Amnewyork 212 239-5555
330 W 34th St Fl 17 New York (10001) *(G-9188)*
Amoroso Wood Products Co Inc 631 249-4998
462 Old Country Rd Melville (11747) *(G-8327)*
Amoseastern Apparel Inc (PA) 212 921-1859
49 W 38th St Fl 7 New York (10018) *(G-9189)*
AMP-Line Corp 845 623-3288
3 Amethyst Ct West Nyack (10994) *(G-16940)*
Ampac Paper LLC (PA) 845 778-5511
30 Coldenham Rd Walden (12586) *(G-16549)*
Ampacet Corporation (PA) 914 631-6600
660 White Plains Rd # 360 Tarrytown (10591) *(G-16110)*
Ampaco, Brooklyn Also called American Package Company Inc *(G-1603)*
Ampex Casting Corporation 212 719-1318
23 W 47th St Unit 3 New York (10036) *(G-9190)*
Amphenol Aerospace Industrial, Sidney Also called Amphenol Corporation *(G-15458)*
Amphenol Corporation 607 563-5364
40-60 Delaware Ave Sidney (13838) *(G-15458)*
Amphenol Corporation 607 563-5011
40-60 Delaware Ave Sidney (13838) *(G-15459)*
Amphenol Intrconnect Pdts Corp (HQ) 607 754-4444
20 Valley St Endicott (13760) *(G-4803)*
Amplitech Inc 631 521-7738
620 Johnson Ave Ste 2 Bohemia (11716) *(G-1010)*
Amplitech Group Inc 631 521-7831
620 Johnson Ave Bohemia (11716) *(G-1011)*
Ampro International Inc 845 278-4910
30 Coventry Ln Brewster (10509) *(G-1207)*
Amri, Albany Also called Albany Molecular Research Inc *(G-39)*
Amri, Rensselaer Also called Albany Molecular Research Inc *(G-14055)*
Amri Rensselaer, Rensselaer Also called Albany Molecular Research Inc *(G-14054)*
Amron Electronics Inc 631 737-1234
160 Gary Way Ronkonkoma (11779) *(G-14898)*
Amsale Aberra LLC 212 695-5936
318 W 39th St Fl 12 New York (10018) *(G-9191)*
Amscan Everyday Warehouse, Chester Also called Amscan Inc *(G-3626)*
Amscan Inc 845 469-9116
47 Elizabeth Dr Chester (10918) *(G-3626)*
Amscan Inc 845 782-0490
2 Commerce Dr S Harriman (10926) *(G-5993)*
Amsco Inc 716 823-4213
925 Bailey Ave Buffalo (14206) *(G-2829)*
Amsco School Publications Inc 212 886-6500
315 Hudson St Fl 5 New York (10013) *(G-9192)*
Amsterdam Oil Heat, Amsterdam Also called J H Buhrmaster Company Inc *(G-351)*
Amsterdam Pharmacy, New York Also called Shrineeta Pharmacy Inc *(G-12079)*
Amsterdam Printing & Litho Inc 518 792-6501
428 Corinth Rd Queensbury (12804) *(G-14002)*
Amsterdam Printing & Litho Inc 518 842-6000
166 Wallins Corners Rd Amsterdam (12010) *(G-333)*
Amsterdam Printing & Litho Inc 518 842-6000
166 Wallins Corners Rd Amsterdam (12010) *(G-334)*
Amsterdam Printing & Litho Inc 518 792-6501
428 Corinth Rd Queensbury (12804) *(G-14003)*
Amstutze Woodworking (PA) 518 946-8206
246 Springfield Rd Upper Jay (12987) *(G-16327)*
Amt Incorporated 518 284-2910
883 Chestnut St Sharon Springs (13459) *(G-15405)*
Amy Pak Publishing Inc 585 964-8188
3997 Roosevelt Hwy Holley (14470) *(G-6515)*
Amy Scherber Inc (PA) 212 462-4338
75 9th Ave New York (10011) *(G-9193)*
Amy's Bread, New York Also called Amy Scherber Inc *(G-9193)*
An Excelsior Elevator Corp 516 408-3070
640 Main St Unit 2 Westbury (11590) *(G-16995)*
An Group Inc 631 549-4090
17 Scott Dr Melville (11747) *(G-8328)*
An-Cor Industrial Plastics Inc 716 695-3141
900 Niagara Falls Blvd North Tonawanda (14120) *(G-12972)*
Anabec Inc 716 759-1674
9393 Main St Clarence (14031) *(G-3683)*
Anacor Pharmaceuticals Inc 212 733-2323
235 E 42nd St New York (10017) *(G-9194)*
Anage Inc 212 944-6533
530 Fashion Ave Frnt 5 New York (10018) *(G-9195)*
Analog Digital Technology LLC 585 698-1845
95 Mount Read Blvd # 149 Rochester (14611) *(G-14219)*
Analysts In Media (aim) Inc 212 488-1777
55 Broad St Fl 9 New York (10004) *(G-9196)*
Analytics Intell, New York Also called Informa Solutions Inc *(G-10640)*
Anand Printing Machinery Inc 631 667-3079
188 W 16th St Deer Park (11729) *(G-4122)*
Anandamali Inc 212 343-8964
35 N Moore St New York (10013) *(G-9197)*
Anaren Inc (PA) 315 432-8909
6635 Kirkville Rd East Syracuse (13057) *(G-4519)*

Anaren Microwave Inc ... 315 432-8909
6635 Kirkville Rd East Syracuse (13057) ***(G-4520)***
Anasia Inc ... 718 588-1407
1175 Jerome Ave Bronx (10452) ***(G-1274)***
Anastasia Furs International (PA) ... 212 868-9241
224 W 30th St Rm 204 New York (10001) ***(G-9198)***
Anatoli Inc ... 845 334-9000
43 Basin Rd Ste 11 West Hurley (12491) ***(G-16931)***
Anchor Canvas LLC ... 631 265-5602
556 W Jericho Tpke Smithtown (11787) ***(G-15505)***
Anchor Commerce Trading Corp ... 516 881-3485
53 Dutchess Blvd Atlantic Beach (11509) ***(G-467)***
Anchor Glass Container Corp ... 607 737-1933
151 E Mccanns Blvd Elmira Heights (14903) ***(G-4721)***
Anchor Tech Products Corp ... 914 592-0240
4 Vernon Ln Ste 2 Elmsford (10523) ***(G-4742)***
Ancient Modern Art LLC ... 212 302-0080
14 E 17th St Ph 1 New York (10003) ***(G-9199)***
Ancon Gear & Instrument Corp (PA) ... 631 694-5255
29 Seabro Ave Amityville (11701) ***(G-275)***
Andela Products, Richfield Springs *Also called Andela Tool & Machine Inc* ***(G-14074)***
Andela Tool & Machine Inc ... 315 858-0055
493 State Route 28 Richfield Springs (13439) ***(G-14074)***
Anderson Equipment Company ... 716 877-1992
2140 Military Rd Tonawanda (14150) ***(G-16160)***
Anderson Instrument Co Inc (HQ) ... 518 922-5315
156 Auriesville Rd Fultonville (12072) ***(G-5491)***
Anderson Precision Inc ... 716 484-1148
20 Livingston Ave Jamestown (14701) ***(G-7007)***
Andes Gold Corporation ... 212 541-2495
405 Lexington Ave New York (10174) ***(G-9200)***
Andex Corp ... 585 328-3790
69 Deep Rock Rd Rochester (14624) ***(G-14220)***
Andigo New Media Inc ... 212 727-8445
150 W 25th St Rm 900 New York (10001) ***(G-9201)***
Andike Millwork Inc (PA) ... 718 894-1796
5818 64th St Fl 2 Maspeth (11378) ***(G-8146)***
Andor Design Corp ... 516 364-1619
20 Pond View Dr Syosset (11791) ***(G-15833)***
Andrea Electronics Corporation (PA) ... 631 719-1800
620 Johnson Ave Ste 1b Bohemia (11716) ***(G-1012)***
Andrea Strongwater ... 212 873-0905
465 W End Ave New York (10024) ***(G-9202)***
Andrea Systems LLC ... 631 390-3140
140 Finn Ct Farmingdale (11735) ***(G-4950)***
Andrew M Schwartz LLC ... 212 391-7070
71 Gansevoort St Ste 2a New York (10014) ***(G-9203)***
Andrew Sapienza Bakery Inc ... 516 437-1715
553 Meacham Ave Elmont (11003) ***(G-4728)***
Andritz Inc ... 518 745-2988
13 Pruyns Island Dr Glens Falls (12801) ***(G-5686)***
Androme Leather Inc ... 518 773-7945
21 Foster St Gloversville (12078) ***(G-5721)***
Andros Bowman Products LLC ... 540 217-4100
151 West Ave Lyndonville (14098) ***(G-7994)***
Andros Manufacturing Corp ... 585 663-5700
30 Hojack Park Rochester (14612) ***(G-14221)***
Andujar Asbestos and Lead ... 716 228-6757
473 4th St Buffalo (14201) ***(G-2830)***
Andy & Evan Industries Inc ... 212 967-7908
261 W 35th St Ste 702 New York (10001) ***(G-9204)***
Andy & Evan Shirt Co., The, New York *Also called Andy & Evan Industries Inc* ***(G-9204)***
Angel Media and Publishing ... 845 727-4949
26 Snake Hill Rd West Nyack (10994) ***(G-16941)***
Angel Textiles Inc ... 212 532-0900
519 8th Ave Fl 21 New York (10018) ***(G-9205)***
Angel Tips Nail Salon ... 718 225-8300
25473 Horace Harding Expy Little Neck (11362) ***(G-7529)***
Angel-Made In Heaven Inc (PA) ... 212 869-5678
525 Fashion Ave Rm 1710 New York (10018) ***(G-9206)***
Angel-Made In Heaven Inc ... 718 832-4778
116 26th St Brooklyn (11232) ***(G-1611)***
Angelic Gourmet, Naples *Also called Naples Vly Mrgers Acqstons LLC* ***(G-8813)***
Angelica Forest Products Inc ... 585 466-3205
54 Closser Ave Angelica (14709) ***(G-376)***
Angelica Spring Company Inc ... 585 466-7892
99 West Ave Angelica (14709) ***(G-377)***
Angie Washroom, New Windsor *Also called Larcent Enterprises Inc* ***(G-8987)***
Angiodynamics Inc ... 518 975-1400
603 Queensbury Ave Queensbury (12804) ***(G-14004)***
Angiodynamics Inc ... 518 792-4112
10 Glens Fls Technical Pa Glens Falls (12801) ***(G-5687)***
Angiodynamics Inc ... 518 742-4430
543 Queensbury Ave Queensbury (12804) ***(G-14005)***
Angiodynamics Inc (PA) ... 518 795-1400
14 Plaza Dr Latham (12110) ***(G-7380)***
Angiogenex Inc (PA) ... 347 468-6799
425 Madison Ave Ste 902 New York (10017) ***(G-9207)***
Angiotech Biocoatings Corp ... 585 321-1130
336 Summit Point Dr Henrietta (14467) ***(G-6315)***
Anglo Apparel Service, New York *Also called Anglo II Ltd* ***(G-9208)***
Anglo II Ltd ... 212 563-4980
224 W 35th St Fl 8 New York (10001) ***(G-9208)***
Ango Home, New York *Also called Feldman Company Inc* ***(G-10203)***
Angola Pennysaver Inc ... 716 549-1164
19 Center St Angola (14006) ***(G-379)***
Angus Buffers & Biochemicals, Niagara Falls *Also called Angus Chemical Company* ***(G-12819)***
Angus Chemical Company ... 716 283-1434
2236 Liberty Dr Niagara Falls (14304) ***(G-12819)***
Anheuser-Busch LLC ... 315 638-0365
2885 Belgium Rd Baldwinsville (13027) ***(G-566)***
Anheuser-Busch LLC ... 212 573-8800
250 Park Ave Fl 2 New York (10177) ***(G-9209)***
Anheuser-Busch Companies LLC ... 718 589-2610
510 Food Center Dr Bronx (10474) ***(G-1275)***
Anheuser-Busch Inbev Fin Inc ... 212 573-8800
250 Park Ave New York (10177) ***(G-9210)***
Anhui Skyworth LLC ... 917 940-6903
44 Kensington Ct Hempstead (11550) ***(G-6288)***
Aniiwe Inc ... 347 683-1891
774 Rockaway Ave Apt 3k Brooklyn (11212) ***(G-1612)***
Anima Group LLC ... 917 913-2053
435 E 79th St Ph H New York (10075) ***(G-9211)***
Anima Mundi Herbals LLC ... 415 279-5727
2323 Borden Ave Long Island City (11101) ***(G-7693)***
Animal Fair Media Inc ... 212 629-0392
545 8th Ave Rm 401 New York (10018) ***(G-9212)***
Anka Tool & Die Inc ... 845 268-4116
150 Wells Ave Congers (10920) ***(G-3875)***
Ankom Development LLC ... 315 986-1937
2052 Oneil Rd Macedon (14502) ***(G-8007)***
Ankom Technology Corp ... 315 986-8090
2052 Oneil Rd Macedon (14502) ***(G-8008)***
Anmar Acquisition LLC (HQ) ... 585 352-7777
35 Vantage Point Dr Rochester (14624) ***(G-14222)***
Ann Gish Inc (PA) ... 212 969-9200
4 W 20th St New York (10011) ***(G-9213)***
Anna B Inc ... 516 680-6609
391 Cold Spring Rd Syosset (11791) ***(G-15834)***
Anna Sui Corp (PA) ... 212 768-1951
250 W 39th St Fl 15 New York (10018) ***(G-9214)***
Anna Young Assoc Ltd ... 516 546-4400
100 Doxsee Dr Freeport (11520) ***(G-5397)***
Anne Taintor Inc ... 718 483-9312
137 Montague St Brooklyn (11201) ***(G-1613)***
Annese & Associates Inc ... 716 972-0076
500 Corporate Pkwy # 106 Buffalo (14226) ***(G-2831)***
Annies Ice ... 585 593-5605
35 Herman Ave Wellsville (14895) ***(G-16774)***
Annointed Buty Ministries LLC ... 646 867-3796
1697 E 54th St Brooklyn (11234) ***(G-1614)***
Annuals Publishing Co Inc ... 212 505-0950
10 E 23rd St Ste 510 New York (10010) ***(G-9215)***
Anorad Corporation ... 631 380-2100
41 Research Way East Setauket (11733) ***(G-4495)***
Another 99 Cent Paradise ... 718 786-4578
4206 Greenpoint Ave Sunnyside (11104) ***(G-15825)***
Ansa Systems of USA Inc ... 718 835-3743
145 Hook Creek Blvd B6a1 Valley Stream (11581) ***(G-16425)***
Ansen Corporation (PA) ... 315 393-3573
100 Chimney Point Dr Ogdensburg (13669) ***(G-13132)***
Ansen Corporation ... 315 393-3573
100 Chimney Point Dr Ogdensburg (13669) ***(G-13133)***
Ansun Graphics Inc ... 315 437-6869
6392 Deere Rd Ste 4 Syracuse (13206) ***(G-15874)***
Answer Printing Inc ... 212 922-2922
505 8th Ave Rm 1101 New York (10018) ***(G-9216)***
Antab Mch Sprfinishing Lab Inc ... 585 865-8290
46 Latta Rd Rochester (14612) ***(G-14223)***
Antenna & Radome Res Assoc (PA) ... 631 231-8400
15 Harold Ct Bay Shore (11706) ***(G-670)***
Anterios Inc ... 212 303-1683
60 E 42nd St Ste 1160 New York (10165) ***(G-9217)***
Anthony Gigi Inc ... 860 984-1943
45 Ramsey Rd Unit 28 Shirley (11967) ***(G-15435)***
Anthony L & S LLC (PA) ... 212 386-7245
500 Fashion Ave Fl 16b New York (10018) ***(G-9218)***
Anthony L&S Footwear Group, New York *Also called Anthony L & S LLC* ***(G-9218)***
Anthony Lawrence of New York ... 212 206-8820
3233 47th Ave Long Island City (11101) ***(G-7694)***
Anthony Manno & Co Inc ... 631 445-1834
307 Skidmore Rd Ste 2 Deer Park (11729) ***(G-4123)***
Anthony Manufacturing Inc ... 631 957-9424
34 Gear Ave Lindenhurst (11757) ***(G-7476)***
Anthony River Inc ... 315 475-1315
116 Granger St Syracuse (13202) ***(G-15875)***
Anthroposophic Press Inc (PA) ... 518 851-2054
15 Greenridge Dr Clifton Park (12065) ***(G-3721)***
Antico Casale Usa LLC ... 914 760-1100
1244 Clintonville St 2c Whitestone (11357) ***(G-17227)***
Antimony New York LLC ... 917 232-1836
120 E 34th St Apt 7g New York (10016) ***(G-9219)***
Antiques & Collectible Autos ... 716 825-3990
35 Dole St Buffalo (14210) ***(G-2832)***

ALPHABETIC

(PA)=Parent Co (HQ)=Headquarters (DH)=Div Headquarters
2018 Harris
New York Manufacturers Directory
893

Anton Community Newspapers, Mineola *Also called Long Island Cmnty Nwsppers Inc* ***(G-8555)***
Antonicelli Vito Race Car...716 684-2205
3883 Broadway St Buffalo (14227) ***(G-2833)***
Antwerp Diamond Distributors...212 319-3300
581 5th Ave Fl 5 New York (10017) ***(G-9220)***
Antwerp Sales Intl Inc...212 354-6515
576 5th Ave New York (10036) ***(G-9221)***
Anvil Knitwear, Inc., New York *Also called Gildan Apparel USA Inc* ***(G-10336)***
Anyelas Vineyards LLC...315 685-3797
2433 W Lake Rd Skaneateles (13152) ***(G-15476)***
Aos, Valley Stream *Also called Automated Office Systems Inc* ***(G-16426)***
APC Paper Company Inc...315 384-4225
100 Remington Ave Norfolk (13667) ***(G-12914)***
APC-Mge, New York *Also called Schneider Electric It Corp* ***(G-12011)***
Apec Paper Industries Ltd...212 730-0088
255 W 88th St Apt 4b New York (10024) ***(G-9222)***
Apex Airtronics Inc (PA)...718 485-8560
2465 Atlantic Ave Brooklyn (11207) ***(G-1615)***
Apex Aridyne Corp...516 239-4400
168 Doughty Blvd Inwood (11096) ***(G-6789)***
Apex Packing & Rubber Co Inc...631 420-8150
1855 New Hwy Ste D Farmingdale (11735) ***(G-4951)***
Apex Real Holdings Inc...877 725-2150
1640 40th St Ste A Brooklyn (11218) ***(G-1616)***
Apex Signal Corporation...631 567-1100
110 Wilbur Pl Bohemia (11716) ***(G-1013)***
Apex Texicon Inc (PA)...516 239-4400
295 Madison Ave New York (10017) ***(G-9223)***
Apexx Omni-Graphics Inc...718 326-3330
5829 64th St Maspeth (11378) ***(G-8147)***
Apf Management Company LLC...914 665-5400
60 Fullerton Ave Yonkers (10704) ***(G-17431)***
Apf Manufacturing Company LLC (PA)...914 963-6300
60 Fullerton Ave Yonkers (10704) ***(G-17432)***
Apf Munn Master Frame Makers, Yonkers *Also called Apf Manufacturing Company LLC* ***(G-17432)***
Apg Neuros, Plattsburgh *Also called Apgn Inc* ***(G-13679)***
Apgn Inc...518 324-4150
160 Banker Rd Plattsburgh (12901) ***(G-13679)***
Aphrodities...718 224-1774
2007 Francis Lewis Blvd Whitestone (11357) ***(G-17228)***
API, Central Islip *Also called Autronic Plastics Inc* ***(G-3510)***
API Heat Transf Thermasys Corp (HQ)...716 684-6700
2777 Walden Ave Buffalo (14225) ***(G-2834)***
API Heat Transfer Company (PA)...716 684-6700
2777 Walden Ave Ste 1 Buffalo (14225) ***(G-2835)***
API Heat Transfer Inc...585 496-5755
91 North St Arcade (14009) ***(G-387)***
API Industries Inc (PA)...845 365-2200
2 Glenshaw St Orangeburg (10962) ***(G-13239)***
API Industries Inc...845 365-2200
2 Glenshaw St Orangeburg (10962) ***(G-13240)***
API Technologies, Fairport *Also called Sendec Corp* ***(G-4883)***
API Technologies Corp, Auburn *Also called Spectrum Microwave Inc* ***(G-517)***
Apicella Jewelers Inc...212 840-2024
40 W 39th St Fl 4 New York (10018) ***(G-9224)***
Apogee Power Usa Inc...202 746-2890
7 Verne Pl Hartsdale (10530) ***(G-6016)***
Apogee Retail NY...516 731-1727
3041 Hempstead Tpke Levittown (11756) ***(G-7445)***
Apogee Translite Inc...631 254-6975
593 Acorn St Ste B Deer Park (11729) ***(G-4124)***
Apogy LLC...866 766-1723
65 N Moore St Fl 2 New York (10013) ***(G-9225)***
Apollo Apparel Group LLC...212 398-6585
1407 Brdway Ste 2000-200 New York (10018) ***(G-9226)***
Apollo Display Tech Corp (PA)...631 580-4360
87 Raynor Ave Ste 1 Ronkonkoma (11779) ***(G-14899)***
Apollo Investment Fund VII LP...212 515-3200
9 W 57th St Fl 43 New York (10019) ***(G-9227)***
Apollo Jeans, New York *Also called Apollo Apparel Group LLC* ***(G-9226)***
Apollo Lighting and Hasco Ltg, Mount Vernon *Also called Luminatta Inc* ***(G-8748)***
Apollo Optical Systems Inc...585 272-6170
925 John St West Henrietta (14586) ***(G-16901)***
Apollo Orthotics Corp...516 333-3223
320 Westbury Ave Carle Place (11514) ***(G-3411)***
Apollo Steel Corporation...716 283-8758
4800 Tomson Ave Niagara Falls (14304) ***(G-12820)***
Apollo Windows & Doors Inc...718 386-3326
1003 Metropolitan Ave Brooklyn (11211) ***(G-1617)***
Apothecus Pharmaceutical Corp (PA)...516 624-8200
220 Townsend Sq Oyster Bay (11771) ***(G-13391)***
Appairent Technologies Inc (PA)...585 214-2460
150 Lucius Gordon Dr West Henrietta (14586) ***(G-16902)***
Apparatus LLC...646 527-9732
122 W 30th St Fl 4 New York (10001) ***(G-9228)***
Apparatus Mfg Inc...845 471-5116
13 Commerce St Poughkeepsie (12603) ***(G-13905)***
Apparatus Studio, New York *Also called Apparatus LLC* ***(G-9228)***
Apparel Group Ltd...212 328-1200
469 7th Ave Fl 8 New York (10018) ***(G-9229)***
Apparel Partnership Group LLC...212 302-7722
250 W 39th St Rm 701 New York (10018) ***(G-9230)***
Apparel Production Inc...212 278-8362
270 W 39th St Rm 1701 New York (10018) ***(G-9231)***
Appfigures Inc...212 343-7900
133 Chrystie St Fl 3 New York (10002) ***(G-9232)***
Applause Coating LLC...631 231-5223
8b Grand Blvd Brentwood (11717) ***(G-1173)***
Apple, Port Washington *Also called US Juice Partners LLC* ***(G-13888)***
Apple & Eve LLC (HQ)...516 621-1122
2 Seaview Blvd Ste 100 Port Washington (11050) ***(G-13822)***
Apple Bank For Savings...718 486-7294
44 Lee Ave Brooklyn (11211) ***(G-1618)***
Apple Commuter Inc...917 299-0066
54 Lake Dr New Hyde Park (11040) ***(G-8861)***
Apple Core Electronics Inc...718 628-4068
991 Flushing Ave Brooklyn (11206) ***(G-1619)***
Apple Digital Printing, Long Island City *Also called Apple Enterprises Inc* ***(G-7695)***
Apple Enterprises Inc...718 361-2200
1308 43rd Ave Long Island City (11101) ***(G-7695)***
Apple Healing & Relaxation...718 278-1089
3114 Broadway Long Island City (11106) ***(G-7696)***
Apple Imprints Apparel Inc...716 893-1130
2336 Bailey Ave Buffalo (14211) ***(G-2836)***
Apple Med Urgent Care PC...914 523-5965
504 Gramatan Ave Mount Vernon (10552) ***(G-8707)***
Apple Press...914 723-6660
23 Harrison Blvd White Plains (10604) ***(G-17106)***
Apple Rubber Products Inc (PA)...716 684-6560
310 Erie St Lancaster (14086) ***(G-7327)***
Apple Rubber Products Inc...716 684-7649
204 Cemetery Rd Lancaster (14086) ***(G-7328)***
Application Security Inc (HQ)...212 912-4100
55 Broad St Rm 10a New York (10004) ***(G-9233)***
Applied Biophysics Inc...518 880-6860
185 Jordan Rd Ste 7 Troy (12180) ***(G-16246)***
Applied Coatings Holding Corp (PA)...585 482-0300
1653 E Main St Ste 1 Rochester (14609) ***(G-14224)***
Applied Concepts Inc...315 696-6676
397 State Route 281 Tully (13159) ***(G-16297)***
Applied Energy Solutions LLC...585 538-3270
1 Technology Pl Caledonia (14423) ***(G-3304)***
Applied Image Inc...585 482-0300
1653 E Main St Ste 1 Rochester (14609) ***(G-14225)***
Applied Minerals Inc (PA)...212 226-4265
55 Washington St Ste 301 Brooklyn (11201) ***(G-1620)***
Applied Power Systems Inc...516 935-2230
124 Charlotte Ave Hicksville (11801) ***(G-6346)***
Applied Safety LLC...718 608-6292
4349 10th St Ste 311 Long Island City (11101) ***(G-7697)***
Applied Technology Mfg Corp...607 687-2200
71 Temple St Owego (13827) ***(G-13375)***
Applied Terminal Systems, Auburn *Also called Daikin Applied Americas Inc* ***(G-490)***
Appliedea Inc...212 920-6822
20 Park Ave New York (10016) ***(G-9234)***
Applince Installation Svc Corp (PA)...716 884-7425
3190 Genesee St Buffalo (14225) ***(G-2837)***
Apprenda Inc (PA)...518 383-2130
433 River St Fl 4 Troy (12180) ***(G-16247)***
Apprise Mobile, New York *Also called Theirapp LLC* ***(G-12333)***
Appsbidder Inc...917 880-4269
55 Clark St 772 Brooklyn (11201) ***(G-1621)***
April Printing Co Inc...212 685-7455
1201 Broadway Ste 403 New York (10001) ***(G-9235)***
APS American Polymers Svcs Inc...212 362-7711
104 W 40th St Rm 500 New York (10018) ***(G-9236)***
APS Enterprise Software Inc...631 784-7720
775 Park Ave Huntington (11743) ***(G-6686)***
Apsco Sports Enterprises Inc...718 965-9500
50th & 1st Ave Bldg 57 Brooklyn (11232) ***(G-1622)***
Apsis USA Inc...631 421-6800
1855 New Hwy Ste B Farmingdale (11735) ***(G-4952)***
Aptar Congers, Congers *Also called Aptargroup Inc* ***(G-3876)***
Aptargroup Inc...845 639-3700
250 N Route 303 Congers (10920) ***(G-3876)***
Apton Door, Islandia *Also called Metro Door Inc* ***(G-6839)***
Apx Arstan Products, Hicksville *Also called Arstan Products International* ***(G-6348)***
Apx Technologies Inc...516 433-1313
264 Duffy Ave Hicksville (11801) ***(G-6347)***
Aquarii Inc...315 672-8807
17 Genesee St Camillus (13031) ***(G-3349)***
Aquarium Pump & Piping Systems...631 567-5555
528 Chester Rd Sayville (11782) ***(G-15232)***
Aquifer Drilling & Testing Inc (PA)...516 616-6026
75 E 2nd St Mineola (11501) ***(G-8528)***
AR & AR Jewelry Inc...212 764-7916
31 W 47th St Fl 15 New York (10036) ***(G-9237)***
AR Media Inc...212 352-0731
601 W 26th St Rm 810 New York (10001) ***(G-9238)***

AR Publishing Company Inc 212 482-0303
55 Broad St Rm 20b New York (10004) **(G-9239)**
Arabella Textiles LLC 212 679-0611
303 5th Ave Rm 1402 New York (10016) **(G-9240)**
Aramsco Inc 718 361-7540
1819 Flushing Ave Ste 2 Ridgewood (11385) **(G-14113)**
Arbe Machinery Inc 631 756-2477
54 Allen Blvd Farmingdale (11735) **(G-4953)**
Arbeit Bros Inc 212 736-9761
345 7th Ave Fl 20 New York (10001) **(G-9241)**
Arbor Books Inc 201 236-9990
244 Madison Ave New York (10016) **(G-9242)**
Arbor Valley Flooring, Salamanca *Also called Norton-Smith Hardwoods Inc* **(G-15130)**
Arborn Printing & Graphics, Mamaroneck *Also called Division Den-Bar Enterprises* **(G-8065)**
ARC of Chemung, The, Elmira *Also called Chemung Cnty Chpter Nysarc Inc* **(G-4688)**
ARC Remanufacturing Inc 718 728-0701
1940 42nd St Long Island City (11105) **(G-7698)**
ARC Systems Inc 631 582-8020
2090 Joshuas Path Hauppauge (11788) **(G-6042)**
ARC TEC Wldg & Fabrication Inc 718 982-9274
15 Harrison Ave Staten Island (10302) **(G-15659)**
Arca Ink LLC 518 798-0100
30 Bluebird Rd South Glens Falls (12803) **(G-15546)**
Arcade Inc 212 541-2600
1740 Broadway Fl 14 New York (10019) **(G-9243)**
Arcade Glass Works, Chaffee *Also called Hart To Hart Industries Inc* **(G-3562)**
Arcade Herald, Arcade *Also called Neighbor To Neighbor News Inc* **(G-397)**
Arcadia Chem Preservative LLC 516 466-5258
100 Great Neck Rd Apt 5b Great Neck (11021) **(G-5806)**
Arcadia Mfg Group Inc (PA) 518 434-6213
80 Cohoes Ave Green Island (12183) **(G-5871)**
Arcadia Mfg Group Inc 518 434-6213
1032 Broadway Menands (12204) **(G-8399)**
Arcangel Inc 347 771-0789
209 W 38th St Rm 1001 New York (10018) **(G-9244)**
Archaelogy Magazine 718 472-3050
3636 33rd St Ste 301 Long Island City (11106) **(G-7699)**
Archer-Daniels-Midland Company 716 849-7333
250 Ganson St Buffalo (14203) **(G-2838)**
Archer-Daniels-Midland Company 518 828-4691
201 State Route 23b Hudson (12534) **(G-6634)**
Archer-Daniels-Midland Company 518 828-4691
Ste B Rr 23 Hudson (12534) **(G-6635)**
Archer-Daniels-Midland Company 585 346-2311
3401 Rochester Rd Lakeville (14480) **(G-7305)**
Archie Comic Publications Inc 914 381-5155
629 Fifth Ave Ste 100 Pelham (10803) **(G-13513)**
Archie Comics Publishers, Pelham *Also called Archie Comic Publications Inc* **(G-13513)**
Archimedes Products Inc 631 589-1215
21 Floyds Run Bohemia (11716) **(G-1014)**
Architctral Dsign Elements LLC 718 218-7800
52 Box St Brooklyn (11222) **(G-1623)**
Architctral Mllwk Installation 631 499-0755
590 Elwood Rd East Northport (11731) **(G-4453)**
Architctral Shetmetal Pdts Inc 518 381-6144
1329 Amsterdam Rd Scotia (12302) **(G-15345)**
Architects Newspaper LLC 212 966-0630
21 Murray St Fl 5 New York (10007) **(G-9245)**
Architectural Coatings Inc 718 418-9584
538 Johnson Ave Brooklyn (11237) **(G-1624)**
Architectural Dctg Co LLC 845 483-1340
130 Salt Point Tpke Poughkeepsie (12603) **(G-13906)**
Architectural Enhancements Inc 845 343-9663
135 Crotty Rd Middletown (10941) **(G-8460)**
Architectural Fiberglass Corp 631 842-4772
1395 Marconi Blvd Copiague (11726) **(G-3918)**
Architectural Glass Inc 845 831-3116
71 Maple St Apt 2 Beacon (12508) **(G-776)**
Architectural Sign Group Inc 516 326-1800
145 Meacham Ave Elmont (11003) **(G-4729)**
Architectural Textiles USA Inc 212 213-6972
36 E 23rd St Ste F New York (10010) **(G-9246)**
Architex International, New York *Also called Architectural Textiles USA Inc* **(G-9246)**
Archive360 Inc 212 731-2438
165 Broadway Fl 23 New York (10006) **(G-9247)**
Arcom Automatics LLC 315 422-1230
185 Ainsley Dr Syracuse (13210) **(G-15876)**
Arcom Labs, Syracuse *Also called Arrow-Communication Labs Inc* **(G-15879)**
Arconic Fstening Systems Rings, Kingston *Also called Huck International Inc* **(G-7220)**
Arconic Inc (PA) 212 836-2758
390 Park Ave New York (10022) **(G-9248)**
Arconic Inc 716 358-6451
2632 S Work St Ste 24 Falconer (14733) **(G-4898)**
Arctic Glacier Minnesota Inc 585 388-0080
900 Turk Hill Rd Fairport (14450) **(G-4849)**
Arctic Glacier Newburgh Inc 718 456-2013
335 Moffat St Brooklyn (11237) **(G-1625)**
Arctic Glacier Newburgh Inc (HQ) 845 561-0549
225 Lake St Newburgh (12550) **(G-12771)**
Arctic Glacier PA Inc 610 494-8200
900 Turk Hill Rd Fairport (14450) **(G-4850)**
Arctic Glacier Texas Inc 215 283-0326
900 Turk Hill Rd Fairport (14450) **(G-4851)**
Arctic Glacier USA 215 283-0326
900 Turk Hill Rd Fairport (14450) **(G-4852)**
Arctic Wholesale Refrigeration, Rochester *Also called East Side Development Corp* **(G-14345)**
Arctix, Locust Valley *Also called Alpha 6 Distributions LLC* **(G-7659)**
Arcy Plastic Laminates Inc (PA) 518 235-0753
555 Patroon Creek Blvd Albany (12206) **(G-45)**
Ardagh Metal Packaging USA Inc 607 584-3300
379 Broome Corporate Pkwy Conklin (13748) **(G-3889)**
Ardent Mills LLC 518 447-1700
101 Normanskill St Albany (12202) **(G-46)**
Ardex Cosmetics of America 518 283-6700
744 Pawling Ave Troy (12180) **(G-16248)**
Area Development Magazine, Westbury *Also called Halcyon Business Publications* **(G-17020)**
Area Inc 212 924-7084
58 E 11th St Fl 2 New York (10003) **(G-9249)**
Area Warehouse, New York *Also called Area Inc* **(G-9249)**
Aremco Products Inc 845 268-0039
707 Executive Blvd Ste B Valley Cottage (10989) **(G-16402)**
Arena Graphics Inc 516 767-5108
52 Main St Frnt Port Washington (11050) **(G-13823)**
Arena Sports Center, Port Washington *Also called Arena Graphics Inc* **(G-13823)**
Ares Box LLC 718 858-8760
63 Flushing Ave Unit 224 Brooklyn (11205) **(G-1626)**
Ares Printing and Packg Corp 718 858-8760
Brooklyn Navy Yard Bldg Brooklyn (11205) **(G-1627)**
Argee America Inc 212 768-9840
1400 Broadway Ste 2307 New York (10018) **(G-9250)**
Argee Sportswear, New York *Also called Argee America Inc* **(G-9250)**
Argencord Machine Corp Inc 631 842-8990
10 Reith St Copiague (11726) **(G-3919)**
Argo Envelope Corp 718 729-2700
4310 21st St Long Island City (11101) **(G-7700)**
Argo General Machine Work Inc 718 392-4605
3816 11th St Long Island City (11101) **(G-7701)**
Argo Lithographers Inc 718 729-2700
4310 21st St Long Island City (11101) **(G-7702)**
Argon Corp (PA) 516 487-5314
160 Great Neck Rd Great Neck (11021) **(G-5807)**
Argon Medical Devices Inc 585 321-1130
336 Summit Point Dr Henrietta (14467) **(G-6316)**
Argos Inc 845 528-0576
58 Seifert Ln Putnam Valley (10579) **(G-13989)**
Argosy Composite Advanced Mate 212 268-0003
225 W 34th St Ste 1106 New York (10122) **(G-9251)**
Arh, Deer Park *Also called American Racing Headers Inc* **(G-4120)**
Ariel Optics Inc 585 265-4820
261 David Pkwy Ontario (14519) **(G-13217)**
Ariel Tian LLC 212 457-1266
253 W 35th St Fl 8 Forest Hills (11375) **(G-5327)**
Ariela and Associates Intl LLC (PA) 212 683-4131
1359 Broadway Fl 21 New York (10018) **(G-9252)**
Aries Precision Products, Rochester *Also called Estebania Enterprises Inc* **(G-14380)**
Ariesun Inc 866 274-3049
160 W 3rd St Mount Vernon (10550) **(G-8708)**
Arimed Orthotics Prosthetics P (PA) 718 875-8754
302 Livingston St Brooklyn (11217) **(G-1628)**
Arimed Orthotics Prosthetics P 718 979-6155
235 Dongan Hills Ave 2d Staten Island (10305) **(G-15660)**
Arista Coffee Inc 347 531-0813
5901 55th St Maspeth (11378) **(G-8148)**
Arista Flag Corporation 845 246-7700
157 W Saugerties Rd Saugerties (12477) **(G-15209)**
Arista Innovations Inc 516 746-2262
131 Liberty Ave Mineola (11501) **(G-8529)**
Arista Printing, Mineola *Also called Arista Innovations Inc* **(G-8529)**
Arista Steel Designs Corp 718 965-7077
788 3rd Ave Brooklyn (11232) **(G-1629)**
Aristocrat Lighting Inc 718 522-0003
104 Halleck St Brooklyn (11231) **(G-1630)**
Arizona Beverage Company LLC (HQ) 516 812-0300
60 Crossways Park Dr W # 400 Woodbury (11797) **(G-17303)**
Arizona Beverages USA, Woodbury *Also called Arizona Beverage Company LLC* **(G-17303)**
Ark Sciences Inc 646 943-1520
1601 Veterans Hwy Ste 315 Islandia (11749) **(G-6825)**
Arkay Packaging Corporation (PA) 631 273-2000
100 Marcus Blvd Ste 2 Hauppauge (11788) **(G-6043)**
Arkema Inc 585 243-6359
3289 Genesee St Piffard (14533) **(G-13573)**
Arkwin Industries Inc (HQ) 516 333-2640
686 Main St Westbury (11590) **(G-16996)**
Arlan Damper Corporation 631 589-7431
1598 Lakeland Ave Bohemia (11716) **(G-1015)**
Arlee Group, New York *Also called Arlee Home Fashions Inc* **(G-9253)**
Arlee Home Fashions Inc (PA) 212 689-0020
261 5th Ave Fl Mezz New York (10016) **(G-9253)**
Arlee Lighting Corp 516 595-8558
125 Doughty Blvd Inwood (11096) **(G-6790)**

Arlington Equipment Corp.....518 798-5867
588 Queensbury Ave Queensbury (12804) ***(G-14006)***
Arlyn Scales, East Rockaway *Also called Circuits & Systems Inc* ***(G-4488)***
Arm & Hammer, Schenectady *Also called Church & Dwight Co Inc* ***(G-15270)***
Arm Construction Company Inc.....646 235-6520
10001 27th Ave East Elmhurst (11369) ***(G-4410)***
Arm Global Solutions Inc.....844 276-4525
138 Joseph Ave Rochester (14605) ***(G-14226)***
Arm Rochester Inc.....585 354-5077
138 Joseph Ave Rochester (14605) ***(G-14227)***
Arma Container Corp.....631 254-1200
65 N Industry Ct Deer Park (11729) ***(G-4125)***
Armacel Armor Corporation.....805 384-1144
745 5th Ave Fl 7 New York (10151) ***(G-9254)***
Armadillo Bar & Grill, Kingston *Also called Tortilla Heaven Inc* ***(G-7245)***
Armento Architectural Arts, Kenmore *Also called Armento Incorporated* ***(G-7173)***
Armento Incorporated.....716 875-2423
1011 Military Rd Kenmore (14217) ***(G-7173)***
Armitron Watch Div, Little Neck *Also called E Gluck Corporation* ***(G-7531)***
Armor Dynamics Inc.....845 658-9200
138 Maple Hill Rd Kingston (12401) ***(G-7207)***
Armor Tile, Buffalo *Also called Engineered Composites Inc* ***(G-2953)***
Armour Bearer Group Inc.....646 812-4487
424 Beach 65th St Arverne (11692) ***(G-421)***
Armstrong Mold Corporation (PA).....315 437-1517
6910 Manlius Center Rd East Syracuse (13057) ***(G-4521)***
Armstrong Mold Corporation.....315 437-1517
5860 Fisher Rd East Syracuse (13057) ***(G-4522)***
Armstrong Pumps Inc.....716 693-8813
93 East Ave North Tonawanda (14120) ***(G-12973)***
Armstrong Transmitter Corp.....315 673-1269
4835 N Street Rd Marcellus (13108) ***(G-8117)***
Arnan Development Corp (PA).....607 432-8391
6459 State Highway 23 Oneonta (13820) ***(G-13194)***
Arnell Inc.....516 486-7098
73 High St Hempstead (11550) ***(G-6289)***
Arnold Magnetic Tech Corp (HQ).....585 385-9010
770 Linden Ave Rochester (14625) ***(G-14228)***
Arnold Printing Corp.....607 272-7800
604 W Green St Ithaca (14850) ***(G-6859)***
Arnold Taylor Printing Inc.....516 781-0564
2218 Brody Ln Bellmore (11710) ***(G-809)***
Arnold-Davis LLC.....607 772-1201
187 Indl Pk Dr Binghamton (13904) ***(G-886)***
Arnolds Meat Food Products.....718 384-8071
274 Heyward St Brooklyn (11206) ***(G-1631)***
Arnouse Digital Devices Corp.....516 673-4444
1983 Marcus Ave Ste 104 New Hyde Park (11042) ***(G-8862)***
Arnprior Rpid Mfg Slutions Inc (PA).....585 617-6301
2400 Mount Read Blvd # 112 Rochester (14615) ***(G-14229)***
Arnprior Rpid Mfg Slutions Inc.....585 617-6301
2400 Mount Read Blvd # 1124 Rochester (14615) ***(G-14230)***
Aro-Graph Corporation.....315 463-8693
847 North Ave Syracuse (13206) ***(G-15877)***
Aro-Graph Displays, Syracuse *Also called Aro-Graph Corporation* ***(G-15877)***
Aromafloria, Huntington Station *Also called California Fragrance Company* ***(G-6736)***
Aromasong Usa Inc.....718 838-9669
35 Frost St Brooklyn (11211) ***(G-1632)***
Aron Streit Inc.....212 475-7000
171 Route 303 Orangeburg (10962) ***(G-13241)***
Aronowitz Metal Works.....845 356-1660
5 Edwin Ln Monsey (10952) ***(G-8603)***
Arpa USA.....212 965-4099
62 Greene St Frnt 1 New York (10012) ***(G-9255)***
Arpac LLC.....315 471-5103
6581 Townline Rd Syracuse (13206) ***(G-15878)***
Arper USA Inc.....212 647-8900
476 Broadway Ste 2f New York (10013) ***(G-9256)***
Array Marketing Group Inc (HQ).....212 750-3367
200 Madison Ave Ste 2121 New York (10016) ***(G-9257)***
Arringement International Inc.....347 323-7974
16015 45th Ave Flushing (11358) ***(G-5234)***
Arro Manufacturing LLC.....716 763-6203
4687 Gleason Rd Lakewood (14750) ***(G-7310)***
Arro Tool & Die Inc.....716 763-6203
4687 Gleason Rd Lakewood (14750) ***(G-7311)***
Arrow Chemical Corp.....516 377-7770
28 Rider Pl Freeport (11520) ***(G-5398)***
Arrow Grinding Inc.....716 693-3333
525 Vicke St Tonaw Ctr Tonawanda (14150) ***(G-16161)***
Arrow Leather Finishing Inc.....518 762-3121
12 W State St Johnstown (12095) ***(G-7138)***
Arrow-Communication Labs Inc.....315 422-1230
185 Ainsley Dr Syracuse (13210) ***(G-15879)***
Arrowear Athletic Apparel, Lynbrook *Also called Valley Stream Sporting Gds Inc* ***(G-7992)***
Arrowhead Spring Vineyards LLC.....716 434-8030
4746 Townline Rd Lockport (14094) ***(G-7598)***
Arrowpak, Richmond Hill *Also called Baralan Usa Inc* ***(G-14080)***
Arstan Products International.....516 433-1313
264 Duffy Ave Hicksville (11801) ***(G-6348)***
Art & Understanding Inc.....518 426-9010
25 Monroe St Ste 205 Albany (12210) ***(G-47)***
Art and Cook Inc.....718 567-7778
14 C 53rd St Fl 2 Brooklyn (11232) ***(G-1633)***
Art Asiapacific Publishing LLC.....212 255-6003
410 W 24th St Apt 14a New York (10011) ***(G-9258)***
Art Bedi-Makky Foundry Corp.....718 383-4191
227 India St Ste 31 Brooklyn (11222) ***(G-1634)***
Art Boards, Brooklyn *Also called Patrick Mackin Custom Furn* ***(G-2423)***
Art Craft Leather Goods Inc.....718 257-7401
1970 Pitkin Ave Brooklyn (11207) ***(G-1635)***
Art Dental Laboratory Inc.....516 437-1882
199 Jericho Tpke Ste 402 Floral Park (11001) ***(G-5201)***
Art Digital Technologies LLC.....646 649-4820
85 Debevoise Ave Brooklyn (11222) ***(G-1636)***
Art Essentials of New York (PA).....845 368-1100
25 Church Rd Airmont (10952) ***(G-11)***
Art Flag Company Inc.....212 334-1890
8 Jay St Frnt 1 New York (10013) ***(G-9259)***
Art Foam, Lindenhurst *Also called Strux Corp* ***(G-7508)***
Art In America, New York *Also called Brant Art Publications Inc* ***(G-9505)***
Art Industries of New York.....212 633-9200
601 W 26th St Rm 1425 New York (10001) ***(G-9260)***
Art Leather Mfg Co Inc.....516 867-4716
69 Hamilton Ave Ste 2 Oyster Bay (11771) ***(G-13392)***
Art of Shaving - Fl LLC.....212 823-9410
10 Columbus Cir Ste 209 New York (10019) ***(G-9261)***
Art of Shaving - Fl LLC.....212 362-1493
2151 Broadway Frnt 2 New York (10023) ***(G-9262)***
Art Parts Signs Inc.....585 381-2134
100 Lincoln Pkwy East Rochester (14445) ***(G-4472)***
Art People Inc.....212 431-4865
594 Broadway Rm 1102 New York (10012) ***(G-9263)***
Art Precision Metal Products.....631 842-8889
1465 S Strong Ave Copiague (11726) ***(G-3920)***
Art Resources Transfer Inc.....212 255-2919
526 W 26th St Rm 614 New York (10001) ***(G-9264)***
Art Scroll Printing Corp.....212 929-2413
230 W 41st St Bsmt 1 New York (10036) ***(G-9265)***
Art-Craft Optical Company Inc.....585 546-6640
57 Goodway Dr S Rochester (14623) ***(G-14231)***
Art-TEC Jewelry Designs Ltd (PA).....212 719-2941
48 W 48th St Ste 401 New York (10036) ***(G-9266)***
Artcraft Building Services.....845 895-3893
85 Old Hoagerburgh Rd Wallkill (12589) ***(G-16561)***
Arteast LLC.....212 965-8787
102 Franklin St Fl 4 New York (10013) ***(G-9267)***
Artemis Inc.....631 232-2424
36 Central Ave Hauppauge (11788) ***(G-6044)***
Artemis Studios Inc.....718 788-6022
34 35th St Ste 2b Brooklyn (11232) ***(G-1637)***
Arthur Brown W Mfg Co.....631 243-5594
49 E Industry Ct Ste I Deer Park (11729) ***(G-4126)***
Arthur Gluck Shirtmakers Inc.....212 755-8165
871 E 24th St Brooklyn (11210) ***(G-1638)***
Arthur Invitation, New York *Also called Exotic Print and Paper Inc* ***(G-10160)***
Arthur Lauer Inc.....845 255-7871
47 Steves Ln Gardiner (12525) ***(G-5560)***
Articulate Global Inc.....800 861-4880
244 5th Ave Ste 2960 New York (10001) ***(G-9268)***
Artifex Press LLC.....212 414-1482
109 W 27th St New York (10001) ***(G-9269)***
Artina Group Inc.....914 592-1850
250 Clearbrook Rd Ste 245 Elmsford (10523) ***(G-4743)***
Artisan Bags, Childwold *Also called Leather Artisan* ***(G-3658)***
Artisan Custom Interiors, West Hempstead *Also called Artisan Woodworking Ltd* ***(G-16880)***
Artisan Machining Inc.....631 589-1416
49 Remington Blvd Ronkonkoma (11779) ***(G-14900)***
Artisan Management Group Inc.....716 569-4094
39 Venman St Frewsburg (14738) ***(G-5462)***
Artisan Woodworking Ltd.....516 486-0818
163 Hempstead Tpke West Hempstead (11552) ***(G-16880)***
Artisanal Brands Inc.....914 441-3591
42 Forest Ln Bronxville (10708) ***(G-1499)***
Artistic Frame Corp (PA).....212 289-2100
979 3rd Ave Ste 1705 New York (10022) ***(G-9270)***
Artistic Group, The, New York *Also called Artistic Typography Corp* ***(G-9272)***
Artistic Ironworks Inc.....631 665-4285
94 Saxon Ave Bay Shore (11706) ***(G-671)***
Artistic Products LLC.....631 435-0200
125 Commerce Dr Hauppauge (11788) ***(G-6045)***
Artistic Ribbon Novelty Co Inc.....212 255-4224
22 W 21st St Fl 3 New York (10010) ***(G-9271)***
Artistic Typography Corp (PA).....212 463-8880
151 W 30th St Fl 8 New York (10001) ***(G-9272)***
Artistics Printing Corp.....516 561-2121
746 Franklin Ave Ste 2 Franklin Square (11010) ***(G-5370)***
Artistry In Wood of Syracuse.....315 431-4022
6804 Manlius Center Rd # 2 East Syracuse (13057) ***(G-4523)***
Artists, Doo Wop, Deer Park *Also called New Wop Records* ***(G-4203)***
Artkraft Sign, New York *Also called Artkraft Strauss LLC* ***(G-9273)***
Artkraft Strauss LLC.....212 265-5155
1776 Broadway Ste 1810 New York (10019) ***(G-9273)***

ALPHABETIC SECTION

Artnews Ltd (PA) 212 398-1690
  110 Greene St Ph 2 New York (10012) *(G-9274)*
Artnewsletter, New York Also called Artnews Ltd *(G-9274)*
Artone Furniture By Design, Jamestown Also called Artone LLC *(G-7008)*
Artone LLC 716 664-2232
  1089 Allen St Jamestown (14701) *(G-7008)*
Artsaics Studios Inc 631 254-2558
  1006 Grand Blvd Deer Park (11729) *(G-4127)*
Artscroll Printing Corp (PA) 212 929-2413
  53 W 23rd St Fl 4 New York (10010) *(G-9275)*
Artube, Great Neck Also called Iridium Industries Inc *(G-5833)*
Artvoice 716 881-6604
  810 Main St Buffalo (14202) *(G-2839)*
Artyarns 914 428-0333
  70 Westmoreland Ave White Plains (10606) *(G-17107)*
Artys Sprnklr Svc Instilation 516 538-4371
  234 E Meadow Ave Unit B East Meadow (11554) *(G-4438)*
Aruba Networks Inc 732 343-1305
  556 W 22nd St New York (10011) *(G-9276)*
Arumai Technologies Inc (PA) 914 217-0038
  175 King St Armonk (10504) *(G-410)*
Arusha Tanzanite, Great Neck Also called Le Vian Corp *(G-5837)*
Aruvil International Inc (PA) 212 447-5020
  185 Madison Ave Rm 1701 New York (10016) *(G-9277)*
Arvos Inc (HQ) 585 593-2700
  3020 Truax Rd Wellsville (14895) *(G-16775)*
Aryzta LLC 310 417-4700
  64 Chester St Rochester (14611) *(G-14232)*
Aryzta LLC 585 235-8160
  235 Buffalo Rd Rochester (14611) *(G-14233)*
Asa Manufacturing Inc 718 853-3033
  3611 14th Ave Brooklyn (11218) *(G-1639)*
Asahi Shimbun America Inc 212 398-0257
  620 8th Ave New York (10018) *(G-9278)*
ASAP Rack Rental Inc 718 499-4495
  33 35th St St5 Brooklyn (11232) *(G-1640)*
Asavings.com, Brooklyn Also called Focus Camera Inc *(G-1990)*
Ascension Industries Inc (PA) 716 693-9381
  1254 Erie Ave North Tonawanda (14120) *(G-12974)*
Ascent Aerospace Holdings LLC (PA) 212 916-8142
  330 Madison Ave Fl 28 New York (10017) *(G-9279)*
Asco Castings Inc (PA) 212 719-9800
  3100 47th Ave Ste G Long Island City (11101) *(G-7703)*
Ascribe Inc 585 413-0298
  383 Buell Rd Rochester (14624) *(G-14234)*
Asence Inc 347 335-2606
  65 Broadway Fl 7 New York (10006) *(G-9280)*
Asept Pak Inc 518 651-2026
  64 West St Malone (12953) *(G-8038)*
Ashburns Inc 212 227-5692
  90 John St Rm 409 New York (10038) *(G-9281)*
Ashburns Engravers, New York Also called Ashburns Inc *(G-9281)*
Asher Collection, Great Neck Also called Asher Jewelry Company Inc *(G-5808)*
Asher Jewelry Company Inc 212 302-6233
  175 Great Neck Rd Ste 201 Great Neck (11021) *(G-5808)*
Ashi Diamonds LLC 212 319-8291
  18 E 48th St Fl 14 New York (10017) *(G-9282)*
Ashko Group LLC 212 594-6050
  10 W 33rd St Rm 1019 New York (10001) *(G-9283)*
Ashland Hercules Water Tech, Liverpool Also called Solenis LLC *(G-7575)*
Ashley Resin Corp 718 851-8111
  1171 59th St Brooklyn (11219) *(G-1641)*
Ashly Audio Inc 585 872-0010
  847 Holt Rd Ste 1 Webster (14580) *(G-16737)*
Ashton-Potter USA Ltd 716 633-2000
  10 Curtwright Dr Williamsville (14221) *(G-17261)*
Asi Sign Systems, New York Also called Modulex New York Inc *(G-11317)*
Asi Sign Systems Inc 646 742-1320
  192 Lexington Ave Rm 1002 New York (10016) *(G-9284)*
Asi Sign Systems Inc 716 775-0104
  2957 Alt Blvd Grand Island (14072) *(G-5765)*
Asia Connection LLC 212 369-4644
  200 E 90th St Apt 4h New York (10128) *(G-9285)*
Asian Global Trading Corp 718 786-0998
  3613 36th Ave Ste 2 Long Island City (11106) *(G-7704)*
Asite LLC 203 545-3089
  245 W 29th St Rm 1601 New York (10001) *(G-9286)*
Ask Chemicals Hi-Tech LLC 607 587-9146
  6329 Rte 21 Alfred Station (14803) *(G-198)*
Asm, Central Bridge Also called American Standard Mfg Inc *(G-3507)*
Asm Mechanical Systems, Ridgewood Also called Aabco Sheet Metal Co Inc *(G-14110)*
Asm USA Inc 212 925-2906
  73 Spring St Rm 309 New York (10012) *(G-9287)*
Asn Inc 718 894-0700
  6020 59th Pl Ste 2 Maspeth (11378) *(G-8149)*
Asp Industries Inc 585 254-9130
  9 Evelyn St Rochester (14606) *(G-14235)*
Aspect Printing Inc 347 789-4284
  904 E 51st St Brooklyn (11203) *(G-1642)*
Aspen Law & Business, New York Also called Aspen Publishers Inc *(G-9288)*
Aspen Publishers Inc (HQ) 212 771-0600
  76 9th Ave Ste 724 New York (10011) *(G-9288)*
Aspen Research Group Ltd 212 425-9588
  17 State St Fl 15 New York (10004) *(G-9289)*
Aspex Incorporated 212 966-0410
  161 Hudson St Apt 1a New York (10013) *(G-9290)*
Aspire One Communications LLC 201 281-2998
  245 Main St Ste 8 Cornwall (12518) *(G-4007)*
Asr Group International Inc (HQ) 914 963-2400
  1 Federal St Yonkers (10705) *(G-17433)*
Assa Abloy Entrance Systems US 315 492-6600
  28 Corporate Cir Ste 1 East Syracuse (13057) *(G-4524)*
Assembly Equipment Division, Rochester Also called High Speed Hammer Company Inc *(G-14456)*
Associated Brands Inc 585 798-3475
  111 8th Ave New York (10011) *(G-9291)*
Associated Drapery & Equipment 516 671-5245
  3 Kosnitz Dr Unit 111 Monroe (10950) *(G-8583)*
Associated Materials LLC 631 467-4535
  1830 Lakeland Ave Ronkonkoma (11779) *(G-14901)*
Associated Publishing Co, Buffalo Also called Mac Innes Enterprises Inc *(G-3072)*
Associated Publishing Company (HQ) 325 676-4032
  61 John Muir Dr Buffalo (14228) *(G-2840)*
Association For Cmpt McHy Inc (PA) 212 869-7440
  2 Penn Plz Rm 701 New York (10121) *(G-9292)*
Assouline Publishing Inc (PA) 212 989-6769
  3 Park Ave Fl 27 New York (10016) *(G-9293)*
Aston Leather Inc 212 481-2760
  153 W 27th St Ste 406 New York (10001) *(G-9294)*
Astor-Honor Division, New York Also called Beauty Fashion Inc *(G-9389)*
Astra Products Inc 631 464-4747
  6 Bethpage Rd Copiague (11726) *(G-3921)*
Astra Tool & Instr Mfg Corp 914 747-3863
  369 Bradhurst Ave Hawthorne (10532) *(G-6266)*
Astro Chemical Company Inc 518 399-5338
  3 Mill Rd Ballston Lake (12019) *(G-578)*
Astro Electroplating Inc 631 968-0656
  171 4th Ave Bay Shore (11706) *(G-672)*
Astro Label & Tag Ltd 718 435-4474
  5820 Fort Hamilton Pkwy Brooklyn (11219) *(G-1643)*
Astrocom Electronics Inc 607 432-1930
  115 Dk Lifgren Dr Oneonta (13820) *(G-13195)*
Astrodyne Inc 516 536-5755
  18 Neil Ct Oceanside (11572) *(G-13092)*
Astron Candle Manufacturing Co 718 728-3330
  1125 30th Ave Long Island City (11102) *(G-7705)*
Astronics Corporation (PA) 716 805-1599
  130 Commerce Way East Aurora (14052) *(G-4391)*
Astucci US Ltd 718 752-9700
  4369 9th St Long Island City (11101) *(G-7706)*
Astucci US Ltd (PA) 212 725-3171
  385 5th Ave Rm 1100 New York (10016) *(G-9295)*
Asur Jewelry Inc 718 472-1687
  4709 30th St Ste 403 Long Island City (11101) *(G-7707)*
AT&T Corp 716 639-0673
  8200 Transit Rd Ste 200 Williamsville (14221) *(G-17262)*
AT&T Corp 212 317-7048
  767 5th Ave Fl 12a New York (10153) *(G-9296)*
Atair Aerospace Inc 718 923-1709
  63 Flushing Ave Unit 262 Brooklyn (11205) *(G-1644)*
Atalla Handbags Inc 718 965-5500
  117 57th St Brooklyn (11220) *(G-1645)*
Atc, Huntington Station Also called American Tchncal Ceramics Corp *(G-6732)*
Atc Plastics LLC 212 375-2515
  555 Madison Ave Fl 5 New York (10022) *(G-9297)*
Atco EZ Dock, Auburn Also called Auburn Tank & Manufacturing Co *(G-480)*
Atd Precision Machining, Rochester Also called Allstate Tool and Die Inc *(G-14206)*
Atech-Seh Metal Fabricator 716 895-8888
  330 Greene St Buffalo (14206) *(G-2841)*
Ateco Products, Bay Shore Also called Sumner Industries Inc *(G-742)*
Atelier Viollet Corp 718 782-1727
  505 Driggs Ave Brooklyn (11211) *(G-1646)*
Ateres Book Binding, Brooklyn Also called Ateres Publishing & Bk Bindery *(G-1647)*
Ateres Publishing & Bk Bindery 718 935-9355
  845 Bedford Ave Brooklyn (11205) *(G-1647)*
Ateret LLC 212 819-0777
  22 W 48th St New York (10036) *(G-9298)*
Aterian Investment Partners LP (PA) 212 547-2806
  11 E 44th St Rm 1803 New York (10017) *(G-9299)*
Aterra Exploration LLC 212 315-0030
  230 W 56th St Apt 53d New York (10019) *(G-9300)*
Athalon Sportgear Inc 212 268-8070
  10 W 33rd St Rm 1012 New York (10001) *(G-9301)*
Athenex Inc 716 427-2950
  1001 Main St Ste 600 Buffalo (14203) *(G-2842)*
Athenex Inc (PA) 716 427-2950
  1001 Main St Ste 600 Buffalo (14203) *(G-2843)*
Athenex Pharma Solutions LLC 877 463-7823
  11342 Main St Clarence (14031) *(G-3684)*
Athletic Cap Co Inc 718 398-1300
  123 Fields Ave Staten Island (10314) *(G-15661)*

Athlon Spt Communications Inc — 212 478-1910
60 E 42nd St Ste 820 New York (10165) *(G-9302)*
ATI, Brooklyn *Also called Anne Taintor Inc (G-1613)*
ATI Model Products Inc (PA) — 631 694-7022
180 Smith St Farmingdale (11735) *(G-4954)*
ATI Specialty Materials, Lockport *Also called Tdy Industries LLC (G-7648)*
ATI Trading Inc — 718 888-7918
13631 41st Ave Ste 5a Flushing (11355) *(G-5235)*
Atis Colojet, Ronkonkoma *Also called Maharlika Holdings LLC (G-14963)*
Atk Gasl Inc — 631 737-6100
77 Raynor Ave Ronkonkoma (11779) *(G-14902)*
Atlantic Business Products, New York *Also called Facsimile Cmmncations Inds Inc (G-10178)*
Atlantic Color Corp — 631 345-3800
14 Ramsey Rd Shirley (11967) *(G-15436)*
Atlantic Electronic Tech LLC — 800 296-2177
285 5th Ave Apt 2b Brooklyn (11215) *(G-1648)*
Atlantic Electronic Technology, Brooklyn *Also called Atlantic Electronic Tech LLC (G-1648)*
Atlantic Engineer Products LLC — 518 822-1800
239 State Route 23b Hudson (12534) *(G-6636)*
Atlantic Essential Pdts Inc — 631 434-8333
7 Oser Ave Ste 1 Hauppauge (11788) *(G-6046)*
Atlantic Farm & Food Inc — 718 441-3152
11415 Atlantic Ave Richmond Hill (11418) *(G-14079)*
Atlantic Industrial Tech Inc — 631 234-3131
90 Precision Dr Shirley (11967) *(G-15437)*
Atlantic Monthly Group Inc — 202 266-7000
60 Madison Ave New York (10010) *(G-9303)*
Atlantic Pork & Provisions Inc — 718 272-9550
14707 94th Ave Jamaica (11435) *(G-6930)*
Atlantic Precious Metal Cast — 718 937-7100
4132 27th St Long Island City (11101) *(G-7708)*
Atlantic Projects Company Inc — 518 878-2065
5 Southside Dr Ste 11s Clifton Park (12065) *(G-3722)*
Atlantic Recording Corp (HQ) — 212 707-2000
1633 Broadway Low 2c1 New York (10019) *(G-9304)*
Atlantic Records, New York *Also called Atlantic Recording Corp (G-9304)*
Atlantic Specialty Co Inc — 845 356-2502
20 Jeffrey Pl Monsey (10952) *(G-8604)*
Atlantic Stairs Corp — 718 417-8818
284a Meserole St Brooklyn (11206) *(G-1649)*
Atlantic States Distributing — 518 427-6364
1325 Broadway Menands (12204) *(G-8400)*
Atlantic States Kitchens Baths, Menands *Also called Atlantic States Distributing (G-8400)*
Atlantic Transformer Inc — 716 795-3258
1674 Quaker Rd Barker (14012) *(G-611)*
Atlantic Trophy Co Inc — 212 684-6020
866 Avenue Of The America New York (10001) *(G-9305)*
Atlantic Ultraviolet Corp — 631 234-3275
375 Marcus Blvd Hauppauge (11788) *(G-6047)*
Atlantic, The, New York *Also called Atlantic Monthly Group Inc (G-9303)*
Atlantis Energy Systems Inc (PA) — 845 486-4052
7 Industry St Poughkeepsie (12603) *(G-13907)*
Atlantis Energy Systems Inc (PA) — 916 438-2930
7 Industry St Poughkeepsie (12603) *(G-13908)*
Atlantis Equipment Corporation (PA) — 518 733-5910
16941 Ny 22 Stephentown (12168) *(G-15778)*
Atlantis Solar and Wind, Potsdam *Also called Atlantis Solar Inc (G-13895)*
Atlantis Solar Inc — 916 226-9183
2302 River Rd Potsdam (13676) *(G-13895)*
Atlas & Company LLC — 212 234-3100
355 Lexington Ave Fl 6 New York (10017) *(G-9306)*
Atlas Bituminous Co Inc — 315 457-2394
173 Farrell Rd Syracuse (13209) *(G-15880)*
Atlas Coatings Corp — 718 402-2000
820 E 140th St Bronx (10454) *(G-1276)*
Atlas Coatings Group Corp (PA) — 718 469-8787
4808 Farragut Rd Brooklyn (11203) *(G-1650)*
Atlas Concrete Batching Corp — 718 523-3000
9511 147th Pl Jamaica (11435) *(G-6931)*
Atlas Copco Comptec LLC (HQ) — 518 765-3344
46 School Rd Voorheesville (12186) *(G-16538)*
Atlas Fence, East Syracuse *Also called Alexscoe LLC (G-4517)*
Atlas Fence & Railing Co Inc — 718 767-2200
15149 7th Ave Whitestone (11357) *(G-17229)*
Atlas Fence Co, Whitestone *Also called Atlas Fence & Railing Co Inc (G-17229)*
Atlas Graphics Inc — 516 997-5527
567 Main St Westbury (11590) *(G-16997)*
Atlas Metal Industries Inc — 607 776-2048
17 Wheeler Ave Hammondsport (14840) *(G-5975)*
Atlas Music Publishing LLC (PA) — 646 502-5170
6 E 39th St Ste 1104 New York (10016) *(G-9307)*
Atlas Print Solutions Inc — 212 949-8775
589 8th Ave Fl 4 New York (10018) *(G-9308)*
Atlas Recycling LLC — 212 925-3280
25 Howard St Fl 2 New York (10013) *(G-9309)*
Atlas Switch Co Inc — 516 222-6280
969 Stewart Ave Garden City (11530) *(G-5509)*
Atlas Transit Mix Corp — 718 523-3000
9511 147th Pl Jamaica (11435) *(G-6932)*

Atlaz International Ltd — 516 239-1854
298 Lawrence Ave Unit 1 Lawrence (11559) *(G-7416)*
Atmost Refrigeration Co Inc (PA) — 518 828-2180
793 Route 66 Hudson (12534) *(G-6637)*
Atomic Signworks — 315 779-7446
1040 Bradley St Ste 3 Watertown (13601) *(G-16657)*
Atr Jewelry Inc — 212 819-0075
71 W 47th St Ste 402 New York (10036) *(G-9310)*
Ats, Yorktown Heights *Also called Advanced Tchncal Solutions Inc (G-17522)*
Attends Healthcare Inc — 212 338-5100
200 Park Ave New York (10166) *(G-9311)*
Attias Oven Corp — 718 499-0145
926 3rd Ave Brooklyn (11232) *(G-1651)*
Attica Millwork Inc — 585 591-2333
71 Market St Attica (14011) *(G-470)*
Attica Package Company Inc — 585 591-0510
45 Windsor St Attica (14011) *(G-471)*
Attitudes Footwear Inc — 212 754-9113
1040 1st Ave Ste 232 New York (10022) *(G-9312)*
Atwater Estate Vineyards LLC — 607 546-8463
5055 State Route 414 Burdett (14818) *(G-3290)*
Atwater Foods, Lyndonville *Also called Shoreline Fruit LLC (G-7996)*
Atwood Tool & Machine Inc — 607 648-6543
39 Kattelville Rd Chenango Bridge (13745) *(G-3623)*
Atypon Systems Inc — 212 524-7060
330 7th Ave Fl 5 New York (10001) *(G-9313)*
Auburn Armature, East Syracuse *Also called Power-Flo Technologies Inc (G-4568)*
Auburn Armature, Rochester *Also called Power-Flo Technologies Inc (G-14609)*
Auburn Bearing & Mfg Inc — 315 986-7600
4 State Route 350 Macedon (14502) *(G-8009)*
Auburn Custom Millwork Inc — 315 253-3843
4022 Technology Park Blvd Auburn (13021) *(G-477)*
Auburn Foundry Inc — 315 253-4441
15 Wadsworth St Auburn (13021) *(G-478)*
Auburn Leathercrafters, Auburn *Also called Finger Lakes Lea Crafters LLC (G-493)*
Auburn Publishing Co — 315 253-5311
25 Dill St Auburn (13021) *(G-479)*
Auburn Tank & Manufacturing Co — 315 255-2788
24 Mcmaster St Auburn (13021) *(G-480)*
Auburn Vacuum Forming Co Inc — 315 253-2440
40 York St Auburn (13021) *(G-481)*
Auburn-Watson Corp (PA) — 716 876-8000
3295 Walden Ave Depew (14043) *(G-4272)*
Audible Difference Inc — 212 662-4848
110 8th St Brooklyn (11215) *(G-1652)*
Audible Difference Inc (PA) — 212 662-4848
110 8th St Brooklyn (11215) *(G-1653)*
Audible Difference Lnc, Brooklyn *Also called Audible Difference Inc (G-1653)*
Audio Technology New York Inc — 718 369-7528
129 31st St Brooklyn (11232) *(G-1654)*
Audio Video Invasion Inc — 516 345-2636
53 Werman Ct Plainview (11803) *(G-13613)*
Audio-Sears Corp — 607 652-7305
2 South St Stamford (12167) *(G-15643)*
Audiology, Brooklyn *Also called Audio Technology New York Inc (G-1654)*
Audiosavings Inc — 888 445-1555
600 Bayview Ave Ste 200 Inwood (11096) *(G-6791)*
Audubon Machinery Corporation (PA) — 716 564-5165
814 Wurlitzer Dr North Tonawanda (14120) *(G-12975)*
Aufhauser Corp Canada, Plainview *Also called Aufhauser Manufacturing Corp (G-13615)*
Aufhauser Corporation (PA) — 516 694-8696
39 West Mall Plainview (11803) *(G-13614)*
Aufhauser Manufacturing Corp — 516 694-8696
39 West Mall Plainview (11803) *(G-13615)*
Augury Inc — 347 699-5011
110 5th Ave Fl 5 New York (10011) *(G-9314)*
August Graphics, Bronx *Also called D B F Associates (G-1310)*
August Silk Inc (PA) — 212 643-2400
499 7th Ave Fl 5s New York (10018) *(G-9315)*
August Silk Inc — 212 643-2400
499 7th Ave Fl 5s New York (10018) *(G-9316)*
August Studios — 718 706-6487
4008 22nd St Fl 3 Long Island City (11101) *(G-7709)*
August Thomsen Corp — 516 676-7100
36 Sea Cliff Ave Glen Cove (11542) *(G-5623)*
Augusta Studios, Long Island City *Also called August Studios (G-7709)*
Aura Detergent LLC (PA) — 718 824-2162
1811 Mayflower Ave Bronx (10461) *(G-1277)*
Aura Essence, Brooklyn *Also called Candle In The Window Inc (G-1755)*
Aura International Mfg Inc — 212 719-1418
512 Fashion Ave Fl 26 New York (10018) *(G-9317)*
Aurafin Oroamerica, New York *Also called Richline Group Inc (G-11892)*
Auratic Inc — 914 413-8154
41 Madison Ave Ste 1402 New York (10010) *(G-9318)*
Aureonic — 518 791-9331
13 Whispering Pines Rd Gansevoort (12831) *(G-5499)*
Aurora Indus Machining Inc — 716 826-7911
3380 N Benzing Rd Orchard Park (14127) *(G-13275)*
Aurora Machine, Rochester *Also called Alkemy Machine LLC (G-14201)*
Aurora Sef, Peekskill *Also called RMS Packaging Inc (G-13506)*

ALPHABETIC SECTION
Awr Energy Inc

Aurora Shoe Company, King Ferry *Also called Lake View Manufacturing LLC* ***(G-7198)***
Aurora Stone Group LLC...315 471-6869
114 Marcy St East Syracuse (13057) ***(G-4525)***
Aurora Technical Services Ltd...716 652-1463
11970 Parker Rd East Aurora (14052) ***(G-4392)***
Aurubis Buffalo Inc...716 879-6700
600 Military Rd Buffalo (14207) ***(G-2844)***
Aurubis Buffalo Inc (HQ)...716 879-6700
70 Sayre St Buffalo (14207) ***(G-2845)***
Ausco Inc...516 944-9882
425 Smith St Ste 1 Farmingdale (11735) ***(G-4955)***
Austin Air Systems Limited...716 856-3700
500 Elk St Buffalo (14210) ***(G-2846)***
Austin Industries Inc (PA)...585 589-1353
3871 Oak Orchard Rd Albion (14411) ***(G-165)***
Austin Mohawk and Company LLC...315 793-3000
2175 Beechgrove Pl Utica (13501) ***(G-16331)***
Austin Nichols & Co Inc (HQ)...519 561-5225
250 Park Ave New York (10177) ***(G-9319)***
Autel North America, Farmingdale *Also called Autel US Inc* ***(G-4956)***
Autel US Inc (HQ)...631 923-2620
175 Central Ave Ste 200 Farmingdale (11735) ***(G-4956)***
Auterra Inc...518 382-9600
2135 Technology Dr Schenectady (12308) ***(G-15260)***
Authentic Parts, Holbrook *Also called Ingham Industries Inc* ***(G-6480)***
Authority On Transportation, Dix Hills *Also called Authority Transportation Inc* ***(G-4314)***
Authority Transportation Inc...888 933-1268
167 Oakfield Ave Dix Hills (11746) ***(G-4314)***
Auto Body Services LLC...631 431-4640
400 W Hoffman Ave Lindenhurst (11757) ***(G-7477)***
Auto Data Labels, Deer Park *Also called Auto Data Systems Inc* ***(G-4128)***
Auto Data Systems Inc (PA)...631 667-2382
2000 Deer Park Ave Deer Park (11729) ***(G-4128)***
Auto Market Publications Inc...631 667-0500
1641 Deer Park Ave Ste 5 Deer Park (11729) ***(G-4129)***
Auto Sport Designs Inc...631 425-1555
203 W Hills Rd Huntington Station (11746) ***(G-6735)***
Auto-Mat Company Inc...516 938-7373
69 Hazel St Hicksville (11801) ***(G-6349)***
Auto-Mate Technologies LLC...631 727-8886
34 Hinda Blvd Riverhead (11901) ***(G-14149)***
Autodyne Manufacturing Co Inc...631 957-5858
200 N Strong Ave Lindenhurst (11757) ***(G-7478)***
Automated & MGT Solutions LLC...518 283-5352
743 Columbia Tpke East Greenbush (12061) ***(G-4420)***
Automated Bldg MGT Systems Inc (PA)...516 216-5603
54 Cherry Ln Floral Park (11001) ***(G-5202)***
Automated Building Controls...914 381-2860
629 N Barry Ave Mamaroneck (10543) ***(G-8055)***
Automated Cells & Eqp Inc...607 936-1341
9699 Enterprise Dr Painted Post (14870) ***(G-13415)***
Automated Control Logic Inc...914 769-8880
578 Commerce St Thornwood (10594) ***(G-16139)***
Automated Dynamics, Niskayuna *Also called ADC Acquisition Company* ***(G-12910)***
Automated Elevator Systems...845 595-1063
659 Jersey Ave Greenwood Lake (10925) ***(G-5916)***
Automated Office Systems Inc...516 396-5555
71 S Central Ave Valley Stream (11580) ***(G-16426)***
Automated Systems Group, Rochester *Also called Micro Instrument Corp* ***(G-14528)***
Automatic Bar Machining Co, Webster *Also called Kathleen B Mead* ***(G-16752)***
Automatic Connector Inc...631 543-5000
375 Oser Ave Hauppauge (11788) ***(G-6048)***
Automation Correct LLC...315 299-3589
405 Parrish Ln Syracuse (13205) ***(G-15881)***
Automation Papers Inc...315 432-0565
6361 Thompson Rd Stop 1 Syracuse (13206) ***(G-15882)***
Automation Source Technologies (PA)...631 643-1678
21 Otis St Unit B West Babylon (11704) ***(G-16797)***
Automationcorrect.com, Syracuse *Also called Automation Correct LLC* ***(G-15881)***
Automecha International Ltd (PA)...607 843-2235
48 S Canal St Oxford (13830) ***(G-13388)***
Automotion Parking Systems LLC...516 565-5600
411 Hempstead Tpke # 200 West Hempstead (11552) ***(G-16881)***
Automotive LLC...248 728-8642
4320 Federal Dr Batavia (14020) ***(G-624)***
Automotive Accessories Group...212 736-8100
505 8th Ave Rm 12a05 New York (10018) ***(G-9320)***
Automotive Filters Mfg Inc...631 435-1010
80a Keyland Ct A Bohemia (11716) ***(G-1016)***
Automotive Leather Group LLC...516 627-4000
17 Barstow Rd Ste 206 Great Neck (11021) ***(G-5809)***
Automtive Uphl Cnvertible Tops...914 961-4242
170 Marbledale Rd Tuckahoe (10707) ***(G-16293)***
Autostat Corporation...516 379-9447
209 Nassau Rd 11 Roosevelt (11575) ***(G-15027)***
Autronic Plastics Inc...516 333-7577
1150 Motor Pkwy Central Islip (11722) ***(G-3510)***
Auven Therapeutics MGT LP...212 616-4000
1325 Ave Of The Amrcas New York (10019) ***(G-9321)***
Auxilium Pharmaceuticals Inc...484 321-2022
70 High St Rye (10580) ***(G-15080)***
AV Denim Inc...212 764-6668
230 W 38th St Fl 8r New York (10018) ***(G-9322)***
AV Therapeutics Inc...917 497-5523
20 E 68th St Ste 204 New York (10065) ***(G-9323)***
Ava Wood Products, Ava *Also called Robert W Still* ***(G-529)***
Avalanche Fabrication Inc...585 545-4000
6314 Dean Pkwy Ontario (14519) ***(G-13218)***
Avalanche Studios New York Inc...212 993-6447
536 Broadway New York (10012) ***(G-9324)***
Avalin LLC...212 842-2286
221 W 37th St Fl 3 New York (10018) ***(G-9325)***
Avalon Copy Centers Amer Inc (PA)...315 471-3333
901 N State St Syracuse (13208) ***(G-15883)***
Avalon Copy Centers Amer Inc...716 995-7777
741 Main St Buffalo (14203) ***(G-2847)***
Avalon Document Services, Syracuse *Also called Avalon Copy Centers Amer Inc* ***(G-15883)***
Avalon Document Services, Buffalo *Also called Avalon Copy Centers Amer Inc* ***(G-2847)***
Avalonbay Communities Inc...516 484-7766
1100 Avalon Sq Glen Cove (11542) ***(G-5624)***
Avalonics Inc...516 238-7074
94 Gardiners Ave Ste 164 Levittown (11756) ***(G-7446)***
Avanel Industries Inc...516 333-0990
121 Hopper St Westbury (11590) ***(G-16998)***
Avant Garde Screen Printing Co, Flushing *Also called Albert Siy* ***(G-5231)***
Avante...516 782-4888
35 Hicks Ln Great Neck (11024) ***(G-5810)***
Avanti Advanced Mfg Corp...716 541-8945
673 Ontario St Buffalo (14207) ***(G-2848)***
Avanti Control Systems Inc...518 921-4368
1 Hamilton St Fl 2 Gloversville (12078) ***(G-5722)***
Avanti Furniture Corp...516 293-8220
497 Main St Farmingdale (11735) ***(G-4957)***
Avanti Press Inc...212 414-1025
6 W 18th St Ste 6l New York (10011) ***(G-9326)***
Avanti U S A Ltd...716 695-5800
412 Young St Tonawanda (14150) ***(G-16162)***
Avaya Services Inc...866 462-8292
2 Penn Plz Rm 702 New York (10121) ***(G-9327)***
Avco Industries Inc...631 851-1555
120 Windsor Pl Central Islip (11722) ***(G-3511)***
Avcom of Virginia Inc...585 924-4560
590 Fishers Station Dr Victor (14564) ***(G-16485)***
Aventura Technologies Inc (PA)...631 300-4000
48 Mall Dr Commack (11725) ***(G-3848)***
Avenue Magazine, New York *Also called Manhattan Media LLC* ***(G-11154)***
Avenue Therapeutics Inc...781 652-4500
2 Gansevoort St Fl 9 New York (10014) ***(G-9328)***
Avery Biomedical Devices Inc...631 864-1600
61 Mall Dr Ste 1 Commack (11725) ***(G-3849)***
Avery Dennison, Orangeburg *Also called Paxar Corporation* ***(G-13260)***
Avery Dennison Corporation...845 680-3873
524 Route 303 Orangeburg (10962) ***(G-13242)***
Avery Dennison Corporation...626 304-2000
218 W 40th St Fl 8 New York (10018) ***(G-9329)***
Avf Inc (PA)...951 360-7111
2775 Broadway St Ste 200 Buffalo (14227) ***(G-2849)***
AVI, Plainview *Also called Audio Video Invasion Inc* ***(G-13613)***
AVI-Spl Employee...212 840-4801
8 W 38th St Rm 1101 New York (10018) ***(G-9330)***
Avid Technology Inc...212 983-2424
90 Park Ave New York (10016) ***(G-9331)***
Avitto Leather Goods Inc...212 219-7501
424 W Broadway Frnt A New York (10012) ***(G-9332)***
Avm Printing Inc...631 351-1331
43 Corporate Dr Hauppauge (11788) ***(G-6049)***
Avocode Inc...646 934-8410
55 E 73rd St Apt Gf New York (10021) ***(G-9333)***
Avon Press, Hauppauge *Also called Avon Reproductions Inc* ***(G-6050)***
Avon Reproductions Inc...631 273-2400
175 Engineers Rd Hauppauge (11788) ***(G-6050)***
Avs Gem Stone Corp...212 944-6380
48 W 48th St Ste 1010 New York (10036) ***(G-9334)***
AVS Laminates Inc...631 286-2136
99 Bellport Ave Bellport (11713) ***(G-821)***
Avstar Fuel Systems Inc...315 255-1955
15 Brookfield Pl Auburn (13021) ***(G-482)***
AVX Corporation...716 372-6611
1695 Seneca Ave Olean (14760) ***(G-13155)***
AW Mack Manufacturing Co Inc...845 452-4050
1098 Dutchess Tpke Poughkeepsie (12603) ***(G-13909)***
Awaken Led Company...802 338-5971
477 State Route 11 # 1050 Champlain (12919) ***(G-3565)***
Award Publishing Limited...212 246-0405
40 W 55th St Apt 9b New York (10019) ***(G-9335)***
Awning Man, The, Yonkers *Also called Fabric Concepts For Industry* ***(G-17458)***
Awning Mart Inc...315 699-5928
5665 State Route 31 Cicero (13039) ***(G-3671)***
Awnings Plus Inc...716 693-3690
363 Delaware St Tonawanda (14150) ***(G-16163)***
Awr Energy Inc...585 469-7750
35 Melody Ln Plattsburgh (12901) ***(G-13680)***

ALPHABETIC

(PA)=Parent Co (HQ)=Headquarters (DH)=Div Headquarters
2018 Harris
New York Manufacturers Directory
899

Awt Supply Corp 516 437-9105
153 Meacham Ave Elmont (11003) *(G-4730)*
Axim Biotechnologies Inc 212 751-0001
5 Rockefeller Plz Fl 20 New York (10111) *(G-9336)*
Axis Denim, New York Also called Axis Na LLC *(G-9337)*
Axis Na LLC (PA) 212 840-4005
70 W 40th St Fl 11 New York (10018) *(G-9337)*
Axle Express 518 347-2220
729 Broadway Schenectady (12305) *(G-15261)*
Axle Teknology LLC (PA) 631 423-3044
113 Woodbury Rd Huntington (11743) *(G-6687)*
Axtell Bradtke Lumber Co 607 265-3850
113 Beals Pond Rd Masonville (13804) *(G-8137)*
Aycan Medical Systems LLC 585 271-3078
693 East Ave Ste 102 Rochester (14607) *(G-14236)*
AZ Yashir Bapaz Inc 212 947-7357
134 W 37th St New York (10018) *(G-9338)*
Azar Displays, Nanuet Also called Azar International Inc *(G-8797)*
Azar International Inc 845 624-8808
31 W Prospect St Nanuet (10954) *(G-8797)*
Azibi Ltd 212 869-6550
270 W 39th St Rm 1501 New York (10018) *(G-9339)*
Aztec Industries Inc 631 585-1331
200 13th Ave Unit 5 Ronkonkoma (11779) *(G-14903)*
Aztec Mfg of Rochester 585 352-8152
19 Hickory Ln Spencerport (14559) *(G-15589)*
Aztec Tool Co Inc 631 243-1144
180 Rodeo Dr Edgewood (11717) *(G-4607)*
Azurrx Biopharma Inc 646 699-7855
760 Parkside Ave Ste 304 Brooklyn (11226) *(G-1655)*
B & B Forest Products Ltd 518 622-0811
251 Route 145 Cairo (12413) *(G-3296)*
B & B Jewelry Mfg Co, New York Also called Barber Brothers Jewelry Mfg *(G-9368)*
B & B Lumber Company Inc (PA) 866 282-0582
4800 Solvay Rd Jamesville (13078) *(G-7077)*
B & B Precision Components Inc 631 273-3321
301 Christopher St # 303 Ronkonkoma (11779) *(G-14904)*
B & B Precision Mfg Inc (PA) 585 226-6226
310 W Main St Avon (14414) *(G-535)*
B & B Sheet Metal Inc 718 433-2501
2540 50th Ave Long Island City (11101) *(G-7710)*
B & B Sweater Mills Inc (PA) 718 456-8693
1160 Flushing Ave Brooklyn (11237) *(G-1656)*
B & D Enterprises of Utica (PA) 315 735-3311
2 Campion Rd Ste 7 New Hartford (13413) *(G-8846)*
B & F Architectural Support Gr 212 279-6488
450 7th Ave Ste 307 New York (10123) *(G-9340)*
B & H Electronics Corp 845 782-5000
308 Museum Village Rd Monroe (10950) *(G-8584)*
B & H Precision Fabricators 631 563-9620
95 Davinci Dr Bohemia (11716) *(G-1017)*
B & J Delivers Inc 631 524-5550
70 Emjay Blvd Bldg D Brentwood (11717) *(G-1174)*
B & J Lumber Co Inc 518 677-3845
1075 State Route 22 Cambridge (12816) *(G-3332)*
B & K Components Ltd 323 776-4277
2100 Old Union Rd Buffalo (14227) *(G-2850)*
B & K Dye Cutting Inc 718 497-5216
245 Varet St Brooklyn (11206) *(G-1657)*
B & P Jays Inc 716 668-8408
19 N Hill Dr Buffalo (14224) *(G-2851)*
B & R Electric Motor Inc 631 752-7533
5919 Central Ave Farmingdale (11735) *(G-4958)*
B & R Industries Inc 631 736-2275
12 Commercial Blvd Medford (11763) *(G-8267)*
B & R Promotional Products 212 563-0040
34 W 120th St Apt 1 New York (10027) *(G-9341)*
B & R Sheet 718 558-5544
10652 157th St Jamaica (11433) *(G-6933)*
B & R Tool Inc 718 948-2729
955 Rensselaer Ave Staten Island (10309) *(G-15662)*
B & S Bialy, Oceanside Also called Bagels By Bell Ltd *(G-13093)*
B & W Heat Treating Company 716 876-8184
2780 Kenmore Ave Tonawanda (14150) *(G-16164)*
B & Z Technologies LLC 631 675-9666
7 Technology Dr East Setauket (11733) *(G-4496)*
B C America, New York Also called Intertex USA Inc *(G-10683)*
B C Manufacturing Inc 585 482-1080
100 Thruway Park Dr West Henrietta (14586) *(G-16903)*
B C T, Holbrook Also called Speedcard Inc *(G-6501)*
B C T, Syosset Also called SDS Business Cards Inc *(G-15860)*
B Cake NY LLC 347 787-7199
702 Washington Ave Brooklyn (11238) *(G-1658)*
B D B Typewriter Supply Works 718 232-4800
6215 14th Ave Brooklyn (11219) *(G-1659)*
B F G Elcpltg and Mfg Co 716 362-0888
3949 Jeffrey Blvd Blasdell (14219) *(G-954)*
B H Aircraft Company Inc (PA) 631 580-9747
2230 Smithtown Ave Ronkonkoma (11779) *(G-14905)*
B H M Metal Products Co 845 292-5297
Horseshoe Lake Rd Kauneonga Lake (12749) *(G-7165)*
B J Long Co, Rochester Also called R V Dow Enterprises Inc *(G-14644)*

B J S Electric 845 774-8166
1000 Craigville Rd Chester (10918) *(G-3627)*
B K Integrity, New York Also called Golden Integrity Inc *(G-10374)*
B K Jewelry Contractor Inc 212 398-9093
71 W 47th St Fl 11 New York (10036) *(G-9342)*
B Live LLC 212 489-0721
347 W 36th St Rm 402 New York (10018) *(G-9343)*
B M P, Medina Also called Bmp America Inc *(G-8300)*
B P I, West Henrietta Also called Brinkman Precision Inc *(G-16905)*
B P Nash Co Inc 315 445-1310
5841 Butternut Dr East Syracuse (13057) *(G-4526)*
B S C, Binghamton Also called Binghamton Simulator Co Inc *(G-891)*
B S J Limited 212 764-4600
1400 Broadway Ste 1702 New York (10018) *(G-9344)*
B S J Limited (PA) 212 221-8403
1375 Broadway Rm 507 New York (10018) *(G-9345)*
B Smith Furs Inc 212 967-5290
224 W 30th St Rm 402 New York (10001) *(G-9346)*
B Tween LLC 212 819-9040
1411 Broadway Rm 2520 New York (10018) *(G-9347)*
B V M Associates 631 254-6220
999-32 Montrell 414 Shirley (11967) *(G-15438)*
B W A, New York Also called Ben Wachter Associates Inc *(G-9401)*
B&B Albany Pallet Company LLC 315 492-1786
4800 Solvay Rd Jamesville (13078) *(G-7078)*
B&K Precision Corporation 631 369-2665
31 Oakwood Dr Manorville (11949) *(G-8110)*
B-Reel Films Inc 917 388-3836
401 Broadway Fl 24 New York (10013) *(G-9348)*
B-Squared Inc 212 777-2044
104 W 29th St Fl 7 New York (10001) *(G-9349)*
B/E Aerospace Inc 631 563-6400
355 Knickerbocker Ave Bohemia (11716) *(G-1018)*
B/E Aerospace Inc 631 589-0877
355 Knickerbocker Ave Bohemia (11716) *(G-1019)*
B2b Cleaning Services, Yonkers Also called Rumsey Corp *(G-17501)*
B3cg Interconnect Usa Inc 450 491-4040
18 Northern Ave 100 Plattsburgh (12903) *(G-13681)*
B601 V2 Inc 646 391-6431
315 5th Ave Rm 903 New York (10016) *(G-9350)*
Ba Sports Nutrition LLC 718 357-7402
1720 Whitestone Expy # 101 Whitestone (11357) *(G-17230)*
Baar & Beards, New York Also called Gce International Inc *(G-10305)*
Babbit Bearings, Syracuse Also called Babbitt Bearings Inc *(G-15884)*
Babbitt Bearings Inc (PA) 315 479-6603
734 Burnet Ave Syracuse (13203) *(G-15884)*
Babbitt Bearings Incorporated 315 479-6603
734 Burnet Ave Syracuse (13203) *(G-15885)*
Babcock Co Inc 607 776-3341
36 Delaware Ave Bath (14810) *(G-653)*
Babula Construction Inc 716 681-0886
5136 William St Lancaster (14086) *(G-7329)*
Baby Central LLC 718 372-2229
2436 Mcdonald Ave Brooklyn (11223) *(G-1660)*
Baby Signature Inc (PA) 212 686-1700
251 5th Ave Fl 2l New York (10016) *(G-9351)*
Baby Uv/Kids Uv Inc (PA) 917 301-9020
11 Hawks Nest Rd Stony Brook (11790) *(G-15787)*
Babydoll, New York Also called Mag Brands LLC *(G-11124)*
Babyfair Inc 212 736-7989
34 W 33rd St Rm 818 New York (10001) *(G-9352)*
Babyganics, Westbury Also called Kas Direct LLC *(G-17028)*
Babylon Iron Works Inc 631 643-3311
205 Edison Ave West Babylon (11704) *(G-16798)*
Babysafe Usa LLC 877 367-4141
251 County Road 17 Afton (13730) *(G-8)*
Backstage LLC (PA) 212 493-4243
45 Main St Ste 416 Brooklyn (11201) *(G-1661)*
Backtech Inc 973 279-0838
2 Peter Cooper Rd Apt Mf New York (10010) *(G-9353)*
Backyard Fence Inc 518 452-9496
4204 Albany St Albany (12205) *(G-48)*
Baco Enterprises Inc (PA) 718 589-6225
1190 Longwood Ave Bronx (10474) *(G-1278)*
Badge Machine Products Inc 585 394-0330
2491 Brickyard Rd Canandaigua (14424) *(G-3364)*
Badger Technologies Inc 585 869-7101
5829 County Road 41 Farmington (14425) *(G-5155)*
Badger Technologies Inc (PA) 585 869-7101
5829 County Road 41 Farmington (14425) *(G-5156)*
Badgley Mischka Licensing LLC 212 921-1585
550 7th Ave Fl 22 New York (10018) *(G-9354)*
Badoud Communications 315 472-7821
750 W Genesee St Syracuse (13204) *(G-15886)*
Bae Systems Controls Inc (HQ) 607 770-2000
1098 Clark St Endicott (13760) *(G-4804)*
Bae Systems Info & Elec Sys 631 912-1525
450 Pulaski Rd Greenlawn (11740) *(G-5891)*
Bag Arts Ltd 212 684-7020
20 W 36th St Rm 5r New York (10018) *(G-9355)*
Bag Arts The Art Packaging LLC 212 684-7020
20 W 36th St Fl 5 New York (10018) *(G-9356)*

Bag Bazaar Ltd 212 689-3508
1 E 33rd St Fl 6 New York (10016) **(G-9357)**
Bagel Club, Bayside *Also called A T A Bagel Shoppe Inc* **(G-759)**
Bagel Club Inc 718 423-6106
20521 35th Ave Bayside (11361) **(G-762)**
Bagel Grove Inc 315 724-8015
7 Burrstone Rd Utica (13502) **(G-16332)**
Bagel Land 585 442-3080
1896 Monroe Ave Rochester (14618) **(G-14237)**
Bagel Lites LLC 855 813-7888
240 51st Ave Apt 1f Long Island City (11101) **(G-7711)**
Bagel Oasis, Flushing *Also called Triboro Bagel Co Inc* **(G-5308)**
Bagel Shoppe, The, Fishkill *Also called Enterprise Bagels Inc* **(G-5190)**
Bagelovers Inc 607 844-3683
42 Elm St Dryden (13053) **(G-4345)**
Bagelry, Cedarhurst *Also called M & M Bagel Corp* **(G-3484)**
Bagels By Bell Ltd 718 272-2780
3333 Royal Ave Oceanside (11572) **(G-13093)**
Bagels On The Square, Staten Island *Also called Carmine Street Bagels Inc* **(G-15676)**
Baggu 347 457-5266
109 Ingraham St Brooklyn (11237) **(G-1662)**
Bags Unlimited Inc 585 436-6282
7 Canal St Rochester (14608) **(G-14238)**
Bagznyc Corp 212 643-8202
19 W 34th St Rm 318 New York (10001) **(G-9358)**
Baikal Inc (PA) 212 239-4650
341 W 38th St Fl 3 New York (10018) **(G-9359)**
Bailey Boonville Mills Inc 315 942-2131
123 Mill St Boonville (13309) **(G-1159)**
Bailey Manufacturing Co LLC 716 965-2731
10987 Bennett State Rd Forestville (14062) **(G-5340)**
Baillie Lumber Co LP 315 942-5284
189 West St Boonville (13309) **(G-1160)**
Bainbridge & Knight LLC 212 986-5100
801 2nd Ave Fl 19 New York (10017) **(G-9360)**
Baird Mold Making Inc 631 667-0322
195 N Fehr Way Ste C Bay Shore (11706) **(G-673)**
Bairnco Corporation (HQ) 914 461-1300
1133 Westchester Ave N-222 White Plains (10604) **(G-17108)**
Bajan Group Inc 518 464-2884
950 New Loudon Rd Ste 280 Latham (12110) **(G-7381)**
Bak USA Technologies Corp 716 248-2704
425 Michigan Ave Ste 4 Buffalo (14203) **(G-2852)**
Baked Cupcakery 716 773-2050
1879 Whitehaven Rd Grand Island (14072) **(G-5766)**
Baker Commodities Inc 585 482-1880
2268 Browncroft Blvd Rochester (14625) **(G-14239)**
Baker Logging & Firewood 585 374-5733
8781 Grlnghuse Atlanta Rd Naples (14512) **(G-8810)**
Baker Products Inc 212 459-2323
5 Oakley Rd White Plains (10606) **(G-17109)**
Baker Tool & Die 716 694-2025
48 Industrial Dr North Tonawanda (14120) **(G-12976)**
Baker Tool & Die & Die 716 694-2025
48 Industrial Dr North Tonawanda (14120) **(G-12977)**
Bakers of All Nations, Mineola *Also called Ericeira Inc* **(G-8543)**
Bakers Pride Oven Co Inc 914 576-0200
145 Huguenot St Ste Mz1 New Rochelle (10801) **(G-8932)**
Bakery & Coffee Shop 315 287-1829
274 W Main St Gouverneur (13642) **(G-5757)**
Bakery Innovative Tech Corp 631 758-3081
139 N Ocean Ave Patchogue (11772) **(G-13440)**
Balajee Enterprises Inc 212 629-6150
150 W 30th St Frnt 2 New York (10001) **(G-9361)**
Balance Enterprises Inc 516 822-3183
12 W Cherry St Hicksville (11801) **(G-6350)**
Balanced Tech Corp 212 768-8330
37 W 37th St Fl 10 New York (10018) **(G-9362)**
Balchem Corporation (PA) 845 326-5600
52 Sunrise Park Rd New Hampton (10958) **(G-8842)**
Baldwin Machine Works Inc 631 842-9110
20 Grant Ave 2040 Copiague (11726) **(G-3922)**
Baldwin Ribbon & Stamping Corp 718 335-6700
3956 63rd St Woodside (11377) **(G-17336)**
Baldwin Richardson Foods Co 315 986-2727
3268 Blue Heron Dr Macedon (14502) **(G-8010)**
Balint Tool, Brooklyn *Also called Tools & Stamping Corp* **(G-2683)**
Baliva Concrete Products Inc 585 328-8442
245 Paul Rd Rochester (14624) **(G-14240)**
Ball Chain Mfg Co Inc (PA) 914 664-7500
741 S Fulton Ave Mount Vernon (10550) **(G-8709)**
Ball Metal Beverage Cont Corp 845 692-3800
95 Ballard Rd Middletown (10941) **(G-8461)**
Ball Metal Beverage Cont Corp 518 587-6030
11 Adams Rd Saratoga Springs (12866) **(G-15172)**
Ball Metal Beverage Cont Div, Middletown *Also called Ball Metal Beverage Cont Corp* **(G-8461)**
Ball Metal Beverage Cont Div, Saratoga Springs *Also called Ball Metal Beverage Cont Corp* **(G-15172)**
Ballantrae Lithographers Inc 914 592-3275
96 Wayside Dr White Plains (10607) **(G-17110)**
Balticare Inc (PA) 646 380-9470
501 Fashion Ave Rm 414 New York (10018) **(G-9363)**
Bam Enterprises Inc (PA) 716 773-7634
2937 Alt Blvd Grand Island (14072) **(G-5767)**
Bam Sales LLC (PA) 212 781-3000
1407 Broadway Rm 2018 New York (10018) **(G-9364)**
Bamberger Polymers Intl Corp 516 622-3600
2 Jericho Plz Ste 109 Jericho (11753) **(G-7094)**
Bamboo Global Industries 973 943-1878
339 E 58th St Apt 7e New York (10022) **(G-9365)**
Bandier Corp 212 242-5400
960 Park Ave Apt 11b New York (10028) **(G-9366)**
Bandit International Ltd 718 402-2100
600 E 132nd St Bronx (10454) **(G-1279)**
Bands N Bows 718 984-4316
34 Fieldway Ave Staten Island (10308) **(G-15663)**
Bangla Patrika Inc 718 482-9923
3806 31st St 2 Long Island City (11101) **(G-7712)**
Bank Displays.com, Deer Park *Also called L Miller Design Inc* **(G-4186)**
Bank-Miller Co Inc 914 227-9357
333 Fifth Ave Pelham (10803) **(G-13514)**
Banner Metalcraft Inc 631 563-7303
300 Trade Zone Dr Ronkonkoma (11779) **(G-14906)**
Banner Smoked Fish Inc 718 449-1992
2715 W 15th St Brooklyn (11224) **(G-1663)**
Banner Transmission & Eng Co 516 221-9459
2765 Broadway Bellmore (11710) **(G-810)**
Banner Transmissions, Bellmore *Also called Banner Transmission & Eng Co* **(G-810)**
Bar Fields Inc 347 587-7795
2614 W 13th St Brooklyn (11223) **(G-1664)**
Bara Fashions, Brooklyn *Also called Matchables Inc* **(G-2285)**
Baralan Usa Inc (HQ) 718 849-5768
12019 89th Ave Richmond Hill (11418) **(G-14080)**
Barbara Matera Ltd 212 475-5006
890 Broadway Fl 5 New York (10003) **(G-9367)**
Barber & Deline Enrgy Svcs LLC 315 696-8961
10 Community Dr Tully (13159) **(G-16298)**
Barber & Deline LLC 607 749-2619
995 State Route 11a Tully (13159) **(G-16299)**
Barber Brothers Jewelry Mfg 212 819-0666
580 5th Ave Ste 725 New York (10036) **(G-9368)**
Barber Welding Inc 315 834-6645
2517 Rte 31 W Weedsport (13166) **(G-16772)**
Barbera Transduser Systems 718 816-3025
21 Louis St Staten Island (10304) **(G-15664)**
Barc Usa Inc 516 719-1052
5 Delaware Dr Ste 2 New Hyde Park (11042) **(G-8863)**
Barclay Brown Corp 718 376-7166
47 Lancaster Ave Brooklyn (11223) **(G-1665)**
Barclay Tagg Racing 631 404-8269
86 Geranium Ave Floral Park (11001) **(G-5203)**
Bardwil Industries Inc (PA) 212 944-1870
1071 Ave Of The Americas New York (10018) **(G-9369)**
Bardwil Linens, New York *Also called Bardwil Industries Inc* **(G-9369)**
Bare Beauty Laser Hair Removal 718 278-2273
5 E 57th St Fl 6 New York (10022) **(G-9370)**
Bare Escentuals Inc 646 537-0070
1140 3rd Ave New York (10065) **(G-9371)**
Bare Minerals, New York *Also called Bare Escentuals Inc* **(G-9371)**
Bare Wire Div, Jordan *Also called Omega Wire Inc* **(G-7158)**
Bare Wire Div, Camden *Also called Omega Wire Inc* **(G-3346)**
Bare Wire Division, Camden *Also called Owi Corporation* **(G-3347)**
Bare Wire Division, Camden *Also called International Wire Group Inc* **(G-3344)**
Bargold Storage Systems LLC 718 247-7000
4141 38th St Long Island City (11101) **(G-7713)**
Bari Engineering Corp 212 966-2080
240 Bowery New York (10012) **(G-9372)**
Bari-Jay Fashions Inc (PA) 212 921-1551
225 W 37th St Fl 7 New York (10018) **(G-9373)**
Barilla America Ny Inc 585 226-5600
100 Horseshoe Blvd Avon (14414) **(G-536)**
Barker Brothers Incorporated 718 456-6400
1666 Summerfield St Ste 1 Ridgewood (11385) **(G-14114)**
Barker Steel LLC 518 465-6221
126 S Port Rd Albany (12202) **(G-49)**
Barnaby Prints Inc (PA) 845 477-2501
673 Jersey Ave Greenwood Lake (10925) **(G-5917)**
Barnes Group Inc 315 457-9200
1225 State Fair Blvd Syracuse (13209) **(G-15887)**
Barnes Metal Finishing Inc 585 798-4817
3932 Salt Works Rd Medina (14103) **(G-8298)**
Barney & Dickenson Inc (PA) 607 729-1536
520 Prentice Rd Vestal (13850) **(G-16462)**
Baroka Creations Inc 212 768-0527
36 W 47th St Ste 1402 New York (10036) **(G-9374)**
Baron Packaging, Hauppauge *Also called J & M Packaging Inc* **(G-6124)**
Barone Offset Printing Corp 212 989-5500
89 Lake Ridge Cv Mohegan Lake (10547) **(G-8577)**
Barra & Trumbore Inc 845 626-5442
40 Old Mine Rd Kerhonkson (12446) **(G-7183)**
Barrage 212 586-9390
401 W 47th St Frnt A New York (10036) **(G-9375)**

ALPHABETIC

Barrasso & Sons Trucking Inc ... 631 581-0360
160 Floral Park St Islip Terrace (11752) ***(G-6854)***
Barrera Jose & Maria Co Ltd ... 212 239-1994
29 W 36th St Fl 8 New York (10018) ***(G-9376)***
Barrett Bronze Inc ... 914 699-6060
115 Miller Pl Mount Vernon (10550) ***(G-8710)***
Barrett Paving Materials Inc ... 315 353-6611
Rr 56 Norwood (13668) ***(G-13058)***
Barrett Paving Materials Inc ... 315 737-9471
363 Rasbach Rd Clayville (13322) ***(G-3712)***
Barrett Paving Materials Inc ... 607 723-5367
14 Brandywine St Binghamton (13901) ***(G-887)***
Barrett Paving Materials Inc ... 315 788-2037
26572 State Route 37 Watertown (13601) ***(G-16658)***
Barrie House Coffee & Tea, Elmsford *Also called Bh Coffee Company LLC* ***(G-4745)***
Barrier Brewing Company LLC ... 516 316-4429
612 W Walnut St Long Beach (11561) ***(G-7668)***
Barron Games Intl Co LLC ... 716 630-0054
84 Aero Dr Ste 5 Buffalo (14225) ***(G-2853)***
Barron Metal Products Inc ... 914 965-1232
286 Nepperhan Ave Yonkers (10701) ***(G-17434)***
Barrons Educational, Hauppauge *Also called Barrons Educational Series Inc* ***(G-6051)***
Barrons Educational Series Inc (PA) ... 631 434-3311
250 Wireless Blvd Hauppauge (11788) ***(G-6051)***
Barry Industries Inc ... 212 242-5200
36 W 17th St Frnt 1 New York (10011) ***(G-9377)***
Barry Steel Fabrication Inc (PA) ... 716 433-2144
30 Simonds St Lockport (14094) ***(G-7599)***
Barry Supply Co Div, New York *Also called Barry Industries Inc* ***(G-9377)***
Bars Precision Inc ... 585 742-6380
5 Charleston Dr Mendon (14506) ***(G-8412)***
Barson Composites Corporation (PA) ... 516 752-7882
160 Bethpage Sweet Old Bethpage (11804) ***(G-13147)***
Bartell Machinery Systems LLC (HQ) ... 315 336-7600
6321 Elmer Hill Rd Rome (13440) ***(G-14833)***
Bartholomew Mazza Ltd Inc ... 212 935-4530
22 W 48th St Ste 805 New York (10036) ***(G-9378)***
Bartizan Data Systems LLC ... 914 965-7977
217 Riverdale Ave Yonkers (10705) ***(G-17435)***
Bartolomeo Publishing Inc ... 631 420-4949
100 Cabot St Unit A West Babylon (11704) ***(G-16799)***
Bartolotta Furniture, Auburn *Also called Matteo & Antonio Bartolotta* ***(G-506)***
Barton International, Glens Falls *Also called Barton Mines Company LLC* ***(G-5688)***
Barton Mines Company LLC (PA) ... 518 798-5462
6 Warren St Glens Falls (12801) ***(G-5688)***
Barton Tool Inc ... 716 665-2801
1864 Lyndon Blvd Falconer (14733) ***(G-4899)***
Basco, Amherst *Also called American Precision Inds Inc* ***(G-227)***
Base Container Inc ... 718 636-2004
180 Classon Ave Brooklyn (11205) ***(G-1666)***
Base Systems Inc ... 845 278-1991
1606 Route 22 Brewster (10509) ***(G-1208)***
BASF Beauty Care Solutions LLC ... 631 689-0200
50 Health Sciences Dr Stony Brook (11790) ***(G-15788)***
BASF Corporation ... 914 737-2554
1057 Lower South St Peekskill (10566) ***(G-13497)***
BASF Corporation ... 518 465-6534
70 Riverside Ave Rensselaer (12144) ***(G-14056)***
BASF Corporation ... 914 785-2000
500 White Plains Rd Tarrytown (10591) ***(G-16111)***
BASF Corporation ... 973 245-6000
560 White Plains Rd Tarrytown (10591) ***(G-16112)***
BASF Corporation ... 914 788-1627
1057 Lower South St Peekskill (10566) ***(G-13498)***
BASF Corporation ... 212 450-8280
545 5th Ave Fl 11 New York (10017) ***(G-9379)***
BASF Corporation ... 631 689-0200
361 Sheep Pasture Rd East Setauket (11733) ***(G-4497)***
BASF The Chemical Company, East Setauket *Also called BASF Corporation* ***(G-4497)***
Basil S Kadhim ... 888 520-5192
280 Madison Ave Rm 912 New York (10016) ***(G-9380)***
Basileus Company LLC ... 315 963-3516
8104 Cazenovia Rd Manlius (13104) ***(G-8101)***
Basilio's, Canastota *Also called Salarinos Italian Foods Inc* ***(G-3398)***
Basiloff LLC ... 646 671-0353
179 Bennett Ave Apt 7f New York (10040) ***(G-9381)***
Basin Holdings US LLC (PA) ... 212 695-7376
200 Park Ave Fl 58 New York (10166) ***(G-9382)***
Bass Oil & Chemical Llc ... 718 628-4444
136 Morgan Ave Brooklyn (11237) ***(G-1667)***
Bass Oil Company Inc ... 718 628-4444
136 Morgan Ave Brooklyn (11237) ***(G-1668)***
Bassin Technical Sales Co ... 914 698-9358
1009 W Boston Post Rd # 2 Mamaroneck (10543) ***(G-8056)***
Batampte Pickle Products Inc (PA) ... 718 251-2100
77 Brooklyn Terminal Mkt Brooklyn (11236) ***(G-1669)***
Batavia Enclosures Inc ... 585 344-1797
636 Main St Arcade (14009) ***(G-388)***
Batavia Legal Printing Inc ... 585 768-2100
7 Bank St Le Roy (14482) ***(G-7428)***
Batavia Precision Glass LLC ... 585 343-6050
231 Currier Ave Buffalo (14212) ***(G-2854)***
Batavia Press LLC ... 585 343-4429
3817 W Main Street Rd Batavia (14020) ***(G-625)***
Bates Industries, South Glens Falls *Also called Mdi East Inc* ***(G-15549)***
Bates Jackson Engraving Co Inc ... 716 854-3000
17 Elm St 21 Buffalo (14203) ***(G-2855)***
Bator Bintor Inc ... 347 546-6503
42 Delevan St Brooklyn (11231) ***(G-1670)***
Battenfeld Grease Oil Corp NY ... 716 695-2100
1174 Erie Ave North Tonawanda (14120) ***(G-12978)***
Battenfeld-American Inc ... 716 822-8410
1575 Clinton St Buffalo (14206) ***(G-2856)***
Battery Energy Storage Systems ... 518 256-7029
291 River St Ste 318 Troy (12180) ***(G-16249)***
Battery Research and Tstg Inc ... 315 342-2373
1313 County Route 1 Oswego (13126) ***(G-13353)***
Battsco LLC ... 516 586-6544
190 Lauman Ln Unit A Hicksville (11801) ***(G-6351)***
Bauble Bar Inc ... 646 664-4803
1115 Broadway Fl 5 New York (10010) ***(G-9383)***
Bauerschmidt & Sons Inc ... 718 528-3500
11920 Merrick Blvd Jamaica (11434) ***(G-6934)***
Baum Christine and John Corp ... 585 621-8910
1577 W Ridge Rd Rochester (14615) ***(G-14241)***
Baums Castorine Company Inc ... 315 336-8154
200 Matthew St Rome (13440) ***(G-14834)***
Bausch & Lomb Holdings Inc (HQ) ... 585 338-6000
450 Lexington Ave New York (10017) ***(G-9384)***
Bausch & Lomb Incorporated (HQ) ... 585 338-6000
1400 N Goodman St Rochester (14609) ***(G-14242)***
Bausch & Lomb Incorporated ... 585 338-6000
1400 N Goodman St Rochester (14609) ***(G-14243)***
Baxter Healthcare Corporation ... 800 356-3454
711 Park Ave Medina (14103) ***(G-8299)***
Baxter International Inc ... 845 457-9370
500 Neelytown Rd Montgomery (12549) ***(G-8627)***
Bay Horse Innovations Nyinc ... 607 898-3337
130 Cayuga St Groton (13073) ***(G-5918)***
Bay Sales Company, New York *Also called Salmco Jewelry Corp* ***(G-11975)***
Bayit Home Automation Corp ... 973 988-2638
2299 Mcdonald Ave Brooklyn (11223) ***(G-1671)***
Bayshore Electric Motors ... 631 475-1397
33 Suffolk Ave Patchogue (11772) ***(G-13441)***
Bayshore Motors, Patchogue *Also called Bayshore Electric Motors* ***(G-13441)***
Bayshore Wire Products Corp ... 631 451-8825
480 Mill Rd Coram (11727) ***(G-3964)***
Bayside Beepers & Cellular ... 718 343-3888
25607 Hillside Ave Glen Oaks (11004) ***(G-5654)***
Bazaar ... 212 903-5497
300 W 57th St Fl 25 New York (10019) ***(G-9385)***
BC Systems Inc ... 631 751-9370
200 N Belle Mead Ave # 2 Setauket (11733) ***(G-15399)***
BCM, Mount Vernon *Also called Ball Chain Mfg Co Inc* ***(G-8709)***
Bco Industries Western NY Inc ... 716 877-2800
77 Oriskany Dr Tonawanda (14150) ***(G-16165)***
Bcp Ingredients Inc (HQ) ... 845 326-5600
52 Sunrise Park Rd New Hampton (10958) ***(G-8843)***
Bd Initiative-Hlthcare Wrkr SA, Nyack *Also called Becton Dickinson and Company* ***(G-13061)***
Bd Projects, New York *Also called Architects Newspaper LLC* ***(G-9245)***
BDB Technologies LLC ... 800 921-4270
768 Bedford Ave Brooklyn (11205) ***(G-1672)***
Bdg Media Inc (PA) ... 917 951-9768
158 W 27th St Fl 11 New York (10001) ***(G-9386)***
Bdm, Syosset *Also called Buffalo Dental Mfg Co Inc* ***(G-15836)***
Bdp Industries Inc (PA) ... 518 695-6851
354 State Route 29 Greenwich (12834) ***(G-5904)***
BDR Creative Concepts Inc ... 516 942-7768
141 Central Ave Ste B Farmingdale (11735) ***(G-4959)***
Be The Media, New Hyde Park *Also called Natural E Creative LLC* ***(G-8895)***
Beaba USA, New York *Also called Peek A Boo USA Inc* ***(G-11612)***
Beachbuttons LLC ... 917 306-9369
6 Greene St Apt 4b New York (10013) ***(G-9387)***
Beacon, Babylon *Also called A C J Communications Inc* ***(G-541)***
Beacon Adhesives Inc ... 914 699-3400
125 S Macquesten Pkwy Mount Vernon (10550) ***(G-8711)***
Beacon Chemical, Mount Vernon *Also called Beacon Adhesives Inc* ***(G-8711)***
Beacon Newspapers, Hempstead *Also called Nassau County Publications* ***(G-6306)***
Beacon Press Inc ... 212 691-5050
32 Cushman Rd White Plains (10606) ***(G-17111)***
Beacon Press News, Wappingers Falls *Also called Wappingers Falls Shopper Inc* ***(G-16598)***
Beacon Spch Lnge Pthlgy Phys ... 516 626-1635
1441 Old Northern Blvd Roslyn (11576) ***(G-15040)***
Beacon Therapy Services, Roslyn *Also called Beacon Spch Lnge Pthlgy Phys* ***(G-15040)***
Beak & Skiff Cider Mill Inc ... 315 677-5105
4472 Us Route 20 La Fayette (13084) ***(G-7265)***
Beal Blocks, New York *Also called B & R Promotional Products* ***(G-9341)***
BEAM Manufacturing Corp ... 631 253-2724
107 Otis St Unit A West Babylon (11704) ***(G-16800)***
Bean King International LLC ... 845 268-3135
36 N Route 9w Congers (10920) ***(G-3877)***

Bear Metal Works Inc 716 824-4350
39 Scoville Ave Buffalo (14206) *(G-2857)*
Bear Port Publishing Company 877 337-8577
45 W 21st St 3b New York (10010) *(G-9388)*
Beardslee Realty 516 747-5557
290 E Jericho Tpke Mineola (11501) *(G-8530)*
Bears Management Group Inc 585 624-5694
7577 E Main St Lima (14485) *(G-7464)*
Bears Playgrounds, Lima *Also called Bears Management Group Inc (G-7464)*
Beast Vapes Nyc 718 714-8139
182 30th St Brooklyn (11232) *(G-1673)*
Beastons Budget Printing 585 244-2721
1260 Scttsvlle Rd Ste 300 Rochester (14624) *(G-14244)*
Beauty America LLC 917 744-1430
10 Bond St Ste 296 Great Neck (11021) *(G-5811)*
Beauty Fashion Inc 212 840-8800
8 W 38th St Frnt 2 New York (10018) *(G-9389)*
Beaver Creek Industries Inc 607 545-6382
11530 White Rd Canaseraga (14822) *(G-3391)*
Bebop Books, New York *Also called Lee & Low Books Incorporated (G-10992)*
BEC Acquisition Co, Melville *Also called Tech Software LLC (G-8389)*
Becca Inc 646 568-6250
142 W 36th St Fl 15 New York (10018) *(G-9390)*
Becca Cosmetics, New York *Also called Becca Inc (G-9390)*
Beck Vault Company 315 337-7590
6648 Shank Ave Rome (13440) *(G-14835)*
Beck, Don, Corfu *Also called Delaval Inc (G-3976)*
Becker Electronics Inc 631 619-9100
50 Alexander Ct Ste 2 Ronkonkoma (11779) *(G-14907)*
Beckmann Converting Inc (PA) 518 842-0073
14 Park Dr Amsterdam (12010) *(G-335)*
Becks Classic Mfg Inc 631 435-3800
50 Emjay Blvd Ste 7 Brentwood (11717) *(G-1175)*
Becton Dickinson and Company 845 353-3371
1 Main St Apt 3307 Nyack (10960) *(G-13061)*
Bedessee Imports Ltd 718 272-1300
140 Varick Ave Brooklyn (11237) *(G-1674)*
Bedford Freeman & Worth (HQ) 212 576-9400
1 New York Plz Ste 4500 New York (10004) *(G-9391)*
Bedford Freeman & Worth 212 375-7000
1 New York Plz Ste 4500 New York (10004) *(G-9392)*
Bedford Communications Inc 212 807-8220
1410 Broadway Frnt 2 New York (10018) *(G-9393)*
Bedford Downing Glass 718 418-6409
220 Ingraham St Ste 2 Brooklyn (11237) *(G-1675)*
Bedford Precision Parts Corp 914 241-2211
290 Adams St Bedford Hills (10507) *(G-796)*
Bedford Pund Rdge Rcord Review, Katonah *Also called Record Review LLC (G-7162)*
Bedford Wdwrk Instllations Inc 914 764-9434
200 Pound Ridge Rd Bedford (10506) *(G-791)*
Bedrock Communications 212 532-4150
152 Madison Ave Rm 802 New York (10016) *(G-9394)*
Bedrock Landscaping Mtls Corp (PA) 631 587-4950
454 Sunrise Hwy Babylon (11704) *(G-543)*
Bedrock Plus, Babylon *Also called Bedrock Landscaping Mtls Corp (G-543)*
Bee Green Industries Inc 516 334-3525
322 Westbury Ave Carle Place (11514) *(G-3412)*
Bee Publications Inc 716 632-4700
5564 Main St Williamsville (14221) *(G-17263)*
Beebie Printing & Art Agcy Inc 518 725-4528
40 E Pine St Gloversville (12078) *(G-5723)*
Beech Grove Technology Inc 845 223-6844
11 Sandy Pines Blvd Hopewell Junction (12533) *(G-6574)*
Beech-Nut Nutrition Company (HQ) 518 839-0300
1 Nutritious Pl Amsterdam (12010) *(G-336)*
Beecher Emssn Sltn Tchnlgs LLC (PA) 607 796-0149
1250 Schweizer Rd Horseheads (14845) *(G-6596)*
Beehive Press Inc 718 654-1200
3742 Boston Rd Bronx (10469) *(G-1280)*
Beer Marketers Insights Inc 845 507-0040
49 E Maple Ave Suffern (10901) *(G-15808)*
Beetins Wholesale Inc 718 524-0899
125 Ravenhurst Ave Staten Island (10310) *(G-15665)*
Beets Love Production LLC 585 270-2471
1150 Lee Rd Rochester (14606) *(G-14245)*
Behance, New York *Also called Adobe Systems Incorporated (G-9078)*
Behlman Electronics Inc (HQ) 631 435-0410
80 Cabot Ct Hauppauge (11788) *(G-6052)*
Beila Group Inc 212 260-1948
285 Mott St New York (10012) *(G-9395)*
Beis Moshiach Inc 718 778-8000
744 Eastern Pkwy Brooklyn (11213) *(G-1676)*
Beitals Aquarium Sales & Svc, Pearl River *Also called C B Management Services Inc (G-13477)*
Beka World LP 905 821-1050
258 Sonwil Dr Buffalo (14225) *(G-2858)*
Bekaert Corporation 716 830-1321
6000 N Bailey Ave Ste 9 Amherst (14226) *(G-229)*
Bektrom Foods Inc (PA) 516 802-3800
6800 Jericho Tpke 207w Syosset (11791) *(G-15835)*
Bel Aire Offset Corp 718 539-8333
1853 College Point Blvd College Point (11356) *(G-3804)*
Bel Aire Printing, College Point *Also called Bel Aire Offset Corp (G-3804)*
Bel Americas Inc 646 454-8220
122 E 42nd St Rm 2715 New York (10168) *(G-9396)*
Bel Art International 718 402-2100
600 E 132nd St Bronx (10454) *(G-1281)*
Bel Transformer Inc (HQ) 516 239-5777
500 Bayview Ave Inwood (11096) *(G-6792)*
Bel-Bee Products Incorporated 845 353-0300
100 Snake Hill Rd Ste 1 West Nyack (10994) *(G-16942)*
Belangers Gravel & Stone Inc 585 728-3906
10184 State Route 21 Wayland (14572) *(G-16733)*
Belden Inc 607 796-5600
224 N Main St Ste 4 Horseheads (14845) *(G-6597)*
Belden Manufacturing Inc 607 238-0998
1813 Us Route 11 Kirkwood (13795) *(G-7259)*
Belfair Draperies, Long Island City *Also called Anthony Lawrence of New York (G-7694)*
Belgian Boys USA, Farmingdale *Also called Merb LLC (G-5057)*
Bell-Pac, East Syracuse *Also called Bellotti Packaging Inc (G-4527)*
Bella International Inc 716 484-0102
111 W 2nd St Ste 4000 Jamestown (14701) *(G-7009)*
Bellarno International Ltd 212 302-4107
1140 Ave Of The Americas New York (10036) *(G-9397)*
Bellataire Diamonds Inc 212 687-8881
19 W 44th St Fl 15 New York (10036) *(G-9398)*
Belle Maison USA Ltd 718 805-0200
8950 127th St Richmond Hill (11418) *(G-14081)*
Bellerophon Publications Inc 212 627-9977
205 Lexington Ave Fl 17 New York (10016) *(G-9399)*
Bellini Collections, New York *Also called Formart Corp (G-10238)*
Bellmore Steel Products Corp 516 785-9667
2282 Bellmore Ave Bellmore (11710) *(G-811)*
Bello LLC 516 623-8800
178 Hanse Ave Freeport (11520) *(G-5399)*
Bellotti Packaging Inc 315 433-0131
6881 Schuyler Rd East Syracuse (13057) *(G-4527)*
Belmay Holding Corporation 914 376-1515
1 Odell Plz Ste 123 Yonkers (10701) *(G-17436)*
Belmet Products Inc (PA) 718 542-8220
1350 Garrison Ave Bronx (10474) *(G-1282)*
Belrix Industries Inc 716 821-5964
3590 Jeffrey Blvd Buffalo (14219) *(G-2859)*
Belsito Communications Inc 845 534-9700
1 Ardmore St New Windsor (12553) *(G-8978)*
BELT DEWATERING PRESS, Greenwich *Also called Bdp Industries Inc (G-5904)*
Belt Maintenance Systems, Buffalo *Also called Rlp Holdings Inc (G-3187)*
Belton Industries, Brooklyn *Also called Filta Clean Co Inc (G-1974)*
Beltran Associates Inc 718 252-2996
1133 E 35th St Ste 1 Brooklyn (11210) *(G-1677)*
Beltran Technologies Inc 718 338-3311
1133 E 35th St Brooklyn (11210) *(G-1678)*
Beluga Inc (PA) 212 594-5511
463 7th Ave Fl 4 New York (10018) *(G-9400)*
Bematech, Bethpage *Also called Logic Controls Inc (G-870)*
Bemco of Western Ny Inc 716 823-8400
122 Roberts Ave Buffalo (14206) *(G-2860)*
Bemis Company Inc 631 794-2900
100 Wilshire Blvd Edgewood (11717) *(G-4608)*
Bemis North America, Edgewood *Also called Bemis Company Inc (G-4608)*
Ben Wachter Associates Inc (PA) 212 736-4064
36 W 44th St Ste 700 New York (10036) *(G-9401)*
Ben Weitsman of Albany LLC 518 462-4444
300 Smith Blvd Albany (12202) *(G-50)*
Ben-Amun Co Inc (PA) 212 944-6480
246 W 38th St Fl 12a New York (10018) *(G-9402)*
Ben-Sak Textile Inc 212 279-5122
307 W 38th St Frnt 9 New York (10018) *(G-9403)*
Benartex Inc 212 840-3250
132 W 36th St Rm 401 New York (10018) *(G-9404)*
Benchemark Printing Inc 518 393-1361
1890 Maxon Rd Ext Schenectady (12308) *(G-15262)*
Benchers Unlimited, Brooklyn *Also called Issacs Yisroel (G-2115)*
Benchmark Books, Tarrytown *Also called Marshall Cavendish Corp (G-16118)*
Benchmark Education Co LLC (PA) 914 637-7200
145 Huguenot St Fl 8 New Rochelle (10801) *(G-8933)*
Benchmark Furniture Mfg 718 257-4707
300 Dewitt Ave Brooklyn (11236) *(G-1679)*
Benchmark Graphics Ltd 212 683-1711
9 E 37th St Fl 5 New York (10016) *(G-9405)*
Benchmark Media Systems Inc 315 437-6300
203 E Hampton Pl Ste 2 Syracuse (13206) *(G-15888)*
Benedictine Hospital, Kingston *Also called Healthalliance Hospital (G-7219)*
Benemy Welding & Fabrication 315 548-8500
8 Pleasant Ave Phelps (14532) *(G-13553)*
Benetton Services, New York *Also called Ramsbury Property Us Inc (G-11823)*
Benetton Trading Usa Inc (PA) 212 593-0290
601 5th Ave Fl 4 New York (10017) *(G-9406)*
Benfield Control Systems Inc 914 948-6660
25 Lafayette Ave White Plains (10603) *(G-17112)*
Benishty Brothers Corp 646 339-9991
233 Mosher Ave Woodmere (11598) *(G-17329)*

ALPHABETIC

Benjamin Moore & Co — 518 736-1723
Union Ave Ext Johnstown (12095) *(G-7139)*

Benjamin Printing Inc — 315 788-7922
60 E Church St Adams (13605) *(G-2)*

Benjamin Sheridan Corporation (HQ) — 585 657-6161
7629 State Route 5 And 20 Bloomfield (14469) *(G-975)*

Benlee Enterprises LLC — 212 730-7330
3100 47th Ave Unit 2 Long Island City (11101) *(G-7714)*

Benners Gardens LLC — 518 828-1055
1 Hudson City Ctr Hudson (12534) *(G-6638)*

Bennett Die & Tool Inc — 607 739-5629
130 Wygant Rd Horseheads (14845) *(G-6598)*

Bennett Die & Tool Inc — 607 273-2836
113 Brewery Ln Ithaca (14850) *(G-6860)*

Bennett Manufacturing Co Inc — 716 937-9161
13315 Railroad St Alden (14004) *(G-178)*

Bennett Multimedia Inc — 718 629-1454
1087 Utica Ave Brooklyn (11203) *(G-1680)*

Bennett Printing Corporation — 718 629-1454
1087 Utica Ave Brooklyn (11203) *(G-1681)*

Bennett Stair Company Inc — 518 384-1554
1021 State Route 50 Ballston Lake (12019) *(G-579)*

Bensak, New York Also called Ben-Sak Textile Inc *(G-9403)*

Benson Industries Inc — 212 779-3230
192 Lexington Ave Rm 502 New York (10016) *(G-9407)*

Benson Mills Inc — 718 236-6743
140 58th St Ste 7j Brooklyn (11220) *(G-1682)*

Benson Sales Co Inc — 718 236-6743
6813 20th Ave Brooklyn (11204) *(G-1683)*

Benson Steel Fabricators, Saugerties Also called Kenbenco Inc *(G-15215)*

Bentley Cravats, New York Also called W B Bow Tie Corp *(G-12601)*

Bentley Manufacturing Inc (PA) — 212 714-1800
10 W 33rd St Rm 220 New York (10001) *(G-9408)*

Benton Announcements Inc — 716 836-4100
3006 Bailey Ave 3010 Buffalo (14215) *(G-2861)*

Bentones Enterprises, New York Also called Hjn Inc *(G-10531)*

Benway-Haworth-Lwlr-Iacosta He — 518 432-4070
21 Everett Rd Albany (12205) *(G-51)*

Benzsay & Harrison Inc — 518 895-2311
Railroad Ave Delanson (12053) *(G-4257)*

Beowawe Binary LLC — 646 829-3900
1095 Avenue Of The Ave New York (10036) *(G-9409)*

Berardi Bakery Inc — 718 746-9529
15045 12th Rd Whitestone (11357) *(G-17231)*

Bereza Iron Works Inc — 585 254-6311
87 Dewey Ave Rochester (14608) *(G-14246)*

Berger & Wild LLC — 646 415-8459
401 Broadway Ste 302 New York (10013) *(G-9410)*

Berjen Metal Industries Ltd — 631 673-7979
645 New York Ave Unit 1 Huntington (11743) *(G-6688)*

Berkman Bros Inc — 718 782-1827
538 Johnson Ave Brooklyn (11237) *(G-1684)*

Berkshire Business Forms Inc — 518 828-2600
829 Route 66 Hudson (12534) *(G-6639)*

Berkshire Transformer (PA) — 631 467-5328
77 Windsor Pl Ste 18 Central Islip (11722) *(G-3512)*

Berkshire Weaving, New York Also called Richloom Fabrics Group Inc *(G-11895)*

Bernan Associates, New York Also called Kraus Organization Limited *(G-10927)*

Bernard Chaus Inc (PA) — 212 354-1280
530 Fashion Ave Fl 18 New York (10018) *(G-9411)*

Bernard Chaus Inc — 646 562-4700
515 7th Ave Ste 18 New York (10018) *(G-9412)*

Bernard Hall — 585 425-3340
10 Perinton Hills Mall Fairport (14450) *(G-4853)*

Bernette Apparel LLC — 212 279-5526
42 W 39th St Fl 2 New York (10018) *(G-9413)*

Bernhard Arnold & Company Inc (PA) — 212 907-1500
485 Lexington Ave Fl 9 New York (10017) *(G-9414)*

Bernstein Display, New York Also called Leo D Bernstein & Sons Inc *(G-11003)*

Berry Global Inc — 315 986-2161
112 Main St Macedon (14502) *(G-8011)*

Berry Global Inc — 315 484-0397
1500 Milton Ave Solvay (13209) *(G-15528)*

Berry Global Group Inc — 315 986-6270
200 Main St Macedon (14502) *(G-8012)*

Berry Industrial Group Inc (PA) — 845 353-8338
30 Main St Nyack (10960) *(G-13062)*

Berry Jewelry Company, New York Also called MJM Jewelry Corp *(G-11311)*

Berry Jewelry Company, Brooklyn Also called MJM Jewelry Corp *(G-2330)*

Berry Plastics Corporation — 315 986-6270
200 Main St Macedon (14502) *(G-8013)*

Berry Plastics Group Inc — 716 366-2112
3565 Chadwick Dr Dunkirk (14048) *(G-4357)*

Berry Specialty Tapes LLC — 631 727-6000
1852 Old Country Rd Riverhead (11901) *(G-14150)*

Berrywild — 212 686-5848
200 E 30th St Bsmt New York (10016) *(G-9415)*

Bert Wassererman — 212 759-5210
370 Lexington Ave New York (10017) *(G-9416)*

Bertelsmann Inc (HQ) — 212 782-1000
1745 Broadway Fl 20 New York (10019) *(G-9417)*

Bertelsmann Pubg Group Inc (HQ) — 212 782-1000
1540 Broadway Fl 24 New York (10036) *(G-9418)*

Beryllium Manufacturing, Copiague Also called Worldwide Arntcal Cmpnents Inc *(G-3963)*

Besam Entrance Solutions, East Syracuse Also called Assa Abloy Entrance Systems US *(G-4524)*

Bescor Video Accessories Ltd — 631 420-1717
244 Route 109 Farmingdale (11735) *(G-4960)*

Besicorp Ltd (PA) — 845 336-7700
1151 Flatbush Rd Kingston (12401) *(G-7208)*

Bespoke Apparel Inc — 212 382-0330
214 W 39th St Rm 200b New York (10018) *(G-9419)*

Besstech, Troy Also called Battery Energy Storage Systems *(G-16249)*

Best Adhesives Company Inc — 718 417-3800
4702 Metropolitan Ave Ridgewood (11385) *(G-14115)*

Best Boilers Inc — 718 372-4210
2402 Neptune Ave Brooklyn (11224) *(G-1685)*

Best Brands Consumer Pdts Inc (PA) — 212 684-7456
20 W 33rd St Fl 5 New York (10001) *(G-9420)*

Best Bread, Port Chester Also called Good Bread Bakery *(G-13775)*

Best Concrete Mix Corp — 718 463-5500
3510 College Point Blvd Flushing (11354) *(G-5236)*

Best Foods Baking Group, Tonawanda Also called Bimbo Bakeries Usa Inc *(G-16166)*

Best Line Inc — 917 670-6210
101 Manila Ave Fl 2 Staten Island (10306) *(G-15666)*

Best Mdlr HMS Afrbe P Q& S In — 631 204-0049
495 County Road 39 Southampton (11968) *(G-15563)*

Best Medical Wear Ltd — 718 858-5544
21 Hall St Brooklyn (11205) *(G-1686)*

Best Pallet & Crate LLC — 518 438-2945
22 Railroad Ave Albany (12205) *(G-52)*

Best Priced Products Inc — 914 345-3800
250 Clearbrook Rd Ste 240 Elmsford (10523) *(G-4744)*

Best Time Processor LLC — 917 455-4126
8746 Van Wyck Expy Richmond Hill (11418) *(G-14082)*

Best Tinsmith Supply Inc — 518 863-2541
4 Zetta Dr Northville (12134) *(G-13036)*

Best Toy Manufacturing Ltd — 718 855-9040
43 Hall St Ste B1 Brooklyn (11205) *(G-1687)*

Best Way Tools By Anderson Inc — 631 586-4702
171 Brook Ave Deer Park (11729) *(G-4130)*

Bestec Concept Inc — 718 937-5848
4310 23rd St Lbby 4 Long Island City (11101) *(G-7715)*

Bestline International RES Inc — 518 631-2177
224 State St Schenectady (12305) *(G-15263)*

Bestway Enterprises Inc (PA) — 607 753-8261
3877 Luker Rd Cortland (13045) *(G-4034)*

Bestway of New York Inc — 607 753-8261
3877 Luker Rd Cortland (13045) *(G-4035)*

Bestype Digital Imaging LLC — 212 966-6886
285 W Broadway Frnt A New York (10013) *(G-9421)*

Bet Networks Incorporated — 212 846-8111
1540 Broadway Fl 26 New York (10036) *(G-9422)*

Beta Transformer Tech Corp (HQ) — 631 244-7393
40 Orville Dr Ste 2 Bohemia (11716) *(G-1020)*

Beth Kobliner Company LLC — 212 501-8407
1995 Broadway Ste 1800 New York (10023) *(G-9423)*

Beth Ward Studios LLC — 646 922-7575
133 W 25th St Rm 8e New York (10001) *(G-9424)*

Beths Farm Kitchen — 518 799-3414
504 Rte 46 Stuyvesant Falls (12174) *(G-15805)*

Betsy & Adam Ltd (PA) — 212 302-3750
1400 Broadway Rm 602 New York (10018) *(G-9425)*

Better Baked Foods Inc — 716 326-4651
25 Jefferson St Westfield (14787) *(G-17075)*

Better Fresh Corp — 718 628-3682
41 Varick Ave Brooklyn (11237) *(G-1688)*

Better Light & Power, Rochester Also called Better Power Inc *(G-14247)*

Better Power Inc — 585 475-1321
508 White Spruce Blvd Rochester (14623) *(G-14247)*

Better Wire Products Inc — 716 883-3377
1255 Niagara St Buffalo (14213) *(G-2862)*

Betterbee, Greenwich Also called Northast Ctr For Bekeeping LLC *(G-5910)*

Betterbee Inc — 518 314-0575
8 Meader Rd Greenwich (12834) *(G-5905)*

Bettertex Inc — 212 431-3373
450 Broadway New York (10013) *(G-9426)*

Bettertex Interiors, New York Also called Bettertex Inc *(G-9426)*

Beval Engine & Machine, Central Islip Also called Abk Enterprises Inc *(G-3508)*

Beverage Media Group Inc (PA) — 212 571-3232
152 Madison Ave Rm 600 New York (10016) *(G-9427)*

Beverage Works Incorporated — 718 834-0500
70 Hamilton Ave 8 Brooklyn (11231) *(G-1689)*

Beverage Works Nj Inc — 631 293-3501
16 Dubon Ct Farmingdale (11735) *(G-4961)*

Beverage Works Ny Inc — 718 812-2034
70 Hamilton Ave 8 Brooklyn (11231) *(G-1690)*

Beverly Creations Inc — 800 439-6855
40 E 34th St Rm 1403 New York (10016) *(G-9428)*

Bevilacque Group LLC — 212 414-8858
19 Norwood Rd Port Washington (11050) *(G-13824)*

Bevilacque Group LLC By Profor, Port Washington *Also called Bevilacque Group LLC (G-13824)*
Beyer Graphics Inc............631 543-3900
30 Austin Blvd Ste A Commack (11725) **(G-3850)**
Beyond Beauty Basics LLC............516 731-7100
3359 Hempstead Tpke Levittown (11756) **(G-7447)**
Beyond Design Inc............607 865-7487
807 Pines Brook Rd Walton (13856) **(G-16568)**
Beyond Loom Inc (PA)............212 575-3100
262 W 38th St Rm 203 New York (10018) **(G-9429)**
Beyond Vape............917 909-1113
602 Pacific St Brooklyn (11217) **(G-1691)**
Beyondly Inc............646 658-3665
20 W 20th St Ste 1004 New York (10011) **(G-9430)**
Beyondspring Inc............646 305-6387
28 Liberty St Fl 39 New York (10005) **(G-9431)**
Beyondspring Phrmceuticals Inc............646 305-6387
28 Liberty St Fl 39 New York (10005) **(G-9432)**
Bfc Print Network Inc (PA)............716 838-4532
455 Commerce Dr Ste 6 Amherst (14228) **(G-230)**
Bfg Manufacturing Services Inc............716 362-0888
3949 Jeffrey Blvd Buffalo (14219) **(G-2863)**
Bfg Marine Inc............631 586-5500
200 Candlewood Rd Bay Shore (11706) **(G-674)**
Bfgg Investors Group LLC............585 424-3456
1900 University Ave Rochester (14610) **(G-14248)**
Bfma Holding Corporation............607 753-6746
37 Huntington St Cortland (13045) **(G-4036)**
Bg Bindery Inc............631 767-4242
5877 57th St Maspeth (11378) **(G-8150)**
Bga Technology LLC............631 750-4600
116 Wilbur Pl Bohemia (11716) **(G-1021)**
Bh Brand Inc............212 239-1635
10 W 33rd St Rm 218 New York (10001) **(G-9433)**
Bh Brands, New York *Also called Bh Brand Inc* **(G-9433)**
Bh Coffee Company LLC (PA)............914 377-2500
4 Warehouse Ln Ste 121 Elmsford (10523) **(G-4745)**
BH Multi Com Corp (PA)............212 944-0020
15 W 46th St Fl 6 New York (10036) **(G-9434)**
Bharat Electronics Limited............516 248-4021
53 Hilton Ave Garden City (11530) **(G-5510)**
Bhi Elevator Cabs Inc............516 431-5665
74 Alabama Ave Island Park (11558) **(G-6818)**
Bi Nutraceuticals Inc............631 232-1105
120 Hoffman Ln Central Islip (11749) **(G-3513)**
Bianca Burgers LLC............516 764-9591
15 S Long Beach Rd Rockville Centre (11570) **(G-14816)**
Bianca Group Ltd............212 768-3011
244 W 39th St Fl 4 New York (10018) **(G-9435)**
Bibo International LLC............617 304-2242
130 Water St Apt 4g New York (10005) **(G-9436)**
Bicker Inc............212 688-0085
425 Madison Ave Fl 12 New York (10017) **(G-9437)**
Bicon Pharmaceutical Inc............631 593-4199
75 N Industry Ct Deer Park (11729) **(G-4131)**
Bidpress LLC............267 973-8876
659 Washington St Apt 5r New York (10014) **(G-9438)**
Bielecky Bros Inc (PA)............718 424-4764
5022 72nd St Woodside (11377) **(G-17337)**
Bielka Inc............212 980-6841
136 E 57th St Ste 907 New York (10022) **(G-9439)**
Bien Cuit LLC............718 852-0200
120 Smith St Brooklyn (11201) **(G-1692)**
Big Apple Elevtr Srv & Consult............212 279-0700
247 W 30th St New York (10001) **(G-9440)**
Big Apple Sign Corp............631 342-0303
3 Oval Dr Islandia (11749) **(G-6826)**
Big Apple Sign Corp (PA)............212 629-3650
247 W 35th St Frnt 1 New York (10001) **(G-9441)**
Big Apple Visual Group, Islandia *Also called Big Apple Sign Corp* **(G-6826)**
Big Apple Visual Group, New York *Also called Big Apple Sign Corp* **(G-9441)**
Big Apple Welding Supply............718 439-3959
236 47th St Brooklyn (11220) **(G-1693)**
Big Bang Clothing Inc............212 221-0379
214 W 39th St Rm 1008 New York (10018) **(G-9442)**
Big Bang Clothing Co, New York *Also called Big Bang Clothing Inc* **(G-9442)**
Big Bear, Buffalo *Also called Stephen M Kiernan* **(G-3224)**
Big City Bagel Lites, Long Island City *Also called Bagel Lites LLC* **(G-7711)**
Big Data Bizviz LLC............716 803-2367
1075 East And West Rd West Seneca (14224) **(G-16968)**
Big Fish Entertainment LLC............646 797-4955
1411 Broadway Fl 16 New York (10018) **(G-9443)**
Big Heart Pet Brands............716 891-6566
243 Urban St Buffalo (14211) **(G-2864)**
Big Idea Brands LLC............212 938-0270
1410 Broadway Frnt 4 New York (10018) **(G-9444)**
Big Indie - Beautiful Boy LLC (PA)............917 464-5599
41 Plochmann Ln Woodstock (12498) **(G-17377)**
Big John's Beef Jerky, Saratoga Springs *Also called Big Johns Adirondack Inc* **(G-15173)**
Big Johns Adirondack Inc............518 587-3680
45 N Milton Rd Saratoga Springs (12866) **(G-15173)**
Big Shine Energy, Newburgh *Also called Big Shine Worldwide Inc* **(G-12772)**
Big Shine Worldwide Inc............845 444-5255
300 Corporate Blvd Newburgh (12550) **(G-12772)**
Big White Wall Holding Inc............917 281-2649
41 E 11th St Fl 11 New York (10003) **(G-9445)**
Bigbee Steel and Tank Company............518 273-0801
958 19th St Watervliet (12189) **(G-16703)**
Bigname Commerce LLC............631 693-1070
5300 New Horizons Blvd Amityville (11701) **(G-276)**
Bignay Inc............786 346-1673
315 E 86th St Apt 21ge New York (10028) **(G-9446)**
Bigrow Paper Mfg Corp............718 624-4439
930 Bedford Ave Brooklyn (11205) **(G-1694)**
Bigrow Paper Product, Brooklyn *Also called Bigrow Paper Mfg Corp* **(G-1694)**
Bigsky Technologies LLC............585 218-9499
1600 N Clinton Ave Ste 11 Rochester (14621) **(G-14249)**
Bigwood Systems Inc............607 257-0915
35 Thornwood Dr Ste 400 Ithaca (14850) **(G-6861)**
Bilbee Controls Inc............518 622-3033
628 Main St Cairo (12413) **(G-3297)**
Bilco Industries Inc............917 783-5008
214 W 39th St Rm 301 New York (10018) **(G-9447)**
Bilinski Sausage Mfg Co, Cohoes *Also called Schonwetter Enterprises Inc* **(G-3782)**
Bill Blass Group LLC............212 689-8957
236 5th Ave Fl 8 New York (10001) **(G-9448)**
Bill Lake Homes Construction............518 673-2424
188 Flanders Rd Sprakers (12166) **(G-15601)**
Bill Shea Enterprises Inc............585 343-2284
8825 Alexander Rd Batavia (14020) **(G-626)**
Billanti Casting Co Inc............516 775-4800
299 S 11th St New Hyde Park (11040) **(G-8864)**
Billanti Jewelry Casting, New Hyde Park *Also called Billanti Casting Co Inc* **(G-8864)**
Billie-Ann Plastics Pkg Corp............718 497-3409
360 Troutman St Brooklyn (11237) **(G-1695)**
Billing Blocks Inc............718 442-5006
147 North Ave Staten Island (10314) **(G-15667)**
Billing Coding and Prtg Inc............718 827-9409
455 Grant Ave Brooklyn (11208) **(G-1696)**
Billion Tower Intl LLC............212 220-0608
989 6th Ave Fl 8 New York (10018) **(G-9449)**
Billion Tower USA LLC............212 220-0608
989 Avenue Of The America New York (10018) **(G-9450)**
Billsboro Winery............315 789-9538
4760 State Route 14 Geneva (14456) **(G-5582)**
Billy Beez Usa LLC............315 741-5099
9090 Destiy Usa Dr L301 Unit L 301 Syracuse (13204) **(G-15889)**
Billy Beez Usa LLC (PA)............646 606-2249
3 W 35th St Fl 3 New York (10001) **(G-9451)**
Billy Beez Usa LLC............845 915-4709
1282 Palisades Center Dr West Nyack (10994) **(G-16943)**
Biltron Automotive Products............631 928-8613
509 Bicycle Path Unit Q Port Jeff STA (11776) **(G-13786)**
Bimbo Bakeries............631 274-4906
955 Grand Blvd Deer Park (11729) **(G-4132)**
Bimbo Bakeries............518 463-2221
78 N Manning Blvd Albany (12206) **(G-53)**
Bimbo Bakeries USA, Bay Shore *Also called Bimbo Foods Bakeries Inc* **(G-676)**
Bimbo Bakeries Usa Inc............716 692-9140
1960 Niagara Falls Blvd Tonawanda (14150) **(G-16166)**
Bimbo Bakeries Usa Inc............718 601-1561
5625 Broadway Frnt 2 Bronx (10463) **(G-1283)**
Bimbo Bakeries Usa Inc............718 545-0291
4011 34th Ave Long Island City (11101) **(G-7716)**
Bimbo Bakeries Usa Inc............516 877-2850
12 E Jericho Tpke Mineola (11501) **(G-8531)**
Bimbo Bakeries Usa Inc............716 372-8444
111 N 2nd St Olean (14760) **(G-13156)**
Bimbo Bakeries Usa Inc............516 887-1024
669 Sunrise Hwy Spc 4 Lynbrook (11563) **(G-7975)**
Bimbo Bakeries Usa Inc............315 379-9069
19 Miner St Ste D Canton (13617) **(G-3406)**
Bimbo Bakeries Usa Inc............718 463-6300
5754 Page Pl Maspeth (11378) **(G-8151)**
Bimbo Bakeries Usa Inc............518 489-4053
40 Fuller Rd Albany (12205) **(G-54)**
Bimbo Bakeries Usa Inc............203 531-2311
30 Inez Dr Bay Shore (11706) **(G-675)**
Bimbo Bakeries Usa Inc............315 253-9782
11 Corcoran Dr Auburn (13021) **(G-483)**
Bimbo Bakeries Usa Inc............716 706-0450
2900 Commerce Pkwy Lancaster (14086) **(G-7330)**
Bimbo Bakeries Usa Inc............315 785-7060
144 Eastern Blvd Watertown (13601) **(G-16659)**
Bimbo Bakeries Usa Inc............845 568-0943
98 Scobie Dr Newburgh (12550) **(G-12773)**
Bimbo Bakeries Usa Inc............800 856-8544
1624 Castle Gardens Rd Vestal (13850) **(G-16463)**
Bimbo Bakeries Usa Inc............315 782-4189
1100 Water St Watertown (13601) **(G-16660)**
Bimbo Bakeries Usa Inc............845 294-5282
9 Police Dr Goshen (10924) **(G-5746)**
Bimbo Foods Bakeries Inc (HQ)............631 273-6000
40 Harold Ct Bay Shore (11706) **(G-676)**

ALPHABETIC

(PA)=Parent Co (HQ)=Headquarters (DH)=Div Headquarters
2018 Harris
New York Manufacturers Directory
905

Binah Magazines Corp 718 305-5200
207 Foster Ave Brooklyn (11230) *(G-1697)*
Bindle and Keep 917 740-5002
47 Hall St Ste 109 Brooklyn (11205) *(G-1698)*
Binghamton Burial Vault Co Inc 607 722-4931
1114 Porter Ave Binghamton (13901) *(G-888)*
Binghamton Knitting Co Inc 607 722-6941
11 Alice St Binghamton (13904) *(G-889)*
Binghamton Precast & Sup Corp 607 722-0334
18 Phelps St Binghamton (13901) *(G-890)*
Binghamton Press, Vestal Also called Gannett Co Inc *(G-16470)*
Binghamton Simulator Co Inc 607 321-2980
151 Court St Binghamton (13901) *(G-891)*
Binoptics LLC (HQ) 607 257-3200
9 Brown Rd Ithaca (14850) *(G-6862)*
Bio Nutrition, Oceanside Also called Only Natural Inc *(G-13110)*
Bio Service, Woodside Also called Firecom Inc *(G-17345)*
Bio-Botanica Inc (PA) 631 231-0987
75 Commerce Dr Hauppauge (11788) *(G-6053)*
Bio-Chem Barrier Systems LLC 631 261-2682
11 W Scudder Pl Northport (11768) *(G-13025)*
Bio-Nutritional Products, White Plains Also called Meta-Therm Corp *(G-17164)*
Biochemical Diagnostics Inc 631 595-9200
180 Heartland Blvd Edgewood (11717) *(G-4609)*
Biocontinuum Group Inc 212 406-1060
116 Chambers St New York (10007) *(G-9452)*
Biodesign Inc of New York (PA) 845 454-6610
1 Sunset Rdg Carmel (10512) *(G-3426)*
Biodex Medical Systems Inc (PA) 631 924-9000
20 Ramsey Rd Shirley (11967) *(G-15439)*
Biodex Medical Systems   Inc 631 924-3146
49 Natcon Dr Shirley (11967) *(G-15440)*
Biodigitalpc, New Hyde Park Also called Arnouse Digital Devices Corp *(G-8862)*
Biofeedback Instrument Corp 212 222-5665
255 W 98th St Apt 3d New York (10025) *(G-9453)*
Bioinformatics Publishing, New York Also called Genomeweb LLC *(G-10322)*
Bioins Inc 646 398-3718
1767 Central Park Ave # 258 Yonkers (10710) *(G-17437)*
Bioivt, Westbury Also called Bioreclamationivt LLC *(G-16999)*
Biolitec Inc 413 525-0600
110 E 42nd St Rm 1800 New York (10017) *(G-9454)*
Biologic Solutions, Purchase Also called FMC International Ltd *(G-13972)*
Biologique Recherche, New York Also called Distribio USA LLC *(G-9941)*
Biomed Pharmaceuticals Inc 914 592-0525
4 Skyline Dr Ste 5 Hawthorne (10532) *(G-6267)*
Bionic Eye Technologies Inc 845 505-5254
4 Willow Lake Dr Fishkill (12524) *(G-5188)*
Biopool Us Inc 716 483-3851
2823 Girts Rd Jamestown (14701) *(G-7010)*
Bioreclamationivt LLC (PA) 516 483-1196
123 Frost St Ste 115 Westbury (11590) *(G-16999)*
Biorem Environmental Inc 585 924-2220
100 Rawson Rd Ste 230 Victor (14564) *(G-16486)*
Bioresearch Inc (PA) 212 734-5315
4 Sunset Ln Pound Ridge (10576) *(G-13958)*
Biospecifics Technologies Corp (PA) 516 593-7000
35 Wilbur St Lynbrook (11563) *(G-7976)*
Biospherix Ltd 315 387-3414
25 Union St Parish (13131) *(G-13439)*
Biospherix Medical, Parish Also called Biospherix Ltd *(G-13439)*
Biotech Energy Inc 800 340-1387
100 Clinton Point Dr Plattsburgh (12901) *(G-13682)*
Biotech Energy Systems, Plattsburgh Also called Biotech Energy Inc *(G-13682)*
Biotemper 516 302-7985
516 Mineola Ave Carle Place (11514) *(G-3413)*
Biotemper Plus, Carle Place Also called Biotemper *(G-3413)*
Bioworks Inc (PA) 585 924-4362
100 Rawson Rd Ste 205 Victor (14564) *(G-16487)*
Birch Coffee, Long Island City Also called Birch Guys LLC *(G-7717)*
Birch Guys LLC 917 763-0751
4035 23rd St Long Island City (11101) *(G-7717)*
Birch Machine & Tool Inc 716 735-9802
80 Telegraph Rd Middleport (14105) *(G-8454)*
Bird Bus Sales, Elmsford Also called JP Bus & Truck Repair Ltd *(G-4767)*
Birdair Inc (HQ) 716 633-9500
65 Lawrence Bell Dr # 100 Amherst (14221) *(G-231)*
Birds Eye Foods Inc 716 988-3218
Mechanic St South Dayton (14138) *(G-15539)*
Birds Eye Holdings Inc 585 383-1850
90 Linden Park Rochester (14625) *(G-14250)*
Birkett Mills (PA) 315 536-3311
163 Main St Ste 2 Penn Yan (14527) *(G-13529)*
Birkett Mills 315 536-4112
163 Main St Ste 3 Penn Yan (14527) *(G-13530)*
Birnbaum & Bullock Ltd 212 242-2914
151 W 25th St Rm 2a New York (10001) *(G-9455)*
Birthstone Enterprises, New York Also called Alchemy Simya Inc *(G-9126)*
Bishop Print Shop Inc 607 965-8155
9 East St Edmeston (13335) *(G-4635)*

Bison Bag Co Inc 716 434-4380
5404 Crown Dr Lockport (14094) *(G-7600)*
Bison Iron & Step, Buffalo Also called M K Ulrich Construction Inc *(G-3071)*
Bison Products, Buffalo Also called Upstate Niagara Coop Inc *(G-3263)*
Bison Steel Incorporated 716 683-0900
2 Main St Ste 103 Depew (14043) *(G-4273)*
Bissel-Babcock Millwork Inc 716 761-6976
3866 Kendrick Rd Sherman (14781) *(G-15423)*
Bistate Oil Management Corp 212 935-4110
10 E 40th St Rm 2705 New York (10016) *(G-9456)*
Bistrian Cement Corporation 631 324-1123
225 Springs Fireplace Rd East Hampton (11937) *(G-4425)*
Bittner Company LLC 585 214-1790
75 Goodway Dr Ste 3 Rochester (14623) *(G-14251)*
Bitzer Scroll Inc 315 463-2101
6055 Court Street Rd Syracuse (13206) *(G-15890)*
Bizbash Masterplanner, New York Also called Bizbash Media Inc *(G-9457)*
Bizbash Media Inc (PA) 646 638-3600
115 W 27th St Fl 8 New York (10001) *(G-9457)*
BJ Magazines Inc 212 367-9705
200 Varick St New York (10014) *(G-9458)*
BJG Services LLC 516 592-5692
237 W 35th St Ste 505 New York (10001) *(G-9459)*
BK Associates Intl Inc 607 432-1499
127 Commerce Rd Oneonta (13820) *(G-13196)*
Bk Printing Inc 315 565-5396
6507 Basile Rowe East Syracuse (13057) *(G-4528)*
Black & Decker (us) Inc 914 235-6300
2 Powers Ln Brewster (10509) *(G-1209)*
Black & Decker (us) Inc 716 884-6220
881 W Delavan Ave Buffalo (14209) *(G-2865)*
Black & Decker (us) Inc 631 952-2008
180 Oser Ave Ste 100 Hauppauge (11788) *(G-6054)*
Black Bear Company Inc 718 784-7330
2710 49th Ave Long Island City (11101) *(G-7718)*
Black Bear Fuels Oil, Harris Also called Jus-Sar Fuel Inc *(G-5997)*
Black Book Photography Inc 212 979-6700
740 Broadway Ste 10 New York (10003) *(G-9460)*
Black Book, The, New York Also called Black Book Photography Inc *(G-9460)*
Black Enterprise, New York Also called Earl G Graves Pubg Co Inc *(G-10012)*
Black Hound, Brooklyn Also called Amiram Dror Inc *(G-1609)*
Black River Brewing Co Inc 315 755-2739
500 Newell St Watertown (13601) *(G-16661)*
Black River Generations LLC 315 773-2314
4515 2nd St Fort Drum (13602) *(G-5345)*
Black River Woodworking Inc 315 376-8405
4773 State Route 410 Castorland (13620) *(G-3450)*
Blackbirds Brooklyn LLC 917 362-4080
597 Sackett St Brooklyn (11217) *(G-1699)*
Blackbook, New York Also called McCarthy LLC *(G-11220)*
Blackbook Media Corp 212 334-1800
32 Union Sq E Ste 4l New York (10003) *(G-9461)*
Blackbox Biometrics Inc 585 329-3399
125 Tech Park Dr Ste 1131 Rochester (14623) *(G-14252)*
Blackheart Records, Brooklyn Also called Lagunatic Music & Filmworks *(G-2191)*
Blackstone Advanced Tech LLC 716 665-5410
86 Blackstone Ave Jamestown (14701) *(G-7011)*
Blackstone Group, New York Also called Grand Slam Holdings LLC *(G-10389)*
Blackswirl, New York Also called Robert Ehrlich *(G-11911)*
Blades 212 477-1059
659 Broadway New York (10012) *(G-9462)*
Blading Services Unlimited LLC 315 875-5313
40 Madison Blvd Canastota (13032) *(G-3392)*
Blair Cnstr Fabrication Sp 315 253-2321
13 Brae Ridge Rd Auburn (13021) *(G-484)*
Blair Industries Inc (PA) 631 924-6600
3671 Horseblock Rd Medford (11763) *(G-8268)*
Blair-Hsm, Medford Also called HSM Machine Works Inc *(G-8281)*
Blanche P Field LLC 212 355-6616
155 E 56th St Ph New York (10022) *(G-9463)*
Blandi Products LLC 908 377-2885
875 3rd Ave Fl 7 New York (10022) *(G-9464)*
Blasch Precision Ceramics Inc (PA) 518 436-1263
580 Broadway Ste 1 Menands (12204) *(G-8401)*
Blaser Production Inc 845 294-3200
31 Hatfield Ln Goshen (10924) *(G-5747)*
Blaser Swisslube Holding Corp (HQ) 845 294-3200
31 Hatfield Ln Goshen (10924) *(G-5748)*
Blatt Searle & Company Ltd (PA) 212 730-7717
4121 28th St Long Island City (11101) *(G-7719)*
Blc Textiles Inc 844 500-7900
330 Old Country Rd # 201 Mineola (11501) *(G-8532)*
Bleecker Pastry Tartufo Inc 718 937-9830
3722 13th St Long Island City (11101) *(G-7720)*
Bleezarde Publishing Inc 518 756-2030
164 Main St Ravena (12143) *(G-14033)*
Blend Smoothie Bar 845 568-7366
25 Creamery Dr New Windsor (12553) *(G-8979)*
Bli International Inc 631 940-9000
75 N Industry Ct Deer Park (11729) *(G-4133)*
Blinds To Go, Hartsdale Also called TLC Vision (usa) Corporation *(G-6021)*

Blinds To Go (us) Inc...718 477-9523
2845 Richmond Ave Staten Island (10314) ***(G-15668)***
Blindtek Designer Systems Inc...914 347-7100
1 Hayes St Elmsford (10523) ***(G-4746)***
Bliss Foods Inc...212 732-8888
275 Greenwich St Frnt 2 New York (10007) ***(G-9465)***
Bliss Foods Inc...212 732-8888
275 Greenwich St Frnt 2 New York (10007) ***(G-9466)***
Bliss Machine Inc...585 492-5128
260 North St Arcade (14009) ***(G-389)***
Bliss-Poston The Second Wind...212 481-1055
928 Broadway Ste 403 New York (10010) ***(G-9467)***
Bloch Industries LLC...585 334-9600
140 Commerce Dr Rochester (14623) ***(G-14253)***
Blondie S Bakeshop Inc...631 424-4545
90 Washington Dr Centerport (11721) ***(G-3500)***
Blood Moon Productions Ltd...718 556-9410
75 Saint Marks Pl Staten Island (10301) ***(G-15669)***
Blooming Grove Stair Co (PA)...845 783-4245
1 Stair Way Monroe (10950) ***(G-8585)***
Blooming Grove Stair Co...845 791-4016
309 E Broadway Monticello (12701) ***(G-8642)***
Bloomsburg Carpet Inds Inc...212 688-7447
49 W 23rd St Fl 4 New York (10010) ***(G-9468)***
Bloomsbury Publishing Inc...212 419-5300
1385 Brdwy Fl 5 New York (10018) ***(G-9469)***
Bloomsbury USA, New York *Also called Bloomsbury Publishing Inc* ***(G-9469)***
Blu Sand LLC...212 564-1147
589 8th Ave Fl 9 New York (10018) ***(G-9470)***
Blue and White Publishing Inc...215 431-3339
425 Riverside Dr Apt 3c New York (10025) ***(G-9471)***
Blue Box, Brooklyn *Also called Pink Box Accessories LLC* ***(G-2435)***
Blue Boy, Staten Island *Also called Rgm Signs Inc* ***(G-15754)***
Blue Cast Denim Co Inc...212 719-1182
10 Blue Grass Ct Huntington (11743) ***(G-6689)***
Blue Chip Mold Inc...585 647-1790
95 Lagrange Ave Rochester (14613) ***(G-14254)***
Blue Horizon Media Inc (PA)...212 661-7878
11 Park Pl Rm 1508 New York (10007) ***(G-9472)***
Blue Manufacturing Co Inc...607 796-2463
3852 Watkins Rd Millport (14864) ***(G-8515)***
Blue Marble Ice Cream...718 858-5551
220 36th St Unit 33 Brooklyn (11232) ***(G-1700)***
Blue Ocean Food Trading LLC...718 689-4291
154 42nd St Brooklyn (11232) ***(G-1701)***
Blue Pig Ice Cream Factory...914 271-3850
121 Maple St Croton On Hudson (10520) ***(G-4088)***
Blue Rhino Global Sourcing Inc...516 752-0670
10 Hub Dr Ste 101 Melville (11747) ***(G-8329)***
Blue Skies...631 392-1140
859 Long Island Ave Deer Park (11729) ***(G-4134)***
Blue Sky Plastic Production...718 366-3966
305 Johnson Ave Brooklyn (11206) ***(G-1702)***
Blue Star Beverages Corp...718 381-3535
1099 Flushing Ave Brooklyn (11237) ***(G-1703)***
Blue Star Products Inc...631 952-3204
355 Marcus Blvd Ste 2 Hauppauge (11788) ***(G-6055)***
Blue Stone Press, High Falls *Also called Ulster County Press Office* ***(G-6429)***
Blue Tee Corp (PA)...212 598-0880
387 Park Ave S Fl 5 New York (10016) ***(G-9473)***
Blue Toad Hard Cider...585 424-5508
120 Mushroom Blvd Rochester (14623) ***(G-14255)***
Blue Tortilla LLC...631 451-0100
1070 Middle Country Rd # 4 Selden (11784) ***(G-15369)***
Blue Wolf Group LLC (HQ)...866 455-9653
11 E 26th St Fl 21 New York (10010) ***(G-9474)***
Bluebar Oil Co Inc...315 245-4328
8446 Mill Pond Way Blossvale (13308) ***(G-991)***
Blueberry Knitting Inc (PA)...718 599-6520
138 Ross St Brooklyn (11211) ***(G-1704)***
Blueduck Trading Ltd...212 268-3122
463 7th Ave Rm 806 New York (10018) ***(G-9475)***
Blueprint Cleanse, New York *Also called Zoe Sakoutis LLC* ***(G-12736)***
Bluesoho (PA)...646 805-2583
160 Varick St Fl 2 New York (10013) ***(G-9476)***
Blum & Fink Inc...212 695-2606
158 W 29th St Fl 12 New York (10001) ***(G-9477)***
Bm America LLC (HQ)...201 438-7733
4 W 58th St Fl 10 New York (10019) ***(G-9478)***
BMA Media Services Inc...585 385-2060
1655 Lyell Ave Rochester (14606) ***(G-14256)***
BMC, Broadalbin *Also called Broadalbin Manufacturing Corp* ***(G-1239)***
BMC LLC...716 681-7755
3155 Broadway St Buffalo (14227) ***(G-2866)***
BMC Software Inc...212 402-1500
1114 Ave Of The Americas New York (10036) ***(G-9479)***
Bmg Chrysalis, New York *Also called Bmg Rights Management (us) LLC* ***(G-9480)***
Bmg Printing and Promotion LLC...631 231-9200
170 Wilbur Pl Ste 700 Bohemia (11716) ***(G-1022)***
Bmg Rights Management (us) LLC (HQ)...212 561-3000
1745 Broadway Fl 19 New York (10019) ***(G-9480)***
Bmp America Inc (HQ)...585 798-0950
11625 Maple Ridge Rd Medina (14103) ***(G-8300)***
Bms Designs Inc...718 828-5792
1385 Seabury Ave Bronx (10461) ***(G-1284)***
Bms Manufacturing Co Inc...607 535-2426
2857 County Line Rd Watkins Glen (14891) ***(G-16718)***
BNC Innovative Woodworking...718 277-2800
555 Liberty Ave Brooklyn (11207) ***(G-1705)***
Bnei Aram Soba Inc...718 645-4460
1616 Ocean Pkwy Brooklyn (11223) ***(G-1706)***
Bnm Product Service...631 750-1586
1561 Lincoln Ave Holbrook (11741) ***(G-6460)***
Bnns Co Inc...212 302-1844
71 W 47th St Ste 600-601 New York (10036) ***(G-9481)***
BNo Intl Trdg Co Inc...716 487-1900
505 Chautauqua Ave Jamestown (14701) ***(G-7012)***
Bnz Tech, East Setauket *Also called B & Z Technologies LLC* ***(G-4496)***
Bo-Mer Plastics LLC...315 252-7216
13 Pulaski St Auburn (13021) ***(G-485)***
Boa Handcuff, Huntington *Also called Boa Security Technologies Corp* ***(G-6690)***
Boa Security Technologies Corp...516 576-0295
586 New York Ave Unit 3 Huntington (11743) ***(G-6690)***
Boardman Simons Publishing (PA)...212 620-7200
55 Broad St Fl 26 New York (10004) ***(G-9482)***
Bob Murphy Inc...607 729-3553
3127 Vestal Rd Vestal (13850) ***(G-16464)***
Bob Perani Sport Shops Inc...585 427-2930
1225 Jefferson Rd Rochester (14623) ***(G-14257)***
Bob's Signs, Syracuse *Also called Wizard Equipment Inc* ***(G-16097)***
Bobbi Brown Prof Cosmt Inc...646 613-6500
575 Broadway Fl 4 New York (10012) ***(G-9483)***
Bobby Jones Sportswear, Rochester *Also called Xmh-Hfi Inc* ***(G-14801)***
Bobley-Harmann Corporation...516 433-3800
200 Trade Zone Dr Unit 2 Ronkonkoma (11779) ***(G-14908)***
Bobrick Washroom Equipment Inc...518 877-7444
200 Commerce Dr Clifton Park (12065) ***(G-3723)***
Boces Business Office...607 763-3300
435 Glenwood Rd Binghamton (13905) ***(G-892)***
Body Builders Inc...718 492-7997
5518 3rd Ave Brooklyn (11220) ***(G-1707)***
Bodyarmor, Whitestone *Also called Ba Sports Nutrition LLC* ***(G-17230)***
Bodycote Syracuse Heat Treatin...315 451-0000
7055 Interstate Island Rd Syracuse (13209) ***(G-15891)***
Bodycote Thermal Proc Inc...585 436-7876
620 Buffalo Rd Rochester (14611) ***(G-14258)***
Boehm Surgical Instrument...585 436-6584
966 Chili Ave Ste 3 Rochester (14611) ***(G-14259)***
Boeing Company...201 259-9400
304 Park Ave S New York (10010) ***(G-9484)***
Boeing Medcl Trtmnt Mltry Arcr, Norwich *Also called Chenango Concrete Corp* ***(G-13039)***
Boka Printing Inc...607 725-3235
12 Hall St Binghamton (13903) ***(G-893)***
Bomac Inc...315 433-9181
6477 Ridings Rd Syracuse (13206) ***(G-15892)***
BOMB MAGAZINE, Brooklyn *Also called New Art Publications Inc* ***(G-2367)***
Bombardier Mass Transit Corp...518 566-0150
71 Wall St Plattsburgh (12901) ***(G-13683)***
Bombardier Transportation...607 324-0216
1 William K Jackson Ln Hornell (14843) ***(G-6586)***
Bombardier Trnsp Holdings USA...607 776-4791
7940 State Route 415 Bath (14810) ***(G-654)***
Bombay Kitchen Foods Inc...516 767-7401
76 S Bayles Ave Port Washington (11050) ***(G-13825)***
Bon Bons Chocolatier, Huntington *Also called Lady-N-Th-wndow Chocolates Inc* ***(G-6702)***
Boncraft Inc...716 662-9720
777 E Park Dr Tonawanda (14150) ***(G-16167)***
Bond No 9, New York *Also called Laurice El Badry Rahme Ltd* ***(G-10974)***
Bonded Concrete Inc (PA)...518 273-5800
303 Watervliet Shaker Rd Watervliet (12189) ***(G-16704)***
Bonded Concrete Inc...518 674-2854
Rr 43 West Sand Lake (12196) ***(G-16960)***
Bondi Digital Publishing LLC...212 405-1655
88 10th Ave Frnt 6 New York (10011) ***(G-9485)***
Bonduelle USA Inc...585 948-5252
40 Stevens St Oakfield (14125) ***(G-13083)***
Bondy Printing Corp...631 242-1510
267 W Main St Bay Shore (11706) ***(G-677)***
Bonelli Foods LLC...212 346-0942
139 Fulton St Rm 314 New York (10038) ***(G-9486)***
Bongenre.com, Brooklyn *Also called Jill Fenichell Inc* ***(G-2141)***
Bonide Products Inc...315 736-8231
6301 Sutliff Rd Oriskany (13424) ***(G-13329)***
Bonjour For Kids, New York *Also called Consolidated Childrens AP Inc* ***(G-9764)***
Bonk Sam Unforms Civilian Cap...718 585-0665
131 Rose Feiss Blvd Fl 2 Bronx (10454) ***(G-1285)***
Bonnie J, New York *Also called Sanoy Inc* ***(G-11987)***
Bonnier Publishing Usa Inc...212 321-0237
251 Park Ave S Fl 12 New York (10010) ***(G-9487)***
Bono Sawdust Co, Corona *Also called Bono Sawdust Supply Co Inc* ***(G-4014)***
Bono Sawdust Supply Co Inc...718 446-1374
3330 127th Pl Corona (11368) ***(G-4014)***

ALPHABETIC

(PA)=Parent Co (HQ)=Headquarters (DH)=Div Headquarters

Bonpoint Inc (PA)...212 246-3291
396 W Broadway Apt 3 New York (10012) ***(G-9488)***
Bonsal American Inc...631 208-8073
931 Burman Blvd Calverton (11933) ***(G-3314)***
Bonura and Sons Iron Works...718 381-4100
957 Lorraine Dr Franklin Square (11010) ***(G-5371)***
Book1one LLC...585 458-2101
655 Driving Park Ave Rochester (14613) ***(G-14260)***
Booklinks Publishing Svcs LLC...718 852-2116
55 Washington St Ste 253c Brooklyn (11201) ***(G-1708)***
Booklyn Artists Alliance...718 383-9621
37 Greenpoint Ave Ste C4 Brooklyn (11222) ***(G-1709)***
Boom Creative Development, New York *Also called Boom LLC* ***(G-9489)***
Boom LLC...646 218-0752
800 3rd Ave Fl 2 New York (10022) ***(G-9489)***
Boonville Herald Inc...315 942-4449
105 E Schuyler St Boonville (13309) ***(G-1161)***
Boonville Manufacturing Corp...315 942-4368
13485 State Route 12 Boonville (13309) ***(G-1162)***
Boonvlle Hrald Adrndack Turist, Boonville *Also called Boonville Herald Inc* ***(G-1161)***
Boosey & Hawkes Inc (HQ)...212 358-5300
229 W 28th St Fl 11 New York (10001) ***(G-9490)***
Borabora Fruit Juices Inc...845 795-1027
255 Milton Highland (12528) ***(G-6430)***
Borden & Riley Paper Co Inc...718 454-9494
18410 Jamaica Ave Ste W3 Hollis (11423) ***(G-6520)***
Borgattis Ravioli Egg Noodles...718 367-3799
632 E 187th St Bronx (10458) ***(G-1286)***
Borghese Inc (PA)...212 659-5318
3 E 54th St Fl 20 New York (10022) ***(G-9491)***
Borgwarner Inc...607 257-1800
780 Warren Rd Ithaca (14850) ***(G-6863)***
Borgwarner Ithaca LLC...607 257-6700
800 Warren Rd Ithaca (14850) ***(G-6864)***
Borgwarner Morse TEC Inc...607 266-5111
780 Warren Rd Ithaca (14850) ***(G-6865)***
Borgwarner Morse TEC LLC (HQ)...607 257-6700
800 Warren Rd Ithaca (14850) ***(G-6866)***
Borgwarner Morse TEC LLC...607 257-6700
3690 Luker Rd Cortland (13045) ***(G-4037)***
Bornomala USA Inc...347 753-2355
3766 72nd St Fl 3 Jackson Heights (11372) ***(G-6921)***
Boro Park Cutting Tool Corp...718 720-0610
106b Wakefield Ave Staten Island (10314) ***(G-15670)***
Boro Park Signs, Brooklyn *Also called Sign Group Inc* ***(G-2580)***
Bos-Hatten Inc...716 662-7030
50 Cobham Dr Orchard Park (14127) ***(G-13276)***
Boss Precision Ltd...585 352-7070
2440 S Union St Spencerport (14559) ***(G-15590)***
Boss Sauce, Rochester *Also called American Specialty Mfg Co* ***(G-14215)***
Boston Valley Pottery Inc (PA)...716 649-7490
6860 S Abbott Rd Orchard Park (14127) ***(G-13277)***
Boston Valley Terra Cotta, Orchard Park *Also called Boston Valley Pottery Inc* ***(G-13277)***
Botify Corporation...617 576-2005
119 W 24th St New York (10011) ***(G-9492)***
Botkier Ny LLC...212 343-2782
19 W 34th St Fl 7 New York (10001) ***(G-9493)***
Bottling Group LLC...315 788-6751
1035 Bradley St Watertown (13601) ***(G-16662)***
Bottling Group LLC...800 789-2626
1111 Westchester Ave White Plains (10604) ***(G-17113)***
Bottling Group LLC (HQ)...914 767-6000
1111 Westchester Ave White Plains (10604) ***(G-17114)***
Boucheron Joaillerie USA Inc...212 715-7330
460 Park Ave Fl 12 New York (10022) ***(G-9494)***
Boulay Fabrication Inc...315 677-5247
Rr 20 Box West La Fayette (13084) ***(G-7266)***
Boulevard Printing...716 837-3800
1330 Niagara Falls Blvd # 2 Tonawanda (14150) ***(G-16168)***
Boundless Spatial Inc...646 831-5531
222 Broadway Fl 19 New York (10038) ***(G-9495)***
Boundless Technologies, Phelps *Also called Z-Axis Inc* ***(G-13563)***
Bourghol Brothers Inc...845 268-9752
73 Lake Rd Congers (10920) ***(G-3878)***
Bourne Co, New York *Also called Bourne Music Publishers* ***(G-9496)***
Bourne Music Publishers...212 391-4300
5 W 37th St Fl 6 New York (10018) ***(G-9496)***
Bovie Medical Corporation (PA)...914 468-4009
4 Manhattanville Rd # 106 Purchase (10577) ***(G-13970)***
Bow Industrial Corporation...518 561-0190
178 W Service Rd Champlain (12919) ***(G-3566)***
Bowe Industries Inc (PA)...718 441-6464
8836 77th Ave Glendale (11385) ***(G-5661)***
Bowe Industries Inc...718 441-6464
8836 77th Ave Glendale (11385) ***(G-5662)***
Bowen Products Corporation...315 498-4481
5084 S Onondaga Rd Nedrow (13120) ***(G-8818)***
Boxbee Inc...646 612-7839
134 W 26th St Rm 404 New York (10001) ***(G-9497)***
Boxcar Press Incorporated...315 473-0930
509 W Fayette St Ste 135 Syracuse (13204) ***(G-15893)***
Boy Scouts of America...212 532-0985
271 Madison Ave Ste 401 New York (10016) ***(G-9498)***
Boyd Printing Company, Latham *Also called William Boyd Printing Co Inc* ***(G-7411)***
Boydell & Brewer Inc...585 275-0419
668 Mount Hope Ave Rochester (14620) ***(G-14261)***
Boylan Bottling Co Inc...800 289-7978
6 E 43rd St Fl 18 New York (10017) ***(G-9499)***
BP Beyond Printing Inc...516 328-2700
117 Fulton Ave Hempstead (11550) ***(G-6290)***
BP Digital Imaging LLC...607 753-0022
87 Main St Cortland (13045) ***(G-4038)***
BP Magazine, Buffalo *Also called Green Apple Courage Inc* ***(G-2999)***
Bpe Studio Inc...212 868-9896
270 W 38th St Rm 702 New York (10018) ***(G-9500)***
Bqp, Glens Falls *Also called Brennans Quick Print Inc* ***(G-5689)***
Bracci Ironworks Inc...718 629-2374
1440 Utica Ave Brooklyn (11203) ***(G-1710)***
Brach Knitting Mills Inc...845 651-4450
12 Roosevelt Ave Florida (10921) ***(G-5217)***
Brach Machine Inc...585 343-9134
4814 Ellicott Street Rd Batavia (14020) ***(G-627)***
Bradford Publications Inc...716 373-2500
639 W Norton Dr Olean (14760) ***(G-13157)***
Bradley Marketing Group Inc...212 967-6100
1431 Broadway Fl 12 New York (10018) ***(G-9501)***
Braga Woodworks...845 342-4636
19 Montgomery St Middletown (10940) ***(G-8462)***
Bragley Mfg Co Inc...718 622-7469
924 Bergen St Brooklyn (11238) ***(G-1711)***
Bragley Shipg Carrying Cases, Brooklyn *Also called Bragley Mfg Co Inc* ***(G-1711)***
Braided Oak Spirits LLC...845 381-1525
12 Roberts St Middletown (10940) ***(G-8463)***
Brainpop Group, New York *Also called Brainpop LLC* ***(G-9502)***
Brainpop LLC...212 574-6017
71 W 23rd St Fl 17 New York (10010) ***(G-9502)***
Brainwave Toys-New York, New York *Also called Vogel Applied Technologies* ***(G-12589)***
Brainworks Software Dev Corp (PA)...631 563-5000
100 S Main St Ste 102 Sayville (11782) ***(G-15233)***
Brakewell Stl Fabricators Inc...845 469-9131
55 Leone Ln Chester (10918) ***(G-3628)***
Bral Nader Fine Jewelry Inc...800 493-1222
576 5th Ave New York (10036) ***(G-9503)***
Bramson House Inc...516 764-5006
151 Albany Ave Freeport (11520) ***(G-5400)***
Brand Box USA LLC...607 584-7682
1 Chamberlain St Binghamton (13904) ***(G-894)***
Brands Within Reach LLC...847 720-9090
141 Halstead Ave Ste 201 Mamaroneck (10543) ***(G-8057)***
Brandt Equipment LLC...718 994-0800
4461 Bronx Blvd Bronx (10470) ***(G-1287)***
Brandt Industries, Bronx *Also called Brandt Equipment LLC* ***(G-1287)***
Brandys Mold and Tool Ctr Ltd (PA)...585 334-8333
10 Riverton Way West Henrietta (14586) ***(G-16904)***
Brannkey Inc (PA)...212 371-1515
1385 Broadway Fl 14 New York (10018) ***(G-9504)***
Brannock Device Co Inc...315 475-9862
116 Luther Ave Liverpool (13088) ***(G-7535)***
Branson Ultrasonics Corp...585 624-8000
475 Quaker Meeting Hse Rd Honeoye Falls (14472) ***(G-6553)***
Brant Art Publications Inc...212 941-2800
110 Greene St Ph 2 New York (10012) ***(G-9505)***
Brant Publications Inc (PA)...212 941-2800
110 Greene St Ph 2 New York (10012) ***(G-9506)***
Brasilans Press Pblcations Inc...212 764-6161
60 W 46th St Rm 302 New York (10036) ***(G-9507)***
Brauen Constrution...585 492-0042
1087 Chaffee Rd Arcade (14009) ***(G-390)***
Braun Bros Brushes Inc...631 667-2179
35 4th St Valley Stream (11581) ***(G-16427)***
Braun Brush Company, Albertson *Also called Braun Industries Inc* ***(G-155)***
Braun Horticulture Inc...716 282-6101
3302 Highland Ave Niagara Falls (14305) ***(G-12821)***
Braun Industries Inc...516 741-6000
43 Albertson Ave Albertson (11507) ***(G-155)***
Brave Chefs Incorporated...347 956-5905
4130 249th St Ste 2 Little Neck (11363) ***(G-7530)***
Brayley Tool & Machine Inc...585 342-7190
1685 Lyell Ave Rochester (14606) ***(G-14262)***
Braze...504 327-7269
263 W 38th St Fl 16 New York (10018) ***(G-9508)***
Braze Alloy Inc...718 815-5757
3075 Richmond Ter Staten Island (10303) ***(G-15671)***
Brazen Street LLC...516 305-7951
734 Pennsylvania Ave Brooklyn (11207) ***(G-1712)***
Bread Factory LLC...914 637-8150
30 Grove Ave New Rochelle (10801) ***(G-8934)***
Bread Market Cafe...212 768-9292
16 W 45th St Fl 5 New York (10036) ***(G-9509)***
Breed Enterprises Inc...585 388-0126
34 Water St Fairport (14450) ***(G-4854)***
Bren-Trnics Batteries Intl Inc...631 499-5155
10 Brayton Ct Commack (11725) ***(G-3851)***

Bren-Trnics Batteries Intl LLC 631 499-5155
10 Brayton Ct Commack (11725) ***(G-3852)***
Bren-Tronics Inc 631 499-5155
10 Brayton Ct Commack (11725) ***(G-3853)***
Brennans Quick Print Inc 518 793-4999
6 Collins Dr Glens Falls (12804) ***(G-5689)***
Brenseke George Wldg Ir Works 631 271-4870
915 Long Island Ave Ste A Deer Park (11729) ***(G-4135)***
Brenseke's, Deer Park *Also called Brenseke George Wldg Ir Works* ***(G-4135)***
Breton Industries Inc (PA) 518 842-3030
1 Sam Stratton Rd Amsterdam (12010) ***(G-337)***
Brewer & Newell Printing, Rochester *Also called Forward Enterprises Inc* ***(G-14401)***
Brewer-Cantelmo Co Inc 212 244-4600
55 W 39th St Rm 205 New York (10018) ***(G-9510)***
Brewerton Special Tee's, Brewerton *Also called Irene Cerone* ***(G-1201)***
Brewery Ommegang Ltd 607 286-4144
656 County Highway 33 Cooperstown (13326) ***(G-3909)***
Brewster Coachworks, Lagrangeville *Also called Graphics Slution Providers Inc* ***(G-7278)***
Brewster Transit Mix Corp (PA) 845 279-3738
31 Fields Ln Brewster (10509) ***(G-1210)***
Brewster Transit Mix Corp 845 279-3738
Fields Ln Brewster (10509) ***(G-1211)***
Brick & Ballerstein Inc 718 497-1400
1085 Irving Ave Ridgewood (11385) ***(G-14116)***
Brickit 631 727-8977
17 Central Ave Hauppauge (11788) ***(G-6056)***
Bridal Guide, New York *Also called Rfp LLC* ***(G-11883)***
Brides Inc 718 435-6092
4817 New Utrecht Ave Brooklyn (11219) ***(G-1713)***
Bridge City Vape Co LLC 845 625-7962
106 Van Wagner Rd Apt 6f Poughkeepsie (12603) ***(G-13910)***
Bridge Components Inc 716 731-1184
2122 Cory Dr Sanborn (14132) ***(G-15140)***
Bridge Enterprises Inc 718 625-6622
544 Park Ave Brooklyn (11205) ***(G-1714)***
Bridge Fulfillment Inc 718 625-6622
493 Flushing Ave Ste 19 Brooklyn (11205) ***(G-1715)***
Bridge Metal Industries LLC 914 663-9200
717 S 3rd Ave Mount Vernon (10550) ***(G-8712)***
Bridge Printing Inc 212 243-5390
4710 32nd Pl Fl 2 Long Island City (11101) ***(G-7721)***
Bridge Records Inc 914 654-9270
200 Clinton Ave New Rochelle (10801) ***(G-8935)***
Bridgehampton Steel & Wldg Inc 631 537-2486
27 Foster Ave Bridgehampton (11932) ***(G-1230)***
Bridgeport Metalcraft Inc 315 623-9597
567 County Route 23 Constantia (13044) ***(G-3906)***
Bridgestone APM Company 419 423-9552
6350 Inducon Dr E Sanborn (14132) ***(G-15141)***
Brigadoon Software Inc (PA) 845 624-0909
119 Rockland Ctr 250 Nanuet (10954) ***(G-8798)***
Brigantine Inc (HQ) 212 354-8550
225 W 37th St New York (10018) ***(G-9511)***
Brigden Memorials, Albion *Also called Woodside Granite Industries* ***(G-174)***
Briggs & Stratton Corporation 315 495-0100
4245 Highbridge Rd Sherrill (13461) ***(G-15426)***
Briggs & Stratton Corporation 315 495-0100
5375 N Main St Munnsville (13409) ***(G-8795)***
Bright Chair Co, Middletown *Also called Princeton Upholstery Co Inc* ***(G-8493)***
Bright Kids Nyc Inc 917 539-4575
225 Broadway Ste 1504 New York (10007) ***(G-9512)***
Bright Line Eting Slutions LLC 585 245-2956
18 Brickston Dr Pittsford (14534) ***(G-13585)***
Bright Way Supply Inc 718 833-2882
6302 Fort Hamilton Pkwy Brooklyn (11219) ***(G-1716)***
Brightline Ventures I LLC 212 626-6829
1120 Avenue Of The Americ New York (10036) ***(G-9513)***
Brighton Bakery 315 475-2948
335 E Brighton Ave Syracuse (13210) ***(G-15894)***
Brighton Design, Tonawanda *Also called Brighton Tool & Die Designers* ***(G-16169)***
Brighton Tool & Die Designers (PA) 716 876-0879
463 Brighton Rd Tonawanda (14150) ***(G-16169)***
Brijon, Ronkonkoma *Also called Lanco Corporation* ***(G-14957)***
Brilliant Jewelers/Mjj Inc 212 353-2326
902 Broadway Fl 18 New York (10010) ***(G-9514)***
Brinkman Intl Group Inc (PA) 585 429-5000
167 Ames St Rochester (14611) ***(G-14263)***
Brinkman Precision Inc 585 429-5001
100 Park Centre Dr West Henrietta (14586) ***(G-16905)***
Brinkman Products Inc (HQ) 585 235-4545
167 Ames St Rochester (14611) ***(G-14264)***
Bristol Boarding Inc 585 271-7860
1336 Culver Rd Rochester (14609) ***(G-14265)***
Bristol Core Inc 585 919-0302
5310 North St Canandaigua (14424) ***(G-3365)***
Bristol Gift Co Inc 845 496-2821
8 North St Washingtonville (10992) ***(G-16620)***
Bristol Instruments Inc 585 924-2620
50 Victor Heights Pkwy Victor (14564) ***(G-16488)***
Bristol Metals Inc 585 657-7665
7817 State Route 5 And 20 Bloomfield (14469) ***(G-976)***
Bristol Seamless Ring Corp 212 874-2645
209 W 86th St Apt 817 New York (10024) ***(G-9515)***
Bristol-Myers Squibb Company (PA) 212 546-4000
345 Park Ave Bsmt Lc3 New York (10154) ***(G-9516)***
Bristol-Myers Squibb Company 315 432-2000
6000 Thompson Rd East Syracuse (13057) ***(G-4529)***
Bristol-Myers Squibb Company 516 832-2191
1000 Stewart Ave Garden City (11530) ***(G-5511)***
Bristol/White Plains 914 681-1800
305 North St White Plains (10605) ***(G-17115)***
British American Publishing 518 786-6000
19 British American Blvd Latham (12110) ***(G-7382)***
British Science Corporation (PA) 212 980-8700
100 Wheeler Ave Staten Island (10314) ***(G-15672)***
Brittish American Envmtl, Clifton Park *Also called Microb Phase Services* ***(G-3728)***
Broadalbin Manufacturing Corp 518 883-5313
8 Pine St Broadalbin (12025) ***(G-1239)***
Broadcast Manager Inc 212 509-1200
65 Broadway Ste 602 New York (10006) ***(G-9517)***
Broadnet Technologies Inc 315 443-3694
2-212 Center For Science Syracuse (13244) ***(G-15895)***
Broadway Knitting Mills Inc 716 692-4421
1333 Strad Ave Ste 216 North Tonawanda (14120) ***(G-12979)***
Broadway National, Ronkonkoma *Also called Broadway Neon Sign Corp* ***(G-14910)***
Broadway National Group LLC 800 797-4467
1900 Ocean Ave Ronkonkoma (11779) ***(G-14909)***
Broadway National Sign & Ltg, Ronkonkoma *Also called Broadway National Group LLC* ***(G-14909)***
Broadway Neon Sign Corp 908 241-4177
1900 Ocean Ave Ronkonkoma (11779) ***(G-14910)***
Broadway Technology LLC (PA) 646 912-6450
28 Liberty St 8 New York (10005) ***(G-9518)***
Brock Awnings Ltd 631 765-5200
211 E Montauk Hwy Ste 1 Hampton Bays (11946) ***(G-5982)***
Brockyn Corporation 631 244-2770
606 Johnson Ave Ste 31 Bohemia (11716) ***(G-1023)***
Broda Machine Co Inc 716 297-3221
8745 Packard Rd Niagara Falls (14304) ***(G-12822)***
Broder Mfg Inc 718 366-1667
566 Johnson Ave Brooklyn (11237) ***(G-1717)***
Brodock Press Inc (PA) 315 735-9577
502 Court St Ste G Utica (13502) ***(G-16333)***
Broetje Automation-Usa Inc 716 204-8640
165 Lawrence Bell Dr # 116 Williamsville (14221) ***(G-17264)***
Broken Threads Inc 212 730-4351
147 W 35th St Ste 501 New York (10001) ***(G-9519)***
Bronson Labrotaries, Hauppauge *Also called Bronson Nutritionals LLC* ***(G-6057)***
Bronson Nutritionals LLC (PA) 631 750-0000
70 Commerce Dr Hauppauge (11788) ***(G-6057)***
Bronx Design Group, The, Bronx *Also called G&J Graphics Inc* ***(G-1342)***
Bronx New Way Corp 347 431-1385
113 E Kingsbridge Rd Bronx (10468) ***(G-1288)***
Bronx Times Reporter, Brooklyn *Also called Community News Group LLC* ***(G-1795)***
Bronx Wstchester Tempering Inc 914 663-9400
160 S Macquesten Pkwy Mount Vernon (10550) ***(G-8713)***
Bronxville Review, New Rochelle *Also called Gannett Co Inc* ***(G-8948)***
Brook North Farms Inc 315 834-9390
89 York St Auburn (13021) ***(G-486)***
Brooke Leigh Ltd (PA) 212 736-9098
520 8th Ave Fl 20 New York (10018) ***(G-9520)***
Brooke Maya Inc 212 279-2340
124 W 36th St Fl 7 New York (10018) ***(G-9521)***
Brookhaven Instruments Corp 631 758-3200
750 Blue Point Rd Holtsville (11742) ***(G-6526)***
Brooklyn Baby Cakes Inc 917 334-2518
411 Hancock St Brooklyn (11216) ***(G-1718)***
Brooklyn Bangers LLC 718 875-3535
111 Atlantic Ave Ste 1r Brooklyn (11201) ***(G-1719)***
Brooklyn Brew Shop LLC 718 874-0119
20 Jay St Ste 410 Brooklyn (11201) ***(G-1720)***
Brooklyn Btlg Milton NY Inc (PA) 845 795-2171
643 South Rd Milton (12547) ***(G-8516)***
Brooklyn Casing Co Inc 718 522-0866
412 3rd St Brooklyn (11215) ***(G-1721)***
Brooklyn Circus (PA) 718 858-0919
150 Nevins St Brooklyn (11217) ***(G-1722)***
Brooklyn Cstm Met Fbrction Inc 718 499-1573
48 Prospect Park Sw Brooklyn (11215) ***(G-1723)***
Brooklyn Denim Co 718 782-2600
85 N 3rd St Brooklyn (11249) ***(G-1724)***
Brooklyn Heights Press, Brooklyn *Also called Brooklyn Journal Publications* ***(G-1728)***
Brooklyn Industries LLC 718 788-5250
328 7th Ave Brooklyn (11215) ***(G-1725)***
Brooklyn Industries LLC 718 486-6464
162 Bedford Ave Ste A Brooklyn (11249) ***(G-1726)***
Brooklyn Industries LLC 718 789-2764
206 5th Ave Ste 1 Brooklyn (11217) ***(G-1727)***
Brooklyn Journal Publications 718 422-7400
16 Court St 30 Brooklyn (11241) ***(G-1728)***
Brooklyn Rail Inc 718 349-8427
99 Commercial St Apt 15 Brooklyn (11222) ***(G-1729)***

ALPHABETIC

Brooklyn Remembers Inc 718 491-1705
9201 4th Ave Brooklyn (11209) ***(G-1730)***
Brooklyn Roasting Works LLC 718 855-1000
45 Washington St Brooklyn (11201) ***(G-1731)***
Brooklyn Signs LLC 718 252-7575
6404 14th Ave Brooklyn (11219) ***(G-1732)***
Brooklyn Store Front Co Inc 718 384-4372
62 Throop Ave Brooklyn (11206) ***(G-1733)***
Brooklyn Sweet Spot Inc 718 522-2577
366 Myrtle Ave Brooklyn (11205) ***(G-1734)***
Brooklyn Vape 917 336-7363
53 5th Ave Brooklyn (11217) ***(G-1735)***
Brooklyn Winery LLC (PA) 347 763-1506
213 N 8th St Brooklyn (11211) ***(G-1736)***
Brooks Bottling Co LLC 607 432-1782
5560 State Highway 7 Oneonta (13820) ***(G-13197)***
Brooks Litho Digital Group Inc 631 789-4500
35 W Jefryn Blvd Ste A Deer Park (11729) ***(G-4136)***
Brooks Woodworking Inc 914 666-2029
15 Kensico Dr Mount Kisco (10549) ***(G-8664)***
Brookside Lumber Inc 315 497-0937
4191 Duryea St Moravia (13118) ***(G-8656)***
Brookvale Records Inc 631 587-7722
31 Brookvale Ave West Babylon (11704) ***(G-16801)***
Broom Tioga Boces, Binghamton *Also called Boces Business Office* ***(G-892)***
Broome County 607 785-9567
2001 E Main St Endicott (13760) ***(G-4805)***
Bross Quality Paving 845 532-7116
4 Kossar Pl Ellenville (12428) ***(G-4646)***
Brotherhood Americas 845 496-3661
100 Brotherhood Plaza Dr Washingtonville (10992) ***(G-16621)***
Brothers Roofing Supplies Co 718 779-0280
10514 Astoria Blvd East Elmhurst (11369) ***(G-4411)***
Brothers-In-Lawn Property 716 279-6191
176 Vulcan Tonawanda (14150) ***(G-16170)***
Brown Printers of Troy Inc 518 235-4080
363 5th Ave Troy (12182) ***(G-16250)***
Brown Printing Co, Troy *Also called Brown Printers of Troy Inc* ***(G-16250)***
Brown Printing Company 212 782-7800
1500 Broadway Ste 505 New York (10036) ***(G-9522)***
Brown Publishing Network Inc 212 682-3330
122 E 42nd St Rm 2810 New York (10168) ***(G-9523)***
Brownstone Capitl Partners LLC 212 889-0069
251 5th Ave Fl 3 New York (10016) ***(G-9524)***
Brownstone Publishers Inc 212 473-8200
149 5th Ave Fl 10 New York (10010) ***(G-9525)***
Brucci Ltd 914 965-0707
861 Nepperhan Ave Yonkers (10703) ***(G-17438)***
Bruce Pierce 716 731-9310
2386 Lockport Rd Sanborn (14132) ***(G-15142)***
Brueton Industries Inc (PA) 516 379-3400
146 Hanse Ave Ste 1 Freeport (11520) ***(G-5401)***
Brunner International Inc 585 798-6000
3959 Bates Rd Medina (14103) ***(G-8301)***
Bruno & Canio Ltd 845 624-3060
130 Blauvelt Rd Nanuet (10954) ***(G-8799)***
Bruno Associates, Altamont *Also called Rsb Associates Inc* ***(G-216)***
Bruno Associates, Fort Edward *Also called Rfb Associates Inc* ***(G-5354)***
Bruno Magli, New York *Also called Bm America LLC* ***(G-9478)***
Brunschwig & Fils LLC (HQ) 800 538-1880
245 Central Ave Bethpage (11714) ***(G-864)***
Brushtech (disc) Inc 518 563-8420
4 Matt Ave Plattsburgh (12901) ***(G-13684)***
Bruynswick Sales Inc 845 789-2049
14 Bruynswick Rd New Paltz (12561) ***(G-8918)***
Bryant Machine & Development 716 894-8282
63 Stanley St Buffalo (14206) ***(G-2867)***
Bryant Machine Co Inc 716 894-8282
63 Stanley St Buffalo (14206) ***(G-2868)***
Bryant Manufacturing Wny Inc 716 894-8282
63 Stanley St Buffalo (14206) ***(G-2869)***
Bryit Group LLC 631 563-6603
1724 Church St Holbrook (11741) ***(G-6461)***
Brzozka Industries Inc 631 588-8164
790 Broadway Ave Holbrook (11741) ***(G-6462)***
BSC Associates LLC 607 321-2980
151 Court St Binghamton (13901) ***(G-895)***
BSD Aluminum Foil LLC 347 689-3875
260 Hewest St Brooklyn (11211) ***(G-1737)***
BSD Top Direct Inc 646 468-0156
68 Route 109 West Babylon (11704) ***(G-16802)***
Bso Energy Corp 212 520-1827
125 Park Ave Ste 2507 New York (10017) ***(G-9526)***
Bst United Corp 631 777-2110
59 Central Ave Farmingdale (11735) ***(G-4962)***
Bsu Inc 607 272-8100
445 E State St Ithaca (14850) ***(G-6867)***
Bsv Enterprises, Spencerport *Also called Bsv Metal Finishers Inc* ***(G-15591)***
Bsv Metal Finishers Inc 585 349-7072
11 Aristocrat Cir Spencerport (14559) ***(G-15591)***
Btween US, New York *Also called B Tween LLC* ***(G-9347)***

Buckeye Corrugated Inc 585 924-1600
797 Old Dutch Rd Victor (14564) ***(G-16489)***
Buckle Down, Farmingdale *Also called Custom Sitecom LLC* ***(G-4981)***
Buckley Qc Fasteners Inc 716 662-1490
3874 California Rd Orchard Park (14127) ***(G-13278)***
Bucksense Inc 877 710-2825
140 West St Fl 2 New York (10007) ***(G-9527)***
Bud Barger Assoc Inc 631 696-6703
3 Mount Mckinley Ave Farmingville (11738) ***(G-5167)***
Budd Woodwork Inc 718 389-1110
54 Franklin St Brooklyn (11222) ***(G-1738)***
Buell Fuel LLC 315 841-3000
2676 State Route 12b Deansboro (13328) ***(G-4109)***
Buffalo Sports Inc 716 826-7700
3840 Mckinley Pkwy Blasdell (14219) ***(G-955)***
Buffalo, New York *Also called Gbg Denim Usa LLC* ***(G-10298)***
Buffalo Abrasives Inc (PA) 716 693-3856
960 Erie Ave North Tonawanda (14120) ***(G-12980)***
Buffalo Armory LLC 716 935-6346
1050 Military Rd Buffalo (14217) ***(G-2870)***
Buffalo Bioblower Tech LLC 716 625-8618
6100 Donner Rd Lockport (14094) ***(G-7601)***
Buffalo Blends Inc (PA) 716 825-4422
1400 William St Buffalo (14206) ***(G-2871)***
Buffalo Circuits Inc 716 662-2113
105 Mid County Dr Orchard Park (14127) ***(G-13279)***
Buffalo Compressed Air Inc 716 783-8673
2727 Broadway St Ste 3a Cheektowaga (14227) ***(G-3591)***
Buffalo Crushed Stone Inc (HQ) 716 826-7310
500 Como Park Blvd Buffalo (14227) ***(G-2872)***
Buffalo Crushed Stone Inc 716 566-9636
Rr 16 Franklinville (14737) ***(G-5378)***
Buffalo Crushed Stone Inc 607 587-8102
638 State Route 244 Alfred Station (14803) ***(G-199)***
Buffalo Dental Mfg Co Inc 516 496-7200
159 Lafayette Dr Syosset (11791) ***(G-15836)***
Buffalo Envelope Company, Depew *Also called Buffalo Envelope Inc* ***(G-4274)***
Buffalo Envelope Inc 716 686-0100
2914 Walden Ave Ste 300 Depew (14043) ***(G-4274)***
Buffalo Filter LLC 716 835-7000
5900 Genesee St Lancaster (14086) ***(G-7331)***
Buffalo Finishing Company, Ithaca *Also called F M Abdulky Inc* ***(G-6876)***
Buffalo Finishing Works Inc 716 893-5266
1255 Niagara St Buffalo (14213) ***(G-2873)***
Buffalo Games Inc 716 827-8393
220 James E Casey Dr Buffalo (14206) ***(G-2874)***
Buffalo Games & Puzzles, Buffalo *Also called Buffalo Games Inc* ***(G-2874)***
Buffalo Gear Inc 716 731-2100
3635 Lockport Rd Sanborn (14132) ***(G-15143)***
Buffalo Hardwood Floor Center, Buffalo *Also called Mm of East Aurora LLC* ***(G-3089)***
Buffalo Hearg & Speech 716 558-1105
1026 Union Rd West Seneca (14224) ***(G-16969)***
Buffalo Law Journal 716 541-1600
465 Main St Ste 100 Buffalo (14203) ***(G-2875)***
Buffalo Lining & Fabricating 716 883-6500
73 Gillette Ave Buffalo (14214) ***(G-2876)***
Buffalo Machine Tls of Niagara 716 201-1310
4935 Lockport Rd Lockport (14094) ***(G-7602)***
Buffalo Metal Casting Co Inc 716 874-6211
1875 Elmwood Ave Buffalo (14207) ***(G-2877)***
Buffalo Metal Finishing Co (PA) 716 883-2751
135 Dart St Buffalo (14213) ***(G-2878)***
Buffalo News Inc 716 849-4401
1 News Plz Buffalo (14203) ***(G-2879)***
Buffalo Newspress Inc 716 852-1600
200 Broadway St Buffalo (14204) ***(G-2880)***
Buffalo Polymer Processors Inc 716 537-3153
42 Edgewood Dr Holland (14080) ***(G-6507)***
Buffalo Power Elec Ctr De 716 651-1600
166 Taylor Dr Ste 1 Depew (14043) ***(G-4275)***
Buffalo Provisions Co Inc 718 292-4300
4009 76th St Elmhurst (11373) ***(G-4671)***
Buffalo Pumps Inc (HQ) 716 693-1850
874 Oliver St North Tonawanda (14120) ***(G-12981)***
Buffalo Rocket, Buffalo *Also called Rocket Communications Inc* ***(G-3190)***
Buffalo Snowmelter, North Tonawanda *Also called Roemac Industrial Sales Inc* ***(G-13009)***
Buffalo Spree Publishing Inc 585 413-0040
100 Allens Creek Rd Ste 8 Rochester (14618) ***(G-14266)***
Buffalo Spree Publishing Inc (PA) 716 783-9119
1738 Elmwood Ave Ste 103 Buffalo (14207) ***(G-2881)***
Buffalo Standard Printing Corp 716 835-9454
3620 Harlem Rd Ste 5 Buffalo (14215) ***(G-2882)***
Buffalo Tungsten Inc 716 759-6353
2 Main St Depew (14043) ***(G-4276)***
Buflovak LLC (PA) 716 895-2100
750 E Ferry St Buffalo (14211) ***(G-2883)***
Building Management Assoc Inc 718 542-4779
998 E 167th St Ofc Bronx (10459) ***(G-1289)***
Bulkley Dunton (HQ) 212 863-1800
1 Penn Plz Ste 2814 New York (10119) ***(G-9528)***
Bull Street LLC 212 495-9855
19 W 69th St Apt 201 New York (10023) ***(G-9529)***

Bullet Industries Inc ...585 352-0836
7 Turner Dr Spencerport (14559) ***(G-15592)***
Bulletin Boards & Dirctry Pdts ...914 248-8008
2986 Navajo Rd Ste 1 Yorktown Heights (10598) ***(G-17523)***
Bullett Media LLC ...212 242-2123
419 Lafayette St Fl 6 New York (10003) ***(G-9530)***
Bullex Inc (HQ) ...518 689-2023
20 Corporate Cir Ste 3 Albany (12203) ***(G-55)***
Bullex Inc ...518 689-2023
20 Corporate Cir Ste 3 Albany (12203) ***(G-56)***
Bullex Digital Safety, Albany *Also called Bullex Inc* ***(G-55)***
Bullex Digital Safety, Albany *Also called Bullex Inc* ***(G-56)***
Bullitt Group, Bohemia *Also called Bullitt Mobile LLC* ***(G-1024)***
Bullitt Mobile LLC ...631 424-1749
80 Orville Dr Ste 100 Bohemia (11716) ***(G-1024)***
Bullock Boys LLC ...518 783-6161
400 Old Loudon Rd Latham (12110) ***(G-7383)***
Bulow & Associates Inc ...716 838-0298
317 Wheeler St Tonawanda (14150) ***(G-16171)***
Buna Besta Tortillas ...347 987-3995
219 Johnson Ave Brooklyn (11206) ***(G-1739)***
Buncee LLC ...631 591-1390
4603 Middle Country Rd Calverton (11933) ***(G-3315)***
Bunge Limited Finance Corp ...914 684-2800
50 Main St White Plains (10606) ***(G-17116)***
Bunger Sayville, Sayville *Also called Bungers Surf Shop* ***(G-15234)***
Bungers Surf Shop ...631 244-3646
247 W Main St Sayville (11782) ***(G-15234)***
Buperiod PBC ...917 406-9804
5414 6th Ave 2 Brooklyn (11220) ***(G-1740)***
Burdick Publications Inc ...315 685-9500
2352 E Lake Rd Skaneateles (13152) ***(G-15477)***
Bureau of National Affairs Inc ...212 687-4530
25 W 43rd St Ste 1007 New York (10036) ***(G-9531)***
Burgess Products Division, New York Mills *Also called Fountainhead Group Inc* ***(G-12742)***
Burgess-Manning Inc (HQ) ...716 662-6540
50 Cobham Dr Orchard Park (14127) ***(G-13280)***
Burke & Bannayan ...585 723-1010
2465 W Ridge Rd Ste 2 Rochester (14626) ***(G-14267)***
Burke Frging Heat Treating Inc ...585 235-6060
30 Sherer St Rochester (14611) ***(G-14268)***
Burlen Corp ...212 684-0052
6 E 32nd St Fl 10 New York (10016) ***(G-9532)***
Burnett Process Inc (HQ) ...585 254-8080
545 Colfax St Rochester (14606) ***(G-14269)***
Burnett Process Inc ...585 277-1623
545 Colfax St Rochester (14606) ***(G-14270)***
Burnham Polymeric Inc ...518 792-3040
1408 Route 9 Fort Edward (12828) ***(G-5348)***
Burnhams, The, Fort Edward *Also called Burnham Polymeric Inc* ***(G-5348)***
Burns Archive Photographic Dis ...212 889-1938
140 E 38th St Frnt 1 New York (10016) ***(G-9533)***
Burnt Hills Fabricators Inc ...518 885-1115
318 Charlton Rd B Ballston Spa (12020) ***(G-591)***
Burnt Mill Smithing ...585 293-2380
127 Burnt Mill Rd Churchville (14428) ***(G-3664)***
Burr & Son Inc ...315 446-1550
119 Seeley Rd Syracuse (13224) ***(G-15896)***
Burrows Paper Corporation ...315 823-2300
730 E Mill St Little Falls (13365) ***(G-7520)***
Burrows Paper Corporation ...315 823-2300
489 W Main St Little Falls (13365) ***(G-7521)***
Burrows Paper Mill, Little Falls *Also called Burrows Paper Corporation* ***(G-7520)***
Burt Millwork Corporation ...718 257-4601
85 Fairview Dr Albertson (11507) ***(G-156)***
Burt Rigid Box Inc ...607 433-2510
58 Browne St Oneonta (13820) ***(G-13198)***
Burt Rigid Box Inc (PA) ...607 433-2510
58 Browne St Oneonta (13820) ***(G-13199)***
Burton Corporation ...802 862-4500
21 Lawrence Paquette Dr Champlain (12919) ***(G-3567)***
Burton Industries Inc ...631 643-6660
243 Wyandanch Ave Ste A West Babylon (11704) ***(G-16803)***
Burton Snowboards, Champlain *Also called Burton Corporation* ***(G-3567)***
Busch Products Inc ...315 474-8422
110 Baker St Syracuse (13206) ***(G-15897)***
Bush Industries Inc (PA) ...716 665-2000
1 Mason Dr Jamestown (14701) ***(G-7013)***
Bushwick Kitchen LLC ...917 297-1045
630 Flushing Ave Fl 5 Brooklyn (11206) ***(G-1741)***
Business Advisory Services ...718 337-3740
1104 Bay 25th St Far Rockaway (11691) ***(G-4926)***
Business Card Express Inc ...631 669-3400
300 Farmingdale Rd West Babylon (11704) ***(G-16804)***
Business Directory Inc ...718 486-8099
137 Division Ave Ste A Brooklyn (11211) ***(G-1742)***
Business First of New York (HQ) ...716 854-5822
465 Main St Ste 100 Buffalo (14203) ***(G-2884)***
Business First of New York ...518 640-6800
40 British American Blvd Latham (12110) ***(G-7384)***
Business Integrity Inc (HQ) ...718 238-2008
79 Madison Ave Fl 2 New York (10016) ***(G-9534)***
Business Journal, Syracuse *Also called CNY Business Review Inc* ***(G-15917)***
Business Journals ...212 790-5100
1166 Ave Of The America New York (10036) ***(G-9535)***
Business Management Systems ...914 245-8558
2404 Loring Pl Yorktown Heights (10598) ***(G-17524)***
Business Review, Latham *Also called Business First of New York* ***(G-7384)***
Busse Hospital Disposables, Hauppauge *Also called Robert Busse & Co Inc* ***(G-6204)***
Bust Inc ...212 675-1707
253 36th St Unit 3 Brooklyn (11232) ***(G-1743)***
Bust Magazine, Brooklyn *Also called Bust Inc* ***(G-1743)***
Bustle Digital Group, New York *Also called Bdg Media Inc* ***(G-9386)***
Butter Cooky Bakery ...516 354-3831
217 Jericho Tpke Floral Park (11001) ***(G-5204)***
Butterck McCall Vogue Pattern, New York *Also called McCall Pattern Company* ***(G-11219)***
Butterfly Beauty LLC ...646 604-4289
150 E 52nd St Fl 14a New York (10022) ***(G-9536)***
Butterwood Desserts Inc ...716 652-0131
1863 Davis Rd West Falls (14170) ***(G-16876)***
Buttons & Trimcom Inc ...212 868-1971
519 8th Ave Rm 26 New York (10018) ***(G-9537)***
Buxton Machine and Tool Co Inc ...716 876-2312
2181 Elmwood Ave Buffalo (14216) ***(G-2885)***
Buxton Medical Equipment Corp ...631 957-4500
1178 Route 109 Lindenhurst (11757) ***(G-7479)***
BW Elliott Mfg Co LLC ...607 772-0404
11 Beckwith Ave Binghamton (13901) ***(G-896)***
Bwog, New York *Also called Blue and White Publishing Inc* ***(G-9471)***
Bws Specialty Fabrication, Orchard Park *Also called Quality Industrial Services* ***(G-13319)***
By Robert James ...212 253-2121
74 Orchard St New York (10002) ***(G-9538)***
Bycmac Corp ...845 255-0884
144 Main St Gardiner (12525) ***(G-5561)***
Byelocorp Scientific Inc (PA) ...212 785-2580
76 Perry St New York (10014) ***(G-9539)***
Byer California ...212 944-8989
1407 Broadway Rm 807 New York (10018) ***(G-9540)***
Byfusion Inc ...347 563-5286
350 Manhattan Ave Apt 104 Brooklyn (11211) ***(G-1744)***
Byk USA Inc ...845 469-5800
48 Leone Ln Chester (10918) ***(G-3629)***
Bylada Foods LLC ...845 623-1300
250 W Nyack Rd Ste 110 West Nyack (10994) ***(G-16944)***
Byliner Inc ...415 680-3608
27 W 24th St Ste 202 New York (10010) ***(G-9541)***
Byram Concrete & Supply LLC ...914 682-4477
145 Virginia Rd White Plains (10603) ***(G-17117)***
Byrne Dairy Inc (PA) ...315 475-2121
2394 Us Route 11 La Fayette (13084) ***(G-7267)***
Byrne Dairy Inc ...315 475-2111
275 Cortland Ave Syracuse (13202) ***(G-15898)***
Byrne Distribution Center, Syracuse *Also called Byrne Dairy Inc* ***(G-15898)***
Bys Publishing LLC ...315 655-9431
118 Albany St Cazenovia (13035) ***(G-3469)***
Bystronic Inc ...631 231-3677
185 Commerce Dr Hauppauge (11788) ***(G-6058)***
Byte Consulting Inc ...646 500-8606
295 Madison Ave Fl 35 New York (10017) ***(G-9542)***
Bytheway Publishing Services ...607 334-8365
365 Follett Hill Rd Norwich (13815) ***(G-13037)***
Bz Media LLC ...631 421-4158
225 Broadhollow Rd 211e Melville (11747) ***(G-8330)***
C & A Atelier, Richmond Hill *Also called Carlos & Alex Atelier Inc* ***(G-14083)***
C & A Service Inc (PA) ...516 354-1200
65 S Tyson Ave Floral Park (11001) ***(G-5205)***
C & C Athletic Inc ...845 713-4670
11 Myrtle Ave Walden (12586) ***(G-16550)***
C & C Bindery Co Inc ...631 752-7078
25 Central Ave Unit B Farmingdale (11735) ***(G-4963)***
C & C Custom Metal Fabricators ...631 235-9646
2 N Hoffman Ln Hauppauge (11788) ***(G-6059)***
C & C Duplicators Inc ...631 244-0800
220 Knickerbocker Ave # 1 Bohemia (11716) ***(G-1025)***
C & C Metal Fabrications Inc ...315 598-7607
159 Hubbard St Fulton (13069) ***(G-5467)***
C & C Ready-Mix Corporation (PA) ...607 797-5108
3112 Vestal Rd Vestal (13850) ***(G-16465)***
C & C Ready-Mix Corporation ...607 687-1690
3818 Rt 17 C Owego (13827) ***(G-13376)***
C & D Assembly Inc ...607 898-4275
107 Corona Ave Groton (13073) ***(G-5919)***
C & F Fabricators & Erectors ...607 432-3520
Rr 7 Colliersville (13747) ***(G-3839)***
C & F Iron Works Inc ...914 592-2450
14 N Payne St Ste 1 Elmsford (10523) ***(G-4747)***
C & F Steel Corp ...914 592-3928
14 N Payne St Ste 2 Elmsford (10523) ***(G-4748)***
C & G of Kingston Inc ...845 331-0148
25 Cornell St Kingston (12401) ***(G-7209)***
C & G Video Systems Inc (PA) ...315 452-1490
7778 Tirrell Hill Cir Liverpool (13090) ***(G-7536)***
C & H Machining Inc ...631 582-6737
281 Knickerbocker Ave Bohemia (11716) ***(G-1026)***

ALPHABETIC

C & H Precision Tools Inc ALPHABETIC SECTION

C & H Precision Tools Inc 631 758-3806
194 Morris Ave Ste 20 Holtsville (11742) ***(G-6527)***
C & M Circuits Inc 631 589-0208
50 Orville Dr Bohemia (11716) ***(G-1027)***
C & M Products Inc 315 471-3303
1209 N Salina St Ste 1 Syracuse (13208) ***(G-15899)***
C & R De Santis Inc 718 447-5076
2645 Forest Ave Ste 2 Staten Island (10303) ***(G-15673)***
C & T Tool & Instrument Co 718 429-1253
4125 58th St Woodside (11377) ***(G-17338)***
C A M Graphics Co Inc 631 842-3400
24 Central Dr Farmingdale (11735) ***(G-4964)***
C B I, Oriskany *Also called Caldwell Bennett Inc* ***(G-13330)***
C B Management Services Inc 845 735-2300
73 S Pearl St Pearl River (10965) ***(G-13477)***
C B S Food Products Corp 718 452-2500
770 Chauncey St Brooklyn (11207) ***(G-1745)***
C C Industries Inc 518 581-7633
344 Burgoyne Rd Saratoga Springs (12866) ***(G-15174)***
C C M, Wolcott *Also called Carballo Contract Machining* ***(G-17299)***
C D A Inc 631 473-1595
66 Southern Blvd Ste A Nesconset (11767) ***(G-8821)***
C E King & Sons Inc 631 324-4944
10 Saint Francis Pl East Hampton (11937) ***(G-4426)***
C F Peters Corp 718 416-7800
7030 80th St Ste 2 Glendale (11385) ***(G-5663)***
C F Print Ltd Inc 631 567-2110
35 W Jefryn Blvd Ste 2 Deer Park (11729) ***(G-4137)***
C G & Son Machining Inc 315 964-2430
87 Nichols Rd Williamstown (13493) ***(G-17257)***
C H Thompson Company Inc 607 724-1094
69-93 Eldredge St Binghamton (13902) ***(G-897)***
C Howard Company Inc 631 286-7940
1007 Station Rd Bellport (11713) ***(G-822)***
C I G, New York *Also called Cambridge Info Group Inc* ***(G-9557)***
C J & C Sheet Metal Corp 631 376-9425
433 Falmouth Rd West Babylon (11704) ***(G-16805)***
C J Logging Equipment Inc 315 942-5431
8730 Industrial Dr Boonville (13309) ***(G-1163)***
C J Winter Machine Tech (HQ) 585 429-5000
167 Ames St Rochester (14611) ***(G-14271)***
C K Printing 718 965-0388
267 41st St Brooklyn (11232) ***(G-1746)***
C L Precision Machine & Tl Co 718 651-8475
5015 70th St Woodside (11377) ***(G-17339)***
C M, Amherst *Also called Columbus McKinnon Corporation* ***(G-235)***
C M E Corp 315 451-7101
1005 W Fayette St Ste 3c Syracuse (13204) ***(G-15900)***
C P Chemical Co Inc 914 428-2517
25 Home St White Plains (10606) ***(G-17118)***
C Q Communications Inc 516 681-2922
17 W John St Unit 1 Hicksville (11801) ***(G-6352)***
C R Bard Inc 518 793-2531
289 Bay Rd Queensbury (12804) ***(G-14007)***
C R Bard Inc 518 793-2531
289 Bay Rd Glens Falls (12804) ***(G-5690)***
C R C Manufacturing Inc 585 254-8820
37 Curlew St Rochester (14606) ***(G-14272)***
C S I G Inc 845 383-3800
721 Broadway 270 Kingston (12401) ***(G-7210)***
C S L, North Creek *Also called Creative Stage Lighting Co Inc* ***(G-12949)***
C S Welding, Ontario *Also called Cs Automation Inc* ***(G-13220)***
C Speed LLC 315 453-1043
316 Commerce Blvd Liverpool (13088) ***(G-7537)***
C T A Digital Inc 845 513-0433
326 State Route 208 Monroe (10950) ***(G-8586)***
C T Hogan, Copake Falls *Also called Alumiseal Corp* ***(G-3914)***
C T M Industries Ltd (HQ) 718 479-3300
22005 97th Ave Jamaica (11429) ***(G-6935)***
C To C Design & Print Inc 631 885-4020
1850 Pond Rd Unit B Ronkonkoma (11779) ***(G-14911)***
C W Sheet Metal, Maspeth *Also called Nelson Air Device Corporation* ***(G-8186)***
C&A Aromatics, Floral Park *Also called Citrus and Allied Essences Ltd* ***(G-5207)***
C&C Automatics Inc 315 331-1436
127 W Shore Blvd Newark (14513) ***(G-12750)***
C&C Diecuts, Farmingdale *Also called C & C Bindery Co Inc* ***(G-4963)***
C&T Tool & Instrmnt, Woodside *Also called C & T Tool & Instrument Co* ***(G-17338)***
C-Air International, Valley Stream *Also called Parnasa International Inc* ***(G-16442)***
C-Flex Bearing Co Inc 315 895-7454
104 Industrial Dr Frankfort (13340) ***(G-5359)***
C.H.thompson Finishing, Binghamton *Also called Tcmf Inc* ***(G-948)***
C/O Court Sq Capitl Partners, New York *Also called Mdi Holdings LLC* ***(G-11228)***
C/O M&M Fowarding, Tonawanda *Also called Fiber Laminations Limited* ***(G-16180)***
C/O Pdell Ndell Fine Winberger, New York *Also called Mom Dad Publishing Inc* ***(G-11321)***
Ca Inc (PA) 800 225-5224
520 Madison Ave Fl 22 New York (10022) ***(G-9543)***
Cab Plastics, Brooklyn *Also called Cab Signs Inc* ***(G-1747)***
Cab Signs Inc 718 479-2424
38 Livonia Ave Brooklyn (11212) ***(G-1747)***
Cab-Network Inc 516 334-8666
1500 Shames Dr Unit B Westbury (11590) ***(G-17000)***
Cabezon Design Group Inc 718 488-9868
197 Waverly Ave Brooklyn (11205) ***(G-1748)***
Cabinet Shapes Corp 718 784-6255
3721 12th St Long Island City (11101) ***(G-7722)***
Cabinetry By Tbr Inc 516 365-8500
1492 Northern Blvd Manhasset (11030) ***(G-8088)***
Cabinets By Stanley Inc 718 222-5861
46 Hall St Brooklyn (11205) ***(G-1749)***
Cable Management Solutions Inc 631 674-0004
291 Skip Ln Bay Shore (11706) ***(G-678)***
Cable Your World Inc 631 509-1180
1075 Route 112 Ste 4 Port Jeff STA (11776) ***(G-13787)***
Cables and Chips Inc (PA) 212 619-3132
121 Fulton St Fl 4 New York (10038) ***(G-9544)***
Cables Unlimited Inc 631 563-6363
3 Old Dock Rd Yaphank (11980) ***(G-17403)***
Caboodle Printing Inc 716 693-6000
1975 Wehrle Dr Ste 120 Williamsville (14221) ***(G-17265)***
Cabot Coach Builders Inc 516 625-4000
77 Carriage Ln Roslyn Heights (11577) ***(G-15049)***
Cabriole Designs Inc 212 593-4528
315 E 91st St Ste 3 New York (10128) ***(G-9545)***
Cachet Industries Inc 212 944-2188
463 Fashion Ave Rm 601 New York (10018) ***(G-9546)***
Caddell Burns Manufacturing Co 631 757-1772
247 Asharoken Ave Northport (11768) ***(G-13026)***
Caddell Dry Dock & Repr Co Inc 718 442-2112
Foot Of Broadway 1 W New Staten Island (10310) ***(G-15674)***
Caddell Ship Yards, Staten Island *Also called Caddell Dry Dock & Repr Co Inc* ***(G-15674)***
Caddy Concepts Inc 516 570-6279
15 Cuttermill Rd Great Neck (11021) ***(G-5812)***
Cadmus Journal Services Inc 607 762-5365
136 Carlin Rd Conklin (13748) ***(G-3890)***
CAF Usa Inc 607 737-3004
300 E 18th St Elmira Heights (14903) ***(G-4722)***
Cafe Kubal 315 278-2812
202 Lockwood Rd Syracuse (13214) ***(G-15901)***
Cahoon Farms Inc 315 594-8081
10951 Lummisville Rd Wolcott (14590) ***(G-17298)***
Cai Inc (PA) 212 819-0008
430 E 56th St New York (10022) ***(G-9547)***
Cai Design Inc 212 401-9973
240 W 37th St Ste 303 New York (10018) ***(G-9548)***
Caithness Equities Corporation (PA) 212 599-2112
565 5th Ave Fl 29 New York (10017) ***(G-9549)***
Cal Blen Electronic Industries 631 242-6243
6 Kenneth Ave Huntington (11743) ***(G-6691)***
Calchem Corporation (PA) 631 423-5696
2001 Ocean Ave Ronkonkoma (11779) ***(G-14912)***
Caldeira USA Inc 212 532-2292
230 5th Ave Ste 300 New York (10001) ***(G-9550)***
Caldwell Bennett Inc 315 337-8540
6152 County Seat Rd Oriskany (13424) ***(G-13330)***
Caldwell Cor, Fairport *Also called Mastercraft Decorators Inc* ***(G-4869)***
Calfonex Company 845 778-2212
121 Orchard St Walden (12586) ***(G-16551)***
Calgon Carbon Corporation 716 531-9113
830 River Rd North Tonawanda (14120) ***(G-12982)***
Calia Consultants, Staten Island *Also called Calia Technical Inc* ***(G-15675)***
Calia Technical Inc 718 447-3928
420 Jefferson Blvd Staten Island (10312) ***(G-15675)***
Caliber Imging Diagnostics Inc (PA) 585 239-9800
50 Methodist Hill Dr Rochester (14623) ***(G-14273)***
Calibrated Instruments Inc 914 741-5700
306 Aerie Ct Manhasset (11030) ***(G-8089)***
Calibration Technologies Inc 631 676-6133
30 Woodland Blvd Centereach (11720) ***(G-3495)***
Calico Cottage Inc 631 841-2100
210 New Hwy Amityville (11701) ***(G-277)***
California Fragrance Company 631 424-4023
171 E 2nd St Huntington Station (11746) ***(G-6736)***
California Petro Trnspt Corp 212 302-5151
114 W 47th St New York (10036) ***(G-9551)***
California US Holdings Inc 212 726-6500
417 5th Ave Lbby 7th New York (10016) ***(G-9552)***
Caliper Architecture PC 718 302-2427
67 Metropolitan Ave Ste 2 Brooklyn (11249) ***(G-1750)***
Caliperstudio Co 718 302-2427
75 Scott Ave Brooklyn (11237) ***(G-1751)***
Call Forwarding Technologies 516 621-3600
55 Northern Blvd Ste 3b Greenvale (11548) ***(G-5897)***
Callahan & Nannini Quarry Inc 845 496-4323
276 Clove Rd Salisbury Mills (12577) ***(G-15139)***
Callanan Industries Inc 315 697-9569
6375 Tuttle Rd Canastota (13032) ***(G-3393)***
Callanan Industries Inc (HQ) 518 374-2222
8 Southwoods Blvd Ste 4 Albany (12211) ***(G-57)***
Callanan Industries Inc 845 457-3158
215 Montgomery Rd Montgomery (12549) ***(G-8628)***
Callanan Industries Inc 845 331-6868
Salem St Kingston (12401) ***(G-7211)***

Callanan Industries Inc 518 785-5666
9 Fonda Rd Latham (12110) **(G-7385)**
Callanan Industries Inc 518 382-5354
145 Cordell Rd Schenectady (12303) **(G-15264)**
Callaway Arts & Entrmt Inc 646 465-4667
41 Union Sq W Ste 1101 New York (10003) **(G-9553)**
Callaway Digital Arts Inc 212 675-3050
41 Union Sq W Ste 1101 New York (10003) **(G-9554)**
Callidus Software Inc 212 554-7300
152 W 57th St Fl 8 New York (10019) **(G-9555)**
Calmetrics Inc 631 580-2522
1340 Lincoln Ave Ste 6 Holbrook (11741) **(G-6463)**
Calpac Incorporated 631 789-0502
44 Seabro Ave Amityville (11701) **(G-278)**
Calspan Corporation (HQ) 716 631-6955
4455 Genesee St Buffalo (14225) **(G-2886)**
Calspan Corporation 716 236-1040
2041 Niagara Falls Blvd Niagara Falls (14304) **(G-12823)**
Calspan Flight Research Center, Niagara Falls *Also called Calspan Corporation* **(G-12823)**
Caltex International Ltd 315 425-1040
60 Presidential Plz # 1405 Syracuse (13202) **(G-15902)**
Calvary Design Team Inc (PA) 585 347-6127
855 Publishers Pkwy Webster (14580) **(G-16738)**
Calvary Robotics, Webster *Also called Calvary Design Team Inc* **(G-16738)**
Calvin Klein Inc 212 292-9000
654 Madison Ave New York (10065) **(G-9556)**
CAM Fuel Inc 718 246-4306
50 Commerce St Brooklyn (11231) **(G-1752)**
CAM Machinery Co, Brooklyn *Also called S & S Machinery Corp* **(G-2541)**
CAM Touchview Products Inc 631 842-3400
51 Division St Sag Harbor (11963) **(G-15103)**
Cama Graphics Inc 718 707-9747
3200 Skillman Ave Ste B Long Island City (11101) **(G-7723)**
Cambridge Info Group Inc (PA) 301 961-6700
888 7th Ave Ste 1701 New York (10106) **(G-9557)**
Cambridge Kitchens Mfg Inc 516 935-5100
280 Duffy Ave Unit 1 Hicksville (11801) **(G-6353)**
Cambridge Manufacturing LLC 516 326-1350
1700 Jericho Tpke New Hyde Park (11040) **(G-8865)**
Cambridge Resources, Brooklyn *Also called Coda Resources Ltd* **(G-1789)**
Cambridge Security Seals LLC 845 520-4111
1 Cambridge Plz Pomona (10970) **(G-13758)**
Cambridge University Press 212 337-5000
165 Broadway Fl 20 New York (10006) **(G-9558)**
Cambridge Whos Who Pubg Inc (PA) 516 833-8440
498 Rxr Plz Fl 4 Uniondale (11556) **(G-16312)**
Cambridge-Pacific Inc 518 677-5988
891 State Rd 22 Cambridge (12816) **(G-3333)**
Camco, Ronkonkoma *Also called Gliptone Manufacturing Inc* **(G-14933)**
Camden House, Rochester *Also called Boydell & Brewer Inc* **(G-14261)**
Camden News Inc 315 245-1849
39 Main St Camden (13316) **(G-3340)**
Camden Wire Co Inc 315 245-3800
12 Masonic Ave Camden (13316) **(G-3341)**
Camellia Foods, Buffalo *Also called Camellia General Provision Co* **(G-2887)**
Camellia General Provision Co 716 893-5352
1333 Genesee St Buffalo (14211) **(G-2887)**
Camelot Print & Copy Centers, Latham *Also called Kjckd Inc* **(G-7395)**
Cameo Metal Products Inc 718 788-1106
127 12th St Brooklyn (11215) **(G-1753)**
Cameo Process Corp 914 948-0082
15 Stewart Pl Apt 7g White Plains (10603) **(G-17119)**
Cameron Bridge Works LLC 607 734-9456
1051 S Main St Elmira (14904) **(G-4685)**
Cameron Mfg & Design Inc (PA) 607 739-3606
727 Blostein Blvd Horseheads (14845) **(G-6599)**
Camfil USA Inc 518 456-6085
6600 Deere Rd Syracuse (13206) **(G-15903)**
Caminus Corporation (HQ) 212 515-3600
340 Madison Ave Fl 8 New York (10173) **(G-9559)**
Campanellis Poultry Farm Inc 845 482-2222
4 Perry Rd Bethel (12720) **(G-859)**
Campbell Alliance Group Inc 212 377-2740
335 Madison Ave Fl 17 New York (10017) **(G-9560)**
Campbell's Print Shop, Bronx *Also called Linda Campbell* **(G-1386)**
Campus Course Paks Inc 516 877-3967
1 South Ave Fl 1 Garden City (11530) **(G-5512)**
Campus Crafts Inc 585 328-6780
160 Murray St Rochester (14606) **(G-14274)**
Camso Manufacturing Usa Ltd (HQ) 518 561-7528
1 Martina Cir Plattsburgh (12901) **(G-13685)**
Canaan Printing Inc 718 729-3100
20007 46th Ave Bayside (11361) **(G-763)**
Canada Goose Inc 888 276-6297
601 W 26th St Rm 1745 New York (10001) **(G-9561)**
Canada Goose Us Inc (HQ) 888 276-6297
300 International Dr Williamsville (14221) **(G-17266)**
Canal Asphalt Inc 914 667-8500
800 Canal St Mount Vernon (10550) **(G-8714)**
Canali USA Inc (HQ) 212 767-0205
415 W 13th St Fl 2 New York (10014) **(G-9562)**

Canalside Creamery Inc 716 695-2876
985 Ruie Rd North Tonawanda (14120) **(G-12983)**
Canandaigua Msgnr Incorported (PA) 585 394-0770
73 Buffalo St Canandaigua (14424) **(G-3366)**
Canandaigua Quick Print, Canandaigua *Also called Carges Entps of Canandaigua* **(G-3367)**
Canandaigua Technology Center, Canandaigua *Also called Pactiv LLC* **(G-3384)**
Canarm Ltd (HQ) 800 267-4427
808 Commerce Park Dr Ogdensburg (13669) **(G-13134)**
Canarsie Courier Inc 718 257-0600
1142 E 92nd St 44 Brooklyn (11236) **(G-1754)**
Canary Connect Inc 212 390-8576
606 W 28th St Fl 7 New York (10001) **(G-9563)**
Canastota Publishing Co Inc 315 697-9010
130 E Center St Canastota (13032) **(G-3394)**
Cancer Targeting Systems 212 965-4534
100 Wall St New York (10005) **(G-9564)**
Candex Solutions Inc 215 650-3214
410 Park Ave New York (10022) **(G-9565)**
Candid Litho Printing Ltd (PA) 212 431-3800
210 Route 109 Farmingdale (11735) **(G-4965)**
Candid Worldwide LLC (HQ) 212 799-5300
210 Route 109 Farmingdale (11735) **(G-4966)**
Candle In The Window Inc 718 852-5743
43 Hall St Ste C10 Brooklyn (11205) **(G-1755)**
Candlelight Cabinetry Inc 716 434-2114
24 Michigan St Lockport (14094) **(G-7603)**
Candles By Foster 914 739-9226
810 South St Peekskill (10566) **(G-13499)**
Candlesticks Inc 212 947-8900
112 W 34th St Fl 18 New York (10120) **(G-9566)**
Candy Kraft, Altamont *Also called Robert Pikcilingis* **(G-215)**
Candy Land, Rome *Also called Noras Candy Shop* **(G-14853)**
Candy Man, Wilmington *Also called Adirondack Chocolate Co Ltd* **(G-17290)**
Candy Planet Division, New York *Also called Toymax Inc* **(G-12405)**
Cane Simple, New York *Also called Cane Sugar LLC* **(G-9567)**
Cane Sugar LLC 212 329-2695
950 3rd Ave Ste 2200 New York (10022) **(G-9567)**
Canfield & Tack Inc 585 235-7710
925 Exchange St Rochester (14608) **(G-14275)**
Canfield Aerospace & Mar Inc 631 648-1050
90 Remington Blvd Ronkonkoma (11779) **(G-14913)**
Canfield Electronics Inc (PA) 631 585-4100
6 Burton Pl Lindenhurst (11757) **(G-7480)**
Canfield Machine & Tool LLC 315 593-8062
121 Howard Rd Fulton (13069) **(G-5468)**
Cannizzaro Seal & Engraving Co 718 513-6125
435 Avenue U Brooklyn (11223) **(G-1756)**
Cannoli Factory Inc 631 643-2700
75 Wyandanch Ave Wyandanch (11798) **(G-17387)**
Cannon Co, Brooklyn *Also called Attias Oven Corp* **(G-1651)**
Cannon Industries Inc (PA) 585 254-8080
525 Lee Rd Rochester (14606) **(G-14276)**
Cannonsville Lumber Inc 607 467-3380
199 Old Route 10 Deposit (13754) **(G-4299)**
Canopy Books LLC (PA) 516 354-4888
28 N Wisconsin Ave 2-1 Massapequa (11758) **(G-8208)**
Canopy Canopy Canopy Inc 347 529-5182
264 Canal St Ste 3w New York (10013) **(G-9568)**
Cant Live Without It LLC 844 517-9355
28 W 23rd St Fl 5 New York (10010) **(G-9569)**
Canton Bio-Medical Inc (PA) 518 283-5963
11 Sicho Rd Poestenkill (12140) **(G-13752)**
Canton Noodle Corporation 212 226-3276
101 Mott St New York (10013) **(G-9570)**
Canvas Products Company Inc 516 742-1058
234 Herricks Rd Mineola (11501) **(G-8533)**
Canyon Publishing Inc 212 334-0227
55 John St Ste 6 New York (10038) **(G-9571)**
Cap USA Jerseyman Harlem Inc (PA) 212 222-7942
112 W 125th St New York (10027) **(G-9572)**
Capco Marketing 315 699-1687
8417 Oswego Rd 177 Baldwinsville (13027) **(G-567)**
Capco Wai Shing LLC 212 268-1976
132 W 36th St Rm 509 New York (10018) **(G-9573)**
Capital Concrete Inc 716 648-8001
5690 Camp Rd Hamburg (14075) **(G-5942)**
Capital District Stairs Inc 518 383-2449
45 Dunsbach Rd Halfmoon (12065) **(G-5931)**
Capital Dst Print & Imaging 518 456-6773
2075 Central Ave Schenectady (12304) **(G-15265)**
Capital E Financial Group 212 319-6550
598 Madison Ave Fl 9 New York (10022) **(G-9574)**
Capital Gold Corporation (PA) 212 668-0842
601 Lexington Ave Fl 36 New York (10022) **(G-9575)**
Capital Kit Cab & Door Mfrs 718 886-0303
1425 128th St College Point (11356) **(G-3805)**
Capital Ktchens Cab Doors Mfrs, College Point *Also called Capital Kit Cab & Door Mfrs* **(G-3805)**
Capital Mercury Shirtmakers Co, New York *Also called Gce International Inc* **(G-10306)**
Capital Programs Inc 212 842-4640
420 Lexington Ave Lbby 6 New York (10170) **(G-9576)**

ALPHABETIC

ALPHABETIC SECTION

Capital Reg Wkly Newsppr Group 518 674-2841
29 Sheer Rd Averill Park (12018) *(G-531)*
Capital Region Wkly Newspapers 518 877-7160
645 Albany Shaker Rd Albany (12211) *(G-58)*
Capital Sawmill Service 518 479-0729
4119 Us Highway 20 Nassau (12123) *(G-8816)*
Capital Stone LLC 518 382-7588
2241 Central Ave Schenectady (12304) *(G-15266)*
Capital Stone Saratoga LLC 518 226-8677
4295 Route 50 Saratoga Springs (12866) *(G-15175)*
Capitol Awning & Shade Co, Jamaica *Also called Capitol Awning Co Inc (G-6936)*
Capitol Awning Co Inc 212 505-1717
10515 180th St Jamaica (11433) *(G-6936)*
Capitol City Specialties Co 518 486-8935
10 Burdick Dr Albany (12205) *(G-59)*
Capitol Cups Inc 518 627-0051
1030 Riverfront Ctr Amsterdam (12010) *(G-338)*
Capitol Eq 2 LLC 518 886-8341
376 Broadway Ste 27 Saratoga Springs (12866) *(G-15176)*
Capitol Newspaper, Albany *Also called Newspaper Times Union (G-108)*
Capitol Plastic Products Inc 518 627-0051
1030 Riverfront Ctr Amsterdam (12010) *(G-339)*
Capitol Poly Corp 718 855-6000
101 Spencer St Brooklyn (11205) *(G-1757)*
Capitol Restoration Corp 516 783-1425
2473 Belmond Ave North Bellmore (11710) *(G-12932)*
Caplugs, Buffalo *Also called Protective Industries Inc (G-3165)*
Caplugs, Buffalo *Also called Protective Industries Inc (G-3166)*
Caps Teamwear Inc 585 663-1750
65 Milburn St Rochester (14607) *(G-14277)*
Capstone Printing, New York *Also called Kallen Corp (G-10841)*
Capstream Technologies LLC 716 945-7100
16 Main St Salamanca (14779) *(G-15126)*
Captech Industries LLC 347 374-1182
6 Revere Park Rome (13440) *(G-14836)*
Captive Plastics LLC 716 366-2112
3565 Chadwick Dr Dunkirk (14048) *(G-4358)*
Capture Globa Integ Solut Inc 718 352-0579
21214 48th Ave Bayside Hills (11364) *(G-773)*
Caputo Bakery Inc 718 875-6871
329 Court St Ste 1 Brooklyn (11231) *(G-1758)*
Caputo's Bake Shop, Brooklyn *Also called Caputo Bakery Inc (G-1758)*
Capy Machine Shop Inc (PA) 631 694-6916
114 Spagnoli Rd Melville (11747) *(G-8331)*
Car Doctor Motor Sports LLC 631 537-1548
610 Scuttle Hole Rd Water Mill (11976) *(G-16625)*
Car Doctor, The, Water Mill *Also called Car Doctor Motor Sports LLC (G-16625)*
Car Engineering and Mfg, Victor *Also called Charles A Rogers Entps Inc (G-16490)*
Car-Freshner Corporation (HQ) 315 788-6250
21205 Little Tree Dr Watertown (13601) *(G-16663)*
Car-Freshner Corporation 315 788-6250
22569 Fisher Cir Watertown (13601) *(G-16664)*
Car-Go Industries Inc (PA) 718 472-1443
5007 49th St Woodside (11377) *(G-17340)*
Caranda Emporium LLC 212 866-7100
2292 Frdrick Douglas Blvd New York (10027) *(G-9577)*
Caraustar Industries Inc 716 874-0393
25 Dewberry Ln Buffalo (14227) *(G-2888)*
Caravan International Corp 212 223-7190
641 Lexington Ave Fl 13 New York (10022) *(G-9578)*
Caravella Food Corp 646 552-0455
16611 Cryders Ln Whitestone (11357) *(G-17232)*
Carballo Contract Machining 315 594-2511
6205 Lake Ave Wolcott (14590) *(G-17299)*
Carbaugh Tool Company Inc 607 739-3293
126 Philo Rd W Elmira (14903) *(G-4686)*
Carbert Music Inc 212 725-9277
126 E 38th St New York (10016) *(G-9579)*
Carbide-Usa LLC 607 331-9353
100 Home St Elmira (14904) *(G-4687)*
Carbon Activated Corporation 716 662-2005
336 Stonehenge Dr Orchard Park (14127) *(G-13281)*
Carbon Copies, Cortland *Also called BP Digital Imaging LLC (G-4038)*
Carbon Graphite Materials Inc 716 792-7979
115 Central Ave Brocton (14716) *(G-1248)*
Carbonfree Chemicals Spe I LLC 914 421-4900
1 N Lexington Ave White Plains (10601) *(G-17120)*
Card Pak Start Up, East Hampton *Also called Luria Communications Inc (G-4433)*
Card Printing.us, Monsey *Also called Tele-Pak Inc (G-8620)*
Cardiac Life Products Inc 585 267-7775
349 W Coml St Ste 1400 East Rochester (14445) *(G-4473)*
Cardinal Boiler and Tank, Brooklyn *Also called Cardinal Tank Corp (G-1759)*
Cardinal Tank Corp 718 625-4350
700 Hicks St Brooklyn (11231) *(G-1759)*
Cardinali Bakery, Carle Place *Also called Gennaris Itln French Bky Inc (G-3415)*
Cardish Machine Works Inc 518 273-2329
7 Elm St Watervliet (12189) *(G-16705)*
Cardona Industries USA Ltd (PA) 516 466-5200
505 Northern Blvd Ste 213 Great Neck (11021) *(G-5813)*
Cardullo, J Iron Works, Bay Shore *Also called Jerry Cardullo Iron Works Inc (G-707)*

Carduner Sales Company, Farmingville *Also called Bud Barger Assoc Inc (G-5167)*
Care Enterprises Inc 631 472-8155
435 Renee Dr Bayport (11705) *(G-749)*
Care/of, New York *Also called Noho Health Inc (G-11467)*
Careconnector 919 360-2987
177 Concord St Apt 2a Brooklyn (11201) *(G-1760)*
Careers and The Disabled, Melville *Also called Equal Opprtnity Pblcations Inc (G-8344)*
Carefree Kitchens Inc 631 567-2120
925 Lincoln Ave Ste 1 Holbrook (11741) *(G-6464)*
Carestream Health Inc 585 627-1800
1669 Lake Ave Rochester (14652) *(G-14278)*
Carges Entps of Canandaigua 585 394-2600
330 S Main St Canandaigua (14424) *(G-3367)*
Cargill Incorporated 607 535-6300
518 E 4th St Watkins Glen (14891) *(G-16719)*
Cargill Incorporated 716 665-6570
1029 Poland Center Rd Kennedy (14747) *(G-7182)*
Cargill Incorporated 315 622-3533
7700 Maltage Dr Liverpool (13090) *(G-7538)*
Carib Prints Ltd 646 210-2863
752 E 137th St Bronx (10454) *(G-1290)*
Caribbean Foods Delight Inc 845 398-3000
117 Route 303 Ste B Tappan (10983) *(G-16103)*
Caribe Bakery, Bronx *Also called 527 Franco Bakery Corporation (G-1250)*
Carl Fischer LLC (PA) 212 777-0900
48 Wall St 28 New York (10005) *(G-9580)*
Carl Zeiss Inc (HQ) 914 747-1800
1 Zeiss Dr Thornwood (10594) *(G-16140)*
Carlara Group Ltd 914 769-2020
467 Bedford Rd Pleasantville (10570) *(G-13744)*
Carleton Technologies Inc (HQ) 716 662-0006
10 Cobham Dr Orchard Park (14127) *(G-13282)*
Carlisle Construction Mtls LLC 386 753-0786
9 Hudson Crossing Dr Montgomery (12549) *(G-8629)*
Carlo Monte Designs Inc 212 935-5611
17 E 48th St Fl 8 New York (10017) *(G-9581)*
Carlos & Alex Atelier Inc 718 441-8911
10010 91st Ave Fl 2 Richmond Hill (11418) *(G-14083)*
Carlson Wood Products Inc (PA) 716 287-2923
1705 Bates Rd Sinclairville (14782) *(G-15473)*
Carlson, L A Co, East Greenbush *Also called Leonard Carlson (G-4423)*
Carlton Ice Cream Co, Brooklyn *Also called Macedonia Ltd (G-2253)*
Carmine Street Bagels Inc 212 691-3041
107 Park Dr N Staten Island (10314) *(G-15676)*
Carmona Nyc LLC 718 227-6662
9830 67th Ave Apt 1d Rego Park (11374) *(G-14043)*
Carnel Printing and Copying, Port Washington *Also called Carnels Printing Inc (G-13826)*
Carnels Printing Inc 516 883-3355
22 Main St Frnt A Port Washington (11050) *(G-13826)*
Carnival, New York *Also called Cookies Inc (G-9776)*
Carnival Inc 415 781-9815
284 Mott St Apt 4d New York (10012) *(G-9582)*
Carob Industries Inc 631 225-0900
215 W Hoffman Ave Lindenhurst (11757) *(G-7481)*
Caroda Inc 212 630-9986
254 W 35th St New York (10001) *(G-9583)*
Carol Dauplaise Ltd 212 997-5290
134 W 37th St Fl 3 New York (10018) *(G-9584)*
Carol For Eva Graham Inc 212 889-8686
366 5th Ave Rm 815 New York (10001) *(G-9585)*
Carol Group Ltd 212 505-2030
150 W 30th St Rm 902 New York (10001) *(G-9586)*
Carol Peretz 516 248-6300
49 Windsor Ave Ste 103 Mineola (11501) *(G-8534)*
Carol Peretz Workshop, Mineola *Also called Carol Peretz (G-8534)*
Carol Vail, Salem *Also called Carolina Eastern-Vail Inc (G-15137)*
Carolina Amato Inc 212 768-9095
270 W 38th St Rm 902 New York (10018) *(G-9587)*
Carolina Eastern-Vail Inc 518 854-9785
4134 State Route 22 Salem (12865) *(G-15137)*
Carolina Herrera Ltd (HQ) 212 944-5757
501 Fashion Ave Fl 17 New York (10018) *(G-9588)*
Carolina Precision Plas LLC 631 981-0743
115 Comac St Ronkonkoma (11779) *(G-14914)*
Carolinas Desserts Inc 914 779-4000
1562 Central Park Ave Yonkers (10710) *(G-17439)*
Carols Polar Parlor 315 468-3404
3800 W Genesee St Syracuse (13219) *(G-15904)*
Carolyn Ray Inc 914 476-0619
578 Nepperhan Ave Ste C10 Yonkers (10701) *(G-17440)*
Caron Distribution Center, New York *Also called National Spinning Co Inc (G-11374)*
Carousel ADS, Brooklyn *Also called Drns Corp (G-1883)*
Carpenter Industries Inc 315 463-4284
1 General Motors Dr # 10 Syracuse (13206) *(G-15905)*
Carpenter Manufacturing Co 315 682-9176
110 Fairgrounds Dr Manlius (13104) *(G-8102)*
Carpentier Industries LLC 585 385-5550
119 Despatch Dr East Rochester (14445) *(G-4474)*
Carpet Beaters LLC 877 375-9336
12163 235th St Rosedale (11422) *(G-15036)*

Carpet Fabrications Intl 914 381-6060
628 Waverly Ave Ste 1 Mamaroneck (10543) ***(G-8058)***
Carr Communications Group LLC 607 748-0481
513 Prentice Rd Vestal (13850) ***(G-16466)***
Carr Jewelers, Latham *Also called Carr Manufacturing Jewelers* ***(G-7386)***
Carr Manufacturing Jewelers 518 783-6093
22 West Ln Latham (12110) ***(G-7386)***
Carr Printing, Vestal *Also called Carr Communications Group LLC* ***(G-16466)***
Carrera Casting Corp 212 382-3296
64 W 48th St Fl 2 New York (10036) ***(G-9589)***
Carrier Corporation 315 432-6000
Carrier Pkwy Trl 20 Syracuse (13221) ***(G-15906)***
Carrier Corporation 315 463-5744
6390 Fly Rd East Syracuse (13057) ***(G-4530)***
Carrier Corporation 315 432-6000
Carrier Pkwy Tr 20 Syracuse (13221) ***(G-15907)***
Carrier Corporation 315 432-6000
Carrier Global Account Syracuse (13221) ***(G-15908)***
Carrier Corporation 315 432-6000
Kinne St East Syracuse (13057) ***(G-4531)***
Carrier Corporation 315 432-3844
Carrier Pkwy Bldg Tr 20 East Syracuse (13057) ***(G-4532)***
Carrier Globl Engrg Conference, Syracuse *Also called Carrier Corporation* ***(G-15906)***
Carrier News, Hicksville *Also called All Island Media Inc* ***(G-6343)***
Carrmet Industries, Farmingdale *Also called Joe P Industries Inc* ***(G-5026)***
Carry Hot Inc 212 279-7535
545 W 45th St Rm 501 New York (10036) ***(G-9590)***
Carry-All Canvas Bag Co Inc 718 375-4230
1983 Coney Island Ave Brooklyn (11223) ***(G-1761)***
Cars Magazine, Roslyn Heights *Also called National Marketing Services* ***(G-15055)***
Carta Usa LLC 585 436-3012
1600 Lexington Ave # 116 Rochester (14606) ***(G-14279)***
Carter Enterprises LLC (PA) 718 853-5052
4610 12th Ave Brooklyn (11219) ***(G-1762)***
Carter Precision Metals LLC 516 333-1917
99 Urban Ave Westbury (11590) ***(G-17001)***
Carter Street Bakery Inc 585 749-7104
580 Child St Rochester (14606) ***(G-14280)***
Carters Inc 585 387-9043
3349 Monroe Ave Rochester (14618) ***(G-14281)***
Carters Inc 315 637-3128
537 Towne Dr Fayetteville (13066) ***(G-5171)***
Carters Inc 718 980-1759
430 New Dorp Ln Staten Island (10306) ***(G-15677)***
Carters Inc 631 549-6781
350 Walt Whitman Rd Huntington Station (11746) ***(G-6737)***
Carthage Fibre Drum Inc (PA) 315 493-2730
14 Hewitt Dr Carthage (13619) ***(G-3436)***
Carthage Specialty Pprbd Inc 315 493-2120
30 Champion St Carthage (13619) ***(G-3437)***
Carts Mobile Food Eqp Corp 718 788-5540
113 8th St Brooklyn (11215) ***(G-1763)***
Carvart Glass Inc (PA) 212 675-0030
1441 Broadway Fl 28 New York (10018) ***(G-9591)***
Carver Creek Enterprises Inc 585 657-7511
2524 Cannan Rd Bloomfield (14469) ***(G-977)***
Carver Sand & Gravel, Schoharie *Also called Masick Soil Conservation Co* ***(G-15339)***
Carvin French Jewelers Inc 212 755-6474
515 Madison Ave Rm 1605 New York (10022) ***(G-9592)***
Cas, Cheektowaga *Also called Culinary Arts Specialties Inc* ***(G-3594)***
Casa Collection Inc 718 694-0272
106 Ferris St Brooklyn (11231) ***(G-1764)***
Casa Innovations Inc 718 965-6600
140 58th St Ste 5h-1 Brooklyn (11220) ***(G-1765)***
Casa Larga Vineyards (PA) 585 223-4210
27 Emerald Hill Cir Fairport (14450) ***(G-4855)***
Casa Larga Vineyards 585 223-4210
2287 Turk Hill Rd Fairport (14450) ***(G-4856)***
Casa Nueva Custom Furnishing 914 476-2272
510 Nepperhan Ave Yonkers (10701) ***(G-17441)***
Casa Redimix Concrete Corp 718 589-1555
886 Edgewater Rd Bronx (10474) ***(G-1291)***
Casablanca Foods LLC 212 317-1111
135 E 57th St Unit 96 New York (10022) ***(G-9593)***
Casablanca Records, New York *Also called Tm Music Inc* ***(G-12376)***
Cascade Helmets Holdings Inc 315 453-3073
4697 Crssrads Pk Dr Ste 1 Liverpool (13088) ***(G-7539)***
Cascade Mountain Winery & Rest 845 373-9021
835 Cascade Rd Amenia (12501) ***(G-218)***
Cascade Technical Services LLC (HQ) 516 596-6300
30 N Prospect Ave Lynbrook (11563) ***(G-7977)***
Cascade Technical Services LLC 518 355-2201
2846 Curry Rd Ste B Schenectady (12303) ***(G-15267)***
Cascades New York Inc 716 285-3681
4001 Packard Rd Niagara Falls (14303) ***(G-12824)***
Cascades New York Inc 718 340-2100
5515 Grand Ave Maspeth (11378) ***(G-8152)***
Cascades New York Inc 518 346-6151
801 Corporation Park Schenectady (12302) ***(G-15268)***
Cascades New York Inc 518 238-1900
148 Hudson River Rd Wynantskill (12198) ***(G-17394)***
Cascades Tssue Group-Sales Inc 518 238-1900
148 Hudson River Rd Waterford (12188) ***(G-16630)***
Cascades Tssue Group-Sales Inc (HQ) 819 363-5100
148 Hudson River Rd Waterford (12188) ***(G-16631)***
Casco Security, Rochester *Also called Custom Sound and Video* ***(G-14317)***
Case Brothers Inc 716 925-7172
370 Quinn Rd Limestone (14753) ***(G-7472)***
Case Group LLC 518 720-3100
195 Cohoes Ave Green Island (12183) ***(G-5872)***
Case Window and Door, Green Island *Also called Case Group LLC* ***(G-5872)***
Casey Machine Co Inc 716 651-0150
74 Ward Rd Lancaster (14086) ***(G-7332)***
Casper Science LLC 212 633-4309
230 Park Ave S Fl 13 New York (10003) ***(G-9594)***
Cassadaga Designs Inc 716 595-3030
309 Maple Ave Cassadaga (14718) ***(G-3442)***
Cassinelli Food Products Inc 718 274-4881
3112 23rd Ave Long Island City (11105) ***(G-7724)***
Cassini Parfums Ltd 212 753-7540
3 W 57th St Fl 8 New York (10019) ***(G-9595)***
Cast-All Corporation (PA) 516 741-4025
229 Liberty Ave Mineola (11501) ***(G-8535)***
Cast-All Corporation 516 741-4025
229 Liberty Ave Mineola (11501) ***(G-8536)***
Castek Inc (HQ) 914 636-1000
20 Jones St New Rochelle (10801) ***(G-8936)***
Castel Grisch Winery, Montour Falls *Also called Malina Management Company Inc* ***(G-8649)***
Castella Imports Inc 631 231-5500
60 Davids Dr Hauppauge (11788) ***(G-6060)***
Castelli America LLC 716 782-2101
5151 Fairbanks Rd Ashville (14710) ***(G-423)***
Casters Custom Sawing 315 387-5104
6323 Us Route 11 Sandy Creek (13145) ***(G-15159)***
Castino Corporation 845 229-0341
1300 Route 9g Hyde Park (12538) ***(G-6772)***
Castle Brands Inc (PA) 646 356-0200
122 E 42nd St Rm 5000 New York (10168) ***(G-9596)***
Castle Connolly Medical Ltd 212 367-8400
42 W 24th St Fl 2 New York (10010) ***(G-9597)***
Castle Fuels Corporation 914 381-6600
440 Mamaroneck Ave Harrison (10528) ***(G-5998)***
Castle Harvester Co Inc 585 526-5884
3165 Seneca Castle Rd Seneca Castle (14547) ***(G-15381)***
Castle Harvstr Met Fabricators, Seneca Castle *Also called Castle Harvester Co Inc* ***(G-15381)***
Castle Power Solutions LLC 518 743-1000
22 Hudson Falls Rd Ste D South Glens Falls (12803) ***(G-15547)***
Castle Reagh Print Craft, Freeport *Also called Castlereagh Printcraft Inc* ***(G-5402)***
Castlereagh Printcraft Inc 516 623-1728
320 Buffalo Ave Freeport (11520) ***(G-5402)***
Castoleum Corporation 914 664-5877
240 E 7th St Mount Vernon (10550) ***(G-8715)***
Casttle Harbor, Plainview *Also called Hot Line Industries Inc* ***(G-13634)***
Casual Friday Inc 585 544-9470
1561 Lyell Ave Rochester (14606) ***(G-14282)***
Casual Home Worldwide Inc 631 789-2999
38 William St Amityville (11701) ***(G-279)***
Casuals Etc Inc 212 838-1319
16 E 52nd St Fl 4 New York (10022) ***(G-9598)***
Caswell Inc 315 946-1213
7696 State Route 31 Lyons (14489) ***(G-7997)***
Catalina Products Corp (PA) 718 336-8288
2455 Mcdonald Ave Brooklyn (11223) ***(G-1766)***
Catalyst Group Design, New York *Also called Catalyst Group Inc* ***(G-9599)***
Catalyst Group Inc 212 243-7777
345 7th Ave Rm 1100 New York (10001) ***(G-9599)***
Catapult 323 839-6204
1140 Broadway Rm 704 New York (10001) ***(G-9600)***
Cataract Hose Co 914 941-9019
6 Waller Ave Ossining (10562) ***(G-13345)***
Cataract Hose Co No 2, Ossining *Also called Cataract Hose Co* ***(G-13345)***
Cataract Steel Industries, Niagara Falls *Also called Costanzos Welding Inc* ***(G-12829)***
Catch Ventures Inc 347 620-4351
30 W 63rd St Apt 14o New York (10023) ***(G-9601)***
Cathay Global Co Inc 718 229-0920
5815 215th St Bayside Hills (11364) ***(G-774)***
Cathay Home Inc (PA) 212 213-0988
230 5th Ave Ste 215 New York (10001) ***(G-9602)***
Cathay Resources Inc 516 922-2839
38 Cord Pl East Norwich (11732) ***(G-4464)***
Cathedral Candle Co 315 422-9119
510 Kirkpatrick St Syracuse (13208) ***(G-15909)***
Cathedral Corporation (PA) 315 338-0021
632 Ellsworth Rd Rome (13441) ***(G-14837)***
Catherine Deane, New York *Also called Arcangel Inc* ***(G-9244)***
Catherine Stein Designs Inc 212 840-1188
411 5th Ave Rm 600 New York (10016) ***(G-9603)***
CATHOLIC COURIER, Rochester *Also called Rochester Catholic Press* ***(G-14659)***
Catholic New York, New York *Also called Ecclesiastical Communications* ***(G-10027)***
Catholic News Publishing Co 914 632-7771
606 Halstead Ave Mamaroneck (10543) ***(G-8059)***

ALPHABETIC

Catholic Sun, The, Syracuse *Also called Syracuse Catholic Press Assn* ***(G-16074)***
Cathy Daniels Ltd (PA)..........212 354-8000
501 Fashion Ave Rm 400 New York (10018) ***(G-9604)***
Catskill Boiler Co., Greenville *Also called Hawkencatskills LLC* ***(G-5903)***
Catskill Castings Co, Bloomville *Also called G Haynes Holdings Inc* ***(G-989)***
Catskill Craftsmen Inc..........607 652-7321
15 W End Ave Stamford (12167) ***(G-15644)***
Catskill Delaware Publications (PA)..........845 887-5200
5 Lower Main St Callicoon (12723) ***(G-3312)***
Catskill Mountain News, Arkville *Also called Catskill Mountain Publishing* ***(G-409)***
Catskill Mountain Publishing..........845 586-2601
43414 State Hwy 28 Arkville (12406) ***(G-409)***
Catsmo LLC..........845 895-2296
25 Myers Rd Wallkill (12589) ***(G-16562)***
Cattaraugus Containers Inc..........716 676-2000
21 Elm St 23 Franklinville (14737) ***(G-5379)***
Cava Spiliadis USA..........212 247-8214
200 W 57th St Ste 908 New York (10019) ***(G-9605)***
Cavalry Solutions..........315 422-1699
449 E Wshngtn St Ste 100 Syracuse (13202) ***(G-15910)***
Cayuga Crushed Stone Inc..........607 533-4273
87 Portland Point Rd Lansing (14882) ***(G-7373)***
Cayuga Press Cortland Inc..........888 229-8421
4707 Dey Rd Liverpool (13088) ***(G-7540)***
Cayuga Tool and Die Inc..........607 533-7400
182 Newman Rd Groton (13073) ***(G-5920)***
Cayuga Wooden Boatworks Inc..........315 253-7447
381 Enfield Main Rd Ithaca (14850) ***(G-6868)***
Cazar Printing & Advertising..........718 446-4606
4215 102nd St Corona (11368) ***(G-4015)***
Cazenovia Equipment Co Inc..........315 736-0898
8186 Seneca Tpke Clinton (13323) ***(G-3742)***
CB Products, Floral Park *Also called CB Publishing LLC* ***(G-5206)***
CB Publishing LLC..........516 354-4888
50 Carnation Ave Bldg 2-1 Floral Park (11001) ***(G-5206)***
CBA Group LLC..........607 779-7522
33 Broome Corporate Pkwy Conklin (13748) ***(G-3891)***
Cbe/New York, Plainview *Also called Conrad Blasius Equipment Co* ***(G-13620)***
CBM Fabrications Inc..........518 399-8023
15 Westside Dr Ballston Lake (12019) ***(G-580)***
Cbord Group Inc (HQ)..........607 257-2410
950 Danby Rd Ste 100c Ithaca (14850) ***(G-6869)***
CCA Holding Inc..........716 446-8800
300 Corporate Pkwy Amherst (14226) ***(G-232)***
CCC Publications Inc..........718 306-1008
12020 Flatlands Ave Brooklyn (11207) ***(G-1767)***
CCL Label Inc..........716 852-2155
685 Howard St Buffalo (14206) ***(G-2889)***
Ccmi Inc..........315 781-3270
88 Middle St Geneva (14456) ***(G-5583)***
Ccn International Inc..........315 789-4400
200 Lehigh St Geneva (14456) ***(G-5584)***
CCS Machinery Inc..........631 968-0900
2175 Union Blvd Bay Shore (11706) ***(G-679)***
CCT (us) Inc..........716 297-7509
2221 Niagara Falls Blvd # 5 Niagara Falls (14304) ***(G-12825)***
Cct Inc..........212 532-3355
60 Madison Ave Ste 1209 New York (10010) ***(G-9606)***
Ccz Ready Mix Concrete Corp..........516 579-7352
2 Loring Rd Levittown (11756) ***(G-7448)***
Cda Machine Inc..........585 671-5959
514 Vosburg Rd Webster (14580) ***(G-16739)***
Cdc Publishing LLC..........215 579-1695
19 North St Morrisville (13408) ***(G-8661)***
Cdj Stamping Inc..........585 224-8120
146 Halstead St Ste 123 Rochester (14610) ***(G-14283)***
Cdl Manufacturing Inc..........585 589-2533
15661 Telegraph Rd Albion (14411) ***(G-166)***
Cdml Computer Services Ltd..........718 428-9063
5343 198th St Fresh Meadows (11365) ***(G-5452)***
Cdnv Wood Carving Frames Inc (PA)..........914 375-3447
498 Nepperhan Ave Yonkers (10701) ***(G-17442)***
Cds Productions Inc..........518 385-8255
108 Erie Blvd Ste 400 Schenectady (12305) ***(G-15269)***
CEC Elevator Cab Corp..........718 328-3632
540 Manida St Bronx (10474) ***(G-1292)***
Cedar West Inc (PA)..........631 467-1444
1700 Ocean Ave Ste 1 Ronkonkoma (11779) ***(G-14915)***
Cegid Corporation..........212 757-9038
274 Madison Ave Rm 1400 New York (10016) ***(G-9607)***
Cego Custom Shirts, New York *Also called Sifonya Inc* ***(G-12087)***
Ceipal LLC..........585 351-2934
722 Weiland Rd Rochester (14626) ***(G-14284)***
Ceipal LLC..........585 584-1316
687 Lee Rd Ste 208a Rochester (14606) ***(G-14285)***
CEIT Corp..........518 825-0649
625 State Route 3 Unit 2 Plattsburgh (12901) ***(G-13686)***
Cell-Nique Corporation..........888 417-9343
22 Hamilton Way Castleton On Hudson (12033) ***(G-3446)***
Cellec Technologies Inc..........585 454-9166
125 Tech Park Dr Ste 2111 Rochester (14623) ***(G-14286)***
Cellect LLC..........508 744-6906
10 New St Saint Johnsville (13452) ***(G-15118)***
Cellect Plastics LLC..........518 568-7036
12 New St Saint Johnsville (13452) ***(G-15119)***
Cellgen Inc..........516 889-9300
55 Commercial St Freeport (11520) ***(G-5403)***
Cellu Tissue - Long Island LLC..........631 232-2626
555 N Research Pl Central Islip (11722) ***(G-3514)***
Cellular Empire Inc..........800 778-3513
2614 W 13th St Brooklyn (11223) ***(G-1768)***
Cellvation Inc..........212 554-4520
2 Gansevoort St Fl 9 New York (10014) ***(G-9608)***
Celonis Inc..........941 615-9670
1820 Avenue M Unit 544 Brooklyn (11230) ***(G-1769)***
Cem Machine Inc (PA)..........315 493-4258
571 W End Ave Carthage (13619) ***(G-3438)***
Cemac Foods Corp..........914 835-0526
8 Cayuga Trl Harrison (10528) ***(G-5999)***
Cementex Latex Corp..........212 741-1770
121 Varick St Frnt 2 New York (10013) ***(G-9609)***
Cemex Cement Inc..........212 317-6000
590 Madison Ave Fl 41 New York (10022) ***(G-9610)***
Cemoi Inc (PA)..........212 583-4920
5 Penn Plz Ste 2325 New York (10001) ***(G-9611)***
Cemtrex Inc (PA)..........631 756-9116
19 Engineers Ln Farmingdale (11735) ***(G-4967)***
Cenere, New York *Also called Precision International Co Inc* ***(G-11719)***
Cenibra Inc..........212 818-8242
335 Madison Ave Fl 23 New York (10017) ***(G-9612)***
Ceno Technologies Inc..........716 885-5050
1234 Delaware Ave Buffalo (14209) ***(G-2890)***
Centar Fuel Co Inc..........516 538-2424
700 Nassau Blvd West Hempstead (11552) ***(G-16882)***
Centennial Media LLC..........646 527-7320
10th Floor 40 Worth St Flr 10 New York (10013) ***(G-9613)***
Center For Inquiry Inc (PA)..........716 636-4869
3965 Rensch Rd Amherst (14228) ***(G-233)***
Center Line Studios Inc (PA)..........845 534-7143
112 Forge Hill Rd New Windsor (12553) ***(G-8980)***
Center Sheet Metal Inc..........718 378-4476
1371 E Bay Ave Bronx (10474) ***(G-1293)***
Center State Propane LLC (PA)..........315 841-4044
1130 Mason Rd Waterville (13480) ***(G-16700)***
Centerra Wine Company, Canandaigua *Also called Constellation Brands US Oprs* ***(G-3370)***
Central Adirondack Textiles, Boonville *Also called S M S C Inc* ***(G-1167)***
Central Apparel Group Ltd..........212 868-6505
16 W 36th St Rm 1202 New York (10018) ***(G-9614)***
Central Asphalt, Oriskany *Also called Suit-Kote Corporation* ***(G-13338)***
Central Asphalt, Watkins Glen *Also called Suit-Kote Corporation* ***(G-16722)***
Central Cnfrnce of Amrcn Rbbis..........212 972-3636
355 Lexington Ave Fl 18 New York (10017) ***(G-9615)***
Central Dover Development..........917 709-3266
247 Dover Furnace Rd Dover Plains (12522) ***(G-4338)***
Central Garden & Pet Company..........631 451-8021
1100 Middle Country Rd Selden (11784) ***(G-15370)***
Central Garden & Pet Company..........212 877-1270
2475 Broadway New York (10025) ***(G-9616)***
Central Island Juice Corp..........516 338-8301
128 Magnolia Ave Westbury (11590) ***(G-17002)***
Central Islip Pharmacy Inc..........631 234-6039
1629 Islip Ave Central Islip (11722) ***(G-3515)***
Central Kitchen Corp..........631 283-1029
871 County Road 39 Southampton (11968) ***(G-15564)***
Central Marking Equipment, Syracuse *Also called C M E Corp* ***(G-15900)***
Central Mills Inc..........212 221-0748
1400 Broadway Rm 1605 New York (10018) ***(G-9617)***
Central Nat Pulp & Ppr Sls Inc..........914 696-9000
3 Manhattanville Rd Purchase (10577) ***(G-13971)***
Central Park Active Wear, New York *Also called Central Apparel Group Ltd* ***(G-9614)***
Central Rede Sign Co Inc..........716 213-0797
317 Wheeler St Tonawanda (14150) ***(G-16172)***
Central Semiconductor Corp..........631 435-1110
145 Adams Ave Hauppauge (11788) ***(G-6061)***
Central Textiles Inc..........212 213-8740
10 E 40th St Rm 3410 New York (10016) ***(G-9618)***
Central Timber Co Inc..........518 638-6338
9088 State Route 22 Granville (12832) ***(G-5789)***
Central Timber Research/Devt, Granville *Also called Central Timber Co Inc* ***(G-5789)***
Central Time Clock Inc..........718 784-4900
523 50th Ave Long Island City (11101) ***(G-7725)***
Centre Interiors Wdwkg Co Inc..........718 323-1343
10001 103rd Ave Ozone Park (11417) ***(G-13402)***
Centrisource Inc..........716 871-1105
777 E Park Dr Tonawanda (14150) ***(G-16173)***
Centro Inc..........212 791-9450
841 Broadway Fl 6 New York (10003) ***(G-9619)***
Centroid Inc..........516 349-0070
111 E Ames Ct Unit 1 Plainview (11803) ***(G-13616)***
Century Awning Concepts, Mount Vernon *Also called Kingston Building Products LLC* ***(G-8744)***
Century Direct LLC..........212 763-0600
15 Enter Ln Islandia (11749) ***(G-6827)***

Century Grand Inc 212 925-3838
302 Grand St New York (10002) ***(G-9620)***
Century Metal Parts Corp 631 667-0800
230 S Fehr Way Bay Shore (11706) ***(G-680)***
Century Mold Company Inc (PA) 585 352-8600
25 Vantage Point Dr Rochester (14624) ***(G-14287)***
Century Mold Mexico LLC (HQ) 585 352-8600
25 Vantage Point Dr Rochester (14624) ***(G-14288)***
Century Pharmacy Three, New York *Also called Century Grand Inc* ***(G-9620)***
Century Ready Mix Inc 631 888-2200
615 Cord Ave West Babylon (11704) ***(G-16806)***
Century Systems Ltd 718 543-5991
485 W 246th St Bronx (10471) ***(G-1294)***
Century Tom Inc 347 654-3179
3344 Farrington St Flushing (11354) ***(G-5237)***
Century-Tech Inc 718 326-9400
32 Intersection St Hempstead (11550) ***(G-6291)***
Century-Tech Inc (PA) 516 493-9800
5825 63rd St Hempstead (11550) ***(G-6292)***
Cenveo Inc 716 662-2800
100 Centre Dr Orchard Park (14127) ***(G-13283)***
Ceo Cast Inc 212 732-4300
211 E 43rd St Rm 400 New York (10017) ***(G-9621)***
Ceoentano, Buffalo *Also called Rosina Food Products Inc* ***(G-3193)***
Cep Technologies Corporation (PA) 914 968-4100
763 Saw Mill River Rd Yonkers (10710) ***(G-17443)***
Ceramaterials LLC 518 701-6722
226 Route 209 Port Jervis (12771) ***(G-13803)***
Ceramica V. A. R. M., New Rochelle *Also called Ceramica Varm* ***(G-8937)***
Ceramica Varm (PA) 914 381-6215
479 5th Ave New Rochelle (10801) ***(G-8937)***
Ceres Technologies Inc 845 247-4701
5 Tower Dr Saugerties (12477) ***(G-15210)***
Cerion Energy Inc 585 271-5630
1 Blossom Rd Rochester (14610) ***(G-14289)***
Cerion LLC 585 271-5630
1 Blossom Rd Rochester (14610) ***(G-14290)***
Ceros Inc (PA) 347 744-9250
151 W 25th St Rm 200 New York (10001) ***(G-9622)***
Cerovene Inc 845 359-1101
10 Corporate Dr Orangeburg (10962) ***(G-13243)***
Cerovene Inc (PA) 845 267-2055
612 Corporate Way Ste 10 Valley Cottage (10989) ***(G-16403)***
Certainteed Corporation 716 823-3684
231 Ship Canal Pkwy Lackawanna (14218) ***(G-7269)***
Certainteed Corporation 716 827-7560
231 Ship Canal Pkwy Buffalo (14218) ***(G-2891)***
Certified Fabrications Inc 716 731-8123
2127 Cory Dr Sanborn (14132) ***(G-15144)***
Certified Flameproofing Corp 631 265-4824
17 N Ingelore Ct Smithtown (11787) ***(G-15506)***
Certified Health Products Inc 718 339-7498
67 35th St Unit 12 Brooklyn (11232) ***(G-1770)***
Certified Prcsion McHining Inc 631 244-3671
70 Knickerbocker Ave # 4 Bohemia (11716) ***(G-1028)***
Ces Industries Inc 631 782-7088
95 Hoffman Ln Ste S Islandia (11749) ***(G-6828)***
Cetek Inc (PA) 845 452-3510
19 Commerce St Poughkeepsie (12603) ***(G-13911)***
Cettel Studio of New York Inc 518 494-3622
636 Atateka Dr Chestertown (12817) ***(G-3649)***
Cfe, Brooklyn *Also called Carts Mobile Food Eqp Corp* ***(G-1763)***
Cffco USA Inc 718 747-1118
55 Jericho Tpke Ste 302 Jericho (11753) ***(G-7095)***
CFI, Perry *Also called Creative Food Ingredients Inc* ***(G-13545)***
Cfo Publishing LLC (PA) 212 459-3004
50 Broad St Frnt New York (10004) ***(G-9623)***
Cfp Purchasing Inc 705 806-0383
4760 197th St Flushing (11358) ***(G-5238)***
CFS Enterprises Inc 718 585-0500
650 E 132nd St Bronx (10454) ***(G-1295)***
CFS Steel Company, Bronx *Also called CFS Enterprises Inc* ***(G-1295)***
Cgi Technologies Solutions Inc 212 682-7411
655 3rd Ave Ste 700 New York (10017) ***(G-9624)***
Cgm, Brocton *Also called Carbon Graphite Materials Inc* ***(G-1248)***
Cgs Fabrication LLC 585 347-6127
855 Publishers Pkwy Webster (14580) ***(G-16740)***
Cgsi Group LLC 516 986-5503
3835 Sedgwick Ave Bronx (10463) ***(G-1296)***
Cgw Corp (PA) 631 472-6600
102 S Gillette Ave Bayport (11705) ***(G-750)***
Chabot Jewelry, Brooklyn *Also called E Chabot Ltd* ***(G-1891)***
Chad Pierson 518 251-0186
Chad Pierson Bakers Mills (12811) ***(G-556)***
Chad Pierson Logging & Trckg, Bakers Mills *Also called Chad Pierson* ***(G-556)***
Chadwicks Town Park, New Hartford *Also called Hartford Hwy Dept* ***(G-8851)***
Chain Store Age Magazine 212 756-5000
425 Park Ave New York (10022) ***(G-9625)***
Chain Stores Age, New York *Also called Lebhar-Friedman Inc* ***(G-10986)***
Chaindom Enterprises Inc 212 719-4778
48 W 48th St Ste 200 New York (10036) ***(G-9626)***
Chair Factory 718 363-2383
1355 Atlantic Ave Brooklyn (11216) ***(G-1771)***
Chakra Communications Inc 607 748-7491
32 Washington Ave Endicott (13760) ***(G-4806)***
Chakra Communications Inc 716 505-7300
80 W Drullard Ave Lancaster (14086) ***(G-7333)***
Challenge Graphics Svcs Inc (PA) 631 586-0171
22 Connor Ln Deer Park (11729) ***(G-4138)***
Chamart Exclusives Inc 914 345-3870
68 Williams St Elmsford (10523) ***(G-4749)***
Chamberlin Rubber Company Inc 585 427-7780
3333 Brighton Henrietta Rochester (14623) ***(G-14291)***
Chambord LLC 718 859-1110
4302 Farragut Rd Brooklyn (11203) ***(G-1772)***
Chameleon Color Cards Ltd 716 625-9452
6530 S Transit Rd Lockport (14094) ***(G-7604)***
Chameleon Gems Inc 516 829-3333
98 Cuttermill Rd Ste 398n Great Neck (11021) ***(G-5814)***
Champion Aluminum Corp 631 656-3424
250 Kennedy Dr Hauppauge (11788) ***(G-6062)***
Champion Cutting Tool Corp 516 536-8200
11-15 Saint Marks Ave Rockville Centre (11570) ***(G-14817)***
Champion Home Builders Inc 315 841-4122
951 Rte 12 S Sangerfield (13455) ***(G-15160)***
Champion Materials Inc (PA) 315 493-2654
502 S Washington St Carthage (13619) ***(G-3439)***
Champion Materials Inc 315 493-2654
21721 Cole Rd Carthage (13619) ***(G-3440)***
Champion Millwork Inc 315 463-0711
140 Hiawatha Pl Syracuse (13208) ***(G-15911)***
Champion Photochemistry Inc 585 760-6444
1669 Lake Ave Rochester (14615) ***(G-14292)***
Champion Window and Door, Hauppauge *Also called Champion Aluminum Corp* ***(G-6062)***
Champion Zipper Corp 212 239-0414
447 W 36th St Fl 2 New York (10018) ***(G-9627)***
Champlain Hanger, Rouses Point *Also called Champlain Plastics Inc* ***(G-15065)***
Champlain Hudson Power Ex Inc 518 465-0710
600 Broadway Fl 3 Albany (12207) ***(G-60)***
Champlain Plastics Inc 518 297-3700
87 Pillsbury Rd Rouses Point (12979) ***(G-15065)***
Champlain Valley Mil Corp Inc 518 962-4711
6679 Main St Westport (12993) ***(G-17096)***
Champs Sports, Hicksville *Also called Foot Locker Retail Inc* ***(G-6374)***
Chams, New York *Also called North American Mills Inc* ***(G-11473)***
Chamtek Mfg Inc 585 328-4900
123 Louise St Rochester (14606) ***(G-14293)***
Chan & Chan (usa) Corp 718 388-9633
2 Rewe St Brooklyn (11211) ***(G-1773)***
Chan Kee Dried Bean Curd Inc 718 622-0820
71 Steuben St Brooklyn (11205) ***(G-1774)***
Chan Luu LLC 212 398-3163
1441 Broadway New York (10018) ***(G-9628)***
Changes, Glendale *Also called Bowe Industries Inc* ***(G-5661)***
Channel Manufacturing Inc (PA) 516 944-6271
55 Channel Dr Port Washington (11050) ***(G-13827)***
Chanse Petroleum Corporation (PA) 212 682-3789
828 5th Ave Apt 1f New York (10065) ***(G-9629)***
Chapin International Inc 585 343-3140
700 Ellicott St Batavia (14020) ***(G-628)***
Chapin Manufacturing Inc (PA) 585 343-3140
700 Ellicott St Ste 3 Batavia (14020) ***(G-629)***
Chapman Skateboard Co Inc 631 321-4773
87 N Industry Ct Ste A Deer Park (11729) ***(G-4139)***
Chapman Stained Glass Studio 518 449-5552
212 Quail St Albany (12203) ***(G-61)***
Charing Cross Music Inc 212 541-7571
3 Columbus Cir Ste 1720 New York (10019) ***(G-9630)***
Charis & Mae Inc 212 641-0816
31 W 34th St Fl 8 New York (10001) ***(G-9631)***
Charl Industries Inc 631 234-0100
225 Engineers Rd Hauppauge (11788) ***(G-6063)***
Charles A Hones Inc 607 273-5720
222 S Albany St Ste 3 Ithaca (14850) ***(G-6870)***
Charles A Rogers Entps Inc 585 924-6400
51 Victor Heights Pkwy Victor (14564) ***(G-16490)***
Charles Freihofer Baking Co 518 463-2221
1 Prospect Rd Albany (12206) ***(G-62)***
Charles H Beckley Inc (PA) 718 665-2218
749 E 137th St Bronx (10454) ***(G-1297)***
Charles Henricks Inc 212 243-5800
121 Varick St Fl 9 New York (10013) ***(G-9632)***
Charles P Rogers Brass Beds (PA) 212 675-4400
26 W 17th St New York (10011) ***(G-9633)***
Charles P Rogers Brass Ir Bed, New York *Also called Charles P Rogers Brass Beds* ***(G-9633)***
Charles Perrella Inc 845 348-4777
78 S Broadway Nyack (10960) ***(G-13063)***
Charles Richter, Wallkill *Also called Richter Metalcraft Corporation* ***(G-16565)***
Charles Ross & Son Company (PA) 631 234-0500
710 Old Willets Path Hauppauge (11788) ***(G-6064)***
Charles V Weber Machine Shop 518 272-8033
2 Campbell Ave Troy (12180) ***(G-16251)***

ALPHABETIC

Charles Vaillant Inc....212 752-4832
37 W 57th St Ste 803 New York (10019) *(G-9634)*
Charlotte Neuville Design LLC....646 530-4570
882 3rd Ave Brooklyn (11232) *(G-1775)*
Charlton Precision Pdts Inc....845 338-2351
461 Sawkill Rd Kingston (12401) *(G-7212)*
Charm Mfg Co Inc....607 565-8161
251 State Route 17c Waverly (14892) *(G-16724)*
Charm Pools, Waverly *Also called Charm Mfg Co Inc (G-16724)*
Charming Fashion Inc....212 730-2872
247 W 38th St Rm 1400 New York (10018) *(G-9635)*
Chart Inc....518 272-3565
302 10th St Troy (12180) *(G-16252)*
Chart Industries Inc....716 691-0202
260 Creekside Dr Ste 100 Amherst (14228) *(G-234)*
Charter Ventures LLC....212 868-0222
135 W 36th St Rm 1800 New York (10018) *(G-9636)*
Chartwell Pharma Nda B2 Holdin....845 268-5000
77 Brenner Dr Congers (10920) *(G-3879)*
Chartwell Pharmaceuticals LLC....845 268-5000
77 Brenner Dr Congers (10920) *(G-3880)*
Chase Corporation....631 827-0476
7 Harbour Point Dr Northport (11768) *(G-13027)*
Chase Instrument Co, West Babylon *Also called Peyser Instrument Corporation (G-16848)*
Chase Media Group....914 962-3871
1520 Front St Yorktown Heights (10598) *(G-17525)*
Chase Partners, Northport *Also called Chase Corporation (G-13027)*
Chase Press, Yorktown Heights *Also called Shop Smart Central Inc (G-17535)*
Chateau La Fayette Reneau, Hector *Also called Lafayette Chateau (G-6283)*
Chatham Courier, The, Hudson *Also called Johnson Acquisition Corp (G-6652)*
Chautauqua Circuits Inc....716 366-5771
855 Main St Dunkirk (14048) *(G-4359)*
Chautauqua Iron Works, Mayville *Also called Kleinfelder John (G-8247)*
Chautauqua Machine Spc LLC....716 782-3276
1880 Open Meadows Rd Ashville (14710) *(G-424)*
Chautauqua Sign Co Inc....716 665-2222
2164 Allen Street Ext Falconer (14733) *(G-4900)*
Chautauqua Wine Company Inc....716 934-9463
2627 Chapin Rd Silver Creek (14136) *(G-15469)*
Chautauqua Woods Corp....716 366-3808
134 Franklin Ave Dunkirk (14048) *(G-4360)*
Chautqua Prcsion Machining Inc....716 763-3752
1287 Hunt Rd Ashville (14710) *(G-425)*
Check Group LLC....212 221-4700
1385 Broadway Fl 16 New York (10018) *(G-9637)*
Check-Mate Industries Inc....631 491-1777
370 Wyandanch Ave West Babylon (11704) *(G-16807)*
Check-O-Matic Inc....845 781-7675
13 D A Weider Blvd # 101 Monroe (10950) *(G-8587)*
Checklist Boards Corporation....585 586-0152
763 Linden Ave Ste 2 Rochester (14625) *(G-14294)*
Checkm8 Inc (PA)....212 268-0048
307 W 36th St Fl 13 New York (10018) *(G-9638)*
Cheese Experts USA Ltd Lblty....908 275-3889
14 Notus Ave Staten Island (10312) *(G-15678)*
Chefs Delight Packing Co....718 388-8581
94 N 8th St Brooklyn (11249) *(G-1776)*
Chelsea Plastics Inc....212 924-4530
200 Lexington Ave Rm 914 New York (10016) *(G-9639)*
Chem-Puter Friendly Inc....631 331-2259
1 Sevilla Walk Mount Sinai (11766) *(G-8696)*
Chem-Tainer Industries Inc (PA)....631 422-8300
361 Neptune Ave West Babylon (11704) *(G-16808)*
Chem-Tek Systems Inc....631 253-3010
208 S Fehr Way Bay Shore (11706) *(G-681)*
Chemark International USA Inc....631 593-4566
729 Acorn St Deer Park (11729) *(G-4140)*
Chembio Diagnostic Systems Inc....631 924-1135
3661 Horseblock Rd Ste A Medford (11763) *(G-8269)*
Chembio Diagnostics Inc (PA)....631 924-1135
3661 Horseblock Rd Ste C Medford (11763) *(G-8270)*
Chemclean Corporation....718 525-4500
13045 180th St Jamaica (11434) *(G-6937)*
Chemicolloid Laboratories Inc....516 747-2666
55 Herricks Rd New Hyde Park (11040) *(G-8866)*
Chemistry Department, Oswego *Also called Energy Nuclear Operations (G-13356)*
Chemite Inc....607 529-3218
407 County Road 60 Waverly (14892) *(G-16725)*
Chemlube International LLC (PA)....914 381-5800
500 Mmaroneck Ave Ste 306 Harrison (10528) *(G-6000)*
Chemlube Marketing Inc....914 381-5800
500 Mamaroneck Ave Harrison (10528) *(G-6001)*
Chemours Company Fc LLC....716 278-5100
3181 Buffalo Ave Niagara Falls (14303) *(G-12826)*
Chemprene Inc....845 831-2800
483 Fishkill Ave Beacon (12508) *(G-777)*
Chemprene Holding Inc....845 831-2800
483 Fishkill Ave Beacon (12508) *(G-778)*
Chemtrade Chemicals US LLC....315 430-7650
1421 Willis Ave Syracuse (13204) *(G-15912)*
Chemtrade Chemicals US LLC....315 478-2323
344 W Genesee St Ste 100 Syracuse (13202) *(G-15913)*
Chemung Cnty Chpter Nysarc Inc (HQ)....607 734-6151
711 Sullivan St Elmira (14901) *(G-4688)*
Chenango Asphalt Products....607 334-3117
23 State St Norwich (13815) *(G-13038)*
Chenango Concrete Corp....607 334-2545
County Rd 32 E River Rd Norwich (13815) *(G-13039)*
Chenango Concrete Corp (PA)....518 294-9964
145 Podpadic Rd Richmondville (12149) *(G-14101)*
Chenango Union Printing Inc....607 334-2112
15 American Ave Norwich (13815) *(G-13040)*
Chenango Valley Tech Inc....607 674-4115
328 Route 12b Sherburne (13460) *(G-15411)*
Chentronics Corporation....607 334-5531
115 County Rd 45 Norwich (13815) *(G-13041)*
Chepaume Industries LLC....315 829-6400
6201 Cooper St Vernon (13476) *(G-16456)*
Chequedcom Inc....888 412-0699
513 Broadway Ste 1 Saratoga Springs (12866) *(G-15177)*
Cheri Mon Baby LLC....212 354-5511
1412 Broadway Rm 1608 New York (10018) *(G-9640)*
Cheribundi Inc (PA)....800 699-0460
500 Technology Farm Dr Geneva (14456) *(G-5585)*
Cherry Creek Woodcraft Inc (PA)....716 988-3211
1 Cherry St South Dayton (14138) *(G-15540)*
Cherry Holding Ltd....516 679-3748
1536 Broad St North Bellmore (11710) *(G-12933)*
Cherry Lane Lithographing Corp....516 293-9294
15 E Bethpage Rd Unit A Plainview (11803) *(G-13617)*
Cherry Lane Magazine LLC....212 561-3000
1745 Broadway 19 New York (10019) *(G-9641)*
Cherry Metal Works, North Bellmore *Also called Cherry Holding Ltd (G-12933)*
Chesky Records Inc....212 586-7799
1650 Broadway Ste 900 New York (10019) *(G-9642)*
Chester Printing Service, Middletown *Also called Triad Printing Inc (G-8501)*
Chester Shred-It/West....914 407-2502
420 Columbus Ave Ste 100 Valhalla (10595) *(G-16391)*
Chester West County Press....914 684-0006
29 W 4th St Mount Vernon (10550) *(G-8716)*
Chester-Jensen Company....610 876-6276
124 S Main St Cattaraugus (14719) *(G-3465)*
Chesu Inc....239 564-2803
81 Newtown Ln East Hampton (11937) *(G-4427)*
Chet Kruszka's Svce, Orchard Park *Also called Chet Kruszkas Service Inc (G-13284)*
Chet Kruszkas Service Inc....716 662-7450
3536 Southwestern Blvd Orchard Park (14127) *(G-13284)*
Chia Company, New York *Also called Chia Usa LLC (G-9643)*
Chia Usa LLC....212 226-7512
379 W Broadway New York (10012) *(G-9643)*
Chicago Watermark Company, New York *Also called Donald Bruhnke (G-9949)*
Chicone Builders LLC....607 535-6540
302 W South St Montour Falls (14865) *(G-8648)*
Chief, The, New York *Also called New York Cvl Srvc Emplys Pblsh (G-11418)*
Child Nutrition Prog Dept Ed....212 371-1000
1011 1st Ave Fl 6 New York (10022) *(G-9644)*
Child's Work-Child's Play, Melville *Also called Guidance Group Inc (G-8354)*
Childrens Progress Inc....212 730-0905
108 W 39th St Rm 1305 New York (10018) *(G-9645)*
Chim-Cap Corp....800 262-9622
120 Schmitt Blvd Farmingdale (11735) *(G-4968)*
Chimney Doctors Americas Corp....631 868-3586
738a Montauk Hwy Bayport (11705) *(G-751)*
China Daily Distribution Corp (HQ)....212 537-8888
1500 Broadway Ste 2800 New York (10036) *(G-9646)*
China Huaren Organic Pdts Inc....212 232-0120
100 Wall St Fl 15 New York (10005) *(G-9647)*
China Imprint LLC....585 563-3391
750 Saint Paul St Rochester (14605) *(G-14295)*
China Industrial Steel Inc....646 328-1502
110 Wall St Fl 11 New York (10005) *(G-9648)*
China Lithium Technologies (PA)....212 391-2688
15 W 39th St Fl 14 New York (10018) *(G-9649)*
China N E Petro Holdings Ltd....212 307-3568
445 Park Ave New York (10022) *(G-9650)*
China Newsweek Corporation....212 481-2510
15 E 40th St Fl 11 New York (10016) *(G-9651)*
China Press....212 683-8282
15 E 40th St Fl 6 New York (10016) *(G-9652)*
China Ruitai Intl Holdings Ltd....718 740-2278
8710 Clover Pl Hollis (11423) *(G-6521)*
China Ting Fashion Group (usa)....212 716-1600
525 7th Ave Rm 1606 New York (10018) *(G-9653)*
China Xd Plastics Company Ltd....212 747-1118
500 5th Ave Ste 960 New York (10110) *(G-9654)*
Chinese Medical Report Inc....718 359-5676
3907 Prince St Ste 5b Flushing (11354) *(G-5239)*
Chip It All Ltd....631 473-2040
366 Sheep Pasture Rd Port Jefferson (11777) *(G-13797)*
Chipita America Inc....845 292-2540
1243 Old Route 17 Ferndale (12734) *(G-5176)*
Chiplogic Inc....631 617-6317
14a Old Dock Rd Yaphank (11980) *(G-17404)*
CHIPTEK, Arcade *Also called Gowanda - Bti LLC (G-394)*

Chivvis Enterprises Inc....631 842-9055
10 Grant St Copiague (11726) *(G-3923)*
Chloe International Inc....212 730-6661
525 Fashion Ave Rm 1601 New York (10018) *(G-9655)*
Chlor Alkali Products & Vinyls, Niagara Falls *Also called Olin Chlor Alkali Logistics (G-12875)*
Chobani LLC (HQ)....607 337-1246
147 State Highway 320 Norwich (13815) *(G-13042)*
Chobani LLC....607 847-6181
669 County Road 25 New Berlin (13411) *(G-8826)*
Chobani Idaho LLC....208 432-2248
147 State Highway 320 Norwich (13815) *(G-13043)*
Chocnyc LLC....917 804-4848
4996 Broadway New York (10034) *(G-9656)*
Choco-Logo, Buffalo *Also called Dilese International Inc (G-2931)*
Chocolat Moderne LLC....212 229-4797
27 W 20th St Ste 904 New York (10011) *(G-9657)*
Chocolate By Design Inc....631 737-0082
660 Sycamore Ave Bohemia (11716) *(G-1029)*
Chocolate Delivery Systems, Buffalo *Also called N Make Mold Inc (G-3101)*
Chocolate Delivery Systems Inc (PA)....716 854-6050
85 River Rock Dr Ste 202 Buffalo (14207) *(G-2892)*
Chocolate Pizza Company Inc....315 673-4098
3774 Lee Mulroy Rd Marcellus (13108) *(G-8118)*
Chocolatier Magazine, New York *Also called Haymarket Group Ltd (G-10474)*
Chocolations LLC....914 777-3600
607 E Boston Post Rd Mamaroneck (10543) *(G-8060)*
Chocomaker Inc....716 877-3146
85 River Rock Dr Ste 202 Buffalo (14207) *(G-2893)*
Chocovision Corporation....845 473-4970
14 Catharine St Poughkeepsie (12601) *(G-13912)*
Chohehco LLC....315 420-4624
78 State St Skaneateles (13152) *(G-15478)*
Choice Magazine Listening Inc....516 883-8280
85 Channel Dr Ste 3 Port Washington (11050) *(G-13828)*
Chomerics Div, Fairport *Also called Parker-Hannifin Corporation (G-4874)*
Choppy V M & Sons LLC....518 266-1444
4 Van Buren St Troy (12180) *(G-16253)*
Chopt Creative Salad Co LLC (PA)....646 233-2923
853 Broadway Ste 606 New York (10003) *(G-9658)*
Christi Plastics Inc....585 436-8510
215 Tremont St Rochester (14608) *(G-14296)*
Christian Book Publishing....646 559-2533
213 Bennett Ave New York (10040) *(G-9659)*
Christian Bus Endeavors Inc (PA)....315 788-8560
210 Court St Ste 10 Watertown (13601) *(G-16665)*
Christian Casey LLC (PA)....212 500-2200
1440 Broadway Frnt 3 New York (10018) *(G-9660)*
Christian Casey LLC....212 500-2200
1440 Broadway Frnt 3 New York (10018) *(G-9661)*
Christian Dior Perfumes LLC (HQ)....212 931-2200
19 E 57th St New York (10022) *(G-9662)*
Christian Fabrication LLC....315 822-0135
122 South St West Winfield (13491) *(G-16986)*
Christian Press Inc....718 886-4400
14317 Franklin Ave Flushing (11355) *(G-5240)*
Christian Siriano Holdings LLC....212 695-5494
260 W 35th St Ste 403 New York (10001) *(G-9663)*
Christiana Millwork Inc (PA)....315 492-9099
4755 Jamesville Rd Jamesville (13078) *(G-7079)*
Christina Sales Inc....212 391-0710
1441 Broadway New York (10018) *(G-9664)*
Christiny, Wantagh *Also called Christopher Anthony Pubg Co (G-16577)*
Christo-Vac, Cornwall *Also called Costume Armour Inc (G-4008)*
Christophe Danhier, New York *Also called Danhier Co LLC (G-9856)*
Christopher Anthony Pubg Co....516 826-9205
2225 Wantagh Ave Wantagh (11793) *(G-16577)*
Christopher Designs Inc....212 382-1013
50 W 47th St Fl 1507 New York (10036) *(G-9665)*
Christos Inc....212 921-0025
318 W 39th St Fl 12 New York (10018) *(G-9666)*
Chroma Communications Inc....631 289-8871
2030 Route 112 Medford (11763) *(G-8271)*
Chroma Logic....716 736-2458
6651 Wiley Rd Ripley (14775) *(G-14147)*
Chromagraphics Press Inc....631 367-6160
3 Martha Dr Melville (11747) *(G-8332)*
Chromalloy American LLC (HQ)....845 230-7355
330 Blaisdell Rd Orangeburg (10962) *(G-13244)*
Chromalloy Gas Turbine LLC....845 359-2462
330 Blaisdell Rd Orangeburg (10962) *(G-13245)*
Chromalloy Gas Turbine LLC....845 692-8912
105 Tower Dr Middletown (10941) *(G-8464)*
Chromalloy Middletown, Middletown *Also called Chromalloy Gas Turbine LLC (G-8464)*
Chromalloy New York, Orangeburg *Also called Chromalloy Gas Turbine LLC (G-13245)*
Chromananotech LLC....607 239-9626
85 Murray Hill Rd Vestal (13850) *(G-16467)*
Chromosense LLC....347 770-5421
1 Metrotech Ctr Fl 19 Brooklyn (11201) *(G-1777)*
Chronicle....347 969-7281
3468 Wilson Ave Apt 2b Bronx (10469) *(G-1298)*
Chronicle Express....315 536-4422
138 Main St Penn Yan (14527) *(G-13531)*
Chronicle, The, Glens Falls *Also called Oak Lone Publishing Co Inc (G-5708)*
Chudnow Manufacturing Co Inc....516 593-4222
3055 New St Oceanside (11572) *(G-13094)*
Chula Girls, New York *Also called Detour Apparel Inc (G-9914)*
Church & Dwight Co Inc....518 887-5109
706 Ennis Rd Schenectady (12306) *(G-15270)*
Church Bulletin Inc....631 249-4994
200 Dale St West Babylon (11704) *(G-16809)*
Church Communities NY Inc....518 589-5103
2255 Platte Clove Rd Elka Park (12427) *(G-4643)*
Church Communities NY Inc....518 589-5103
Platte Clove Rd Elka Park (12427) *(G-4644)*
Church Publishing Incorporated (HQ)....212 592-1800
445 5th Ave Frnt 1 New York (10016) *(G-9667)*
CHv Printed Company....516 997-1101
1905 Hempstead Tpke B East Meadow (11554) *(G-4439)*
Chyronhego Corporation (HQ)....631 845-2000
5 Hub Dr Melville (11747) *(G-8333)*
Cibao Meat Products Inc....718 993-5072
630 Saint Anns Ave Bronx (10455) *(G-1299)*
CIC International Ltd....212 213-0089
1118 42nd St Brooklyn (11219) *(G-1778)*
Ciccarelli Custom Taylor, Long Island City *Also called Primo Coat Corp (G-7877)*
Cid Technologies, Liverpool *Also called Thermo Cidtec Inc (G-7580)*
CIDC Corp....718 342-5820
2015 Pitkin Ave Brooklyn (11207) *(G-1779)*
Cidega American Trim, Durham *Also called Advanced Yarn Technologies Inc (G-4378)*
Cierra Industries Inc....315 252-6630
491 Grant Avenue Rd Auburn (13021) *(G-487)*
Cigar Box Studios Inc....845 236-9283
24 Riverview Dr Marlboro (12542) *(G-8135)*
Cigar Oasis Inc....516 520-5258
79 Heisser Ct Farmingdale (11735) *(G-4969)*
Cilyox Inc....716 853-3809
345 Broadway St Buffalo (14204) *(G-2894)*
Ciment St-Laurent Inc....518 943-4040
6446 Route 9w Catskill (12414) *(G-3454)*
Cimline Inc....518 880-4073
21 Railroad Ave Albany (12205) *(G-63)*
Cinch Technologies Inc....212 266-0022
7 World Trade Ctr New York (10007) *(G-9668)*
Cinderella Press Ltd....212 431-3130
327 Canal St 3 New York (10013) *(G-9669)*
Cinderellas Sweets Ltd....516 374-7976
874 Lakeside Dr Woodmere (11598) *(G-17330)*
Cine Design Group LLC....646 747-0734
15 Park Row Lbby L New York (10038) *(G-9670)*
Cinedeck, New York *Also called Cine Design Group LLC (G-9670)*
Cinedigm Software....212 206-9001
45 W 36th St Fl 7 New York (10018) *(G-9671)*
Ciner Manufacturing Co Inc....212 947-3770
20 W 37th St Fl 10 New York (10018) *(G-9672)*
Cintube Ltd....518 324-3333
139 Distribution Way Plattsburgh (12901) *(G-13687)*
Circle 5 Deli Corp....718 525-5687
13440 Guy R Brewer Blvd Jamaica (11434) *(G-6938)*
Circle Peak Capital MGT LLC (PA)....646 230-8812
1325 Ave Of The Americas New York (10019) *(G-9673)*
Circle Press Inc (PA)....212 924-4277
121 Varick St Fl 7 New York (10013) *(G-9674)*
Circo File Corp....516 922-1848
69 Hamilton Ave Ste 1 Oyster Bay (11771) *(G-13393)*
Circo-O-File, Oyster Bay *Also called Circo File Corp (G-13393)*
Circor Aerospace Inc....631 737-1900
425 Rabro Dr Ste 1 Hauppauge (11788) *(G-6065)*
Circuits & Systems Inc....516 593-4301
59 2nd St East Rockaway (11518) *(G-4488)*
Circulation Dept, New York *Also called Lebhar-Friedman Inc (G-10987)*
Cirrus Healthcare Products LLC (PA)....631 692-7600
60 Main St Cold Spring Harbor (11724) *(G-3792)*
Cisco Systems Inc....212 714-4000
1 Penn Plz Ste 3306 New York (10119) *(G-9675)*
Citation Manufacturing Co Inc....845 425-6868
42 Harmony Rd Spring Valley (10977) *(G-15602)*
Citiforms Inc....212 334-9671
134 W 29th St Rm 704 New York (10001) *(G-9676)*
Citigroup Inc....212 816-6000
388 Greenwich St New York (10013) *(G-9677)*
Citisource Industries Inc....212 683-1033
244 5th Ave Ste 229 New York (10001) *(G-9678)*
Citixsys Technologies Inc....212 745-1365
1 Rockefeller Plz Fl 11 New York (10020) *(G-9679)*
Citizen, The, Auburn *Also called Auburn Publishing Co (G-479)*
Citizen Publishing Corp....845 627-1414
119 Main St Ste 2 Nanuet (10954) *(G-8800)*
Citros Building Materials Co....718 779-0727
10514 Astoria Blvd East Elmhurst (11369) *(G-4412)*
Citrus and Allied Essences, Floral Park *Also called C & A Service Inc (G-5205)*
Citrus and Allied Essences Ltd (PA)....516 354-1200
65 S Tyson Ave Floral Park (11001) *(G-5207)*

ALPHABETIC

(PA)=Parent Co (HQ)=Headquarters (DH)=Div Headquarters
2018 Harris
New York Manufacturers Directory
919

City and State Ny LLC 212 268-0442
61 Broadway Rm 1315 New York (10006) ***(G-9680)***
City Bakery Inc (PA) 212 366-1414
3 W 18th St Frnt 1 New York (10011) ***(G-9681)***
City Baking LLC 718 392-8514
1041 45th Ave Long Island City (11101) ***(G-7726)***
City Casting Corp 212 938-0511
151 W 46th St Fl 5 New York (10036) ***(G-9682)***
City Cooling Enterprises Inc 718 331-7400
1624 61st St Brooklyn (11204) ***(G-1780)***
City Evolutionary 718 861-7585
336 Barretto St Bronx (10474) ***(G-1300)***
City Fashion, The, Brooklyn *Also called Amj DOT LLC* ***(G-1610)***
City Gear Inc 914 450-4746
213 Taxter Rd Irvington (10533) ***(G-6809)***
City Hats, New York *Also called Beila Group Inc* ***(G-9395)***
City Jeans Inc 718 239-5353
845 White Plins Rd Frnt 1 Bronx (10473) ***(G-1301)***
City Mason Corp 718 658-3796
10417 148th St Jamaica (11435) ***(G-6939)***
City Newspaper 585 244-3329
250 N Goodman St Ste 1 Rochester (14607) ***(G-14297)***
City of Kingston 845 331-2490
91 E Strand St Kingston (12401) ***(G-7213)***
City of New York 718 965-8787
4014 1st Ave Fl 3 Brooklyn (11232) ***(G-1781)***
City of New York 718 236-2693
5602 19th Ave Brooklyn (11204) ***(G-1782)***
City of Olean 716 376-5694
174 S 19th St Olean (14760) ***(G-13158)***
City of Oneonta 607 433-3470
110 East St Oneonta (13820) ***(G-13200)***
City Pattern Shop Inc 315 463-5239
4052 New Court Ave Syracuse (13206) ***(G-15914)***
City Post Express Inc 718 995-8690
17518 147th Ave Jamaica (11434) ***(G-6940)***
City Real Estate Book Inc 516 593-2949
9831 S Franklin Ave Valley Stream (11580) ***(G-16428)***
City Signs Inc 718 375-5933
1940 Mcdonald Ave Brooklyn (11223) ***(G-1783)***
City Sites Sportswear Inc (PA) 718 375-2990
2421 Mcdonald Ave Brooklyn (11223) ***(G-1784)***
City Sports Inc 212 730-2009
64 W 48th St Frnt B New York (10036) ***(G-9683)***
City Sports Imaging Inc 212 481-3600
20 E 46th St Rm 200 New York (10017) ***(G-9684)***
City Store Gates Mfg Corp 718 939-9700
1520 129th St College Point (11356) ***(G-3806)***
City Winery Napa LLC 212 633-4399
155 Varick St New York (10013) ***(G-9685)***
Cityscape Ob/Gyn PLLC 212 683-3595
38 E 32nd St Fl 4 New York (10016) ***(G-9686)***
Cives Corporation 315 287-2200
8 Church St Gouverneur (13642) ***(G-5758)***
Cives Corporation 315 543-2321
14331 Mill St Harrisville (13648) ***(G-6014)***
Cives Steel Company Nthrn Div, Gouverneur *Also called Cives Corporation* ***(G-5758)***
Civil Svc Rtred Employees Assn 718 937-0290
3427 Steinway St Ste 1 Long Island City (11101) ***(G-7727)***
CJ Component Products LLC 631 567-3733
624 Tower Mews Oakdale (11769) ***(G-13074)***
CJ Indstries A Div Smrset Inds, Gloversville *Also called Somerset Industries Inc* ***(G-5737)***
CJ Jewelry Inc 212 719-2464
2 W 47th St Ste 1106 New York (10036) ***(G-9687)***
CJ Motor Sports, Boonville *Also called C J Logging Equipment Inc* ***(G-1163)***
Cjk Manufacturing LLC 585 663-6370
160 Commerce Dr Rochester (14623) ***(G-14298)***
Cjn Machinery Corp 631 244-8030
917 Lincoln Ave Ste 13 Holbrook (11741) ***(G-6465)***
CK Coatings 585 502-0425
57 North St Ste 150 Le Roy (14482) ***(G-7429)***
Clad Industries LLC 585 413-4359
1704 Wayneport Rd Ste 1 Macedon (14502) ***(G-8014)***
Clad Metal Specialties Inc 631 666-7750
1516 5th Industrial Ct Bay Shore (11706) ***(G-682)***
Claddagh Electronics Ltd 718 784-0571
1032 47th Rd Long Island City (11101) ***(G-7728)***
Clapper Hollow Designs Inc 518 234-9561
369 N Grand St Cobleskill (12043) ***(G-3759)***
Clara Papa 315 733-2660
1323 Blandina St 1 Utica (13501) ***(G-16334)***
Clarence Resins and Chemicals 716 406-9804
9585 Keller Rd Clarence Center (14032) ***(G-3699)***
Clarion Publications Inc 585 243-3530
38 Main St Geneseo (14454) ***(G-5579)***
Clarityad Inc 646 397-4198
833 Broadway Apt 2 New York (10003) ***(G-9688)***
Clark Botanicals Inc 914 826-4319
9 Paradise Rd Bronxville (10708) ***(G-1500)***
Clark Concrete Co Inc (PA) 315 478-4101
434 E Brighton Ave Syracuse (13210) ***(G-15915)***
Clark Laboratories Inc (HQ) 716 483-3851
2823 Girts Rd Jamestown (14701) ***(G-7014)***
Clark Rigging & Rental Corp 585 265-2910
680 Basket Rd Webster (14580) ***(G-16741)***
Clark Specialty Co Inc 607 776-3193
7185 State Route 54 Bath (14810) ***(G-655)***
Clark Trucking Co Div, Syracuse *Also called Clark Concrete Co Inc* ***(G-15915)***
Clarke Hess Communication RES 631 698-3350
3243 Route 112 Ste 1 Medford (11763) ***(G-8272)***
Clarke-Boxit Corporation 716 487-1950
45 Norwood Ave Jamestown (14701) ***(G-7015)***
Clarkson N Potter Inc 212 782-9000
1745 Broadway New York (10019) ***(G-9689)***
Clarsons Corp 585 235-8775
215 Tremont St Ste 8 Rochester (14608) ***(G-14299)***
Classic & Performance Spc 716 759-1800
80 Rotech Dr Lancaster (14086) ***(G-7334)***
Classic Album 718 388-2818
343 Lorimer St Brooklyn (11206) ***(G-1785)***
Classic Album LLC 718 388-2818
343 Lorimer St Brooklyn (11206) ***(G-1786)***
Classic Auto Crafts Inc 518 966-8003
6501 State Route 32 Greenville (12083) ***(G-5902)***
Classic Automation LLC (PA) 585 241-6010
800 Salt Rd Webster (14580) ***(G-16742)***
Classic Awnings Inc 716 649-0390
1 Elmview Ave Hamburg (14075) ***(G-5943)***
Classic Awnings & Party Tents, Hamburg *Also called Classic Awnings Inc* ***(G-5943)***
Classic Brass Inc 716 763-1400
2051 Stoneman Cir Lakewood (14750) ***(G-7312)***
Classic Cabinets 845 357-4331
375 Spook Rock Rd Suffern (10901) ***(G-15809)***
Classic Collections Fine Art 914 591-4500
20 Haarlem Ave Ste 408 White Plains (10603) ***(G-17121)***
Classic Color Graphics Inc (PA) 516 822-9090
268 N Broadway Unit 8 Hicksville (11801) ***(G-6354)***
Classic Color Graphics Inc 516 822-9090
87 Broadway Hicksville (11801) ***(G-6355)***
Classic Concrete Corp 516 822-1800
29a Midland Ave Hicksville (11801) ***(G-6356)***
Classic Cooking LLC 718 439-0200
16535 145th Dr Jamaica (11434) ***(G-6941)***
Classic Creations Inc 516 498-1991
1 Linden Pl Ste 409 Great Neck (11021) ***(G-5815)***
Classic Designer Workshop Inc 212 730-8480
265 W 37th St Rm 703 New York (10018) ***(G-9690)***
Classic Flavors Fragrances Inc 212 777-0004
878 W End Ave Apt 12b New York (10025) ***(G-9691)***
Classic Hosiery Inc 845 342-6661
33 Mulberry St Ste 4 Middletown (10940) ***(G-8465)***
Classic Labels Inc 631 467-2300
217 River Ave Patchogue (11772) ***(G-13442)***
Classic Medallics Inc 718 392-5410
520 S Fulton Ave Mount Vernon (10550) ***(G-8717)***
Classic Sofa Ltd 212 620-0485
130 E 63rd St Ph B New York (10065) ***(G-9692)***
Classic Tool Design Inc 845 562-8700
31 Walnut St New Windsor (12553) ***(G-8981)***
Classic Tube, Lancaster *Also called Classic & Performance Spc* ***(G-7334)***
Classified Advertising, Troy *Also called Want-Ad Digest Inc* ***(G-16287)***
Classpass Inc (PA) 888 493-5953
275 7th Ave Fl 11 New York (10001) ***(G-9693)***
Classroom Inc 212 545-8400
245 5th Ave Fl 20 New York (10016) ***(G-9694)***
Claude Tribastone Inc 585 265-3776
6367 Dean Pkwy Ontario (14519) ***(G-13219)***
Clayton Dubilier & Rice Fun (PA) 212 407-5200
375 Park Ave Fl 18 New York (10152) ***(G-9695)***
Clayville Ice Co Inc 315 839-5405
2514 Foundry Pl Clayville (13322) ***(G-3713)***
Clean All of Syracuse LLC 315 472-9189
838 Erie Blvd W Syracuse (13204) ***(G-15916)***
Clean Gas Systems Inc 631 467-1600
380 Townline Rd Ste 120 Hauppauge (11788) ***(G-6066)***
Clean Room Depot Inc 631 589-3033
1730 Church St Holbrook (11741) ***(G-6466)***
Cleaning Tech Group LLC 716 665-2340
9 N Main St Jamestown (14701) ***(G-7016)***
Cleanroom Systems Inc 315 452-7400
7000 Performance Dr North Syracuse (13212) ***(G-12957)***
Cleanse TEC 718 346-9111
1000 Linwood St Brooklyn (11208) ***(G-1787)***
Clear Cast Technologies Inc (PA) 914 945-0848
99 N Water St Ossining (10562) ***(G-13346)***
Clear Channel Outdoor Inc 212 812-0000
99 Park Ave Fl 2 New York (10016) ***(G-9696)***
Clear Edge Crosible Inc 315 685-3466
4653 Jordan Rd Skaneateles Falls (13153) ***(G-15489)***
Clear Edge Filtration, Skaneateles Falls *Also called Clear Edge Crosible Inc* ***(G-15489)***
Clear View Bag Company Inc 518 458-7153
5 Burdick Dr Albany (12205) ***(G-64)***
Clearcove Systems Inc 585 734-3012
7910 Rae Blvd Victor (14564) ***(G-16491)***
Clearlake Land Co Inc 315 848-2427
Hanks Rd Star Lake (13690) ***(G-15648)***

Clearstep Technologies LLC 315 952-3628
213 Emann Dr Camillus (13031) ***(G-3350)***
Clearview Glass & Mirror, Monroe *Also called G & M Clearview Inc* ***(G-8590)***
Clearview Social Inc 801 414-7675
77 Goodell St Ste 430 Buffalo (14203) ***(G-2895)***
Clearwater Paper Corporation 315 287-1200
4921 State Highway 58 Gouverneur (13642) ***(G-5759)***
Clearweld, Binghamton *Also called Crysta-Lyn Chemical Company* ***(G-901)***
Clearwood Custom Carpentry and 315 432-8422
617 W Manlius St Ste 1 East Syracuse (13057) ***(G-4533)***
Cleary Custom Cabinets Inc 516 939-2475
794 S Broadway Hicksville (11801) ***(G-6357)***
Clemente Latham Concrete, Latham *Also called Callanan Industries Inc* ***(G-7385)***
Clemente Latham Concrete Corp 518 374-2222
1245 Kings Rd Schenectady (12303) ***(G-15271)***
Clemente Latham North Div, Schenectady *Also called Clemente Latham Concrete Corp* ***(G-15271)***
Clements Burrville Sawmill 315 782-4549
18181 Van Allen Rd N Watertown (13601) ***(G-16666)***
Clerio Vision Inc 617 216-7881
312 Susquehanna Rd Rochester (14618) ***(G-14300)***
Cleveland Biolabs Inc 716 849-6810
73 High St Buffalo (14203) ***(G-2896)***
Cleveland Polymer Tech LLC (PA) 518 326-9146
125 Monroe St Bldg 125 Watervliet (12189) ***(G-16706)***
Clever Devices Ltd (PA) 516 433-6100
300 Crossways Park Dr Woodbury (11797) ***(G-17304)***
Clever Fellows I, Troy *Also called Chart Inc* ***(G-16252)***
Clever Goats Media LLC 917 512-0340
40 Exchange Pl Ste 1602 New York (10005) ***(G-9697)***
Click It Inc 631 686-2900
85 Corporate Dr Hauppauge (11788) ***(G-6067)***
Clifford H Jones Inc 716 693-2444
608 Young St Tonawanda (14150) ***(G-16174)***
Cliffstar LLC (HQ) 716 366-6100
1 Cliffstar Dr Dunkirk (14048) ***(G-4361)***
Climatronics Corp (HQ) 541 471-7111
606 Johnson Ave Ste 28 Bohemia (11716) ***(G-1030)***
Climax Packaging Inc 315 376-8000
7840 State Route 26 Lowville (13367) ***(G-7963)***
Climax Paperboard, Carthage *Also called Carthage Specialty Pprbd Inc* ***(G-3437)***
Clinique Laboratories LLC (HQ) 212 572-4200
767 5th Ave Fl 41 New York (10153) ***(G-9698)***
Clinique Laboratories, Inc., New York *Also called Clinique Laboratories LLC* ***(G-9698)***
Clinique Services Inc (HQ) 212 572-4200
767 5th Ave New York (10153) ***(G-9699)***
Clinton Clrs & EMB Shoppe Inc 315 853-8421
43 College St Clinton (13323) ***(G-3743)***
Clinton Creamery Inc 917 324-9699
13221 220th St Laurelton (11413) ***(G-7412)***
Clinton Signs Inc 585 482-1620
1407 Empire Blvd Webster (14580) ***(G-16743)***
Clinton Vineyards Inc 845 266-5372
450 Schultzville Rd Clinton Corners (12514) ***(G-3748)***
Clintons Ditch Coop Co Inc 315 699-2695
8478 Pardee Rd Cicero (13039) ***(G-3672)***
Clintrak Clinical Labeling S (PA) 888 479-3900
2800 Veterans Hwy Bohemia (11716) ***(G-1031)***
Clique Apparel Inc 516 375-7969
2034 Green Acres Mall Valley Stream (11581) ***(G-16429)***
Cliquer's, New York *Also called Colors Fashion Inc* ***(G-9733)***
Clo-Shure Intl Inc (PA) 212 268-5029
224 W 35th St Ste 1000 New York (10001) ***(G-9700)***
Clopay Ames True Tmper Hldng (HQ) 516 938-5544
100 Jericho Quadrangle # 224 Jericho (11753) ***(G-7096)***
Closet Systems Group, The, Brooklyn *Also called Designs By Robert Scott Inc* ***(G-1856)***
Cloud Printing 212 775-0888
66 W Broadway Frnt E New York (10007) ***(G-9701)***
Cloud Rock Group LLC 516 967-6023
525 Bryant Ave Roslyn (11576) ***(G-15041)***
Cloud Toronto Inc 408 569-4542
1967 Wehrle Dr Ste 1 Williamsville (14221) ***(G-17267)***
Cloudparc Inc 954 665-5962
122 W 27th St Fl 10 New York (10001) ***(G-9702)***
Cloudsense Inc 917 880-6195
1325 Avenue Of The Flr 28 New York (10019) ***(G-9703)***
Clover Wire Forming Co Inc 914 375-0400
1021 Saw Mill River Rd Yonkers (10710) ***(G-17444)***
Clovis Point, Queens Village *Also called East End Vineyards LLC* ***(G-13992)***
Clp Pb LLC (PA) 212 340-8100
1290 Ave Of The Amrcas New York (10104) ***(G-9704)***
Clpa Embroidery 516 409-0002
2635 Pettit Ave Bellmore (11710) ***(G-812)***
Club 1100 ....585 235-3478
1100 Jay St Rochester (14611) ***(G-14301)***
Club Protector Inc 716 652-4787
191 Buffalo Creek Rd Elma (14059) ***(G-4659)***
Clyde Duneier Inc (PA) 212 398-1122
415 Madison Ave Fl 6 New York (10017) ***(G-9705)***
Cmb Wireless Group LLC (PA) 631 750-4700
116 Wilbur Pl Bohemia (11716) ***(G-1032)***
Cmc-Kuhnke Inc 518 694-3310
1060 Brdwy Albany (12204) ***(G-65)***
Cmp Adaptive Equipment Supply, Deer Park *Also called Crosley Medical Products Inc* ***(G-4144)***
Cmp Advnced Mech Sltons NY LLC 607 352-1712
90 Bevier St Binghamton (13904) ***(G-898)***
Cmp Industries LLC (PA) 518 434-3147
413 N Pearl St Albany (12207) ***(G-66)***
Cmp Industries LLC 518 434-3147
413 N Pearl St Albany (12207) ***(G-67)***
Cmp Media, New York *Also called Ubm LLC* ***(G-12459)***
Cmp New York, Binghamton *Also called Cmp Advnced Mech Sltons NY LLC* ***(G-898)***
CMS Heat Transfer Division Inc 631 968-0084
273 Knickerbocker Ave Bohemia (11716) ***(G-1033)***
CMX Media LLC 917 793-5831
1271 Av Of The Americas New York (10020) ***(G-9706)***
CN Group Incorporated 914 358-5690
76 Mamaroneck Ave White Plains (10601) ***(G-17122)***
CNA Specialties Inc 631 567-7929
226 Mcneil St Sayville (11782) ***(G-15235)***
Cnc Manufacturing Corp 718 728-6800
3214 49th St Long Island City (11103) ***(G-7729)***
Cni Meat & Produce Inc 516 599-5929
500 W Merrick Rd Valley Stream (11580) ***(G-16430)***
Cntry Cross Communications LLC 386 758-9696
106 W 3rd St Ste 106 Jamestown (14701) ***(G-7017)***
Cnv Architectural Coatings Inc 718 418-9584
538 Johnson Ave Brooklyn (11237) ***(G-1788)***
CNY Business Review Inc 315 472-3104
269 W Jefferson St Syracuse (13202) ***(G-15917)***
CNy Business Solutions 315 733-5031
502 Court St Ste 206 Utica (13502) ***(G-16335)***
Co-Op City News, New Rochelle *Also called Hagedorn Communications Inc* ***(G-8951)***
Co-Optics America Lab Inc 607 432-0557
297 River Street Svc Rd Service Oneonta (13820) ***(G-13201)***
Co-Optics Groups, The, Oneonta *Also called Co-Optics America Lab Inc* ***(G-13201)***
Co2 Textiles LLC (PA) 212 269-2222
88 Greenwich St Apt 1507 New York (10006) ***(G-9707)***
Coach Inc 212 615-2082
515 W 33rd St New York (10001) ***(G-9708)***
Coach Inc 212 581-4115
10 Columbus Cir Ste 101a New York (10019) ***(G-9709)***
Coach Inc 718 760-0624
90 Queens Blvd Elmhurst (11373) ***(G-4672)***
Coach Inc 585 425-7720
7979 Pittsford Victor Rd Victor (14564) ***(G-16492)***
Coach Inc 212 245-4148
620 5th Ave Frnt 3 New York (10020) ***(G-9710)***
Coach Inc 212 473-6925
143 Prince St Frnt A New York (10012) ***(G-9711)***
Coach Inc 212 754-0041
595 Madison Ave Frnt 1 New York (10022) ***(G-9712)***
Coach Inc 212 675-6403
79 5th Ave Frnt 3 New York (10003) ***(G-9713)***
Coach Inc (PA) 212 594-1850
10 Hudson Yards New York (10001) ***(G-9714)***
Coach Inc 518 456-5657
120 Washington Avenue Ext # 57 Albany (12203) ***(G-68)***
Coach Leatherware Company, New York *Also called Coach Stores Inc* ***(G-9717)***
Coach Leatherware Intl 212 594-1850
516 W 34th St Bsmt 5 New York (10001) ***(G-9715)***
Coach Services Inc 212 594-1850
10 Hudson Yards New York (10001) ***(G-9716)***
Coach Stores Inc 212 643-9727
516 W 34th St Bsmt 5 New York (10001) ***(G-9717)***
Coalition On Positive Health 212 633-2500
1751 Park Ave Fl 4 New York (10035) ***(G-9718)***
Coast To Coast Circuits Inc 585 254-2980
205 Lagrange Ave Rochester (14613) ***(G-14302)***
Coastal Pipeline Products Corp 631 369-4000
55 Twomey Ave Calverton (11933) ***(G-3316)***
Coastal Publications Inc 631 725-1700
22 Division St Sag Harbor (11963) ***(G-15104)***
Coastel Cable Tools Inc 315 471-5361
344 E Brighton Ave Syracuse (13210) ***(G-15918)***
Coastel Cable Tools Intl, Syracuse *Also called Coastel Cable Tools Inc* ***(G-15918)***
Coated Abrasive Division, Watervliet *Also called Saint-Gobain Abrasives Inc* ***(G-16712)***
Coating Technology Inc 585 546-7170
800 Saint Paul St Rochester (14605) ***(G-14303)***
Cobbe Industries Inc 716 287-2661
1397 Harris Hollow Rd Gerry (14740) ***(G-5604)***
Cobblestone Bakery Corp 631 491-3777
39 Wyandanch Ave Wyandanch (11798) ***(G-17388)***
Cobblestone Frm Winery Vinyrd 315 549-1004
5102 State Route 89 Romulus (14541) ***(G-14869)***
Cobey Inc (PA) 716 362-9550
1 Ship Canal Pkwy Buffalo (14218) ***(G-2897)***
Cobham Holdings (us) Inc 716 662-0006
10 Cobham Dr Orchard Park (14127) ***(G-13285)***
Cobham Holdings Inc (HQ) 716 662-0006
10 Orchard Park Dr Orchard Park (14127) ***(G-13286)***

ALPHABETIC

Cobham Management Services Inc....716 662-0006
10 Cobham Dr Orchard Park (14127) ***(G-13287)***
Cobham Mission Systems Div, Orchard Park *Also called Cobham Management Services Inc* ***(G-13287)***
Cobleskill Concrete Ready Mix, Amsterdam *Also called Cobleskill Red E Mix & Supply* ***(G-340)***
Cobleskill Red E Mix & Supply (PA)....518 234-2015
774 State Highway 5s Amsterdam (12010) ***(G-340)***
Cobleskill Stone Products Inc....518 299-3066
395 Falke Rd Prattsville (12468) ***(G-13961)***
Cobleskill Stone Products Inc....518 295-7121
163 Eastern Ave Schoharie (12157) ***(G-15338)***
Cobleskill Stone Products Inc (PA)....518 234-0221
112 Rock Rd Cobleskill (12043) ***(G-3760)***
Cobleskill Stone Products Inc....607 432-8321
57 Ceperley Ave Oneonta (13820) ***(G-13202)***
Cobleskill Stone Products Inc....607 637-4271
1565 Green Flats Rd Hancock (13783) ***(G-5984)***
Cobra Manufacturing Corp....845 514-2505
68 Leggs Mills Rd Lake Katrine (12449) ***(G-7294)***
Cobra Operating Industries LLC....607 639-1700
37 Main St Afton (13730) ***(G-9)***
Cobra Systems Inc....845 338-6675
2669 New York 32 Bloomington (12411) ***(G-987)***
Coca-Cola, Horseheads *Also called Rochester Coca Cola Bottling* ***(G-6620)***
Coca-Cola, Rochester *Also called Rochester Coca Cola Bottling* ***(G-14660)***
Coca-Cola Bottling Co of NY....518 459-2010
38 Warehouse Row Albany (12205) ***(G-69)***
Coca-Cola Bottling Company....518 483-0422
15 Ida Pkwy Malone (12953) ***(G-8039)***
Coca-Cola Btlg Co Buffalo Inc....716 874-4610
200 Milens Rd Tonawanda (14150) ***(G-16175)***
Coca-Cola Btlg Co of NY Inc....845 562-3037
10 Heampstead Rd New Windsor (12553) ***(G-8982)***
Coca-Cola Btlg Co of NY Inc....718 326-3334
5902 Borden Ave Maspeth (11378) ***(G-8153)***
Coca-Cola Btlg Co of NY Inc....914 592-4574
111 Fairview Pk Dr Ste 1 Elmsford (10523) ***(G-4750)***
Coca-Cola Btlg Co of NY Inc....718 416-7575
5840 Borden Ave Maspeth (11378) ***(G-8154)***
Coca-Cola Btlg Co of NY Inc....315 457-9221
298 Farrell Rd Syracuse (13209) ***(G-15919)***
Coca-Cola Btlg Co of NY Inc....631 434-3535
375 Wireless Blvd Hauppauge (11788) ***(G-6068)***
Coca-Cola Btlg Co of NY Inc....718 420-6800
400 Western Ave Staten Island (10303) ***(G-15679)***
Coca-Cola Btlg Co of NY Inc....914 789-1580
115 Fairview Pk Dr Ste 1 Elmsford (10523) ***(G-4751)***
Coca-Cola Refreshments USA Inc....718 401-5200
977 E 149th St Bronx (10455) ***(G-1302)***
Coca-Cola Refreshments USA Inc....315 785-8907
22614 County Route 51 Watertown (13601) ***(G-16667)***
Coca-Cola Refreshments USA Inc....914 592-0806
3 Skyline Dr Hawthorne (10532) ***(G-6268)***
Coccadotts Inc....518 438-4937
1179 Central Ave Albany (12205) ***(G-70)***
Cochecton Mills Inc (PA)....845 932-8282
30 Depot Rd Cochecton (12726) ***(G-3765)***
Cockpit Usa Inc....212 575-1616
15 W 39th St Fl 12 New York (10018) ***(G-9719)***
Cockpit Usa Inc (PA)....212 575-1616
15 W 39th St Fl 12 New York (10018) ***(G-9720)***
Cockpit Usa Inc....908 558-9704
15 W 39th St Fl 12 New York (10018) ***(G-9721)***
Cockpit, The, New York *Also called Cockpit Usa Inc* ***(G-9720)***
Coco Architectureal Grilles....631 482-9449
173 Allen Blvd Farmingdale (11735) ***(G-4970)***
Coco Rico Southeast, Bronx *Also called Goodo Beverage Company* ***(G-1348)***
Coda Media Inc....917 478-2565
108 W 39th St Rm 1000 New York (10018) ***(G-9722)***
Coda Resources Ltd (PA)....718 649-1666
960 Alabama Ave Brooklyn (11207) ***(G-1789)***
Coda Story, New York *Also called Coda Media Inc* ***(G-9722)***
Codesters Inc....646 232-1025
900 Broadway Ste 903 New York (10003) ***(G-9723)***
Codinos Limited Inc....518 372-3308
704 Corporation Park # 5 Schenectady (12302) ***(G-15272)***
Cody Printing Corp....718 651-8854
3728 56th St Woodside (11377) ***(G-17341)***
Coe Displays Inc....718 937-5658
4301 22nd St Ste 603 Long Island City (11101) ***(G-7730)***
Coecles Hbr Marina & Boat Yard....631 749-0856
68 Cartwright Rd Shelter Island (11964) ***(G-15408)***
Coffee Holding Co Inc (PA)....718 832-0800
3475 Victory Blvd Ste 4 Staten Island (10314) ***(G-15680)***
Coffing, Getzville *Also called Columbus McKinnon Corporation* ***(G-5608)***
Cofire Paving Corporation....718 463-1403
12030 28th Ave Flushing (11354) ***(G-5241)***
Cognigen Acquisition, Buffalo *Also called Cognigen Corporation* ***(G-2898)***
Cognigen Corporation....716 633-3463
1780 Wehrle Dr Ste 110 Buffalo (14221) ***(G-2898)***
Cognitiveflow Sensor Tech....631 513-9369
9 Melville Ct Stony Brook (11790) ***(G-15789)***
Cognotion Inc....347 692-0640
1407 Broadway Fl 24 New York (10018) ***(G-9724)***
Coham/Rvrdale Dcrative Fabrics, New York *Also called Richloom Home Fashions Corp* ***(G-11896)***
Cohber Press Inc (PA)....585 475-9100
1000 John St West Henrietta (14586) ***(G-16906)***
Cohens Bakery Inc....716 892-8149
1132 Broadway St Buffalo (14212) ***(G-2899)***
Coil Stamping Inc....631 588-3040
1340 Lincoln Ave Ste 1 Holbrook (11741) ***(G-6467)***
Coinmach Service Corp....516 349-8555
303 Sunnyside Blvd # 70 Plainview (11803) ***(G-13618)***
Colad Group LLC (HQ)....716 961-1776
693 Seneca St Fl 5 Buffalo (14210) ***(G-2900)***
Colarusso Blacktop Co, Hudson *Also called A Colarusso and Son Inc* ***(G-6631)***
Colburns AC Rfrgn....716 569-3695
17 White Dr Frewsburg (14738) ***(G-5463)***
Cold Mix Manufacturing Corp....718 463-1444
65 Edison Ave Mount Vernon (10550) ***(G-8718)***
Cold Point Corporation....315 339-2331
7500 Cold Point Dr Rome (13440) ***(G-14838)***
Cold Spring Granite Company....518 647-8191
Hc 9 Box N Au Sable Forks (12912) ***(G-474)***
Cold Springs R & D Inc....315 413-1237
1207 Van Vleck Rd Ste A Syracuse (13209) ***(G-15920)***
Colden Closet LLC....716 713-6125
1375 Boies Rd East Aurora (14052) ***(G-4393)***
Coldstream Group Inc (PA)....914 698-5959
420 Railroad Way Mamaroneck (10543) ***(G-8061)***
Colgat-Plmolive Centl Amer Inc (HQ)....212 310-2000
300 Park Ave New York (10022) ***(G-9725)***
Colgate-Palmolive Company (PA)....212 310-2000
300 Park Ave Fl 5 New York (10022) ***(G-9726)***
Colgate-Palmolive Company....718 506-3961
21818 100th Ave Queens Village (11429) ***(G-13991)***
Colgate-Palmolive Globl Trdg....212 310-2000
300 Park Ave Fl 8 New York (10022) ***(G-9727)***
Colgate-Palmolive Nj Inc....212 310-2000
300 Park Ave Fl 8 New York (10022) ***(G-9728)***
Coliseum, New York *Also called Plugg LLC* ***(G-11700)***
Collaborative Laboratories (HQ)....631 689-0200
3 Technology Dr Ste 400 East Setauket (11733) ***(G-4498)***
Collection Xiix Ltd (PA)....212 686-8990
1370 Broadway Fl 17 New York (10018) ***(G-9729)***
College Calendar Company....315 768-8242
148 Clinton St Whitesboro (13492) ***(G-17220)***
College Nnoscale Science Engrg, Albany *Also called University At Albany* ***(G-147)***
Collegebound Teen Magazine, Staten Island *Also called Ramholtz Publishing Inc* ***(G-15749)***
Collegeville Imagineering, Bay Shore *Also called Rubies Costume Company Inc* ***(G-736)***
Collinite Corporation....315 732-2282
1520 Lincoln Ave Utica (13502) ***(G-16336)***
Collins Pet & Garden Center, Malone *Also called Scotts Feed Inc* ***(G-8046)***
Colonial Electric, Farmingdale *Also called Colonial Precision Machinery* ***(G-4971)***
Colonial Group LLC....516 349-8010
150 Express St Ste 2 Plainview (11803) ***(G-13619)***
Colonial Label, Patchogue *Also called Depot Label Company Inc* ***(G-13443)***
Colonial Label Systems Inc....631 254-0111
50 Corbin Ave Ste L Bay Shore (11706) ***(G-683)***
Colonial Precision Machinery....631 249-0738
134 Rome St Farmingdale (11735) ***(G-4971)***
Colonial Rapid, Bay Shore *Also called Colonial Label Systems Inc* ***(G-683)***
Colonial Redi Record Corp....718 972-7433
1225 36th St Brooklyn (11218) ***(G-1790)***
Colonial Tag & Label Co Inc....516 482-0508
425 Northern Blvd Ste 36 Great Neck (11021) ***(G-5816)***
Colonial Tanning Corporation (PA)....518 725-7171
8 Wilson St 810 Gloversville (12078) ***(G-5724)***
Colonial Terrace Hotel, Cortlandt Manor *Also called Terrace Management Inc* ***(G-4080)***
Colonial Wire & Cable Co Inc (PA)....631 234-8500
40 Engineers Rd Hauppauge (11788) ***(G-6069)***
Colonie Block and Supply Co....518 869-8411
124 Lincoln Ave Colonie (12205) ***(G-3845)***
Colonie Plastics Corp....631 434-6969
188 Candlewood Rd Bay Shore (11706) ***(G-684)***
Colony Holdings Intl LLC....212 868-2800
131 W 35th St Fl 6 New York (10001) ***(G-9730)***
Color Card LLC....631 232-1300
1065 Islip Ave Central Islip (11722) ***(G-3516)***
Color Carton Corp....718 665-0840
341 Canal Pl Bronx (10451) ***(G-1303)***
Color Craft Finishing Corp....631 563-3230
30 Floyds Run Ste A Bohemia (11716) ***(G-1034)***
Color Fx, New York *Also called Joseph Industries Inc* ***(G-10804)***
Color Industries LLC....718 392-8301
3002 48th Ave Ste H Long Island City (11101) ***(G-7731)***
Color ME Mine....585 383-8420
3349 Monroe Ave Ste 32 Rochester (14618) ***(G-14304)***
Color Pro Sign, Schenectady *Also called Ray Sign Inc* ***(G-15313)***

Color Story, New York *Also called Leser Enterprises Ltd* ***(G-11009)***
Color Unlimited Inc...212 802-7547
244 5th Ave Frnt New York (10001) ***(G-9731)***
Color-Aid Corporation...212 673-5500
38 La Fayette St Ste 2 Hudson Falls (12839) ***(G-6670)***
Colorfast...212 929-2440
121 Varick St Fl 9 New York (10013) ***(G-9732)***
Colorfully Yours Inc...631 242-8600
11 Grant Ave Bay Shore (11706) ***(G-685)***
Colorpak, Melville *Also called Poly-Pak Industries Inc* ***(G-8377)***
Colors Fashion Inc...212 629-0401
901 Avenue Of The Ste 153 New York (10001) ***(G-9733)***
Colors In Optics Ltd...718 845-0300
120 Broadway G New Hyde Park (11040) ***(G-8867)***
Colorspec Coatings Intl Inc...631 472-8251
1716 Church St Holbrook (11741) ***(G-6468)***
Colortex Inc...212 564-2000
1202 Lexington Ave 115 New York (10028) ***(G-9734)***
Columbia, Macedon *Also called Water Technologies Inc* ***(G-8022)***
Columbia Button Nailhead Corp...718 386-3414
306 Stagg St 316 Brooklyn (11206) ***(G-1791)***
Columbia Cabinets LLC (PA)...212 972-7550
332 E Main St Mount Kisco (10549) ***(G-8665)***
Columbia Cabinets LLC...518 283-1700
489 Broadway Saratoga Springs (12866) ***(G-15178)***
Columbia Daily Spectator...212 854-9550
2875 Broadway Ste 303 New York (10025) ***(G-9735)***
Columbia Dentoform Corporation (PA)...718 482-1569
3110 37th Ave Ste 307 Long Island City (11101) ***(G-7732)***
Columbia Metal Fabricators...631 476-7527
801 Hallock Ave Port Jeff STA (11776) ***(G-13788)***
Columbia Pool Accessories Inc...718 993-0389
111 Bruckner Blvd Bronx (10454) ***(G-1304)***
Columbia Records Inc...212 833-8000
25 Madison Ave Fl 19 New York (10010) ***(G-9736)***
Columbia Seal N Sew, Brooklyn *Also called Dlx Industries Inc* ***(G-1870)***
Columbia Sportswear Company...631 274-6091
152 The Arches Cir Deer Park (11729) ***(G-4141)***
Columbia Telecom Group...631 501-5000
200 5th Ave Ste 651 New York (10010) ***(G-9737)***
Columbia Univ Publications, New York *Also called Trust of Colum Unive In The Ci* ***(G-12434)***
Columbia University Press (HQ)...212 459-0600
61 W 62nd St Fl 3 New York (10023) ***(G-9738)***
Columbia University Press...212 459-0600
61 W 62nd St Fl 3 New York (10023) ***(G-9739)***
Columbia University Press...212 459-0600
61 W 62nd St Fl 3 New York (10023) ***(G-9740)***
Columbus Accessories, New York *Also called Columbus Trading Corp* ***(G-9741)***
Columbus Baking Co, Syracuse *Also called George Retzos* ***(G-15973)***
Columbus McKinnon Corporation...716 689-5400
470 John Jmes Adubon Pkwy Amherst (14228) ***(G-235)***
Columbus McKinnon Corporation (PA)...716 689-5400
205 Crosspoint Pkwy Getzville (14068) ***(G-5607)***
Columbus McKinnon Corporation...716 689-5400
205 Crosspoint Pkwy Getzville (14068) ***(G-5608)***
Columbus McKinnon Corporation...716 689-5400
205 Crosspoint Pkwy Getzville (14068) ***(G-5609)***
Columbus McKinnon Corporation...716 689-5400
205 Crosspoint Pkwy Getzville (14068) ***(G-5610)***
Columbus McKnnon- Lift TEC Div, Getzville *Also called Columbus McKinnon Corporation* ***(G-5610)***
Columbus Trading Corp...212 564-1780
120 W 31st St Rm 600 New York (10001) ***(G-9741)***
Columbus Woodworking Inc...607 674-4546
164 Casey Cheese Fctry Rd Sherburne (13460) ***(G-15412)***
Comairco Equipment Inc (HQ)...716 656-0211
3250 Union Rd Cheektowaga (14227) ***(G-3592)***
Comander Terminals LLC...516 922-7600
1 Commander Sq Oyster Bay (11771) ***(G-13394)***
Comax Aromatics Corporation...631 249-0505
130 Baylis Rd Melville (11747) ***(G-8334)***
Comax Flavors, Melville *Also called Comax Manufacturing Corp* ***(G-8335)***
Comax Manufacturing Corp...631 249-0505
130 Baylis Rd Melville (11747) ***(G-8335)***
Combe Incorporated (PA)...914 694-5454
1101 Westchester Ave White Plains (10604) ***(G-17123)***
Combine Graphics Corp...212 695-4044
10714 Queens Blvd Forest Hills (11375) ***(G-5328)***
Comboland Packing Corp...718 858-4200
2 Cumberland St Brooklyn (11205) ***(G-1792)***
Comco Plastics Inc...718 849-9000
11 Stepar Pl Huntington Station (11746) ***(G-6738)***
Comely International Trdg Inc...212 683-1240
303 5th Ave Rm 1903 New York (10016) ***(G-9742)***
Comerford Collection, Bridgehampton *Also called Comerford Hennessy At Home Inc* ***(G-1231)***
Comerford Hennessy At Home Inc...631 537-6200
2442 Main St Bridgehampton (11932) ***(G-1231)***
Comet Flasher Inc (PA)...716 821-9595
1 Babcock St Buffalo (14210) ***(G-2901)***
Comet Informatics LLC...585 385-2310
642 Kreag Rd Ste 300 Pittsford (14534) ***(G-13586)***
Comfort Bedding Inc...718 485-7662
13 Christopher Ave Brooklyn (11212) ***(G-1793)***
Comfort Care Textiles Inc (HQ)...631 543-0531
368 Veterans Memorial Hwy # 5 Commack (11725) ***(G-3854)***
Comfort Wax Incorporated...718 204-7028
3174 Steinway St Fl 5 Astoria (11103) ***(G-431)***
Comfortex Corporation (HQ)...518 273-3333
21 Elm St Watervliet (12189) ***(G-16707)***
Comfortex Window Fashions, Watervliet *Also called Comfortex Corporation* ***(G-16707)***
Comgraph Sales Service...716 601-7243
7491 Clinton St Elma (14059) ***(G-4660)***
Comint Apparel Group LLC (PA)...212 947-7474
463 7th Ave Fl 4 New York (10018) ***(G-9743)***
Command Components Corporation...631 666-4411
6 Cherry St Bay Shore (11706) ***(G-686)***
Command Systems Division, Farmingdale *Also called Telephonics Corporation* ***(G-5138)***
Comme-Ci Comme-CA AP Group...631 300-1035
380 Rabo Dr Hauppauge (11788) ***(G-6070)***
Commentary Inc...212 891-1400
165 E 56th St Fl 16 New York (10022) ***(G-9744)***
Commentary Magazine, New York *Also called American Jewish Committee* ***(G-9171)***
Commerce Offset Ltd...914 769-6671
657 Commerce St Thornwood (10594) ***(G-16141)***
Commerce Spring Corp...631 293-4844
143 Allen Blvd Farmingdale (11735) ***(G-4972)***
Commercehub Inc (PA)...518 810-0700
201 Fuller Rd Fl 6 Albany (12203) ***(G-71)***
Commercial Communications LLC...845 343-9078
14 Montgomery St Middletown (10940) ***(G-8466)***
Commercial Concrete, Westbury *Also called New York Ready Mix Inc* ***(G-17042)***
Commercial Display Design LLC...607 336-7353
120 Kemper Ln Norwich (13815) ***(G-13044)***
Commercial Draperies Unlimited, Mamaroneck *Also called White Plains Drapery Uphl Inc* ***(G-8083)***
Commercial Fabrics Inc...716 694-0641
908 Niagara Falls Blvd North Tonawanda (14120) ***(G-12984)***
Commercial Gaskets New York...212 244-8130
247 W 38th St Rm 409 New York (10018) ***(G-9745)***
Commercial Millworks Inc...315 475-7479
221 W Division St Syracuse (13204) ***(G-15921)***
Commercial Press Inc...315 274-0028
6589 Us Highway 11 Canton (13617) ***(G-3407)***
Commercial Print & Imaging...716 597-0100
4778 Main St Buffalo (14226) ***(G-2902)***
Commify Technology...917 603-1822
228 Park Ave S New York (10003) ***(G-9746)***
Commitment 2000 Inc...716 439-1206
105 Msgr Valente Dr Buffalo (14206) ***(G-2903)***
Committee For Color & Trends, New York *Also called Cct Inc* ***(G-9606)***
Commodity Resource Corporation...585 538-9500
2773 Caledonia Leroy Rd Caledonia (14423) ***(G-3305)***
Commodore Chocolatier USA Inc...845 561-3960
482 Broadway Newburgh (12550) ***(G-12774)***
Commodore Machine Co Inc...585 657-6916
26 Maple Ave Bloomfield (14469) ***(G-978)***
Commodore Manufacutring Corp...718 788-2600
3913 2nd Ave Brooklyn (11232) ***(G-1794)***
Commodore Plastics LLC...585 657-7777
26 Maple Ave Bloomfield (14469) ***(G-979)***
Commodore Tool, Brooklyn *Also called Commodore Manufacutring Corp* ***(G-1794)***
Common Sense Natural Soap, Cambridge *Also called Robert Racine* ***(G-3338)***
Common Sense Natural Soap...518 677-0224
7 Pearl St Cambridge (12816) ***(G-3334)***
Commonweal Foundation Inc...212 662-4200
475 Riverside Dr Rm 405 New York (10115) ***(G-9747)***
COMMONWEAL MAGAZINE, New York *Also called Commonweal Foundation Inc* ***(G-9747)***
Commonwealth Home Fashion Inc...514 384-8290
31 Station Rd Willsboro (12996) ***(G-17288)***
Commonwealth Toy Novelty Inc (PA)...212 242-4070
980 Ave Of The Amer # 3 New York (10018) ***(G-9748)***
Communication Power Corp...631 434-7306
80 Davids Dr Ste 3 Hauppauge (11788) ***(G-6071)***
Communications & Energy Corp...315 446-5723
204 Ambergate Rd Syracuse (13214) ***(G-15922)***
Communications Systems Div, Farmingdale *Also called Telephonics Corporation* ***(G-5136)***
Community Cpons Frnchising Inc...516 277-1968
100 Carney St Ste 2 Glen Cove (11542) ***(G-5625)***
Community Directory, Brooklyn *Also called Business Directory Inc* ***(G-1742)***
Community Glass Inc...607 737-8860
139 W 17th St Elmira (14903) ***(G-4689)***
Community Magazine, Brooklyn *Also called Bnei Aram Soba Inc* ***(G-1706)***
Community Media Group LLC (PA)...518 439-4949
125 Adams St Delmar (12054) ***(G-4269)***
Community Media LLC...212 229-1890
515 Canal St Fl 1 New York (10013) ***(G-9749)***
Community News Group LLC (PA)...718 260-2500
1 Metrotech Ctr Fl 10 Brooklyn (11201) ***(G-1795)***
Community Newspaper Group LLC...607 432-1000
102 Chestnut St Oneonta (13820) ***(G-13203)***

ALPHABETIC

Community Newspaper Group LLC 518 565-4114
170 Margaret St Plattsburgh (12901) *(G-13688)*
Community Newspapers, Moravia *Also called Republican Registrar Inc (G-8658)*
Community Newsppr Holdings Inc 585 798-1400
541-543 Main St Medina (14103) *(G-8302)*
Community Newsppr Holdings Inc 716 693-1000
473 3rd St Ste 201 Niagara Falls (14301) *(G-12827)*
Community Newsppr Holdings Inc 716 282-2311
473 3rd St Ste 201 Niagara Falls (14301) *(G-12828)*
Community Newsppr Holdings Inc 716 439-9222
135 Main St Ste 1 Lockport (14094) *(G-7605)*
Community Playthings, Chester *Also called Community Products LLC (G-3630)*
Community Playthings, Elka Park *Also called Church Communities NY Inc (G-4643)*
Community Playthings, Elka Park *Also called Church Communities NY Inc (G-4644)*
Community Plythings Rifton Eqp, Rifton *Also called Community Products LLC (G-14144)*
Community Products LLC (PA) 845 658-8799
2032 Route 213 St Rifton (12471) *(G-14144)*
Community Products LLC 845 658-7720
359 Gibson Hill Rd Chester (10918) *(G-3630)*
Community Products LLC 845 572-3433
24 Elizabeth Dr Chester (10918) *(G-3631)*
Community Products LLC 845 658-8351
2032 Route 213 St Rifton (12471) *(G-14145)*
Community Products LLC 518 589-5103
2255 Platte Clove Rd Elka Park (12427) *(G-4645)*
Compac Development Corporation 631 881-4903
110 Plant Ave Ste 1 Hauppauge (11788) *(G-6072)*
Compar Manufacturing Corp 212 304-2777
308 Dyckman St New York (10034) *(G-9750)*
Compass Printing Plus 518 891-7050
42 Main St Saranac Lake (12983) *(G-15163)*
Compass Printing Plus (PA) 518 523-3308
42 Main St Saranac Lake (12983) *(G-15164)*
Competicion Mower Repair 516 280-6584
75 Windsor Ave Mineola (11501) *(G-8537)*
Complemar Print LLC 716 875-7238
3034 Genesee St Buffalo (14225) *(G-2904)*
Complete Fiber Solutions Inc 718 828-8900
1459 Bassett Ave Bronx (10461) *(G-1305)*
Complete Orthopedic Svcs Inc 516 357-9113
2094 Front St East Meadow (11554) *(G-4440)*
Complete Publishing Solutions 212 242-7321
350 W 51st St Apt 13b New York (10019) *(G-9751)*
Complete SEC & Contrls Inc 631 421-7200
100 Hillwood Dr Huntington Station (11746) *(G-6739)*
Complex Biosystems Inc 315 464-8007
8266 Warbler Way Apt C6 Liverpool (13090) *(G-7541)*
Complex Magazine, New York *Also called CMX Media LLC (G-9706)*
Complex Media Inc (PA) 917 793-5831
1271 6th Ave Fl 35 New York (10020) *(G-9752)*
Complystream, New York *Also called Thinktrek Inc (G-12339)*
Composite Forms Inc 914 937-1808
7 Merritt St Port Chester (10573) *(G-13768)*
Composite Materials Division, New York *Also called Mitsubishi Chemical Amer Inc (G-11710)*
Compositech Ltd 516 835-1458
4 Fairbanks Blvd Woodbury (11797) *(G-17305)*
Compoz A Puzzle Inc 516 883-2311
2 Secatoag Ave Port Washington (11050) *(G-13829)*
Comprehensive Dental Tech 607 467-4456
Rr 1 Box 69 Hancock (13783) *(G-5985)*
Comps Inc 516 676-0400
3 School St Ste 101b Glen Cove (11542) *(G-5626)*
Compucolor Associates Inc 516 358-0000
2200 Marcus Ave Ste C New Hyde Park (11042) *(G-8868)*
Computer Conversions Corp 631 261-3300
6 Dunton Ct East Northport (11731) *(G-4454)*
Computer Instruments Corp 631 876-8400
963a Brush Hollow Rd Westbury (11590) *(G-17003)*
Computerized Metal Bending Ser 631 249-1177
91 Cabot St Unit A West Babylon (11704) *(G-16810)*
Comsec Ventures International 518 523-1600
17 Tamarack Ave Lake Placid (12946) *(G-7297)*
Comstock Food, Leicester *Also called Seneca Foods Corporation (G-7444)*
Comstock Foods Division, South Dayton *Also called Birds Eye Foods Inc (G-15539)*
Comtech PST Corp (HQ) 631 777-8900
105 Baylis Rd Melville (11747) *(G-8336)*
Comtech Telecom Corp (PA) 631 962-7000
68 S Service Rd Ste 230 Melville (11747) *(G-8337)*
Con Rel Auto Electric Inc 518 356-1646
3637 Carman Rd Schenectady (12303) *(G-15273)*
Conagra Brands Inc 212 461-2410
405 Lexington Ave New York (10174) *(G-9753)*
Conax Technologies LLC (PA) 716 684-4500
2300 Walden Ave Buffalo (14225) *(G-2905)*
Concept Components, Bohemia *Also called McGuigan Inc (G-1098)*
Concept One Accessories, New York *Also called Uspa Accessories LLC (G-12513)*
Concept Printing and Promotion, Nyack *Also called Concept Printing Inc (G-13064)*
Concept Printing Inc 845 353-4040
40 Lydecker St Nyack (10960) *(G-13064)*
Conceptronic, Central Islip *Also called Cvd Equipment Corporation (G-3519)*

Concepts In Wood of CNY 315 463-8084
4021 New Court Ave Syracuse (13206) *(G-15923)*
Concepts New York, The, Brooklyn *Also called Milla Global Inc (G-2319)*
Concepts Nyc Inc 212 244-1033
20 W 33rd St Fl 9 New York (10001) *(G-9754)*
Concinnity Division, Melville *Also called I W Industries Inc (G-8359)*
Concord Express Cargo Inc 718 276-7200
17214 119th Ave Jamaica (11434) *(G-6942)*
Concord Jewelry Mfg Co LLC 212 719-4030
64 W 48th St Ste 1004 New York (10036) *(G-9755)*
Concord Jwlry Mfrs, New York *Also called Concord Jewelry Mfg Co LLC (G-9755)*
Concord Settings, New York *Also called Kaprielian Enterprises Inc (G-10845)*
Concorde Apparel Company LLC (PA) 212 307-7848
55 W 39th St Fl 11 New York (10018) *(G-9756)*
Concrete Mixer Supplycom Inc (PA) 716 375-5565
1721 Cornell Dr Olean (14760) *(G-13159)*
Cond Nast's, New York *Also called Conde Nast International Inc (G-9758)*
Conde Nast (PA) 212 630-3642
750 3rd Ave Fl 8 New York (10017) *(G-9757)*
Conde Nast International Inc (PA) 212 286-2860
1 World Trade Ctr New York (10007) *(G-9758)*
Conde Nast Publications, New York *Also called Advance Magazine Publs Inc (G-9085)*
Conde Nast Publications Div, New York *Also called Advance Magazine Publs Inc (G-9086)*
Conde Pumps Div, Sherrill *Also called Westmoor Ltd (G-15433)*
Condeco Software Inc (HQ) 917 677-7600
1350 Broadway Rm 1712 New York (10018) *(G-9759)*
Condor Electronics Corp 585 235-1500
295 Mount Read Blvd Rochester (14611) *(G-14305)*
Cone Buddy System Inc 585 427-9940
3495 Winton Pl Ste E290 Rochester (14623) *(G-14306)*
Conesus Lake Association Inc 585 346-6864
5828 Big Tree Rd Lakeville (14480) *(G-7306)*
Confer Plastics Inc 800 635-3213
97 Witmer Rd North Tonawanda (14120) *(G-12985)*
Conference Board Inc (PA) 212 759-0900
845 3rd Ave Fl 2 New York (10022) *(G-9760)*
Conformer Products Inc 516 504-6300
60 Cuttermill Rd Ste 411 Great Neck (11021) *(G-5817)*
Confrtrnity of Prescious Blood 718 436-1120
5300 Fort Hamilton Pkwy Brooklyn (11219) *(G-1796)*
Congress For Jewish Culture 212 505-8040
1133 Broadway Ste 1019 New York (10010) *(G-9761)*
Conic Systems Inc 845 856-4053
11 Rebel Ln Port Jervis (12771) *(G-13804)*
Conkur Printing Co Inc 212 541-5980
121 Varick St Rm 400 New York (10013) *(G-9762)*
Conmed Andover Medical Inc (HQ) 315 797-8375
525 French Rd Ste 3 Utica (13502) *(G-16337)*
Conmed Corporation 315 797-8375
525 French Rd Utica (13502) *(G-16338)*
Conmed Corporation 315 797-8375
525 French Rd Utica (13502) *(G-16339)*
Connection Mold Inc 585 458-6463
585 Ling Rd Rochester (14612) *(G-14307)*
Connectiva Systems Inc (PA) 646 722-8741
19 W 44th St Ste 611 New York (10036) *(G-9763)*
Connex Grinding & Machining 315 946-4340
65 Clyde Rd Lyons (14489) *(G-7998)*
Connie Cleaners, Great Neck *Also called Connie French Cleaners Inc (G-5818)*
Connie French Cleaners Inc 516 487-1343
801 Middle Neck Rd Great Neck (11024) *(G-5818)*
Connie's T Shirt Shop, East Northport *Also called Island Silkscreen Inc (G-4458)*
Connies Laundry 716 822-2800
1494 S Park Ave Buffalo (14220) *(G-2906)*
Connover Packaging Inc 585 377-2510
119 Despatch Dr East Rochester (14445) *(G-4475)*
Conopco Inc 585 647-8322
28 Mansfield St Rochester (14606) *(G-14308)*
Conrad Blasius Equipment Co 516 753-1200
199 Newtown Rd Plainview (11803) *(G-13620)*
Consoldted Precision Pdts Corp 315 687-0014
901 E Genesee St Chittenango (13037) *(G-3660)*
Consolidated Barricades Inc 518 922-7944
179 Dillenbeck Rd Fultonville (12072) *(G-5492)*
Consolidated Childrens AP Inc (HQ) 212 239-8615
100 W 33rd St Ste 1105 New York (10001) *(G-9764)*
Consolidated Color Press Inc 212 929-8197
307 7th Ave Rm 607 New York (10001) *(G-9765)*
Consolidated Container Co LLC 585 262-6470
18 Champeney Ter Rochester (14605) *(G-14309)*
Consolidated Container Co LLC 585 343-9351
14 Hall St Batavia (14020) *(G-630)*
Consolidated Edison Co NY Inc 914 933-2936
511 Theodore Fremd Ave Rye (10580) *(G-15081)*
Consolidated Fashion Corp 212 719-3000
225 W 39th St Fl 12 New York (10018) *(G-9766)*
Consolidated Loose Leaf Inc (PA) 212 924-5800
989 Avnue Of The Americas New York (10018) *(G-9767)*
Constas Printing Corporation 315 474-2176
1120 Burnet Ave Syracuse (13203) *(G-15924)*
Constellation Brands Inc (PA) 585 678-7100
207 High Point Dr # 100 Victor (14564) *(G-16493)*

ALPHABETIC SECTION
Coral Graphic Services Inc

Constellation Brands Inc 585 393-4880
3325 Marvin Sands Dr Canandaigua (14424) **(G-3368)**
Constellation Brands Smo LLC 585 396-7161
111 8th Ave New York (10011) **(G-9768)**
Constellation Brands US Oprs 585 396-7600
116 Buffalo St Canandaigua (14424) **(G-3369)**
Constellation Brands US Oprs (HQ) 585 396-7600
235 N Bloomfield Rd Canandaigua (14424) **(G-3370)**
Constellium 212 675-5087
830 3rd Ave Rm 901 New York (10022) **(G-9769)**
Construction Parts Whse Inc 315 445-1310
5841 Butternut Dr East Syracuse (13057) **(G-4534)**
Construction Technology Inc (PA) 914 747-8900
400 Columbus Ave Ste 110s Valhalla (10595) **(G-16392)**
Consumer Flavoring Extract Co 718 435-0201
921 Mcdonald Ave Brooklyn (11218) **(G-1797)**
Consumer Reports Inc (PA) 914 378-2000
101 Truman Ave Yonkers (10703) **(G-17445)**
Consumers Beverages Inc 716 837-3087
3025 Sheridan Dr Buffalo (14226) **(G-2907)**
Consumers Beverages Inc 716 675-4934
1375 Union Rd West Seneca (14224) **(G-16970)**
Consumers Union, Yonkers *Also called Consumer Reports Inc* **(G-17445)**
Contactive Inc 646 476-9059
137 Varick St Ste 605 New York (10013) **(G-9770)**
Container Tstg Solutions LLC 716 487-3300
17 Tiffany Ave Jamestown (14701) **(G-7018)**
Container Tstg Solutions LLC (PA) 716 487-3300
17 Lester St Sinclairville (14782) **(G-15474)**
Contech Engnered Solutions LLC 716 870-9091
34 Birdsong Pkwy Orchard Park (14127) **(G-13288)**
Contempra Design Inc 718 984-8586
20 Grille Ct Staten Island (10309) **(G-15681)**
Conti Auto Body Corp 516 921-6435
44 Jericho Tpke Syosset (11791) **(G-15837)**
Continental Access, Amityville *Also called Continental Instruments LLC* **(G-280)**
Continental Buchanan LLC 703 480-3800
350 Broadway Buchanan (10511) **(G-2799)**
Continental Cordage Corp (HQ) 315 655-9800
75 Burton St Cazenovia (13035) **(G-3470)**
Continental Instruments LLC (HQ) 631 842-9400
355 Bayview Ave Amityville (11701) **(G-280)**
Continental Knitting Mills 631 242-5330
156 Brook Ave Deer Park (11729) **(G-4142)**
Continental Kraft Corp 516 681-9090
100 Jericho Quadrangle # 219 Jericho (11753) **(G-7097)**
Continental Latex Corp 718 783-7883
1489 Shore Pkwy Apt 1g Brooklyn (11214) **(G-1798)**
Continental Lift Truck Inc 718 738-4738
12718 Foch Blvd South Ozone Park (11420) **(G-15556)**
Continental Quilting Co Inc 718 499-9100
3000 Marcus Ave Ste 3e6 New Hyde Park (11042) **(G-8869)**
Continuity Publishing Inc 212 869-4170
15 W 39th St Fl 9 New York (10018) **(G-9771)**
Continuity Software Inc 646 216-8628
5 Penn Plz Fl 23 New York (10001) **(G-9772)**
Continuum Intl Pubg Group Inc 646 649-4215
15 W 26th St Fl 8 New York (10010) **(G-9773)**
Contract Pharmacal Corp 631 231-4610
110 Plant Ave Hauppauge (11788) **(G-6073)**
Contract Pharmacal Corp 631 231-4610
1324 Motor Pkwy Hauppauge (11749) **(G-6074)**
Contract Pharmacal Corp 631 231-4610
250 Kennedy Dr Hauppauge (11788) **(G-6075)**
Contract Pharmacal Corp 631 231-4610
145 Oser Ave Hauppauge (11788) **(G-6076)**
Contract Pharmacal Corp 631 231-4610
160 Commerce Dr Hauppauge (11788) **(G-6077)**
Contract Pharmacal Corp 631 231-4610
150 Commerce Dr Hauppauge (11788) **(G-6078)**
Contract Phrmctcals Ltd Nagara 716 887-3400
100 Forest Ave Buffalo (14213) **(G-2908)**
Control Elec Div Fil-Coil, Sayville *Also called Esc Control Electronics LLC* **(G-15236)**
Control Electropolishing Corp 718 858-6634
109 Walworth St Brooklyn (11205) **(G-1799)**
Control Global Solutions, Halfmoon *Also called Ebeling Associates Inc* **(G-5932)**
Control Logic Corporation 607 965-6423
2533 State Highway 80 West Burlington (13482) **(G-16874)**
Control Research Inc 631 225-1111
385 Bayview Ave Unit C Amityville (11701) **(G-281)**
Controlled Castings Corp 516 349-1718
31 Commercial Ct Plainview (11803) **(G-13621)**
Convenience Store News 214 217-7800
770 Broadway Fl 5 New York (10003) **(G-9774)**
Convergent Audio Tech Inc 585 359-2700
85 High Tech Dr Rush (14543) **(G-15070)**
Convergent Cnnctivity Tech Inc 845 651-5250
1751 State Route 17a Florida (10921) **(G-5218)**
Convergent Med MGT Svcs LLC 718 921-6159
7513 3rd Ave Brooklyn (11209) **(G-1800)**
Conversant LLC 212 471-9570
150 E 62nd St New York (10065) **(G-9775)**

Converter Design Inc (PA) 518 745-7138
25 Murdock Ave Glens Falls (12801) **(G-5691)**
Coocoo SMS Inc 646 459-4260
356 New York Ave Ste 1 Huntington (11743) **(G-6692)**
Cookie Connection Inc 315 422-2253
705 Park Ave Syracuse (13204) **(G-15925)**
Cookie Factory, Bronx *Also called Golden Glow Cookie Co Inc* **(G-1347)**
Cookie Factory LLC 518 268-1060
520 Congress St Troy (12180) **(G-16254)**
Cookiebaker LLC 716 878-8000
1 Robert Rich Way Buffalo (14213) **(G-2909)**
Cookies Inc 646 452-5552
1 E 33rd St Fl 6 New York (10016) **(G-9776)**
Cookies United LLC 631 581-4000
141 Freeman Ave Islip (11751) **(G-6846)**
Cooking With Chef Michelle LLC 516 662-2324
4603 Middle Country Rd Calverton (11933) **(G-3317)**
Cooks Intl Ltd Lblty Co 212 741-4407
7 World Trade Ctr Fl 46 New York (10007) **(G-9777)**
Cooper & Clement Inc 315 454-8135
1840 Lemoyne Ave Syracuse (13208) **(G-15926)**
Cooper Crouse Hinds Elec Pdts, Syracuse *Also called Cooper Crouse-Hinds LLC* **(G-15927)**
Cooper Crouse-Hinds LLC (HQ) 866 764-5454
1201 Wolf St Syracuse (13208) **(G-15927)**
Cooper Industries LLC 315 477-7000
Wolf & 7th North St Syracuse (13208) **(G-15928)**
Cooper Lighting LLC 516 470-1000
100 Andrews Rd Ste 1 Hicksville (11801) **(G-6358)**
Cooper Lighting LLC 315 579-2873
125 E Jefferson St Syracuse (13202) **(G-15929)**
Cooper Molded Products, Syracuse *Also called Cooper Industries LLC* **(G-15928)**
Cooper Power Systems LLC 716 375-7100
1648 Dugan Rd Olean (14760) **(G-13160)**
Cooper Turbocompressor Inc (HQ) 716 896-6600
3101 Broadway St Buffalo (14227) **(G-2910)**
Cooperfriedman Elc Sup Co Inc 718 269-4906
2219 41st Ave Long Island City (11101) **(G-7733)**
Coopers Cave Ale Co S-Corp 518 792-0007
2 Sagamore St Glens Falls (12801) **(G-5692)**
Cooperstown Bat Co Inc (PA) 607 547-2415
Rr 28 Fly Creek (13337) **(G-5318)**
Cooperstown Bat Co Inc 607 547-2415
118 Main St Cooperstown (13326) **(G-3910)**
Cooperstown Brewing Co LLC 607 286-9330
41 Browne St Oneonta (13820) **(G-13204)**
Coopervision Inc 585 385-6810
180 Thruway Park Dr West Henrietta (14586) **(G-16907)**
Coopervision Inc 585 889-3301
711 North Rd Scottsville (14546) **(G-15357)**
Coopervision Inc 585 385-6810
209 High Point Dr Victor (14564) **(G-16494)**
Coopervision Inc (HQ) 585 385-6810
209 High Point Dr Victor (14564) **(G-16495)**
Copeland Coating Company Inc 518 766-2932
3600 Us Highway 20 Nassau (12123) **(G-8817)**
Copen International Limited, New York *Also called Cai Inc* **(G-9547)**
Copen United LLC 212 819-0008
37 W 39th St Fl 6 New York (10018) **(G-9778)**
Copesetic Inc 315 684-7780
62 E Main St Morrisville (13408) **(G-8662)**
Copia Interactive LLC 212 481-0520
105 Madison Ave New York (10016) **(G-9779)**
Copper John Corporation 315 258-9269
173 State St Auburn (13021) **(G-488)**
Copper Ridge Oil Inc 716 372-4021
111 W 2nd St Ste 404 Jamestown (14701) **(G-7019)**
Copra 917 224-1727
215 E Broadway Apt 2r New York (10002) **(G-9780)**
Copy Cat 718 934-2192
3177 Coney Island Ave A Brooklyn (11235) **(G-1801)**
Copy Corner Inc 718 388-4545
200 Division Ave Brooklyn (11211) **(G-1802)**
Copy Room Inc 212 371-8600
885 3rd Ave Lowr 2ll New York (10022) **(G-9781)**
Copy Stop Inc 914 428-5188
50 Main St Ste 32 White Plains (10606) **(G-17124)**
Copy X/Press Ltd 631 585-2200
700 Union Pkwy Ste 5 Ronkonkoma (11779) **(G-14916)**
Copy4les Inc 212 487-9778
146 W 29th St Rm 9w New York (10001) **(G-9782)**
Cora Materials Corp 516 488-6300
30 Nassau Terminal Rd New Hyde Park (11040) **(G-8870)**
Cora Matrls, New Hyde Park *Also called Cora Materials Corp* **(G-8870)**
Coral Blood Service 800 483-4888
525 Executive Blvd # 285 Elmsford (10523) **(G-4752)**
Coral Cast LLC 516 349-1300
31 Commercial Ct Plainview (11803) **(G-13622)**
Coral Color Process Ltd 631 543-5200
50 Mall Dr Commack (11725) **(G-3855)**
Coral Graphic Services Inc (HQ) 516 576-2100
840 S Broadway Hicksville (11801) **(G-6359)**
Coral Graphic Services Inc 516 576-2100
840 S Broadway Hicksville (11801) **(G-6360)**

ALPHABETIC

(PA)=Parent Co (HQ)=Headquarters (DH)=Div Headquarters
2018 Harris
New York Manufacturers Directory
925

Coral Graphic Svce, Hicksville *Also called Coral Graphic Services Inc* ***(G-6359)***
Coral Management Corp...718 893-9286
923 Bryant Ave Bronx (10474) ***(G-1306)***
Corbertex LLC...212 971-0008
1412 Broadway Rm 1100 New York (10018) ***(G-9783)***
Corbett Hill Gravel Products, Jamestown *Also called Jamestown Macadam Inc* ***(G-7042)***
Corbett Stves Pttern Works Inc...585 546-7109
80 Lowell St Rochester (14605) ***(G-14310)***
Core Group Displays Inc...845 876-5109
41 Pitcher Rd Rhinebeck (12572) ***(G-14067)***
Core Welding, Sanborn *Also called Bruce Pierce* ***(G-15142)***
Coremet Trading Inc...212 964-3600
160 Brdwy Ste 1107 New York (10038) ***(G-9784)***
Corey Creek Vineyards, Cutchogue *Also called Vedell North Fork LLC* ***(G-4100)***
Corey Rugs, Great Neck *Also called Rosecore Division* ***(G-5852)***
Corfu Machine Inc (PA)...585 418-4083
1977 Genesee St Corfu (14036) ***(G-3975)***
Corinne McCormack Inc...212 868-7919
7 W 36th St Fl 9 New York (10018) ***(G-9785)***
Corinthian Cast Stone Inc...631 920-2340
115 Wyandanch Ave Wyandanch (11798) ***(G-17389)***
Corium Corporation (PA)...914 381-0100
147 Palmer Ave Mamaroneck (10543) ***(G-8062)***
Corkhill Grp, Jamaica *Also called Corkhill Manufacturing Co Inc* ***(G-6943)***
Corkhill Manufacturing Co Inc...718 528-7413
13121 Merrick Blvd Jamaica (11434) ***(G-6943)***
Corman USA Inc...718 727-7455
1140 Bay St Ste 2c Staten Island (10305) ***(G-15682)***
Corneal Design Corporation...301 670-7076
3288 Plank Rd Lima (14485) ***(G-7465)***
Cornell Beverages Inc...718 381-3000
105 Harrison Pl Brooklyn (11237) ***(G-1803)***
Cornell Laboratory Ornithology, Ithaca *Also called Cornell University* ***(G-6872)***
Cornell University...607 277-2338
512 E State St Ithaca (14850) ***(G-6871)***
Cornell University...607 254-2473
159 Sapsucker Woods Rd Ithaca (14850) ***(G-6872)***
Cornell University Press, Ithaca *Also called Cornell University* ***(G-6871)***
Corning Cable Systems Cr Un...607 974-9000
1 Riverfront Plz Corning (14831) ***(G-3982)***
Corning Consumer Products Co, Corning *Also called Corning Vitro Corporation* ***(G-3992)***
Corning Incorporated (PA)...607 974-9000
1 Riverfront Plz Corning (14831) ***(G-3983)***
Corning Incorporated...607 974-9000
Decker Bldg Corning (14831) ***(G-3984)***
Corning Incorporated...607 974-1274
905 Addison Rd Painted Post (14870) ***(G-13416)***
Corning Incorporated...607 974-9000
1 Riverfront Plz Corning (14831) ***(G-3985)***
Corning Incorporated...315 379-3200
334 County Route 16 Canton (13617) ***(G-3408)***
Corning Incorporated...607 433-3100
275 River St Oneonta (13820) ***(G-13205)***
Corning Incorporated...607 248-1200
Hp-Ab-01-A9b Corning (14831) ***(G-3986)***
Corning Incorporated...646 521-9600
767 5th Ave Ste 2301 New York (10153) ***(G-9786)***
Corning Incorporated...607 974-6729
9261 Addison Rd Painted Post (14870) ***(G-13417)***
Corning Incorporated...607 974-4488
1 W Market St Ste 601 Corning (14830) ***(G-3987)***
Corning Incorporated...607 974-8496
1 Museum Way Corning (14830) ***(G-3988)***
Corning International Corp (HQ)...607 974-9000
1 Riverfront Plz Corning (14831) ***(G-3989)***
Corning Optcal Cmmncations LLC...607 974-7543
22 W 3rd St Corning (14830) ***(G-3990)***
Corning Rubber Company Inc...631 738-0041
1744 Julia Goldbach Ave Ronkonkoma (11779) ***(G-14917)***
Corning Specialty Mtls Inc...607 974-9000
1 Riverfront Plz Corning (14831) ***(G-3991)***
Corning Tropel Corporation...585 377-3200
60 Oconnor Rd Fairport (14450) ***(G-4857)***
Corning Vitro Corporation...607 974-8605
1 Riverfront Plz Corning (14830) ***(G-3992)***
Corning Wax, Ronkonkoma *Also called Corning Rubber Company Inc* ***(G-14917)***
Cornwall Local, Cornwall *Also called News of The Highlands Inc* ***(G-4011)***
Corona Plumbing & Htg Sup Inc...718 424-4133
10466 Roosevelt Ave Corona (11368) ***(G-4016)***
Corona Ready Mix Inc...718 271-5940
5025 97th Pl Corona (11368) ***(G-4017)***
Coronet Kitchen & Bath, Ronkonkoma *Also called Dak Mica and Wood Products* ***(G-14920)***
Coronet Parts Mfg Co Inc (PA)...718 649-1750
883 Elton St Brooklyn (11208) ***(G-1804)***
Coronet Parts Mfg Co Inc...718 649-1750
901 Elton St Fl 1 Brooklyn (11208) ***(G-1805)***
Corpkit Legal Supplies, Islip *Also called Rike Enterprises Inc* ***(G-6851)***
Corporate News, Pearl River *Also called 21st Century Fox America Inc* ***(G-13476)***
Cort Contracting...845 758-1190
188 W Market St Red Hook (12571) ***(G-14041)***

Cortice Biosciences Inc...646 747-9090
1345 Avenue Of The Americ New York (10105) ***(G-9787)***
Cortland, Cortland *Also called Actuant Corporation* ***(G-4033)***
Cortland Cable Company Inc...607 753-8276
44 River St Cortland (13045) ***(G-4039)***
Cortland Company Inc (HQ)...607 753-8276
44 River St Cortland (13045) ***(G-4040)***
Cortland Industries Inc...212 575-2710
1400 Broadway New York (10018) ***(G-9788)***
Cortland Line Mfg LLC...607 756-2851
3736 Kellogg Rd Cortland (13045) ***(G-4041)***
Cortland Machine and Tool Co...607 756-5852
60 Grant St Cortland (13045) ***(G-4042)***
Cortland Plastics Intl LLC...607 662-0120
211 S Main St Cortland (13045) ***(G-4043)***
Cortland Ready Mix, Cortland *Also called Saunders Concrete Co Inc* ***(G-4067)***
Cortland Ready Mix Inc...607 753-3063
6 Locust Ave Ofc Rte 13 Cortland (13045) ***(G-4044)***
Cortland Standard Printing Co...607 756-5665
110 Main St Cortland (13045) ***(G-4045)***
Cortland-Ithaca Subn Shopper, Freeville *Also called Freeville Publishing Co Inc* ***(G-5447)***
Cortlandt Smoke and Vape...914 930-7592
2153 Albany Post Rd Montrose (10548) ***(G-8652)***
Corzane Cabinets, Farmingdale *Also called Kazac Inc* ***(G-5031)***
Cos TEC Manufacturing Corp...631 589-7170
390 Knickerbocker Ave # 1 Bohemia (11716) ***(G-1035)***
Cosa Xentaur Corporation (PA)...631 345-3434
84 Horseblock Rd Unit G Yaphank (11980) ***(G-17405)***
Cosco Enterprises Inc...718 383-4488
1930 Troutman St Ridgewood (11385) ***(G-14117)***
Cosco Soap & Detergent, Ridgewood *Also called Cosco Enterprises Inc* ***(G-14117)***
Cosense Inc...516 364-9161
125 Coachman Pl W Syosset (11791) ***(G-15838)***
Cosmetic World, New York *Also called Ledes Group Inc* ***(G-10991)***
Cosmetics Plus Ltd...516 768-7250
23 Deep Wood Ln Amagansett (11930) ***(G-217)***
Cosmic Enterprise...718 342-6257
147 Rockaway Ave Ste A Brooklyn (11233) ***(G-1806)***
Cosmicoat of Wny Inc...716 772-2644
8419 East Ave Gasport (14067) ***(G-5571)***
Cosmo Electronic Machine Corp...631 249-2535
113 Gazza Blvd Farmingdale (11735) ***(G-4973)***
Cosmo Optics, Albany *Also called Ion Optics Inc* ***(G-89)***
Cosmopolitan Cabinet Company...631 467-4960
40 Fleetwood Ct Ste 1 Ronkonkoma (11779) ***(G-14918)***
Cosmos Communications Inc...718 482-1800
1105 44th Dr Long Island City (11101) ***(G-7734)***
Cosmos Electronic Machine Corp (PA)...631 249-2535
140 Schmitt Blvd Farmingdale (11735) ***(G-4974)***
Cossitt Concrete Products Inc...315 824-2700
6543 Middleport Rd Hamilton (13346) ***(G-5970)***
Costanza Ready Mix Inc...516 783-4444
1345 Newbridge Rd North Bellmore (11710) ***(G-12934)***
Costanzos Bakery Inc...716 656-9093
30 Innsbruck Dr Buffalo (14227) ***(G-2911)***
Costanzos Welding Inc (PA)...716 282-0845
22nd Allen St Niagara Falls (14302) ***(G-12829)***
Costello Bros Petroleum Corp (PA)...914 237-3189
990 Mclean Ave Ste 3 Yonkers (10704) ***(G-17446)***
Costello Tagliapietra, New York *Also called CTS LLC* ***(G-9820)***
Costume Armour Inc...845 534-9120
2 Mill St Stop 4 Cornwall (12518) ***(G-4008)***
Costume Culture By Franco LLC...718 821-7100
7017 83rd St Glendale (11385) ***(G-5664)***
Cote Hardwood Products Inc (PA)...607 898-5737
4725 Cat Path Rd Locke (13092) ***(G-7595)***
Cote Wood Products, Locke *Also called Cote Hardwood Products Inc* ***(G-7595)***
Coto Technology, New York *Also called Kearney-National Inc* ***(G-10868)***
Cotswolt Industries, New York *Also called Central Textiles Inc* ***(G-9618)***
Cott Beverages, Dunkirk *Also called Cliffstar LLC* ***(G-4361)***
Cotton Emporium Inc (PA)...718 894-3365
8000 Cooper Ave Glendale (11385) ***(G-5665)***
Cotton Well Drilling Co Inc...716 672-2788
Center Rd Sheridan (14135) ***(G-15422)***
Cottonwood Metals Inc...646 807-8674
1625 Sycamore Ave Ste A Bohemia (11716) ***(G-1036)***
Cottrell Paper Company Inc...518 885-1702
1135 Rock City Rd Rock City Falls (12863) ***(G-14807)***
Coty Inc...212 389-7000
1 Park Ave Fl 4 New York (10016) ***(G-9789)***
Coty Inc (HQ)...212 389-7300
350 5th Ave Ste 2700 New York (10118) ***(G-9790)***
Coty US LLC (HQ)...212 389-7000
350 5th Ave New York (10118) ***(G-9791)***
Coty US LLC...212 389-7000
726 Eab Plz Uniondale (11556) ***(G-16313)***
Cougar Sport Inc...212 947-3054
55 W 39th St Rm 305 New York (10018) ***(G-9792)***
Coughlin Printing Group, Watertown *Also called Christian Bus Endeavors Inc* ***(G-16665)***
Coughlin Printing Group...315 788-8560
210 Court St Ste 10 Watertown (13601) ***(G-16668)***

Councel For Sclar Hmnism Cscop, Amherst *Also called Center For Inquiry Inc* ***(G-233)***
Counter Evolution...212 647-7505
37 W 17th St New York (10011) ***(G-9793)***
Countertop Creations, Rochester *Also called Frank J Martello* ***(G-14403)***
Countertops & Cabinets Inc...315 433-1038
4073 New Court Ave Syracuse (13206) ***(G-15930)***
Countess Corporation...212 869-7070
225 W 37th St Fl 12 New York (10018) ***(G-9794)***
Countess Mara Inc...212 768-7300
120 W 45th St Fl 37 New York (10036) ***(G-9795)***
Country Coin-Op, Newport *Also called Reynolds Drapery Service Inc* ***(G-12816)***
Country Folks...585 343-9721
123 N Spruce St Batavia (14020) ***(G-631)***
Country Printer, The, Huntington *Also called Photo Agents Ltd* ***(G-6709)***
Country Side Sand & Gravel (HQ)...716 988-3271
Taylor Hollow Rd Collins (14034) ***(G-3840)***
Country Side Sand & Gravel...716 988-3271
8458 Route 62 South Dayton (14138) ***(G-15541)***
County Draperies Inc...845 342-9009
64 Genung St Middletown (10940) ***(G-8467)***
County Energy Corp...718 626-7000
65 S 11th St Apt 1e Brooklyn (11249) ***(G-1807)***
County Fabricators...914 741-0219
175 Marble Ave Pleasantville (10570) ***(G-13745)***
County Line Stone Co Inc...716 542-5435
4515 Crittenden Rd Akron (14001) ***(G-18)***
County Waste Management Inc...914 592-5007
565 Harrison Ave Harrison (10528) ***(G-6002)***
County WD Applnc & TV Srvc of...585 328-7417
95 Mount Read Blvd Ste 14 Rochester (14611) ***(G-14311)***
Courage Clothing Co Inc...212 354-5690
1407 Broadway Rm 3604 New York (10018) ***(G-9796)***
Courier Life Publications, Brooklyn *Also called Courier-Life Inc* ***(G-1809)***
Courier Observer, Ogdensburg *Also called St Lawrence County Newspapers* ***(G-13143)***
Courier Packaging Inc...718 349-2390
220 West St Brooklyn (11222) ***(G-1808)***
Courier Printing Corp...607 467-2191
24 Laurel Bank Ave Ste 2 Deposit (13754) ***(G-4300)***
Courier-Life Inc...718 260-2500
1 Metrotech Ctr Brooklyn (11201) ***(G-1809)***
Courser Inc...607 739-3861
802 County Road 64 # 100 Elmira (14903) ***(G-4690)***
Courtaulds Textiles Ltd...212 946-8000
358 5th Ave Fl 6 New York (10001) ***(G-9797)***
Courtlandt Boot Jack Co Inc...718 445-6200
3334 Prince St Flushing (11354) ***(G-5242)***
Cousin's Furniture, Deer Park *Also called Cousins Furniture & Hm Imprvs* ***(G-4143)***
Cousins Furniture & Hm Imprvs...631 254-3752
515 Acorn St Deer Park (11729) ***(G-4143)***
Couture Inc...212 921-1166
16 W 37th St Frnt 1 New York (10018) ***(G-9798)***
Couture Logging Inc...607 753-6445
3060 State Route 13 Cortland (13045) ***(G-4046)***
Couture Press...310 734-4831
200 Park Ave New York (10166) ***(G-9799)***
Couture Timber Harvesting...607 836-4719
2760 Phelps Rd Mc Graw (13101) ***(G-8252)***
Cove Point Holdings LLC (PA)...212 599-3388
60 E 42nd St Rm 3210 New York (10165) ***(G-9800)***
Coventry Manufacturing Co Inc (PA)...914 668-2212
115 E 3rd St Mount Vernon (10550) ***(G-8719)***
Covergrip Corporation...855 268-3747
30 Aero Rd Bohemia (11716) ***(G-1037)***
Covington Sound...646 256-7486
2705 Kingsbridge Ter Bronx (10463) ***(G-1307)***
Cowee Forest Products Inc...518 658-2233
28 Taylor Ave Berlin (12022) ***(G-854)***
Cox & Company Inc...212 366-0200
1664 Old Country Rd Plainview (11803) ***(G-13623)***
Coyote Moon LLC (PA)...315 686-5600
17371 County Route 3 Clayton (13624) ***(G-3711)***
Coyote Moon Vineyards, Clayton *Also called Coyote Moon LLC* ***(G-3711)***
Coyote Motorsports, Spencerport *Also called Bullet Industries Inc* ***(G-15592)***
Cpac Inc (HQ)...585 382-3223
2364 State Route 20a Leicester (14481) ***(G-7442)***
Cpac Equipment Inc...585 382-3223
2364 State Route 20a Leicester (14481) ***(G-7443)***
CPI, New York *Also called Capital Programs Inc* ***(G-9576)***
CPI Aerostructures Inc...631 586-5200
91 Heartland Blvd Edgewood (11717) ***(G-4610)***
CPI Industries Inc...631 909-3434
275 Dayton Ave Manorville (11949) ***(G-8111)***
CPI of Falconer Inc...716 664-4444
1890 Lyndon Blvd Falconer (14733) ***(G-4901)***
Cpp - Guaymas...315 687-0014
901 E Genesee St Chittenango (13037) ***(G-3661)***
Cpp - Steel Treaters...315 736-3081
100 Furnace St Oriskany (13424) ***(G-13331)***
Cpp Global, Ronkonkoma *Also called Carolina Precision Plas LLC* ***(G-14914)***
Cpp-Syracuse Inc (HQ)...315 687-0014
901 E Genesee St Chittenango (13037) ***(G-3662)***
CPS Creative, New York *Also called Complete Publishing Solutions* ***(G-9751)***
CPT Usa LLC (PA)...212 575-1616
15 W 39th St Fl 12 New York (10018) ***(G-9801)***
CPW Direct Mail Group LLC...631 588-6565
110 Schmitt Blvd Farmingdale (11735) ***(G-4975)***
Cq Magazine, Hicksville *Also called C Q Communications Inc* ***(G-6352)***
Cq Traffic Control Devices LLC...518 767-0057
1521 Us Rte 9w Selkirk (12158) ***(G-15376)***
Cq Traffic Control Products, Selkirk *Also called Cq Traffic Control Devices LLC* ***(G-15376)***
Crabtree & Evelyn Ltd...845 928-4831
928 Adirondack Way Central Valley (10917) ***(G-3548)***
Crabtree Publishing Inc...212 496-5040
350 5th Ave Ste 3304 New York (10118) ***(G-9802)***
Craft Atlantic, New York *Also called Craftatlantic LLC* ***(G-9804)***
Craft Clerical Clothes Inc (PA)...212 764-6122
247 W 37th St Rm 1700 New York (10018) ***(G-9803)***
Craft Custom Woodwork Co Inc...718 821-2162
5949 56th Ave Maspeth (11378) ***(G-8155)***
Craft Packaging Inc...718 633-4045
1274 49th St Ste 350 Brooklyn (11219) ***(G-1810)***
Craft Pak Inc...718 257-2700
67 Gateway Dr Staten Island (10304) ***(G-15683)***
Craft Robe Co., New York *Also called Craft Clerical Clothes Inc* ***(G-9803)***
Craft-Tech Mfg Corp...631 563-4949
1750 Artic Ave Bohemia (11716) ***(G-1038)***
Craftatlantic LLC...646 726-4205
115 Greenwich Ave New York (10014) ***(G-9804)***
Craftech...518 828-5011
5 Dock St Chatham (12037) ***(G-3585)***
Craftech Industries Inc...518 828-5001
8 Dock St Hudson (12534) ***(G-6640)***
Crafters Workshop Inc...914 345-2838
116 S Central Ave Ste 1 Elmsford (10523) ***(G-4753)***
Craftmaster Flavor Technology...631 789-8607
23 Albany Ave Amityville (11701) ***(G-282)***
Craftsman Manufacturing Co In...585 426-5780
1279 Mount Read Blvd Rochester (14606) ***(G-14312)***
Craftsmen Woodworkers Ltd...718 326-3350
5865 Maspeth Ave Maspeth (11378) ***(G-8156)***
Craig Envelope Corp...718 786-4277
220 Miller Pl Hicksville (11801) ***(G-6361)***
Crain Communications Inc...212 210-0100
685 3rd Ave New York (10017) ***(G-9805)***
Crains New York Business...212 210-0250
711 3rd Ave New York (10017) ***(G-9806)***
Crainville Block Co, Queensbury *Also called Glens Falls Ready Mix Inc* ***(G-14010)***
Crandall Filling Machinery Inc...716 897-3486
80 Gruner Rd Buffalo (14227) ***(G-2912)***
Crane Equipment & Service Inc (HQ)...716 689-5400
140 John Jmes Adubon Pkwy Amherst (14228) ***(G-236)***
Cranesville Block Co Inc (PA)...518 684-6154
1250 Riverfront Ctr Amsterdam (12010) ***(G-341)***
Cranesville Block Co Inc...315 732-2135
895 Catherine St Utica (13501) ***(G-16340)***
Cranesville Block Co Inc...845 292-1585
1794 State Route 52 Liberty (12754) ***(G-7458)***
Cranesville Block Co Inc...845 896-5687
70 Route 9 Fishkill (12524) ***(G-5189)***
Cranesville Block Co Inc...315 773-2296
23903 Cemetery Rd Felts Mills (13638) ***(G-5175)***
Cranesville Block Co Inc...845 331-1775
637 E Chester St Kingston (12401) ***(G-7214)***
Cranesville Block Co Inc...315 384-4000
8405 State Highway 56 Norfolk (13667) ***(G-12915)***
Cranesville Concrete, Norfolk *Also called Cranesville Block Co Inc* ***(G-12915)***
Cranesville Concrete Co, Utica *Also called Cranesville Block Co Inc* ***(G-16340)***
Cranesville Concrete Co, Liberty *Also called Cranesville Block Co Inc* ***(G-7458)***
Cranesville Ready-Mix, Amsterdam *Also called Cranesville Block Co Inc* ***(G-341)***
Cranial Technologies Inc...914 472-0975
495 Central Park Ave Scarsdale (10583) ***(G-15246)***
Crawford Furniture Mfg Corp...716 483-2102
347 Broadhead Ave Jamestown (14701) ***(G-7020)***
Crawford Print Shop Inc...607 359-4970
6120 Herrington Rd Addison (14801) ***(G-5)***
Craz Woodworking Assoc Inc...631 205-1890
24 Sawgrass Dr Bellport (11713) ***(G-823)***
Crazy Cowboy Brewing Co LLC...516 812-0576
60 Crossways Park Dr W # 400 Woodbury (11797) ***(G-17306)***
Crazy Hatter, Holtsville *Also called Screen The World Inc* ***(G-6534)***
Cream Bebe...917 578-2088
694 Myrtle Ave Ste 220 Brooklyn (11205) ***(G-1811)***
Create-A-Card Inc...631 584-2273
16 Brasswood Rd Saint James (11780) ***(G-15114)***
Creation Baumann USA Inc...516 764-7431
114 N Centre Ave Rockville Centre (11570) ***(G-14818)***
Creations In Canvas, Yonkers *Also called Dalee Bookbinding Co Inc* ***(G-17449)***
Creations In Lucite Inc...718 871-2000
165 Franklin Ave Apt 5 Brooklyn (11205) ***(G-1812)***
Creative Cabinet Corp America...631 751-5768
3 Onyx Dr Stony Brook (11790) ***(G-15790)***

ALPHABETIC

Creative Cabinetry Corporation 914 963-6061
42 Morsemere Pl Yonkers (10701) *(G-17447)*
Creative Compositions, Amityville Also called Jeffrey John *(G-299)*
Creative Costume Co 212 564-5552
3804 Rivers Pointe Way Liverpool (13090) *(G-7542)*
Creative Counter Tops Inc 845 471-6480
17 Van Kleeck Dr Poughkeepsie (12601) *(G-13913)*
Creative Custom Shades, Brooklyn Also called Custom Lampshades Inc *(G-1826)*
Creative Design and Mch Inc 845 778-9001
197 Stone Castle Rd Rock Tavern (12575) *(G-14809)*
Creative Food Ingredients Inc 585 237-2213
1 Lincoln Ave Perry (14530) *(G-13545)*
Creative Forms Inc 212 431-7540
80 Varick St Apt 10a New York (10013) *(G-9807)*
Creative Gold LLC 718 686-2225
1425 37th St Ste 5 Brooklyn (11218) *(G-1813)*
Creative Home Furnishings (PA) 631 582-8000
250 Creative Dr Central Islip (11722) *(G-3517)*
Creative Images & Applique 718 821-8700
5208 Grand Ave Ste 2 Maspeth (11378) *(G-8157)*
Creative Laminates Inc 315 463-7580
4003 Eastbourne Dr Syracuse (13206) *(G-15931)*
Creative Magazine Inc 516 378-0800
31 Merrick Ave Ste 60 Merrick (11566) *(G-8415)*
Creative Metal Fabricators 631 567-2266
360 Knickerbocker Ave # 13 Bohemia (11716) *(G-1039)*
Creative Models & Prototypes 516 433-6828
160 Lauman Ln Unit A Hicksville (11801) *(G-6362)*
Creative Orthotics & Prosthet (HQ) 607 734-7215
1300 College Ave Ste 1 Elmira (14901) *(G-4691)*
Creative Orthotics Prosthetics, Ithaca Also called Hanger Prsthetcs & Ortho Inc *(G-6882)*
Creative Orthotics Prosthetics 607 771-4672
65 Pennsylvania Ave 207 Binghamton (13903) *(G-899)*
Creative Orthotics Prosthetics 607 431-2526
37 Associate Dr Oneonta (13820) *(G-13206)*
Creative Printing Corp 212 226-3870
121 Varick St Fl 9 New York (10013) *(G-9808)*
Creative Prntng, New York Also called Creative Printing Corp *(G-9808)*
Creative Relations LLC 212 462-4392
425 W 23rd St Rm 1f New York (10011) *(G-9809)*
Creative Scents USA Inc 718 522-5901
183 Wilson St Ste 106 Brooklyn (11211) *(G-1814)*
Creative Solutions Group Inc (PA) 914 771-4200
555 Tuckahoe Rd Yonkers (10710) *(G-17448)*
Creative Stage Lighting Co Inc 518 251-3302
149 State Route 28n North Creek (12853) *(G-12949)*
Creative Stone & Cabinets 631 772-6548
448 Middle Country Rd # 1 Selden (11784) *(G-15371)*
Creative Tools & Supply Inc 212 279-7077
135 W 29th St Rm 205 New York (10001) *(G-9810)*
Creative Vape 347 927-0982
894 Wyckoff Ave Brooklyn (11237) *(G-1815)*
Creative Window Fashions Inc 718 746-5817
315 Cresthaven Ln Whitestone (11357) *(G-17233)*
Creative Yard Designs Inc 315 706-6143
8329 Us Route 20 Manlius (13104) *(G-8103)*
Creatron Services Inc 516 437-5119
504 Cherry Ln Floral Park (11001) *(G-5208)*
Credit Union Journal Inc (PA) 212 803-8200
1 State St Fl 26 New York (10004) *(G-9811)*
Creditiq Inc 888 988-4223
270 Lafayette St Ste 608 New York (10012) *(G-9812)*
Crepe Team, The, Brooklyn Also called Crepini LLC *(G-1816)*
Crepini LLC 347 422-0829
5600 1st Ave Brooklyn (11220) *(G-1816)*
Crescent Duck Farm Inc 631 722-8700
10 Edgar Ave Aquebogue (11931) *(G-384)*
Crescent Manufacturing, North Collins Also called Crescent Marketing Inc *(G-12943)*
Crescent Marketing Inc (PA) 716 337-0145
10285 Eagle Dr North Collins (14111) *(G-12943)*
Crescent Wedding Rings Inc 212 869-8296
36 W 47th St Ste 306 New York (10036) *(G-9813)*
Crest Haven Precast Inc 518 483-4750
4925 State Route 11 Burke (12917) *(G-3292)*
Crest Lock Co Inc 718 345-9898
342 Herzl St Brooklyn (11212) *(G-1817)*
Crest Mills, New York Also called Jbl Trading LLC *(G-10749)*
Cri Graphic, Amityville Also called Control Research Inc *(G-281)*
Crisada Inc 718 729-9730
3913 23rd St Long Island City (11101) *(G-7735)*
Crisray Printing Corp 631 293-3770
50 Executive Blvd Ste A Farmingdale (11735) *(G-4976)*
Cristina, Hempstead Also called King Cracker Corp *(G-6301)*
Criterion Bell & Specialty 718 788-2600
4312 2nd Ave Brooklyn (11232) *(G-1818)*
Critical Imaging LLC 315 732-5020
2428 Chenango Rd Utica (13502) *(G-16341)*
Critical Link LLC 315 425-4045
6712 Brooklawn Pkwy # 203 Syracuse (13211) *(G-15932)*
Crocs Inc 845 928-3002
498 Red Apple Ct Central Valley (10917) *(G-3549)*
Crocs Medical Apparel, New York Also called Icer Scrubs LLC *(G-10597)*

Cromwell Group, Mamaroneck Also called Corium Corporation *(G-8062)*
Cronin Enterprises Inc 914 345-9600
70 E Main St Ste 2 Elmsford (10523) *(G-4754)*
Crosby Company 716 852-3522
183 Pratt St Buffalo (14204) *(G-2913)*
Croscill Home Fashions, New York Also called Mistdoda Inc *(G-11309)*
Crosley Medical Products Inc 631 595-2547
60 S 2nd St Ste E Deer Park (11729) *(G-4144)*
Crosman Corporation (HQ) 585 657-6161
7629 State Route 5 And 20 Bloomfield (14469) *(G-980)*
Crosman Corporation 585 398-3920
1360 Rural Rte 8 Farmington (14425) *(G-5157)*
Cross Border Transactions LLC 646 767-7342
580 White Plains Rd # 660 Tarrytown (10591) *(G-16113)*
Cross Country Mfg Inc 607 656-4103
2355 Rte 206 Greene (13778) *(G-5881)*
Cross Country Mfg Inc (PA) 607 656-4103
2355 State Highway 206 Greene (13778) *(G-5882)*
Cross Filtration Ltd Lblty Co 315 412-1539
87 W Cayuga St Moravia (13118) *(G-8657)*
Crosstex International Inc (HQ) 631 582-6777
10 Ranick Rd Hauppauge (11788) *(G-6079)*
Crosstex International Inc 631 582-6777
2095 Express Dr N Hauppauge (11788) *(G-6080)*
Crosswinds Farm & Creamery 607 327-0363
6762 Log City Rd Ovid (14521) *(G-13370)*
Crosswinds Sourcing LLC 646 438-6904
260 W 39th St Fl 10 New York (10018) *(G-9814)*
Croton Watch Co Inc 800 443-7639
250 W Nyack Rd Ste 114 West Nyack (10994) *(G-16945)*
Crowley Fabg Machining Co Inc (PA) 607 484-0299
403 N Nanticoke Ave Endicott (13760) *(G-4807)*
Crowley Foods, Binghamton Also called HP Hood LLC *(G-916)*
Crowley Foods Inc (HQ) 800 637-0019
93 Pennsylvania Ave Binghamton (13903) *(G-900)*
Crowley Tar Products Co Inc (PA) 212 682-1200
305 Madison Ave Ste 1035 New York (10165) *(G-9815)*
Crown Aircraft Lighting Inc 718 767-3410
1021 Clintonville St # 4 Whitestone (11357) *(G-17234)*
Crown Brand Twine, Maspeth Also called A & A Line & Wire Corp *(G-8139)*
Crown Delta Corporation 914 245-8910
1550 Front St Yorktown Heights (10598) *(G-17526)*
Crown Die Casting Corp 914 667-5400
268 W Lincoln Ave Mount Vernon (10550) *(G-8720)*
Crown Equipment Corporation 516 822-5100
5 Charlotte Ave Ste 1 Hicksville (11801) *(G-6363)*
Crown Hill Stone Inc 716 326-4601
59 Franklin St Westfield (14787) *(G-17076)*
Crown Industrial 607 745-8709
839 State Route 13 Cortland (13045) *(G-4047)*
Crown Jewelers Intl Inc 212 420-7800
168 7th Ave S New York (10014) *(G-9816)*
Crown Lift Trucks, Hicksville Also called Crown Equipment Corporation *(G-6363)*
Crown Medical Products, Suffern Also called Advanced Medical Mfg Corp *(G-15806)*
Crown Mill Work Corp 845 371-2200
12 Melnick Dr Monsey (10952) *(G-8605)*
Crown Novelty Works Inc 631 253-0949
42 Elkland Rd Melville (11747) *(G-8338)*
Crown Sign Systems Inc 914 375-2118
2 South St Mount Vernon (10550) *(G-8721)*
Crown Tank Company LLC 855 276-9682
60 Electric Pkwy Horseheads (14845) *(G-6600)*
Crown Woodworking Corp 718 974-6415
583 Montgomery St Brooklyn (11225) *(G-1819)*
Crownlite Mfg Corp 631 589-9100
1650 Sycamore Ave Ste 24 Bohemia (11716) *(G-1040)*
CRS Nuclear Services LLC 716 810-0688
840 Aero Dr Ste 150 Cheektowaga (14225) *(G-3593)*
CRS Remanufacturing Co Inc 718 739-1720
9440 158th St Jamaica (11433) *(G-6944)*
Crucible Industries LLC 800 365-1180
575 State Fair Blvd Syracuse (13209) *(G-15933)*
Cruise Industry News, New York Also called Mathisen Ventures Inc *(G-11203)*
Crumbrubber Technology Inc 718 468-3988
18740 Hollis Ave Hollis (11423) *(G-6522)*
Crunched Inc 415 484-9909
41 E 11th St New York (10003) *(G-9817)*
Crusader Candle Co Inc 718 625-0005
325 Nevins St Ste 327329 Brooklyn (11215) *(G-1820)*
Cruzin Management Inc (HQ) 212 641-8700
401 Park Ave S Fl 7 New York (10016) *(G-9818)*
Cryomech Inc 315 455-2555
113 Falso Dr Syracuse (13211) *(G-15934)*
Cryovac Inc 585 436-3211
1525 Brooks Ave Rochester (14624) *(G-14313)*
Crysta-Lyn Chemical Company 607 296-4721
6 Emma St Binghamton (13905) *(G-901)*
Crystal Ceres Industries Inc 716 283-0445
2250 Liberty Dr Niagara Falls (14304) *(G-12830)*
Crystal Fusion Tech Inc 631 253-9800
185 W Montauk Hwy Lindenhurst (11757) *(G-7482)*

Crystal Is Inc (HQ).....518 271-7375
70 Cohoes Ave Ste 1b Troy (12183) ***(G-16240)***
Crystal Linton Technologies.....585 444-8784
2180 Brigh Henri Town Lin Rochester (14623) ***(G-14314)***
Crystal Rock LLC.....716 626-7460
100 Stradtman St Ste 1 Buffalo (14206) ***(G-2914)***
Crystalizations Systems Inc.....631 467-0090
1401 Lincoln Ave Holbrook (11741) ***(G-6469)***
Crystalonics Inc.....631 981-6140
2805 Veterans Mem Hwy 14 Ronkonkoma (11779) ***(G-14919)***
Cs Automation Inc.....315 524-5123
518 Berg Rd Ontario (14519) ***(G-13220)***
Cs Manufacturing Limited.....607 587-8154
56 S Main St Alfred (14802) ***(G-196)***
CSC Serviceworks Inc (HQ).....516 349-8555
303 Sunnyside Blvd # 70 Plainview (11803) ***(G-13624)***
CSC Serviceworks Holdings (PA).....516 349-8555
303 Sunnyside Blvd # 70 Plainview (11803) ***(G-13625)***
Csco LLC (PA).....212 221-5100
525 7th Ave Rm 1006 New York (10018) ***(G-9819)***
Csi, Falconer *Also called Reynolds Packaging McHy Inc* ***(G-4918)***
Csi International Inc.....800 441-2895
1001 Main St Niagara Falls (14301) ***(G-12831)***
CSP Technologies Inc (HQ).....518 627-0051
1031 Riverfront Ctr Amsterdam (12010) ***(G-342)***
Csrea, Long Island City *Also called Civil Svc Rtred Employees Assn* ***(G-7727)***
Csw Inc.....585 247-4010
70 Pixley Industrial Pkwy Rochester (14624) ***(G-14315)***
CT Industrial Supply Co Inc.....718 417-3226
305 Ten Eyck St Brooklyn (11206) ***(G-1821)***
CT Publications Co.....718 592-2196
4808 111th St Corona (11368) ***(G-4018)***
Ctac Holdings LLC.....212 924-2280
68 35th Street Brooklyn Brooklyn (11232) ***(G-1822)***
CTB Enterprise LLC.....631 563-0088
1170 Lincoln Ave Unit 7 Holbrook (11741) ***(G-6470)***
CTI Software Inc.....631 253-3550
44 W Jefryn Blvd Ste P Deer Park (11729) ***(G-4145)***
CTS LLC.....212 278-0058
211 E 18th St Apt 4d New York (10003) ***(G-9820)***
CTX Printing, Cambridge *Also called Cambridge-Pacific Inc* ***(G-3333)***
Cuba Specialty Mfg Co Inc.....585 567-4176
81 S Genesee St Fillmore (14735) ***(G-5183)***
Cubbies Unlimited Corporation.....631 586-8572
74 N Industry Ct Deer Park (11729) ***(G-4146)***
Cubic Trnsp Systems Inc.....212 255-1810
245 W 17th St Fl 8 New York (10011) ***(G-9821)***
Cubitek Inc.....631 665-6900
95 Emjay Blvd Ste 2 Brentwood (11717) ***(G-1176)***
Cuccio-Zanetti Inc.....518 587-1363
455 Middle Grove Rd Middle Grove (12850) ***(G-8437)***
Cuddeback Machining Inc.....585 392-5889
18 Draffin Rd Hilton (14468) ***(G-6443)***
Cuffs Planning & Models Ltd.....914 632-1883
317 Beechmont Dr New Rochelle (10804) ***(G-8938)***
Culicover & Shapiro Inc.....516 597-4888
270 Duffy Ave Ste K Hicksville (11801) ***(G-6364)***
Culin/Colella Inc.....914 698-7727
632 Center Ave Mamaroneck (10543) ***(G-8063)***
Culinary Arts Specialties Inc.....716 656-8943
2268 Union Rd Cheektowaga (14227) ***(G-3594)***
Cult Records LLC.....718 395-2077
263 Bowery Apt 3 New York (10002) ***(G-9822)***
Cultureiq Inc (PA).....212 755-8633
7 Penn Plz Ste 1112 New York (10001) ***(G-9823)***
Cumberland Packing Corp (PA).....718 858-4200
2 Cumberland St Brooklyn (11205) ***(G-1823)***
Cummins - Allison Corp.....718 263-2482
8002 Kew Gardens Rd # 402 Kew Gardens (11415) ***(G-7188)***
Cummins Eng Company/James Town, Lakewood *Also called Cummins Inc* ***(G-7314)***
Cummins Inc.....716 456-2676
4720 Baker St Lakewood (14750) ***(G-7313)***
Cummins Inc.....716 456-2111
4720 Baker St Lakewood (14750) ***(G-7314)***
Cummins Inc.....812 377-5000
101-133 Jackson Ave Jamestown (14701) ***(G-7021)***
Cummins Inc.....718 892-2400
890 Zerega Ave Bronx (10473) ***(G-1308)***
Cummins Northeast LLC.....315 437-2296
6193 Eastern Ave Syracuse (13211) ***(G-15935)***
Cuore Technology, Cheektowaga *Also called Leo Schultz* ***(G-3606)***
Cupcake Contessas Corporation.....516 307-1222
1242 Julia Ln North Bellmore (11710) ***(G-12935)***
Cupid Foundations Inc (PA).....212 686-6224
475 Park Ave S Manhattan New York (10022) ***(G-9824)***
Cupid Intimates, New York *Also called Cupid Foundations Inc* ***(G-9824)***
Curaegis Technologies Inc (PA).....585 254-1100
1999 Mount Read Blvd # 3 Rochester (14615) ***(G-14316)***
Curbell Medical Products Inc.....716 667-2520
20 Centre Dr Orchard Park (14127) ***(G-13289)***
Curbell Medical Products Inc (HQ).....716 667-2520
7 Cobham Dr Orchard Park (14127) ***(G-13290)***
Cureatr Inc.....212 203-3927
222 Broadway Fl 201919 New York (10038) ***(G-9825)***
Curemdcom Inc.....212 509-6200
120 Broadway Fl 35 New York (10271) ***(G-9826)***
Curran Manufacturing Corp (PA).....631 273-1010
200 Oser Ave Hauppauge (11788) ***(G-6081)***
Curran Manufacturing Corp.....631 273-1010
210 Oser Ave Hauppauge (11788) ***(G-6082)***
Curran Renewable Energy LLC.....315 769-2000
20 Commerce Dr Massena (13662) ***(G-8225)***
Currant Company LLC.....845 266-8999
59 Walnut Ln Staatsburg (12580) ***(G-15637)***
Currantc, Staatsburg *Also called Currant Company LLC* ***(G-15637)***
Current Applications Inc.....315 788-4689
275 Bellew Ave S Watertown (13601) ***(G-16669)***
Current Controls Inc.....585 593-1544
353 S Brooklyn Ave Wellsville (14895) ***(G-16776)***
Curriculum Associates LLC.....978 313-1355
55 Prospect St Brooklyn (11201) ***(G-1824)***
Currier Plastics Inc.....315 255-1779
101 Columbus St Auburn (13021) ***(G-489)***
Curtin-Hebert Co Inc.....518 725-7157
11 Forest St Gloversville (12078) ***(G-5725)***
Curtin-Hebert Machines, Gloversville *Also called Curtin-Hebert Co Inc* ***(G-5725)***
Curtis Instruments Inc (PA).....914 666-2971
200 Kisco Ave Mount Kisco (10549) ***(G-8666)***
Curtis L Maclean L C (HQ).....716 898-7800
50 Thielman Dr Buffalo (14206) ***(G-2915)***
Curtis PMC Division, Mount Kisco *Also called Curtis Instruments Inc* ***(G-8666)***
Curtis Prtg Co The Del Press.....518 477-4820
711 Columbia Tpke East Greenbush (12061) ***(G-4421)***
Curtis Screw Co Inc.....716 898-7800
50 Thielman Dr Buffalo (14206) ***(G-2916)***
Curtis/Palmer Hydroelectric LP.....518 654-6297
15 Pine St Corinth (12822) ***(G-3979)***
Curtiss-Wrght Intgrted Sensing, Farmingdale *Also called Curtiss-Wright Controls* ***(G-4977)***
Curtiss-Wright Controls.....631 756-4740
175 Central Ave Ste 100 Farmingdale (11735) ***(G-4977)***
Curtiss-Wright Flow Ctrl Corp (HQ).....631 293-3800
1966 Broadhollow Rd Ste E Farmingdale (11735) ***(G-4978)***
Curtiss-Wright Flow Ctrl Corp.....631 293-3800
1966 Broadhollow Rd Ste E Farmingdale (11735) ***(G-4979)***
Cusimano, Michael, Rochester *Also called Empire Fabricators Inc* ***(G-14366)***
Custom 101 Prints Inc.....718 708-4425
3601 Bronxwood Ave Bronx (10469) ***(G-1309)***
Custom Bags Unlimited, Hamburg *Also called Kragel Co Inc* ***(G-5955)***
Custom Brewcrafters Inc.....585 624-4386
300 Village Square Blvd Honeoye Falls (14472) ***(G-6554)***
Custom Candy Concepts Inc.....516 824-3228
50 Inip Dr Inwood (11096) ***(G-6793)***
Custom Canvas Manufacturing Co.....716 852-6372
775 Seneca St Buffalo (14210) ***(G-2917)***
Custom CAS Inc.....718 726-3575
2631 1st St Long Island City (11102) ***(G-7736)***
Custom Coatings, Farmingdale *Also called Time-Cap Laboratories Inc* ***(G-5141)***
Custom Controls.....315 253-4785
2804 Skillett Rd Scipio Center (13147) ***(G-15343)***
Custom Cool, Bronx *Also called S & V Restaurant Eqp Mfrs Inc* ***(G-1444)***
Custom Countertops Inc.....716 646-1579
5260 Armor Duells Rd Orchard Park (14127) ***(G-13291)***
Custom Countertops Inc (PA).....716 685-2871
3192 Walden Ave Depew (14043) ***(G-4277)***
Custom Design Kitchens Inc.....518 355-4446
1700 Duanesburg Rd Duanesburg (12056) ***(G-4350)***
Custom Design Metals Inc.....631 563-2444
1612 Locust Ave Ste C Bohemia (11716) ***(G-1041)***
Custom Display Manufacture.....516 783-6491
1686 Logan St North Bellmore (11710) ***(G-12936)***
Custom Door & Mirror Inc.....631 414-7725
148 Milbar Blvd Farmingdale (11735) ***(G-4980)***
Custom Eco Friendly Bags, Roslyn *Also called Custom Eco Friendly LLC* ***(G-15042)***
Custom Eco Friendly LLC (PA).....347 227-0229
50 Spruce Dr Roslyn (11576) ***(G-15042)***
Custom Electronics Inc.....607 432-3880
87 Browne St Oneonta (13820) ***(G-13207)***
Custom European Imports Inc.....845 357-5718
100 Sterling Mine Rd Sloatsburg (10974) ***(G-15502)***
Custom Fixtures Inc.....718 965-1141
129 13th St Brooklyn (11215) ***(G-1825)***
Custom Frame & Molding Co.....631 491-9091
97 Lamar St 101 West Babylon (11704) ***(G-16811)***
Custom House Engravers Inc.....631 567-3004
104 Keyland Ct Bohemia (11716) ***(G-1042)***
Custom Klean Corp.....315 865-8101
8890 Boak Rd E Holland Patent (13354) ***(G-6513)***
Custom Lampshades Inc.....718 254-0500
544 Park Ave Ste 503 Brooklyn (11205) ***(G-1826)***
Custom Laser Inc.....716 434-8600
6747 Akron Rd Lockport (14094) ***(G-7606)***
Custom Lucite Creations Inc.....718 871-2000
165 Franklin Ave Apt 5 Brooklyn (11205) ***(G-1827)***

A L P H A B E T I C

(PA)=Parent Co (HQ)=Headquarters (DH)=Div Headquarters

2018 Harris
New York Manufacturers Directory

929

Custom Manufacturing Inc 607 569-2738
93 Lake St Hammondsport (14840) ***(G-5976)***
Custom Metal Fabrication, West Babylon *Also called Custom Metal Incorporated* ***(G-16812)***
Custom Metal Incorporated 631 643-4075
72 Otis St West Babylon (11704) ***(G-16812)***
Custom Mix Inc 516 797-7090
31 Clark Blvd Massapequa Park (11762) ***(G-8218)***
Custom Molding Solutions Inc 585 293-1702
456 Sanford Rd N Churchville (14428) ***(G-3665)***
Custom Patches Inc 845 679-6320
1760 Glasco Tpke Woodstock (12498) ***(G-17378)***
Custom Pins Inc 914 690-9378
150 Clearbrook Rd Ste 139 Elmsford (10523) ***(G-4755)***
Custom Power System, Sayville *Also called Fil-Coil (fc) Corp* ***(G-15237)***
Custom Power Systems, Central Islip *Also called Berkshire Transformer* ***(G-3512)***
Custom Prtrs Guilderland Inc 518 456-2811
2210 Western Ave Guilderland (12084) ***(G-5924)***
Custom Publishing Group Ltd 212 840-8800
8 W 38th St 204 New York (10018) ***(G-9827)***
Custom Service Solutions Inc 585 637-3760
1900 Transit Way Brockport (14420) ***(G-1242)***
Custom Sheet Metal Corp 315 463-9105
1 General Motors Dr Ste 5 Syracuse (13206) ***(G-15936)***
Custom Shipping Products Inc 716 355-4437
8661 Knowlton Rd Clymer (14724) ***(G-3758)***
Custom Sitecom LLC 631 420-4238
470 Smith St Farmingdale (11735) ***(G-4981)***
Custom Sound and Video 585 424-5000
40 Rutter St Rochester (14606) ***(G-14317)***
Custom Sports Lab Inc 212 832-1648
515 Madison Ave Rm 1204 New York (10022) ***(G-9828)***
Custom Sportswear Corp 914 666-9200
375 Adams St Bedford Hills (10507) ***(G-797)***
Custom Stair & Millwork Co 315 839-5793
6 Gridley Pl Sauquoit (13456) ***(G-15228)***
Custom Studio Division, Tappan *Also called Nationwide Custom Services* ***(G-16105)***
Custom Wood Inc 718 927-4700
770 E 94th St Brooklyn (11236) ***(G-1828)***
Custom Woodcraft LLC 315 843-4234
2525 Perry Schumaker Rd Munnsville (13409) ***(G-8796)***
Custom Woodwork Ltd 631 727-5260
205 Marcy Ave Riverhead (11901) ***(G-14151)***
Customize Elite Socks LLC 212 533-8551
156 2nd Ave Apt 2c New York (10003) ***(G-9829)***
Customshow Inc 800 255-5303
216 E 45th St Fl 17 New York (10017) ***(G-9830)***
Cutco Cutlery Corporation (HQ) 716 372-3111
1116 E State St Olean (14760) ***(G-13161)***
Cutting Edge Metal Works 631 981-8333
12 Long Island Ave Holtsville (11742) ***(G-6528)***
Cuzins Duzin Corp 347 724-6200
8420 Austin St Apt 3a Kew Gardens (11415) ***(G-7189)***
Cvd Equipment Corporation 845 246-3631
1117 Kings Hwy Saugerties (12477) ***(G-15211)***
Cvd Equipment Corporation (PA) 631 981-7081
355 S Technology Dr Central Islip (11722) ***(G-3518)***
Cvd Equipment Corporation 631 582-4365
355 S Technology Dr Central Islip (11722) ***(G-3519)***
CVI Laser LLC 585 244-7220
55 Science Pkwy Rochester (14620) ***(G-14318)***
Cw Fasteners & Zippers Corp 212 594-3203
142 W 36th St Fl 5 New York (10018) ***(G-9831)***
Cw Metals Inc 917 416-7906
3421 Greenpoint Ave Long Island City (11101) ***(G-7737)***
Cws Powder Coatings Company LP 845 398-2911
2234 Bradley Hill Rd # 12 Blauvelt (10913) ***(G-964)***
Cy Fashion Corp 212 730-8600
525 7th Ave Rm 811 New York (10018) ***(G-9832)***
Cy Plastics Works Inc 585 229-2555
8601 Main St Honeoye (14471) ***(G-6551)***
Cya Action Funwell, Patchogue *Also called Gem West Inc* ***(G-13445)***
Cyandia Inc 315 679-4268
843 Malden Rd Syracuse (13211) ***(G-15937)***
Cyber Knit, New York *Also called Lifestyle Design Usa Ltd* ***(G-11021)***
Cyber Swag Merchandise of NY, Maspeth *Also called Creative Images & Applique* ***(G-8157)***
Cyberlimit Inc 212 840-9597
257 W 38th St Fl 6 New York (10018) ***(G-9833)***
Cybersports Inc (PA) 315 737-7150
11 Avery Pl Utica (13502) ***(G-16342)***
Cyclone Air Power Inc 718 447-3038
12 Van St Staten Island (10310) ***(G-15684)***
Cyclotherm of Watertown Inc 315 782-1100
787 Pearl St Watertown (13601) ***(G-16670)***
Cygnet Studio Inc 646 450-4550
251 W 39th St Fl 17 New York (10018) ***(G-9834)***
Cygnus Automation Inc 631 981-0909
1605 9th Ave Bohemia (11716) ***(G-1043)***
Cyncal Steel Fabricators Inc 631 254-5600
225 Pine Aire Dr Bay Shore (11706) ***(G-687)***
Cynosure Inc 516 594-3333
400 Karin Ln Hicksville (11801) ***(G-6365)***
Cynthia Rowley Inc (PA) 212 242-3803
376 Bleecker St New York (10014) ***(G-9835)***
Cynthia Steffe, New York *Also called Bernard Chaus Inc* ***(G-9412)***
Cypress Bioscience Inc 858 452-2323
110 E 59th St Fl 33 New York (10022) ***(G-9836)***
Cypress Semiconductor Corp 631 261-1358
34 Rowley Dr Northport (11768) ***(G-13028)***
Cytec Industries Inc 716 372-9650
1405 Buffalo St Olean (14760) ***(G-13162)***
Cytec Olean Inc 716 372-9650
1405 Buffalo St Olean (14760) ***(G-13163)***
Cytec Solvay Group, Olean *Also called Cytec Industries Inc* ***(G-13162)***
Cz USA Dwf Dan Wesson Firearm, Norwich *Also called Dan Wesson Corp* ***(G-13045)***
D & A Offset Services Inc 212 924-0612
185 Varick St Ste 3 New York (10014) ***(G-9837)***
D & C Cleaning Inc 631 789-5659
1095 Campagnoli Ave Copiague (11726) ***(G-3924)***
D & D Motor Systems Inc 315 701-0861
215 Park Ave Syracuse (13204) ***(G-15938)***
D & D Printing, Buffalo *Also called Dan Trent Company Inc* ***(G-2920)***
D & D Window Tech Inc (PA) 212 308-2822
979 3rd Ave Lbby 132 New York (10022) ***(G-9838)***
D & E Industrial, Akron *Also called Re-Al Industrial Corp* ***(G-25)***
D & F Pallet Inc 716 672-2984
134 Clinton Ave Fredonia (14063) ***(G-5381)***
D & G Sheet Metal Co Inc 718 326-9111
5400 Grand Ave Maspeth (11378) ***(G-8158)***
D & G Welding Inc 716 873-3088
249 Hertel Ave Buffalo (14207) ***(G-2918)***
D & I Finishing Inc 631 471-3034
1560 Ocean Ave Ste 7 Bohemia (11716) ***(G-1044)***
D & L Electronic Die, Farmingdale *Also called Cosmo Electronic Machine Corp* ***(G-4973)***
D & L Manufacturing, Bronx *Also called L & D Manufacturing Corp* ***(G-1379)***
D & M Custom Cabinets Inc 516 678-2818
2994 Long Beach Rd Oceanside (11572) ***(G-13095)***
D & M Enterprises Incorporated 914 937-6430
1 Mill St Ste 2 Port Chester (10573) ***(G-13769)***
D & R Silk Screening Ltd 631 234-7464
201 Creative Dr Central Islip (11722) ***(G-3520)***
D & S Supplies Inc 718 721-5256
2067 21st St Astoria (11105) ***(G-432)***
D & W Design Inc (PA) 845 343-3366
62 Industrial Pl Middletown (10940) ***(G-8468)***
D & W Diesel Inc 518 437-1300
51 Sicker Rd Ste 3 Latham (12110) ***(G-7387)***
D & W Enterprises LLC 585 590-6727
10775 W Shelby Rd Medina (14103) ***(G-8303)***
D and D Sheet Metal Corp 718 465-7585
9510 218th St Ste 4 Jamaica (11429) ***(G-6945)***
D B F Associates 718 328-0005
1150 E 156th St Bronx (10474) ***(G-1310)***
D Bag Lady Inc 585 425-8095
183 Perinton Pkwy Fairport (14450) ***(G-4858)***
D Best Glass & Mirror, Brooklyn *Also called D Best Service Co Inc* ***(G-1829)***
D Best Service Co Inc 718 972-6133
729 Church Ave Brooklyn (11218) ***(G-1829)***
D C C, New York *Also called Digital Color Concepts Inc* ***(G-9928)***
D C I Plasma Center Inc (PA) 914 241-1646
71 S Bedford Rd Mount Kisco (10549) ***(G-8667)***
D C I Technical Inc 516 355-0464
475 Franklin Ave Fl 2 Franklin Square (11010) ***(G-5372)***
D C M, West Babylon *Also called Display Components Mfg Inc* ***(G-16814)***
D D & L Inc 607 729-9131
3 Alice St Binghamton (13904) ***(G-902)***
D D C, Mechanicville *Also called Decrescente Distributing Co* ***(G-8257)***
D F Stauffer Biscuit Co Inc 585 968-2700
8670 Farnsworth Rd Cuba (14727) ***(G-4094)***
D G M Graphics Inc 516 223-2220
55 Merrick Ave Merrick (11566) ***(G-8416)***
D J Crowell Co Inc 716 684-3343
2815 Town Line Rd Alden (14004) ***(G-179)***
D J Night Ltd 212 302-9050
225 W 37th St Fl 6 New York (10018) ***(G-9839)***
D K Machine Inc 518 747-0626
48 Sullivan Pkwy Fort Edward (12828) ***(G-5349)***
D K P Wood Railings & Stairs 631 665-8656
1971 Union Blvd Bay Shore (11706) ***(G-688)***
D M J Casting Inc 212 719-1951
62 W 47th St Ste 508 New York (10036) ***(G-9840)***
D Maldari & Sons Inc 718 499-3555
557 3rd Ave Brooklyn (11215) ***(G-1830)***
D N Gannon Fabricating Inc 315 463-7466
404 Wavel St Syracuse (13206) ***(G-15939)***
D Oro Onofrio Inc 718 491-2961
1051 73rd St Apt 1 Brooklyn (11228) ***(G-1831)***
D P Mount Vernon, Mount Vernon *Also called Sentage Corporation* ***(G-8779)***
D R Cornue Woodworks 315 655-9463
3206 Us Route 20 Cazenovia (13035) ***(G-3471)***
D R M Management Inc (PA) 716 668-0333
3430 Transit Rd Depew (14043) ***(G-4278)***

ALPHABETIC SECTION
Danisco US Inc

D R S Watch Materials......212 819-0470
56 W 47th St Fl 2 New York (10036) ***(G-9841)***
D S I, Poestenkill *Also called Dynamic Systems Inc* ***(G-13753)***
D Squared Technologies Inc......516 932-7319
71 Birchwood Park Dr Jericho (11753) ***(G-7098)***
D T B, Bohemia *Also called Dayton T Brown Inc* ***(G-1048)***
D T I, Rochester *Also called Dimension Technologies Inc* ***(G-14330)***
D V S Iron & Aluminum Works......718 768-7961
117 14th St Brooklyn (11215) ***(G-1832)***
D W Haber & Son Inc......718 993-6405
825 E 140th St Bronx (10454) ***(G-1311)***
D W S Associates Inc......631 667-6666
89 N Industry Ct Deer Park (11729) ***(G-4147)***
D W S Printing, Deer Park *Also called D W S Associates Inc* ***(G-4147)***
D'Addario & Company Inc, Brooklyn *Also called DAddario & Company Inc* ***(G-1833)***
D-Best Equipment Corp......516 358-0965
77 Hempstead Gardens Dr West Hempstead (11552) ***(G-16883)***
D-C Theatricks......716 847-0180
747 Main St Buffalo (14203) ***(G-2919)***
D-K Manufacturing Corp......315 592-4327
551 W 3rd St S Fulton (13069) ***(G-5469)***
D-Lite Donuts......718 626-5953
4519 Broadway Astoria (11103) ***(G-433)***
D.A.M. Construction, Company, Arverne *Also called Darrell Mitchell* ***(G-422)***
D3 Repro Group......347 507-1075
3401 38th Ave Long Island City (11101) ***(G-7738)***
Da Electric......347 270-3422
6 E Clarke Pl Bronx (10452) ***(G-1312)***
Dab-O-Matic Corp (PA)......914 699-7070
896 S Columbus Ave Mount Vernon (10550) ***(G-8722)***
Dabby-Reid Ltd......212 356-0040
347 W 36th St Rm 701 New York (10018) ***(G-9842)***
DAc Lighting Inc......914 698-5959
420 Railroad Way Mamaroneck (10543) ***(G-8064)***
Dacobe Enterprises LLC......315 368-0093
325 Lafayette St Utica (13502) ***(G-16343)***
Dada Group US Inc......631 888-0818
22104 67th Ave Apt B Bayside (11364) ***(G-764)***
DAddario & Company Inc......631 439-3300
99 Marcus Dr Melville (11747) ***(G-8339)***
DAddario & Company Inc......718 599-6660
1000 Dean St Ste 410 Brooklyn (11238) ***(G-1833)***
DAddario & Company Inc (PA)......631 439-3300
595 Smith St Farmingdale (11735) ***(G-4982)***
DAF Office Networks Inc......315 699-7070
6121 Jemola Runne Cicero (13039) ***(G-3673)***
DAgostino Iron Works Inc......585 235-8850
10 Deep Rock Rd Rochester (14624) ***(G-14319)***
Daheshist Publishing Co Ltd......212 581-8360
1775 Broadway 501 New York (10019) ***(G-9843)***
Dahill Distributors Inc......347 371-9453
975 Dahill Rd Brooklyn (11204) ***(G-1834)***
Dahlstrom Roll Form, Jamestown *Also called Lakeside Capital Corporation* ***(G-7048)***
Dahua Electronics Corporation......718 886-2188
13412 59th Ave Flushing (11355) ***(G-5243)***
Daige Products Inc......516 621-2100
1 Albertson Ave Ste 3 Albertson (11507) ***(G-157)***
Daikin Applied Americas Inc......315 253-2771
4900 Technology Park Blvd Auburn (13021) ***(G-490)***
Dail Cornell Sun, The, Ithaca *Also called Daily Cornell Sun* ***(G-6873)***
Daily Beast Company LLC (HQ)......212 445-4600
7 Hanover Sq New York (10004) ***(G-9844)***
Daily Cornell Sun......607 273-0746
139 W State St Ithaca (14850) ***(G-6873)***
Daily Freeman......845 331-5000
79 Hurley Ave Kingston (12401) ***(G-7215)***
Daily Gazette Company (PA)......518 374-4141
2345 Maxon Rd Ext Schenectady (12308) ***(G-15274)***
Daily Gazette Company......518 395-3060
2345 Maxon Rd Ext Schenectady (12308) ***(G-15275)***
Daily Mail & Greene Cnty News (HQ)......518 943-2100
414 Main St Catskill (12414) ***(G-3455)***
Daily Media, Rochester *Also called Daily Record* ***(G-14320)***
Daily Messenger, Canandaigua *Also called Canandaigua Msgnr Incorporated* ***(G-3366)***
Daily News LP (HQ)......212 210-2100
4 New York Plz Fl 6 New York (10004) ***(G-9845)***
Daily Newsppr For Torah Jewry, Brooklyn *Also called Hamodia Corp* ***(G-2063)***
Daily Orange Corporation......315 443-2314
744 Ostrom Ave Syracuse (13210) ***(G-15940)***
Daily Racing Form Inc (HQ)......212 366-7600
708 3rd Ave Fl 12 New York (10017) ***(G-9846)***
Daily Racing Form LLC......212 514-2180
75 Broad St New York (10004) ***(G-9847)***
Daily Record (PA)......585 232-2035
16 W Main St Ste G9 Rochester (14614) ***(G-14320)***
Daily Sun New York, New York *Also called Daily World Press Inc* ***(G-9848)***
Daily Voice, Armonk *Also called Main Street Connect LLC* ***(G-415)***
Daily Wear Sportswear Corp (PA)......718 972-0533
2308 Mcdonald Ave Brooklyn (11223) ***(G-1835)***
Daily World Press Inc......212 922-9201
228 E 45th St Rm 700 New York (10017) ***(G-9848)***
Dailycandy Inc......646 230-8719
584 Broadway Rm 510 New York (10012) ***(G-9849)***
Daimler Buses North Amer Inc......315 768-8101
165 Base Rd Oriskany (13424) ***(G-13332)***
Dainty Home, New York *Also called Baby Signature Inc* ***(G-9351)***
Dairy Conveyor Corp (PA)......845 278-7878
38 Mount Ebo Rd S Brewster (10509) ***(G-1212)***
Dairy Delite, Farmingdale *Also called Noga Dairies Inc* ***(G-5076)***
Dairy Farmers America Inc......816 801-6440
5001 Brittonfield Pkwy East Syracuse (13057) ***(G-4535)***
Dairy Farmers America Inc......585 409-2200
5140 Agi Business Pk Dr W Batavia (14020) ***(G-632)***
Dairy Maid Raviolo Mfg (PA)......718 449-2620
216 Avenue U Fl 1 Brooklyn (11223) ***(G-1836)***
Daisy Brand Confectionery, Bronx *Also called Scaccianoce Inc* ***(G-1449)***
Daisy Memory Products, Roslyn *Also called Dynamic Photography Inc* ***(G-15043)***
Dak Mica and Wood Products......631 467-0749
2147 5th Ave Ronkonkoma (11779) ***(G-14920)***
Dakota Systems Mfg Corp......631 249-5811
1885 New Hwy Ste 2 Farmingdale (11735) ***(G-4983)***
Dakota Wall, Farmingdale *Also called Dakota Systems Mfg Corp* ***(G-4983)***
Dakotah, Central Islip *Also called Creative Home Furnishings* ***(G-3517)***
Dakott LLC......888 805-6795
244 Madison Ave Ste 211 New York (10016) ***(G-9850)***
Dal-Tile Corporation......718 894-9574
5840 55th Dr Maspeth (11378) ***(G-8159)***
Dal-Tile Corporation......914 835-1801
31 Oakland Ave Harrison (10528) ***(G-6003)***
Dalcom USA Ltd......516 466-7733
11 Middle Neck Rd Ste 301 Great Neck (11021) ***(G-5819)***
Dale Press Inc......718 543-6200
5676 Riverdale Ave # 311 Bronx (10471) ***(G-1313)***
Dalee Bookbinding Co Inc......914 965-1660
129 Clinton Pl Yonkers (10701) ***(G-17449)***
Dalfon, Great Neck *Also called Dalcom USA Ltd* ***(G-5819)***
Dalma Dress Mfg Co Inc......212 391-8296
3 Carman Rd Greenvale (11548) ***(G-5898)***
Dalrymple Grav & Contg Co Inc (HQ)......607 739-0391
2105 S Broadway Pine City (14871) ***(G-13577)***
Dalrymple Grav & Contg Co Inc......607 529-3235
Chemung Flats Rd Chemung (14825) ***(G-3621)***
Dalrymple Holding Corp (PA)......607 737-6200
2105 S Broadway Pine City (14871) ***(G-13578)***
Daly Meghan......347 699-3259
78 5th Ave Brooklyn (11217) ***(G-1837)***
Damascus Bakery Inc......718 855-1456
56 Gold St Brooklyn (11201) ***(G-1838)***
Damianou Sportswear Inc......718 204-5600
6001 31st Ave Ste 2 Woodside (11377) ***(G-17342)***
Dampits International Inc......212 581-3047
425 W 57th St New York (10019) ***(G-9851)***
Dan Ann Associates, Kirkwood *Also called Belden Manufacturing Inc* ***(G-7259)***
Dan Beers......607 316-8895
807 County Road 22 Earlville (13332) ***(G-4384)***
Dan Kane Plating Co Inc......212 675-4947
357 W 36th St New York (10018) ***(G-9852)***
Dan Trent Company Inc......716 822-1422
1728 Clinton St Buffalo (14206) ***(G-2920)***
Dan Wesson Corp......607 336-1174
65 Borden Ave Norwich (13815) ***(G-13045)***
Dana Michele LLC......917 757-7777
3 E 84th St New York (10028) ***(G-9853)***
Danaher Corporation......516 443-9432
445 E 14th St Apt 3f New York (10009) ***(G-9854)***
Danbury Pharma LLC......631 393-6333
220 Smith St Farmingdale (11735) ***(G-4984)***
Dancker Sellew & Douglas Inc......908 231-1600
6067 Corporate Dr East Syracuse (13057) ***(G-4536)***
DAndrea Inc......516 496-2200
115 Eileen Way Ste 106 Syosset (11791) ***(G-15839)***
Danet Inc......718 266-4444
8518 17th Ave Fl 2 Brooklyn (11214) ***(G-1839)***
DAngelico Guitars of America......732 380-0995
141 W 28th St Fl 4 New York (10001) ***(G-9855)***
DAngelo Home Collections Inc......917 267-8920
39 Warwick Tpke Warwick (10990) ***(G-16609)***
Danhier Co LLC......212 563-7683
380 Rector Pl Apt 3d New York (10280) ***(G-9856)***
Dani Accessories Inc......631 692-4505
204 Lawrence Hill Rd Cold Spring Harbor (11724) ***(G-3793)***
Dani II Inc (PA)......212 869-5999
231 W 39th St Rm 1002 New York (10018) ***(G-9857)***
Danice Stores Inc......212 665-0389
305 W 125th St New York (10027) ***(G-9858)***
Daniel & Lois Lyndaker Logging......315 346-6527
10460 Monnat School Rd Castorland (13620) ***(G-3451)***
Daniel Demarco and Assoc Inc......631 598-7000
25 Greene Ave Amityville (11701) ***(G-283)***
Daniel M Friedman & Assoc Inc......212 695-5545
19 W 34th St Fl 4 New York (10001) ***(G-9859)***
Danisco US Inc......585 256-5200
3490 Winton Pl Rochester (14623) ***(G-14321)***

ALPHABETIC

Danisco US Inc 585 277-4300
1700 Lexington Ave Rochester (14606) *(G-14322)*
Danner, Eg Mfg, Central Islip *Also called Eugene G Danner Mfg Inc (G-3521)*
Dannon Company Inc (HQ) 914 872-8400
100 Hillside Ave Fl 3 White Plains (10603) *(G-17125)*
Dannonewave, White Plains *Also called Dannon Company Inc (G-17125)*
Danny & Nicole, New York *Also called Kelly Grace Corp (G-10870)*
Danny Couture, New York *Also called Danny R Couture Corp (G-9861)*
Danny Macaroons Inc 260 622-8463
2191 3rd Ave Ste 3 New York (10035) *(G-9860)*
Danny R Couture Corp (PA) 212 594-1095
261 W 35th St Ground Fl New York (10001) *(G-9861)*
Danone Nutricia Early 914 872-8556
100 Hillside Ave White Plains (10603) *(G-17126)*
Danray Textiles Corp (PA) 212 354-5213
270 W 39th St Fl 5 New York (10018) *(G-9862)*
Dans Paper Inc 631 537-0500
158 County Road 39 Southampton (11968) *(G-15565)*
Dansville Logging & Lumber 585 335-5879
10903 State Route 36 Dansville (14437) *(G-4102)*
Dantex Trimming & Textile Co, New York *Also called Danray Textiles Corp (G-9862)*
Dapper Dads Inc 917 903-8045
45 Rochester Ave Brooklyn (11233) *(G-1840)*
Darby Dental Supply 516 688-6421
105 Executive Ct Jericho (11753) *(G-7099)*
Darco Manufacturing Inc 315 432-8905
6756 Thompson Rd Syracuse (13211) *(G-15941)*
DArcy Printing and Lithog 212 924-1554
121 Varick St Fl 9 New York (10013) *(G-9863)*
Dark Star Lithograph Corp 845 634-3780
9 Perth Ln New City (10956) *(G-8829)*
Darman Manufacturing Coinc 315 724-9632
1410 Lincoln Ave Utica (13502) *(G-16344)*
Darmiyan LLC 917 689-0389
450 E 63rd St Apt 5a New York (10065) *(G-9864)*
Darrell Mitchell 646 659-7075
704 Beach 67th St Arverne (11692) *(G-422)*
Dart Awning Inc 718 945-4224
365 S Main St Freeport (11520) *(G-5404)*
Dart Communications, New Hartford *Also called Dartcom Incorporated (G-8847)*
Dartcom Incorporated 315 790-5456
2 Oxford Xing Ste 1 New Hartford (13413) *(G-8847)*
Das Yidishe Licht Inc 718 387-3166
66 Middleton St Apt 1 Brooklyn (11206) *(G-1841)*
Dasan Inc 212 244-5410
54 W 39th St Fl 8 New York (10018) *(G-9865)*
Dash Printing Inc 212 643-8534
153 W 27th St New York (10001) *(G-9866)*
Dashlane Inc 212 596-7510
156 5th Ave New York (10010) *(G-9867)*
Data Control Inc 585 265-2980
277 David Pkwy Ontario (14519) *(G-13221)*
Data Device Corporation (HQ) 631 567-5600
105 Wilbur Pl Bohemia (11716) *(G-1045)*
Data Display USA Inc 631 218-2130
1330 Lincoln Ave Ste 2 Holbrook (11741) *(G-6471)*
Data Flow Inc 631 436-9200
6 Balsam Dr Medford (11763) *(G-8273)*
Data Implementation Inc 212 979-2015
5 E 22nd St Apt 14t New York (10010) *(G-9868)*
Data Interchange Systems Inc 914 277-7775
9 Ridge Way Purdys (10578) *(G-13988)*
Data Key Communication LLC 315 445-2347
7573 Hunt Ln Fayetteville (13066) *(G-5172)*
Data Max, New York *Also called Datamax International Inc (G-9870)*
Data Palette Info Svcs LLC 718 433-1060
35 Marino Ave Port Washington (11050) *(G-13830)*
Data-Pac Mailing Systems Corp 585 671-0210
1217 Bay Rd Ste 12 Webster (14580) *(G-16744)*
Datacom Systems Inc 315 463-9541
9 Adler Dr East Syracuse (13057) *(G-4537)*
Datadog Inc (PA) 866 329-4466
620 8th Ave Fl 45 New York (10018) *(G-9869)*
Datagraphic Business Systems 516 485-9069
79 Emjay Blvd Brentwood (11717) *(G-1177)*
Datalink Computer Products 914 666-2358
165 E Main St 175 Mount Kisco (10549) *(G-8668)*
Datamax International Inc 212 693-0933
132 Nassau St Rm 511 New York (10038) *(G-9870)*
Datasonic Inc 516 248-7330
1413 Cleveland Ave East Meadow (11554) *(G-4441)*
Datatran Labs Inc 845 856-4313
11 Rebel Ln Port Jervis (12771) *(G-13805)*
Dates Weiser Furniture Corp 716 891-1700
1700 Broadway St Buffalo (14212) *(G-2921)*
Datorib Inc 631 698-6222
974 Middle Country Rd Selden (11784) *(G-15372)*
Datum Alloys Inc 607 239-6274
407 Airport Rd Endicott (13760) *(G-4808)*
Dau Thrmal Slutions N Amer Inc 585 678-9025
1657 E Park Dr Macedon (14502) *(G-8015)*
Dave & Johnny Ltd 212 302-9050
225 W 37th St Fl 6 New York (10018) *(G-9871)*
Dave Sandel Cranes Inc 631 325-5588
56 S Country Rd Westhampton (11977) *(G-17085)*
Davel Systems Inc 718 382-6024
1314 Avenue M Brooklyn (11230) *(G-1842)*
Davenport, Rochester *Also called Brinkman Products Inc (G-14264)*
Daves Electric Motors & Pumps 212 982-2930
282 E 7th St Apt 1 New York (10009) *(G-9872)*
Daves Precision Machine Shop 845 626-7263
56 Webster Ave Kerhonkson (12446) *(G-7184)*
David & Young Co Inc 212 594-6034
366 5th Ave Rm 707 New York (10001) *(G-9873)*
David Christy 607 863-4610
2810 Cincinnatus Rd Cincinnatus (13040) *(G-3681)*
David Fehlman 315 455-8888
6729 Pickard Dr Syracuse (13211) *(G-15942)*
David Flatt Furniture Ltd 718 937-7944
3842 Review Ave Ste 2 Long Island City (11101) *(G-7739)*
David Friedman and Sons, New York *Also called David Friedman Chain Co Inc (G-9874)*
David Friedman Chain Co Inc 212 684-1760
10 E 38th St Fl 6 New York (10016) *(G-9874)*
David Helsing 607 796-2681
2077 Grand Central Ave Horseheads (14845) *(G-6601)*
David Howell & Company, Bedford Hills *Also called David Howell Product Design (G-798)*
David Howell Product Design 914 666-4080
405 Adams St Bedford Hills (10507) *(G-798)*
David Isseks & Sons Inc 212 966-8694
298 Broome St New York (10002) *(G-9875)*
David Johnson 315 493-4735
Deer River Rd Carthage (13619) *(G-3441)*
David King Linen Inc 718 241-7298
295 5th Ave Ste 1202 New York (10016) *(G-9876)*
David Kucera Inc 845 255-1044
42 Steves Ln Gardiner (12525) *(G-5562)*
David Peyser Sportswear Inc (PA) 631 231-7788
90 Spence St Bay Shore (11706) *(G-689)*
David Peyser Sportswear Inc 212 695-7716
4 Bryant Park Fl 12 New York (10018) *(G-9877)*
David S Diamonds Inc 212 921-8029
546 5th Ave Fl 7 New York (10036) *(G-9878)*
David Sutherland Showrooms - N (PA) 212 871-9717
D&D Building 979 3rd New York (10022) *(G-9879)*
David Weeks Studio 212 966-3433
38 Walker St Frnt 1 New York (10013) *(G-9880)*
David Weisz & Sons Inc 212 840-4747
20 W 47th St Ste 601 New York (10036) *(G-9881)*
David Yurman, New York *Also called Yurman Retail Inc (G-12720)*
David Yurman Enterprises LLC 914 539-4444
125 Westchester Ave # 1060 White Plains (10601) *(G-17127)*
David Yurman Enterprises LLC (PA) 212 896-1550
24 Vestry St New York (10013) *(G-9882)*
David Yurman Enterprises LLC 516 627-1700
2046 Northern Blvd Manhasset (11030) *(G-8090)*
David Yurman Enterprises LLC 845 928-8660
484 Evergreen Ct Central Valley (10917) *(G-3550)*
David Yurman Retail LLC 877 226-1400
712 Madison Ave New York (10065) *(G-9883)*
Davidoff Gneva Madison Ave Inc 212 751-9060
515 Madison Ave New York (10022) *(G-9884)*
Davidoff of Geneva Ny., Inc, New York *Also called Davidoff Gneva Madison Ave Inc (G-9884)*
Davidson Publishing, New York *Also called Boardman Simons Publishing (G-9482)*
Davies Office Refurbishing Inc (PA) 518 426-7188
40 Loudonville Rd Albany (12204) *(G-72)*
Davinci Designs Inc 631 595-1095
20 Lucon Dr Unit A Deer Park (11729) *(G-4148)*
Davinci Dsgns Distinctive Furn, Deer Park *Also called Davinci Designs Inc (G-4148)*
Davis 716 833-4678
283 Minnesota Ave Buffalo (14215) *(G-2922)*
Davis Aircraft Products Co Inc 631 563-1500
1150 Walnut Ave Ste 1 Bohemia (11716) *(G-1046)*
Davis International Inc 585 421-8175
388 Mason Rd Fairport (14450) *(G-4859)*
Davis Logging & Lumber 315 245-1040
1450 Curtiss Rd Camden (13316) *(G-3342)*
Davis Restraint Systems Inc 631 563-1500
1150 Walnut Ave Bohemia (11716) *(G-1047)*
Davis Trailer World LLC 585 538-6640
1640 Main St York (14592) *(G-17521)*
Davis Trlr World & Cntry Mall, York *Also called Davis Trailer World LLC (G-17521)*
Davis Ziff Publishing Inc (HQ) 212 503-3500
28 E 28th St Fl 10 New York (10016) *(G-9885)*
Davler Media Group LLC (PA) 212 315-0800
498 Fashion Ave Fl 10 New York (10018) *(G-9886)*
Davos Brands LLC 212 779-1911
381 Park Ave S Rm 1015 New York (10016) *(G-9887)*
Dawn Food Products Inc 716 830-8214
160 Lawrence Bell Dr # 120 Williamsville (14221) *(G-17268)*
Dawn Paper Co Inc (PA) 516 596-9110
4 Leonard Dr East Rockaway (11518) *(G-4489)*
Dawn Printing Company, East Rockaway *Also called Dawn Paper Co Inc (G-4489)*

ALPHABETIC SECTION

Delivery Systems Inc

Dawnex Industries Inc............718 384-0199
861 Park Ave Brooklyn (11206) *(G-1843)*
Dawson Doors, Jamestown *Also called Dawson Metal Company Inc (G-7022)*
Dawson Metal Company Inc............716 664-3811
825 Allen St Jamestown (14701) *(G-7022)*
Daxor Corporation (PA)............212 244-0555
350 5th Ave Ste 4740 New York (10118) *(G-9888)*
Day Automation Systems Inc (PA)............585 924-4630
7931 Rae Blvd Victor (14564) *(G-16496)*
Day One Lighting, Suffern *Also called E-Ffinergy Group LLC (G-15811)*
Dayleen Intimates Inc............914 969-5900
540 Nepperhan Ave Yonkers (10701) *(G-17450)*
Daylight Technology USA Inc............973 255-8100
5971 59th St Maspeth (11378) *(G-8160)*
Dayton Industries Inc............718 542-8144
1350 Garrison Ave Bronx (10474) *(G-1314)*
Dayton Rogers New York LLC............585 349-4040
150 Fedex Way Rochester (14624) *(G-14323)*
Dayton T Brown Inc (PA)............631 589-6300
1175 Church St Bohemia (11716) *(G-1048)*
Dbase LLC............607 729-0234
31 Front St Binghamton (13905) *(G-903)*
Dbg Media............718 599-6828
358 Classon Ave Brooklyn (11238) *(G-1844)*
Dbs Interiors Corp............631 491-3013
81 Otis St West Babylon (11704) *(G-16813)*
DC Contracting & Building Corp............631 385-1117
136 Railroad St Huntington Station (11746) *(G-6740)*
DC Fabrication & Welding Inc............845 295-0215
17 Radcliff Rd Ferndale (12734) *(G-5177)*
Dcl Furniture Manufacturing............516 248-2683
96 Windsor Ave Mineola (11501) *(G-8538)*
Ddc Technologies Inc............516 594-1533
311 Woods Ave Oceanside (11572) *(G-13096)*
De Ans Pork Products Inc (PA)............718 788-2464
899 4th Ave Brooklyn (11232) *(G-1845)*
De Iorio's Bakery, Utica *Also called Deiorio Foods Inc (G-16345)*
De Luxe Packaging Corp............416 754-4633
63 North St Saugerties (12477) *(G-15212)*
De Meo Brothers Hair, New York *Also called De Meo Brothers Inc (G-9889)*
De Meo Brothers Inc (PA)............212 268-1400
129 W 29th St Fl 5 New York (10001) *(G-9889)*
De Originals Ltd............516 474-6544
22 Laurel Ln Old Westbury (11568) *(G-13153)*
De Santis Holster and Lea Gds, Amityville *Also called Helgen Industries Inc (G-292)*
Dead Ringer LLC............585 355-4685
2100 Brghton Hnrtta St375 Ste 375 Rochester (14623) *(G-14324)*
Deakon Homes and Interiors............518 271-0342
16 Industrial Park Rd Troy (12180) *(G-16255)*
Deal, New York *Also called Dnp Electronics America LLC (G-9944)*
Deal International Inc............585 288-4444
110 Halstead St Ste 1 Rochester (14610) *(G-14325)*
Dealer-Presscom Inc............631 589-0434
1595 Smithtown Ave Ste A Bohemia (11716) *(G-1049)*
Dean Foods Company............315 452-5001
6867 Schuyler Rd East Syracuse (13057) *(G-4538)*
Dean Manufacturing Inc............607 770-1300
413 Commerce Rd Vestal (13850) *(G-16468)*
Dean Trading Corp............718 485-0600
200 Junius St Brooklyn (11212) *(G-1846)*
Deanco Digital Printing LLC............212 371-2025
4545 39th St Sunnyside (11104) *(G-15826)*
Deangelis Ltd............212 348-8225
262 Glen Head Rd Glen Head (11545) *(G-5645)*
Deans Paving Inc............315 736-7601
6002 Cavanaugh Rd Marcy (13403) *(G-8121)*
Dearfoams Div, New York *Also called RG Barry Corporation (G-11884)*
Death Wish Coffee Company LLC............518 400-1050
19 Wood Rd Ste 500 Round Lake (12151) *(G-15061)*
Debmar-Mercury............212 669-5025
75 Rockefeller Plz # 1600 New York (10019) *(G-9890)*
Deborah Connolly & Associates, New York *Also called Arabella Textiles LLC (G-9240)*
Debra Fisher, Valley Stream *Also called Ready To Assemble Company Inc (G-16448)*
Debrucque Cleveland Tramrail S............315 697-5160
3 Technology Blvd Canastota (13032) *(G-3395)*
Debt Resolve Inc............914 949-5500
1133 Westchester Ave S-223 White Plains (10604) *(G-17128)*
Decal Makers Inc............516 221-7200
2477 Merrick Rd Bellmore (11710) *(G-813)*
Decal Techniques Inc............631 491-1800
40 Corbin Ave Ste I Bay Shore (11706) *(G-690)*
Deck Bros Inc............716 852-0262
222 Chicago St Buffalo (14204) *(G-2923)*
Decker Forest Products Inc............607 563-2345
New York State Rte 8 Sidney (13838) *(G-15460)*
Decor By Dene Inc............718 376-5566
2569 Mcdonald Ave Brooklyn (11223) *(G-1847)*
Decorated Cookie Company LLC............315 487-2111
314 Lakeside Rd Syracuse (13209) *(G-15943)*
Decorative Hardeware............914 238-5251
180 Hunts Ln Chappaqua (10514) *(G-3579)*
Decorative Novelty Co Inc............718 965-8600
74 20th St Brooklyn (11232) *(G-1848)*
Decree Signs & Graphics Inc............973 278-3603
91 Tulip Ave Apt Kd1 Floral Park (11001) *(G-5209)*
Decrescente Distributing Co............518 664-9866
211 N Main St Mechanicville (12118) *(G-8257)*
Dedeco International Sales Inc (PA)............845 887-4840
11617 State Route 97 Long Eddy (12760) *(G-7674)*
Deedee Desserts LLC............716 627-2330
6969 Southwestern Blvd Lake View (14085) *(G-7303)*
Deejays, Monsey *Also called DJS Nyc Inc (G-8606)*
Deelka Vision Corp............718 937-4121
4502 Queens Blvd Sunnyside (11104) *(G-15827)*
Deep Dyeing Inc............718 418-7187
120 Bayview Ave Manhasset (11030) *(G-8091)*
Deer Park Driveshaft & Hose............631 667-4091
85 Brook Ave Ste C Deer Park (11729) *(G-4149)*
Deer Park Drv Shaft & Hose Co, Deer Park *Also called Deer Park Driveshaft & Hose (G-4149)*
Deer Park Macaroni Co Inc (PA)............631 667-4600
1882 Deer Park Ave Deer Park (11729) *(G-4150)*
Deer Park Macaroni Co Inc............631 667-4600
1882 Deer Park Ave Deer Park (11729) *(G-4151)*
Deer Park Ravioli & Macaroni, Deer Park *Also called Deer Park Macaroni Co Inc (G-4151)*
Deer Park Sand & Gravel Corp............631 586-2323
145 S 4th St Bay Shore (11706) *(G-691)*
Deer Pk Stair Bldg Mllwk Inc............631 363-5000
51 Kennedy Ave Blue Point (11715) *(G-993)*
Deer Run Enterprises Inc............585 346-0850
3772 W Lake Rd Geneseo (14454) *(G-5580)*
Deer Run Winery, Geneseo *Also called Deer Run Enterprises Inc (G-5580)*
Deerfield Millwork Inc............631 726-9663
58 Deerfield Rd Unit 2 Water Mill (11976) *(G-16626)*
Dees Audio & Vision............585 719-9256
347 Seneca Pkwy Rochester (14613) *(G-14326)*
Defelsko Corporation............315 393-4450
800 Proctor Ave Ogdensburg (13669) *(G-13135)*
Definition Press Inc............212 777-4490
141 Greene St New York (10012) *(G-9891)*
Defran Systems Inc............212 727-8342
1 Penn Plz Ste 1700 New York (10119) *(G-9892)*
Degennaro Fuel Service LLC............518 239-6350
242 County Route 357 Medusa (12120) *(G-8318)*
Deiorio Foods Inc (PA)............315 732-7612
2200 Bleecker St Utica (13501) *(G-16345)*
Dejah Associates Inc............631 265-2185
1515 5th Industrial Ct Bay Shore (11706) *(G-692)*
Dejah Enterprises, Bay Shore *Also called Dejah Associates Inc (G-692)*
Dejana Trck Utility Eqp Co LLC (HQ)............631 544-9000
490 Pulaski Rd Kings Park (11754) *(G-7200)*
Dejana Trck Utility Eqp Co LLC............631 549-0944
743 Park Ave Huntington (11743) *(G-6693)*
Dejana Truck & Utility Eqp Co, Huntington *Also called Dejana Trck Utility Eqp Co LLC (G-6693)*
Dejay Litho Inc............631 319-6916
230 Knickerbocker Ave Bohemia (11716) *(G-1050)*
Delaney Books Inc............516 921-8888
212 Michael Dr Syosset (11791) *(G-15840)*
Delaney Machine Products Ltd............631 225-1032
150 S Alleghany Ave Ste A Lindenhurst (11757) *(G-7483)*
Delaval Inc............585 599-4696
850 Main Rd Corfu (14036) *(G-3976)*
Delaware County Times Inc............607 746-2176
56 Main St Delhi (13753) *(G-4262)*
Delaware Manufacturing Inds, North Tonawanda *Also called Dmic Inc (G-12987)*
Delaware Mfg Inds Corp (PA)............716 743-4360
3776 Commerce Ct North Tonawanda (14120) *(G-12986)*
Delaware Valley Forge Inc............716 447-9140
241 Rano St Buffalo (14207) *(G-2924)*
Delbia Do Company Inc (PA)............718 585-2226
2550 Park Ave Bronx (10451) *(G-1315)*
Delbia Do Company Inc............718 585-2226
11 Canal Pl Bronx (10451) *(G-1316)*
Delcath Systems Inc (PA)............212 489-2100
1633 Broadway Fl 22c New York (10019) *(G-9893)*
Delectable, New York *Also called Vinous Group LLC (G-12571)*
Delfingen Us-New York Inc............716 215-0300
2221 Niagara Falls Blvd # 12 Niagara Falls (14304) *(G-12832)*
Delford Industries Inc............845 342-3901
82 Washington St 84 Middletown (10940) *(G-8469)*
Delft Blue LLC............315 768-7100
36 Garden St A New York Mills (13417) *(G-12740)*
Delft Printing Inc............716 683-1100
1000 Commerce Pkwy Lancaster (14086) *(G-7335)*
Delicias Andinas Food Corp............718 416-2922
5750 Maspeth Ave Flushing (11378) *(G-5244)*
Delicioso Coco Helado Inc............718 292-1930
849 Saint Anns Ave Bronx (10456) *(G-1317)*
Delicious Foods Inc............718 446-9352
11202 Roosevelt Ave Corona (11368) *(G-4019)*
Delivery Systems Inc............212 221-7007
19 W 44th St New York (10036) *(G-9894)*

ALPHABETIC

(PA)=Parent Co (HQ)=Headquarters (DH)=Div Headquarters

2018 Harris
New York Manufacturers Directory

933

Dell Communications Inc...212 989-3434
109 W 27th St Frnt 2 New York (10001) ***(G-9895)***
Dell Graphics, New York *Also called Dell Communications Inc* ***(G-9895)***
Dell's Maraschino Cherries Co, Brooklyn *Also called Dells Cherries LLC* ***(G-1850)***
Della Systems Inc...631 580-0010
951 S 2nd St Ronkonkoma (11779) ***(G-14921)***
Dellas Graphics, Rochester *Also called Canfield & Tack Inc* ***(G-14275)***
Dellet Industries Inc...718 965-0101
1 43rd St Ste L8 Brooklyn (11232) ***(G-1849)***
Dells Cherries LLC...718 624-4380
175 Dikeman St Ste 177 Brooklyn (11231) ***(G-1850)***
Dells Cherries LLC...718 624-4380
81 Ferris St Brooklyn (11231) ***(G-1851)***
Delocon Wholesale Inc...716 592-2711
270 W Main St Springville (14141) ***(G-15630)***
Deloka LLC...315 946-6910
150 Dunn Rd Lyons (14489) ***(G-7999)***
Delphi Amherst Test Operations, Amherst *Also called Delphi Automotive LLP* ***(G-237)***
Delphi Automotive LLP...716 438-4886
4326 Ridge Lea Rd Amherst (14226) ***(G-237)***
Delphi Automotive Systems LLC...585 359-6000
5500 W Henrietta Rd West Henrietta (14586) ***(G-16908)***
Delphi Automotive Systems LLC...585 359-6000
5500 W Henrietta Rd West Henrietta (14586) ***(G-16909)***
Delphi Automotive Systems LLC...585 359-6000
5500 W Henrietta Rd West Henrietta (14586) ***(G-16910)***
Delphi Powertrain Systems, West Henrietta *Also called Delphi Automotive Systems LLC* ***(G-16910)***
Delphi Thermal Systems...716 439-2454
350 Upper Mountain Rd Lockport (14094) ***(G-7607)***
Delphi Thrmal Lckport Model Sp, Lockport *Also called Mahle Behr USA Inc* ***(G-7627)***
Delphi-T Compressor Engrg Ctr, Amherst *Also called Mahle Indstrbeteiligungen GMBH* ***(G-248)***
Delroyd Worm Gear, Niagara Falls *Also called Nuttall Gear L L C* ***(G-12872)***
Delsur Parts...631 630-1606
112 Pheasant Cir Brentwood (11717) ***(G-1178)***
Delta Lock Company LLC...631 238-7035
366 Central Ave Bohemia (11716) ***(G-1051)***
Delta Metal Products Co Inc...718 855-4200
476 Flushing Ave Brooklyn (11205) ***(G-1852)***
Delta Polymers Inc...631 254-6240
130 S 2nd St Bay Shore (11706) ***(G-693)***
Delta Press Inc...212 989-3445
2426 Lucas Tpke High Falls (12440) ***(G-6427)***
Delta Sheet Metal Corp...718 429-5805
3935 Skillman Ave Long Island City (11104) ***(G-7740)***
Delta Upholsterers, New York *Also called Henry B Urban Inc* ***(G-10500)***
Delta Upholsterers Inc...212 489-3308
619 W 54th St Fl 6 New York (10019) ***(G-9896)***
Deltacraft Paper Company, Buffalo *Also called Millcraft Paper Company* ***(G-3086)***
Deltacraft Paper Company LLC...716 856-5135
99 Bud Mil Dr Buffalo (14206) ***(G-2925)***
Deluxe Corporation...845 362-4054
9 Lincoln Ave Spring Valley (10977) ***(G-15603)***
Deluxe Machine & Tool Co, Batavia *Also called Bill Shea Enterprises Inc* ***(G-626)***
Deluxe Packaging Corp...845 246-6090
63 North St Saugerties (12477) ***(G-15213)***
Deluxe Passport Express, Brooklyn *Also called Deluxe Travel Store Inc* ***(G-1853)***
Deluxe Travel Store Inc...718 435-8111
5014 12th Ave Brooklyn (11219) ***(G-1853)***
Demartini Oil Equipment Svc...518 463-5752
214 River Rd Glenmont (12077) ***(G-5683)***
Demets Candy Company LLC...607 562-8600
1 Turtle Cir Horseheads (14845) ***(G-6602)***
Democrat & Chronicle, Rochester *Also called Gannett Co Inc* ***(G-14408)***
Democrat & Chronicle, Farmington *Also called Gannett Co Inc* ***(G-5160)***
Democrat & Chronicle, Lakeville *Also called Gannett Co Inc* ***(G-7307)***
Demos Medical Publishing LLC...516 889-1791
11 W 42nd St Ste 15c New York (10036) ***(G-9897)***
Deniz Information Systems...212 750-5199
208 E 51st St Ste 129 New York (10022) ***(G-9898)***
Denmar Electric...845 624-4430
202 Main St Nanuet (10954) ***(G-8801)***
Dennies Manufacturing Inc...585 393-4646
2543 State Route 21 Canandaigua (14424) ***(G-3371)***
Dennis Basso Couture Inc...212 794-4500
825 Madison Ave New York (10065) ***(G-9899)***
Dennis Basso Furs, New York *Also called Dennis Basso Couture Inc* ***(G-9899)***
Dennis Publishing Inc...646 717-9500
55 W 39th St Fl 5 New York (10018) ***(G-9900)***
Denny Machine Co Inc...716 873-6865
20 Norris St Buffalo (14207) ***(G-2926)***
Dennys Drive Shaft Service...716 875-6640
1189 Military Rd Kenmore (14217) ***(G-7174)***
Dental Tribune America LLC...212 244-7181
116 W 23rd St Ste 500 New York (10011) ***(G-9901)***
Dentek Oral Care Inc (HQ)...865 983-1300
660 White Plains Rd # 250 Tarrytown (10591) ***(G-16114)***
Denton Advertising Inc...631 586-4333
1650 Sycamore Ave Ste 28 Bohemia (11716) ***(G-1052)***
Denton Publications Inc (PA)...518 873-6368
14 Hand Ave Elizabethtown (12932) ***(G-4640)***
Denton Publications Inc...518 561-9680
21 Mckinley Ave Ste 3 Plattsburgh (12901) ***(G-13689)***
Denton Stoneworks Inc...516 746-1500
94 Denton Ave Garden City Park (11040) ***(G-5553)***
Denvin Inc...718 232-3389
6520 New Utrecht Ave Brooklyn (11219) ***(G-1854)***
Department of Sanitation, Brooklyn *Also called City of New York* ***(G-1782)***
Departures Magazine...212 382-5600
1120 Ave Of The Amrcs 9 New York (10036) ***(G-9902)***
Depco Inc...631 582-1995
20 Newton Pl Hauppauge (11788) ***(G-6083)***
Dependable Acme Threaded Pdts...516 338-4700
167 School St Westbury (11590) ***(G-17004)***
Dependable Lithographers Inc...718 472-4200
3200 Skillman Ave Long Island City (11101) ***(G-7741)***
Dependable Tool & Die Co Inc...315 453-5696
129 Dwight Park Cir # 2 Syracuse (13209) ***(G-15944)***
Depot Label Company Inc...631 467-2952
217 River Ave Patchogue (11772) ***(G-13443)***
Depp Glass Inc...718 784-8500
4140 38th St Long Island City (11101) ***(G-7742)***
Depuy Synthes Inc...607 271-2500
35 Airport Rd Horseheads (14845) ***(G-6603)***
Der Blatt Inc...845 783-1148
6 Taitch Ct Unit 112 Monroe (10950) ***(G-8588)***
Der Yid Inc...718 797-3900
84 Bay St Brooklyn (11231) ***(G-1855)***
DER YID PUBLICATION, Brooklyn *Also called Der Yid Inc* ***(G-1855)***
Deraffele Mfg Co Inc...914 636-6850
2525 Palmer Ave Ste 4 New Rochelle (10801) ***(G-8939)***
Derby Fashion Center, Conklin *Also called S & T Knitting Co Inc* ***(G-3900)***
Derecktor Shipyards, Mamaroneck *Also called Robert E Derecktor Inc* ***(G-8078)***
Dereon/24 K Style, New York *Also called Rvc Enterprises LLC* ***(G-11957)***
Derm/Buro Inc (PA)...516 694-8300
229 Newtown Rd Plainview (11803) ***(G-13626)***
Dermatech Labs Inc...631 225-1700
165 S 10th St Lindenhurst (11757) ***(G-7484)***
Dern Moore Machine Company Inc...716 433-6243
151 S Niagara St Lockport (14094) ***(G-7608)***
Deronde Doors and Frames Inc...716 895-8888
330 Greene St Buffalo (14206) ***(G-2927)***
Derosa Fabrications Inc...631 563-0640
250 Knickerbocker Ave Bohemia (11716) ***(G-1053)***
Derrick Corporation (PA)...716 683-9010
590 Duke Rd Buffalo (14225) ***(G-2928)***
Derrick Corporation...716 685-4892
2540 Walden Ave Cheektowaga (14225) ***(G-3595)***
Derrick Equipment, Buffalo *Also called Derrick Corporation* ***(G-2928)***
Desi Talk LLC...212 675-7515
115 W 30th St Rm 1206 New York (10001) ***(G-9903)***
Design A Sign of Putnam Inc...845 279-5328
1456 Route 22 Ste A102 Brewster (10509) ***(G-1213)***
Design Archives Inc...212 768-0617
1460 Broadway New York (10036) ***(G-9904)***
Design Craft Division, Jamestown *Also called Larson Metal Manufacturing Co* ***(G-7049)***
Design Distributors Inc...631 242-2000
300 Marcus Blvd Deer Park (11729) ***(G-4152)***
Design For All LLC...212 523-0021
240 W 37th St Rm 601 New York (10018) ***(G-9905)***
Design Interiors, Brooklyn *Also called Atlantic Stairs Corp* ***(G-1649)***
Design Lithographers Inc...212 645-8900
519 8th Ave Ste 3 New York (10018) ***(G-9906)***
Design Research Ltd...212 228-7675
243 Centre St New York (10013) ***(G-9907)***
Design Solutions LI Inc...631 656-8700
711 Middle Country Rd Saint James (11780) ***(G-15115)***
Design Source By Lg Inc...212 274-0022
115 Bowery Frnt 1 New York (10002) ***(G-9908)***
Design Works Craft Inc (PA)...631 244-5749
70 Orville Dr Ste 1 Bohemia (11716) ***(G-1054)***
Design-A-Sign, Brewster *Also called Design A Sign of Putnam Inc* ***(G-1213)***
Design/OI Inc...631 474-5536
200 Wilson St Unit D2 Port Jeff STA (11776) ***(G-13789)***
Designatronics Incorporated (PA)...516 328-3300
250 Duffy Ave Unit A Hicksville (11801) ***(G-6366)***
Designatronics Incorporated...516 328-3300
250 Duffy Ave Unit A Hicksville (11801) ***(G-6367)***
Designatronics Incorporated...516 328-3970
250 Duffy Ave Unit A Hicksville (11801) ***(G-6368)***
Designatronics Incorporated...516 328-3300
250 Duffy Ave Unit A Hicksville (11801) ***(G-6369)***
Designer Epoxy Finishes Inc...646 943-6044
445 Broadhollow Rd Ste 25 Melville (11747) ***(G-8340)***
Designer Glass, College Point *Also called Gmd Industries Inc* ***(G-3810)***
Designer Hardwood Flrg CNY Inc...315 207-0044
193 E Seneca St Oswego (13126) ***(G-13354)***
Designers Folding Box Corp...716 853-5141
84 Tennessee St Buffalo (14204) ***(G-2929)***
Designers Touch Inc (PA)...718 641-3718
750 Shore Rd Apt 6b Long Beach (11561) ***(G-7669)***

Designlogocom Inc 212 564-0200
200 W 37th St New York (10018) ***(G-9909)***
Designplex LLC 845 358-6647
107 Cedar Hill Ave Nyack (10960) ***(G-13065)***
Designs By Hc, New York *Also called Horo Creations LLC* ***(G-10551)***
Designs By Novello Inc 914 934-7711
505 N Main St Port Chester (10573) ***(G-13770)***
Designs By Robert Scott Inc 718 609-2535
810 Humboldt St Ste 3 Brooklyn (11222) ***(G-1856)***
Designs For Vision Inc 631 585-3300
760 Koehler Ave Ronkonkoma (11779) ***(G-14922)***
Designs On Fifth Ltd 212 921-4162
20 W 47th St Ste 701 New York (10036) ***(G-9910)***
Designway Ltd 212 254-2220
27 E 21st St Fl 7 New York (10010) ***(G-9911)***
Desiron, New York *Also called F&M Ornamental Designs LLC* ***(G-10170)***
Desiron, New York *Also called F&M Ornamental Designs LLC* ***(G-10171)***
Desktop Publishing Concepts 631 752-1934
855 Conklin St Ste T Farmingdale (11735) ***(G-4985)***
Desku Group Inc 646 436-1464
7206 7th Ave Brooklyn (11209) ***(G-1857)***
Deslauriers, Brooklyn *Also called Interntnal Strpping Diecutting* ***(G-2112)***
Desmi-Afti Inc 716 662-0632
227 Thorn Ave Bldg C Orchard Park (14127) ***(G-13292)***
Dessin/Fournir Inc 212 758-0844
232 E 59th St Fl 2 New York (10022) ***(G-9912)***
Dessy Creations, New York *Also called A & M Rosenthal Entps Inc* ***(G-9028)***
Desu Machinery Corporation 716 681-5798
200 Gould Ave Depew (14043) ***(G-4279)***
Detector Pro 845 635-3488
1447 Route 44 Pleasant Valley (12569) ***(G-13742)***
Detekion Security Systems Inc 607 729-7179
200 Plaza Dr Ste 1 Vestal (13850) ***(G-16469)***
Detny Footwear Inc 212 423-1040
1 River Pl Apt 1224 New York (10036) ***(G-9913)***
Detour Apparel Inc (PA) 212 221-3265
530 7th Ave Rm 608 New York (10018) ***(G-9914)***
Detox Water, Brooklyn *Also called Superleaf LLC* ***(G-2650)***
Deunall Corporation 516 667-8875
147 Blacksmith Rd E Levittown (11756) ***(G-7449)***
Deutsch Relays 631 342-1700
55 Engineers Rd Hauppauge (11788) ***(G-6084)***
Deux Lux Inc 212 620-0801
37 W 20th St Ste 1204 New York (10011) ***(G-9915)***
Deva Concepts LLC 212 343-0344
75 Spring St Fl 8 New York (10012) ***(G-9916)***
Devacurl, New York *Also called Deva Concepts LLC* ***(G-9916)***
Devil Dog Manufacturing Co Inc (PA) 845 647-4411
23 Market St Ellenville (12428) ***(G-4647)***
Devin Mfg Inc 585 496-5770
40 Edward St Arcade (14009) ***(G-391)***
Devonian Stone New York Inc 607 655-2600
463 Atwell Hill Rd Windsor (13865) ***(G-17294)***
Dew Graphics, New York *Also called DEW Graphics Inc* ***(G-9917)***
DEW Graphics Inc 212 727-8820
519 8th Ave Fl 18 New York (10018) ***(G-9917)***
Dewes Gumbs Die Co Inc 718 784-9755
3833 24th St Long Island City (11101) ***(G-7743)***
Dewey Machine & Tool Inc 607 749-3930
49 James St Homer (13077) ***(G-6544)***
Dewitt Plastics Inc 315 255-1209
28 Aurelius Ave Auburn (13021) ***(G-491)***
Dezawy LLC 917 436-8820
55 W 116th St Ste 327 New York (10026) ***(G-9918)***
Df Mavens Inc 347 813-4705
2420 49th St Astoria (11103) ***(G-434)***
DFA New York LLC 212 523-0021
318 W 39th St Fl 10 New York (10018) ***(G-9919)***
Dhs Systems LLC (HQ) 845 359-6066
560 Route 303 Ste 206 Orangeburg (10962) ***(G-13246)***
Di Borghese Castello LLC 631 734-5111
17150 County Road 48 Cutchogue (11935) ***(G-4097)***
Di Domenico Packaging Co Inc 718 727-5454
304 Bertram Ave Staten Island (10312) ***(G-15685)***
Di Fiore and Sons Custom Wdwkg 718 278-1663
4202 Astoria Blvd Long Island City (11103) ***(G-7744)***
Di Highway Sign Structure Corp 315 736-8312
40 Greenman Ave New York Mills (13417) ***(G-12741)***
Di Sanos Creative Canvas Inc 315 894-3137
113 W Main St Frankfort (13340) ***(G-5360)***
Di Vico Craft Products Ltd 845 265-9390
3441 Route 9 Cold Spring (10516) ***(G-3787)***
Di Zukunft, New York *Also called Congress For Jewish Culture* ***(G-9761)***
Dia 212 675-4097
535 W 22nd St Fl 4 New York (10011) ***(G-9920)***
Dia-Nielsen USA Incorporated (HQ) 856 642-9700
400 Exchange St Buffalo (14204) ***(G-2930)***
Dialase Inc 212 575-8833
36 W 47th St Ste 709 New York (10036) ***(G-9921)***
Diam International, Yonkers *Also called Creative Solutions Group Inc* ***(G-17448)***
Diamex Inc 212 575-8145
580 5th Ave Ste 625 New York (10036) ***(G-9922)***
Diamond Boutique 516 444-3373
77 Main St Port Washington (11050) ***(G-13831)***
Diamond Bridal Collection Ltd 212 302-0210
260 W 39th St Fl 17 New York (10018) ***(G-9923)***
Diamond Constellation Corp 212 819-0324
37 W 47th St Ste 506 New York (10036) ***(G-9924)***
Diamond Coring & Cutting Inc 718 381-4545
5919 55th St Maspeth (11378) ***(G-8161)***
Diamond Dimensions, Mount Vernon *Also called Aaron Group LLC* ***(G-8701)***
Diamond Distributors Inc (PA) 212 921-9188
608 5th Ave Fl 10 New York (10020) ***(G-9925)***
Diamond Inscription Tech 646 366-7944
36 W 47th St Ste 1008 New York (10036) ***(G-9926)***
Diamond Packaging Holdings LLC 585 334-8030
111 Commerce Dr Rochester (14623) ***(G-14327)***
Diamond Precast Products Inc 631 874-3777
170 Railroad Ave Center Moriches (11934) ***(G-3489)***
Diamond Saw Works Inc (PA) 716 496-7417
12290 Olean Rd Chaffee (14030) ***(G-3560)***
Diamond Venetian Blind Shade, Long Beach *Also called Designers Touch Inc* ***(G-7669)***
Diana Kane Incorporated 718 638-6520
229 5th Ave Ste B Brooklyn (11215) ***(G-1858)***
Diane Artemis Studios, Brooklyn *Also called Artemis Studios Inc* ***(G-1637)***
Diane Studios Inc (PA) 718 788-6007
34 35th St Ste 2b Brooklyn (11232) ***(G-1859)***
Diane Von Furstenberg The Shop, New York *Also called Dvf Studio LLC* ***(G-9993)***
Dianos Kathryn Designs 212 267-1584
376 Broadway Apt 13b New York (10013) ***(G-9927)***
Dib Managmnt Inc 718 439-8190
251 53rd St Brooklyn (11220) ***(G-1860)***
Dicamillo Marble and Granite 845 878-0078
20 Jon Barrett Rd Patterson (12563) ***(G-13462)***
Dice America Inc 585 869-6200
7676 Netlink Dr Victor (14564) ***(G-16497)***
Dick Bailey Printers, Brooklyn *Also called Dick Bailey Service Inc* ***(G-1861)***
Dick Bailey Service Inc 718 522-4363
25 Chapel St Ste 602 Brooklyn (11201) ***(G-1861)***
Dicks Concrete Co Inc (PA) 845 374-5966
1053 County Route 37 New Hampton (10958) ***(G-8844)***
Dico Products, Utica *Also called Divine Brothers Company* ***(G-16350)***
Dico Products Corporation 315 797-0470
200 Seward Ave Utica (13502) ***(G-16346)***
Didco Inc 212 997-5022
8570 67th Ave Rego Park (11374) ***(G-14044)***
Die-Matic Products LLC 516 433-7900
130 Express St Plainview (11803) ***(G-13627)***
Diegraphics Group, Rochester *Also called Csw Inc* ***(G-14315)***
Diehl Development Inc 585 494-2920
5922 N Lake Rd Bergen (14416) ***(G-843)***
Diehl Sand & Gravel, Bergen *Also called Diehl Development Inc* ***(G-843)***
Diemax of Rochester Inc 585 288-3912
1555 Lyell Ave Ste 141 Rochester (14606) ***(G-14328)***
Diemolding Corporation (PA) 315 363-4710
100 Donald Hicks Dew Dr Wampsville (13163) ***(G-16574)***
Diemolding Corporation 315 363-4710
N Court St Wampsville (13163) ***(G-16575)***
Dietooling, Wampsville *Also called Diemolding Corporation* ***(G-16575)***
Digicom International Inc 631 249-8999
145 Rome St Farmingdale (11735) ***(G-4986)***
Digiday, New York *Also called Dm2 Media LLC* ***(G-9943)***
Digiorange Inc 718 787-1500
5620 1st Ave Ste 4 Brooklyn (11220) ***(G-1862)***
Digitac Inc (PA) 732 215-4020
2076 Ocean Pkwy Brooklyn (11223) ***(G-1863)***
Digital Analysis Corporation 315 685-0760
716 Visions Dr Skaneateles (13152) ***(G-15479)***
Digital Associates LLC 631 983-6075
50 Karl Ave Ste 303 Smithtown (11787) ***(G-15507)***
Digital Brewery LLC 646 665-2106
3537 36th St Ste 4 Astoria (11106) ***(G-435)***
Digital Color Concepts Inc (PA) 212 989-4888
30 W 21st St Fl 5 New York (10010) ***(G-9928)***
Digital Evolution Inc (PA) 212 732-2722
123 William St Fl 26 New York (10038) ***(G-9929)***
Digital Fabrication Wkshp Inc 518 249-6500
99 S 3rd St Ste 2 Hudson (12534) ***(G-6641)***
Digital Governance Division, New York *Also called Evidon Inc* ***(G-10148)***
Digital Home Creations Inc 585 576-7070
350 Shadowbrook Dr Webster (14580) ***(G-16745)***
Digital Imaging Tech LLC 518 885-4400
425 Eastline Rd D Ballston Spa (12020) ***(G-592)***
Digital Imiging Technologies, Ballston Spa *Also called Dit Prints Incorporated* ***(G-593)***
Digital Instruments Inc 716 874-5848
580 Ensminger Rd Tonawanda (14150) ***(G-16176)***
Digital Matrix Corp 516 481-7990
34 Sarah Dr Ste B Farmingdale (11735) ***(G-4987)***
Digital One USA Inc 718 396-4890
7230 Roosevelt Ave Flushing (11372) ***(G-5245)***
Digital Page LLC 518 446-9129
75 Benjamin St Albany (12202) ***(G-73)***
Digital Printing, Conklin *Also called Cadmus Journal Services Inc* ***(G-3890)***

ALPHABETIC

Digital United Color Prtg Inc 845 986-9846
33 South St Warwick (10990) *(G-16610)*
Digitech Printers, New York *Also called Balajee Enterprises Inc (G-9361)*
Digitronik Dev Labs Inc 585 360-0043
181 Saint Paul St Apt 6d Rochester (14604) *(G-14329)*
Dijifi LLC 646 519-2447
1166 Manhattan Ave # 100 Brooklyn (11222) *(G-1864)*
Dilese International Inc 716 855-3500
141 Broadway St Buffalo (14203) *(G-2931)*
Diligent Board Member Svcs LLC 212 741-8181
310 5th Ave Fl 7 New York (10001) *(G-9930)*
Diligent Corporation (PA) 212 741-8181
1385 Brdwy Fl 19 New York (10018) *(G-9931)*
Dillner Precast Inc (PA) 631 421-9130
14 Meadow Ln Lloyd Harbor (11743) *(G-7593)*
Dillner Precast Inc 631 421-9130
200 W 9th St Huntington Station (11746) *(G-6741)*
Dimaio Millwork Corporation 914 476-1937
12 Bright Pl Yonkers (10705) *(G-17451)*
Dimanco Inc (PA) 315 797-0470
200 Seward Ave Utica (13502) *(G-16347)*
Dimar Manufacturing Corp 716 759-0351
10123 Main St Clarence (14031) *(G-3685)*
Dimarzio Inc 718 442-6655
1388 Richmond Ter Staten Island (10310) *(G-15686)*
Dimension Development Corp 718 361-8825
3630 37th St Fl 1 Long Island City (11101) *(G-7745)*
Dimension Fabricators Inc 518 374-1936
2000 7th St Scotia (12302) *(G-15346)*
Dimension Technologies Inc 585 436-3530
315 Mount Read Blvd Ste 5 Rochester (14611) *(G-14330)*
Dimensional Mills, Hudson Falls *Also called Dwa Pallet Inc (G-6672)*
Dimensional Mills Inc 518 746-1047
337 Main St Hudson Falls (12839) *(G-6671)*
Dimoda Designs Inc 212 355-8166
48 W 48th St Ste 403 New York (10036) *(G-9932)*
Dine Right Seating, West Babylon *Also called Excel Commercial Seating (G-16816)*
Dine Rite Seating Products Inc 631 226-8899
165 E Hoffman Ave Unit 3 Lindenhurst (11757) *(G-7485)*
Dinette Depot Ltd 516 515-9623
350 Dewitt Ave Brooklyn (11207) *(G-1865)*
Dining Furniture, Brooklyn *Also called Dinette Depot Ltd (G-1865)*
Dinos Sausage & Meat Co Inc 315 732-2661
722 Catherine St Utica (13501) *(G-16348)*
Dinosaw Inc (PA) 518 828-9942
340 Power Ave Hudson (12534) *(G-6642)*
Dionics-Usa Inc 516 997-7474
96b Urban Ave Westbury (11590) *(G-17005)*
Dipaolo Baking Co Inc 585 303-5013
598 Plymouth Ave N Rochester (14608) *(G-14331)*
Direct 2 Market Solutions, Fairport *Also called Selby Marketing Associates Inc (G-4882)*
Direct Alliance, New York *Also called T & R Knitting Mills Inc (G-12287)*
Direct Mktg Edctl Fndation Inc 212 790-1512
1333 Broadway Rm 301 New York (10018) *(G-9933)*
Direct Print Inc (PA) 212 987-6003
77 E 125th St New York (10035) *(G-9934)*
Direkt Force LLC 716 652-3022
455 Olean Rd Ste 3 East Aurora (14052) *(G-4394)*
Dirt T Shirts Inc 845 336-4230
444 Old Neighborhood Rd Kingston (12401) *(G-7216)*
Dirty Lemon Beverages LLC 877 897-7784
95 Grand St Apt 5 New York (10013) *(G-9935)*
Dis, Islandia *Also called Duetto Integrated Systems Inc (G-6830)*
Dis, New York *Also called Deniz Information Systems (G-9898)*
Disc Graphics Inc 631 300-1129
30 Gilpin Ave Hauppauge (11788) *(G-6085)*
Disc Graphics Inc (PA) 631 234-1400
10 Gilpin Ave Hauppauge (11788) *(G-6086)*
Discountclocks.com, Long Island City *Also called Central Time Clock Inc (G-7725)*
Discover Casting Inc 212 302-5060
17 W 45th St Ste 701 New York (10036) *(G-9936)*
Discover Magazine, New York *Also called Discover Media LLC (G-9937)*
Discover Media LLC 212 624-4800
90 5th Ave Ste 1100 New York (10011) *(G-9937)*
Dispatch Graphics Inc 212 307-5943
344 W 38th St Fl 4r New York (10018) *(G-9938)*
Dispatch Letter Service, New York *Also called Dispatch Graphics Inc (G-9938)*
Dispersion Technology Inc 914 241-4777
364 Adams St Bedford Hills (10507) *(G-799)*
Display Components Mfg Inc 631 420-0600
267 Edison Ave West Babylon (11704) *(G-16814)*
Display Fireworks, Canandaigua *Also called Young Explosives Corp (G-3390)*
Display Logic USA Inc 631 406-1922
40 Oser Ave Ste 4 Hauppauge (11788) *(G-6087)*
Display Marketing Group Inc 631 348-4450
170 Oval Dr Ste B Islandia (11749) *(G-6829)*
Display Presentations Ltd 631 951-4050
16 Court St Fl 14 Brooklyn (11241) *(G-1866)*
Display Producers Inc 718 904-1200
40 Winding Brook Rd New Rochelle (10804) *(G-8940)*
Display Technologies LLC (HQ) 718 321-3100
1111 Marcus Ave Ste M68 New Hyde Park (11042) *(G-8871)*
Displays & Beyond Inc 718 805-7786
8816 77th Ave Glendale (11385) *(G-5666)*
Displays By Rioux Inc 315 458-3639
6090 E Taft Rd North Syracuse (13212) *(G-12958)*
Dissent Magazine 212 316-3120
120 Wall St Fl 31 New York (10005) *(G-9939)*
Distech Systems Inc (HQ) 585 254-7020
1000 University Ave # 400 Rochester (14607) *(G-14332)*
Distinction Magazine Inc 631 843-3522
235 Pinelawn Rd Melville (11747) *(G-8341)*
Distinctive Printing Inc 212 727-3000
225 W 37th St Fl 16 New York (10018) *(G-9940)*
Distribio USA LLC 212 989-6077
261 5th Ave Rm 1612 New York (10016) *(G-9941)*
Dit Prints Incorporated 518 885-4400
425 Eastline Rd Ste D Ballston Spa (12020) *(G-593)*
Diva Farms Ltd 315 735-4397
1301 Broad St Utica (13501) *(G-16349)*
Diversified Envelope Ltd 585 615-4697
95 Mount Read Blvd # 103 Rochester (14611) *(G-14333)*
Diversified Manufacturing Inc 716 681-7670
4401 Walden Ave Lancaster (14086) *(G-7336)*
Diversify Apparel, New York *Also called Babyfair Inc (G-9352)*
Diversion Magazine, New York *Also called Hearst Business Publishing Inc (G-10479)*
Diversity Best Practices, New York *Also called Working Mother Media Inc (G-12686)*
Divico Products, Cold Spring *Also called Di Vico Craft Products Ltd (G-3787)*
Divine Art Furniture Inc 718 834-0111
43 Hall St Ste C9 Brooklyn (11205) *(G-1867)*
Divine Bros, Utica *Also called Dimanco Inc (G-16347)*
Divine Brothers Company 315 797-0470
200 Seward Ave Utica (13502) *(G-16350)*
Divine Phoenix LLC 585 737-1482
2985 Benson Rd Skaneateles (13152) *(G-15480)*
Divine Phoenix Books, Skaneateles *Also called Divine Phoenix LLC (G-15480)*
Division Den-Bar Enterprises 914 381-2220
745 W Boston Post Rd Mamaroneck (10543) *(G-8065)*
Division of Emergency Services, Holbrook *Also called M C Products (G-6488)*
Division Street News Corp 518 234-2515
108 Division St Apt 7 Cobleskill (12043) *(G-3761)*
Dixie Foam Ltd 212 645-8999
1205 Manhattan Ave # 311 Brooklyn (11222) *(G-1868)*
Dixiefoam Beds, Brooklyn *Also called Dixie Foam Ltd (G-1868)*
Dixon Tool and Manufacturing 585 235-1352
240 Burrows St Rochester (14606) *(G-14334)*
Diyzeitung, Brooklyn *Also called News Report Inc (G-2379)*
Dj Acquisition Management Corp 585 265-3000
6364 Dean Pkwy Ontario (14519) *(G-13222)*
Dj Pirrone Industries Inc 518 864-5496
8865 Mariaville Rd Pattersonville (12137) *(G-13471)*
Dj Publishing Inc 516 767-2500
25 Willowdale Ave Port Washington (11050) *(G-13832)*
DJS Nyc Inc 845 445-8618
15 S Remsen St Monsey (10952) *(G-8606)*
DK, Fulton *Also called D-K Manufacturing Corp (G-5469)*
DK Publishing 212 366-2000
345 Hudson St New York (10014) *(G-9942)*
Dkm Ad Art, Buffalo *Also called Dkm Sales LLC (G-2932)*
Dkm Sales LLC 716 893-7777
1352 Genesee St Buffalo (14211) *(G-2932)*
Dkny, New York *Also called Donna Karan Company LLC (G-9953)*
Dkny Jeans, New York *Also called Donna Karan Company LLC (G-9951)*
Dkny Underwear, New York *Also called Wacoal America Inc (G-12604)*
Dl Manufacturing Inc 315 432-8977
340 Gateway Park Dr North Syracuse (13212) *(G-12959)*
Dlc Comprehensive Medical PC 718 857-1200
979 Fulton St Brooklyn (11238) *(G-1869)*
Dlh Energy Service LLC 716 410-0028
4422 W Fairmount Ave Lakewood (14750) *(G-7315)*
Dli, Cazenovia *Also called Knowles Cazenovia Inc (G-3473)*
Dlr Enterprises LLC 315 813-2911
104 E Seneca St Sherrill (13461) *(G-15427)*
Dlx Industries Inc 718 272-9420
225 25th St Brooklyn (11232) *(G-1870)*
Dm2 Media LLC 646 419-4357
26 Mercer St Apt 4 New York (10013) *(G-9943)*
DMD Machining Technology Inc 585 659-8180
17231 Roosevelt Hwy Kendall (14476) *(G-7171)*
Dmef/Edge, New York *Also called Direct Mktg Edctl Fndation Inc (G-9933)*
Dmic Inc 716 743-4360
3776 Commerce Ct North Tonawanda (14120) *(G-12987)*
Dnp Electronics America LLC 212 503-1060
335 Madison Ave Fl 3 New York (10017) *(G-9944)*
Do It Different Inc 917 842-0230
59 W 71st St New York (10023) *(G-9945)*
Dobrin Industries Inc (PA) 800 353-2229
210 Walnut St Ste 22 Lockport (14094) *(G-7609)*
Docchat, Rye *Also called Smn Medical PC (G-15094)*

Dock Hardware Incorporated 585 266-7920
24 Seneca Ave Ste 4 Rochester (14621) ***(G-14335)***
Doco Quick Print Inc 315 782-6623
808 Huntington St Watertown (13601) ***(G-16671)***
Doctor Pavers 516 342-6016
2 Mack Pl Bethpage (11714) ***(G-865)***
Doctor Print Inc (PA) 631 873-4560
18 Commerce Dr Ste 1 Hauppauge (11788) ***(G-6088)***
Doctorow Communications Inc 845 708-5166
180 Phillips Hill Rd 1b New City (10956) ***(G-8830)***
Document Journal Inc 646 586-3099
264 Canal St New York (10013) ***(G-9946)***
Document Strategies LLC 585 506-9000
185 Gibbs St Rochester (14605) ***(G-14336)***
Doery Awning Co, Lawrence *Also called TG Peppe Inc* ***(G-7426)***
Dog Good Products LLC 212 789-7000
1407 Broadway Fl 41 New York (10018) ***(G-9947)***
Dog Guard, Troy *Also called Sunward Electronics Inc* ***(G-16281)***
Doheny Nice and Easy 518 793-1733
150 Broad St Glens Falls (12801) ***(G-5693)***
Doheny's Mobil, Glens Falls *Also called Doheny Nice and Easy* ***(G-5693)***
Dohnsco Inc 516 773-4800
19 Gracewood Dr Manhasset (11030) ***(G-8092)***
Dolby Laboratories Inc 212 767-1700
1350 6th Ave Fl 28 New York (10019) ***(G-9948)***
Dolce Vite International LLC 713 962-5767
386 12th St Brooklyn (11215) ***(G-1871)***
Dollar Popular Inc 914 375-0361
473 S Broadway Yonkers (10705) ***(G-17452)***
Dolmen 912 596-1537
216 Broome Corporate Pkwy Conklin (13748) ***(G-3892)***
Dolomite Group, Walworth *Also called Rochester Asphalt Materials* ***(G-16572)***
Dolomite Products Company Inc (HQ) 315 524-1998
1150 Penfield Rd Rochester (14625) ***(G-14337)***
Dolomite Products Company Inc 607 324-3636
7610 County Road 65 Hornell (14843) ***(G-6587)***
Dolomite Products Company Inc 585 586-2568
746 Whalen Rd Penfield (14526) ***(G-13522)***
Dolomite Products Company Inc 585 768-7295
8250 Golf Rd Le Roy (14482) ***(G-7430)***
Dolomite Products Company Inc 585 352-0460
2540 S Union St Spencerport (14559) ***(G-15593)***
Doma Marketing Inc 516 684-1111
28 Haven Ave Ste 226 Port Washington (11050) ***(G-13833)***
Domain, Brooklyn *Also called Sweater Brand Inc* ***(G-2655)***
Domani Fashions Corp 718 797-0505
86 S 1st St Brooklyn (11249) ***(G-1872)***
Domenick Denigris Inc (PA) 718 823-2264
1485 Bassett Ave Bronx (10461) ***(G-1318)***
Domestic Casing Co 718 522-1902
410 3rd Ave Brooklyn (11215) ***(G-1873)***
Dominic De Nigris Inc 718 597-4460
3255 E Tremont Ave Frnt Bronx (10461) ***(G-1319)***
Dominion Voting Systems Inc 404 955-9799
221 Hopkins Ave Jamestown (14701) ***(G-7023)***
Dominique Intimate Apparel, Yonkers *Also called Dayleen Intimates Inc* ***(G-17450)***
Domino Foods Inc 800 729-4840
1 Federal St Yonkers (10705) ***(G-17453)***
Domino Sugar, Yonkers *Also called Domino Foods Inc* ***(G-17453)***
Domoteck Interiors Inc 718 433-4300
2430 Brooklyn Queens Expy # 1 Woodside (11377) ***(G-17343)***
Don Beck Inc 585 493-3040
5249 State Route 39 Castile (14427) ***(G-3444)***
Donald Bruhnke 212 600-1260
455 W 37th St Apt 1018 New York (10018) ***(G-9949)***
Donald R Husband Inc 607 770-1990
1140 E Maine Rd Johnson City (13790) ***(G-7122)***
Donald Snyder Jr 315 265-4485
528 Allen Falls Rd Potsdam (13676) ***(G-13896)***
Donald Snyder Jr Logging, Potsdam *Also called Donald Snyder Jr* ***(G-13896)***
Donald Stefan 716 492-1110
3428 W Yorkshire Rd Chaffee (14030) ***(G-3561)***
Donmaar Enterprises, Barneveld *Also called Sampo Inc* ***(G-617)***
Donmar Printing Co 516 280-2239
90 2nd St Ste 2 Mineola (11501) ***(G-8539)***
Donna Degan, New York *Also called Leslie Stuart Co Inc* ***(G-11011)***
Donna Distefano Ltd (PA) 212 594-3757
37 W 20th St Ste 1106 New York (10011) ***(G-9950)***
Donna Karan Company LLC 212 372-6500
240 W 40th St Bsmt 2 New York (10018) ***(G-9951)***
Donna Karan Company LLC 212 789-1500
240 W 40th St Bsmt New York (10018) ***(G-9952)***
Donna Karan Company LLC 716 297-0752
1900 Military Rd Niagara Falls (14304) ***(G-12833)***
Donna Karan Company LLC (HQ) 212 789-1500
240 W 40th St New York (10018) ***(G-9953)***
Donna Karan International Inc (HQ) 212 789-1500
240 W 40th St New York (10018) ***(G-9954)***
Donna Karan International Inc 212 768-5800
240 W 40th St Bsmt New York (10018) ***(G-9955)***
Donna Morgan LLC 212 575-2550
132 W 36th St Rm 801 New York (10018) ***(G-9956)***
Donne Dieu 212 226-0573
63 Flushing Ave Unit 112 Brooklyn (11205) ***(G-1874)***
Donnelley Financial LLC (HQ) 212 425-0298
55 Water St Lowr L1 New York (10041) ***(G-9957)***
Donorwall Inc 212 766-9670
125 Maiden Ln Rm 205 New York (10038) ***(G-9958)***
Donver Incorporated 716 945-1910
4185 Killbuck Rd Kill Buck (14748) ***(G-7195)***
Door Dam, Wassaic *Also called Presray Corporation* ***(G-16623)***
Doortec Archtctural Met GL LLC 718 567-2730
234 46th St Brooklyn (11220) ***(G-1875)***
Dor-A-Mar Canvas Products Co 631 750-9202
182 Cherry Ave West Sayville (11796) ***(G-16963)***
Doral Apparel Group Inc 917 208-5652
498 Fashion Ave Fl 10 New York (10018) ***(G-9959)***
Doral Refining Corp 516 223-3684
533 Atlantic Ave Freeport (11520) ***(G-5405)***
Doreen Interiors Ltd 212 255-9008
76 Nottingham Rd New Hyde Park (11040) ***(G-8872)***
Dorel Hat Co (PA) 845 831-5231
1 Main St Beacon (12508) ***(G-779)***
Doremus FP LLC 212 366-3800
228 E 45th St Fl 10 New York (10017) ***(G-9960)***
Dorgan Welding Service 315 462-9030
1378 White Rd Phelps (14532) ***(G-13554)***
Doric Vault of Wny Inc 716 828-1776
73 Gilbert St Buffalo (14206) ***(G-2933)***
Doris Panos Designs Ltd 631 245-0580
130 Old East Neck Rd Melville (11747) ***(G-8342)***
Dorling Kindersley Publishing (HQ) 212 213-4800
375 Hudson St New York (10014) ***(G-9961)***
Dorm Co., Cheektowaga *Also called Dorm Company Corporation* ***(G-3596)***
Dorm Company Corporation 502 551-6195
575 Kennedy Rd Ste 2 Cheektowaga (14227) ***(G-3596)***
Dormitory Authority - State NY 631 434-1487
998 Crooked Hill Rd # 26 Brentwood (11717) ***(G-1179)***
Dorose Albums, East Elmhurst *Also called Dorose Novelty Co Inc* ***(G-4413)***
Dorose Novelty Co Inc 718 451-3088
3107 103rd St East Elmhurst (11369) ***(G-4413)***
Dorset Farms Inc 631 734-6010
38355 Main Rd Peconic (11958) ***(G-13494)***
Dorsey Metrology Intl Inc 845 229-2929
53 Oakley St Poughkeepsie (12601) ***(G-13914)***
Dortronics Systems Inc 631 725-0505
1668 Bhmpton Sag Hbr Tpke Sag Harbor (11963) ***(G-15105)***
Dory Enterprises Inc 607 565-7079
184 Sr 17c Waverly (14892) ***(G-16726)***
DOT Publishing 315 593-2510
117 Cayuga St Fulton (13069) ***(G-5470)***
DOT Tool Co Inc 607 724-7001
131 Nowlan Rd Binghamton (13901) ***(G-904)***
Dotto Wagner 315 342-8020
185 E Seneca St Oswego (13126) ***(G-13355)***
Double Star USA Inc 212 929-2210
307 Kingsland Ave Brooklyn (11222) ***(G-1876)***
Double Take Fashions Inc 718 832-9000
1407 Broadway Rm 712 New York (10018) ***(G-9962)***
Doug Lambertson Od 718 698-9300
2555 Richmond Ave Ste 4 Staten Island (10314) ***(G-15687)***
Dougs Machine Shop Inc 585 905-0004
5300 North St Canandaigua (14424) ***(G-3372)***
Dovelin Printing Company Inc 718 302-3951
43 Hall St Ste C2 Brooklyn (11205) ***(G-1877)***
Dover Corporation 212 922-1640
500 5th Ave Ste 1828 New York (10110) ***(G-9963)***
Dover Enterprises, Syracuse *Also called Burr & Son Inc* ***(G-15896)***
Dover Global Holdings Inc (HQ) 212 922-1640
280 Park Ave New York (10017) ***(G-9964)***
Dover Marine Mfg & Sup Co Inc 631 667-4300
98 N Industry Ct Deer Park (11729) ***(G-4153)***
Dow Jones & Company Inc (HQ) 609 627-2999
1211 Avenue Of The Americ New York (10036) ***(G-9965)***
Dow Jones & Company Inc 212 597-5983
1211 Avenue Of The Americ New York (10036) ***(G-9966)***
Dow Jones Aer Company Inc 212 416-2000
1211 Av Of The Am Lwr C3r New York (10036) ***(G-9967)***
Dowa International Corp 212 697-3217
370 Lexington Ave Rm 1002 New York (10017) ***(G-9968)***
Dowd - Witbeck Printing Corp 518 274-2421
599 Pawling Ave Troy (12180) ***(G-16256)***
Downtown Express Newspaper, New York *Also called Community Media LLC* ***(G-9749)***
Downtown Interiors Inc 212 337-0230
250 Hudson St Lbby 1 New York (10013) ***(G-9969)***
Downtown Media Group LLC 646 723-4510
12 W 27th St Ste 1000 New York (10001) ***(G-9970)***
Downtown Music LLC 212 625-2980
485 Broadway Fl 3 New York (10013) ***(G-9971)***
Doyle & Roth Mfg Co Inc (PA) 212 269-7840
39 Broad St Ste 710 New York (10004) ***(G-9972)***
Doyle Sails, Huntington Station *Also called Melbourne C Fisher Yacht Sails* ***(G-6753)***
Doyle-Hild Sailmakers 718 885-2255
225 Fordham St Bronx (10464) ***(G-1320)***

ALPHABETIC

(PA)=Parent Co (HQ)=Headquarters (DH)=Div Headquarters
2018 Harris
New York Manufacturers Directory
937

DP Murphy Co Inc...631 673-9400
945 Grand Blvd Deer Park (11729) ***(G-4154)***
Dpr Food Service, Deer Park *Also called Deer Park Macaroni Co Inc* ***(G-4150)***
Dr Jacobs Naturals LLC...718 265-1522
2615 Coney Island Ave 2nd Brooklyn (11223) ***(G-1878)***
Dr Jayscom...888 437-5297
853 Broadway Ste 1900 New York (10003) ***(G-9973)***
Dr Mineral, Westbury *Also called Mineralbious Corp* ***(G-17040)***
Dr Pepper Snapple Group Inc...315 589-4911
4363 State Route 104 Williamson (14589) ***(G-17251)***
Dr Pepper Snapple Group Inc...914 846-2300
55 Hunter Ln Elmsford (10523) ***(G-4756)***
Dr Pepper Snapple Group Inc...718 246-6200
212 Wolcott St Brooklyn (11231) ***(G-1879)***
Dr Print, Hauppauge *Also called Doctor Print Inc* ***(G-6088)***
Dr Reddys Laboratories NY Inc...518 827-7702
1974 State Route 145 Middleburgh (12122) ***(G-8452)***
Dr Sofa, Bronx *Also called Sofa Doctor Inc* ***(G-1456)***
Dra Imaging PC...845 296-1057
169 Myers Corners Rd # 250 Wappingers Falls (12590) ***(G-16586)***
Drag Specialties, Ballston Spa *Also called Lemans Corporation* ***(G-600)***
DRAGON STEEL PRODUCTS, New York *Also called Dragon Trading Inc* ***(G-9974)***
Dragon Trading Inc...212 717-1496
211 E 70th St Apt 20d New York (10021) ***(G-9974)***
Dragon Vapes Nyc...718 801-7855
13527 Roosevelt Ave Flushing (11354) ***(G-5246)***
Draper Associates Incorporated...212 255-2727
121 Varick St Rm 203 New York (10013) ***(G-9975)***
Drapery Industries Inc...585 232-2992
175 Humboldt St Ste 222 Rochester (14610) ***(G-14338)***
Drasgow Inc...585 786-3603
4150 Poplar Tree Rd Gainesville (14066) ***(G-5497)***
Dray Enterprises Inc...585 768-2201
1 Church St Le Roy (14482) ***(G-7431)***
Dream Fabric Printing, Warwick *Also called Dream Green Productions* ***(G-16611)***
Dream Green Productions...917 267-8920
39 Warwick Tpke Warwick (10990) ***(G-16611)***
Dream Statuary Inc...718 647-2024
251 Cleveland St Brooklyn (11208) ***(G-1880)***
Dreams To Print...718 483-8020
10101 Foster Ave Brooklyn (11236) ***(G-1881)***
Dreamseats LLC...631 656-1066
60 Austin Blvd Commack (11725) ***(G-3856)***
Dreamwave LLC...212 594-4250
34 W 33rd St Fl 2 New York (10001) ***(G-9976)***
Drescher Paper Box Inc...716 854-0288
459 Broadway St Buffalo (14204) ***(G-2934)***
Dresdiam Inc...212 819-2217
36 W 47th St Ste 1008 New York (10036) ***(G-9977)***
Dresser-Argus Inc...718 643-1540
36 Bridge St Brooklyn (11201) ***(G-1882)***
Dresser-Rand Company...585 596-3100
37 Coats St Wellsville (14895) ***(G-16777)***
Dresser-Rand Group Inc...716 375-3000
500 Paul Clark Dr Olean (14760) ***(G-13164)***
Dressy Tessy Inc (PA)...212 869-0750
1410 Broadway Rm 502 New York (10018) ***(G-9978)***
Drew Philips Corp (PA)...212 354-0095
231 W 39th St New York (10018) ***(G-9979)***
Dreyfus Ashby Inc (HQ)...212 818-0770
630 3rd Ave Rm 1501 New York (10017) ***(G-9980)***
DRG New York Holdings Corp (PA)...914 668-9000
700 S Fulton Ave Mount Vernon (10550) ***(G-8723)***
Dri Relays Inc (HQ)...631 342-1700
60 Commerce Dr Hauppauge (11788) ***(G-6089)***
Drill America Inc...516 764-5700
3574 Lawson Blvd Oceanside (11572) ***(G-13097)***
Drillco Equipment Co Inc...718 777-5986
3452 11th St Long Island City (11106) ***(G-7746)***
Drillco National Group Inc (PA)...718 726-9801
2432 44th St Long Island City (11103) ***(G-7747)***
Drive / Devilbiss Healthcare, Port Washington *Also called Medical Depot Inc* ***(G-13862)***
Drive Shaft Shop Inc...631 348-1818
210 Blydenburg Rd Unit A Hauppauge (11749) ***(G-6090)***
Drns Corp...718 369-4530
140 58th St Ste 3f Brooklyn (11220) ***(G-1883)***
Drone Usa Inc (PA)...212 220-8795
1 World Trade Ctr 285f New York (10007) ***(G-9981)***
Dropcar Inc (PA)...646 342-1595
1412 Broadway Ste 2100 New York (10018) ***(G-9982)***
Drt Laboratories LLC...845 547-2034
331 Spook Rock Rd Airmont (10901) ***(G-12)***
Drum Ready-Mix, Felts Mills *Also called Cranesville Block Co Inc* ***(G-5175)***
Drummond Framing Inc...212 647-1701
38 W 21st St Fl 10 New York (10010) ***(G-9983)***
Dryden & Palmer Co, Canajoharie *Also called Gravymaster Inc* ***(G-3360)***
Dryve LLC...646 279-3648
4515 Waldo Ave Bronx (10471) ***(G-1321)***
DSI Group Inc...800 553-2202
5713 49th St Maspeth (11378) ***(G-8162)***
DSM Nutritional Products LLC...518 372-5155
2105 Technology Dr Schenectady (12308) ***(G-15276)***
DSM Nutritional Products LLC...518 372-5155
300 Tech Park Glenville (12302) ***(G-5716)***
Dsr International Corp...631 427-2600
107 Northern Blvd Ste 401 Great Neck (11021) ***(G-5820)***
Dsti Inc...716 557-2362
301 W Franklin St Olean (14760) ***(G-13165)***
Dt Industry, New York *Also called Dressy Tessy Inc* ***(G-9978)***
Du Monde Trading Inc...212 944-1306
1407 Brrdwy Rm 1905 New York (10018) ***(G-9984)***
Du Serv Development Co, Troy *Also called George M Dujack* ***(G-16258)***
Dual Print & Mail LLC (HQ)...716 775-8001
3235 Grand Island Blvd Grand Island (14072) ***(G-5768)***
Dual Print & Mail LLC...716 684-3825
340 Nagel Dr Cheektowaga (14225) ***(G-3597)***
Duall Finishing Inc...716 827-1707
53 Hopkins St Buffalo (14220) ***(G-2935)***
Dualtron Manufacturing, West Babylon *Also called Vandilay Industries Inc* ***(G-16870)***
Duane Park Patisserie Inc...212 274-8447
179 Duane St Frnt 1 New York (10013) ***(G-9985)***
Ducduc LLC (PA)...212 226-1868
200 Lexington Ave Rm 715 New York (10016) ***(G-9986)***
Ducduc Nyc, New York *Also called Ducduc LLC* ***(G-9986)***
Duck Flats Pharma...315 689-3407
245 E Main St Elbridge (13060) ***(G-4638)***
Duck River Textiles Inc (PA)...212 679-2980
295 5th Ave New York (10016) ***(G-9987)***
Duck Walk Vinyards...631 726-7555
231 Montauk Hwy Water Mill (11976) ***(G-16627)***
Ducommun Aerostructures NY Inc...518 731-2791
171 Stacey Rd Coxsackie (12051) ***(G-4082)***
Ducon Technologies Inc (PA)...631 694-1700
5 Penn Plz Ste 2403 New York (10001) ***(G-9988)***
Ducon Technologies Inc...631 420-4900
19 Engineers Ln Farmingdale (11735) ***(G-4988)***
Duetto Integrated Systems Inc...631 851-0102
85 Hoffman Ln Ste Q Islandia (11749) ***(G-6830)***
Dufour Pastry Kitchens Inc...718 402-8800
251 Locust Ave Bronx (10454) ***(G-1322)***
Duke Company...607 347-4455
7 Hall Rd Ithaca (14850) ***(G-6874)***
Duke Concrete Products Inc...518 793-7743
50 Duke Dr Queensbury (12804) ***(G-14008)***
Duke of Iron Inc...631 543-3600
1039 W Jericho Tpke Smithtown (11787) ***(G-15508)***
Dun-Rite Spclized Carriers LLC...718 991-1100
1561 Southern Blvd Bronx (10460) ***(G-1323)***
Duncan & Son Carpentry Inc...914 664-4311
1 W Prospect Ave Mount Vernon (10550) ***(G-8724)***
Dundas-Jafine Inc...716 681-9690
11099 Broadway St Alden (14004) ***(G-180)***
Dundee Foods LLC (PA)...585 377-7700
815 Whitney Rd W Fairport (14450) ***(G-4860)***
Dundeespirits, Fairport *Also called Dundee Foods LLC* ***(G-4860)***
Dundy Glass & Mirror Corp...718 723-5800
12252 Montauk St Springfield Gardens (11413) ***(G-15629)***
Dune Inc...212 925-6171
200 Lexington Ave Rm 200 New York (10016) ***(G-9989)***
Dune Woodworking...631 996-2482
723 Pulaski St Riverhead (11901) ***(G-14152)***
Dunkirk Construction Products...716 366-5220
852 Main St Dunkirk (14048) ***(G-4362)***
Dunkirk Metal Products Wny LLC (PA)...716 366-2555
3575 Chadwick Dr Dunkirk (14048) ***(G-4363)***
Dunkirk Specialty Steel LLC...716 366-1000
830 Brigham Rd Dunkirk (14048) ***(G-4364)***
Dunlea Whl GL & Mirror Inc...914 664-5277
147 S Macquesten Pkwy Mount Vernon (10550) ***(G-8725)***
Dunmore Corporation...845 279-5061
3633 Danbury Rd Brewster (10509) ***(G-1214)***
Dunn Paper - Natural Dam Inc...315 287-1200
4921 St Rt 58 Gouverneur (13642) ***(G-5760)***
Dupli Envelope & Graphics, Syracuse *Also called Dupli Graphics Corporation* ***(G-15945)***
Dupli Graphics Corporation (HQ)...315 234-7286
6761 Thompson Rd Syracuse (13211) ***(G-15945)***
Dupli Graphics Corporation...315 422-4732
Dupli Park Dr Syracuse (13218) ***(G-15946)***
Dupont, Buffalo *Also called E I Du Pont De Nemours & Co* ***(G-2938)***
Dupont, Rochester *Also called E I Du Pont De Nemours & Co* ***(G-14342)***
Dura Architectural Signage, Long Island City *Also called Dura Engraving Corporation* ***(G-7748)***
Dura Engraving Corporation...718 706-6400
4815 32nd Pl Long Island City (11101) ***(G-7748)***
Dura Foam Inc...718 894-2488
6302 59th Ave Maspeth (11378) ***(G-8163)***
Dura Spec Inc...718 526-3053
1239 Village Ct North Baldwin (11510) ***(G-12921)***
Dura-Mill Inc...518 899-2255
16 Stonebreak Rd Ballston Spa (12020) ***(G-594)***
Dural Door Company Inc...718 729-1333
3128 Greenpoint Ave Long Island City (11101) ***(G-7749)***
Durall Dolly LLC...802 728-7122
48 Spencer St Brooklyn (11205) ***(G-1884)***

Duran Jewelry Inc ... 212 431-1959
36 W 47th St Ste 1205 New York (10036) ***(G-9990)***
Duranm Inc ... 914 774-3367
101 Dale Ave Cortlandt Manor (10567) ***(G-4073)***
Durasol Systems Inc (HQ) ... 845 610-1100
445 Bellvale Rd Chester (10918) ***(G-3632)***
Durata Therapeutics Inc ... 646 871-6400
7 Times Sq Ste 3502 New York (10036) ***(G-9991)***
Durez Corporation ... 716 286-0100
5000 Packard Rd Niagara Falls (14304) ***(G-12834)***
Duro Dyne Corporation (HQ) ... 631 249-9000
130 Broadhollow Rd Farmingdale (11735) ***(G-4989)***
Duro Dyne Machinery Corp ... 631 249-9000
81 Spence St Bay Shore (11706) ***(G-694)***
Duro Dyne National Corp (PA) ... 631 249-9000
81 Spence St Bay Shore (11706) ***(G-695)***
Duro-Shed Inc (PA) ... 585 344-0800
721 Center Rd Buffalo (14224) ***(G-2936)***
Dutch Spirits LLC ... 518 398-1022
98 Ryan Rd Pine Plains (12567) ***(G-13582)***
Dutch's Spirits, Pine Plains *Also called Dutch Spirits LLC* ***(G-13582)***
Dutchess Plumbing & Heating ... 845 889-8255
28 Reservoir Rd Staatsburg (12580) ***(G-15638)***
Dutchess Wines LLC ... 845 876-1319
39 Lorraine Dr Rhinebeck (12572) ***(G-14068)***
Dutchland Plastics LLC ... 315 280-0247
102 E Seneca St Sherrill (13461) ***(G-15428)***
Dutchtreat, Buffalo *Also called Pdi Cone Co Inc* ***(G-3139)***
Duvel Mortgage USA Inc ... 607 267-6121
656 County Highway 33 Cooperstown (13326) ***(G-3911)***
Duxiana Dux Bed ... 212 755-2600
235 E 58th St New York (10022) ***(G-9992)***
Duzmor Painting Inc ... 585 768-4760
7959 E Main Rd Le Roy (14482) ***(G-7432)***
Dvash Foods Inc ... 845 578-1959
2 Brewer Rd Monsey (10952) ***(G-8607)***
Dvf Studio LLC (PA) ... 212 741-6607
440 W 14th St New York (10014) ***(G-9993)***
Dvf Studio LLC (PA) ... 646 576-8009
252 W 37th St Fl 14 New York (10018) ***(G-9994)***
Dvmax, New York *Also called Sneakers Software Inc* ***(G-12141)***
Dwa Pallet Inc ... 518 746-1047
337 Main St Hudson Falls (12839) ***(G-6672)***
Dweck Industries Inc (PA) ... 718 615-1695
2455 Mcdonald Ave Fl 2 Brooklyn (11223) ***(G-1885)***
Dweck Industries Inc ... 718 615-1695
2247 E 16th St Fl 2 Brooklyn (11229) ***(G-1886)***
Dwell Life Inc ... 212 382-2010
60 Broad St Fl 24 New York (10004) ***(G-9995)***
Dwell Store The, New York *Also called Dwell Life Inc* ***(G-9995)***
Dwm International Inc ... 646 290-7448
37-18 Nthrn Blvd Ste 516 Long Island City (11101) ***(G-7750)***
Dwnld Inc ... 484 483-6572
601394 Broadway Fl 6 New York (10013) ***(G-9996)***
Dwyer Farm LLC ... 914 456-2742
40 Bowman Ln Walden (12586) ***(G-16552)***
Dyco Electronics Inc ... 607 324-2030
7775 Industrial Park Rd Hornell (14843) ***(G-6588)***
Dyenamix Inc ... 212 941-6642
359 Broadway Frnt 2 New York (10013) ***(G-9997)***
Dylans Candy Bar Inc ... 646 735-0078
315 E 62nd St Fl 6 New York (10065) ***(G-9998)***
Dylix Corporation ... 719 773-2985
347 Lang Blvd Grand Island (14072) ***(G-5769)***
Dyna-Empire Inc ... 516 222-2700
1075 Stewart Ave Garden City (11530) ***(G-5513)***
Dyna-Tech Quality Inc ... 585 458-9970
1570 Emerson St Rochester (14606) ***(G-14339)***
Dyna-Vac Equipment Inc ... 315 865-8084
8963 State Route 365 Stittville (13469) ***(G-15784)***
Dynabrade Inc (PA) ... 716 631-0100
8989 Sheridan Dr Clarence (14031) ***(G-3686)***
Dynak Inc ... 585 271-2255
530 Savage Rd Churchville (14428) ***(G-3666)***
Dynamasters Inc ... 585 458-9970
1570 Emerson St Rochester (14606) ***(G-14340)***
Dynamic Decisions Inc (PA) ... 908 755-5000
18519 64th Ave Fresh Meadows (11365) ***(G-5453)***
Dynamic Design Group Inc ... 212 840-9400
15 W 47th St Ste 801 New York (10036) ***(G-9999)***
Dynamic Dies Inc ... 585 247-4010
70 Pixley Industrial Pkwy Rochester (14624) ***(G-14341)***
Dynamic Health Labs Inc ... 718 858-0100
110 Bridge St Ste 2 Brooklyn (11201) ***(G-1887)***
Dynamic Hybirds Inc ... 315 426-8110
1201 E Fayette St Ste 11 Syracuse (13210) ***(G-15947)***
Dynamic Intl Mfrs & Distrs Inc ... 347 993-1914
78 Lafayette Ave Ste 201 Suffern (10901) ***(G-15810)***
Dynamic Laboratories Inc ... 631 231-7474
30 Haynes Ct Ronkonkoma (11779) ***(G-14923)***
Dynamic Labs, Ronkonkoma *Also called Dynamic Laboratories Inc* ***(G-14923)***
Dynamic Packaging Inc ... 718 388-0800
1567 39th St Brooklyn (11218) ***(G-1888)***
Dynamic Pak, Syracuse *Also called Weather Products Corporation* ***(G-16094)***
Dynamic Photography Inc ... 516 381-2951
48 Flamingo Rd N Roslyn (11576) ***(G-15043)***
Dynamic Printing, Central Islip *Also called Richard Ruffner* ***(G-3536)***
Dynamic Screenprinting ... 518 487-4256
12 Vatrano Rd Albany (12205) ***(G-74)***
Dynamic Sealing Tech Inc ... 716 376-0708
301 W Franklin St Olean (14760) ***(G-13166)***
Dynamic Systems Inc ... 518 283-5350
323 Rte 355 Poestenkill (12140) ***(G-13753)***
Dynamica Inc ... 212 818-1900
930 5th Ave Apt 3f New York (10021) ***(G-10000)***
Dynamo Development Inc ... 212 385-1552
860 Broadway Fl 5 New York (10003) ***(G-10001)***
Dynasty Belts Inc ... 516 625-6280
161 Railroad Ave New Hyde Park (11040) ***(G-8873)***
Dynasty Chemical Corp ... 518 463-1146
444 N Pearl St Menands (12204) ***(G-8402)***
Dynasty Metal Works Inc ... 631 284-3719
787 Raynor Ave Riverhead (11901) ***(G-14153)***
Dynasty Stainless Steel & Meta ... 718 205-6623
5985 Maurice Ave Maspeth (11378) ***(G-8164)***
Dynatabs LLC ... 718 376-6084
1600 Ocean Pkwy Apt 1f Brooklyn (11230) ***(G-1889)***
Dynax Corporation ... 914 764-0202
79 Westchester Ave Pound Ridge (10576) ***(G-13959)***
Dyno Nobel Inc ... 845 338-2144
161 Ulster Ave Ulster Park (12487) ***(G-16308)***
Dynocoat Inc ... 631 244-9344
1738 Church St Holbrook (11741) ***(G-6472)***
Dyson-Kissner-Moran Corp (PA) ... 212 661-4600
2515 South Rd Ste 5 Poughkeepsie (12601) ***(G-13915)***
Dz9 Power LLC ... 877 533-5530
408 Wayne St Olean (14760) ***(G-13167)***
E & D Specialty Stands Inc ... 716 337-0161
2081 Franklin St North Collins (14111) ***(G-12944)***
E & G Bedding Corp ... 718 369-1092
1901 8th Ave Brooklyn (11215) ***(G-1890)***
E & G Press, Catskill *Also called Hill Crest Press* ***(G-3457)***
E & J Iron Works Inc ... 718 665-6040
801 E 136th St Bronx (10454) ***(G-1324)***
E & O Mari Inc ... 845 562-4400
256 Broadway Newburgh (12550) ***(G-12775)***
E & R Machine Inc ... 716 434-6639
211 Grand St Lockport (14094) ***(G-7610)***
E & T Plastic Mfg Co Inc (PA) ... 718 729-6226
4545 37th St Long Island City (11101) ***(G-7751)***
E & W Manufacturing Co Inc ... 516 367-8571
15 Pine Dr Woodbury (11797) ***(G-17307)***
E and V Energy Corporation ... 315 786-2067
22925 State Route 12 Watertown (13601) ***(G-16672)***
E B Atlas Steel Corp ... 716 876-0900
120 Tonawanda St Buffalo (14207) ***(G-2937)***
E B B Graphics Inc ... 516 750-5510
75 State St Westbury (11590) ***(G-17006)***
E B Industries LLC (PA) ... 631 293-8565
90 Carolyn Blvd Farmingdale (11735) ***(G-4990)***
E B Industries LLC ... 631 293-8565
90 Carolyn Blvd Farmingdale (11735) ***(G-4991)***
E B Trottnow Machine Spc ... 716 694-0600
8955 Woodside Dr Eden (14057) ***(G-4598)***
E C C Corp ... 518 873-6494
7 Church St Elizabethtown (12932) ***(G-4641)***
E C Lyons, Bronx *Also called Edward C Lyons Company Inc* ***(G-1327)***
E C S, Brooklyn *Also called Ecs Global* ***(G-1903)***
E C Sumereau & Sons, Huntington Station *Also called John Larocca & Son Inc* ***(G-6750)***
E Chabot Ltd ... 212 575-1026
1544 E 13th St Apt 1a Brooklyn (11230) ***(G-1891)***
E D I, Yonkers *Also called Electronic Devices Inc* ***(G-17456)***
E D I Window Systems, Binghamton *Also called D D & L Inc* ***(G-902)***
E F Iron Works & Construction ... 631 242-4766
241 N Fehr Way Ste 3 Bay Shore (11706) ***(G-696)***
E F Lippert Co Inc ... 716 373-1100
4451 S Nine Mile Rd Allegany (14706) ***(G-202)***
E F Thresh Inc ... 315 437-7301
6000 Galster Rd East Syracuse (13057) ***(G-4539)***
E G M Restaurant Equipment Mfg ... 718 782-9800
688 Flushing Ave Brooklyn (11206) ***(G-1892)***
E G S, Port Washington *Also called E Global Solutions Inc* ***(G-13834)***
E Global Solutions Inc ... 516 767-5138
8 Haven Ave Ste 221 Port Washington (11050) ***(G-13834)***
E Gluck Corporation (PA) ... 718 784-0700
6015 Little Neck Pkwy Little Neck (11362) ***(G-7531)***
E Graphics Corporation ... 718 486-9767
160 Havemeyer St Brooklyn (11211) ***(G-1893)***
E H Hurwitz & Associates ... 718 884-3766
3000 Kingsbridge Ave Bronx (10463) ***(G-1325)***
E I Du Pont De Nemours & Co ... 716 876-4420
3115 River Rd Buffalo (14207) ***(G-2938)***
E I Du Pont De Nemours & Co ... 718 761-0043
10 Teleport Dr Staten Island (10311) ***(G-15688)***

ALPHABETIC

(PA)=Parent Co (HQ)=Headquarters (DH)=Div Headquarters
2018 Harris
New York Manufacturers Directory
939

E I Du Pont De Nemours & Co...585 339-4200
69 Seneca Ave Rochester (14621) ***(G-14342)***
E J Manufacturing Inc...516 313-9380
2935 Charlotte Dr Merrick (11566) ***(G-8417)***
E J Willis Company Inc...315 891-7602
37 N Main St Middleville (13406) ***(G-8508)***
E L Smith Printing Co Inc...201 373-0111
3 Lisa Ct New City (10956) ***(G-8831)***
E M G Creations Inc...212 643-0960
8 W 37th St New York (10018) ***(G-10002)***
E M I, Rome *Also called Enviromaster International LLC* ***(G-14839)***
E M T Manufacturing Inc...516 333-1917
273 Cherry Pl East Meadow (11554) ***(G-4442)***
E P Sewing Pleating Inc...212 967-2575
327 W 36th St Frnt 2 New York (10018) ***(G-10003)***
E S M, Amherst *Also called Esm Group Inc* ***(G-239)***
E S P Metal Crafts Inc...718 381-2443
379 Harman St Brooklyn (11237) ***(G-1894)***
E Schreiber Inc...212 382-0280
580 5th Ave Fl 32a New York (10036) ***(G-10004)***
E T C, New York *Also called Casuals Etc Inc* ***(G-9598)***
E Tetz & Sons Inc (PA)...845 692-4486
130 Crotty Rd Middletown (10941) ***(G-8470)***
E V G Division, Lynbrook *Also called Russell Industries Inc* ***(G-7986)***
E W Smith Publishing Co...845 562-1218
36 Meriline Ave New Windsor (12553) ***(G-8983)***
E W Williams Publications...212 661-1516
370 Lexington Ave Rm 1409 New York (10017) ***(G-10005)***
E Z Entry Doors Inc...716 434-3440
5299 Enterprise Dr Lockport (14094) ***(G-7611)***
E&I Printing...212 206-0506
545 8th Ave Rm 5e New York (10018) ***(G-10006)***
E&M Power, Binghamton *Also called Mechanical Pwr Conversion LLC* ***(G-930)***
E&T Plastics, Long Island City *Also called E & T Plastic Mfg Co Inc* ***(G-7751)***
E-Beam Services Inc (PA)...516 622-1422
270 Duffy Ave Ste H Hicksville (11801) ***(G-6370)***
E-Ffinergy Group LLC...845 547-2424
355 Spook Rock Rd Suffern (10901) ***(G-15811)***
E-Front, New York *Also called Efront Financial Solutions Inc* ***(G-10039)***
E-One Inc...716 646-6790
4760 Camp Rd Hamburg (14075) ***(G-5944)***
E-Play Brands LLC...212 563-2646
25 W 39th St Fl 5 New York (10018) ***(G-10007)***
E-Quest Lighting, Ronkonkoma *Also called Vision Quest Lighting Inc* ***(G-15022)***
E-Systems Group LLC (HQ)...607 775-1100
100 Progress Pkwy Conklin (13748) ***(G-3893)***
E-Won Industrial Co Inc...212 750-9610
625 Main St Apt 1532 New York (10044) ***(G-10008)***
E-Z Global Wholesale Inc...888 769-7888
925 E 14th St Brooklyn (11230) ***(G-1895)***
E-Z Red Co, Deposit *Also called Walter R Tucker Entps Ltd* ***(G-4305)***
E-Z Ware Dishes Inc...718 376-3244
1002 Quentin Rd Brooklyn (11223) ***(G-1896)***
E-Z-Em Inc (HQ)...609 524-2864
155 Pinelawn Rd Ste 230n Melville (11747) ***(G-8343)***
E-Zoil Products Inc...716 213-0103
234 Fillmore Ave Tonawanda (14150) ***(G-16177)***
E.J. McKenica & Sons Inc, Buffalo *Also called Edwin J McKenica & Sons Inc* ***(G-2946)***
E/One Utility Systems, Schenectady *Also called Environment-One Corporation* ***(G-15279)***
EAC Holdings of NY Corp...716 822-2500
701 Willet Rd Buffalo (14218) ***(G-2939)***
Ead Cases...845 343-2111
43 Smith St Middletown (10940) ***(G-8471)***
Eag Electric Inc...201 376-5103
496 Mosel Ave Staten Island (10304) ***(G-15689)***
Eagle Art Publishing Inc...212 685-7411
475 Park Ave S Rm 2800 New York (10016) ***(G-10009)***
Eagle Bridge Machine & Tl Inc...518 686-4541
135 State Route 67 Eagle Bridge (12057) ***(G-4380)***
Eagle Business Systems, Bohemia *Also called Clintrak Clinical Labeling S* ***(G-1031)***
Eagle Comtronics Inc...315 451-3313
7665 Henry Clay Blvd Liverpool (13088) ***(G-7543)***
Eagle Crest Vineyard LLC...585 346-5760
7107 Vineyard Rd Conesus (14435) ***(G-3874)***
Eagle Envelope Company Inc (HQ)...607 387-3195
1 Dupli Park Dr Syracuse (13204) ***(G-15948)***
Eagle Fashions U S A, Brooklyn *Also called Eagle Finishing* ***(G-1897)***
Eagle Finishing...718 497-7875
49 Wyckoff Ave Brooklyn (11237) ***(G-1897)***
Eagle Graphics Inc...585 244-5006
149 Anderson Ave Rochester (14607) ***(G-14343)***
Eagle Harbor Sand & Gravel Inc...585 798-4501
4780 Eagle Harbour Rd Albion (14411) ***(G-167)***
Eagle Instruments Inc...914 939-6843
35 Grove St Port Chester (10573) ***(G-13771)***
Eagle International LLC...917 282-2536
228 E Route 59 Ste 50 Nanuet (10954) ***(G-8802)***
Eagle Lace Dyeing Corp...212 947-2712
335 W 35th St Fl 2 New York (10001) ***(G-10010)***
Eagle Media Partners LP (PA)...315 434-8889
2501 James St Ste 100 Syracuse (13206) ***(G-15949)***
Eagle Nesher, Brooklyn *Also called Imperial Sweater Mills Inc* ***(G-2098)***
Eagle Newspapers, Syracuse *Also called Eagle Media Partners LP* ***(G-15949)***
Eagle Regalia Co Inc...845 425-2245
747 Chestnut Ridge Rd # 101 Spring Valley (10977) ***(G-15604)***
Eagle Telephonics Inc...631 471-3600
3880 Veterans Mem Hwy Bohemia (11716) ***(G-1055)***
Eagle Welding Machine...315 594-1845
13458 Ridge Rd Wolcott (14590) ***(G-17300)***
Eagle Zinc Co Div, New York *Also called T L Diamond & Company Inc* ***(G-12288)***
Eagles Nest Holdings LLC (PA)...513 874-5270
455 E 86th St New York (10028) ***(G-10011)***
Earl G Graves Pubg Co Inc (HQ)...212 242-8000
260 Madison Ave Ste 11 New York (10016) ***(G-10012)***
Earlville Paper Box Co Inc...315 691-2131
19 Clyde St Earlville (13332) ***(G-4385)***
Earring King Jewelry Mfg Inc...718 544-7947
62 W 47th St Ste 1202 New York (10036) ***(G-10013)***
Earth Spectrum, New York *Also called Spectrum Prtg Lithography Inc* ***(G-12182)***
Easco Boiler, Bronx *Also called A L Eastmond & Sons Inc* ***(G-1254)***
Easco Boiler Corp...718 378-3000
1175 Leggett Ave Bronx (10474) ***(G-1326)***
Easel, New York *Also called Ksk International Inc* ***(G-10930)***
East Aurora Advertiser, East Aurora *Also called Grant Hamilton* ***(G-4396)***
East Branch Winery Inc (PA)...607 292-3999
5503 Dutch St Dundee (14837) ***(G-4351)***
East Cast Clor Compounding Inc...631 491-9000
15 Kean St West Babylon (11704) ***(G-16815)***
East Cast Envlope Graphics LLC...718 326-2424
5615 55th Dr Maspeth (11378) ***(G-8165)***
East Cast Orthtics Prosthetics...716 856-5192
505 Delaware Ave Buffalo (14202) ***(G-2940)***
East Coast Cultures LLC...917 261-3010
906 State Route 28 Kingston (12401) ***(G-7217)***
East Coast Cycle LLC...631 780-5360
80 Smith St Ste 1 Farmingdale (11735) ***(G-4992)***
East Coast Embroidery Ltd...631 254-3878
74 Brook Ave Ste 1 Deer Park (11729) ***(G-4155)***
East Coast Envmtl Group Inc...516 352-1946
136 Allen Blvd Farmingdale (11735) ***(G-4993)***
East Coast Intl Tire Inc...718 386-9088
5746 Flushing Ave Bldg C Maspeth (11378) ***(G-8166)***
East Coast Mines & Material, East Quogue *Also called East Coast Mines Ltd* ***(G-4469)***
East Coast Mines Ltd...631 653-5445
2 Lewis Rd East Quogue (11942) ***(G-4469)***
East Coast Molders Inc...516 240-6000
3001 New St Ste F Oceanside (11572) ***(G-13098)***
East Coast Orthoic & Pros Cor (PA)...516 248-5566
75 Burt Dr Deer Park (11729) ***(G-4156)***
East Coast Orthoic & Pros Cor...212 923-2161
3927 Broadway New York (10032) ***(G-10014)***
East Coast Spring Mix Inc...845 355-1215
211 Lynch Ave New Hampton (10958) ***(G-8845)***
East Coast Thermographers Inc...718 321-3211
1558 127th St Ste 1 College Point (11356) ***(G-3807)***
East Coast Tool & Mfg...716 826-5183
1 Alliance Dr Buffalo (14218) ***(G-2941)***
East End...716 532-2622
1995 Lenox Rd Collins (14034) ***(G-3841)***
East End Country Kitchens Inc...631 727-2258
121 Edwards Ave Calverton (11933) ***(G-3318)***
East End Sign Design Inc...631 399-2574
1161 Montauk Hwy Mastic (11950) ***(G-8234)***
East End Vineyards LLC...718 468-0500
21548 Jamaica Ave Queens Village (11428) ***(G-13992)***
East Hampton Ind News Inc...631 324-2500
74 Montauk Hwy Unit 19 East Hampton (11937) ***(G-4428)***
East Hampton Independent The, East Hampton *Also called East Hampton Ind News Inc* ***(G-4428)***
East Hampton Star Inc...631 324-0002
153 Main St East Hampton (11937) ***(G-4429)***
East Hill Creamery LLC...585 237-3622
346 Main St S Perry (14530) ***(G-13546)***
East Hills Instrument Inc...516 621-8686
60 Shames Dr Westbury (11590) ***(G-17007)***
East Hudson Watershed Corp...845 319-6349
2 Route 164 Patterson (12563) ***(G-13463)***
East Main Associates...585 624-1990
7520 E Main St Lima (14485) ***(G-7466)***
East Meet East Inc...646 481-0033
32 W 39th St Fl 4 New York (10018) ***(G-10015)***
East Pattern & Model Corp (PA)...585 461-3240
75 N Main St Fairport (14450) ***(G-4861)***
East Penn Manufacturing Co...631 321-7161
790 Railroad Ave Babylon (11704) ***(G-544)***
East Ridge Quick Print...585 266-4911
1249 Ridgeway Ave Ste Y Rochester (14615) ***(G-14344)***
East Side Development Corp...585 242-9219
274 N Goodman St Rochester (14607) ***(G-14345)***
East Side Machine Inc...585 265-4560
625 Phillips Rd Webster (14580) ***(G-16746)***
East Side Printers, East Syracuse *Also called Eastside Printers* ***(G-4540)***

East To West Architectral Pdts 631 433-9690
103 Tinton Pl Ste 1a East Northport (11731) ***(G-4455)***
East West Global Sourcing Inc 917 887-2286
425 Neptune Ave Apt 22a Brooklyn (11224) ***(G-1898)***
East/West Industries Inc 631 981-5900
2002 Orville Dr N Ronkonkoma (11779) ***(G-14924)***
Eastchester Photo Services 914 961-6596
132 Fisher Ave Eastchester (10709) ***(G-4594)***
Eastchester Photo Svce, Eastchester *Also called Eastchester Photo Services* ***(G-4594)***
Eastco Manufacturing Corp 914 738-5667
323 Fifth Ave Pelham (10803) ***(G-13515)***
Eastend Enforcement Products 631 878-8424
24 Chichester Ave Center Moriches (11934) ***(G-3490)***
Eastern Air Products LLC 716 391-1866
41 Ward Rd Lancaster (14086) ***(G-7337)***
Eastern Castings Co 518 677-5610
2 Pearl St Cambridge (12816) ***(G-3335)***
Eastern Color Imaging, Bohemia *Also called Eastern Color Stripping Inc* ***(G-1056)***
Eastern Color Stripping Inc 631 563-3700
666 Lanson St Bohemia (11716) ***(G-1056)***
Eastern Company 315 468-6251
3000 Milton Ave Solvay (13209) ***(G-15529)***
Eastern Concepts Ltd 718 472-3377
4125 39th St Sunnyside (11104) ***(G-15828)***
Eastern Enterprise Corp 718 727-8600
465 Bay St Ste 2 Staten Island (10304) ***(G-15690)***
Eastern Exterior Wall 631 589-3880
869 Lincoln Ave Bohemia (11716) ***(G-1057)***
Eastern Feather & Down Corp 718 387-4100
1027 Metropolitan Ave Brooklyn (11211) ***(G-1899)***
Eastern Finding Corp 516 747-6640
116 County Courthouse Rd New Hyde Park (11040) ***(G-8874)***
Eastern Granite Inc 718 356-9139
6228 Amboy Rd Staten Island (10309) ***(G-15691)***
Eastern Hills Printing (PA) 716 741-3300
9195 Main St Clarence (14031) ***(G-3687)***
Eastern Industrial Steel Corp (PA) 845 639-9749
4 Fringe Ct New City (10956) ***(G-8832)***
Eastern Jewelry Mfg Co Inc 212 840-0001
48 W 48th St Ste 707 New York (10036) ***(G-10016)***
Eastern Jungle Gym Inc (PA) 845 878-9800
30 Commerce Dr Carmel (10512) ***(G-3427)***
Eastern Machine and Electric 716 284-8271
1041 Niagara Ave Niagara Falls (14305) ***(G-12835)***
Eastern Manufacturing Inc 716 741-4572
9760 County Rd Clarence Center (14032) ***(G-3700)***
Eastern Metal of Elmira Inc (PA) 607 734-2295
1430 Sullivan St Elmira (14901) ***(G-4692)***
Eastern Niagra Radiology 716 882-6544
899 Main St Buffalo (14203) ***(G-2942)***
Eastern Offset, Albany *Also called Northeast Commercial Prtg Inc* ***(G-110)***
Eastern Precision Machining 631 286-4758
11 Farber Dr Ste I Bellport (11713) ***(G-824)***
Eastern Precision Mfg 845 358-1951
76 S Franklin St 78 Nyack (10960) ***(G-13066)***
Eastern Silk Mills Inc 212 730-1300
148 W 37th St Fl 3 New York (10018) ***(G-10017)***
Eastern Silver of Boro Park 718 854-5600
4901 16th Ave Brooklyn (11204) ***(G-1900)***
Eastern Storefronts & Mtls Inc 631 471-7065
1739 Julia Goldbach Ave Ronkonkoma (11779) ***(G-14925)***
Eastern Strategic Materials 212 332-1619
45 Rockefeller Plz # 2000 New York (10111) ***(G-10018)***
Eastern Unit Exch Rmnfacturing 718 739-7113
186 Beech St Floral Park (11001) ***(G-5210)***
Eastern Welding Inc 631 727-0306
274 Mill Rd Riverhead (11901) ***(G-14154)***
Eastland Electronics Co Inc 631 580-3800
700 Union Pkwy Ste 9 Ronkonkoma (11779) ***(G-14926)***
Eastman Chemical Company 585 722-2905
2255 Mount Read Blvd Rochester (14615) ***(G-14346)***
Eastman Kodak Company 585 722-2187
233 Olde Harbour Trl Rochester (14612) ***(G-14347)***
Eastman Kodak Company (PA) 585 724-4000
343 State St Rochester (14650) ***(G-14348)***
Eastman Kodak Company 585 724-5600
1669 Lake Ave Bldg 31-4 Rochester (14652) ***(G-14349)***
Eastman Kodak Company 585 722-9695
1818 W Jefferson Rd Pittsford (14534) ***(G-13587)***
Eastman Kodak Company 585 726-6261
39 Kaywood Dr Rochester (14626) ***(G-14350)***
Eastman Kodak Company 585 724-4000
2600 Manitou Rd Rochester (14650) ***(G-14351)***
Eastman Kodak Company 800 698-3324
343 State St Rochester (14650) ***(G-14352)***
Eastman Kodak Company 585 722-4385
1999 Lake Ave 6/83/Rl Rochester (14650) ***(G-14353)***
Eastman Kodak Company 585 588-5598
300 Weiland Road Rochester (14650) ***(G-14354)***
Eastman Kodak Company 585 726-7000
343 State St Rochester (14650) ***(G-14355)***
Eastman Kodak Company 585 722-4007
2400 Mount Read Blvd Rochester (14615) ***(G-14356)***
Eastman Kodak Company 585 588-3896
100 Latona Rd Gate 340 Rochester (14652) ***(G-14357)***
Eastman Kodak Company 585 724-4000
343 State St Rochester (14650) ***(G-14358)***
Eastman Machine Company 716 856-2200
779 Washington St Buffalo (14203) ***(G-2943)***
Eastman Park Micrographics Inc 866 934-4376
100 Latona Rd Bldg 318 Rochester (14652) ***(G-14359)***
Eastnets Americas Corp 212 631-0666
450 Fashion Ave Ste 1509 New York (10123) ***(G-10019)***
Easton Pharmaceuticals Inc 347 284-0192
736 Center St Ste 5 Lewiston (14092) ***(G-7454)***
Eastport Management, New York *Also called Eastport Operating Partners LP* ***(G-10020)***
Eastport Operating Partners LP (PA) 212 387-8791
204 E 20th St Fl 3 New York (10003) ***(G-10020)***
Eastside Orthotics Prosthetics, New York *Also called Manhattan Eastside Dev Corp* ***(G-11153)***
Eastside Oxide Co 607 734-1253
211 Judson St Elmira (14901) ***(G-4693)***
Eastside Printers 315 437-6515
6163 E Molloy Rd East Syracuse (13057) ***(G-4540)***
Eastwood Litho Inc 315 437-2626
4020 New Court Ave Syracuse (13206) ***(G-15950)***
Easy Book Publishing Inc 518 459-6281
260 Osborne Rd Ste 3 Albany (12211) ***(G-75)***
Easy H2b, Hudson *Also called Micosta Enterprises Inc* ***(G-6657)***
Eating Evolved Inc 516 510-2601
10 Technology Dr Unit 4 East Setauket (11733) ***(G-4499)***
Eatingevolved LLC 631 675-2440
10 Technology Dr Unit 4 Setauket (11733) ***(G-15400)***
Eaton Brothers Corp 716 649-8250
3530 Lakeview Rd Hamburg (14075) ***(G-5945)***
Eaton Corporation 212 319-2100
830 3rd Ave Fl 7 New York (10022) ***(G-10021)***
Eaton Corporation 585 394-1780
2375 State Route 332 # 250 Canandaigua (14424) ***(G-3373)***
Eaton Corporation 516 353-3017
280 Bellmore Rd East Meadow (11554) ***(G-4443)***
Eaton Corporation 315 579-2872
125 E Jefferson St Syracuse (13202) ***(G-15951)***
Eaton Corporation 716 691-0008
55 Pineview Dr Ste 600 Buffalo (14228) ***(G-2944)***
Eaton Crouse-Hinds 315 477-7000
500 7th North St Syracuse (13208) ***(G-15952)***
Eaton Hydraulics LLC 716 375-7132
1648 Dugan Rd Olean (14760) ***(G-13168)***
Eatons Crouse Hinds Business 315 477-7000
1201 Wolf St Syracuse (13208) ***(G-15953)***
Eaw Electronic Systems Inc 845 471-5290
16 Victory Ln Ste 3 Poughkeepsie (12603) ***(G-13916)***
Eazy Locks LLC 718 327-7770
1914 Mott Ave Far Rockaway (11691) ***(G-4927)***
Eazy Movements 716 837-2083
337 Hoyt St Buffalo (14213) ***(G-2945)***
Eazylift Albany LLC 518 452-6929
836 Troy Schenectady Rd Latham (12110) ***(G-7388)***
EB Acquisitions LLC 212 355-3310
444 Madison Ave Ste 501 New York (10022) ***(G-10022)***
Eb Automation Industries, West Hempstead *Also called Genesis One Unlimeted* ***(G-16885)***
Eb Couture Ltd 212 912-0190
110 W 34th St Rm 1002 New York (10001) ***(G-10023)***
EB&I Marketing, Skaneateles *Also called Burdick Publications Inc* ***(G-15477)***
Ebc Technologies LLC 631 729-8182
200 Motor Pkwy Ste D26 Hauppauge (11788) ***(G-6091)***
Ebeling Associates Inc (PA) 518 688-8700
9 Corporate Dr Ste 1 Halfmoon (12065) ***(G-5932)***
Ebenezer Railcar Services Inc 716 674-5650
1005 Indian Church Rd West Seneca (14224) ***(G-16971)***
Eberhardt Enterprises Inc 585 458-7681
1325 Mount Read Blvd Rochester (14606) ***(G-14360)***
EBM, Westbury *Also called Executive Business Media Inc* ***(G-17010)***
EBM Care Inc 212 500-5000
317 Madison Ave New York (10017) ***(G-10024)***
Ebner Publishing International 646 742-0740
37 W 26th St Rm 412 New York (10010) ***(G-10025)***
Eboost, New York *Also called Vitalize Labs LLC* ***(G-12584)***
Ebsco Industries Inc 585 398-2000
5815 County Road 41 Farmington (14425) ***(G-5158)***
EBY Electro Inc 516 576-7777
210 Express St Plainview (11803) ***(G-13628)***
EC Wood & Company Inc 718 388-2287
110 E Industry Ct Deer Park (11729) ***(G-4157)***
Eccella Corporation 855 879-3223
545 8th Ave Rm 850 New York (10018) ***(G-10026)***
Ecclesiastical Communications 212 688-2399
1011 1st Ave Fl 6 New York (10022) ***(G-10027)***
Ecclesiastical Press, Edmeston *Also called Bishop Print Shop Inc* ***(G-4635)***
Ecco Bay Sportswear, New York *Also called Cathy Daniels Ltd* ***(G-9604)***
Echo Appellate Press Inc 516 432-3601
30 W Park Ave Ste 200 Long Beach (11561) ***(G-7670)***
Echo Group Inc 917 608-7440
62 W 39th St Ste 1005 New York (10018) ***(G-10028)***

ALPHABETIC

(PA)=Parent Co (HQ)=Headquarters (DH)=Div Headquarters

Eci, Norwich *Also called Electron Coil Inc* ***(G-13046)***
Eck Plastic Arts Inc 607 722-3227
87 Prospect Ave Binghamton (13901) ***(G-905)***
Ecker Window Corp 914 776-0000
1 Odell Plz Yonkers (10701) ***(G-17454)***
Eckerson Drugs Inc 845 352-1800
275 N Main St Ste 12 Spring Valley (10977) ***(G-15605)***
Ecko Fin & Tooling Inc 716 487-0200
221 Hopkins Ave Ste 2 Jamestown (14701) ***(G-7024)***
Eclectic Cntract Furn Inds Inc 212 967-5504
450 Fashion Ave Ste 2710 New York (10123) ***(G-10029)***
Eclipse Collection Jewelers 212 764-6883
7 W 45th St Ste 1401 New York (10036) ***(G-10030)***
Eco-Bat America LLC 845 692-4414
65 Ballard Rd Middletown (10941) ***(G-8472)***
Ecolab Inc 716 683-6298
3719 Union Rd Ste 121 Cheektowaga (14225) ***(G-3598)***
Ecological Laboratories Inc (PA) 516 823-3441
13 Hendrickson Ave Lynbrook (11563) ***(G-7978)***
Econocraft Worldwide Mfg Inc 914 966-2280
56 Worth St Frnt Unit Yonkers (10701) ***(G-17455)***
Economist Group, The, New York *Also called Economist Newspaper Group Inc* ***(G-10032)***
Economist Intelligence Unit NA 212 554-0600
750 3rd Ave Fl 5 New York (10017) ***(G-10031)***
Economist Magazine, The, New York *Also called Economist Newspaper NA Inc* ***(G-10033)***
Economist Newspaper Group Inc (HQ) 212 541-0500
750 3rd Ave Fl 5 New York (10017) ***(G-10032)***
Economist Newspaper NA Inc (HQ) 212 554-0676
750 3rd Ave Fl 5 New York (10017) ***(G-10033)***
Economy 24/7 Inc 917 403-8876
167 6th Ave Brooklyn (11217) ***(G-1901)***
Economy Energy LLC 845 222-3384
500 Highland Ave Peekskill (10566) ***(G-13500)***
Economy Pump & Motor Repair 718 433-2600
3652 36th St Astoria (11106) ***(G-436)***
Ecoplast & Packaging LLC 718 996-0800
4619 Surf Ave Brooklyn (11224) ***(G-1902)***
Ecosmartplastics, Bohemia *Also called Repellem Consumer Pdts Corp* ***(G-1122)***
ECR International Inc (PA) 315 797-1310
2201 Dwyer Ave Utica (13501) ***(G-16351)***
ECR International Inc 716 366-5500
85 Middle Rd Dunkirk (14048) ***(G-4365)***
Ecs Global 718 855-5888
55 Washington St Ste 302a Brooklyn (11201) ***(G-1903)***
Ecto Tech Automation, Buffalo *Also called Multisorb Technologies Inc* ***(G-3100)***
Ecuador News Inc 718 205-7014
6403 Roosevelt Ave Fl 2 Woodside (11377) ***(G-17344)***
Ed Beach Forest Management 607 538-1745
2042 Scott Rd Bloomville (13739) ***(G-988)***
Ed Levin Inc 518 677-8595
52 W Main St Cambridge (12816) ***(G-3336)***
Ed Levin Jewelry, Cambridge *Also called Ed Levin Inc* ***(G-3336)***
Ed Negron Fine Woodworking 718 246-1016
43 Hall St Fl 5 Brooklyn (11205) ***(G-1904)***
Edco Supply Corporation 718 788-8108
323 36th St Brooklyn (11232) ***(G-1905)***
Eden Tool & Die Inc 716 992-4240
2721 Hemlock Rd Eden (14057) ***(G-4599)***
Edge Display Group Entp Inc 631 498-1373
35 Sawgrass Dr Ste 2 Bellport (11713) ***(G-825)***
Edge-Craft Process Co, West Babylon *Also called Flexene Corp* ***(G-16818)***
Edgewood Industries Inc 516 227-2447
635 Commercial Ave Garden City (11530) ***(G-5514)***
Edgian Press Inc 516 931-2114
10 Bethpage Rd Hicksville (11801) ***(G-6371)***
Edible Arragement, Babylon *Also called Nsj Group Ltd* ***(G-548)***
Edible Arrangement Store 1373, Hicksville *Also called Noaspence Inc* ***(G-6401)***
Edison Power & Light Co Inc 718 522-0002
204 Van Dyke St Ste 207 Brooklyn (11231) ***(G-1906)***
Edison Price Lighting Inc (PA) 718 685-0700
4150 22nd St Long Island City (11101) ***(G-7752)***
Edison Price Lighting Inc 718 685-0700
4105 21st St Long Island City (11101) ***(G-7753)***
Edith Lances Corp 212 683-1990
247 W 35th St Fl 2 New York (10001) ***(G-10034)***
Editions De Prfums Madison LLC (HQ) 646 666-0527
654 Madison Ave Rm 1609 New York (10065) ***(G-10035)***
Editorial America S A, New York *Also called Et Publishing Intl LLC* ***(G-10129)***
Edlaw Pharmaceuticals Inc 631 454-6888
195 Central Ave Ste B Farmingdale (11735) ***(G-4994)***
EDM Mfg 631 669-1966
141 John St Ste 600 Babylon (11702) ***(G-545)***
Edo Corporation, Amityville *Also called Edo LLC* ***(G-284)***
Edo Crprtion-Fiber Science Div, Bohemia *Also called Edo LLC* ***(G-1058)***
Edo LLC (HQ) 631 630-4000
1500 New Horizons Blvd Amityville (11701) ***(G-284)***
Edo LLC 631 218-1413
5852 Johnson Ave Bohemia (11716) ***(G-1058)***
Edo LLC 631 630-4200
1500 New Horizons Blvd Amityville (11701) ***(G-285)***
Edo LLC 631 630-4000
1500 New Horizons Blvd Amityville (11701) ***(G-286)***
EDP Renewables North Amer LLC 518 426-1650
1971 Western Ave 230 Albany (12203) ***(G-76)***
Edr Industries Inc 516 868-1928
100 Commercial St Freeport (11520) ***(G-5406)***
Edrington Group Usa LLC (PA) 212 352-6000
150 5th Ave Fl 11 New York (10011) ***(G-10036)***
Edroy Products Co Inc 845 358-6600
245 N Midland Ave Nyack (10960) ***(G-13067)***
Edsal Machine Products Inc (PA) 718 439-9163
126 56th St Brooklyn (11220) ***(G-1907)***
Edsim Leather Co Inc (PA) 212 695-8500
131 W 35th St Fl 14 New York (10001) ***(G-10037)***
Edward C Lyons Company Inc 718 515-5361
3646 White Plains Rd Frnt Bronx (10467) ***(G-1327)***
Edward C Muller Corp 718 881-7270
3646 White Plains Rd Frnt Bronx (10467) ***(G-1328)***
Edward C. Lyons, Bronx *Also called Edward C Muller Corp* ***(G-1328)***
Edward Fields Incorporated (PA) 212 310-0400
150 E 58th St Ste 1101 New York (10155) ***(G-10038)***
Edwards Graphic Co Inc 718 548-6858
3801 Hudson Manor Ter 4s Bronx (10463) ***(G-1329)***
Edwards Vacuum LLC (HQ) 800 848-9800
6416 Inducon Dr W Sanborn (14132) ***(G-15145)***
Edwin H Morris & Co, New York *Also called Mpl Communications Inc* ***(G-11338)***
Edwin J McKenica & Sons Inc 716 823-4646
1200 Clinton St Buffalo (14206) ***(G-2946)***
Edwin Mellen Press Inc 716 754-2796
442 Center St Lewiston (14092) ***(G-7455)***
Eeg Enterprises Inc 516 293-7472
586 Main St Farmingdale (11735) ***(G-4995)***
Eele Laboratories LLC 631 244-0051
50 Orville Dr Bohemia (11716) ***(G-1059)***
Efam Enterprises LLC 718 204-1760
3731 29th St Long Island City (11101) ***(G-7754)***
Effanjay Pens Inc 212 316-9565
2109 Borden Ave Fl 2 Long Island City (11101) ***(G-7755)***
Efficiency Printing Co Inc 914 949-8611
126 S Lexington Ave White Plains (10606) ***(G-17129)***
Efficient Automated Mch Corp 718 937-9393
3913 23rd St Fl 1 Long Island City (11101) ***(G-7756)***
Efficient Mach Shop, Long Island City *Also called Efficient Automated Mch Corp* ***(G-7756)***
Efj Inc 518 234-4799
128 Macarthur Ave Cobleskill (12043) ***(G-3762)***
Efron Designs Ltd 718 482-8440
2121 41st Ave Ste 5b Long Island City (11101) ***(G-7757)***
Efront Financial Solutions Inc 212 220-0660
11 E 44th St Fl 15 New York (10017) ***(G-10039)***
Efs Designs 718 852-9511
610 Smith St Ste 3 Brooklyn (11231) ***(G-1908)***
Eft Analytics Inc 212 290-2300
350 5th Ave Ste 4810 New York (10118) ***(G-10040)***
Eg Indsturies, Rochester *Also called Ernie Green Industries Inc* ***(G-14379)***
Eg Industries, Rochester *Also called Ernie Green Industries Inc* ***(G-14378)***
Egg Low Farms Inc 607 674-4653
35 W State St Sherburne (13460) ***(G-15413)***
Egli Machine Company Inc 607 563-3663
240 State Highway 7 Sidney (13838) ***(G-15461)***
Egmont US Inc 212 685-0102
443 Park Ave S Rm 806 New York (10016) ***(G-10041)***
Ehrlich Enterprises Inc 631 956-0690
91 Marcus Blvd Hauppauge (11788) ***(G-6092)***
Ehs Group LLC 914 937-6162
69 Townsend St Port Chester (10573) ***(G-13772)***
Ei, Endicott *Also called Endicott Interconnect Tech Inc* ***(G-4810)***
El Electronics Inc 516 334-0870
1800 Shames Dr Westbury (11590) ***(G-17008)***
Eidosmedia Inc 646 795-2100
14 Wall St Ste 6c New York (10005) ***(G-10042)***
Eighteen Liana Trading Inc 718 369-4247
110 W 40th St Rm 606 New York (10018) ***(G-10043)***
Eileen Fisher Inc (PA) 914 591-5700
2 Bridge St Ste 230 Irvington (10533) ***(G-6810)***
Eileen Fisher Womens Apparel, Irvington *Also called Eileen Fisher Inc* ***(G-6810)***
Eileens Special Cheesecake 212 966-5585
17 Cleveland Pl Frnt A New York (10012) ***(G-10044)***
Eis Inc 585 426-5330
40 Hytec Cir Rochester (14606) ***(G-14361)***
Eiseman-Ludmar Co Inc 516 932-6990
56 Bethpage Dr Hicksville (11801) ***(G-6372)***
Eisen Bros, Brooklyn *Also called National Die & Button Mould Co* ***(G-2357)***
Ej Group Inc 315 699-2601
6177 S Bay Rd Cicero (13039) ***(G-3674)***
Eko-Blu, New York *Also called N Y Winstons Inc* ***(G-11361)***
Ekostinger Inc 585 739-0450
140 Despatch Dr East Rochester (14445) ***(G-4476)***
Eks Manufacturing Inc 917 217-0784
577 Wortman Ave Brooklyn (11208) ***(G-1909)***
El Aguila 212 410-2450
137 E 116th St Frnt 1 New York (10029) ***(G-10045)***

El Diario LLC 212 807-4600
1 Metrotech Ctr Fl 1801 Brooklyn (11201) *(G-1910)*
EL Erman International Ltd 212 444-9440
1205 E 29th St Brooklyn (11210) *(G-1911)*
El Greco Woodworking Inc (PA) 716 483-0315
106 E 1st St Ste 1 Jamestown (14701) *(G-7025)*
El-Don Battery Post Inc 716 627-3697
4109 Saint Francis Dr Hamburg (14075) *(G-5946)*
El-Gen LLC 631 218-3400
7 Shirley St Unit 1 Bohemia (11716) *(G-1060)*
El-La Design Inc 212 382-1080
209 W 38th St Rm 901 New York (10018) *(G-10046)*
Ela, New York *Also called Electric Lighting Agencies (G-10049)*
Elab Smokers Boutique 585 865-4513
4373 Lake Ave Rochester (14612) *(G-14362)*
Elam Sand & Gravel Corp (PA) 585 657-8000
8222 State Route 5 And 20 Bloomfield (14469) *(G-981)*
Elan Upholstery Inc 631 563-0650
120b Wilbur Pl Ste B Bohemia (11716) *(G-1061)*
Elana Laderos Ltd 212 764-0840
230 W 38th St Fl 15 New York (10018) *(G-10047)*
Elanco Animal Health, New Hyde Park *Also called Eli Lilly and Company (G-8876)*
Elara Fdsrvice Disposables LLC 877 893-3244
420 Jericho Tpke Ste 320 Jericho (11753) *(G-7100)*
Elastomers Inc 716 633-4883
2095 Wehrle Dr Williamsville (14221) *(G-17269)*
Elco Manufacturing Co Inc (PA) 516 767-3577
26 Ivy Way Port Washington (11050) *(G-13835)*
Elderlee Incorporated (HQ) 315 789-6670
729 Cross Rd Oaks Corners (14518) *(G-13088)*
Eldorado Coffee Distributors, Maspeth *Also called Eldorado Coffee Roasters Ltd (G-8167)*
Eldorado Coffee Roasters Ltd 718 418-4100
5675 49th St Maspeth (11378) *(G-8167)*
Eleanor Ettinger Inc 212 925-7474
24 W 57th St Ste 609 New York (10019) *(G-10048)*
Eleanors Best 845 809-5621
15 Peacock Way Garrison (10524) *(G-5569)*
Electomechanical Componets, Auburn *Also called Emcom Inc (G-492)*
Electrcal Instrumentation Ctrl 518 861-5789
1253 Youngs Rd Delanson (12053) *(G-4258)*
Electric City Concrete Co Inc (HQ) 518 887-5560
774 State Highway 5s Amsterdam (12010) *(G-343)*
Electric Lighting Agencies (PA) 212 645-4580
36 W 25th St Fl 6 New York (10010) *(G-10049)*
Electric Motor Specialties, Jamestown *Also called Electric Motor Specialty Inc (G-7026)*
Electric Motor Specialty, Jamestown *Also called Sunset Ridge Holdings Inc (G-7066)*
Electric Motor Specialty Inc 716 487-1458
490 Crescent St Jamestown (14701) *(G-7026)*
Electric Motors and Pumps Inc 718 935-9118
466 Carroll St Brooklyn (11215) *(G-1912)*
Electric Swtchbard Sltions LLC 718 643-1105
270 Park Ave New Hyde Park (11040) *(G-8875)*
Electrical Controls Link 585 924-7010
100 Rawson Rd Ste 220 Victor (14564) *(G-16498)*
Electro Abrasives LLC 716 822-2500
701 Willet Rd Buffalo (14218) *(G-2947)*
Electro Alloy Recovery Inc 631 879-7530
130 Knickerbocker Ave M Bohemia (11716) *(G-1062)*
Electro Form Corp 607 722-6404
128 Bevier St Binghamton (13904) *(G-906)*
Electro Industries, Westbury *Also called El Electronics Inc (G-17008)*
Electro Plating Service Inc 914 948-3777
127 Oakley Ave White Plains (10601) *(G-17130)*
Electro Waste Systems, Bohemia *Also called Electro Alloy Recovery Inc (G-1062)*
Electro-Harmonix, Long Island City *Also called New Sensor Corporation (G-7856)*
Electro-Kinetics Inc 845 887-4930
51 Creamery Rd Callicoon (12723) *(G-3313)*
Electro-Metrics Corporation 518 762-2600
231 Enterprise Rd Johnstown (12095) *(G-7140)*
Electro-Optical Products Corp 718 456-6000
6240 Forest Ave Fl 2 Ridgewood (11385) *(G-14118)*
Electrochem Solutions Inc (HQ) 716 759-5800
10000 Wehrle Dr Clarence (14031) *(G-3688)*
Electron Coil Inc 607 336-7414
141 Barr Rd Norwich (13815) *(G-13046)*
Electron Top Mfg Co Inc 718 846-7400
12615 89th Ave Richmond Hill (11418) *(G-14084)*
Electronic Arts Inc 212 672-0722
1515 Broadway Rm 3601 New York (10036) *(G-10050)*
Electronic Coating Tech Inc (PA) 518 688-2048
1 Mustang Dr Ste 4 Cohoes (12047) *(G-3771)*
Electronic Devices Inc (HQ) 914 965-4400
21 Gray Oaks Ave Yonkers (10710) *(G-17456)*
Electronic Die Corp 718 455-3200
19th St Fl 2 Brooklyn (11232) *(G-1913)*
Electronic Machine Parts LLC 631 434-3700
400 Oser Ave Ste 2000 Hauppauge (11788) *(G-6093)*
Electronic Printing Inc 631 218-2200
1200 Prime Pl Hauppauge (11788) *(G-6094)*
Electronic Systems Inc 631 589-4389
1742 Church St Holbrook (11741) *(G-6473)*
Electronic Tech Briefs, New York *Also called Abp International Inc (G-9051)*
Electronics & Innovation Ltd 585 214-0598
150 Research Blvd Rochester (14623) *(G-14363)*
Electronics Systems Division, Hauppauge *Also called Parker-Hannifin Corporation (G-6183)*
Electrosurgical Instrument Co, Rochester *Also called Ftt Medical Inc (G-14406)*
Electrotech Service Eqp Corp 718 626-7700
2450 46th St Astoria (11103) *(G-437)*
Elegance Coating Ltd 386 668-8379
33 W Service Rd 100 Champlain (12919) *(G-3568)*
Elegance Lighting Ltd 631 509-0640
2426 Middle Country Rd Centereach (11720) *(G-3496)*
Elegant Desserts By Metro Inc 718 388-1323
868 Kent Ave Brooklyn (11205) *(G-1914)*
Elegant Headwear Co Inc 212 695-8520
10 W 33rd St Rm 1122 New York (10001) *(G-10051)*
Elegant Jewelers Mfg Co Inc 212 869-4951
31 W 47th St Ste 301 New York (10036) *(G-10052)*
Elegant Linen Inc 718 492-0297
200 60th St Brooklyn (11220) *(G-1915)*
Elegant Linen Inc (PA) 718 871-3535
5719 New Utrecht Ave Brooklyn (11219) *(G-1916)*
Elegant Sportswear, Brooklyn *Also called K & S Childrens Wear Inc (G-2162)*
Element K, Rochester *Also called Skillsoft Corporation (G-14712)*
Eleni's Cookies, Long Island City *Also called Elenis Nyc Inc (G-7758)*
Elenis Nyc Inc (PA) 718 361-8136
4725 34th St Ste 305 Long Island City (11101) *(G-7758)*
Elepath Inc 347 417-4975
110 Kent Ave 9 Brooklyn (11249) *(G-1917)*
Elephants Custom Furniture Inc 917 509-3581
67 Van Dam St Brooklyn (11222) *(G-1918)*
Elevator Accessories Mfg 914 739-7004
1035 Howard St 37 Peekskill (10566) *(G-13501)*
Elevator Systems Inc 516 239-4044
465 Endo Blvd Unit 1 Garden City (11530) *(G-5515)*
Elevator Ventures Corporation 212 375-1900
9720 99th St Ozone Park (11416) *(G-13403)*
Elevondata Labs Inc 470 222-5438
1350 Ave Of The Amrcs 2nd New York (10019) *(G-10053)*
Elg Utica Alloys Inc (HQ) 315 733-0475
378 Gros Blvd Ste 3 Herkimer (13350) *(G-6324)*
Elg Utica Alloys Holdings Inc 315 733-0475
91 Wurz Ave Utica (13502) *(G-16352)*
Eli Lilly and Company 516 622-2244
1979 Marcus Ave New Hyde Park (11042) *(G-8876)*
Elias Artmetal Inc 516 873-7501
70 E 2nd St Mineola (11501) *(G-8540)*
Elias Fragrances Inc (PA) 718 693-6400
3 Hunter Dr Rye Brook (10573) *(G-15096)*
Elie Balleh Couture, New York *Also called Eb Couture Ltd (G-10023)*
Elie Tahari Ltd 212 398-2622
501 5th Ave Fl 2 New York (10017) *(G-10054)*
Elie Tahari Ltd 212 398-2622
510 5th Ave Fl 3 New York (10036) *(G-10055)*
Elie Tahari Ltd 631 329-8883
1 Main St East Hampton (11937) *(G-4430)*
Elie Tahari Ltd 212 763-2000
1114 Ave Of The Americas New York (10036) *(G-10056)*
Elie Tahari Ltd 973 671-6300
11 W 42nd St Fl 14 New York (10036) *(G-10057)*
Elima-Draft Incorporated 631 375-2830
3 Bancroft St Setauket (11733) *(G-15401)*
Elis Bread (eli Zabar) Inc (PA) 212 772-2011
1064 Madison Ave Apt 5 New York (10028) *(G-10058)*
Elite Cellular Accessories Inc 877 390-2502
61 E Industry Ct Deer Park (11729) *(G-4158)*
Elite Coffee Roasters, East Amherst *Also called Elite Roasters Inc (G-4386)*
Elite Daily Inc 212 402-9097
53 W 23rd St Fl 12 New York (10010) *(G-10059)*
Elite Machine Inc 585 289-4733
3 Merrick Cir Manchester (14504) *(G-8084)*
Elite Medical Supply of NY 716 712-0881
1900 Ridge Rd West Seneca (14224) *(G-16972)*
Elite Parfums Ltd (HQ) 212 983-2640
551 5th Ave Rm 1500 New York (10176) *(G-10060)*
Elite Precise Manufacturer LLC 518 993-3040
55 Willett St Fort Plain (13339) *(G-5356)*
Elite Roasters Inc (PA) 716 626-0307
8600 Transit Rd Ste 1b East Amherst (14051) *(G-4386)*
Elite Semi Conductor Products 631 884-8400
860 N Richmond Ave Lindenhurst (11757) *(G-7486)*
Elite Traveler LLC 646 430-7900
441 Lexington Ave Fl 3 New York (10017) *(G-10061)*
Elite Traveler Magazine, New York *Also called Universal Cmmncations of Miami (G-12489)*
Elite Uniforms Ltd 516 487-5481
310 Northern Blvd Ste A Great Neck (11021) *(G-5821)*
Elizabeth Arden, New York *Also called Unilever United States Inc (G-12475)*
Elizabeth Eakins Inc (PA) 212 628-1950
654 Madison Ave Rm 1409 New York (10065) *(G-10062)*
Elizabeth Fillmore LLC 212 647-0863
27 W 20th St Ste 705 New York (10011) *(G-10063)*
Elizabeth Gillett Ltd 212 629-7993
260 W 36th St Rm 802 New York (10018) *(G-10064)*
Elizabeth Gillett Designs, New York *Also called Elizabeth Gillett Ltd (G-10064)*

ALPHABETIC

Alphabetic Section

Elizabeth Wilson 516 486-2157
579 Edgemere Ave Uniondale (11553) *(G-16314)*
Elizabeth Wood 315 492-5470
4900 Broad Rd Syracuse (13215) *(G-15954)*
Elizabeth's, Uniondale Also called Elizabeth Wilson *(G-16314)*
Ella Design, New York Also called Lai Apparel Design Inc *(G-10954)*
Elle Magazine, New York Also called Hearst Corporation *(G-10485)*
Eller, New York Also called Clear Channel Outdoor Inc *(G-9696)*
Ellicottville Kitchen Eqp, Salamanca Also called Strategies North America Inc *(G-15135)*
Elliot Gantz & Company Inc 631 249-0680
115 Schmitt Blvd Farmingdale (11735) *(G-4996)*
Elliot Industries Inc 716 287-3100
Leach Rd Ellington (14732) *(G-4658)*
Elliot Lauren, New York Also called I S C A Corp *(G-10587)*
Elliot Lucca, New York Also called Indonesian Imports Inc *(G-10633)*
Elliquence LLC 516 277-9000
2455 Grand Ave Baldwin (11510) *(G-557)*
Ellis Products Corp (PA) 516 791-3732
628 Golf Dr Valley Stream (11581) *(G-16431)*
Ellison Bronze Inc 716 665-6522
125 W Main St Falconer (14733) *(G-4902)*
Ellman International, Hicksville Also called Cynosure Inc *(G-6365)*
Elm Graphics Inc 315 737-5984
9694 Mallory Rd New Hartford (13413) *(G-8848)*
Elma Press, Elma Also called Frederick Coon Inc *(G-4661)*
Elmar Industries Inc 716 681-5650
200 Gould Ave Depew (14043) *(G-4280)*
Elmat Quality Printing Ltd 516 569-5722
79 Columbia Ave Cedarhurst (11516) *(G-3483)*
Elmgang Enterprises I Inc 212 868-4142
354 W 38th St Frnt New York (10018) *(G-10065)*
Elmgrove Technologies Div, Rochester Also called Photonamics Inc *(G-14602)*
Elmhurst Dairy Inc 718 526-3442
15602 Liberty Ave Ste 2 Jamaica (11433) *(G-6946)*
Elmira Country Club Inc 607 734-6251
1538 W Church St Elmira (14905) *(G-4694)*
Elmira Grinding Works Inc 607 734-1579
311 Main St Wellsburg (14894) *(G-16773)*
Elmira Heat Treating Inc 607 734-1577
407 S Kinyon St Elmira (14904) *(G-4695)*
Elmira Metal Works Inc 607 734-9813
1493 Cedar St Elmira (14904) *(G-4696)*
Elmira Star-Gazette, Elmira Also called Star-Gazette Fund Inc *(G-4715)*
Elmont North Little League 516 775-8210
1532 Clay St Elmont (11003) *(G-4731)*
Elmsford Sheet Metal Works Inc........................... 914 739-6300
23 Arlo Ln Cortlandt Manor (10567) *(G-4074)*
Elo Touch Solutions Inc 585 427-2802
2245 Brdgtn Hnrtta Twn Ln Rochester (14623) *(G-14364)*
Elodina Inc 646 402-5202
222 Broadway Fl 19 New York (10038) *(G-10066)*
Elramida Holdings Inc 646 280-0503
2555 E 29th St Brooklyn (11235) *(G-1919)*
Elrene Home Fashions, New York Also called Josie Accessories Inc *(G-10807)*
Elsag North America LLC 877 773-5724
7 Sutton Pl Ste A Brewster (10509) *(G-1215)*
Elsener Organ Works Inc 631 254-2744
120 E Jefryn Blvd Ste A Deer Park (11729) *(G-4159)*
Elsevier Inc (HQ) 212 633-3773
230 Park Ave Fl 8 New York (10169) *(G-10067)*
Eltee Tool & Die Co 607 748-4301
404 E Franklin St Endicott (13760) *(G-4809)*
Elton El Mantle Inc 315 432-9067
6072 Court Street Rd Syracuse (13206) *(G-15955)*
Eluminocity US Inc 651 528-1165
80 Pine St Fl 24 New York (10005) *(G-10068)*
Elvo, Mount Kisco Also called Zumbach Electronics Corp *(G-8691)*
Elwood International Inc 631 842-6600
89 Hudson St Copiague (11726) *(G-3925)*
Elwood Specialty Products Inc 716 877-6622
2180 Elmwood Ave Buffalo (14216) *(G-2948)*
Elwood, William J, Copiague Also called Elwood International Inc *(G-3925)*
Ely Beach Solar LLC 718 796-9400
5030 Broadway Ste 819 New York (10034) *(G-10069)*
EM Pfaff & Son Inc 607 739-3691
204 E Franklin St Horseheads (14845) *(G-6604)*
Em-Kay Molds Inc 716 895-6180
398 Ludington St Buffalo (14206) *(G-2949)*
Ema Jewelry Inc 212 575-8989
246 W 38th St Fl 6 New York (10018) *(G-10070)*
Emagin Corporation (PA) 845 838-7900
2070 Route 52 Hopewell Junction (12533) *(G-6575)*
Embassy Apparel Inc 212 768-8330
37 W 37th St Fl 10 New York (10018) *(G-10071)*
Embassy Dinettes Inc 631 253-2292
78 E Industry Ct Deer Park (11729) *(G-4160)*
Embassy Industries Inc 631 435-0209
315 Oser Ave Ste 1 Hauppauge (11788) *(G-6095)*
Embassy Millwork Inc 518 839-0965
3 Sam Stratton Rd Amsterdam (12010) *(G-344)*
Emblaze Systems Inc (HQ) 212 371-1100
424 Madison Ave Fl 16 New York (10017) *(G-10072)*
Embroidery Screen Prtg Netwrk, Vestal Also called Spst Inc *(G-16477)*
EMC Fintech 716 488-9071
1984 Allen Street Ext Falconer (14733) *(G-4903)*
Emco Chemical (usa) Corp 718 797-3652
334 Douglass St Brooklyn (11217) *(G-1920)*
Emco Electric Services LLC 212 420-9766
526 W 26th St Rm 1012 New York (10001) *(G-10073)*
Emco Finishing Products Inc 716 483-1176
470 Crescent St Jamestown (14701) *(G-7027)*
Emcom Inc 315 255-5300
62 Columbus St Ste 4 Auburn (13021) *(G-492)*
Emcom Industries Inc 716 852-3711
235 Genesee St Buffalo (14204) *(G-2950)*
Emcs LLC 716 523-2002
4414 Manor Ln Hamburg (14075) *(G-5947)*
EMD Millipore Corporation 845 621-6560
118 Eleanor Dr Mahopac (10541) *(G-8025)*
Emda Inc 631 243-6363
250 Executive Dr Ste J Edgewood (11717) *(G-4611)*
Emdroidme, Poughkeepsie Also called Sciane Enterprises Inc *(G-13949)*
Emerald Holdings Inc 718 797-4404
63 Flushing Ave Unit 201 Brooklyn (11205) *(G-1921)*
Emerald Knitting, Brooklyn Also called Emerald Holdings Inc *(G-1921)*
Emergency Beacon Corp 914 576-2700
15 River St New Rochelle (10801) *(G-8941)*
Emergent Power Inc (HQ) 201 441-3590
968 Albany Shaker Rd Latham (12110) *(G-7389)*
Emerson & Oliver LLC 585 775-9929
44 Elton St Rochester (14607) *(G-14365)*
Emerson Control Techniques, Grand Island Also called Nidec Indus Automtn USA LLC *(G-5778)*
Emerson Electric Co 212 244-2490
1250 Broadway Ste 2300 New York (10001) *(G-10074)*
Emes Motor Inc 718 387-2445
876 Metropolitan Ave Brooklyn (11211) *(G-1922)*
Emhart Glass Manufacturing Inc 607 734-3671
74 Kahler Rd Horseheads (14845) *(G-6605)*
EMI Music Publishing, New York Also called Screen Gems-EMI Music Inc *(G-12026)*
Emilia Interiors Inc (PA) 718 629-4202
867 E 52nd St Brooklyn (11203) *(G-1923)*
Emily and Ashley, New York Also called Greenbeads Llc *(G-10402)*
Emitled Inc 516 531-3533
2300 Shames Dr Westbury (11590) *(G-17009)*
Emkay Bordeaux, Arcade Also called Emkay Trading Corp *(G-392)*
Emkay Candle Company, Syracuse Also called Muench-Kreuzer Candle Company *(G-16014)*
Emkay Trading Corp (PA) 914 592-9000
250 Clearbrook Rd Ste 127 Elmsford (10523) *(G-4757)*
Emkay Trading Corp 585 492-3800
58 Church St Arcade (14009) *(G-392)*
Emmi USA Inc 845 268-9990
100 Dutch Hill Rd Ste 220 Orangeburg (10962) *(G-13247)*
Emoji, New York Also called Leng Universal Inc *(G-11000)*
Emory Machine & Tool Co Inc 585 436-9610
6176 Hunters Dr Farmington (14425) *(G-5159)*
Emp, Hauppauge Also called Electronic Machine Parts LLC *(G-6093)*
Empire Air Hvac, Brooklyn Also called Empire Air Systems LLC *(G-1924)*
Empire Air Specialties Inc 518 689-4440
40 Kraft Ave Albany (12205) *(G-77)*
Empire Air Systems LLC 718 377-1549
2535 65th St Brooklyn (11204) *(G-1924)*
Empire Archtctural Systems Inc 518 773-5109
125 Belzano Rd Johnstown (12095) *(G-7141)*
Empire Bias Binding Co Inc 718 545-0300
3439 31st St Long Island City (11106) *(G-7759)*
Empire Brewing Company Inc 315 925-8308
120 Walton St Syracuse (13202) *(G-15956)*
Empire Building Products Inc 518 695-6094
12 Spring St Schuylerville (12871) *(G-15340)*
Empire Business Forms Inc (PA) 845 471-5666
15 Olympic Way Poughkeepsie (12603) *(G-13917)*
Empire Central, Deer Park Also called Empire Scientific *(G-4162)*
Empire Cheese Inc 585 968-1552
4520 County Road 6 Cuba (14727) *(G-4095)*
Empire City Vape LLC 718 676-6166
535 Neptune Ave Apt 20e Brooklyn (11224) *(G-1925)*
Empire Coachworks Intl LLC 732 257-7981
475 Haverstraw Rd Suffern (10901) *(G-15812)*
Empire Coffee Company Inc 914 934-1100
106 Purdy Ave Port Chester (10573) *(G-13773)*
Empire Devleopment 716 789-2097
5889 Magnolia Stedman Rd Mayville (14757) *(G-8246)*
Empire Division 315 476-6273
201 Kirkpatrick St # 207 Syracuse (13208) *(G-15957)*
Empire Exhibits & Displays Inc 518 266-9362
131 Round Lake Ave Mechanicville (12118) *(G-8258)*
Empire Exhibits and Displays, Mechanicville Also called Empire Exhibits & Displays Inc *(G-8258)*

Empire Fabricators Inc....585 235-3050
95 Saginaw Dr Rochester (14623) *(G-14366)*
Empire Gypsum Pdts & Sup Corp....914 592-8141
25 Haven St Elmsford (10523) *(G-4758)*
Empire Industrial Burner Svc....631 242-4619
550 Brook Ave Deer Park (11729) *(G-4161)*
Empire Industrial Systems Corp (PA)....631 242-4619
40 Corbin Ave Bay Shore (11706) *(G-697)*
Empire Innovation Group LLC....716 852-5000
410 Main St Ste 5 Buffalo (14202) *(G-2951)*
Empire Metal Fabricators Inc....585 288-2140
1385 Empire Blvd Ste 3 Rochester (14609) *(G-14367)*
Empire Metal Finishing Inc....718 545-6700
2469 46th St Astoria (11103) *(G-438)*
Empire National, Brooklyn *Also called A To Z Kosher Meat Products Co (G-1535)*
Empire Open Mri....914 961-1777
1915 Central Park Ave # 25 Yonkers (10710) *(G-17457)*
Empire Optical Inc....585 454-4470
1249 Ridgeway Ave Ste P Rochester (14615) *(G-14368)*
Empire Plastics Inc....607 754-9132
2011 E Main St Endwell (13760) *(G-4840)*
Empire Precision Plastics, Rochester *Also called Epp Team Inc (G-14375)*
Empire Press Co (PA)....718 756-9500
550 Empire Blvd Brooklyn (11225) *(G-1926)*
Empire Publishing Inc....516 829-4000
1525 Central Ave Ste 1 Far Rockaway (11691) *(G-4928)*
Empire Scientific, Deer Park *Also called TAe Trans Atlantic Elec Inc (G-4240)*
Empire Scientific....630 510-8636
151 E Industry Ct Deer Park (11729) *(G-4162)*
Empire Signs, East Elmhurst *Also called Liberty Awnings & Signs Inc (G-4416)*
Empire State Metal Pdts Inc....718 847-1617
10110 Jamaica Ave Richmond Hill (11418) *(G-14085)*
Empire State Pipeline (HQ)....585 321-1560
6685 W Henrietta Rd Rush (14543) *(G-15071)*
Empire State Weeklies Inc....585 671-1533
46 North Ave Webster (14580) *(G-16747)*
Empire Transit Mix Inc....718 384-3000
430 Maspeth Ave Brooklyn (11211) *(G-1927)*
Empire Ventilation Eqp Co Inc (PA)....718 728-2143
9 Industrial Dr Florida (10921) *(G-5219)*
Empowrx LLC....212 755-3577
249 E 53rd St Apt 2a New York (10022) *(G-10075)*
Empro Niagara Inc....716 433-2769
5027 Ridge Rd Lockport (14094) *(G-7612)*
Ems Development Corporation (HQ)....631 924-4736
95 Horseblock Rd Unit 2 Yaphank (11980) *(G-17406)*
Ems Development Corporation....631 345-6200
95 Horseblock Rd Unit 2a Yaphank (11980) *(G-17407)*
Ems Technologies Inc....607 723-3676
71 Frederick St Binghamton (13901) *(G-907)*
Emsaru USA Corp....212 459-9355
608 5th Ave Ste 500 New York (10020) *(G-10076)*
Emsig Manufacturing Corp (PA)....718 784-7717
263 W 38th St Fl 5 New York (10018) *(G-10077)*
Emsig Manufacturing Corp....518 828-7301
160 Fairview Ave Ste 916 Hudson (12534) *(G-6643)*
Emsig Manufacturing Corp....718 784-7717
263 W 38th St Fl 5 New York (10018) *(G-10078)*
Emt, Albany *Also called Engineered Molding Tech LLC (G-78)*
Emtron Hybrids Inc....631 924-9668
86 Horseblock Rd Unit G Yaphank (11980) *(G-17408)*
Emulso Corp....716 854-2889
2750 Kenmore Ave Tonawanda (14150) *(G-16178)*
Emunas Sales Inc....718 621-3138
947 E 27th St Brooklyn (11210) *(G-1928)*
Emusiccom Inc (PA)....212 201-9240
215 Lexington Ave Fl 18 New York (10016) *(G-10079)*
Emvi Chocolate, Broadalbin *Also called Emvi Inc (G-1240)*
Emvi Inc....518 883-5111
111 Bellen Rd Ste 2 Broadalbin (12025) *(G-1240)*
En Tech Corp....845 398-0776
375 Western Hwy Tappan (10983) *(G-16104)*
Enable Labs, Troy *Also called Vita Rara Inc (G-16285)*
Enbi Indiana Inc....585 647-1627
1661 Lyell Ave Rochester (14606) *(G-14369)*
Enchante Accessories Inc (PA)....212 689-6008
16 E 34th St Fl 16 New York (10016) *(G-10080)*
Enchante Lites LLC (HQ)....212 602-1818
15 W 34th St Fl 8 New York (10001) *(G-10081)*
Encore Chocolates Inc....585 266-2970
147 Pattonwood Dr Rochester (14617) *(G-14370)*
Encore Electronics Inc....518 584-5354
4400 Route 50 Saratoga Springs (12866) *(G-15179)*
Encore Refining and Recycleing....631 319-1910
1120 Lincoln Ave Holbrook (11741) *(G-6474)*
Encore Retail Systems Inc (PA)....718 385-3443
180 E Prospect Ave Mamaroneck (10543) *(G-8066)*
Encysive Pharmaceuticals Inc (HQ)....212 733-2323
235 E 42nd St New York (10017) *(G-10082)*
Endava Inc (HQ)....212 920-7240
441 Lexington Ave Rm 702 New York (10017) *(G-10083)*
Endeavor Printing LLC....718 570-2720
3704 29th St Long Island City (11101) *(G-7760)*
Endicott Interconnect Tech Inc....866 820-4820
1701 North St Endicott (13760) *(G-4810)*
Endicott Precision Inc....607 754-7076
1328-30 Campville Rd Endicott (13760) *(G-4811)*
Endicott Research Group Inc....607 754-9187
2601 Wayne St Endicott (13760) *(G-4812)*
Endoscopic Procedure Center, Syracuse *Also called Elizabeth Wood (G-15954)*
Endovor Inc....214 679-7385
1330 1st Ave Apt 1119 New York (10021) *(G-10084)*
Endovor LLC....214 679-7385
525 E 68th St A1027 New York (10065) *(G-10085)*
Endres Knitwear Co Inc....718 933-8687
3020 Jerome Ave Bronx (10468) *(G-1330)*
Endurance LLC....212 719-2500
530 7th Ave Rm 902 New York (10018) *(G-10086)*
Endurart Inc....212 473-7000
132 Nassau St Rm 1100 New York (10038) *(G-10087)*
Enecon Corporation (PA)....516 349-0022
6 Platinum Ct Medford (11763) *(G-8274)*
Eneflux Armtek Magnetics Inc (HQ)....516 576-3434
6 Platinum Ct Medford (11763) *(G-8275)*
Ener-G Cogen LLC....718 551-7170
1261 Broadway New York (10001) *(G-10088)*
Ener-G-Rotors Inc....518 372-2608
17 Fern Ave Schenectady (12306) *(G-15277)*
Enerac Inc....516 997-1554
1320 Lincoln Ave Ste 1 Holbrook (11741) *(G-6475)*
Energy Brands Inc (HQ)....212 545-6000
260 Madison Ave Fl 10 New York (10016) *(G-10089)*
Energy Harvesters LLC....617 325-9852
63 Garden Dr Rochester (14609) *(G-14371)*
Energy Intelligence Group Inc (PA)....212 532-1112
270 Madison Ave Fl 19 New York (10016) *(G-10090)*
Energy Nuclear Operations....315 342-0055
268 Lake Rd Oswego (13126) *(G-13356)*
Energy Panel Structures Inc....315 923-7777
10269 Old Route 31 Clyde (14433) *(G-3750)*
Energy Panel Structures Inc....585 343-1777
10269 Old Route 31 Clyde (14433) *(G-3751)*
Energy Panel Structures Inc....518 355-6708
864 Burdeck St Schenectady (12306) *(G-15278)*
Enertech Labs Inc....716 332-9074
714 Northland Ave Buffalo (14211) *(G-2952)*
Enertiv Inc....646 350-3525
555 W 23rd St Ph M New York (10011) *(G-10091)*
Enetics Inc....585 924-5010
830 Canning Pkwy Victor (14564) *(G-16499)*
Engagement Technology LLC....914 591-7600
33 W Main St Ste 303 Elmsford (10523) *(G-4759)*
Engelack Gem Corporation....212 719-3094
36 W 47th St Ste 601 New York (10036) *(G-10092)*
Engineered Air Products, Lancaster *Also called Eastern Air Products LLC (G-7337)*
Engineered Composites Inc....716 362-0295
55 Roberts Ave Buffalo (14206) *(G-2953)*
Engineered Lifting Tech, Orchard Park *Also called Kinedyne Inc (G-13303)*
Engineered Metal Products Inc....631 842-3780
10 Reith St Copiague (11726) *(G-3926)*
Engineered Molding Tech LLC....518 482-2004
59 Exchange St Albany (12205) *(G-78)*
Engineered Plastics Inc....800 682-2525
300 International Dr # 100 Williamsville (14221) *(G-17270)*
Engineered Polymer Systems Div, Marion *Also called Parker-Hannifin Corporation (G-8127)*
Engineered Products Oper Epo, Rochester *Also called Pulsafeeder Inc (G-14632)*
Engineering Educational Eqp Co, New Paltz *Also called Kevco Industries (G-8920)*
Engineering Maint Pdts Inc....516 624-9774
250 Berry Hill Rd Oyster Bay (11771) *(G-13395)*
Engineering Mfg & Tech, East Meadow *Also called E M T Manufacturing Inc (G-4442)*
Engineering Mfg Tech LLC....607 754-7111
101 Delaware Ave Endicott (13760) *(G-4813)*
Engrav-O-Type Press Inc....585 262-7590
30 Bermar Park Ste 2 Rochester (14624) *(G-14372)*
Enhance A Colour Corp....212 490-3620
211 E 43rd St Rm 700 New York (10017) *(G-10093)*
Enhanced Tool Inc....716 691-5200
90 Pineview Dr Amherst (14228) *(G-238)*
Eni Mks Products Group....585 427-8300
100 Highpower Rd Rochester (14623) *(G-14373)*
Eni Technology Inc (HQ)....585 427-8300
100 Highpower Rd Rochester (14623) *(G-14374)*
Enivate - Aerospace Division, Orchard Park *Also called ITT Enidine Inc (G-13299)*
Enjoy, Scarsdale *Also called Japan America Learning Ctr Inc (G-15248)*
Enjoy City North Inc....607 584-5061
31 Front St Binghamton (13905) *(G-908)*
Enlighten Air Inc....917 656-1248
23 E 81st St Apt 10 New York (10028) *(G-10094)*
Enplas America Inc....646 892-7811
299 Park Ave Fl 41 New York (10171) *(G-10095)*
Enrg Inc....716 873-2939
155 Rano St Ste 300 Buffalo (14207) *(G-2954)*

ALPHABETIC

(PA)=Parent Co (HQ)=Headquarters (DH)=Div Headquarters
2018 Harris
New York Manufacturers Directory
945

Ensil Technical Services Inc.....716 282-1020
1901 Maryland Ave Niagara Falls (14305) ***(G-12836)***
Entermarket.....914 437-7268
280 N Bedford Rd Ste 305 Mount Kisco (10549) ***(G-8669)***
Enterprise Bagels Inc.....845 896-3823
986 Main St Ste 3 Fishkill (12524) ***(G-5190)***
Enterprise Container LLC.....631 253-4400
44 Island Container Plz Wyandanch (11798) ***(G-17390)***
Enterprise Folding Box Co Inc.....716 876-6421
75 Isabelle St Buffalo (14207) ***(G-2955)***
Enterprise Network NY Inc.....516 263-0641
1407 E 101st St Ste B Brooklyn (11236) ***(G-1929)***
Enterprise Press Inc.....212 741-2111
627 Greenwich St New York (10014) ***(G-10096)***
Enterprise Tech Group Inc.....914 588-0327
15 Irving Pl New Rochelle (10801) ***(G-8942)***
Enterprise Wood Products Inc.....718 853-9243
4712 18th Ave Brooklyn (11204) ***(G-1930)***
Entertainment Weekly Inc (HQ).....212 522-5600
135 W 50th St Frnt 3 New York (10020) ***(G-10097)***
Entertron Industries Inc.....716 772-7216
99 Robinson Pl Lockport (14094) ***(G-7613)***
Enticing Lingerie Inc.....718 998-8625
166 Gravesend Neck Rd Brooklyn (11223) ***(G-1931)***
Entrainant Inc.....212 946-4724
1 World Trade Ctr Fl 85 New York (10007) ***(G-10098)***
Enumeral Biomedical Corp (PA).....347 227-4787
1370 Broadway Fl 5 New York (10018) ***(G-10099)***
Envent Systems Inc.....646 294-6980
62 Harmon Ave Pelham (10803) ***(G-13516)***
Enviro Service & Supply Corp.....347 838-6500
45b Marble Loop Staten Island (10309) ***(G-15692)***
Enviroform Recycled Pdts Inc.....315 789-1810
287 Gambee Rd Geneva (14456) ***(G-5586)***
Enviromaster International LLC.....315 336-3716
5780 Success Dr Rome (13440) ***(G-14839)***
Environment-One Corporation.....518 346-6161
2773 Balltown Rd Schenectady (12309) ***(G-15279)***
Environmental Closures, Mineola *Also called Geotechnical Drilling Inc* ***(G-8546)***
Environmental Temp Systems LLC.....516 640-5818
111 Roosevelt Ave Ste C Mineola (11501) ***(G-8541)***
Envy Publishing Group Inc.....212 253-9874
118 E 25th St Bsmt Ll New York (10010) ***(G-10100)***
Enyce, New York *Also called 5 Star Apparel LLC* ***(G-9022)***
Enzo Diagnostics, Farmingdale *Also called Enzo Life Sciences Inc* ***(G-4997)***
Enzo Life Sciences Inc (HQ).....631 694-7070
10 Executive Blvd Farmingdale (11735) ***(G-4997)***
Enzo Life Sciences Intl Inc.....610 941-0430
10 Executive Blvd Farmingdale (11735) ***(G-4998)***
Enzo Manzoni LLC.....212 464-7000
2896 W 12th St Brooklyn (11224) ***(G-1932)***
Eon Collections.....212 695-1263
247 W 35th St Rm 401 New York (10001) ***(G-10101)***
Eon Labs Inc (HQ).....516 478-9700
1999 Marcus Ave Ste 300 New Hyde Park (11042) ***(G-8877)***
Ephesus Lighting, Syracuse *Also called Eaton Corporation* ***(G-15951)***
Epi Printing & Finishing, Rochester *Also called Engrav-O-Type Press Inc* ***(G-14372)***
Epic Pharma LLC.....718 276-8600
22715 N Conduit Ave Laurelton (11413) ***(G-7413)***
Epicor Software Corporation.....805 496-6789
2165 Technology Dr Schenectady (12308) ***(G-15280)***
Epl, Long Island City *Also called Edison Price Lighting Inc* ***(G-7752)***
Epner Technology Incorporated (PA).....718 782-5948
78 Kingsland Ave Brooklyn (11222) ***(G-1933)***
Epner Technology Incorporated.....718 782-8722
78 Kingsland Ave Brooklyn (11222) ***(G-1934)***
Epoch Microelectronics Inc.....914 332-8570
420 Columbus Ave Ste 204 Valhalla (10595) ***(G-16393)***
Epoch Times International Inc.....212 239-2808
229 W 28th St Fl 5 New York (10001) ***(G-10102)***
Epost International Inc.....212 352-9390
483 10th Ave New York (10018) ***(G-10103)***
Epp Team Inc.....585 454-4995
500 Lee Rd Ste 400 Rochester (14606) ***(G-14375)***
Eps Iron Works Inc.....516 294-5840
38 Windsor Ave Ste 101 Mineola (11501) ***(G-8542)***
Epuffer Inc.....718 374-6030
2348 80th St Fl 1 Brooklyn (11214) ***(G-1935)***
Equal Opprtnity Pblcations Inc.....631 421-9421
445 Broadhollow Rd # 425 Melville (11747) ***(G-8344)***
Equicenter Inc.....585 742-2522
3247 Rush Mendon Rd Honeoye Falls (14472) ***(G-6555)***
Equicheck LLC.....631 987-6356
20 Medford Ave Ste 7 Patchogue (11772) ***(G-13444)***
Equilend Holdings LLC (PA).....212 901-2200
225 Liberty St Fl 10 New York (10281) ***(G-10104)***
Equilibrium Brewery LLC.....201 245-0292
22 Henry St Middletown (10940) ***(G-8473)***
Equipment Apparel LLC.....212 502-1890
19 W 34th St Fl 8 New York (10001) ***(G-10105)***
Equissentials LLC.....607 432-2856
3200 Chestnut St Ste 5 Oneonta (13820) ***(G-13208)***
Equityarcade LLC.....678 232-1301
33 Nassau Ave Brooklyn (11222) ***(G-1936)***
Equivital Inc.....646 513-4169
19 W 34th St Rm 1018 New York (10001) ***(G-10106)***
ER Butler & Co Inc (PA).....212 925-3565
55 Prince St New York (10012) ***(G-10107)***
Erbessd Reliability LLC.....518 874-2700
2c Glens Falls Tech Park Glens Falls (12801) ***(G-5694)***
Erbessd Reliability Instrs, Glens Falls *Also called Erbessd Reliability LLC* ***(G-5694)***
Ercole Nyc Inc (PA).....212 675-2218
142 26th St Brooklyn (11232) ***(G-1937)***
Erdle Perforating Holdings Inc (PA).....585 247-4700
100 Pixley Indus Pkwy Rochester (14624) ***(G-14376)***
Ergun Inc.....631 721-0049
10 Mineola Ave Unit B Roslyn Heights (11577) ***(G-15050)***
Erhard & Gilcher Inc.....315 474-1072
235 Cortland Ave Syracuse (13202) ***(G-15958)***
Eric S Turner & Company Inc.....914 235-7114
3335 Centre Ave New Rochelle (10801) ***(G-8943)***
Eric Signature, New York *Also called Harrison Sportswear Inc* ***(G-10463)***
Eric Winterling Inc.....212 629-7686
20 W 20th St Fl 5 New York (10011) ***(G-10108)***
Ericeira Inc.....516 294-4034
54 E Jericho Tpke Mineola (11501) ***(G-8543)***
Erickson Beamon Ltd.....212 643-4810
498 Fashion Ave Rm 2406 New York (10018) ***(G-10109)***
Erie Engineered Products Inc.....716 206-0204
3949 Walden Ave Lancaster (14086) ***(G-7338)***
Erika T Schwartz MD PC.....212 873-3420
724 5th Ave Fl 10 New York (10019) ***(G-10110)***
Erin Fetherston, New York *Also called Fetherston Design Group LLC* ***(G-10208)***
Ernex Chocolate, Brooklyn *Also called Ernex Corporation Inc* ***(G-1938)***
Ernex Corporation Inc.....718 951-2251
5518 Avenue N Brooklyn (11234) ***(G-1938)***
Ernie Green Industries Inc.....585 295-8951
85 Pixley Industrial Pkwy Rochester (14624) ***(G-14377)***
Ernie Green Industries Inc.....585 647-2300
1667 Emerson St Rochester (14606) ***(G-14378)***
Ernie Green Industries Inc.....585 647-2300
460 Buffalo Rd Ste 220 Rochester (14611) ***(G-14379)***
Ernst Publishing Co, Albany *Also called Ucc Guide Inc* ***(G-145)***
Ert Software Inc.....845 358-5721
4 Pine Glen Dr Blauvelt (10913) ***(G-965)***
Ertel Alsop, Kingston *Also called Stavo Industries Inc* ***(G-7241)***
Ertel Engineering Co, Kingston *Also called Stavo Industries Inc* ***(G-7242)***
Es Beta Inc.....631 582-6740
125 Comac St Ronkonkoma (11779) ***(G-14927)***
Esc Control Electronics LLC.....631 467-5328
98 Lincoln Ave Sayville (11782) ***(G-15236)***
Eschen Prosthetic & Orthotic L.....212 606-1262
510 E 73rd St Ste 201 New York (10021) ***(G-10111)***
Escholar LLC.....914 989-2900
222 Bloomingdale Rd # 107 White Plains (10605) ***(G-17131)***
Eser Realty Corp (PA).....718 383-0565
62 Greenpoint Ave 64 Brooklyn (11222) ***(G-1939)***
Eshel Jewelry Mfg Co Inc.....212 588-8800
17 E 48th St Fl 9 New York (10017) ***(G-10112)***
Esi, Holbrook *Also called Electronic Systems Inc* ***(G-6473)***
ESi Cases & Accessories Inc.....212 883-8838
44 E 32nd St Rm 601 New York (10016) ***(G-10113)***
Eskay Metal Fabricating, Buffalo *Also called Schuler-Subra Inc* ***(G-3206)***
Eskayel Inc.....347 703-8084
75 S 6th St Brooklyn (11249) ***(G-1940)***
Esm Group Inc (HQ).....716 446-8914
300 Corporate Pkwy 118n Amherst (14226) ***(G-239)***
Esm II Inc (HQ).....716 446-8888
300 Corporate Pkwy 118n Amherst (14226) ***(G-240)***
Esm Special Metals & Tech Inc.....716 446-8914
300 Corporate Pkwy 118n Amherst (14226) ***(G-241)***
Espey Mfg & Electronics Corp (PA).....518 584-4100
233 Ballston Ave Saratoga Springs (12866) ***(G-15180)***
Espostos Fnest Qlty Ssage Pdts, New York *Also called Elmgang Enterprises I Inc* ***(G-10065)***
Esquire Magazine, New York *Also called Hearst Corporation* ***(G-10488)***
Esquire Mechanical Corp.....718 625-4006
79 Sandford St Brooklyn (11205) ***(G-1941)***
Ess Bee Industries Inc.....718 894-5202
95 Evergreen Ave Brooklyn (11206) ***(G-1942)***
Essar Americas.....212 292-2600
277 Park Ave 47th New York (10172) ***(G-10114)***
Essar Steel Minnesota LLC (PA).....212 292-2600
277 Park Ave Fl 35l New York (10172) ***(G-10115)***
Essence Communications Inc (HQ).....212 522-1212
225 Liberty St Fl 9 New York (10281) ***(G-10116)***
Essence Magazine, New York *Also called Essence Communications Inc* ***(G-10116)***
Essential Homme Magazine, New York *Also called Essential Publications US LLC* ***(G-10117)***
Essential Publications US LLC.....646 707-0898
14 E 4th St Rm 604 New York (10012) ***(G-10117)***
Essential Ribbons Inc.....212 967-4173
53 W 36th St Rm 405 New York (10018) ***(G-10118)***
Essex Box & Pallet Co Inc.....518 834-7279
49 Industrial Park Rd Keeseville (12944) ***(G-7166)***

Essex Industries.....518 942-6671
17 Pilfershire Rd Mineville (12956) *(G-8573)*
Essex Manufacturing Inc.....212 239-0080
350 5th Ave Ste 2400 New York (10118) *(G-10119)*
Essex Works Ltd.....718 495-4575
446 Riverdale Ave Brooklyn (11207) *(G-1943)*
Essie Cosmetics Ltd.....212 818-1500
575 5th Ave New York (10017) *(G-10120)*
Essilor Laboratories Amer Inc.....845 365-6700
165 Route 303 Orangeburg (10962) *(G-13248)*
Estebania Enterprises Inc.....585 529-9330
15 Mcardle St Ste A Rochester (14611) *(G-14380)*
Estee Lauder Companies Inc.....917 606-3240
9 W 22nd St New York (10010) *(G-10121)*
Estee Lauder Companies Inc.....212 756-4800
655 Madison Ave Fl 15 New York (10065) *(G-10122)*
Estee Lauder Companies Inc.....212 572-4200
767 5th Ave Fl 37 New York (10153) *(G-10123)*
Estee Lauder Companies Inc (PA).....212 572-4200
767 5th Ave Fl 37 New York (10153) *(G-10124)*
Estee Lauder Companies Inc.....646 602-7590
65 Bleecker St Frnt 1 New York (10012) *(G-10125)*
Estee Lauder Inc (HQ).....212 572-4200
767 5th Ave Fl 37 New York (10153) *(G-10126)*
Estee Lauder Inc.....631 531-1000
125 Pinelawn Rd Melville (11747) *(G-8345)*
Estee Lauder Inc.....631 454-7000
350 S Service Rd Melville (11747) *(G-8346)*
Estee Lauder Inc.....212 756-4800
655 Madison Ave Fl 10 New York (10065) *(G-10127)*
Estee Lauder International Inc (HQ).....212 572-4200
767 5th Ave Bsmt 1 New York (10153) *(G-10128)*
Estiator, New York *Also called Interhellenic Publishing Inc* ***(G-10671)***
ET Oakes Corporation.....631 232-0002
686 Old Willets Path Hauppauge (11788) *(G-6096)*
ET Precision Optics Inc.....585 254-2560
33 Curlew St Rochester (14606) *(G-14381)*
Et Publishing Intl LLC.....212 838-7220
150 E 58th St Ste 2200 New York (10155) *(G-10129)*
Etc Hosiery & Underwear Ltd.....212 947-5151
350 5th Ave Ste 2525 New York (10118) *(G-10130)*
Etcetera Wallpapers, Glen Cove *Also called Sunnyside Decorative Prints Co* ***(G-5643)***
Eternal Fortune Fashion LLC.....212 965-5322
135 W 36th St Fl 5 New York (10018) *(G-10131)*
Eternal Line.....845 856-1999
1237 State Route 42 Sparrow Bush (12780) *(G-15586)*
Eternal Love Parfums Corp.....516 921-6100
485 Underhill Blvd # 207 Syosset (11791) *(G-15841)*
Eternal Love Perfumes, Syosset *Also called Eternal Love Parfums Corp* ***(G-15841)***
Ethis Communications Inc.....212 791-1440
44 Church St Ste 200 White Plains (10601) *(G-17132)*
Etna Products Co Inc (PA).....212 989-7591
99 Madison Ave Fl 11 New York (10016) *(G-10132)*
Etna Tool & Die Corporation.....212 475-4350
42 Bond St Frnt A New York (10012) *(G-10133)*
Eton Institute.....855 334-3688
1 Rockefeller Plz Fl 11 New York (10020) *(G-10134)*
Eton International, New York *Also called Basil S Kadhim* ***(G-9380)***
Ets, Mineola *Also called Environmental Temp Systems LLC* ***(G-8541)***
Eu Design LLC.....212 420-7788
73 Spring St Rm 506 New York (10012) *(G-10135)*
Euchner USA Inc.....315 701-0315
6723 Lyons St East Syracuse (13057) *(G-4541)*
Eugene G Danner Mfg Inc.....631 234-5261
160 Oval Dr Central Islip (11749) *(G-3521)*
Eugenia Selective Living Inc.....631 277-1461
122 Freeman Ave Islip (11751) *(G-6847)*
Euphorbia Productions Ltd.....212 533-1700
632 Broadway Fl 9 New York (10012) *(G-10136)*
Euphrates Inc.....518 762-3488
230 Enterprise Rd Johnstown (12095) *(G-7142)*
Euro Bands Inc.....212 719-9777
247 W 37th St Rm 700 New York (10018) *(G-10137)*
Euro Fine Paper Inc.....516 238-5253
220 Nassau Blvd Garden City (11530) *(G-5516)*
Euro Gear (usa) Inc.....518 578-1775
1 Cumberland Ave Plattsburgh (12901) *(G-13690)*
Euro Pacific Precious Metals.....212 481-0310
152 Madison Ave Rm 1003 New York (10016) *(G-10138)*
Euro Woodworking Inc.....718 246-9172
303 Park Ave Fl 8 Brooklyn (11205) *(G-1944)*
Euroco Costumes Inc.....212 629-9665
254 W 35th St Fl 15 New York (10001) *(G-10139)*
Eurocraft Custom Furniture.....718 956-0600
3425 11th St Long Island City (11106) *(G-7761)*
Euromed Inc.....845 359-4039
25 Corporate Dr Orangeburg (10962) *(G-13249)*
Europadisk LLC.....718 407-7300
2402 Queens Plz S Long Island City (11101) *(G-7762)*
European Marble Works Co Inc.....718 387-9778
54 Nassau Blvd Garden City (11530) *(G-5517)*
Europrojects Intl Inc.....917 262-0795
152 W 25th St Fl 8b New York (10001) *(G-10140)*
Eurotex Inc.....716 205-8861
4600 Witmer Rd Niagara Falls (14305) *(G-12837)*
Eurotex North America, Niagara Falls *Also called Eurotex Inc* ***(G-12837)***
Ev-Box North America Inc.....646 930-6305
335 Madison Ave 335 New York (10017) *(G-10141)*
Eva Fehren, New York *Also called Gorga Fehren Fine Jewelry LLC* ***(G-10379)***
Evado Filip.....917 774-8666
159 Bleecker St New York (10012) *(G-10142)*
EVANGELIST, THE, Albany *Also called Albany Catholic Press Assoc* ***(G-35)***
Evans & Paul LLC.....516 576-0800
140 Dupont St Plainview (11803) *(G-13629)*
Evans Chemetics LP.....315 539-9221
228 E Main St Waterloo (13165) *(G-16646)*
Evans Manufacturing LLC.....631 439-3300
595 Smith St Farmingdale (11735) *(G-4999)*
Eve Sales Corp.....718 589-6800
945 Close Ave Bronx (10473) *(G-1331)*
Evelo Inc.....917 251-8743
327 Beach 101st St Rockaway Park (11694) *(G-14813)*
Evenhouse Printing.....716 649-2666
4783 Southwestern Blvd Hamburg (14075) *(G-5948)*
Evening Telegram, Herkimer *Also called Gatehouse Media LLC* ***(G-6325)***
Evening Tribune, Hornell *Also called Gatehouse Media LLC* ***(G-6590)***
Event Journal Inc.....516 470-1811
700 Hicksville Rd Bethpage (11714) *(G-866)*
Event Services Corporation.....315 488-9357
6171 Airport Rd Solvay (13209) *(G-15530)*
Ever-Nu-Metal Products Inc.....646 423-5833
471 20th St Brooklyn (11215) *(G-1945)*
Everblock Systems LLC.....844 422-5625
790 Madison Ave Rm 200 New York (10065) *(G-10143)*
Evercore Partners Svcs E LLC.....212 857-3100
55 E 52nd St New York (10055) *(G-10144)*
Everest Bbn Inc.....212 268-7979
42 Broadway Ste 1736 New York (10004) *(G-10145)*
Everfab Inc.....716 655-1550
12928 Big Tree Rd East Aurora (14052) *(G-4395)*
Evergreen, New York *Also called Integrated Copyright Group* ***(G-10658)***
Evergreen Bleachers Inc.....518 654-9084
122 Maple St Corinth (12822) *(G-3980)*
Evergreen Corp Central NY.....315 454-4175
235 Cortland Ave Syracuse (13202) *(G-15959)*
Evergreen High Voltage LLC.....281 814-9973
140 Peninsula Way Lake Placid (12946) *(G-7298)*
Evergreen Manufacturing, Syracuse *Also called Evergreen Corp Central NY* ***(G-15959)***
Evergreen Slate Company Inc.....518 642-2530
2027 County Route 23 Middle Granville (12849) *(G-8431)*
Everlast Seals and Supply LLC.....718 388-7373
41 Montrose Ave Brooklyn (11206) *(G-1946)*
Everlast Sports Mfg Corp (HQ).....212 239-0990
42 W 39th St New York (10018) *(G-10146)*
Everlast Worldwide Inc (HQ).....212 239-0990
42 W 39th St Fl 3 New York (10018) *(G-10147)*
Everlasting Images.....607 785-8743
504 Shady Dr Endicott (13760) *(G-4814)*
Everlasting Memories.....716 833-1111
3701 Mckinley Pkwy # 210 Blasdell (14219) *(G-956)*
Everplans, New York *Also called Beyondly Inc* ***(G-9430)***
Eversan Inc.....315 736-3967
34 Main St Ste 3 Whitesboro (13492) *(G-17221)*
Every Toe Covered, New York *Also called Etc Hosiery & Underwear Ltd* ***(G-10130)***
Everybodys Carribbean Magazine, Brooklyn *Also called Herman Hall Communications* ***(G-2075)***
Evidon Inc (HQ).....917 262-2530
10 E 39th St Fl 8 New York (10016) *(G-10148)*
Evolution Impressions Inc.....585 473-6600
160 Commerce Dr Rochester (14623) *(G-14382)*
Evolution Spirits Inc.....917 543-7880
401 Park Ave S New York (10016) *(G-10149)*
Evolve Guest Controls LLC (PA).....855 750-9090
16 S Maryland Ave Port Washington (11050) *(G-13836)*
Evonik Corporation.....518 233-7090
7 Schoolhouse Ln Waterford (12188) *(G-16632)*
Ewatchfactory Corp (PA).....212 564-8318
390 5th Ave Rm 910 New York (10018) *(G-10150)*
Ewt Holdings III Corp (HQ).....212 644-5900
666 5th Ave Fl 36 New York (10103) *(G-10151)*
Ex El Enterprises Ltd.....212 489-4500
630 Fort Washington Ave New York (10040) *(G-10152)*
Ex-It Medical Devices Inc.....212 653-0637
1330 Ave Of The Americas New York (10019) *(G-10153)*
Exact Machining & Mfg.....585 334-7090
305 Commerce Dr Ste 7 Rochester (14623) *(G-14383)*
Exact Solutions Inc.....212 707-8627
139 Fulton St Rm 511 New York (10038) *(G-10154)*
Exacta LLC.....716 406-2303
8955 Williams Ct Clarence Center (14032) *(G-3701)*
Excalbur Brnze Sculpture Fndry.....718 366-3444
309 Starr St Brooklyn (11237) *(G-1947)*
Excel Aluminum Products Inc.....315 471-0925
563 N Salina St Syracuse (13208) *(G-15960)*

ALPHABETIC

Excel Commercial Seating — ALPHABETIC SECTION

Excel Commercial Seating 828 428-8338
190 Field St West Babylon (11704) *(G-16816)*

Excel Graphics Services Inc 212 929-2183
519 8th Ave Fl 18 New York (10018) *(G-10155)*

Excel Industries Inc 716 542-5468
11737 Main St Clarence (14031) *(G-3689)*

Excel Paint Applicators Inc 347 221-1968
555 Doughty Blvd Inwood (11096) *(G-6794)*

Excel Technology Inc 212 355-3400
780 3rd Ave New York (10017) *(G-10156)*

Excelco Developments Inc 716 934-2651
65 Main St Silver Creek (14136) *(G-15470)*

Excelco/Newbrook Inc 716 934-2644
16 Mechanic St Silver Creek (14136) *(G-15471)*

Excell Print & Promotions Inc 914 437-8668
50 Main St Ste 100 White Plains (10606) *(G-17133)*

Excelled Sheepskin & Lea Coat (PA) 212 594-5843
1400 Broadway Fl 31 New York (10018) *(G-10157)*

Excellent Art Mfg Corp 718 388-7075
531 Bayview Ave Inwood (11096) *(G-6795)*

Excellent Photocopies, Brooklyn Also called Excellent Printing Inc *(G-1949)*

Excellent Poly Inc 718 768-6555
820 4th Ave Brooklyn (11232) *(G-1948)*

Excellent Printing Inc 718 384-7272
165 Hooper St Brooklyn (11211) *(G-1949)*

Excelsior Graphics Inc 212 730-6200
485 Madison Ave Fl 13 New York (10022) *(G-10158)*

Excelsior Mlt-Cltural Inst Inc 706 627-4285
13340 Roosevelt Ave 7g Flushing (11354) *(G-5247)*

Excelsior Publications 607 746-7600
133 Main St Delhi (13753) *(G-4263)*

Excelsus Solutions LLC 585 533-0003
300b Commerce Dr Rochester (14623) *(G-14384)*

Exchange My Mail Inc 516 605-1835
30 Jericho Executive Plz 100c Jericho (11753) *(G-7101)*

Exclusive Designs 516 378-5258
84 Albany Ave Freeport (11520) *(G-5407)*

Execuprint Inc 585 288-5570
111 Humboldt St Rochester (14609) *(G-14385)*

Executive Business Media Inc 516 334-3030
825 Old Country Rd Westbury (11590) *(G-17010)*

Executive Machines Inc 718 965-6600
882 3rd Ave Unit 8 Brooklyn (11232) *(G-1950)*

Executive Mirror Doors Inc 631 234-1090
1 Comac Loop Unit 7 Ronkonkoma (11779) *(G-14928)*

Executive Prtg & Direct Mail 914 592-3200
8 Westchester Plz Ste 117 Elmsford (10523) *(G-4760)*

Executive Sign Corp 212 397-4050
43 Boulevard Cornwall On Hudson (12520) *(G-4013)*

Executive Sign Corporation 212 397-4050
347 W 36th St Rm 902 New York (10018) *(G-10159)*

Exelis, Rochester Also called Harris Corporation *(G-14444)*

Exelis Geospatial Systems, Rochester Also called Harris Corporation *(G-14442)*

Exelis Geospatial Systems, Rochester Also called Harris Corporation *(G-14443)*

Exergy LLC 516 832-9300
320 Endo Blvd Unit 1 Garden City (11530) *(G-5518)*

Exfo Burleigh Pdts Group Inc 585 301-1530
181 S Main St Ste 10 Canandaigua (14424) *(G-3374)*

Exhibit Corporation America 718 937-2600
4623 Crane St Ste 3 Long Island City (11101) *(G-7763)*

Exhibit Portables, Long Island City Also called Exhibit Corporation America *(G-7763)*

Exhibits & More 585 924-4040
7615 Omnitech Pl Ste 4a Victor (14564) *(G-16500)*

Exide Batteries, Batavia Also called Exide Technologies *(G-633)*

Exide Technologies 585 344-0656
4330 Commerce Dr Batavia (14020) *(G-633)*

Exigo Precision Inc 585 254-5818
190 Murray St Rochester (14606) *(G-14386)*

Exotic Print and Paper Inc 212 807-0465
15 E 13th St New York (10003) *(G-10160)*

Expedi-Printing Inc 516 513-0919
41 Red Brook Rd Great Neck (11024) *(G-5822)*

Expedient Heat Treating Corp 716 433-1177
61 Dale Dr North Tonawanda (14120) *(G-12988)*

Experiment LLC 212 889-1659
260 5th Ave Fl 3 New York (10001) *(G-10161)*

Experiment Publishing LLC 212 889-1273
220 E 23rd St Ste 301 New York (10010) *(G-10162)*

Expert Industries Inc 718 434-6060
848 E 43rd St Brooklyn (11210) *(G-1951)*

Expert Machine Services Inc 718 786-1200
3944a 28th St Long Island City (11101) *(G-7764)*

Expert Metal Slitters Corp 718 361-2735
3740 12th St Long Island City (11101) *(G-7765)*

Expo Furniture Designs Inc 516 674-1420
1 Garvies Point Rd Glen Cove (11542) *(G-5627)*

Expo Lighting Design, Glen Cove Also called Expo Furniture Designs Inc *(G-5627)*

Expositor Newspapers Inc 585 427-2468
2535 Brighton Henrietta Rochester (14623) *(G-14387)*

Express Building Supply Inc 516 608-0379
3550 Lawson Blvd Oceanside (11572) *(G-13099)*

Express Checkout LLC 646 512-2068
110 E 1st St Apt 20 New York (10009) *(G-10163)*

Express Concrete Inc 631 273-4224
1250 Suffolk Ave Brentwood (11717) *(G-1180)*

Express Mart, Watertown Also called Petre Alii Petroleum *(G-16693)*

Express Press, Rochester Also called Clarsons Corp *(G-14299)*

Express Seal Div, Lancaster Also called Apple Rubber Products Inc *(G-7327)*

Express Tag & Label, Brooklyn Also called Jerry Tomaselli *(G-2136)*

Expresseal, Lancaster Also called Apple Rubber Products Inc *(G-7328)*

Expression Embroidery, Jamaica Also called Expressions Punching & Digitiz *(G-6947)*

Expressions Punching & Digitiz 718 291-1177
9315 179th Pl Jamaica (11433) *(G-6947)*

Expressive Scent, Brooklyn Also called Jacmax Industries LLC *(G-2129)*

Exquisite Glass & Stone Inc 718 937-9266
3117 12th St Astoria (11106) *(G-439)*

Extek Inc 585 533-1672
7500 W Henrietta Rd Rush (14543) *(G-15072)*

Exten II LLC 716 895-2214
50 Stradtman St Buffalo (14206) *(G-2956)*

Extreme Auto Accessories Corp (PA) 718 978-6722
12019 Rockaway Blvd South Ozone Park (11420) *(G-15557)*

Extreme Group Holdings LLC (HQ) 212 833-8000
550 Madison Ave Fl 6 New York (10022) *(G-10164)*

Extreme Molding LLC 518 326-9319
25 Gibson St Ste 2 Watervliet (12189) *(G-16708)*

Extreme Spices Inc (PA) 917 496-4081
5634 56th St Ste 36 Maspeth (11378) *(G-8168)*

Extreme Streetwear, Batavia Also called Alicia F Herdlein *(G-621)*

Exxelia-Raf Tabtronics LLC 585 243-4331
2854 Genesee St Piffard (14533) *(G-13574)*

Exxonmobil Chemical Company 315 966-1000
729 State Route 31 Macedon (14502) *(G-8016)*

EY Industries Inc 718 624-9122
63 Flushing Ave Unit 331 Brooklyn (11205) *(G-1952)*

Eye Deal Eyewear Inc 716 297-1500
4611 Military Rd Niagara Falls (14305) *(G-12838)*

Eye Graphics & Printing Inc 718 488-0606
499 Van Brunt St Ste 3a Brooklyn (11231) *(G-1953)*

Eye Shadow, New York Also called Stony Apparel Corp *(G-12232)*

Eyeglass Service Industries 914 666-3150
777 Bedford Rd Bedford Hills (10507) *(G-800)*

Eyelock Corporation 855 393-5625
355 Lexington Ave New York (10017) *(G-10165)*

Eyelock LLC (HQ) 855 393-5625
355 Lexington Ave Fl 12 New York (10017) *(G-10166)*

Eyeworks Inc 585 454-4470
1249 Ridgeway Ave Ste M Rochester (14615) *(G-14388)*

EZ CMS Systems US, Brooklyn Also called EZ Systems US Inc *(G-1955)*

EZ Lift Garage Door Service, Spring Valley Also called EZ Lift Operator Corp *(G-15606)*

EZ Lift Operator Corp 845 356-1676
111 S Main St Spring Valley (10977) *(G-15606)*

EZ Newsletter LLC 412 943-7777
1449 Bay Ridge Ave 2 Brooklyn (11219) *(G-1954)*

EZ Systems US Inc 212 634-6899
35 Meadow St Ste 103 Brooklyn (11206) *(G-1955)*

F & B Photo Offset Co Inc (PA) 516 431-5433
4 California Pl N Island Park (11558) *(G-6819)*

F & D Printing, Staten Island Also called F & D Services Inc *(G-15693)*

F & D Services Inc 718 984-1635
34 E Augusta Ave Staten Island (10308) *(G-15693)*

F & H Metal Finishing Co Inc 585 798-2151
700 Genesee St Medina (14103) *(G-8304)*

F & J Designs Inc 212 302-8755
526 Fashion Ave Fl 8 New York (10018) *(G-10167)*

F & M Precise Metals Co, Farmingdale Also called Pirnat Precise Metals Inc *(G-5090)*

F & R Enterprises Inc (PA) 315 841-8189
1594 State Route 315 Waterville (13480) *(G-16701)*

F & T Graphics Inc 631 643-1000
690 Old Willets Path Hauppauge (11788) *(G-6097)*

F & V Distribution Company LLC 516 812-0393
1 Arizona Plz Woodbury (11797) *(G-17308)*

F A Alpine Windows Mfg 845 469-5700
1683 State Route 17m Chester (10918) *(G-3633)*

F A Printing 212 974-5982
690 10th Ave Frnt 1 New York (10019) *(G-10168)*

F C W Division, Uniondale Also called Hearst Business Media *(G-16318)*

F Cappiello Dairy Pdts Inc 518 374-5064
115 Van Guysling Ave Schenectady (12305) *(G-15281)*

F E Hale Mfg Co 315 894-5490
120 Benson Pl Frankfort (13340) *(G-5361)*

F H Stickles & Son Inc 518 851-9048
2590 Rr 9 Livingston (12541) *(G-7587)*

F I S, Oriskany Also called Fiber Instrument Sales Inc *(G-13333)*

F J Remey Co Inc 516 741-5112
121 Willis Ave Mineola (11501) *(G-8544)*

F K Williams Division, North Tonawanda Also called Gardei Industries LLC *(G-12991)*

F L Demeter Inc 516 487-5187
12 N Gate Rd Great Neck (11023) *(G-5823)*

F Logic, Hastings On Hudson Also called Flogic Inc *(G-6023)*

F M Abdulky Inc (PA)............607 272-7373
527 W Seneca St Ithaca (14850) ***(G-6875)***
F M Abdulky Inc............607 272-7373
527 W Seneca St Ithaca (14850) ***(G-6876)***
F M C Aricultural Chem Group, Middleport *Also called FMC Corporation* ***(G-8455)***
F M C Peroxygen Chemicals Div, Tonawanda *Also called FMC Corporation* ***(G-16181)***
F M Group Inc............845 589-0102
100 Wells Ave Congers (10920) ***(G-3881)***
F M Howell & Company (PA)............607 734-6291
79 Pennsylvania Ave Elmira (14904) ***(G-4697)***
F M L Industries Inc............607 749-7273
10 Hudson St Homer (13077) ***(G-6545)***
F Olivers LLC............585 244-2585
747 Park Ave Rochester (14607) ***(G-14389)***
F P H Communications............212 528-1728
225 Broadway Ste 2008 New York (10007) ***(G-10169)***
F R A M Technologies Inc............718 338-6230
3048 Bedford Ave Brooklyn (11210) ***(G-1956)***
F W Roberts Mfg Co Inc............716 434-3555
73 Lock St Lockport (14094) ***(G-7614)***
F X Graphix Inc............716 871-1511
3043 Delaware Ave Buffalo (14217) ***(G-2957)***
F&M Ornamental Designs LLC............212 353-2600
200 Lexington Ave Rm 702 New York (10016) ***(G-10170)***
F&M Ornamental Designs LLC (PA)............908 241-7776
200 Lexington Ave Rm 702 New York (10016) ***(G-10171)***
F+w Media Inc............212 447-1400
1140 Broadway Fl 14 New York (10001) ***(G-10172)***
F-O-R Software LLC............212 231-9506
757 3rd Ave Fl 20 New York (10017) ***(G-10173)***
F-O-R Software LLC (PA)............914 220-8800
10 Bank St Ste 880 White Plains (10606) ***(G-17134)***
F-O-R Software LLC............212 724-3920
100 Park Ave Rm 1600 New York (10017) ***(G-10174)***
F5 Networks Inc............888 882-7535
600 Lexington Ave Fl 5 New York (10022) ***(G-10175)***
Fab Industries Corp (HQ)............516 498-3200
98 Cuttermill Rd Ste 412 Great Neck (11021) ***(G-5824)***
Fabbian USA Corp............973 882-3824
307 W 38th St Rm 1103 New York (10018) ***(G-10176)***
Fabric Concepts For Industry............914 375-2565
354 Ashburton Ave Yonkers (10701) ***(G-17458)***
Fabric Quilters Unlimited Inc............516 333-2866
1400 Shames Dr Westbury (11590) ***(G-17011)***
Fabric Resources Intl Ltd (PA)............516 829-4550
9 Park Pl Great Neck (11021) ***(G-5825)***
Fabrication Enterprises Inc............914 591-9300
250 Clearbrook Rd Ste 240 Elmsford (10523) ***(G-4761)***
Fabrication Specialties Corp............631 242-0326
2 Saxwood St Ste G Deer Park (11729) ***(G-4163)***
Fabritex Inc............706 376-6584
215 W 40th St Fl 9 New York (10018) ***(G-10177)***
Faces Magazine Inc (PA)............201 843-4004
46 Violet Ave Poughkeepsie (12601) ***(G-13918)***
Faces Magazine Inc............845 454-7420
40 Violet Ave Poughkeepsie (12601) ***(G-13919)***
Facilamatic Instrument Corp............516 825-6300
39 Clinton Ave Valley Stream (11580) ***(G-16432)***
Facilities, New York *Also called Bedrock Communications* ***(G-9394)***
Facilities Exchange, New York *Also called FX INC* ***(G-10277)***
Facsimile Cmmncations Inds Inc (PA)............212 741-6400
134 W 26th St Fl 3 New York (10001) ***(G-10178)***
Factory East............718 280-1558
723 Kent Ave Brooklyn (11249) ***(G-1957)***
Factory Nyc, Brooklyn *Also called Factory East* ***(G-1957)***
Factory Wheel Warehouse Inc............516 605-2131
30 W Ames Ct Plainview (11803) ***(G-13630)***
Facts On File Inc (HQ)............212 967-8800
132 W 31st St Rm 1600 New York (10001) ***(G-10179)***
Fad Inc............631 385-2460
630 New York Ave Ste B Huntington (11743) ***(G-6694)***
Fad Treasures, Huntington *Also called Fad Inc* ***(G-6694)***
Fage USA Dairy Industry Inc............518 762-5912
1 Opportunity Dr Johnstown (12095) ***(G-7143)***
Fage USA Holdings (HQ)............518 762-5912
1 Opportunity Dr Johnstown (12095) ***(G-7144)***
Fage USA Yogurt Mfg Plant, Johnstown *Also called Fage USA Dairy Industry Inc* ***(G-7143)***
Fahrenheit NY Inc............212 354-6554
315 W 39th St Rm 803 New York (10018) ***(G-10180)***
Fahy-Williams Publishing Inc............315 781-6820
171 Reed St Geneva (14456) ***(G-5587)***
Fair-Rite Products Corp (PA)............845 895-2055
1 Commercial Row Wallkill (12589) ***(G-16563)***
Fairbank Farms, Ashville *Also called Fairbank Reconstruction Corp* ***(G-426)***
Fairbank Reconstruction Corp............800 628-3276
5151 Fairbanks Rd Ashville (14710) ***(G-426)***
Fairbanks Mfg LLC............845 341-0002
79 Industrial Pl Middletown (10940) ***(G-8474)***
Fairchild Publications Inc (HQ)............212 630-4000
475 5th Ave New York (10017) ***(G-10181)***
Fairchild Publishing LLC............212 286-3897
4 Times Sq Fl 17 New York (10036) ***(G-10182)***
Fairmount Press............212 255-2300
121 Varick St Fl 9 New York (10013) ***(G-10183)***
Fairview Bell and Intercom............718 627-8621
502 Gravesend Neck Rd B Brooklyn (11223) ***(G-1958)***
Fairview Fitting & Mfg Inc............716 614-0320
3777 Commerce Ct North Tonawanda (14120) ***(G-12989)***
Fairview Paper Box Corp............585 786-5230
200 Allen St Warsaw (14569) ***(G-16604)***
Fait Usa Inc............215 674-5310
350 5th Ave Fl 41 New York (10118) ***(G-10184)***
Fal Coffee Inc............718 305-4255
240 Kent Ave Ste A8 Brooklyn (11249) ***(G-1959)***
Fala Technologies Inc............845 336-4000
430 Old Neighborhood Rd Kingston (12401) ***(G-7218)***
Falcon Chair and Table Inc............716 664-7136
121 S Work St Falconer (14733) ***(G-4904)***
Falcon Perspectives Inc............718 706-9168
28 Vernon Blvd Ste 45 Long Island City (11101) ***(G-7766)***
Falcone Food Distribution, Brooklyn *Also called Falcones Cookie Land Ltd* ***(G-1960)***
Falconer Electronics Inc (PA)............716 665-4176
421 W Everett St Falconer (14733) ***(G-4905)***
Falconer Printing & Design Inc............716 665-2121
66 E Main St Falconer (14733) ***(G-4906)***
Falcones Cookie Land Ltd (PA)............718 236-4200
1648 61st St Brooklyn (11204) ***(G-1960)***
Falconstor Software Inc (PA)............631 777-5188
2 Huntington Quadrangle 2s Melville (11747) ***(G-8347)***
Falk Industries Inc............518 725-2777
179 Corporate Dr Johnstown (12095) ***(G-7145)***
Falke's Quarry, Prattsville *Also called Cobleskill Stone Products Inc* ***(G-13961)***
Fallon Inc............718 326-7226
5930 56th Rd Maspeth (11378) ***(G-8169)***
Falls Manufacturing Inc (PA)............518 672-7189
95 Main St Philmont (12565) ***(G-13565)***
Falso Industries Inc............315 463-0266
4100 New Court Ave Syracuse (13206) ***(G-15961)***
Falso Metal Fabricating, Syracuse *Also called Falso Industries Inc* ***(G-15961)***
Falvo Manufacturing Co Inc............315 738-7682
20 Harbor Point Rd Utica (13502) ***(G-16353)***
Fam Creations............212 869-4833
7 W 45th St Ste 1404 New York (10036) ***(G-10185)***
Fambus Inc............607 785-3700
2800 Watson Blvd Endicott (13760) ***(G-4815)***
Fame Construction Inc............718 626-1000
2388 Brklyn Queens Expy W Astoria (11103) ***(G-440)***
Family Hearing Center............845 897-3059
18 Westage Dr Ste 16 Fishkill (12524) ***(G-5191)***
Family Publications Ltd............212 947-2177
325 W 38th St Rm 804 New York (10018) ***(G-10186)***
Family Publishing Group Inc............914 381-7474
141 Halstead Ave Mamaroneck (10543) ***(G-8067)***
Famous Box Scooter Co............631 943-2013
75 Rogers Ct West Babylon (11704) ***(G-16817)***
Famous Doughnuts Inc............716 834-6356
3043 Main St Buffalo (14214) ***(G-2958)***
Famous Manhattan Soup Chef, Staten Island *Also called Interntional Gourmet Soups Inc* ***(G-15709)***
Fancy, New York *Also called Thing Daemon Inc* ***(G-12338)***
Fancy Flamingo LLC............516 209-7306
450 W 17th St Apt 528 New York (10011) ***(G-10187)***
Fancy Window & Door, Brooklyn *Also called Fancy Windows & Doors Mfg Corp* ***(G-1961)***
Fancy Windows & Doors Mfg Corp............718 366-7800
312 Ten Eyck St Brooklyn (11206) ***(G-1961)***
Fanshawe Foods LLC............212 757-3130
5 Columbus Cir New York (10019) ***(G-10188)***
Fantasia Jewelry Inc............212 921-9590
42 W 39th St Fl 14 New York (10018) ***(G-10189)***
Fantasy Fireworks Display............518 664-1809
28 Flike Rd Stillwater (12170) ***(G-15781)***
Fantasy Glass Compan............845 786-5818
61 Beach Rd Stony Point (10980) ***(G-15794)***
Fantasy Home Improvement Corp............718 277-4021
2731 Atlantic Ave Brooklyn (11207) ***(G-1962)***
Fantasy Sports Media Group Inc............416 917-6002
27 W 20th St Ste 900 New York (10011) ***(G-10190)***
Fantasy Sports Network, New York *Also called Fantasy Sports Media Group Inc* ***(G-10190)***
Fanvision Entertainment LLC (PA)............917 297-7428
33 W 17th St Ste 901 New York (10011) ***(G-10191)***
Fao Printing, Brooklyn *Also called Phillip Tissicher* ***(G-2431)***
Far East Industries Inc (PA)............718 687-2482
118 Stephan Marc Ln New Hyde Park (11040) ***(G-8878)***
Far Eastern Coconut Company............631 851-8800
200 Corporate Plz 201a Central Islip (11749) ***(G-3522)***
Far Rockaway Drugs Inc............718 471-2500
1727 Seagirt Blvd Far Rockaway (11691) ***(G-4929)***
Faradyne Motors LLC............315 331-5985
2077 Division St Palmyra (14522) ***(G-13430)***
Farber Plastics Inc............516 378-4860
162 Hanse Ave Freeport (11520) ***(G-5408)***
Farber Trucking Corp............516 378-4860
162 Hanse Ave Freeport (11520) ***(G-5409)***
Farino & Sons Asphalt, Kings Park *Also called Amfar Asphalt Corp* ***(G-7199)***

ALPHABETIC

Farmers Hub LLC (HQ) ALPHABETIC SECTION

Farmers Hub LLC (HQ)....914 380-2945
8 Francine Ct White Plains (10607) ***(G-17135)***
Farmingdale Iron Works Inc....631 249-5995
105 Florida St Farmingdale (11735) ***(G-5000)***
Farney Lumber Corporation....315 346-6013
7194 Brewery Rd Lowville (13367) ***(G-7964)***
Faro Industries Inc....585 647-6000
340 Lyell Ave Rochester (14606) ***(G-14390)***
Farrand Controls Division, Valhalla *Also called Ruhle Companies Inc* ***(G-16398)***
Farrant Screw Machine Products....585 457-3213
Gulf Rd Java Village (14083) ***(G-7087)***
Farrar Straus and Giroux LLC (HQ)....212 741-6900
18 W 18th St Fl 7 New York (10011) ***(G-10192)***
Farrington Packaging Corp....315 733-4600
2007 Beechgrove Pl Utica (13501) ***(G-16354)***
Farrow and Ball Inc (HQ)....212 752-5544
979 3rd Ave Ste 1519 New York (10022) ***(G-10193)***
Farthing Press Inc....716 852-4674
260 Oak St Buffalo (14203) ***(G-2959)***
Fashion Accents LLC....401 331-6626
366 5th Ave Rm 802 New York (10001) ***(G-10194)***
Fashion Ave Sweater Knits LLC....212 302-8282
525 7th Ave Fl 4 New York (10018) ***(G-10195)***
Fashion Avenue Knits Inc....718 456-9000
1400 Broadway Rm 2401 New York (10018) ***(G-10196)***
Fashion Calendar International....212 289-0420
153 E 87th St Apt 6a New York (10128) ***(G-10197)***
Fashion Chef, The, Brooklyn *Also called Charlotte Neuville Design LLC* ***(G-1775)***
Fashion Ribbon Co Inc (PA)....718 482-0100
3401 38th Ave Long Island City (11101) ***(G-7767)***
Fashiondex Inc....914 271-6121
153 W 27th St Ste 701 New York (10001) ***(G-10198)***
Fasprint....518 483-4631
20 Finney Blvd Malone (12953) ***(G-8040)***
Fast By Gast Inc....716 773-1536
120 Industrial Dr Grand Island (14072) ***(G-5770)***
Fast Company Magazine, New York *Also called Mansueto Ventures LLC* ***(G-11166)***
Fast-Trac Entertainment Ltd....888 758-8886
7 E 74th St Apt 5 New York (10021) ***(G-10199)***
Fastener Dimensions Inc....718 847-6321
9403 104th St Ozone Park (11416) ***(G-13404)***
Fasteners Depot LLC....718 622-4222
5308 13th Ave Brooklyn (11219) ***(G-1963)***
Faster-Form Corp....800 327-3676
1 Faster Form Cir Ste 1 New Hartford (13413) ***(G-8849)***
Fastnet Software Intl Inc....888 740-7790
459 Elwood Rd East Northport (11731) ***(G-4456)***
Fastsigns, Buffalo *Also called Fletcher Enterprises Inc* ***(G-2963)***
Fastsigns, Staten Island *Also called Vez Inc* ***(G-15774)***
Fastsigns....518 456-7446
1593 Central Ave Albany (12205) ***(G-79)***
Fat Baby, New York *Also called Nycjbs LLC* ***(G-11496)***
Father Sam's Bakery, Buffalo *Also called Commitment 2000 Inc* ***(G-2903)***
Faulkner Truss Company Inc....315 536-8894
1830 King Hill Rd Dresden (14441) ***(G-4343)***
Faviana International Inc (PA)....212 594-4422
320 W 37th St Fl 10 New York (10018) ***(G-10200)***
Favorite Plastic Corp....718 253-7000
1465 Utica Ave Brooklyn (11234) ***(G-1964)***
Fay Da Mott St, Brooklyn *Also called Fayda Manufacturing Corp* ***(G-1965)***
Fayda Manufacturing Corp....718 456-9331
259 Meserole St Brooklyn (11206) ***(G-1965)***
Faye Bernard Loungewear....718 951-7245
2604 Avenue M Brooklyn (11210) ***(G-1966)***
Fayette Street Coatings Inc (HQ)....315 488-5401
1970 W Fayette St Syracuse (13204) ***(G-15962)***
Fayette Street Coatings Inc....315 488-5401
1 Burr Dr Liverpool (13088) ***(G-7544)***
FB Laboratories Inc....631 750-0000
70 Commerce Dr Hauppauge (11788) ***(G-6098)***
FB Sale LLC....315 986-9999
1688 Wayneport Rd Macedon (14502) ***(G-8017)***
FBC Chemical Corporation....716 681-1581
4111 Walden Ave Lancaster (14086) ***(G-7339)***
Fbm Galaxy Inc....315 463-5144
6741 Old Collamer Rd East Syracuse (13057) ***(G-4542)***
Fcmp Inc....716 692-4623
230 Fire Tower Dr Tonawanda (14150) ***(G-16179)***
Fcr LLC....845 926-1071
508 Fishkill Ave Beacon (12508) ***(G-780)***
Fearby Enterprises, Medina *Also called F & H Metal Finishing Co Inc* ***(G-8304)***
Fedders Islandaire Inc....631 471-2900
22 Research Way East Setauket (11733) ***(G-4500)***
Fedders Islandaire Company, East Setauket *Also called Fedders Islandaire Inc* ***(G-4500)***
Federal Contract MGT Svcs, Brooklyn *Also called It Commodity Sourcing Inc* ***(G-2116)***
Federal Envelope Inc....212 243-8380
22 W 32nd St New York (10001) ***(G-10201)***
Federal Prison Industries....845 386-6819
2 Mile Dr Otisville (10963) ***(G-13369)***
Federal Prison Industries....518 897-4000
Old Ray Brook Rd Ray Brook (12977) ***(G-14037)***
Federal Pump Corporation (PA)....718 451-2000
1144 Utica Ave Brooklyn (11203) ***(G-1967)***
Federal Sample Card Corp....718 458-1344
4520 83rd St Elmhurst (11373) ***(G-4673)***
Federal Sheet Metal Works Inc....315 735-4730
1416 Dudley Ave Utica (13501) ***(G-16355)***
Federal Yellow Book, New York *Also called Leadership Directories Inc* ***(G-10982)***
Federated Media Publishing LLC....917 677-7976
31 W 27th St Fl 8 New York (10001) ***(G-10202)***
Fedex Ground Package Sys Inc....800 463-3339
82 Gateway Dr Plattsburgh (12901) ***(G-13691)***
Fedex Office & Print Svcs Inc....718 982-5223
2456 Richmond Ave Ste C Staten Island (10314) ***(G-15694)***
Fei Communications Inc....516 794-4500
55 Charles Lindbergh Blvd Uniondale (11553) ***(G-16315)***
Fei Products LLC (PA)....716 693-6230
825 Wurlitzer Dr North Tonawanda (14120) ***(G-12990)***
Fei-Zyfer Inc....714 933-4045
55 Charles Lindbergh Blvd Uniondale (11553) ***(G-16316)***
Feinkind Inc....800 289-6136
17 Algonquin Dr Irvington (10533) ***(G-6811)***
Feinstein Iron Works Inc....516 997-8300
990 Brush Hollow Rd Westbury (11590) ***(G-17012)***
Felber Metal Fabricators, Holbrook *Also called Brzozka Industries Inc* ***(G-6462)***
Felchar Manufacturing Corp (HQ)....607 723-3106
196 Corporate Dr Binghamton (13904) ***(G-909)***
Feldheim Publishers, Nanuet *Also called Philipp Feldheim Inc* ***(G-8806)***
Feldman Company Inc....212 966-1303
241 W 37th St Rm 1001 New York (10018) ***(G-10203)***
Feldman Jewelry Creations Inc....718 438-8895
4821 16th Ave Brooklyn (11204) ***(G-1968)***
Feldman Manufacturing Corp....718 433-1700
3010 41st Ave Ste 3fl Long Island City (11101) ***(G-7768)***
Feldmeier Equipment Inc (PA)....315 823-2000
6800 Townline Rd Syracuse (13211) ***(G-15963)***
Feldware Inc....718 372-0486
250 Avenue W Brooklyn (11223) ***(G-1969)***
Felicetti Concrete Products....716 284-5740
4129 Hyde Park Blvd Niagara Falls (14305) ***(G-12839)***
Felix Roma & Sons Inc....607 748-3336
2 S Page Ave Endicott (13760) ***(G-4816)***
Felix Schoeller North Amer Inc....315 298-8425
179 County Route 2a Pulaski (13142) ***(G-13962)***
Felix Schoeller North Amer Inc....315 298-5133
179 County Route 2a Pulaski (13142) ***(G-13963)***
Felix Schoeller Technical Pprs, Pulaski *Also called Felix Schoeller North Amer Inc* ***(G-13963)***
Felix Storch Inc (PA)....718 893-3900
770 Garrison Ave Bronx (10474) ***(G-1332)***
Felluss Recording....212 727-8055
36 E 23rd St Rm 9l New York (10010) ***(G-10204)***
Felton Machine Co Inc....716 215-9001
2221 Niagara Falls Blvd Niagara Falls (14304) ***(G-12840)***
Feminist Press Inc....212 817-7915
365 5th Ave Ste 5406 New York (10016) ***(G-10205)***
Femtech Women Powered Software....516 328-2631
1230 Hempstead Tpke Franklin Square (11010) ***(G-5373)***
Fenbar Prcision Machinists Inc....914 769-5506
633 Commerce St Thornwood (10594) ***(G-16142)***
Fence Plaza Corp....718 469-2200
1601 Nostrand Ave Brooklyn (11226) ***(G-1970)***
Fenix Furniture Co....631 273-3500
35 Drexel Dr Bay Shore (11706) ***(G-698)***
Fennell Industries LLC (PA)....607 733-6693
108 Stephens Pl Elmira (14901) ***(G-4698)***
Fennell Spring Company LLC....607 739-3541
295 Hemlock St Horseheads (14845) ***(G-6606)***
Feraco Industries....631 547-8120
3 Plumb Ct Huntington Station (11746) ***(G-6742)***
Ferguson....718 937-9500
5722 49th St Maspeth (11378) ***(G-8170)***
Ferguson Enterprises Inc....800 437-1146
200 Atlantic Ave New Hyde Park (11040) ***(G-8879)***
Fermer Precision Inc....315 822-6371
114 Johnson Rd Ilion (13357) ***(G-6779)***
Ferrara Bakery & Cafe Inc (PA)....212 226-6150
195 Grand St New York (10013) ***(G-10206)***
Ferrara Bros LLC (HQ)....718 939-3030
12005 31st Ave Flushing (11354) ***(G-5248)***
Ferrara Manufacturing, New York *Also called Rogers Group Inc* ***(G-11928)***
Ferrara Manufacturing Company, New York *Also called HC Contracting Inc* ***(G-10477)***
Ferraro Manufacturing Company....631 752-1509
150 Central Ave Farmingdale (11735) ***(G-5001)***
Ferris USA LLC....617 895-8102
18 W 108th St New York (10025) ***(G-10207)***
Ferro Corporation....585 586-8770
603 W Commercial St East Rochester (14445) ***(G-4477)***
Ferro Corporation....315 536-3357
1789 Transelco Dr Penn Yan (14527) ***(G-13532)***
Ferro Electronic Mtl Systems, Penn Yan *Also called Ferro Electronics Materials* ***(G-13533)***
Ferro Electronic Mtl Systems, Penn Yan *Also called Ferro Electronics Materials* ***(G-13534)***
Ferro Electronics Materials....716 278-9400
4511 Hyde Park Blvd Niagara Falls (14305) ***(G-12841)***

ALPHABETIC SECTION
Fire Island Tide Publication

Ferro Electronics Materials (HQ) 315 536-3357
1789 Transelco Dr Penn Yan (14527) ***(G-13533)***
Ferro Electronics Materials 315 536-3357
1789 Transelco Dr Penn Yan (14527) ***(G-13534)***
Ferro Fabricators Inc 718 703-0007
1117 38th St Brooklyn (11218) ***(G-1971)***
Ferro Machine Co Inc 845 398-3641
70 S Greenbush Rd Orangeburg (10962) ***(G-13250)***
Festival Bakers, Bronx *Also called Waldorf Bakers Inc* ***(G-1492)***
Fetherston Design Group LLC 212 643-7537
225 W Broadway New York (10013) ***(G-10208)***
Feyem USA Inc 845 363-6253
7 Sutton Pl Brewster (10509) ***(G-1216)***
Ffc Holding Corp Subsidiaries (PA) 716 366-5400
1 Ice Cream Dr Dunkirk (14048) ***(G-4366)***
FG Galassi Moulding Co Inc 845 258-2100
699 Pulaski Hwy Goshen (10924) ***(G-5749)***
Fgi, Amsterdam *Also called Fiber Glass Industries Inc* ***(G-345)***
Fiber Foot Appliances Inc 631 465-9199
34 Sarah Dr Ste A Farmingdale (11735) ***(G-5002)***
Fiber Glass Industries Inc (PA) 518 842-4000
69 Edson St Amsterdam (12010) ***(G-345)***
Fiber Glass Industries Inc 518 843-3533
1 Homestead Pl Amsterdam (12010) ***(G-346)***
Fiber Instrument Sales Inc (PA) 315 736-2206
161 Clear Rd Oriskany (13424) ***(G-13333)***
Fiber Laminations Limited 716 692-1825
600 Main St Tonawanda (14150) ***(G-16180)***
Fiber Optics Schott America, Auburn *Also called Schott Corporation* ***(G-514)***
Fiber USA Corp 718 888-1512
13620 38th Ave Ste 11f Flushing (11354) ***(G-5249)***
Fiber-Seal of New York Inc (PA) 212 888-5580
979 3rd Ave Ste 903 New York (10022) ***(G-10209)***
Fiberall Corp 516 371-5200
449 Sheridan Blvd Inwood (11096) ***(G-6796)***
Fibercel Packaging LLC (HQ) 716 933-8703
46 Brooklyn St Portville (14770) ***(G-13892)***
Fiberdyne Labs Inc 315 895-8470
127 Business Park Dr Frankfort (13340) ***(G-5362)***
Fiberglass Replacement Parts 716 893-6471
200 Colorado Ave Buffalo (14215) ***(G-2960)***
Fiberone LLC 315 434-8877
5 Technology Pl Ste 4 East Syracuse (13057) ***(G-4543)***
Fiberwave Corporation 718 802-9011
140 58th St Ste 37 Brooklyn (11220) ***(G-1972)***
Fibre Case & Novelty Co Inc (PA) 212 254-6060
270 Lafayette St Ste 1510 New York (10012) ***(G-10210)***
Fibre Materials Corp 516 349-1660
40 Dupont St Plainview (11803) ***(G-13631)***
Fibrix LLC 716 683-4100
3307 Walden Ave Depew (14043) ***(G-4281)***
Fibron Products Inc 716 886-2378
170 Florida St Buffalo (14208) ***(G-2961)***
Fics Inc 607 359-4474
25 Community Dr Addison (14801) ***(G-6)***
Fidazzel Inc 917 557-3860
2280 Olinville Ave # 409 Bronx (10467) ***(G-1333)***
Fidelus Technologies LLC 212 616-7800
240 W 35th St Fl 6 New York (10001) ***(G-10211)***
Fidesa US Corporation 212 269-9000
17 State St Unit 122 New York (10004) ***(G-10212)***
Field Company, High Falls *Also called Field Wares LLC* ***(G-6428)***
Field Trip Jerky, Brooklyn *Also called Provisionaire & Co LLC* ***(G-2473)***
Field Wares LLC 508 380-6545
244 Rock Hill Rd High Falls (12440) ***(G-6428)***
Fieldbrook Foods Corporation (HQ) 716 366-5400
1 Ice Cream Dr Dunkirk (14048) ***(G-4367)***
Fieldtex Products Inc 585 427-2940
3055 Brighton Henrietta Rochester (14623) ***(G-14391)***
Fierce Fun Toys LLC 646 322-7172
100 Riverside Dr Ste 2 New York (10024) ***(G-10213)***
Fil Doux Inc 212 202-1459
227 5th Ave Brooklyn (11215) ***(G-1973)***
Fil-Coil (fc) Corp (PA) 631 467-5328
98 Lincoln Ave Sayville (11782) ***(G-15237)***
Fil-Coil International LLC 631 467-5328
98 Lincoln Ave Sayville (11782) ***(G-15238)***
Filestream Inc 516 759-4100
257 Buckram Rd Locust Valley (11560) ***(G-7660)***
Filling Equipment Co Inc 718 445-2111
1539 130th St College Point (11356) ***(G-3808)***
Fillmore Greenhouses Inc 585 567-2678
11589 State Route 19a Portageville (14536) ***(G-13890)***
Filmpak Extrusion LLC 631 293-6767
125 Spagnoli Rd Melville (11747) ***(G-8348)***
Films Media Group, New York *Also called Infobase Publishing Company* ***(G-10637)***
Filta Clean Co Inc 718 495-3800
107 Georgia Ave Brooklyn (11207) ***(G-1974)***
Filter Tech Inc (PA) 315 682-8815
113 Fairgrounds Dr Manlius (13104) ***(G-8104)***
Filtros Ltd 585 586-8770
603 W Commercial St East Rochester (14445) ***(G-4478)***
Filtros Plant, East Rochester *Also called Filtros Ltd* ***(G-4478)***
Fina Cabinet Corp 718 409-2900
20 N Macquesten Pkwy Mount Vernon (10550) ***(G-8726)***
Final Dimension Inc 718 786-0100
57-401 59th St Fl 1 Maspeth (11378) ***(G-8171)***
Final Touch Printing Inc 845 352-2677
29 Decatur Ave Unit 1 Spring Valley (10977) ***(G-15607)***
Finals, The, Port Jervis *Also called Swimwear Anywhere Inc* ***(G-13817)***
Finance Manager, East Setauket *Also called Mml Software Ltd* ***(G-4506)***
Financial Times, New York *Also called FT Publications Inc* ***(G-10266)***
Financial Times Newspaper, New York *Also called FT Publications Inc* ***(G-10267)***
Findmine Inc 925 787-6181
137 Varick St Fl 2 New York (10013) ***(G-10214)***
Fine and Raw Chocolate 718 366-3633
288 Seigel St Brooklyn (11206) ***(G-1975)***
Fine Architectural Met Smiths, Florida *Also called New England Tool Co Ltd* ***(G-5221)***
Fine Arts Furniture Inc 212 744-9139
3872 13th St Long Island City (11101) ***(G-7769)***
Fine Cut Diamonds Corporation 212 575-8780
580 5th Ave Ste 901 New York (10036) ***(G-10215)***
Fine Sheer Industries Inc (PA) 212 594-4224
350 5th Ave Ste 4710 New York (10118) ***(G-10216)***
Fine Sounds Group Inc (PA) 212 364-0219
214 Lafayette St New York (10012) ***(G-10217)***
Fineline Thermographers Inc 718 643-1100
544 Park Ave Ste 308 Brooklyn (11205) ***(G-1976)***
Finer Touch Printing Corp 516 944-8000
4 Yennicock Ave Port Washington (11050) ***(G-13837)***
Finesse Accessories, Plainview *Also called Mgd Brands Inc* ***(G-13648)***
Finesse Creations Inc 718 692-2100
3004 Avenue J Brooklyn (11210) ***(G-1977)***
Finest Cc Corp 917 574-4525
3111 E Tremont Ave Bronx (10461) ***(G-1334)***
Finestar, Long Island City *Also called Efam Enterprises LLC* ***(G-7754)***
Finger Food Products Inc 716 297-4888
6400 Inducon Dr W Sanborn (14132) ***(G-15146)***
Finger Lakes Cheese Trail 607 857-5726
4970 County Road 14 Odessa (14869) ***(G-13129)***
Finger Lakes Chemicals Inc (PA) 585 454-4760
420 Saint Paul St Rochester (14605) ***(G-14392)***
Finger Lakes Conveyors Inc 315 539-9246
2359 State Route 414 E Waterloo (13165) ***(G-16647)***
Finger Lakes Distilling 607 546-5510
4676 State Route 414 Burdett (14818) ***(G-3291)***
Finger Lakes Extrusion Corp 585 905-0632
2437 State Route 21 Canandaigua (14424) ***(G-3375)***
Finger Lakes Lea Crafters LLC 315 252-4107
42 Washington St Auburn (13021) ***(G-493)***
Finger Lakes Massage Group (PA) 607 272-9024
215 E State St Ste 2 Ithaca (14850) ***(G-6877)***
Finger Lakes Media Inc 607 243-7600
45 Water St Dundee (14837) ***(G-4352)***
Finger Lakes Printing Co Inc (HQ) 315 789-3333
218 Genesee St Geneva (14456) ***(G-5588)***
Finger Lakes Radiology LLC 315 787-5399
196 North St Geneva (14456) ***(G-5589)***
Finger Lakes School of Massage, Ithaca *Also called Finger Lakes Massage Group* ***(G-6877)***
Finger Lakes Stone Co Inc 607 273-4646
33 Quarry Rd Ithaca (14850) ***(G-6878)***
Finger Lakes Timber Co Inc 585 346-2990
6274 Decker Rd Livonia (14487) ***(G-7591)***
Finger Lakes Trellis Supply 315 904-4007
4041a Railroad Ave Williamson (14589) ***(G-17252)***
Finger Lakes/Castle, Rochester *Also called Finger Lakes Chemicals Inc* ***(G-14392)***
Fingerlakes Construction, Clyde *Also called Energy Panel Structures Inc* ***(G-3750)***
Fingerlakes Construction, Clyde *Also called Energy Panel Structures Inc* ***(G-3751)***
Fingerlakes Construction, Schenectady *Also called Energy Panel Structures Inc* ***(G-15278)***
Fingerprint America Inc 518 435-1609
1843 Central Ave Albany (12205) ***(G-80)***
Fingertech USA, Brooklyn *Also called BDB Technologies LLC* ***(G-1672)***
Finish Line Technologies Inc (PA) 631 666-7300
50 Wireless Blvd Hauppauge (11788) ***(G-6099)***
Finishing Line, The, Le Roy *Also called Duzmor Painting Inc* ***(G-7432)***
Finzer Holding LLC 315 597-1147
2085 Division St Palmyra (14522) ***(G-13431)***
Finzer Roller New York, Palmyra *Also called Finzer Holding LLC* ***(G-13431)***
Fiora Italy, Bay Shore *Also called Innovative Jewelry Inc* ***(G-703)***
Fiorentina LLC 516 208-5448
1519 Hendrickson Ave Merrick (11566) ***(G-8418)***
Fire Apparatus Service Tech 716 753-3538
7895 Lyons Rd Sherman (14781) ***(G-15424)***
Fire Fox Security Corp 917 981-9280
2070 72nd St Apt B1 Brooklyn (11204) ***(G-1978)***
Fire Island Fuel 631 772-1482
106 Parkwood Dr Shirley (11967) ***(G-15441)***
Fire Island News, Bronx *Also called Five Islands Publishing Inc* ***(G-1335)***
Fire Island Sea Clam Co Inc 631 589-2199
132 Atlantic Ave West Sayville (11796) ***(G-16964)***
Fire Island Tide Publication 631 567-7470
40 Main St Sayville (11782) ***(G-15239)***

ALPHABETIC

(PA)=Parent Co (HQ)=Headquarters (DH)=Div Headquarters
2018 Harris
New York Manufacturers Directory
951

Fire Island Tide The, Sayville *Also called Fire Island Tide Publication* ***(G-15239)***
Firecom Inc (PA)...718 899-6100
3927 59th St Woodside (11377) ***(G-17345)***
Firefighters Journal...718 391-0283
2420 Jackson Ave Long Island City (11101) ***(G-7770)***
Firematic Supply Co Inc (PA)...631 924-3181
10 Ramsey Rd East Yaphank (11967) ***(G-4593)***
Firetronics Inc (PA)...516 997-5151
50 Jericho Tpke Jericho (11753) ***(G-7102)***
Fireworks By Grucci Inc...631 286-0088
20 Pinehurst Dr Bellport (11713) ***(G-826)***
First Choice News Inc...212 477-2044
639 1/2 Broadway New York (10012) ***(G-10218)***
First Displays Inc...347 642-5972
2415 43rd Ave Fl 2 Long Island City (11101) ***(G-7771)***
First Due Fire Equipment Inc...845 222-1329
130 W Ramapo Rd Garnerville (10923) ***(G-5568)***
First Games Publr Netwrk Inc...212 983-0501
420 Lexington Ave Rm 412 New York (10170) ***(G-10219)***
First Image Design Corp...212 221-8282
98 Cuttrmill Rd Ste 231 New York (10036) ***(G-10220)***
First Impressions Finishing...631 467-2244
132 Remington Blvd Ronkonkoma (11779) ***(G-14929)***
First Light Farm & Creamery, East Bethany *Also called Sandvoss Farms LLC* ***(G-4406)***
First Line Printing Inc...718 606-0860
3728 56th St Woodside (11377) ***(G-17346)***
First Love Fashions LLC...212 256-1089
1407 Broadway Rm 2010 New York (10018) ***(G-10221)***
First Presbyterian Church...315 252-3861
112 South St Auburn (13021) ***(G-494)***
First Qlty Packg Solutions LLC (PA)...516 829-3030
80 Cuttermill Rd Ste 500 Great Neck (11021) ***(G-5826)***
First Quality Hygienic Inc...516 829-3030
80 Cuttermill Rd Ste 500 Great Neck (11021) ***(G-5827)***
First Quality Products Inc (HQ)...516 829-4949
80 Cuttermill Rd Ste 500 Great Neck (11021) ***(G-5828)***
First Sbf Holding Inc (PA)...845 425-9882
9 Pinecrest Rd Ste 101 Valley Cottage (10989) ***(G-16404)***
First View, New York *Also called Viewfinder Inc* ***(G-12567)***
First2print Inc...212 868-6886
494 8th Ave Fl 12 New York (10001) ***(G-10222)***
Firth Rixson Inc (HQ)...585 328-1383
181 Mckee Rd Rochester (14611) ***(G-14393)***
Firth Rixson Monroe, Rochester *Also called Firth Rixson Inc* ***(G-14393)***
Fisau, Yorktown Heights *Also called Business Management Systems* ***(G-17524)***
Fischer Diamonds Inc...212 869-1990
1212 Avenue Of The Americ New York (10036) ***(G-10223)***
Fischler Diamonds Inc...212 921-8196
580 5th Ave Ste 3100 New York (10036) ***(G-10224)***
Fischler Hockey Service...212 749-4152
200 W 109th St Apt C5 New York (10025) ***(G-10225)***
Fish & Crown Ltd (PA)...212 707-9603
42 W 39th St New York (10018) ***(G-10226)***
Fish To Dish Inc...718 972-7600
5516 16th Ave Brooklyn (11204) ***(G-1979)***
Fishing Valley LLC...716 523-6158
7217 N Canal Rd Lockport (14094) ***(G-7615)***
Fisonic Corp...212 732-3777
4402 23rd St Long Island City (11101) ***(G-7772)***
Fisonic Corp (PA)...716 763-0295
31-00 47th Ave Ste 106 New York (10023) ***(G-10227)***
Fisonic Technology, New York *Also called Fisonic Corp* ***(G-10227)***
Fitch Graphics Ltd...212 619-3800
229 W 28th St Fl 9 New York (10001) ***(G-10228)***
Fitch Group, New York *Also called Francis Emory Fitch Inc* ***(G-10248)***
Fitzgerald Publishing Co Inc...914 793-5016
1853 Central Park Ave # 8 Yonkers (10710) ***(G-17459)***
Fitzpatrick and Weller Inc...716 699-2393
12 Mill St Ellicottville (14731) ***(G-4655)***
Fitzsimmons Systems Inc...315 214-7010
53 Nelson St Cazenovia (13035) ***(G-3472)***
Five Boro Doors Mouldings Inc...718 865-9371
3569 Maple Ct Oceanside (11572) ***(G-13100)***
Five Boro Holding LLC...718 431-9500
1425 37th St Ste 3 Brooklyn (11218) ***(G-1980)***
Five Burroughs Brewing Co...718 355-8575
215 47th St Brooklyn (11220) ***(G-1981)***
Five Corners Repair Inc...585 322-7369
6653 Hardys Rd Bliss (14024) ***(G-974)***
Five Islands Publishing Inc...631 583-5345
8 Fort Charles Pl Bronx (10463) ***(G-1335)***
Five Star Awnings Inc...718 860-6070
5923 Decatur St Ridgewood (11385) ***(G-14119)***
Five Star Creations Inc...845 783-1187
4 Preshburg Blvd Unit 302 Monroe (10950) ***(G-8589)***
Five Star Field Services...347 446-6816
535 W Penn St Long Beach (11561) ***(G-7671)***
Five Star Industries Inc...716 674-2589
114 Willowdale Dr West Seneca (14224) ***(G-16973)***
Five Star Measurement, Long Beach *Also called Five Star Field Services* ***(G-7671)***
Five Star Millwork LLC...845 920-0247
6 E Dexter Plz Pearl River (10965) ***(G-13478)***
Five Star Printing, Jamaica *Also called Ssrja LLC* ***(G-6987)***
Five Star Prtg & Mailing Svcs...212 929-0300
225 W 37th St Fl 16 New York (10018) ***(G-10229)***
Five Star Tool Co Inc...585 328-9580
125 Elmgrove Park Rochester (14624) ***(G-14394)***
Fixtures 2000 Inc...631 236-4100
400 Oser Ave Ste 350 Hauppauge (11788) ***(G-6100)***
Fiz Beverages, Rochester *Also called Load/N/Go Beverage Corp* ***(G-14502)***
Fjs Industries Inc...917 428-3797
970 E 92nd St Brooklyn (11236) ***(G-1982)***
Flado Enterprises Inc...716 668-6400
1380 French Rd Ste 6 Depew (14043) ***(G-4282)***
Flagpoles Incorporated...631 751-5500
95 Gnarled Hollow Rd East Setauket (11733) ***(G-4501)***
Flair Display Inc...718 324-9330
3920 Merritt Ave Bronx (10466) ***(G-1336)***
Flair Printers, Brooklyn *Also called Printing Sales Group Limited* ***(G-2464)***
Flame Control Coatings LLC...716 282-1399
4120 Hyde Park Blvd Niagara Falls (14305) ***(G-12842)***
Flanagan Electric Corp...631 567-2976
630 Broadway Ave Ste 7 Holbrook (11741) ***(G-6476)***
Flanagans Creative Disp Inc...845 858-2542
55 Jersey Ave Port Jervis (12771) ***(G-13806)***
Flare Multi Copy, Brooklyn *Also called Flare Multicopy Corp* ***(G-1983)***
Flare Multicopy Corp...718 258-8860
1840 Flatbush Ave Brooklyn (11210) ***(G-1983)***
Flash Ventures Inc...212 255-7070
853 Broadway Ste 400 New York (10003) ***(G-10230)***
Flashflo Manufacturing Inc...716 826-9500
88 Hopkins St Buffalo (14220) ***(G-2962)***
Flatcut LLC...212 542-5732
68 Jay St Ste 901 Brooklyn (11201) ***(G-1984)***
Flaum Appetizing, Brooklyn *Also called M & M Food Products Inc* ***(G-2246)***
Flavor League, Brooklyn *Also called Flavor Paper Ltd* ***(G-1985)***
Flavor Paper Ltd...718 422-0230
216 Pacific St Brooklyn (11201) ***(G-1985)***
Flavormatic Industries Inc...845 297-9100
90 Brentwood Dr Wappingers Falls (12590) ***(G-16587)***
Flavors Holdings Inc (HQ)...212 572-8677
35 E 62nd St New York (10065) ***(G-10231)***
Fleetcom Inc...914 776-5582
1081 Yonkers Ave Yonkers (10704) ***(G-17460)***
Fleetwood Cabinet Co Inc (PA)...516 379-2139
673 Livonia Ave Brooklyn (11207) ***(G-1986)***
Fleischman Vinegar, North Rose *Also called Fleischmanns Vinegar Co Inc* ***(G-12952)***
Fleischmanns Vinegar Co Inc...315 587-4414
4754 State Route 414 North Rose (14516) ***(G-12952)***
Fletcher Enterprises Inc...716 837-7446
4913 Genesee St Buffalo (14225) ***(G-2963)***
Flex Enterprises Inc...585 742-1000
820 Canning Pkwy Victor (14564) ***(G-16501)***
Flex Supply, Farmingdale *Also called Custom Door & Mirror Inc* ***(G-4980)***
Flex Tubing, Canandaigua *Also called Finger Lakes Extrusion Corp* ***(G-3375)***
Flex-Hose Company Inc...315 437-1903
6801 Crossbow Dr East Syracuse (13057) ***(G-4544)***
Flexbar Machine Corporation...631 582-8440
250 Gibbs Rd Islandia (11749) ***(G-6831)***
Flexene Corp...631 491-0580
108 Lamar St West Babylon (11704) ***(G-16818)***
Flexfit Llc...516 932-8800
350 Karin Ln Unit A Hicksville (11801) ***(G-6373)***
Flexible Lifeline Systems Inc...716 896-4949
100 Stradtman St Buffalo (14206) ***(G-2964)***
Flexim Americas Corporation (HQ)...631 492-2300
250 Executive Dr Ste V Edgewood (11717) ***(G-4612)***
Flexlume Sign Corporation...716 884-2020
1464 Main St Buffalo (14209) ***(G-2965)***
Flexo Transparent LLC...716 825-7710
28 Wasson St Buffalo (14210) ***(G-2966)***
Flexographic Printing, Rochester *Also called American Packaging Corporation* ***(G-14214)***
Flextrade Systems Inc (PA)...516 627-8993
111 Great Neck Rd Ste 314 Great Neck (11021) ***(G-5829)***
Flickinger Glassworks Inc...718 875-1531
175 Van Dyke St Ste 321ap Brooklyn (11231) ***(G-1987)***
Flightline Electronics Inc (HQ)...585 742-5340
7625 Omnitech Pl Victor (14564) ***(G-16502)***
Flik International/Compass...212 450-4750
450 Lexington Ave New York (10017) ***(G-10232)***
Flint Group Incorporated...585 458-1223
1128 Lexington Ave Bldg 3 Rochester (14606) ***(G-14395)***
Flint Ink North America Div, Rochester *Also called Flint Group Incorporated* ***(G-14395)***
Flirtatious, New York *Also called Soho Apparel Ltd* ***(G-12146)***
Flo-Tech Orthotic & Prosthetic...607 387-3070
7325 Halseyville Rd Trumansburg (14886) ***(G-16290)***
Float Tech Inc...518 266-0964
216 River St Ste 1 Troy (12180) ***(G-16257)***
Flogic Inc...914 478-1352
25 Chestnut Dr Hastings On Hudson (10706) ***(G-6023)***
Flomatic Corporation...518 761-9797
15 Pruyns Island Dr Glens Falls (12801) ***(G-5695)***
Flomatic Valves, Glens Falls *Also called Flomatic Corporation* ***(G-5695)***

Florelle Tissue Corporation 647 997-7405
1 Bridge St Brownville (13615) ***(G-2797)***
Florida North Inc 518 868-2888
134 Vanderwerken Rd Sloansville (12160) ***(G-15501)***
Flour Power Bakery Cafe 917 747-6895
87 Debruce Rd Livingston Manor (12758) ***(G-7588)***
Flow Control LLC (HQ) 914 323-5700
1 International Dr Rye Brook (10573) ***(G-15097)***
Flow Dental, Deer Park *Also called Flow X Ray Corporation* ***(G-4164)***
Flow Society, New York *Also called Big Idea Brands LLC* ***(G-9444)***
Flow X Ray Corporation 631 242-9729
100 W Industry Ct Deer Park (11729) ***(G-4164)***
Flow-Safe Inc 716 662-2585
3865 Taylor Rd Orchard Park (14127) ***(G-13293)***
Flower City Printing Inc (PA) 585 663-9000
1725 Mount Read Blvd Rochester (14606) ***(G-14396)***
Flower City Printing Inc 585 512-1235
1001 Lee Rd Rochester (14606) ***(G-14397)***
Flower Cy Tissue Mills Co Inc (PA) 585 458-9200
700 Driving Park Ave Rochester (14613) ***(G-14398)***
Flownet LLC 716 685-4036
580 Lake Ave Lancaster (14086) ***(G-7340)***
Floymar Manufacturing, Hauppauge *Also called Ehrlich Enterprises Inc* ***(G-6092)***
Flp Group LLC 315 252-7583
301 Clark St Auburn (13021) ***(G-495)***
Fluid Handling LLC 716 897-2800
175 Standard Pkwy Cheektowaga (14227) ***(G-3599)***
Fluid Handling LLC (HQ) 716 897-2800
175 Standard Pkwy Cheektowaga (14227) ***(G-3600)***
Fluid Mechanisms Hauppauge Inc 631 234-0100
225 Engineers Rd Hauppauge (11788) ***(G-6101)***
Fluid Metering Inc (HQ) 516 922-6050
5 Aerial Way Ste 500 Syosset (11791) ***(G-15842)***
Fluoro Seal, Buffalo *Also called Inhance Technologies LLC* ***(G-3026)***
Fluorologic Inc 585 248-2796
33 Bishops Ct Pittsford (14534) ***(G-13588)***
Flushing Boiler & Welding Co 718 463-1266
8720 Ditmas Ave Brooklyn (11236) ***(G-1988)***
Flushing Iron Weld Inc 718 359-2208
13125 Maple Ave Flushing (11355) ***(G-5250)***
Flushing Pharmacy Inc 718 260-8999
414 Flushing Ave Ste 1 Brooklyn (11205) ***(G-1989)***
Flushing Terminal, Flushing *Also called Tilcon New York Inc* ***(G-5306)***
Fluxdata Incorporated 800 425-0176
176 Anderson Ave Ste F304 Rochester (14607) ***(G-14399)***
Fly Creek Cder Mill Orchrd Inc 607 547-9692
288 Goose St Fly Creek (13337) ***(G-5319)***
Fly-Tyers Carry-All LLC 607 821-1460
112 Meade Rd Charlotteville (12036) ***(G-3583)***
Flycell Inc 212 400-1212
80 Pine St Fl 29 New York (10005) ***(G-10233)***
Flynn Burner Corporation 914 636-1320
425 Fifth Ave New Rochelle (10801) ***(G-8944)***
Flynn's Xerox, New York *Also called Flynns Inc* ***(G-10234)***
Flynns Inc (PA) 212 339-8700
115 W 30th St New York (10001) ***(G-10234)***
FM Brush Co Inc 718 821-5939
7002 72nd Pl Glendale (11385) ***(G-5667)***
FMC Corporation 716 735-3761
100 Niagara St Middleport (14105) ***(G-8455)***
FMC Corporation 716 879-0400
78 Sawyer Ave Ste 1 Tonawanda (14150) ***(G-16181)***
FMC International Ltd 914 935-0918
2975 Westchester Ave Purchase (10577) ***(G-13972)***
Foam Products Inc 718 292-4830
360 Southern Blvd Bronx (10454) ***(G-1337)***
Focus Camera Inc (PA) 718 437-8800
895 Mcdonald Ave Brooklyn (11218) ***(G-1990)***
Focus Point Windows & Doors, Long Beach *Also called Air Tite Manufacturing Inc* ***(G-7667)***
Fodera Guitars Inc 718 832-3455
68 34th St Unit 3 Brooklyn (11232) ***(G-1991)***
Fog Creek Software Inc 866 364-2733
1 Exchange Plz Fl 25 New York (10006) ***(G-10235)***
Fogel Neckwear Corp 212 686-7673
44 W 28th St Fl 15 New York (10001) ***(G-10236)***
Folene Packaging LLC 917 626-6740
2509 Avenue M Brooklyn (11210) ***(G-1992)***
Folio Graphics Co Inc 718 763-2076
2759 E 66th St Brooklyn (11234) ***(G-1993)***
Folstaf Company, The, Charlotteville *Also called Fly-Tyers Carry-All LLC* ***(G-3583)***
Fonar Corporation (PA) 631 694-2929
110 Marcus Dr Melville (11747) ***(G-8349)***
Fontrick Door Inc 585 345-6032
9 Apollo Dr Batavia (14020) ***(G-634)***
Foo Yuan Food Products Co Inc 212 925-2840
2301 Borden Ave Long Island City (11101) ***(G-7773)***
Food Gems Ltd 718 296-7788
8423 Rockaway Blvd Ozone Park (11416) ***(G-13405)***
Foot Locker Retail Inc 516 827-5306
358 Broadway Mall Hicksville (11801) ***(G-6374)***
For A Safer America, Amsterdam *Also called Keep America Beautiful Inc* ***(G-354)***
Forbes Precision Inc 585 865-7069
100 Boxart St Ste 105 Rochester (14612) ***(G-14400)***
Forbes Products, Dansville *Also called GPM Associates LLC* ***(G-4103)***
Force Digital Media Inc 631 243-0243
39 W Jefryn Blvd Ste 2 Deer Park (11729) ***(G-4165)***
Force Dynamics Inc 607 546-5023
4995 Voorheis Rd Trumansburg (14886) ***(G-16291)***
Ford Gum & Machine Company Inc (PA) 716 542-4561
18 Newton Ave Akron (14001) ***(G-19)***
Ford Motor Company 716 821-4000
3663 Lake Shore Rd Buffalo (14219) ***(G-2967)***
Ford Regulator Valve Corp 718 497-3255
199 Varet St Brooklyn (11206) ***(G-1994)***
Fordham Marble Co Inc 914 682-6699
45 Crane Ave White Plains (10603) ***(G-17136)***
Forecast Consoles Inc 631 253-9000
681 Old Willets Path Hauppauge (11788) ***(G-6102)***
Forerunner Technologies Inc (PA) 631 337-2100
1430 Church St Unit A Bohemia (11716) ***(G-1063)***
Forest Hills Courier, Bayside *Also called Schneps Publications Inc* ***(G-769)***
Forest Iron Works Inc 516 671-4229
3 Elm St Ste A Locust Valley (11560) ***(G-7661)***
Forest Laboratories LLC (HQ) 212 421-7850
909 3rd Ave Fl 23 New York (10022) ***(G-10237)***
Forest Laboratories LLC 212 421-7850
45 Adams Ave Hauppauge (11788) ***(G-6103)***
Forest Laboratories LLC 631 858-6010
500 Commack Rd Commack (11725) ***(G-3857)***
Forest Medical LLC 315 434-9000
6700 Old Collamer Rd # 114 East Syracuse (13057) ***(G-4545)***
Forest Uniforms, New York *Also called Urban Textiles Inc* ***(G-12501)***
Forkey Construction & Fabg Inc 607 849-4879
3690 Luker Rd Cortland (13045) ***(G-4048)***
Form A Rockland Plastics Inc 315 848-3300
7152 Main St Cranberry Lake (12927) ***(G-4083)***
Form-Tec Inc 516 867-0200
216 N Main St Ste E Freeport (11520) ***(G-5410)***
Formac Welding Inc 631 421-5525
42 W Hills Rd Huntington Station (11746) ***(G-6743)***
Formaggio Italian Cheese, Hurleyville *Also called Mongiellos Itln Cheese Spc LLC* ***(G-6770)***
Formart Corp 212 819-1819
312 5th Ave Fl 6 New York (10001) ***(G-10238)***
Formatix Corp 631 467-3399
9 Colt Ct Ronkonkoma (11779) ***(G-14930)***
Formats Unlimited Inc 631 249-9200
19 W Jefryn Blvd Ste 2 Deer Park (11729) ***(G-4166)***
Formcraft Display Products 914 632-1410
42 Beverly Rd New Rochelle (10804) ***(G-8945)***
Formed Plastics Inc 516 334-2300
207 Stonehinge Ln Carle Place (11514) ***(G-3414)***
Forms For You Division, Poughkeepsie *Also called Empire Business Forms Inc* ***(G-13917)***
Foro Marble Co Inc 718 852-2322
166 2nd Ave Brooklyn (11215) ***(G-1995)***
Forrest Engravg, New Rochelle *Also called Forrest Engraving Co Inc* ***(G-8946)***
Forrest Engraving Co Inc 845 228-0200
92 1st St New Rochelle (10801) ***(G-8946)***
Forsyth Industries Inc 716 652-1070
1195 Colvin Blvd Buffalo (14223) ***(G-2968)***
Forsythe Cosmetic Group Ltd 516 239-4200
10 Niagara Ave Freeport (11520) ***(G-5411)***
Forsythe Licensing, Freeport *Also called Forsythe Cosmetic Group Ltd* ***(G-5411)***
Fort Miller Group Inc 518 695-5000
688 Wilbur Ave Greenwich (12834) ***(G-5906)***
Fort Miller Service Corp (PA) 518 695-5000
688 Wilbur Ave Greenwich (12834) ***(G-5907)***
Fort Orange Press Inc 518 489-3233
11 Sand Creek Rd Albany (12205) ***(G-81)***
Forte Network 631 390-9050
75 Lockfield Rd East Northport (11731) ***(G-4457)***
Forte Security Group, East Northport *Also called Forte Network* ***(G-4457)***
Forteq North America Inc 585 427-9410
150 Park Centre Dr West Henrietta (14586) ***(G-16911)***
Fortitude Industries 607 324-1500
7200 County Route 70a Hornell (14843) ***(G-6589)***
Fortress Biotech Inc (PA) 781 652-4500
3 Columbus Cir Fl 15 New York (10019) ***(G-10239)***
Fortune Poly Products Inc 718 361-0767
17910 93rd Ave Jamaica (11433) ***(G-6948)***
Fortune Sign 646 383-8682
1334 39th St Brooklyn (11218) ***(G-1996)***
Forum Publishing Co 631 754-5000
383 E Main St Centerport (11721) ***(G-3501)***
Forum South, The, Howard Beach *Also called Vpj Publication Inc* ***(G-6628)***
Forward Enterprises Inc 585 235-7670
215 Tremont St Ste 8 Rochester (14608) ***(G-14401)***
Forwear, New York *Also called A and J Apparel Corp* ***(G-9030)***
Foscarini Inc 212 257-4412
20 Greene St New York (10013) ***(G-10240)***
Foscarini Showroom, New York *Also called Foscarini Inc* ***(G-10240)***
Foseco Inc 914 345-4760
777 Old Saw Mill River Rd Tarrytown (10591) ***(G-16115)***

ALPHABETIC

Fossil Industries Inc ...631 254-9200
44 W Jefryn Blvd Ste A Deer Park (11729) ***(G-4167)***
Foster - Gordon Manufacturing ...631 589-6776
55 Knickerbocker Ave G Bohemia (11716) ***(G-1064)***
Foster Reeve & Associates Inc (PA) ...718 609-0090
1155 Manhattan Ave # 1011 Brooklyn (11222) ***(G-1997)***
Foster Refrigerators Entp ...518 671-6036
300 Fairview Ave Hudson (12534) ***(G-6644)***
Fotis Oneonta Italian Bakery ...607 432-3871
42 River St Oneonta (13820) ***(G-13209)***
Fotofiles, Vestal *Also called Truebite Inc* ***(G-16479)***
Fougera Pharmaceuticals Inc (HQ) ...631 454-7677
60 Baylis Rd Melville (11747) ***(G-8350)***
Fougera Pharmaceuticals Inc ...631 454-7677
55 Cantiague Rock Rd Hicksville (11801) ***(G-6375)***
Foundation Center Inc (PA) ...212 620-4230
1 Financial Sq Fl 24 New York (10005) ***(G-10241)***
Fountain Tile Outlet Inc ...718 927-4555
609 Fountain Ave Ste A Brooklyn (11208) ***(G-1998)***
Fountainhead Group Inc (PA) ...315 736-0037
23 Garden St New York Mills (13417) ***(G-12742)***
Fountainhead Group Inc ...708 598-7100
3 Graden St New York Mills (13417) ***(G-12743)***
Four &TWenty Blackbirds, Brooklyn *Also called Blackbirds Brooklyn LLC* ***(G-1699)***
Four Brothers Italian Bakery ...914 741-5434
332 Elwood Ave Hawthorne (10532) ***(G-6269)***
Four Dee Inc ...718 615-1695
2247 E 16th St Brooklyn (11229) ***(G-1999)***
Four Directions Inc ...315 829-8388
4677 State Route 5 Vernon (13476) ***(G-16457)***
Four Fat Fowl Inc ...518 733-5230
324 State Route 43 Stop B Stephentown (12168) ***(G-15779)***
Four K Machine Shop Inc ...516 997-0752
54 Brooklyn Ave Westbury (11590) ***(G-17013)***
Four Paws Products Ltd ...631 436-7421
3125 Vtrans Mem Hwy Ste 1 Ronkonkoma (11779) ***(G-14931)***
Four Quarter, Westbury *Also called Cab-Network Inc* ***(G-17000)***
Four S Showcase Manufacturing ...718 649-4900
1044 Linwood St Brooklyn (11208) ***(G-2000)***
Four Sasons Multi-Services Inc ...347 843-6262
3525 Decatur Ave Apt 2k Bronx (10467) ***(G-1338)***
Four Seasons Buildings Pdts, Holbrook *Also called Latium USA Trading LLC* ***(G-6484)***
Four Seasons Fashion Mfg Inc ...212 947-6820
270 W 39th St Fl 12 New York (10018) ***(G-10242)***
Four Square Tool, Conklin *Also called Toolroom Express Inc* ***(G-3902)***
Four Star, New York *Also called Vanity Room Inc* ***(G-12526)***
Four Wheel Drive, Staten Island *Also called Cyclone Air Power Inc* ***(G-15684)***
Four-Way Pallet Corp ...631 351-3401
191 E 2nd St Huntington Station (11746) ***(G-6744)***
Fourteen Arnold Ave Corp ...315 272-1700
14 Arnold Ave Utica (13502) ***(G-16356)***
Fourtys Ny Inc ...212 382-0301
231 W 39th St Rm 806 New York (10018) ***(G-10243)***
Fowler Route Co Inc ...917 653-4640
25 Sunnyside Dr Yonkers (10705) ***(G-17461)***
Fownes Brothers & Co Inc (PA) ...212 683-0150
16 E 34th St Fl 5 New York (10016) ***(G-10244)***
Fownes Brothers & Co Inc ...518 752-4411
204 County Highway 157 Gloversville (12078) ***(G-5726)***
Fox 416 Corp ...718 385-4600
416 Thatford Ave Brooklyn (11212) ***(G-2001)***
Fox Run Vineyards Inc ...315 536-4616
670 State Route 14 Penn Yan (14527) ***(G-13535)***
Fox Unlimited Inc ...212 736-3071
345 7th Ave Rm 2b New York (10001) ***(G-10245)***
Fox's U-Bet Syrups, Brooklyn *Also called Fox 416 Corp* ***(G-2001)***
Foxhill Press Inc ...212 995-9620
37 E 7th St Ste 2 New York (10003) ***(G-10246)***
Fppf Chemical Co Inc (PA) ...716 856-9607
117 W Tupper St Ste 1 Buffalo (14201) ***(G-2969)***
Fra-Rik Formica Fabg Co Inc ...718 597-3335
1464 Blondell Ave Fl 2 Bronx (10461) ***(G-1339)***
Fradan Manufacturing Corp ...914 632-3653
499 5th Ave New Rochelle (10801) ***(G-8947)***
Fragrance Acquisitions LLC ...845 534-9172
1900 Corporate Blvd Newburgh (12550) ***(G-12776)***
Fragrance Outlet Inc ...845 928-1408
404 Dune Rd Central Valley (10917) ***(G-3551)***
Fralo, Syracuse *Also called Roth Global Plastics Inc* ***(G-16048)***
Frame Shoppe & Art Gallery ...516 365-6014
447 Plandome Rd Manhasset (11030) ***(G-8093)***
Frame Shoppe & Gallery, Manhasset *Also called Frame Shoppe & Art Gallery* ***(G-8093)***
Frame Works America Inc ...631 288-1300
146 Mill Rd Westhampton Beach (11978) ***(G-17087)***
Framerica Corporation ...631 650-1000
2 Todd Ct Yaphank (11980) ***(G-17409)***
Frames Plus Inc ...518 462-1842
991 Broadway Ste 208 Menands (12204) ***(G-8403)***
Framing Technology Inc ...585 464-8470
137 Syke St Rochester (14611) ***(G-14402)***
Francepress LLC (PA) ...646 202-9828
115 E 57th St Fl 11 New York (10022) ***(G-10247)***
Franchet Metal Craft Inc ...718 658-6400
17832 93rd Ave Jamaica (11433) ***(G-6949)***
Francis Emory Fitch Inc (PA) ...212 619-3800
229 W 28th St Fl 9 New York (10001) ***(G-10248)***
Franco Apparel Group Inc ...212 967-7272
1407 Broadway New York (10018) ***(G-10249)***
Franco Apparel Group Team, New York *Also called Franco Apparel Group Inc* ***(G-10249)***
Franetta, New York *Also called Beyond Loom Inc* ***(G-9429)***
Frank Billanti Casting Co Inc ...212 221-0440
42 W 38th St Rm 204 New York (10018) ***(G-10250)***
Frank Blancato Inc ...212 768-1495
64 W 48th St Fl 16 New York (10036) ***(G-10251)***
Frank J Martello ...585 235-2780
1227 Maple St Rochester (14611) ***(G-14403)***
Frank Lowe Rbr & Gasket Co Inc ...631 777-2707
44 Ramsey Rd Shirley (11967) ***(G-15442)***
Frank Merriwell Inc ...516 921-8888
212 Michael Dr Syosset (11791) ***(G-15843)***
Frank Murken Products, Schenectady *Also called Tattersall Industries LLC* ***(G-15327)***
Frank Torrone & Sons Inc ...718 273-7600
400 Broadway Staten Island (10310) ***(G-15695)***
Frank Wardynski & Sons Inc ...716 854-6083
336 Peckham St Buffalo (14206) ***(G-2970)***
Frank Wines Inc ...646 765-6637
345 E 80th St Apt 8b New York (10075) ***(G-10252)***
Franklin Electric Co Inc ...718 244-7744
17501 Rockaway Blvd # 309 Jamaica (11434) ***(G-6950)***
Franklin Manufacturing Div, Hauppauge *Also called Embassy Industries Inc* ***(G-6095)***
Franklin Packaging Inc (PA) ...631 582-8900
96 Sea Cove Rd Northport (11768) ***(G-13029)***
Franklin Poly Film Inc ...718 492-3523
1149 56th St Brooklyn (11219) ***(G-2002)***
Franklin Report LLC ...212 639-9100
201 E 69th St Apt 14j New York (10021) ***(G-10253)***
Franklin's Printing, Cheektowaga *Also called Hugh F McPherson Inc* ***(G-3604)***
Franklin-Douglas Inc ...516 883-0121
52 Main St Side Port Washington (11050) ***(G-13838)***
Franks Cushions Inc ...718 848-1216
6302 59th Ave Maspeth (11378) ***(G-8172)***
Franz Fischer Inc ...718 821-1300
1267 Flushing Ave Brooklyn (11237) ***(G-2003)***
Frasier and Jones, Syracuse *Also called Frazer & Jones Co* ***(G-15964)***
Fratellis LLC ...607 722-5663
20 Campbell Rd Binghamton (13905) ***(G-910)***
Frazer & Jones Co ...315 468-6251
3000 Milton Ave Syracuse (13209) ***(G-15964)***
Frazer & Jones Division, Solvay *Also called Eastern Company* ***(G-15529)***
Frazer Computing Inc ...315 379-3500
6196 Us Highway 11 Canton (13617) ***(G-3409)***
Frazier Industrial Company ...315 539-9256
1291 Waterloo Geneva Rd Waterloo (13165) ***(G-16648)***
Fred A Nudd Corporation (PA) ...315 524-2531
1743 State Route 104 Ontario (14519) ***(G-13223)***
Fred Lawrence Co, Bay Shore *Also called Lanwood Industries Inc* ***(G-709)***
Fred M Lawrence Co Inc (PA) ...718 786-7227
45 Drexel Dr Bay Shore (11706) ***(G-699)***
Fred M Velepec Co Inc ...718 821-6636
7172 70th St Glendale (11385) ***(G-5668)***
Fred Schulz Inc ...845 724-3409
4 Jordan Ct Poughquag (12570) ***(G-13957)***
Fred Weidner & Son Printers ...212 964-8676
15 Maiden Ln Ste 1505 New York (10038) ***(G-10254)***
Frederick Coon Inc ...716 683-6812
5751 Clinton St Elma (14059) ***(G-4661)***
Frederick Cowan & Company Inc ...631 369-0360
48 Kroemer Ave Riverhead (11901) ***(G-14155)***
Frederick Machine Repair Inc ...716 332-0104
405 Ludington St Buffalo (14206) ***(G-2971)***
Fredonia Pennysaver Inc (PA) ...716 679-1509
276 W Main St Ste 1 Fredonia (14063) ***(G-5382)***
Free Trader, Elizabethtown *Also called Denton Publications Inc* ***(G-4640)***
Free Trader, Plattsburgh *Also called Denton Publications Inc* ***(G-13689)***
Freeda Vitamins Inc (PA) ...718 433-4337
4725 34th St Ste 303 Long Island City (11101) ***(G-7774)***
Freedom Mfg LLC ...518 584-0441
3 Duplainville Rd Apt C Saratoga Springs (12866) ***(G-15181)***
Freedom Rains Inc ...646 710-4512
230 W 39th St Fl 7 New York (10018) ***(G-10255)***
Freedom Run Winery Inc ...716 433-4136
5138 Lower Mountain Rd Lockport (14094) ***(G-7616)***
Freeman Technology Inc ...732 829-8345
2355 Bell Blvd Apt 2h Bayside (11360) ***(G-765)***
Freeport Baldwin Leader, Garden City *Also called L & M Publications Inc* ***(G-5525)***
Freeport Paper Industries Inc ...631 851-1555
120 Windsor Pl Central Islip (11722) ***(G-3523)***
Freeport Screen & Stamping ...516 379-0330
31 Hanse Ave Freeport (11520) ***(G-5412)***
Freetime Magazine Inc ...585 473-2266
1255 University Ave # 270 Rochester (14607) ***(G-14404)***
Freeville Publishing Co Inc ...607 844-9119
9 Main St Freeville (13068) ***(G-5447)***

ALPHABETIC SECTION
Furniture Dsign By Knossos Inc

Freeze Clothing, New York *Also called Central Mills Inc* ***(G-9617)***
Freeze-Dry Foods Inc 585 589-6399
111 West Ave Ste 2 Albion (14411) ***(G-168)***
Freirich Julian Co Inc (PA) 718 361-9111
815 Kerr St Long Island City (11101) ***(G-7775)***
French & Itln Furn Craftsmen 718 599-5000
999 Grand St Brooklyn (11211) ***(G-2004)***
French Accnt Rugs & Tapestries 212 686-6097
36 E 31st St Frnt B New York (10016) ***(G-10256)***
French Associates Inc 718 387-9880
7339 172nd St Fresh Meadows (11366) ***(G-5454)***
French Atmosphere Inc (PA) 516 371-9100
421 7th Ave 525 New York (10001) ***(G-10257)***
French Itln Furn Craftsmen Cor, Brooklyn *Also called French & Itln Furn Craftsmen* ***(G-2004)***
French Morning LLC 646 290-7463
27 W 20th St Ste 800 New York (10011) ***(G-10258)***
French Pdts Frnch Pickle Works, Fresh Meadows *Also called French Associates Inc* ***(G-5454)***
French Toast, New York *Also called Lollytogs Ltd* ***(G-11053)***
Frenz Group LLC 212 465-0908
14932 3rd Ave Whitestone (11357) ***(G-17235)***
Frequency Electronics Inc (PA) 516 794-4500
55 Charles Lindbergh Blvd # 2 Uniondale (11553) ***(G-16317)***
Frequency Selective Networks 718 424-7500
12 N Cottage St Valley Stream (11580) ***(G-16433)***
Fresenius Kabi Usa LLC 716 773-0053
3159 Staley Rd Grand Island (14072) ***(G-5771)***
Fresenius Kabi USA LLC 716 773-0800
3159 Staley Rd Grand Island (14072) ***(G-5772)***
Fresh Bake Pizza Co, Depew *Also called D R M Management Inc* ***(G-4278)***
Fresh Fanatic Inc 516 521-6574
88 Washington Ave Brooklyn (11205) ***(G-2005)***
Fresh Harvest Incorporated 845 296-1024
1574 Route 9 Wappingers Falls (12590) ***(G-16588)***
Fresh Ice Cream Company LLC 347 603-6021
630 Flushing Ave 4 Brooklyn (11206) ***(G-2006)***
Fresh Prints LLC 917 826-2752
134 E 70th St New York (10021) ***(G-10259)***
Fresh Tortillas Si Inc 718 979-6666
304 New Dorp Ln Staten Island (10306) ***(G-15696)***
Freshop Inc 585 738-6035
3246 Monroe Ave Ste 1 Rochester (14618) ***(G-14405)***
Freshway Distributors, Hicksville *Also called Kozy Shack Enterprises LLC* ***(G-6388)***
Frew Run Gravel Products Inc 716 569-4712
984 Frew Run Rd Frewsburg (14738) ***(G-5464)***
Frey Concrete Incoprorated, Orchard Park *Also called United Materials LLC* ***(G-13326)***
Fridge Magazine Inc 212 997-7673
108 W 39th St Fl 4 New York (10018) ***(G-10260)***
Friedel Paper Box & Converting 315 437-3325
7596 Rania Rd Baldwinsville (13027) ***(G-568)***
Friendly Fuel Incorporated 518 581-7036
54 Church St Saratoga Springs (12866) ***(G-15182)***
Friendly Star Fuel Inc 718 369-8801
889 3rd Ave Brooklyn (11232) ***(G-2007)***
Friendship Dairies LLC 585 973-3031
6701 County Road 20 Friendship (14739) ***(G-5466)***
Frieslndcmpina Ingrdnts N Amer 607 746-0196
40196 State Hwy 10 Delhi Delhi (13753) ***(G-4264)***
Frigo Design, Brewerton *Also called Ae Fund Inc* ***(G-1199)***
Frisch Plastics Corp 973 685-5936
7 Joyce Rd Hartsdale (10530) ***(G-6017)***
Frito-Lay North America Inc 716 631-2360
25 Curtwright Dr Williamsville (14221) ***(G-17271)***
Frito-Lay North America Inc 585 343-5456
8063 Kelsey Rd Batavia (14020) ***(G-635)***
Frito-Lay North America Inc 607 775-7000
10 Spud Ln Binghamton (13904) ***(G-911)***
Fritters & Buns Inc 845 227-6609
236 Blue Hill Rd Hopewell Junction (12533) ***(G-6576)***
Froebe Group LLC 646 649-2150
154 W 27th St Rm 4 New York (10001) ***(G-10261)***
Frog International, Hauppauge *Also called Organic Frog Inc* ***(G-6182)***
Fronhofer Tool Company Inc 518 692-2496
4197 County Rd 48 Cossayuna (12823) ***(G-4081)***
Frontier Ht-Dip Glvanizing Inc 716 875-2091
1740 Elmwood Ave Buffalo (14207) ***(G-2972)***
Frontier Hydraulics Corp 716 694-2070
1738 Elmwood Ave Ste 2 Buffalo (14207) ***(G-2973)***
Frontier Plating 716 896-2811
68 Dignity Cir Buffalo (14211) ***(G-2974)***
Frontier Plating Co, Buffalo *Also called Frontier Plating* ***(G-2974)***
Frontiers Unlimited Inc 631 283-4663
52 Jagger Ln Southampton (11968) ***(G-15566)***
Fross Industries Inc 716 297-0652
3315 Haseley Dr Niagara Falls (14304) ***(G-12843)***
Frost Publications Inc 845 726-3232
55 Laurel Hill Dr Westtown (10998) ***(G-17097)***
Frozen Food Digest Inc 212 557-8600
271 Madison Ave Ste 805 New York (10016) ***(G-10262)***
Frozen Pastry Products Corp 845 364-9833
41 Lincoln Ave Spring Valley (10977) ***(G-15608)***
Frp Apparel Group LLC 212 695-8000
110 W 40th St Fl 26 New York (10018) ***(G-10263)***
Fruit St Hlth Pub Beneft Corp 347 960-6400
85 Broad St Fl 18 New York (10004) ***(G-10264)***
Fruitcrown Products Corp (PA) 631 694-5800
250 Adams Blvd Farmingdale (11735) ***(G-5003)***
Fsr Beauty Ltd 212 447-0036
411 5th Ave Rm 804 New York (10016) ***(G-10265)***
FT Publications Inc (HQ) 212 641-6500
330 Hudson St New York (10013) ***(G-10266)***
FT Publications Inc 212 641-2420
330 Hudson St New York (10013) ***(G-10267)***
FT Seismic Support Inc 607 527-8595
5596 Mills Rd Campbell (14821) ***(G-3357)***
Fts Systems Inc (HQ) 845 687-5300
3538 Main St Stone Ridge (12484) ***(G-15785)***
Ftt Manufacturing, Rochester *Also called Ppi Corp* ***(G-14611)***
Ftt Medical Inc 585 444-0980
275 Commerce Dr Rochester (14623) ***(G-14406)***
Ftt Mfg, Rochester *Also called Ppi Corp* ***(G-14612)***
Fuccillo Ford Nelliston Inc 518 993-5555
6500 State Hwy 5 Nelliston (13410) ***(G-8820)***
Fuda Group (usa) Corporation 646 751-7488
48 Wall St Fl 11 New York (10005) ***(G-10268)***
Fuel Data Systems Inc 800 447-7870
772 Greenville Tpke Middletown (10940) ***(G-8475)***
Fuel Efficiency LLC 315 923-2511
101 Davis Pkwy Clyde (14433) ***(G-3752)***
Fuel Energy Services USA Ltd 607 846-2650
250 Ltta Brook Indus Pkwy Horseheads (14845) ***(G-6607)***
Fuel Soul 516 379-0810
188 Merrick Rd Merrick (11566) ***(G-8419)***
Fuel Tank Envmtl Svcs Corp 631 374-9083
674 Washington Dr Centerport (11721) ***(G-3502)***
Fuel Watchman Sales & Service 718 665-6100
364 Jackson Ave Bronx (10454) ***(G-1340)***
Fujitsu Ntwrk Cmmnications Inc 845 731-2000
2 Blue Hill Plz Ste 1609 Pearl River (10965) ***(G-13479)***
Fulcrum Promos, New York *Also called Fulcrum Promotions & Prtg LLC* ***(G-10269)***
Fulcrum Promotions & Prtg LLC 203 909-6362
1460 Broadway New York (10036) ***(G-10269)***
Full Circle Home LLC 212 432-0001
146 W 29th St Rm 9w New York (10001) ***(G-10270)***
Full Circle Studios LLC 716 875-7740
710 Main St Buffalo (14202) ***(G-2975)***
Full Motion Beverage Inc (PA) 631 585-1100
998 Old Country Rd Plainview (11803) ***(G-13632)***
Full Service Auto Body Inc 718 831-9300
25601 Jericho Tpke Floral Park (11001) ***(G-5211)***
Full Timer, Bronx *Also called Fuel Watchman Sales & Service* ***(G-1340)***
Fuller Fabrications 315 469-7415
3915 State Route 91 Jamesville (13078) ***(G-7080)***
Fuller Sportswear Co Inc 516 773-3353
10 Grenfell Dr Great Neck (11020) ***(G-5830)***
Fuller Tool Incorporated 315 891-3183
225 Platform Rd Newport (13416) ***(G-12814)***
Fulmont Ready-Mix Company Inc (PA) 518 887-5560
774 State Highway 5s Amsterdam (12010) ***(G-347)***
Fulton Boiler Works Inc (PA) 315 298-5121
3981 Port St Pulaski (13142) ***(G-13964)***
Fulton Boiler Works Inc 315 298-5121
972 Centerville Rd Pulaski (13142) ***(G-13965)***
Fulton Companies, Pulaski *Also called Fulton Volcanic Inc* ***(G-13967)***
Fulton Daily News, Fulton *Also called DOT Publishing* ***(G-5470)***
Fulton Heating Solutions Inc 315 298-5121
972 Centerville Rd Pulaski (13142) ***(G-13966)***
Fulton Newspapers Inc 315 598-6397
67 S 2nd St Fulton (13069) ***(G-5471)***
Fulton Patriot, Fulton *Also called Fulton Newspapers Inc* ***(G-5471)***
Fulton Tool Co Inc 315 598-2900
802 W Broadway Ste 1 Fulton (13069) ***(G-5472)***
Fulton Volcanic Inc (PA) 315 298-5121
3981 Port St Pulaski (13142) ***(G-13967)***
Fultonville Machine & Tool Co 518 853-4441
73 Union St Fultonville (12072) ***(G-5493)***
Fun Industries of NY 631 845-3805
111 Milbar Blvd Farmingdale (11735) ***(G-5004)***
Fun Media Inc 646 472-0135
1001 Ave Of The Americas New York (10018) ***(G-10271)***
Funda-Mantels LLC 631 924-1404
659 Mastic Rd Mastic (11950) ***(G-8235)***
Fung Wong Bakery Inc 212 267-4037
30 Mott St Frnt New York (10013) ***(G-10272)***
Fung Wong Bakery Shop, New York *Also called Fung Wong Bakery Inc* ***(G-10272)***
Fungilab Inc 631 750-6361
89 Cabot Ct Ste K Hauppauge (11788) ***(G-6104)***
Furniture By Craftmaster Ltd 631 750-0658
1595 Ocean Ave Ste A9 Bohemia (11716) ***(G-1065)***
Furniture Doctor Inc 585 657-6941
7007 State Route 5 And 20 Bloomfield (14469) ***(G-982)***
Furniture Dsign By Knossos Inc 718 729-0404
2430 Bklyn Qns Expy Ste 3 Woodside (11377) ***(G-17347)***

ALPHABETIC

(PA)=Parent Co (HQ)=Headquarters (DH)=Div Headquarters
2018 Harris
New York Manufacturers Directory
955

Furniture World, New Rochelle *Also called Towse Publishing Co* ***(G-8971)***
Fuse Electronics Inc...607 352-3222
1223 Us Route 11 Kirkwood (13795) ***(G-7260)***
Fusion Brands America Inc...212 269-1387
444 Madison Ave Ste 700 New York (10022) ***(G-10273)***
Fusion Pro Performance Ltd...917 833-0761
16 W 36th St Rm 1205 New York (10018) ***(G-10274)***
Fusion Telecom Intl Inc (PA)...212 201-2400
420 Lexington Ave Rm 1718 New York (10170) ***(G-10275)***
Futon City Discounters Inc...315 437-1328
6361 Thompson Rd Syracuse (13206) ***(G-15965)***
Future Diagnostics LLC...347 434-6700
266 47th St Brooklyn (11220) ***(G-2008)***
Future Mobility Products Inc...716 783-9130
1 Buffalo River Pl Buffalo (14210) ***(G-2976)***
Future Screw Machine Pdts Inc...631 765-1610
41155 County Road 48 Southold (11971) ***(G-15582)***
Future Spray Finishing Co...631 242-6252
78 Brook Ave Ste A Deer Park (11729) ***(G-4168)***
Future Star Digatech...718 666-0350
713 Monroe St Brooklyn (11221) ***(G-2009)***
Future Us Inc...844 779-2822
79 Madison Ave Fl 2 New York (10016) ***(G-10276)***
Futurebiotics, Hauppauge *Also called FB Laboratories Inc* ***(G-6098)***
Futurebiotics LLC...631 273-6300
70 Commerce Dr Hauppauge (11788) ***(G-6105)***
FWC Networks Inc...718 408-1558
1615 Carroll St Brooklyn (11213) ***(G-2010)***
FX INC...212 244-2240
1 Penn Plz Ste 6238 New York (10119) ***(G-10277)***
G & C Welding Co Inc...516 883-3228
39 Annette Dr Port Washington (11050) ***(G-13839)***
G & G C Machine & Tool Co Inc...516 873-0999
18 Sylvester St Westbury (11590) ***(G-17014)***
G & G Window Repair Inc...585 334-3370
6710 W Henrietta Rd Ste 4 Rush (14543) ***(G-15073)***
G & H Wood Products LLC...716 372-5510
2427 N Union Street Ext Olean (14760) ***(G-13169)***
G & J Rdymx & Masnry Sup Inc...718 454-0800
18330 Jamaica Ave Hollis (11423) ***(G-6523)***
G & M Clearview Inc...845 781-4877
112 Spring St Monroe (10950) ***(G-8590)***
G & M Dege Inc...631 475-1450
250 Orchard Rd Bldg 1 East Patchogue (11772) ***(G-4466)***
G & O Equipment Corp...718 218-7844
1211 Oakpoint Ave Bronx (10474) ***(G-1341)***
G & P Printing Inc...212 274-8092
142 Baxter St New York (10013) ***(G-10278)***
G & S Farm & Home Inc...716 542-9922
13550 Bloomingdale Rd Akron (14001) ***(G-20)***
G & W Tool & Die Co, Valley Stream *Also called Precision Tl Die & Stamping Co* ***(G-16444)***
G A Braun Inc (PA)...315 475-3123
79 General Irwin Blvd North Syracuse (13212) ***(G-12960)***
G A Braun Inc...315 475-3123
461 E Brighton Ave Syracuse (13210) ***(G-15966)***
G A Richards & Co Inc...516 334-5412
18 Sylvester St Westbury (11590) ***(G-17015)***
G and G Service...518 785-9247
21 Nelson Ave Latham (12110) ***(G-7390)***
G B International Trdg Co Ltd...607 785-0938
408 Airport Rd Endicott (13760) ***(G-4817)***
G Bopp USA Inc...845 296-1065
4 Bill Horton Way Wappingers Falls (12590) ***(G-16589)***
G C Casting, Oneonta *Also called American Blade Mfg LLC* ***(G-13193)***
G C Controls Inc...607 656-4117
1408 County Road 2 Greene (13778) ***(G-5883)***
G C D M Ironworks Inc...914 347-2058
55 N Evarts Ave Elmsford (10523) ***(G-4762)***
G C Hanford Manufacturing Co (PA)...315 476-7418
304 Oneida St Syracuse (13202) ***(G-15967)***
G C Ironworks, Elmsford *Also called G C D M Ironworks Inc* ***(G-4762)***
G C Mobile Svces, Cortlandt Manor *Also called Gc Mobile Services Inc* ***(G-4075)***
G E Inspection Technologies LP...315 554-2000
721 Visions Dr Skaneateles (13152) ***(G-15481)***
G F Labels, Queensbury *Also called Glens Falls Business Forms Inc* ***(G-14009)***
G Fried Carpert Service...516 333-3900
800 Old Country Rd Westbury (11590) ***(G-17016)***
G Fried Carpet and Design Ctr, Westbury *Also called G Fried Carpert Service* ***(G-17016)***
G Haynes Holdings Inc...607 538-1160
51971 State Highway 10 Bloomville (13739) ***(G-989)***
G I Certified Inc...212 397-1945
623 W 51st St New York (10019) ***(G-10279)***
G J C Ltd Inc...607 770-4500
6 Emma St Binghamton (13905) ***(G-912)***
G J Olney Inc...315 827-4208
9057 Dopp Hill Rd Westernville (13486) ***(G-17072)***
G L 7 Sales Plus Ltd...631 696-8290
125 Middle Country Rd F Coram (11727) ***(G-3965)***
G M I, Hornell *Also called Gray Manufacturing Inds LLC* ***(G-6591)***
G Marks Hdwr Liquidating Corp...631 225-5400
333 Bayview Ave Amityville (11701) ***(G-287)***
G N R Co, Smithtown *Also called G N R Plastics Inc* ***(G-15509)***
G N R Plastics Inc...631 724-8758
11 Wandering Way Smithtown (11787) ***(G-15509)***
G Pesso & Sons Inc...718 224-9130
20320 35th Ave Bayside (11361) ***(G-766)***
G R M, Bellmore *Also called Rush Gold Manufacturing Ltd* ***(G-816)***
G S Communications USA Inc...718 389-7371
179 Greenpoint Ave Brooklyn (11222) ***(G-2011)***
G Schirmer Inc (HQ)...212 254-2100
180 Madison Ave Ste 2400 New York (10016) ***(G-10280)***
G Schirmer Inc...845 469-4699
2 Old Rt 17 Chester (10918) ***(G-3634)***
G Sicuranza Ltd...516 759-0259
4 East Ave Glen Cove (11542) ***(G-5628)***
G T Machine & Tool, Long Island City *Also called Theodosiou Inc* ***(G-7927)***
G Tech Natureal Gasses Systems, Buffalo *Also called Gas Tchnlogy Enrgy Cncepts LLC* ***(G-2980)***
G W Canfield & Son Inc...315 735-5522
600 Plant St Utica (13502) ***(G-16357)***
G W Manufacturing, Ridgewood *Also called Gw Manufacturing* ***(G-14122)***
G X Electric Corporation...212 921-0400
8 W 38th St New York (10018) ***(G-10281)***
G Z G Rest & Kit Met Works...718 788-8621
120 13th St Brooklyn (11215) ***(G-2012)***
G&G Sealcoating and Paving Inc...585 787-1500
1449 Ontario Ontario (14519) ***(G-13224)***
G&J Graphics Inc...718 409-9874
2914 Westchester Ave Bronx (10461) ***(G-1342)***
G&W Industries, New York *Also called Gw Acquisition LLC* ***(G-10430)***
G-III Apparel Group, New York *Also called G-III Leather Fashions Inc* ***(G-10284)***
G-III Apparel Group Ltd (PA)...212 403-0500
512 7th Ave Fl 35 New York (10018) ***(G-10282)***
G-III Apparel Group Ltd...212 403-0500
512 Fashion Ave Fl 35 New York (10018) ***(G-10283)***
G-III Leather Fashions Inc...212 403-0500
512 7th Ave Fl 35 New York (10018) ***(G-10284)***
G-S Plastic Optics, Rochester *Also called Germanow-Simon Corporation* ***(G-14420)***
G18 Corporation...212 869-0010
215 W 40th St Fl 9 New York (10018) ***(G-10285)***
G4i, Rensselaer *Also called Great 4 Image Inc* ***(G-14058)***
Gabani Inc...631 283-4930
81 Lee Ave Southampton (11968) ***(G-15567)***
Gabbagoods, New York *Also called M&S Accessory Network Corp* ***(G-11107)***
Gabila & Sons Mfg Inc...631 789-2220
100 Wartburg Ave Copiague (11726) ***(G-3927)***
Gabila Food Products Inc...631 789-2220
100 Wartburg Ave Copiague (11726) ***(G-3928)***
Gabila's Knishes, Copiague *Also called Gabila & Sons Mfg Inc* ***(G-3927)***
Gabriela Systems Ltd...631 225-7952
135 Bangor St Lindenhurst (11757) ***(G-7487)***
Gabriella Importers Inc (PA)...212 579-3945
481 Johnson Ave Ste D Bohemia (11716) ***(G-1066)***
Gabriella Importers Inc...212 579-3945
305 W 87th St New York (10024) ***(G-10286)***
Gabrielle Andra...212 366-9624
305 W 21st St New York (10011) ***(G-10287)***
Gad Systems, Lawrence *Also called John J Richardson* ***(G-7417)***
Gadabout USA Wheelchairs Inc...585 338-2110
892 E Ridge Rd Rochester (14621) ***(G-14407)***
Gaddis Engineering, Glen Cove *Also called Gaddis Industrial Equipment* ***(G-5629)***
Gaddis Industrial Equipment...516 759-3100
140 Pratt Oval Glen Cove (11542) ***(G-5629)***
Gaebel Enterprises, East Syracuse *Also called Gei International Inc* ***(G-4546)***
Gaffney Kroese Electrial, Garden City *Also called Gaffney Kroese Supply Corp* ***(G-5519)***
Gaffney Kroese Supply Corp...516 228-5091
377 Oak St Ste 202 Garden City (11530) ***(G-5519)***
Gagne Associates Inc...800 800-5954
41 Commercial Dr Johnson City (13790) ***(G-7123)***
Galas Framing Services...718 706-0007
4224 Orchard St Fl 4 Long Island City (11101) ***(G-7776)***
Galaxy Knitting Mills, Long Island City *Also called In Toon Amkor Fashions Inc* ***(G-7793)***
Galaxy Software LLC...631 244-8405
154 Middlesex Ave Oakdale (11769) ***(G-13075)***
Galian Handbags, New York *Also called Rodem Incorporated* ***(G-11922)***
Galison Publishing LLC...212 354-8840
70 W 36th St Fl 11 New York (10018) ***(G-10288)***
Galison/Mudpuppy, New York *Also called Galison Publishing LLC* ***(G-10288)***
Galiva Inc...903 600-5755
236 Broadway Ste 214 Brooklyn (11211) ***(G-2013)***
Gallagher Printing Inc...716 873-2434
2518 Delaware Ave Buffalo (14216) ***(G-2977)***
Gallant Graphics Ltd...845 868-1166
242 Attlebury Hill Rd Stanfordville (12581) ***(G-15647)***
Galle & Zinter Inc...716 833-4212
3405 Harlem Rd Buffalo (14225) ***(G-2978)***
Galle Mamorial, Buffalo *Also called Galle & Zinter Inc* ***(G-2978)***
Gallery 57 Dental...212 246-8700
24 W 57th St Ste 701 New York (10019) ***(G-10289)***
Galli Shirts and Sports AP...845 226-7305
246 Judith Dr Stormville (12582) ***(G-15801)***

ALPHABETIC SECTION

Galmer Ltd 718 392-4609
  4301 21st St Ste 130b Long Island City (11101) *(G-7777)*
Galmer Silversmiths, Long Island City Also called Galmer Ltd *(G-7777)*
Galt Industries Inc 212 758-0770
  121 E 71st St New York (10021) *(G-10290)*
Gamble & Gamble Inc (PA) 716 731-3239
  5890 West St Sanborn (14132) *(G-15147)*
GAME Sportswear Ltd (PA) 914 962-1701
  1401 Front St Yorktown Heights (10598) *(G-17527)*
Game Time LLC 914 557-9662
  1407 Broadway Rm 400 New York (10018) *(G-10291)*
Games For Change Inc 212 242-4922
  205 E 42nd St Fl 20 New York (10017) *(G-10292)*
Gametime Media Inc 212 860-2090
  120 E 87th St Apt R8e New York (10128) *(G-10293)*
Gametime Sportswear Plus LLC 315 724-5893
  1206 Belle Ave Utica (13501) *(G-16358)*
Gamma Enterprises LLC 631 755-1080
  113 Alder St West Babylon (11704) *(G-16819)*
Gamma Instrument Co Inc 516 486-5526
  52 Chasner St Hempstead (11550) *(G-6293)*
Gamma Lab, West Babylon Also called Gamma Enterprises LLC *(G-16819)*
Gamma North Corporation 716 902-5100
  13595 Broadway St Alden (14004) *(G-181)*
Gamma Products Inc 845 562-3332
  509 Temple Hill Rd New Windsor (12553) *(G-8984)*
Gan Kavod Inc 315 797-3114
  2050 Tilden Ave New Hartford (13413) *(G-8850)*
Ganesh Foods, Waterloo Also called Gharana Industries LLC *(G-16649)*
Gangi Distributors Inc 718 442-5745
  135 Mcclean Ave Staten Island (10305) *(G-15697)*
Gannett Co Inc 516 484-7510
  99 Seaview Blvd Ste 200 Port Washington (11050) *(G-13840)*
Gannett Co Inc 585 232-7100
  245 E Main St Rochester (14604) *(G-14408)*
Gannett Co Inc 585 924-3406
  6300 Collett Rd Farmington (14425) *(G-5160)*
Gannett Co Inc 914 278-9315
  92 North Ave New Rochelle (10801) *(G-8948)*
Gannett Co Inc 607 798-1234
  4421 Vestal Pkwy E Vestal (13850) *(G-16470)*
Gannett Co Inc 607 352-2702
  10 Gannett Dr Johnson City (13790) *(G-7124)*
Gannett Co Inc 585 346-4150
  3155 Rochester Rd Bldg E Lakeville (14480) *(G-7307)*
Gannett NY Production Facility, Johnson City Also called Gannett Co Inc *(G-7124)*
Gannett Stllite Info Ntwrk Inc 914 965-5000
  1 Odell Plz Yonkers (10701) *(G-17462)*
Gannett Stllite Info Ntwrk Inc 585 798-1400
  413 Main St Medina (14103) *(G-8305)*
Gannett Stllite Info Ntwrk Inc 914 381-3400
  700 Waverly Ave Mamaroneck (10543) *(G-8068)*
Gannett Stllite Info Ntwrk LLC 845 578-2300
  1 Crosfield Ave West Nyack (10994) *(G-16946)*
Gannett Stllite Info Ntwrk LLC 845 454-2000
  85 Civic Center Plz Poughkeepsie (12601) *(G-13920)*
Gannett Suburban Newspapers, Mamaroneck Also called Gannett Stllite Info Ntwrk Inc *(G-8068)*
Gar Wood Custom Boats 518 494-2966
  20 Duell Hill Rd Brant Lake (12815) *(G-1170)*
Garan Incorporated (HQ) 212 563-1292
  200 Madison Ave Fl 4 New York (10016) *(G-10294)*
Garan Manufacturing Co (HQ) 212 563-2000
  200 Madison Ave Fl 4 New York (10016) *(G-10295)*
Garb-El Products Co, Lockport Also called 240 Michigan Street Inc *(G-7596)*
Garb-O-Liner Inc 914 235-1585
  64 Drake Ave New Rochelle (10805) *(G-8949)*
Garco, Penfield Also called Robinson Tools LLC *(G-13526)*
Garco Manufacturing Corp Inc 718 287-3330
  4802 Farragut Rd Brooklyn (11203) *(G-2014)*
Gardall Safe Corporation 315 432-9115
  219 Lamson St Ste 1 Syracuse (13206) *(G-15968)*
Gardei Industries LLC (PA) 716 693-7100
  1087 Erie Ave North Tonawanda (14120) *(G-12991)*
Gardei Manufacturing, North Tonawanda Also called Pioneer Printers Inc *(G-13004)*
Garden City Printers & Mailers 516 485-1600
  144 Cherry Valley Ave West Hempstead (11552) *(G-16884)*
Garden State Shavings Inc 845 544-2835
  16 Almond Tree Ln Warwick (10990) *(G-16612)*
Gardner Dnver Oberdorfer Pumps 315 437-0361
  5900 Firestone Dr Syracuse (13206) *(G-15969)*
Gardner The Train Doctor, North Rose Also called Gargraves Trackage Corporation *(G-12953)*
Garelick Farms Inc 518 283-0820
  504 Third Avenue Ext East Greenbush (12061) *(G-4422)*
Gargraves Trackage Corporation (PA) 315 483-6577
  8967 Ridge Rd North Rose (14516) *(G-12953)*
Garland Logging Inc 518 483-1170
  587 County Route 26 Malone (12953) *(G-8041)*
Garland Technology LLC (PA) 716 242-8500
  199 Delaware Ave Buffalo (14202) *(G-2979)*

Garlock Sealing Tech LLC 315 597-4811
  1666 Division St Palmyra (14522) *(G-13432)*
Garment Care Systems LLC 518 674-1826
  50 Blue Heron Dr Averill Park (12018) *(G-532)*
Garrett J Cronin 914 761-9299
  1 Stuart Way White Plains (10607) *(G-17137)*
Garrison Woodworking Inc 845 726-3525
  226 Hoslers Rd Westtown (10998) *(G-17098)*
Gary Gelbfish MD 718 258-3004
  2502 Avenue I Brooklyn (11210) *(G-2015)*
Gary Plastic, Bronx Also called Viele Manufacturing Corp *(G-1490)*
Gary Plastic Packaging Corp (PA) 718 893-2200
  1340 Viele Ave Bronx (10474) *(G-1343)*
Gary Roth & Associates Ltd 516 333-1000
  1400 Old Country Rd # 305 Westbury (11590) *(G-17017)*
Gary Stock Corporation 914 276-2700
  597 Rte 22 Croton Falls (10519) *(G-4087)*
Garyline, Bronx Also called Gary Plastic Packaging Corp *(G-1343)*
Garys Loft 212 244-0970
  28 W 36th St New York (10018) *(G-10296)*
Gas Field Specialists Inc 716 378-6422
  224 N Main St Horseheads (14845) *(G-6608)*
Gas Recovery Systems LLC (HQ) 914 421-4903
  1 N Lexington Ave Ste 620 White Plains (10601) *(G-17138)*
Gas Recovery Systems Illinois, White Plains Also called Gas Recovery Systems LLC *(G-17138)*
Gas Tchnlgy Enrgy Cncepts LLC 716 831-9695
  201 Dutton Ave Buffalo (14211) *(G-2980)*
Gas Turbine Controls Corp 914 693-0830
  6 Skyline Dr Ste 150 Hawthorne (10532) *(G-6270)*
Gasoft Equipment Inc 845 863-1010
  231 Dubois St Newburgh (12550) *(G-12777)*
Gasport Welding & Fabg Inc 716 772-7205
  8430 Telegraph Rd Gasport (14067) *(G-5572)*
Gasser & Sons Inc (PA) 631 543-6600
  440 Moreland Rd Commack (11725) *(G-3858)*
Gassho Body & Mind Inc 518 695-9991
  76 Broad St Schuylerville (12871) *(G-15341)*
Gatecomusa, Flushing Also called Yellow E House Inc *(G-5315)*
Gatehouse Media LLC (HQ) 585 598-0030
  175 Sullys Trl Ste 300 Pittsford (14534) *(G-13589)*
Gatehouse Media LLC 315 792-5000
  350 Willowbrook Office Pa Utica (13501) *(G-16359)*
Gatehouse Media LLC 607 776-2121
  10 W Steuben St Bath (14810) *(G-656)*
Gatehouse Media LLC 315 866-2220
  111 Green St Herkimer (13350) *(G-6325)*
Gatehouse Media LLC 607 936-4651
  34 W Pulteney St Corning (14830) *(G-3993)*
Gatehouse Media LLC 585 394-0770
  73 Buffalo St Canandaigua (14424) *(G-3376)*
Gatehouse Media LLC 607 324-1425
  32 Broadway Mall Hornell (14843) *(G-6590)*
Gatehouse Media MO Holdings 530 846-3661
  175 Sullys Trl Ste 300 Pittsford (14534) *(G-13590)*
Gatehuse Media PA Holdings Inc (HQ) 585 598-0030
  175 Sullys Trl Fl 3 Pittsford (14534) *(G-13591)*
Gateway Newspapers Inc 845 628-8400
  928 S Lake Blvd Apt 1e Mahopac (10541) *(G-8026)*
Gateway Prtg & Graphics Inc 716 823-3873
  3970 Big Tree Rd Hamburg (14075) *(G-5949)*
Gatherer's Gourmet Granola, Delmar Also called Sanzdranz LLC *(G-4271)*
Gatti Tool & Mold Inc 585 328-1350
  997 Beahan Rd Rochester (14624) *(G-14409)*
Gaughan Construction Corp 718 850-9577
  13034 90th Ave Richmond Hill (11418) *(G-14086)*
Gavin Mfg Corp 631 467-0040
  25 Central Ave Unit A Farmingdale (11735) *(G-5005)*
Gay Sheet Metal Dies Inc 716 877-0208
  301 Hinman Ave Buffalo (14216) *(G-2981)*
Gaylord Archival, North Syracuse Also called Gaylord Bros Inc *(G-12961)*
Gaylord Bros Inc 315 457-5070
  7282 William Barry Blvd North Syracuse (13212) *(G-12961)*
Gaymar Industries Inc 800 828-7341
  10 Centre Dr Orchard Park (14127) *(G-13294)*
Gazette & Press, Rye Also called Mason & Gore Inc *(G-15089)*
Gazette Press Inc 914 963-8300
  2 Clinton Ave Rye (10580) *(G-15082)*
Gb Aero Engine LLC 914 925-9600
  555 Theodore Fremd Ave Rye (10580) *(G-15083)*
Gb Group Inc 212 594-3748
  Umpire State Bldg 1808 New York (10021) *(G-10297)*
Gbf, Tonawanda Also called Green Buffalo Fuel LLC *(G-16185)*
Gbg Denim Usa LLC (HQ) 646 839-7000
  350 5th Ave Lbby 9 New York (10118) *(G-10298)*
Gbg National Brands Group LLC 646 839-7000
  350 5th Ave Lbby 9 New York (10118) *(G-10299)*
Gbg Socks LLC 646 839-7000
  350 5th Ave Lbby 9 New York (10118) *(G-10300)*
Gbg USA Inc 646 839-7083
  350 5th Ave Fl 7 New York (10118) *(G-10301)*

(PA)=Parent Co (HQ)=Headquarters (DH)=Div Headquarters

Gbg USA Inc 212 615-3400
261 W 35th St Fl 15 New York (10001) *(G-10302)*
Gbg West LLC (HQ) 646 839-7000
350 5th Ave Lbby 11 New York (10118) *(G-10303)*
Gbv Promotions Inc 631 231-7300
44 Drexel Dr Bay Shore (11706) *(G-700)*
Gc Mobile Services Inc 914 736-9730
32 William Puckey Dr Cortlandt Manor (10567) *(G-4075)*
Gce International Inc (PA) 212 704-4800
1385 Broadway Fl 21 New York (10018) *(G-10304)*
Gce International Inc 212 868-0500
350 5th Ave Ste 616 New York (10118) *(G-10305)*
Gce International Inc 773 263-1210
1359 Broadway Rm 2000 New York (10018) *(G-10306)*
GCM Metal Industries Inc 718 386-4059
454 Troutman St Brooklyn (11237) *(G-2016)*
Gcm Steel Products Inc 718 386-3346
454 Troutman St Brooklyn (11237) *(G-2017)*
Gcns Technology Group Inc (PA) 347 713-8160
597 Rutland Rd Brooklyn (11203) *(G-2018)*
Gds Publishing Inc 212 796-2000
40 Wall St Fl 5 New York (10005) *(G-10307)*
GE Aviation Systems LLC 631 467-5500
1000 Macarthur Mem Hwy Bohemia (11716) *(G-1067)*
GE Global Research 518 387-5000
1 Research Cir Niskayuna (12309) *(G-12911)*
GE Healthcare Fincl Svcs Inc 212 713-2000
299 Park Ave Fl 3 New York (10171) *(G-10308)*
GE Healthcare Inc 516 626-2799
80 Seaview Blvd Ste E Port Washington (11050) *(G-13841)*
GE Mds LLC (HQ) 585 242-9600
175 Science Pkwy Rochester (14620) *(G-14410)*
GE Plastics 518 475-5011
1 Noryl Ave Selkirk (12158) *(G-15377)*
GE Polymershapes 516 433-4092
120 Andrews Rd Hicksville (11801) *(G-6376)*
GE Transportation Energy, Schenectady Also called GE Transportation Eng Systems *(G-15282)*
GE Transportation Eng Systems 518 258-9276
1 River Rd Bldg 2-333d Schenectady (12345) *(G-15282)*
Gear Motions Incorporated 716 885-1080
1120 Niagara St Buffalo (14213) *(G-2982)*
Gear Motions Incorporated (PA) 315 488-0100
1750 Milton Ave Syracuse (13209) *(G-15970)*
Geddes Bakery Co Inc 315 437-8084
421 S Main St North Syracuse (13212) *(G-12962)*
Gefa Instrument Corp 516 420-4419
205 Bethpage Sweet Old Bethpage (11804) *(G-13148)*
Gehring Textiles, Garden City Also called Gehring Tricot Corporation *(G-5520)*
Gehring Tricot Corporation (PA) 315 429-8551
1225 Franklin Ave Ste 300 Garden City (11530) *(G-5520)*
Gehring Tricot Corporation 315 429-8551
68 Ransom St Ste 272 Dolgeville (13329) *(G-4329)*
Gei International Inc (PA) 315 463-9261
100 Ball St East Syracuse (13057) *(G-4546)*
Geier Bindery Co, Farmingdale Also called Mid Island Group *(G-5063)*
Geliko LLC 212 876-5620
1751 2nd Ave Rm 102 New York (10128) *(G-10309)*
Gem Fabrication of NC 704 278-6713
586 Commercial Ave Garden City (11530) *(G-5521)*
Gem Manufacturing Inc 585 235-1670
853 West Ave Bldg 17a Rochester (14611) *(G-14411)*
Gem Metal Spinning & Stamping 718 729-7014
517 47th Rd Long Island City (11101) *(G-7778)*
Gem Mine Corp 516 367-1075
84 Cypress Dr Woodbury (11797) *(G-17309)*
Gem Reproduction Services Corp 845 298-0172
1299 Route 9 Ste 105 Wappingers Falls (12590) *(G-16590)*
Gem West Inc 631 567-4228
433 E Main St Unit 1 Patchogue (11772) *(G-13445)*
Gem-Bar Setting Inc 212 869-9238
15 W 46th St New York (10036) *(G-10310)*
Gemcor Automation LLC 716 674-9300
100 Gemcor Dr West Seneca (14224) *(G-16974)*
Gemfields USA Incorporated 212 398-5400
589 5th Ave Rm 909 New York (10017) *(G-10311)*
Gemini Manufactures 716 633-0306
160 Holtz Dr Cheektowaga (14225) *(G-3601)*
Gemini Manufacturing LLC 914 375-0855
56 Lafayette Ave Ste 380 White Plains (10603) *(G-17139)*
Gemini Pharmaceuticals Inc 631 543-3334
87 Modular Ave Ste 1 Commack (11725) *(G-3859)*
Gemoro Inc 212 768-8844
48 W 48th St Ste 1102 New York (10036) *(G-10312)*
Gemprint Corporation 212 997-0007
580 5th Ave Bsmt Ll05 New York (10036) *(G-10313)*
Gemson Graphics Inc 516 873-8400
820 Willis Ave Ste 2c Albertson (11507) *(G-158)*
Gemtrol Inc 716 894-0716
1800 Broadway St Bldg 1c Buffalo (14212) *(G-2983)*
Gemveto Jewelry Company Inc 212 755-2522
18 E 48th St Rm 501 New York (10017) *(G-10314)*

Gen Publishing Inc 914 834-3880
140 Huguenot St Fl 3 New Rochelle (10801) *(G-8950)*
Gen-West Associates LLC 315 255-1779
101 Columbus St Auburn (13021) *(G-496)*
Genco John 716 483-5446
71 River St Jamestown (14701) *(G-7028)*
Genencor Division Danisco US, Rochester Also called Danisco US Inc *(G-14321)*
Genencor International, Rochester Also called Danisco US Inc *(G-14322)*
General Art Company Inc 212 255-1298
14 E 38th St Fl 6 New York (10016) *(G-10315)*
General Art Framing, New York Also called General Art Company Inc *(G-10315)*
General Bearing Corporation (HQ) 845 358-6000
44 High St West Nyack (10994) *(G-16947)*
General Business Supply Inc 518 720-3939
2550 9th Ave Watervliet (12189) *(G-16709)*
General Chemical, Syracuse Also called Chemtrade Chemicals US LLC *(G-15912)*
General Cinema Bevs of Ohio 914 767-6000
1 Pepsi Way Ste 1 Somers (10589) *(G-15531)*
General Coatings Tech Inc (PA) 718 821-1232
24 Woodward Ave Ridgewood (11385) *(G-14120)*
General Composites Inc 518 963-7333
39 Myers Way Willsboro (12996) *(G-17289)*
General Control Systems Inc 518 270-8045
60 Cohoes Ave Ste 101 Green Island (12183) *(G-5873)*
General Cryogenic Tech LLC 516 334-8200
400 Shames Dr Westbury (11590) *(G-17018)*
General Cutting Inc 631 580-5011
90 13th Ave Unit 10 Ronkonkoma (11779) *(G-14932)*
General Diaries Corporation 516 371-2244
56 John St Inwood (11096) *(G-6797)*
General Die and Die Cutng Inc 516 665-3584
151 Babylon Tpke Roosevelt (11575) *(G-15028)*
General Electric Company 315 456-3304
5990 E Molloy Rd Syracuse (13211) *(G-15971)*
General Electric Company 315 554-2000
721 Visions Dr Skaneateles (13152) *(G-15482)*
General Electric Company 518 385-4022
1 River Rd Bldg 55 Schenectady (12305) *(G-15283)*
General Electric Company 518 385-2211
1 River Rd Bldg 33 Schenectady (12305) *(G-15284)*
General Electric Company 518 459-4110
11 Anderson Dr Albany (12205) *(G-82)*
General Electric Company 203 373-2756
1 River Rd Bldg 43 Schenectady (12345) *(G-15285)*
General Electric Company 518 385-3716
1 River Rd Schenectady (12345) *(G-15286)*
General Electric Company 585 593-2700
372 Andover Rd Wellsville (14895) *(G-16778)*
General Electric Company 518 746-5750
446 Lock 8 Way 8th Hudson Falls (12839) *(G-6673)*
General Electric Company 518 385-2211
1 River Rd Bldg 37 Schenectady (12345) *(G-15287)*
General Electric Company 845 567-7410
169 New York 17k 17 K Newburgh (12550) *(G-12778)*
General Electric Company 518 387-5000
1 Research Cir Schenectady (12309) *(G-15288)*
General Electric Company 518 385-7620
2690 Balltown Rd Bldg 600 Niskayuna (12309) *(G-12912)*
General Electric Company 518 385-3439
705 Corporation Park Schenectady (12302) *(G-15289)*
General Fibre Products Corp 516 358-7500
170 Nassau Terminal Rd New Hyde Park (11040) *(G-8880)*
General Fire-Proof Door Corp 718 893-5500
913 Edgewater Rd Bronx (10474) *(G-1344)*
General Galvanizing Sup Co Inc (PA) 718 589-4300
652 Whittier St Fl Mezz Bronx (10474) *(G-1345)*
General Led Corp 516 280-2854
206 E Jericho Tpke Mineola (11501) *(G-8545)*
General Media Strategies Inc 212 586-4141
483 10th Ave Rm 325 New York (10018) *(G-10316)*
General Microwave Corporation (HQ) 516 802-0900
227a Michael Dr Syosset (11791) *(G-15844)*
General Mills Inc 716 856-6060
54 S Michigan Ave Buffalo (14203) *(G-2984)*
General Mills Inc 716 856-6060
315 Ship Canal Pkwy Buffalo (14218) *(G-2985)*
General Motors LLC 315 764-2000
56 Chevrolet Rd Massena (13662) *(G-8226)*
General Motors LLC 716 879-5000
2995 River Rd 2 Buffalo (14207) *(G-2986)*
General Mtr Cmponents Holdings, Lockport Also called GM Components Holdings LLC *(G-7620)*
General Oil Equipment Co Inc (PA) 716 691-7012
60 John Glenn Dr Amherst (14228) *(G-242)*
General Plating Inc 585 423-0830
850 Saint Paul St Ste 10 Rochester (14605) *(G-14412)*
General Refining & Smelting 516 538-4747
106 Taft Ave Hempstead (11550) *(G-6294)*
General Refining Corporation 516 538-4747
59 Madison Ave Hempstead (11550) *(G-6295)*
General Semiconductor Inc 631 300-3818
150 Motor Pkwy Ste 101 Hauppauge (11788) *(G-6106)*

General Specialties, Shokan *Also called Mack Wood Working* ***(G-15455)***
General Splice Corporation....914 271-5131
Hwy 129 Croton On Hudson (10520) ***(G-4089)***
General Sportwear Company Inc (PA)....212 764-5820
230 W 38th St Fl 4 New York (10018) ***(G-10317)***
General Trade Mark La....718 979-7261
31 Hylan Blvd Apt 14c Staten Island (10305) ***(G-15698)***
General Traffic Equipment Corp....845 569-9000
259 Broadway Newburgh (12550) ***(G-12779)***
General Vy-Coat LLC....718 266-6002
1636 Coney Island Ave 2b Brooklyn (11230) ***(G-2019)***
General Welding & Fabg Inc (PA)....716 652-0033
991 Maple Rd Elma (14059) ***(G-4662)***
General Welding & Fabg Inc....716 681-8200
1 Walden Galleria Buffalo (14225) ***(G-2987)***
General Welding & Fabg Inc....585 697-7660
60 Saginaw Dr Ste 4 Rochester (14623) ***(G-14413)***
Generation Power LLC....315 234-2451
238 W Division St Syracuse (13204) ***(G-15972)***
Generic Compositors, Stamford *Also called Stone Crest Industries Inc* ***(G-15646)***
Generics Bidco I LLC....256 859-4011
1 Ram Ridge Rd Chestnut Ridge (10977) ***(G-3651)***
Genesco Inc....585 227-3080
271 Greece Rdg 69a Rochester (14626) ***(G-14414)***
Genesee Building Products LLC....585 548-2726
7982 Byron Stafford Rd Stafford (14143) ***(G-15640)***
Genesee County Express, Hornell *Also called Seneca Media Inc* ***(G-6593)***
Genesee Manufacturing Co Inc....585 266-3201
566 Hollenbeck St Rochester (14621) ***(G-14415)***
Genesee Metal Products Inc....585 968-6000
106 Railroad Ave Wellsville (14895) ***(G-16779)***
Genesee Metal Stampings Inc....585 475-0450
975 John St West Henrietta (14586) ***(G-16912)***
Genesee Plant, Piffard *Also called Arkema Inc* ***(G-13573)***
Genesee Precision Inc....585 344-0385
4300 Commerce Dr Batavia (14020) ***(G-636)***
Genesee Reserve Buffalo LLC....716 824-3116
300 Bailey Ave Buffalo (14210) ***(G-2988)***
Genesee Vly Met Finshg Co Inc....585 232-4412
244 Verona St Rochester (14608) ***(G-14416)***
Genesis Digital Imaging Inc....310 305-7358
150 Verona St Rochester (14608) ***(G-14417)***
Genesis Electl Motor, Woodside *Also called Genesis Electrical Motors* ***(G-17348)***
Genesis Electrical Motors....718 274-7030
6010 32nd Ave Woodside (11377) ***(G-17348)***
Genesis Machining Corp....516 377-1197
725 Brooklyn Ave North Baldwin (11510) ***(G-12922)***
Genesis Mannequins USA II Inc....212 505-6600
151 W 25th St Fl 4 New York (10001) ***(G-10318)***
Genesis One Unlimited....516 208-5863
600 Pinebrook Ave West Hempstead (11552) ***(G-16885)***
Genesis Vision Inc....585 254-0193
1260 Lyell Ave Rochester (14606) ***(G-14418)***
Genetic Engineering News, New Rochelle *Also called Gen Publishing Inc* ***(G-8950)***
Geneva Granite Co Inc (PA)....315 789-8142
272 Border City Rd Geneva (14456) ***(G-5590)***
Geneva Home Fashion LLC....212 213-8323
230 5th Ave Ste 612 New York (10001) ***(G-10319)***
Geneva Printing Company Inc....315 789-8191
40 Castle St Geneva (14456) ***(G-5591)***
Geneva Watch Company Inc (HQ)....212 221-1177
1407 Broadway Rm 400 New York (10018) ***(G-10320)***
Genie Fastener Mfg Co, Bohemia *Also called Treo Industries Inc* ***(G-1142)***
Genie Instant Printing Center, New York *Also called Genie Instant Printing Co Inc* ***(G-10321)***
Genie Instant Printing Co Inc....212 575-8258
37 W 43rd St New York (10036) ***(G-10321)***
Genius Media Group Inc....509 670-7502
92 3rd St Brooklyn (11231) ***(G-2020)***
Genius Tool Americas, Orchard Park *Also called Genius Tools Americas Corp* ***(G-13295)***
Genius Tools Americas Corp....716 662-6872
15 Cobham Dr Orchard Park (14127) ***(G-13295)***
Gennaris Itln French Bky Inc....516 997-8968
465 Westbury Ave Carle Place (11514) ***(G-3415)***
Genoa Sand & Gravel Lnsg....607 533-4551
390 Peruville Rd Freeville (13068) ***(G-5448)***
Genomeweb LLC....212 651-5636
40 Fulton St Rm 1002 New York (10038) ***(G-10322)***
Genpak, Glens Falls *Also called Great Pacific Entps US Inc* ***(G-5698)***
Genpak LLC....845 343-7971
Republic Plz Middletown (10940) ***(G-8476)***
Gentner Precision Components....315 597-5734
406 Stafford Rd Palmyra (14522) ***(G-13433)***
Geo Publishing, New York *Also called Emblaze Systems Inc* ***(G-10072)***
Geoffrey Beene Inc....212 371-5570
37 W 57th St Frnt 2 New York (10019) ***(G-10323)***
Geometric Circuits Inc....631 249-0230
920 Lincoln Ave Unit 1 Holbrook (11741) ***(G-6477)***
Geonex International Corp....212 473-4555
200 Park Ave S Ste 920 New York (10003) ***(G-10324)***
Geopump Inc....585 798-6666
213 State St Medina (14103) ***(G-8306)***
Geordie Magee Uphl & Canvas....315 676-7679
Weber Rd Brewerton (13029) ***(G-1200)***
George Basch Co Inc....516 378-8100
1554 Peapond Rd North Bellmore (11710) ***(G-12937)***
George Chilson Logging....607 732-1558
54 Franklin St Elmira (14904) ***(G-4699)***
George G Sharp Inc (PA)....212 732-2800
160 Broadway New York (10038) ***(G-10325)***
George Industries LLC....607 748-3371
1 S Page Ave Endicott (13760) ***(G-4818)***
George Knitting Mills Corp....212 242-3300
116 W 23rd St Fl 4 New York (10011) ***(G-10326)***
George Lederman Inc....212 753-4556
515 Madison Ave Rm 1218 New York (10022) ***(G-10327)***
George M Dujack....518 279-1303
80 Town Office Rd Troy (12180) ***(G-16258)***
George Ponte Inc....914 243-4202
500 E Main St Jefferson Valley (10535) ***(G-7090)***
George Raum Manufacturing, Central Islip *Also called Gmr Manufacturing Inc* ***(G-3524)***
George Retzos....315 422-2913
502 Pearl St Syracuse (13203) ***(G-15973)***
Georgia-Pacific LLC....518 561-3500
327 Margaret St Plattsburgh (12901) ***(G-13692)***
Georgia-Pacific LLC....518 346-6151
801 Corporation Park Schenectady (12302) ***(G-15290)***
Georgia-Pacific Corrugared LLC....585 343-3800
4 Etreadeasy Ave Batavia (14020) ***(G-637)***
Georgie Kaye, New York *Also called Georgy Creative Fashions Inc* ***(G-10328)***
Georgy Creative Fashions Inc....212 279-4885
249 W 29th St New York (10001) ***(G-10328)***
Geospatial Systems Inc (HQ)....585 427-8310
150 Lucius Gordon Dr # 211 West Henrietta (14586) ***(G-16913)***
Geosync Microwave Inc....631 760-5567
320 Oser Ave Hauppauge (11788) ***(G-6107)***
Geotec, Westbury *Also called Tishcon Corp* ***(G-17062)***
Geotech Associates Ltd....631 286-0251
20 Stiriz Rd Brookhaven (11719) ***(G-1507)***
Geotechnical Drilling Inc....516 616-6055
75 E 2nd St Mineola (11501) ***(G-8546)***
Geoweb3d Inc....607 323-1114
4104 Vestal Rd Ste 202 Vestal (13850) ***(G-16471)***
Gerald Frd Packg Display LLC (PA)....716 692-2705
550 Fillmore Ave Tonawanda (14150) ***(G-16182)***
Gerald McGlone....518 482-2613
17 Zoar Ave Colonie (12205) ***(G-3846)***
Geri-Gentle Corporation (PA)....917 804-7807
3841 Ocean View Ave Brooklyn (11224) ***(G-2021)***
Geritrex LLC....914 668-4003
144 E Kingsbridge Rd Mount Vernon (10550) ***(G-8727)***
Geritrex Holdings Inc (PA)....914 668-4003
144 E Kingsbridge Rd Mount Vernon (10550) ***(G-8728)***
Gerli & Co Inc (PA)....212 213-1919
41 Madison Ave Ste 4101 New York (10010) ***(G-10329)***
German Machine & Assembly Inc....585 546-4200
226 Jay St Rochester (14608) ***(G-14419)***
Germanium Corp America Inc....315 853-4900
34 Robinson Rd Clinton (13323) ***(G-3744)***
Germanium Corp America Inc....315 732-3744
1634 Lincoln Ave Utica (13502) ***(G-16360)***
Germanow-Simon Corporation....585 232-1440
408 Saint Paul St Rochester (14605) ***(G-14420)***
Gernatt Asphalt Products Inc (PA)....716 532-3371
13870 Taylor Hollow Rd Collins (14034) ***(G-3842)***
Gernatt Asphalt Products Inc....716 496-5111
Benz Dr Springville (14141) ***(G-15631)***
Gernatt Companies, Collins *Also called Gernatt Asphalt Products Inc* ***(G-3842)***
Gerome Technologies Inc....518 463-1324
85 Broadway Ste 1 Menands (12204) ***(G-8404)***
Gerson & Gerson Inc (PA)....212 244-6775
100 W 33rd St Ste 911 New York (10001) ***(G-10330)***
Gertrude Hawk Chocolates Inc....
21182 Salmon Run Mall Loo Watertown (13601) ***(G-16673)***
Get Real Surfaces Inc (PA)....845 337-4483
121 Washington St Poughkeepsie (12601) ***(G-13921)***
Getec Inc....845 292-0800
624 Harris Rd Ferndale (12734) ***(G-5178)***
Getinge Sourcing LLC....585 475-1400
1777 E Henrietta Rd Rochester (14623) ***(G-14421)***
Getinge Usa Inc (HQ)....800 475-9040
1777 E Henrietta Rd Rochester (14623) ***(G-14422)***
Getting The Word Out Inc....518 891-9352
36 Church St Apt 106 Saranac Lake (12983) ***(G-15165)***
Gevril, Valley Cottage *Also called First Sbf Holding Inc* ***(G-16404)***
Gfb Fashions Ltd....212 239-9230
463 Fashion Ave Rm 1502 New York (10018) ***(G-10331)***
Gfh Orthotic & Prosthetic Labs....631 467-3725
161 Keyland Ct Bohemia (11716) ***(G-1068)***
Gfl Amenities, Brooklyn *Also called Gfl USA Inc* ***(G-2022)***
Gfl USA Inc....917 297-8701
81 Prospect St Brooklyn (11201) ***(G-2022)***
Gg Design and Printing....718 321-3220
93 Henry St Frnt 1 New York (10002) ***(G-10332)***

ALPHABETIC

Ggp Publishing Inc 914 834-8896
105 Calvert St Ste 201 Harrison (10528) *(G-6004)*
GH Bass & Co (HQ) 646 768-4600
512 7th Ave Fl 28 New York (10018) *(G-10333)*
Gh Induction Atmospheres LLC 585 368-2120
35 Industrial Park Cir Rochester (14624) *(G-14423)*
Ghani Textiles Inc 718 859-4561
2459 Coyle St Fl 2 Brooklyn (11235) *(G-2023)*
Gharana Industries LLC 315 651-4004
61 Swift St Waterloo (13165) *(G-16649)*
Giagni Enterprises, Mount Vernon *Also called Promptus Electronic Hdwr Inc (G-8767)*
Giagni Enterprises LLC 914 699-6500
550 S Columbus Ave Mount Vernon (10550) *(G-8729)*
Giagni International Corp 914 699-6500
548 S Columbus Ave Mount Vernon (10550) *(G-8730)*
Gibar Inc 315 452-5656
7838 Brewerton Rd Cicero (13039) *(G-3675)*
Gibraltar Industries Inc (PA) 716 826-6500
3556 Lake Shore Rd # 100 Buffalo (14219) *(G-2989)*
Gifford Group Inc 212 569-8500
250 Dyckman St New York (10034) *(G-10334)*
Gift Valleys.com, Ronkonkoma *Also called Bobley-Harmann Corporation (G-14908)*
Gifts Software Inc 904 438-6000
360 Lexington Ave Rm 601 New York (10017) *(G-10335)*
Gig-It, New York *Also called 212 Db Corp (G-9011)*
Gigi New York, Melville *Also called Graphic Image Incorporated (G-8353)*
Gilber Braid, New York *Also called Tamber Knits Inc (G-12298)*
Gild-Rite Inc 631 752-9000
51 Carolyn Blvd Farmingdale (11735) *(G-5006)*
Gildan Apparel USA Inc (HQ) 212 476-0341
48 W 38th St Fl 8 New York (10018) *(G-10336)*
Gildan Media Corp 718 459-6299
6631 Wetherole St Flushing (11374) *(G-5251)*
Gilded Otter Brewing Co 845 256-1700
3 Main St New Paltz (12561) *(G-8919)*
Giliberto Designs Inc 212 695-0216
142 W 36th St Fl 8 New York (10018) *(G-10337)*
Gillette Creamery, Albany *Also called Phyljohn Distributors Inc (G-120)*
Gillies Coffee Company 718 499-7766
150 19th St Brooklyn (11232) *(G-2024)*
Gillinder Brothers Inc 845 856-5375
39 Erie St 55 Port Jervis (12771) *(G-13807)*
Gillinder Glass, Port Jervis *Also called Gillinder Brothers Inc (G-13807)*
Gilmores Sound Advice Inc 212 265-4445
599 11th Ave Fl 5 New York (10036) *(G-10338)*
Gim Electronics Corp 516 942-3382
270 Duffy Ave Ste H Hicksville (11801) *(G-6377)*
Gimbel & Associates, Garden City *Also called H&E Service Corp (G-5522)*
Gina Group LLC 212 947-2445
10 W 33rd St Ph 3 New York (10001) *(G-10339)*
Gina Hosiery, New York *Also called Gina Group LLC (G-10339)*
Ginny Lee Cafe, Lodi *Also called Wagner Vineyards & Brewing Co (G-7666)*
Giovane Ltd 212 332-7373
592 5th Ave Ste L New York (10036) *(G-10340)*
Giovane Piranesi, New York *Also called Giovane Ltd (G-10340)*
Giovanni Bakery Corp 212 695-4296
476 9th Ave New York (10018) *(G-10341)*
Giovanni Food Co Inc (PA) 315 457-2373
8800 Sixty Rd Baldwinsville (13027) *(G-569)*
Giuliante Machine Tool Inc 914 835-0008
12 John Walsh Blvd Peekskill (10566) *(G-13502)*
Giulietta LLC 212 334-1859
649 Morgan Ave Ste 3h Brooklyn (11222) *(G-2025)*
Giumenta Corp (PA) 718 832-1200
42 2nd Ave Brooklyn (11215) *(G-2026)*
Givaudan Fragrances Corp 212 649-8800
40 W 57th St Fl 11 New York (10019) *(G-10342)*
Givi Inc 212 586-5029
16 W 56th St Fl 4 New York (10019) *(G-10343)*
Gizmo Products Inc 585 301-0970
205 Seneca Pkwy Rochester (14613) *(G-14424)*
GKN Aerospace Monitor Inc 562 619-8558
1000 New Horizons Blvd Amityville (11701) *(G-288)*
GL & RL Logging Inc 518 883-3936
713 Union Mills Rd Broadalbin (12025) *(G-1241)*
GL&v USA Inc 518 747-2444
27 Allen St Hudson Falls (12839) *(G-6674)*
GL&v USA Inc (HQ) 518 747-2444
27 Allen St Hudson Falls (12839) *(G-6675)*
Glaceau, New York *Also called Energy Brands Inc (G-10089)*
Glacee Skincare LLC 212 690-7632
611 W 136th St Apt 4 New York (10031) *(G-10344)*
Gladding Braided Products LLC 315 653-7211
1 Gladding St South Otselic (13155) *(G-15555)*
Glamour Magazine 212 286-2860
4 Times Sq Fl 16 New York (10036) *(G-10345)*
Glamourpuss Nyc LLC 212 722-1370
1305 Madison Ave New York (10128) *(G-10346)*
Glaro Inc 631 234-1717
735 Calebs Path Ste 1 Hauppauge (11788) *(G-6108)*
Glasbau Hahn America LLC 845 566-3331
15 Little Brook Ln Ste 2 Newburgh (12550) *(G-12780)*
Glasgow Products Inc 516 374-5937
886 Lakeside Dr Woodmere (11598) *(G-17331)*
Glass Apps LLC (PA) 310 987-1536
11 Times Sq Ste 15 New York (10036) *(G-10347)*
Glass Star America Inc 631 291-9432
15 Frowein Rd Bldg E2 Center Moriches (11934) *(G-3491)*
Glassbox US Inc 917 378-2933
234 5th Ave Ste 207 New York (10001) *(G-10348)*
Glasses USA LLC 212 784-6094
954 Lexington Ave Ste 537 New York (10021) *(G-10349)*
Glassesusa.com, New York *Also called Glasses USA LLC (G-10349)*
Glassfab Inc 585 262-4000
257 Ormond St Rochester (14605) *(G-14425)*
Glassteel Parts and Services, Rochester *Also called Pfaudler Inc (G-14598)*
Glassview LLC (PA) 646 844-4922
25 E 67th St Ph A New York (10065) *(G-10350)*
Glasteel Parts & Services Inc (HQ) 585 235-1010
1000 West Ave Rochester (14611) *(G-14426)*
Glaxosmithkline LLC 845 341-7590
3 Tyler St Montgomery (12549) *(G-8630)*
Glaxosmithkline LLC 845 797-3259
6 Alpert Dr Wappingers Falls (12590) *(G-16591)*
Glaxosmithkline LLC 585 738-9025
1177 Winton Rd S Rochester (14618) *(G-14427)*
Glaxosmithkline LLC 716 913-5679
17 Mahogany Dr Buffalo (14221) *(G-2990)*
Glaxosmithkline LLC 518 239-6901
3169 Route 145 East Durham (12423) *(G-4409)*
Glaxosmithkline LLC 518 852-9637
108 Woodfield Blvd Mechanicville (12118) *(G-8259)*
Glaxosmthkline Cnsmr Heathcare, East Durham *Also called Glaxosmithkline LLC (G-4409)*
Gleaner Company Ltd 718 657-0788
9205 172nd St Fl 2 Jamaica (11433) *(G-6951)*
Gleason Corporation (PA) 585 473-1000
1000 University Ave Rochester (14607) *(G-14428)*
Gleason Works (HQ) 585 473-1000
1000 University Ave Rochester (14607) *(G-14429)*
Gleason-Avery, Auburn *Also called John G Rubino Inc (G-502)*
Glen Plaza Marble & Gran Inc 516 671-1100
75 Glen Cove Ave Ste A Glen Cove (11542) *(G-5630)*
Glenda Inc 718 442-8981
1732 Victory Blvd Staten Island (10314) *(G-15699)*
Glendale Architectural WD Pdts 718 326-2700
7102 80th St Glendale (11385) *(G-5669)*
Glendale Products, Glendale *Also called Glendale Architectural WD Pdts (G-5669)*
Glenn Foods Inc (PA) 516 377-1400
371 S Main St Ste 119-405 Freeport (11520) *(G-5413)*
Glenn Wayne Bakery, Bohemia *Also called Glenn Wayne Wholesale Bky Inc (G-1069)*
Glenn Wayne Wholesale Bky Inc 631 289-9200
1800 Artic Ave Bohemia (11716) *(G-1069)*
Glenny's, Freeport *Also called Glenn Foods Inc (G-5413)*
Glennys Inc 516 377-1400
1960 59th St Brooklyn (11204) *(G-2027)*
Glenora Wine Cellars Inc 607 243-9500
5435 State Route 14 Dundee (14837) *(G-4353)*
Glenridge Fabricators Inc 718 456-2297
7945 77th Ave Glendale (11385) *(G-5670)*
Glens Falls Business Forms Inc 518 798-6643
10 Ferguson Ln Queensbury (12804) *(G-14009)*
Glens Falls Newspapers Inc 518 792-3131
76 Lawrence St Glens Falls (12801) *(G-5696)*
Glens Falls Printing LLC 518 793-0555
51 Hudson Ave Glens Falls (12801) *(G-5697)*
Glens Falls Ready Mix Inc (HQ) 518 793-1695
774 State Highway 5s Amsterdam (12010) *(G-348)*
Glens Falls Ready Mix Inc 518 793-1695
112 Big Boom Rd Queensbury (12804) *(G-14010)*
Glenwood Cast Stone Inc 718 859-6500
4106 Glenwood Rd Brooklyn (11210) *(G-2028)*
Glenwood Mason Supply, Brooklyn *Also called Glenwood Cast Stone Inc (G-2028)*
Glenwood Masonry Products, Brooklyn *Also called Superior Block Corp (G-2647)*
Gli-Dex Sales Corp 716 692-6501
855 Wurlitzer Dr North Tonawanda (14120) *(G-12992)*
Glidden Machine & Tool, North Tonawanda *Also called Gli-Dex Sales Corp (G-12992)*
Glidden Professional Paint Ctr, Rochester *Also called PPG Architectural Finishes Inc (G-14610)*
Gliptone Manufacturing Inc 631 285-7250
1740 Julia Goldbach Ave Ronkonkoma (11779) *(G-14933)*
Glissade New York LLC 631 756-4800
399 Smith St Farmingdale (11735) *(G-5007)*
Glissen Chemical Co Inc (PA) 718 436-4200
1321 58th St Brooklyn (11219) *(G-2029)*
Glitner Ticketing, Levittown *Also called Glitnir Ticketing Inc (G-7450)*
Glitnir Ticketing Inc 516 390-5168
3 Snapdragon Ln Levittown (11756) *(G-7450)*
Glitter, New York *Also called Magic Numbers Inc (G-11132)*
Glk Foods LLC 585 289-4414
11 Clark St Shortsville (14548) *(G-15456)*

Globa Phoni Compu Techn Solut (PA)....607 257-7279
21 Dutch Mill Rd Ithaca (14850) ***(G-6879)***
Global Abrasive Products Inc (PA)....716 438-0047
62 Mill St Lockport (14094) ***(G-7617)***
Global Alliance For Tb....212 227-7540
40 Wall St Fl 24 New York (10005) ***(G-10351)***
Global Alumina Corporation (PA)....212 351-0000
277 Park Ave Fl 40 New York (10172) ***(G-10352)***
Global Alumina Services Co....212 309-8060
277 Park Ave Fl 40 New York (10172) ***(G-10353)***
Global Applctions Solution LLC....212 741-9595
125 Park Ave Fl 25 New York (10017) ***(G-10354)***
Global Brands Inc....845 358-1212
1031 Route 9w S Nyack (10960) ***(G-13068)***
Global Creations, New York *Also called Global Gem Corporation* ***(G-10358)***
Global Earth Energy....716 332-7150
534 Delaware Ave Ste 412 Buffalo (14202) ***(G-2991)***
Global Entity Media Inc....631 580-7772
2090 5th Ave Ste 2 Ronkonkoma (11779) ***(G-14934)***
Global Finance Magazine....212 524-3223
7 E 20th St New York (10003) ***(G-10355)***
Global Finance Magazine., New York *Also called Global Finance Media Inc* ***(G-10356)***
Global Finance Magazine., New York *Also called Global Finance Magazine* ***(G-10355)***
Global Finance Media Inc....212 447-7900
7 E 20th St Fl 2 New York (10003) ***(G-10356)***
Global Financial Shared Svcs, Seneca Falls *Also called Xylem Inc* ***(G-15397)***
Global Fire Corporation....888 320-1799
244 5th Ave Ste 2238 New York (10001) ***(G-10357)***
Global Food Source & Co Inc....914 320-9615
114 Carpenter Ave Tuckahoe (10707) ***(G-16294)***
Global Gem Corporation....212 350-9936
425 Madison Ave Rm 400 New York (10017) ***(G-10358)***
Global Glass Corp....516 681-2309
134 Woodbury Rd Hicksville (11801) ***(G-6378)***
Global Gold Inc....212 239-4657
1410 Broadway Fl 8 New York (10018) ***(G-10359)***
Global Gold Corporation (PA)....914 925-0020
555 Theodore Fremd Ave C208 Rye (10580) ***(G-15084)***
Global Graphics Inc....718 939-4967
3711 Prince St Ste D Flushing (11354) ***(G-5252)***
Global Grind Digital....212 840-9399
512 Fashion Ave Fl 42 New York (10018) ***(G-10360)***
Global Instrumentation LLC....315 682-0272
8104 Cazenovia Rd Ste 2/3 Manlius (13104) ***(G-8105)***
Global Lighting Inc....914 591-4095
201 Saw Mill River Rd 3 Yonkers (10701) ***(G-17463)***
Global Marine Power Inc....631 208-2933
221 Scott Ave Calverton (11933) ***(G-3319)***
Global Market Development Inc....631 667-1002
200 Executive Dr Ste G Edgewood (11717) ***(G-4613)***
Global Natural Foods Inc....845 439-3292
672 Old Route 17 Rear Ofc Livingston Manor (12758) ***(G-7589)***
Global Payment Tech Inc....516 887-0700
20 E Sunrise Hwy Valley Stream (11581) ***(G-16434)***
Global Payment Tech Inc (PA)....631 563-2500
170 Wilbur Pl Ste 600 Bohemia (11716) ***(G-1070)***
Global Plastics LP....800 417-4605
21 Downing St Frnt 1 New York (10014) ***(G-10361)***
Global Precision Products, Rush *Also called Gpp Post-Closing Inc* ***(G-15075)***
Global Resources Sg Inc....212 686-1411
267 5th Ave Rm 506 New York (10016) ***(G-10362)***
Global Security Tech LLC....917 838-4507
1407 Broadway Fl 30 New York (10018) ***(G-10363)***
Global Steel Products Corp (HQ)....631 586-3455
95 Marcus Blvd Deer Park (11729) ***(G-4169)***
Global Textile, New York *Also called Himatsingka America Inc* ***(G-10524)***
Global Tissue Group Inc (PA)....631 924-3019
870 Expressway Dr S Medford (11763) ***(G-8276)***
Global Video LLC (HQ)....516 222-2600
1000 Woodbury Rd Ste 1 Woodbury (11797) ***(G-17310)***
Globalfoundries US 2 LLC (HQ)....512 457-3900
2070 Route 52 Hopewell Junction (12533) ***(G-6577)***
Globalfoundries US Inc....512 457-3900
2070 Route 52 Hopewell Junction (12533) ***(G-6578)***
Globalfoundries US Inc....518 305-9013
400 Stone Break Rd Ext Malta (12020) ***(G-8051)***
Globalfoundries US Inc....408 462-3900
107 Hermes Rd Ballston Spa (12020) ***(G-595)***
Globalquest Solutions Inc....716 601-3524
2813 Wehrle Dr Ste 3 Buffalo (14221) ***(G-2992)***
Globe Electronic Hardware Inc....718 457-0303
3424 56th St Woodside (11377) ***(G-17349)***
Globe Grinding Corp....631 694-1970
1365 Akron St Copiague (11726) ***(G-3929)***
Globe Metallurgical Inc....716 804-0862
3807 Highland Ave Niagara Falls (14305) ***(G-12844)***
Globe Specialty Metals, Niagara Falls *Also called Globe Metallurgical Inc* ***(G-12844)***
Globe-Tex, New Rochelle *Also called HB Athletic Inc* ***(G-8955)***
Globe-Tex Apparal, New York *Also called Tbhl International LLC* ***(G-12307)***
Globecomm Systems Inc (HQ)....631 231-9800
45 Oser Ave Hauppauge (11788) ***(G-6109)***
Globex Kosher Foods Inc....718 630-5555
5600 1st Ave Ste 19 Brooklyn (11220) ***(G-2030)***
Globmarble LLC....347 717-4088
2201 Neptune Ave Ste 5 Brooklyn (11224) ***(G-2031)***
Globus Cork Inc....347 963-4059
741 E 136th St Bronx (10454) ***(G-1346)***
Gloede Neon Signs Ltd Inc....845 471-4366
97 N Clinton St Poughkeepsie (12601) ***(G-13922)***
Glopak USA Corp (PA)....347 869-9252
1816 127th St Ste 2 College Point (11356) ***(G-3809)***
Glopak USA Corp....516 433-3214
35 Engel St Ste B Hicksville (11801) ***(G-6379)***
Gloria Apparel Inc....212 947-0869
256 W 38th St Fl 700 New York (10018) ***(G-10364)***
Glowa Manufacturing Inc....607 770-0811
6 Emma St Binghamton (13905) ***(G-913)***
Gluck Orgelbau Inc....212 233-2684
170 Park Row Apt 20a New York (10038) ***(G-10365)***
Gluten Free Bake Shop Inc....845 782-5307
19 Industry Dr Mountainville (10953) ***(G-8793)***
Glycobia Inc....607 339-0051
33 Thornwood Dr Ste 104 Ithaca (14850) ***(G-6880)***
Glyph Production Technologies, Cortland *Also called Technologies Application LLC* ***(G-4070)***
GM Components Holdings LLC....716 439-2237
200 Upper Mountain Rd Lockport (14094) ***(G-7618)***
GM Components Holdings LLC....585 647-7000
1000 Lexington Ave Rochester (14606) ***(G-14430)***
GM Components Holdings LLC....716 439-2463
200 Upper Mountain Rd Lockport (14094) ***(G-7619)***
GM Components Holdings LLC....716 439-2011
200 Upper Mountain Rd # 7 Lockport (14094) ***(G-7620)***
GM Components Holdings LLC....716 439-2402
200 Upper Mountain Rd # 10 Lockport (14094) ***(G-7621)***
GM Ice Cream Inc....646 236-7383
8911 207th St Queens Village (11427) ***(G-13993)***
GM Insulation Corp....516 354-6000
1345 Rosser Ave Elmont (11003) ***(G-4732)***
GM Palmer Inc....585 492-2990
51 Edward St Arcade (14009) ***(G-393)***
GM Pre Cast Products, Jamestown *Also called Suhor Industries Inc* ***(G-7064)***
GM Printing, Long Island City *Also called Grand Meridian Printing Inc* ***(G-7781)***
GM Sheet Metal Inc....718 349-2830
193 Newell St Brooklyn (11222) ***(G-2032)***
GMC Mercantile Corp....212 498-9488
231 W 39th St Rm 612 New York (10018) ***(G-10366)***
Gmch Lockport, Lockport *Also called GM Components Holdings LLC* ***(G-7619)***
Gmch Lockport Ptc, Lockport *Also called GM Components Holdings LLC* ***(G-7618)***
Gmch Rochester, Rochester *Also called GM Components Holdings LLC* ***(G-14430)***
Gmd Industries Inc....718 445-8779
12920 18th Ave College Point (11356) ***(G-3810)***
Gmp LLC....914 939-0571
47 Purdy Ave Port Chester (10573) ***(G-13774)***
Gmr Manufacturing Inc....631 582-2600
101 Windsor Pl Unit D Central Islip (11722) ***(G-3524)***
Gms Hicks Street Corporation....718 858-1010
214 Hicks St Brooklyn (11201) ***(G-2033)***
Gn Printing....718 784-1713
4216 34th Ave Long Island City (11101) ***(G-7779)***
Gncc Capital Inc (PA)....702 951-9793
244 5th Ave Ste 2525 New York (10001) ***(G-10367)***
GNI Commerce Inc....347 275-1155
458 Neptune Ave Apt 11f Brooklyn (11224) ***(G-2034)***
Gnosis Chocolate Inc....646 688-5549
4003 27th St Long Island City (11101) ***(G-7780)***
Gny Equipment LLC....631 667-1010
20 Drexel Dr Bay Shore (11706) ***(G-701)***
Go Blue Technologies Ltd....631 404-6285
325 August Rd North Babylon (11703) ***(G-12918)***
Go Go Apple Inc....646 264-8909
4126 Benham St Elmhurst (11373) ***(G-4674)***
Go Mobo, New York *Also called Mobo Systems Inc* ***(G-11314)***
Gocare247, Brooklyn *Also called Mdcare911 LLC* ***(G-2291)***
Goddard Design Co....718 599-0170
51 Nassau Ave Ste 1b Brooklyn (11222) ***(G-2035)***
Godiva Chocolatier Inc (HQ)....212 984-5900
333 W 34th St Fl 6 New York (10001) ***(G-10368)***
Godiva Chocolatier Inc....718 271-3603
9015 Queens Blvd Ste 2045 Elmhurst (11373) ***(G-4675)***
Godiva Chocolatier Inc....718 677-1452
5378 Kings Plz Brooklyn (11234) ***(G-2036)***
Godiva Chocolatier Inc....212 809-8990
33 Maiden Ln Frnt 1 New York (10038) ***(G-10369)***
Goergen-Mackwirth Co Inc....716 874-4800
765 Hertel Ave Buffalo (14207) ***(G-2993)***
Gold & Diamonds Wholesale Outl....718 438-7888
4417 5th Ave Brooklyn (11220) ***(G-2037)***
Gold Coast Gazette, Glen Cove *Also called Kch Publications Inc* ***(G-5632)***
Gold Mark Mfg Co, Brooklyn *Also called Goldmark Inc* ***(G-2039)***
Gold Medal Packing Inc....315 337-1911
8301 Old River Rd Oriskany (13424) ***(G-13334)***
Gold Pride Press Inc....585 224-8800
12 Pixley Industrial Pkwy # 40 Rochester (14624) ***(G-14431)***

ALPHABETIC

Gold Pure Food Products Co Inc — 516 483-5600
1 Brooklyn Rd Hempstead (11550) *(G-6296)*

Goldarama Company Inc — 212 730-7299
56 W 45th St Ste 1504 New York (10036) *(G-10370)*

Goldberg Prosthetic & Orthotic — 631 689-6606
9 Technology Dr East Setauket (11733) *(G-4502)*

Goldberger Company LLC (PA) — 212 924-1194
36 W 25th St Fl 14 New York (10010) *(G-10371)*

Goldberger International, New York Also called Goldberger Company LLC *(G-10371)*

Golden Artist Colors Inc — 607 847-6154
188 Bell Rd New Berlin (13411) *(G-8827)*

Golden Bridge Group Inc — 718 335-8882
7416 Grand Ave Elmhurst (11373) *(G-4676)*

Golden Eagle Marketing LLC — 212 726-1242
244 5th Ave New York (10001) *(G-10372)*

Golden Egret LLC — 516 922-2839
38 Cord Pl East Norwich (11732) *(G-4465)*

Golden Glow Cookie Co Inc — 718 379-6223
1844 Givan Ave Bronx (10469) *(G-1347)*

Golden Group International Ltd — 845 440-1025
305 Quaker Rd Patterson (12563) *(G-13464)*

Golden Horse Enterprise NY Inc — 212 594-3339
70 W 36th St Rm 12e New York (10018) *(G-10373)*

Golden Integrity Inc — 212 764-6753
37 W 47th St Ste 1601 New York (10036) *(G-10374)*

Golden Leaves Knitwear Inc — 718 875-8235
43 Hall St Ste B3 Brooklyn (11205) *(G-2038)*

Golden Legacy Ilstrd Histry, Yonkers Also called Fitzgerald Publishing Co Inc *(G-17459)*

Golden Pacific Lxj Inc — 267 975-6537
156 W 56th St Ste 2002 New York (10019) *(G-10375)*

Golden Renewable Energy LLC — 914 920-9800
700 Nepperhan Ave Yonkers (10703) *(G-17464)*

Golden Taste Inc — 845 356-4133
318 Roosevelt Ave Spring Valley (10977) *(G-15609)*

Goldmark Inc — 718 438-0295
3611 14th Ave Ste B01 Brooklyn (11218) *(G-2039)*

Goldmark Products Inc — 631 777-3343
855 Conklin St Ste D Farmingdale (11735) *(G-5008)*

Goldmont Enterprises Inc — 212 947-3633
7603 Caldwell Ave Middle Village (11379) *(G-8444)*

Goldsmith, Binghamton Also called Mellem Corporation *(G-931)*

Goldstar Lighting LLC — 646 543-6811
1407 Broadway Fl 30 New York (10018) *(G-10376)*

Golf Directories USA Inc — 516 365-5351
39 Orchard St Ste 7 Manhasset (11030) *(G-8094)*

Golfing Magazine — 516 822-5446
22 W Nicholai St Ste 200 Hicksville (11801) *(G-6380)*

Golos Printing Inc — 607 732-1896
110 E 9th St Elmira Heights (14903) *(G-4723)*

Golub Corporation — 518 943-3903
320 W Bridge St Catskill (12414) *(G-3456)*

Golub Corporation — 518 899-6063
3 Hemphill Pl Ste 116 Malta (12020) *(G-8052)*

Golub Corporation — 315 363-0679
142 Genesee St Oneida (13421) *(G-13177)*

Golub Corporation — 607 336-2588
5631 State Highway 12 Norwich (13815) *(G-13047)*

Golub Corporation — 518 583-3697
3045 Route 50 Saratoga Springs (12866) *(G-15183)*

Golub Corporation — 518 822-0076
351 Fairview Ave Ste 3 Hudson (12534) *(G-6645)*

Golub Corporation — 607 235-7240
33 Chenango Bridge Rd Binghamton (13901) *(G-914)*

Golub Corporation — 845 344-0327
511 Schutt Road Ext Middletown (10940) *(G-8477)*

Gone South Concrete Block Inc — 315 598-2141
2809 State Route 3 Fulton (13069) *(G-5473)*

Good Bread Bakery — 914 939-3900
33 New Broad St Ste 1 Port Chester (10573) *(G-13775)*

Good Earth Inc — 716 684-8111
5960 Broadway St Lancaster (14086) *(G-7341)*

Good Earth Organics Corp (PA) — 716 684-8111
5960 Broadway St Lancaster (14086) *(G-7342)*

Good Health Healthcare Newsppr — 585 421-8109
106 Cobblestone Court Dr Victor (14564) *(G-16503)*

Good Home Co Inc — 212 352-1509
132 W 24th St New York (10011) *(G-10377)*

Good Show Sportswear, New York Also called Good Show Sportwear Inc *(G-10378)*

Good Show Sportwear Inc — 212 334-8751
132 Mulberry St 3 New York (10013) *(G-10378)*

Good Times Magazine — 516 280-2100
346 Westbury Ave Ste Ll Carle Place (11514) *(G-3416)*

Gooding & Associates Inc — 631 749-3313
15 Dinah Rock Rd Shelter Island (11964) *(G-15409)*

Gooding Co Inc — 716 434-5501
5568 Davison Rd Lockport (14094) *(G-7622)*

Goodman Main Stopper Mfg Co — 718 875-5140
523 Atlantic Ave Brooklyn (11217) *(G-2040)*

Goodnature Products Inc (PA) — 716 855-3325
3860 California Rd Orchard Park (14127) *(G-13296)*

Goodo Beverage Company — 718 328-6400
1801 Boone Ave Bronx (10460) *(G-1348)*

Goodrich Corporation — 315 838-1200
104 Otis St Rome (13441) *(G-14840)*

Goodwill Inds of Greater NY — 914 621-0781
80 Route 6 Unit 605 Baldwin Place (10505) *(G-562)*

Goodwill Wstn NY Inc — 716 633-3305
4311 Transit Rd Williamsville (14221) *(G-17272)*

Goodyear, Tonawanda Also called Sumitomo Rubber Usa LLC *(G-16223)*

Gorbel Inc (PA) — 585 924-6262
600 Fishers Run Fishers (14453) *(G-5186)*

Gorbel Inc — 800 821-0086
600 Fishers Run Victor (14564) *(G-16504)*

Gorden Automotive Equipment — 716 674-2700
60 N America Dr West Seneca (14224) *(G-16975)*

Gordon Fire Equipment LLC — 845 691-5700
3199 Us Highway 9w Highland (12528) *(G-6431)*

Gordon S Anderson Mfg Co — 845 677-3304
215 N Mabbettsville Rd Millbrook (12545) *(G-8511)*

Gorga Fehren Fine Jewelry LLC — 646 861-3595
153 E 88th St New York (10128) *(G-10379)*

Gorilla Coffee Inc — 917 297-8947
472 Bergen St Ste A Brooklyn (11217) *(G-2041)*

Gorilla Coffee Inc (PA) — 718 230-3244
97 5th Ave Brooklyn (11217) *(G-2042)*

Goshen Quarry, Goshen Also called Tilcon New York Inc *(G-5754)*

Got Power Inc — 631 767-9493
5 Campus Ln Ronkonkoma (11779) *(G-14935)*

Got Wood LLC — 315 440-8857
28 North St Cleveland (13042) *(G-3718)*

Gotenna Inc — 415 894-2616
81 Willoughby St Fl 3 Brooklyn (11201) *(G-2043)*

Gotham City Industries Inc — 914 713-0979
372 Fort Hill Rd Scarsdale (10583) *(G-15247)*

Gotham Diamonds, New York Also called American Originals Corporation *(G-9177)*

Gotham Energy 360 LLC — 917 338-1023
48 Wall St Fl 5 New York (10005) *(G-10380)*

Gotham Ink & Color Co Inc — 845 947-4000
19 Holt Dr Stony Point (10980) *(G-15795)*

Gotham Ink Corp — 516 677-1969
19 Teibrook Ave Syosset (11791) *(G-15845)*

Gotham Pen and Pencil, Yonkers Also called Gotham Pen Co Inc *(G-17465)*

Gotham Pen Co Inc — 212 675-7904
1 Roundtop Rd Yonkers (10710) *(G-17465)*

Gotham T-Shirt Corp — 516 676-0900
211 Glen Cove Ave Unit 5 Sea Cliff (11579) *(G-15363)*

Gotham Veterinary Center PC — 212 222-1900
700 Columbus Ave Frnt 5 New York (10025) *(G-10381)*

Gottavape — 518 945-8273
1870 Altamont Ave Schenectady (12303) *(G-15291)*

Gottlieb & Sons Inc — 212 575-1907
21 W 47th St Fl 4 New York (10036) *(G-10382)*

Gottlieb Jewelery Mfg, New York Also called Gottlieb & Sons Inc *(G-10382)*

Gottlieb Schwartz Family — 718 761-2010
724 Collfield Ave Staten Island (10314) *(G-15700)*

Goulds Pumps, Seneca Falls Also called ITT Water Technology Inc *(G-15388)*

Goulds Pumps Incorporated, Seneca Falls Also called Goulds Pumps LLC *(G-15382)*

Goulds Pumps Incorporated — 315 258-4949
1 Goulds Dr Auburn (13021) *(G-497)*

Goulds Pumps LLC (HQ) — 315 568-2811
240 Fall St Seneca Falls (13148) *(G-15382)*

Gourmet Boutique LLC (PA) — 718 977-1200
14402 158th St Jamaica (11434) *(G-6952)*

Gourmet Connection, Baldwinsville Also called Capco Marketing *(G-567)*

Gourmet Crafts Inc — 718 372-0505
152 Highlawn Ave Brooklyn (11223) *(G-2044)*

Gourmet Guru Inc — 718 842-2828
1123 Worthen St Bronx (10474) *(G-1349)*

Gourmet Toast Corp — 718 852-4536
345 Park Ave Brooklyn (11205) *(G-2045)*

Government Data Publication — 347 789-8719
1661 Mcdonald Ave Brooklyn (11230) *(G-2046)*

Gowanda - Bti LLC — 716 492-4081
7426a Tanner Pkwy Arcade (14009) *(G-394)*

Goya Foods Inc — 716 549-0076
200 S Main St Angola (14006) *(G-380)*

Goya Foods Great Lakes, Angola Also called Goya Foods Inc *(G-380)*

Goyard Inc (HQ) — 212 813-0005
20 E 63rd St New York (10065) *(G-10383)*

Goyard Miami LLC (HQ) — 212 813-0005
20 E 63rd St New York (10065) *(G-10384)*

Goyard US, New York Also called Goyard Inc *(G-10383)*

Gpc International Inc (PA) — 631 752-9600
510 Broadhollow Rd # 205 Melville (11747) *(G-8351)*

Gpi Equipment Company, Jefferson Valley Also called George Ponte Inc *(G-7090)*

GPM Associates LLC — 585 335-3940
10 Forbes St Dansville (14437) *(G-4103)*

GPM Associates LLC — 585 359-1770
45 High Tech Dr Ste 100 Rush (14543) *(G-15074)*

Gpp Post-Closing Inc — 585 334-4640
90 High Tech Dr Rush (14543) *(G-15075)*

Gpt, Bohemia Also called Global Payment Tech Inc *(G-1070)*

ALPHABETIC SECTION — Great North Road Media Inc

Gq Magazine 212 286-2860
  4 Times Sq Fl 9 New York (10036) *(G-10385)*
Grace Associates Inc 718 767-9000
  470 West St Harrison (10528) *(G-6005)*
Grace Ryan & Magnus Mllwk LLC 914 665-0902
  17 N Bleeker St Mount Vernon (10550) *(G-8731)*
Grace Wheeler 716 664-6501
  118 E 1st St Jamestown (14701) *(G-7029)*
Gradian Health Systems Inc 212 537-0340
  915 Broadway Ste 1001 New York (10010) *(G-10386)*
Gradient Lens Corporation 585 235-2620
  207 Tremont St Ste 1 Rochester (14608) *(G-14432)*
Grado Group Inc 718 556-4200
  66 Willow Ave Staten Island (10305) *(G-15701)*
Grado Laboratories Inc 718 435-5340
  4614 7th Ave Ste 1 Brooklyn (11220) *(G-2047)*
Graham Corporation (PA) 585 343-2216
  20 Florence Ave Batavia (14020) *(G-638)*
Gramco Inc (PA) 716 592-2845
  299 Waverly St Springville (14141) *(G-15632)*
Gramercy Jewelry Mfg Corp 212 268-0461
  35 W 45th St Fl 5 New York (10036) *(G-10387)*
Granada Electronics Inc 718 387-1157
  485 Kent Ave Brooklyn (11249) *(G-2048)*
Grand Central Publishing (HQ) 212 364-1200
  1290 Ave Of The Americas New York (10104) *(G-10388)*
Grand Island Animal Hospital 716 773-7645
  2323 Whitehaven Rd Grand Island (14072) *(G-5773)*
Grand Island Research & Dev, Grand Island Also called Grand Island Animal Hospital *(G-5773)*
Grand Knitting Mills Inc (PA) 631 226-5000
  7050 New Horizons Blvd # 1 Amityville (11701) *(G-289)*
Grand Marnier, New York Also called Marnier-Lapostolle Inc *(G-11187)*
Grand Meridian Printing Inc 718 937-3888
  3116 Hunters Point Ave Long Island City (11101) *(G-7781)*
Grand Prix Litho Inc 631 242-4182
  101 Colin Dr Unit 5 Holbrook (11741) *(G-6478)*
Grand Processing Inc 718 388-0600
  1050 Grand St Brooklyn (11211) *(G-2049)*
Grand Slam Holdings LLC (HQ) 212 583-5000
  345 Park Ave Bsmt Lb4 New York (10154) *(G-10389)*
Grand Slam Safety LLC 315 766-7008
  9793 S Bridge St Croghan (13327) *(G-4084)*
Grandeur Creations Inc 212 643-1277
  146 W 29th St Rm 9e New York (10001) *(G-10390)*
Grandma Browns Beans Inc 315 963-7221
  5837 Scenic Ave Mexico (13114) *(G-8430)*
Grandma Maes Cntry Nturals LLC 212 348-8171
  340 E 93rd St Apt 30h New York (10128) *(G-10391)*
Grandview Block & Supply Co 518 346-7981
  1705 Hamburg St Schenectady (12304) *(G-15292)*
Grandview Concrete Corp 518 346-7981
  1705 Hamburg St Schenectady (12304) *(G-15293)*
Granite & Marble Works Inc 518 584-2800
  8 Commerce Park Dr Gansevoort (12831) *(G-5500)*
Granite Tops Inc 914 699-2909
  716 S Columbus Ave Mount Vernon (10550) *(G-8732)*
Granite Works LLC 607 565-7012
  133 William Donnelly Waverly (14892) *(G-16727)*
Grannys Kitchens, Frankfort Also called Maplehurst Bakeries LLC *(G-5364)*
Grant Hamilton (PA) 716 652-0320
  710 Main St East Aurora (14052) *(G-4396)*
Grant's Interest Rate Observer, New York Also called Grants Financial Publishing *(G-10393)*
Grant-Noren 845 726-4281
  83 Ridge Rd Westtown (10998) *(G-17099)*
Grantoo LLC 646 356-0460
  60 Broad St Ste 3502 New York (10004) *(G-10392)*
Grants Financial Publishing 212 809-7994
  2 Wall St Ste 603 New York (10005) *(G-10393)*
Granville Glass & Granite 518 812-0492
  131 Revere Rd Hudson Falls (12839) *(G-6676)*
Grapes & Grains 518 283-9463
  279 Troy Rd Ste 4 Rensselaer (12144) *(G-14057)*
Graph-Tex Inc 607 756-7791
  46 Elm St Cortland (13045) *(G-4049)*
Graph-Tex Inc (PA) 607 756-1875
  24 Court St Cortland (13045) *(G-4050)*
Graphalloy, Yonkers Also called Graphite Metallizing Corp *(G-17466)*
Graphic Cntrls Acqisition Corp (HQ) 716 853-7500
  400 Exchange St Buffalo (14204) *(G-2994)*
Graphic Concepts, Plainview Also called Steval Graphics Concepts Inc *(G-13663)*
Graphic Connections, Geneva Also called Tramwell Inc *(G-5599)*
Graphic Controls Holdings Inc (HQ) 716 853-7500
  400 Exchange St Buffalo (14204) *(G-2995)*
Graphic Design U S A, New York Also called American Graphic Design Awards *(G-9167)*
Graphic Fabrications Inc 516 763-3222
  488a Sunrise Hwy Rockville Centre (11570) *(G-14819)*
Graphic For Industry, New York Also called Graphics For Industry Inc *(G-10395)*
Graphic Image Associates LLC 631 249-9600
  305 Spagnoli Rd Melville (11747) *(G-8352)*
Graphic Image Incorporated 631 249-9600
  305 Spagnoli Rd Melville (11747) *(G-8353)*

Graphic Lab Inc 212 682-1815
  228 E 45th St Fl 4 New York (10017) *(G-10394)*
Graphic Management Partners, Port Chester Also called Gmp LLC *(G-13774)*
Graphic Printing 718 701-4433
  2376 Jerome Ave Bronx (10468) *(G-1350)*
Graphic Signs & Awnings Ltd 718 227-6000
  165 Industrial Loop Ste 1 Staten Island (10309) *(G-15702)*
Graphicomm Inc 716 283-0830
  7703 Niagara Falls Blvd Niagara Falls (14304) *(G-12845)*
Graphics 247 Corp 718 729-2470
  4402 23rd St Ste 113 Long Island City (11101) *(G-7782)*
Graphics For Industry Inc 212 889-6202
  307 W 36th St Fl 10 New York (10018) *(G-10395)*
Graphics of Utica 315 797-4868
  10436 Dustin Rd Remsen (13438) *(G-14052)*
Graphics Plus Printing Inc 607 299-0500
  215 S Main St Cortland (13045) *(G-4051)*
Graphics Slution Providers Inc (PA) 845 677-5088
  115 Barmore Rd Lagrangeville (12540) *(G-7278)*
Graphis Inc 212 532-9387
  389 5th Ave Rm 1105 New York (10016) *(G-10396)*
Graphite Metallizing Corp (PA) 914 968-8400
  1050 Nepperhan Ave Yonkers (10703) *(G-17466)*
Graphitek Inc 518 686-5966
  4883 State Route 67 Hoosick Falls (12090) *(G-6566)*
Graphtex A Div of Htc, Utica Also called Human Technologies Corporation *(G-16364)*
Grasers Dental Ceramics 716 649-5100
  5020 Armor Duells Rd # 2 Orchard Park (14127) *(G-13297)*
Gratitude & Company Inc 607 277-3188
  215 N Cayuga St Ste 71 Ithaca (14850) *(G-6881)*
Graver Technologies LLC 585 624-1330
  300 W Main St Honeoye Falls (14472) *(G-6556)*
Gravity East Village Inc 212 388-9788
  515 E 5th St New York (10009) *(G-10397)*
Gravymaster Inc 203 453-1893
  101 Erie Blvd Canajoharie (13317) *(G-3360)*
Gray Glass Inc 718 217-2943
  21744 98th Ave Ste C Queens Village (11429) *(G-13994)*
Gray Manufacturing Inds LLC 607 281-1325
  6258 Ice House Rd Hornell (14843) *(G-6591)*
Grayhawk Leasing LLC (HQ) 914 767-6000
  1 Pepsi Way Somers (10589) *(G-15532)*
Graymont Materials Inc 518 561-5200
  111 Quarry Rd Plattsburgh (12901) *(G-13693)*
Graywood Companies Inc (PA) 585 254-7000
  1390 Mount Read Blvd Rochester (14606) *(G-14433)*
Grc, Hempstead Also called General Refining & Smelting *(G-6294)*
Great 4 Image Inc 518 424-2058
  5 Forest Hills Blvd Rensselaer (12144) *(G-14058)*
Great Adirondack Yarn Company 518 843-3381
  950 County Highway 126 Amsterdam (12010) *(G-349)*
Great American Awning & Patio 518 899-2300
  43 Round Lake Rd Ballston Spa (12020) *(G-596)*
Great American Bicycle LLC 518 584-8100
  41 Geyser Rd Saratoga Springs (12866) *(G-15184)*
Great American Dessert Co LLC 718 894-3494
  5842 Maurice Ave Maspeth (11378) *(G-8173)*
Great American Industries Inc (HQ) 607 729-9331
  300 Plaza Dr Vestal (13850) *(G-16472)*
Great American Tool Co Inc 716 646-5700
  7223 Boston State Rd Hamburg (14075) *(G-5950)*
Great Arrow Graphics, Buffalo Also called Massimo Friedman Inc *(G-3078)*
Great ATL Pr-Cast Con Statuary 718 948-5677
  225 Ellis St Staten Island (10307) *(G-15703)*
Great Brands of Europe Inc 914 872-8804
  100 Hillside Ave Fl 3 White Plains (10603) *(G-17140)*
Great China Empire, New York Also called Gce International Inc *(G-10304)*
Great Eastern Color Lith (PA) 845 454-7420
  46 Violet Ave Poughkeepsie (12601) *(G-13923)*
Great Eastern Pasta Works LLC 631 956-0889
  385 Sheffield Ave West Babylon (11704) *(G-16820)*
Great Gates Etc, New York Also called North Eastern Fabricators Inc *(G-11474)*
Great Impressions, South Dayton Also called Cherry Creek Woodcraft Inc *(G-15540)*
Great Jones Lumber Corp 212 254-5560
  45 Great Jones St New York (10012) *(G-10398)*
Great Lakes Cheese NY Inc 315 232-4511
  23 Phelps St Adams (13605) *(G-3)*
Great Lakes Gear Co Inc 716 694-0715
  126 E Niagara St Ste 2 Tonawanda (14150) *(G-16183)*
Great Lakes Metal Treating 716 694-1240
  300 E Niagara St Tonawanda (14150) *(G-16184)*
Great Lakes Orthopedic Labs 716 878-7307
  219 Bryant St Buffalo (14222) *(G-2996)*
Great Lakes Plastics Co Inc 716 896-3100
  2371 Broadway St Buffalo (14212) *(G-2997)*
Great Lakes Pressed Steel Corp 716 885-4037
  1400 Niagara St Buffalo (14213) *(G-2998)*
Great Lakes Specialites 716 672-4622
  9491 Route 60 Fredonia (14063) *(G-5383)*
Great Lakes Technologies, Liverpool Also called Scapa North America *(G-7573)*
Great North Road Media Inc 646 619-1355
  3115 Broadway Apt 61 New York (10027) *(G-10399)*

(PA)=Parent Co (HQ)=Headquarters (DH)=Div Headquarters

Great Northern Printing Co, Potsdam *Also called Randy Sixberry* ***(G-13901)***
Great Pacific Entps US Inc (HQ).......518 761-2593
68 Warren St Glens Falls (12801) ***(G-5698)***
Great Universal Corp.......917 302-0065
1441 Broadway Fl 5 New York (10018) ***(G-10400)***
Great Wall Corp.......212 704-4372
4727 36th St Long Island City (11101) ***(G-7783)***
Great Western Malting Co.......800 496-7732
16 Beeman Way Champlain (12919) ***(G-3569)***
Greatbatch Medical, Alden *Also called Integer Holdings Corporation* ***(G-183)***
Greatbatch Medical, Clarence *Also called Precimed Inc* ***(G-3696)***
Greater Niagara Bldg Ctr Inc.......716 299-0543
9540 Niagara Falls Blvd Niagara Falls (14304) ***(G-12846)***
Greater Niagara Newspaper, Medina *Also called Gannett Stllite Info Ntwrk Inc* ***(G-8305)***
Greater Rchster Advertiser Inc.......585 385-1974
201 Main St East Rochester (14445) ***(G-4479)***
Greco Bros Rdymx Con Co Inc.......718 855-6271
381 Hamilton Ave Brooklyn (11231) ***(G-2050)***
Greek Nat Hrald Dily Nwsppr In, Long Island City *Also called National Herald Inc* ***(G-7851)***
Green Apple Courage Inc.......716 614-4673
374 Delaware Ave Ste 240 Buffalo (14202) ***(G-2999)***
Green Beam Led Inc.......718 439-6262
4601b 1st Ave Brooklyn (11232) ***(G-2051)***
Green Buffalo Fuel LLC.......716 768-0600
720 Riverview Blvd Tonawanda (14150) ***(G-16185)***
Green Energy Concepts Inc.......845 238-2574
37 Elkay Dr Ste 51 Chester (10918) ***(G-3635)***
Green Girl Prtg & Msgnr Inc.......212 575-0357
44 W 39th St New York (10018) ***(G-10401)***
Green Global Energy Inc.......716 501-9770
2526 Niagara Falls Blvd Niagara Falls (14304) ***(G-12847)***
Green Island Power Authority.......518 273-0661
20 Clinton St Green Island (12183) ***(G-5874)***
Green Mountain Graphics, Sunnyside *Also called Eastern Concepts Ltd* ***(G-15828)***
Green Prosthetics & Orthotics.......716 484-1088
1290 E 2nd St Jamestown (14701) ***(G-7030)***
Green Renewable Inc.......518 658-2233
28 Taylor Ave Berlin (12022) ***(G-855)***
Green Valley Foods LLC.......315 926-4280
3736 S Main St Marion (14505) ***(G-8124)***
Green Wave International Inc.......718 499-3371
5423 1st Ave Brooklyn (11220) ***(G-2052)***
Green Zone Food Service Inc.......917 709-1728
9906 Christie Ave 3a Corona (11368) ***(G-4020)***
Greenbeads Llc.......212 327-2765
220 E 72nd St Apt 17d New York (10021) ***(G-10402)***
Greenbeam Led, Brooklyn *Also called Green Beam Led Inc* ***(G-2051)***
Greenbelt Industries Inc.......800 668-1114
45 Comet Ave Buffalo (14216) ***(G-3000)***
Greenbuds LLC.......718 483-9212
1434 57th St Brooklyn (11219) ***(G-2053)***
Greenbush Tape & Label Inc.......518 465-2389
40 Broadway Unit 31 Albany (12202) ***(G-83)***
Greene Brass & Alum Fndry LLC.......607 656-4204
51971 State Highway 10 Bloomville (13739) ***(G-990)***
Greene Brass & Aluminum Fndry, Greene *Also called American Blade Mfg LLC* ***(G-5880)***
Greene Lumber Co LP.......607 278-6101
16991 State Highway 23 Davenport (13750) ***(G-4105)***
Greene Technologies Inc.......607 656-4166
Grand & Clinton St Greene (13778) ***(G-5884)***
Greenebuild LLC.......917 562-0556
390a Lafayette Ave Brooklyn (11238) ***(G-2054)***
Greenfiber Albany Inc.......518 842-1470
210 County Highway 102 Gloversville (12078) ***(G-5727)***
Greenfield Die Casting Corp.......516 623-9230
99 Doxsee Dr Freeport (11520) ***(G-5414)***
Greenfield Industries Inc.......516 623-9230
99 Doxsee Dr Freeport (11520) ***(G-5415)***
Greenfield Manufacturing Inc.......518 581-2368
25 Freedom Way Saratoga Springs (12866) ***(G-15185)***
Greenfield Martin Clothiers, Brooklyn *Also called Martin Greenfield Clothiers* ***(G-2279)***
Greenkissny Inc.......914 304-4323
75 S Broadway White Plains (10601) ***(G-17141)***
Greenleaf Cabinet Makers LLC.......315 432-4600
6691 Pickard Dr Syracuse (13211) ***(G-15974)***
Greenmaker Industries LLC.......866 684-7800
885 Conklin St Farmingdale (11735) ***(G-5009)***
Greenpac Mill LLC (HQ).......716 299-0560
4400 Royal Ave Niagara Falls (14303) ***(G-12848)***
Greentree Pharmacy Inc.......718 768-2700
291 7th Ave Brooklyn (11215) ***(G-2055)***
Greenvale Bagel Inc.......516 221-8221
3060 Merrick Rd Wantagh (11793) ***(G-16578)***
Greenville Local, Ravena *Also called Bleezarde Publishing Inc* ***(G-14033)***
Greenway Cabinetry Inc.......516 877-0009
485 Willis Ave Williston Park (11596) ***(G-17285)***
Greenwood Graphics Inc.......516 822-4856
960 S Broadway Ste 106 Hicksville (11801) ***(G-6381)***
Greenwood Winery LLC.......315 432-8132
6475 Collamer Rd East Syracuse (13057) ***(G-4547)***
Gregg Sadwick, Rochester *Also called Jml Optical Industries LLC* ***(G-14484)***
Gregson-Clark, Caledonia *Also called Rhett M Clark Inc* ***(G-3309)***
Greif Inc.......716 836-4200
2122 Colvin Blvd Tonawanda (14150) ***(G-16186)***
Greno Industries Inc (PA).......518 393-4195
2820 Amsterdam Rd Scotia (12302) ***(G-15347)***
Grey House Publishing Inc.......845 483-3535
84 Patrick Ln Stop 3 Poughkeepsie (12603) ***(G-13924)***
Grey House Publishing Inc (PA).......518 789-8700
4919 Route 22 Amenia (12501) ***(G-219)***
Grey State Apparel LLC.......212 255-4216
305 7th Ave Ste 13a New York (10001) ***(G-10403)***
Greyhouse Publshng, Poughkeepsie *Also called Grey House Publishing Inc* ***(G-13924)***
Greyline Signs Inc.......716 947-4526
6681 Schuyler Dr Derby (14047) ***(G-4306)***
Greyston Bakery Inc.......914 375-1510
104 Alexander St Yonkers (10701) ***(G-17467)***
Grid Typographic Services Inc.......212 627-0303
27 W 24th St Ste 9c New York (10010) ***(G-10404)***
Grid Typographic Svces, New York *Also called Grid Typographic Services Inc* ***(G-10404)***
Griffin Automation Inc.......716 674-2300
240 Westminster Rd West Seneca (14224) ***(G-16976)***
Griffin Chemical Company LLC.......716 693-2465
889 Erie Ave Ste 1 North Tonawanda (14120) ***(G-12993)***
Griffin Manufacturing Company.......585 265-1991
1656 Ridge Rd Webster (14580) ***(G-16748)***
Griffon Corporation (PA).......212 957-5000
712 5th Ave Fl 18 New York (10019) ***(G-10405)***
Grillbot LLC.......646 258-5639
1562 1st Ave Ste 251 New York (10028) ***(G-10406)***
Grillmaster Inc.......718 272-9191
15314 83rd St Howard Beach (11414) ***(G-6625)***
Grimaldi Bakery, Ridgewood *Also called Grimaldis Home Bread Inc* ***(G-14121)***
Grimaldis Home Bread Inc.......718 497-1425
2101 Menahan St Ridgewood (11385) ***(G-14121)***
Grimble Bakery, Bronx *Also called Miss Grimble Associates Inc* ***(G-1402)***
Grind.......646 558-3250
419 Park Ave S Fl 2 New York (10016) ***(G-10407)***
Grinnell Designs Ltd.......212 391-5277
260 W 39th St Rm 302 New York (10018) ***(G-10408)***
Grit Energy Services Inc.......212 701-4500
100 Wall St Fl 11 New York (10005) ***(G-10409)***
Grohe America Inc.......212 206-8820
160 5th Ave Fl 4 New York (10010) ***(G-10410)***
Grolier International Inc (HQ).......212 343-6100
557 Broadway New York (10012) ***(G-10411)***
Grom Columbus LLC.......212 974-3444
1796 Broadway New York (10019) ***(G-10412)***
Grosso Materials Inc.......845 361-5211
90 Collabar Rd Montgomery (12549) ***(G-8631)***
Group Commerce Inc (PA).......646 346-0598
902 Broadway Fl 6 New York (10010) ***(G-10413)***
Group Enterainment LLC.......212 868-5233
115 W 29th St Rm 1102 New York (10001) ***(G-10414)***
Group International LLC.......718 475-8805
14711 34th Ave Flushing (11354) ***(G-5253)***
Groupe 16sur20 LLC (PA).......212 625-1620
198 Bowery New York (10012) ***(G-10415)***
Grover Aluminum Products Inc.......631 475-3500
577 Medford Ave Patchogue (11772) ***(G-13446)***
Grover Cleveland Press Inc.......716 564-2222
2676 Sweet Home Rd Amherst (14228) ***(G-243)***
Grover Home Headquarters, Patchogue *Also called Grover Aluminum Products Inc* ***(G-13446)***
Growmark Fs LLC.......585 538-2186
2936 Telephone Rd Caledonia (14423) ***(G-3306)***
Grownbeans Inc.......212 989-3486
110 Bank St Apt 2j New York (10014) ***(G-10416)***
Growth Products Ltd.......914 428-1316
80 Lafayette Ave White Plains (10603) ***(G-17142)***
Grphics Grafek, Syracuse *Also called Matt Industries Inc* ***(G-16005)***
Gruber Display Co Inc.......718 882-8220
3920g Merritt Ave Bronx (10466) ***(G-1351)***
Grumman Field Support Services.......516 575-0574
S Oyster Bay Rd Bethpage (11714) ***(G-867)***
Gruner & Jahr USA.......212 782-7870
375 Lexington Ave New York (10017) ***(G-10417)***
Gruner + Jahr Prtg & Pubg Co.......212 463-1000
110 5th Ave Fl 7 New York (10011) ***(G-10418)***
Gruner + Jahr USA Group Inc (PA).......866 323-9336
1745 Broadway Fl 16 New York (10019) ***(G-10419)***
Gruner Jahr USA Publishing Div, New York *Also called Gruner + Jahr USA Group Inc* ***(G-10419)***
Gryphon Sensors LLC.......315 452-8882
7351 Round Pond Rd North Syracuse (13212) ***(G-12963)***
Gs Communications USA, Brooklyn *Also called G S Communications USA Inc* ***(G-2011)***
Gs Direct LLC.......212 902-1000
85 Broad St New York (10004) ***(G-10420)***
Gsa Upstate NY (PA).......631 244-5744
755 Montauk Hwy Oakdale (11769) ***(G-13076)***
Gschwind Group, Patchogue *Also called Suffolk McHy & Pwr Tl Corp* ***(G-13460)***

ALPHABETIC SECTION
Habitat Magazine, New York

Gscp Emax Acquisition LLC 212 902-1000
85 Broad St New York (10004) ***(G-10421)***
GSE Composites Inc 631 389-1300
110 Oser Ave Hauppauge (11788) ***(G-6110)***
Gsn Government Security News, Massapequa Park *Also called World Business Media LLC* ***(G-8224)***
Gsp Components Inc 585 436-3377
1190 Brooks Ave Rochester (14624) ***(G-14434)***
Gt Innovations LLC 585 739-7659
7674 Swamp Rd Bergen (14416) ***(G-844)***
Gt Machine & Tool, Long Island City *Also called Cnc Manufacturing Corp* ***(G-7729)***
Gt Parts & Services, Clifton Park *Also called Worldwide Gas Turbine Pdts Inc* ***(G-3737)***
Gti Graphic Technology Inc (PA) 845 562-7066
211 Dupont Ave Newburgh (12550) ***(G-12781)***
Guaranteed Printing Svc Co Inc 212 929-2410
4710 33rd St Long Island City (11101) ***(G-7784)***
Guardian Booth LLC 844 992-6684
29 Roosevelt Ave Ste 301 Spring Valley (10977) ***(G-15610)***
Guardian Concrete Inc 518 372-0080
2140 Maxon Rd Ext Schenectady (12308) ***(G-15294)***
Guardian Concrete Steps, Schenectady *Also called Guardian Concrete Inc* ***(G-15294)***
Guardian Industries LLC 315 787-7000
50 Forge Ave Geneva (14456) ***(G-5592)***
Guardian Systems Tech Inc 716 481-5597
659 Oakwood Ave East Aurora (14052) ***(G-4397)***
Guernica 914 414-7318
63 3rd Pl Apt 4r Brooklyn (11231) ***(G-2056)***
Guernica Magazine, Brooklyn *Also called Guernica* ***(G-2056)***
Guess Inc 845 928-3930
498 Red Apple Ct Central Valley (10917) ***(G-3552)***
Guess Inc 315 539-5634
655 State Route 318 # 96 Waterloo (13165) ***(G-16650)***
Guess Inc 212 286-9856
575 5th Ave Lbby 1 New York (10017) ***(G-10422)***
Guess Inc 716 298-3561
1826 Military Rd Spc 113 Niagara Falls (14304) ***(G-12849)***
Guest Informat LLC 212 557-3010
110 E 42nd St Rm 1714 New York (10017) ***(G-10423)***
Guesthouse Division, Brooklyn *Also called R H Guest Incorporated* ***(G-2490)***
Guidance Channel, Woodbury *Also called Global Video LLC* ***(G-17310)***
Guidance Group Inc 631 756-4618
1 Huntington Quad 1n03 Melville (11747) ***(G-8354)***
Guild Diamond Products Inc (PA) 212 871-0007
1212 Avenue Of The Americ New York (10036) ***(G-10424)***
Guilderland Printing, Guilderland *Also called Custom Prtrs Guilderland Inc* ***(G-5924)***
Guilford Press, New York *Also called Guilford Publications Inc* ***(G-10425)***
Guilford Press, New York *Also called Guilford Publications Inc* ***(G-10426)***
Guilford Publications Inc 212 431-9800
7 Penn Plz Ste 1200 New York (10001) ***(G-10425)***
Guilford Publications Inc 800 365-7006
370 7th Ave Ste 1200 New York (10001) ***(G-10426)***
Guitar Specialist Inc 914 533-5589
219 Oakridge Cmn South Salem (10590) ***(G-15559)***
Guldenschuh Logging & Lbr LLC 585 538-4750
143 Wheatland Center Rd Caledonia (14423) ***(G-3307)***
Gullo Machine & Tool Inc 585 657-7318
4 E Main St Bloomfield (14469) ***(G-983)***
Gumbusters of New York, Brooklyn *Also called Metro Products & Services LLC* ***(G-2311)***
Gumuchian Fils Ltd 212 593-3118
16 E 52nd St Ste 701 New York (10022) ***(G-10427)***
Gun Week, Buffalo *Also called Second Amendment Foundation* ***(G-3209)***
Gunlocke Company LLC (HQ) 585 728-5111
1 Gunlocke Dr Wayland (14572) ***(G-16734)***
Gunther Partners LLC (HQ) 212 521-2930
655 Madison Ave Fl 11 New York (10065) ***(G-10428)***
Guosa Life Sciences Inc 718 813-7806
846 Center Dr North Baldwin (11510) ***(G-12923)***
Gurley Precision Instrs Inc 518 272-6300
514 Fulton St Troy (12180) ***(G-16259)***
Gurwitch Products LLC (HQ) 281 275-7000
135 E 57th St Unit 106 New York (10022) ***(G-10429)***
Gustbuster Ltd 631 391-9000
855 Conklin St Ste O Farmingdale (11735) ***(G-5010)***
Gutchess Freedom Inc 716 492-2824
10699 Maple Grove Rd Freedom (14065) ***(G-5387)***
Gutchess Lumber Co Inc (PA) 607 753-3393
890 Mclean Rd Cortland (13045) ***(G-4052)***
Guthrie Heli-ARC Inc 585 548-5053
6276 Clinton Street Rd Bergen (14416) ***(G-845)***
Gutts Corporation of America, Irvington *Also called Guttz Corporation of America* ***(G-6812)***
Guttz Corporation of America 914 591-9600
50 S Buckhout St Ste 104 Irvington (10533) ***(G-6812)***
Guyson Corporation of USa (HQ) 518 587-7894
13 Grande Blvd Saratoga Springs (12866) ***(G-15186)***
Gw Acquisition LLC 212 736-4848
1370 Broadway Rm 1100 New York (10018) ***(G-10430)***
GW Lisk Company Inc 315 548-2165
1369 Phelps Junction Rd Phelps (14532) ***(G-13555)***
Gw Manufacturing 718 386-8078
24a Woodward Ave Ridgewood (11385) ***(G-14122)***
Gym Store Inc 718 366-7804
5889 57th St Maspeth (11378) ***(G-8174)***
Gym Store.com, Maspeth *Also called Gym Store Inc* ***(G-8174)***
H & H Furniture Co 718 850-5252
11420 101st Ave Jamaica (11419) ***(G-6953)***
H & H Hulls Inc 518 828-1339
35 Industrial Tract Anx Hudson (12534) ***(G-6646)***
H & H Laboratories Inc (PA) 718 624-8041
61 4th St Brooklyn (11231) ***(G-2057)***
H & H Laboratories Inc 718 624-8041
409 Hoyt St Brooklyn (11231) ***(G-2058)***
H & H Metal Specialty Inc 716 665-2110
153 Hopkins Ave Jamestown (14701) ***(G-7031)***
H & H Technologies Inc 631 567-3526
10 Colt Ct Ronkonkoma (11779) ***(G-14936)***
H & M Leasing Corp 631 225-5246
1245 Marconi Blvd Copiague (11726) ***(G-3930)***
H & R Precision, Farmingdale *Also called Precision Envelope Co Inc* ***(G-5096)***
H & S Edible Products Corp 914 413-3489
119 Fulton Ln Mount Vernon (10550) ***(G-8733)***
H & T Goldman Corporation 800 822-0272
2 W 46th St Ste 607 New York (10036) ***(G-10431)***
H A Guden Company Inc 631 737-2900
99 Raynor Ave Ronkonkoma (11779) ***(G-14937)***
H and B Digital, New York *Also called A & M LLC* ***(G-9027)***
H B Millwork Inc (PA) 631 289-8086
500 Long Island Ave Medford (11763) ***(G-8277)***
H B Millwork Inc 631 924-4195
9 Old Dock Rd Yaphank (11980) ***(G-17410)***
H Best Ltd 212 354-2400
1411 Broadway Fl 8 New York (10018) ***(G-10432)***
H C Kionka & Co Inc 212 227-3155
15 Maiden Ln Ste 908 New York (10038) ***(G-10433)***
H C Young Tool & Machine Co 315 463-0663
3700 New Court Ave Syracuse (13206) ***(G-15975)***
H D M Labs Inc 516 431-8357
153 Kingston Blvd Island Park (11558) ***(G-6820)***
H F Brown Machine Co Inc 315 732-6129
708 State St Utica (13502) ***(G-16361)***
H F Cary & Sons 607 598-2563
70 Reniff Rd Lockwood (14859) ***(G-7658)***
H F W Communications Inc (HQ) 315 703-7979
6437 Collamer Rd Ste 1 East Syracuse (13057) ***(G-4548)***
H Freund Woodworking Co Inc 516 334-3774
589 Main St Westbury (11590) ***(G-17019)***
H G Maybeck Co Inc 718 297-4410
17930 93rd Ave Ste 2 Jamaica (11433) ***(G-6954)***
H Group Inc 212 719-5500
462 7th Ave Fl 9 New York (10018) ***(G-10434)***
H H B Bakery of Little Neck 718 631-7004
24914 Horace Harding Expy Flushing (11362) ***(G-5254)***
H K Technologies Inc 212 779-0100
303 5th Ave Rm 1707 New York (10016) ***(G-10435)***
H L Robinson Sand & Gravel (PA) 607 659-5153
535 Ithaca Rd Candor (13743) ***(G-3403)***
H M W, Brewster *Also called Hudson Machine Works Inc* ***(G-1218)***
H Risch Inc 585 442-0110
44 Saginaw Dr Rochester (14623) ***(G-14435)***
H S Assembly Inc 585 266-4287
570 Hollandback Rochester (14605) ***(G-14436)***
H T L & S Ltd 718 435-4474
5820 Fort Hamilton Pkwy Brooklyn (11219) ***(G-2059)***
H T Specialty Inc 585 458-4060
70 Bermar Park Rochester (14624) ***(G-14437)***
H THEOPHILE, New York *Also called Kathmando Valley Preservation* ***(G-10856)***
H W Naylor Co Inc 607 263-5145
121 Main St Morris (13808) ***(G-8660)***
H W Wilson Company Inc 718 588-8635
950 University Ave Bronx (10452) ***(G-1352)***
H&E Service Corp 646 472-1936
400 Garden Cy Plz Ste 405 Garden City (11530) ***(G-5522)***
H&F Products Inc 845 651-6100
51 Forest Rd Ste 360 Monroe (10950) ***(G-8591)***
H&L Computers Inc 516 873-8088
13523 Northern Blvd Flushing (11354) ***(G-5255)***
H2 At Hammerman, New York *Also called Hammerman Bros Inc* ***(G-10445)***
H2o Solutions Inc 518 527-0915
61 Major Dickinson Ave Stillwater (12170) ***(G-15782)***
Haagen-Dazs, Farmingdale *Also called Nestle Healthcare Ntrtn Inc* ***(G-5074)***
Haanen Packard Machinery Inc (PA) 518 747-2330
16 Allen St Hudson Falls (12839) ***(G-6677)***
Haba USA 800 468-6873
4407 Jordan Rd Skaneateles (13152) ***(G-15483)***
Habasit America Inc 716 824-8484
1400 Clinton St Buffalo (14206) ***(G-3001)***
Habco Corp 631 789-1400
41 Ranick Dr E Amityville (11701) ***(G-290)***
Habco Sales, Amityville *Also called Habco Corp* ***(G-290)***
Habermaass Corporation 315 685-8919
4407 Jordan Rd Skaneateles (13152) ***(G-15484)***
Habitat Magazine, New York *Also called Carol Group Ltd* ***(G-9586)***

ALPHABETIC

(PA)=Parent Co (HQ)=Headquarters (DH)=Div Headquarters
2018 Harris
New York Manufacturers Directory
965

Hachette Book Group Inc (HQ)...800 759-0190
1290 Ave Of The Americas New York (10104) ***(G-10436)***
Hacker Boat Company Inc (PA)...518 543-6731
8 Delaware Ave Silver Bay (12874) ***(G-15468)***
Haculla Nyc Inc...718 886-3163
6805 Fresh Meadow Ln Fresh Meadows (11365) ***(G-5455)***
Hadco Metal Trading Co LLC...631 270-9724
120 Spagnoli Rd Ste 1 Melville (11747) ***(G-8355)***
Haddad Bros Inc (PA)...212 563-2117
28 W 36th St Rm 1026 New York (10018) ***(G-10437)***
Haddad Bros Inc...718 377-5505
1200 Mcdonald Ave Brooklyn (11230) ***(G-2060)***
Haddad Hosiery LLC...212 251-0022
34 W 33rd St Rm 401 New York (10001) ***(G-10438)***
Hadeka Stone Corp (PA)...518 282-9605
115 Staso Ln Hampton (12837) ***(G-5981)***
Hades Manufacturing Corp...631 249-4244
135 Florida St Farmingdale (11735) ***(G-5011)***
Hadfield Inc...631 981-4314
840 S 2nd St Ronkonkoma (11779) ***(G-14938)***
Hadley Exhibits Inc (PA)...716 874-3666
1700 Elmwood Ave Buffalo (14207) ***(G-3002)***
Hadleys Fab-Weld Inc...315 926-5101
4202 Sunset Dr Marion (14505) ***(G-8125)***
Hadp LLC...518 831-6824
602 Potential Pkwy Scotia (12302) ***(G-15348)***
Hagadah Passover Bakery...718 638-1589
814 Bergen St Brooklyn (11238) ***(G-2061)***
Hagedorn Communications Inc (PA)...914 636-7400
662 Main St Ste 1 New Rochelle (10801) ***(G-8951)***
Hagner Industries Inc...716 873-5720
95 Botsford Pl Buffalo (14216) ***(G-3003)***
Hahns Old Fashioned Cake Co...631 249-3456
75 Allen Blvd Farmingdale (11735) ***(G-5012)***
Haig Graphic Communications, Hauppauge *Also called Haig Press Inc* ***(G-6111)***
Haig Press Inc...631 582-5800
690 Old Willets Path Hauppauge (11788) ***(G-6111)***
Haights Cross Cmmnications Inc (PA)...212 209-0500
136 Madison Ave Fl 8 New York (10016) ***(G-10439)***
Haights Cross Operating Co (HQ)...914 289-9400
10 New King St Ste 102 White Plains (10604) ***(G-17143)***
Hailo Network Usa Inc...646 561-8552
568 Broadway Fl 11 New York (10012) ***(G-10440)***
Hain Blueprint Inc...212 414-5741
1111 Marcus Ave Ste 100 New Hyde Park (11042) ***(G-8881)***
Hain Celestial Group Inc (PA)...516 587-5000
1111 Marcus Ave Ste 100 New Hyde Park (11042) ***(G-8882)***
Haines Equipment Inc...607 566-8531
20 Carrington St Avoca (14809) ***(G-534)***
Hair Color Research Group Inc...718 445-6026
13320 Whitestone Expy Flushing (11354) ***(G-5256)***
Hair Ventures LLC...718 664-7689
94 Fargo Ln Irvington (10533) ***(G-6813)***
Hairstory, Irvington *Also called Hair Ventures LLC* ***(G-6813)***
Haitian Times Inc...718 230-8700
80 Lakeside Dr New Rochelle (10801) ***(G-8952)***
Hal-Hen Company Inc...516 294-3200
180 Atlantic Ave New Hyde Park (11040) ***(G-8883)***
Halcyon Business Publications...800 735-2732
400 Post Ave Ste 304 Westbury (11590) ***(G-17020)***
Hale Electrical Dist Svcs Inc...716 818-7595
12088 Big Tree Rd Wales Center (14169) ***(G-16560)***
Haley Concrete Inc (PA)...716 492-0849
10413 Delevan Elton Rd Delevan (14042) ***(G-4260)***
Haleys Comet Seafood Corp...212 571-1828
605 3rd Ave Fl 34 New York (10158) ***(G-10441)***
Half Time, Poughkeepsie *Also called Quench It Inc* ***(G-13945)***
Halfmoon Town Water Department...518 233-7489
8 Brookwood Rd Waterford (12188) ***(G-16633)***
Halfway House LLC...518 873-2198
7158 Us Route 9 Elizabethtown (12932) ***(G-4642)***
Hall Construction Pdts & Svcs...518 747-7047
31 Allen St Hudson Falls (12839) ***(G-6678)***
Hallagan Manufacturing Co Inc...315 331-4640
500 Hoffman St Newark (14513) ***(G-12751)***
Hallock Fabricating Corp...631 727-2441
324 Doctors Path Riverhead (11901) ***(G-14156)***
Halm Industries Co Inc (PA)...516 676-6700
180 Glen Head Rd Glen Head (11545) ***(G-5646)***
Halm Instrument Co Inc...516 676-6700
180 Glen Head Rd Glen Head (11545) ***(G-5647)***
Halmark Architectural Finshg...718 272-1831
353 Stanley Ave Brooklyn (11207) ***(G-2062)***
Halmode Apparel Inc...212 819-9114
1400 Brdwy 11th & Fl 16 New York (10018) ***(G-10442)***
Halmode Petite Div, New York *Also called Halmode Apparel Inc* ***(G-10442)***
Halo Associates...212 691-9549
289 Bleecker St Fl 5 New York (10014) ***(G-10443)***
Halo Optical Products Inc...518 773-4256
9 Phair St Ste 1 Gloversville (12078) ***(G-5728)***
Halpern Tool Corp (PA)...914 633-0038
111 Plain Ave New Rochelle (10801) ***(G-8953)***
Hamil America Inc...212 244-2645
42 W 39th St Fl 15 New York (10018) ***(G-10444)***
Hamilton County News, Amsterdam *Also called William J Kline & Son Inc* ***(G-374)***
Hamilton Design Kit Homes, Queensbury *Also called Northern Design & Bldg Assoc* ***(G-14019)***
Hamilton Marketing Corporation...585 395-0678
5211 Lake Rd S Brockport (14420) ***(G-1243)***
Hamilton Printing Company Inc...518 732-2161
22 Hamilton Ave Troy (12180) ***(G-16260)***
Hamlet Products Inc...914 665-0307
221 N Macquesten Pkwy Mount Vernon (10550) ***(G-8734)***
Hamlin Bottle & Can Return Inc...585 259-1301
3423 Redman Rd Brockport (14420) ***(G-1244)***
Hammer Communications Inc...631 261-5806
28 Sunken Meadow Rd Northport (11768) ***(G-13030)***
Hammer Magazine, Northport *Also called Hammer Communications Inc* ***(G-13030)***
Hammer Packaging Corp (PA)...585 424-3880
200 Lucius Gordon Dr West Henrietta (14586) ***(G-16914)***
Hammerman Bros Inc...212 956-2800
50 W 57th St Fl 12 New York (10019) ***(G-10445)***
Hammond & Irving Inc (PA)...315 253-6265
254 North St Auburn (13021) ***(G-498)***
Hammond Manufacturing Co Inc...716 630-7030
475 Cayuga Rd Cheektowaga (14225) ***(G-3602)***
Hamodia Corp...718 853-9094
207 Foster Ave Brooklyn (11230) ***(G-2063)***
Hampshire Chemical Corp...315 539-9221
228 E Main St Waterloo (13165) ***(G-16651)***
Hampshire Jewels, New York *Also called Emsaru USA Corp* ***(G-10076)***
Hampshire Lithographers, New York *Also called Advantage Quick Print Inc* ***(G-9095)***
Hampshire Sub II Inc (HQ)...631 321-0923
114 W 41st St Fl 5 New York (10036) ***(G-10446)***
Hampton Art LLC...631 924-1335
19 Scouting Blvd Medford (11763) ***(G-8278)***
Hampton Press Incorporated...646 638-3800
307 7th Ave Rm 506 New York (10001) ***(G-10447)***
Hampton Sand Corp...631 325-5533
1 High St Westhampton (11977) ***(G-17086)***
Hampton Shipyards Inc...631 653-6777
7 Carter Ln East Quogue (11942) ***(G-4470)***
Hampton Technologies LLC...631 924-1335
19 Scouting Blvd Medford (11763) ***(G-8279)***
Hampton Transport Inc...631 716-4445
3655 Route 112 Coram (11727) ***(G-3966)***
Hamptons Magazine, Southampton *Also called Hamptons Media LLC* ***(G-15569)***
Hamptons Magazine...631 283-7125
67 Hampton Rd Unit 5 Southampton (11968) ***(G-15568)***
Hamptons Media LLC...631 283-6900
67 Hampton Rd Unit 5 Southampton (11968) ***(G-15569)***
Hamtronics Inc...585 392-9430
39 Willnick Cir Rochester (14626) ***(G-14438)***
Han-Kraft Uniform Headwear, Buffalo *Also called Hankin Brothers Cap Co* ***(G-3004)***
Hana Pastries Inc...718 369-7593
34 35th St Unit 9 Brooklyn (11232) ***(G-2064)***
Hana Sheet Metal Inc...914 377-0773
9 Celli Pl 11 Yonkers (10701) ***(G-17468)***
Hana Sportswear Inc...315 639-6332
321 Lakeview Dr Dexter (13634) ***(G-4308)***
Hanan Products Company Inc...516 938-1000
196 Miller Pl Hicksville (11801) ***(G-6382)***
Hanco Metal Products Inc...212 787-5992
25 Jay St Brooklyn (11201) ***(G-2065)***
Hancock Quarry/Asphalt, Hancock *Also called Cobleskill Stone Products Inc* ***(G-5984)***
Hancor Inc...607 565-3033
1 William Donnly Inds Waverly (14892) ***(G-16728)***
Hand Care Inc...516 747-5649
42 Sugar Maple Dr Roslyn (11576) ***(G-15044)***
Hand Held Products Inc (HQ)...315 554-6000
700 Visions Dr Skaneateles Falls (13153) ***(G-15490)***
Hand Held Products Inc...315 554-6000
700 Visions Dr Skaneateles Falls (13153) ***(G-15491)***
Handcraft Cabinetry Inc...914 681-9437
230 Ferris Ave Ste 1 White Plains (10603) ***(G-17144)***
Handcraft Manufacturing Corp (PA)...212 251-0022
34 W 33rd St Rm 401 New York (10001) ***(G-10448)***
Handmade Frames Inc...718 782-8364
1013 Grand St Ste 2 Brooklyn (11211) ***(G-2066)***
Handone Studios Inc...585 421-8175
388 Mason Rd Fairport (14450) ***(G-4862)***
Handsome Dans LLC (PA)...917 965-2499
186 1st Ave New York (10009) ***(G-10449)***
Handy & Harman (HQ)...914 461-1300
1133 Westchester Ave N-222 White Plains (10604) ***(G-17145)***
Handy & Harman Group Ltd (HQ)...914 461-1300
1133 Westchester Ave N-222 White Plains (10604) ***(G-17146)***
Handy & Harman Ltd (HQ)...212 520-2300
590 Madison Ave Rm 3202 New York (10022) ***(G-10450)***
Handy Laundry Products Corp (PA)...800 263-5973
382 Route 59 Ste 318 Airmont (10952) ***(G-13)***
Handy Tool & Mfg Co Inc...718 478-9203
1205 Rockaway Ave Brooklyn (11236) ***(G-2067)***

Hanes Supply Inc 518 438-0139
156 Railroad Ave Ste 3 Albany (12205) *(G-84)*
Hanesbrands Inc 646 472-4117
16 E 34th St New York (10016) *(G-10451)*
Hanesbrands Inc 212 576-9300
260 Madison Ave Fl 6 New York (10016) *(G-10452)*
Hanet Plastics Usa Inc 518 324-5850
139 Distribution Way Plattsburgh (12901) *(G-13694)*
Hanford Pharmaceuticals, Syracuse *Also called G C Hanford Manufacturing Co (G-15967)*
Hanger Inc 718 575-5504
11835 Queens Blvd Ste Ll3 Forest Hills (11375) *(G-5329)*
Hanger Inc 516 678-3650
556 Merrick Rd Ste 101 Rockville Centre (11570) *(G-14820)*
Hanger Clinic, Oneonta *Also called Creative Orthotics Prosthetics (G-13206)*
Hanger Prosthectics Orthotics, Forest Hills *Also called Hanger Inc (G-5329)*
Hanger Prsthetcs & Ortho Inc 607 277-6620
310 Taughannock Blvd 1a Ithaca (14850) *(G-6882)*
Hanger Prsthetcs & Ortho Inc 607 776-8013
47 W Steuben St Bath (14810) *(G-657)*
Hanger Prsthetcs & Ortho Inc 607 771-4672
65 Pennsylvania Ave Binghamton (13903) *(G-915)*
Hanger Prsthetcs & Ortho Inc 315 472-5200
910 Erie Blvd E Ste 3 Syracuse (13210) *(G-15976)*
Hanger Prsthetcs & Ortho Inc 585 292-9510
333 Metro Park Ste F200 Rochester (14623) *(G-14439)*
Hanger Prsthetcs & Ortho Inc 607 795-1220
1300 College Ave Ste 1 Elmira (14901) *(G-4700)*
Hanger Prsthetcs & Ortho Inc 315 789-4810
787 State Route 5 And 20 Geneva (14456) *(G-5593)*
Hania By Anya Cole LLC 212 302-3550
16 W 56th St Fl 4 New York (10019) *(G-10453)*
Hankin Brothers Cap Co 716 892-8840
1910 Genesee St Buffalo (14211) *(G-3004)*
Hanna Altinis Co Inc 718 706-1134
3601 48th Ave Long Island City (11101) *(G-7785)*
Hannay Reels Inc 518 797-3791
553 State Route 143 Westerlo (12193) *(G-17071)*
Hansa Plastics Inc 631 269-9050
8 Meadow Glen Rd Kings Park (11754) *(G-7201)*
Hansa Usa LLC 646 412-6407
18 E 48th St Fl 3 New York (10017) *(G-10454)*
Hansae Co Ltd 212 354-6690
501 Fashion Ave Rm 208 New York (10018) *(G-10455)*
Hansel n Gretel Brand Inc 718 326-0041
7936 Cooper Ave Glendale (11385) *(G-5671)*
Hansen & Hansen Qulty Prtg Div, Syracuse *Also called Syracuse Computer Forms Inc (G-16075)*
Hansen Metal Fabrications, Farmington *Also called Hansen Steel (G-5161)*
Hansen Steel 585 398-2020
6021 County Road 41 Farmington (14425) *(G-5161)*
Hanson Aggregates East LLC 716 372-1574
4419 S Nine Mile Rd Allegany (14706) *(G-203)*
Hanson Aggregates East LLC 585 798-0762
Glenwood Ave Medina (14103) *(G-8307)*
Hanson Aggregates East LLC 716 372-1574
4419 S 9 Mile Rd Falconer (14733) *(G-4907)*
Hanson Aggregates East LLC 585 343-1787
5870 Main Rd Stafford (14143) *(G-15641)*
Hanson Aggregates East LLC 315 536-9391
131 Garfield Ave Penn Yan (14527) *(G-13536)*
Hanson Aggregates East LLC 315 548-2911
392 State Route 96 Phelps (14532) *(G-13556)*
Hanson Aggregates East LLC 315 493-3721
County Rt 47 Great Bend (13643) *(G-5798)*
Hanson Aggregates New York LLC 716 665-4620
2237 Allen St Jamesville (13078) *(G-7081)*
Hanson Aggregates New York LLC 716 665-4620
2237 Allen Street Ext Jamestown (14701) *(G-7032)*
Hanson Aggregates New York LLC 585 638-5841
6895 Ellicott Street Rd Pavilion (14525) *(G-13472)*
Hanson Aggregates New York LLC 315 469-5501
4800 Jamesville Rd Jamesville (13078) *(G-7082)*
Hanson Aggregates New York LLC 607 276-5881
546 Clark Rd Almond (14804) *(G-206)*
Hanson Aggregates PA Inc 315 858-1100
237 Kingdom Rd Jordanville (13361) *(G-7160)*
Hanson Aggregates PA Inc 518 568-2444
7904 St Hwy 5 Saint Johnsville (13452) *(G-15120)*
Hanson Aggregates PA LLC 585 624-3800
2049 County Rd 6 Honeoye Falls (14472) *(G-6557)*
Hanson Aggregates PA LLC 585 624-1220
2049 Honeoye Falls 6 Rd Honeoye Falls (14472) *(G-6558)*
Hanson Aggregates PA LLC 315 469-5501
4800 Jamesville Rd Jamesville (13078) *(G-7083)*
Hanson Aggregates PA LLC 315 685-3321
Rr 321 Skaneateles (13152) *(G-15485)*
Hanson Aggregates PA LLC 315 782-2300
25133 Nys Rt 3 Watertown (13601) *(G-16674)*
Hanson Aggregates PA LLC 315 821-7222
1780 State Route 12b Oriskany Falls (13425) *(G-13342)*
Hanson Aggregates PA LLC 315 393-3743
701 Cedar St Ogdensburg (13669) *(G-13136)*
Hanson Aggregates PA LLC 315 789-6202
2026 County Rd Ste 6 Oaks Corners (14518) *(G-13089)*
Hanson Aggregates PA LLC 585 436-3250
1535 Scottsville Rd Rochester (14623) *(G-14440)*
Hanson Ready Mix Concrete, Almond *Also called Hanson Aggregates New York LLC (G-206)*
Hanson Sign Companies, Falconer *Also called Hanson Sign Screen Prcess Corp (G-4908)*
Hanson Sign Screen Prcess Corp 716 661-3900
82 Carter St Falconer (14733) *(G-4908)*
Hansteel (usa) Inc 212 226-0105
230 Grand St Ste 602 New York (10013) *(G-10456)*
Hanyan & Higgins Company Inc 315 769-8838
9772 State Highway 56 Massena (13662) *(G-8227)*
Hanzlian Sausage Deli, Cheektowaga *Also called Hanzlian Sausage Incorporated (G-3603)*
Hanzlian Sausage Incorporated 716 891-5247
2351 Genesee St Cheektowaga (14225) *(G-3603)*
Happy Fella, New York *Also called Hf Mfg Corp (G-10513)*
Happy Sock, New York *Also called United Retail II (G-12485)*
Happy Software Inc 518 584-4668
11 Federal St Saratoga Springs (12866) *(G-15187)*
Harbec Inc 585 265-0010
358 Timothy Ln Ontario (14519) *(G-13225)*
Harbor Elc Fabrication Tls Inc 914 636-4400
29 Portman Rd New Rochelle (10801) *(G-8954)*
Harbor Wldg & Fabrication Corp 631 667-1880
208 S Fehr Way Bay Shore (11706) *(G-702)*
Harbors Maine Lobster LLC 516 775-2400
969 Lakeville Rd New Hyde Park (11040) *(G-8884)*
Harborside Press 631 470-4967
94 N Woodhull Rd Huntington (11743) *(G-6695)*
Harbour Roads, Albany *Also called Kal-Harbour Inc (G-93)*
Hard Copy Printing, New York *Also called Top Copi Reproductions Inc (G-12389)*
Hard Manufacturing Co Inc 716 893-1800
230 Grider St Buffalo (14215) *(G-3005)*
Hard Ten, Brooklyn *Also called Dreams To Print (G-1881)*
Hard Ten Clothing Inc 212 302-1321
231 W 39th St Rm 606 New York (10018) *(G-10457)*
Harden Furniture LLC (PA) 315 675-3600
8550 Mill Pond Way Mc Connellsville (13401) *(G-8251)*
Hardinge Inc (PA) 607 734-2281
1 Hardinge Dr Elmira (14902) *(G-4701)*
Hardware Specialty Co Inc 315 434-9093
23 Corporate Cir Ste 5 East Syracuse (13057) *(G-4549)*
Hargrave Development 716 877-7880
84 Shepard Ave Kenmore (14217) *(G-7175)*
Hargraves Bus MGT Consulting, Kenmore *Also called Hargrave Development (G-7175)*
Haring, J V & Son, Staten Island *Also called J V Haring & Son (G-15713)*
Harley Robert D Company Ltd 212 947-1872
240 W 35th St Ste 1005 New York (10001) *(G-10458)*
Harmac Medical Products Inc (PA) 716 897-4500
2201 Bailey Ave Buffalo (14211) *(G-3006)*
Harmon and Castella Printing 845 471-9163
164 Garden St Poughkeepsie (12601) *(G-13925)*
Harmonic Drive LLC 631 231-6630
89 Cabot Ct Ste A Hauppauge (11788) *(G-6112)*
Harold Wood Co Inc 716 873-1535
329 Hinman Ave Buffalo (14216) *(G-3007)*
Harome Designs LLC 631 864-1900
75 Modular Ave Commack (11725) *(G-3860)*
Harper International Corp 716 276-9900
4455 Genesee St Ste 123 Buffalo (14225) *(G-3008)*
Harper Products Ltd 516 997-2330
117 State St Westbury (11590) *(G-17021)*
Harper's Bazaar, New York *Also called Hearst Corporation (G-10490)*
Harpercollins 212 207-7000
195 Broadway Fl 2 New York (10007) *(G-10459)*
Harpercollins Publishers LLC (HQ) 212 207-7000
195 Broadway Fl 2 New York (10007) *(G-10460)*
Harpercollins Publishers LLC 212 553-4200
233 Broadway Rm 1001 New York (10279) *(G-10461)*
Harpers Magazine Foundation 212 420-5720
666 Broadway Fl 11 New York (10012) *(G-10462)*
Harris Assembly Group, Binghamton *Also called Arnold-Davis LLC (G-886)*
Harris Broadcast, New York *Also called Imagine Communications Corp (G-10614)*
Harris Corporation, Rome *Also called Peraton Inc (G-14857)*
Harris Corporation 585 244-5830
1680 University Ave Rochester (14610) *(G-14441)*
Harris Corporation 585 269-6600
400 Initiative Dr Rochester (14624) *(G-14442)*
Harris Corporation 585 269-5001
800 Lee Rd Bldg 601 Rochester (14606) *(G-14443)*
Harris Corporation 413 263-6200
800 Lee Rd Rochester (14606) *(G-14444)*
Harris Corporation 703 668-6239
474 Phoenix Dr Rome (13441) *(G-14841)*
Harris Corporation 585 269-5000
2696 Manitou Rd Bldg 101 Rochester (14624) *(G-14445)*
Harris Corporation 585 244-5830
570 Culver Rd Rochester (14609) *(G-14446)*
Harris Corporation 585 244-5830
50 Carlson Rd Rochester (14610) *(G-14447)*

ALPHABETIC

Harris Corporation 718 767-1100
1902 Whitestone Expy # 204 Whitestone (11357) *(G-17236)*

Harris Corporation 585 244-5830
1350 Jefferson Rd Rochester (14623) *(G-14448)*

Harris Logging Inc 518 792-1083
39 Mud Pond Rd Queensbury (12804) *(G-14011)*

Harris Machine, Newark *Also called Van Laeken Richard (G-12768)*

Harris Rf Communications, Rochester *Also called Harris Corporation (G-14448)*

Harrison Bakery West 315 422-1468
1306 W Genesee St Syracuse (13204) *(G-15977)*

Harrison Sportswear Inc 212 391-1051
260 W 39th St Fl 7 New York (10018) *(G-10463)*

Harry N Abrams Incorporated 212 206-7715
195 Broadway Fl 9 New York (10007) *(G-10464)*

Harry Winston Inc (HQ) 212 399-1000
718 5th Ave New York (10019) *(G-10465)*

Harry's Razor Company, New York *Also called Harrys Inc (G-10466)*

Harrys Inc (PA) 888 212-6855
161 Ave Of The New York (10013) *(G-10466)*

Hart Energy Publishing Lllp 212 621-4621
110 William St Fl 18 New York (10038) *(G-10467)*

Hart Reproduction Services 212 704-0556
242 W 36th St Rm 801 New York (10018) *(G-10468)*

Hart Rifle Barrel Inc 315 677-9841
1680 Jamesville Ave Syracuse (13210) *(G-15978)*

Hart Specialties Inc 631 226-5600
5000 New Horizons Blvd Amityville (11701) *(G-291)*

Hart Sports Inc 631 385-1805
4 Roxanne Ct Huntington Station (11746) *(G-6745)*

Hart To Hart Industries Inc 716 492-2709
13520 Chaffee Curriers Rd Chaffee (14030) *(G-3562)*

Hartchrom Inc 518 880-0411
25 Gibson St Ste 1 Watervliet (12189) *(G-16710)*

Hartford Hwy Dept 315 724-0654
48 Genesee St New Hartford (13413) *(G-8851)*

Hartman Enterprises Inc 315 363-7300
455 Elizabeth St Oneida (13421) *(G-13178)*

Harvard Maintenance Inc 212 682-2617
245 Park Ave New York (10167) *(G-10469)*

Harvard University Press 212 337-0280
150 5th Ave Ste 632 New York (10011) *(G-10470)*

Harvard Woven Label, New York *Also called Imperial-Harvard Label Co (G-10620)*

Harvest Homes Inc 518 895-2341
1331 Cole Rd Delanson (12053) *(G-4259)*

Harvest Technologies Inc 518 899-7124
36 Featherfoil Way Ballston Spa (12020) *(G-597)*

Harvy Canes, Flushing *Also called Harvy Surgical Supply Corp (G-5257)*

Harvy Surgical Supply Corp 718 939-1122
3435 Collins Pl Flushing (11354) *(G-5257)*

Harwitt Industries Inc 516 623-9787
61 S Main St Unit A Freeport (11520) *(G-5416)*

Hasco Componets 516 328-9292
906 Jericho Tpke New Hyde Park (11040) *(G-8885)*

Haskell Jewels Ltd (PA) 212 764-3332
390 5th Ave Fl 2 New York (10018) *(G-10471)*

Haskell Machine & Tool Inc 607 749-2421
5 S Fulton St Homer (13077) *(G-6546)*

Hastings Hide Inc 516 295-2400
372 Doughty Blvd Inwood (11096) *(G-6798)*

Hastings Tile & Bath Inc (PA) 516 379-3500
711 Koehler Ave Ste 8 Ronkonkoma (11779) *(G-14939)*

Hat Attack I Bujibaja, Bronx *Also called Hat Attack Inc (G-1353)*

Hat Attack Inc (PA) 718 994-1000
4643 Bullard Ave Ste A Bronx (10470) *(G-1353)*

Hat Depot, Brooklyn *Also called Room At The Top Inc (G-2526)*

Hat Factory Furniture Co 914 788-6288
1000 N Division St Ste 8 Peekskill (10566) *(G-13503)*

Hat World & Lids, Rochester *Also called Genesco Inc (G-14414)*

Hatfield Metal Fab Inc 845 454-9078
16 Hatfield Ln Poughkeepsie (12603) *(G-13926)*

Hathaway Prcess Instrmentation, Amherst *Also called Allied Motion Systems Corp (G-223)*

Hatherleigh Company Ltd 607 538-1092
62545 State Highway 10 Hobart (13788) *(G-6451)*

Haun Welding Supply Inc 607 846-2289
1100 Sullivan St Elmira (14901) *(G-4702)*

Haun Welding Supply Inc 315 592-5012
214 N 4th St Fulton (13069) *(G-5474)*

Hauppauge Computer Works Inc (HQ) 631 434-1600
909 Motor Pkwy Hauppauge (11788) *(G-6113)*

Hauppauge Digital Inc (PA) 631 434-1600
909 Motor Pkwy Hauppauge (11788) *(G-6114)*

Hauppuge Cmpt Dgtal Erope Sarl, Hauppauge *Also called Hauppauge Computer Works Inc (G-6113)*

Haute By Blair Stanley LLC 212 557-7868
330 E 38th St Apt 23e New York (10016) *(G-10472)*

Havaianas, New York *Also called Alpargatas Usa Inc (G-9149)*

Hawk-I Security Inc 631 656-1056
355 Oser Ave Hauppauge (11788) *(G-6115)*

Hawkencatskills LLC 518 966-8900
18 Shultes Rd Greenville (12083) *(G-5903)*

Hawkeye Forest Products, Hamburg *Also called Hawkeye Forest Products LP (G-5951)*

Hawkeye Forest Products LP (PA) 608 534-6156
4002 Legion Dr Hamburg (14075) *(G-5951)*

Hawkins Fabrics Inc (PA) 518 773-9550
111 Woodside Ave Ste 1 Gloversville (12078) *(G-5729)*

Hawver Display Inc (PA) 585 544-2290
140 Carter St Rochester (14621) *(G-14449)*

Hayman-Chaffey Designs Inc 212 889-7771
137 E 25th St New York (10010) *(G-10473)*

Haymarket Group Ltd 212 239-0855
12 W 37th St 9 New York (10018) *(G-10474)*

Haymarket Media Inc (HQ) 646 638-6000
275 7th Ave Fl 10 New York (10001) *(G-10475)*

Haynes Roberts Inc 212 989-1901
601 W 26th St Rm 1655 New York (10001) *(G-10476)*

Hazlitt 1852 Vineyards, Hector *Also called Hazlitts 1852 Vineyards Inc (G-6282)*

Hazlitts 1852 Vineyards Inc 607 546-9463
5712 State Route 414 Hector (14841) *(G-6282)*

Hazlow Electronics Inc 585 325-5323
49 Saint Bridgets Dr Rochester (14605) *(G-14450)*

HB, Hauppauge *Also called Hohmann & Barnard Inc (G-6118)*

HB Architectural Lighting Inc 347 851-4123
862 E 139th St Bronx (10454) *(G-1354)*

HB Athletic Inc (PA) 914 560-8422
56 Harrison St Fl 4 New Rochelle (10801) *(G-8955)*

Hbs, Great Neck *Also called Toni Industries Inc (G-5864)*

Hc Brill Co Inc 716 685-4000
3765 Walden Ave Lancaster (14086) *(G-7343)*

HC Contracting Inc 212 643-9292
318 W 39th St Fl 4 New York (10018) *(G-10477)*

Hci Engineering 315 336-3450
5880 Bartlett Rd Rome (13440) *(G-14842)*

Hdm Hydraulics LLC 716 694-8004
125 Fire Tower Dr Tonawanda (14150) *(G-16187)*

Heads & Tails Lure Co 607 739-7900
283 Hibbard Rd Horseheads (14845) *(G-6609)*

Health Care Compliance (HQ) 516 478-4100
30 Jericho Executive Plz 400c Jericho (11753) *(G-7103)*

Health Care Originals Inc 585 471-8215
1 Pleasant St Ste 442 Rochester (14604) *(G-14451)*

Health Matters America Inc 716 235-8772
2501 Broadway St Unit 2 Buffalo (14227) *(G-3009)*

Healthalliance Hospital 845 338-2500
105 Marys Ave Kingston (12401) *(G-7219)*

Healthcare Consulting Svcs Inc 860 740-8660
974 Little East Neck Rd West Babylon (11704) *(G-16821)*

Healthee Endeavors Inc 718 653-5499
3565c Boston Rd Bronx (10469) *(G-1355)*

Healthone Pharmacy Inc 718 495-9015
119 Pennsylvania Ave Brooklyn (11207) *(G-2068)*

Healthway Home Products Inc 315 298-2904
3420 Maple Ave Pulaski (13142) *(G-13968)*

Healthway Products Company 315 207-1410
249a Mitchell St Oswego (13126) *(G-13357)*

Healthy Basement Systems LLC 516 650-9046
79 Cedarhurst Ave Medford (11763) *(G-8280)*

Healthy Brand Oil Corp (PA) 718 937-0806
5215 11th St Ste 3 Long Island City (11101) *(G-7786)*

Healthy N Fit Intl Inc 914 271-6040
435 Yorktown Rd Croton On Hudson (10520) *(G-4090)*

Healthy Way of Life Magazine 718 616-1681
1529 Voorhies Ave Brooklyn (11235) *(G-2069)*

Heany Industries Inc 585 889-2700
249 Briarwood Ln Scottsville (14546) *(G-15358)*

Hearing Aid Office, The, Albany *Also called Benway-Haworth-Lwlr-Iacosta He (G-51)*

Hearing Spech Ctr of Rochester 585 286-9373
1170 Ridge Rd Ste 2 Webster (14580) *(G-16749)*

Hearst Bus Communications Inc (PA) 212 649-2000
300 W 57th St New York (10019) *(G-10478)*

Hearst Business Media (HQ) 516 227-1300
50 Charles Lindbergh Blvd # 100 Uniondale (11553) *(G-16318)*

Hearst Business Media Corp 631 650-6151
3500 Sunrise Hwy Ste 100 Great River (11739) *(G-5869)*

Hearst Business Media Corp 631 650-4441
3500 Sunrise Hwy Great River (11739) *(G-5870)*

Hearst Business Publishing Inc 212 969-7500
888 7th Ave Fl 2 New York (10106) *(G-10479)*

Hearst Communications Inc (PA) 415 777-7825
300 W 57th St New York (10019) *(G-10480)*

Hearst Communications Inc (HQ) 212 649-2000
300 W 57th St New York (10019) *(G-10481)*

Hearst Corporation (PA) 212 649-2000
300 W 57th St Fl 42 New York (10019) *(G-10482)*

Hearst Corporation 212 649-3100
300 W 57th St Fl 29 New York (10019) *(G-10483)*

Hearst Corporation 212 903-5366
224 W 57th St Frnt 1 New York (10019) *(G-10484)*

Hearst Corporation 212 767-5800
1633 Broadway Fl 44 New York (10019) *(G-10485)*

Hearst Corporation 516 382-4580
810 7th Ave New York (10019) *(G-10486)*

Hearst Corporation 212 830-2980
1790 Broadway New York (10019) *(G-10487)*

Hearst Corporation.....518 454-5694
645 Albany Shaker Rd Albany (12211) *(G-85)*
Hearst Corporation.....212 649-4271
300 W 57th St Fl 21 New York (10019) *(G-10488)*
Hearst Corporation.....212 204-4300
1440 Broadway Fl 13 New York (10018) *(G-10489)*
Hearst Corporation.....212 903-5000
300 W 57th St Fl 42 New York (10019) *(G-10490)*
Hearst Corporation.....212 649-2275
300 W 57th St Fl 42 New York (10019) *(G-10491)*
Hearst Digital Studios Inc.....212 969-7552
300 W 57th St New York (10019) *(G-10492)*
Hearst Holdings Inc (HQ).....212 649-2000
300 W 57th St New York (10019) *(G-10493)*
Hearst Interactive Media, New York *Also called Hearst Communications Inc (G-10481)*
Hearst Magazines, New York *Also called Hearst Corporation (G-10482)*
Heart of Tea.....917 725-3164
419 Lafayette St Fl 2f New York (10003) *(G-10494)*
Hearth Cabinets and More Ltd.....315 641-1197
4483 Buckley Rd Liverpool (13088) *(G-7545)*
Heartland Commerce Inc.....845 920-0800
1 Blue Hill Plz Ste 16 Pearl River (10965) *(G-13480)*
Hearts of Palm LLC.....212 944-6660
1411 Broadway Fl 23 New York (10018) *(G-10495)*
Hearts of Palm LLC (PA).....212 944-6660
1411 Broadway Fl 25 New York (10018) *(G-10496)*
Heartwood Specialties Inc.....607 654-0102
10249 Gibson Rd Hammondsport (14840) *(G-5977)*
Heary Bros Lghtning Protection.....716 941-6141
11291 Moore Rd Springville (14141) *(G-15633)*
Heat and Frost Inslatrs & Asbs.....718 784-3456
3553 24th St Astoria (11106) *(G-441)*
Heat USA II LLC (PA).....212 254-4328
11902 23rd Ave College Point (11356) *(G-3811)*
Heat USA II LLC.....212 564-4328
35 E 21st St New York (10010) *(G-10497)*
Heat-Timer Corporation.....212 481-2020
79 Alexander Ave Ste 36a Bronx (10454) *(G-1356)*
Heat-Timer Service, Bronx *Also called Heat-Timer Corporation (G-1356)*
Heath Manufacturing Company.....800 444-3140
700 Ellicott St Batavia (14020) *(G-639)*
Heath Outdoors Products, Batavia *Also called Heath Manufacturing Company (G-639)*
Heatherdell RB Hammers, Blauvelt *Also called Rbhammers Corp (G-968)*
Heating & Burner Supply Inc.....718 665-0006
479 Walton Ave Bronx (10451) *(G-1357)*
Heaven Fresh USA Inc.....800 642-0367
4600 Witmer Industrial Es Niagara Falls (14305) *(G-12850)*
Hebeler LLC (PA).....716 873-9300
2000 Military Rd Tonawanda (14150) *(G-16188)*
Hebeler Process Solutions LLC.....716 873-9300
2000 Military Rd Tonawanda (14150) *(G-16189)*
Hecht & Sohn Glass Co Inc.....718 782-8295
406 Willoughby Ave Brooklyn (11205) *(G-2070)*
Hector Pt Sr Rehab Svc Pllc.....518 371-5554
1 Wall St Clifton Park (12065) *(G-3724)*
Hedges and Gardens, East Hampton *Also called Irony Limited Inc (G-4431)*
Hedonist Artisan Chocolates.....585 461-2815
674 South Ave Ste B Rochester (14620) *(G-14452)*
Hefti, New Rochelle *Also called Harbor Elc Fabrication Tls Inc (G-8954)*
Heidelberg Group Inc.....315 866-0999
3056 State Hwy Rte 28 N Herkimer (13350) *(G-6326)*
Heidenhain International Inc (HQ).....716 661-1700
1 Precision Way Jamestown (14701) *(G-7033)*
Heindl Printers, Rochester *Also called Louis Heindl & Son Inc (G-14504)*
Heineck Associates Inc.....631 207-2347
28 Curtis Ave Bellport (11713) *(G-827)*
Heintz & Weber Co Inc.....716 852-7171
150 Reading St Buffalo (14220) *(G-3010)*
Heleo.com, New York *Also called Helium Media Inc (G-10498)*
Helgen Industries Inc.....631 841-6300
431 Bayview Ave Amityville (11701) *(G-292)*
Heliojet Cleaning Tech Inc.....585 768-8710
57 North St Ste 120 Le Roy (14482) *(G-7433)*
Helium Media Inc.....917 596-4081
165 Duane St Apt 7b New York (10013) *(G-10498)*
Hellas Stone Inc.....718 545-4716
3344 9th St Astoria (11106) *(G-442)*
Heller Performance Polymers, New York *Also called Atc Plastics LLC (G-9297)*
Hello and Hola Media Inc.....212 807-4795
1 Metrotech Ctr Fl 18 Brooklyn (11201) *(G-2071)*
Helmel Engineering Pdts Inc.....716 297-8644
6520 Lockport Rd Niagara Falls (14305) *(G-12851)*
Helmer Avenue, West Winfield *Also called Precisionmatics Co Inc (G-16987)*
Helmont Mills Inc (HQ).....518 568-7913
15 Lion Ave Saint Johnsville (13452) *(G-15121)*
Helvetica Press Incorporated.....212 737-1857
244 5th Ave New York (10001) *(G-10499)*
Hemisphere Novelties Inc.....914 378-4100
167 Saw Mill River Rd 3c Yonkers (10701) *(G-17469)*
Hempstead Sentinel Inc.....516 486-5000
55 Chasner St Hempstead (11550) *(G-6297)*
Hemstrought's Bakeries, New Hartford *Also called B & D Enterprises of Utica (G-8846)*
Henderson Products Inc.....315 785-0994
22686 Fisher Rd Ste A Watertown (13601) *(G-16675)*
Henderson Truck Equipment, Watertown *Also called Henderson Products Inc (G-16675)*
Hendrickson Custom Cabinetry.....718 401-0137
132 Saint Anns Ave Fl 2 Bronx (10454) *(G-1358)*
Hengyuan Copper USA Inc.....718 357-6666
14107 20th Ave Ste 506 Whitestone (11357) *(G-17237)*
Hennig Custom Woodwork Corp.....516 536-3460
2497 Long Beach Rd Oceanside (11572) *(G-13101)*
Hennig Custom Woodworking, Oceanside *Also called Hennig Custom Woodwork Corp (G-13101)*
Henpecked Husband Farms Corp.....631 728-2800
1212 Speonk Riverhead Rd Speonk (11972) *(G-15599)*
Henry B Urban Inc.....212 489-3308
619 W 54th St Ste 6l New York (10019) *(G-10500)*
Henry Design Studios Inc.....516 801-2760
129 Birch Hill Rd Ste 2 Locust Valley (11560) *(G-7662)*
Henry Dunay Designs Inc.....212 768-9700
10 W 46th St Ste 1200 New York (10036) *(G-10501)*
Henry Holt and Company LLC.....646 307-5095
175 5th Ave Ste 400 New York (10010) *(G-10502)*
Henry Morgan.....718 317-5013
433 Tennyson Dr Staten Island (10312) *(G-15704)*
Henry Newman LLC.....607 273-8512
312 4th St Ithaca (14850) *(G-6883)*
Henry Schein Inc.....315 431-0340
6057 Corporate Dr Ste 2 East Syracuse (13057) *(G-4550)*
Henry Schein Fincl Svcs LLC (HQ).....631 843-5500
135 Duryea Rd Melville (11747) *(G-8356)*
Henry Schein International Inc, Melville *Also called Henry Schein Fincl Svcs LLC (G-8356)*
Henry Segal Co, Hempstead *Also called Shane Tex Inc (G-6309)*
Henrys Deals Inc.....347 821-4685
1002 Quentin Rd Ste 2009 Brooklyn (11223) *(G-2072)*
Herald Press Inc.....718 784-5255
3710 30th St Long Island City (11101) *(G-7787)*
Herald Publishing Company LLC.....315 470-2022
4 Times Sq Fl 23 New York (10036) *(G-10503)*
Herald Statesman, Yonkers *Also called Gannett Stllite Info Ntwrk Inc (G-17462)*
Herbert Jaffe Inc.....718 392-1956
4011 Skillman Ave Long Island City (11104) *(G-7788)*
Herbert Wolf Corp.....212 242-0300
95 Vandam St Apt C New York (10013) *(G-10504)*
Hercules, Huntington Station *Also called I A S National Inc (G-6748)*
Hercules Candy Co.....315 463-4339
209 W Heman St East Syracuse (13057) *(G-4551)*
Hercules Gift & Gormet, East Syracuse *Also called Hercules Candy Co (G-4551)*
Hercules Group Inc.....212 813-8000
27 Seaview Blvd Port Washington (11050) *(G-13842)*
Hercules Heat Treating Corp.....718 625-1266
101 Classon Ave 113 Brooklyn (11205) *(G-2073)*
Hercules International Inc.....631 423-6900
95 W Hills Rd Huntington Station (11746) *(G-6746)*
Herff Jones LLC.....607 936-2366
262 W 2nd St Corning (14830) *(G-3994)*
Hergo Ergonomic Support (PA).....718 894-0639
5601 55th Ave Maspeth (11378) *(G-8175)*
Heritage Contract Flooring LLC.....716 853-1555
29 Depot St Buffalo (14206) *(G-3011)*
Heritage Packaging, Victor *Also called W Stuart Smith Inc (G-16535)*
Heritage Printing Center.....518 563-8240
94 Margaret St Plattsburgh (12901) *(G-13695)*
Heritage Wide Plank Flooring, Riverhead *Also called Custom Woodwork Ltd (G-14151)*
Herkimer Cheese, Ilion *Also called Original Hrkmer Cnty Chese Inc (G-6782)*
Herkimer Diamond Mines Inc.....315 891-7355
800 Mohawk St Herkimer (13350) *(G-6327)*
Herkimer Tool & Equipment Co, Herkimer *Also called Herkimer Tool & Machining Corp (G-6328)*
Herkimer Tool & Machining Corp.....315 866-2110
125 Marginal Rd Herkimer (13350) *(G-6328)*
Herman H Sticht Company Inc.....718 852-7602
45 Main St Ste 401 Brooklyn (11201) *(G-2074)*
Herman Hall Communications.....718 941-1879
1630 Nostrand Ave Brooklyn (11226) *(G-2075)*
Herman Kay, New York *Also called Mystic Inc (G-11358)*
Herman Kay Company Ltd.....212 239-2025
463 7th Ave Fl 12 New York (10018) *(G-10505)*
Hermann Gerdens Inc.....631 841-3132
1725 N Strongs Rd Copiague (11726) *(G-3931)*
Hermann J Wiemer Vineyard.....607 243-7971
3962 Rte 14 Dundee (14837) *(G-4354)*
Hermosa Corp.....315 768-4320
102 Main St New York Mills (13417) *(G-12744)*
Heron Hill Vineyards Inc (PA).....607 868-4241
9301 County Route 76 Hammondsport (14840) *(G-5978)*
Heron Hill Winery, Hammondsport *Also called Heron Hill Vineyards Inc (G-5978)*
Herr Manufacturing Co Inc.....716 754-4341
17 Pearce Ave Tonawanda (14150) *(G-16190)*
Herris Gourmet Inc.....917 578-2308
536 Grand St Brooklyn (11211) *(G-2076)*

ALPHABETIC

(PA)=Parent Co (HQ)=Headquarters (DH)=Div Headquarters
2018 Harris
New York Manufacturers Directory
969

Herrmann Group LLC 716 876-9798
2320 Elmwood Ave Kenmore (14217) *(G-7176)*
Hersco-Arch Products, Long Island City Also called Hersco-Orthotic Labs Corp *(G-7789)*
Hersco-Orthotic Labs Corp 718 391-0416
3928 Crescent St Long Island City (11101) *(G-7789)*
Hershel Horowitz Corp 212 719-1710
580 5th Ave Ste 901 New York (10036) *(G-10506)*
Hershey Kiss 203 Inc 516 503-3740
3536 Bunker Ave Wantagh (11793) *(G-16579)*
Hertling Trousers Inc 718 784-6100
236 Greenpoint Ave Brooklyn (11222) *(G-2077)*
Hes Inc 607 359-2974
6303 Symonds Hill Rd Addison (14801) *(G-7)*
Hess Corporation (PA) 212 997-8500
1185 Ave Of The Amer New York (10036) *(G-10507)*
Hess Energy Exploration Ltd (HQ) 732 750-6500
1185 Ave Of The Americas New York (10036) *(G-10508)*
Hess Explrtion Prod Hldngs Ltd (HQ) 732 750-6000
1185 Ave Of The Americas New York (10036) *(G-10509)*
Hess Oil Virgin Island Corp 212 997-8500
1185 Ave Of The Amer 39 New York (10036) *(G-10510)*
Hess Pipeline Corporation 212 997-8500
1185 Ave Of The Amer 39 New York (10036) *(G-10511)*
Hess Tioga Gas Plant LLC 212 997-8500
1185 Ave Of The Americas New York (10036) *(G-10512)*
Heterochemical Corporation 516 561-8225
111 E Hawthorne Ave Valley Stream (11580) *(G-16435)*
Hexion Inc 518 792-8040
64 Fernan Rd South Glens Falls (12803) *(G-15548)*
Hey Doll, New York Also called Lesilu Productions Inc *(G-11010)*
Hf Mfg Corp (PA) 212 594-9142
1460 Broadway New York (10036) *(G-10513)*
Hf Technologies LLC 585 254-5030
810 Martin Rd Hamlin (14464) *(G-5973)*
HFC Prestige Intl US LLC 212 389-7800
350 5th Ave New York (10118) *(G-10514)*
Hfi, New York Also called Home Fashions Intl LLC *(G-10545)*
Hgi Skydyne, Port Jervis Also called Hornet Group Inc *(G-13808)*
Hh Liquidating Corp 646 282-2500
110 E 59th St Fl 34 New York (10022) *(G-10515)*
HHS Pharmaceuticals Inc 347 674-1670
107 Hamilton Pl New York (10031) *(G-10516)*
HI Speed Envelope Co Inc 718 617-1600
560 S 3rd Ave Ste 1 Mount Vernon (10550) *(G-8735)*
HI Tech Signs of NY Inc 516 794-7880
415 E Meadow Ave East Meadow (11554) *(G-4444)*
HI Wines, New York Also called Frank Wines Inc *(G-10252)*
Hi-Lites, Watkins Glen Also called Skylark Publications Ltd *(G-16721)*
Hi-Med, Old Bethpage Also called Hitemco Medical Applications *(G-13149)*
Hi-Tech Advanced Solutions Inc 718 926-3488
10525 65th Ave Apt 4h Forest Hills (11375) *(G-5330)*
Hi-Tech Cnc Machining Corp 914 668-5090
13 Elm Ave Mount Vernon (10550) *(G-8736)*
Hi-Tech Industries NY Inc 607 217-7361
23 Ozalid Rd Johnson City (13790) *(G-7125)*
Hi-Tech Metals Inc 718 894-1212
5920 56th Ave Maspeth (11378) *(G-8176)*
Hi-Tech Packg World-Wide LLC 845 947-1912
110 Corporate Dr New Windsor (12553) *(G-8985)*
Hi-Tech Pharmacal - An Akorn, Amityville Also called Hi-Tech Pharmacal Co Inc *(G-293)*
Hi-Tech Pharmacal Co Inc (HQ) 631 789-8228
369 Bayview Ave Amityville (11701) *(G-293)*
Hi-Temp Brazing Inc 631 491-4917
539 Acorn St Deer Park (11729) *(G-4170)*
Hi-Temp Fabrication Inc 716 852-5655
15 Lawrence Bell Dr Buffalo (14221) *(G-3012)*
Hi-Tron Semiconductor Corp 631 231-1500
85 Engineers Rd Hauppauge (11788) *(G-6116)*
Hibert Publishing LLC 914 381-7474
222 Purchase St Rye (10580) *(G-15085)*
Hibu Inc (HQ) 516 730-1900
90 Merrick Ave Ste 530 East Meadow (11554) *(G-4445)*
Hickey Freeman Tailored CL Inc 585 467-7240
1155 N Clinton Ave Rochester (14621) *(G-14453)*
Hickory Hollow Wind Cellars, Dundee Also called Hickory Road Land Co LLC *(G-4355)*
Hickory Road Land Co LLC 607 243-9114
5289 Route 14 Dundee (14837) *(G-4355)*
Hicksville Machine Works Corp 516 931-1524
761 S Broadway Hicksville (11801) *(G-6383)*
Hig Capital, Williamsville Also called Ashton-Potter USA Ltd *(G-17261)*
Higgins Supl Co, Mc Graw Also called Higgins Supply Company Inc *(G-8253)*
Higgins Supply Company Inc 607 836-6474
18-23 South St Mc Graw (13101) *(G-8253)*
High Energy U. S. A., New York Also called Kidz World Inc *(G-10883)*
High Falls Brewing Company LLC (HQ) 585 546-1030
445 Saint Paul St Rochester (14605) *(G-14454)*
High Falls Operating Co LLC 585 546-1030
445 Saint Paul St Rochester (14605) *(G-14455)*
High Frequency Tech Co Inc 631 242-3020
172 Brook Ave Ste D Deer Park (11729) *(G-4171)*

High Performance Sftwr USA Inc 866 616-4958
145 Hook Creek Blvd Valley Stream (11581) *(G-16436)*
High Point Design LLC 212 354-2400
1411 Broadway Fl 8 New York (10018) *(G-10517)*
High Prfmce Plymr Cmposits Div, Medford Also called Enecon Corporation *(G-8274)*
High Quality Video Inc (PA) 212 686-9534
12 W 27th St Fl 7 New York (10001) *(G-10518)*
High Ridge News LLC 718 548-7412
5818 Broadway Bronx (10463) *(G-1359)*
High Speed Hammer Company Inc 585 266-4287
313 Norton St Rochester (14621) *(G-14456)*
High Times Vape 631 569-5322
500 Medford Ave Ste 1 Patchogue (11772) *(G-13447)*
High Voltage Inc 518 329-3275
31 County Route 7a Copake (12516) *(G-3913)*
Highcrest Investors LLC (HQ) 212 702-4323
445 Hamilton Ave Ste 1210 New York (10153) *(G-10519)*
Higher Power Industries Inc 914 709-9800
11 Sunny Slope Ter Yonkers (10703) *(G-17470)*
Highland Injection Molding 716 945-2424
175 Rochester St Salamanca (14779) *(G-15127)*
Highland Museum & Lighthouse 508 487-1121
111 M Simons Rd Cairo (12413) *(G-3298)*
Highland Organization Corp 631 991-3240
435 Unit 23 Brook Ave Deer Park (11729) *(G-4172)*
Highland Valley Supply Inc 845 849-2863
30 Airport Dr Wappingers Falls (12590) *(G-16592)*
Highlander Realty Inc 914 235-8073
70 Church St New Rochelle (10805) *(G-8956)*
Highline Media LLC 859 692-2100
375 Park Ave New York (10152) *(G-10520)*
Highrange Fuels Inc 914 930-8300
96 Oregon Rd Cortlandt Manor (10567) *(G-4076)*
Highway Garage 518 568-2837
110 State Highway 331 Saint Johnsville (13452) *(G-15122)*
Highway Toll ADM LLC 516 684-9584
66 Powerhouse Rd Ste 301 Roslyn Heights (11577) *(G-15051)*
Hill Crest Press 518 943-0671
138 Grandview Ave Catskill (12414) *(G-3457)*
Hill Knitting Mills Inc 718 846-5000
10005 92nd Ave Ste Mgmt Richmond Hill (11418) *(G-14087)*
Hill, Lois Accessories, New York Also called Ancient Modern Art LLC *(G-9199)*
Hillary Merchant Inc 646 575-9242
2 Wall St Ste 807 New York (10005) *(G-10521)*
Hillburn Granite Company Inc 845 357-8900
166 Sixth St Hillburn (10931) *(G-6441)*
Hilliard Corporation (PA) 607 733-7121
100 W 4th St Elmira (14901) *(G-4703)*
Hilliard Corporation 607 733-7121
1420 College Ave Elmira (14901) *(G-4704)*
Hills Pet Products Inc (HQ) 212 310-2000
300 Park Ave New York (10022) *(G-10522)*
Hillside Iron Works, Waterford Also called Maximum Security Products Corp *(G-16634)*
Hillside Printing Inc 718 658-6719
16013 Hillside Ave Jamaica (11432) *(G-6955)*
Hilltop Slate Inc 518 642-1453
Rr 22 Box A Middle Granville (12849) *(G-8432)*
Hilltown Pork Inc (PA) 518 781-4050
12948 State Route 22 Canaan (12029) *(G-3359)*
Hilord Chemical Corporation 631 234-7373
70 Engineers Rd Hauppauge (11788) *(G-6117)*
Himatsingka America Inc (HQ) 212 545-8929
261 5th Ave Rm 1400 New York (10016) *(G-10523)*
Himatsingka America Inc 212 252-0802
261 5th Ave Rm 501 New York (10016) *(G-10524)*
Himatsingka Holdings NA Inc (HQ) 212 545-8929
261 5th Ave Rm 1400 New York (10016) *(G-10525)*
Hinge Inc 502 445-3111
137 5th Ave Fl 5 New York (10010) *(G-10526)*
Hinspergers Poly Industries 585 798-6625
430 W Oak Orchard St Medina (14103) *(G-8308)*
Hipotronics Inc (HQ) 845 279-8091
1650 Route 22 Brewster (10509) *(G-1217)*
Hippo Industries, Oyster Bay Also called Engineering Maint Pdts Inc *(G-13395)*
Hippocrene Books Inc (PA) 212 685-4371
171 Madison Ave Rm 1605 New York (10016) *(G-10527)*
Hipshot Products Inc 607 532-9404
8248 State Route 96 Interlaken (14847) *(G-6786)*
Hirsch Optical Corp 516 752-2211
91 Carolyn Blvd Farmingdale (11735) *(G-5013)*
His Productions USA Inc 212 594-3737
139 Fulton St Rm 317 New York (10038) *(G-10528)*
His Vision Inc 585 254-0022
1260 Lyell Ave Rochester (14606) *(G-14457)*
Hispanica Intl Delights Amer, New York Also called Hispanica Intl Dlghts Amer Inc *(G-10529)*
Hispanica Intl Dlghts Amer Inc 866 928-5070
575 Lexington Ave Fl 4 New York (10022) *(G-10529)*
Historcal Soc of Mddltown Walk 845 342-0941
25 East Ave Middletown (10940) *(G-8478)*
Historic TW Inc (HQ) 212 484-8000
75 Rockefeller Plz New York (10019) *(G-10530)*
History Publishing Company LLC 845 398-8161
173 Route 9w Palisades (10964) *(G-13426)*

Hisun Led, Flushing *Also called Hisun Optoelectronics Co Ltd (G-5258)*
Hisun Optoelectronics Co Ltd....718 886-6966
4109 College Point Blvd Flushing (11355) *(G-5258)*
Hitachi Cable America Inc (HQ)....914 694-9200
2 Manhattanville Rd # 301 Purchase (10577) *(G-13973)*
Hitachi Metals America Ltd....914 694-9200
2 Manhattanville Rd # 301 Purchase (10577) *(G-13974)*
Hitachi Metals America Ltd (HQ)....914 694-9200
2 Manhattanville Rd # 301 Purchase (10577) *(G-13975)*
Hitemco, Old Bethpage *Also called Barson Composites Corporation (G-13147)*
Hitemco Medical Applications....516 752-7882
160 Sweet Hollow Rd Old Bethpage (11804) *(G-13149)*
Hje Company Inc....518 792-8733
820 Quaker Rd Queensbury (12804) *(G-14012)*
Hjn Inc (PA)....212 398-9564
16 W 46th St Ste 900 New York (10036) *(G-10531)*
HK Metal Trading Ltd....212 868-3333
450 Fashion Ave Ste 2300 New York (10123) *(G-10532)*
Hks Printing Company Inc....212 675-2529
115 E 27th St New York (10016) *(G-10533)*
Hlp Klearfold Packaging Pdts....718 554-3271
75 Maiden Ln Rm 808 New York (10038) *(G-10534)*
Hlp Klearfold Visualize, New York *Also called Hlp Klearfold Packaging Pdts (G-10534)*
Hlw Acres LLC....585 591-0795
1727 Exchange Street Rd Attica (14011) *(G-472)*
Hlw Acres Poultry Processing, Attica *Also called Hlw Acres LLC (G-472)*
Hmi Metal Powders, Clayville *Also called Homogeneous Metals Inc (G-3715)*
Hmi Metal Powders....315 839-5421
2395 Main St Clayville (13322) *(G-3714)*
Hmo Beverage Corp....917 371-6100
68 33rd St Unit 4 Brooklyn (11232) *(G-2078)*
HMS Productions Inc (PA)....212 719-9190
250 W 39th St Fl 12 New York (10018) *(G-10535)*
Hn Precision-Ny, Rochester *Also called Nationwide Precision Pdts Corp (G-14549)*
Hnh, New York *Also called Handy & Harman Ltd (G-10450)*
Hni Corporation....212 683-2232
200 Lexington Ave Rm 1112 New York (10016) *(G-10536)*
HNST Mold Inspections LLC (PA)....845 215-9258
6 Kevin Ct Nanuet (10954) *(G-8803)*
Hobart Corporation....631 864-3440
71 Mall Dr Ste 1 Commack (11725) *(G-3861)*
Hobart Corporation....585 427-9000
3495 Winton Pl Rochester (14623) *(G-14458)*
Hockey Facility....518 452-7396
830 Albany Shaker Rd Albany (12211) *(G-86)*
Hodgins Engraving Co Inc....585 343-4444
3817 W Main Street Rd Batavia (14020) *(G-640)*
Hoehn Inc....518 463-8900
159 Chestnut St Albany (12210) *(G-87)*
Hoehn.us, Albany *Also called Hoehn Inc (G-87)*
Hoercher Industries Inc....585 398-2982
A1 Country Club Rd Ste 1 East Rochester (14445) *(G-4480)*
Hoffman & Hoffman....315 536-4773
489 State Route 54 Penn Yan (14527) *(G-13537)*
Hoffmans Trade Group LLC....518 250-5556
64 2nd St Troy (12180) *(G-16261)*
Hogan Flavors & Fragrances....212 598-4310
130 E 18th St Frnt New York (10003) *(G-10537)*
Hogan Fragrances International, New York *Also called Hogan Flavors & Fragrances (G-10537)*
Hogil Pharmaceutical Corp....914 681-1800
237 Mmaroneck Ave Ste 207 White Plains (10605) *(G-17147)*
Hohenforst Splitting Co Inc....518 725-0012
152 W Fulton St Gloversville (12078) *(G-5730)*
Hohl Machine & Conveyor Co Inc....716 882-7210
1580 Niagara St Buffalo (14213) *(G-3013)*
Hohlveyor, Buffalo *Also called Hohl Machine & Conveyor Co Inc (G-3013)*
Hohmann & Barnard Inc (HQ)....631 234-0600
30 Rasons Ct Hauppauge (11788) *(G-6118)*
Hohmann & Barnard Inc....518 357-9757
310 Wayto Rd Schenectady (12303) *(G-15295)*
Hola Publishing Co....718 424-3129
2932 Northern Blvd Long Island City (11101) *(G-7790)*
Holbrooke By Sberry, New York *Also called Holbrooke Inc (G-10538)*
Holbrooke Inc....646 397-4674
444 E 20th St Apt 1b New York (10009) *(G-10538)*
Holdens Screen Supply Corp....212 627-2727
121 Varick St New York (10013) *(G-10539)*
Holiday House Publishing, New York *Also called Bicker Inc (G-9437)*
Holistic Blends Inc....315 468-4300
6726 Townline Rd Stop 1 Syracuse (13211) *(G-15979)*
Holland & Sherry Inc (PA)....212 542-8410
330 E 59th St Ph New York (10022) *(G-10540)*
Holland & Sherry Intr Design, New York *Also called Holland & Sherry Inc (G-10540)*
Hollander HM Fshons Hldngs LLC....212 575-0400
440 Park Ave S Fl 10 New York (10016) *(G-10541)*
Hollander Sleep Products LLC....212 575-0400
440 Park Ave S New York (10016) *(G-10542)*
Hollingsworth & Vose Company....518 695-8000
3235 County Rte 113 Greenwich (12834) *(G-5908)*
Hollywood Advertising Banners....631 842-3000
539 Oak St Copiague (11726) *(G-3932)*
Hollywood Banners, Copiague *Also called Hollywood Advertising Banners (G-3932)*
Hollywood Banners Inc....631 842-3000
539 Oak St Copiague (11726) *(G-3933)*
Hollywood Cabinets Co....516 354-0857
182 Hendrickson Ave Elmont (11003) *(G-4733)*
Hollywood Signs Inc....917 577-7333
388 3rd Ave Brooklyn (11215) *(G-2079)*
Holmes Group The Inc....212 333-2300
271 W 47th St Apt 23a New York (10036) *(G-10543)*
Holstein World, East Syracuse *Also called H F W Communications Inc (G-4548)*
Holy Cow Kosher LLC....347 788-8620
750 Chestnut Ridge Rd Spring Valley (10977) *(G-15611)*
Holyoke Fittings Inc....718 649-0710
850 Stanley Ave Brooklyn (11208) *(G-2080)*
Home Depot USA Inc....845 561-6540
1220 New York 300 Newburgh (12550) *(G-12782)*
Home Depot, The, Newburgh *Also called Home Depot USA Inc (G-12782)*
Home Fashions Intl LLC (PA)....212 689-3579
295 5th Ave Ste 1520 New York (10016) *(G-10544)*
Home Fashions Intl LLC....212 684-0091
295 5th Ave Ste 1520 New York (10016) *(G-10545)*
Home Ideal Inc....718 762-8998
4528 159th St Flushing (11358) *(G-5259)*
Home Lighting & Accessories, New City *Also called Doctorow Communications Inc (G-8830)*
Home Maide Inc....845 837-1700
1 Short St Harriman (10926) *(G-5994)*
Home Reporter & Sunset News, Brooklyn *Also called Home Reporter Inc (G-2081)*
Home Reporter Inc....718 238-6600
8723 3rd Ave Brooklyn (11209) *(G-2081)*
Home Service Publications (HQ)....914 238-1000
1 Readers Digest Rd Pleasantville (10570) *(G-13746)*
Home4u Inc....347 262-7214
152 Skillman St Apt 8 Brooklyn (11205) *(G-2082)*
Homegrown For Good LLC....857 540-6361
29 Beechwood Ave New Rochelle (10801) *(G-8957)*
Homer Iron Works LLC....607 749-3963
5130 Us Route 11 Homer (13077) *(G-6547)*
Homer Logging Contractor....607 753-8553
6176 Sunnyside Dr Homer (13077) *(G-6548)*
Homes Land Eastrn Long Island, Southampton *Also called Frontiers Unlimited Inc (G-15566)*
Homesell Inc....718 514-0346
4010 Hylan Blvd Staten Island (10308) *(G-15705)*
Homogeneous Metals Inc....315 839-5421
2395 Main St Clayville (13322) *(G-3715)*
Honeoye Falls Distillery LLC (PA)....201 780-4618
168 W Main St Honeoye Falls (14472) *(G-6559)*
Honeybee Rbtics Cft Mechanisms, Brooklyn *Also called Honeybee Robotics Ltd (G-2083)*
Honeybee Robotics Ltd (PA)....212 966-0661
Suit Bldg 128 Brooklyn (11205) *(G-2083)*
Honeywell Imaging and Mobility, Skaneateles Falls *Also called Hand Held Products Inc (G-15490)*
Honeywell International Inc....518 270-0200
3 Tibbits Ave Troy (12183) *(G-16241)*
Honeywell International Inc....315 554-6643
700 Visions Dr Skaneateles Falls (13153) *(G-15492)*
Honeywell International Inc....845 342-4400
13 Bedford Ave Middletown (10940) *(G-8479)*
Honeywell International Inc....212 964-5111
263 Old Country Rd Melville (11747) *(G-8357)*
Honeywell International Inc....516 577-2000
2 Corporate Center Dr # 100 Melville (11747) *(G-8358)*
Honeywell Scanning & Mobility, Skaneateles Falls *Also called Hand Held Products Inc (G-15491)*
Hong Hop Co Inc....212 962-1735
10 Bowery New York (10013) *(G-10546)*
Hong Hop Noodle Company, New York *Also called Hong Hop Co Inc (G-10546)*
Honor Brand Feeds, Narrowsburg *Also called Narrowsburg Feed & Grain Co (G-8814)*
Honora, New York *Also called Brannkey Inc (G-9504)*
Hood Industries Inc....716 836-0301
580 Tifft St Buffalo (14220) *(G-3014)*
Hooek Produktion Inc....212 367-9111
147 W 26th St Fl 6 New York (10001) *(G-10547)*
Hoosier Magnetics Inc....315 323-5832
110 Denny St Ogdensburg (13669) *(G-13137)*
Hootz Family Bowling Inc....518 756-4668
100 Main St Ravena (12143) *(G-14034)*
Hope International Productions....212 247-3188
315 W 57th St Apt 6h New York (10019) *(G-10548)*
Hopes Windows Inc....716 665-5124
84 Hopkins Ave Jamestown (14701) *(G-7034)*
Hopewell Precision Inc....845 221-2737
19 Ryan Rd Hopewell Junction (12533) *(G-6579)*
Hopp Companies Inc....516 358-4170
815 2nd Ave New Hyde Park (11040) *(G-8886)*
Hoptron Brewtique....631 438-0296
22 W Main St Ste 11 Patchogue (11772) *(G-13448)*

ALPHABETIC

Horace J Metz ... 716 873-9103
2385 Elmwood Ave Kenmore (14217) *(G-7177)*
Horizon Apparel Mfg Inc ... 516 361-4878
115 Bayside Dr Atlantic Beach (11509) *(G-468)*
Horizon Floors I LLC ... 212 509-9686
11 Broadway Lbby 5 New York (10004) *(G-10549)*
Horizon Power Source LLC ... 877 240-0580
50 Glen St Glen Cove (11542) *(G-5631)*
Horizons Magazine, Brooklyn *Also called Targum Press USA Inc (G-2668)*
Horly Novelty Co Inc ... 212 226-4800
17 Ludlow St Frnt 2 New York (10002) *(G-10550)*
Horne Organization Inc (PA) ... 914 572-1330
15 Arthur Pl Yonkers (10701) *(G-17471)*
Horne Products Inc ... 631 293-0773
144 Verdi St Farmingdale (11735) *(G-5014)*
Hornell Brewing Co Inc ... 914 597-7911
222 Bloomingdale Rd Ste 4 White Plains (10605) *(G-17148)*
Hornet Group Inc ... 845 858-6400
100 River Rd Port Jervis (12771) *(G-13808)*
Horns & Halos Cft Brewing LLC ... 585 507-7248
3154 State St Caledonia (14423) *(G-3308)*
Horo Creations LLC ... 212 719-4818
71 W 47th St Ste 404 New York (10036) *(G-10551)*
Horseheads Printing, Horseheads *Also called David Helsing (G-6601)*
Hosel & Ackerson Inc (PA) ... 212 575-1490
570 Fashion Ave Rm 805 New York (10018) *(G-10552)*
Hoshizaki Nrtheastern Dist Ctr ... 516 605-1411
150 Dupont St Ste 100 Plainview (11803) *(G-13633)*
Hoskie Co Inc ... 718 628-8672
132 Harrison Pl Brooklyn (11237) *(G-2084)*
Hosmer Inc ... 888 467-9463
6999 State Route 89 Ovid (14521) *(G-13371)*
Hosmer's Winery, Ovid *Also called Hosmer Inc (G-13371)*
Hospira Inc ... 716 684-9400
2501 Walden Ave Buffalo (14225) *(G-3015)*
Hospitality Graphics Inc ... 212 643-6700
545 8th Ave Rm 401 New York (10018) *(G-10553)*
Hospitality Inc ... 212 268-1930
247 W 35th St 4 New York (10001) *(G-10554)*
Hot Cashews, New York *Also called Just Bottoms & Tops Inc (G-10825)*
Hot Kiss Inc ... 212 730-0404
1407 Brdwy Ste 2000 New York (10018) *(G-10555)*
Hot Line Industries Inc (PA) ... 516 764-0400
28 South Mall Plainview (11803) *(G-13634)*
Hot Shot Hk LLC ... 212 921-1111
1407 Broadway Rm 2018 New York (10018) *(G-10556)*
Hot Sox Company Incorporated (PA) ... 212 957-2000
95 Madison Ave Fl 15 New York (10016) *(G-10557)*
Hotel Business, Islandia *Also called Icd Publications Inc (G-6833)*
Hotelexpert, New York *Also called Tyme Global Technologies LLC (G-12455)*
Hotelinteractive Inc ... 631 424-7755
155 E Main St Ste 140 Smithtown (11787) *(G-15510)*
Houghton Mifflin Clarion Books, New York *Also called Houghton Mifflin Harcourt Pubg (G-10558)*
Houghton Mifflin Harcourt Pubg ... 212 420-5800
3 Park Ave Fl 18 New York (10016) *(G-10558)*
Houghton Mifflin Harcourt Pubg ... 914 747-2709
28 Claremont Ave Thornwood (10594) *(G-16143)*
Houles USA Inc ... 212 935-3900
979 3rd Ave Ste 1200 New York (10022) *(G-10559)*
Hound & Gatos Pet Foods Corp ... 212 618-1917
14 Wall St Fl 20 New York (10005) *(G-10560)*
House O'Weenies, Bronx *Also called Marathon Enterprises Inc (G-1389)*
House of Heydenryk Jr Inc ... 212 206-9611
601 W 26th St Rm 305 New York (10001) *(G-10561)*
House of Heydenryk The, New York *Also called House of Heydenryk Jr Inc (G-10561)*
House of Portfolios Co Inc (PA) ... 212 206-7323
37 W 26th St Rm 305 New York (10010) *(G-10562)*
House of Portfolios Co Inc ... 212 206-7323
48 W 21st St New York (10010) *(G-10563)*
House of Serengeti, White Plains *Also called Farmers Hub LLC (G-17135)*
House of Stone Inc ... 845 782-7271
1015 State Route 17m Monroe (10950) *(G-8592)*
House of The Foaming Case Inc ... 718 454-0101
110 08 Dunkirk St Saint Albans (11412) *(G-15110)*
House Pearl Fashions (us) Ltd ... 212 840-3183
1410 Broadway Rm 1501 New York (10018) *(G-10564)*
Hovee Inc ... 646 249-6200
722 Saint Nicholas Ave New York (10031) *(G-10565)*
Hover-Davis Inc (HQ) ... 585 352-9590
100 Paragon Dr Rochester (14624) *(G-14459)*
Howard Charles Inc ... 917 902-6934
180 Froehlich Farm Blvd Woodbury (11797) *(G-17311)*
Howard Formed Steel Pdts Div, Bronx *Also called Truxton Corp (G-1479)*
Howard J Moore Company Inc ... 631 351-8467
210 Terminal Dr Ste B Plainview (11803) *(G-13635)*
Howden Fan Company, Depew *Also called Howden North America Inc (G-4284)*
Howden North America Inc (HQ) ... 803 741-2700
2475 George Urban Blvd # 120 Depew (14043) *(G-4283)*
Howden North America Inc ... 716 817-6900
2475 George Urban Blvd Depew (14043) *(G-4284)*

Howdens, Depew *Also called Howden North America Inc (G-4283)*
Howe Machine & Tool Corp ... 516 931-5687
236 Park Ave Bethpage (11714) *(G-868)*
Howell Packaging, Elmira *Also called F M Howell & Company (G-4697)*
Howmedica Osteonics Corp ... 518 783-1880
2 Northway Ln Latham (12110) *(G-7391)*
HP Hood LLC ... 607 295-8134
25 Hurlbut St Arkport (14807) *(G-408)*
HP Hood LLC ... 315 363-3870
252 Genesee St Oneida (13421) *(G-13179)*
HP Hood LLC ... 315 658-2132
20700 State Route 411 La Fargeville (13656) *(G-7262)*
HP Hood LLC ... 518 218-9097
9 Norman Dr Albany (12205) *(G-88)*
HP Hood LLC ... 315 829-3339
19 Ward St Vernon (13476) *(G-16458)*
HP Hood LLC ... 607 772-6580
93 Pennsylvania Ave Binghamton (13903) *(G-916)*
HP Inc ... 212 835-1640
5 Penn Plz Ste 1912 New York (10001) *(G-10566)*
Hpce, Pearl River *Also called Hunts Point Clean Energy LLC (G-13483)*
Hpi Co Inc (PA) ... 718 851-2753
1656 41st St Brooklyn (11218) *(G-2085)*
Hpk Industries LLC ... 315 724-0196
1208 Broad St Utica (13501) *(G-16362)*
HRA Poster Project, Brooklyn *Also called City of New York (G-1781)*
Hrd Metal Products Inc ... 631 243-6700
120 E Jefryn Blvd Ste A Deer Park (11729) *(G-4173)*
Hrg Group Inc (PA) ... 212 906-8555
450 Park Ave Fl 29 New York (10022) *(G-10567)*
Hs Homeworx LLC ... 646 870-0406
18 E 74th St Fl 5 New York (10021) *(G-10568)*
HSM Machine Works Inc (PA) ... 631 924-6600
3671 Horseblock Rd Medford (11763) *(G-8281)*
HSM Packaging Corporation ... 315 476-7996
4529 Crown Rd Liverpool (13090) *(G-7546)*
HSN, New York *Also called Macfadden Cmmnctions Group LLC (G-11111)*
Htf Components Inc ... 914 703-6795
134 Bowbell Rd White Plains (10607) *(G-17149)*
Hti Recycling LLC ... 716 433-9294
490 Ohio St Lockport (14094) *(G-7623)*
Hubbard Tool and Die Corp ... 315 337-7840
Rome Indus Ctr Bldg 5 Rome (13440) *(G-14843)*
Hubbell Galvanising, Yorkville *Also called O W Hubbell & Sons Inc (G-17540)*
Hubbell Galvanizing Inc ... 315 736-8311
5124 Commercial Dr Yorkville (13495) *(G-17539)*
Hubco Inc ... 716 683-5940
2885 Commerce Dr Alden (14004) *(G-182)*
Hubray Inc ... 800 645-2855
2045 Grand Ave North Baldwin (11510) *(G-12924)*
Huck International Inc ... 845 331-7300
1 Corporate Dr Kingston (12401) *(G-7220)*
Huckleberry Inc ... 631 630-5450
655 Old Willets Path Hauppauge (11788) *(G-6119)*
Huda Kawshai LLC ... 929 255-7009
8514 168th St Ste 3 Jamaica (11432) *(G-6956)*
Hudson Cabinetry Design, Peekskill *Also called Hat Factory Furniture Co (G-13503)*
Hudson Dying & Finishing LLC ... 518 752-4389
68 Harrison St Gloversville (12078) *(G-5731)*
Hudson Eastern Industries Inc ... 917 295-5818
1118 143rd Pl Whitestone (11357) *(G-17238)*
Hudson Energy Services LLC (PA) ... 630 300-0013
4 Executive Blvd Ste 301 Suffern (10901) *(G-15813)*
Hudson Envelope Corporation (PA) ... 212 473-6666
135 3rd Ave New York (10003) *(G-10569)*
Hudson Fabrics LLC ... 518 671-6100
128 2nd Street Ext Hudson (12534) *(G-6647)*
Hudson Industries Corporation ... 518 762-4638
100 Maple Ave Johnstown (12095) *(G-7146)*
Hudson Machine Works Inc ... 845 279-1413
30 Branch Rd Brewster (10509) *(G-1218)*
Hudson Mirror LLC ... 914 930-8906
710 Washington St Peekskill (10566) *(G-13504)*
Hudson News Inc ... 212 971-6800
250 Greenwich St New York (10007) *(G-10570)*
Hudson Park Press Inc ... 212 929-8898
232 Madison Ave Rm 1400 New York (10016) *(G-10571)*
Hudson Power Transmission Co ... 718 622-3869
241 Halsey St Brooklyn (11216) *(G-2086)*
Hudson Printing Co Inc ... 718 937-8600
747 3rd Ave Lbby 3 New York (10017) *(G-10572)*
Hudson River Met Detector Sls, Pleasant Valley *Also called Detector Pro (G-13742)*
Hudson Scenic Studio Inc (PA) ... 914 375-0900
130 Fernbrook St Yonkers (10705) *(G-17472)*
Hudson Software Corporation ... 914 773-0400
3 W Main St Ste 106 Elmsford (10523) *(G-4763)*
Hudson Steel Fabricators ... 585 454-3923
444 Hudson Ave Rochester (14605) *(G-14460)*
Hudson Technologies Company (PA) ... 845 735-6000
1 Blue Hill Plz Ste 1541 Pearl River (10965) *(G-13481)*
Hudson Valley Apple Products, Milton *Also called Brooklyn Btlg Milton NY Inc (G-8516)*
Hudson Valley Baking Co, Mamaroneck *Also called Richard Engdal Baking Corp (G-8077)*

Hudson Valley Black Press....845 562-1313
343 Broadway Newburgh (12550) *(G-12783)*
Hudson Valley Chocolatier Inc (PA)....845 831-8240
269 Main St Beacon (12508) *(G-781)*
Hudson Valley Coatings LLC....845 398-1778
175 N Route 9w Ste 12 Congers (10920) *(G-3882)*
Hudson Valley Creamery LLC....518 851-2570
2986 Us Route 9 Hudson (12534) *(G-6648)*
Hudson Valley Foie Gras LLC....845 292-2500
80 Brooks Rd Ferndale (12734) *(G-5179)*
Hudson Valley Lighting Inc....845 561-0300
151 Airport Dr Wappingers Falls (12590) *(G-16593)*
Hudson Valley Magazine, Fishkill *Also called Suburban Publishing Inc (G-5196)*
Hudson Valley Office Furn Inc....845 565-6673
7 Wisner Ave Newburgh (12550) *(G-12784)*
Hudson Valley Paper Works Inc....845 569-8883
8 Lander St 15 Newburgh (12550) *(G-12785)*
Hudson Xinde Energy Inc (PA)....212 220-7112
1 World Trade Ctr Fl 85 New York (10007) *(G-10573)*
Huersch Marketing Group LLC....518 874-1045
70 Cohoes Ave Ste 4 Green Island (12183) *(G-5875)*
Huffington Post, The, New York *Also called Thehuffingtonpostcom Inc (G-12332)*
Hugh F McPherson Inc....716 668-6107
70 Innsbruck Dr Cheektowaga (14227) *(G-3604)*
Hughes-Treitler, Garden City *Also called Ametek Inc (G-5508)*
Hugo Boss Usa Inc (HQ)....212 940-0600
55 Water St Fl 48 New York (10041) *(G-10574)*
Huhtamaki Inc....315 593-5311
100 State St Fulton (13069) *(G-5475)*
Hulley Holding Company Inc (PA)....716 332-3982
2500 Elmwood Ave Kenmore (14217) *(G-7178)*
Hulley Woodworking Company, Kenmore *Also called Hulley Holding Company Inc (G-7178)*
Hum Limited Liability Corp....631 525-2174
70 Deer Valley Dr Nesconset (11767) *(G-8822)*
Human Condition Safety Inc....646 867-0644
61 Broadway Fl 31 New York (10006) *(G-10575)*
Human Electronics Inc....315 724-9850
155 Genesee St Utica (13501) *(G-16363)*
Human Life Foundation Inc....212 685-5210
271 Madison Ave Ste 1005 New York (10016) *(G-10576)*
Human Technologies Corporation....315 735-3532
2260 Dwyer Ave Utica (13501) *(G-16364)*
Humana Press Inc....212 460-1500
233 Spring St Fl 6 New York (10013) *(G-10577)*
Humanscale Corporation (PA)....212 725-4749
11 E 26th St Fl 8 New York (10010) *(G-10578)*
Humanware USA Inc (PA)....800 722-3393
1 Ups Way Champlain (12919) *(G-3570)*
Humor Rainbow Incorporated....646 402-9113
129 W 29th St Fl 10 New York (10001) *(G-10579)*
Hunt Country Furniture Inc (PA)....845 832-6601
19 Dog Tail Corners Rd Wingdale (12594) *(G-17296)*
Hunt Country Vineyards....315 595-2812
4021 Italy Hill Rd Branchport (14418) *(G-1169)*
Hunt Graphics Inc....631 751-5349
43 Pineview Ln Coram (11727) *(G-3967)*
Hunter Displays, East Patchogue *Also called Hunter Metal Industries Inc (G-4467)*
Hunter Douglas Inc (HQ)....845 664-7000
1 Blue Hill Plz Ste 1569 Pearl River (10965) *(G-13482)*
Hunter Douglas Inc....212 588-0564
979 3rd Ave New York (10022) *(G-10580)*
Hunter Machine Inc....585 924-7480
6551 Anthony Dr Victor (14564) *(G-16505)*
Hunter Metal Industries Inc....631 475-5900
14 Hewlett Ave East Patchogue (11772) *(G-4467)*
Huntington Ice & Cube Corp (PA)....718 456-2013
335 Moffat St Brooklyn (11237) *(G-2087)*
Huntington Ingalls Inc....518 884-3834
33 Cady Hill Blvd Saratoga Springs (12866) *(G-15188)*
Huntington Services Inc....516 795-8500
727 N Broadway Ste A4 Massapequa (11758) *(G-8209)*
Huntington Welding & Iron....631 423-3331
139 W Pulaski Rd Huntington Station (11746) *(G-6747)*
Hunts Point Clean Energy LLC....203 451-5143
401 N Middletown Rd Pearl River (10965) *(G-13483)*
Huron Tl Cutter Grinding Inc....631 420-7000
2045 Wellwood Ave Farmingdale (11735) *(G-5015)*
Hurryworks LLC....516 998-4600
990 Seaview Blvd Port Washington (11050) *(G-13843)*
Hustler Powerboats, Calverton *Also called Global Marine Power Inc (G-3319)*
Hutchinson Industries Inc....716 852-1435
92 Msgr Valente Dr Buffalo (14206) *(G-3016)*
Hutnick Rehab, Bohemia *Also called Gfh Orthotic & Prosthetic Labs (G-1068)*
Hvr Advnced Pwr Components Inc....716 693-4700
2090 Old Union Rd Cheektowaga (14227) *(G-3605)*
Hw Holdings Inc (HQ)....212 399-1000
718 5th Ave New York (10019) *(G-10581)*
Hw Specialties Co Inc....631 589-0745
210 Knickerbocker Ave B Bohemia (11716) *(G-1071)*
Hy Gold Jewelers Inc....212 744-3202
1070 Madison Ave Frnt 4 New York (10028) *(G-10582)*
Hy-Grade Metal Products Corp....315 475-4221
906 Burnet Ave Syracuse (13203) *(G-15980)*
Hy-Tech Mold Inc....585 247-2450
60 Elmgrove Park Rochester (14624) *(G-14461)*
Hybrid Cases, Holbrook *Also called Roadie Products Inc (G-6497)*
Hyde Park, Poughkeepsie *Also called Architectural Dctg Co LLC (G-13906)*
Hyde Park Brewing Co Inc....845 229-8277
4076 Albany Post Rd Hyde Park (12538) *(G-6773)*
Hydra Technology Corp....716 896-8316
179 Grider St Buffalo (14215) *(G-3017)*
Hydramec Inc....585 593-5190
4393 River St Scio (14880) *(G-15342)*
Hydrive Energy....914 925-9100
350 Theodore Fremd Ave Rye (10580) *(G-15086)*
Hydro-Air Components Inc....716 827-6510
100 Rittling Blvd Buffalo (14220) *(G-3018)*
Hydroacoustics Inc....585 359-1000
999 Lehigh Station Rd # 100 Henrietta (14467) *(G-6317)*
Hygrade....718 488-9000
30 Warsoff Pl Brooklyn (11205) *(G-2088)*
Hygrade Fuel Inc....516 741-0723
260 Columbus Pkwy Mineola (11501) *(G-8547)*
Hyman Podrusnick Co Inc....718 853-4502
212 Foster Ave Brooklyn (11230) *(G-2089)*
Hyperbaric Technologies Inc....518 842-3030
1 Sam Stratton Rd Amsterdam (12010) *(G-350)*
Hyperlaw Inc....212 873-6982
17 W 70th St Apt 4 New York (10023) *(G-10583)*
Hyperline Systems Inc....613 736-8500
9322 3rd Ave Ste 406 Brooklyn (11209) *(G-2090)*
Hypoxico Inc....212 972-1009
50 Lexington Ave Ste 249 New York (10010) *(G-10584)*
Hypres Inc (PA)....914 592-1190
175 Clearbrook Rd Elmsford (10523) *(G-4764)*
Hypur Precision Machining Inc....631 584-8498
10 Technology Dr Unit 8 East Setauket (11733) *(G-4503)*
Hytech Tool & Die Inc....716 488-2796
2202 Washington St Jamestown (14701) *(G-7035)*
I & I Systems....845 753-9126
66 Table Rock Rd Tuxedo Park (10987) *(G-16306)*
I & S of NY Inc....716 373-7001
4174 Route 417 Allegany (14706) *(G-204)*
I 2 Print Inc....718 937-8800
3819 24th St Long Island City (11101) *(G-7791)*
I 3 Manufacturing Services Inc....607 238-7077
100 Eldredge St Binghamton (13901) *(G-917)*
I A S National Inc....631 423-6900
95 W Hills Rd Huntington Station (11746) *(G-6748)*
I ABC Corporation....315 639-3100
349 Lakeview Dr Dexter (13634) *(G-4309)*
I C M, Woodside *Also called International Creative Met Inc (G-17350)*
I C S, New York *Also called Integrated Graphics Inc (G-10659)*
I D E Processes Corporation (PA)....718 544-1177
106 81st Ave Kew Gardens (11415) *(G-7190)*
I D Machine Inc....607 796-2549
1580 Lake St Elmira (14901) *(G-4705)*
I D Tel Corp....718 876-6000
55 Canal St Staten Island (10304) *(G-15706)*
I Do Machining, Elmira *Also called I D Machine Inc (G-4705)*
I E D Corp....631 348-0424
88 Bridge Rd Islandia (11749) *(G-6832)*
I E M, Troy *Also called Interntnal Elctronic Mchs Corp (G-16263)*
I Fix Screen....631 421-1938
203 Centereach Mall Centereach (11720) *(G-3497)*
I J White Corporation....631 293-3788
20 Executive Blvd Farmingdale (11735) *(G-5016)*
I L C, Bohemia *Also called Ilc Industries LLC (G-1073)*
I Love Accessories Inc....212 239-1875
10 W 33rd St Rm 210 New York (10001) *(G-10585)*
I Meglio Corp....631 617-6900
151 Alkier St Brentwood (11717) *(G-1181)*
I N K T Inc....212 957-2700
250 W 54th St Fl 9 New York (10019) *(G-10586)*
I On Youth....716 832-6509
115 Godfrey St Buffalo (14215) *(G-3019)*
I P A, Woodstock *Also called Innovative Pdts of Amer Inc (G-17379)*
I R M, Plainview *Also called Aufhauser Corporation (G-13614)*
I Rauchs Sons Inc....718 507-8844
3220 112th St East Elmhurst (11369) *(G-4414)*
I S C A Corp (PA)....212 719-5123
512 7th Ave Fl 7 New York (10018) *(G-10587)*
I Spiewak & Sons Inc....212 695-1620
225 W 37th St Fl 15l New York (10018) *(G-10588)*
I Trade Technology Ltd....615 348-7233
400 Rella Blvd Ste 165 Suffern (10901) *(G-15814)*
I Triple E Spectrum, New York *Also called Magazine I Spectrum E (G-11125)*
I W Industries Inc (PA)....631 293-9494
35 Melville Park Rd Melville (11747) *(G-8359)*
I W M, Dryden *Also called Integrated Water Management (G-4346)*
I'M Nuts, Hewlett *Also called Yes Were Nuts Ltd (G-6341)*

ALPHABETIC

I-Evolve Techonology Services (PA)....801 566-5268
501 John James Audubon Pk Amherst (14228) ***(G-244)***
I3 Assembly LLC....607 238-7077
100 Eldredge St Binghamton (13901) ***(G-918)***
I3 Electronics Inc (PA)....607 238-7077
100 Eldredge St Binghamton (13901) ***(G-919)***
IA Construction Corporation....716 933-8787
Rr 305 Box S Portville (14770) ***(G-13893)***
Iaas , The, Flushing *Also called Intercultural Alliance Artists* ***(G-5261)***
IAC Search LLC (HQ)....212 314-7300
555 W 18th St New York (10011) ***(G-10589)***
Iac/Interactivecorp (PA)....212 314-7300
555 W 18th St New York (10011) ***(G-10590)***
Iadc Inc....718 238-0623
845 Father Capodanno Blvd Staten Island (10305) ***(G-15707)***
IaMmaliamills LLC....805 845-2137
32 33rd St Unit 13 Brooklyn (11232) ***(G-2091)***
Iat Interactive LLC....914 273-2233
333 N Bedford Rd Ste 110 Mount Kisco (10549) ***(G-8670)***
Iba Industrial Inc....631 254-6800
151 Heartland Blvd Edgewood (11717) ***(G-4614)***
IBC/ Worldwide, New Hyde Park *Also called Interntnal Bus Cmmncations Inc* ***(G-8887)***
Iberia Foods Corp (HQ)....718 272-8900
1900 Linden Blvd Brooklyn (11207) ***(G-2092)***
Ibio Inc....302 355-0650
600 Madison Ave Ste 1601 New York (10022) ***(G-10591)***
IBlt Inc....212 768-0292
257 W 38th St Fl 2 New York (10018) ***(G-10592)***
IBM, Endicott *Also called International Bus Mchs Corp* ***(G-4819)***
IBM, New York *Also called International Bus Mchs Corp* ***(G-10673)***
IBM, Armonk *Also called International Bus Mchs Corp* ***(G-412)***
IBM, Poughkeepsie *Also called International Bus Mchs Corp* ***(G-13927)***
IBM, Hopewell Junction *Also called International Bus Mchs Corp* ***(G-6580)***
IBM, Armonk *Also called International Bus Mchs Corp* ***(G-413)***
IBM World Trade Corporation (HQ)....914 765-1900
1 New Orchard Rd Ste 1 Armonk (10504) ***(G-411)***
Ibrands International LLC....212 354-1330
230 W 39th St New York (10018) ***(G-10593)***
Ibt Media Inc (PA)....646 867-7100
7 Hanover Sq Fl 5 New York (10004) ***(G-10594)***
Ic Optics, New Hyde Park *Also called Colors In Optics Ltd* ***(G-8867)***
Ic Technologies LLC....212 966-7895
475 Greenwich St New York (10013) ***(G-10595)***
Icarus Enterprises Inc....917 969-4461
568 Broadway Fl 11 New York (10012) ***(G-10596)***
Icd Publications Inc (PA)....631 246-9300
1377 Motor Pkwy Ste 410 Islandia (11749) ***(G-6833)***
Ice Air LLC....914 668-4700
80 Hartford Ave Mount Vernon (10553) ***(G-8737)***
Ice Box Water, Cold Spring Harbor *Also called Water Resources Group LLC* ***(G-3796)***
Ice Cream Man Inc....518 692-8382
417 State Route 29 Greenwich (12834) ***(G-5909)***
Ice Cube Inc (PA)....613 254-0071
171 E Industry Ct Ste B Deer Park (11729) ***(G-4174)***
Icell Inc....516 590-0007
133 Fulton Ave Hempstead (11550) ***(G-6298)***
Icer Scrubs LLC....212 221-4700
1385 Broadway Fl 16 New York (10018) ***(G-10597)***
Ices Queen, Brooklyn *Also called Primo Frozen Desserts Inc* ***(G-2456)***
Icestone LLC....718 624-4900
63 Flushing Ave Unit 283b Brooklyn (11205) ***(G-2093)***
ICM, North Syracuse *Also called Interntnal Cntrls Msrmnts Corp* ***(G-12965)***
ICM Controls Corp....315 233-5266
7313 William Barry Blvd North Syracuse (13212) ***(G-12964)***
Icommunicator, Brooklyn *Also called Ppr Direct Inc* ***(G-2446)***
Icon Design LLC....585 768-6040
9 Lent Ave Le Roy (14482) ***(G-7434)***
Icon Enterprises Intl Inc....718 752-9764
2653 Stoney St Mohegan Lake (10547) ***(G-8578)***
Icon-TV, Mohegan Lake *Also called Icon Enterprises Intl Inc* ***(G-8578)***
Iconix Inc....516 513-1420
40 Oser Ave Ste 4 Hauppauge (11788) ***(G-6120)***
ICP, West Seneca *Also called International Control Products* ***(G-16977)***
ICP, Depew *Also called Pcb Group Inc* ***(G-4292)***
Icpme-Ithaca Center, Ithaca *Also called International Center For Postg* ***(G-6886)***
Icy Hot Lingerie, New York *Also called Sensual Inc* ***(G-12048)***
Icynene US Acquisition Corp (HQ)....800 758-7325
438 Main St Ste 100 Buffalo (14202) ***(G-3020)***
ID Signsystems Inc....585 266-5750
410 Atlantic Ave Rochester (14609) ***(G-14462)***
Idalia Solar Technologies LLC....212 792-3913
270 Lafayette St Ste 1402 New York (10012) ***(G-10598)***
Idc, West Babylon *Also called Isolation Dynamics Corp* ***(G-16823)***
Idc Printing & Sty Co Inc (PA)....516 599-0400
536 Merrick Rd Lynbrook (11563) ***(G-7979)***
Ideal Brilliant Co Inc....212 840-2044
580 5th Ave Ste 600 New York (10036) ***(G-10599)***
Ideal Burial Vault Company....585 599-2242
1166 Vision Pkwy Corfu (14036) ***(G-3977)***
Ideal Creations Inc....212 563-5928
10 W 33rd St Rm 708 New York (10001) ***(G-10600)***
Ideal Manufacturing Inc....585 872-7190
80 Bluff Dr East Rochester (14445) ***(G-4481)***
Ideal Signs Inc....718 292-9196
538 Wales Ave Bronx (10455) ***(G-1360)***
Ideal Snacks Corporation....845 292-7000
89 Mill St Liberty (12754) ***(G-7459)***
Ideal Stair Parts, Little Falls *Also called Ideal Wood Products Inc* ***(G-7522)***
Ideal Wood Products Inc....315 823-1124
225 W Main St Little Falls (13365) ***(G-7522)***
Identfication Data Imaging LLC....516 484-6500
26 Harbor Park Dr Port Washington (11050) ***(G-13844)***
Identifycom Inc....212 235-0000
120 W 45th St Ste 2701 New York (10036) ***(G-10601)***
Identity Ink & Custom Tee, Kenmore *Also called Herrmann Group LLC* ***(G-7176)***
Ideoli Group Inc....212 705-8769
938 Port Washington Blvd # 1 Port Washington (11050) ***(G-13845)***
Idesco Corp....212 889-2530
37 W 26th St Fl 10 New York (10010) ***(G-10602)***
Idex Corporation....585 292-8121
2883 Brghtn Hnretta Tl Rd Rochester (14623) ***(G-14463)***
Idg, New York *Also called International Direct Group Inc* ***(G-10676)***
Idg LLC....315 797-1000
31 Faass Ave Utica (13502) ***(G-16365)***
Idg Technetwork, New York *Also called International Data Group Inc* ***(G-10674)***
IDI, Port Washington *Also called Identfication Data Imaging LLC* ***(G-13844)***
Idl, Ronkonkoma *Also called Ingenious Designs LLC* ***(G-14941)***
Idoc Software Inc....516 680-9090
191 Sint Nchlas Ave Apt 3 New York (10026) ***(G-10603)***
Idonethis, New York *Also called West Internet Trading Company* ***(G-12640)***
Idra Alta Moda LLC....914 644-8202
200 West St 305 New York (10282) ***(G-10604)***
IEC Electronics Corp (PA)....315 331-7742
105 Norton St Newark (14513) ***(G-12752)***
IEC Electronics Corp....585 647-1760
1365 Emerson St Rochester (14606) ***(G-14464)***
IEC Electronics Wire Cable Inc....585 924-9010
105 Norton St Newark (14513) ***(G-12753)***
IEC Holden Corporation....518 213-3991
51 Distribution Way Plattsburgh (12901) ***(G-13696)***
Ieh Corporation....718 492-4440
140 58th St Ste 8e Brooklyn (11220) ***(G-2094)***
Iet Labs Inc (PA)....516 334-5959
1 Expressway Plz Ste 120 Roslyn Heights (11577) ***(G-15052)***
IFF, New York *Also called Interntnal Flvors Frgrnces Inc* ***(G-10681)***
Ifg Corp....212 629-9600
1372 Brdwy 12ae 12 Ae New York (10018) ***(G-10605)***
Ifg Corp....212 239-8615
463 7th Ave Fl 4 New York (10018) ***(G-10606)***
Igambit Inc (PA)....631 670-6777
1050 W Jericho Tpke Ste A Smithtown (11787) ***(G-15511)***
Igc New York Inc....212 764-0949
580 5th Ave Ste 708 New York (10036) ***(G-10607)***
Ignelzi Interiors Inc....718 464-0279
9805 217th St Queens Village (11429) ***(G-13995)***
Igniter Systems Inc....716 542-5511
12600 Clarence Center Rd Akron (14001) ***(G-21)***
Igo Inc (PA)....408 596-0061
590 Madison Ave Rm 3202 New York (10022) ***(G-10608)***
Igt Global Solutions Corp....518 382-2900
1 Broadway Ctr Fl 2 Schenectady (12305) ***(G-15296)***
Ihd Motorsports LLC....979 690-1669
1152 Upper Front St Binghamton (13905) ***(G-920)***
Iheartcommunications Inc....585 454-4884
100 Chestnut St Ste 1700 Rochester (14604) ***(G-14465)***
Iheartcommunications Inc....212 603-4660
1133 Ave Americas Fl 34 New York (10036) ***(G-10609)***
Ihi Inc (HQ)....212 599-8100
150 E 52nd St Fl 24 New York (10022) ***(G-10610)***
Iim Global, Long Beach *Also called Innovation In Motion Inc* ***(G-7672)***
Iimak, Amherst *Also called International Imaging Mtls Inc* ***(G-245)***
Ik Supply, Farmingdale *Also called International Key Supply LLC* ***(G-5020)***
Ikeddi Enterprises Inc (PA)....212 302-7644
1407 Brdwy Ste 2900 New York (10018) ***(G-10611)***
Ikeddi Enterprises Inc....212 302-7644
1407 Broadway Rm 1805 New York (10018) ***(G-10612)***
Ilab America Inc....631 615-5053
45 Hemlock St Selden (11784) ***(G-15373)***
Ilc Holdings Inc (HQ)....631 567-5600
105 Wilbur Pl Bohemia (11716) ***(G-1072)***
Ilc Industries LLC (HQ)....631 567-5600
105 Wilbur Pl Bohemia (11716) ***(G-1073)***
Ilico Jewelry Inc....516 482-0201
98 Cuttermill Rd Ste 396 Great Neck (11021) ***(G-5831)***
Ilion Plastics Inc....315 894-4868
27 Pleasant Ave Ilion (13357) ***(G-6780)***
Illinois Tool Works Inc....860 435-2574
5979 N Elm Ave Millerton (12546) ***(G-8514)***
Illinois Tool Works Inc....716 681-8222
4471 Walden Ave Lancaster (14086) ***(G-7344)***

ALPHABETIC SECTION

Industrial Finishing Products

Illinois Tool Works Inc....607 770-4945
33 Lewis Rd Binghamton (13905) *(G-921)*
Illumination Technologies Inc....315 463-4673
5 Adler Dr East Syracuse (13057) *(G-4552)*
Iluv, Port Washington *Also called Jwin Electronics Corp (G-13852)*
Ima Life North America Inc....716 695-6354
2175 Military Rd Tonawanda (14150) *(G-16191)*
Imacor Inc....516 393-0970
821 Franklin Ave Ste 301 Garden City (11530) *(G-5523)*
Image Iron Works Inc....718 592-8276
5050 98th St Corona (11368) *(G-4021)*
Image Press, The, Cicero *Also called Add Associates Inc (G-3670)*
Image Sales & Marketing Inc....516 238-7023
106 Thornwood Rd Massapequa Park (11762) *(G-8219)*
Image Specialists Inc....631 475-0867
80 Elderwood Dr Saint James (11780) *(G-15116)*
Image Tech....716 635-0167
96 Donna Lea Blvd Buffalo (14221) *(G-3021)*
Image Typography Inc....631 218-6932
751 Coates Ave Ste 31 Holbrook (11741) *(G-6479)*
Image360....585 272-1234
275 Marketplace Dr Rochester (14623) *(G-14466)*
Imaginant Inc....585 264-0480
3800 Monroe Ave Ste 29 Pittsford (14534) *(G-13592)*
Imagination Playground LLC....212 463-0334
5 Union Sq W New York (10003) *(G-10613)*
Imagine Communications Corp....212 303-4200
1 Penn Plz Fl 39 New York (10119) *(G-10614)*
Imaging and Sensing Technology, Horseheads *Also called Mirion Technologies Ist Corp (G-6612)*
Imago Recording Company (PA)....212 751-3033
240 E 47th St Apt 20f New York (10017) *(G-10615)*
IMC Teddy Food Service....631 789-8881
50 Ranick Dr E Amityville (11701) *(G-294)*
Imco Inc....585 352-7810
15 Turner Dr Spencerport (14559) *(G-15594)*
Imek Media LLC....212 422-9000
32 Broadway Ste 511 New York (10004) *(G-10616)*
Imena Jewelry Manufacturer Inc....212 827-0073
2 W 45th St Ste 1000 New York (10036) *(G-10617)*
Imerys Fsed Mnrl Ngara FLS Inc (HQ)....716 286-1250
2000 College Ave Niagara Falls (14305) *(G-12852)*
Imerys Steelcasting Usa Inc (HQ)....716 278-1634
4111 Witmer Rd Niagara Falls (14305) *(G-12853)*
Imerys Usa Inc....315 287-0780
16a Main St Hailesboro Rd Gouverneur (13642) *(G-5761)*
IMG The Daily....212 541-5640
432 W 45th St Fl 5 New York (10036) *(G-10618)*
Immco Diagnostics Inc (HQ)....716 691-6911
60 Pineview Dr Buffalo (14228) *(G-3022)*
Immudyne Inc....914 244-1777
50 Spring Meadow Rd Mount Kisco (10549) *(G-8671)*
Imobile of Ny LLC....212 505-3355
649 Broadway New York (10012) *(G-10619)*
Imobile of Ny-Sprint, New York *Also called Imobile of Ny LLC (G-10619)*
Impact Journals LLC....800 922-0957
6666 E Quaker St Ste 1 Orchard Park (14127) *(G-13298)*
Impact Tech A Skrsky Innvtions, Rochester *Also called Sikorsky Aircraft Corporation (G-14710)*
Impala Press Ltd....631 588-4262
931 S 2nd St Ronkonkoma (11779) *(G-14940)*
Imperia Masonry Supply Corp (PA)....914 738-0900
57 Canal Rd Pelham (10803) *(G-13517)*
Imperial Color, Brentwood *Also called Lauricella Press Inc (G-1186)*
Imperial Damper & Louver Co....718 731-3800
907 E 141st St Bronx (10454) *(G-1361)*
Imperial Frames & Albums LLC....718 832-9793
8200 21st Ave Brooklyn (11214) *(G-2095)*
Imperial Instrmnt & Mach, Westbury *Also called Imperial Instrument Corp (G-17022)*
Imperial Instrument Corp....516 739-6644
18 Sylvester St Westbury (11590) *(G-17022)*
Imperial Laminators Co Inc....718 272-9500
961 Elton St Brooklyn (11208) *(G-2096)*
Imperial Polymers Inc....718 387-4741
534 Grand St Brooklyn (11211) *(G-2097)*
Imperial Pools Inc (PA)....518 786-1200
33 Wade Rd Latham (12110) *(G-7392)*
Imperial Sweater Mills Inc....718 871-4414
1365 38th St Brooklyn (11218) *(G-2098)*
Imperial-Harvard Label Co....212 736-8420
236 W 40th St Fl 3 New York (10018) *(G-10620)*
Impladent Ltd (PA)....718 465-1810
19845 Foothill Ave Jamaica (11423) *(G-6957)*
Import-Export Corporation....718 707-0880
3814 30th St Long Island City (11101) *(G-7792)*
Impremedia LLC (HQ)....212 807-4785
1 Metrotech Ctr Fl 18 Brooklyn (11201) *(G-2099)*
Impress Graphic Technologies....516 781-0845
141 Linden Ave Westbury (11590) *(G-17023)*
Impressions Inc....212 594-5954
36 W 37th St Rm 400 New York (10018) *(G-10621)*
Impressions International Inc....585 442-5240
1255 University Ave # 150 Rochester (14607) *(G-14467)*
Impressions Prtg & Graphics, New York *Also called Designlogocom Inc (G-9909)*
Impressive Imprints....716 692-0905
601 Division St North Tonawanda (14120) *(G-12994)*
Impressive Imprints Inc....631 293-6161
195 Central Ave Ste N Farmingdale (11735) *(G-5017)*
Imprinted Sportswear, Camillus *Also called Steve Poli Sales (G-3352)*
IMR Test Labs, Lansing *Also called Metal Improvement Company LLC (G-7374)*
Imrex LLC (PA)....516 479-3675
55 Sandy Hill Rd Oyster Bay (11771) *(G-13396)*
In Mocean Group LLC (PA)....212 944-0317
463 Fashion Ave Fl 21 New York (10018) *(G-10622)*
In Moda com Inc....718 788-4466
241 W 37th St Rm 803 New York (10018) *(G-10623)*
In Northeast Precision Welding....518 441-2260
1177 Route 9 Castleton On Hudson (12033) *(G-3447)*
In Room Plus Inc....716 838-9433
2495 Main St Ste 217 Buffalo (14214) *(G-3023)*
In The Crease, Penn Yan *Also called Warrior Sports Inc (G-13544)*
In Toon Amkor Fashions Inc....718 937-4546
4809 34th St Long Island City (11101) *(G-7793)*
In-House Inc....718 445-9007
1535 126th St Ste 3 College Point (11356) *(G-3812)*
In-Step Marketing Inc (PA)....212 797-3450
39 Broadway Fl 32 New York (10006) *(G-10624)*
Incentivate Health LLC....518 469-8491
60 Railroad Pl Ste 101 Saratoga Springs (12866) *(G-15189)*
Incisive Rwg, Inc., New York *Also called Infopro Digital Inc (G-10638)*
Incitec Pivot Limited....212 238-3010
120 Broadway Fl 32 New York (10271) *(G-10625)*
Incodema Inc....607 277-7070
407 Cliff St Ithaca (14850) *(G-6884)*
Incodema3d LLC....607 269-4390
330 Main St Freeville (13068) *(G-5449)*
Incon Gems Inc....212 221-8560
2 W 46th St Ste 603 New York (10036) *(G-10626)*
Incredible Scents Inc....516 656-3300
1009 Glen Cove Ave Ste 6 Glen Head (11545) *(G-5648)*
Incycle Software Corp (PA)....212 626-2608
1120 Ave Of The Americas New York (10036) *(G-10627)*
Ind Rev LLC....212 221-4700
1385 Broadway Fl 16 New York (10018) *(G-10628)*
Indegy Inc....866 801-5394
154 Grand St New York (10013) *(G-10629)*
Independence Harley-Davidson, Binghamton *Also called Ihd Motorsports LLC (G-920)*
Independent Baptist Voice, Conklin *Also called Newspaper Publisher LLC (G-3896)*
Independent Brewers Untd Corp....585 263-9308
445 Saint Paul St Rochester (14605) *(G-14468)*
Independent Field Svc LLC (PA)....315 559-9243
6744 Pickard Dr Syracuse (13211) *(G-15981)*
Independent Home Products LLC....718 541-1256
59 Hempstead Gardens Dr West Hempstead (11552) *(G-16886)*
Index Incorporated....440 632-5400
415 Concord Ave Bronx (10455) *(G-1362)*
Index Magazine....212 243-1428
526 W 26th St Rm 920 New York (10001) *(G-10630)*
India Abroad Publications Inc....212 929-1727
102 Madison Ave Frnt B New York (10016) *(G-10631)*
Indian Ladder Farmstead Brewer....518 577-1484
287 Altamont Rd Altamont (12009) *(G-210)*
Indian Larry Legacy....718 609-9184
400 Union Ave Brooklyn (11211) *(G-2100)*
Indian Springs Mfg Co Inc....315 635-6101
2095 W Genesee Rd Baldwinsville (13027) *(G-570)*
Indian Valley, Binghamton *Also called Ivi Services Inc (G-924)*
Indian Water Treatment Plant, Ossining *Also called Ossining Village of Inc (G-13349)*
Indigo Home Inc....212 684-4146
230 5th Ave Ste 1916 New York (10001) *(G-10632)*
Indigo Rein, New York *Also called Jrg Apparel Group Company Ltd (G-10812)*
Indikon Company, New Hartford *Also called Riverhawk Company LP (G-8854)*
Indira Foods Inc....718 343-1500
25503 Hillside Ave # 255 Floral Park (11004) *(G-5215)*
Indium Corporation of America (PA)....800 446-3486
34 Robinson Rd Clinton (13323) *(G-3745)*
Indium Corporation of America....315 793-8200
1676 Lincoln Ave Utica (13502) *(G-16366)*
Indium Corporation of America....315 381-2330
111 Business Park Dr Utica (13502) *(G-16367)*
Indonesian Imports Inc (PA)....888 800-5899
339 5th Ave Fl 2 New York (10016) *(G-10633)*
Industrial Cables, Chester *Also called Nexans Energy USA Inc (G-3637)*
Industrial Elec & Automtn, Buffalo *Also called 4695 Main Street Snyder Inc (G-2803)*
Industrial Electronic Hardware....718 492-4440
140 58th St Ste 8e Brooklyn (11220) *(G-2101)*
Industrial Fabricating Corp (PA)....315 437-3353
6201 E Molloy Rd East Syracuse (13057) *(G-4553)*
Industrial Fabricating Corp....315 437-8234
4 Collamer Cir East Syracuse (13057) *(G-4554)*
Industrial Finishing Products....718 342-4871
820 Remsen Ave Brooklyn (11236) *(G-2102)*

ALPHABETIC

(PA)=Parent Co (HQ)=Headquarters (DH)=Div Headquarters

2018 Harris
New York Manufacturers Directory

975

Industrial Handling Svcs Inc 518 399-0488
209 Alplaus Ave Alplaus (12008) ***(G-207)***
Industrial Indxing Systems Inc 585 924-9181
626 Fishers Run Victor (14564) ***(G-16506)***
Industrial Machine Repair 607 272-0717
1144 Taughannock Blvd Ithaca (14850) ***(G-6885)***
Industrial Oil Tank Service 315 736-6080
120 Dry Rd Oriskany (13424) ***(G-13335)***
Industrial Paint Services Corp 607 687-0107
60 W Main St 62 Owego (13827) ***(G-13377)***
Industrial Paper Tube Inc 718 893-5000
1335 E Bay Ave Bronx (10474) ***(G-1363)***
Industrial Precision Pdts Inc 315 343-4421
350 Mitchell St Oswego (13126) ***(G-13358)***
Industrial Raw Materials LLC 212 688-8080
39 West Mall Plainview (11803) ***(G-13636)***
Industrial Raw Materials LLC 212 688-8080
112 W 56th St New York (10019) ***(G-10634)***
Industrial SEC Systems Contrls, Garden City *Also called Issco Corporation* ***(G-5524)***
Industrial Services of Wny 716 799-7788
7221 Niagara Falls Blvd Niagara Falls (14304) ***(G-12854)***
Industrial Support Inc 716 662-2954
36 Depot St Buffalo (14206) ***(G-3024)***
Industrial Test Eqp Co Inc 516 883-6423
2 Manhasset Ave Port Washington (11050) ***(G-13846)***
Industrial Tool & Die Co Inc 518 273-7383
14 Industrial Park Rd Troy (12180) ***(G-16262)***
Industrial Wax, Plainview *Also called Industrial Raw Materials LLC* ***(G-13636)***
Industrial Welding & Fabg Co, Jamestown *Also called Wilston Enterprises Inc* ***(G-7076)***
Industry Forecast, Mount Kisco *Also called Jerome Levy Forecasting Center* ***(G-8673)***
Inertia Switch Inc 845 359-8300
70 S Greenbush Rd Orangeburg (10962) ***(G-13251)***
Inex Inc 716 537-2270
9229 Olean Rd Holland (14080) ***(G-6508)***
Infant Formula Laboratory Svc 718 257-3000
711 Livonia Ave Brooklyn (11207) ***(G-2103)***
Inficon Inc (HQ) 315 434-1149
2 Technology Pl East Syracuse (13057) ***(G-4555)***
Inficon Holding AG 315 434-1100
2 Technology Pl East Syracuse (13057) ***(G-4556)***
Infimed Inc (PA) 315 453-4545
121 Metropolitan Park Dr Liverpool (13088) ***(G-7547)***
Infimed Inc 585 383-1710
15 Fishers Rd Pittsford (14534) ***(G-13593)***
Infinite Software Solutions 718 982-1315
1110 South Ave Ste 303 Staten Island (10314) ***(G-15708)***
Infinitlink Corporation 934 777-0180
455 Sunrise Hwy Ste 2r West Babylon (11704) ***(G-16822)***
Infinity Augmented Reality Inc 917 677-2084
228 Park Ave S 61130 New York (10003) ***(G-10635)***
Infinity Sourcing Services LLC 212 868-2900
224 W 35th St Ste 902 New York (10001) ***(G-10636)***
Infitec Inc 315 433-1150
6500 Badgley Rd East Syracuse (13057) ***(G-4557)***
Inflation Systems Inc 914 381-8070
500 Ogden Ave Mamaroneck (10543) ***(G-8069)***
Influence Graphics, Long Island City *Also called Sizzal LLC* ***(G-7907)***
Info Label Inc 518 664-0791
12 Enterprise Ave Halfmoon (12065) ***(G-5933)***
Info Quick Solutions 315 463-1400
7460 Morgan Rd Liverpool (13090) ***(G-7548)***
Infobase Publishing Company (PA) 212 967-8800
132 W 31st St Fl 17 New York (10001) ***(G-10637)***
Infopro Digital Inc 212 457-9400
55 Broad St Fl 22 New York (10004) ***(G-10638)***
Infor Global Solutions Inc (HQ) 646 336-1700
641 Avenue Of Americas New York (10011) ***(G-10639)***
Inform Studio Inc 718 401-6149
480 Austin Pl Frnt E Bronx (10455) ***(G-1364)***
Informa Solutions Inc 516 543-3733
45 Rockefeller Plz # 2000 New York (10111) ***(G-10640)***
Informatica LLC 212 845-7650
810 7th Ave Ste 1100c New York (10019) ***(G-10641)***
Informerly Inc 646 238-7137
35 Essex St New York (10002) ***(G-10642)***
Infoservices International 631 549-1805
1 Saint Marks Pl Cold Spring Harbor (11724) ***(G-3794)***
Infrared Components Corp 315 732-1544
2306 Bleecker St Utica (13501) ***(G-16368)***
Ingenious Designs LLC 631 254-3376
2060 9th Ave Ronkonkoma (11779) ***(G-14941)***
Ingersoll-Rand Company 716 896-6600
3101 Broadway St Buffalo (14227) ***(G-3025)***
Ingham Industries Inc 631 242-2493
1363 Lincoln Ave Ste 1 Holbrook (11741) ***(G-6480)***
Ingleside Machine Co Inc 585 924-3046
1120 Hook Rd Farmington (14425) ***(G-5162)***
Inglis Co Inc 315 475-1315
116 Granger St Syracuse (13202) ***(G-15982)***
Ings Mata Stone, New York *Also called Mata Ig* ***(G-11200)***
Inhance Technologies LLC 716 825-9031
1951 Hamburg Tpke Ste 5 Buffalo (14218) ***(G-3026)***
Ink Publishing Corporation 347 294-1220
68 Jay St Ste 315 Brooklyn (11201) ***(G-2104)***
Ink Well 718 253-9736
1440 Coney Island Ave Brooklyn (11230) ***(G-2105)***
Ink-It Printing Inc 718 229-5590
1535 126th St Ste 1 College Point (11356) ***(G-3813)***
Ink-It Prtg Inc/Angle Offset, College Point *Also called Ink-It Printing Inc* ***(G-3813)***
Inkkas LLC 646 845-9803
38 E 29th St Rm 6r New York (10016) ***(G-10643)***
Inland Paper Products Corp 718 827-8150
444 Liberty Ave Brooklyn (11207) ***(G-2106)***
Inland Vacuum Industries Inc (PA) 585 293-3330
35 Howard Ave Churchville (14428) ***(G-3667)***
Inner-Pak Container Inc 631 289-9700
116 West Ave Patchogue (11772) ***(G-13449)***
Innex Industries Inc 585 247-3575
6 Marway Dr Rochester (14624) ***(G-14469)***
Innogenix Inc 631 450-4704
8200 New Horizons Blvd Amityville (11701) ***(G-295)***
Innotech Graphic Eqp Corp 845 268-6900
614 Corporate Way Ste 5 Valley Cottage (10989) ***(G-16405)***
Innova Interiors Inc 718 401-2122
780 E 134th St Fl 2 Bronx (10454) ***(G-1365)***
Innovant Inc (PA) 631 348-1900
135 Oval Dr Islandia (11749) ***(G-6834)***
Innovant Inc 212 929-4883
37 W 20th St Ste 209 New York (10011) ***(G-10644)***
Innovant Inc 212 929-4883
37 W 20th St Ste 1101 New York (10011) ***(G-10645)***
Innovant Group, Islandia *Also called Innovant Inc* ***(G-6834)***
Innovation Associates Inc 607 798-9376
530 Columbia Dr Ste 101 Johnson City (13790) ***(G-7126)***
Innovation In Motion Inc 407 878-7561
780 Long Beach Blvd Long Beach (11561) ***(G-7672)***
Innovation MGT Group Inc 800 889-0987
999 Montauk Hwy Shirley (11967) ***(G-15443)***
Innovative Automation Inc 631 439-3300
595 Smith St Farmingdale (11735) ***(G-5018)***
Innovative Cleaning Solutions 716 731-4408
2990 Carney Dr Sanborn (14132) ***(G-15148)***
Innovative Designs LLC 212 695-0892
141 W 36th St Fl 8 New York (10018) ***(G-10646)***
Innovative Industries LLC 718 784-7300
4322 22nd St Ste 205 Long Island City (11101) ***(G-7794)***
Innovative Jewelry Inc (PA) 718 408-8950
5 Inez Dr Bay Shore (11706) ***(G-703)***
Innovative Labs LLC 631 231-5522
85 Commerce Dr Hauppauge (11788) ***(G-6121)***
Innovative Municipal Pdts US 800 387-5777
454 River Rd Glenmont (12077) ***(G-5684)***
Innovative Pdts of Amer Inc 845 679-4500
234 Tinker St Woodstock (12498) ***(G-17379)***
Innovative Plastics Corp (PA) 845 359-7500
400 Route 303 Orangeburg (10962) ***(G-13252)***
Innovative Power Products Inc 631 563-0088
1170 Lincoln Ave Unit 7 Holbrook (11741) ***(G-6481)***
Innovative Surface Solutions, Glenmont *Also called Innovative Municipal Pdts US* ***(G-5684)***
Innovative Systems of New York 516 541-7410
201 Rose St Massapequa Park (11762) ***(G-8220)***
Innovative Video Tech Inc 631 388-5700
355 Oser Ave Hauppauge (11788) ***(G-6122)***
Ino-Tex LLC 212 400-2205
135 W 36th St Fl 6 New York (10018) ***(G-10647)***
Inolife Technologies Inc (PA) 212 348-5600
11 E 86th St Ste 19b New York (10028) ***(G-10648)***
Inori Jewels 347 703-5078
580 5th Ave New York (10036) ***(G-10649)***
Inova LLC 866 528-2804
6032 Depot Rd Altamont (12009) ***(G-211)***
Inova LLC 518 861-3400
6032 Depot Rd Altamont (12009) ***(G-212)***
Inpora Technologies LLC 646 838-2474
1501 Broadway New York (10036) ***(G-10650)***
Inpro Corporation 716 332-4699
250 Cooper Ave Ste 102 Tonawanda (14150) ***(G-16192)***
Inprotopia Corporation 917 338-7501
401 W 110th St Apt 2001 New York (10025) ***(G-10651)***
Inquiring Minds Inc (PA) 845 246-5775
65 S Partition St Saugerties (12477) ***(G-15214)***
Inscape (new York) Inc (HQ) 716 665-6210
221 Lister Ave 1 Falconer (14733) ***(G-4909)***
Inscape Archtectural Interiors, Falconer *Also called Inscape (new York) Inc* ***(G-4909)***
Inscape Inc 716 665-6210
221 Lister Ave Falconer (14733) ***(G-4910)***
Insert Outsert Experts, The, Lockport *Also called Gooding Co Inc* ***(G-7622)***
Insight Unlimited Inc 914 861-2090
660 Quaker Rd Chappaqua (10514) ***(G-3580)***
Insight Venture Partners IV 212 230-9200
1114 Avenue Of The Americ New York (10036) ***(G-10652)***
Inspired Entertainment Inc (PA) 646 565-3861
250 W 57th St Ste 2223 New York (10107) ***(G-10653)***
Instant Again LLC 585 436-8003
1277 Mount Read Blvd # 2 Rochester (14606) ***(G-14470)***

Instant Monogramming Inc.....585 654-5550
1150 University Ave Ste 5 Rochester (14607) *(G-14471)*
Instant Printing Service, Ithaca *Also called Madison Printing Corp (G-6893)*
Instant Stream Inc.....917 438-7182
1271 Ave Of The Americas New York (10020) *(G-10654)*
Instant Verticals Inc.....631 501-0001
330 Broadhollow Rd Farmingdale (11735) *(G-5019)*
Instantwhip of Buffalo Inc.....716 892-7031
2117 Genesee St Buffalo (14211) *(G-3027)*
Institute of Electrical and El.....212 705-8900
3 Park Ave Fl 17 New York (10016) *(G-10655)*
Institutional Invester.....212 224-3300
1120 Ave Of The Amrcs Fl New York (10036) *(G-10656)*
Instrumental Software Tech.....518 602-0001
77 Van Dam St Ste 9 Saratoga Springs (12866) *(G-15190)*
Instrumentation Laboratory Co.....845 680-0028
526 Route 303 Orangeburg (10962) *(G-13253)*
Instruments For Industry, Inc., Ronkonkoma *Also called Ametek CTS Us Inc (G-14897)*
Insty Trints, Kenmore *Also called Horace J Metz (G-7177)*
Insty-Prints, Niagara Falls *Also called Graphicomm Inc (G-12845)*
Insulating Coatings Corp.....607 723-1727
27 Link Dr Ste D Binghamton (13904) *(G-922)*
Insulators Local 12, Astoria *Also called Heat and Frost Inslatrs & Asbs (G-441)*
Insultech, North Tonawanda *Also called Shannon Entps Wstn NY Inc (G-13011)*
Int Trading USA LLC.....212 760-2338
261 W 35th St Ste 1100 New York (10001) *(G-10657)*
Intech 21 Inc.....516 626-7221
21 Harbor Park Dr Port Washington (11050) *(G-13847)*
Inteco Intimates, New York *Also called Intimateco LLC (G-10686)*
Integer Holdings Corporation.....716 937-5100
11900 Walden Ave Alden (14004) *(G-183)*
Integer Holdings Corporation.....716 759-5200
4098 Barton Rd Clarence (14031) *(G-3690)*
Integra Microsystem 1988 Inc.....718 609-6099
61 Greenpoint Ave Ste 412 Brooklyn (11222) *(G-2107)*
Integrated Control Corp.....631 673-5100
748 Park Ave Huntington (11743) *(G-6696)*
Integrated Copyright Group.....615 329-3999
1745 Broadway 19 New York (10019) *(G-10658)*
Integrated Graphics Inc (PA).....212 592-5600
7 W 36th St Fl 12 New York (10018) *(G-10659)*
Integrated Indus Resources, Lockport *Also called GM Components Holdings LLC (G-7621)*
Integrated Liner Tech Inc (PA).....518 621-7422
45 Discovery Dr Rensselaer (12144) *(G-14059)*
Integrated Medical Devices.....315 457-4200
549 Electronics Pkwy # 200 Liverpool (13088) *(G-7549)*
Integrated Solar Tech LLC.....914 249-9364
181 Westchester Ave # 409 Port Chester (10573) *(G-13776)*
Integrated Tech Support Svcs.....718 454-2497
18616 Jordan Ave Saint Albans (11412) *(G-15111)*
Integrated Water Management.....607 844-4276
289 Cortland Rd Dryden (13053) *(G-4346)*
Integrated Wood Components Inc.....607 467-1739
791 Airport Rd Deposit (13754) *(G-4301)*
Integrity Tool Incorporated.....315 524-4409
6485 Furnace Rd Ontario (14519) *(G-13226)*
Integrted Work Envronments LLC.....716 725-5088
6346 Everwood Ct N East Amherst (14051) *(G-4387)*
Integument Technologies Inc.....716 873-1199
72 Pearce Ave Tonawanda (14150) *(G-16193)*
Intek Precision.....585 293-0853
539 Attridge Rd Churchville (14428) *(G-3668)*
INTEL Corporation.....408 765-8080
55 Dodge Rd Getzville (14068) *(G-5611)*
Intelibs Inc.....877 213-2640
1500 Stony Brook Rd Ste 3 Stony Brook (11794) *(G-15791)*
Intellicell Biosciences Inc.....646 576-8700
460 Park Ave Fl 17 New York (10022) *(G-10660)*
Intellicheck Mobilisa Inc (PA).....516 992-1900
100 Jericho Quadrangle # 202 Jericho (11753) *(G-7104)*
Intellidyne LLC.....516 676-0777
303 Sunnyside Blvd # 75 Plainview (11803) *(G-13637)*
Intelligen Power Systems LLC.....212 750-0373
301 Winding Rd Old Bethpage (11804) *(G-13150)*
Intelligence Newsletter, New York *Also called Intellignc The Ftr Cmptng Nwsl (G-10662)*
Intelligent Ctrl Systems LLC.....516 340-1011
6 Inlet Pl Huntington (11743) *(G-6697)*
Intelligent Traffic Systems.....631 567-5994
140 Keyland Ct Unit 1 Bohemia (11716) *(G-1074)*
Intelligize Incorporated (PA).....571 612-8580
230 Park Ave Fl 7 New York (10169) *(G-10661)*
Intellignc The Ftr Cmptng Nwsl.....212 222-1123
360 Central Park W New York (10025) *(G-10662)*
Intellimetal Inc.....585 424-3260
2025 Brighton Henrietta Rochester (14623) *(G-14472)*
Intellitravel Media Inc (HQ).....646 695-6700
530 Fashion Ave Rm 201 New York (10018) *(G-10663)*
Intentions Jewelry LLC.....845 226-4650
83 Miller Hill Dr Lagrangeville (12540) *(G-7279)*
Inter Craft Custom Furniture.....718 278-2573
1431 Astoria Blvd Astoria (11102) *(G-443)*
Inter Molds Inc.....631 667-8580
26 Cleveland Ave Bay Shore (11706) *(G-704)*
Inter Pacific Consulting Corp.....718 460-2787
14055 34th Ave Apt 3n Flushing (11354) *(G-5260)*
Inter Parfums Inc (PA).....212 983-2640
551 5th Ave New York (10176) *(G-10664)*
Inter State Laminates Inc.....518 283-8355
44 Main St Poestenkill (12140) *(G-13754)*
Inter-Fence Co Inc.....718 939-9700
1520 129th St College Point (11356) *(G-3814)*
Interaction Insight Corp.....800 285-2950
750 3rd Ave Fl 9 New York (10017) *(G-10665)*
Interactive Instruments Inc.....518 347-0955
704 Corporation Park # 1 Scotia (12302) *(G-15349)*
Interaxissourcingcom Inc.....212 905-6001
41 E 11th St Fl 11 New York (10003) *(G-10666)*
Interbrand LLC.....212 840-9595
1 W 37th St Fl 9 New York (10018) *(G-10667)*
Intercall of New York, Mineola *Also called Intercall Systems Inc (G-8548)*
Intercall Systems Inc.....516 294-4524
150 Herricks Rd Mineola (11501) *(G-8548)*
Intercept Pharmaceuticals Inc (PA).....646 747-1000
10 Hudson Yards Fl 37 New York (10001) *(G-10668)*
Intercos America Inc.....845 732-3910
120 Brookhill Dr West Nyack (10994) *(G-16948)*
Intercotton Company Inc.....212 265-3809
888 7th Ave Fl 29 New York (10106) *(G-10669)*
Intercultural Alliance Artists.....917 406-1202
4510 165th St Flushing (11358) *(G-5261)*
Interdgital Communications LLC.....631 622-4000
2 Huntington Quad Ste 4s Melville (11747) *(G-8360)*
Interdynamics.....914 241-1423
100 S Bedford Rd Ste 300 Mount Kisco (10549) *(G-8672)*
Interface Performance Mtls.....315 346-3100
9635 Main St Beaver Falls (13305) *(G-789)*
Interface Performance Mtls Inc.....315 592-8100
2885 State Route 481 Fulton (13069) *(G-5476)*
Interface Performance Mtls Inc.....518 686-3400
12 Davis St Hoosick Falls (12090) *(G-6567)*
Interface Products Co Inc.....631 242-4605
215 N Fehr Way Ste C Bay Shore (11706) *(G-705)*
Interfaceflor LLC.....212 686-8284
330 5th Ave Fl 12 New York (10001) *(G-10670)*
Interhellenic Publishing Inc.....212 967-5016
421 7th Ave Ste 810 New York (10001) *(G-10671)*
Interior Metals.....718 439-7324
255 48th St Brooklyn (11220) *(G-2108)*
Interior Solutions of Wny LLC.....716 332-0372
472 Franklin St Buffalo (14202) *(G-3028)*
Interiors By Robert, Richmond Hill *Also called Terbo Ltd (G-14099)*
Interiors-Pft Inc.....212 244-9600
3200 Skillman Ave Fl 3 Long Island City (11101) *(G-7795)*
International Aids Vaccine Ini (PA).....212 847-1111
125 Broad St Fl 9 New York (10004) *(G-10672)*
International Aids Vaccine Ini.....646 381-8066
140 58th St Brooklyn (11220) *(G-2109)*
International Bus Mchs Corp.....607 754-9558
1701 North St Endicott (13760) *(G-4819)*
International Bus Mchs Corp.....212 324-5000
55 Broad St Fl 27 New York (10004) *(G-10673)*
International Bus Mchs Corp.....914 345-5219
1 New Orchard Rd Ste 1 Armonk (10504) *(G-412)*
International Bus Mchs Corp.....845 433-1234
2455 South Rd Poughkeepsie (12601) *(G-13927)*
International Bus Mchs Corp.....800 426-4968
10 North Dr Hopewell Junction (12533) *(G-6580)*
International Bus Mchs Corp.....914 499-2000
20 Old Post Rd Armonk (10504) *(G-413)*
International Business Times, New York *Also called Ibt Media Inc (G-10594)*
International Casein Corp Cal.....516 466-4363
111 Great Neck Rd Ste 218 Great Neck (11021) *(G-5832)*
International Center For Postg.....607 257-5860
179 Graham Rd Ste E Ithaca (14850) *(G-6886)*
International Climbing Mchs.....607 288-4001
630 Elmira Rd Ithaca (14850) *(G-6887)*
International Control Products.....716 558-4400
1700 Union Rd Ste 2 West Seneca (14224) *(G-16977)*
International Creative Met Inc.....718 424-8179
3728 61st St Woodside (11377) *(G-17350)*
International Data Group Inc.....212 331-7883
117 E 55th St Ste 204 New York (10022) *(G-10674)*
International Design Assoc Ltd.....212 687-0333
747 3rd Ave Rm 218 New York (10017) *(G-10675)*
International Direct Group Inc.....212 921-9036
525 7th Ave Rm 208 New York (10018) *(G-10676)*
International Fiber Corp (PA).....716 693-4040
50 Bridge St North Tonawanda (14120) *(G-12995)*
International Fire-Shield Inc.....315 255-1006
194 Genesee St Auburn (13021) *(G-499)*
International Imaging Mtls Inc (PA).....716 691-6333
310 Commerce Dr Amherst (14228) *(G-245)*
International Inspirations Ltd (PA).....212 465-8500
358 5th Ave Rm 501 New York (10001) *(G-10677)*

ALPHABETIC

International Insurance Soc 212 815-9291
101 Murray St Fl 4 New York (10007) *(G-10678)*
International Key Supply LLC 631 983-6096
32 Gazza Blvd Farmingdale (11735) *(G-5020)*
International Leisure Pdts Inc 631 254-2155
191 Rodeo Dr Edgewood (11717) *(G-4615)*
International Life Science 631 549-0471
23 Gloria Ln Huntington (11743) *(G-6698)*
International Mdse Svcs Inc 914 699-4000
336 S Fulton Ave Fl 1 Mount Vernon (10553) *(G-8738)*
International Metals Trdg LLC 866 923-0182
25 Melville Park Rd # 114 Melville (11747) *(G-8361)*
International MGT Netwrk 646 401-0032
445 Park Ave Fl 9 New York (10022) *(G-10679)*
International Mtls & Sups Inc 518 834-9899
56 Industrial Park Rd Keeseville (12944) *(G-7167)*
International Newspaper Prntng, Glen Head *Also called International Newsppr Prtg Co (G-5649)*
International Newsppr Prtg Co 516 626-6095
18 Carlisle Dr Glen Head (11545) *(G-5649)*
International Ord Tech Inc 716 664-1100
101 Harrison St Jamestown (14701) *(G-7036)*
International Paper Company 518 585-6761
568 Shore Airport Rd Ticonderoga (12883) *(G-16148)*
International Paper Company 585 663-1000
200 Boxart St Rochester (14612) *(G-14473)*
International Paper Company 845 986-6409
1422 Long Meadow Rd Tuxedo Park (10987) *(G-16307)*
International Paper Company 607 775-1550
1240 Conklin Rd Conklin (13748) *(G-3894)*
International Paper Company 315 797-5120
50 Harbor Point Rd Utica (13502) *(G-16369)*
International Paper Company 716 852-2144
100 Bud Mil Dr Buffalo (14206) *(G-3029)*
International Paper Company 518 372-6461
803 Corporation Park Glenville (12302) *(G-5717)*
International Patterns Inc 631 952-2000
8 Arthur Ct Plainview (11803) *(G-13638)*
International Robotics Inc 914 630-1060
2001 Palmer Ave Ste Ll1 Larchmont (10538) *(G-7375)*
International Stone Accessrs 718 522-5399
703 Myrtle Ave Brooklyn (11205) *(G-2110)*
International Time Products 516 931-0005
410 Jericho Tpke Ste 110 Jericho (11753) *(G-7105)*
International Tool & Mch Inc 585 654-6955
121 Lincoln Ave Rochester (14611) *(G-14474)*
International Wire Group, Camden *Also called Camden Wire Co Inc (G-3341)*
International Wire Group (PA) 315 245-3800
12 Masonic Ave Camden (13316) *(G-3343)*
International Wire Group Inc (HQ) 315 245-2000
12 Masonic Ave Camden (13316) *(G-3344)*
Internationl Studios Inc 212 819-1616
108 W 39th St Rm 1300 New York (10018) *(G-10680)*
Internodal International Inc 631 765-0037
54800 Route 25 Southold (11971) *(G-15583)*
Interntional Fireprof Door Inc 718 783-1310
1005 Greene Ave Brooklyn (11221) *(G-2111)*
Interntional Gourmet Soups Inc 212 768-7687
1110 South Ave Ste 300 Staten Island (10314) *(G-15709)*
Interntnal Bus Cmmncations Inc (PA) 516 352-4505
1981 Marcus Ave Ste C105 New Hyde Park (11042) *(G-8887)*
Interntnal Cntrls Msrmnts Corp (PA) 315 233-5266
7313 William Barry Blvd North Syracuse (13212) *(G-12965)*
Interntnal Elctronic Mchs Corp 518 268-1636
850 River St Troy (12180) *(G-16263)*
Interntnal Flvors Frgrnces Inc (PA) 212 765-5500
521 W 57th St New York (10019) *(G-10681)*
Interntnal Strpping Diecutting 718 383-7720
200 Franklin St Brooklyn (11222) *(G-2112)*
Interntnl Publcatns Media Grup 917 604-9602
708 3rd Ave Ste 145 New York (10017) *(G-10682)*
Interntonal Consmr Connections 516 481-3438
5 Terminal Rd Unit A West Hempstead (11552) *(G-16887)*
Interntonal Glatt Kosher Meats, Brooklyn *Also called Globex Kosher Foods Inc (G-2030)*
Interparts International Inc (PA) 516 576-2000
190 Express St Plainview (11803) *(G-13639)*
Interplex Nas Electronics, College Point *Also called Nas CP Corp (G-3823)*
Interstate Chemical Co Inc 585 344-2822
4 Treadeasy Ave Batavia (14020) *(G-641)*
Interstate Litho Corp 631 232-6025
151 Alkier St Brentwood (11717) *(G-1182)*
Interstate Thermographers Corp 914 948-1745
70 Westmoreland Ave White Plains (10606) *(G-17150)*
Interstate Window Corporation 631 231-0800
345 Crooked Hill Rd Ste 1 Brentwood (11717) *(G-1183)*
Interstate Wood & Vinyl Pdts, Amityville *Also called Interstate Wood Products Inc (G-296)*
Interstate Wood Products Inc 631 842-4488
1084 Sunrise Hwy Amityville (11701) *(G-296)*
Intersurgical Incorporated (PA) 315 451-2900
6757 Kinne St East Syracuse (13057) *(G-4558)*
Intertex USA Inc 212 279-3601
131 W 35th St Fl 10 New York (10001) *(G-10683)*
Interview Inc 212 941-2900
575 Broadway Fl 5 New York (10012) *(G-10684)*
Interview Magazine, New York *Also called Interview Inc (G-10684)*
Inteva Products LLC 248 655-8886
30 Rockefeller Plz New York (10112) *(G-10685)*
Intex Company Inc (PA) 516 223-0200
80 Commercial St Freeport (11520) *(G-5417)*
Intimateco LLC 212 239-4411
149 Madison Ave Rm 300 New York (10016) *(G-10686)*
Intra-Cellular Therapies Inc 212 923-3344
430 E 29th St New York (10016) *(G-10687)*
Intralinks Holdings Inc (HQ) 212 543-7700
150 E 42nd St Fl 8 New York (10017) *(G-10688)*
Intrapac International Corp 518 561-2030
4 Plant St Plattsburgh (12901) *(G-13697)*
Intrepid Control Service Inc 718 886-8771
2904 Francis Lewis Blvd Flushing (11358) *(G-5262)*
Intri-Cut Inc 716 691-5200
90 Pineview Dr Amherst (14228) *(G-246)*
Intrigue Concepts Inc 800 424-8170
8 Gilbert Pl Ste 8 Roosevelt (11575) *(G-15029)*
Intriguing Threads Apparel Inc (PA) 212 768-8733
552 Fashion Ave Rm 603 New York (10018) *(G-10689)*
Intrinsiq Materials Inc 585 301-4432
1200 Ridgeway Ave Ste 110 Rochester (14615) *(G-14475)*
Intstrux LLC 646 688-2782
15 W 39th St Fl 13 New York (10018) *(G-10690)*
Intuition Publishing Limited 212 838-7115
40 E 34th St Rm 1101 New York (10016) *(G-10691)*
Invagen Pharmaceuticals Inc 631 949-6367
550 S Research Pl Central Islip (11722) *(G-3525)*
Invagen Pharmaceuticals Inc (HQ) 631 231-3233
7 Oser Ave Ste 4 Hauppauge (11788) *(G-6123)*
Investars, New York *Also called Netologic Inc (G-11394)*
Investment News 212 210-0100
711 3rd Ave Fl 3 New York (10017) *(G-10692)*
Investors Business Daily Inc 212 626-7676
1501 Broadway Fl 12 New York (10036) *(G-10693)*
Invid Tech, Hauppauge *Also called Innovative Video Tech Inc (G-6122)*
Invision Inc (HQ) 212 557-5554
25 W 43rd St Ste 609 New York (10036) *(G-10694)*
Inwood Material 516 371-1842
1 Sheridan Blvd Inwood (11096) *(G-6799)*
Ion Optics Inc 518 339-6853
75 Benjamin St Albany (12202) *(G-89)*
Ip Med Inc 516 766-3800
3571 Hargale Rd Oceanside (11572) *(G-13102)*
IPC/Razor LLC (PA) 212 551-4500
277 Park Ave Fl 39 New York (10172) *(G-10695)*
Ipcc, Flushing *Also called Inter Pacific Consulting Corp (G-5260)*
Ipe, Orchard Park *Also called Bos-Hatten Inc (G-13276)*
Ipm US Inc 212 481-7967
276 5th Ave Rm 203 New York (10001) *(G-10696)*
Ipp Energy LLC 607 773-3307
22 Charles St Binghamton (13905) *(G-923)*
Ipsidy Inc (PA) 407 951-8640
780 Long Beach Blvd Long Beach (11561) *(G-7673)*
Iquit Cig LLC 718 475-1422
4014 13th Ave Brooklyn (11218) *(G-2113)*
Ir Media Group (usa) Inc 212 425-9649
25 Broadway Fl 9 New York (10004) *(G-10697)*
Iradj Moini Couture Ltd 212 594-9242
403 W 46th St New York (10036) *(G-10698)*
Irene Cerone 315 668-2899
9600 Brewerton Rd Brewerton (13029) *(G-1201)*
Irene Goodman Literary Agency 212 604-0330
27 W 24th St Ste 700b New York (10010) *(G-10699)*
Iridesse Inc 212 230-6000
600 Madison Ave Fl 5 New York (10022) *(G-10700)*
Iridium Industries Inc 516 504-9700
17 Barstow Rd Ste 302 Great Neck (11021) *(G-5833)*
Iriniri Designs Ltd 845 469-7934
1358 Kings Hwy Sugar Loaf (10981) *(G-15824)*
Irish America Inc 212 725-2993
875 Americas Rm 2100 New York (10001) *(G-10701)*
Irish America Magazine, New York *Also called Irish America Inc (G-10701)*
Irish Echo Newspaper Corp 212 482-4818
165 Madison Ave Rm 302 New York (10016) *(G-10702)*
Irish Tribune Inc 212 684-3366
875 Avenue Of The Amerrm2 Rm 2100 New York (10001) *(G-10703)*
Irish Voice Newspaper, New York *Also called Irish Tribune Inc (G-10703)*
Iron Art Inc 914 592-7977
14 N Payne St Elmsford (10523) *(G-4765)*
Iron Eagle Group Inc (PA) 888 481-4445
160 W 66th St Apt 41g New York (10023) *(G-10704)*
Iron Flamingo Brewery, Corning *Also called Rising Sons 6 Brewing Coinc (G-3999)*
Iron Horse Graphics Ltd 631 537-3400
112 Maple Ln Bridgehampton (11932) *(G-1232)*
Iron Smoke Whiskey LLC 585 388-7584
111 Parce Ave Ste 5 Fairport (14450) *(G-4863)*
Iron Worker 516 338-2756
1039 W Jericho Tpke Smithtown (11787) *(G-15512)*

Ironshore Holdings Inc 315 457-1052
290 Elwood Davis Rd Liverpool (13088) ***(G-7550)***
Irony Limited Inc (PA)....631 329-4065
53 Sag Harbor Tpke East Hampton (11937) ***(G-4431)***
Iroquois Rock Products Inc (HQ) 585 381-7010
1150 Penfield Rd Rochester (14625) ***(G-14476)***
Irpenscom 585 507-7997
4 Katsura Ct Penfield (14526) ***(G-13523)***
Irtronics Instruments Inc 914 693-6291
132 Forest Blvd Ardsley (10502) ***(G-404)***
Irv Inc....212 334-4507
540 Broadway Fl 4 New York (10012) ***(G-10705)***
Irv & Vic Sportswear Co, Yonkers *Also called Robert Viggiani* ***(G-17500)***
Irv Schroder & Sons Inc....518 828-0194
2906 Atlantic Ave Stottville (12172) ***(G-15803)***
Irving Consumer Products Inc (HQ) 518 747-4151
1 Eddy St Fort Edward (12828) ***(G-5350)***
Irving Farm Coffee Co Inc (PA) 212 206-0707
151 W 19th St Fl 6 New York (10011) ***(G-10706)***
Irving Tissue Div, Fort Edward *Also called Irving Consumer Products Inc* ***(G-5350)***
Irving Woodlands LLC 607 723-4862
53 Shaw Rd Conklin (13748) ***(G-3895)***
Isabel and Nina, New York *Also called Travis Ayers Inc* ***(G-12416)***
Isabel Toledo Enterprises Inc....212 685-0948
1181 Broadway Fl 7 New York (10001) ***(G-10707)***
Isfel Co Inc (PA) 212 736-6216
110 W 34th St Rm 1101 New York (10001) ***(G-10708)***
Ish Precision Machine Corp (PA) 718 436-8858
786 Mcdonald Ave Brooklyn (11218) ***(G-2114)***
Isimulate LLC....877 947-2831
90 State St Ste 700 Albany (12207) ***(G-90)***
Isine Inc (PA)....631 913-4400
4155 Veterans Memorial Hw Ronkonkoma (11779) ***(G-14942)***
Isis/Koppermann, New York *Also called Isisnet LLC* ***(G-10709)***
Isisnet LLC....212 239-1205
53 W 36th St Rm 502 New York (10018) ***(G-10709)***
Island Audio Engineering 631 543-2372
7 Glenmere Ct Commack (11725) ***(G-3862)***
Island Automated Gate Co LLC....631 425-0196
125 W Hills Rd Huntington Station (11746) ***(G-6749)***
Island Chimney Service, Bohemia *Also called Ace Cntracting Consulting Corp* ***(G-1001)***
Island Circuits International 516 625-5555
1318 130th St Fl 2 College Point (11356) ***(G-3815)***
Island Components Group Inc 631 563-4224
101 Colin Dr Unit 4 Holbrook (11741) ***(G-6482)***
Island Container Corp....631 253-4400
44 Island Container Plz Wyandanch (11798) ***(G-17391)***
Island Custom Stairs Inc....631 205-5335
23 Scouting Blvd Unit C Medford (11763) ***(G-8282)***
Island Industries Corp....631 451-8825
480 Mill Rd Coram (11727) ***(G-3968)***
Island Instrument Corp....631 243-0550
65 Burt Dr Deer Park (11729) ***(G-4175)***
Island Interiors, West Babylon *Also called Dbs Interiors Corp* ***(G-16813)***
Island Lite Louvers Inc....631 608-4250
35 Albany Ave Amityville (11701) ***(G-297)***
Island Machine Inc....518 562-1232
86 Boynton Ave Plattsburgh (12901) ***(G-13698)***
Island Marketing Corp....516 739-0500
95 Searing Ave Ste 2 Mineola (11501) ***(G-8549)***
Island Nameplate Inc....845 651-4005
124 S Main St Florida (10921) ***(G-5220)***
Island Ordnance Systems LLC....516 746-2100
267 E Jericho Tpke Ste 2 Mineola (11501) ***(G-8550)***
Island Precision, Ronkonkoma *Also called Roger Latari* ***(G-15004)***
Island Publications, Melville *Also called Distinction Magazine Inc* ***(G-8341)***
Island Pyrochemical Inds Corp (PA)....516 746-2100
267 E Jericho Tpke Ste 2 Mineola (11501) ***(G-8551)***
Island Ready Mix Inc....631 874-3777
170 Railroad Ave Center Moriches (11934) ***(G-3492)***
Island Recycling Corp....631 234-6688
228 Blydenburg Rd Central Islip (11749) ***(G-3526)***
Island Research and Dev Corp....631 471-7100
200 13th Ave Unit 12 Ronkonkoma (11779) ***(G-14943)***
Island Silkscreen Inc....631 757-4567
328 Larkfield Rd East Northport (11731) ***(G-4458)***
Island Stairs Corp....347 645-0560
178 Industrial Loop Staten Island (10309) ***(G-15710)***
Island Street Lumber Co Inc....716 692-4127
11 Felton St North Tonawanda (14120) ***(G-12996)***
Island Technology, Ronkonkoma *Also called Island Research and Dev Corp* ***(G-14943)***
Island Vitamin, Farmingdale *Also called Maxus Pharmaceuticals Inc* ***(G-5054)***
Islandaire, East Setauket *Also called RE Hansen Industries Inc* ***(G-4510)***
Islandia Mri Associates PC....631 234-2828
200 Corporate Plz Ste 203 Central Islip (11749) ***(G-3527)***
Islechem LLC 716 773-8401
2801 Long Rd Grand Island (14072) ***(G-5774)***
Islip Bulletin, Patchogue *Also called John Lor Publishing Ltd* ***(G-13451)***
Islip Miniture Golf 631 940-8900
500 E Main St Bay Shore (11706) ***(G-706)***
ISO Plastics Corp 914 663-8300
160 E 1st St Mount Vernon (10550) ***(G-8739)***
Isolation Dynamics Corp 631 491-5670
66 Otis St Unit A West Babylon (11704) ***(G-16823)***
Isolation Systems Inc....716 694-6390
889 Erie Ave Ste 1 North Tonawanda (14120) ***(G-12997)***
Isolation Technology Inc....631 253-3314
73 Nancy St Unit A West Babylon (11704) ***(G-16824)***
Isonics Corporation (PA) 212 356-7400
535 8th Ave Fl 3 New York (10018) ***(G-10710)***
Isp Optics Corporation (HQ)....914 591-3070
50 S Buckhout St Irvington (10533) ***(G-6814)***
Israeli Yellow Pages 718 520-1000
12510 Queens Blvd Ste 14 Kew Gardens (11415) ***(G-7191)***
Issacs Yisroel....718 851-7430
4424 18th Ave Brooklyn (11204) ***(G-2115)***
Issco Corporation (PA)....212 732-8748
111 Cherry Valley Ave # 410 Garden City (11530) ***(G-5524)***
Ist Conax Nuclear, Buffalo *Also called Mirion Tech Conax Nuclear Inc* ***(G-3088)***
It Commodity Sourcing Inc....718 677-1577
1640 E 22nd St Brooklyn (11210) ***(G-2116)***
It's About Time, Mount Kisco *Also called Iat Interactive LLC* ***(G-8670)***
It's About Time Publishing, Mount Kisco *Also called Laurtom Inc* ***(G-8677)***
Itac Label & Tag Corp....718 625-2148
179 Lexington Ave Brooklyn (11216) ***(G-2117)***
Italian Marble & Granite Inc 716 741-1800
8526 Roll Rd Clarence Center (14032) ***(G-3702)***
Itc Mfg Group Inc....212 684-3696
109 W 38th St Rm 701 New York (10018) ***(G-10711)***
Itelinso, Cold Spring Harbor *Also called Infoservices International* ***(G-3794)***
Ithaca Beer Company Inc....607 272-1305
122 Ithaca Beer Dr Ithaca (14850) ***(G-6888)***
Ithaca Ice Company, The, Ithaca *Also called Henry Newman LLC* ***(G-6883)***
Ithaca Journal News Co Inc....607 272-2321
123 W State St Ste 1 Ithaca (14850) ***(G-6889)***
Ithaca Peripherals, Ithaca *Also called Transact Technologies Inc* ***(G-6914)***
Ithaca Pregancy Center....607 753-3909
4 Church St Cortland (13045) ***(G-4053)***
Ithaca Times, Ithaca *Also called New Ski Inc* ***(G-6902)***
Itin Scale Co Inc....718 336-5900
4802 Glenwood Rd Brooklyn (11234) ***(G-2118)***
ITR Industries Inc (PA)....914 964-7063
441 Saw Mill River Rd Yonkers (10701) ***(G-17473)***
Its Our Time, New York *Also called Fashion Avenue Knits Inc* ***(G-10196)***
Itss, Saint Albans *Also called Integrated Tech Support Svcs* ***(G-15111)***
ITT Aerospace Controls LLC....914 641-2000
4 W Red Oak Ln White Plains (10604) ***(G-17151)***
ITT Corporation....585 269-7109
4847 Main St Hemlock (14466) ***(G-6287)***
ITT Corporation....315 568-2811
240 Fall St Seneca Falls (13148) ***(G-15383)***
ITT Engineered Valves LLC (HQ)....662 257-6982
240 Fall St Seneca Falls (13148) ***(G-15384)***
ITT Enidine Inc (HQ)....716 662-1900
7 Centre Dr Orchard Park (14127) ***(G-13299)***
ITT Goulds Pumps Inc....914 641-2129
240 Fall St Seneca Falls (13148) ***(G-15385)***
ITT Inc (PA)....914 641-2000
1133 Westchester Ave N-100 White Plains (10604) ***(G-17152)***
ITT Industries Holdings Inc (HQ)....914 641-2000
1133 Westchester Ave N-100 White Plains (10604) ***(G-17153)***
ITT LLC (HQ)....914 641-2000
1133 Westchester Ave N-100 White Plains (10604) ***(G-17154)***
ITT LLC....315 568-4733
240 Fall St Seneca Falls (13148) ***(G-15386)***
ITT LLC....315 258-4904
1 Goulds Dr Auburn (13021) ***(G-500)***
ITT LLC....914 641-2000
2881 E Bayard Street Ext Seneca Falls (13148) ***(G-15387)***
ITT Monitoring Control, Seneca Falls *Also called ITT LLC* ***(G-15386)***
ITT Water Technology, Auburn *Also called ITT LLC* ***(G-500)***
ITT Water Technology Inc 315 568-2811
2881 E Bayard Street Ext Seneca Falls (13148) ***(G-15388)***
Itts Industrial Inc....718 605-6934
165 Industrial Loop Ste C Staten Island (10309) ***(G-15711)***
Ivalua Inc 650 930-9710
195 Montague St Brooklyn (11201) ***(G-2119)***
Iver Printing Inc....718 275-2070
124 N 12th St New Hyde Park (11040) ***(G-8888)***
Ives Farm Market....315 592-4880
2652 Rr 176 Fulton (13069) ***(G-5477)***
Ives Slaughterhouse, Fulton *Also called Ives Farm Market* ***(G-5477)***
Ivi Services Inc....607 729-5111
5 Pine Camp Dr Binghamton (13904) ***(G-924)***
Ivy Classic Industries Inc....914 632-8200
40 Plain Ave New Rochelle (10801) ***(G-8958)***
Ivy Enterprises Inc (HQ)....516 621-9779
3 Seaview Blvd Port Washington (11050) ***(G-13848)***
Iwci, Deposit *Also called Integrated Wood Components Inc* ***(G-4301)***
Iwe, East Amherst *Also called Integrted Work Envronments LLC* ***(G-4387)***

ALPHABETIC

Iweb Design Inc 805 243-8305
1491 Metro Ave Ste 3i Bronx (10462) ***(G-1366)***
Izi Creations, New York *Also called Adamor Inc* ***(G-9072)***
Izquierdo Studios Ltd 212 807-9757
34 W 28th St 6 New York (10001) ***(G-10712)***
Izun Pharmaceuticals Corp (PA) 212 618-6357
1 Rockefeller Plz Fl 11 New York (10020) ***(G-10713)***
J & A Usa Inc 631 243-3336
335 Crooked Hill Rd Brentwood (11717) ***(G-1184)***
J & C Finishing 718 456-1087
1067 Wyckoff Ave Ridgewood (11385) ***(G-14123)***
J & E Talit Inc 718 850-1333
13011 Atlantic Ave Fl 2 Richmond Hill (11418) ***(G-14088)***
J & F Advertising, Carle Place *Also called Market Place Publications* ***(G-3421)***
J & G Machine & Tool Co Inc 315 310-7130
4510 Smith Rd Marion (14505) ***(G-8126)***
J & H Creations Inc 212 465-0962
19 W 36th St Fl 3 New York (10018) ***(G-10714)***
J & J Bronze & Aluminum Cast 718 383-2111
249 Huron St Brooklyn (11222) ***(G-2120)***
J & J Log & Lumber Corp 845 832-6535
528 Old State Route 22 Dover Plains (12522) ***(G-4339)***
J & J Printing Inc (PA) 315 458-7411
500 Cambridge Ave Syracuse (13208) ***(G-15983)***
J & J Swiss Precision Inc 631 243-5584
160 W Industry Ct Ste F Deer Park (11729) ***(G-4176)***
J & J Tl Die Mfg & Stampg Corp 845 228-0242
594 Horsepound Rd Carmel (10512) ***(G-3428)***
J & L Precision Co Inc 585 768-6388
9222 Summit Street Rd Le Roy (14482) ***(G-7435)***
J & M Feed Corporation 631 281-2152
675 Montauk Hwy Shirley (11967) ***(G-15444)***
J & M Packaging Inc 631 608-3069
21 Newton Rd Hauppauge (11788) ***(G-6124)***
J & M Textile Co Inc 212 268-8000
505 8th Ave Rm 701 New York (10018) ***(G-10715)***
J & N Computer Services Inc 585 388-8780
1387 Fairport Rd Ste 900j Fairport (14450) ***(G-4864)***
J & R Unique Giftware 718 821-0398
5863 56th St Maspeth (11378) ***(G-8177)***
J & S Logging Inc 315 262-2112
3860 State Highway 56 South Colton (13687) ***(G-15537)***
J & T Metal Products Co Inc 631 226-7400
89 Eads St West Babylon (11704) ***(G-16825)***
J & X Production Inc 718 200-1228
327 W 36th St 7f New York (10018) ***(G-10716)***
J A G Diamond Manufacturers 212 575-0660
580 5th Ave Ste 905b New York (10036) ***(G-10717)***
J A T Printing Inc 631 427-1155
46 Gerard St Unit 2 Huntington (11743) ***(G-6699)***
J A Yansick Lumber Co Inc 585 492-4312
16 Rule Dr Arcade (14009) ***(G-395)***
J and M Schwarz, Albany *Also called Smiths Gas Service Inc* ***(G-134)***
J B S, Scotia *Also called Jbs LLC* ***(G-15350)***
J B Tool & Die Co Inc 516 333-1480
629 Main St Westbury (11590) ***(G-17024)***
J C Industries Inc 631 420-1920
89 Eads St West Babylon (11704) ***(G-16826)***
J D Calato Manufacturing Co (PA) 716 285-3546
4501 Hyde Park Blvd Niagara Falls (14305) ***(G-12855)***
J D Cousins Inc 716 824-1098
667 Tifft St Buffalo (14220) ***(G-3030)***
J D Handling Systems Inc 518 828-9676
1346 State Route 9h Ghent (12075) ***(G-5620)***
J D Steward Inc 718 358-0169
4537 162nd St Flushing (11358) ***(G-5263)***
J Davis Manufacturing Co Inc 315 337-7574
222 Erie Blvd E Rome (13440) ***(G-14844)***
J E T, Ronkonkoma *Also called Jet Redi Mix Concrete Inc* ***(G-14947)***
J Edlin Interiors Ltd 212 243-2111
122 W 27th St Fl 2 New York (10001) ***(G-10718)***
J F B & Sons Lithographers 631 467-1444
1700 Ocean Ave Lake Ronkonkoma (11779) ***(G-7302)***
J F M Sheet Metal Inc 631 737-8494
2090 Pond Rd Ronkonkoma (11779) ***(G-14944)***
J F Machining Company Inc 716 791-3910
2382 Balmer Rd Ransomville (14131) ***(G-14032)***
J Gimbel Inc 718 296-5200
275 Hempstead Tpke Ste A West Hempstead (11552) ***(G-16888)***
J H Buhrmaster Company Inc 518 843-1700
164 W Main St Amsterdam (12010) ***(G-351)***
J H Buscher Inc 716 667-2003
227 Thorn Ave Ste 30 Orchard Park (14127) ***(G-13300)***
J H C Fabrications Inc (PA) 718 649-0065
595 Berriman St Brooklyn (11208) ***(G-2121)***
J H Jewelry Co Inc 212 239-1330
12 W 32nd St Fl 12 New York (10001) ***(G-10719)***
J H M Engineering 718 871-1810
4014 8th Ave Brooklyn (11232) ***(G-2122)***
J H Rhodes Company Inc 315 829-3600
10 Ward St Vernon (13476) ***(G-16459)***
J H Robotics Inc 607 729-3758
109 Main St Johnson City (13790) ***(G-7127)***
J I Intrntnal Contact Lens Lab 718 997-1212
6352 Saunders St Ste A Rego Park (11374) ***(G-14045)***
J Ironwork, Brooklyn *Also called Railings By New Star Brass* ***(G-2493)***
J J Creations Inc 718 392-2828
4742 37th St Long Island City (11101) ***(G-7796)***
J K Fertility, Yonkers *Also called J Kendall LLC* ***(G-17474)***
J K J, Rochester *Also called JK Jewelry Inc* ***(G-14483)***
J Kendall LLC 646 739-4956
71 Belvedere Dr Yonkers (10705) ***(G-17474)***
J Klagsbrun Inc (PA) 212 712-9388
25 E 86th St 6f New York (10028) ***(G-10720)***
J L M, New York *Also called Jlm Couture Inc* ***(G-10780)***
J Lowy Co 718 338-7324
940 E 19th St Brooklyn (11230) ***(G-2123)***
J Lowy Lea Skullcaps Mfg Co, Brooklyn *Also called J Lowy Co* ***(G-2123)***
J M C Bow Co Inc 718 686-8110
1271 39th St Ste 3 Brooklyn (11218) ***(G-2124)***
J M Canty Inc 716 625-4227
6100 Donner Rd Lockport (14094) ***(G-7624)***
J M Haley Corp 631 845-5200
151 Toledo St Ste 1 Farmingdale (11735) ***(G-5021)***
J M L Productions Inc 718 643-1674
162 Spencer St Brooklyn (11205) ***(G-2125)***
J M P Display Fixture Co Inc 718 649-0333
760 E 96th St Brooklyn (11236) ***(G-2126)***
J M R Plastics Corporation 718 898-9825
5847 78th St Middle Village (11379) ***(G-8445)***
J Mackenzie Ltd 585 321-1770
234 Wallace Way Rochester (14624) ***(G-14477)***
J N White Associates Inc 585 237-5191
129 N Center St Perry (14530) ***(G-13547)***
J P Installations Warehouse 914 576-3188
29 Portman Rd New Rochelle (10801) ***(G-8959)***
J P Machine Products Inc 631 249-9229
144 Rome St Farmingdale (11735) ***(G-5022)***
J P Printing Inc (PA) 516 293-6110
331 Main St Farmingdale (11735) ***(G-5023)***
J P R Pharmacy Inc 718 327-0600
529 Beach 20th St Far Rockaway (11691) ***(G-4930)***
J Pahura Contractors 585 589-5793
415 East Ave Albion (14411) ***(G-169)***
J Percoco Industries Inc 631 312-4572
1546 Ocean Ave Ste 4 Bohemia (11716) ***(G-1075)***
J Percy For Mrvin Rchards Ltd (HQ) 212 944-5300
512 Fashion Ave New York (10018) ***(G-10721)***
J Petrocelli Wine Cellars LLC 631 765-1100
39390 Route 25 Peconic (11958) ***(G-13495)***
J R Gold Designs Ltd 212 922-9292
555 5th Ave Fl 19 New York (10017) ***(G-10722)***
J R Nites (PA) 212 354-9670
1400 Broadway Rm 601 New York (10018) ***(G-10723)***
J R Products Inc 716 633-7565
9680 County Rd Clarence Center (14032) ***(G-3703)***
J R S Precision Machining 631 737-1330
40 Raynor Ave Ste 2 Ronkonkoma (11779) ***(G-14945)***
J Rivera, Bohemia *Also called Pro Torque* ***(G-1118)***
J Soehner Corporation 516 599-2534
200 Brower Ave Rockville Centre (11570) ***(G-14821)***
J Sussman Inc 718 297-0228
10910 180th St Jamaica (11433) ***(G-6958)***
J T D Stamping Co Inc 631 643-4144
403 Wyandanch Ave West Babylon (11704) ***(G-16827)***
J T Printing 21 .... 718 484-3939
304 Broad St Staten Island (10304) ***(G-15712)***
J T Systematic 607 754-0929
39 Valley St Endwell (13760) ***(G-4841)***
J V Haring & Son 718 720-1947
1277 Clove Rd Ste 2 Staten Island (10301) ***(G-15713)***
J V Precision Inc 518 851-3200
3031 Us Route 9 Hudson (12534) ***(G-6649)***
J Valdi, New York *Also called Lgb Inc* ***(G-11016)***
J Vogler Enterprise LLC 585 247-1625
15 Evelyn St Rochester (14606) ***(G-14478)***
J W Stevens Co Inc 315 472-6311
6059 Corporate Dr East Syracuse (13057) ***(G-4559)***
J Zeluck Inc (PA) 718 251-8060
5300 Kings Hwy Brooklyn (11234) ***(G-2127)***
J&R Fuel of LI Inc 631 234-1959
97 W Suffolk Ave Central Islip (11722) ***(G-3528)***
J&T Macquesten Realty, Mount Vernon *Also called Dunlea Whl GL & Mirror Inc* ***(G-8725)***
J-K Prosthetics & Orthotics 914 699-2077
699 N Macquesten Pkwy Mount Vernon (10552) ***(G-8740)***
J.hoaglund, New York *Also called THE Design Group Inc* ***(G-12330)***
J.N. White Designs, Perry *Also called J N White Associates Inc* ***(G-13547)***
J9 Technologies Inc 412 586-5038
25 Broadway Fl 9 New York (10004) ***(G-10724)***
Jaab Precision Inc 631 218-3725
180 Gary Way Ronkonkoma (11779) ***(G-14946)***
Jab Concrete Supply Corp 718 842-5250
1465 Bronx River Ave Bronx (10472) ***(G-1367)***
Jabil Circuit Inc 845 471-9237
2455 South Rd Poughkeepsie (12601) ***(G-13928)***

Jabo Agricultural Inc....631 475-1800
9 Northwood Ln Patchogue (11772) **(G-13450)**
Jac Usa Inc....212 841-7430
45 Broadway Ste 1810 New York (10006) **(G-10725)**
Jack J Florio Jr....716 434-9123
36b Main St Lockport (14094) **(G-7625)**
Jack L Popkin & Co Inc....718 361-6700
12510 84th Rd Kew Gardens (11415) **(G-7192)**
Jack Luckner Steel Shelving Co....718 363-0500
5454 43rd St Maspeth (11378) **(G-8178)**
Jack Merkel Inc....631 234-2600
1720 Express Dr S Hauppauge (11788) **(G-6125)**
Jack W Miller....585 538-2399
2339 North Rd Scottsville (14546) **(G-15359)**
Jackel Inc....908 359-2039
1359 Broadway Fl 17 New York (10018) **(G-10726)**
Jackel International, New York *Also called Jackel Inc* **(G-10726)**
Jackie's Girls, New York *Also called Waterbury Garment LLC* **(G-12625)**
Jacknob International Ltd....631 546-6560
290 Oser Ave Hauppauge (11788) **(G-6126)**
Jacks and Jokers 52 LLC....917 740-2595
215 E 68th St Apt 5o New York (10065) **(G-10727)**
Jacks Gourmet LLC....718 954-4681
1000 Dean St Ste 214 Brooklyn (11238) **(G-2128)**
Jackson Dakota Inc....718 786-8600
3010 41st Ave Ste 3 Long Island City (11101) **(G-7797)**
Jackson Dakota Inc (PA)....212 838-9444
979 3rd Ave Ste 503 New York (10022) **(G-10728)**
Jacksons Welding LLC....607 756-2725
215 N Homer Ave Cortland (13045) **(G-4054)**
Jacksons Welding Service & Sls, Cortland *Also called Jacksons Welding LLC* **(G-4054)**
Jaclyn Inc....212 736-5657
330 5th Ave Rm 1305 New York (10001) **(G-10729)**
Jacmax Industries LLC....718 439-3743
473 Wortman Ave Brooklyn (11208) **(G-2129)**
Jacmel Jewelry Inc (PA)....718 349-4300
1385 Broadway Fl 8 New York (10018) **(G-10730)**
Jacob Dresdner Co, New York *Also called Dresdiam Inc* **(G-9977)**
Jacob Hidary Foundation Inc....212 736-6540
10 W 33rd St Rm 900 New York (10001) **(G-10731)**
Jacob Inc....646 450-3067
287 Keap St Brooklyn (11211) **(G-2130)**
Jacobi Industries, Medford *Also called Jacobi Tool & Die Mfg Inc* **(G-8283)**
Jacobi Tool & Die Mfg Inc....631 736-5394
131 Middle Island Rd Medford (11763) **(G-8283)**
Jacobs & Cohen Inc....212 714-2702
255 W 36th St Fl 9 New York (10018) **(G-10732)**
Jacobs Juice Corp....646 255-2860
388 Avenue X Apt 2h Brooklyn (11223) **(G-2131)**
Jacobs Manufacturing, Hogansburg *Also called Jacobs Tobacco Company* **(G-6453)**
Jacobs Press Inc....315 252-4861
87 Columbus St Auburn (13021) **(G-501)**
Jacobs Tobacco Company....518 358-4948
344 Frogtown Rd Hogansburg (13655) **(G-6453)**
Jacobs Woodworking LLC....315 427-8999
801 W Fayette St Syracuse (13204) **(G-15984)**
Jacoby Enterprises LLC....718 435-0289
1615 54th St Brooklyn (11204) **(G-2132)**
Jacques Torres Chocolate, Brooklyn *Also called Mrchocolatecom LLC* **(G-2347)**
Jacques Torres Chocolate LLC (PA)....212 414-2462
350 Hudson St Frnt 1 New York (10014) **(G-10733)**
Jad Corp of America....718 762-8900
2048 119th St College Point (11356) **(G-3816)**
Jadak LLC (HQ)....315 701-0678
7279 William Barry Blvd North Syracuse (13212) **(G-12966)**
Jadak Technologies Inc (HQ)....315 701-0678
7279 William Barry Blvd North Syracuse (13212) **(G-12967)**
Jado Sewing Machines Inc....718 784-2314
4008 22nd St Long Island City (11101) **(G-7798)**
Jaf Converters Inc....631 842-3131
60 Marconi Blvd Copiague (11726) **(G-3934)**
Jag Manufacturing Inc....518 762-9558
26 Grecco Dr Johnstown (12095) **(G-7147)**
Jags Manufacturing Network Inc....631 750-6367
13403 Lincoln Ave Holbrook (11741) **(G-6483)**
Jaguar Casting Co Inc....212 869-0197
100 United Nations Plz New York (10017) **(G-10734)**
Jaguar Industries Inc....845 947-1800
89 Broadway Haverstraw (10927) **(G-6261)**
Jaguar Jewelry Casting NY Inc....212 768-4848
48 W 48th St Ste 500 New York (10036) **(G-10735)**
Jaidan Industries Inc....516 944-3650
16 Capi Ln Port Washington (11050) **(G-13849)**
Jain Irrigation Inc....315 755-4400
740 Water St Watertown (13601) **(G-16676)**
Jakes Sneakers Inc....718 233-1132
845 Classon Ave Brooklyn (11238) **(G-2133)**
Jakob Schlaepfer Inc....212 221-2323
37 W 26th St Rm 208 New York (10010) **(G-10736)**
Jal Signs Inc....516 536-7280
540 Merrick Rd Baldwin (11510) **(G-558)**
Jalex Industries Ltd....631 491-5072
86 Nancy St West Babylon (11704) **(G-16828)**
Jam Industries Inc....585 458-9830
9 Marway Cir Rochester (14624) **(G-14479)**
Jam Paper, New York *Also called Hudson Envelope Corporation* **(G-10569)**
Jam Printing Publishing Inc....914 345-8400
11 Clearbrook Rd Ste 133 Elmsford (10523) **(G-4766)**
Jamaica Electroplating, North Baldwin *Also called Dura Spec Inc* **(G-12921)**
Jamaica Iron Works Inc....718 657-4849
10847 Merrick Blvd Jamaica (11433) **(G-6959)**
Jamaica Lamp Corp....718 776-5039
21220 Jamaica Ave Queens Village (11428) **(G-13996)**
Jamaican Weekly Gleaner, Jamaica *Also called Gleaner Company Ltd* **(G-6951)**
Jamar Precision Products Co....631 254-0234
5 Lucon Dr Deer Park (11729) **(G-4177)**
Jamco Aerospace Inc....631 586-7900
121a E Industry Ct Deer Park (11729) **(G-4178)**
James A Staley Co Inc....845 878-3344
5 Bowen Ct Carmel (10512) **(G-3429)**
James B Crowell & Sons Inc....845 895-3464
242 Lippincott Rd Wallkill (12589) **(G-16564)**
James Conolly Printing Co....585 426-4150
72 Marway Cir Rochester (14624) **(G-14480)**
James D Rubino Inc....631 244-8730
20 Jules Ct Ste 5 Bohemia (11716) **(G-1076)**
James King Woodworking Inc....518 761-6091
656 County Line Rd Queensbury (12804) **(G-14013)**
James L Taylor Mfg Co (PA)....845 452-3780
130 Salt Point Tpke Poughkeepsie (12603) **(G-13929)**
James L Taylor Mfg Co....845 452-3780
130 Salt Point Tpke Poughkeepsie (12603) **(G-13930)**
James L. Taylor Mfg., Poughkeepsie *Also called James L Taylor Mfg Co* **(G-13929)**
James Morgan Publishing (PA)....212 655-5470
5 Penn Plz Ste 2300 New York (10001) **(G-10737)**
James Morris....315 824-8519
6697 Airport Rd Hamilton (13346) **(G-5971)**
James Richard Specialty Chem....914 478-7500
24 Ridge St Hastings On Hudson (10706) **(G-6024)**
James Thompson & Company Inc (PA)....212 686-4242
463 7th Ave Rm 1603 New York (10018) **(G-10738)**
James Town Macadam Inc....716 665-4504
1946 New York Ave Falconer (14733) **(G-4911)**
James Wire Die Co....315 894-3233
138 West St Ilion (13357) **(G-6781)**
James Woerner Inc....631 454-9330
130 Allen Blvd Farmingdale (11735) **(G-5024)**
Jamesport Vineyards, Jamesport *Also called North House Vineyards Inc* **(G-7002)**
Jamestown Advanced Pdts Corp....716 483-3406
2855 Girts Rd Jamestown (14701) **(G-7037)**
Jamestown Awning Inc....716 483-1435
313 Steele St Jamestown (14701) **(G-7038)**
Jamestown Bronze Works Inc....716 665-2302
174 Hopkins Ave Jamestown (14701) **(G-7039)**
Jamestown Cont of Rochester....585 254-9190
82 Edwards Deming Dr Rochester (14606) **(G-14481)**
Jamestown Container Corp (PA)....716 665-4623
14 Deming Dr Falconer (14733) **(G-4912)**
Jamestown Engine Plant, Lakewood *Also called Cummins Inc* **(G-7313)**
Jamestown Envelope, Falconer *Also called Falconer Printing & Design Inc* **(G-4906)**
Jamestown Fab Stl & Sup Inc....716 665-2227
1034 Allen St Jamestown (14701) **(G-7040)**
Jamestown Iron Works Inc....716 665-2818
2022 Allen Street Ext Falconer (14733) **(G-4913)**
Jamestown Kitchen & Bath Inc....716 665-2299
1085 E 2nd St Jamestown (14701) **(G-7041)**
Jamestown Macadam Inc (PA)....716 664-5108
74 Walden Ave Jamestown (14701) **(G-7042)**
Jamestown Mattress Co....716 665-2247
150 Blackstone Ave Jamestown (14701) **(G-7043)**
Jamestown Metal Products LLC....716 665-5313
178 Blackstone Ave Jamestown (14701) **(G-7044)**
Jamestown Plastics Inc (PA)....716 792-4144
8806 Highland Ave Brocton (14716) **(G-1249)**
Jamestown Scientific Inds LLC....716 665-3224
1300 E 2nd St Jamestown (14701) **(G-7045)**
Jana Kos Collection, The, New York *Also called Style Partners Inc* **(G-12245)**
Janco Press Inc....631 563-3003
20 Floyds Run Bohemia (11716) **(G-1077)**
Jane Bohan Inc....212 529-6090
611 Broadway New York (10012) **(G-10739)**
Jane Knitting Kit, New York *Also called Janes Designer Yrn Pttrns Inc* **(G-10740)**
Jane Lewis....607 722-0584
82 Castle Creek Rd Binghamton (13901) **(G-925)**
Janed Enterprises....631 694-4494
48 Allen Blvd Unit B Farmingdale (11735) **(G-5025)**
Janes Designer Yrn Pttrns Inc....347 260-3071
1745 Broadway Ste 1750 New York (10019) **(G-10740)**
Janlynn Corporation, The, Bohemia *Also called Spectrum Crafts Inc* **(G-1133)**
Janowski Hamburger, Rockville Centre *Also called Bianca Burgers LLC* **(G-14816)**
Japan America Learning Ctr Inc (PA)....914 723-7600
81 Montgomery Ave Scarsdale (10583) **(G-15248)**

ALPHABETIC

Japan Printing & Graphics Inc ALPHABETIC SECTION

Japan Printing & Graphics Inc 212 406-2905
160 Broadway Lbby D New York (10038) **(G-10741)**
Jaquith Industries Inc 315 478-5700
600 E Brighton Ave Syracuse (13210) **(G-15985)**
Jar Metals Inc 845 425-8901
50 2nd Ave Nanuet (10954) **(G-8804)**
Jaracz Jr Joseph Paul 716 533-1377
64 Ferndale Dr Orchard Park (14127) **(G-13301)**
Jarets Stuffed Cupcakes 607 658-9096
116 Oak Hill Ave Endicott (13760) **(G-4820)**
Jarvik Heart Inc 212 397-3911
333 W 52nd St Ste 700 New York (10019) **(G-10742)**
Jasani Designs Usa Inc 212 257-6465
25 W 43rd St Ste 1014 New York (10036) **(G-10743)**
Jasco Cutting Tools, Rochester *Also called Graywood Companies Inc* **(G-14433)**
Jasco Heat Treating Inc 585 388-0071
75 Macedon Center Rd Fairport (14450) **(G-4865)**
Jason & Jean Products Inc 718 271-8300
104 Corona Ave Corona (11368) **(G-4022)**
Jason Ladanye Guitar Piano & H 518 527-3973
605 Park Ave Albany (12208) **(G-91)**
Jason Manufacturing Company, Rochester *Also called Three R Enterprises Inc* **(G-14752)**
Jasper Transport LLC 315 729-5760
1680 Flat St Penn Yan (14527) **(G-13538)**
Javcon Machine Inc 631 586-1890
255 Skidmore Rd Deer Park (11729) **(G-4179)**
Javin Machine Corp 631 643-3322
31 Otis St West Babylon (11704) **(G-16829)**
Javlyn Process Systems LLC 585 424-5580
3136 Winton Rd S Ste 102 Rochester (14623) **(G-14482)**
Jax Coco USA LLC 347 688-8198
5 Penn Plz Ste 2300 New York (10001) **(G-10744)**
Jax Signs and Neon Inc 607 727-3420
108 Odell Ave Endicott (13760) **(G-4821)**
Jaxi's Sportswear, Brooklyn *Also called Jaxis Inc* **(G-2134)**
Jaxis Inc (PA) 212 302-7611
1365 38th St Brooklyn (11218) **(G-2134)**
Jaxson Rollforming Inc 631 842-7775
145 Dixon Ave Ste 1 Amityville (11701) **(G-298)**
Jay Bags Inc 845 459-6500
55 Union Rd Ste 107 Spring Valley (10977) **(G-15612)**
Jay Little Oil Well Servi 716 925-8905
5460 Nichols Run Limestone (14753) **(G-7473)**
Jay Moulding Corporation 518 237-4200
7 Bridge Ave Ste 1 Cohoes (12047) **(G-3772)**
Jay Strongwater Holdings LLC (HQ) 646 657-0558
230 W 39th St Fl 8 New York (10018) **(G-10745)**
Jay Turoff 718 856-7300
681 Coney Island Ave Brooklyn (11218) **(G-2135)**
Jay-Aimee Designs Inc 718 609-0333
99 Railroad Station Plz # 200 Hicksville (11801) **(G-6384)**
Jay-Art Nvelties/Tower Grafics, Brooklyn *Also called Jay Turoff* **(G-2135)**
Jaya Apparel Group LLC 212 764-4980
1384 Broadway Fl 18 New York (10018) **(G-10746)**
Jayden Star LLC 212 686-0400
385 5th Ave Rm 507 New York (10016) **(G-10747)**
Jaymar Jewelry Co Inc 212 564-4788
69 5th Ave Apt 8d New York (10003) **(G-10748)**
Jays Furniture Products Inc 716 876-8854
321 Ramsdell Ave Buffalo (14216) **(G-3031)**
Jazzles, White Plains *Also called Readent Inc* **(G-17189)**
Jbf Stainless LLC 315 569-2800
148 Industrial Park Dr Frankfort (13340) **(G-5363)**
Jbl Trading LLC 347 394-5592
43 W 33rd St Rm 603 New York (10001) **(G-10749)**
Jbren Corp 716 332-5928
107 Dorothy St Buffalo (14206) **(G-3032)**
Jbs LLC 518 346-0001
6 Maple Ave Scotia (12302) **(G-15350)**
JC Crystal Inc 212 594-0858
260 W 35th St Fl 10 New York (10001) **(G-10750)**
Jcdecaux Mallscape LLC (HQ) 646 834-1200
350 5th Ave Fl 73 New York (10118) **(G-10751)**
JD Tool Inc 607 786-3129
521 E Main St Endicott (13760) **(G-4822)**
Jds Graphics, New York *Also called JDS Graphics Inc* **(G-10752)**
JDS Graphics Inc 973 330-3300
226 W 37th St Fl 10 New York (10018) **(G-10752)**
Jdt International LLC 212 400-7570
276 5th Ave Rm 704 New York (10001) **(G-10753)**
JE Miller Inc 315 437-6811
747 W Manlius St East Syracuse (13057) **(G-4560)**
JE Monahan Fabrications LLC 518 761-0414
559 Queensbury Ave 1/2 Queensbury (12804) **(G-14014)**
Jeam Imports, Brooklyn *Also called Executive Machines Inc* **(G-1950)**
Jean & Alex Jewelry Mfg & Cons 212 935-7621
587 5th Ave Fl 2 New York (10017) **(G-10754)**
Jean Philippe Fragrances LLC 212 983-2640
551 5th Ave Rm 1500 New York (10176) **(G-10755)**
Jeanjer LLC 212 944-1330
1400 Broadway Fl 15 New York (10018) **(G-10756)**
Jeans Inc 646 223-1122
1357 Broadway Ste 411 New York (10018) **(G-10757)**
Jed Lights Inc (HQ) 516 812-5001
10 Connor Ln Deer Park (11729) **(G-4180)**
Jeff Cooper Inc 516 333-8200
288 Westbury Ave Carle Place (11514) **(G-3417)**
Jefferson Concrete Corp 315 788-4171
22850 County Route 51 Watertown (13601) **(G-16677)**
Jeffersonville Volunteer 845 482-3110
49 Callicoon Center Rd Jeffersonville (12748) **(G-7093)**
Jeffrey D Menoff 716 665-1468
785 Fairmount Ave Jamestown (14701) **(G-7046)**
Jeffrey John 631 842-2850
25 Elm Pl Amityville (11701) **(G-299)**
Jeffrey Spring Modern Art, Astoria *Also called Modern Art Foundry Inc* **(G-448)**
Jekerda Sales, Jericho *Also called North American Pipe Corp* **(G-7111)**
Jem Container Corp 800 521-0145
151 Fairchild Ave Ste 1 Plainview (11803) **(G-13640)**
Jem Sign Corp (PA) 516 867-4466
470 S Franklin St Hempstead (11550) **(G-6299)**
Jem Threading Specialties Inc 718 665-3341
1059 Washington Ave Bronx (10456) **(G-1368)**
Jem Tool & Die Corp 631 539-8734
81 Paris Ct West Islip (11795) **(G-16934)**
JEm Wdwkg & Cabinets Inc 518 828-5361
250 Falls Rd Hudson (12534) **(G-6650)**
Jemcap Servicing LLC 212 213-9353
360 Madison Ave Rm 1902 New York (10017) **(G-10758)**
Jenalex Creative Marketing Inc 212 935-2266
116 E 57th St Fl 3 New York (10022) **(G-10759)**
Jenlor Ltd 315 637-9080
523 E Genesee St Fayetteville (13066) **(G-5173)**
Jenmar Door & Glass Inc 718 767-7900
15038 12th Ave Whitestone (11357) **(G-17239)**
Jenna Concrete Corporation 718 842-5250
1465 Bronx River Ave Bronx (10472) **(G-1369)**
Jenna Harlem River Inc 718 842-5997
1465 Bronx River Ave Bronx (10472) **(G-1370)**
Jenray Products Inc 914 375-5596
252 Lake Ave Fl 2a Yonkers (10701) **(G-17475)**
Jentronics, Holbrook *Also called Bryit Group LLC* **(G-6461)**
Jentsch & Co Inc 716 852-4111
107 Dorothy St Buffalo (14206) **(G-3033)**
JEnvie Sport Inc 212 967-2322
255 W 36th St 6 New York (10018) **(G-10760)**
Jeric Knit Wear 631 979-8827
61 Hofstra Dr Smithtown (11787) **(G-15513)**
Jerome Levy Forecasting Center 914 244-8617
69 S Moger Ave Ste 202 Mount Kisco (10549) **(G-8673)**
Jerome Stvens Phrmcuticals Inc 631 567-1113
60 Davinci Dr Bohemia (11716) **(G-1078)**
Jerry Cardullo Iron Works Inc 631 242-8881
101 Spence St Bay Shore (11706) **(G-707)**
Jerry Miller I.D. Shoes, Buffalo *Also called Jerry Miller Molded Shoes Inc* **(G-3034)**
Jerry Miller Molded Shoes Inc (PA) 716 881-3920
36 Mason St Buffalo (14213) **(G-3034)**
Jerry Sorbara Furs Inc 212 594-3897
39 W 32nd St Rm 1400 New York (10001) **(G-10761)**
Jerry Tomaselli 718 965-1400
141 32nd St Brooklyn (11232) **(G-2136)**
Jerry's Bagels & Bakery, Valley Stream *Also called Jerrys Bagels* **(G-16437)**
Jerrys Bagels 516 791-0063
951 Rosedale Rd Valley Stream (11581) **(G-16437)**
Jersey Express Inc 716 834-6151
3080 Main St Buffalo (14214) **(G-3035)**
Jesco Lighting Inc 718 366-3211
15 Harbor Park Dr Port Washington (11050) **(G-13850)**
Jesco Lighting Group LLC (PA) 718 366-3211
15 Harbor Park Dr Port Washington (11050) **(G-13851)**
Jesse Joeckel 631 668-2772
65 Tuthill Rd Montauk (11954) **(G-8623)**
Jessel Marking Equipment, Syracuse *Also called New York Marking Devices Corp* **(G-16018)**
Jessica Michelle, New York *Also called Orchid Manufacturing Co Inc* **(G-11536)**
Jet Components Inc 631 436-7300
62 Bridge Rd Islandia (11749) **(G-6835)**
Jet Line, White Plains *Also called Gemini Manufacturing LLC* **(G-17139)**
Jet Redi Mix Concrete Inc 631 580-3640
2101 Pond Rd Ste 1 Ronkonkoma (11779) **(G-14947)**
Jet Sew Corporation 315 896-2683
8119 State Route 12 Barneveld (13304) **(G-613)**
Jet-Black Sealers Inc 716 891-4197
555 Ludwig Ave Buffalo (14227) **(G-3036)**
Jets Lefrois Corp 585 637-5003
56 High St Brockport (14420) **(G-1245)**
Jets Lefrois Foods, Brockport *Also called Jets Lefrois Corp* **(G-1245)**
Jette Group, Bay Shore *Also called Cable Management Solutions Inc* **(G-678)**
Jetwrx Rotable Services, Elmira *Also called Jrsmm LLC* **(G-4706)**
Jewelers Machinist Co Inc 631 661-5020
400 Columbus Ave Babylon (11704) **(G-546)**
Jewelers Solder Supply Inc 718 637-1256
1362 54th St Brooklyn (11219) **(G-2137)**

ALPHABETIC SECTION
John Patrick, Germantown

Jewelmak Inc 212 398-2999
344 E 59th St Fl 1&2 New York (10022) *(G-10762)*
Jewelry Arts Manufacturing 212 382-3583
151 W 46th St Fl 12 New York (10036) *(G-10763)*
Jewels By Star Ltd 212 308-3490
555 5th Ave Fl 7 New York (10017) *(G-10764)*
Jeweltex Mfg Corp 212 921-8188
48 W 48th St Ste 507 New York (10036) *(G-10765)*
Jewish Heritage For Blind 718 338-4999
1655 E 24th St Brooklyn (11229) *(G-2138)*
Jewish Journal 718 630-9350
7014 13th Ave Brooklyn (11228) *(G-2139)*
Jewish Press Inc 718 330-1100
4915 16th Ave Brooklyn (11204) *(G-2140)*
Jewish Week Inc (PA) 212 921-7822
1501 Broadway Ste 505 New York (10036) *(G-10766)*
Jewler's Solder Sheet & Wire, Brooklyn *Also called Jewelers Solder Supply Inc (G-2137)*
Jeypore Group, New York *Also called Incon Gems Inc (G-10626)*
JF Machine Shop Inc 631 491-7273
89 Otis St Unit A West Babylon (11704) *(G-16830)*
Jf Rafter The Lexington Co, Eden *Also called John F Rafter Inc (G-4600)*
Jfb Print Solutions Inc 631 694-8300
21 Park Dr Lido Beach (11561) *(G-7462)*
Jfe Engineering Corporation 212 310-9320
350 Park Ave Fl 27th New York (10022) *(G-10767)*
Jfe Steel America Inc (HQ) 212 310-9320
600 3rd Ave Rm 1201 New York (10016) *(G-10768)*
Jfs Inc 646 264-1200
531 W 26th St Unit 531 New York (10001) *(G-10769)*
JG Innovative Industries Inc 718 784-7300
8002 Kew Gardens Rd # 5002 Kew Gardens (11415) *(G-7193)*
Jgx LLC 212 575-1244
1407 Broadway Rm 1416 New York (10018) *(G-10770)*
Jhc Labresin, Brooklyn *Also called J H C Fabrications Inc (G-2121)*
Jill Fagin Enterprises Inc (PA) 212 674-9383
107 Avenue B New York (10009) *(G-10771)*
Jill Fenichell Inc 718 237-2490
169 Prospect Pl Brooklyn (11238) *(G-2141)*
Jillery, New York *Also called Jill Fagin Enterprises Inc (G-10771)*
Jim Henson Company Inc 212 794-2400
117 E 69th St New York (10021) *(G-10772)*
Jim Henson Productions, New York *Also called Jim Henson Company Inc (G-10772)*
Jim Quinn 518 356-0398
12 Morningside Dr Schenectady (12303) *(G-15297)*
Jim Quinn and Associates, Schenectady *Also called Jim Quinn (G-15297)*
Jim Romas Bakery Inc 607 748-7425
202 N Nanticoke Ave Endicott (13760) *(G-4823)*
Jim Wachtler Inc 212 755-4367
1212 Avenue Of The Ste 2200 New York (10036) *(G-10773)*
Jimco Lamp & Manufacturing Co 631 218-2152
181 Freeman Ave Islip (11751) *(G-6848)*
Jimco Lamp Company, Islip *Also called Jimco Lamp & Manufacturing Co (G-6848)*
Jimeale Incorporated 917 686-5383
130 Church St Ste 163 New York (10007) *(G-10774)*
Jimmy Crystal New York Co Ltd 212 594-0858
47 W 37th St Fl 3 New York (10018) *(G-10775)*
Jimmy Sales, Brooklyn *Also called Tie King Inc (G-2679)*
Jin Pin Market Inc 718 898-0788
8220 Roosevelt Ave Jackson Heights (11372) *(G-6922)*
Jinglebell Inc 914 219-5395
190 Byram Lake Rd Armonk (10504) *(G-414)*
JINGLENOG DBA, Armonk *Also called Jinglebell Inc (G-414)*
Jiranimo Industries Ltd 212 921-5106
49a W 37th St New York (10018) *(G-10776)*
Jisan Trading Corporation 212 244-1269
519 8th Ave Rm 810 New York (10018) *(G-10777)*
Jj Basics LLC (PA) 212 768-4779
525 7th Ave Rm 307 New York (10018) *(G-10778)*
JJ Cassone Bakery Inc 914 939-1568
202 S Regent St Port Chester (10573) *(G-13777)*
Jj Fantasia Inc 212 868-1198
38 W 32nd St New York (10001) *(G-10779)*
Jj Marco, New York *Also called Hy Gold Jewelers Inc (G-10582)*
JK Jewelry Inc 585 292-0770
1500 Brighton Henrietta Rochester (14623) *(G-14483)*
JK Manufacturing Inc 212 683-3535
115 Forest Ave Unit 22 Locust Valley (11560) *(G-7663)*
Jlm Couture Inc (PA) 212 921-7058
525 Fashion Ave Rm 1703 New York (10018) *(G-10780)*
Jlt Lancaster Clamps Div, Poughkeepsie *Also called James L Taylor Mfg Co (G-13930)*
JM Manufacturer Inc 212 869-0626
241 W 37th St Rm 924 New York (10018) *(G-10781)*
JM Murray Center Inc (PA) 607 756-9913
823 State Route 13 Ste 1 Cortland (13045) *(G-4055)*
JM Murray Center Inc 607 756-0246
4057 West Rd Cortland (13045) *(G-4056)*
JM Originals Inc 845 647-3003
70 Berme Rd Ellenville (12428) *(G-4648)*
JM Studio Inc 646 546-5514
247 W 35th St Fl 3 New York (10001) *(G-10782)*
Jma Wireless, Liverpool *Also called John Mezzalingua Assoc LLC (G-7551)*

Jmg Fuel Inc 631 579-4319
3 Fowler Ave Ronkonkoma (11779) *(G-14948)*
Jmk Enterprises LLC 845 634-8100
301 N Main St Ste 1 New City (10956) *(G-8833)*
Jml Optical Industries LLC 585 248-8900
820 Linden Ave Rochester (14625) *(G-14484)*
Jml Quarries Inc 845 932-8206
420 Bernas Rd Cochecton (12726) *(G-3766)*
JMS Ices Inc 718 448-0853
501 Port Richmond Ave Staten Island (10302) *(G-15714)*
Jn Marina, New York *Also called Marina Jewelry Co Inc (G-11175)*
Jo Mart Chocolates, Brooklyn *Also called Jo-Mart Candies Corp (G-2142)*
Jo-Mart Candies Corp 718 375-1277
2917 Avenue R Brooklyn (11229) *(G-2142)*
Jo-Vin Decorators Inc 718 441-9350
9423 Jamaica Ave Woodhaven (11421) *(G-17324)*
Joan Boyce Ltd (PA) 212 867-7474
19 W 44th St Ste 417 New York (10036) *(G-10783)*
Joanna Mastroianni, New York *Also called Elana Laderos Ltd (G-10047)*
Jobs Weekly Inc 716 648-5627
31 Buffalo St Ste 2 Hamburg (14075) *(G-5952)*
Jobson Medical Information LLC (PA) 212 274-7000
440 9th Ave Fl 14 New York (10001) *(G-10784)*
Jockey International Inc 212 840-4900
1411 Broadway Rm 1010 New York (10018) *(G-10785)*
Jockey International Inc 518 761-0965
1439 State Route 9 Ste 10 Lake George (12845) *(G-7286)*
Jockey Store, New York *Also called Jockey International Inc (G-10785)*
Joe Benbasset Inc (PA) 212 268-4920
213 W 35th St Rm 803 New York (10001) *(G-10786)*
Joe Fresh, New York *Also called Jfs Inc (G-10769)*
Joe Moro 607 272-0591
214 Fayette St Ithaca (14850) *(G-6890)*
Joe P Industries Inc 631 293-7889
6 Commerce Dr Farmingdale (11735) *(G-5026)*
Joe Pietryka Incorporated (PA) 845 855-1201
85 Charles Colman Blvd Pawling (12564) *(G-13473)*
Joed Press 212 243-3620
242 W 36th St Fl 8 New York (10018) *(G-10787)*
Joel Kiryas Meat Market Corp 845 782-9194
51 Forest Rd Ste 345 Monroe (10950) *(G-8593)*
Joel Zelcer 917 525-6790
102 S 8th St Brooklyn (11249) *(G-2143)*
Joes Jeans, New York *Also called Gbg West LLC (G-10303)*
John A Eberly Inc 315 449-3034
136 Beattie St Syracuse (13224) *(G-15986)*
John A Vassilaros & Son Inc 718 886-4140
2905 120th St Flushing (11354) *(G-5264)*
John Auguliaro Printing Co 718 382-5283
2533 Mcdonald Ave Brooklyn (11223) *(G-2144)*
John Bossone, Glendale *Also called New Day Woodwork Inc (G-5674)*
John C Dolph Company Inc 732 329-2333
200 Von Roll Dr Schenectady (12306) *(G-15298)*
John Crane Inc 315 593-6237
2314 County Route 4 Fulton (13069) *(G-5478)*
John Deere Authorized Dealer, Fulton *Also called Gone South Concrete Block Inc (G-5473)*
John E Potente & Sons Inc 516 935-8585
114 Woodbury Rd Unit 1 Hicksville (11801) *(G-6385)*
John F Krell Jr 315 492-3201
4046 W Seneca Trpk Syracuse (13215) *(G-15987)*
John F Rafter Inc 716 992-3425
2746 W Church St Eden (14057) *(G-4600)*
John G Rubino Inc 315 253-7396
45 Aurelius Ave Auburn (13021) *(G-502)*
John Gailer Inc 212 243-5662
3718 Northern Blvd Ste 3 Long Island City (11101) *(G-7799)*
John Hassall LLC (HQ) 516 334-6200
609 Cantiague Rock Rd # 1 Westbury (11590) *(G-17025)*
John Hassall LLC 323 869-0150
609 Cantiague Rock Rd # 1 Westbury (11590) *(G-17026)*
John J Mazur Inc 631 242-4554
94 E Jefryn Blvd Ste K Deer Park (11729) *(G-4181)*
John J Richardson 516 538-6339
12 Bernard St Lawrence (11559) *(G-7417)*
John Kochis Custom Designs 212 244-6046
237 W 35th St Ste 702 New York (10001) *(G-10788)*
John Kristiansen New York Inc 212 388-1097
665 Broadway Frnt New York (10012) *(G-10789)*
John Langenbacher Co Inc 718 328-0141
888 Longfellow Ave Bronx (10474) *(G-1371)*
John Larocca & Son Inc 631 423-5256
290 Broadway Huntington Station (11746) *(G-6750)*
John Lor Publishing Ltd 631 475-1000
20 Medford Ave Ste 1 Patchogue (11772) *(G-13451)*
John Marshall Sound Inc 212 265-6066
630 9th Ave Ste 1108 New York (10036) *(G-10790)*
John Mezzalingua Assoc LLC (PA) 315 431-7100
7645 Henry Clay Blvd # 678 Liverpool (13088) *(G-7551)*
John N Fehlinger Co Inc (PA) 212 233-5656
20 Vesey St Rm 1000 New York (10007) *(G-10791)*
John Patrick, Germantown *Also called On The Double Inc (G-5603)*

ALPHABETIC

(PA)=Parent Co (HQ)=Headquarters (DH)=Div Headquarters
2018 Harris
New York Manufacturers Directory
983

John Prior ALPHABETIC SECTION

John Prior...516 520-9801
2545 Hempstead Tpke # 402 East Meadow (11554) **(G-4446)**
John R Robinson Inc...718 786-6088
3805 30th St Long Island City (11101) **(G-7800)**
John Ramsey Elec Svcs LLC...585 298-9596
7940 Rae Blvd Victor (14564) **(G-16507)**
John Szoke Editions, New York *Also called John Szoke Graphics Inc* **(G-10792)**
John Szoke Graphics Inc...212 219-8300
24 W 57th St Ste 304 New York (10019) **(G-10792)**
John T Montecalvo Inc...631 325-1492
1233 Speonk River Head Rd Speonk (11972) **(G-15600)**
John V Agugliaro Printing, Brooklyn *Also called John Auguliaro Printing Co* **(G-2144)**
John Varvatos Company...212 812-8000
26 W 17th St Fl 12 New York (10011) **(G-10793)**
John Vespa Inc (PA)...315 788-6330
19626 Overlook Dr Watertown (13601) **(G-16678)**
John Wiley & Sons Inc...845 457-6250
46 Wavey Willow Ln Montgomery (12549) **(G-8632)**
Johnnie Ryan Co Inc...716 282-1606
3084 Niagara St Niagara Falls (14303) **(G-12856)**
Johnny Bienstock Music...212 779-7977
126 E 38th St New York (10016) **(G-10794)**
Johnny Mica Inc...631 225-5213
116 E Hoffman Ave Lindenhurst (11757) **(G-7488)**
Johnny's Ideal Prntng Co, Hudson *Also called Johnnys Ideal Printing Co* **(G-6651)**
Johnnys Ideal Printing Co...518 828-6666
352 Warren St Hudson (12534) **(G-6651)**
Johnnys Machine Shop...631 338-9733
81 Mahan St West Babylon (11704) **(G-16831)**
Johns Manville Corporation...518 565-3000
1 Kaycee Loop Rd Plattsburgh (12901) **(G-13699)**
Johns Ravioli Company Inc...914 576-7030
15 Drake Ave New Rochelle (10805) **(G-8960)**
Johnson & Hoffman LLC...516 742-3333
40 Voice Rd Carle Place (11514) **(G-3418)**
Johnson Acquisition Corp (HQ)...518 828-1616
364 Warren St Hudson (12534) **(G-6652)**
Johnson Bros Lumber, Cazenovia *Also called PDJ Inc* **(G-3476)**
Johnson Contrls Authorized Dlr, North Baldwin *Also called Split Systems Corp* **(G-12926)**
Johnson Controls Inc...585 924-9346
7612 Main Street Fishers Victor (14564) **(G-16508)**
Johnson Controls Inc...518 884-8313
339 Brownell Rd Ballston Spa (12020) **(G-598)**
Johnson Controls Inc...518 694-4822
130 Railroad Ave Albany (12205) **(G-92)**
Johnson Controls Inc...585 671-1930
237 Birch Ln Webster (14580) **(G-16750)**
Johnson Controls Inc...914 593-5200
8 Skyline Dr Ste 115 Hawthorne (10532) **(G-6271)**
Johnson Controls Inc...716 688-7340
130 John Muir Dr Ste 100 Buffalo (14228) **(G-3037)**
Johnson Controls Inc...585 724-2232
1669 Lake Ave Bldg 333 Rochester (14652) **(G-14485)**
Johnson Manufacturing Co...631 472-1184
326 3rd Ave Bayport (11705) **(G-752)**
Johnson Manufacturing Company...716 881-3030
1489 Niagara St Buffalo (14213) **(G-3038)**
Johnson Mch & Fibr Pdts Co Inc...716 665-2003
142 Hopkins Ave Jamestown (14701) **(G-7047)**
Johnson Newspaper Corporation...518 483-4700
469 E Main St Ste 2 Malone (12953) **(G-8042)**
Johnson Outdoors Inc...607 779-2200
625 Conklin Rd Binghamton (13903) **(G-926)**
Johnson S Sand Gravel Inc...315 771-1450
23284 County Route 3 La Fargeville (13656) **(G-7263)**
Johnston Dandy Company...315 455-5773
100 Dippold Ave Syracuse (13208) **(G-15988)**
Johnston Precision Inc...315 253-4181
7 Frank Smith St Auburn (13021) **(G-503)**
Joka Industries Inc...631 589-0444
65 Knickerbocker Ave A Bohemia (11716) **(G-1079)**
Joldeson One Aerospace Inds, Ozone Park *Also called Joldeson One Aerospace Inds* **(G-13406)**
Joldeson One Aerospace Inds...718 848-7396
10002 103rd Ave Ozone Park (11417) **(G-13406)**
Jolibe Atelier LLC...347 882-6617
325 W 38th St New York (10018) **(G-10795)**
Jolin Machining Corp...631 589-1305
1561 Smithtown Ave Bohemia (11716) **(G-1080)**
Jomar Industries Inc...845 357-5773
382 Route 59 Ste 352 Airmont (10952) **(G-14)**
Jomart Associates Inc...212 627-2153
170 Oval Dr Ste A Islandia (11749) **(G-6836)**
Jomat New York Inc...718 369-7641
4100 1st Ave Ste 3 Brooklyn (11232) **(G-2145)**
Jon Barry Company Division, Brooklyn *Also called Kwik Ticket Inc* **(G-2183)**
Jon Lyn Ink Inc...516 546-2312
255 Sunrise Hwy Ste 1 Merrick (11566) **(G-8420)**
Jon Teri Sports Inc (PA)...212 398-0657
241 W 37th St Frnt 2 New York (10018) **(G-10796)**
Jonas Louis Paul Studios Inc...518 851-2211
304 Miller Rd Hudson (12534) **(G-6653)**
Jonathan David Publishers Inc...718 456-8611
6822 Eliot Ave Middle Village (11379) **(G-8446)**
Jonathan Lord Corp...631 563-4445
87 Carlough Rd Unit A Bohemia (11716) **(G-1081)**
Jonathan Meizler LLC...212 213-2977
37 W 26th St Ph New York (10010) **(G-10797)**
Jonathan Metal & Glass Ltd...718 846-8000
17818 107th Ave Jamaica (11433) **(G-6960)**
Jonathan Michael Coat Corp...212 239-9230
463 Fashion Ave Rm 1502 New York (10018) **(G-10798)**
Jonathan Michael Coats, New York *Also called Gfb Fashions Ltd* **(G-10331)**
Jonden Manufacturing Co Inc...516 442-4895
3069 Lawson Blvd Oceanside (11572) **(G-13103)**
Jones Humdinger...607 771-6501
204 Hayes Rd Binghamton (13905) **(G-927)**
Jones Jeanswear Group, New York *Also called One Jeanswear Group Inc* **(G-11520)**
Jones New York, New York *Also called Nine West Holdings Inc* **(G-11455)**
Jones New York, New York *Also called Nine West Holdings Inc* **(G-11459)**
Jones New York, New York *Also called Nine West Holdings Inc* **(G-11457)**
Jonice Industires...516 640-4283
95 Angevine Ave Hempstead (11550) **(G-6300)**
Jordache Enterprises Inc...212 944-1330
1400 Broadway Rm 1415 New York (10018) **(G-10799)**
Jordache Enterprises Inc (PA)...212 643-8400
1400 Broadway Rm 1404b New York (10018) **(G-10800)**
Jordache Woodworking Corp...718 349-3373
276 Greenpoint Ave # 1303 Brooklyn (11222) **(G-2146)**
Jordan Box Co, Syracuse *Also called Jordon Box Company Inc* **(G-15989)**
Jordan Machine Inc...585 647-3585
1241 Ridgeway Ave Ste I Rochester (14615) **(G-14486)**
Jordan Panel Systems Corp (PA)...631 754-4900
196 Laurel Rd Unit 2 East Northport (11731) **(G-4459)**
Jordan Scott Designs Ltd...212 947-4250
25 W 36th St Fl 12 New York (10018) **(G-10801)**
Jordon Box Company Inc...315 422-3419
140 Dickerson St Syracuse (13202) **(G-15989)**
Jordon Controls, Rochester *Also called Rotork Controls Inc* **(G-14680)**
Jos H Lowenstein and Sons Inc...718 218-8013
420 Morgan Ave Brooklyn (11222) **(G-2147)**
Joseph (uk) Inc...212 570-0077
1061 Madison Ave Grnd New York (10028) **(G-10802)**
Joseph A Filippazzo Software...718 987-1626
106 Lovell Ave Staten Island (10314) **(G-15715)**
Joseph Abboud Manufacturing...212 586-9140
650 5th Ave Fl 20 New York (10019) **(G-10803)**
Joseph Fedele...718 448-3658
1950b Richmond Ter Staten Island (10302) **(G-15716)**
Joseph H Navaie...607 936-9030
81 W Market St Corning (14830) **(G-3995)**
Joseph Industries Inc (PA)...212 764-0010
1410 Broadway Rm 1201 New York (10018) **(G-10804)**
Joseph Paul...718 693-4269
1064 Rogers Ave Apt 5 Brooklyn (11226) **(G-2148)**
Joseph Shalhoub & Son Inc...718 871-6300
1258 Prospect Ave Brooklyn (11218) **(G-2149)**
Joseph Struhl Co Inc...516 741-3660
195 Atlantic Ave New Hyde Park (11040) **(G-8889)**
Joseph Treu Successors Inc...212 691-7026
104 W 27th St Rm 5b New York (10001) **(G-10805)**
Joseph Zakon Winery Ltd...718 604-1430
586 Montgomery St Brooklyn (11225) **(G-2150)**
Joseph's Cloak, New York *Also called Americo Group Inc* **(G-9182)**
Josh Packaging Inc...631 822-1660
245 Marcus Blvd Ste 1 Hauppauge (11788) **(G-6127)**
Joshua Liner Gallery LLC...212 244-7415
540 W 28th St Frnt New York (10001) **(G-10806)**
Josie Accessories Inc (PA)...212 889-6376
261 5th Ave Fl 10 New York (10016) **(G-10807)**
Jotaly Inc...212 886-6000
1385 Broadway Fl 12 New York (10018) **(G-10808)**
Journal and Republican, Lowville *Also called Lowville Newspaper Corporation* **(G-7967)**
Journal News...914 694-5000
1133 Westchester Ave N-110 White Plains (10604) **(G-17155)**
Journal Register Company...518 584-4242
20 Lake Ave Saratoga Springs (12866) **(G-15191)**
Journal Register Company (PA)...212 257-7212
5 Hanover Sq Fl 25 New York (10004) **(G-10809)**
Journal Stationers, Greenwich *Also called Tefft Publishers Inc* **(G-5914)**
Jovani Fashion Ltd...212 279-0222
1370 Broadway Fl 4 New York (10018) **(G-10810)**
Joy Edward Company...315 474-3360
6747 W Benedict Rd East Syracuse (13057) **(G-4561)**
Joy of Learning...718 443-6463
992 Gates Ave Brooklyn (11221) **(G-2151)**
Joy Process Mechanical, East Syracuse *Also called Joy Edward Company* **(G-4561)**
Joya LLC...718 852-6979
19 Vanderbilt Ave Brooklyn (11205) **(G-2152)**
Joya Studio, Brooklyn *Also called Joya LLC* **(G-2152)**
Joyce Center, Manhasset *Also called Advanced Prosthetics Orthotics* **(G-8087)**
Joyce Trimming Inc...212 719-3110
109 W 38th St New York (10018) **(G-10811)**

ALPHABETIC SECTION

Joyva Corp (PA) 718 497-0170
  53 Varick Ave Brooklyn (11237) *(G-2153)*
JP Bus & Truck Repair Ltd (PA) 914 592-2872
  1 Warehouse Ln Elmsford (10523) *(G-4767)*
JP Filling Inc 845 534-4793
  20 Industry Dr Mountainville (10953) *(G-8794)*
JP Oil Group Inc 607 563-1360
  49 Union St Sidney (13838) *(G-15462)*
JP Signs 518 569-3907
  9592 State Route 9 Chazy (12921) *(G-3589)*
Jpm and Associates 516 483-4699
  639 Nostrand Ave Uniondale (11553) *(G-16319)*
Jpm Fine Woodworking LLC 516 236-7605
  103 Estate Dr Jericho (11753) *(G-7106)*
Jpmorgan Chase Bank Nat Assn 718 944-7964
  3514 White Plains Rd Bronx (10467) *(G-1372)*
Jpmorgan Chase Bank Nat Assn 718 767-3592
  13207 14th Ave College Point (11356) *(G-3817)*
Jpmorgan Chase Bank Nat Assn 845 298-2461
  1460 Route 9 Wappingers Falls (12590) *(G-16594)*
Jpmorgan Chase Bank Nat Assn 718 668-0346
  1690 Hylan Blvd Staten Island (10305) *(G-15717)*
Jpw Riggers & Erectors, Syracuse *Also called Jpw Structural Contracting Inc (G-15990)*
Jpw Structural Contracting Inc 315 432-1111
  6376 Thompson Rd Syracuse (13206) *(G-15990)*
Jq Woodworking Inc 516 766-3424
  3085 New St Oceanside (11572) *(G-13104)*
Jre Test, Victor *Also called John Ramsey Elec Svcs LLC (G-16507)*
Jre Test LLC 585 298-9736
  7940 Rae Blvd Victor (14564) *(G-16509)*
Jrg Apparel Group Company Ltd 212 997-0900
  1407 Broadway Rm 817 New York (10018) *(G-10812)*
Jrlon Inc 315 597-4067
  4344 Fox Rd Palmyra (14522) *(G-13434)*
JRs Fuels Inc 518 622-9939
  8037 Route 32 Cairo (12413) *(G-3299)*
JRS Pharma LP (HQ) 845 878-8300
  2981 Route 22 Ste 1 Patterson (12563) *(G-13465)*
Jrsmm LLC 607 331-1549
  1316 College Ave Elmira (14901) *(G-4706)*
JS Blank & Co Inc 212 689-4835
  112 Madison Ave Fl 7 New York (10016) *(G-10813)*
Jsc Design, New York *Also called Badgley Mischka Licensing LLC (G-9354)*
Jsc Designs Ltd 212 302-1001
  550 Fashion Ave Fl 22 New York (10018) *(G-10814)*
JSD Communications Inc 914 588-1841
  10 Colonel Thomas Ln Bedford (10506) *(G-792)*
JSM Vinyl Products Inc 516 775-4520
  44 Orchid Ln New Hyde Park (11040) *(G-8890)*
Jsp, Bohemia *Also called Jerome Stvens Phrmcuticals Inc (G-1078)*
Jsr Ultrasonics Division, Pittsford *Also called Imaginant Inc (G-13592)*
Jt Precision Inc 716 795-3860
  8701 Haight Rd Barker (14012) *(G-612)*
Jt Roselle Lighting & Sup Inc 914 666-3700
  333 N Bedford Rd Ste 120 Mount Kisco (10549) *(G-8674)*
JT Systems Inc 315 622-1980
  8132 Oswego Rd Liverpool (13090) *(G-7552)*
Jta USA Inc 718 722-0902
  63 Flushing Ave Unit 339 Brooklyn (11205) *(G-2154)*
Jtekt Torsen North America 585 464-5000
  2 Jetview Dr Rochester (14624) *(G-14487)*
Juan Motors, Palmyra *Also called Faradyne Motors LLC (G-13430)*
Judaica Press Inc 718 972-6202
  123 Ditmas Ave Brooklyn (11218) *(G-2155)*
Judi Boisson American Country, Southampton *Also called American Country Quilts & Lin (G-15562)*
Judis Lampshades Inc 917 561-3921
  1495 E 22nd St Brooklyn (11210) *(G-2156)*
Judith Lewis Printer Inc 516 997-7777
  1915 Ladenburg Dr Westbury (11590) *(G-17027)*
Judith N Graham Inc 914 921-5446
  64 Halls Ln Rye (10580) *(G-15087)*
Judscott Handprints Ltd (PA) 914 347-5515
  2269 Saw Mill River Rd 4d Elmsford (10523) *(G-4768)*
Judys Group Inc 212 921-0515
  1400 Broadway Rm 919 New York (10018) *(G-10815)*
Juice Press LLC (PA) 212 777-0034
  7 W 18th St Fl 6 New York (10011) *(G-10816)*
Juices Enterprises Inc 718 953-1860
  1142 Nostrand Ave Brooklyn (11225) *(G-2157)*
Julia Jordan Corporation 646 214-3090
  530 Fashion Ave Rm 505 New York (10018) *(G-10817)*
Julia Knit Inc 718 848-1900
  8050 Pitkin Ave Ozone Park (11417) *(G-13407)*
Julian A McDermott Corporation 718 456-3606
  1639 Stephen St Ridgewood (11385) *(G-14124)*
Julians Recipe LLC 888 640-8880
  128 Norman Ave Brooklyn (11222) *(G-2158)*
Julius Cohen Jewelers Inc 212 371-3050
  169 Richardson St Brooklyn (11222) *(G-2159)*
Julius Klein Group 212 719-1811
  580 5th Ave Ste 500 New York (10036) *(G-10818)*

Julius Lowy Frame Restoring Co 212 861-8585
  232 E 59th St 4fn New York (10022) *(G-10819)*
Jumo, New York *Also called Medikidz Usa Inc (G-11242)*
Jump Design Group Inc 212 869-3300
  1400 Broadway Fl 2 New York (10018) *(G-10820)*
Jump Design Group, The, New York *Also called Jump Design Group Inc (G-10820)*
Jump Ramp Games Inc 212 500-1456
  307 W 38th St Rm 1101 New York (10018) *(G-10821)*
Jumprope Inc 347 927-5867
  121 W 27th St Ste 1204 New York (10001) *(G-10822)*
June Jacobs Labs LLC 212 471-4830
  460 Park Ave Fl 16 New York (10022) *(G-10823)*
Junior Achevement of Eastrn NY 518 783-4336
  8 Stanley Cir Ste 8 Latham (12110) *(G-7393)*
Juniors Cheesecake Inc 212 302-2000
  386 Flatbush Avenue Ext Brooklyn (11201) *(G-2160)*
Juniper Elbow Co Inc (PA) 718 326-2546
  7215 Metropolitan Ave Middle Village (11379) *(G-8447)*
Juniper Industries, Middle Village *Also called Juniper Elbow Co Inc (G-8447)*
Juniper Industries Florida Inc 718 326-2546
  7215 Metropolitan Ave Middle Village (11379) *(G-8448)*
Junk In My Trunk Inc 631 420-5865
  266 Route 109 Farmingdale (11735) *(G-5027)*
Juno Chefs 845 294-5400
  1 6 1/2 Station Rd Goshen (10924) *(G-5750)*
Jupiter Creations Inc 917 493-9393
  330 7th Ave Ste 901 New York (10001) *(G-10824)*
Juris Publishing Inc 631 351-5430
  71 New St Ste 1 Huntington (11743) *(G-6700)*
Jurist Company Inc 212 243-8008
  1105 44th Dr Long Island City (11101) *(G-7801)*
Jus-Sar Fuel Inc 845 791-8900
  884 Old Route 17 Harris (12742) *(G-5997)*
Just Beverages LLC 480 388-1133
  31 Broad St Glens Falls (12801) *(G-5699)*
Just Bottoms & Tops Inc (PA) 212 564-3202
  1412 Broadway Rm 1808 New York (10018) *(G-10825)*
Just Brass Inc 212 724-5447
  215 W 90th St Apt 9a New York (10024) *(G-10826)*
Just For Men Div, New York *Also called Jeanjer LLC (G-10756)*
Just In Time Cnc Machining 585 335-2010
  88 Ossian St Dansville (14437) *(G-4104)*
Just In Time Company, Endwell *Also called J T Systematic (G-4841)*
Just Lamps of New York Inc 716 626-2240
  334 Harris Hill Rd Apt 1 Buffalo (14221) *(G-3039)*
Just Plastics, New York *Also called Gifford Group Inc (G-10334)*
Just Press Print LLC 585 783-1300
  304 Whitney St Rochester (14606) *(G-14488)*
Just Right Carbines LLC 585 261-5331
  231 Saltonstall St Canandaigua (14424) *(G-3377)*
Just Wood Pallets Inc 718 644-7013
  78 Vails Gate Heights Dr New Windsor (12553) *(G-8986)*
Justa Company 718 932-6139
  3464 9th St Long Island City (11106) *(G-7802)*
Justin Ashley Designs Inc 718 707-0200
  4301 21st St Ste 212a Long Island City (11101) *(G-7803)*
Justin Gregory Inc 631 249-5187
  94 E Jefryn Blvd Ste E Deer Park (11729) *(G-4182)*
Justperfectmsp Ltd 877 201-0005
  48 W 48th St Ste 401 New York (10036) *(G-10827)*
Justyna Kaminska NY Inc 917 423-5527
  1270 Broadway Rm 708 New York (10001) *(G-10828)*
Juvly Aesthetics Inc 614 686-3627
  18 E 41st St Rm 406 New York (10017) *(G-10829)*
JW Burg Machine & Tool Inc 716 434-0015
  7430 Rapids Rd Clarence Center (14032) *(G-3704)*
JW Consulting Inc 845 325-7070
  20 Chevron Rd Unit 201 Monroe (10950) *(G-8594)*
Jwin Electronics Corp (PA) 516 626-7188
  2 Harbor Park Dr Port Washington (11050) *(G-13852)*
K & B Signs, Mount Vernon *Also called K & B Stamping Co Inc (G-8741)*
K & B Stamping Co Inc 914 664-8555
  29 Mount Vernon Ave Mount Vernon (10550) *(G-8741)*
K & B Woodworking Inc 518 634-7253
  133 Rolling Meadow Rd Cairo (12413) *(G-3300)*
K & E Fabricating Company Inc 716 829-1829
  40 Stanley St Buffalo (14206) *(G-3040)*
K & H Industries Inc (PA) 716 312-0088
  160 Elmview Ave Hamburg (14075) *(G-5953)*
K & H Industries Inc 716 312-0088
  160 Elmview Ave Hamburg (14075) *(G-5954)*
K & H Precision Products Inc 585 624-4894
  45 Norton St Honeoye Falls (14472) *(G-6560)*
K & R Allied Inc 718 625-6610
  39 Pearl St Fl 2 Brooklyn (11201) *(G-2161)*
K & S & East, Pelham *Also called Eastco Manufacturing Corp (G-13515)*
K & S Childrens Wear Inc 718 624-0006
  204 Wallabout St Brooklyn (11206) *(G-2162)*
K Barthelmes Mfg Co Inc 585 328-8140
  61 Brooklea Dr Rochester (14624) *(G-14489)*
K C Technical Services, Bohemia *Also called Cos TEC Manufacturing Corp (G-1035)*

K C Technical Services Inc 631 589-7170
390 Knickerbocker Ave # 1 Bohemia (11716) ***(G-1082)***
K D Dance, Bronx *Also called KD Dids Inc* ***(G-1373)***
K D M Die Company Inc 716 828-9000
620 Elk St Buffalo (14210) ***(G-3041)***
K Displays 718 854-6045
1363 47th St Brooklyn (11219) ***(G-2163)***
K F I Inc 516 546-2904
33 Debevoise Ave Roosevelt (11575) ***(G-15030)***
K Hein Machines Inc 607 748-1546
341 Vestal Pkwy E Vestal (13850) ***(G-16473)***
K Industries Inc (PA) 631 897-2125
1107 Station Rd Ste 5a Bellport (11713) ***(G-828)***
K Kitchen, Buffalo *Also called Kalnitz Kitchens Inc* ***(G-3043)***
K M Drive Line Inc 718 599-0628
966 Grand St Brooklyn (11211) ***(G-2164)***
K P I Plastics, Howes Cave *Also called W Kintz Plastics Inc* ***(G-6629)***
K P Signs, North Bellmore *Also called KP Industries Inc* ***(G-12938)***
K Pat Incorporated 212 688-5728
77 Columbia St New York (10002) ***(G-10830)***
K Road Moapa Solar LLC 212 351-0535
295 Madison Ave Fl 37 New York (10017) ***(G-10831)***
K Road Power Management LLC (PA) 212 351-0535
767 3rd Ave Fl 37 New York (10017) ***(G-10832)***
K Sidrane Inc 631 393-6974
24 Baiting Place Rd Farmingdale (11735) ***(G-5028)***
K T A V Publishing House Inc 201 963-9524
527 Empire Blvd Brooklyn (11225) ***(G-2165)***
K T P Design Co Inc 212 481-6613
118 E 28th St Rm 707 New York (10016) ***(G-10833)***
K Tooling LLC 607 637-3781
396 E Front St Hancock (13783) ***(G-5986)***
K Z Precision, Lancaster *Also called Kz Precision Inc* ***(G-7345)***
K&G of Syracuse Inc 315 446-1921
2500 Erie Blvd E Syracuse (13224) ***(G-15991)***
K&Ns Foods Usa LLC 315 598-8080
607 Phillips St Fulton (13069) ***(G-5479)***
K-Binet Inc 845 348-1149
624 Route 303 Blauvelt (10913) ***(G-966)***
K-D Stone Inc 518 642-2082
Rr 22 Middle Granville (12849) ***(G-8433)***
K-Technologies Inc 716 828-4444
4090 Jeffrey Blvd Buffalo (14219) ***(G-3042)***
K.E.Y.S. Publishers, Brooklyn *Also called Kwesi Legesse LLC* ***(G-2182)***
K2 International Corp 212 947-1734
22 W 32nd St Fl 9 New York (10001) ***(G-10834)***
K2 Plastics Inc 585 494-2727
8210 Buffalo Rd Bergen (14416) ***(G-846)***
Kabar Manufacturing Corp (HQ) 631 694-6857
140 Schmitt Blvd Farmingdale (11735) ***(G-5029)***
Kabar Manufacturing Corp 631 694-1036
113 Gazza Blvd Farmingdale (11735) ***(G-5030)***
Kabbalah Centre, Richmond Hill *Also called Research Centre of Kabbalah* ***(G-14091)***
Kabco Pharmaceuticals Inc 631 842-3600
2000 New Horizons Blvd Amityville (11701) ***(G-300)***
Kabrics 607 962-6344
2737 Forest Hill Dr Corning (14830) ***(G-3996)***
Kadant Inc 518 793-8801
436 Quaker Rd Glens Falls (12804) ***(G-5700)***
Kadco Usa Inc 518 661-6068
17 W Main St Mayfield (12117) ***(G-8244)***
Kaddis Manufacturing Corp 585 624-3070
1175 Bragg St Honeoye Falls (14472) ***(G-6561)***
Kader Lithograph Company Inc 917 664-4380
3002 48th Ave Ste C Long Island City (11101) ***(G-7804)***
Kadmon Corporation LLC (PA) 212 308-6000
450 E 29th St Fl 5 New York (10016) ***(G-10835)***
Kadmon Holdings Inc 212 308-6000
450 E 29th St New York (10016) ***(G-10836)***
Kaffeto Gourmet, Tarrytown *Also called Altaro Corp* ***(G-16109)***
Kafko (us) Corp 877 721-7665
787 Watervliet Shaker Rd Latham (12110) ***(G-7394)***
Kahn-Lucas-Lancaster Inc 212 239-2407
112 W 34th St Ste 600 New York (10120) ***(G-10837)***
Kaitery Furs Ltd 718 204-1396
2529 49th St Long Island City (11103) ***(G-7805)***
Kal Manufacturing Corporation 585 265-4310
657 Basket Rd Webster (14580) ***(G-16751)***
Kal Pac Corp 845 457-7013
10 Factory St Montgomery (12549) ***(G-8633)***
Kal-Harbour Inc 518 266-0690
11 Villa Rd Albany (12204) ***(G-93)***
Kalati Company Inc 516 423-9132
14 Bond St Ste 152 Great Neck (11021) ***(G-5834)***
Kale Factory Inc 917 363-6361
790 Washington Ave Brooklyn (11238) ***(G-2166)***
Kaleidoscope Imaging Inc 212 631-9947
251 W 39th St Fl 4 New York (10018) ***(G-10838)***
Kaleko Bros 212 819-0100
62 W 47th St Ste 1504 New York (10036) ***(G-10839)***
Kalel Partners LLC 347 561-7804
7012 170th St Ste 101 Flushing (11365) ***(G-5265)***
Kalikow Brothers LP 212 643-0315
34 W 33rd St Fl 4n New York (10001) ***(G-10840)***
Kallen Corp 212 242-1470
99 Hudson St New York (10013) ***(G-10841)***
Kalnitz Kitchens Inc 716 684-1700
2620 Walden Ave Buffalo (14225) ***(G-3043)***
Kaltec Food Packaging Inc 845 856-9888
36 Center St 40 Port Jervis (12771) ***(G-13809)***
Kaltech Food Packaging Inc 845 856-1210
3640 Center St Port Jervis (12771) ***(G-13810)***
Kaltex America Inc 212 971-0575
350 5th Ave Ste 7100 New York (10118) ***(G-10842)***
Kaltex North America Inc (HQ) 212 894-3200
350 5th Ave Ste 7100 New York (10118) ***(G-10843)***
Kamali Automotive Group Inc 516 627-4000
17 Barstow Rd Ste 206 Great Neck (11021) ***(G-5835)***
Kamali Group Inc 516 627-4000
17 Barstow Rd Ste 206 Great Neck (11021) ***(G-5836)***
Kamali Leather Corp 518 762-2522
204 Harrison St Johnstown (12095) ***(G-7148)***
Kaman Automation Inc 585 254-8840
1000 University Ave Rochester (14607) ***(G-14490)***
Kamerys Wholesale Meats Inc 716 372-6756
322 E Riverside Dr Olean (14760) ***(G-13170)***
Kammetal Inc (PA) 718 722-9991
29 Imlay St Brooklyn (11231) ***(G-2167)***
Kane-M Inc 973 777-2797
135 W 29th St Rm 1003 New York (10001) ***(G-10844)***
Kangaroo Crossing, Manlius *Also called Mayberry Shoe Company Inc* ***(G-8107)***
Kannalife Sciences Inc 516 669-3219
4 Knoll Ct Lloyd Harbor (11743) ***(G-7594)***
Kantek Inc 516 594-4600
3460a Hampton Rd Oceanside (11572) ***(G-13105)***
Kantian Skincare LLC 631 780-4711
496 Smithtown Byp Smithtown (11787) ***(G-15514)***
Kaprielian Enterprises Inc 212 645-6623
207 W 25th St Fl 8 New York (10001) ***(G-10845)***
Kaps-All Packaging Systems 631 574-8778
200 Mill Rd Riverhead (11901) ***(G-14157)***
Kapstone Container Corporation 518 842-2450
28 Park Dr Amsterdam (12010) ***(G-352)***
Karbra Company 212 736-9300
151 W 46th St Fl 10 New York (10036) ***(G-10846)***
Karen Kane Inc 212 827-0980
1441 Broadway Fl 33 New York (10018) ***(G-10847)***
Karey Kassl Corp 516 349-8484
180 Terminal Dr Plainview (11803) ***(G-13641)***
Karey Products, Plainview *Also called Karey Kassl Corp* ***(G-13641)***
Karishma Fashions Inc 718 565-5404
3708 74th St Jackson Heights (11372) ***(G-6923)***
Karlyn Industries Inc 845 351-2249
16 Spring St Southfields (10975) ***(G-15580)***
Karo Sheet Metal Inc 718 542-8420
229 Russell St Brooklyn (11222) ***(G-2168)***
Karosheet Metal, Brooklyn *Also called Karo Sheet Metal Inc* ***(G-2168)***
Karp Associates Inc (PA) 631 768-8300
260 Spagnoli Rd Melville (11747) ***(G-8362)***
Karp Overseas Corporation 718 784-2105
5454 43rd St Maspeth (11378) ***(G-8179)***
Karr Graphics Corp 212 645-6000
2219 41st Ave Ste 2a Long Island City (11101) ***(G-7806)***
Kart, Maspeth *Also called Jack Luckner Steel Shelving Co* ***(G-8178)***
Kartell Us Inc 212 966-6665
39 Greene St New York (10013) ***(G-10848)***
Karter Bias Binding, Long Island City *Also called Empire Bias Binding Co Inc* ***(G-7759)***
Kas Direct LLC 516 934-0541
1600 Stewart Ave Ste 411 Westbury (11590) ***(G-17028)***
Kas-Kel, Fonda *Also called Kasson & Keller Inc* ***(G-5320)***
Kas-Ray Industries Inc 212 620-3144
122 W 26th St New York (10001) ***(G-10849)***
Kaseya US Sales LLC 415 694-5700
62 W 22nd St Ste 2r New York (10010) ***(G-10850)***
Kasisto Inc 917 734-4750
43 W 24th St Rm 8b New York (10010) ***(G-10851)***
Kasper Group LLC (HQ) 212 354-4311
1412 Broadway Fl 5 New York (10018) ***(G-10852)***
Kasper Group LLC 212 354-4311
1412 Broadway Fl 5 New York (10018) ***(G-10853)***
Kassis Superior Sign Co Inc 315 463-7446
6699 Old Thompson Rd Syracuse (13211) ***(G-15992)***
Kasson & Keller Inc 518 853-3421
60 School St Fonda (12068) ***(G-5320)***
Kastor Consulting Inc 718 224-9109
3919 218th St Bayside (11361) ***(G-767)***
Kat Nap Products, Brooklyn *Also called Steinbock-Braff Inc* ***(G-2627)***
Kate Spade & Company (HQ) 212 354-4900
2 Park Ave Fl 8 New York (10016) ***(G-10854)***
Kates Kakes 518 466-8671
987 Kings Rd Schenectady (12303) ***(G-15299)***
Kates Paperie Ltd 212 966-3904
188 Lafayette St Frnt A New York (10013) ***(G-10855)***

Katherine Blizniak (PA) 716 674-8545
525 Bullis Rd West Seneca (14224) *(G-16978)*
Kathleen B Mead 585 247-0146
393 Coastal View Dr Webster (14580) *(G-16752)*
Kathmando Valley Preservation 212 727-0074
36 W 25th St Fl 17 New York (10010) *(G-10856)*
Katikati Inc 585 678-1764
150 Lucius Gordon Dr West Henrietta (14586) *(G-16915)*
Katz Americas, Sanborn *Also called Katz Group Americas Inc (G-15149)*
Katz Gluten Free, Mountainville *Also called Gluten Free Bake Shop Inc (G-8793)*
Katz Group Americas Inc (HQ) 716 995-3059
3685 Lockport Rd Sanborn (14132) *(G-15149)*
Katz Martell Fashion Trdg Intl 212 840-0070
1385 Broadway Rm 1401 New York (10018) *(G-10857)*
Kaufman Brothers Printing 212 563-1854
327 W 36th St Rm 403 New York (10018) *(G-10858)*
Kawasaki Rail Car Inc (HQ) 914 376-4700
29 Wells Ave Bldg 4 Yonkers (10701) *(G-17476)*
Kawasho Foods USA Inc 212 841-7400
45 Broadway Fl 18 New York (10006) *(G-10859)*
Kay See Dental Mfg Co 816 842-2817
777 Avenue Of The Apt 32 New York (10001) *(G-10860)*
Kay Unger, New York *Also called Phoebe Company LLC (G-11669)*
Kay-Ray Industries, New York *Also called Kas-Ray Industries Inc (G-10849)*
Kaymil Printing Company Inc 212 594-3718
140 W 30th St Frnt New York (10001) *(G-10861)*
Kaymil Ticket Company, New York *Also called Kaymil Printing Company Inc (G-10861)*
Kayo of California 212 354-6336
525 Fashion Ave Rm 309 New York (10018) *(G-10862)*
Kays Caps Inc (PA) 518 273-6079
65 Arch St Troy (12183) *(G-16242)*
Kazac Inc 631 249-7299
55 Allen Blvd Ste C Farmingdale (11735) *(G-5031)*
KB Millwork Inc 516 280-2183
36 Grey Ln Levittown (11756) *(G-7451)*
Kbc, Bronx *Also called Kirschner Brush LLC (G-1377)*
Kbl Healthcare LP 212 319-5555
757 3rd Ave Fl 20 New York (10017) *(G-10863)*
Kbs Communications LLC 212 765-7124
331 W 57th St Ste 148 New York (10019) *(G-10864)*
Kc Collections LLC 212 302-4412
1407 Broadway Rm 1710 New York (10018) *(G-10865)*
Kc Tag Co 518 842-6666
108 Edson St Amsterdam (12010) *(G-353)*
Kch Publications Inc 516 671-2360
57 Glen St Ste 1 Glen Cove (11542) *(G-5632)*
Kcp Holdco Inc (PA) 212 265-1500
603 W 50th St New York (10019) *(G-10866)*
Kcp Operating Company LLC 212 265-1500
603 W 50th St New York (10019) *(G-10867)*
KD Dids Inc (PA) 718 402-2012
140 E 144th St Bronx (10451) *(G-1373)*
KDI Paragon, Lagrangeville *Also called Paragon Aquatics (G-7282)*
KDO Industries Inc 631 608-4612
32 Ranick Dr W Amityville (11701) *(G-301)*
Ke Durasol Awnings Inc 845 610-1100
445 Bellvale Rd Chester (10918) *(G-3636)*
Kearney-National Inc (HQ) 212 661-4600
565 5th Ave Fl 4 New York (10017) *(G-10868)*
Keck Group Inc (PA) 845 988-5757
314 State Route 94 S Warwick (10990) *(G-16613)*
Kedco Inc 516 454-7800
564 Smith St Farmingdale (11735) *(G-5032)*
Kedco Wine Storage Systems, Farmingdale *Also called Kedco Inc (G-5032)*
Keebler Company 585 948-8010
2999 Judge Rd Oakfield (14125) *(G-13084)*
Keebler Company 631 234-3700
55 Gilpin Ave Hauppauge (11788) *(G-6128)*
Keebler Company 845 365-5200
29 Corporate Dr Orangeburg (10962) *(G-13254)*
Keegan Ales LLC 845 331-2739
20 Saint James St Kingston (12401) *(G-7221)*
Keeler Services 607 776-5757
47 W Steuben St Ste 4 Bath (14810) *(G-658)*
Keeners East End Litho Inc 631 324-8565
10 Prospect Blvd East Hampton (11937) *(G-4432)*
Keep America Beautiful Inc 518 842-4388
1 Prospect St Amsterdam (12010) *(G-354)*
Keep Healthy Inc 631 651-9090
1019 Fort Salonga Rd Northport (11768) *(G-13031)*
Kefa Industries Group Inc 718 568-9297
9219 63rd Dr Rego Park (11374) *(G-14046)*
Kehr-Buffalo Wire Frame Co Inc 716 897-2288
127 Kehr St Buffalo (14211) *(G-3044)*
Keilhauer 646 742-0192
200 Lexington Ave Rm 1101 New York (10016) *(G-10869)*
Keith Grimes, Bridgehampton *Also called Sagaponack Sand & Gravel Corp (G-1233)*
Keith Lewis Studio Inc 845 339-5629
35 Rifton Ter Rifton (12471) *(G-14146)*
Keller Bros & Miller Inc 716 854-2374
401 Franklin St Buffalo (14202) *(G-3045)*
Keller International Pubg LLC (PA) 516 829-9210
150 Main St Ste 10 Port Washington (11050) *(G-13853)*
Keller Technology Corporation (PA) 716 693-3840
2320 Military Rd Tonawanda (14150) *(G-16194)*
Kelley Bros Hardware Corp 315 852-3302
1714 Albany St De Ruyter (13052) *(G-4106)*
Kelley Farm & Garden Inc 518 234-2332
239 W Main St Cobleskill (12043) *(G-3763)*
Kellogg Company 315 452-0310
7350 Round Pond Rd North Syracuse (13212) *(G-12968)*
Kellogg Company 845 365-5284
29 Corporate Dr Orangeburg (10962) *(G-13255)*
Kelly Foundry & Machine Co 315 732-8313
300 Hubbell St Ste 308 Utica (13501) *(G-16370)*
Kelly Grace Corp (PA) 212 704-9603
49 W 37th St Fl 10 New York (10018) *(G-10870)*
Kelly Window Systems Inc 631 420-8500
460 Smith St Farmingdale (11735) *(G-5033)*
Kelmar Systems Inc 631 421-1230
284 Broadway Huntington Station (11746) *(G-6751)*
Kelson Products Inc 716 825-2585
3300 N Benzing Rd Orchard Park (14127) *(G-13302)*
Kelta Inc (PA) 631 789-5000
141 Rodeo Dr Edgewood (11717) *(G-4616)*
Keltron Connector Co., Ronkonkoma *Also called Keltron Electronics (de Corp) (G-14949)*
Keltron Electronics (de Corp) 631 567-6300
3385 Vtrans Mem Hwy Ste E Ronkonkoma (11779) *(G-14949)*
Kem Medical Products Corp (PA) 631 454-6565
400 Broadhollow Rd Ste 2 Farmingdale (11735) *(G-5034)*
Kemco Sales LLC 203 762-1902
119 Despatch Dr East Rochester (14445) *(G-4482)*
Kemet Properties LLC 718 654-8079
1179 E 224th St Bronx (10466) *(G-1374)*
Kemp Metal Products Inc 516 997-8860
2300 Shames Dr Westbury (11590) *(G-17029)*
Kemp Technologies Inc (PA) 631 345-5292
1540 Broadway Fl 23 New York (10036) *(G-10871)*
Kemper System America Inc (HQ) 716 558-2971
1200 N America Dr West Seneca (14224) *(G-16979)*
Ken-Ton Open Mri PC 716 876-7000
2882 Elmwood Ave Kenmore (14217) *(G-7179)*
Kenal Services Corp 315 788-9226
1109 Water St Watertown (13601) *(G-16679)*
Kenan International Trading 718 672-4922
10713 Northern Blvd Corona (11368) *(G-4023)*
Kenbenco Inc 845 246-3066
437 Route 212 Saugerties (12477) *(G-15215)*
Kendall Circuits Inc 631 473-3636
5507-10 Nesconset Hwy 105 Mount Sinai (11766) *(G-8697)*
Kendi Iron Works Inc (PA) 718 821-2722
236 Johnson Ave Brooklyn (11206) *(G-2169)*
Kendor Music Inc 716 492-1254
21 Grove St Delevan (14042) *(G-4261)*
Kenmar Shirts Inc (PA) 718 824-3880
1415 Blondell Ave Bronx (10461) *(G-1375)*
Kennedy Valve Division, Elmira *Also called McWane Inc (G-4708)*
Kennel Klub, Utica *Also called Clara Papa (G-16334)*
Kenneth Cole Productions LP (HQ) 212 265-1500
603 W 50th St New York (10019) *(G-10872)*
Kenneth Cole Productions Inc (HQ) 212 265-1500
603 W 50th St New York (10019) *(G-10873)*
Kenneth J Lane Inc 212 868-1780
20 W 37th St Fl 9 New York (10018) *(G-10874)*
Kenney Manufacturing Displays 631 231-5563
12 Grand Blvd Brentwood (11717) *(G-1185)*
Kenny Mfg, Brentwood *Also called Kenney Manufacturing Displays (G-1185)*
Kens Service & Sales Inc 716 683-1155
11500 Clinton St Elma (14059) *(G-4663)*
Kensington & Sons LLC 646 430-8298
270 Lafayette St Ste 200 New York (10012) *(G-10875)*
Kensington Publishing Corp 212 407-1500
119 W 40th St Fl 21 New York (10018) *(G-10876)*
Kenstan Lock & Hardware Co Inc 631 423-1977
101 Commercial St Ste 100 Plainview (11803) *(G-13642)*
Kenstan Lock Co., Plainview *Also called Kenstan Lock & Hardware Co Inc (G-13642)*
Kent Associates Inc 212 675-0722
99 Battery Pl Apt 11p New York (10280) *(G-10877)*
Kent Chemical Corporation 212 521-1700
460 Park Ave Fl 7 New York (10022) *(G-10878)*
Kent Electro-Plating Corp 718 358-9599
5 Dupont Ct Dix Hills (11746) *(G-4315)*
Kent Gage & Tool Company, Poughkeepsie *Also called Stanfordville Mch & Mfg Co Inc (G-13951)*
Kent Nutrition Group Inc 315 788-0032
810 Waterman Dr Watertown (13601) *(G-16680)*
Kent Optronics Inc 845 897-0138
40 Corporate Park Rd Hopewell Junction (12533) *(G-6581)*
Kentronics Inc 631 567-5994
140 Keyland Ct Unit 1 Bohemia (11716) *(G-1083)*
Kenwell Corporation 315 592-4263
871 Hannibal St Fulton (13069) *(G-5480)*

ALPHABETIC

(PA)=Parent Co (HQ)=Headquarters (DH)=Div Headquarters
2018 Harris
New York Manufacturers Directory
987

Kenwin Sales Corp 516 933-7553
1100 Shames Dr Westbury (11590) ***(G-17030)***
Kenyon Press Inc 607 674-9066
1 Kenyon Press Dr Sherburne (13460) ***(G-15414)***
Keon Optics Inc 845 429-7103
30 John F Kennedy Dr Stony Point (10980) ***(G-15796)***
Kepco Inc (PA) 718 461-7000
13138 Sanford Ave Flushing (11355) ***(G-5266)***
Kepco Inc 718 461-7000
13140 Maple Ave Flushing (11355) ***(G-5267)***
Kepco Inc 718 461-7000
13138 Sanford Ave Flushing (11355) ***(G-5268)***
Kerner and Merchant 315 463-8023
104 Johnson St East Syracuse (13057) ***(G-4562)***
Kernow North America 585 586-3590
5 Park Forest Dr Pittsford (14534) ***(G-13594)***
Kerns Manufacturing Corp (PA) 718 784-4044
3714 29th St Long Island City (11101) ***(G-7807)***
Kerry Bfnctnal Ingredients Inc (HQ) 607 334-1700
158 State Highway 320 Norwich (13815) ***(G-13048)***
Kerry Bio-Science, Norwich *Also called Kerry Bfnctnal Ingredients Inc* ***(G-13048)***
Kerry Inc 845 584-3081
225 N Route 303 Ste 109 Congers (10920) ***(G-3883)***
Keryakos Inc 518 344-7092
1080 Catalyn St Fl 2 Schenectady (12303) ***(G-15300)***
Kesser Wine, Brooklyn *Also called Joseph Zakon Winery Ltd* ***(G-2150)***
Kessler Thermometer Corp 631 841-5500
40 Gleam St West Babylon (11704) ***(G-16832)***
Kesso Foods Inc 718 777-5303
7720 21st Ave East Elmhurst (11370) ***(G-4415)***
Ketcham Medicine Cabinets 631 615-6151
3505 Vtrans Mem Hwy Ste L Ronkonkoma (11779) ***(G-14950)***
Ketcham Pump Co Inc 718 457-0800
3420 64th St Woodside (11377) ***(G-17351)***
Ketchum Manufacturing Co Inc 518 696-3331
11 Town Shed Rd Lake Luzerne (12846) ***(G-7296)***
Keuka Brewing Co LLC 607 868-4648
8572 Briglin Rd Hammondsport (14840) ***(G-5979)***
Keuka Studios Inc 585 624-5960
1011 Rush Henrietta Townl Rush (14543) ***(G-15076)***
Kevco Industries 845 255-7407
6 Millbrook Rd New Paltz (12561) ***(G-8920)***
Kevin Freeman 631 447-5321
414 S Service Rd Ste 119 Patchogue (11772) ***(G-13452)***
Kevin J Kassman 585 529-4245
1408 Buffalo Rd Rochester (14624) ***(G-14491)***
Kevin Regan Logging Ltd 315 245-3890
1011 Hillsboro Rd Camden (13316) ***(G-3345)***
Key Brand Entertainment Inc 212 966-5400
104 Franklin St New York (10013) ***(G-10879)***
Key Cast Stone Company Inc 631 789-2145
113 Albany Ave Amityville (11701) ***(G-302)***
Key Computer Svcs of Chelsea 212 206-8060
227 E 56th St New York (10022) ***(G-10880)***
Key Container Corp 631 582-3847
135 Hollins Ln East Islip (11730) ***(G-4437)***
Key Digital Systems Inc 914 667-9700
521 E 3rd St Mount Vernon (10553) ***(G-8742)***
Key Foods, Valley Stream *Also called Cni Meat & Produce Inc* ***(G-16430)***
Key High Vacuum Products Inc 631 584-5959
36 Southern Blvd Nesconset (11767) ***(G-8823)***
Key Signals 631 433-2962
47 Tuthill Point Rd East Moriches (11940) ***(G-4449)***
Key Tech Finishing 716 832-1232
2929 Main St Ste 2 Buffalo (14214) ***(G-3046)***
Keyes Machine Works Inc 585 426-5059
147 Park Ave Gates (14606) ***(G-5576)***
Keymark Corporation 518 853-3421
1188 Cayadutta St Fonda (12068) ***(G-5321)***
Keynote Systems Corporation 716 564-1332
2810 Sweet Home Rd Buffalo (14228) ***(G-3047)***
Keystone Corporation (PA) 716 832-1232
2929 Main St Buffalo (14214) ***(G-3048)***
Keystone Electronics Corp (PA) 718 956-8900
3107 20th Rd Astoria (11105) ***(G-444)***
Keystone Iron & Wire Works Inc 844 258-7986
15 Main St East Rockaway (11518) ***(G-4490)***
Keystone Iron Elevator, East Rockaway *Also called Keystone Iron & Wire Works Inc* ***(G-4490)***
Khk Usa Inc 516 248-3850
259 Elm Pl Ste 2 Mineola (11501) ***(G-8552)***
Ki Pro Performance, New York *Also called Fusion Pro Performance Ltd* ***(G-10274)***
Kicks Closet Sportswear Inc 347 577-0857
1031 Southern Blvd Frnt 2 Bronx (10459) ***(G-1376)***
Kids, New York *Also called Bagznyc Corp* ***(G-9358)***
Kids Discover, New York *Also called Mark Levine* ***(G-11178)***
Kidtellect Inc 617 803-1456
222 Broadway Level19 New York (10038) ***(G-10881)***
Kidz Concepts LLC 212 398-1110
1412 Brdwy Fl 3 New York (10018) ***(G-10882)***
Kidz Toyz Inc 914 261-4453
280 N Bedford Rd Ste 203 Mount Kisco (10549) ***(G-8675)***
Kidz World Inc 212 563-4949
226 W 37th St Fl 12 New York (10018) ***(G-10883)***
Kilian Manufacturing Corp (HQ) 315 432-0700
1728 Burnet Ave Syracuse (13206) ***(G-15993)***
Killer Motor Sports, New York *Also called Vertana Group LLC* ***(G-12553)***
Kiltronx Enviro Systems LLC 917 971-7177
330 Motor Pkwy Ste 201 Hauppauge (11788) ***(G-6129)***
Kim Eugenia Inc 212 674-1345
347 W 36th St Rm 502 New York (10018) ***(G-10884)***
Kim Jae Printing Co Inc 212 691-6289
249 Parkside Dr Roslyn Heights (11577) ***(G-15053)***
Kim Seybert Inc (PA) 212 564-7850
37 W 37th St Fl 9 New York (10018) ***(G-10885)***
Kimball Office Inc 212 753-6161
215 Park Ave S Fl 3 New York (10003) ***(G-10886)***
Kimber Mfg 914 721-8417
1120 Saw Mill River Rd Yonkers (10710) ***(G-17477)***
Kimber Mfg Inc 914 965-0753
16 Harrison Ave Yonkers (10705) ***(G-17478)***
Kimber Mfg Inc (PA) 914 964-0771
1 Lawton St Yonkers (10705) ***(G-17479)***
Kimber Mfg Inc 406 758-2222
555 Taxter Rd Ste 235 Elmsford (10523) ***(G-4769)***
Kimberley Diamond, New York *Also called H C Kionka & Co Inc* ***(G-10433)***
Kimbri Liquor, Mohegan Lake *Also called Shopping Center Wine & Liquor* ***(G-8579)***
Kimmeridge Energy MGT Co LLC (PA) 646 517-7252
400 Madison Ave Rm 14c New York (10017) ***(G-10887)***
Kinaneco Inc (PA) 315 468-6201
2925 Milton Ave Syracuse (13209) ***(G-15994)***
Kinaneco Printing Systems, Syracuse *Also called Kinaneco Inc* ***(G-15994)***
Kind Group LLC (PA) 212 645-0800
19 W 44th St Ste 811 New York (10036) ***(G-10888)***
Kindling Inc 212 400-6296
440 Park Ave S Fl 14 New York (10016) ***(G-10889)***
Kinedyne Inc 716 667-6833
3566 S Benzing Rd Orchard Park (14127) ***(G-13303)***
Kinemotive Corporation 631 249-6440
222 Central Ave Ste 1 Farmingdale (11735) ***(G-5035)***
Kinequip Inc 716 694-5000
365 Old Niagara Fls Blvd Buffalo (14228) ***(G-3049)***
Kinetic Fuel Technology Inc 716 745-1461
1205 Balmer Rd Youngstown (14174) ***(G-17548)***
Kinetic Laboratories, Youngstown *Also called Kinetic Fuel Technology Inc* ***(G-17548)***
Kinetic Marketing Inc 212 620-0600
1133 Broadway Ste 221 New York (10010) ***(G-10890)***
Kinfolk Studios Inc 347 799-2946
90 Wythe Ave Brooklyn (11249) ***(G-2170)***
King Album Inc 631 253-9500
20 Kean St West Babylon (11704) ***(G-16833)***
King Cracker Corp 516 539-9251
307 Peninsula Blvd Hempstead (11550) ***(G-6301)***
King Displays Inc 212 629-8455
333 W 52nd St New York (10019) ***(G-10891)***
King Lithographers Inc (PA) 914 667-4200
245 S 4th Ave Mount Vernon (10550) ***(G-8743)***
King Paving, Albany *Also called King Road Materials Inc* ***(G-94)***
King Research Inc 718 788-0122
114 12th St Ste 1 Brooklyn (11215) ***(G-2171)***
King Road Materials Inc (HQ) 518 381-9995
8 Southwoods Blvd Albany (12211) ***(G-94)***
King Road Materials Inc 518 382-5354
145 Cordell Rd Schenectady (12303) ***(G-15301)***
King Road Materials Inc 518 382-5354
Cordell Rd Albany (12212) ***(G-95)***
King Sales Inc 718 301-9862
284 Wallabout St Brooklyn (11206) ***(G-2172)***
King Steel Iron Work Corp 718 384-7500
2 Seneca Ave Brooklyn (11237) ***(G-2173)***
Kingform Cap Company Inc 516 822-2501
121 New South Rd Hicksville (11801) ***(G-6386)***
Kinglift Elevator Inc 917 923-3517
1 Maiden Ln Fl 5 New York (10038) ***(G-10892)***
Kings Film & Sheet Inc 718 624-7510
482 Baltic St Brooklyn (11217) ***(G-2174)***
Kings Material, Brooklyn *Also called US Concrete Inc* ***(G-2731)***
Kings Park Asphalt Corporation 631 269-9774
201 Moreland Rd Ste 2 Hauppauge (11788) ***(G-6130)***
Kings Park Ready Mix Corp 631 269-4330
140 Old Northport Rd E Kings Park (11754) ***(G-7202)***
Kings Quarry, Adams Center *Also called R G King General Construction* ***(G-4)***
Kings Quartet Corp 845 986-9090
270 Kings Hwy Warwick (10990) ***(G-16614)***
Kings Ready Mix, Roslyn Heights *Also called US Concrete Inc* ***(G-15058)***
Kings Specialty Co, Brooklyn *Also called Kings Film & Sheet Inc* ***(G-2174)***
Kingsbury Printing Co Inc 518 747-6606
813 Bay Rd Queensbury (12804) ***(G-14015)***
Kingston Building Products LLC 914 665-0707
11 Brookdale Pl Ste 101 Mount Vernon (10550) ***(G-8744)***
Kingston Hoops Summer 845 401-6830
68 Glen St Kingston (12401) ***(G-7222)***
Kingston Pharma LLC 315 705-4019
5 County Route 42 Massena (13662) ***(G-8228)***

ALPHABETIC SECTION

Kingston Pharmaceuticals, Massena Also called Kingston Pharma LLC *(G-8228)*
Kingston Wste Wtr Trment Plant, Kingston Also called City of Kingston *(G-7213)*
Kingstreet Sounds, New York Also called His Productions USA Inc *(G-10528)*
Kinplex Corp (PA) 631 242-4800
  200 Heartland Blvd Edgewood (11717) *(G-4617)*
Kinplex Corp 631 242-4800
  200 Heartland Blvd Edgewood (11717) *(G-4618)*
Kinro Manufacturing Inc (HQ) 817 483-7791
  200 Mmaroneck Ave Ste 301 White Plains (10601) *(G-17156)*
Kinshofer Usa Inc 716 731-4333
  6420 Inducon Dr W Ste G Sanborn (14132) *(G-15150)*
Kintex Inc 716 297-0652
  3315 Haseley Dr Niagara Falls (14304) *(G-12857)*
Kionix Inc 607 257-1080
  36 Thornwood Dr Ithaca (14850) *(G-6891)*
Kirays & Joel Meat Market, Monroe Also called Joel Kiryas Meat Market Corp *(G-8593)*
Kirschner Brush LLC 718 292-1809
  605 E 132nd St Frnt 3 Bronx (10454) *(G-1377)*
Kirtas Inc 585 924-5999
  749 Phillips Rd Ste 300 Victor (14564) *(G-16510)*
Kirtas Inc 585 924-2420
  7620 Omnitech Pl Victor (14564) *(G-16511)*
Kiss My Face, Gardiner Also called Bycmac Corp *(G-5561)*
Kissle, Jamaica Also called Whitney Foods Inc *(G-7000)*
Kitchen Cabinet Co, Poughkeepsie Also called Modern Cabinet Company Inc *(G-13936)*
Kitchen Design Center, Sauquoit Also called Custom Stair & Millwork Co *(G-15228)*
Kitchen Specialty Craftsmen 607 739-0833
  2366 Corning Rd Elmira (14903) *(G-4707)*
Kiton Building Corp 212 486-3224
  4 E 54th St New York (10022) *(G-10893)*
Kittinger Company Inc 716 876-1000
  4675 Transit Rd Buffalo (14221) *(G-3050)*
Kittywalk Systems Inc 516 627-8418
  10 Farmview Rd Port Washington (11050) *(G-13854)*
KJ MEAT DIRECT, Monroe Also called JW Consulting Inc *(G-8594)*
Kjckd Inc (PA) 518 435-9696
  630 Columbia St Ext Ste 2 Latham (12110) *(G-7395)*
KKR Millennium GP LLC 212 750-8300
  9 W 57th St Ste 4150 New York (10019) *(G-10894)*
KKR Ntral Rsources Fund I-A LP (HQ) 212 750-8300
  9 W 57th St Ste 4200 New York (10019) *(G-10895)*
Kkw Corp 631 589-5454
  90 Bourne Blvd Sayville (11782) *(G-15240)*
Klara Technologies Inc 844 215-5272
  1 State St Fl 25 New York (10004) *(G-10896)*
Klauber Brothers Inc (PA) 212 686-2531
  980 Ave Of The Ave Frnt 2 New York (10018) *(G-10897)*
Kld Labs Inc 631 549-4222
  55 Cabot Ct Hauppauge (11788) *(G-6131)*
Klearbar Inc 516 684-9892
  8 Graywood Rd Port Washington (11050) *(G-13855)*
Klee Corp 585 272-0320
  340 Jefferson Rd Rochester (14623) *(G-14492)*
Kleen Stik Industries Inc 718 984-5031
  44 Lenzie St Staten Island (10312) *(G-15718)*
Kleer-Fax Inc 631 225-1100
  750 New Horizons Blvd Amityville (11701) *(G-303)*
Klees Car Wash and Detailing, Rochester Also called Klee Corp *(G-14492)*
Klein & Company, Massapequa Also called R Klein Jewelry Co Inc *(G-8214)*
Klein & Sons Logging Inc 845 292-6682
  3114 State Route 52 Wht Sphr Spgs (12787) *(G-17250)*
Klein Cutlery LLC 585 928-2500
  7971 Refinery Rd Bolivar (14715) *(G-1156)*
Klein Reinforcing Services Inc 585 352-9433
  11 Turner Dr Spencerport (14559) *(G-15595)*
Kleinfelder John 716 753-3163
  5239 W Lake Rd Mayville (14757) *(G-8247)*
Klemmt Orthopaedic Services, Johnson City Also called Klemmt Orthotics & Prosthetics *(G-7128)*
Klemmt Orthotics & Prosthetics 607 770-4400
  130 Oakdale Rd Johnson City (13790) *(G-7128)*
Klg Usa LLC 845 856-5311
  20 W King St Port Jervis (12771) *(G-13811)*
Kling Magnetics Inc 518 392-4000
  343 State Route 295 Chatham (12037) *(G-3586)*
Klutz (HQ) 650 687-2600
  568 Broadway Rm 503 New York (10012) *(G-10898)*
Klutz Store, New York Also called Klutz *(G-10898)*
KMA Corporation 518 743-1330
  153 Maple St Ste 5 Glens Falls (12801) *(G-5701)*
Kms Contracting Inc 718 495-6500
  86 Georgia Ave Brooklyn (11207) *(G-2175)*
Knf Clean Room Products Corp 631 588-7000
  1800 Ocean Ave Ronkonkoma (11779) *(G-14951)*
Kng Construction Co Inc 212 595-1451
  19 Silo Ln Warwick (10990) *(G-16615)*
Knickerbocker Graphics Svcs 212 244-7485
  256 W 38th St Rm 504 New York (10018) *(G-10899)*
Knickerbocker Partition Corp (PA) 516 546-0550
  193 Hanse Ave Freeport (11520) *(G-5418)*
Knight Life Entertainment 646 733-8911
  674 Lincoln Pl Apt 9 Brooklyn (11216) *(G-2176)*
Knight Sttlement Sand Grav LLC 607 776-2048
  7291 County Route 15 Bath (14810) *(G-659)*
Knightly Endeavors 845 340-0949
  319 Wall St Ste 2 Kingston (12401) *(G-7223)*
Knise & Krick Inc 315 422-3516
  324 Pearl St Syracuse (13203) *(G-15995)*
Knit Illustrated Inc 212 268-9054
  247 W 37th St Frnt 3 New York (10018) *(G-10900)*
Knit Resource Center Ltd 212 221-1990
  250 W 39th St Rm 207 New York (10018) *(G-10901)*
Knitty City, New York Also called A Thousand Cranes Inc *(G-9039)*
Knj Fabricators LLC 347 234-6985
  4341 Wickham Ave Bronx (10466) *(G-1378)*
Knogo, Ronkonkoma Also called Sentry Technology Corporation *(G-15006)*
Knoll Inc 716 891-1700
  1700 Broadway St Buffalo (14212) *(G-3051)*
Knoll Inc 212 343-4124
  1330 Ave Of The A New York (10019) *(G-10902)*
Knoll Printing & Packaging Inc 516 621-0100
  149 Eileen Way Syosset (11791) *(G-15846)*
Knoll Textile, New York Also called Knoll Inc *(G-10902)*
Knoll Worldwide, Syosset Also called Knoll Printing & Packaging Inc *(G-15846)*
Knorr Brake Company LLC 518 561-1387
  613 State Route 3 Unit 1 Plattsburgh (12901) *(G-13700)*
Knorr Brake Holding Corp (HQ) 315 786-5356
  748 Starbuck Ave Watertown (13601) *(G-16681)*
Knorr Brake Truck Systems Co (HQ) 315 786-5200
  748 Starbuck Ave Watertown (13601) *(G-16682)*
Knothe Apparel Group, New York Also called Sleepwear Holdings Inc *(G-12126)*
Knowles Cazenovia Inc (HQ) 315 655-8710
  2777 Us Route 20 Cazenovia (13035) *(G-3473)*
Knowlton Technologies LLC 315 782-0600
  213 Factory St Watertown (13601) *(G-16683)*
Knucklehead Embroidery Inc 607 797-2725
  800 Valley Plz Ste 4 Johnson City (13790) *(G-7129)*
Ko Fro Foods Inc 718 972-6480
  4418 18th Ave 4420 Brooklyn (11204) *(G-2177)*
Ko-Sure Food Distributors, Brooklyn Also called Taam Tov Foods Inc *(G-2662)*
Kobalt Music Pubg Amer Inc (PA) 212 247-6204
  220 W 42nd St Fl 11 New York (10036) *(G-10903)*
Kobe Steel USA Holdings Inc (HQ) 212 751-9400
  535 Madison Ave Fl 5 New York (10022) *(G-10904)*
Koch Container Div, Victor Also called Buckeye Corrugated Inc *(G-16489)*
Koch Metal Spinning Co Inc 716 835-3631
  74 Jewett Ave Buffalo (14214) *(G-3052)*
Koch Supply & Trading LP 212 319-4895
  667 Madison Ave Fl 22 New York (10065) *(G-10905)*
Kodak Alaris Inc (HQ) 585 290-2891
  2400 Mount Read Blvd # 1175 Rochester (14615) *(G-14493)*
Kodak Gallery - Cohber, West Henrietta Also called Cohber Press Inc *(G-16906)*
Kodansha USA Inc 917 322-6200
  451 Park Ave S Fl 7 New York (10016) *(G-10906)*
Kodiak Studios Inc 718 769-5399
  3030 Emmons Ave Apt 3t Brooklyn (11235) *(G-2178)*
Koehler Instrument Company Inc 631 589-3800
  85 Corporate Dr Holtsville (11742) *(G-6529)*
Koehler-Gibson Mkg & Graphics, Buffalo Also called Koehlr-Gibson Mkg Graphics Inc *(G-3053)*
Koehlr-Gibson Mkg Graphics Inc 716 838-5960
  875 Englewood Ave Buffalo (14223) *(G-3053)*
Koenig Iron Works Inc 718 433-0900
  814 37th Ave Long Island City (11101) *(G-7808)*
Koeppels Kustom Kitchens Inc 518 489-0092
  16 Van Rensselaer Rd Albany (12205) *(G-96)*
Kogeto Inc (PA) 646 490-8169
  51 Wooster St Fl 2 New York (10013) *(G-10907)*
Kohlberg Sports Group Inc (HQ) 914 241-7430
  111 Radio Circle Dr Mount Kisco (10549) *(G-8676)*
Kohler Awning Inc 716 685-3333
  2600 Walden Ave Buffalo (14225) *(G-3054)*
Koke Inc 800 535-5303
  582 Queensbury Ave Queensbury (12804) *(G-14016)*
Kokin Inc 212 643-8225
  247 W 38th St Rm 701 New York (10018) *(G-10908)*
Kokoroko Bakery, Woodside Also called Kokoroko Corporation *(G-17352)*
Kokoroko Corporation 718 433-4321
  4755 47th St Woodside (11377) *(G-17352)*
Kolcorp Industries Ltd (PA) 212 354-0400
  10 E 36th St New York (10016) *(G-10909)*
Kollage Work Too Ltd 212 695-1821
  261 W 35th St Ste 302 New York (10001) *(G-10910)*
Komar Kids LLC (HQ) 212 725-1500
  16 E 34th St Fl 14 New York (10016) *(G-10911)*
Komar Layering LLC (HQ) 212 725-1500
  16 E 34th St Fl 10 New York (10016) *(G-10912)*
Komar Luxury Brands 646 472-0060
  16 E 34th St Fl 10 New York (10016) *(G-10913)*
Kon Tat Group Corporation 718 207-5022
  1491 E 34th St Brooklyn (11234) *(G-2179)*

(PA)=Parent Co (HQ)=Headquarters (DH)=Div Headquarters

Konar Precision Mfg Inc..........631 242-4466
62 S 2nd St Ste F Deer Park (11729) ***(G-4183)***
Kondor Technologies Inc..........631 471-8832
206 Christopher St Ronkonkoma (11779) ***(G-14952)***
Konecranes Inc..........585 359-4450
1020 Lehigh Station Rd # 4 Henrietta (14467) ***(G-6318)***
Kong Kee Food Corp..........718 937-2746
4831 Van Dam St Long Island City (11101) ***(G-7809)***
Konica Mnolta Sups Mfg USA Inc..........845 294-8400
51 Hatfield Ln Goshen (10924) ***(G-5751)***
Konrad Design, Farmingdale *Also called T A Tool & Molding Inc* ***(G-5133)***
Konrad Prosthetics & Orthotics (PA)..........516 485-9164
596 Jennings Ave West Hempstead (11552) ***(G-16889)***
Konstantin D FRAnk& Sons Vini..........607 868-4884
9749 Middle Rd Hammondsport (14840) ***(G-5980)***
Koon Enterprises LLC..........718 886-3163
6805 Fresh Madow Ln Ste B Fresh Meadows (11365) ***(G-5456)***
Koonichi Inc..........718 886-8338
6805 Fresh Madow Ln Ste B Fresh Meadows (11365) ***(G-5457)***
Koral Industries..........212 719-0392
1384 Broadway Fl 18 New York (10018) ***(G-10914)***
Korangy Publishing Inc (PA)..........212 260-1332
450 W 31st St Fl 4 New York (10001) ***(G-10915)***
Kore Infrastructure LLC (PA)..........646 532-9060
4 High Pine Glen Cove (11542) ***(G-5633)***
Korea Central Daily News Inc (HQ)..........718 361-7700
4327 36th St Long Island City (11101) ***(G-7810)***
Korea Times New York Inc (HQ)..........718 784-4526
3710 Skillman Ave Long Island City (11101) ***(G-7811)***
Korea Times New York Inc..........718 729-5555
3710 Skillman Ave Long Island City (11101) ***(G-7812)***
Korea Times New York Inc..........718 961-7979
15408 Nthrn Blvd Ste 2b Flushing (11354) ***(G-5269)***
Korean New York Daily, The, Flushing *Also called New York IL Bo Inc* ***(G-5279)***
Korean Yellow Pages..........718 461-0073
14809 Northern Blvd Flushing (11354) ***(G-5270)***
Koregon Enterprises Inc..........450 218-6836
102 W Service Rd Champlain (12919) ***(G-3571)***
Korin Japanese Trading Corp..........212 587-7021
57 Warren St Frnt A New York (10007) ***(G-10916)***
Koring Bros Inc..........888 233-1292
30 Pine St New Rochelle (10801) ***(G-8961)***
Koshii Maxelum America Inc..........845 471-0500
12 Van Kleeck Dr Poughkeepsie (12601) ***(G-13931)***
Kossars Bialys LLC..........212 473-4810
367 Grand St New York (10002) ***(G-10917)***
Kossars On Grand LLC..........212 473-4810
367 Grand St New York (10002) ***(G-10918)***
Koster Keunen Waxes, Sayville *Also called Kkw Corp* ***(G-15240)***
Koster Keunen Waxes Ltd..........631 589-0400
90 Bourne Blvd Sayville (11782) ***(G-15241)***
Kotel Importers Inc..........212 245-6200
22 W 48th St Ste 607 New York (10036) ***(G-10919)***
Kourosh, College Point *Also called Lahoya Enterprise Inc* ***(G-3818)***
Kowa American Corporation (HQ)..........212 303-7800
55 E 59th St Fl 19 New York (10022) ***(G-10920)***
Kozinn+sons Merchant Tailors..........212 643-1916
22 W 32nd St Fl 5 New York (10001) ***(G-10921)***
Kozy Shack Enterprises LLC (HQ)..........516 870-3000
83 Ludy St Hicksville (11801) ***(G-6387)***
Kozy Shack Enterprises LLC..........516 870-3000
50 Ludy St Hicksville (11801) ***(G-6388)***
KP Industries Inc..........516 679-3161
2481 Charles Ct Ste 1 North Bellmore (11710) ***(G-12938)***
KPP Ltd..........516 338-5201
81 Urban Ave Westbury (11590) ***(G-17031)***
Kps Capital Partners LP (PA)..........212 338-5100
485 Lexington Ave Fl 31 New York (10017) ***(G-10922)***
Kraft Hat Manufacturers Inc..........845 735-6200
7 Veterans Pkwy Pearl River (10965) ***(G-13484)***
Kraft Heinz Foods Company..........607 865-7131
261 Delaware St Walton (13856) ***(G-16569)***
Kraft Heinz Foods Company..........315 376-6575
7388 Utica Blvd Lowville (13367) ***(G-7965)***
Kraft Heinz Foods Company..........914 335-2500
555 S Broadway Tarrytown (10591) ***(G-16116)***
Kraft Heinz Foods Company..........607 527-4584
8596 Main St Campbell (14821) ***(G-3358)***
Kraft Heinz Foods Company..........585 226-4400
140 Spring St Avon (14414) ***(G-537)***
Kragel Co Inc..........716 648-1344
23 Lake St Hamburg (14075) ***(G-5955)***
Krainz Creations Inc..........212 583-1555
589 5th Ave New York (10017) ***(G-10923)***
Kraman Iron Works Inc..........212 460-8400
410 E 10th St New York (10009) ***(G-10924)***
Kramartron Precision Inc..........845 368-3668
2 Spook Rock Rd Unit 107 Tallman (10982) ***(G-16101)***
Krasner Group Inc (PA)..........212 268-4100
40 W 37th St Ph A New York (10018) ***(G-10925)***
Kraus & Sons Inc..........212 620-0408
355 S End Ave Apt 10j New York (10280) ***(G-10926)***
Kraus Organization Limited (PA)..........212 686-5411
181 Hudson St Ste 2a New York (10013) ***(G-10927)***
Kraus USA Inc..........800 775-0703
12 Harbor Park Dr Port Washington (11050) ***(G-13856)***
Kravitz Design Inc (PA)..........212 625-1644
13 Crosby St Rm 401 New York (10013) ***(G-10928)***
Krefab Corporation..........631 842-5151
125 Chichester Rd Huntington (11743) ***(G-6701)***
Krengel Manufacturing Co Inc..........212 227-1901
121 Fulton Ave Fl 2 Fulton (13069) ***(G-5481)***
Kreon Inc..........516 470-9522
999 S Oyster Bay Rd # 105 Bethpage (11714) ***(G-869)***
Krepe Kraft Inc..........716 826-7086
1801 Elmwood Ave Buffalo (14207) ***(G-3055)***
Krepe-Kraft, Buffalo *Also called Krepe Kraft Inc* ***(G-3055)***
Kris-Tech Wire Company Inc (PA)..........315 339-5268
80 Otis St Rome (13441) ***(G-14845)***
Kroger Packaging Inc..........631 249-6690
215 Central Ave Ste M Farmingdale (11735) ***(G-5036)***
Kronenberger Mfg Corp..........585 385-2340
115 Despatch Dr East Rochester (14445) ***(G-4483)***
Kronos Incorporated..........518 459-5545
16 Sage Est Ste 206 Albany (12204) ***(G-97)***
Krug Precision Inc..........516 944-9350
7 Carey Pl Port Washington (11050) ***(G-13857)***
Kryten Iron Works Inc..........914 345-0990
3 Browns Ln Ste 201 Hawthorne (10532) ***(G-6272)***
KSA Manufacturing LLC..........315 488-0809
5050 Smoral Rd Camillus (13031) ***(G-3351)***
Kse Sportsman Media Inc (PA)..........212 852-6600
1040 Ave Of The Americas New York (10018) ***(G-10929)***
Ksk International Inc (PA)..........212 354-7770
450 Park Ave Ste 2703 New York (10022) ***(G-10930)***
Ksm Group Ltd..........716 751-6006
2905 Beebe Rd Newfane (14108) ***(G-12811)***
Kt Group Inc..........212 760-2500
13 W 36th St Fl 3 New York (10018) ***(G-10931)***
Ktd Screw Machine Inc..........631 243-6861
70 E Jefryn Blvd Ste D Deer Park (11729) ***(G-4184)***
Kubota Authorized Dealer, Mendon *Also called Saxby Implement Corp* ***(G-8414)***
Kuno Steel Products Corp..........516 938-8500
132 Duffy Ave Hicksville (11801) ***(G-6389)***
Kuraray America Inc..........212 986-2230
33 Maiden Ln Fl 6 New York (10038) ***(G-10932)***
Kureha Advanced Materials Inc..........724 295-3352
420 Lexington Ave Rm 2510 New York (10170) ***(G-10933)***
Kurrier Inc..........718 389-3018
145 Java St Brooklyn (11222) ***(G-2180)***
Kurt Gaum Inc..........212 719-2836
580 5th Ave Ste 303 New York (10036) ***(G-10934)***
Kurtz Truck Equipment Inc..........607 849-3468
1085 Mcgraw Marathon Rd Marathon (13803) ***(G-8115)***
Kurz and Zobel Inc..........585 254-9060
688 Colfax St Rochester (14606) ***(G-14494)***
Kush Oasis Enterprises LLC..........516 513-1316
228 Martin Dr Syosset (11791) ***(G-15847)***
Kussmaul Electronics Co Inc..........631 218-0298
170 Cherry Ave West Sayville (11796) ***(G-16965)***
Kustom Collabo, Brooklyn *Also called Vsg International LLC* ***(G-2756)***
Kustom Korner..........716 646-0173
5140 Camp Rd Hamburg (14075) ***(G-5956)***
Kutters Cheese Factory Inc..........585 599-3693
857 Main Rd Corfu (14036) ***(G-3978)***
Kw Distributors Group Inc..........718 843-3500
9018 Liberty Ave Ozone Park (11417) ***(G-13408)***
Kwadair LLC..........646 824-2511
137 Kent St Brooklyn (11222) ***(G-2181)***
Kwesi Legesse LLC..........347 581-9872
203 Remsen Ave Brooklyn (11212) ***(G-2182)***
Kwik Kut Manufacturing Co, Mohawk *Also called Mary F Morse* ***(G-8575)***
Kwik Ticket Inc (PA)..........718 421-3800
4101 Glenwood Rd Brooklyn (11210) ***(G-2183)***
Kwong CHI Metal Fabrication..........718 369-6429
166 41st St Brooklyn (11232) ***(G-2184)***
Kww Productions Corp..........212 398-8181
1410 Broadway Fl 24 New York (10018) ***(G-10935)***
Kybod Group LLC..........408 306-1657
222 E 34th St Apt 1005 New York (10016) ***(G-10936)***
Kyle Editing LLC..........212 675-3464
15 W 26th St Fl 8 New York (10010) ***(G-10937)***
Kyle R Lawrence Electric Inc..........315 502-4181
101 Hyde Pkwy Palmyra (14522) ***(G-13435)***
Kyntec Corporation..........716 810-6956
2100 Old Union Rd Buffalo (14227) ***(G-3056)***
Kyocera Precision Tools Inc..........607 687-0012
1436 Taylor Rd Owego (13827) ***(G-13378)***
Kyra Communications Corp..........516 783-6244
3864 Bayberry Ln Seaford (11783) ***(G-15366)***
Kz Precision Inc..........716 683-3202
1 Mason Pl Lancaster (14086) ***(G-7345)***
L & D Acquisition LLC..........585 531-9000
1 Lake Niagara Ln Naples (14512) ***(G-8811)***

L & D Manufacturing Corp 718 665-5226
366 Canal Pl Frnt Bronx (10451) *(G-1379)*
L & J Interiors Inc 631 218-0838
35 Orville Dr Ste 3 Bohemia (11716) *(G-1084)*
L & K Graphics Inc 631 667-2269
1917 Deer Park Ave Deer Park (11729) *(G-4185)*
L & L Overhead Garage Doors (PA) 718 721-2518
3125 45th St Long Island City (11103) *(G-7813)*
L & L Trucking Inc 315 339-2550
1 Revere Park Rome (13440) *(G-14846)*
L & M Optical Disc LLC 718 649-3500
65 W 36th St Fl 11 New York (10018) *(G-10938)*
L & M Publications Inc 516 378-3133
2 Endo Blvd Garden City (11530) *(G-5525)*
L & M Uniserv Corp 718 854-3700
4416 18th Ave Pmb 133 Brooklyn (11204) *(G-2185)*
L & M West, New York *Also called L & M Optical Disc LLC (G-10938)*
L & S Metals Inc 716 692-6865
111 Witmer Rd North Tonawanda (14120) *(G-12998)*
L A R Electronics Corp 716 285-0555
2733 Niagara St Niagara Falls (14303) *(G-12858)*
L A S Replacement Parts Inc 718 583-4700
1645 Webster Ave Bronx (10457) *(G-1380)*
L American Ltd 716 372-9480
222 Homer St Olean (14760) *(G-13171)*
L and S Packing Co 631 845-1717
101 Central Ave Farmingdale (11735) *(G-5037)*
L D Flecken Inc 631 777-4881
11 Old Dock Rd Unit 11 Yaphank (11980) *(G-17411)*
L F Fashion Orient Intl Co Ltd 917 667-3398
32 W 40th St Apt 2l New York (10018) *(G-10939)*
L F International Inc 212 756-5000
425 Park Ave Fl 5 New York (10022) *(G-10940)*
L I C Screen Printing Inc 516 546-7289
2949 Joyce Ln Merrick (11566) *(G-8421)*
L I F Publishing Corp (PA) 631 345-5200
14 Ramsey Rd Shirley (11967) *(G-15445)*
L I Stamp, Ridgewood *Also called Long Island Stamp & Seal Co (G-14126)*
L J Valente Inc 518 674-3750
8957 Ny Highway 66 Averill Park (12018) *(G-533)*
L K Manufacturing Corp 631 243-6910
56 Eads St West Babylon (11704) *(G-16834)*
L K Printing, White Plains *Also called Copy Stop Inc (G-17124)*
L K Printing Corp 914 761-1944
50 Main St Ste 32 White Plains (10606) *(G-17157)*
L LLC 716 885-3918
106 Soldiers Pl Buffalo (14222) *(G-3057)*
L M N Printing Company Inc 516 285-8526
23 W Merrick Rd Ste A Valley Stream (11580) *(G-16438)*
L M R, New York *Also called Lefrak Entertainment Co Ltd (G-10995)*
L Magazine LLC 212 807-1254
45 Main St Ste 806 Brooklyn (11201) *(G-2186)*
L Miller Design Inc 631 242-1163
100 E Jefryn Blvd Ste F Deer Park (11729) *(G-4186)*
L N D Incorporated 516 678-6141
3230 Lawson Blvd Oceanside (11572) *(G-13106)*
L P R Precision Parts & Tls Co 631 293-7334
108 Rome St Ste 1 Farmingdale (11735) *(G-5038)*
L P Transportation, Selkirk *Also called Palpross Incorporated (G-15379)*
L S I, East Aurora *Also called Luminescent Systems Inc (G-4398)*
L S Sign Co Inc 718 469-8600
1030 Wyckoff Ave Ridgewood (11385) *(G-14125)*
L S Z Inc 914 948-4040
30 Glenn St Ste 309 White Plains (10603) *(G-17158)*
L V D, Akron *Also called Strippit Inc (G-26)*
L VII Resilient LLC 631 987-5819
108 Cherry Ln Medford (11763) *(G-8284)*
L W S Inc 631 580-0472
125 Gary Way Ste 1 Ronkonkoma (11779) *(G-14953)*
L Y Z Creations Ltd Inc 718 768-2977
78 18th St Brooklyn (11232) *(G-2187)*
L& JG Stickley Incorporated (PA) 315 682-5500
1 Stickley Dr Manlius (13104) *(G-8106)*
L'Etoile Jewelers, Lynbrook *Also called Master Craft Jewelry Co Inc (G-7981)*
L'Oreal Paris, New York *Also called LOreal Usa Inc (G-11067)*
L-3 Cmmnctons Fgn Holdings Inc (HQ) 212 697-1111
600 3rd Ave Fl 32 New York (10016) *(G-10941)*
L-3 Cmmnctons Ntronix Holdings 212 697-1111
600 3rd Ave Fl 34 New York (10016) *(G-10942)*
L-3 Narda-Miteq, Hauppauge *Also called L3 Technologies Inc (G-6133)*
L-3 Narda-Miteq, Hauppauge *Also called L3 Technologies Inc (G-6135)*
L3 Communication, New York *Also called L-3 Cmmnctons Fgn Holdings Inc (G-10941)*
L3 Technologies Inc (PA) 212 697-1111
600 3rd Ave Fl 34 New York (10016) *(G-10943)*
L3 Technologies Inc 631 231-1700
435 Moreland Rd Hauppauge (11788) *(G-6132)*
L3 Technologies Inc 631 436-7400
100 Davids Dr Hauppauge (11788) *(G-6133)*
L3 Technologies Inc 631 289-0363
49 Rider Ave Patchogue (11772) *(G-13453)*
L3 Technologies Inc 607 721-5465
265 Industrial Park Dr Kirkwood (13795) *(G-7261)*
L3 Technologies Inc 631 231-1700
435 Moreland Rd Hauppauge (11788) *(G-6134)*
L3 Technologies Inc 631 436-7400
330 Oser Ave Hauppauge (11788) *(G-6135)*
La Bella Strings, Newburgh *Also called E & O Mari Inc (G-12775)*
La Calenita Bakery & Cafeteria 718 205-8273
4008 83rd St Elmhurst (11373) *(G-4677)*
La Cola 1 Inc 917 509-6669
529 W 42nd St Apt 5b New York (10036) *(G-10944)*
La Cremeria 212 226-6758
178 Mulberry St New York (10012) *(G-10945)*
La Escondida Inc 845 562-1387
129 Lake St Newburgh (12550) *(G-12786)*
La Fina Design Inc 212 689-6725
42 W 38th St Rm 1200 New York (10018) *(G-10946)*
La Flor Products Company Inc (PA) 631 851-9601
25 Hoffman Ave Hauppauge (11788) *(G-6136)*
La Flor Spices, Hauppauge *Also called La Flor Products Company Inc (G-6136)*
La Forge Francaise Ltd Inc 631 591-0572
100 Kroemer Ave Riverhead (11901) *(G-14158)*
La Lame Inc 212 921-9770
215 W 40th St Fl 5 New York (10018) *(G-10947)*
La Lame Importers, New York *Also called La Lame Inc (G-10947)*
La Mar Lighting Co Inc 631 777-7700
485 Smith St Farmingdale (11735) *(G-5039)*
La Nuit Collection, New York *Also called Patra Ltd (G-11596)*
La Prima Bakery Inc (PA) 718 584-4442
765 E 182nd St Bronx (10460) *(G-1381)*
La Raza, Brooklyn *Also called Impremedia LLC (G-2099)*
La Strada Dance Footwear Inc 631 242-1401
770 Grand Blvd Ste 1 Deer Park (11729) *(G-4187)*
La Vita Health Foods Ltd 845 368-4101
257 Route 59 Suffern (10901) *(G-15815)*
La Voz Hispana, New York *Also called Nick Lugo Inc (G-11445)*
La-Mar Fashions, Deer Park *Also called Continental Knitting Mills (G-4142)*
Lab Crafters Inc 631 471-7755
2085 5th Ave Ronkonkoma (11779) *(G-14954)*
Lab-Aids Inc 631 737-1133
17 Colt Ct Ronkonkoma (11779) *(G-14955)*
Labatt USA LLC 716 604-1050
50 Fountain Plz Ste 900 Buffalo (14202) *(G-3058)*
Labco of Palmyra Inc 315 597-5202
904 Canandaigua Rd Palmyra (14522) *(G-13436)*
Label Gallery Inc 607 334-3244
1 Lee Ave 11 Norwich (13815) *(G-13049)*
Label Makers Inc 631 319-6329
170 Wilbur Pl Ste 100 Bohemia (11716) *(G-1085)*
Label Source Inc 212 244-1403
321 W 35th St New York (10001) *(G-10948)*
Labella Pasta Inc 845 331-9130
906 State Route 28 Kingston (12401) *(G-7224)*
Labels I-G, New York *Also called Labels Inter-Global Inc (G-10949)*
Labels Inter-Global Inc 212 398-0006
109 W 38th St Rm 701 New York (10018) *(G-10949)*
Labels X Press, Buffalo *Also called Magazines & Brochures Inc (G-3074)*
Labels, Stickers and More, Bayport *Also called Stickershopcom Inc (G-755)*
Labeltex Mills Inc 212 279-6165
1430 Broadway Rm 1510 New York (10018) *(G-10950)*
Labgrafix Printing Inc 516 280-8300
43 Rocklyn Ave Unit B Lynbrook (11563) *(G-7980)*
Labhar - Freidman, New York *Also called L F International Inc (G-10940)*
Labortory For Laser Energetics, Rochester *Also called University of Rochester (G-14772)*
Labrador Stone Inc 570 465-2120
11 Dutchess Rd Binghamton (13901) *(G-928)*
Lace Marble & Granite Inc 347 425-1645
1465 39th St Brooklyn (11218) *(G-2188)*
Lackawanna Hot Rolled Plant, Blasdell *Also called Republic Steel Inc (G-958)*
Lactalis American Group Inc 716 827-2622
2375 S Park Ave Buffalo (14220) *(G-3059)*
Lactalis American Group Inc (HQ) 716 823-6262
2376 S Park Ave Buffalo (14220) *(G-3060)*
Lady Brass Co Inc 516 887-8040
1717 Broadway Unit 2 Hewlett (11557) *(G-6332)*
Lady Burd Exclusive Cosmt Inc (PA) 631 454-0444
44 Executive Blvd Ste 1 Farmingdale (11735) *(G-5040)*
Lady Burd Private Label Cosmt, Farmingdale *Also called Lady Burd Exclusive Cosmt Inc (G-5040)*
Lady Ester Lingerie Corp 212 689-1729
33 E 33rd St Rm 800 New York (10016) *(G-10951)*
Lady Linda Cakes, Bronx *Also called Operative Cake Corp (G-1418)*
Lady-N-Th-wndow Chocolates Inc 631 549-1059
319 Main St Huntington (11743) *(G-6702)*
Ladybird Bakery Inc 718 499-8108
1112 8th Ave Brooklyn (11215) *(G-2189)*
Lafarge Building Materials Inc 518 756-5000
Rr Ravena (12143) *(G-14035)*
Lafarge North America Inc 716 651-9235
6125 Genesee St Lancaster (14086) *(G-7346)*

ALPHABETIC

Lafarge North America Inc 716 854-5791
575 Ohio St Buffalo (14203) *(G-3061)*
Lafarge North America Inc 716 772-2621
400 Hinman Rd Lockport (14094) *(G-7626)*
Lafarge North America Inc 914 930-3027
350 Broadway Buchanan (10511) *(G-2800)*
Lafarge North America Inc 518 756-5000
1916 Route 9 W Ravena (12143) *(G-14036)*
Lafarge North America Inc 716 876-8788
4001 River Rd Tonawanda (14150) *(G-16195)*
Lafayette Chateau 607 546-2062
Rr 414 Hector (14841) *(G-6283)*
Lafayette Mirror & Glass Co 718 768-0660
2300 Marcus Ave New Hyde Park (11042) *(G-8891)*
Lafayette Pub Inc 212 925-4242
332 Lafayette St New York (10012) *(G-10952)*
Lagardere North America Inc (HQ) 212 477-7373
60 E 42nd St Ste 1940 New York (10165) *(G-10953)*
Lagasse Works Inc 315 946-9202
5 Old State Route 31 Lyons (14489) *(G-8000)*
Lage Industries Corporation 718 342-3400
9814 Ditmas Ave Brooklyn (11236) *(G-2190)*
Lagoe-Oswego Corp 315 343-3160
429 Antlers Dr Rochester (14618) *(G-14495)*
Lagoner Farms Inc 315 589-4899
6954 Tuckahoe Rd Williamson (14589) *(G-17253)*
Lagunatic Music & Filmworks 212 353-9600
456 Johnson Ave 202 Brooklyn (11237) *(G-2191)*
Lahoya Enterprise Inc 718 886-8799
1842 College Point Blvd College Point (11356) *(G-3818)*
Lahr Plastics, Fairport *Also called Lahr Recycling & Resins Inc* *(G-4866)*
Lahr Recycling & Resins Inc 585 425-8608
164 Daley Rd Fairport (14450) *(G-4866)*
Lai Apparel Design Inc 212 382-1075
209 W 38th St Rm 901 New York (10018) *(G-10954)*
Lai International Inc 763 780-0060
1 Tibbits Ave Green Island (12183) *(G-5876)*
Laird Telemedia 845 339-9555
2000 Sterling Rd Mount Marion (12456) *(G-8692)*
Lake Champlain Weekly, Plattsburgh *Also called Studley Printing & Publishing* *(G-13730)*
Lake Country Media, Albion *Also called Albion-Holley Pennysaver Inc* *(G-164)*
Lake Country Woodworkers Ltd 585 374-6353
12 Clark St Naples (14512) *(G-8812)*
Lake Image Systems Inc 585 321-3630
205 Summit Point Dr Ste 2 Henrietta (14467) *(G-6319)*
Lake Immunogenics Inc 585 265-1973
348 Berg Rd Ontario (14519) *(G-13227)*
Lake Placid Advertisers Wkshp 518 523-3359
Cold Brook Plz Lake Placid (12946) *(G-7299)*
Lake Region Medical Inc 716 662-5025
3902 California Rd Orchard Park (14127) *(G-13304)*
Lake View Manufacturing LLC 315 364-7892
1690 State Route 90 N King Ferry (13081) *(G-7198)*
Lakeland Industries Inc (PA) 631 981-9700
3555 Vtrans Mem Hwy Ste C Ronkonkoma (11779) *(G-14956)*
Lakelands Concrete, Lima *Also called East Main Associates* *(G-7466)*
Lakelands Concrete Pdts Inc 585 624-1990
7520 E Main St Lima (14485) *(G-7467)*
Lakeshore Carbide Inc 716 462-4349
5696 Minerva Dr Lake View (14085) *(G-7304)*
Lakeshore Pennysaver, Fredonia *Also called Fredonia Pennysaver Inc* *(G-5382)*
Lakeside Capital Corporation 716 664-2555
402 Chandler St Ste 2 Jamestown (14701) *(G-7048)*
Lakeside Cider Mill Farm Inc 518 399-8359
336 Schauber Rd Ballston Lake (12019) *(G-581)*
Lakeside Container Corp (PA) 518 561-6150
299 Arizona Ave Plattsburgh (12903) *(G-13701)*
Lakeside Industries Inc 716 386-3031
2 Lakeside Dr Bemus Point (14712) *(G-842)*
Lakeside Precision Inc 716 366-5030
208 Dove St Dunkirk (14048) *(G-4368)*
Lakestar Semi Inc (PA) 212 974-6254
888 7th Ave Ste 3300 New York (10106) *(G-10955)*
Lakeview Innovations Inc 212 502-6702
112 W 34th St Ste 18030 New York (10120) *(G-10956)*
Lakeview Sportswear Corp 800 965-6550
1425 37th St Ste 607 Brooklyn (11218) *(G-2192)*
Lakeville Service Station, Floral Park *Also called Full Service Auto Body Inc* *(G-5211)*
Lakewood Vineyards Inc 607 535-9252
4024 State Route 14 Watkins Glen (14891) *(G-16720)*
Lali Jewelry Inc 212 944-2277
50 W 47th St Ste 1610 New York (10036) *(G-10957)*
Lali Jewels, New York *Also called Lali Jewelry Inc* *(G-10957)*
Lalique Boutique, New York *Also called Lalique North America Inc* *(G-10958)*
Lalique North America Inc 212 355-6550
609 Madison Ave New York (10022) *(G-10958)*
Lam Research Corporation 845 896-0606
300 Westage Bus Ctr Dr # 190 Fishkill (12524) *(G-5192)*
Lamar Plastics Packaging Ltd 516 378-2500
216 N Main St Ste F Freeport (11520) *(G-5419)*
Lambro Industries Inc (PA) 631 842-8088
115 Albany Ave Amityville (11701) *(G-304)*
Laminated Window Products Inc 631 242-6883
211 N Fehr Way Bay Shore (11706) *(G-708)*
Lamm Audio Lab, Brooklyn *Also called Lamm Industries Inc* *(G-2193)*
Lamm Industries Inc 718 368-0181
2621 E 24th St Ste 1 Brooklyn (11235) *(G-2193)*
Lamontage, New York *Also called Mgk Group Inc* *(G-11273)*
Lamoreaux Landing Wl 607 582-6162
9224 State Route 414 Lodi (14860) *(G-7665)*
Lamothermic Corp 845 278-6118
391 Route 312 Brewster (10509) *(G-1219)*
Lamparts Co Inc 914 723-8986
160 E 3rd St Ste 2 Mount Vernon (10550) *(G-8745)*
Lams Foods Inc 718 217-0476
9723 218th St Queens Village (11429) *(G-13997)*
Lancaster Knives Inc (PA) 716 683-5050
165 Court St Lancaster (14086) *(G-7347)*
Lancaster Quality Pork Inc 718 439-8822
5600 1st Ave Ste 6 Brooklyn (11220) *(G-2194)*
Lancaster Tanks and Steel Pdts, Buffalo *Also called Jbren Corp* *(G-3032)*
Lance Valves 716 681-5825
15 Enterprise Dr Lancaster (14086) *(G-7348)*
Lanco Corporation 631 231-2300
2905 Vtrans Mem Hwy Ste 3 Ronkonkoma (11779) *(G-14957)*
Lanco Manufacturing Co 516 292-8953
384 Hempstead Tpke West Hempstead (11552) *(G-16890)*
Land and Sea Trailer Shop, Coram *Also called G L 7 Sales Plus Ltd* *(G-3965)*
Land n Sea Inc (PA) 212 703-2980
1375 Broadway Fl 2 New York (10018) *(G-10959)*
Land OLakes Inc 516 681-2980
50 Ludy St Hicksville (11801) *(G-6390)*
Land Packaging Corp 914 472-5976
7 Black Birch Ln Scarsdale (10583) *(G-15249)*
Land Self Prtction Systems Div, Buffalo *Also called Northrop Grumman Intl Trdg Inc* *(G-3118)*
Landies Candies Co Inc 716 834-8212
2495 Main St Ste 350 Buffalo (14214) *(G-3062)*
Landlord Guard Inc 212 695-6505
1 Maiden Ln Fl 7 New York (10038) *(G-10960)*
Landmark Group Inc 845 358-0350
709 Executive Blvd Ste A Valley Cottage (10989) *(G-16406)*
Landpro Equipment LLC 716 665-3110
1756 Lindquist Dr Falconer (14733) *(G-4914)*
Lane Enterprises Inc 607 776-3366
16 May St Bath (14810) *(G-660)*
Lane Enterprises Inc 518 885-4385
825 State Route 67 Ballston Spa (12020) *(G-599)*
Lane Metal Products, Bath *Also called Lane Enterprises Inc* *(G-660)*
Lane Park Graphics Inc 914 273-5898
93 Mcmanus Rd S Patterson (12563) *(G-13466)*
Lane Park Litho Plate 212 255-9100
155 Ave Of The Amer Fl 8 New York (10013) *(G-10961)*
Lanel, Floral Park *Also called Creatron Services Inc* *(G-5208)*
Lanel Inc 516 437-5119
504 Cherry Ln Ste 3 Floral Park (11001) *(G-5212)*
Lanes Flr Cvrngs Intriors Inc 212 532-5200
30 W 26th St Fl 11r New York (10010) *(G-10962)*
Langer Biomechanics Inc 800 645-5520
2905 Vtrans Mem Hwy Ste 2 Ronkonkoma (11779) *(G-14958)*
Language and Graphics Inc 212 315-5266
350 W 57th St Apt 14i New York (10019) *(G-10963)*
Lanier Clothes, New York *Also called Oxford Industries Inc* *(G-11553)*
Lannett Company, Carmel *Also called Silarx Pharmaceuticals Inc* *(G-3433)*
Lanoves Inc 718 384-1880
72 Anthony St Brooklyn (11222) *(G-2195)*
Lantern Hall LLC 718 381-2122
52 Harrison Pl Brooklyn (11237) *(G-2196)*
Lanwood Industries Inc 718 786-3000
45 Drexel Dr Bay Shore (11706) *(G-709)*
Lanza Corp 914 937-6360
404 Willett Ave Port Chester (10573) *(G-13778)*
Lapp Insulators LLC 585 768-6221
130 Gilbert St Le Roy (14482) *(G-7436)*
Lapp Management Corp 607 243-5141
3700 Route 14 Himrod (14842) *(G-6448)*
Larcent Enterprises Inc 845 562-3332
509 Temple Hill Rd New Windsor (12553) *(G-8987)*
Laregence Inc 212 736-2548
34 W 27th St Fl 2 New York (10001) *(G-10964)*
Largo Music Inc 212 756-5080
425 Park Ave Ste 501 New York (10022) *(G-10965)*
Larkin Anya Ltd 718 361-1827
4310 23rd St Ste 2b Long Island City (11101) *(G-7814)*
Larosa Cupcakes 347 866-3920
314 Lake Ave Staten Island (10303) *(G-15719)*
Larry Kings Corporation 718 481-8741
13708 250th St Rosedale (11422) *(G-15037)*
Larson Metal Manufacturing Co 716 665-6807
1831 Mason Dr Jamestown (14701) *(G-7049)*
LArte Del Gelato Gruppo Inc 718 383-6600
3100 47th Ave Long Island City (11101) *(G-7815)*
Larte Del Gelato Inc 212 366-0570
75 9th Ave Frnt 38 New York (10011) *(G-10966)*

Laser & Electron Beam Inc.....603 626-6080
77 7th Ave Apt 3h New York (10011) *(G-10967)*
Laser and Varicose Vein Trtmnt.....718 667-1777
500 Seaview Ave Ste 240 Staten Island (10305) *(G-15720)*
Laser Printer Checks Corp.....845 782-5837
7 Vayoel Moshe Ct # 101 Monroe (10950) *(G-8595)*
Lasermax Inc.....585 272-5420
3495 Winton Pl Ste A37 Rochester (14623) *(G-14496)*
Lasermaxdefense, Rochester *Also called Lasermax Inc (G-14496)*
Lasertech Crtridge RE-Builders.....518 373-1246
7 Longwood Dr Clifton Park (12065) *(G-3725)*
Last Magazine, The, New York *Also called Berger & Wild LLC (G-9410)*
Last N Last, New Rochelle *Also called Paint Over Rust Products Inc (G-8964)*
Last Resort, The, Rouses Point *Also called Sandys Deli Inc (G-15068)*
Last Straw Inc.....516 371-2727
22 Lawrence Ln Unit 1 Lawrence (11559) *(G-7418)*
Lasticks Aerospace Inc.....631 242-8484
35 Washington Ave Ste E Bay Shore (11706) *(G-710)*
Lasvit Inc.....212 219-3043
51 Wooster St Fl 1 New York (10013) *(G-10968)*
Latchable Inc.....646 833-0604
450 W 33rd St Fl 12 New York (10001) *(G-10969)*
Latham International Inc (PA).....518 783-7776
787 Watervliet Shaker Rd Latham (12110) *(G-7396)*
Latham International Inc.....518 346-5292
706 Corporation Park 1 Schenectady (12302) *(G-15302)*
Latham Manufacturing, Schenectady *Also called Latham International Inc (G-15302)*
Latham Manufacturing, Latham *Also called Latham Pool Products Inc (G-7398)*
Latham Pool Products Inc (PA).....518 951-1000
787 Watervliet Shaker Rd Latham (12110) *(G-7397)*
Latham Pool Products Inc.....260 432-8731
787 Watervliet Shaker Rd Latham (12110) *(G-7398)*
Latham Seamless Gutters, Altamont *Also called Alfred B Parella (G-208)*
Latham Software Sciences Inc.....518 785-1100
678 Troy Schenectady Rd # 104 Latham (12110) *(G-7399)*
Latina Media Ventures LLC (PA).....212 642-0200
120 Broadway Fl 34 New York (10271) *(G-10970)*
Latino Show Magazine Inc.....718 709-1151
8025 88th Rd Woodhaven (11421) *(G-17325)*
Latium USA Trading LLC (PA).....631 563-4000
5005 Veterans Mem Hwy Holbrook (11741) *(G-6484)*
Latorre Orthopedic Laboratory.....518 786-8655
960 Troy Schenectady Rd Latham (12110) *(G-7400)*
Laufer Wind Group LLC.....212 792-3912
270 Lafayette St Ste 1402 New York (10012) *(G-10971)*
Laumont Editions, New York *Also called Laumont Labs Inc (G-10972)*
Laumont Labs Inc.....212 664-0595
333 W 52nd St Fl 14 New York (10019) *(G-10972)*
Laundress Inc.....212 209-0074
247 W 30th St Ste 7l New York (10001) *(G-10973)*
Laura Star Service Center, Averill Park *Also called Garment Care Systems LLC (G-532)*
Laurice El Badry Rahme Ltd.....212 633-1641
399 Bleecker St New York (10014) *(G-10974)*
Lauricella Press Inc.....516 931-5906
81 Emjay Blvd Brentwood (11717) *(G-1186)*
Laurtom Inc.....914 273-2233
333 N Bedford Rd Ste 100 Mount Kisco (10549) *(G-8677)*
Laurus Development Inc.....716 823-1202
3556 Lake Shore Rd # 121 Buffalo (14219) *(G-3063)*
Lavanya, Jackson Heights *Also called Karishma Fashions Inc (G-6923)*
Law360, New York *Also called Portfolio Media Inc (G-11708)*
Lawdy Miss Clawdy, Pound Ridge *Also called Lloyd Price Icon Food Brands (G-13960)*
Lawn Elements Inc.....631 656-9711
1150 Lincoln Ave Ste 4 Holbrook (11741) *(G-6485)*
Lawson M Whiting Inc.....315 986-3064
15 State Route 350 Macedon (14502) *(G-8018)*
Lawton Electric Co, Ogdensburg *Also called Lawtons Electric Motor Service (G-13138)*
Lawtons Electric Motor Service.....315 393-2728
148 Cemetery Rd Ogdensburg (13669) *(G-13138)*
Layton Manufacturing Corp (PA).....718 498-6000
864 E 52nd St Brooklyn (11203) *(G-2197)*
Lazare Kaplan Intl Inc (PA).....212 972-9700
19 W 44th St Fl 16 New York (10036) *(G-10975)*
Lazarek Inc.....315 343-1242
209 Erie St Oswego (13126) *(G-13359)*
Lazer Incorporated (PA).....336 744-8047
1465 Jefferson Rd Ste 110 Rochester (14623) *(G-14497)*
Lazer Marble & Granite Corp.....718 859-9644
1053 Dahill Rd Brooklyn (11204) *(G-2198)*
Lazer Photo Engraving, Rochester *Also called Lazer Incorporated (G-14497)*
Lazo Setter Company, New York *Also called Mataci Inc (G-11201)*
Lb Furniture Industries LLC.....518 828-1501
99 S 3rd St Hudson (12534) *(G-6654)*
Lb Laundry Inc.....347 399-8030
4431 Kissena Blvd Flushing (11355) *(G-5271)*
Lbg Acquisition LLC.....212 226-1276
158 Bowery New York (10012) *(G-10976)*
Lcdrives Corp.....860 712-8926
65 Main St Pytn Hl 3204 Rm 3204 Peyton Hall Potsdam (13676) *(G-13897)*
Lco Destiny LLC.....315 782-3302
22476 Fisher Rd Watertown (13601) *(G-16684)*
LD McCauley LLC.....716 662-6744
3875 California Rd Orchard Park (14127) *(G-13305)*
LDB Interior Textiles, New York *Also called E W Williams Publications (G-10005)*
LDI Lighting Inc (PA).....718 384-4490
240 Broadway Ste C Brooklyn (11211) *(G-2199)*
LDI Lighting Inc.....718 384-4490
193 Williamsburg St W A Brooklyn (11211) *(G-2200)*
Le Book Publishing Inc (HQ).....212 334-5252
552 Broadway Apt 6s New York (10012) *(G-10977)*
Le Chocolat LLC.....845 352-8301
41 Main St Monsey (10952) *(G-8608)*
Le Chocolate of Rockland LLC.....845 533-4125
1 Ramapo Ave Suffern (10901) *(G-15816)*
Le Creuset, Riverhead *Also called Schiller Stores Inc (G-14168)*
Le Hook Rouge LLC.....212 947-6272
275 Conover St Ste 3q-3p Brooklyn (11231) *(G-2201)*
Le Lab, Valley Stream *Also called Lelab Dental Laboratory Inc (G-16439)*
Le Labo Fragrances, New York *Also called Le Labo Holding LLC (G-10978)*
Le Labo Holding LLC (HQ).....844 316-9319
233 Elizabeth St New York (10012) *(G-10978)*
Le Labo Holding LLC.....646 719-1740
80 39th St Fl Ground Brooklyn (11232) *(G-2202)*
Le Paveh Ltd.....212 736-6110
23 W 47th St Ste 501 New York (10036) *(G-10979)*
Le Roi Inc.....315 342-3681
21 S 2nd St Fulton (13069) *(G-5482)*
Le Roy Pennysaver, Le Roy *Also called Dray Enterprises Inc (G-7431)*
Le Vian Corp (PA).....516 466-7200
235 Great Neck Rd Great Neck (11021) *(G-5837)*
Le Vian Corp.....516 466-7200
10 W 46th St New York (10036) *(G-10980)*
Lea & Viola Inc.....646 918-6866
525 Fashion Ave Rm 1401 New York (10018) *(G-10981)*
Lea Apparel Inc.....718 418-2800
6126 Cooper Ave Glendale (11385) *(G-5672)*
Leader Herald, The, Gloversville *Also called William B Collins Company (G-5744)*
Leader Printing Inc.....516 546-1544
2272 Babylon Tpke Merrick (11566) *(G-8422)*
Leader Sheet Metal Inc.....347 271-4961
759 E 133rd St 2 Bronx (10454) *(G-1382)*
Leader, The, Corning *Also called Gatehouse Media LLC (G-3993)*
Leadership Directories Inc (PA).....212 627-4140
1407 Broadway Rm 318 New York (10018) *(G-10982)*
Leadertex Group, New York *Also called Leadertex Intl Inc (G-10983)*
Leadertex Intl Inc.....212 563-2242
135 W 36th St Fl 12 New York (10018) *(G-10983)*
Leading Edge Fabrication.....631 274-9797
699 Acorn St Ste B Deer Park (11729) *(G-4188)*
Leape Resources,, Alexander *Also called Lenape Energy Inc (G-190)*
Learn360, New York *Also called Facts On File Inc (G-10179)*
Learnimation.....917 868-7261
55 Washington St Ste 454 Brooklyn (11201) *(G-2203)*
Learningateway LLC.....212 920-7969
106 Saint James Pl Brooklyn (11238) *(G-2204)*
Learningexpress LLC.....646 274-6454
224 W 29th St Fl 3 New York (10001) *(G-10984)*
Leather Artisan.....518 359-3102
9740 State Highway 3 Childwold (12922) *(G-3658)*
Leather Craftsmen Inc (PA).....631 752-9000
6 Dubon Ct Farmingdale (11735) *(G-5041)*
Leather Craftsmen Inc.....714 429-9763
6 Dubon Ct Farmingdale (11735) *(G-5042)*
Leather Craftsmen West, Farmingdale *Also called Leather Craftsmen Inc (G-5042)*
Leather Impact Inc.....212 382-2788
525 Fashion Ave Rm 1012 New York (10018) *(G-10985)*
Leather Indexes Corp.....516 827-1900
174a Miller Pl Hicksville (11801) *(G-6391)*
Leather Outlet.....518 668-0328
1656 State Route 9 Lake George (12845) *(G-7287)*
Leatherstocking Mobile Home PA.....315 839-5691
2089 Doolittle Rd Sauquoit (13456) *(G-15229)*
Lebhar-Friedman Inc (PA).....212 756-5000
150 W 30th St Fl 19 New York (10001) *(G-10986)*
Lebhar-Friedman Inc.....212 756-5000
425 Park Ave Fl 6 New York (10022) *(G-10987)*
Leblon Cachaca, New York *Also called Leblon LLC (G-10989)*
Leblon Holdings LLC.....212 741-2675
33 Irving Pl Fl 3 New York (10003) *(G-10988)*
Leblon LLC.....954 649-0148
33 Irving Pl Fl 3 New York (10003) *(G-10989)*
Leblon LLC.....786 281-5672
266 W 26th St Ste 801 New York (10001) *(G-10990)*
Lebron Equipment Supply, New York *Also called 3835 Lebron Rest Eqp & Sup Inc (G-9019)*
Lechler Laboratories Inc.....845 426-6800
100 Red Schoolhse Rd C2 Spring Valley (10977) *(G-15613)*
Lechler Labs, Chestnut Ridge *Also called Mehron Inc (G-3652)*
Lechler Labs, Spring Valley *Also called Lechler Laboratories Inc (G-15613)*
Lecreuset of America, Central Valley *Also called Schiller Stores Inc (G-3555)*

(PA)=Parent Co (HQ)=Headquarters (DH)=Div Headquarters
2018 Harris
New York Manufacturers Directory
993

Led Lumina USA LLC 631 750-4433
116 Wilbur Pl Bohemia (11716) *(G-1086)*

Led Next, Westbury *Also called Emitled Inc (G-17009)*

Led Waves, Brooklyn *Also called Light Waves Concept Inc (G-2223)*

Led Waves Inc 347 416-6182
4100 1st Ave Ste 3n Brooklyn (11232) *(G-2205)*

Ledan Inc 631 239-1226
6 Annetta Ave Northport (11768) *(G-13032)*

Ledan Design Group, Northport *Also called Ledan Inc (G-13032)*

Ledes Group Inc 212 840-8800
85 5th Ave Fl 12 New York (10003) *(G-10991)*

Lee & Low Books Incorporated 212 779-4400
95 Madison Ave Rm 1205 New York (10016) *(G-10992)*

Lee Dyeing Company NC Inc 518 736-5232
328 N Perry St Johnstown (12095) *(G-7149)*

Lee Enterprises Incorporated 518 792-3131
76 Lawrence St Glens Falls (12801) *(G-5702)*

Lee Newspapers Inc 518 673-3237
6113 State Highway 5 Palatine Bridge (13428) *(G-13421)*

Lee Philips Packaging Inc 631 580-3306
750 Union Pkwy Ronkonkoma (11779) *(G-14959)*

Lee Printing Inc 718 237-1651
188 Lee Ave Brooklyn (11211) *(G-2206)*

Lee Publications Inc (PA) 518 673-3237
6113 State Highway 5 Palatine Bridge (13428) *(G-13422)*

Lee Spring Company Div, New York *Also called Unimex Corporation (G-12477)*

Lee Spring Company LLC (HQ) 718 362-5183
140 58th St Ste 3c Brooklyn (11220) *(G-2207)*

Lee Spring LLC (PA) 718 236-2222
140 58th St Ste 3c Brooklyn (11220) *(G-2208)*

Lee World Industries LLC 212 265-8866
150 Broadway Ste 1608 New York (10038) *(G-10993)*

Lee Yuen Fung Trading Co Inc (PA) 212 594-9595
125 W 29th St Fl 5 New York (10001) *(G-10994)*

Leesa Designs Ltd 631 261-3991
31 Glenn Cres Centerport (11721) *(G-3503)*

Leetech Manufacturing Inc 631 563-1442
105 Carlough Rd Unit C Bohemia (11716) *(G-1087)*

Lefrak Entertainment Co Ltd 212 586-3600
40 W 57th St Fl 4 New York (10019) *(G-10995)*

Legacy Manufacturing, Bronx *Also called Legacy USA LLC (G-1383)*

Legacy USA LLC 888 383-3330
415 Concord Ave Bronx (10455) *(G-1383)*

Legacy Valve LLC 914 403-5075
14 Railroad Ave Valhalla (10595) *(G-16394)*

Legal Servicing LLC 716 565-9300
2801 Wehrle Dr Ste 5 Williamsville (14221) *(G-17273)*

Legal Strategies Inc 516 377-3940
1795 Harvard Ave Merrick (11566) *(G-8423)*

Legendary Auto Interiors Ltd 315 331-1212
121 W Shore Blvd Newark (14513) *(G-12754)*

Legge System, Peekskill *Also called Walter G Legge Company Inc (G-13510)*

Leggiadro International Inc (PA) 212 997-8766
8 W 36th St Fl 9 New York (10018) *(G-10996)*

Legion Lighting Co Inc 718 498-1770
221 Glenmore Ave Brooklyn (11207) *(G-2209)*

Legno Veneto USA 716 651-9169
3283 Walden Ave Depew (14043) *(G-4285)*

Lehigh Cement Company (HQ) 518 792-1137
313 Warren St Glens Falls (12801) *(G-5703)*

Lehigh Cement Company 518 943-5940
120 Alpha Rd Catskill (12414) *(G-3458)*

Lehigh Northeast Cement, Glens Falls *Also called Lehigh Cement Company (G-5703)*

Lehmann Printing Company Inc 212 929-2395
247 W 37th St Rm 2a New York (10018) *(G-10997)*

Lehneis Orthotics Prosthetic 631 369-3115
518 E Main St Riverhead (11901) *(G-14159)*

Leica Microsystems Inc 716 686-3000
3362 Walden Ave Depew (14043) *(G-4286)*

Leidel Corporation (PA) 631 244-0900
95 Orville Dr Bohemia (11716) *(G-1088)*

Leigh Scott Enterprises Inc 718 343-5440
24802 Union Tpke Bellerose (11426) *(G-806)*

Leiter Sukkahs Inc 718 436-0303
1346 39th St Brooklyn (11218) *(G-2210)*

Lela Rose, New York *Also called Stitch & Couture Inc (G-12229)*

Lelab Dental Laboratory Inc 516 561-5050
550 W Merrick Rd Ste 8 Valley Stream (11580) *(G-16439)*

Lemans Corporation 518 885-7500
10 Mccrea Hill Rd Ballston Spa (12020) *(G-600)*

Lemetric Hair Centers Inc 212 986-5620
124 E 40th St Rm 601 New York (10016) *(G-10998)*

Lemode Concepts Inc 631 841-0796
19 Elm Pl Amityville (11701) *(G-305)*

Lemode Plumbing & Heating 718 545-3336
3455 11th St Astoria (11106) *(G-445)*

Lemon Brothers Foundation Inc 347 920-2749
23b Debs Pl Bronx (10475) *(G-1384)*

Lemoyne Machine Products Corp 315 454-0708
106 Evelyn Ter Syracuse (13208) *(G-15996)*

Lemral Knitwear Inc 718 210-0175
70 Franklin Ave Brooklyn (11205) *(G-2211)*

Lenape Energy Inc (PA) 585 344-1200
9489 Alexander Rd Alexander (14005) *(G-190)*

Lenape Resources Inc 585 344-1200
9489 Alexander Rd Alexander (14005) *(G-191)*

Lenaro Paper Co Inc 631 439-8800
31 Windsor Pl Central Islip (11722) *(G-3529)*

Lenco, Amityville *Also called Saraga Industries Corp (G-324)*

Lencore Acoustics Corp (PA) 516 682-9292
1 Crossways Park Dr W Woodbury (11797) *(G-17312)*

Lencore Acoustics Corp 315 384-9114
1 S Main St Norfolk (13667) *(G-12916)*

Lending Trimming Co Inc 212 242-7502
179 Christopher St New York (10014) *(G-10999)*

Leng Universal Inc 212 398-6800
530 7th Ave Rm 1101 New York (10018) *(G-11000)*

Lennons Litho Inc 315 866-3156
234 Kast Hill Rd Herkimer (13350) *(G-6329)*

Lenon Models Inc 212 229-1581
236 W 27th St Rm 900 New York (10001) *(G-11001)*

Lenore Marshall Inc 212 947-5945
231 W 29th St Frnt 1 New York (10001) *(G-11002)*

Lens Lab 718 379-2020
2124 Bartow Ave Bronx (10475) *(G-1385)*

Lens Lab Express 718 921-5488
482 86th St Brooklyn (11209) *(G-2212)*

Lens Lab Express of Graham Ave 718 486-0117
28 Graham Ave Brooklyn (11206) *(G-2213)*

Lens Lab Express Southern Blvd 718 626-5184
3097 Steinway St Ste 301 Astoria (11103) *(G-446)*

Lens Triptar Co Inc 585 473-4470
439 Monroe Ave Ste 1 Rochester (14607) *(G-14498)*

Lenz, Peconic *Also called Dorset Farms Inc (G-13494)*

Leo D Bernstein & Sons Inc (PA) 212 337-9578
151 W 25th St Frnt 1 New York (10001) *(G-11003)*

Leo Diamond, The, New York *Also called Leo Schachter Diamonds LLC (G-11007)*

Leo Ingwer Inc 212 719-1342
62 W 47th St Ste 1004 New York (10036) *(G-11004)*

Leo International Inc 718 290-8005
471 Sutter Ave Brooklyn (11207) *(G-2214)*

Leo P Callahan Inc 607 797-7314
229 Lwer Stlla Ireland Rd Binghamton (13905) *(G-929)*

Leo Paper Inc 917 305-0708
286 5th Ave Fl 6 New York (10001) *(G-11005)*

Leo Schachter & Co Inc 212 688-2000
529 5th Ave New York (10017) *(G-11006)*

Leo Schachter Diamonds LLC 212 688-2000
50 W 47th St Fl 2100 New York (10036) *(G-11007)*

Leo Schultz 716 969-0945
1144 Maryvale Dr Cheektowaga (14225) *(G-3606)*

Leonard Bus Sales Inc 607 467-3100
730 Ellsworth Rd Rome (13441) *(G-14847)*

Leonard Carlson 518 477-4710
90 Waters Rd East Greenbush (12061) *(G-4423)*

Leonardo Printing Corp 914 664-7890
529 E 3rd St Mount Vernon (10553) *(G-8746)*

Leonardo Prntng, Mount Vernon *Also called Leonardo Printing Corp (G-8746)*

Leonore Doskow Inc 914 737-1335
1 Juniper Ln Cortlandt Manor (10567) *(G-4077)*

Lep, Hawthorne *Also called Ludl Electronic Products Ltd (G-6274)*

Leprino Foods Company 570 888-9658
400 Leprino Ave Waverly (14892) *(G-16729)*

Leray Homes Inc 315 788-6087
22732 Duffy Rd Watertown (13601) *(G-16685)*

Leroux Fuels 518 563-3653
994 Military Tpke Plattsburgh (12901) *(G-13702)*

Leroy Plastics Inc 585 768-8158
20 Lent Ave Le Roy (14482) *(G-7437)*

Les Ateliers Tamalet 929 325-7976
37 W 39th St New York (10018) *(G-11008)*

Les Chateaux De France Inc 516 239-6795
1 Craft Ave Inwood (11096) *(G-6800)*

Lesanne Life Sciences LLC 914 234-0860
47 Brook Farm Rd Bedford (10506) *(G-793)*

Leser Enterprises Ltd 212 644-8921
18 E 48th St Rm 1104 New York (10017) *(G-11009)*

Lesilu Productions Inc 212 947-6419
60 W 38th St Rm 302 New York (10018) *(G-11010)*

Leslie Stuart Co Inc 212 629-4551
149 W 36th St Fl 8 New York (10018) *(G-11011)*

Lesly Enterprise & Associates 631 988-1301
29 Columbo Dr Deer Park (11729) *(G-4189)*

Lessoilcom 516 319-5052
672 Dogwood Ave Franklin Square (11010) *(G-5374)*

Let Water Be Water LLC 212 627-2630
40 W 27th St Fl 3 New York (10001) *(G-11012)*

Letigre, New York *Also called Lt2 LLC (G-11086)*

Letterama Inc (PA) 516 349-0800
111 Cabot St West Babylon (11704) *(G-16835)*

Lettergraphics, Bridgeport *Also called Syracuse Letter Company Inc (G-1236)*

Level Wear, Cheektowaga *Also called Accolade USA Inc (G-3590)*

Levi Strauss & Co 212 944-8555
1501 Broadway New York (10036) *(G-11013)*

ALPHABETIC SECTION — Lighting Services Inc (PA)

Levi Strauss & Co 917 213-6263
　13432 Blossom Ave Flushing (11355) *(G-5272)*
Leviton Manufacturing Co Inc (PA) 631 812-6000
　201 N Service Rd Melville (11747) *(G-8363)*
Levitt Industrial Textile, Westbury Also called Kenwin Sales Corp *(G-17030)*
Levolor Window Furnishings Inc (HQ) 845 664-7000
　1 Blue Hill Plz Pearl River (10965) *(G-13485)*
Levon Graphics Corp 631 753-2022
　210 Route 109 Farmingdale (11735) *(G-5043)*
Levy Group Inc (PA) 212 398-0707
　1333 Broadway Fl 9 New York (10018) *(G-11014)*
Lewbro Ready Mix Inc (PA) 315 497-0498
　502 Locke Rd Groton (13073) *(G-5921)*
Lewis & Myers Inc (PA) 585 494-1410
　7307 S Lake Rd Bergen (14416) *(G-847)*
Lewis Machine Co Inc 718 625-0799
　209 Congress St Brooklyn (11201) *(G-2215)*
Lewis Sand & Gravel, Lewis Also called Upstone Materials Inc *(G-7452)*
Lewis, S J Machine Co, Brooklyn Also called Lewis Machine Co Inc *(G-2215)*
Lexan Industries Inc 631 434-7586
　15 Harold Ct Bay Shore (11706) *(G-711)*
Lexar Global LLC 845 352-9700
　711 Executive Blvd Ste K Valley Cottage (10989) *(G-16407)*
Lexington Machining LLC 585 235-0880
　677 Buffalo Rd Rochester (14611) *(G-14499)*
Lexington Machining LLC (PA) 585 235-0880
　677 Buffalo Rd Rochester (14611) *(G-14500)*
Lexis Nexis Mathew Bender, Menands Also called Lexis Publishing *(G-8405)*
Lexis Publishing 518 487-3000
　1275 Broadway Menands (12204) *(G-8405)*
Lexisnexis, Conklin Also called Relx Inc *(G-3899)*
Lexstar Inc (PA) 845 947-1415
　25 Lincoln St Haverstraw (10927) *(G-6262)*
Lf Outerwear LLC 212 239-2025
　463 7th Ave Fl 12 New York (10018) *(G-11015)*
Lgb Inc 212 278-8280
　1410 Broadway Rm 3205 New York (10018) *(G-11016)*
Lgn Materials & Solutions 888 414-0005
　149 Esplanade Mount Vernon (10553) *(G-8747)*
Lhv Precast Inc 845 336-8880
　540 Ulster Landing Rd Kingston (12401) *(G-7225)*
LI Community Newspapers Inc 516 747-8282
　132 E 2nd St Mineola (11501) *(G-8553)*
LI Fireproof Door, Whitestone Also called Lif Industries Inc *(G-17240)*
LI Pipe Supply, Garden City Also called Long Island Pipe Supply Inc *(G-5528)*
LI Script LLC 631 321-3850
　333 Crossways Park Dr Woodbury (11797) *(G-17313)*
Liana Uniforms, New York Also called Eighteen Liana Trading Inc *(G-10043)*
Libbys Bakery Cafe LLC 603 918-8825
　92 Montcalm St Ticonderoga (12883) *(G-16149)*
Liberty Apparel Company Inc (PA) 718 625-4000
　1407 Broadway Rm 1500 New York (10018) *(G-11017)*
Liberty Awnings & Signs Inc 347 203-1470
　7705 21st Ave East Elmhurst (11370) *(G-4416)*
Liberty Brass Turning Co Inc 718 784-2911
　1200 Shames Dr Unit C Westbury (11590) *(G-17032)*
Liberty Controls Inc 718 461-0600
　1505 132nd St Fl 2 College Point (11356) *(G-3819)*
Liberty Displays Inc 716 743-1757
　4230b Ridge Lea Rd # 110 Amherst (14226) *(G-247)*
Liberty Fabrication Inc 718 495-5735
　226 Glenmore Ave Brooklyn (11207) *(G-2216)*
Liberty Food and Fuel 315 299-4039
　1131 N Salina St Syracuse (13208) *(G-15997)*
Liberty Install Inc 631 651-5655
　100 Centershore Rd Centerport (11721) *(G-3504)*
Liberty Label Mfg Inc 631 737-2365
　21 Peachtree Ct Holbrook (11741) *(G-6486)*
Liberty Machine & Tool 315 699-3242
　7908 Ontario Ave Cicero (13039) *(G-3676)*
Liberty Panel & Home Center, Brooklyn Also called Liberty Panel Center Inc *(G-2217)*
Liberty Panel Center Inc (PA) 718 647-2763
　1009 Liberty Ave Brooklyn (11208) *(G-2217)*
Liberty Pipe Incorporated 516 747-2472
　128 Liberty Ave Mineola (11501) *(G-8554)*
Liberty Pumps Inc 800 543-2550
　7000 Appletree Ave Bergen (14416) *(G-848)*
Library of America, New York Also called Literary Classics of US *(G-11036)*
Library Tales Publishing Inc 347 394-2629
　244 5th Ave Ste Q222 New York (10001) *(G-11018)*
Licenders (PA) 212 759-5200
　939 8th Ave New York (10019) *(G-11019)*
Lickity Splits 585 345-6091
　238 East Ave Batavia (14020) *(G-642)*
Liddabit Sweets 917 912-1370
　330 Wythe Ave Apt 2g Brooklyn (11249) *(G-2218)*
Liddell Corporation 716 297-8557
　4600 Witmer Ind Est 5 Niagara Falls (14305) *(G-12859)*
Lidestri Food and Drink, Fairport Also called Lidestri Foods Inc *(G-4867)*
Lidestri Foods Inc (PA) 585 377-7700
　815 Whitney Rd W Fairport (14450) *(G-4867)*

Lids Corporation 718 338-7790
　5385 Kings Plz Brooklyn (11234) *(G-2219)*
Lids Corporation 518 459-7060
　131 Colonie Ctr Spc 429 Albany (12205) *(G-98)*
Lieb Cellars LLC 631 298-1942
　35 Cox Neck Rd Mattituck (11952) *(G-8239)*
Lieb Cellars Tasting Room, Mattituck Also called Lieb Cellars LLC *(G-8239)*
Liebe NY, Perry Also called R J Liebe Athletic Company *(G-13548)*
Lif Distributing Inc 631 630-6900
　155 Oval Dr Islandia (11749) *(G-6837)*
Lif Industries Inc (PA) 516 390-6800
　5 Harbor Park Dr Ste 1 Port Washington (11050) *(G-13858)*
Lif Industries Inc 718 767-8800
　1105 Clintonville St Whitestone (11357) *(G-17240)*
Lifc Corp 516 426-5737
　101 Haven Ave Port Washington (11050) *(G-13859)*
Life Juice Brands LLC 585 944-7982
　115 Brook Rd Pittsford (14534) *(G-13595)*
Life Medical Technologies LLC 845 894-2121
　2070 Rte 52 21a Bldg 320a Hopewell Junction (12533) *(G-6582)*
Life Pill Laboratories LLC 914 682-2146
　50 Main St Ste 100 White Plains (10606) *(G-17159)*
Life Plus Style, New York Also called International Design Assoc Ltd *(G-10675)*
Life Style Design Group 212 391-8666
　1441 Broadway Fl 7 New York (10018) *(G-11020)*
Life Technologies Corporation 716 774-6700
　3175 Staley Rd Grand Island (14072) *(G-5775)*
Life Watch Technology Inc 917 669-2428
　42-10 Polen St Ste 412 Flushing (11355) *(G-5273)*
Lifeforms Printing 716 685-4500
　786 Terrace Blvd Ste 2 Depew (14043) *(G-4287)*
Lifegas, Cohoes Also called Linde Gas North America LLC *(G-3773)*
Lifegas, Syracuse Also called Linde Gas North America LLC *(G-15999)*
Lifelink Monitoring Corp (PA) 845 336-2098
　3201 Route 212 Bearsville (12409) *(G-787)*
Lifesake Division, New Hartford Also called Faster-Form Corp *(G-8849)*
Lifescan Inc 516 557-2693
　15 Tardy Ln N Wantagh (11793) *(G-16580)*
Lifestyle Design Usa Ltd 212 279-9400
　315 W 39th St Rm 709 New York (10018) *(G-11021)*
Lifestyle International LLC 917 757-0067
　469 7th Ave New York (10018) *(G-11022)*
Lifestyle-Trimco (PA) 718 257-9101
　323 Malta St Brooklyn (11207) *(G-2220)*
Lifestyle-Trimco Viaggo, Brooklyn Also called Lifestyle-Trimco *(G-2220)*
Lifetime Brands Inc (PA) 516 683-6000
　1000 Stewart Ave Garden City (11530) *(G-5526)*
Lifetime Chimney Supply LLC 516 576-8144
　171 E Ames Ct Plainview (11803) *(G-13643)*
Lifetime Stainless Steel Corp 585 924-9393
　7387 Ny 96 850 Victor (14564) *(G-16512)*
Lifewatch Inc 800 716-1433
　1344 Broadway Ste 106 Hewlett (11557) *(G-6333)*
Lifewatch Personal Mergency, Hewlett Also called Lifewatch Inc *(G-6333)*
Liffey Sheet Metal Corp 347 381-1134
　4555 36th St Long Island City (11101) *(G-7816)*
Lift Safe - Fuel Safe Inc 315 423-7702
　212 W Seneca Tpke Syracuse (13205) *(G-15998)*
Liftforward Inc 917 693-4993
　180 Maiden Ln Fl 10 New York (10038) *(G-11023)*
Light Blue USA LLC 718 475-2515
　1421 Locust Ave Brooklyn (11230) *(G-2221)*
Light Dental Labs Inc 516 785-7730
　250 N Syracuse Ave Massapequa (11758) *(G-8210)*
Light Fabrications, Rochester Also called Eis Inc *(G-14361)*
Light House Hill Marketing 212 354-1338
　38 W 39th St Fl 4l New York (10018) *(G-11024)*
Light Inc 212 629-3255
　530 Fashion Ave Rm 1002 New York (10018) *(G-11025)*
Light Phone Inc (PA) 415 595-0044
　49 Bogart St Apt 44 Brooklyn (11206) *(G-2222)*
Light Waves Concept Inc 212 677-6400
　4100 1st Ave Brooklyn (11232) *(G-2223)*
Lightbulb Press Inc 212 485-8800
　39 W 28th St New York (10001) *(G-11026)*
Lighthouse Components 917 993-6820
　14 Wall St New York (10005) *(G-11027)*
Lighting By Dom Yonkers Inc 914 968-8700
　253 S Broadway Yonkers (10705) *(G-17480)*
Lighting By Gregory, New York Also called Lbg Acquisition LLC *(G-10976)*
Lighting Collaborative Inc 212 253-7220
　275 Park Ave Apt 6k Brooklyn (11205) *(G-2224)*
Lighting Holdings Intl LLC (PA) 845 306-1850
　4 Manhattanville Rd Purchase (10577) *(G-13976)*
Lighting N Beyond LLC 718 669-9142
　628 Ste 303 Blauvelt (10913) *(G-967)*
Lighting Products Division, Skaneateles Falls Also called Welch Allyn Inc *(G-15495)*
Lighting Sculptures Inc 631 242-3387
　66 N Industry Ct Deer Park (11729) *(G-4190)*
Lighting Services Inc (PA) 845 942-2800
　2 Holt Dr Stony Point (10980) *(G-15797)*

Lightron Corporation 516 938-5544
100 Jericho Quadrangle Jericho (11753) ***(G-7107)***
Lightspin Technologies Inc 301 656-7600
616 Lowell Dr Endwell (13760) ***(G-4842)***
Lik LLC 516 848-5135
6 Bluff Point Rd Northport (11768) ***(G-13033)***
Lilac Quarries LLC 607 867-4016
1702 State Highway 8 Mount Upton (13809) ***(G-8700)***
Lilly Collection, New York *Also called Lily & Taylor Inc* ***(G-11028)***
Lillys Homestyle Bakeshop Inc 718 491-2904
6210 9th Ave Brooklyn (11220) ***(G-2225)***
Lily & Taylor Inc 212 564-5459
247 W 37th St Frnt 6 New York (10018) ***(G-11028)***
Lime Energy Co 704 892-4442
1a Elk Terminal Buffalo (14204) ***(G-3064)***
Limo-Print.com, Central Islip *Also called Color Card LLC* ***(G-3516)***
Lin Jin Feng 718 232-3039
7718 18th Ave Brooklyn (11214) ***(G-2226)***
Lincdoc LLC 585 563-1669
401 Main St East Rochester (14445) ***(G-4484)***
Linco Printing Inc 718 937-5141
5022 23rd St Long Island City (11101) ***(G-7817)***
Lincware, East Rochester *Also called Lincdoc LLC* ***(G-4484)***
Linda Campbell 718 994-4026
4420 Richardson Ave Bronx (10470) ***(G-1386)***
Linda Richards, New York *Also called Linrich Designs Inc* ***(G-11031)***
Linda Tool & Die Corporation 718 522-2066
163 Dwight St Brooklyn (11231) ***(G-2227)***
Linda Wine & Spirit 718 703-5707
1219 Flatbush Ave Brooklyn (11226) ***(G-2228)***
Linde Gas North America LLC 518 713-2015
10 Arrowhead Ln Cohoes (12047) ***(G-3773)***
Linde Gas North America LLC 315 431-4081
147 Midler Park Dr Syracuse (13206) ***(G-15999)***
Linde LLC 716 847-0748
101 Katherine St Buffalo (14210) ***(G-3065)***
Linde LLC 518 439-8187
76 W Yard Rd Feura Bush (12067) ***(G-5180)***
Linde LLC 716 773-7552
3279 Grand Island Blvd Grand Island (14072) ***(G-5776)***
Linde Merchant Production Inc 315 593-1360
370 Owens Rd Fulton (13069) ***(G-5483)***
Linden Cookies Inc 845 268-5050
25 Brenner Dr Congers (10920) ***(G-3884)***
Linden Forms & Systems Inc 212 219-1100
40 S 6th St Brooklyn (11249) ***(G-2229)***
Lindenhurst Fabricators Inc 631 226-3737
117 S 13th St Lindenhurst (11757) ***(G-7489)***
Linder New York LLC 646 678-5819
195 Chrystie St Rm 900 New York (10002) ***(G-11029)***
Lindley Wood Works Inc 607 523-7786
9625 Morgan Creek Rd Lindley (14858) ***(G-7519)***
Lindsay & Co, New York *Also called Lindsay-Hoenig Ltd* ***(G-11030)***
Lindsay Lyn Accessories Div, New York *Also called Jaclyn Inc* ***(G-10729)***
Lindsay-Hoenig Ltd 212 575-9711
64 W 48th St Ste 1306 New York (10036) ***(G-11030)***
Lindsey Adelman 718 623-3013
27 Prospect Park W Brooklyn (11215) ***(G-2230)***
Line Ward Corporation 716 675-7373
157 Seneca Creek Rd Buffalo (14224) ***(G-3066)***
Linear Lighting Corporation 718 361-7552
3130 Hunters Point Ave Long Island City (11101) ***(G-7818)***
Linear Signs Inc 631 532-5330
275 W Hoffman Ave Ste 1 Lindenhurst (11757) ***(G-7490)***
Linita Design & Mfg Corp 716 566-7753
1951 Hamburg Tpke Ste 24 Lackawanna (14218) ***(G-7270)***
Link Control Systems Inc 631 471-3950
16 Colt Ct Ronkonkoma (11779) ***(G-14960)***
Linli Color, West Babylon *Also called East Cast Clor Compounding Inc* ***(G-16815)***
Lino International Inc 516 482-7100
111 Great Neck Rd 300a Great Neck (11021) ***(G-5838)***
Lino Metal, Great Neck *Also called Lino International Inc* ***(G-5838)***
Lino Press Inc 718 665-2625
652 Southern Blvd Bronx (10455) ***(G-1387)***
Linrich Designs Inc 212 382-2257
256 W 38th St Fl 8 New York (10018) ***(G-11031)***
Lintex Linens Inc 212 679-8046
295 5th Ave Ste 1702 New York (10016) ***(G-11032)***
Linzer Products Corp (HQ) 631 253-3333
248 Wyandanch Ave West Babylon (11704) ***(G-16836)***
Lion & Bear Distributors, Jericho *Also called Satnam Distributors LLC* ***(G-7116)***
Lion Die-Cutting Co Inc 718 383-8841
95 Dobbin St Ste 1 Brooklyn (11222) ***(G-2231)***
Lion In The Sun Park Slope Ltd 718 369-4006
232 7th Ave Brooklyn (11215) ***(G-2232)***
Lionel Habas Associates Inc 212 860-8454
1601 3rd Ave Apt 22d New York (10128) ***(G-11033)***
Lipe Automation, Liverpool *Also called Ironshore Holdings Inc* ***(G-7550)***
Lippincott Massie McQuilkin L 212 352-2055
27 W 20th St Ste 305 New York (10011) ***(G-11034)***
Liptis Pharmaceuticals USA Inc 845 627-0260
110 Red Schoolhouse Rd Spring Valley (10977) ***(G-15614)***
Liquid Industries Inc 716 628-2999
7219 New Jersey Ave Niagara Falls (14305) ***(G-12860)***
Liquid Knits Inc 718 706-6600
3200 Skillman Ave Fl 2 Long Island City (11101) ***(G-7819)***
Liquid Management Partners LLC 516 775-5050
1983 Marcus Ave Ste E138 New Hyde Park (11042) ***(G-8892)***
Liquitane, Rochester *Also called Consolidated Container Co LLC* ***(G-14309)***
Liquitane, Batavia *Also called Consolidated Container Co LLC* ***(G-630)***
Liquor Bottle Packg Intl Inc 212 922-2813
305 Madison Ave Ste 1357 New York (10165) ***(G-11035)***
Lisk Coils, Phelps *Also called GW Lisk Company Inc* ***(G-13555)***
Listec Video Corp (PA) 631 273-3029
90 Oser Ave Hauppauge (11788) ***(G-6137)***
Liston Manufacturing Inc 716 695-2111
421 Payne Ave North Tonawanda (14120) ***(G-12999)***
Litchfield Fabrics of NC (PA) 518 773-9500
111 Woodside Ave Gloversville (12078) ***(G-5732)***
Lite Brite Manufacturing Inc 718 855-9797
575 President St Brooklyn (11215) ***(G-2233)***
Lite FM Radio, New York *Also called Iheartcommunications Inc* ***(G-10609)***
Lite-Makers Inc 718 739-9300
10715 180th St Jamaica (11433) ***(G-6961)***
Litelab Corp 718 361-6829
540 54th Ave Long Island City (11101) ***(G-7820)***
Litelab Corp (PA) 716 856-4300
251 Elm St Buffalo (14203) ***(G-3067)***
Literary Classics of US 212 308-3360
14 E 60th St Ste 1101 New York (10022) ***(G-11036)***
Lites On West Soho, Haverstraw *Also called Lexstar Inc* ***(G-6262)***
Litho Dynamics Inc 914 769-1759
17 Saw Mill River Rd Hawthorne (10532) ***(G-6273)***
Lithomatic Business Forms Inc 212 255-6700
233 W 18th St Frnt A New York (10011) ***(G-11037)***
Litmor Publications, Garden City *Also called Litmor Publishing Corp* ***(G-5527)***
Litmor Publishing Corp (PA) 516 931-0012
821 Franklin Ave Ste 208 Garden City (11530) ***(G-5527)***
Little Bird Chocolates Inc 646 620-6395
25 Fairchild Ave Ste 200 Massapequa (11758) ***(G-8211)***
Little Curios Confections, Massapequa *Also called Little Bird Chocolates Inc* ***(G-8211)***
Little Eric Shoes On Madison 212 717-1513
1118 Madison Ave New York (10028) ***(G-11038)***
Little Store, The, Roscoe *Also called Roscoe Little Store Inc* ***(G-15035)***
Little Trees, Watertown *Also called Car-Freshner Corporation* ***(G-16663)***
Little Valley Sand & Gravel 716 938-6676
8984 New Albion Rd Little Valley (14755) ***(G-7534)***
Little Wolf Cabinet Shop Inc 212 734-1116
1583 1st Ave Frnt 1 New York (10028) ***(G-11039)***
Littlebits Electronics Inc 917 464-4577
601 W 26th St Ste M274 New York (10001) ***(G-11040)***
Live Oak Media, Pine Plains *Also called ABRA Media Inc* ***(G-13581)***
Live Vote II Inc 646 343-9053
105 W 86th St 322 New York (10024) ***(G-11041)***
Liveright Publishing Corp 212 354-5500
500 5th Ave Fl 6 New York (10110) ***(G-11042)***
Livermoore Logging, Cassadaga *Also called Wrights Hardwoods Inc* ***(G-3443)***
Livetiles Corp 917 472-7887
60 Madison Ave Fl 8 New York (10010) ***(G-11043)***
Livid Magazine 929 340-7123
1055 Bedford Ave Apt 4c Brooklyn (11216) ***(G-2234)***
Living Doors Inc 631 924-5393
22 Scouting Blvd Ste 3 Medford (11763) ***(G-8285)***
Living Media, Long Island City *Also called Thomson Press (india) Limited* ***(G-7929)***
Living Well Innovations Inc 646 517-3200
115 Engineers Rd Hauppauge (11788) ***(G-6138)***
Livingston County News 585 243-1234
122 Main St Geneseo (14454) ***(G-5581)***
Livingston Lighting and Power, Scottsville *Also called Power and Cnstr Group Inc* ***(G-15360)***
Liz Claiborne Coats, New York *Also called Levy Group Inc* ***(G-11014)***
Liz Claiborne Swimwear, Farmingdale *Also called Swimwear Anywhere Inc* ***(G-5131)***
Liz Lange, Brooklyn *Also called Zoomers Inc* ***(G-2796)***
Lizotte Logging Inc 518 359-2200
50 Haymeadow Rd Tupper Lake (12986) ***(G-16300)***
Ljmm Inc 845 454-5876
188 Washington St Poughkeepsie (12601) ***(G-13932)***
Lk Industries Inc 716 941-9202
9731 Center St Glenwood (14069) ***(G-5718)***
Llcs Publishing Corp 718 569-2703
2071 Flatbush Ave Ste 189 Brooklyn (11234) ***(G-2235)***
Lloyd Price Icon Food Brands 914 764-8624
95 Horseshoe Hill Rd Pound Ridge (10576) ***(G-13960)***
Lloyds Fashions Inc (PA) 631 435-3353
335 Crooked Hill Rd Brentwood (11717) ***(G-1187)***
Lm Mignon LLC 212 730-9221
499 Fashion Ave Fl 4n New York (10018) ***(G-11044)***
Lmg National Publishing Inc (HQ) 585 598-6874
350 Willowbrook Office Pa Fairport (14450) ***(G-4868)***
Lmgi, Liverpool *Also called Lockheed Martin Global Inc* ***(G-7555)***
LMI, Bergen *Also called Lewis & Myers Inc* ***(G-847)***

ALPHABETIC SECTION

Loom Concepts LLC

Lmr Group Inc....212 730-9221
463 7th Ave Fl 4 New York (10018) *(G-11045)*
Lmt Technology Solutions....585 784-7470
4 Commercial St Ste 400 Rochester (14614) *(G-14501)*
Lnd, Oceanside *Also called L N D Incorporated* *(G-13106)*
LNK International Inc....631 435-3500
22 Arkay Dr Hauppauge (11788) *(G-6139)*
LNK International Inc....631 435-3500
100 Ricefield Ln Hauppauge (11788) *(G-6140)*
LNK International Inc....631 435-3500
325 Kennedy Dr Hauppauge (11788) *(G-6141)*
LNK International Inc....631 543-3787
145 Ricefield Ln Hauppauge (11788) *(G-6142)*
LNK International Inc....631 435-3500
40 Arkay Dr Hauppauge (11788) *(G-6143)*
LNK International Inc....631 231-3415
2095 Expressway Dr N Hauppauge (11788) *(G-6144)*
LNK International Inc....631 231-4020
55 Arkay Dr Hauppauge (11788) *(G-6145)*
Lo & Sons Inc....917 775-4025
55 Prospect St Brooklyn (11201) *(G-2236)*
Lo-Co Fuel Corp....631 929-5086
10 Stephen Dr Wading River (11792) *(G-16544)*
Load/N/Go Beverage Corp (PA)....585 218-4019
355 Portland Ave Rochester (14605) *(G-14502)*
Loar Group Inc (PA)....212 210-9348
450 Lexington Ave Fl 31 New York (10017) *(G-11046)*
Local Media Group Inc....845 341-1100
40 Mulberry St Middletown (10940) *(G-8480)*
Local Media Group Inc (HQ)....845 341-1100
40 Mulberry St Middletown (10940) *(G-8481)*
Local Media Group Inc....845 341-1100
60 Brookline Ave Middletown (10940) *(G-8482)*
Local Media Group Inc....845 794-3712
479 Broadway Monticello (12701) *(G-8643)*
Local Media Group Inc....845 340-4910
34 John St Kingston (12401) *(G-7226)*
Local News, Oswego *Also called Dotto Wagner* *(G-13355)*
Locations Magazine....212 288-4745
124 E 79th St New York (10075) *(G-11047)*
Locker Masters Inc....518 288-3203
10329 State Route 22 Granville (12832) *(G-5790)*
Lockheed Martin....315 456-3333
497 Electronics Pkwy Syracuse (13221) *(G-16000)*
Lockheed Martin Corporation....716 297-1000
2221 Niagara Falls Blvd Niagara Falls (14304) *(G-12861)*
Lockheed Martin Corporation....212 953-1510
420 Lexington Ave Rm 2601 New York (10170) *(G-11048)*
Lockheed Martin Corporation....315 456-1548
497 Electronics Pkwy Liverpool (13088) *(G-7553)*
Lockheed Martin Corporation....315 793-5800
8373 Seneca Tpke New Hartford (13413) *(G-8852)*
Lockheed Martin Corporation....516 228-2000
55 Charles Lindbergh Blvd # 1 Uniondale (11553) *(G-16320)*
Lockheed Martin Corporation....607 751-2000
1801 State Route 17 Owego (13827) *(G-13379)*
Lockheed Martin Corporation....607 751-7434
1801 State Rd 17c 17 C Owego (13827) *(G-13380)*
Lockheed Martin Corporation....315 456-0123
497 Electronics Pkwy # 5 Liverpool (13088) *(G-7554)*
Lockheed Martin Corporation....315 456-6604
6060 Tarbell Rd Syracuse (13206) *(G-16001)*
Lockheed Martin Corporation....212 697-1105
600 3rd Ave Fl 35 New York (10016) *(G-11049)*
Lockheed Martin Global Inc (HQ)....315 456-2982
497 Electronics Pkwy # 5 Liverpool (13088) *(G-7555)*
Lockheed Martin Overseas....315 456-0123
497 Electronics Pkwy # 7 Liverpool (13088) *(G-7556)*
Lockheed Martin Overseas LLC....301 897-6923
497 Electronics Pkwy Ep5 Liverpool (13088) *(G-7557)*
Lockhouse Distillery....716 768-4898
41 Columbia St Ste 200 Buffalo (14204) *(G-3068)*
Lockwood Trade Journal Co Inc....212 391-2060
3743 Crescent St Fl 2 Long Island City (11101) *(G-7821)*
Lodi Down & Feather, New York *Also called Sleepable Sofas Ltd* *(G-12125)*
Lodolce Machine Co Inc....845 246-7017
196 Malden Tpke Saugerties (12477) *(G-15216)*
Loffreno Cstm Interiors Contg....718 981-0319
33 Ada Pl Staten Island (10301) *(G-15721)*
Logic Controls Inc....516 248-0400
999 S Oyster Bay Rd Bethpage (11714) *(G-870)*
Logical Control Solutions Inc....585 424-5340
829 Phillips Rd Ste 100 Victor (14564) *(G-16513)*
Logical Operations Inc....585 350-7000
3535 Winton Pl Rochester (14623) *(G-14503)*
Logitek Inc....631 567-1100
110 Wilbur Pl Bohemia (11716) *(G-1089)*
Logo....212 846-2568
1515 Broadway New York (10036) *(G-11050)*
Logo Print Company....607 324-5403
135 Seneca St Hornell (14843) *(G-6592)*
Logomax Inc....631 420-0484
242 Route 109 Ste B Farmingdale (11735) *(G-5044)*

Lois Kitchen LLC....216 308-9335
206 Avenue A Apt 2a New York (10009) *(G-11051)*
Lokai Holdings LLC....646 979-3474
36 E 31st St Rm 602 New York (10016) *(G-11052)*
Lola, New York *Also called Alyk Inc* *(G-9158)*
Lollipop Tree Inc....845 471-8733
181 York St Auburn (13021) *(G-504)*
Lollytogs Ltd (PA)....212 502-6000
100 W 33rd St Ste 1012 New York (10001) *(G-11053)*
Lomak Petroleum, Mayville *Also called Range Rsurces - Appalachia LLC* *(G-8249)*
Lombardi Design & Mfg, Freeport *Also called Anna Young Assoc Ltd* *(G-5397)*
Lomin Construction Company....516 759-5734
328 Glen Cove Rd Glen Head (11545) *(G-5650)*
Lomir Inc....518 483-7697
213 W Main St Malone (12953) *(G-8043)*
Lomir Biomedical Inc, Malone *Also called Lomir Inc* *(G-8043)*
London Paris Ltd....718 564-4793
4211 13th Ave Brooklyn (11219) *(G-2237)*
London Theater News Ltd....212 517-8608
12 E 86th St Apt 620 New York (10028) *(G-11054)*
Long Ireland Brewing LLC....631 403-4303
723 Pulaski St Riverhead (11901) *(G-14160)*
Long Island Advance, Patchogue *Also called Patchogue Advance Inc* *(G-13456)*
Long Island Analytical Labs....631 472-3400
110 Colin Dr Holbrook (11741) *(G-6487)*
Long Island Brand Bevs LLC....855 542-2832
3788 Review Ave Long Island City (11101) *(G-7822)*
Long Island Business News....631 737-1700
2150 Smithtown Ave Ste 7 Ronkonkoma (11779) *(G-14961)*
Long Island Catholic Newspaper....516 594-1212
50 N Park Ave Rockville Centre (11570) *(G-14822)*
Long Island Cmnty Nwsppers Inc (PA)....516 482-4490
132 E 2nd St Mineola (11501) *(G-8555)*
Long Island Cmnty Nwsppers Inc....631 427-7000
322 Main St Huntington (11743) *(G-6703)*
Long Island Compost Corp....516 334-6600
100 Urban Ave Westbury (11590) *(G-17033)*
Long Island Fireproof Door, Port Washington *Also called Lif Industries Inc* *(G-13858)*
Long Island Geotech....631 473-1044
6 Berkshire Ct Port Jefferson (11777) *(G-13798)*
Long Island Golfer Magazine, Hicksville *Also called Golfing Magazine* *(G-6380)*
Long Island Green Guys....631 664-4306
26 Silverbrook Dr Riverhead (11901) *(G-14161)*
Long Island Iced Tea Corp (PA)....855 542-2832
12 Dubon Ct Ste 1 Farmingdale (11735) *(G-5045)*
Long Island Metalform Inc....631 242-9088
12 Lucon Dr Deer Park (11729) *(G-4191)*
Long Island Pipe Supply Inc (PA)....516 222-8008
586 Commercial Ave Garden City (11530) *(G-5528)*
Long Island Pipe Supply Inc....718 456-7877
5858 56th St Flushing (11378) *(G-5274)*
Long Island Pipe Supply Inc....518 270-2159
60 Cohoes Ave Troy (12183) *(G-16243)*
Long Island Pipe Supply Inc (PA)....516 222-8008
586 Commercial Ave Garden City (11530) *(G-5529)*
Long Island Precast Inc....631 286-0240
20 Stiriz Rd Brookhaven (11719) *(G-1508)*
Long Island Press, Farmingdale *Also called Morey Publishing* *(G-5069)*
Long Island Radiant Heat, Mastic Beach *Also called Vincent Genovese* *(G-8237)*
Long Island Spirits Inc....631 630-9322
2182 Sound Ave Calverton (11933) *(G-3320)*
Long Island Stamp & Seal Co....718 628-8550
5431 Myrtle Ave Ste 2 Ridgewood (11385) *(G-14126)*
Long Island Tool & Die Inc....631 225-0600
1445 S Strong Ave Copiague (11726) *(G-3935)*
Long Islander Newspapers LLC....631 427-7000
14 Wall St Ste A Huntington (11743) *(G-6704)*
Long Islands Best Inc....855 542-3785
1650 Sycamore Ave Ste 4b Bohemia (11716) *(G-1090)*
Long Islndr Nrth/Sth Pblctns, Huntington *Also called Long Island Cmnty Nwsppers Inc* *(G-6703)*
Long Lumber and Supply Corp....518 439-1661
2100 New Scotland Rd Slingerlands (12159) *(G-15499)*
Long Paige, New York *Also called Jiranimo Industries Ltd* *(G-10776)*
Longo Cabinets, Lindenhurst *Also called Longo Commercial Cabinets Inc* *(G-7491)*
Longo Commercial Cabinets Inc....631 225-4290
829 N Richmond Ave Lindenhurst (11757) *(G-7491)*
Longo New York Inc....212 929-7128
444 W 17th St New York (10011) *(G-11055)*
Longstem Organizers Inc....914 777-2174
380 E Main St Jefferson Valley (10535) *(G-7091)*
Longtail Studios Inc....646 443-8146
180 Varick St Rm 820 New York (10014) *(G-11056)*
Loobrica International Corp....347 997-0296
41 Darnell Ln Staten Island (10309) *(G-15722)*
Look By M Inc....212 213-4019
838 Avenue Of The America New York (10001) *(G-11057)*
Lookbooks Media Inc....646 737-3360
208 W 30th St Rm 802 New York (10001) *(G-11058)*
Loom Concepts LLC....212 813-9586
767 Lexington Ave Rm 405 New York (10065) *(G-11059)*

ALPHABETIC

Loominus Handwoven, Woodstock *Also called Marsha Fleisher* ***(G-17380)***
Loomstate LLC....212 219-2300
270 Bowery Fl 3 New York (10012) ***(G-11060)***
Looney Tunes CD Store, West Babylon *Also called Brookvale Records Inc* ***(G-16801)***
Looseleaf Law Publications Inc....718 359-5559
4308 162nd St Flushing (11358) ***(G-5275)***
Loosesleeve Law Publications, Flushing *Also called Warodean Corporation* ***(G-5312)***
Lopez Restorations Inc (PA)....718 383-1555
394 Mcguinness Blvd Ste 4 Brooklyn (11222) ***(G-2238)***
Lopopolo Iron Works Inc....718 339-0572
2495 Mcdonald Ave Brooklyn (11223) ***(G-2239)***
Loral Space & Commnctns Holdng....212 697-1105
600 5th Ave Fl 16 New York (10020) ***(G-11061)***
Loral Space Communications Inc (PA)....212 697-1105
600 5th Ave Fl 16 New York (10020) ***(G-11062)***
Loral Spacecom Corporation (HQ)....212 697-1105
565 5th Ave Fl 19 New York (10017) ***(G-11063)***
LOreal Usa Inc....212 818-1500
575 5th Ave Bsmt New York (10017) ***(G-11064)***
LOreal Usa Inc....917 606-9554
435 Hudson St New York (10014) ***(G-11065)***
LOreal Usa Inc....212 389-4201
575 5th Ave Fl 20 New York (10017) ***(G-11066)***
LOreal Usa Inc....212 984-4704
575 5th Ave Fl 23 New York (10017) ***(G-11067)***
LOreal Usa Inc....646 658-5477
575 5th Ave Fl 25 New York (10017) ***(G-11068)***
LOreal USA Products Inc (HQ)....212 818-1500
10 Hudson Yards New York (10001) ***(G-11069)***
Lorelei Orthotics Prosthetics....212 727-2011
19 W 21st St Rm 204 New York (10010) ***(G-11070)***
Loreman's, Keeseville *Also called Loremanss Embroidery Engrav* ***(G-7168)***
Loremanss Embroidery Engrav....518 834-9205
1599 Front St Keeseville (12944) ***(G-7168)***
Loremi Jewelry Inc....212 840-3429
17 W 45th St Ste 501 New York (10036) ***(G-11071)***
Lorena Canals USA Inc....844 567-3622
104 Burnside Dr Hastings On Hudson (10706) ***(G-6025)***
Lori Silverman Shoes, White Plains *Also called Lsil & Co Inc* ***(G-17160)***
Lornamead Inc....716 874-7190
175 Cooper Ave Tonawanda (14150) ***(G-16196)***
Lornamead Inc (HQ)....716 874-7190
175 Cooper St New York (10034) ***(G-11072)***
Los Olivos Ltd....631 773-6439
105 Bi County Blvd Farmingdale (11735) ***(G-5046)***
Lost Worlds Inc....212 923-3423
920 Riverside Dr Apt 68 New York (10032) ***(G-11073)***
Losurdo Foods Inc....518 842-1500
78 Sam Stratton Rd Amsterdam (12010) ***(G-355)***
Lots O' Luv, Syosset *Also called Bektrom Foods Inc* ***(G-15835)***
Lotta Luv Beauty LLC....646 786-2847
1359 Broadway Fl 17 New York (10018) ***(G-11074)***
Lotus Apparel Designs Inc....646 236-9363
661 Oakwood Ct Westbury (11590) ***(G-17034)***
Lotus Awnings Enterprises Inc....718 965-4824
157 11th St Brooklyn (11215) ***(G-2240)***
Lou Sally Fashions Corp (HQ)....212 354-9670
1400 Broadway Lbby 6 New York (10018) ***(G-11075)***
Lou Sally Fashions Corp....212 354-1283
1400 Broadway Lbby 3 New York (10018) ***(G-11076)***
Loudon Ltd....631 757-4447
281 Larkfield Rd East Northport (11731) ***(G-4460)***
Loughlin Manufacturing Corp....631 585-4422
1601 9th Ave Bohemia (11716) ***(G-1091)***
Louis Heindl & Son Inc....585 454-5080
306 Central Ave Rochester (14605) ***(G-14504)***
Louis Hornick & Co Inc....212 679-2448
117 E 38th St New York (10016) ***(G-11077)***
Louis Iannettoni....315 454-3231
1841 Lemoyne Ave Syracuse (13208) ***(G-16002)***
Louis Schwartz....845 356-6624
28 Lawrence St Spring Valley (10977) ***(G-15615)***
Louis Tamis & Sons Inc....212 684-1760
10 E 38th St Fl 6 New York (10016) ***(G-11078)***
Louis Vuitton North Amer Inc....212 644-2574
1000 3rd Ave New York (10022) ***(G-11079)***
Louise Blouin Media, Southampton *Also called Ltb Media (usa) Inc* ***(G-15570)***
Loungehouse LLC....646 524-2965
34 W 33rd St Fl 11 New York (10001) ***(G-11080)***
Lourdes Industries Inc (PA)....631 234-6600
65 Hoffman Ave Hauppauge (11788) ***(G-6146)***
Lourdes Systems Inc....631 234-7077
21 Newton Pl Hauppauge (11788) ***(G-6147)***
Love & Quiches Desserts, Freeport *Also called Saj of Freeport Corp* ***(G-5435)***
Love Bright Jewelry Inc....516 620-2509
3446 Frederick St Oceanside (11572) ***(G-13107)***
Love Unlimited NY Inc....718 359-8500
762 Summa Ave Westbury (11590) ***(G-17035)***
Lovebrightjewelry.com, Oceanside *Also called Love Bright Jewelry Inc* ***(G-13107)***
Lovee Doll & Toy Co Inc....212 242-1545
39 W 38th St Rm 4w New York (10018) ***(G-11081)***
Lovejoy Chaplet Corporation....518 686-5232
12 River St Hoosick Falls (12090) ***(G-6568)***
Lovely Bride LLC....212 924-2050
182 Duane St Frnt A New York (10013) ***(G-11082)***
Lovingly LLC....845 977-0775
1399 Route 52 Ste 100 Fishkill (12524) ***(G-5193)***
Low-Cost Mfg Co Inc....516 627-3282
318 Westbury Ave Carle Place (11514) ***(G-3419)***
Lowel-Light Manufacturing Inc....718 921-0600
140 58th St Ste 8c Brooklyn (11220) ***(G-2241)***
Lowville Farmers Coop Inc....315 376-6587
5500 Shady Ave Lowville (13367) ***(G-7966)***
Lowville Newspaper Corporation....315 376-3525
7567 S State St Lowville (13367) ***(G-7967)***
Loy L Press Inc....716 634-5966
3959 Union Rd Buffalo (14225) ***(G-3069)***
Loyaltyplant Inc (PA)....551 221-2701
70 23 Juno St Forest Hills (11375) ***(G-5331)***
Lr Acquisition LLC....212 301-8765
1407 Broadway Rm 1207 New York (10018) ***(G-11083)***
Lr Paris LLC....703 652-1132
345 7th Ave Fl 7 New York (10001) ***(G-11084)***
Lrc Electronics, Horseheads *Also called Belden Inc* ***(G-6597)***
Ls Power Equity Partners LP (PA)....212 615-3456
1700 Broadway Fl 35 New York (10019) ***(G-11085)***
Lsc Peripherals Incorporated....631 244-0707
415 Central Ave Ste F Bohemia (11716) ***(G-1092)***
LSI Computer Systems....631 271-0400
1235 Walt Whitman Rd Melville (11747) ***(G-8364)***
LSI Lightron Inc....845 562-5500
500 Hudson Valley Ave New Windsor (12553) ***(G-8988)***
Lsil & Co Inc....914 761-0998
2 Greene Ln White Plains (10605) ***(G-17160)***
Lt2 LLC....212 684-1510
250 Park Ave S Fl 10 New York (10003) ***(G-11086)***
Ltb Media (usa) Inc....212 447-9555
376 Gin Ln Southampton (11968) ***(G-15570)***
LTS (chemical) Inc....845 494-2940
37 Ramland Rd 2 Orangeburg (10962) ***(G-13256)***
Lu Biscuits, White Plains *Also called Great Brands of Europe Inc* ***(G-17140)***
Lubow Machine Corp....631 226-1700
1700 N Strongs Rd Copiague (11726) ***(G-3936)***
Lucas Dental Equipment Co Inc....631 244-2807
360 Knickerbocker Ave # 4 Bohemia (11716) ***(G-1093)***
Lucas Electric....516 809-8619
3524 Merrick Rd Seaford (11783) ***(G-15367)***
Lucas Vineyards & Winery....607 532-4825
3862 County Road 150 Interlaken (14847) ***(G-6787)***
Lucia Group Inc....631 392-4900
45 W Jefryn Blvd Ste 108 Deer Park (11729) ***(G-4192)***
Lucideon....518 382-0082
2210 Technology Dr Schenectady (12308) ***(G-15303)***
Lucinas Gourmet Food Inc....646 835-9784
3646 37th St Long Island City (11101) ***(G-7823)***
Lucky Brand, New York *Also called Trebbianno LLC* ***(G-12418)***
Lucky Brand Dungarees LLC....631 350-7358
100 Walt Whitman Rd 1090b Huntington Station (11746) ***(G-6752)***
Lucky Magazine....212 286-6220
4 Times Sq Fl 22 New York (10036) ***(G-11087)***
Lucky Peach LLC....212 228-0031
60 E 11th St Fl 5 New York (10003) ***(G-11088)***
Ludl Electronic Products Ltd....914 769-6111
171 Brady Ave Hawthorne (10532) ***(G-6274)***
Ludlow Music Inc....212 594-9795
266 W 37th St Fl 17 New York (10018) ***(G-11089)***
Ludwig Holdings Corp....845 340-9727
20 Kieffer Ln Kingston (12401) ***(G-7227)***
Lugo Nutrition Inc....302 573-2503
51 N Broadway Unit 2b Nyack (10960) ***(G-13069)***
Luitpold Pharmaceuticals Inc (HQ)....631 924-4000
5 Ramsey Rd Shirley (11967) ***(G-15446)***
Luitpold Pharmaceuticals Inc....631 924-4000
5 Ramsey Rd Shirley (11967) ***(G-15447)***
Lukas Lighting Inc....800 841-4011
4020 22nd St Ste 11 Long Island City (11101) ***(G-7824)***
Luke's Copy Shop, Staten Island *Also called R & L Press of SI Inc* ***(G-15748)***
Lukoil Americas Corporation (HQ)....212 421-4141
505 5th Ave Fl 9 New York (10017) ***(G-11090)***
Lukoil North America LLC (HQ)....212 421-4141
505 5th Ave Fl 9 New York (10017) ***(G-11091)***
Lulu DK LLC....212 223-4234
245 E 60th St Apt 1 New York (10022) ***(G-11092)***
Luluvise Inc....914 309-7812
229 W 116th St Apt 5a New York (10026) ***(G-11093)***
Lumazu LLC....518 623-3372
141 Garnet Lake Rd Warrensburg (12885) ***(G-16600)***
Lumazu LLC (PA)....518 623-3372
484 S Johnsburg Rd Warrensburg (12885) ***(G-16601)***
Lumetrics Inc....585 214-2455
1565 Jefferson Rd Ste 420 Rochester (14623) ***(G-14505)***
Lumia Energy Solutions LLC....516 478-5795
48 Jericho Tpke Jericho (11753) ***(G-7108)***

Luminary Publishing Inc.....845 334-8600
314 Wall St Kingston (12401) *(G-7228)*
Luminati Aerospace LLC.....631 574-2616
400 David Ct Calverton (11933) *(G-3321)*
Luminatta Inc.....914 664-3600
717 S 3rd Ave Mount Vernon (10550) *(G-8748)*
Luminescent Systems Inc (HQ).....716 655-0800
130 Commerce Way East Aurora (14052) *(G-4398)*
Luna Luz, New York *Also called Azibi Ltd (G-9339)*
Luria Communications Inc.....631 329-4922
31 Shorewood Dr Fl 1 East Hampton (11937) *(G-4433)*
Luthier Musical Corp.....212 397-6038
49 W 24th St Fl 4 New York (10010) *(G-11094)*
Luvente, Long Island City *Also called Benlee Enterprises LLC (G-7714)*
Lux Accessories, New York *Also called International Inspirations Ltd (G-10677)*
Lux Mundi Corp.....631 244-4596
10 Colt Ct Ronkonkoma (11779) *(G-14962)*
Luxe Imagine Consulting LLC.....212 273-9770
261 W 35th St Ste 404 New York (10001) *(G-11095)*
Luxerdame Co Inc.....718 752-9800
4315 Queens St Ste A Long Island City (11101) *(G-7825)*
Luxfer Magtech Inc.....631 727-8600
680 Elton St Riverhead (11901) *(G-14162)*
Luxo Corporation.....914 345-0067
5 Westchester Plz Ste 110 Elmsford (10523) *(G-4770)*
Lwa Works Inc.....518 271-8360
2622 7th Ave Ste 50s Watervliet (12189) *(G-16711)*
Lycian Stage Lighting, Chester *Also called Ric-Lo Productions Ltd (G-3640)*
Lydall Performance Mtl Inc.....518 273-6320
68 George St Green Island (12183) *(G-5877)*
Lydall Performance Mtls Inc.....518 273-6320
68 George St Green Island (12183) *(G-5878)*
Lydia H Soifer & Assoc Inc.....914 683-5401
1025 Westchester Ave White Plains (10604) *(G-17161)*
Lyn Jo Enterprises Ltd.....716 753-2776
Rr 394 Box 147 Mayville (14757) *(G-8248)*
Lyn Jo Kitchens Inc.....718 336-6060
1679 Mcdonald Ave Brooklyn (11230) *(G-2242)*
Lynch Knitting Mills Inc.....718 821-3436
538 Johnson Ave Brooklyn (11237) *(G-2243)*
Lyndaker Timber Harvesting LLC.....315 346-1328
10204 State Route 812 Castorland (13620) *(G-3452)*
Lynmar Printing Corp.....631 957-8500
8600 New Horizons Blvd Amityville (11701) *(G-306)*
Lyntronics Inc.....631 205-1061
7 Old Dock Rd Unit 1 Yaphank (11980) *(G-17412)*
Lynx Analytics Inc.....475 227-7347
32 W 39th St Fl 4 New York (10018) *(G-11096)*
Lynx Product Group LLC.....716 751-3100
650 Lake St Wilson (14172) *(G-17291)*
Lyons & Sullivan Inc.....518 584-1523
376 Caroline St Saratoga Springs (12866) *(G-15192)*
Lyophilization Systems Inc.....845 338-0456
14 Hickory Hill Rd New Paltz (12561) *(G-8921)*
Lyric Lighting Ltd Inc.....718 497-0109
4825 Metro Ave Ste 3 Ridgewood (11385) *(G-14127)*
M & C Furniture.....718 422-2136
375 Park Ave Brooklyn (11205) *(G-2244)*
M & D Fire Door, Brooklyn *Also called M & D Installers Inc (G-2245)*
M & D Installers Inc (PA).....718 782-6978
70 Flushing Ave Brooklyn (11205) *(G-2245)*
M & D Millwork LLC.....631 789-1439
178 New Hwy Amityville (11701) *(G-307)*
M & E Mfg Co Inc.....845 331-7890
19 Progress St Kingston (12401) *(G-7229)*
M & H Research and Dev Corp.....607 734-2346
471 Post Creek Rd Beaver Dams (14812) *(G-788)*
M & J Custom Lampshade Company, Brooklyn *Also called Mjk Enterprises LLC (G-2329)*
M & L Steel & Ornamental Iron.....718 816-8660
27 Housman Ave Staten Island (10303) *(G-15723)*
M & M Bagel Corp.....516 295-1222
507 Central Ave Cedarhurst (11516) *(G-3484)*
M & M Canvas & Awnings Inc.....631 424-5370
180 Oval Dr Islandia (11749) *(G-6838)*
M & M Food Products Inc.....718 821-1970
286 Scholes St Brooklyn (11206) *(G-2246)*
M & M Molding Corp.....631 582-1900
250 Creative Dr Central Islip (11722) *(G-3530)*
M & M Signs & Awnings, Islandia *Also called M & M Canvas & Awnings Inc (G-6838)*
M & R Design, New York *Also called Mrinalini Inc (G-11339)*
M & R Woodworking & Finishing.....718 486-5480
49 Withers St Brooklyn (11211) *(G-2247)*
M & S Precision Machine Co LLC.....518 747-1193
27 Casey Rd Queensbury (12804) *(G-14017)*
M & S Quality Co Ltd.....212 302-8757
26 W 47th St Ste 502 New York (10036) *(G-11097)*
M & S Schmalberg Inc.....212 244-2090
242 W 36th St Rm 700 New York (10018) *(G-11098)*
M & W Aluminum Products Inc.....315 414-0005
321 Wavel St Syracuse (13206) *(G-16003)*
M &L Industry of NY Inc.....845 827-6255
583 State Route 32 Ste 1u Highland Mills (10930) *(G-6439)*
M A C, Elmsford *Also called Magnetic Analysis Corporation (G-4771)*
M A M Knitting Mills Corp.....800 570-0093
43 Hall St Brooklyn (11205) *(G-2248)*
M A Moslow & Bros Inc.....716 896-2950
375 Norfolk Ave Buffalo (14215) *(G-3070)*
M A R A Metals Ltd.....718 786-7868
2520 40th Ave Long Island City (11101) *(G-7826)*
M and J Hair Center Inc.....516 872-1010
1103 Stewart Ave Ste 100 Garden City (11530) *(G-5530)*
M and M Industrial Welding.....631 451-6044
2890 Route 112 Medford (11763) *(G-8286)*
M B C Metal Inc.....718 384-6713
68 Lombardy St Brooklyn (11222) *(G-2249)*
M B M Manufacturing Inc.....718 769-4148
331 Rutledge St Ste 203 Brooklyn (11211) *(G-2250)*
M C Kitchen & Bath, Brooklyn *Also called M & C Furniture (G-2244)*
M C Packaging Corp Plant, Babylon *Also called M C Packaging Corporation (G-547)*
M C Packaging Corporation (PA).....631 694-3012
200 Adams Blvd Farmingdale (11735) *(G-5047)*
M C Packaging Corporation.....631 643-3763
300 Governor Ave Babylon (11704) *(G-547)*
M C Products.....631 471-4070
1330 Lincoln Ave Ste 2 Holbrook (11741) *(G-6488)*
M D I, Shirley *Also called Modular Devices Inc (G-15449)*
M D I Industries, Deer Park *Also called MD International Industries (G-4197)*
M D L, New York *Also called Meryl Diamond Ltd (G-11262)*
M F L B Inc.....631 254-8300
7 Grant Ave Bay Shore (11706) *(G-712)*
M F Manufacturing Enterprises.....516 822-5135
2 Ballad Ln Hicksville (11801) *(G-6392)*
M Factory USA Inc (HQ).....917 410-7878
32 33rd St Unit 5 Brooklyn (11232) *(G-2251)*
M G New York Inc.....212 371-5566
14 E 60th St Ste 400 New York (10022) *(G-11099)*
M H Mandelbaum Orthotic.....631 473-8668
116 Oakland Ave Port Jefferson (11777) *(G-13799)*
M H Manufacturing Incorporated.....212 461-6900
50 W 47th St New York (10036) *(G-11100)*
M H Stryke Co Inc.....631 242-2660
181 E Industry Ct Ste A Deer Park (11729) *(G-4193)*
M Heskia Company Inc.....212 768-1845
98 Cutter Rd Ste 125 New York (10036) *(G-11101)*
M Hidary & Co Inc.....212 736-6540
10 W 33rd St Rm 900 New York (10001) *(G-11102)*
M I, Hauppauge *Also called Mason Industries Inc (G-6152)*
M I I, Mamaroneck *Also called Marval Industries Inc (G-8071)*
M I T Poly-Cart Corp.....212 724-7290
211 Central Park W New York (10024) *(G-11103)*
M J K, Brooklyn *Also called Mjk Cutting Inc (G-2328)*
M J M Tooling Corp.....718 292-3590
1059 Washington Ave Bronx (10456) *(G-1388)*
M K S, Rochester *Also called Mks Medical Electronics (G-14538)*
M K Ulrich Construction Inc.....716 893-5777
1601 Harlem Rd Buffalo (14206) *(G-3071)*
M L A, New York *Also called Modern Language Assn Amer Inc (G-11315)*
M L Design Inc (PA).....212 233-0213
77 Ludlow St Frnt 1 New York (10002) *(G-11104)*
M M Tool and Manufacturing.....845 691-4140
175 Chapel Hill Rd Highland (12528) *(G-6432)*
M M Welding.....315 363-3980
558 Lenox Ave Oneida (13421) *(G-13180)*
M Manastrip-M Corporation.....518 664-2089
821 Main St Clifton Park (12065) *(G-3726)*
M O S S Communications, Franklin Square *Also called Movin On Sounds and SEC Inc (G-5375)*
M P I, Tarrytown *Also called Micro Powders Inc (G-16120)*
M R C, Buffalo *Also called Tchnologies N MRC Ameerica LLC (G-3235)*
M R C Industries Inc.....516 328-6900
99 Seaview Blvd Ste 210 Port Washington (11050) *(G-13860)*
M S B International Ltd (PA).....212 302-5551
1412 Broadway Rm 1210 New York (10018) *(G-11105)*
M Santoliquido Corp.....914 375-6674
925 Saw Mill River Rd Yonkers (10710) *(G-17481)*
M Shanken Communications Inc (PA).....212 684-4224
825 8th Ave Fl 33 New York (10019) *(G-11106)*
M Squared Graphics, Oyster Bay *Also called Miroddi Imaging Inc (G-13398)*
M T D Corporation.....631 491-3905
41 Otis St West Babylon (11704) *(G-16837)*
M T M Printing Co Inc.....718 353-3297
2321 College Point Blvd College Point (11356) *(G-3820)*
M V Sport, Bay Shore *Also called Mv Corp Inc (G-717)*
M W Microwave Corp.....516 295-1814
45 Auerbach Ln Lawrence (11559) *(G-7419)*
M&A Metals, Brooklyn *Also called Interior Metals (G-2108)*
M&C Associates LLC.....631 467-8760
700 Vets Memrl Hwy 335 Hauppauge (11788) *(G-6148)*
M&F Stringing LLC.....914 664-1600
2 Cortlandt St Mount Vernon (10550) *(G-8749)*
M&G Duravent Inc.....518 463-7284
10 Jupiter Ln Albany (12205) *(G-99)*

M&H Soaring, Beaver Dams *Also called M & H Research and Dev Corp* **(G-788)**
M&M Printing Inc 516 796-3020
245 Westbury Ave Carle Place (11514) **(G-3420)**
M&S Accessory Network Corp 347 492-7790
10 W 33rd St Rm 718 New York (10001) **(G-11107)**
M. C. Container, Brooklyn *Also called Base Container Inc* **(G-1666)**
M/Wbe, Brooklyn *Also called Active World Solutions Inc* **(G-1558)**
M2 Apparel, New York *Also called M2 Fashion Group Holdings Inc* **(G-11108)**
M2 Fashion Group Holdings Inc 917 208-2948
153 E 87th St Apt 10d New York (10128) **(G-11108)**
M2 Race Systems Inc 607 882-9078
53 Enfield Main Rd Ithaca (14850) **(G-6892)**
M3 Graphic Group Ltd 212 366-0863
150 W 28th St Ste 504 New York (10001) **(G-11109)**
M3 Promotion, New York *Also called M3 Graphic Group Ltd* **(G-11109)**
Mac Artspray Finishing Corp 718 649-3800
799 Sheffield Ave Brooklyn (11207) **(G-2252)**
Mac Crete Corporation 718 932-1803
3412 10th St Long Island City (11106) **(G-7827)**
Mac Donuts of New York, Long Island City *Also called Mac Crete Corporation* **(G-7827)**
Mac Innes Enterprises Inc 325 676-4032
61 John Muir Dr Buffalo (14228) **(G-3072)**
Mac Swed Inc 212 684-7730
20 W 36th St Rm 5l New York (10018) **(G-11110)**
Mac-Artspray Finshg, Brooklyn *Also called Mac Artspray Finishing Corp* **(G-2252)**
Macadoodles 607 652-9019
26 River St Stamford (12167) **(G-15645)**
Macaran Printed Products, Cohoes *Also called W N Vanalstine & Sons Inc* **(G-3786)**
Macauto Usa Inc 585 342-2060
80 Excel Dr Rochester (14621) **(G-14506)**
Macedonia Ltd 718 462-3596
34 E 29th St Brooklyn (11226) **(G-2253)**
Macfadden Cmmnctions Group LLC 212 979-4800
333 7th Ave Fl 11 New York (10001) **(G-11111)**
Machias Furniture Factory Inc (PA) 716 353-8687
3638 Route 242 Machias (14101) **(G-8023)**
Machida Incorporated 845 365-0600
40 Ramland Rd S Ste 1 Orangeburg (10962) **(G-13257)**
Machina Deus Lex Inc 917 577-0972
15921 Grand Central Pkwy Jamaica (11432) **(G-6962)**
Machine Clothing Company, New York *Also called Billion Tower Intl LLC* **(G-9449)**
Machine Components Corp 516 694-7222
70 Newtown Rd Plainview (11803) **(G-13644)**
Machine Technology Inc 845 454-4030
104 Bushwick Rd Poughkeepsie (12603) **(G-13933)**
Machine Tool Repair & Sales 631 580-2550
1537 Lincoln Ave Holbrook (11741) **(G-6489)**
Machine Tool Specialty 315 699-5287
8125 Thompson Rd Cicero (13039) **(G-3677)**
Machinecraft Inc 585 436-1070
1645 Lyell Ave Ste 125 Rochester (14606) **(G-14507)**
Machinery Mountings Inc 631 851-0480
41 Sarah Dr Hauppauge (11788) **(G-6149)**
Machinit Inc 631 454-9297
400 Smith St Farmingdale (11735) **(G-5048)**
Machoonjdgroup 856 345-4689
18 Victorian Ln Medford (11763) **(G-8287)**
Macinnes Tool Corporation 585 467-1920
1700 Hudson Ave Ste 3 Rochester (14617) **(G-14508)**
Mack Studios Displays Inc 315 252-7542
5500 Technology Park Blvd Auburn (13021) **(G-505)**
Mack Wood Working 845 657-6625
2792 State Route 28 Shokan (12481) **(G-15455)**
Mackenzie-Childs LLC (PA) 315 364-6118
3260 State Route 90 Aurora (13026) **(G-528)**
Maclean Curtis, Buffalo *Also called Curtis L Maclean L C* **(G-2915)**
Macmillan Academic Pubg Inc (HQ) 212 226-1476
75 Varick St Fl 9 New York (10013) **(G-11112)**
Macmillan College Pubg Co Inc 212 702-2000
866 3rd Ave Frnt 2 New York (10022) **(G-11113)**
Macmillan Holdings LLC 212 576-9428
1 New York Plz Ste 4500 New York (10004) **(G-11114)**
Macmillan Publishers Inc 646 307-5151
175 5th Ave Ste 400 New York (10010) **(G-11115)**
Macmillan Publishing Group LLC (HQ) 212 674-5151
175 5th Ave New York (10010) **(G-11116)**
Macneil Polymers Inc (PA) 716 681-7755
3155 Broadway St Buffalo (14227) **(G-3073)**
Maco Bag Corporation 315 226-1000
412 Van Buren St Newark (14513) **(G-12755)**
Macro Tool & Machine Company 845 223-3824
1397 Route 55 Lagrangeville (12540) **(G-7280)**
Macrochem Corporation (HQ) 212 514-8094
80 Broad St Ste 2210 New York (10004) **(G-11117)**
Macrodyne Inc 518 383-3800
1 Fairchild Sq Ste 5 Clifton Park (12065) **(G-3727)**
Macrolink Inc 631 924-8200
25 Scouting Blvd Ste 1 Medford (11763) **(G-8288)**
Mad Scntsts Brwing Prtners LLC 347 766-2739
40 Van Dyke St Brooklyn (11231) **(G-2254)**
Madame Alexander Doll Co LLC 212 244-4500
112 W 34th St Ste 1207 New York (10120) **(G-11118)**
Madden Zone, New York *Also called Steven Madden Ltd* **(G-12225)**
Made Close LLC 917 837-1357
141 Meserole Ave Brooklyn (11222) **(G-2255)**
Made Fresh Daily 212 285-2253
226 Front St New York (10038) **(G-11119)**
Madelaine Chocolate Company, Rockaway Beach *Also called Madelaine Chocolate Novlt Inc* **(G-14810)**
Madelaine Chocolate Novlt Inc (PA) 718 945-1500
9603 Beach Channel Dr Rockaway Beach (11693) **(G-14810)**
Madhat Inc 518 947-0732
149 Sullivan St Apt 3e New York (10012) **(G-11120)**
Madison & Dunn 585 563-7760
850 Saint Paul St Ste 29 Rochester (14605) **(G-14509)**
Madison County Distillery LLC 315 391-6070
2420 Rte 20 Cazenovia (13035) **(G-3474)**
Madison Electric 718 358-4121
21916 Linden Blvd Cambria Heights (11411) **(G-3331)**
Madison Industries Inc (PA) 212 679-5110
295 5th Ave Ste 512 New York (10016) **(G-11121)**
Madison Manufacturing, Hamilton *Also called James Morris* **(G-5971)**
Madison Printing Corp 607 273-3535
704 W Buffalo St Ithaca (14850) **(G-6893)**
Madison Square Press, New York *Also called Annuals Publishing Co Inc* **(G-9215)**
Madisons Delight LLC 718 720-8900
711 Forest Ave Staten Island (10310) **(G-15724)**
Madjek Inc 631 842-4475
185 Dixon Ave Amityville (11701) **(G-308)**
Madoff Energy III LLC 212 744-1918
319 Lafayette St New York (10012) **(G-11122)**
Madonna, New York *Also called Haddad Bros Inc* **(G-10437)**
Madrid Fire District 315 322-4346
26 10 Church St Madrid (13660) **(G-8024)**
Maehr Industries Inc 631 924-1661
14 Sawgrass Dr Bellport (11713) **(G-829)**
Mafco Consolidated Group Inc (HQ) 212 572-8600
35 E 62nd St New York (10065) **(G-11123)**
Mag Brands LLC 212 629-9600
463 7th Ave Fl 4 New York (10018) **(G-11124)**
Mag Inc 607 257-6970
20 Eastlake Rd Ithaca (14850) **(G-6894)**
Magazine Antiques, The, New York *Also called Brant Publications Inc* **(G-9506)**
Magazine Group, New York *Also called Thomas Publishing Company LLC* **(G-12344)**
Magazine I Spectrum E 212 419-7555
3 Park Ave Fl 17 New York (10016) **(G-11125)**
Magazines & Brochures Inc 716 875-9699
2205 Kenmore Ave Ste 107 Buffalo (14207) **(G-3074)**
Magcrest Packaging Inc 845 425-0451
5 Highview Rd Monsey (10952) **(G-8609)**
Mageba USA LLC 212 317-1991
575 Lexington Ave Fl 4 New York (10022) **(G-11126)**
Magee Canvas & Trailer Sales, Brewerton *Also called Geordie Magee Uphl & Canvas* **(G-1200)**
Magellan Aerospace Bethel Inc 203 798-9373
9711 50th Ave Corona (11368) **(G-4024)**
Magellan Aerospace NY Inc (HQ) 718 699-4000
9711 50th Ave Corona (11368) **(G-4025)**
Magellan Aerospace NY Inc 631 589-2440
25 Aero Rd Bohemia (11716) **(G-1094)**
Magellan Aerospace Processing 631 694-1818
165 Field St West Babylon (11704) **(G-16838)**
Mager & Gougelman Inc (PA) 212 661-3939
345 E 37th St Rm 316 New York (10016) **(G-11127)**
Mager & Gougelman Inc 212 661-3939
230 Hilton Ave Ste 112 Hempstead (11550) **(G-6302)**
Mager & Gougelman Inc 516 489-0202
230 Hilton Ave Ste 112 Hempstead (11550) **(G-6303)**
Maggio Data Forms Printing Ltd 631 348-0343
1735 Express Dr N Hauppauge (11788) **(G-6150)**
Maggy Boutique Ltd 212 997-5222
530 Fashion Ave Fl 6 New York (10018) **(G-11128)**
Maggy London, New York *Also called Maggy Boutique Ltd* **(G-11128)**
Maggy London Blouse Div, New York *Also called Maggy London International Ltd* **(G-11129)**
Maggy London International Ltd (PA) 212 944-7199
530 Fashion Ave Fl 16 New York (10018) **(G-11129)**
Magic Brands International LLC 212 563-4999
31 W 34th St Rm 401 New York (10001) **(G-11130)**
Magic Maestro Music, New York *Also called Simon & Simon LLC* **(G-12103)**
Magic Novelty Co Inc (PA) 212 304-2777
308 Dyckman St New York (10034) **(G-11131)**
Magic Numbers Inc 646 839-8578
29 Little West 12th St New York (10014) **(G-11132)**
Magic Tank LLC 877 646-2442
80 Maiden Ln Rm 2204 New York (10038) **(G-11133)**
Magic Tech Co Ltd 516 539-7944
401 Hempstead Tpke West Hempstead (11552) **(G-16891)**
Magic Touch Icewares Intl 212 794-2852
220 E 72nd St Apt 11g New York (10021) **(G-11134)**
Magna Products Corp 585 647-2280
777 Mount Read Blvd Rochester (14606) **(G-14510)**
Magnaworks Technology Inc 631 218-3431
36 Carlough Rd Unit H Bohemia (11716) **(G-1095)**

Magnet Wire Division, Edgewood *Also called Weico Wire & Cable Inc* ***(G-4634)***
Magnet-Ndctive Systems Ltd USA.....585 924-4000
7625 Omnitech Pl Victor (14564) ***(G-16514)***
Magnetic Aids Inc.....845 863-1400
201 Ann St Newburgh (12550) ***(G-12787)***
Magnetic Analysis Corporation (PA).....914 530-2000
103 Fairview Pk Dr Ste 2 Elmsford (10523) ***(G-4771)***
Magnetic Technologies Corp (HQ).....585 385-9010
770 Linden Ave Rochester (14625) ***(G-14511)***
Magnetic Technology, Rochester *Also called Arnold Magnetic Tech Corp* ***(G-14228)***
Magnificat Inc.....914 502-1820
86 Main St Ste 303 Yonkers (10701) ***(G-17482)***
Magniflood Inc.....631 226-1000
7200 New Horizons Blvd Amityville (11701) ***(G-309)***
Magnolia Bakery, New York *Also called Magnolia Operating LLC* ***(G-11135)***
Magnolia Operating LLC (PA).....212 265-2777
1841 Broadway New York (10023) ***(G-11135)***
Magnum Creation Inc.....212 642-0993
23 W 47th St Fl 5 New York (10036) ***(G-11136)***
Magnum Energy Partners, Brooklyn *Also called Mep Alaska LLC* ***(G-2302)***
Magnum Shielding Corporation.....585 381-9957
3800 Monroe Ave Ste 14f Pittsford (14534) ***(G-13596)***
Magnus Precision Mfg Inc.....315 548-8032
1912 State Route 96 Phelps (14532) ***(G-13557)***
Magnus Sands Point Shop, Port Washington *Also called Robert Bartholomew Ltd* ***(G-13876)***
Magpump LLC.....585 444-9812
235 Middle Rd Ste 600 Henrietta (14467) ***(G-6320)***
Magsoft Corporation.....518 877-8390
2715 State Route 9 # 102 Ballston Spa (12020) ***(G-601)***
Magtrol Inc.....716 668-5555
70 Gardenville Pkwy W Buffalo (14224) ***(G-3075)***
Maharam Fabric Corporation.....631 582-3434
74 Horseblock Rd Yaphank (11980) ***(G-17413)***
Maharlika Holdings LLC.....631 319-6203
111 Trade Zone Ct Unit A Ronkonkoma (11779) ***(G-14963)***
Mahin Impressions Inc.....212 871-9777
30 W Main St Ste 301 Riverhead (11901) ***(G-14163)***
Mahle Behr USA Inc.....716 439-2011
350 Upper Mountain Rd Lockport (14094) ***(G-7627)***
Mahle Indstrbeteiligungen GMBH.....716 319-6700
4236 Ridge Lea Rd Amherst (14226) ***(G-248)***
Mahle Industries Incorporated.....248 735-3623
4236 Ridge Lea Rd Amherst (14226) ***(G-249)***
Maia Systems LLC.....718 206-0100
8344 Parsons Blvd Ste 101 Jamaica (11432) ***(G-6963)***
Maidenform LLC.....201 436-9200
260 Madison Ave Fl 6 New York (10016) ***(G-11137)***
Maidstone Coffee Co.....585 272-1040
60 Mushroom Blvd Rochester (14623) ***(G-14512)***
Mailers-Pblsher Wlfare Tr Fund.....212 869-5986
1501 Broadway New York (10036) ***(G-11138)***
Main Street Connect LLC.....203 803-4110
200 Business Park Dr # 209 Armonk (10504) ***(G-415)***
Main Street Sweets.....914 332-5757
35 Main St Tarrytown (10591) ***(G-16117)***
Maine Coil & Transformer Co, Johnson City *Also called Donald R Husband Inc* ***(G-7122)***
Mainly Monograms Inc.....845 624-4923
260 W Nyack Rd Ste 1 West Nyack (10994) ***(G-16949)***
Maio Fuel Company LP.....914 683-1154
46 Fairview Ave White Plains (10603) ***(G-17162)***
Maison Goyard, New York *Also called Goyard Miami LLC* ***(G-10384)***
Maiyet Inc.....212 343-9999
16 Crosby St Apt Corp New York (10013) ***(G-11139)***
Maizteca Foods Inc.....718 641-3933
13005 Liberty Ave South Richmond Hill (11419) ***(G-15558)***
Majestic Curtains LLC.....718 898-0774
4410 Ketcham St Apt 2g Elmhurst (11373) ***(G-4678)***
Majestic Home Imprvs Distr.....718 853-5079
5902 Fort Hamilton Pkwy Brooklyn (11219) ***(G-2256)***
Majestic Mold & Tool Inc.....315 695-2079
177 Volney St Phoenix (13135) ***(G-13569)***
Majestic Rayon Corporation.....212 929-6443
116 W 23rd St Fl 4 New York (10011) ***(G-11140)***
Majic Corrugated Inc, Batavia *Also called Georgia-Pacific Corrugared LLC* ***(G-637)***
Major-IPC Inc.....845 292-2200
53 Webster Ave Liberty (12754) ***(G-7460)***
Makarenko Studios Inc.....914 968-7673
2984 Saddle Ridge Dr Yorktown Heights (10598) ***(G-17528)***
Makari, New York *Also called Victoria Albi Intl Inc* ***(G-12563)***
Make My Cake II Inc.....212 234-2344
2380 Adam Clytn Powll Jr New York (10030) ***(G-11141)***
Make-Waves Instrument Corp (PA).....716 681-7524
4172 Vinewood Dr Buffalo (14221) ***(G-3076)***
Makerbot Industries LLC (HQ).....347 334-6800
1 Metrotech Ctr Fl 21 Brooklyn (11201) ***(G-2257)***
Makerbot Industries LLC.....347 457-5758
298 Mulberry St New York (10012) ***(G-11142)***
Makers Nutrition LLC (PA).....631 456-5397
315 Oser Ave Ste 3 Hauppauge (11788) ***(G-6151)***
Makins Hats Ltd.....212 594-6666
212 W 35th St Fl 12 New York (10001) ***(G-11143)***
Makiplastic.....716 772-2222
4904 Gasport Rd Gasport (14067) ***(G-5573)***
Malcon Inc.....914 666-7146
405 Adams St Bedford Hills (10507) ***(G-801)***
Male Power Apparel, Hauppauge *Also called Comme-Ci Comme-CA AP Group* ***(G-6070)***
Maler Technologies Inc.....212 391-2070
337 E 81st St Bsmt New York (10028) ***(G-11144)***
Malhame Publs & Importers Inc.....631 694-8600
180 Orville Dr Unit A Bohemia (11716) ***(G-1096)***
Malia Mills, Brooklyn *Also called IaMmaliamills LLC* ***(G-2091)***
Malia Mills Inc.....212 354-4200
32 33rd St Unit 13 Brooklyn (11232) ***(G-2258)***
Malibu Cabinets, Suffern *Also called American Best Cabinets Inc* ***(G-15807)***
Malin + Goetz Inc (PA).....212 244-7771
330 7th Ave Ste 2100 New York (10001) ***(G-11145)***
Malina Management Company Inc.....607 535-9614
3620 County Road 16 Montour Falls (14865) ***(G-8649)***
Malisa Branko Inc.....631 225-9741
95 Garfield Ave Copiague (11726) ***(G-3937)***
Mallery Lumber LLC.....607 637-2236
158 Labarre St Hancock (13783) ***(G-5987)***
Mallinckrodt LLC.....607 538-9124
172 Railroad Ave Hobart (13788) ***(G-6452)***
Mallinckrodt Pharmaceuticals, Hobart *Also called Mallinckrodt LLC* ***(G-6452)***
Mallory & Church LLC.....212 868-7888
552 Fashion Ave Rm 202 New York (10018) ***(G-11146)***
Malone Concrete Products Div, Malone *Also called Upstone Materials Inc* ***(G-8050)***
Malone Industrial Press Inc.....518 483-5880
10 Stevens St Malone (12953) ***(G-8044)***
Malone News, Malone *Also called Johnson Newspaper Corporation* ***(G-8042)***
Malone Newspapers Corp.....518 483-2000
469 E Main St Ste 2 Malone (12953) ***(G-8045)***
Malone Telegram, Malone *Also called Malone Newspapers Corp* ***(G-8045)***
Malone Welding, Montour Falls *Also called Robert M Brown* ***(G-8650)***
Malouf Colette Inc.....212 941-9588
594 Broadway Rm 1216 New York (10012) ***(G-11147)***
Maloya Laser Inc.....631 543-2327
65a Mall Dr Ste 1 Commack (11725) ***(G-3863)***
Malyn Industrial Ceramics Inc.....716 741-1510
8640 Roll Rd Clarence Center (14032) ***(G-3705)***
Mam Knitg, Brooklyn *Also called M A M Knitting Mills Corp* ***(G-2248)***
Mam USA Corporation.....914 269-2500
2700 Westchester Ave # 315 Purchase (10577) ***(G-13977)***
Mama Luca Production Inc.....212 582-9700
156 W 56th St Ste 1803 New York (10019) ***(G-11148)***
Mamas.....518 399-2828
119 Lake Hill Rd Burnt Hills (12027) ***(G-3293)***
Mamco, Oneonta *Also called Mold-A-Matic Corporation* ***(G-13211)***
Mamitas Ices Ltd.....718 738-3238
10411 100th St Ozone Park (11417) ***(G-13409)***
Mamma Says, Ferndale *Also called Chipita America Inc* ***(G-5176)***
Man of World.....212 915-0017
25 W 39th St Fl 5 New York (10018) ***(G-11149)***
Man Products Inc.....631 789-6500
99 Milbar Blvd Unit 1 Farmingdale (11735) ***(G-5049)***
Mana Products Inc (PA).....718 361-2550
3202 Queens Blvd Fl 6 Long Island City (11101) ***(G-7828)***
Mana Products Inc.....718 361-5204
3202 Queens Blvd Fl 6 Long Island City (11101) ***(G-7829)***
Manacraft Precision Inc.....914 654-0967
945 Spring Rd Pelham (10803) ***(G-13518)***
Manchester Newspaper Inc (PA).....518 642-1234
14 E Main St Granville (12832) ***(G-5791)***
Manchester Wood Inc.....518 642-9518
1159 County Route 24 Granville (12832) ***(G-5792)***
Manchu New York Inc.....212 921-5050
530 Fashion Ave Rm 1906 New York (10018) ***(G-11150)***
Manchu Times Fashion Inc.....212 921-5050
530 Sventh Ave Ste 1906 New York (10018) ***(G-11151)***
Mancum Graphics, New York *Also called Mc Squared Nyc Inc* ***(G-11217)***
Mandalay Food Products Inc.....718 230-3370
640 Dean St Brooklyn (11238) ***(G-2259)***
Mandarin Soy Sauce Inc.....845 343-1505
4 Sands Station Rd Middletown (10940) ***(G-8483)***
MANE Enterprises Inc.....718 472-4955
3100 47th Ave Ste 5100 Long Island City (11101) ***(G-7830)***
Mango Usa Inc.....718 998-6050
5620 1st Ave Ste 1 Brooklyn (11220) ***(G-2260)***
Manhasset Tool & Die Co Inc.....716 684-6066
4270 Walden Ave Lancaster (14086) ***(G-7349)***
Manhattan Cabinets, Island Park *Also called A-1 Manhattan Custom Furn Inc* ***(G-6817)***
Manhattan Cabinets Inc.....212 548-2436
1349 2nd Ave New York (10021) ***(G-11152)***
Manhattan Cooling Towers Inc.....212 279-1045
1142 46th Rd Long Island City (11101) ***(G-7831)***
Manhattan Display Inc.....718 392-1365
1215 Jackson Ave Ste B Long Island City (11101) ***(G-7832)***
Manhattan Eastside Dev Corp.....212 305-3275
622 W 168th St Ste Vc333 New York (10032) ***(G-11153)***
Manhattan Map Co, New York *Also called Yale Robbins Inc* ***(G-12709)***

ALPHABETIC

Manhattan Media LLC (PA)...212 268-8600
72 Madison Ave Fl 11 New York (10016) **(G-11154)**
Manhattan Milling & Drying Co...516 496-1041
78 Pond Rd Woodbury (11797) **(G-17314)**
Manhattan Neon Sign Corp...212 714-0430
640 W 28th St Fl 2 New York (10001) **(G-11155)**
Manhattan Poly Bag Corporation...917 689-7549
1228 47th St Brooklyn (11219) **(G-2261)**
Manhattan Scientifics Inc (PA)...212 541-2405
405 Lexington Ave Fl 26 New York (10174) **(G-11156)**
Manhattan Shade & Glass Co Inc (PA)...212 288-5616
1299 3rd Ave Frnt New York (10021) **(G-11157)**
Manhattan Signs, Floral Park *Also called Decree Signs & Graphics Inc* **(G-5209)**
Manhattan Special Bottling...718 388-4144
342 Manhattan Ave Brooklyn (11211) **(G-2262)**
Manhattan Times Inc...212 569-5800
5030 Broadway Ste 801 New York (10034) **(G-11158)**
Manhole Brrier SEC Systems Inc...516 741-1032
8002 Kew Gardens Rd # 901 Kew Gardens (11415) **(G-7194)**
Manifestation-Glow Press Inc...718 380-5259
7740 164th St Fresh Meadows (11366) **(G-5458)**
Manifold Center, The, Medford *Also called B & R Industries Inc* **(G-8267)**
Manitou Concrete...585 424-6040
1260 Jefferson Rd Rochester (14623) **(G-14513)**
Mann Consultants LLC...914 763-0512
67 Chapel Rd Waccabuc (10597) **(G-16541)**
Mann Publications Inc...212 840-6266
450 Fashion Ave Ste 2306 New York (10123) **(G-11159)**
Mannesmann Corporation...212 258-4000
601 Lexington Ave Fl 56 New York (10022) **(G-11160)**
Manning Lewis Div Rubicon Inds...908 687-2400
848 E 43rd St Brooklyn (11210) **(G-2263)**
Mannington Mills Inc...212 251-0290
200 Lexington Ave Rm 430 New York (10016) **(G-11161)**
Mannix, Brentwood *Also called Interstate Window Corporation* **(G-1183)**
Manny Grunberg Inc...212 302-6173
62 W 47th St Ste 703 New York (10036) **(G-11162)**
Manor Electric Supply Corp...718 648-8003
2737 Ocean Ave Brooklyn (11229) **(G-2264)**
Manrico Cashmere, New York *Also called Manrico Usa Inc* **(G-11163)**
Manrico Usa Inc...212 794-4200
922 Madison Ave New York (10021) **(G-11163)**
Manrico Usa Inc (PA)...212 794-4200
922 Madison Ave New York (10021) **(G-11164)**
Mansfield Press Inc...212 265-5411
599 11th Ave Fl 3 New York (10036) **(G-11165)**
Mansueto Ventures LLC...212 389-5300
7 World Trade Ctr Fl 29 New York (10007) **(G-11166)**
Mantel & Mantel Stamping Corp...631 467-1916
802 S 4th St Ronkonkoma (11779) **(G-14964)**
Manth Mfg Inc...716 693-6525
131 Fillmore Ave Tonawanda (14150) **(G-16197)**
Manth-Brownell Inc...315 687-7263
1120 Fyler Rd Kirkville (13082) **(G-7254)**
Manuf Appld Renova Sys...518 654-9084
105 Mill St Corinth (12822) **(G-3981)**
Manufacturers Indexing Pdts...631 271-0956
53 Gristmill Ln Halesite (11743) **(G-5928)**
Manufacturers Tool & Die Co...585 352-1080
3 Turner Dr Spencerport (14559) **(G-15596)**
Manufacturing, Lockport *Also called Hti Recycling LLC* **(G-7623)**
Manufacturing Facility, Middletown *Also called President Cont Group II LLC* **(G-8492)**
Manufacturing Resources Inc...631 481-0041
2392 Innovation Way # 4 Rochester (14624) **(G-14514)**
Manufacturing Solutions Inc...585 235-3320
850 Saint Paul St Ste 11 Rochester (14605) **(G-14515)**
Manzella Knitting...716 825-0808
3345 N Benzing Rd Orchard Park (14127) **(G-13306)**
Manzione Enterprises, Brooklyn *Also called Manzione Ready Mix Corp* **(G-2265)**
Manzione Ready Mix Corp...718 628-3837
46 Knickerbocker Ave Brooklyn (11237) **(G-2265)**
Mapeasy Inc...631 537-6213
54 Industrial Rd Wainscott (11975) **(G-16548)**
Maple Grove and Enterprises, Arcade *Also called Maple Grove Corp* **(G-396)**
Maple Grove Corp...585 492-5286
7075 Route 98 Arcade (14009) **(G-396)**
Maple Hill Creamery LLC (PA)...518 758-7777
285 Allendale Rd W Stuyvesant (12173) **(G-15804)**
Maple Hill Creamery LLC...518 758-7777
5 Hudson St Kinderhook (12106) **(G-7197)**
Maplehurst Bakeries LLC...315 735-5000
178 Industrial Park Dr Frankfort (13340) **(G-5364)**
Mapleland Farms LLC...518 854-7669
647 Bunker Hill Rd Salem (12865) **(G-15138)**
Maplewood Ice Co Inc...518 499-2345
9785 State Route 4 Whitehall (12887) **(G-17218)**
Mar-A-Thon Filters Inc...631 957-4774
369 41st St Lindenhurst (11757) **(G-7492)**
Maracle Industrial Finshg Co...585 387-9077
93 Kilbourn Rd Rochester (14618) **(G-14516)**
Maramont Corporation (PA)...718 439-8900
5600 1st Ave Brooklyn (11220) **(G-2266)**
Marathon Boat Group Inc...607 849-3211
1 Grumman Way Marathon (13803) **(G-8116)**
Marathon Enterprises Inc...718 665-2560
787 E 138th St Bronx (10454) **(G-1389)**
Marathon Heater Co Inc...607 657-8113
13 Town Barn Rd Richford (13835) **(G-14076)**
Marathon Roofing Products Inc...716 685-3340
3310 N Benzing Rd Orchard Park (14127) **(G-13307)**
Marble Doctors LLC...203 628-8339
244 5th Ave Ste 2608 New York (10001) **(G-11167)**
Marble Knits Inc...718 237-7990
544 Park Ave Ste 3 Brooklyn (11205) **(G-2267)**
Marble Knitting Mills, Brooklyn *Also called Marble Knits Inc* **(G-2267)**
Marble Works Inc...914 376-3653
660 Saw Mill River Rd Yonkers (10710) **(G-17483)**
Marcal Printing Inc...516 942-9500
85 N Broadway Hicksville (11801) **(G-6393)**
Marcasiano Inc...212 614-9412
296 Elizabeth St Apt 2f New York (10012) **(G-11168)**
Marcel Finishing Corp...718 381-2889
4 David Ct Plainview (11803) **(G-13645)**
Marcellus Energy Services LLC...607 236-0038
3 Mill St Ste 6 Candor (13743) **(G-3404)**
Marchesa Accesories, New York *Also called Akh Group LLC* **(G-9118)**
Marco Hi-Tech JV LLC (PA)...212 798-8100
475 Park Ave S Fl 10 New York (10016) **(G-11169)**
Marco Manufacturing Inc...845 485-1571
55 Page Park Dr Poughkeepsie (12603) **(G-13934)**
Marco Moore Inc...212 575-2090
825 Northern Blvd Ste 201 Great Neck (11021) **(G-5839)**
Marcon Electronic Systems LLC...516 633-6396
152 Westend Ave Freeport (11520) **(G-5420)**
Marcon Services...516 223-8019
152 Westend Ave Freeport (11520) **(G-5421)**
Marconi Intl USA Co Ltd...212 391-2626
214 W 39th St Rm 1100 New York (10018) **(G-11170)**
Marcovicci-Wenz Engineering...631 467-9040
33 Comac Loop Unit 10 Ronkonkoma (11779) **(G-14965)**
Marcus Goldman Inc...212 431-0707
37 W 39th St Rm 1201 New York (10018) **(G-11171)**
Marcy Business Forms Inc...718 935-9100
1468 40th St Brooklyn (11218) **(G-2268)**
Marcy Printing Inc...718 935-9100
777 Kent Ave Ste A Brooklyn (11205) **(G-2269)**
Mardek LLC...585 735-9333
73 N Wilmarth Rd Pittsford (14534) **(G-13597)**
Mardon Tool & Die Co Inc...585 254-4545
19 Lois St Rochester (14606) **(G-14517)**
Marex Aquisition Corp...585 458-3940
1385 Emerson St Rochester (14606) **(G-14518)**
Mari Strings Inc...212 799-6781
14 W 71st St New York (10023) **(G-11172)**
Maria Dionisio Welding Inc...631 956-0815
71 W Montauk Hwy Lindenhurst (11757) **(G-7493)**
Mariah Metal Products Inc...516 938-9783
89 Tec St Hicksville (11801) **(G-6394)**
Marie Claire, New York *Also called Hearst Corporation* **(G-10487)**
Marie Claire USA...212 841-8493
300 W 57th St Fl 34 New York (10019) **(G-11173)**
Marietta Corporation (HQ)...607 753-6746
37 Huntington St Cortland (13045) **(G-4057)**
Marietta Corporation...607 753-0982
106 Central Ave Cortland (13045) **(G-4058)**
Marigold Signs Inc...516 433-7446
485 S Broadway Ste 34 Hicksville (11801) **(G-6395)**
Marilyn Model Management Inc...646 556-7587
32 Union Sq E Ph 1 New York (10003) **(G-11174)**
Marina Holding Corp...718 646-9283
3939 Emmons Ave Brooklyn (11235) **(G-2270)**
Marina Ice Cream...718 235-3000
888 Jamaica Ave Brooklyn (11208) **(G-2271)**
Marina Jewelry Co Inc...212 354-5027
42 W 48th St Ste 804 New York (10036) **(G-11175)**
Marine & Indus Hydraulics Inc...914 698-2036
329 Center Ave Mamaroneck (10543) **(G-8070)**
Marine Boiler & Welding Inc...718 378-1900
1428 Sheridan Expy Bronx (10459) **(G-1390)**
Marine Park Appliances LLC...718 513-1808
3412 Avenue N Brooklyn (11234) **(G-2272)**
Marinos Italian Ices, Richmond Hill *Also called Olympic Ice Cream Co Inc* **(G-14089)**
Marion's Italian Ices, Jamaica *Also called Olympic Ice Cream Co Inc* **(G-6974)**
Maripharm Laboratories...716 984-6520
2045 Niagara Falls Blvd Niagara Falls (14304) **(G-12862)**
Maritime Activity Reports (PA)...212 477-6700
118 E 25th St Fl 2 New York (10010) **(G-11176)**
Maritime Broadband Inc...347 404-6041
1143 47th Ave Long Island City (11101) **(G-7833)**
Mark - 10 Corporation...631 842-9200
11 Dixon Ave Copiague (11726) **(G-3938)**
Mark Dri Products Inc...516 484-6200
999 S Oyster Bay Rd # 312 Bethpage (11714) **(G-871)**
Mark Ecko Enterprises, New York *Also called Mee Accessories LLC* **(G-11244)**

Mark F Rosenhaft N A O.....516 374-1010
538 Central Ave Cedarhurst (11516) *(G-3485)*
Mark I Publications Inc.....718 205-8000
7119 80th St Ste 8201 Glendale (11385) *(G-5673)*
Mark King Jewelry Inc.....212 921-0746
62 W 47th St Ste 310r New York (10036) *(G-11177)*
Mark Levine.....212 677-4457
149 5th Ave Fl 10 New York (10010) *(G-11178)*
Mark Nelson Designs LLC.....646 422-7020
404 E 55th St Fl 4 New York (10022) *(G-11179)*
Mark Peri International.....516 208-6824
3516 Hargale Rd Oceanside (11572) *(G-13108)*
Mark Posner.....718 258-6241
1950 52nd St Brooklyn (11204) *(G-2273)*
Mark Robinson Inc.....212 223-3515
18 E 48th St Rm 1102 New York (10017) *(G-11180)*
Mark T Westinghouse.....518 678-3262
138 Grandview Ave Catskill (12414) *(G-3459)*
Markar Architectural Products.....716 685-4104
68 Ward Rd Lancaster (14086) *(G-7350)*
Marken LLP.....631 396-7454
123 Smith St Farmingdale (11735) *(G-5050)*
Market Factory Inc.....212 625-9988
425 Broadway Fl 3 New York (10013) *(G-11181)*
Market Logic Software Inc.....646 405-1041
80 Pine St Fl 24 New York (10005) *(G-11182)*
Market Place Publications.....516 997-7909
234 Silverlake Blvd Ste 2 Carle Place (11514) *(G-3421)*
Marketer's Forum Magazine, Centerport *Also called Forum Publishing Co* *(G-3501)*
Marketfax Information Services, Hastings On Hudson *Also called Alternative Technology Corp* *(G-6022)*
Marketing Action Xecutives Inc.....212 971-9155
50 W 96th St Apt 7b New York (10025) *(G-11183)*
Marketing Group International.....631 754-8095
1 Stargazer Ct Northport (11768) *(G-13034)*
Marketplace Slutions Group LLC.....631 868-0111
48 Nimbus Rd Ste 303 Holbrook (11741) *(G-6490)*
Marketplace, The, Chester *Also called Advertiser Publications Inc* *(G-3625)*
Marketresearchcom Inc.....212 807-2600
641 Ave Of The America New York (10011) *(G-11184)*
Markets Media LLC.....646 442-4646
110 Wall St Fl 15 New York (10005) *(G-11185)*
Marketshare LLC.....631 273-0598
90 Cain Dr Brentwood (11717) *(G-1188)*
Markin Tubing LP (PA).....585 495-6211
1 Markin Ln Wyoming (14591) *(G-17396)*
Markin Tubing LP.....585 495-6211
400 Ingham Ave Buffalo (14218) *(G-3077)*
Markin Tubing Division, Buffalo *Also called Markin Tubing LP* *(G-3077)*
Markin Tubing Inc.....585 495-6211
Pearl Creek Rd Wyoming (14591) *(G-17397)*
Markowitz Jewelry Co Inc.....845 774-1175
53 Forest Rd Ste 104 Monroe (10950) *(G-8596)*
Markpericom.....516 208-6824
3516 Hargale Rd Oceanside (11572) *(G-13109)*
Marks Corpex Banknote Co (PA).....631 968-0277
1440 5th Ave Bay Shore (11706) *(G-713)*
Marks USA, Amityville *Also called G Marks Hdwr Liquidating Corp* *(G-287)*
Marksmen Manufacturing Corp.....800 305-6942
355 Marcus Blvd Deer Park (11729) *(G-4194)*
Marktech International Corp (PA).....518 956-2980
3 Northway Ln N Latham (12110) *(G-7401)*
Marktech Optoelectronics, Latham *Also called Marktech International Corp* *(G-7401)*
Markwik Corp.....516 470-1990
309 W John St Hicksville (11801) *(G-6396)*
Marlborough Jewels Inc.....718 768-2000
67 35th St Unit 2 Brooklyn (11232) *(G-2274)*
Marley Spoon Inc.....646 934-6970
601 W 26th St Rm 900 New York (10001) *(G-11186)*
Marlou Garments Inc.....516 739-7100
2115 Jericho Tpke New Hyde Park (11040) *(G-8893)*
Marlow Printing Co Inc.....718 625-4948
667 Kent Ave Brooklyn (11249) *(G-2275)*
Marly Home Industries USA Inc.....718 388-3030
181 Lombardy St Brooklyn (11222) *(G-2276)*
Marmach Machine Inc.....585 768-8800
11 Lent Ave Le Roy (14482) *(G-7438)*
Marnier-Lapostolle Inc.....212 207-4350
183 Madison Ave New York (10016) *(G-11187)*
Marotta Dental Studio Inc.....631 249-7520
130 Finn Ct Farmingdale (11735) *(G-5051)*
Marovato Industries Inc.....718 389-0800
100 Dobbin St Brooklyn (11222) *(G-2277)*
Marplex Furniture Corporation.....914 969-7755
167 Saw Mill Rver Rd Fl 1 Yonkers (10701) *(G-17484)*
Marquardt Switches Inc (HQ).....315 655-8050
2711 Us Route 20 Cazenovia (13035) *(G-3475)*
Marretti USA Inc.....212 255-5565
101 Ave Of The Americas New York (10013) *(G-11188)*
Marros Equipment & Trucks.....315 539-8702
2354 State Route 414 Waterloo (13165) *(G-16652)*
Mars, Corinth *Also called Manuf Appld Renova Sys* *(G-3981)*
Mars Fashions Inc.....718 402-2200
780 E 134th St Fl 5 Bronx (10454) *(G-1391)*
Marsal & Sons, Lindenhurst *Also called Middleby Corporation* *(G-7495)*
Marsha Fleisher.....845 679-6500
18 Tinker St Woodstock (12498) *(G-17380)*
Marshall Cavendish Corp.....914 332-8888
99 White Plains Rd Tarrytown (10591) *(G-16118)*
Marshall Ingredients LLC.....800 796-9353
5786 Limekiln Rd Wolcott (14590) *(G-17301)*
Marsid Group Ltd.....516 334-1603
245 Westbury Ave Carle Place (11514) *(G-3422)*
Marsid Press, Carle Place *Also called Marsid Group Ltd* *(G-3422)*
MARsid-M&m Group, The, Carle Place *Also called M&M Printing Inc* *(G-3420)*
Mart-Tex Athletics Inc.....631 454-9583
180 Allen Blvd Farmingdale (11735) *(G-5052)*
Martec Industries.....585 458-3940
1385 Emerson St Rochester (14606) *(G-14519)*
Martens Country Kit Pdts LLC.....315 776-8821
1323 Towpath Rd Port Byron (13140) *(G-13762)*
Martha & Marley Spoon, New York *Also called Marley Spoon Inc* *(G-11186)*
Martha Stewart Living (HQ).....212 827-8000
601 W 26th St Rm 900 New York (10001) *(G-11189)*
Martha Stewart Living Omni LLC.....212 827-8000
20 W 43rd St New York (10036) *(G-11190)*
Martin Brass Works Inc.....718 523-3146
17544 Liberty Ave Jamaica (11433) *(G-6964)*
Martin Chafkin.....718 383-1155
1155 Manhattan Ave # 431 Brooklyn (11222) *(G-2278)*
Martin D Whitbeck.....607 746-7642
68 Meredith St Delhi (13753) *(G-4265)*
Martin Dental Studio, Watertown *Also called Martins Dental Studio* *(G-16686)*
Martin Flyer Incorporated.....212 840-8899
70 W 36th St Rm 602 New York (10018) *(G-11191)*
Martin Greenfield Clothiers.....718 497-5480
239 Varet St Brooklyn (11206) *(G-2279)*
Martin Orna Ir Works II Inc.....516 354-3923
266 Elmont Rd Elmont (11003) *(G-4734)*
Martinelli Holdings LLC.....302 504-1361
2 Clinton Ave Rye (10580) *(G-15088)*
Martinelli Publications, Yonkers *Also called Yonkers Time Publishing Co* *(G-17519)*
Martinez Hand Made Cigars.....212 239-4049
171 W 29th St Frnt A New York (10001) *(G-11192)*
Martinez Specialties Inc.....607 898-3053
205 Bossard Rd Groton (13073) *(G-5922)*
Martins Dental Studio.....315 788-0800
162 Sterling St Watertown (13601) *(G-16686)*
Marval Industries Inc.....914 381-2400
315 Hoyt Ave Mamaroneck (10543) *(G-8071)*
Marvel Dairy Whip Inc.....516 889-4232
258 Lido Blvd Lido Beach (11561) *(G-7463)*
Marvel Entertainment LLC (HQ).....212 576-4000
135 W 50th St Fl 7 New York (10020) *(G-11193)*
Marvel Equipment Corp Inc.....718 383-6597
215 Eagle St Brooklyn (11222) *(G-2280)*
Marvellissima Intl Ltd.....212 682-7306
333 E 46th St Apt 20a New York (10017) *(G-11194)*
Marx Myles Graphic Services, New York *Also called X Myles Mar Inc* *(G-12699)*
Mary Ann Liebert Inc.....914 740-2100
140 Huguenot St Fl 3 New Rochelle (10801) *(G-8962)*
Mary Bright Inc.....212 677-1970
269 E 10th St Apt 7 New York (10009) *(G-11195)*
Mary F Morse.....315 866-2741
125 Columbia St Ste 1 Mohawk (13407) *(G-8575)*
Marzullo Electric LLC.....315 455-1050
103 Oliva Dr Syracuse (13211) *(G-16004)*
Mas Cutting Inc.....212 869-0826
257 W 39th St Rm 11e New York (10018) *(G-11196)*
Masick Soil Conservation Co.....518 827-5354
4860 State Route 30 Schoharie (12157) *(G-15339)*
Mason & Gore Inc.....914 921-1025
2 Clinton Ave Rye (10580) *(G-15089)*
Mason Carvings Inc.....716 484-7884
2871 Ivystone Dr Jamestown (14701) *(G-7050)*
Mason Contract Products LLC.....516 328-6900
85 Denton Ave New Hyde Park (11040) *(G-8894)*
Mason Industries Inc (PA).....631 348-0282
350 Rabro Dr Hauppauge (11788) *(G-6152)*
Mason Industries Inc.....631 348-0282
33 Ranick Rd Ste 1 Hauppauge (11788) *(G-6153)*
Mason Medical Products, Port Washington *Also called M R C Industries Inc* *(G-13860)*
Mason Scott Industries LLC.....516 349-1800
159 Westwood Cir Roslyn Heights (11577) *(G-15054)*
Mason Transparent Package Inc.....718 792-6000
1180 Commerce Ave Bronx (10462) *(G-1392)*
Mason Woodworks LLC.....917 363-7052
127 Chester Ave Brooklyn (11218) *(G-2281)*
Masonville Stone Incorporated.....607 265-3597
12999 State Highway 8 Masonville (13804) *(G-8138)*
Maspeth Press Inc.....718 429-2363
6620 Grand Ave Maspeth (11378) *(G-8180)*
Maspeth Steel Fabricators Inc.....718 361-9192
5215 11th St Ste 21 Long Island City (11101) *(G-7834)*

ALPHABETIC

Maspeth Welding Inc...718 497-5430
5930 54th St Maspeth (11378) ***(G-8181)***
Mass Appeal Magazine...718 858-0979
261 Vandervoort Ave Brooklyn (11211) ***(G-2282)***
Mass Mdsg Self Selection Eqp...631 234-3300
35 Orville Dr Ste 2 Bohemia (11716) ***(G-1097)***
Massapequa Post...516 798-5100
1045b Park Blvd Massapequa Park (11762) ***(G-8221)***
Massapqua Prcsion McHining Ltd...631 789-1485
30 Seabro Ave Amityville (11701) ***(G-310)***
Massena Metals Inc...315 769-3846
86 S Racquette River Rd Massena (13662) ***(G-8229)***
Massena Ready Mix, Massena *Also called Upstone Materials Inc* ***(G-8233)***
Massimo Friedman Inc...716 836-0408
2495 Main St Ste 457 Buffalo (14214) ***(G-3078)***
Mast Brothers Inc...718 388-2625
63 Flushing Ave Unit 341 Brooklyn (11205) ***(G-2283)***
Masten Enterprises LLC (PA)...845 932-8206
420 Bernas Rd Cochecton (12726) ***(G-3767)***
Master & Dynamics, New York *Also called New Audio LLC* ***(G-11402)***
Master Art Corp...845 362-6430
131 Clinton Ln Ste E Spring Valley (10977) ***(G-15616)***
Master Craft Finishers Inc...631 586-0540
30 W Jefryn Blvd Ste 1 Deer Park (11729) ***(G-4195)***
Master Craft Jewelry Co Inc...516 599-1012
150 Vincent Ave Lynbrook (11563) ***(G-7981)***
Master Image Printing Inc...914 347-4400
75 N Central Ave Ste 202 Elmsford (10523) ***(G-4772)***
Master Juvenile Products Inc...845 647-8400
70 Berme Rd Ellenville (12428) ***(G-4649)***
Master Machine Incorporated...716 487-2555
155 Blackstone Ave Jamestown (14701) ***(G-7051)***
Master Molding Inc...631 694-1444
97 Gazza Blvd Farmingdale (11735) ***(G-5053)***
Master Window & Door Corp...718 782-5407
199 Starr St Brooklyn (11237) ***(G-2284)***
Master-Halco Inc...631 585-8150
54 Union Ave Ste B Ronkonkoma (11779) ***(G-14966)***
Mastercraft Decorators Inc...585 223-5150
320 Macedon Center Rd Fairport (14450) ***(G-4869)***
Mastercraft Manufacturing Co...718 729-5620
3715 11th St Long Island City (11101) ***(G-7835)***
Masterdisk Corporation...212 541-5022
134 S Central Ave Ste C Elmsford (10523) ***(G-4773)***
Masterpiece Color LLC...917 279-6056
12 E 46th St Fl 2 New York (10017) ***(G-11197)***
Masterpiece Diamonds LLC...212 986-1515
12 E 46th St Fl 2 New York (10017) ***(G-11198)***
Mastro Concrete Inc...718 528-6788
15433 Brookville Blvd Rosedale (11422) ***(G-15038)***
Mastro Graphic Arts Inc...585 436-7570
67 Deep Rock Rd Rochester (14624) ***(G-14520)***
Mata Fashions LLC...917 716-7894
222 W 37th St Fl 4 New York (10018) ***(G-11199)***
Mata Ig...212 979-7921
332 Bleecker St New York (10014) ***(G-11200)***
Mataci Inc...212 502-1899
247 W 35th St Fl 15 New York (10001) ***(G-11201)***
Match Eyewear LLC...516 877-0170
1600 Shames Dr Westbury (11590) ***(G-17036)***
Matchables Inc...718 389-9318
106 Green St Ste G1 Brooklyn (11222) ***(G-2285)***
Material Measuring Corporation...516 334-6167
121 Hopper St Westbury (11590) ***(G-17037)***
Material Process Systems Inc...718 302-3081
87 Richardson St Ste 2 Brooklyn (11211) ***(G-2286)***
Materials Design Workshop...718 893-1954
830 Barry St Bronx (10474) ***(G-1393)***
Materials Recovery Company...518 274-3681
8000 Main St Troy (12180) ***(G-16264)***
Materion Advanced Materials (HQ)...800 327-1355
2978 Main St Buffalo (14214) ***(G-3079)***
Materion Advanced Materials...800 327-1355
42 Mount Ebo Rd S Brewster (10509) ***(G-1220)***
Materion Brewster LLC...845 279-0900
42 Mount Ebo Rd S Brewster (10509) ***(G-1221)***
Materne North America Corp (HQ)...212 675-7881
20 W 22nd St Fl 12 New York (10010) ***(G-11202)***
Matheson Tri-Gas Inc...518 203-5003
15 Green Mountain Dr Cohoes (12047) ***(G-3774)***
Matheson Tri-Gas Inc...518 439-0362
1297 Feura Bush Rd Feura Bush (12067) ***(G-5181)***
Mathisen Ventures Inc...212 986-1025
441 Lexington Ave Rm 809 New York (10017) ***(G-11203)***
Matic Industries Inc...718 886-5470
1540 127th St College Point (11356) ***(G-3821)***
Matov Industries Inc...718 392-5060
1011 40th Ave Long Island City (11101) ***(G-7836)***
Matrix Machining Corp...631 643-6690
69 B Nancy St Unitb West Babylon (11704) ***(G-16839)***
Matrix Railway Corp...631 643-1483
69 Nancy St Unit A West Babylon (11704) ***(G-16840)***
Matrix Steel Company Inc...718 381-6800
50 Bogart St Brooklyn (11206) ***(G-2287)***
Matrixcare Inc...518 583-6400
575 8th Ave Fl 15 New York (10018) ***(G-11204)***
Matrox Graphics Inc...518 561-4417
625 State Route 3 1/2 Plattsburgh (12901) ***(G-13703)***
Matt Industries Inc (PA)...315 472-1316
6761 Thompson Rd Syracuse (13211) ***(G-16005)***
Matt Textile Inc...212 967-6010
142 W 36th St Fl 3 New York (10018) ***(G-11205)***
Mattel Inc...716 714-8514
609 Girard Ave East Aurora (14052) ***(G-4399)***
Matteo & Antonio Bartolotta...315 252-2220
282 State St Auburn (13021) ***(G-506)***
Matteson Logging Inc...585 593-3037
2808 Beech Hill Rd Wellsville (14895) ***(G-16780)***
Mattessich Iron LLC...315 409-8496
1484 New State Route 31 Memphis (13112) ***(G-8394)***
Matthew Shively LLC...914 937-3531
28 Bulkley Ave Port Chester (10573) ***(G-13779)***
Matthew-Lee Corporation...631 226-0100
149 Pennsylvania Ave Lindenhurst (11757) ***(G-7494)***
Matthews Hats...718 859-4683
99 Kenilworth Pl Fl 1 Brooklyn (11210) ***(G-2288)***
Mauceri Sign & Awning Co, Jamaica *Also called Mauceri Sign Inc* ***(G-6965)***
Mauceri Sign Inc...718 656-7700
16725 Rockaway Blvd Jamaica (11434) ***(G-6965)***
Maurice Max Inc...212 334-6573
49 W 27th St Fl 5 New York (10001) ***(G-11206)***
Maury's Cookie Dough, New York *Also called City Bakery Inc* ***(G-9681)***
Mausner Equipment Co Inc...631 689-7358
8 Heritage Ln Setauket (11733) ***(G-15402)***
Maven Marketing LLC (PA)...615 510-3248
349 5th Ave Fl 8 New York (10016) ***(G-11207)***
Maverik Lacrosse LLC...516 213-3050
535 W 24th St Fl 5 New York (10011) ***(G-11208)***
Maviano Corp...845 494-2598
21 Robert Pitt Dr Ste 207 Monsey (10952) ***(G-8610)***
Mavito Fine Jewelry Ltd Inc...212 398-9384
37 W 47th St Ste 500 New York (10036) ***(G-11209)***
Max 200 Performance Dog Eqp...315 776-9588
2113 State Route 31 Port Byron (13140) ***(G-13763)***
Max Brenner Union Square LLC...646 467-8803
841 Broadway New York (10003) ***(G-11210)***
Max Kahan Inc...212 575-4646
20 W 47th St Ste 300 New York (10036) ***(G-11211)***
Max Leon Inc...845 928-8201
825 Adirondack Way Central Valley (10917) ***(G-3553)***
Maxam North America Inc...313 322-8651
3 Cemetary Dr Ogdensburg (13669) ***(G-13139)***
Maxi Companies Inc...315 446-1002
4317 E Genesee St De Witt (13214) ***(G-4108)***
Maxim Hygiene Products Inc (PA)...516 621-3323
121 E Jericho Tpke Mineola (11501) ***(G-8556)***
Maximillion Communications LLC...212 564-3945
245 W 17th St Fl 2 New York (10011) ***(G-11212)***
Maximum Security Products Corp...518 233-1800
3 Schoolhouse Ln Waterford (12188) ***(G-16634)***
Maxine Denker Inc (PA)...212 689-1440
212 Manhattan St Staten Island (10307) ***(G-15725)***
Maxivision, Long Island City *Also called Bestec Concept Inc* ***(G-7715)***
Maxsecure Systems Inc...800 657-4336
300 International Dr # 100 Buffalo (14221) ***(G-3080)***
Maxsun Corporation (PA)...718 418-6800
5711 49th St Maspeth (11378) ***(G-8182)***
Maxsun Furnishings, Maspeth *Also called Maxsun Corporation* ***(G-8182)***
Maxus Pharmaceuticals Inc...631 249-0003
50 Executive Blvd Ste B Farmingdale (11735) ***(G-5054)***
Maxwell Bakery Inc...718 498-2200
2700 Atlantic Ave Brooklyn (11207) ***(G-2289)***
Maxworld Inc...212 242-7588
213 W 14th St New York (10011) ***(G-11213)***
May Ship Repair Contg Corp...718 442-9700
3075 Richmond Ter Ste 3 Staten Island (10303) ***(G-15726)***
May Tool & Die Inc...716 695-1033
9 Hackett Dr Tonawanda (14150) ***(G-16198)***
Maybelline Inc...212 885-1310
575 5th Ave Bsmt Fl New York (10017) ***(G-11214)***
Mayberry Shoe Company Inc...315 692-4086
131 W Seneca St Ste B Manlius (13104) ***(G-8107)***
Maybrook Asphalt, Montgomery *Also called Tilcon New York Inc* ***(G-8639)***
Mayer Bros Apple Products Inc (PA)...716 668-1787
3300 Transit Rd West Seneca (14224) ***(G-16980)***
Mayfair Machine Company Inc...631 981-6644
128 Remington Blvd Ronkonkoma (11779) ***(G-14967)***
Mayflower Splint Co...631 549-5131
16 Arbor Ln Dix Hills (11746) ***(G-4316)***
Mayim Chaim Beverages, Bronx *Also called New York Bottling Co Inc* ***(G-1410)***
Maz Digital Inc (PA)...646 692-9799
135 W 26th St Ste 10a New York (10001) ***(G-11215)***
Mazel Supply...212 947-2213
1439 Ocean Ave Apt B10 Brooklyn (11230) ***(G-2290)***

ALPHABETIC SECTION
Medek Laboratories Inc

Mazza Classics Incorporated 631 390-9060
117 Gazza Blvd Farmingdale (11735) *(G-5055)*
Mazza Co, The, North Baldwin *Also called W & B Mazza & Sons Inc (G-12930)*
Mazzella Blasting Mat Co, Bronx *Also called T M International LLC (G-1469)*
MB Food Processing Inc 845 436-5001
5190 S Fallsburg Main St South Fallsburg (12779) *(G-15543)*
MB Plastics Inc (PA) 718 523-1180
130 Stony Hollow Rd Greenlawn (11740) *(G-5892)*
MBA Orthotics Inc 631 392-4755
60 Corbin Ave Unit 60g Bay Shore (11706) *(G-714)*
Mbh Furniture Innovations Inc 845 354-8202
28 Lincoln Ave Spring Valley (10977) *(G-15617)*
MBI Firearms, Mineola *Also called Michael Britt Inc (G-8558)*
Mbny LLC (PA) 646 467-8810
260 5th Ave Fl 9 New York (10001) *(G-11216)*
Mbss, Kew Gardens *Also called Manhole Brrier SEC Systems Inc (G-7194)*
Mc Coy Tops and Covers, Woodside *Also called Mc Coy Tops and Interiors Inc (G-17353)*
Mc Coy Tops and Interiors Inc 718 458-5800
6914 49th Ave Woodside (11377) *(G-17353)*
Mc Duffies Bakery, Clarence *Also called McDuffies of Scotland Inc (G-3691)*
Mc Gregor Vineyard Winery, Dundee *Also called East Branch Winery Inc (G-4351)*
Mc Ivor Manufacturing Inc 716 825-1808
400 Ingham Ave Buffalo (14218) *(G-3081)*
Mc Squared Nyc Inc 212 947-2260
121 Varick St Frnt B New York (10013) *(G-11217)*
McAfee LLC 646 728-1440
1133 Avenue Of The Americ New York (10036) *(G-11218)*
McAllisters Precision Wldg Inc 518 221-3455
47 Broadway Menands (12204) *(G-8406)*
McAlpin Industries Inc (PA) 585 266-3060
255 Hollenbeck St Rochester (14621) *(G-14521)*
McAlpin Industries Inc 585 544-5335
265 Hollenbeck St Rochester (14621) *(G-14522)*
McAuliffe Paper Inc 315 453-2222
100 Commerce Blvd Liverpool (13088) *(G-7558)*
McBooks Press Inc 607 272-2114
520 N Meadow St 2 Ithaca (14850) *(G-6895)*
McCall Pattern Company (HQ) 212 465-6800
120 Broadway Fl 34 New York (10271) *(G-11219)*
McCarroll Uphl Designs LLC 518 828-0500
743 Columbia St Hudson (12534) *(G-6655)*
McCarthy LLC 646 862-5354
32 Union Sq E New York (10003) *(G-11220)*
McCarthy Tire and Auto Ctr, Menands *Also called McCarthy Tire Svc Co NY Inc (G-8407)*
McCarthy Tire Svc Co NY Inc 518 449-5185
980 Broadway Menands (12204) *(G-8407)*
McCullagh Coffee, Buffalo *Also called S J McCullagh Inc (G-3201)*
McD Metals LLC 518 456-9694
20 Corporate Cir Ste 2 Albany (12203) *(G-100)*
McDermott Light & Signal, Ridgewood *Also called Julian A McDermott Corporation (G-14124)*
McDonough Hardwoods Ltd 315 829-3449
6426 Skinner Rd Vernon Center (13477) *(G-16460)*
McDowell Research Co Inc (HQ) 315 332-7100
2000 Technology Pkwy Newark (14513) *(G-12756)*
McDuffies of Scotland Inc 716 759-8510
9920 Main St Clarence (14031) *(G-3691)*
McEwan Trucking & Grav Produc 716 609-1828
11696 Route 240 East Concord (14055) *(G-4407)*
McG Electronics Inc 631 586-5125
12 Burt Dr Deer Park (11729) *(G-4196)*
McG Graphics Inc 631 499-0730
101 Village Hill Dr Dix Hills (11746) *(G-4317)*
McG Surge Protection, Deer Park *Also called McG Electronics Inc (G-4196)*
McGaw Framed Art, New York *Also called McGaw Group LLC (G-11221)*
McGaw Group LLC 212 876-8822
233 E 93rd St New York (10128) *(G-11221)*
McGraw Wood Products LLC (PA) 607 836-6465
1 Charles St Mc Graw (13101) *(G-8254)*
McGraw-Hill Education Inc (PA) 646 766-2000
2 Penn Plz Fl 20 New York (10121) *(G-11222)*
McGraw-Hill Glbl Edctn Hldngs (PA) 646 766-2000
2 Penn Plz Fl 20 New York (10121) *(G-11223)*
McGraw-Hill School Education H (PA) 646 766-2000
2 Penn Plz Fl 20 New York (10121) *(G-11224)*
McGraw-Hill School Educatn LLC 646 766-2060
2 Penn Plz Fl 20 New York (10121) *(G-11225)*
McGuigan Inc 631 750-6222
210 Knickerbocker Ave Bohemia (11716) *(G-1098)*
McHone Industries Inc 716 945-3380
110 Elm St Salamanca (14779) *(G-15128)*
McHugh Painting Co Inc 716 741-8077
10335 Clarence Center Rd Clarence (14031) *(G-3692)*
McIntosh Box & Pallet Co Inc 315 789-8750
40 Doran Ave Geneva (14456) *(G-5594)*
McIntosh Box & Pallet Co Inc 315 675-8511
741 State Route 49 Bernhards Bay (13028) *(G-857)*
McIntosh Box & Pallet Co Inc 315 446-9350
200 6th St Rome (13440) *(G-14848)*
McKee Foods Corporation 631 979-9364
111 Serene Pl Hauppauge (11788) *(G-6154)*

McKeon Rolling Stl Door Co Inc (PA) 631 803-3000
44 Sawgrass Dr Bellport (11713) *(G-830)*
MCM Natural Stone Inc 585 586-6510
860 Linden Ave Ste 1 Rochester (14625) *(G-14523)*
McM Products USA Inc 646 756-4090
681 5th Ave Fl 10 New York (10022) *(G-11226)*
McMahon Group LLC (PA) 212 957-5300
545 W 45th St New York (10036) *(G-11227)*
MCMAHON PUBLISHING GROUP, New York *Also called McMahon Group LLC (G-11227)*
McQuilling Partners Inc (PA) 516 227-5718
1035 Stewart Ave Ste 100 Garden City (11530) *(G-5531)*
McWane Inc 607 734-2211
1021 E Water St Elmira (14901) *(G-4708)*
MD Electronics Corporation 716 488-0300
33 Precision Way Jamestown (14701) *(G-7052)*
MD Electronics of Illinois, Jamestown *Also called MD Electronics Corporation (G-7052)*
MD International Industries 631 254-3100
120 E Jefryn Blvd Ste Aa Deer Park (11729) *(G-4197)*
Md-Reports, Staten Island *Also called Infinite Software Solutions (G-15708)*
Md4 Holdings Inc 315 434-1869
6713 Collamer Rd East Syracuse (13057) *(G-4563)*
Mdamerica Wellness Inc 631 396-0991
225 Broadhollow Rd 110e Melville (11747) *(G-8365)*
Mdcare911 LLC 917 640-4869
30 Main St Apt 5c Brooklyn (11201) *(G-2291)*
Mdek Inc 347 569-7318
9728 3rd Ave Brooklyn (11209) *(G-2292)*
Mdi, Hauppauge *Also called Metal Dynamics Intl Corp (G-6160)*
Mdi East Inc 518 747-8730
22 Hudson Falls Rd Ste 6 South Glens Falls (12803) *(G-15549)*
Mdi Holdings LLC 212 559-1127
399 Park Ave Fl 14 New York (10022) *(G-11228)*
Mdj Sales Associates Inc 914 420-5897
27 Doris Rd Mamaroneck (10543) *(G-8072)*
Mdr Printing Corp 516 627-3221
125 Plandome Rd Manhasset (11030) *(G-8095)*
Mds Hot Bagels Deli Inc 718 438-5650
127 Church Ave Brooklyn (11218) *(G-2293)*
Mds USA Inc 718 358-5588
13244 Booth Memorial Ave Flushing (11355) *(G-5276)*
ME & Ro Inc (PA) 212 431-8744
241 Elizabeth St Frnt A New York (10012) *(G-11229)*
Me-J, New York *Also called Mej Beats LLC (G-11247)*
Meade Machine Co Inc 315 923-1703
31 Ford St Clyde (14433) *(G-3753)*
Meades Welding and Fabricating 631 581-1555
331 Islip Ave Islip (11751) *(G-6849)*
Meadowbrook Distributing Corp 516 226-9000
95 Jefferson St Garden City (11530) *(G-5532)*
Meadowwood NY LLC 212 729-5400
1 Penn Plz Ste 4000 New York (10119) *(G-11230)*
Mealplan Corp 909 706-8398
203 E 4th St Apt 6 New York (10009) *(G-11231)*
Measupro Inc (PA) 845 425-8777
1 Alpine Ct Spring Valley (10977) *(G-15618)*
Measurement Incorporated 914 682-1969
7-11 S Broadway Ste 402 White Plains (10601) *(G-17163)*
Meat Industry Newsletter, West Islip *Also called Spc Marketing Company (G-16937)*
Mecca Printing, Buffalo *Also called B & P Jays Inc (G-2851)*
Mechanical Displays Inc 718 258-5588
4420 Farragut Rd Brooklyn (11203) *(G-2294)*
Mechanical Pwr Conversion LLC 607 766-9620
6 Emma St Binghamton (13905) *(G-930)*
Mechanical Rubber Pdts Co Inc 845 986-2271
77 Forester Ave Ste 1 Warwick (10990) *(G-16616)*
Mechanical Specialties Co, Binghamton *Also called Ms Machining Inc (G-934)*
Mechanical Technology Inc (PA) 518 218-2550
325 Washington Avenue Ext Albany (12205) *(G-101)*
Mecho Systems 718 729-8373
3708 34th St Long Island City (11101) *(G-7837)*
Mechoshade Systems Inc (HQ) 718 729-2020
4203 35th St Long Island City (11101) *(G-7838)*
Mechtronics Corporation (PA) 845 231-1400
511 Fishkill Ave Beacon (12508) *(G-782)*
Mechtronics Corporation 845 831-9300
511 Fishkill Ave Beacon (12508) *(G-783)*
Med Reviews LLC 212 239-5860
1370 Broadway Fl 5 New York (10018) *(G-11232)*
Med Services Inc 631 218-6450
100 Knickerbocker Ave C Bohemia (11716) *(G-1099)*
Med-Eng LLC 315 713-0103
103 Tulloch Dr Ogdensburg (13669) *(G-13140)*
Medallion Associates Inc 212 929-9130
37 W 20th St Fl 4 New York (10011) *(G-11233)*
Medallion Security Door & Win, New Hyde Park *Also called Texas Home Security Inc (G-8910)*
Medco, Edgewood *Also called Merit Electronic Design Co Inc (G-4619)*
Medco Machine LLC 315 986-2109
2320 Walworth Marion Rd Walworth (14568) *(G-16571)*
Medek Laboratories Inc 845 943-4988
63 First Ave Monroe (10950) *(G-8597)*

ALPHABETIC

(PA)=Parent Co (HQ)=Headquarters (DH)=Div Headquarters
2018 Harris
New York Manufacturers Directory
1005

Meder Textile Co Inc 516 883-0409
20 Lynn Rd Port Washington (11050) ***(G-13861)***

Medi-Physics, Port Washington *Also called GE Healthcare Inc* ***(G-13841)***

Medi-Ray Inc 877 898-3003
150 Marbledale Rd Tuckahoe (10707) ***(G-16295)***

Medi-Tech International Corp (PA) 800 333-0109
26 Court St Ste 1301 Brooklyn (11242) ***(G-2295)***

Media Press Corp 212 791-6347
55 John St 520 New York (10038) ***(G-11234)***

Media Signs LLC 718 252-7575
6404 14th Ave Brooklyn (11219) ***(G-2296)***

Media Technologies Ltd 631 467-7900
220 Sonata Ct Eastport (11941) ***(G-4596)***

Media Transcripts Inc 212 362-1481
41 W 83rd St Apt 1b New York (10024) ***(G-11235)***

Media Trust LLC (PA) 212 802-1162
404 Park Ave S Fl 2 New York (10016) ***(G-11236)***

Mediaplanet Publishing Hse Inc (PA) 646 922-1400
350 7th Ave Fl 18 New York (10001) ***(G-11237)***

Mediapost Communications LLC 212 204-2000
1460 Broadway Fl 12 New York (10036) ***(G-11238)***

Medical Acoustics LLC 716 218-7353
640 Ellicott St Ste 407 Buffalo (14203) ***(G-3082)***

Medical Action Industries Inc 631 231-4600
150 Motor Pkwy Ste 205 Hauppauge (11788) ***(G-6155)***

Medical Coaches Incorporated (PA) 607 432-1333
399 County Highway 58 Oneonta (13820) ***(G-13210)***

Medical Daily Inc 646 867-7100
7 Hanover Sq Fl 6 New York (10004) ***(G-11239)***

Medical Depot Inc (PA) 516 998-4600
99 Seaview Blvd Ste 210 Port Washington (11050) ***(G-13862)***

Medical Information Systems 516 621-7200
2 Seaview Blvd Ste 104 Port Washington (11050) ***(G-13863)***

Medical Technology Products 631 285-6640
33a Smith St Greenlawn (11740) ***(G-5893)***

Medical Transcription Billing 631 863-1198
237 W 35th St Ste 1202 New York (10001) ***(G-11240)***

Medicine Rules Inc 631 334-5395
2 Constance Ct East Setauket (11733) ***(G-4504)***

Medico, New Windsor *Also called S M Frank & Company Inc* ***(G-8997)***

Medidata Solutions Inc (PA) 212 918-1800
350 Hudson St Fl 9 New York (10014) ***(G-11241)***

Mediflex, Islandia *Also called Flexbar Machine Corporation* ***(G-6831)***

Medikidz Usa Inc 646 895-9319
205 Lexington Ave Rm 1601 New York (10016) ***(G-11242)***

Medima LLC 716 741-0400
5727 Strickler Rd Clarence (14031) ***(G-3693)***

Medima Metals, Clarence *Also called Medima LLC* ***(G-3693)***

Medina Journal Register, Medina *Also called Community Newsppr Holdings Inc* ***(G-8302)***

Medina Millworks LLC 585 798-2969
10694 Ridge Rd Medina (14103) ***(G-8309)***

Medipoint Inc 516 294-8822
72 E 2nd St Mineola (11501) ***(G-8557)***

Medipoint International,, Mineola *Also called Medipoint Inc* ***(G-8557)***

Mediterranean Thick Yogurt, East Elmhurst *Also called Kesso Foods Inc* ***(G-4415)***

Mediterrean Dyro Company 718 786-4888
1102 38th Ave Long Island City (11101) ***(G-7839)***

Meditub Incorporated 866 633-4882
11 Wedgewood Ln Lawrence (11559) ***(G-7420)***

Medius North America, New York *Also called Medius Software Inc* ***(G-11243)***

Medius Software Inc 877 295-0058
12 E 49th St Fl 11 New York (10017) ***(G-11243)***

Medline Industries Inc 845 344-3301
3301 Route 6 Middletown (10940) ***(G-8484)***

Medsafe Systems Inc 516 883-8222
46 Orchard Farm Rd Port Washington (11050) ***(G-13864)***

Medsim-Eagle Simulation Inc 607 658-9354
811 North St Endicott (13760) ***(G-4824)***

Medsource Technologies LLC 716 662-5025
3902 California Rd Orchard Park (14127) ***(G-13308)***

Medsurg Direct, Plainview *Also called Peter Digioia* ***(G-13656)***

Medtech Products Inc (HQ) 914 524-6810
660 White Plains Rd Tarrytown (10591) ***(G-16119)***

Medtek Lighting Corporation (PA) 518 745-7264
206 Glen St Ste 5 Glens Falls (12801) ***(G-5704)***

Mee Accessories LLC (PA) 917 262-1000
475 10th Ave Fl 9 New York (10018) ***(G-11244)***

Meeco Sullivan LLC 800 232-3625
3 Chancellor Ln Warwick (10990) ***(G-16617)***

Meegenius Inc 212 283-7285
151 W 25th St Fl 3 New York (10001) ***(G-11245)***

Meeker Sales Corp 718 384-5400
551 Sutter Ave Brooklyn (11207) ***(G-2297)***

Meethappy Inc 917 903-0591
2122 Bit Path Seaford (11783) ***(G-15368)***

Mega Apparel International, Merrick *Also called Mega Sourcing Inc* ***(G-8424)***

Mega Cabinets Inc 631 789-4112
51 Ranick Dr E Amityville (11701) ***(G-311)***

Mega Graphics Inc 914 962-1402
1725 Front St Ste 1 Yorktown Heights (10598) ***(G-17529)***

Mega Power Sports Corporation 212 627-3380
1123 Broadway Ph New York (10010) ***(G-11246)***

Mega Sourcing Inc (PA) 646 682-0304
1929 Edward Ln Merrick (11566) ***(G-8424)***

Mega Tool & Mfg Corp 607 734-8398
1023 Caton Ave Elmira (14904) ***(G-4709)***

Mega Vision Inc 718 228-1065
1274 Flushing Ave Brooklyn (11237) ***(G-2298)***

Megamatt Inc 516 536-3541
35 Vassar Pl Rockville Centre (11570) ***(G-14823)***

Megohmer Vbrating Reed Standco, Brooklyn *Also called Herman H Sticht Company Inc* ***(G-2074)***

Mehron Inc 845 426-1700
100 Red Schoolhouse Rd C2 Chestnut Ridge (10977) ***(G-3652)***

Meisel-Peskin Co Inc (PA) 718 497-1840
349 Scholes St 353 Brooklyn (11206) ***(G-2299)***

Mej Beats LLC 516 707-6655
180 E 64th St New York (10065) ***(G-11247)***

Mekanism Inc 212 226-2772
80 Broad St Fl 35 New York (10004) ***(G-11248)***

Mekatronics Incorporated 516 883-6805
85 Channel Dr Ste 2 Port Washington (11050) ***(G-13865)***

Melbourne C Fisher Yacht Sails 631 673-5055
1345 New York Ave Ste 2 Huntington Station (11746) ***(G-6753)***

Melcher Media Inc 212 727-2322
124 W 13th St New York (10011) ***(G-11249)***

Meliorum Technologies Inc 585 313-0616
620 Park Ave 145 Rochester (14607) ***(G-14524)***

Melissa, Interlaken *Also called Hipshot Products Inc* ***(G-6786)***

Melita Corp 718 392-7280
3330 14th St Astoria (11106) ***(G-447)***

Melland Gear Instr of Huppauge 631 234-0100
225 Engineers Rd Hauppauge (11788) ***(G-6156)***

Mellem Corporation 607 723-0001
31 Lewis St Ste 1 Binghamton (13901) ***(G-931)***

Mellen Press, The, Lewiston *Also called PSR Press Ltd* ***(G-7457)***

Mellen Pressroom & Bindery, Lewiston *Also called 450 Ridge St Inc* ***(G-7453)***

Melles Griot, Rochester *Also called CVI Laser LLC* ***(G-14318)***

Melmont Fine Pringng/Graphics 516 939-2253
6 Robert Ct Ste 24 Bethpage (11714) ***(G-872)***

Meloon Foundries LLC 315 454-3231
1841 Lemoyne Ave Syracuse (13208) ***(G-16006)***

Melto Metal Products Co Inc 516 546-8866
37 Hanse Ave Freeport (11520) ***(G-5422)***

Meltz Lumber Co of Mellenville 518 672-7021
483 Route 217 Hudson (12534) ***(G-6656)***

Melwood Partners Inc (PA) 516 307-8030
100 Qentin Roosevelt Blvd Garden City (11530) ***(G-5533)***

Memorial Sloan Kttering Cancer, New York *Also called Mskcc Rmipc* ***(G-11342)***

Memory Md Inc 917 318-0215
205 E 42nd St Fl 14 New York (10017) ***(G-11250)***

Memory Protection Devices Inc 631 249-0001
200 Broadhollow Rd Ste 4 Farmingdale (11735) ***(G-5056)***

Menpin Supply Corp 718 415-4168
1229 60th St Brooklyn (11219) ***(G-2300)***

Mens Journal, New York *Also called Straight Arrow Publishing Co* ***(G-12233)***

Mens Journal LLC 212 484-1616
1290 Ave Of The Americas New York (10104) ***(G-11251)***

Mentholatum Company (HQ) 716 677-2500
707 Sterling Dr Orchard Park (14127) ***(G-13309)***

Menu Solutions Inc 718 575-5160
4510 White Plains Rd Bronx (10470) ***(G-1394)***

Menucha Publishers Inc 718 232-0856
1221 38th St Brooklyn (11218) ***(G-2301)***

Meopta USA Inc 631 436-5900
50 Davids Dr Hauppauge (11788) ***(G-6157)***

Mep Alaska LLC 646 535-9005
3619 Bedford Ave Apt 4e Brooklyn (11210) ***(G-2302)***

Mer Gems Corp 212 714-9129
62 W 47th St Ste 614 New York (10036) ***(G-11252)***

Merb LLC 631 393-3621
140 Carolyn Blvd Farmingdale (11735) ***(G-5057)***

Mercer Milling Co 315 701-1334
4698 Crossroads Park Dr Liverpool (13088) ***(G-7559)***

Mercer Rubber Co 631 348-0282
350 Rabro Dr Hauppauge (11788) ***(G-6158)***

Mercer's Dairy, Boonville *Also called Quality Dairy Farms Inc* ***(G-1166)***

Merchandiser Inc 315 462-6411
70 Stephens St Clifton Springs (14432) ***(G-3739)***

Merchant Publishing Inc 212 691-6666
34 W 13th St Bsmt New York (10011) ***(G-11253)***

Merchant Service Pymnt Access 212 561-5516
626 Rxr Plz Uniondale (11556) ***(G-16321)***

Merco Hackensack Inc 845 357-3699
201 Route 59 Ste D2 Hillburn (10931) ***(G-6442)***

Merco Tape, Hillburn *Also called Merco Hackensack Inc* ***(G-6442)***

Mercury Apparel, West Nyack *Also called Mainly Monograms Inc* ***(G-16949)***

Mercury Envelope Co Inc 516 678-6744
100 Merrick Rd Ste 204e Rockville Centre (11570) ***(G-14824)***

Mercury Envelope Printing, Rockville Centre *Also called Mercury Envelope Co Inc* ***(G-14824)***

Mercury Lock and Door Service 718 542-7048
529 C Wortham St Bronx (10474) ***(G-1395)***

ALPHABETIC SECTION

Mercury Paint Corporation (PA) 718 469-8787
 4808 Farragut Rd Brooklyn (11203) *(G-2303)*
Mercury Pen Company Inc 518 899-9653
 245 Eastline Rd Ballston Lake (12019) *(G-582)*
Mercury Plastics Corp 718 498-5400
 989 Utica Ave 995 Brooklyn (11203) *(G-2304)*
Mercury Print Productions Inc (PA) 585 458-7900
 2332 Innovation Way 4 Rochester (14624) *(G-14525)*
Meredith Corporate Solutions, New York *Also called Meredith Corporation* *(G-11255)*
Meredith Corporation 212 557-6600
 125 Park Ave Fl 20 New York (10017) *(G-11254)*
Meredith Corporation 212 499-2000
 805 3rd Ave Fl 22 New York (10022) *(G-11255)*
Meredith Corporation 515 284-2157
 805 3rd Ave Fl 29 New York (10022) *(G-11256)*
Meredith Hispanic Ventures, New York *Also called Meredith Corporation* *(G-11256)*
Mergence Studios Ltd 212 288-5616
 135 Ricefield Ln Hauppauge (11788) *(G-6159)*
Mergent Inc 212 413-7700
 444 Madison Ave Ste 502 New York (10022) *(G-11257)*
Meridian Manufacturing Inc 518 885-0450
 27 Kent St Ste 103a Ballston Spa (12020) *(G-602)*
Meridian Technologies Inc 516 285-1000
 700 Elmont Rd Elmont (11003) *(G-4735)*
Merit Electronic Design Co Inc 631 667-9699
 190 Rodeo Dr Edgewood (11717) *(G-4619)*
Meritool LLC 716 699-6005
 5 Park Ave Ste 1 Ellicottville (14731) *(G-4656)*
Merkos Bookstore, Brooklyn *Also called Merkos LInyonei Chinuch Inc* *(G-2305)*
Merkos LInyonei Chinuch Inc 718 778-0226
 291 Kingston Ave Brooklyn (11213) *(G-2305)*
Merlin Printing Inc 631 842-6666
 215 Dixon Ave Amityville (11701) *(G-312)*
Merrill Communications, New York *Also called Merrill New York Company Inc* *(G-11261)*
Merrill Communications LLC 212 620-5600
 1345 Ave Of The Amrcs 1 New York (10105) *(G-11258)*
Merrill Corporation 917 934-7300
 25 W 45th St Fl 10 New York (10036) *(G-11259)*
Merrill Corporation Inc 212 620-5600
 1345 Ave Of The Ave Fl 17 New York (10105) *(G-11260)*
Merrill New York Company Inc 212 229-6500
 246 W 54th St New York (10019) *(G-11261)*
Merrill Press, Buffalo *Also called Complemar Print LLC* *(G-2904)*
Merrimac Leasing, Johnstown *Also called Lee Dyeing Company NC Inc* *(G-7149)*
Merritt Estate Winery Inc 716 965-4800
 2264 King Rd Forestville (14062) *(G-5341)*
Merritt Machinery LLC 716 434-5558
 10 Simonds St Lockport (14094) *(G-7628)*
Meryl Diamond Ltd (PA) 212 730-0333
 1375 Broadway Fl 9 New York (10018) *(G-11262)*
Merz Metal & Machine Corp 716 893-7786
 237 Chelsea Pl Buffalo (14211) *(G-3083)*
Merzon Leather Co Inc 718 782-6260
 810 Humboldt St Ste 2 Brooklyn (11222) *(G-2306)*
Mesh LLC 646 839-7000
 350 5th Ave Lbby 9 New York (10118) *(G-11263)*
Meskita Lifestyle Brands LLC 212 695-5054
 336 W 37th St New York (10018) *(G-11264)*
Mesoblast Inc 212 880-2060
 505 5th Ave Fl 3 New York (10017) *(G-11265)*
Mesorah Publications Ltd 718 921-9000
 4401 2nd Ave Brooklyn (11232) *(G-2307)*
Messenger Post Media, Canandaigua *Also called Wolfe Publications Inc* *(G-3389)*
Messenger Press 518 885-9231
 1826 Amsterdam Rd Ballston Spa (12020) *(G-603)*
Messex Group Inc 646 229-2582
 244 5th Ave Ste D256 New York (10001) *(G-11266)*
Mestel Brothers Stairs & Rails 516 496-4127
 11 Gary Rd Ste 102 Syosset (11791) *(G-15848)*
Met Weld International LLC 518 765-2318
 5727 Ostrander Rd Altamont (12009) *(G-213)*
Meta Pharmacy Systems Inc 516 488-6189
 401 Franklin Ave Ste 106 Garden City (11530) *(G-5534)*
Meta-Therm Corp 914 697-4840
 70 W Red Oak Ln White Plains (10604) *(G-17164)*
Metadure Defense & SEC LLC 631 249-2141
 165 Gazza Blvd Farmingdale (11735) *(G-5058)*
Metadure Parts & Sales Inc 631 249-2141
 165 Gazza Blvd Farmingdale (11735) *(G-5059)*
Metal Cladding Inc 716 434-5513
 230 S Niagara St Lockport (14094) *(G-7629)*
Metal Coated Fibers Inc 518 280-8514
 679 Mariaville Rd Schenectady (12306) *(G-15304)*
Metal Concepts 845 592-1863
 9 Hanna Ln 12 Beacon (12508) *(G-784)*
Metal Container Corporation 845 567-1500
 1000 Breunig Rd New Windsor (12553) *(G-8989)*
Metal Crafts Inc 718 443-3333
 650 Berriman St Brooklyn (11208) *(G-2308)*
Metal Dynamics Intl Corp 631 231-1153
 25 Corporate Dr Hauppauge (11788) *(G-6160)*

Metal Fab LLC 607 775-3200
 13 Spud Ln Binghamton (13904) *(G-932)*
Metal Improvement Company LLC 607 533-7000
 131 Woodsedge Dr Lansing (14882) *(G-7374)*
Metal Man Restoration 914 662-4218
 254 E 3rd St Fl 1 Mount Vernon (10553) *(G-8750)*
Metal Man Services, Watertown *Also called Kenal Services Corp* *(G-16679)*
Metal Parts Manufacturing Inc 315 831-2530
 119 Remsen Rd Barneveld (13304) *(G-614)*
Metal Products Intl LLC 716 215-1930
 7510 Porter Rd Ste 4 Niagara Falls (14304) *(G-12863)*
Metal Solutions Inc 315 732-6271
 1821 Broad St Ste 5 Utica (13501) *(G-16371)*
Metal Stampings, Honeoye Falls *Also called Stever-Locke Industries Inc* *(G-6565)*
Metal Tek Products 516 586-4514
 100 Express St Plainview (11803) *(G-13646)*
Metal Works of NY Inc 718 525-9440
 11603 Merrick Blvd Jamaica (11434) *(G-6966)*
Metalcraft By N Barzel, Brooklyn *Also called Metal Crafts Inc* *(G-2308)*
Metalcraft Marine Us Inc 315 501-4015
 583 E Broadway St Cape Vincent (13618) *(G-3410)*
Metalico Aluminum Recovery Inc 315 463-9500
 6223 Thompson Rd Syracuse (13206) *(G-16007)*
Metallic Ladder Mfg Corp 716 358-6201
 41 S Washington St Randolph (14772) *(G-14029)*
Metalline Fire Door Co Inc (PA) 718 583-2320
 4110 Park Ave Bronx (10457) *(G-1396)*
Metallized Carbon Corporation (PA) 914 941-3738
 19 S Water St Ossining (10562) *(G-13347)*
Metalocke Industries Inc 718 267-9200
 3202 57th St Woodside (11377) *(G-17354)*
Metals Building Products 844 638-2527
 5005 Veterans Mem Hwy Holbrook (11741) *(G-6491)*
Metalsigma Usa Inc 212 731-4346
 350 5th Ave New York (10118) *(G-11267)*
Metalsmith Inc 631 467-1500
 1340 Lincoln Ave Ste 13 Holbrook (11741) *(G-6492)*
Metalworks Inc 718 319-0011
 1303 Herschell St Bronx (10461) *(G-1397)*
Metavac LLC 631 207-2344
 4000 Point St Holtsville (11742) *(G-6530)*
Metcar Products, Ossining *Also called Metallized Carbon Corporation* *(G-13347)*
Meteor Express Inc 718 551-9177
 16801 Rockaway Blvd # 202 Jamaica (11434) *(G-6967)*
Methods Tooling & Mfg Inc 845 246-7100
 635 Glasco Tpke Mount Marion (12456) *(G-8693)*
Metpak Inc 917 309-0196
 320 Roebling St Ste 601 Brooklyn (11211) *(G-2309)*
Metpar Corp 516 333-2600
 95 State St Westbury (11590) *(G-17038)*
Metro Center Western New York, Buffalo *Also called William S Hein & Co Inc* *(G-3282)*
Metro City Group Inc 516 781-2500
 2283 Bellmore Ave Bellmore (11710) *(G-814)*
Metro Creative Graphics Inc (PA) 212 947-5100
 519 8th Ave Fl 18 New York (10018) *(G-11268)*
Metro Door Inc (HQ) 800 669-3667
 2929 Express Dr N 300b Islandia (11749) *(G-6839)*
Metro Duct Systems Inc 718 278-4294
 1219 Astoria Blvd Apt 2 Long Island City (11102) *(G-7840)*
Metro Dynmc Scntific Instr Lab 631 842-4300
 20 Nancy St West Babylon (11704) *(G-16841)*
Metro Group Inc (PA) 718 392-3616
 5023 23rd St Long Island City (11101) *(G-7841)*
Metro Group Inc 716 434-4055
 8 South St Lockport (14094) *(G-7630)*
Metro Grouping, Long Island City *Also called Metro Group Inc* *(G-7841)*
Metro Kitchens Corp 718 434-1166
 1040 E 45th St Brooklyn (11203) *(G-2310)*
Metro Knitting Corp 718 894-0765
 6325 70th St Middle Village (11379) *(G-8449)*
Metro Lube (PA) 718 947-1167
 9110 Metropolitan Ave Rego Park (11374) *(G-14047)*
Metro Machining & Fabricating 718 545-0104
 3234 61st St Woodside (11377) *(G-17355)*
Metro Mattress Corp 716 205-2300
 2212 Military Rd Niagara Falls (14304) *(G-12864)*
Metro Millwork, North Salem *Also called Metropolitan Fine Mllwk Corp* *(G-12955)*
Metro Nespaper, New York *Also called Seabay Media Holdings LLC* *(G-12028)*
Metro New York, New York *Also called Sb New York Inc* *(G-12000)*
Metro Products & Services LLC (PA) 866 846-8486
 1424 74th St Brooklyn (11228) *(G-2311)*
Metro Service Center, Elmsford *Also called Westinghouse A Brake Tech Corp* *(G-4800)*
Metro Storage Center, Getzville *Also called William S Hein & Co Inc* *(G-5619)*
Metro Tel Communications, Staten Island *Also called I D Tel Corp* *(G-15706)*
Metrofab Pipe Incorporated 516 349-7373
 15 Fairchild Ct Plainview (11803) *(G-13647)*
Metropltan Data Sltons MGT Inc 516 586-5520
 279 Conklin St Farmingdale (11735) *(G-5060)*
Metropolis Magazine, New York *Also called Bellerophon Publications Inc* *(G-9399)*
Metropolitan Fine Mllwk Corp 914 669-4900
 230 Hardscrabble Rd North Salem (10560) *(G-12955)*

(PA)=Parent Co (HQ)=Headquarters (DH)=Div Headquarters

Metropolitan Granite & MBL Inc — 585 342-7020
860 Maple St Ste 100 Rochester (14611) *(G-14526)*

Metropolitan Packg Mfg Corp — 718 383-2700
68 Java St Brooklyn (11222) *(G-2312)*

Metropolitan Sign & Riggin — 718 231-0010
330 Casanova St Bronx (10474) *(G-1398)*

Metropolitan Signs Inc (PA) — 315 638-1448
3760 Patchett Rd Baldwinsville (13027) *(G-571)*

Metrosource Publishing Inc — 212 691-5127
498 Fashion Ave Fl 10 New York (10018) *(G-11269)*

Mettle Concept Inc — 888 501-0680
545 8th Ave Rm 401 New York (10018) *(G-11270)*

Mettler-Toledo Inc — 607 257-6000
5 Barr Rd Ithaca (14850) *(G-6896)*

Mettowee Lumber & Plastics Co — 518 642-1100
82 Church St Granville (12832) *(G-5793)*

Metzger Speciality Brands — 212 957-0055
161 W 54th St Apt 802 New York (10019) *(G-11271)*

Mexico Independent Inc (PA) — 315 963-3763
260 Washington St Watertown (13601) *(G-16687)*

Meyco Products Inc (PA) — 631 421-9800
1225 Walt Whitman Rd Melville (11747) *(G-8366)*

Mezmeriz Inc — 607 216-8140
33 Thornwood Dr Ste 100 Ithaca (14850) *(G-6897)*

Mf Digital, Deer Park Also called Formats Unlimited Inc *(G-4166)*

Mg Imaging — 212 704-4073
229 W 28th St Rm 300 New York (10001) *(G-11272)*

Mgd Brands Inc — 516 545-0150
30 Commercial Ct Plainview (11803) *(G-13648)*

Mgi, Hauppauge Also called Mini Graphics Inc *(G-6165)*

Mgi, Northport Also called Marketing Group International *(G-13034)*

Mgk Group Inc — 212 989-2732
979 3rd Ave Ste 1811 New York (10022) *(G-11273)*

MGM, Buffalo Also called Tyson Deli Inc *(G-3255)*

Mgr Equipment Corp — 516 239-3030
22 Gates Ave Inwood (11096) *(G-6801)*

Mgs Group, The, Rome Also called MGS Manufacturing Inc *(G-14849)*

MGS Manufacturing Inc (PA) — 315 337-3350
122 Otis St Rome (13441) *(G-14849)*

Mht Lighting, Staten Island Also called North American Mfg Entps Inc *(G-15733)*

Mhxco Foam Company LLC — 518 843-8400
120 Edson St Amsterdam (12010) *(G-356)*

Miami Media LLC (HQ) — 212 268-8600
72 Madison Ave Fl 11 New York (10016) *(G-11274)*

Mibro Group — 716 631-5713
4039 Genesee St Buffalo (14225) *(G-3084)*

Mica America, Bay Shore Also called Fenix Furniture Co *(G-698)*

Mica International Ltd — 516 378-3400
126 Albany Ave Freeport (11520) *(G-5423)*

Micatu Inc — 888 705-8836
315 Daniel Zenker Dr #202 Horseheads (14845) *(G-6610)*

Micelli Chocalate Mold Co, West Babylon Also called Sweet Tooth Enterprises LLC *(G-16867)*

Michael Andrews Bespoke, New York Also called Michael Andrews LLC *(G-11275)*

Michael Andrews LLC — 212 677-1755
680 Broadway Fl Mezz New York (10012) *(G-11275)*

Michael Anthony Jewelers LLC (HQ) — 914 699-0000
115 S Macquesten Pkwy Mount Vernon (10550) *(G-8751)*

Michael Benalt Inc — 845 628-1008
100 Buckshollow Rd Mahopac (10541) *(G-8027)*

Michael Bernstein Design Assoc — 718 456-9277
361 Stagg St Fl 4 Brooklyn (11206) *(G-2313)*

Michael Bondanza Inc — 212 869-0043
10 E 38th St Fl 6 New York (10016) *(G-11276)*

Michael Britt Inc — 516 248-2010
89 Mineola Blvd Fl 1 Mineola (11501) *(G-8558)*

Michael Feldman Inc — 718 433-1700
3010 41st Ave Ste 3 Long Island City (11101) *(G-7842)*

Michael Fiore Ltd — 516 561-8238
126 E Fairview Ave Valley Stream (11580) *(G-16440)*

Michael K Lennon Inc — 631 288-5200
851 Riverhead Rd Westhampton Beach (11978) *(G-17088)*

Michael Karp Music Inc — 212 840-3285
59 W 71st St Apt 7a New York (10023) *(G-11277)*

Michael Kors, New York Also called Herman Kay Company Ltd *(G-10505)*

Michael Neuman, Rye Also called Western Oil and Gas JV Inc *(G-15095)*

Michael P Mmarr — 315 623-9380
1358 State Route 49 Constantia (13044) *(G-3907)*

Michael Stuart Inc — 718 821-0704
199 Cook St Brooklyn (11206) *(G-2314)*

Michael Todd Stevens — 585 436-9957
95 Mount Read Blvd #125 Rochester (14611) *(G-14527)*

Michaelian & Kohlberg Inc — 212 431-9009
225 E 59th St New York (10022) *(G-11278)*

Michbi Doors Inc — 631 231-9050
75 Emjay Blvd Brentwood (11717) *(G-1189)*

Mick Radio Nuclear Instrument — 718 597-3999
521 Homestead Ave Mount Vernon (10550) *(G-8752)*

Mickelberry Communications Inc (PA) — 212 832-0303
405 Park Ave New York (10022) *(G-11279)*

Micosta Enterprises Inc — 518 822-9708
3007 County Route 20 Hudson (12534) *(G-6657)*

Micro Centric Corporation (PA) — 800 573-1139
25 S Terminal Dr Plainview (11803) *(G-13649)*

Micro Contacts Inc (PA) — 516 433-4830
1 Enterprise Pl Unit E Hicksville (11801) *(G-6397)*

Micro Contract Manufacturing — 631 738-7874
27 Scouting Blvd Unit E Medford (11763) *(G-8289)*

Micro Essential Laboratory — 718 338-3618
4224 Avenue H Brooklyn (11210) *(G-2315)*

Micro Graphics, Lockport Also called Jack J Florio Jr *(G-7625)*

Micro Instrument Corp — 585 458-3150
1199 Emerson St Rochester (14606) *(G-14528)*

Micro Photo Acoustics Inc — 631 750-6035
105 Comac St Ronkonkoma (11779) *(G-14968)*

Micro Powders Inc (PA) — 914 332-6400
580 White Plains Rd #400 Tarrytown (10591) *(G-16120)*

Micro Publishing Inc — 212 533-9180
71 W 23rd St Lbby A New York (10010) *(G-11280)*

Micro Semicdtr Researches LLC (PA) — 646 863-6070
310 W 52nd St Apt 12b New York (10019) *(G-11281)*

Micro Systems Specialists Inc — 845 677-6150
3280 Franklin Ave Fl 2 Millbrook (12545) *(G-8512)*

Micro Threaded Products Inc — 585 288-0080
325 Mount Read Blvd Ste 4 Rochester (14611) *(G-14529)*

Micro-Tech Machine Inc — 315 331-6671
301 W Shore Blvd Newark (14513) *(G-12757)*

Microb Phase Services — 518 877-8948
14 Nottingham Way S Clifton Park (12065) *(G-3728)*

Microcad Trning Consulting Inc — 617 923-0500
1110 Route 55 Ste 209 Lagrangeville (12540) *(G-7281)*

Microcad Trning Consulting Inc — 631 291-9484
77 Arkay Dr Ste C2 Hauppauge (11788) *(G-6161)*

Microchip Technology Inc — 631 233-3280
80 Arkay Dr Ste 100 Hauppauge (11788) *(G-6162)*

Microchip Technology Inc — 607 785-5992
3301 Country Club Rd Endicott (13760) *(G-4825)*

Microera Printers Inc — 585 783-1300
304 Whitney St Rochester (14606) *(G-14530)*

Microfoam, Utica Also called Idg LLC *(G-16365)*

Microgen Systems Inc — 585 214-2426
150 Lucius Gordon Dr #117 West Henrietta (14586) *(G-16916)*

Micromem Technologies — 212 672-1806
245 Park Ave Fl 24 New York (10167) *(G-11282)*

Micromod Automation Inc — 585 321-9200
3 Townline Cir Ste 4 Rochester (14623) *(G-14531)*

Micromod Automtn & Contrls Inc — 585 321-9209
3 Townline Cir Ste 4 Rochester (14623) *(G-14532)*

Micromold Products Inc — 914 969-2850
7 Odell Plz 133 Yonkers (10701) *(G-17485)*

Micron Inds Rochester Inc — 585 247-6130
31 Industrial Park Cir Rochester (14624) *(G-14533)*

Micropage, New York Also called Micro Publishing Inc *(G-11280)*

MICROPEN DIVISION, Honeoye Falls Also called Micropen Technologies Corp *(G-6562)*

Micropen Technologies Corp — 585 624-2610
93 Papermill St Honeoye Falls (14472) *(G-6562)*

Microsoft Corporation — 914 323-2150
125 Westchester Ave White Plains (10601) *(G-17165)*

Microsoft Corporation — 631 760-2340
160 Walt Whitman Rd 1006b Huntington Station (11746) *(G-6754)*

Microsoft Corporation — 212 245-2100
11 Times Sq Fl 9 New York (10036) *(G-11283)*

Microsoft Corporation — 516 380-1531
2929 Expressway Dr N #300 Hauppauge (11749) *(G-6163)*

Microstrategy Incorporated — 888 537-8135
5 Penn Plz Ste 901 New York (10001) *(G-11284)*

Microwave Circuit Tech Inc — 631 845-1041
45 Central Dr Farmingdale (11735) *(G-5061)*

Microwave Filter Company Inc (PA) — 315 438-4700
6743 Kinne St East Syracuse (13057) *(G-4564)*

Mid Atlantic Graphics Corp — 631 345-3800
14 Ramsey Rd Shirley (11967) *(G-15448)*

Mid Enterprise Inc — 631 924-3933
809 Middle Country Rd Middle Island (11953) *(G-8440)*

Mid Hdson Wkshp For The Dsbled — 845 471-3820
188 Washington St Poughkeepsie (12601) *(G-13935)*

Mid Island Die Cutting Corp — 631 293-0180
77 Schmitt Blvd Farmingdale (11735) *(G-5062)*

Mid Island Group — 631 293-0180
77 Schmitt Blvd Farmingdale (11735) *(G-5063)*

Mid-Hudson Concrete Pdts Inc — 845 265-3141
3504 Route 9 Cold Spring (10516) *(G-3788)*

Mid-Island Bindery Inc — 631 293-0180
77 Schmitt Blvd Farmingdale (11735) *(G-5064)*

Mid-State Ready Mix, Central Square Also called Torrington Industries Inc *(G-3545)*

Mid-York Press Inc — 607 674-4491
2808 State Highway 80 Sherburne (13460) *(G-15415)*

Midas Mdici Group Holdings Inc (PA) — 212 792-0920
445 Park Ave Frnt 5 New York (10022) *(G-11285)*

Midbury Industries Inc — 516 868-0600
86 E Merrick Rd Freeport (11520) *(G-5424)*

Middle Ages Brewing Company — 315 476-4250
120 Wilkinson St Ste 3 Syracuse (13204) *(G-16008)*

Middleby Corporation 631 226-6688
175 E Hoffman Ave Lindenhurst (11757) ***(G-7495)***
Middletown Press (PA) 845 343-1895
20 W Main St 26 Middletown (10940) ***(G-8485)***
Midgley Printing Corp 315 475-1864
433 W Onondaga St Ste B Syracuse (13202) ***(G-16009)***
Midland Farms Inc (PA) 518 436-7038
375 Broadway Menands (12204) ***(G-8408)***
Midland Machinery Co Inc 716 692-1200
101 Cranbrook Road Ext Exd Tonawanda (14150) ***(G-16199)***
Midstate Printing Corp 315 475-4101
4707 Dey Rd Liverpool (13088) ***(G-7560)***
Midstate Spring Inc 315 437-2623
4054 New Court Ave Syracuse (13206) ***(G-16010)***
Midura Jewels Inc 213 265-8090
36 W 47th St Ste 809i New York (10036) ***(G-11286)***
Midwood Signs & Design Inc 718 499-9041
202 28th St Brooklyn (11232) ***(G-2316)***
Miggins Screw Products Inc 845 279-2307
66 Putnam Ave Brewster (10509) ***(G-1222)***
Mighty Quinns Barbeque LLC 973 777-8340
103 2nd Ave Frnt 1 New York (10003) ***(G-11287)***
Mignon Group, The, New York *Also called Lm Mignon LLC* ***(G-11044)***
Miguelina Inc 212 925-0320
325 W 37th St Fl 2 New York (10018) ***(G-11288)***
Mikael Aghal LLC 212 596-4010
49 W 38th St Fl 4 New York (10018) ***(G-11289)***
Mikam Graphics LLC 212 684-9393
1440 Broadway Fl 22 New York (10018) ***(G-11290)***
Mike's Custom Cabinets, Constantia *Also called Michael P Mmarr* ***(G-3907)***
Miken Companies Inc 716 668-6311
75 Boxwood Ln Buffalo (14227) ***(G-3085)***
Mil & Mir Steel Products Co 718 328-7596
1210 Randall Ave Bronx (10474) ***(G-1399)***
Mil-Spec Industries Corp 516 625-5787
42 Herb Hill Rd Glen Cove (11542) ***(G-5634)***
Mil-Spec. Enterprises, Brooklyn *Also called Carter Enterprises LLC* ***(G-1762)***
Milaaya Embroideries, New York *Also called Milaaya Inc* ***(G-11291)***
Milaaya Inc 212 764-6386
566 Fashion Ave Rm 805 New York (10018) ***(G-11291)***
Milan Accessories, New York *Also called AKOS Group Ltd* ***(G-9119)***
Milan Provision Co Inc 718 899-7678
10815 Roosevelt Ave Corona (11368) ***(G-4026)***
Milanese Commercial Door LLC 518 658-0398
28 Taylor Ave Berlin (12022) ***(G-856)***
Milano Granite and Marble Corp 718 477-7200
3521 Victory Blvd Staten Island (10314) ***(G-15727)***
Milburn Printing, Bohemia *Also called Mpe Graphics Inc* ***(G-1101)***
Miles Machine Inc 716 484-6026
85 Jones And Gifford Ave Jamestown (14701) ***(G-7053)***
Milestone Construction Corp 718 459-8500
9229 Queens Blvd Ste C2 Rego Park (11374) ***(G-14048)***
Milex Precision Inc 631 595-2393
66 S 2nd St Ste G Bay Shore (11706) ***(G-715)***
Milgo Industrial, Brooklyn *Also called M B C Metal Inc* ***(G-2249)***
Milgo Industrial Inc (PA) 718 388-6476
68 Lombardy St Brooklyn (11222) ***(G-2317)***
Milgo Industrial Inc 718 387-0406
514 Varick Ave Brooklyn (11222) ***(G-2318)***
Milgo/Bufkin, Brooklyn *Also called Milgo Industrial Inc* ***(G-2317)***
Mill Services, Cobleskill *Also called Efj Inc* ***(G-3762)***
Mill, The, Corning *Also called Ryers Creek Corp* ***(G-4000)***
Mill-Max Mfg Corp 516 922-6000
190 Pine Hollow Rd Oyster Bay (11771) ***(G-13397)***
Milla Global Inc 516 488-3601
1301 Metropolitan Ave Brooklyn (11237) ***(G-2319)***
Millbrook Vineyard, Millbrook *Also called Millbrook Winery Inc* ***(G-8513)***
Millbrook Winery Inc 845 677-8383
26 Wing Rd Millbrook (12545) ***(G-8513)***
Millco Woodworking LLC 585 526-6844
1710 Railroad Pl Hall (14463) ***(G-5940)***
Millcraft Paper Company 716 856-5135
99 Bud Mil Dr Buffalo (14206) ***(G-3086)***
Millennium Antenna Corp 315 798-9374
1001 Broad St Ste 401 Utica (13501) ***(G-16372)***
Millennium Medical Publishing 212 995-2211
611 Broadway Rm 310 New York (10012) ***(G-11292)***
Millennium Productions Inc 212 944-6203
265 W 37th St 11 New York (10018) ***(G-11293)***
Millennium Rmnfctred Toner Inc 718 585-9887
7 Bruckner Blvd Bronx (10454) ***(G-1400)***
Millennium Signs & Display Inc 516 292-8000
90 W Graham Ave Hempstead (11550) ***(G-6304)***
Millennium Stl Rack Rntals Inc (PA) 718 965-4736
253 Bond St Brooklyn (11217) ***(G-2320)***
Miller & Berkowitz Ltd 212 244-5459
345 7th Ave Fl 20 New York (10001) ***(G-11294)***
Miller & Veit Inc 212 247-2275
22 W 48th St Ste 703 New York (10036) ***(G-11295)***
Miller & Weber Inc 718 821-7110
507 Davie St Westbury (11590) ***(G-17039)***
Miller Blaker Inc 718 665-3930
620 E 132nd St Bronx (10454) ***(G-1401)***
Miller Enterprises CNY Inc 315 682-4999
131 W Seneca St Ste B Manlius (13104) ***(G-8108)***
Miller Mechanical Services Inc 518 792-0430
55-57 Walnut St Glens Falls (12801) ***(G-5705)***
Miller Metal Fabricating Inc 585 359-3400
315 Commerce Dr Rochester (14623) ***(G-14534)***
Miller Mohr Display Inc 631 941-2769
12 Technology Dr Unit 6 East Setauket (11733) ***(G-4505)***
Miller Printing & Litho Inc 518 842-0001
97 Guy Park Ave Amsterdam (12010) ***(G-357)***
Miller Stuart, Hauppauge *Also called Compac Development Corporation* ***(G-6072)***
Miller Technology Inc 631 694-2224
61 Gazza Blvd Farmingdale (11735) ***(G-5065)***
Miller Truck Rental, Scottsville *Also called Jack W Miller* ***(G-15359)***
Miller's Ready Mix, Gloversville *Also called Stephen Miller Gen Contrs Inc* ***(G-5738)***
Millercoors LLC 585 385-0670
1000 Pittsford Victor Rd Pittsford (14534) ***(G-13598)***
Millers Bulk Food and Bakery 585 798-9700
10858 Ridge Rd Medina (14103) ***(G-8310)***
Millers Millworks Inc 585 494-1420
29 N Lake Ave Bergen (14416) ***(G-849)***
Millers Presentation Furniture, Bergen *Also called Millers Millworks Inc* ***(G-849)***
Milli Home, New York *Also called Global Resources Sg Inc* ***(G-10362)***
Milligan & Higgins Div, Johnstown *Also called Hudson Industries Corporation* ***(G-7146)***
Milliore Fashion Inc 212 302-0001
250 W 39th St Rm 506 New York (10018) ***(G-11296)***
Millivac Instruments Inc 518 355-8300
2818 Curry Rd Schenectady (12303) ***(G-15305)***
Millrock Technology Inc 845 339-5700
39 Kieffer Ln Ste 2 Kingston (12401) ***(G-7230)***
Mills, William J & Company, Greenport *Also called 125-127 Main Street Corp* ***(G-5894)***
Millwood Inc 518 233-1475
430 Hudson River Rd Waterford (12188) ***(G-16635)***
Millwright Wdwrk Installetion 631 587-2635
991 Peconic Ave West Babylon (11704) ***(G-16842)***
Milmar Food Group, Goshen *Also called Juno Chefs* ***(G-5750)***
Milmar Food Group II LLC 845 294-5400
1 6 1/2 Station Rd Goshen (10924) ***(G-5752)***
Milne Mfg Inc 716 772-2536
8411 State St Gasport (14067) ***(G-5574)***
Milnot Holding Corporation 518 839-0300
1 Nutritious Pl Amsterdam (12010) ***(G-358)***
Milso Industries Inc 631 234-1133
25 Engineers Rd Hauppauge (11788) ***(G-6164)***
Milton Merl & Associates Inc 212 634-9292
647 W 174th St Bsmt B New York (10033) ***(G-11297)***
Miltons of New York Inc 212 997-3359
110 W 40th St Rm 1001 New York (10018) ***(G-11298)***
Milward Alloys Inc 716 434-5536
500 Mill St Lockport (14094) ***(G-7631)***
Mima S Bakery, Brooklyn *Also called Vito & Sons Bakery* ***(G-2752)***
Mimeocom Inc (PA) 212 847-3000
3 Park Ave Fl 22 New York (10016) ***(G-11299)***
Mimi So International LLC 212 300-8600
22 W 48th St Ste 902 New York (10036) ***(G-11300)***
Mimi So New York, New York *Also called Mimi So International LLC* ***(G-11300)***
Min Ho Designs Inc 212 838-3667
425 Madison Ave Rm 1703 New York (10017) ***(G-11301)***
Min New York, New York *Also called Salonclick LLC* ***(G-11976)***
Min-Max Machine Ltd 631 585-4378
1971 Pond Rd Ronkonkoma (11779) ***(G-14969)***
Mind Designs Inc (PA) 631 563-3644
5 Gregory Ct Farmingville (11738) ***(G-5168)***
Mindbodygreen LLC 347 529-6952
45 Main St Ste 422 Brooklyn (11201) ***(G-2321)***
Mineo & Sapio Meats Inc 716 884-2398
410 Connecticut St Buffalo (14213) ***(G-3087)***
Mineralbious Corp 516 498-9715
28 Northcote Rd Westbury (11590) ***(G-17040)***
Minerals Technologies Inc (PA) 212 878-1800
622 3rd Ave Fl 38 New York (10017) ***(G-11302)***
Minero & Sapio Sausage, Buffalo *Also called Mineo & Sapio Meats Inc* ***(G-3087)***
Mines Press Inc 914 788-1800
231 Croton Ave Cortlandt Manor (10567) ***(G-4078)***
Ming Pao (new York) Inc 718 786-2888
4331 33rd St Fl 2 Long Island City (11101) ***(G-7843)***
Ming Pao (new York) Inc 212 334-2220
265 Canal St Ste 403 New York (10013) ***(G-11303)***
Ming Pao (new York) Inc (HQ) 718 786-2888
4331 33rd St Long Island City (11101) ***(G-7844)***
Ming Pao Daily News, New York, Long Island City *Also called Ming Pao (new York) Inc* ***(G-7843)***
Ming Pay N Y, Long Island City *Also called Ming Pao (new York) Inc* ***(G-7844)***
Mini Circuits, Brooklyn *Also called Scientific Components Corp* ***(G-2564)***
Mini Circuits Lab, Deer Park *Also called Scientific Components Corp* ***(G-4231)***
Mini Graphics Inc 516 223-6464
140 Commerce Dr Hauppauge (11788) ***(G-6165)***
Mini-Circuits, Brooklyn *Also called Scientific Components Corp* ***(G-2563)***

ALPHABETIC

Mini-Circuits Fort Wayne LLC 718 934-4500
13 Neptune Ave Brooklyn (11235) **(G-2322)**
Mini-Max Dntl Repr Eqpmnts Inc 631 242-0322
25 W Jefryn Blvd Ste B Deer Park (11729) **(G-4198)**
Minico Industries Inc 631 595-1455
66a S 2nd St Ste A Bay Shore (11706) **(G-716)**
Minimax Concrete Corp 716 444-8908
2735 Bedell Rd Grand Island (14072) **(G-5777)**
Minimill Technologies Inc 315 692-4557
5792 Widewaters Pkwy # 1 Syracuse (13214) **(G-16011)**
Minisink Rubber, Warwick *Also called Mechanical Rubber Pdts Co Inc* **(G-16616)**
Minitec Framing Systems LLC 585 924-4690
100 Rawson Rd Ste 228 Victor (14564) **(G-16515)**
Mink Mart Inc 212 868-2785
345 7th Ave Fl 9 New York (10001) **(G-11304)**
Minority Reporter Inc (PA) 585 225-3628
19 Borrowdale Dr Rochester (14626) **(G-14535)**
Mint-X Products Corporation 877 646-8224
2048 119th St College Point (11356) **(G-3822)**
Minted Green Inc 845 458-1845
85 Regina Rd Airmont (10952) **(G-15)**
Minute Man Printing Company, White Plains *Also called Garrett J Cronin* **(G-17137)**
Minuteman Press, Manhasset *Also called Mdr Printing Corp* **(G-8095)**
Minuteman Press, Hewlett *Also called Torsaf Printers Inc* **(G-6337)**
Minuteman Press, Glen Oaks *Also called Wynco Press One Inc* **(G-5656)**
Minuteman Press, Deer Park *Also called L & K Graphics Inc* **(G-4185)**
Minuteman Press, Huntington *Also called J A T Printing Inc* **(G-6699)**
Minuteman Press, Liverpool *Also called Seaboard Graphic Services LLC* **(G-7574)**
Minuteman Press, Hauppauge *Also called Huckleberry Inc* **(G-6119)**
Minuteman Press, Bellerose *Also called Leigh Scott Enterprises Inc* **(G-806)**
Minuteman Press, Adams *Also called Benjamin Printing Inc* **(G-2)**
Minuteman Press, Rockville Centre *Also called Graphic Fabrications Inc* **(G-14819)**
Minuteman Press, Elmsford *Also called Cronin Enterprises Inc* **(G-4754)**
Minuteman Press, Rochester *Also called Baum Christine and John Corp* **(G-14241)**
Minuteman Press, Selden *Also called Datorib Inc* **(G-15372)**
Minuteman Press, Rochester *Also called Multiple Imprssons of Rchester* **(G-14545)**
Minuteman Press, Fairport *Also called Bernard Hall* **(G-4853)**
Minuteman Press, Farmingdale *Also called J P Printing Inc* **(G-5023)**
Minuteman Press, Bayside *Also called Alexander Polakovich* **(G-761)**
Minuteman Press, Merrick *Also called Jon Lyn Ink Inc* **(G-8420)**
Minuteman Press, East Northport *Also called Loudon Ltd* **(G-4460)**
Minuteman Press, Port Washington *Also called Sammba Printing Inc* **(G-13879)**
Minuteman Press Inc 845 623-2277
121 W Nyack Rd Ste 3 Nanuet (10954) **(G-8805)**
Minuteman Press Intl Inc 718 343-5440
24814 Union Tpke Jamaica (11426) **(G-6968)**
Minutemen Precision Mch & Tl, Ronkonkoma *Also called Minutemen Precsn McHning Tool* **(G-14970)**
Minutemen Precsn McHning Tool 631 467-4900
135 Raynor Ave Ronkonkoma (11779) **(G-14970)**
Miny Group Inc 212 925-6722
148 Lafayette St Fl 2 New York (10013) **(G-11305)**
Minyanville Media Inc 212 991-6200
708 3rd Ave Fl 6 New York (10017) **(G-11306)**
Mip, Halesite *Also called Manufacturers Indexing Pdts* **(G-5928)**
Mirage Moulding & Supply, Farmingdale *Also called Mirage Moulding Mfg Inc* **(G-5066)**
Mirage Moulding Mfg Inc 631 843-6168
160 Milbar Blvd Farmingdale (11735) **(G-5066)**
Mirandy Products Ltd 516 489-6800
1078 Grand Ave South Hempstead (11550) **(G-15554)**
Mirion Tech Conax Nuclear Inc 716 681-1973
402 Sonwil Dr Buffalo (14225) **(G-3088)**
Mirion Tech Imaging LLC 607 562-4300
315 Daniel Zenker Dr Horseheads (14845) **(G-6611)**
Mirion Tech Imging Systems Div, Horseheads *Also called Mirion Tech Imaging LLC* **(G-6611)**
Mirion Technologies Ist Corp (HQ) 607 562-4300
315 Daniel Zenker Dr # 204 Horseheads (14845) **(G-6612)**
Miroddi Imaging Inc (PA) 516 624-6898
27 Centre View Dr Oyster Bay (11771) **(G-13398)**
Mirror-Tech Manufacturing Co 914 965-1232
286 Nepperhan Ave Yonkers (10701) **(G-17486)**
Mirrorlite Superscript, Peekskill *Also called Hudson Mirror LLC* **(G-13504)**
Miscellnous Ir Fabricators Inc 518 355-1822
1404 Dunnsville Rd Schenectady (12306) **(G-15306)**
Mishpacha Magazine Inc 718 686-9339
5809 16th Ave Brooklyn (11204) **(G-2323)**
Mison Concepts Inc 516 933-8000
485 S Broadway Ste 33 Hicksville (11801) **(G-6398)**
Misonix Inc (PA) 631 694-9555
1938 New Hwy Farmingdale (11735) **(G-5067)**
Miss Grimble Associates Inc 718 665-2253
909 E 135th St Bronx (10454) **(G-1402)**
Miss Group (PA) 212 391-2535
1410 Broadway Rm 703 New York (10018) **(G-11307)**
Miss Group, The, Brooklyn *Also called MISS Sportswear Inc* **(G-2325)**
Miss Group, The, Brooklyn *Also called MISS Sportswear Inc* **(G-2326)**
Miss Jessies LLC 718 643-9016
441 Broadway Fl 2 New York (10013) **(G-11308)**
Miss Jessies Products, New York *Also called Miss Jessies LLC* **(G-11308)**
MISS Sportswear Inc 212 391-2535
117 9th St Brooklyn (11215) **(G-2324)**
MISS Sportswear Inc (PA) 212 391-2535
117 9th St Brooklyn (11215) **(G-2325)**
MISS Sportswear Inc 718 369-6012
117 9th St Brooklyn (11215) **(G-2326)**
Mission Crane Service Inc (PA) 718 937-3333
4700 33rd St Long Island City (11101) **(G-7845)**
Mission Critical Energy Inc 716 276-8465
1801 N French Rd Getzville (14068) **(G-5612)**
Mission Systems & Training, Owego *Also called Lockheed Martin Corporation* **(G-13380)**
Missiontex Inc 718 532-9053
236 Greenpoint Ave Ste 12 Brooklyn (11222) **(G-2327)**
Mistdoda Inc (HQ) 919 735-7111
261 5th Ave Fl 25 New York (10016) **(G-11309)**
Mitchell Electronics Corp 914 699-3800
85 W Grand St Mount Vernon (10552) **(G-8753)**
Mitchell Gold Co 516 627-3525
1900 Northern Blvd Ste F Manhasset (11030) **(G-8096)**
Mitchell Machine Tool LLC 585 254-7520
190 Murray St Rochester (14606) **(G-14536)**
Mitchell Prtg & Mailing Inc (PA) 315 343-3531
1 Burkle St Oswego (13126) **(G-13360)**
Mitchell Stone Products LLC 518 359-7029
161 Main St Tupper Lake (12986) **(G-16301)**
Mitchell's Speedway Press, Oswego *Also called Speedway Press Inc* **(G-13366)**
Mitco Manufacturing 800 338-8908
605 Locust St Garden City (11530) **(G-5535)**
Mitegen LLC 607 266-8877
95 Brown Rd Ste 1034 Ithaca (14850) **(G-6898)**
Mitsubishi Chemical Amer Inc (PA) 212 223-3043
655 3rd Ave Fl 15 New York (10017) **(G-11310)**
Mitsubishi Elc Pwr Pdts Inc 516 962-2813
55 Marcus Dr Melville (11747) **(G-8367)**
Mitsui Chemicals America Inc (HQ) 914 253-0777
800 Westchester Ave N607 Rye Brook (10573) **(G-15098)**
Mitten Manufacturing Inc 315 437-7564
5960 Court Street Rd Syracuse (13206) **(G-16012)**
Mix N Mac LLC 845 381-5536
280 Route 211 E Middletown (10940) **(G-8486)**
Mixture Screen Printing 845 561-2857
1607 Route 300 100 Newburgh (12550) **(G-12788)**
Mizkan America Inc 585 798-5720
711 Park Ave Medina (14103) **(G-8311)**
Mizkan America Inc 585 765-9171
247 West Ave Lyndonville (14098) **(G-7995)**
Mizkan Americas Inc 315 483-6944
7673 Sodus Center Rd Sodus (14551) **(G-15525)**
MJB Printing Corp 631 581-0177
280 Islip Ave Islip (11751) **(G-6850)**
Mjj Brilliant, New York *Also called Brilliant Jewelers/Mjj Inc* **(G-9514)**
Mjk Cutting Inc 718 384-7613
117 9th St Brooklyn (11215) **(G-2328)**
Mjk Enterprises LLC 917 653-9042
34 35th St Brooklyn (11232) **(G-2329)**
MJM Jewelry Corp (PA) 212 354-5014
29 W 38th St Rm 1601 New York (10018) **(G-11311)**
MJM Jewelry Corp 718 596-1600
400 3rd Ave Brooklyn (11215) **(G-2330)**
Mjs Woodworking, Bohemia *Also called J Percoco Industries Inc* **(G-1075)**
Mkj Communications Corp 212 206-0072
174 Hudson St Fl 2 New York (10013) **(G-11312)**
Mks Instruments Inc 585 292-7472
100 Highpower Rd Rochester (14623) **(G-14537)**
Mks Medical Electronics 585 292-7400
100 Highpower Rd Rochester (14623) **(G-14538)**
Mkt329 Inc 631 249-5500
565 Broadhollow Rd Ste 5 Farmingdale (11735) **(G-5068)**
MLS Sales 516 681-2736
226 10th St Bethpage (11714) **(G-873)**
Mm of East Aurora LLC 716 651-9663
3801 Harlem Rd Buffalo (14215) **(G-3089)**
MMC Enterprises Corp 800 435-1088
175 Commerce Dr Ste E Hauppauge (11788) **(G-6166)**
MMC Magnetics Corp 631 435-9888
175 Commerce Dr Ste E Hauppauge (11788) **(G-6167)**
Mml Software Ltd 631 941-1313
45 Research Way Ste 207 East Setauket (11733) **(G-4506)**
Mmo Music Group Inc 914 592-1188
50 Executive Blvd Ste 236 Elmsford (10523) **(G-4774)**
MMS H& F Inc 718 785-6663
8745 144th St Jamaica (11435) **(G-6969)**
Mnm Service Distributors Inc 914 337-5268
1 Greystone Cir Bronxville (10708) **(G-1501)**
Mnn Holding Company LLC 404 558-5251
155 Water St Ste 616 Brooklyn (11201) **(G-2331)**
MNS Fuel Corp 516 735-3835
2154 Pond Rd Ronkonkoma (11779) **(G-14971)**
Mobile Data Systems Inc 631 360-3400
110 Lake Ave S Ste 35 Nesconset (11767) **(G-8824)**

ALPHABETIC SECTION
Moneypaper Inc

Mobile Fleet Inc (PA)..........631 206-2920
10 Commerce Dr Hauppauge (11788) ***(G-6168)***
Mobile Hatch Inc..........212 314-7300
555 W 18th St New York (10011) ***(G-11313)***
Mobile Media Inc (PA)..........845 744-8080
24 Center St Pine Bush (12566) ***(G-13575)***
Mobile Mini Inc..........315 732-4555
2222 Oriskany St W Ste 3 Utica (13502) ***(G-16373)***
Mobile Mini Inc..........631 543-4900
1158 Jericho Tpke Commack (11725) ***(G-3864)***
Mobileapp Systems LLC..........716 667-2780
4 Grand View Trl Buffalo (14217) ***(G-3090)***
Mobius Labs Inc..........518 961-2600
37 Vischer Ferry Rd Rexford (12148) ***(G-14065)***
Mobo Systems Inc..........212 260-0895
26 Broadway Fl 24 New York (10004) ***(G-11314)***
Mod Printing, Islip *Also called MJB Printing Corp* ***(G-6850)***
Mod-A-Can Inc (PA)..........516 931-8545
178 Miller Pl Hicksville (11801) ***(G-6399)***
Mod-Pac Corp (PA)..........716 898-8480
1801 Elmwood Ave Ste 1 Buffalo (14207) ***(G-3091)***
Mod-Pac Corp..........716 447-9013
1801 Elmwood Ave Ste 1 Buffalo (14207) ***(G-3092)***
Model Power, Farmingdale *Also called ATI Model Products Inc* ***(G-4954)***
Modern Art Foundry Inc..........718 728-2030
1870 41st St Astoria (11105) ***(G-448)***
Modern Block LLC..........315 923-7443
2440 Wyne Zandra Rose Vly Clyde (14433) ***(G-3754)***
Modern Cabinet Company Inc..........845 473-4900
17 Van Kleeck Dr Poughkeepsie (12601) ***(G-13936)***
Modern Coating and Research..........315 597-3517
400 E Main St Palmyra (14522) ***(G-13437)***
Modern Craft Bar Rest Equip, Lindenhurst *Also called Modern Craft Bar Rest Equip* ***(G-7496)***
Modern Craft Bar Rest Equip..........631 226-5647
165 E Hoffman Ave Unit 3 Lindenhurst (11757) ***(G-7496)***
Modern Decal Co..........315 622-2778
8146 Soule Rd Liverpool (13090) ***(G-7561)***
Modern Farmer Media Inc..........518 828-7447
403 Warren St Hudson (12534) ***(G-6658)***
Modern Heat Trting Forging Inc (PA)..........716 884-2176
1112 Niagara St Buffalo (14213) ***(G-3093)***
Modern Itln Bky of W Babylon..........631 589-7300
301 Locust Ave Oakdale (11769) ***(G-13077)***
Modern Language Assn Amer Inc..........646 576-5000
85 Broad St Fl 5 New York (10004) ***(G-11315)***
Modern Mechanical Fab Inc..........518 298-5177
100 Walnut St Ste 7 Champlain (12919) ***(G-3572)***
Modern Metal Fabricators Inc..........518 966-4142
799 Cr 111 Hannacroix (12087) ***(G-5991)***
Modern Packaging Inc..........631 595-2437
505 Acorn St Deer Park (11729) ***(G-4199)***
Modern Plastic Bags Mfg Inc..........718 237-2985
63 Flushing Ave Unit 303 Brooklyn (11205) ***(G-2332)***
Modern Publishing, New York *Also called Unisystems Inc* ***(G-12482)***
Modern-TEC Manufacturing Inc..........716 625-8700
4935 Lockport Rd Lockport (14094) ***(G-7632)***
Modo Eyeware, New York *Also called Modo Retail LLC* ***(G-11316)***
Modo Retail LLC..........212 965-4900
252 Mott St New York (10012) ***(G-11316)***
Modu-Craft Inc (PA)..........716 694-0709
276 Creekside Dr Tonawanda (14150) ***(G-16200)***
Modu-Craft Inc..........716 694-0709
337 Payne Ave North Tonawanda (14120) ***(G-13000)***
Modular Devices Inc..........631 345-3100
1 Roned Rd Shirley (11967) ***(G-15449)***
Modular Medical Corp..........718 829-2626
1513 Olmstead Ave Bronx (10462) ***(G-1403)***
Modulex New York Inc..........646 742-1320
192 Lexington Ave Rm 1002 New York (10016) ***(G-11317)***
Modulightor Inc..........212 371-0336
246 E 58th St New York (10022) ***(G-11318)***
Modutank Inc..........718 392-1112
4104 35th Ave Long Island City (11101) ***(G-7846)***
Moes Wear Apparel Inc..........718 940-1597
1020 E 48th St Ste 8 Brooklyn (11203) ***(G-2333)***
Moffett Turf Equipment Inc..........585 334-0100
33 Thruway Park Dr West Henrietta (14586) ***(G-16917)***
Moffitt Fan Corporation..........585 768-7010
54 Church St Le Roy (14482) ***(G-7439)***
Mogen David Winegroup, Westfield *Also called Wine Group Inc* ***(G-17084)***
Mohawk Cabinet Company Inc..........518 725-0645
137 E State St Gloversville (12078) ***(G-5733)***
Mohawk Electro Techniques Inc..........315 896-2661
7677 Cameron Hill Rd Barneveld (13304) ***(G-615)***
Mohawk Fabric Company Inc..........518 842-3090
96 Guy Park Ave Amsterdam (12010) ***(G-359)***
Mohawk Fine Papers Inc (PA)..........518 237-1740
465 Saratoga St Cohoes (12047) ***(G-3775)***
Mohawk Fine Papers Inc..........518 237-1741
465 Saratoga St Cohoes (12047) ***(G-3776)***
Mohawk Metal Mfg & Sls..........315 853-7663
4901 State Route 233 Westmoreland (13490) ***(G-17091)***
Mohawk Resources Ltd..........518 842-1431
65 Vrooman Ave Amsterdam (12010) ***(G-360)***
Mohawk River Leather Works..........518 853-3900
32 Broad St Fultonville (12072) ***(G-5494)***
Mohawk Sign Systems Inc..........518 842-5303
5 Dandreano Dr Amsterdam (12010) ***(G-361)***
Mohawk Valley Knt McHy Co Inc..........315 736-3038
561 Main St New York Mills (13417) ***(G-12745)***
Mohawk Valley Manufacturing..........315 797-0851
2237 Broad St Frankfort (13340) ***(G-5365)***
Mohawk Valley Mill, Little Falls *Also called Burrows Paper Corporation* ***(G-7521)***
Mohawk Valley Printing Co, Herkimer *Also called Lennons Litho Inc* ***(G-6329)***
Moira New Hope Food Pantry..........518 529-6524
2341 County Route 5 Moira (12957) ***(G-8581)***
Mokai Manufacturing Inc..........845 566-8287
13 Jeanne Dr Newburgh (12550) ***(G-12789)***
Molabs Inc..........310 721-6828
32 Little West 12th St New York (10014) ***(G-11319)***
Mold-A-Matic Corporation..........607 433-2121
147 River St Oneonta (13820) ***(G-13211)***
Mold-Rite Plastics LLC..........518 561-1812
1 Plant St Plattsburgh (12901) ***(G-13704)***
Moldcraft Inc..........716 684-1126
240 Gould Ave Depew (14043) ***(G-4288)***
Moldedtanks.com, Bay Shore *Also called Chem-Tek Systems Inc* ***(G-681)***
Moldova Pickles & Salads Inc..........718 284-2220
1060 E 46th St Brooklyn (11203) ***(G-2334)***
Moldtech Inc..........716 685-3344
1900 Commerce Pkwy Lancaster (14086) ***(G-7351)***
Molecular Glasses Inc..........585 210-2861
1667 Lake Ave Ste 278b Rochester (14615) ***(G-14539)***
Moley Magnetics Inc..........716 434-4023
5202 Commerce Dr Lockport (14094) ***(G-7633)***
Molly Vapes Inc..........718 743-0120
3235 Emmons Ave Apt 608 Brooklyn (11235) ***(G-2335)***
Mollys Cupcakes New York..........212 255-5441
228 Bleecker St New York (10014) ***(G-11320)***
Mom Dad Publishing Inc..........646 476-9170
59 Maiden Ln Fl 27 New York (10038) ***(G-11321)***
Mom Sas, New York *Also called Materne North America Corp* ***(G-11202)***
Momentive, Waterford *Also called Mpm Silicones LLC* ***(G-16641)***
Momentive Performance (HQ)..........281 325-3536
260 Hudson River Rd Waterford (12188) ***(G-16636)***
Momentive Performance Mtls Inc..........614 986-2495
260 Hudson River Rd Waterford (12188) ***(G-16637)***
Momentive Performance Mtls Inc..........914 784-4807
769 Old Saw Mill River Rd Tarrytown (10591) ***(G-16121)***
Momentive Performance Mtls Inc (HQ)..........518 237-3330
260 Hudson River Rd Waterford (12188) ***(G-16638)***
Momentive Prfmce Mtls Holdings, Albany *Also called Momentive Prfmce Mtls Holdings* ***(G-102)***
Momentive Prfmce Mtls Holdings..........518 533-4600
22 Corporate Woods Blvd Albany (12211) ***(G-102)***
Momentummedia Sports Pubg, Ithaca *Also called Mag Inc* ***(G-6894)***
Momn Pops Inc..........845 567-0640
13 Orr Hatch Cornwall (12518) ***(G-4009)***
Momofuku 171 First Avenue LLC..........212 777-7773
171 1st Ave New York (10003) ***(G-11322)***
Mona Belts, Bronx *Also called Mona Slide Fasteners Inc* ***(G-1404)***
Mona Slide Fasteners Inc (PA)..........718 325-7700
4510 White Plains Rd Bronx (10470) ***(G-1404)***
Monacelli Press LLC..........212 229-9925
236 W 27th St Rm 4a New York (10001) ***(G-11323)***
Monaghan Medical Corporation (PA)..........518 561-7330
5 Latour Ave Ste 1600 Plattsburgh (12901) ***(G-13705)***
Monaghan Medical Corporation..........315 472-2136
327 W Fayette St Ste 212 Syracuse (13202) ***(G-16013)***
Monarch Electric Products Inc..........718 583-7996
4077 Park Ave Fl 5 Bronx (10457) ***(G-1405)***
Monarch Graphics Inc..........631 232-1300
1065 Islip Ave Central Islip (11722) ***(G-3531)***
Monarch Metal Fabrication Inc..........631 563-8967
1625 Sycamore Ave Ste A Bohemia (11716) ***(G-1100)***
Monarch Plastics Inc..........716 569-2175
225 Falconer St Frewsburg (14738) ***(G-5465)***
Monasani Signs Inc..........631 266-2635
22 Compton St East Northport (11731) ***(G-4461)***
Mondelez Global LLC..........845 567-4701
800 Corporate Blvd Newburgh (12550) ***(G-12790)***
Mondelez Global LLC..........585 345-3300
4303 Federal Dr Batavia (14020) ***(G-643)***
Mondo Publishing Inc (PA)..........212 268-3560
980 Avenue Of The America New York (10018) ***(G-11324)***
Moneast Inc..........845 298-8898
1708 Route 9 Ste 3 Wappingers Falls (12590) ***(G-16595)***
Monelle Jewelry..........212 977-9535
608 5th Ave Ste 504 New York (10020) ***(G-11325)***
Moneypaper Inc..........914 925-0022
411 Theodore Fremd Ave # 132 Rye (10580) ***(G-15090)***

ALPHABETIC

(PA)=Parent Co (HQ)=Headquarters (DH)=Div Headquarters
2018 Harris
New York Manufacturers Directory
1011

Moneysaver Advertising Inc....585 593-1275
639 W Norton Dr Olean (14760) *(G-13172)*
Moneysaver Shopping News, Olean *Also called Moneysaver Advertising Inc (G-13172)*
Monfefo LLC....347 779-2600
630 Flushing Ave 5q Brooklyn (11206) *(G-2336)*
Mongiello Sales Inc....845 436-4200
250 Hilldale Rd Hurleyville (12747) *(G-6769)*
Mongiellos Itln Cheese Spc LLC....845 436-4200
250 Hilldale Rd Hurleyville (12747) *(G-6770)*
Mongodb Inc....646 727-4092
229 W 43rd St Fl 5 New York (10036) *(G-11326)*
Mongru Neckwear Inc....718 706-0406
1010 44th Ave Fl 2 Long Island City (11101) *(G-7847)*
Monitor Controls, Hauppauge *Also called Monitor Elevator Products LLC (G-6169)*
Monitor Elevator Products LLC....631 543-4334
125 Ricefield Ln Hauppauge (11788) *(G-6169)*
Monkey Joe Roasting Company....845 331-4598
478 Broadway Ste A Kingston (12401) *(G-7231)*
Monkey Rum, New York *Also called Evolution Spirits Inc (G-10149)*
Mono-Systems Inc....716 821-1344
180 Hopkins St Buffalo (14220) *(G-3094)*
Monofrax LLC....716 483-7200
1870 New York Ave Falconer (14733) *(G-4915)*
Monolithic Coatings Inc....914 621-2765
916 Highway Route 20 Sharon Springs (13459) *(G-15406)*
Monroe Cable Company Inc....845 692-2800
14 Commercial Ave Middletown (10941) *(G-8487)*
Monroe County Auto Svcs Inc (PA)....585 764-3741
1505 Lyell Ave Rochester (14606) *(G-14540)*
Monroe Fluid Technology Inc....585 392-3434
36 Draffin Rd Hilton (14468) *(G-6444)*
Monroe Industries Inc....585 226-8230
5611 Tec Dr Avon (14414) *(G-538)*
Monroe Plating Div, Rochester *Also called McAlpin Industries Inc (G-14522)*
Monroe Stair Products Inc (PA)....845 783-4245
1 Stair Way Monroe (10950) *(G-8598)*
Monroe Stair Products Inc....845 791-4016
309 E Broadway Monticello (12701) *(G-8644)*
Monroe Table Company Inc....716 945-7700
255 Rochester St Ste 15 Salamanca (14779) *(G-15129)*
Montana Global LLC....212 213-1572
9048 160th St Jamaica (11432) *(G-6970)*
Montauk Brewing Company Inc....631 668-8471
62 S Erie Ave Montauk (11954) *(G-8624)*
Montauk Inlet Seafood Inc....631 668-3419
E Lake Dr Ste 540-541 Montauk (11954) *(G-8625)*
Monte Goldman Embroidery Co....212 874-5397
15 W 72nd St Apt 11n New York (10023) *(G-11327)*
Monte Press Inc....718 325-4999
4808 White Plains Rd Bronx (10470) *(G-1406)*
Montero International Inc....212 695-1787
149 Sullivan Ln Unit 1 Westbury (11590) *(G-17041)*
Montezuma Winery LLC....315 568-8190
2981 Us Route 20 Seneca Falls (13148) *(G-15389)*
Montfort Brothers Inc....845 896-6694
44 Elm St Fishkill (12524) *(G-5194)*
Monthly Gift Inc....888 444-9661
401 Park Ave S New York (10016) *(G-11328)*
Monticello Black Top Corp....845 434-7280
80 Patio Dr Thompsonville (12784) *(G-16138)*
Montly Gift, New York *Also called Monthly Gift Inc (G-11328)*
Montrose Equipment Sales Inc....718 388-7446
202 N 10th St Brooklyn (11211) *(G-2337)*
Moo Goong Hwa, Corona *Also called Kenan International Trading (G-4023)*
Moog - Isp, Niagara Falls *Also called Moog Inc (G-12865)*
Moog Inc (PA)....716 652-2000
400 Jamison Rd Plant26 Elma (14059) *(G-4664)*
Moog Inc....716 687-4954
300 Jamison Rd East Aurora (14052) *(G-4400)*
Moog Inc....716 805-8100
7021 Sneca St At Jmson Rd East Aurora (14052) *(G-4401)*
Moog Inc....716 731-6300
6686 Walmore Rd Niagara Falls (14304) *(G-12865)*
Moog Inc....716 687-4778
160 Jamison Rd Elma (14059) *(G-4665)*
Moon Gates Company....718 426-0023
3243 104th St East Elmhurst (11369) *(G-4417)*
Moon, Wm, Catskill *Also called William Moon Iron Works Inc (G-3462)*
Mooney-Keehley Inc....585 271-1573
38 Saginaw Dr Rochester (14623) *(G-14541)*
Moonlight Creamery....585 223-0880
36 West Ave Fairport (14450) *(G-4870)*
Moor Electronics Inc....716 821-5304
95 Dorothy St Ste 6 Buffalo (14206) *(G-3095)*
Mooradian Hydraulics & Eqp Co (PA)....518 766-3866
1190 Route 9 Castleton On Hudson (12033) *(G-3448)*
Moore Business Forms, Lakewood *Also called R R Donnelley & Sons Company (G-7317)*
Moore Business Forms, Grand Island *Also called RR Donnelley & Sons Company (G-5781)*
Moore Printing Company Inc....585 394-1533
9 Coy St Canandaigua (14424) *(G-3378)*
Moore Research Center, Grand Island *Also called RR Donnelley & Sons Company (G-5782)*
Mooseberry Soap Co LLC....315 332-8913
513 W Union St Ste B Newark (14513) *(G-12758)*
Moran Ship Yard, Staten Island *Also called Moran Towing Corporation (G-15729)*
Moran Shipyard Corporation (HQ)....718 981-5600
2015 Richmond Ter Staten Island (10302) *(G-15728)*
Moran Towing Corporation....718 981-5600
2015 Richmond Ter Staten Island (10302) *(G-15729)*
Morania Oil of Long Island, Farmingdale *Also called O C P Inc (G-5079)*
Morco, Plainview *Also called Howard J Moore Company Inc (G-13635)*
Morco Products Corp....718 853-4005
556 39th St Brooklyn (11232) *(G-2338)*
Morcon Inc (PA)....518 677-8511
879 State Rd 22 Cambridge (12816) *(G-3337)*
Mordechai Collection, New York *Also called Ada Gems Corp (G-9070)*
Morehouse Publishing, New York *Also called Church Publishing Incorporated (G-9667)*
Moreland Hose & Belting Corp....631 563-7071
4118 Sunrise Hwy Oakdale (11769) *(G-13078)*
Morelle Products Ltd....212 391-8070
211 E 18th St Apt 4d New York (10003) *(G-11329)*
Moresca Clothing and Costume....845 331-6012
361 Union Center Rd Ulster Park (12487) *(G-16309)*
Morey Publishing....516 284-3300
20 Hempstead Tpke Unit B Farmingdale (11735) *(G-5069)*
Morgan Fuel & Heating Co Inc....845 856-7831
6 Sleepy Hollow Rd Port Jervis (12771) *(G-13812)*
Morgan Fuel & Heating Co Inc....845 246-4931
240 Ulster Ave Saugerties (12477) *(G-15217)*
Morgan Fuel & Heating Co Inc....845 626-7766
5 Webster Ave Kerhonkson (12446) *(G-7185)*
Morgik Metal Designs....212 463-0304
145 Hudson St Frnt 4 New York (10013) *(G-11330)*
Morgood Tools Inc....585 436-8828
940 Millstead Way Rochester (14624) *(G-14542)*
Morito/Kane-M, New York *Also called Kane-M Inc (G-10844)*
Morlyn Asphalt Corp....845 888-2695
420 Bernas Rd Cochecton (12726) *(G-3768)*
Morningstar Concrete Products....716 693-4020
528 Young St Tonawanda (14150) *(G-16201)*
Morningstar Foods, Delhi *Also called Saputo Dairy Foods Usa LLC (G-4267)*
Moro Corporation....607 724-4241
23 Griswold St Binghamton (13904) *(G-933)*
Moro Design, Ithaca *Also called Joe Moro (G-6890)*
Morris Brothers Sign Svc Inc....212 675-9130
37 W 20th St Ste 708 New York (10011) *(G-11331)*
Morris Fine Furniture Workshop, Brooklyn *Also called Walter P Sauer LLC (G-2759)*
Morris Golf Ventures....631 283-0559
Sebonac Inlet Rd Southampton (11968) *(G-15571)*
Morris Kitchen Inc....646 413-5186
30 Chester Ct Brooklyn (11225) *(G-2339)*
Morris Machining Service Inc....585 527-8100
95 Mount Read Blvd Rochester (14611) *(G-14543)*
Morris Products Inc....518 743-0523
53 Carey Rd Queensbury (12804) *(G-14018)*
Morse Systems, Ithaca *Also called Borgwarner Ithaca LLC (G-6864)*
Mortech Industries Inc....845 628-6138
961 Route 6 Mahopac (10541) *(G-8028)*
Mortgage Press Ltd....516 409-1400
1220 Wantagh Ave Wantagh (11793) *(G-16581)*
Morton Buildings Inc....585 786-8191
5616 Route 20a E Warsaw (14569) *(G-16605)*
Morton Salt Inc....585 493-2511
45 Ribaud Ave Silver Springs (14550) *(G-15472)*
Mosby Holdings Corp (HQ)....212 309-8100
125 Park Ave New York (10017) *(G-11332)*
Moschos Furs Inc....212 244-0255
345 7th Ave Rm 1501 New York (10001) *(G-11333)*
Moscot Wholesale Corp....212 647-1550
69 W 14th St Fl 2 New York (10011) *(G-11334)*
Motema Music LLC....212 860-6969
8 W 127th St Apt 2 New York (10027) *(G-11335)*
Mother Mousse Ltd (PA)....718 983-8366
3767 Victory Blvd Ste D Staten Island (10314) *(G-15730)*
Mother Nature & Partners, Brooklyn *Also called Mnn Holding Company LLC (G-2331)*
Moti Inc....718 436-4280
4118 13th Ave Brooklyn (11219) *(G-2340)*
Motion Message Inc....631 924-9500
22 Sawgrass Dr Ste 4 Bellport (11713) *(G-831)*
Motivair Corporation....716 691-9222
85 Woodridge Dr Amherst (14228) *(G-250)*
Motor Components LLC....607 737-8011
2243 Corning Rd Elmira Heights (14903) *(G-4724)*
Motorad of America, Niagara Falls *Also called Transcedar Industries Ltd (G-12901)*
Motorola Solutions Inc....518 348-0833
7 Deer Run Holw Halfmoon (12065) *(G-5934)*
Motorola Solutions Inc....718 330-2163
335 Adams St Fl 7 Brooklyn (11201) *(G-2341)*
Motorola Solutions Inc....518 869-9517
251 New Karner Rd Albany (12205) *(G-103)*
Mott's, Williamson *Also called Dr Pepper Snapple Group Inc (G-17251)*
Motts, Elmsford *Also called Motts LLP (G-4775)*

ALPHABETIC SECTION
Mustang Bio Inc

Motts LLP (HQ) 972 673-8088
55 Hunter Ln Elmsford (10523) ***(G-4775)***
Mount Kisco Transfer Stn Inc 914 666-6350
10 Lincoln Pl Mount Kisco (10549) ***(G-8678)***
Mount Vernon Iron Works Inc 914 668-7064
130 Miller Pl Mount Vernon (10550) ***(G-8754)***
Mount Vernon Machine Inc 845 268-9400
614 Corporate Way Ste 8 Valley Cottage (10989) ***(G-16408)***
Mountain Forest Products Inc 518 597-3674
3281 Nys Route 9n Crown Point (12928) ***(G-4093)***
Mountain Side Farms Inc 718 526-3442
15504 Liberty Ave Jamaica (11433) ***(G-6971)***
Mountain T-Shirts Inc 518 943-4533
8 W Bridge St Catskill (12414) ***(G-3460)***
Mountain T-Shirts & Sign Works, Catskill *Also called Mountain T-Shirts Inc* ***(G-3460)***
Movin On Sounds and SEC Inc 516 489-2350
636 Hempstead Tpke Franklin Square (11010) ***(G-5375)***
Movinads & Signs LLC 518 378-3000
1771 Route 9 Halfmoon (12065) ***(G-5935)***
Moznaim Co, Brooklyn *Also called Moznaim Publishing Co Inc* ***(G-2342)***
Moznaim Publishing Co Inc 718 853-0525
4304 12th Ave Brooklyn (11219) ***(G-2342)***
Mozzarella Fresca Incorporated 559 752-4823
2376 S Park Ave Buffalo (14220) ***(G-3096)***
MP Caroll Inc 716 683-8520
4822 Genesee St Cheektowaga (14225) ***(G-3607)***
Mp Displays LLC 845 268-4113
704 Executive Blvd Ste 1 Valley Cottage (10989) ***(G-16409)***
Mp Studio Inc 212 302-5666
147 W 35th St Ste 1603 New York (10001) ***(G-11336)***
Mpdraw LLC 212 228-8383
109 Ludlow St New York (10002) ***(G-11337)***
Mpe Graphics Inc 631 582-8900
120 Wilbur Pl Ste A Bohemia (11716) ***(G-1101)***
Mpi Consulting Incorporated 631 253-2377
87 Jersey St West Babylon (11704) ***(G-16843)***
Mpi Consulting Incorporated 631 253-2377
87 Jersey St West Babylon (11704) ***(G-16844)***
Mpi Incorporated 845 471-7630
165 Smith St Stop 5 Poughkeepsie (12601) ***(G-13937)***
Mpl Inc 607 266-0480
41 Dutch Mill Rd Ithaca (14850) ***(G-6899)***
Mpl Communications Inc (HQ) 212 246-5881
41 W 54th St New York (10019) ***(G-11338)***
Mpm Holdings Inc (PA) 518 237-3330
260 Hudson River Rd Waterford (12188) ***(G-16639)***
Mpm Intermediate Holdings Inc (HQ) 518 237-3330
260 Hudson River Rd Waterford (12188) ***(G-16640)***
Mpm Silicones LLC 518 233-3330
260 Hudson River Rd Waterford (12188) ***(G-16641)***
Mpr Magazine App Inc 718 403-0303
2653 E 19th St Fl 2 Brooklyn (11235) ***(G-2343)***
Mr Disposable Inc 718 388-8574
101 Richardson St Ste 2 Brooklyn (11211) ***(G-2344)***
Mr Pierogi LLC 718 499-7821
126 12th St Brooklyn (11215) ***(G-2345)***
Mr Sign, East Northport *Also called Monasani Signs Inc* ***(G-4461)***
Mr Sign, Brooklyn *Also called Penn Signs Inc* ***(G-2427)***
Mr Sign Usa Inc 718 218-3321
1920 Atlantic Ave Brooklyn (11233) ***(G-2346)***
Mr Smoothie 845 296-1686
207 South Ave Ste F102 Poughkeepsie (12601) ***(G-13938)***
Mr Steam, Long Island City *Also called Sussman-Automatic Corporation* ***(G-7925)***
Mr Vape Guru 845 796-2274
73 Pleasant St Monticello (12701) ***(G-8645)***
Mr.-Bar-B-q-, Melville *Also called Blue Rhino Global Sourcing Inc* ***(G-8329)***
MRC Bearings, Jamestown *Also called SKF USA Inc* ***(G-7060)***
MRC Global (us) Inc 607 739-8575
224 N Main St Bldg 13-1 Horseheads (14845) ***(G-6613)***
Mrchocolatecom LLC 718 875-9772
66 Water St Ste 2 Brooklyn (11201) ***(G-2347)***
Mri Northtowns Group PC 716 836-4646
199 Park Club Ln Ste 300 Buffalo (14221) ***(G-3097)***
Mrinalini Inc 646 510-2747
469 7th Ave Rm 1254 New York (10018) ***(G-11339)***
Mrs John L Strong & Co LLC 212 838-3775
699 Madison Ave Fl 5 New York (10065) ***(G-11340)***
Mrt Textile Inc 800 674-1073
350 5th Ave New York (10118) ***(G-11341)***
Ms Machining Inc 607 723-1105
2 William St Binghamton (13904) ***(G-934)***
Ms Paper Products Co Inc 718 624-0248
930 Bedford Ave Brooklyn (11205) ***(G-2348)***
Ms Spares LLC 607 223-3024
8055 Evesborough Dr Clay (13041) ***(G-3709)***
Ms. Michelles, Calverton *Also called Cooking With Chef Michelle LLC* ***(G-3317)***
Msdivisions, Middletown *Also called Commercial Communications LLC* ***(G-8466)***
Msi Inc 845 639-6683
329 Strawtown Rd New City (10956) ***(G-8834)***
Msi-Molding Solutions Inc 315 736-2412
6247 State Route 233 Rome (13440) ***(G-14850)***
Mskcc Rmipc 212 639-6212
1250 1st Ave Ste S-C24 New York (10065) ***(G-11342)***
MSP Technologycom LLC 631 424-7542
77 Bankside Dr Centerport (11721) ***(G-3505)***
MSQ Corporation 718 465-0900
21504 Hempstead Ave Queens Village (11429) ***(G-13998)***
Mssi, Millbrook *Also called Micro Systems Specialists Inc* ***(G-8512)***
Mt Fuel Corp 631 445-2047
7 Bridge Rd Setauket (11733) ***(G-15403)***
Mt Morris Shopper Inc 585 658-3520
85 N Main St Mount Morris (14510) ***(G-8695)***
MTI, Albany *Also called Mechanical Technology Inc* ***(G-101)***
MTI, New York *Also called Minerals Technologies Inc* ***(G-11302)***
MTI Instruments Inc 518 218-2550
325 Washington Ave 3 Albany (12206) ***(G-104)***
MTK Electronics Inc 631 924-7666
1 National Blvd Medford (11763) ***(G-8290)***
Mtm Publishing Inc 212 242-6930
435 W 23rd St New York (10011) ***(G-11343)***
MTS Systems Corporation 518 899-2140
30 Gleneagles Blvd Ballston Lake (12019) ***(G-583)***
Mtwli Precision Corp 631 244-3767
1605 Sycamore Ave Unit B Bohemia (11716) ***(G-1102)***
Mualema LLC 609 820-6098
128 W 112th St Apt 1a New York (10026) ***(G-11344)***
Mud Puddle Books Inc 212 647-9168
36 W 25th St Fl 5 New York (10010) ***(G-11345)***
Muench-Kreuzer Candle Company (PA) 315 471-4515
617 Hiawatha Blvd E Syracuse (13208) ***(G-16014)***
Mulitex Usa Inc 212 398-0440
215 W 40th St Fl 7 New York (10018) ***(G-11346)***
Muller Quaker Dairy, Batavia *Also called Dairy Farmers America Inc* ***(G-632)***
Muller Tool Inc 716 895-3658
74 Anderson Rd Buffalo (14225) ***(G-3098)***
Mullers Cider House LLC 585 287-5875
1344 University Ave # 180 Rochester (14607) ***(G-14544)***
Mullican Flooring LP 716 537-2642
209 Vermont St Holland (14080) ***(G-6509)***
Multi Packaging Solutions Inc 516 488-2000
325 Duffy Ave Unit 1 Hicksville (11801) ***(G-6400)***
Multi Packaging Solutions Inc (HQ) 646 885-0005
150 E 52nd St Ste 2800 New York (10022) ***(G-11347)***
Multi Packg Solutions Intl Ltd (HQ) 646 885-0005
885 3rd Ave Fl 28 New York (10022) ***(G-11348)***
Multi Tech Electric 718 606-2695
2526 50th St Woodside (11377) ***(G-17356)***
Multi-Health Systems Inc 800 456-3003
Indus Pkwy Ste 70660 60 Cheektowaga (14227) ***(G-3608)***
Multifold Die Ctng Finshg Corp 631 232-1235
120 Ricefield Ln Ste B Hauppauge (11788) ***(G-6170)***
Multimatic Products Inc 800 767-7633
900 Marconi Ave Ronkonkoma (11779) ***(G-14972)***
Multimedia Plus Inc 212 982-3229
853 Broadway Ste 1605 New York (10003) ***(G-11349)***
Multimedia Services Inc 607 936-3186
11136 River Rd 40 Corning (14830) ***(G-3997)***
Multiple Imprssons of Rchester (PA) 585 546-1160
41 Chestnut St Rochester (14604) ***(G-14545)***
Multisorb Tech Intl LLC (PA) 716 824-8900
325 Harlem Rd Buffalo (14224) ***(G-3099)***
Multisorb Technologies Inc 716 668-4191
20 French Rd Cheektowaga (14227) ***(G-3609)***
Multisorb Technologies Inc 716 656-1402
10 French Rd Buffalo (14227) ***(G-3100)***
Multitone Finishing Co Inc 516 485-1043
56 Hempstead Gardens Dr West Hempstead (11552) ***(G-16892)***
Multiwire Laboratories Ltd 607 257-3378
95 Brown Rd 1018266a Ithaca (14850) ***(G-6900)***
Munn Works LLC 914 665-6100
150 N Macquesten Pkwy Mount Vernon (10550) ***(G-8755)***
Munson Machinery Company Inc 315 797-0090
210 Seward Ave Utica (13502) ***(G-16374)***
Murphy Manufacturing Co Inc 585 223-0100
38 West Ave Fairport (14450) ***(G-4871)***
Murray Bresky Consultants Ltd (PA) 845 436-5001
5190 Main St South Fallsburg (12779) ***(G-15544)***
Murray Logging LLC 518 834-7372
1535 Route 9 Keeseville (12944) ***(G-7169)***
Murray's Chicken, South Fallsburg *Also called Murray Bresky Consultants Ltd* ***(G-15544)***
Music & Sound Retailer Inc 516 767-2500
25 Willowdale Ave Port Washington (11050) ***(G-13866)***
Music Library, New York *Also called Boosey & Hawkes Inc* ***(G-9490)***
Music Minus One, Elmsford *Also called Mmo Music Group Inc* ***(G-4774)***
Music Sales, New York *Also called G Schirmer Inc* ***(G-10280)***
Music Sales, Chester *Also called G Schirmer Inc* ***(G-3634)***
Music Sales Corporation (PA) 212 254-2100
180 Madison Ave Ste 2400 New York (10016) ***(G-11350)***
Musicskins LLC 646 827-4271
140 58th St Ste 197 Brooklyn (11220) ***(G-2349)***
Mustang Bio Inc 781 652-4500
2 Gansevoort St Fl 9 New York (10014) ***(G-11351)***

ALPHABETIC

Mustang-Major Tool & Die Co............716 992-9200
3243 N Boston Rd Eden (14057) **(G-4601)**
Mutual Engraving Company Inc............516 489-0534
497 Hempstead Ave West Hempstead (11552) **(G-16893)**
Mutual Harware, Long Island City *Also called Mutual Sales Corp* **(G-7848)**
Mutual Library Bindery Inc............315 455-6638
6295 E Molloy Rd Ste 3 East Syracuse (13057) **(G-4565)**
Mutual Sales Corp............718 361-8373
545 49th Ave Long Island City (11101) **(G-7848)**
Muzet Inc............315 452-0050
104 S Main St Syracuse (13212) **(G-16015)**
Mv Corp Inc............631 273-8020
88 Spence St Ste 90 Bay Shore (11706) **(G-717)**
Mwi Inc (PA)............585 424-4200
1269 Brighton Henrietta T Rochester (14623) **(G-14546)**
Mwsi Inc (PA)............914 347-4200
12 Skyline Dr Ste 230 Hawthorne (10532) **(G-6275)**
Mx Solar USA LLC............732 356-7300
100 Wall St Ste 1000 New York (10005) **(G-11352)**
My Apparel, New York *Also called El-La Design Inc* **(G-10046)**
My Hanky Inc............646 321-0869
680 81st St Apt 4d Brooklyn (11228) **(G-2350)**
My Industries Inc............845 638-2257
368 New Hempstead Rd New City (10956) **(G-8835)**
My Life My Health, Flushing *Also called Life Watch Technology Inc* **(G-5273)**
My Most Favorite Food............212 580-5130
247 W 72nd St Frnt 1 New York (10023) **(G-11353)**
My Publisher Inc............212 935-5215
845 3rd Ave Rm 1410 New York (10022) **(G-11354)**
Mycra Pac Designer Wear Inc (PA)............925 631-6878
158 W 29th St Fl 12 New York (10001) **(G-11355)**
Myers Group LLC (PA)............973 761-6414
257 W 38th St New York (10018) **(G-11356)**
Myles Tool Company Inc............716 731-1300
6300 Inducon Corporate Dr Sanborn (14132) **(G-15151)**
Mypublisher Inc (HQ)............914 773-4312
8 Westchester Plz Ste 145 Elmsford (10523) **(G-4776)**
Mystery Scene Magazine, New York *Also called Kbs Communications LLC* **(G-10864)**
Mystic Apparel Company, New York *Also called Mystic Apparel LLC* **(G-11357)**
Mystic Apparel LLC (PA)............212 279-2466
1333 Broadway Fl 6 New York (10018) **(G-11357)**
Mystic Display Co Inc............718 485-2651
909 Remsen Ave Brooklyn (11236) **(G-2351)**
Mystic Inc (PA)............212 239-2025
463 7th Ave Fl 12 New York (10018) **(G-11358)**
MZB Accessories LLC............718 472-7500
2976 Northern Blvd Fl 4 Long Island City (11101) **(G-7849)**
N & G of America Inc............516 428-3414
28 W Lane Dr Plainview (11803) **(G-13650)**
N & L Fuel Corp............718 863-3538
2014 Blackrock Ave Bronx (10472) **(G-1407)**
N & L Instruments Inc............631 471-4000
90 13th Ave Unit 1 Ronkonkoma (11779) **(G-14973)**
N A Alumil Corporation............718 355-9393
4401 21st St Ste 203 Long Island City (11101) **(G-7850)**
N A P, Brooklyn *Also called Nap Industries Inc* **(G-2355)**
N A R Associates Inc............845 557-8713
128 Rte 55 Barryville (12719) **(G-620)**
N A S C O, Watertown *Also called Northern Awning & Sign Company* **(G-16690)**
N C Iron Works Inc............718 633-4660
1117 60th St Brooklyn (11219) **(G-2352)**
N E Controls LLC............315 626-2480
7048 Interstate Island Rd Syracuse (13209) **(G-16016)**
N I Boutique, Long Island City *Also called Nazim Izzak Inc* **(G-7852)**
N I T, New York *Also called Network Infrstructure Tech Inc* **(G-11396)**
N Make Mold Inc............716 877-3146
85 River Rock Dr Ste 202 Buffalo (14207) **(G-3101)**
N Pologeorgis Furs Inc............212 563-2250
143 W 29th St Fl 8 New York (10001) **(G-11359)**
N R S I, Syosset *Also called National Rding Styles Inst Inc* **(G-15851)**
N Sketch Build Inc............800 975-0597
982 Main St Ste 4-130 Fishkill (12524) **(G-5195)**
N V Magazine, New York *Also called Envy Publishing Group Inc* **(G-10100)**
N Y B P Inc............585 624-2541
1355 Pittsford Mendon Rd Mendon (14506) **(G-8413)**
N Y Bijoux Corp............212 244-9585
1261 Broadway Rm 606 New York (10001) **(G-11360)**
N Y Contract Seating Inc............718 417-9298
5560 60th St Maspeth (11378) **(G-8183)**
N Y Elli Design Corp............718 228-0014
5105 Flushing Ave 2 Maspeth (11378) **(G-8184)**
N Y Western Concrete Corp............585 343-6850
638 E Main St Batavia (14020) **(G-644)**
N Y Winstons Inc............212 665-3166
5 W 86th St Apt 9e New York (10024) **(G-11361)**
N3a Corporation............516 284-6799
345 Doughty Blvd Inwood (11096) **(G-6802)**
Nabisco, Newburgh *Also called Mondelez Global LLC* **(G-12790)**
Nabisco, Batavia *Also called Mondelez Global LLC* **(G-643)**
Nadcor, Plattsburgh *Also called North American Door Corp* **(G-13707)**
Nae, Central Islip *Also called North American Enclosures Inc* **(G-3534)**
Nafco, Newark *Also called North American Filter Corp* **(G-12760)**
Nagad Cabinets Inc............718 382-7200
1039 Mcdonald Ave Brooklyn (11230) **(G-2353)**
Nagle Fuel Corporation............212 304-4618
265 Nagle Ave New York (10034) **(G-11362)**
Nak International Corp (PA)............516 997-4212
131 Jericho Tpke Ste 204 Jericho (11753) **(G-7109)**
Nakano Foods, Medina *Also called Mizkan America Inc* **(G-8311)**
Nakano Foods, Lyndonville *Also called Mizkan America Inc* **(G-7995)**
Nalco Company LLC............518 796-1985
6 Butler Pl 2 Saratoga Springs (12866) **(G-15193)**
Nalge Nunc International Corp (HQ)............585 498-2661
1600 Lexington Ave # 107 Rochester (14606) **(G-14547)**
Name Base Inc............212 545-1400
172 Lexington Ave Apt 1 New York (10016) **(G-11363)**
Nameplate Mfrs of Amer............631 752-0055
65 Toledo St Farmingdale (11735) **(G-5070)**
NAMSNET, Long Island City *Also called Toweriq Inc* **(G-7931)**
Nanette Lepore, New York *Also called Nlhe LLC* **(G-11460)**
Nanette Lepore, New York *Also called Robespierre Inc* **(G-11914)**
Nanette Lepore Showroom, New York *Also called Robespierre Inc* **(G-11913)**
Nannit, New York *Also called Udisense Inc* **(G-12460)**
Nano Vibronix Inc............516 374-8330
601 Chestnut St Cedarhurst (11516) **(G-3486)**
Nanobionovum LLC............518 581-1171
117 Grand Ave Saratoga Springs (12866) **(G-15194)**
Nanomas Technologies Inc............607 821-4208
1093 Clark St Endicott (13760) **(G-4826)**
Nanoprobes Inc............631 205-9490
95 Horseblock Rd Unit 1 Yaphank (11980) **(G-17414)**
Nanopv Corporation............609 851-3666
7526 Morgan Rd Liverpool (13090) **(G-7562)**
Nanorx Inc............914 671-0224
6 Devoe Pl Chappaqua (10514) **(G-3581)**
Nanotronics Imaging Inc............212 401-6209
63 Flushing Ave Unit 128 Brooklyn (11205) **(G-2354)**
Nanovibronix Inc............914 233-3004
525 Executive Blvd Elmsford (10523) **(G-4777)**
Nantier Ball Minoustchine Pubg, New York *Also called NBM Publishing Inc* **(G-11384)**
Nantucket Allserve Inc............914 612-4000
55 Hunter Ln Elmsford (10523) **(G-4778)**
Nantucket Nectars, Elmsford *Also called Nantucket Allserve Inc* **(G-4778)**
Nanz Company, The, New York *Also called Nanz Custom Hardware Inc* **(G-11364)**
Nanz Custom Hardware Inc (PA)............212 367-7000
20 Vandam St Fl 5l New York (10013) **(G-11364)**
Nanz Custom Hardware Inc............212 367-7000
105 E Jefryn Blvd Deer Park (11729) **(G-4200)**
Naomi Manufacturing, Island Park *Also called Nathan Berrie & Sons Inc* **(G-6821)**
Nap Industries, Brooklyn *Also called Marlow Printing Co Inc* **(G-2275)**
Nap Industries Inc............718 625-4948
667 Kent Ave Brooklyn (11249) **(G-2355)**
Napco Security Tech Inc (PA)............631 842-9400
333 Bayview Ave Amityville (11701) **(G-313)**
Naples Vly Mrgers Acqstons LLC............585 490-1339
154 N Main St Naples (14512) **(G-8813)**
Narda Satellite Networks, Hauppauge *Also called L3 Technologies Inc* **(G-6134)**
Narde Paving Company Inc............607 737-7177
400 E 14th St Elmira (14903) **(G-4710)**
Narratively Inc............203 536-0332
697 Hancock St 2 Brooklyn (11233) **(G-2356)**
Narrowsburg Feed & Grain Co............845 252-3936
Fifth And Main St Narrowsburg (12764) **(G-8814)**
Nas CP Corp (HQ)............718 961-6757
1434 110th St Apt 4a College Point (11356) **(G-3823)**
Nas Quick Sign Inc............716 876-7599
1628 Elmwood Ave Buffalo (14207) **(G-3102)**
Nas-Tra Automotive Inds Inc............631 225-1225
3 Sidney Ct Lindenhurst (11757) **(G-7497)**
Nasco Enterprises Inc............516 921-9696
95 Woodcrest Dr Syosset (11791) **(G-15849)**
Nasdaq Omx, New York *Also called Omx (us) Inc* **(G-11518)**
Nash Electric Services Inc............914 226-8375
3 Glover Ave Yonkers (10704) **(G-17487)**
Nash Metalware Co Inc............315 339-5794
200 Railroad St Rome (13440) **(G-14851)**
Nash Printing Inc............516 935-4567
101 Dupont St Ste 2 Plainview (11803) **(G-13651)**
Nasiff Associates Inc............315 676-2346
841 County Route 37 Central Square (13036) **(G-3544)**
Nassau Auto Remanufacturer............516 485-4500
25 Chasner St Hempstead (11550) **(G-6305)**
Nassau Auto Remanufacturers, Hempstead *Also called Nassau Auto Remanufacturer* **(G-6305)**
Nassau Chromium Plating Co Inc............516 746-6666
122 2nd St Mineola (11501) **(G-8559)**
Nassau County Publications............516 481-5400
5 Centre St Hempstead (11550) **(G-6306)**
Nassau Suffolk Brd of Womens............631 666-8835
145 New York Ave Bay Shore (11706) **(G-718)**

Nassau Tool Works Inc 631 328-7031
34 Lamar St West Babylon (11704) *(G-16845)*
Nastel Technologies Inc (PA)....631 761-9100
88 Sunnyside Blvd Ste 101 Plainview (11803) *(G-13652)*
Nastra Automotive, Lindenhurst *Also called Nas-Tra Automotive Inds Inc (G-7497)*
Nat Nast Company Inc (PA)....212 575-1186
1370 Broadway Rm 900 New York (10018) *(G-11365)*
Natalie Creations, New York *Also called Beverly Creations Inc (G-9428)*
Natech Plastics Inc....631 580-3506
85 Remington Blvd Ronkonkoma (11779) *(G-14974)*
Nathan Berrie & Sons Inc 516 432-8500
3956 Long Beach Rd Island Park (11558) *(G-6821)*
Nathan Love LLC 212 925-7111
407 Broome St Rm 6r New York (10013) *(G-11366)*
Nathan Printing Express Inc....914 472-0914
740 Central Park Ave Scarsdale (10583) *(G-15250)*
Nathan Steel Corp 315 797-1335
36 Wurz Ave Utica (13502) *(G-16375)*
Nation Company LP 212 209-5400
520 8th Ave Rm 2100 New York (10018) *(G-11367)*
Nation Magazine....212 209-5400
33 Irving Pl Fl 8 New York (10003) *(G-11368)*
Nation, The, New York *Also called Nation Company LP (G-11367)*
National Advertising & Prtg....212 629-7650
231 W 29th St Rm 1408 New York (10001) *(G-11369)*
National Catholic Wkly Review, New York *Also called America Press Inc (G-9162)*
National Computer & Electronic 631 242-7222
367 Bay Shore Rd Ste D Deer Park (11729) *(G-4201)*
National Contract Industries....212 249-0045
510 E 86th St Apt 16b New York (10028) *(G-11370)*
National Die & Button Mould Co 201 939-7800
1 Kent Ave Brooklyn (11249) *(G-2357)*
National Elev Cab & Door Corp....718 478-5900
5315 37th Ave Woodside (11377) *(G-17357)*
National Equipment Corporation (PA)....718 585-0200
600 Mmaroneck Ave Ste 400 Harrison (10528) *(G-6006)*
National Equipment Corporation....718 585-0200
801 E 141st St Bronx (10454) *(G-1408)*
National Flag & Display Co Inc (PA) 212 228-6600
30 E 21st St Apt 2b New York (10010) *(G-11371)*
National Grape Coop Assn Inc (PA)....716 326-5200
80 State St Westfield (14787) *(G-17077)*
National Health Prom Assoc....914 421-2525
711 Westchester Ave # 301 White Plains (10604) *(G-17166)*
National Herald Inc....718 784-5255
3710 30th St Long Island City (11101) *(G-7851)*
National Learning Corp (PA)....516 921-8888
212 Michael Dr Syosset (11791) *(G-15850)*
National Maint Contg Corp....716 285-1583
5600 Niagara Falls Blvd Niagara Falls (14304) *(G-12866)*
National Marketing Services....516 942-9595
200 S Service Rd Ste 203 Roslyn Heights (11577) *(G-15055)*
National Pad & Paper, Syracuse *Also called Automation Papers Inc (G-15882)*
National Paper Converting Inc....607 687-6049
207 Corporate Dr Owego (13827) *(G-13381)*
National Parachute Industries....908 782-1646
78 White Rd Extensio Palenville (12463) *(G-13423)*
National Parachute Industry, Palenville *Also called National Parachute Industries (G-13423)*
National Pipe & Plastics Inc (PA) 607 729-9381
3421 Vestal Rd Vestal (13850) *(G-16474)*
National Prfmce Solutions Inc....718 833-4767
7106 13th Ave Brooklyn (11228) *(G-2358)*
National Prosthetic Orthot....718 767-8400
21441 42nd Ave Ste 3a Bayside (11361) *(G-768)*
National Ramp, Valley Cottage *Also called Landmark Group Inc (G-16406)*
National Rding Styles Inst Inc....516 921-5500
179 Lafayette Dr Syosset (11791) *(G-15851)*
National Reproductions Inc....212 619-3800
229 W 28th St Fl 9 New York (10001) *(G-11372)*
National Review Inc (PA)....212 679-7330
19 W 44th St Ste 1701 New York (10036) *(G-11373)*
National Review Online, New York *Also called National Review Inc (G-11373)*
National Security Systems Inc 516 627-2222
511 Manhasset Woods Rd Manhasset (11030) *(G-8097)*
National Spinning Co Inc....212 382-6400
1212 Ave Of The Americ St New York (10036) *(G-11374)*
National Steel Rule Die Inc....718 402-1396
2407 3rd Ave Bronx (10451) *(G-1409)*
National Time Recording Eqp Co....212 227-3310
64 Reade St Fl 2 New York (10007) *(G-11375)*
National Tobacco Company LP 212 253-8185
257 Park Ave S Fl 7 New York (10010) *(G-11376)*
National Vac Envmtl Svcs Corp 518 743-0563
80 Park Rd Glens Falls (12804) *(G-5706)*
National Wire & Metal Tech Inc 716 661-9180
22 Carolina St Jamestown (14701) *(G-7054)*
Nationwide Circuits Inc....585 328-0791
1444 Emerson St Rochester (14606) *(G-14548)*
Nationwide Coils Inc (PA) 914 277-7396
24 Foxwood Cir Mount Kisco (10549) *(G-8679)*
Nationwide Custom Services....845 365-0414
77 Main St Tappan (10983) *(G-16105)*
Nationwide Dairy Inc 347 689-8148
792 E 93rd St Brooklyn (11236) *(G-2359)*
Nationwide Displays, Central Islip *Also called Nationwide Exhibitor Svcs Inc (G-3532)*
Nationwide Exhibitor Svcs Inc 631 467-2034
110 Windsor Pl Central Islip (11722) *(G-3532)*
Nationwide Lifts, Queensbury *Also called S & H Enterprises Inc (G-14023)*
Nationwide Precision Pdts Corp....585 272-7100
200 Tech Park Dr Rochester (14623) *(G-14549)*
Nationwide Sales and Service....631 491-6625
303 Smith St Ste 4 Farmingdale (11735) *(G-5071)*
Nationwide Tarps Incorporated (PA)....518 843-1545
50 Willow St Amsterdam (12010) *(G-362)*
Native Amercn Enrgy Group Inc (PA)....718 408-2323
7211 Austin St Ste 288 Forest Hills (11375) *(G-5332)*
Native Textiles Inc (PA) 212 951-5100
411 5th Ave Rm 901 New York (10016) *(G-11377)*
Natori Company Incorporated (PA)....212 532-7796
180 Madison Ave Fl 19 New York (10016) *(G-11378)*
Natori Company Incorporated....212 532-7796
180 Madison Ave Fl 19 New York (10016) *(G-11379)*
Natori Company, The, New York *Also called Natori Company Incorporated (G-11379)*
Natural Dreams LLC....718 760-4202
5312 104th St Corona (11368) *(G-4027)*
Natural E Creative LLC....516 488-1143
1110 Jericho Tpke New Hyde Park (11040) *(G-8895)*
Natural Image Hair Concepts, Garden City *Also called M and J Hair Center Inc (G-5530)*
Natural Lab Inc....718 321-8848
13538 39th Ave Ste 4 Flushing (11354) *(G-5277)*
Natural Organics Inc (PA) 631 293-0030
548 Broadhollow Rd Melville (11747) *(G-8368)*
Natural Organics Laboratories....631 957-5600
9500 New Horizons Blvd Amityville (11701) *(G-314)*
Natural Stone & Cabinet Inc....718 388-2988
1365 Halsey St Brooklyn (11237) *(G-2360)*
Naturally Free Food Inc....631 361-9710
35 Roundabout Rd Smithtown (11787) *(G-15515)*
Nature America Inc (HQ)....212 726-9200
1 New York Plz Ste 4500 New York (10004) *(G-11380)*
Nature Only Inc....917 922-6539
10420 Queens Blvd Apt 3b Forest Hills (11375) *(G-5333)*
Nature Publishing Group, New York *Also called Nature America Inc (G-11380)*
Nature's Bounty, Inc., Ronkonkoma *Also called Natures Bounty (ny) Inc (G-14975)*
Nature's Plus, Melville *Also called Natural Organics Inc (G-8368)*
Natures Bounty (ny) Inc....631 567-9500
90 Orville Dr Bohemia (11716) *(G-1103)*
Natures Bounty (ny) Inc (HQ) 631 580-6137
2100 Smithtown Ave Ronkonkoma (11779) *(G-14975)*
Natures Bounty Co....631 200-2000
10 Vitamin Dr Bayport (11705) *(G-753)*
Natures Bounty Co....631 244-2065
2100 Smithtown Ave Ronkonkoma (11779) *(G-14976)*
Natures Bounty Co....518 452-5813
120 Wash Ave Ext Ste 110 Albany (12203) *(G-105)*
Natures Bounty Co....631 244-2021
2100 Smithtown Ave Ronkonkoma (11779) *(G-14977)*
Natures Bounty Co (HQ) 631 200-2000
2100 Smithtown Ave Ronkonkoma (11779) *(G-14978)*
Natures Bounty Co....631 200-7338
2145 9th Ave Ronkonkoma (11779) *(G-14979)*
Natures Bounty Co....631 588-3492
4320 Veterans Mem Hwy Holbrook (11741) *(G-6493)*
Natures Value Inc (PA) 631 846-2500
468 Mill Rd Coram (11727) *(G-3969)*
Natures Warehouse....800 215-4372
55 Main St Philadelphia (13673) *(G-13564)*
Naturpathica Holistic Hlth Inc....631 329-8792
74 Montauk Hwy Unit 23 East Hampton (11937) *(G-4434)*
Natus Medical Incorporated 631 457-4430
150 Motor Pkwy Ste 106 Hauppauge (11788) *(G-6171)*
Nautica International Inc (HQ)....212 541-5757
40 W 57th St Fl 3 New York (10019) *(G-11381)*
Nautical Marine Paint Corp....718 462-7000
4802 Farragut Rd Brooklyn (11203) *(G-2361)*
Nautical Paint, Brooklyn *Also called Nautical Marine Paint Corp (G-2361)*
Navas Designs Inc....818 988-9050
200 E 58th St Apt 17b New York (10022) *(G-11382)*
Navatar Group Inc (HQ)....212 863-9655
90 Broad St Ste 1703 New York (10004) *(G-11383)*
Navilyst Medical Inc 800 833-9973
10 Glens Fls Technical Pa Glens Falls (12801) *(G-5707)*
Navitar Inc 585 359-4000
200 Commerce Dr Rochester (14623) *(G-14550)*
Navy Plum LLC....845 641-7441
47 Plum Rd Monsey (10952) *(G-8611)*
Nazim Izzak Inc 212 920-5546
4402 23rd St Ste 517 Long Island City (11101) *(G-7852)*
Nb Elctrcal Enclsures Mfrs Inc....718 272-8792
902 903 Shepherd Ave Brooklyn (11208) *(G-2362)*
NBC Universal LLC....718 482-8310
210 54th Ave Long Island City (11101) *(G-7853)*
Nbets Corporation....516 785-1259
1901 Wantagh Ave Wantagh (11793) *(G-16582)*

ALPHABETIC

(PA)=Parent Co (HQ)=Headquarters (DH)=Div Headquarters
2018 Harris
New York Manufacturers Directory
1015

NBM Publishing Inc............212 643-5407
160 Broadway Ste 700e New York (10038) ***(G-11384)***
Nbn Technologies LLC............585 355-5556
136 Wilshire Rd Rochester (14618) ***(G-14551)***
Nbs, Amityville *Also called New Business Solutions Inc* ***(G-315)***
Nbty Manufacturing LLC (HQ)............631 567-9500
2100 Smithtown Ave Ronkonkoma (11779) ***(G-14980)***
NC Industries Inc (PA)............248 528-5200
200 John James Audubon Buffalo (14228) ***(G-3103)***
Ncc Ny LLC............718 943-7000
1840 Mcdonald Ave Brooklyn (11223) ***(G-2363)***
Nceec, Deer Park *Also called National Computer & Electronic* ***(G-4201)***
Nci, New York *Also called National Contract Industries* ***(G-11370)***
Nci Group Inc............315 339-1245
6168 State Route 233 Rome (13440) ***(G-14852)***
Nci Panel Systems, Montgomery *Also called Northeast Cnstr Inds Inc* ***(G-8634)***
NCM Publishers Inc............212 691-9100
200 Varick St Rm 608 New York (10014) ***(G-11385)***
NCR Corporation............607 273-5310
950 Danby Rd Ithaca (14850) ***(G-6901)***
NCR Corporation............516 876-7200
30 Jericho Executive Plz Jericho (11753) ***(G-7110)***
ND Labs Inc............516 612-4900
202 Merrick Rd Lynbrook (11563) ***(G-7982)***
Ne & Ws Inc............718 326-4699
6085 60th St Maspeth (11378) ***(G-8185)***
NEa Manufacturing Corp............516 371-4200
345 Doughty Blvd Inwood (11096) ***(G-6803)***
Necd, Woodside *Also called National Elev Cab & Door Corp* ***(G-17357)***
Necessary Objects Ltd (PA)............212 334-9888
3030 47th Ave Fl 6 Long Island City (11101) ***(G-7854)***
Neenah Northeast LLC............315 376-3571
5492 Bostwick St Lowville (13367) ***(G-7968)***
Neenah Northeast LLC............315 782-5800
101 Bridge St Brownville (13615) ***(G-2798)***
Nefab Packaging North East LLC............518 346-9105
203 Glenville Indus Park Scotia (12302) ***(G-15351)***
Nefco, Copiague *Also called North East Finishing Co Inc* ***(G-3941)***
Negys New Land Vinyrd Winery............315 585-4432
623 Lerch Rd Ste 1 Geneva (14456) ***(G-5595)***
Neighbor Newspapers............631 226-2636
565 Broadhollow Rd Ste 3 Farmingdale (11735) ***(G-5072)***
Neighbor To Neighbor News Inc............585 492-2525
223 Main St Arcade (14009) ***(G-397)***
Neil Savalia Inc............212 869-0123
15 W 47th St Ste 903 New York (10036) ***(G-11386)***
Neilson International Inc............631 454-0400
144 Allen Blvd Ste B Farmingdale (11735) ***(G-5073)***
Nelco Laboratories Inc............631 242-0082
154 Brook Ave Deer Park (11729) ***(G-4202)***
Nell-Joy Industries Inc (PA)............631 842-8989
8 Reith St Ste 10 Copiague (11726) ***(G-3939)***
Nelson Air Device Corporation............718 729-3801
4628 54th Ave Maspeth (11378) ***(G-8186)***
Nelson Holdings Ltd (PA)............607 772-1794
71 Frederick St Binghamton (13901) ***(G-935)***
Nelson Prsthtics Orthotics Lab, Cheektowaga *Also called Prosthetics By Nelson Inc* ***(G-3614)***
Nemaris Inc............646 794-8648
475 Park Ave S Fl 11 New York (10016) ***(G-11387)***
Neo Cabinetry LLC............718 403-0456
400 Liberty Ave Brooklyn (11207) ***(G-2364)***
Neo Ray Lighting Products, Hicksville *Also called Cooper Lighting LLC* ***(G-6358)***
Neometrics, Hauppauge *Also called Natus Medical Incorporated* ***(G-6171)***
Neon............212 727-5628
1400 Broadway Rm 300 New York (10018) ***(G-11388)***
Neopost USA Inc............631 435-9100
415 Oser Ave Ste K Hauppauge (11788) ***(G-6172)***
Nepco, Warrensburg *Also called Northeastern Products Corp* ***(G-16602)***
Nepenthes America Inc............212 343-4262
307 W 38th St Rm 201 New York (10018) ***(G-11389)***
Neptune Machine Inc............718 852-4100
521 Carroll St Brooklyn (11215) ***(G-2365)***
Neptune Soft Water Inc............315 446-5151
1201 E Fayette St Ste 6 Syracuse (13210) ***(G-16017)***
Nervecom Inc............212 625-9914
199 Lafayette St Apt 3b New York (10012) ***(G-11390)***
Nervve Technologies Inc (PA)............716 800-2250
450 Park Ave Fl 30 New York (10022) ***(G-11391)***
Nes Bearing Company Inc............716 372-6532
1601 Johnson St Olean (14760) ***(G-13173)***
Nes Costume, New York *Also called Nes Jewelry Inc* ***(G-11392)***
Nes Jewelry Inc (PA)............212 502-0025
20 W 33rd St Fl 6 New York (10001) ***(G-11392)***
Nesher Printing Inc............212 760-2521
30 E 33rd St Frnt A New York (10016) ***(G-11393)***
Nessen Lighting, The, Mamaroneck *Also called Coldstream Group Inc* ***(G-8061)***
Nestle Healthcare Ntrtn Inc............516 249-5085
565 Broadhollow Rd Farmingdale (11735) ***(G-5074)***
Nestle Purina Factory, Dunkirk *Also called Nestle Purina Petcare Company* ***(G-4369)***
Nestle Purina Petcare Company............716 366-8080
3800 Middle Rd Dunkirk (14048) ***(G-4369)***
Nestle Usa Inc............914 272-4021
1311 Mmroneck Ave Ste 350 White Plains (10605) ***(G-17167)***
NET & Die Inc............315 592-4311
24 Foster St Fulton (13069) ***(G-5484)***
Netech Corporation............631 531-0100
110 Toledo St Farmingdale (11735) ***(G-5075)***
Netegrity Inc (HQ)............631 342-6000
1 Ca Plz Central Islip (11749) ***(G-3533)***
Netologic Inc............212 269-3796
17 State St Fl 38 New York (10004) ***(G-11394)***
Netsuite Inc............646 652-5700
8 W 40th St 5f New York (10018) ***(G-11395)***
Nettle Meadow Farm, Warrensburg *Also called Lumazu LLC* ***(G-16601)***
Network Infrstructure Tech Inc............212 404-7340
90 John St Fl 7 New York (10038) ***(G-11396)***
Network Journal Inc............212 962-3791
39 Broadway Rm 2120 New York (10006) ***(G-11397)***
Neumann Jutta New York Inc............212 982-7048
355 E 4th St New York (10009) ***(G-11398)***
Neurotrope Inc............973 242-0005
205 E 42nd St Fl 16 New York (10017) ***(G-11399)***
Neva Slip, Inwood *Also called Excellent Art Mfg Corp* ***(G-6795)***
Nevaeh Jeans Company............845 641-4255
450 W 152nd St Apt 31 New York (10031) ***(G-11400)***
Neverware Inc............516 302-3223
112 W 27th St Ste 201 New York (10001) ***(G-11401)***
Neville Mfg Svc & Dist Inc (PA)............716 834-3038
2320 Clinton St Cheektowaga (14227) ***(G-3610)***
New Age Ironworks Inc............718 277-1895
183 Van Siclen Ave Brooklyn (11207) ***(G-2366)***
New Age Precision Tech Inc............631 471-4000
151 Remington Blvd Ronkonkoma (11779) ***(G-14981)***
New American, Brooklyn *Also called Afro Times Newspaper* ***(G-1568)***
New Art Publications Inc............718 636-9100
80 Hanson Pl Ste 703 Brooklyn (11217) ***(G-2367)***
New Art Signs Co Inc............718 443-0900
78 Plymouth Dr N Glen Head (11545) ***(G-5651)***
New Atlantic Ready Mix Corp............718 812-0739
18330 Jamaica Ave Hollis (11423) ***(G-6524)***
New Audio LLC............212 213-6060
132 W 31st St Rm 701 New York (10001) ***(G-11402)***
New Avon LLC............716 572-4842
433 Thorncliff Rd Buffalo (14223) ***(G-3104)***
New Avon LLC (HQ)............212 282-8500
1 Liberty Plz New York (10006) ***(G-11403)***
New Balance Underwear, New York *Also called Balanced Tech Corp* ***(G-9362)***
New Berlin Gazette............607 847-6131
29 Lackawanna Ave Norwich (13815) ***(G-13050)***
New Bgnnngs Win Door Dstrs LLC............845 214-0698
28 Willowbrook Hts Poughkeepsie (12603) ***(G-13939)***
New Buffalo Shirt Factory Inc............716 436-5839
1979 Harlem Rd Buffalo (14212) ***(G-3105)***
New Business Solutions Inc............631 789-1500
31 Sprague Ave Amityville (11701) ***(G-315)***
New City Press Inc............845 229-0335
202 Comforter Blvd Hyde Park (12538) ***(G-6774)***
New Classic Inc............718 609-1100
4143 37th St Long Island City (11101) ***(G-7855)***
New Classic Trade Inc............347 822-9052
17211 93rd Ave Jamaica (11433) ***(G-6972)***
New Concepts of New York LLC............212 695-4999
89 19th St 91 Brooklyn (11232) ***(G-2368)***
New Cov Manufacturing, West Henrietta *Also called Semans Enterprises Inc* ***(G-16925)***
New Day Woodwork Inc............718 275-1721
8861 76th Ave Glendale (11385) ***(G-5674)***
New Deal Printing Corp (PA)............718 729-5800
420 E 55th St Apt Grdp New York (10022) ***(G-11404)***
New Dimension Awards Inc (PA)............718 236-8200
6505 11th Ave Brooklyn (11219) ***(G-2369)***
New Dimension Trophies, Brooklyn *Also called New Dimension Awards Inc* ***(G-2369)***
New Dimensions Office Group............718 387-0995
540 Morgan Ave Brooklyn (11222) ***(G-2370)***
New Dimensions Research Corp............631 694-1356
260 Spagnoli Rd Melville (11747) ***(G-8369)***
New Directions Publishing............212 255-0230
80 8th Ave Fl 19 New York (10011) ***(G-11405)***
New Dynamics Corporation............845 692-0022
15 Fortune Rd W Middletown (10941) ***(G-8488)***
New Eagle Silo Corp............585 492-1300
7648 Hurdville Rd Arcade (14009) ***(G-398)***
New Energy Systems Group............917 573-0302
116 W 23rd St Fl 5 New York (10011) ***(G-11406)***
New England Barns Inc............631 445-1461
45805 Route 25 Southold (11971) ***(G-15584)***
New England Orthotic & Prost............212 682-9313
235 E 38th St New York (10016) ***(G-11407)***
New England Reclamation Inc............914 949-2000
20 Haarlem Ave White Plains (10603) ***(G-17168)***
New England Tool Co Ltd............845 651-7550
44 Jayne St Florida (10921) ***(G-5221)***

New ERA Cap Co Inc.....716 604-9000
160 Delaware Ave Buffalo (14202) ***(G-3106)***
New ERA Cap Co Inc (PA).....716 604-9000
160 Delaware Ave Buffalo (14202) ***(G-3107)***
New ERA Cap Co Inc.....716 549-0445
8061 Erie Rd Derby (14047) ***(G-4307)***
New Fine Chemicals Inc.....631 321-8151
35 W Hoffman Ave Lindenhurst (11757) ***(G-7498)***
New Generation Lighting Inc.....212 966-0328
144 Bowery Frnt 1 New York (10013) ***(G-11408)***
New Goldstar 1 Printing Corp.....212 343-3909
63 Orchard St New York (10002) ***(G-11409)***
New Hampton Creations Inc.....212 244-7474
237 W 35th St Ste 502 New York (10001) ***(G-11410)***
New Hope Media LLC.....646 366-0830
108 W 39th St Rm 805 New York (10018) ***(G-11411)***
New Hope Mills Inc.....315 252-2676
181 York St Auburn (13021) ***(G-507)***
New Hope Mills Mfg Inc (PA).....315 252-2676
181 York St Auburn (13021) ***(G-508)***
New Horizon Graphics Inc.....631 231-8055
1200 Prime Pl Hauppauge (11788) ***(G-6173)***
New Horizons Bakery, Binghamton *Also called Fratellis LLC* ***(G-910)***
New Jersey Pulverizing Co Inc (PA).....516 921-9595
4 Rita St Syosset (11791) ***(G-15852)***
New Kit On The Block.....631 757-5655
100 Knickerbocker Ave K Bohemia (11716) ***(G-1104)***
New Living Inc.....631 751-8819
99 Waverly Ave Apt 6d Patchogue (11772) ***(G-13454)***
New Market Products Co Inc.....607 292-6226
9671 Back St Wayne (14893) ***(G-16736)***
New Media Investment Group Inc (PA).....212 479-3160
1345 Avenue Of The Americ New York (10105) ***(G-11412)***
New Mount Pleasant Bakery.....518 374-7577
941 Crane St Schenectady (12303) ***(G-15307)***
New Paltz Times, New Paltz *Also called Ulster Publishing Co Inc* ***(G-8926)***
New Press.....212 629-8802
120 Wall St Fl 31 New York (10005) ***(G-11413)***
New Primecare.....516 822-4031
1184 Broadway Hewlett (11557) ***(G-6334)***
New Rosen Printing, Buffalo *Also called Cilyox Inc* ***(G-2894)***
New Scale Technologies Inc.....585 924-4450
121 Victor Heights Pkwy Victor (14564) ***(G-16516)***
New Sensor Corporation (PA).....718 937-8300
5501 2nd St Long Island City (11101) ***(G-7856)***
New Ski Inc.....607 277-7000
109 N Cayuga St Ste A Ithaca (14850) ***(G-6902)***
New Skin, Tarrytown *Also called Medtech Products Inc* ***(G-16119)***
New Star Bakery.....718 961-8868
4121a Kissena Blvd Flushing (11355) ***(G-5278)***
New Style Signs Limited Inc.....212 242-7848
149 Madison Ave Rm 606 New York (10016) ***(G-11414)***
New Triad For Collaborative.....212 873-9610
205 W 86th St Apt 911 New York (10024) ***(G-11415)***
New Vision Industries Inc.....607 687-7700
1239 Campville Rd Endicott (13760) ***(G-4827)***
New Windsor Waste Water Plant.....845 561-2550
145 Caesars Ln New Windsor (12553) ***(G-8990)***
New Wop Records.....631 617-9732
317 W 14th St Deer Park (11729) ***(G-4203)***
New World Records, Brooklyn *Also called Recorded Anthlogy of Amrcn Mus* ***(G-2503)***
New York Accessories Group, New York *Also called New York Accessory Group Inc* ***(G-11416)***
New York Accessory Group Inc (PA).....212 532-7911
411 5th Ave Fl 4 New York (10016) ***(G-11416)***
New York Air Brake, Watertown *Also called Knorr Brake Truck Systems Co* ***(G-16682)***
New York Air Brake LLC (HQ).....315 786-5219
748 Starbuck Ave Watertown (13601) ***(G-16688)***
New York Binding Co Inc.....718 729-2454
2121 41st Ave Ste A Long Island City (11101) ***(G-7857)***
New York Blood Pressure, Mendon *Also called N Y B P Inc* ***(G-8413)***
New York Bottling Co Inc.....718 963-3232
626 Whittier St Bronx (10474) ***(G-1410)***
New York Christan Times Inc.....718 638-6397
1061 Atlantic Ave Brooklyn (11238) ***(G-2371)***
New York CT Loc246 Seiu Wel BF.....212 233-0616
217 Broadway New York (10007) ***(G-11417)***
New York Cutting & Gumming Co.....212 563-4146
265 Ballard Rd Middletown (10941) ***(G-8489)***
New York Cvl Srvc Emplys Pblsh.....212 962-2690
277 Broadway Ste 1506 New York (10007) ***(G-11418)***
New York Daily Challenge Inc (PA).....718 636-9500
1195 Atlantic Ave Fl 2 Brooklyn (11216) ***(G-2372)***
New York Daily News, New York *Also called Daily News LP* ***(G-9845)***
New York Daily News.....212 248-2100
4 New York Plz Fl 6 New York (10004) ***(G-11419)***
New York Digital Corporation.....631 630-9798
33 Walt Whitman Rd # 117 Huntington Station (11746) ***(G-6755)***
New York Digital Print Center.....718 767-1953
15050 14th Rd Ste 1 Whitestone (11357) ***(G-17241)***
New York Division, Owego *Also called Kyocera Precision Tools Inc* ***(G-13378)***

New York Elegance Entps Inc.....212 685-3088
385 5th Ave Rm 709 New York (10016) ***(G-11420)***
New York Embroidery & Monogram, Hicksville *Also called NY Embroidery Inc* ***(G-6403)***
New York Enrgy Synthetics Inc.....212 634-4787
375 Park Ave Ste 2607 New York (10152) ***(G-11421)***
New York Enterprise Report, New York *Also called Rsl Media LLC* ***(G-11949)***
New York Eye, Amityville *Also called Hart Specialties Inc* ***(G-291)***
New York Familypublications, Mamaroneck *Also called Family Publishing Group Inc* ***(G-8067)***
New York Fan Coil LLC.....646 580-1344
7 Chesapeake Bay Rd Coram (11727) ***(G-3970)***
New York Findings Corp.....212 925-5745
70 Bowery Unit 8 New York (10013) ***(G-11422)***
New York Gourmet Coffee Inc.....631 254-0076
204 N Fehr Way Ste C Bay Shore (11706) ***(G-719)***
New York Hospital Disposable.....718 384-1620
101 Richardson St Ste 1 Brooklyn (11211) ***(G-2373)***
New York IL Bo Inc.....718 961-1538
4522 162nd St Fl 2 Flushing (11358) ***(G-5279)***
New York Imaging Service Inc.....716 834-8022
255 Cooper Ave Tonawanda (14150) ***(G-16202)***
New York Industrial Works Inc (PA).....718 292-0615
796 E 140th St Bronx (10454) ***(G-1411)***
New York Laser & Aestheticks.....516 627-7777
1025 Nthrn Blvd Ste 206 Roslyn (11576) ***(G-15045)***
New York Law Journal, New York *Also called Alm Media LLC* ***(G-9146)***
New York Legal Publishing.....518 459-1100
120 Broadway Ste 1a Menands (12204) ***(G-8409)***
New York Manufactured Products.....585 254-9353
6 Cairn St Rochester (14611) ***(G-14552)***
New York Manufacturing Corp.....585 254-9353
6 Cairn St Rochester (14611) ***(G-14553)***
New York Marble and Stone Corp.....718 729-7272
4411 55th Ave Maspeth (11378) ***(G-8187)***
New York Marine Elec Inc.....631 734-6050
124 Springville Rd Ste 1 Hampton Bays (11946) ***(G-5983)***
New York Marking Devices Corp.....585 454-5188
700 Clinton Ave S Ste 2 Rochester (14620) ***(G-14554)***
New York Marking Devices Corp (PA).....315 463-8641
2207 Teall Ave Syracuse (13206) ***(G-16018)***
New York Media LLC.....212 508-0700
75 Varick St Ste 1404 New York (10013) ***(G-11423)***
New York Nautical Inc.....212 962-4522
200 Church St Frnt 4 New York (10013) ***(G-11424)***
New York Packaging Corp.....516 746-0600
135 Fulton Ave New Hyde Park (11040) ***(G-8896)***
New York Packaging II LLC.....516 746-0600
135 Fulton Ave Garden City (11530) ***(G-5536)***
New York Pasta Authority Inc.....347 787-2130
640 Parkside Ave Brooklyn (11226) ***(G-2374)***
New York Poplin LLC.....718 768-3296
4611 1st Ave Brooklyn (11232) ***(G-2375)***
New York Popular Inc.....718 499-2020
168 39th St Unit 3 Brooklyn (11232) ***(G-2376)***
New York Post, Brooklyn *Also called Nyp Holdings Inc* ***(G-2396)***
New York Post, New York *Also called Nyp Holdings Inc* ***(G-11500)***
New York Press & Graphics Inc.....518 489-7089
12 Interstate Ave Albany (12205) ***(G-106)***
New York Press Inc.....212 268-8600
72 Madison Ave Fl 11 New York (10016) ***(G-11425)***
New York Qrtrly Foundation Inc.....917 843-8825
322 76th St Brooklyn (11209) ***(G-2377)***
New York Quarries Inc.....518 756-3138
305 Rte 111 Alcove (12007) ***(G-175)***
New York Ravioli Pasta Co Inc.....516 270-2852
12 Denton Ave S New Hyde Park (11040) ***(G-8897)***
New York Ready Mix Inc.....516 338-6969
120 Rushmore St Westbury (11590) ***(G-17042)***
New York Review of Books, New York *Also called Nyrev Inc* ***(G-11501)***
New York Rhbilitative Svcs LLC.....516 239-0990
135 Rockaway Tpke Ste 107 Lawrence (11559) ***(G-7421)***
New York Running Co, New York *Also called PRC Liquidating Company* ***(G-11716)***
New York Sample Card Co Inc.....212 242-1242
151 W 26th St Fl 12 New York (10001) ***(G-11426)***
New York Sand & Stone LLC.....718 596-2897
5700 47th St Maspeth (11378) ***(G-8188)***
New York Skateboards, Deer Park *Also called Chapman Skateboard Co Inc* ***(G-4139)***
New York Spring Water Inc.....212 777-4649
517 W 36th St New York (10018) ***(G-11427)***
New York State Foam Enrgy LLC.....845 534-4656
2 Commercial Dr Cornwall (12518) ***(G-4010)***
New York State Tool Co Inc.....315 737-8985
3343 Oneida St Chadwicks (13319) ***(G-3558)***
New York Steel Services Co.....718 291-7770
18009 Liberty Ave Jamaica (11433) ***(G-6973)***
New York Style Eats, Sunnyside *Also called Deelka Vision Corp* ***(G-15827)***
New York Sweater Company Inc.....845 629-9533
141 W 36th St Rm 17 New York (10018) ***(G-11428)***
New York Tank Co, Watervliet *Also called Bigbee Steel and Tank Company* ***(G-16703)***

ALPHABETIC

New York Times Co Mag Group, New York *Also called Gruner + Jahr Prtg & Pubg Co* ***(G-10418)***
New York Times Company (PA)....212 556-1234
620 8th Ave New York (10018) ***(G-11429)***
New York Times Company....718 281-7000
1 New York Times Plz Flushing (11354) ***(G-5280)***
New York Times Company....212 556-4300
620 8th Ave Bsmt 1 New York (10018) ***(G-11430)***
New York Trading Co, New York *Also called E-Won Industrial Co Inc* ***(G-10008)***
New York Typing & Printing Co....718 268-7900
10816 72nd Ave Forest Hills (11375) ***(G-5334)***
New York University....212 998-4300
7 E 12th St Ste 800 New York (10003) ***(G-11431)***
New York Vanity and Mfg Co....718 417-1010
10 Henry St Freeport (11520) ***(G-5425)***
New York1 News Operations....212 379-3311
75 9th Ave Frnt 6 New York (10011) ***(G-11432)***
Newburgh Brewing Company LLC....845 569-2337
88 S Colden St Newburgh (12550) ***(G-12791)***
Newburgh Distribution Corp (PA)....845 561-6330
463 Temple Hill Rd New Windsor (12553) ***(G-8991)***
Newburgh Envelope Corp....845 566-4211
1720 Route 300 Newburgh (12550) ***(G-12792)***
Newcastle Fabrics Corp....718 388-6600
86 Beadel St Brooklyn (11222) ***(G-2378)***
Newchem Inc....315 331-7680
434 E Union St Newark (14513) ***(G-12759)***
Newco Products Division, Ballston Spa *Also called Dura-Mill Inc* ***(G-594)***
Newcut, Newark *Also called Newchem Inc* ***(G-12759)***
Newkirk Products Inc (HQ)....518 862-3200
15 Corporate Cir Albany (12203) ***(G-107)***
Newline Products Inc....972 881-3318
509 Temple Hill Rd New Windsor (12553) ***(G-8992)***
Newmat Northeast Corp....631 253-9277
81b Mahan St West Babylon (11704) ***(G-16846)***
Newport Business Solutions Inc....631 319-6129
61 Keyland Ct Bohemia (11716) ***(G-1105)***
Newport Corporation....585 248-4246
705 Saint Paul St Rochester (14605) ***(G-14555)***
Newport Graphics Inc....212 924-2600
121 Varick St Rm 302 New York (10013) ***(G-11433)***
Newport Magnetics Inc....315 845-8878
396 Old State Rd Newport (13416) ***(G-12815)***
Newport Rochester Inc....585 262-1325
705 Saint Paul St Rochester (14605) ***(G-14556)***
News Communications Inc (PA)....212 689-2500
501 Madison Ave Fl 23 New York (10022) ***(G-11434)***
News Corporation (PA)....212 416-3400
1211 Ave Of The Americas New York (10036) ***(G-11435)***
News India Times, New York *Also called News India USA Inc* ***(G-11437)***
News India Times, New York *Also called News India Usa LLC* ***(G-11436)***
News India Usa LLC....212 675-7515
37 W 20th St Ste 1109 New York (10011) ***(G-11436)***
News India USA Inc....212 675-7515
37 W 20th St Ste 1109 New York (10011) ***(G-11437)***
News of The Highlands Inc (PA)....845 534-7771
35 Hasbrouck Ave Cornwall (12518) ***(G-4011)***
News Report Inc....718 851-6607
1281 49th St Ste 3 Brooklyn (11219) ***(G-2379)***
News Review, The, Mattituck *Also called Times Review Newspaper Corp* ***(G-8243)***
News/Sprts Microwave Rentl Inc....619 670-0572
415 Madison Ave Fl 11 New York (10017) ***(G-11438)***
Newsday LLC (HQ)....631 843-4050
235 Pinelawn Rd Melville (11747) ***(G-8370)***
Newsday LLC....631 843-3135
25 Deshon Dr Melville (11747) ***(G-8371)***
Newsday Media Group, Melville *Also called Newsday LLC* ***(G-8370)***
Newsgraphics of Delmar Inc....518 439-5363
125 Adams St Delmar (12054) ***(G-4270)***
Newspaper Delivery Solutions....718 370-1111
309 Bradley Ave Staten Island (10314) ***(G-15731)***
Newspaper Publisher LLC....607 775-0472
1035 Conklin Rd Conklin (13748) ***(G-3896)***
Newspaper Times Union....518 454-5676
645 Albany Shaker Rd Albany (12211) ***(G-108)***
Newsweek LLC....646 867-7100
7 Hanover Sq Fl 5 New York (10004) ***(G-11439)***
Newtex Industries Inc (PA)....585 924-9135
8050 Victor Mendon Rd Victor (14564) ***(G-16517)***
Newtown Finishing, Brooklyn *Also called Newcastle Fabrics Corp* ***(G-2378)***
Newyork Pedorthic Associates....718 236-7700
2102 63rd St Brooklyn (11204) ***(G-2380)***
Nex-Gen Ready Mix Corp....347 231-0073
530 Faile St Bronx (10474) ***(G-1412)***
Nexans Energy USA Inc....845 469-2141
25 Oakland Ave Chester (10918) ***(G-3637)***
Nexbev Industries LLC....917 626-5255
1 Blue Hill Plz Ste 1564 Pearl River (10965) ***(G-13486)***
Nexgen Enviro Systems Inc....631 226-2930
190 E Hoffman Ave Ste D Lindenhurst (11757) ***(G-7499)***
Nexstar Holding Corp....716 929-9000
275 Northpointe Pkwy Amherst (14228) ***(G-251)***
Next Advance Inc (PA)....518 674-3510
2113 Ny 7 Troy (12180) ***(G-16265)***
Next Big Sound Inc....646 657-9837
125 Park Ave Fl 19 New York (10017) ***(G-11440)***
Next Magazine, New York *Also called Rnd Enterprises Inc* ***(G-11907)***
Next Potential LLC....401 742-5190
278 E 10th St Apt 5b New York (10009) ***(G-11441)***
Next Step Magazine, The, Victor *Also called Next Step Publishing Inc* ***(G-16518)***
Next Step Publishing Inc....585 742-1260
2 W Main St Ste 200 Victor (14564) ***(G-16518)***
Nextpotential, New York *Also called Next Potential LLC* ***(G-11441)***
Nfe Management LLC....212 798-6100
1345 Ave Of The Americas New York (10105) ***(G-11442)***
Nfk International, Brooklyn *Also called Slava Industries Incorporated* ***(G-2595)***
Niabraze LLC....716 447-1082
675 Ensminger Rd Tonawanda (14150) ***(G-16203)***
Niagara Blower Company (HQ)....800 426-5169
91 Sawyer Ave Tonawanda (14150) ***(G-16204)***
Niagara Chocolates, Buffalo *Also called Sweetworks Inc* ***(G-3230)***
Niagara Cooler Inc....716 434-1235
6605 Slyton Settlement Rd Lockport (14094) ***(G-7634)***
Niagara Cutter, Buffalo *Also called NC Industries Inc* ***(G-3103)***
Niagara Development & Mfg Div, Niagara Falls *Also called Fross Industries Inc* ***(G-12843)***
Niagara Dispensing Tech Inc....716 636-9827
170 Northpointe Pkwy Buffalo (14228) ***(G-3108)***
Niagara Falls Plant, Niagara Falls *Also called Tulip Molded Plastics Corp* ***(G-12902)***
Niagara Fiberboard Inc....716 434-8881
140 Van Buren St Lockport (14094) ***(G-7635)***
Niagara Fiberglass Inc....716 822-3921
88 Okell St Buffalo (14220) ***(G-3109)***
Niagara Gazette, Niagara Falls *Also called Community Newsppr Holdings Inc* ***(G-12828)***
Niagara Gear Corporation....716 874-3131
941 Military Rd Buffalo (14217) ***(G-3110)***
Niagara Label Company Inc....716 542-3000
12715 Lewis Rd Akron (14001) ***(G-22)***
Niagara Lasalle Corporation....716 827-7010
110 Hopkins St Buffalo (14220) ***(G-3111)***
Niagara Precision Inc....716 439-0956
233 Market St Lockport (14094) ***(G-7636)***
Niagara Printing, Niagara Falls *Also called Quantum Color Inc* ***(G-12883)***
Niagara Punch & Die Corp....716 896-7619
176 Gruner Rd Buffalo (14227) ***(G-3112)***
Niagara Refining LLC....716 706-1400
5661 Transit Rd Depew (14043) ***(G-4289)***
Niagara Sample Book Co Inc....716 284-6151
1717 Mackenna Ave Niagara Falls (14303) ***(G-12867)***
Niagara Scientific Inc....315 437-0821
6743 Kinne St East Syracuse (13057) ***(G-4566)***
Niagara Sheets LLC....716 692-1129
7393 Shawnee Rd North Tonawanda (14120) ***(G-13001)***
Niagara Specialty Metals Inc....716 542-5552
12600 Clarence Center Rd Akron (14001) ***(G-23)***
Niagara Thermo Products, Niagara Falls *Also called Kintex Inc* ***(G-12857)***
Niagara Transformer Corp....716 896-6500
1747 Dale Rd Buffalo (14225) ***(G-3113)***
Niagara Truss & Pallet LLC....716 433-5400
5626 Old Saunders Settle Lockport (14094) ***(G-7637)***
Niagara Tying Service Inc....716 825-0066
176 Dingens St Buffalo (14206) ***(G-3114)***
Nibble Inc Baking Co....518 334-3950
451 Broadway Apt 5 Troy (12180) ***(G-16266)***
Nibmor Project LLC....718 374-5091
11 Middle Neck Rd Great Neck (11021) ***(G-5840)***
Nice-Pak Products Inc (PA)....845 365-2772
2 Nice Pak Park Orangeburg (10962) ***(G-13258)***
Nice-Pak Products Inc....845 353-6090
100 Brookhill Dr West Nyack (10994) ***(G-16950)***
Niche Media Holdings LLc (HQ)....702 990-2500
257 Park Ave S Fl 5 New York (10010) ***(G-11443)***
Nicholas Dfine Furn Decorators....914 245-8982
546 E 170th St 48 Bronx (10456) ***(G-1413)***
Nicholas Kirkwood LLC (PA)....646 559-5239
807 Washington St New York (10014) ***(G-11444)***
Nicholson Steam Trap, Walden *Also called Spence Engineering Company Inc* ***(G-16556)***
Nick Lugo Inc....212 348-2100
159 E 116th St Fl 2 New York (10029) ***(G-11445)***
Nickel City Studios Photo Jour....716 200-0956
45 Linwood Ave Buffalo (14209) ***(G-3115)***
Nickel Group LLC....212 706-7906
212 Beach 141st St Rockaway Park (11694) ***(G-14814)***
Nickelodeon Magazines Inc (HQ)....212 541-1949
1633 Broadway Fl 7 New York (10019) ***(G-11446)***
Nicoform Inc....585 454-5530
72 Cascade Dr Ste 12 Rochester (14614) ***(G-14557)***
Nicolia Concrete Products Inc....631 669-0700
640 Muncy St Lindenhurst (11757) ***(G-7500)***
Nicolia of Long Island, Lindenhurst *Also called Nicolia Concrete Products Inc* ***(G-7500)***
Nicolia Ready Mix Inc....631 669-7000
615 Cord Ave Lindenhurst (11757) ***(G-7501)***
Nicolo Raineri....212 925-6128
82 Bowery New York (10013) ***(G-11447)***

Nicolo Raineri Jeweler, New York *Also called Nicolo Raineri* ***(G-11447)***
Nicraft, Buffalo *Also called Deltacraft Paper Company LLC* ***(G-2925)***
Nidec Indus Automtn USA LLC 716 774-1193
359 Lang Blvd Bldg B Grand Island (14072) ***(G-5778)***
Nidec Motor Corporation 315 434-9303
6268 E Molloy Rd East Syracuse (13057) ***(G-4567)***
Niebylski Bakery Inc 718 721-5152
2364 Steinway St Astoria (11105) ***(G-449)***
Nielsen Hardware Corporation (PA) 607 821-1475
71 Frederick St Binghamton (13901) ***(G-936)***
Nielsen/Sessions, Binghamton *Also called Nielsen Hardware Corporation* ***(G-936)***
Nift Group Inc 504 505-1144
14 Woodbine St Brooklyn (11221) ***(G-2381)***
Nifty Bar Grinding & Cutting 585 381-0450
450 Whitney Rd Penfield (14526) ***(G-13524)***
Nightingale Food Entps Inc 347 577-1630
2306 1st Ave New York (10035) ***(G-11448)***
Nijon Tool Co Inc 631 242-3434
12 Evergreen Pl 12 Deer Park (11729) ***(G-4204)***
Nike Inc 212 226-5433
21 Mercer St Frnt A New York (10013) ***(G-11449)***
Nike Inc 631 242-3014
102 The Arches Cir Deer Park (11729) ***(G-4205)***
Nike Inc 631 960-0184
2675 Sunrise Hwy Islip Terrace (11752) ***(G-6855)***
Nike Inc 716 298-5615
1886 Military Rd Niagara Falls (14304) ***(G-12868)***
Nikish Software Corp 631 754-1618
801 Motor Pkwy Hauppauge (11788) ***(G-6174)***
Nikkei America Inc (HQ) 212 261-6200
1325 Avenue Of The Americ New York (10019) ***(G-11450)***
Nikon Instruments Inc (HQ) 631 547-4200
1300 Walt Whitman Rd Fl 2 Melville (11747) ***(G-8372)***
Nilda Desserts, Poughkeepsie *Also called Ljmm Inc* ***(G-13932)***
Nildas Desserts Limited 845 454-5876
188 Washington St Poughkeepsie (12601) ***(G-13940)***
Nimbletv Inc 646 502-7010
450 Fashion Ave Fl 43 New York (10123) ***(G-11451)***
Ninas Custard 716 636-0345
2577 Millersport Hwy Getzville (14068) ***(G-5613)***
Nine Pin Ciderworks LLC 518 449-9999
929 Broadway Albany (12207) ***(G-109)***
Nine West Footwear Corporation (PA) 800 999-1877
1411 Broadway Fl 20 New York (10018) ***(G-11452)***
Nine West Holdings Inc 212 642-3860
1411 Broadway Fl 38 New York (10018) ***(G-11453)***
Nine West Holdings Inc 212 221-6376
1411 Broadway Fl 38 New York (10018) ***(G-11454)***
Nine West Holdings Inc 212 575-2571
1441 Broadway Fl 20 New York (10018) ***(G-11455)***
Nine West Holdings Inc 212 822-1300
1441 Broadway New York (10018) ***(G-11456)***
Nine West Holdings Inc 215 785-4000
1441 Broadway Fl 10 New York (10018) ***(G-11457)***
Nine West Holdings Inc 212 642-3860
1411 Broadway Fl 15 New York (10018) ***(G-11458)***
Nine West Holdings Inc 212 642-3860
575 Fashion Ave Frnt 1 New York (10018) ***(G-11459)***
Nireco America, Port Jervis *Also called Datatran Labs Inc* ***(G-13805)***
Nirvana Inc 315 942-4900
1 Nirvana Plz Forestport (13338) ***(G-5338)***
Nirx Medical Technologies LLC 516 676-6479
15 Cherry Ln Glen Head (11545) ***(G-5652)***
Nis Manufacturing Inc 518 456-2566
1 Mustang Dr Ste 5 Cohoes (12047) ***(G-3777)***
Nisonger Instrument Sls & Svc, Mamaroneck *Also called Secor Marketing Group Inc* ***(G-8079)***
Nite Train R, Champlain *Also called Koregon Enterprises Inc* ***(G-3571)***
Nitel Inc 347 731-1558
199 Lee Ave Ste 119 Brooklyn (11211) ***(G-2382)***
Nitram Energy Inc 716 662-6540
50 Cobham Dr Orchard Park (14127) ***(G-13310)***
Nitro Manufacturing LLC 716 646-9900
440 Shirley Rd North Collins (14111) ***(G-12945)***
Nitro Manufacturing LLC 716 646-9900
106 Evans St Ste E Hamburg (14075) ***(G-5957)***
Nitro Wheels Inc 716 337-0709
4440 Shirley Rd North Collins (14111) ***(G-12946)***
Nixon Gear, Syracuse *Also called Gear Motions Incorporated* ***(G-15970)***
Njf Publishing Corp 631 345-5200
14 Ramsey Rd Shirley (11967) ***(G-15450)***
Njr Medical Devices 440 258-8204
390 Oak Ave Cedarhurst (11516) ***(G-3487)***
Nk Electric LLC 914 271-0222
22 Scenic Dr Croton On Hudson (10520) ***(G-4091)***
NK Medical Products Inc (PA) 716 759-7200
80 Creekside Dr Amherst (14228) ***(G-252)***
Nlhe LLC 212 594-0012
225 W 35th St New York (10001) ***(G-11460)***
Nlr Counter Tops LLC 347 295-0410
902 E 92nd St New York (10128) ***(G-11461)***
Nmcc, Niagara Falls *Also called National Maint Contg Corp* ***(G-12866)***
Nmny Group LLC 212 944-6500
1410 Broadway Fl 16 New York (10018) ***(G-11462)***
No Longer Empty Inc 202 413-4262
122 W 27th St Fl 10 New York (10001) ***(G-11463)***
Noah Enterprises Ltd (PA) 212 736-2888
520 8th Ave Lbby 2 New York (10018) ***(G-11464)***
Noaspence Inc 516 433-7848
1040 S Broadway Unit 6 Hicksville (11801) ***(G-6401)***
Nobilium, Albany *Also called Cmp Industries LLC* ***(G-67)***
Noble Checks Inc 212 537-6241
1682 43rd St Apt 2 Brooklyn (11204) ***(G-2383)***
Noble Pine Products Co Inc 914 664-5877
240 E 7th St Mount Vernon (10550) ***(G-8756)***
Noble Vintages, Fredonia *Also called Woodbury Vineyards Inc* ***(G-5386)***
Noble Wood Shavings, Sherrill *Also called Dlr Enterprises LLC* ***(G-15427)***
Nochairs Inc 917 748-8731
325 W 38th St Rm 310 New York (10018) ***(G-11465)***
Nochem Paint Stripping Inc 631 563-2750
32 Bergen Ln Blue Point (11715) ***(G-994)***
Noco Incorporated (PA) 716 833-6626
2440 Sheridan Dr Ste 202 Tonawanda (14150) ***(G-16205)***
Nodus Noodle Corporation 718 309-3725
4504 Queens Blvd Sunnyside (11104) ***(G-15829)***
Noel Assoc 516 371-5420
114 Henry St Ste A Inwood (11096) ***(G-6804)***
Noetic Partners Inc 212 836-4351
445 Park Ave Frnt 1 New York (10022) ***(G-11466)***
Noga Dairies Inc 516 293-5448
175 Price Pkwy Farmingdale (11735) ***(G-5076)***
Noho Health Inc 877 227-3631
9 Great Jones St Apt 4 New York (10012) ***(G-11467)***
Noir Jewelry LLC 212 465-8500
358 5th Ave Rm 501 New York (10001) ***(G-11468)***
Nola Speaker, Holbrook *Also called Accent Speaker Technology Ltd* ***(G-6455)***
Noll Reynolds Met Fabrication 315 422-3333
554 E Brighton Ave Ste 1 Syracuse (13210) ***(G-16019)***
Nomad Editions LLC 212 918-0992
123 Ellison Ave Bronxville (10708) ***(G-1502)***
None, College Point *Also called City Store Gates Mfg Corp* ***(G-3806)***
Noodle Education Inc 646 289-7800
59 Charles St Suite200 New York (10014) ***(G-11469)***
Norampac New England Inc 860 923-9563
801 Corporation Park Schenectady (12302) ***(G-15308)***
Norampac New York City Inc 718 340-2100
5515 Grand Ave Maspeth (11378) ***(G-8189)***
Norampac Thompson Inc., Schenectady *Also called Norampac New England Inc* ***(G-15308)***
Norandex Inc Vestal 607 786-0778
2300 Vestal Rd Vestal (13850) ***(G-16475)***
Noras Candy Shop 315 337-4530
321 N Doxtator St Rome (13440) ***(G-14853)***
Norazza Inc (PA) 716 706-1160
3938 Broadway St Buffalo (14227) ***(G-3116)***
Norcatec LLC (PA) 516 222-7070
100 Garden Cy Plz Ste 530 Garden City (11530) ***(G-5537)***
Norcorp Inc 914 666-1310
400 E Main St Mount Kisco (10549) ***(G-8680)***
Nordic Interior Inc 718 456-7000
11025 14th Ave College Point (11356) ***(G-3824)***
Nordic Press Inc 212 686-3356
243 E 34th St New York (10016) ***(G-11470)***
Nordon Inc (PA) 585 546-6200
691 Exchange St Rochester (14608) ***(G-14558)***
Noresco Industrial Group Inc 516 759-3355
3 School St Ste 103 Glen Cove (11542) ***(G-5635)***
Norjac Boxes Inc 631 842-1300
570 Oak St Copiague (11726) ***(G-3940)***
Norlite LLC 518 235-0030
628 Saratoga St Cohoes (12047) ***(G-3778)***
Norlite Corporation, Cohoes *Also called Norlite LLC* ***(G-3778)***
Noroc Enterprises Inc 718 585-3230
415 Concord Ave Bronx (10455) ***(G-1414)***
Norse Energy Corp USA 716 568-2048
3556 Lake Shore Rd # 700 Buffalo (14219) ***(G-3117)***
Norsk Titanium US Inc (HQ) 949 735-9463
44 Martina Cir Plattsburgh (12901) ***(G-13706)***
Nortech Laboratories Inc 631 501-1452
125 Sherwood Ave Farmingdale (11735) ***(G-5077)***
Nortek Powder Coating LLC 315 337-2339
5900 Success Dr Rome (13440) ***(G-14854)***
North America Pastel Artists 718 463-4701
13303 41st Ave Apt 1a Flushing (11355) ***(G-5281)***
North American Bear Co Inc 212 388-0700
1261 Broadway Rm 815 New York (10001) ***(G-11471)***
North American Breweries Inc (HQ) 585 546-1030
445 Saint Paul St Rochester (14605) ***(G-14559)***
North American Carbide, Orchard Park *Also called Transport National Dev Inc* ***(G-13324)***
North American Carbide of NY, Orchard Park *Also called Transport National Dev Inc* ***(G-13325)***
North American DF Inc (PA) 718 698-2500
280 Watchogue Rd Staten Island (10314) ***(G-15732)***
North American Door Corp 518 566-0161
1471 Military Tpke Plattsburgh (12901) ***(G-13707)***

ALPHABETIC

North American Enclosures Inc (PA) 631 234-9500
85 Jetson Ln Ste B Central Islip (11722) ***(G-3534)***
North American Filter Corp (PA) 800 265-8943
200 W Shore Blvd Newark (14513) ***(G-12760)***
North American Graphics Inc 212 725-2200
150 Varick St Rm 303 New York (10013) ***(G-11472)***
North American Hoganas Inc 716 285-3451
5950 Packard Rd Niagara Falls (14304) ***(G-12869)***
North American MBL Systems Inc 718 898-8700
3354 62nd St Woodside (11377) ***(G-17358)***
North American Mfg Entps Inc (PA) 718 524-4370
1961 Richmond Ter Staten Island (10302) ***(G-15733)***
North American Mfg Entps Inc 718 524-4370
1961 Richmond Ter Staten Island (10302) ***(G-15734)***
North American Mills Inc 212 695-6146
1370 Broadway Rm 1101 New York (10018) ***(G-11473)***
North American Mint Inc 585 654-8500
1600 Lexington Ave 240a Rochester (14606) ***(G-14560)***
North American Pipe Corp 516 338-2863
420 Jericho Tpke Ste 222 Jericho (11753) ***(G-7111)***
North American Service Group, Ballston Spa *Also called North American Svcs Group LLC* ***(G-604)***
North American Signs Buffalo, Buffalo *Also called Nas Quick Sign Inc* ***(G-3102)***
North American Slate Inc 518 642-1702
50 Columbus St Granville (12832) ***(G-5794)***
North American Stone Inc 585 266-4020
1358 E Ridge Rd Rochester (14621) ***(G-14561)***
North American Svcs Group LLC (HQ) 518 885-1820
1240 Saratoga Rd Ballston Spa (12020) ***(G-604)***
North Americas Breweries, Rochester *Also called High Falls Brewing Company LLC* ***(G-14454)***
North Amrcn Brwries Hldngs LLC (PA) 585 546-1030
445 Saint Paul St Rochester (14605) ***(G-14562)***
North Atlantic Industries Inc (PA) 631 567-1100
110 Wilbur Pl Bohemia (11716) ***(G-1106)***
North Atlantic Trading Co, New York *Also called National Tobacco Company LP* ***(G-11376)***
North Bronx Retinal & Ophthlmi 347 535-4932
3725 Henry Hudson Pkwy Bronx (10463) ***(G-1415)***
North Coast Outfitters Ltd 631 727-5580
1015 E Main St Ste 1 Riverhead (11901) ***(G-14164)***
NORTH COUNTRY BEHAVIORAL HEALT, Saranac Lake *Also called Northern New York Rural* ***(G-15166)***
North Country Books Inc 315 735-4877
220 Lafayette St Utica (13502) ***(G-16376)***
North Country Dairy, North Lawrence *Also called Upstate Niagara Coop Inc* ***(G-12951)***
North Country This Week 315 265-1000
19 Depot St Ste 1 Potsdam (13676) ***(G-13898)***
North Country Welding Inc 315 788-9718
904 Leray St Watertown (13601) ***(G-16689)***
North County News, Yorktown Heights *Also called Northern Tier Publishing Corp* ***(G-17530)***
North Delaware Printing Inc 716 692-0576
645 Delaware St Ste 1 Tonawanda (14150) ***(G-16206)***
North E Rggers Erectors NY Inc 518 842-6377
178 Clizbe Ave Amsterdam (12010) ***(G-363)***
North East Finishing Co Inc 631 789-8000
245 Ralph Ave Copiague (11726) ***(G-3941)***
North East Fuel Group Inc 718 984-6774
51 Stuyvesant Ave Staten Island (10312) ***(G-15735)***
North Eastern Fabricators Inc 718 542-0450
910 Park Ave Ph Ph New York (10075) ***(G-11474)***
North End Paper Co Inc 315 593-8100
702 Hannibal St Fulton (13069) ***(G-5485)***
North Face, Central Valley *Also called Vf Outdoor LLC* ***(G-3556)***
NORTH FIELD, Island Park *Also called Northfeld Precision Instr Corp* ***(G-6822)***
North Fork Wood Works Inc 631 255-4028
5175 Route 48 Mattituck (11952) ***(G-8240)***
North Hills Signal Proc Corp (HQ) 516 682-7700
6851 Jericho Tpke Ste 170 Syosset (11791) ***(G-15853)***
North Hills Signal Proc Corp 516 682-7740
6851 Jericho Tpke Ste 170 Syosset (11791) ***(G-15854)***
North House Vineyards Inc 631 779-2817
1216 Main Rd Rte 25a Jamesport (11947) ***(G-7002)***
North Hudson Woodcraft Corp 315 429-3105
152 N Helmer Ave Dolgeville (13329) ***(G-4330)***
North Pk Innovations Group Inc (PA) 716 699-2031
6442 Route 242 E Ellicottville (14731) ***(G-4657)***
North Point Press, New York *Also called Farrar Straus and Giroux LLC* ***(G-10192)***
North Point Technologies 607 238-1114
520 Columbia Dr Ste 105 Johnson City (13790) ***(G-7130)***
North Point Technology LLC 866 885-3377
816 Buffalo St Endicott (13760) ***(G-4828)***
North Salina Cigar Store, Syracuse *Also called Saakshi Inc* ***(G-16050)***
North Shore Farms Two Ltd 516 280-6880
330 E Jericho Tpke Mineola (11501) ***(G-8560)***
North Shore Home Improver 631 474-2824
200 Wilson St Port Jeff STA (11776) ***(G-13790)***
North Shore Monuments Inc 516 759-2156
667 Cedar Swamp Rd Ste 5 Glen Head (11545) ***(G-5653)***
North Shore Neon Sign Co Inc 718 937-4848
4649 54th Ave Flushing (11378) ***(G-5282)***
North Shore News Group, Smithtown *Also called Smithtown News Inc* ***(G-15521)***
North Shore Orthtics Prsthtics 631 928-3040
591 Bicycle Path Ste D Port Jeff STA (11776) ***(G-13791)***
North Shore Pallet Inc 631 673-4700
191 E 2nd St Huntington Station (11746) ***(G-6756)***
North Six Inc 212 463-7227
159 Bleecker St Frnt A New York (10012) ***(G-11475)***
North Star Knitting Mills Inc 718 894-4848
7030 80th St Glendale (11385) ***(G-5675)***
North Sunshine LLC 307 027-1634
616 Corporate Way Ste 2-3 Valley Cottage (10989) ***(G-16410)***
North-East Machine Inc 518 746-1837
4160 State Route 4 Hudson Falls (12839) ***(G-6679)***
North-South Books Inc 212 706-4545
600 3rd Ave Fl 2 New York (10016) ***(G-11476)***
Northamerican Breweries, Rochester *Also called North American Breweries Inc* ***(G-14559)***
Northast Coml Win Trtments Inc 845 331-0148
25 Cornell St Kingston (12401) ***(G-7232)***
Northast Ctr For Bekeeping LLC 800 632-3379
8 Meader Rd Greenwich (12834) ***(G-5910)***
Northeast Cnstr Inds Inc 845 565-1000
657 Rte 17 K S St Ste 2 Montgomery (12549) ***(G-8634)***
Northeast Commercial Prtg Inc (PA) 518 459-5047
1237 Central Ave Ste 3 Albany (12205) ***(G-110)***
Northeast Concrete Pdts Inc 518 563-0700
1024 Military Tpke Plattsburgh (12901) ***(G-13708)***
Northeast Conveyors Inc 585 768-8912
7620 Evergreen St Lima (14485) ***(G-7468)***
Northeast Data 845 331-5554
619 State Route 28 Kingston (12401) ***(G-7233)***
Northeast Doulas 845 621-0654
23 Hilltop Dr Mahopac (10541) ***(G-8029)***
Northeast Fabricators LLC 607 865-4031
30-35 William St Walton (13856) ***(G-16570)***
Northeast Group 518 563-8214
12 Nepco Way Plattsburgh (12903) ***(G-13709)***
Northeast Group, The, Plattsburgh *Also called Northeast Prtg & Dist Co Inc* ***(G-13711)***
Northeast Hardware Specialties 516 487-6868
393 Jericho Tpke Ste 103 Mineola (11501) ***(G-8561)***
Northeast Mesa LLC (PA) 845 878-9344
10 Commerce Dr Carmel (10512) ***(G-3430)***
Northeast Metrology Corp 716 827-3770
4490 Broadway Depew (14043) ***(G-4290)***
Northeast Pallet & Cont Co Inc 518 271-0535
1 Mann Ave Bldg 300 Troy (12180) ***(G-16267)***
Northeast Panel & Truss LLC 845 339-3656
2 Kieffer Ln Kingston (12401) ***(G-7234)***
Northeast Promotional Group In 518 793-1024
75 Main St South Glens Falls (12803) ***(G-15550)***
Northeast Prtg & Dist Co Inc 514 577-3545
163 Idaho Ave Plattsburgh (12903) ***(G-13710)***
Northeast Prtg & Dist Co Inc (PA) 518 563-8214
12 Nepco Way Plattsburgh (12903) ***(G-13711)***
Northeast Solite Corporation (PA) 845 246-2646
1135 Kings Hwy Saugerties (12477) ***(G-15218)***
Northeast Solite Corporation 845 246-2177
962 Kings Hwy Mount Marion (12456) ***(G-8694)***
Northeast Stitches & Ink Inc 518 798-5549
95 Main St South Glens Falls (12803) ***(G-15551)***
Northeast Toner Inc 518 899-5545
26 Walden Gln Fl 2 Ballston Lake (12019) ***(G-584)***
Northeast Treaters Inc 518 945-2660
796 Schoharie Tpke Athens (12015) ***(G-463)***
Northeast Treaters NY LLC 518 945-2660
796 Schoharie Tpke Athens (12015) ***(G-464)***
Northeast Water Systems LLC 585 943-9225
2338 W Kendall Rd Kendall (14476) ***(G-7172)***
Northeast Windows Usa Inc 516 378-6577
1 Kees Pl Merrick (11566) ***(G-8425)***
Northeast Wire and Cable Co 716 297-8483
8635 Packard Rd Niagara Falls (14304) ***(G-12870)***
Northeastern Air Quality Inc 518 857-3641
730 3rd St Albany (12206) ***(G-111)***
Northeastern Electric Motors 518 793-5939
34 Hollow Rd Hadley (12835) ***(G-5926)***
Northeastern Fuel Corp 917 560-6241
51 Stuyvesant Ave Staten Island (10312) ***(G-15736)***
Northeastern Paper Corp 631 659-3634
2 Lilac Ct Huntington (11743) ***(G-6705)***
Northeastern Products Corp (PA) 518 623-3161
115 Sweet Rd Warrensburg (12885) ***(G-16602)***
Northeastern Sealcoat Inc 585 544-4372
470 Hollenbeck St Bldg 3 Rochester (14621) ***(G-14563)***
Northeastern Sign Corp 315 265-6657
102 Cold Brook Dr South Colton (13687) ***(G-15538)***
Northeastern Transparts Inc 716 833-0792
5727 S Park Ave Hamburg (14075) ***(G-5958)***
Northeastern Water Jet Inc 518 843-4988
4 Willow St Amsterdam (12010) ***(G-364)***
Northern Adhesives Inc 718 388-5834
97 Apollo St Brooklyn (11222) ***(G-2384)***
Northern Air Systems Inc (PA) 585 594-5050
3605 Buffalo Rd Rochester (14624) ***(G-14564)***

ALPHABETIC SECTION

Nucare Pharmacy & Surgical, New York

Northern Air Technology Inc (PA) 585 594-5050
3605 Buffalo Rd Rochester (14624) ***(G-14565)***

Northern Awning & Sign Company 315 782-8515
22891 County Route 51 Watertown (13601) ***(G-16690)***

Northern Biodiesel Inc 585 545-4534
317 State Route 104 Ontario (14519) ***(G-13228)***

Northern Bituminous Mix Inc 315 598-2141
32 Silk Rd Fulton (13069) ***(G-5486)***

Northern Design & Bldg Assoc 518 747-2200
100 Park Rd Queensbury (12804) ***(G-14019)***

Northern Design Inc 716 652-7071
12990 Old Big Tree Rd East Aurora (14052) ***(G-4402)***

Northern Forest Pdts Co Inc 315 942-6955
9833 Crolius Dr Boonville (13309) ***(G-1164)***

Northern Goose Polar Project, New York *Also called Freedom Rains Inc* ***(G-10255)***

Northern Indus Svces Mech Div, Cohoes *Also called Nis Manufacturing Inc* ***(G-3777)***

Northern King Lures Inc (PA) 585 865-3373
167 Armstrong Rd Rochester (14616) ***(G-14566)***

Northern Lifts Elevator Co LLC (PA) 518 644-2831
45 Indian Brook Hollow Rd Bolton Landing (12814) ***(G-1157)***

Northern Lights Candles, Wellsville *Also called Northern Lights Entps Inc* ***(G-16781)***

Northern Lights Entps Inc 585 593-1200
3474 Andover Rd Wellsville (14895) ***(G-16781)***

Northern Machining Inc 315 384-3189
2a N Main St Norfolk (13667) ***(G-12917)***

Northern Metalworks Corp 646 523-1689
15 King Ave Selden (11784) ***(G-15374)***

Northern New York Rural 518 891-9460
126 Kiwassa Rd Saranac Lake (12983) ***(G-15166)***

Northern NY Newspapers Corp 315 782-1000
260 Washington St Watertown (13601) ***(G-16691)***

Northern Ready-Mix Inc (PA) 315 598-2141
32 Silk Rd Fulton (13069) ***(G-5487)***

Northern Tier Cnc Inc (PA) 518 236-4702
733 Woods Falls Rd Mooers Forks (12959) ***(G-8655)***

Northern Tier Publishing Corp 914 962-4748
1520 Front St Yorktown Heights (10598) ***(G-17530)***

Northern Timber Harvesting LLC 585 233-7330
6042 State Route 21 Alfred Station (14803) ***(G-200)***

NORTHERN WESTCHESTER HOSPITAL, Mount Kisco *Also called Norcorp Inc* ***(G-8680)***

Northfeld Precision Instr Corp 516 431-1112
4400 Austin Blvd Island Park (11558) ***(G-6822)***

Northknight Logistics Inc 716 283-3090
7724 Buffalo Ave Niagara Falls (14304) ***(G-12871)***

Northland Filter Intl LLC 315 207-1410
249a Mitchell St Oswego (13126) ***(G-13361)***

Northpoint Digital LLC 212 819-1700
1540 Broadway Fl 41 New York (10036) ***(G-11477)***

Northpoint Trading Inc (PA) 212 481-8001
347 5th Ave New York (10016) ***(G-11478)***

Northport Printing, West Babylon *Also called Bartolomeo Publishing Inc* ***(G-16799)***

Northrock Industries Inc 631 924-6130
31 Crossway E Bohemia (11716) ***(G-1107)***

Northrop Grumman Corporation 703 280-2900
660 Grumman Rd W Bethpage (11714) ***(G-874)***

Northrop Grumman Intl Trdg Inc 716 626-7233
1740 Wehrle Dr Buffalo (14221) ***(G-3118)***

Northrop Grumman Systems Corp 516 575-0574
925 S Oyster Bay Rd Bethpage (11714) ***(G-875)***

Northrop Grumman Systems Corp 716 626-4600
1740 Wehrle Dr Buffalo (14221) ***(G-3119)***

Northrop Grumman Systems Corp 631 423-1014
70 Dewey St Huntington (11743) ***(G-6706)***

Northrop Grumman Systems Corp 315 336-0500
Rr 26 Box N Rome (13440) ***(G-14855)***

Northside Media Group LLC (HQ) 917 318-6513
55 Washington St Ste 652 Brooklyn (11201) ***(G-2385)***

Northside Media Group LLC 917 318-6513
55 Washington St Ste 652 Brooklyn (11201) ***(G-2386)***

Northtown Imaging, Buffalo *Also called Mri Northtowns Group PC* ***(G-3097)***

Northwell Health Inc 888 387-5811
521 Park Ave New York (10065) ***(G-11479)***

Northwest Textile Holding Inc (PA) 516 484-6996
49 Bryant Ave Roslyn (11576) ***(G-15046)***

Northwind Graphics 518 899-9651
2453 State Route 9 Ballston Spa (12020) ***(G-605)***

Norton Performance Plas Corp 518 642-2200
1 Sealants Park Granville (12832) ***(G-5795)***

Norton Pulpstones Incorporated 716 433-9400
53 Caledonia St Lockport (14094) ***(G-7638)***

Norton, Ww & Company,, New York *Also called Liveright Publishing Corp* ***(G-11042)***

Norton-Smith Hardwoods Inc (PA) 716 945-0346
25 Morningside Ave Salamanca (14779) ***(G-15130)***

Norwesco Inc 607 687-8081
263 Corporate Dr Owego (13827) ***(G-13382)***

Norwich Aero, Norwich *Also called Sureseal Corporation* ***(G-13056)***

Norwich Aero Products Inc (HQ) 607 336-7636
50 Ohara Dr Norwich (13815) ***(G-13051)***

Norwich Manufacturing Division, Binghamton *Also called Felchar Manufacturing Corp* ***(G-909)***

Norwich Pharma Services, Norwich *Also called Norwich Pharmaceuticals Inc* ***(G-13052)***

Norwich Pharmaceuticals Inc 607 335-3000
6826 State Highway 12 Norwich (13815) ***(G-13052)***

Norwood Quar Btmnous Con Plnts, Norwood *Also called Barrett Paving Materials Inc* ***(G-13058)***

Norwood Screw Machine Parts 516 481-6644
200 E 2nd St Ste 2 Mineola (11501) ***(G-8562)***

Nostrand Pharmacy LLC 718 282-2956
1913 Nostrand Ave Brooklyn (11226) ***(G-2387)***

Not For Profit Chari, Bronx *Also called Lemon Brothers Foundation Inc* ***(G-1384)***

Noteworthy Company, The, Amsterdam *Also called Noteworthy Industries Inc* ***(G-365)***

Noteworthy Industries Inc 518 842-2662
336 Forest Ave Amsterdam (12010) ***(G-365)***

Noticia Hispanoamericana Inc 516 223-5678
53 E Merrick Rd Ste 353 Baldwin (11510) ***(G-559)***

Noto Industrial Corp 631 736-7600
11 Thomas St Coram (11727) ***(G-3971)***

Nova Bus Lfs, A Division of PR, Plattsburgh *Also called Prevost Car US Inc* ***(G-13717)***

Nova Health Systems Inc 315 798-9018
1001 Broad St Ste 3 Utica (13501) ***(G-16377)***

Nova Optical, Orangeburg *Also called Essilor Laboratories Amer Inc* ***(G-13248)***

Nova Pack, Philmont *Also called Pvc Container Corporation* ***(G-13566)***

Nova Packaging Ltd Inc 914 232-8406
7 Sunrise Ave Katonah (10536) ***(G-7161)***

Nova Science Publishers Inc 631 231-7269
400 Oser Ave Ste 1600 Hauppauge (11788) ***(G-6175)***

Novamed-Usa Inc 914 789-2100
4 Westchester Plz Ste 137 Elmsford (10523) ***(G-4779)***

Novanta Inc 818 341-5151
7279 William Barry Blvd Syracuse (13212) ***(G-16020)***

Novartis Corporation 914 592-7476
711 Old Saw Mill River Rd Tarrytown (10591) ***(G-16122)***

Novartis Corporation 718 276-8600
22715 N Conduit Ave Laurelton (11413) ***(G-7414)***

Novartis Pharmaceuticals Corp 888 669-6682
230 Park Ave New York (10169) ***(G-11480)***

Novartis Pharmaceuticals Corp 718 276-8600
22715 N Conduit Ave Laurelton (11413) ***(G-7415)***

Novatech Inc 716 892-6682
190 Gruner Rd Cheektowaga (14227) ***(G-3611)***

Novel Box Company Ltd 718 965-2222
659 Berriman St Brooklyn (11208) ***(G-2388)***

Novelis Corporation 315 342-1036
448 County Route 1a Oswego (13126) ***(G-13362)***

Novelis Corporation 315 349-0121
72 Alcan W Entrance Rd Oswego (13126) ***(G-13363)***

Novelis Inc 315 349-0121
448 County Route 1a Oswego (13126) ***(G-13364)***

Novelty Crystal Corp (PA) 718 458-6700
3015 48th Ave Long Island City (11101) ***(G-7858)***

Novelty Scenic Studios Inc, Monroe *Also called Associated Drapery & Equipment* ***(G-8583)***

Noven Pharmaceuticals Inc 212 682-4420
350 5th Ave Ste 3700 New York (10118) ***(G-11481)***

Novetree Coffee, Brooklyn *Also called Fal Coffee Inc* ***(G-1959)***

Novita Fabrics Furnishing Corp 516 299-4500
1 Brewster St Glen Cove (11542) ***(G-5636)***

Novoye Rsskoye Slovo Pubg Corp 646 460-4566
2614 Voorhies Ave Brooklyn (11235) ***(G-2389)***

Novum Medical Products Inc 716 759-7200
80 Creekside Dr Amherst (14228) ***(G-253)***

NP Roniet Creations Inc 212 302-1847
10 W 46th St Ste 1708 New York (10036) ***(G-11482)***

Nppi, Vestal *Also called National Pipe & Plastics Inc* ***(G-16474)***

Nrd LLC 716 773-7634
2937 Alt Blvd Grand Island (14072) ***(G-5779)***

Nsgv Inc 212 367-3167
90 5th Ave New York (10011) ***(G-11483)***

Nsgv Inc 212 367-3100
90 5th Ave New York (10011) ***(G-11484)***

Nsh, Menands *Also called Simmons Machine Tool Corp* ***(G-8410)***

Nsi Industries LLC 800 841-2505
50 S Macquesten Pkwy Mount Vernon (10550) ***(G-8757)***

Nsj Group Ltd 631 893-9300
80 W Main St Ste A Babylon (11702) ***(G-548)***

NSM Surveillance, New York *Also called News/Sprts Microwave Rentl Inc* ***(G-11438)***

Nsusa, Deer Park *Also called Nutra Solutions USA Inc* ***(G-4207)***

NTI Global, Amsterdam *Also called Nationwide Tarps Incorporated* ***(G-362)***

Nu - Communitek LLC 516 433-3553
108 New South Rd Ste A Hicksville (11801) ***(G-6402)***

Nu Life Restorations of L I 516 489-5200
51 Valley Rd Old Westbury (11568) ***(G-13154)***

Nu Ways Inc 585 254-7510
655 Pullman Ave Rochester (14615) ***(G-14567)***

Nu-Chem Laboratories, Bellport *Also called Optisource International Inc* ***(G-832)***

Nu-Life Long Island, Old Westbury *Also called Nu Life Restorations of L I* ***(G-13154)***

Nu2 Systems LLC 914 719-7272
155 Lafayette Ave White Plains (10603) ***(G-17169)***

Nubian Heritage 631 265-3551
367 Old Willets Path Hauppauge (11788) ***(G-6176)***

Nucare Pharmacy & Surgical, New York *Also called Nucare Pharmacy West LLC* ***(G-11486)***

Nucare Pharmacy & Surgical, New York *Also called Nucare Pharmacy Inc* ***(G-11485)***

ALPHABETIC

Nucare Pharmacy Inc......212 426-9300
1789 1st Ave New York (10128) ***(G-11485)***
Nucare Pharmacy West LLC......212 462-2525
250 9th Ave New York (10001) ***(G-11486)***
Nuclear Diagnostic Pdts NY Inc......516 575-4201
130 Commercial St Plainview (11803) ***(G-13653)***
Nucor Steel Auburn Inc......315 253-4561
25 Quarry Rd Auburn (13021) ***(G-509)***
Nugent Printing Company, Oceanside *Also called The Nugent Organization Inc* ***(G-13123)***
Nuhart & Co Inc......718 383-8484
49 Dupont St Brooklyn (11222) ***(G-2390)***
Nuk USA LLC......914 366-2820
303 S Broadway Ste 450 Tarrytown (10591) ***(G-16123)***
Nulux Inc......718 383-1112
1717 Troutman St Ridgewood (11385) ***(G-14128)***
Numed Pharmaceuticals, Brooklyn *Also called Ys Marketing Inc* ***(G-2791)***
Numerix LLC (PA)......212 302-2220
99 Park Ave Fl 5 New York (10016) ***(G-11487)***
Nupro Technologies LLC......412 422-5922
23 Coach St Ste 2a Canandaigua (14424) ***(G-3379)***
Nutec Components Inc......631 242-1224
81 E Jefryn Blvd Ste A Deer Park (11729) ***(G-4206)***
Nutek Disposables Inc......516 829-3030
80 Cuttermill Rd Ste 500 Great Neck (11021) ***(G-5841)***
Nutra Solutions USA Inc......631 392-1900
1019 Grand Blvd Deer Park (11729) ***(G-4207)***
Nutra-Scientifics LLC......917 238-8510
108 Overlook Rd Pomona (10970) ***(G-13759)***
Nutra-Vet Research Corp......845 473-1900
201 Smith St Poughkeepsie (12601) ***(G-13941)***
Nutraceutical Wellness LLC......888 454-3320
28 W 27th St Fl 2 New York (10001) ***(G-11488)***
Nutrafol, New York *Also called Nutraceutical Wellness LLC* ***(G-11488)***
Nutraqueen LLC......347 368-6568
138 E 34th St Apt 2f New York (10016) ***(G-11489)***
Nutrascience Labs Inc......631 247-0660
70 Carolyn Blvd Farmingdale (11735) ***(G-5078)***
Nutrifast LLC......347 671-3181
244 5th Ave Ste W249 New York (10001) ***(G-11490)***
Nutritional Designs, Lynbrook *Also called ND Labs Inc* ***(G-7982)***
Nuttall Gear L L C (HQ)......716 298-4100
2221 Niagara Falls Blvd # 17 Niagara Falls (14304) ***(G-12872)***
Nuvite Chemical Compounds Corp......718 383-8351
213 Freeman St 215 Brooklyn (11222) ***(G-2391)***
NV Prrcone MD Cosmeceuticals......212 734-2537
1745 Broadway New York (10019) ***(G-11491)***
Nxxi Inc......914 701-4500
4 Manhattanville Rd # 205 Purchase (10577) ***(G-13978)***
NY 1 Art Gallery Inc......917 698-0626
32 3rd St New Hyde Park (11040) ***(G-8898)***
NY Cabinet Factory Inc......718 256-6541
6901 14th Ave Brooklyn (11228) ***(G-2392)***
NY Denim Inc......212 764-6668
1407 Broadway Rm 1021 New York (10018) ***(G-11492)***
NY Embroidery Inc......516 822-6456
25 Midland Ave Hicksville (11801) ***(G-6403)***
NY Froyo LLC......516 312-4588
324 W 19th St Deer Park (11729) ***(G-4208)***
NY Iron Inc......718 302-9000
3131 48th Ave Ste 2 Long Island City (11101) ***(G-7859)***
NY Orthopedic Usa Inc......718 852-5330
63 Flushing Ave Unit 333 Brooklyn (11205) ***(G-2393)***
NY Phrmacy Compounding Ctr Inc......201 403-5151
3715 23rd Ave Astoria (11105) ***(G-450)***
NY Print Partners, Sunnyside *Also called Deanco Digital Printing LLC* ***(G-15826)***
NY Tempering LLC......718 326-8989
6021 Flushing Ave Maspeth (11378) ***(G-8190)***
NY Tilemakers......989 278-8453
331 Grand St Brooklyn (11211) ***(G-2394)***
NY Titanium Inc......718 227-4244
63 Robin Ct Staten Island (10309) ***(G-15737)***
Nyc Community Media LLC......212 229-1890
1 Metrotech Ctr N Fl 10 Brooklyn (11201) ***(G-2395)***
Nyc Design Co, New York *Also called M S B International Ltd* ***(G-11105)***
Nyc District Council Ubcja......212 366-7500
395 Hudson St Lbby 3 New York (10014) ***(G-11493)***
Nyc Fireplaces & Kitchens......718 326-4328
5830 Maspeth Ave Maspeth (11378) ***(G-8191)***
Nyc Idol Apparel Inc......212 997-9797
214 W 39th St Rm 807 New York (10018) ***(G-11494)***
Nyc Knitwear Inc......212 840-1313
525 Fashion Ave Rm 701 New York (10018) ***(G-11495)***
Nyc Thermography, New York *Also called Hart Reproduction Services* ***(G-10468)***
Nyc Trade Printers Corp......718 606-0610
3245 62nd St Woodside (11377) ***(G-17359)***
Nycjbs LLC......212 533-1888
112 Rivington St Frnt New York (10002) ***(G-11496)***
Nycom Business Solutions Inc......516 345-6000
804 Hempstead Tpke Franklin Square (11010) ***(G-5376)***
Nycon Diamond & Tools Corp......855 937-6922
55 Knickerbocker Ave Bohemia (11716) ***(G-1108)***

Nyemac Inc......631 668-1303
Paradise Ln Montauk (11954) ***(G-8626)***
Nyi Building Products Inc (PA)......518 458-7500
5 Southside Dr Ste 204 Clifton Park (12065) ***(G-3729)***
Nykon Inc......315 483-0504
8175 Stell Rd Sodus (14551) ***(G-15526)***
Nylon LLc......212 226-6454
110 Greene St Ste 607 New York (10012) ***(G-11497)***
Nylon Magazine, New York *Also called Nylon LLc* ***(G-11497)***
Nylon Media Inc (PA)......212 226-6454
110 Greene St Ste 607 New York (10012) ***(G-11498)***
Nylonshop, New York *Also called Nylon Media Inc* ***(G-11498)***
Nyman Jewelry Inc (PA)......212 944-1976
66 W 9th St New York (10011) ***(G-11499)***
Nyp Holdings Inc......718 260-2500
1 Metrotech Ctr N Fl 10 Brooklyn (11201) ***(G-2396)***
Nyp Holdings Inc (HQ)......212 997-9272
1211 Ave Of The Americas New York (10036) ***(G-11500)***
Nyrev Inc......212 757-8070
435 Hudson St Rm 300 New York (10014) ***(G-11501)***
Nys Nyu-Cntr Intl Cooperation......212 998-3680
418 Lafayette St New York (10003) ***(G-11502)***
Nysco Products LLC......718 792-9000
2350 Lafayette Ave Bronx (10473) ***(G-1416)***
Nyt Capital LLC (HQ)......212 556-1234
620 8th Ave New York (10018) ***(G-11503)***
O & S Machine & Tool Co Inc......716 941-5542
8143 State Rd Colden (14033) ***(G-3797)***
O Brien Gere Mfg Inc......315 437-6100
7600 Morgan Rd Ste 1 Liverpool (13090) ***(G-7563)***
O C Choppers, Newburgh *Also called Orange County Choppers Inc* ***(G-12793)***
O C P Inc......516 679-2000
500 Bi County Blvd # 209 Farmingdale (11735) ***(G-5079)***
O C Tanner Company......914 921-2025
27 Park Dr S Rye (10580) ***(G-15091)***
O P I Industries, Ronkonkoma *Also called Paramount Equipment Inc* ***(G-14988)***
O Rama Light Inc......518 539-9000
22 Hudson Falls Rd Ste 52 South Glens Falls (12803) ***(G-15552)***
O Tex, Rochester *Also called Robert J Faraone* ***(G-14653)***
O Val Nick Music Co Inc......212 873-2179
254 W 72nd St Apt 1a New York (10023) ***(G-11504)***
O W Hubbell & Sons Inc......315 736-8311
5124 Commercial Dr Yorkville (13495) ***(G-17540)***
O'Bryan Bros, New York *Also called Komar Layering LLC* ***(G-10912)***
O'Neil Construction, Glen Head *Also called Lomin Construction Company* ***(G-5650)***
O-At-Ka Milk Products Coop Inc (PA)......585 343-0536
700 Ellicott St Batavia (14020) ***(G-645)***
O-Neh-Da Vineyard, Conesus *Also called Eagle Crest Vineyard LLC* ***(G-3874)***
Oak Lone Publishing Co Inc......518 792-1126
15 Ridge St Glens Falls (12801) ***(G-5708)***
Oak Valley Logging Inc......518 622-8249
558 Frank Hitchcock Rd Cairo (12413) ***(G-3301)***
Oak-Bark Corporation......518 372-5691
37 Maple Ave Scotia (12302) ***(G-15352)***
Oak-Mitsui Inc......518 686-8060
1 Mechanic St Bldg 2 Hoosick Falls (12090) ***(G-6569)***
Oak-Mitsui Technologies LLC......518 686-4961
80 1st St Hoosick Falls (12090) ***(G-6570)***
Oakdale Industrial Elec Corp......631 737-4090
1995 Pond Rd Ronkonkoma (11779) ***(G-14982)***
Oakhurst Partners LLC......212 502-3220
148 Madison Ave Fl 13 New York (10016) ***(G-11505)***
Oaklee International Inc......631 436-7900
125 Raynor Ave Ronkonkoma (11779) ***(G-14983)***
Oakley Inc......212 575-0960
1515 Broadway Frnt 4 New York (10036) ***(G-11506)***
Oakwood Publishing Co......516 482-7720
14 Bond St Ste 386 Great Neck (11021) ***(G-5842)***
Oasis Cosmetic Labs Inc......631 758-0038
182 Long Island Ave Holtsville (11742) ***(G-6531)***
Oberdorfer Pumps Inc......315 437-0361
5900 Firestone Dr Syracuse (13206) ***(G-16021)***
Oberon, New York *Also called Tabrisse Collections Inc* ***(G-12293)***
Observer......347 915-5638
81 Prospect St Fl 4 Brooklyn (11201) ***(G-2397)***
Observer Daily Sunday Newsppr......716 366-3000
10 E 2nd St Dunkirk (14048) ***(G-4370)***
Observer Dispatch, Utica *Also called Gatehouse Media LLC* ***(G-16359)***
Ocala Group LLC......516 233-2750
1981 Marcus Ave Ste 227 New Hyde Park (11042) ***(G-8899)***
Occhioerosso John......718 541-7025
75 Santa Monica Ln Staten Island (10309) ***(G-15738)***
Occidental Chemical Corp......716 278-7795
4700 Buffalo Ave Niagara Falls (14304) ***(G-12873)***
Occidental Chemical Corp......716 773-8100
2801 Long Rd Grand Island (14072) ***(G-5780)***
Occidental Chemical Corp......716 278-7794
56 Street & Energy Blvd Niagara Falls (14302) ***(G-12874)***
Occidental Chemical Corp......716 694-3827
3780 Commerce Ct Ste 600 North Tonawanda (14120) ***(G-13002)***
Occidental Energy Mktg Inc......212 632-4950
1230 Av Of The Amrcs 80 New York (10020) ***(G-11507)***

ALPHABETIC SECTION **Omx (us) Inc**

Occunomix International LLC....631 741-1940
585 Bicycle Path Ste 52 Port Jeff STA (11776) ***(G-13792)***
Ocean Cardiac Monitoring....631 777-3700
38 W 17th St Deer Park (11729) ***(G-4209)***
Ocean Park Drugs & Surgical, Far Rockaway *Also called Far Rockaway Drugs Inc* ***(G-4929)***
Ocean Printing, Ronkonkoma *Also called Copy X/Press Ltd* ***(G-14916)***
Ocean Steel Corporation....607 584-7500
53 Shaw Rd Conklin (13748) ***(G-3897)***
Ocean Waves Swim LLC....212 967-4481
231 W 39th St Rm 500 New York (10018) ***(G-11508)***
Oceans Cuisine Ltd....631 209-9200
367 Sheffield Ct Ridge (11961) ***(G-14105)***
Oceanside-Island Park Herald, Lawrence *Also called Richner Communications Inc* ***(G-7424)***
Ocip Holding LLC (PA)....646 589-6180
660 Madison Ave Fl 19 New York (10065) ***(G-11509)***
Ocs, Brooklyn *Also called Original Convector Specialist* ***(G-2406)***
Ocs Industries, Brooklyn *Also called CIDC Corp* ***(G-1779)***
Octagon Process LLC (HQ)....845 680-8800
30 Ramland Rd S Ste 103 Orangeburg (10962) ***(G-13259)***
Octopus Advanced Systems Inc....914 771-6110
27 Covington Rd Yonkers (10710) ***(G-17488)***
Ocular Sciences A Coopervision, Victor *Also called Coopervision Inc* ***(G-16495)***
Odegard Inc....212 545-0069
3030 47th Ave Ste 700 Long Island City (11101) ***(G-7860)***
Oden Machinery Inc (PA)....716 874-3000
600 Ensminger Rd Tonawanda (14150) ***(G-16207)***
ODY Accessories Inc....212 239-0580
1239 Broadway New York (10001) ***(G-11510)***
Odyssey Controls Inc....585 548-9800
6256 Clinton Street Rd Bergen (14416) ***(G-850)***
Odyssey Mag Pubg Group Inc....212 545-4800
4 New York Plz New York (10004) ***(G-11511)***
Oehlers Wldg & Fabrication Inc....716 821-1800
242 Elk St Buffalo (14210) ***(G-3120)***
OEM Solutions Inc....716 864-9324
4995 Rockhaven Dr Clarence (14031) ***(G-3694)***
Oerlikon Blzers Cating USA Inc....716 270-2228
6000 N Bailey Ave Ste 9 Amherst (14226) ***(G-254)***
Oerlikon Blzers Cating USA Inc....716 270-2228
6000 N Bailey Ave Ste 9 Amherst (14226) ***(G-255)***
Oerlikon Blzers Cating USA Inc....716 564-8557
6000 N Bailey Ave Ste 3 Buffalo (14226) ***(G-3121)***
Oerlikon Metco (us) Inc....716 270-2228
6000 N Bailey Ave Amherst (14226) ***(G-256)***
Oestreich Metal Works Inc....315 463-4268
6131 Court Street Rd Syracuse (13206) ***(G-16022)***
Off State Water Group, Montgomery *Also called On Point Reps Inc* ***(G-8635)***
Office Grabs NY Inc....212 444-1331
1303 53rd St 105 Brooklyn (11219) ***(G-2398)***
Official Offset Corporation....631 957-8500
8600 New Horizons Blvd Amityville (11701) ***(G-316)***
Official Press, The, New York *Also called Hks Printing Company Inc* ***(G-10533)***
Ogd V-Hvac Inc....315 858-1002
174 Pumkinhook Rd Van Hornesville (13475) ***(G-16455)***
Ogden Newspapers Inc....716 487-1111
15 W 2nd St Jamestown (14701) ***(G-7055)***
Ogi Limited, New York *Also called Osnat Gad Inc* ***(G-11544)***
Ogilvie Press, Lancaster *Also called Rmf Printing Technologies Inc* ***(G-7364)***
Ogosport LLC....718 554-0777
63 Flushing Ave Unit 137 Brooklyn (11205) ***(G-2399)***
Ogulnick Uniforms, New York *Also called Tailored Sportsman LLC* ***(G-12297)***
OH How Cute Inc....347 838-6031
38 Androvette St Staten Island (10309) ***(G-15739)***
Ohio Baking Company Inc....315 724-2033
10585 Cosby Manor Rd Utica (13502) ***(G-16378)***
Ohr Pharmaceutical Inc (PA)....212 682-8452
800 3rd Ave Fl 11 New York (10022) ***(G-11512)***
Ohserase Manufacturing LLC....518 358-9309
26 Eagle Dr Akwesasne (13655) ***(G-29)***
Ohserase Manufacturing LLC....518 358-9309
393 Frogtown Rd Hogansburg (13655) ***(G-6454)***
Oil and Lubricant Depot LLC....718 258-9220
61 Ranick Dr S Amityville (11701) ***(G-317)***
Oil Depot, The, Amityville *Also called Oil and Lubricant Depot LLC* ***(G-317)***
Oil Solutions Intl Inc....631 608-8889
35 Mill St Amityville (11701) ***(G-318)***
Olan Laboratories Inc....631 582-2082
20 Newton Pl Hauppauge (11788) ***(G-6177)***
Old Castle Precast, Middle Island *Also called Afco Precast Sales Corp* ***(G-8438)***
Old Dutch Mustard Co Inc (PA)....516 466-0522
98 Cuttermill Rd Ste 260s Great Neck (11021) ***(G-5843)***
Old Dutchmans Wrough Iron Inc....716 688-2034
2800 Millersport Hwy Getzville (14068) ***(G-5614)***
Old Poland Foods LLC....718 486-7700
149 N 8th St Brooklyn (11249) ***(G-2400)***
Old Ue LLC....718 707-0700
4511 33rd St Long Island City (11101) ***(G-7861)***
Old Williamsburgh Candle Corp....718 566-1500
143 Alabama Ave Brooklyn (11207) ***(G-2401)***
Old World Mouldings Inc....631 563-8660
821 Lincoln Ave Bohemia (11716) ***(G-1109)***
Old World Provisions Inc (PA)....518 465-7307
12 Industrial Park Rd Troy (12180) ***(G-16268)***
Oldcastle Building Envelope (HQ)....212 957-5400
1350 Ave Of The Americas New York (10019) ***(G-11513)***
Oldcastle Buildingenvelope Inc....631 234-2200
895 Motor Pkwy Hauppauge (11788) ***(G-6178)***
Oldcastle Precast Inc....518 767-2116
100 S County Rte 101 South Bethlehem (12161) ***(G-15536)***
Oldcastle Precast Inc....518 767-2112
123 County Route 101 Selkirk (12158) ***(G-15378)***
Oldcastle Precast Bldg Systems, Selkirk *Also called Oldcastle Precast Inc* ***(G-15378)***
Olde Chtqua Vneyards Ltd Lblty....716 792-2749
6654 W Main Rd Portland (14769) ***(G-13891)***
Olde Saratoga Brewing....518 581-0492
131 Excelsior Ave Saratoga Springs (12866) ***(G-15195)***
Olean Advanced Products, Olean *Also called AVX Corporation* ***(G-13155)***
Olean Waste Water Treatment, Olean *Also called City of Olean* ***(G-13158)***
Oledworks LLC (PA)....585 287-6802
1645 Lyell Ave Ste 140 Rochester (14606) ***(G-14568)***
Oligomerix Inc....914 997-8877
3960 Broadway Ste 340d New York (10032) ***(G-11514)***
Olin Chlor Alkali Logistics....716 278-6411
2400 Buffalo Ave Niagara Falls (14303) ***(G-12875)***
Olive Led Lighting Inc....718 746-0830
1310 111th St College Point (11356) ***(G-3825)***
OLIVEA MATHEWS, New York *Also called Pride & Joys Inc* ***(G-11729)***
Oliver Gear, Buffalo *Also called Gear Motions Incorporated* ***(G-2982)***
Oliver Gear Inc....716 885-1080
1120 Niagara St Buffalo (14213) ***(G-3122)***
Olmstead Machine Inc....315 587-9864
10399 Warehouse Ave North Rose (14516) ***(G-12954)***
Olmstead Products Corp....516 681-3700
1 Jefry Ln Hicksville (11801) ***(G-6404)***
Olollo Inc....877 701-0110
43 Hall St Ste B8 Brooklyn (11205) ***(G-2402)***
Olson Sign Company Inc....518 370-2118
1750 Valley Rd Ext Schenectady (12302) ***(G-15309)***
Olson Signs & Graphics, Schenectady *Also called Olson Sign Company Inc* ***(G-15309)***
Olympia Company, Elmsford *Also called Olympia Sports Company Inc* ***(G-4780)***
Olympia Sports Company Inc....914 347-4737
500 Executive Blvd # 170 Elmsford (10523) ***(G-4780)***
Olympic Ice Cream Co Inc (PA)....718 849-6200
12910 91st Ave Richmond Hill (11418) ***(G-14089)***
Olympic Ice Cream Co Inc....718 849-6200
12910 91st Ave Jamaica (11418) ***(G-6974)***
Olympic Jewelry Inc....212 768-7004
62 W 47th St Ste 509 New York (10036) ***(G-11515)***
Olympic Manufacturing Inc....631 231-8900
195 Marcus Blvd Hauppauge (11788) ***(G-6179)***
Olympic Press Inc....212 242-4934
950 3rd Ave Fl 7 New York (10022) ***(G-11516)***
Olympic Software & Consulting....631 351-0655
290 Broadhollow Rd 130e Melville (11747) ***(G-8373)***
Omc Inc....718 731-5001
4010 Park Ave Bronx (10457) ***(G-1417)***
Omega Consolidated Corporation....585 392-9262
101 Heinz St Hilton (14468) ***(G-6445)***
Omega Die Casting Co, Hauppauge *Also called Jacknob International Ltd* ***(G-6126)***
Omega Furniture Manufacturing....315 463-7428
102 Wavel St Syracuse (13206) ***(G-16023)***
Omega Heater Company Inc....631 588-8820
2059 9th Ave Ronkonkoma (11779) ***(G-14984)***
Omega Industries & Development....516 349-8010
150 Express St Ste 2 Plainview (11803) ***(G-13654)***
Omega Tool Measuring Mchs Inc (PA)....585 598-7800
101 Perinton Pkwy Fairport (14450) ***(G-4872)***
Omega Wire Inc....315 337-4300
900 Railroad St Rome (13440) ***(G-14856)***
Omega Wire Inc....315 689-7115
24 N Beaver St Jordan (13080) ***(G-7158)***
Omega Wire Inc (HQ)....315 245-3800
12 Masonic Ave Camden (13316) ***(G-3346)***
Omg Desserts Inc....585 698-1561
1227 Ridgeway Ave Ste J Rochester (14615) ***(G-14569)***
Omicron Technologies Inc....631 434-7697
1736 Church St Holbrook (11741) ***(G-6494)***
Omni-ID Usa Inc....585 697-9913
1200 Ridgeway Ave Ste 106 Rochester (14615) ***(G-14570)***
Omniafiltra LLC....315 346-7300
9567 Main St Beaver Falls (13305) ***(G-790)***
Omnicare Anesthesia PC (PA)....718 433-0044
3636 33rd St Ste 211 Astoria (11106) ***(G-451)***
Omnimusic, Port Washington *Also called Franklin-Douglas Inc* ***(G-13838)***
Omntec Mfg Inc....631 981-2001
1993 Pond Rd Ronkonkoma (11779) ***(G-14985)***
Omp Printing & Graphics, Clinton *Also called Tenney Media Group* ***(G-3747)***
Omrix Biopharmaceuticals Inc....908 218-0707
1 Rckfller Ctr Ste 2322 New York (10020) ***(G-11517)***
Omt, Yorkville *Also called Oriskany Mfg Tech LLC* ***(G-17542)***
Omx (us) Inc....646 428-2800
140 Broadway Fl 25 New York (10005) ***(G-11518)***

ALPHABETIC

On Demand Books LLC 212 966-2222
939 Lexington Ave New York (10065) *(G-11519)*
On Line Power Technologies 914 968-4440
113 Sunnyside Dr Yonkers (10705) *(G-17489)*
On Montauk, Montauk *Also called Nyemac Inc (G-8626)*
On Point Reps Inc 518 258-2268
20a Wellroad Ave Montgomery (12549) *(G-8635)*
On Semiconductor Corporation 585 784-5770
1964 Lake Ave Rochester (14615) *(G-14571)*
On The Double Inc 518 431-3571
178 Viewmont Rd Germantown (12526) *(G-5603)*
On The Job Embroidery & AP 914 381-3556
154 E Boston Post Rd # 1 Mamaroneck (10543) *(G-8073)*
On The Mark Digital Printing & 716 823-3373
5758 S Park Ave Hamburg (14075) *(G-5959)*
On The Spot Binding Inc 718 497-2200
4805 Metropolitan Ave Ridgewood (11385) *(G-14129)*
On Time Plastics Inc 516 442-4280
121 Henry St Freeport (11520) *(G-5426)*
Once Again Nut Butter Collectv (PA) 585 468-2535
12 S State St Nunda (14517) *(G-13059)*
Ondrivesus Corp 516 771-6777
216 N Main St Bldg B2 Freeport (11520) *(G-5427)*
One Girl Cookies Ltd 212 675-4996
68 Dean St Ste A Brooklyn (11201) *(G-2403)*
One In A Million Inc 516 829-1111
51 Franklin Ave Valley Stream (11580) *(G-16441)*
One Jeanswear Group Inc (HQ) 212 835-3500
1441 Broadway New York (10018) *(G-11520)*
One Step Up Kids, New York *Also called Kidz Concepts LLC (G-10882)*
One Step Up Ltd 212 398-1110
1412 Broadway Fl 3 New York (10018) *(G-11521)*
One Story Inc 917 816-3659
232 3rd St Ste A108 Brooklyn (11215) *(G-2404)*
One Technologies LLC 718 509-0704
44 Court St Ste 1217 Brooklyn (11201) *(G-2405)*
One Tree Dist 315 701-2924
200 Midler Park Dr Syracuse (13206) *(G-16024)*
One-Blue LLC 212 223-4380
1350 Broadway Rm 1406 New York (10018) *(G-11522)*
Oneida Air Systems Inc 315 476-5151
1001 W Fayette St Ste 2a Syracuse (13204) *(G-16025)*
Oneida Concrete Products, Buffalo *Also called Oneida Sales & Service Inc (G-3123)*
Oneida Concrete Products, Lackawanna *Also called Oneida Sales & Service Inc (G-7271)*
Oneida Dispatch, Oneida *Also called Oneida Publications Inc (G-13185)*
Oneida Foundries Inc 315 363-4570
559 Fitch St Oneida (13421) *(G-13181)*
Oneida International Inc 315 361-3000
163-181 Kenwood Ave Oneida (13421) *(G-13182)*
Oneida Molded Plastics LLC (PA) 315 363-7980
104 S Warner St Oneida (13421) *(G-13183)*
Oneida Molded Plastics LLC 315 363-7990
104 S Warner St Oneida (13421) *(G-13184)*
Oneida Publications Inc 315 363-5100
130 Broad St Oneida (13421) *(G-13185)*
Oneida Sales & Service Inc (PA) 716 822-8205
155 Commerce Dr Buffalo (14218) *(G-3123)*
Oneida Sales & Service Inc 716 270-0433
155 Commerce Dr Lackawanna (14218) *(G-7271)*
Oneida Silversmiths Inc 315 361-3000
163 Kenwood Ave 181 Oneida (13421) *(G-13186)*
Oneonta Asphalt, Oneonta *Also called Cobleskill Stone Products Inc (G-13202)*
Oneonta City Wtr Trtmnt Plant, Oneonta *Also called City of Oneonta (G-13200)*
Oneonta Fence 607 433-6707
2 Washburn St Oneonta (13820) *(G-13212)*
Ongweoweh Corp (PA) 607 266-7070
767 Warren Rd Ithaca (14850) *(G-6903)*
Only Hearts Ltd (PA) 718 783-3218
134 W 37th St Fl 9 New York (10018) *(G-11523)*
Only Natural Inc 516 897-7001
3580 Oceanside Rd Unit 5 Oceanside (11572) *(G-13110)*
Ontario Knife Company 716 676-5527
26 Empire St Ste 1 Franklinville (14737) *(G-5380)*
Ontario Label Graphics Inc 716 434-8505
6444 Ridge Rd Lockport (14094) *(G-7639)*
Ontario Plastics Inc 585 663-2644
2503 Dewey Ave Rochester (14616) *(G-14572)*
Ontra Presentations LLC 212 213-1315
440 Park Ave S Fl 3 New York (10016) *(G-11524)*
Ony Biotech Inc 716 636-9096
1576 Sweet Home Rd Amherst (14228) *(G-257)*
Ony Inc Baird Researchpark 716 636-9096
1576 Sweet Home Rd Buffalo (14228) *(G-3124)*
Onyx Solar Group LLC (PA) 917 951-9732
1123 Broadway Ste 908 New York (10010) *(G-11525)*
Opd, Depew *Also called Leica Microsystems Inc (G-4286)*
Open & Shut Doors, Brentwood *Also called Michbi Doors Inc (G-1189)*
Open-Xchange Inc 914 332-5720
303 S Broadway Ste 224 Tarrytown (10591) *(G-16124)*
Openfin Inc 917 450-8822
25 Broadway Fl 9 New York (10004) *(G-11526)*
Openroad Integrated Media Inc 212 691-0900
180 Maiden Ln Ste 2803 New York (10038) *(G-11527)*
Operative Cake Corp 718 278-5600
711 Brush Ave Bronx (10465) *(G-1418)*
Operative Media Inc (HQ) 212 994-8930
6 E 32nd St Fl 3 New York (10016) *(G-11528)*
Ophthotech Corporation 212 845-8200
1 Penn Plz Ste 1924 New York (10119) *(G-11529)*
Opposuits USA Inc 917 438-8878
228 E 45th St Ste 9e New York (10017) *(G-11530)*
Oprah Magazine, New York *Also called Hearst Corporation (G-10484)*
Opta Minerals 905 689-7361
266 Elmwood Ave Buffalo (14222) *(G-3125)*
Optic Solution LLC 518 293-4034
133 Standish Rd Saranac (12981) *(G-15161)*
Optical Gaging Products Div, Rochester *Also called Quality Vision Intl Inc (G-14637)*
Opticool Solutions LLC 585 347-6127
855 Publishers Pkwy Webster (14580) *(G-16753)*
Opticool Technologies, Webster *Also called Opticool Solutions LLC (G-16753)*
Optics Plus Inc 716 744-2636
4291 Delaware Ave Tonawanda (14150) *(G-16208)*
Optics Technology Inc 585 586-0950
3800 Monroe Ave Ste 3 Pittsford (14534) *(G-13599)*
Optika Eyes Ltd 631 567-8852
153 Main St Unit 1 Sayville (11782) *(G-15242)*
Optimax Systems Inc (PA) 585 265-1020
6367 Dean Pkwy Ontario (14519) *(G-13229)*
Optimized Devices Inc 914 769-6100
220 Marble Ave Pleasantville (10570) *(G-13747)*
Optimum Applied Systems Inc 845 471-3333
16 Victory Ln Ste 5 Poughkeepsie (12603) *(G-13942)*
Optimum Window Mfg Corp 845 647-1900
28 Canal St Ellenville (12428) *(G-4650)*
Optionline LLC 516 218-3225
100 Hilton Ave Apt 23 Garden City (11530) *(G-5538)*
Options Publishing, New York *Also called Triumph Learning LLC (G-12430)*
Optipro Systems LLC 585 265-0160
6368 Dean Pkwy Ontario (14519) *(G-13230)*
Optisource International Inc 631 924-8360
40 Sawgrass Dr Ste 1 Bellport (11713) *(G-832)*
Optogenics of Syracuse Inc 315 446-3000
2840 Erie Blvd E Syracuse (13224) *(G-16026)*
Opus Technology Corporation 631 271-1883
10 Gwynne Rd Melville (11747) *(G-8374)*
Oracle America Inc 518 427-9353
7 Southwoods Blvd Ste 1 Albany (12211) *(G-112)*
Oracle America Inc 585 317-4648
345 Woodcliff Dr Ste 1 Fairport (14450) *(G-4873)*
Oracle Corporation 212 508-7700
120 Park Ave Fl 26 New York (10017) *(G-11531)*
Orafol Americas Inc 585 272-0290
200 Park Centre Dr West Henrietta (14586) *(G-16918)*
Orafol Americas Inc 585 272-0309
200 Park Centre Dr Henrietta (14467) *(G-6321)*
Oramaax Dental Products Inc 516 771-8514
216 N Main St Ste A Freeport (11520) *(G-5428)*
Orange County Choppers Inc 845 522-5200
14 Crossroads Ct Newburgh (12550) *(G-12793)*
Orange County Ironworks LLC 845 769-3000
36 Maybrook Rd Montgomery (12549) *(G-8636)*
Orange Die Cutting Corp 845 562-0900
1 Favoriti Ave Newburgh (12550) *(G-12794)*
Orange Packaging, Newburgh *Also called Orange Die Cutting Corp (G-12794)*
Orangenius Inc 631 742-0648
115 W 18th St Fl 2 New York (10011) *(G-11532)*
Orbcomm Inc 703 433-6396
125 Business Park Dr Utica (13502) *(G-16379)*
Orbis Brynmore Lithographics 212 987-2100
1735 2nd Ave Frnt 1 New York (10128) *(G-11533)*
Orbit Industries LLC 914 244-1500
116 Radio Circle Dr # 302 Mount Kisco (10549) *(G-8681)*
Orbit International Corp (PA) 631 435-8300
80 Cabot Ct Hauppauge (11788) *(G-6180)*
Orbit International Corp 631 435-8300
80 Cabot Ct Hauppauge (11788) *(G-6181)*
Orbital Holdings Inc 951 360-7100
2775 Broadway St Ste 200 Buffalo (14227) *(G-3126)*
Orcam Inc 800 713-3741
1350 Broadway Rm 1600 New York (10018) *(G-11534)*
Orchard Apparel Group Ltd 212 268-8701
212 W 35th St Fl 7 New York (10001) *(G-11535)*
Orchard Hill Mch & Tl Co Inc 315 245-0015
2855 State Route 49 Blossvale (13308) *(G-992)*
Orchid Manufacturing Co Inc 212 840-5700
77 W 55th St Apt 4k New York (10019) *(G-11536)*
Ore-Lube Corporation 631 205-0030
20 Sawgrass Dr Bellport (11713) *(G-833)*
Orege North America Inc (PA) 770 862-9388
575 Madison Ave Fl 25 New York (10022) *(G-11537)*
Orelube, Bellport *Also called Ore-Lube Corporation (G-833)*
Orens Daily Roast Inc (PA) 212 348-5400
12 E 46th St Fl 6 New York (10017) *(G-11538)*

Orffeo Printing & Imaging Inc......716 681-5757
99 Cambria St Lancaster (14086) *(G-7352)*
Orfit Industries America, Jericho *Also called SC Medical Overseas Inc (G-7117)*
Organic Frog Inc......516 897-0369
85 Commerce Dr Hauppauge (11788) *(G-6182)*
Organic Peak, Mineola *Also called Maxim Hygiene Products Inc (G-8556)*
Orics Industries Inc......718 461-8613
240 Smith St Farmingdale (11735) *(G-5080)*
Origin Press Inc......516 746-2262
131 Liberty Ave Mineola (11501) *(G-8563)*
Original Convector Specialist......718 342-5820
2015 Pitkin Ave Brooklyn (11207) *(G-2406)*
Original Crunch Roll Fctry LLC......716 402-5030
90 Sylvan Pkwy Amherst (14228) *(G-258)*
Original Dream Statuary, Brooklyn *Also called Dream Statuary Inc (G-1880)*
Original Fowlers Choclat Inc......716 668-2113
2563 Union Rd Ste 101 Cheektowaga (14227) *(G-3612)*
Original Hrkmer Cnty Chese Inc......315 895-7428
2745 State Route 51 Ilion (13357) *(G-6782)*
Orion Fashions Holdings LLC......212 764-3332
390 5th Ave New York (10018) *(G-11539)*
Oriskany Arms Inc......315 737-2196
175 Clear Rd Oriskany (13424) *(G-13336)*
Oriskany Manufacturing LLC......315 732-4962
2 Wurz Ave Yorkville (13495) *(G-17541)*
Oriskany Mfg Tech LLC......315 732-4962
2 Wurz Ave Yorkville (13495) *(G-17542)*
Orlandi Inc (PA)......631 756-0110
131 Executive Blvd Farmingdale (11735) *(G-5081)*
Orlandi Inc......631 756-0110
121 Executive Blvd Farmingdale (11735) *(G-5082)*
Orlandi Scented Products, Farmingdale *Also called Orlandi Inc (G-5081)*
Orleans Custom Packing Inc......585 314-8227
101 Cadbury Way Holley (14470) *(G-6516)*
Orleans Pallet Company Inc......585 589-0781
227 West Ave Albion (14411) *(G-170)*
Ormec Systems Corp (PA)......585 385-3520
19 Linden Park Rochester (14625) *(G-14573)*
Ornametal Inc......845 562-5151
216 S William St Newburgh (12550) *(G-12795)*
Oro Avanti Inc (PA)......516 487-5185
250 Kings Point Rd Great Neck (11024) *(G-5844)*
Orolia Usa Inc......585 321-5800
1565 Jefferson Rd Ste 460 Rochester (14623) *(G-14574)*
Orpheo USA Corp......212 464-8255
315 Madison Ave Rm 2601 New York (10017) *(G-11540)*
Ortex Home Textile Inc......718 241-7298
523 E 82nd St Brooklyn (11236) *(G-2407)*
Ortex Home Textiles, Brooklyn *Also called Ortex Home Textile Inc (G-2407)*
Ortho Dent Laboratory Inc......716 839-1900
6325 Sheridan Dr Williamsville (14221) *(G-17274)*
Ortho Medical Products (PA)......212 879-3700
315 E 83rd St New York (10028) *(G-11541)*
Ortho Rite Inc......914 235-9100
65 Plain Ave New Rochelle (10801) *(G-8963)*
Ortho-Clinical Diagnostics Inc......585 453-4771
100 Latona Rd Bldg 313 Rochester (14626) *(G-14575)*
Ortho-Clinical Diagnostics Inc......585 453-5200
2402 Innovation Way # 3 Rochester (14624) *(G-14576)*
Ortho-Clinical Diagnostics Inc......716 631-1281
15 Limestone Dr Williamsville (14221) *(G-17275)*
Ortho-Clinical Diagnostics Inc......585 453-3000
1000 Lee Rd Rochester (14626) *(G-14577)*
Ortho/Rochester Tech, Rochester *Also called Ortho-Clinical Diagnostics Inc (G-14576)*
Orthocon Inc......914 357-2600
1 Bridge St Ste 121 Irvington (10533) *(G-6815)*
Orthocraft Inc......718 951-1700
1477 E 27th St Brooklyn (11210) *(G-2408)*
Orthogonal......585 254-2775
1999 Lake Ave Rochester (14650) *(G-14578)*
Orthopedic Arts Laboratory Inc......718 858-2400
141 Atlantic Ave Apt 1 Brooklyn (11201) *(G-2409)*
Orthopedic Treatment Facility......718 898-7326
4906 Queens Blvd Woodside (11377) *(G-17360)*
Orthotics & Prosthetics Dept......585 341-9299
4901 Lac De Ville Blvd Rochester (14618) *(G-14579)*
Orthstar Enterprises Inc......607 562-2100
119 Sing Sing Rd Horseheads (14845) *(G-6614)*
Orza Bakery Inc......914 965-5736
261 New Main St Ste 263 Yonkers (10701) *(G-17490)*
Os33 Inc......708 336-3466
16 W 22nd St Fl 6 New York (10010) *(G-11542)*
Osaka Gas Energy America Corp......914 253-5500
1 N Lexington Ave Ste 504 White Plains (10601) *(G-17170)*
Oscar Blandi, New York *Also called Blandi Products LLC (G-9464)*
Oscar Heyman & Bros Inc (PA)......212 593-0400
501 Madison Ave Fl 15 New York (10022) *(G-11543)*
OSI Pharmaceuticals LLC......631 847-0175
500 Bi County Blvd # 118 Farmingdale (11735) *(G-5083)*
OSI Pharmaceuticals LLC (HQ)......631 962-2000
1 Bioscience Way Dr Farmingdale (11735) *(G-5084)*
OSI Specialties, Tarrytown *Also called Momentive Performance Mtls Inc (G-16121)*
Osmose Holdings Inc......716 882-5905
2475 George Urban Blvd # 160 Depew (14043) *(G-4291)*
Osnat Gad Inc......212 957-0535
608 5th Ave Ste 609 New York (10020) *(G-11544)*
Oso Industries Inc......917 709-2050
1205 Manhattan Ave Brooklyn (11222) *(G-2410)*
Osprey Boat......631 331-4153
96 Mount Sinai Ave Mount Sinai (11766) *(G-8698)*
Osprey Publishing Inc......212 419-5300
1385 Broadway Fl 5 New York (10018) *(G-11545)*
Ossining Bakery Lmp Inc......914 941-2654
50 N Highland Ave Ossining (10562) *(G-13348)*
Ossining Village of Inc......914 202-9668
25 Fowler Ave Ossining (10562) *(G-13349)*
Oswald Manufacturing Co Inc......516 883-8850
65 Channel Dr Port Washington (11050) *(G-13867)*
Otex Protective Inc......585 232-7160
2180 Brighton Henrietta Rochester (14623) *(G-14580)*
Other Half Brewing Co......347 987-3527
195 Centre St Brooklyn (11231) *(G-2411)*
Other Press LLC......212 414-0054
267 5th Ave Fl 6 New York (10016) *(G-11546)*
Otis Bedding Mfg Co Inc (PA)......716 825-2599
80 James E Casey Dr Buffalo (14206) *(G-3127)*
Otis Elevator Company......315 736-0167
5172 Commercial Dr Yorkville (13495) *(G-17543)*
Otis Elevator Company......917 339-9600
1 Penn Plz Ste 410 New York (10119) *(G-11547)*
Otis Elevator Company......914 375-7800
1 Odell Plz Ste 120 Yonkers (10701) *(G-17491)*
Otis Elevator Company......518 426-4006
20 Loudonville Rd Ste 1 Albany (12204) *(G-113)*
Otis Products Inc (PA)......315 348-4300
6987 Laura St Lyons Falls (13368) *(G-8004)*
Otis Technology, Lyons Falls *Also called Otis Products Inc (G-8004)*
Otiwti, Fairport *Also called Qualitrol Company LLC (G-4879)*
Otsego Ready Mix Inc......607 432-3400
2 Wells Ave Oneonta (13820) *(G-13213)*
Ottaway Newspapers Inc......845 343-2181
40 Mulberry St Middletown (10940) *(G-8490)*
Our Daily Eats LLC......518 810-8412
10 Burdick Dr Ste 1 Albany (12205) *(G-114)*
Our Own Candle Company Inc (PA)......716 769-5000
10349 Main St Findley Lake (14736) *(G-5185)*
Our Terms Fabricators Inc......631 752-1517
48 Cabot St West Babylon (11704) *(G-16847)*
Ourem Iron Works Inc......914 476-4856
498 Nepperhan Ave Ste 5 Yonkers (10701) *(G-17492)*
Out of Print, New York *Also called Sputnick 84 LLC (G-12200)*
Outdoor Group LLC......585 201-5358
1325 John St West Henrietta (14586) *(G-16919)*
Outdoor Lightning Perspectives......631 266-6200
1 Warner Ct Huntington (11743) *(G-6707)*
Outerstuff LLC (PA)......212 594-9700
1412 Broadway Fl 18 New York (10018) *(G-11548)*
Outlook Newspaper......845 356-6261
145 College Rd Suffern (10901) *(G-15817)*
Outreach Publishing Corp......718 773-0525
546 Montgomery St Brooklyn (11225) *(G-2412)*
Ovation Instore, Maspeth *Also called DSI Group Inc (G-8162)*
Overhead Door Corporation......518 828-7652
1 Hudson Ave Hudson (12534) *(G-6659)*
Overlook Press, The, New York *Also called Peter Mayer Publishers Inc (G-11652)*
Overnight Labels Inc......631 242-4240
151 W Industry Ct Ste 15 Deer Park (11729) *(G-4210)*
Overnight Mountings Inc......516 865-3000
1400 Plaza Ave New Hyde Park (11040) *(G-8900)*
Overture Media Inc......917 446-7455
411 Lafayette St Ste 638 New York (10003) *(G-11549)*
Ovid Therapeutics Inc......646 661-7661
1460 Broadway Fl 4 New York (10036) *(G-11550)*
Ovitz Corporation......585 474-4695
150 Lucius Gordon Dr # 123 West Henrietta (14586) *(G-16920)*
OWayne Enterprises Inc......718 326-2200
4901 Maspeth Ave Maspeth (11378) *(G-8192)*
Owego Pennysaver Press Inc......607 687-2434
181 Front St Owego (13827) *(G-13383)*
Owens Corning Sales LLC......518 475-3600
1277 Feura Bush Rd Feura Bush (12067) *(G-5182)*
Owens-Brockway Glass Cont Inc......315 258-3211
7134 County House Rd Auburn (13021) *(G-510)*
Owi Corporation......315 245-4305
12 Masonic Ave Camden (13316) *(G-3347)*
Owl Books Div, New York *Also called Henry Holt and Company LLC (G-10502)*
Owl Wire & Cable LLC......315 697-2011
3127 Seneca Tpke Canastota (13032) *(G-3396)*
Owletts Saw Mills......607 525-6340
4214 Cook Rd Woodhull (14898) *(G-17327)*
Own Instrument Inc......914 668-6546
250 E 7th St Mount Vernon (10550) *(G-8758)*
Oxair Ltd......716 298-8288
8320 Quarry Rd Niagara Falls (14304) *(G-12876)*

ALPHABETIC

Oxbo International Corporation (HQ) 585 548-2665
7275 Batavia Byron Rd Byron (14422) *(G-3295)*
Oxford Book Company Inc 212 227-2120
9 Pine St New York (10005) *(G-11551)*
Oxford Cleaners 212 734-0006
847 Lexington Ave Frnt New York (10065) *(G-11552)*
Oxford Industries Inc 212 247-7712
600 5th Ave Fl 12 New York (10020) *(G-11553)*
Oxford Industries Inc 212 840-2288
25 W 39th St New York (10018) *(G-11554)*
Oxford University Press LLC (HQ) 212 726-6000
198 Madison Ave Fl 8 New York (10016) *(G-11555)*
Oxford University Press LLC 212 726-6000
198 Madison Ave Fl 8 New York (10016) *(G-11556)*
Oxford University Press, Inc., New York *Also called Oxford University Press LLC (G-11555)*
Oxo International Inc 212 242-3333
601 W 26th St Rm 1050 New York (10001) *(G-11557)*
Oxygen Inc (PA) 516 433-1144
6 Midland Ave Hicksville (11801) *(G-6405)*
Oxygen Generating Systems Intl, North Tonawanda *Also called Audubon Machinery Corporation (G-12975)*
Oyster Bay Pump Works Inc 516 933-4500
78 Midland Ave Unit 1 Hicksville (11801) *(G-6406)*
Oz Baking Company Ltd 516 466-5114
114 Middle Neck Rd Great Neck (11021) *(G-5845)*
Ozipko Enterprises Inc 585 424-6740
125 White Spruce Blvd # 5 Rochester (14623) *(G-14581)*
Ozmodyl Ltd 212 226-0622
233 Broadway Rm 707 New York (10279) *(G-11558)*
Ozteck Industries Inc 516 883-8857
65 Channel Dr Port Washington (11050) *(G-13868)*
P & B Woodworking Inc 845 744-2508
2415 State Route 52 Pine Bush (12566) *(G-13576)*
P & C Gas Measurements Service 716 257-3412
9505 Tannery Rd Cattaraugus (14719) *(G-3466)*
P & C Service, Cattaraugus *Also called P & C Gas Measurements Service (G-3466)*
P & D Equipment Sales LLC 585 343-2394
10171 Brookville Rd Alexander (14005) *(G-192)*
P & F Bakers Inc 516 931-6821
640 S Broadway Hicksville (11801) *(G-6407)*
P & F Industries Inc (PA) 631 694-9800
445 Broadhollow Rd # 100 Melville (11747) *(G-8375)*
P & F Industries of NY Corp 718 894-3501
6006 55th Dr Maspeth (11378) *(G-8193)*
P & H Machine Shop Inc 585 247-5500
40 Industrial Park Cir Rochester (14624) *(G-14582)*
P & H Thermotech Inc 585 624-1310
1883 Heath Markham Rd Lima (14485) *(G-7469)*
P & I Sportswear Inc 718 934-4587
384 5th Ave New York (10018) *(G-11559)*
P & L Development LLC 516 986-1700
200 Hicks St Westbury (11590) *(G-17043)*
P & L Development LLC 516 986-1700
275 Grand Blvd Unit 1 Westbury (11590) *(G-17044)*
P & L Development LLC (PA) 516 986-1700
200 Hicks St Westbury (11590) *(G-17045)*
P & M LLC 631 842-2200
50 Ranick Dr E Amityville (11701) *(G-319)*
P & R Industries Inc (PA) 585 266-6725
1524 N Clinton Ave Rochester (14621) *(G-14583)*
P & R Industries Inc 585 544-1811
1524 N Clinton Ave Rochester (14621) *(G-14584)*
P & R Truss Co 716 496-5484
13989 E Schutt Rd Chaffee (14030) *(G-3563)*
P & W Press Inc 646 486-3417
20 W 22nd St Ste 710 New York (10010) *(G-11560)*
P and F Machine Industries, Maspeth *Also called P & F Industries of NY Corp (G-8193)*
P B & H Moulding Corporation 315 455-1756
7121 Woodchuck Hill Rd Fayetteville (13066) *(G-5174)*
P C I Manufacturing Div, Westbury *Also called Procomponents Inc (G-17051)*
P C I Paper Conversions Inc (PA) 315 437-1641
3584 Walters Rd Syracuse (13209) *(G-16027)*
P C I Paper Conversions Inc 315 703-8300
6761 Thompson Rd Syracuse (13211) *(G-16028)*
P C I Paper Conversions Inc 315 634-3317
6761 Thompson Rd Syracuse (13211) *(G-16029)*
P C I Paper Conversions Inc 315 437-1641
6761 Thompson Rd Syracuse (13211) *(G-16030)*
P C Rfrs Radiology 212 586-5700
3630 37th St Frnt Long Island City (11101) *(G-7862)*
P C T, Amsterdam *Also called Power and Composite Tech LLC (G-366)*
P D A Panache, Bohemia *Also called Pda Panache Corp (G-1112)*
P D I, Brooklyn *Also called Promotional Development Inc (G-2471)*
P D R Inc 516 829-5300
101 Dupont St Plainview (11803) *(G-13655)*
P E Guerin (PA) 212 243-5270
23 Jane St New York (10014) *(G-11561)*
P E Machine Works, Plainview *Also called Port Everglades Machine Works (G-13658)*
P G I, Forest Hills *Also called Preston Glass Industries Inc (G-5335)*
P G M, Rochester *Also called Precision Grinding & Mfg Corp (G-14615)*
P G Media, New York *Also called Parents Guide Network Corp (G-11584)*
P H Custom Woodworking Corp 917 801-1444
830 Barry St Fl 2nd Bronx (10474) *(G-1419)*
P J D Publications Ltd 516 626-0650
1315 Jericho Tpke New Hyde Park (11040) *(G-8901)*
P J R Industries Inc 716 825-9300
1951 Hamburg Tpke Ste 17 Buffalo (14218) *(G-3128)*
P K G Equipment Incorporated 585 436-4650
367 Paul Rd Rochester (14624) *(G-14585)*
P L X, Deer Park *Also called Plx Inc (G-4214)*
P M Belts Usa Inc 800 762-3580
131 32nd St Brooklyn (11232) *(G-2413)*
P M Plastics Inc 716 662-1255
1 Bank St Ste 1 Orchard Park (14127) *(G-13311)*
P P I Business Forms Inc 716 825-1241
94 Spaulding St Buffalo (14220) *(G-3129)*
P Pascal Coffee Roasters, Yonkers *Also called P Pascal Inc (G-17493)*
P Pascal Inc 914 969-7933
960 Nepperhan Ave Yonkers (10703) *(G-17493)*
P R B Metal Products Inc 631 467-1800
200 Christopher St Ronkonkoma (11779) *(G-14986)*
P Ryton Corp 718 937-7052
504 50th Ave Long Island City (11101) *(G-7863)*
P S M Group Inc 716 532-6686
17 Main St Forestville (14062) *(G-5342)*
P S Pibbs Inc 718 445-8046
13315 32nd Ave Flushing (11354) *(G-5283)*
P T E Inc 516 775-3839
36 Ontario Rd Floral Park (11001) *(G-5213)*
P Tool & Die Co Inc 585 889-1340
3535 Union St North Chili (14514) *(G-12941)*
P V C Molding Technologies 315 331-1212
122 W Shore Blvd Newark (14513) *(G-12761)*
P&F, Melville *Also called P & F Industries Inc (G-8375)*
P&G Metal Components Corp 716 896-7900
54 Gruner Rd Buffalo (14227) *(G-3130)*
P&I, Pper P I Daily P I People, New York *Also called Pensions & Investments (G-11626)*
P-Hgh 2 Co Inc 954 534-6058
180 Cambridge Ave Buffalo (14215) *(G-3131)*
P.A.t, Bohemia *Also called Precision Assembly Tech Inc (G-1115)*
P3 Technologies 585 730-7340
383 Buell Rd Rochester (14624) *(G-14586)*
P8h Inc 212 343-1142
81 Prospect St 7 Brooklyn (11201) *(G-2414)*
PA Pellets LLC (HQ) 814 848-9970
1 Fischers Rd Ste 160 Pittsford (14534) *(G-13600)*
Paal Technologies Inc 631 319-6262
152 Remington Blvd Ste 1 Ronkonkoma (11779) *(G-14987)*
Pacamor/Kubar Bearings, Troy *Also called S/N Precision Enterprises Inc (G-16276)*
Pace Editions Inc (PA) 212 421-3237
32 E 57th St Fl 3 New York (10022) *(G-11562)*
Pace Editions Inc 212 675-7431
44 W 18th St Fl 5 New York (10011) *(G-11563)*
Pace Manufacturing Company 607 936-0431
894 Addison Rd Painted Post (14870) *(G-13418)*
Pace Polyethylene Mfg Co Inc (PA) 914 381-3000
46 Calvert St Harrison (10528) *(G-6007)*
Pace Prints, New York *Also called Pace Editions Inc (G-11562)*
Pace Up Pharmaceuticals LLC 631 450-4495
200 Bangor St Lindenhurst (11757) *(G-7502)*
Pace Walkers of America Inc 631 444-2147
105 Washington Ave Port Jefferson (11777) *(G-13800)*
Pace Window & Door, Victor *Also called Pace Window and Door Corp (G-16519)*
Pace Window and Door Corp (PA) 585 924-8350
7224 State Route 96 Victor (14564) *(G-16519)*
Pacemaker Packaging Corp 718 458-1188
7200 51st Rd Woodside (11377) *(G-17361)*
Pacific Alliance Usa Inc 336 500-8184
350 5th Ave Fl 5 New York (10118) *(G-11564)*
Pacific Alliance Usa Inc (HQ) 646 839-7000
350 5th Ave Lbby 9 New York (10118) *(G-11565)*
Pacific City International 646 309-1250
265 W 37th St New York (10018) *(G-11566)*
Pacific Concepts, New York *Also called Ewatchfactory Corp (G-10150)*
Pacific Designs Intl Inc 718 364-2867
2743 Webster Ave Bronx (10458) *(G-1420)*
Pacific Die Cast Inc 845 778-6374
827 Route 52 Ste 2 Walden (12586) *(G-16553)*
Pacific Poly Product Corp 718 786-7129
3934 Crescent St Long Island City (11101) *(G-7864)*
Pacific Worldwide Inc 212 502-3360
20 W 33rd St Fl 11 New York (10001) *(G-11567)*
Pack America Corp (HQ) 212 508-6666
108 W 39th St Fl 16 New York (10018) *(G-11568)*
Package One Inc (PA) 518 344-5425
414 Union St Schenectady (12305) *(G-15310)*
Package Pavement Company Inc 845 221-2224
3530 Route 52 Stormville (12582) *(G-15802)*
Package Print Technologies 716 871-9905
1831 Niagara St Buffalo (14207) *(G-3132)*
Packaging Corporation America 315 457-6780
4471 Steelway Blvd S Liverpool (13090) *(G-7564)*

Packaging Corporation America.....315 785-9083
20400 Old Rome State Rd Watertown (13601) ***(G-16692)***
Packaging Dynamics Ltd.....631 563-4499
35 Carlough Rd Ste 2 Bohemia (11716) ***(G-1110)***
Packstar Group Inc.....716 853-1688
215 John Glenn Dr Buffalo (14228) ***(G-3133)***
Pacs Switchgear LLC (PA).....516 465-7100
1211 Stewart Ave Bethpage (11714) ***(G-876)***
Pactech Packaging LLC.....585 458-8008
2605 Manitou Rd Rochester (14624) ***(G-14587)***
Pactiv Corporation.....518 743-3100
6 Haskell Ave Glens Falls (12801) ***(G-5709)***
Pactiv LLC.....518 562-6101
74 Weed St Plattsburgh (12901) ***(G-13712)***
Pactiv LLC.....585 394-1525
2480 Sommers Dr Canandaigua (14424) ***(G-3380)***
Pactiv LLC.....315 457-6780
4471 Steelway Blvd S Liverpool (13090) ***(G-7565)***
Pactiv LLC.....585 394-5125
2651 Brickyard Rd Canandaigua (14424) ***(G-3381)***
Pactiv LLC.....518 793-2524
18 Peck Ave Glens Falls (12801) ***(G-5710)***
Pactiv LLC.....847 482-2000
5310 North St Canandaigua (14424) ***(G-3382)***
Pactiv LLC.....518 562-6120
74 Weed St Plattsburgh (12901) ***(G-13713)***
Pactiv LLC.....585 393-3229
5250 North St Canandaigua (14424) ***(G-3383)***
Pactiv LLC.....585 248-1213
1169 Pittsford Victor Rd Pittsford (14534) ***(G-13601)***
Pactiv LLC.....585 393-3149
5250 North St Canandaigua (14424) ***(G-3384)***
Paddle8, Brooklyn *Also called P8h Inc* ***(G-2414)***
Paddock Chevrolet Golf Dome.....716 504-4059
175 Brompton Rd Tonawanda (14150) ***(G-16209)***
Paddy Lee Fashions Inc.....718 786-6020
4709 36th St Fl 2nd Long Island City (11101) ***(G-7865)***
Paesana, Farmingdale *Also called L and S Packing Co* ***(G-5037)***
Page Front Group Inc.....716 823-8222
2703 S Park Ave Lackawanna (14218) ***(G-7272)***
Paint Over Rust Products Inc.....914 636-0700
38 Portman Rd New Rochelle (10801) ***(G-8964)***
Paiping Carpets, New York *Also called Edward Fields Incorporated* ***(G-10038)***
Pak 21, Brooklyn *Also called Apex Real Holdings Inc* ***(G-1616)***
Paklab, Hauppauge *Also called Universal Packg Systems Inc* ***(G-6245)***
Pal Aluminum Inc (PA).....516 937-1990
230 Duffy Ave Unit B Hicksville (11801) ***(G-6408)***
Pal Aluminum Inc.....718 262-0091
10620 180th St Jamaica (11433) ***(G-6975)***
Pal Industries, Hicksville *Also called Pal Aluminum Inc* ***(G-6408)***
Pal Industries, Jamaica *Also called Pal Aluminum Inc* ***(G-6975)***
Pal Manufacturing Corp.....516 937-1990
230 Duffy Ave Unit B Hicksville (11801) ***(G-6409)***
Paladino Prtg & Graphics Inc.....718 279-6000
20009 32nd Ave Flushing (11361) ***(G-5284)***
Palagonia Bakery Co Inc.....718 272-5400
508 Junius St Brooklyn (11212) ***(G-2415)***
Palagonia Italian Bread, Brooklyn *Also called Palagonia Bakery Co Inc* ***(G-2415)***
Palagrave Macmillan, New York *Also called Macmillan Publishing Group LLC* ***(G-11116)***
Paleteria Fernandez Inc.....914 315-1598
350 Mamaroneck Ave Mamaroneck (10543) ***(G-8074)***
Paletot Ltd.....212 268-3774
499 Fashion Ave Rm 25s New York (10018) ***(G-11569)***
Paley Studios Ltd.....585 232-5260
1677 Lyell Ave A Rochester (14606) ***(G-14588)***
Palgrave Macmillan Ltd.....646 307-5028
175 5th Ave Frnt 4 New York (10010) ***(G-11570)***
Palisades Paper Inc.....845 354-0333
13 Jackson Ave Spring Valley (10977) ***(G-15619)***
Pall Biomedical Inc.....516 484-3600
25 Harbor Park Dr Port Washington (11050) ***(G-13869)***
Pall Corporation (HQ).....516 484-5400
25 Harbor Park Dr Port Washington (11050) ***(G-13870)***
Pall Corporation.....607 753-6041
3643 State Route 281 Cortland (13045) ***(G-4059)***
Pall Corporation.....607 753-6041
3669 State Route 281 Cortland (13045) ***(G-4060)***
Pall Corporation.....516 484-2818
25 Harbor Park Dr Port Washington (11050) ***(G-13871)***
Pall Corporation.....607 753-6041
839 State Route 13 Ste 12 Cortland (13045) ***(G-4061)***
Pall Life Sciences, Port Washington *Also called Pall Corporation* ***(G-13871)***
Pall Medical, Port Washington *Also called Pall Biomedical Inc* ***(G-13869)***
Pall Trinity Micro, Cortland *Also called Pall Corporation* ***(G-4059)***
Pall's Advnced Sprtons Systems, Cortland *Also called Pall Corporation* ***(G-4061)***
Palladia Inc.....212 206-3669
105 W 17th St New York (10011) ***(G-11571)***
Palladium Times, Oswego *Also called Sample News Group LLC* ***(G-13365)***
Pallet Division Inc.....585 328-3780
40 Silver St Rochester (14611) ***(G-14589)***
Pallet Services Inc.....585 647-4020
1681 Lyell Ave Rochester (14606) ***(G-14590)***
Pallets Inc.....518 747-4177
99 1/2 East St Fort Edward (12828) ***(G-5351)***
Pallets Plus, Olean *Also called G & H Wood Products LLC* ***(G-13169)***
Pallets R US Inc.....631 758-2360
555 Woodside Ave Bellport (11713) ***(G-834)***
Pallette Stone Corporation.....518 584-2421
269 Ballard Rd Gansevoort (12831) ***(G-5501)***
Palma Tool & Die Company Inc.....716 681-4685
40 Ward Rd Lancaster (14086) ***(G-7353)***
Palmbay Ltd.....718 424-3388
4459 Kissena Blvd Apt 6h Flushing (11355) ***(G-5285)***
Palmer Industries Inc.....607 754-8741
2320 Lewis St Endicott (13760) ***(G-4829)***
Palmer Industries Inc (PA).....607 754-2957
509 Paden St Endicott (13760) ***(G-4830)***
Palmer Industries Inc.....607 754-1954
1 Heath St Endicott (13760) ***(G-4831)***
Palpross Incorporated.....845 469-2188
Maple Ave Rr 396 Selkirk (12158) ***(G-15379)***
Palumbo Block, Dover Plains *Also called Palumbo Sand & Gravel Company* ***(G-4341)***
Palumbo Block Co Inc.....845 832-6100
365 Dover Furnace Rd Dover Plains (12522) ***(G-4340)***
Palumbo Sand & Gravel Company.....845 832-3356
155 Sherman Hill Rd Dover Plains (12522) ***(G-4341)***
Pama Enterprises Inc.....516 504-6300
60 Cuttermill Rd Ste 411 Great Neck (11021) ***(G-5846)***
Pan American Leathers Inc (PA).....978 741-4150
347 W 36th St Rm 1204 New York (10018) ***(G-11572)***
Pan American Roller Inc.....914 762-8700
5 Broad Ave Ossining (10562) ***(G-13350)***
Panagraphics Inc.....716 312-8088
30 Quail Run Orchard Park (14127) ***(G-13312)***
Panasonic Corp North America.....888 765-2489
1339 S Park Ave Buffalo (14220) ***(G-3134)***
Pane DOro.....914 964-0043
166 Ludlow St Yonkers (10705) ***(G-17494)***
Panelogic Inc.....607 962-6319
366 Baker Street Ext Corning (14830) ***(G-3998)***
Pangea Brands LLC (PA).....617 638-0001
6 W 20th St Fl 3 New York (10011) ***(G-11573)***
Pangea Brands LLC.....617 638-0001
6 W 20th St Fl 3 New York (10011) ***(G-11574)***
Panoply Media LLC (HQ).....646 382-5423
15 Metrotech Ctr Fl 8 Brooklyn (11201) ***(G-2416)***
Panther Graphics Inc (PA).....585 546-7163
465 Central Ave Rochester (14605) ***(G-14591)***
Pap Chat Inc.....516 350-1888
3105 Quentin Rd Brooklyn (11234) ***(G-2417)***
Papa Bubble.....212 966-2599
380 Broome St Frnt A New York (10013) ***(G-11575)***
Paper Box Corp.....212 226-7490
1751 2nd Ave Apt 10a New York (10128) ***(G-11576)***
Paper House Productions Inc.....845 246-7261
160 Malden Tpke Bldg 2 Saugerties (12477) ***(G-15219)***
Paper Magazine, New York *Also called Paper Publishing Company Inc* ***(G-11578)***
Paper Magic Group Inc.....631 521-3682
345 7th Ave Fl 6 New York (10001) ***(G-11577)***
Paper Publishing Company Inc.....212 226-4405
15 E 32nd St New York (10016) ***(G-11578)***
Paper Solutions Inc.....718 499-4226
342 37th St Brooklyn (11232) ***(G-2418)***
Papercutz Inc.....646 559-4681
160 Broadway Rm 700e New York (10038) ***(G-11579)***
Paperworks, Baldwinsville *Also called Specialized Packg Group Inc* ***(G-574)***
Paperworks Industries Inc.....913 621-0922
2900 Mclane Rd Baldwinsville (13027) ***(G-572)***
Paperworld Inc.....516 221-2702
3054 Lee Pl Bellmore (11710) ***(G-815)***
Par Pharmaceutical, Chestnut Ridge *Also called Generics Bidco I LLC* ***(G-3651)***
Par Pharmaceutical Inc (HQ).....845 573-5500
1 Ram Ridge Rd Chestnut Ridge (10977) ***(G-3653)***
Par Phrmceutical Companies Inc (HQ).....845 573-5500
1 Ram Ridge Rd Chestnut Ridge (10977) ***(G-3654)***
Par Sterile Products LLC (HQ).....845 573-5500
1 Ram Ridge Rd Chestnut Ridge (10977) ***(G-3655)***
Par Technology Corporation (PA).....315 738-0600
8383 Seneca Tpke Ste 2 New Hartford (13413) ***(G-8853)***
Par-Foam Products Inc.....716 855-2066
239 Van Rensselaer St Buffalo (14210) ***(G-3135)***
Parabit Systems Inc.....516 378-4800
35 Debevoise Ave Roosevelt (11575) ***(G-15031)***
PARABOLA, New York *Also called Society For The Study* ***(G-12144)***
Parace Bionics LLC.....877 727-2231
276 Landmark Ct Yorktown Heights (10598) ***(G-17531)***
Parachute Publishing LLC.....212 337-6743
322 8th Ave Ste 702 New York (10001) ***(G-11580)***
Paraco Gas Corporation.....845 279-8414
4 Joes Hill Rd Brewster (10509) ***(G-1223)***
Paraco Gas Corporation (PA).....800 647-4427
800 Westchester Ave S604 Rye Brook (10573) ***(G-15099)***

A L P H A B E T I C

Parade Magazine, New York *Also called Parade Publications Inc* **(G-11581)**
Parade Publications Inc (HQ)...212 450-7000
711 3rd Ave New York (10017) **(G-11581)**
Paradigm Group LLC...718 860-1538
1357 Lafayette Ave Frnt 1 Bronx (10474) **(G-1421)**
Paradigm Mktg Consortium Inc...516 677-6012
350 Michael Dr Syosset (11791) **(G-15855)**
Paradigm Spine LLC...888 273-9897
505 Park Ave Fl 14 New York (10022) **(G-11582)**
Paradise Plastics LLC...718 788-3733
116 39th St Brooklyn (11232) **(G-2419)**
Paragon Aquatics...845 452-5500
1351 Route 55 Unit 1 Lagrangeville (12540) **(G-7282)**
Paragon Corporation...516 484-6090
21 Forest Dr Port Washington (11050) **(G-13872)**
Paragon Publishing Inc...718 302-2093
97 Harrison Ave Brooklyn (11206) **(G-2420)**
Paragon Steel Rule Dies Inc...585 254-3395
979 Mount Read Blvd Rochester (14606) **(G-14592)**
Paramount Cord & Brackets...212 325-9100
6 Tournament Dr White Plains (10605) **(G-17171)**
Paramount Equipment Inc...631 981-4422
201 Christopher St Ronkonkoma (11779) **(G-14988)**
Paramount Graphix...845 367-5003
26 Hill St Port Jervis (12771) **(G-13813)**
Paramount Textiles Inc...212 966-1040
34 Walker St New York (10013) **(G-11583)**
Paratore Signs Inc...315 455-5551
1551 Brewerton Rd Syracuse (13208) **(G-16031)**
Paratus Industries Inc...716 826-2000
6659 E Quaker St Orchard Park (14127) **(G-13313)**
Pardazzio Uomo, Westbury *Also called Montero International Inc* **(G-17041)**
Parents Guide Network Corp...212 213-8840
419 Park Ave S Rm 505 New York (10016) **(G-11584)**
Pareteum Corporation...212 984-1096
100 Park Ave New York (10017) **(G-11585)**
Parfums Boucheron Jewelry, New York *Also called Boucheron Joaillerie USA Inc* **(G-9494)**
Parfuse Corp...516 997-1795
65 Kinkel St Westbury (11590) **(G-17046)**
Parikh Worldwide Media, LLC, New York *Also called Desi Talk LLC* **(G-9903)**
Paris Art Label Co Inc...631 467-2300
217 River Ave Patchogue (11772) **(G-13455)**
Paris Wedding Center Corp (PA)...347 368-4085
42-53 42 55 Main St Flushing (11355) **(G-5286)**
Paris Wedding Center Corp...212 267-8088
45 E Broadway Fl 2 New York (10002) **(G-11586)**
Park Assist LLC...646 666-7525
57 W 38th St Fl 11 New York (10018) **(G-11587)**
Park Ave Bldg & Roofg Sups LLC...718 403-0100
2120 Atlantic Ave Brooklyn (11233) **(G-2421)**
Park Avenue Imprints LLC (PA)...716 822-5737
2955 S Park Ave Buffalo (14218) **(G-3136)**
Park Avenue Nutrition, Richmond Hill *Also called Womens Health Care PC* **(G-14100)**
Park Avenue Sportswear Ltd (PA)...718 369-0520
820 4th Ave Brooklyn (11232) **(G-2422)**
Park Electrochemical Corp (PA)...631 465-3600
48 S Service Rd Ste 300 Melville (11747) **(G-8376)**
Park Enterprises Rochester Inc...585 546-4200
226 Jay St Rochester (14608) **(G-14593)**
Park West Jewelery Inc...646 329-6145
565 W End Ave Apt 8b New York (10024) **(G-11588)**
Park's Department, Williamsville *Also called Town of Amherst* **(G-17283)**
Parkchester Dps LLC...718 823-4411
2000 E Tremont Ave Bronx (10462) **(G-1422)**
Parker Machine Company Inc...518 747-0675
28 Sullivan Pkwy Fort Edward (12828) **(G-5352)**
Parker Warby Retail Inc (PA)...646 517-5223
161 Ave Of The Amer Fl 6f New York (10013) **(G-11589)**
Parker-Hannifin Aerospace, Clyde *Also called Parker-Hannifin Corporation* **(G-3755)**
Parker-Hannifin Corporation...716 686-6400
4087 Walden Ave Lancaster (14086) **(G-7354)**
Parker-Hannifin Corporation...631 231-3737
124 Columbia St Clyde (14433) **(G-3755)**
Parker-Hannifin Corporation...248 628-6017
4087 Walden Ave Lancaster (14086) **(G-7355)**
Parker-Hannifin Corporation...631 231-3737
300 Marcus Blvd Hauppauge (11788) **(G-6183)**
Parker-Hannifin Corporation...585 425-7000
83 Estates Dr W Fairport (14450) **(G-4874)**
Parker-Hannifin Corporation...315 926-4211
3967 Buffalo St Marion (14505) **(G-8127)**
Parker-Hannifin Corporation...716 685-4040
4087 Walden Ave Lancaster (14086) **(G-7356)**
Parks Paving & Sealing Inc...315 737-5761
3220 Valley Pl Sauquoit (13456) **(G-15230)**
Parks TRUcking&paving, Sauquoit *Also called Parks Paving & Sealing Inc* **(G-15230)**
Parkside Candy Co Inc (PA)...716 833-7540
3208 Main St Ste 1 Buffalo (14214) **(G-3137)**
Parkside Printing Co Inc...516 933-5423
4 Tompkins Ave Jericho (11753) **(G-7112)**
Parkway Bread Distributors Inc...845 362-1221
15 Conklin Rd Pomona (10970) **(G-13760)**
Parlor City Paper Box Co Inc...607 772-0600
2 Eldredge St Binghamton (13901) **(G-937)**
Parlor Labs Inc...866 801-7323
515 W 19th St New York (10011) **(G-11590)**
Parnasa International Inc...516 394-0400
181 S Franklin Ave # 400 Valley Stream (11581) **(G-16442)**
Parrinello Printing Inc...716 633-7780
84 Aero Dr Buffalo (14225) **(G-3138)**
Parry's Hardware, Hamilton *Also called Parrys Incorporated* **(G-5972)**
Parrys Incorporated...315 824-0002
100 Utica St Hamilton (13346) **(G-5972)**
Parsley Apparel Corp...631 981-7181
2153 Pond Rd Ronkonkoma (11779) **(G-14989)**
Parsons & Whittemore Inc...914 937-9009
4 International Dr # 300 Port Chester (10573) **(G-13780)**
Parsons Whittemore Entps Corp (PA)...914 937-9009
4 International Dr # 300 Port Chester (10573) **(G-13781)**
Parsons-Meares Ltd...212 242-3378
2107 41st Ave Ste 1l Long Island City (11101) **(G-7866)**
Partlow Corporation...518 922-5315
156 Auriesville Rd Fultonville (12072) **(G-5495)**
Partlow West, Fultonville *Also called Partlow Corporation* **(G-5495)**
Pasabahce USA...212 683-1600
41 Madison Ave Fl 7 New York (10010) **(G-11591)**
Pascale Madonna, Long Island City *Also called Fashion Ribbon Co Inc* **(G-7767)**
Pass & Seymour Inc (HQ)...315 468-6211
50 Boyd Ave Syracuse (13209) **(G-16032)**
Pass Em-Entries Inc (PA)...718 392-0100
3914 Crescent St Long Island City (11101) **(G-7867)**
Passive-Plus Inc...631 425-0938
48 Elm St Huntington (11743) **(G-6708)**
Passport Brands Inc (PA)...646 459-2625
240 Madison Ave Fl 8 New York (10016) **(G-11592)**
Passport Magazine, New York *Also called Q Communications Inc* **(G-11786)**
Passur Aerospace Inc...631 589-6800
35 Orville Dr Ste 1 Bohemia (11716) **(G-1111)**
Pasta People, West Babylon *Also called Great Eastern Pasta Works LLC* **(G-16820)**
Pat & Rose Dress Inc...212 279-1357
327 W 36th St Rm 3a New York (10018) **(G-11593)**
Patchogue Advance Inc...631 475-1000
20 Medford Ave Ste 1 Patchogue (11772) **(G-13456)**
Patco Group, Maspeth *Also called Patco Tapes Inc* **(G-8194)**
PATCO PACKAGING, Copiague *Also called Norjac Boxes Inc* **(G-3940)**
Patco Tapes Inc...718 497-1527
5927 56th St Maspeth (11378) **(G-8194)**
Patdan Fuel Corporation...718 326-3668
7803 68th Rd Middle Village (11379) **(G-8450)**
Pathfinder 103 Inc...315 363-4260
229 Park Ave Oneida (13421) **(G-13187)**
Pathfinder Industries Inc...315 593-2483
117 N 3rd St Fulton (13069) **(G-5488)**
Pati Inc...718 244-6788
Jfk Intl Airprt Hngar 16 Jamaica (11430) **(G-6976)**
Patience Brewster Inc...315 685-8336
3872 Jordan Rd Skaneateles (13152) **(G-15486)**
Patient Portal Tech Inc (PA)...315 638-2030
8276 Willett Pkwy Ste 200 Baldwinsville (13027) **(G-573)**
Patient-Wear LLC...914 740-7770
3940 Merritt Ave Bronx (10466) **(G-1423)**
Patla Enterprises Inc...315 790-0143
190 E State St Sherrill (13461) **(G-15429)**
Patmian LLC...212 758-0770
655 Madison Ave Fl 24 New York (10065) **(G-11594)**
Patra Ltd...212 764-6575
318 W 39th St Fl 2 New York (10018) **(G-11595)**
Patra Ltd...212 764-6575
318 W 39th St New York (10018) **(G-11596)**
Patra Ltd (PA)...212 764-6575
318 W 39th St New York (10018) **(G-11597)**
Patricia Underwood, New York *Also called Paletot Ltd* **(G-11569)**
Patrick Rohan...718 781-2573
9 Green St Monticello (12701) **(G-8646)**
Patrick Mackin Custom Furn...718 237-2592
612 Degraw St Brooklyn (11217) **(G-2423)**
Patrick Ryans Modern Press...518 434-2921
1 Colonie St Albany (12207) **(G-115)**
Patron Technology Inc...212 271-4328
850 7th Ave Ste 704 New York (10019) **(G-11598)**
Patsy Strocchia & Sons Iron Wo...516 625-8800
175 I U Willets Rd Ste 4 Albertson (11507) **(G-159)**
Patterson Blacktop Corp...845 628-3425
1181 Route 6 Carmel (10512) **(G-3431)**
Patterson Blacktop Corp (HQ)...914 949-2000
20 Haarlem Ave White Plains (10603) **(G-17172)**
Patterson Materials Corp...845 832-6000
322 Walsh Ave New Windsor (12553) **(G-8993)**
Patterson Materials Corp (HQ)...914 949-2000
20 Haarlem Ave White Plains (10603) **(G-17173)**
Patuga LLC...716 204-7220
7954 Transit Rd 316 Williamsville (14221) **(G-17276)**
Paul Bunyan Products Inc...315 696-6164
890 Mclean Rd Cortland (13045) **(G-4062)**

ALPHABETIC SECTION
Peelle Company (PA)

Paul David Enterprises Inc....646 667-5530
19 W 34th St Rm 1018 New York (10001) ***(G-11599)***
Paul De Lima Coffee Company, Liverpool *Also called Paul De Lima Company Inc* ***(G-7566)***
Paul De Lima Company Inc (PA)....315 457-3725
7546 Morgan Rd Ste 1 Liverpool (13090) ***(G-7566)***
Paul De Lima Company Inc....315 457-3725
8550 Pardee Rd Cicero (13039) ***(G-3678)***
Paul Delima Coffee Company....315 457-3725
8550 Pardee Rd Cicero (13039) ***(G-3679)***
Paul J Mitchell Logging Inc....518 359-7029
15 Mitchell Ln Tupper Lake (12986) ***(G-16302)***
Paul Michael Group Inc....631 585-5700
460 Hawkins Ave Ronkonkoma (11779) ***(G-14990)***
Paul T Freund Corporation (PA)....315 597-4873
216 Park Dr Palmyra (14522) ***(G-13438)***
Paula Dorf Cosmetics Inc....212 582-0073
850 7th Ave Ste 801 New York (10019) ***(G-11600)***
Paula Varsalona Ltd....212 570-9100
552 Fashion Ave Rm 602 New York (10018) ***(G-11601)***
Paulin Investment Company....631 957-8500
8600 New Horizons Blvd Amityville (11701) ***(G-320)***
Paulpac LLC....631 283-7610
104 Foster Xing Southampton (11968) ***(G-15572)***
Pauls Rods & Restos Inc....631 665-7637
131 Brook Ave Ste 13 Deer Park (11729) ***(G-4211)***
Paumanok Vineyards Ltd....631 722-8800
1074 Main Rd Rte 25 Aquebogue (11931) ***(G-385)***
Pavana USA Inc....646 833-8811
10 W 33rd St Rm 408 New York (10001) ***(G-11602)***
Pavco Asphalt Inc....631 289-3223
615 Furrows Rd Holtsville (11742) ***(G-6532)***
Pavmed Inc....212 401-1951
60 E 42nd St Fl 46 New York (10165) ***(G-11603)***
Pawling Corporation (PA)....845 855-1000
157 Charles Colman Blvd Pawling (12564) ***(G-13474)***
Pawling Corporation....845 373-9300
32 Nelson Hill Rd Wassaic (12592) ***(G-16622)***
Pawling Engineered Pdts Inc....845 855-1000
157 Charles Colman Blvd Pawling (12564) ***(G-13475)***
Pawling Engineered Products, Pawling *Also called Pawling Corporation* ***(G-13474)***
Paxar Corporation (HQ)....845 398-3229
524 Route 303 Orangeburg (10962) ***(G-13260)***
Paxton Metal Craft Division, Peekskill *Also called Elevator Accessories Mfg* ***(G-13501)***
Paya Printing of NY Inc....516 625-8346
87 Searingtown Rd Albertson (11507) ***(G-160)***
Pb Industries, Homer *Also called Solidus Industries Inc* ***(G-6550)***
Pb Mapinfo Corporation....518 285-6000
1 Global Vw Troy (12180) ***(G-16269)***
Pb08 Inc....347 866-7353
40 Bloomingdale Rd Hicksville (11801) ***(G-6410)***
Pbi Media Inc., New York *Also called Access Intelligence LLC* ***(G-9057)***
PBL Industries Corp....631 979-4266
49 Dillmont Dr Smithtown (11787) ***(G-15516)***
PBR Graphics Inc....518 458-2909
20 Railroad Ave Ste 1 Albany (12205) ***(G-116)***
PC Solutions & Consulting....607 735-0466
407 S Walnut St Elmira (14904) ***(G-4711)***
Pca/Syracuse, 384, Liverpool *Also called Packaging Corporation America* ***(G-7564)***
Pca/Watertown 393, Watertown *Also called Packaging Corporation America* ***(G-16692)***
Pcamerica, Pearl River *Also called Heartland Commerce Inc* ***(G-13480)***
Pcb Coach Builders Corp....718 897-7606
6334 Austin St Rego Park (11374) ***(G-14049)***
Pcb Group Inc (HQ)....716 684-0001
3425 Walden Ave Depew (14043) ***(G-4292)***
Pcb Piezotronics Inc....716 684-0001
3425 Walden Ave Depew (14043) ***(G-4293)***
Pcb Piezotronics Inc....716 684-0003
3425 Walden Ave Depew (14043) ***(G-4294)***
PCI, Bohemia *Also called Precision Charts Inc* ***(G-1116)***
PCI Industries Corp....914 662-2700
550 Franklin Ave Mount Vernon (10550) ***(G-8759)***
Pcore Electric Company Inc....585 768-1200
135 Gilbert St Le Roy (14482) ***(G-7440)***
Pcx Aerostructures LLC....631 249-7901
70 Raynor Ave Ronkonkoma (11779) ***(G-14991)***
Pcx Aerostructures LLC....631 467-2632
60 Milbar Blvd Farmingdale (11735) ***(G-5085)***
Pda Panache Corp....631 776-0523
70 Knickerbocker Ave # 7 Bohemia (11716) ***(G-1112)***
Pdf Seal Incorporated....631 595-7035
503 Acorn St Deer Park (11729) ***(G-4212)***
Pdi, New York *Also called Props Displays & Interiors* ***(G-11759)***
Pdi Cone Co Inc....716 825-8750
69 Leddy St Buffalo (14210) ***(G-3139)***
Pdj Components Inc....845 469-9191
35 Brookside Ave Chester (10918) ***(G-3638)***
PDJ Inc....315 655-8824
2550 E Ballina Rd Cazenovia (13035) ***(G-3476)***
Pdk Labs Inc....631 273-2630
145 Ricefield Ln Hauppauge (11788) ***(G-6184)***
PDM Studios Inc....716 694-8337
510 Main St Tonawanda (14150) ***(G-16210)***
PDQ Manufacturing Co Inc....845 889-3123
29 Hilee Rd Rhinebeck (12572) ***(G-14069)***
PDQ Printing, New Paltz *Also called PDQ Shipping Services* ***(G-8922)***
PDQ Shipping Services....845 255-5500
8 New Paltz Plz 299 New Paltz (12561) ***(G-8922)***
Peace Times Weekly Inc....718 762-6500
14527 33rd Ave Flushing (11354) ***(G-5287)***
Peaceful Valley Maple Farm (PA)....518 762-0491
116 Lagrange Rd Johnstown (12095) ***(G-7150)***
Peachtree Enterprises Inc....212 989-3445
2219 41st Ave Ste 4a Long Island City (11101) ***(G-7868)***
Peak Motion Inc....716 534-4925
11190 Main St Clarence (14031) ***(G-3695)***
Peaks Coffee Company....315 565-1900
3264 Rte 20 Cazenovia (13035) ***(G-3477)***
Peanut Butter & Co Inc....212 757-3130
119 W 57th St Ste 300 New York (10019) ***(G-11604)***
Pearl Erwin Inc (PA)....212 889-7410
389 5th Ave Rm 1100 New York (10016) ***(G-11605)***
Pearl Erwin Inc....212 883-0650
300 Madison Ave Frnt 1 New York (10017) ***(G-11606)***
Pearl Leather Finishers Inc....518 762-4543
11 Industrial Pkwy 21 Johnstown (12095) ***(G-7151)***
Pearl Leather Group LLC....516 627-4047
17 Barstow Rd Ste 206 Great Neck (11021) ***(G-5847)***
Pearl River Pastries LLC....845 735-5100
389 W Nyack Rd West Nyack (10994) ***(G-16951)***
Pearl River Pastry Chocolates, West Nyack *Also called Pearl River Pastries LLC* ***(G-16951)***
Pearl Technologies Inc....315 365-2632
13297 Seneca St Savannah (13146) ***(G-15231)***
Pearltek, New York *Also called Robin Stanley Inc* ***(G-11915)***
Pearson Education Inc....845 340-8700
317 Wall St Kingston (12401) ***(G-7235)***
Pearson Education Inc....212 782-3337
1185 Avenue Of The Americ New York (10036) ***(G-11607)***
Pearson Education Inc....212 366-2000
375 Hudson St New York (10014) ***(G-11608)***
Pearson Education Inc....201 236-7000
59 Brookhill Dr West Nyack (10994) ***(G-16952)***
Pearson Education Holdings Inc (HQ)....201 236-6716
330 Hudson St Fl 9 New York (10013) ***(G-11609)***
Pearson Inc (HQ)....212 641-2400
1330 Hudson St New York (10013) ***(G-11610)***
Pearson Longman LLC....917 981-2200
51 Madison Ave Fl 27 New York (10010) ***(G-11611)***
Pearson Longman LLC (HQ)....212 641-2400
10 Bank St Ste 1030 White Plains (10606) ***(G-17174)***
Peck & Hale LLC....631 589-2510
180 Division Ave West Sayville (11796) ***(G-16966)***
Pecker Iron Works LLC....914 665-0100
137 Ruxton Rd Mount Kisco (10549) ***(G-8682)***
Peckham Industries Inc (PA)....914 949-2000
20 Haarlem Ave Ste 200 White Plains (10603) ***(G-17175)***
Peckham Industries Inc....518 943-0155
7065 Us Highway 9w Catskill (12414) ***(G-3461)***
Peckham Industries Inc....518 893-2176
430 Coy Rd Greenfield Center (12833) ***(G-5889)***
Peckham Industries Inc....518 945-1120
Uninn St Athens (12015) ***(G-465)***
Peckham Materials, Carmel *Also called Patterson Blacktop Corp* ***(G-3431)***
Peckham Materials Corp....845 562-5370
322 Walsh Ave Newburgh (12553) ***(G-12796)***
Peckham Materials Corp (HQ)....914 686-2045
20 Haarlem Ave Ste 200 White Plains (10603) ***(G-17176)***
Peckham Materials Corp....518 747-3353
438 Vaughn Rd Hudson Falls (12839) ***(G-6680)***
Peckham Materials Corp....518 945-1120
2 Union St Ext Athens (12015) ***(G-466)***
Peckham Materials Corp....518 494-2313
5983 State Route 9 Chestertown (12817) ***(G-3650)***
Peco Conduit Fittings, Orangeburg *Also called Producto Electric Corp* ***(G-13265)***
Peco Pallet Inc (HQ)....914 376-5444
2 Bridge St Ste 210 Irvington (10533) ***(G-6816)***
Peconic B Shopper, Southold *Also called Academy Printing Services Inc* ***(G-15581)***
Peconic Ironworks Ltd....631 204-0323
33 Flying Point Rd # 108 Southampton (11968) ***(G-15573)***
Peconic Plastics Inc....631 653-3676
6062 Old Country Rd Quogue (11959) ***(G-14028)***
Pecoraro Dairy Products Inc (PA)....718 388-2379
287 Leonard St Brooklyn (11211) ***(G-2424)***
Pedifix Inc....845 277-2850
281 Fields Ln Brewster (10509) ***(G-1224)***
Pedre Corp (PA)....212 868-2935
270 Duffy Ave Ste G Hicksville (11801) ***(G-6411)***
Pedre Watch, Hicksville *Also called Pedre Corp* ***(G-6411)***
Peek A Boo USA Inc....201 533-8700
555 8th Ave Rm 403 New York (10018) ***(G-11612)***
Peeled Inc....212 706-2001
65 15th St Ste 1 Brooklyn (11215) ***(G-2425)***
Peeled Snacks, Brooklyn *Also called Peeled Inc* ***(G-2425)***
Peelle Company (PA)....631 231-6000
373 Smithtown Byp 311 Hauppauge (11788) ***(G-6185)***

ALPHABETIC

(PA)=Parent Co (HQ)=Headquarters (DH)=Div Headquarters
2018 Harris
New York Manufacturers Directory
1029

Peer International Corp (HQ) 212 265-3910
250 W 57th St Ste 820 New York (10107) *(G-11613)*
Peer Software Incorporated (PA) 631 979-1770
1363 Veterans Hwy Ste 44 Hauppauge (11788) *(G-6186)*
Peer-Southern Productions Inc (HQ) 212 265-3910
250 W 57th St New York (10107) *(G-11614)*
Peerless Envelopes & Prtg Co, Brooklyn *Also called H T L & S Ltd (G-2059)*
Peerless Instrument Co Inc 631 396-6500
1966 Broadhollow Rd Ste D Farmingdale (11735) *(G-5086)*
Peerless Mfg Co 716 539-7400
50 Cobham Dr Orchard Park (14127) *(G-13314)*
Peerless-Winsmith Inc 716 592-9311
172 Eaton St Springville (14141) *(G-15634)*
Peermusic III Ltd (PA) 212 265-3910
250 W 57th St Ste 820 New York (10107) *(G-11615)*
Peermusic Ltd (HQ) 212 265-3910
250 W 57th St Ste 820 New York (10107) *(G-11616)*
Pefin Technologies LLC 917 715-3720
39 W 32nd St Rm 1500 New York (10001) *(G-11617)*
Pegasus Books NY Ltd 646 343-9502
148 W 37th St Fl 13 New York (10018) *(G-11618)*
Pegasystems Inc 212 626-6550
1120 Ave Of The Americas New York (10036) *(G-11619)*
Peggy Jennings Designs, New York *Also called PJ Designs Inc (G-11691)*
Pei/Genesis Inc 631 256-1747
2410 N Ocean Ave Ste 401 Farmingville (11738) *(G-5169)*
Peking Food LLC 718 628-8080
47 Stewart Ave Brooklyn (11237) *(G-2426)*
Peko Precision Products Inc 585 301-1386
70 Holworthy St Rochester (14606) *(G-14594)*
Pelican Bay Ltd 718 729-9300
3901 22nd St Long Island City (11101) *(G-7869)*
Pelican Products Co Inc (PA) 718 860-3220
1049 Lowell St Bronx (10459) *(G-1424)*
Pelkowski Precast Corp 631 269-5727
294a Old Northport Rd Kings Park (11754) *(G-7203)*
Pella Corporation 607 223-2023
800 Valley Plz Ste 5 Johnson City (13790) *(G-7131)*
Pella Corporation 607 231-8550
800 Valley Plz Ste 5 Johnson City (13790) *(G-7132)*
Pella Corporation 607 238-2812
800 Valley Plz Ste 5 Johnson City (13790) *(G-7133)*
Pella Corporation 516 385-3622
77 Albertson Ave Ste 2 Albertson (11507) *(G-161)*
Pella Corporation 607 238-2812
800 Valley Plz Ste 5 Johnson City (13790) *(G-7134)*
Pella Corporation 516 385-3622
77 Albertson Ave Ste 2 Albertson (11507) *(G-162)*
Pella Corporation 607 231-8550
800 Valley Plz Ste 5 Johnson City (13790) *(G-7135)*
Pella Corporation 631 208-0710
901 Burman Blvd Calverton (11933) *(G-3322)*
Pella Window Door, Johnson City *Also called Pella Corporation (G-7131)*
Pella Window Door, Johnson City *Also called Pella Corporation (G-7132)*
Pella Window Door, Johnson City *Also called Pella Corporation (G-7133)*
Pella Window Door, Albertson *Also called Pella Corporation (G-161)*
Pella Window Door, Johnson City *Also called Pella Corporation (G-7134)*
Pella Window Door, Albertson *Also called Pella Corporation (G-162)*
Pella Window Door, Johnson City *Also called Pella Corporation (G-7135)*
Pellegrini Vineyards LLC 631 734-4111
23005 Main Rd Cutchogue (11935) *(G-4098)*
Pellets LLC 716 693-1750
63 Industrial Dr Ste 3 North Tonawanda (14120) *(G-13003)*
Pellicano Specialty Foods Inc 716 822-2366
195 Reading St Buffalo (14220) *(G-3140)*
Peloton Interactive Inc (PA) 866 650-1996
125 W 25th St Fl 11 New York (10001) *(G-11620)*
Peltrix, Purdys *Also called Data Interchange Systems Inc (G-13988)*
Pems Tool & Machine Inc 315 823-3595
125 Southern Ave Little Falls (13365) *(G-7523)*
Pemystifying Diital, Woodbury *Also called Photo Industry Inc (G-17315)*
Penasack Machine Company Inc 585 589-7044
49 Sanford St Albion (14411) *(G-171)*
Pencoa, Westbury *Also called Harper Products Ltd (G-17021)*
Penetradar Corporation 716 731-2629
2509 Niagara Falls Blvd Niagara Falls (14304) *(G-12877)*
Penetron International Ltd 631 941-9700
45 Research Way Ste 203 East Setauket (11733) *(G-4507)*
Penfli Industries Inc 212 947-6080
11 Woodland Pl Great Neck (11021) *(G-5848)*
Penguin Random House LLC 212 782-1000
1540 Broadway New York (10036) *(G-11621)*
Penguin Random House LLC (HQ) 212 782-9000
1745 Broadway New York (10019) *(G-11622)*
Penguin Random House LLC 212 572-6162
1745 Broadway Frnt 3 New York (10019) *(G-11623)*
Penguin Random House LLC 212 782-9000
1745 Broadway Frnt 3 New York (10019) *(G-11624)*
Penguin Random House LLC 212 366-2377
80 State St Albany (12207) *(G-117)*
Penhouse Media Group Inc (PA) 212 702-6000
11 Penn Plz Fl 12 New York (10001) *(G-11625)*
Peninsula Plastics Ltd 716 854-3050
161 Marine Dr Apt 6e Buffalo (14202) *(G-3141)*
Penn & Fletcher Inc 212 239-6868
2107 41st Ave Fl 5 Long Island City (11101) *(G-7870)*
Penn Can Asphalt Materials, Lyons *Also called Penn Can Equipment Corporation (G-8001)*
Penn Can Equipment Corporation 315 378-0337
300 Cole Rd Lyons (14489) *(G-8001)*
Penn Enterprises Inc 845 446-0765
845 Washington Rd West Point (10996) *(G-16959)*
Penn Signs Inc 718 797-1112
1920 Atlantic Ave Brooklyn (11233) *(G-2427)*
Penn State Metal Fabri 718 786-8814
810 Humboldt St Ste 9 Brooklyn (11222) *(G-2428)*
Pennant Foods, Rochester *Also called Aryzta LLC (G-14233)*
Pennant Ingredients Inc (HQ) 585 235-8160
64 Chester St Rochester (14611) *(G-14595)*
Penner Elbow Company Inc 718 526-9000
4700 76th St Elmhurst (11373) *(G-4679)*
Pennsauken Packing Company LLC 585 377-7700
815 Whitney Rd W Fairport (14450) *(G-4875)*
Penny Express, Avon *Also called Penny Lane Printing Inc (G-539)*
Penny Lane Printing Inc 585 226-8111
1471 Rte 15 Avon (14414) *(G-539)*
Penny Saver News, Edgewood *Also called S G New York LLC (G-4623)*
Pennysaver Group Inc 914 966-1400
80 Alexander St Yonkers (10701) *(G-17495)*
Pennysaver News, Bohemia *Also called S G New York LLC (G-1124)*
Pennysaver/Town Crier, Edgewood *Also called All Island Media Inc (G-4606)*
Pennysavers Rw Publications, Elma *Also called R W Publications Div of Wtrhs (G-4667)*
Pensions & Investments 212 210-0763
711 3rd Ave New York (10017) *(G-11626)*
Pensrus, Staten Island *Also called Henry Morgan (G-15704)*
Penta-Tech Coated Products LLC 315 986-4098
1610 Commons Pkwy Macedon (14502) *(G-8019)*
Pentair Water Pool and Spa Inc 845 452-5500
341 Route 55 Lagrangeville (12540) *(G-7283)*
Pentaplastics, Bohemia *Also called Leidel Corporation (G-1088)*
Penthouse Group, The, Freeport *Also called Penthouse Manufacturing Co Inc (G-5429)*
Penthouse Manufacturing Co Inc 516 379-1300
225 Buffalo Ave Freeport (11520) *(G-5429)*
Penton Business Media Inc 914 949-8500
707 Westchester Ave # 101 White Plains (10604) *(G-17177)*
Penton Media Inc (HQ) 212 204-4200
1166 Avenue Of The Americ New York (10036) *(G-11627)*
Penton Media Inc 212 204-4200
1166 Avenue Of The Americ New York (10036) *(G-11628)*
Penton Media - Aviation Week, New York *Also called Penton Media Inc (G-11627)*
Peoples Choice M R I 716 681-7377
125 Galileo Dr Buffalo (14221) *(G-3142)*
Pep Realty, New York *Also called Atlas Recycling LLC (G-9309)*
Pepe Creations Inc 212 391-1514
2 W 45th St Ste 1003 New York (10036) *(G-11629)*
Peppermints Salon Inc 718 357-6304
15722 Powells Cove Blvd Whitestone (11357) *(G-17242)*
Pepsi Beverages Co 518 782-2150
421 Old Niskayuna Rd Latham (12110) *(G-7402)*
Pepsi Beverages Company, Watertown *Also called Bottling Group LLC (G-16662)*
Pepsi Beverages Company, White Plains *Also called Bottling Group LLC (G-17113)*
Pepsi Beverages Company, White Plains *Also called Bottling Group LLC (G-17114)*
Pepsi Bottle and Group, Somers *Also called General Cinema Bevs of Ohio (G-15531)*
Pepsi Bottling Ventures LLC 631 772-6144
4141 Parklane Ave Ste 600 Patchogue (11772) *(G-13457)*
Pepsi Bottling Ventures LLC 631 226-9000
550 New Horizons Blvd Amityville (11701) *(G-321)*
Pepsi Btlg Group Globl Fin LLC (HQ) 914 767-6000
1 Pepsi Way Ste 1 Somers (10589) *(G-15533)*
Pepsi-Cola, Patchogue *Also called Pepsi Bottling Ventures LLC (G-13457)*
Pepsi-Cola Bottling Co NY Inc 718 649-2465
11202 15th Ave College Point (11356) *(G-3826)*
Pepsi-Cola Bottling Co NY Inc 914 699-2600
601 S Fulton Ave Mount Vernon (10550) *(G-8760)*
Pepsi-Cola Bottling Co NY Inc 718 786-8550
5035 56th Rd Maspeth (11378) *(G-8195)*
Pepsi-Cola Bottling Co NY Inc 718 892-1570
650 Brush Ave Bronx (10465) *(G-1425)*
Pepsi-Cola Bottling Group (HQ) 914 767-6000
1111 Westchester Ave White Plains (10604) *(G-17178)*
Pepsi-Cola Metro Btlg Co Inc (HQ) 914 767-6000
1111 Westchester Ave White Plains (10604) *(G-17179)*
Pepsi-Cola Metro Btlg Co Inc 914 253-2000
700 Anderson Hill Rd Purchase (10577) *(G-13979)*
Pepsi-Cola Metro Btlg Co Inc 607 795-1399
140 Wygant Rd Horseheads (14845) *(G-6615)*
Pepsi-Cola Newburgh Btlg Inc 845 562-5400
1 Pepsi Way Newburgh (12550) *(G-12797)*
Pepsi-Cola Operating Company (HQ) 914 767-6000
1111 Westchester Ave White Plains (10604) *(G-17180)*

ALPHABETIC SECTION

Pepsi-Cola Sales and Dist Inc (HQ) 914 253-2000
 700 Anderson Hill Rd Purchase (10577) *(G-13980)*
Pepsico, White Plains *Also called Pepsi-Cola Metro Btlg Co Inc (G-17179)*
Pepsico, Newburgh *Also called Pepsi-Cola Newburgh Btlg Inc (G-12797)*
Pepsico, Latham *Also called Pepsi Beverages Co (G-7402)*
Pepsico, Horseheads *Also called Pepsi-Cola Metro Btlg Co Inc (G-6615)*
Pepsico, White Plains *Also called Pepsi-Cola Bottling Group (G-17178)*
Pepsico, Amityville *Also called Pepsi Bottling Ventures LLC (G-321)*
Pepsico 419 252-0247
 3 Skyline Dr Hawthorne (10532) *(G-6276)*
Pepsico 914 801-1500
 100 Summit Lake Dr # 103 Valhalla (10595) *(G-16395)*
Pepsico Inc (PA) 914 253-2000
 700 Anderson Hill Rd Purchase (10577) *(G-13981)*
Pepsico Inc 914 253-2000
 1111 Westchester Ave White Plains (10604) *(G-17181)*
Pepsico Inc 914 742-4500
 100 E Stevens Ave Valhalla (10595) *(G-16396)*
Pepsico Inc 914 253-2000
 Anderson Hill Rd Purchase (10577) *(G-13982)*
Pepsico Inc 914 253-3474
 150 Airport Rd Hngr V White Plains (10604) *(G-17182)*
Pepsico Inc 914 253-2713
 700 Anderson Hill Rd Purchase (10577) *(G-13983)*
Pepsico Inc 914 767-6976
 1111 Westchester Ave White Plains (10604) *(G-17183)*
Pepsico Capital Resources Inc 914 253-2000
 700 Anderson Hill Rd Purchase (10577) *(G-13984)*
Pepsico Sales Inc 914 253-2000
 700 Anderson Hill Rd Purchase (10577) *(G-13985)*
Pepsico World Trading Co Inc 914 767-6000
 1111 Westchester Ave White Plains (10604) *(G-17184)*
Per Annum Inc 212 647-8700
 555 8th Ave Rm 202 New York (10018) *(G-11630)*
Peraflex Hose Inc 716 876-8806
 155 Great Arrow Ave Ste 4 Buffalo (14207) *(G-3143)*
Peralta Metal Works Inc 718 649-8661
 602 Atkins Ave Brooklyn (11208) *(G-2429)*
Peraton Inc 315 838-7000
 474 Phoenix Dr Rome (13441) *(G-14857)*
Perception Imaging Inc 631 676-5262
 90 Colin Dr Unit 11 Holbrook (11741) *(G-6495)*
Perceptive Pixel Inc (HQ) 701 367-5845
 641 Avenue Of The Ste 7 New York (10011) *(G-11631)*
Peregrine Industries Inc 631 838-2870
 40 Wall St New York (10005) *(G-11632)*
Pereira & ODell LLC 212 897-1000
 5 Crosby St Rm 5h New York (10013) *(G-11633)*
Perfect Form Manufacturing LLC 585 500-5923
 1325 John St West Henrietta (14586) *(G-16921)*
Perfect Forms and Systems Inc 631 462-1100
 35 Riverview Ter Smithtown (11787) *(G-15517)*
Perfect Gear & Instrument (HQ) 516 328-3330
 55 Denton Ave S New Hyde Park (11040) *(G-8902)*
Perfect Gear & Instrument 516 873-6122
 125 Railroad Ave Garden City Park (11040) *(G-5554)*
Perfect Poly Inc 631 265-0539
 1 Gina Ct Nesconset (11767) *(G-8825)*
Perfect Print Inc 718 832-5280
 220 36th St Unit 2a Brooklyn (11232) *(G-2430)*
Perfect Publications, Brooklyn *Also called Joseph Paul (G-2148)*
Perfect Shoulder Company Inc 914 699-8100
 2 Cortlandt St Mount Vernon (10550) *(G-8761)*
Perfection Electricks, Brooklyn *Also called Martin Chafkin (G-2278)*
Perfection Gear Inc 716 592-9310
 172 Eaton St Springville (14141) *(G-15635)*
Perfex Corporation 315 826-3600
 32 Case St Poland (13431) *(G-13757)*
Perforated Screen Surfaces 866 866-8690
 216 Broome Corporate Pkwy Conklin (13748) *(G-3898)*
Performance Advantage Co Inc 716 683-7413
 6 W Main St Lowr Rear Lancaster (14086) *(G-7357)*
Performance Custom Trailer 518 504-4021
 230 Lockhart Mountain Rd Lake George (12845) *(G-7288)*
Performance Designed By Peters 585 223-9062
 7 Duxbury Hts Fairport (14450) *(G-4876)*
Performance Diesel Service LLC 315 854-5269
 24 Latour Ave Plattsburgh (12901) *(G-13714)*
Performance Lacrosse Group Inc (HQ) 315 453-3073
 4697 Crossroads Park Dr Liverpool (13088) *(G-7567)*
Performance Mfg Inc 716 735-3500
 80 Telegraph Rd Middleport (14105) *(G-8456)*
Performance Precision Mfg LLC 518 993-3033
 55 Willett St Fort Plain (13339) *(G-5357)*
Performance Sourcing Group Inc 914 636-2100
 109 Montgomery Ave Scarsdale (10583) *(G-15251)*
Performance Systems Contg Inc 607 277-6240
 124 Brindley St Ithaca (14850) *(G-6904)*
Performance Technologies Inc (HQ) 585 256-0200
 3500 Winton Pl Ste 4 Rochester (14623) *(G-14596)*
Performance Wire & Cable Inc 315 245-2594
 9482 State Route 13 Camden (13316) *(G-3348)*

Perfume Americana Inc (PA) 212 683-8029
 1216 Broadway New York (10001) *(G-11634)*
Perfume Americana Wholesale, New York *Also called Perfume Americana Inc (G-11634)*
Perfume Amrcana Whlesalers Inc 212 683-8029
 11 W 30th St Betwe Broad Between New York (10001) *(G-11635)*
Perfumers Workshop Intl Ltd (PA) 212 644-8950
 350 7th Ave Rm 802 New York (10001) *(G-11636)*
Peri, Pearl River *Also called Piezo Electronics Research (G-13487)*
Peri-Facts Academy 585 275-6037
 601 Elmwood Ave Rochester (14642) *(G-14597)*
Perimondo LLC 212 749-0721
 331 W 84th St Apt 2 New York (10024) *(G-11637)*
Periodical Services Co Inc 518 822-9300
 351 Fairview Ave Ste 300 Hudson (12534) *(G-6660)*
Perkins International Inc (HQ) 309 675-1000
 672 Delaware Ave Buffalo (14209) *(G-3144)*
Perma Glow Ltd Inc 212 575-9677
 48 W 48th St Ste 301 New York (10036) *(G-11638)*
Perma Tech Inc 716 854-0707
 363 Hamburg St Buffalo (14204) *(G-3145)*
Permanent Press, Sag Harbor *Also called Second Chance Press Inc (G-15108)*
Permit Fashion Group Inc 212 912-0988
 135 W 36th St Fl 16 New York (10018) *(G-11639)*
Pernod Ricard Usa LLC (HQ) 212 372-5400
 250 Park Ave Ste 17a New York (10177) *(G-11640)*
Perretta Graphics Corp 845 473-0550
 46 Violet Ave Poughkeepsie (12601) *(G-13943)*
Perrigo Company 718 960-9900
 1625 Bathgate Ave Bronx (10457) *(G-1426)*
Perrigo New York Inc 718 901-2800
 455 Claremont Pkwy Bronx (10457) *(G-1427)*
Perrigo New York Inc (HQ) 718 960-9900
 1700 Bathgate Ave Bronx (10457) *(G-1428)*
Perrone Aerospace, Fultonville *Also called Perrone Leather LLC (G-5496)*
Perrone Leather LLC (PA) 518 853-4300
 182a Riverside Dr Fultonville (12072) *(G-5496)*
Perrottas Bakery Inc 518 283-4711
 766 Pawling Ave Troy (12180) *(G-16270)*
Perry Ellis America, New York *Also called Perry Ellis Menswear LLC (G-11643)*
Perry Ellis International Inc 212 536-5400
 1126 Avenue Of The Americ New York (10036) *(G-11641)*
Perry Ellis International Inc 212 536-5499
 42 W 39th St Fl 4 New York (10018) *(G-11642)*
Perry Ellis Menswear LLC (HQ) 212 221-7500
 1120 Ave Of The Americas New York (10036) *(G-11643)*
Perry Plastics Inc 718 747-5600
 3050 Whitestone Expy # 300 Flushing (11354) *(G-5288)*
Perry Street Software Inc 415 935-1429
 489 5th Ave Rm 2900 New York (10017) *(G-11644)*
Perrys Ice Cream Company Inc 716 542-5492
 1 Ice Cream Plz Akron (14001) *(G-24)*
Persch Service Print Inc (PA) 716 366-2677
 11 W 3rd St Dunkirk (14048) *(G-4371)*
Perseus Books Group, New York *Also called Clp Pb LLC (G-9704)*
Perseus Fisher Books LLC 212 340-8100
 387 Park Ave S Fl 12 New York (10016) *(G-11645)*
Persistent Systems LLC 212 561-5895
 303 5th Ave Rm 306 New York (10016) *(G-11646)*
Personal Alarm SEC Systems 212 448-1944
 379 5th Ave Fl 3 New York (10016) *(G-11647)*
Personal Graphics Corporation 315 853-3421
 5123 State Route 233 Westmoreland (13490) *(G-17092)*
Pervi Precision Company Inc 631 589-5557
 220 Knickerbocker Ave # 1 Bohemia (11716) *(G-1113)*
PES Group, Brooklyn *Also called Project Energy Savers LLC (G-2470)*
Pesce Bakery, Saugerties *Also called Pesces Bakery Inc (G-15220)*
Pesces Bakery Inc 845 246-4730
 20 Pesce Ct Saugerties (12477) *(G-15220)*
Pesselnik & Cohen Inc 212 925-0287
 82 Bowery Unit 10 New York (10013) *(G-11648)*
Pet Authority, Brooklyn *Also called Dynamic Health Labs Inc (G-1887)*
Pet Proteins LLC 888 293-1029
 347 W 36th St Rm 1204 New York (10018) *(G-11649)*
Petcap Press Corporation 718 609-0910
 3200 Skillman Ave Ste F Long Island City (11101) *(G-7871)*
Pete Levin Music Inc 845 247-9211
 598 Schoolhouse Rd Saugerties (12477) *(G-15221)*
Peter Atman Inc 212 644-8882
 6 E 45th St Rm 1100 New York (10017) *(G-11650)*
Peter C Herman Inc 315 926-4100
 5395 Skinner Rd Marion (14505) *(G-8128)*
Peter Digioia 516 644-5517
 7 Sherwood Dr Plainview (11803) *(G-13656)*
Peter Kwasny Inc 727 641-1462
 400 Oser Ave Ste 1650 Hauppauge (11788) *(G-6187)*
Peter Lang Publishing Inc (HQ) 212 647-7700
 29 Broadway Rm 1800 New York (10006) *(G-11651)*
Peter Mayer Publishers Inc 212 673-2210
 141 Wooster St Fl 4 New York (10012) *(G-11652)*
Peter Papastrat 607 723-8112
 193 Main St Binghamton (13905) *(G-938)*

Peter Pauper Press Inc.....914 681-0144
202 Mmaroneck Ave Ste 400 White Plains (10601) ***(G-17185)***
Peter Productions Devivi Inc.....315 568-8484
2494 Kingdom Rd Waterloo (13165) ***(G-16653)***
Peter Thomas Roth Labs LLC (PA).....212 581-5800
460 Park Ave Fl 16 New York (10022) ***(G-11653)***
Peters LLC.....607 637-5470
5259 Peas Eddy Rd Hancock (13783) ***(G-5988)***
Petersons Nelnet LLC.....609 896-1800
3 Columbia Cir Ste 205 Albany (12203) ***(G-118)***
Petit Printing Corp.....716 871-9490
42 Hunters Gln Getzville (14068) ***(G-5615)***
Petland Discounts Inc.....516 821-3194
1340 Peninsula Blvd Hewlett (11557) ***(G-6335)***
Petnet Solutions Inc.....865 218-2000
660 1st Ave Rm 140 New York (10016) ***(G-11654)***
Petre Alii Petroleum.....315 785-1037
1268 Arsenal St Watertown (13601) ***(G-16693)***
Petrillo's Bakery, Rochester *Also called Scaife Enterprises Inc* ***(G-14693)***
Petro Inc.....516 686-1717
3 Fairchild Ct Plainview (11803) ***(G-13657)***
Petro Inc.....516 686-1900
477 W John St Hicksville (11801) ***(G-6412)***
Petrune, Ithaca *Also called Petrunia LLC* ***(G-6905)***
Petrunia LLC.....607 277-1930
126 E State St Ithaca (14850) ***(G-6905)***
Pets n People Inc.....631 232-1200
2100 Pacific St Hauppauge (11788) ***(G-6188)***
Petteys Lumber.....518 792-5943
10247 State Route 149 Fort Ann (12827) ***(G-5344)***
Pexip Inc (HQ).....703 338-3544
240 W 35th St Ste 1002 New York (10001) ***(G-11655)***
Peyser Instrument Corporation.....631 841-3600
40 Gleam St West Babylon (11704) ***(G-16848)***
Pezera Associates, Calverton *Also called East End Country Kitchens Inc* ***(G-3318)***
Pfannenberg Inc.....716 685-6866
68 Ward Rd Lancaster (14086) ***(G-7358)***
Pfannenberg Manufacturing LLC.....716 685-6866
68 Ward Rd Lancaster (14086) ***(G-7359)***
Pfaudler Inc (HQ).....585 464-5663
1000 West Ave Rochester (14611) ***(G-14598)***
Pfaudler US Inc.....585 235-1000
1000 West Ave Rochester (14611) ***(G-14599)***
Pfeil & Holing Inc.....718 545-4600
5815 Northern Blvd Woodside (11377) ***(G-17362)***
Pfizer HCP Corporation (HQ).....212 733-2323
235 E 42nd St New York (10017) ***(G-11656)***
Pfizer Inc (PA).....212 733-2323
235 E 42nd St New York (10017) ***(G-11657)***
Pfizer Inc.....518 297-6611
64 Maple St Rouses Point (12979) ***(G-15066)***
Pfizer Inc.....914 437-5868
4 Martine Ave White Plains (10606) ***(G-17186)***
Pfizer Inc.....937 746-3603
150 E 42nd St Fl 38 New York (10017) ***(G-11658)***
Pfizer Inc.....212 733-6276
150 E 42nd St Bsmt 2 New York (10017) ***(G-11659)***
Pfizer Inc.....804 257-2000
235 E 42nd St New York (10017) ***(G-11660)***
Pfizer Inc.....212 733-2323
235 E 42nd St New York (10017) ***(G-11661)***
Pfizer Overseas LLC.....212 733-2323
235 E 42nd St New York (10017) ***(G-11662)***
Pgs Millwork Inc (PA).....212 244-6610
535 8th Ave Rm 20n New York (10018) ***(G-11663)***
Phaidon Press Inc.....212 652-5400
65 Bleecker St Fl 8 New York (10012) ***(G-11664)***
Phantom Laboratory Inc.....518 692-1190
2727 State Route 29 Greenwich (12834) ***(G-5911)***
Phantom Laboratory, The, Greenwich *Also called Phantom Laboratory Inc* ***(G-5911)***
Pharbest Pharmaceuticals Inc.....631 249-5130
14 Engineers Ln Ste 1 Farmingdale (11735) ***(G-5087)***
Pharma-Smart International Inc.....585 427-0730
Rochester Tech Park 773 E Rochester (14624) ***(G-14600)***
Pharmacena Labs, Carle Place *Also called Stamapro Inc* ***(G-3424)***
Pharmaceutic Labs LLC.....518 608-1060
15 Walker Way Albany (12205) ***(G-119)***
Pharmaderm, Melville *Also called Fougera Pharmaceuticals Inc* ***(G-8350)***
Pharmadva LLC.....585 469-1410
150 Lucius Gordon Dr # 211 West Henrietta (14586) ***(G-16922)***
Pharmalife Inc.....631 249-4040
130 Gazza Blvd Farmingdale (11735) ***(G-5088)***
Pharmasmart, Rochester *Also called Pharma-Smart International Inc* ***(G-14600)***
Pharmavantage LLC.....631 321-8171
15 Lakeland Ave Babylon (11702) ***(G-549)***
Pharmline, Florida *Also called Stauber California Inc* ***(G-5222)***
PHASE IL MARKETING DBA, Amherst *Also called Nexstar Holding Corp* ***(G-251)***
PHC Restoration Holdings LLC.....212 643-0517
147 W 29th St Fl 4 New York (10001) ***(G-11665)***
Phelinger Tool & Die Corp.....716 685-1780
1254 Town Line Rd Alden (14004) ***(G-184)***
Phelps Cement Products Inc.....315 548-9415
5 S Newark St Phelps (14532) ***(G-13558)***
Pheonix Custom Furniture Ltd.....212 727-2648
2107 41st Ave Fl 2 Long Island City (11101) ***(G-7872)***
Philcom Ltd.....716 875-8005
1144 Military Rd Buffalo (14217) ***(G-3146)***
Philip Crangi, New York *Also called PHC Restoration Holdings LLC* ***(G-11665)***
Philip Morris Intl Inc (PA).....917 663-2000
120 Park Ave Fl 6 New York (10017) ***(G-11666)***
Philipp Feldheim Inc (PA).....845 356-2282
208 Airport Executive Par Nanuet (10954) ***(G-8806)***
Philippe Adec Paris, New York *Also called Morelle Products Ltd* ***(G-11329)***
Philips Elec N Amer Corp.....607 776-3692
7265 State Route 54 Bath (14810) ***(G-661)***
Philips Healthcare, Latham *Also called Philips Medical Systems Mr* ***(G-7403)***
Philips Lighting N Amer Corp.....646 265-7170
267 5th Ave New York (10016) ***(G-11667)***
Philips Medical Systems Mr (HQ).....518 782-1122
450 Old Niskayuna Rd Latham (12110) ***(G-7403)***
Phillip J Ortiz Manufacturing.....845 226-7030
44 Railroad Ave Hopewell Junction (12533) ***(G-6583)***
Phillip Juan.....800 834-4543
9 Union Ave Staten Island (10303) ***(G-15740)***
Phillip Tissicher.....718 282-3310
5107 Avenue H Brooklyn (11234) ***(G-2431)***
Phillips-Van Heusen Europe.....212 381-3500
200 Madison Ave Bsmt 1 New York (10016) ***(G-11668)***
Philpac Corporation (PA).....716 875-8005
1144 Military Rd Buffalo (14217) ***(G-3147)***
Phoebe Company LLC.....212 302-5556
230 W 38th St Fl 11 New York (10018) ***(G-11669)***
Phoenix Cables Corporation.....845 691-6253
131 Tillson Avenue Ext Highland (12528) ***(G-6433)***
Phoenix Graphics Inc.....585 232-4040
464 State St 470 Rochester (14608) ***(G-14601)***
Phoenix Laboratories Inc.....516 822-1230
200 Adams Blvd Farmingdale (11735) ***(G-5089)***
Phoenix Material Handling, Phoenix *Also called Phoenix Welding & Fabg Inc* ***(G-13570)***
Phoenix Mch Pdts of Hauppauge.....631 234-0100
225 Engineers Rd Hauppauge (11788) ***(G-6189)***
Phoenix Metal Designs Inc.....516 597-4100
175 Lauman Ln Hicksville (11801) ***(G-6413)***
Phoenix Ribbon Co Inc.....212 239-0155
20 W 36th St Fl 7 New York (10018) ***(G-11670)***
Phoenix Services Group LLC.....518 828-6611
1 Hudson City Ctr Hudson (12534) ***(G-6661)***
Phoenix Usa LLC.....646 351-6598
315 W 33rd St Apt 30h New York (10001) ***(G-11671)***
Phoenix Venture Fund LLC.....212 759-1909
70 E 55th St Fl 10 New York (10022) ***(G-11672)***
Phoenix Welding & Fabg Inc.....315 695-2223
10 County Route 6 Phoenix (13135) ***(G-13570)***
Phoenix Wood Wrights Ltd.....631 727-9691
132 Kroemer Ave 3 Riverhead (11901) ***(G-14165)***
Photo Agents Ltd.....631 421-0258
716 New York Ave Huntington (11743) ***(G-6709)***
Photo Industry Inc.....516 364-0016
7600 Jericho Tpke Ste 301 Woodbury (11797) ***(G-17315)***
Photo Medic Equipment Inc.....631 242-6600
3 Saxwood St Ste E Deer Park (11729) ***(G-4213)***
Photo Research, Syracuse *Also called Novanta Inc* ***(G-16020)***
Photograve Corporation.....718 667-4825
1140 S Railroad Ave Staten Island (10306) ***(G-15741)***
Photomedex Inc (HQ).....888 966-1010
40 Ramland Rd S Fl 2 Orangeburg (10962) ***(G-13261)***
PHOTOMEDEX SURGICAL PRODUCTS, Orangeburg *Also called Photomedex Inc* ***(G-13261)***
Photon Gear Inc.....585 265-3360
245 David Pkwy Ontario (14519) ***(G-13231)***
Photon Vision Systems Inc (PA).....607 749-2689
1 Technology Pl Homer (13077) ***(G-6549)***
Photonamics Inc.....585 426-3774
558 Elmgrove Rd Rochester (14606) ***(G-14602)***
Photonic Controls LLC.....607 562-4585
500 1st Ctr Ste 2 Horseheads (14845) ***(G-6616)***
Photonics Industries Intl Inc (PA).....631 218-2240
1800 Ocean Ave Unit A Ronkonkoma (11779) ***(G-14992)***
Photonix Technologies Inc.....607 786-4600
48 Washington Ave Endicott (13760) ***(G-4832)***
Phototherapeutix, Glens Falls *Also called Medtek Lighting Corporation* ***(G-5704)***
Phreesia New York.....888 654-7473
432 Park Ave S Fl 12 New York (10016) ***(G-11673)***
Phyljohn Distributors Inc.....518 459-2775
6 Interstate Ave Albany (12205) ***(G-120)***
Phymetrix Inc.....631 627-3950
28 Scouting Blvd Ste C Medford (11763) ***(G-8291)***
Physical Review, Ridge *Also called American Physical Society* ***(G-14104)***
Physicalmind Institute.....212 343-2150
84 Wooster St Ste 605 New York (10012) ***(G-11674)***
Physiologics LLC.....800 765-6775
2100 Smithtown Ave Ronkonkoma (11779) ***(G-14993)***

Phytofilter Technologies Inc.....518 507-6399
9 Kirby Rd Apt 19 Saratoga Springs (12866) *(G-15196)*
Piaget.....212 355-6444
663 5th Ave Fl 7 New York (10022) *(G-11675)*
Piaggio Group Americas Inc.....212 380-4400
257 Park Ave S Fl 4 New York (10010) *(G-11676)*
Piano Software Inc.....646 350-1999
1 World Trade Ctr Ste 46d New York (10007) *(G-11677)*
Piazzas Ice Cream Ice Hse Inc.....718 818-8811
41 Housman Ave Staten Island (10303) *(G-15742)*
Pibbs Industries, Flushing *Also called P S Pibbs Inc (G-5283)*
Pic A Poc Enterprises Inc.....631 981-2094
53 Union Ave Ronkonkoma (11779) *(G-14994)*
Pic Nic LLC.....914 245-6500
123 Holmes Ct Yorktown Heights (10598) *(G-17532)*
Picador USA.....646 307-5629
175 5th Ave New York (10010) *(G-11678)*
Picasso Coach Builders, Rego Park *Also called Pcb Coach Builders Corp (G-14049)*
Piccini Industries Ltd.....845 365-0614
37 Ramland Rd Orangeburg (10962) *(G-13262)*
Piccini Mnm Inc.....845 741-6770
35 Highland Ave West Nyack (10994) *(G-16953)*
PICKETT BUILDING MATERIALS, Oneonta *Also called Arnan Development Corp (G-13194)*
Picone Meat Specialties Ltd.....914 381-3002
180 Jefferson Ave Mamaroneck (10543) *(G-8075)*
Picone's Sausage, Mamaroneck *Also called Picone Meat Specialties Ltd (G-8075)*
Picture Perfect Framing.....718 851-1884
1758 50th St Brooklyn (11204) *(G-2432)*
Pidyon Controls Inc (PA).....212 683-9523
141 W 24th St Apt 4 New York (10011) *(G-11679)*
Pie, Webster *Also called Practical Instrument Elec Inc (G-16755)*
Piedmont Plastics Inc.....518 724-0563
4 Access Rd Albany (12205) *(G-121)*
Piemonte Company, Woodside *Also called Piemonte Home Made Ravioli Co (G-17363)*
Piemonte Home Made Ravioli Co (PA).....718 429-1972
3436 65th St Woodside (11377) *(G-17363)*
Piemonte Home Made Ravioli Co.....212 226-0475
190 Grand St New York (10013) *(G-11680)*
Pier-Tech Inc.....516 442-5420
7 Hampton Rd Oceanside (11572) *(G-13111)*
Pierce Arrow Draperies, Buffalo *Also called Pierce Arrow Drapery Mfg (G-3148)*
Pierce Arrow Drapery Mfg.....716 876-3023
1685 Elmwood Ave Ste 312 Buffalo (14207) *(G-3148)*
Pierce Industries LLC.....585 458-0888
465 Paul Rd Rochester (14624) *(G-14603)*
Pierce Steel Fabricators.....716 372-7652
430 N 7th St Olean (14760) *(G-13174)*
Pierrepont Visual Graphics.....585 305-9672
15 Elser Ter Rochester (14611) *(G-14604)*
Pietro Demarco Importers Inc.....914 969-3201
1185 Saw Mill River Rd # 4 Yonkers (10710) *(G-17496)*
Piezo Electronics Research.....845 735-9349
30 Walter St Pearl River (10965) *(G-13487)*
Pii Holdings Inc (HQ).....716 876-9951
2150 Elmwood Ave Buffalo (14207) *(G-3149)*
Pilgrim Foods Co, Great Neck *Also called Old Dutch Mustard Co Inc (G-5843)*
Pilgrim Surf & Supply.....718 218-7456
68 N 3rd St Brooklyn (11249) *(G-2433)*
Pilkington North America Inc.....315 438-3341
6412 Deere Rd Ste 1 Syracuse (13206) *(G-16033)*
Piller Power Systems Inc (HQ).....845 695-6658
45 Wes Warren Dr Middletown (10941) *(G-8491)*
Pillow Perfections Ltd Inc.....718 383-2259
252 Norman Ave Ste 101 Brooklyn (11222) *(G-2434)*
Pilot Inc (PA).....212 951-1133
421 W 24th St Apt 4c New York (10011) *(G-11681)*
Pilot Inc.....212 951-1133
110 E 25th St New York (10010) *(G-11682)*
Pilot Products Inc.....718 728-2141
2413 46th St Long Island City (11103) *(G-7873)*
Pin Pharma Inc.....212 543-2583
3960 Broadway Fl 2 New York (10032) *(G-11683)*
Pincharming Inc.....516 663-5115
215 Brixton Rd Garden City (11530) *(G-5539)*
Pindar Vineyards LLC.....631 734-6200
37645 Route 25 Peconic (11958) *(G-13496)*
Pinder International Inc (PA).....631 273-0324
1140 Motor Pkwy Ste A Hauppauge (11788) *(G-6190)*
Pine Barrens Printing, Westhampton Beach *Also called Michael K Lennon Inc (G-17088)*
Pine Bush Printing Co Inc.....518 456-2431
2005 Western Ave Albany (12203) *(G-122)*
Pine Hill Fabricators.....716 823-2474
2731 Seneca St Buffalo (14224) *(G-3150)*
Pine Pharmaceuticals LLC.....716 248-1025
100 Colvin Woods Pkwy Tonawanda (14150) *(G-16211)*
Pine Tree Farms Inc.....607 532-4312
3714 Cayuga St Interlaken (14847) *(G-6788)*
Pinewood Marketing, Hartsdale *Also called Richard Edelson (G-6018)*
Pingmd Inc.....212 632-2665
136 Madison Ave Fl 6 New York (10016) *(G-11684)*
Pink Inc.....212 352-8282
23 E 10th St Apt 1b New York (10003) *(G-11685)*
Pink and Palmer, Rye *Also called Judith N Graham Inc (G-15087)*
Pink Box Accessories LLC.....716 777-4477
1170 72nd St Brooklyn (11228) *(G-2435)*
Pink Crush LLC.....718 788-6978
1410 Broadway Rm 1002 New York (10018) *(G-11686)*
Pinnacle Manufacturing Co Inc.....585 343-5664
56 Harvester Ave Batavia (14020) *(G-646)*
Pinos Press Inc.....315 935-0110
201 E Jefferson St Syracuse (13202) *(G-16034)*
Pinpoint Systems Intl Inc (PA).....631 775-2100
10 Pinehurst Dr Bellport (11713) *(G-835)*
Pins and Lanes, Lowville *Also called Qubicaamf Worldwide LLC (G-7969)*
Pins N Needles.....212 535-6222
1045 Lexington Ave New York (10021) *(G-11687)*
Pioneer Printers Inc.....716 693-7100
1087 Erie Ave North Tonawanda (14120) *(G-13004)*
Pioneer Window Holdings Inc (PA).....516 822-7000
15 Frederick Pl Hicksville (11801) *(G-6414)*
Pioneer Window Holdings Inc.....518 762-5526
200 Union Ave Johnstown (12095) *(G-7152)*
Pioneer Windows Manufacturing, Hicksville *Also called Pioneer Window Holdings Inc (G-6414)*
PIP Printing, Oceanside *Also called Ahw Printing Corp (G-13091)*
PIP Printing, Lynbrook *Also called Pro Printing (G-7983)*
PIP Printing, Syosset *Also called Vivona Business Printers Inc (G-15862)*
PIP Printing, White Plains *Also called Alamar Printing Inc (G-17102)*
PIP Printing, Hicksville *Also called Marcal Printing Inc (G-6393)*
Piper Plastics Corp.....631 842-6889
102 Ralph Ave Copiague (11726) *(G-3942)*
Pipkarnia Starodolska, Brooklyn *Also called Old Poland Foods LLC (G-2400)*
Pirnat Precise Metals Inc.....631 293-9169
127 Marine St Farmingdale (11735) *(G-5090)*
Pirod Inc.....631 231-7660
15 Oser Ave Hauppauge (11788) *(G-6191)*
Piroke Trade Inc.....646 515-1537
1430 35th St Fl 2 Brooklyn (11218) *(G-2436)*
Pit Stop Motorsports, Forestville *Also called P S M Group Inc (G-5342)*
Pitney Bowes Inc.....212 564-7548
637 W 27th St Fl 8 New York (10001) *(G-11688)*
Pitney Bowes Inc.....203 356-5000
90 Park Ave Rm 1110 New York (10016) *(G-11689)*
Pitney Bowes Inc.....518 283-0345
350 Jordan Rd Ste 1 Troy (12180) *(G-16271)*
Pitney Bowes Inc.....516 822-0900
200 Robbins Ln Unit B2 Jericho (11753) *(G-7113)*
Pitney Bowes Software Inc.....518 272-0014
350 Jordan Rd Ste 1 Troy (12180) *(G-16272)*
Pivot Punch Corporation.....716 625-8000
6550 Campbell Blvd Lockport (14094) *(G-7640)*
Pivot Records LLC.....718 417-1213
600 Johnson Ave Brooklyn (11237) *(G-2437)*
Piwik Pro LLC.....888 444-0049
222 Broadway Fl 19 New York (10038) *(G-11690)*
Pixacore, New York *Also called Intstrux LLC (G-10690)*
Pixy Dust, Amagansett *Also called Cosmetics Plus Ltd (G-217)*
Pj Decorators Inc.....516 735-9693
257 Pontiac Pl East Meadow (11554) *(G-4447)*
PJ Designs Inc.....212 355-3100
100 E 50th St Ste 38a New York (10022) *(G-11691)*
Pk Metals, Coram *Also called Suffolk Indus Recovery Corp (G-3974)*
Pk30 System LLC.....212 473-8050
3607 Atwood Rd Stone Ridge (12484) *(G-15786)*
Pkg Group.....212 965-0112
560 Broadway Rm 406 New York (10012) *(G-11692)*
Pl Developments, Westbury *Also called P & L Development LLC (G-17045)*
Pl Developments New York, Westbury *Also called P & L Development LLC (G-17044)*
Place Vendome Holding Co Inc.....212 696-0765
230 5th Ave Ste 1107 New York (10001) *(G-11693)*
Placid Baker.....518 326-2657
250 Broadway Troy (12180) *(G-16273)*
Plain Digital Inc.....914 310-0280
235 Garth Rd Apt D6a Scarsdale (10583) *(G-15252)*
Planar Optics Inc.....585 671-0100
858 Hard Rd Webster (14580) *(G-16754)*
Planet Embroidery.....718 381-4827
6695 Forest Ave Ridgewood (11385) *(G-14130)*
Plant Office, Wyoming *Also called Texas Brine Company LLC (G-17398)*
Plant-Tech2o Inc.....516 483-7845
30 Chasner St Hempstead (11550) *(G-6307)*
Plascal Corp.....516 249-2200
361 Eastern Pkwy Farmingdale (11735) *(G-5091)*
Plascoline Inc.....917 410-5754
275 Madison Ave Fl 14th New York (10016) *(G-11694)*
Plaslok Corp.....716 681-7755
3155 Broadway St Buffalo (14227) *(G-3151)*
Plasti-Vue Corp.....718 463-2300
4130 Murray St Flushing (11355) *(G-5289)*
Plastic & Reconstructive Svcs.....914 584-5605
333 N Bedford Rd Mount Kisco (10549) *(G-8683)*

ALPHABETIC

Plastic Solutions Inc 631 234-9013
158 Schenck Ave Bayport (11705) *(G-754)*
Plastic Sys/Gr Bflo Inc 716 835-7555
465 Cornwall Ave Buffalo (14215) *(G-3152)*
Plastic Works 914 576-2050
26 Garden St New Rochelle (10801) *(G-8965)*
Plastic-Craft Products Corp 845 358-3010
744 W Nyack Rd West Nyack (10994) *(G-16954)*
Plasticware LLC (PA) 845 267-0790
13 Wilsher Dr Monsey (10952) *(G-8612)*
Plasticweld Systems, Newfane *Also called Vante Inc* *(G-12813)*
Plasticycle Corporation (PA) 914 997-6882
245 Main St Ste 430 White Plains (10601) *(G-17187)*
Plastifold Industries Division, Brooklyn *Also called Visitainer Corp* *(G-2749)*
Plastirun Corporation 631 273-2626
70 Emjay Blvd Bldg A Brentwood (11717) *(G-1190)*
Platform Experts Inc 646 843-7100
2938 Quentin Rd Brooklyn (11229) *(G-2438)*
Platina, New York *Also called Alexander Primak Jewelry Inc* *(G-9132)*
Platinum Carting Corp 631 649-4322
1806 Carleton Ave Bay Shore (11706) *(G-720)*
Platinum Printing & Graphics 631 249-3325
70 Carolyn Blvd Ste C Farmingdale (11735) *(G-5092)*
Platinum Sales Promotion Inc 718 361-0200
3514a Crescent St Long Island City (11106) *(G-7874)*
Plattco Corporation (PA) 518 563-4640
7 White St Plattsburgh (12901) *(G-13715)*
Platter's Chocolates, North Tonawanda *Also called Roger L Urban Inc* *(G-13010)*
Plattsburgh Press-Republican, Plattsburgh *Also called Community Newspaper Group LLC* *(G-13688)*
Plattsburgh Quarry, Plattsburgh *Also called Graymont Materials Inc* *(G-13693)*
Plattsburgh Sheet Metal Inc 518 561-4930
95 Sailly Ave Plattsburgh (12901) *(G-13716)*
Play-It Productions Inc 212 695-6530
735 Port Washington Blvd Port Washington (11050) *(G-13873)*
Playbill Incorporated (PA) 212 557-5757
729 7th Ave Fl 4 New York (10019) *(G-11695)*
Playbill Incorporated 718 335-4033
3715 61st St Woodside (11377) *(G-17364)*
Playfitness Corp 917 497-5443
27 Palisade St Staten Island (10305) *(G-15743)*
Playground NY Inc 505 920-7236
55 Hope St Apt 212 Brooklyn (11211) *(G-2439)*
Playlife LLC 646 207-9082
297 Church St Fl 5 New York (10013) *(G-11696)*
Plaza Braceltte Mounting, New Hyde Park *Also called Satco Castings Service Inc* *(G-8905)*
Plaza Group Creation, New York *Also called Jordan Scott Designs Ltd* *(G-10801)*
Pleasure Chest Sales Ltd 212 242-4185
156 7th Ave S New York (10014) *(G-11697)*
Pleatco LLC 516 609-0200
28 Garvies Point Rd Glen Cove (11542) *(G-5637)*
Plectica LLC 917 304-7052
175 Varick St New York (10014) *(G-11698)*
Plexi Craft Quality Products 212 924-3244
200 Lexington Ave Rm 914 New York (10016) *(G-11699)*
Pliant LLC 315 986-6286
200 Main St Macedon (14502) *(G-8020)*
Pliotron Company America LLC 716 298-4457
4650 Witmer Indus Est Niagara Falls (14305) *(G-12878)*
Plt, Rochester *Also called Precision Laser Technology LLC* *(G-14616)*
Plug Power Inc (PA) 518 782-7700
968 Albany Shaker Rd Latham (12110) *(G-7404)*
Plugg LLC 212 840-6655
1410 Broadway Frnt 2 New York (10018) *(G-11700)*
Plura Broadcast Inc (PA) 516 997-5675
67 Grand Ave Massapequa (11758) *(G-8212)*
Plures Technologies Inc (PA) 585 905-0554
4070 County Road 16 Canandaigua (14424) *(G-3385)*
Pluribus Products Inc 718 852-1614
1 Overlook Ave Bayville (11709) *(G-775)*
Pluslux LLC 516 371-4400
461 Doughty Blvd Inwood (11096) *(G-6805)*
Plx Inc (PA) 631 586-4190
25 W Jefryn Blvd Ste A Deer Park (11729) *(G-4214)*
Pmb Precision Products Inc 631 491-6753
725 Mount Ave North Babylon (11703) *(G-12919)*
Pmd, Victor *Also called Progressive Mch & Design LLC* *(G-16521)*
PMF, Brooklyn *Also called Precision Mtal Fabricators Inc* *(G-2449)*
PMG, Ronkonkoma *Also called Paul Michael Group Inc* *(G-14990)*
PMI Global Services Inc 917 663-2000
120 Park Ave Fl 6 New York (10017) *(G-11701)*
PMI Industries LLC 585 464-8050
350 Buell Rd Rochester (14624) *(G-14605)*
Pmrnyc, Brooklyn *Also called Total Metal Resource* *(G-2688)*
PNC Sports 516 665-2244
1880 Deer Park Ave Deer Park (11729) *(G-4215)*
Pneumercator Company Inc 631 293-8450
1785 Express Dr N Hauppauge (11788) *(G-6192)*
Pni Capital Partners 516 466-7120
1400 Old Country Rd # 103 Westbury (11590) *(G-17047)*
Pocono Pool Products-North 518 283-1023
15 Krey Blvd Rensselaer (12144) *(G-14060)*
Poerformance Design, Fairport *Also called Performance Designed By Peters* *(G-4876)*
Poetry Mailing List Marsh Hawk 516 766-1891
2823 Rockaway Ave Oceanside (11572) *(G-13112)*
Poets House Inc 212 431-7920
10 River Ter New York (10282) *(G-11702)*
Point Canvas Company Inc 607 692-4381
5952 State Route 26 Whitney Point (13862) *(G-17249)*
Point Electric Div, Blauvelt *Also called Swivelier Company Inc* *(G-970)*
Point Industrial, Bemus Point *Also called Lakeside Industries Inc* *(G-842)*
Point of Sale Outfitters, Geneva *Also called R M Reynolds* *(G-5596)*
Pointman LLC 716 842-1439
403 Main St Ste 200 Buffalo (14203) *(G-3153)*
Pointwise Information Service 315 457-4111
223 1st St Liverpool (13088) *(G-7568)*
Pol-Tek Industries Ltd 716 823-1502
2300 Clinton St Buffalo (14227) *(G-3154)*
Pole Position Raceway 716 683-7223
1 Walden Galleria Cheektowaga (14225) *(G-3613)*
Pole-Tech Co Inc 631 689-5525
97 Gnarled Hollow Rd East Setauket (11733) *(G-4508)*
Poletech Flagpole Manufaturer, East Setauket *Also called Pole-Tech Co Inc* *(G-4508)*
Polich Tallix Inc 845 567-9464
39 Edmunds Ln Walden (12586) *(G-16554)*
Policy ADM Solutions Inc 914 332-4320
505 White Plains Rd Tarrytown (10591) *(G-16125)*
Polish American Journal, Orchard Park *Also called Panagraphics Inc* *(G-13312)*
Political Risk Services, The, East Syracuse *Also called The PRS Group Inc* *(G-4583)*
POLITICAL SCIENCE QUARTERLY, New York *Also called Academy of Political Science* *(G-9055)*
Polkadot Usa Inc 914 835-3697
33 Country Rd Mamaroneck (10543) *(G-8076)*
Pollack Graphics Inc 212 727-8400
601 W 26th St Ste M204 New York (10001) *(G-11703)*
Pollardwater, New Hyde Park *Also called Ferguson Enterprises Inc* *(G-8879)*
Polly Treating, New York *Also called Xinya International Trading Co* *(G-12704)*
Polo Ralph Lauren Hosiery Div, New York *Also called Hot Sox Company Incorporated* *(G-10557)*
Polska Gazeta, Brooklyn *Also called Spring Publishing Corporation* *(G-2614)*
Poly Can, Carthage *Also called David Johnson* *(G-3441)*
Poly Craft Industries Corp 631 630-6731
40 Ranick Rd Hauppauge (11788) *(G-6193)*
Poly Scientific R&D Corp 631 586-0400
70 Cleveland Ave Bay Shore (11706) *(G-721)*
Poly Software International 845 735-9301
7 Kerry Ct Pearl River (10965) *(G-13488)*
Poly-Flex Corp (PA) 631 586-9500
250 Executive Dr Ste S Edgewood (11717) *(G-4620)*
Poly-Pak Industries Inc (PA) 631 293-6767
125 Spagnoli Rd Melville (11747) *(G-8377)*
Polycast Industries Inc 631 595-2530
130 S 2nd St Bay Shore (11706) *(G-722)*
Polygen Pharmaceuticals Inc 631 392-4044
41 Mercedes Way Unit 17 Edgewood (11717) *(G-4621)*
Polymag Inc 631 286-4111
685 Station Rd Ste 2 Bellport (11713) *(G-836)*
Polymag Tek Inc 585 235-8390
215 Tremont St Ste 2 Rochester (14608) *(G-14606)*
Polymer Conversions Inc 716 662-8550
5732 Big Tree Rd Orchard Park (14127) *(G-13315)*
Polymer Engineered Pdts Inc 585 426-1811
23 Moonlanding Rd Rochester (14624) *(G-14607)*
Polymer Slutions Group Fin LLC (PA) 212 771-1717
100 Park Ave Fl 31 New York (10017) *(G-11704)*
Polyplastic Forms Inc 631 249-5011
49 Gazza Blvd Farmingdale (11735) *(G-5093)*
Polyseal Packaging Corp 718 792-5530
1178 E 180th St Bronx (10460) *(G-1429)*
Polyset Company Inc 518 664-6000
65 Hudson Ave Mechanicville (12118) *(G-8260)*
Polyshot Corporation 585 292-5010
75 Lucius Gordon Dr West Henrietta (14586) *(G-16923)*
Polytech Pool Mfg Inc 718 492-8991
262 48th St 262 Brooklyn (11220) *(G-2440)*
Polytex Inc 716 549-5100
1305 Eden Evans Center Rd Angola (14006) *(G-381)*
Pom Gear, Brooklyn *Also called Cellular Empire Inc* *(G-1768)*
Pompian Manufacturing Co Inc 914 476-7076
280 Nepperhan Ave Yonkers (10701) *(G-17497)*
Poncio Signs 718 543-4851
3007 Albany Cres Bronx (10463) *(G-1430)*
Ponder, New York *Also called Parlor Labs Inc* *(G-11590)*
Ponti Rossi Inc 347 506-9616
186 Franklin St Apt C16 Brooklyn (11222) *(G-2441)*
Pony Farm Press & Graphics 607 432-9020
330 Pony Farm Rd Oneonta (13820) *(G-13214)*
Pooran Pallet Inc 718 938-7970
319 Barretto St Bronx (10474) *(G-1431)*
Pop A2z, New York *Also called Sky Frame & Art Inc* *(G-12120)*

Pop Bar LLC ... 212 255-4874
5 Carmine St Frnt 6 New York (10014) *(G-11705)*
Pop Nyc, New York *Also called Popnyc 1 LLC (G-11706)*
Pop Printing Incorporated ... 212 808-7800
288 Hamilton Ave Brooklyn (11231) *(G-2442)*
Popnyc 1 LLC ... 646 684-4600
75 Saint Nicholas Pl 2e New York (10032) *(G-11706)*
Poppin Inc ... 212 391-7200
1115 Broadway Fl 3 New York (10010) *(G-11707)*
Popular Mechanics, New York *Also called Hearst Corporation (G-10486)*
Popular Pattern, New York *Also called Stephen Singer Pattern Co Inc (G-12220)*
Popularity Products, Brooklyn *Also called New York Popular Inc (G-2376)*
Porcelain Refinishing Corp ... 516 352-4841
19905 32nd Ave Flushing (11358) *(G-5290)*
Pork King Sausage Inc ... 718 542-2810
F22 Hunts Point Co Op Mkt Bronx (10474) *(G-1432)*
Porous Materials Inc (PA) ... 607 257-5544
20 Dutch Mill Rd Ithaca (14850) *(G-6906)*
Port Authority of NY & NJ ... 718 390-2534
2777 Goethals Rd N Fl 2 Staten Island (10303) *(G-15744)*
Port Everglades Machine Works ... 516 367-2280
57 Colgate Dr Plainview (11803) *(G-13658)*
Port Jervis Machine Corp ... 845 856-6210
176 1/2 Jersey Ave Port Jervis (12771) *(G-13814)*
Porta Decor ... 516 826-6900
290 Duffy Ave Unit 3 Hicksville (11801) *(G-6415)*
Portable Tech Solutions LLC ... 631 727-8084
221 David Ct Calverton (11933) *(G-3323)*
Portequip Work Stations, Niagara Falls *Also called Stephenson Custom Case Company (G-12895)*
Portfab LLC ... 718 542-3600
45 Ranick Dr E Amityville (11701) *(G-322)*
Portfolio Media Inc ... 646 783-7100
111 W 19th St Fl 5 New York (10011) *(G-11708)*
Portville Sand & Gravel Div, Portville *Also called IA Construction Corporation (G-13893)*
Portware LLC (HQ) ... 212 425-5233
233 Broadway Fl 24 New York (10279) *(G-11709)*
Poseidon Systems LLC ... 585 239-6025
200 Canal View Blvd # 300 Rochester (14623) *(G-14608)*
Posillico Materials LLC ... 631 249-1872
1750 New Hwy Farmingdale (11735) *(G-5094)*
Posimech Inc ... 631 924-5959
15 Scouting Blvd Unit 3 Medford (11763) *(G-8292)*
Positive Print Litho Offset ... 212 431-4850
121 Varick St Rm 204 New York (10013) *(G-11710)*
Post Journal ... 716 487-1111
412 Murray Ave Jamestown (14701) *(G-7056)*
Post Modern Productions Inc (PA) ... 212 719-3916
20 Orchard St Apt 2f New York (10002) *(G-11711)*
Post Road ... 203 545-2122
101 E 16th St Apt 4b New York (10003) *(G-11712)*
Post Star, Glens Falls *Also called Lee Enterprises Incorporated (G-5702)*
Post-Journal, The, Jamestown *Also called Ogden Newspapers Inc (G-7055)*
Potential Poly Bag Inc ... 718 258-0800
1253 Coney Island Ave Brooklyn (11230) *(G-2443)*
Potsdam Specialty Paper Inc (HQ) ... 315 265-4000
547a Sissonville Rd Potsdam (13676) *(G-13899)*
Potsdam Specialty Paper, Inc., Potsdam *Also called Potsdam Specialty Paper Inc (G-13899)*
Potsdam Stone Concrete, Plattsburgh *Also called Upstone Materials Inc (G-13736)*
Potter Lumber Co Inc ... 716 373-1260
3786 Potter Rd Allegany (14706) *(G-205)*
Potter Lumber Co LLC ... 814 438-7888
4002 Legion Dr Hamburg (14075) *(G-5960)*
Potters Industries LLC ... 315 265-4920
72 Reynolds Rd Potsdam (13676) *(G-13900)*
Poughkeepsie Journal, Poughkeepsie *Also called Gannett Stllite Info Ntwrk LLC (G-13920)*
Poultry Dist, Brooklyn *Also called Vineland Kosher Poultry Inc (G-2746)*
Powa Technologies Inc ... 347 344-7848
1 Bryant Park Ste 39 New York (10036) *(G-11713)*
Power and Cnstr Group Inc ... 585 889-6020
86 River Rd Scottsville (14546) *(G-15360)*
Power and Composite Tech LLC ... 518 843-6825
200 Wallins Corners Rd Amsterdam (12010) *(G-366)*
Power Connector Inc ... 631 563-7878
140 Wilbur Pl Ste 4 Bohemia (11716) *(G-1114)*
Power Drives Inc (PA) ... 716 822-3600
801 Exchange St Buffalo (14210) *(G-3155)*
Power Gneration Indus Engs Inc ... 315 633-9389
8927 Tyler Rd Bridgeport (13030) *(G-1234)*
Power Line Constructors Inc ... 315 853-6183
24 Robinson Rd Clinton (13323) *(G-3746)*
Power Scrub It Inc ... 516 997-2500
75 Urban Ave Westbury (11590) *(G-17048)*
Power Up Manufacturing Inc ... 716 876-4890
275 N Pointe Pkwy Ste 100 Buffalo (14228) *(G-3156)*
Power-Flo Technologies Inc ... 315 399-5801
6500 New Venture Gear Dr East Syracuse (13057) *(G-4568)*
Power-Flo Technologies Inc ... 585 426-4607
62 Marway Cir Rochester (14624) *(G-14609)*
Powercomplete LLC ... 212 228-4129
636 Broadway Rm 300 New York (10012) *(G-11714)*
Powerflow Inc ... 716 892-1014
1714 Broadway St Buffalo (14212) *(G-3157)*
Powerhouse Books, Brooklyn *Also called Powerhouse Cultural Entrmt Inc (G-2444)*
Powerhouse Cultural Entrmt Inc ... 212 604-9074
126a Front St Brooklyn (11201) *(G-2444)*
Powermate Cellular ... 718 833-9400
140 58th St Ste 1d Brooklyn (11220) *(G-2445)*
Powers Fasteners, Brewster *Also called Black & Decker (us) Inc (G-1209)*
Powertex Inc (PA) ... 518 297-4000
1 Lincoln Blvd Ste 101 Rouses Point (12979) *(G-15067)*
Powr-UPS Corp ... 631 345-5700
1 Roned Rd Shirley (11967) *(G-15451)*
Poz Publishing, New York *Also called Smart & Strong LLC (G-12129)*
Ppc Broadband Inc (HQ) ... 315 431-7200
6176 E Molloy Rd East Syracuse (13057) *(G-4569)*
PPG Architectural Finishes Inc ... 585 271-1363
566 Clinton Ave S Rochester (14620) *(G-14610)*
Ppi Corp ... 585 880-7277
275 Commerce Dr Rochester (14623) *(G-14611)*
Ppi Corp ... 585 243-0300
275 Commerce Dr Rochester (14623) *(G-14612)*
Ppr Direct Inc ... 718 965-8600
74 20th St Fl 2 Brooklyn (11232) *(G-2446)*
Ppr Direct Marketing LLC (PA) ... 718 965-8600
74 20th St Brooklyn (11232) *(G-2447)*
PR & Stone & Tile Inc ... 718 383-1115
17 Beadel St Brooklyn (11222) *(G-2448)*
Practical Instrument Elec Inc ... 585 872-9350
82 E Main St Ste 3 Webster (14580) *(G-16755)*
Practicepro Software Systems ... 516 222-0010
666 Old Country Rd Bsmt Garden City (11530) *(G-5540)*
Prager Metis Cpas LLC ... 212 972-7555
225 W 34th St Ste 1800 New York (10122) *(G-11715)*
Pragmatics Technology Inc ... 845 795-5071
14 Old Indian Trl Milton (12547) *(G-8517)*
Pratt With ME Hmi Met Powders, Clayville *Also called Hmi Metal Powders (G-3714)*
Praxair Inc ... 716 879-2000
175 E Park Dr Tonawanda (14150) *(G-16212)*
Praxair Inc ... 845 267-2337
614 Corporate Way Ste 4 Valley Cottage (10989) *(G-16411)*
Praxair Inc ... 716 649-1600
5322 Scranton Rd Hamburg (14075) *(G-5961)*
Praxair Inc ... 518 482-4360
116 Railroad Ave Albany (12205) *(G-123)*
Praxair Inc ... 716 286-4600
4501 Royal Ave Niagara Falls (14303) *(G-12879)*
Praxair Inc ... 845 359-4200
542 Route 303 Orangeburg (10962) *(G-13263)*
Praxair Inc ... 716 879-4000
135 E Park Dr Tonawanda (14150) *(G-16213)*
Praxair Distribution Inc ... 315 457-5821
4560 Morgan Pl Liverpool (13090) *(G-7569)*
Praxair Distribution Inc ... 315 735-6153
9432 State Route 49 Marcy (13403) *(G-8122)*
Praxair Surface Tech Inc ... 845 398-8322
560 Route 303 Orangeburg (10962) *(G-13264)*
Praxis Powder Technology Inc ... 518 812-0112
604 Queensbury Ave Queensbury (12804) *(G-14020)*
PRC Liquidating Company ... 212 823-9626
10 Columbus Cir New York (10019) *(G-11716)*
Pre Cycled Inc ... 845 278-7611
1689 Route 22 Brewster (10509) *(G-1225)*
Pre-Tech Plastics Inc ... 518 942-5950
3085 Plank Rd Mineville (12956) *(G-8574)*
Precare Corp ... 631 524-5171
400 Wireless Blvd Hauppauge (11788) *(G-6194)*
Precare Corp (PA) ... 631 667-1055
100 Oser Ave Hauppauge (11788) *(G-6195)*
Precimed Inc ... 716 759-5600
10000 Wehrle Dr Clarence (14031) *(G-3696)*
Precious Plate Inc ... 716 283-0690
2124 Liberty Dr Niagara Falls (14304) *(G-12880)*
Precipart Corporation ... 631 694-3100
120 Finn Ct Ste 2 Farmingdale (11735) *(G-5095)*
Precise Optics, Deer Park *Also called Photo Medic Equipment Inc (G-4213)*
Precise Punch Corporation ... 716 625-8000
6550 Campbell Blvd Lockport (14094) *(G-7641)*
Precise Tool & Mfg Inc ... 585 247-0700
9 Coldwater Cres Rochester (14624) *(G-14613)*
Preciseled Inc ... 516 418-5337
52 Railroad Ave Valley Stream (11580) *(G-16443)*
Precision Abrasives Corp ... 716 826-5833
3176 Abbott Rd Orchard Park (14127) *(G-13316)*
Precision Arms Inc ... 845 225-1130
421 Route 52 Carmel (10512) *(G-3432)*
Precision Assembly Tech Inc ... 631 699-9400
160 Wilbur Pl Ste 500 Bohemia (11716) *(G-1115)*
Precision Built Tops LLC ... 607 336-5417
89 Borden Ave Norwich (13815) *(G-13053)*
Precision Charts Inc ... 631 244-8295
130 Wilbur Pl Dept Pc Bohemia (11716) *(G-1116)*
Precision Cnc ... 631 847-3999
71 E Jefryn Blvd Deer Park (11729) *(G-4216)*

ALPHABETIC

Precision Co., Menands *Also called McAllisters Precision Wldg Inc* ***(G-8406)***
Precision Cosmetics Mfg Co 914 667-1200
519 S 5th Ave Ste 6 Mount Vernon (10550) ***(G-8762)***
Precision Custom Coatings LLC 212 868-5770
234 W 39th St New York (10018) ***(G-11717)***
Precision Dental Cabinets Inc (PA) 631 543-3870
900 W Jericho Tpke Smithtown (11787) ***(G-15518)***
Precision Dental Ceramics of B 716 681-4133
5204 Genesee St Bowmansville (14026) ***(G-1168)***
Precision Design Systems Inc 585 426-4500
1645 Lyell Ave Ste 136 Rochester (14606) ***(G-14614)***
Precision Diamond Cutters Inc 212 719-4438
2 W 46th St Ste 1007 New York (10036) ***(G-11718)***
Precision Diecutting Inc 315 776-8465
1381 Spring Lake Rd Port Byron (13140) ***(G-13764)***
Precision Disc Grinding Corp 516 747-5450
255 E 2nd St Mineola (11501) ***(G-8564)***
Precision Eforming LLC 607 753-7730
839 State Route 13 Ste 1 Cortland (13045) ***(G-4063)***
Precision Elctro Mnrl Pmco Inc 716 284-2484
150 Portage Rd Niagara Falls (14303) ***(G-12881)***
Precision Electronics Inc 631 842-4900
1 Di Tomas Ct Copiague (11726) ***(G-3943)***
Precision Engraving Company, Amityville *Also called Precision Signscom Inc* ***(G-323)***
Precision Envelope Co Inc 631 694-3990
110 Schmitt Blvd 7a Farmingdale (11735) ***(G-5096)***
Precision Extrusion Inc 518 792-1199
12 Glens Fls Technical Pa Glens Falls (12801) ***(G-5711)***
Precision Fabrication LLC 585 591-3449
40 S Pearl St Attica (14011) ***(G-473)***
Precision Filters Inc (PA) 607 277-3550
240 Cherry St Ithaca (14850) ***(G-6907)***
Precision Furniture, Bronx *Also called Precision Orna Ir Works Inc* ***(G-1433)***
Precision Gear Incorporated 718 321-7200
11207 14th Ave College Point (11356) ***(G-3827)***
Precision Grinding & Mfg Corp (PA) 585 458-4300
1305 Emerson St Rochester (14606) ***(G-14615)***
Precision International Co Inc 212 268-9090
201 E 28th St 9n New York (10016) ***(G-11719)***
Precision Label Corporation 631 270-4490
175 Marine St Farmingdale (11735) ***(G-5097)***
Precision Laser Technology LLC 585 458-6208
1001 Lexington Ave Ste 4 Rochester (14606) ***(G-14616)***
Precision Locker, Jamestown *Also called Rollform of Jamestown Inc* ***(G-7058)***
Precision Machine Parts, Valatie *Also called Weiss Industries Inc* ***(G-16390)***
Precision Machine Tech LLC 585 467-1840
85 Excel Dr Rochester (14621) ***(G-14617)***
Precision Machining and Mfg 845 647-5380
190 Port Ben Rd Wawarsing (12489) ***(G-16732)***
Precision Magnetics LLC 585 385-9010
770 Linden Ave Rochester (14625) ***(G-14618)***
Precision Mechanisms Corp 516 333-5955
50 Bond St Westbury (11590) ***(G-17049)***
Precision Metals Corp 631 586-5032
221 Skip Ln Bay Shore (11706) ***(G-723)***
Precision Mtal Fabricators Inc 718 832-9805
236 39th St Brooklyn (11232) ***(G-2449)***
Precision Orna Ir Works Inc 718 379-5200
1838 Adee Ave Bronx (10469) ***(G-1433)***
Precision Packaging Pdts Inc 585 638-8200
88 Nesbitt Dr Holley (14470) ***(G-6517)***
Precision Pharma Services Inc 631 752-7314
155 Duryea Rd Melville (11747) ***(G-8378)***
Precision Photo-Fab Inc 716 821-9393
4020 Jeffrey Blvd Buffalo (14219) ***(G-3158)***
Precision Plus Vacuum Parts 716 297-2039
6416 Inducon Dr W Sanborn (14132) ***(G-15152)***
Precision Polish LLC 315 894-3792
144 Adams St Frankfort (13340) ***(G-5366)***
Precision Process Inc (PA) 716 731-1587
2111 Liberty Dr Niagara Falls (14304) ***(G-12882)***
Precision Product Inc 718 852-7127
18 Steuben St Brooklyn (11205) ***(G-2450)***
Precision Ready Mix Inc 718 658-5600
14707 Liberty Ave Jamaica (11435) ***(G-6977)***
Precision Signscom Inc 631 842-5060
243 Dixon Ave Amityville (11701) ***(G-323)***
Precision Spclty Fbrctions LLC 716 824-2108
51 N Gates Ave Buffalo (14218) ***(G-3159)***
Precision Systems Mfg Inc 315 451-3480
4855 Executive Dr Liverpool (13088) ***(G-7570)***
Precision Techniques Inc 718 991-1440
25 Holt Dr Stony Point (10980) ***(G-15798)***
Precision Tl Die & Stamping Co 516 561-0041
68 Franklin Ave Valley Stream (11580) ***(G-16444)***
Precision Tool and Mfg 518 678-3130
314 Pennsylvania Ave Palenville (12463) ***(G-13424)***
Precision Valve & Automtn Inc (PA) 518 371-2684
1 Mustang Dr Ste 3 Cohoes (12047) ***(G-3779)***
Precisionmatics Co Inc 315 822-6324
1 Helmer Ave West Winfield (13491) ***(G-16987)***
Preebro Printing 718 633-7300
5319 Fort Hamilton Pkwy Brooklyn (11219) ***(G-2451)***
Prefab Construction Inc 631 821-9613
16 Jackson Ave Sound Beach (11789) ***(G-15535)***
Prefered Directors Share, Amityville *Also called Casual Home Worldwide Inc* ***(G-279)***
Preferred Wholesale, New York *Also called R-S Restaurant Eqp Mfg Corp* ***(G-11811)***
Pregis LLC 518 743-3100
18 Peck Ave Glens Falls (12801) ***(G-5712)***
Prejean Winery Inc 315 536-7524
2634 State Route 14 Penn Yan (14527) ***(G-13539)***
Preload Concrete Structures 631 231-8100
60 Commerce Dr Hauppauge (11788) ***(G-6196)***
Premco Inc 914 636-7095
11 Beechwood Ave New Rochelle (10801) ***(G-8966)***
Premier, Richmond Hill *Also called 131-11 Atlantic RE Inc* ***(G-14077)***
Premier Brands of America Inc (PA) 914 667-6200
31 South St Ste 2s Mount Vernon (10550) ***(G-8763)***
Premier Brands of America Inc 718 325-3000
120 Pearl St Mount Vernon (10550) ***(G-8764)***
Premier Cabinet Wholesalers, Rochester *Also called Rochester Countertop Inc* ***(G-14662)***
Premier Care Industries, Hauppauge *Also called Precare Corp* ***(G-6194)***
Premier Group NY 212 229-1200
18 W 23rd St Fl 3 New York (10010) ***(G-11720)***
Premier Hardwood Products Inc 315 492-1786
4800 Solvay Rd Jamesville (13078) ***(G-7084)***
Premier Ingridients Inc 516 641-6763
3 Johnstone Rd Great Neck (11021) ***(G-5849)***
Premier Ink Systems Inc 845 782-5802
2 Commerce Dr S Harriman (10926) ***(G-5995)***
Premier Knits Ltd 718 323-8264
9735 133rd Ave Ozone Park (11417) ***(G-13410)***
Premier Machining Tech Inc 716 608-1311
2100 Old Union Rd Buffalo (14227) ***(G-3160)***
Premier Metals Group 585 436-4020
11 Cairn St Rochester (14611) ***(G-14619)***
Premier Packaging Corporation 585 924-8460
6 Framark Dr Victor (14564) ***(G-16520)***
Premier Paint Roller Co LLC 718 441-7700
13111 Atlantic Ave Richmond Hill (11418) ***(G-14090)***
Premier Sign Systems LLC 585 235-0390
10 Excel Dr Rochester (14621) ***(G-14620)***
Premier Skirting Products Inc 516 239-6581
241 Mill St Lawrence (11559) ***(G-7422)***
Premier Skrting Tblecloths Too, Lawrence *Also called Premier Skirting Products Inc* ***(G-7422)***
Premier Store Fixtures, Hauppauge *Also called Fixtures 2000 Inc* ***(G-6100)***
Premier Supplies, New York *Also called Print By Premier LLC* ***(G-11736)***
Premier Systems LLC 631 587-9700
41 John St Ste 6 Babylon (11702) ***(G-550)***
Premier Woodcraft Ltd 610 383-6624
277 Martine Ave 214 White Plains (10601) ***(G-17188)***
Premier Woodworking Inc 631 236-4100
400 Oser Ave Hauppauge (11788) ***(G-6197)***
Premiere Living Products LLC 631 873-4337
22 Branwood Dr Dix Hills (11746) ***(G-4318)***
Premium 5 Kids LLC 212 563-4999
31 W 34th St New York (10001) ***(G-11721)***
Premium Assure Inc 605 252-9999
1726 Mcdonald Ave Ste 201 Brooklyn (11230) ***(G-2452)***
Premium Bldg Components Inc 518 885-0194
831 Rt 67 Bldg 46 Ballston Spa (12020) ***(G-606)***
Premium Mulch & Materials Inc 631 320-3666
482 Mill Rd Coram (11727) ***(G-3972)***
Premium Ocean LLC 917 231-1061
1271 Ryawa Ave Bronx (10474) ***(G-1434)***
Premium Processing Corp 631 232-1105
30 Kittiwake Ln Babylon (11702) ***(G-551)***
Premium Shirts Lerma Mexico, New York *Also called American T Shirts Inc* ***(G-9180)***
Premium Sweets USA Inc 718 739-6000
16803 Hillside Ave Jamaica (11432) ***(G-6978)***
Premium Wine Group LLC 631 298-1900
35 Cox Neck Rd Mattituck (11952) ***(G-8241)***
Premium Woodworking LLC 631 485-3133
108 Lamar St West Babylon (11704) ***(G-16849)***
Prepac Designs Inc 914 524-7800
25 Abner Pl Yonkers (10704) ***(G-17498)***
Preparatory Magazine Group 718 761-4800
1200 South Ave Ste 202 Staten Island (10314) ***(G-15745)***
Preplay Inc 917 297-7428
33 W 17th St Ste 901 New York (10011) ***(G-11722)***
Presbrey- Leland Memorials, Valhalla *Also called Presbrey-Leland Inc* ***(G-16397)***
Presbrey-Leland Inc 914 949-2264
250 Lakeview Ave Valhalla (10595) ***(G-16397)***
Prescribing Reference Inc 646 638-6000
275 7th Ave Fl 10 New York (10001) ***(G-11723)***
Preserving Chrstn Publications (PA) 315 942-6617
12614 State Route 46 Boonville (13309) ***(G-1165)***
President Cont Group II LLC 845 516-1600
290 Ballard Rd Middletown (10941) ***(G-8492)***
Presray Corporation 845 373-9300
32 Nelson Hill Rd Wassaic (12592) ***(G-16623)***
Press Air, Mamaroneck *Also called Bassin Technical Sales Co* ***(G-8056)***

Press Express....914 592-3790
400 Executive Blvd # 146 Elmsford (10523) *(G-4781)*
Press of Fremont Payne Inc....212 966-6570
55 Broad St Frnt 3 New York (10004) *(G-11724)*
Press of Manorville & Moriches, Southampton *Also called Southampton Town Newspapers (G-15576)*
Press Room New York Division, New York *Also called Circle Press Inc (G-9674)*
Presser Kosher Baking Corp....718 375-5088
1720 Avenue M Brooklyn (11230) *(G-2453)*
Presstek Printing LLC....585 467-8140
521 E Ridge Rd Rochester (14621) *(G-14621)*
Presstek Printing LLC....585 266-2770
20 Balfour Dr Rochester (14621) *(G-14622)*
Pressure Washer Sales, Holland Patent *Also called Custom Klean Corp (G-6513)*
Pressure Washing Services Inc....607 286-7458
26 Maple St Milford (13807) *(G-8509)*
Prestel Publishing LLC....212 995-2720
900 Broadway Ste 603 New York (10003) *(G-11725)*
Presti Ready Mix Concrete Inc....516 378-6006
210 E Merrick Rd Freeport (11520) *(G-5430)*
Presti Stone and Mason, Freeport *Also called Presti Ready Mix Concrete Inc (G-5430)*
Prestige Box Corporation (PA)....516 773-3115
115 Cuttermill Rd Great Neck (11021) *(G-5850)*
Prestige Brands Intl LLC....914 524-6810
660 White Plains Rd Tarrytown (10591) *(G-16126)*
Prestige Envelope & Lithograph....631 521-7043
1745 Merrick Ave Ste 2 Merrick (11566) *(G-8426)*
Prestige Global NY Sls Corp....212 776-4322
102 W 38th St Fl 8 New York (10018) *(G-11726)*
Prestige Hangers Str Fixs Corp....718 522-6777
1026 55th St Brooklyn (11219) *(G-2454)*
Prestige Litho & Graphics, Merrick *Also called Prestige Envelope & Lithograph (G-8426)*
Prestige Printing Company, Brooklyn *Also called 6727 11th Ave Corp (G-1520)*
Prestigeline Inc....631 273-3636
5 Inez Dr Bay Shore (11706) *(G-724)*
Preston Glass Industries Inc....718 997-8888
10420 Queens Blvd Apt 17a Forest Hills (11375) *(G-5335)*
Prestone Press LLC....347 468-7900
4750 30th St Long Island City (11101) *(G-7875)*
Prestone Printing Company, Long Island City *Also called Prestone Press LLC (G-7875)*
Pretlist....646 368-1849
545 W 110th St Apt 2b New York (10025) *(G-11727)*
Prevost Car US Inc....518 957-2052
260 Banker Rd Plattsburgh (12901) *(G-13717)*
Prg Integrated Solutions, Armonk *Also called Production Resource Group LLC (G-416)*
Price Chopper Operating Co....518 562-3565
19 Centre Dr Plattsburgh (12901) *(G-13718)*
Price Chopper Operating Co....518 456-5115
2080 Western Ave Ste 160 Guilderland (12084) *(G-5925)*
Price Chopper Pharmacy, Catskill *Also called Golub Corporation (G-3456)*
Price Chopper Pharmacy, Oneida *Also called Golub Corporation (G-13177)*
Price Chopper Pharmacy, Norwich *Also called Golub Corporation (G-13047)*
Price Chopper Pharmacy, Hudson *Also called Golub Corporation (G-6645)*
Price Chopper Pharmacy, Middletown *Also called Golub Corporation (G-8477)*
Price Chopper Pharmacy 184, Malta *Also called Golub Corporation (G-8052)*
Price Chopper Pharmacy 234, Binghamton *Also called Golub Corporation (G-914)*
Pricet Printing....315 655-0369
3852 Charles Rd Cazenovia (13035) *(G-3478)*
Pricing Engine Inc....917 549-3289
175 Varick St Fl 4 New York (10014) *(G-11728)*
Pride & Joys Inc....212 594-9820
1400 Broadway Rm 503 New York (10018) *(G-11729)*
Pride Lines Ltd....631 225-0033
651 W Hoffman Ave Lindenhurst (11757) *(G-7503)*
Prim Hall Enterprises Inc....518 561-7408
11 Spellman Rd Plattsburgh (12901) *(G-13719)*
Prima Asphalt and Concrete....631 289-3223
615 Furrows Rd Holtsville (11742) *(G-6533)*
Primary Plastics Inc....607 785-4865
315 Scarborough Dr Endwell (13760) *(G-4843)*
Primary Wave Publishing LLC....212 661-6990
116 E 16th St Fl 9 New York (10003) *(G-11730)*
Prime Components, Deer Park *Also called Prime Electronic Components (G-4217)*
Prime Electric Motors Inc....718 784-1124
4850 33rd St Long Island City (11101) *(G-7876)*
Prime Electronic Components....631 254-0101
150 W Industry Ct Deer Park (11729) *(G-4217)*
Prime Feather Industries Ltd....718 326-8701
7-11 Suffern Pl Suffern (10901) *(G-15818)*
Prime Food Processing Corp....718 963-2323
300 Vandervoort Ave Brooklyn (11211) *(G-2455)*
Prime Garments Inc....212 354-7294
1407 Broadway Rm 1200 New York (10018) *(G-11731)*
Prime Materials Recovery Inc....315 697-5251
51 Madison Blvd Canastota (13032) *(G-3397)*
Prime Pack LLC....732 253-7734
303 5th Ave Rm 1007 New York (10016) *(G-11732)*
Prime Pharmaceutical, New York *Also called Prime Pack LLC (G-11732)*
Prime Research Solutions LLC....917 836-7941
7328 136th St Flushing (11367) *(G-5291)*
Prime Time, Garden City *Also called Richner Communications Inc (G-5543)*
Prime Tool & Die LLC....607 334-5435
6277 County Road 32 Norwich (13815) *(G-13054)*
Prime Turbine Parts LLC....518 306-7306
85 Railroad Pl Saratoga Springs (12866) *(G-15197)*
Prime View USA Inc....212 730-4905
36 W 44th St Ste 812 New York (10036) *(G-11733)*
Prime Wood Products....518 792-1407
1288 Vaughn Rd Queensbury (12804) *(G-14021)*
Primelite Manufacturing Corp....516 868-4411
407 S Main St Freeport (11520) *(G-5431)*
Primesouth Inc....585 567-4191
11537 Route 19 Fillmore (14735) *(G-5184)*
Primo Coat Corp....718 349-2070
4315 Queens St Fl 3 Long Island City (11101) *(G-7877)*
Primo Frozen Desserts Inc....718 252-2312
1633 Utica Ave Brooklyn (11234) *(G-2456)*
Primo Plastics Inc....718 349-1000
162 Russell St Brooklyn (11222) *(G-2457)*
Primoplast Inc....631 750-0680
1555 Ocean Ave Ste E Bohemia (11716) *(G-1117)*
Prince Minerals, New York *Also called American Minerals Inc (G-9176)*
Prince of The Sea Ltd....516 333-6344
28 Urban Ave Westbury (11590) *(G-17050)*
Prince Rubber & Plas Co Inc (PA)....225 272-1653
137 Arthur St Buffalo (14207) *(G-3161)*
Prince Seating Corp....718 363-2300
1355 Atlantic Ave Brooklyn (11216) *(G-2458)*
Princess Marcella Borghese, New York *Also called Borghese Inc (G-9491)*
Princess Music Publishing Co....212 586-0240
1650 Broadway Ste 701 New York (10019) *(G-11734)*
Princetel Inc....914 579-2410
200 Saw Mill River Rd Hawthorne (10532) *(G-6277)*
Princeton Label & Packaging....609 490-0800
217 River Ave Patchogue (11772) *(G-13458)*
Princeton Sciences....845 368-1214
386 Route 59 Ste 402 Airmont (10952) *(G-16)*
Princeton Upholstery Co Inc (PA)....845 343-2196
51 Railroad Ave Middletown (10940) *(G-8493)*
Principia Partners LLC....212 480-2270
140 Broadway Fl 46 New York (10005) *(G-11735)*
Princton Archtctural Press LLC (HQ)....518 671-6100
202 Warren St Hudson (12534) *(G-6662)*
Print & Graphics Group....518 371-4649
12 Fire Rd Clifton Park (12065) *(G-3730)*
Print Better Inc....347 348-1841
5939 Myrtle Ave Ridgewood (11385) *(G-14131)*
Print By Premier LLC....212 947-1365
212 W 35th St Fl 2 New York (10001) *(G-11736)*
Print Center Inc....718 643-9559
3 Harbor Rd Ste 21 Cold Spring Harbor (11724) *(G-3795)*
Print City Corp....212 487-9778
165 W 29th St New York (10001) *(G-11737)*
Print Cottage LLC....516 369-1749
1138 Lakeshore Dr Massapequa Park (11762) *(G-8222)*
Print House Inc....718 443-7500
538 Johnson Ave Brooklyn (11237) *(G-2459)*
Print It Here....516 308-7785
185 Jerusalem Ave Massapequa (11758) *(G-8213)*
Print It Inc....845 371-2227
59 Route 59 Ste 141 Monsey (10952) *(G-8613)*
Print Mall....718 437-7700
4122 16th Ave Brooklyn (11204) *(G-2460)*
Print Management Group Inc....212 213-1555
33 E 33rd St Fl 3 New York (10016) *(G-11738)*
Print Market Inc....631 940-8181
66 E Jefryn Blvd Ste 1 Deer Park (11729) *(G-4218)*
Print Media Inc....212 563-4040
350 7th Ave Fl 12 New York (10001) *(G-11739)*
Print On Demand Initiative Inc....585 239-6044
1240 Jefferson Rd Rochester (14623) *(G-14623)*
Print Pack Inc (HQ)....404 460-7000
70 Schmitt Blvd Farmingdale (11735) *(G-5098)*
Print Seforim Bzul Inc....718 679-1011
8 Lynch St Apt 6r Brooklyn (11206) *(G-2461)*
Print Shop....607 734-4937
3153 Lake Rd Horseheads (14845) *(G-6617)*
Print Shoppe....315 792-9585
311 Turner St Ste 310 Utica (13501) *(G-16380)*
Print Solutions Plus Inc....315 234-3801
7325 Oswego Rd Liverpool (13090) *(G-7571)*
Print-O-Rama Copy Center, Merrick *Also called Leader Printing Inc (G-8422)*
Printcorp Inc....631 696-0641
2050 Ocean Ave Ronkonkoma (11779) *(G-14995)*
Printech Business Systems Inc....212 290-2542
519 8th Ave Fl 3 New York (10018) *(G-11740)*
Printed Deals, Rochester *Also called Valassis Communications Inc (G-14778)*
Printed Image....716 821-1880
1906 Clinton St Buffalo (14206) *(G-3162)*
Printer Components Inc (HQ)....585 924-5190
100 Photikon Dr Ste 2 Fairport (14450) *(G-4877)*
Printers 3, Hauppauge *Also called Avm Printing Inc (G-6049)*

ALPHABETIC

(PA)=Parent Co (HQ)=Headquarters (DH)=Div Headquarters
2018 Harris
New York Manufacturers Directory
1037

Printers 3 Inc 631 351-1331
  43 Corporate Dr Ste 2 Hauppauge (11788) *(G-6198)*
Printery 516 922-3250
  43 W Main St Oyster Bay (11771) *(G-13399)*
Printery 315 253-7403
  55 Arterial W Auburn (13021) *(G-511)*
Printex Packaging Corporation 631 234-4300
  555 Raymond Dr Islandia (11749) *(G-6840)*
Printfacility Inc 212 349-4009
  225 Broadway Fl 3 New York (10007) *(G-11741)*
Printhouse, The, Brooklyn *Also called Print House Inc (G-2459)*
Printing, Brooklyn *Also called Reliable Press II Inc (G-2508)*
Printing Emporium, Merrick *Also called D G M Graphics Inc (G-8416)*
Printing Express, Jamaica *Also called Hillside Printing Inc (G-6955)*
Printing Factory LLC 718 451-0500
  1940 Utica Ave Brooklyn (11234) *(G-2462)*
Printing House of W S Miller, Oyster Bay *Also called Printery (G-13399)*
Printing Max New York Inc 718 692-1400
  2282 Flatbush Ave Brooklyn (11234) *(G-2463)*
Printing Plus, Rochester *Also called Ozipko Enterprises Inc (G-14581)*
Printing Prep Inc 716 852-5071
  707 Washington St Buffalo (14203) *(G-3163)*
Printing Prmtnl Solutions LLC 315 474-1110
  2320 Milton Ave Ste 5 Syracuse (13209) *(G-16035)*
Printing Promotional Solutions, Syracuse *Also called Printing Prmtnl Solutions LLC (G-16035)*
Printing Resources Inc 518 482-2470
  100 Fuller Rd Ste 1 Albany (12205) *(G-124)*
Printing Sales Group Limited 718 258-8860
  1856 Flatbush Ave Brooklyn (11210) *(G-2464)*
Printing Spectrum Inc 631 689-1010
  12 Research Way Ste 1 East Setauket (11733) *(G-4509)*
Printing X Press Ions 631 242-1992
  5 Dix Cir Dix Hills (11746) *(G-4319)*
Printinghouse Press Ltd 212 719-0990
  10 E 39th St Rm 700 New York (10016) *(G-11742)*
Printout Copy Corp 718 855-4040
  829 Bedford Ave Brooklyn (11205) *(G-2465)*
Printroc Inc 585 461-2556
  620 South Ave Rochester (14620) *(G-14624)*
Printutopia 718 788-1545
  393 Prospect Ave Brooklyn (11215) *(G-2466)*
Printworks Printing & Design 315 433-8587
  5982 E Molloy Rd Syracuse (13211) *(G-16036)*
Printz and Patternz LLC 518 944-6020
  1550 Altamont Ave Schenectady (12303) *(G-15311)*
Printz Pttrnz Scrn-Prnting EMB, Schenectady *Also called Printz and Patternz LLC (G-15311)*
Priority Enterprise, New York *Also called Priority Printing Entps Inc (G-11743)*
Priority Printing Entps Inc 646 285-0684
  315 W 36th St New York (10018) *(G-11743)*
Priscilla Quart Co Firts 516 365-2755
  160 Plandome Rd Fl 2 Manhasset (11030) *(G-8098)*
Prism Solar Technologies Inc (PA) 845 883-4200
  180 South St Highland (12528) *(G-6434)*
Prisma Glass & Mirror Inc 718 366-7191
  1815 Decatur St Ridgewood (11385) *(G-14132)*
Prismatic Dyeing & Finshg Inc 845 561-1800
  40 Wisner Ave Newburgh (12550) *(G-12798)*
Private Lbel Fods Rchester Inc 585 254-9205
  1686 Lyell Ave Rochester (14606) *(G-14625)*
Private Portfolio, New York *Also called Coty US LLC (G-9791)*
Prms Inc 631 851-7945
  45 Ramsey Rd Unit 26 Shirley (11967) *(G-15452)*
Prms Electronic Components, Shirley *Also called Prms Inc (G-15452)*
Pro Drones Usa LLC 718 530-3558
  115 E 57th St Fl 11 New York (10022) *(G-11744)*
Pro Hitter Corp 845 358-8670
  170 S Main St New City (10956) *(G-8836)*
Pro Line Manufacturing Co LLC 973 692-9696
  500 Fashion Ave Fl 16 New York (10018) *(G-11745)*
Pro Metal of NY Corp 516 285-0440
  814 W Merrick Rd Valley Stream (11580) *(G-16445)*
Pro Pack, Eagle Bridge *Also called Professional Packg Svcs Inc (G-4381)*
Pro Printers of Greene County, Catskill *Also called Mark T Westinghouse (G-3459)*
Pro Printing 516 561-9700
  359 Merrick Rd Lynbrook (11563) *(G-7983)*
Pro Publica Inc 212 514-5250
  155 Ave Of The Americas New York (10013) *(G-11746)*
Pro Torque 631 218-8700
  1440 Church St Bohemia (11716) *(G-1118)*
Pro-Gear Co Inc 716 684-3811
  1120 Niagara St Buffalo (14213) *(G-3164)*
Pro-Line Solutions Inc 914 664-0002
  18 Sargent Pl Mount Vernon (10550) *(G-8765)*
Pro-Print, New York *Also called Kolcorp Industries Ltd (G-10909)*
Pro-TEC V I P, Gloversville *Also called Protech (llc) (G-5734)*
Pro-Tech Sno Pusher, Rochester *Also called Pro-Tech Wldg Fabrication Inc (G-14626)*
Pro-Tech Wldg Fabrication Inc 585 436-9755
  711 West Ave Rochester (14611) *(G-14626)*
Pro-Teck Coating Inc 716 537-2619
  7785 Olean Rd Holland (14080) *(G-6510)*
Pro-Tek Packaging Group, Ronkonkoma *Also called Oaklee International Inc (G-14983)*
Pro-Value Distribution Inc 585 783-1461
  1547 Lyell Ave Ste 3 Rochester (14606) *(G-14627)*
Proactive Medical Products LLC 845 205-6004
  270 Washington St Mount Vernon (10553) *(G-8766)*
Procab, Woodridge *Also called Professional Cab Detailing Co (G-17333)*
Procomponents Inc (PA) 516 683-0909
  900 Merchants Concourse Westbury (11590) *(G-17051)*
Procter & Gamble Company 646 885-4201
  120 W 45th St Fl 3 New York (10036) *(G-11747)*
Product Development Intl LLC 212 279-6170
  215 W 40th St Fl 8 New York (10018) *(G-11748)*
Product Integration & Mfg Inc 585 436-6260
  55 Fessenden St Rochester (14611) *(G-14628)*
Product Station Inc 516 942-4220
  366 N Broadway Ste 410 Jericho (11753) *(G-7114)*
Productand Design Inc 718 858-2440
  63 Flushing Ave Unit 322 Brooklyn (11205) *(G-2467)*
Production Metal Cutting Inc 585 458-7136
  1 Curlew St Rochester (14606) *(G-14629)*
Production Milling Company 914 666-0792
  364 Adams St Ste 5 Bedford Hills (10507) *(G-802)*
Production Resource Group LLC (PA) 877 774-7088
  200 Business Park Dr # 109 Armonk (10504) *(G-416)*
Production Resource Group LLC 845 567-5700
  539 Temple Hill Rd New Windsor (12553) *(G-8994)*
Producto Corporation 716 484-7131
  2980 Turner Rd Jamestown (14701) *(G-7057)*
Producto Electric Corp 845 359-4900
  11 Kings Hwy Orangeburg (10962) *(G-13265)*
Products Superb Inc 315 923-7057
  231 Clyde Marengo Rd Clyde (14433) *(G-3756)*
Professional Access LLC 212 432-2844
  88 Old Farm Rd N Chappaqua (10514) *(G-3582)*
Professional Buty Holdings Inc 631 787-8576
  150 Motor Pkwy Ste 401 Hauppauge (11788) *(G-6199)*
Professional Cab Detailing Co 845 436-7282
  Navograrsky Rd Woodridge (12789) *(G-17333)*
Professional Disposables Inc 845 365-1700
  2 Nice Pak Park Orangeburg (10962) *(G-13266)*
Professional Health Imaging, Wantagh *Also called R M F Health Management L L C (G-16583)*
Professional Manufacturers 631 586-2440
  475 Brook Ave Deer Park (11729) *(G-4219)*
Professional Medical Devices 914 835-0614
  10 Century Trl Harrison (10528) *(G-6008)*
Professional Packg Svcs Inc 518 677-5100
  62 Owlkill Rd Eagle Bridge (12057) *(G-4381)*
Professional Pavers Corp 718 784-7853
  6605 Woodhaven Blvd Bsmt Rego Park (11374) *(G-14050)*
Professional Remodelers Inc 516 565-9300
  340 Hempstead Ave Unit A West Hempstead (11552) *(G-16894)*
Professional Solutions Print 631 231-9300
  125 Wireless Blvd Ste E Hauppauge (11788) *(G-6200)*
Professional Tape Corporation 516 656-5519
  100 Pratt Oval Glen Cove (11542) *(G-5638)*
Professional Technologies, Rome *Also called Professional Technology Inc (G-14858)*
Professional Technology Inc 315 337-4156
  5433 Lowell Rd Rome (13440) *(G-14858)*
Profesnal Spt Pblications Inc (PA) 212 697-1460
  519 8th Ave New York (10018) *(G-11749)*
Profesnal Spt Pblications Inc 516 327-9500
  570 Elmont Rd Elmont (11003) *(G-4736)*
Profesnal Spt Pblications Inc 516 327-9500
  570 Elmont Rd Ste 202 Elmont (11003) *(G-4737)*
Proficient Surgical Eqp Inc 516 487-1175
  99 Seaview Blvd Ste 1c Port Washington (11050) *(G-13874)*
Profile, New York *Also called Eternal Fortune Fashion LLC (G-10131)*
Profile Printing & Graphics (PA) 631 273-2727
  275 Marcus Blvd Hauppauge (11788) *(G-6201)*
Profits Direct Inc 631 851-4083
  200 Trade Zone Dr Unit 2 Ronkonkoma (11779) *(G-14996)*
Profoot Inc 718 965-8600
  74 20th St Fl 2 Brooklyn (11232) *(G-2468)*
Proformance Foods Inc 703 869-3413
  44 Dobbin St Fl 1 Brooklyn (11222) *(G-2469)*
Progenics Pharmaceuticals Inc (PA) 646 975-2500
  1 World Trade Ctr Fl 47 New York (10007) *(G-11750)*
Proginet Corporation 516 535-3600
  200 Garden Cy Plz Ste 220 Garden City (11530) *(G-5541)*
PROGRESS INDUSTRIES SALES, Utica *Also called Fourteen Arnold Ave Corp (G-16356)*
Progressive Color Graphics 212 292-8787
  122 Station Rd Great Neck (11023) *(G-5851)*
Progressive Fibre Products Co 212 566-2720
  160 Broadway Rm 1105 New York (10038) *(G-11751)*
Progressive Graphics & Prtg 315 331-3635
  1171 E Union St Newark (14513) *(G-12762)*
Progressive Hardware Co Inc 631 445-1826
  63 Brightside Ave East Northport (11731) *(G-4462)*

Progressive Mch & Design LLC (PA) 585 924-5250
727 Rowley Rd Victor (14564) *(G-16521)*
Progressive Orthotics Ltd (PA) 631 732-5556
280 Middle Country Rd G Selden (11784) *(G-15375)*
Progressive Orthotics Ltd 631 447-3860
285 Sills Rd Bldg 8c East Patchogue (11772) *(G-4468)*
Progressive Products LLC 914 417-6022
4 International Dr # 224 Rye Brook (10573) *(G-15100)*
Progressive Tool Company Inc 607 748-8294
3221 Lawndale St Endwell (13760) *(G-4844)*
Progressus Company Inc 516 255-0245
100 Merrick Rd Ste 510w Rockville Centre (11570) *(G-14825)*
Prohibition Distillery LLC 917 685-8989
10 Union St Roscoe (12776) *(G-15034)*
Project Energy Savers LLC 718 596-4231
68 Jay St Ste 516 Brooklyn (11201) *(G-2470)*
Project Visual, Islandia *Also called Zahk Sales Inc (G-6844)*
Projector Lamp Services LLC 631 244-0051
120 Wilbur Pl Ste C Bohemia (11716) *(G-1119)*
Prokosch and Sonn Sheet Metal 845 562-4211
772 South St Newburgh (12550) *(G-12799)*
Prolink Industries Inc 212 354-5690
1407 Broadway Rm 3605 New York (10018) *(G-11752)*
Prolocksusa, Hauppauge *Also called Olan Laboratories Inc (G-6177)*
Promats Athletics LLC (PA) 607 746-8911
41155 State Highway 10 Delhi (13753) *(G-4266)*
Prometheus Books Inc 716 691-2158
59 John Glenn Dr Amherst (14228) *(G-259)*
Prometheus International Inc 718 472-0700
4502 11th St Long Island City (11101) *(G-7878)*
Promolines, New York *Also called Maxworld Inc (G-11213)*
Promosuite, New York *Also called Broadcast Manager Inc (G-9517)*
Promotional Development Inc 718 485-8550
909 Remsen Ave Brooklyn (11236) *(G-2471)*
Promotional Sales Books LLC 212 675-0364
30 W 26th St Frnt New York (10010) *(G-11753)*
Prompt Bindery Co Inc 212 675-5181
350 W 38th St New York (10018) *(G-11754)*
Prompt Printing Inc 631 454-6524
160 Rome St Farmingdale (11735) *(G-5099)*
Promptus Electronic Hdwr Inc 914 699-4700
520 Homestead Ave Mount Vernon (10550) *(G-8767)*
Pronovias USA Inc 212 897-6393
14 E 52nd St New York (10022) *(G-11755)*
Pronto Jewelry Inc 212 719-9455
23 W 47th St New York (10036) *(G-11756)*
Pronto Printer 914 737-0800
2085 E Main St Ste 3 Cortlandt Manor (10567) *(G-4079)*
Pronto Tool & Die Co Inc 631 981-8920
50 Remington Blvd Ronkonkoma (11779) *(G-14997)*
Proof 7 Ltd 212 680-1843
121 Varick St Rm 301 New York (10013) *(G-11757)*
Proof Industries Inc 631 694-7663
125 Rome St Farmingdale (11735) *(G-5100)*
Proof Magazine, New York *Also called Rough Draft Publishing LLC (G-11940)*
Propak Inc 518 677-5100
70 Owlkill Rd Eagle Bridge (12057) *(G-4382)*
Proper Chemical Ltd 631 420-8000
280 Smith St Farmingdale (11735) *(G-5101)*
Proper Cloth LLC 646 964-4221
495 Broadway Fl 6 New York (10012) *(G-11758)*
Props Displays & Interiors 212 620-3840
132 W 18th St New York (10011) *(G-11759)*
Props For Today, Long Island City *Also called Interiors-Pft Inc (G-7795)*
Prospect News 212 374-2800
6 Maiden Ln Fl 9 New York (10038) *(G-11760)*
Prospector Network 212 601-2781
350 5th Ave Fl 59 New York (10118) *(G-11761)*
Prosthetic Rehabilitation Ctr (PA) 845 565-8255
2 Winding Ln Newburgh (12550) *(G-12800)*
Prosthetics By Nelson Inc (PA) 716 894-6666
2959 Genesee St Cheektowaga (14225) *(G-3614)*
Prosthodontic & Implant Den 212 319-6363
693 5th Ave New York (10022) *(G-11762)*
Protec Friction Supply, Mount Kisco *Also called Rpb Distributors LLC (G-8687)*
Protech (llc) 518 725-7785
11 Cayadutta St Gloversville (12078) *(G-5734)*
Protective Industries Inc (HQ) 716 876-9951
2150 Elmwood Ave Buffalo (14207) *(G-3165)*
Protective Industries Inc 716 876-9855
2150 Elmwood Ave Buffalo (14207) *(G-3166)*
Protective Industries Inc 716 876-9951
2510 Elmwood Ave Buffalo (14217) *(G-3167)*
Protective Lining Corp 718 854-3838
601 39th St Brooklyn (11232) *(G-2472)*
Protective Power Systms & Cntr 845 773-9016
259 N Grand Ave Poughkeepsie (12603) *(G-13944)*
Protege, Brooklyn *Also called Schwartz Textile Converting Co (G-2562)*
Protex International Corp 631 563-4250
366 Central Ave Bohemia (11716) *(G-1120)*
Proto Machine Inc 631 392-1159
60 Corbin Ave Ste D Bay Shore (11706) *(G-725)*
Protocase Incorporated 866 849-3911
210 S 8th St Lewiston (14092) *(G-7456)*
Protofast Holding Corp 631 753-2549
182 N Oak St Copiague (11726) *(G-3944)*
Prototype Manufacturing Corp 716 695-1700
836 Wurlitzer Dr North Tonawanda (14120) *(G-13005)*
Provident Fuel Inc 516 224-4427
4 Stillwell Ln Woodbury (11797) *(G-17316)*
Provisionaire & Co LLC 646 681-8600
630 Flushing Ave Fl 4 Brooklyn (11206) *(G-2473)*
PRSA, New York *Also called Public Relations Soc Amer Inc (G-11767)*
Prweek/Prescribing Reference, New York *Also called Haymarket Media Inc (G-10475)*
Pry Care Products, Mount Vernon *Also called Pro-Line Solutions Inc (G-8765)*
Prz Technologies Inc 716 683-1300
5490 Broadway St Lancaster (14086) *(G-7360)*
Ps38 LLC 212 819-1123
545 8th Ave Rm 350 New York (10018) *(G-11763)*
Psb Ltd 585 654-7078
543 Atlantic Ave Ste 2 Rochester (14609) *(G-14630)*
Psg Innovations Inc 917 299-8986
924 Kilmer Ln Valley Stream (11581) *(G-16446)*
PSI Transit Mix Corp 631 382-7930
34 E Main St Smithtown (11787) *(G-15519)*
Pspi, Elmont *Also called Professnal Spt Pblications Inc (G-4737)*
PSR Press Ltd 716 754-2266
415 Ridge St Lewiston (14092) *(G-7457)*
Psychology Today, New York *Also called Sussex Publishers LLC (G-12269)*
Psychonomic Society Inc 512 381-1494
233 Spring St Fl 7 New York (10013) *(G-11764)*
Ptc Precision LLC 607 748-8294
3221 Lawndale St Endwell (13760) *(G-4845)*
Pti-Pacific Inc 212 414-8495
166 5th Ave Fl 4t New York (10010) *(G-11765)*
Pts Financial Technology LLC 844 825-7634
1001 Ave Of The Americas New York (10018) *(G-11766)*
Public Relations Soc Amer Inc (PA) 212 460-1400
120 Wall St Fl 21 New York (10005) *(G-11767)*
Public School, New York *Also called Ps38 LLC (G-11763)*
Public School 212 302-1108
209 W 38th St Rm 501 New York (10018) *(G-11768)*
Publimax Printing Corp 718 366-7133
6615 Traffic Ave Ridgewood (11385) *(G-14133)*
Publishers Clearing House LLC 516 249-4063
265 Spagnoli Rd Ste 1 Melville (11747) *(G-8379)*
Publishers Weekly, New York *Also called Pwxyz LLC (G-11785)*
Publishing Group America Inc 646 658-0550
60 E 42nd St Ste 1146 New York (10165) *(G-11769)*
Publishing Medical Journals, Orchard Park *Also called Impact Journals LLC (G-13298)*
Publishing Synthesis Ltd 212 219-0135
39 Crosby St Apt 2n New York (10013) *(G-11770)*
Puccio Design International 516 248-6426
54 Nassau Blvd Garden City (11530) *(G-5542)*
Puccio European Marble & Onyx, Garden City *Also called Puccio Design International (G-5542)*
Puccio Marble and Onyx, Garden City *Also called European Marble Works Co Inc (G-5517)*
Pugliese Vineyards Inc 631 734-4057
34515 Main Rd Rr 25 Cutchogue (11935) *(G-4099)*
Puig Usa Inc (PA) 212 271-5940
40 E 34th St Fl 19 New York (10016) *(G-11771)*
Pullman Mfg Corporation 585 334-1350
77 Commerce Dr Rochester (14623) *(G-14631)*
Pulmuone Foods Usa Inc 845 365-3300
30 Rockland Park Ave Tappan (10983) *(G-16106)*
Pulsafeeder Inc (HQ) 585 292-8000
2883 Brighton Henrietta T Rochester (14623) *(G-14632)*
Pulsar Technology Systems Inc 718 361-9292
2720 42nd Rd Long Island City (11101) *(G-7879)*
Pulse Insights LLC 888 718-6860
175 Varick St Fl 4 New York (10014) *(G-11772)*
Pulse Plastics Products Inc 718 328-5224
1156 E 165th St Bronx (10459) *(G-1435)*
Pumilia's Pizza Shell, Waterville *Also called F & R Enterprises Inc (G-16701)*
Punch Fashions LLC 646 519-7333
3 W 35th St New York (10001) *(G-11773)*
Pupa Tek Inc 631 664-7817
6 Queens St Huntington (11743) *(G-6710)*
Pupellos Organic Chips Inc 718 710-9154
509 Ockers Dr Oakdale (11769) *(G-13079)*
Pura Fruta LLC 415 279-5727
2323 Borden Ave Long Island City (11101) *(G-7880)*
Pure Acoustics Inc 718 788-4411
18 Fuller Pl Brooklyn (11215) *(G-2474)*
Pure Ghee Inc (PA) 718 224-7399
5701 225th St Flushing (11364) *(G-5292)*
Pure Kemika LLC 718 745-2200
6228 136th St Apt 2 Flushing (11367) *(G-5293)*
Pure Planet Waters LLC 718 676-7900
4809 Avenue N Ste 185 Brooklyn (11234) *(G-2475)*
Pure Trade Us Inc 212 256-1600
347 5th Ave Rm 604 New York (10016) *(G-11774)*

ALPHABETIC

Purebase Networks Inc....646 670-8964
37 Wall St Apt 9a New York (10005) *(G-11775)*
Purely Maple Inc....646 524-7135
159 Bleecker St Apt 2b New York (10012) *(G-11776)*
Purely Maple LLC....203 997-9309
902 Broadway Fl 6 New York (10010) *(G-11777)*
Pureology Research LLC....212 984-4360
565 5th Ave New York (10017) *(G-11778)*
Purespice LLC....617 549-8400
173 Shagbark Ln Hopewell Junction (12533) *(G-6584)*
Purest of America, Saint Albans *Also called Zzz Mattress Manufacturing (G-15112)*
Purine Pharma LLC....315 705-4030
144 E Kingsbridge Rd Mount Vernon (10550) *(G-8768)*
Purinepharma LLC....732 485-1400
5 County Route 42 Massena (13662) *(G-8230)*
Purity Ice Cream Co Inc (PA)....607 272-1545
700 Cascadilla St Ste A Ithaca (14850) *(G-6908)*
Purity Products Inc....516 767-1967
200 Terminal Dr Plainview (11803) *(G-13659)*
Purvi Enterprises Incorporated....347 808-9448
5556 44th St Maspeth (11378) *(G-8196)*
Putnam Cnty News Recorder LLC....845 265-2468
144 Main St Ste 1 Cold Spring (10516) *(G-3789)*
Putnam Press, Mahopac *Also called Gateway Newspapers Inc (G-8026)*
Putnam Rolling Ladder Co Inc (PA)....212 226-5147
32 Howard St New York (10013) *(G-11779)*
Putnam Rolling Ladder Co Inc....718 381-8219
444 Jefferson St Brooklyn (11237) *(G-2476)*
PVA, Cohoes *Also called Precision Valve & Automtn Inc (G-3779)*
Pvc Container Corporation....518 672-7721
370 Stevers Crossing Rd Philmont (12565) *(G-13566)*
Pvh Corp (PA)....212 381-3500
200 Madison Ave Bsmt 1 New York (10016) *(G-11780)*
Pvh Corp....845 561-0233
1073 State Route 94 New Windsor (12553) *(G-8995)*
Pvh Corp....631 254-8200
1358 The Arches Cir Deer Park (11729) *(G-4220)*
Pvh Corp....212 381-3800
200 Madison Ave Bsmt 1 New York (10016) *(G-11781)*
Pvh Corp....212 502-6300
404 5th Ave Fl 4 New York (10018) *(G-11782)*
Pvh Corp....212 719-2600
205 W 39th St Fl 4 New York (10018) *(G-11783)*
Pvh Europe, New York *Also called Phillips-Van Heusen Europe (G-11668)*
Pvi Solar Inc....212 280-2100
599 11th Ave Bby New York (10036) *(G-11784)*
PVS Chemical Solutions, Buffalo *Also called PVS Technologies Inc (G-3169)*
PVS Chemical Solutions Inc....716 825-5762
55 Lee St Buffalo (14210) *(G-3168)*
PVS Technologies Inc....716 825-5762
55 Lee St Buffalo (14210) *(G-3169)*
Pwxyz LLC....212 377-5500
71 W 23rd St Ste 1608 New York (10010) *(G-11785)*
Pylantis New York LLC....310 429-5911
102 E Cortland St Groton (13073) *(G-5923)*
Pyrotechnique By Grucci Inc (PA)....540 639-8800
20 Pinehurst Dr Bellport (11713) *(G-837)*
Pyrotek Incorporated....607 756-3050
641 State Route 13 Cortland (13045) *(G-4064)*
Pyrotek Incorporated....716 731-3221
2040 Cory Dr Sanborn (14132) *(G-15153)*
Pyx Enterprise, Brooklyn *Also called Pyx Inc (G-2477)*
Pyx Inc....718 469-4253
143 E 29th St Brooklyn (11226) *(G-2477)*
Q Communications Inc....212 594-6520
247 W 35th St Rm 1200 New York (10001) *(G-11786)*
Q Ed Creations....212 391-1155
2 W 46th St Ste 1408 New York (10036) *(G-11787)*
Q Omni Inc....914 962-2726
1994 Commerce St Yorktown Heights (10598) *(G-17533)*
Q Squared Design LLC....212 686-8860
41 Madison Ave Ste 1905 New York (10010) *(G-11788)*
Q.E.d, Rochester *Also called QED Technologies Intl Inc (G-14633)*
Qca, Rochester *Also called Quality Contract Assemblies (G-14636)*
Qcr Express Corp....888 924-5888
2565 23rd St Apt 3d Astoria (11102) *(G-452)*
QED Technologies Intl Inc....585 256-6540
1040 University Ave Rochester (14607) *(G-14633)*
Qes Solutions Inc (PA)....585 783-1455
1547 Lyell Ave Rochester (14606) *(G-14634)*
Qhi Group Incorporated....646 512-5727
40 Wall St Ste 2866 New York (10005) *(G-11789)*
Qioptiq Inc (HQ)....585 223-2370
78 Schuyler Baldwin Dr Fairport (14450) *(G-4878)*
Qlc, Long Island City *Also called Quadlogic Controls Corporation (G-7882)*
Qlogix Entertainment LLC....215 459-6315
600 W 113th St 7b4 New York (10025) *(G-11790)*
Qls Solutions Group Inc....716 852-2203
701 Seneca St Ste 600 Buffalo (14210) *(G-3170)*
Qmc Technologies Inc....716 681-0810
4388 Broadway Depew (14043) *(G-4295)*
Qmi, Mount Vernon *Also called Giagni Enterprises LLC (G-8729)*
Qna Tech, Ridge *Also called Quality and Asrn Tech Corp (G-14106)*
Qps Die Cutters Finishers Corp....718 966-1811
140 Alverson Ave Staten Island (10309) *(G-15746)*
Qsf Inc....585 247-6200
140 Cherry Rd Gates (14624) *(G-5577)*
Qsr Medical Communications, Westhampton Beach *Also called Shugar Publishing (G-17089)*
Qssi, Walden *Also called Pacific Die Cast Inc (G-16553)*
Qta Machining Inc....716 862-8108
876 Bailey Ave Buffalo (14206) *(G-3171)*
Quad/Graphics Inc....718 706-7600
4402 11th St Fl 1 Long Island City (11101) *(G-7881)*
Quad/Graphics Inc....518 581-4000
56 Duplainville Rd Saratoga Springs (12866) *(G-15198)*
Quad/Graphics Inc....212 206-5535
60 5th Ave Lowr Level New York (10011) *(G-11791)*
Quad/Graphics Inc....212 741-1001
375 Hudson St New York (10014) *(G-11792)*
Quadlogic Controls Corporation....212 930-9300
3300 Northern Blvd Fl 2 Long Island City (11101) *(G-7882)*
Quadra Flex Corp....607 758-7066
1955 State Route 13 Cortland (13045) *(G-4065)*
Quadra Flex Quality Labels, Cortland *Also called Quadra Flex Corp (G-4065)*
Quadrangle Quick Print, Melville *Also called Quadrangle Quickprints Ltd (G-8380)*
Quadrangle Quickprints Ltd....631 694-4464
1 Huntington Quad Ll04 Melville (11747) *(G-8380)*
Quadrant Biosciences Inc....315 614-2325
505 Irving Ave Ste 3100ab Syracuse (13210) *(G-16037)*
Quadristi LLC....585 279-3318
275 Mount Read Blvd Rochester (14611) *(G-14635)*
Quaker Bonnet Inc....716 885-7208
54 Irving Pl Buffalo (14201) *(G-3172)*
Quaker Boy Inc (PA)....716 662-3979
5455 Webster Rd Orchard Park (14127) *(G-13317)*
Quaker Boy Turkey Calls, Orchard Park *Also called Quaker Boy Inc (G-13317)*
Quaker Millwork & Lumber Inc....716 662-3388
77 S Davis St Orchard Park (14127) *(G-13318)*
Qualbuys LLC....855 884-3274
6800 Jericho Tpke 120w Syosset (11791) *(G-15856)*
Qualicoat Inc....585 293-2650
14 Sanford Rd N Churchville (14428) *(G-3669)*
Qualified Manufacturing Corp....631 249-4440
134 Toledo St Farmingdale (11735) *(G-5102)*
Qualitrol Company LLC (HQ)....586 643-3717
1385 Fairport Rd Fairport (14450) *(G-4879)*
Quality and Asrn Tech Corp....646 450-6762
18 Marginwood Dr Ridge (11961) *(G-14106)*
Quality Bindery Service Inc....716 883-5185
501 Amherst St Buffalo (14207) *(G-3173)*
Quality Candle Mfg Co Inc....631 842-8475
121 Cedar St Copiague (11726) *(G-3945)*
Quality Carpet One Floor & HM....718 941-4200
214 Ditmas Ave Brooklyn (11218) *(G-2478)*
Quality Castings Inc....732 409-3203
3100 47th Ave Ste 2120b Long Island City (11101) *(G-7883)*
Quality Circle Products Inc....914 736-6600
2108 Albany Post Rd Montrose (10548) *(G-8653)*
Quality Components Framing Sys....315 768-1167
44 Mohawk St Bldg 10 Whitesboro (13492) *(G-17222)*
Quality Contract Assemblies....585 663-9030
100 Boxart St Ste 251 Rochester (14612) *(G-14636)*
Quality Dairy Farms Inc....315 942-2611
13584 State Route 12 Boonville (13309) *(G-1166)*
Quality Embedments Mfg Co, New York *Also called Endurart Inc (G-10087)*
Quality Enclosures Inc (PA)....631 234-0115
101 Windsor Pl Unit H Central Islip (11722) *(G-3535)*
Quality Fence, Merrick *Also called Quality Lineals Usa Inc (G-8427)*
Quality Foam Inc....718 381-3644
137 Gardner Ave Brooklyn (11237) *(G-2479)*
Quality Fuel 1 Corporation....631 392-4090
1235 Deer Park Ave North Babylon (11703) *(G-12920)*
Quality Graphics Tri State....845 735-2523
171 Center St Pearl River (10965) *(G-13489)*
Quality Graphics West Seneca....716 668-4528
2460 Union Rd Cheektowaga (14227) *(G-3615)*
Quality Guides....716 326-3163
39 E Main St Westfield (14787) *(G-17078)*
Quality HM Brands Holdings LLC (PA)....718 292-2024
125 Rose Feiss Blvd Bronx (10454) *(G-1436)*
Quality Impressions Inc....646 613-0002
163 Varick St Fl 6 New York (10013) *(G-11793)*
Quality Industrial Services....716 667-7703
75 Bank St Orchard Park (14127) *(G-13319)*
Quality King Distributors Inc....631 439-2027
201 Comac St Ronkonkoma (11779) *(G-14998)*
Quality Life Inc....718 939-5787
2047 129th St College Point (11356) *(G-3828)*
Quality Lineals Usa Inc....516 378-6577
105 Bennington Ave Ste 1 Freeport (11520) *(G-5432)*
Quality Lineals Usa Inc (PA)....516 378-6577
1 Kees Pl Merrick (11566) *(G-8427)*

ALPHABETIC SECTION — R D A Container Corporation

Quality Machining Service Inc 315 736-5774
  70 Sauquoit St New York Mills (13417) *(G-12746)*
Quality Manufacturing Sys LLC 716 763-0988
  1995 Stoneman Cir Lakewood (14750) *(G-7316)*
Quality Metal Stamping LLC (PA) 516 255-9000
  100 Merrick Rd Ste 310w Rockville Centre (11570) *(G-14826)*
Quality Millwork Corp 718 892-2250
  425 Devoe Ave Bronx (10460) *(G-1437)*
Quality Nature Inc 718 484-4666
  8225 5th Ave Ste 215 Brooklyn (11209) *(G-2480)*
Quality Offset LLC 347 342-4660
  4750 30th St Long Island City (11101) *(G-7884)*
Quality One Wireless LLC 631 233-3337
  2127 Lakeland Ave Unit 2 Ronkonkoma (11779) *(G-14999)*
Quality Patterns Inc 212 704-0355
  246 W 38th St Fl 9 New York (10018) *(G-11794)*
Quality Plus, Rochester *Also called Rapid Precision Machining Inc (G-14645)*
Quality Quick Signs, Depew *Also called Flado Enterprises Inc (G-4282)*
Quality Ready Mix Inc 516 437-0100
  1824 Gilford Ave New Hyde Park (11040) *(G-8903)*
Quality Saw & Knife Inc 631 491-4747
  115 Otis St West Babylon (11704) *(G-16850)*
Quality Stainless Fabrication, Gates *Also called Qsf Inc (G-5577)*
Quality Stainless Steel NY Inc (PA) 718 748-1785
  865 63rd St Brooklyn (11220) *(G-2481)*
Quality Stair Builders Inc 631 694-0711
  95 Schmitt Blvd Farmingdale (11735) *(G-5103)*
Quality Strapping Inc 718 418-1111
  55 Meadow St Brooklyn (11206) *(G-2482)*
Quality Vision International, Rochester *Also called Quality Vision Services Inc (G-14638)*
Quality Vision Intl Inc (PA) 585 544-0400
  850 Hudson Ave Rochester (14621) *(G-14637)*
Quality Vision Services Inc 585 544-0450
  1175 North St Rochester (14621) *(G-14638)*
Quality Woodworking Corp 718 875-3437
  260 Butler St Brooklyn (11217) *(G-2483)*
Qualtech Tool & Machine Inc 585 223-9227
  1000 Turk Hill Rd Ste 292 Fairport (14450) *(G-4880)*
Qualtronic Devices Inc 631 360-0859
  130 Oakside Dr Smithtown (11787) *(G-15520)*
Quanta Electronics Inc 631 961-9953
  48 Fran Ln Centereach (11720) *(G-3498)*
Quantum Asset Recovery 716 393-2712
  482 Niagara Falls Blvd Buffalo (14223) *(G-3174)*
Quantum Color Inc 716 283-8700
  8742 Buffalo Ave Niagara Falls (14304) *(G-12883)*
Quantum Knowledge LLC 631 727-6111
  356 Reeves Ave Riverhead (11901) *(G-14166)*
Quantum Logic Corp 516 746-1380
  91 5th Ave New Hyde Park (11040) *(G-8904)*
Quantum Mechanics Ny LLC 917 519-7077
  40 Hennessey Dr Huntington (11743) *(G-6711)*
Quantum Medical Imaging LLC 631 567-5800
  150 Verona St Rochester (14608) *(G-14639)*
Quantum Sails Rochester LLC 585 342-5200
  1461 Hudson Ave Rochester (14621) *(G-14640)*
Quartet Financial Systems Inc (PA) 845 358-6071
  1412 Broadway Rm 2300 New York (10018) *(G-11795)*
Quarto Group Inc (HQ) 212 779-0700
  276 5th Ave Rm 205 New York (10001) *(G-11796)*
Quattro Frameworks Inc 718 361-2620
  4310 23rd St Ste 307 Long Island City (11101) *(G-7885)*
Qub9 Inc 585 484-1808
  181 Saint Paul St Apt 3a Rochester (14604) *(G-14641)*
Qubicaamf Worldwide LLC 315 376-6541
  7412 Utica Blvd Lowville (13367) *(G-7969)*
Quebracho Inc 718 326-3605
  421 Troutman St Brooklyn (11237) *(G-2484)*
Queen Ann Macaroni Mfg Co Inc 718 256-1061
  7205 18th Ave Brooklyn (11204) *(G-2485)*
Queen Ann Ravioli, Brooklyn *Also called Queen Ann Macaroni Mfg Co Inc (G-2485)*
Queen City Malting LLC 716 481-1313
  644 N Forest Rd Buffalo (14221) *(G-3175)*
Queen City Manufacturing Inc 716 877-1102
  333 Henderson Ave Buffalo (14217) *(G-3176)*
Queenaire Technologies Inc 315 393-5454
  9483 State Highway 37 Ogdensburg (13669) *(G-13141)*
Queens Central News, Camden *Also called Camden News Inc (G-3340)*
Queens Chronicle, Glendale *Also called Mark I Publications Inc (G-5673)*
Queens Ready Mix Inc 718 526-4919
  14901 95th Ave Jamaica (11435) *(G-6979)*
Queens Times, Corona *Also called CT Publications Co (G-4018)*
Queens Tribune, Whitestone *Also called Tribco LLC (G-17245)*
Quemere International LLC 914 934-8366
  330 N Main St Port Chester (10573) *(G-13782)*
Quench It Inc 845 462-5400
  2290 South Rd Poughkeepsie (12601) *(G-13945)*
Quest Bead & Cast Inc 212 354-1737
  49 W 37th St Fl 16 New York (10018) *(G-11797)*
Quest Beads, New York *Also called Quest Bead & Cast Inc (G-11797)*
Quest Magazine, New York *Also called Quest Media Llc (G-11798)*

Quest Manufacturing Inc 716 312-8000
  5600 Camp Rd Hamburg (14075) *(G-5962)*
Quest Media Llc 646 840-3404
  920 3rd Ave Fl 6 New York (10022) *(G-11798)*
Queue Solutions LLC 631 750-6440
  250 Knickerbocker Ave Bohemia (11716) *(G-1121)*
Quick Cut Gasket & Rubber 716 684-8628
  192 Erie St Lancaster (14086) *(G-7361)*
Quick Frzen Foods Annual Prcss, New York *Also called Frozen Food Digest Inc (G-10262)*
Quick Guide, New York *Also called Guest Informat LLC (G-10423)*
Quick Roll Leaf Mfg Co Inc (PA) 845 457-1500
  118 Bracken Rd Montgomery (12549) *(G-8637)*
Quick Sign F X 516 249-6531
  6 Powell St Farmingdale (11735) *(G-5104)*
Quick Turn Around Machining, Buffalo *Also called Qta Machining Inc (G-3171)*
Quicker Printer Inc 607 734-8622
  210 W Gray St Elmira (14901) *(G-4712)*
Quickprint 585 394-2600
  330 S Main St Canandaigua (14424) *(G-3386)*
Quikrete Companies Inc 716 213-2027
  11 N Steelawanna Ave Lackawanna (14218) *(G-7273)*
Quikrete Companies Inc 315 673-2020
  4993 Limeledge Rd Ste 560 Marcellus (13108) *(G-8119)*
Quikrete-Buffalo, Lackawanna *Also called Quikrete Companies Inc (G-7273)*
Quilted Koala Ltd 800 223-5678
  1384 Broadway Ste 15 New York (10018) *(G-11799)*
Quinn and Co of NY Ltd 212 868-1900
  48 W 38th St Ph New York (10018) *(G-11800)*
Quintel Usa Inc 585 420-8364
  1200 Ridgeway Ave Ste 132 Rochester (14615) *(G-14642)*
Quip Nyc Inc 703 615-1076
  45 Main St Ste 628 Brooklyn (11201) *(G-2486)*
Quist Industries Ltd 718 243-2800
  204 Van Dyke St Ste 320a Brooklyn (11231) *(G-2487)*
Quo Vadis Editions Inc 716 648-2602
  120 Elmview Ave Hamburg (14075) *(G-5963)*
Quogue Capital LLC 212 554-4475
  1285 Ave Of The Ave Fl 35 New York (10019) *(G-11801)*
Quoin LLC 914 967-9400
  555 Theodore Fremd Ave B302 Rye (10580) *(G-15092)*
Quoizel Inc 631 436-4402
  590 Old Willets Path # 1 Hauppauge (11788) *(G-6202)*
Quorum Group LLC 585 798-8888
  11601 Maple Ridge Rd Medina (14103) *(G-8312)*
Quotable Cards Inc 212 420-7552
  611 Broadway Rm 810 New York (10012) *(G-11802)*
Quovo Inc 646 216-9437
  29 W 30th St Fl 2 New York (10001) *(G-11803)*
Quva Pharma Inc 973 224-7795
  135 Central Park W New York (10023) *(G-11804)*
Qworldstar Inc 212 768-4500
  200 Park Ave S Fl 8 New York (10003) *(G-11805)*
R & A Industrial Products 716 823-4300
  30 Cornelia St Buffalo (14210) *(G-3177)*
R & B Machinery Corp 716 894-3332
  400 Kennedy Rd Ste 3 Buffalo (14227) *(G-3178)*
R & F Boards & Dividers Inc 718 331-1529
  1678 57th St Brooklyn (11204) *(G-2488)*
R & F Handmade Paints Inc 845 331-3112
  84 Ten Broeck Ave Kingston (12401) *(G-7236)*
R & F Marketing, New York *Also called Place Vendome Holding Co Inc (G-11693)*
R & H Baking Co Inc 718 852-1768
  19 5th St Brooklyn (11231) *(G-2489)*
R & J Displays Inc 631 491-3500
  96 Otis St West Babylon (11704) *(G-16851)*
R & J Graphics Inc 631 293-6611
  45 Central Ave Farmingdale (11735) *(G-5105)*
R & J Sheet Metal Distrs Inc 518 433-1525
  119 Sheridan Ave Albany (12210) *(G-125)*
R & L Press Inc 718 447-8557
  896 Forest Ave Staten Island (10310) *(G-15747)*
R & L Press of SI Inc 718 667-3258
  2506 Hylan Blvd Staten Island (10306) *(G-15748)*
R & M Graphics of New York 212 929-0294
  121 Varick St Fl 9 New York (10013) *(G-11806)*
R & M Industries Inc 212 366-6414
  111 Broadway Rm 1112 New York (10006) *(G-11807)*
R & M Richards Inc (PA) 212 921-8820
  1400 Broadway Fl 9 New York (10018) *(G-11808)*
R & M Thermofoil Doors Inc 718 206-4991
  14830 94th Ave Jamaica (11435) *(G-6980)*
R & R Grosbard Inc 212 575-0077
  1156 Avenue Of The Americ New York (10036) *(G-11809)*
R & S Machine Center Inc 518 563-4016
  4398 Route 22 Plattsburgh (12901) *(G-13720)*
R and J Sheet Metal, Albany *Also called R & J Sheet Metal Distrs Inc (G-125)*
R C Henderson Stair Builders 516 876-9898
  100 Summa Ave Westbury (11590) *(G-17052)*
R C Kolstad Water Corp 585 216-2230
  73 Lake Rd Ontario (14519) *(G-13232)*
R D A Container Corporation 585 247-2323
  70 Cherry Rd Gates (14624) *(G-5578)*

(PA)=Parent Co (HQ)=Headquarters (DH)=Div Headquarters

R D Drive and Shop, Little Falls *Also called R D S Mountain View Trucking* ***(G-7524)***
R D Printing Associates Inc....631 390-5964
1865 New Hwy Ste 1 Farmingdale (11735) ***(G-5106)***
R D R Industries Inc....315 866-5020
146 W Main St Mohawk (13407) ***(G-8576)***
R D S Mountain View Trucking....315 823-4265
1600 State Route 5s Little Falls (13365) ***(G-7524)***
R D Specialties Inc....585 265-0220
560 Salt Rd Webster (14580) ***(G-16756)***
R E F Precision Products....631 242-4471
517 Acorn St Ste A Deer Park (11729) ***(G-4221)***
R F Giardina Co....516 922-1364
200 Lexington Ave Apt 3a Oyster Bay (11771) ***(G-13400)***
R G Flair Co Inc....631 586-7311
199 S Fehr Way Bay Shore (11706) ***(G-726)***
R G Glass, New York *Also called RG Glass Creations Inc* ***(G-11885)***
R G King General Construction....315 583-3560
13018 County Route 155 Adams Center (13606) ***(G-4)***
R Goldsmith....718 239-1396
1974 Mayflower Ave Bronx (10461) ***(G-1438)***
R H Crown Co Inc....518 762-4589
100 N Market St Johnstown (12095) ***(G-7153)***
R H Guest Incorporated....718 675-7600
1300 Church Ave Brooklyn (11226) ***(G-2490)***
R Hochman Papers Incorporated....516 466-6414
1000 Dean St Ste 315 Brooklyn (11238) ***(G-2491)***
R I C, Ontario *Also called Rochester Industrial Ctrl Inc* ***(G-13235)***
R I R Communications Systems (PA)....718 706-9957
20 Nuvern Ave Mount Vernon (10550) ***(G-8769)***
R I R Communications Systems....718 706-9957
20 Nuvern Ave Mount Vernon (10550) ***(G-8770)***
R J Liebe Athletic Company....585 237-6111
200 Main St N Perry (14530) ***(G-13548)***
R J Reynolds Tobacco Company....716 871-1553
275 Cooper Ave Ste 116 Tonawanda (14150) ***(G-16214)***
R J S Direct Marketing Inc....631 667-5768
561 Acorn St Ste E Deer Park (11729) ***(G-4222)***
R J Valente Gravel Inc....518 279-1001
3349 Rte 2 Cropseyville (12052) ***(G-4085)***
R K B Opto-Electronics Inc (PA)....315 455-6636
6677 Moore Rd Syracuse (13211) ***(G-16038)***
R Klein Jewelry Co Inc....516 482-3260
39 Brockmeyer Dr Massapequa (11758) ***(G-8214)***
R L C Electronics Inc....914 241-1334
83 Radio Circle Dr Mount Kisco (10549) ***(G-8684)***
R M F Health Management L L C....718 854-5400
3361 Park Ave Wantagh (11793) ***(G-16583)***
R M Reynolds (PA)....315 789-7365
504 Exchange St Geneva (14456) ***(G-5596)***
R M S Motor Corporation....607 723-2323
41 Travis Dr Binghamton (13904) ***(G-939)***
R P Fedder Corp (PA)....585 288-1600
740 Driving Park Ave B Rochester (14613) ***(G-14643)***
R P M, Bay Shore *Also called Rinaldi Precision Machine* ***(G-730)***
R P M Industries Inc....315 255-1105
26 Aurelius Ave Auburn (13021) ***(G-512)***
R P M Machine Co....585 671-3744
755 Gravel Rd Webster (14580) ***(G-16757)***
R P O, West Henrietta *Also called Rochester Precision Optics LLC* ***(G-16924)***
R R Donnelley & Sons Company....716 763-2613
112 Winchester Rd Lakewood (14750) ***(G-7317)***
R R Donnelley & Sons Company....518 438-9722
4 Executive Park Dr Ste 2 Albany (12203) ***(G-126)***
R S T Cable and Tape Inc....631 981-0096
2130 Pond Rd Ste B Ronkonkoma (11779) ***(G-15000)***
R Schleider Contracting Corp....631 269-4249
135 Old Northport Rd Kings Park (11754) ***(G-7204)***
R Steiner Technologies Inc....585 425-5912
180 Perinton Pkwy Fairport (14450) ***(G-4881)***
R T C A, Elmsford *Also called Radon Testing Corp of America* ***(G-4782)***
R T F Manufacturing, Hudson *Also called Atmost Refrigeration Co Inc* ***(G-6637)***
R V Dow Enterprises Inc....585 454-5862
466 Central Ave Rochester (14605) ***(G-14644)***
R V H Estates Inc....914 664-9888
138 Mount Vernon Ave Mount Vernon (10550) ***(G-8771)***
R W Publications Div of Wtrhs (PA)....716 714-5620
6091 Seneca St Bldg C Elma (14059) ***(G-4666)***
R W Publications Div of Wtrhs....716 714-5620
6091 Seneca St Bldg C Elma (14059) ***(G-4667)***
R&A Prods, Buffalo *Also called R & A Industrial Products* ***(G-3177)***
R&S Machine, Plattsburgh *Also called R & S Machine Center Inc* ***(G-13720)***
R&S Steel LLC....315 281-0123
412 Canal St Rome (13440) ***(G-14859)***
R-Co Products Corporation....800 854-7657
1855 Big Tree Rd Lakewood (14750) ***(G-7318)***
R-Pac International Corp (PA)....212 465-1818
132 W 36th St Fl 7 New York (10018) ***(G-11810)***
R-S Restaurant Eqp Mfg Corp (PA)....212 925-0335
272 Bowery New York (10012) ***(G-11811)***
R-Tronics, Rome *Also called J Davis Manufacturing Co Inc* ***(G-14844)***
RA Newhouse Inc (PA)....516 248-6670
110 Liberty Ave Mineola (11501) ***(G-8565)***
Racing Industries Inc....631 905-0100
901 Scott Ave Calverton (11933) ***(G-3324)***
Radar Sports LLC....516 678-1919
2660 Washington Ave Oceanside (11572) ***(G-13113)***
Radarsport.com, Oceanside *Also called Radar Sports LLC* ***(G-13113)***
Radax Industries Inc....585 265-2055
700 Basket Rd Ste A Webster (14580) ***(G-16758)***
Radiancy Inc (HQ)....845 398-1647
40 Ramland Rd S Ste 200 Orangeburg (10962) ***(G-13267)***
Radiant Pro Ltd....516 763-5678
245 Merrick Rd Oceanside (11572) ***(G-13114)***
Radiation Shielding Systems....888 631-2278
415 Spook Rock Rd Suffern (10901) ***(G-15819)***
Radicle Farm Company, New York *Also called Radicle Farm LLC* ***(G-11812)***
Radicle Farm LLC....315 226-3294
394 Broadway Fl 5 New York (10013) ***(G-11812)***
Radio Circle Realty Inc....914 241-8742
136 Radio Circle Dr Mount Kisco (10549) ***(G-8685)***
Radiology Film Reading Svcs, Long Island City *Also called P C Rfrs Radiology* ***(G-7862)***
Radnor-Wallace (PA)....516 767-2131
921 Port Washington Blvd # 1 Port Washington (11050) ***(G-13875)***
Radon Testing Corp of America (PA)....914 345-3380
2 Hayes St Elmsford (10523) ***(G-4782)***
Raff Enterprises....518 218-7883
12 Petra Ln Ste 6 Albany (12205) ***(G-127)***
Raffettos Corp....212 777-1261
144 W Houston St New York (10012) ***(G-11813)***
Rag & Bone Industries LLC....212 249-3331
416 W 13th St New York (10014) ***(G-11814)***
Rag & Bone Industries LLC (PA)....212 278-8214
425 W 13th St Ofc 2 New York (10014) ***(G-11815)***
Rago Foundations LLC....718 728-8436
1815 27th Ave Astoria (11102) ***(G-453)***
Rago Shapewear, Astoria *Also called Rago Foundations LLC* ***(G-453)***
Ragozin Data....212 674-3123
4402 11th St Ste 613 Long Island City (11101) ***(G-7886)***
Rags Knitwear Ltd....718 782-8417
850 Metropolitan Ave Brooklyn (11211) ***(G-2492)***
Railings By New Star Brass....516 358-1153
26 Cobeck Ct Brooklyn (11223) ***(G-2493)***
Railtech Composites Inc....518 324-6190
80 Montana Dr Plattsburgh (12903) ***(G-13721)***
Railworks Transit Systems Inc (HQ)....212 502-7900
5 Penn Plz New York (10001) ***(G-11816)***
Rain Catchers Seamless Gutters....516 520-1956
39 Park Ln Bethpage (11714) ***(G-877)***
Rainbeau Ridge Farm....914 234-2197
49 Davids Way Bedford Hills (10507) ***(G-803)***
Rainbow Custom Counter Tops, Staten Island *Also called Joseph Fedele* ***(G-15716)***
Rainbow Leather Inc....718 939-8762
1415 112th St College Point (11356) ***(G-3829)***
Rainbow Lettering....607 732-5751
1329 College Ave Elmira (14901) ***(G-4713)***
Rainbow Plastics Inc....718 218-7288
371 Vandervoort Ave Brooklyn (11211) ***(G-2494)***
Rainbow Poly Bag Co Inc....718 386-3500
179 Morgan Ave Brooklyn (11237) ***(G-2495)***
Rainbow Powder Coating Corp....631 586-4019
86 E Industry Ct Deer Park (11729) ***(G-4223)***
Rainforest Apothecary, Long Island City *Also called Anima Mundi Herbals LLC* ***(G-7693)***
Rainforest Apparel LLC....212 840-0880
1385 Broadway Fl 24 New York (10018) ***(G-11817)***
Raith America Inc....518 874-3000
300 Jordan Rd Troy (12180) ***(G-16274)***
Rajbhog Foods Inc....718 358-5105
4123 Murray St Flushing (11355) ***(G-5294)***
RAK Finishing Corp....718 416-4242
15934 83rd St Howard Beach (11414) ***(G-6626)***
Raleigh and Drake Pbc....212 625-8212
110 E 25th St Fl 3 New York (10010) ***(G-11818)***
Raloid Tool Co Inc....518 664-4261
Hc 146 Mechanicville (12118) ***(G-8261)***
Ralph Lauren Corporation (PA)....212 318-7000
650 Madison Ave Fl C1 New York (10022) ***(G-11819)***
Ralph Lauren Corporation....212 421-1570
979 3rd Ave Ste 404 New York (10022) ***(G-11820)***
Ralph Lauren Corporation....917 934-4200
205 W 39th St Fl 13 New York (10018) ***(G-11821)***
Ralph Lauren Corporation....212 221-7751
25 W 39th St Fl 8 New York (10018) ***(G-11822)***
Ralph Martinelli....914 345-3055
100 Clearbrook Rd Ste 170 Elmsford (10523) ***(G-4783)***
Ralph Payne....718 222-4200
475 Van Buren St Ste 11c Brooklyn (11221) ***(G-2496)***
Ralph's Ices, Staten Island *Also called JMS Ices Inc* ***(G-15714)***
Ram Fabricating LLC....315 437-6654
412 Wavel St Syracuse (13206) ***(G-16039)***
Ram Precision Tool Inc....716 759-8722
139 Gunnville Rd Lancaster (14086) ***(G-7362)***
Ram Transformer Technologies....914 632-3988
11 Beechwood Ave New Rochelle (10801) ***(G-8967)***

Rambachs International Bakery....518 563-1721
65 S Peru St Plattsburgh (12901) *(G-13722)*
Ramco Arts, Sodus *Also called Nykon Inc (G-15526)*
Ramholtz Publishing Inc....718 761-4800
1200 South Ave Ste 202 Staten Island (10314) *(G-15749)*
Rami Sheet Metal Inc....845 426-2948
25 E Hickory St Spring Valley (10977) *(G-15620)*
Ramick Welding, Farmingdale *Also called W R P Welding Ltd (G-5149)*
Ramler International Ltd....516 353-3106
485 Underhill Blvd # 100 Syosset (11791) *(G-15857)*
Ramsbury Property Us Inc (HQ)....212 223-6250
601 5th Ave Fl 4 New York (10017) *(G-11823)*
Ramsey Electronics, Victor *Also called Avcom of Virginia Inc (G-16485)*
Ramsey Electronics LLC....585 924-4560
590 Fishers Station Dr Victor (14564) *(G-16522)*
Ramy Brook LLC....212 744-2789
231 W 39th St Rm 720 New York (10018) *(G-11824)*
Ran Mar Enterprises Ltd....631 666-4754
143 Anchor Ln Bay Shore (11706) *(G-727)*
Rand & Paseka Mfg Co Inc....516 867-1500
10 Hanse Ave Freeport (11520) *(G-5433)*
Rand Machine Products Inc (PA)....716 665-5217
2072 Allen Street Ext Falconer (14733) *(G-4916)*
Rand Machine Products Inc....716 985-4681
5035 Route 60 Sinclairville (14782) *(G-15475)*
Rand Mfg, Schenectady *Also called Rand Products Manufacturing Co (G-15312)*
Rand Products Manufacturing Co....518 374-9871
1602 Van Vranken Ave Schenectady (12308) *(G-15312)*
Randa Accessories Lea Gds LLC....212 354-5100
417 5th Ave Fl 11 New York (10016) *(G-11825)*
Randall Loeffler Inc....212 226-8787
588 Broadway Rm 1203 New York (10012) *(G-11826)*
Randgold Resources Ltd....212 815-2129
101 Barclay St New York (10007) *(G-11827)*
Randob Labs Ltd....845 534-2197
45 Quaker Ave Ste 207 Cornwall (12518) *(G-4012)*
Randolph Dimension Corporation....716 358-6901
216 Main St Ste 216 Randolph (14772) *(G-14030)*
Randy Sixberry....315 265-6211
6 Main St Ste 101 Potsdam (13676) *(G-13901)*
Range Repair Warehouse....585 235-0980
421 Penbrooke Dr Ste 2 Penfield (14526) *(G-13525)*
Range Rsurces - Appalachia LLC....716 753-3385
100 E Chautauqua St Mayville (14757) *(G-8249)*
Ranger Design Us Inc....800 565-5321
6377 Dean Pkwy Ontario (14519) *(G-13233)*
Ranney Precision....716 731-6418
6421 Wendt Dr Niagara Falls (14304) *(G-12884)*
Ranney Precision Machining, Niagara Falls *Also called Ranney Precision (G-12884)*
Rap Genius, Brooklyn *Also called Genius Media Group Inc (G-2020)*
Rapa Independent North America....518 561-0513
124 Connecticut Rd Plattsburgh (12903) *(G-13723)*
Raphael, Peconic *Also called J Petrocelli Wine Cellars LLC (G-13495)*
Rapid Fan & Blower Inc....718 786-2060
2314 39th Ave Long Island City (11101) *(G-7887)*
Rapid Intellect Group Inc....518 929-3210
77b Church St Chatham (12037) *(G-3587)*
Rapid Precision Machining Inc....585 467-0780
50 Lafayette Rd Rochester (14609) *(G-14645)*
Rapid Print and Marketing Inc....585 924-1520
8 High St Victor (14564) *(G-16523)*
Rapid Rays Printing & Copying....716 852-0550
300 Broadway St Buffalo (14204) *(G-3179)*
Rapid Removal LLC....716 665-4663
1599 Route 394 Falconer (14733) *(G-4917)*
Rapid Reproductions LLC....607 843-2221
4511 State Hwy 12 Oxford (13830) *(G-13389)*
Rapid Service Engraving Co....716 896-4555
1593 Genesee St Buffalo (14211) *(G-3180)*
Rapid-Lite Fixture Corporation....347 599-2600
249 Huron St Brooklyn (11222) *(G-2497)*
Rapistak Corporation....716 822-2804
2025 Electric Ave Blasdell (14219) *(G-957)*
Rapp Signs Inc....607 656-8167
3979 State Route 206 Greene (13778) *(G-5885)*
Rare Editions, New York *Also called Star Childrens Dress Co Inc (G-12208)*
Rasco Graphics Inc....212 206-0447
519 8th Ave Fl 18 New York (10018) *(G-11828)*
Rasjada Enterprises Ltd....631 242-1055
1337 Richland Blvd Bay Shore (11706) *(G-728)*
Rason Asphalt Inc (PA)....631 293-6210
Rr 110 Farmingdale (11735) *(G-5107)*
Rason Asphalt Inc....516 239-7880
4 Johnson Rd Lawrence (11559) *(G-7423)*
Rason Asphalt Inc....516 671-1500
44 Morris Ave Glen Cove (11542) *(G-5639)*
Rasp Incorporated....518 747-8020
8 Dukes Way Gansevoort (12831) *(G-5502)*
Ratan Ronkonkoma....631 588-6800
3055 Veterans Mem Hwy Ronkonkoma (11779) *(G-15001)*
Rational Enterprises, Albany *Also called Rational Retention LLC (G-128)*
Rational Retention LLC (PA)....518 489-3000
2 Tower Pl Ste 13 Albany (12203) *(G-128)*
Rational Retention LLC....518 489-3000
2 Tower Pl Ste 13 Albany (12203) *(G-129)*
Rauch Industries Inc....704 867-5333
828 S Broadway Tarrytown (10591) *(G-16127)*
Raulli and Sons Inc (PA)....315 479-6693
213 Teall Ave Syracuse (13210) *(G-16040)*
Raulli and Sons Inc....315 474-1370
660 Burnet Ave Syracuse (13203) *(G-16041)*
Raulli and Sons Inc....315 479-2515
920 Canal St Syracuse (13210) *(G-16042)*
Raulli Iron Works Inc....315 337-8070
133 Mill St Rome (13440) *(G-14860)*
Raven New York LLC....212 584-9690
450 W 15th St New York (10011) *(G-11829)*
Ravioli Store Inc....718 729-9300
4344 21st St Long Island City (11101) *(G-7888)*
Ravioli Store, The, Long Island City *Also called Pelican Bay Ltd (G-7869)*
Raw Indulgence Ltd....866 498-4671
200 Saw Mill River Rd Hawthorne (10532) *(G-6278)*
Raw Revolution, Hawthorne *Also called Raw Indulgence Ltd (G-6278)*
Rawlings Sporting Goods Co Inc....315 429-8511
52 Mckinley Ave Dolgeville (13329) *(G-4331)*
Rawpothecary Inc....917 783-7770
630 Flushing Ave Brooklyn (11206) *(G-2498)*
Raxon Fabrics Corp (HQ)....212 532-6816
261 5th Ave New York (10016) *(G-11830)*
Ray Gold Shade Inc....718 377-8892
16 Wellington Ct Brooklyn (11230) *(G-2499)*
Ray Griffiths Inc....212 689-7209
303 5th Ave Rm 1901 New York (10016) *(G-11831)*
Ray Medica Inc....952 885-0500
505 Park Ave Ste 1400 New York (10022) *(G-11832)*
Ray Sign Inc....518 377-1371
28 Colonial Ave Schenectady (12304) *(G-15313)*
Rayana Designs Inc....718 786-2040
2520 40th Ave Long Island City (11101) *(G-7889)*
Rayco Manufacturing Co Inc....516 431-2006
10715 180th St Jamaica (11433) *(G-6981)*
Rayco Manufacturing Div, Jamaica *Also called Rayco Manufacturing Co Inc (G-6981)*
Rayco of Schenectady Inc....518 212-5113
4 Sam Stratton Rd Amsterdam (12010) *(G-367)*
Raydon Precision Bearing Co....516 887-2582
75 Merrick Rd Lynbrook (11563) *(G-7984)*
Raydoor Inc....212 421-0641
134 W 29th St Rm 909 New York (10001) *(G-11833)*
Raymond Consolidated Corp (HQ)....800 235-7200
22 S Canal St Greene (13778) *(G-5886)*
Raymond Corporation (HQ)....800 235-7200
22 S Canal St Greene (13778) *(G-5887)*
Raymond Corporation....607 656-2311
6650 Kirkville Rd East Syracuse (13057) *(G-4570)*
Raymond Corporation....315 463-5000
6517 Chrysler Ln East Syracuse (13057) *(G-4571)*
Raymond Corporation....315 643-5000
6533 Chrysler Ln East Syracuse (13057) *(G-4572)*
Raymond Leasing, East Syracuse *Also called Raymond Corporation (G-4570)*
Raymond Sales Corporation....607 656-2311
22 S Canal St Greene (13778) *(G-5888)*
Rays Italian Bakery Inc....516 825-9170
45 Railroad Ave Valley Stream (11580) *(G-16447)*
Rays Restaurant & Bakery Inc....718 441-7707
12325 Jamaica Ave Jamaica (11418) *(G-6982)*
Raytech Corp Asbestos Personal (PA)....516 747-0300
190 Willis Ave Mineola (11501) *(G-8566)*
Raytech Corporation (HQ)....718 259-7388
97 Froehlich Farm Blvd Woodbury (11797) *(G-17317)*
Razorfish LLC....212 798-6600
1440 Broadway Fl 18 New York (10018) *(G-11834)*
RB Converting Inc....607 777-1325
28 Track Dr Binghamton (13904) *(G-940)*
RB Diamond Inc....212 398-4560
22 W 48th St Ste 904 New York (10036) *(G-11835)*
RB Woodcraft Inc....315 474-2429
1860 Erie Blvd E Ste 1 Syracuse (13210) *(G-16043)*
Rbhammers Corp....845 353-5042
500 Bradley Hill Rd Blauvelt (10913) *(G-968)*
RBHM Incorporated....609 259-4900
1885 E 2nd St Brooklyn (11223) *(G-2500)*
Rbw Studio LLC....212 388-1621
67 34th St Unit 5 Brooklyn (11232) *(G-2501)*
RC Entps Bus & Trck Inc....518 568-5753
5895 State Highway 29 Saint Johnsville (13452) *(G-15123)*
RC Imaging Inc....585 392-4336
50 Old Hojack Ln Hilton (14468) *(G-6446)*
Rce Manufacturing LLC....631 856-9005
10 Brayton Ct Commack (11725) *(G-3865)*
RD Intrntnl Style....212 382-2360
275 W 39th St Fl 7 New York (10018) *(G-11836)*
Rd Publications Inc (HQ)....914 238-1000
1 Readers Digest Rd Pleasantville (10570) *(G-13748)*

ALPHABETIC

(PA)=Parent Co (HQ)=Headquarters (DH)=Div Headquarters
2018 Harris
New York Manufacturers Directory
1043

Rd2 Construction & Dem LLC — 718 980-1650
63 Trossach Rd Staten Island (10304) *(G-15750)*

Rda Holding Co (PA) — 914 238-1000
750 3rd Ave New York (10017) *(G-11837)*

Rdd Pharma Inc — 302 319-9970
3 Columbus Cir Fl 15 New York (10019) *(G-11838)*

Rdi, Edgewood Also called Iba Industrial Inc *(G-4614)*

Rdi Inc (PA) — 914 773-1000
333 N Bedford Rd Ste 135 Mount Kisco (10549) *(G-8686)*

RDI ELECTRONICS, Mount Kisco Also called Rdi Inc *(G-8686)*

RE 99 Cents Inc — 718 639-2325
4905 Roosevelt Ave Woodside (11377) *(G-17365)*

RE Fuel — 631 909-3316
210 Montauk Hwy Moriches (11955) *(G-8659)*

RE Hansen Industries Inc (PA) — 631 471-2900
22 Research Way East Setauket (11733) *(G-4510)*

Re-Al Industrial Corp — 716 542-4556
5391 Crittenden Rd Akron (14001) *(G-25)*

Read Manufacturing Company Inc — 631 567-4487
330 Dante Ct Holbrook (11741) *(G-6496)*

Readent Inc — 212 710-3004
445 Hamilton Ave Ste 1102 White Plains (10601) *(G-17189)*

Reader's Digest, New York Also called Trusted Media Brands Inc *(G-12435)*

Readers Dgest Yung Fmilies Inc — 914 238-1000
Readers Digest Rd Pleasantville (10570) *(G-13749)*

Readers Digest Assn Incthe — 414 423-0100
16 E 34th St Fl 14 New York (10016) *(G-11839)*

Reading Room Inc (PA) — 212 463-1029
48 Wall St Fl 5 New York (10005) *(G-11840)*

Ready Check Glo Inc — 516 547-1849
23 Bruce Ln Ste E East Northport (11731) *(G-4463)*

Ready Egg Farms Inc — 607 674-4653
35 W State St Sherburne (13460) *(G-15416)*

Ready To Assemble Company Inc — 516 825-4397
115 S Corona Ave Valley Stream (11580) *(G-16448)*

Readyjet Technical Svcs Inc — 518 705-4019
1 Warren St Johnstown (12095) *(G-7154)*

Real Bark Mulch LLC — 518 747-3650
1380 Towpath Ln Fort Edward (12828) *(G-5353)*

Real Co Inc — 347 433-8549
616 Corporate Way Valley Cottage (10989) *(G-16412)*

Real Deal, The, New York Also called Korangy Publishing Inc *(G-10915)*

Real Design Inc — 315 429-3071
187 S Main St Dolgeville (13329) *(G-4332)*

Real Est Book of Long Island — 516 364-5000
575 Underhill Blvd # 110 Syosset (11791) *(G-15858)*

Real Estate Media Inc — 212 929-6976
120 Broadway Fl 5 New York (10271) *(G-11841)*

Real Goods Solar Inc — 845 708-0800
22 Third St New City (10956) *(G-8837)*

Real Industry Inc (PA) — 805 435-1255
17 State St Ste 3811 New York (10004) *(G-11842)*

Real Wood Tiles, Buffalo Also called Fibron Products Inc *(G-2961)*

Reality Ai, New York Also called Reality Analytics Inc *(G-11843)*

Reality Analytics Inc — 347 363-2200
157 Columbus Ave New York (10023) *(G-11843)*

Realtimetraderscom — 716 632-6600
1325 N Forest Rd Ste 240 Buffalo (14221) *(G-3181)*

Rear View Safety Inc — 855 815-3842
1797 Atlantic Ave Brooklyn (11233) *(G-2502)*

Reason Software Company Inc — 646 664-1038
228 Park Ave S Unit 74122 New York (10003) *(G-11844)*

Recommunity, Beacon Also called Fcr LLC *(G-780)*

Recon Construction Corp — 718 939-1305
1108 Shore Rd Little Neck (11363) *(G-7532)*

Record — 518 270-1200
20 Lake Ave Saratoga Springs (12866) *(G-15199)*

Record Advertiser — 716 693-1000
435 River Rd North Tonawanda (14120) *(G-13006)*

Record Review LLC — 914 244-0533
16 The Pkwy Fl 3 Katonah (10536) *(G-7162)*

Recorded Anthology of Amrcn Mus — 212 290-1695
20 Jay St Ste 1001 Brooklyn (11201) *(G-2503)*

Recorder, The, Amsterdam Also called Tri-Village Publishers Inc *(G-371)*

Recreational Equipment Inc — 914 410-9500
49 Fitzgerald St Yonkers (10710) *(G-17499)*

Recycled Brooklyn Group LLC — 917 902-0662
236 Van Brunt St Brooklyn (11231) *(G-2504)*

Red Creek Cold Storage LLC (PA) — 315 576-2069
14127 Keeley St Red Creek (13143) *(G-14038)*

Red Line Networx Screen Prtg, Brooklyn Also called Body Builders Inc *(G-1707)*

Red Newt Cellars Inc — 607 546-4100
3675 Tichenor Rd Hector (14841) *(G-6284)*

Red Oak Software Inc — 585 454-3170
3349 Monroe Ave Ste 175 Rochester (14618) *(G-14646)*

Red Onyx Industrial Pdts LLC — 516 459-6035
23 Green St Ste 310 Huntington (11743) *(G-6712)*

Red Tail Moulding & Mllwk LLC — 516 852-4613
23 Frowein Rd Ste 1 Center Moriches (11934) *(G-3493)*

Red Tail Ridge Inc — 315 536-4580
846 State Route 14 Penn Yan (14527) *(G-13540)*

Red Tail Ridge Winery, Penn Yan Also called Red Tail Ridge Inc *(G-13540)*

Red White & Blue Entps Corp — 718 565-8080
3443 56th St Woodside (11377) *(G-17366)*

Redbook Magazine — 212 649-3331
224 W 57th St Lbby Fl22 New York (10019) *(G-11845)*

Redco Foods Inc — 315 823-1300
1 Hansen Is Little Falls (13365) *(G-7525)*

Redcom Laboratories Inc — 585 924-6567
1 Redcom Ctr Victor (14564) *(G-16524)*

Reddi Car Corp — 631 589-3141
174 Greeley Ave Sayville (11782) *(G-15243)*

Redding Reloading Equipment, Cortland Also called Redding-Hunter Inc *(G-4066)*

Redding-Hunter Inc — 607 753-3331
1089 Starr Rd Cortland (13045) *(G-4066)*

Redi Bag Brand, Garden City Also called New York Packaging II LLC *(G-5536)*

Redi Records Payroll — 718 854-6990
1225 36th St Brooklyn (11218) *(G-2505)*

Redi-Bag USA, New Hyde Park Also called New York Packaging Corp *(G-8896)*

Redken 5th Avenue Nyc LLC — 212 984-5113
565 5th Ave New York (10017) *(G-11846)*

Redland Foods Corp — 716 288-9061
40 Sonwil Dr Cheektowaga (14225) *(G-3616)*

Redspring Communications Inc — 518 587-0547
125 High Rock Ave Saratoga Springs (12866) *(G-15200)*

Reebok International Ltd — 212 221-6375
1185 Av Of The Amrcs Lbby New York (10036) *(G-11847)*

Reebok International Ltd — 914 948-3719
125 Westchester Ave White Plains (10601) *(G-17190)*

Reebok International Ltd — 718 370-0471
2655 Richmond Ave Staten Island (10314) *(G-15751)*

Reed Business Information, New York Also called Relx Inc *(G-11858)*

Reed Systems Ltd — 845 647-3660
17 Edwards Pl Ellenville (12428) *(G-4651)*

Reefer Tek Llc — 347 590-1067
885a E 149th St Fl 2 Bronx (10455) *(G-1439)*

Reelcology Inc — 845 258-1880
39 Transport Ln Pine Island (10969) *(G-13580)*

Reelex Packaging Solutions Inc — 845 878-7878
39 Jon Barrett Rd Patterson (12563) *(G-13467)*

Reenergy Black River, Fort Drum Also called Black River Generations LLC *(G-5345)*

Reenergy Black River LLC — 315 773-2314
4515 Ephrtes River Vly Rd Fort Drum (13602) *(G-5346)*

Reentry Games Inc — 646 421-0080
215 E 5th St New York (10003) *(G-11848)*

Reese Manufacturing Inc — 631 842-3780
16 Reith St Copiague (11726) *(G-3946)*

Refill Services LLC — 607 369-5864
16 Winkler Rd Sidney (13838) *(G-15463)*

REFINEDKIND PET PRODUCTS, Irvington Also called Feinkind Inc *(G-6811)*

Refinery 29 Inc (PA) — 212 966-3112
225 Broadway Fl 23 New York (10007) *(G-11849)*

Reflective Shopper Usa LLC — 855 735-3222
251 W Nyack Rd Ste C West Nyack (10994) *(G-16955)*

Reflex Offset Inc — 516 746-4142
305 Suburban Ave Deer Park (11729) *(G-4224)*

Reflexite Precision Tech Ctr, Henrietta Also called Orafol Americas Inc *(G-6321)*

Refuel Inc (PA) — 917 645-2974
1384 Broadway Rm 407 New York (10018) *(G-11850)*

Refuel Jeans, New York Also called Refuel Inc *(G-11850)*

Regal Commodities, Purchase Also called Regal Trading Inc *(G-13986)*

Regal Emblem Co Inc — 212 925-8833
250 W Broadway Fl 2 New York (10013) *(G-11851)*

Regal Jewelry Inc — 212 382-1695
39 W 32nd St Rm 1004 New York (10001) *(G-11852)*

Regal Screen Printing Intl — 845 356-8181
42 Grove St Spring Valley (10977) *(G-15621)*

Regal Tip, Niagara Falls Also called J D Calato Manufacturing Co *(G-12855)*

Regal Trading Inc — 914 694-6100
2975 Westchester Ave # 210 Purchase (10577) *(G-13986)*

Regan Arts LLC — 646 488-6610
65 Bleecker St Fl 8 New York (10012) *(G-11853)*

Rege Inc — 845 565-7772
110 Corporate Dr New Windsor (12553) *(G-8996)*

Regence Picture Frames Inc — 718 779-0888
12 Cherry Ln Lynbrook (11563) *(G-7985)*

Regeneron Pharmaceuticals Inc (PA) — 914 847-7000
777 Old Saw Mill River Rd # 10 Tarrytown (10591) *(G-16128)*

Regeneron Pharmaceuticals Inc — 518 488-6000
81 Columbia Tpke Rensselaer (12144) *(G-14061)*

Regenron Hlthcare Slutions Inc — 914 847-7000
745 Old Saw Mill River Rd Tarrytown (10591) *(G-16129)*

Regent Paints Inc — 917 966-6011
6944 Cooper Ave Glendale (11385) *(G-5676)*

Regina Press, Bohemia Also called Malhame Publs & Importers Inc *(G-1096)*

Regional MGT & Consulting Inc — 718 599-3718
79 Bridgewater St Brooklyn (11222) *(G-2506)*

Register Graphics Inc — 716 358-2921
220 Main St Randolph (14772) *(G-14031)*

Regulus Energy LLC — 716 200-7417
250 Cooper Ave Ste 106 Tonawanda (14150) *(G-16215)*

Rehab Tech, Syracuse Also called Rehabilitation Tech of Syracuse *(G-16044)*

Rehabilitation International......212 420-1500
15350 89th Ave Apt 1101 Jamaica (11432) *(G-6983)*
Rehablitation Tech of Syracuse......315 426-9920
1101 Erie Blvd E Ste 209 Syracuse (13210) *(G-16044)*
Reichert Inc......716 686-4500
3362 Walden Ave Depew (14043) *(G-4296)*
Reichert Technologies, Depew *Also called Reichert Inc (G-4296)*
Reilly Windows & Doors, Calverton *Also called Pella Corporation (G-3322)*
Reimann & Georger Corporation......716 895-1156
1849 Harlem Rd Buffalo (14212) *(G-3182)*
Reinhold Brothers Inc......212 867-8310
799 Park Ave New York (10021) *(G-11854)*
Reino Manufacturing Co Inc......914 636-8990
34 Circuit Rd New Rochelle (10805) *(G-8968)*
Reis D Furniture Mfg......516 248-5676
327 Sagamore Ave Ste 2 Mineola (11501) *(G-8567)*
Reisman Bros Bakery Inc......718 331-1975
110 Avenue O Brooklyn (11204) *(G-2507)*
Reismans Bros. Bakery, Brooklyn *Also called Reisman Bros Bakery Inc (G-2507)*
Relavis Corporation......212 995-2900
40 Wall St Ste 3300 New York (10005) *(G-11855)*
Release Coatings New York Inc......585 593-2335
125 S Brooklyn Ave Wellsville (14895) *(G-16782)*
Reliable Autmtc Sprnklr Co Inc (PA)......800 431-1588
103 Fairview Pk Dr Ste 1 Elmsford (10523) *(G-4784)*
Reliable Brothers Inc......518 273-6732
185 Cohoes Ave Green Island (12183) *(G-5879)*
Reliable Elec Mt Vernon Inc......914 668-4440
519 S 5th Ave Mount Vernon (10550) *(G-8772)*
Reliable Press II Inc......718 840-5812
148 39th St Unit 6 Brooklyn (11232) *(G-2508)*
Reliable Welding & Fabrication......631 758-2637
214 W Main St Patchogue (11772) *(G-13459)*
Reliance Fluid Tech LLC......716 332-0988
3943 Buffalo Ave Niagara Falls (14303) *(G-12885)*
Reliance Gayco, Kingston *Also called Universal Metal Fabricators (G-7248)*
Reliance Machining Inc......718 784-0314
4335 Vernon Blvd Long Island City (11101) *(G-7890)*
Reliance Mica Co Inc......718 788-0282
336 Beach 149th St Rockaway Park (11694) *(G-14815)*
Reliant Security......917 338-2200
450 Fashion Ave Ste 503 New York (10123) *(G-11856)*
Relmada Therapeutics Inc......646 677-3853
750 3rd Ave Fl 9 New York (10017) *(G-11857)*
Relx Inc (HQ)......212 309-8100
230 Park Ave Ste 700 New York (10169) *(G-11858)*
Relx Inc......212 463-6644
249 W 17th St New York (10011) *(G-11859)*
Relx Inc......212 633-3900
655 6th Ave New York (10010) *(G-11860)*
Relx Inc......607 772-2600
136 Carlin Rd Conklin (13748) *(G-3899)*
REM Printing Inc......518 438-7338
55 Railroad Ave Albany (12205) *(G-130)*
Rem-Tronics Inc......716 934-2697
659 Brigham Rd Dunkirk (14048) *(G-4372)*
Remains Lighting, Brooklyn *Also called Aesthonics Inc (G-1567)*
Remains Lighting......212 675-8051
130 W 28th St Frnt 1 New York (10001) *(G-11861)*
Remarkable Liquids LLC......518 861-5351
6032 Depot Rd Altamont (12009) *(G-214)*
Rembar Company LLC......914 693-2620
67 Main St Dobbs Ferry (10522) *(G-4326)*
Remedies Surgical Supplies......718 599-5301
331 Rutledge St Ste 204 Brooklyn (11211) *(G-2509)*
Remington Arms Company LLC......315 895-3482
14 Hoefler Ave Ilion (13357) *(G-6783)*
Remodeling News, Bedford *Also called JSD Communications Inc (G-792)*
Remsen Fuel Inc......718 984-9551
4668 Amboy Rd Staten Island (10312) *(G-15752)*
Remsen Graphics Corp......718 643-7500
52 Court St 2 Brooklyn (11201) *(G-2510)*
Remus Industries......914 906-1544
11 Oakbrook Rd Ossining (10562) *(G-13351)*
Ren Tool & Manufacturing Co......518 377-2123
1801 Chrisler Ave Schenectady (12303) *(G-15314)*
Renaissance Bijou Ltd......212 869-1969
20 W 47th St Ste 18 New York (10036) *(G-11862)*
Renaissance Global, New York *Also called Renaissnce Crpt Tapestries Inc (G-11863)*
Renaissance Import, Lockport *Also called Candlelight Cabinetry Inc (G-7603)*
Renaissnce Crpt Tapestries Inc......212 696-0080
200 Lexington Ave Rm 1006 New York (10016) *(G-11863)*
Renaldos Sales and Service Ctr......716 337-3760
1770 Milestrip Rd North Collins (14111) *(G-12947)*
Renanssance The Book, Port Chester *Also called Albumx Corp (G-13766)*
Renco Group Inc (PA)......212 541-6000
1 Rockefeller Plz Fl 29 New York (10020) *(G-11864)*
Renco Manufacturing Inc......718 392-8877
1040 45th Ave Fl 2 Long Island City (11101) *(G-7891)*
Rene Portier Inc......718 853-7896
3611 14th Ave Ste 6 Brooklyn (11218) *(G-2511)*
Renegade Nation Ltd......212 868-9000
434 Av Of The Amercs Fl 6 New York (10011) *(G-11865)*
Renegade Nation Online LLC......212 868-9000
434 Ave Of The Americas # 6 New York (10011) *(G-11866)*
Renewable Energy Inc......718 690-2691
6 Cornell Ln Little Neck (11363) *(G-7533)*
Renewal By Andersen LLC......631 843-1716
2029 New Hwy Farmingdale (11735) *(G-5108)*
Renewal By Andrsen Long Island, Farmingdale *Also called Renewal By Andersen LLC (G-5108)*
Rennen International, South Ozone Park *Also called Extreme Auto Accessories Corp (G-15557)*
Renold Ajax, Westfield *Also called Renold Holdings Inc (G-17079)*
Renold Holdings Inc (HQ)......716 326-3121
100 Bourne St Westfield (14787) *(G-17079)*
Renold Inc......716 326-3121
100 Bourne St Westfield (14787) *(G-17080)*
Renovatio Med & Surgical Sups, Buffalo *Also called Yr Blanc & Co LLC (G-3287)*
Rent-A-Center Inc......718 322-2400
11211 Liberty Ave Jamaica (11419) *(G-6984)*
Rentschler Biotechnologie GMBH......631 656-7137
400 Oser Ave Ste 1650 Hauppauge (11788) *(G-6203)*
REO Welding Inc......518 238-1022
5 New Cortland St Cohoes (12047) *(G-3780)*
Repapers Corporation (PA)......305 691-1635
268 N Broadway Unit 9 Hicksville (11801) *(G-6416)*
Repellem Consumer Pdts Corp......631 273-3992
1626 Locust Ave Ste 6 Bohemia (11716) *(G-1122)*
Repertoire International De LI......212 817-1990
365 5th Ave Fl 3 New York (10016) *(G-11867)*
Repro Med Systems Inc......845 469-2042
24 Carpenter Rd Ste 1 Chester (10918) *(G-3639)*
Repsol Oil & Gas Usa LLC......607 562-4000
337 Daniel Zenker Dr Horseheads (14845) *(G-6618)*
Republic Clothing Corporation......212 719-3000
1411 Broadway Fl 37 New York (10018) *(G-11868)*
Republic Clothing Group, New York *Also called Republic Clothing Corporation (G-11868)*
Republic Clothing Group Inc......212 719-3000
1411 Broadway Fl 37 New York (10018) *(G-11869)*
Republic Construction Co Inc......914 235-3654
305 North Ave New Rochelle (10801) *(G-8969)*
Republic Steel Inc......716 827-2800
3049 Lake Shore Rd Blasdell (14219) *(G-958)*
Republican Registrar Inc......315 497-1551
6 Central St Moravia (13118) *(G-8658)*
Request Inc......518 899-1254
14 Corporate Dr Ste 6 Halfmoon (12065) *(G-5936)*
Request Jeans, New York *Also called US Design Group Ltd (G-12505)*
Request Multimedia, Halfmoon *Also called Request Inc (G-5936)*
Request Serious Play LLC......518 899-1254
14 Corporate Dr Halfmoon (12065) *(G-5937)*
RES Magazine, New York *Also called Res Media Group Inc (G-11870)*
Res Media Group Inc......212 320-3750
601 W 26th St Fl 11 New York (10001) *(G-11870)*
Rescuestuff Inc......718 318-7570
962 Washington St Peekskill (10566) *(G-13505)*
Research Centre of Kabbalah......718 805-0380
8384 115th St Richmond Hill (11418) *(G-14091)*
Research Frontiers Inc (PA)......516 364-1902
240 Crossways Park Dr Woodbury (11797) *(G-17318)*
Reserve Confections Chocolate, Spring Valley *Also called Reserve Confections Inc (G-15622)*
Reserve Confections Inc......845 371-7744
3 Perlman Dr Ste 105 Spring Valley (10977) *(G-15622)*
Reserve Gas Company, Alden *Also called Alden Aurora Gas Company Inc (G-177)*
Reserve Gas Company Inc......716 937-9484
13441 Railroad St Alden (14004) *(G-185)*
Reservoir Media Management Inc (PA)......212 675-0541
225 Varick St Fl 6 New York (10014) *(G-11871)*
Residential Fences Corp......631 205-9758
1760 Middle Country Rd Ridge (11961) *(G-14107)*
Resonance Technologies Inc......631 237-4901
109 Comac St Ronkonkoma (11779) *(G-15002)*
Resonant Legal Media LLC......212 687-7100
1040 Av Of The Amrcs 18 New York (10018) *(G-11872)*
Resonant Legal Media LLC (PA)......800 781-3591
1 Penn Plz Ste 1514 New York (10119) *(G-11873)*
Resource Capital Funds LP......631 692-9111
224 Wall St Ste 202 Huntington (11743) *(G-6713)*
Resource PTRlm&ptrochmcl Intl......212 537-3856
3 Columbus Cir Fl 15 New York (10019) *(G-11874)*
Response Care Inc......585 671-4144
38 Commercial St Webster (14580) *(G-16759)*
Responselink Inc......518 424-7776
31 Dussault Dr Latham (12110) *(G-7405)*
Responselink of Albany, Latham *Also called Responselink Inc (G-7405)*
Restaurant 570 8th Avenue LLC......646 722-8191
213 W 40th St Fl 3 New York (10018) *(G-11875)*
Restonic, Buffalo *Also called Royal Bedding Co Buffalo Inc (G-3197)*
Retailer, Lockport *Also called Metro Group Inc (G-7630)*

ALPHABETIC

(PA)=Parent Co (HQ)=Headquarters (DH)=Div Headquarters
2018 Harris
New York Manufacturers Directory
1045

Retailer, The, Port Washington *Also called Music & Sound Retailer Inc* ***(G-13866)***
Retrophin LLC....646 564-3680
777 3rd Ave Fl 22 New York (10017) ***(G-11876)***
Return Textiles LLC....646 408-0108
187 Lafayette St Fl 5 New York (10013) ***(G-11877)***
Reuse Action Incorporated....716 949-0900
279 Northampton St Buffalo (14208) ***(G-3183)***
Reuter Pallet Pkg Sys Inc....845 457-9937
272 Neelytown Rd Montgomery (12549) ***(G-8638)***
Revival Industries Inc....315 868-1085
126 Old Forge Rd Ilion (13357) ***(G-6784)***
Revivn Inc....347 762-8193
63 Flushing Ave Unit 231 Brooklyn (11205) ***(G-2512)***
Revlon Inc (PA)....212 527-4000
1 New York Plz New York (10004) ***(G-11878)***
Revlon Consumer Products Corp (HQ)....212 527-4000
1 New York Plz New York (10004) ***(G-11879)***
Revman International Inc (HQ)....212 894-3100
350 5th Ave Fl 70 New York (10118) ***(G-11880)***
Revolution Golf, New York *Also called Maven Marketing LLC* ***(G-11207)***
Revolutionwear Inc....617 669-9191
1745 Broadway Fl 17 New York (10019) ***(G-11881)***
Revonate Manufacturing LLC....315 433-1160
7401 Round Pond Rd Syracuse (13212) ***(G-16045)***
Rexford Services Inc....716 366-6671
4849 W Lake Rd Dunkirk (14048) ***(G-4373)***
Reynolds Book Bindery LLC....607 772-8937
37 Milford St Binghamton (13904) ***(G-941)***
Reynolds Drapery Service Inc....315 845-8632
7440 Main St Newport (13416) ***(G-12816)***
Reynolds Manufacturing Inc....607 562-8936
3298 State Rte 352 Big Flats (14814) ***(G-879)***
Reynolds Metals Company LLC (HQ)....212 518-5400
390 Park Ave New York (10022) ***(G-11882)***
Reynolds Packaging McHy Inc....716 358-6451
2632 S Work St Ste 24 Falconer (14733) ***(G-4918)***
Reynolds Shipyard Corporation....718 981-2800
200 Edgewater St Staten Island (10305) ***(G-15753)***
Reynolds Tech Fabricators Inc....315 437-0532
6895 Kinne St East Syracuse (13057) ***(G-4573)***
Rf Communications, Rochester *Also called Harris Corporation* ***(G-14446)***
Rf Inter Science Co, Patchogue *Also called Kevin Freeman* ***(G-13452)***
Rfb Associates Inc....518 271-0551
35 Sullivan Pkwy Fort Edward (12828) ***(G-5354)***
Rfn Inc....516 764-5100
40 Drexel Dr Bay Shore (11706) ***(G-729)***
Rfp LLC....212 838-7733
228 E 45th St Fl 11 New York (10017) ***(G-11883)***
RG, Buffalo *Also called Roberts-Gordon LLC* ***(G-3188)***
RG Apparel Group, New York *Also called Excelled Sheepskin & Lea Coat* ***(G-10157)***
RG Barry Corporation....212 244-3145
9 E 37th St Fl 11 New York (10016) ***(G-11884)***
RG Glass Creations Inc....212 675-0030
1441 Broadway 28 New York (10018) ***(G-11885)***
RGH Associates Inc....631 643-1111
86 Nancy St West Babylon (11704) ***(G-16852)***
Rgm Signs Inc....718 442-0598
1234 Castleton Ave Staten Island (10310) ***(G-15754)***
Rheinwald Printing Co Inc....585 637-5100
15 Main St Brockport (14420) ***(G-1246)***
Rheonix Inc (PA)....607 257-1242
10 Brown Rd Ste 103 Ithaca (14850) ***(G-6909)***
Rhett M Clark Inc....585 538-9570
3213 Lehigh St Caledonia (14423) ***(G-3309)***
Rhino Trunk & Case Inc....585 244-4553
565 Blossom Rd Ste J Rochester (14610) ***(G-14647)***
Rhoda Lee Inc....212 840-5700
77 W 55th St Apt 4k New York (10019) ***(G-11886)***
Ribble Lumber Inc....315 536-6221
249 1/2 Lake St Penn Yan (14527) ***(G-13541)***
Ribz LLC....212 764-9595
1407 Broadway Rm 1402 New York (10018) ***(G-11887)***
Ric-Lo Productions Ltd....845 469-2285
1144 Kings Hwy Chester (10918) ***(G-3640)***
Rich Brilliant Willing, Brooklyn *Also called Rbw Studio LLC* ***(G-2501)***
Rich Holdings Inc....716 878-8000
1 Robert Rich Way Buffalo (14213) ***(G-3184)***
Rich Products Corporation (PA)....716 878-8000
1 Robert Rich Way Buffalo (14213) ***(G-3185)***
Richard Anthony Corp....914 922-7141
1500 Front St Ste 12 Yorktown Heights (10598) ***(G-17534)***
Richard Anthony Custom Mllwk, Yorktown Heights *Also called Richard Anthony Corp* ***(G-17534)***
Richard Bauer Logging....585 343-4149
3936 Cookson Rd Alexander (14005) ***(G-193)***
Richard C Owen Publishers Inc....914 232-3903
243 Route 100 Somers (10589) ***(G-15534)***
Richard Edelson....914 428-7573
80 Pinewood Rd Hartsdale (10530) ***(G-6018)***
Richard Engdal Baking Corp....914 777-9600
421 Waverly Ave Mamaroneck (10543) ***(G-8077)***
Richard Leeds Intl Inc (PA)....212 532-4546
135 Madison Ave Fl 10 New York (10016) ***(G-11888)***
Richard Manno & Company Inc....631 643-2200
42 Lamar St West Babylon (11704) ***(G-16853)***
Richard Manufacturing Co Inc....718 254-0958
63 Flushing Ave Unit 327 Brooklyn (11205) ***(G-2513)***
Richard R Cain Inc....845 229-7410
50 Scenic Dr Hyde Park (12538) ***(G-6775)***
Richard Rothbard Inc....845 355-2300
1866 Route 284 Slate Hill (10973) ***(G-15496)***
Richard Ruffner....631 234-4600
69 Carleton Ave Central Islip (11722) ***(G-3536)***
Richard Stacey Rs Automation, Albion *Also called Rs Automation* ***(G-172)***
Richard Stewart....518 632-5363
4495 State Rte 149 Hartford (12838) ***(G-6015)***
Richards & West Inc....585 461-4088
501 W Commercial St Ste 1 East Rochester (14445) ***(G-4485)***
Richards Logging LLC....518 359-2775
201 State Route 3 Tupper Lake (12986) ***(G-16303)***
Richards Machine Tool Co Inc....716 683-3380
3753 Walden Ave Lancaster (14086) ***(G-7363)***
Richards Screw Machine, West Babylon *Also called RGH Associates Inc* ***(G-16852)***
Richardson Brands Company (HQ)....800 839-8938
101 Erie Blvd Canajoharie (13317) ***(G-3361)***
Richardson Foods, Canajoharie *Also called Richardson Brands Company* ***(G-3361)***
Richemont North America Inc....212 891-2440
645 5th Ave Fl 6 New York (10022) ***(G-11889)***
Richer's Bakery, Flushing *Also called H H B Bakery of Little Neck* ***(G-5254)***
Richlar Custom Foam Div, East Syracuse *Also called Richlar Industries Inc* ***(G-4574)***
Richlar Industries Inc....315 463-5144
6741 Old Collamer Rd East Syracuse (13057) ***(G-4574)***
Richline Group Inc....212 643-2908
245 W 29th St Rm 900 New York (10001) ***(G-11890)***
Richline Group Inc....212 764-8454
1385 Broadway Fl 12 New York (10018) ***(G-11891)***
Richline Group Inc....914 699-0000
1385 Broadway Fl 12 New York (10018) ***(G-11892)***
Richloom Corp....212 685-5400
261 5th Ave Fl 12 New York (10016) ***(G-11893)***
Richloom Fabrics Corp (PA)....212 685-5400
261 5th Ave Fl 12 New York (10016) ***(G-11894)***
Richloom Fabrics Group Inc (HQ)....212 685-5400
261 5th Ave Fl 12 New York (10016) ***(G-11895)***
Richloom Home Fashion, New York *Also called Richloom Corp* ***(G-11893)***
Richloom Home Fashions Corp....212 685-5400
261 5th Ave Fl 12 New York (10016) ***(G-11896)***
Richmond Ready Mix Corp....917 731-8400
328 Park St Staten Island (10306) ***(G-15755)***
Richner Communications Inc (PA)....516 569-4000
2 Endo Blvd Garden City (11530) ***(G-5543)***
Richner Communications Inc....516 569-4000
379 Central Ave Lawrence (11559) ***(G-7424)***
Richs Sttches EMB Screenprint....845 621-2175
407 Route 6 Mahopac (10541) ***(G-8030)***
Richter Metalcraft Corporation....845 895-2025
80 Cottage St Wallkill (12589) ***(G-16565)***
Rick-Mic Industries Inc....631 563-8389
1951 Ocean Ave Ste 6 Ronkonkoma (11779) ***(G-15003)***
Rico International....818 767-7711
8484 San Fernando Rd Farmingdale (11735) ***(G-5109)***
Rid Lom Precision Mfg....585 594-8600
50 Regency Oaks Blvd Rochester (14624) ***(G-14648)***
Ridge Cabinet & Showcase Inc....585 663-0560
1545 Mount Read Blvd # 2 Rochester (14606) ***(G-14649)***
Ridgewood Times Prtg & Pubg....718 821-7500
6071 Woodbine St Fl 1 Ridgewood (11385) ***(G-14134)***
Riefler Concrete Products LLC....716 649-3260
5690 Camp Rd Hamburg (14075) ***(G-5964)***
Right World View....914 406-2994
2900 Purchase St 528 Purchase (10577) ***(G-13987)***
Rigidized Metals Corporation....716 849-4703
658 Ohio St Buffalo (14203) ***(G-3186)***
Rigidized-Metal, Buffalo *Also called Rigidized Metals Corporation* ***(G-3186)***
Rij Pharmaceutical Corporation....845 692-5799
40 Commercial Ave Middletown (10941) ***(G-8494)***
Rike Enterprises Inc....631 277-8338
46 Taft Ave Islip (11751) ***(G-6851)***
Riley Gear Corporation....716 694-0900
61 Felton St North Tonawanda (14120) ***(G-13007)***
RILM, New York *Also called Repertoire International De Ll* ***(G-11867)***
Rimco Plastics Corp....607 739-3864
316 Colonial Dr Horseheads (14845) ***(G-6619)***
Rims Like New Inc....845 537-0396
507 Union School Rd Middletown (10941) ***(G-8495)***
Rina, Plattsburgh *Also called Rapa Independent North America* ***(G-13723)***
Rinaldi Precision Machine....631 242-4141
60 Corbin Ave Ste F Bay Shore (11706) ***(G-730)***
Ring Division Producto Machine, Jamestown *Also called Producto Corporation* ***(G-7057)***
Ringhoff Fuel Inc....631 878-0663
72 Atlantic Ave East Moriches (11940) ***(G-4450)***
Ringlead Inc....310 906-0545
205 E Main St Ste 2-3a Huntington (11743) ***(G-6714)***

ALPHABETIC SECTION

Rings Wire Inc 212 741-9779
246 W 38th St Rm 501 New York (10018) *(G-11897)*

Rini Tank & Truck Service 718 384-6606
327 Nassau Ave Brooklyn (11222) *(G-2514)*

Rino, Freeport Also called Ondrivesus Corp *(G-5427)*

Rio Apparel USA Inc 212 869-9150
237 W 37th St Rm 13l New York (10018) *(G-11898)*

Riot New Media Group Inc 604 700-4896
147 Prince St Ste 1 Brooklyn (11201) *(G-2515)*

Rip Van Wafels Inc 415 529-5403
67 West St Ste 705 Brooklyn (11222) *(G-2516)*

Ripak Aerospace Processing, West Babylon Also called Magellan Aerospace Processing *(G-16838)*

Ripi Precision Co Inc (PA) 631 694-2453
92 Toledo St Farmingdale (11735) *(G-5110)*

Ripley Machine & Tool Co Inc 716 736-3205
9825 E Main Rd Ripley (14775) *(G-14148)*

Riri USA Inc (HQ) 212 268-3866
350 5th Ave Ste 6700 New York (10018) *(G-11899)*

Risa Management Corp 718 361-2606
5501 43rd St Fl 3 Maspeth (11378) *(G-8197)*

Risa's, Maspeth Also called Risa Management Corp *(G-8197)*

Rising Sons 6 Brewing Coinc 607 368-4836
196 Baker St Corning (14830) *(G-3999)*

Rising Stars Soccer Club CNY 315 381-3096
4980 State Route 233 Westmoreland (13490) *(G-17093)*

Rision Inc 212 987-2628
306 E 78th St Apt 1b New York (10075) *(G-11900)*

Risk Management Magazine, New York Also called Risk Society Management Pubg *(G-11901)*

Risk Society Management Pubg 212 286-9364
655 3rd Ave Fl 2 New York (10017) *(G-11901)*

RIT Printing Corp 631 586-6220
250 N Fairway Bay Shore (11706) *(G-731)*

Ritchie Brothers Slate Co, Middle Granville Also called Vermont Natural Stoneworks *(G-8436)*

Ritchie Corp 212 768-0083
263 W 38th St Fl 13 New York (10018) *(G-11902)*

Ritnoa Inc 212 660-2148
24019 Jamaica Ave Fl 2 Bellerose (11426) *(G-807)*

Rittlewood Holding Co, New York Also called Rda Holding Co *(G-11837)*

Riva Jewelry Manufacturing Inc 718 361-3100
140 58th St Ste 8b Brooklyn (11220) *(G-2517)*

River Rat Design 315 393-4770
1801 Ford St Ste A Ogdensburg (13669) *(G-13142)*

Rivera 718 458-1488
3330 109th St Flushing (11368) *(G-5295)*

Riverdale Press, The, Bronx Also called Dale Press Inc *(G-1313)*

Riverfront Costume Design 716 693-2501
200 River Rd North Tonawanda (14120) *(G-13008)*

Riverhawk Company LP 315 624-7171
215 Clinton Rd New Hartford (13413) *(G-8854)*

Riverside Automation, Rochester Also called Riverview Associates Inc *(G-14651)*

Riverside Iron LLC 315 535-4864
26 Water St Gouverneur (13642) *(G-5762)*

Riverside Machinery Company (PA) 718 492-7400
140 53rd St Brooklyn (11232) *(G-2518)*

Riverside Machinery Company 718 492-7400
132 54th St Brooklyn (11220) *(G-2519)*

Riverside Mfg Acquisition LLC 585 458-2090
655 Driving Park Ave Rochester (14613) *(G-14650)*

Rivertowns Enterprise, Dobbs Ferry Also called W H White Publications Inc *(G-4328)*

Riverview Associates Inc 585 235-5980
1040 Jay St Rochester (14611) *(G-14651)*

Riverview Industries Inc 845 265-5284
3012 Route 9 Ste 1 Cold Spring (10516) *(G-3790)*

Riverwood Signs By Dandev Desi 845 229-0282
7 Maple Ln Hyde Park (12538) *(G-6776)*

Rizzoli Intl Publications Inc (HQ) 212 387-3400
300 Park Ave S Fl 4 New York (10010) *(G-11903)*

Rizzoli Intl Publications Inc 212 387-3572
300 Park Ave S Fl 3 New York (10010) *(G-11904)*

Rizzoli Intl Publications Inc 212 308-2000
300 Park Ave Frnt 4 New York (10022) *(G-11905)*

RJ Harvey Instrument Corp 845 359-3943
11 Jane St Tappan (10983) *(G-16107)*

Rj Millworkers Inc 607 433-0525
12 Lewis St Oneonta (13820) *(G-13215)*

RJ Precision LLC 585 768-8030
6662 Main Rd Stafford (14143) *(G-15642)*

Rj Welding & Fabricating Inc 315 523-1288
2300 Wheat Rd Clifton Springs (14432) *(G-3740)*

Rjm2 Inc 212 944-1660
241 W 37th St Rm 926 New York (10018) *(G-11906)*

Rjs Machine Works Inc 716 826-1778
1611 Electric Ave Lackawanna (14218) *(G-7274)*

RKI Building Spc Co Inc 718 728-7788
1530 131st St College Point (11356) *(G-3830)*

Rlp Holdings Inc 716 852-0832
1049 Military Rd Buffalo (14217) *(G-3187)*

Rls Holdings Inc 716 418-7274
11342 Main St Clarence (14031) *(G-3697)*

Rm Bakery LLC 718 472-3036
4425 54th Dr Maspeth (11378) *(G-8198)*

Rmb Embroidery Service 585 271-5560
176 Anderson Ave Ste F110 Rochester (14607) *(G-14652)*

Rmd Holding Inc 845 628-0030
593 Route 6 Mahopac (10541) *(G-8031)*

Rmf Print Management Group 716 683-4351
786 Terrace Blvd Ste 3 Depew (14043) *(G-4297)*

Rmf Printing Technologies Inc 716 683-7500
50 Pearl St Lancaster (14086) *(G-7364)*

Rmi Printing, New York Also called Rosen Mandell & Immerman Inc *(G-11936)*

RMS Medical Products, Chester Also called Repro Med Systems Inc *(G-3639)*

RMS Packaging Inc 914 205-2070
1050 Lower South St Peekskill (10566) *(G-13506)*

Rmw Filtration Products Co LLC 631 226-9412
230 Lambert Ave Copiague (11726) *(G-3947)*

Rn Furniture Corp 347 960-9622
11409 Atlantic Ave Richmond Hill (11418) *(G-14092)*

Rnd Enterprises Inc 212 627-0165
446 W 33rd St New York (10001) *(G-11907)*

Road Cases USA Inc 631 563-0633
1625 Sycamore Ave Ste A Bohemia (11716) *(G-1123)*

Roadie Products Inc 631 567-8588
1121 Lincoln Ave Unit 20 Holbrook (11741) *(G-6497)*

Roadrunner Records Inc (PA) 212 274-7500
1290 Avenue Of The Americ New York (10104) *(G-11908)*

Roanwell Corporation 718 401-0288
2564 Park Ave Bronx (10451) *(G-1440)*

Roar Beverages LLC (PA) 631 683-5565
125 W Shore Rd Huntington (11743) *(G-6715)*

Roar Biomedical Inc 631 591-2749
4603 Middle Country Rd Calverton (11933) *(G-3325)*

Rob Herschenfeld Design Inc 718 456-6801
304 Boerum St Brooklyn (11206) *(G-2520)*

Rob Salamida Company Inc 607 729-4868
71 Pratt Ave Ste 1 Johnson City (13790) *(G-7136)*

Robat Inc 518 812-6244
1 Fairchild Sq Ste 114 Clifton Park (12065) *(G-3731)*

Robeco/Ascot Products Inc 516 248-1521
100 Ring Rd W Garden City (11530) *(G-5544)*

Robell Research Inc 212 755-6577
635 Madison Ave Fl 13 New York (10022) *(G-11909)*

Robert & William Inc (PA) 631 727-5780
224 Griffing Ave Riverhead (11901) *(G-14167)*

Robert Abady Dog Food Co Ltd 845 473-1900
201 Smith St Poughkeepsie (12601) *(G-13946)*

Robert Bartholomew Ltd 516 767-2970
15 Main St Port Washington (11050) *(G-13876)*

Robert Bosch LLC 315 733-3312
2118 Beechgrove Pl Utica (13501) *(G-16381)*

Robert Busse & Co Inc 631 435-4711
75 Arkay Dr Hauppauge (11788) *(G-6204)*

Robert Cohen 718 789-0996
10540 Rockaway Blvd Ste A Ozone Park (11417) *(G-13411)*

Robert Danes Danes Inc (PA) 212 226-1351
481 Greenwich St Apt 5b New York (10013) *(G-11910)*

Robert E Derecktor Inc 914 698-0962
311 E Boston Post Rd Mamaroneck (10543) *(G-8078)*

Robert Ehrlich 516 353-4617
75 Saint Marks Pl New York (10003) *(G-11911)*

Robert Greenburg (PA) 845 586-2226
Cross Rd Margaretville (12455) *(G-8123)*

Robert J Faraone 585 232-7160
1600 N Clinton Ave Rochester (14621) *(G-14653)*

Robert M Brown 607 426-6250
150 Mill St Montour Falls (14865) *(G-8650)*

Robert M Vault 315 243-1447
1360 Lestina Beach Rd Bridgeport (13030) *(G-1235)*

Robert Miller Associates LLC 718 392-1640
4310 23rd St Long Island City (11101) *(G-7892)*

Robert Pikcilingis 518 355-1860
2575 Western Ave Altamont (12009) *(G-215)*

Robert Portegello Graphics 718 241-8118
2028 Utica Ave Brooklyn (11234) *(G-2521)*

Robert Racine (PA) 518 677-0224
41 N Union St Cambridge (12816) *(G-3338)*

Robert Tabatznik Assoc Inc (PA) 845 336-4555
867 Flatbush Rd Kingston (12401) *(G-7237)*

Robert Viggiani 914 423-4046
37 Vredenburgh Ave Ste B Yonkers (10704) *(G-17500)*

Robert W Butts Logging Co 518 643-2897
420 Mannix Rd Peru (12972) *(G-13550)*

Robert W Still 315 942-5594
11755 State Route 26 Ava (13303) *(G-529)*

Robert-Masters Corp 718 545-1030
3217 61st St Woodside (11377) *(G-17367)*

Roberto Coin Inc (PA) 212 486-4545
579 5th Ave Fl 17 New York (10017) *(G-11912)*

Roberts Nichols Fire Apparatus 518 431-1945
84 Island View Rd Cohoes (12047) *(G-3781)*

Roberts Office Furn Cncpts Inc 315 451-9185
7327 Henry Clay Blvd Liverpool (13088) ***(G-7572)***
Roberts-Gordon LLC (HQ) 716 852-4400
1250 William St Buffalo (14206) ***(G-3188)***
Robespierre Inc 212 764-8810
214 W 39th St Ph Ste 602 New York (10018) ***(G-11913)***
Robespierre Inc (PA) 212 594-0012
225 W 35th St Ste 600 New York (10001) ***(G-11914)***
Robin Industries Ltd 718 218-9616
56 N 3rd St Brooklyn (11249) ***(G-2522)***
Robin Stanley Inc 212 871-0007
1212 Avenue Of The Americ New York (10036) ***(G-11915)***
Robinson Concrete Inc (PA) 315 253-6666
3486 Franklin Street Rd Auburn (13021) ***(G-513)***
Robinson Concrete Inc 315 492-6200
3537 Apulia Rd Jamesville (13078) ***(G-7085)***
Robinson Concrete Inc 315 676-4662
7020 Corporate Park Dr Brewerton (13029) ***(G-1202)***
Robinson Knife 716 685-6300
2615 Walden Ave Buffalo (14225) ***(G-3189)***
Robinson Tools LLC 585 586-5432
477 Whitney Rd Penfield (14526) ***(G-13526)***
Robly Digital Marketing LLC 917 238-0730
93 Leonard St Apt 6 New York (10013) ***(G-11916)***
Robo Self Serve, Williamsville *Also called Schmitt Sales Inc* ***(G-17277)***
Robocom Systems International, Farmingdale *Also called Robocom Us LLC* ***(G-5111)***
Robocom Us LLC (HQ) 631 861-2045
1111 Broadhollow Rd # 100 Farmingdale (11735) ***(G-5111)***
Roboshop Inc 315 437-6454
226 Midler Park Dr Syracuse (13206) ***(G-16046)***
Robot Fruit Inc 631 423-7250
40 Radcliff Dr Huntington (11743) ***(G-6716)***
Robs Cycle Supply 315 292-6878
613 Wolf St Syracuse (13208) ***(G-16047)***
Robs Really Good LLC 516 671-4411
100 Roslyn Ave Sea Cliff (11579) ***(G-15364)***
Roccera LLC 585 426-0887
771 Elmgrove Rd Bldg No2 Rochester (14624) ***(G-14654)***
Rocco Bormioli Glass Co Inc (PA) 212 719-0606
41 Madison Ave Ste 1603 New York (10010) ***(G-11917)***
Rochester 100 Inc 585 475-0200
40 Jefferson Rd Rochester (14623) ***(G-14655)***
Rochester Asphalt Materials (HQ) 585 381-7010
1150 Penfield Rd Rochester (14625) ***(G-14656)***
Rochester Asphalt Materials 315 524-4619
1200 Atlantic Ave Walworth (14568) ***(G-16572)***
Rochester Asphalt Materials 585 924-7360
5929 Loomis Rd Farmington (14425) ***(G-5163)***
Rochester Atomated Systems Inc 585 594-3222
40 Regency Oaks Blvd Rochester (14624) ***(G-14657)***
Rochester Business Journal 585 546-8303
16 W Main St Ste 341 Rochester (14614) ***(G-14658)***
Rochester Catholic Press (PA) 585 529-9530
1150 Buffalo Rd Rochester (14624) ***(G-14659)***
Rochester Coca Cola Bottling 607 739-5678
210 Industrial Park Rd Horseheads (14845) ***(G-6620)***
Rochester Coca Cola Bottling 585 546-3900
123 Upper Falls Blvd Rochester (14605) ***(G-14660)***
Rochester Colonial Mfg Corp (PA) 585 254-8191
1794 Lyell Ave Rochester (14606) ***(G-14661)***
Rochester Countertop Inc (PA) 585 338-2260
3300 Monroe Ave Ste 212 Rochester (14618) ***(G-14662)***
Rochester Democrat & Chronicle 585 232-7100
55 Exchange Blvd Rochester (14614) ***(G-14663)***
Rochester Gear Inc 585 254-5442
213 Norman St Rochester (14613) ***(G-14664)***
Rochester Golf Week, Rochester *Also called Expositor Newspapers Inc* ***(G-14387)***
Rochester Industrial Ctrl Inc (PA) 315 524-4555
6400 Furnace Rd Ontario (14519) ***(G-13234)***
Rochester Industrial Ctrl Inc 315 524-4555
6345 Furnace Rd Ontario (14519) ***(G-13235)***
Rochester Insulated Glass Inc 585 289-3611
73 Merrick Cir Manchester (14504) ***(G-8085)***
Rochester Lumber Company 585 924-7171
6080 Collett Rd Farmington (14425) ***(G-5164)***
Rochester Magnet, East Rochester *Also called Carpentier Industries LLC* ***(G-4474)***
Rochester Midland Corporation (PA) 585 336-2200
155 Paragon Dr Rochester (14624) ***(G-14665)***
Rochester Optical, Rochester *Also called Genesis Vision Inc* ***(G-14418)***
Rochester Orthopedic Labs (PA) 585 272-1060
300 Airpark Dr Ste 100 Rochester (14624) ***(G-14666)***
Rochester Overnight Pltg LLC 585 328-4590
2 Cairn St Rochester (14611) ***(G-14667)***
Rochester Photonics Corp 585 387-0674
115 Canal Landing Blvd Rochester (14626) ***(G-14668)***
Rochester Precision Optics LLC 585 292-5450
850 John St West Henrietta (14586) ***(G-16924)***
Rochester Screen Printing, Rochester *Also called Michael Todd Stevens* ***(G-14527)***
Rochester Seal Pro LLC 585 594-3818
53 Northwind Way Rochester (14624) ***(G-14669)***
Rochester Silver Works LLC 585 477-9501
100 Latona Rd Bldg 110 Rochester (14652) ***(G-14670)***
Rochester Silver Works LLC 585 743-1610
240 Aster St Rochester (14615) ***(G-14671)***
Rochester Stampings Inc 585 467-5241
400 Trade Ct Rochester (14624) ***(G-14672)***
Rochester Steel Treating Works 585 546-3348
962 E Main St Rochester (14605) ***(G-14673)***
Rochester Structural LLC 585 436-1250
961 Lyell Ave Bldg 5 Rochester (14606) ***(G-14674)***
Rochester Technology Park, Rochester *Also called Tech Park Food Services LLC* ***(G-14745)***
Rochester Tool and Mold Inc 585 464-9336
515 Lee Rd Rochester (14606) ***(G-14675)***
Rochester Tube Fabricators 585 254-0290
1128 Lexington Ave 5d Rochester (14606) ***(G-14676)***
Rochling Advent Tool & Mold LP 585 254-2000
999 Ridgeway Ave Rochester (14615) ***(G-14677)***
Rock Hill Bakehouse Ltd 518 743-1627
21 Saratoga Rd Gansevoort (12831) ***(G-5503)***
Rock Iroquois Products Inc 585 637-6834
5251 Sweden Walker Rd Brockport (14420) ***(G-1247)***
Rock Mountain Farms Inc 845 647-9084
11 Spring St Ellenville (12428) ***(G-4652)***
Rock Stream Vineyards 607 243-8322
162 Fir Tree Point Rd Rock Stream (14878) ***(G-14808)***
Rockaloid, Piermont *Also called Rockland Colloid Corp* ***(G-13572)***
Rockaway Stairs Ltd 718 945-0047
1011 Bay 24th St Far Rockaway (11691) ***(G-4931)***
Rockefeller University 212 327-8568
950 3rd Ave Fl 2 New York (10022) ***(G-11918)***
Rocket Communications, Buffalo *Also called Gallagher Printing Inc* ***(G-2977)***
Rocket Communications Inc 716 873-2594
2507 Delaware Ave Buffalo (14216) ***(G-3190)***
Rocket Fuel Inc 212 594-8888
195 Broadway Fl 10 New York (10007) ***(G-11919)***
Rocket Tech Fuel Corp 516 810-8947
20 Corbin Ave Bay Shore (11706) ***(G-732)***
Rocking The Boat Inc 718 466-5799
812 Edgewater Rd Bronx (10474) ***(G-1441)***
Rockland Bakery Inc (PA) 845 623-5800
94 Demarest Mill Rd W Nanuet (10954) ***(G-8807)***
Rockland Colloid Corp (PA) 845 359-5559
44 Franklin St Piermont (10968) ***(G-13572)***
Rockland County Times, Nanuet *Also called Citizen Publishing Corp* ***(G-8800)***
Rockland Insulated Wire Cable 845 429-3103
87 Broadway Haverstraw (10927) ***(G-6263)***
Rockland Review Publishing, West Nyack *Also called Angel Media and Publishing* ***(G-16941)***
Rockmills Steel Products Corp 718 366-8300
5912 54th St Maspeth (11378) ***(G-8199)***
Rockport Company LLC 631 243-0418
1288 The Arches Cir Deer Park (11729) ***(G-4225)***
Rockport Company LLC 718 271-3627
9015 Queens Blvd Ste 1025 Elmhurst (11373) ***(G-4680)***
Rockport Pa LLC 212 482-8580
477 Madison Ave Fl 18 New York (10022) ***(G-11920)***
Rockville Pro, Inwood *Also called Audiosavings Inc* ***(G-6791)***
Rockwell Automation Inc 585 487-2700
1000 Pittsford Victor Rd # 17 Pittsford (14534) ***(G-13602)***
Rockwell Collins Simulation 607 352-1298
31 Lewis Rd Binghamton (13905) ***(G-942)***
Rockwell Video Solutions LLC 631 745-0582
10 Koral Dr Southampton (11968) ***(G-15574)***
Rodac USA Corp 716 741-3931
5605 Kraus Rd Clarence (14031) ***(G-3698)***
Rodale Electronics, Hauppauge *Also called Rodale Wireless Inc* ***(G-6205)***
Rodale Inc 212 697-2040
733 3rd Ave Fl 15 New York (10017) ***(G-11921)***
Rodale Wireless Inc 631 231-0044
20 Oser Ave Ste 2 Hauppauge (11788) ***(G-6205)***
Rodan, Hicksville *Also called Oxygen Inc* ***(G-6405)***
Rodem Incorporated 212 779-7122
120 W 29th St Frnt A New York (10001) ***(G-11922)***
Rodeo of NY Inc 212 730-0744
62 W 47th St New York (10036) ***(G-11923)***
Rodgard Corporation 716 852-1435
92 Msgr Valente Dr Buffalo (14206) ***(G-3191)***
Roemac Industrial Sales Inc 716 692-7332
27 Fredericka St North Tonawanda (14120) ***(G-13009)***
Roessel & Co Inc 585 458-5560
199 Lagrange Ave Rochester (14613) ***(G-14678)***
Roethel, Ogdensburg *Also called River Rat Design* ***(G-13142)***
Roffe Accessories Inc (PA) 212 213-1440
833 Broadway Apt 4 New York (10003) ***(G-11924)***
Rogan LLC 212 680-1407
330 Bowery New York (10012) ***(G-11925)***
Rogan LLC (PA) 646 496-9339
270 Bowery 3 New York (10012) ***(G-11926)***
Roger & Sons Inc (PA) 212 226-4734
268 Bowery Frnt 6 New York (10012) ***(G-11927)***
Roger L Urban Inc (PA) 716 693-5391
908 Niagara Falls Blvd # 107 North Tonawanda (14120) ***(G-13010)***
Roger Latari 631 580-2422
30 Raynor Ave Ste 1 Ronkonkoma (11779) ***(G-15004)***

ALPHABETIC SECTION
Rotron Incorporated (HQ)

Roger Michael Press Inc (PA).....732 752-0800
499 Van Brunt St Ste 6b Brooklyn (11231) ***(G-2523)***
Rogers Enterprises, Rochester *Also called Dock Hardware Incorporated* ***(G-14335)***
Rogers Group Inc.....212 643-9292
318 W 39th St Fl 4 New York (10018) ***(G-11928)***
Rogers Industrial Spring, Buffalo *Also called Kehr-Buffalo Wire Frame Co Inc* ***(G-3044)***
Rohlfs Stined Leaded GL Studio.....914 699-4848
783 S 3rd Ave Mount Vernon (10550) ***(G-8773)***
Rohto USA Inc (HQ).....716 677-2500
707 Sterling Dr Orchard Park (14127) ***(G-13320)***
Rokon Tech LLC.....718 429-0729
5223 74th St Elmhurst (11373) ***(G-4681)***
Roli Retreads Inc.....631 694-7670
212 E Carmans Rd Unit A Farmingdale (11735) ***(G-5112)***
Roli Tire and Auto Repair, Farmingdale *Also called Roli Retreads Inc* ***(G-5112)***
Roli USA Inc.....412 600-4840
100 5th Ave New York (10011) ***(G-11929)***
Rolite Mfg Inc.....716 683-0259
10 Wendling Ct Lancaster (14086) ***(G-7365)***
Roll Lock Truss, Waddington *Also called Structural Wood Corporation* ***(G-16542)***
Rolla Daily News Plus, Pittsford *Also called Gatehouse Media MO Holdings* ***(G-13590)***
Rollers Inc.....716 837-0700
2495 Main St Ste 359 Buffalo (14214) ***(G-3192)***
Rollers Unlimited, Syracuse *Also called David Fehlman* ***(G-15942)***
Rolliform of Jamestown Inc.....716 665-5310
181 Blackstone Ave Jamestown (14701) ***(G-7058)***
Rollhaus Seating Products Inc.....718 729-9111
4310 21st St Long Island City (11101) ***(G-7893)***
Rolling Gate Supply Corp.....718 366-5258
7919 Cypress Ave Glendale (11385) ***(G-5677)***
Rolling Star Manufacturing Inc.....315 896-4767
125 Liberty Ln Barneveld (13304) ***(G-616)***
Rolling Stone, New York *Also called Wenner Media LLC* ***(G-12639)***
Rolling Stone Magazine.....212 484-1616
1290 Ave Of The Amer Fl 2 New York (10104) ***(G-11930)***
Rollo Mio Artisan Bakery, Maspeth *Also called Rm Bakery LLC* ***(G-8198)***
Rollson Inc.....631 423-9578
10 Smugglers Cv Huntington (11743) ***(G-6717)***
Roly Door Sales Inc.....716 877-1515
5659 Herman Hill Rd Hamburg (14075) ***(G-5965)***
Roma Bakery Inc.....516 825-9170
45 Railroad Ave Valley Stream (11580) ***(G-16449)***
Roma Industries LLC.....212 268-0723
12 W 37th St Fl 10 New York (10018) ***(G-11931)***
Roma Ray Bakery, Valley Stream *Also called Rays Italian Bakery Inc* ***(G-16447)***
Romac Electronics Inc.....516 349-7900
155 E Ames Ct Unit 1 Plainview (11803) ***(G-13660)***
Roman Stone Construction Co.....631 667-0566
85 S 4th St Bay Shore (11706) ***(G-733)***
Romance & Co Inc.....212 382-0337
2 W 47th St Ste 1111 New York (10036) ***(G-11932)***
Romantic Times Inc.....718 237-1097
81 Willoughby St Ste 701 Brooklyn (11201) ***(G-2524)***
Romantic Times Magazine, Brooklyn *Also called Romantic Times Inc* ***(G-2524)***
Romar Contracting Inc.....845 778-2737
630 State Route 52 Walden (12586) ***(G-16555)***
Romark Diagnostics, Tappan *Also called RJ Harvey Instrument Corp* ***(G-16107)***
Rome Fastener, New York *Also called Rings Wire Inc* ***(G-11897)***
Rome Sign & Display Co.....315 336-0550
510 Erie Blvd W Rome (13440) ***(G-14861)***
Rome Specialty Company Inc.....315 337-8200
501 W Embargo St Rome (13440) ***(G-14862)***
Romir Enterprises, New York *Also called Mer Gems Corp* ***(G-11252)***
Romold Inc.....585 529-4440
5 Moonlanding Rd Rochester (14624) ***(G-14679)***
Rona Precision Inc.....631 737-4034
142 Remington Blvd Ste 2 Ronkonkoma (11779) ***(G-15005)***
Rona Precision Mfg, Ronkonkoma *Also called Rona Precision Inc* ***(G-15005)***
Ronan Paints, Bronx *Also called T J Ronan Paint Corp* ***(G-1468)***
Ronbar Laboratories Inc.....718 937-6755
5202 Van Dam St Long Island City (11101) ***(G-7894)***
Roner Inc (PA).....718 392-6020
3553 24th St Long Island City (11106) ***(G-7895)***
Roner Inc.....718 392-6020
1433 31st Ave Long Island City (11106) ***(G-7896)***
Ronmar, Flushing *Also called United Steel Products Inc* ***(G-5311)***
Ronni Nicole Group LLC.....212 764-1000
1400 Broadway Rm 2102 New York (10018) ***(G-11933)***
Roode Hoek & Co Inc.....718 522-5921
55 Ferris St Brooklyn (11231) ***(G-2525)***
Roofing Consultant, Buffalo *Also called Tiedemann Waldemar Inc* ***(G-3244)***
Room At The Top Inc.....718 257-0766
632 Hegeman Ave Brooklyn (11207) ***(G-2526)***
Roomactually LLC.....646 388-1922
175 Varick St New York (10014) ***(G-11934)***
Roome Technologies Inc.....585 229-4437
4796 Honeoye Business Par Honeoye (14471) ***(G-6552)***
Rooster Hill Vineyards, Penn Yan *Also called Hoffman & Hoffman* ***(G-13537)***
Ropack USA Inc.....631 482-7777
49 Mall Dr Commack (11725) ***(G-3866)***

Rosco Inc (PA).....718 526-2601
9021 144th Pl Jamaica (11435) ***(G-6985)***
Rosco Div, Rome *Also called Rome Specialty Company Inc* ***(G-14862)***
Roscoe Brothers Inc.....607 844-3750
15 Freeville Rd Dryden (13053) ***(G-4347)***
Roscoe Little Store Inc.....607 498-5553
59 Stewart Ave Roscoe (12776) ***(G-15035)***
Rose Cumming, New York *Also called Dessin/Fournir Inc* ***(G-9912)***
Rose Fence Inc (PA).....516 223-0777
345 W Sunrise Hwy Freeport (11520) ***(G-5434)***
Rose Fence Inc.....516 790-2308
356 Bay Ave Halesite (11743) ***(G-5929)***
Rose Fence Inc.....516 223-0777
345 Sunrise Hwy Baldwin (11510) ***(G-560)***
Rose Graphics LLC.....516 547-6142
109 Kean St West Babylon (11704) ***(G-16854)***
Rose Solomon Co.....718 855-1788
63 Flushing Ave Unit 330 Brooklyn (11205) ***(G-2527)***
Rose Trunk Mfg Co Inc.....516 766-6686
3935 Sally Ln Oceanside (11572) ***(G-13115)***
Rose-Ann Division, New York *Also called Texport Fabrics Corp* ***(G-12326)***
Rosecore Division.....516 504-4530
11 Grace Ave Ste 100 Great Neck (11021) ***(G-5852)***
Rosedub, South Fallsburg *Also called Allied Wine Corp* ***(G-15542)***
Rosemont Press Incorporated (PA).....212 239-4770
253 Church St Apt 2 New York (10013) ***(G-11935)***
Rosemont Press Incorporated.....212 239-4770
35 W Jefryn Blvd Ste A Deer Park (11729) ***(G-4226)***
Rosen Mandell & Immerman Inc.....212 691-2277
121 Varick St Rm 301 New York (10013) ***(G-11936)***
Rosen Publishing Group Inc.....212 777-3017
29 E 21st St Fl 2 New York (10010) ***(G-11937)***
Rosenau Beck Inc.....212 279-6202
135 W 36th St Rm 10l New York (10018) ***(G-11938)***
Rosenbaum Foot, Brooklyn *Also called Newyork Pedorthic Associates* ***(G-2380)***
Rosenwach Group, The, Astoria *Also called Rosenwach Tank Co Inc* ***(G-454)***
Rosenwach Tank Co, Astoria *Also called Sitecraft Inc* ***(G-456)***
Rosenwach Tank Co Inc (PA).....212 972-4411
4302 Ditmars Blvd Astoria (11105) ***(G-454)***
Rosetti Handbags and ACC (HQ).....212 273-3765
1333 Broadway Fl 9 New York (10018) ***(G-11939)***
Rosina Food Products Inc (HQ).....716 668-0123
170 French Rd Buffalo (14227) ***(G-3193)***
Rosina Holding Inc (PA).....716 668-0123
170 French Rd Buffalo (14227) ***(G-3194)***
Roslyn Bread Company Inc.....516 625-1470
190 Mineola Ave Roslyn Heights (11577) ***(G-15056)***
Ross Communications Associates.....631 393-5089
200 Broadhollow Rd # 207 Melville (11747) ***(G-8381)***
Ross Electronics Ltd.....718 569-6643
12 Maple Ave Haverstraw (10927) ***(G-6264)***
Ross JC Inc.....716 439-1161
6722 Lincoln Ave Lockport (14094) ***(G-7642)***
Ross L Sports Screening Inc.....716 824-5350
2756 Seneca St Buffalo (14224) ***(G-3195)***
Ross Metal Fabricators Div, Hauppauge *Also called Charles Ross & Son Company* ***(G-6064)***
Ross Metal Fabricators Inc.....631 586-7000
225 Marcus Blvd Deer Park (11729) ***(G-4227)***
Ross Valve Mfg.....518 274-0961
75 102nd St Troy (12180) ***(G-16275)***
Rossi Tool & Dies Inc.....845 267-8246
161 Route 303 Valley Cottage (10989) ***(G-16413)***
Rossiter & Schmitt Co Inc.....516 937-3610
220 S Fehr Way Bay Shore (11706) ***(G-734)***
Rota File Corporation.....516 496-7200
159 Lafayette Dr Syosset (11791) ***(G-15859)***
Rota Pack Inc.....631 274-1037
34 Sarah Dr Ste B Farmingdale (11735) ***(G-5113)***
Rota Tool, Syosset *Also called Rota File Corporation* ***(G-15859)***
Rotation Dynamics Corporation.....585 352-9023
3581 Big Ridge Rd Spencerport (14559) ***(G-15597)***
Roth Clothing Co Inc (PA).....718 384-4927
300 Penn St Brooklyn (11211) ***(G-2528)***
Roth Design & Consulting Inc.....718 209-0193
132 Bogart St Brooklyn (11206) ***(G-2529)***
Roth Global Plastics Inc.....315 475-0100
1 General Motors Dr Syracuse (13206) ***(G-16048)***
Roth's Metal Works, Brooklyn *Also called Roth Design & Consulting Inc* ***(G-2529)***
Rothe Welding Inc.....845 246-3051
1455 Route 212 Saugerties (12477) ***(G-15222)***
Rothschild Mens Div, New York *Also called S Rothschild & Co Inc* ***(G-11964)***
Roto Salt Company Inc.....315 536-3742
118 Monell St Penn Yan (14527) ***(G-13542)***
Rotork Controls Inc.....585 328-1550
675 Mile Crossing Blvd Rochester (14624) ***(G-14680)***
Rotork Controls Inc (HQ).....585 328-1550
675 Mile Crossing Blvd Rochester (14624) ***(G-14681)***
Rotron, Saugerties *Also called Ametek Technical & Indus Pdts* ***(G-15208)***
Rotron Incorporated (HQ).....845 679-2401
55 Hasbrouck Ln Woodstock (12498) ***(G-17381)***

ALPHABETIC

(PA)=Parent Co (HQ)=Headquarters (DH)=Div Headquarters
2018 Harris
New York Manufacturers Directory
1049

Rotron Incorporated....845 679-2401
9 Hasbrouck Ln Woodstock (12498) ***(G-17382)***
Rotronic Instrument Corp (HQ)....631 348-6844
135 Engineers Rd Ste 150 Hauppauge (11788) ***(G-6206)***
Rottkamp Tennis Inc....631 421-0040
100 Broadway Huntington Station (11746) ***(G-6757)***
Rough Brothers Holding Co (HQ)....716 826-6500
3556 Lake Shore Rd # 100 Buffalo (14219) ***(G-3196)***
Rough Draft Publishing LLC....212 741-4773
1916 Old Chelsea Sta New York (10113) ***(G-11940)***
Rough Guides US Ltd....212 414-3635
345 Hudson St Fl 4 New York (10014) ***(G-11941)***
Round Top Knit & Screening....518 622-3600
Rr 31 Round Top (12473) ***(G-15064)***
Roust USA, New York *Also called Russian Standard Vodka USA Inc* ***(G-11955)***
Rovel Manufacturing Co Inc....516 365-2752
52 Wimbledon Dr Roslyn (11576) ***(G-15047)***
Row, The, New York *Also called Tr Apparel LLC* ***(G-12407)***
Roxanne Assoulin, New York *Also called Maurice Max Inc* ***(G-11206)***
Roxter Lighting, Long Island City *Also called Matov Industries Inc* ***(G-7836)***
Royal Adhesives & Sealants LLC....315 451-1755
3584 Walters Rd Rsd Syracuse (13209) ***(G-16049)***
Royal Bedding Co Buffalo Inc....716 895-1414
201 James E Casey Dr Buffalo (14206) ***(G-3197)***
Royal Caribbean Bakery, Mount Vernon *Also called Royal Caribbean Jamaican Bky* ***(G-8774)***
Royal Caribbean Jamaican Bky (PA)....914 668-6868
620 S Fulton Ave Mount Vernon (10550) ***(G-8774)***
Royal Clothing Corp....718 436-5841
1316 48th St Apt 1 Brooklyn (11219) ***(G-2530)***
Royal Copenhagen Inc (PA)....845 454-4442
63 Page Park Dr Poughkeepsie (12603) ***(G-13947)***
Royal Custom Cabinets....315 376-6042
6149 Patty St Lowville (13367) ***(G-7970)***
Royal Engraving, Brooklyn *Also called Tripi Engraving Co Inc* ***(G-2700)***
Royal Fireworks Printing Co....845 726-3333
First Ave Unionville (10988) ***(G-16326)***
Royal Home Fashions Inc (HQ)....212 689-7222
261 5th Ave Fl 25 New York (10016) ***(G-11942)***
Royal Industries Inc (PA)....718 369-3046
225 25th St Brooklyn (11232) ***(G-2531)***
Royal Jewelry Mfg Inc (PA)....212 302-2500
825 Northern Blvd Fl 2 Great Neck (11021) ***(G-5853)***
Royal Kedem Wine, Marlboro *Also called Royal Wine Corporation* ***(G-8136)***
Royal Line The, Brooklyn *Also called Royal Industries Inc* ***(G-2531)***
Royal Marble & Granite Inc....516 536-5900
3295 Royal Ave Oceanside (11572) ***(G-13116)***
Royal Media Group, New York *Also called Royal News Corp* ***(G-11944)***
Royal Metal Products Inc....518 966-4442
463 West Rd Surprise (12176) ***(G-15832)***
Royal Miracle Corp....212 921-5797
2 W 46th St Rm 9209 New York (10036) ***(G-11943)***
Royal Molds Inc....718 382-7686
1634 Marine Pkwy Brooklyn (11234) ***(G-2532)***
Royal News Corp....212 564-8972
8 W 38th St Rm 901 New York (10018) ***(G-11944)***
Royal Paint Roller Corp....516 367-4370
1 Harvard Dr Woodbury (11797) ***(G-17319)***
Royal Paint Roller Mfg, Woodbury *Also called Royal Paint Roller Corp* ***(G-17319)***
Royal Plastics Corp....718 647-7500
2840 Atlantic Ave Ste 1 Brooklyn (11207) ***(G-2533)***
Royal Press, Staten Island *Also called C & R De Santis Inc* ***(G-15673)***
Royal Press, White Plains *Also called L K Printing Corp* ***(G-17157)***
Royal Prestige Lasting Co....516 280-5148
198 Jerusalem Ave Hempstead (11550) ***(G-6308)***
Royal Products, Hauppauge *Also called Curran Manufacturing Corp* ***(G-6081)***
Royal Products, Hauppauge *Also called Curran Manufacturing Corp* ***(G-6082)***
Royal Promotion Group Inc....212 246-3780
119 W 57th St Ste 906 New York (10019) ***(G-11945)***
Royal Sweet Bakery Inc....718 567-7770
119 49th St Brooklyn (11232) ***(G-2534)***
Royal Tees Inc....845 357-9448
29 Lafayette Ave Suffern (10901) ***(G-15820)***
Royal Windows and Doors, Bay Shore *Also called Royal Windows Mfg Corp* ***(G-735)***
Royal Windows Mfg Corp....631 435-8888
1769 5th Ave Unit A Bay Shore (11706) ***(G-735)***
Royal Wine Corporation....845 236-4000
1519 Route 9w Marlboro (12542) ***(G-8136)***
Royale Limousine Manufacturers, Roslyn Heights *Also called Cabot Coach Builders Inc* ***(G-15049)***
Royalton Millwork & Design....716 439-4092
7526 Tonawanda Creek Rd Lockport (14094) ***(G-7643)***
Royalty Network Inc (PA)....212 967-4300
224 W 30th St Rm 1007 New York (10001) ***(G-11946)***
Royce Associates A Ltd Partnr....516 367-6298
366 N Broadway Ste 400 Jericho (11753) ***(G-7115)***
Rozal Industries Inc....631 420-4277
151 Marine St Farmingdale (11735) ***(G-5114)***
Rp55 Inc....212 840-4035
230 W 39th St Fl 7 New York (10018) ***(G-11947)***
Rpb Distributors LLC....914 244-3600
45 Kensico Dr Mount Kisco (10549) ***(G-8687)***
Rpc Inc....347 873-3935
165 Emporia Ave Elmont (11003) ***(G-4738)***
RPC Car Service, Elmont *Also called Rpc Inc* ***(G-4738)***
RPC Photonics Inc....585 272-2840
330 Clay Rd Rochester (14623) ***(G-14682)***
Rpf Associates Inc....631 462-7446
2155 Jericho Tpke Ste A Commack (11725) ***(G-3867)***
Rpg, New York *Also called Royal Promotion Group Inc* ***(G-11945)***
RPM Displays, Auburn *Also called R P M Industries Inc* ***(G-512)***
RPS Holdings Inc....607 257-7778
2415 N Triphammer Rd # 2 Ithaca (14850) ***(G-6910)***
RR Donnelley & Sons Company....716 773-0647
300 Lang Blvd Grand Island (14072) ***(G-5781)***
RR Donnelley & Sons Company....646 755-8125
250 W 26th St Rm 402 New York (10001) ***(G-11948)***
RR Donnelley & Sons Company....716 773-0300
300 Lang Blvd Grand Island (14072) ***(G-5782)***
RR Donnelley Financial, Inc., New York *Also called Donnelley Financial LLC* ***(G-9957)***
Rs Automation....585 589-0199
4015 Oak Orchard Rd Albion (14411) ***(G-172)***
RS Precision Industries Inc....631 420-0424
295 Adams Blvd Farmingdale (11735) ***(G-5115)***
Rsb Associates Inc....518 281-5067
488 Picard Rd Altamont (12009) ***(G-216)***
Rsl Media LLC....212 307-6760
1001 Ave Of The Ave Fl 11 New York (10018) ***(G-11949)***
RSM Electron Power Inc (PA)....631 586-7600
221 W Industry Ct Deer Park (11729) ***(G-4228)***
RSM Electron Power Inc....631 586-7600
100 Engineers Rd Ste 100 Hauppauge (11788) ***(G-6207)***
Rsquared Ny Inc....631 521-8700
100 Heartland Blvd Edgewood (11717) ***(G-4622)***
RSR, Middletown *Also called Eco-Bat America LLC* ***(G-8472)***
Rt Machined Specialties....716 731-2055
2221 Niagara Falls Blvd Niagara Falls (14304) ***(G-12886)***
Rt Solutions LLC....585 245-3456
80 Linden Oaks Ste 210 Rochester (14625) ***(G-14683)***
RTD Manufacturing Inc....315 337-3151
6273 State Route 233 Rome (13440) ***(G-14863)***
Rtr Bag & Co Ltd....212 620-0011
27 W 20th St New York (10011) ***(G-11950)***
Rubber Stamp X Press....631 423-1322
7 Bradford Pl Huntington Station (11747) ***(G-6758)***
Rubber Stamps Inc....212 675-1180
174 Herricks Rd Mineola (11501) ***(G-8568)***
Rubberform Recycled Pdts LLC....716 478-0404
75 Michigan St Lockport (14094) ***(G-7644)***
Rubicon Industries Corp (PA)....718 434-4700
848 E 43rd St Brooklyn (11210) ***(G-2535)***
Rubie's Distribution Center, Bay Shore *Also called Rubies Costume Company Inc* ***(G-737)***
Rubies Costume Company Inc (PA)....718 846-1008
12008 Jamaica Ave Richmond Hill (11418) ***(G-14093)***
Rubies Costume Company Inc....631 777-3300
158 Candlewood Rd Bay Shore (11706) ***(G-736)***
Rubies Costume Company Inc....718 441-0834
12017 Jamaica Ave Richmond Hill (11418) ***(G-14094)***
Rubies Costume Company Inc....631 951-3688
1 Holloween Hwy Bay Shore (11706) ***(G-737)***
Rubies Costume Company Inc....516 326-1500
1770 Walt Whitman Rd Melville (11747) ***(G-8382)***
Rubies Costume Company Inc....718 846-1008
1 Rubie Plz Richmond Hill (11418) ***(G-14095)***
Rubies Masquerade Company LLC (PA)....718 846-1008
1 Rubie Plz Richmond Hill (11418) ***(G-14096)***
Rubinstein Jewelry Mfg Co....718 784-8650
3100 47th Ave Long Island City (11101) ***(G-7897)***
Ruby Engineering LLC....646 391-4600
354 Sackett St Brooklyn (11231) ***(G-2536)***
Ruby Newco LLC....212 852-7000
1211 Ave Of The Americas New York (10036) ***(G-11951)***
Ruby Road, New York *Also called Hearts of Palm LLC* ***(G-10495)***
Ruby Road, New York *Also called Hearts of Palm LLC* ***(G-10496)***
Ruckel Manufacturing Co, Brooklyn *Also called EY Industries Inc* ***(G-1952)***
Rudolf Friedman Inc....212 869-5070
42 W 48th St Ste 1102 New York (10036) ***(G-11952)***
Rudy Stempel & Family Sawmill....518 872-0431
73 Stemple Rd East Berne (12059) ***(G-4405)***
Ruga Grinding & Mfg Corp....631 924-5067
84 Horseblock Rd Unit A Yaphank (11980) ***(G-17415)***
Rugby Magazine, White Plains *Also called American Intl Media LLC* ***(G-17105)***
Ruggeri Manufacturing, Rochester *Also called Van Thomas Inc* ***(G-14780)***
Ruhle Companies Inc....914 287-4000
99 Wall St Valhalla (10595) ***(G-16398)***
Rui Xing International Trdg Co....516 298-2667
89 Jerusalem Ave Hicksville (11801) ***(G-6417)***
Ruleville Manufacturing Co Inc (PA)....212 695-1620
469 Fashion Ave Fl 10 New York (10018) ***(G-11953)***
Rumsey Corp....914 751-3640
15 Rumsey Rd Yonkers (10705) ***(G-17501)***

Rumson Acquisition LLC......718 349-4300
1385 Broadway Fl 9 New York (10018) ***(G-11954)***
Run It Systems, New York *Also called Marcus Goldman Inc* ***(G-11171)***
Rural Hill Sand and Grav Corp......315 846-5212
10262 County Route 79 Woodville (13650) ***(G-17383)***
Rus Industries Inc......716 284-7828
3255 Lockport Rd Niagara Falls (14305) ***(G-12887)***
Rush Gold Manufacturing Ltd......516 781-3155
2400 Merrick Rd Bellmore (11710) ***(G-816)***
Rush Gravel Corp......585 533-1740
130 Kavanaugh Rd Honeoye Falls (14472) ***(G-6563)***
Rush Machinery Inc......585 554-3070
4761 State Route 364 Rushville (14544) ***(G-15078)***
Russco Metal Spinning Co Inc......516 872-6055
3064 Lawson Blvd Oceanside (11572) ***(G-13117)***
Russell Bass......607 637-5253
59 Saw Mill Rd Hancock (13783) ***(G-5989)***
Russell Bass & Son Lumber, Hancock *Also called Russell Bass* ***(G-5989)***
Russell Industries Inc......516 536-5000
40 Horton Ave Lynbrook (11563) ***(G-7986)***
Russell Plastics Tech Co Inc......631 963-8602
521 W Hoffman Ave Lindenhurst (11757) ***(G-7504)***
Russian Bazaar, Brooklyn *Also called Danet Inc* ***(G-1839)***
Russian Daily, Brooklyn *Also called Novoye Rsskoye Slovo Pubg Corp* ***(G-2389)***
Russian Mix Inc......347 385-7198
2225 Benson Ave Apt 74 Brooklyn (11214) ***(G-2537)***
Russian Standard Vodka USA Inc......212 679-1894
232 Madison Ave Fl 16 New York (10016) ***(G-11955)***
Russin Lumber Corp......845 457-4000
75 Pierces Rd Newburgh (12550) ***(G-12801)***
Russkaya Reklama Inc......718 769-3000
2699 Coney Island Ave Brooklyn (11235) ***(G-2538)***
Russo's Gluten Free Gourmet, Shirley *Also called Anthony Gigi Inc* ***(G-15435)***
Rutcarele Inc......347 830-5353
3449 110th St Corona (11368) ***(G-4028)***
Ruthy's Bakery & Cafe, New York *Also called Ruthys Cheesecake Rugelach Bky* ***(G-11956)***
Ruthys Cheesecake Rugelach Bky......212 463-8800
300 E 54th St Apt 31b New York (10022) ***(G-11956)***
Rv Printing......631 567-8658
39 Portside Dr Holbrook (11741) ***(G-6498)***
Rvc Enterprises LLC (PA)......212 391-4600
1384 Broadway Fl 17 New York (10018) ***(G-11957)***
Rw Manufacturing Company, East Rochester *Also called Richards & West Inc* ***(G-4485)***
Rwb Controls Inc......716 897-4341
471 Connecticut St Buffalo (14213) ***(G-3198)***
RWS Manufacturing Inc......518 361-1657
22 Ferguson Ln Queensbury (12804) ***(G-14022)***
Ry-Gan Printing Inc......585 482-7770
111 Humboldt St Rochester (14609) ***(G-14684)***
Ryan Gems Inc......212 697-0149
20 E 46th St Rm 200 New York (10017) ***(G-11958)***
Ryan Printing, Hilton *Also called William J Ryan* ***(G-6447)***
Ryan Printing Inc......845 535-3235
300 Corporate Dr Ste 6 Blauvelt (10913) ***(G-969)***
Ryba General Merchandise Inc......718 522-2028
63 Flushing Ave Unit 332 Brooklyn (11205) ***(G-2539)***
Ryba Software Inc......718 264-9352
7359 186th St Fresh Meadows (11366) ***(G-5459)***
Rye Record......914 713-3213
14 Elm Pl Ste 200 Rye (10580) ***(G-15093)***
Ryers Creek Corp......607 523-6617
1330 Mill Dr Corning (14830) ***(G-4000)***
Ryland Peters & Small Inc......646 791-5410
341 E 116th St New York (10029) ***(G-11959)***
Rynone Manufacturing Corp......607 565-8187
229 Howard St Waverly (14892) ***(G-16730)***
Rynone Packaging Corp......607 565-8173
184 State Route 17c Waverly (14892) ***(G-16731)***
S & B Fashion Inc......718 482-1386
4315 Queens St Ste B Long Island City (11101) ***(G-7898)***
S & B Machine Works Inc......516 997-2666
111 New York Ave Westbury (11590) ***(G-17053)***
S & C Bridals LLC (PA)......212 789-7000
1407 Broadway Fl 41 New York (10018) ***(G-11960)***
S & D Welding Corp......631 454-0383
229 Edison Ave Ste A West Babylon (11704) ***(G-16855)***
S & H Enterprises Inc......888 323-8755
10b Holden Ave Queensbury (12804) ***(G-14023)***
S & H Machine Company Inc......716 834-1194
83 Clyde Ave Buffalo (14215) ***(G-3199)***
S & H Uniform Corp......914 937-6800
1 Aqueduct Rd White Plains (10606) ***(G-17191)***
S & J Sheet Metal Supply......718 384-0800
70 Grand Ave Brooklyn (11205) ***(G-2540)***
S & J Trading Inc......718 347-1323
8030 263rd St Floral Park (11004) ***(G-5216)***
S & K Counter Tops Inc......716 662-7986
4708 Duerr Rd Orchard Park (14127) ***(G-13321)***
S & L Aerospace Metals LLC......718 326-1821
12012 28th Ave Flushing (11354) ***(G-5296)***
S & M Ring Corp......212 382-0900
1080 Channel Dr Hewlett (11557) ***(G-6336)***
S & R Tool Inc......585 346-2029
6066 Stone Hill Rd Lakeville (14480) ***(G-7308)***
S & S Enterprises, Jamestown *Also called Genco John* ***(G-7028)***
S & S Fashions Inc......718 328-0001
941 Longfellow Ave Bronx (10474) ***(G-1442)***
S & S Graphics Inc......914 668-4230
521 E 3rd St Mount Vernon (10553) ***(G-8775)***
S & S Machinery Corp (PA)......718 492-7400
140 53rd St Brooklyn (11232) ***(G-2541)***
S & S Machinery Corp......718 492-7400
132 54th St Brooklyn (11220) ***(G-2542)***
S & S Manufacturing Co Inc (PA)......212 444-6000
1375 Broadway Fl 2 New York (10018) ***(G-11961)***
S & S Prtg Die-Cutting Co Inc......718 388-8990
488 Morgan Ave Ste A Brooklyn (11222) ***(G-2543)***
S & S Soap Co Inc......718 585-2900
815 E 135th St Bronx (10454) ***(G-1443)***
S & T Knitting Co Inc (PA)......607 722-7558
1010 Conklin Rd Conklin (13748) ***(G-3900)***
S & T Machine, Brooklyn *Also called Fjs Industries Inc* ***(G-1982)***
S & T Machine Inc......718 272-2484
970 E 92nd St Fl 1 Brooklyn (11236) ***(G-2544)***
S & V Custom Furniture Mfg......516 746-8299
75 Windsor Ave Unit E Mineola (11501) ***(G-8569)***
S & V Knits Inc......631 752-1595
117 Marine St Farmingdale (11735) ***(G-5116)***
S & V Restaurant Eqp Mfrs Inc......718 220-1140
4320 Park Ave Bronx (10457) ***(G-1444)***
S & W Knitting Mills Inc......718 237-2416
703 Bedford Ave Fl 3 Brooklyn (11206) ***(G-2545)***
S & W Ladies Wear......718 431-2800
3611 14th Ave Ste 601 Brooklyn (11218) ***(G-2546)***
S & W Metal Trading Corp......212 719-5070
1601 E 7th St Brooklyn (11230) ***(G-2547)***
S A Baxter LLC (PA)......845 469-7995
37 Elkay Dr Ste 33 Chester (10918) ***(G-3641)***
S A S Industries Inc......631 727-1441
939 Wding River Manor Rd Manorville (11949) ***(G-8112)***
S A W, Kingston *Also called Spiegel Woodworks Inc* ***(G-7239)***
S and G Imaging, Walworth *Also called Software & General Services Co* ***(G-16573)***
S B B, Syracuse *Also called Sullivan Bazinet Bongio Inc* ***(G-16070)***
S B Manufacturing LLC......845 352-3700
161 Route 59 Monsey (10952) ***(G-8614)***
S B Whistler & Sons Inc......585 798-3000
11023 W Center Street Ext Medina (14103) ***(G-8313)***
S Broome and Co Inc......718 663-6800
3300 47th Ave Fl 1 Long Island City (11101) ***(G-7899)***
S C T......585 467-7740
3000 E Ridge Rd Rochester (14622) ***(G-14685)***
S D C, Armonk *Also called Surgical Design Corp* ***(G-418)***
S D I, Binghamton *Also called Sensor & Decontamination Inc* ***(G-944)***
S D S of Long Island, Bay Shore *Also called M F L B Inc* ***(G-712)***
S D Warren Company......914 696-5544
925 Westchester Ave # 115 White Plains (10604) ***(G-17192)***
S D Z Metal Spinning Stamping......718 778-3600
1807 Pacific St Brooklyn (11233) ***(G-2548)***
S Donadic Woodworking Inc......718 361-9888
4525 39th St Sunnyside (11104) ***(G-15830)***
S E A Supls, Plainview *Also called S E A Supplies Ltd* ***(G-13661)***
S E A Supplies Ltd......516 694-6677
1670 Old Country Rd # 104 Plainview (11803) ***(G-13661)***
S G I......917 386-0385
40 E 52nd St Frnt A New York (10022) ***(G-11962)***
S G New York LLC......631 698-8400
1 Rodeo Dr Edgewood (11717) ***(G-4623)***
S G New York LLC (PA)......631 665-4000
2950 Vtrans Mem Hwy Ste 1 Bohemia (11716) ***(G-1124)***
S Hellerman Inc (PA)......718 622-2995
242 Green St Brooklyn (11222) ***(G-2549)***
S I Communications Inc......914 725-2500
8 Harwood Ct Scarsdale (10583) ***(G-15253)***
S J B Fabrication......716 895-0281
430 Kennedy Rd Buffalo (14227) ***(G-3200)***
S J McCullagh Inc (PA)......716 856-3473
245 Swan St Buffalo (14204) ***(G-3201)***
S K Circuits Inc (PA)......703 376-8718
483 Foxwood Ter Oneida (13421) ***(G-13188)***
S Kashi & Sons Inc......212 869-9393
175 Great Neck Rd Ste 204 Great Neck (11021) ***(G-5854)***
S L C Industries Incorporated......607 775-2299
63 Barlow Rd Binghamton (13904) ***(G-943)***
S L Fashions Group, New York *Also called Lou Sally Fashions Corp* ***(G-11075)***
S M Frank & Company Inc......914 739-3100
1073 State Route 94 Ste 7 New Windsor (12553) ***(G-8997)***
S M I, New York *Also called Specialty Minerals Inc* ***(G-12178)***
S M P, Pearl River *Also called Strategic Mktg Promotions Inc* ***(G-13491)***
S M S C Inc......315 942-4394
101 Water St Boonville (13309) ***(G-1167)***
S P Books Inc......212 431-5011
99 Spring St Fl 3 New York (10012) ***(G-11963)***

ALPHABETIC

(PA)=Parent Co (HQ)=Headquarters (DH)=Div Headquarters
2018 Harris
New York Manufacturers Directory
1051

S P Industries Inc 845 255-5000
815 Rte 208 Gardiner (12525) ***(G-5563)***
S R & R Industries Inc 845 692-8329
45 Enterprise Pl Middletown (10941) ***(G-8496)***
S R Instruments Inc (PA) 716 693-5977
600 Young St Tonawanda (14150) ***(G-16216)***
S R S Inc 732 548-6630
5920 56th Ave Maspeth (11378) ***(G-8200)***
S R Sloan Inc (PA) 315 736-7730
8111 Halsey Rd Whitesboro (13492) ***(G-17223)***
S Rothschild & Co Inc (PA) 212 354-8550
1407 Broadway Fl 10 New York (10018) ***(G-11964)***
S S I, Rochester *Also called Schlegel Systems Inc* ***(G-14695)***
S S Precision Gear & Instr 718 457-7474
4512 104th St Corona (11368) ***(G-4029)***
S Scharf Inc 516 541-9552
278 N Richmond Ave Massapequa (11758) ***(G-8215)***
S T J Orthotic Svces, Lindenhurst *Also called Stj Orthotic Services Inc* ***(G-7507)***
S Z Design & Prints, Monsey *Also called Sz - Design & Print Inc* ***(G-8618)***
S&B Alternative Fuels Inc 631 585-6637
1232 Stony Brook Rd Lake Grove (11755) ***(G-7290)***
S&D Welding, West Babylon *Also called S & D Welding Corp* ***(G-16855)***
S&G Optical, Long Island City *Also called 21st Century Optics Inc* ***(G-7675)***
S/N Precision Enterprises Inc 518 283-8002
145 Jordan Rd Ste 1 Troy (12180) ***(G-16276)***
S1 Biopharma Inc 201 839-0941
7 World Trade Ctr 250g New York (10007) ***(G-11965)***
S2 Sportswear Inc 347 335-0713
4100 1st Ave Ste 5n Brooklyn (11232) ***(G-2550)***
S3j Electronics LLC 716 206-1309
2000 Commerce Pkwy Lancaster (14086) ***(G-7366)***
SA Day Buffalo Flux Facility, Buffalo *Also called Johnson Manufacturing Company* ***(G-3038)***
Saab Defense and SEC USA LLC 315 445-5009
5717 Enterprise Pkwy East Syracuse (13057) ***(G-4575)***
Saad Collection Inc (PA) 212 937-0341
1165 Broadway Ste 305 New York (10001) ***(G-11966)***
Saakshi Inc 315 475-3988
851 N Salina St Syracuse (13208) ***(G-16050)***
Sabbsons International Inc 718 360-1947
474 50th St Brooklyn (11220) ***(G-2551)***
Saber Awards, New York *Also called Holmes Group The Inc* ***(G-10543)***
Sabic Innovative Plas US LLC 518 475-5011
1 Noryl Ave Selkirk (12158) ***(G-15380)***
Sabic Innovative Plastics 713 448-7474
1 Gail Ct East Greenbush (12061) ***(G-4424)***
Sabin Metal Corporation (PA) 631 329-1695
300 Pantigo Pl Ste 102 East Hampton (11937) ***(G-4435)***
Sabin Metal Corporation 585 538-2194
1647 Wheatland Center Rd Scottsville (14546) ***(G-15361)***
Sabin Robbins, New York *Also called Eagles Nest Holdings LLC* ***(G-10011)***
Sabin Robbins Paper Company 513 874-5270
455 E 86th St New York (10028) ***(G-11967)***
Sabon Management LLC 212 982-0968
123 Prince St Frnt A New York (10012) ***(G-11968)***
Sabra Dental Products 914 945-0836
24 Quail Hollow Rd Ossining (10562) ***(G-13352)***
Sabra Dipping Company LLC (HQ) 914 372-3900
777 Westchester Ave Fl 3 White Plains (10604) ***(G-17193)***
Sabra Dipping Company LLC 516 249-0151
535 Smith St Farmingdale (11735) ***(G-5117)***
Sabre Energy Services LLC 518 514-1572
1891 New Scotland Rd Slingerlands (12159) ***(G-15500)***
Sabre Enterprises Inc 315 430-3127
1813 Lemoyne Ave Syracuse (13208) ***(G-16051)***
Saccomize Inc 818 287-3000
1554 Stillwell Ave Bronx (10461) ***(G-1445)***
Sacks and Company New York (PA) 212 741-1000
119 W 57th St Ph N New York (10019) ***(G-11969)***
Sadowsky Guitars Ltd 718 433-1990
2107 41st Ave Fl 4 Long Island City (11101) ***(G-7900)***
Saes Memry, New Hartford *Also called Saes Smart Materials Inc* ***(G-8855)***
Saes Smart Materials Inc 315 266-2026
4355 Middle Settlement Rd New Hartford (13413) ***(G-8855)***
Safavieh Inc 516 945-1900
40 Harbor Park Dr Port Washington (11050) ***(G-13877)***
Safcore LLC 917 627-5263
23 Van Dam St Brooklyn (11222) ***(G-2552)***
Safe Circuits Inc 631 586-3682
15 Shoreham Dr W Dix Hills (11746) ***(G-4320)***
Safe Flight Instrument Corp 914 220-1125
20 New King St White Plains (10604) ***(G-17194)***
Safe Passage International Inc 585 292-4910
333 Metro Park Ste F204 Rochester (14623) ***(G-14686)***
Safe Skies LLC (PA) 888 632-5027
954 3rd Ave Ste 504 New York (10022) ***(G-11970)***
Safe-Dent Enterprises LLC 845 362-0141
4 Orchard Hill Dr Monsey (10952) ***(G-8615)***
Safeguard Inc 631 929-3273
578 Sound Ave Wading River (11792) ***(G-16545)***
Safelite Glass Corp 716 685-1358
2918 Walden Ave Depew (14043) ***(G-4298)***
Safespan Platform Systems Inc 716 694-1100
237 Fillmore Ave Tonawanda (14150) ***(G-16217)***
Safespan Platform Systems Inc (PA) 716 694-3332
252 Fillmore Ave Tonawanda (14150) ***(G-16218)***
Safetec of America Inc 716 895-1822
887 Kensington Ave Buffalo (14215) ***(G-3202)***
Safety-Kleen Systems Inc 716 855-2212
60 Katherine St Buffalo (14210) ***(G-3203)***
Safeworks LLC 800 696-5577
3030 60th St Ste 1 Woodside (11377) ***(G-17368)***
Safina Center 808 888-9440
118 Administration Stony Brook (11794) ***(G-15792)***
Sag Harbor, New York *Also called Life Style Design Group* ***(G-11020)***
Sag Harbor Express 631 725-1700
35 Main St Sag Harbor (11963) ***(G-15106)***
Sag Harbor Industries Inc (PA) 631 725-0440
1668 Bhmpton Sag Hbr Tpke Sag Harbor (11963) ***(G-15107)***
Saga International Recycl LLC 718 621-5900
6623 13th Ave Brooklyn (11219) ***(G-2553)***
Sagaponack Sand & Gravel Corp (PA) 631 537-2424
Haines Path Bridgehampton (11932) ***(G-1233)***
Sage Knitwear Inc 718 628-7902
103 Jersey St Unit D West Babylon (11704) ***(G-16856)***
Sage Parts Plus 718 651-1898
1 Main Terminal Ste 1 Flushing (11371) ***(G-5297)***
Sagelife Parenting LLC 315 299-5713
235 Harrison St Ste 2 Syracuse (13202) ***(G-16052)***
Sagemylife, Syracuse *Also called Sagelife Parenting LLC* ***(G-16052)***
Sahadi Fine Foods Inc 718 369-0100
4215 1st Ave Brooklyn (11232) ***(G-2554)***
Sahlen Packing Company Inc 716 852-8677
318 Howard St Buffalo (14206) ***(G-3204)***
Saint Gobain Grains & Powders 716 731-8200
6600 Walmore Rd Niagara Falls (14304) ***(G-12888)***
Saint Honore Pastry Shop Inc 516 767-2555
993 Port Washington Blvd Port Washington (11050) ***(G-13878)***
Saint Laurie, New York *Also called Kozinn+sons Merchant Tailors* ***(G-10921)***
Saint Martins Press, New York *Also called Bedford Freeman & Worth* ***(G-9392)***
Saint-Gbain Advnced Crmics LLC 716 691-2000
168 Creekside Dr Amherst (14228) ***(G-260)***
Saint-Gbain Advnced Crmics LLC (HQ) 716 278-6066
23 Acheson Dr Niagara Falls (14303) ***(G-12889)***
Saint-Gobain Abrasives Inc 518 266-2200
2600 10th Ave Watervliet (12189) ***(G-16712)***
Saint-Gobain Adfors Amer Inc (HQ) 716 775-3900
1795 Baseline Rd Grand Island (14072) ***(G-5783)***
Saint-Gobain Adfors Amer Inc 585 589-4401
14770 East Ave Albion (14411) ***(G-173)***
Saint-Gobain Dynamics Inc 716 278-6007
23 Acheson Dr Niagara Falls (14303) ***(G-12890)***
Saint-Gobain Performance Plas, Poestenkill *Also called Canton Bio-Medical Inc* ***(G-13752)***
Saint-Gobain Prfmce Plas Corp 518 642-2200
1 Sealants Park Granville (12832) ***(G-5796)***
Saint-Gobain Prfmce Plas Corp 518 686-7301
14 Mccaffrey St Hoosick Falls (12090) ***(G-6571)***
Saint-Gobain Prfmce Plas Corp 518 283-5963
11 Sicho Rd Poestenkill (12140) ***(G-13755)***
Saint-Gobain Prfmce Plas Corp 518 686-7301
1 Liberty St Hoosick Falls (12090) ***(G-6572)***
Saint-Gobain Strl Ceramics 716 278-6233
23 Acheson Dr Niagara Falls (14303) ***(G-12891)***
Saint-Gobain-Paris France, Grand Island *Also called Saint-Gobain Adfors Amer Inc* ***(G-5783)***
Saj of Freeport Corp 516 623-8800
178 Hanse Ave Freeport (11520) ***(G-5435)***
Sakonnet Technology LLC 212 849-9267
11 E 44th St Fl 1000 New York (10017) ***(G-11971)***
Sal MA Instrument Corp 631 242-2227
10 Clearwater Ln West Islip (11795) ***(G-16935)***
Salamanca Daily Reporter, Salamanca *Also called Sun-Times Media Group Inc* ***(G-15136)***
Salamanca Lumber Company Inc 716 945-4810
59 Rochester St Salamanca (14779) ***(G-15131)***
Salamanca Penny Saver, Salamanca *Also called Salamanca Press Penny Saver* ***(G-15132)***
Salamanca Press Penny Saver 716 945-1500
36 River St Salamanca (14779) ***(G-15132)***
Salarinos Italian Foods Inc 315 697-9766
110 James St Canastota (13032) ***(G-3398)***
Sale 121 Corp 240 855-8988
1324 Lexington Ave # 111 New York (10128) ***(G-11972)***
Salentica Systems Inc 212 672-1777
245 Park Ave Fl 39 New York (10167) ***(G-11973)***
Salerno Packaging Inc (HQ) 518 563-3636
14 Gus Lapham Ln Plattsburgh (12901) ***(G-13724)***
Salerno Plastic Film and Bags, Plattsburgh *Also called Salerno Packaging Inc* ***(G-13724)***
Sales & Marketing Office, Syracuse *Also called Monaghan Medical Corporation* ***(G-16013)***
Sales Department, Floral Park *Also called Allomatic Products Company* ***(G-5200)***
Sales Office, Northport *Also called Cypress Semiconductor Corp* ***(G-13028)***
Sales Tax Asset Rceivable Corp 212 788-5874
255 Greenwich St Fl 6 New York (10007) ***(G-11974)***
Salisbury Sportswear Inc 516 221-9519
2523 Marine Pl Bellmore (11710) ***(G-817)***

Salko Kitchens Inc ... 845 565-4420
256 Walsh Ave New Windsor (12553) *(G-8998)*

Sally Beauty Supply LLC ... 716 831-3286
310 Main St West Seneca (14224) *(G-16981)*

Sally Sherman Foods, Mount Vernon *Also called UFS Industries Inc (G-8790)*

Salmco Jewelry Corp ... 212 695-8792
22 W 32nd St Fl 16 New York (10001) *(G-11975)*

Salmon Crek Cabinetry Inc ... 315 589-5419
6687 Salmon Creek Rd Williamson (14589) *(G-17254)*

Salmon River News, Watertown *Also called Mexico Independent Inc (G-16687)*

Salonclick LLC ... 718 643-6793
117 Crosby St New York (10012) *(G-11976)*

Salsburg Dimensional Stone ... 631 653-6790
18 Pine St Brookhaven (11719) *(G-1509)*

Salty Road Inc ... 347 673-3925
190 Bedford Ave 404 Brooklyn (11249) *(G-2555)*

Salutem Group LLC ... 347 620-2640
44 Wall St Fl 12 New York (10005) *(G-11977)*

Salvador Colletti Blank ... 718 217-6725
25141 Van Zandt Ave Douglaston (11362) *(G-4334)*

Salvin Company, Kingston *Also called Vincent Conigliaro (G-7251)*

Sam A Lupo & Sons Inc (PA) ... 800 388-5352
1219 Campville Rd Endicott (13760) *(G-4833)*

Sam Bonk Uniform, Bronx *Also called Bonk Sam Unforms Civilian Cap (G-1285)*

Sam Hee International Inc ... 212 594-7815
213 W 35th St Ste 503 New York (10001) *(G-11978)*

Sam NY, New York *Also called Andrew M Schwartz LLC (G-9203)*

Sam Salem & Son LLC ... 212 695-6020
302 5th Ave Fl 4 New York (10001) *(G-11979)*

Samaki Inc ... 845 858-1012
62 Jersey Ave Port Jervis (12771) *(G-13815)*

Samco LLC ... 518 725-4705
122 S Main St Ste 2 Gloversville (12078) *(G-5735)*

Samco Scientific Corporation ... 800 522-3359
75 Panorama Creek Dr Rochester (14625) *(G-14687)*

Sammba Printing Inc ... 516 944-4449
437 Port Washington Blvd Port Washington (11050) *(G-13879)*

Sampla Belting North Amer LLC ... 716 667-7450
61 N Gates Ave Lackawanna (14218) *(G-7275)*

Sample News Group LLC ... 315 343-3800
140 W 1st St Oswego (13126) *(G-13365)*

Sampo Inc ... 315 896-2606
119 Remsen Rd Barneveld (13304) *(G-617)*

Sampsons Prsthtic Orthotic Lab, Schenectady *Also called Sampsons Prsthtic Orthotic Lab (G-15315)*

Sampsons Prsthtic Orthotic Lab ... 518 374-6011
1737 State St Schenectady (12304) *(G-15315)*

Samscreen Inc ... 607 722-3979
216 Broome Corporate Pkwy Conklin (13748) *(G-3901)*

Samson Technologies Corp (HQ) ... 631 784-2200
278 Duffy Ave Unit B Hicksville (11801) *(G-6418)*

Samuel B Collection Inc ... 516 466-1826
98 Cuttermill Rd Great Neck (11021) *(G-5855)*

Samuel Broome Uniform ACC, Long Island City *Also called S Broome and Co Inc (G-7899)*

Samuel French Inc (PA) ... 212 206-8990
235 Park Ave S Fl 5 New York (10003) *(G-11980)*

Samuel Schulman Furs Inc ... 212 736-5550
150 W 30th St Fl 13 New York (10001) *(G-11981)*

Samuel Son & Co Inc ... 716 856-6500
250 Lake Ave Ste 3 Blasdell (14219) *(G-959)*

San Francisco Chronicle, New York *Also called Hearst Communications Inc (G-10480)*

San Jae Educational Resou ... 845 364-5458
9 Chamberlain Ct Pomona (10970) *(G-13761)*

San Signs & Awnings, Yonkers *Also called M Santoliquido Corp (G-17481)*

Sanaa Spices, Maspeth *Also called Extreme Spices Inc (G-8168)*

Sanctuary Brands LLC (PA) ... 212 704-4014
70 W 40th St Fl 5 New York (10018) *(G-11982)*

Sand Hill Industries Inc ... 518 885-7991
12 Grove St Ballston Spa (12020) *(G-607)*

Sandberg & Sikorski Corp, New York *Also called A Jaffe Inc (G-9038)*

Sandbox Brands Inc ... 212 647-8877
26 W 17th St Lbby New York (10011) *(G-11983)*

Sandford Blvd Donuts Inc ... 914 663-7708
440 E Sandford Blvd Mount Vernon (10550) *(G-8776)*

Sandle Custom Bearing Corp ... 585 593-7000
1110 State Route 19 Wellsville (14895) *(G-16783)*

Sandow Media LLC ... 646 805-0200
1271 Ave Of The Ave Fl 17 New York (10020) *(G-11984)*

Sandstone Technologies Corp (PA) ... 585 785-5537
2117 Buffalo Rd 245 Rochester (14624) *(G-14688)*

Sandstone Technologies Corp ... 585 785-5537
2117 Buffalo Rd Unit 245 Rochester (14624) *(G-14689)*

Sandvoss Farms LLC ... 585 297-7044
10198 East Rd East Bethany (14054) *(G-4406)*

Sandy Dalal Ltd ... 212 532-5822
220 Central Park S 10f New York (10019) *(G-11985)*

Sandy Duftler Designs Ltd ... 516 379-3084
775 Brooklyn Ave Ste 105 North Baldwin (11510) *(G-12925)*

Sandy Littman Inc ... 845 562-1112
420 N Montgomery St Newburgh (12550) *(G-12802)*

Sandys Bumper Mart Inc ... 315 472-8149
120 Wall St Syracuse (13204) *(G-16053)*

Sandys Deli Inc ... 518 297-6951
90 Montgomery St Rouses Point (12979) *(G-15068)*

Sanford Printing Inc ... 718 461-1202
13335 41st Rd Flushing (11355) *(G-5298)*

Sanford Stone LLC ... 607 467-1313
185 Latham Rd Deposit (13754) *(G-4302)*

Sangster Foods Inc ... 212 993-9129
225 Parkside Ave Apt 3p Brooklyn (11226) *(G-2556)*

Sanguine Gas Exploration LLC ... 212 582-8555
152 W 57th St Fl 4100 New York (10019) *(G-11986)*

Sanjay Pallets Inc ... 347 590-2485
424 Coster St Bronx (10474) *(G-1446)*

Sanmina Corporation ... 607 689-5000
1200 Taylor Rd Owego (13827) *(G-13384)*

Sanoy Inc ... 212 695-6384
19 W 36th St Fl 11 New York (10018) *(G-11987)*

Santa Fe Manufacturing Corp ... 631 234-0100
225 Engineers Rd Hauppauge (11788) *(G-6208)*

Santee Print Works (PA) ... 212 997-1570
58 W 40th St Fl 11 New York (10018) *(G-11988)*

Santoro Signs Inc ... 716 895-8875
3180 Genesee St Ste 1 Buffalo (14225) *(G-3205)*

Sanzdranz LLC (PA) ... 518 894-8625
83 Dumbarton Dr Delmar (12054) *(G-4271)*

Sanzdranz LLC ... 518 894-8625
388 Broadway Schenectady (12305) *(G-15316)*

Sapienza Bake Shop, Elmont *Also called Sapienza Pastry Inc (G-4739)*

Sapienza Pastry Inc ... 516 352-5232
1376 Hempstead Tpke Elmont (11003) *(G-4739)*

Sapphire Systems Inc (PA) ... 212 905-0100
405 Lexington Ave Fl 49 New York (10174) *(G-11989)*

Saptalis Pharmaceuticals LLC ... 631 231-2751
45 Davids Dr Hauppauge (11788) *(G-6209)*

Saputo Dairy Foods Usa LLC ... 607 746-2141
40236 State Highway 10 Delhi (13753) *(G-4267)*

Sara Lee Courtaulds USA, New York *Also called Courtaulds Textiles Ltd (G-9797)*

Sarabeth's Bakery, Bronx *Also called Sbk Preserves Inc (G-1448)*

Sarabeths Kitchen LLC ... 718 589-2900
1161 E 156th St Bronx (10474) *(G-1447)*

Saraga Industries Corp ... 631 842-4049
690 Albany Ave Unit D Amityville (11701) *(G-324)*

Sarar Usa Inc ... 845 928-8874
873 Adirondack Way Central Valley (10917) *(G-3554)*

Saratoga Chips LLC ... 877 901-6950
63 Putnam St Ste 202 Saratoga Springs (12866) *(G-15201)*

Saratoga Horseworks Ltd ... 518 843-6756
57 Edson St Amsterdam (12010) *(G-368)*

Saratoga Lighting Holdings LLC (PA) ... 212 906-7800
535 Madison Ave Fl 4 New York (10022) *(G-11990)*

Saratoga Spring Water Company ... 518 584-6363
11 Geyser Rd Saratoga Springs (12866) *(G-15202)*

Saratoga Trunk and Furniture ... 518 463-3252
5 Macaffer Dr Albany (12204) *(G-131)*

Saratogian USA Today, Saratoga Springs *Also called Journal Register Company (G-15191)*

Saraval Industries ... 516 768-9033
348 N Midland Ave Nyack (10960) *(G-13070)*

Sares International Inc ... 718 366-8412
95 Evergreen Ave Ste 5 Brooklyn (11206) *(G-2557)*

Sargent Manufacturing Inc ... 212 722-7000
120 E 124th St New York (10035) *(G-11991)*

Sargento Foods Inc ... 920 893-8484
498 7th Ave New York (10018) *(G-11992)*

Sarina Accessories LLC ... 212 239-8106
15 W 36th St Fl 5 New York (10018) *(G-11993)*

Sarkisians Jewelry Co ... 212 869-1060
17 W 45th St Ste 201 New York (10036) *(G-11994)*

Sartek Industries Inc (PA) ... 631 473-3555
34 Jamaica Ave Ste 1 Port Jefferson (11777) *(G-13801)*

Sarug Inc ... 718 339-2791
2055 Mcdonald Ave Brooklyn (11223) *(G-2558)*

Sarug Inc ... 718 381-7300
1616 Summerfield St Ridgewood (11385) *(G-14135)*

Sarug Knitwear, Ridgewood *Also called Sarug Inc (G-14135)*

Sas Institute Inc ... 212 757-3826
787 Seventh Ave Fl 47 New York (10019) *(G-11995)*

Sas Maintenance Services Inc ... 718 837-2124
8435 Bay 16th St Ste A Brooklyn (11214) *(G-2559)*

Sassy Sauce Inc ... 585 621-1050
740 Driving Park Ave F Rochester (14613) *(G-14690)*

Satco Castings Service Inc ... 516 354-1500
1400 Plaza Ave New Hyde Park (11040) *(G-8905)*

Satco Lighting, Edgewood *Also called Satco Products Inc (G-4624)*

Satco Products Inc (PA) ... 631 243-2022
110 Heartland Blvd Edgewood (11717) *(G-4624)*

Satellite Incorporated ... 212 221-6687
43 W 46th St Ste 503 New York (10036) *(G-11996)*

Satellite Network Inc ... 718 336-2698
2030 Mcdonald Ave Brooklyn (11223) *(G-2560)*

Satin Fine Foods Inc ... 845 469-1034
32 Leone Ln Chester (10918) *(G-3642)*

A
L
P
H
A
B
E
T
I
C

ALPHABETIC SECTION

Satispie LLC..716 982-4600
155 Balta Dr Rochester (14623) *(G-14691)*
Satnam Distributors LLC..................................516 802-0600
200 Robbins Ln Unit B Jericho (11753) *(G-7116)*
Saturn Industries Inc (PA)................................518 828-9956
157 Union Tpke Hudson (12534) *(G-6663)*
Saturn Sales Inc..519 658-5125
4500 Witmer Indstrl 202 Niagara Falls (14305) *(G-12892)*
Saunders Concrete Co Inc.................................607 756-7905
6 Locust Ave Cortland (13045) *(G-4067)*
Sausbiers Awning Shop Inc...............................518 828-3748
43 8th St Hudson (12534) *(G-6664)*
SAV Thermo Inc..631 249-9444
133 Cabot St West Babylon (11704) *(G-16857)*
Savaco Inc...716 751-9455
2905 Beebe Rd Newfane (14108) *(G-12812)*
Savage & Son Installations LLC..........................585 342-7533
676 Pullman Ave Rochester (14615) *(G-14692)*
Save Around, Binghamton Also called Enjoy City North Inc *(G-908)*
Save More Beverage Corp..................................518 371-2520
1512 Route 9 Ste 1 Halfmoon (12065) *(G-5938)*
Save O Seal Corporation Inc..............................914 592-3031
90 E Main St Elmsford (10523) *(G-4785)*
Savenergy Inc...516 239-1958
645 South St Unit A Garden City (11530) *(G-5545)*
Saveur Magazine...212 219-7400
304 Park Ave S Fl 8 New York (10010) *(G-11997)*
Savoritefactory, New York Also called Q Ed Creations *(G-11787)*
Savwatt Usa Inc (PA)......................................646 478-2676
475 Park Ave S Fl 30 New York (10016) *(G-11998)*
Saw Mill Pediatrics Pllc...................................914 449-6064
95 Locust Rd Pleasantville (10570) *(G-13750)*
Saxby Implement Corp (PA)..............................585 624-2938
180 Mendon Victor Rd Mendon (14506) *(G-8414)*
Saxon Glass Technologies Inc............................607 587-9630
200 N Main St Ste 114 Alfred (14802) *(G-197)*
Saxton Corporation...518 732-7705
1320 Route 9 Castleton On Hudson (12033) *(G-3449)*
Sayeda Manufacturing Corp..............................631 345-2525
20 Scouting Blvd Medford (11763) *(G-8293)*
Sb Corporation...212 822-3166
114 W 41st St Fl 4 New York (10036) *(G-11999)*
Sb Molds LLC...845 352-3700
161 Route 59 Ste 203a Monsey (10952) *(G-8616)*
Sb New York Inc (HQ)....................................212 457-7790
120 Broadway New York (10271) *(G-12000)*
Sbb Inc...315 422-2376
1 Gm Dr Ste 5 East Syracuse (13057) *(G-4576)*
Sbcontract.com, Farmingdale Also called Metadure Parts & Sales Inc *(G-5059)*
Sbi Enterprises, Ellenville Also called Master Juvenile Products Inc *(G-4649)*
Sbi Enterprises, Ellenville Also called JM Originals Inc *(G-4648)*
Sbk Preserves Inc..800 773-7378
1161 E 156th St Bronx (10474) *(G-1448)*
SC Medical Overseas Inc..................................516 935-8500
350 Jericho Tpke Ste 302 Jericho (11753) *(G-7117)*
SC Supply Chain Management LLC....................212 344-3322
90 Broad St Ste 1504 New York (10004) *(G-12001)*
SC Textiles Inc...631 944-6262
434 New York Ave Huntington (11743) *(G-6718)*
Sca Tissue North America LLC.........................518 692-8434
72 County Route 53 Greenwich (12834) *(G-5912)*
Sca Tissue North America LLC.........................518 583-2785
49 Geyser Rd Saratoga Springs (12866) *(G-15203)*
Scaccianoce Inc..718 991-4462
1165 Burnett Pl Bronx (10474) *(G-1449)*
Scaife Enterprises Inc.....................................585 454-5231
67 Lyell Ave Rochester (14608) *(G-14693)*
Scala Furniture Industries NY, Bronx Also called Bel Art International *(G-1281)*
Scalamandre Silks, Hauppauge Also called Scalamandre Wallpaper Inc *(G-6210)*
Scalamandre Silks Inc (PA)..............................212 980-3888
979 3rd Ave Ste 202 New York (10022) *(G-12002)*
Scalamandre Wallpaper Inc...............................631 467-8800
350 Wireless Blvd Hauppauge (11788) *(G-6210)*
Scale-Tronix Inc (PA).....................................914 948-8117
4341 State Street Rd Skaneateles (13152) *(G-15487)*
Scan-A-Chrome Color Inc..................................631 532-6146
555 Oak St Copiague (11726) *(G-3948)*
Scancorp Inc..315 454-5596
1840 Lemoyne Ave Syracuse (13208) *(G-16054)*
Scanga Woodworking Corp...............................845 265-9115
22 Corporate Park W Cold Spring (10516) *(G-3791)*
Scapa North America.......................................315 413-1111
1111 Vine St Liverpool (13088) *(G-7573)*
Scara-Mix Inc..718 442-7357
2537 Richmond Ter Staten Island (10303) *(G-15756)*
Scarano Boat Building Inc................................518 463-3401
194 S Port Rd Albany (12202) *(G-132)*
Scarano Boatbuilding Inc..................................518 463-3401
194 S Port Rd Albany (12202) *(G-133)*
Scarguard Labs LLC..516 482-8050
15 Barstow Rd Great Neck (11021) *(G-5856)*
Scarsdale Inquirer, Scarsdale Also called S I Communications Inc *(G-15253)*

Scehenvus Fire Dist...607 638-9017
40 Main St Schenevus (12155) *(G-15337)*
Scehenvus Gram Hose Co, Schenevus Also called Schenevus Fire Dist *(G-15337)*
Scent 2 Market, Yonkers Also called Belmay Holding Corporation *(G-17436)*
Scent-A-Vision Inc..631 424-4905
171 E 2nd St Huntington Station (11746) *(G-6759)*
Scepter Inc..315 568-4225
11 Lamb Rd Seneca Falls (13148) *(G-15390)*
Scepter New York, Seneca Falls Also called Scepter Inc *(G-15390)*
Scepter Publishers Inc....................................212 354-0670
56 Harrison St Ste 401 New Rochelle (10801) *(G-8970)*
Scerri Quality Wood Floors, New York Also called Wood Floor Expo Inc *(G-12683)*
Sch Dpx Corporation.......................................917 405-5377
22 W 21st St Ste 700 New York (10010) *(G-12003)*
Schaefer Entps of Deposit...............................607 467-4990
315 Old Route 10 Deposit (13754) *(G-4303)*
Schaefer Logging Inc......................................607 467-4990
315 Old Route 10 Deposit (13754) *(G-4304)*
Schaefer Machine Co Inc.................................516 248-6880
100 Hudson St Mineola (11501) *(G-8570)*
Schaller & Weber, New York Also called Schaller Manufacturing Corp *(G-12004)*
Schaller Manufacturing Corp (PA).....................718 721-5480
1654 2nd Ave Apt 2n New York (10028) *(G-12004)*
Scharf and Breit Inc.......................................516 282-0287
2 Hillside Ave Ste F Williston Park (11596) *(G-17286)*
Schatz Bearing Corporation..............................845 452-6000
10 Fairview Ave Poughkeepsie (12601) *(G-13948)*
Schenck Corporation (HQ)...............................631 242-4010
535 Acorn St Deer Park (11729) *(G-4229)*
Schenck Trebel Corp (HQ)...............................631 242-4397
535 Acorn St Deer Park (11729) *(G-4230)*
SCHENECTADY HERALD PRINTING CO, Troy Also called Dowd - Witbeck Printing Corp *(G-16256)*
Schenectady Steel Co Inc.................................518 355-3220
18 Mariaville Rd Schenectady (12306) *(G-15317)*
Schiller Stores Inc..845 928-4316
869 Adirondack Way Central Valley (10917) *(G-3555)*
Schiller Stores Inc (PA)..................................631 208-9400
509 Tanger Mall Dr Riverhead (11901) *(G-14168)*
Schilling Forge Inc..315 454-4421
606 Factory Ave Syracuse (13208) *(G-16055)*
Schindler Elevator Corporation..........................212 708-1000
620 12th Ave Fl 4 New York (10036) *(G-12005)*
Schindler Elevator Corporation..........................718 417-3131
8400 72nd Dr Ste 2 Glendale (11385) *(G-5678)*
Schindler Elevator Corporation..........................516 860-1321
7 Midland Ave Hicksville (11801) *(G-6419)*
Schindler Elevator Corporation..........................800 225-3123
1211 6th Ave Ste 2950 New York (10036) *(G-12006)*
Schlegel Electronic Mtls Inc (PA)......................585 295-2030
1600 Lexington Ave 236a Rochester (14606) *(G-14694)*
Schlegel Systems Inc (HQ).............................585 427-7200
1555 Jefferson Rd Rochester (14623) *(G-14695)*
Schlesinger Siemans Elec LLC..........................718 386-6230
527 Madison Ave Fl 8 New York (10022) *(G-12007)*
Schless Bottles Inc (PA).................................718 236-2790
4616 16th Ave Brooklyn (11204) *(G-2561)*
Schlumberger Technology Corp.........................607 378-0105
224 N Main St Bldg S Horseheads (14845) *(G-6621)*
Schmersal Inc...914 347-4775
15 Skyline Dr Ste 230 Hawthorne (10532) *(G-6279)*
Schmitt Sales Inc...716 632-8595
5095 Main St Williamsville (14221) *(G-17277)*
Schneeman Studio Limited...............................212 244-3330
330 W 38th St Rm 505 New York (10018) *(G-12008)*
Schneider Amalco Inc......................................917 470-9674
600 3rd Ave Fl 2 New York (10016) *(G-12009)*
Schneider Brothers Corporation........................315 458-8369
7371 Eastman Rd Syracuse (13212) *(G-16056)*
Schneider Elc Systems USA Inc........................214 527-3099
7 E 8th St New York (10003) *(G-12010)*
Schneider Electric It Corp................................646 335-0216
520 8th Ave Rm 2103 New York (10018) *(G-12011)*
Schneider Electric Usa Inc...............................646 335-0220
112 W 34th St Ste 908 New York (10120) *(G-12012)*
Schneider Electric Usa Inc...............................585 377-1313
441 Penbrooke Dr Ste 9 Penfield (14526) *(G-13527)*
Schneider M Soap & Chemical Co.....................718 389-1000
1930 Troutman St Ridgewood (11385) *(G-14136)*
Schneider Mills Inc...828 632-0801
1430 Broadway Rm 1202 New York (10018) *(G-12013)*
Schneps Publications Inc (PA).........................718 224-5863
3815 Bell Blvd Ste 38 Bayside (11361) *(G-769)*
Schoen Trimming & Cord Co Inc......................212 255-3949
151 W 25th St Fl 10 New York (10001) *(G-12014)*
Schoharie Quarry/Asphalt, Schoharie Also called Cobleskill Stone Products Inc *(G-15338)*
Scholastic Copy Center, New York Also called Scholastic Inc *(G-12017)*
Scholastic Corporation (PA).............................212 343-6100
557 Broadway Lbby 1 New York (10012) *(G-12015)*
Scholastic Inc (HQ).......................................800 724-6527
557 Broadway Lbby 1 New York (10012) *(G-12016)*

ALPHABETIC SECTION
Sean John Clothing Inc (PA)

Scholastic Inc 212 343-6100
557 Broadway Lbby 1 New York (10012) *(G-12017)*

Scholastic Inc 212 343-7100
568 Broadway Rm 809 New York (10012) *(G-12018)*

Scholium International Inc 516 883-8032
151 Cow Neck Rd Port Washington (11050) *(G-13880)*

Schonbek, Plattsburgh *Also called Swarovski Lighting Ltd (G-13731)*

Schonbek Shipping Bldg, Plattsburgh *Also called Swarovski Lighting Ltd (G-13732)*

Schonwetter Enterprises Inc 518 237-0171
41 Lark St Cohoes (12047) *(G-3782)*

School Guide Publications, Mamaroneck *Also called Catholic News Publishing Co (G-8059)*

School of Management, Binghamton *Also called Suny At Binghamton (G-946)*

Schoolnet Inc (HQ) 646 496-9000
525 Fashion Ave Fl 4 New York (10018) *(G-12019)*

Schott Corporation (HQ) 914 831-2200
555 Taxter Rd Ste 470 Elmsford (10523) *(G-4786)*

Schott Corporation 315 255-2791
62 Columbus St Auburn (13021) *(G-514)*

Schott Defense, Elmsford *Also called Schott Government Services LLC (G-4788)*

Schott Gemtron Corporation 423 337-3522
555 Taxter Rd Ste 470 Elmsford (10523) *(G-4787)*

Schott Government Services LLC 703 418-1409
555 Taxter Rd Ste 470 Elmsford (10523) *(G-4788)*

Schott Lithotec USA Corp 845 463-5300
555 Taxter Rd Ste 470 Elmsford (10523) *(G-4789)*

Schott Solar Pv Inc 888 457-6527
555 Taxter Rd Ste 470 Elmsford (10523) *(G-4790)*

Schrader Meat Market 607 869-6328
1937 Summerville Rd Romulus (14541) *(G-14870)*

Schroeder Machine Div, East Syracuse *Also called Niagara Scientific Inc (G-4566)*

Schuler-Haas Electric Corp 607 936-3514
598 Ritas Way Painted Post (14870) *(G-13419)*

Schuler-Subra Inc 716 893-3100
83 Doat St Buffalo (14211) *(G-3206)*

Schulz Interiors, Poughquag *Also called Fred Schulz Inc (G-13957)*

Schurman Fine Papers 212 206-0067
275 7th Ave Frnt 6 New York (10001) *(G-12020)*

Schuster & Richard Lab, College Point *Also called Schuster & Richard Labortories (G-3831)*

Schuster & Richard Labortories 718 358-8607
1420 130th St College Point (11356) *(G-3831)*

Schutt Cider Mill 585 872-2924
1063 Plank Rd Webster (14580) *(G-16760)*

Schutte-Buffalo Hammer Mill, Buffalo *Also called Schutte-Buffalo Hammermill LLC (G-3207)*

Schutte-Buffalo Hammermill LLC 716 855-1202
61 Depot St Buffalo (14206) *(G-3207)*

Schwab Corp (HQ) 585 381-4900
900 Linden Ave Rochester (14625) *(G-14696)*

Schwabel Fabricating Co Inc (PA) 716 876-2086
349 Sawyer Ave Tonawanda (14150) *(G-16219)*

Schwartz Textile Converting Co 718 499-8243
160 7th St Brooklyn (11215) *(G-2562)*

Schweitzer-Mauduit Intl Inc 518 329-4222
2424 Route 82 Ancram (12502) *(G-375)*

SCI Bore Inc 212 674-7128
70 Irving Pl Apt 5c New York (10003) *(G-12021)*

Sciane Enterprises Inc 845 452-2400
2600 South Rd Ste 37 Poughkeepsie (12601) *(G-13949)*

Sciarra Laboratories Inc 516 933-7853
48509 S Broadway Hicksville (11801) *(G-6420)*

Sciegen Pharmaceuticals Inc (PA) 631 434-2723
330 Oser Ave Hauppauge (11788) *(G-6211)*

Scienta Pharmaceuticals LLC 845 589-0774
612 Corporate Way Ste 9 Valley Cottage (10989) *(G-16414)*

Scientific American Library, New York *Also called Bedford Freeman & Worth (G-9391)*

Scientific Components Corp (PA) 718 934-4500
13 Neptune Ave Brooklyn (11235) *(G-2563)*

Scientific Components Corp 631 243-4901
161 E Industry Ct Deer Park (11729) *(G-4231)*

Scientific Components Corp 718 368-2060
2450 Knapp St Brooklyn (11235) *(G-2564)*

Scientific Industries Inc (PA) 631 567-4700
80 Orville Dr Ste 102 Bohemia (11716) *(G-1125)*

Scientific Plastics Inc 212 967-1199
243 W 30th St Fl 8 New York (10001) *(G-12022)*

Scientific Polymer Products 585 265-0413
6265 Dean Pkwy Ontario (14519) *(G-13236)*

Scientific Solutions Globl LLC 516 543-3376
326 Westbury Ave Carle Place (11514) *(G-3423)*

Scientific Tool Co Inc (PA) 315 431-4243
101 Arterial Rd Syracuse (13206) *(G-16057)*

Scientifics Direct Inc 716 773-7500
532 Main St Tonawanda (14150) *(G-16220)*

Scissor Online, Bolivar *Also called Klein Cutlery LLC (G-1156)*

Sciterra LLC 646 883-3724
244 5th Ave Ste L280 New York (10001) *(G-12023)*

Scj Associates Inc 585 359-0600
60 Commerce Dr Rochester (14623) *(G-14697)*

SCM, New York *Also called SC Supply Chain Management LLC (G-12001)*

SCM, Suffern *Also called Super Conductor Materials Inc (G-15821)*

Scomac Inc 585 494-2200
8629 Buffalo Rd Bergen (14416) *(G-851)*

Scooby Dog Food, Utica *Also called Scooby Rendering & Inc (G-16382)*

Scooby Rendering & Inc 315 793-1014
1930 Oriskany St W Utica (13502) *(G-16382)*

Scoops R US Incorporated 212 730-7959
1514 Broadway New York (10036) *(G-12024)*

Scorpion Security Products Inc 607 724-9999
330 N Jensen Rd Vestal (13850) *(G-16476)*

Scotia Beverages Inc 518 370-3621
701 Corporation Park Schenectady (12302) *(G-15318)*

Scotsman Press, Syracuse *Also called Badoud Communications Inc (G-15886)*

Scott Kay Inc 201 287-0100
154 W 14th St Fl 6 New York (10011) *(G-12025)*

Scott Rotary Seals, Olean *Also called Dsti Inc (G-13165)*

Scott Rotary Seals, Olean *Also called Dynamic Sealing Tech Inc (G-13166)*

Scotti Graphics Inc 212 367-9602
3200 Skillman Ave Fl 1 Long Island City (11101) *(G-7901)*

Scotts Company LLC 631 478-6843
65 Engineers Rd Hauppauge (11788) *(G-6212)*

Scotts Company LLC 631 289-7444
445 Horseblock Rd Yaphank (11980) *(G-17416)*

Scotts Feed Inc 518 483-3110
245 Elm St Malone (12953) *(G-8046)*

Screen Gems Inc 845 561-0036
41 Windsor Hwy New Windsor (12553) *(G-8999)*

Screen Gems-EMI Music Inc (HQ) 212 786-8000
150 5th Ave Fl 7 New York (10011) *(G-12026)*

Screen Team Inc 718 786-2424
3402c Review Ave Long Island City (11101) *(G-7902)*

Screen The World Inc 631 475-0023
658 Blue Point Rd Holtsville (11742) *(G-6534)*

Screw Compressor Tech Inc 716 827-6600
158 Ridge Rd Buffalo (14218) *(G-3208)*

Script-Master Div, New York *Also called Brewer-Cantelmo Co Inc (G-9510)*

Scriven Duplicating Service 518 233-8180
100 Eastover Rd Troy (12182) *(G-16277)*

Scriven Press, Troy *Also called Scriven Duplicating Service (G-16277)*

Scroll Media Inc 617 395-8904
235 W 102nd St Apt 14i New York (10025) *(G-12027)*

Scully Sanitation 315 899-8996
11146 Skaneateles Tpke West Edmeston (13485) *(G-16875)*

Sculptgraphicz Inc 646 837-7302
67 35th St Unit B520 Brooklyn (11232) *(G-2565)*

Scy Manufacturing Inc 516 986-3083
600 Bayview Ave Ste 200 Inwood (11096) *(G-6806)*

SD Christie Associates Inc 914 734-1800
424 Central Ave Ste 5 Peekskill (10566) *(G-13507)*

SD Eagle Global Inc 516 822-1778
2 Kay St Jericho (11753) *(G-7118)*

SD Times, Melville *Also called Bz Media LLC (G-8330)*

SDC, Saugerties *Also called Stainless Design Concepts Ltd (G-15224)*

Sdi Cable, Bohemia *Also called Security Dynamics Inc (G-1126)*

SDJ Machine Shop Inc 585 458-1236
1215 Mount Read Blvd # 1 Rochester (14606) *(G-14698)*

Sdp/Si, Hicksville *Also called Designatronics Incorporated (G-6366)*

Sdr Technology Inc 716 583-1249
1613 Lindan Dr Alden (14004) *(G-186)*

SDS Business Cards Inc 516 747-3131
170 The Vale Syosset (11791) *(G-15860)*

Se-Mar Electric Co Inc 716 674-7404
101 South Ave West Seneca (14224) *(G-16982)*

Sea Isle Custom Rod Builders 516 868-8855
495 Guy Lombardo Ave Freeport (11520) *(G-5436)*

Sea Mats, Malone *Also called Seaway Mats Inc (G-8047)*

Sea Waves Inc (PA) 516 766-4201
2425 Long Beach Rd Oceanside (11572) *(G-13118)*

Seabay Media Holdings LLC (PA) 212 457-7790
120 Broadway Fl 6 New York (10271) *(G-12028)*

Seaboard Electronics, New Rochelle *Also called Highlander Realty Inc (G-8956)*

Seaboard Graphic Services LLC 315 652-4200
7570 Oswego Rd Liverpool (13090) *(G-7574)*

Seabreeze Pavement of Ny LLC 585 338-2333
14 Maryknoll Park Rochester (14622) *(G-14699)*

Seal & Design Inc 315 432-8021
6741 Thompson Rd Syracuse (13211) *(G-16058)*

Seal Reinforced Fiberglass Inc (PA) 631 842-2230
19 Bethpage Rd Copiague (11726) *(G-3949)*

Seal Reinforced Fiberglass Inc 631 842-2230
23 Bethpage Rd Copiague (11726) *(G-3950)*

Sealcraft Industries Inc 718 517-2000
5308 13th Ave Ste 251 Brooklyn (11219) *(G-2566)*

Sealmaster, Buffalo *Also called Jet-Black Sealers Inc (G-3036)*

Sealtest Dairy Products, Rochester *Also called Upstate Niagara Coop Inc (G-14775)*

Sealy Mattress Co Albany Inc 518 880-1600
30 Veterans Memorial Dr Troy (12183) *(G-16244)*

Sean John, New York *Also called Christian Casey LLC (G-9660)*

Sean John Clothing, New York *Also called Christian Casey LLC (G-9661)*

Sean John Clothing Inc 212 500-2200
1710 Broadway Frnt 1 New York (10019) *(G-12029)*

Sean John Clothing Inc (PA) 212 500-2200
1440 Broadway Frnt 3 New York (10018) *(G-12030)*

ALPHABETIC

Seanair Machine Co Inc 631 694-2820
95 Verdi St Farmingdale (11735) *(G-5118)*
Searles Graphics Inc (PA) 631 345-2202
56 Old Dock Rd Yaphank (11980) *(G-17417)*
Seasons Soyfood Inc 718 797-9896
605 Degraw St Brooklyn (11217) *(G-2567)*
Seating Inc 800 468-2475
60 N State St Nunda (14517) *(G-13060)*
Seaward Candies 585 638-6761
3588 N Main Street Rd Holley (14470) *(G-6518)*
Seaway Mats Inc 518 483-2560
252 Park St Malone (12953) *(G-8047)*
Seaway Timber Harvesting Inc (PA) 315 769-5970
15121 State Highway 37 Massena (13662) *(G-8231)*
Sebby Clothing, New York *Also called Comint Apparel Group LLC (G-9743)*
Second Amendment Foundation 716 885-6408
267 Linwood Ave Ste A Buffalo (14209) *(G-3209)*
Second Chance Press Inc 631 725-1101
4170 Noyac Rd Sag Harbor (11963) *(G-15108)*
Second Generation Wood Stairs 718 370-0085
2581 Richmond Ter Ste 3 Staten Island (10303) *(G-15757)*
Secondary Services Inc 716 896-4000
757 E Ferry St Buffalo (14211) *(G-3210)*
Secor Marketing Group Inc 914 381-3600
225 Hoyt Ave Mamaroneck (10543) *(G-8079)*
Secret Celebrity Licensing LLC 212 812-9277
1431 Broadway Fl 10 New York (10018) *(G-12031)*
Secs Inc (PA) 914 667-5600
550 S Columbus Ave Mount Vernon (10550) *(G-8777)*
Secs Inc 914 667-5600
550 S Columbus Ave Mount Vernon (10550) *(G-8778)*
Sector Microwave Inds Inc 631 242-2245
999 Grand Blvd Deer Park (11729) *(G-4232)*
Sector4vapes 607 377-2224
106 Bridge St Corning (14830) *(G-4001)*
Secuprint Inc 585 341-3100
1560 Emerson St Rochester (14606) *(G-14700)*
Securax, Bohemia *Also called Protex International Corp (G-1120)*
Secured Services Inc (PA) 866 419-3900
110 William St Fl 14 New York (10038) *(G-12032)*
Secureit Tactical Inc (PA) 800 651-8835
6691 Commerce Blvd Syracuse (13211) *(G-16059)*
Securevue Inc 631 587-5850
28 Trues Dr West Islip (11795) *(G-16936)*
Securities Data Publishing Inc (PA) 212 631-1411
11 Penn Plz Fl 17 New York (10001) *(G-12033)*
Security Defense System 718 769-7900
15038 12th Ave Whitestone (11357) *(G-17243)*
Security Dynamics Inc 631 392-1701
217 Knickerbocker Ave Bohemia (11716) *(G-1126)*
Security Letter 212 348-1553
166 E 96th St Apt 3b New York (10128) *(G-12034)*
Security Offset Services Inc 631 944-6031
11 Grandview St Huntington (11743) *(G-6719)*
Seed Media Group LLC 646 502-7050
405 Greenwich St Apt 2 New York (10013) *(G-12035)*
Seedlngs Lf Scnce Ventures LLC 917 913-8511
230 E 15th St Apt 1a New York (10003) *(G-12036)*
Seeley Machine Inc 518 798-9510
75 Big Boom Rd Queensbury (12804) *(G-14024)*
Seeley Machine & Fabrication, Queensbury *Also called Seeley Machine Inc (G-14024)*
Seetin Design Group Inc 718 486-5610
57 Grand Street Ext Brooklyn (11211) *(G-2568)*
Sefaira Inc 855 733-2472
135 E 57th St Fl 6 New York (10022) *(G-12037)*
Sefi Fabricator, Amityville *Also called IMC Teddy Food Service (G-294)*
Sefi Fabricators, Amityville *Also called P & M LLC (G-319)*
Segovia Technology Co 212 868-4412
115 W 18th St Fl 2 New York (10011) *(G-12038)*
Seibel Modern Mfg & Wldg Corp 716 683-1536
38 Palmer Pl Lancaster (14086) *(G-7367)*
Seidlin Consulting 212 496-2043
580 W End Ave New York (10024) *(G-12039)*
Seifert Graphics Inc 315 736-2744
6133 Judd Rd Oriskany (13424) *(G-13337)*
Seifert Transit Graphics, Oriskany *Also called Seifert Graphics Inc (G-13337)*
Seisenbacher Inc 585 730-4960
175 Humboldt St Ste 250 Rochester (14610) *(G-14701)*
Seize Sur Vingt, New York *Also called Groupe 16sur20 LLC (G-10415)*
Sekas International Ltd 212 629-6095
345 7th Ave Fl 9 New York (10001) *(G-12040)*
Selby Marketing Associates Inc (PA) 585 377-0750
1387 Fairport Rd Ste 800 Fairport (14450) *(G-4882)*
Select Controls Inc 631 567-9010
45 Knickerbocker Ave # 3 Bohemia (11716) *(G-1127)*
Select Door, North Java *Also called Select Interior Door Ltd (G-12950)*
Select Fabricators Inc 585 393-0650
5310 North St Bldg 5 Canandaigua (14424) *(G-3387)*
Select Industries New York Inc 800 723-5333
450 Fashion Ave Ste 3002 New York (10123) *(G-12041)*
Select Information Exchange 212 496-6435
175 W 79th St 3a New York (10024) *(G-12042)*
Select Interior Door Ltd 585 535-9900
2074 Perry Rd North Java (14113) *(G-12950)*
Select Jewelry Inc 718 784-3626
4728 37th St Fl 3 Long Island City (11101) *(G-7903)*
Select Products Holdings LLC 855 777-3532
1 Arnold Dr Unit 3 Huntington (11743) *(G-6720)*
Select-A-Form Inc 631 981-3076
4717 Veterans Mem Hwy Holbrook (11741) *(G-6499)*
Select-Tech Inc 845 895-8111
3050 State Route 208 Wallkill (12589) *(G-16566)*
Selective Beauty Corporation 585 336-7600
315 Bleecker St 109 New York (10014) *(G-12043)*
Selectrode Industries Inc (PA) 631 547-5470
230 Broadway Huntington Station (11746) *(G-6760)*
Selflock Screw Products Co Inc 315 541-4464
461 E Brighton Ave Syracuse (13210) *(G-16060)*
Selini Neckwear Inc 212 268-5488
248 W 37th St New York (10018) *(G-12044)*
Sellco Industries Inc 607 756-7594
58 Grant St Cortland (13045) *(G-4068)*
Selux Corporation 845 691-7723
5 Lumen Ln Highland (12528) *(G-6435)*
Semans Enterprises Inc 585 444-0097
25 Hendrix Rd Ste E West Henrietta (14586) *(G-16925)*
Semco Ceramics Inc (HQ) 315 782-3000
363 Eastern Blvd Watertown (13601) *(G-16694)*
Semec Corp 518 825-0160
20 Gateway Dr Plattsburgh (12901) *(G-13725)*
Semi-Linear Inc 212 243-2108
1123 Broadway Ste 718 New York (10010) *(G-12045)*
Semitronics Corp (HQ) 516 223-0200
80 Commercial St Freeport (11520) *(G-5437)*
Semrock, Rochester *Also called Semrok Inc (G-14702)*
Semrok Inc (HQ) 585 594-7050
3625 Buffalo Rd Ste 6 Rochester (14624) *(G-14702)*
Semtex Industrial, Freeport *Also called Intex Company Inc (G-5417)*
Sendec Corp (HQ) 585 425-3390
72 Perinton Pkwy Fairport (14450) *(G-4883)*
Sendec Corp 585 425-5965
151 Perinton Pkwy Fairport (14450) *(G-4884)*
Sendyne Corp 212 966-0663
250 W Broadway Fl 6 New York (10013) *(G-12046)*
Seneca Ceramics Corp 315 781-0100
835 Mcivor Rd Phelps (14532) *(G-13559)*
Seneca County Area Shopper 607 532-4333
1885 State Route 96a Ovid (14521) *(G-13372)*
Seneca Falls Capital Inc (PA) 315 568-5804
314 Fall St Seneca Falls (13148) *(G-15391)*
Seneca Falls Machine, Seneca Falls *Also called Seneca Falls Capital Inc (G-15391)*
Seneca Falls Machine Tool Co 315 568-5804
314 Fall St Seneca Falls (13148) *(G-15392)*
Seneca Falls Technology Group, Seneca Falls *Also called Seneca Falls Machine Tool Co (G-15392)*
Seneca FLS Spc & Logistics Co (PA) 315 568-4139
50 Johnston St Seneca Falls (13148) *(G-15393)*
Seneca Foods Corporation (PA) 315 926-8100
3736 S Main St Marion (14505) *(G-8129)*
Seneca Foods Corporation 315 781-8733
100 Gambee Rd Geneva (14456) *(G-5597)*
Seneca Foods Corporation 315 926-0531
3709 Mill St Marion (14505) *(G-8130)*
Seneca Foods Corporation 315 926-4277
3732 S Main St Marion (14505) *(G-8131)*
Seneca Foods Corporation 585 658-2211
5705 Rte 36 Leicester (14481) *(G-7444)*
Seneca Manufacturing Company 716 945-4400
175 Rochester St Salamanca (14779) *(G-15133)*
Seneca Media Inc (PA) 607 324-1425
32 Broadway Mall Hornell (14843) *(G-6593)*
Seneca Media Inc 585 593-5300
159 N Main St Wellsville (14895) *(G-16784)*
Seneca Nation Enterprise 716 934-7430
11482 Route 20 Irving (14081) *(G-6807)*
Seneca Resources Corporation 716 630-6750
165 Lawrence Bell Dr Williamsville (14221) *(G-17278)*
Seneca Signs LLC 315 446-9420
102 Headson Dr Syracuse (13214) *(G-16061)*
Seneca Stone Corporation 315 549-8253
Cty Rd 121 Hoster Cors Rd Fayette (13065) *(G-5170)*
Seneca Stone Corporation (HQ) 607 737-6200
2105 S Broadway Pine City (14871) *(G-13579)*
Seneca TEC Inc 585 381-2645
73 Country Corner Ln Fairport (14450) *(G-4885)*
Seneca Truck & Trailer Inc 315 781-1100
2200 State Route 14 Geneva (14456) *(G-5598)*
Seneca West Printing Inc 716 675-8010
860 Center Rd West Seneca (14224) *(G-16983)*
Senera Co Inc 516 639-3774
834 Glenridge Ave Valley Stream (11581) *(G-16450)*
Senneth LLC 347 232-3170
26 Ronald Dr Ste 500 Monsey (10952) *(G-8617)*
Sensational Collection Inc (PA) 212 840-7388
1410 Broadway Rm 505 New York (10018) *(G-12047)*

Sensio America...877 501-5337
800 Route 146 Clifton Park (12065) ***(G-3732)***
Sensitron Semiconductor, Deer Park *Also called RSM Electron Power Inc* ***(G-4228)***
Sensitron Semiconductor, Hauppauge *Also called RSM Electron Power Inc* ***(G-6207)***
Sensor & Decontamination Inc...301 526-8389
892 Powderhouse Rd Binghamton (13903) ***(G-944)***
Sensor Films Incorporated...585 738-3500
687 Rowley Rd Victor (14564) ***(G-16525)***
Sensormatic Electronics LLC...845 365-3125
10 Corporate Dr Orangeburg (10962) ***(G-13268)***
Sensual Inc...212 869-1450
463 7th Ave New York (10018) ***(G-12048)***
Sentage Corporation...914 664-2200
161 S Macquesten Pkwy 2 Mount Vernon (10550) ***(G-8779)***
Sentimental Inc...212 221-0282
214 W 39th St Rm 504a New York (10018) ***(G-12049)***
Sentimental NY, New York *Also called Sentimental Inc* ***(G-12049)***
Sentinel Printing, Hempstead *Also called Hempstead Sentinel Inc* ***(G-6297)***
Sentinel Printing Inc...516 334-7400
75 State St Westbury (11590) ***(G-17054)***
Sentinel Printing Services Inc...845 562-1218
36 Meriline Ave New Windsor (12553) ***(G-9000)***
Sentinel Products Corp...518 568-7036
12 New St Saint Johnsville (13452) ***(G-15124)***
Sentinel, The, New Windsor *Also called E W Smith Publishing Co* ***(G-8983)***
Sentry Automatic Sprinkler...631 723-3095
735 Flanders Rd Riverhead (11901) ***(G-14169)***
Sentry Devices Corp...631 491-3191
33 Rustic Gate Ln Dix Hills (11746) ***(G-4321)***
Sentry Funding Partnership, Ronkonkoma *Also called Sentry Technology Corporation* ***(G-15007)***
Sentry Metal Blast Inc...716 285-5241
553 West Ave Lockport (14094) ***(G-7645)***
Sentry Metal Services, Lockport *Also called Sentry Metal Blast Inc* ***(G-7645)***
Sentry Technology Corporation...631 739-2000
1881 Lakeland Ave Ronkonkoma (11779) ***(G-15006)***
Sentry Technology Corporation (PA)...800 645-4224
1881 Lakeland Ave Ronkonkoma (11779) ***(G-15007)***
Sepac Inc...607 732-2030
1580 Lake St Elmira (14901) ***(G-4714)***
Sepco-Sturges Electronics, Dryden *Also called Sturges Elec Pdts Co Inc* ***(G-4348)***
Sephardic Yellow Pages...718 998-0299
2150 E 4th St Brooklyn (11223) ***(G-2569)***
Sepsa North America, Ballston Spa *Also called Albatros North America Inc* ***(G-589)***
September Associates, Oakdale *Also called Steel-Brite Ltd* ***(G-13082)***
Sequa Corporation...201 343-1122
300 Blaisdell Rd Orangeburg (10962) ***(G-13269)***
Sequential Electronics Systems...914 592-1345
399 Executive Blvd Elmsford (10523) ***(G-4791)***
Serendipity Consulting Corp...914 763-8251
48 Twin Lakes Rd South Salem (10590) ***(G-15560)***
Serengeti Teas and Spices, New York *Also called Caranda Emporium LLC* ***(G-9577)***
Serge Duct Designs Inc...718 783-7799
535 Dean St Apt 124 Brooklyn (11217) ***(G-2570)***
Seri Systems Inc...585 272-5515
172 Metro Park Rochester (14623) ***(G-14703)***
Sermoneta Gloves, New York *Also called Shadal LLC* ***(G-12057)***
Serraview America Inc...800 903-3716
2 Wall St Fl 10 New York (10005) ***(G-12050)***
Service Advertising Group Inc...718 361-6161
4216 34th Ave Long Island City (11101) ***(G-7904)***
Service Canvas Co Inc...716 853-0558
149 Swan St Unit 155 Buffalo (14203) ***(G-3211)***
Service Education Incorporated...585 264-9240
790 Canning Pkwy Ste 1 Victor (14564) ***(G-16526)***
Service Filtration Corp...716 877-2608
225 E Park Dr Tonawanda (14150) ***(G-16221)***
Service Machine & Tool Company...607 732-0413
206 E Mccanns Blvd Elmira Heights (14903) ***(G-4725)***
Service Mfg Group Inc (PA)...716 893-1482
400 Scajaquada St Buffalo (14211) ***(G-3212)***
Service Mfg Group Inc...716 893-1482
400 Scajaquada St Buffalo (14211) ***(G-3213)***
Servicenow Inc...914 318-1168
60 E 42nd St Ste 1230 New York (10165) ***(G-12051)***
Servo Reeler System, Queens Village *Also called Xedit Corp* ***(G-14000)***
Servotec Usa LLC...518 671-6120
1 Industrial Tract Anx # 3 Hudson (12534) ***(G-6665)***
Servotronics Inc (PA)...716 655-5990
1110 Maple Rd Elma (14059) ***(G-4668)***
Serway Bros Inc (PA)...315 337-0601
Plant 2 Rome Indus Ctr Rome (13440) ***(G-14864)***
Serway Cabinet Trends, Rome *Also called Serway Bros Inc* ***(G-14864)***
Sesco Industries Inc...718 939-5137
11019 15th Ave College Point (11356) ***(G-3832)***
Setauket Manufacturing Co...631 231-7272
202 Christopher St Ronkonkoma (11779) ***(G-15008)***
Settapani Bakery, Brooklyn *Also called Settepani Inc* ***(G-2571)***
Settepani Inc (PA)...718 349-6524
602 Lorimer St Brooklyn (11211) ***(G-2571)***
Setton Farms, Commack *Also called Settons Intl Foods Inc* ***(G-3868)***
Settons Intl Foods Inc (PA)...631 543-8090
85 Austin Blvd Commack (11725) ***(G-3868)***
Seven Springs Gravel Pdts LLC...585 343-4336
8479 Seven Springs Rd Batavia (14020) ***(G-647)***
Seven Stories Press Inc...212 226-8760
140 Watts St New York (10013) ***(G-12052)***
Seventeen Magazine, New York *Also called Hearst Corporation* ***(G-10489)***
Seville Central Mix Corp (PA)...516 868-3000
157 Albany Ave Freeport (11520) ***(G-5438)***
Seville Central Mix Corp...516 293-6190
495 Wining Rd Old Bethpage (11804) ***(G-13151)***
Seville Central Mix Corp...516 239-8333
101 Johnson Rd Lawrence (11559) ***(G-7425)***
Seviroli Foods Inc (PA)...516 222-6220
601 Brook St Garden City (11530) ***(G-5546)***
Sew True, New York *Also called Champion Zipper Corp* ***(G-9627)***
Sextet Fabrics Inc...516 593-0608
21 Ryder Pl Ste 4 East Rockaway (11518) ***(G-4491)***
Sfoglini LLC...646 872-1035
630 Flushing Ave Fl 2 Brooklyn (11206) ***(G-2572)***
Sg Blocks Inc (PA)...615 585-2639
195 Montague St Fl 14 Brooklyn (11201) ***(G-2573)***
Sg Nyc LLC...310 210-1837
28 W 27th St Fl 12 New York (10001) ***(G-12053)***
Sg-TEC LLC...631 750-6161
1520 Ocean Ave Bohemia (11716) ***(G-1128)***
SGD North America...212 753-4200
900 3rd Ave Fl 4 New York (10022) ***(G-12054)***
SGD Pharma Packaging Inc...212 223-7100
900 3rd Ave Fl 4 New York (10022) ***(G-12055)***
Sgg, Long Island City *Also called Stanley Creations Inc* ***(G-7913)***
Sgl Services Corp...718 630-0392
1221 Ave Of Americas 42 New York (10020) ***(G-12056)***
Sgt Dresser-Rand, Wellsville *Also called Siemens Government Tech Inc* ***(G-16785)***
Sh Leather Novelty Company...718 387-7742
123 Clymer St Bsmt Brooklyn (11249) ***(G-2574)***
Shaant Industries Inc...716 366-3654
134 Franklin Ave Dunkirk (14048) ***(G-4374)***
Shabtai Gourmet, Woodmere *Also called Cinderellas Sweets Ltd* ***(G-17330)***
Shad Industries Inc...631 504-6028
7 Old Dock Rd Unit 1 Yaphank (11980) ***(G-17418)***
Shadal LLC...212 319-5946
609 Madison Ave Ste 611 New York (10022) ***(G-12057)***
Shade & Shutter Systems of NY...631 208-0275
260 Hampton Rd Southampton (11968) ***(G-15575)***
Shadow Lake Golf & Racquet CLB, Rochester *Also called Dolomite Products Company Inc* ***(G-14337)***
Shadowtv Inc...212 445-2540
630 9th Ave Ste 202 New York (10036) ***(G-12058)***
Shafer & Sons...315 853-5285
4932 State Route 233 Westmoreland (13490) ***(G-17094)***
Shah Diamonds Inc...212 888-9393
22 W 48th St Ste 600 New York (10036) ***(G-12059)***
Shahin Designs Ltd...212 737-7225
766 Madison Ave Fl 3 New York (10065) ***(G-12060)***
Shake Inc...650 544-5479
175 Varick St Fl 4 New York (10014) ***(G-12061)***
Shake-N-Go Fashion Inc...516 944-7777
83 Harbor Rd Port Washington (11050) ***(G-13881)***
Shake-N-Go Fashion Inc (PA)...516 944-7777
85 Harbor Rd Port Washington (11050) ***(G-13882)***
Shako Inc...315 437-1294
6191 E Molloy Rd East Syracuse (13057) ***(G-4577)***
Shakuff LLC...212 675-0383
34 35th St Unit 29 Brooklyn (11232) ***(G-2575)***
Shalam Imports Inc (PA)...718 686-6271
1552 Dahill Rd Ste B Brooklyn (11204) ***(G-2576)***
Shalamex, Brooklyn *Also called Shalam Imports Inc* ***(G-2576)***
Shamrock Plastic Corporation...585 328-6040
95 Mount Read Blvd Rochester (14611) ***(G-14704)***
Shamrock Plastics & Tool Inc...585 328-6040
95 Mount Read Blvd # 149 Rochester (14611) ***(G-14705)***
Shamron Mills Ltd...212 354-0430
242 W 38th St Fl 14 New York (10018) ***(G-12062)***
Shane & Shawn, New York *Also called Detny Footwear Inc* ***(G-9913)***
Shane Tex Inc...516 486-7522
50 Polk Ave Hempstead (11550) ***(G-6309)***
Shanghai Stove Inc...718 599-4583
78 Gerry St 82 Brooklyn (11206) ***(G-2577)***
Shanker Industries Inc (PA)...631 940-9889
301 Suburban Ave Deer Park (11729) ***(G-4233)***
Shannon Entps Wstn NY Inc...716 693-7954
75 Main St North Tonawanda (14120) ***(G-13011)***
Shanu Gems Inc...212 921-4470
1212 Ave Of The Americas New York (10036) ***(G-12063)***
Shapeways Inc (PA)...914 356-5816
419 Park Ave S Fl 9 New York (10016) ***(G-12064)***
Shapiro Bernstein & Co Inc...212 588-0878
488 Madison Ave Fl 1201 New York (10022) ***(G-12065)***
Shapiro Wlliam NY Univ Med Ctr, New York *Also called William H Shapiro* ***(G-12662)***

Shar-Mar Machine Company 631 567-8040
1648 Locust Ave Ste F Bohemia (11716) *(G-1129)*
Sharedbook Inc 646 442-8840
110 William St Fl 30 New York (10038) *(G-12066)*
Sharenet Inc 315 477-1100
214 Solar St Ste 110 Syracuse (13204) *(G-16062)*
Sharodine Inc 516 767-3548
18 Haven Ave Frnt 2 Port Washington (11050) *(G-13883)*
Sharon Manufacturing Co Inc 631 242-8870
540 Brook Ave Deer Park (11729) *(G-4234)*
Sharon Metal Stamping Corp 718 828-4510
1457 Bassett Ave Bronx (10461) *(G-1450)*
Sharonana Enterprises Inc 631 875-5619
52 Sharon Dr Coram (11727) *(G-3973)*
Sharp Printing Inc 716 731-3994
3477 Lockport Rd Sanborn (14132) *(G-15154)*
Shaw Contract Flrg Svcs Inc 212 953-7429
521 5th Ave Fl 37 New York (10175) *(G-12067)*
Shawmut Woodworking & Sup Inc 212 920-8900
3 E 54th St Fl 8 New York (10022) *(G-12068)*
Shawmutdesign and Construction, New York Also called *Shawmut Woodworking & Sup Inc (G-12068)*
Sheets, The, Long Island City Also called *Ragozin Data (G-7886)*
Shehawken Archery Co Inc 607 967-8333
40 S Main St Bainbridge (13733) *(G-553)*
Shelby Crushed Stone Inc 585 798-4501
10830 Blair Rd Medina (14103) *(G-8314)*
Sheldon Slate Products Co Inc 518 642-1280
Fox Rd Middle Granville (12849) *(G-8434)*
Sheldrake Point Vineyard LLC 607 532-8967
7448 County Road 153 Ovid (14521) *(G-13373)*
Sheldrake Point Winery, Ovid Also called *Sheldrake Point Vineyard LLC (G-13373)*
Shell Ann Printing, Stony Point Also called *Stony Point Graphics Ltd (G-15799)*
Shell Containers Inc (ny) 516 352-4505
1981 Marcus Ave Ste C105 New Hyde Park (11042) *(G-8906)*
Shelley Promotions Inc 212 924-4987
87 5th Ave New York (10003) *(G-12069)*
Shelter Enterprises Inc 518 237-4100
8 Saratoga St Cohoes (12047) *(G-3783)*
Shelter Island Cmnty Nwspapers, Shelter Island Also called *Shelter Island Reporter Inc (G-15410)*
Shelter Island Reporter Inc 631 749-1000
50 N Ferry Rd Shelter Island (11964) *(G-15410)*
Shenfeld Studio Tile, Syracuse Also called *Shenfield Studio LLC (G-16063)*
Shenfield Studio LLC 315 436-8869
6361 Thompson Rd Stop 12 Syracuse (13206) *(G-16063)*
Shennong Pharmaceuticals Inc 347 422-2200
110 Wall St New York (10005) *(G-12070)*
Shepherds Flat, New York Also called *Caithness Equities Corporation (G-9549)*
Sheppard Grain Enterprises LLC 315 548-9271
1615 Maryland Rd Phelps (14532) *(G-13560)*
Sherburne Metal Sales Inc (PA) 607 674-4441
40 S Main St Sherburne (13460) *(G-15417)*
Sherco Services LLC 516 676-3028
2 Park Pl Ste A Glen Cove (11542) *(G-5640)*
Sheridan House Inc 914 725-5431
230 Nelson Rd Scarsdale (10583) *(G-15254)*
Sherrill Manufacturing Inc 315 280-0727
102 E Seneca St Sherrill (13461) *(G-15430)*
Sherry-Mica Products Inc 631 471-7513
45 Remington Blvd Ste D Ronkonkoma (11779) *(G-15009)*
Sherwin Commerce, New York Also called *AT&T Corp (G-9296)*
Shhhmouse, Brooklyn Also called *Digiorange Inc (G-1862)*
Shield Press Inc 212 431-7489
9 Lispenard St Fl 1 New York (10013) *(G-12071)*
Shield Security Doors Ltd 202 468-3308
124 W 60th St New York (10023) *(G-12072)*
Shimada Shoji (hk) Limited 212 268-0465
501 5th Ave Rm 1105 New York (10017) *(G-12073)*
Shindo Usa Inc 212 868-9311
162 W 36th St New York (10018) *(G-12074)*
Shine Foods USA Inc 516 784-9674
7824 266th St Glen Oaks (11004) *(G-5655)*
Shining Creations Inc 845 358-4911
40 S Main St Ste 1 New City (10956) *(G-8838)*
Shinn Vineyard, Mattituck Also called *Shinn Winery LLC (G-8242)*
Shinn Winery LLC 631 804-0367
2000 Oregon Rd Mattituck (11952) *(G-8242)*
Shipman Print Solutions, Niagara Falls Also called *Shipman Printing Inds Inc (G-12893)*
Shipman Printing Inds Inc 716 504-7700
2424 Niagara Falls Blvd Niagara Falls (14304) *(G-12893)*
Shipman Printing Inds Inc 716 504-7700
6120 Lendell Dr Sanborn (14132) *(G-15155)*
Shipmtes/Printmates Holdg Corp (PA) 518 370-1158
705 Corporation Park # 2 Scotia (12302) *(G-15353)*
Shiprite Software Inc 315 733-6191
1312 Genesee St Utica (13502) *(G-16383)*
Shira Accessories Ltd 212 594-4455
30 W 36th St Rm 504 New York (10018) *(G-12075)*
Shirl-Lynn of New York (PA) 315 363-5898
266 Wilson St Oneida (13421) *(G-13189)*

Shiro Limited 212 780-0007
928 Broadway Ste 806 New York (10010) *(G-12076)*
Shirt Shack, Spring Valley Also called *Regal Screen Printing Intl (G-15621)*
Shiseido Americas Corporation (HQ) 212 805-2300
900 3rd Ave Fl 15 New York (10022) *(G-12077)*
Shiseido Cosmetics, New York Also called *Shiseido Americas Corporation (G-12077)*
Shop Smart Central Inc 914 962-3871
1520 Front St Yorktown Heights (10598) *(G-17535)*
Shopping Bag, The, East Rochester Also called *Greater Rchster Advertiser Inc (G-4479)*
Shopping Center Wine & Liquor 914 528-1600
3008 E Main St Mohegan Lake (10547) *(G-8579)*
Shore Line Momogramming & EMB, Mamaroneck Also called *Shore Line Monogramming Inc (G-8080)*
Shore Line Monogramming Inc 914 698-8000
115 Hoyt Ave Mamaroneck (10543) *(G-8080)*
Shore Products Co, Auburn Also called *T Shore Products Ltd (G-519)*
Shoreline Fruit LLC 585 765-2639
10190 Route 18 Lyndonville (14098) *(G-7996)*
Shoreline Publishing Inc 914 738-7869
629 Fifth Ave Ste B01 Pelham (10803) *(G-13519)*
Shoretel Inc 877 654-3573
300 State St Ste 100 Rochester (14614) *(G-14706)*
Short Jj Associates Inc (PA) 315 986-3511
1645 Wayneport Rd Macedon (14502) *(G-8021)*
Short Run Forms Inc 631 567-7171
171 Keyland Ct Bohemia (11716) *(G-1130)*
Showeray Co (PA) 718 965-3633
225 25th St Brooklyn (11232) *(G-2578)*
Shred Center 716 664-3052
20 Carroll St Jamestown (14701) *(G-7059)*
Shredder Essentials, Brooklyn Also called *Casa Innovations Inc (G-1765)*
Shrineeta Pharmacy 212 234-7959
1749 Amsterdam Ave Frnt New York (10031) *(G-12078)*
Shrineeta Pharmacy Inc 212 234-7959
1743 Amsterdam Ave New York (10031) *(G-12079)*
Shritec Consultants Inc 516 621-7072
91 Searingtown Rd Albertson (11507) *(G-163)*
Shugar Publishing 631 288-4404
99b Main St Westhampton Beach (11978) *(G-17089)*
Shugaray Division of Zaralo, New York Also called *Zaralo LLC (G-12724)*
Shyam Ahuja Limited 212 644-5910
201 E 56th St Frnt A New York (10022) *(G-12080)*
Shyk International Corp 212 663-3302
258 Riverside Dr Apt 7b New York (10025) *(G-12081)*
Shykat Promotions 866 574-2757
10561 Creek Rd Forestville (14062) *(G-5343)*
Si Funeral Services, Fairport Also called *Suhor Industries Inc (G-4890)*
Si Group Inc (PA) 518 347-4200
2750 Balltown Rd Schenectady (12309) *(G-15319)*
Si Group Inc 518 347-4200
1000 Main St Rotterdam Junction (12150) *(G-15059)*
Si Group Inc 518 347-4200
Rr 5 Box South Rotterdam Junction (12150) *(G-15060)*
Si Group Global Manufacturing, Rotterdam Junction Also called *Si Group Inc (G-15059)*
SI Partners Inc 516 433-1415
15 E Carl St Unit 1 Hicksville (11801) *(G-6421)*
Sick Inc 585 347-2000
855 Publishers Pkwy Webster (14580) *(G-16761)*
Sidco Filter Corporation 585 289-3100
58 North Ave Manchester (14504) *(G-8086)*
Sidco Food Distribution Corp 718 733-3939
2324 Webster Ave Bronx (10458) *(G-1451)*
Side Hill Farmers Coop Inc 315 447-4693
8275 State Route 13 Canastota (13032) *(G-3399)*
Side Hustle Music Group LLC 800 219-4003
600 3rd Ave Fl 2 New York (10016) *(G-12082)*
Sidney Favorite Printing Div, Sidney Also called *Tri-Town News Inc (G-15464)*
Siegel & Stockman Inc 212 633-1508
126 W 25th St Frnt 1 New York (10001) *(G-12083)*
Siegfrieds Call Inc 845 765-2275
20 Kent St 109 Beacon (12508) *(G-785)*
Siemens Corporation 202 434-7800
527 Madison Ave Fl 8 New York (10022) *(G-12084)*
Siemens Electro Industrial Sa 212 258-4000
527 Madison Ave Fl 8 New York (10022) *(G-12085)*
Siemens Government Tech Inc 585 593-1234
37 Coats St Wellsville (14895) *(G-16785)*
Siemens Hlthcare Dgnostics Inc 914 631-0475
511 Benedict Ave Tarrytown (10591) *(G-16130)*
Siemens Industry Inc 716 568-0983
85 Northpointe Pkwy Amherst (14228) *(G-261)*
Siemens Industry Inc 607 936-9512
23 W Market St Ste 3 Corning (14830) *(G-4002)*
Siemens Industry Inc 716 568-0983
85 Northpointe Pkwy Ste 8 Buffalo (14228) *(G-3214)*
Siemens Industry Inc 631 218-1000
50 Orville Dr Ste 2 Bohemia (11716) *(G-1131)*
Siemens Industry Inc 585 797-2300
50 Methodist Hill Dr # 1500 Rochester (14623) *(G-14707)*
Siemens Industry Inc 631 231-3600
155 Plant Ave Hauppauge (11788) *(G-6213)*

Siemens Product Life Mgmt Sftw......585 389-8699
345 Woodcliff Dr Fairport (14450) *(G-4886)*
Siemens USA Holdings Inc......212 258-4000
601 Lexington Ave Fl 56 New York (10022) *(G-12086)*
Sierra Processing LLC......518 433-0020
2 Moyer Ave Schenectady (12306) *(G-15320)*
Sierson Crane & Welding Inc......315 723-6914
4822 State Route 233 Westmoreland (13490) *(G-17095)*
Sifonya Inc......212 620-4512
303 Park Ave S Frnt 2 New York (10010) *(G-12087)*
Siga Technologies Inc (PA)......212 672-9100
27 E 62nd St Apt 5a New York (10065) *(G-12088)*
Sigma Intl Gen Med Apprtus LLC......585 798-3901
711 Park Ave Medina (14103) *(G-8315)*
Sigma Manufacturing Inds Inc......718 842-9180
1361 E Bay Ave Bronx (10474) *(G-1452)*
Sigma Worldwide LLC (PA)......646 217-0629
65 W 83rd St Apt 5 New York (10024) *(G-12089)*
Sigmacare, New York Also called Matrixcare Inc *(G-11204)*
Sigmamotor Inc......716 735-3115
3 N Main St Middleport (14105) *(G-8457)*
Sigmund Cohn Corp......914 664-5300
121 S Columbus Ave Mount Vernon (10553) *(G-8780)*
Sign & Signs......718 941-6200
785 Coney Island Ave Brooklyn (11218) *(G-2579)*
Sign A Rama Inc......631 952-3324
663 Old Willets Path C Hauppauge (11788) *(G-6214)*
Sign A Rama of Syracuse......315 446-9420
3060 Erie Blvd E Ste 1 Syracuse (13224) *(G-16064)*
Sign Center Inc......212 967-2113
15 W 39th St Fl 7 New York (10018) *(G-12090)*
Sign City of New York Inc......718 661-1118
13212 11th Ave College Point (11356) *(G-3833)*
Sign Company......212 967-2113
15 W 39th St Fl 7 New York (10018) *(G-12091)*
Sign Company, The, New York Also called Sign Center Inc *(G-12090)*
Sign Design, Port Chester Also called Lanza Corp *(G-13778)*
Sign Design Group New York Inc......718 392-0779
3326 Northern Blvd Long Island City (11101) *(G-7905)*
Sign Expo, New York Also called Signexpo Enterprises Inc *(G-12095)*
Sign Group Inc......718 438-7103
5215 New Utrecht Ave Brooklyn (11219) *(G-2580)*
Sign Guys LLC......315 253-4276
67 Franklin St Auburn (13021) *(G-515)*
Sign Here Enterprises LLC......914 328-3111
28 N Central Ave Rear Hartsdale (10530) *(G-6019)*
Sign Impressions Inc......585 723-0420
2590 W Ridge Rd Ste 6 Rochester (14626) *(G-14708)*
Sign Language Custom WD Signs, Perry Also called Sign Language Inc *(G-13549)*
Sign Language Inc......585 237-2620
6491 State Route 20a Perry (14530) *(G-13549)*
Sign Shop Inc......631 226-4145
1272 Montauk Hwy Copiague (11726) *(G-3951)*
Sign Studio Inc......518 266-0877
1 Ingalls Ave Troy (12180) *(G-16278)*
Sign Works Incorporated......914 592-0700
150 Clearbrook Rd Ste 118 Elmsford (10523) *(G-4792)*
Sign World Inc......212 619-9000
1194 Utica Ave Brooklyn (11203) *(G-2581)*
Sign-A-Rama, Hartsdale Also called Sign Here Enterprises LLC *(G-6019)*
Sign-A-Rama, Baldwin Also called Jal Signs Inc *(G-558)*
Sign-A-Rama, Mount Kisco Also called Westchester Signs Inc *(G-8688)*
Sign-A-Rama, Syracuse Also called Sign A Rama of Syracuse *(G-16064)*
Sign-A-Rama, Huntington Station Also called Z-Car-D Corp *(G-6768)*
Sign-A-Rama, Bellmore Also called Speedy Sign A Rama USA Inc *(G-818)*
Sign-A-Rama, Hicksville Also called Marigold Signs Inc *(G-6395)*
Sign-A-Rama, New Hyde Park Also called Three Gems Inc *(G-8911)*
Sign-A-Rama, Hauppauge Also called Sign A Rama Inc *(G-6214)*
Signa Chemistry Inc (PA)......212 933-4101
400 Madison Ave Fl 21 New York (10017) *(G-12092)*
Signal Graphics Printing, Wappingers Falls Also called Gem Reproduction Services Corp *(G-16590)*
Signal Transformer, Inwood Also called Bel Transformer Inc *(G-6792)*
Signature Diamond Entps LLC......212 869-5115
15 W 47th St Ste 203 New York (10036) *(G-12093)*
Signature Industries Inc......516 679-5177
32 Saint Johns Pl Freeport (11520) *(G-5439)*
Signature Metal MBL Maint LLC......718 292-8280
791 E 132nd St Bronx (10454) *(G-1453)*
Signature Name Plate Co Inc......585 321-9960
292 Commerce Dr Rochester (14623) *(G-14709)*
Signature Systems Group LLC......800 569-2751
38 E 29th St Fl 3l New York (10016) *(G-12094)*
Signatures, New York Also called Light House Hill Marketing *(G-11024)*
Signexpo Enterprises Inc (PA)......212 925-8585
127 W 26th St Rm 401 New York (10001) *(G-12095)*
Signpost Inc......877 334-2837
127 W 26th St Fl 2 New York (10001) *(G-12096)*
Signs & Decal Corp......718 486-6400
410 Morgan Ave Brooklyn (11211) *(G-2582)*

Signs By Sunrise, Jamaica Also called Tru-Art Sign Co Inc *(G-6995)*
Signs By Tomorrow, Commack Also called Rpf Associates Inc *(G-3867)*
Signs Inc......518 483-4759
2 Boyer Ave Malone (12953) *(G-8048)*
Signs Ink Ltd......914 739-9059
3255 Crompond Rd Yorktown Heights (10598) *(G-17536)*
Signs New York, Brooklyn Also called Brooklyn Signs LLC *(G-1732)*
Signs Now, Rochester Also called Image360 *(G-14466)*
Signs of Success Ltd......516 295-6000
247 Merrick Rd Ste 101 Lynbrook (11563) *(G-7987)*
Sigro Precision, West Babylon Also called BEAM Manufacturing Corp *(G-16800)*
Sihi Pumps Inc (HQ)......716 773-6450
303 Industrial Dr Grand Island (14072) *(G-5784)*
Sikorsky Aircraft Corporation......585 424-1990
300 Canal View Blvd Rochester (14623) *(G-14710)*
Silar Laboratories Division, Scotia Also called Oak-Bark Corporation *(G-15352)*
Silarx Pharmaceuticals Inc (HQ)......845 352-4020
1033 Stoneleigh Ave Carmel (10512) *(G-3433)*
Silgan Containers Mfg Corp......315 946-4826
8673 Lyons Marengo Rd Lyons (14489) *(G-8002)*
Silgan Plastics LLC......315 536-5690
40 Powell Ln Penn Yan (14527) *(G-13543)*
Silicon Carbide Products Inc......607 562-8599
361 Daniel Zenker Dr Horseheads (14845) *(G-6622)*
Silicon Imaging Inc......518 374-3367
25 Covington Ct Niskayuna (12309) *(G-12913)*
Silicon Pulsed Power LLC......610 407-4700
958 Main St Ste A Clifton Park (12065) *(G-3733)*
Silicone Products & Technology......716 684-1155
4471 Walden Ave Lancaster (14086) *(G-7368)*
Silipos Holding LLC......716 283-0700
7049 Williams Rd Niagara Falls (14304) *(G-12894)*
Silk Screen Art Inc......518 762-8423
1 School St Johnstown (12095) *(G-7155)*
Silly Phillie Creations Inc......718 492-6300
140 58th St Ste 6f Brooklyn (11220) *(G-2583)*
Silva Cabinetry Inc......914 737-7697
12 White St Ste C Buchanan (10511) *(G-2801)*
Silvatrim Corp......212 675-0933
324 W 22nd St New York (10011) *(G-12097)*
Silvatrim Corporation America, New York Also called Silvatrim Corp *(G-12097)*
Silver City Group Inc......315 363-0344
27577 W Seneca St Sherrill (13461) *(G-15431)*
Silver City Metals, Sherrill Also called Silver City Group Inc *(G-15431)*
Silver Creek Carpet, New York Also called Bloomsburg Carpet Inds Inc *(G-9468)*
Silver Griffin Inc......518 272-7771
691 Hoosick Rd Troy (12180) *(G-16279)*
Silver Oak Pharmacy Inc......718 922-3400
5105 Church Ave Brooklyn (11203) *(G-2584)*
Silverman & Gorf Inc......718 625-1309
60 Franklin Ave Brooklyn (11205) *(G-2585)*
Silverstone Shtmtl Fbrications......718 422-0380
66 Huntington St Brooklyn (11231) *(G-2586)*
Silvertique Fine Jewelry, New York Also called Goldarama Company Inc *(G-10370)*
Sima Technologies LLC......412 828-9130
125 Commerce Dr Hauppauge (11788) *(G-6215)*
Simcha Candle Co Inc......845 783-0406
244 Mac Arthur Ave New Windsor (12553) *(G-9001)*
Simco Leather Corporation......518 762-7100
99 Pleasant Ave Johnstown (12095) *(G-7156)*
Simco Manufacturing Jewelers......212 575-8390
62 W 47th St Ste 903 New York (10036) *(G-12098)*
Similarweb Inc......347 685-5422
50 W 17th St Fl 9 New York (10011) *(G-12099)*
Simka Diamond Corp......212 921-4420
580 5th Ave Ste 709 New York (10036) *(G-12100)*
Simmons Fabricating Svc Inc......845 635-3755
1558 Main St Pleasant Valley (12569) *(G-13743)*
Simmons Machine Tool Corp (PA)......518 462-5431
1700 Broadway Menands (12204) *(G-8410)*
Simmons-Boardman Pubg Corp (HQ)......212 620-7200
55 Broad St Fl 26 New York (10004) *(G-12101)*
Simon & Schuster Inc......212 698-7000
1230 Ave Of The Americas New York (10020) *(G-12102)*
Simon & Simon LLC......202 419-0490
1745 Broadway Fl 17 New York (10019) *(G-12103)*
Simon Defense Inc......516 217-6000
1533 Rocky Point Rd Middle Island (11953) *(G-8441)*
Simon Liu Inc......718 567-2011
5113 2nd Ave Brooklyn (11232) *(G-2587)*
Simon S Decorating Inc......718 339-2931
1670 E 19th St Brooklyn (11229) *(G-2588)*
Simon Schuster Digital Sls Inc......212 698-4391
51 W 52d St New York (10019) *(G-12104)*
Simple Elegance New York, Brooklyn Also called Sabbsons International Inc *(G-2551)*
Simple Elegance New York Inc......718 360-1947
474 50th St Brooklyn (11220) *(G-2589)*
Simplex Manufacturing Co Inc......315 252-7524
105 Dunning Ave Auburn (13021) *(G-516)*
Simplexgrinnell LP......585 288-6200
90 Goodway Dr Rochester (14623) *(G-14711)*

Simplexgrinnell LP 518 952-6040
1399 Vischer Ferry Rd Clifton Park (12065) *(G-3734)*
Simplexgrinnell LP 845 774-4120
4 Commerce Dr S Ste 3 Harriman (10926) *(G-5996)*
Simplexgrinnell LP 315 437-4660
6731 Collamer Rd Ste 4 East Syracuse (13057) *(G-4578)*
Simplexgrinnell LP 607 338-5100
6731 Collamer Rd Ste 4 East Syracuse (13057) *(G-4579)*
Simplicity Bandsaw Inc 716 557-8805
3674 Main St Hinsdale (14743) *(G-6450)*
Simplicity Creative Group Inc (HQ) 212 686-7676
261 Madison Ave Fl 4 New York (10016) *(G-12105)*
Simply Amazing Enterprises Inc 631 503-6452
68 S Service Rd Ste 1 Melville (11747) *(G-8383)*
Simply Gum Inc 917 721-8032
270 Lafayette St Ste 1301 New York (10012) *(G-12106)*
Simply Lite Foods, Commack *Also called Simply Natural Foods LLC (G-3869)*
Simply Natural Foods LLC 631 543-9600
74 Mall Dr Commack (11725) *(G-3869)*
Simpore Inc 585 748-5980
150 Lucius Gordon Dr # 121 West Henrietta (14586) *(G-16926)*
Simrex Corporation 716 206-0174
1223 William St Buffalo (14206) *(G-3215)*
Sims Group USA Holdings Corp 718 786-6031
3027 Greenpoint Ave Long Island City (11101) *(G-7906)*
Sims Metal Management, New York *Also called Smm - North America Trade Corp (G-12136)*
Sims Steel Corporation 631 587-8670
650 Muncy St Lindenhurst (11757) *(G-7505)*
Simtec Industries Corporation 631 293-0080
65 Marine St Ste A Farmingdale (11735) *(G-5119)*
Simulaids Inc 845 679-2475
16 Simulaids Dr Saugerties (12477) *(G-15223)*
Sin Yang Yang Company, Jackson Heights *Also called Jin Pin Market Inc (G-6922)*
Sinapi's Italian Ice, Hawthorne *Also called Four Brothers Italian Bakery (G-6269)*
Sincerus LLC 800 419-2804
2478 Mcdonald Ave Brooklyn (11223) *(G-2590)*
Sinclair International Company (PA) 518 798-2361
85 Boulevard Queensbury (12804) *(G-14025)*
Sinclair Technologies Inc (HQ) 716 874-3682
5811 S Park Ave 3 Hamburg (14075) *(G-5966)*
Sing Ah Poultry 718 625-7253
114 Sackett St Brooklyn (11231) *(G-2591)*
Sing Tao Daily, New York *Also called Sing Tao Newspapers NY Ltd (G-12107)*
Sing Tao Newspapers NY Ltd 212 431-9030
5317 8th Ave Brooklyn (11220) *(G-2592)*
Sing Tao Newspapers NY Ltd 718 821-0123
905 Flushing Ave Fl 2 Brooklyn (11206) *(G-2593)*
Sing Tao Newspapers NY Ltd (PA) 212 699-3800
188 Lafayette St New York (10013) *(G-12107)*
Sing Trix 212 352-1500
118 W 22nd St Fl 3 New York (10011) *(G-12108)*
Singlecut Beersmiths LLC 718 606-0788
1933 37th St Astoria (11105) *(G-455)*
Sinn- Tech Industries Inc 631 643-1171
48 Gleam St West Babylon (11704) *(G-16858)*
Sinn-Tech Industries Inc 631 643-1171
48 Gleam St West Babylon (11704) *(G-16859)*
Sinnara, Maspeth *Also called Purvi Enterprises Incorporated (G-8196)*
Sino Printing Inc 212 334-6896
30 Allen St Frnt A New York (10002) *(G-12109)*
Sir Industries Inc 631 234-2444
208 Blydenburg Rd Unit C Hauppauge (11749) *(G-6216)*
Sir Kensington's, New York *Also called Kensington & Sons LLC (G-10875)*
Sir Speedy, Bay Shore *Also called Bondy Printing Corp (G-677)*
Sir Speedy, Rochester *Also called Beastons Budget Printing (G-14244)*
Sir Speedy, Westbury *Also called E B B Graphics Inc (G-17006)*
Sir Speedy, Plainview *Also called Nash Printing Inc (G-13651)*
Sir Speedy, Wappingers Falls *Also called Moneast Inc (G-16595)*
Sir Speedy, Pleasantville *Also called Carlara Group Ltd (G-13744)*
Sir Speedy, Westbury *Also called Sentinel Printing Inc (G-17054)*
Sir Speedy, Lake Placid *Also called Lake Placid Advertisers Wkshp (G-7299)*
Sir Speedy, Plainview *Also called P D R Inc (G-13655)*
Sirianni Hardwoods Inc 607 962-4688
912 Addison Rd Painted Post (14870) *(G-13420)*
Sister Sister Inc (PA) 212 629-9600
463 7th Ave Fl 4 New York (10018) *(G-12110)*
Sita Finishing Inc 718 417-5295
207 Starr St Ste 1 Brooklyn (11237) *(G-2594)*
Sita Knitting, Brooklyn *Also called Sita Finishing Inc (G-2594)*
Sitecompli LLC 800 564-1152
53 W 23rd St Fl 12 New York (10010) *(G-12111)*
Sitecraft Inc 718 729-4900
4302 Ditmars Blvd Astoria (11105) *(G-456)*
Sitewatch Technology LLC 207 778-3246
22 Sunset Ave East Quogue (11942) *(G-4471)*
Sivko Furs Inc 607 698-4827
3089 County Route 119 Canisteo (14823) *(G-3405)*
Siw Inc 631 888-0130
271 Skip Ln Bay Shore (11706) *(G-738)*
Six Boro Publishing 347 589-6756
221 E 122nd St Apt 1703 New York (10035) *(G-12112)*
Sixnet LLC 518 877-5173
331 Ushers Rd Ste 14 Ballston Lake (12019) *(G-585)*
Sixnet Holdings LLC 518 877-5173
331 Ushers Rd Ste 10 Ballston Lake (12019) *(G-586)*
Sixpoint Brewery, Brooklyn *Also called Mad Scntsts Brwing Prtners LLC (G-2254)*
Sixteen Markets Inc 347 759-1024
110 Wall St Ste 1502 New York (10005) *(G-12113)*
Sizzal LLC 212 354-6123
1105 44th Rd Fl 2 Long Island City (11101) *(G-7907)*
Sj Associates Inc (PA) 516 942-3232
500 N Broadway Ste 159 Jericho (11753) *(G-7119)*
Sjm Interface, New York *Also called Sign Company (G-12091)*
Sk Energy Shots, New York *Also called Street King LLC (G-12235)*
Skae Power Solutions LLC (PA) 845 365-9103
348 Route 9w Palisades (10964) *(G-13427)*
Skd Distribution Corp 718 525-6000
28 Westchester Ave Jericho (11753) *(G-7120)*
Skd Tactical Inc 845 897-2889
291 Main St Highland Falls (10928) *(G-6437)*
Skechers Factory Outlet 315, Bronx *Also called Skechers USA Inc (G-1454)*
Skechers USA Inc 718 585-3024
651 River Ave Bronx (10451) *(G-1454)*
Skelton Screw Products Co, Westbury *Also called All Type Screw Machine Pdts (G-16992)*
Sketch Studio Trading Inc 212 244-2875
221 W 37th St Ste 600 New York (10018) *(G-12114)*
SKF Aeroengine North America, Falconer *Also called SKF USA Inc (G-4919)*
SKF Aeroengine North America, Falconer *Also called SKF USA Inc (G-4920)*
SKF USA Inc 716 661-2869
1 Maroco St Falconer (14733) *(G-4919)*
SKF USA Inc 716 661-2600
402 Chandler St Jamestown (14701) *(G-7060)*
SKF USA Inc 716 661-2600
1 Maroco St Falconer (14733) *(G-4920)*
Skil-Care Corporation 914 963-2040
29 Wells Ave Bldg 4 Yonkers (10701) *(G-17502)*
Skills Alliance Inc 646 492-5300
135 W 29th St Rm 201 New York (10001) *(G-12115)*
Skillsoft Corporation 585 240-7500
500 Canal View Blvd Rochester (14623) *(G-14712)*
Skimovex USA, Orchard Park *Also called Burgess-Manning Inc (G-13280)*
Skin Atelier Inc 845 294-1202
1997 Route 17m Goshen (10924) *(G-5753)*
Skin Nutrition Intl Inc 212 231-8355
410 Park Ave Fl 15 New York (10022) *(G-12116)*
Skin Prints Inc 845 920-8756
63 Walter St Pearl River (10965) *(G-13490)*
Skincare Products Inc 917 837-5255
118 E 57th St New York (10022) *(G-12117)*
Skinprint, Goshen *Also called Skin Atelier Inc (G-5753)*
Skinz Inc 516 593-3139
156 Union Ave Lynbrook (11563) *(G-7988)*
Skinz Mfg, Lynbrook *Also called Skinz Inc (G-7988)*
Skip Hop Inc 646 902-9874
50 W 23rd St Fl 10 New York (10010) *(G-12118)*
Skip Hop Holdings Inc (HQ) 212 868-9850
50 W 23rd St Fl 10 New York (10010) *(G-12119)*
Skooba Design, Rochester *Also called Three Point Ventures LLC (G-14751)*
Sky Aerospace Products, Westbury *Also called John Hassall LLC (G-17026)*
Sky Frame & Art Inc (PA) 212 925-7856
141 W 28th St Fl 12 New York (10001) *(G-12120)*
Sky Geek, Lagrangeville *Also called Styles Aviation Inc (G-7284)*
Sky Laundromat Inc 718 639-7070
8615 Ava Pl Apt 4e Jamaica (11432) *(G-6986)*
Skydyne Company 845 858-6400
100 River Rd Port Jervis (12771) *(G-13816)*
Skyguard, Hauppauge *Also called Vehicle Manufacturers Inc (G-6247)*
Skyhorse Publishing Inc 212 643-6816
307 W 36th St Fl 11 New York (10018) *(G-12121)*
Skylark Publications Ltd 607 535-9866
217 N Franklin St Watkins Glen (14891) *(G-16721)*
Skyler Brand Ventures LLC 646 979-5904
590 Madison Ave Fl 19 New York (10022) *(G-12122)*
Skyline Custom Cabinetry Inc 631 393-2983
200 Verdi St Unit A Farmingdale (11735) *(G-5120)*
Skyline LLC 631 403-4131
16 Hulse Rd Ste 1 East Setauket (11733) *(G-4511)*
Skyline New York, Hauppauge *Also called Watson Productions LLC (G-6255)*
Skystem LLC 877 778-3320
100 W 92nd St Apt 20d New York (10025) *(G-12123)*
Skytravel (usa) LLC 518 888-2610
20 Talon Dr Schenectady (12309) *(G-15321)*
SL Industries Inc (HQ) 212 520-2300
590 Madison Ave Fl 32 New York (10022) *(G-12124)*
Slant/Fin Corporation (PA) 516 484-2600
100 Forest Dr Greenvale (11548) *(G-5899)*
Slantco Manufacturing Inc (HQ) 516 484-2600
100 Forest Dr Greenvale (11548) *(G-5900)*

Slanto Manufacturing Inc ... 516 759-5721
40 Garvies Point Rd Glen Cove (11542) ***(G-5641)***
Slava Industries Incorporated (PA) ... 718 499-4850
555 16th St Brooklyn (11215) ***(G-2595)***
SLC, Auburn *Also called Auburn Custom Millwork Inc* ***(G-477)***
Sleep Improvement Center Inc ... 516 536-5799
178 Sunrise Hwy Fl 2 Rockville Centre (11570) ***(G-14827)***
Sleep Master, Syracuse *Also called Futon City Discounters Inc* ***(G-15965)***
Sleepable Sofas Ltd ... 973 546-4502
600 3rd Ave Fl 15 New York (10016) ***(G-12125)***
Sleeping Partners Home Fashion, Brooklyn *Also called Sleeping Partners Intl Inc* ***(G-2596)***
Sleeping Partners Intl Inc ... 212 254-1515
140 58th St Ste 11 Brooklyn (11220) ***(G-2596)***
Sleepwear Holdings Inc ... 516 466-4738
1372 Broadway Fl 18 New York (10018) ***(G-12126)***
Sleepy Head Inc ... 718 237-9655
230 3rd St Brooklyn (11215) ***(G-2597)***
Sleepy Hollow Chimney Sup Ltd ... 631 231-2333
85 Emjay Blvd Brentwood (11717) ***(G-1191)***
Slidebean Incorporated ... 866 365-0588
25 Broadway New York (10004) ***(G-12127)***
Slim Line Case Co Inc ... 585 546-3639
64 Spencer St Rochester (14608) ***(G-14713)***
Slims Bagels Unlimited Inc (PA) ... 718 229-1140
22118 Horace Harding Expy Oakland Gardens (11364) ***(G-13086)***
Sliperfection, New York *Also called Lady Ester Lingerie Corp* ***(G-10951)***
Sln Group Inc ... 718 677-5969
2172 E 26th St Brooklyn (11229) ***(G-2598)***
Sloane Design Inc ... 212 539-0184
226 52nd St Brooklyn (11220) ***(G-2599)***
Slosson Edctl Publications Inc ... 716 652-0930
538 Buffalo Rd East Aurora (14052) ***(G-4403)***
Slv Labs LLC ... 631 901-1170
320 Oser Ave Hauppauge (11788) ***(G-6217)***
Slyde Inc ... 917 331-2114
474 48th Ave Apt 18a Long Island City (11109) ***(G-7908)***
SM News Plus Incorporated ... 212 888-0153
346 E 59th St Frnt 1 New York (10022) ***(G-12128)***
Small Business Advisors Inc ... 516 374-1387
2005 Park St Atlantic Beach (11509) ***(G-469)***
Small Packages Inc ... 845 255-7710
119 Hasbrouck Rd New Paltz (12561) ***(G-8923)***
Smart & Strong LLC ... 212 938-2051
212 W 35th St Fl 8 New York (10001) ***(G-12129)***
Smart High Voltage Solutions ... 631 563-6724
390 Knickerbocker Ave # 6 Bohemia (11716) ***(G-1132)***
Smart Space Products LLC (PA) ... 877 777-2441
244 5th Ave Ste 2487 New York (10001) ***(G-12130)***
Smart Systems Inc ... 607 776-5380
320 E Washington St Bath (14810) ***(G-662)***
Smart USA Inc ... 718 416-4400
6907 69th Pl Glendale (11385) ***(G-5679)***
Smart Weigh, Spring Valley *Also called Measupro Inc* ***(G-15618)***
Smartoners Inc (PA) ... 718 975-0197
289 Keap St Ste A Brooklyn (11211) ***(G-2600)***
Smartpill Corporation ... 716 882-0701
847 Main St Buffalo (14203) ***(G-3216)***
Smartys Corner ... 607 239-5276
501 W Main St Endicott (13760) ***(G-4834)***
SMC, Conklin *Also called E-Systems Group LLC* ***(G-3893)***
Smg Control Systems, Buffalo *Also called Service Mfg Group Inc* ***(G-3213)***
SMI, Salamanca *Also called Snyder Manufacturing Inc* ***(G-15134)***
Smidgens Inc ... 585 624-1486
7336 Community Dr Lima (14485) ***(G-7470)***
Smile Specialists ... 877 337-6135
236 E 36th St New York (10016) ***(G-12131)***
Smith & Sons Fuels Inc ... 518 661-6112
36 2nd Ave Mayfield (12117) ***(G-8245)***
Smith & Watson ... 212 686-6444
200 Lexington Ave Rm 805 New York (10016) ***(G-12132)***
Smith Control Systems Inc ... 518 828-7646
1839 Route 9h Hudson (12534) ***(G-6666)***
Smith Graphics Inc ... 631 420-4180
40 Florida St Farmingdale (11735) ***(G-5121)***
Smith International Inc ... 585 265-2330
1915 Lake Rd Ontario (14519) ***(G-13237)***
Smith International Inc ... 212 350-9400
601 Lexington Ave Fl 57 New York (10022) ***(G-12133)***
Smith Metal Works Newark Inc ... 315 331-1651
1000 E Union St Newark (14513) ***(G-12763)***
Smith Sand & Gravel Inc ... 315 673-4124
4782 Shepard Rd Marcellus (13108) ***(G-8120)***
Smith Service Corps, Ontario *Also called Smith International Inc* ***(G-13237)***
Smith Street Bread Co LLC ... 718 797-9712
17 5th St Brooklyn (11231) ***(G-2601)***
Smith Tool & Die Inc ... 607 674-4165
714 Pleasant Valley Rd Sherburne (13460) ***(G-15418)***
Smith, E W Publishing, New Windsor *Also called Sentinel Printing Services Inc* ***(G-9000)***
Smithers Tools & Mch Pdts Inc ... 845 876-3063
3718 Route 9g Rhinebeck (12572) ***(G-14070)***
Smiths Gas Service Inc ... 518 438-0400
5 Walker Way Ste 1 Albany (12205) ***(G-134)***

Smithtown Concrete Products ... 631 265-1815
441 Middle Country Rd Saint James (11780) ***(G-15117)***
Smithtown News Inc ... 631 265-2100
1 Brooksite Dr Smithtown (11787) ***(G-15521)***
SMK Wines & Liquors LLC ... 212 685-7651
23 E 28th St New York (10016) ***(G-12134)***
Sml Acquisition LLC ... 914 592-3130
33 W Main St Ste 505 Elmsford (10523) ***(G-4793)***
Sml Brothers Holding Corp ... 718 402-2000
820 E 140th St Bronx (10454) ***(G-1455)***
Sml USA Inc (PA) ... 212 736-8800
5 Penn Plz Ste 1500 New York (10001) ***(G-12135)***
Smm - North America Trade Corp ... 212 604-0710
16 W 22nd St Fl 10 New York (10010) ***(G-12136)***
Smn Medical PC ... 844 362-2428
2 Allendale Dr Rye (10580) ***(G-15094)***
Smoke N Vape ... 212 390-1654
644 9th Ave Frnt 1 New York (10036) ***(G-12137)***
Smokey Joes, Oceanside *Also called Yale Trouser Corporation* ***(G-13128)***
Smooth Industries Incorporated ... 212 869-1080
1411 Broadway Rm 3000 New York (10018) ***(G-12138)***
Smooth Magazine ... 212 925-1150
55 John St Ste 800 New York (10038) ***(G-12139)***
Smoothbore International Inc ... 315 754-8124
13881 Westbury Cutoff Rd Red Creek (13143) ***(G-14039)***
SMS, Huntington Station *Also called Super Sweep Inc* ***(G-6761)***
Smsc, Hauppauge *Also called Standard Microsystems Corp* ***(G-6223)***
Snapp Too Enterprise ... 718 224-5252
3312 211th St Flushing (11361) ***(G-5299)***
Snapple Beverage Corp (del) (HQ) ... 914 612-4000
900 King St Rye Brook (10573) ***(G-15101)***
Snapple Distributors, Staten Island *Also called Gangi Distributors Inc* ***(G-15697)***
Snapple Distributors, Ronkonkoma *Also called American Bottling Company* ***(G-14894)***
Sneaker News Inc ... 347 687-1588
41 Elizabeth St Ste 301 New York (10013) ***(G-12140)***
Sneakers Software Inc ... 800 877-9221
519 8th Ave Rm 812 New York (10018) ***(G-12141)***
Sneaky Chef Foods LLC ... 914 301-3277
520 White Plains Rd Tarrytown (10591) ***(G-16131)***
Snow Craft Co Inc ... 516 739-1399
200 Fulton Ave New Hyde Park (11040) ***(G-8907)***
Snowman ... 212 239-8818
1181 Broadway Fl 6 New York (10001) ***(G-12142)***
Snr Cctv Systems Division, Port Jefferson *Also called Sartek Industries Inc* ***(G-13801)***
Sns Machinery, Brooklyn *Also called Riverside Machinery Company* ***(G-2518)***
Snyder Industries Inc (PA) ... 716 694-1240
340 Wales Ave Tonawanda (14150) ***(G-16222)***
Snyder Logging ... 315 265-1462
528 Allen Falls Rd Potsdam (13676) ***(G-13902)***
Snyder Manufacturing Inc ... 716 945-0354
255 Rochester St Unit 1 Salamanca (14779) ***(G-15134)***
Snyder Neon & Plastic Signs, Colonie *Also called Snyders Neon Displays Inc* ***(G-3847)***
Snyders Neon Displays Inc ... 518 857-4100
5 Highland Ave Colonie (12205) ***(G-3847)***
Sobi, Brooklyn *Also called Social Bicycles Inc* ***(G-2602)***
Soc America Inc ... 631 472-6666
3505 Veterans Memorial Hw Ronkonkoma (11779) ***(G-15010)***
Social Bicycles Inc ... 917 746-7624
55 Prospect St Ste 304 Brooklyn (11201) ***(G-2602)***
Social Register Association ... 646 612-7314
14 Wall St Ste 3f New York (10005) ***(G-12143)***
Social Science Electronic Pubg ... 585 442-8170
1239 University Ave Rochester (14607) ***(G-14714)***
Society Awards, Long Island City *Also called Dwm International Inc* ***(G-7750)***
Society For The Study ... 212 822-8806
20 W 20th St Fl 2 New York (10011) ***(G-12144)***
Socket Products Mfg Corp ... 631 232-9870
175 Bridge Rd Islandia (11749) ***(G-6841)***
Socks and More of NY Inc ... 718 769-1785
1605 Avenue Z Fl 1 Brooklyn (11235) ***(G-2603)***
Sofa Doctor Inc ... 718 292-6300
220 E 134th St Frnt 1b Bronx (10451) ***(G-1456)***
Sofanou, Niagara Falls *Also called Delfingen Us-New York Inc* ***(G-12832)***
Soft Sheen Products Inc (HQ) ... 212 818-1500
575 5th Ave New York (10017) ***(G-12145)***
Soft-Noze Usa Inc ... 315 732-2726
2216 Broad St Frankfort (13340) ***(G-5367)***
Soft-Tex International Inc ... 800 366-2324
428 Hudson River Rd Waterford (12188) ***(G-16642)***
Soft-Tex Manufacturing Co, Waterford *Also called Soft-Tex International Inc* ***(G-16642)***
Softlink International ... 914 574-8197
297 Knollwood Rd Ste 301 White Plains (10607) ***(G-17195)***
Softpack International Inc ... 631 544-7014
279 Kohr Rd Kings Park (11754) ***(G-7205)***
Software & General Services Co ... 315 986-4184
1365 Fairway 5 Cir Walworth (14568) ***(G-16573)***
Soggy Doggy Productions LLC ... 877 504-4811
50 Chestnut Ave Larchmont (10538) ***(G-7376)***
Sogimex, New York *Also called Myers Group LLC* ***(G-11356)***
Sohha Savory Yogurt, New York *Also called Mualema LLC* ***(G-11344)***

Soho and Tribeca Map, New York *Also called Ozmodyl Ltd* ***(G-11558)***
Soho Apparel Ltd 212 840-1109
525 Fashion Ave Fl 6 New York (10018) ***(G-12146)***
Soho Editions Inc 914 591-5100
2641 Deer St Mohegan Lake (10547) ***(G-8580)***
Soho Guilds, Kew Gardens *Also called A & B Color Corp (del)* ***(G-7186)***
Soho Letterpress Inc 718 788-2518
68 35th St Unit 6 Brooklyn (11232) ***(G-2604)***
Soho Press Inc 212 260-1900
853 Broadway Ste 1402 New York (10003) ***(G-12147)***
Soifer Center, The, White Plains *Also called Lydia H Soifer & Assoc Inc* ***(G-17161)***
Sokolin LLC (PA) 631 537-4434
445 Sills Rd Unit K Yaphank (11980) ***(G-17419)***
Sokolin Wine, Yaphank *Also called Sokolin LLC* ***(G-17419)***
SOL MARKOWITZ, Monroe *Also called C T A Digital Inc* ***(G-8586)***
Sola Home Expo Inc 718 646-3383
172 Neptune Ave Brooklyn (11235) ***(G-2605)***
Solabia USA Inc 212 847-2397
28 W 44th St New York (10036) ***(G-12148)***
Solar Energy Systems LLC (PA) 718 389-1545
1205 Manhattan Ave # 1210 Brooklyn (11222) ***(G-2606)***
Solar Metrology LLC 845 247-4701
1340 Lincoln Ave Ste 6 Holbrook (11741) ***(G-6500)***
Solar Screen Co Inc 718 592-8222
5311 105th St Corona (11368) ***(G-4030)***
Solar Thin Films Inc (PA) 516 341-7787
1136 Rxr Plz Uniondale (11556) ***(G-16322)***
Solarelectricway, Brooklyn *Also called Solarwaterway Inc* ***(G-2607)***
Solarpath Inc 201 490-4499
415 Madison Ave Fl 14 New York (10017) ***(G-12149)***
Solarpath Sun Solutions, New York *Also called Solarpath Inc* ***(G-12149)***
Solarwaterway Inc 888 998-5337
882 3rd Ave Ste 353 Brooklyn (11232) ***(G-2607)***
Solarz Bros Printing Corp 718 383-1330
231 Norman Ave Ste 105 Brooklyn (11222) ***(G-2608)***
Solata Foods LLC 845 245-4812
20 Governor Dr Newburgh (12550) ***(G-12803)***
Soldi, Brooklyn *Also called Mpr Magazine App Inc* ***(G-2343)***
Solenis LLC 315 461-4730
911 Old Liverpool Rd Liverpool (13088) ***(G-7575)***
Soleo Health, Hawthorne *Also called Biomed Pharmaceuticals Inc* ***(G-6267)***
Solepoxy Inc 716 372-6300
211 W Franklin St Olean (14760) ***(G-13175)***
Solex Catsmo Fine Foods, Wallkill *Also called Catsmo LLC* ***(G-16562)***
Solid Cell Inc (PA) 585 426-5000
771 Elmgrove Rd Rochester (14624) ***(G-14715)***
Solid Sealing Technology Inc 518 266-6019
44 Dalliba Ave Ste 240 Watervliet (12189) ***(G-16713)***
Solid Surface Acrylics Inc 716 743-1870
800 Walck Rd Ste 14 North Tonawanda (14120) ***(G-13012)***
Solid Surface Acrylics LLC 716 743-1870
800 Walck Rd Ste 14 North Tonawanda (14120) ***(G-13013)***
Solid Surfaces Inc 585 292-5340
1 Townline Cir Rochester (14623) ***(G-14716)***
Solid-Look Corporation 917 683-1780
4628 243rd St Douglaston (11362) ***(G-4335)***
Solidus Industries Inc 607 749-4540
6849 N Glen Haven Rd Homer (13077) ***(G-6550)***
Solitec Incorporated 315 298-4213
3981 Port St Pulaski (13142) ***(G-13969)***
Solivaira Specialties Inc 716 693-4009
4 Detroit St North Tonawanda (14120) ***(G-13014)***
Solmac Inc 716 630-7061
1975 Wehrle Dr Ste 130 Williamsville (14221) ***(G-17279)***
Solo, Brooklyn *Also called Air Skate & Air Jump Corp* ***(G-1571)***
Solo Licensing Corp 212 244-5505
358 5th Ave Rm 1205 New York (10001) ***(G-12150)***
Solstarny, New York *Also called Solstars Inc* ***(G-12151)***
Solstars Inc 212 605-0430
575 Madison Ave Ste 1006 New York (10022) ***(G-12151)***
Solstiss Inc 212 719-9194
561 Fashion Ave Fl 16 New York (10018) ***(G-12152)***
Soludos LLC 212 219-1101
520 Broadway Fl 5 New York (10012) ***(G-12153)***
Solutia Business Entps Inc 314 674-1000
111 8th Ave New York (10011) ***(G-12154)***
Solvaira Specialties Inc (PA) 716 693-4040
50 Bridge St North Tonawanda (14120) ***(G-13015)***
Solve Advisors Inc 646 699-5041
265 Sunrise Hwy Ste 22 Rockville Centre (11570) ***(G-14828)***
Solvents Company Inc 631 595-9300
9 Cornell St Kingston (12401) ***(G-7238)***
Somers Stain Glass Inc 631 586-7772
108 Brook Ave Ste A Deer Park (11729) ***(G-4235)***
Somerset Dyeing & Finishing 518 773-7383
68 Harrison St Gloversville (12078) ***(G-5736)***
Somerset Industries Inc (PA) 518 773-7383
68 Harrison St Gloversville (12078) ***(G-5737)***
Somerset Manufacturers Inc 516 626-3832
36 Glen Cove Rd Roslyn Heights (11577) ***(G-15057)***
Somerset Production Co LLC 716 932-6480
338 Harris Hill Rd # 102 Buffalo (14221) ***(G-3217)***
Somerville Acquisitions Co Inc 845 856-5261
15 Big Pond Rd Huguenot (12746) ***(G-6682)***
Somerville Tech Group Inc 908 782-9500
15 Big Pond Rd Huguenot (12746) ***(G-6683)***
Sommer, Amherst *Also called Sterling United Inc* ***(G-262)***
Sommer and Sons Printing Inc 716 822-4311
2222 S Park Ave Buffalo (14220) ***(G-3218)***
Somml Health LLC 518 880-2170
43 New Scotland Ave Mc25 Albany (12208) ***(G-135)***
Sonaal Industries Inc 718 383-3860
210 Kingsland Ave Brooklyn (11222) ***(G-2609)***
Sonaer Inc 631 756-4780
68 Lamar St Unit D West Babylon (11704) ***(G-16860)***
Sonicor Inc 631 920-6555
82 Otis St West Babylon (11704) ***(G-16861)***
Sonneman-A Way of Light 845 926-5469
151 Airport Dr Wappingers Falls (12590) ***(G-16596)***
Sono-Tek Corporation (PA) 845 795-2020
2012 Route 9w Stop 3 Milton (12547) ***(G-8518)***
Sonoco-Crellin Intl Inc (HQ) 518 392-2000
87 Center St Chatham (12037) ***(G-3588)***
Sonomed Inc 516 354-0900
1979 Marcus Ave Ste C105 New Hyde Park (11042) ***(G-8908)***
Sonomed Escalon, New Hyde Park *Also called Sonomed Inc* ***(G-8908)***
Sonotec US Inc 631 415-4758
190 Blydenburg Rd Islandia (11749) ***(G-6842)***
Sontek Industries Inc (PA) 781 749-3055
36 E 12th St Fl 6 New York (10003) ***(G-12155)***
Sonus-USA, Webster *Also called Hearing Spech Ctr of Rochester* ***(G-16749)***
Sony Broadband Entertainment (HQ) 212 833-6800
550 Madison Ave Fl 6 New York (10022) ***(G-12156)***
Sony Corporation of America (HQ) 212 833-8000
25 Madison Ave Fl 27 New York (10010) ***(G-12157)***
Sony Dadc US Inc 212 833-8800
550 Madison Ave New York (10022) ***(G-12158)***
Sony Music Entertainment, New York *Also called Sony Corporation of America* ***(G-12157)***
Sony Music Entertainment (HQ) 212 833-8500
25 Madison Ave Fl 19 New York (10010) ***(G-12159)***
Sony Music Entertainment Inc 212 833-8000
25 Madison Ave Fl 19 New York (10010) ***(G-12160)***
Sony Music Entertainment Inc 212 833-5057
79 5th Ave Fl 16 New York (10003) ***(G-12161)***
Sony Music Holdings, New York *Also called Sony Music Entertainment Inc* ***(G-12160)***
Sony Music Holdings Inc (HQ) 212 833-8000
25 Madison Ave Fl 26 New York (10010) ***(G-12162)***
Sony Style, New York *Also called Sony Dadc US Inc* ***(G-12158)***
Sony Wonder, New York *Also called Sony Music Entertainment* ***(G-12159)***
Sony/Atv Music Publishing LLC (HQ) 212 833-7730
25 Madison Ave Fl 24 New York (10010) ***(G-12163)***
Sopark Corp (PA) 716 822-0434
3300 S Park Ave Buffalo (14218) ***(G-3219)***
Soper Designs, New York *Also called Kurt Gaum Inc* ***(G-10934)***
Sorfin Yoshimura Ltd 516 802-4600
100 Crossways Park Dr W # 215 Woodbury (11797) ***(G-17320)***
Soroc Technology Corp 716 849-5913
1051 Clinton St Buffalo (14206) ***(G-3220)***
Sorrento Lactalis, Buffalo *Also called Lactalis American Group Inc* ***(G-3060)***
Sorrento Lactalis Inc 716 823-6262
2375 S Park Ave Buffalo (14220) ***(G-3221)***
SOS Chefs of New York Inc 212 505-5813
104 Avenue B Apt 1 New York (10009) ***(G-12164)***
SOS International LLC 212 742-2410
40 Fulton St Fl 26 New York (10038) ***(G-12165)***
SOS International LLC 212 742-2410
40 Fulton St Fl 26 New York (10038) ***(G-12166)***
Sosi, New York *Also called SOS International LLC* ***(G-12166)***
Sotek Inc 716 821-5961
3590 Jeffrey Blvd Blasdell (14219) ***(G-960)***
Soterix Medical Inc 888 990-8327
237 W 35th St Ste 1401 New York (10001) ***(G-12167)***
Soterix Medical Technologies, New York *Also called Soterix Medical Inc* ***(G-12167)***
Soul Full Cup, Corning *Also called Joseph H Navaie* ***(G-3995)***
Sound & Communication, Port Washington *Also called Testa Communications Inc* ***(G-13886)***
Sound Communications Inc 516 767-2500
25 Willowdale Ave Port Washington (11050) ***(G-13884)***
Sound Source Inc 585 271-5370
161 Norris Dr Rochester (14610) ***(G-14717)***
Sound Video Systems Wny LLC 716 684-8200
1720 Military Rd Buffalo (14217) ***(G-3222)***
Soundcoat Company Inc (HQ) 631 242-2200
1 Burt Dr Deer Park (11729) ***(G-4236)***
Source Envelope Inc 866 284-0707
104 Allen Blvd Ste I Farmingdale (11735) ***(G-5122)***
Source Media, New York *Also called Credit Union Journal Inc* ***(G-9811)***
Source Media LLC (HQ) 212 803-8200
1 State St Fl 27 New York (10004) ***(G-12168)***

Source One Promotional Product.....516 208-6996
2024 Brian Dr Merrick (11566) *(G-8428)*
Source Technologies.....718 708-0305
9728 3rd Ave Brooklyn (11209) *(G-2610)*
South Bridge Press Inc.....212 233-4047
122 W 26th St Fl 3 New York (10001) *(G-12169)*
South Brooklyn Book Company, New York *Also called Welcome Rain Publishers LLC* *(G-12634)*
South Central Boyz.....718 496-7270
2568 Bedford Ave Apt 1a Brooklyn (11226) *(G-2611)*
South of The Highway, Southampton *Also called Dans Paper Inc* *(G-15565)*
South Seneca Vinyl LLC.....315 585-6050
1585 Yale Farm Rd Romulus (14541) *(G-14871)*
South Shore Ice Co Inc.....516 379-2056
89 E Fulton Ave Roosevelt (11575) *(G-15032)*
South Shore Ready Mix Inc.....516 872-3049
116 E Hawthorne Ave Valley Stream (11580) *(G-16451)*
Southampton Town Newspapers (PA).....631 283-4100
135 Windmill Ln Southampton (11968) *(G-15576)*
Southampton Town Newspapers.....631 288-1100
12 Mitchell Rd Westhampton Beach (11978) *(G-17090)*
Southbay Fuel Injectors.....516 442-4707
566 Merrick Rd Ste 3 Rockville Centre (11570) *(G-14829)*
Southco Inc.....585 624-2545
250 East St Honeoye Falls (14472) *(G-6564)*
Southern Adirondack Honey Co., Greenwich *Also called Betterbee Inc* *(G-5905)*
Southern Adrndck Fbr Prdcrs CP.....518 692-2700
2532 State Route 40 Greenwich (12834) *(G-5913)*
Southern Graphic Systems LLC.....315 695-7079
67 County Route 59 Phoenix (13135) *(G-13571)*
Southern Standard Cartons, Great Neck *Also called Standard Group* *(G-5859)*
Southern Standard Cartoons, Great Neck *Also called Standard Group LLC* *(G-5860)*
Southern States Coop Inc.....315 438-4500
6701 Manlius Center Rd # 240 East Syracuse (13057) *(G-4580)*
Southern Tier Pennysaver, Jamestown *Also called Spartan Publishing Inc* *(G-7061)*
Southern Tier Plastics Inc.....607 723-2601
Kirkwood Industrial Park Binghamton (13902) *(G-945)*
Southside Precast Products, Buffalo *Also called P J R Industries Inc* *(G-3128)*
Soutine Inc.....212 496-1450
104 W 70th St Frnt 1 New York (10023) *(G-12170)*
Sovereign Brands LLC (PA).....212 343-8366
81 Greene St Apt 2 New York (10012) *(G-12171)*
Sovereign Servicing System LLC.....914 779-1400
1 Stone Pl Ste 200 Bronxville (10708) *(G-1503)*
Sp Scientific, Gardiner *Also called S P Industries Inc* *(G-5563)*
Spa Sciara, Mount Kisco *Also called Plastic & Reconstructive Svcs* *(G-8683)*
Space 150.....612 332-6458
20 Jay St Ste 928 Brooklyn (11201) *(G-2612)*
Space Age Plstic Fbrcators Inc.....718 324-4062
4519 White Plains Rd Bronx (10470) *(G-1457)*
Space Coast Semiconductor Inc.....631 414-7131
1111 Broadhollow Rd Fl 3 Farmingdale (11735) *(G-5123)*
Space Sign.....718 961-1112
1525 132nd St College Point (11356) *(G-3834)*
Space-Craft Worldwide Inc.....631 603-3000
91 Rodeo Dr Edgewood (11717) *(G-4625)*
Spaeth Design Inc.....718 606-9685
6006 37th Ave Woodside (11377) *(G-17369)*
Spancraft Ltd.....516 295-0055
920 Railroad Ave Woodmere (11598) *(G-17332)*
Spandage, Brooklyn *Also called Medi-Tech International Corp* *(G-2295)*
Spanish Artisan Wine Group LLC.....914 414-6982
370 Cushman Rd Patterson (12563) *(G-13468)*
Spanish Artisan Wine Group Ltd, Patterson *Also called Spanish Artisan Wine Group LLC* *(G-13468)*
Spanish Tele Dirctry Hola 912, Long Island City *Also called Hola Publishing Co* *(G-7790)*
Spanjer Corp.....347 448-8033
3856 11th St Long Island City (11101) *(G-7909)*
Spanjer Signs, Long Island City *Also called Spanjer Corp* *(G-7909)*
Spano's Bread, Utica *Also called Ohio Baking Company Inc* *(G-16378)*
Sparclean MBL Refinishing Inc.....718 445-2351
6915 64th Pl Ridgewood (11385) *(G-14137)*
Spark Creations Inc.....212 575-8385
10 W 46th St Fl 9 New York (10036) *(G-12172)*
Sparkle Light Manufacturing, Yonkers *Also called Lighting By Dom Yonkers Inc* *(G-17480)*
Sparkspread, New York *Also called Great North Road Media Inc* *(G-10399)*
Sparrow Mining Co (PA).....718 519-6600
3743 White Plains Rd Bronx (10467) *(G-1458)*
Spartacist Publishing Co.....212 732-7860
48 Warren St New York (10007) *(G-12173)*
Spartan Brands Inc (PA).....212 340-0320
451 Park Ave S Fl 5 New York (10016) *(G-12174)*
Spartan Brands Inc.....212 340-0320
451 Park Ave S Fl 5 New York (10016) *(G-12175)*
Spartan Instruments, North Babylon *Also called Pmb Precision Products Inc* *(G-12919)*
Spartan Precision Machining.....516 546-5171
56 Cabot St West Babylon (11704) *(G-16862)*
Spartan Publishing Inc.....716 664-7373
2 Harding Ave Jamestown (14701) *(G-7061)*
Spatula LLC.....917 582-8684
2165 Broadway New York (10024) *(G-12176)*
Spaulding & Rogers Mfg Inc.....518 768-2070
3252 New Scotland Rd Voorheesville (12186) *(G-16539)*
Spaulding Law Printing Inc.....315 422-4805
231 Walton St Ste 103 Syracuse (13202) *(G-16065)*
Spc Global LLC.....646 723-3238
1270 Broadway Rm 710 New York (10001) *(G-12177)*
Spc Marketing Company.....631 661-2727
191 Norma Ave West Islip (11795) *(G-16937)*
Speaqua Corp.....858 334-9042
46 W Jefryn Blvd Deer Park (11729) *(G-4237)*
Special Circle Inc.....516 595-9988
123 Shelter Rock Rd New Hyde Park (11040) *(G-8909)*
Special Metals Corporation.....315 798-2900
4317 Middle Settlement Rd New Hartford (13413) *(G-8856)*
Special Metals Corporation.....716 366-5663
100 Willowbrook Ave Dunkirk (14048) *(G-4375)*
Special Tees.....718 980-0987
250 Buel Ave Staten Island (10305) *(G-15758)*
Speciality Quality Packaging, Schenectady *Also called Sqp Inc* *(G-15322)*
Specialized Packg Group Inc (HQ).....315 638-4355
2900 Mclane Rd Baldwinsville (13027) *(G-574)*
Specialized Packg Radisson LLC.....315 638-4355
8800 Sixty Rd Baldwinsville (13027) *(G-575)*
Specialized Printed Forms Inc.....585 538-2381
352 Center St Caledonia (14423) *(G-3310)*
Specialty Bldg Solutions Inc.....631 393-6918
Eads St Ste 165a West Babylon (11704) *(G-16863)*
Specialty Fabricators.....631 256-6982
4120 Sunrise Hwy Oakdale (11769) *(G-13080)*
Specialty Ink Co Inc (PA).....631 586-3666
40 Harbour Dr Blue Point (11715) *(G-995)*
Specialty Microwave Corp.....631 737-2175
120 Raynor Ave Ronkonkoma (11779) *(G-15011)*
Specialty Minerals Inc.....518 585-7982
35 Highland St Ticonderoga (12883) *(G-16150)*
Specialty Minerals Inc (HQ).....212 878-1800
622 3rd Ave Fl 38 New York (10017) *(G-12178)*
Specialty Quality Packg LLC.....914 580-3200
602 Potential Pkwy Scotia (12302) *(G-15354)*
Specialty Services.....585 728-5650
2631e Naples St Wayland (14572) *(G-16735)*
Specialty Signs Co Inc.....212 243-8521
15 W 39th St Fl 7 New York (10018) *(G-12179)*
Specialty Silicone Pdts Inc.....518 885-8826
3 Mccrea Hill Rd Ballston Spa (12020) *(G-608)*
Specialty Steel Fabg Corp.....718 893-6326
544 Casanova St Bronx (10474) *(G-1459)*
Specialty Steel of America., Bronx *Also called Specialty Steel Fabg Corp* *(G-1459)*
Specialty Wldg & Fabg NY Inc (PA).....315 426-1807
1025 Hiawatha Blvd E Syracuse (13208) *(G-16066)*
Specilty Bus Mchs Holdings LLC.....212 587-9600
260 W 35th St Fl 11 New York (10001) *(G-12180)*
Spectacle Optical Inc.....646 706-1015
9801 67th Ave Apt 7f Rego Park (11374) *(G-14051)*
Spectaculars, Westhampton Beach *Also called Frame Works America Inc* *(G-17087)*
Spectra Vista Corporation.....845 471-7007
29 Firemens Way Stop 3 Poughkeepsie (12603) *(G-13950)*
Spectracom, Rochester *Also called Orolia Usa Inc* *(G-14574)*
Spectracom Corporation (HQ).....585 321-5800
1565 Jefferson Rd Ste 460 Rochester (14623) *(G-14718)*
Spectral Systems LLC (PA).....845 896-2200
35 Corporate Park Rd Hopewell Junction (12533) *(G-6585)*
Spectron Glass & Electronics.....631 582-5600
595 Old Willets Path A Hauppauge (11788) *(G-6218)*
Spectron Systems Technology (PA).....631 582-5600
595 Old Willets Path A Hauppauge (11788) *(G-6219)*
Spectronics Corporation.....516 333-4840
956 Brush Hollow Rd Westbury (11590) *(G-17055)*
Spectrum, Oceanside *Also called Kantek Inc* *(G-13105)*
Spectrum Apparel Inc.....212 239-2025
463 Fashion Ave Fl 12 New York (10018) *(G-12181)*
Spectrum Brands Inc.....631 232-1200
2100 Pacific St Hauppauge (11788) *(G-6220)*
Spectrum Cable Corporation.....585 235-7714
295 Mount Read Blvd Ste 2 Rochester (14611) *(G-14719)*
Spectrum Catalysts Inc.....631 560-3683
69 Windsor Pl Central Islip (11722) *(G-3537)*
Spectrum Crafts Inc.....631 244-5749
70 Orville Dr Ste 1 Bohemia (11716) *(G-1133)*
Spectrum Microwave Inc.....315 253-6241
23 N Division St Auburn (13021) *(G-517)*
Spectrum On Broadway.....718 932-5388
6106 34th Ave Woodside (11377) *(G-17370)*
Spectrum Prtg Lithography Inc.....212 255-3131
505 8th Ave Rm 1802 New York (10018) *(G-12182)*
Spectrum Signs Inc.....631 756-1010
6106 34th Ave Woodside (11377) *(G-17371)*
Spectrum Thin Films Inc.....631 901-1010
135 Marcus Blvd Hauppauge (11788) *(G-6221)*
Speedcard Inc.....631 472-1904
133 Glenmere Way Holbrook (11741) *(G-6501)*

ALPHABETIC

(PA)=Parent Co (HQ)=Headquarters (DH)=Div Headquarters
2018 Harris
New York Manufacturers Directory
1063

Speedpro Imaging, East Syracuse *Also called Bk Printing Inc* ***(G-4528)***
Speedway LLC...631 738-2536
2825 Middle Country Rd Lake Grove (11755) ***(G-7291)***
Speedway LLC...718 815-6897
951 Bay St Staten Island (10305) ***(G-15759)***
Speedway Press Inc...315 343-3531
1 Burkle St Oswego (13126) ***(G-13366)***
Speedways Conveyors Inc...716 893-2222
1210 E Ferry St Buffalo (14211) ***(G-3223)***
Speedy Enterprise of USA Corp...718 463-3000
4120 162nd St Flushing (11358) ***(G-5300)***
Speedy Sign A Rama USA Inc...516 783-1075
2956 Merrick Rd Bellmore (11710) ***(G-818)***
Speedzone Inc...631 750-1973
937 Montauk Hwy Oakdale (11769) ***(G-13081)***
Speedzone Raceway Hobbies, Oakdale *Also called Speedzone Inc* ***(G-13081)***
Spektrix Inc...646 741-5110
115 W 30th St Rm 501 New York (10001) ***(G-12183)***
Spellman High Vltage Elec Corp (PA)...631 630-3000
475 Wireless Blvd Hauppauge (11788) ***(G-6222)***
Spence Engineering Company Inc...845 778-5566
150 Coldenham Rd Walden (12586) ***(G-16556)***
Spencer AB Inc...646 831-3728
265 W 37th St Rm 2388 New York (10018) ***(G-12184)***
Spencer Jeremy, New York *Also called HMS Productions Inc* ***(G-10535)***
Sperry Advertising, South Glens Falls *Also called Northeast Stitches & Ink Inc* ***(G-15551)***
Spex, Rochester *Also called Precision Machine Tech LLC* ***(G-14617)***
Speyside Holdings LLC...845 928-2221
911 State Route 32 Highland Mills (10930) ***(G-6440)***
Spf Holdings II LLC (HQ)...212 750-8300
9 W 57th St Ste 4200 New York (10019) ***(G-12185)***
Spfm Corp (PA)...718 788-6800
162 2nd Ave Brooklyn (11215) ***(G-2613)***
Spforms, Caledonia *Also called Specialized Printed Forms Inc* ***(G-3310)***
Sph Group Holdings LLC (HQ)...212 520-2300
590 Madison Ave Fl 32 New York (10022) ***(G-12186)***
Spic and Span Company...914 524-6823
660 White Plains Rd # 250 Tarrytown (10591) ***(G-16132)***
Spider, Woodside *Also called Safeworks LLC* ***(G-17368)***
Spiegel Woodworks Inc...845 336-8090
418 Old Neighborhood Rd Kingston (12401) ***(G-7239)***
Spin Holdco Inc (HQ)...516 349-8555
303 Sunnyside Blvd # 70 Plainview (11803) ***(G-13662)***
Spin Magazine Media...212 231-7400
276 5th Ave Rm 800 New York (10001) ***(G-12187)***
Spin-Rite Corporation...585 266-5200
30 Dubelbeiss Ln Rochester (14622) ***(G-14720)***
Spinco Metal Products Inc...315 331-6285
1 Country Club Dr Newark (14513) ***(G-12764)***
Spinergy, Rochester *Also called BMA Media Services Inc* ***(G-14256)***
Spirent Inc (HQ)...631 208-0680
303 Griffing Ave Riverhead (11901) ***(G-14170)***
Spirit Music Group Inc (HQ)...212 533-7672
235 W 23rd St Fl 4 New York (10011) ***(G-12188)***
Splice Technologies Inc...631 924-8108
625 North St Manorville (11949) ***(G-8113)***
Split Rock Trading Co Inc...631 929-3261
22 Creek Rd Wading River (11792) ***(G-16546)***
Split Systems Corp (PA)...516 223-5511
1593 Grand Ave North Baldwin (11510) ***(G-12926)***
Spongebath LLC...917 475-1347
2334 28th St Apt 2r Astoria (11105) ***(G-457)***
Sport Athleisure Ltd...212 868-6505
16 W 36th St Rm 1205 New York (10018) ***(G-12189)***
Sports Illustrated For Kids...212 522-1212
1271 Ave Of The Americas New York (10020) ***(G-12190)***
Sports Pblications Prod NY LLC...212 366-7700
708 3rd Ave Fl 12 New York (10017) ***(G-12191)***
Sports Products America LLC...212 594-5511
34 W 33rd St Fl 2 New York (10001) ***(G-12192)***
Sports Reporter Inc...212 737-2750
527 3rd Ave Ste 327 New York (10016) ***(G-12193)***
Sportsfield Specialties Inc...607 746-8911
41155 State Highway 10 Delhi (13753) ***(G-4268)***
Sportsmaster Apparel, Troy *Also called Standard Manufacturing Co Inc* ***(G-16280)***
Sportswear Unlimited, Bedford Hills *Also called Custom Sportswear Corp* ***(G-797)***
Spotlight Newspaper, Delmar *Also called Community Media Group LLC* ***(G-4269)***
Spotlight Publications LLC...914 345-9473
100 Clearbrook Rd Ste 170 Elmsford (10523) ***(G-4794)***
Spray Market, The, Brooklyn *Also called Spfm Corp* ***(G-2613)***
Spray Nine Corporation...800 477-7299
309 W Montgomery St Johnstown (12095) ***(G-7157)***
Spray-Tech Finishing Inc...716 664-6317
443 Buffalo St Jamestown (14701) ***(G-7062)***
Spring Inc...646 732-0323
41 E 11th St Fl 11 New York (10003) ***(G-12194)***
Spring Publishing Corporation...718 782-0881
419 Manhattan Ave Brooklyn (11222) ***(G-2614)***
Spring Street Design Group, New York *Also called Vetta Jewelry Inc* ***(G-12556)***
Springer Adis Us LLC (HQ)...212 460-1500
233 Spring St Fl 6 New York (10013) ***(G-12195)***
Springer Business Media, New York *Also called Springer Scnce + Bus Media LLC* ***(G-12199)***
Springer Customer Svc Ctr LLC...212 460-1500
233 Spring St Fl 6 New York (10013) ***(G-12196)***
Springer Healthcare LLC...212 460-1500
233 Spring St Fl 6 New York (10013) ***(G-12197)***
Springer Publishing Co LLC...212 431-4370
11 W 42nd St Ste 15a New York (10036) ***(G-12198)***
Springer Scnce + Bus Media LLC (HQ)...781 871-6600
233 Spring St Fl 6 New York (10013) ***(G-12199)***
Springfield Control Systems...718 631-0870
4056 Douglaston Pkwy Douglaston (11363) ***(G-4336)***
Springfield Oil Services Inc (PA)...914 315-6812
550 Mmaroneck Ave Ste 503 Harrison (10528) ***(G-6009)***
Springfield Oil Services Inc...516 482-5995
40 Cuttermill Rd Ste 201 Great Neck (11021) ***(G-5857)***
Springville Mfg Co Inc...716 592-4957
8798 North St Springville (14141) ***(G-15636)***
SPS Medical Supply Corp (HQ)...585 359-0130
6789 W Henrietta Rd Rush (14543) ***(G-15077)***
SPS Medical Supply Corp...585 968-2377
31 Water St Ste 1 Cuba (14727) ***(G-4096)***
Spst Inc...607 798-6952
119b Rano Blvd Vestal (13850) ***(G-16477)***
Sputnick 84 LLC...844 667-7468
127 W 26th St Rm 400 New York (10001) ***(G-12200)***
SPX Corporation...585 436-5550
135 Mount Read Blvd Rochester (14611) ***(G-14721)***
SPX Flow Tech Systems Inc, Getzville *Also called SPX Flow Tech Systems Inc* ***(G-5616)***
SPX Flow Tech Systems Inc (HQ)...716 692-3000
105 Crosspoint Pkwy Getzville (14068) ***(G-5616)***
SPX Flow Technology, Rochester *Also called SPX Flow Us LLC* ***(G-14722)***
SPX Flow Us LLC...585 436-5550
135 Mount Read Blvd Rochester (14611) ***(G-14722)***
Sqp, Scotia *Also called Specialty Quality Packg LLC* ***(G-15354)***
Sqp Inc...518 831-6800
602 Potential Pkwy Schenectady (12302) ***(G-15322)***
Square One Publishers Inc...516 535-2010
115 Herricks Rd Garden City Park (11040) ***(G-5555)***
Square Stamping Mfg Corp...315 896-2641
108 Old Remsen Rd Barneveld (13304) ***(G-618)***
Squeaky Clean, Brooklyn *Also called National Prfmce Solutions Inc* ***(G-2358)***
Squond Inc...718 778-6630
185 Marcy Ave Ste 302 Brooklyn (11211) ***(G-2615)***
SRC Liquidation Company...716 631-3900
435 Lawrence Bell Dr # 4 Williamsville (14221) ***(G-17280)***
Srctec LLC...315 452-8700
5801 E Taft Rd Ste 6 Syracuse (13212) ***(G-16067)***
Sriracha2go, New York *Also called Kybod Group LLC* ***(G-10936)***
SRP, New York *Also called Structured Retail Products* ***(G-12239)***
SRP Apparel Group Inc...212 764-4810
525 7th Ave Rm 1808 New York (10018) ***(G-12201)***
SRS, Maspeth *Also called Stain Rail Systems Inc* ***(G-8201)***
Srtech Industry Corp...718 496-7001
5022 201st St Oakland Gardens (11364) ***(G-13087)***
SS&c Financial Services LLC (HQ)...914 670-3600
1 South Rd Harrison (10528) ***(G-6010)***
Ssa Trading Ltd...646 465-9500
226 W 37th St Fl 6 New York (10018) ***(G-12202)***
Ssac Inc...800 843-8848
8242 Loop Rd Baldwinsville (13027) ***(G-576)***
Ssf Production LLC...518 324-3407
194 Pleasant Ridge Rd Plattsburgh (12901) ***(G-13726)***
SSG Fashions Ltd...212 221-0933
27 E 37th St Frnt 1 New York (10016) ***(G-12203)***
Ssjjj Manufacturing LLC (PA)...516 498-3200
98 Cuttermill Rd Ste 412 Great Neck (11021) ***(G-5858)***
SSP, Syracuse *Also called Selflock Screw Products Co Inc* ***(G-16060)***
SSP, Ballston Spa *Also called Specialty Silicone Pdts Inc* ***(G-608)***
Ssrja LLC...718 725-7020
10729 180th St Jamaica (11433) ***(G-6987)***
St Gerard Enterprises Inc...631 473-2003
507 Bicycle Path Port Jeff STA (11776) ***(G-13793)***
St Gerard Printing, Port Jeff STA *Also called St Gerard Enterprises Inc* ***(G-13793)***
St James Printing Inc...631 981-2095
656 Rosevale Ave Ronkonkoma (11779) ***(G-15012)***
St John...718 720-8367
229 Morrison Ave Staten Island (10310) ***(G-15760)***
St John...718 771-4541
1700 Saint Johns Pl Brooklyn (11233) ***(G-2616)***
St Lawrence Cement Co, Catskill *Also called Ciment St-Laurent Inc* ***(G-3454)***
St Lawrence County Newspapers (HQ)...315 393-1003
230 Caroline St Ste 1 Ogdensburg (13669) ***(G-13143)***
St Lawrence Lumber Inc...315 649-2990
27140 County Route 57 Three Mile Bay (13693) ***(G-16145)***
St Raymond Monument Co...718 824-3600
2727 Lafayette Ave Bronx (10465) ***(G-1460)***
St Silicones Corporation...518 406-3208
821 Main St Clifton Park (12065) ***(G-3735)***
St Silicones Inc...518 664-0745
95 N Central Ave Mechanicville (12118) ***(G-8262)***

ALPHABETIC SECTION | **Stauber California Inc**

St Tropez Inc.......800 366-6383
530 Broadway Fl 10 New York (10012) ***(G-12204)***
St Vincent Press Inc.......585 325-5320
250 Cumberland St Ste 260 Rochester (14605) ***(G-14723)***
Stack Electronics, Deer Park *Also called Veja Electronics Inc* ***(G-4247)***
Stafford Labs Orthotics/Prosth.......845 692-5227
189 Monhagen Ave Middletown (10940) ***(G-8497)***
Stag Brothers Cast Stone Co.......718 629-0975
909 E 51st St Brooklyn (11203) ***(G-2617)***
Stain Rail Systems Inc.......732 548-6630
5920 56th Ave Maspeth (11378) ***(G-8201)***
Staining Plant, Newburgh *Also called Russin Lumber Corp* ***(G-12801)***
Stainless Design Concepts Ltd.......845 246-3631
1117 Kings Hwy Saugerties (12477) ***(G-15224)***
Stainless Metals Inc.......718 784-1454
6001 31st Ave Ste 1 Woodside (11377) ***(G-17372)***
Stairworld Inc.......718 441-9722
10114 Jamaica Ave Richmond Hill (11418) ***(G-14097)***
Stallion Inc (PA).......718 706-0111
3620 34th St Long Island City (11106) ***(G-7910)***
Stallion Technologies Inc.......315 622-1176
4324 Loveland Dr Liverpool (13090) ***(G-7576)***
Stamapro Inc.......888 623-5003
516 Mineola Ave Carle Place (11514) ***(G-3424)***
Stamp, Rhinebeck *Also called Smithers Tools & Mch Pdts Inc* ***(G-14070)***
Stamp Rite Tool & Die Inc.......718 752-0334
4311 35th St Long Island City (11101) ***(G-7911)***
Stampcrete Decorative Concrete, Liverpool *Also called Stampcrete International Ltd* ***(G-7577)***
Stampcrete International Ltd.......315 451-2837
325 Commerce Blvd Liverpool (13088) ***(G-7577)***
Stamped Fittings Inc.......607 733-9988
217 Lenox Ave Elmira Heights (14903) ***(G-4726)***
Stamper Technology Inc.......585 247-8370
232 Wallace Way Rochester (14624) ***(G-14724)***
Stand Up Mri of Lynbrook PC.......516 256-1558
229 Broadway Lynbrook (11563) ***(G-7989)***
Standard Analytics Io Inc.......917 882-5422
7 World Trade Ctr 46th New York (10007) ***(G-12205)***
Standard Group (PA).......718 335-5500
1010 Nthrn Blvd Ste 236 Great Neck (11021) ***(G-5859)***
Standard Group LLC (HQ).......718 507-6430
1010 Nthrn Blvd Ste 236 Great Neck (11021) ***(G-5860)***
Standard Industrial Works Inc.......631 888-0130
271 Skip Ln Bay Shore (11706) ***(G-739)***
Standard Manufacturing Co Inc (PA).......518 235-2200
750 2nd Ave Troy (12182) ***(G-16280)***
Standard Microsystems Corp (HQ).......631 435-6000
80 Arkay Dr Ste 100 Hauppauge (11788) ***(G-6223)***
Standard Motor Products Inc (PA).......718 392-0200
3718 Northern Blvd # 600 Long Island City (11101) ***(G-7912)***
Standard Paper Box Machine Co.......718 328-3300
347 Coster St Fl 2 Bronx (10474) ***(G-1461)***
Standard Portable, Mayville *Also called Lyn Jo Enterprises Ltd* ***(G-8248)***
Standard Products Division, Wassaic *Also called Pawling Corporation* ***(G-16622)***
Standard Screen Supply Corp (PA).......212 627-2727
121 Varick St Rm 200 New York (10013) ***(G-12206)***
Standard Steel Fabricators.......518 765-4820
Dutch Hill Rd Voorheesville (12186) ***(G-16540)***
Standard Wedding Band Co.......516 294-0954
951 Franklin Ave Garden City (11530) ***(G-5547)***
Standing Stone Vineyards.......607 582-6051
9934 State Route 414 Hector (14841) ***(G-6285)***
Standwill Packaging Inc.......631 752-1236
220 Sherwood Ave Farmingdale (11735) ***(G-5124)***
Stanfordville Mch & Mfg Co Inc (PA).......845 868-2266
29 Victory Ln Poughkeepsie (12603) ***(G-13951)***
Stanley Creations Inc.......718 361-6100
3100 47th Ave Ste 4105 Long Island City (11101) ***(G-7913)***
Stanley Home Products, Leicester *Also called Cpac Inc* ***(G-7442)***
Stanley Industrial Eqp LLC.......315 656-8733
8094 Saintsville Rd Kirkville (13082) ***(G-7255)***
Stanley M Indig.......718 692-0648
2173 E 38th St Brooklyn (11234) ***(G-2618)***
Stanley Paper Co Inc.......518 489-1131
1 Terminal St Albany (12206) ***(G-136)***
Stanley Pleating Stitching Co.......718 392-2417
2219 41st Ave Fl 3 Long Island City (11101) ***(G-7914)***
Stanmark Jewelry Inc.......212 730-2557
64 W 48th St Ste 1303 New York (10036) ***(G-12207)***
Stanson Automated LLC.......866 505-7826
145 Saw Mill River Rd # 2 Yonkers (10701) ***(G-17503)***
Staplex Company Inc.......718 768-3333
777 5th Ave Brooklyn (11232) ***(G-2619)***
Star Childrens Dress Co Inc (PA).......212 279-1524
1250 Broadway Fl 18 New York (10001) ***(G-12208)***
Star Communications, Hauppauge *Also called Star Quality Printing Inc* ***(G-6224)***
Star Community Pubg Group LLC, Melville *Also called Star Community Publishing* ***(G-8384)***
Star Community Publishing.......631 843-4050
235 Pinelawn Rd Melville (11747) ***(G-8384)***
Star Corrugated Box Co Inc.......718 386-3200
5515 Grand Ave Flushing (11378) ***(G-5301)***
Star Desk Pad Co Inc.......914 963-9400
60 Mclean Ave Yonkers (10705) ***(G-17504)***
Star Draperies Inc.......631 756-7121
24 Florida St Farmingdale (11735) ***(G-5125)***
Star Headlight Lantern Co Inc (PA).......585 226-9500
455 Rochester St Avon (14414) ***(G-540)***
Star Kay White Inc (PA).......845 268-2600
151 Wells Ave Congers (10920) ***(G-3885)***
Star Mold Co Inc.......631 694-2283
125 Florida St Farmingdale (11735) ***(G-5126)***
Star Mountain Coffee, Jamaica *Also called Star Mountain JFK Inc* ***(G-6988)***
Star Mountain JFK Inc.......718 553-6787
Federal Cir Bldg 141 Jamaica (11430) ***(G-6988)***
Star Poly Bag Inc (PA).......718 384-3130
200 Liberty Ave Brooklyn (11207) ***(G-2620)***
Star Press Pearl River Inc.......845 268-2294
614 Corporate Way Ste 8 Valley Cottage (10989) ***(G-16415)***
Star Quality Printing Inc.......631 273-1900
270 Oser Ave Hauppauge (11788) ***(G-6224)***
Star Ready Mix East Inc.......631 289-8787
225 Springs Fireplace Rd East Hampton (11937) ***(G-4436)***
Star Ready Mix Inc.......631 289-8787
172 Peconic Ave Medford (11763) ***(G-8294)***
Star Seal of New York, Gasport *Also called Cosmicoat of Wny Inc* ***(G-5571)***
Star Sports Corp.......516 773-4075
747 Middle Neck Rd # 103 Great Neck (11024) ***(G-5861)***
Star Tubing Corp.......716 483-1703
53 River St Jamestown (14701) ***(G-7063)***
Star Wire Mesh Fabricators.......212 831-4133
518 E 119th St New York (10035) ***(G-12209)***
Star-Gazette Fund Inc.......607 734-5151
310 E Church St Elmira (14901) ***(G-4715)***
Starboard Sun, Getzville *Also called Mission Critical Energy Inc* ***(G-5612)***
Starcraft Press Inc.......718 383-6700
4402 11th St Ste 311 Long Island City (11101) ***(G-7915)***
Starcyl USA Corp.......877 782-7295
348 State Route 11 Champlain (12919) ***(G-3573)***
Starfire Holding Corporation (PA).......914 614-7000
445 Hamilton Ave Ste 1210 White Plains (10601) ***(G-17196)***
Starfire Printing, Holbrook *Also called Image Typography Inc* ***(G-6479)***
Starfire Printing Inc.......631 736-1495
28 Washington Ave Holtsville (11742) ***(G-6535)***
Starfire Swords Ltd Inc.......607 589-7244
74 Railroad Ave Spencer (14883) ***(G-15588)***
Starfire Systems Inc.......518 899-9336
8 Sarnowski Dr Schenectady (12302) ***(G-15323)***
Starfuels Inc (HQ).......914 289-4800
50 Main St White Plains (10606) ***(G-17197)***
Stargate Computer Corp.......516 474-4799
24 Harmony Dr Port Jeff STA (11776) ***(G-13794)***
Stark Aquarium Products Co Inc.......718 445-5357
2914 122nd St Flushing (11354) ***(G-5302)***
Stark Fish, Flushing *Also called Stark Aquarium Products Co Inc* ***(G-5302)***
Stark Scalamandre Fabric LLC.......212 376-2900
942 3rd Ave New York (10022) ***(G-12210)***
Starkey & Henricks, New York *Also called Charles Henricks Inc* ***(G-9632)***
Starlight Paint Factory, Bronx *Also called Starlite Pnt & Varnish Co Inc* ***(G-1462)***
Starlight Properties, Bellport *Also called Pyrotechnique By Grucci Inc* ***(G-837)***
Starline Usa Inc.......716 773-0100
3036 Alt Blvd Grand Island (14072) ***(G-5785)***
Starliner Shipping & Travel.......718 385-1515
5305 Church Ave Ste 1 Brooklyn (11203) ***(G-2621)***
Starlite Media LLC (PA).......212 909-7700
118 E 28th St Rm 601 New York (10016) ***(G-12211)***
Starlite Pnt & Varnish Co Inc.......718 292-6420
724 E 140th St Bronx (10454) ***(G-1462)***
Staroba Plastics Inc.......716 537-3153
42 Edgewood Dr Holland (14080) ***(G-6511)***
Statebook LLC.......845 383-1991
185 Fair St Ste 2 Kingston (12401) ***(G-7240)***
Stated Island Stair Inc.......718 317-9276
439 Sharrotts Rd Staten Island (10309) ***(G-15761)***
Staten Island Advance, Staten Island *Also called Advance Publications Inc* ***(G-15653)***
Staten Island Parent Magazine.......718 761-4800
16 Shenandoah Ave Ste 2 Staten Island (10314) ***(G-15762)***
Staten Island Stair Inc.......718 317-9276
439 Sharrotts Rd Staten Island (10309) ***(G-15763)***
Statewide Fireproof Door Co.......845 268-6043
178 Charles Blvd Valley Cottage (10989) ***(G-16416)***
Station Hill of Barrytown.......845 758-5293
120 Station Hill Rd Barrytown (12507) ***(G-619)***
Stature Electric, Watertown *Also called Allied Motion Technologies Inc* ***(G-16656)***
Stature Electric Inc.......315 782-5910
22543 Fisher Rd Watertown (13601) ***(G-16695)***
Staub Machine Company Inc.......716 649-4211
206 Lake St Hamburg (14075) ***(G-5967)***
Staub Square, Hamburg *Also called Staub Machine Company Inc* ***(G-5967)***
Staub Usa Inc.......914 747-0300
270 Marble Ave Pleasantville (10570) ***(G-13751)***
Stauber California Inc.......845 651-4443
41 Bridge St Florida (10921) ***(G-5222)***

ALPHABETIC

(PA)=Parent Co (HQ)=Headquarters (DH)=Div Headquarters
2018 Harris
New York Manufacturers Directory
1065

Stavo Industries Inc (PA) 845 331-4552
132 Flatbush Ave Kingston (12401) ***(G-7241)***
Stavo Industries Inc 845 331-5389
132 Flatbush Ave Kingston (12401) ***(G-7242)***
Stealth Archtctral Windows Inc 718 821-6666
232 Varet St Brooklyn (11206) ***(G-2622)***
Stealth Inc 718 252-7900
1129 E 27th St Brooklyn (11210) ***(G-2623)***
Stealth Window, Brooklyn *Also called Stealth Archtctral Windows Inc* ***(G-2622)***
Steamline Machine, Fairport *Also called Streamline Precision Inc* ***(G-4889)***
Stebe Shcjhjff 839 383-9833
18 Lynbrook Rd Poughkeepsie (12603) ***(G-13952)***
Stedman Energy Inc 716 789-3018
4411 Canterbury Dr Mayville (14757) ***(G-8250)***
Steel & Obrien Mfg Inc 585 492-5800
274 Rte 98 S Arcade (14009) ***(G-399)***
Steel City Salt LLC 716 532-0000
13870 Taylor Hollow Rd Collins (14034) ***(G-3843)***
Steel Craft, Brooklyn *Also called Steelcraft Manufacturing Co* ***(G-2624)***
Steel Craft Rolling Door 631 608-8662
5 Di Tomas Ct Copiague (11726) ***(G-3952)***
Steel Excel Inc (HQ) 914 461-1300
1133 Westchester Ave N-222 White Plains (10604) ***(G-17198)***
Steel Partners Holdings LP (PA) 212 520-2300
590 Madison Ave Rm 3202 New York (10022) ***(G-12212)***
Steel Sales Inc 607 674-6363
8085 New York St Hwy 12 Sherburne (13460) ***(G-15419)***
Steel Tech SA LLC 845 786-3691
7 Hillside Dr Thiells (10984) ***(G-16137)***
Steel Work Inc 585 232-1555
340 Oak St Rochester (14608) ***(G-14725)***
Steel-Brite Ltd 631 589-4044
2 Dawn Dr Oakdale (11769) ***(G-13082)***
Steelcraft Manufacturing Co 718 277-2404
352 Pine St Brooklyn (11208) ***(G-2624)***
Steeldeck Ny Inc 718 599-3700
141 Banker St Brooklyn (11222) ***(G-2625)***
Steele Truss Company Inc 518 562-4663
118 Trade Rd Plattsburgh (12901) ***(G-13727)***
Steelflex Electro Corp 516 226-4466
145 S 13th St Lindenhurst (11757) ***(G-7506)***
Steelmasters Inc 718 498-2854
135 Liberty Ave Brooklyn (11212) ***(G-2626)***
Steelways Inc 845 562-0860
401 S Water St Newburgh (12553) ***(G-12804)***
Steelways Shipyard, Newburgh *Also called Steelways Inc* ***(G-12804)***
Steering Columns Galore Inc 845 278-5762
8 Vine Rd Mahopac (10541) ***(G-8032)***
Steezys LLC 646 276-5333
80 8th Ave 202 New York (10011) ***(G-12213)***
Stefan & Sons Welding, Chaffee *Also called Donald Stefan* ***(G-3561)***
Stefan Furs Inc 212 594-2788
150 W 30th St Fl 15 New York (10001) ***(G-12214)***
Stefan Sydor Optics Inc 585 271-7300
31 Jetview Dr Rochester (14624) ***(G-14726)***
Steffen Publishing Inc 315 865-4100
9584 Main St Holland Patent (13354) ***(G-6514)***
Steigercraft, Bellport *Also called AVS Laminates Inc* ***(G-821)***
Steilmann European Selections 914 997-0015
354 N Main St Port Chester (10573) ***(G-13783)***
Stein Fibers Ltd (PA) 518 489-5700
4 Computer Dr W Ste 200 Albany (12205) ***(G-137)***
Stein Industries Inc 631 789-2222
22 Sprague Ave Amityville (11701) ***(G-325)***
Steinbock-Braff Inc 718 972-6500
3611 14th Ave Brooklyn (11218) ***(G-2627)***
Steindl Cast Stone Co Inc 718 296-8530
9107 76th St Woodhaven (11421) ***(G-17326)***
Steiner Doors, Brooklyn *Also called A G M Deco Inc* ***(G-1533)***
Steiner Technologies Inc 585 425-5910
180 Perinton Pkwy Fairport (14450) ***(G-4887)***
Steinway Inc (HQ) 718 721-2600
1 Steinway Pl Long Island City (11105) ***(G-7916)***
Steinway and Sons (HQ) 718 721-2600
1 Steinway Pl Long Island City (11105) ***(G-7917)***
Steinway Awning II LLC (PA) 718 729-2965
4230 24th St Astoria (11101) ***(G-458)***
Steinway Awnings, Astoria *Also called Steinway Awning II LLC* ***(G-458)***
Steinway Hall, Long Island City *Also called Steinway Inc* ***(G-7916)***
Steinway Musical Instrs Inc (HQ) 781 894-9770
1133 Ave Of The Americas New York (10036) ***(G-12215)***
Steinway Pasta & Gelati Inc 718 246-5414
37 Grand Ave Ste 1 Brooklyn (11205) ***(G-2628)***
Stellar Alliance, New York *Also called Alen Sands York Associates Ltd* ***(G-9130)***
Stellar Printing Inc 718 361-1600
3838 9th St Long Island City (11101) ***(G-7918)***
Stemcultures LLC 518 621-0848
1 Discovery Dr Rensselaer (12144) ***(G-14062)***
Stemline Therapeutics Inc 646 502-2311
750 Lexington Ave Fl 11 New York (10022) ***(G-12216)***
Stensul Inc 212 380-8620
150 W 25th St Fl 3 New York (10001) ***(G-12217)***

Stephan & Company ACC Ltd (PA) 212 481-3888
10 E 38th St Fl 9 New York (10016) ***(G-12218)***
Stephen Bader Company Inc 518 753-4456
10 Charles St Valley Falls (12185) ***(G-16422)***
Stephen Dweck, New York *Also called Rumson Acquisition LLC* ***(G-11954)***
Stephen Dweck Industries, Brooklyn *Also called Dweck Industries Inc* ***(G-1885)***
Stephen Gould Corporation 212 497-8180
450 7th Ave Fl 32 New York (10123) ***(G-12219)***
Stephen J Lipkins Inc 631 249-8866
855 Conklin St Ste A Farmingdale (11735) ***(G-5127)***
Stephen M Kiernan 716 836-6300
701 Seneca St Ste 300 Buffalo (14210) ***(G-3224)***
Stephen Miller Gen Contrs Inc 518 661-5601
301 Riceville Rd Gloversville (12078) ***(G-5738)***
Stephen Singer Pattern Co Inc 212 947-2902
340 W 39th St Fl 4 New York (10018) ***(G-12220)***
Stephenson Custom Case Company 905 542-8762
1623 Military Rd Niagara Falls (14304) ***(G-12895)***
Stephenson Lumber Company Inc 518 548-7521
Rr 8 Speculator (12164) ***(G-15587)***
Stepping Stones One Day Signs 518 237-5774
105 Broad St Waterford (12188) ***(G-16643)***
Steps Plus Inc 315 432-0885
6375 Thompson Rd Syracuse (13206) ***(G-16068)***
Stereo Advantage Inc 716 656-7161
45 Boxwood Ln Cheektowaga (14227) ***(G-3617)***
Steri-Pharma LLC 315 473-7180
429 S West St Syracuse (13202) ***(G-16069)***
Sterilator Company, Cuba *Also called SPS Medical Supply Corp* ***(G-4096)***
Steriliz LLC 585 415-5411
150 Linden Oaks Rochester (14625) ***(G-14727)***
Steris Corporation 877 887-1788
40 Melville Park Rd Melville (11747) ***(G-8385)***
Sterling Industries Inc 631 753-3070
410 Eastern Pkwy Farmingdale (11735) ***(G-5128)***
Sterling Instruments Div, Hicksville *Also called Designatronics Incorporated* ***(G-6369)***
Sterling Molded Products Inc 845 344-4546
9-17 Oliver Ave Middletown (10940) ***(G-8498)***
Sterling North America Inc 631 243-6933
270 Oser Ave Hauppauge (11788) ***(G-6225)***
Sterling Pierce Company Inc 516 593-1170
395 Atlantic Ave East Rockaway (11518) ***(G-4492)***
Sterling Possessions Ltd 212 594-0418
251 W 39th St New York (10018) ***(G-12221)***
Sterling Sound Inc 212 604-9433
88 10th Ave Frnt 6 New York (10011) ***(G-12222)***
Sterling Toggle Inc 631 491-0500
99 Mahan St West Babylon (11704) ***(G-16864)***
Sterling United Inc 716 835-9290
6030 N Bailey Ave Ste 1 Amherst (14226) ***(G-262)***
Stern & Stern Industries Inc 607 324-4485
188 Thacher St Hornell (14843) ***(G-6594)***
Sterrx LLC (PA) 518 324-7879
141 Idaho Ave Plattsburgh (12903) ***(G-13728)***
Sterrx LLC 518 324-7879
141 Idaho Ave Ste 1 Plattsburgh (12903) ***(G-13729)***
Sterrx Cmo, Plattsburgh *Also called Sterrx LLC* ***(G-13729)***
Stetron International Inc (PA) 716 854-3443
90 Broadway St Ste 1 Buffalo (14203) ***(G-3225)***
Steuben Courier Advocate, Bath *Also called Gatehouse Media LLC* ***(G-656)***
Steuben Foods Incorporated (PA) 718 291-3333
15504 Liberty Ave Jamaica (11433) ***(G-6989)***
Steuben Foods Incorporated 716 655-4000
1150 Maple Rd Elma (14059) ***(G-4669)***
Steval Graphics Concepts Inc 516 576-0220
7 Fairchild Ct Ste 200 Plainview (11803) ***(G-13663)***
Steve & Andys Organics Inc 718 499-7933
630 Flushing Ave Brooklyn (11206) ***(G-2629)***
Steve Madden, Long Island City *Also called Steven Madden Ltd* ***(G-7919)***
Steve Poli Sales 315 487-0394
102 Farmington Dr Camillus (13031) ***(G-3352)***
Steven Coffey Pallet S Inc 585 261-6783
3376 Edgemere Dr Rochester (14612) ***(G-14728)***
Steven Galapo Diamonds LLC 212 221-3000
15 W 47th St Ste 1204 New York (10036) ***(G-12223)***
Steven John Opticians 718 543-3336
5901 Riverdale Ave Bronx (10471) ***(G-1463)***
Steven Kraus Associates Inc 631 923-2033
9 Private Rd Huntington (11743) ***(G-6721)***
Steven Madden Ltd 845 348-7026
1661 Palisades Center Dr West Nyack (10994) ***(G-16956)***
Steven Madden Ltd 212 736-3283
41 W 34th St New York (10001) ***(G-12224)***
Steven Madden Ltd (PA) 718 446-1800
5216 Barnett Ave Long Island City (11104) ***(G-7919)***
Steven Madden Ltd 212 695-5545
19 W 34th St Fl 4 New York (10001) ***(G-12225)***
Stevens Bandes Graphics Corp 212 675-1128
333 Hudson St Fl 3 New York (10013) ***(G-12226)***
Stevenson Printing Co Inc 516 676-1233
1 Brewster St Ste 2 Glen Cove (11542) ***(G-5642)***

Stever-Locke Industries Inc 585 624-3450
179 N Main St Honeoye Falls (14472) ***(G-6565)***
Steves Original Furs Inc 212 967-8007
345 7th Ave Fl 9 New York (10001) ***(G-12227)***
Stewart Tobori & Chang Div, New York *Also called Harry N Abrams Incorporated* ***(G-10464)***
Stewarts Processing Corp (PA)....518 581-1200
2907 State Route 9 Ballston Spa (12020) ***(G-609)***
Stf, Uniondale *Also called Solar Thin Films Inc* ***(G-16322)***
STf Services Inc....315 463-8506
26 Corporate Cir Ste 2 East Syracuse (13057) ***(G-4581)***
STI-Co Industries Inc....716 662-2680
11 Cobham Dr Ste A Orchard Park (14127) ***(G-13322)***
Stickershopcom Inc....631 563-4323
582 Middle Rd Bayport (11705) ***(G-755)***
Sticky Socks LLC 212 541-5927
200 W 60th St Apt 7g New York (10023) ***(G-12228)***
Stidd Systems Inc....631 477-2400
220 Carpenter St Greenport (11944) ***(G-5895)***
Stiegelbauer Associates Inc (PA)....718 624-0835
Bldg 280 Brooklyn (11205) ***(G-2630)***
Stillwater Wood & Iron 518 664-4501
114 N Hudson Ave Stillwater (12170) ***(G-15783)***
Stitch & Couture Inc (PA)....212 947-9204
224 W 30th St Fl 14 New York (10001) ***(G-12229)***
Stj Enterprises 516 612-0110
540 Willow Ave Cedarhurst (11516) ***(G-3488)***
Stj Orthotic Services Inc (PA)....631 956-0181
920 Wellwood Ave Ste B Lindenhurst (11757) ***(G-7507)***
Stk Electronics Inc 315 655-8476
2747 Rte 20 Cazenovia (13035) ***(G-3479)***
Stock Drive Products Div, Hicksville *Also called Designatronics Incorporated* ***(G-6367)***
Stoffel Polygon Systems Inc 914 961-2000
199 Marbledale Rd Tuckahoe (10707) ***(G-16296)***
Stone & Terrazzo World Inc....718 361-6899
5132 35th St Long Island City (11101) ***(G-7920)***
Stone and Bath Gallery....718 438-4500
856 39th St Brooklyn (11232) ***(G-2631)***
Stone Bridge Iron and Stl Inc 518 695-3752
426 Purinton Rd Gansevoort (12831) ***(G-5504)***
Stone Crafters International, Brooklyn *Also called PR & Stone & Tile Inc* ***(G-2448)***
Stone Crest Industries Inc....607 652-2665
152 Starheim Rd Stamford (12167) ***(G-15646)***
Stone Expo & Cabinetry LLC....516 292-2988
7 Terminal Rd West Hempstead (11552) ***(G-16895)***
Stone Glo Products, Bronx *Also called TWI-Laq Industries Inc* ***(G-1481)***
Stone House Associates Inc....212 221-7447
37 W 47th St Ste 910 New York (10036) ***(G-12230)***
Stone Well Bodies & Mch Inc 315 497-3512
625 Sill Rd Genoa (13071) ***(G-5602)***
Stonegate Stabless 518 746-7133
106 Reynolds Rd Fort Edward (12828) ***(G-5355)***
Stones Homemade Candies Inc....315 343-8401
145 W Bridge St Oswego (13126) ***(G-13367)***
Stonesong Press LLC 212 929-4600
270 W 39th St Rm 201 New York (10018) ***(G-12231)***
Stoney Croft Converters Inc....718 608-9800
364 Sharrotts Rd Staten Island (10309) ***(G-15764)***
Stony Apparel Corp....212 391-0022
1407 Broadway Rm 3300 New York (10018) ***(G-12232)***
Stony Brook Mfg Co Inc (PA)....631 369-9530
652 Scott Ave Calverton (11933) ***(G-3326)***
Stony Brook University....631 632-6434
310 Administration Bldg Stony Brook (11794) ***(G-15793)***
Stony Manufacturing Inc....716 652-6730
591 Pound Rd Elma (14059) ***(G-4670)***
Stony Point Graphics Ltd 845 786-3322
1 S Liberty Dr Stony Point (10980) ***(G-15799)***
Stop Entertainment Inc 212 242-7867
408 Rye Hill Rd Monroe (10950) ***(G-8599)***
Stop N Shop LLC....518 512-9657
911 Central Ave Ste 149 Albany (12206) ***(G-138)***
Storage Sheds, Westmoreland *Also called Shafer & Sons* ***(G-17094)***
Storflex Fixture, Corning *Also called Storflex Holdings Inc* ***(G-4003)***
Storflex Holdings Inc....607 962-2137
392 Pulteney St Corning (14830) ***(G-4003)***
Stork H & E Turbo Blading Inc 607 277-4968
334 Comfort Rd Ithaca (14850) ***(G-6911)***
Stromberg Brand, Valley Cottage *Also called Stromberg Brand Corporation* ***(G-16417)***
Storybooks Forever....716 822-7845
4 Magnolia Ave Buffalo (14220) ***(G-3226)***
Strada Soft Inc 718 556-6940
20 Clifton Ave Staten Island (10305) ***(G-15765)***
Strahl & Pitsch Inc....631 669-0175
230 Great East Neck Rd West Babylon (11704) ***(G-16865)***
Straight Arrow Publishing Co....212 484-1616
1290 Ave Of The Amer Fl 2 New York (10104) ***(G-12233)***
Strassburg Medical LLC 716 433-9368
525 Wheatfield St North Tonawanda (14120) ***(G-13016)***
Stratconglobal Inc 212 989-2355
685 3rd Ave Fl 4 New York (10017) ***(G-12234)***
Strategic Mktg Promotions Inc (PA) 845 623-7777
1 Blue Hill Plz Ste 1561 Pearl River (10965) ***(G-13491)***
Strategic Pharma Services Inc 631 231-5424
58 Bradley St Brentwood (11717) ***(G-1192)***
Strategic Signage Sourcing LLC....518 450-1093
2 Gilbert Rd Saratoga Springs (12866) ***(G-15204)***
Strategies North America Inc 716 945-6053
150 Elm St Salamanca (14779) ***(G-15135)***
Stratford Oriented, Macedon *Also called Exxonmobil Chemical Company* ***(G-8016)***
Strathmore Directories Ltd 516 997-2525
26 Bond St Westbury (11590) ***(G-17056)***
Strathmore Products, Inc., Syracuse *Also called Fayette Street Coatings Inc* ***(G-15962)***
Strathmore Publications, Westbury *Also called Strathmore Directories Ltd* ***(G-17056)***
Strativa Pharmaceuticals....201 802-4000
1 Ram Ridge Rd Spring Valley (10977) ***(G-15623)***
Strato Transit Components LLC 518 686-4541
155 State Route 67 Eagle Bridge (12057) ***(G-4383)***
Straus Communications 845 782-4000
20 West Ave Ste 201 Chester (10918) ***(G-3643)***
Straus Newspaper, Chester *Also called Straus Communications* ***(G-3643)***
Straus Newspapers Inc 845 782-4000
20 West Ave Chester (10918) ***(G-3644)***
Strauss Eye Prosthetics Inc 585 424-1350
360 White Spruce Blvd Rochester (14623) ***(G-14729)***
Strawtown Jewelry, New City *Also called Shining Creations Inc* ***(G-8838)***
Stream Police, New York *Also called Instant Stream Inc* ***(G-10654)***
Streamline Plastics Co Inc....718 401-4000
2590 Park Ave Bronx (10451) ***(G-1464)***
Streamline Precision Inc 585 421-9050
205 Turk Hill Park Fairport (14450) ***(G-4888)***
Streamline Precision Inc....585 421-9050
1000 Turk Hill Rd Ste 205 Fairport (14450) ***(G-4889)***
Streck's Machinery, Watervliet *Also called Strecks Inc* ***(G-16714)***
Strecks Inc 518 273-4410
800 1st St Watervliet (12189) ***(G-16714)***
Street Beat Sportswear Inc (PA)....718 302-1500
462 Kent Ave Fl 2 Brooklyn (11249) ***(G-2632)***
Street King LLC 212 400-2200
575 Madison Ave Fl 24 New York (10022) ***(G-12235)***
Street Smart Designs Inc....646 865-0056
29 W 35th St Fl 6 New York (10001) ***(G-12236)***
Streit Matzoh Co, Orangeburg *Also called Aron Streit Inc* ***(G-13241)***
Striano Electric Co Inc 516 408-4969
246 Park Ave Garden City Park (11040) ***(G-5556)***
Striata Inc 212 918-4677
48 Wall St Ste 1100 New York (10005) ***(G-12237)***
Strictly Business, Plattsburgh *Also called Northeast Group* ***(G-13709)***
Strider Global LLC 212 726-1302
261 W 28th St Apt 6a New York (10001) ***(G-12238)***
Strippit Inc (HQ)....716 542-5500
12975 Clarence Center Rd Akron (14001) ***(G-26)***
Strocchia Iron Works, Albertson *Also called Patsy Strocchia & Sons Iron Wo* ***(G-159)***
Stroehmann Bakeries 33, Maspeth *Also called Bimbo Bakeries Usa Inc* ***(G-8151)***
Stroehmann Bakeries 56, Olean *Also called Bimbo Bakeries Usa Inc* ***(G-13156)***
Stroehmann Bakeries 72, Goshen *Also called Bimbo Bakeries Usa Inc* ***(G-5746)***
Stroehmann Bakeries 90, Vestal *Also called Bimbo Bakeries Usa Inc* ***(G-16463)***
Stromberg Brand Corporation 914 739-7410
12 Ford Products Rd Valley Cottage (10989) ***(G-16417)***
Strong Forge & Fabrication 585 343-5251
20 Liberty St Batavia (14020) ***(G-648)***
Strong Group Inc....516 766-6300
222 Atlantic Ave Unit B Oceanside (11572) ***(G-13119)***
Strong Hospital, Rochester *Also called Orthotics & Prosthetics Dept* ***(G-14579)***
Strong Tempering GL Indust LLC 718 765-0007
530 63rd St Ste B Brooklyn (11220) ***(G-2633)***
Strong Ventures, New York *Also called Mrs John L Strong & Co LLC* ***(G-11340)***
Structural Ceramics Division, Niagara Falls *Also called Saint-Gbain Advnced Crmics LLC* ***(G-12889)***
Structural Ceramics Group, Niagara Falls *Also called Saint-Gobain Dynamics Inc* ***(G-12890)***
Structural Industries Inc 631 471-5200
2950 Veterans Memorial Hw Bohemia (11716) ***(G-1134)***
Structural Wood Corporation....315 388-4442
243 Lincoln Ave Waddington (13694) ***(G-16542)***
Structured 3d Inc....346 704-2614
188 Dixon Ave Amityville (11701) ***(G-326)***
Structured Retail Products....212 224-3692
225 Park Ave S Fl 8 New York (10003) ***(G-12239)***
Structuredweb Inc 201 325-3110
20 W 20th St Ste 402 New York (10011) ***(G-12240)***
Struthers Electronics, Bay Shore *Also called Lexan Industries Inc* ***(G-711)***
Strux Corp....516 768-3969
100 Montauk Hwy Lindenhurst (11757) ***(G-7508)***
STS Refill America LLC....516 934-8008
399 W John St Unit A Hicksville (11801) ***(G-6422)***
STS Steel Inc....518 370-2693
301 Nott St Ste 2 Schenectady (12305) ***(G-15324)***
Stu-Art Supplies, North Baldwin *Also called Hubray Inc* ***(G-12924)***
Stuart Communications Inc....845 252-7414
93 Erie Ave Narrowsburg (12764) ***(G-8815)***
Stuart Mold & Manufacturing 716 488-9765
560 N Work St Falconer (14733) ***(G-4921)***

ALPHABETIC

Stuart Spector Designs Ltd **ALPHABETIC SECTION**

Stuart Spector Designs Ltd 845 246-6124
1450 Route 212 Saugerties (12477) ***(G-15225)***
Stuart Tool & Die Inc 716 488-1975
600 N Work St Falconer (14733) ***(G-4922)***
Stuart-Dean Co Inc 718 472-1326
4350 10th St Long Island City (11101) ***(G-7921)***
Stubbs Printing Inc 315 769-8641
271 E Orvis St Ste B Massena (13662) ***(G-8232)***
Stucki Embroidery Works Inc (PA) 845 657-2308
Rr 28 Box W Boiceville (12412) ***(G-1155)***
Studco Building Systems US LLC 585 545-3000
1700 Boulter Indus Park Webster (14580) ***(G-16762)***
Student Lifeline Inc 516 327-0800
922 Hempstead Tpke Franklin Square (11010) ***(G-5377)***
Student Safety Books, Franklin Square *Also called Student Lifeline Inc* ***(G-5377)***
Studio 21 LA Inc 718 965-6579
13 42nd St Fl 5 Brooklyn (11232) ***(G-2634)***
Studio 26, New York *Also called RR Donnelley & Sons Company* ***(G-11948)***
Studio 40 Inc 212 420-8631
810 Humboldt St Ste 4 Brooklyn (11222) ***(G-2635)***
Studio Associates of New York 212 268-1163
242 W 30th St Rm 604 New York (10001) ***(G-12241)***
Studio Dellarte 718 599-3715
74 Bayard St Brooklyn (11222) ***(G-2636)***
Studio Fun International Inc 914 238-1000
44 S Broadway Fl 7 White Plains (10601) ***(G-17199)***
Studio Krp LLC 310 589-5777
210 11th Ave Rm 500 New York (10001) ***(G-12242)***
Studio One Leather Design Inc 212 760-1701
270 W 39th St Rm 505 New York (10018) ***(G-12243)***
Studio Silversmiths Inc 718 418-6785
6315 Traffic Ave Ridgewood (11385) ***(G-14138)***
Studley Printing & Publishing 518 563-1414
4701 State Route 9 Plattsburgh (12901) ***(G-13730)***
Stuff Magazine 212 302-2626
1040 Ave Of The Amrcas New York (10018) ***(G-12244)***
Stuhrling Original LLC 718 840-5760
449 20th St Brooklyn (11215) ***(G-2637)***
Sturdy Store Displays Inc 718 389-9919
110 Beard St Brooklyn (11231) ***(G-2638)***
Sturges Elec Pdts Co Inc 607 844-8604
23 North St Dryden (13053) ***(G-4348)***
Sturges Manufacturing Co Inc 315 732-6159
2030 Sunset Ave Utica (13502) ***(G-16384)***
Stutzman Management Corp 800 735-2013
11 Saint Joseph St Lancaster (14086) ***(G-7369)***
Style Partners Inc 212 904-1499
318 W 39th St Fl 7 New York (10018) ***(G-12245)***
Style Plus Hosiery Mills, Valley Stream *Also called Ellis Products Corp* ***(G-16431)***
Stylebuilt Accessories Inc (PA) 917 439-0578
45 Rose Ln East Rockaway (11518) ***(G-4493)***
Stylebuilt Acesries, East Rockaway *Also called Stylebuilt Accessories Inc* ***(G-4493)***
Styleclick Inc (HQ) 212 329-0300
810 7th Ave Fl 18 New York (10019) ***(G-12246)***
Stylecraft Interiors Inc 516 487-2133
22 Watermill Ln Great Neck (11021) ***(G-5862)***
Stylemaster, Richmond Hill *Also called Belle Maison USA Ltd* ***(G-14081)***
Styles Aviation Inc (PA) 845 677-8185
30 Airway Dr Ste 2 Lagrangeville (12540) ***(G-7284)***
Styles Manufacturing Corp 516 763-5303
3571 Hargale Rd Oceanside (11572) ***(G-13120)***
Stylesprit, New York *Also called Entrainant Inc* ***(G-10098)***
Stylist Pleating Corp 718 384-8181
109 S 5th St Brooklyn (11249) ***(G-2639)***
Stylistic Press Inc 212 675-0797
99 Battery Pl Apt 11p New York (10280) ***(G-12247)***
Suburban Marketing Assoc, Elmsford *Also called Ralph Martinelli* ***(G-4783)***
Suburban News, Spencerport *Also called Westside News Inc* ***(G-15598)***
Suburban Publishing Inc (PA) 845 463-0542
1 Summit Ct Ste 200a Fishkill (12524) ***(G-5196)***
Success Apparel LLC 212 502-1890
19 W 34th St Fl 7 New York (10001) ***(G-12248)***
Successware Inc 716 565-2338
8860 Main St 102 Williamsville (14221) ***(G-17281)***
Sue & Sam Co Inc (PA) 718 436-1672
720 39th St 720 Brooklyn (11232) ***(G-2640)***
Suffolk Cement Precast Inc (PA) 631 727-4432
1813 Middle Rd Calverton (11933) ***(G-3327)***
Suffolk Cement Products Inc 631 727-2317
1843 Middle Rd Calverton (11933) ***(G-3328)***
Suffolk Community Council Inc (PA) 631 434-9277
819 Grand Blvd Ste 1 Deer Park (11729) ***(G-4238)***
Suffolk Copy Center Inc 631 665-0570
26 W Main St Bay Shore (11706) ***(G-740)***
Suffolk Granite Manufacturing 631 226-4774
25 Gear Ave Lindenhurst (11757) ***(G-7509)***
Suffolk Indus Recovery Corp 631 732-6403
3542 Route 112 Coram (11727) ***(G-3974)***
Suffolk McHy & Pwr Tl Corp (PA) 631 289-7153
12 Waverly Ave Patchogue (11772) ***(G-13460)***
Suffolk Monument Mfg, Lindenhurst *Also called Suffolk Granite Manufacturing* ***(G-7509)***
Suffolk Printing, Bay Shore *Also called Suffolk Copy Center Inc* ***(G-740)***
Sugar Foods Corporation (PA) 212 753-6900
950 3rd Ave Fl 21 New York (10022) ***(G-12249)***
Sugar Shack Desert Company Inc 518 523-7540
2567 Main St Lake Placid (12946) ***(G-7300)***
Sugarbear Cupcakes 917 698-9005
14552 159th St Jamaica (11434) ***(G-6990)***
Suhor Industries Inc (PA) 585 377-5100
72 Oconnor Rd Fairport (14450) ***(G-4890)***
Suhor Industries Inc 716 483-6818
584 Buffalo St Jamestown (14701) ***(G-7064)***
Suit-Kote Corporation (PA) 607 753-1100
1911 Lorings Crossing Rd Cortland (13045) ***(G-4069)***
Suit-Kote Corporation 315 735-8501
191 Dry Rd Oriskany (13424) ***(G-13338)***
Suit-Kote Corporation 585 473-6321
2 Rockwood St Frnt Rochester (14610) ***(G-14730)***
Suit-Kote Corporation 607 535-2743
20 Fairgrounds Ln Watkins Glen (14891) ***(G-16722)***
Suit-Kote Corporation 585 268-7127
5628 Tuckers Corners Rd Belmont (14813) ***(G-841)***
Suit-Kote Corporation 716 664-3750
57 Lister St Jamestown (14701) ***(G-7065)***
Suit-Kote Corporation 716 683-8850
505 Como Park Blvd Buffalo (14227) ***(G-3227)***
Suite Solutions Inc 716 929-3050
100 Corporate Pkwy # 338 Amherst (14226) ***(G-263)***
Sukkah Center, Brooklyn *Also called Y & A Trading Inc* ***(G-2785)***
Sullivan Bazinet Bongio Inc 315 437-6500
1 General Motors Dr Ste 5 Syracuse (13206) ***(G-16070)***
Sullivan Concrete Inc 845 888-2235
420 Bernas Rd Cochecton (12726) ***(G-3769)***
Sullivan County Democrat, Callicoon *Also called Catskill Delaware Publications* ***(G-3312)***
Sullivan St Bky - Hlls Kit Inc 212 265-5580
533 W 47th St New York (10036) ***(G-12250)***
Sullivan Structures, Cochecton *Also called Sullivan Concrete Inc* ***(G-3769)***
Sulphur Creations Inc 212 719-2223
71 W 47th St Ste 402 New York (10036) ***(G-12251)***
Sum Sum LLC 516 812-3959
3595 Lawson Blvd Whse D Warehouse D Oceanside (11572) ***(G-13121)***
Suma Industries Inc 646 436-5202
345 E 52nd St Apt 9d New York (10022) ***(G-12252)***
Sumax Cycle Products Inc 315 768-1058
122 Clear Rd Oriskany (13424) ***(G-13339)***
Sumer Gold Ltd 212 354-8677
33 W 46th St Fl 4 New York (10036) ***(G-12253)***
Sumitomo Elc USA Holdings Inc (HQ) 212 490-6610
600 5th Ave Fl 18 New York (10020) ***(G-12254)***
Sumitomo Rubber Usa LLC (HQ) 716 879-8200
10 Sheridan Dr Tonawanda (14150) ***(G-16223)***
Summit Aerospace Inc 718 433-1326
4301 21st St Ste 203 Long Island City (11101) ***(G-7922)***
Summit Apparel Inc (PA) 631 213-8299
91 Cabot Ct Hauppauge (11788) ***(G-6226)***
Summit Appliances, Bronx *Also called Felix Storch Inc* ***(G-1332)***
Summit Communications 914 273-5504
28 Half Mile Rd Armonk (10504) ***(G-417)***
Summit Fincl Disclosure LLC 212 913-0510
216 E 45th St Fl 15 New York (10017) ***(G-12255)***
Summit Instrument Corp 516 433-0140
99 Engineers Dr Hicksville (11801) ***(G-6423)***
Summit Laser Products, Holbrook *Also called Summit Technologies LLC* ***(G-6502)***
Summit Lubricants Inc 585 815-0798
4d Treadeasy Ave Batavia (14020) ***(G-649)***
Summit Manufacturing LLC (HQ) 631 952-1570
100 Spence St Bay Shore (11706) ***(G-741)***
Summit MSP LLC 716 433-1014
6042 Old Beattie Rd Lockport (14094) ***(G-7646)***
Summit Plastics, Bay Shore *Also called Summit Manufacturing LLC* ***(G-741)***
Summit Print & Mail LLC 716 433-1014
6042 Old Beattie Rd Lockport (14094) ***(G-7647)***
Summit Professional Networks 212 557-7480
469 Fashion Ave Fl 10 New York (10018) ***(G-12256)***
Summit Research Laboratories, Huguenot *Also called Somerville Acquisitions Co Inc* ***(G-6682)***
Summit Research Labs Inc (PA) 845 856-5261
15 Big Pond Rd Huguenot (12746) ***(G-6684)***
Summit Technologies LLC 631 590-1040
723 Broadway Ave Holbrook (11741) ***(G-6502)***
Summitreheis, Huguenot *Also called Summit Research Labs Inc* ***(G-6684)***
Sumner Industries Inc 631 666-7290
309 Orinoco Dr Bay Shore (11706) ***(G-742)***
Sun Microsystems, Albany *Also called Oracle America Inc* ***(G-112)***
Sun Ming Jan Inc 718 418-8221
145 Noll St Brooklyn (11206) ***(G-2641)***
Sun Printing Incorporated 607 337-3034
57 Borden Ave 65 Norwich (13815) ***(G-13055)***
Sun Scientific Inc 914 479-5108
145 Palisade St Dobbs Ferry (10522) ***(G-4327)***
Sun Source, New York *Also called Jacobs & Cohen Inc* ***(G-10732)***
Sun Valley Printing, Binghamton *Also called Jane Lewis* ***(G-925)***

Sun-Times Media Group Inc 716 945-1644
36 River St Salamanca (14779) ***(G-15136)***
Suna Bros Inc 212 869-5670
10 W 46th St Fl 5 New York (10036) ***(G-12257)***
Sunbelt Industries Inc (PA) 315 823-2947
540 E Mill St Little Falls (13365) ***(G-7526)***
Sunbilt Solar Pdts By Sussman 718 297-0228
10910 180th St Jamaica (11433) ***(G-6991)***
Sunburst Studios Inc 718 768-6360
584 3rd Ave Brooklyn (11215) ***(G-2642)***
Sunbuster, Farmingdale *Also called Gustbuster Ltd* ***(G-5010)***
Sundance Industries Inc 845 795-5809
36 Greentree Ln Milton (12547) ***(G-8519)***
Sunday Record, The, Saratoga Springs *Also called Record* ***(G-15199)***
Sundial Brands LLC 631 842-8800
11 Ranick Dr S Amityville (11701) ***(G-327)***
Sundial Creations, Amityville *Also called Sundial Group LLC* ***(G-329)***
Sundial Editions, Ronkonkoma *Also called Profits Direct Inc* ***(G-14996)***
Sundial Fragrances & Flavors 631 842-8800
11 Ranick Dr S Amityville (11701) ***(G-328)***
Sundial Group LLC 631 842-8800
11 Ranick Dr S Amityville (11701) ***(G-329)***
Sundown Ski & Sport Shop Inc (PA) 631 737-8600
3060 Middle Country Rd Lake Grove (11755) ***(G-7292)***
Sunfeather Herbal Soap, Potsdam *Also called Sunfeather Natural Soap Co Inc* ***(G-13903)***
Sunfeather Natural Soap Co Inc 315 265-1776
1551 State Highway 72 Potsdam (13676) ***(G-13903)***
Sunham Home Fashions LLC (PA) 212 695-1218
136 Madison Ave Fl 16 New York (10016) ***(G-12258)***
Sunlight US Co., Inc., Buffalo *Also called Rough Brothers Holding Co* ***(G-3196)***
Sunny Names, New York *Also called Sunynams Fashions Ltd* ***(G-12262)***
Sunny Scuba Inc (PA) 212 333-4915
454 9th Ave New York (10018) ***(G-12259)***
Sunny Sports, New York *Also called Sunny Scuba Inc* ***(G-12259)***
Sunnycrest Inc (PA) 315 252-7214
58 Prospect St Auburn (13021) ***(G-518)***
Sunnyside Decorative Prints Co 516 671-1935
67 Robinson Ave Glen Cove (11542) ***(G-5643)***
Sunquest Pharmaceuticals Inc 855 478-6779
385 W John St Ste 1 Hicksville (11801) ***(G-6424)***
Sunrise Baking Co LLC 718 499-0800
4564 2nd Ave Brooklyn (11232) ***(G-2643)***
Sunrise Door Solutions 631 464-4139
1215 Sunrise Hwy Copiague (11726) ***(G-3953)***
Sunrise Installation, Copiague *Also called Sunrise Door Solutions* ***(G-3953)***
Sunrise Jewelers of NY Inc 516 541-1302
1220 Sunrise Hwy Massapequa (11758) ***(G-8216)***
Sunrise Tile Inc 718 939-0538
13309 35th Ave Flushing (11354) ***(G-5303)***
Sunset Ridge Holdings Inc 716 487-1458
490-496 Crescent St Jamestown (14701) ***(G-7066)***
Sunshine Diamond Cutter Inc 212 221-1028
38 W 48th St Ste 905 New York (10036) ***(G-12260)***
Sunward Electronics Inc 518 687-0030
258 Broadway Ste 2a Troy (12180) ***(G-16281)***
Sunwin Global Industry Inc 646 370-6196
295 5th Ave Ste 515 New York (10016) ***(G-12261)***
Sunwire Electric Corp 718 456-7500
70 Wyckoff Ave Apt 4h Brooklyn (11237) ***(G-2644)***
Suny At Binghamton 607 777-2316
Vestal Pkwy E Binghamton (13901) ***(G-946)***
Sunynams Fashions Ltd 212 268-5200
270 W 38th St Fl 2 New York (10018) ***(G-12262)***
Supdates, New York *Also called Bull Street LLC* ***(G-9529)***
Super Company Inc 315 569-5153
235 Harrison St Mail Drop Syracuse (13202) ***(G-16071)***
Super Conductor Materials Inc 845 368-0240
391 Spook Rock Rd Suffern (10901) ***(G-15821)***
Super Express USA Pubg Corp 212 227-5800
8410 101st St Apt 4l Richmond Hill (11418) ***(G-14098)***
Super Moderna/Magic Master, New Hyde Park *Also called Joseph Struhl Co Inc* ***(G-8889)***
Super Neon Light Co Inc 718 236-5667
7813 16th Ave Brooklyn (11214) ***(G-2645)***
Super Price Chopper Inc 716 893-3323
1580 Genesee St Buffalo (14211) ***(G-3228)***
Super Software 845 735-0000
151 S Main St Ste 303 New City (10956) ***(G-8839)***
Super Steelworks Corporation 718 386-4770
12 Lucon Dr Deer Park (11729) ***(G-4239)***
Super Stud Building Products, Long Island City *Also called Superior Metals & Processing* ***(G-7923)***
Super Sweep Inc (PA) 631 223-8205
20 Railroad St Unit 1 Huntington Station (11746) ***(G-6761)***
Super Web Inc 631 643-9100
97 Lamar St West Babylon (11704) ***(G-16866)***
Super-Tek Products Inc 718 278-7900
2544 Borough Pl Woodside (11377) ***(G-17373)***
Super-Trim Inc 212 255-2370
30 W 24th St Fl 4 New York (10010) ***(G-12263)***
Superboats Inc 631 226-1761
694 Roosevelt Ave Lindenhurst (11757) ***(G-7510)***
Superchat LLC 212 352-8581
310 E 70th St Apt 6lm New York (10021) ***(G-12264)***
Superflex Ltd 718 768-1400
152 44th St Brooklyn (11232) ***(G-2646)***
Supergen Products LLC 315 573-7887
320 Hoffman St Newark (14513) ***(G-12765)***
Superior Aggregates Supply LLC 516 333-2923
612 Muncy St Lindenhurst (11757) ***(G-7511)***
Superior Bat Company, Jamestown *Also called Grace Wheeler* ***(G-7029)***
Superior Block Corp 718 421-0900
4106 Glenwood Rd Brooklyn (11210) ***(G-2647)***
Superior Confections Inc 718 698-3300
1150 South Ave Staten Island (10314) ***(G-15766)***
Superior Decorators Inc 718 381-4793
7416 Cypress Hills St Glendale (11385) ***(G-5680)***
Superior Elec Enclosure Inc 718 797-9090
16 Spencer St Brooklyn (11205) ***(G-2648)***
Superior Energy Services Inc 716 483-0100
1720 Foote Avenue Ext Jamestown (14701) ***(G-7067)***
Superior Exteriors of Buffalo 716 873-1000
57 Insbrook Ct East Amherst (14051) ***(G-4388)***
Superior Fiber Mills Inc 718 782-7500
181 Lombardy St Brooklyn (11222) ***(G-2649)***
Superior Furs Inc 516 365-4123
1697 Northern Blvd Manhasset (11030) ***(G-8099)***
Superior Metal & Woodwork Inc 631 465-9004
70 Central Ave Farmingdale (11735) ***(G-5129)***
Superior Metals & Processing 718 545-7500
801 26th Ave Long Island City (11102) ***(G-7923)***
Superior Model Form Co, Middle Village *Also called Goldmont Enterprises Inc* ***(G-8444)***
Superior Motion Controls Inc 516 420-2921
40 Smith St Farmingdale (11735) ***(G-5130)***
Superior Packaging, Farmingdale *Also called Mkt329 Inc* ***(G-5068)***
Superior Plastic Slipcovers, Glendale *Also called Superior Decorators Inc* ***(G-5680)***
Superior Print On Demand 607 240-5231
165 Charles St Vestal (13850) ***(G-16478)***
Superior Printing Ink Co Inc 716 685-6763
2483 Walden Ave Cheektowaga (14225) ***(G-3618)***
Superior Stl Door Trim Co Inc 716 665-3256
154 Fairmount Ave Jamestown (14701) ***(G-7068)***
Superior Technology Inc 585 352-6556
200 Paragon Dr Rochester (14624) ***(G-14731)***
Superior Tool Company, North Tonawanda *Also called Ameri-Cut Tool Grinding Inc* ***(G-12971)***
Superior Walls of Hudson Vly, Poughkeepsie *Also called Superior Wlls of Hdson Vly Inc* ***(G-13953)***
Superior Walls Upstate NY Inc 585 624-9390
7574 E Main St Lima (14485) ***(G-7471)***
Superior Washer & Gasket Corp (PA) 631 273-8282
170 Adams Ave Hauppauge (11788) ***(G-6227)***
Superior Welding 631 676-2751
331 Dante Ct Ste G Holbrook (11741) ***(G-6503)***
Superior Wlls of Hdson Vly Inc 845 485-4033
68 Violet Ave Poughkeepsie (12601) ***(G-13953)***
Superior Wood Turnings 716 483-1254
118 E 1st St Jamestown (14701) ***(G-7069)***
Superite Gear Instr of Hppauge (PA) 631 234-0100
225 Engineers Rd Hauppauge (11788) ***(G-6228)***
Superleaf LLC 888 887-4318
212 7th St 1 Brooklyn (11215) ***(G-2650)***
Supermarket Equipment Depo Inc 718 665-6200
1135 Bronx River Ave Bronx (10472) ***(G-1465)***
Supermedia LLC 212 513-9700
2 Penn Plz Fl 22 New York (10121) ***(G-12265)***
Superpower Inc 518 346-1414
450 Duane Ave Ste 1 Schenectady (12304) ***(G-15325)***
Supersmile, New York *Also called Robell Research Inc* ***(G-11909)***
Supply & Demand, New York *Also called Drew Philips Corp* ***(G-9979)***
Supply Technologies (ny) (HQ) 212 966-3310
80 State St Albany (12207) ***(G-139)***
Supplynet Inc (PA) 800 826-0279
706 Executive Blvd Ste B Valley Cottage (10989) ***(G-16418)***
Suppositoria Laboratory, Bronx *Also called Perrigo New York Inc* ***(G-1428)***
Supreme Boilers Inc 718 342-2220
9221 Ditmas Ave Brooklyn (11236) ***(G-2651)***
Supreme Chocolatier LLC 718 761-9600
1150 South Ave Fl 1 Staten Island (10314) ***(G-15767)***
Supreme Fire-Proof Door Co Inc 718 665-4224
391 Rider Ave Bronx (10451) ***(G-1466)***
Supreme Leather Products, Spring Valley *Also called Louis Schwartz* ***(G-15615)***
Supreme Poly Plastics Inc 718 456-9300
299 Meserole St Brooklyn (11206) ***(G-2652)***
Supreme Poultry Inc 718 472-0300
3788 Review Ave Long Island City (11101) ***(G-7924)***
Supreme Screw Products Inc 718 293-6600
10 Skyline Dr Unit B Plainview (11803) ***(G-13664)***
Supreme Steel Inc 631 884-1320
690 N Jefferson Ave Lindenhurst (11757) ***(G-7512)***
Supresta US LLC (HQ) 914 674-9434
420 Saw Mill River Rd Ardsley (10502) ***(G-405)***

ALPHABETIC

ALPHABETIC SECTION

Sure Fit Inc 212 395-9340
58 W 40th St Rm 2a New York (10018) *(G-12266)*
Sure Flow Equipment Inc 800 263-8251
250 Cooper Ave Ste 102 Tonawanda (14150) *(G-16224)*
Sure Iron Works, Brooklyn *Also called Kms Contracting Inc (G-2175)*
Sure-Kol Refrigerator Co Inc 718 625-0601
490 Flushing Ave Brooklyn (11205) *(G-2653)*
Sure-Lock Industries LLC 315 207-0044
193 E Seneca St Oswego (13126) *(G-13368)*
Surepure Inc 917 368-8480
405 Lexington Ave Fl 25 New York (10174) *(G-12267)*
Surescan Corporation 607 321-0042
100 Eldredge St Binghamton (13901) *(G-947)*
Sureseal Corporation 607 336-6676
50 Ohara Dr Norwich (13815) *(G-13056)*
Surf-Tech Manufacturing Corp 631 589-1194
80 Orville Dr Ste 115 Bohemia (11716) *(G-1135)*
Surface Finish Technology 607 732-2909
215 Judson St Elmira (14901) *(G-4716)*
Surface Magazine 646 805-0200
134 W 26th St Frnt 1 New York (10001) *(G-12268)*
Surface Publishing, New York *Also called Surface Magazine (G-12268)*
Surgical Design Corp 914 273-2445
3 Macdonald Ave Armonk (10504) *(G-418)*
Surmet Ceramics Corporation 716 875-4091
699 Hertel Ave Ste 290 Buffalo (14207) *(G-3229)*
Surmotech LLC 585 742-1220
7676 Netlink Dr Victor (14564) *(G-16527)*
Surprise Plastics Inc 718 492-6355
124 57th St Brooklyn (11220) *(G-2654)*
Surving Studios 845 355-1430
17 Millsburg Rd Middletown (10940) *(G-8499)*
Survival Inc 631 385-5060
90 Washington Dr Ste C Centerport (11721) *(G-3506)*
Sussex Publishers LLC (PA) 212 260-7210
115 E 23rd St Fl 9 New York (10010) *(G-12269)*
Sussman-Automatic Corporation (PA) 347 609-7652
4320 34th St Long Island City (11101) *(G-7925)*
Sutter Machine Tool and Die, Bronx *Also called M J M Tooling Corp (G-1388)*
Sutton Place Software Inc 631 421-1737
13 Tappen Dr Melville (11747) *(G-8386)*
Svyz Trading Corp 718 220-1140
4320 Park Ave Bronx (10457) *(G-1467)*
Swagelok Western NY 585 359-8470
10 Thruway Park Dr West Henrietta (14586) *(G-16927)*
Swain Technology Inc 585 889-2786
963 North Rd Scottsville (14546) *(G-15362)*
Swamp Island Dessert Co, West Falls *Also called Butterwood Desserts Inc (G-16876)*
Swank Inc 212 867-2600
90 Park Ave Rm 1302 New York (10016) *(G-12270)*
Swanson Lumber 716 499-1726
5273 N Hill Rd Gerry (14740) *(G-5605)*
Swaps Monitor Publications Inc 212 742-8550
29 Broadway Rm 1315 New York (10006) *(G-12271)*
Swarovski Lighting Ltd (PA) 518 563-7500
61 Industrial Blvd Plattsburgh (12901) *(G-13731)*
Swarovski Lighting Ltd 518 324-6378
1483 Military Tpke Ste B Plattsburgh (12901) *(G-13732)*
Swarovski North America Ltd 914 423-4132
6080 Mall Walk Yonkers (10704) *(G-17505)*
Swarovski North America Ltd 212 695-1502
1 Penn Plz Frnt 4 New York (10119) *(G-12272)*
Swatfame Inc 212 944-8022
530 Fashion Ave Rm 1204 New York (10018) *(G-12273)*
Swatt Baking Co, Olean *Also called L American Ltd (G-13171)*
Sweater Brand Inc 718 797-0505
86 S 1st St Brooklyn (11249) *(G-2655)*
Swed Masters Workshop LLC 212 644-8822
214 E 82nd St Frnt 1 New York (10028) *(G-12274)*
Swedish Hill Vineyard Inc 607 403-0029
4565 State Route 414 Romulus (14541) *(G-14872)*
Swedish Hill Winery, Romulus *Also called Swedish Hill Vineyard Inc (G-14872)*
Sweet Apparel Inc 212 221-3321
525 7th Ave Rm 513 New York (10018) *(G-12275)*
Sweet Melodys LLC 716 580-3227
8485 Transit Rd East Amherst (14051) *(G-4389)*
Sweet Mouth Inc 800 433-7758
244 5th Ave Ste L243 New York (10001) *(G-12276)*
Sweet Tooth Enterprises LLC 631 752-2888
135 Dale St West Babylon (11704) *(G-16867)*
Sweeteners Plus Inc 585 728-3770
5768 Sweeteners Blvd Lakeville (14480) *(G-7309)*
Sweetriot Inc 212 431-7468
131 Varick St Ste 936 New York (10013) *(G-12277)*
Sweetwater Energy Inc 585 647-5760
500 Lee Rd Ste 200 Rochester (14606) *(G-14732)*
Sweetworks Inc (PA) 716 634-4545
3500 Genesee St Buffalo (14225) *(G-3230)*
Swell Bottle, New York *Also called Cant Live Without It LLC (G-9569)*
Swift Fulfillment Services 516 593-1198
290 Broadway Lynbrook (11563) *(G-7990)*

Swift Glass Co Inc 607 733-7166
131 22nd St Elmira Heights (14903) *(G-4727)*
Swift Multigraphics LLC 585 442-8000
55 Southwood Ln Rochester (14618) *(G-14733)*
Swift River Associates Inc (PA) 716 875-0902
4051 River Rd Tonawanda (14150) *(G-16225)*
Swimline Corp (PA) 631 254-2155
191 Rodeo Dr Edgewood (11717) *(G-4626)*
Swimline International Corp 631 254-2155
191 Rodeo Dr Edgewood (11717) *(G-4627)*
Swimwear Anywhere Inc (PA) 631 420-1400
85 Sherwood Ave Farmingdale (11735) *(G-5131)*
Swimwear Anywhere Inc 845 858-4141
21 Minisink Ave Port Jervis (12771) *(G-13817)*
Swing Frame, Freeport *Also called Access Display Group Inc (G-5389)*
Swirl Bliss LLC 516 867-9475
1777 Grand Ave North Baldwin (11510) *(G-12927)*
Swiss Madison LLC 434 623-4766
498 Liberty Ave Brooklyn (11207) *(G-2656)*
Swiss Specialties Inc 631 567-8800
15 Crescent Ct Wading River (11792) *(G-16547)*
Swiss Tool Corporation 631 842-7766
100 Court St Copiague (11726) *(G-3954)*
Swissbit Na Inc 914 935-1400
18 Willett Ave 202 Port Chester (10573) *(G-13784)*
Swisse Cheeks, Brooklyn *Also called Silly Phillie Creations Inc (G-2583)*
Swissmar Inc 905 764-1121
6391 Walmore Rd Niagara Falls (14304) *(G-12896)*
Swissway Inc 631 351-5350
123 W Hills Rd Huntington Station (11746) *(G-6762)*
Switch Beverage Company LLC 203 202-7383
2 Seaview Blvd Fl 3 Port Washington (11050) *(G-13885)*
Switches and Sensors Inc 631 924-2167
86 Horseblock Rd Unit J Yaphank (11980) *(G-17420)*
Switching Power Inc 631 981-7231
3601 Veterans Mem Hwy Ronkonkoma (11779) *(G-15013)*
Switzer, Buffalo *Also called Precision Photo-Fab Inc (G-3158)*
Swivelier Company Inc 845 353-1455
600 Bradley Hill Rd Ste 3 Blauvelt (10913) *(G-970)*
Swremote, Buffalo *Also called Pointman LLC (G-3153)*
Sycamore Hill Designs Inc 585 820-7322
7585 Modock Rd Victor (14564) *(G-16528)*
Sylhan LLC (PA) 631 243-6600
210 Rodeo Dr Edgewood (11717) *(G-4628)*
Sylvia Heisel, New York *Also called Post Modern Productions Inc (G-11711)*
Symantec Corporation 646 487-6000
1 Penn Plz Ste 5420 New York (10119) *(G-12278)*
Symbio Technologies LLC 914 576-1205
333 Mamaroneck Ave White Plains (10605) *(G-17200)*
Symbol Technologies LLC (HQ) 631 737-6851
1 Zebra Plz Holtsville (11742) *(G-6536)*
Symbol Technologies LLC 631 738-2400
110 Orville Dr Bohemia (11716) *(G-1136)*
Symbol Technologies LLC 631 738-3346
1 Zebra Plz Holtsville (11742) *(G-6537)*
Symbol Technologies LLC 631 218-3907
25 Andrea Rd Holbrook (11741) *(G-6504)*
Symbol Technologies Delaware, Holtsville *Also called Symbol Technologies LLC (G-6536)*
Symphony Talent LLC (PA) 212 999-9000
19 W 34th St Fl 10 New York (10001) *(G-12279)*
Symrise Inc 646 459-5000
505 Park Ave Fl 15 New York (10022) *(G-12280)*
Symrise Inc 845 469-7675
45 Leone Ln Chester (10918) *(G-3645)*
Symwave Inc (HQ) 949 542-4400
80 Arkay Dr Hauppauge (11788) *(G-6229)*
Synaptics Incorporated 585 899-4300
90 Linden Oaks Ste 100 Rochester (14625) *(G-14734)*
Synced Inc 917 565-5591
120 Walker St Ste 4 New York (10013) *(G-12281)*
Synco Chemical Corporation 631 567-5300
24 Davinci Dr Bohemia (11716) *(G-1137)*
Synco Technologies Inc 212 255-2031
54 W 21st St Rm 602 New York (10010) *(G-12282)*
Synergx Systems Inc (HQ) 516 433-4700
3927 59th St Woodside (11377) *(G-17374)*
Synergy Digital 718 643-2742
43 Hall St Brooklyn (11205) *(G-2657)*
Synergy Flavors NY Company LLC 585 232-6648
86 White St Rochester (14608) *(G-14735)*
Synergy Intrntnal Optrnics LLC 631 277-0500
101 Comac St Ronkonkoma (11779) *(G-15014)*
Synergy Pharmaceuticals Inc (HQ) 212 227-8611
420 Lexington Ave Rm 2500 New York (10170) *(G-12283)*
Synergy Pharmaceuticals Inc (PA) 212 297-0020
420 Lexington Ave Rm 2012 New York (10170) *(G-12284)*
Synergy Resources Inc 631 665-2050
320 Carleton Ave Ste 6200 Central Islip (11722) *(G-3538)*
Synergy Tooling Systems Inc (PA) 716 834-4457
287 Commerce Dr Amherst (14228) *(G-264)*
Syntec Optics, Rochester *Also called Syntec Technologies Inc (G-14736)*
Syntec Optics, Rochester *Also called Syntec Technologies Inc (G-14737)*

ALPHABETIC SECTION

Syntec Technologies Inc (PA) 585 768-2513
  515 Lee Rd Rochester (14606) *(G-14736)*
Syntec Technologies Inc 585 464-9336
  515 Lee Rd Rochester (14606) *(G-14737)*
Syntel Inc 212 785-9810
  1 Exchange Plz Ste 2001 New York (10006) *(G-12285)*
Synthes USA, Horseheads Also called Depuy Synthes Inc *(G-6603)*
Synthetic Textiles Inc (PA) 716 842-2598
  398 Broadway St Buffalo (14204) *(G-3231)*
Syntho Pharmaceuticals Inc 631 755-9898
  230 Sherwood Ave Farmingdale (11735) *(G-5132)*
Syraco Products Inc 315 476-5306
  1054 S Clinton St Syracuse (13202) *(G-16072)*
Syracusa Sand and Gravel Inc 585 924-7146
  1389 Malone Rd Victor (14564) *(G-16529)*
Syracuse Casing Co Inc 315 475-0309
  528 Erie Blvd W Syracuse (13204) *(G-16073)*
Syracuse Catholic Press Assn 315 422-8153
  421 S Warren St Fl 2 Syracuse (13202) *(G-16074)*
Syracuse Computer Forms Inc 315 478-0108
  216 Burnet Ave Syracuse (13203) *(G-16075)*
Syracuse Corrugated Box Corp 315 437-9901
  302 Stoutenger St East Syracuse (13057) *(G-4582)*
Syracuse Cultural Workers Prj 315 474-1132
  400 Lodi St Syracuse (13203) *(G-16076)*
Syracuse Hvac, Syracuse Also called John F Krell Jr *(G-15987)*
Syracuse Industrial Sls Co Ltd 315 478-5751
  1850 Lemoyne Ave Syracuse (13208) *(G-16077)*
Syracuse Label & Surround Prtg, Syracuse Also called Syracuse Label Co Inc *(G-16078)*
Syracuse Label Co Inc 315 422-1037
  200 Stewart Dr Syracuse (13212) *(G-16078)*
Syracuse Letter Company Inc 315 476-8328
  1179 Oak Ln Bridgeport (13030) *(G-1236)*
Syracuse Midstate Spring, Syracuse Also called Midstate Spring Inc *(G-16010)*
Syracuse New Times, Syracuse Also called All Times Publishing LLC *(G-15868)*
Syracuse New Times, Syracuse Also called A Zimmer Ltd *(G-15866)*
Syracuse Plastics LLC 315 637-9881
  7400 Morgan Rd Liverpool (13090) *(G-7578)*
Syracuse Prosthetic Center Inc 315 476-9697
  1124 E Fayette St Syracuse (13210) *(G-16079)*
Syracuse Sand & Gravel LLC 315 548-8207
  1902 County Route 57 Fulton (13069) *(G-5489)*
Syracuse Stamping Company, Syracuse Also called Syraco Products Inc *(G-16072)*
Syracuse Technical Center, Syracuse Also called Chemtrade Chemicals US LLC *(G-15913)*
Syracuse University Press Inc 315 443-5534
  621 Skytop Rd Ste 110 Syracuse (13244) *(G-16080)*
Syrasoft LLC 315 708-0341
  6 Canton St Baldwinsville (13027) *(G-577)*
System of AME Binding 631 390-8560
  95 Hoffman Ln Central Islip (11749) *(G-3539)*
Systems Drs C3 Inc (HQ) 716 631-6200
  485 Cayuga Rd Buffalo (14225) *(G-3232)*
Systems Trading Inc 718 261-8900
  48 S Svc Rd Ste Ll90 Melville (11747) *(G-8387)*
Sz - Design & Print Inc 845 352-0395
  33 Rita Ave Monsey (10952) *(G-8618)*
T & C Power Conversion Inc 585 482-5551
  132 Humboldt St Rochester (14610) *(G-14738)*
T & K Printing, Brooklyn Also called T&K Printing Inc *(G-2661)*
T & L Automatics Inc 585 647-3717
  770 Emerson St Rochester (14613) *(G-14739)*
T & L Trading Co 718 782-5550
  17 Meserole St Brooklyn (11206) *(G-2658)*
T & M Plating Inc 212 967-1110
  357 W 36th St Fl 7 New York (10018) *(G-12286)*
T & R Knitting Mills Inc (PA) 718 497-4017
  8000 Cooper Ave Ste 6 Glendale (11385) *(G-5681)*
T & R Knitting Mills Inc 212 840-8665
  214 W 39th St New York (10018) *(G-12287)*
T & Smoothie Inc 631 804-6653
  499 N Service Rd Ste 83 Patchogue (11772) *(G-13461)*
T A S Sales Service LLC 518 234-4919
  105 Kenyon Rd Cobleskill (12043) *(G-3764)*
T A Tool & Molding Inc 631 293-0172
  185 Marine St Farmingdale (11735) *(G-5133)*
T C Dunham Paint Company Inc 914 969-4202
  581 Saw Mill River Rd Yonkers (10701) *(G-17506)*
T C I, Whitesboro Also called Telecommunication Concepts *(G-17224)*
T C Peters Printing Co Inc 315 724-4149
  2336 W Whitesboro St Utica (13502) *(G-16385)*
T C Timber, Skaneateles Also called Habermaass Corporation *(G-15484)*
T E Q, Huntington Station Also called Tequipment Inc *(G-6764)*
T Eason Land Surveyor 631 474-2200
  27 Poplar St Port Jeff STA (11776) *(G-13795)*
T G M Products Inc 631 491-0515
  90 Wyandanch Ave Unit E Wyandanch (11798) *(G-17392)*
T G S Inc 516 629-6905
  6 Wildwood Ct Locust Valley (11560) *(G-7664)*
T J Ronan Paint Corp 718 292-1100
  749 E 135th St Bronx (10454) *(G-1468)*

T J Signs Unlimited LLC (PA) 631 273-4800
  171 Freeman Ave Islip (11751) *(G-6852)*
T Jn Electric 917 560-0981
  116 Cortlandt Rd Mahopac (10541) *(G-8033)*
T Jn Electric Inc 845 628-6970
  901 Route 6 Mahopac (10541) *(G-8034)*
T L Diamond & Company Inc (PA) 212 249-6660
  116 E 68th St Apt 5a New York (10065) *(G-12288)*
T L F Graphics Inc 585 272-5500
  235 Metro Park Rochester (14623) *(G-14740)*
T L X, Plainview Also called Xpress Printing Inc *(G-13675)*
T Lemme Mechanical Inc 518 436-4136
  1074 Broadway Menands (12204) *(G-8411)*
T M Design Screen Printing, Rochester Also called Todd Walbridge *(G-14755)*
T M I of New York, Brooklyn Also called Technipoly Manufacturing Inc *(G-2671)*
T M I Plastics Industries Inc 718 383-0363
  28 Wythe Ave Brooklyn (11249) *(G-2659)*
T M International LLC 718 842-0949
  413 Faile St 15 Bronx (10474) *(G-1469)*
T M Machine Inc 716 822-0817
  176 Reading St Buffalo (14220) *(G-3233)*
T M W Diamonds Mfg Co (PA) 212 869-8444
  15 W 47th St Ste 302 New York (10036) *(G-12289)*
T Mix Inc 646 379-6814
  6217 5th Ave Brooklyn (11220) *(G-2660)*
T O Dey Service Corp 212 683-6300
  151 W 46th St Fl 3 New York (10036) *(G-12290)*
T O Gronlund Company Inc 212 679-3535
  200 Lexington Ave Rm 1515 New York (10016) *(G-12291)*
T R P Machine Inc 631 567-9620
  35 Davinci Dr Ste B Bohemia (11716) *(G-1138)*
T R W Automotive, Auburn Also called TRW Automotive US LLC *(G-523)*
T Rj Shirts Inc 347 642-3071
  3050 90th St East Elmhurst (11369) *(G-4418)*
T RS Great American Rest 516 294-1680
  17 Hillside Ave Williston Park (11596) *(G-17287)*
T S B A Group Inc (PA) 718 565-6000
  3830 Woodside Ave Sunnyside (11104) *(G-15831)*
T S O General Corp 631 952-5320
  81 Emjay Blvd Unit 1 Brentwood (11717) *(G-1193)*
T S P Corp 585 768-6769
  78 One Half Lake St Le Roy (14482) *(G-7441)*
T S Pink Corp 607 432-1100
  139 Pony Farm Rd Oneonta (13820) *(G-13216)*
T Shore Products Ltd 315 252-9174
  5 Eagle Dr Auburn (13021) *(G-519)*
T T I, Oriskany Also called Terahertz Technologies Inc *(G-13340)*
T V Trade Media Inc 212 288-3933
  216 E 75th St Apt 1w New York (10021) *(G-12292)*
T&B Bakery Corp 646 642-4300
  5870 56th St Maspeth (11378) *(G-8202)*
T&K Printing Inc 718 439-9454
  262 44th St Brooklyn (11232) *(G-2661)*
T-Base Communications USA Inc 315 713-0013
  806 Commerce Park Dr Ogdensburg (13669) *(G-13144)*
T-Company LLC 646 290-6365
  16 Monitor Rd Smithtown (11787) *(G-15522)*
T-Rex Supply Corporation 516 308-0505
  1 Fulton Ave Ste 120 Hempstead (11550) *(G-6310)*
T-S-K Electronics Inc 716 693-3916
  908 Niagara Falls Blvd # 122 North Tonawanda (14120) *(G-13017)*
T-Shirt Graphics, Ballston Spa Also called Sand Hill Industries Inc *(G-607)*
Taam Tov Foods Inc 718 788-8880
  188 28th St Brooklyn (11232) *(G-2662)*
Taber Acquisition Corp 716 694-4000
  455 Bryant St North Tonawanda (14120) *(G-13018)*
Taber Industries, North Tonawanda Also called Taber Acquisition Corp *(G-13018)*
Tabi Inc 347 701-1051
  488 Onderdonk Ave Apt 1l Flushing (11385) *(G-5304)*
Table Tops Paper Corp 718 831-6440
  47 Hall St Ste C-2 Brooklyn (11205) *(G-2663)*
Tablecloths For Granted Ltd 518 370-5481
  510 Union St Schenectady (12305) *(G-15326)*
Tables Manufacturing, Edgewood Also called Kinplex Corp *(G-4618)*
Tablet Newspaper, The, Brooklyn Also called Tablet Publishing Company Inc *(G-2664)*
Tablet Publishing Company Inc 718 965-7333
  1712 10th Ave Brooklyn (11215) *(G-2664)*
Tabrisse Collections Inc 212 921-1014
  1412 Broadway New York (10018) *(G-12293)*
TAC Screw Products Inc 585 663-5840
  170 Bennington Dr Rochester (14616) *(G-14741)*
Tackle Factory, Fillmore Also called Cuba Specialty Mfg Co Inc *(G-5183)*
Taconic, Petersburg Also called Tonoga Inc *(G-13551)*
Tacr, Middletown Also called Turbine Arfoil Cating Repr LLC *(G-8502)*
Tactair Fluid Controls Inc 315 451-3928
  4806 W Taft Rd Liverpool (13088) *(G-7579)*
Tactica International Inc (PA) 212 575-0500
  11 W 42nd St New York (10036) *(G-12294)*
TAe Trans Atlantic Elec Inc (PA) 631 595-9206
  151 E Industry Ct Deer Park (11729) *(G-4240)*

(PA)=Parent Co (HQ)=Headquarters (DH)=Div Headquarters

Tag Dental Implant Solutions, Valley Stream *Also called Total Dntl Implant Sltions LLC* ***(G-16453)***
Tag Envelope Co Inc 718 389-6844
1419 128th St College Point (11356) ***(G-3835)***
Tag Flange & Machining Inc 516 536-1300
3375 Royal Ave Oceanside (11572) ***(G-13122)***
Tahari Arthur S Levine, New York *Also called Tahari ASL LLC* ***(G-12295)***
Tahari ASL LLC 212 763-2800
1114 Ave Of The Americas New York (10036) ***(G-12295)***
Tai Seng 718 399-6311
106 Lexington Ave Brooklyn (11238) ***(G-2665)***
Taikoh USA Inc 646 556-6652
369 Lexington Ave Fl 2 New York (10017) ***(G-12296)***
Tailorbyrd, New York *Also called Sanctuary Brands LLC* ***(G-11982)***
Tailored Coatings Inc 716 893-4869
1800 Brdwy St Bldg 2a Buffalo (14212) ***(G-3234)***
Tailored Sportsman LLC 646 366-8733
230 W 38th St Fl 6 New York (10018) ***(G-12297)***
Takeform Architectural Graphics, Medina *Also called Quorum Group LLC* ***(G-8312)***
Talaera 206 229-0631
81 Fleet Pl Apt 11a Brooklyn (11201) ***(G-2666)***
Talas, Brooklyn *Also called Technical Library Service Inc* ***(G-2670)***
Talbots Inc 914 328-1034
125 Westchester Ave # 2460 White Plains (10601) ***(G-17201)***
Tallmans Express Lube 315 266-1033
8421 Seneca Tpke New Hartford (13413) ***(G-8857)***
Talyarps Corporation (PA) 914 699-3030
143 Sparks Ave Pelham (10803) ***(G-13520)***
Talyarps Corporation 914 699-3030
716 S Columbus Ave Mount Vernon (10550) ***(G-8781)***
Tam Ceramics Group of Ny LLC 716 278-9400
4511 Hyde Park Blvd Niagara Falls (14305) ***(G-12897)***
Tam Ceramics LLC 716 278-9480
4511 Hyde Park Blvd Niagara Falls (14305) ***(G-12898)***
Tamber Knits Inc 212 730-1121
231 W 39th St Fl 8 New York (10018) ***(G-12298)***
Tambetti Inc 212 751-9584
48 W 48th St Ste 501 New York (10036) ***(G-12299)***
Tami Great Food Corp 845 352-7901
22 Briarcliff Dr Monsey (10952) ***(G-8619)***
Tamka Sport LLC 718 224-7820
225 Beverly Rd Douglaston (11363) ***(G-4337)***
Tamperproof Screw Company Inc 516 931-1616
30 Laurel St Hicksville (11801) ***(G-6425)***
Tamsen Z LLC 212 292-6412
350 Park Ave Fl 4 New York (10022) ***(G-12300)***
Tanagro Jewelry Corp 212 753-2817
36 W 44th St Ste 1101 New York (10036) ***(G-12301)***
Tandus Centiva Inc 212 206-7170
71 5th Ave Fl 2 New York (10003) ***(G-12302)***
Tandy Leather Factory Inc 845 480-3588
298 Main St Nyack (10960) ***(G-13071)***
Tanen & Co, Brooklyn *Also called Tanen Cap Co* ***(G-2667)***
Tanen Cap Co 212 254-7100
397 Bridge St Fl 8 Brooklyn (11201) ***(G-2667)***
Tangent Machine & Tool Corp 631 249-3088
108 Gazza Blvd Farmingdale (11735) ***(G-5134)***
Tangram Company LLC 631 758-0460
125 Corporate Dr Holtsville (11742) ***(G-6538)***
Tao Group LLC 646 625-4818
355 W 16th St New York (10011) ***(G-12303)***
Tap2play LLC 914 960-6232
110 W 40th St Rm 1902 New York (10018) ***(G-12304)***
Tape Printers Inc 631 249-5585
155 Allen Blvd Ste A Farmingdale (11735) ***(G-5135)***
Tape Systems Inc 914 668-3700
630 S Columbus Ave Mount Vernon (10550) ***(G-8782)***
Tape-It Inc 631 243-4100
233 N Fehr Way Bay Shore (11706) ***(G-743)***
Tapemaker Sales Co Inc 516 333-0592
48 Urban Ave Westbury (11590) ***(G-17057)***
Tapemaker Supply Company LLC 914 693-3407
22 Sherbrooke Rd Hartsdale (10530) ***(G-6020)***
Tapestries Etc, New York *Also called Vander Heyden Woodworking* ***(G-12523)***
Tappan Wire & Cable Inc (HQ) 845 353-9000
100 Bradley Pkwy Blauvelt (10913) ***(G-971)***
Taqa Entertainment, Valley Stream *Also called Taste and See Entrmt Inc* ***(G-16452)***
Tara Rific Screen Printing Inc 718 583-6864
4197 Park Ave Bronx (10457) ***(G-1470)***
Target Rock, Farmingdale *Also called Curtiss-Wright Flow Ctrl Corp* ***(G-4978)***
Targetprocess Inc (PA) 877 718-2617
1325 Millersport Hwy Amherst (14221) ***(G-265)***
Targum Press USA Inc 248 355-2266
1946 59th St Brooklyn (11204) ***(G-2668)***
Taro Manufacturing Company Inc 315 252-9430
114 Clark St Auburn (13021) ***(G-520)***
Tarrytown Bakery Inc 914 631-0209
150 Wildey St Tarrytown (10591) ***(G-16133)***
Tarsia Technical Industries 631 231-8322
93 Marcus Blvd Hauppauge (11788) ***(G-6230)***
Tarsier Ltd 212 401-6181
655 Madison Ave Frnt 3 New York (10065) ***(G-12305)***
Taste and See Entrmt Inc 516 285-3010
255 Dogwood Rd Valley Stream (11580) ***(G-16452)***
Tate's Bake Shop, East Moriches *Also called Tates Wholesale LLC* ***(G-4451)***
Tates Wholesale LLC 631 780-6511
62 Pine St East Moriches (11940) ***(G-4451)***
Tatra Mfg Corporation 631 691-1184
30 Railroad Ave Copiague (11726) ***(G-3955)***
Tattersall Industries LLC 518 381-4270
2125 Technology Dr Schenectady (12308) ***(G-15327)***
Taumel Assembly Systems, Patterson *Also called Taumel Metalforming Corp* ***(G-13469)***
Taumel Metalforming Corp 845 878-3100
25 Jon Barrett Rd Patterson (12563) ***(G-13469)***
Taylor 518 954-2832
166 Wallins Corners Rd Amsterdam (12010) ***(G-369)***
Taylor & Francis Group LLC 212 216-7800
711 3rd Ave Fl 8 New York (10017) ***(G-12306)***
Taylor Communications Inc 937 221-1303
155 Pinelawn Rd Ste 120s Melville (11747) ***(G-8388)***
Taylor Communications Inc 718 352-0220
1600 Stewart Ave Ste 301 Westbury (11590) ***(G-17058)***
Taylor Concrete Products Inc 315 788-2191
20475 Old Rome Rd Watertown (13601) ***(G-16696)***
Taylor Copy Services, Syracuse *Also called Constas Printing Corporation* ***(G-15924)***
Taylor Devices Inc (PA) 716 694-0800
90 Taylor Dr North Tonawanda (14120) ***(G-13019)***
Taylor Made Group LLC (HQ) 518 725-0681
66 Kingsboro Ave Gloversville (12078) ***(G-5739)***
Taylor Metalworks Inc 716 662-3113
3925 California Rd Orchard Park (14127) ***(G-13323)***
Taylor Precision Machining 607 535-3101
3921 Dug Rd Montour Falls (14865) ***(G-8651)***
Taylor Products Inc (PA) 518 773-9312
66 Kingsboro Ave Gloversville (12078) ***(G-5740)***
Taylor Tank Company Inc 718 434-1300
848 E 43rd St Brooklyn (11210) ***(G-2669)***
Tb, Rochester *Also called Turner Bellows Inc* ***(G-14763)***
Tbhl International LLC 212 799-2007
252 W 38th St Fl 11 New York (10018) ***(G-12307)***
Tc Transcontinental USA Inc 818 993-4767
67 Irving Pl Fl 2 New York (10003) ***(G-12308)***
Tchnologies N MRC Ameerica LLC 716 822-4300
25 Roberts Ave Buffalo (14206) ***(G-3235)***
Tcmf Inc 607 724-1094
69-93 Eldredge St Binghamton (13901) ***(G-948)***
TCS Electronics Inc 585 337-4301
1124 Corporate Dr Farmington (14425) ***(G-5165)***
TCS Industries Inc 585 426-1160
400 Trabold Rd Rochester (14624) ***(G-14742)***
Tdg Operations LLC 212 779-4300
200 Lexington Ave Rm 1314 New York (10016) ***(G-12309)***
Tdk USA Corporation (HQ) 516 535-2600
455 Rxr Plz Uniondale (11556) ***(G-16323)***
Tdk-Lambda Americas Inc 631 967-3000
145 Marcus Blvd Ste 3 Hauppauge (11788) ***(G-6231)***
Tdl Manufacturing Inc 215 538-8820
80 Cabot Ct Hauppauge (11788) ***(G-6232)***
Tdo Sandblasting, Roosevelt *Also called Tropical Driftwood Originals* ***(G-15033)***
TDS Fitness Equipment 607 733-6789
160 Home St Elmira (14904) ***(G-4717)***
TDS Woodcraft, Staten Island *Also called TDS Woodworking Inc* ***(G-15768)***
TDS Woodworking Inc 718 442-5298
104 Port Richmond Ave Staten Island (10302) ***(G-15768)***
Tdy Industries LLC 716 433-4411
695 Ohio St Lockport (14094) ***(G-7648)***
Te Connectivity Corporation 585 785-2500
2245 Brighton Henrta Twn Rochester (14623) ***(G-14743)***
Te Neues Publishing Company (PA) 212 627-9090
350 7th Ave Rm 301 New York (10001) ***(G-12310)***
Tea & Coffee Trade Journal, Long Island City *Also called Lockwood Trade Journal Co Inc* ***(G-7821)***
Tea Life LLC 516 365-7711
73 Plandome Rd Manhasset (11030) ***(G-8100)***
Teachergaming LLC 866 644-9323
809 W 181st St 231 New York (10033) ***(G-12311)***
Teachers College Columbia Univ 212 678-3929
1234 Amsterdam Ave New York (10027) ***(G-12312)***
Teachers College Press, New York *Also called Teachers College Columbia Univ* ***(G-12312)***
Teachley LLC 347 552-1272
25 Broadway Fl 13 New York (10004) ***(G-12313)***
Teachspin Inc 716 725-6116
2495 Main St Ste 409 Buffalo (14214) ***(G-3236)***
Teale Machine Company Inc 585 244-6700
1425 University Ave Rochester (14607) ***(G-14744)***
Tealeafs 716 688-8022
5416 Main St Williamsville (14221) ***(G-17282)***
Team Builders Inc 718 979-1005
88 New Dorp Plz S Ste 303 Staten Island (10306) ***(G-15769)***
Team Builders Management, Staten Island *Also called Team Builders Inc* ***(G-15769)***
Team Fabrication Inc 716 655-4038
1055 Davis Rd West Falls (14170) ***(G-16877)***
Tebbens Steel LLC 631 208-8330
800 Burman Blvd Calverton (11933) ***(G-3329)***

TEC - Crete Transit Mix Corp 718 657-6880
4673 Metropolitan Ave Ridgewood (11385) ***(G-14139)***
TEC Glass & Inst LLC 315 926-7639
4211 Sunset Dr Marion (14505) ***(G-8132)***
Tech Lube, Yaphank *Also called Tribology Inc* ***(G-17421)***
Tech Park Food Services LLC 585 295-1250
789 Elmgrove Rd Rochester (14624) ***(G-14745)***
Tech Products Inc 718 442-4900
105 Willow Ave Staten Island (10305) ***(G-15770)***
Tech Software LLC 516 986-3050
270 Spagnoli Rd Ste 102 Melville (11747) ***(G-8389)***
Tech Valley Printing, Watervliet *Also called General Business Supply Inc* ***(G-16709)***
Techgrass 646 719-2000
77 Water St New York (10005) ***(G-12314)***
Technapulse LLC 631 234-8700
400 Oser Ave Ste 1950 Hauppauge (11788) ***(G-6233)***
Technic Inc 516 349-0700
111 E Ames Ct Unit 2 Plainview (11803) ***(G-13665)***
Technical Library Service Inc 212 219-0770
330 Morgan Ave Brooklyn (11211) ***(G-2670)***
Technical Packaging Inc 516 223-2300
2365 Milburn Ave Baldwin (11510) ***(G-561)***
Technical Service Industries 212 719-9800
17506 Devonshire Rd 5n Jamaica (11432) ***(G-6992)***
Technical Wldg Fabricators LLC 518 463-2229
27 Thatcher St Albany (12207) ***(G-140)***
Techniflo Corporation 716 741-3500
9730 County Rd Clarence Center (14032) ***(G-3706)***
Technimetal Precision Inds 631 231-8900
195 Marcus Blvd Hauppauge (11788) ***(G-6234)***
Technipoly Manufacturing Inc 718 383-0363
20 Wythe Ave Brooklyn (11249) ***(G-2671)***
Technologies Application LLC 607 275-0345
3736 Kellogg Rd Cortland (13045) ***(G-4070)***
Technology Desking Inc 212 257-6998
39 Broadway Rm 1640 New York (10006) ***(G-12315)***
Technomag Inc 631 246-6142
12 Technology Dr Unit 5 East Setauket (11733) ***(G-4512)***
Technopaving New York Inc 631 351-6472
270 Broadway Huntington Station (11746) ***(G-6763)***
Tecmotiv (usa) Inc 905 669-5911
1500 James Ave Niagara Falls (14305) ***(G-12899)***
Tecnofil Chenango SAC 607 674-4441
40 S Main St Sherburne (13460) ***(G-15420)***
Tecnolux Incorporated 718 369-3900
103 14th St Brooklyn (11215) ***(G-2672)***
Tectonic Flooring USA LLC 212 686-2700
1140 1st Ave Frnt 1 New York (10065) ***(G-12316)***
Tectran Inc 800 776-5549
2345 Walden Ave Ste 100 Cheektowaga (14225) ***(G-3619)***
Tectran Mfg Inc (HQ) 800 776-5549
2345 Walden Ave Ste 1 Buffalo (14225) ***(G-3237)***
Ted Westbrook 716 625-4443
4736 Mapleton Rd Lockport (14094) ***(G-7649)***
Ted-Steel Indstries, New York *Also called Ted-Steel Industries Ltd* ***(G-12317)***
Ted-Steel Industries Ltd 212 279-3878
361 W 36th St Frnt A New York (10018) ***(G-12317)***
Tee Pee Auto Sales Corp 516 338-9333
52 Swan St Westbury (11590) ***(G-17059)***
Tee Pee Fence & Rail, Jamaica *Also called Tee Pee Fence and Railing* ***(G-6993)***
Tee Pee Fence and Railing 718 658-8323
9312 179th Pl Jamaica (11433) ***(G-6993)***
Tee Pee Signs, Hempstead *Also called Jem Sign Corp* ***(G-6299)***
Teena Creations Inc 516 867-1500
10 Hanse Ave Freeport (11520) ***(G-5440)***
Tefft Publishers Inc 518 692-9290
35 Salem St Greenwich (12834) ***(G-5914)***
Tegna Inc 716 849-2222
259 Delaware Ave Buffalo (14202) ***(G-3238)***
Tek Precision Co Ltd 631 242-0330
205 W Industry Ct Deer Park (11729) ***(G-4241)***
Tek Weld 631 694-5503
45 Rabro Dr Unit 1 Hauppauge (11788) ***(G-6235)***
Teka Fine Line Brushes Inc 718 692-2928
3691 Bedford Ave Brooklyn (11229) ***(G-2673)***
Teka Precision Inc 845 753-1900
251 Mountainview Ave Nyack (10960) ***(G-13072)***
Teknic Inc 585 784-7454
115 Victor Heights Pkwy Victor (14564) ***(G-16530)***
Tel Tech International 516 393-5174
200 Broadhollow Rd # 207 Melville (11747) ***(G-8390)***
Tel Technology Center Amer LLC (HQ) 512 424-4200
255 Fuller Rd Ste 244 Albany (12203) ***(G-141)***
Tel-Tru Inc (PA) 585 295-0225
408 Saint Paul St Rochester (14605) ***(G-14746)***
Tel-Tru Manufacturing Company, Rochester *Also called Tel-Tru Inc* ***(G-14746)***
Tele-Pak Inc 845 426-2300
421 Route 59 Monsey (10952) ***(G-8620)***
Tele-Vue Optics Inc 845 469-4551
32 Elkay Dr Chester (10918) ***(G-3646)***
Telebyte Inc (PA) 631 423-3232
355 Marcus Blvd Ste 2 Hauppauge (11788) ***(G-6236)***
Telechemische Inc 845 561-3237
222 Dupont Ave Newburgh (12550) ***(G-12805)***
Telecommunication Concepts 315 736-8523
329 Oriskany Blvd Whitesboro (13492) ***(G-17224)***
Teledyne Lecroy Inc (HQ) 845 425-2000
700 Chestnut Ridge Rd Chestnut Ridge (10977) ***(G-3656)***
Teledyne Optech Inc 585 427-8310
1046 University Ave # 147 Rochester (14607) ***(G-14747)***
Telemergency Ltd 914 629-4222
3 Quincy Ln White Plains (10605) ***(G-17202)***
Telephone Sales & Service Co (PA) 212 233-8505
132 W Broadway New York (10013) ***(G-12318)***
Telephonics Corporation 631 755-7659
815 Broadhollow Rd Farmingdale (11735) ***(G-5136)***
Telephonics Corporation 631 549-6000
770 Park Ave Huntington (11743) ***(G-6722)***
Telephonics Corporation (HQ) 631 755-7000
815 Broadhollow Rd Farmingdale (11735) ***(G-5137)***
Telephonics Corporation 631 755-7000
815 Broadhollow Rd Farmingdale (11735) ***(G-5138)***
Telephonics Corporation 631 755-7000
770 Park Ave Huntington (11743) ***(G-6723)***
Telephonics Corporation 631 470-8800
780 Park Ave Huntington (11743) ***(G-6724)***
Telephonics Tlsi Corp 631 470-8854
780 Park Ave Huntington (11743) ***(G-6725)***
Telesca-Heyman Inc 212 534-3442
304 E 94th St 6 New York (10128) ***(G-12319)***
Telesite USA Inc 631 952-2288
89 Arkay Dr Hauppauge (11788) ***(G-6237)***
Teller Printing Corp 718 486-3662
317 Division Ave Brooklyn (11211) ***(G-2674)***
Telmar Information Services (PA) 212 725-3000
711 3rd Ave Rm 1500 New York (10017) ***(G-12320)***
Telog Instruments Inc 585 742-3000
830 Canning Pkwy Victor (14564) ***(G-16531)***
Telxon Corporation (HQ) 631 738-2400
1 Zebra Plz Holtsville (11742) ***(G-6539)***
Tempco Glass Fabrication LLC 718 461-6888
13110 Maple Ave Flushing (11355) ***(G-5305)***
Temper Corporation (PA) 518 853-3467
544 Persse Rd Fonda (12068) ***(G-5322)***
Temper Corporation 518 853-3467
544 Persse Rd Fonda (12068) ***(G-5323)***
Temple Bar, New York *Also called Lafayette Pub Inc* ***(G-10952)***
Temple St Clair LLC 212 219-8664
594 Broadway Rm 306 New York (10012) ***(G-12321)***
Tempo Industries Inc 516 334-6900
90 Hopper St Westbury (11590) ***(G-17060)***
Tempo Paris, New York *Also called 6th Avenue Showcase Inc* ***(G-9024)***
Temptu Inc 718 937-9503
522 46th Ave Ste B Long Island City (11101) ***(G-7926)***
Temrex Corporation (PA) 516 868-6221
300 Buffalo Ave Freeport (11520) ***(G-5441)***
Temrick Inc 631 567-8860
1605 Sycamore Ave Unit B Bohemia (11716) ***(G-1139)***
Tenby LLC 646 863-5890
344 W 38th St Fl 3 New York (10018) ***(G-12322)***
Tenney Media Group (PA) 315 853-5569
28 Robinson Rd Clinton (13323) ***(G-3747)***
Tennyson Machine Co Inc 914 668-5468
535 S 5th Ave Mount Vernon (10550) ***(G-8783)***
Tens Machine Company Inc 631 981-3321
800 Grundy Ave Holbrook (11741) ***(G-6505)***
Tensa Software 914 686-5376
66 Greenvale Cir White Plains (10607) ***(G-17203)***
Tensator Group, Bay Shore *Also called Tensator Inc* ***(G-744)***
Tensator Inc 631 666-0300
260 Spur Dr S Bay Shore (11706) ***(G-744)***
Tent and Table Com LLC 716 570-0258
2845 Bailey Ave Buffalo (14215) ***(G-3239)***
Tentina Window Fashions Inc 631 957-9585
1186 Route 109 Lindenhurst (11757) ***(G-7513)***
Tequipment Inc 516 922-3508
7 Norden Ln Huntington Station (11746) ***(G-6764)***
Terahertz Technologies Inc 315 736-3642
169 Clear Rd Oriskany (13424) ***(G-13340)***
Terani Couture, New York *Also called Countess Corporation* ***(G-9794)***
Terbo Ltd 718 847-2860
8905 130th St Richmond Hill (11418) ***(G-14099)***
Termatec Molding Inc 315 483-4150
28 Foley Dr Sodus (14551) ***(G-15527)***
Terphane Holdings LLC (HQ) 585 657-5800
2754 W Park Dr Bloomfield (14469) ***(G-984)***
Terphane Inc 585 657-5800
2754 W Park Dr Bloomfield (14469) ***(G-985)***
Terra Enrgy Resource Tech Inc (PA) 212 286-9197
99 Park Ave Ph A New York (10016) ***(G-12323)***
Terrace Management Inc 914 737-0400
119 Oregon Rd Cortlandt Manor (10567) ***(G-4080)***
Terranua US Corp 212 852-9028
535 5th Ave Fl 4 New York (10017) ***(G-12324)***

ALPHABETIC

(PA)=Parent Co (HQ)=Headquarters (DH)=Div Headquarters
2018 Harris New York Manufacturers Directory
1073

Terrapin Station Ltd.....716 874-6677
1172 Hertel Ave Buffalo (14216) ***(G-3240)***
Terrells Potato Chip Co Inc.....315 437-2786
218 Midler Park Dr Syracuse (13206) ***(G-16081)***
Terrys Transmission.....315 458-4333
6217 E Taft Rd North Syracuse (13212) ***(G-12969)***
Tesla Motors Inc.....212 206-1204
10 Columbus Cir Ste 102d New York (10019) ***(G-12325)***
Tessy Plastics Corp (PA).....315 689-3924
700 Visions Dr Skaneateles (13152) ***(G-15488)***
Tessy Plastics Corp.....315 689-3924
488 State Route 5 Elbridge (13060) ***(G-4639)***
Test Cloud, Huntington *Also called Pupa Tek Inc* ***(G-6710)***
Testa Communications Inc.....516 767-2500
25 Willowdale Ave Port Washington (11050) ***(G-13886)***
Testori Interiors Inc.....518 298-4400
107 Lwrnce Paqtte Indstrl Champlain (12919) ***(G-3574)***
Teva Womens Health Inc.....716 693-6230
825 Wurlitzer Dr North Tonawanda (14120) ***(G-13020)***
Texas Brine Company LLC.....585 495-6228
1346 Saltvale Rd Wyoming (14591) ***(G-17398)***
Texas Home Security Inc (PA).....516 747-2100
50 Rose Pl New Hyde Park (11040) ***(G-8910)***
Texport Fabrics Corp.....212 226-6066
495 Broadway Fl 7 New York (10012) ***(G-12326)***
Texray, New York *Also called Z-Ply Corp* ***(G-12721)***
Texture Plus Inc.....631 218-9200
1611 Lakeland Ave Bohemia (11716) ***(G-1140)***
Texwood Inc (u S A).....212 262-8383
850 7th Ave Ste 1000 New York (10019) ***(G-12327)***
TG Peppe Inc.....516 239-7852
299 Rockaway Tpke Unit B Lawrence (11559) ***(G-7426)***
Tg Therapeutics Inc.....212 554-4484
2 Gansevoort St Fl 9 New York (10014) ***(G-12328)***
Tgp Flying Cloud Holdings LLC.....646 829-3900
565 5th Ave Fl 27 New York (10017) ***(G-12329)***
Thales Laser SA.....585 223-2370
78 Schuyler Baldwin Dr Fairport (14450) ***(G-4891)***
Thalian, New York *Also called F & J Designs Inc* ***(G-10167)***
Thalle Industries Inc (PA).....914 762-3415
51 Route 100 Briarcliff Manor (10510) ***(G-1229)***
Thatcher Company New York Inc.....315 589-9330
4135 Rte 104 Williamson (14589) ***(G-17255)***
Thats My Girl Inc (PA).....212 695-0020
80 39th St Ste 501 Brooklyn (11232) ***(G-2675)***
Thayer Tool & Die Inc.....716 782-4841
1718 Blckvlle Watts Flts Ashville (14710) ***(G-427)***
The Caldwell Manufacturing Co (PA).....585 352-3790
2605 Manitou Rd Ste 100 Rochester (14624) ***(G-14748)***
The Caldwell Manufacturing Co.....585 352-2803
Holland Industrial Park Victor (14564) ***(G-16532)***
The Centro Company Inc.....914 533-2200
215 Silver Spring Rd South Salem (10590) ***(G-15561)***
The Chocolate Shop.....716 882-5055
871 Niagara St Buffalo (14213) ***(G-3241)***
THE Design Group Inc.....212 681-1548
240 Madison Ave Fl 8 New York (10016) ***(G-12330)***
The Earth Times Foundation.....718 297-0488
195 Adams St Apt 6j Brooklyn (11201) ***(G-2676)***
The Fisherman, Shirley *Also called L I F Publishing Corp* ***(G-15445)***
The Fisherman, Shirley *Also called Njf Publishing Corp* ***(G-15450)***
The Gramecy Group.....518 348-1325
4 Gramecy Ct Clifton Park (12065) ***(G-3736)***
The Hacker Quarterly, Saint James *Also called 2600 Enterprises Inc* ***(G-15113)***
The Kingsbury Printing Co Inc.....518 747-6606
110 Franklin St Hudson Falls (12839) ***(G-6681)***
The Nugent Organization Inc.....212 645-6600
3433 Ocean Harbor Dr Oceanside (11572) ***(G-13123)***
The Observer, Dundee *Also called Finger Lakes Media Inc* ***(G-4352)***
The Observer, Dunkirk *Also called Observer Daily Sunday Newsppr* ***(G-4370)***
The Printing Company, Albany *Also called Printing Resources Inc* ***(G-124)***
The PRS Group Inc (PA).....315 431-0511
5800 Hrtge Lndng Dr Ste E East Syracuse (13057) ***(G-4583)***
The River Reporter, Narrowsburg *Also called Stuart Communications Inc* ***(G-8815)***
The Sandhar Corp.....718 523-0819
16427 Highland Ave Jamaica (11432) ***(G-6994)***
The Smoke House of Catskills.....845 246-8767
724 Route 212 Saugerties (12477) ***(G-15226)***
The Spirited Shipper, Long Island City *Also called Platinum Sales Promotion Inc* ***(G-7874)***
The Spotlight, Delmar *Also called Newsgraphics of Delmar Inc* ***(G-4270)***
The Swatch Group U S Inc.....212 297-9192
56 Grand Central Terminal New York (10017) ***(G-12331)***
Theautopartsshop.com, Hauppauge *Also called Ebc Technologies LLC* ***(G-6091)***
Thego Corporation.....631 776-2472
2 Mooring Dr Bellport (11713) ***(G-838)***
Thehuffingtonpostcom Inc (HQ).....212 245-7844
770 Broadway Fl 4 New York (10003) ***(G-12332)***
Theirapp LLC.....212 896-1255
880 3rd Ave New York (10022) ***(G-12333)***
Themis Chimney Inc.....718 937-4716
190 Morgan Ave Brooklyn (11237) ***(G-2677)***
Theodore A Rapp Associates.....845 469-2100
728 Craigville Rd Chester (10918) ***(G-3647)***
Theodosiou Inc.....718 728-6800
3214 49th St Long Island City (11103) ***(G-7927)***
Theory LLC.....212 762-2300
1114 Avenue Of The Americ New York (10036) ***(G-12334)***
Theory LLC.....212 879-0265
1157 Madison Ave New York (10028) ***(G-12335)***
Theory LLC.....631 204-0231
98 Main St Southampton (11968) ***(G-15577)***
Therese The Childrens Collectn.....518 346-2315
301 Nott St Schenectady (12305) ***(G-15328)***
Therm Incorporated.....607 272-8500
1000 Hudson Street Ext Ithaca (14850) ***(G-6912)***
Thermal Foams/Syracuse Inc (PA).....716 874-6474
2101 Kenmore Ave Buffalo (14207) ***(G-3242)***
Thermal Foams/Syracuse Inc.....315 699-8734
6173 S Bay Rd Cicero (13039) ***(G-3680)***
Thermal Process Cnstr Co.....631 293-6400
19 Engineers Ln Farmingdale (11735) ***(G-5139)***
Thermal Tech Doors Inc (PA).....516 745-0100
576 Brook St Garden City (11530) ***(G-5548)***
Thermo Cidtec Inc.....315 451-9410
101 Commerce Blvd Liverpool (13088) ***(G-7580)***
Thermo Fisher Scientific Inc.....716 774-6700
3175 Staley Rd Grand Island (14072) ***(G-5786)***
Thermo Fisher Scientific Inc.....585 458-8008
1999 Mnt Rd Blvd 1-3 Bldg 13 Rochester (14615) ***(G-14749)***
Thermo Fisher Scientific Inc.....585 899-7610
75 Panorama Creek Dr Rochester (14625) ***(G-14750)***
Thermoaura Inc.....518 813-4997
132b Railroad Ave Ste B Albany (12205) ***(G-142)***
Thermold Corporation.....315 697-3924
7059 Harp Rd Canastota (13032) ***(G-3400)***
Thermopatch Corporation (PA).....315 446-8110
2204 Erie Blvd E Syracuse (13224) ***(G-16082)***
Thermotech Corp.....716 823-3311
3 Bradford St Buffalo (14210) ***(G-3243)***
Theskimm Inc.....212 228-4628
49 W 23rd St Fl 10 New York (10010) ***(G-12336)***
Thestreet Inc (PA).....212 321-5000
14 Wall St Fl 15 New York (10005) ***(G-12337)***
Theta Industries Inc.....516 883-4088
26 Valley Rd Ste 1 Port Washington (11050) ***(G-13887)***
Thewritedeal, New York *Also called Dezawy LLC* ***(G-9918)***
Thing Daemon Inc.....917 746-9895
96 Spring St Fl 5 New York (10012) ***(G-12338)***
Think Green Junk Removal Inc.....845 297-7771
29 Meadow Wood Ln Wappingers Falls (12590) ***(G-16597)***
Think Tank, New York *Also called City and State Ny LLC* ***(G-9680)***
Thinktrek Inc.....212 884-8399
420 Lexington Ave Rm 300 New York (10170) ***(G-12339)***
Thirsty Owl Wine Company.....607 869-5805
6861 State Route 89 Ovid (14521) ***(G-13374)***
This Business Is Tribaly Owned, Irving *Also called Seneca Nation Enterprise* ***(G-6807)***
Thistle Hill Weavers.....518 284-2729
101 Chestnut Ridge Rd Cherry Valley (13320) ***(G-3624)***
Thom McGinnes Excavating Plbg, Le Roy *Also called T S P Corp* ***(G-7441)***
Thomas C Wilson, Long Island City *Also called Thomas C Wilson LLC* ***(G-7928)***
Thomas C Wilson LLC.....718 729-3360
2111 44th Ave Long Island City (11101) ***(G-7928)***
Thomas Electronics Inc (PA).....315 923-2051
208 Davis Pkwy Clyde (14433) ***(G-3757)***
Thomas Enterprise Solutions, New York *Also called Thomas Publishing Company LLC* ***(G-12342)***
Thomas Foundry LLC.....315 361-9048
559 Fitch St Oneida (13421) ***(G-13190)***
Thomas Group Inc.....212 947-6400
131 Varick St Rm 1016 New York (10013) ***(G-12340)***
Thomas Group, The, New York *Also called Thomas Group Inc* ***(G-12340)***
Thomas International Pubg Co (HQ).....212 613-3441
5 Penn Plz Fl 15 New York (10001) ***(G-12341)***
Thomas Jefferson Press, Port Jefferson *Also called Pace Walkers of America Inc* ***(G-13800)***
Thomas Matthews Wdwkg Ltd.....631 287-3657
15 Powell Ave Southampton (11968) ***(G-15578)***
Thomas Matthews Wdwkg Ltd (PA).....631 287-2023
225 Ocean View Pkwy Southampton (11968) ***(G-15579)***
Thomas Publishing Company LLC (PA).....212 695-0500
5 Penn Plz Fl 9 New York (10001) ***(G-12342)***
Thomas Publishing Company LLC.....212 695-0500
5 Penn Plz Fl 9 New York (10001) ***(G-12343)***
Thomas Publishing Company LLC.....212 695-0500
5 Penn Plz Fl 8 New York (10001) ***(G-12344)***
Thomas Publishing Company LLC.....212 695-0500
5 Penn Plz Fl 9 New York (10001) ***(G-12345)***
Thomas R Schul TEC GL & Inst, Marion *Also called TEC Glass & Inst LLC* ***(G-8132)***
Thomas Sasson Co Inc.....212 697-4998
555 5th Ave Rm 1900 New York (10017) ***(G-12346)***
Thompson Ferrier LLC.....212 244-2212
230 5th Ave Ste 1004 New York (10001) ***(G-12347)***
Thompson Group, Troy *Also called Pitney Bowes Software Inc* ***(G-16272)***

Thompson Overhead Door Co Inc 718 788-2470
47 16th St Brooklyn (11215) *(G-2678)*
Thomson Industries Inc (PA) 716 691-9100
45 Hazelwood Dr Amherst (14228) *(G-266)*
Thomson Press (india) Limited 646 318-0369
4 Court Sq Fl 3rm2 Long Island City (11101) *(G-7929)*
Thomson Reuters Corporation 212 393-9461
500 Pearl St New York (10007) *(G-12348)*
Thomson Reuters Corporation (HQ) 646 223-4000
3 Times Sq New York (10036) *(G-12349)*
Thor Marketing Corp 201 247-7103
616 Corporate Way Ste 2 Valley Cottage (10989) *(G-16419)*
Thornwillow Press Ltd 212 980-0738
57 W 58th St Ste 11e New York (10019) *(G-12350)*
Thornwood Products Ltd 914 769-9161
401 Claremont Ave Ste 7 Thornwood (10594) *(G-16144)*
Thousand Island Ready Mix Con 315 686-3203
38760 State Route 180 La Fargeville (13656) *(G-7264)*
Thousand Islands Printing Co 315 482-2581
45501 St Rt 12 Alexandria Bay (13607) *(G-194)*
Thousand Islands Sun, Alexandria Bay *Also called Thousand Islands Printing Co (G-194)*
Thousand Islands Winery LLC 315 482-9306
43298 Seaway Ave Ste 1 Alexandria Bay (13607) *(G-195)*
Thread Check Inc 631 231-1515
390 Oser Ave Ste 2 Hauppauge (11788) *(G-6238)*
Thread LLC (PA) 212 414-8844
26 W 17th St Rm 301 New York (10011) *(G-12351)*
Three Brothers Winery, Geneva *Also called Negys New Land Vinyrd Winery (G-5595)*
Three Five III-V Materials Inc 212 213-8290
19 W 21st St Rm 203 New York (10010) *(G-12352)*
Three Gems Inc 516 248-0388
2201 Hillside Ave New Hyde Park (11040) *(G-8911)*
Three Point Ventures LLC 585 697-3444
3495 Winton Pl Ste E120 Rochester (14623) *(G-14751)*
Three R Enterprises Inc 585 254-5050
447 Adirondack St Rochester (14606) *(G-14752)*
Three Star Offset Printing 516 867-8223
188 N Main St Freeport (11520) *(G-5442)*
Three Star Supply, Jamaica *Also called City Mason Corp (G-6939)*
Three Tarts, New York *Also called Creative Relations LLC (G-9809)*
Three V, Brooklyn *Also called 3v Company Inc (G-1516)*
Three Village Times, Mineola *Also called Westbury Times (G-8572)*
Thuro Metal Products Inc (PA) 631 435-0444
21-25 Grand Blvd N Brentwood (11717) *(G-1194)*
Thyssenkrupp Elevator Corp 212 268-2020
519 8th Ave Fl 6 New York (10018) *(G-12353)*
Thyssenkrupp Materials NA Inc 212 972-8800
489 5th Ave Fl 20 New York (10017) *(G-12354)*
Thyssenkrupp Materials NA Inc 585 279-0000
1673 Lyell Ave Rochester (14606) *(G-14753)*
TI Group Auto Systems LLC 315 568-7042
240 Fall St Seneca Falls (13148) *(G-15394)*
Tia Lattrell 845 373-9494
13 Powder House Rd Amenia (12501) *(G-220)*
Tibana Finishing Inc 718 417-5375
1630 Cody Ave Ridgewood (11385) *(G-14140)*
Tibro Water Technologies Ltd 647 426-3415
106 E Seneca St Unit 25 Sherrill (13461) *(G-15432)*
Tic TAC Toes Mfg Corp 518 773-8187
1 Hamilton St Gloversville (12078) *(G-5741)*
Tickle Hill Winery 607 546-7740
3831 Ball Diamond Rd Hector (14841) *(G-6286)*
Ticonderoga Mch & Wldg Corp 518 585-7444
55 Race Track Rd Ticonderoga (12883) *(G-16151)*
Ticonium Division, Albany *Also called Cmp Industries LLC (G-66)*
Tie King Inc (PA) 718 768-8484
243 44th St Brooklyn (11232) *(G-2679)*
Tie King Inc 212 714-9611
42 W 38th St Rm 1200 New York (10018) *(G-12355)*
Tie View Neckwear Co Inc 718 853-4156
1559 58th St Brooklyn (11219) *(G-2680)*
Tiedemann Waldemar Inc 716 875-5665
1720 Military Rd Ste 2 Buffalo (14217) *(G-3244)*
Tien Wah Press, New York *Also called Twp America Inc (G-12453)*
Tiffen Co, The, Hauppauge *Also called Tiffen Company LLC (G-6239)*
Tiffen Company LLC 631 273-2500
80 Oser Ave Hauppauge (11788) *(G-6239)*
Tiffen Company LLC (PA) 631 273-2500
90 Oser Ave Hauppauge (11788) *(G-6240)*
Tiga Holdings Inc 845 838-3000
74 Dennings Ave Beacon (12508) *(G-786)*
Tiger 21 LLC 212 360-1700
1995 Broadway Fl 6 New York (10023) *(G-12356)*
Tiger Fashion Inc 212 244-1175
20 W 36th St Frnt New York (10018) *(G-12357)*
Tiger J LLC (PA) 212 465-9300
1430 Broadway Rm 1900 New York (10018) *(G-12358)*
Tiger Supply Inc 631 293-2700
99 Sherwood Ave Farmingdale (11735) *(G-5140)*
Tigerstar Records, New York *Also called Imago Recording Company (G-10615)*
Tii Industries Inc 631 789-5000
1385 Akron St Copiague (11726) *(G-3956)*
Tii Technologies Inc (HQ) 516 364-9300
141 Rodeo Dr Edgewood (11717) *(G-4629)*
Tika Mobile Inc (PA) 646 650-5545
902 Broadway Fl 6 New York (10010) *(G-12359)*
Tikamobile, New York *Also called Tika Mobile Inc (G-12359)*
Tiki Industries Inc 516 779-3629
8 Tree Haven Ln Riverhead (11901) *(G-14171)*
Tilaros Bakery Inc 716 488-3209
32 Willard St Ste 34 Jamestown (14701) *(G-7070)*
Tilcon New York Inc (HQ) 845 358-4500
162 Old Mill Rd West Nyack (10994) *(G-16957)*
Tilcon New York Inc 845 778-5591
272 Berea Rd Walden (12586) *(G-16557)*
Tilcon New York Inc 845 480-3249
3466 College Point Blvd Flushing (11354) *(G-5306)*
Tilcon New York Inc 845 615-0216
2 Quarry Rd Goshen (10924) *(G-5754)*
Tilcon New York Inc 845 457-3158
215 Montgomery Rd Montgomery (12549) *(G-8639)*
Tilcon New York Inc 845 942-0602
Fort Of Elm Tomkins Cove (10986) *(G-16153)*
Tilcon New York Inc 845 358-3100
1 Crusher Rd West Nyack (10994) *(G-16958)*
Tile Shop Inc 585 424-2180
420 Jefferson Rd Ste 3 Rochester (14623) *(G-14754)*
Tillsonburg Company USA Inc 267 994-8096
37 W 39th St Rm 1101 New York (10018) *(G-12360)*
Tim Cretin Logging & Sawmill 315 946-4476
3607 Wayne Center Rd Lyons (14489) *(G-8003)*
Timber Frames Inc 585 374-6405
5557 State Route 64 Canandaigua (14424) *(G-3388)*
Time Base Consoles, Edgewood *Also called Time Base Corporation (G-4630)*
Time Base Corporation (PA) 631 293-4068
170 Rodeo Dr Edgewood (11717) *(G-4630)*
Time Home Entertainment Inc 212 522-1212
1271 Ave Of The Americas New York (10020) *(G-12361)*
Time Inc 212 522-1212
1271 Avenue Of The Americ New York (10020) *(G-12362)*
Time Inc (PA) 212 522-1212
225 Liberty St Ste C2 New York (10281) *(G-12363)*
Time Inc 212 522-0361
1271 Ave Of The Amer Sb7 New York (10020) *(G-12364)*
Time Inc Affluent Media Group (HQ) 212 382-5600
1120 Ave Of The Americas New York (10036) *(G-12365)*
Time Inc Affluent Media Group (HQ) 212 382-5600
1120 Ave Of The Americas New York (10036) *(G-12366)*
Time Journal, Cobleskill *Also called Division Street News Corp (G-3761)*
Time Out New York Partners LP 646 432-3000
475 10th Ave Fl 12 New York (10018) *(G-12367)*
Time Precision, Carmel *Also called Precision Arms Inc (G-3432)*
Time Release Sciences Inc 716 823-4580
205 Dingens St Buffalo (14206) *(G-3245)*
Time Square Lighting, Stony Point *Also called Times Square Stage Ltg Co Inc (G-15800)*
Time To Know Inc 212 230-1210
655 3rd Ave Fl 21 New York (10017) *(G-12368)*
Time Warner Companies Inc (HQ) 212 484-8000
1 Time Warner Ctr Bsmt B New York (10019) *(G-12369)*
Time-Cap Laboratories Inc 631 753-9090
7 Michael Ave Farmingdale (11735) *(G-5141)*
Time2vape LLC 718 335-0401
9219 Roosevelt Ave Jackson Heights (11372) *(G-6924)*
Timeless Decor LLC 315 782-5759
22419 Fisher Rd Watertown (13601) *(G-16697)*
Timeless Fashions LLC 212 730-9328
100 United Nations Plz New York (10017) *(G-12370)*
Timeless Frames, Watertown *Also called Lco Destiny LLC (G-16684)*
Timely Signs Inc 516 285-5339
2135 Linden Blvd Elmont (11003) *(G-4740)*
Timely Signs of Kingston Inc 845 331-8710
154 Clinton Ave Fl 1 Kingston (12401) *(G-7243)*
Times Beacon Record Newspapers (PA) 631 331-1154
185 Route 25a Ste 4 East Setauket (11733) *(G-4513)*
Times Center, The, New York *Also called New York Times Company (G-11430)*
Times Herald, The, Olean *Also called Bradford Publications Inc (G-13157)*
Times Herald-Record, Middletown *Also called Local Media Group Inc (G-8482)*
Times Herald-Record, Monticello *Also called Local Media Group Inc (G-8643)*
Times Herald-Record, Kingston *Also called Local Media Group Inc (G-7226)*
Times News Weekly, Ridgewood *Also called Ridgewood Times Prtg & Pubg (G-14134)*
Times Review Newspaper Corp 631 354-8031
7780 Main Rd Mattituck (11952) *(G-8243)*
Times Square Stage Ltg Co Inc 845 947-3034
5 Holt Dr Stony Point (10980) *(G-15800)*
Times Square Studios Ltd 212 930-7720
1500 Broadway Fl 2 New York (10036) *(G-12371)*
Timing Group LLC 646 878-2600
237 W 37th St Ste 1100 New York (10018) *(G-12372)*
Timothy L Simpson 518 234-1401
5819 State Route 145 Sharon Springs (13459) *(G-15407)*
Tin Box Company of America Inc (PA) 631 845-1600
216 Sherwood Ave Farmingdale (11735) *(G-5142)*

ALPHABETIC

(PA)=Parent Co (HQ)=Headquarters (DH)=Div Headquarters
2018 Harris
New York Manufacturers Directory
1075

Tint World ALPHABETIC SECTION

Tint World.....631 458-1999
3165 Route 112 Medford (11763) ***(G-8295)***
Tio Foods LLC.....305 672-6645
115 W 18th St Fl 2 New York (10011) ***(G-12373)***
Tio Gazpacho, New York *Also called Tio Foods LLC **(G-12373)***
Tioga County Courier.....607 687-0108
59 Church St Owego (13827) ***(G-13385)***
Tioga County Waste Wood Recycl, Owego *Also called Wholesale Mulch & Sawdust Inc **(G-13387)***
Tioga Hardwoods Inc (PA).....607 657-8686
12685 State Route 38 Berkshire (13736) ***(G-852)***
Tioga Tool Inc (PA).....607 785-6005
160 Glendale Dr Endicott (13760) ***(G-4835)***
Tips & Dies Inc.....315 337-4161
505 Rome Industrial Park Rome (13440) ***(G-14865)***
Tire Conversion Tech Inc.....518 372-1600
874 Albany Shaker Rd Latham (12110) ***(G-7406)***
Tishcon Corp (PA).....516 333-3056
30 New York Ave Westbury (11590) ***(G-17061)***
Tishcon Corp.....516 333-3056
30 New York Ave Westbury (11590) ***(G-17062)***
Tishcon Corp.....516 333-3050
41 New York Ave Westbury (11590) ***(G-17063)***
Tishcon Corp.....516 333-3050
36 New York Ave Westbury (11590) ***(G-17064)***
Titan Controls Inc.....516 358-2407
122 W 27th St Fl 5 New York (10001) ***(G-12374)***
Titan Steel Corp.....315 656-7046
6333 N Kirkville Rd Kirkville (13082) ***(G-7256)***
Titan Technology Group, New York *Also called Ttg LLC **(G-12440)***
Titanium Dem Remediation Group.....716 433-4100
4907 I D A Park Dr Lockport (14094) ***(G-7650)***
Titanx Engine Cooling Inc.....716 665-7129
2258 Allen Street Ext Jamestown (14701) ***(G-7071)***
Titchener Iron Works Division, Binghamton *Also called Moro Corporation **(G-933)***
Titherington Design & Mfg.....518 324-2205
102 Sharron Ave Unit 1 Plattsburgh (12901) ***(G-13733)***
Title of Work, New York *Also called Jonathan Meizler LLC **(G-10797)***
Tito Moldmaker Co, New York *Also called Vasquez Tito **(G-12533)***
Titus Mountain Sand & Grav LLC.....518 483-3740
17 Junction Rd Malone (12953) ***(G-8049)***
Tj Powder Coaters LLC.....607 724-4779
24 Broad St Binghamton (13904) ***(G-949)***
Tj Signs Unlimited LLC.....631 273-4800
171 Freeman Ave Islip (11751) ***(G-6853)***
Tjb Sunshine Enterprises.....518 384-6483
6 Redwood Dr Ballston Lake (12019) ***(G-587)***
Tkm Technologies Inc.....631 474-4700
623 Bicycle Path Ste 5 Port Jeff STA (11776) ***(G-13796)***
TLC Vision (usa) Corporation.....914 395-3949
150 Central Park Ave Hartsdale (10530) ***(G-6021)***
TLC-Lc Inc (PA).....212 756-8900
115 E 57th St Bsmt New York (10022) ***(G-12375)***
TLC-The Light Connection Inc.....315 736-7384
132 Base Rd Oriskany (13424) ***(G-13341)***
Tlf Graphics, Rochester *Also called T L F Graphics Inc **(G-14740)***
Tli Import Inc.....917 578-4568
151 2nd Ave Brooklyn (11215) ***(G-2681)***
Tlsi Incorporated.....631 470-8880
780 Park Ave Huntington (11743) ***(G-6726)***
Tm Music Inc.....212 471-4000
9 E 63rd St Apt 2-3 New York (10065) ***(G-12376)***
TMC Usa LLC (PA).....518 587-8920
60 Railroad Pl Ste 501 Saratoga Springs (12866) ***(G-15205)***
Tmp Technologies Inc (PA).....716 895-6100
1200 Northland Ave Buffalo (14215) ***(G-3246)***
Tmp Technologies Inc.....585 495-6231
6110 Lamb Rd Wyoming (14591) ***(G-17399)***
Tms Development, Westbury *Also called Vescom Structural Systems Inc **(G-17070)***
Tntpaving.....607 372-4911
1077 Taft Ave Endicott (13760) ***(G-4836)***
To Dey, New York *Also called T O Dey Service Corp **(G-12290)***
Tobay Printing Co Inc.....631 842-3300
1361 Marconi Blvd Copiague (11726) ***(G-3957)***
Tobeyco Manufacturing Co Inc.....607 962-2446
165 Cedar St Corning (14830) ***(G-4004)***
Tocare LLC.....718 767-0618
15043b 14th Ave Fl 1 Whitestone (11357) ***(G-17244)***
Today Media, Rye *Also called Martinelli Holdings LLC **(G-15088)***
Todaysgentleman.com, Lynbrook *Also called Adf Accessories Inc **(G-7971)***
Todd Enterprises, West Babylon *Also called Chem-Tainer Industries Inc **(G-16808)***
Todd Enterprises Inc.....516 773-8087
747 Middle Neck Rd # 103 Great Neck (11024) ***(G-5863)***
Todd Systems Inc.....914 963-3400
50 Ash St Yonkers (10701) ***(G-17507)***
Todd Walbridge.....585 254-3018
1916 Lyell Ave Rochester (14606) ***(G-14755)***
Todt Hill Audiological Svcs.....718 816-1952
78 Todt Hill Rd Ste 202 Staten Island (10314) ***(G-15771)***
Toga Manufacturing Inc (HQ).....631 242-4800
200 Heartland Blvd Edgewood (11717) ***(G-4631)***
Toho Shoji (new York) Inc.....212 868-7466
990 Avenue Of The America New York (10018) ***(G-12377)***
Token, Brooklyn *Also called 3phase Industries LLC **(G-1514)***
Tokens, Staten Island *Also called Maxine Denker Inc **(G-15725)***
Tokion Magazine, New York *Also called Downtown Media Group LLC **(G-9970)***
Tokyo Electron America Inc.....518 289-3100
2 Bayberry Dr Malta (12020) ***(G-8053)***
Tokyo Electron America Inc.....518 292-4200
255 Fuller Rd Ste 214 Albany (12203) ***(G-143)***
Toledo Graphics Group, Farmingdale *Also called Desktop Publishing Concepts **(G-4985)***
Toltec Fabrics Inc.....212 706-9310
437 5th Ave Fl 10 New York (10016) ***(G-12378)***
Tom & Jerry Printcraft Forms (PA).....914 777-7468
960 Mamaroneck Ave Mamaroneck (10543) ***(G-8081)***
Tom & Linda Platt Inc.....212 221-7208
29 W 38th St Rm 6l New York (10018) ***(G-12379)***
Tom Dixon, New York *Also called Design Research Ltd **(G-9907)***
Tom Doherty Associates Inc.....212 388-0100
175 5th Ave Frnt 1 New York (10010) ***(G-12380)***
Tom James Company.....212 581-6968
641 Lexington Ave Fl 19 New York (10022) ***(G-12381)***
Tom James Company.....212 593-0204
717 5th Ave New York (10022) ***(G-12382)***
Tom Moriber Furs Inc.....212 244-2180
345 7th Ave Fl 19 New York (10001) ***(G-12383)***
Tomas Maier.....212 988-8686
956 Madison Ave Frnt 1 New York (10021) ***(G-12384)***
Tomia Beauty Brands LLC.....917 301-0125
38 W 21st St New York (10010) ***(G-12385)***
Tomia Beauty Supply, New York *Also called Tomia Beauty Brands LLC **(G-12385)***
Tomkins USA, Syracuse *Also called Tompkins Srm LLC **(G-16083)***
Tommy Boy Entertainment LLC.....212 388-8300
220 E 23rd St Ste 400 New York (10010) ***(G-12386)***
Tommy John Inc.....800 708-3490
100 Broadway Ste 1101 New York (10005) ***(G-12387)***
Tomorrow Group, The, Albany *Also called Saratoga Trunk and Furniture **(G-131)***
Tompkins Metal Finishing Inc.....585 344-2600
6 Apollo Dr Batavia (14020) ***(G-650)***
Tompkins Srm LLC.....315 422-8763
623 Oneida St Syracuse (13202) ***(G-16083)***
Tompkins Weekly Inc.....607 539-7100
36 Besemer Rd Ithaca (14850) ***(G-6913)***
Tomric Plastic, Buffalo *Also called Chocolate Delivery Systems Inc **(G-2892)***
Tomric Systems Inc.....716 854-6050
85 River Rock Dr Buffalo (14207) ***(G-3247)***
Tonanwanda News, Niagara Falls *Also called Community Newsppr Holdings Inc **(G-12827)***
Tonawanda Coke Corporation (PA).....716 876-6222
3875 River Rd Tonawanda (14150) ***(G-16226)***
Tonawanda Limb & Brace Inc.....716 695-1131
545 Delaware St Tonawanda (14150) ***(G-16227)***
Tonche Timber LLC.....845 389-3489
3959 State Highway 30 Amsterdam (12010) ***(G-370)***
Toner-N-More Inc.....718 232-6200
2220 65th St Ste 103 Brooklyn (11204) ***(G-2682)***
Tongli Pharmaceuticals USA Inc (PA).....212 842-8837
4260 Main St Apt 6f Flushing (11355) ***(G-5307)***
Toni Industries Inc.....212 921-0700
111 Great Neck Rd Ste 305 Great Neck (11021) ***(G-5864)***
Tonix Phrmceuticals Holdg Corp (PA).....212 980-9155
509 Madison Ave Rm 306 New York (10022) ***(G-12388)***
Tonner Doll Company Inc (PA).....845 339-9537
1094 Morton Blvd Kingston (12401) ***(G-7244)***
Tonoga Inc (PA).....518 658-3202
136 Coon Brook Rd Petersburg (12138) ***(G-13551)***
Tony Baird Electronics Inc.....315 422-4430
461 E Brighton Ave Syracuse (13210) ***(G-16084)***
Tonys Ornamental Ir Works Inc.....315 337-3730
6757 Martin St Rome (13440) ***(G-14866)***
Tooling Enterprises Inc.....716 842-0445
680 New Babcock St Ste 1 Buffalo (14206) ***(G-3248)***
Toolroom Express Inc.....607 723-5373
1010 Conklin Rd Conklin (13748) ***(G-3902)***
Tools & Stamping Corp.....718 392-4040
48 Eagle St Brooklyn (11222) ***(G-2683)***
Tootter Inc.....212 204-7937
1470 Royce St Brooklyn (11234) ***(G-2684)***
Top Copi Reproductions Inc.....212 571-4141
160 Broadway Fl 3 New York (10038) ***(G-12389)***
Top Fortune Usa Ltd.....516 608-2694
100 Atlantic Ave Ste 2 Lynbrook (11563) ***(G-7991)***
Top Line, New York *Also called Pro Line Manufacturing Co LLC **(G-11745)***
Top Quality Products Inc.....212 213-1988
1173 Broadway New York (10001) ***(G-12390)***
Top Shelf Jewelry Inc.....845 647-4661
206 Canal St Ellenville (12428) ***(G-4653)***
Top Stuff, New York *Also called Isfel Co Inc **(G-10708)***
Topaz Industries Inc.....631 207-0700
130 Corporate Dr Holtsville (11742) ***(G-6540)***
Topiderm Inc (PA).....631 226-7979
5200 New Horizons Blvd Amityville (11701) ***(G-330)***

ALPHABETIC SECTION

Trane US Inc

Topix Pharmaceuticals Inc (PA) 631 226-7979
5200 New Horizons Blvd Amityville (11701) *(G-331)*
Topoo Industries Incorporated 718 331-3755
7815 16th Ave Brooklyn (11214) *(G-2685)*
Toppan Printing Co Amer Inc (HQ) 212 596-7747
747 3rd Ave Fl 7 New York (10017) *(G-12391)*
Toppan Vintage Inc (PA) 212 596-7747
747 3rd Ave Fl 7 New York (10017) *(G-12392)*
Topps-All Products of Yonkers 914 968-4226
148 Ludlow St Ste 2 Yonkers (10705) *(G-17508)*
Toprint Ltd 718 439-0469
6110 7th Ave Brooklyn (11220) *(G-2686)*
Toptec Products LLC 631 421-9800
1225 Walt Whitman Rd Melville (11747) *(G-8391)*
Tor Books, New York *Also called Tom Doherty Associates Inc (G-12380)*
Toray Holding (usa) Inc (HQ) 212 697-8150
461 5th Ave Fl 9 New York (10017) *(G-12393)*
Toray Industries Inc 212 697-8150
600 3rd Ave Fl 5 New York (10016) *(G-12394)*
Torch Graphics Inc 212 679-4334
1001 Ave Of The Americas New York (10018) *(G-12395)*
Torino Indus Fabrication Inc 631 509-1640
4 Pinehurst Dr Bellport (11713) *(G-839)*
Torino Industrial Inc 631 509-1640
4 Pinehurst Dr Bellport (11713) *(G-840)*
Torino Industrial Fabrication, Bellport *Also called Torino Industrial Inc (G-840)*
Tork Inc (PA) 914 664-3542
50 S Macquesten Pkwy Mount Vernon (10550) *(G-8784)*
Toronto Metal Spinning and Ltg 905 793-1174
4500 Witmer Indus Ests Niagara Falls (14305) *(G-12900)*
Torotron Corporation 718 428-6992
18508 Union Tpke Ste 101 Fresh Meadows (11366) *(G-5460)*
Torre Products Co Inc 212 925-8989
479 Washington St New York (10013) *(G-12396)*
Torrent Ems LLC 716 312-4099
190 Walnut St Lockport (14094) *(G-7651)*
Torrington Industries Inc 315 676-4662
90 Corporate Park Dr Central Square (13036) *(G-3545)*
Torrone Outdoor Displays, Staten Island *Also called Frank Torrone & Sons Inc (G-15695)*
Torsaf Printers Inc 516 569-5577
1315 Broadway Unit B Hewlett (11557) *(G-6337)*
Tortilla Heaven Inc 845 339-1550
97 Abeel St Kingston (12401) *(G-7245)*
Tortilleria Chinantla Inc 718 302-0101
975 Grand St Brooklyn (11211) *(G-2687)*
Tory Electric 914 292-5036
641 Old Post Rd Bedford (10506) *(G-794)*
Tosca Brick Oven Pizza Real 718 430-0026
4038 E Tremont Ave Bronx (10465) *(G-1471)*
Tosch Products Ltd 315 672-3040
25 Main St Camillus (13031) *(G-3353)*
Toshiba Amer Info Systems Inc (HQ) 949 583-3000
1251 Ave Of The Ste 4110 New York (10020) *(G-12397)*
Toshiba America Inc (HQ) 212 596-0600
1251 Ave Of Ameri Ste 4100 New York (10020) *(G-12398)*
Total Concept Graphic Inc 212 229-2626
519 8th Ave Rm 805a New York (10018) *(G-12399)*
Total Display Solutions Inc 607 724-9999
1429 Upper Front St Binghamton (13901) *(G-950)*
Total Dntl Implant Sltions LLC 212 877-3777
260 W Sunrise Hwy Valley Stream (11581) *(G-16453)*
Total Energy Fabrication Corp 580 363-1500
2 Hardscrabble Rd North Salem (10560) *(G-12956)*
Total Machine and Welding, Bronx *Also called Coral Management Corp (G-1306)*
Total Metal Resource 718 384-7818
175 Bogart St Brooklyn (11206) *(G-2688)*
Total Offset Graphic, New York *Also called Total Offset Inc (G-12400)*
Total Offset Inc 212 966-4482
200 Hudson St Fl 11 New York (10013) *(G-12400)*
Total Piping Solutions Inc 716 372-0160
1760 Haskell Rd Olean (14760) *(G-13176)*
Total Solution Graphics Inc 718 706-1540
2511 49th Ave Long Island City (11101) *(G-7930)*
Total Webcasting Inc 845 883-0909
8 Bruce St New Paltz (12561) *(G-8924)*
Toto USA Inc 917 237-0665
20 W 22nd St Frnt 2 New York (10010) *(G-12401)*
Toto USA Inc 770 282-8686
20 W 22nd St Frnt 2 New York (10010) *(G-12402)*
Totowa Asphalt, West Nyack *Also called Tilcon New York Inc (G-16957)*
Touch Adjust Clip Co Inc 631 589-3077
1687 Roosevelt Ave Bohemia (11716) *(G-1141)*
Touch By A Memory, Ellenville *Also called Top Shelf Jewelry Inc (G-4653)*
Touch Tunes, New York *Also called Touchtunes Music Corporation (G-12403)*
Touchdown, New York *Also called Professnal Spt Pblications Inc (G-11749)*
Touchstone Technology Inc 585 458-2690
350 Mile Crossing Blvd Rochester (14624) *(G-14756)*
Touchtunes Music Corporation (HQ) 847 419-3300
850 3rd Ave Ste 15c New York (10022) *(G-12403)*
Toura LLC 646 652-8668
392 2nd St 2 Brooklyn (11215) *(G-2689)*
Tovie Asarese Royal Prtg Co 716 885-7692
351 Grant St Buffalo (14213) *(G-3249)*
Tower Computers, Brewster *Also called Base Systems Inc (G-1208)*
Tower Insulating Glass LLC 516 887-3300
2485 Charles Ct North Bellmore (11710) *(G-12939)*
Tower Isles Frozen Foods Ltd 718 495-2626
2025 Atlantic Ave Brooklyn (11233) *(G-2690)*
Tower Isles Patties, Brooklyn *Also called Tower Isles Frozen Foods Ltd (G-2690)*
Tower Sales Co, Brooklyn *Also called Turoff Tower Graphics Inc (G-2707)*
Toweriq Inc 844 626-7638
37-18 Nthrn Blvd Ste 421 Long Island City (11101) *(G-7931)*
Town Food Service Eqp Co Inc (PA) 718 388-5650
72 Beadel St Brooklyn (11222) *(G-2691)*
Town Line Auto, Greenville *Also called Classic Auto Crafts Inc (G-5902)*
Town of Amherst 716 631-7113
450 Maple Rd Williamsville (14221) *(G-17283)*
Town of Ohio 315 392-2055
N Lake Rd Forestport (13338) *(G-5339)*
Town of Ohio Highway Garage, Forestport *Also called Town of Ohio (G-5339)*
Towne House Restorations Inc 718 497-9200
4309 Vernon Blvd Long Island City (11101) *(G-7932)*
Townley Inc 212 779-0544
10 W 33rd St Rm 418 New York (10001) *(G-12404)*
Townley Cosmetics, New York *Also called Townley Inc (G-12404)*
Townline Machine Co Inc 315 462-3413
3151 Manchester Clifton Springs (14432) *(G-3741)*
Towpath Machine Corp 315 252-0112
31 Allen St Auburn (13021) *(G-521)*
Towse Publishing Co 914 235-3095
1333a North Ave New Rochelle (10804) *(G-8971)*
Toy Admiration Co Inc 914 963-9400
60 Mclean Ave Yonkers (10705) *(G-17509)*
Toymax Inc (HQ) 212 633-6611
200 5th Ave New York (10010) *(G-12405)*
Tpa Computer Corp 877 866-6044
531 Route 52 Apt 4 Carmel (10512) *(G-3434)*
TPC Inc 315 438-8605
6780 Nthrn Blvd Ste 401 East Syracuse (13057) *(G-4584)*
Tpi Arcade Inc 585 492-0122
7888 Route 98 Arcade (14009) *(G-400)*
Tpi Industries LLC (HQ) 845 692-2820
265 Ballard Rd Middletown (10941) *(G-8500)*
Tr Apparel LLC 310 595-4337
609 Greenwich St Fl 3 New York (10014) *(G-12406)*
Tr Apparel LLC (HQ) 646 358-3888
609 Greenwich St Fl 3 New York (10014) *(G-12407)*
TR Designs Inc 212 398-9300
260 W 39th St Fl 19 New York (10018) *(G-12408)*
Trac Medical Solutions Inc 518 346-7799
2165 Technology Dr Schenectady (12308) *(G-15329)*
Trac Regulators Inc 914 699-9352
160 S Terrace Ave Mount Vernon (10550) *(G-8785)*
Tracey Welding Co Inc 518 756-6309
29 Riverview Dr Coeymans (12045) *(G-3770)*
Track 7 Inc 845 544-1810
3 Forester Ave Warwick (10990) *(G-16618)*
Traco Manufacturing Inc 585 343-2434
4300 Commerce Dr Batavia (14020) *(G-651)*
Tracy Reese, New York *Also called TR Designs Inc (G-12408)*
Trade Mark Graphics Inc 718 306-0001
4502 Avenue N Brooklyn (11234) *(G-2692)*
Tradepaq Corporation 914 332-9174
220 White Plains Rd # 360 Tarrytown (10591) *(G-16134)*
Trader Interntnal Publications 914 631-6856
50 Fremont Rd Sleepy Hollow (10591) *(G-15497)*
Trader Joe's 541, New York *Also called Trader Joes Company (G-12409)*
Trader Joes Company 212 529-6326
138 E 14th St New York (10003) *(G-12409)*
Tradewins Publishing Corp 631 361-6916
19 Bellemeade Ave Ste B Smithtown (11787) *(G-15523)*
Trading Edge Ltd 347 699-7079
1923 Bleecker St Apt 1r Ridgewood (11385) *(G-14141)*
Trading Services International 212 501-0142
133 W 72nd St Rm 601 New York (10023) *(G-12410)*
Trafalgar Company LLC (HQ) 212 768-8800
417 5th Ave Fl 11 New York (10016) *(G-12411)*
Traffic Lane Closures LLC 845 228-6100
3620 Danbury Rd Brewster (10509) *(G-1226)*
Traffic Logix Corporation 866 915-6449
3 Harriet Ln Spring Valley (10977) *(G-15624)*
Tramwell Inc 315 789-2762
70 State St Geneva (14456) *(G-5599)*
Trane US Inc 718 721-8844
4518 Court Sq Ste 100 Long Island City (11101) *(G-7933)*
Trane US Inc 914 593-0303
3 Westchester Plz Ste 198 Elmsford (10523) *(G-4795)*
Trane US Inc 315 234-1500
15 Technology Pl East Syracuse (13057) *(G-4585)*
Trane US Inc 518 785-1315
301 Old Niskayuna Rd # 1 Latham (12110) *(G-7407)*
Trane US Inc 585 256-2500
75 Town Centre Dr Ste I Rochester (14623) *(G-14757)*

ALPHABETIC

(PA)=Parent Co (HQ)=Headquarters (DH)=Div Headquarters

2018 Harris
New York Manufacturers Directory

1077

Trane US Inc......716 626-1260
45 Earhart Dr Ste 103 Buffalo (14221) **(G-3250)**
Trane US Inc......631 952-9477
245 Newtown Rd Ste 500 Plainview (11803) **(G-13666)**
Trans Tech Bus, Warwick *Also called Transprttion Collaborative Inc* **(G-16619)**
Trans-High Corporation......212 387-0500
250 W 57th St Ste 920 New York (10107) **(G-12412)**
Trans-Lux Corporation (PA)......800 243-5544
445 Park Ave Ste 2001 New York (10022) **(G-12413)**
Transact Technologies Inc......607 257-8901
20 Bomax Dr Ithaca (14850) **(G-6914)**
Transaction Printer Group......607 274-2500
108 Woodcrest Ter Ithaca (14850) **(G-6915)**
Transalta, Binghamton *Also called Ipp Energy LLC* **(G-923)**
Transcedar Industries Ltd......716 731-6442
6292 Walmore Rd Niagara Falls (14304) **(G-12901)**
Transcntinental Ultra Flex Inc......718 272-9100
975 Essex St Brooklyn (11208) **(G-2693)**
Transco Railway Products Inc......716 824-1219
Milestrip Rd Blasdell (14219) **(G-961)**
Transcolux Corp......315 768-1500
587 Main St Ste 303 New York Mills (13417) **(G-12747)**
Transcontinental Printing GP......716 626-3078
300 International Dr # 200 Amherst (14221) **(G-267)**
Transcontinental Ross-Ellis, New York *Also called Tc Transcontinental USA Inc* **(G-12308)**
Transistor Devices Inc......631 471-7492
125 Comac St Ronkonkoma (11779) **(G-15015)**
Transit Air Inc......607 324-0216
1 William K Jackson Ln Hornell (14843) **(G-6595)**
Transitair Systems, Hornell *Also called Transit Air Inc* **(G-6595)**
Transland Sourcing LLC......718 596-5704
5 Lynch St Brooklyn (11249) **(G-2694)**
Transparency Life Sciences LLC......862 252-1216
225 W 60th St Apt 15d New York (10023) **(G-12414)**
Transpo Industries Inc (PA)......914 636-1000
20 Jones St Ste 3 New Rochelle (10801) **(G-8972)**
Transport National Dev Inc (PA)......716 662-0270
5720 Ellis Rd Orchard Park (14127) **(G-13324)**
Transport National Dev Inc......716 662-0270
5720 Ellis Rd Orchard Park (14127) **(G-13325)**
Transportgistics Inc......631 567-4100
28 N Country Rd Ste 103 Mount Sinai (11766) **(G-8699)**
Transprttion Collaborative Inc......845 988-2333
7 Lake Station Rd Warwick (10990) **(G-16619)**
Transtech Systems Inc (PA)......518 370-5558
900 Albany Shaker Rd Latham (12110) **(G-7408)**
Trash and Vaudeville Inc......212 777-1727
96 E 7th St Frnt A New York (10009) **(G-12415)**
Travel & Leisure, New York *Also called Departures Magazine* **(G-9902)**
Travel Leisure Magazine, New York *Also called Time Inc Affluent Media Group* **(G-12366)**
Travis Ayers Inc......212 921-5165
1412 Broadway Fl 8 New York (10018) **(G-12416)**
Tread Quarters (PA)......800 876-6676
200 Holleder Pkwy Rochester (14615) **(G-14758)**
Treauu Inc......703 731-0196
60 E 120th St Fl 2 New York (10035) **(G-12417)**
Trebbianno LLC (PA)......212 868-2770
19 W 34th St Fl 7 New York (10001) **(G-12418)**
Trebor Instrument Corp......631 423-7026
39 Balsam Dr Dix Hills (11746) **(G-4322)**
Treehouse Private Brands Inc......716 693-4715
570 Fillmore Ave Tonawanda (14150) **(G-16228)**
Treiman Publications Corp......607 657-8473
12724 State Route 38 Berkshire (13736) **(G-853)**
Trek Inc (PA)......716 438-7555
190 Walnut St Lockport (14094) **(G-7652)**
Tremont Offset Inc......718 892-7333
1500 Ericson Pl Bronx (10461) **(G-1472)**
Trench & Marine Pump Co Inc......212 423-9098
3466 Park Ave Bronx (10456) **(G-1473)**
Trendsformers Ltd Liability Co......888 700-2423
150 W 56th St Apt 6406 New York (10019) **(G-12419)**
Trensdformers, New York *Also called Trendsformers Ltd Liability Co* **(G-12419)**
Treo Brands LLC......914 341-1850
106 Calvert St Harrison (10528) **(G-6011)**
Treo Industries Inc......631 737-4022
35 Carlough Rd Ste 1 Bohemia (11716) **(G-1142)**
Treyco Products Corp......716 693-6525
131 Fillmore Ave Tonawanda (14150) **(G-16229)**
Tri City Highway Products Inc......607 722-2967
111 Bevier St Binghamton (13904) **(G-951)**
Tri County Advertiser, Brockport *Also called Rheinwald Printing Co Inc* **(G-1246)**
Tri County Custom Vacuum......845 774-7595
653 State Route 17m Monroe (10950) **(G-8600)**
Tri Kolor Printing & Sty......315 474-6753
1035 Montgomery St Syracuse (13202) **(G-16085)**
Tri Star, Maspeth *Also called Asn Inc* **(G-8149)**
Tri Star Label Inc......914 237-4800
630 S Columbus Ave Mount Vernon (10550) **(G-8786)**
Tri State Shearing Bending Inc......718 485-2200
366 Herzl St Brooklyn (11212) **(G-2695)**
Tri Supreme Optical, Farmingdale *Also called Tri-Supreme Optical LLC* **(G-5144)**
Tri Valley Iron Inc......845 365-1013
700 Oak Tree Rd Palisades (10964) **(G-13428)**
Tri-Boro Shlving Prtition Corp......718 782-8527
1940 Flushing Ave Ridgewood (11385) **(G-14142)**
Tri-City Highway Products Inc......518 294-9964
145 Podpadic Rd Richmondville (12149) **(G-14102)**
Tri-Flex Label Corp......631 293-0411
48 Allen Blvd Unit A Farmingdale (11735) **(G-5143)**
Tri-Force Sales LLC......732 261-5507
767 3rd Ave Rm 35b New York (10017) **(G-12420)**
Tri-Lon Clor Lithographers Ltd......212 255-6140
233 Spring St Frnt 9th New York (10013) **(G-12421)**
Tri-Metal Industries Inc......716 691-3323
100 Pineview Dr Amherst (14228) **(G-268)**
Tri-Plex Packaging Corporation......212 481-6070
307 5th Ave Fl 7 New York (10016) **(G-12422)**
Tri-Seal Holdings Inc......845 353-3300
900 Bradley Hill Rd Blauvelt (10913) **(G-972)**
Tri-Star Offset Corp......718 894-5555
6020 59th Pl Ste 3 Maspeth (11378) **(G-8203)**
Tri-State Biodiesel LLC......718 860-6600
531 Barretto St Bronx (10474) **(G-1474)**
Tri-State Brick & Stone NY Inc (PA)......212 366-0300
333 7th Ave Fl 5 New York (10001) **(G-12423)**
Tri-State Food Jobbers Inc......718 921-1211
5600 1st Ave Unit A5 Brooklyn (11220) **(G-2696)**
Tri-State Metals LLC......914 347-8157
41 N Lawn Ave Elmsford (10523) **(G-4796)**
Tri-State Towing Equipment NY, Westbury *Also called Tee Pee Auto Sales Corp* **(G-17059)**
Tri-State Window Factory Corp......631 667-8600
360 Marcus Blvd Deer Park (11729) **(G-4242)**
Tri-Supreme Optical LLC......631 249-2020
91 Carolyn Blvd Farmingdale (11735) **(G-5144)**
Tri-Technologies Inc......914 699-2001
40 Hartford Ave Mount Vernon (10553) **(G-8787)**
Tri-Town News Inc (PA)......607 561-3515
74 Main St Sidney (13838) **(G-15464)**
Tri-Town Packing Corp......315 389-5101
Helena Rd Brasher Falls (13613) **(G-1171)**
Tri-Village Publishers Inc......518 843-1100
1 Venner Rd Amsterdam (12010) **(G-371)**
Triad Counter Corp......631 750-0615
1225 Church St Bohemia (11716) **(G-1143)**
Triad Network Technologies......585 924-8505
75b Victor Heights Pkwy Victor (14564) **(G-16533)**
Triad Printing Inc......845 343-2722
7 Prospect St Middletown (10940) **(G-8501)**
Trialgraphix, New York *Also called Resonant Legal Media LLC* **(G-11873)**
Triangle Grinding Machine Corp......631 643-3636
66 Nancy St Unit A West Babylon (11704) **(G-16868)**
Triangle Label Tag Inc......718 875-3030
525 Dekalb Ave Brooklyn (11205) **(G-2697)**
Triangle Rubber Co Inc......631 589-9400
50 Aero Rd Bohemia (11716) **(G-1144)**
Trianon Collection Inc......212 921-9450
16 W 46th St Fl 10 New York (10036) **(G-12424)**
Tribco LLC......718 357-7400
15050 14th Rd Ste 2 Whitestone (11357) **(G-17245)**
Tribeca, New York *Also called Flash Ventures Inc* **(G-10230)**
Tribology Inc......631 345-3000
35 Old Dock Rd Yaphank (11980) **(G-17421)**
Triboro Bagel Co Inc......718 359-9245
18312 Horace Harding Expy Flushing (11365) **(G-5308)**
Triboro Iron Works Inc......718 361-9600
3830 31st St Long Island City (11101) **(G-7934)**
Triborough Electric......718 321-2144
15044 11th Ave Whitestone (11357) **(G-17246)**
Tribune Entertainment Co Del......203 866-2204
220 E 42nd St Fl 26 New York (10017) **(G-12425)**
Tribune Media Services Inc (HQ)......518 792-9914
40 Media Dr Queensbury (12804) **(G-14026)**
Triceutical Inc......631 249-0003
1652 Hering Ave Bronx (10461) **(G-1475)**
Trico Manufacturing Corp......718 349-6565
196 Dupont St Brooklyn (11222) **(G-2698)**
Tricon Des LLC......619 227-0778
2428 Tiemann Ave Bronx (10469) **(G-1476)**
Tricon Machine LLC......585 671-0679
820 Coventry Dr Webster (14580) **(G-16763)**
Tricon Piping Systems Inc......315 655-4178
2 Technology Blvd Canastota (13032) **(G-3401)**
Tricycle Foundation Inc......800 873-9871
89 5th Ave Ste 301 New York (10003) **(G-12426)**
Trident Partners III, Victor *Also called Newtex Industries Inc* **(G-16517)**
Trident Precision Mfg Inc......585 265-2010
734 Salt Rd Webster (14580) **(G-16764)**
Trident Valve Actuator Co......914 698-2650
329 Center Ave Mamaroneck (10543) **(G-8082)**
Trihex Manufacturing Inc......315 589-9331
6708 Pound Rd Williamson (14589) **(G-17256)**
Tril Inc......631 645-7989
320 Pioxi St Copiague (11726) **(G-3958)**

ALPHABETIC SECTION
Tumble Forms Inc (PA)

Trilake Three Press Corp 518 359-2462
136 Park St Tupper Lake (12986) *(G-16304)*
Trilon Color Lithographers, New York *Also called Tri-Lon Clor Lithographers Ltd (G-12421)*
Trimac Molding Services 607 967-2900
13 Pruyn St Bainbridge (13733) *(G-554)*
Trimaster/Htech Holding LLC (HQ) 212 257-6772
590 Madison Ave Fl 27 New York (10022) *(G-12427)*
Trimet Coal LLC 718 951-3654
1615 Avenue I Apt 420 Brooklyn (11230) *(G-2699)*
Trimmer Capacitor Company, The, Cazenovia *Also called Voltronics LLC (G-3481)*
Trine Rolled Moulding Corp 718 828-5200
1421 Ferris Pl Bronx (10461) *(G-1477)*
Trinity Biotech Distribution, Jamestown *Also called Biopool Us Inc (G-7010)*
Trinity Biotech USA, Jamestown *Also called Clark Laboratories Inc (G-7014)*
Trinity Packaging Corporation 716 668-3111
55 Innsbruck Dr Buffalo (14227) *(G-3251)*
Trinity Packaging Corporation (HQ) 914 273-4111
357 Main St Armonk (10504) *(G-419)*
Trinity Tools Inc 716 694-1111
261 Main St North Tonawanda (14120) *(G-13021)*
Trio French Bakery, New York *Also called Giovanni Bakery Corp (G-10341)*
Tripar Manufacturing Co Inc 631 563-0855
1620 Ocean Ave Ste 1 Bohemia (11716) *(G-1145)*
Tripi Engraving Co Inc 718 383-6500
60 Meserole Ave Brooklyn (11222) *(G-2700)*
Triple Canopy, New York *Also called Canopy Canopy Canopy Inc (G-9568)*
Triple E Manufacturing 716 761-6996
117 Osborn St Sherman (14781) *(G-15425)*
Triple H Construction Inc 516 280-8252
832 Bethlynn Ct East Meadow (11554) *(G-4448)*
Triple J Bedding LLC 718 643-8005
63 Flushing Ave Unit 331 Brooklyn (11205) *(G-2701)*
Triple Point Manufacturing 631 218-4988
1371 Church St Ste 6 Bohemia (11716) *(G-1146)*
Triplett Machine Inc 315 548-3198
1374 Phelps Junction Rd Phelps (14532) *(G-13561)*
Triplex Industries Inc 585 621-6920
100 Boxart St Ste 27 Rochester (14612) *(G-14759)*
Tripp Plating Works Inc 716 894-2424
1491 William St Buffalo (14206) *(G-3252)*
Tristate Contract Sales LLC 845 782-2614
164 Dug Rd Chester (10918) *(G-3648)*
Triton Builders Inc 631 841-2534
645 Broadway Ste T Amityville (11701) *(G-332)*
Triton Infosys Inc 877 308-2388
1230 Avenue Of The Americ New York (10020) *(G-12428)*
Trium Strs-Lg Isld LLC 516 997-5757
717 Main St Westbury (11590) *(G-17065)*
Triumph Actuation Systems LLC 516 378-0162
417 S Main St Freeport (11520) *(G-5443)*
Triumph Apparel Corporation (PA) 212 302-2606
530 Fashion Ave Ste M1 New York (10018) *(G-12429)*
Triumph Group Inc 516 997-5757
717 Main St Westbury (11590) *(G-17066)*
Triumph Learning LLC (HQ) 212 652-0200
136 Madison Ave New York (10016) *(G-12430)*
Triumph Structures-Long Island, Westbury *Also called Triumph Group Inc (G-17066)*
TRM Linen Inc 718 686-6075
1546 59th St Brooklyn (11219) *(G-2702)*
Trojan Metal Fabrication Inc (PA) 631 968-5040
2215 Union Blvd Bay Shore (11706) *(G-745)*
Trojan Powder Coating, Bay Shore *Also called Trojan Metal Fabrication Inc (G-745)*
Trojan Steel 518 686-7426
48 Factory Hill Rd Hoosick Falls (12090) *(G-6573)*
Tronic Plating Co Inc 516 293-7883
37 Potter St Farmingdale (11735) *(G-5145)*
Tronser Inc 315 655-9528
3066 John Trush Jr Blvd Cazenovia (13035) *(G-3480)*
Tropical Driftwood Originals 516 623-0980
499 Nassau Rd Roosevelt (11575) *(G-15033)*
Tropp Printing Corp 212 233-4519
181 Broadway Fl 3 New York (10007) *(G-12431)*
Tropp Prntng, New York *Also called Tropp Printing Corp (G-12431)*
Trove Inc 212 268-2046
20 Jay St Ste 846 Brooklyn (11201) *(G-2703)*
Trovvit Inc 718 908-5376
445 7th St Brooklyn (11215) *(G-2704)*
Troy Belting and Supply Co 518 272-4920
70 Cohoes Rd Watervliet (12189) *(G-16715)*
Troy Boiler Works Inc 518 274-2650
2800 7th Ave Troy (12180) *(G-16282)*
Troy Cabinet Manufacturing Div, Troy *Also called Deakon Homes and Interiors (G-16255)*
Troy Sand & Gravel Co Inc 518 674-2854
Rr 43 West Sand Lake (12196) *(G-16961)*
Troy Sign & Printing 718 994-4482
4827 White Plains Rd Bronx (10470) *(G-1478)*
Troy Sign Printing Center, Bronx *Also called Troy Sign & Printing (G-1478)*
Troyer Inc 585 352-5590
4555 Lyell Rd Rochester (14606) *(G-14760)*
Troys Landscape Supply Co Inc 518 785-1526
1266 Loudon Rd Cohoes (12047) *(G-3784)*

Trs Packaging, Buffalo *Also called Time Release Sciences Inc (G-3245)*
Tru Mold Shoes Inc 716 881-4484
42 Breckenridge St Buffalo (14213) *(G-3253)*
Tru-Art Sign Co Inc 718 658-5068
10515 180th St Jamaica (11433) *(G-6995)*
Tru-Tone Metal Products Inc 718 386-5960
1261 Willoughby Ave Brooklyn (11237) *(G-2705)*
Truarc Fabrication 518 691-0430
1 Commerce Park Dr Gansevoort (12831) *(G-5505)*
Truck-Lite Co LLC 716 665-2614
310 E Elmwood Ave Falconer (14733) *(G-4923)*
Truck-Lite Co LLC (PA) 716 665-6214
310 E Elmwood Ave Falconer (14733) *(G-4924)*
Truck-Lite Sub Inc 800 888-7095
310 E Elmwood Ave Falconer (14733) *(G-4925)*
True Colors, New York *Also called Richard Leeds Intl Inc (G-11888)*
True Erp New York 631 582-7210
2150 Joshuas Path Ste 11f Hauppauge (11788) *(G-6241)*
Truebite Inc 607 785-7664
2590 Glenwood Rd Vestal (13850) *(G-16479)*
Truebite Inc 607 786-3184
129 Squires Ave Endicott (13760) *(G-4837)*
Trueex LLC 646 786-8526
162 5th Ave Ste 900 New York (10010) *(G-12432)*
Trueforge Global McHy Corp 516 825-7040
100 Merrick Rd Ste 208e Rockville Centre (11570) *(G-14830)*
Truemade Products Inc 631 981-4755
910 Marconi Ave Ronkonkoma (11779) *(G-15016)*
Truesense Imaging Inc 585 784-5500
1964 Lake Ave Rochester (14615) *(G-14761)*
Truform Manufacturing Corp 585 458-1090
1500 N Clinton Ave Rochester (14621) *(G-14762)*
Truly Tubular Fitting Corp 914 664-8686
115 E 3rd St Mount Vernon (10550) *(G-8788)*
Trunk & Trolley LLC 212 947-9001
15 W 34th St New York (10001) *(G-12433)*
Trunk Outlet, Rochester *Also called Rhino Trunk & Case Inc (G-14647)*
Trusses & Trim Division, Farmington *Also called Rochester Lumber Company (G-5164)*
Trust of Colum Unive In The Ci 212 854-2793
2929 Broadway Fl 3 New York (10025) *(G-12434)*
Trusted Media Brands Inc (HQ) 914 238-1000
750 3rd Ave Fl 3 New York (10017) *(G-12435)*
Trusted Media Brands Inc 646 293-6025
750 3rd Ave Fl 4 New York (10017) *(G-12436)*
Trusted Media Brands Inc 914 244-5244
44 S Broadway Fl 7 White Plains (10601) *(G-17204)*
Truxton Corp 718 842-6000
1357 Lafayette Ave Bronx (10474) *(G-1479)*
TRW Automotive Inc 315 255-3311
2150 Crane Brook Dr Auburn (13021) *(G-522)*
TRW Automotive US LLC 315 255-3311
2150 Crane Brook Dr Auburn (13021) *(G-523)*
Trylon Wire & Metal Works Inc 718 542-4472
526 Tiffany St Bronx (10474) *(G-1480)*
Tryp Times Square 212 246-8800
234 W 48th St New York (10036) *(G-12437)*
TS Manufactoring, New York *Also called Alpine Creations Ltd (G-9154)*
TS Pink, Oneonta *Also called T S Pink Corp (G-13216)*
TSA Luggage Locks, New York *Also called Safe Skies LLC (G-11970)*
Tsar USA LLC 646 415-7968
99 Madison Ave Fl 5 New York (10016) *(G-12438)*
Tsi Technologies, New York *Also called Trading Services International (G-12410)*
Tsm, Elmsford *Also called Tri-State Metals LLC (G-4796)*
TSS Foam Industries Corp 585 538-2321
2770 W Main St Caledonia (14423) *(G-3311)*
Tss-Transport Snltn Sstms 917 267-8534
20 W 22nd St Ste 612 New York (10010) *(G-12439)*
Tte Filters LLC (HQ) 716 532-2234
1 Magnetic Pkwy Gowanda (14070) *(G-5763)*
Ttg LLC 917 777-0959
115 W 30th St Rm 209 New York (10001) *(G-12440)*
TTI, Hauppauge *Also called Tarsia Technical Industries (G-6230)*
Tube Fabrication Company Inc 716 673-1871
183 E Main St Ste 10 Fredonia (14063) *(G-5384)*
Tucano Usa Inc 212 966-9211
77 Bleecker St Apt C212 New York (10012) *(G-12441)*
Tucker Jones House Inc 631 642-9092
1 Enterprise Dr East Setauket (11733) *(G-4514)*
Tucker Printers Inc 585 359-3030
270 Middle Rd Henrietta (14467) *(G-6322)*
Tudor Electrical Supply Co Inc 212 867-7550
137 W 24th St New York (10011) *(G-12442)*
Tula Life LLC 201 895-3309
660 Madison Ave Ste 1600 New York (10065) *(G-12443)*
Tulip Development Labs, Hauppauge *Also called Tdl Manufacturing Inc (G-6232)*
Tulip Molded Plastics Corp 716 282-1261
3123 Highland Ave Niagara Falls (14305) *(G-12902)*
Tully Products Inc 716 773-3166
2065 Baseline Rd Grand Island (14072) *(G-5787)*
Tumble Forms Inc (PA) 315 429-3101
1013 Barker Rd Dolgeville (13329) *(G-4333)*

ALPHABETIC

Tumblehome Boatshop 518 623-5050
684 State Route 28 Warrensburg (12885) *(G-16603)*
Tumi Inc 212 447-8747
261 5th Ave Rm 2010 New York (10016) *(G-12444)*
Tumi Inc 212 742-8020
67 Wall St Frnt 3 New York (10005) *(G-12445)*
Tumi Stores, New York *Also called Tumi Inc (G-12445)*
Tunaverse Media Inc 631 778-8350
750 Veterans Hwy Ste 200 Hauppauge (11788) *(G-6242)*
Tunecore Inc (PA) 646 651-1060
45 Main St Ste 705 Brooklyn (11201) *(G-2706)*
Tupper Lake Hardwoods Inc 518 359-8248
167 Pitchfork Pond Rd Tupper Lake (12986) *(G-16305)*
Turbine Arfoil Cating Repr LLC 845 692-8912
105 Tower Dr Middletown (10941) *(G-8502)*
Turbine Engine Comp Utica 315 768-8070
8273 Halsey Rd Whitesboro (13492) *(G-17225)*
Turbo Dynamics, Plainview *Also called Omega Industries & Development (G-13654)*
Turbo Express Inc 718 723-3686
16019 Rockaway Blvd Ste D Jamaica (11434) *(G-6996)*
Turbo Machined Products LLC 315 895-3010
102 Industrial Dr Frankfort (13340) *(G-5368)*
Turbo Plastics Corp Inc 631 345-9768
18 Old Dock Rd 20 Yaphank (11980) *(G-17422)*
Turbofil Packaging Mchs LLC 914 239-3878
30 Beach St Mount Vernon (10550) *(G-8789)*
Turbopro Inc 716 681-8651
1284 Town Line Rd Alden (14004) *(G-187)*
Turn On Products Inc (PA) 212 764-2121
270 W 38th St Rm 1200 New York (10018) *(G-12446)*
Turn On Products Inc 212 764-4545
525 7th Ave Rm 1403 New York (10018) *(G-12447)*
Turner Bellows Inc 585 235-4456
526 Child St Ste 1 Rochester (14606) *(G-14763)*
Turner Plating, New Rochelle *Also called Eric S Turner & Company Inc (G-8943)*
Turner Undgrd Instllations Inc 585 739-0238
1233 Lehigh Station Rd Henrietta (14467) *(G-6323)*
Turning Point Tool LLC 585 288-7380
135 Dodge St Rochester (14606) *(G-14764)*
Turoff Tower Graphics Inc 718 856-7300
681 Coney Island Ave Brooklyn (11218) *(G-2707)*
Tusk Manufacturing Inc 631 567-3349
1371 Church St Ste 1 Bohemia (11716) *(G-1147)*
Tuthill Corporation 631 727-1097
75 Kings Dr Riverhead (11901) *(G-14172)*
Tuthilltown Spirits LLC 845 255-1527
14 Gristmill Ln Gardiner (12525) *(G-5564)*
Tuv Taam Corp 718 855-2207
502 Flushing Ave Brooklyn (11205) *(G-2708)*
TV Data, Queensbury *Also called Tribune Media Services Inc (G-14026)*
TV Executive, New York *Also called T V Trade Media Inc (G-12292)*
TV Guide Magazine LLC (HQ) 800 866-1400
50 Rockefeller Plz Fl 14 New York (10020) *(G-12448)*
TV Guide Magazine Group Inc (HQ) 212 852-7500
1211 Ave Of The Americas New York (10036) *(G-12449)*
TV Guilfoil & Associates Inc (PA) 315 453-0920
121 Dwight Park Cir Syracuse (13209) *(G-16086)*
TVI Imports LLC 631 793-3077
178 Abbey St Massapequa Park (11762) *(G-8223)*
Twcc Product and Sales 212 614-9364
122 5th Ave New York (10011) *(G-12450)*
Twenty-First Century Press Inc 716 837-0800
501 Cornwall Ave Buffalo (14215) *(G-3254)*
Twentyone Brix Winery, Portland *Also called Olde Chtqua Vneyards Ltd Lblty (G-13891)*
TWI Watches LLC 718 663-3969
4014 1st Ave Brooklyn (11232) *(G-2709)*
TWI-Laq Industries Inc 718 638-5860
1345 Seneca Ave Bronx (10474) *(G-1481)*
Twin Counties Pro Printers Inc 518 828-3278
59 Fairview Ave Hudson (12534) *(G-6667)*
Twin County Recycling Corp (PA) 516 827-6900
113 Magnolia Ave Westbury (11590) *(G-17067)*
Twin Lake Chemical Inc 716 433-3824
520 Mill St Lockport (14094) *(G-7653)*
Twin Marquis Inc (HQ) 718 386-6868
7 Bushwick Pl Brooklyn (11206) *(G-2710)*
Twin Pane Insulated GL Co Inc 631 924-1060
86 Horseblock Rd Unit D Yaphank (11980) *(G-17423)*
Twin Rivers Paper Company LLC 315 348-8491
Lyonsdale Rd Lyons Falls (13368) *(G-8005)*
Twin Rivers Paper Company LLC 315 823-2300
501 W Main St Little Falls (13365) *(G-7527)*
Twinco Mfg Co Inc 631 231-0022
30 Commerce Dr Hauppauge (11788) *(G-6243)*
Twinkle Lighting Inc 718 225-0939
13114 40th Rd Flushing (11354) *(G-5309)*
Twist Intimate Apparel, New York *Also called Twist Intimate Group LLC (G-12451)*
Twist Intimate Group LLC (PA) 212 695-5990
35 W 35th St Rm 903 New York (10001) *(G-12451)*
Twist It Top It 718 793-8947
10309 Metropolitan Ave Forest Hills (11375) *(G-5336)*
Twisters 585 346-3730
13 Commercial St Livonia (14487) *(G-7592)*
Two Bills Machine & Tool Co 516 437-2585
17 Concord St Floral Park (11001) *(G-5214)*
Two Palms Press Inc 212 965-8598
476 Broadway Ste 3f New York (10013) *(G-12452)*
Two Rivers Computing Inc 914 968-9239
976 Mclean Ave Yonkers (10704) *(G-17510)*
Two Sisters Kiev Bakery Inc (PA) 718 769-2626
2737 W 15th St Brooklyn (11224) *(G-2711)*
Two Sisters Kiev Bakery Inc 718 627-5438
1627 E 18th St Brooklyn (11229) *(G-2712)*
Two Worlds Arts Ltd 212 929-2210
307 Kingsland Ave Brooklyn (11222) *(G-2713)*
Two-Four Software, New York *Also called F-O-R Software LLC (G-10173)*
Two-Four Software, White Plains *Also called F-O-R Software LLC (G-17134)*
Twp America Inc (HQ) 212 274-8090
299 Broadway Ste 720 New York (10007) *(G-12453)*
TX Rx Systems Inc 716 549-4700
8625 Industrial Pkwy Angola (14006) *(G-382)*
Tyco Simplexgrinnell 315 437-9664
6731 Collamer Rd Ste 4 East Syracuse (13057) *(G-4586)*
Tyco Simplexgrinnell 716 483-0079
527 Foote Ave Jamestown (14701) *(G-7072)*
Tyco Simplexgrinnell 315 337-6333
4057 Wilson Rd E Taberg (13471) *(G-16100)*
Tycoon International Inc 212 563-7107
3436 W 32nd St Fl 4 New York (10001) *(G-12454)*
Tyme Global Technologies LLC 212 796-1950
60 W 66th St Apt 15a New York (10023) *(G-12455)*
Tyme Technologies Inc (PA) 646 205-1603
44 Wall St Fl 12 New York (10005) *(G-12456)*
Tymetal Corp (HQ) 518 692-9930
678 Wilbur Ave Greenwich (12834) *(G-5915)*
Tymor Park 845 724-5691
249 Duncan Rd Lagrangeville (12540) *(G-7285)*
Tyrolit Company, Hauppauge *Also called Meopta USA Inc (G-6157)*
Tyson Deli Inc (HQ) 716 826-6400
665 Perry St Buffalo (14210) *(G-3255)*
U All Inc 518 438-2558
9 Interstate Ave Albany (12205) *(G-144)*
U B J, New York *Also called United Brothers Jewelry Inc (G-12483)*
U E Systems Incorporated (PA) 914 592-1220
14 Hayes St Elmsford (10523) *(G-4797)*
U K Sailmakers, Bronx *Also called Ulmer Sales LLC (G-1483)*
U S A Today, Port Washington *Also called Gannett Co Inc (G-13840)*
U S Air Tool Co Inc (PA) 631 471-3300
60 Fleetwood Ct Ronkonkoma (11779) *(G-15017)*
U S Air Tool International, Ronkonkoma *Also called U S Air Tool Co Inc (G-15017)*
U S Embroidery Inc 718 585-9662
728 E 136th St Ste 1 Bronx (10454) *(G-1482)*
U S Energy Development Corp (PA) 716 636-0401
2350 N Forest Rd Getzville (14068) *(G-5617)*
U S Japan Publication NY Inc 212 252-8833
147 W 35th St Ste 1705 New York (10001) *(G-12457)*
U S Orthotic Center, New York *Also called Custom Sports Lab Inc (G-9828)*
U S Plychmical Overseas Corp 845 356-5530
584 Chestnut Ridge Rd # 586 Chestnut Ridge (10977) *(G-3657)*
U S Sugar Co Inc 716 828-1170
692 Bailey Ave Buffalo (14206) *(G-3256)*
U S TEC, Victor *Also called 331 Holding Inc (G-16482)*
U S Tech Corporation 315 437-7207
6511 Basile Rowe East Syracuse (13057) *(G-4587)*
U X World Inc 914 375-6167
245 Saw Mill River Rd # 106 Hawthorne (10532) *(G-6280)*
U-Cut Enterprises Inc 315 492-9316
4800 Solvay Rd Jamesville (13078) *(G-7086)*
U2o Usa, LLC, Plainview *Also called 5yz Logistics LLC (G-13605)*
Ubec, Salamanca *Also called Highland Injection Molding (G-15127)*
Ubm Inc 212 600-3000
2 Penn Plz New York (10121) *(G-12458)*
Ubm LLC (HQ) 516 562-7800
1983 Marcus Ave Ste 250 New Hyde Park (11042) *(G-8912)*
Ubm LLC 516 562-5000
2 Penn Plz Fl 15 New York (10121) *(G-12459)*
Ubm Tech, New Hyde Park *Also called Ubm LLC (G-8912)*
Uc Coatings Corporation 716 833-9366
2250 Fillmore Ave Buffalo (14214) *(G-3257)*
Ucb Pharma Inc (PA) 919 767-2555
755 Jefferson Rd Rochester (14623) *(G-14765)*
Ucc Guide Inc (PA) 518 434-0909
99 Washington Ave Albany (12210) *(G-145)*
Ucr Steel Group LLC (PA) 718 764-3414
405 Rxr Plz Uniondale (11556) *(G-16324)*
Ucr Steel Group LLC 718 764-3414
90 Trade Zone Ct Ronkonkoma (11779) *(G-15018)*
Udisense Inc 858 442-9875
620 8th Ave Fl 38 New York (10018) *(G-12460)*
Ue Music, New York *Also called Universal Edition Inc (G-12490)*
Ufc Biotechnology 716 777-3776
1576 Sweet Home Rd # 225 Amherst (14228) *(G-269)*

Ufo Contemporary Inc 212 226-5400
42 W 38th St Rm 1204 New York (10018) *(G-12461)*
Ufp New York LLC 716 496-5484
13989 E Schutt Rd Chaffee (14030) *(G-3564)*
Ufp New York LLC 518 828-2888
11 Falls Industrial Pk Rd Hudson (12534) *(G-6668)*
Ufp New York LLC (HQ) 315 253-2758
11 Allen St Auburn (13021) *(G-524)*
Ufp New York LLC 607 563-1556
13 Winkler Rd Sidney (13838) *(G-15465)*
UFS Industries Inc 718 822-1100
300 N Macquesten Pkwy Mount Vernon (10550) *(G-8790)*
Uft New York, Chaffee *Also called P & R Truss Co (G-3563)*
Ufx Holding I Corporation (HQ) 212 644-5900
55 E 52nd St Fl 35 New York (10055) *(G-12462)*
Ufx Holding II Corporation (HQ) 212 644-5900
55 E 52nd St Fl 35 New York (10055) *(G-12463)*
Uge, New York *Also called Urban Green Energy Inc (G-12499)*
UGI, Brooklyn *Also called United Gemdiam Inc (G-2720)*
Uhmac Inc 716 537-2343
136 N Main St Holland (14080) *(G-6512)*
Ui Acquisition Holding Co (PA) 607 779-7522
33 Broome Corporate Pkwy Conklin (13748) *(G-3903)*
Ui Holding Company (HQ) 607 779-7522
33 Broome Corporate Pkwy Conklin (13748) *(G-3904)*
Uipath 844 432-0455
311 W 43rd St Fl 13 New York (10036) *(G-12464)*
Ul Corp 201 203-4453
3812 Corporal Stone St # 2 Bayside (11361) *(G-770)*
Ul Information & Insights Inc (HQ) 518 640-9200
23 British American Blvd # 2 Latham (12110) *(G-7409)*
Ulano Product Inc 718 622-5200
110 3rd Ave Brooklyn (11217) *(G-2714)*
Ulmer Sales LLC 718 885-1700
175 City Island Ave Bronx (10464) *(G-1483)*
Ulrich Planfiling Eqp Corp 716 763-1815
2120 4th Ave Lakewood (14750) *(G-7319)*
Ulrich Sign Co Inc 716 434-0167
177 Oakhurst St Lockport (14094) *(G-7654)*
Ulster County Iron Works LLC 845 255-0003
64 N Putt Corners Rd New Paltz (12561) *(G-8925)*
Ulster County Press Office 845 687-4480
1209 State Route 213 High Falls (12440) *(G-6429)*
Ulster Precision Inc 845 338-0995
57 Teller St Kingston (12401) *(G-7246)*
Ulster Publishing Co Inc (PA) 845 334-8205
322 Wall St Fl 1 Kingston (12401) *(G-7247)*
Ulster Publishing Co Inc 845 255-7005
29 S Chestnut St Ste 101 New Paltz (12561) *(G-8926)*
Ultimate Pavers Corp 917 417-2652
659 Quincy Ave Staten Island (10305) *(G-15772)*
Ultimate Prcision Met Pdts Inc 631 249-9441
200 Finn Ct Farmingdale (11735) *(G-5146)*
Ultimate Signs & Designs Inc 516 481-0800
86 Sewell St Hempstead (11550) *(G-6311)*
Ultimate Styles of America 631 254-0219
27 Garfield Ave Unit A Bay Shore (11706) *(G-746)*
Ultra Clarity Corp 719 470-1010
3101 Parkview Dr Spring Valley (10977) *(G-15625)*
Ultra Elec Flightline Systems, Victor *Also called Flightline Electronics Inc (G-16502)*
Ultra Electronics Inc, Victor *Also called Magnet-Ndctive Systems Ltd USA (G-16514)*
Ultra Electronics, Ems, Yaphank *Also called Ems Development Corporation (G-17406)*
Ultra Fine Jewelry Mfg 516 349-2848
180 Dupont St Unit C Plainview (11803) *(G-13667)*
Ultra Thin Pzza Shlls Fltbrads, Deer Park *Also called Ultra Thin Ready To Bake Pizza (G-4243)*
Ultra Thin Ready To Bake Pizza 516 679-6655
151 E Industry Ct Deer Park (11729) *(G-4243)*
Ultra Tool and Manufacturing 585 467-3700
159 Lagrange Ave Rochester (14613) *(G-14766)*
Ultra-Scan Corporation 716 832-6269
4240 Ridge Lea Rd Ste 10 Amherst (14226) *(G-270)*
Ultradian Diagnostics LLC 518 618-0046
5 University Pl A324 Rensselaer (12144) *(G-14063)*
Ultraflex Power Technologies 631 467-6814
158 Remington Blvd Ste 2 Ronkonkoma (11779) *(G-15019)*
Ultralife Corporation (PA) 315 332-7100
2000 Technology Pkwy Newark (14513) *(G-12766)*
Ultrapedics Ltd (PA) 718 748-4806
355 Ovington Ave Ste 104 Brooklyn (11209) *(G-2715)*
Ultravolt Inc 631 471-4444
1800 Ocean Ave Unit A Ronkonkoma (11779) *(G-15020)*
Ultrepet LLC 781 275-6400
136c Fuller Rd Albany (12205) *(G-146)*
Umbro Machine & Tool Co Inc 845 876-4669
3811 Route 9g Rhinebeck (12572) *(G-14071)*
Umi, New York *Also called Urban Mapping Inc (G-12500)*
Umicore Technical Materials 518 792-7700
9 Pruyns Island Dr Glens Falls (12801) *(G-5713)*
Umicore USA Inc 919 874-7171
9 Pruyns Island Dr Glens Falls (12801) *(G-5714)*
Ums Manufacturing LLC 518 562-2410
194 Pleasant Ridge Rd Plattsburgh (12901) *(G-13734)*
Unadilla Laminated Products, Sidney *Also called Unadilla Silo Company Inc (G-15466)*
Unadilla Silo Company Inc 607 369-9341
100 West Rd Sidney (13838) *(G-15466)*
Uncharted Play Inc 646 675-7783
246 Lenox Ave New York (10027) *(G-12465)*
Uncle Wallys LLC 631 205-0455
41 Natcon Dr Shirley (11967) *(G-15453)*
Unco United Oil Holdings LLC 212 481-1003
100 Park Ave Fl 16 New York (10017) *(G-12466)*
Under Armour Inc 518 761-6787
1444 State Route 9 Lake George (12845) *(G-7289)*
Underline Communications LLC 212 994-4340
12 W 27th St Fl 14 New York (10001) *(G-12467)*
Uneeda Enterprizes Inc 800 431-2494
640 Chestnut Ridge Rd Spring Valley (10977) *(G-15626)*
UNI Jewelry Inc 212 398-1818
48 W 48th St Ste 1401 New York (10036) *(G-12468)*
UNI Source Technology 514 748-8888
1320 Rt 9 Champlain (12919) *(G-3575)*
Unicell Body Company Inc (PA) 716 853-8628
571 Howard St Buffalo (14206) *(G-3258)*
Unicell Body Company Inc 716 853-8628
170 Cordell Rd Schenectady (12303) *(G-15330)*
Unicell Body Company Inc 585 424-2660
1319 Brighton Henrietta Rochester (14623) *(G-14767)*
Unicenter Millwork Inc 716 741-8201
9605 Clarence Center Rd Clarence Center (14032) *(G-3707)*
Unico Inc 845 562-9255
25 Renwick St Newburgh (12550) *(G-12806)*
Unico Special Products Inc 845 562-9255
25 Renwick St Newburgh (12550) *(G-12807)*
Unicom Graphic Communications 212 221-2456
230 Park Ave Rm 1000 New York (10169) *(G-12469)*
Unicor, Otisville *Also called Federal Prison Industries (G-13369)*
Unicor, Ray Brook *Also called Federal Prison Industries (G-14037)*
Unicorn Graphics, Garden City *Also called Won & Lee Inc (G-5552)*
Unidex Company, Warsaw *Also called Unidex Corporation Western NY (G-16606)*
Unidex Corporation Western NY 585 786-3170
2416 State Route 19 N Warsaw (14569) *(G-16606)*
Unifab Inc 585 235-1760
215 Tremont St Ste 31 Rochester (14608) *(G-14768)*
Unified Inc led 646 370-4650
35 W 36th St New York (10018) *(G-12470)*
Unified Media Inc 917 595-2710
180 Madison Ave Lbby L New York (10016) *(G-12471)*
Unified Solutions For Clg Inc 718 782-8800
1829 Pacific St Brooklyn (11233) *(G-2716)*
Unifor Inc 212 673-3434
149 5th Ave Ste 3r New York (10010) *(G-12472)*
Uniform Express, Rochester *Also called Kevin J Kassman (G-14491)*
Uniform Namemakers Inc 716 626-5474
55 Amherst Villa Rd Buffalo (14225) *(G-3259)*
Uniform Professionals, Cincinnatus *Also called David Christy (G-3681)*
Uniforms By Park Coats Inc 718 499-1182
790 3rd Ave Brooklyn (11232) *(G-2717)*
Unifrax Corporation 716 278-3800
2351 Whirlpool St Niagara Falls (14305) *(G-12903)*
Unifrax Holding Co (HQ) 212 644-5900
55 E 52nd St Fl 35 New York (10055) *(G-12473)*
Unifrax I LLC 716 696-3000
360 Fire Tower Dr Tonawanda (14150) *(G-16230)*
Unifrax I LLC (HQ) 716 768-6500
600 Rverwalk Pkwy Ste 120 Tonawanda (14150) *(G-16231)*
Unifuse LLC 845 889-4000
2092 Route 9g Staatsburg (12580) *(G-15639)*
Unilever United States Inc 212 546-0200
390 Park Ave New York (10022) *(G-12474)*
Unilever United States Inc 212 546-0200
663 5th Ave Fl 8 New York (10022) *(G-12475)*
Unilock Ltd 716 822-6074
510 Smith St Buffalo (14210) *(G-3260)*
Unilock New York Inc (HQ) 845 278-6700
51 International Blvd Brewster (10509) *(G-1227)*
Unilux Advanced Mfg LLC 518 344-7490
30 Commerce Park Rd Schenectady (12309) *(G-15331)*
Unimar Inc 315 699-4400
3195 Vickery Rd Syracuse (13212) *(G-16087)*
Unimax Supply Co Inc (PA) 212 925-1051
269 Canal St New York (10013) *(G-12476)*
Unimed Optical (PA) 718 384-3600
175 Marcy Ave Brooklyn (11211) *(G-2718)*
Unimex Corporation (PA) 212 755-8800
54 E 64th St New York (10065) *(G-12477)*
Unimex Corporation 718 236-2222
1462 62nd St Brooklyn (11219) *(G-2719)*
Union Standard & Un Conf McHy, Bronx *Also called National Equipment Corporation (G-1408)*
Union Standard Eqp Co Div, Harrison *Also called National Equipment Corporation (G-6006)*
Union Sun & Journal, Lockport *Also called Community Newsppr Holdings Inc (G-7605)*

ALPHABETIC

(PA)=Parent Co (HQ)=Headquarters (DH)=Div Headquarters
2018 Harris New York Manufacturers Directory
1081

Unipharm Inc (PA) 212 564-3634
350 5th Ave Ste 6701 New York (10118) ***(G-12478)***
Uniqlo USA LLC 877 486-4756
546 Broadway New York (10012) ***(G-12479)***
Unique Designs Inc 212 575-7701
521 5th Ave Rm 820 New York (10175) ***(G-12480)***
Unique Display Mfg Corp (PA) 516 546-3800
216 N Main St Ste D Freeport (11520) ***(G-5444)***
Unique MBL Gran Orgnztion Corp 718 482-0440
3831 9th St Long Island City (11101) ***(G-7935)***
Unique Overseas Inc 516 466-9792
425 Northern Blvd Ste 22 Great Neck (11021) ***(G-5865)***
Unique Packaging Corporation 514 341-5872
1320 State Route 9 # 3807 Champlain (12919) ***(G-3576)***
Unique Petz LLC 212 714-1800
10 W 33rd St Rm 220 New York (10001) ***(G-12481)***
Unique Quality Fabrics Inc 845 343-3070
115 Wisner Ave Middletown (10940) ***(G-8503)***
Unisend LLC 585 414-9575
249 Gallant Fox Ln Webster (14580) ***(G-16765)***
Unison Industries LLC 607 335-5000
5345 State Highway 12 Norwich (13815) ***(G-13057)***
Unisource Food Eqp Systems Inc 516 681-0537
1505 Lincoln Ave Holbrook (11741) ***(G-6506)***
Unistel LLC 585 341-4600
860 Hard Rd Webster (14580) ***(G-16766)***
Unisystems Inc (PA) 212 826-0850
155 E 55th St Apt 203 New York (10022) ***(G-12482)***
Unit Step Company, Sanborn *Also called Gamble & Gamble Inc* ***(G-15147)***
United Baking Co Inc 631 413-5116
16 Bronx Ave Central Islip (11722) ***(G-3540)***
United Baking Co Inc (PA) 631 205-0455
41 Natcon Dr Shirley (11967) ***(G-15454)***
United Biochemicals LLC 716 731-5161
6351 Inducon Dr E Sanborn (14132) ***(G-15156)***
United Brothers Jewelry Inc 212 921-2558
48 W 48th St Ste 700 New York (10036) ***(G-12483)***
United Business Forms, Long Island City *Also called United Print Group Inc* ***(G-7936)***
United Data Forms Inc 631 218-0104
500 Johnson Ave Ste B Bohemia (11716) ***(G-1148)***
United Dividers, Elmira *Also called Fennell Industries LLC* ***(G-4698)***
United Farm Processing Corp (PA) 718 933-6060
4366 Park Ave Bronx (10457) ***(G-1484)***
United Gemdiam Inc 718 851-5083
1537 52nd St Brooklyn (11219) ***(G-2720)***
United Iron Inc 914 667-5700
6 Roslyn Pl Mount Vernon (10550) ***(G-8791)***
United Knitwear International (PA) 212 354-2920
1384 Broadway Rm 1210 New York (10018) ***(G-12484)***
United Machining Inc 631 589-6751
1595 Smithtown Ave Ste D Bohemia (11716) ***(G-1149)***
United Materials LLC (PA) 716 683-1432
3949 Frest Pk Way Ste 400 North Tonawanda (14120) ***(G-13022)***
United Materials LLC 716 731-2332
2186 Cory Dr Sanborn (14132) ***(G-15157)***
United Materials LLC 716 662-0564
75 Bank St Orchard Park (14127) ***(G-13326)***
United Metal Industries Inc 516 354-6800
1008 3rd Ave New Hyde Park (11040) ***(G-8913)***
United Pet Group, Hauppauge *Also called Spectrum Brands Inc* ***(G-6220)***
United Pickle Products Corp 718 933-6060
4366 Park Ave Bronx (10457) ***(G-1485)***
United Pipe Nipple Co Inc 516 295-2468
1602 Lakeview Dr Hewlett (11557) ***(G-6338)***
United Plastics Inc 718 389-2255
640 Humboldt St Ste 1 Brooklyn (11222) ***(G-2721)***
United Print Group Inc 718 392-4242
3636 33rd St Ste 303 Long Island City (11106) ***(G-7936)***
United Rbotic Integrations LLC 716 683-8334
2781 Town Line Rd Alden (14004) ***(G-188)***
United Retail II 212 966-9692
436 W Broadway New York (10012) ***(G-12485)***
United Richter Electrical Mtrs 716 855-1945
106 Michigan Ave Buffalo (14204) ***(G-3261)***
United Rockland Holding Co Inc 845 357-1900
9 N Airmont Rd Suffern (10901) ***(G-15822)***
United Satcom Inc 718 359-4100
4555 Robinson St Flushing (11355) ***(G-5310)***
United Sheet Metal Corp 718 482-1197
4602 28th St Long Island City (11101) ***(G-7937)***
United Ship Repair Inc 718 237-2800
54 Richards St Brooklyn (11231) ***(G-2722)***
United Silicone Inc 716 681-8222
4471 Walden Ave Lancaster (14086) ***(G-7370)***
United States Gypsum Company 585 948-5221
2750 Maple Ave Oakfield (14125) ***(G-13085)***
United Steel Products Inc 914 968-7782
3340 127th Pl Flushing (11368) ***(G-5311)***
United Steel Products Inc 718 478-5330
3340 127th Pl Corona (11368) ***(G-4031)***
United Structure Solution Inc 347 227-7526
240 W 65th St Apt 26c New York (10023) ***(G-12486)***
United Sttes Brnze Sign of Fla 516 352-5155
811 2nd Ave New Hyde Park (11040) ***(G-8914)***
United Supply Systems, Syosset *Also called Paradigm Mktg Consortium Inc* ***(G-15855)***
United Synggue Cnsrvtive Jdism (PA) 212 533-7800
120 Broadway Ste 1540 New York (10271) ***(G-12487)***
United Technologies Corp 315 432-7849
6304 Carrier Pkwy East Syracuse (13057) ***(G-4588)***
United Technologies Corp 866 788-5095
1212 Pittsford Victor Rd Pittsford (14534) ***(G-13603)***
United Thread Mills Corp (PA) 516 536-3900
3530 Lawson Blvd Gf Oceanside (11572) ***(G-13124)***
United Transit Mix Inc 718 416-3400
318 Boerum St Brooklyn (11206) ***(G-2723)***
United Wind Inc 800 268-9896
20 Jay St Ste 928 Brooklyn (11201) ***(G-2724)***
United Wire Technologies Inc 315 623-7203
1804 State Route 49 Constantia (13044) ***(G-3908)***
United-Guardian Inc (PA) 631 273-0900
230 Marcus Blvd Hauppauge (11788) ***(G-6244)***
Unither Manufacturing LLC 585 475-9000
755 Jefferson Rd Rochester (14623) ***(G-14769)***
Unither Manufacturing LLC 585 274-5430
331 Clay Rd Rochester (14623) ***(G-14770)***
Unitone Communication Systems 212 777-9090
220 E 23rd St Ste 411 New York (10010) ***(G-12488)***
Universal 3d Innovation Inc 516 837-9423
1085 Rockaway Ave Valley Stream (11581) ***(G-16454)***
Universal Builders Supply Inc 845 758-8801
45 Ocallaghan Ln Red Hook (12571) ***(G-14042)***
Universal Cmmncations of Miami 212 986-5100
801 2nd Ave Lbby New York (10017) ***(G-12489)***
Universal Coolers Inc 718 788-8621
120 13th St Brooklyn (11215) ***(G-2725)***
Universal Custom Millwork Inc 518 330-6622
3 Sam Stratton Rd Amsterdam (12010) ***(G-372)***
Universal Designs Inc 718 721-1111
3517 31st St Long Island City (11106) ***(G-7938)***
Universal Edition Inc 917 213-2177
331 W 57th St Ste 380 New York (10019) ***(G-12490)***
Universal Elliot Corp 212 736-8877
327 W 36th St Rm 700 New York (10018) ***(G-12491)***
Universal Fire Proof Door 718 455-8442
1171 Myrtle Ave Brooklyn (11206) ***(G-2726)***
Universal Forest Products, Chaffee *Also called Ufp New York LLC* ***(G-3564)***
Universal Forest Products, Hudson *Also called Ufp New York LLC* ***(G-6668)***
Universal Forest Products, Auburn *Also called Ufp New York LLC* ***(G-524)***
Universal Instruments Corp (HQ) 800 842-9732
33 Broome Corporate Pkwy Conklin (13748) ***(G-3905)***
Universal Metal Fabricators 845 331-8248
27 Emerick St Kingston (12401) ***(G-7248)***
Universal Metal Works LLC 315 598-7607
159 Hubbard St Fulton (13069) ***(G-5490)***
Universal Metals Inc 516 829-0896
98 Cuttermill Rd Ste 428 Great Neck (11021) ***(G-5866)***
Universal Music Group Inc 212 333-8237
825 8th Ave Fl C2b New York (10019) ***(G-12492)***
Universal Packg Systems Inc (PA) 631 543-2277
380 Townline Rd Ste 130 Hauppauge (11788) ***(G-6245)***
Universal Parent and Youth 917 754-2426
1530 Pa Ave Apt 17e Brooklyn (11239) ***(G-2727)***
Universal Precision Corp 585 321-9760
40 Commerce Dr Rochester (14623) ***(G-14771)***
Universal Proteins, Amityville *Also called Natural Organics Labroratories* ***(G-314)***
Universal Ready Mix Inc 516 746-4535
197 Atlantic Ave New Hyde Park (11040) ***(G-8915)***
Universal Remote Control Inc (PA) 914 630-4343
500 Mmaroneck Ave Ste 502 Harrison (10528) ***(G-6012)***
Universal Screening Associates 718 232-2744
6509 11th Ave Brooklyn (11219) ***(G-2728)***
Universal Shielding Corp 631 667-7900
20 W Jefryn Blvd Deer Park (11729) ***(G-4244)***
Universal Signs and Svc Inc 631 446-1121
435 Brook Ave Unit 2 Deer Park (11729) ***(G-4245)***
Universal Stainless & Alloy 716 366-1000
830 Brigham Rd Dunkirk (14048) ***(G-4376)***
Universal Steel Fabricators 718 342-0782
90 Junius St Brooklyn (11212) ***(G-2729)***
Universal Step Inc 315 437-7611
5970 Butternut Dr East Syracuse (13057) ***(G-4589)***
Universal Strapping Inc 845 268-2500
630 Corporate Way Valley Cottage (10989) ***(G-16420)***
Universal Thin Film Lab Corp 845 562-0601
232 N Plank Rd Newburgh (12550) ***(G-12808)***
Universal Tooling Corporation 716 985-4691
4533 Route 60 Gerry (14740) ***(G-5606)***
Universal Water Technology, Far Rockaway *Also called Business Advisory Services* ***(G-4926)***
Universe Publishing, New York *Also called Rizzoli Intl Publications Inc* ***(G-11904)***
University Advertising Agency, Stony Brook *Also called Stony Brook University* ***(G-15793)***
University At Albany 518 437-8686
257 Fuller Rd Albany (12203) ***(G-147)***
University of Rochester 585 275-3483
250 E River Rd Rochester (14623) ***(G-14772)***

University Table Cloth Company 845 371-3876
10 Centre St Spring Valley (10977) *(G-15627)*
Uniware Houseware Corp 631 242-7400
120 Wilshire Blvd Ste B Brentwood (11717) *(G-1195)*
Unlimited Industries Inc 631 666-9483
234 Orinoco Dr Brightwaters (11718) *(G-1238)*
Unlimited Ink Inc 631 582-0696
595 Old Willets Path B Hauppauge (11788) *(G-6246)*
Unlimited Jeans Co Inc 212 661-6355
401 Broadway Frnt A New York (10013) *(G-12493)*
Untuckit LLC 201 214-9054
220 Lafayette St New York (10012) *(G-12494)*
UOP LLC 716 879-7600
175 E Park Dr Tonawanda (14150) *(G-16232)*
Up Country, New York *Also called Du Monde Trading Inc (G-9984)*
Upayori, Brooklyn *Also called Universal Parent and Youth (G-2727)*
Upholstery Unlimited, Hudson *Also called McCarroll Uphl Designs LLC (G-6655)*
Upper Ninty LLC 646 863-3105
697 Amsterdam Ave New York (10025) *(G-12495)*
Upper Ninty Soccer and Sport, New York *Also called Upper Ninty LLC (G-12495)*
UPS, Manlius *Also called Miller Enterprises CNY Inc (G-8108)*
Upstate Cabinet Co Inc 585 429-5090
32 Marway Cir Rochester (14624) *(G-14773)*
Upstate Door Inc 585 786-3880
26 Industrial St Warsaw (14569) *(G-16607)*
Upstate Increte Incorporated 585 254-2010
49 Adelaide St Rochester (14606) *(G-14774)*
Upstate Insulated Glass Inc 315 475-4960
47 Weber Rd Central Square (13036) *(G-3546)*
Upstate Medical Solutions Inc 716 799-3782
25 Minnetonka Rd Buffalo (14220) *(G-3262)*
Upstate Milk Co-Operatives, Buffalo *Also called Upstate Niagara Coop Inc (G-3264)*
Upstate Niagara Coop Inc (PA) 716 892-3156
25 Anderson Rd Buffalo (14225) *(G-3263)*
Upstate Niagara Coop Inc 716 892-2121
1730 Dale Rd Buffalo (14225) *(G-3264)*
Upstate Niagara Coop Inc 585 458-1880
45 Fulton Ave Rochester (14608) *(G-14775)*
Upstate Niagara Coop Inc 716 484-7178
223 Fluvanna Ave Jamestown (14701) *(G-7073)*
Upstate Niagara Coop Inc 315 389-5111
22 County Route 52 North Lawrence (12967) *(G-12951)*
Upstate Office Furniture, Johnson City *Also called Upstate Office Liquidators Inc (G-7137)*
Upstate Office Liquidators Inc 607 722-9234
718 Azon Rd Johnson City (13790) *(G-7137)*
Upstate Piping Products Inc 518 238-3457
95 Hudson River Rd Waterford (12188) *(G-16644)*
Upstate Printing Inc 315 475-6140
433 W Onondaga St Syracuse (13202) *(G-16088)*
Upstate Records Management LLC 518 834-1144
1729 Front St Keeseville (12944) *(G-7170)*
Upstate Refractory Svcs Inc 315 331-2955
100 Erie Blvd Newark (14513) *(G-12767)*
Upstate Tube Inc 315 488-5636
5050 Smoral Rd Camillus (13031) *(G-3354)*
Upstone Materials Inc 518 873-2275
Rr 9 Lewis (12950) *(G-7452)*
Upstone Materials Inc 518 891-0236
909 State Route 3 Saranac Lake (12983) *(G-15167)*
Upstone Materials Inc (HQ) 518 561-5321
111 Quarry Rd Plattsburgh (12901) *(G-13735)*
Upstone Materials Inc 518 483-2671
359 Elm St Malone (12953) *(G-8050)*
Upstone Materials Inc 315 265-8036
111 Quarry Rd Plattsburgh (12901) *(G-13736)*
Upstone Materials Inc 315 764-0251
539 S Main St Massena (13662) *(G-8233)*
Uptek Solutions Corp 631 256-5565
130 Knickerbocker Ave A Bohemia (11716) *(G-1150)*
Uptown, Halfmoon *Also called Save More Beverage Corp (G-5938)*
Uptown Media Group LLC 212 360-5073
113 E 125th St Frnt 1 New York (10035) *(G-12496)*
Uptown Nails LLC 800 748-1881
500 5th Ave New York (10110) *(G-12497)*
Upturn Industries Inc 607 967-2923
2-4 Whitney Way Bainbridge (13733) *(G-555)*
Urban Apparel Group Inc 212 947-7009
226 W 37th St Fl 17 New York (10018) *(G-12498)*
Urban Green Energy Inc 917 720-5681
330 W 38th St Rm 1103 New York (10018) *(G-12499)*
Urban Mapping Inc 415 946-8170
295 Madison Ave Rm 1010 New York (10017) *(G-12500)*
Urban Racercom 718 279-2202
21333 39th Ave Bayside (11361) *(G-771)*
Urban Rose, New York *Also called French Atmosphere Inc (G-10257)*
Urban Technologies Inc 716 672-2709
3451 Stone Quarry Rd Fredonia (14063) *(G-5385)*
Urban Textiles Inc 212 777-1900
49 Elizabeth St Fl 6 New York (10013) *(G-12501)*
Urban Woodworks Ltd 718 827-1570
18 Crescent St Brooklyn (11208) *(G-2730)*
Urbandaddy Inc 212 929-7905
900 Broadway Ste 1003 New York (10003) *(G-12502)*
Urdu Times 718 297-8700
16920 Hillside Ave Jamaica (11432) *(G-6997)*
Urrey Lumber 518 827-4851
663 Clauverwie Rd Middleburgh (12122) *(G-8453)*
Ursula Company Store, Waterford *Also called Ursula of Switzerland Inc (G-16645)*
Ursula of Switzerland Inc (PA) 518 237-2580
31 Mohawk Ave Waterford (12188) *(G-16645)*
Urthworx Inc 646 373-7535
320 W 106th St Apt 2f New York (10025) *(G-12503)*
US Airports Flight Support Svc, Rochester *Also called Usairports Services Inc (G-14776)*
US Allegro Inc 347 408-6601
5430 44th St Maspeth (11378) *(G-8204)*
US Alliance Paper Inc 631 254-3030
101 Heartland Blvd Edgewood (11717) *(G-4632)*
US Angels, New York *Also called S & C Bridals LLC (G-11960)*
US Authentic LLC 914 767-0295
11 Mt Holly Rd E Katonah (10536) *(G-7163)*
US Beverage Net Inc 315 579-2025
225 W Jefferson St Syracuse (13202) *(G-16089)*
US China Magazine 212 663-4333
200 W 95th St Apt 21 New York (10025) *(G-12504)*
US Clothing Company, Bronx *Also called U S Embroidery Inc (G-1482)*
US Concrete Inc 718 853-4644
10 Powerhouse Rd Roslyn Heights (11577) *(G-15058)*
US Concrete Inc 718 438-6800
692 Mcdonald Ave Brooklyn (11218) *(G-2731)*
US Design Group Ltd 212 354-4070
1385 Broadway Rm 1905 New York (10018) *(G-12505)*
US Diagnostics Inc 866 216-5308
711 3rd Ave Rm 1502 New York (10017) *(G-12506)*
US Drives Inc 716 731-1606
2221 Niagara Falls Blvd # 41 Niagara Falls (14304) *(G-12904)*
US Electroplating Corp 631 293-1998
100 Field St Unit A West Babylon (11704) *(G-16869)*
US Energy Group, New Hyde Park *Also called Use Acquisition LLC (G-8916)*
US Frontline News Inc 212 922-9090
228 E 45th St Rm 700 New York (10017) *(G-12507)*
US Greenfiber, Gloversville *Also called Greenfiber Albany Inc (G-5727)*
US Health Equipment Company 845 658-7576
138 Maple Hill Rd Kingston (12401) *(G-7249)*
US Hispanic Media Inc (HQ) 212 885-8000
1 Metrotech Ctr Fl 18 Brooklyn (11201) *(G-2732)*
US Hoists Corp 631 472-3030
800 Burman Blvd Calverton (11933) *(G-3330)*
US Home Textiles Group LLC 212 768-3030
1400 Broadway Fl 18 New York (10018) *(G-12508)*
US Juice Partners LLC (HQ) 516 621-1122
2 Seaview Blvd Port Washington (11050) *(G-13888)*
US News & World Report Inc (PA) 212 716-6800
4 New York Plz Fl 6 New York (10004) *(G-12509)*
US Nonwovens Corp (PA) 631 952-0100
100 Emjay Blvd Brentwood (11717) *(G-1196)*
US Optical LLC 315 463-4800
6848 Ellicott Dr East Syracuse (13057) *(G-4590)*
US Peroxide 716 775-5585
1815 Love Rd Ste 1 Grand Island (14072) *(G-5788)*
US Polychemical Holding Corp 845 356-5530
584 Chestnut Ridge Rd Spring Valley (10977) *(G-15628)*
US Pump Corp 516 303-7799
707 Woodfield Rd West Hempstead (11552) *(G-16896)*
US Salt LLC 607 535-2721
Salt Point Rd Watkins Glen (14891) *(G-16723)*
US Sander LLC 518 875-9157
4131 Rte 20 Esperance (12066) *(G-4846)*
US Weekly LLC 212 484-1616
1290 Ave Of The Americas New York (10104) *(G-12510)*
USA Body Inc 315 852-6123
994 Middle Lake Rd De Ruyter (13052) *(G-4107)*
USA Custom Pad Corp (PA) 607 563-9550
16 Winkler Rd Sidney (13838) *(G-15467)*
USA Foil Inc 631 234-5252
70 Emjay Blvd Bldg C Brentwood (11717) *(G-1197)*
USA Furs By George Inc 212 643-1415
212 W 30th St New York (10001) *(G-12511)*
USA Halal Foods Inc 718 291-9111
4700 Northern Blvd Long Island City (11101) *(G-7939)*
USA Illumination Inc 845 565-8500
1126 River Rd New Windsor (12553) *(G-9002)*
USA Sealing Inc 716 288-9952
356 Sonwil Dr Cheektowaga (14225) *(G-3620)*
USA Sewing Inc 315 792-8017
901 Broad St Ste 2 Utica (13501) *(G-16386)*
USA Signs of America Inc 631 254-6900
172 E Industry Ct Deer Park (11729) *(G-4246)*
USA Tees.com, Brooklyn *Also called Universal Screening Associates (G-2728)*
USA Today International Corp 703 854-3400
535 Madison Ave Fl 27 New York (10022) *(G-12512)*
Usai, New Windsor *Also called USA Illumination Inc (G-9002)*
Usairports Services Inc 585 527-6835
1295 Scottsville Rd Rochester (14624) *(G-14776)*

ALPHABETIC

Use Acquisition LLC — 270 Park Ave New Hyde Park (11040) *(G-8916)* 516 812-6800

Used Equipment Directory, New York Also called Penton Media Inc *(G-11628)*

Usheco Inc — 138 Maple Hill Rd Kingston (12401) *(G-7250)* 845 658-9200

Ushers Machine and Tool Co Inc — 180 Ushers Rd Round Lake (12151) *(G-15062)* 518 877-5501

Uspa Accessories LLC — 119 W 40th St Fl 3 New York (10018) *(G-12513)* 212 868-2590

Usq Group LLC — 222 Broadway Fl 19 New York (10038) *(G-12514)* 212 777-7751

UTC Fire SEC Americas Corp Inc — 10 Walker Way Ste 3 Albany (12205) *(G-148)* 518 456-0444

Utica Boilers, Utica Also called ECR International Inc *(G-16351)*

Utica Cutlery Company — 820 Noyes St Utica (13502) *(G-16387)* 315 733-4663

Utica Metal Products Inc — 1526 Lincoln Ave Utica (13502) *(G-16388)* 315 732-6163

Utility Brass & Bronze Div, Brooklyn Also called Giumenta Corp *(G-2026)*

Utility Canvas Inc (PA) — 2686 Route 44 55 Gardiner (12525) *(G-5565)* 845 255-9290

Utility Engineering Co — 40 Walter St Pearl River (10965) *(G-13492)* 845 735-8900

Utility Manufacturing Co Inc — 700 Main St Westbury (11590) *(G-17068)* 516 997-6300

Utility Systems Tech Inc — 70 Cohoes Rd Watervliet (12189) *(G-16716)* 518 326-4142

Utleys Incorporated — 3123 61st St Woodside (11377) *(G-17375)* 718 956-1661

Utrecht Art Supplies, New York Also called Utrecht Manufacturing Corp *(G-12515)*

Utrecht Manufacturing Corp — 237 W 23rd St New York (10011) *(G-12515)* 212 675-8699

V & E Kohnstamm & Co Div, Brooklyn Also called Virginia Dare Extract Co Inc *(G-2747)*

V & J Graphics Inc — 153 Phelps St Oneida (13421) *(G-13191)* 315 363-1933

V A I, Ronkonkoma Also called Vormittag Associates Inc *(G-15023)*

V A P Tool & Dye — 436 W 4th St West Islip (11795) *(G-16938)* 631 587-5262

V C N Group Ltd Inc — 1 Clifton St North Baldwin (11510) *(G-12928)* 516 223-4812

V E Power Door Co Inc — 140 Emjay Blvd Brentwood (11717) *(G-1198)* 631 231-4500

V E W, New York Also called Vera Wang Group LLC *(G-12542)*

V Lake Industries Inc — 1555 Niagara St Buffalo (14213) *(G-3265)* 716 885-9141

V M Choppy & Sons, Troy Also called Choppy V M & Sons LLC *(G-16253)*

V Magazine, New York Also called Visionaire Publishing LLC *(G-12581)*

Va Inc — 803 Linden Ave Ste 1 Rochester (14625) *(G-14777)* 585 385-5930

Vaad LHafotzas Sichoes — 788 Eastern Pkwy Brooklyn (11213) *(G-2733)* 718 778-5436

Vac Air Service Inc — 1295 E 2nd St Jamestown (14701) *(G-7074)* 716 665-2206

Vactronics, Bayside Hills Also called Cathay Global Co Inc *(G-774)*

Vacuum Instrument Corporation (PA) — 2101 9th Ave Ste A Ronkonkoma (11779) *(G-15021)* 631 737-0900

Vader Systems LLC — 385 Crsspint Pkwy Ste 104 Getzville (14068) *(G-5618)* 716 688-1600

Vaire LLC — 200 E 2nd St Ste 34 Huntington Station (11746) *(G-6765)* 631 271-4933

Valad Electric Heating Corp — 65 Leonards Dr Montgomery (12549) *(G-8640)* 888 509-4927

Valair Inc — 87 Harbor St Wilson (14172) *(G-17292)* 716 751-9480

Valassis Communications Inc — 5 Marway Cir Ste 8 Rochester (14624) *(G-14778)* 585 627-4138

Valencia Bakery Inc (PA) — 801 Edgewater Rd Bronx (10474) *(G-1486)* 718 991-6400

Valenti Distributing — 84 Maple Ave Blasdell (14219) *(G-962)* 716 824-2304

Valenti Neckwear Co Inc — 540 Nepperhan Ave Ste 564 Yonkers (10701) *(G-17511)* 914 969-0700

Valentin & Kalich Jwly Mfg Ltd — 42 W 48th St Ste 903 New York (10036) *(G-12516)* 212 575-9044

Valentin Magro, New York Also called Valentin & Kalich Jwly Mfg Ltd *(G-12516)*

Valentine Jewelry Mfg Co Inc — 31 W 47th St Ste 602 New York (10036) *(G-12517)* 212 382-0606

Valentine Packaging Corp — 6020 59th Pl Ste 7 Maspeth (11378) *(G-8205)* 718 418-6000

Valentine Printing Corp — 509 E 79th St Brooklyn (11236) *(G-2734)* 718 444-4400

Valeo — 4 Executive Plz Ste 114 Yonkers (10701) *(G-17512)* 800 634-2704

Valerie Bohigian — 225 Hunter Ave Sleepy Hollow (10591) *(G-15498)* 914 631-8866

Valian Associates, Sleepy Hollow Also called Valerie Bohigian *(G-15498)*

Valiant Entertainment LLC — 350 7th Ave Rm 300 New York (10001) *(G-12518)* 212 972-0361

Valid Electric Corp — 65 Leonards Dr Montgomery (12549) *(G-8641)* 914 631-9436

Valle Signs and Awnings — 889 Nassau Rd Uniondale (11553) *(G-16325)* 516 408-3440

Valley Creek Side Inc — 1960 State Route 8 Clayville (13322) *(G-3716)* 315 839-5526

Valley Industrial Products Inc — 152 New York Ave Huntington (11743) *(G-6727)* 631 385-9300

Valley Industries, Gerry Also called Cobbe Industries Inc *(G-5604)*

Valley Signs, Clayville Also called Valley Creek Side Inc *(G-3716)*

Valley Stream Sporting Gds Inc — 325 Hendrickson Ave Lynbrook (11563) *(G-7992)* 516 593-7800

Valmont Inc (PA) — 1 W 34th St Rm 303 New York (10001) *(G-12519)* 212 685-1653

Valmont Site Pro 1, Hauppauge Also called Pirod Inc *(G-6191)*

Valois of America Inc — 250 N Route 303 Congers (10920) *(G-3886)* 845 639-3700

Valplast International Corp — 200 Shames Dr Westbury (11590) *(G-17069)* 516 442-3923

Value Fragrances & Flavors, Goshen Also called Value Fragrances Inc *(G-5756)*

Value Fragrances & Flavors Inc — 7 Musket Ct Goshen (10924) *(G-5755)* 845 294-5726

Value Fragrances Inc — 7 Musket Ct Goshen (10924) *(G-5756)* 845 294-5726

Value Line Inc (HQ) — 551 5th Ave Rm 300 New York (10176) *(G-12520)* 212 907-1500

Value Line Publishing LLC — 551 5th Ave Rm 300 New York (10176) *(G-12521)* 201 842-8054

Value Spring Technology Inc — 521 Harrison Ave Harrison (10528) *(G-6013)* 917 705-4658

Valvetech Inc — 1391 Phelps Junction Rd Phelps (14532) *(G-13562)* 315 548-4551

Valvoline Inc — 374 Central Ave White Plains (10606) *(G-17205)* 914 684-0170

Van Alphen & Doran Corp — 3098 Guilderland Ave Schenectady (12306) *(G-15332)* 518 782-9242

Van Blarcom Closures Inc (PA) — 156 Sanford St Brooklyn (11205) *(G-2735)* 718 855-3810

Van Cpeters Logging Inc — 4480 Peas Eddy Rd Hancock (13783) *(G-5990)* 607 637-3574

Van De Mark Chemical Co Inc (PA) — 1 N Transit Rd Lockport (14094) *(G-7655)* 716 433-6764

Van Heusen, New Windsor Also called Pvh Corp *(G-8995)*

Van Heusen, Deer Park Also called Pvh Corp *(G-4220)*

Van Heusen, New York Also called Pvh Corp *(G-11782)*

Van Heusen, New York Also called Pvh Corp *(G-11783)*

Van Laeken Richard — 2680 Parker Rd Newark (14513) *(G-12768)* 315 331-0289

Van Leeuwen Artisan Ice Cream — 56 Dobbin St Brooklyn (11222) *(G-2736)* 718 701-1630

Van Reenen Tool & Die Inc — 350 Commerce Dr 4 Rochester (14623) *(G-14779)* 585 288-6000

Van Slyke Belting LLC — 606 Snyders Corners Rd Poestenkill (12140) *(G-13756)* 518 283-5479

Van Thomas Inc — 740 Driving Park Ave G1 Rochester (14613) *(G-14780)* 585 426-1414

Vanberg & Dewulf Co Inc — 52 Pioneer St Ste 4 Cooperstown (13326) *(G-3912)* 607 547-8184

Vance Metal Fabricators Inc — 251 Gambee Rd Geneva (14456) *(G-5600)* 315 789-5626

Vanchlor Company Inc (PA) — 45 Main St Lockport (14094) *(G-7656)* 716 434-2624

Vanchlor Company Inc — 555 W Jackson St Lockport (14094) *(G-7657)* 716 434-2624

Vandam Inc — 121 W 27th St Ste 1102 New York (10001) *(G-12522)* 212 929-0416

Vander Heyden Woodworking — 151 W 25th St Fl 8 New York (10001) *(G-12523)* 212 242-0525

Vanderveer Pharmacy, Brooklyn Also called Nostrand Pharmacy LLC *(G-2387)*

Vandilay Industries Inc — 60 Bell St Unit A West Babylon (11704) *(G-16870)* 631 226-3064

Vanec, Orchard Park Also called Vibration & Noise Engrg Corp *(G-13327)*

Vanguard Graphics LLC — 17 Hallwoods Rd Ithaca (14850) *(G-6916)* 607 272-1212

Vanguard Metals Inc — 135 Brightside Ave Central Islip (11722) *(G-3541)* 631 234-6500

Vanguard Printing, Ithaca Also called Vanguard Graphics LLC *(G-6916)*

Vanhouten Motorsports — 27 Center Rd Lacona (13083) *(G-7277)* 315 387-6312

Vanity Fair — 4 Times Sq Bsmt C1b New York (10036) *(G-12524)* 212 286-6052

Vanity Fair Bathmart Inc — 2971 Webster Ave Bronx (10458) *(G-1487)* 718 584-6700

Vanity Fair Brands LP — 25 W 39th St New York (10018) *(G-12525)* 212 548-1548

Vanity Room Inc — 230 W 39th St Fl 9 New York (10018) *(G-12526)* 212 921-7154

Vanlab, Rochester Also called Synergy Flavors NY Company LLC *(G-14735)*

Vans Inc — 313 Smith Haven Mall Lake Grove (11755) *(G-7293)* 631 724-1011

Vans Inc — 25 Franklin St Brooklyn (11222) *(G-2737)* 718 349-2311

Vansantis Development Inc 315 461-0113
4595 Morgan Pl Liverpool (13090) *(G-7581)*
Vansridge Dairy LLC 315 364-8569
2831 Black St Scipio Center (13147) *(G-15344)*
Vantage Mfg & Assembly LLC 845 471-5290
900 Dutchess Tpke Poughkeepsie (12603) *(G-13954)*
Vantage Press Inc 212 736-1767
419 Park Ave S Fl 18 New York (10016) *(G-12527)*
Vante Inc 716 778-7691
3600 Coomer Rd Newfane (14108) *(G-12813)*
Vape Flavorium 607 346-7276
940c Chemung St Horseheads (14845) *(G-6623)*
Vape Paradise Inc 845 467-4517
47 Bennett St Middletown (10940) *(G-8504)*
Vape4style Inc 718 395-0406
1762 Gerritsen Ave Brooklyn (11229) *(G-2738)*
Varflex Corporation 315 336-4400
512 W Court St Rome (13440) *(G-14867)*
Variable Graphics LLC 212 691-2323
15 W 36th St Rm 601 New York (10018) *(G-12528)*
Varian Medical Systems, Liverpool *Also called Infimed Inc (G-7547)*
Varick Street Litho Inc 646 843-0800
121 Varick St New York (10013) *(G-12529)*
Variety Gem Co Inc (PA) 212 921-1820
295 Northern Blvd Ste 208 Great Neck (11021) *(G-5867)*
Varnish Software Inc 201 857-2832
85 Broad St Fl 18 New York (10004) *(G-12530)*
Varonis Systems Inc (PA) 877 292-8767
1250 Broadway Fl 29 New York (10001) *(G-12531)*
Varsity Monitor LLC 212 691-6292
50 5th Ave Fl 3 New York (10011) *(G-12532)*
Vasomedical Inc (PA) 516 997-4600
137 Commercial St Ste 200 Plainview (11803) *(G-13668)*
Vasomedical Solutions Inc 516 997-4600
137 Commercial St Ste 200 Plainview (11803) *(G-13669)*
Vasquez Tito 212 944-0441
36 W 47th St Ste 206 New York (10036) *(G-12533)*
Vassilaros Coffee, Flushing *Also called John A Vassilaros & Son Inc (G-5264)*
Vaughan Designs Inc (HQ) 212 319-7070
979 3rd Ave Ste 1511 New York (10022) *(G-12534)*
Vault.com, Vault Media, New York *Also called Vaultcom Inc (G-12535)*
Vaultcom Inc (PA) 212 366-4212
132 W 31st St Rm 1501 New York (10001) *(G-12535)*
Vcp Mobility Inc 718 356-7827
4131 Richmond Ave Staten Island (10312) *(G-15773)*
Vdc Electronics Inc 631 683-5850
155 W Carver St Ste 2 Huntington (11743) *(G-6728)*
VDO Lab Inc 914 949-1741
400 Tarrytown Rd White Plains (10607) *(G-17206)*
Vector Group Ltd 212 409-2800
712 5th Ave New York (10019) *(G-12536)*
Vector Magnetics LLC 607 273-8351
236 Cherry St Ithaca (14850) *(G-6917)*
Vectra Inc 718 361-1000
3200 Skillman Ave Fl 3 Long Island City (11101) *(G-7940)*
Vectra Visual, Long Island City *Also called Vectra Inc (G-7940)*
Vedell North Fork LLC 631 323-3526
36225 Main Rd Cutchogue (11935) *(G-4100)*
Veeco Instruments Inc 516 677-0200
100 Sunnyside Blvd Ste B Woodbury (11797) *(G-17321)*
Veeco Instruments Inc 516 349-8300
1 Terminal Dr Plainview (11803) *(G-13670)*
Veeco Instruments Inc (PA) 516 677-0200
1 Terminal Dr Plainview (11803) *(G-13671)*
Veeco Process Equipment, Plainview *Also called Veeco Instruments Inc (G-13670)*
Veeco Process Equipment Inc (HQ) 516 677-0200
1 Terminal Dr Plainview (11803) *(G-13672)*
Veerhouse Voda Haiti LLC 917 353-5944
42 Broadway Fl 12 New York (10004) *(G-12537)*
Veerhouse Voda Haiti SA, New York *Also called Veerhouse Voda Haiti LLC (G-12537)*
Vega Coffee Inc 415 881-7969
325 N End Ave Apt 4b New York (10282) *(G-12538)*
Vegetable Operations, Geneva *Also called Seneca Foods Corporation (G-5597)*
Vegetable Operations, Marion *Also called Seneca Foods Corporation (G-8131)*
Vehicle Manufacturers Inc 631 851-1700
400 Oser Ave Ste 100 Hauppauge (11788) *(G-6247)*
Vehicle Safety Dept 315 458-6683
5801 E Taft Rd Ste 4 Syracuse (13212) *(G-16090)*
Vehicle Tracking Solutions LLC 631 586-7400
152 Veterans Memorial Hwy Commack (11725) *(G-3870)*
Veja Electronics Inc (PA) 631 321-6086
46 W Jefryn Blvd Ste A Deer Park (11729) *(G-4247)*
Velis Associates Inc (PA) 631 225-4220
151 S 14th St Lindenhurst (11757) *(G-7514)*
Vell Company Inc 845 365-1013
700 Oak Tree Rd Palisades (10964) *(G-13429)*
Velmex Inc 585 657-6151
7550 State Route 5 And 20 Bloomfield (14469) *(G-986)*
Velocity Outsourcing LLC 212 891-4043
750 3rd Ave New York (10017) *(G-12539)*
Velocity Pharma LLC 516 312-7585
226 Sherwood Ave Unit B Farmingdale (11735) *(G-5147)*
Velocity Print Solutions, Scotia *Also called Shipmtes/Printmates Holdg Corp (G-15353)*
Velvet Healing By Alma Corp 347 271-4220
645 Melrose Ave Frnt 1 Bronx (10455) *(G-1488)*
Velvetop Products, Huntington Station *Also called Walsh & Hughes Inc (G-6766)*
Venco Sales Inc 631 754-0782
755 Park Ave Ste 300 Huntington (11743) *(G-6729)*
Vending Times Inc 516 442-1850
55 Maple Ave Ste 304 Rockville Centre (11570) *(G-14831)*
Vendome Group LLC 646 795-3899
216 E 45th St Fl 6 New York (10017) *(G-12540)*
Vendome Press, New York *Also called Helvetica Press Incorporated (G-10499)*
Veneer One Inc 516 536-6480
3415 Hampton Rd Oceanside (11572) *(G-13125)*
Vengo Inc 866 526-7054
4550 30th St Ste 41 Long Island City (11101) *(G-7941)*
Venice Marina, Brooklyn *Also called Marina Holding Corp (G-2270)*
Vent-A-Fume, Buffalo *Also called Vent-A-Kiln Corporation (G-3266)*
Vent-A-Kiln Corporation 716 876-2023
51 Botsford Pl Buffalo (14216) *(G-3266)*
Ventura Enterprise Co Inc 212 391-0170
512 Fashion Ave Fl 38 New York (10018) *(G-12541)*
Venture Economics, New York *Also called Securities Data Publishing Inc (G-12033)*
Venture Respiratory Inc 718 437-3633
1413 38th St Brooklyn (11218) *(G-2739)*
Venue Graphics Supply Inc 718 361-1690
1120 46th Rd Long Island City (11101) *(G-7942)*
Venus, New York *Also called Shah Diamonds Inc (G-12059)*
Venus Manufacturing Co Inc (PA) 315 639-3100
349 Lakeview Dr Dexter (13634) *(G-4310)*
Venus Pharmaceuticals Intl Inc 631 249-4140
55a Kennedy Dr Hauppauge (11788) *(G-6248)*
Venus Printing Company 212 967-8900
1420 Kew Ave Hewlett (11557) *(G-6339)*
Vepo Solutions LLC 914 384-2121
3 Fairview Ct Cross River (10518) *(G-4086)*
Ver-Tech Elevator, Ozone Park *Also called Elevator Ventures Corporation (G-13403)*
Vera Wang Group LLC (PA) 212 575-6400
15 E 26th St Fl 4 New York (10010) *(G-12542)*
Veranda Magazine, New York *Also called Veranda Publications Inc (G-12543)*
Veranda Publications Inc 212 903-5206
300 W 57th St Fl 28 New York (10019) *(G-12543)*
Veratex Inc (PA) 212 683-9300
254 5th Ave Fl 3 New York (10001) *(G-12544)*
Verdonette Inc 212 719-2003
270 W 39th St Fl 5 New York (10018) *(G-12545)*
Veriled Inc 877 521-5520
100 Church St Ste 871 New York (10007) *(G-12546)*
Verizon, New York *Also called Supermedia LLC (G-12265)*
Verla International Ltd 845 561-2440
463 Temple Hill Rd New Windsor (12553) *(G-9003)*
Vermed Inc 800 669-6905
400 Exchange St Buffalo (14204) *(G-3267)*
Vermont Multicolor Slate 518 642-2400
146 State Route 22a Middle Granville (12849) *(G-8435)*
Vermont Natural Stoneworks 518 642-2460
146 State Route 22a Middle Granville (12849) *(G-8436)*
Vermont Structural Slate Co 518 499-1912
Buckley Rd Whitehall (12887) *(G-17219)*
Vernon Devices, New Rochelle *Also called Halpern Tool Corp (G-8953)*
Vernon Plating Works Inc 718 639-1124
3318 57th St Woodside (11377) *(G-17376)*
Vernon Wine & Liquor Inc 718 784-5096
5006 Vernon Blvd Long Island City (11101) *(G-7943)*
Verns Machine Co Inc 315 926-4223
4929 Steel Point Rd Marion (14505) *(G-8133)*
Verona Pharma Inc 914 797-5007
50 Main St Ste 1000 White Plains (10606) *(G-17207)*
Verragio Ltd (PA) 212 868-8181
132 W 36th St Bsmt New York (10018) *(G-12547)*
Verris Inc 201 565-1648
99 Wall St Unit 236 New York (10005) *(G-12548)*
Versailles Drapery Upholstery 212 533-2059
4709 30th St Ste 200 Long Island City (11101) *(G-7944)*
Versailles Industries LLC 212 792-9615
485 Fashion Ave Rm 500 New York (10018) *(G-12549)*
Versaponents, Deer Park *Also called Lighting Sculptures Inc (G-4190)*
Versaponents Inc 631 242-3387
66 N Industry Ct Deer Park (11729) *(G-4248)*
Verso Inc 718 246-8160
20 Jay St Ste 1010 Brooklyn (11201) *(G-2740)*
Verso Corporation 212 599-2700
370 Lexington Ave Rm 802 New York (10017) *(G-12550)*
Verso Paper Management LP 781 320-8660
370 Lexington Ave Rm 802 New York (10017) *(G-12551)*
Verso Paper Management LP (PA) 212 599-2700
60 W 42nd Ste 1942 New York (10165) *(G-12552)*
Vertaloc, New York *Also called US Diagnostics Inc (G-12506)*
Vertana Group LLC (PA) 646 430-8226
37 W 20th St Ste 804 New York (10011) *(G-12553)*
Vertex Innovative Solutions In 315 437-6711
6671 Commerce Blvd Syracuse (13211) *(G-16091)*

ALPHABETIC

Vertical Apparel, New York *Also called American Apparel Trading Corp* ***(G-9163)***
Vertical Lax Inc 518 669-3699
20 Corporate Cir Ste 4 Albany (12203) ***(G-149)***
Vertical Research Partners LLC 212 257-6499
52 Vanderbilt Ave Rm 200 New York (10017) ***(G-12554)***
Vertiv Services Inc 516 349-8500
79 Express St Fl 14 Plainview (11803) ***(G-13673)***
Very Best Irtj 914 271-6585
435 Yorktown Rd Croton On Hudson (10520) ***(G-4092)***
Vescom Structural Systems Inc 516 876-8100
100 Shames Dr Unit 1 Westbury (11590) ***(G-17070)***
Vespa Sand & Stone, Watertown *Also called John Vespa Inc* ***(G-16678)***
Vestal Asphalt Inc (PA) 607 785-3393
201 Stage Rd Vestal (13850) ***(G-16480)***
Vestal Electronic Devices LLC 607 773-8461
635 Dickson St Endicott (13760) ***(G-4838)***
Veteran Air LLC 315 720-1101
7174 State Fair Blvd Syracuse (13209) ***(G-16092)***
Veteran Air Filtration, Syracuse *Also called Veteran Air LLC* ***(G-16092)***
Veteran Offset Printing, Rochester *Also called Veterans Offset Printing Inc* ***(G-14781)***
Veterans Offset Printing Inc 585 288-2900
500 N Goodman St Rochester (14609) ***(G-14781)***
Veterinary Biochemical Ltd 845 473-1900
201 Smith St Poughkeepsie (12601) ***(G-13955)***
Vetra Systems Corporation 631 434-3185
275 Marcus Blvd Unit J Hauppauge (11788) ***(G-6249)***
Vetroelite Inc 925 724-7900
115 W 30th St Rm 402 New York (10001) ***(G-12555)***
Vetta Jewelry Inc (PA) 212 564-8250
70 W 36th St Fl 9 New York (10018) ***(G-12556)***
Vez Inc 718 273-7002
1209 Forest Ave Staten Island (10310) ***(G-15774)***
Vf Imagewear Inc 718 352-2363
333 Pratt Ave Bayside (11359) ***(G-772)***
Vf Outdoor Inc 718 698-6215
2655 Richmond Ave # 1570 Staten Island (10314) ***(G-15775)***
Vf Outdoor LLC 845 928-4900
461 Dune Rd Central Valley (10917) ***(G-3556)***
Vf Sportswear Inc 212 541-5757
40 W 57th St Fl 3 New York (10019) ***(G-12557)***
Vgg Holding LLC 212 415-6700
590 Madison Ave Fl 41 New York (10022) ***(G-12558)***
Vhx Corporation 347 689-1446
555 W 18th St New York (10011) ***(G-12559)***
Via America Fine Jewelry Inc 212 302-1218
578 5th Ave Unit 26 New York (10036) ***(G-12560)***
Viamedia Corporation 718 485-7792
2610 Atlantic Ave Brooklyn (11207) ***(G-2741)***
Viana Signs Corp 516 887-2000
3520 Lawson Blvd Oceanside (11572) ***(G-13126)***
Viatech Pubg Solutions Inc 631 968-8500
1440 5th Ave Bay Shore (11706) ***(G-747)***
Viatran Corporation (HQ) 716 564-7813
199 Fire Tower Dr Tonawanda (14150) ***(G-16233)***
Vibe Magazine, New York *Also called Vibe Media Group LLC* ***(G-12561)***
Vibe Media Group LLC 212 448-7300
120 Wall St Fl 21 New York (10005) ***(G-12561)***
Vibra Tech Industries Inc 914 946-1916
126 Oakley Ave White Plains (10601) ***(G-17208)***
Vibration & Noise Engrg Corp 716 827-4959
3374 N Benzing Rd Orchard Park (14127) ***(G-13327)***
Vibration Eliminator Co Inc (PA) 631 841-4000
15 Dixon Ave Copiague (11726) ***(G-3959)***
Vibro-Laser Instrs Corp LLC 518 874-2700
2c Glens Falls Tech Park Glens Falls (12801) ***(G-5715)***
Vic Demayos Inc 845 626-4343
4967 Us Highway 209 Accord (12404) ***(G-1)***
Vic Leak Detection, Ronkonkoma *Also called Vacuum Instrument Corporation* ***(G-15021)***
Vic-Gina Printing Company Inc 914 636-0200
1299 North Ave New Rochelle (10804) ***(G-8973)***
Vicarious Visions Inc 518 283-4090
350 Jordan Rd Troy (12180) ***(G-16283)***
Vickers Stock Research Corp (HQ) 212 425-7500
61 Broadway Rm 1910 New York (10006) ***(G-12562)***
Vicks Lithograph & Prtg Corp (PA) 315 272-2401
5166 Commercial Dr Yorkville (13495) ***(G-17544)***
Vicks Lithograph & Prtg Corp 315 736-9344
5210 Commercial Dr Yorkville (13495) ***(G-17545)***
Vicon Industries Inc (PA) 631 952-2288
135 Fell Ct Hauppauge (11788) ***(G-6250)***
Vicron Electronic Mfg, Bronx *Also called Monarch Electric Products Inc* ***(G-1405)***
Victoire Latam Asset MGT LLC, New York *Also called Capital E Financial Group* ***(G-9574)***
Victor Insulators Inc 585 924-2127
280 Maple Ave Victor (14564) ***(G-16534)***
Victoria Albi Intl Inc 212 689-2600
1178 Broadway Fl 5 New York (10001) ***(G-12563)***
Victoria Dngelo Intr Cllctions, Warwick *Also called DAngelo Home Collections Inc* ***(G-16609)***
Victoria Fine Foods LLC (HQ) 718 649-1635
443 E 100th St Brooklyn (11236) ***(G-2742)***
Victoria Plating Co Inc 718 589-1550
650 Tiffany St Bronx (10474) ***(G-1489)***
Victoria Precision Inc 845 473-9309
78 Travis Rd Hyde Park (12538) ***(G-6777)***
Victoria Stilwell Positevely, New York *Also called Dog Good Products LLC* ***(G-9947)***
Victory Garden 212 206-7273
31 Carmine St Frnt A New York (10014) ***(G-12564)***
Victory Signs Inc 315 762-0220
8915 Old State Route 13 Canastota (13032) ***(G-3402)***
Victory Sports, Staten Island *Also called Glenda Inc* ***(G-15699)***
Victory Vision Care Inc 718 622-2020
565 Atlantic Ave Brooklyn (11217) ***(G-2743)***
Vida-Blend LLC 518 627-4138
1430 State Highway 5s Amsterdam (12010) ***(G-373)***
Vidal Candies USA Inc 609 781-8169
845 3rd Ave Fl 6 New York (10022) ***(G-12565)***
Vidbolt Inc 716 560-8944
4 Elam Pl Buffalo (14214) ***(G-3268)***
Videk Inc 585 377-0377
1387 Fairport Rd 1000c Fairport (14450) ***(G-4892)***
Video Technology Services Inc 516 937-9700
5 Aerial Way Ste 300 Syosset (11791) ***(G-15861)***
Videotec Security Inc 518 825-0020
35 Gateway Dr Ste 100 Plattsburgh (12901) ***(G-13737)***
Viducci, Great Neck *Also called Classic Creations Inc* ***(G-5815)***
Viele Manufacturing Corp 718 893-2200
1340 Viele Ave Bronx (10474) ***(G-1490)***
View Collections Inc 212 944-4030
265 W 37th St Rm 5w New York (10018) ***(G-12566)***
Viewfinder Inc 212 831-0939
101 W 23rd St Ste 2303 New York (10011) ***(G-12567)***
Viewsport International Inc 585 259-1562
11 Feathery Cir Penfield (14526) ***(G-13528)***
Vigliotti's Great Garden, Yaphank *Also called Scotts Company LLC* ***(G-17416)***
Vigneri Chocolate Inc 585 254-6160
810 Emerson St Rochester (14613) ***(G-14782)***
Viking Athletics Ltd 631 957-8000
80 Montauk Hwy Ste 1 Lindenhurst (11757) ***(G-7515)***
Viking Industries Inc 845 883-6325
89 S Ohioville Rd New Paltz (12561) ***(G-8927)***
Viking Iron Works Inc 845 471-5010
37 Hatfield Ln Poughkeepsie (12603) ***(G-13956)***
Viking Jackets & Athletic Wear, Walden *Also called C & C Athletic Inc* ***(G-16550)***
Viking Mar Wldg Ship Repr LLC 718 758-4116
14 Raleigh Pl Brooklyn (11226) ***(G-2744)***
Viking Technologies Ltd 631 957-8000
80 E Montauk Hwy Lindenhurst (11757) ***(G-7516)***
Viking-Cives, Harrisville *Also called Cives Corporation* ***(G-6014)***
Viktor Gold Enterprise Corp 212 768-8885
58 W 47th St Unit 36 New York (10036) ***(G-12568)***
Village Decoration Ltd 315 437-2522
20 Corporate Cir East Syracuse (13057) ***(G-4591)***
Village Lantern Baking Corp 631 225-1690
155 N Wellwood Ave Lindenhurst (11757) ***(G-7517)***
Village Plaquesmith, Ththe, Bohemia *Also called Custom House Engravers Inc* ***(G-1042)***
Village Print Room, Oneonta *Also called Pony Farm Press & Graphics* ***(G-13214)***
Village Printing, Endicott *Also called Fambus Inc* ***(G-4815)***
Village Times, The, East Setauket *Also called Times Beacon Record Newspapers* ***(G-4513)***
Village Video News, West Babylon *Also called Village Video Productions Inc* ***(G-16871)***
Village Video Productions Inc 631 752-9311
107 Alder St West Babylon (11704) ***(G-16871)***
Village Wrought Iron Inc 315 683-5589
7756 Main St Fabius (13063) ***(G-4848)***
Villager, The, Brooklyn *Also called Nyc Community Media LLC* ***(G-2395)***
Villeroy & Boch Usa Inc 212 213-8149
41 Madison Ave Ste 1801 New York (10010) ***(G-12569)***
Vin Mar Precision Metal Inc 631 563-6608
1465 S Strong Ave Copiague (11726) ***(G-3960)***
Vin-Clair Bindery, West Haverstraw *Also called Vin-Clair Inc* ***(G-16878)***
Vin-Clair Inc 845 429-4998
132 E Railroad Ave West Haverstraw (10993) ***(G-16878)***
Vincent Associates, Rochester *Also called Va Inc* ***(G-14777)***
Vincent Conigliaro 845 340-0489
308 State Route 28 Kingston (12401) ***(G-7251)***
Vincent Genovese 631 281-8170
19 Woodmere Dr Mastic Beach (11951) ***(G-8237)***
Vincent Manufacturing Co Inc 315 823-0280
560 E Mill St Little Falls (13365) ***(G-7528)***
Vincent Martino Dental Lab 716 674-7800
74 Ransier Dr Buffalo (14224) ***(G-3269)***
Vincents Food Corp 516 481-3544
179 Old Country Rd Carle Place (11514) ***(G-3425)***
Vinci Enterprise Corp 212 768-7888
110 W 40th St Rm 209 New York (10018) ***(G-12570)***
Vincys Printing Ltd 518 355-4363
1832 Curry Rd Schenectady (12306) ***(G-15333)***
Vindagra USA Incorporated 516 605-1960
1121 Walt Whitman Rd Melville (11747) ***(G-8392)***
Vinegar Hill Asset LLC 718 469-0342
436 E 34th St Brooklyn (11203) ***(G-2745)***
Vineland Kosher Poultry Inc 718 921-1347
5600 1st Ave A7 Brooklyn (11220) ***(G-2746)***

Vinevrest Co, Washingtonville *Also called Brotherhood Americas (G-16621)*
Vinifera Wine Cellard, Hammondsport *Also called Konstantin D FRAnk& Sons Vini (G-5980)*
Vinous Group LLC......917 275-5184
54 W 40th St New York (10018) *(G-12571)*
Vinyl Materials Inc......631 586-9444
365 Bay Shore Rd Deer Park (11729) *(G-4249)*
Vinyl Tech Window, Staten Island *Also called Eastern Enterprise Corp (G-15690)*
Vinyl Works Inc......518 786-1200
33 Wade Rd Latham (12110) *(G-7410)*
Vinyline Window and Door Inc......914 476-3500
636 Saw Mill River Rd Yonkers (10710) *(G-17513)*
Viola Cabinet Corporation......716 284-6327
4205 Hyde Park Blvd Niagara Falls (14305) *(G-12905)*
Viola Construction, Niagara Falls *Also called Viola Cabinet Corporation (G-12905)*
Violife LLC......914 207-1820
3 W 35th St Fl 7 New York (10001) *(G-12572)*
VIP Foods Inc......718 821-5330
1080 Wyckoff Ave Ridgewood (11385) *(G-14143)*
VIP Paper Trading Inc......212 382-4642
1140 Ave Of The New York (10036) *(G-12573)*
VIP Printing......718 641-9361
16040 95th St Howard Beach (11414) *(G-6627)*
Viraj - USA Inc (HQ)......516 280-8380
100 Quentin Roosevelt Blv Garden City (11530) *(G-5549)*
Virgil Mountain Inc (PA)......212 378-0007
1 E 28th St Fl 4 New York (10016) *(G-12574)*
Virginia Dare Extract Co Inc (PA)......718 788-6320
882 3rd Ave Unit 2 Brooklyn (11232) *(G-2747)*
Viridis Learning Inc......347 420-9181
2 Gold St Apt 4005 New York (10038) *(G-12575)*
Viropro Inc......650 300-5190
49 W 38th St Fl 11 New York (10018) *(G-12576)*
Virtual Frameworks Inc......646 690-8207
841 Broadway Ste 504 New York (10003) *(G-12577)*
Virtual Super LLC......212 685-6400
116 E 27th St Fl 3 New York (10016) *(G-12578)*
Virtualapt Corp......917 293-3173
45 Main St Ste 613 Brooklyn (11201) *(G-2748)*
Virtue Paintball LLC (PA)......631 617-5560
40 Oser Ave Ste 14 Hauppauge (11788) *(G-6251)*
Virtusphere Inc......607 760-2207
7 Hillside Ave Binghamton (13903) *(G-952)*
Virtuvent Inc......646 845-0387
1221 Av Of The Amrcas4200 New York (10020) *(G-12579)*
Visage Swiss Watch LLC......212 594-7991
29 W 30th St Rm 701 New York (10001) *(G-12580)*
Visage Watches, New York *Also called Visage Swiss Watch LLC (G-12580)*
Visant Secondary Holdings Corp (HQ)......914 595-8200
357 Main St Armonk (10504) *(G-420)*
Vishay Americas Inc......315 938-7575
14992 Snowshoe Rd Henderson (13650) *(G-6313)*
Vishay Thin Film LLC......716 283-4025
2160 Liberty Dr Niagara Falls (14304) *(G-12906)*
Visible Systems Corporation (PA)......508 628-1510
248 Main St Ste 2 Oneida (13421) *(G-13192)*
Visimetrics Corporation......716 871-7070
2290 Kenmore Ave Buffalo (14207) *(G-3270)*
Vision Quest, Brooklyn *Also called Lens Lab Express (G-2212)*
Vision Quest Lighting Inc......631 737-4800
90 13th Ave Unit 1 Ronkonkoma (11779) *(G-15022)*
Vision World, Bedford Hills *Also called Eyeglass Service Industries (G-800)*
Vision-Sciences, Orangeburg *Also called Machida Incorporated (G-13257)*
Visionaire Publishing LLC......646 434-6091
30 W 24th St New York (10010) *(G-12581)*
Visiontron Corp......631 582-8600
720 Old Willets Path Hauppauge (11788) *(G-6252)*
Visiplex Instruments Corp......845 365-0190
250 Clearbrook Rd Elmsford (10523) *(G-4798)*
Visitainer Corp......718 636-0300
148 Classon Ave Brooklyn (11205) *(G-2749)*
Vista Packaging Inc......718 854-9200
1425 37th St Ste 6 Brooklyn (11218) *(G-2750)*
Vista Pharmacy & Surgical, Far Rockaway *Also called J P R Pharmacy Inc (G-4930)*
Vista Visual Group, Lindenhurst *Also called Linear Signs Inc (G-7490)*
Vistalab Technologies Inc......914 244-6226
2 Geneva Rd Brewster (10509) *(G-1228)*
Vistec Lithography, Troy *Also called Raith America Inc (G-16274)*
Vistec Lithography Inc......518 874-3184
300 Jordan Rd Troy (12180) *(G-16284)*
Visual Citi Inc (PA)......631 482-3030
305 Henry St Lindenhurst (11757) *(G-7518)*
Visual Effects Inc......718 324-0011
15929 Jamaica Ave 2 Jamaica (11432) *(G-6998)*
Visual F-X, Brooklyn *Also called Street Beat Sportswear Inc (G-2632)*
Visual ID Source Inc......516 307-9759
65 E 2nd St Mineola (11501) *(G-8571)*
Visual Impact Graphics Inc......585 548-7118
653 Ellicott St Ste 6 Batavia (14020) *(G-652)*
Visual Listing Systems Inc......631 689-7222
19 Technology Dr East Setauket (11733) *(G-4515)*
Visual Millwork & Fix Mfg Inc......718 267-7800
95 Marcus Blvd Deer Park (11729) *(G-4250)*
Vita Rara Inc......518 369-7356
415 River St Ste 4 Troy (12180) *(G-16285)*
Vita-Nat Inc......631 293-6000
298 Adams Blvd Farmingdale (11735) *(G-5148)*
Vitafede (PA)......213 488-0136
25 W 26th St Fl 5 New York (10010) *(G-12582)*
Vitakem Nutraceutical Inc......631 956-8343
811 W Jericho Tpke Smithtown (11787) *(G-15524)*
Vital Signs & Graphics Co Inc......518 237-8372
251 Saratoga St Cohoes (12047) *(G-3785)*
Vital Vio Inc......914 245-6048
185 Jordan Rd Ste 1 Troy (12180) *(G-16286)*
Vitale Ready Mix Concrete, Auburn *Also called Robinson Concrete Inc (G-513)*
Vitalis LLC......646 831-7338
902 Broadway Fl 6 New York (10010) *(G-12583)*
Vitalize Labs LLC......212 966-6130
134 Spring St Ste 502 New York (10012) *(G-12584)*
Vitamin Power Incororated......631 676-5790
75 Commerce Dr Hauppauge (11788) *(G-6253)*
Vitamix Laboratories, Farmingdale *Also called Wellmill LLC (G-5152)*
Vitamix Laboratories Inc......631 465-9245
69 Mall Dr Commack (11725) *(G-3871)*
Vitane Pharmaceuticals Inc......845 267-6700
125 Wells Ave Congers (10920) *(G-3887)*
Vitarose Corp of America......718 951-9700
2615 Nostrand Ave Ste 1 Brooklyn (11210) *(G-2751)*
Viterion Corporation......914 333-6033
565 Taxter Rd Ste 175 Elmsford (10523) *(G-4799)*
Vito & Sons Bakery......201 617-8501
1423 72nd St Brooklyn (11228) *(G-2752)*
Vitobob Furniture Inc......516 676-1696
3879 13th St Long Island City (11101) *(G-7945)*
Vitra Inc (HQ)......212 463-5700
29 9th Ave New York (10014) *(G-12585)*
Vitrix Hot Glass and Crafts, Corning *Also called Vitrix Inc (G-4005)*
Vitrix Inc......607 936-8707
77 W Market St Corning (14830) *(G-4005)*
Vits International Inc......845 353-5000
200 Corporate Dr Blauvelt (10913) *(G-973)*
Vivid Rgb Lighting LLC......718 635-0817
824 Main St Ste 1 Peekskill (10566) *(G-13508)*
Vivona Business Printers Inc......516 496-3453
343 Jackson Ave Syosset (11791) *(G-15862)*
Vivus Technologies LLC......585 798-6658
591 Mahar St Medina (14103) *(G-8316)*
Vizbee Inc......650 787-1424
120 E 23rd St Fl 5 New York (10010) *(G-12586)*
Vizio Medical Devices LLC......646 845-7382
200 Chambers St Apt 28a New York (10007) *(G-12587)*
VJ Technologies Inc (PA)......631 589-8800
89 Carlough Rd Bohemia (11716) *(G-1151)*
Vjt, Bohemia *Also called VJ Technologies Inc (G-1151)*
Vline Inc......512 222-5464
81 Prospect St Brooklyn (11201) *(G-2753)*
Vma, Poughkeepsie *Also called Vantage Mfg & Assembly LLC (G-13954)*
Vnovom Svete......212 302-9480
55 Broad St Fl 20 New York (10004) *(G-12588)*
Vogel Applied Technologies......212 677-3136
36 E 12th St Fl 7 New York (10003) *(G-12589)*
Vogue China, New York *Also called Advance Magazine Publs Inc (G-9089)*
Vogue Magazine......212 286-2860
1 World Trade Ctr Fl 25 New York (10007) *(G-12590)*
Vogue Too Plting Stitching EMB......212 354-1022
265 W 37th St Fl 14 New York (10018) *(G-12591)*
Voice Analysis Clinic......212 245-3803
326 W 55th St Apt 4d New York (10019) *(G-12592)*
Voices For All LLC......518 261-1664
29 Moreland Dr Mechanicville (12118) *(G-8263)*
Volckening Inc (PA)......718 748-0294
6700 3rd Ave Brooklyn (11220) *(G-2754)*
Volkert Precision Tech Inc......718 464-9500
22240 96th Ave Ste 3 Queens Village (11429) *(G-13999)*
Volpi Manufacturing USA Co Inc......315 255-1737
5 Commerce Way Auburn (13021) *(G-525)*
Volt Tek Inc......585 377-2050
111 Parce Ave Fairport (14450) *(G-4893)*
Voltronics LLC......410 749-2424
2777 Us Route 20 Cazenovia (13035) *(G-3481)*
Von Musulin Patricia......212 206-8345
148 W 24th St Fl 10 New York (10011) *(G-12593)*
Von Pok & Chang New York Inc......212 599-0556
4 E 43rd St Fl 7 New York (10017) *(G-12594)*
Von Roll Usa Inc (HQ)......518 344-7100
200 Von Roll Dr Schenectady (12306) *(G-15334)*
Vondom LLC......212 207-3252
979 3rd Ave Ste 1532 New York (10022) *(G-12595)*
Vonn Lighting, Long Island City *Also called Vonn LLC (G-7946)*
Vonn LLC......888 604-8666
3245 Hunters Point Ave # 2 Long Island City (11101) *(G-7946)*

ALPHABETIC

Voodoo Manufacturing Inc 646 893-8366
361 Stagg St Ste 408 Brooklyn (11206) *(G-2755)*
Vormittag Associates Inc (PA) 800 824-7776
120 Comac St Ste 1 Ronkonkoma (11779) *(G-15023)*
Vortex Ventures Inc 516 946-8345
857 Newton Ave North Baldwin (11510) *(G-12929)*
Vosky Precision Machining Corp 631 737-3200
70 Air Park Dr Ronkonkoma (11779) *(G-15024)*
Voss Manufacturing Inc 716 731-5062
2345 Lockport Rd Sanborn (14132) *(G-15158)*
Voss Signs LLC 315 682-6418
112 Fairgrounds Dr Ste 2 Manlius (13104) *(G-8109)*
Voss Usa Inc 212 995-2255
236 W 30th St Rm 900 New York (10001) *(G-12596)*
Vox Systems, Massapequa Also called *Huntington Services Inc* *(G-8209)*
Voyager Custom Products, Buffalo Also called *Voyager Emblems Inc* *(G-3271)*
Voyager Emblems Inc 416 255-3421
701 Seneca St Ste D Buffalo (14210) *(G-3271)*
Vpj Publication Inc 718 845-3221
15519 Lahn St Howard Beach (11414) *(G-6628)*
Vr Containment LLC 917 972-3441
17625 Union Tpke Ste 175 Fresh Meadows (11366) *(G-5461)*
Vr Food Equipment Inc 315 531-8133
5801 County Road 41 Farmington (14425) *(G-5166)*
Vsg International LLC 718 300-8171
196 Clinton Ave Apt A2 Brooklyn (11205) *(G-2756)*
Vship Co 718 706-8566
3636 33rd St Ste 207 Astoria (11106) *(G-459)*
VSM Investors LLC (PA) 212 351-1600
245 Park Ave Fl 41 New York (10167) *(G-12597)*
Vtb Holdings Inc (HQ) 914 345-2255
100 Summit Lake Dr Valhalla (10595) *(G-16399)*
Vts Medical Systems, Melville Also called *Steris Corporation* *(G-8385)*
Vulcan Iron Works Inc 631 395-6846
190 Weeks Ave Manorville (11949) *(G-8114)*
Vulcan Steam Forging Co 716 875-3680
247 Rano St Buffalo (14207) *(G-3272)*
Vulcraft of New York Inc (HQ) 607 529-9000
621 M St Chemung (14825) *(G-3622)*
Vuum LLC 212 868-3459
249 W 34th St Rm 703 New York (10001) *(G-12598)*
Vuzix Corporation (PA) 585 359-5900
25 Hendrix Rd Ste A West Henrietta (14586) *(G-16928)*
Vvs International Inc 212 302-5410
2 W 46th St New York (10036) *(G-12599)*
VWR Chemicals LLC (HQ) 518 297-4444
3 Lincoln Blvd Rouses Point (12979) *(G-15069)*
VWR Education LLC 585 359-2502
5100 W Henrietta Rd West Henrietta (14586) *(G-16929)*
Vybion Inc 607 266-0860
33 Thornwood Dr Ste 104 Ithaca (14850) *(G-6918)*
Vyera Pharmaceuticals LLC 646 356-5577
600 3rd Ave Fl 10 New York (10016) *(G-12600)*
Vytek Inc 631 750-1770
271 Knickerbocker Ave Bohemia (11716) *(G-1152)*
W & B Mazza & Sons Inc 516 379-4130
2145 Marion Pl North Baldwin (11510) *(G-12930)*
W & G Manufacturing, Brooklyn Also called *Sue & Sam Co Inc* *(G-2640)*
W & H Stampings Inc 631 234-6161
45 Engineers Rd Hauppauge (11788) *(G-6254)*
W & W Manufacturing Co 516 942-0011
239 Higbie Ln West Islip (11795) *(G-16939)*
W A Baum Co Inc 631 226-3940
620 Oak St Copiague (11726) *(G-3961)*
W B Bow Tie Corp 212 683-6130
521 W 26th St Fl 6 New York (10001) *(G-12601)*
W D Technology Inc 914 779-8738
42 Water St Ste B Eastchester (10709) *(G-4595)*
W Designe Inc 914 736-1058
5 John Walsh Blvd Peekskill (10566) *(G-13509)*
W E W Container Corporation 718 827-8150
189 Wyona St Brooklyn (11207) *(G-2757)*
W F Saunders & Sons Inc (PA) 315 469-3217
5126 S Onondaga Rd Nedrow (13120) *(G-8819)*
W G R Z - T V Channel 2, Buffalo Also called *Tegna Inc* *(G-3238)*
W H Jones & Son Inc 716 875-8233
1208 Military Rd Kenmore (14217) *(G-7180)*
W H White Publications Inc 914 725-2500
95 Main St Dobbs Ferry (10522) *(G-4328)*
W Hubbell & Sons Inc (PA) 315 736-8311
5124 Commercial Dr Yorkville (13495) *(G-17546)*
W J Albro Machine Works Inc 631 345-0657
86 Horseblock Rd Unit L Yaphank (11980) *(G-17424)*
W K Z A 106.9 K I S S-F M, Jamestown Also called *Cntry Cross Communications LLC* *(G-7017)*
W Kintz Plastics Inc (PA) 518 296-8513
165 Caverns Rd Howes Cave (12092) *(G-6629)*
W M T Publications Inc 585 244-3329
250 N Goodman St Ste 1 Rochester (14607) *(G-14783)*
W M W, Buffalo Also called *West Metal Works Inc* *(G-3278)*
W N R Pattern & Tool Inc 716 681-9334
21 Pavement Rd Lancaster (14086) *(G-7371)*

W N Vanalstine & Sons Inc (PA) 518 237-1436
18 New Cortland St Cohoes (12047) *(G-3786)*
W R P Welding Ltd 631 249-8859
126 Toledo St Farmingdale (11735) *(G-5149)*
W Stuart Smith Inc 585 742-3310
625 Fishers Run Victor (14564) *(G-16535)*
W W Custom Clad Inc 518 673-3322
75 Creek St Canajoharie (13317) *(G-3362)*
W W Norton & Company Inc (PA) 212 354-5500
500 5th Ave Fl 6 New York (10110) *(G-12602)*
W W Norton & Company Inc 212 354-5500
500 5th Ave Lbby 1 New York (10110) *(G-12603)*
W.O.w Brand Products, North Tonawanda Also called *Griffin Chemical Company LLC* *(G-12993)*
Wacf Enterprise Inc 631 745-5841
275 Asharoken Ave Northport (11768) *(G-13035)*
Wacoal America Inc 718 794-1032
1543 Saint Lawrence Ave Bronx (10460) *(G-1491)*
Wacoal America Inc 212 743-9600
136 Madison Ave Fl 15 New York (10016) *(G-12604)*
Wacoal International Corp 212 532-6100
136 Madison Ave Fl 15 New York (10016) *(G-12605)*
Wadadda.com, Monticello Also called *Patrick Rohan* *(G-8646)*
Waddington North America Inc 585 638-8200
88 Nesbitt Dr Holley (14470) *(G-6519)*
Wadsworth Logging Inc 518 863-6870
3095 State Highway 30 Gloversville (12078) *(G-5742)*
Waffenbauch USA 716 326-4508
165 Academy St Westfield (14787) *(G-17081)*
Wagner Farms, Lodi Also called *Lamoreaux Landing WI* *(G-7665)*
Wagner Hardwoods LLC 607 594-3321
6307 St Route 224 Cayuta (14824) *(G-3467)*
Wagner Hardwoods LLC 607 594-3321
6307 St Route 224 Cayuta (14824) *(G-3468)*
Wagner Lumber, Owego Also called *Wagner Millwork Inc* *(G-13386)*
Wagner Millwork Inc 607 687-5362
4060 Gaskill Rd Owego (13827) *(G-13386)*
Wagner Technical Services Inc 845 566-4018
1658 Route 300 Newburgh (12550) *(G-12809)*
Wagner Vineyards & Brewing Co 607 582-6574
9322 State Route 414 Lodi (14860) *(G-7666)*
Wagners LLC (PA) 516 933-6580
366 N Broadway Ste 402 Jericho (11753) *(G-7121)*
Waguya News, Wolcott Also called *Wayuga Community Newspapers* *(G-17302)*
Wainland Inc 718 626-2233
2460 47th St Astoria (11103) *(G-460)*
Wal Machine, West Babylon Also called *Mpi Consulting Incorporated* *(G-16843)*
Wal Machine, West Babylon Also called *Mpi Consulting Incorporated* *(G-16844)*
Walco Leather Co Inc 212 243-2244
5 Banks Farm Rd Bedford (10506) *(G-795)*
Walco Stainless, Utica Also called *Utica Cutlery Company* *(G-16387)*
Waldman Alexander M Diamond Co 212 921-8098
30 W 47th St Ste 805 New York (10036) *(G-12606)*
Waldman Diamond Company, New York Also called *Waldman Alexander M Diamond Co* *(G-12606)*
Waldman Publishing Corporation (PA) 212 730-9590
570 Fashion Ave Rm 800 New York (10018) *(G-12607)*
Waldorf Bakers Inc 718 665-2253
909 E 135th St Bronx (10454) *(G-1492)*
Walking Charger, The, Rochester Also called *Energy Harvesters LLC* *(G-14371)*
Wall Protection Products LLC 877 943-6826
32 Nelson Hill Rd Wassaic (12592) *(G-16624)*
Wall Street Business Pdts Inc 212 563-4014
151 W 30th St Fl 8 New York (10001) *(G-12608)*
Wall Street Reporter Magazine 212 363-2600
419 Lafayette St Fl 2 New York (10003) *(G-12609)*
Wall Tool & Tape Corp 718 641-6813
8111 101st Ave Ozone Park (11416) *(G-13412)*
Wall Tool Manufacturing, Ozone Park Also called *Wall Tool & Tape Corp* *(G-13412)*
Wallace Home Design Ctr 631 765-3890
44500 County Road 48 Southold (11971) *(G-15585)*
Wallace Refiners Inc 212 391-2649
15 W 47th St Ste 808 New York (10036) *(G-12610)*
Wallguard.com, Wassaic Also called *Wall Protection Products LLC* *(G-16624)*
Wallico Shoes Corp 212 826-7171
32 E 57th St Fl 14 New York (10022) *(G-12611)*
Wallkill Lodge No 627 F&Am 845 778-7148
61 Main St Walden (12586) *(G-16558)*
Wallkill Valley Publications 845 561-0170
300 Stony Brook Ct Ste B Newburgh (12550) *(G-12810)*
Wallkill Valley Times, Newburgh Also called *Wallkill Valley Publications* *(G-12810)*
Wally Packaging, Monsey Also called *Magcrest Packaging Inc* *(G-8609)*
Wally Packaging Inc (HQ) 718 377-5323
1168 E 21st St Brooklyn (11210) *(G-2758)*
Walnut Packaging Inc 631 293-3836
450 Smith St Farmingdale (11735) *(G-5150)*
Walnut Printing Inc 718 707-0100
2812 41st Ave Long Island City (11101) *(G-7947)*
Walpole Woodworkers Inc 631 726-2859
779 Montauk Hwy Water Mill (11976) *(G-16628)*

ALPHABETIC SECTION
Web Graphics, Queensbury

Walsh & Hughes Inc (PA)....631 427-5904
1455 New York Ave Huntington Station (11746) ***(G-6766)***
Walsh & Sons Machine Inc....845 526-0301
15 Secor Rd Ste 5 Mahopac (10541) ***(G-8035)***
Walter Edbril Inc....212 532-3253
10 E 38th St Fl 6 New York (10016) ***(G-12612)***
Walter G Legge Company Inc....914 737-5040
444 Central Ave Peekskill (10566) ***(G-13510)***
Walter P Sauer LLC....718 937-0600
276 Greenpoint Ave # 8400 Brooklyn (11222) ***(G-2759)***
Walter R Tucker Entps Ltd....607 467-2866
8 Leonard Way Deposit (13754) ***(G-4305)***
Walters & Walters Inc....347 202-8535
961 E 224th St Bronx (10466) ***(G-1493)***
Wan Ja Shan, Middletown *Also called Mandarin Soy Sauce Inc* ***(G-8483)***
Wanjashan International LLC....845 343-1505
4 Sands Station Rd Middletown (10940) ***(G-8505)***
Want-Ad Digest Inc....518 279-1181
870 Hoosick Rd Ste 1 Troy (12180) ***(G-16287)***
Wantagh 5 & 10, Wantagh *Also called Nbets Corporation* ***(G-16582)***
Wantagh Computer Center....516 826-2189
10 Stanford Ct Wantagh (11793) ***(G-16584)***
Wappingers Falls Shopper Inc....845 297-3723
84 E Main St Wappingers Falls (12590) ***(G-16598)***
Warby Parker Eyewear, New York *Also called Parker Warby Retail Inc* ***(G-11589)***
Ward Diesel Filter Systems, Horseheads *Also called Beecher Emssn Sltn Tchnlgs LLC* ***(G-6596)***
Ward Industrial Equipment Inc (PA)....716 856-6966
1051 Clinton St Buffalo (14206) ***(G-3273)***
Ward Iron Works Limited, Buffalo *Also called Ward Industrial Equipment Inc* ***(G-3273)***
Ward Lafrance Truck Corp....518 893-1865
26 Congress St Ste 259f Saratoga Springs (12866) ***(G-15206)***
Ward Sales Co Inc....315 476-5276
1117 W Fayette St Ste 1 Syracuse (13204) ***(G-16093)***
Ward Steel Company Inc....315 451-4566
4591 Morgan Pl Liverpool (13090) ***(G-7582)***
Warm....212 925-1200
181 Mott St Frnt 1 New York (10012) ***(G-12613)***
Warnaco Group Inc (HQ)....212 287-8000
501 Fashion Ave New York (10018) ***(G-12614)***
Warnaco Inc (HQ)....212 287-8000
501 Fashion Ave Fl 14 New York (10018) ***(G-12615)***
Warnaco Inc....718 722-3000
70 Washington St Fl 10 Brooklyn (11201) ***(G-2760)***
Warner....716 446-0663
514 Hopkins Rd Buffalo (14221) ***(G-3274)***
Warner Energy LLC (PA)....315 457-3828
7526 Morgan Rd Liverpool (13090) ***(G-7583)***
Warner Music Group Corp (HQ)....212 275-2000
1633 Broadway New York (10019) ***(G-12616)***
Warner Music Inc (HQ)....212 275-2000
75 Rockefeller Plz Bsmt 1 New York (10019) ***(G-12617)***
Warner S, New York *Also called Warnaco Inc* ***(G-12615)***
Warodean Corporation....718 359-5559
4308 162nd St Flushing (11358) ***(G-5312)***
Warren Corporation (HQ)....917 379-3434
711 5th Ave Fl 11 New York (10022) ***(G-12618)***
Warren Cutlery Corp....845 876-3444
3584 Route 9g Rhinebeck (12572) ***(G-14072)***
Warren Energy Services LLC....212 697-9660
1114 Ave Of The Americas New York (10036) ***(G-12619)***
Warren Printing Inc....212 627-5000
3718 Northern Blvd # 418 Long Island City (11101) ***(G-7948)***
Warrior Sports Inc....315 536-0937
26 Powell Ln Penn Yan (14527) ***(G-13544)***
Warshaw Jacobson Group, New York *Also called Irv Inc* ***(G-10705)***
Warwick Press, Warwick *Also called Digital United Color Prtg Inc* ***(G-16610)***
Wascomat of America, Inwood *Also called Pluslux LLC* ***(G-6805)***
Wash Quarters LLC....989 802-2017
680 Hoagerburgh Rd Wallkill (12589) ***(G-16567)***
Washburn Litho Envirgo Prtg, Rochester *Also called Presstek Printing LLC* ***(G-14622)***
Washburn Manufacturing Tech....607 387-3991
9828 State Route 96 Trumansburg (14886) ***(G-16292)***
Washburns Dairy Inc....518 725-0629
145 N Main St Gloversville (12078) ***(G-5743)***
Washer Solutions Inc....585 742-6388
760 Canning Pkwy Ste A Victor (14564) ***(G-16536)***
Washington Mills Elec Mnrls (HQ)....716 278-6600
1801 Buffalo Ave Niagara Falls (14303) ***(G-12907)***
Washington Foundries Inc....516 374-8447
1434 Vian Ave Hewlett (11557) ***(G-6340)***
Washington Mills Tonawanda Inc (HQ)....716 693-4550
1000 E Niagara St Tonawanda (14150) ***(G-16234)***
Washington Square News, New York *Also called New York University* ***(G-11431)***
Waste Management, Palatine Bridge *Also called Lee Publications Inc* ***(G-13422)***
Wastecorp Pumps LLC (PA)....888 829-2783
345 W 85th St Apt 23 New York (10024) ***(G-12620)***
Wataah, New York *Also called Let Water Be Water LLC* ***(G-11012)***
Watch Journal LLC....212 229-1500
110 E 25th St Fl 4 New York (10010) ***(G-12621)***
Watchanish LLC....917 558-0404
1 Rockefeller Plz Fl 11 New York (10020) ***(G-12622)***
Watchcraft Inc....347 531-0382
2214 40th Ave Ste 4 Long Island City (11101) ***(G-7949)***
Watchitoo Inc....212 354-5888
24 W 40th St Fl 14 New York (10018) ***(G-12623)***
Watchtime Magazine, New York *Also called Ebner Publishing International* ***(G-10025)***
Watec America Corporation....702 434-6111
720 Route 17m Ste 4 Middletown (10940) ***(G-8506)***
Water Cooling Corp....718 723-6500
24520 Merrick Blvd Rosedale (11422) ***(G-15039)***
Water Energy Systems LLC....844 822-7665
1 Maiden Ln New York (10038) ***(G-12624)***
Water Oracle....845 876-8327
41 E Market St Rhinebeck (12572) ***(G-14073)***
Water Resources Group LLC....631 824-9088
84 Main St Cold Spring Harbor (11724) ***(G-3796)***
Water Splash Inc....800 936-3430
25 Locust St Ste 421 Champlain (12919) ***(G-3577)***
Water Street Brass Corporation....716 763-0059
4515 Gleason Rd Lakewood (14750) ***(G-7320)***
Water Technologies Inc (PA)....315 986-0000
1635 Commons Pkwy Macedon (14502) ***(G-8022)***
Water Treatment Services Inc....914 241-2261
395 Adams St Bedford Hills (10507) ***(G-804)***
Water Treatment Svce, Bedford Hills *Also called Water Treatment Services Inc* ***(G-804)***
Water Wise of America Inc....585 232-1210
90 Canal St Rochester (14608) ***(G-14784)***
Water Wise of America Inc (PA)....585 232-1210
75 Bermar Park Ste 5 Rochester (14624) ***(G-14785)***
Waterbury Garment LLC....212 725-1500
16 E 34th St Fl 10 New York (10016) ***(G-12625)***
Watermark Designs Holdings Ltd....718 257-2800
350 Dewitt Ave Brooklyn (11207) ***(G-2761)***
Watertown Concrete Inc....315 788-1040
24471 State Route 12 Watertown (13601) ***(G-16698)***
Watertown Daily Times, Watertown *Also called Northern NY Newspapers Corp* ***(G-16691)***
Watkins Welding and Mch Sp Inc....914 949-6168
87 Westmoreland Ave White Plains (10606) ***(G-17209)***
Watson Adventures LLC....212 564-8293
330 W 38th St Rm 407 New York (10018) ***(G-12626)***
Watson Bowman Acme Corp....716 691-8162
95 Pineview Dr Amherst (14228) ***(G-271)***
Watson Productions LLC....516 334-9766
740 Old Willets Path # 400 Hauppauge (11788) ***(G-6255)***
Wave of Long Island, The, Rockaway Beach *Also called Wave Publishing Co Inc* ***(G-14811)***
Wave Publishing Co Inc....718 634-4000
8808 Rockaway Beach Blvd Rockaway Beach (11693) ***(G-14811)***
Waverly Iron Corp....631 732-2800
25 Commercial Blvd Medford (11763) ***(G-8296)***
Wavodyne Therapeutics Inc....954 632-6630
150 Lucius Gordon Dr West Henrietta (14586) ***(G-16930)***
Way Out Toys Inc....212 689-9094
230 5th Ave Ste 800 New York (10001) ***(G-12627)***
Waymor1 Inc....518 677-8511
Hc 22 Cambridge (12816) ***(G-3339)***
Wayne County Mail, Webster *Also called Empire State Weeklies Inc* ***(G-16747)***
Wayne Decorators Inc....718 529-4200
14409 Rockaway Blvd Apt 1 Jamaica (11436) ***(G-6999)***
Wayne Integrated Tech Corp....631 242-0213
160 Rodeo Dr Edgewood (11717) ***(G-4633)***
Wayne Printing Inc....914 761-2400
70 W Red Oak Ln Fl 4 White Plains (10604) ***(G-17210)***
Wayne Printing & Lithographic, White Plains *Also called Wayne Printing Inc* ***(G-17210)***
Waynes Welding Inc....315 768-6146
66 Calder Ave Yorkville (13495) ***(G-17547)***
Wayuga Community Newspapers (PA)....315 754-6229
6784 Main St Red Creek (13143) ***(G-14040)***
Wayuga Community Newspapers....315 594-2506
12039 E Main St Wolcott (14590) ***(G-17302)***
Wayuga News, Red Creek *Also called Wayuga Community Newspapers* ***(G-14040)***
Wcd Window Coverings Inc....845 336-4511
1711 Ulster Ave Lake Katrine (12449) ***(G-7295)***
We Work....877 673-6628
1 Little West 12th St New York (10014) ***(G-12628)***
Wea International Inc (HQ)....212 275-1300
75 Rockefeller Plz New York (10019) ***(G-12629)***
Wear Abouts Apparel Inc....212 827-0888
260 W 36th St Rm 602 New York (10018) ***(G-12630)***
Weather Products Corporation....315 474-8593
102 W Division St Fl 1 Syracuse (13204) ***(G-16094)***
Weather Tight Exteriors....631 375-5108
8 Woodbrook Dr Ridge (11961) ***(G-14108)***
Weatherproof, Bay Shore *Also called David Peyser Sportswear Inc* ***(G-689)***
Weaver Machine & Tool Co Inc....315 253-4422
44 York St Auburn (13021) ***(G-526)***
Weaver Wind Energy LLC....607 379-9463
7 Union St Freeville (13068) ***(G-5450)***
Web Associates Inc....716 883-3377
1255 Niagara St Buffalo (14213) ***(G-3275)***
Web Graphics, Queensbury *Also called Amsterdam Printing & Litho Inc* ***(G-14003)***

ALPHABETIC

Web Seal Inc (PA) ALPHABETIC SECTION

Web Seal Inc (PA) 585 546-1320
15 Oregon St Rochester (14605) *(G-14786)*
Web-Tech Packaging Inc 716 684-4520
500 Commerce Pkwy Lancaster (14086) *(G-7372)*
Webb-Mason Inc 716 276-8792
300 Airborne Pkwy Ste 210 Buffalo (14225) *(G-3276)*
Weber Intl Packg Co LLC 518 561-8282
318 Cornelia St Plattsburgh (12901) *(G-13738)*
Weber's Mach Shop, Troy *Also called Charles V Weber Machine Shop (G-16251)*
Weber-Knapp Company (PA) 716 484-9135
441 Chandler St Jamestown (14701) *(G-7075)*
Webster Ontrio Wlwrth Pnnysver 585 265-3620
164 E Main St Webster (14580) *(G-16767)*
Webster Printing Corporation 585 671-1533
46 North Ave Webster (14580) *(G-16768)*
Wecare Organics LLC 315 689-1937
9293 Bonta Bridge Rd Jordan (13080) *(G-7159)*
Weco Metal Products, Ontario *Also called Dj Acquisition Management Corp (G-13222)*
Wedco Fabrications Inc 718 852-6330
2016 130th St College Point (11356) *(G-3836)*
Wedding Gown Preservation Co 607 748-7999
707 North St Endicott (13760) *(G-4839)*
Wedel Sign Company Inc 631 727-4577
705 W Main St Riverhead (11901) *(G-14173)*
Week Publications, The, New York *Also called Dennis Publishing Inc (G-9900)*
Weekly Ajkal 718 565-2100
3707 74th St Ste 8 Jackson Heights (11372) *(G-6925)*
Weekly Bornomal, Jackson Heights *Also called Bornomala USA Inc (G-6921)*
Weekly Business News Corp 212 689-5888
274 Madison Ave Rm 1101 New York (10016) *(G-12631)*
Weeks & Reichel Printing Inc 631 589-1443
131 Railroad Ave Sayville (11782) *(G-15244)*
Wego International Floors LLC 516 487-3510
239 Great Neck Rd Great Neck (11021) *(G-5868)*
Weico Wire & Cable Inc 631 254-2970
161 Rodeo Dr Edgewood (11717) *(G-4634)*
Weicro Graphics Inc 631 253-3360
95 Mahan St West Babylon (11704) *(G-16872)*
Weider Publications LLC 212 545-4800
1 Park Ave Fl 10 New York (10016) *(G-12632)*
Weighing & Systems Tech Inc 518 274-2797
274 2nd St Troy (12180) *(G-16288)*
Weisbeck Publishing Printing 716 937-9226
13200 Broadway St Alden (14004) *(G-189)*
Weisco Inc 212 575-8989
246 W 38th St Fl 6 New York (10018) *(G-12633)*
Weiss Industries Inc 518 784-9643
27 Blossom Ln Valatie (12184) *(G-16390)*
Weiss Instruments Inc 631 207-1200
905 Waverly Ave Holtsville (11742) *(G-6541)*
Wel Made Enterprises Inc 631 752-1238
1630 New Hwy Farmingdale (11735) *(G-5151)*
Welch Allyn Inc 315 685-4100
4341 State Street Rd Skaneateles Falls (13153) *(G-15493)*
Welch Allyn Inc (HQ) 315 685-4100
4341 State Street Rd Skaneateles Falls (13153) *(G-15494)*
Welch Allyn Inc 315 685-4347
4619 Jordan Rd Skaneateles Falls (13153) *(G-15495)*
Welch Foods Inc A Cooperative 716 326-5252
2 S Portage St Westfield (14787) *(G-17082)*
Welch Foods Inc A Cooperative 716 326-3131
100 N Portage St Westfield (14787) *(G-17083)*
Welch Machine Inc 585 647-3578
961 Lyell Ave Bldg 1-6 Rochester (14606) *(G-14787)*
Welcome Magazine Inc 716 839-3121
4511 Harlem Rd Amherst (14226) *(G-272)*
Welcome Rain Publishers LLC 212 686-1909
230 5th Ave New York (10001) *(G-12634)*
Weld-Built Body Co Inc 631 643-9700
276 Long Island Ave Wyandanch (11798) *(G-17393)*
Weldcomputer Corporation 518 283-2897
105 Jordan Rd Ste 1 Troy (12180) *(G-16289)*
Welded Tube Usa Inc 716 828-1111
2537 Hamburg Tpke Lackawanna (14218) *(G-7276)*
Welding and Brazing Svcs Inc 607 397-1009
2761 County Highway 26 Richfield Springs (13439) *(G-14075)*
Welding Chapter of New York 212 481-1496
44 W 28th St Fl 12 New York (10001) *(G-12635)*
Welding Metallurgy Inc (HQ) 631 253-0500
110 Plant Ave Ste 1 Hauppauge (11788) *(G-6256)*
Weldrite Closures Inc 585 429-8790
2292 Innovation Way Rochester (14624) *(G-14788)*
Well-Made Toy Mfg Corporation 718 381-4225
146 Soundview Dr Port Washington (11050) *(G-13889)*
Wellmill LLC 631 465-9245
141 Central Ave Ste B Farmingdale (11735) *(G-5152)*
Wellquest International Inc (PA) 212 689-9094
230 5th Ave Ste 800 New York (10001) *(G-12636)*
Wells Rugs Inc 516 676-2056
44 Sea Cliff Ave Glen Cove (11542) *(G-5644)*
Wells, George Ruggery, Glen Cove *Also called Wells Rugs Inc (G-5644)*
Wellspring Corp (PA) 212 529-5454
54a Ludlow St New York (10002) *(G-12637)*
Wellspring Omni Holdings Corp 212 318-9800
390 Park Ave New York (10022) *(G-12638)*
Wellsville Daily Reporter, Wellsville *Also called Seneca Media Inc (G-16784)*
Welsh Gold Stampers Inc 718 984-5031
44 Lenzie St Staten Island (10312) *(G-15776)*
Wemco Casting LLC 631 563-8050
20 Jules Ct Ste 2 Bohemia (11716) *(G-1153)*
Wen Hwa Printing, Flushing *Also called Global Graphics Inc (G-5252)*
Wendels Poultry Farm 716 592-2299
12466 Vaughn St East Concord (14055) *(G-4408)*
Wendon Engineering, Hawthorne *Also called Princetel Inc (G-6277)*
Wendt Corporation 716 391-1200
2555 Walden Ave Buffalo (14225) *(G-3277)*
Wendys Auto Express Inc 845 624-6100
121 Main St Nanuet (10954) *(G-8808)*
Wenig Company, The, Amityville *Also called Portfab LLC (G-322)*
Wenig Corporation 718 542-3600
230 Manida St Fl 2 Bronx (10474) *(G-1494)*
Wenner Bread Products Inc (PA) 800 869-6262
33 Rajon Rd Bayport (11705) *(G-756)*
Wenner Media LLC (PA) 212 484-1616
1290 Ave Of The Amer Fl 2 New York (10104) *(G-12639)*
Were Forms Inc 585 482-4400
500 Helendale Rd Ste 190 Rochester (14609) *(G-14789)*
Werlatone Inc 845 278-2220
17 Jon Barrett Rd Patterson (12563) *(G-13470)*
Werma (usa) Inc 315 414-0200
6731 Collamer Rd Ste 1 East Syracuse (13057) *(G-4592)*
Werner Brothers Electric Inc 518 377-3056
677 Riverview Rd Rexford (12148) *(G-14066)*
Wessie Machine Inc 315 926-4060
5229 Steel Point Rd Marion (14505) *(G-8134)*
West African Movies 718 731-2190
1692 Webster Ave Bronx (10457) *(G-1495)*
West End Iron Works Inc 518 456-1105
4254 Albany St Albany (12205) *(G-150)*
West End Journal, Far Rockaway *Also called Empire Publishing Inc (G-4928)*
West Falls Machine Co Inc 716 655-0440
11692 E Main Rd East Aurora (14052) *(G-4404)*
West Falls Machine Co 1, East Aurora *Also called West Falls Machine Co Inc (G-4404)*
West Herr Automotive Group, Hamburg *Also called Kustom Korner (G-5956)*
West Information Center, New York *Also called West Publishing Corporation (G-12642)*
West Internet Trading Company 415 484-5848
47 Great Jones St Fl 5 New York (10012) *(G-12640)*
West Metal Works Inc 716 895-4900
68 Hayes Pl Buffalo (14210) *(G-3278)*
West Pacific Enterprises Corp 212 564-6800
260 W 39th St Rm 5w New York (10018) *(G-12641)*
West Publishing Corporation 212 922-1920
530 5th Ave Fl 7 New York (10036) *(G-12642)*
West Seneca Bee Inc 716 632-4700
5564 Main St Williamsville (14221) *(G-17284)*
Westbrook Machinery, Lockport *Also called Ted Westbrook (G-7649)*
Westbury Times 516 747-8282
132 E 2nd St Mineola (11501) *(G-8572)*
Westchester County Bus Jurnl, White Plains *Also called Westfair Communications Inc (G-17214)*
Westchester Law Journal Inc 914 948-0715
199 Main St Ste 301 White Plains (10601) *(G-17211)*
Westchester Mailing Service 914 948-1116
39 Westmoreland Ave Fl 2 White Plains (10606) *(G-17212)*
Westchester Modular Homes Inc 845 832-9400
30 Reagans Mill Rd Wingdale (12594) *(G-17297)*
Westchester Signs Inc 914 666-7446
145 Kisco Ave Mount Kisco (10549) *(G-8688)*
Westchester Technologies Inc 914 736-1034
8 John Walsh Blvd Ste 311 Peekskill (10566) *(G-13511)*
Westchester Wine Warehouse LLC 914 824-1400
53 Tarrytown Rd Ste 1 White Plains (10607) *(G-17213)*
Westchster Crankshaft Grinding, East Elmhurst *Also called Westchstr Crnkshft Grndng (G-4419)*
Westchstr Crnkshft Grndng 718 651-3900
3263 110th St East Elmhurst (11369) *(G-4419)*
Westcode Incorporated 607 766-9881
2226 Airport Rd Binghamton (13905) *(G-953)*
Western Bituminous, Rochester *Also called Suit-Kote Corporation (G-14730)*
Western Edition, Westhampton Beach *Also called Southampton Town Newspapers (G-17090)*
Western New York Energy LLC 585 798-9693
4141 Bates Rd Medina (14103) *(G-8317)*
Western New York Family Mag 716 836-3486
3147 Delaware Ave Ste B Buffalo (14217) *(G-3279)*
Western Oil and Gas JV Inc 914 967-4758
7 Mccullough Pl Rye (10580) *(G-15095)*
Western Queens Gazette, Long Island City *Also called Service Advertising Group Inc (G-7904)*
Western Synthetic Felt, Jericho *Also called Lightron Corporation (G-7107)*
Westfair Communications Inc 914 694-3600
3 Westchester Park Dr G7 White Plains (10604) *(G-17214)*

Westfield Publication, Westfield *Also called Quality Guides* ***(G-17078)***
Westinghouse A Brake Tech Corp 518 561-0044
72 Arizona Ave Plattsburgh (12903) ***(G-13739)***
Westinghouse A Brake Tech Corp 914 347-8650
4 Warehouse Ln Ste 144 Elmsford (10523) ***(G-4800)***
Westmail Press, White Plains *Also called Westchester Mailing Service* ***(G-17212)***
Westmoor Ltd 315 363-1500
906 W Hamilton Ave Sherrill (13461) ***(G-15433)***
Westmore Litho Corp 718 361-9403
4017 22nd St Long Island City (11101) ***(G-7950)***
Westmore Litho Printing Co, Long Island City *Also called Westmore Litho Corp* ***(G-7950)***
Westpoint Home LLC (HQ) 212 930-2074
28 E 28th St Cncrse Level New York (10016) ***(G-12643)***
Westpoint International Inc (HQ) 212 930-2044
28 E 28th St Bsmt 2 New York (10016) ***(G-12644)***
Westrock - Solvay Llc (HQ) 315 484-9050
53 Indl Dr Syracuse (13204) ***(G-16095)***
Westrock - Southern Cont LLC 315 487-6111
100 Southern Dr Camillus (13031) ***(G-3355)***
Westrock Cp LLC 770 448-2193
45 Campion Rd New Hartford (13413) ***(G-8858)***
Westrock CP LLC 315 484-9050
53 Industrial Dr Syracuse (13204) ***(G-16096)***
Westrock CP LLC 716 694-1000
51 Robinson St North Tonawanda (14120) ***(G-13023)***
Westrock CP LLC 716 692-6510
51 Robinson St North Tonawanda (14120) ***(G-13024)***
Westrock Mwv LLC 212 688-5000
299 Park Ave Fl 13 New York (10171) ***(G-12645)***
Westrock Rkt Company 330 296-5155
140 W Industry Ct Deer Park (11729) ***(G-4251)***
Westrock Rkt Company 770 448-2193
4914 W Genesee St Camillus (13031) ***(G-3356)***
Westron Corporation 516 678-2300
18 Neil Ct Oceanside (11572) ***(G-13127)***
Westron Lighting, Oceanside *Also called Westron Corporation* ***(G-13127)***
Westside Clothing Co Inc 212 273-9898
240 W 35th St Ste 1000 New York (10001) ***(G-12646)***
Westside News Inc 585 352-3411
1835 N Union St Spencerport (14559) ***(G-15598)***
Westypo Printers Inc 914 737-7394
540 Harrison Ave Peekskill (10566) ***(G-13512)***
Wet & Wild Pools & Spas, Brooklyn *Also called Polytech Pool Mfg Inc* ***(G-2440)***
Wet Paint, New York *Also called Wetpaintcom Inc* ***(G-12647)***
Wetherall Contracting NY Inc 718 894-7011
8312 Penelope Ave Ste 101 Middle Village (11379) ***(G-8451)***
Wetlook Detailing Inc 212 390-8877
1125 Banner Ave Apt 11a Brooklyn (11235) ***(G-2762)***
Wetpaintcom Inc 206 859-6300
902 Broadway Fl 11 New York (10010) ***(G-12647)***
Wew Container, Brooklyn *Also called Inland Paper Products Corp* ***(G-2106)***
Wey Inc 212 532-3299
21 W 39th St Fl 6 New York (10018) ***(G-12648)***
WF Lake Corp 518 798-9934
65 Park Rd Queensbury (12804) ***(G-14027)***
Wg Sheet Metal Corp 718 235-3093
341 Amber St Brooklyn (11208) ***(G-2763)***
WGB Industries Inc 716 693-5527
233 Fillmore Ave Ste 23 Tonawanda (14150) ***(G-16235)***
Whalebone Creative, Montauk *Also called Jesse Joeckel* ***(G-8623)***
Whalens Horseradish Products 518 587-6404
1710 Route 29 Galway (12074) ***(G-5498)***
Wham 1180 AM, Rochester *Also called Iheartcommunications Inc* ***(G-14465)***
Whats Next Manufacturing Inc 585 492-1014
4 Rule Dr Arcade (14009) ***(G-401)***
Whats The Big Idea, Huntington Station *Also called Wtbi Inc* ***(G-6767)***
Wheel & Tire Depot Ex Corp 914 375-2100
584 Yonkers Ave Yonkers (10704) ***(G-17514)***
Wheeler/Rinstar Ltd 212 244-1130
242 W 30th St New York (10001) ***(G-12649)***
Whentech LLC (HQ) 212 571-0042
55 E 52nd St Fl 40 New York (10055) ***(G-12650)***
Where Is Utica Cof Rasting Inc 315 269-8898
92 Genesee St Utica (13502) ***(G-16389)***
Whirlwind Music Distrs Inc 800 733-9473
99 Ling Rd Rochester (14612) ***(G-14790)***
Whispr Group Inc 212 924-3979
72 Allen St Fl 3 New York (10002) ***(G-12651)***
Whistle Stop Bakery, Rockville Centre *Also called Megamatt Inc* ***(G-14823)***
Whitacre Engineering Company 315 622-1075
4522 Wetzel Rd Liverpool (13090) ***(G-7584)***
White Coffee Corp 718 204-7900
1835 38th St Astoria (11105) ***(G-461)***
White Eagle Packing Co Inc 518 374-4366
922 Congress St Schenectady (12303) ***(G-15335)***
White Gate Holdings Inc (PA) 212 564-3266
22 W 38th St Fl 6 New York (10018) ***(G-12652)***
White House Cabinet Shop LLC 607 674-9358
11 Knapp St Sherburne (13460) ***(G-15421)***
White Label Partners LLC 917 445-6650
250 Mercer St Apt B1205 New York (10012) ***(G-12653)***
White Plains Drapery Uphl Inc 914 381-0908
801 E Boston Post Rd Mamaroneck (10543) ***(G-8083)***
White Plains Marble Inc 914 347-6000
186 E Main St Elmsford (10523) ***(G-4801)***
White Plains Rd & E 211th St, Bronx *Also called Jpmorgan Chase Bank Nat Assn* ***(G-1372)***
White Workroom Inc 212 941-5910
40 W 27th St Fl 11 New York (10001) ***(G-12654)***
Whiteboard Ventures Inc 855 972-6346
315 W 36th St Fl 10 New York (10018) ***(G-12655)***
Whitehall Times, Granville *Also called Manchester Newspaper Inc* ***(G-5791)***
Whitesboro Spring & Alignment (PA) 315 736-4441
247 Oriskany Blvd Whitesboro (13492) ***(G-17226)***
Whitesboro Spring Svce, Whitesboro *Also called Whitesboro Spring & Alignment* ***(G-17226)***
Whitestone Pharmacy, Whitestone *Also called Tocare LLC* ***(G-17244)***
Whitford Development Inc 631 471-7711
646 Main St Ste 301 Port Jefferson (11777) ***(G-13802)***
Whiting Door Mfg Corp (PA) 716 542-5427
113 Cedar St Akron (14001) ***(G-27)***
Whiting Door Mfg Corp 716 542-3070
13550 Bloomingdale Rd Akron (14001) ***(G-28)***
Whitley East LLC 718 403-0050
Brooklyn Navy Yd Bg 2 Fl Brooklyn (11205) ***(G-2764)***
Whitney Boin Studio Inc 914 377-4385
42 Warburton Ave Ste 1 Yonkers (10701) ***(G-17515)***
Whitney Foods Inc 718 291-3333
15504 Liberty Ave Jamaica (11433) ***(G-7000)***
Whitsons Food Svc Bronx Corp 631 424-2700
1800 Motor Pkwy Islandia (11749) ***(G-6843)***
Whittall & Shon (PA) 212 594-2626
1201 Broadway Ste 904a New York (10001) ***(G-12656)***
Wholesale Mulch & Sawdust Inc 607 687-2637
3711 Waverly Rd Owego (13827) ***(G-13387)***
Wholesale Window Warehouse, Oceanside *Also called Express Building Supply Inc* ***(G-13099)***
Wicked Smart LLC 518 459-2855
700 5th Ave Watervliet (12189) ***(G-16717)***
Wicked Spoon Inc 646 335-2890
127 W 24th St Fl 6 New York (10011) ***(G-12657)***
Wickers Performance Wear, Commack *Also called Wickers Sportswear Inc* ***(G-3872)***
Wickers Sportswear Inc (PA) 631 543-1700
88 Wyandanch Blvd Commack (11725) ***(G-3872)***
Wide Flange Inc 718 492-8705
176 27th St Brooklyn (11232) ***(G-2765)***
Widetronix Inc 607 330-4752
950 Danby Rd Ste 139 Ithaca (14850) ***(G-6919)***
Widex International, Hauppauge *Also called Widex Usa Inc* ***(G-6257)***
Widex Usa Inc (HQ) 718 360-1000
185 Commerce Dr Hauppauge (11788) ***(G-6257)***
Widmer Time Recorder Company 212 227-0405
27 Park Pl Rm 219 New York (10007) ***(G-12658)***
Wiggby Precision Machine Corp 718 439-6900
140 58th St Ste 56 Brooklyn (11220) ***(G-2766)***
Wikoff Color Corporation 585 458-0653
686 Pullman Ave Rochester (14615) ***(G-14791)***
Wil-Nic, Freeport *Also called Edr Industries Inc* ***(G-5406)***
Wilbar International Inc 631 951-9800
50 Cabot Ct Hauppauge (11788) ***(G-6258)***
Wilbedone Inc 607 756-8813
1133 State Route 222 Cortland (13045) ***(G-4071)***
Wilco Finishing Corp 718 417-6405
1288 Willoughby Ave Brooklyn (11237) ***(G-2767)***
Wilco Industries Inc 631 676-2593
788 Marconi Ave Ronkonkoma (11779) ***(G-15025)***
Wilcro Inc 716 632-4204
90 Earhart Dr Ste 19 Buffalo (14221) ***(G-3280)***
Wild Turkey, New York *Also called Austin Nichols & Co Inc* ***(G-9319)***
Wild Works Incorporated 716 891-4197
30 Railroad Ave Albany (12205) ***(G-151)***
Wilda, Long Island City *Also called Import-Export Corporation* ***(G-7792)***
Wilder Manufacturing Co Inc 516 222-0433
439 Oak St Garden City (11530) ***(G-5550)***
Wilkesboro Road, New York *Also called Schneider Mills Inc* ***(G-12013)***
Willard Machine 716 885-1630
73 Forest Ave Buffalo (14213) ***(G-3281)***
Willco Fine Art Ltd 718 935-9567
145 Nassau St Apt 9c New York (10038) ***(G-12659)***
Willemin Macodel Incorporated 914 345-3504
10 Skyline Dr Ste 132 Hawthorne (10532) ***(G-6281)***
William B Collins Company (HQ) 518 773-8272
8 E Fulton St Gloversville (12078) ***(G-5744)***
William Boyd Printing Co Inc 518 339-5832
4 Weed Rd Ste 1 Latham (12110) ***(G-7411)***
William Brooks Woodworking 718 495-9767
856 Saratoga Ave Brooklyn (11212) ***(G-2768)***
William Charles Prtg Co Inc 516 349-0900
7 Fairchild Ct Ste 100 Plainview (11803) ***(G-13674)***
William E Williams Valve Corp 718 392-1660
3850 Review Ave Long Island City (11101) ***(G-7951)***
William Goldberg Diamond Corp 212 980-4343
589 5th Ave Fl 14 New York (10017) ***(G-12660)***

ALPHABETIC

(PA)=Parent Co (HQ)=Headquarters (DH)=Div Headquarters
2018 Harris
New York Manufacturers Directory
1091

ALPHABETIC SECTION

William H Jackson Company 718 784-4482
  3629 23rd St Long Island City (11106) *(G-7952)*
William H Sadlier Inc (PA) 212 233-3646
  9 Pine St New York (10005) *(G-12661)*
William H Shapiro 212 263-7037
  530 1st Ave Ste 3e New York (10016) *(G-12662)*
William Harvey Studio Inc 718 599-4343
  214 N 8th St Brooklyn (11211) *(G-2769)*
William J Kline & Son Inc (PA) 518 843-1100
  1 Venner Rd Amsterdam (12010) *(G-374)*
William J Ryan 585 392-6200
  1365 Hamlin Parma Townlne Hilton (14468) *(G-6447)*
William Kanes Mfg Corp 718 346-1515
  23 Alabama Ave Brooklyn (11207) *(G-2770)*
William Moon Iron Works Inc 518 943-3861
  80 Main St Catskill (12414) *(G-3462)*
William Morrow Publishing, New York Also called Harpercollins Publishers LLC *(G-10460)*
William R Shoemaker Inc 716 649-0511
  399 Pleasant Ave Hamburg (14075) *(G-5968)*
William S Hein & Co Inc (PA) 716 882-2600
  2350 N Forest Rd Ste 14a Getzville (14068) *(G-5619)*
William S Hein & Co Inc 716 882-2600
  1575 Main St Buffalo (14209) *(G-3282)*
William Somerville Maintenance 212 534-4600
  166 E 124th St New York (10035) *(G-12663)*
William Ward Logging 518 946-7826
  Valley Rd Jay (12941) *(G-7089)*
Williams Tool Inc 315 737-7226
  9372 Elm St Chadwicks (13319) *(G-3559)*
Williams-Sonoma Store 154, New York Also called Williams-Sonoma Stores Inc *(G-12664)*
Williams-Sonoma Stores Inc 212 633-2203
  110 7th Ave New York (10011) *(G-12664)*
Williamsburg Branch, Brooklyn Also called Apple Bank For Savings *(G-1618)*
Williamsburg Bulletin 718 387-0123
  136 Ross St Brooklyn (11211) *(G-2771)*
Williamson Law Book Co 585 924-3400
  790 Canning Pkwy Ste 2 Victor (14564) *(G-16537)*
Willis Mc Donald Co Inc 212 366-1526
  44 W 62nd St Ph A New York (10023) *(G-12665)*
Willow Creek Winery, Silver Creek Also called Chautauqua Wine Company Inc *(G-15469)*
Wilmax Usa LLC 917 388-2790
  315 5th Ave Rm 505 New York (10016) *(G-12666)*
Wilmington Products USA, Roslyn Also called Northwest Textile Holding Inc *(G-15046)*
Wilson & Wilson Group 212 729-4736
  6514 110th St Forest Hills (11375) *(G-5337)*
Wilson Electroplating, Binghamton Also called G J C Ltd Inc *(G-912)*
Wilson N Wilson Group & RES, Forest Hills Also called Wilson & Wilson Group *(G-5337)*
Wilson Picture Frames, West Hempstead Also called Interntonal Consmr Connections *(G-16887)*
Wilson Press LLC 315 568-9693
  56 Miller St Seneca Falls (13148) *(G-15395)*
Wilsonart Intl Holdings LLC 516 935-6980
  999 S Oyster Bay Rd # 3305 Bethpage (11714) *(G-878)*
Wilston Enterprises Inc 716 483-1411
  121 Jackson Ave Jamestown (14701) *(G-7076)*
Wilt Industries Inc 518 548-4961
  2452 State Route 8 Lake Pleasant (12108) *(G-7301)*
Win Set Technologies LLC 631 234-7077
  2364 Middle Country Rd Centereach (11720) *(G-3499)*
Win Wood Cabinetry Inc 516 304-2216
  200 Forest Dr Ste 7 Greenvale (11548) *(G-5901)*
Win-Holt Equipment Corp (PA) 516 222-0335
  20 Crossways Park Dr N # 205 Woodbury (11797) *(G-17322)*
Win-Holt Equipment Corp 516 222-0433
  439 Oak St Ste 1 Garden City (11530) *(G-5551)*
Win-Holt Equipment Group, Woodbury Also called Win-Holt Equipment Corp *(G-17322)*
Winchester Optical Company (HQ) 607 734-4251
  1935 Lake St Elmira (14901) *(G-4718)*
Wind Products Inc 212 292-3135
  20 Jay St Ste 936 Brooklyn (11201) *(G-2772)*
Wind Solutions LLC 518 813-8029
  251 County Road 156 Esperance (12066) *(G-4847)*
Windiam Usa Inc 212 542-0949
  580 5th Ave Ste 2907 New York (10036) *(G-12667)*
Window Rama Enterprises Inc 631 462-9054
  6333 Jericho Tpke Ste 11 Commack (11725) *(G-3873)*
Window Tech Systems Inc 518 899-9000
  15 Old Stonebreak Rd Ballston Spa (12020) *(G-610)*
Window Technologies LLC 402 464-0202
  555 5th Ave Fl 14 New York (10017) *(G-12668)*
Window-Fix Inc 718 854-3475
  331 37th St Fl 1 Brooklyn (11232) *(G-2773)*
Windowcraft Inc 516 294-3580
  77 2nd Ave Garden City Park (11040) *(G-5557)*
Windowman Inc (usa) 718 246-2626
  460 Kingsland Ave Brooklyn (11222) *(G-2774)*
Windows Media Publishing LLC 917 732-7892
  369 Remsen Ave Brooklyn (11212) *(G-2775)*
Windowtex Inc 877 294-3580
  77 2nd Ave Garden City Park (11040) *(G-5558)*
Windsor Technology LLC 585 461-2500
  1527 Lyell Ave Rochester (14606) *(G-14792)*
Windsor United Industries LLC 607 655-3300
  10 Park St Windsor (13865) *(G-17295)*
Wine & Spirits Magazine Inc (PA) 212 695-4660
  2 W 32nd St Ste 601 New York (10001) *(G-12669)*
Wine Group Inc 716 326-3151
  85 Bourne St Westfield (14787) *(G-17084)*
Wine Market 516 328-8800
  2337 New Hyde Park Rd New Hyde Park (11042) *(G-8917)*
Wine Services Inc 631 722-3800
  1129 Cross River Dr Ste A Riverhead (11901) *(G-14174)*
Wineracks.com Inc 845 658-7181
  819 Route 32 Tillson (12486) *(G-16152)*
Winesoft International Corp 914 400-6247
  503 S Broadway Ste 220 Yonkers (10705) *(G-17516)*
Wing Heung Noodle Inc 212 966-7496
  144 Baxter St New York (10013) *(G-12670)*
Wing Kei Noodle Inc 212 226-1644
  102 Canal St New York (10002) *(G-12671)*
Winghing 8 Ltd 718 439-0021
  6215 6th Ave Brooklyn (11220) *(G-2776)*
Wink Acquisition Corp., New York Also called Wink Labs Inc *(G-12673)*
Wink Inc 212 389-1382
  606 W 28th St Fl 6 New York (10001) *(G-12672)*
Wink Labs Inc (HQ) 916 717-0437
  606 W 28th St Fl 7 New York (10001) *(G-12673)*
Winn Manufacturing Inc 518 642-3515
  12 Burtis Ave Granville (12832) *(G-5797)*
Winner Press Inc 718 937-7715
  4331 33rd St 1 Long Island City (11101) *(G-7953)*
Winsight LLC 646 708-7309
  90 Broad St Ste 402 New York (10004) *(G-12674)*
Winson Surnamer Inc 718 729-8787
  4402 11th St Ste 601 Long Island City (11101) *(G-7954)*
Winter Water Factory 646 387-3247
  191 33rd St Brooklyn (11232) *(G-2777)*
Winterling, Eric Costumes, New York Also called Eric Winterling Inc *(G-10108)*
Winters Instruments, Buffalo Also called Winters Instruments Inc *(G-3283)*
Winters Instruments Inc (HQ) 281 880-8607
  455 Cayuga Rd Ste 650 Buffalo (14225) *(G-3283)*
Winters Railroad Service Inc 716 337-2668
  11309 Sisson Hwy North Collins (14111) *(G-12948)*
Wipesplus, Rye Brook Also called Progressive Products LLC *(G-15100)*
Wired Coffee and Bagel Inc 518 506-3194
  Rr 9 Malta (12020) *(G-8054)*
Wireless Communications Inc 845 353-5921
  4 Chemong Ct Nyack (10960) *(G-13073)*
Wizard Equipment Inc 315 414-9999
  10 Dwight Park Dr Ste 3 Syracuse (13209) *(G-16097)*
Wizer Equipment, Rochester Also called Woerner Industries Inc *(G-14793)*
Wizq Inc 586 381-9048
  307 5th Ave Fl 8 New York (10016) *(G-12675)*
Wl Concepts & Production Inc 516 538-5300
  1 Bennington Ave Freeport (11520) *(G-5445)*
Wlj Printers, White Plains Also called Westchester Law Journal Inc *(G-17211)*
Wm E Martin and Sons Co Inc 516 605-2444
  55 Bryant Ave Ste 300 Roslyn (11576) *(G-15048)*
Wmg Acquisition Corp (HQ) 212 275-2000
  75 Rockefeller Plz New York (10019) *(G-12676)*
Wmg Holding Company Inc 212 275-2000
  75 Rockefeller Plz New York (10019) *(G-12677)*
Wmw Machinery Company, Deer Park Also called World LLC *(G-4254)*
Wna Holley, Holley Also called Waddington North America Inc *(G-6519)*
Wny Jobs.com, Hamburg Also called Jobs Weekly Inc *(G-5952)*
Wobbleworks Inc (PA) 718 618-9904
  89 5th Ave Ste 802 New York (10003) *(G-12678)*
Wochit Inc (PA) 212 979-8343
  12 E 33rd St Fl 4 New York (10016) *(G-12679)*
Woerner Industries Inc 585 436-1934
  485 Hague St Rochester (14606) *(G-14793)*
Wok To Walk, New York Also called Restaurant 570 8th Avenue LLC *(G-11875)*
Wolak Inc 315 839-5366
  2360 King Rd Clayville (13322) *(G-3717)*
Wolf X-Ray Corporation 631 242-9729
  100 W Industry Ct Deer Park (11729) *(G-4252)*
Wolf-TEC, Kingston Also called Ludwig Holdings Corp *(G-7227)*
Wolfe Lumber Mill Inc 716 772-7750
  8416 Ridge Rd Gasport (14067) *(G-5575)*
Wolfe Publications Inc (PA) 585 394-0770
  73 Buffalo St Canandaigua (14424) *(G-3389)*
Wolff & Dungey Inc 315 475-2105
  325 Temple St Syracuse (13202) *(G-16098)*
Wolffer Estate Vineyard Inc 631 537-5106
  139 Sagg Rd Sagaponack (11962) *(G-15109)*
Wolffer Estate Winery, Sagaponack Also called Wolffer Estate Vineyard Inc *(G-15109)*
Wolfgang B Gourmet Foods Inc 518 719-1727
  117 Cauterskill Ave Catskill (12414) *(G-3463)*
Wolo Mfg Corp 631 242-0333
  1 Saxwood St Ste 1 Deer Park (11729) *(G-4253)*
Wolski Wood Works Inc 718 577-9816
  14134 78th Rd Apt 3c Flushing (11367) *(G-5313)*

Wolters Kluwer US Inc 212 894-8920
111 8th Ave Fl 13 New York (10011) ***(G-12680)***
Wolters Kluwer US Inc 631 517-8060
400 W Main St Ste 244 Babylon (11702) ***(G-552)***
Women's Health Magazine, New York *Also called Rodale Inc* ***(G-11921)***
Womens E News Inc 212 244-1720
6 Barclay St Fl 6 New York (10007) ***(G-12681)***
Womens Health Care PC (PA) 718 850-0009
11311 Jamaica Ave Ste C Richmond Hill (11418) ***(G-14100)***
Womens Wear Daily, New York *Also called Fairchild Publications Inc* ***(G-10181)***
Won & Lee Inc 516 222-0712
971 Stewart Ave Garden City (11530) ***(G-5552)***
Wonder Natural Foods Corp (PA) 631 726-4433
30 Blank Ln Water Mill (11976) ***(G-16629)***
Wonder Products, Middletown *Also called Advanced Enterprises Inc* ***(G-8459)***
Wonderly Company, The, Kingston *Also called Northast Coml Win Trtments Inc* ***(G-7232)***
Wonton Food Inc 718 784-8178
5210 37th St Long Island City (11101) ***(G-7955)***
Wonton Food Inc (PA) 718 628-6868
220 Moore St 222 Brooklyn (11206) ***(G-2778)***
Wonton Food Inc 212 677-8865
183 E Broadway New York (10002) ***(G-12682)***
Wood & Hyde Leather Co Inc 518 725-7105
68 Wood St Gloversville (12078) ***(G-5745)***
Wood Design, Peekskill *Also called W Designe Inc* ***(G-13509)***
Wood Designs Deluxe Corp 917 414-4640
4090 Austin Blvd Island Park (11558) ***(G-6823)***
Wood Etc Inc 315 484-9663
1175 State Fair Blvd # 3 Syracuse (13209) ***(G-16099)***
Wood Floor Expo Inc 212 472-0671
426 E 73rd St Frnt 1 New York (10021) ***(G-12683)***
Wood Innovations of Suffolk 631 698-2345
266 Middle Island Rd # 8 Medford (11763) ***(G-8297)***
Wood Talk 631 940-3085
203 N Fehr Way Ste C Bay Shore (11706) ***(G-748)***
Wood Tex Products LLC 607 243-5141
3700 Route 14 Himrod (14842) ***(G-6449)***
Wood-Tex Products, Himrod *Also called Lapp Management Corp* ***(G-6448)***
Woodards Concrete Products Inc 845 361-3471
629 Lybolt Rd Bullville (10915) ***(G-3289)***
Woodbine Products Inc 631 586-3770
110 Plant Ave Hauppauge (11788) ***(G-6259)***
Woodbury Cmmon Premium Outlets, Central Valley *Also called Sarar Usa Inc* ***(G-3554)***
Woodbury Printing Plus + Inc 845 928-6610
96 Turner Rd Central Valley (10917) ***(G-3557)***
Woodbury Systems Group Inc 516 364-2653
30 Glenn Dr Woodbury (11797) ***(G-17323)***
Woodbury Vineyards Inc 716 679-9463
3215 S Roberts Rd Fredonia (14063) ***(G-5386)***
Woodcock Brothers Brewing Comp 716 333-4000
638 Lake St Wilson (14172) ***(G-17293)***
Woodcraft, Rochester *Also called Aces Over Eights Inc* ***(G-14184)***
Wooden Boatworks 631 477-6507
190 Sterling St Unit 2 Greenport (11944) ***(G-5896)***
Woodfalls Industries 518 236-7201
434 Burke Rd Plattsburgh (12901) ***(G-13740)***
Woodmaster Industries, Jamaica *Also called Abbott Industries Inc* ***(G-6926)***
Woodmere Fabrics Inc 212 695-0144
35 W 35th St New York (10001) ***(G-12684)***
Woodmotif Inc 516 564-8325
42 Chasner St Hempstead (11550) ***(G-6312)***
Woodmotif Cabinetry, Hempstead *Also called Woodmotif Inc* ***(G-6312)***
Woods Knife Corporation 516 798-4972
19 Brooklyn Ave Massapequa (11758) ***(G-8217)***
Woods Machine and Tool LLC 607 699-3253
150 Howell St Nichols (13812) ***(G-12909)***
Woodside Decorator, Staten Island *Also called All Signs* ***(G-15656)***
Woodside Granite Industries (PA) 585 589-6500
13890 Ridge Rd W Albion (14411) ***(G-174)***
Woodstock Times, Kingston *Also called Ulster Publishing Co Inc* ***(G-7247)***
Woodtalk Stairs & Rails, Bay Shore *Also called Wood Talk* ***(G-748)***
Woodtronics Inc 914 962-5205
1661 Front St Ste 3 Yorktown Heights (10598) ***(G-17537)***
Woodward Industries Inc 716 692-2242
233 Fillmore Ave Ste 23 Tonawanda (14150) ***(G-16236)***
Woodward/White Inc 718 509-6082
45 Main St Ste 820 Brooklyn (11201) ***(G-2779)***
Woolmark Americas Inc 347 767-3160
110 E 25th St Fl 3 New York (10010) ***(G-12685)***
WOOLMARK COMPANY, THE, New York *Also called Woolmark Americas Inc* ***(G-12685)***
Wordingham Machine Co Inc 585 924-2294
515 Lee Rd Rochester (14606) ***(G-14794)***
Wordingham Technologies, Rochester *Also called Wordingham Machine Co Inc* ***(G-14794)***
Wordwise Inc 914 232-5366
1 Brady Ln Katonah (10536) ***(G-7164)***
Working Family Solutions Inc 845 802-6182
359 Washington Avenue Ext Saugerties (12477) ***(G-15227)***
Working Mother Media Inc 212 351-6400
2 Park Ave Fl 10 New York (10016) ***(G-12686)***
Workman Publishing Co Inc (PA) 212 254-5900
225 Varick St Fl 9 New York (10014) ***(G-12687)***
Workman Publishing Co Inc 212 254-5900
708 Broadway Fl 6 New York (10003) ***(G-12688)***
Workplace Interiors LLC 585 425-7420
400 Packetts Lndg Fairport (14450) ***(G-4894)***
Workshop Art Fabrication 845 331-0385
117 Tremper Ave Kingston (12401) ***(G-7252)***
Worksman Cycles, Ozone Park *Also called Worksman Trading Corp* ***(G-13413)***
Worksman Trading Corp 718 322-2000
9415 100th St Ozone Park (11416) ***(G-13413)***
World Business Media LLC 212 344-0759
4770 Sunrise Hwy Ste 105 Massapequa Park (11762) ***(G-8224)***
World Cheese Co Inc 718 965-1700
178 28th St Brooklyn (11232) ***(G-2780)***
World Guide Publishing 800 331-7840
1271 Ave Of The Americas New York (10020) ***(G-12689)***
World Journal Book Store, Flushing *Also called World Journal LLC* ***(G-5314)***
World Journal LLC 212 879-3933
205 E 78th St New York (10075) ***(G-12690)***
World Journal LLC (HQ) 718 746-8889
14107 20th Ave Fl 2 Whitestone (11357) ***(G-17247)***
World Journal LLC 718 445-2277
13619 39th Ave Flushing (11354) ***(G-5314)***
World Journal LLC 718 871-5000
6007 8th Ave Brooklyn (11220) ***(G-2781)***
World LLC 631 940-9121
513 Acorn St Ste B Deer Park (11729) ***(G-4254)***
World of McIntosh, New York *Also called Fine Sounds Group Inc* ***(G-10217)***
World Screen News, New York *Also called Wsn Inc* ***(G-12696)***
World Trading Center Inc 631 273-3330
115 Engineers Rd Fl 2 Hauppauge (11788) ***(G-6260)***
Worlds Finest Chocolate Inc 718 332-2442
73 Exeter St Brooklyn (11235) ***(G-2782)***
Worldwide Arntcal Cmpnents Inc (PA) 631 842-3780
10 Reith St Copiague (11726) ***(G-3962)***
Worldwide Arntcal Cmpnents Inc 631 842-3780
10 Reith St Copiague (11726) ***(G-3963)***
Worldwide Gas Turbine Pdts Inc 518 877-7200
300 Commerce Dr Clifton Park (12065) ***(G-3737)***
Worldwide Protective Pdts LLC 877 678-4568
4255 Mckinley Pkwy Hamburg (14075) ***(G-5969)***
Worldwide Resources Inc 718 760-5000
1908 Avenue O Brooklyn (11230) ***(G-2783)***
Worldwide Ticket Craft 516 538-6200
1390 Jerusalem Ave Merrick (11566) ***(G-8429)***
Worm Power, Rochester *Also called Rt Solutions LLC* ***(G-14683)***
Worth Collection Ltd (PA) 212 268-0312
520 8th Ave Rm 2301 New York (10018) ***(G-12691)***
Worth Publishers Inc 212 475-6000
1 New York Plz Ste 4500 New York (10004) ***(G-12692)***
Worthington Industries Inc 315 336-5500
530 Henry St Rome (13440) ***(G-14868)***
Worzalla Publishing Company 212 967-7909
222 W 37th St Fl 10 New York (10018) ***(G-12693)***
Wp Lavori USA Inc (HQ) 212 244-6074
597 Broadway Fl 2 New York (10012) ***(G-12694)***
WR Design Corp 212 354-9000
230 W 39th St Fl 5f New York (10018) ***(G-12695)***
WR Smith & Sons Inc 845 620-9400
121 W Nyack Rd Nanuet (10954) ***(G-8809)***
Wr9000, New York *Also called WR Design Corp* ***(G-12695)***
Wrightcut EDM & Machine Inc 607 733-5018
951 Carl St Elmira (14904) ***(G-4719)***
Wrights Hardwoods Inc 716 595-2345
6868 Route 60 Cassadaga (14718) ***(G-3443)***
Writing Sculptures, Deer Park *Also called Versaponents Inc* ***(G-4248)***
Wrkbook LLC 914 355-1293
19 Brookdale Ave White Plains (10603) ***(G-17215)***
Wsf Industries Inc 716 692-4930
7 Hackett Dr Tonawanda (14150) ***(G-16237)***
Wsn Inc 212 924-7620
1123 Broadway Ste 1207 New York (10010) ***(G-12696)***
Wtbi Inc 631 547-1993
200 E 2nd St Ste 12 Huntington Station (11746) ***(G-6767)***
Www.dynatabs.com, Brooklyn *Also called Dynatabs LLC* ***(G-1889)***
Www.picturesongold.com, Staten Island *Also called Photograve Corporation* ***(G-15741)***
Www.poppin.com, New York *Also called Poppin Inc* ***(G-11707)***
Wyde Lumber 845 513-5571
419 State Route 17b Monticello (12701) ***(G-8647)***
Wyeth, Rouses Point *Also called Pfizer Inc* ***(G-15066)***
Wyeth Holdings LLC 845 602-5000
401 N Middletown Rd Pearl River (10965) ***(G-13493)***
Wyeth LLC (HQ) 973 660-5000
235 E 42nd St New York (10017) ***(G-12697)***
Wyeth Pharmaceutical Division, Pearl River *Also called Wyeth Holdings LLC* ***(G-13493)***
Wynco Press One Inc 516 354-6145
7839 268th St Glen Oaks (11004) ***(G-5656)***
Wynn Starr Flavors Inc (PA) 845 584-3080
225 N Route 303 Ste 109 Congers (10920) ***(G-3888)***

ALPHABETIC

Wyrestorm Technologies LLC 518 289-1293
23 Wood Rd Round Lake (12151) ***(G-15063)***
X Brand Editions 718 482-7646
4020 22nd St Ste 1 Long Island City (11101) ***(G-7956)***
X Function Inc (PA) 212 231-0092
902 Broadway Fl 11 New York (10010) ***(G-12698)***
X Myles Mar Inc 212 683-2015
875 Av Of The Americas New York (10001) ***(G-12699)***
X Press Screen Printing 716 679-7788
4867 W Lake Rd Dunkirk (14048) ***(G-4377)***
X Press Signs Inc 716 892-3000
1780 Union Rd Ste 106 West Seneca (14224) ***(G-16984)***
X-Gen Pharmaceuticals Inc (PA) 607 562-2700
300 Daniel Zenker Dr Big Flats (14814) ***(G-880)***
X-Gen Pharmaceuticals Inc 631 261-8188
744 Baldwin St Elmira (14901) ***(G-4720)***
X-Gen Pharmaceuticals Inc 607 562-2700
300 Daniel Zenker Dr Horseheads (14845) ***(G-6624)***
X-L Envelope and Printing Inc 716 852-2135
701 Seneca St Ste 100 Buffalo (14210) ***(G-3284)***
X-Press Printing & Office Sup, Mahopac *Also called Rmd Holding Inc* ***(G-8031)***
X-Treme Ready Mix Inc 718 739-3384
17801 Liberty Ave Jamaica (11433) ***(G-7001)***
X1000, Binghamton *Also called Surescan Corporation* ***(G-947)***
Xactra Technologies Inc 585 426-2030
105 Mcloughlin Rd Ste F Rochester (14615) ***(G-14795)***
Xanadu 212 465-0580
150 W 30th St Rm 702 New York (10001) ***(G-12700)***
Xania Labs Inc 718 361-2550
3202 Queens Blvd Fl 6 Long Island City (11101) ***(G-7957)***
Xborder Entertainment LLC 518 726-7036
568 State Route 3 Plattsburgh (12901) ***(G-13741)***
Xedit Corp 718 380-1592
21831 97th Ave Queens Village (11429) ***(G-14000)***
Xeku Corporation 607 761-1447
2520 Vestal Pkwy E222 Vestal (13850) ***(G-16481)***
Xeleum Lighting LLC 954 617-8170
333 N Bedford Rd Ste 135 Mount Kisco (10549) ***(G-8689)***
Xelic Incorporated 585 415-2764
1250 Pittsford Victor Rd # 370 Pittsford (14534) ***(G-13604)***
Xentaur Corporation 631 345-3434
84 Horseblock Rd Unit G Yaphank (11980) ***(G-17425)***
Xerox Corporation 585 423-4711
100 S Clinton Ave Fl 4 Rochester (14604) ***(G-14796)***
Xerox Corporation 585 422-4564
800 Phillips Rd Ste 20599 Webster (14580) ***(G-16769)***
Xerox Corporation 212 716-4000
245 Park Ave Fl 21 New York (10167) ***(G-12701)***
Xerox Corporation 914 397-1319
8 Hangar Rd White Plains (10604) ***(G-17216)***
Xerox Corporation 585 425-6100
1387 Fairport Rd Ste 200 Fairport (14450) ***(G-4895)***
Xerox Corporation 516 677-1500
155 Pinelawn Rd Ste 200n Melville (11747) ***(G-8393)***
Xerox Corporation 212 330-1386
485 Lexington Ave Fl 10 New York (10017) ***(G-12702)***
Xerox Corporation 845 918-3147
30 Dunnigan Dr Ste 3 Suffern (10901) ***(G-15823)***
Xerox Corporation 518 434-6543
80 State St Ste 3 Albany (12207) ***(G-152)***
Xerox Corporation 585 427-4500
225 Tech Park Dr Rochester (14623) ***(G-14797)***
Xerox Corporation 585 423-3538
100 S Clinton Ave Rochester (14604) ***(G-14798)***
Xerox Corporation 585 423-5090
800 Phillips Rd Webster (14580) ***(G-16770)***
Xerox Corporation 585 264-5584
80 Linden Oaks Rochester (14625) ***(G-14799)***
Xerox Corporation 716 831-3300
450 Corporate Pkwy # 100 Buffalo (14226) ***(G-3285)***
Xing Lin USA Intl Corp 212 947-4846
1410 Broadway New York (10018) ***(G-12703)***
Xinya International Trading Co 212 216-9681
115 W 30th St Rm 1109 New York (10001) ***(G-12704)***
Xl Graphics Inc 212 929-8700
121 Varick St Rm 300 New York (10013) ***(G-12705)***
Xli Corporation 585 436-2250
55 Vanguard Pkwy Rochester (14606) ***(G-14800)***
Xmh-Hfi Inc (PA) 585 467-7240
1155 N Clinton Ave Rochester (14621) ***(G-14801)***
Xomox Jewelry Inc 212 944-8428
151 W 46th St Fl 15 New York (10036) ***(G-12706)***
Xpand, New York *Also called Whiteboard Ventures Inc* ***(G-12655)***
Xpress Printing Inc 516 605-1000
7 Fairchild Ct Ste 100 Plainview (11803) ***(G-13675)***
Xstatic Pro Inc 718 237-2299
901 Essex St Brooklyn (11208) ***(G-2784)***
Xstelos Holdings Inc 212 729-4962
630 5th Ave Ste 2600 New York (10111) ***(G-12707)***
Xto Incorporated (PA) 315 451-7807
110 Wrentham Dr Liverpool (13088) ***(G-7585)***
Xylem, Cheektowaga *Also called Fluid Handling LLC* ***(G-3600)***
Xylem Inc 716 862-4123
2881 E Bayard Street Ext Seneca Falls (13148) ***(G-15396)***
Xylem Inc 315 258-4949
1 Goulds Dr Auburn (13021) ***(G-527)***
Xylem Inc 315 239-2499
2881 E Bayard Street Ext Seneca Falls (13148) ***(G-15397)***
Xylem Inc (PA) 914 323-5700
1 International Dr Rye Brook (10573) ***(G-15102)***
Xylon Industries Inc 631 293-4717
79 Florida St Farmingdale (11735) ***(G-5153)***
Y & A Trading Inc 718 436-6333
1365 38th St Brooklyn (11218) ***(G-2785)***
Y & Z Precision Inc 516 349-8243
155 E Ames Ct Unit 4 Plainview (11803) ***(G-13676)***
Y & Z Precision Machine Shop, Plainview *Also called Y & Z Precision Inc* ***(G-13676)***
Yacoubian Jewelers Inc 212 302-6729
2 W 45th St Ste 1104 New York (10036) ***(G-12708)***
Yale, Getzville *Also called Columbus McKinnon Corporation* ***(G-5609)***
Yale Robbins Inc 212 683-5700
205 Lexington Ave Fl 12 New York (10016) ***(G-12709)***
Yale Trouser Corporation 516 255-0700
3670 Oceanside Rd W Ste 6 Oceanside (11572) ***(G-13128)***
Yaloz Mold & Die, Brooklyn *Also called Yaloz Mould & Die Co Inc* ***(G-2786)***
Yaloz Mould & Die Co Inc 718 389-1131
239 Java St Fl 2 Brooklyn (11222) ***(G-2786)***
Yam TV LLC 917 932-5418
144 W 23rd St Apt 8e New York (10011) ***(G-12710)***
Yankee Corp 718 589-1377
1180 Randall Ave Bronx (10474) ***(G-1496)***
Yankee Fuel Inc 631 880-8810
780 Sunrise Hwy West Babylon (11704) ***(G-16873)***
Yankee Wiping Cloth, Bronx *Also called Yankee Corp* ***(G-1496)***
Yarnz International Inc 212 868-5883
260 W 36th St Rm 201 New York (10018) ***(G-12711)***
Yated Neeman Inc 845 369-1600
53 Olympia Ln Monsey (10952) ***(G-8621)***
Yellow E House Inc 718 888-2000
18812 Northern Blvd Flushing (11358) ***(G-5315)***
Yellow Pages Inc (PA) 845 639-6060
222 N Main St New City (10956) ***(G-8840)***
Yellowpagecitycom 585 410-6688
280 Kenneth Dr Ste 300 Rochester (14623) ***(G-14802)***
Yeohlee Inc 212 631-8099
12 W 29th St New York (10001) ***(G-12712)***
Yepes Fine Furniture 718 383-0221
72 Van Dam St Brooklyn (11222) ***(G-2787)***
Yes Dental Laboratory Inc 914 333-7550
155 White Plains Rd # 223 Tarrytown (10591) ***(G-16135)***
Yes Were Nuts Ltd 516 374-1940
1215 Broadway Hewlett (11557) ***(G-6341)***
Yesteryears Vintage Doors LLC 315 324-5250
66 S Main St Hammond (13646) ***(G-5974)***
Yewtree Millworks Corp 914 320-5851
372 Ashburton Ave Yonkers (10701) ***(G-17517)***
Yfd Cabinetry, West Haverstraw *Also called Your Furniture Designers Inc* ***(G-16879)***
Yigal-Azrouel Inc 212 302-1194
225 W 39th St Fl 5 New York (10018) ***(G-12713)***
Ying Ke Youth Age Group Inc 929 402-8458
1 Campbell Dr Dix Hills (11746) ***(G-4323)***
Yingli Green Enrgy Amricas Inc (HQ) 888 686-8820
33 Irving Pl Fl 3 New York (10003) ***(G-12714)***
Yingli Solar, New York *Also called Yingli Green Enrgy Amricas Inc* ***(G-12714)***
Yiwen Usa Inc 212 370-0828
60 E 42nd St Ste 1030 New York (10165) ***(G-12715)***
Yo Fresh Inc 845 634-1616
170 S Main St New City (10956) ***(G-8841)***
Yo Fresh Inc 518 982-0659
5 Southside Dr Clifton Park (12065) ***(G-3738)***
Yofah Religious Articles Inc 718 435-3288
2001 57th St Ste 1 Brooklyn (11204) ***(G-2788)***
Yog N Go Inc 585 319-8110
163 W Commercial St East Rochester (14445) ***(G-4486)***
Yoga In Daily Life - NY Inc 718 539-8548
1438 132nd St College Point (11356) ***(G-3837)***
Yohay Baking Company, Lindenhurst *Also called Alrajs Inc* ***(G-7474)***
Yoland Corporation 718 499-4803
253 36th St Unit 2 Brooklyn (11232) ***(G-2789)***
Yomiuri International Inc 212 752-2196
747 3rd Ave Fl 28 New York (10017) ***(G-12716)***
Yong Ji Productions Inc 917 559-4616
10219 44th Ave Corona (11368) ***(G-4032)***
Yong Xin Kitchen Supplies Inc 212 995-8908
50 Delancey St Frnt A New York (10002) ***(G-12717)***
Yonkers Cabinets Inc 914 668-2133
1179 Yonkers Ave Yonkers (10704) ***(G-17518)***
Yonkers Time Publishing Co 914 965-4000
40 Larkin Plz Yonkers (10701) ***(G-17519)***
Yonkers Whl Beer Distrs Inc 914 963-8600
424 Riverdale Ave Yonkers (10705) ***(G-17520)***
Yorganic, New York *Also called Bliss Foods Inc* ***(G-9465)***
Yorganic, New York *Also called Bliss Foods Inc* ***(G-9466)***

York Fuel Incorporated 718 951-0202
1760 Flatbush Ave Brooklyn (11210) ***(G-2790)***
York Industries Inc 516 746-3736
303 Nassau Blvd Garden City Park (11040) ***(G-5559)***
York International Corporation 718 389-4152
1130 45th Rd Long Island City (11101) ***(G-7958)***
York Ladder Inc 718 784-6666
3720 12th St Long Island City (11101) ***(G-7959)***
York Ladders, Long Island City *Also called AAAA York Inc* ***(G-7677)***
Yorktown Printing Corp 914 962-2526
1520 Front St Yorktown Heights (10598) ***(G-17538)***
Yorkville Sound Inc 716 297-2920
4625 Witmer Indus Est Niagara Falls (14305) ***(G-12908)***
Yost Neon Displays Inc 716 674-6780
20 Ransier Dr West Seneca (14224) ***(G-16985)***
You and ME Legwear LLC 212 279-9292
10 W 33rd St Rm 300 New York (10001) ***(G-12718)***
Young & Franklin Inc (HQ) 315 457-3110
942 Old Liverpool Rd Liverpool (13088) ***(G-7586)***
Young & Swartz Inc 716 852-2171
39 Cherry St Buffalo (14204) ***(G-3286)***
Young Explosives Corp 585 394-1783
2165 New Michigan Rd Canandaigua (14424) ***(G-3390)***
Younique Clothing, New York *Also called Turn On Products Inc* ***(G-12447)***
Your Furniture Designers Inc 845 947-3046
118 E Railroad Ave West Haverstraw (10993) ***(G-16879)***
Your Name Professional Brand, Long Island City *Also called Mana Products Inc* ***(G-7828)***
Your Way Custom Cabinets Inc 914 371-1870
20 N Macquesten Pkwy Mount Vernon (10550) ***(G-8792)***
Yourhealth911.com, Brooklyn *Also called GNI Commerce Inc* ***(G-2034)***
Yoyo Lip Gloss Inc 718 357-6304
2438 47th St Astoria (11103) ***(G-462)***
Ypis of Staten Island Inc 718 815-4557
130 Stuyvesant Pl Ste 5 Staten Island (10301) ***(G-15777)***
Yr Blanc & Co LLC 716 800-3999
1275 Main St Ste 120 Buffalo (14209) ***(G-3287)***
Ys Marketing Inc 718 778-6080
2004 Mcdonald Ave Brooklyn (11223) ***(G-2791)***
Ys Metal 518 512-5275
54 Dott Ave Albany (12205) ***(G-153)***
YS Publishing Co Inc 212 682-9360
228 E 45th St Rm 700 New York (10017) ***(G-12719)***
Yugo Landau, Brooklyn *Also called Eastern Feather & Down Corp* ***(G-1899)***
Yula Corporation 718 991-0900
330 Bryant Ave Bronx (10474) ***(G-1497)***
Yum Yum Noodle Bar 845 679-7992
275 Fair St Ste 17 Kingston (12401) ***(G-7253)***
Yurman Retail Inc 888 398-7626
712 Madison Ave New York (10065) ***(G-12720)***
Z Best Printing Inc 631 595-1400
699 Acorn St Ste B Deer Park (11729) ***(G-4255)***
Z Card North America, New York *Also called In-Step Marketing Inc* ***(G-10624)***
Z Vape Station/Atlantic Smoke 516 442-0548
384 Atlantic Ave Freeport (11520) ***(G-5446)***
Z Works Inc 631 750-0612
1395 Lakeland Ave Ste 10 Bohemia (11716) ***(G-1154)***
Z-Axis Inc 315 548-5000
1916 State Route 96 Phelps (14532) ***(G-13563)***
Z-Car-D Corp 631 424-2077
403 Oakwood Rd Huntington Station (11746) ***(G-6768)***
Z-Ply Corp 212 398-7011
213 W 35th St Ste 5w New York (10001) ***(G-12721)***
Z-Studios Dsign Fbrication LLC 347 512-4210
30 Haven Pl Brooklyn (11233) ***(G-2792)***
Zacks Enterprises Inc 800 366-4924
33 Corporate Dr Orangeburg (10962) ***(G-13270)***
Zacmel Graphics LLC 631 944-6031
500 Brook Ave Ste B Deer Park (11729) ***(G-4256)***
Zadig and Voltaire, New York *Also called Arteast LLC* ***(G-9267)***
Zagwear, Orangeburg *Also called Zacks Enterprises Inc* ***(G-13270)***
Zahk Sales Inc 631 348-9300
75 Hoffman Ln Ste A Islandia (11749) ***(G-6844)***
Zak Jewelry Tools Inc 212 768-8122
55 W 47th St Fl 2 New York (10036) ***(G-12722)***
Zam Barrett Dialogue Inc 646 649-0140
128 32nd St 112 Brooklyn (11232) ***(G-2793)***
Zan Optics Products Inc 718 435-0533
982 39th St Brooklyn (11219) ***(G-2794)***
Zanetti Millwork, Middle Grove *Also called Cuccio-Zanetti Inc* ***(G-8437)***
Zanzano Woodworking Inc 914 725-6025
91 Locust Ave Scarsdale (10583) ***(G-15255)***
Zappala Farms AG Systems Inc 315 626-6293
11404 Schuler Rd Cato (13033) ***(G-3453)***
Zappone Chrysler Jeep Ddge Inc 518 982-0610
1780 Route 9 Halfmoon (12065) ***(G-5939)***
Zar Apparel Group, New York *Also called Zar Group LLC* ***(G-12723)***
Zar Group LLC (PA) 212 944-2510
1375 Broadway Fl 12 New York (10018) ***(G-12723)***
Zaralo LLC 212 764-4590
500 7th Ave Fl 18 New York (10018) ***(G-12724)***
Zaro Bake Shop Inc (PA) 718 993-7327
138 Bruckner Blvd Bronx (10454) ***(G-1498)***
Zaro Bake Shop Inc 212 292-0175
370 Lexington Ave New York (10017) ***(G-12725)***
Zaro's Bread Basket, Bronx *Also called Zaro Bake Shop Inc* ***(G-1498)***
Zaro's Bread Basket, New York *Also called Zaro Bake Shop Inc* ***(G-12725)***
Zastech Inc 516 496-4777
15 Ryan St Syosset (11791) ***(G-15863)***
Zazoom LLC (PA) 212 321-2100
1 Exchange Plz Ste 801 New York (10006) ***(G-12726)***
Zazoom Media Group, New York *Also called Zazoom LLC* ***(G-12726)***
Zebra Books, New York *Also called Kensington Publishing Corp* ***(G-10876)***
Zebra Environmental Corp (PA) 516 596-6300
30 N Prospect Ave Lynbrook (11563) ***(G-7993)***
Zebra Technologies Entp Corp 800 722-6234
1 Zebra Plz Holtsville (11742) ***(G-6542)***
Zebrowski Industries Inc 716 532-3911
4345 Route 39 Collins (14034) ***(G-3844)***
Zedge Inc 330 577-3424
22 Cortlandt St Fl 14 New York (10007) ***(G-12727)***
Zeeba Jewelry Manufacturing, New York *Also called Zeeba Jewelry Mfg Inc* ***(G-12728)***
Zeeba Jewelry Mfg Inc 212 997-1009
36 W 47th St Ste 902 New York (10036) ***(G-12728)***
Zehnder Rittling, Buffalo *Also called Hydro-Air Components Inc* ***(G-3018)***
Zela International Co 518 436-1833
13 Manor St Albany (12207) ***(G-154)***
Zeller Woodworks LLC 585 254-7607
35 Norman St Rochester (14613) ***(G-14803)***
Zelman & Friedman Jwly Mfg Co 718 349-3400
4722 37th St Long Island City (11101) ***(G-7960)***
Zenger Group Inc 716 871-1058
777 E Park Dr Tonawanda (14150) ***(G-16238)***
Zenger Partners LLC 716 876-2284
1881 Kenmore Ave Kenmore (14217) ***(G-7181)***
Zenith Autoparts Corp 845 344-1382
20 Industrial Pl Middletown (10940) ***(G-8507)***
Zenith Color Comm Group Inc (PA) 212 989-4400
4710 33rd St Long Island City (11101) ***(G-7961)***
Zenith Promotions, Lawrence *Also called Last Straw Inc* ***(G-7418)***
Zenith Solutions 718 575-8570
6922 Manse St Flushing (11375) ***(G-5316)***
Zeo Health Ltd 845 353-5185
159 Route 303 Valley Cottage (10989) ***(G-16421)***
Zeppelin Electric Company Inc 631 928-9467
26 Deer Ln East Setauket (11733) ***(G-4516)***
Zeptometrix Corporation (PA) 716 882-0920
847 Main St Buffalo (14203) ***(G-3288)***
Zered Inc (PA) 718 353-7464
12717 20th Ave College Point (11356) ***(G-3838)***
Zerovalent Nanometals Inc 585 298-8592
693 East Ave Ste 103 Rochester (14607) ***(G-14804)***
Zeta Machine Corp 631 471-8832
206 Christopher St Ronkonkoma (11779) ***(G-15026)***
Zeteck, New York *Also called Zetek Corporation* ***(G-12729)***
Zetek Corporation 212 668-1485
13 E 37th St Ste 701 New York (10016) ***(G-12729)***
Zg Apparel Group LLC 212 944-2510
1375 Broadway Fl 12 New York (10018) ***(G-12730)***
Zia Power Inc 845 661-8388
116 E 27th St New York (10016) ***(G-12731)***
ZIC Sportswear Inc (PA) 718 361-9022
2107 41st Ave Fl 3 Long Island City (11101) ***(G-7962)***
Ziebart, Rochester *Also called Monroe County Auto Svcs Inc* ***(G-14540)***
Ziegler Truck & Diesl Repr Inc 315 782-7278
22249 Fabco Rd Watertown (13601) ***(G-16699)***
Zielinskis Asphalt Inc 315 306-4057
4989 State Route 12b Oriskany Falls (13425) ***(G-13343)***
Zierick Manufacturing Corp (PA) 800 882-8020
131 Radio Circle Dr Mount Kisco (10549) ***(G-8690)***
Ziff-Davis Publishing, New York *Also called Davis Ziff Publishing Inc* ***(G-9885)***
Zinc Corporation America Div, New York *Also called Hh Liquidating Corp* ***(G-10515)***
Zinepak LLC 212 706-8621
349 5th Ave New York (10016) ***(G-12732)***
Zinerva Pharmaceuticals LLC 630 729-4184
6017 Corinne Ln Clarence Center (14032) ***(G-3708)***
Zings Company LLC 631 454-0339
250 Adams Blvd Farmingdale (11735) ***(G-5154)***
Zinnias Inc 718 746-8551
24520 Grand Central Pkwy 4l Bellerose (11426) ***(G-808)***
Zip Jack Custom Umbrellas, Tarrytown *Also called Zip-Jack Industries Ltd* ***(G-16136)***
Zip Products Inc 585 482-0044
565 Blossom Rd Ste E Rochester (14610) ***(G-14805)***
Zip-Jack Industries Ltd 914 592-2000
73 Carrollwood Dr Tarrytown (10591) ***(G-16136)***
Zipari Inc 855 558-7884
45 Main St Ste 406 Brooklyn (11201) ***(G-2795)***
Ziptswitch, Bay Shore *Also called Adeptronics Incorporated* ***(G-665)***
Zircar Ceramics Inc (PA) 845 651-6600
100 N Main St Ste 2 Florida (10921) ***(G-5223)***
Zircar Refr Composites Inc 845 651-2200
14 Golden Hill Ter Florida (10921) ***(G-5224)***
Zircar Refr Composites Inc (PA) 845 651-4481
46 Jayne St Florida (10921) ***(G-5225)***

ALPHABETIC

Zircar Zirconia Inc 845 651-3040
87 Meadow Rd Florida (10921) *(G-5226)*
Zirconia Creations Intl 212 239-3730
134 W 29th St Rm 801 New York (10001) *(G-12733)*
Zitomer LLC 212 737-5560
969 Madison Ave Fl 1 New York (10021) *(G-12734)*
Ziva Gem LLC (PA) 646 416-5828
200 Madison Ave Ste 2225 New York (10016) *(G-12735)*
Zmz Mfg Inc 518 234-4336
300 Mickle Hollow Rd Warnerville (12187) *(G-16599)*
Zoe, Long Island City *Also called ZIC Sportswear Inc (G-7962)*
Zoe Sakoutis LLC 212 414-5741
135 W 29th St Rm 704 New York (10001) *(G-12736)*
Zographos Designs Ltd 212 545-0227
300 E 33rd St Apt 9m New York (10016) *(G-12737)*
Zola Books Inc (PA) 917 822-4950
242 W 38th St Fl 2 New York (10018) *(G-12738)*
Zomega Terahertz Corporation 585 347-4337
806 Admiralty Way Webster (14580) *(G-16771)*
Zone Fabricators Inc 718 272-0200
10780 101st St Ozone Park (11417) *(G-13414)*
Zoomers Inc (PA) 718 369-2656
32 33rd St Brooklyn (11232) *(G-2796)*
Zorlu USA Inc (PA) 212 689-4622
295 5th Ave Ste 503 New York (10016) *(G-12739)*

Zotos International Inc 315 781-3207
300 Forge Ave Geneva (14456) *(G-5601)*
Zuant, Valley Stream *Also called High Performance Sftwr USA Inc (G-16436)*
Zuckerbakers Inc 516 785-6900
2845 Jerusalem Ave Wantagh (11793) *(G-16585)*
Zumbach Electronics Corp 914 241-7080
140 Kisco Ave Mount Kisco (10549) *(G-8691)*
Zumtobel Lighting Inc (HQ) 845 691-6262
3300 Route 9w Highland (12528) *(G-6436)*
Zwack Incorporated 518 733-5135
15875 Ny 22 Stephentown (12168) *(G-15780)*
Zweigles Inc 585 546-1740
651 Plymouth Ave N Rochester (14608) *(G-14806)*
Zylon Corporation 845 425-9469
23 Mountain Ave Monsey (10952) *(G-8622)*
Zylon Polymers, Monsey *Also called Zylon Corporation (G-8622)*
Zyloware Corporation (PA) 914 708-1200
8 Slater St Ste 1 Port Chester (10573) *(G-13785)*
Zyloware Eyewear, Port Chester *Also called Zyloware Corporation (G-13785)*
Zymtrnix Catalytic Systems Inc 918 694-8206
405 Will Hall Crnell Univ Ithaca (14853) *(G-6920)*
Zyp Precision LLC 315 539-3667
1098 Birdsey Rd Waterloo (13165) *(G-16654)*
Zzz Mattress Manufacturing 718 454-1468
11080 Dunkirk St Saint Albans (11412) *(G-15112)*

PRODUCT INDEX

• Product categories are listed in alphabetical order.

A

ABRASIVES
ABRASIVES: Coated
ABRASIVES: Grains
ACADEMIC TUTORING SVCS
ACCELERATION INDICATORS & SYSTEM COMPONENTS: Aerospace
ACCELERATORS: Electron Linear
ACCELERATORS: Particle, High Voltage
ACCOUNTING MACHINES & CASH REGISTERS
ACID RESIST: Etching
ACIDS
ACIDS: Battery
ACOUSTICAL BOARD & TILE
ACRYLIC RESINS
ACTUATORS: Indl, NEC
ADDITIVE BASED PLASTIC MATERIALS: Plasticizers
ADHESIVES
ADHESIVES & SEALANTS
ADHESIVES & SEALANTS WHOLESALERS
ADHESIVES: Epoxy
ADVERTISING AGENCIES
ADVERTISING AGENCIES: Consultants
ADVERTISING DISPLAY PRDTS
ADVERTISING MATERIAL DISTRIBUTION
ADVERTISING REPRESENTATIVES: Electronic Media
ADVERTISING REPRESENTATIVES: Magazine
ADVERTISING REPRESENTATIVES: Media
ADVERTISING REPRESENTATIVES: Newspaper
ADVERTISING REPRESENTATIVES: Printed Media
ADVERTISING SPECIALTIES, WHOLESALE
ADVERTISING SVCS: Direct Mail
ADVERTISING SVCS: Display
ADVERTISING SVCS: Outdoor
ADVERTISING SVCS: Sample Distribution
ADVERTISING SVCS: Transit
AERIAL WORK PLATFORMS
AEROSOLS
AGENTS & MANAGERS: Entertainers
AGENTS, BROKERS & BUREAUS: Personal Service
AGRICULTURAL EQPT: BARN, SILO, POULTRY, DAIRY/LIVESTOCK MACH
AGRICULTURAL EQPT: Fertilizng, Sprayng, Dustng/Irrigatn Mach
AGRICULTURAL EQPT: Milking Machines
AGRICULTURAL EQPT: Planting Machines
AGRICULTURAL EQPT: Spreaders, Fertilizer
AGRICULTURAL EQPT: Trailers & Wagons, Farm
AGRICULTURAL EQPT: Turf & Grounds Eqpt
AGRICULTURAL EQPT: Turf Eqpt, Commercial
AIR CLEANING SYSTEMS
AIR CONDITIONERS, AUTOMOTIVE: Wholesalers
AIR CONDITIONING & VENTILATION EQPT & SPLYS: Wholesales
AIR CONDITIONING EQPT
AIR CONDITIONING UNITS: Complete, Domestic Or Indl
AIR COOLERS: Metal Plate
AIR DUCT CLEANING SVCS
AIR MATTRESSES: Plastic
AIR POLLUTION MEASURING SVCS
AIR PREHEATERS: Nonrotating, Plate Type
AIR PURIFICATION EQPT
AIRCRAFT & AEROSPACE FLIGHT INSTRUMENTS & GUIDANCE SYSTEMS
AIRCRAFT & HEAVY EQPT REPAIR SVCS
AIRCRAFT ASSEMBLY PLANTS
AIRCRAFT CONTROL SYSTEMS: Electronic Totalizing Counters
AIRCRAFT ENGINES & PARTS
AIRCRAFT EQPT & SPLYS WHOLESALERS
AIRCRAFT FLIGHT INSTRUMENT REPAIR SVCS
AIRCRAFT FLIGHT INSTRUMENTS
AIRCRAFT LIGHTING
AIRCRAFT PARTS & AUXILIARY EQPT: Accumulators, Propeller
AIRCRAFT PARTS & AUXILIARY EQPT: Assys, Subassemblies/Parts
AIRCRAFT PARTS & AUXILIARY EQPT: Body Assemblies & Parts
AIRCRAFT PARTS & AUXILIARY EQPT: Gears, Power Transmission
AIRCRAFT PARTS & AUXILIARY EQPT: Landing Assemblies & Brakes
AIRCRAFT PARTS & AUXILIARY EQPT: Military Eqpt & Armament
AIRCRAFT PARTS & AUXILIARY EQPT: Refueling Eqpt, In Flight
AIRCRAFT PARTS & AUXILIARY EQPT: Seat Ejector Devices
AIRCRAFT PARTS & EQPT, NEC
AIRCRAFT SEATS
AIRCRAFT: Airplanes, Fixed Or Rotary Wing
AIRCRAFT: Gliders
AIRCRAFT: Motorized
AIRCRAFT: Research & Development, Manufacturer
ALARM SYSTEMS WHOLESALERS
ALARMS: Burglar
ALARMS: Fire
ALCOHOL: Methyl & Methanol, Synthetic
ALKALIES & CHLORINE
ALKALOIDS & OTHER BOTANICAL BASED PRDTS
ALLERGENS & ALLERGENIC EXTRACTS
ALLOYS: Additive, Exc Copper Or Made In Blast Furnaces
ALTERNATORS & GENERATORS: Battery Charging
ALTERNATORS: Automotive
ALUMINUM
ALUMINUM ORE MINING
ALUMINUM PRDTS
ALUMINUM: Rolling & Drawing
AMMONIUM NITRATE OR AMMONIUM SULFATE
AMMUNITION
AMMUNITION: Components
AMMUNITION: Pellets & BB's, Pistol & Air Rifle
AMMUNITION: Small Arms
AMPLIFIERS
AMPLIFIERS: Parametric
AMPLIFIERS: Pulse Amplifiers
AMPLIFIERS: RF & IF Power
AMUSEMENT & RECREATION SVCS: Amusement Ride
AMUSEMENT & RECREATION SVCS: Arcades
AMUSEMENT & RECREATION SVCS: Art Gallery, Commercial
AMUSEMENT & RECREATION SVCS: Arts & Crafts Instruction
AMUSEMENT & RECREATION SVCS: Exposition Operation
AMUSEMENT & RECREATION SVCS: Gambling & Lottery Svcs
AMUSEMENT & RECREATION SVCS: Game Machines
AMUSEMENT & RECREATION SVCS: Golf Club, Membership
AMUSEMENT & RECREATION SVCS: Gun Club, Membership
AMUSEMENT & RECREATION SVCS: Physical Fitness Instruction
AMUSEMENT & RECREATION SVCS: Tennis & Professionals
AMUSEMENT MACHINES: Coin Operated
AMUSEMENT PARK DEVICES & RIDES
ANALGESICS
ANALYZERS: Moisture
ANALYZERS: Network
ANESTHESIA EQPT
ANESTHETICS: Bulk Form
ANIMAL FEED & SUPPLEMENTS: Livestock & Poultry
ANIMAL FEED: Wholesalers
ANIMAL FOOD & SUPPLEMENTS: Bird Food, Prepared
ANIMAL FOOD & SUPPLEMENTS: Dog
ANIMAL FOOD & SUPPLEMENTS: Dog & Cat
ANIMAL FOOD & SUPPLEMENTS: Feed Concentrates
ANIMAL FOOD & SUPPLEMENTS: Feed Premixes
ANIMAL FOOD & SUPPLEMENTS: Feed Supplements
ANIMAL FOOD & SUPPLEMENTS: Mineral feed supplements
ANIMAL FOOD & SUPPLEMENTS: Pet, Exc Dog & Cat, Canned
ANIMAL FOOD & SUPPLEMENTS: Poultry
ANODIZING SVC
ANTENNAS: Radar Or Communications
ANTENNAS: Receiving
ANTIBIOTICS
ANTIBIOTICS, PACKAGED
ANTIFREEZE
ANTIQUE FURNITURE RESTORATION & REPAIR
ANTIQUE REPAIR & RESTORATION SVCS, EXC FURNITURE & AUTOS
ANTIQUE SHOPS
APPAREL ACCESS STORES
APPAREL DESIGNERS: Commercial
APPAREL FILLING MATERIALS: Cotton Waste, Kapok/Related Matl
APPAREL: Hand Woven
APPLIANCE CORDS: Household Electrical Eqpt
APPLIANCES, HOUSEHOLD: Kitchen, Major, Exc Refrigs & Stoves
APPLIANCES, HOUSEHOLD: Refrigerator Cabinets, Metal Or Wood
APPLIANCES, HOUSEHOLD: Refrigs, Mechanical & Absorption
APPLIANCES, HOUSEHOLD: Sewing Machines & Attchmnts, Domestic
APPLIANCES: Household, Refrigerators & Freezers
APPLIANCES: Major, Cooking
APPLIANCES: Small, Electric
APPLICATIONS SOFTWARE PROGRAMMING
AQUARIUM ACCESS, METAL
AQUARIUM DESIGN & MAINTENANCE SVCS
AQUARIUMS & ACCESS: Glass
AQUARIUMS & ACCESS: Plastic
ARCHITECTURAL SVCS
ARMATURE REPAIRING & REWINDING SVC
AROMATIC CHEMICAL PRDTS
ART & ORNAMENTAL WARE: Pottery
ART DEALERS & GALLERIES
ART DESIGN SVCS
ART GOODS & SPLYS WHOLESALERS
ART MARBLE: Concrete
ART NEEDLEWORK, MADE FROM PURCHASED MATERIALS
ART RELATED SVCS
ART RESTORATION SVC
ART SPLY STORES
ARTISTS' EQPT
ARTISTS' MATERIALS, WHOLESALE
ARTISTS' MATERIALS: Frames, Artists' Canvases
ARTISTS' MATERIALS: Ink, Drawing, Black & Colored
ARTISTS' MATERIALS: Paints, Exc Gold & Bronze
ARTISTS' MATERIALS: Pastels
ARTISTS' MATERIALS: Pencils & Leads
ARTISTS' MATERIALS: Wax
ARTWORK: Framed
ASBESTOS PRODUCTS
ASPHALT & ASPHALT PRDTS
ASPHALT COATINGS & SEALERS
ASPHALT MIXTURES WHOLESALERS
ASPHALT PLANTS INCLUDING GRAVEL MIX TYPE
ASSEMBLING SVC: Plumbing Fixture Fittings, Plastic
ASSOCIATIONS: Engineering
ASSOCIATIONS: Scientists'
ATOMIZERS
ATTENUATORS
AUDIO & VIDEO EQPT, EXC COMMERCIAL
AUDIO COMPONENTS
AUDIO ELECTRONIC SYSTEMS
AUDIO-VISUAL PROGRAM PRODUCTION SVCS
AUDIOLOGISTS' OFFICES
AUDITING SVCS
AUTO & HOME SUPPLY STORES: Auto & Truck Eqpt & Parts
AUTO & HOME SUPPLY STORES: Automotive Access
AUTO & HOME SUPPLY STORES: Speed Shops, Incl Race Car Splys
AUTO & HOME SUPPLY STORES: Trailer Hitches, Automotive
AUTO & HOME SUPPLY STORES: Truck Eqpt & Parts
AUTOCLAVES: Indl
AUTOCLAVES: Laboratory

PRODUCT INDEX

AUTOMATIC REGULATING CONTROL: Building Svcs Monitoring, Auto
AUTOMATIC REGULATING CONTROLS: AC & Refrigeration
AUTOMATIC REGULATING CONTROLS: Elect Air Cleaner, Automatic
AUTOMATIC REGULATING CONTROLS: Energy Cutoff, Residtl/Comm
AUTOMATIC REGULATING CONTROLS: Ice Maker
AUTOMATIC REGULATING CONTROLS: Pneumatic Relays, Air-Cond
AUTOMATIC REGULATING CONTROLS: Refrig/Air-Cond Defrost
AUTOMATIC REGULATING CTRLS: Damper, Pneumatic Or Electric
AUTOMATIC TELLER MACHINES
AUTOMATIC VENDING MACHINES: Mechanisms & Parts
AUTOMOBILES: Off-Highway, Electric
AUTOMOBILES: Wholesalers
AUTOMOTIVE & TRUCK GENERAL REPAIR SVC
AUTOMOTIVE BODY SHOP
AUTOMOTIVE BODY, PAINT & INTERIOR REPAIR & MAINTENANCE SVC
AUTOMOTIVE CUSTOMIZING SVCS, NONFACTORY BASIS
AUTOMOTIVE PARTS, ACCESS & SPLYS
AUTOMOTIVE PARTS: Plastic
AUTOMOTIVE PRDTS: Rubber
AUTOMOTIVE REPAIR SHOPS: Brake Repair
AUTOMOTIVE REPAIR SHOPS: Diesel Engine Repair
AUTOMOTIVE REPAIR SHOPS: Electrical Svcs
AUTOMOTIVE REPAIR SHOPS: Engine Repair
AUTOMOTIVE REPAIR SHOPS: Machine Shop
AUTOMOTIVE REPAIR SHOPS: Trailer Repair
AUTOMOTIVE REPAIR SVC
AUTOMOTIVE SPLYS & PARTS, NEW, WHOL: Testing Eqpt, Electric
AUTOMOTIVE SPLYS & PARTS, NEW, WHOLESALE: Brakes
AUTOMOTIVE SPLYS & PARTS, NEW, WHOLESALE: Clutches
AUTOMOTIVE SPLYS & PARTS, NEW, WHOLESALE: Engines/Eng Parts
AUTOMOTIVE SPLYS & PARTS, NEW, WHOLESALE: Splys
AUTOMOTIVE SPLYS & PARTS, NEW, WHOLESALE: Trim
AUTOMOTIVE SPLYS & PARTS, NEW, WHOLESALE: Wheels
AUTOMOTIVE SPLYS & PARTS, USED, WHOLESALE: Wheels
AUTOMOTIVE SPLYS & PARTS, WHOLESALE, NEC
AUTOMOTIVE SPLYS/PARTS, NEW, WHOL: Body Rpr/Paint Shop Splys
AUTOMOTIVE SVCS, EXC REPAIR & CARWASHES: Maintenance
AUTOMOTIVE SVCS, EXC REPAIR: Washing & Polishing
AUTOMOTIVE SVCS, EXC RPR/CARWASHES: High Perf Auto Rpr/Svc
AUTOMOTIVE TOPS INSTALLATION OR REPAIR: Canvas Or Plastic
AUTOMOTIVE TOWING & WRECKING SVC
AUTOMOTIVE UPHOLSTERY SHOPS
AUTOMOTIVE WELDING SVCS
AUTOMOTIVE: Bodies
AUTOMOTIVE: Seating
AUTOTRANSFORMERS: Electric
AWNING REPAIR SHOP
AWNINGS & CANOPIES
AWNINGS & CANOPIES: Awnings, Fabric, From Purchased Matls
AWNINGS & CANOPIES: Fabric
AWNINGS: Fiberglass
AWNINGS: Metal
AWNINGS: Wood
AXLES

B

BABY FORMULA
BABY PACIFIERS: Rubber
BADGES, WHOLESALE
BADGES: Identification & Insignia
BAGS & BAGGING: Knit
BAGS & CONTAINERS: Textile, Exc Sleeping
BAGS & SACKS: Shipping & Shopping
BAGS: Canvas
BAGS: Cellophane
BAGS: Duffle, Canvas, Made From Purchased Materials
BAGS: Food Storage & Frozen Food, Plastic
BAGS: Food Storage & Trash, Plastic
BAGS: Garment Storage Exc Paper Or Plastic Film
BAGS: Grocers', Made From Purchased Materials
BAGS: Knapsacks, Canvas, Made From Purchased Materials
BAGS: Laundry, Garment & Storage
BAGS: Paper
BAGS: Paper, Made From Purchased Materials
BAGS: Plastic
BAGS: Plastic & Pliofilm
BAGS: Plastic, Made From Purchased Materials
BAGS: Rubber Or Rubberized Fabric
BAGS: Shipping
BAGS: Shopping, Made From Purchased Materials
BAGS: Tea, Fabric, Made From Purchased Materials
BAGS: Textile
BAGS: Trash, Plastic Film, Made From Purchased Materials
BAGS: Wardrobe, Closet Access, Made From Purchased Materials
BAKERIES, COMMERCIAL: On Premises Baking Only
BAKERIES: On Premises Baking & Consumption
BAKERY FOR HOME SVC DELIVERY
BAKERY MACHINERY
BAKERY PRDTS, FROZEN: Wholesalers
BAKERY PRDTS: Bagels, Fresh Or Frozen
BAKERY PRDTS: Bakery Prdts, Partially Cooked, Exc frozen
BAKERY PRDTS: Bread, All Types, Fresh Or Frozen
BAKERY PRDTS: Buns, Sweet, Frozen
BAKERY PRDTS: Cakes, Bakery, Exc Frozen
BAKERY PRDTS: Cakes, Bakery, Frozen
BAKERY PRDTS: Cones, Ice Cream
BAKERY PRDTS: Cookies
BAKERY PRDTS: Cookies & crackers
BAKERY PRDTS: Cracker Meal & Crumbs
BAKERY PRDTS: Doughnuts, Exc Frozen
BAKERY PRDTS: Doughnuts, Frozen
BAKERY PRDTS: Dry
BAKERY PRDTS: Frozen
BAKERY PRDTS: Matzoth
BAKERY PRDTS: Pastries, Danish, Frozen
BAKERY PRDTS: Pastries, Exc Frozen
BAKERY PRDTS: Pies, Bakery, Exc Frozen
BAKERY PRDTS: Rolls, Bread Type, Fresh Or Frozen
BAKERY PRDTS: Wholesalers
BAKERY: Wholesale Or Wholesale & Retail Combined
BANDAGES
BANDS: Copper & Copper Alloy
BANDS: Plastic
BANNERS: Fabric
BANQUET HALL FACILITIES
BAR FIXTURES: Wood
BARBECUE EQPT
BARRICADES: Metal
BARS & BAR SHAPES: Steel, Hot-Rolled
BARS, COLD FINISHED: Steel, From Purchased Hot-Rolled
BARS: Concrete Reinforcing, Fabricated Steel
BARS: Iron, Made In Steel Mills
BASEBOARDS: Metal
BASEMENT WINDOW AREAWAYS: Concrete
BASES, BEVERAGE
BASKETS: Steel Wire
BATCHING PLANTS: Cement Silos
BATH SALTS
BATHING SUIT STORES
BATHMATS, COTTON
BATHROOM ACCESS & FITTINGS: Vitreous China & Earthenware
BATHTUBS: Concrete
BATTERIES, EXC AUTOMOTIVE: Wholesalers
BATTERIES: Alkaline, Cell Storage
BATTERIES: Lead Acid, Storage
BATTERIES: Rechargeable
BATTERIES: Storage
BATTERIES: Wet
BATTERY CASES: Plastic Or Plastics Combination
BATTERY CHARGERS
BATTERY CHARGERS: Storage, Motor & Engine Generator Type
BATTERY CHARGING GENERATORS
BATTS & BATTING: Cotton
BAUXITE MINING
BEARINGS & PARTS Ball
BEARINGS: Ball & Roller
BEAUTY & BARBER SHOP EQPT
BEAUTY SALONS
BED & BREAKFAST INNS
BEDDING, BEDSPREADS, BLANKETS & SHEETS
BEDDING, BEDSPREADS, BLANKETS & SHEETS: Comforters & Quilts
BEDDING, FROM SILK OR MANMADE FIBER
BEDS & ACCESS STORES
BEDS: Hospital
BEDSPREADS & BED SETS, FROM PURCHASED MATERIALS
BEDSPREADS, COTTON
BEEKEEPERS' SPLYS
BEER & ALE WHOLESALERS
BEER & ALE, WHOLESALE: Beer & Other Fermented Malt Liquors
BEER, WINE & LIQUOR STORES
BEER, WINE & LIQUOR STORES: Beer, Packaged
BEER, WINE & LIQUOR STORES: Wine
BELLOWS
BELTING: Rubber
BELTING: Transmission, Rubber
BELTS: Conveyor, Made From Purchased Wire
BELTS: Indl
BELTS: Seat, Automotive & Aircraft
BENCHES: Seating
BEVERAGE BASES & SYRUPS
BEVERAGE, NONALCOHOLIC: Iced Tea/Fruit Drink, Bottled/Canned
BEVERAGES, ALCOHOLIC: Ale
BEVERAGES, ALCOHOLIC: Applejack
BEVERAGES, ALCOHOLIC: Beer
BEVERAGES, ALCOHOLIC: Beer & Ale
BEVERAGES, ALCOHOLIC: Bourbon Whiskey
BEVERAGES, ALCOHOLIC: Brandy
BEVERAGES, ALCOHOLIC: Cocktails
BEVERAGES, ALCOHOLIC: Distilled Liquors
BEVERAGES, ALCOHOLIC: Gin
BEVERAGES, ALCOHOLIC: Liquors, Malt
BEVERAGES, ALCOHOLIC: Near Beer
BEVERAGES, ALCOHOLIC: Neutral Spirits, Fruit
BEVERAGES, ALCOHOLIC: Rum
BEVERAGES, ALCOHOLIC: Vodka
BEVERAGES, ALCOHOLIC: Wines
BEVERAGES, MALT
BEVERAGES, NONALCOHOLIC: Bottled & canned soft drinks
BEVERAGES, NONALCOHOLIC: Carbonated
BEVERAGES, NONALCOHOLIC: Carbonated, Canned & Bottled, Etc
BEVERAGES, NONALCOHOLIC: Cider
BEVERAGES, NONALCOHOLIC: Flavoring extracts & syrups, nec
BEVERAGES, NONALCOHOLIC: Fruit Drnks, Under 100% Juice, Can
BEVERAGES, NONALCOHOLIC: Lemonade, Bottled & Canned, Etc
BEVERAGES, NONALCOHOLIC: Soft Drinks, Canned & Bottled, Etc
BEVERAGES, NONALCOHOLIC: Tea, Iced, Bottled & Canned, Etc
BEVERAGES, WINE & DISTILLED ALCOHOLIC, WHOLESALE: Liquor
BEVERAGES, WINE & DISTILLED ALCOHOLIC, WHOLESALE: Neutral Sp
BEVERAGES, WINE & DISTILLED ALCOHOLIC, WHOLESALE: Wine
BEVERAGES, WINE WHOLESALE : Wine Coolers
BICYCLE SHOPS
BICYCLES WHOLESALERS
BICYCLES, PARTS & ACCESS
BILLETS: Steel
BILLFOLD INSERTS: Plastic
BILLIARD & POOL TABLES & SPLYS
BINDING SVC: Books & Manuals
BINDING SVC: Magazines
BINDING SVC: Pamphlets
BINDING SVC: Trade
BINDINGS: Bias, Made From Purchased Materials
BINS: Prefabricated, Sheet Metal
BIOLOGICAL PRDTS: Bacterial Vaccines
BIOLOGICAL PRDTS: Blood Derivatives
BIOLOGICAL PRDTS: Exc Diagnostic
BIOLOGICAL PRDTS: Extracts
BIOLOGICAL PRDTS: Vaccines
BIOLOGICAL PRDTS: Vaccines & Immunizing
BLADES: Saw, Chain Type
BLADES: Saw, Hand Or Power

PRODUCT INDEX

BLANKBOOKS
BLANKBOOKS & LOOSELEAF BINDERS
BLANKBOOKS: Albums
BLANKBOOKS: Albums, Record
BLANKBOOKS: Checkbooks & Passbooks, Bank
BLANKBOOKS: Diaries
BLANKBOOKS: Memorandum, Printed
BLANKETS & BLANKETING, COTTON
BLASTING SVC: Sand, Metal Parts
BLINDS & SHADES: Vertical
BLINDS : Window
BLOCK & BRICK: Sand Lime
BLOCKS & BRICKS: Concrete
BLOCKS: Chimney Or Fireplace, Concrete
BLOCKS: Landscape Or Retaining Wall, Concrete
BLOCKS: Paving, Concrete
BLOCKS: Paving, Cut Stone
BLOCKS: Radiation-Proof, Concrete
BLOCKS: Standard, Concrete Or Cinder
BLOWERS & FANS
BLOWERS & FANS
BLUEPRINTING SVCS
BOAT BUILDING & REPAIR
BOAT BUILDING & REPAIRING: Fiberglass
BOAT BUILDING & REPAIRING: Motorized
BOAT BUILDING & REPAIRING: Non-Motorized
BOAT BUILDING & RPRG: Fishing, Small, Lobster, Crab, Oyster
BOAT DEALERS
BOAT DEALERS: Canoe & Kayak
BOAT LIFTS
BOAT REPAIR SVCS
BOAT YARD: Boat yards, storage & incidental repair
BOATS & OTHER MARINE EQPT: Plastic
BODIES: Truck & Bus
BODY PARTS: Automobile, Stamped Metal
BOILER REPAIR SHOP
BOILERS & BOILER SHOP WORK
BOILERS: Low-Pressure Heating, Steam Or Hot Water
BOLTS: Metal
BONDERIZING: Bonderizing, Metal Or Metal Prdts
BOOK STORES
BOOKS, WHOLESALE
BOOTHS: Spray, Sheet Metal, Prefabricated
BOOTS: Women's
BOTTLE CAPS & RESEALERS: Plastic
BOTTLED GAS DEALERS: Propane
BOTTLED WATER DELIVERY
BOTTLES: Plastic
BOTTLES: Vacuum
BOUTIQUE STORES
BOWLING EQPT & SPLYS
BOX & CARTON MANUFACTURING EQPT
BOXES & CRATES: Rectangular, Wood
BOXES & SHOOK: Nailed Wood
BOXES: Corrugated
BOXES: Filing, Paperboard Made From Purchased Materials
BOXES: Mail Or Post Office, Collection/Storage, Sheet Metal
BOXES: Packing & Shipping, Metal
BOXES: Paperboard, Folding
BOXES: Paperboard, Set-Up
BOXES: Plastic
BOXES: Solid Fiber
BOXES: Stamped Metal
BOXES: Switch, Electric
BOXES: Wooden
BRAKES & BRAKE PARTS
BRAKES: Electromagnetic
BRASS FOUNDRY, NEC
BRAZING SVCS
BRAZING: Metal
BRIC-A-BRAC
BRICK, STONE & RELATED PRDTS WHOLESALERS
BRICKS & BLOCKS: Structural
BRICKS: Concrete
BRIDAL SHOPS
BRIDGE COMPONENTS: Bridge sections, prefabricated, highway
BRIEFCASES
BROADCASTING & COMMS EQPT: Antennas, Transmitting/Comms
BROADCASTING & COMMS EQPT: Rcvr-Transmitter Unt, Transceiver
BROADCASTING & COMMUNICATION EQPT: Transmit-Receiver, Radio
BROADCASTING & COMMUNICATIONS EQPT: Cellular Radio Telephone
BROADCASTING & COMMUNICATIONS EQPT: Studio Eqpt, Radio & TV
BROADCASTING & COMMUNICATIONS EQPT: Transmitting, Radio/TV
BROKERS' SVCS
BROKERS: Automotive
BROKERS: Business
BROKERS: Food
BROKERS: Loan
BROKERS: Printing
BRONZE FOUNDRY, NEC
BROOMS & BRUSHES
BROOMS & BRUSHES: Hair Pencils Or Artists' Brushes
BROOMS & BRUSHES: Household Or Indl
BROOMS & BRUSHES: Paint & Varnish
BROOMS & BRUSHES: Paint Rollers
BROOMS & BRUSHES: Paintbrushes
BRUSH BLOCKS: Carbon Or Molded Graphite
BRUSHES
BUCKLES & PARTS
BUILDING & OFFICE CLEANING SVCS
BUILDING & STRUCTURAL WOOD MBRS: Timbers, Struct, Lam Lumber
BUILDING & STRUCTURAL WOOD MEMBERS
BUILDING & STRUCTURAL WOOD MEMBERS: Arches, Laminated Lumber
BUILDING BOARD & WALLBOARD, EXC GYPSUM
BUILDING BOARD: Gypsum
BUILDING CLEANING & MAINTENANCE SVCS
BUILDING COMPONENTS: Structural Steel
BUILDING ITEM REPAIR SVCS, MISCELLANEOUS
BUILDING PRDTS & MATERIALS DEALERS
BUILDING PRDTS: Concrete
BUILDING PRDTS: Stone
BUILDING STONE, ARTIFICIAL: Concrete
BUILDINGS & COMPONENTS: Prefabricated Metal
BUILDINGS, PREFABRICATED: Wholesalers
BUILDINGS: Portable
BUILDINGS: Prefabricated, Metal
BUILDINGS: Prefabricated, Plastic
BUILDINGS: Prefabricated, Wood
BUILDINGS: Prefabricated, Wood
BULLETIN BOARDS: Wood
BUMPERS: Motor Vehicle
BURIAL VAULTS: Concrete Or Precast Terrazzo
BURLAP & BURLAP PRDTS
BURNERS: Gas, Indl
BUSES: Wholesalers
BUSHINGS & BEARINGS: Copper, Exc Machined
BUSHINGS: Cast Steel, Exc Investment
BUSINESS ACTIVITIES: Non-Commercial Site
BUSINESS FORMS WHOLESALERS
BUSINESS FORMS: Printed, Continuous
BUSINESS FORMS: Printed, Manifold
BUSINESS MACHINE REPAIR, ELECTRIC
BUSINESS SUPPORT SVCS
BUTADIENE: Indl, Organic, Chemical
BUTTONS

C

CABINETS & CASES: Show, Display & Storage, Exc Wood
CABINETS: Bathroom Vanities, Wood
CABINETS: Entertainment
CABINETS: Entertainment Units, Household, Wood
CABINETS: Factory
CABINETS: Filing, Metal
CABINETS: Filing, Wood
CABINETS: Kitchen, Metal
CABINETS: Kitchen, Wood
CABINETS: Office, Metal
CABINETS: Office, Wood
CABINETS: Radio & Television, Metal
CABINETS: Show, Display, Etc, Wood, Exc Refrigerated
CABLE TELEVISION
CABLE TELEVISION PRDTS
CABLE: Coaxial
CABLE: Fiber
CABLE: Fiber Optic
CABLE: Nonferrous, Shipboard
CABLE: Noninsulated
CABLE: Ropes & Fiber
CABLE: Steel, Insulated Or Armored
CAGES: Wire
CALCULATING & ACCOUNTING EQPT
CALIBRATING SVCS, NEC
CAMERA & PHOTOGRAPHIC SPLYS STORES
CAMERAS & RELATED EQPT: Photographic
CANDLE SHOPS
CANDLES
CANDLES: Wholesalers
CANDY & CONFECTIONS: Cake Ornaments
CANDY & CONFECTIONS: Candy Bars, Including Chocolate Covered
CANDY & CONFECTIONS: Chocolate Candy, Exc Solid Chocolate
CANDY & CONFECTIONS: Fudge
CANDY, NUT & CONFECTIONERY STORES: Candy
CANDY, NUT & CONFECTIONERY STORES: Confectionery
CANDY: Chocolate From Cacao Beans
CANNED SPECIALTIES
CANOPIES: Sheet Metal
CANS: Aluminum
CANS: Metal
CANVAS PRDTS
CANVAS PRDTS, WHOLESALE
CANVAS PRDTS: Convertible Tops, Car/Boat, Fm Purchased Mtrl
CANVAS PRDTS: Shades, Made From Purchased Materials
CAPACITORS: Fixed Or Variable
CAPACITORS: NEC
CAPS & PLUGS: Electric, Attachment
CAR WASH EQPT
CARBIDES
CARBON & GRAPHITE PRDTS, NEC
CARBONS: Electric
CARDBOARD PRDTS, EXC DIE-CUT
CARDBOARD: Waterproof, Made From Purchased Materials
CARDIOVASCULAR SYSTEM DRUGS, EXC DIAGNOSTIC
CARDS: Color
CARDS: Greeting
CARDS: Identification
CARDS: Playing
CARPET DYEING & FINISHING
CARPETS & RUGS: Tufted
CARPETS, RUGS & FLOOR COVERING
CARPETS: Hand & Machine Made
CARPETS: Textile Fiber
CARRIAGES: Horse Drawn
CARRYING CASES, WHOLESALE
CASEMENTS: Aluminum
CASES, WOOD
CASES: Attache'
CASES: Carrying
CASES: Carrying, Clothing & Apparel
CASES: Jewelry
CASES: Nonrefrigerated, Exc Wood
CASES: Packing, Nailed Or Lock Corner, Wood
CASES: Plastic
CASES: Sample Cases
CASES: Shipping, Nailed Or Lock Corner, Wood
CASH REGISTER REPAIR SVCS
CASING-HEAD BUTANE & PROPANE PRODUCTION
CASINGS: Sheet Metal
CASKETS & ACCESS
CASKETS WHOLESALERS
CAST STONE: Concrete
CASTERS
CASTINGS GRINDING: For The Trade
CASTINGS: Aerospace Investment, Ferrous
CASTINGS: Aerospace, Aluminum
CASTINGS: Aerospace, Nonferrous, Exc Aluminum
CASTINGS: Aluminum
CASTINGS: Brass, Bronze & Copper
CASTINGS: Brass, NEC, Exc Die
CASTINGS: Bronze, NEC, Exc Die
CASTINGS: Commercial Investment, Ferrous
CASTINGS: Die, Aluminum
CASTINGS: Die, Lead
CASTINGS: Die, Nonferrous
CASTINGS: Die, Zinc
CASTINGS: Ductile
CASTINGS: Gray Iron
CASTINGS: Machinery, Aluminum
CASTINGS: Machinery, Nonferrous, Exc Die or Aluminum Copper
CASTINGS: Precision
CASTINGS: Steel
CATALOG & MAIL-ORDER HOUSES

PRODUCT INDEX

CATALOG SHOWROOMS
CATALYSTS: Chemical
CATAPULTS
CATERERS
CEILING SYSTEMS: Luminous, Commercial
CEMENT & CONCRETE RELATED PRDTS & EQPT: Bituminous
CEMENT ROCK: Crushed & Broken
CEMENT: Heat Resistant
CEMENT: Hydraulic
CEMENT: Masonry
CEMENT: Natural
CEMENT: Portland
CEMETERY MEMORIAL DEALERS
CERAMIC FIBER
CERAMIC FLOOR & WALL TILE WHOLESALERS
CHAIN: Welded, Made From Purchased Wire
CHAMBERS & CAISSONS
CHANDELIERS: Commercial
CHANDELIERS: Residential
CHARCOAL: Activated
CHASSIS: Motor Vehicle
CHEESE WHOLESALERS
CHEMICAL ELEMENTS
CHEMICAL INDICATORS
CHEMICAL PROCESSING MACHINERY & EQPT
CHEMICAL: Sodm Compnds/Salts, Inorg, Exc Rfnd Sodm Chloride
CHEMICALS & ALLIED PRDTS WHOLESALERS, NEC
CHEMICALS & ALLIED PRDTS, WHOLESALE: Alkalines & Chlorine
CHEMICALS & ALLIED PRDTS, WHOLESALE: Anti-Corrosion Prdts
CHEMICALS & ALLIED PRDTS, WHOLESALE: Aromatic
CHEMICALS & ALLIED PRDTS, WHOLESALE: Chemical Additives
CHEMICALS & ALLIED PRDTS, WHOLESALE: Chemicals, Indl
CHEMICALS & ALLIED PRDTS, WHOLESALE: Dry Ice
CHEMICALS & ALLIED PRDTS, WHOLESALE: Essential Oils
CHEMICALS & ALLIED PRDTS, WHOLESALE: Oxygen
CHEMICALS & ALLIED PRDTS, WHOLESALE: Plastics Materials, NEC
CHEMICALS & ALLIED PRDTS, WHOLESALE: Plastics Prdts, NEC
CHEMICALS & ALLIED PRDTS, WHOLESALE: Plastics Sheets & Rods
CHEMICALS & ALLIED PRDTS, WHOLESALE: Polyurethane Prdts
CHEMICALS & ALLIED PRDTS, WHOLESALE: Salts & Polishes, Indl
CHEMICALS & ALLIED PRDTS, WHOLESALE: Syn Resin, Rub/Plastic
CHEMICALS & ALLIED PRDTS, WHOLESALE: Waxes, Exc Petroleum
CHEMICALS/ALLIED PRDTS, WHOL: Coal Tar Prdts, Prim/Intermdt
CHEMICALS: Agricultural
CHEMICALS: Alcohols
CHEMICALS: Aluminum Chloride
CHEMICALS: Aluminum Compounds
CHEMICALS: Aluminum Oxide
CHEMICALS: Brine
CHEMICALS: Calcium & Calcium Compounds
CHEMICALS: Compounds Or Salts, Iron, Ferric Or Ferrous
CHEMICALS: Fire Retardant
CHEMICALS: Formaldehyde
CHEMICALS: High Purity Grade, Organic
CHEMICALS: High Purity, Refined From Technical Grade
CHEMICALS: Hydrogen Peroxide
CHEMICALS: Inorganic, NEC
CHEMICALS: Isotopes, Radioactive
CHEMICALS: Lithium Compounds, Inorganic
CHEMICALS: Medicinal
CHEMICALS: Medicinal, Organic, Uncompounded, Bulk
CHEMICALS: Metal Salts/Compounds, Exc Sodium, Potassium/Alum
CHEMICALS: NEC
CHEMICALS: Organic, NEC
CHEMICALS: Phenol
CHEMICALS: Silica Compounds
CHEMICALS: Sodium Bicarbonate
CHEMICALS: Sodium/Potassium Cmpnds,Exc Bleach,Alkalies/Alum
CHEMICALS: Sulfur Chloride

CHEMICALS: Water Treatment
CHEWING GUM
CHILD DAY CARE SVCS
CHILDREN'S & INFANTS' CLOTHING STORES
CHILDREN'S WEAR STORES
CHIMES: Electric
CHIMNEY CAPS: Concrete
CHIMNEYS & FITTINGS
CHINA COOKWARE
CHLORINE
CHOCOLATE, EXC CANDY FROM BEANS: Chips, Powder, Block, Syrup
CHOCOLATE, EXC CANDY FROM PURCH CHOC: Chips, Powder, Block
CHRISTMAS TREE LIGHTING SETS: Electric
CHUCKS
CHURCHES
CHUTES & TROUGHS
CIGAR & CIGARETTE HOLDERS
CIGAR LIGHTERS EXC PRECIOUS METAL
CIGARETTE & CIGAR PRDTS & ACCESS
CIRCUIT BOARDS, PRINTED: Television & Radio
CIRCUIT BOARDS: Wiring
CIRCUIT BREAKERS
CIRCUITS, INTEGRATED: Hybrid
CIRCUITS: Electronic
CIRCULAR KNIT FABRICS DYEING & FINISHING
CLAMPS & COUPLINGS: Hose
CLAY PRDTS: Architectural
CLAYS, EXC KAOLIN & BALL
CLEANING EQPT: Blast, Dustless
CLEANING EQPT: Carpet Sweepers, Exc Household Elec Vacuum
CLEANING EQPT: Commercial
CLEANING EQPT: High Pressure
CLEANING OR POLISHING PREPARATIONS, NEC
CLEANING PRDTS: Degreasing Solvent
CLEANING PRDTS: Deodorants, Nonpersonal
CLEANING PRDTS: Disinfectants, Household Or Indl Plant
CLEANING PRDTS: Drycleaning Preparations
CLEANING PRDTS: Indl Plant Disinfectants Or Deodorants
CLEANING PRDTS: Laundry Preparations
CLEANING PRDTS: Metal Polish
CLEANING PRDTS: Polishing Preparations & Related Prdts
CLEANING PRDTS: Rug, Upholstery/Dry Clng Detergents/Spotters
CLEANING PRDTS: Sanitation Preparations
CLEANING PRDTS: Sanitation Preps, Disinfectants/Deodorants
CLEANING PRDTS: Shoe Polish Or Cleaner
CLEANING PRDTS: Specialty
CLEANING PRDTS: Window Cleaning Preparations
CLEANING SVCS: Industrial Or Commercial
CLIPPERS: Fingernail & Toenail
CLIPS & FASTENERS, MADE FROM PURCHASED WIRE
CLOSURES: Closures, Stamped Metal
CLOSURES: Plastic
CLOTHING & ACCESS, WOMEN, CHILD & INFANT, WHOL: Diapers
CLOTHING & ACCESS, WOMEN, CHILD & INFANT, WHOL: Scarves
CLOTHING & ACCESS, WOMEN, CHILD & INFANT, WHOLESALE: Under
CLOTHING & ACCESS, WOMEN, CHILD & INFANT, WHSLE: Sportswear
CLOTHING & ACCESS, WOMEN, CHILDREN & INFANT, WHOL: Access
CLOTHING & ACCESS, WOMEN, CHILDREN & INFANT, WHOL: Gloves
CLOTHING & ACCESS, WOMEN, CHILDREN & INFANT, WHOL: Handbags
CLOTHING & ACCESS, WOMEN, CHILDREN & INFANT, WHOL: Sweaters
CLOTHING & ACCESS, WOMEN, CHILDREN & INFANTS, WHOL: Purses
CLOTHING & ACCESS, WOMEN, CHILDREN/INFANT, WHOL: Baby Goods
CLOTHING & ACCESS, WOMEN, CHILDREN/INFANT, WHOL: Nightwear
CLOTHING & ACCESS, WOMEN, CHILDREN/INFANT, WHOL: Outerwear
CLOTHING & ACCESS, WOMEN, CHILDREN/INFANT, WHOL: Swimsuits
CLOTHING & ACCESS, WOMENS, CHILDRE'S & INFANTS, WHOL: Suits

CLOTHING & ACCESS, WOMENS, CHILDREN & INFANTS, WHOL: Hats
CLOTHING & ACCESS: Costumes, Masquerade
CLOTHING & ACCESS: Costumes, Theatrical
CLOTHING & ACCESS: Cummerbunds
CLOTHING & ACCESS: Footlets
CLOTHING & ACCESS: Handicapped
CLOTHING & ACCESS: Handkerchiefs, Exc Paper
CLOTHING & ACCESS: Hospital Gowns
CLOTHING & ACCESS: Men's Miscellaneous Access
CLOTHING & ACCESS: Suspenders
CLOTHING & APPAREL STORES: Custom
CLOTHING & FURNISHINGS, MEN & BOY, WHOLESALE: Suits/Trousers
CLOTHING & FURNISHINGS, MEN'S & BOYS', WHOLESALE: Fur
CLOTHING & FURNISHINGS, MEN'S & BOYS', WHOLESALE: Gloves
CLOTHING & FURNISHINGS, MEN'S & BOYS', WHOLESALE: Hats
CLOTHING & FURNISHINGS, MEN'S & BOYS', WHOLESALE: Neckwear
CLOTHING & FURNISHINGS, MEN'S & BOYS', WHOLESALE: Scarves
CLOTHING & FURNISHINGS, MEN'S & BOYS', WHOLESALE: Shirts
CLOTHING & FURNISHINGS, MEN'S & BOYS', WHOLESALE: Trousers
CLOTHING & FURNISHINGS, MEN'S & BOYS', WHOLESALE: Umbrellas
CLOTHING & FURNISHINGS, MEN'S & BOYS', WHOLESALE: Uniforms
CLOTHING & FURNISHINGS, MENS & BOYS, WHOL: Sportswear/Work
CLOTHING & FURNISHINGS, MENS & BOYS, WHOLESALE: Apprl Belts
CLOTHING ACCESS STORES: Umbrellas
CLOTHING STORES, NEC
CLOTHING STORES: Dancewear
CLOTHING STORES: Designer Apparel
CLOTHING STORES: Jeans
CLOTHING STORES: Leather
CLOTHING STORES: T-Shirts, Printed, Custom
CLOTHING STORES: Uniforms & Work
CLOTHING STORES: Unisex
CLOTHING STORES: Work
CLOTHING, WOMEN & CHILD, WHLSE: Dress, Suit, Skirt & Blouse
CLOTHING/ACCESS, WOMEN, CHILDREN/INFANT, WHOL: Apparel Belt
CLOTHING/FURNISHINGS, MEN/BOY, WHOL: Furnishings, Exc Shoes
CLOTHING: Academic Vestments
CLOTHING: Access
CLOTHING: Access, Women's & Misses'
CLOTHING: Aprons, Exc Rubber/Plastic, Women, Misses, Junior
CLOTHING: Aprons, Harness
CLOTHING: Aprons, Work, Exc Rubberized & Plastic, Men's
CLOTHING: Athletic & Sportswear, Men's & Boys'
CLOTHING: Athletic & Sportswear, Women's & Girls'
CLOTHING: Baker, Barber, Lab/Svc Ind Apparel, Washable, Men
CLOTHING: Bathing Suits & Beachwear, Children's
CLOTHING: Bathing Suits & Swimwear, Girls, Children & Infant
CLOTHING: Bathing Suits & Swimwear, Knit
CLOTHING: Bathrobes, Mens & Womens, From Purchased Materials
CLOTHING: Beachwear, Knit
CLOTHING: Belts
CLOTHING: Blouses & Shirts, Girls' & Children's
CLOTHING: Blouses, Boys', From Purchased Materials
CLOTHING: Blouses, Women's & Girls'
CLOTHING: Blouses, Womens & Juniors, From Purchased Mtrls
CLOTHING: Brassieres
CLOTHING: Bridal Gowns
CLOTHING: Burial
CLOTHING: Capes & Jackets, Women's & Misses'
CLOTHING: Capes, Exc Fur/Rubber, Womens, Misses & Juniors
CLOTHING: Chemises, Camisoles/Teddies, Women, Misses/Junior
CLOTHING: Children & Infants'

PRODUCT INDEX

CLOTHING: Children's, Girls'
CLOTHING: Clergy Vestments
CLOTHING: Coats & Jackets, Leather & Sheep-Lined
CLOTHING: Coats & Suits, Men's & Boys'
CLOTHING: Coats, Leatherette, Oiled Fabric, Etc, Mens & Boys
CLOTHING: Coats, Tailored, Mens/Boys, From Purchased Mtls
CLOTHING: Cold Weather Knit Outerwear, Including Ski Wear
CLOTHING: Corset Access, Clasps & Stays
CLOTHING: Costumes
CLOTHING: Diaper Covers, Waterproof, From Purchased Material
CLOTHING: Disposable
CLOTHING: Down-Filled, Men's & Boys'
CLOTHING: Dresses
CLOTHING: Dresses & Skirts
CLOTHING: Dresses, Knit
CLOTHING: Dressing Gowns, Mens/Womens, From Purchased Matls
CLOTHING: Foundation Garments, Women's
CLOTHING: Furs
CLOTHING: Garments, Indl, Men's & Boys
CLOTHING: Girdles & Other Foundation Garments, Knit
CLOTHING: Girdles & Panty Girdles
CLOTHING: Gloves, Knit, Exc Dress & Semidress
CLOTHING: Gowns & Dresses, Wedding
CLOTHING: Gowns, Formal
CLOTHING: Hats & Caps, Leather
CLOTHING: Hats & Caps, NEC
CLOTHING: Hats & Caps, Uniform
CLOTHING: Hats & Headwear, Knit
CLOTHING: Hosiery, Men's & Boys'
CLOTHING: Hosiery, Pantyhose & Knee Length, Sheer
CLOTHING: Hospital, Men's
CLOTHING: Housedresses
CLOTHING: Jackets & Vests, Exc Fur & Leather, Women's
CLOTHING: Jackets, Knit
CLOTHING: Jeans, Men's & Boys'
CLOTHING: Knit Underwear & Nightwear
CLOTHING: Leather
CLOTHING: Leather & sheep-lined clothing
CLOTHING: Leg Warmers
CLOTHING: Maternity
CLOTHING: Men's & boy's clothing, nec
CLOTHING: Men's & boy's underwear & nightwear
CLOTHING: Mens & Boys Jackets, Sport, Suede, Leatherette
CLOTHING: Millinery
CLOTHING: Neckties, Knit
CLOTHING: Neckwear
CLOTHING: Outerwear, Knit
CLOTHING: Outerwear, Lthr, Wool/Down-Filled, Men, Youth/Boy
CLOTHING: Outerwear, Women's & Misses' NEC
CLOTHING: Overcoats & Topcoats, Men/Boy, Purchased Materials
CLOTHING: Pants, Work, Men's, Youths' & Boys'
CLOTHING: Panty Hose
CLOTHING: Raincoats, Exc Vulcanized Rubber, Purchased Matls
CLOTHING: Robes & Dressing Gowns
CLOTHING: Robes & Housecoats, Children's
CLOTHING: Scarves & Mufflers, Knit
CLOTHING: Service Apparel, Women's
CLOTHING: Shawls, Knit
CLOTHING: Sheep-Lined
CLOTHING: Shirts
CLOTHING: Shirts, Dress, Men's & Boys'
CLOTHING: Shirts, Knit
CLOTHING: Shirts, Sports & Polo, Men & Boy, Purchased Mtrl
CLOTHING: Shirts, Sports & Polo, Men's & Boys'
CLOTHING: Shirts, Women's & Juniors', From Purchased Mtrls
CLOTHING: Skirts
CLOTHING: Slacks & Shorts, Dress, Men's, Youths' & Boys'
CLOTHING: Slacks, Girls' & Children's
CLOTHING: Sleeping Garments, Men's & Boys'
CLOTHING: Sleeping Garments, Women's & Children's
CLOTHING: Slipper Socks
CLOTHING: Socks
CLOTHING: Sportswear, Women's
CLOTHING: Suits & Skirts, Women's & Misses'
CLOTHING: Suits, Men's & Boys', From Purchased Materials
CLOTHING: Sweaters & Sweater Coats, Knit
CLOTHING: Sweaters, Men's & Boys'
CLOTHING: Sweatshirts & T-Shirts, Men's & Boys'
CLOTHING: Swimwear, Men's & Boys'
CLOTHING: Swimwear, Women's & Misses'
CLOTHING: T-Shirts & Tops, Knit
CLOTHING: T-Shirts & Tops, Women's & Girls'
CLOTHING: Tailored Suits & Formal Jackets
CLOTHING: Ties, Bow, Men's & Boys', From Purchased Materials
CLOTHING: Ties, Handsewn, From Purchased Materials
CLOTHING: Ties, Neck & Bow, Men's & Boys'
CLOTHING: Ties, Neck, Men's & Boys', From Purchased Material
CLOTHING: Tights & Leg Warmers
CLOTHING: Trousers & Slacks, Men's & Boys'
CLOTHING: Underwear, Knit
CLOTHING: Underwear, Men's & Boys'
CLOTHING: Underwear, Women's & Children's
CLOTHING: Uniforms & Vestments
CLOTHING: Uniforms, Ex Athletic, Women's, Misses' & Juniors'
CLOTHING: Uniforms, Men's & Boys'
CLOTHING: Uniforms, Military, Men/Youth, Purchased Materials
CLOTHING: Uniforms, Policemen's, From Purchased Materials
CLOTHING: Uniforms, Team Athletic
CLOTHING: Uniforms, Work
CLOTHING: Warm Weather Knit Outerwear, Including Beachwear
CLOTHING: Waterproof Outerwear
CLOTHING: Work Apparel, Exc Uniforms
CLOTHING: Work, Men's
CLUTCHES OR BRAKES: Electromagnetic
CLUTCHES, EXC VEHICULAR
COAL MINING SERVICES
COAL MINING SVCS: Bituminous, Contract Basis
COAL MINING: Anthracite
COATING COMPOUNDS: Tar
COATING OR WRAPPING SVC: Steel Pipe
COATING SVC
COATING SVC: Electrodes
COATING SVC: Hot Dip, Metals Or Formed Prdts
COATING SVC: Metals & Formed Prdts
COATING SVC: Metals, With Plastic Or Resins
COATING SVC: Rust Preventative
COATING SVC: Silicon
COATINGS: Air Curing
COATINGS: Epoxy
COATINGS: Polyurethane
COFFEE SVCS
COILS & TRANSFORMERS
COILS: Electric Motors Or Generators
COILS: Pipe
COIN OPERATED LAUNDRIES & DRYCLEANERS
COIN-OPERATED LAUNDRY
COKE: Calcined Petroleum, Made From Purchased Materials
COKE: Produced In Chemical Recovery Coke Ovens
COLLECTION AGENCY, EXC REAL ESTATE
COLLEGES, UNIVERSITIES & PROFESSIONAL SCHOOLS
COLLETS
COLOR SEPARATION: Photographic & Movie Film
COLORS: Pigments, Inorganic
COLORS: Pigments, Organic
COMFORTERS & QUILTS, FROM MANMADE FIBER OR SILK
COMMERCIAL & INDL SHELVING WHOLESALERS
COMMERCIAL & OFFICE BUILDINGS RENOVATION & REPAIR
COMMERCIAL ART & GRAPHIC DESIGN SVCS
COMMERCIAL EQPT WHOLESALERS, NEC
COMMERCIAL EQPT, WHOLESALE: Bakery Eqpt & Splys
COMMERCIAL EQPT, WHOLESALE: Comm Cooking & Food Svc Eqpt
COMMERCIAL EQPT, WHOLESALE: Display Eqpt, Exc Refrigerated
COMMERCIAL EQPT, WHOLESALE: Mannequins
COMMERCIAL EQPT, WHOLESALE: Restaurant, NEC
COMMERCIAL EQPT, WHOLESALE: Scales, Exc Laboratory
COMMERCIAL EQPT, WHOLESALE: Store Fixtures & Display Eqpt
COMMERCIAL LAUNDRY EQPT
COMMERCIAL PHOTOGRAPHIC STUDIO
COMMERCIAL PRINTING & NEWSPAPER PUBLISHING COMBINED
COMMON SAND MINING
COMMUNICATION HEADGEAR: Telephone
COMMUNICATIONS CARRIER: Wired
COMMUNICATIONS EQPT & SYSTEMS, NEC
COMMUNICATIONS EQPT REPAIR & MAINTENANCE
COMMUNICATIONS EQPT WHOLESALERS
COMMUNICATIONS EQPT: Microwave
COMMUNICATIONS EQPT: Radio, Marine
COMMUNICATIONS SVCS
COMMUNICATIONS SVCS: Cellular
COMMUNICATIONS SVCS: Data
COMMUNICATIONS SVCS: Facsimile Transmission
COMMUNICATIONS SVCS: Internet Host Svcs
COMMUNICATIONS SVCS: Online Svc Providers
COMMUNICATIONS SVCS: Proprietary Online Svcs Networks
COMMUNICATIONS SVCS: Satellite Earth Stations
COMMUNICATIONS SVCS: Signal Enhancement Network Svcs
COMMUNICATIONS SVCS: Telephone, Data
COMMUNICATIONS SVCS: Telephone, Local
COMMUNICATIONS SVCS: Telephone, Voice
COMMUNITY CHESTS
COMMUTATORS: Electronic
COMPACT DISCS OR CD'S, WHOLESALE
COMPACT LASER DISCS: Prerecorded
COMPACTORS: Trash & Garbage, Residential
COMPARATORS: Optical
COMPOSITION STONE: Plastic
COMPOST
COMPRESSORS, AIR CONDITIONING: Wholesalers
COMPRESSORS: Air & Gas
COMPRESSORS: Air & Gas, Including Vacuum Pumps
COMPRESSORS: Refrigeration & Air Conditioning Eqpt
COMPUTER & COMPUTER SOFTWARE STORES
COMPUTER & COMPUTER SOFTWARE STORES: Peripheral Eqpt
COMPUTER & COMPUTER SOFTWARE STORES: Software, Bus/Non-Game
COMPUTER & COMPUTER SOFTWARE STORES: Software, Computer Game
COMPUTER & OFFICE MACHINE MAINTENANCE & REPAIR
COMPUTER DISKETTES WHOLESALERS
COMPUTER FORMS
COMPUTER GRAPHICS SVCS
COMPUTER HARDWARE REQUIREMENTS ANALYSIS
COMPUTER INTERFACE EQPT: Indl Process
COMPUTER PERIPHERAL EQPT REPAIR & MAINTENANCE
COMPUTER PERIPHERAL EQPT, NEC
COMPUTER PERIPHERAL EQPT, WHOLESALE
COMPUTER PERIPHERAL EQPT: Encoders
COMPUTER PERIPHERAL EQPT: Film Reader Devices
COMPUTER PERIPHERAL EQPT: Graphic Displays, Exc Terminals
COMPUTER PERIPHERAL EQPT: Input Or Output
COMPUTER PROGRAMMING SVCS
COMPUTER PROGRAMMING SVCS: Custom
COMPUTER RELATED MAINTENANCE SVCS
COMPUTER SERVICE BUREAU
COMPUTER SOFTWARE DEVELOPMENT
COMPUTER SOFTWARE DEVELOPMENT & APPLICATIONS
COMPUTER SOFTWARE SYSTEMS ANALYSIS & DESIGN: Custom
COMPUTER STORAGE DEVICES, NEC
COMPUTER TERMINALS
COMPUTER TERMINALS: CRT
COMPUTER-AIDED DESIGN SYSTEMS SVCS
COMPUTER-AIDED ENGINEERING SYSTEMS SVCS
COMPUTERS, NEC
COMPUTERS, NEC, WHOLESALE
COMPUTERS, PERIPHERALS & SOFTWARE, WHOLESALE: Disk Drives
COMPUTERS, PERIPHERALS & SOFTWARE, WHOLESALE: Printers
COMPUTERS, PERIPHERALS & SOFTWARE, WHOLESALE: Software
COMPUTERS: Indl, Process, Gas Flow
COMPUTERS: Mainframe
COMPUTERS: Mini
COMPUTERS: Personal
CONCENTRATES, DRINK
CONCENTRATES, FLAVORING, EXC DRINK
CONCRETE CURING & HARDENING COMPOUNDS

PRODUCT INDEX

CONCRETE MIXERS
CONCRETE PLANTS
CONCRETE PRDTS
CONCRETE PRDTS, PRECAST, NEC
CONCRETE: Asphaltic, Not From Refineries
CONCRETE: Bituminous
CONCRETE: Ready-Mixed
CONDENSERS & CONDENSING UNITS: Air Conditioner
CONDENSERS: Fixed Or Variable
CONDENSERS: Heat Transfer Eqpt, Evaporative
CONDENSERS: Motors Or Generators
CONDUITS & FITTINGS: Electric
CONDUITS: Pressed Pulp Fiber, Made From Purchased Materials
CONFECTIONERY PRDTS WHOLESALERS
CONFECTIONS & CANDY
CONFINEMENT SURVEILLANCE SYS MAINTENANCE & MONITORING SVCS
CONNECTORS & TERMINALS: Electrical Device Uses
CONNECTORS: Cord, Electric
CONNECTORS: Electrical
CONNECTORS: Electronic
CONNECTORS: Solderless, Electric-Wiring Devices
CONSTRUCTION & MINING MACHINERY WHOLESALERS
CONSTRUCTION & ROAD MAINTENANCE EQPT: Drags, Road
CONSTRUCTION EQPT: Attachments
CONSTRUCTION EQPT: Attachments, Snow Plow
CONSTRUCTION EQPT: Crane Carriers
CONSTRUCTION EQPT: Cranes
CONSTRUCTION EQPT: Dozers, Tractor Mounted, Material Moving
CONSTRUCTION EQPT: Hammer Mills, Port, Incl Rock/Ore Crush
CONSTRUCTION EQPT: Rakes, Land Clearing, Mechanical
CONSTRUCTION EQPT: Rollers, Sheepsfoot & Vibratory
CONSTRUCTION EQPT: SCRAPERS, GRADERS, ROLLERS & SIMILAR EQPT
CONSTRUCTION EQPT: Wrecker Hoists, Automobile
CONSTRUCTION MATERIALS, WHOLESALE: Aggregate
CONSTRUCTION MATERIALS, WHOLESALE: Awnings
CONSTRUCTION MATERIALS, WHOLESALE: Block, Concrete & Cinder
CONSTRUCTION MATERIALS, WHOLESALE: Blocks, Building, NEC
CONSTRUCTION MATERIALS, WHOLESALE: Building Stone, Granite
CONSTRUCTION MATERIALS, WHOLESALE: Building Stone, Marble
CONSTRUCTION MATERIALS, WHOLESALE: Building, Exterior
CONSTRUCTION MATERIALS, WHOLESALE: Building, Interior
CONSTRUCTION MATERIALS, WHOLESALE: Cement
CONSTRUCTION MATERIALS, WHOLESALE: Clay, Exc Refractory
CONSTRUCTION MATERIALS, WHOLESALE: Concrete Mixtures
CONSTRUCTION MATERIALS, WHOLESALE: Door Frames
CONSTRUCTION MATERIALS, WHOLESALE: Glass
CONSTRUCTION MATERIALS, WHOLESALE: Gravel
CONSTRUCTION MATERIALS, WHOLESALE: Lime Building Prdts
CONSTRUCTION MATERIALS, WHOLESALE: Limestone
CONSTRUCTION MATERIALS, WHOLESALE: Masons' Materials
CONSTRUCTION MATERIALS, WHOLESALE: Millwork
CONSTRUCTION MATERIALS, WHOLESALE: Molding, All Materials
CONSTRUCTION MATERIALS, WHOLESALE: Paving Materials
CONSTRUCTION MATERIALS, WHOLESALE: Paving Mixtures
CONSTRUCTION MATERIALS, WHOLESALE: Prefabricated Structures
CONSTRUCTION MATERIALS, WHOLESALE: Roof, Asphalt/Sheet Metal
CONSTRUCTION MATERIALS, WHOLESALE: Roofing & Siding Material
CONSTRUCTION MATERIALS, WHOLESALE: Sand
CONSTRUCTION MATERIALS, WHOLESALE: Septic Tanks
CONSTRUCTION MATERIALS, WHOLESALE: Siding, Exc Wood
CONSTRUCTION MATERIALS, WHOLESALE: Stone, Crushed Or Broken
CONSTRUCTION MATERIALS, WHOLESALE: Tile, Clay/Other Ceramic
CONSTRUCTION MATERIALS, WHOLESALE: Windows
CONSTRUCTION MATLS, WHOL: Lumber, Rough, Dressed/Finished
CONSTRUCTION SAND MINING
CONSTRUCTION SITE PREPARATION SVCS
CONSTRUCTION: Bridge
CONSTRUCTION: Commercial & Institutional Building
CONSTRUCTION: Dry Cleaning Plant
CONSTRUCTION: Food Prdts Manufacturing or Packing Plant
CONSTRUCTION: Guardrails, Highway
CONSTRUCTION: Heavy Highway & Street
CONSTRUCTION: Indl Building & Warehouse
CONSTRUCTION: Indl Building, Prefabricated
CONSTRUCTION: Indl Buildings, New, NEC
CONSTRUCTION: Pharmaceutical Manufacturing Plant
CONSTRUCTION: Religious Building
CONSTRUCTION: Single-Family Housing
CONSTRUCTION: Single-family Housing, New
CONSTRUCTION: Steel Buildings
CONSTRUCTION: Street Surfacing & Paving
CONSTRUCTION: Tennis Court
CONSTRUCTION: Warehouse
CONSTRUCTION: Waste Water & Sewage Treatment Plant
CONSULTING SVC: Business, NEC
CONSULTING SVC: Computer
CONSULTING SVC: Educational
CONSULTING SVC: Engineering
CONSULTING SVC: Financial Management
CONSULTING SVC: Human Resource
CONSULTING SVC: Management
CONSULTING SVC: Marketing Management
CONSULTING SVC: Online Technology
CONSULTING SVC: Sales Management
CONSULTING SVCS, BUSINESS: Communications
CONSULTING SVCS, BUSINESS: Energy Conservation
CONSULTING SVCS, BUSINESS: Publishing
CONSULTING SVCS, BUSINESS: Safety Training Svcs
CONSULTING SVCS, BUSINESS: Sys Engnrg, Exc Computer/Prof
CONSULTING SVCS, BUSINESS: Systems Analysis & Engineering
CONSULTING SVCS, BUSINESS: Systems Analysis Or Design
CONSULTING SVCS, BUSINESS: Test Development & Evaluation
CONSULTING SVCS, BUSINESS: Testing, Educational Or Personnel
CONSULTING SVCS: Oil
CONSULTING SVCS: Scientific
CONTACT LENSES
CONTACTS: Electrical
CONTAINERS, GLASS: Cosmetic Jars
CONTAINERS, GLASS: Food
CONTAINERS, GLASS: Medicine Bottles
CONTAINERS: Cargo, Wood & Metal Combination
CONTAINERS: Cargo, Wood & Wood With Metal
CONTAINERS: Corrugated
CONTAINERS: Foil, Bakery Goods & Frozen Foods
CONTAINERS: Food & Beverage
CONTAINERS: Food, Folding, Made From Purchased Materials
CONTAINERS: Food, Liquid Tight, Including Milk
CONTAINERS: Glass
CONTAINERS: Laminated Phenolic & Vulcanized Fiber
CONTAINERS: Liquid Tight Fiber, From Purchased Materials
CONTAINERS: Metal
CONTAINERS: Plastic
CONTAINERS: Sanitary, Food
CONTAINERS: Shipping & Mailing, Fiber
CONTAINERS: Shipping, Bombs, Metal Plate
CONTAINERS: Shipping, Wood
CONTAINERS: Wood
CONTRACT FOOD SVCS
CONTRACTOR: Framing
CONTRACTOR: Rigging & Scaffolding
CONTRACTORS: Acoustical & Ceiling Work
CONTRACTORS: Acoustical & Insulation Work
CONTRACTORS: Antenna Installation
CONTRACTORS: Awning Installation
CONTRACTORS: Boiler & Furnace
CONTRACTORS: Boiler Maintenance Contractor
CONTRACTORS: Building Eqpt & Machinery Installation
CONTRACTORS: Building Sign Installation & Mntnce
CONTRACTORS: Carpentry Work
CONTRACTORS: Carpentry, Cabinet & Finish Work
CONTRACTORS: Carpentry, Cabinet Building & Installation
CONTRACTORS: Carpentry, Finish & Trim Work
CONTRACTORS: Ceramic Floor Tile Installation
CONTRACTORS: Closed Circuit Television Installation
CONTRACTORS: Commercial & Office Building
CONTRACTORS: Communications Svcs
CONTRACTORS: Concrete
CONTRACTORS: Concrete Pumping
CONTRACTORS: Concrete Repair
CONTRACTORS: Construction Site Cleanup
CONTRACTORS: Countertop Installation
CONTRACTORS: Demountable Partition Installation
CONTRACTORS: Directional Oil & Gas Well Drilling Svc
CONTRACTORS: Drywall
CONTRACTORS: Electrical
CONTRACTORS: Electronic Controls Installation
CONTRACTORS: Energy Management Control
CONTRACTORS: Excavating
CONTRACTORS: Excavating Slush Pits & Cellars Svcs
CONTRACTORS: Exterior Wall System Installation
CONTRACTORS: Fence Construction
CONTRACTORS: Fiber Optic Cable Installation
CONTRACTORS: Fiberglass Work
CONTRACTORS: Fire Detection & Burglar Alarm Systems
CONTRACTORS: Fire Escape Installation
CONTRACTORS: Fire Sprinkler System Installation Svcs
CONTRACTORS: Floor Laying & Other Floor Work
CONTRACTORS: Garage Doors
CONTRACTORS: Gas Field Svcs, NEC
CONTRACTORS: Gasoline Condensation Removal Svcs
CONTRACTORS: Glass, Glazing & Tinting
CONTRACTORS: Heating & Air Conditioning
CONTRACTORS: Highway & Street Construction, General
CONTRACTORS: Highway & Street Paving
CONTRACTORS: Home & Office Intrs Finish, Furnish/Remodel
CONTRACTORS: Hydraulic Eqpt Installation & Svcs
CONTRACTORS: Hydronics Heating
CONTRACTORS: Insulation Installation, Building
CONTRACTORS: Kitchen & Bathroom Remodeling
CONTRACTORS: Lighting Syst
CONTRACTORS: Machinery Installation
CONTRACTORS: Marble Installation, Interior
CONTRACTORS: Masonry & Stonework
CONTRACTORS: Mechanical
CONTRACTORS: Multi-Family Home Remodeling
CONTRACTORS: Office Furniture Installation
CONTRACTORS: Oil & Gas Building, Repairing & Dismantling Svc
CONTRACTORS: Oil & Gas Field Geological Exploration Svcs
CONTRACTORS: Oil & Gas Field Geophysical Exploration Svcs
CONTRACTORS: Oil & Gas Well Casing Cement Svcs
CONTRACTORS: Oil & Gas Well Drilling Svc
CONTRACTORS: Oil & Gas Well Flow Rate Measurement Svcs
CONTRACTORS: Oil & Gas Wells Svcs
CONTRACTORS: Oil Field Haulage Svcs
CONTRACTORS: Oil Field Lease Tanks: Erectg, Clng/Rprg Svcs
CONTRACTORS: Oil Sampling Svcs
CONTRACTORS: Oil/Gas Well Construction, Rpr/Dismantling Svcs
CONTRACTORS: On-Site Welding
CONTRACTORS: Ornamental Metal Work
CONTRACTORS: Paint & Wallpaper Stripping
CONTRACTORS: Painting & Wall Covering
CONTRACTORS: Pipe Laying
CONTRACTORS: Plastering, Plain or Ornamental
CONTRACTORS: Plumbing
CONTRACTORS: Power Generating Eqpt Installation
CONTRACTORS: Prefabricated Fireplace Installation
CONTRACTORS: Prefabricated Window & Door Installation
CONTRACTORS: Refrigeration
CONTRACTORS: Roofing
CONTRACTORS: Roustabout Svcs
CONTRACTORS: Safety & Security Eqpt
CONTRACTORS: Sandblasting Svc, Building Exteriors
CONTRACTORS: Seismograph Survey Svcs
CONTRACTORS: Sheet Metal Work, NEC
CONTRACTORS: Sheet metal Work, Architectural
CONTRACTORS: Siding

PRODUCT INDEX

CONTRACTORS: Single-family Home General Remodeling
CONTRACTORS: Solar Energy Eqpt
CONTRACTORS: Sound Eqpt Installation
CONTRACTORS: Stone Masonry
CONTRACTORS: Store Fixture Installation
CONTRACTORS: Store Front Construction
CONTRACTORS: Structural Iron Work, Structural
CONTRACTORS: Structural Steel Erection
CONTRACTORS: Svc Station Eqpt Installation, Maint & Repair
CONTRACTORS: Textile Warping
CONTRACTORS: Tile Installation, Ceramic
CONTRACTORS: Ventilation & Duct Work
CONTRACTORS: Water Intake Well Drilling Svc
CONTRACTORS: Water Well Drilling
CONTRACTORS: Water Well Servicing
CONTRACTORS: Waterproofing
CONTRACTORS: Well Chemical Treating Svcs
CONTRACTORS: Well Logging Svcs
CONTRACTORS: Window Treatment Installation
CONTRACTORS: Windows & Doors
CONTRACTORS: Wood Floor Installation & Refinishing
CONTROL CIRCUIT DEVICES
CONTROL EQPT: Electric
CONTROL EQPT: Noise
CONTROL PANELS: Electrical
CONTROLS & ACCESS: Indl, Electric
CONTROLS & ACCESS: Motor
CONTROLS: Access, Motor
CONTROLS: Automatic Temperature
CONTROLS: Electric Motor
CONTROLS: Environmental
CONTROLS: Marine & Navy, Auxiliary
CONTROLS: Numerical
CONTROLS: Positioning, Electric
CONTROLS: Relay & Ind
CONTROLS: Thermostats, Exc Built-in
CONTROLS: Voice
CONVENIENCE STORES
CONVENTION & TRADE SHOW SVCS
CONVERTERS: Data
CONVERTERS: Frequency
CONVERTERS: Phase Or Rotary, Electrical
CONVERTERS: Power, AC to DC
CONVERTERS: Torque, Exc Auto
CONVEYOR SYSTEMS: Belt, General Indl Use
CONVEYOR SYSTEMS: Bulk Handling
CONVEYOR SYSTEMS: Pneumatic Tube
CONVEYOR SYSTEMS: Robotic
CONVEYORS & CONVEYING EQPT
COOKING & FOOD WARMING EQPT: Commercial
COOKING & FOODWARMING EQPT: Coffee Brewing
COOKING & FOODWARMING EQPT: Commercial
COOKING WARE, EXC PORCELAIN ENAMELED
COOKING WARE: Cooking Ware, Porcelain Enameled
COOKWARE, STONEWARE: Coarse Earthenware & Pottery
COOKWARE: Fine Earthenware
COOLING TOWERS: Metal
COPPER ORES
COPPER PRDTS: Refined, Primary
COPPER: Rolling & Drawing
COPYRIGHT BUYING & LICENSING
CORD & TWINE
CORE WASH OR WAX
CORES: Magnetic
CORK & CORK PRDTS: Tiles
CORRESPONDENCE SCHOOLS
CORRUGATED PRDTS: Boxes, Partition, Display Items, Sheet/Pad
COSMETIC PREPARATIONS
COSMETICS & TOILETRIES
COSMETICS WHOLESALERS
COSTUME JEWELRY & NOVELTIES: Apparel, Exc Precious Metals
COSTUME JEWELRY & NOVELTIES: Bracelets, Exc Precious Metals
COSTUME JEWELRY & NOVELTIES: Costume Novelties
COSTUME JEWELRY & NOVELTIES: Earrings, Exc Precious Metals
COSTUME JEWELRY & NOVELTIES: Exc Semi & Precious
COSTUME JEWELRY & NOVELTIES: Pins, Exc Precious Metals
COUGH MEDICINES
COUNTER & SINK TOPS
COUNTERS & COUNTING DEVICES

COUNTERS OR COUNTER DISPLAY CASES, EXC WOOD
COUNTERS OR COUNTER DISPLAY CASES, WOOD
COUNTERS: Mechanical
COUNTING DEVICES: Controls, Revolution & Timing
COUNTING DEVICES: Electromechanical
COUNTING DEVICES: Speed Indicators & Recorders, Vehicle
COUPLINGS: Shaft
COUPON REDEMPTION SVCS
COURIER SVCS, AIR: Package Delivery, Private
COURIER SVCS: Ground
COVERS: Automobile Seat
COVERS: Automotive, Exc Seat & Tire
COVERS: Canvas
COVERS: Hot Tub & Spa
COVERS: Slip Made Of Fabric, Plastic, Etc.
CRANE & AERIAL LIFT SVCS
CRANES & MONORAIL SYSTEMS
CRANES: Indl Plant
CRANKSHAFTS & CAMSHAFTS: Machining
CRATES: Fruit, Wood Wirebound
CREDIT BUREAUS
CROWNS & CLOSURES
CRUDE PETROLEUM & NATURAL GAS PRODUCTION
CRUDE PETROLEUM & NATURAL GAS PRODUCTION
CRUDE PETROLEUM PRODUCTION
CRUDES: Cyclic, Organic
CRYOGENIC COOLING DEVICES: Infrared Detectors, Masers
CRYSTALS
CULTURE MEDIA
CULVERTS: Metal Plate
CUPS: Plastic Exc Polystyrene Foam
CURBING: Granite Or Stone
CURTAIN & DRAPERY FIXTURES: Poles, Rods & Rollers
CURTAIN WALLS: Building, Steel
CURTAINS & BEDDING: Knit
CURTAINS & CURTAIN FABRICS: Lace
CURTAINS: Cottage Sets, From Purchased Materials
CURTAINS: Shower
CURTAINS: Window, From Purchased Materials
CUSHIONS & PILLOWS
CUSHIONS & PILLOWS: Bed, From Purchased Materials
CUSHIONS: Textile, Exc Spring & Carpet
CUSTOM COMPOUNDING OF RUBBER MATERIALS
CUT STONE & STONE PRODUCTS
CUTLERY
CUTLERY WHOLESALERS
CUTOUTS: Cardboard, Die-Cut, Made From Purchased Materials
CUTOUTS: Distribution
CUTTING SVC: Paper, Exc Die-Cut
CYCLIC CRUDES & INTERMEDIATES
CYLINDER & ACTUATORS: Fluid Power
CYLINDERS: Pressure

D

DAIRY EQPT
DAIRY PRDTS STORE: Cheese
DAIRY PRDTS STORE: Ice Cream, Packaged
DAIRY PRDTS STORES
DAIRY PRDTS WHOLESALERS: Fresh
DAIRY PRDTS: Bakers' Cheese
DAIRY PRDTS: Bottled Baby Formula
DAIRY PRDTS: Butter
DAIRY PRDTS: Canned Baby Formula
DAIRY PRDTS: Cheese
DAIRY PRDTS: Cheese, Cottage
DAIRY PRDTS: Concentrated Skim Milk
DAIRY PRDTS: Cream Substitutes
DAIRY PRDTS: Cream, Sweet
DAIRY PRDTS: Dairy Based Desserts, Frozen
DAIRY PRDTS: Dietary Supplements, Dairy & Non-Dairy Based
DAIRY PRDTS: Dips & Spreads, Cheese Based
DAIRY PRDTS: Dried & Powdered Milk & Milk Prdts
DAIRY PRDTS: Evaporated Milk
DAIRY PRDTS: Farmers' Cheese
DAIRY PRDTS: Fermented & Cultured Milk Prdts
DAIRY PRDTS: Frozen Desserts & Novelties
DAIRY PRDTS: Ice Cream & Ice Milk
DAIRY PRDTS: Ice Cream, Bulk
DAIRY PRDTS: Ice Cream, Packaged, Molded, On Sticks, Etc.
DAIRY PRDTS: Milk, Condensed & Evaporated
DAIRY PRDTS: Milk, Fluid

DAIRY PRDTS: Milk, Processed, Pasteurized, Homogenized/Btld
DAIRY PRDTS: Natural Cheese
DAIRY PRDTS: Processed Cheese
DAIRY PRDTS: Pudding Pops, Frozen
DAIRY PRDTS: Sherbets, Dairy Based
DAIRY PRDTS: Spreads, Cheese
DAIRY PRDTS: Whipped Topping, Exc Frozen Or Dry Mix
DAIRY PRDTS: Yogurt, Exc Frozen
DAIRY PRDTS: Yogurt, Frozen
DATA PROCESSING & PREPARATION SVCS
DATA PROCESSING SVCS
DECORATIVE WOOD & WOODWORK
DEFENSE SYSTEMS & EQPT
DEGREASING MACHINES
DEHYDRATION EQPT
DELAY LINES
DENTAL EQPT
DENTAL EQPT & SPLYS
DENTAL EQPT & SPLYS WHOLESALERS
DENTAL EQPT & SPLYS: Cabinets
DENTAL EQPT & SPLYS: Compounds
DENTAL EQPT & SPLYS: Cutting Instruments
DENTAL EQPT & SPLYS: Dental Materials
DENTAL EQPT & SPLYS: Enamels
DENTAL EQPT & SPLYS: Laboratory
DENTAL EQPT & SPLYS: Orthodontic Appliances
DENTAL EQPT & SPLYS: Sterilizers
DENTAL EQPT & SPLYS: Teeth, Artificial, Exc In Dental Labs
DENTAL EQPT & SPLYS: Wax
DENTISTS' OFFICES & CLINICS
DEPILATORIES, COSMETIC
DERMATOLOGICALS
DERRICKS: Oil & Gas Field
DESALTER KITS: Sea Water
DESIGN SVCS, NEC
DESIGN SVCS: Commercial & Indl
DESIGN SVCS: Computer Integrated Systems
DESIGN SVCS: Shoe
DETECTION APPARATUS: Electronic/Magnetic Field, Light/Heat
DIAGNOSTIC SUBSTANCES
DIAGNOSTIC SUBSTANCES OR AGENTS: Blood Derivative
DIAGNOSTIC SUBSTANCES OR AGENTS: In Vivo
DIAGNOSTIC SUBSTANCES OR AGENTS: Microbiology & Virology
DIAGNOSTIC SUBSTANCES OR AGENTS: Veterinary
DIAMOND MINING SVCS: Indl
DIAMOND SETTER SVCS
DIAMONDS, GEMS, WHOLESALE
DIAMONDS: Cutting & Polishing
DIAPERS: Cloth
DIAPERS: Disposable
DIE CUTTING SVC: Paper
DIE SETS: Presses, Metal Stamping
DIES & TOOLS: Special
DIES: Cutting, Exc Metal
DIES: Extrusion
DIES: Paper Cutting
DIES: Plastic Forming
DIES: Steel Rule
DIODES: Light Emitting
DIODES: Solid State, Germanium, Silicon, Etc
DIRECT SELLING ESTABLISHMENTS: Beverage Svcs
DIRECT SELLING ESTABLISHMENTS: Encyclopedias & Publications
DIRECT SELLING ESTABLISHMENTS: Food Svcs
DISCOUNT DEPARTMENT STORES
DISCS & TAPE: Optical, Blank
DISHWASHING EQPT: Commercial
DISINFECTING SVCS
DISK & DRUM DRIVES & COMPONENTS: Computers
DISK DRIVES: Computer
DISPENSING EQPT & PARTS, BEVERAGE: Beer
DISPENSING EQPT & PARTS, BEVERAGE: Cold, Exc Coin-Operated
DISPENSING EQPT & PARTS, BEVERAGE: Fountain/Other Beverage
DISPENSING EQPT & SYSTEMS, BEVERAGE: Liquor
DISPLAY CASES: Refrigerated
DISPLAY FIXTURES: Showcases, Wood, Exc Refrigerated
DISPLAY FIXTURES: Wood
DISPLAY ITEMS: Corrugated, Made From Purchased Materials
DISPLAY STANDS: Merchandise, Exc Wood

PRODUCT INDEX

DISTILLATES: Hardwood
DOCK OPERATION SVCS, INCL BLDGS, FACILITIES, OPERS & MAINT
DOCKS: Floating, Wood
DOCKS: Prefabricated Metal
DOCUMENT EMBOSSING SVCS
DOLLIES: Mechanics'
DOLOMITE: Crushed & Broken
DOLOMITIC MARBLE: Crushed & Broken
DOMESTIC HELP SVCS
DOOR & WINDOW REPAIR SVCS
DOOR OPERATING SYSTEMS: Electric
DOORS & WINDOWS WHOLESALERS: All Materials
DOORS & WINDOWS: Screen & Storm
DOORS & WINDOWS: Storm, Metal
DOORS: Dormers, Wood
DOORS: Fiberglass
DOORS: Fire, Metal
DOORS: Folding, Plastic Or Plastic Coated Fabric
DOORS: Garage, Overhead, Metal
DOORS: Garage, Overhead, Wood
DOORS: Glass
DOORS: Rolling, Indl Building Or Warehouse, Metal
DOORS: Wooden
DOWN FEATHERS
DRAPERIES & CURTAINS
DRAPERIES & DRAPERY FABRICS, COTTON
DRAPERIES: Plastic & Textile, From Purchased Materials
DRAPERY & UPHOLSTERY STORES: Draperies
DRAPERY & UPHOLSTERY STORES: Slip Covers
DRAPES & DRAPERY FABRICS, FROM MANMADE FIBER
DRIED FRUITS WHOLESALERS
DRILL BITS
DRILLING MACHINERY & EQPT: Water Well
DRINK MIXES, NONALCOHOLIC: Cocktail
DRINKING PLACES: Alcoholic Beverages
DRINKING PLACES: Night Clubs
DRINKING PLACES: Tavern
DRINKING PLACES: Wine Bar
DRINKING WATER COOLERS WHOLESALERS: Mechanical
DRIVE SHAFTS
DRIVES: High Speed Indl, Exc Hydrostatic
DRONES: Target, Used By Ships, Metal
DROP CLOTHS: Fabric
DRUG TESTING KITS: Blood & Urine
DRUGS & DRUG PROPRIETARIES, WHOL: Biologicals/Allied Prdts
DRUGS & DRUG PROPRIETARIES, WHOLESALE
DRUGS & DRUG PROPRIETARIES, WHOLESALE: Blood Plasma
DRUGS & DRUG PROPRIETARIES, WHOLESALE: Pharmaceuticals
DRUGS & DRUG PROPRIETARIES, WHOLESALE: Vitamins & Minerals
DRUGS ACTING ON THE CENTRAL NERVOUS SYSTEM & SENSE ORGANS
DRUGS AFFECTING NEOPLASMS & ENDOCRINE SYSTEMS
DRUGS/DRUG PROPRIETARIES, WHOL: Proprietary/Patent Medicines
DRUGS: Parasitic & Infective Disease Affecting
DRUMS: Fiber
DRYCLEANING EQPT & SPLYS: Commercial
DRYCLEANING SVC: Drapery & Curtain
DUCTS: Sheet Metal
DUMPSTERS: Garbage
DYES & PIGMENTS: Organic
DYES & TINTS: Household
DYES: Synthetic Organic

E

EATING PLACES
EDUCATIONAL PROGRAM ADMINISTRATION, GOVERNMENT: State
EDUCATIONAL PROGRAMS ADMINISTRATION SVCS
EDUCATIONAL SVCS
EDUCATIONAL SVCS, NONDEGREE GRANTING: Continuing Education
ELASTOMERS
ELECTRIC MOTOR & GENERATOR AUXILIARY PARTS
ELECTRIC MOTOR REPAIR SVCS
ELECTRIC SERVICES
ELECTRIC SVCS, NEC Power Transmission
ELECTRIC SVCS, NEC: Power Generation
ELECTRICAL APPARATUS & EQPT WHOLESALERS

ELECTRICAL APPLIANCES, TELEVISIONS & RADIOS WHOLESALERS
ELECTRICAL CONSTRUCTION MATERIALS WHOLESALERS
ELECTRICAL CURRENT CARRYING WIRING DEVICES
ELECTRICAL DISCHARGE MACHINING, EDM
ELECTRICAL EQPT & SPLYS
ELECTRICAL EQPT FOR ENGINES
ELECTRICAL EQPT REPAIR & MAINTENANCE
ELECTRICAL EQPT REPAIR SVCS
ELECTRICAL EQPT REPAIR SVCS: High Voltage
ELECTRICAL EQPT: Automotive, NEC
ELECTRICAL EQPT: Household
ELECTRICAL GOODS, WHOLESALE: Batteries, Dry Cell
ELECTRICAL GOODS, WHOLESALE: Burglar Alarm Systems
ELECTRICAL GOODS, WHOLESALE: Capacitors
ELECTRICAL GOODS, WHOLESALE: Connectors
ELECTRICAL GOODS, WHOLESALE: Electronic Parts
ELECTRICAL GOODS, WHOLESALE: Facsimile Or Fax Eqpt
ELECTRICAL GOODS, WHOLESALE: Fans, Household
ELECTRICAL GOODS, WHOLESALE: Fittings & Construction Mat
ELECTRICAL GOODS, WHOLESALE: Household Appliances, NEC
ELECTRICAL GOODS, WHOLESALE: Intercommunication Eqpt
ELECTRICAL GOODS, WHOLESALE: Light Bulbs & Related Splys
ELECTRICAL GOODS, WHOLESALE: Lighting Fittings & Access
ELECTRICAL GOODS, WHOLESALE: Lighting Fixtures, Comm & Indl
ELECTRICAL GOODS, WHOLESALE: Lighting Fixtures, Residential
ELECTRICAL GOODS, WHOLESALE: Mobile telephone Eqpt
ELECTRICAL GOODS, WHOLESALE: Motors
ELECTRICAL GOODS, WHOLESALE: Semiconductor Devices
ELECTRICAL GOODS, WHOLESALE: Signaling, Eqpt
ELECTRICAL GOODS, WHOLESALE: Sound Eqpt
ELECTRICAL GOODS, WHOLESALE: Telephone Eqpt
ELECTRICAL GOODS, WHOLESALE: Transformers
ELECTRICAL GOODS, WHOLESALE: VCR & Access
ELECTRICAL GOODS, WHOLESALE: Vacuum Cleaners, Household
ELECTRICAL GOODS, WHOLESALE: Video Eqpt
ELECTRICAL GOODS, WHOLESALE: Wire & Cable
ELECTRICAL GOODS, WHOLESALE: Wire & Cable, Electronic
ELECTRICAL HOUSEHOLD APPLIANCE REPAIR
ELECTRICAL INDL APPARATUS, NEC
ELECTRICAL SPLYS
ELECTRICAL SUPPLIES: Porcelain
ELECTROCARS: Golfer Transportation
ELECTRODES: Fluorescent Lamps
ELECTRODES: Thermal & Electrolytic
ELECTROMEDICAL EQPT
ELECTRON TUBES
ELECTRON TUBES: Cathode Ray
ELECTRONIC COMPONENTS
ELECTRONIC DETECTION SYSTEMS: Aeronautical
ELECTRONIC DEVICES: Solid State, NEC
ELECTRONIC EQPT REPAIR SVCS
ELECTRONIC LOADS & POWER SPLYS
ELECTRONIC PARTS & EQPT WHOLESALERS
ELECTRONIC SHOPPING
ELECTRONIC TRAINING DEVICES
ELECTROPLATING & PLATING SVC
ELEVATORS & EQPT
ELEVATORS WHOLESALERS
ELEVATORS: Installation & Conversion
ELEVATORS: Stair, Motor Powered
EMBLEMS: Embroidered
EMBOSSING SVC: Paper
EMBROIDERING & ART NEEDLEWORK FOR THE TRADE
EMBROIDERING SVC
EMBROIDERING SVC: Schiffli Machine
EMBROIDERING: Swiss Loom
EMBROIDERY ADVERTISING SVCS
EMERGENCY ALARMS
EMPLOYMENT AGENCY SVCS
ENAMELING SVC: Metal Prdts, Including Porcelain
ENAMELS
ENCLOSURES: Electronic
ENERGY MEASUREMENT EQPT

ENGINE REBUILDING: Diesel
ENGINE REBUILDING: Gas
ENGINEERING SVCS
ENGINEERING SVCS: Building Construction
ENGINEERING SVCS: Electrical Or Electronic
ENGINEERING SVCS: Heating & Ventilation
ENGINEERING SVCS: Industrial
ENGINEERING SVCS: Marine
ENGINEERING SVCS: Mechanical
ENGINEERING SVCS: Petroleum
ENGINEERING SVCS: Pollution Control
ENGINEERING SVCS: Professional
ENGINEERING SVCS: Sanitary
ENGINEERING SVCS: Structural
ENGINES: Internal Combustion, NEC
ENGINES: Jet Propulsion
ENGRAVING SVC, NEC
ENGRAVING SVC: Jewelry & Personal Goods
ENGRAVING SVCS
ENGRAVING: Steel line, For The Printing Trade
ENGRAVINGS: Plastic
ENTERTAINERS & ENTERTAINMENT GROUPS
ENTERTAINMENT SVCS
ENVELOPES
ENVELOPES WHOLESALERS
ENVIRONMENTAL QUALITY PROGS ADMIN, GOVT: Waste Management
ENZYMES
EPOXY RESINS
EQUIPMENT: Pedestrian Traffic Control
EQUIPMENT: Rental & Leasing, NEC
ESCALATORS: Passenger & Freight
ETCHING & ENGRAVING SVC
ETCHING SVC: Metal
ETCHING SVC: Photochemical
ETHANOLAMINES
ETHYLENE-PROPYLENE RUBBERS: EPDM Polymers
EXCAVATING EQPT
EXPANSION JOINTS: Rubber
EXPLOSIVES
EXPLOSIVES, EXC AMMO & FIREWORKS WHOLESALERS
EXTENSION CORDS
EXTRACTS, FLAVORING
EXTRACTS: Dying Or Tanning, Natural
EYEGLASS CASES
EYEGLASSES
EYEGLASSES: Sunglasses
EYES: Artificial

F

FABRIC FINISHING: Mending, Wool
FABRIC STORES
FABRICATED METAL PRODUCTS, NEC
FABRICS & CLOTH: Quilted
FABRICS: Alpacas, Mohair, Woven
FABRICS: Apparel & Outerwear, Broadwoven
FABRICS: Apparel & Outerwear, Cotton
FABRICS: Apparel & Outerwear, From Manmade Fiber Or Silk
FABRICS: Automotive, From Manmade Fiber
FABRICS: Bags & Bagging, Cotton
FABRICS: Bonded-Fiber, Exc Felt
FABRICS: Broad Woven, Goods, Cotton
FABRICS: Broadwoven, Cotton
FABRICS: Broadwoven, Synthetic Manmade Fiber & Silk
FABRICS: Broadwoven, Wool
FABRICS: Brocade, Cotton
FABRICS: Canvas
FABRICS: Chemically Coated & Treated
FABRICS: Coated Or Treated
FABRICS: Cords
FABRICS: Corduroys, Cotton
FABRICS: Denims
FABRICS: Elastic, From Manmade Fiber Or Silk
FABRICS: Fiberglass, Broadwoven
FABRICS: Glass, Narrow
FABRICS: Glove, Lining
FABRICS: Hand Woven
FABRICS: Handkerchief, Cotton
FABRICS: Jacquard Woven, From Manmade Fiber Or Silk
FABRICS: Jean
FABRICS: Jersey Cloth
FABRICS: Lace & Decorative Trim, Narrow
FABRICS: Lace & Lace Prdts
FABRICS: Lace, Knit, NEC
FABRICS: Laminated

PRODUCT INDEX

FABRICS: Linings & Interlinings, Cotton
FABRICS: Long Cloth, Cotton
FABRICS: Nonwoven
FABRICS: Nylon, Broadwoven
FABRICS: Paper, Broadwoven
FABRICS: Pile Warp or Flat Knit
FABRICS: Pile, Circular Knit
FABRICS: Pocketing Twill, Cotton
FABRICS: Polyester, Broadwoven
FABRICS: Print, Cotton
FABRICS: Resin Or Plastic Coated
FABRICS: Rubberized
FABRICS: Shirting, Cotton
FABRICS: Shoe
FABRICS: Silk, Broadwoven
FABRICS: Silk, Narrow
FABRICS: Spandex, Broadwoven
FABRICS: Specialty Including Twisted Weaves, Broadwoven
FABRICS: Stretch, Cotton
FABRICS: Surgical Fabrics, Cotton
FABRICS: Tapestry, Cotton
FABRICS: Tricot
FABRICS: Trimmings
FABRICS: Trimmings, Textile
FABRICS: Upholstry, Cotton
FABRICS: Varnished Glass & Coated Fiberglass
FABRICS: Wall Covering, From Manmade Fiber Or Silk
FABRICS: Warp & Flat Knit Prdts
FABRICS: Warp Knit, Lace & Netting
FABRICS: Weft Or Circular Knit
FABRICS: Woven, Narrow Cotton, Wool, Silk
FACILITIES SUPPORT SVCS
FACSIMILE COMMUNICATION EQPT
FAMILY CLOTHING STORES
FANS, BLOWING: Indl Or Commercial
FANS, EXHAUST: Indl Or Commercial
FANS, VENTILATING: Indl Or Commercial
FARM & GARDEN MACHINERY WHOLESALERS
FARM PRDTS, RAW MATERIALS, WHOLESALE: Bristles
FARM PRDTS, RAW MATERIALS, WHOLESALE: Hides
FARM SPLY STORES
FARM SPLYS, WHOLESALE: Beekeeping Splys, Nondurable
FASTENERS: Metal
FASTENERS: Metal
FASTENERS: Notions, NEC
FASTENERS: Notions, Snaps
FASTENERS: Notions, Zippers
FAUCETS & SPIGOTS: Metal & Plastic
FEATHERS: Renovating
FELT: Acoustic
FENCE POSTS: Iron & Steel
FENCES & FENCING MATERIALS
FENCES OR POSTS: Ornamental Iron Or Steel
FENCING DEALERS
FENCING MATERIALS: Docks & Other Outdoor Prdts, Wood
FENCING MATERIALS: Plastic
FENCING MATERIALS: Wood
FENCING: Chain Link
FERRITES
FERROALLOYS
FERROMANGANESE, NOT MADE IN BLAST FURNACES
FERTILIZERS: NEC
FERTILIZERS: Nitrogenous
FERTILIZERS: Phosphatic
FIBER & FIBER PRDTS: Acrylic
FIBER & FIBER PRDTS: Fluorocarbon
FIBER & FIBER PRDTS: Organic, Noncellulose
FIBER & FIBER PRDTS: Polyester
FIBER & FIBER PRDTS: Protein
FIBER & FIBER PRDTS: Synthetic Cellulosic
FIBER OPTICS
FIBERS: Carbon & Graphite
FILLERS & SEALERS: Wood
FILM & SHEET: Unsupported Plastic
FILM BASE: Cellulose Acetate Or Nitrocellulose Plastics
FILM PROCESSING & FINISHING LABORATORY
FILM: Motion Picture
FILTERS
FILTERS & SOFTENERS: Water, Household
FILTERS: Air
FILTERS: Air Intake, Internal Combustion Engine, Exc Auto
FILTERS: General Line, Indl
FILTERS: Motor Vehicle
FILTRATION DEVICES: Electronic

FINANCIAL INVESTMENT ACTIVITIES, NEC: Financial Reporting
FINANCIAL INVESTMENT ADVICE
FINANCIAL SVCS
FINDINGS & TRIMMINGS Fabric, NEC
FINDINGS & TRIMMINGS Waistbands, Trouser
FINDINGS & TRIMMINGS: Apparel
FINDINGS & TRIMMINGS: Fabric
FINGERNAILS, ARTIFICIAL
FINGERPRINT EQPT
FINISHING AGENTS: Leather
FIRE ARMS, SMALL: Guns Or Gun Parts, 30 mm & Below
FIRE ARMS, SMALL: Pellet & BB guns
FIRE ARMS, SMALL: Rifles Or Rifle Parts, 30 mm & below
FIRE CONTROL OR BOMBING EQPT: Electronic
FIRE DETECTION SYSTEMS
FIRE ESCAPES
FIRE EXTINGUISHERS: Portable
FIRE OR BURGLARY RESISTIVE PRDTS
FIRE PROTECTION EQPT
FIREARMS & AMMUNITION, EXC SPORTING, WHOLESALE
FIREARMS: Small, 30mm or Less
FIREFIGHTING APPARATUS
FIREPLACE & CHIMNEY MATERIAL: Concrete
FIREPLACE EQPT & ACCESS
FIREWORKS
FIREWORKS DISPLAY SVCS
FISH & SEAFOOD PROCESSORS: Canned Or Cured
FISH & SEAFOOD PROCESSORS: Fresh Or Frozen
FISHING EQPT: Lures
FITTINGS & ASSEMBLIES: Hose & Tube, Hydraulic Or Pneumatic
FITTINGS: Pipe
FITTINGS: Pipe, Fabricated
FIXTURES & EQPT: Kitchen, Metal, Exc Cast Aluminum
FIXTURES: Bank, Metal, Ornamental
FIXTURES: Cut Stone
FLAGPOLES
FLAGS: Fabric
FLAT GLASS: Antique
FLAT GLASS: Building
FLAT GLASS: Construction
FLAT GLASS: Laminated
FLAT GLASS: Plate, Polished & Rough
FLAT GLASS: Strengthened Or Reinforced
FLAT GLASS: Tempered
FLAT GLASS: Window, Clear & Colored
FLATWARE, STAINLESS STEEL
FLAVORS OR FLAVORING MATERIALS: Synthetic
FLOOR COMPOSITION: Magnesite
FLOOR COVERING STORES
FLOOR COVERING STORES: Carpets
FLOOR COVERING: Plastic
FLOOR COVERINGS WHOLESALERS
FLOOR COVERINGS: Textile Fiber
FLOOR COVERINGS: Tile, Support Plastic
FLOORING & GRATINGS: Open, Construction Applications
FLOORING: Hard Surface
FLOORING: Hardwood
FLOORING: Tile
FLORISTS
FLOWER ARRANGEMENTS: Artificial
FLOWER POTS Plastic
FLOWERS: Artificial & Preserved
FLUID METERS & COUNTING DEVICES
FLUID POWER PUMPS & MOTORS
FLUID POWER VALVES & HOSE FITTINGS
FLUORO RUBBERS
FLUXES
FOAM CHARGE MIXTURES
FOAM RUBBER
FOIL & LEAF: Metal
FOIL OR LEAF: Gold
FOIL: Aluminum
FOIL: Copper
FOIL: Laminated To Paper Or Other Materials
FOOD CASINGS: Plastic
FOOD PRDTS, BREAKFAST: Cereal, Infants' Food
FOOD PRDTS, BREAKFAST: Cereal, Wheat Flakes
FOOD PRDTS, CANNED OR FRESH PACK: Fruit Juices
FOOD PRDTS, CANNED OR FRESH PACK: Vegetable Juices
FOOD PRDTS, CANNED, NEC
FOOD PRDTS, CANNED: Baby Food
FOOD PRDTS, CANNED: Barbecue Sauce

FOOD PRDTS, CANNED: Beans & Bean Sprouts
FOOD PRDTS, CANNED: Catsup
FOOD PRDTS, CANNED: Ethnic
FOOD PRDTS, CANNED: Fruit Juices, Concentrated
FOOD PRDTS, CANNED: Fruit Juices, Fresh
FOOD PRDTS, CANNED: Fruit Purees
FOOD PRDTS, CANNED: Fruits
FOOD PRDTS, CANNED: Fruits
FOOD PRDTS, CANNED: Fruits & Fruit Prdts
FOOD PRDTS, CANNED: Italian
FOOD PRDTS, CANNED: Jams, Including Imitation
FOOD PRDTS, CANNED: Jams, Jellies & Preserves
FOOD PRDTS, CANNED: Maraschino Cherries
FOOD PRDTS, CANNED: Mexican, NEC
FOOD PRDTS, CANNED: Olives
FOOD PRDTS, CANNED: Puddings, Exc Meat
FOOD PRDTS, CANNED: Ravioli
FOOD PRDTS, CANNED: Sauerkraut
FOOD PRDTS, CANNED: Soup, Chicken
FOOD PRDTS, CANNED: Spaghetti & Other Pasta Sauce
FOOD PRDTS, CANNED: Tomato Sauce.
FOOD PRDTS, CANNED: Tomatoes
FOOD PRDTS, CANNED: Vegetables
FOOD PRDTS, CONFECTIONERY, WHOLESALE: Candy
FOOD PRDTS, CONFECTIONERY, WHOLESALE: Nuts, Salted/Roasted
FOOD PRDTS, CONFECTIONERY, WHOLESALE: Snack Foods
FOOD PRDTS, DAIRY, WHOLESALE: Milk & Cream, Fluid
FOOD PRDTS, FISH & SEAFOOD, WHOLESALE: Fresh
FOOD PRDTS, FISH & SEAFOOD: Canned & Jarred, Etc
FOOD PRDTS, FISH & SEAFOOD: Fish, Fresh, Prepared
FOOD PRDTS, FISH & SEAFOOD: Fish, Smoked
FOOD PRDTS, FISH & SEAFOOD: Fresh, Prepared
FOOD PRDTS, FISH & SEAFOOD: Fresh/Frozen Chowder, Soup/Stew
FOOD PRDTS, FISH & SEAFOOD: Salmon, Smoked
FOOD PRDTS, FISH & SEAFOOD: Seafood, Frozen, Prepared
FOOD PRDTS, FROZEN: Breakfasts, Packaged
FOOD PRDTS, FROZEN: Dinners, Packaged
FOOD PRDTS, FROZEN: Ethnic Foods, NEC
FOOD PRDTS, FROZEN: Fruits & Vegetables
FOOD PRDTS, FROZEN: Fruits, Juices & Vegetables
FOOD PRDTS, FROZEN: NEC
FOOD PRDTS, FROZEN: Pizza
FOOD PRDTS, FROZEN: Snack Items
FOOD PRDTS, FROZEN: Soups
FOOD PRDTS, FROZEN: Vegetables, Exc Potato Prdts
FOOD PRDTS, FROZEN: Whipped Topping
FOOD PRDTS, MEAT & MEAT PRDTS, WHOLESALE: Fresh
FOOD PRDTS, WHOL: Canned Goods, Fruit, Veg, Seafood/Meats
FOOD PRDTS, WHOLESALE: Beverage Concentrates
FOOD PRDTS, WHOLESALE: Beverages, Exc Coffee & Tea
FOOD PRDTS, WHOLESALE: Chocolate
FOOD PRDTS, WHOLESALE: Coffee, Green Or Roasted
FOOD PRDTS, WHOLESALE: Condiments
FOOD PRDTS, WHOLESALE: Cookies
FOOD PRDTS, WHOLESALE: Flour
FOOD PRDTS, WHOLESALE: Grains
FOOD PRDTS, WHOLESALE: Health
FOOD PRDTS, WHOLESALE: Juices
FOOD PRDTS, WHOLESALE: Organic & Diet
FOOD PRDTS, WHOLESALE: Pasta & Rice
FOOD PRDTS, WHOLESALE: Sandwiches
FOOD PRDTS, WHOLESALE: Sausage Casings
FOOD PRDTS, WHOLESALE: Specialty
FOOD PRDTS, WHOLESALE: Tea
FOOD PRDTS: Almond Pastes
FOOD PRDTS: Bran, Rice
FOOD PRDTS: Bread Crumbs, Exc Made In Bakeries
FOOD PRDTS: Breakfast Bars
FOOD PRDTS: Cane Syrup, From Purchased Raw Sugar
FOOD PRDTS: Cereals
FOOD PRDTS: Cheese Curls & Puffs
FOOD PRDTS: Chicken, Processed, Frozen
FOOD PRDTS: Chocolate Bars, Solid
FOOD PRDTS: Chocolate Coatings & Syrup
FOOD PRDTS: Coconut Oil
FOOD PRDTS: Coconut, Desiccated & Shredded
FOOD PRDTS: Coffee
FOOD PRDTS: Coffee Extracts
FOOD PRDTS: Coffee Roasting, Exc Wholesale Grocers
FOOD PRDTS: Cooking Oils, Refined Vegetable, Exc Corn

PRODUCT INDEX

FOOD PRDTS: Corn Chips & Other Corn-Based Snacks
FOOD PRDTS: Corn Sugars & Syrups
FOOD PRDTS: Cottonseed Lecithin
FOOD PRDTS: Dessert Mixes & Fillings
FOOD PRDTS: Desserts, Ready-To-Mix
FOOD PRDTS: Dough, Pizza, Prepared
FOOD PRDTS: Doughs & Batters
FOOD PRDTS: Doughs & Batters From Purchased Flour
FOOD PRDTS: Dressings, Salad, Raw & Cooked Exc Dry Mixes
FOOD PRDTS: Dried & Dehydrated Fruits, Vegetables & Soup Mix
FOOD PRDTS: Ducks, Processed, Fresh
FOOD PRDTS: Ducks, Processed, NEC
FOOD PRDTS: Edible Oil Prdts, Exc Corn Oil
FOOD PRDTS: Edible fats & oils
FOOD PRDTS: Egg Substitutes, Made From Eggs
FOOD PRDTS: Eggs, Processed
FOOD PRDTS: Emulsifiers
FOOD PRDTS: Flavored Ices, Frozen
FOOD PRDTS: Flour & Other Grain Mill Products
FOOD PRDTS: Flour Mixes & Doughs
FOOD PRDTS: Fruit Juices
FOOD PRDTS: Fruits & Vegetables, Pickled
FOOD PRDTS: Fruits, Dehydrated Or Dried
FOOD PRDTS: Fruits, Dried Or Dehydrated, Exc Freeze-Dried
FOOD PRDTS: Gelatin Dessert Preparations
FOOD PRDTS: Gluten Meal
FOOD PRDTS: Horseradish, Exc Sauce
FOOD PRDTS: Ice, Blocks
FOOD PRDTS: Ice, Cubes
FOOD PRDTS: Instant Coffee
FOOD PRDTS: Jelly, Corncob
FOOD PRDTS: Juice Pops, Frozen
FOOD PRDTS: Macaroni Prdts, Dry, Alphabet, Rings Or Shells
FOOD PRDTS: Macaroni, Noodles, Spaghetti, Pasta, Etc
FOOD PRDTS: Malt
FOOD PRDTS: Mayonnaise & Dressings, Exc Tomato Based
FOOD PRDTS: Mixes, Bread & Bread-Type Roll
FOOD PRDTS: Mixes, Bread & Roll From Purchased Flour
FOOD PRDTS: Mixes, Doughnut From Purchased Flour
FOOD PRDTS: Mixes, Pancake From Purchased Flour
FOOD PRDTS: Molasses, Mixed/Blended, Purchased Ingredients
FOOD PRDTS: Mustard, Prepared
FOOD PRDTS: Nuts & Seeds
FOOD PRDTS: Olive Oil
FOOD PRDTS: Oriental Noodles
FOOD PRDTS: Pasta, Rice/Potatoes, Uncooked, Pkgd
FOOD PRDTS: Pasta, Uncooked, Packaged With Other Ingredients
FOOD PRDTS: Peanut Butter
FOOD PRDTS: Pickles, Vinegar
FOOD PRDTS: Pizza Doughs From Purchased Flour
FOOD PRDTS: Pizza, Refrigerated
FOOD PRDTS: Potato & Corn Chips & Similar Prdts
FOOD PRDTS: Potato Chips & Other Potato-Based Snacks
FOOD PRDTS: Potato Sticks
FOOD PRDTS: Potatoes, Dried, Packaged With Other Ingredients
FOOD PRDTS: Poultry, Processed, NEC
FOOD PRDTS: Poultry, Slaughtered & Dressed
FOOD PRDTS: Preparations
FOOD PRDTS: Prepared Meat Sauces Exc Tomato & Dry
FOOD PRDTS: Prepared Sauces, Exc Tomato Based
FOOD PRDTS: Raw cane sugar
FOOD PRDTS: Relishes, Vinegar
FOOD PRDTS: Rice, Milled
FOOD PRDTS: Salads
FOOD PRDTS: Sauerkraut, Bulk
FOOD PRDTS: Seasonings & Spices
FOOD PRDTS: Soup Mixes, Dried
FOOD PRDTS: Soy Sauce
FOOD PRDTS: Spices, Including Ground
FOOD PRDTS: Spreads, Sandwich, Salad Dressing Base
FOOD PRDTS: Starches
FOOD PRDTS: Sugar
FOOD PRDTS: Sugar, Beet
FOOD PRDTS: Sugar, Cane
FOOD PRDTS: Sugar, Corn
FOOD PRDTS: Sugar, Granulated Cane, Purchd Raw Sugar/Syrup
FOOD PRDTS: Syrup, Maple
FOOD PRDTS: Syrups
FOOD PRDTS: Tea
FOOD PRDTS: Tofu Desserts, Frozen
FOOD PRDTS: Tofu, Exc Frozen Desserts
FOOD PRDTS: Tortilla Chips
FOOD PRDTS: Tortillas
FOOD PRDTS: Vegetables, Dried or Dehydrated Exc Freeze-Dried
FOOD PRDTS: Vegetables, Pickled
FOOD PRDTS: Vinegar
FOOD PRODUCTS MACHINERY
FOOD STORES: Delicatessen
FOOD STORES: Grocery, Independent
FOOD STORES: Supermarkets
FOOTWEAR, WHOLESALE: Athletic
FOOTWEAR, WHOLESALE: Shoe Access
FOOTWEAR, WHOLESALE: Shoes
FOOTWEAR: Cut Stock
FORGINGS
FORGINGS: Aluminum
FORGINGS: Armor Plate, Iron Or Steel
FORGINGS: Automotive & Internal Combustion Engine
FORGINGS: Gear & Chain
FORGINGS: Machinery, Ferrous
FORGINGS: Nonferrous
FORGINGS: Pump & compressor, Nonferrous
FORMS: Concrete, Sheet Metal
FOUNDRIES: Aluminum
FOUNDRIES: Brass, Bronze & Copper
FOUNDRIES: Gray & Ductile Iron
FOUNDRIES: Iron
FOUNDRIES: Nonferrous
FOUNDRIES: Steel
FOUNDRIES: Steel Investment
FRAMES & FRAMING WHOLESALE
FRANCHISES, SELLING OR LICENSING
FREIGHT CONSOLIDATION SVCS
FREIGHT FORWARDING ARRANGEMENTS
FRICTION MATERIAL, MADE FROM POWDERED METAL
FRUITS & VEGETABLES WHOLESALERS: Fresh
FUEL ADDITIVES
FUEL BRIQUETTES & WAXES
FUEL BRIQUETTES OR BOULETS, MADE WITH PETROLEUM BINDER
FUEL CELL FORMS: Cardboard, Made From Purchased Materials
FUEL CELLS: Solid State
FUEL DEALERS: Wood
FUEL OIL DEALERS
FUELS: Diesel
FUELS: Ethanol
FUELS: Jet
FUELS: Oil
FUNDRAISING SVCS
FUNERAL HOMES & SVCS
FUNGICIDES OR HERBICIDES
FUR APPAREL STORES
FUR CLOTHING WHOLESALERS
FUR FINISHING & LINING: For The Fur Goods Trade
FUR: Apparel
FUR: Coats
FUR: Coats & Other Apparel
FUR: Hats
FUR: Jackets
FURNACES & OVENS: Indl
FURNACES: Indl, Electric
FURNACES: Warm Air, Electric
FURNITURE & CABINET STORES: Cabinets, Custom Work
FURNITURE & CABINET STORES: Custom
FURNITURE & FIXTURES Factory
FURNITURE PARTS: Metal
FURNITURE REFINISHING SVCS
FURNITURE STOCK & PARTS: Carvings, Wood
FURNITURE STOCK & PARTS: Dimension Stock, Hardwood
FURNITURE STOCK & PARTS: Frames, Upholstered Furniture, Wood
FURNITURE STOCK & PARTS: Hardwood
FURNITURE STORES
FURNITURE STORES: Cabinets, Kitchen, Exc Custom Made
FURNITURE STORES: Custom Made, Exc Cabinets
FURNITURE STORES: Juvenile
FURNITURE STORES: Office
FURNITURE STORES: Outdoor & Garden
FURNITURE STORES: Unfinished
FURNITURE UPHOLSTERY REPAIR SVCS
FURNITURE WHOLESALERS
FURNITURE, HOUSEHOLD: Wholesalers
FURNITURE, OFFICE: Wholesalers
FURNITURE, WHOLESALE: Beds & Bedding
FURNITURE, WHOLESALE: Racks
FURNITURE, WHOLESALE: Tables, Occasional
FURNITURE: Bed Frames & Headboards, Wood
FURNITURE: Bedroom, Wood
FURNITURE: Beds, Household, Incl Folding & Cabinet, Metal
FURNITURE: Bookcases, Office, Wood
FURNITURE: Box Springs, Assembled
FURNITURE: Cabinets & Filing Drawers, Office, Exc Wood
FURNITURE: Cabinets & Vanities, Medicine, Metal
FURNITURE: Chairs & Couches, Wood, Upholstered
FURNITURE: Chairs, Household Upholstered
FURNITURE: Chairs, Household Wood
FURNITURE: Chairs, Office Exc Wood
FURNITURE: Chairs, Office Wood
FURNITURE: China Closets
FURNITURE: Church
FURNITURE: Console Tables, Wood
FURNITURE: Couches, Sofa/Davenport, Upholstered Wood Frames
FURNITURE: Cribs, Metal
FURNITURE: Cut Stone
FURNITURE: Desks & Tables, Office, Exc Wood
FURNITURE: Desks & Tables, Office, Wood
FURNITURE: Desks, Wood
FURNITURE: Dinette Sets, Metal
FURNITURE: Dining Room, Wood
FURNITURE: Foundations & Platforms
FURNITURE: Garden, Exc Wood, Metal, Stone Or Concrete
FURNITURE: Hospital
FURNITURE: Hotel
FURNITURE: Household, Metal
FURNITURE: Household, NEC
FURNITURE: Household, Upholstered On Metal Frames
FURNITURE: Household, Upholstered, Exc Wood Or Metal
FURNITURE: Household, Wood
FURNITURE: Hydraulic Barber & Beauty Shop Chairs
FURNITURE: Institutional, Exc Wood
FURNITURE: Juvenile, Wood
FURNITURE: Kitchen & Dining Room
FURNITURE: Kitchen & Dining Room, Metal
FURNITURE: Laboratory
FURNITURE: Living Room, Upholstered On Wood Frames
FURNITURE: Mattresses & Foundations
FURNITURE: Mattresses, Box & Bedsprings
FURNITURE: Mattresses, Innerspring Or Box Spring
FURNITURE: NEC
FURNITURE: Novelty, Wood
FURNITURE: Office Panel Systems, Exc Wood
FURNITURE: Office, Exc Wood
FURNITURE: Office, Wood
FURNITURE: Outdoor, Wood
FURNITURE: Pews, Church
FURNITURE: Picnic Tables Or Benches, Park
FURNITURE: Rattan
FURNITURE: Restaurant
FURNITURE: School
FURNITURE: Ship
FURNITURE: Silverware Chests, Wood
FURNITURE: Sleep
FURNITURE: Sofa Beds Or Convertible Sofas)
FURNITURE: Storage Chests, Household, Wood
FURNITURE: Tables & Table Tops, Wood
FURNITURE: Tables, Office, Exc Wood
FURNITURE: Tables, Office, Wood
FURNITURE: Theater
FURNITURE: Upholstered
FURNITURE: Vehicle
FURRIERS
FUSES: Electric

G

GAMES & TOYS: Baby Carriages & Restraint Seats
GAMES & TOYS: Banks
GAMES & TOYS: Child Restraint Seats, Automotive
GAMES & TOYS: Craft & Hobby Kits & Sets
GAMES & TOYS: Doll Hats
GAMES & TOYS: Dolls & Doll Clothing
GAMES & TOYS: Dolls, Exc Stuffed Toy Animals
GAMES & TOYS: Electronic
GAMES & TOYS: Game Machines, Exc Coin-Operated
GAMES & TOYS: Miniature Dolls, Collectors'

PRODUCT INDEX

GAMES & TOYS: Puzzles
GAMES & TOYS: Scooters, Children's
GAMES & TOYS: Trains & Eqpt, Electric & Mechanical
GARBAGE CONTAINERS: Plastic
GARBAGE DISPOSALS: Household
GARBAGE DISPOSERS & COMPACTORS: Commercial
GARNET MINING SVCS
GAS & OIL FIELD EXPLORATION SVCS
GAS & OIL FIELD SVCS, NEC
GAS STATIONS
GASES & LIQUIFIED PETROLEUM GASES
GASES: Carbon Dioxide
GASES: Flourinated Hydrocarbon
GASES: Indl
GASES: Neon
GASES: Nitrogen
GASES: Oxygen
GASKET MATERIALS
GASKETS
GASKETS & SEALING DEVICES
GASOLINE FILLING STATIONS
GASOLINE WHOLESALERS
GATES: Dam, Metal Plate
GATES: Ornamental Metal
GAUGES
GEARS
GEARS & GEAR UNITS: Reduction, Exc Auto
GEARS: Power Transmission, Exc Auto
GELATIN
GEM STONES MINING, NEC: Natural
GEMSTONE & INDL DIAMOND MINING SVCS
GENERAL & INDUSTRIAL LOAN INSTITUTIONS
GENERAL MERCHANDISE, NONDURABLE, WHOLESALE
GENERATING APPARATUS & PARTS: Electrical
GENERATION EQPT: Electronic
GENERATORS: Electric
GENERATORS: Electrochemical, Fuel Cell
GENERATORS: Gas
GENERATORS: Ultrasonic
GIFT SHOP
GIFT, NOVELTY & SOUVENIR STORES: Artcraft & carvings
GIFT, NOVELTY & SOUVENIR STORES: Gifts & Novelties
GIFT, NOVELTY & SOUVENIR STORES: Party Favors
GIFTS & NOVELTIES: Wholesalers
GIFTWARE: Brass
GLASS FABRICATORS
GLASS PRDTS, FROM PURCHASED GLASS: Art
GLASS PRDTS, FROM PURCHASED GLASS: Glass Beads, Reflecting
GLASS PRDTS, FROM PURCHASED GLASS: Glassware
GLASS PRDTS, FROM PURCHASED GLASS: Insulating
GLASS PRDTS, FROM PURCHASED GLASS: Mirrored
GLASS PRDTS, FROM PURCHASED GLASS: Mirrors, Framed
GLASS PRDTS, FROM PURCHASED GLASS: Ornaments, Christmas Tree
GLASS PRDTS, FROM PURCHASED GLASS: Sheet, Bent
GLASS PRDTS, FROM PURCHASED GLASS: Watch Crystals
GLASS PRDTS, FROM PURCHASED GLASS: Windshields
GLASS PRDTS, FROM PURCHD GLASS: Strengthened Or Reinforced
GLASS PRDTS, PRESSED OR BLOWN: Bulbs, Electric Lights
GLASS PRDTS, PRESSED OR BLOWN: Chimneys, Lamp
GLASS PRDTS, PRESSED OR BLOWN: Glassware, Art Or Decorative
GLASS PRDTS, PRESSED OR BLOWN: Lens Blanks, Optical
GLASS PRDTS, PRESSED OR BLOWN: Optical
GLASS PRDTS, PRESSED OR BLOWN: Ornaments, Christmas Tree
GLASS PRDTS, PRESSED OR BLOWN: Scientific Glassware
GLASS PRDTS, PRESSED/BLOWN: Glassware, Art, Decor/Novelty
GLASS PRDTS, PURCHASED GLASS: Glassware, Scientific/Tech
GLASS PRDTS, PURCHASED GLASS: Insulating, Multiple-Glazed
GLASS PRDTS, PURCHD GLASS: Furniture Top, Cut, Beveld/Polshd
GLASS PRDTS, PURCHSD GLASS: Ornamental, Cut, Engraved/D-cor
GLASS STORE: Leaded Or Stained
GLASS STORES

GLASS: Fiber
GLASS: Flat
GLASS: Insulating
GLASS: Leaded
GLASS: Pressed & Blown, NEC
GLASS: Stained
GLASS: Structural
GLASS: Tempered
GLASSWARE STORES
GLASSWARE WHOLESALERS
GLASSWARE: Laboratory
GLASSWARE: Laboratory & Medical
GLOBAL POSITIONING SYSTEMS & EQPT
GLOVE MENDING, FACTORY BASIS
GLOVES: Fabric
GLOVES: Leather
GLOVES: Leather, Dress Or Semidress
GLOVES: Leather, Work
GLOVES: Plastic
GLOVES: Safety
GLOVES: Work
GLOVES: Woven Or Knit, From Purchased Materials
GLUE
GOLD ORE MINING
GOLD ORES
GOLD RECOVERY FROM TAILINGS
GOLD STAMPING, EXC BOOKS
GOLF CARTS: Powered
GOLF EQPT
GOURMET FOOD STORES
GOVERNMENT, EXECUTIVE OFFICES: Mayors'
GOVERNMENT, GENERAL: Administration
GRANITE: Crushed & Broken
GRANITE: Cut & Shaped
GRANITE: Dimension
GRANITE: Dimension
GRAPHIC ARTS & RELATED DESIGN SVCS
GRAPHIC LAYOUT SVCS: Printed Circuitry
GRASSES: Artificial & Preserved
GRATINGS: Tread, Fabricated Metal
GRAVE MARKERS: Concrete
GRAVEL MINING
GREASE CUPS: Metal
GREASE TRAPS: Concrete
GREASES: Lubricating
GREENHOUSES: Prefabricated Metal
GREETING CARDS WHOLESALERS
GRILLS & GRILLWORK: Woven Wire, Made From Purchased Wire
GRINDING BALLS: Ceramic
GRINDING SVC: Precision, Commercial Or Indl
GRINDING SVCS: Ophthalmic Lens, Exc Prescription
GRIT: Steel
GRITS: Crushed & Broken
GROCERIES WHOLESALERS, NEC
GROCERIES, GENERAL LINE WHOLESALERS
GUARDRAILS
GUIDANCE SYSTEMS & EQPT: Space Vehicle
GUIDED MISSILES & SPACE VEHICLES
GUM & WOOD CHEMICALS
GUN STOCKS: Wood
GUNSMITHS
GUTTERS: Sheet Metal
GYPSUM PRDTS

H

HAIR & HAIR BASED PRDTS
HAIR ACCESS WHOLESALERS
HAIR CARE PRDTS
HAIR CARE PRDTS: Hair Coloring Preparations
HAIRPIN MOUNTINGS
HANDBAG STORES
HANDBAGS
HANDBAGS: Women's
HANDCUFFS & LEG IRONS
HANDLES: Brush Or Tool, Plastic
HANDLES: Wood
HANGERS: Garment, Plastic
HANGERS: Garment, Wire
HANGERS: Garment, Wire
HARDBOARD & FIBERBOARD PRDTS
HARDWARE
HARDWARE & BUILDING PRDTS: Plastic
HARDWARE & EQPT: Stage, Exc Lighting

HARDWARE CLOTH: Woven Wire, Made From Purchased Wire
HARDWARE STORES
HARDWARE STORES: Builders'
HARDWARE STORES: Pumps & Pumping Eqpt
HARDWARE STORES: Tools
HARDWARE WHOLESALERS
HARDWARE, WHOLESALE: Bolts
HARDWARE, WHOLESALE: Builders', NEC
HARDWARE, WHOLESALE: Screws
HARDWARE, WHOLESALE: Security Devices, Locks
HARDWARE: Aircraft
HARDWARE: Builders'
HARDWARE: Cabinet
HARDWARE: Door Opening & Closing Devices, Exc Electrical
HARDWARE: Furniture
HARDWARE: Furniture, Builders' & Other Household
HARDWARE: Luggage
HARDWARE: Piano
HARNESS ASSEMBLIES: Cable & Wire
HARNESSES, HALTERS, SADDLERY & STRAPS
HAT BOXES
HEADPHONES: Radio
HEALTH AIDS: Exercise Eqpt
HEALTH SCREENING SVCS
HEARING AIDS
HEAT EMISSION OPERATING APPARATUS
HEAT EXCHANGERS
HEAT EXCHANGERS: After Or Inter Coolers Or Condensers, Etc
HEAT TREATING: Metal
HEATERS: Space, Exc Electric
HEATERS: Swimming Pool, Oil Or Gas
HEATERS: Unit, Domestic
HEATING & AIR CONDITIONING EQPT & SPLYS WHOLESALERS
HEATING & AIR CONDITIONING UNITS, COMBINATION
HEATING EQPT & SPLYS
HEATING EQPT: Complete
HEATING EQPT: Induction
HEATING SYSTEMS: Radiant, Indl Process
HEATING UNITS & DEVICES: Indl, Electric
HELICOPTERS
HELMETS: Athletic
HIDES & SKINS
HIGH ENERGY PARTICLE PHYSICS EQPT
HIGHWAY SIGNALS: Electric
HOBBY & CRAFT SPLY STORES
HOBBY, TOY & GAME STORES: Ceramics Splys
HOBBY, TOY & GAME STORES: Toys & Games
HOISTS
HOLDING COMPANIES: Banks
HOLDING COMPANIES: Investment, Exc Banks
HOLDING COMPANIES: Personal, Exc Banks
HOME DELIVERY NEWSPAPER ROUTES
HOME ENTERTAINMENT EQPT: Electronic, NEC
HOME FOR THE MENTALLY RETARDED
HOME FURNISHINGS WHOLESALERS
HOME HEALTH CARE SVCS
HOMEBUILDERS & OTHER OPERATIVE BUILDERS
HOMEFURNISHING STORES: Beddings & Linens
HOMEFURNISHING STORES: Lighting Fixtures
HOMEFURNISHING STORES: Mirrors
HOMEFURNISHING STORES: Vertical Blinds
HOMEFURNISHING STORES: Window Furnishings
HOMEFURNISHINGS & SPLYS, WHOLESALE: Decorative
HOMEFURNISHINGS, WHOLESALE: Bedspreads
HOMEFURNISHINGS, WHOLESALE: Blinds, Venetian
HOMEFURNISHINGS, WHOLESALE: Blinds, Vertical
HOMEFURNISHINGS, WHOLESALE: Carpets
HOMEFURNISHINGS, WHOLESALE: Curtains
HOMEFURNISHINGS, WHOLESALE: Draperies
HOMEFURNISHINGS, WHOLESALE: Kitchenware
HOMEFURNISHINGS, WHOLESALE: Linens, Table
HOMEFURNISHINGS, WHOLESALE: Mirrors/Pictures, Framed/Unframd
HOMEFURNISHINGS, WHOLESALE: Pillowcases
HOMEFURNISHINGS, WHOLESALE: Rugs
HOMEFURNISHINGS, WHOLESALE: Sheets, Textile
HOMEFURNISHINGS, WHOLESALE: Stainless Steel Flatware
HOMEFURNISHINGS, WHOLESALE: Window Covering Parts & Access
HOMEFURNISHINGS, WHOLESALE: Wood Flooring
HOMES, MODULAR: Wooden

PRODUCT INDEX

HOMES: Log Cabins
HONES
HORMONE PREPARATIONS
HORSE & PET ACCESSORIES: Textile
HORSE ACCESS: Harnesses & Riding Crops, Etc, Exc Leather
HOSE: Air Line Or Air Brake, Rubber Or Rubberized Fabric
HOSE: Automobile, Plastic
HOSE: Fire, Rubber
HOSE: Flexible Metal
HOSE: Plastic
HOSE: Pneumatic, Rubber Or Rubberized Fabric, NEC
HOSE: Rubber
HOSE: Vacuum Cleaner, Rubber
HOSES & BELTING: Rubber & Plastic
HOSPITALS: Cancer
HOSPITALS: Medical & Surgical
HOT TUBS
HOT TUBS: Plastic & Fiberglass
HOUSEHOLD APPLIANCE STORES: Air Cond Rm Units, Self-Contnd
HOUSEHOLD APPLIANCE STORES: Electric Household Appliance, Sm
HOUSEHOLD APPLIANCE STORES: Fans, Electric
HOUSEHOLD APPLIANCE STORES: Garbage Disposals
HOUSEHOLD ARTICLES: Metal
HOUSEHOLD FURNISHINGS, NEC
HOUSEWARE STORES
HOUSEWARES, ELECTRIC, EXC COOKING APPLIANCES & UTENSILS
HOUSEWARES, ELECTRIC: Air Purifiers, Portable
HOUSEWARES, ELECTRIC: Cooking Appliances
HOUSEWARES, ELECTRIC: Extractors, Juice
HOUSEWARES, ELECTRIC: Fryers
HOUSEWARES, ELECTRIC: Heaters, Sauna
HOUSEWARES, ELECTRIC: Heaters, Space
HOUSEWARES, ELECTRIC: Heating, Bsbrd/Wall, Radiant Heat
HOUSEWARES, ELECTRIC: Humidifiers, Household
HOUSEWARES, ELECTRIC: Massage Machines, Exc Beauty/Barber
HOUSEWARES: Dishes, China
HOUSEWARES: Dishes, Earthenware
HOUSEWARES: Dishes, Plastic
HOUSEWARES: Kettles & Skillets, Cast Iron
HOUSEWARES: Pots & Pans, Glass
HUMIDIFIERS & DEHUMIDIFIERS
HYDRAULIC EQPT REPAIR SVC
Hard Rubber & Molded Rubber Prdts

I

ICE
ICE CREAM & ICES WHOLESALERS
IDENTIFICATION TAGS, EXC PAPER
IGNEOUS ROCK: Crushed & Broken
IGNITION APPARATUS & DISTRIBUTORS
IGNITION SYSTEMS: High Frequency
IGNITION SYSTEMS: Internal Combustion Engine
INCINERATORS
INDICATORS: Cabin Environment
INDL & PERSONAL SVC PAPER WHOLESALERS
INDL & PERSONAL SVC PAPER, WHOL: Bags, Paper/Disp Plastic
INDL & PERSONAL SVC PAPER, WHOL: Boxes, Corrugtd/Solid Fiber
INDL & PERSONAL SVC PAPER, WHOL: Container, Paper/Plastic
INDL & PERSONAL SVC PAPER, WHOL: Cups, Disp, Plastic/Paper
INDL & PERSONAL SVC PAPER, WHOLESALE: Boxes & Containers
INDL & PERSONAL SVC PAPER, WHOLESALE: Press Sensitive Tape
INDL EQPT SVCS
INDL GASES WHOLESALERS
INDL MACHINERY & EQPT WHOLESALERS
INDL MACHINERY REPAIR & MAINTENANCE
INDL PATTERNS: Foundry Patternmaking
INDL PROCESS INSTRUMENTS: Analyzers
INDL PROCESS INSTRUMENTS: Control
INDL PROCESS INSTRUMENTS: Controllers, Process Variables
INDL PROCESS INSTRUMENTS: Digital Display, Process Variables
INDL PROCESS INSTRUMENTS: Elements, Primary
INDL PROCESS INSTRUMENTS: Fluidic Devices, Circuit & Systems
INDL PROCESS INSTRUMENTS: Indl Flow & Measuring
INDL PROCESS INSTRUMENTS: Level & Bulk Measuring
INDL PROCESS INSTRUMENTS: On-Stream Gas Or Liquid Analysis
INDL PROCESS INSTRUMENTS: Temperature
INDL PROCESS INSTRUMENTS: Water Quality Monitoring/Cntrl Sys
INDL SALTS WHOLESALERS
INDL SPLYS WHOLESALERS
INDL SPLYS, WHOL: Fasteners, Incl Nuts, Bolts, Screws, Etc
INDL SPLYS, WHOLESALE: Abrasives
INDL SPLYS, WHOLESALE: Adhesives, Tape & Plasters
INDL SPLYS, WHOLESALE: Bearings
INDL SPLYS, WHOLESALE: Bins & Containers, Storage
INDL SPLYS, WHOLESALE: Brushes, Indl
INDL SPLYS, WHOLESALE: Clean Room Splys
INDL SPLYS, WHOLESALE: Fasteners & Fastening Eqpt
INDL SPLYS, WHOLESALE: Gears
INDL SPLYS, WHOLESALE: Knives, Indl
INDL SPLYS, WHOLESALE: Power Transmission, Eqpt & Apparatus
INDL SPLYS, WHOLESALE: Rubber Goods, Mechanical
INDL SPLYS, WHOLESALE: Seals
INDL SPLYS, WHOLESALE: Springs
INDL SPLYS, WHOLESALE: Tools
INDL SPLYS, WHOLESALE: Valves & Fittings
INDUCTORS
INFORMATION RETRIEVAL SERVICES
INFRARED OBJECT DETECTION EQPT
INK OR WRITING FLUIDS
INK: Letterpress Or Offset
INK: Printing
INK: Screen process
INSECTICIDES
INSPECTION & TESTING SVCS
INSTR, MEASURE & CONTROL: Gauge, Oil Pressure & Water Temp
INSTRUMENTS & METERS: Measuring, Electric
INSTRUMENTS, LABORATORY: Differential Thermal Analysis
INSTRUMENTS, LABORATORY: Magnetic/Elec Properties Measuring
INSTRUMENTS, LABORATORY: Spectrometers
INSTRUMENTS, MEASURING & CNTRL: Gauges, Auto, Computer
INSTRUMENTS, MEASURING & CNTRL: Radiation & Testing, Nuclear
INSTRUMENTS, MEASURING & CNTRL: Testing, Abrasion, Etc
INSTRUMENTS, MEASURING & CNTRLG: Aircraft & Motor Vehicle
INSTRUMENTS, MEASURING & CNTRLG: Stress, Strain & Measure
INSTRUMENTS, MEASURING & CNTRLG: Tensile Strength Testing
INSTRUMENTS, MEASURING & CNTRLG: Thermometers/Temp Sensors
INSTRUMENTS, MEASURING & CONTROLLING: Gas Detectors
INSTRUMENTS, MEASURING & CONTROLLING: Magnetometers
INSTRUMENTS, MEASURING & CONTROLLING: Photogrammetrical
INSTRUMENTS, MEASURING & CONTROLLING: Toll Booths, Automatic
INSTRUMENTS, MEASURING & CONTROLLING: Ultrasonic Testing
INSTRUMENTS, MEASURING/CNTRL: Hydrometers, Exc Indl Process
INSTRUMENTS, MEASURING/CNTRLG: Fare Registers, St Cars/Buses
INSTRUMENTS, MEASURING/CNTRLNG: Med Diagnostic Sys, Nuclear
INSTRUMENTS, OPTICAL: Borescopes
INSTRUMENTS, OPTICAL: Elements & Assemblies, Exc Ophthalmic
INSTRUMENTS, OPTICAL: Gratings, Diffraction
INSTRUMENTS, OPTICAL: Lenses, All Types Exc Ophthalmic
INSTRUMENTS, OPTICAL: Mirrors
INSTRUMENTS, OPTICAL: Prisms
INSTRUMENTS, OPTICAL: Sights, Telescopic
INSTRUMENTS, OPTICAL: Spyglasses
INSTRUMENTS, OPTICAL: Test & Inspection
INSTRUMENTS, SURGICAL & MEDICAL: Blood & Bone Work
INSTRUMENTS, SURGICAL & MEDICAL: Blood Pressure
INSTRUMENTS, SURGICAL & MEDICAL: Catheters
INSTRUMENTS, SURGICAL & MEDICAL: IV Transfusion
INSTRUMENTS, SURGICAL & MEDICAL: Inhalation Therapy
INSTRUMENTS, SURGICAL & MEDICAL: Inhalators
INSTRUMENTS, SURGICAL & MEDICAL: Knives
INSTRUMENTS, SURGICAL & MEDICAL: Lasers, Surgical
INSTRUMENTS, SURGICAL & MEDICAL: Muscle Exercise, Ophthalmic
INSTRUMENTS, SURGICAL & MEDICAL: Ophthalmic
INSTRUMENTS, SURGICAL & MEDICAL: Physiotherapy, Electrical
INSTRUMENTS, SURGICAL & MEDICAL: Skin Grafting
INSTRUMENTS, SURGICAL & MEDICAL: Suction Therapy
INSTRUMENTS: Analytical
INSTRUMENTS: Colonoscopes, Electromedical
INSTRUMENTS: Combustion Control, Indl
INSTRUMENTS: Electrocardiographs
INSTRUMENTS: Electrolytic Conductivity, Indl
INSTRUMENTS: Electrolytic Conductivity, Laboratory
INSTRUMENTS: Endoscopic Eqpt, Electromedical
INSTRUMENTS: Function Generators
INSTRUMENTS: Generators Tachometer
INSTRUMENTS: Indl Process Control
INSTRUMENTS: Laser, Scientific & Engineering
INSTRUMENTS: Measurement, Indl Process
INSTRUMENTS: Measuring & Controlling
INSTRUMENTS: Measuring Electricity
INSTRUMENTS: Measuring, Electrical Energy
INSTRUMENTS: Measuring, Electrical Power
INSTRUMENTS: Measuring, Electrical Quantities
INSTRUMENTS: Medical & Surgical
INSTRUMENTS: Meteorological
INSTRUMENTS: Microwave Test
INSTRUMENTS: Nautical
INSTRUMENTS: Optical, Analytical
INSTRUMENTS: Oscillographs & Oscilloscopes
INSTRUMENTS: Pressure Measurement, Indl
INSTRUMENTS: Radar Testing, Electric
INSTRUMENTS: Radio Frequency Measuring
INSTRUMENTS: Signal Generators & Averagers
INSTRUMENTS: Standards & Calibration, Electrical Measuring
INSTRUMENTS: Telemetering, Indl Process
INSTRUMENTS: Temperature Measurement, Indl
INSTRUMENTS: Test, Electronic & Electric Measurement
INSTRUMENTS: Test, Electronic & Electrical Circuits
INSTRUMENTS: Testing, Semiconductor
INSTRUMENTS: Thermal Conductive, Indl
INSTRUMENTS: Vibration
INSTRUMENTS: Viscometer, Indl Process
INSULATING COMPOUNDS
INSULATION & CUSHIONING FOAM: Polystyrene
INSULATION MATERIALS WHOLESALERS
INSULATION: Felt
INSULATION: Fiberglass
INSULATORS & INSULATION MATERIALS: Electrical
INSULATORS, PORCELAIN: Electrical
INSULIN PREPARATIONS
INSURANCE CARRIERS: Life
INTEGRATED CIRCUITS, SEMICONDUCTOR NETWORKS, ETC
INTERCOMMUNICATIONS SYSTEMS: Electric
INTERIOR DECORATING SVCS
INTERIOR DESIGN SVCS, NEC
INTERIOR DESIGNING SVCS
INTERIOR REPAIR SVCS
INTRAVENOUS SOLUTIONS
INVERTERS: Nonrotating Electrical
INVERTERS: Rotating Electrical
INVESTMENT ADVISORY SVCS
INVESTMENT FUNDS: Open-Ended
INVESTORS, NEC
INVESTORS: Real Estate, Exc Property Operators
INVESTORS: Security Speculators For Own Account
IRON & STEEL PRDTS: Hot-Rolled
IRON & STEEL: Corrugating, Cold-Rolled
IRON ORE MINING
IRON OXIDES
IRONING BOARDS

J

JANITORIAL & CUSTODIAL SVCS

PRODUCT INDEX

JANITORIAL EQPT & SPLYS WHOLESALERS
JEWELERS' FINDINGS & MATERIALS
JEWELERS' FINDINGS & MATERIALS: Castings
JEWELERS' FINDINGS & MATERIALS: Parts, Unassembled
JEWELERS' FINDINGS & MTLS: Jewel Prep, Instr, Tools, Watches
JEWELERS' FINDINGS/MTRLS: Gem Prep, Settings, Real/Imitation
JEWELRY & PRECIOUS STONES WHOLESALERS
JEWELRY APPAREL
JEWELRY FINDINGS & LAPIDARY WORK
JEWELRY FINDINGS WHOLESALERS
JEWELRY REPAIR SVCS
JEWELRY STORES
JEWELRY STORES: Precious Stones & Precious Metals
JEWELRY STORES: Silverware
JEWELRY, PREC METAL: Mountings, Pens, Lthr, Etc, Gold/Silver
JEWELRY, PRECIOUS METAL: Bracelets
JEWELRY, PRECIOUS METAL: Cases
JEWELRY, PRECIOUS METAL: Cigar & Cigarette Access
JEWELRY, PRECIOUS METAL: Earrings
JEWELRY, PRECIOUS METAL: Medals, Precious Or Semi-precious
JEWELRY, PRECIOUS METAL: Mountings & Trimmings
JEWELRY, PRECIOUS METAL: Necklaces
JEWELRY, PRECIOUS METAL: Pearl, Natural Or Cultured
JEWELRY, PRECIOUS METAL: Pins
JEWELRY, PRECIOUS METAL: Rings, Finger
JEWELRY, PRECIOUS METAL: Rosaries/Other Sm Religious Article
JEWELRY, PRECIOUS METAL: Settings & Mountings
JEWELRY, PRECIOUS METAL: Trimmings, Canes, Umbrellas, Etc
JEWELRY, WHOLESALE
JEWELRY: Decorative, Fashion & Costume
JEWELRY: Precious Metal
JIGS & FIXTURES
JOB PRINTING & NEWSPAPER PUBLISHING COMBINED
JOB TRAINING & VOCATIONAL REHABILITATION SVCS
JOINTS: Ball Except aircraft & Auto
JOINTS: Expansion
JOINTS: Expansion, Pipe

K

KEYBOARDS: Computer Or Office Machine
KEYS, KEY BLANKS
KILNS
KITCHEN CABINET STORES, EXC CUSTOM
KITCHEN CABINETS WHOLESALERS
KITCHEN UTENSILS: Bakers' Eqpt, Wood
KITCHEN UTENSILS: Food Handling & Processing Prdts, Wood
KITCHEN UTENSILS: Wooden
KITCHENWARE STORES
KITCHENWARE: Plastic
KNIT GOODS, WHOLESALE
KNIT OUTERWEAR DYEING & FINISHING, EXC HOSIERY & GLOVE
KNIVES: Agricultural Or indl

L

LABELS: Cotton, Printed
LABELS: Paper, Made From Purchased Materials
LABELS: Woven
LABORATORIES, TESTING: Forensic
LABORATORIES, TESTING: Pollution
LABORATORIES, TESTING: Product Testing, Safety/Performance
LABORATORIES: Biological Research
LABORATORIES: Biotechnology
LABORATORIES: Commercial Nonphysical Research
LABORATORIES: Dental
LABORATORIES: Dental Orthodontic Appliance Production
LABORATORIES: Electronic Research
LABORATORIES: Medical
LABORATORIES: Noncommercial Research
LABORATORIES: Physical Research, Commercial
LABORATORIES: Testing
LABORATORIES: Testing
LABORATORY APPARATUS & FURNITURE
LABORATORY APPARATUS: Furnaces
LABORATORY APPARATUS: Pipettes, Hemocytometer
LABORATORY APPARATUS: Shakers & Stirrers
LABORATORY EQPT, EXC MEDICAL: Wholesalers
LABORATORY EQPT: Chemical
LABORATORY EQPT: Clinical Instruments Exc Medical
LABORATORY EQPT: Measuring
LABORATORY EQPT: Sterilizers
LABORATORY INSTRUMENT REPAIR SVCS
LACE GOODS & WARP KNIT FABRIC DYEING & FINISHING
LACQUERING SVC: Metal Prdts
LADDERS: Metal
LADDERS: Portable, Metal
LADDERS: Wood
LAMINATED PLASTICS: Plate, Sheet, Rod & Tubes
LAMINATING SVCS
LAMP & LIGHT BULBS & TUBES
LAMP BULBS & TUBES, ELECTRIC: For Specialized Applications
LAMP BULBS & TUBES, ELECTRIC: Light, Complete
LAMP BULBS & TUBES/PARTS, ELECTRIC: Generalized Applications
LAMP FRAMES: Wire
LAMP SHADES: Glass
LAMP SHADES: Metal
LAMP STORES
LAMPS: Floor, Residential
LAMPS: Fluorescent
LAMPS: Ultraviolet
LAND SUBDIVIDERS & DEVELOPERS: Commercial
LAND SUBDIVISION & DEVELOPMENT
LANGUAGE SCHOOLS
LANTERNS
LAPIDARY WORK & DIAMOND CUTTING & POLISHING
LAPIDARY WORK: Contract Or Other
LAPIDARY WORK: Jewel Cut, Drill, Polish, Recut/Setting
LARD: From Slaughtering Plants
LASER SYSTEMS & EQPT
LASERS: Welding, Drilling & Cutting Eqpt
LAUNDRY & DRYCLEANER AGENTS
LAUNDRY & GARMENT SVCS, NEC: Fur Cleaning, Repairing/Storage
LAUNDRY & GARMENT SVCS, NEC: Garment Alteration & Repair
LAUNDRY & GARMENT SVCS, NEC: Reweaving, Textiles
LAUNDRY & GARMENT SVCS: Dressmaking, Matl Owned By Customer
LAUNDRY EQPT: Commercial
LAUNDRY EQPT: Household
LAUNDRY SVC: Wiping Towel Sply
LAWN & GARDEN EQPT
LAWN & GARDEN EQPT STORES
LAWN & GARDEN EQPT: Carts Or Wagons
LAWN & GARDEN EQPT: Tractors & Eqpt
LAWN & GARDEN EQPT: Trimmers
LAWN MOWER REPAIR SHOP
LEAD & ZINC
LEAD PENCILS & ART GOODS
LEASING & RENTAL SVCS: Earth Moving Eqpt
LEASING & RENTAL: Computers & Eqpt
LEASING & RENTAL: Construction & Mining Eqpt
LEASING & RENTAL: Other Real Estate Property
LEASING: Laundry Eqpt
LEASING: Shipping Container
LEATHER GOODS, EXC FOOTWEAR, GLOVES, LUGGAGE/BELTING, WHOL
LEATHER GOODS: Belt Laces
LEATHER GOODS: Belting & Strapping
LEATHER GOODS: Boxes
LEATHER GOODS: Cases
LEATHER GOODS: Corners, Luggage
LEATHER GOODS: Cosmetic Bags
LEATHER GOODS: Desk Sets
LEATHER GOODS: Garments
LEATHER GOODS: Holsters
LEATHER GOODS: Key Cases
LEATHER GOODS: Personal
LEATHER GOODS: Transmission Belting
LEATHER GOODS: Wallets
LEATHER TANNING & FINISHING
LEATHER, LEATHER GOODS & FURS, WHOLESALE
LEATHER: Accessory Prdts
LEATHER: Artificial
LEATHER: Bag
LEATHER: Bookbinders'
LEATHER: Case
LEATHER: Colored
LEATHER: Cut
LEATHER: Die-cut
LEATHER: Embossed
LEATHER: Finished
LEATHER: Glove
LEATHER: Handbag
LEATHER: Processed
LEATHER: Specialty, NEC
LEATHER: Upholstery
LEGAL & TAX SVCS
LEGAL OFFICES & SVCS
LEGITIMATE LIVE THEATER PRODUCERS
LENS COATING: Ophthalmic
LESSORS: Landholding Office
LIFESAVING & SURVIVAL EQPT, EXC MEDICAL, WHOLESALE
LIGHT SENSITIVE DEVICES
LIGHTING EQPT: Flashlights
LIGHTING EQPT: Motor Vehicle, Headlights
LIGHTING EQPT: Motor Vehicle, NEC
LIGHTING EQPT: Outdoor
LIGHTING EQPT: Reflectors, Metal, For Lighting Eqpt
LIGHTING EQPT: Streetcar Fixtures
LIGHTING EQPT: Strobe Lighting Systems
LIGHTING FIXTURES WHOLESALERS
LIGHTING FIXTURES, NEC
LIGHTING FIXTURES: Decorative Area
LIGHTING FIXTURES: Fluorescent, Commercial
LIGHTING FIXTURES: Fluorescent, Residential
LIGHTING FIXTURES: Indl & Commercial
LIGHTING FIXTURES: Motor Vehicle
LIGHTING FIXTURES: Ornamental, Commercial
LIGHTING FIXTURES: Public
LIGHTING FIXTURES: Residential
LIGHTING FIXTURES: Residential, Electric
LIGHTING FIXTURES: Street
LIGHTS: Trouble lights
LIME
LIME: Agricultural
LIMESTONE & MARBLE: Dimension
LIMESTONE: Crushed & Broken
LIMESTONE: Cut & Shaped
LIMESTONE: Dimension
LIMESTONE: Ground
LINEN SPLY SVC: Coat
LINENS & TOWELS WHOLESALERS
LINENS: Napkins, Fabric & Nonwoven, From Purchased Materials
LINENS: Tablecloths, From Purchased Materials
LINERS & COVERS: Fabric
LINERS & LINING
LINERS: Indl, Metal Plate
LININGS: Apparel, Made From Purchased Materials
LININGS: Fabric, Apparel & Other, Exc Millinery
LIP BALMS
LIPSTICK
LIQUEFIED PETROLEUM GAS DEALERS
LIQUID CRYSTAL DISPLAYS
LITHOGRAPHIC PLATES
LOCK & KEY SVCS
LOCKERS
LOCKERS: Refrigerated
LOCKS
LOCKS: Coin-Operated
LOCKS: Safe & Vault, Metal
LOCKSMITHS
LOG LOADING & UNLOADING SVCS
LOGGING
LOGGING CAMPS & CONTRACTORS
LOGGING: Timber, Cut At Logging Camp
LOGGING: Wood Chips, Produced In The Field
LOGGING: Wooden Logs
LOOSELEAF BINDERS
LOTIONS OR CREAMS: Face
LOTIONS: SHAVING
LOUDSPEAKERS
LOUVERS: Ventilating
LOZENGES: Pharmaceutical
LUBRICANTS: Corrosion Preventive
LUBRICATING EQPT: Indl
LUBRICATING OIL & GREASE WHOLESALERS
LUBRICATION SYSTEMS & EQPT
LUGGAGE & BRIEFCASES
LUGGAGE & LEATHER GOODS STORES: Leather, Exc Luggage & Shoes
LUGGAGE WHOLESALERS
LUGGAGE: Traveling Bags

PRODUCT INDEX

LUGGAGE: Wardrobe Bags
LUMBER & BLDG MATLS DEALER, RET: Garage Doors, Sell/Install
LUMBER & BLDG MATRLS DEALERS, RET: Bath Fixtures, Eqpt/Sply
LUMBER & BLDG MTRLS DEALERS, RET: Closets, Interiors/Access
LUMBER & BLDG MTRLS DEALERS, RET: Doors, Storm, Wood/Metal
LUMBER & BLDG MTRLS DEALERS, RET: Windows, Storm, Wood/Metal
LUMBER & BUILDING MATERIALS DEALER, RET: Door & Window Prdts
LUMBER & BUILDING MATERIALS DEALER, RET: Masonry Matls/Splys
LUMBER & BUILDING MATERIALS DEALERS, RETAIL: Brick
LUMBER & BUILDING MATERIALS DEALERS, RETAIL: Countertops
LUMBER & BUILDING MATERIALS DEALERS, RETAIL: Paving Stones
LUMBER & BUILDING MATERIALS DEALERS, RETAIL: Sand & Gravel
LUMBER & BUILDING MATERIALS DEALERS, RETAIL: Tile, Ceramic
LUMBER & BUILDING MATERIALS RET DEALERS: Millwork & Lumber
LUMBER & BUILDING MATLS DEALERS, RET: Concrete/Cinder Block
LUMBER: Dimension, Hardwood
LUMBER: Fiberboard
LUMBER: Fuelwood, From Mill Waste
LUMBER: Furniture Dimension Stock, Softwood
LUMBER: Hardwood Dimension
LUMBER: Hardwood Dimension & Flooring Mills
LUMBER: Kiln Dried
LUMBER: Plywood, Hardwood
LUMBER: Plywood, Hardwood or Hardwood Faced
LUMBER: Plywood, Prefinished, Hardwood
LUMBER: Plywood, Softwood
LUMBER: Poles, Wood, Untreated
LUMBER: Siding, Dressed
LUMBER: Silo Stock, Sawn
LUMBER: Treated
LUNCHROOMS & CAFETERIAS

M

MACHINE PARTS: Stamped Or Pressed Metal
MACHINE SHOPS
MACHINE TOOL ACCESS: Balancing Machines
MACHINE TOOL ACCESS: Cams
MACHINE TOOL ACCESS: Cutting
MACHINE TOOL ACCESS: Diamond Cutting, For Turning, Etc
MACHINE TOOL ACCESS: Dies, Thread Cutting
MACHINE TOOL ACCESS: Dressing/Wheel Crushing Attach, Diamond
MACHINE TOOL ACCESS: Drills
MACHINE TOOL ACCESS: Knives, Shear
MACHINE TOOL ACCESS: Milling Machine Attachments
MACHINE TOOL ACCESS: Sockets
MACHINE TOOL ACCESS: Tool Holders
MACHINE TOOL ACCESS: Tools & Access
MACHINE TOOL ATTACHMENTS & ACCESS
MACHINE TOOLS & ACCESS
MACHINE TOOLS, METAL CUTTING: Centering
MACHINE TOOLS, METAL CUTTING: Exotic, Including Explosive
MACHINE TOOLS, METAL CUTTING: Grind, Polish, Buff, Lapp
MACHINE TOOLS, METAL CUTTING: Lathes
MACHINE TOOLS, METAL CUTTING: Numerically Controlled
MACHINE TOOLS, METAL CUTTING: Tool Replacement & Rpr Parts
MACHINE TOOLS, METAL FORMING: Die Casting & Extruding
MACHINE TOOLS, METAL FORMING: Electroforming
MACHINE TOOLS, METAL FORMING: Forging Machinery & Hammers
MACHINE TOOLS, METAL FORMING: Forming, Metal Deposit
MACHINE TOOLS, METAL FORMING: Headers
MACHINE TOOLS, METAL FORMING: High Energy Rate
MACHINE TOOLS, METAL FORMING: Presses, Hyd & Pneumatic
MACHINE TOOLS, METAL FORMING: Pressing
MACHINE TOOLS, METAL FORMING: Punching & Shearing
MACHINE TOOLS, METAL FORMING: Rebuilt
MACHINE TOOLS, METAL FORMING: Spinning, Spline Rollg/Windg
MACHINE TOOLS: Metal Cutting
MACHINE TOOLS: Metal Forming
MACHINERY & EQPT, AGRICULTURAL, WHOLESALE: Dairy
MACHINERY & EQPT, AGRICULTURAL, WHOLESALE: Landscaping Eqpt
MACHINERY & EQPT, AGRICULTURAL, WHOLESALE: Lawn & Garden
MACHINERY & EQPT, INDL, WHOL: Controlling Instruments/Access
MACHINERY & EQPT, INDL, WHOL: Recording Instruments/Access
MACHINERY & EQPT, INDL, WHOLESALE: Conveyor Systems
MACHINERY & EQPT, INDL, WHOLESALE: Countersinks
MACHINERY & EQPT, INDL, WHOLESALE: Fans
MACHINERY & EQPT, INDL, WHOLESALE: Food Manufacturing
MACHINERY & EQPT, INDL, WHOLESALE: Food Product Manufacturng
MACHINERY & EQPT, INDL, WHOLESALE: Heat Exchange
MACHINERY & EQPT, INDL, WHOLESALE: Hydraulic Systems
MACHINERY & EQPT, INDL, WHOLESALE: Indl Machine Parts
MACHINERY & EQPT, INDL, WHOLESALE: Instruments & Cntrl Eqpt
MACHINERY & EQPT, INDL, WHOLESALE: Machine Tools & Access
MACHINERY & EQPT, INDL, WHOLESALE: Measure/Test, Electric
MACHINERY & EQPT, INDL, WHOLESALE: Packaging
MACHINERY & EQPT, INDL, WHOLESALE: Paint Spray
MACHINERY & EQPT, INDL, WHOLESALE: Pneumatic Tools
MACHINERY & EQPT, INDL, WHOLESALE: Power Plant Machinery
MACHINERY & EQPT, INDL, WHOLESALE: Processing & Packaging
MACHINERY & EQPT, INDL, WHOLESALE: Robots
MACHINERY & EQPT, INDL, WHOLESALE: Safety Eqpt
MACHINERY & EQPT, INDL, WHOLESALE: Textile
MACHINERY & EQPT, INDL, WHOLESALE: Water Pumps
MACHINERY & EQPT, INDL, WHOLESALE: Woodworking
MACHINERY & EQPT, WHOLESALE: Construction, General
MACHINERY & EQPT, WHOLESALE: Contractors Materials
MACHINERY & EQPT, WHOLESALE: Crushing, Pulverizng & Screeng
MACHINERY & EQPT, WHOLESALE: Masonry
MACHINERY & EQPT: Electroplating
MACHINERY & EQPT: Farm
MACHINERY & EQPT: Gas Producers, Generators/Other Rltd Eqpt
MACHINERY & EQPT: Liquid Automation
MACHINERY & EQPT: Metal Finishing, Plating Etc
MACHINERY BASES
MACHINERY, COMMERCIAL LAUNDRY: Dryers, Incl Coin-Operated
MACHINERY, COMMERCIAL LAUNDRY: Washing, Incl Coin-Operated
MACHINERY, EQPT & SUPPLIES: Parking Facility
MACHINERY, FOOD PRDTS: Beverage
MACHINERY, FOOD PRDTS: Choppers, Commercial
MACHINERY, FOOD PRDTS: Cutting, Chopping, Grinding, Mixing
MACHINERY, FOOD PRDTS: Dairy & Milk
MACHINERY, FOOD PRDTS: Dairy, Pasteurizing
MACHINERY, FOOD PRDTS: Food Processing, Smokers
MACHINERY, FOOD PRDTS: Juice Extractors, Fruit & Veg, Comm
MACHINERY, FOOD PRDTS: Milk Processing, NEC
MACHINERY, FOOD PRDTS: Mixers, Commercial
MACHINERY, FOOD PRDTS: Oilseed Crushing & Extracting
MACHINERY, FOOD PRDTS: Ovens, Bakery
MACHINERY, FOOD PRDTS: Packing House
MACHINERY, FOOD PRDTS: Presses, Cheese, Beet, Cider & Sugar
MACHINERY, FOOD PRDTS: Roasting, Coffee, Peanut, Etc.
MACHINERY, MAILING: Canceling
MACHINERY, MAILING: Mailing
MACHINERY, MAILING: Postage Meters
MACHINERY, METALWORKING: Assembly, Including Robotic
MACHINERY, METALWORKING: Cutting & Slitting
MACHINERY, OFFICE: Perforators
MACHINERY, OFFICE: Stapling, Hand Or Power
MACHINERY, OFFICE: Time Clocks &Time Recording Devices
MACHINERY, OFFICE: Typing & Word Processing
MACHINERY, PACKAGING: Canning, Food
MACHINERY, PACKAGING: Carton Packing
MACHINERY, PACKAGING: Packing & Wrapping
MACHINERY, PAPER INDUSTRY: Converting, Die Cutting & Stampng
MACHINERY, PAPER INDUSTRY: Paper Mill, Plating, Etc
MACHINERY, PRINTING TRADES: Copy Holders
MACHINERY, PRINTING TRADES: Plates
MACHINERY, PRINTING TRADES: Plates, Offset
MACHINERY, PRINTING TRADES: Presses, Envelope
MACHINERY, PRINTING TRADES: Printing Trade Parts & Attchts
MACHINERY, PRINTING TRADES: Sticks
MACHINERY, SEWING: Sewing & Hat & Zipper Making
MACHINERY, TEXTILE: Card Cutting, Jacquard
MACHINERY, TEXTILE: Embroidery
MACHINERY, TEXTILE: Silk Screens
MACHINERY, TEXTILE: Thread Making Or Spinning
MACHINERY, WOODWORKING: Bandsaws
MACHINERY, WOODWORKING: Cabinet Makers'
MACHINERY, WOODWORKING: Furniture Makers
MACHINERY, WOODWORKING: Lathes, Wood Turning Includes Access
MACHINERY, WOODWORKING: Pattern Makers'
MACHINERY, WOODWORKING: Sanding, Exc Portable Floor Sanders
MACHINERY: Ammunition & Explosives Loading
MACHINERY: Assembly, Exc Metalworking
MACHINERY: Automotive Maintenance
MACHINERY: Automotive Related
MACHINERY: Billing
MACHINERY: Brewery & Malting
MACHINERY: Bridge Or Gate, Hydraulic
MACHINERY: Concrete Prdts
MACHINERY: Construction
MACHINERY: Cryogenic, Industrial
MACHINERY: Custom
MACHINERY: Drill Presses
MACHINERY: Electronic Component Making
MACHINERY: Extruding
MACHINERY: Fiber Optics Strand Coating
MACHINERY: Gear Cutting & Finishing
MACHINERY: General, Industrial, NEC
MACHINERY: Glassmaking
MACHINERY: Grinding
MACHINERY: Ice Cream
MACHINERY: Ice Crushers
MACHINERY: Ice Making
MACHINERY: Industrial, NEC
MACHINERY: Jewelers
MACHINERY: Logging Eqpt
MACHINERY: Marking, Metalworking
MACHINERY: Metalworking
MACHINERY: Milling
MACHINERY: Mining
MACHINERY: Optical Lens
MACHINERY: Ozone
MACHINERY: Packaging
MACHINERY: Paper Industry Miscellaneous
MACHINERY: Pharmaciutical
MACHINERY: Photographic Reproduction
MACHINERY: Plastic Working
MACHINERY: Printing Presses
MACHINERY: Recycling
MACHINERY: Riveting
MACHINERY: Road Construction & Maintenance
MACHINERY: Rubber Working
MACHINERY: Screening Eqpt, Electric
MACHINERY: Semiconductor Manufacturing
MACHINERY: Separation Eqpt, Magnetic
MACHINERY: Sheet Metal Working
MACHINERY: Specialty
MACHINERY: Textile
MACHINERY: Tire Shredding
MACHINERY: Voting
MACHINERY: Wire Drawing
MACHINERY: Woodworking
MACHINES: Forming, Sheet Metal
MACHINISTS' TOOLS: Measuring, Precision
MACHINISTS' TOOLS: Precision
MAGAZINES, WHOLESALE

PRODUCT INDEX

MAGNETIC INK & OPTICAL SCANNING EQPT
MAGNETIC RESONANCE IMAGING DEVICES: Nonmedical
MAGNETIC TAPE, AUDIO: Prerecorded
MAGNETOHYDRODYNAMIC DEVICES OR MHD
MAGNETS: Ceramic
MAGNETS: Permanent
MAGNIFIERS
MAIL-ORDER BOOK CLUBS
MAIL-ORDER HOUSE, NEC
MAIL-ORDER HOUSES: Book & Record Clubs
MAIL-ORDER HOUSES: Books, Exc Book Clubs
MAIL-ORDER HOUSES: Cards
MAIL-ORDER HOUSES: Clothing, Exc Women's
MAIL-ORDER HOUSES: Computer Eqpt & Electronics
MAIL-ORDER HOUSES: Cosmetics & Perfumes
MAIL-ORDER HOUSES: Fitness & Sporting Goods
MAIL-ORDER HOUSES: Food
MAIL-ORDER HOUSES: Furniture & Furnishings
MAIL-ORDER HOUSES: Gift Items
MAIL-ORDER HOUSES: Jewelry
MAIL-ORDER HOUSES: Magazines
MAILING LIST: Brokers
MAILING LIST: Compilers
MAILING SVCS, NEC
MANAGEMENT CONSULTING SVCS: Automation & Robotics
MANAGEMENT CONSULTING SVCS: Business
MANAGEMENT CONSULTING SVCS: Construction Project
MANAGEMENT CONSULTING SVCS: Distribution Channels
MANAGEMENT CONSULTING SVCS: Food & Beverage
MANAGEMENT CONSULTING SVCS: Foreign Trade
MANAGEMENT CONSULTING SVCS: Industrial
MANAGEMENT CONSULTING SVCS: Industrial & Labor
MANAGEMENT CONSULTING SVCS: Industry Specialist
MANAGEMENT CONSULTING SVCS: Real Estate
MANAGEMENT CONSULTING SVCS: Training & Development
MANAGEMENT SERVICES
MANAGEMENT SVCS: Administrative
MANAGEMENT SVCS: Circuit, Motion Picture Theaters
MANAGEMENT SVCS: Construction
MANAGEMENT SVCS: Restaurant
MANDRELS
MANHOLES COVERS: Concrete
MANICURE PREPARATIONS
MANIFOLDS: Pipe, Fabricated From Purchased Pipe
MANNEQUINS
MANUFACTURING INDUSTRIES, NEC
MAPS
MARBLE BOARD
MARBLE, BUILDING: Cut & Shaped
MARBLE: Crushed & Broken
MARINAS
MARINE HARDWARE
MARINE RELATED EQPT
MARINE SVC STATIONS
MARKERS
MARKETS: Meat & fish
MARKING DEVICES
MARKING DEVICES: Date Stamps, Hand, Rubber Or Metal
MARKING DEVICES: Embossing Seals & Hand Stamps
MARKING DEVICES: Embossing Seals, Corporate & Official
MARKING DEVICES: Figures, Metal
MARKING DEVICES: Irons, Marking Or Branding
MARKING DEVICES: Letters, Metal
MARKING DEVICES: Numbering Machines
MARKING DEVICES: Pads, Inking & Stamping
MARKING DEVICES: Postmark Stamps, Hand, Rubber Or Metal
MARKING DEVICES: Screens, Textile Printing
MASKS: Gas
MASQUERADE OR THEATRICAL COSTUMES STORES
MASTIC ROOFING COMPOSITION
MATERIALS HANDLING EQPT WHOLESALERS
MATS & MATTING, MADE FROM PURCHASED WIRE
MATS OR MATTING, NEC: Rubber
MATS, MATTING & PADS: Auto, Floor, Exc Rubber Or Plastic
MATS, MATTING & PADS: Nonwoven
MATS: Blasting, Rope
MATTRESS RENOVATING & REPAIR SHOP
MATTRESS STORES
MEAT & MEAT PRDTS WHOLESALERS
MEAT CUTTING & PACKING
MEAT MARKETS
MEAT PRDTS: Bologna, From Purchased Meat
MEAT PRDTS: Boneless Meat, From Purchased Meat
MEAT PRDTS: Canned
MEAT PRDTS: Dried Beef, From Purchased Meat
MEAT PRDTS: Frankfurters, From Purchased Meat
MEAT PRDTS: Frozen
MEAT PRDTS: Meat By-Prdts, From Slaughtered Meat
MEAT PRDTS: Meat Extracts, From Purchased Meat
MEAT PRDTS: Pork, From Slaughtered Meat
MEAT PRDTS: Prepared Beef Prdts From Purchased Beef
MEAT PRDTS: Prepared Pork Prdts, From Purchased Meat
MEAT PRDTS: Sausage Casings, Natural
MEAT PRDTS: Sausages & Related Prdts, From Purchased Meat
MEAT PRDTS: Sausages, From Purchased Meat
MEAT PRDTS: Sausages, From Slaughtered Meat
MEAT PRDTS: Snack Sticks, Incl Jerky, From Purchased Meat
MEAT PRDTS: Variety, Fresh Edible Organs
MEAT PRDTS: Veal, From Slaughtered Meat
MEAT PROCESSED FROM PURCHASED CARCASSES
MED, DENTAL & HOSPITAL EQPT, WHOL: Incontinent Prdts/Splys
MEDIA BUYING AGENCIES
MEDIA: Magnetic & Optical Recording
MEDICAL & HOSPITAL EQPT WHOLESALERS
MEDICAL & HOSPITAL SPLYS: Radiation Shielding Garments
MEDICAL & SURGICAL SPLYS: Bandages & Dressings
MEDICAL & SURGICAL SPLYS: Braces, Orthopedic
MEDICAL & SURGICAL SPLYS: Clothing, Fire Resistant & Protect
MEDICAL & SURGICAL SPLYS: Cosmetic Restorations
MEDICAL & SURGICAL SPLYS: Cotton & Cotton Applicators
MEDICAL & SURGICAL SPLYS: Ear Plugs
MEDICAL & SURGICAL SPLYS: Foot Appliances, Orthopedic
MEDICAL & SURGICAL SPLYS: Gynecological Splys & Appliances
MEDICAL & SURGICAL SPLYS: Limbs, Artificial
MEDICAL & SURGICAL SPLYS: Models, Anatomical
MEDICAL & SURGICAL SPLYS: Orthopedic Appliances
MEDICAL & SURGICAL SPLYS: Personal Safety Eqpt
MEDICAL & SURGICAL SPLYS: Prosthetic Appliances
MEDICAL & SURGICAL SPLYS: Respiratory Protect Eqpt, Personal
MEDICAL & SURGICAL SPLYS: Sponges
MEDICAL & SURGICAL SPLYS: Suspensories
MEDICAL & SURGICAL SPLYS: Technical Aids, Handicapped
MEDICAL EQPT REPAIR SVCS, NON-ELECTRIC
MEDICAL EQPT: Diagnostic
MEDICAL EQPT: Electromedical Apparatus
MEDICAL EQPT: Electrotherapeutic Apparatus
MEDICAL EQPT: Heart-Lung Machines, Exc Iron Lungs
MEDICAL EQPT: Laser Systems
MEDICAL EQPT: MRI/Magnetic Resonance Imaging Devs, Nuclear
MEDICAL EQPT: PET Or Position Emission Tomography Scanners
MEDICAL EQPT: Patient Monitoring
MEDICAL EQPT: Sterilizers
MEDICAL EQPT: Ultrasonic Scanning Devices
MEDICAL EQPT: Ultrasonic, Exc Cleaning
MEDICAL EQPT: X-Ray Apparatus & Tubes, Radiographic
MEDICAL EQPT: X-Ray Apparatus & Tubes, Therapeutic
MEDICAL PHOTOGRAPHY & ART SVCS
MEDICAL, DENTAL & HOSPITAL EQPT, WHOL: Dentists' Prof Splys
MEDICAL, DENTAL & HOSPITAL EQPT, WHOL: Hosptl Eqpt/Furniture
MEDICAL, DENTAL & HOSPITAL EQPT, WHOL: Surgical Eqpt & Splys
MEDICAL, DENTAL & HOSPITAL EQPT, WHOLESALE: Diagnostic, Med
MEDICAL, DENTAL & HOSPITAL EQPT, WHOLESALE: Med Eqpt & Splys
MEDICAL, DENTAL & HOSPITAL EQPT, WHOLESALE: Medical Lab
MELAMINE RESINS: Melamine-Formaldehyde
MEMBERSHIP ORGANIZATIONS, PROFESSIONAL: Health Association
MEMBERSHIP ORGS, BUSINESS: Growers' Marketing Advisory Svc
MEMBERSHIP ORGS, CIVIC, SOCIAL/FRAT: Educator's Assoc
MEMORIALS, MONUMENTS & MARKERS
MEMORY DEVICES: Magnetic Bubble
MEN'S & BOYS' CLOTHING ACCESS STORES
MEN'S & BOYS' CLOTHING STORES
MEN'S & BOYS' CLOTHING WHOLESALERS, NEC
MEN'S & BOYS' SPORTSWEAR CLOTHING STORES
MEN'S & BOYS' SPORTSWEAR WHOLESALERS
MEN'S & BOYS' UNDERWEAR WHOLESALERS
MEN'S SUITS STORES
MERCHANDISING MACHINE OPERATORS: Vending
METAL & STEEL PRDTS: Abrasive
METAL COMPONENTS: Prefabricated
METAL CUTTING SVCS
METAL DETECTORS
METAL FABRICATORS: Architechtural
METAL FABRICATORS: Plate
METAL FABRICATORS: Sheet
METAL FABRICATORS: Structural, Ship
METAL FINISHING SVCS
METAL RESHAPING & REPLATING SVCS
METAL SERVICE CENTERS & OFFICES
METAL SPINNING FOR THE TRADE
METAL STAMPING, FOR THE TRADE
METAL STAMPINGS: Patterned
METAL STAMPINGS: Perforated
METAL STAMPINGS: Rigidized
METAL TREATING COMPOUNDS
METAL, TITANIUM: Sponge & Granules
METAL: Heavy, Perforated
METALLIC ORES WHOLESALERS
METALS SVC CENTERS & WHOL: Structural Shapes, Iron Or Steel
METALS SVC CENTERS & WHOLESALERS: Cable, Wire
METALS SVC CENTERS & WHOLESALERS: Iron & Steel Prdt, Ferrous
METALS SVC CENTERS & WHOLESALERS: Misc Nonferrous Prdts
METALS SVC CENTERS & WHOLESALERS: Nonferrous Sheets, Etc
METALS SVC CENTERS & WHOLESALERS: Pipe & Tubing, Steel
METALS SVC CENTERS & WHOLESALERS: Sheets, Metal
METALS SVC CENTERS & WHOLESALERS: Steel
METALS SVC CENTERS & WHOLESALERS: Tin & Tin Base Metals
METALS SVC CENTERS & WHOLESALERS: Tubing, Metal
METALS: Precious NEC
METALS: Precious, Secondary
METALS: Primary Nonferrous, NEC
METALWORK: Miscellaneous
METALWORK: Ornamental
METALWORKING MACHINERY WHOLESALERS
METER READERS: Remote
METERING DEVICES: Flow Meters, Impeller & Counter Driven
METERING DEVICES: Totalizing, Consumption
METERING DEVICES: Water Quality Monitoring & Control Systems
METERS: Elasped Time
METERS: Liquid
METHANOL: Natural
MICA PRDTS
MICROCIRCUITS, INTEGRATED: Semiconductor
MICROFILM EQPT
MICROMANIPULATOR
MICROPHONES
MICROPROCESSORS
MICROWAVE COMPONENTS
MICROWAVE OVENS: Household
MILITARY INSIGNIA
MILITARY INSIGNIA, TEXTILE
MILL PRDTS: Structural & Rail
MILLINERY SUPPLIES: Veils & Veiling, Bridal, Funeral, Etc
MILLING: Grain Cereals, Cracked
MILLWORK
MINE DEVELOPMENT SVCS: Nonmetallic Minerals
MINERAL ABRASIVES MINING SVCS
MINERAL MINING: Nonmetallic
MINERAL PRODUCTS
MINERAL WOOL
MINERAL WOOL INSULATION PRDTS
MINERALS: Ground or Treated
MINIATURES
MINING EXPLORATION & DEVELOPMENT SVCS
MINING SVCS, NEC: Lignite
MINING: Sand & Shale Oil
MIRROR REPAIR SHOP
MIRRORS: Motor Vehicle

PRODUCT INDEX

MIXING EQPT
MIXTURES & BLOCKS: Asphalt Paving
MOBILE COMMUNICATIONS EQPT
MOBILE HOMES
MOBILE HOMES WHOLESALERS
MODELS
MODELS: General, Exc Toy
MODULES: Computer Logic
MODULES: Solid State
MOLDED RUBBER PRDTS
MOLDING COMPOUNDS
MOLDINGS, ARCHITECTURAL: Plaster Of Paris
MOLDINGS: Picture Frame
MOLDS: Indl
MOLDS: Plastic Working & Foundry
MONORAIL SYSTEMS
MONUMENTS & GRAVE MARKERS, EXC TERRAZZO
MONUMENTS: Concrete
MONUMENTS: Cut Stone, Exc Finishing Or Lettering Only
MOPS: Floor & Dust
MORTGAGE BANKERS
MOTION PICTURE & VIDEO PRODUCTION SVCS
MOTION PICTURE & VIDEO PRODUCTION SVCS: Non-Theatrical, TV
MOTION PICTURE PRODUCTION & DISTRIBUTION
MOTION PICTURE PRODUCTION & DISTRIBUTION: Television
MOTION PICTURE PRODUCTION ALLIED SVCS
MOTION PICTURE PRODUCTION SVCS
MOTOR & GENERATOR PARTS: Electric
MOTOR HOMES
MOTOR REPAIR SVCS
MOTOR SCOOTERS & PARTS
MOTOR VEHICLE ASSEMBLY, COMPLETE: Autos, Incl Specialty
MOTOR VEHICLE ASSEMBLY, COMPLETE: Buses, All Types
MOTOR VEHICLE ASSEMBLY, COMPLETE: Cars, Armored
MOTOR VEHICLE ASSEMBLY, COMPLETE: Fire Department Vehicles
MOTOR VEHICLE ASSEMBLY, COMPLETE: Military Motor Vehicle
MOTOR VEHICLE ASSEMBLY, COMPLETE: Motor Buses
MOTOR VEHICLE ASSEMBLY, COMPLETE: Snow Plows
MOTOR VEHICLE ASSEMBLY, COMPLETE: Truck & Tractor Trucks
MOTOR VEHICLE ASSEMBLY, COMPLETE: Trucks, Pickup
MOTOR VEHICLE DEALERS: Automobiles, New & Used
MOTOR VEHICLE DEALERS: Cars, Used Only
MOTOR VEHICLE PARTS & ACCESS: Acceleration Eqpt
MOTOR VEHICLE PARTS & ACCESS: Air Conditioner Parts
MOTOR VEHICLE PARTS & ACCESS: Bearings
MOTOR VEHICLE PARTS & ACCESS: Body Components & Frames
MOTOR VEHICLE PARTS & ACCESS: Cylinder Heads
MOTOR VEHICLE PARTS & ACCESS: Electrical Eqpt
MOTOR VEHICLE PARTS & ACCESS: Engines & Parts
MOTOR VEHICLE PARTS & ACCESS: Fuel Systems & Parts
MOTOR VEHICLE PARTS & ACCESS: Gears
MOTOR VEHICLE PARTS & ACCESS: Power Steering Eqpt
MOTOR VEHICLE PARTS & ACCESS: Propane Conversion Eqpt
MOTOR VEHICLE PARTS & ACCESS: Sanders, Safety
MOTOR VEHICLE PARTS & ACCESS: Tops
MOTOR VEHICLE PARTS & ACCESS: Transmission Housings Or Parts
MOTOR VEHICLE PARTS & ACCESS: Transmissions
MOTOR VEHICLE PARTS & ACCESS: Wheel rims
MOTOR VEHICLE PARTS & ACCESS: Wiring Harness Sets
MOTOR VEHICLE SPLYS & PARTS WHOLESALERS: New
MOTOR VEHICLE: Hardware
MOTOR VEHICLE: Radiators
MOTOR VEHICLE: Steering Mechanisms
MOTOR VEHICLES & CAR BODIES
MOTOR VEHICLES, WHOLESALE: Recreational, All-Terrain
MOTOR VEHICLES, WHOLESALE: Truck bodies
MOTORCYCLE & BICYCLE PARTS: Gears
MOTORCYCLE DEALERS
MOTORCYCLE DEALERS: Bicycles, Motorized
MOTORCYCLES & RELATED PARTS
MOTORS: Electric
MOTORS: Generators
MOTORS: Torque
MOVIE THEATERS, EXC DRIVE-IN
MOWERS & ACCESSORIES
MULTIPLEXERS: Telephone & Telegraph

MUSEUMS
MUSEUMS & ART GALLERIES
MUSIC BROADCASTING SVCS
MUSIC COPYING SVCS
MUSIC DISTRIBUTION APPARATUS
MUSIC LICENSING & ROYALTIES
MUSIC LICENSING TO RADIO STATIONS
MUSIC RECORDING PRODUCER
MUSICAL ENTERTAINERS
MUSICAL INSTRUMENT PARTS & ACCESS, WHOLESALE
MUSICAL INSTRUMENT REPAIR
MUSICAL INSTRUMENTS & ACCESS: Carrying Cases
MUSICAL INSTRUMENTS & ACCESS: NEC
MUSICAL INSTRUMENTS & ACCESS: Pianos
MUSICAL INSTRUMENTS & ACCESS: Pipe Organs
MUSICAL INSTRUMENTS & PARTS: Brass
MUSICAL INSTRUMENTS & PARTS: String
MUSICAL INSTRUMENTS & SPLYS STORES
MUSICAL INSTRUMENTS & SPLYS STORES: Pianos
MUSICAL INSTRUMENTS WHOLESALERS
MUSICAL INSTRUMENTS: Blowers, Pipe Organ
MUSICAL INSTRUMENTS: Electric & Electronic
MUSICAL INSTRUMENTS: Guitars & Parts, Electric & Acoustic
MUSICAL INSTRUMENTS: Harmonicas
MUSICAL INSTRUMENTS: Organs
MUSICAL INSTRUMENTS: Reeds
MUSICAL INSTRUMENTS: Strings, Instrument

N

NAIL SALONS
NAME PLATES: Engraved Or Etched
NAMEPLATES
NATIONAL SECURITY FORCES
NATURAL BUTANE PRODUCTION
NATURAL GAS DISTRIBUTION TO CONSUMERS
NATURAL GAS LIQUIDS PRODUCTION
NATURAL GAS PRODUCTION
NATURAL GAS TRANSMISSION & DISTRIBUTION
NATURAL GASOLINE PRODUCTION
NATURAL PROPANE PRODUCTION
NAUTICAL & NAVIGATIONAL INSTRUMENT REPAIR SVCS
NAVIGATIONAL SYSTEMS & INSTRUMENTS
NET & NETTING PRDTS
NETS: Laundry
NEW & USED CAR DEALERS
NEWS DEALERS & NEWSSTANDS
NEWS FEATURE SYNDICATES
NEWS PICTURES GATHERING & DISTRIBUTING SVCS
NEWS SYNDICATES
NEWSPAPERS & PERIODICALS NEWS REPORTING SVCS
NEWSPAPERS, WHOLESALE
NEWSSTAND
NICKEL ALLOY
NONCURRENT CARRYING WIRING DEVICES
NONFERROUS: Rolling & Drawing, NEC
NONMETALLIC MINERALS: Support Activities, Exc Fuels
NOTARIES PUBLIC
NOTEBOOKS, MADE FROM PURCHASED MATERIALS
NOTIONS: Button Blanks & Molds
NOTIONS: Pins, Straight, Steel Or Brass
NOTIONS: Studs, Shirt, Exc Precious/Semi Metal/Stone
NOVELTIES
NOVELTIES & SPECIALTIES: Metal
NOVELTIES: Leather
NOVELTIES: Paper, Made From Purchased Materials
NOVELTIES: Plastic
NOVELTY SHOPS
NOZZLES & SPRINKLERS Lawn Hose
NOZZLES: Spray, Aerosol, Paint Or Insecticide
NUCLEAR REACTORS: Military Or Indl
NURSERIES & LAWN & GARDEN SPLY STORES, RETAIL: Fertilizer
NURSERIES & LAWN & GARDEN SPLY STORES, RETAIL: Sod
NURSERIES & LAWN & GARDEN SPLY STORES, RETAIL: Top Soil
NURSERIES & LAWN/GARDEN SPLY STORE, RET: Lawnmowers/Tractors
NURSERY & GARDEN CENTERS
NUTS: Metal

O

OFFICE EQPT WHOLESALERS
OFFICE EQPT, WHOLESALE: Duplicating Machines

OFFICE FIXTURES: Exc Wood
OFFICE FIXTURES: Wood
OFFICE FURNITURE REPAIR & MAINTENANCE SVCS
OFFICE SPLY & STATIONERY STORES
OFFICE SPLY & STATIONERY STORES: Office Forms & Splys
OFFICE SPLY & STATIONERY STORES: Writing Splys
OFFICE SPLYS, NEC, WHOLESALE
OFFICES & CLINICS OF DENTISTS: Prosthodontist
OFFICES & CLINICS OF DRS, MED: Specialized Practitioners
OFFICES & CLINICS OF HEALTH PRACTITIONERS: Nutritionist
OIL & GAS FIELD MACHINERY
OIL FIELD MACHINERY & EQPT
OIL FIELD SVCS, NEC
OIL ROYALTY TRADERS
OILS & GREASES: Blended & Compounded
OILS & GREASES: Lubricating
OILS: Essential
OILS: Lubricating
OILS: Lubricating
OILS: Orange
OILS: Still
OINTMENTS
ON-LINE DATABASE INFORMATION RETRIEVAL SVCS
OPERATOR: Apartment Buildings
OPERATOR: Nonresidential Buildings
OPHTHALMIC GOODS
OPHTHALMIC GOODS WHOLESALERS
OPHTHALMIC GOODS: Frames & Parts, Eyeglass & Spectacle
OPHTHALMIC GOODS: Frames, Lenses & Parts, Eyeglasses
OPHTHALMIC GOODS: Lenses, Ophthalmic
OPHTHALMIC GOODS: Spectacles
OPHTHALMIC GOODS: Temples & Fronts, Ophthalmic
OPTICAL GOODS STORES
OPTICAL GOODS STORES: Opticians
OPTICAL INSTRUMENTS & APPARATUS
OPTICAL INSTRUMENTS & LENSES
OPTICAL SCANNING SVCS
OPTOMETRIC EQPT & SPLYS WHOLESALERS
ORAL PREPARATIONS
ORDNANCE
ORGAN TUNING & REPAIR SVCS
ORGANIZATIONS: Medical Research
ORGANIZATIONS: Noncommercial Biological Research
ORGANIZATIONS: Professional
ORGANIZATIONS: Religious
ORGANIZATIONS: Research Institute
ORGANIZATIONS: Scientific Research Agency
ORGANIZERS, CLOSET & DRAWER Plastic
ORNAMENTS: Christmas Tree, Exc Electrical & Glass
ORTHOPEDIC SUNDRIES: Molded Rubber
OSCILLATORS
OUTLETS: Electric, Convenience

P

PACKAGE DESIGN SVCS
PACKAGED FROZEN FOODS WHOLESALERS, NEC
PACKAGING & LABELING SVCS
PACKAGING MATERIALS, INDL: Wholesalers
PACKAGING MATERIALS, WHOLESALE
PACKAGING MATERIALS: Paper
PACKAGING MATERIALS: Paper, Coated Or Laminated
PACKAGING MATERIALS: Paper, Thermoplastic Coated
PACKAGING MATERIALS: Plastic Film, Coated Or Laminated
PACKAGING MATERIALS: Polystyrene Foam
PACKAGING MATERIALS: Resinous Impregnated Paper
PACKAGING: Blister Or Bubble Formed, Plastic
PACKING & CRATING SVC
PACKING MATERIALS: Mechanical
PACKING SVCS: Shipping
PACKING: Metallic
PADDING: Foamed Plastics
PADS: Desk, Exc Paper
PADS: Desk, Paper, Made From Purchased Materials
PADS: Mattress
PAGERS: One-way
PAINT STORE
PAINTING SVC: Metal Prdts
PAINTS & ADDITIVES
PAINTS & ALLIED PRODUCTS
PAINTS & VARNISHES: Plastics Based
PAINTS, VARNISHES & SPLYS WHOLESALERS

PRODUCT INDEX

PAINTS, VARNISHES & SPLYS, WHOLESALE: Paints
PALLET REPAIR SVCS
PALLETIZERS & DEPALLETIZERS
PALLETS
PALLETS & SKIDS: Wood
PALLETS: Wood & Metal Combination
PALLETS: Wooden
PANEL & DISTRIBUTION BOARDS: Electric
PANELS: Building, Wood
PANELS: Cardboard, Die-Cut, Made From Purchased Materials
PANELS: Wood
PAPER & BOARD: Die-cut
PAPER CONVERTING
PAPER MANUFACTURERS: Exc Newsprint
PAPER PRDTS
PAPER PRDTS: Feminine Hygiene Prdts
PAPER PRDTS: Infant & Baby Prdts
PAPER PRDTS: Molded Pulp Prdts
PAPER PRDTS: Napkins, Sanitary, Made From Purchased Material
PAPER PRDTS: Pattern Tissue
PAPER PRDTS: Pressed & Molded Pulp & Fiber Prdts
PAPER PRDTS: Pressed Pulp Prdts
PAPER PRDTS: Sanitary
PAPER PRDTS: Tampons, Sanitary, Made From Purchased Material
PAPER PRDTS: Toilet Paper, Made From Purchased Materials
PAPER PRDTS: Toweling Tissue
PAPER PRDTS: Towels, Napkins/Tissue Paper, From Purchd Mtrls
PAPER, WHOLESALE: Fine
PAPER, WHOLESALE: Printing
PAPER: Absorbent
PAPER: Adding Machine Rolls, Made From Purchased Materials
PAPER: Adhesive
PAPER: Art
PAPER: Bristols
PAPER: Building, Insulating & Packaging
PAPER: Business Form
PAPER: Card
PAPER: Chemically Treated, Made From Purchased Materials
PAPER: Cigarette
PAPER: Cloth, Lined, Made From Purchased Materials
PAPER: Coated & Laminated, NEC
PAPER: Corrugated
PAPER: Envelope
PAPER: Filter
PAPER: Kraft
PAPER: Parchment
PAPER: Printer
PAPER: Specialty
PAPER: Tissue
PAPER: Wrapping
PAPER: Wrapping & Packaging
PAPER: Writing
PAPERBOARD
PAPERBOARD CONVERTING
PAPERBOARD PRDTS: Building Insulating & Packaging
PAPERBOARD PRDTS: Container Board
PAPERBOARD PRDTS: Folding Boxboard
PAPERBOARD PRDTS: Kraft Linerboard
PAPERBOARD PRDTS: Packaging Board
PAPERBOARD PRDTS: Pressboard
PAPERBOARD: Boxboard
PAPERBOARD: Liner Board
PAPIER-MACHE PRDTS, EXC STATUARY & ART GOODS
PARACHUTES
PARKING LOTS
PARTITIONS & FIXTURES: Except Wood
PARTITIONS WHOLESALERS
PARTITIONS: Nonwood, Floor Attached
PARTITIONS: Solid Fiber, Made From Purchased Materials
PARTITIONS: Wood & Fixtures
PARTITIONS: Wood, Floor Attached
PARTS: Metal
PARTY & SPECIAL EVENT PLANNING SVCS
PASTES, FLAVORING
PATENT OWNERS & LESSORS
PATTERNS: Indl
PAVERS
PAVING MATERIALS: Prefabricated, Concrete
PAVING MIXTURES

PENCILS & PENS WHOLESALERS
PENS & PARTS: Ball Point
PENS & PARTS: Cartridges, Refill, Ball Point
PENS & PENCILS: Mechanical, NEC
PERFUME: Concentrated
PERFUME: Perfumes, Natural Or Synthetic
PERFUMES
PERLITE: Processed
PERSONAL APPEARANCE SVCS
PERSONAL CREDIT INSTITUTIONS: Consumer Finance Companies
PET ACCESS: Collars, Leashes, Etc, Exc Leather
PET COLLARS, LEASHES, MUZZLES & HARNESSES: Leather
PET SPLYS
PET SPLYS WHOLESALERS
PETROLEUM & PETROLEUM PRDTS, WHOLESALE Engine Fuels & Oils
PETROLEUM & PETROLEUM PRDTS, WHOLESALE: Bulk Stations
PETROLEUM PRDTS WHOLESALERS
PEWTER WARE
PHARMACEUTICAL PREPARATIONS: Adrenal
PHARMACEUTICAL PREPARATIONS: Barbituric Acid
PHARMACEUTICAL PREPARATIONS: Digitalis
PHARMACEUTICAL PREPARATIONS: Druggists' Preparations
PHARMACEUTICAL PREPARATIONS: Medicines, Capsule Or Ampule
PHARMACEUTICAL PREPARATIONS: Penicillin
PHARMACEUTICAL PREPARATIONS: Pills
PHARMACEUTICAL PREPARATIONS: Proprietary Drug PRDTS
PHARMACEUTICAL PREPARATIONS: Solutions
PHARMACEUTICAL PREPARATIONS: Tablets
PHARMACEUTICAL PREPARATIONS: Water, Sterile, For Injections
PHARMACEUTICALS
PHARMACEUTICALS: Mail-Order Svc
PHARMACEUTICALS: Medicinal & Botanical Prdts
PHARMACIES & DRUG STORES
PHONOGRAPH NEEDLES
PHONOGRAPH RECORDS WHOLESALERS
PHONOGRAPH RECORDS: Prerecorded
PHOSPHATES
PHOTOCOPY MACHINES
PHOTOCOPYING & DUPLICATING SVCS
PHOTOELECTRIC DEVICES: Magnetic
PHOTOENGRAVING SVC
PHOTOFINISHING LABORATORIES
PHOTOGRAPH DEVELOPING & RETOUCHING SVCS
PHOTOGRAPHIC EQPT & SPLY: Sound Recordg/Reprod Eqpt, Motion
PHOTOGRAPHIC EQPT & SPLYS
PHOTOGRAPHIC EQPT & SPLYS WHOLESALERS
PHOTOGRAPHIC EQPT & SPLYS: Cameras, Aerial
PHOTOGRAPHIC EQPT & SPLYS: Cameras, Still & Motion Pictures
PHOTOGRAPHIC EQPT & SPLYS: Developers, Not Chemical Plants
PHOTOGRAPHIC EQPT & SPLYS: Editing Eqpt, Motion Picture
PHOTOGRAPHIC EQPT & SPLYS: Film, Sensitized
PHOTOGRAPHIC EQPT & SPLYS: Graphic Arts Plates, Sensitized
PHOTOGRAPHIC EQPT & SPLYS: Plates, Sensitized
PHOTOGRAPHIC EQPT & SPLYS: Printing Eqpt
PHOTOGRAPHIC EQPT & SPLYS: Processing Eqpt
PHOTOGRAPHIC EQPT & SPLYS: Shutters, Camera
PHOTOGRAPHIC EQPT & SPLYS: Toners, Prprd, Not Chem Plnts
PHOTOGRAPHIC EQPT/SPLYS, WHOL: Cameras/Projectors/Eqpt/Splys
PHOTOGRAPHIC LIBRARY SVCS
PHOTOGRAPHIC PEOCESSING CHEMICALS
PHOTOGRAPHIC PROCESSING EQPT & CHEMICALS
PHOTOGRAPHIC SENSITIZED GOODS, NEC
PHOTOGRAPHIC SVCS
PHOTOGRAPHY SVCS: Commercial
PHOTOGRAPHY SVCS: Portrait Studios
PHOTOGRAPHY SVCS: Still Or Video
PHOTOTYPESETTING SVC
PHOTOVOLTAIC Solid State
PHYSICAL FITNESS CENTERS
PHYSICIANS' OFFICES & CLINICS: Medical doctors

PICTURE FRAMES: Metal
PICTURE FRAMES: Wood
PICTURE FRAMING SVCS, CUSTOM
PICTURE PROJECTION EQPT
PIECE GOODS & NOTIONS WHOLESALERS
PIECE GOODS, NOTIONS & DRY GOODS, WHOL: Textile Converters
PIECE GOODS, NOTIONS & DRY GOODS, WHOL: Textiles, Woven
PIECE GOODS, NOTIONS & DRY GOODS, WHOLESALE: Fabrics, Knit
PIECE GOODS, NOTIONS & DRY GOODS, WHOLESALE: Fabrics, Lace
PIECE GOODS, NOTIONS & DRY GOODS, WHOLESALE: Sewing Access
PIECE GOODS, NOTIONS & OTHER DRY GOODS, WHOLESALE: Bridal
PIECE GOODS, NOTIONS & OTHER DRY GOODS, WHOLESALE: Buttons
PIECE GOODS, NOTIONS & OTHER DRY GOODS, WHOLESALE: Fabrics
PIECE GOODS, NOTIONS & OTHER DRY GOODS, WHOLESALE: Woven
PIECE GOODS, NOTIONS/DRY GOODS, WHOL: Drapery Mtrl, Woven
PIECE GOODS, NOTIONS/DRY GOODS, WHOL: Linen Piece, Woven
PIECE GOODS, NOTIONS/DRY GOODS, WHOL: Sewing Splys/Notions
PILLOW FILLING MTRLS: Curled Hair, Cotton Waste, Moss
PILLOWS: Sponge Rubber
PINS
PIPE & FITTING: Fabrication
PIPE & FITTINGS: Cast Iron
PIPE & FITTINGS: Pressure, Cast Iron
PIPE CLEANERS
PIPE JOINT COMPOUNDS
PIPE: Concrete
PIPE: Extruded, Aluminum
PIPE: Plastic
PIPE: Sheet Metal
PIPES & TUBES: Steel
PIPES & TUBES: Welded
PIPES: Steel & Iron
PIPES: Tobacco
PISTONS & PISTON RINGS
PLACEMATS: Plastic Or Textile
PLANING MILLS: Independent, Exc Millwork
PLANING MILLS: Millwork
PLANT CARE SVCS
PLAQUES: Clay, Plaster/Papier-Mache, Factory Production
PLAQUES: Picture, Laminated
PLASMAS
PLASTER WORK: Ornamental & Architectural
PLASTIC COLORING & FINISHING
PLASTIC PRDTS
PLASTIC PRDTS REPAIR SVCS
PLASTICIZERS, ORGANIC: Cyclic & Acyclic
PLASTICS FILM & SHEET
PLASTICS FILM & SHEET: Polyethylene
PLASTICS FILM & SHEET: Polyvinyl
PLASTICS FILM & SHEET: Vinyl
PLASTICS FINISHED PRDTS: Laminated
PLASTICS MATERIAL & RESINS
PLASTICS MATERIALS, BASIC FORMS & SHAPES WHOLESALERS
PLASTICS PROCESSING
PLASTICS SHEET: Packing Materials
PLASTICS: Blow Molded
PLASTICS: Cast
PLASTICS: Extruded
PLASTICS: Finished Injection Molded
PLASTICS: Injection Molded
PLASTICS: Molded
PLASTICS: Polystyrene Foam
PLASTICS: Thermoformed
PLATE WORK: Metalworking Trade
PLATEMAKING SVC: Color Separations, For The Printing Trade
PLATEMAKING SVC: Embossing, For The Printing Trade
PLATEMAKING SVC: Gravure, Plates Or Cylinders
PLATES
PLATES: Paper, Made From Purchased Materials
PLATES: Plastic Exc Polystyrene Foam
PLATING & FINISHING SVC: Decorative, Formed Prdts

PRODUCT INDEX

PLATING & POLISHING SVC
PLATING SVC: Chromium, Metals Or Formed Prdts
PLATING SVC: Electro
PLATING SVC: Gold
PLATING SVC: NEC
PLAYGROUND EQPT
PLEATING & STITCHING FOR THE TRADE: Decorative & Novelty
PLEATING & STITCHING FOR TRADE: Permanent Pleating/Pressing
PLEATING & STITCHING SVC
PLEATING & TUCKING FOR THE TRADE
PLUGS: Electric
PLUMBING & HEATING EQPT & SPLY, WHOL: Htg Eqpt/Panels, Solar
PLUMBING & HEATING EQPT & SPLY, WHOLESALE: Hydronic Htg Eqpt
PLUMBING & HEATING EQPT & SPLYS WHOLESALERS
PLUMBING & HEATING EQPT & SPLYS, WHOL: Plumbing Fitting/Sply
PLUMBING & HEATING EQPT & SPLYS, WHOL: Plumbng/Heatng Valves
PLUMBING & HEATING EQPT & SPLYS, WHOL: Water Purif Eqpt
PLUMBING & HEATING EQPT & SPLYS, WHOLESALE: Brass/Fittings
PLUMBING & HEATING EQPT & SPLYS, WHOLESALE: Sanitary Ware
PLUMBING FIXTURES
PLUMBING FIXTURES: Brass, Incl Drain Cocks, Faucets/Spigots
PLUMBING FIXTURES: Plastic
POINT OF SALE DEVICES
POLISHING SVC: Metals Or Formed Prdts
POLYESTERS
POLYETHYLENE RESINS
POLYPROPYLENE RESINS
POLYTETRAFLUOROETHYLENE RESINS
POLYVINYL CHLORIDE RESINS
POPCORN & SUPPLIES WHOLESALERS
PORCELAIN ENAMELED PRDTS & UTENSILS
POSTERS
POTTERY: Laboratory & Indl
POULTRY & POULTRY PRDTS WHOLESALERS
POULTRY & SMALL GAME SLAUGHTERING & PROCESSING
POULTRY SLAUGHTERING & PROCESSING
POWDER PUFFS & MITTS
POWDER: Metal
POWDER: Silver
POWER GENERATORS
POWER SPLY CONVERTERS: Static, Electronic Applications
POWER SUPPLIES: All Types, Static
POWER SUPPLIES: Transformer, Electronic Type
POWER SWITCHING EQPT
POWER TOOLS, HAND: Grinders, Portable, Electric Or Pneumatic
POWER TOOLS, HAND: Hammers, Portable, Elec/Pneumatic, Chip
POWER TRANSMISSION EQPT WHOLESALERS
POWER TRANSMISSION EQPT: Aircraft
POWER TRANSMISSION EQPT: Mechanical
PRECAST TERRAZZO OR CONCRETE PRDTS
PRECIOUS METALS
PRECIOUS METALS WHOLESALERS
PRECIOUS STONES & METALS, WHOLESALE
PRECIOUS STONES WHOLESALERS
PRECIPITATORS: Electrostatic
PRERECORDED TAPE, CD & RECORD STORES: Video Discs/Tapes
PRERECORDED TAPE, CD/RECORD STORES: Video Tapes, Prerecorded
PRERECORDED TAPE, COMPACT DISC & RECORD STORES
PRERECORDED TAPE, COMPACT DISC & RECORD STORES: Records
PRESSED FIBER & MOLDED PULP PRDTS, EXC FOOD PRDTS
PRESSES
PRIMARY METAL PRODUCTS
PRINT CARTRIDGES: Laser & Other Computer Printers
PRINTED CIRCUIT BOARDS
PRINTERS & PLOTTERS
PRINTERS' SVCS: Folding, Collating, Etc
PRINTERS: Computer
PRINTERS: Magnetic Ink, Bar Code
PRINTING & BINDING: Book Music
PRINTING & BINDING: Books
PRINTING & BINDING: Pamphlets
PRINTING & EMBOSSING: Plastic Fabric Articles
PRINTING & ENGRAVING: Card, Exc Greeting
PRINTING & ENGRAVING: Financial Notes & Certificates
PRINTING & ENGRAVING: Invitation & Stationery
PRINTING & ENGRAVING: Plateless
PRINTING & ENGRAVING: Poster & Decal
PRINTING & STAMPING: Fabric Articles
PRINTING & WRITING PAPER WHOLESALERS
PRINTING EQPT & SUPPLIES: Illustration & Poster Woodcuts
PRINTING INKS WHOLESALERS
PRINTING MACHINERY
PRINTING MACHINERY, EQPT & SPLYS: Wholesalers
PRINTING TRADES MACHINERY & EQPT REPAIR SVCS
PRINTING, COMMERCIAL Newspapers, NEC
PRINTING, COMMERCIAL: Announcements, NEC
PRINTING, COMMERCIAL: Bags, Plastic, NEC
PRINTING, COMMERCIAL: Business Forms, NEC
PRINTING, COMMERCIAL: Calendars, NEC
PRINTING, COMMERCIAL: Cards, Visiting, Incl Business, NEC
PRINTING, COMMERCIAL: Circulars, NEC
PRINTING, COMMERCIAL: Coupons, NEC
PRINTING, COMMERCIAL: Decals, NEC
PRINTING, COMMERCIAL: Envelopes, NEC
PRINTING, COMMERCIAL: Imprinting
PRINTING, COMMERCIAL: Invitations, NEC
PRINTING, COMMERCIAL: Labels & Seals, NEC
PRINTING, COMMERCIAL: Letterpress & Screen
PRINTING, COMMERCIAL: Literature, Advertising, NEC
PRINTING, COMMERCIAL: Magazines, NEC
PRINTING, COMMERCIAL: Periodicals, NEC
PRINTING, COMMERCIAL: Post Cards, Picture, NEC
PRINTING, COMMERCIAL: Promotional
PRINTING, COMMERCIAL: Publications
PRINTING, COMMERCIAL: Screen
PRINTING, COMMERCIAL: Stamps, Trading, NEC
PRINTING, COMMERCIAL: Stationery, NEC
PRINTING, COMMERCIAL: Tags, NEC
PRINTING, LITHOGRAPHIC: Advertising Posters
PRINTING, LITHOGRAPHIC: Calendars
PRINTING, LITHOGRAPHIC: Color
PRINTING, LITHOGRAPHIC: Decals
PRINTING, LITHOGRAPHIC: Fashion Plates
PRINTING, LITHOGRAPHIC: Forms & Cards, Business
PRINTING, LITHOGRAPHIC: Forms, Business
PRINTING, LITHOGRAPHIC: Letters, Circular Or Form
PRINTING, LITHOGRAPHIC: Menus
PRINTING, LITHOGRAPHIC: Offset & photolithographic printing
PRINTING, LITHOGRAPHIC: On Metal
PRINTING, LITHOGRAPHIC: Periodicals
PRINTING, LITHOGRAPHIC: Post Cards, Picture
PRINTING, LITHOGRAPHIC: Promotional
PRINTING, LITHOGRAPHIC: Publications
PRINTING, LITHOGRAPHIC: Tags
PRINTING, LITHOGRAPHIC: Tickets
PRINTING, LITHOGRAPHIC: Transfers, Decalcomania Or Dry
PRINTING: Books
PRINTING: Books
PRINTING: Broadwoven Fabrics. Cotton
PRINTING: Checkbooks
PRINTING: Commercial, NEC
PRINTING: Engraving & Plate
PRINTING: Flexographic
PRINTING: Gravure, Business Form & Card
PRINTING: Gravure, Color
PRINTING: Gravure, Forms, Business
PRINTING: Gravure, Imprinting
PRINTING: Gravure, Job
PRINTING: Gravure, Labels
PRINTING: Gravure, Promotional
PRINTING: Gravure, Rotogravure
PRINTING: Gravure, Stamps, Trading
PRINTING: Gravure, Stationery
PRINTING: Laser
PRINTING: Letterpress
PRINTING: Lithographic
PRINTING: Offset
PRINTING: Pamphlets
PRINTING: Photo-Offset
PRINTING: Photogravure
PRINTING: Photolithographic
PRINTING: Rotary Photogravure
PRINTING: Rotogravure
PRINTING: Screen, Broadwoven Fabrics, Cotton
PRINTING: Screen, Fabric
PRINTING: Screen, Manmade Fiber & Silk, Broadwoven Fabric
PRINTING: Thermography
PROFESSIONAL EQPT & SPLYS, WHOLESALE: Analytical Instruments
PROFESSIONAL EQPT & SPLYS, WHOLESALE: Engineers', NEC
PROFESSIONAL EQPT & SPLYS, WHOLESALE: Optical Goods
PROFESSIONAL EQPT & SPLYS, WHOLESALE: Scientific & Engineerg
PROFESSIONAL EQPT & SPLYS, WHOLESALE: Theatrical
PROFILE SHAPES: Unsupported Plastics
PROGRAM ADMIN, GOVT: Air, Water & Solid Waste Mgmt, Local
PROMOTION SVCS
PROPERTY DAMAGE INSURANCE
PROTECTION EQPT: Lightning
PUBLIC RELATIONS & PUBLICITY SVCS
PUBLISHERS: Art Copy
PUBLISHERS: Art Copy & Poster
PUBLISHERS: Book
PUBLISHERS: Book Clubs, No Printing
PUBLISHERS: Books, No Printing
PUBLISHERS: Catalogs
PUBLISHERS: Comic Books, No Printing
PUBLISHERS: Directories, NEC
PUBLISHERS: Directories, Telephone
PUBLISHERS: Guides
PUBLISHERS: Magazines, No Printing
PUBLISHERS: Maps
PUBLISHERS: Miscellaneous
PUBLISHERS: Music Book
PUBLISHERS: Music Book & Sheet Music
PUBLISHERS: Music, Book
PUBLISHERS: Music, Sheet
PUBLISHERS: Newsletter
PUBLISHERS: Newspaper
PUBLISHERS: Newspapers, No Printing
PUBLISHERS: Pamphlets, No Printing
PUBLISHERS: Periodical, With Printing
PUBLISHERS: Periodicals, Magazines
PUBLISHERS: Periodicals, No Printing
PUBLISHERS: Posters
PUBLISHERS: Racing Forms & Programs
PUBLISHERS: Sheet Music
PUBLISHERS: Shopping News
PUBLISHERS: Technical Manuals
PUBLISHERS: Technical Manuals & Papers
PUBLISHERS: Technical Papers
PUBLISHERS: Telephone & Other Directory
PUBLISHERS: Textbooks, No Printing
PUBLISHERS: Trade journals, No Printing
PUBLISHING & BROADCASTING: Internet Only
PUBLISHING & PRINTING: Art Copy
PUBLISHING & PRINTING: Book Clubs
PUBLISHING & PRINTING: Book Music
PUBLISHING & PRINTING: Books
PUBLISHING & PRINTING: Catalogs
PUBLISHING & PRINTING: Comic Books
PUBLISHING & PRINTING: Directories, NEC
PUBLISHING & PRINTING: Guides
PUBLISHING & PRINTING: Magazines: publishing & printing
PUBLISHING & PRINTING: Music, Book
PUBLISHING & PRINTING: Newsletters, Business Svc
PUBLISHING & PRINTING: Newspapers
PUBLISHING & PRINTING: Pamphlets
PUBLISHING & PRINTING: Patterns, Paper
PUBLISHING & PRINTING: Periodical Statistical Reports
PUBLISHING & PRINTING: Posters
PUBLISHING & PRINTING: Shopping News
PUBLISHING & PRINTING: Technical Manuals
PUBLISHING & PRINTING: Textbooks
PUBLISHING & PRINTING: Trade Journals
PUBLISHING & PRINTING: Yearbooks
PULP MILLS
PULP MILLS: Mech Pulp, Incl Groundwood & Thermomechanical
PULP MILLS: Mechanical & Recycling Processing

PRODUCT INDEX

PULP MILLS: Soda Pulp
PUMICE
PUMP GOVERNORS: Gas Machines
PUMPS
PUMPS & PARTS: Indl
PUMPS & PUMPING EQPT REPAIR SVCS
PUMPS & PUMPING EQPT WHOLESALERS
PUMPS, HEAT: Electric
PUMPS: Domestic, Water Or Sump
PUMPS: Fluid Power
PUMPS: Measuring & Dispensing
PUMPS: Vacuum, Exc Laboratory
PUNCHES: Forming & Stamping
PURIFICATION & DUST COLLECTION EQPT
PURSES: Women's
PUSHCARTS & WHEELBARROWS

Q

QUICKLIME

R

RACE TRACK OPERATION
RACEWAYS
RACKS & SHELVING: Household, Wood
RACKS: Display
RACKS: Garment, Exc Wood
RACKS: Garment, Wood
RACKS: Pallet, Exc Wood
RADAR SYSTEMS & EQPT
RADIATORS, EXC ELECTRIC
RADIO & TELEVISION COMMUNICATIONS EQUIPMENT
RADIO & TELEVISION REPAIR
RADIO BROADCASTING & COMMUNICATIONS EQPT
RADIO BROADCASTING STATIONS
RADIO COMMUNICATIONS: Airborne Eqpt
RADIO RECEIVER NETWORKS
RADIO, TELEVISION & CONSUMER ELECTRONICS STORES: Eqpt, NEC
RADIO, TV & CONSUMER ELECTRONICS: VCR & Access
RADIO, TV/CONSUMER ELEC STORES: Antennas, Satellite Dish
RAILINGS: Prefabricated, Metal
RAILINGS: Wood
RAILROAD CAR RENTING & LEASING SVCS
RAILROAD CAR REPAIR SVCS
RAILROAD CARGO LOADING & UNLOADING SVCS
RAILROAD EQPT
RAILROAD EQPT & SPLYS WHOLESALERS
RAILROAD EQPT, EXC LOCOMOTIVES
RAILROAD EQPT: Brakes, Air & Vacuum
RAILROAD EQPT: Cars & Eqpt, Dining
RAILROAD EQPT: Cars & Eqpt, Rapid Transit
RAILROAD EQPT: Cars & Eqpt, Train, Freight Or Passenger
RAILROAD EQPT: Cars, Maintenance
RAILROAD EQPT: Locomotives & Parts, Indl
RAILROAD EQPT: Lubrication Systems, Locomotive
RAILROAD RELATED EQPT: Railway Track
RAILS: Steel Or Iron
RAMPS: Prefabricated Metal
RAZORS, RAZOR BLADES
RAZORS: Electric
REAL ESTATE AGENCIES & BROKERS
REAL ESTATE OPERATORS, EXC DEVELOPERS: Apartment Hotel
REAL ESTATE OPERATORS, EXC DEVELOPERS: Commercial/Indl Bldg
RECLAIMED RUBBER: Reworked By Manufacturing Process
RECORD BLANKS: Phonographic
RECORDERS: Sound
RECORDING HEADS: Speech & Musical Eqpt
RECORDING TAPE: Video, Blank
RECORDS & TAPES: Prerecorded
RECORDS OR TAPES: Masters
RECOVERY SVCS: Metal
RECREATIONAL & SPORTING CAMPS
RECTIFIERS: Electrical Apparatus
RECTIFIERS: Solid State
RECYCLABLE SCRAP & WASTE MATERIALS WHOLESALERS
RECYCLING: Paper
REELS: Cable, Metal
REFINERS & SMELTERS: Aluminum
REFINERS & SMELTERS: Antimony, Primary
REFINERS & SMELTERS: Cobalt, Primary
REFINERS & SMELTERS: Copper

REFINERS & SMELTERS: Copper, Secondary
REFINERS & SMELTERS: Germanium, Primary
REFINERS & SMELTERS: Gold
REFINERS & SMELTERS: Lead, Secondary
REFINERS & SMELTERS: Nonferrous Metal
REFINERS & SMELTERS: Platinum Group Metal Refining, Primary
REFINERS & SMELTERS: Silicon, Primary, Over 99% Pure
REFINERS & SMELTERS: Silver
REFINERS & SMELTERS: Zinc, Primary, Including Slabs & Dust
REFINING LUBRICATING OILS & GREASES, NEC
REFINING: Petroleum
REFRACTORIES: Alumina Fused
REFRACTORIES: Brick
REFRACTORIES: Brick
REFRACTORIES: Clay
REFRACTORIES: Graphite, Carbon Or Ceramic Bond
REFRACTORIES: Nonclay
REFRACTORIES: Plastic
REFRACTORY CASTABLES
REFRACTORY MATERIALS WHOLESALERS
REFRIGERATION & HEATING EQUIPMENT
REFRIGERATION EQPT & SPLYS WHOLESALERS
REFRIGERATION EQPT: Complete
REFRIGERATION REPAIR SVCS
REFRIGERATION SVC & REPAIR
REFRIGERATORS & FREEZERS WHOLESALERS
REFUSE SYSTEMS
REGULATORS: Generator Voltage
REGULATORS: Power
REGULATORS: Transmission & Distribution Voltage
REGULATORS: Transmission & Distribution Voltage
RELAYS & SWITCHES: Indl, Electric
RELAYS: Electronic Usage
RELIGIOUS SPLYS WHOLESALERS
REMOVERS & CLEANERS
REMOVERS: Paint
RENTAL CENTERS: General
RENTAL SVCS: Business Machine & Electronic Eqpt
RENTAL SVCS: Costume
RENTAL SVCS: Electronic Eqpt, Exc Computers
RENTAL SVCS: Eqpt, Theatrical
RENTAL SVCS: Invalid Splys
RENTAL SVCS: Live Plant
RENTAL SVCS: Pallet
RENTAL SVCS: Tent & Tarpaulin
RENTAL: Video Tape & Disc
REPEATERS: Passive
REPRODUCTION SVCS: Video Tape Or Disk
RESEARCH, DEV & TESTING SVCS, COMM: Chem Lab, Exc Testing
RESEARCH, DEVELOPMENT & TEST SVCS, COMM: Business Analysis
RESEARCH, DEVELOPMENT & TEST SVCS, COMM: Cmptr Hardware Dev
RESEARCH, DEVELOPMENT & TEST SVCS, COMM: Research, Exc Lab
RESEARCH, DEVELOPMENT & TESTING SVCS, COMM: Research Lab
RESEARCH, DEVELOPMENT & TESTING SVCS, COMMERCIAL: Medical
RESEARCH, DEVELOPMENT & TESTING SVCS, COMMERCIAL: Opinion
RESEARCH, DVLPMT & TESTING SVCS, COMM: Merger, Acq & Reorg
RESEARCH, DVLPT & TEST SVCS, COMM: Mkt Analysis or Research
RESIDENTIAL REMODELERS
RESINS: Custom Compound Purchased
RESISTORS
RESISTORS & RESISTOR UNITS
RESORT HOTELS
RESPIRATORS
RESTAURANT EQPT REPAIR SVCS
RESTAURANT EQPT: Carts
RESTAURANT EQPT: Food Wagons
RESTAURANT EQPT: Sheet Metal
RESTAURANTS:Full Svc, American
RESTAURANTS:Full Svc, Mexican
RESTAURANTS:Full Svc, Seafood
RESTAURANTS:Limited Svc, Coffee Shop
RESTAURANTS:Limited Svc, Ice Cream Stands Or Dairy Bars
RESTAURANTS:Limited Svc, Lunch Counter

RESTAURANTS:Ltd Svc, Ice Cream, Soft Drink/Fountain Stands
RESUME WRITING SVCS
RETAIL BAKERY: Bagels
RETAIL BAKERY: Bread
RETAIL LUMBER YARDS
RETAIL STORES, NEC
RETAIL STORES: Alarm Signal Systems
RETAIL STORES: Alcoholic Beverage Making Eqpt & Splys
RETAIL STORES: Aquarium Splys
RETAIL STORES: Artificial Limbs
RETAIL STORES: Audio-Visual Eqpt & Splys
RETAIL STORES: Awnings
RETAIL STORES: Cake Decorating Splys
RETAIL STORES: Canvas Prdts
RETAIL STORES: Cleaning Eqpt & Splys
RETAIL STORES: Concrete Prdts, Precast
RETAIL STORES: Cosmetics
RETAIL STORES: Electronic Parts & Eqpt
RETAIL STORES: Engine & Motor Eqpt & Splys
RETAIL STORES: Farm Eqpt & Splys
RETAIL STORES: Fiberglass Materials, Exc Insulation
RETAIL STORES: Fire Extinguishers
RETAIL STORES: Gravestones, Finished
RETAIL STORES: Hearing Aids
RETAIL STORES: Ice
RETAIL STORES: Infant Furnishings & Eqpt
RETAIL STORES: Medical Apparatus & Splys
RETAIL STORES: Mobile Telephones & Eqpt
RETAIL STORES: Monuments, Finished To Custom Order
RETAIL STORES: Motors, Electric
RETAIL STORES: Orthopedic & Prosthesis Applications
RETAIL STORES: Pet Food
RETAIL STORES: Photocopy Machines
RETAIL STORES: Religious Goods
RETAIL STORES: Stones, Crystalline, Rough
RETAIL STORES: Telephone Eqpt & Systems
RETAIL STORES: Tents
RETAIL STORES: Water Purification Eqpt
RETAIL STORES: Welding Splys
REUPHOLSTERY & FURNITURE REPAIR
REUPHOLSTERY SVCS
RIBBONS & BOWS
RIBBONS, NEC
RIBBONS: Machine, Inked Or Carbon
RIDING APPAREL STORES
RIVETS: Metal
ROAD MATERIALS: Bituminous, Not From Refineries
ROBOTS: Assembly Line
ROCK SALT MINING
ROCKET LAUNCHERS
ROCKETS: Space & Military
RODS: Extruded, Aluminum
RODS: Plastic
RODS: Steel & Iron, Made In Steel Mills
RODS: Welding
ROLL COVERINGS: Rubber
ROLL FORMED SHAPES: Custom
ROLLED OR DRAWN SHAPES, NEC: Copper & Copper Alloy
ROLLERS & FITTINGS: Window Shade
ROLLING MILL MACHINERY
ROLLS & BLANKETS, PRINTERS': Rubber Or Rubberized Fabric
ROLLS: Rubber, Solid Or Covered
ROOFING MATERIALS: Asphalt
ROOFING MATERIALS: Sheet Metal
ROPE
ROTORS: Motor
RUBBER
RUBBER PRDTS: Automotive, Mechanical
RUBBER PRDTS: Mechanical
RUBBER PRDTS: Medical & Surgical Tubing, Extrudd & Lathe-Cut
RUBBER PRDTS: Oil & Gas Field Machinery, Mechanical
RUBBER PRDTS: Reclaimed
RUBBER PRDTS: Silicone
RUBBER PRDTS: Sponge
RUBBER PRDTS: Wet Suits
RUBBER STRUCTURES: Air-Supported
RUGS : Hand & Machine Made
RULERS: Metal

S

SAFES & VAULTS: Metal
SAFETY EQPT & SPLYS WHOLESALERS

PRODUCT INDEX

SAILBOAT BUILDING & REPAIR
SAILS
SALES PROMOTION SVCS
SALT
SALT & SULFUR MINING
SAMPLE BOOKS
SAND & GRAVEL
SAND MINING
SAND: Hygrade
SANDSTONE: Crushed & Broken
SANITARY SVCS: Environmental Cleanup
SANITARY SVCS: Waste Materials, Recycling
SANITARY WARE: Metal
SANITATION CHEMICALS & CLEANING AGENTS
SASHES: Door Or Window, Metal
SATCHELS
SATELLITES: Communications
SAW BLADES
SAWDUST & SHAVINGS
SAWDUST, WHOLESALE
SAWING & PLANING MILLS
SAWING & PLANING MILLS: Custom
SAWMILL MACHINES
SAWS & SAWING EQPT
SCAFFOLDS: Mobile Or Stationary, Metal
SCALES & BALANCES, EXC LABORATORY
SCALES: Baby
SCALP TREATMENT SVCS
SCANNING DEVICES: Optical
SCISSORS: Hand
SCRAP & WASTE MATERIALS, WHOLESALE: Ferrous Metal
SCRAP & WASTE MATERIALS, WHOLESALE: Metal
SCRAP & WASTE MATERIALS, WHOLESALE: Plastics Scrap
SCRAP & WASTE MATERIALS, WHOLESALE: Rags
SCREENS: Projection
SCREENS: Window, Metal
SCREENS: Woven Wire
SCREW MACHINE PRDTS
SCREW MACHINES
SCREWS: Metal
SEALANTS
SEARCH & DETECTION SYSTEMS, EXC RADAR
SEARCH & NAVIGATION SYSTEMS
SEAT BELTS: Automobile & Aircraft
SEATING: Bleacher, Portable
SEATING: Chairs, Table & Arm
SECRETARIAL SVCS
SECURITY CONTROL EQPT & SYSTEMS
SECURITY DEVICES
SECURITY EQPT STORES
SECURITY PROTECTIVE DEVICES MAINTENANCE & MONITORING SVCS
SECURITY SYSTEMS SERVICES
SEMICONDUCTOR & RELATED DEVICES: Read-Only Memory Or ROM
SEMICONDUCTOR CIRCUIT NETWORKS
SEMICONDUCTOR DEVICES: Wafers
SEMICONDUCTORS & RELATED DEVICES
SENSORS: Temperature For Motor Windings
SENSORS: Temperature, Exc Indl Process
SEPARATORS: Metal Plate
SEPTIC TANKS: Concrete
SEPTIC TANKS: Plastic
SERVICES, NEC
SERVOMOTORS: Electric
SEWAGE & WATER TREATMENT EQPT
SEWAGE TREATMENT SYSTEMS & EQPT
SEWER CLEANING EQPT: Power
SEWING CONTRACTORS
SEWING MACHINES & PARTS: Indl
SEWING, NEEDLEWORK & PIECE GOODS STORE: Needlework Gds/Sply
SEWING, NEEDLEWORK & PIECE GOODS STORES: Sewing & Needlework
SHADES: Lamp & Light, Residential
SHADES: Lamp Or Candle
SHADES: Window
SHALE MINING, COMMON
SHALE: Expanded
SHAPES & PILINGS, STRUCTURAL: Steel
SHEATHING: Paper
SHEET METAL SPECIALTIES, EXC STAMPED
SHEET MUSIC STORES
SHEET MUSIC, WHOLESALE

SHEETING: Laminated Plastic
SHEETS & STRIPS: Aluminum
SHEETS: Fabric, From Purchased Materials
SHELVES & SHELVING: Wood
SHELVING: Office & Store, Exc Wood
SHERARDIZING SVC: Metals Or Metal Prdts
SHIELDS OR ENCLOSURES: Radiator, Sheet Metal
SHIMS: Metal
SHIP BLDG & RPRG: Drilling & Production Platforms, Oil/Gas
SHIP BUILDING & REPAIRING: Cargo Vessels
SHIP BUILDING & REPAIRING: Cargo, Commercial
SHIP BUILDING & REPAIRING: Ferryboats
SHIP BUILDING & REPAIRING: Lighthouse Tenders
SHIP BUILDING & REPAIRING: Offshore Sply Boats
SHIP BUILDING & REPAIRING: Rigging, Marine
SHIP BUILDING & REPAIRING: Tankers
SHIPBUILDING & REPAIR
SHIPPING AGENTS
SHOCK ABSORBERS: Indl
SHOE & BOOT ACCESS
SHOE MATERIALS: Counters
SHOE MATERIALS: Plastic
SHOE MATERIALS: Quarters
SHOE MATERIALS: Sole Parts
SHOE MATERIALS: Uppers
SHOE REPAIR SHOP
SHOE STORES
SHOE STORES: Children's
SHOE STORES: Custom
SHOE STORES: Orthopedic
SHOE STORES: Women's
SHOES & BOOTS WHOLESALERS
SHOES: Athletic, Exc Rubber Or Plastic
SHOES: Ballet Slippers
SHOES: Canvas, Rubber Soled
SHOES: Infants' & Children's
SHOES: Men's
SHOES: Men's, Sandals
SHOES: Orthopedic, Men's
SHOES: Orthopedic, Women's
SHOES: Plastic Or Rubber
SHOES: Plastic Or Rubber Soles With Fabric Uppers
SHOES: Rubber Or Rubber Soled Fabric Uppers
SHOES: Women's
SHOES: Women's, Dress
SHOES: Women's, Sandals
SHOPPING CENTERS & MALLS
SHOT PEENING SVC
SHOWCASES & DISPLAY FIXTURES: Office & Store
SHOWER STALLS: Metal
SHOWER STALLS: Plastic & Fiberglass
SHREDDERS: Indl & Commercial
SIDING & STRUCTURAL MATERIALS: Wood
SIDING MATERIALS
SIGN LETTERING & PAINTING SVCS
SIGN PAINTING & LETTERING SHOP
SIGNALING APPARATUS: Electric
SIGNALING DEVICES: Sound, Electrical
SIGNALS: Railroad, Electric
SIGNALS: Traffic Control, Electric
SIGNALS: Transportation
SIGNS & ADVERTISING SPECIALTIES
SIGNS & ADVERTISING SPECIALTIES: Artwork, Advertising
SIGNS & ADVERTISING SPECIALTIES: Displays, Paint Process
SIGNS & ADVERTISING SPECIALTIES: Letters For Signs, Metal
SIGNS & ADVERTISING SPECIALTIES: Novelties
SIGNS & ADVERTISING SPECIALTIES: Scoreboards, Electric
SIGNS & ADVERTSICAL SPECIALTIES: Signs
SIGNS & ADVERTSG SPECIALTIES: Displays/Cutouts Window/Lobby
SIGNS, EXC ELECTRIC, WHOLESALE
SIGNS: Electrical
SIGNS: Neon
SILICA MINING
SILICON & CHROMIUM
SILICON WAFERS: Chemically Doped
SILICONE RESINS
SILICONES
SILK SCREEN DESIGN SVCS
SILVER ORES
SILVER ORES PROCESSING
SILVERSMITHS

SILVERWARE
SILVERWARE & PLATED WARE
SILVERWARE, SILVER PLATED
SIMULATORS: Flight
SINKS: Vitreous China
SKIN CARE PRDTS: Suntan Lotions & Oils
SKYLIGHTS
SLAB & TILE: Precast Concrete, Floor
SLABS: Steel
SLATE PRDTS
SLATE: Dimension
SLINGS: Rope
SLIP RINGS
SLIPPERS: House
SMOKE DETECTORS
SNOW PLOWING SVCS
SOAPS & DETERGENTS
SOAPS & DETERGENTS: Textile
SOCIAL SERVICES INFORMATION EXCHANGE
SOCIAL SVCS, HANDICAPPED
SOCIAL SVCS: Individual & Family
SOFT DRINKS WHOLESALERS
SOFTWARE PUBLISHERS: Application
SOFTWARE PUBLISHERS: Business & Professional
SOFTWARE PUBLISHERS: Computer Utilities
SOFTWARE PUBLISHERS: Education
SOFTWARE PUBLISHERS: Home Entertainment
SOFTWARE PUBLISHERS: NEC
SOFTWARE PUBLISHERS: Operating Systems
SOFTWARE PUBLISHERS: Publisher's
SOFTWARE PUBLISHERS: Word Processing
SOFTWARE TRAINING, COMPUTER
SOLAR CELLS
SOLAR HEATING EQPT
SOLDERS
SOLID CONTAINING UNITS: Concrete
SOLVENTS
SONAR SYSTEMS & EQPT
SOUND EQPT: Electric
SOUND EQPT: Underwater
SOUND REPRODUCING EQPT
SPACE VEHICLE EQPT
SPACE VEHICLES
SPARK PLUGS: Internal Combustion Engines
SPAS
SPEAKER SYSTEMS
SPECIAL EVENTS DECORATION SVCS
SPECIALTY FOOD STORES: Coffee
SPECIALTY FOOD STORES: Health & Dietetic Food
SPECIALTY FOOD STORES: Juices, Fruit Or Vegetable
SPECIALTY FOOD STORES: Vitamin
SPERM BANK
SPONGES: Plastic
SPOOLS: Fiber, Made From Purchased Materials
SPOOLS: Indl
SPORTING & ATHLETIC GOODS: Bags, Golf
SPORTING & ATHLETIC GOODS: Bowling Alleys & Access
SPORTING & ATHLETIC GOODS: Bowling Pins
SPORTING & ATHLETIC GOODS: Bows, Archery
SPORTING & ATHLETIC GOODS: Boxing Eqpt & Splys, NEC
SPORTING & ATHLETIC GOODS: Camping Eqpt & Splys
SPORTING & ATHLETIC GOODS: Cartridge Belts
SPORTING & ATHLETIC GOODS: Driving Ranges, Golf, Electronic
SPORTING & ATHLETIC GOODS: Dumbbells & Other Weight Eqpt
SPORTING & ATHLETIC GOODS: Fishing Bait, Artificial
SPORTING & ATHLETIC GOODS: Fishing Eqpt
SPORTING & ATHLETIC GOODS: Fishing Tackle, General
SPORTING & ATHLETIC GOODS: Game Calls
SPORTING & ATHLETIC GOODS: Gymnasium Eqpt
SPORTING & ATHLETIC GOODS: Hockey Eqpt & Splys, NEC
SPORTING & ATHLETIC GOODS: Lacrosse Eqpt & Splys, NEC
SPORTING & ATHLETIC GOODS: Pools, Swimming, Exc Plastic
SPORTING & ATHLETIC GOODS: Pools, Swimming, Plastic
SPORTING & ATHLETIC GOODS: Shafts, Golf Club
SPORTING & ATHLETIC GOODS: Shooting Eqpt & Splys, General
SPORTING & ATHLETIC GOODS: Skateboards
SPORTING & ATHLETIC GOODS: Skates & Parts, Roller
SPORTING & ATHLETIC GOODS: Target Shooting Eqpt
SPORTING & ATHLETIC GOODS: Team Sports Eqpt
SPORTING & ATHLETIC GOODS: Tennis Eqpt & Splys

PRODUCT INDEX

SPORTING & REC GOODS, WHOLESALE: Camping Eqpt & Splys
SPORTING & RECREATIONAL GOODS & SPLYS WHOLESALERS
SPORTING & RECREATIONAL GOODS, WHOL: Sharpeners, Sporting
SPORTING & RECREATIONAL GOODS, WHOLESALE: Bicycle
SPORTING & RECREATIONAL GOODS, WHOLESALE: Boat Access & Part
SPORTING & RECREATIONAL GOODS, WHOLESALE: Fishing
SPORTING & RECREATIONAL GOODS, WHOLESALE: Fishing Tackle
SPORTING & RECREATIONAL GOODS, WHOLESALE: Fitness
SPORTING & RECREATIONAL GOODS, WHOLESALE: Hot Tubs
SPORTING & RECREATIONAL GOODS, WHOLESALE: Skiing
SPORTING & RECREATIONAL GOODS, WHOLESALE: Watersports
SPORTING GOODS
SPORTING GOODS STORES, NEC
SPORTING GOODS STORES: Camping Eqpt
SPORTING GOODS STORES: Fishing Eqpt
SPORTING GOODS STORES: Playground Eqpt
SPORTING GOODS STORES: Skateboarding Eqpt
SPORTING GOODS STORES: Tennis Goods & Eqpt
SPORTING GOODS: Archery
SPORTING GOODS: Fishing Nets
SPORTING GOODS: Sailboards
SPORTING GOODS: Skin Diving Eqpt
SPORTING GOODS: Surfboards
SPORTING/ATHLETIC GOODS: Gloves, Boxing, Handball, Etc
SPORTS APPAREL STORES
SPORTS PROMOTION SVCS
SPOUTING: Plastic & Fiberglass Reinforced
SPRAYING & DUSTING EQPT
SPRAYING EQPT: Agricultural
SPRAYS: Artificial & Preserved
SPRINGS: Coiled Flat
SPRINGS: Leaf, Automobile, Locomotive, Etc
SPRINGS: Mechanical, Precision
SPRINGS: Precision
SPRINGS: Sash Balances
SPRINGS: Steel
SPRINGS: Wire
SPRINKLING SYSTEMS: Fire Control
STAGE LIGHTING SYSTEMS
STAINLESS STEEL
STAIRCASES & STAIRS, WOOD
STAMPED ART GOODS FOR EMBROIDERING
STAMPING SVC: Book, Gold
STAMPINGS: Automotive
STAMPINGS: Metal
STANDS & RACKS: Engine, Metal
STARTERS: Motor
STATIC ELIMINATORS: Ind
STATIONARY & OFFICE SPLYS, WHOLESALE: Laser Printer Splys
STATIONARY & OFFICE SPLYS, WHOLESALE: Stationery
STATIONER'S SUNDRIES: Rubber
STATIONARY & OFFICE SPLYS WHOLESALERS
STATIONERY PRDTS
STATIONERY: Made From Purchased Materials
STATUARY & OTHER DECORATIVE PRDTS: Nonmetallic
STATUES: Nonmetal
STEAM SPLY SYSTEMS SVCS INCLUDING GEOTHERMAL
STEAM, HEAT & AIR CONDITIONING DISTRIBUTION SVC
STEEL & ALLOYS: Tool & Die
STEEL FABRICATORS
STEEL MILLS
STEEL, COLD-ROLLED: Sheet Or Strip, From Own Hot-Rolled
STEEL, COLD-ROLLED: Strip NEC, From Purchased Hot-Rolled
STEEL, HOT-ROLLED: Sheet Or Strip
STEEL: Cold-Rolled
STEEL: Galvanized
STEEL: Laminated
STENCILS
STONE: Cast Concrete
STONE: Crushed & Broken, NEC

STONE: Dimension, NEC
STONE: Quarrying & Processing, Own Stone Prdts
STONEWARE CLAY MINING
STORE FIXTURES, EXC REFRIGERATED: Wholesalers
STORE FIXTURES: Exc Wood
STORE FIXTURES: Wood
STORE FRONTS: Prefabricated, Metal
STORE FRONTS: Prefabricated, Wood
STRAPPING
STRAPS: Apparel Webbing
STRAPS: Bindings, Textile
STRAPS: Braids, Textile
STRAPS: Cotton Webbing
STRAWS: Drinking, Made From Purchased Materials
STRUCTURAL SUPPORT & BUILDING MATERIAL: Concrete
STUDIOS: Artist's
STUDIOS: Sculptor's
STUDS & JOISTS: Sheet Metal
SUBSCRIPTION FULFILLMENT SVCS: Magazine, Newspaper, Etc
SUGAR SUBSTITUTES: Organic
SUNDRIES & RELATED PRDTS: Medical & Laboratory, Rubber
SUNROOMS: Prefabricated Metal
SUPERMARKETS & OTHER GROCERY STORES
SURFACE ACTIVE AGENTS
SURFACE ACTIVE AGENTS: Oils & Greases
SURGICAL & MEDICAL INSTRUMENTS WHOLESALERS
SURGICAL APPLIANCES & SPLS
SURGICAL APPLIANCES & SPLYS
SURGICAL EQPT: See Also Instruments
SURGICAL IMPLANTS
SURVEYING SVCS: Aerial Digital Imaging
SVC ESTABLISHMENT EQPT & SPLYS WHOLESALERS
SVC ESTABLISHMENT EQPT, WHOL: Cleaning & Maint Eqpt & Splys
SVC ESTABLISHMENT EQPT, WHOLESALE: Beauty Parlor Eqpt & Sply
SVC ESTABLISHMENT EQPT, WHOLESALE: Firefighting Eqpt
SVC ESTABLISHMENT EQPT, WHOLESALE: Laundry Eqpt & Splys
SWEEPING COMPOUNDS
SWIMMING POOL ACCESS: Leaf Skimmers Or Pool Rakes
SWIMMING POOL EQPT: Filters & Water Conditioning Systems
SWIMMING POOL SPLY STORES
SWIMMING POOLS, EQPT & SPLYS: Wholesalers
SWITCHBOARDS & PARTS: Power
SWITCHES
SWITCHES: Electric Power
SWITCHES: Electric Power, Exc Snap, Push Button, Etc
SWITCHES: Electronic
SWITCHES: Electronic Applications
SWITCHES: Silicon Control
SWITCHES: Starting, Fluorescent
SWITCHES: Time, Electrical Switchgear Apparatus
SWITCHGEAR & SWITCHBOARD APPARATUS
SWITCHGEAR & SWITCHGEAR ACCESS, NEC
SWORDS
SYNTHETIC RESIN FINISHED PRDTS, NEC
SYRUPS, DRINK
SYRUPS, FLAVORING, EXC DRINK
SYSTEMS INTEGRATION SVCS
SYSTEMS INTEGRATION SVCS: Local Area Network
SYSTEMS SOFTWARE DEVELOPMENT SVCS

T

TABLE OR COUNTERTOPS, PLASTIC LAMINATED
TABLECLOTHS & SETTINGS
TABLES: Lift, Hydraulic
TABLETS & PADS: Book & Writing, Made From Purchased Material
TABLEWARE OR KITCHEN ARTICLES: Commercial, Fine Earthenware
TABLEWARE: Household & Commercial, Semivitreous
TABLEWARE: Plastic
TABLEWARE: Vitreous China
TAGS & LABELS: Paper
TAGS: Paper, Blank, Made From Purchased Paper
TAILORS: Custom
TALLOW: Animal
TANK REPAIR SVCS
TANKS & OTHER TRACKED VEHICLE CMPNTS
TANKS: Concrete

TANKS: Cryogenic, Metal
TANKS: Fuel, Including Oil & Gas, Metal Plate
TANKS: Lined, Metal
TANKS: Military, Including Factory Rebuilding
TANKS: Plastic & Fiberglass
TANKS: Standard Or Custom Fabricated, Metal Plate
TANKS: Storage, Farm, Metal Plate
TANKS: Water, Metal Plate
TANKS: Wood
TANNERIES: Leather
TAPE DRIVES
TAPES, ADHESIVE: Medical
TAPES: Audio Range, Blank
TAPES: Coated Fiberglass, Pipe Sealing Or Insulating
TAPES: Gummed, Cloth Or Paper Based, From Purchased Matls
TAPES: Magnetic
TAPES: Pressure Sensitive
TARGET DRONES
TELECOMMUNICATION SYSTEMS & EQPT
TELECOMMUNICATIONS CARRIERS & SVCS: Wired
TELEMARKETING BUREAUS
TELEMETERING EQPT
TELEPHONE ANSWERING SVCS
TELEPHONE BOOTHS, EXC WOOD
TELEPHONE EQPT INSTALLATION
TELEPHONE EQPT: Modems
TELEPHONE EQPT: NEC
TELEPHONE SVCS
TELEPHONE SWITCHING EQPT
TELEPHONE: Fiber Optic Systems
TELEPHONE: Headsets
TELEPHONE: Sets, Exc Cellular Radio
TELEVISION BROADCASTING & COMMUNICATIONS EQPT
TELEVISION BROADCASTING STATIONS
TELEVISION SETS
TELEVISION: Cameras
TELEVISION: Closed Circuit Eqpt
TEMPERING: Metal
TENT REPAIR SHOP
TENTS: All Materials
TERMINAL BOARDS
TERRA COTTA: Architectural
TEST KITS: Pregnancy
TESTERS: Battery
TESTERS: Environmental
TESTERS: Integrated Circuit
TESTERS: Physical Property
TESTERS: Water, Exc Indl Process
TEXTILE & APPAREL SVCS
TEXTILE BAGS WHOLESALERS
TEXTILE CONVERTERS: Knit Goods
TEXTILE FABRICATORS
TEXTILE FINISH: Chem Coat/Treat, Fire Resist, Manmade
TEXTILE FINISHING: Chemical Coating Or Treating
TEXTILE FINISHING: Chemical Coating Or Treating, Narrow
TEXTILE FINISHING: Dyeing, Broadwoven, Cotton
TEXTILE FINISHING: Dyeing, Finishing & Printng, Linen Fabric
TEXTILE FINISHING: Dyeing, Manmade Fiber & Silk, Broadwoven
TEXTILE FINISHING: Embossing, Cotton, Broadwoven
TEXTILE FINISHING: Embossing, Man Fiber & Silk, Broadwoven
TEXTILE FINISHING: Silk, Broadwoven
TEXTILE FINISHING: Sponging, Cotton, Broadwoven, Trade
TEXTILE PRDTS: Hand Woven & Crocheted
TEXTILE: Finishing, Cotton Broadwoven
TEXTILE: Finishing, Raw Stock NEC
TEXTILE: Goods, NEC
TEXTILES
TEXTILES: Bagging, Jute
TEXTILES: Fibers, Textile, Rcvrd From Mill Waste/Rags
TEXTILES: Flock
TEXTILES: Linen Fabrics
TEXTILES: Linings, Carpet, Exc Felt
TEXTILES: Mill Waste & Remnant
TEXTILES: Tops & Top Processing, Manmade Or Other Fiber
THEATRICAL LIGHTING SVCS
THEATRICAL PRODUCERS & SVCS
THEATRICAL SCENERY
THERMOMETERS: Indl
THERMOMETERS: Liquid-In-Glass & Bimetal
THERMOMETERS: Medical, Digital
THERMOPLASTIC MATERIALS

PRODUCT INDEX

THERMOPLASTICS
THERMOSETTING MATERIALS
THIN FILM CIRCUITS
THREAD: All Fibers
THREAD: Embroidery
TICKET OFFICES & AGENCIES: Theatrical
TIES, FORM: Metal
TILE: Asphalt, Floor
TILE: Brick & Structural, Clay
TILE: Drain, Clay
TILE: Fireproofing, Clay
TILE: Mosaic, Ceramic
TILE: Stamped Metal, Floor Or Wall
TILE: Terrazzo Or Concrete, Precast
TILE: Wall & Floor, Ceramic
TILE: Wall & Floor, clay
TIMBER PRDTS WHOLESALERS
TIMING DEVICES: Electronic
TIRE & INNER TUBE MATERIALS & RELATED PRDTS
TIRE CORD & FABRIC
TIRE INFLATORS: Hand Or Compressor Operated
TIRES & INNER TUBES
TIRES: Auto
TITANIUM MILL PRDTS
TOBACCO LEAF PROCESSING
TOBACCO: Chewing
TOBACCO: Chewing & Snuff
TOBACCO: Cigarettes
TOBACCO: Cigars
TOBACCO: Smoking
TOILET FIXTURES: Plastic
TOILET PREPARATIONS
TOILET SEATS: Wood
TOILETRIES, COSMETICS & PERFUME STORES
TOILETRIES, WHOLESALE: Hair Preparations
TOILETRIES, WHOLESALE: Perfumes
TOILETRIES, WHOLESALE: Toilet Preparations
TOILETRIES, WHOLESALE: Toiletries
TOMBSTONES: Terrazzo Or Concrete, Precast
TOOL & DIE STEEL
TOOLS: Carpenters', Including Levels & Chisels, Exc Saws
TOOLS: Hand
TOOLS: Hand, Engravers'
TOOLS: Hand, Jewelers'
TOOLS: Hand, Mechanics
TOOLS: Hand, Plumbers'
TOOLS: Hand, Power
TOOTHBRUSHES: Electric
TOOTHBRUSHES: Exc Electric
TOOTHPASTES, GELS & TOOTHPOWDERS
TOWELS: Indl
TOWELS: Linen & Linen & Cotton Mixtures
TOWERS, SECTIONS: Transmission, Radio & Television
TOYS
TOYS & HOBBY GOODS & SPLYS, WHOLESALE: Arts/Crafts Eqpt/Sply
TOYS & HOBBY GOODS & SPLYS, WHOLESALE: Balloons, Novelty
TOYS & HOBBY GOODS & SPLYS, WHOLESALE: Educational Toys
TOYS & HOBBY GOODS & SPLYS, WHOLESALE: Toys & Games
TOYS & HOBBY GOODS & SPLYS, WHOLESALE: Toys, NEC
TOYS & HOBBY GOODS & SPLYS, WHOLESALE: Video Games
TOYS, HOBBY GOODS & SPLYS WHOLESALERS
TOYS: Dolls, Stuffed Animals & Parts
TOYS: Electronic
TOYS: Video Game Machines
TRADE SHOW ARRANGEMENT SVCS
TRADERS: Commodity, Contracts
TRAILERS & PARTS: Boat
TRAILERS & PARTS: Truck & Semi's
TRAILERS & TRAILER EQPT
TRAILERS: Bus, Tractor Type
TRAILERS: Semitrailers, Truck Tractors
TRANSDUCERS: Electrical Properties
TRANSDUCERS: Pressure
TRANSFORMERS: Control
TRANSFORMERS: Distribution
TRANSFORMERS: Distribution, Electric
TRANSFORMERS: Electric
TRANSFORMERS: Electronic
TRANSFORMERS: Ignition, Domestic Fuel Burners

TRANSFORMERS: Power Related
TRANSFORMERS: Specialty
TRANSLATION & INTERPRETATION SVCS
TRANSMISSIONS: Motor Vehicle
TRANSPORTATION EPQT & SPLYS, WHOLESALE: Acft/Space Vehicle
TRANSPORTATION EQPT & SPLYS WHOLESALERS, NEC
TRANSPORTATION EQUIPMENT, NEC
TRANSPORTATION: Local Passenger, NEC
TRAP ROCK: Crushed & Broken
TRAPS: Animal & Fish, Wire
TRAPS: Stem
TRAVEL AGENCIES
TRAVEL TRAILERS & CAMPERS
TRAYS: Cable, Metal Plate
TRAYS: Plastic
TROPHIES, NEC
TROPHIES, PEWTER
TROPHIES, PLATED, ALL METALS
TROPHIES, SILVER
TROPHIES: Metal, Exc Silver
TROPHY & PLAQUE STORES
TRUCK & BUS BODIES: Ambulance
TRUCK & BUS BODIES: Motor Vehicle, Specialty
TRUCK & BUS BODIES: Truck, Motor Vehicle
TRUCK BODIES: Body Parts
TRUCK GENERAL REPAIR SVC
TRUCK PAINTING & LETTERING SVCS
TRUCK PARTS & ACCESSORIES: Wholesalers
TRUCKING & HAULING SVCS: Garbage, Collect/Transport Only
TRUCKING, DUMP
TRUCKING: Except Local
TRUCKING: Local, Without Storage
TRUCKS & TRACTORS: Industrial
TRUCKS: Forklift
TRUCKS: Indl
TRUNKS
TRUSSES: Wood, Floor
TRUSSES: Wood, Roof
TUBE & TUBING FABRICATORS
TUBES: Finned, For Heat Transfer
TUBES: Generator, Electron Beam, Beta Ray
TUBES: Paper
TUBES: Paper Or Fiber, Chemical Or Electrical Uses
TUBES: Steel & Iron
TUBES: Vacuum
TUBES: Wrought, Welded Or Lock Joint
TUBING: Flexible, Metallic
TUBING: Glass
TUBING: Plastic
TUBING: Seamless
TUNGSTEN CARBIDE
TUNGSTEN CARBIDE POWDER
TURBINE GENERATOR SET UNITS: Hydraulic, Complete
TURBINES & TURBINE GENERATOR SET UNITS, COMPLETE
TURBINES & TURBINE GENERATOR SET UNITS: Gas, Complete
TURBINES & TURBINE GENERATOR SETS
TURBINES & TURBINE GENERATOR SETS & PARTS
TURBINES: Gas, Mechanical Drive
TURBINES: Hydraulic, Complete
TURBINES: Steam
TURBO-GENERATORS
TURKEY PROCESSING & SLAUGHTERING
TWINE PRDTS
TYPESETTING SVC
TYPESETTING SVC: Computer
TYPOGRAPHY

U

ULTRASONIC EQPT: Cleaning, Exc Med & Dental
UMBRELLAS & CANES
UMBRELLAS: Garden Or Wagon
UNIFORM STORES
UNIVERSITY
UNSUPPORTED PLASTICS: Floor Or Wall Covering
UPHOLSTERY FILLING MATERIALS
UPHOLSTERY MATERIALS, BROADWOVEN
UPHOLSTERY WORK SVCS
URANIUM ORE MINING, NEC
USED CAR DEALERS
USED MERCHANDISE STORES: Building Materials
UTENSILS: Cast Aluminum, Cooking Or Kitchen

UTENSILS: Household, Cooking & Kitchen, Metal
UTENSILS: Household, Cooking & Kitchen, Porcelain Enameled
UTENSILS: Household, Metal, Exc Cast
UTENSILS: Household, Porcelain Enameled
UTILITY TRAILER DEALERS

V

VACUUM CLEANER STORES
VACUUM CLEANERS: Household
VACUUM CLEANERS: Indl Type
VACUUM SYSTEMS: Air Extraction, Indl
VALUE-ADDED RESELLERS: Computer Systems
VALVES & PIPE FITTINGS
VALVES & REGULATORS: Pressure, Indl
VALVES: Aerosol, Metal
VALVES: Aircraft
VALVES: Aircraft, Control, Hydraulic & Pneumatic
VALVES: Aircraft, Fluid Power
VALVES: Control, Automatic
VALVES: Fluid Power, Control, Hydraulic & pneumatic
VALVES: Gas Cylinder, Compressed
VALVES: Hard Rubber
VALVES: Indl
VALVES: Plumbing & Heating
VALVES: Regulating & Control, Automatic
VALVES: Water Works
VARNISHES, NEC
VEGETABLE STANDS OR MARKETS
VEHICLES: All Terrain
VEHICLES: Recreational
VENDING MACHINES & PARTS
VENTILATING EQPT: Metal
VENTILATING EQPT: Sheet Metal
VENTURE CAPITAL COMPANIES
VETERINARY PHARMACEUTICAL PREPARATIONS
VIBRATORS: Concrete Construction
VIDEO & AUDIO EQPT, WHOLESALE
VIDEO CAMERA-AUDIO RECORDERS: Household Use
VIDEO EQPT
VIDEO PRODUCTION SVCS
VIDEO REPAIR SVCS
VIDEO TAPE PRODUCTION SVCS
VINYL RESINS, NEC
VISUAL COMMUNICATIONS SYSTEMS
VITAMINS: Natural Or Synthetic, Uncompounded, Bulk
VITAMINS: Pharmaceutical Preparations

W

WALL COVERINGS WHOLESALERS
WALLBOARD: Decorated, Made From Purchased Materials
WALLPAPER & WALL COVERINGS
WALLPAPER: Made From Purchased Paper
WALLS: Curtain, Metal
WAREHOUSE CLUBS STORES
WAREHOUSING & STORAGE FACILITIES, NEC
WAREHOUSING & STORAGE, REFRIGERATED: Frozen Or Refrig Goods
WAREHOUSING & STORAGE: General
WAREHOUSING & STORAGE: General
WAREHOUSING & STORAGE: Refrigerated
WARM AIR HEATING & AC EQPT & SPLYS, WHOLESALE Air Filters
WARM AIR HEATING/AC EQPT/SPLYS, WHOL Dehumidifiers, Exc Port
WARM AIR HEATING/AC EQPT/SPLYS, WHOL: Ventilating Eqpt/Sply
WASHCLOTHS
WASHERS: Metal
WASHERS: Plastic
WASHERS: Spring, Metal
WATCH STRAPS, EXC METAL
WATCHCASES
WATCHES
WATCHES & PARTS, WHOLESALE
WATER PURIFICATION EQPT: Household
WATER SUPPLY
WATER TREATMENT EQPT: Indl
WATER: Mineral, Carbonated, Canned & Bottled, Etc
WATER: Pasteurized & Mineral, Bottled & Canned
WATER: Pasteurized, Canned & Bottled, Etc
WATERPROOFING COMPOUNDS
WAVEGUIDES & FITTINGS
WAX REMOVERS
WAXES: Mineral, Natural

PRODUCT INDEX

WAXES: Paraffin
WAXES: Petroleum, Not Produced In Petroleum Refineries
WEATHER STRIPS: Metal
WEAVING MILL, BROADWOVEN FABRICS: Wool Or Similar Fabric
WEDDING CHAPEL: Privately Operated
WEIGHING MACHINERY & APPARATUS
WELDING & CUTTING APPARATUS & ACCESS, NEC
WELDING EQPT
WELDING EQPT & SPLYS WHOLESALERS
WELDING EQPT: Electrical
WELDING MACHINES & EQPT: Ultrasonic
WELDING REPAIR SVC
WELDING SPLYS, EXC GASES: Wholesalers
WELDING TIPS: Heat Resistant, Metal
WELDMENTS
WHEELBARROWS
WHEELCHAIR LIFTS
WHEELCHAIRS
WHEELS
WHEELS & PARTS
WHEELS: Abrasive
WHEELS: Buffing & Polishing
WHEELS: Iron & Steel, Locomotive & Car
WHEELS: Rolled, Locomotive
WIGS & HAIRPIECES
WIND TUNNELS
WINDINGS: Coil, Electronic
WINDMILLS: Electric Power Generation
WINDOW & DOOR FRAMES
WINDOW BLIND REPAIR SVCS
WINDOW FRAMES & SASHES: Plastic
WINDOW FRAMES, MOLDING & TRIM: Vinyl
WINDOW TRIMMING SVCS
WINDOWS, LOUVER: Metal
WINDOWS: Wood
WINE & DISTILLED ALCOHOLIC BEVERAGES WHOLESALERS
WINE CELLARS, BONDED: Wine, Blended
WIRE
WIRE & CABLE: Aluminum
WIRE & WIRE PRDTS
WIRE CLOTH & WOVEN WIRE PRDTS, MADE FROM PURCHASED WIRE
WIRE FABRIC: Welded Steel
WIRE FENCING & ACCESS WHOLESALERS
WIRE MATERIALS: Copper
WIRE MATERIALS: Steel
WIRE PRDTS: Ferrous Or Iron, Made In Wiredrawing Plants
WIRE PRDTS: Steel & Iron
WIRE WHOLESALERS
WIRE: Barbed
WIRE: Barbed & Twisted
WIRE: Communication
WIRE: Mesh
WIRE: Nonferrous
WIRE: Nonferrous, Appliance Fixture
WIRE: Steel, Insulated Or Armored
WOMEN'S & CHILDREN'S CLOTHING WHOLESALERS, NEC
WOMEN'S & GIRLS' SPORTSWEAR WHOLESALERS
WOMEN'S CLOTHING STORES
WOMEN'S CLOTHING STORES: Ready-To-Wear
WOMEN'S SPECIALTY CLOTHING STORES
WOMEN'S SPORTSWEAR STORES
WOOD FENCING WHOLESALERS
WOOD PRDTS
WOOD PRDTS: Beekeeping Splys
WOOD PRDTS: Clothespins
WOOD PRDTS: Display Forms, Boot & Shoe
WOOD PRDTS: Engraved
WOOD PRDTS: Furniture Inlays, Veneers
WOOD PRDTS: Jalousies, Glass, Wood Framed
WOOD PRDTS: Ladders & Stepladders
WOOD PRDTS: Laundry
WOOD PRDTS: Mantels
WOOD PRDTS: Moldings, Unfinished & Prefinished
WOOD PRDTS: Mulch Or Sawdust
WOOD PRDTS: Novelties, Fiber
WOOD PRDTS: Outdoor, Structural
WOOD PRDTS: Panel Work
WOOD PRDTS: Rulers & Rules
WOOD PRDTS: Shavings & Packaging, Excelsior
WOOD PRDTS: Shoe Trees
WOOD PRDTS: Signboards
WOOD PRDTS: Silo Staves
WOOD PRDTS: Survey Stakes
WOOD PRDTS: Trellises
WOOD PRDTS: Trophy Bases
WOOD PRDTS: Window Backs, Store Or Lunchroom, Prefabricated
WOOD PRDTS: Yard Sticks
WOOD PRODUCTS: Reconstituted
WOOD TREATING: Creosoting
WOOD TREATING: Flooring, Block
WOOD TREATING: Structural Lumber & Timber
WOODWORK & TRIM: Interior & Ornamental
WOODWORK: Carved & Turned
WOODWORK: Interior & Ornamental, NEC
WOOL: Grease
WOVEN WIRE PRDTS, NEC
WRITING FOR PUBLICATION SVCS

X

X-RAY EQPT & TUBES
X-RAY EQPT REPAIR SVCS

Y

YARN & YARN SPINNING
YARN MILLS: Twisting
YARN WHOLESALERS
YARN: Embroidery, Spun
YARN: Natural & Animal Fiber, Spun
YARN: Specialty & Novelty
YARN: Weaving, Twisting, Winding Or Spooling
YOGURT WHOLESALERS

PRODUCT SECTION

```
                    ┌─────────────────────────────────────┐
Product category ───┤ BOXES: Folding                      │      Indicates approximate employment figure
                    │ Edgar & Son Paperboard ........G....│      A = Over 500 employees, B = 251-500
                    │   Yourtown (G-11480)       999 999-9999   C = 101-250, D = 51-100, E = 20-50
                    │ Ready Box Co ..................E....│      F = 10-19, G = 5-9
                    │   Anytown (G-7097)         999 999-9999 ── Business phone
City ───────────────┤                                     │
                    │                                     │ ──── Geographic Section entry number where full
                    └─────────────────────────────────────┘      company information appears.
```

See footnotes for symbols and codes identification.
• Refer to the Industrial Product Index preceding this section to locate product headings.

ABRASIVES

American Douglas Metals Inc .... F 716 856-3170
  Buffalo *(G-2824)*
Buffalo Abrasives Inc .... E 716 693-3856
  North Tonawanda *(G-12980)*
Dedeco International Sales Inc .... E 845 887-4840
  Long Eddy *(G-7674)*
Dico Products Corporation .... F 315 797-0470
  Utica *(G-16346)*
Electro Abrasives LLC .... E 716 822-2500
  Buffalo *(G-2947)*
Imerys Fsed Mnrl Ngara FLS Inc .... E 716 286-1250
  Niagara Falls *(G-12852)*
Meloon Foundries LLC .... E 315 454-3231
  Syracuse *(G-16006)*
Precision Elctro Mnrl Pmco Inc .... E 716 284-2484
  Niagara Falls *(G-12881)*
Saint-Gbain Advnced Crmics LLC ..... E 716 691-2000
  Amherst *(G-260)*
Saint-Gobain Abrasives Inc .... B 518 266-2200
  Watervliet *(G-16712)*
Select-Tech Inc .... G 845 895-8111
  Wallkill *(G-16566)*
Uneeda Enterprizes Inc .... C 800 431-2494
  Spring Valley *(G-15626)*
Warren Cutlery Corp .... F 845 876-3444
  Rhinebeck *(G-14072)*
Washington Mills Tonawanda Inc ..... E 716 693-4550
  Tonawanda *(G-16234)*

ABRASIVES: Coated

Barton Mines Company LLC .... C 518 798-5462
  Glens Falls *(G-5688)*
Conrad Blasius Equipment Co .... G 516 753-1200
  Plainview *(G-13620)*
Global Abrasive Products Inc .... E 716 438-0047
  Lockport *(G-7617)*
Precision Abrasives Corp .... E 716 826-5833
  Orchard Park *(G-13316)*

ABRASIVES: Grains

EAC Holdings of NY Corp .... E 716 822-2500
  Buffalo *(G-2939)*
Sunbelt Industries Inc .... F 315 823-2947
  Little Falls *(G-7526)*
Washingtom Mills Elec Mnrls .... D 716 278-6600
  Niagara Falls *(G-12907)*

ACADEMIC TUTORING SVCS

Bright Kids Nyc Inc .... E 917 539-4575
  New York *(G-9512)*

ACCELERATION INDICATORS & SYSTEM COMPONENTS: Aerospace

Aeroflex Incorporated .... B 516 694-6700
  Plainview *(G-13608)*
Cobham Holdings (us) Inc .... A 716 662-0006
  Orchard Park *(G-13285)*
Cobham Holdings Inc 716 662-0006
  Orchard Park *(G-13286)*
Ihi Inc .... E 212 599-8100
  New York *(G-10610)*
Inertia Switch Inc .... E 845 359-8300
  Orangeburg *(G-13251)*
Woodbine Products Inc .... E 631 586-3770
  Hauppauge *(G-6259)*

ACCELERATORS: Electron Linear

Iba Industrial Inc .... E 631 254-6800
  Edgewood *(G-4614)*

ACCELERATORS: Particle, High Voltage

Evergreen High Voltage LLC .... G 281 814-9973
  Lake Placid *(G-7298)*

ACCOUNTING MACHINES & CASH REGISTERS

Logic Controls Inc .... E 516 248-0400
  Bethpage *(G-870)*

ACID RESIST: Etching

Greenfield Manufacturing Inc .... F 518 581-2368
  Saratoga Springs *(G-15185)*

ACIDS

Evans Chemetics LP .... D 315 539-9221
  Waterloo *(G-16646)*

ACIDS: Battery

Horizon Power Source LLC .... E 877 240-0580
  Glen Cove *(G-5631)*

ACOUSTICAL BOARD & TILE

Lencore Acoustics Corp .... F 315 384-9114
  Norfolk *(G-12916)*
Mecho Systems .... F 718 729-8373
  Long Island City *(G-7837)*
Ssf Production LLC .... F 518 324-3407
  Plattsburgh *(G-13726)*

ACRYLIC RESINS

Creations In Lucite Inc .... G 718 871-2000
  Brooklyn *(G-1812)*

ACTUATORS: Indl, NEC

Makerbot Industries LLC .... C 347 334-6800
  Brooklyn *(G-2257)*
Marine & Indus Hydraulics Inc .... F 914 698-2036
  Mamaroneck *(G-8070)*
Rotork Controls Inc .... F 585 328-1550
  Rochester *(G-14680)*
Rotork Controls Inc .... C 585 328-1550
  Rochester *(G-14681)*
Trident Valve Actuator Co .... F 914 698-2650
  Mamaroneck *(G-8082)*
Young & Franklin Inc .... D 315 457-3110
  Liverpool *(G-7586)*

ADDITIVE BASED PLASTIC MATERIALS: Plasticizers

Bamberger Polymers Intl Corp .... F 516 622-3600
  Jericho *(G-7094)*
Dewitt Plastics Inc .... F 315 255-1209
  Auburn *(G-491)*
Fougera Pharmaceuticals Inc .... C 631 454-7677
  Melville *(G-8350)*

ADHESIVES

Adirondack Spclty Adhsives Inc .... F 518 869-5736
  Albany *(G-32)*
Aremco Products Inc .... F 845 268-0039
  Valley Cottage *(G-16402)*
Beacon Adhesives Inc .... E 914 699-3400
  Mount Vernon *(G-8711)*
Best Adhesives Company Inc .... G 718 417-3800
  Ridgewood *(G-14115)*
Northern Adhesives Inc .... E 718 388-5834
  Brooklyn *(G-2384)*
PPG Architectural Finishes Inc .... G 585 271-1363
  Rochester *(G-14610)*
Ran Mar Enterprises Ltd .... F 631 666-4754
  Bay Shore *(G-727)*
Saint Gobain Grains & Powders .... A 716 731-8200
  Niagara Falls *(G-12888)*
Solenis LLC .... G 315 461-4730
  Liverpool *(G-7575)*

ADHESIVES & SEALANTS

Able National Corp .... E 718 386-8801
  Brooklyn *(G-1549)*
Advanced Polymer Solutions LLC .... G 516 621-5800
  Port Washington *(G-13819)*
All Out Die Cutting Inc .... E 718 346-6666
  Brooklyn *(G-1586)*
Angiotech Biocoatings Corp .... E 585 321-1130
  Henrietta *(G-6315)*
Classic Labels Inc .... E 631 467-2300
  Patchogue *(G-13442)*
Hexion Inc .... E 518 792-8040
  South Glens Falls *(G-15548)*
Legacy USA LLC .... F 888 383-3330
  Bronx *(G-1383)*
P C I Paper Conversions Inc .... D 315 703-8300
  Syracuse *(G-16028)*
P C I Paper Conversions Inc .... E 315 634-3317
  Syracuse *(G-16029)*
Polycast Industries Inc .... G 631 595-2530
  Bay Shore *(G-722)*
Polyset Company Inc .... E 518 664-6000
  Mechanicville *(G-8260)*
Royal Adhesives & Sealants LLC ..... F 315 451-1755
  Syracuse *(G-16049)*
Super-Tek Products Inc .... E 718 278-7900
  Woodside *(G-17373)*
Utility Manufacturing Co Inc .... E 516 997-6300
  Westbury *(G-17068)*
Wild Works Incorporated .... G 716 891-4197
  Albany *(G-151)*

ADHESIVES & SEALANTS WHOLESALERS

Nyi Building Products Inc .... F 518 458-7500
  Clifton Park *(G-3729)*

ADHESIVES: Epoxy

Sg-TEC LLC .... G 631 750-6161
  Bohemia *(G-1128)*

ADVERTISING AGENCIES

Act Communications Group Inc .... F 631 669-2403
  West Islip *(G-16932)*
Ad Makers Long Island Inc .... F 631 595-9100
  Deer Park *(G-4112)*
AR Media Inc .... E 212 352-0731
  New York *(G-9238)*
Gatehouse Media LLC .... C 585 598-0030
  Pittsford *(G-13589)*
Gruner + Jahr Prtg & Pubg Co .... C 212 463-1000
  New York *(G-10418)*
Kinaneco Inc .... E 315 468-6201
  Syracuse *(G-15994)*
Luria Communications Inc .... G 631 329-4922
  East Hampton *(G-4433)*

Employee Codes: A=Over 500 employees, B=251-500
C=101-250, D=51-100, E=20-50, F=10-19, G=5-9

2018 Harris
New York Manufacturers Directory

ADVERTISING AGENCIES

Media Trust LLC .... G 212 802-1162
  New York *(G-11236)*
Mickelberry Communications Inc .... G 212 832-0303
  New York *(G-11279)*
Middletown Press .... G 845 343-1895
  Middletown *(G-8485)*
Perception Imaging Inc .... F 631 676-5262
  Holbrook *(G-6495)*
Scholastic Corporation .... G 212 343-6100
  New York *(G-12015)*
Service Advertising Group Inc .... F 718 361-6161
  Long Island City *(G-7904)*
Stop Entertainment Inc .... F 212 242-7867
  Monroe *(G-8599)*

ADVERTISING AGENCIES: Consultants

Eye Graphics & Printing Inc .... F 718 488-0606
  Brooklyn *(G-1953)*
Galli Shirts and Sports AP .... G 845 226-7305
  Stormville *(G-15801)*
Mason & Gore Inc .... E 914 921-1025
  Rye *(G-15089)*
Whispr Group Inc .... F 212 924-3979
  New York *(G-12651)*

ADVERTISING DISPLAY PRDTS

Accenta Incorporated .... G 716 565-6262
  Buffalo *(G-2808)*
Arnprior Rpid Mfg Slutions Inc .... C 585 617-6301
  Rochester *(G-14229)*
Arnprior Rpid Mfg Slutions Inc .... G 585 617-6301
  Rochester *(G-14230)*
Federal Sample Card Corp .... D 718 458-1344
  Elmhurst *(G-4673)*
JG Innovative Industries Inc .... G 718 784-7300
  Kew Gardens *(G-7193)*
Mack Studios Displays Inc .... E 315 252-7542
  Auburn *(G-505)*
Nationwide Exhibitor Svcs Inc .... F 631 467-2034
  Central Islip *(G-3532)*
Promotional Development Inc .... D 718 485-8550
  Brooklyn *(G-2471)*
Qps Die Cutters Finishers Corp .... E 718 966-1811
  Staten Island *(G-15746)*
Strategic Mktg Promotions Inc .... F 845 623-7777
  Pearl River *(G-13491)*
Swift Multigraphics LLC .... G 585 442-8000
  Rochester *(G-14733)*
Tri-Plex Packaging Corporation .... E 212 481-6070
  New York *(G-12422)*

ADVERTISING MATERIAL DISTRIBUTION

Penny Lane Printing Inc .... D 585 226-8111
  Avon *(G-539)*
Real Est Book of Long Island .... F 516 364-5000
  Syosset *(G-15858)*
Shipmtes/Printmates Holdg Corp .... D 518 370-1158
  Scotia *(G-15353)*
Technomag Inc .... G 631 246-6142
  East Setauket *(G-4512)*

ADVERTISING REPRESENTATIVES: Electronic Media

World Business Media LLC .... F 212 344-0759
  Massapequa Park *(G-8224)*

ADVERTISING REPRESENTATIVES: Magazine

Icd Publications Inc .... E 631 246-9300
  Islandia *(G-6833)*

ADVERTISING REPRESENTATIVES: Media

Redbook Magazine .... F 212 649-3331
  New York *(G-11845)*

ADVERTISING REPRESENTATIVES: Newspaper

Advertiser Publications Inc .... F 845 783-1111
  Chester *(G-3625)*
Bradford Publications Inc .... C 716 373-2500
  Olean *(G-13157)*
Community Cpons Frnchising Inc .... E 516 277-1968
  Glen Cove *(G-5625)*
Fire Island Tide Publication .... F 631 567-7470
  Sayville *(G-15239)*

L & M Publications Inc .... E 516 378-3133
  Garden City *(G-5525)*
Local Media Group Inc .... E 845 341-1100
  Middletown *(G-8481)*
Long Island Cmnty Nwsppers Inc .... D 516 482-4490
  Mineola *(G-8555)*
Market Place Publications .... E 516 997-7909
  Carle Place *(G-3421)*
Service Advertising Group Inc .... F 718 361-6161
  Long Island City *(G-7904)*

ADVERTISING REPRESENTATIVES: Printed Media

Economist Newspaper Group Inc .... C 212 541-0500
  New York *(G-10032)*
Penton Media Inc .... B 212 204-4200
  New York *(G-11627)*
Press Express .... G 914 592-3790
  Elmsford *(G-4781)*

ADVERTISING SPECIALTIES, WHOLESALE

A Trusted Name Inc .... F 716 326-7400
  Westfield *(G-17074)*
Advantage Printing Inc .... F 718 820-0688
  Kew Gardens *(G-7187)*
All American Awards Inc .... F 631 567-2025
  Bohemia *(G-1007)*
Concept Printing Inc .... G 845 353-4040
  Nyack *(G-13064)*
Elco Manufacturing Co Inc .... E 516 767-3577
  Port Washington *(G-13835)*
In-Step Marketing Inc .... F 212 797-3450
  New York *(G-10624)*
Middletown Press .... G 845 343-1895
  Middletown *(G-8485)*
U All Inc .... E 518 438-2558
  Albany *(G-144)*
Ward Sales Co Inc .... G 315 476-5276
  Syracuse *(G-16093)*
Whispr Group Inc .... F 212 924-3979
  New York *(G-12651)*

ADVERTISING SVCS: Direct Mail

Advertiser Publications Inc .... F 845 783-1111
  Chester *(G-3625)*
Century Direct LLC .... C 212 763-0600
  Islandia *(G-6827)*
Design Distributors Inc .... D 631 242-2000
  Deer Park *(G-4152)*
Gotham Ink Corp .... G 516 677-1969
  Syosset *(G-15845)*
Orffeo Printing & Imaging Inc .... G 716 681-5757
  Lancaster *(G-7352)*
Perception Imaging Inc .... F 631 676-5262
  Holbrook *(G-6495)*
Shipmtes/Printmates Holdg Corp .... D 518 370-1158
  Scotia *(G-15353)*
Syracuse Letter Company Inc .... F 315 476-8328
  Bridgeport *(G-1236)*
Thomas Publishing Company LLC .... B 212 695-0500
  New York *(G-12342)*

ADVERTISING SVCS: Display

Apple Imprints Apparel Inc .... E 716 893-1130
  Buffalo *(G-2836)*
Exhibits & More .... G 585 924-4040
  Victor *(G-16500)*
Greenwood Graphics Inc .... F 516 822-4856
  Hicksville *(G-6381)*
L Miller Design Inc .... G 631 242-1163
  Deer Park *(G-4186)*
Mystic Display Co Inc .... G 718 485-2651
  Brooklyn *(G-2351)*

ADVERTISING SVCS: Outdoor

Artkraft Strauss LLC .... E 212 265-5155
  New York *(G-9273)*

ADVERTISING SVCS: Sample Distribution

Instantwhip of Buffalo Inc .... E 716 892-7031
  Buffalo *(G-3027)*

ADVERTISING SVCS: Transit

Danet Inc .... F 718 266-4444
  Brooklyn *(G-1839)*

PRODUCT SECTION

Fun Media Inc .... E 646 472-0135
  New York *(G-10271)*

AERIAL WORK PLATFORMS

Park Ave Bldg & Roofg Sups LLC .... E 718 403-0100
  Brooklyn *(G-2421)*

AEROSOLS

Fountainhead Group Inc .... C 708 598-7100
  New York Mills *(G-12743)*

AGENTS & MANAGERS: Entertainers

Fast-Trac Entertainment Ltd 888 758-8886
  New York *(G-10199)*

AGENTS, BROKERS & BUREAUS: Personal Service

Superior Print On Demand .... G 607 240-5231
  Vestal *(G-16478)*
T J Signs Unlimited LLC .... E 631 273-4800
  Islip *(G-6852)*

AGRICULTURAL EQPT: BARN, SILO, POULTRY, DAIRY/LIVESTOCK MACH

P & D Equipment Sales LLC .... G 585 343-2394
  Alexander *(G-192)*
Vansridge Dairy LLC .... E 315 364-8569
  Scipio Center *(G-15344)*

AGRICULTURAL EQPT: Fertilizng, Sprayng, Dustng/Irrigatn Mach

Jain Irrigation Inc .... D 315 755-4400
  Watertown *(G-16676)*

AGRICULTURAL EQPT: Milking Machines

Westmoor Ltd .... F 315 363-1500
  Sherrill *(G-15433)*

AGRICULTURAL EQPT: Planting Machines

Good Earth Organics Corp .... E 716 684-8111
  Lancaster *(G-7342)*

AGRICULTURAL EQPT: Spreaders, Fertilizer

Chapin Manufacturing Inc .... C 585 343-3140
  Batavia *(G-629)*

AGRICULTURAL EQPT: Trailers & Wagons, Farm

Renaldos Sales and Service Ctr .... G 716 337-3760
  North Collins *(G-12947)*

AGRICULTURAL EQPT: Turf & Grounds Eqpt

Bdp Industries Inc .... E 518 695-6851
  Greenwich *(G-5904)*

AGRICULTURAL EQPT: Turf Eqpt, Commercial

Moffett Turf Equipment Inc .... E 585 334-0100
  West Henrietta *(G-16917)*

AIR CLEANING SYSTEMS

Acme Engineering Products Inc .... E 518 236-5659
  Mooers *(G-8654)*
Veteran Air LLC .... G 315 720-1101
  Syracuse *(G-16092)*

AIR CONDITIONERS, AUTOMOTIVE: Wholesalers

American Comfort Direct LLC .... E 201 364-8309
  New York *(G-9165)*

AIR CONDITIONING & VENTILATION EQPT & SPLYS: Wholesales

Elima-Draft Incorporated .... G 631 375-2830
  Setauket *(G-15401)*
Layton Manufacturing Corp .... E 718 498-6000
  Brooklyn *(G-2197)*

PRODUCT SECTION

AIRCRAFT PARTS & AUXILIARY EQPT: Accumulators, Propeller

AIR CONDITIONING EQPT

Company	Code	Phone
Carrier Corporation Syracuse *(G-15906)*	E	315 432-6000
Carrier Corporation East Syracuse *(G-4530)*	B	315 463-5744
Carrier Corporation East Syracuse *(G-4531)*	B	315 432-6000
Duro Dyne Corporation Farmingdale *(G-4989)*	C	631 249-9000
Duro Dyne Machinery Corp Bay Shore *(G-694)*	E	631 249-9000
Duro Dyne National Corp Bay Shore *(G-695)*	C	631 249-9000
Elima-Draft Incorporated Setauket *(G-15401)*	G	631 375-2830
EMC Fintech Falconer *(G-4903)*	F	716 488-9071
Empire Air Systems LLC Brooklyn *(G-1924)*	F	718 377-1549
Fedders Islandaire Inc East Setauket *(G-4500)*	D	631 471-2900
Layton Manufacturing Corp Brooklyn *(G-2197)*	E	718 498-6000
M M Tool and Manufacturing Highland *(G-6432)*	G	845 691-4140
RE Hansen Industries Inc East Setauket *(G-4510)*	C	631 471-2900
Split Systems Corp North Baldwin *(G-12926)*	G	516 223-5511
Transit Air Inc Hornell *(G-6595)*	E	607 324-0216

AIR CONDITIONING UNITS: Complete, Domestic Or Indl

Company	Code	Phone
AC Air Cooling Co Inc Bronx *(G-1259)*	F	718 933-1011
Balticare Inc New York *(G-9363)*	F	646 380-9470
Ice Air LLC Mount Vernon *(G-8737)*	E	914 668-4700
JE Miller Inc East Syracuse *(G-4560)*	F	315 437-6811
Pfannenberg Inc Lancaster *(G-7358)*	D	716 685-6866

AIR COOLERS: Metal Plate

Company	Code	Phone
Thermotech Corp Buffalo *(G-3243)*	G	716 823-3311

AIR DUCT CLEANING SVCS

Company	Code	Phone
Filta Clean Co Inc Brooklyn *(G-1974)*	E	718 495-3800

AIR MATTRESSES: Plastic

Company	Code	Phone
Berry Plastics Group Inc Dunkirk *(G-4357)*	G	716 366-2112
Diamond Packaging Holdings LLC Rochester *(G-14327)*	G	585 334-8030

AIR POLLUTION MEASURING SVCS

Company	Code	Phone
Cemtrex Inc Farmingdale *(G-4967)*	C	631 756-9116
Clean Gas Systems Inc Hauppauge *(G-6066)*	E	631 467-1600

AIR PREHEATERS: Nonrotating, Plate Type

Company	Code	Phone
General Electric Company Wellsville *(G-16778)*	G	585 593-2700

AIR PURIFICATION EQPT

Company	Code	Phone
Aeromed Inc Utica *(G-16330)*	G	518 843-9144
Airgle Corporation Ronkonkoma *(G-14884)*	E	866 501-7750
Austin Air Systems Limited Buffalo *(G-2846)*	D	716 856-3700
Beecher Emssn Sltn Tchnlgs LLC Horseheads *(G-6596)*	F	607 796-0149
Beltran Associates Inc Brooklyn *(G-1677)*	E	718 252-2996
Clean Gas Systems Inc Hauppauge *(G-6066)*	E	631 467-1600
JT Systems Inc Liverpool *(G-7552)*	F	315 622-1980

Company	Code	Phone
Phytofilter Technologies Inc Saratoga Springs *(G-15196)*	G	518 507-6399
Sbb Inc East Syracuse *(G-4576)*	G	315 422-2376
Sullivan Bazinet Bongio Inc Syracuse *(G-16070)*	E	315 437-6500

AIRCRAFT & AEROSPACE FLIGHT INSTRUMENTS & GUIDANCE SYSTEMS

Company	Code	Phone
Atair Aerospace Inc Brooklyn *(G-1644)*	F	718 923-1709
Bae Systems Controls Inc Endicott *(G-4804)*	A	607 770-2000
CIC International Ltd Brooklyn *(G-1778)*	D	212 213-0089
Facilamatic Instrument Corp Valley Stream *(G-16432)*	F	516 825-6300
Kwadair LLC Brooklyn *(G-2181)*	G	646 824-2511
No Longer Empty Inc New York *(G-11463)*	G	202 413-4262
Select Fabricators Inc Canandaigua *(G-3387)*	F	585 393-0650

AIRCRAFT & HEAVY EQPT REPAIR SVCS

Company	Code	Phone
Binghamton Simulator Co Inc Binghamton *(G-891)*	E	607 321-2980
James A Staley Co Inc Carmel *(G-3429)*	F	845 878-3344

AIRCRAFT ASSEMBLY PLANTS

Company	Code	Phone
Altius Aviation LLC Syracuse *(G-15873)*	G	315 455-7555
Ascent Aerospace Holdings LLC New York *(G-9279)*	A	212 916-8142
Barclay Tagg Racing Floral Park *(G-5203)*	E	631 404-8269
Grumman Field Support Services Bethpage *(G-867)*	D	516 575-0574
Joka Industries Inc Bohemia *(G-1079)*	E	631 589-0444
Lesly Enterprise & Associates Deer Park *(G-4189)*	G	631 988-1301
Lockheed Martin Corporation New York *(G-11048)*	A	212 953-1510
Lockheed Martin Corporation Liverpool *(G-7553)*	E	315 456-1548
Lockheed Martin Corporation New Hartford *(G-8852)*	D	315 793-5800
Moog Inc East Aurora *(G-4400)*	B	716 687-4954
Northrop Grumman Systems Corp Bethpage *(G-875)*	A	516 575-0574
Northrop Grumman Systems Corp Buffalo *(G-3119)*	D	716 626-4600
Northrop Grumman Systems Corp Huntington *(G-6706)*	G	631 423-1014
Pro Drones Usa LLC New York *(G-11744)*	F	718 530-3558
Sikorsky Aircraft Corporation Rochester *(G-14710)*	D	585 424-1990
Trium Strs-Lg Isld LLC Westbury *(G-17065)*	D	516 997-5757

AIRCRAFT CONTROL SYSTEMS: Electronic Totalizing Counters

Company	Code	Phone
Moog Inc Elma *(G-4664)*	A	716 652-2000
Moog Inc Elma *(G-4665)*	E	716 687-4778

AIRCRAFT ENGINES & PARTS

Company	Code	Phone
Advanced Atomization Tech LLC Clyde *(G-3749)*	B	315 923-2341
ARC Systems Inc Hauppauge *(G-6042)*	E	631 582-8020
B H Aircraft Company Inc Ronkonkoma *(G-14905)*	D	631 580-9747
Chromalloy American LLC Orangeburg *(G-13244)*	E	845 230-7355
Chromalloy Gas Turbine LLC Orangeburg *(G-13245)*	C	845 359-2462
Chromalloy Gas Turbine LLC Middletown *(G-8464)*	E	845 692-8912
Colonial Group LLC Plainview *(G-13619)*	E	516 349-8010

Company	Code	Phone
Davis Aircraft Products Co Inc Bohemia *(G-1046)*	C	631 563-1500
Dyna-Empire Inc Garden City *(G-5513)*	D	516 222-2700
Gb Aero Engine LLC Rye *(G-15083)*	B	914 925-9600
General Electric Company Schenectady *(G-15283)*	A	518 385-4022
General Electric Company Niskayuna *(G-12912)*	E	518 385-7620
Honeywell International Inc Skaneateles Falls *(G-15492)*	A	315 554-6643
Honeywell International Inc Middletown *(G-8479)*	A	845 342-4400
Honeywell International Inc Melville *(G-8357)*	A	212 964-5111
Howe Machine & Tool Corp Bethpage *(G-868)*	F	516 931-5687
ITT Enidine Inc Orchard Park *(G-13299)*	B	716 662-1900
Kerns Manufacturing Corp Long Island City *(G-7807)*	C	718 784-4044
Lourdes Industries Inc Hauppauge *(G-6146)*	D	631 234-6600
Magellan Aerospace Bethel Inc Corona *(G-4024)*	C	203 798-9373
Magellan Aerospace Processing West Babylon *(G-16838)*	G	631 694-1818
McGuigan Inc Bohemia *(G-1098)*	F	631 750-6222
Nell-Joy Industries Inc Copiague *(G-3939)*	E	631 842-8989
Omega Industries & Development Plainview *(G-13654)*	E	516 349-8010
SOS International LLC New York *(G-12165)*	B	212 742-2410
SOS International LLC New York *(G-12166)*	E	212 742-2410
Therm Incorporated Ithaca *(G-6912)*	E	607 272-8500
Triumph Actuation Systems LLC Freeport *(G-5443)*	D	516 378-0162
Triumph Group Inc Westbury *(G-17066)*	E	516 997-5757
Turbine Engine Comp Utica Whitesboro *(G-17225)*	A	315 768-8070
United Technologies Corp East Syracuse *(G-4588)*	G	315 432-7849

AIRCRAFT EQPT & SPLYS WHOLESALERS

Company	Code	Phone
Fastener Dimensions Inc Ozone Park *(G-13404)*	E	718 847-6321
Magellan Aerospace NY Inc Bohemia *(G-1094)*	C	631 589-2440
Styles Aviation Inc Lagrangeville *(G-7284)*	G	845 677-8185
Worldwide Arntcal Cmpnents Inc Copiague *(G-3962)*	F	631 842-3780

AIRCRAFT FLIGHT INSTRUMENT REPAIR SVCS

Company	Code	Phone
Safe Flight Instrument Corp White Plains *(G-17194)*	C	914 220-1125

AIRCRAFT FLIGHT INSTRUMENTS

Company	Code	Phone
Mod-A-Can Inc Hicksville *(G-6399)*	E	516 931-8545
Optic Solution LLC Saranac *(G-15161)*	F	518 293-4034
Safe Flight Instrument Corp White Plains *(G-17194)*	C	914 220-1125

AIRCRAFT LIGHTING

Company	Code	Phone
Aerospace Lighting Corporation Bohemia *(G-1004)*	D	631 563-6400
Astronics Corporation East Aurora *(G-4391)*	C	716 805-1599
B/E Aerospace Inc Bohemia *(G-1018)*	E	631 563-6400
Luminescent Systems Inc East Aurora *(G-4398)*	B	716 655-0800

AIRCRAFT PARTS & AUXILIARY EQPT: Accumulators, Propeller

Company	Code	Phone
Honeywell International Inc Melville *(G-8358)*	B	516 577-2000

Employee Codes: A=Over 500 employees, B=251-500
C=101-250, D=51-100, E=20-50, F=10-19, G=5-9

AIRCRAFT PARTS & AUXILIARY EQPT: Assys, Subassemblies/Parts

AIRCRAFT PARTS & AUXILIARY EQPT: Assys, Subassemblies/Parts

Company	Col	Phone
Aero Trades Mfg Corp — Mineola (G-8523)	E	516 746-3360
Alro Machine Tool & Die Co Inc — Lindenhurst (G-7475)	F	631 226-5020
Design/OI Inc — Port Jeff STA (G-13789)	F	631 474-5536
Excelco Developments Inc — Silver Creek (G-15470)	E	716 934-2651
Excelco/Newbrook Inc — Silver Creek (G-15471)	D	716 934-2644
GKN Aerospace Monitor Inc — Amityville (G-288)	B	562 619-8558
Handy Tool & Mfg Co Inc — Brooklyn (G-2067)	G	718 478-9203
Lai International Inc — Green Island (G-5876)	D	763 780-0060
Magellan Aerospace Bethel Inc — Corona (G-4024)	C	203 798-9373
Norsk Titanium US Inc — Plattsburgh (G-13706)	G	949 735-9463
Posimech Inc — Medford (G-8292)	E	631 924-5959
Superior Motion Controls Inc — Farmingdale (G-5130)	C	516 420-2921
Tek Precision Co Ltd — Deer Park (G-4241)	E	631 242-0330
Wilco Industries Inc — Ronkonkoma (G-15025)	G	631 676-2593

AIRCRAFT PARTS & AUXILIARY EQPT: Body Assemblies & Parts

Company	Col	Phone
Air Industries Group — Hauppauge (G-6032)	D	631 881-4920
Reese Manufacturing Inc — Copiague (G-3946)	G	631 842-3780

AIRCRAFT PARTS & AUXILIARY EQPT: Gears, Power Transmission

Company	Col	Phone
Gleason Works — Rochester (G-14429)	A	585 473-1000
W J Albro Machine Works Inc — Yaphank (G-17424)	G	631 345-0657

AIRCRAFT PARTS & AUXILIARY EQPT: Landing Assemblies & Brakes

Company	Col	Phone
Dyna-Empire Inc — Garden City (G-5513)	C	516 222-2700

AIRCRAFT PARTS & AUXILIARY EQPT: Military Eqpt & Armament

Company	Col	Phone
Armacel Armor Corporation — New York (G-9254)	E	805 384-1144
Dresser-Argus Inc — Brooklyn (G-1882)	G	718 643-1540
Edo LLC — Amityville (G-284)	G	631 630-4000
Metadure Parts & Sales Inc — Farmingdale (G-5059)	F	631 249-2141

AIRCRAFT PARTS & AUXILIARY EQPT: Refueling Eqpt, In Flight

Company	Col	Phone
Gny Equipment LLC — Bay Shore (G-701)	F	631 667-1010
Usairports Services Inc — Rochester (G-14776)	E	585 527-6835

AIRCRAFT PARTS & AUXILIARY EQPT: Seat Ejector Devices

Company	Col	Phone
East/West Industries Inc — Ronkonkoma (G-14924)	E	631 981-5900

AIRCRAFT PARTS & EQPT, NEC

Company	Col	Phone
Air Industries Machining Corp — Bay Shore (G-666)	C	631 968-5000
Alcoa Fastening Systems — Kingston (G-7206)	A	845 334-7203
Alken Industries Inc — Ronkonkoma (G-14886)	D	631 467-2000
Arkwin Industries Inc — Westbury (G-16996)	C	516 333-2640
Astronics Corporation — East Aurora (G-4391)	C	716 805-1599
Ausco Inc — Farmingdale (G-4955)	D	516 944-9882
B & B Precision Components Inc — Ronkonkoma (G-14904)	G	631 273-3321
B/E Aerospace Inc — Bohemia (G-1018)	E	631 563-6400
Bar Fields Inc — Brooklyn (G-1664)	E	347 587-7795
Blair Industries Inc — Medford (G-8268)	E	631 924-6600
Canfield Aerospace & Mar Inc — Ronkonkoma (G-14913)	F	631 648-1050
Caravan International Corp — New York (G-9578)	E	212 223-7190
Carleton Technologies Inc — Orchard Park (G-13282)	B	716 662-0006
Circor Aerospace Inc — Hauppauge (G-6065)	D	631 737-1900
Cox & Company Inc — Plainview (G-13623)	C	212 366-0200
CPI Aerostructures Inc — Edgewood (G-4610)	B	631 586-5200
Crown Aircraft Lighting Inc — Whitestone (G-17234)	E	718 767-3410
Davis Aircraft Products Co Inc — Bohemia (G-1046)	C	631 563-1500
Ducommun Aerostructures NY Inc — Coxsackie (G-4082)	B	518 731-2791
Eastern Precision Machining — Bellport (G-824)	G	631 286-4758
Engineered Metal Products Inc — Copiague (G-3926)	G	631 842-3780
Ensil Technical Services Inc — Niagara Falls (G-12836)	E	716 282-1020
Fluid Mechanisms Hauppauge Inc — Hauppauge (G-6101)	E	631 234-0100
GE Aviation Systems LLC — Bohemia (G-1067)	C	631 467-5500
Goodrich Corporation — Rome (G-14840)	C	315 838-1200
Hicksville Machine Works Corp — Hicksville (G-6383)	F	516 931-1524
HSM Machine Works Inc — Medford (G-8281)	E	631 924-6600
Jac Usa Inc — New York (G-10725)	G	212 841-7430
Jamco Aerospace Inc — Deer Park (G-4178)	E	631 586-7900
Jaquith Industries Inc — Syracuse (G-15985)	E	315 478-5700
Joldeson One Aerospace Inds — Ozone Park (G-13406)	D	718 848-7396
Jrsmm LLC — Elmira (G-4706)	C	607 331-1549
Loar Group Inc — New York (G-11046)	C	212 210-9348
Magellan Aerospace NY Inc — Corona (G-4025)	F	718 699-4000
Magellan Aerospace NY Inc — Bohemia (G-1094)	C	631 589-2440
MD International Industries — Deer Park (G-4197)	N	631 254-3100
Metal Dynamics Intl Corp — Hauppauge (G-6160)	G	631 231-1153
Milex Precision Inc — Bay Shore (G-715)	F	631 595-2393
Min-Max Machine Ltd — Ronkonkoma (G-14969)	E	631 585-4378
Minutemen Precsn McHning Tool — Ronkonkoma (G-14970)	E	631 467-4900
Moog Inc — Elma (G-4664)	A	716 652-2000
Nassau Tool Works Inc — West Babylon (G-16845)	E	631 328-7031
Omega Industries & Development — Plainview (G-13654)	E	516 349-8010
Parker-Hannifin Corporation — Clyde (G-3755)	C	631 231-3737
Precision Cnc — Deer Park (G-4216)	G	631 847-3999
Ripi Precision Co Inc — Farmingdale (G-5110)	G	631 694-2453
S & L Aerospace Metals LLC — Flushing (G-5296)	D	718 326-1821
Santa Fe Manufacturing Corp — Hauppauge (G-6208)	G	631 234-0100
Servotronics Inc — Elma (G-4668)	G	631 655-5990
Styles Aviation Inc — Lagrangeville (G-7284)	G	845 677-8185
Sumner Industries Inc — Bay Shore (G-742)	F	631 666-7290
Tangent Machine & Tool Corp — Farmingdale (G-5134)	E	631 249-3088
Tdl Manufacturing Inc — Hauppauge (G-6232)	F	215 538-8820
Tens Machine Company Inc — Holbrook (G-6505)	E	631 981-3321
TPC Inc — East Syracuse (G-4584)	G	315 438-8605
Triumph Actuation Systems LLC — Freeport (G-5443)	D	516 378-0162
Vosky Precision Machining Corp — Ronkonkoma (G-15024)	F	631 737-3200
Young & Franklin Inc — Liverpool (G-7586)	D	315 457-3110

AIRCRAFT SEATS

Company	Col	Phone
B/E Aerospace Inc — Bohemia (G-1018)	E	631 563-6400
B/E Aerospace Inc — Bohemia (G-1019)	C	631 589-0877
East/West Industries Inc — Ronkonkoma (G-14924)	E	631 981-5900
Readyjet Technical Svcs Inc — Johnstown (G-7154)	F	518 705-4019

AIRCRAFT: Airplanes, Fixed Or Rotary Wing

Company	Col	Phone
Boeing Company — New York (G-9484)	A	201 259-9400

AIRCRAFT: Gliders

Company	Col	Phone
M & H Research and Dev Corp — Beaver Dams (G-788)	G	607 734-2346

AIRCRAFT: Motorized

Company	Col	Phone
Drone Usa Inc — New York (G-9981)	E	212 220-8795
Lockheed Martin Corporation — Niagara Falls (G-12861)	E	716 297-1000

AIRCRAFT: Research & Development, Manufacturer

Company	Col	Phone
Alliant Tchsystems Oprtons LLC — Ronkonkoma (G-14890)	E	631 737-6100
Atk Gasl Inc — Ronkonkoma (G-14902)	G	631 737-6100
Calspan Corporation — Buffalo (G-2886)	C	716 631-6955
Calspan Corporation — Niagara Falls (G-12823)	F	716 236-1040
Luminati Aerospace LLC — Calverton (G-3321)	F	631 574-2616
Tech Park Food Services LLC — Rochester (G-14745)	G	585 295-1250

ALARM SYSTEMS WHOLESALERS

Company	Col	Phone
Lifewatch Inc — Hewlett (G-6333)	F	800 716-1433

ALARMS: Burglar

Company	Col	Phone
Datasonic Inc — East Meadow (G-4441)	G	516 248-7330
Harris Corporation — Rochester (G-14444)	A	413 263-6200
Sentry Devices Corp — Dix Hills (G-4321)	G	631 491-3191
Unitone Communication Systems — New York (G-12488)	G	212 777-9090
UTC Fire SEC Americas Corp Inc — Albany (G-148)	D	518 456-0444

ALARMS: Fire

Company	Col	Phone
Fire Apparatus Service Tech — Sherman (G-15424)	G	716 753-3538
Toweriq Inc — Long Island City (G-7931)	F	844 626-7638

ALCOHOL: Methyl & Methanol, Synthetic

Company	Col	Phone
Hunts Point Clean Energy LLC — Pearl River (G-13483)	G	203 451-5143

PRODUCT SECTION

ALKALIES & CHLORINE
Chemours Company Fc LLC .... E 716 278-5100
  Niagara Falls *(G-12826)*
Occidental Chemical Corp .... E 716 278-7795
  Niagara Falls *(G-12873)*
Occidental Chemical Corp .... E 716 773-8100
  Grand Island *(G-5780)*
Occidental Chemical Corp .... C 716 278-7794
  Niagara Falls *(G-12874)*
Olin Chlor Alkali Logistics .... C 716 278-6411
  Niagara Falls *(G-12875)*

ALKALOIDS & OTHER BOTANICAL BASED PRDTS
Bio-Botanica Inc .... D 631 231-0987
  Hauppauge *(G-6053)*

ALLERGENS & ALLERGENIC EXTRACTS
Nelco Laboratories Inc .... E 631 242-0082
  Deer Park *(G-4202)*

ALLOYS: Additive, Exc Copper Or Made In Blast Furnaces
Real Industry Inc .... F 805 435-1255
  New York *(G-11842)*

ALTERNATORS & GENERATORS: Battery Charging
ARC Systems Inc .... E 631 582-8020
  Hauppauge *(G-6042)*

ALTERNATORS: Automotive
Con Rel Auto Electric Inc .... E 518 356-1646
  Schenectady *(G-15273)*
Eastern Unit Exch Rmnfacturing .... F 718 739-7113
  Floral Park *(G-5210)*

ALUMINUM
Alcoa USA Corp .... F 212 518-5400
  New York *(G-9127)*
Greene Brass & Alum Fndry LLC ..... G 607 656-4204
  Bloomville *(G-990)*

ALUMINUM ORE MINING
American Douglas Metals Inc .... F 716 856-3170
  Buffalo *(G-2824)*

ALUMINUM PRDTS
A-Fab Initiatives Inc .... G 716 877-5257
  Buffalo *(G-2807)*
Alumi-Tech LLC .... G 585 663-7010
  Penfield *(G-13521)*
Amt Incorporated .... E 518 284-2910
  Sharon Springs *(G-15405)*
Arconic Inc .... D 212 836-2758
  New York *(G-9248)*
Constellium .... E 212 675-5087
  New York *(G-9769)*
Flagpoles Incorporated .... D 631 751-5500
  East Setauket *(G-4501)*
Itts Industrial Inc .... G 718 605-6934
  Staten Island *(G-15711)*
J Sussman Inc .... E 718 297-0228
  Jamaica *(G-6958)*
Keymark Corporation .... A 518 853-3421
  Fonda *(G-5321)*
Minitec Framing Systems LLC .... F 585 924-4690
  Victor *(G-16515)*
North Coast Outfitters Ltd .... E 631 727-5580
  Riverhead *(G-14164)*
Pioneer Window Holdings Inc .... E 518 762-5526
  Johnstown *(G-7152)*
Super Sweep Inc .... F 631 223-8205
  Huntington Station *(G-6761)*
Swiss Tool Corporation .... E 631 842-7466
  Copiague *(G-3954)*

ALUMINUM: Rolling & Drawing
Arconic Inc .... D 212 836-2758
  New York *(G-9248)*
Mitsubishi Chemical Amer Inc .... E 212 223-3043
  New York *(G-11310)*

N A Alumil Corporation .... G 718 355-9393
  Long Island City *(G-7850)*
Novelis Inc .... E 315 349-0121
  Oswego *(G-13364)*

AMMONIUM NITRATE OR AMMONIUM SULFATE
Ocip Holding LLC .... G 646 589-6180
  New York *(G-11509)*

AMMUNITION
Circor Aerospace Inc .... D 631 737-1900
  Hauppauge *(G-6065)*

AMMUNITION: Components
CIC International Ltd .... D 212 213-0089
  Brooklyn *(G-1778)*

AMMUNITION: Pellets & BB's, Pistol & Air Rifle
Benjamin Sheridan Corporation .... G 585 657-6161
  Bloomfield *(G-975)*
Crosman Corporation .... E 585 657-6161
  Bloomfield *(G-980)*
Crosman Corporation .... E 585 398-3920
  Farmington *(G-5157)*

AMMUNITION: Small Arms
CIC International Ltd .... D 212 213-0089
  Brooklyn *(G-1778)*

AMPLIFIERS
Aguilar Amplification LLC .... F 212 431-9109
  New York *(G-9110)*
Amplitech Group Inc .... G 631 521-7831
  Bohemia *(G-1011)*
Broadcast Manager Inc .... G 212 509-1200
  New York *(G-9517)*
Ilab America Inc .... G 631 615-5053
  Selden *(G-15373)*

AMPLIFIERS: Parametric
Electronics & Innovation Ltd .... F 585 214-0598
  Rochester *(G-14363)*

AMPLIFIERS: Pulse Amplifiers
AMP-Line Corp .... F 845 623-3288
  West Nyack *(G-16940)*

AMPLIFIERS: RF & IF Power
Ametek CTS Us Inc .... E 631 467-8400
  Ronkonkoma *(G-14897)*
B & H Electronics Corp .... E 845 782-5000
  Monroe *(G-8584)*
Communication Power Corp .... E 631 434-7306
  Hauppauge *(G-6071)*
Mks Medical Electronics .... C 585 292-7400
  Rochester *(G-14538)*
Srtech Industry Corp .... E 718 496-7001
  Oakland Gardens *(G-13087)*

AMUSEMENT & RECREATION SVCS: Amusement Ride
Billy Beez Usa LLC .... G 315 741-5099
  Syracuse *(G-15889)*
Billy Beez Usa LLC .... F 646 606-2249
  New York *(G-9451)*
Billy Beez Usa LLC .... G 845 915-4709
  West Nyack *(G-16943)*

AMUSEMENT & RECREATION SVCS: Arcades
Inspired Entertainment Inc .... G 646 565-3861
  New York *(G-10653)*

AMUSEMENT & RECREATION SVCS: Art Gallery, Commercial
Pace Editions Inc .... E 212 421-3237
  New York *(G-11562)*

ANESTHESIA EQPT

AMUSEMENT & RECREATION SVCS: Arts & Crafts Instruction
Donne Dieu .... G 212 226-0573
  Brooklyn *(G-1874)*

AMUSEMENT & RECREATION SVCS: Exposition Operation
Family Publications Ltd .... F 212 947-2177
  New York *(G-10186)*

AMUSEMENT & RECREATION SVCS: Gambling & Lottery Svcs
Inspired Entertainment Inc .... G 646 565-3861
  New York *(G-10653)*

AMUSEMENT & RECREATION SVCS: Game Machines
Mission Crane Service Inc .... D 718 937-3333
  Long Island City *(G-7845)*

AMUSEMENT & RECREATION SVCS: Golf Club, Membership
Dolomite Products Company Inc ..... E 315 524-1998
  Rochester *(G-14337)*

AMUSEMENT & RECREATION SVCS: Gun Club, Membership
Michael Britt Inc .... G 516 248-2010
  Mineola *(G-8558)*

AMUSEMENT & RECREATION SVCS: Physical Fitness Instruction
Playfitness Corp .... G 917 497-5443
  Staten Island *(G-15743)*

AMUSEMENT & RECREATION SVCS: Tennis & Professionals
Paddock Chevrolet Golf Dome .... E 716 504-4059
  Tonawanda *(G-16209)*

AMUSEMENT MACHINES: Coin Operated
Mission Crane Service Inc .... D 718 937-3333
  Long Island City *(G-7845)*

AMUSEMENT PARK DEVICES & RIDES
Acro Industries Inc .... C 585 254-3661
  Rochester *(G-14186)*
Lakeside Industries Inc .... F 716 386-3031
  Bemus Point *(G-842)*
Macro Tool & Machine Company .... G 845 223-3824
  Lagrangeville *(G-7280)*

ANALGESICS
Wyeth LLC .... A 973 660-5000
  New York *(G-12697)*

ANALYZERS: Moisture
Phymetrix Inc .... G 631 627-3950
  Medford *(G-8291)*

ANALYZERS: Network
Cgw Corp .... G 631 472-6600
  Bayport *(G-750)*
Everest Bbn Inc .... F 212 268-7979
  New York *(G-10145)*
Gcns Technology Group Inc .... G 347 713-8160
  Brooklyn *(G-2018)*
International Insurance Soc .... G 212 815-9291
  New York *(G-10678)*

ANESTHESIA EQPT
Gradian Health Systems Inc .... G 212 537-0340
  New York *(G-10386)*
Omnicare Anesthesia PC .... E 718 433-0044
  Astoria *(G-451)*

ANESTHETICS: Bulk Form

Ucb Pharma Inc .... B 919 767-2555
Rochester (G-14765)

ANIMAL FEED & SUPPLEMENTS: Livestock & Poultry

Archer-Daniels-Midland Company .... D 716 849-7333
Buffalo (G-2838)
Bailey Boonville Mills Inc .... G 315 942-2131
Boonville (G-1159)
Baker Commodities Inc .... E 585 482-1880
Rochester (G-14239)
Cargill Incorporated .... E 315 622-3533
Liverpool (G-7538)
Central Garden & Pet Company .... G 631 451-8021
Selden (G-15370)
Central Garden & Pet Company .... G 212 877-1270
New York (G-9616)
J & M Feed Corporation .... G 631 281-2152
Shirley (G-15444)
Kent Nutrition Group Inc .... F 315 788-0032
Watertown (G-16680)
Lowville Farmers Coop Inc .... E 315 376-6587
Lowville (G-7966)
Narrowsburg Feed & Grain Co .... F 845 252-3936
Narrowsburg (G-8814)
Pace Manufacturing Company .... G 607 936-0431
Painted Post (G-13418)
Scotts Feed Inc .... E 518 483-3110
Malone (G-8046)
Southern States Coop Inc .... F 315 438-4500
East Syracuse (G-4580)

ANIMAL FEED: Wholesalers

Kelley Farm & Garden Inc .... E 518 234-2332
Cobleskill (G-3763)
Pace Manufacturing Company .... G 607 936-0431
Painted Post (G-13418)
Scotts Feed Inc .... E 518 483-3110
Malone (G-8046)

ANIMAL FOOD & SUPPLEMENTS: Bird Food, Prepared

Heath Manufacturing Company .... G 800 444-3140
Batavia (G-639)
Pine Tree Farms Inc .... E 607 532-4312
Interlaken (G-6788)
Wagners LLC .... G 516 933-6580
Jericho (G-7121)

ANIMAL FOOD & SUPPLEMENTS: Dog

Dog Good Products LLC .... G 212 789-7000
New York (G-9947)
Robert Abady Dog Food Co Ltd .... F 845 473-1900
Poughkeepsie (G-13946)
Scooby Rendering & Inc .... G 315 793-1014
Utica (G-16382)

ANIMAL FOOD & SUPPLEMENTS: Dog & Cat

Colgate-Palmolive Company .... A 212 310-2000
New York (G-9726)
Hills Pet Products Inc .... G 212 310-2000
New York (G-10522)
Hound & Gatos Pet Foods Corp .... G 212 618-1917
New York (G-10560)
Nestle Purina Petcare Company .... B 716 366-8080
Dunkirk (G-4369)
Pet Proteins LLC .... G 888 293-1029
New York (G-11649)

ANIMAL FOOD & SUPPLEMENTS: Feed Concentrates

Gramco Inc .... G 716 592-2845
Springville (G-15632)

ANIMAL FOOD & SUPPLEMENTS: Feed Premixes

Commodity Resource Corporation ..... F 585 538-9500
Caledonia (G-3305)

ANIMAL FOOD & SUPPLEMENTS: Feed Supplements

Veterinary Biochemical Ltd .... G 845 473-1900
Poughkeepsie (G-13955)

ANIMAL FOOD & SUPPLEMENTS: Mineral feed supplements

Nutra-Vet Research Corp .... F 845 473-1900
Poughkeepsie (G-13941)

ANIMAL FOOD & SUPPLEMENTS: Pet, Exc Dog & Cat, Canned

Grandma Maes Cntry Nturals LLC ..... G 212 348-8171
New York (G-10391)

ANIMAL FOOD & SUPPLEMENTS: Poultry

Cochecton Mills Inc .... E 845 932-8282
Cochecton (G-3765)

ANODIZING SVC

Able Anodizing Corp .... F 718 252-0660
Brooklyn (G-1548)
C H Thompson Company Inc .... D 607 724-1094
Binghamton (G-897)
Fallon Inc .... E 718 326-7226
Maspeth (G-8169)
Keymark Corporation .... A 518 853-3421
Fonda (G-5321)
P3 Technologies .... G 585 730-7340
Rochester (G-14586)
Tru-Tone Metal Products Inc .... E 718 386-5960
Brooklyn (G-2705)
Utica Metal Products Inc .... D 315 732-6163
Utica (G-16388)

ANTENNAS: Radar Or Communications

B & Z Technologies LLC .... G 631 675-9666
East Setauket (G-4496)
Gryphon Sensors LLC .... F 315 452-8882
North Syracuse (G-12963)
Srctec LLC .... C 315 452-8700
Syracuse (G-16067)

ANTENNAS: Receiving

901 D LLC .... E 845 369-1111
Airmont (G-10)
Ampro International Inc .... G 845 278-4910
Brewster (G-1207)
Russell Industries Inc .... F 516 536-5000
Lynbrook (G-7986)

ANTIBIOTICS

G C Hanford Manufacturing Co .... C 315 476-7418
Syracuse (G-15967)
Pfizer Inc .... A 212 733-2323
New York (G-11657)
Pfizer Overseas LLC .... G 212 733-2323
New York (G-11662)

ANTIBIOTICS, PACKAGED

Durata Therapeutics Inc .... G 646 871-6400
New York (G-9991)

ANTIFREEZE

BASF Corporation .... B 914 785-2000
Tarrytown (G-16111)
Bass Oil Company Inc .... E 718 628-4444
Brooklyn (G-1668)
Fppf Chemical Co Inc .... G 716 856-9607
Buffalo (G-2969)

ANTIQUE FURNITURE RESTORATION & REPAIR

Irony Limited Inc .... G 631 329-4065
East Hampton (G-4431)
Nicholas Dfine Furn Decorators .... F 914 245-8982
Bronx (G-1413)

ANTIQUE REPAIR & RESTORATION SVCS, EXC FURNITURE & AUTOS

A W R Group Inc .... F 718 729-0412
Long Island City (G-7676)

ANTIQUE SHOPS

American Country Quilts & Lin .... G 631 283-5466
Southampton (G-15562)
Blanche P Field LLC .... E 212 355-6616
New York (G-9463)

APPAREL ACCESS STORES

Nazim Izzak Inc .... G 212 920-5546
Long Island City (G-7852)
Nine West Footwear Corporation ...... B 800 999-1877
New York (G-11452)

APPAREL DESIGNERS: Commercial

Arteast LLC .... G 212 965-8787
New York (G-9267)
Dianos Kathryn Designs .... G 212 267-1584
New York (G-9927)

APPAREL FILLING MATERIALS: Cotton Waste, Kapok/Related Matl

Return Textiles LLC .... G 646 408-0108
New York (G-11877)

APPAREL: Hand Woven

Jeans Inc .... G 646 223-1122
New York (G-10757)
K Pat Incorporated .... G 212 688-5728
New York (G-10830)

APPLIANCE CORDS: Household Electrical Eqpt

All Shore Industries Inc .... F 718 720-0018
Staten Island (G-15655)

APPLIANCES, HOUSEHOLD: Kitchen, Major, Exc Refrigs & Stoves

Ajmadison Corp .... D 718 532-1800
Brooklyn (G-1572)
Barrage .... E 212 586-9390
New York (G-9375)
Design Solutions LI Inc .... G 631 656-8700
Saint James (G-15115)
Hobart Corporation .... E 631 864-3440
Commack (G-3861)
Marine Park Appliances LLC .... G 718 513-1808
Brooklyn (G-2272)

APPLIANCES, HOUSEHOLD: Refrigerator Cabinets, Metal Or Wood

Ae Fund Inc .... E 315 698-7650
Brewerton (G-1199)

APPLIANCES, HOUSEHOLD: Refrigs, Mechanical & Absorption

General Electric Company .... A 518 385-4022
Schenectady (G-15283)

APPLIANCES, HOUSEHOLD: Sewing Machines & Attchmnts, Domestic

Jado Sewing Machines Inc .... E 718 784-2314
Long Island City (G-7798)

APPLIANCES: Household, Refrigerators & Freezers

Acme Kitchenettes Corp .... E 518 828-4191
Hudson (G-6632)
Dover Corporation .... G 212 922-1640
New York (G-9963)
Felix Storch Inc .... C 718 893-3900
Bronx (G-1332)
Robin Industries Ltd .... F 718 218-9616
Brooklyn (G-2522)
Sure-Kol Refrigerator Co Inc .... F 718 625-0601
Brooklyn (G-2653)

PRODUCT SECTION

APPLIANCES: Major, Cooking

Applince Installation Svc Corp ....E 716 884-7425
  Buffalo *(G-2837)*
Bakers Pride Oven Co Inc ....C 914 576-0200
  New Rochelle *(G-8932)*
Oxo International Inc ....C 212 242-3333
  New York *(G-11557)*

APPLIANCES: Small, Electric

A & M LLC ....G 212 354-1341
  New York *(G-9027)*
Algonquin Power ....G 315 393-5595
  Ogdensburg *(G-13131)*
Fulton Volcanic Inc ....D 315 298-5121
  Pulaski *(G-13967)*
General Electric Company ....G 315 554-2000
  Skaneateles *(G-15482)*
Schlesinger Siemans Elec LLC ....F 718 386-6230
  New York *(G-12007)*
Tactica International Inc ....F 212 575-0500
  New York *(G-12294)*
Uniware Houseware Corp ....E 631 242-7400
  Brentwood *(G-1195)*

APPLICATIONS SOFTWARE PROGRAMMING

Galaxy Software LLC ....G 631 244-8405
  Oakdale *(G-13075)*
Maven Marketing LLC ....G 615 510-3248
  New York *(G-11207)*

AQUARIUM ACCESS, METAL

Aquarium Pump & Piping Systems ......F 631 567-5555
  Sayville *(G-15232)*

AQUARIUM DESIGN & MAINTENANCE SVCS

C B Management Services Inc ....F 845 735-2300
  Pearl River *(G-13477)*

AQUARIUMS & ACCESS: Glass

C B Management Services Inc ....F 845 735-2300
  Pearl River *(G-13477)*

AQUARIUMS & ACCESS: Plastic

Aquarium Pump & Piping Systems ......F 631 567-5555
  Sayville *(G-15232)*
Eugene G Danner Mfg Inc ....E 631 234-5261
  Central Islip *(G-3521)*

ARCHITECTURAL SVCS

B & F Architectural Support Gr ....E 212 279-6488
  New York *(G-9340)*
Deerfield Millwork Inc ....F 631 726-9663
  Water Mill *(G-16626)*
George G Sharp Inc ....E 212 732-2800
  New York *(G-10325)*
Productand Design Inc ....F 718 858-2440
  Brooklyn *(G-2467)*

ARMATURE REPAIRING & REWINDING SVC

Ener-G-Rotors Inc ....G 518 372-2608
  Schenectady *(G-15277)*
Power-Flo Technologies Inc ....D 315 399-5801
  East Syracuse *(G-4568)*
Power-Flo Technologies Inc ....E 585 426-4607
  Rochester *(G-14609)*
Sunset Ridge Holdings Inc ....G 716 487-1458
  Jamestown *(G-7066)*

AROMATIC CHEMICAL PRDTS

C & A Service Inc ....G 516 354-1200
  Floral Park *(G-5205)*
Citrus and Allied Essences Ltd ....E 516 354-1200
  Floral Park *(G-5207)*

ART & ORNAMENTAL WARE: Pottery

American Country Quilts & Lin ....G 631 283-5466
  Southampton *(G-15562)*

ART DEALERS & GALLERIES

Frame Shoppe & Art Gallery ....G 516 365-6014
  Manhasset *(G-8093)*
Penhouse Media Group Inc ....C 212 702-6000
  New York *(G-11625)*

ART DESIGN SVCS

Adflex Corporation ....E 585 454-2950
  Rochester *(G-14189)*
Dwm International Inc ....F 646 290-7448
  Long Island City *(G-7750)*
Graphics Plus Printing Inc ....E 607 299-0500
  Cortland *(G-4051)*

ART GOODS & SPLYS WHOLESALERS

Gei International Inc ....F 315 463-9261
  East Syracuse *(G-4546)*
Golden Group International Ltd ....G 845 440-1025
  Patterson *(G-13464)*
Lifestyle Design Usa Ltd ....F 212 279-9400
  New York *(G-11021)*

ART MARBLE: Concrete

Fordham Marble Co Inc ....F 914 682-6699
  White Plains *(G-17136)*
Milano Granite and Marble Corp ....F 718 477-7200
  Staten Island *(G-15727)*
Royal Marble & Granite Inc ....G 516 536-5900
  Oceanside *(G-13116)*

ART NEEDLEWORK, MADE FROM PURCHASED MATERIALS

Clpa Embroidery ....G 516 409-0002
  Bellmore *(G-812)*
Jomar Industries Inc ....E 845 357-5773
  Airmont *(G-14)*
Knucklehead Embroidery Inc ....G 607 797-2725
  Johnson City *(G-7129)*
Screen The World Inc ....F 631 475-0023
  Holtsville *(G-6534)*
Verdonette Inc ....G 212 719-2003
  New York *(G-12545)*

ART RELATED SVCS

Halo Associates ....G 212 691-9549
  New York *(G-10443)*

ART RESTORATION SVC

Julius Lowy Frame Restoring Co ....E 212 861-8585
  New York *(G-10819)*
Sunburst Studios Inc ....G 718 768-6360
  Brooklyn *(G-2642)*

ART SPLY STORES

Simon Liu Inc ....F 718 567-2011
  Brooklyn *(G-2587)*

ARTISTS' EQPT

Simon Liu Inc ....F 718 567-2011
  Brooklyn *(G-2587)*
Spaulding & Rogers Mfg Inc ....D 518 768-2070
  Voorheesville *(G-16539)*

ARTISTS' MATERIALS, WHOLESALE

R & F Handmade Paints Inc ....F 845 331-3112
  Kingston *(G-7236)*

ARTISTS' MATERIALS: Frames, Artists' Canvases

Clapper Hollow Designs Inc ....E 518 234-9561
  Cobleskill *(G-3759)*
Frames Plus Inc ....F 518 462-1842
  Menands *(G-8403)*
Handmade Frames Inc ....F 718 782-8364
  Brooklyn *(G-2066)*
Lopez Restorations Inc ....F 718 383-1555
  Brooklyn *(G-2238)*
Timeless Decor LLC ....C 315 782-5759
  Watertown *(G-16697)*

ARTISTS' MATERIALS: Ink, Drawing, Black & Colored

Sml Brothers Holding Corp ....D 718 402-2000
  Bronx *(G-1455)*

ARTISTS' MATERIALS: Paints, Exc Gold & Bronze

Golden Artist Colors Inc ....C 607 847-6154
  New Berlin *(G-8827)*

ARTISTS' MATERIALS: Pastels

North America Pastel Artists ....G 718 463-4701
  Flushing *(G-5281)*

ARTISTS' MATERIALS: Pencils & Leads

Gotham Pen Co Inc ....E 212 675-7904
  Yonkers *(G-17465)*

ARTISTS' MATERIALS: Wax

Micro Powders Inc ....E 914 332-6400
  Tarrytown *(G-16120)*

ARTWORK: Framed

Handmade Frames Inc ....F 718 782-8364
  Brooklyn *(G-2066)*
McGaw Group LLC ....F 212 876-8822
  New York *(G-11221)*

ASBESTOS PRODUCTS

Andujar Asbestos and Lead ....G 716 228-6757
  Buffalo *(G-2830)*
Regional MGT & Consulting Inc ....F 718 599-3718
  Brooklyn *(G-2506)*

ASPHALT & ASPHALT PRDTS

A Colarusso and Son Inc ....E 518 828-3218
  Hudson *(G-6631)*
Amfar Asphalt Corp ....G 631 269-9660
  Kings Park *(G-7199)*
Atlas Bituminous Co Inc ....F 315 457-2394
  Syracuse *(G-15880)*
Barrett Paving Materials Inc ....F 315 737-9471
  Clayville *(G-3712)*
C & C Ready-Mix Corporation ....E 607 797-5108
  Vestal *(G-16465)*
Callanan Industries Inc ....E 845 457-3158
  Montgomery *(G-8628)*
Cobleskill Stone Products Inc ....E 607 432-8321
  Oneonta *(G-13202)*
Cobleskill Stone Products Inc ....F 607 637-4271
  Hancock *(G-5984)*
Cosmicoat of Wny Inc ....G 716 772-2644
  Gasport *(G-5571)*
Hanson Aggregates PA LLC ....E 585 624-3800
  Honeoye Falls *(G-6557)*
King Road Materials Inc ....E 518 381-9995
  Albany *(G-94)*
King Road Materials Inc ....F 518 382-5354
  Schenectady *(G-15301)*
Northern Bituminous Mix Inc ....G 315 598-2141
  Fulton *(G-5486)*
Parks Paving & Sealing Inc ....F 315 737-5761
  Sauquoit *(G-15230)*
Peckham Materials Corp ....G 845 562-5370
  Newburgh *(G-12796)*
Peckham Materials Corp ....D 914 686-2045
  White Plains *(G-17176)*
Posillico Materials LLC ....F 631 249-1872
  Farmingdale *(G-5094)*
Rason Asphalt Inc ....G 516 239-7880
  Lawrence *(G-7423)*
Suit-Kote Corporation ....C 607 753-1100
  Cortland *(G-4069)*
Suit-Kote Corporation ....F 585 473-6321
  Rochester *(G-14730)*
Suit-Kote Corporation ....E 716 664-3750
  Jamestown *(G-7065)*
Upstone Materials Inc ....D 518 561-5321
  Plattsburgh *(G-13735)*
Vestal Asphalt Inc ....F 607 785-3393
  Vestal *(G-16480)*

ASPHALT COATINGS & SEALERS

Barrett Paving Materials Inc ....E 315 353-6611
  Norwood *(G-13058)*
Callanan Industries Inc ....E 845 457-3158
  Montgomery *(G-8628)*
Northeastern Sealcoat Inc ....F 585 544-4372
  Rochester *(G-14563)*

ASPHALT COATINGS & SEALERS

Peckham Materials Corp .... E 518 747-3353
  Hudson Falls *(G-6680)*
Sheldon Slate Products Co Inc .... E 518 642-1280
  Middle Granville *(G-8434)*
Suit-Kote Corporation .... E 607 535-2743
  Watkins Glen *(G-16722)*
Tntpaving .... G 607 372-4911
  Endicott *(G-4836)*

ASPHALT MIXTURES WHOLESALERS

A Colarusso and Son Inc .... E 518 828-3218
  Hudson *(G-6631)*
County Line Stone Co Inc .... E 716 542-5435
  Akron *(G-18)*
Hanson Aggregates PA LLC .... E 585 624-1220
  Honeoye Falls *(G-6558)*
Suit-Kote Corporation .... E 585 473-6321
  Rochester *(G-14730)*

ASPHALT PLANTS INCLUDING GRAVEL MIX TYPE

Midland Machinery Co Inc .... D 716 692-1200
  Tonawanda *(G-16199)*
Patterson Blacktop Corp .... G 845 628-3425
  Carmel *(G-3431)*
Peckham Materials Corp .... E 518 747-3353
  Hudson Falls *(G-6680)*
Penn Can Equipment Corporation .... G 315 378-0337
  Lyons *(G-8001)*
Rochester Asphalt Materials .... G 315 524-4619
  Walworth *(G-16572)*

ASSEMBLING SVC: Plumbing Fixture Fittings, Plastic

Mark Posner .... G 718 258-6241
  Brooklyn *(G-2273)*

ASSOCIATIONS: Engineering

American Inst Chem Engineers .... D 646 495-1355
  New York *(G-9170)*

ASSOCIATIONS: Scientists'

Association For Cmpt McHy Inc .... D 212 869-7440
  New York *(G-9292)*

ATOMIZERS

Aloi Solutions LLC .... E 585 292-0920
  Rochester *(G-14207)*
Ascribe Inc .... E 585 413-0298
  Rochester *(G-14234)*
Avanti Advanced Mfg Corp .... G 716 541-8945
  Buffalo *(G-2848)*
Boom LLC .... E 646 218-0752
  New York *(G-9489)*
Chan & Chan (usa) Corp .... G 718 388-9633
  Brooklyn *(G-1773)*
Christian Dior Perfumes LLC .... C 212 931-2200
  New York *(G-9662)*
Deva Concepts LLC .... E 212 343-0344
  New York *(G-9916)*
Givi Inc .... F 212 586-5029
  New York *(G-10343)*
Hoskie Co Inc .... D 718 628-8672
  Brooklyn *(G-2084)*
Mitten Manufacturing Inc .... E 315 437-7564
  Syracuse *(G-16012)*
Shyam Ahuja Limited .... G 212 644-5910
  New York *(G-12080)*
Trendsformers Ltd Liability Co .... G 888 700-2423
  New York *(G-12419)*

ATTENUATORS

Mini-Circuits Fort Wayne LLC .... B 718 934-4500
  Brooklyn *(G-2322)*

AUDIO & VIDEO EQPT, EXC COMMERCIAL

Accent Speaker Technology Ltd .... G 631 738-2540
  Holbrook *(G-6455)*
All In Audio Inc .... F 718 506-0948
  Brooklyn *(G-1585)*
Audio Video Invasion Inc .... F 516 345-2636
  Plainview *(G-13613)*
Audiosavings Inc .... F 888 445-1555
  Inwood *(G-6791)*
Avcom of Virginia Inc .... D 585 924-4560
  Victor *(G-16485)*
AVI-Spl Employee .... B 212 840-4801
  New York *(G-9330)*
B & H Electronics Corp .... G 845 782-5000
  Monroe *(G-8584)*
Bayit Home Automation Corp .... E 973 988-2638
  Brooklyn *(G-1671)*
Communication Power Corp .... E 631 434-7306
  Hauppauge *(G-6071)*
Digital Home Creations Inc .... G 585 576-7070
  Webster *(G-16745)*
G E Inspection Technologies LP .... E 315 554-2000
  Skaneateles *(G-15481)*
General Electric Company .... G 315 554-2000
  Skaneateles *(G-15482)*
Key Digital Systems Inc .... E 914 667-9700
  Mount Vernon *(G-8742)*
L3 Technologies Inc .... A 631 436-7400
  Hauppauge *(G-6133)*
Laird Telemedia .... C 845 339-9555
  Mount Marion *(G-8692)*
Masterdisk Corporation .... F 212 541-5022
  Elmsford *(G-4773)*
Navitar Inc .... D 585 359-4000
  Rochester *(G-14550)*
NEa Manufacturing Corp .... E 516 371-4200
  Inwood *(G-6803)*
New Audio LLC .... E 212 213-6060
  New York *(G-11402)*
New Wop Records .... G 631 617-9732
  Deer Park *(G-4203)*
Scy Manufacturing Inc .... G 516 986-3083
  Inwood *(G-6806)*
Sima Technologies LLC .... G 412 828-9130
  Hauppauge *(G-6215)*
Sony Corporation of America .... C 212 833-8000
  New York *(G-12157)*
Sound Video Systems Wny LLC .... F 716 684-8200
  Buffalo *(G-3222)*
Tkm Technologies Inc .... G 631 474-4700
  Port Jeff STA *(G-13796)*
Touchtunes Music Corporation .... D 847 419-3300
  New York *(G-12403)*
Wyrestorm Technologies LLC .... F 518 289-1293
  Round Lake *(G-15063)*

AUDIO COMPONENTS

Ashly Audio Inc .... E 585 872-0010
  Webster *(G-16737)*
Convergent Audio Tech Inc .... C 585 359-2700
  Rush *(G-15070)*

AUDIO ELECTRONIC SYSTEMS

Audio Technology New York Inc .... F 718 369-7528
  Brooklyn *(G-1654)*
B & K Components Ltd .... D 323 776-4277
  Buffalo *(G-2850)*
Data Interchange Systems Inc .... G 914 277-7775
  Purdys *(G-13988)*
Gilmores Sound Advice Inc .... F 212 265-4445
  New York *(G-10338)*
Granada Electronics Inc .... G 718 387-1157
  Brooklyn *(G-2048)*
Lamm Industries Inc .... G 718 368-0181
  Brooklyn *(G-2193)*
Vincent Conigliaro .... F 845 340-0489
  Kingston *(G-7251)*
Whirlwind Music Distrs Inc .... D 800 733-9473
  Rochester *(G-14790)*
Yorkville Sound Inc .... G 716 297-2920
  Niagara Falls *(G-12908)*

AUDIO-VISUAL PROGRAM PRODUCTION SVCS

ABRA Media Inc .... G 518 398-1010
  Pine Plains *(G-13581)*
Guilford Publications Inc .... D 212 431-9800
  New York *(G-10425)*
Hatherleigh Company Ltd .... G 607 538-1092
  Hobart *(G-6451)*
Play-It Productions Inc .... G 212 695-6530
  Port Washington *(G-13873)*

AUDIOLOGISTS' OFFICES

Family Hearing Center .... G 845 897-3059
  Fishkill *(G-5191)*
Todt Hill Audiological Svcs .... G 718 816-1952
  Staten Island *(G-15771)*

AUDITING SVCS

Advance Finance Group LLC .... D 212 630-5900
  New York *(G-9084)*

AUTO & HOME SUPPLY STORES: Auto & Truck Eqpt & Parts

K M Drive Line Inc .... G 718 599-0628
  Brooklyn *(G-2164)*

AUTO & HOME SUPPLY STORES: Automotive Access

Legendary Auto Interiors Ltd .... E 315 331-1212
  Newark *(G-12754)*
Split Rock Trading Co Inc .... G 631 929-3261
  Wading River *(G-16546)*
Zappala Farms AG Systems Inc .... E 315 626-6293
  Cato *(G-3453)*

AUTO & HOME SUPPLY STORES: Speed Shops, Incl Race Car Splys

Auto Sport Designs Inc .... F 631 425-1555
  Huntington Station *(G-6735)*
Marcovicci-Wenz Engineering .... G 631 467-9040
  Ronkonkoma *(G-14965)*
Troyer Inc .... F 585 352-5590
  Rochester *(G-14760)*

AUTO & HOME SUPPLY STORES: Trailer Hitches, Automotive

General Welding & Fabg Inc .... G 585 697-7660
  Rochester *(G-14413)*

AUTO & HOME SUPPLY STORES: Truck Eqpt & Parts

Agri Services Co .... G 716 937-6618
  Alden *(G-176)*
Chet Kruszkas Service Inc .... F 716 662-7450
  Orchard Park *(G-13284)*
Dejana Trck Utility Eqp Co LLC .... C 631 544-9000
  Kings Park *(G-7200)*
General Welding & Fabg Inc .... G 716 652-0033
  Elma *(G-4662)*

AUTOCLAVES: Indl

Wsf Industries Inc .... E 716 692-4930
  Tonawanda *(G-16237)*

AUTOCLAVES: Laboratory

SPS Medical Supply Corp .... F 585 968-2377
  Cuba *(G-4096)*
Vivus Technologies LLC .... G 585 798-6658
  Medina *(G-8316)*

AUTOMATIC REGULATING CONTROL: Building Svcs Monitoring, Auto

Building Management Assoc Inc .... E 718 542-4779
  Bronx *(G-1289)*
Johnson Controls Inc .... C 585 724-2232
  Rochester *(G-14485)*
Reuse Action Incorporated .... G 716 949-0900
  Buffalo *(G-3183)*
Unisend LLC .... G 585 414-9575
  Webster *(G-16765)*
Virtual Super LLC .... G 212 685-6400
  New York *(G-12578)*

AUTOMATIC REGULATING CONTROLS: AC & Refrigeration

Bitzer Scroll Inc .... D 315 463-2101
  Syracuse *(G-15890)*
Care Enterprises Inc .... G 631 472-8155
  Bayport *(G-749)*
Siemens Industry Inc .... D 716 568-0983
  Amherst *(G-261)*

PRODUCT SECTION

AUTOMOTIVE REPAIR SHOPS: Diesel Engine Repair

AUTOMATIC REGULATING CONTROLS: Elect Air Cleaner, Automatic

Biorem Environmental Inc ....E 585 924-2220
 Victor *(G-16486)*

AUTOMATIC REGULATING CONTROLS: Energy Cutoff, Residtl/Comm

Black River Generations LLC ....E 315 773-2314
 Fort Drum *(G-5345)*
Eastern Strategic Materials ....E 212 332-1619
 New York *(G-10018)*
Johnson Controls Inc ....E 914 593-5200
 Hawthorne *(G-6271)*

AUTOMATIC REGULATING CONTROLS: Ice Maker

Henderson Products Inc ....E 315 785-0994
 Watertown *(G-16675)*

AUTOMATIC REGULATING CONTROLS: Pneumatic Relays, Air-Cond

A K Allen Co Inc ....C 516 747-5450
 Mineola *(G-8522)*

AUTOMATIC REGULATING CONTROLS: Refrig/Air-Cond Defrost

Carrier Corporation ....B 315 432-6000
 Syracuse *(G-15907)*
Svyz Trading Corp ....E 718 220-1140
 Bronx *(G-1467)*

AUTOMATIC REGULATING CTRLS: Damper, Pneumatic Or Electric

Air Louver & Damper Inc ....E 718 392-3232
 Maspeth *(G-8141)*
Air Louver & Damper Inc ....F 718 392-3232
 Long Island City *(G-7681)*
Airflex Industrial Inc ....E 631 752-1234
 Farmingdale *(G-4940)*

AUTOMATIC TELLER MACHINES

International Mdse Svcs Inc ....G 914 699-4000
 Mount Vernon *(G-8738)*
Jpmorgan Chase Bank Nat Assn ....G 718 944-7964
 Bronx *(G-1372)*
Jpmorgan Chase Bank Nat Assn ....G 718 767-3592
 College Point *(G-3817)*
Jpmorgan Chase Bank Nat Assn ....G 718 668-0346
 Staten Island *(G-15717)*
K&G of Syracuse Inc ....G 315 446-1921
 Syracuse *(G-15991)*
Mid Enterprise Inc ....G 631 924-3933
 Middle Island *(G-8440)*
Parabit Systems Inc ....E 516 378-4800
 Roosevelt *(G-15031)*
Sharenet Inc ....G 315 477-1100
 Syracuse *(G-16062)*
Stanson Automated LLC ....F 866 505-7826
 Yonkers *(G-17503)*

AUTOMATIC VENDING MACHINES: Mechanisms & Parts

Global Payment Tech Inc ....F 516 887-0700
 Valley Stream *(G-16434)*
Global Payment Tech Inc ....E 631 563-2500
 Bohemia *(G-1070)*

AUTOMOBILES: Off-Highway, Electric

Bombardier Trnsp Holdings USA ....D 607 776-4791
 Bath *(G-654)*

AUTOMOBILES: Wholesalers

Split Rock Trading Co Inc ....G 631 929-3261
 Wading River *(G-16546)*

AUTOMOTIVE & TRUCK GENERAL REPAIR SVC

Automotive Filters Mfg Inc ....F 631 435-1010
 Bohemia *(G-1016)*
Dennys Drive Shaft Service ....G 716 875-6640
 Kenmore *(G-7174)*
Homer Iron Works LLC ....G 607 749-3963
 Homer *(G-6547)*
James Woerner Inc ....G 631 454-9330
 Farmingdale *(G-5024)*
Whitesboro Spring & Alignment ....F 315 736-4441
 Whitesboro *(G-17226)*

AUTOMOTIVE BODY SHOP

Chet Kruszkas Service Inc ....F 716 662-7450
 Orchard Park *(G-13284)*
Nochem Paint Stripping Inc ....G 631 563-2750
 Blue Point *(G-994)*

AUTOMOTIVE BODY, PAINT & INTERIOR REPAIR & MAINTENANCE SVC

Conti Auto Body Corp ....G 516 921-6435
 Syosset *(G-15837)*

AUTOMOTIVE CUSTOMIZING SVCS, NONFACTORY BASIS

Apsis USA Inc ....F 631 421-6800
 Farmingdale *(G-4952)*

AUTOMOTIVE PARTS, ACCESS & SPLYS

Actasys Inc ....G 617 834-0666
 Watervliet *(G-16702)*
Allomatic Products Company ....G 516 775-0330
 Floral Park *(G-5200)*
Alloy Metal Products LLC ....F 315 676-2405
 Central Square *(G-3542)*
American Auto ACC Incrporation ....E 718 886-6600
 Flushing *(G-5233)*
American Refuse Supply Inc ....G 718 893-8157
 Bronx *(G-1273)*
Anchor Commerce Trading Corp ....G 516 881-3485
 Atlantic Beach *(G-467)*
Apsis USA Inc ....F 631 421-6800
 Farmingdale *(G-4952)*
Automotive Accessories Group ....B 212 736-8100
 New York *(G-9320)*
Axle Express ....E 518 347-2220
 Schenectady *(G-15261)*
Bigbee Steel and Tank Company ....E 518 273-0801
 Watervliet *(G-16703)*
Borgwarner Inc ....E 607 257-1800
 Ithaca *(G-6863)*
Borgwarner Morse TEC Inc ....D 607 266-5111
 Ithaca *(G-6865)*
Borgwarner Morse TEC LLC ....C 607 257-6700
 Ithaca *(G-6866)*
Borgwarner Morse TEC LLC ....D 607 257-6700
 Cortland *(G-4037)*
Car-Go Industries Inc ....G 718 472-1443
 Woodside *(G-17340)*
Classic & Performance Spc ....E 716 759-1800
 Lancaster *(G-7334)*
Cubic Trnsp Systems Inc ....F 212 255-1810
 New York *(G-9821)*
Cummins Inc ....A 716 456-2111
 Lakewood *(G-7314)*
Cummins Inc ....B 812 377-5000
 Jamestown *(G-7021)*
Custom Sitecom LLC ....F 631 420-4238
 Farmingdale *(G-4981)*
Delphi Automotive LLP ....G 716 438-4886
 Amherst *(G-237)*
Delphi Automotive Systems LLC ....C 585 359-6000
 West Henrietta *(G-16908)*
Delphi Automotive Systems LLC ....A 585 359-6000
 West Henrietta *(G-16909)*
Delphi Automotive Systems LLC ....E 585 359-6000
 West Henrietta *(G-16910)*
Delphi Thermal Systems ....F 716 439-2454
 Lockport *(G-7607)*
Dmic Inc ....F 716 743-4360
 North Tonawanda *(G-12987)*
Electronic Machine Parts LLC ....F 631 434-3700
 Hauppauge *(G-6093)*
Exten II LLC ....F 716 895-2214
 Buffalo *(G-2956)*
Fast By Gast Inc. ....G 716 773-1536
 Grand Island *(G-5770)*
General Motors LLC ....B 315 764-2000
 Massena *(G-8226)*
GM Components Holdings LLC ....B 585 647-7000
 Rochester *(G-14430)*
GM Components Holdings LLC ....B 716 439-2463
 Lockport *(G-7619)*
GM Components Holdings LLC ....B 716 439-2011
 Lockport *(G-7620)*
ITT Enidine Inc ....B 716 662-1900
 Orchard Park *(G-13299)*
Jtekt Torsen North America ....F 585 464-5000
 Rochester *(G-14487)*
Karlyn Industries Inc ....F 845 351-2249
 Southfields *(G-15580)*
Kerns Manufacturing Corp ....C 718 784-4044
 Long Island City *(G-7807)*
Lee World Industries LLC ....C 212 265-8866
 New York *(G-10993)*
Magtrol Inc ....E 716 668-5555
 Buffalo *(G-3075)*
Mahle Behr USA Inc ....B 716 439-2011
 Lockport *(G-7627)*
Mahle Industries Incorporated ....F 248 735-3623
 Amherst *(G-249)*
Nas-Tra Automotive Inds Inc ....C 631 225-1225
 Lindenhurst *(G-7497)*
Norcatec LLC ....E 516 222-7070
 Garden City *(G-5537)*
Omega Industries & Development ....E 516 349-8010
 Plainview *(G-13654)*
Par-Foam Products Inc ....C 716 855-2066
 Buffalo *(G-3135)*
Parker-Hannifin Corporation ....D 248 628-6017
 Lancaster *(G-7355)*
Performance Designed By Peters ....F 585 223-9062
 Fairport *(G-4876)*
Phillip J Ortiz Manufacturing ....G 845 226-7030
 Hopewell Junction *(G-6583)*
Powerflow Inc ....D 716 892-1014
 Buffalo *(G-3157)*
Pro-Value Distribution Inc ....G 585 783-1461
 Rochester *(G-14627)*
Rosco Inc ....C 718 526-2601
 Jamaica *(G-6985)*
Secor Marketing Group Inc ....G 914 381-3600
 Mamaroneck *(G-8079)*
Specialty Silicone Pdts Inc ....E 518 885-8826
 Ballston Spa *(G-608)*
Tesla Motors Inc ....A 212 206-1204
 New York *(G-12325)*
Troyer Inc ....F 585 352-5590
 Rochester *(G-14760)*
TRW Automotive Inc ....B 315 255-3311
 Auburn *(G-522)*
Whiting Door Mfg Corp ....B 716 542-5427
 Akron *(G-27)*
Wolo Mfg Corp ....E 631 242-0333
 Deer Park *(G-4253)*
Yomiuri International Inc ....G 212 752-2196
 New York *(G-12716)*

AUTOMOTIVE PARTS: Plastic

CN Group Incorporated ....A 914 358-5690
 White Plains *(G-17122)*
Fiber Laminations Limited ....F 716 692-1825
 Tonawanda *(G-16180)*
Koonichi Inc ....G 718 886-8338
 Fresh Meadows *(G-5457)*
Macauto Usa Inc ....E 585 342-2060
 Rochester *(G-14506)*
Tint World ....G 631 458-1999
 Medford *(G-8295)*

AUTOMOTIVE PRDTS: Rubber

Chamberlin Rubber Company Inc ....E 585 427-7780
 Rochester *(G-14291)*
Vehicle Manufacturers Inc ....E 631 851-1700
 Hauppauge *(G-6247)*

AUTOMOTIVE REPAIR SHOPS: Brake Repair

Whitesboro Spring & Alignment ....F 315 736-4441
 Whitesboro *(G-17226)*

AUTOMOTIVE REPAIR SHOPS: Diesel Engine Repair

Jack W Miller ....G 585 538-2399
 Scottsville *(G-15359)*

Employee Codes: A=Over 500 employees, B=251-500
C=101-250, D=51-100, E=20-50, F=10-19, G=5-9

AUTOMOTIVE REPAIR SHOPS: Electrical Svcs

Gerome Technologies Inc .... D 518 463-1324
  Menands (G-8404)

AUTOMOTIVE REPAIR SHOPS: Engine Repair

Jack Merkel Inc .... G 631 234-2600
  Hauppauge (G-6125)

AUTOMOTIVE REPAIR SHOPS: Machine Shop

Bullet Industries Inc .... G 585 352-0836
  Spencerport (G-15592)
Meade Machine Co Inc .... G 315 923-1703
  Clyde (G-3753)
Vytek Inc .... F 631 750-1770
  Bohemia (G-1152)

AUTOMOTIVE REPAIR SHOPS: Trailer Repair

General Welding & Fabg Inc .... G 585 697-7660
  Rochester (G-14413)

AUTOMOTIVE REPAIR SVC

Banner Transmission & Eng Co ...... F 516 221-9459
  Bellmore (G-810)
Cyclone Air Power Inc .... G 718 447-3038
  Staten Island (G-15684)

AUTOMOTIVE SPLYS & PARTS, NEW, WHOL: Testing Eqpt, Electric

Katikati Inc .... G 585 678-1764
  West Henrietta (G-16915)

AUTOMOTIVE SPLYS & PARTS, NEW, WHOLESALE: Brakes

Interparts International Inc .... E 516 576-2000
  Plainview (G-13639)

AUTOMOTIVE SPLYS & PARTS, NEW, WHOLESALE: Clutches

Rpb Distributors LLC .... G 914 244-3600
  Mount Kisco (G-8687)

AUTOMOTIVE SPLYS & PARTS, NEW, WHOLESALE: Engines/Eng Parts

Cummins Northeast LLC .... E 315 437-2296
  Syracuse (G-15935)

AUTOMOTIVE SPLYS & PARTS, NEW, WHOLESALE: Splys

Extreme Auto Accessories Corp ...... F 718 978-6722
  South Ozone Park (G-15557)

AUTOMOTIVE SPLYS & PARTS, NEW, WHOLESALE: Trim

Legendary Auto Interiors Ltd .... E 315 331-1212
  Newark (G-12754)

AUTOMOTIVE SPLYS & PARTS, NEW, WHOLESALE: Wheels

Factory Wheel Warehouse Inc .... G 516 605-2131
  Plainview (G-13630)

AUTOMOTIVE SPLYS & PARTS, USED, WHOLESALE: Wheels

Factory Wheel Warehouse Inc .... G 516 605-2131
  Plainview (G-13630)

AUTOMOTIVE SPLYS & PARTS, WHOLESALE, NEC

Auto-Mat Company Inc .... E 516 938-7373
  Hicksville (G-6349)
Automotive Filters Mfg Inc .... F 631 435-1010
  Bohemia (G-1016)

Axle Teknology LLC .... G 631 423-3044
  Huntington (G-6687)
Deer Park Driveshaft & Hose .... G 631 667-4091
  Deer Park (G-4149)
Depot Label Company Inc .... G 631 467-2952
  Patchogue (G-13443)
Noresco Industrial Group Inc .... E 516 759-3355
  Glen Cove (G-5635)
Split Rock Trading Co Inc .... G 631 929-3261
  Wading River (G-16546)
Tint World .... G 631 458-1999
  Medford (G-8295)

AUTOMOTIVE SPLYS/PARTS, NEW, WHOL: Body Rpr/Paint Shop Splys

Auto Body Services LLC .... F 631 431-4640
  Lindenhurst (G-7477)

AUTOMOTIVE SVCS, EXC REPAIR & CARWASHES: Maintenance

Roli Retreads Inc .... E 631 694-7670
  Farmingdale (G-5112)

AUTOMOTIVE SVCS, EXC REPAIR: Washing & Polishing

Saccomize Inc .... G 818 287-3000
  Bronx (G-1445)

AUTOMOTIVE SVCS, EXC RPR/CARWASHES: High Perf Auto Rpr/Svc

Riverview Industries Inc .... G 845 265-5284
  Cold Spring (G-3790)

AUTOMOTIVE TOPS INSTALLATION OR REPAIR: Canvas Or Plastic

Quantum Sails Rochester LLC .... G 585 342-5200
  Rochester (G-14640)

AUTOMOTIVE TOWING & WRECKING SVC

American Towman Network Inc .... F 845 986-4546
  Warwick (G-16608)

AUTOMOTIVE UPHOLSTERY SHOPS

Sausbiers Awning Shop Inc .... G 518 828-3748
  Hudson (G-6664)

AUTOMOTIVE WELDING SVCS

Big Apple Welding Supply .... G 718 439-3959
  Brooklyn (G-1693)
Chautauqua Machine Spc LLC .... F 716 782-3276
  Ashville (G-424)
In Northeast Precision Welding .... G 518 441-2260
  Castleton On Hudson (G-3447)

AUTOMOTIVE: Bodies

Antiques & Collectible Autos .... G 716 825-3990
  Buffalo (G-2832)
Conti Auto Body Corp .... G 516 921-6435
  Syosset (G-15837)
Empire Coachworks Intl LLC .... D 732 257-7981
  Suffern (G-15812)

AUTOMOTIVE: Seating

Johnson Controls Inc .... D 518 884-8313
  Ballston Spa (G-598)
Johnson Controls Inc .... G 518 694-4822
  Albany (G-92)
Johnson Controls Inc .... E 585 671-1930
  Webster (G-16750)
Johnson Controls Inc .... C 585 724-2232
  Rochester (G-14485)

AUTOTRANSFORMERS: Electric

General Electric Company .... A 518 385-4022
  Schenectady (G-15283)
General Electric Company .... E 518 385-7620
  Niskayuna (G-12912)

AWNING REPAIR SHOP

Kohler Awning Inc .... E 716 685-3333
  Buffalo (G-3054)

TG Peppe Inc .... G 516 239-7852
  Lawrence (G-7426)

AWNINGS & CANOPIES

Five Star Awnings Inc .... F 718 860-6070
  Ridgewood (G-14119)
Hart To Hart Industries Inc .... G 716 492-2709
  Chaffee (G-3562)
Ke Durasol Awnings Inc .... G 845 610-1100
  Chester (G-3636)
Lotus Awnings Enterprises Inc .... G 718 965-4824
  Brooklyn (G-2240)
Superior Exteriors of Buffalo .... F 716 873-1000
  East Amherst (G-4388)
Vitarose Corp of America .... G 718 951-9700
  Brooklyn (G-2751)

AWNINGS & CANOPIES: Awnings, Fabric, From Purchased Matls

125-127 Main Street Corp .... F 631 477-1500
  Greenport (G-5894)
Abble Awning Co Inc .... G 516 822-1200
  Bethpage (G-861)
Acme Awning Co Inc .... F 718 409-1881
  Bronx (G-1263)
Awning Mart Inc .... G 315 699-5928
  Cicero (G-3671)
Awnings Plus Inc .... F 716 693-3690
  Tonawanda (G-16163)
C E King & Sons Inc .... G 631 324-4944
  East Hampton (G-4426)
Canvas Products Company Inc ...... F 516 742-1058
  Mineola (G-8533)
Capitol Awning Co Inc .... F 212 505-1717
  Jamaica (G-6936)
Classic Awnings Inc .... F 716 649-0390
  Hamburg (G-5943)
Di Sanos Creative Canvas Inc .... G 315 894-3137
  Frankfort (G-5360)
Durasol Systems Inc .... D 845 610-1100
  Chester (G-3632)
Fabric Concepts For Industry .... F 914 375-2565
  Yonkers (G-17458)
Jamestown Awning Inc .... G 716 483-1435
  Jamestown (G-7038)
Kohler Awning Inc .... E 716 685-3333
  Buffalo (G-3054)
Mauceri Sign Inc .... F 718 656-7700
  Jamaica (G-6965)
Perma Tech Inc .... F 716 854-0707
  Buffalo (G-3145)
Sausbiers Awning Shop Inc .... G 518 828-3748
  Hudson (G-6664)
Steinway Awning II LLC .... F 718 729-2965
  Astoria (G-458)
TG Peppe Inc .... G 516 239-7852
  Lawrence (G-7426)

AWNINGS & CANOPIES: Fabric

Kingston Building Products LLC ..... G 914 665-0707
  Mount Vernon (G-8744)
Lanza Corp .... G 914 937-6360
  Port Chester (G-13778)

AWNINGS: Fiberglass

Acme Awning Co Inc .... F 718 409-1881
  Bronx (G-1263)
Space Sign .... F 718 961-1112
  College Point (G-3834)
Vitarose Corp of America .... G 718 951-9700
  Brooklyn (G-2751)

AWNINGS: Metal

Dart Awning Inc .... F 718 945-4224
  Freeport (G-5404)
Kenan International Trading .... G 718 672-4922
  Corona (G-4023)
Space Sign .... F 718 961-1112
  College Point (G-3834)

AWNINGS: Wood

Midwood Signs & Design Inc .... G 718 499-9041
  Brooklyn (G-2316)

PRODUCT SECTION

AXLES
Axle Teknology LLC .... G 631 423-3044
  Huntington *(G-6687)*
Temper Corporation .... G 518 853-3467
  Fonda *(G-5323)*

BABY FORMULA
Baby Central LLC .... G 718 372-2229
  Brooklyn *(G-1660)*

BABY PACIFIERS: Rubber
Mam USA Corporation .... F 914 269-2500
  Purchase *(G-13977)*

BADGES, WHOLESALE
Paragon Corporation .... F 516 484-6090
  Port Washington *(G-13872)*

BADGES: Identification & Insignia
Identfication Data Imaging LLC .... G 516 484-6500
  Port Washington *(G-13844)*

BAGS & BAGGING: Knit
Nochairs Inc .... G 917 748-8731
  New York *(G-11465)*

BAGS & CONTAINERS: Textile, Exc Sleeping
Carry Hot Inc .... F 212 279-7535
  New York *(G-9590)*

BAGS & SACKS: Shipping & Shopping
Kapstone Container Corporation .... D 518 842-2450
  Amsterdam *(G-352)*

BAGS: Canvas
Aka Sport Inc .... F 631 858-9888
  Dix Hills *(G-4312)*
H G Maybeck Co Inc .... E 718 297-4410
  Jamaica *(G-6954)*
Reflective Shopper Usa LLC .... G 855 735-3222
  West Nyack *(G-16955)*

BAGS: Cellophane
Aladdin Packaging LLC .... D 631 273-4747
  Hauppauge *(G-6033)*

BAGS: Duffle, Canvas, Made From Purchased Materials
Select Fabricators Inc .... F 585 393-0650
  Canandaigua *(G-3387)*

BAGS: Food Storage & Frozen Food, Plastic
Pactiv LLC .... C 585 394-5125
  Canandaigua *(G-3381)*

BAGS: Food Storage & Trash, Plastic
Bag Arts The Art Packaging LLC .... G 212 684-7020
  New York *(G-9356)*
Mint-X Products Corporation .... F 877 646-8224
  College Point *(G-3822)*
Pactiv LLC .... C 518 793-2524
  Glens Falls *(G-5710)*

BAGS: Garment Storage Exc Paper Or Plastic Film
Apex Real Holdings Inc .... G 877 725-2150
  Brooklyn *(G-1616)*

BAGS: Grocers', Made From Purchased Materials
333 J & M Food Corp .... F 718 381-1493
  Ridgewood *(G-14109)*
Bag Arts The Art Packaging LLC .... G 212 684-7020
  New York *(G-9356)*
Lin Jin Feng .... G 718 232-3039
  Brooklyn *(G-2226)*

BAGS: Knapsacks, Canvas, Made From Purchased Materials
Johnson Outdoors Inc .... C 607 779-2200
  Binghamton *(G-926)*

BAGS: Laundry, Garment & Storage
Handy Laundry Products Corp .... G 800 263-5973
  Airmont *(G-13)*

BAGS: Paper
American Packaging Corporation .... C 585 254-9500
  Rochester *(G-14214)*
APC Paper Company Inc .... D 315 384-4225
  Norfolk *(G-12914)*
R P Fedder Corp .... E 585 288-1600
  Rochester *(G-14643)*

BAGS: Paper, Made From Purchased Materials
Polyseal Packaging Corp .... E 718 792-5530
  Bronx *(G-1429)*

BAGS: Plastic
Adart Polyethylene Bag Mfg .... G 516 932-1001
  Plainview *(G-13606)*
American Packaging Corporation .... G 585 254-2002
  Rochester *(G-14213)*
American Packaging Corporation .... C 585 254-9500
  Rochester *(G-14214)*
Berry Global Inc .... C 315 986-2161
  Macedon *(G-8011)*
Capitol Poly Corp .... E 718 855-6000
  Brooklyn *(G-1757)*
Clear View Bag Company Inc .... C 518 458-7153
  Albany *(G-64)*
Craft Pak Inc .... G 718 257-2700
  Staten Island *(G-15683)*
Ecoplast & Packaging LLC .... G 718 996-0800
  Brooklyn *(G-1902)*
Edco Supply Corporation .... D 718 788-8108
  Brooklyn *(G-1905)*
Filmpak Extrusion LLC .... D 631 293-6767
  Melville *(G-8348)*
H G Maybeck Co Inc .... E 718 297-4410
  Jamaica *(G-6954)*
Ivi Services Inc .... D 607 729-5111
  Binghamton *(G-924)*
Jay Bags Inc .... G 845 459-6500
  Spring Valley *(G-15612)*
JM Murray Center Inc .... C 607 756-9913
  Cortland *(G-4055)*
JM Murray Center Inc .... C 607 756-0246
  Cortland *(G-4056)*
Kemco Sales LLC .... F 203 762-1902
  East Rochester *(G-4482)*
Magcrest Packaging Inc .... G 845 425-0451
  Monsey *(G-8609)*
Metpak Inc .... G 917 309-0196
  Brooklyn *(G-2309)*
Milla Global Inc .... G 516 488-3601
  Brooklyn *(G-2319)*
Noteworthy Industries Inc .... C 518 842-2662
  Amsterdam *(G-365)*
Nova Packaging Ltd Inc .... E 914 232-8406
  Katonah *(G-7161)*
Select Fabricators Inc .... F 585 393-0650
  Canandaigua *(G-3387)*
Tai Seng .... G 718 399-6311
  Brooklyn *(G-2665)*
Trinity Packaging Corporation .... E 716 668-3111
  Buffalo *(G-3251)*
W E W Container Corporation .... E 718 827-8150
  Brooklyn *(G-2757)*
Wally Packaging Inc .... G 718 377-5323
  Brooklyn *(G-2758)*

BAGS: Plastic & Pliofilm
Maco Bag Corporation .... C 315 226-1000
  Newark *(G-12755)*
Modern Plastic Bags Mfg Inc .... G 718 237-2985
  Brooklyn *(G-2332)*
Primo Plastics Inc .... E 718 349-1000
  Brooklyn *(G-2457)*

BAGS: Plastic, Made From Purchased Materials
Alco Plastics Inc .... E 716 683-3020
  Lancaster *(G-7325)*
Allied Converters Inc .... E 914 235-1585
  New Rochelle *(G-8931)*
Amby International Inc .... G 718 645-0964
  Brooklyn *(G-1595)*
API Industries Inc .... B 845 365-2200
  Orangeburg *(G-13239)*
API Industries Inc .... C 845 365-2200
  Orangeburg *(G-13240)*
Baggu .... G 347 457-5266
  Brooklyn *(G-1662)*
Bags Unlimited Inc .... E 585 436-6282
  Rochester *(G-14238)*
Bison Bag Co Inc .... D 716 434-4380
  Lockport *(G-7600)*
Connover Packaging Inc .... G 585 377-2510
  East Rochester *(G-4475)*
Courier Packaging Inc .... E 718 349-2390
  Brooklyn *(G-1808)*
Excellent Poly Inc .... E 718 768-6555
  Brooklyn *(G-1948)*
Fortune Poly Products Inc .... F 718 361-0767
  Jamaica *(G-6948)*
Franklin Poly Film Inc .... E 718 492-3523
  Brooklyn *(G-2002)*
Josh Packaging Inc .... E 631 822-1660
  Hauppauge *(G-6127)*
Manhattan Poly Bag Corporation .... E 917 689-7549
  Brooklyn *(G-2261)*
Mason Transparent Package Inc .... E 718 792-6000
  Bronx *(G-1392)*
Metropolitan Packg Mfg Corp .... E 718 383-2700
  Brooklyn *(G-2312)*
Nap Industries Inc .... D 718 625-4948
  Brooklyn *(G-2355)*
New York Packaging Corp .... D 516 746-0600
  New Hyde Park *(G-8896)*
New York Packaging II LLC .... C 516 746-0600
  Garden City *(G-5536)*
Pacific Poly Product Corp .... F 718 786-7129
  Long Island City *(G-7864)*
Pack America Corp .... G 212 508-6666
  New York *(G-11568)*
Paradise Plastics LLC .... E 718 788-3733
  Brooklyn *(G-2419)*
Paramount Equipment Inc .... E 631 981-4422
  Ronkonkoma *(G-14988)*
Poly Craft Industries Corp .... E 631 630-6731
  Hauppauge *(G-6193)*
Poly-Pak Industries Inc .... B 631 293-6767
  Melville *(G-8377)*
Polyseal Packaging Corp .... E 718 792-5530
  Bronx *(G-1429)*
Protective Lining Corp .... D 718 854-3838
  Brooklyn *(G-2472)*
Rainbow Poly Bag Co Inc .... E 718 386-3500
  Brooklyn *(G-2495)*
Rege Inc .... F 845 565-7772
  New Windsor *(G-8996)*
Rtr Bag & Co Ltd .... G 212 620-0011
  New York *(G-11950)*
Salerno Packaging Inc .... F 518 563-3636
  Plattsburgh *(G-13724)*
Star Poly Bag Inc .... F 718 384-3130
  Brooklyn *(G-2620)*
Supreme Poly Plastics Inc .... E 718 456-9300
  Brooklyn *(G-2652)*
T M I Plastics Industries Inc .... F 718 383-0363
  Brooklyn *(G-2659)*
Technipoly Manufacturing Inc .... E 718 383-0363
  Brooklyn *(G-2671)*
Trinity Packaging Corporation .... F 914 273-4111
  Armonk *(G-419)*
United Plastics Inc .... G 718 389-2255
  Brooklyn *(G-2721)*

BAGS: Rubber Or Rubberized Fabric
Adam Scott Designs Inc .... E 212 420-8866
  New York *(G-9071)*

BAGS: Shipping
Shalam Imports Inc .... F 718 686-6271
  Brooklyn *(G-2576)*

BAGS: Shopping, Made From Purchased Materials

Ampac Paper LLC....B....845 778-5511
Walden *(G-16549)*
Custom Eco Friendly LLC....G....347 227-0229
Roslyn *(G-15042)*
Rtr Bag & Co Ltd....G....212 620-0011
New York *(G-11950)*

BAGS: Tea, Fabric, Made From Purchased Materials

Health Matters America Inc....F....716 235-8772
Buffalo *(G-3009)*

BAGS: Textile

Ace Drop Cloth Canvas Pdts Inc....E....718 731-1550
Bronx *(G-1261)*
Clear Edge Crosible Inc....D....315 685-3466
Skaneateles Falls *(G-15489)*
GPM Associates LLC....G....585 359-1770
Rush *(G-15074)*
GPM Associates LLC....E....585 335-3940
Dansville *(G-4103)*
Ivi Services Inc....D....607 729-5111
Binghamton *(G-924)*
Jag Manufacturing Inc....E....518 762-9558
Johnstown *(G-7147)*
Kragel Co Inc....G....716 648-1344
Hamburg *(G-5955)*
Kush Oasis Enterprises LLC....G....516 513-1316
Syosset *(G-15847)*
Mgk Group Inc....E....212 989-2732
New York *(G-11273)*
Paulpac LLC....G....631 283-7610
Southampton *(G-15572)*
Redco Foods Inc....D....315 823-1300
Little Falls *(G-7525)*

BAGS: Trash, Plastic Film, Made From Purchased Materials

Garb-O-Liner Inc....G....914 235-1585
New Rochelle *(G-8949)*
Golden Group International Ltd....G....845 440-1025
Patterson *(G-13464)*
Jad Corp of America....E....718 762-8900
College Point *(G-3816)*
Repellem Consumer Pdts Corp....F....631 273-3992
Bohemia *(G-1122)*

BAGS: Wardrobe, Closet Access, Made From Purchased Materials

Colden Closet LLC....G....716 713-6125
East Aurora *(G-4393)*

BAKERIES, COMMERCIAL: On Premises Baking Only

40 Street Baking Inc....G....212 683-4700
Brooklyn *(G-1517)*
527 Franco Bakery Corporation....G....718 993-4200
Bronx *(G-1250)*
A & M Appel Distributing Inc....G....516 735-1172
Massapequa *(G-8206)*
A Angonoa Inc....D....718 762-4466
College Point *(G-3798)*
American Vintage Wine Biscuit....G....718 361-1003
Long Island City *(G-7690)*
Amincor Inc....C....347 821-3452
New York *(G-9186)*
Amy Scherber Inc....F....212 462-4338
New York *(G-9193)*
Andrew Sapienza Bakery Inc....E....516 437-1715
Elmont *(G-4728)*
Aphrodities....G....718 224-1774
Whitestone *(G-17228)*
Aryzta LLC....C....585 235-8160
Rochester *(G-14233)*
Aryzta LLC....D....310 417-4700
Rochester *(G-14232)*
B & D Enterprises of Utica....D....315 735-3311
New Hartford *(G-8846)*
Baked Cupcakery....G....716 773-2050
Grand Island *(G-5766)*
Better Baked Foods Inc....D....716 326-4651
Westfield *(G-17075)*
Bimbo Bakeries....G....631 274-4906
Deer Park *(G-4132)*
Bimbo Bakeries....F....518 463-2221
Albany *(G-53)*
Bimbo Bakeries Usa Inc....G....716 692-9140
Tonawanda *(G-16166)*
Bimbo Bakeries Usa Inc....G....718 601-1561
Bronx *(G-1283)*
Bimbo Bakeries Usa Inc....F....516 887-1024
Lynbrook *(G-7975)*
Bimbo Bakeries Usa Inc....F....315 379-9069
Canton *(G-3406)*
Bimbo Bakeries Usa Inc....F....518 489-4053
Albany *(G-54)*
Bimbo Bakeries Usa Inc....F....716 706-0450
Lancaster *(G-7330)*
Bimbo Bakeries Usa Inc....F....315 785-7060
Watertown *(G-16659)*
Bimbo Bakeries Usa Inc....D....845 568-0943
Newburgh *(G-12773)*
Bimbo Bakeries Usa Inc....C....315 782-4189
Watertown *(G-16660)*
Bimbo Foods Bakeries Inc....C....631 273-6000
Bay Shore *(G-676)*
Bread Factory LLC....E....914 637-8150
New Rochelle *(G-8934)*
Bread Market Cafe....G....212 768-9292
New York *(G-9509)*
Chambord LLC....E....718 859-1110
Brooklyn *(G-1772)*
Cohens Bakery Inc....E....716 892-8149
Buffalo *(G-2899)*
Costanzos Bakery Inc....C....716 656-9093
Buffalo *(G-2911)*
Damascus Bakery Inc....C....718 855-1456
Brooklyn *(G-1838)*
Delicias Andinas Food Corp....E....718 416-2922
Flushing *(G-5244)*
Felix Roma & Sons Inc....D....607 748-3336
Endicott *(G-4816)*
Food Gems Ltd....E....718 296-7788
Ozone Park *(G-13405)*
Fratellis LLC....E....607 722-5663
Binghamton *(G-910)*
Gabila & Sons Mfg Inc....E....631 789-2220
Copiague *(G-3927)*
Gennaris Itln French Bky Inc....G....516 997-8968
Carle Place *(G-3415)*
Glenn Wayne Wholesale Bky Inc....D....631 289-9200
Bohemia *(G-1069)*
Golden Glow Cookie Co Inc....E....718 379-6223
Bronx *(G-1347)*
Gourmet Toast Corp....G....718 852-4536
Brooklyn *(G-2045)*
Grimaldis Home Bread Inc....D....718 497-1425
Ridgewood *(G-14121)*
H & S Edible Products Corp....E....914 413-3489
Mount Vernon *(G-8733)*
Hagadah Passover Bakery....G....718 638-1589
Brooklyn *(G-2061)*
Hana Pastries Inc....G....718 369-7593
Brooklyn *(G-2064)*
Heidelberg Group Inc....E....315 866-0999
Herkimer *(G-6326)*
Herris Gourmet Inc....G....917 578-2308
Brooklyn *(G-2076)*
Jarets Stuffed Cupcakes....G....607 658-9096
Endicott *(G-4820)*
JJ Cassone Bakery Inc....B....914 939-1568
Port Chester *(G-13777)*
Jonathan Lord Corp....F....631 563-4445
Bohemia *(G-1081)*
King Cracker Corp....F....516 539-9251
Hempstead *(G-6301)*
La Calenita Bakery & Cafeteria....G....718 205-8273
Elmhurst *(G-4677)*
Larosa Cupcakes....G....347 866-3920
Staten Island *(G-15719)*
Make My Cake II Inc....G....212 234-2344
New York *(G-11141)*
Maplehurst Bakeries LLC....B....315 735-5000
Frankfort *(G-5364)*
Megamatt Inc....F....516 536-3541
Rockville Centre *(G-14823)*
Melita Corp....C....718 392-7280
Astoria *(G-447)*
New Mount Pleasant Bakery....E....518 374-7577
Schenectady *(G-15307)*
New Star Bakery....E....718 961-8868
Flushing *(G-5278)*
Nibble Inc Baking Co....G....518 334-3950
Troy *(G-16266)*
Nightingale Food Entps Inc....G....347 577-1630
New York *(G-11448)*
Operative Cake Corp....E....718 278-5600
Bronx *(G-1418)*
Ossining Bakery Lmp Inc....G....914 941-2654
Ossining *(G-13348)*
Oz Baking Company Ltd....G....516 466-5114
Great Neck *(G-5845)*
Palagonia Bakery Co Inc....D....718 272-5400
Brooklyn *(G-2415)*
Parkway Bread Distributors Inc....G....845 362-1221
Pomona *(G-13760)*
Peking Food LLC....E....718 628-8080
Brooklyn *(G-2426)*
R & H Baking Co Inc....E....718 852-1768
Brooklyn *(G-2489)*
Rays Italian Bakery Inc....F....516 825-9170
Valley Stream *(G-16447)*
Reisman Bros Bakery Inc....F....718 331-1975
Brooklyn *(G-2507)*
Rm Bakery LLC....E....718 472-3036
Maspeth *(G-8198)*
Rockland Bakery Inc....D....845 623-5800
Nanuet *(G-8807)*
Roma Bakery Inc....F....516 825-9170
Valley Stream *(G-16449)*
Royal Caribbean Jamaican Bky....E....914 668-6868
Mount Vernon *(G-8774)*
Royal Sweet Bakery Inc....F....718 567-7770
Brooklyn *(G-2534)*
Ruthys Cheesecake Rugelach Bky....F....212 463-8800
New York *(G-11956)*
Saint Honore Pastry Shop Inc....G....516 767-2555
Port Washington *(G-13878)*
Smith Street Bread Co LLC....F....718 797-9712
Brooklyn *(G-2601)*
Sugarbear Cupcakes....G....917 698-9005
Jamaica *(G-6990)*
Sullivan St Bky - Hlls Kit Inc....E....212 265-5580
New York *(G-12250)*
Uncle Wallys LLC....E....631 205-0455
Shirley *(G-15453)*
Valencia Bakery Inc....E....718 991-6400
Bronx *(G-1486)*
Village Lantern Baking Corp....G....631 225-1690
Lindenhurst *(G-7517)*
Vito & Sons Bakery....F....201 617-8501
Brooklyn *(G-2752)*
Waldorf Bakers Inc....F....718 665-2253
Bronx *(G-1492)*
Zaro Bake Shop Inc....C....718 993-7327
Bronx *(G-1498)*
Zuckerbakers Inc....F....516 785-6900
Wantagh *(G-16585)*

BAKERIES: On Premises Baking & Consumption

B & D Enterprises of Utica....D....315 735-3311
New Hartford *(G-8846)*
Bagel Land....E....585 442-3080
Rochester *(G-14237)*
Brighton Bakery....G....315 475-2948
Syracuse *(G-15894)*
Caputo Bakery Inc....G....718 875-6871
Brooklyn *(G-1758)*
Costanzos Bakery Inc....C....716 656-9093
Buffalo *(G-2911)*
Dipaolo Baking Co Inc....D....585 303-5013
Rochester *(G-14331)*
Ferrara Bakery & Cafe Inc....D....212 226-6150
New York *(G-10206)*
Geddes Bakery Co Inc....E....315 437-8084
North Syracuse *(G-12962)*
Gennaris Itln French Bky Inc....G....516 997-8968
Carle Place *(G-3415)*
JJ Cassone Bakery Inc....B....914 939-1568
Port Chester *(G-13777)*
L American Ltd....F....716 372-9480
Olean *(G-13171)*
Megamatt Inc....F....516 536-3541
Rockville Centre *(G-14823)*
New Hope Mills Mfg Inc....E....315 252-2676
Auburn *(G-508)*
New Mount Pleasant Bakery....E....518 374-7577
Schenectady *(G-15307)*
Niebylski Bakery Inc....G....718 721-5152
Astoria *(G-449)*

PRODUCT SECTION

BAKERY PRDTS: Dry

Ohio Baking Company Inc .... E 315 724-2033
  Utica *(G-16378)*
Perrottas Bakery Inc .... G 518 283-4711
  Troy *(G-16270)*
Pesces Bakery Inc .... G 845 246-4730
  Saugerties *(G-15220)*
Presser Kosher Baking Corp .... E 718 375-5088
  Brooklyn *(G-2453)*
Ruthys Cheesecake Rugelach Bky ..... F 212 463-8800
  New York *(G-11956)*
Saint Honore Pastry Shop Inc .... G 516 767-2555
  Port Washington *(G-13878)*
Sapienza Pastry Inc .... E 516 352-5232
  Elmont *(G-4739)*
Settepani Inc .... E 718 349-6524
  Brooklyn *(G-2571)*
T Shore Products Ltd .... G 315 252-9174
  Auburn *(G-519)*
Tarrytown Bakery Inc .... F 914 631-0209
  Tarrytown *(G-16133)*
Wenner Bread Products Inc .... B 800 869-6262
  Bayport *(G-756)*

BAKERY FOR HOME SVC DELIVERY

Circle 5 Deli Corp .... G 718 525-5687
  Jamaica *(G-6938)*

BAKERY MACHINERY

Fresh Harvest Incorporated .... G 845 296-1024
  Wappingers Falls *(G-16588)*
Unisource Food Eqp Systems Inc ..... G 516 681-0537
  Holbrook *(G-6506)*

BAKERY PRDTS, FROZEN: Wholesalers

Fratellis LLC .... E 607 722-5663
  Binghamton *(G-910)*
Modern Itln Bky of W Babylon .... C 631 589-7300
  Oakdale *(G-13077)*

BAKERY PRDTS: Bagels, Fresh Or Frozen

999 Bagels Inc .... G 718 915-0742
  Brooklyn *(G-1523)*
A T A Bagel Shoppe Inc .... G 718 352-4948
  Bayside *(G-759)*
Bagel Club Inc .... F 718 423-6106
  Bayside *(G-762)*
Bagel Grove Inc .... E 315 724-8015
  Utica *(G-16332)*
Bagel Land .... E 585 442-3080
  Rochester *(G-14237)*
Bagel Lites LLC .... G 855 813-7888
  Long Island City *(G-7711)*
Bagelovers Inc .... F 607 844-3683
  Dryden *(G-4345)*
Bagels By Bell Ltd .... E 718 272-2780
  Oceanside *(G-13093)*
Enterprise Bagels Inc .... F 845 896-3823
  Fishkill *(G-5190)*
FB Sale LLC .... G 315 986-9999
  Macedon *(G-8017)*
Greenvale Bagel Inc .... E 516 221-8221
  Wantagh *(G-16578)*
M & M Bagel Corp .... F 516 295-1222
  Cedarhurst *(G-3484)*
Mds Hot Bagels Deli Inc .... G 718 438-5650
  Brooklyn *(G-2293)*

BAKERY PRDTS: Bakery Prdts, Partially Cooked, Exc frozen

New Hope Mills Mfg Inc .... E 315 252-2676
  Auburn *(G-508)*
T&B Bakery Corp .... G 646 642-4300
  Maspeth *(G-8202)*

BAKERY PRDTS: Bread, All Types, Fresh Or Frozen

Addeo Bakers Inc .... F 718 367-8316
  Bronx *(G-1264)*
Aladdin Bakers Inc .... C 718 499-1818
  Brooklyn *(G-1573)*
Bimbo Bakeries Usa Inc .... C 718 463-6300
  Maspeth *(G-8151)*
Brighton Bakery .... G 315 475-2948
  Syracuse *(G-15894)*
Commitment 2000 Inc .... E 716 439-1206
  Buffalo *(G-2903)*
Dipaolo Baking Co Inc .... D 585 303-5013
  Rochester *(G-14331)*
George Retzos .... G 315 422-2913
  Syracuse *(G-15973)*
Giovanni Bakery Corp .... F 212 695-4296
  New York *(G-10341)*
Harrison Bakery West .... E 315 422-1468
  Syracuse *(G-15977)*
L American Ltd .... F 716 372-9480
  Olean *(G-13171)*
La Prima Bakery Inc .... F 718 584-4442
  Bronx *(G-1381)*
Modern Itln Bky of W Babylon .... C 631 589-7300
  Oakdale *(G-13077)*
Ohio Baking Company Inc .... E 315 724-2033
  Utica *(G-16378)*
Rock Hill Bakehouse Ltd .... E 518 743-1627
  Gansevoort *(G-5503)*
Roslyn Bread Company Inc .... E 516 625-1470
  Roslyn Heights *(G-15056)*
Tarrytown Bakery Inc .... F 914 631-0209
  Tarrytown *(G-16133)*
Wenner Bread Products Inc .... B 800 869-6262
  Bayport *(G-756)*

BAKERY PRDTS: Buns, Sweet, Frozen

Liddabit Sweets 917 912-1370
  Brooklyn *(G-2218)*

BAKERY PRDTS: Cakes, Bakery, Exc Frozen

Always Baked Fresh .... G 631 648-0811
  Holbrook *(G-6459)*
Butter Cooky Bakery .... G 516 354-3831
  Floral Park *(G-5204)*
Charlotte Neuville Design LLC .... G 646 530-4570
  Brooklyn *(G-1775)*
Chocnyc LLC .... G 917 804-4848
  New York *(G-9656)*
Coccadotts Inc .... F 518 438-4937
  Albany *(G-70)*
Cupcake Contessas Corporation .... G 516 307-1222
  North Bellmore *(G-12935)*
Ferrara Bakery & Cafe Inc .... D 212 226-6150
  New York *(G-10206)*
Great American Dessert Co LLC ...... D 718 894-3494
  Maspeth *(G-8173)*
Hahns Old Fashioned Cake Co .... F 631 249-3456
  Farmingdale *(G-5012)*
McKee Foods Corporation .... A 631 979-9364
  Hauppauge *(G-6154)*
Pane DOro .... F 914 964-0043
  Yonkers *(G-17494)*
Placid Baker .... G 518 326-2657
  Troy *(G-16273)*
Scaife Enterprises Inc .... F 585 454-5231
  Rochester *(G-14693)*

BAKERY PRDTS: Cakes, Bakery, Frozen

Culinary Arts Specialties Inc .... D 716 656-8943
  Cheektowaga *(G-3594)*
Kates Kakes .... G 518 466-8671
  Schenectady *(G-15299)*
LArte Del Gelato Gruppo Inc .... F 718 383-6600
  Long Island City *(G-7815)*

BAKERY PRDTS: Cones, Ice Cream

Alrajs Inc .... E 631 225-0300
  Lindenhurst *(G-7474)*
Cone Buddy System Inc .... F 585 427-9940
  Rochester *(G-14306)*
Larte Del Gelato Inc .... G 212 366-0570
  New York *(G-10966)*
Pdi Cone Co Inc .... D 716 825-8750
  Buffalo *(G-3139)*

BAKERY PRDTS: Cookies

212kiddish Inc .... G 718 705-7227
  Brooklyn *(G-1512)*
AAA Noodle Products Mfg .... G 212 431-4090
  New York *(G-9045)*
Chipita America Inc .... E 845 292-2540
  Ferndale *(G-5176)*
Cookie Factory LLC .... E 518 268-1060
  Troy *(G-16254)*
Cooking With Chef Michelle LLC ..... G 516 662-2324
  Calverton *(G-3317)*
D F Stauffer Biscuit Co Inc .... E 585 968-2700
  Cuba *(G-4094)*
Decorated Cookie Company LLC ..... E 315 487-2111
  Syracuse *(G-15943)*
Elenis Nyc Inc .... E 718 361-8136
  Long Island City *(G-7758)*
Falcones Cookie Land Ltd .... G 718 236-4200
  Brooklyn *(G-1960)*
Golden Glow Cookie Co Inc .... E 718 379-6223
  Bronx *(G-1347)*
Keebler Company .... F 585 948-8010
  Oakfield *(G-13084)*
Keebler Company 631 234-3700
  Hauppauge *(G-6128)*
Keebler Company 845 365-5200
  Orangeburg *(G-13254)*
La Vita Health Foods Ltd .... E 845 368-4101
  Suffern *(G-15815)*
Linden Cookies Inc .... E 845 268-5050
  Congers *(G-3884)*
Lloyd Price Icon Food Brands .... F 914 764-8624
  Pound Ridge *(G-13960)*
McDuffies of Scotland Inc .... E 716 759-8510
  Clarence *(G-3691)*
One Girl Cookies Ltd .... F 212 675-4996
  Brooklyn *(G-2403)*
Quaker Bonnet Inc .... G 716 885-7208
  Buffalo *(G-3172)*
Treehouse Private Brands Inc .... C 716 693-4715
  Tonawanda *(G-16228)*
Wonton Food Inc .... C 718 628-6868
  Brooklyn *(G-2778)*

BAKERY PRDTS: Cookies & crackers

Butterwood Desserts Inc .... E 716 652-0131
  West Falls *(G-16876)*
Cookies United LLC .... C 631 581-4000
  Islip *(G-16876)*
Danny Macaroons Inc .... G 260 622-8463
  New York *(G-9860)*
Great Brands of Europe Inc .... G 914 872-8804
  White Plains *(G-17140)*
Jonathan Lord Corp .... F 631 563-4445
  Bohemia *(G-1081)*
Kaltec Food Packaging Inc .... E 845 856-9888
  Port Jervis *(G-13809)*
Ladybird Bakery Inc .... G 718 499-8108
  Brooklyn *(G-2189)*
New Mount Pleasant Bakery .... E 518 374-7577
  Schenectady *(G-15307)*
Pepsico Inc .... A 914 253-2000
  Purchase *(G-13981)*
Sapienza Pastry Inc .... E 516 352-5232
  Elmont *(G-4739)*
United Baking Co Inc .... F 631 413-5116
  Central Islip *(G-3540)*
United Baking Co Inc .... G 631 205-0455
  Shirley *(G-15454)*
Zaro Bake Shop Inc .... C 718 993-7327
  Bronx *(G-1498)*

BAKERY PRDTS: Cracker Meal & Crumbs

Wonton Food Inc .... E 718 784-8178
  Long Island City *(G-7955)*

BAKERY PRDTS: Doughnuts, Exc Frozen

3rd Avenue Doughnut Inc .... F 718 748-3294
  Brooklyn *(G-1515)*
Alicias Bakery Inc .... G 914 235-4689
  New Rochelle *(G-8930)*
Bimbo Bakeries Usa Inc .... E 203 531-2311
  Bay Shore *(G-675)*
Cuzins Duzin Corp .... G 347 724-6200
  Kew Gardens *(G-7189)*
D-Lite Donuts .... G 718 626-5953
  Astoria *(G-433)*
Famous Doughnuts Inc .... E 716 834-6356
  Buffalo *(G-2958)*
Sandford Blvd Donuts Inc .... G 914 663-7708
  Mount Vernon *(G-8776)*

BAKERY PRDTS: Doughnuts, Frozen

Maplehurst Bakeries LLC .... B 315 735-5000
  Frankfort *(G-5364)*

BAKERY PRDTS: Dry

17 Bakers LLC .... F 844 687-6836
  Williamsville *(G-17258)*
Aryzta LLC .... C 585 235-8160
  Rochester *(G-14233)*

Employee Codes: A=Over 500 employees, B=251-500
C=101-250, D=51-100, E=20-50, F=10-19, G=5-9

BAKERY PRDTS: Dry

City Baking LLC .... G 718 392-8514
  Long Island City *(G-7726)*
Creative Food Ingredients Inc .... C 585 237-2213
  Perry *(G-13545)*
My Most Favorite Food .... G 212 580-5130
  New York *(G-11353)*

BAKERY PRDTS: Frozen

Bello LLC .... C 516 623-8800
  Freeport *(G-5399)*
Brooklyn Baby Cakes Inc .... G 917 334-2518
  Brooklyn *(G-1718)*
Butterwood Desserts Inc .... E 716 652-0131
  West Falls *(G-16876)*
Deiorio Foods Inc .... E 315 732-7612
  Utica *(G-16345)*
Dufour Pastry Kitchens Inc .... E 718 402-8800
  Bronx *(G-1322)*
Fratellis LLC .... E 607 722-5663
  Binghamton *(G-910)*
Ko Fro Foods Inc .... E 718 972-6480
  Brooklyn *(G-2177)*
Rich Holdings Inc .... D 716 878-8000
  Buffalo *(G-3184)*
Rich Products Corporation .... A 716 878-8000
  Buffalo *(G-3185)*
Saj of Freeport Corp .... C 516 623-8800
  Freeport *(G-5435)*
Wenner Bread Products Inc .... B 800 869-6262
  Bayport *(G-756)*

BAKERY PRDTS: Matzoth

Aron Streit Inc .... E 212 475-7000
  Orangeburg *(G-13241)*

BAKERY PRDTS: Pastries, Danish, Frozen

Pearl River Pastries LLC .... E 845 735-5100
  West Nyack *(G-16951)*

BAKERY PRDTS: Pastries, Exc Frozen

Alrajs Inc .... E 631 225-0300
  Lindenhurst *(G-7474)*
Cannoli Factory Inc .... E 631 643-2700
  Wyandanch *(G-17387)*
Old Poland Foods LLC .... F 718 486-7700
  Brooklyn *(G-2400)*

BAKERY PRDTS: Pies, Bakery, Frozen

Circle Peak Capital MGT LLC .... E 646 230-8812
  New York *(G-9673)*
Cobblestone Bakery Corp .... E 631 491-3777
  Wyandanch *(G-17388)*
Micosta Enterprises Inc .... G 518 822-9708
  Hudson *(G-6657)*

BAKERY PRDTS: Rolls, Bread Type, Fresh Or Frozen

Kossars On Grand LLC .... F 212 473-4810
  New York *(G-10918)*

BAKERY PRDTS: Wholesalers

A & M Appel Distributing Inc .... G 516 735-1172
  Massapequa *(G-8206)*
Aron Streit Inc .... E 212 475-7000
  Orangeburg *(G-13241)*
B & D Enterprises of Utica .... D 315 735-3311
  New Hartford *(G-8846)*
Cannoli Factory Inc .... E 631 643-2700
  Wyandanch *(G-17387)*
Costanzos Bakery Inc .... C 716 656-9093
  Buffalo *(G-2911)*
Damascus Bakery Inc .... C 718 855-1456
  Brooklyn *(G-1838)*
Fratellis LLC .... E 607 722-5663
  Binghamton *(G-910)*
Hahns Old Fashioned Cake Co .... F 631 249-3456
  Farmingdale *(G-5012)*
King Cracker Corp .... F 516 539-9251
  Hempstead *(G-6301)*
Mac Crete Corporation .... F 718 932-1803
  Long Island City *(G-7827)*
Modern Itln Bky of W Babylon .... C 631 589-7300
  Oakdale *(G-13077)*
Ohio Baking Company Inc .... E 315 724-2033
  Utica *(G-16378)*
Operative Cake Corp .... E 718 278-5600
  Bronx *(G-1418)*
Roslyn Bread Company Inc .... E 516 625-1470
  Roslyn Heights *(G-15056)*
Royal Caribbean Jamaican Bky .... E 914 668-6868
  Mount Vernon *(G-8774)*

BAKERY: Wholesale Or Wholesale & Retail Combined

3 Bears Gluten Free Bakery .... F 315 323-0277
  Potsdam *(G-13894)*
Above The Rest Baking Corp .... D 718 313-9222
  Bronx *(G-1258)*
Allies GF Goodies LLC .... F 516 216-1719
  Hicksville *(G-6345)*
Amiram Dror Inc .... F 212 979-9505
  Brooklyn *(G-1609)*
Bakery & Coffee Shop .... G 315 287-1829
  Gouverneur *(G-5757)*
Berardi Bakery Inc .... G 718 746-9529
  Whitestone *(G-17231)*
Bien Cuit LLC .... E 718 852-0200
  Brooklyn *(G-1692)*
Bimbo Bakeries Usa Inc .... E 516 877-2850
  Mineola *(G-8531)*
Bimbo Bakeries Usa Inc .... C 716 372-8444
  Olean *(G-13156)*
Blackbirds Brooklyn LLC .... G 917 362-4080
  Brooklyn *(G-1699)*
Blondie S Bakeshop Inc .... G 631 424-4545
  Centerport *(G-3500)*
Caputo Bakery Inc .... G 718 875-6871
  Brooklyn *(G-1758)*
Carmine Street Bagels Inc .... F 212 691-3041
  Staten Island *(G-15676)*
Carolinas Desserts Inc .... G 914 779-4000
  Yonkers *(G-17439)*
Carter Street Bakery Inc .... G 585 749-7104
  Rochester *(G-14280)*
Cinderellas Sweets Ltd .... E 516 374-7976
  Woodmere *(G-17330)*
City Bakery Inc .... E 212 366-1414
  New York *(G-9681)*
Cookie Connection Inc .... G 315 422-2253
  Syracuse *(G-15925)*
Creative Relations LLC .... E 212 462-4392
  New York *(G-9809)*
Daly Meghan .... F 347 699-3259
  Brooklyn *(G-1837)*
Duane Park Patisserie Inc .... F 212 274-8447
  New York *(G-9985)*
Eileens Special Cheesecake .... E 212 966-5585
  New York *(G-10044)*
Ericeira Inc .... G 516 294-4034
  Mineola *(G-8543)*
Fayda Manufacturing Corp .... E 718 456-9331
  Brooklyn *(G-1965)*
Flour Power Bakery Cafe .... E 917 747-6895
  Livingston Manor *(G-7588)*
Fotis Oneonta Italian Bakery .... G 607 432-3871
  Oneonta *(G-13209)*
Fung Wong Bakery Inc .... E 212 267-4037
  New York *(G-10272)*
Geddes Bakery Co Inc .... E 315 437-8084
  North Syracuse *(G-12962)*
Gluten Free Bake Shop Inc .... E 845 782-5307
  Mountainville *(G-8793)*
Good Bread Bakery .... G 914 939-3900
  Port Chester *(G-13775)*
H H B Bakery of Little Neck .... G 718 631-7004
  Flushing *(G-5254)*
Hum Limited Liability Corp .... G 631 525-2174
  Nesconset *(G-8822)*
Jerrys Bagels .... G 516 791-0063
  Valley Stream *(G-16437)*
Jim Romas Bakery Inc .... E 607 748-7425
  Endicott *(G-4823)*
Kokoroko Corporation .... G 718 433-4321
  Woodside *(G-17352)*
Kossars Bialys LLC .... G 212 473-4810
  New York *(G-10917)*
Ladybird Bakery Inc .... G 718 499-8108
  Brooklyn *(G-2189)*
Lillys Homestyle Bakeshop Inc .... D 718 491-2904
  Brooklyn *(G-2225)*
Ljmm Inc .... E 845 454-5876
  Poughkeepsie *(G-13932)*
Made Close LLC .... G 917 837-1357
  Brooklyn *(G-2255)*
Magnolia Operating LLC .... E 212 265-2777
  New York *(G-11135)*
Maxwell Bakery Inc .... E 718 498-2200
  Brooklyn *(G-2289)*
Millers Bulk Food and Bakery .... G 585 798-9700
  Medina *(G-8310)*
Miss Grimble Associates Inc .... F 718 665-2253
  Bronx *(G-1402)*
Mollys Cupcakes New York .... G 212 255-5441
  New York *(G-11320)*
Mother Mousse Ltd .... G 718 983-8366
  Staten Island *(G-15730)*
Niebylski Bakery Inc .... G 718 721-5152
  Astoria *(G-449)*
Nildas Desserts Limited .... G 845 454-5876
  Poughkeepsie *(G-13940)*
Perrottas Bakery Inc .... G 518 283-4711
  Troy *(G-16270)*
Pesces Bakery Inc .... G 845 246-4730
  Saugerties *(G-15220)*
Presser Kosher Baking Corp .... E 718 375-5088
  Brooklyn *(G-2453)*
Quaker Bonnet Inc .... G 716 885-7208
  Buffalo *(G-3172)*
Rambachs International Bakery .... F 518 563-1721
  Plattsburgh *(G-13722)*
Rays Restaurant & Bakery Inc .... G 718 441-7707
  Jamaica *(G-6982)*
Richard Engdal Baking Corp .... F 914 777-9600
  Mamaroneck *(G-8077)*
Sapienza Pastry Inc .... E 516 352-5232
  Elmont *(G-4739)*
Settepani Inc .... E 718 349-6524
  Brooklyn *(G-2571)*
Slims Bagels Unlimited Inc .... E 718 229-1140
  Oakland Gardens *(G-13086)*
Soutine Inc .... G 212 496-1450
  New York *(G-12170)*
Stebe Shcjhjff .... F 839 383-9833
  Poughkeepsie *(G-13952)*
Sunrise Baking Co LLC .... C 718 499-0800
  Brooklyn *(G-2643)*
Tates Wholesale LLC .... C 631 780-6511
  East Moriches *(G-4451)*
Tilaros Bakery Inc .... G 716 488-3209
  Jamestown *(G-7070)*
Triboro Bagel Co Inc .... E 718 359-9245
  Flushing *(G-5308)*
Two Sisters Kiev Bakery Inc .... G 718 769-2626
  Brooklyn *(G-2711)*
Two Sisters Kiev Bakery Inc .... F 718 627-5438
  Brooklyn *(G-2712)*

BANDAGES

Medi-Tech International Corp .... E 800 333-0109
  Brooklyn *(G-2295)*

BANDS: Copper & Copper Alloy

Milward Alloys Inc .... E 716 434-5536
  Lockport *(G-7631)*

BANDS: Plastic

Universal Strapping Inc .... E 845 268-2500
  Valley Cottage *(G-16420)*

BANNERS: Fabric

Ace Banner & Flag Company .... F 212 620-9111
  New York *(G-9062)*
Arista Flag Corporation .... F 845 246-7700
  Saugerties *(G-15209)*
Big Apple Sign Corp .... E 212 629-3650
  New York *(G-9441)*
Big Apple Sign Corp .... E 631 342-0303
  Islandia *(G-6826)*
Dkm Sales LLC .... E 716 893-7777
  Buffalo *(G-2932)*
Hollywood Banners Inc .... E 631 842-3000
  Copiague *(G-3933)*
Kraus & Sons Inc .... F 212 620-0408
  New York *(G-10926)*
Sellco Industries Inc .... E 607 756-7594
  Cortland *(G-4068)*

BANQUET HALL FACILITIES

Casa Larga Vineyards .... G 585 223-4210
  Fairport *(G-4855)*

PRODUCT SECTION

BAR FIXTURES: Wood
Modern Craft Bar Rest Equip .... G 631 226-5647
   Lindenhurst *(G-7496)*

BARBECUE EQPT
Korin Japanese Trading Corp .... E 212 587-7021
   New York *(G-10916)*

BARRICADES: Metal
Backyard Fence Inc .... F 518 452-9496
   Albany *(G-48)*
Consolidated Barricades Inc .... G 518 922-7944
   Fultonville *(G-5492)*
Inpro Corporation .... G 716 332-4699
   Tonawanda *(G-16192)*

BARS & BAR SHAPES: Steel, Hot-Rolled
Vell Company Inc .... G 845 365-1013
   Palisades *(G-13429)*

BARS, COLD FINISHED: Steel, From Purchased Hot-Rolled
Niagara Lasalle Corporation .... D 716 827-7010
   Buffalo *(G-3111)*

BARS: Concrete Reinforcing, Fabricated Steel
Agl Industries Inc .... E 718 326-7597
   Maspeth *(G-8140)*
Arista Steel Designs Corp .... G 718 965-7077
   Brooklyn *(G-1629)*
Baco Enterprises Inc .... D 718 589-6225
   Bronx *(G-1278)*
Barker Steel LLC .... E 518 465-6221
   Albany *(G-49)*
City Evolutionary .... G 718 861-7585
   Bronx *(G-1300)*
Dimension Fabricators Inc .... E 518 374-1936
   Scotia *(G-15346)*
Ferro Fabricators Inc .... F 718 703-0007
   Brooklyn *(G-1971)*
GCM Metal Industries Inc .... F 718 386-4059
   Brooklyn *(G-2016)*
Harbor Wldg & Fabrication Corp .... F 631 667-1880
   Bay Shore *(G-702)*
Klein Reinforcing Services Inc .... F 585 352-9433
   Spencerport *(G-15595)*
New York Steel Services Co .... G 718 291-7770
   Jamaica *(G-6973)*
Siw Inc .... F 631 888-0130
   Bay Shore *(G-738)*
Steel Sales Inc .... E 607 674-6363
   Sherburne *(G-15419)*
Torino Industrial Inc .... F 631 509-1640
   Bellport *(G-840)*
Wide Flange Inc .... F 718 492-8705
   Brooklyn *(G-2765)*

BARS: Iron, Made In Steel Mills
Crucible Industries LLC .... B 800 365-1180
   Syracuse *(G-15933)*
Tri Valley Iron Inc .... F 845 365-1013
   Palisades *(G-13428)*

BASEBOARDS: Metal
Slanto Manufacturing Inc .... E 516 759-5721
   Glen Cove *(G-5641)*

BASEMENT WINDOW AREAWAYS: Concrete
Healthy Basement Systems LLC .... F 516 650-9046
   Medford *(G-8280)*

BASES, BEVERAGE
Better Fresh Corp .... G 718 628-3682
   Brooklyn *(G-1688)*
Hispanica Intl Dlghts Amer Inc .... F 866 928-5070
   New York *(G-10529)*
Tealeafs .... G 716 688-8022
   Williamsville *(G-17282)*

BASKETS: Steel Wire
Braun Horticulture Inc .... G 716 282-6101
   Niagara Falls *(G-12821)*

BATCHING PLANTS: Cement Silos
New Eagle Silo Corp .... G 585 492-1300
   Arcade *(G-398)*

BATH SALTS
Aromasong Usa Inc .... F 718 838-9669
   Brooklyn *(G-1632)*

BATHING SUIT STORES
Malia Mills Inc .... F 212 354-4200
   Brooklyn *(G-2258)*
Shirl-Lynn of New York .... F 315 363-5898
   Oneida *(G-13189)*

BATHMATS, COTTON
Michael Stuart Inc .... E 718 821-0704
   Brooklyn *(G-2314)*

BATHROOM ACCESS & FITTINGS: Vitreous China & Earthenware
AMG Global LLC .... G 212 602-1818
   New York *(G-9185)*
Gamma Products Inc .... D 845 562-3332
   New Windsor *(G-8984)*
Larcent Enterprises Inc .... E 845 562-3332
   New Windsor *(G-8987)*
Stone and Bath Gallery .... G 718 438-4500
   Brooklyn *(G-2631)*

BATHTUBS: Concrete
Meditub Incorporated .... F 866 633-4882
   Lawrence *(G-7420)*

BATTERIES, EXC AUTOMOTIVE: Wholesalers
El-Don Battery Post Inc .... G 716 627-3697
   Hamburg *(G-5946)*
TAe Trans Atlantic Elec Inc .... E 631 595-9206
   Deer Park *(G-4240)*

BATTERIES: Alkaline, Cell Storage
Bren-Trnics Batteries Intl LLC .... E 631 499-5155
   Commack *(G-3852)*

BATTERIES: Lead Acid, Storage
Exide Technologies .... G 585 344-0656
   Batavia *(G-633)*
Johnson Controls Inc .... C 585 724-2232
   Rochester *(G-14485)*

BATTERIES: Rechargeable
Bren-Trnics Batteries Intl Inc .... G 631 499-5155
   Commack *(G-3851)*
Synergy Digital .... F 718 643-2742
   Brooklyn *(G-2657)*

BATTERIES: Storage
Amco Intl Mfg & Design Inc .... E 718 388-8668
   Brooklyn *(G-1596)*
Battery Energy Storage Systems .... G 518 256-7029
   Troy *(G-16249)*
Battery Research and Tstg Inc .... F 315 342-2373
   Oswego *(G-13353)*
Battsco LLC .... G 516 586-6544
   Hicksville *(G-6351)*
Bren-Tronics Inc .... C 631 499-5155
   Commack *(G-3853)*
Cellec Technologies Inc .... G 585 454-9166
   Rochester *(G-14286)*
China Lithium Technologies .... G 212 391-2688
   New York *(G-9649)*
El-Don Battery Post Inc .... G 716 627-3697
   Hamburg *(G-5946)*
Hrg Group Inc .... E 212 906-8555
   New York *(G-10567)*
New Energy Systems Group .... C 917 573-0302
   New York *(G-11406)*
Ultralife Corporation .... A 315 332-7100
   Newark *(G-12766)*
W & W Manufacturing Co .... F 516 942-0011
   West Islip *(G-16939)*

BATTERIES: Wet
Bren-Tronics Inc .... C 631 499-5155
   Commack *(G-3853)*
Electrochem Solutions Inc .... D 716 759-5800
   Clarence *(G-3688)*
Empire Scientific .... G 630 510-8636
   Deer Park *(G-4162)*
Shad Industries Inc .... G 631 504-6028
   Yaphank *(G-17418)*
TAe Trans Atlantic Elec Inc .... E 631 595-9206
   Deer Park *(G-4240)*

BATTERY CASES: Plastic Or Plastics Combination
Memory Protection Devices Inc .... F 631 249-0001
   Farmingdale *(G-5056)*

BATTERY CHARGERS
Applied Energy Solutions LLC .... E 585 538-3270
   Caledonia *(G-3304)*
China Lithium Technologies .... G 212 391-2688
   New York *(G-9649)*
Eluminocity US Inc .... G 651 528-1165
   New York *(G-10068)*
Kussmaul Electronics Co Inc .... E 631 218-0298
   West Sayville *(G-16965)*
Walter R Tucker Entps Ltd .... E 607 467-2866
   Deposit *(G-4305)*

BATTERY CHARGERS: Storage, Motor & Engine Generator Type
Apogee Power Usa Inc .... F 202 746-2890
   Hartsdale *(G-6016)*
Vdc Electronics Inc .... F 631 683-5850
   Huntington *(G-6728)*

BATTERY CHARGING GENERATORS
Eluminocity US Inc .... G 651 528-1165
   New York *(G-10068)*

BATTS & BATTING: Cotton
Ino-Tex LLC .... G 212 400-2205
   New York *(G-10647)*
Rovel Manufacturing Co Inc .... G 516 365-2752
   Roslyn *(G-15047)*
Superior Fiber Mills Inc .... E 718 782-7500
   Brooklyn *(G-2649)*
Vincent Manufacturing Co Inc .... F 315 823-0280
   Little Falls *(G-7528)*

BAUXITE MINING
Alcoa USA Corp .... F 212 518-5400
   New York *(G-9127)*

BEARINGS & PARTS Ball
A Hyatt Ball Co Ltd .... G 518 747-0272
   Fort Edward *(G-5347)*
Kilian Manufacturing Corp .... D 315 432-0700
   Syracuse *(G-15993)*
Mageba USA LLC .... E 212 317-1991
   New York *(G-11126)*
Nes Bearing Company Inc .... E 716 372-6532
   Olean *(G-13173)*
S/N Precision Enterprises Inc .... E 518 283-8002
   Troy *(G-16276)*
Schatz Bearing Corporation .... D 845 452-6000
   Poughkeepsie *(G-13948)*
SKF USA Inc .... D 716 661-2869
   Falconer *(G-4919)*
SKF USA Inc .... D 716 661-2600
   Falconer *(G-4920)*

BEARINGS: Ball & Roller
American Refuse Supply Inc .... G 718 893-8157
   Bronx *(G-1273)*
David Fehlman .... G 315 455-8888
   Syracuse *(G-15942)*
General Bearing Corporation .... C 845 358-6000
   West Nyack *(G-16947)*
Lemoyne Machine Products Corp .... G 315 454-0708
   Syracuse *(G-15996)*
Raydon Precision Bearing Co .... G 516 887-2582
   Lynbrook *(G-7984)*

BEARINGS: Ball & Roller

Sandle Custom Bearing Corp ....G....... 585 593-7000
  Wellsville *(G-16783)*
SKF USA Inc ....D....... 716 661-2600
  Jamestown *(G-7060)*

BEAUTY & BARBER SHOP EQPT

Accurate Pnt Powdr Coating Inc ....F....... 585 235-1650
  Rochester *(G-14182)*
Adults and Children With Learn ....E....... 516 593-8230
  East Rockaway *(G-4487)*
Blackbox Biometrics Inc ....E....... 585 329-3399
  Rochester *(G-14252)*
Brooklyn Industries LLC ....G....... 718 788-5250
  Brooklyn *(G-1725)*
Brooklyn Industries LLC ....F....... 718 486-6464
  Brooklyn *(G-1726)*
Brooklyn Industries LLC ....F....... 718 789-2764
  Brooklyn *(G-1727)*
Callanan Industries Inc ....G....... 518 382-5354
  Schenectady *(G-15264)*
East Penn Manufacturing Co ....G....... 631 321-7161
  Babylon *(G-544)*
Goodwill Inds of Greater NY ....C....... 914 621-0781
  Baldwin Place *(G-562)*
Goodwill Inds Wstn NY Inc ....F....... 716 633-3305
  Williamsville *(G-17272)*
Innovative Industries LLC ....E....... 718 784-7300
  Long Island City *(G-7794)*
J & A Usa Inc ....G....... 631 243-3336
  Brentwood *(G-1184)*
Jags Manufacturing Network Inc ......G....... 631 750-6367
  Holbrook *(G-6483)*
Nitro Manufacturing LLC ....F....... 716 646-9900
  Hamburg *(G-5957)*
Ohserase Manufacturing LLC ....E....... 518 358-9309
  Akwesasne *(G-29)*
Oledworks LLC ....E....... 585 287-6802
  Rochester *(G-14568)*
P S Pibbs Inc ....D....... 718 445-8046
  Flushing *(G-5283)*
Paperworks Industries Inc ....F....... 913 621-0922
  Baldwinsville *(G-572)*
PCI Industries Corp ....E....... 914 662-2700
  Mount Vernon *(G-8759)*
Qualbuys LLC ....G....... 855 884-3274
  Syosset *(G-15856)*
S B Manufacturing LLC ....F....... 845 352-3700
  Monsey *(G-8614)*

BEAUTY SALONS

Lemetric Hair Centers Inc ....F....... 212 986-5620
  New York *(G-10998)*

BED & BREAKFAST INNS

Malina Management Company Inc ...E....... 607 535-9614
  Montour Falls *(G-8649)*
Newspaper Publisher LLC ....F....... 607 775-0472
  Conklin *(G-3896)*

BEDDING, BEDSPREADS, BLANKETS & SHEETS

Cathay Home Inc ....E....... 212 213-0988
  New York *(G-9602)*
Indigo Home Inc ....G....... 212 684-4146
  New York *(G-10632)*
Jdt International LLC ....G....... 212 400-7570
  New York *(G-10753)*
Northpoint Trading Inc ....F....... 212 481-8001
  New York *(G-11478)*
Richloom Fabrics Group Inc ....F....... 212 685-5400
  New York *(G-11895)*
Sunham Home Fashions LLC ....D....... 212 695-1218
  New York *(G-12258)*
Thor Marketing Corp ....G....... 201 247-7103
  Valley Cottage *(G-16419)*

BEDDING, BEDSPREADS, BLANKETS & SHEETS: Comforters & Quilts

Alen Sands York Associates Ltd ....F....... 212 563-6305
  New York *(G-9130)*
EY Industries Inc ....F....... 718 624-9122
  Brooklyn *(G-1952)*
Kaltex North America Inc ....F....... 212 894-3200
  New York *(G-10843)*
Revman International Inc ....E....... 212 894-3100
  New York *(G-11880)*

Royal Home Fashions Inc ....G....... 212 689-7222
  New York *(G-11942)*

BEDDING, FROM SILK OR MANMADE FIBER

Greenbuds LLC ....G....... 718 483-9212
  Brooklyn *(G-2053)*
Westpoint Home LLC ....A....... 212 930-2074
  New York *(G-12643)*

BEDS & ACCESS STORES

Charles P Rogers Brass Beds ....F....... 212 675-4400
  New York *(G-9633)*
Duxiana Dux Bed ....E....... 212 755-2600
  New York *(G-9992)*
Metro Mattress Corp ....E....... 716 205-2300
  Niagara Falls *(G-12864)*

BEDS: Hospital

Hard Manufacturing Co Inc ....D....... 716 893-1800
  Buffalo *(G-3005)*
NK Medical Products Inc ....F....... 716 759-7200
  Amherst *(G-252)*
Novum Medical Products Inc ....F....... 716 759-7200
  Amherst *(G-253)*
VSM Investors LLC ....E....... 212 351-1600
  New York *(G-12597)*

BEDSPREADS & BED SETS, FROM PURCHASED MATERIALS

Belle Maison USA Ltd ....E....... 718 805-0200
  Richmond Hill *(G-14081)*
Bramson House Inc ....C....... 516 764-5006
  Freeport *(G-5400)*
C & G of Kingston Inc ....E....... 845 331-0148
  Kingston *(G-7209)*
County Draperies Inc ....E....... 845 342-9009
  Middletown *(G-8467)*
Fabric Quilters Unlimited Inc ....E....... 516 333-2866
  Westbury *(G-17011)*
Himatsingka America Inc ....E....... 212 545-8929
  New York *(G-10523)*
Jo-Vin Decorators Inc ....E....... 718 441-9350
  Woodhaven *(G-17324)*
Richloom Corp ....F....... 212 685-5400
  New York *(G-11893)*
Wayne Decorators Inc ....G....... 718 529-4200
  Jamaica *(G-6999)*

BEDSPREADS, COTTON

Mason Contract Products LLC ....D....... 516 328-6900
  New Hyde Park *(G-8894)*

BEEKEEPERS' SPLYS

Northast Ctr For Bekeeping LLC ....F....... 800 632-3379
  Greenwich *(G-5910)*

BEER & ALE WHOLESALERS

Olde Saratoga Brewing ....F....... 518 581-0492
  Saratoga Springs *(G-15195)*

BEER & ALE, WHOLESALE: Beer & Other Fermented Malt Liquors

Constellation Brands Inc ....D....... 585 678-7100
  Victor *(G-16493)*
Load/N/Go Beverage Corp ....F....... 585 218-4019
  Rochester *(G-14502)*
Save More Beverage Corp ....G....... 518 371-2520
  Halfmoon *(G-5938)*

BEER, WINE & LIQUOR STORES

City Winery Napa LLC ....F....... 212 633-4399
  New York *(G-9685)*
Lucas Vineyards & Winery ....F....... 607 532-4825
  Interlaken *(G-6787)*

BEER, WINE & LIQUOR STORES: Beer, Packaged

Load/N/Go Beverage Corp ....F....... 585 218-4019
  Rochester *(G-14502)*
Save More Beverage Corp ....G....... 518 371-2520
  Halfmoon *(G-5938)*

BEER, WINE & LIQUOR STORES: Wine

Casa Larga Vineyards ....G....... 585 223-4210
  Fairport *(G-4855)*
Coyote Moon LLC ....F....... 315 686-5600
  Clayton *(G-3711)*
J Petrocelli Wine Cellars LLC ....E....... 631 765-1100
  Peconic *(G-13495)*
Negys New Land Vinyrd Winery ....G....... 315 585-4432
  Geneva *(G-5595)*
Olde Chtqua Vneyards Ltd Lblty ......F....... 716 792-2749
  Portland *(G-13891)*
Standing Stone Vineyards ....G....... 607 582-6051
  Hector *(G-6285)*

BELLOWS

Kinemotive Corporation ....E....... 631 249-6440
  Farmingdale *(G-5035)*
Nicoform Inc ....E....... 585 454-5530
  Rochester *(G-14557)*

BELTING: Rubber

Van Slyke Belting LLC ....G....... 518 283-5479
  Poestenkill *(G-13756)*

BELTING: Transmission, Rubber

Sampla Belting North Amer LLC ....E....... 716 667-7450
  Lackawanna *(G-7275)*

BELTS: Conveyor, Made From Purchased Wire

Chemprene Inc ....C....... 845 831-2800
  Beacon *(G-777)*
Chemprene Holding Inc ....C....... 845 831-2800
  Beacon *(G-778)*
Habasit America Inc ....D....... 716 824-8484
  Buffalo *(G-3001)*

BELTS: Indl

DC Fabrication & Welding Inc ....G....... 845 295-0215
  Ferndale *(G-5177)*

BELTS: Seat, Automotive & Aircraft

Davis Restraint Systems Inc ....F....... 631 563-1500
  Bohemia *(G-1047)*

BENCHES: Seating

Jays Furniture Products Inc ....E....... 716 876-8854
  Buffalo *(G-3031)*
Jcdecaux Mallscape LLC ....F....... 646 834-1200
  New York *(G-10751)*

BEVERAGE BASES & SYRUPS

Agua Enerviva LLC ....F....... 516 597-5440
  Bethpage *(G-863)*
Boylan Bottling Co Inc ....E....... 800 289-7978
  New York *(G-9499)*
Buffalo Blends Inc ....E....... 716 825-4422
  Buffalo *(G-2871)*
Flavormatic Industries Inc ....E....... 845 297-9100
  Wappingers Falls *(G-16587)*

BEVERAGE, NONALCOHOLIC: Iced Tea/Fruit Drink, Bottled/Canned

Arizona Beverage Company LLC ......G....... 516 812-0300
  Woodbury *(G-17303)*
Cell-Nique Corporation ....G....... 888 417-9343
  Castleton On Hudson *(G-3446)*
F & V Distribution Company LLC .....E....... 516 812-0393
  Woodbury *(G-17308)*
Hain Celestial Group Inc ....C....... 516 587-5000
  New Hyde Park *(G-8882)*
Heart of Tea ....F....... 917 725-3164
  New York *(G-10494)*
Long Island Brand Bevs LLC ....D....... 855 542-2832
  Long Island City *(G-7822)*
Long Island Iced Tea Corp ....E....... 855 542-2832
  Farmingdale *(G-5045)*

BEVERAGES, ALCOHOLIC: Ale

Empire Brewing Company Inc ....D....... 315 925-8308
  Syracuse *(G-15956)*

PRODUCT SECTION

BEVERAGES, ALCOHOLIC: Applejack

Company	Code	Phone
Honeoye Falls Distillery LLC	F	201 780-4618
Honeoye Falls (G-6559)		

BEVERAGES, ALCOHOLIC: Beer

Company	Code	Phone
Anheuser-Busch LLC	C	315 638-0365
Baldwinsville (G-566)		
Anheuser-Busch LLC	C	212 573-8800
New York (G-9209)		
Anheuser-Busch Companies LLC	G	718 589-2610
Bronx (G-1275)		
Anheuser-Busch Inbev Fin Inc	F	212 573-8800
New York (G-9210)		
Brazen Street LLC	E	516 305-7951
Brooklyn (G-1712)		
Constellation Brands Inc	D	585 678-7100
Victor (G-16493)		
Decrescente Distributing Co	D	518 664-9866
Mechanicville (G-8257)		
Five Burroughs Brewing Co	G	718 355-8575
Brooklyn (G-1981)		
Gilded Otter Brewing Co	D	845 256-1700
New Paltz (G-8919)		
High Falls Brewing Company LLC	C	585 546-1030
Rochester (G-14454)		
Hoptron Brewtique	G	631 438-0296
Patchogue (G-13448)		
Indian Ladder Farmstead Brewer	G	518 577-1484
Altamont (G-210)		
Ithaca Beer Company Inc	E	607 272-1305
Ithaca (G-6888)		
Keegan Ales LLC	F	845 331-2739
Kingston (G-7221)		
Labatt USA LLC	D	716 604-1050
Buffalo (G-3058)		
Middle Ages Brewing Company	G	315 476-4250
Syracuse (G-16008)		
Montauk Brewing Company Inc	F	631 668-8471
Montauk (G-8624)		
Newburgh Brewing Company LLC	F	845 569-2337
Newburgh (G-12791)		
North American Breweries Inc	F	585 546-1030
Rochester (G-14559)		
North Amrcn Brwries Hldngs LLC	E	585 546-1030
Rochester (G-14562)		
Remarkable Liquids LLC	D	518 861-5351
Altamont (G-214)		
Vanberg & Dewulf Co Inc	G	607 547-8184
Cooperstown (G-3912)		
Yonkers Whl Beer Distrs Inc	G	914 963-8600
Yonkers (G-17520)		

BEVERAGES, ALCOHOLIC: Beer & Ale

Company	Code	Phone
Barrier Brewing Company LLC	G	516 316-4429
Long Beach (G-7668)		
Black River Brewing Co Inc	G	315 755-2739
Watertown (G-16661)		
Brewery Ommegang Ltd	G	607 286-4144
Cooperstown (G-3909)		
Castle Brands Inc	D	646 356-0200
New York (G-9596)		
Coopers Cave Ale Co S-Corp	F	518 792-0007
Glens Falls (G-5692)		
Cooperstown Brewing Co LLC	G	607 286-9330
Oneonta (G-13204)		
Custom Brewcrafters Inc	F	585 624-4386
Honeoye Falls (G-6554)		
Duvel Mortgage USA Inc	G	607 267-6121
Cooperstown (G-3911)		
Equilibrium Brewery LLC	G	201 245-0292
Middletown (G-8473)		
Hornell Brewing Co Inc	G	914 597-7911
White Plains (G-17148)		
Hyde Park Brewing Co Inc	E	845 229-8277
Hyde Park (G-6773)		
Independent Brewers Untd Corp	G	585 263-9308
Rochester (G-14468)		
Keuka Brewing Co LLC	G	607 868-4648
Hammondsport (G-5979)		
Long Ireland Brewing LLC	G	631 403-4303
Riverhead (G-14160)		
Mad Scntsts Brwing Prtners LLC	E	347 766-2739
Brooklyn (G-2254)		
Millercoors LLC	E	585 385-0670
Pittsford (G-13598)		
Olde Saratoga Brewing	F	518 581-0492
Saratoga Springs (G-15195)		
Other Half Brewing Co	G	347 987-3527
Brooklyn (G-2411)		
Rising Sons 6 Brewing Coinc	G	607 368-4836
Corning (G-3999)		
Wagner Vineyards & Brewing Co	E	607 582-6574
Lodi (G-7666)		
Woodcock Brothers Brewing Comp	G	716 333-4000
Wilson (G-17293)		

BEVERAGES, ALCOHOLIC: Bourbon Whiskey

Company	Code	Phone
Iron Smoke Whiskey LLC	G	585 388-7584
Fairport (G-4863)		

BEVERAGES, ALCOHOLIC: Brandy

Company	Code	Phone
Cruzin Management Inc	E	212 641-8700
New York (G-9818)		

BEVERAGES, ALCOHOLIC: Cocktails

Company	Code	Phone
Dutch Spirits LLC	F	518 398-1022
Pine Plains (G-13582)		

BEVERAGES, ALCOHOLIC: Distilled Liquors

Company	Code	Phone
Austin Nichols & Co Inc	F	519 561-5225
New York (G-9319)		
Braided Oak Spirits LLC	F	845 381-1525
Middletown (G-8463)		
Constellation Brands Inc	D	585 678-7100
Victor (G-16493)		
Finger Lakes Distilling	F	607 546-5510
Burdett (G-3291)		
Leblon LLC	F	954 649-0148
New York (G-10989)		
Leblon LLC		786 281-5672
New York (G-10990)		
Long Island Spirits Inc	F	631 630-9322
Calverton (G-3320)		
Marnier-Lapostolle Inc	D	212 207-4350
New York (G-11187)		
Pernod Ricard Usa LLC	D	212 372-5400
New York (G-11640)		
Prohibition Distillery LLC	F	917 685-8989
Roscoe (G-15034)		
Sovereign Brands LLC	G	212 343-8366
New York (G-12171)		
Tuthilltown Spirits LLC	F	845 255-1527
Gardiner (G-5564)		

BEVERAGES, ALCOHOLIC: Gin

Company	Code	Phone
Madison County Distillery LLC	G	315 391-6070
Cazenovia (G-3474)		

BEVERAGES, ALCOHOLIC: Liquors, Malt

Company	Code	Phone
Marnier-Lapostolle Inc	D	212 207-4350
New York (G-11187)		
Vernon Wine & Liquor Inc	G	718 784-5096
Long Island City (G-7943)		

BEVERAGES, ALCOHOLIC: Near Beer

Company	Code	Phone
Horns & Halos Cft Brewing LLC	E	585 507-7248
Caledonia (G-3308)		

BEVERAGES, ALCOHOLIC: Neutral Spirits, Fruit

Company	Code	Phone
Davos Brands LLC	F	212 779-1911
New York (G-9887)		
Dutch Spirits LLC	F	518 398-1022
Pine Plains (G-13582)		

BEVERAGES, ALCOHOLIC: Rum

Company	Code	Phone
Castle Brands Inc	D	646 356-0200
New York (G-9596)		
Cruzin Management Inc	E	212 641-8700
New York (G-9818)		
Evolution Spirits Inc	G	917 543-7880
New York (G-10149)		
Leblon Holdings LLC	E	212 741-2675
New York (G-10988)		

BEVERAGES, ALCOHOLIC: Vodka

Company	Code	Phone
Russian Standard Vodka USA Inc	G	212 679-1894
New York (G-11955)		

BEVERAGES, ALCOHOLIC: Wines

Company	Code	Phone
Allied Wine Corp	F	845 796-4160
South Fallsburg (G-15542)		
Americana Vineyards & Winery	F	607 387-6801
Interlaken (G-6785)		
Anyelas Vineyards LLC	F	315 685-3797
Skaneateles (G-15476)		
Arrowhead Spring Vineyards LLC	G	716 434-8030
Lockport (G-7598)		
Atwater Estate Vineyards LLC	E	607 546-8463
Burdett (G-2290)		
Billsboro Winery		315 789-9538
Geneva (G-5582)		
Brotherhood Americas	E	845 496-3661
Washingtonville (G-16621)		
Casa Larga Vineyards	G	585 223-4210
Fairport (G-4855)		
Casa Larga Vineyards	G	585 223-4210
Fairport (G-4856)		
Cascade Mountain Winery & Rest	F	845 373-9021
Amenia (G-218)		
Cava Spiliadis USA	E	212 247-8214
New York (G-9605)		
Chautauqua Wine Company Inc	G	716 934-9463
Silver Creek (G-15469)		
Clinton Vineyards Inc	G	845 266-5372
Clinton Corners (G-3748)		
Constellation Brands US Oprs	A	585 396-7600
Canandaigua (G-3369)		
Constellation Brands US Oprs	B	585 396-7600
Canandaigua (G-3370)		
Coyote Moon LLC	G	315 686-5600
Clayton (G-3711)		
Deer Run Enterprises Inc	G	585 346-0850
Geneseo (G-5580)		
Dorset Farms Inc	F	631 734-6010
Peconic (G-13494)		
Duck Walk Vinyards	G	631 726-7555
Water Mill (G-16627)		
Eagle Crest Vineyard LLC	G	585 346-5760
Conesus (G-3874)		
East End Vineyards LLC	G	718 468-0500
Queens Village (G-13992)		
Fly Creek Cder Mill Orchrd Inc	G	607 547-9692
Fly Creek (G-5319)		
Fox Run Vineyards Inc	F	315 536-4616
Penn Yan (G-13535)		
Frank Wines Inc	G	646 765-6637
New York (G-10252)		
Freedom Run Winery Inc	G	716 433-4136
Lockport (G-7616)		
Gabriella Importers Inc	G	212 579-3945
Bohemia (G-1066)		
Gabriella Importers Inc	G	212 579-3945
New York (G-10286)		
Glenora Wine Cellars Inc	F	607 243-9500
Dundee (G-4353)		
Grapes & Grains	F	518 283-9463
Rensselaer (G-14057)		
Greenwood Winery LLC	E	315 432-8132
East Syracuse (G-4547)		
Hermann J Wiemer Vineyard	G	607 243-7971
Dundee (G-4354)		
Heron Hill Vineyards Inc	E	607 868-4241
Hammondsport (G-5978)		
Hosmer Inc	F	888 467-9463
Ovid (G-13371)		
J Petrocelli Wine Cellars LLC	F	631 765-1100
Peconic (G-13495)		
Joseph Zakon Winery Ltd	G	718 604-1430
Brooklyn (G-2150)		
Konstantin D FRAnk& Sons Vini	E	607 868-4884
Hammondsport (G-5980)		
Lafayette Chateau	E	607 546-2062
Hector (G-6283)		
Lakewood Vineyards Inc	F	607 535-9252
Watkins Glen (G-16720)		
Lamoreaux Landing WI	D	607 582-6162
Lodi (G-7665)		
Lieb Cellars LLC	E	631 298-1942
Mattituck (G-8239)		
Lucas Vineyards & Winery	F	607 532-4825
Interlaken (G-6787)		
Merritt Estate Winery Inc	F	716 965-4800
Forestville (G-5341)		
Millbrook Winery Inc	F	845 677-8383
Millbrook (G-8513)		
Montezuma Winery LLC	G	315 568-8190
Seneca Falls (G-15389)		

Employee Codes: A=Over 500 employees, B=251-500
C=101-250, D=51-100, E=20-50, F=10-19, G=5-9

Negys New Land Vinyrd Winery..........G....... 315 585-4432
Geneva *(G-5595)*
North House Vineyards Inc..........G....... 631 779-2817
Jamesport *(G-7002)*
Olde Chtqua Vneyards Ltd Lblty..........F....... 716 792-2749
Portland *(G-13891)*
Paumanok Vineyards Ltd..........E....... 631 722-8800
Aquebogue *(G-385)*
Pellegrini Vineyards LLC..........G....... 631 734-4111
Cutchogue *(G-4098)*
Pindar Vineyards LLC..........E....... 631 734-6200
Peconic *(G-13496)*
Prejean Winery Inc..........F....... 315 536-7524
Penn Yan *(G-13539)*
Premium Wine Group LLC..........E....... 631 298-1900
Mattituck *(G-8241)*
Pugliese Vineyards Inc..........G....... 631 734-4057
Cutchogue *(G-4099)*
Red Newt Cellars Inc..........F....... 607 546-4100
Hector *(G-6284)*
Red Tail Ridge Inc..........G....... 315 536-4580
Penn Yan *(G-13540)*
Rock Stream Vineyards..........G....... 607 243-8322
Rock Stream *(G-14808)*
Royal Wine Corporation..........F....... 845 236-4000
Marlboro *(G-8136)*
Sheldrake Point Vineyard LLC..........F....... 607 532-8967
Ovid *(G-13373)*
Sokolin LLC..........E....... 631 537-4434
Yaphank *(G-17419)*
Spanish Artisan Wine Group LLC..........G....... 914 414-6982
Patterson *(G-13468)*
Standing Stone Vineyards..........G....... 607 582-6051
Hector *(G-6285)*
Swedish Hill Vineyard Inc..........D....... 607 403-0029
Romulus *(G-14872)*
Thirsty Owl Wine Company..........G....... 607 869-5805
Ovid *(G-13374)*
Thousand Islands Winery LLC..........E....... 315 482-9306
Alexandria Bay *(G-195)*
Trader Joes Company..........E....... 212 529-6326
New York *(G-12409)*
Vedell North Fork LLC..........G....... 631 323-3526
Cutchogue *(G-4100)*
Wagner Vineyards & Brewing Co..........E....... 607 582-6574
Lodi *(G-7666)*
Westchester Wine Warehouse LLC..........F....... 914 824-1400
White Plains *(G-17213)*
Wine Group Inc..........D....... 716 326-3151
Westfield *(G-17084)*
Wine Market..........G....... 516 328-8800
New Hyde Park *(G-8917)*
Woodbury Vineyards Inc..........G....... 716 679-9463
Fredonia *(G-5386)*

BEVERAGES, MALT

Crazy Cowboy Brewing Co LLC..........E....... 516 812-0576
Woodbury *(G-17306)*
High Falls Operating Co LLC..........A....... 585 546-1030
Rochester *(G-14455)*

BEVERAGES, NONALCOHOLIC: Bottled & canned soft drinks

3v Company Inc..........E....... 718 858-7333
Brooklyn *(G-1516)*
American Bottling Company..........F....... 516 714-0002
Ronkonkoma *(G-14894)*
Beverage Works Nj Inc..........E....... 631 293-3501
Farmingdale *(G-4961)*
Beverage Works Ny Inc..........E....... 718 812-2034
Brooklyn *(G-1690)*
Borabora Fruit Juices Inc..........G....... 845 795-1027
Highland *(G-6430)*
Bottling Group LLC..........G....... 914 767-6000
White Plains *(G-17114)*
Brands Within Reach LLC..........E....... 847 720-9090
Mamaroneck *(G-8057)*
Brooklyn Btlg Milton NY Inc..........C....... 845 795-2171
Milton *(G-8516)*
Cliffstar LLC..........A....... 716 366-6100
Dunkirk *(G-4361)*
Coca-Cola Bottling Co of NY..........F....... 518 459-2010
Albany *(G-69)*
Coca-Cola Bottling Company..........E....... 518 483-0422
Malone *(G-8039)*
Coca-Cola Btlg Co Buffalo Inc..........C....... 716 874-4610
Tonawanda *(G-16175)*
Coca-Cola Btlg Co of NY Inc..........F....... 845 562-3037
New Windsor *(G-8982)*
Coca-Cola Btlg Co of NY Inc..........C....... 718 326-3334
Maspeth *(G-8153)*
Coca-Cola Btlg Co of NY Inc..........F....... 914 592-4574
Elmsford *(G-4750)*
Coca-Cola Btlg Co of NY Inc..........E....... 718 416-7575
Maspeth *(G-8154)*
Coca-Cola Btlg Co of NY Inc..........F....... 315 457-9221
Syracuse *(G-15919)*
Coca-Cola Btlg Co of NY Inc..........E....... 631 434-3535
Hauppauge *(G-6068)*
Coca-Cola Btlg Co of NY Inc..........F....... 718 420-6800
Staten Island *(G-15679)*
Coca-Cola Btlg Co of NY Inc..........F....... 914 789-1580
Elmsford *(G-4751)*
Coca-Cola Refreshments USA Inc..........E....... 718 401-5200
Bronx *(G-1302)*
Coca-Cola Refreshments USA Inc..........E....... 315 785-8907
Watertown *(G-16667)*
Coca-Cola Refreshments USA Inc..........G....... 914 592-0806
Hawthorne *(G-6268)*
Consumers Beverages Inc..........E....... 716 837-3087
Buffalo *(G-2907)*
Consumers Beverages Inc..........G....... 716 675-4934
West Seneca *(G-16970)*
Doheny Nice and Easy..........G....... 518 793-1733
Glens Falls *(G-5693)*
Dr Pepper Snapple Group Inc..........D....... 914 846-2300
Elmsford *(G-4756)*
Dr Pepper Snapple Group Inc..........G....... 718 246-6200
Brooklyn *(G-1879)*
Fancy Flamingo LLC..........G....... 516 209-7306
New York *(G-10187)*
Gangi Distributors Inc..........F....... 718 442-5745
Staten Island *(G-15697)*
Grayhawk Leasing LLC..........G....... 914 767-6000
Somers *(G-15532)*
Kraft Heinz Foods Company..........A....... 914 335-2500
Tarrytown *(G-16116)*
Linda Wine & Spirit..........G....... 718 703-5707
Brooklyn *(G-2228)*
N Y Winstons Inc..........G....... 212 665-3166
New York *(G-11361)*
Pepsi Bottling Ventures LLC..........D....... 631 772-6144
Patchogue *(G-13457)*
Pepsi-Cola Operating Company..........E....... 914 767-6000
White Plains *(G-17180)*
Pepsico Inc..........A....... 914 253-2000
Purchase *(G-13981)*
Pepsico Capital Resources Inc..........G....... 914 253-2000
Purchase *(G-13984)*
Quench It Inc..........E....... 845 462-5400
Poughkeepsie *(G-13945)*
Rochester Coca Cola Bottling..........E....... 607 739-5678
Horseheads *(G-6620)*
Rochester Coca Cola Bottling..........D....... 585 546-3900
Rochester *(G-14660)*
Shopping Center Wine & Liquor..........G....... 914 528-1600
Mohegan Lake *(G-8579)*
Snapp Too Enterprise..........G....... 718 224-5252
Flushing *(G-5299)*
Snapple Beverage Corp (del)..........D....... 914 612-4000
Rye Brook *(G-15101)*
Street King LLC..........G....... 212 400-2200
New York *(G-12235)*
Unilever United States Inc..........F....... 212 546-0200
New York *(G-12474)*
Unilever United States Inc..........C....... 212 546-0200
New York *(G-12475)*

BEVERAGES, NONALCOHOLIC: Carbonated

Bottling Group LLC..........E....... 315 788-6751
Watertown *(G-16662)*
Clintons Ditch Coop Co Inc..........C....... 315 699-2695
Cicero *(G-3672)*
Goodo Beverage Company..........F....... 718 328-6400
Bronx *(G-1348)*
Meadowbrook Distributing Corp..........D....... 516 226-9000
Garden City *(G-5532)*
Pepsi Beverages Co..........G....... 518 782-2150
Latham *(G-7402)*
Pepsi Bottling Ventures LLC..........E....... 631 226-9000
Amityville *(G-321)*
Pepsi Btlg Group Globl Fin LLC..........G....... 914 767-6000
Somers *(G-15533)*
Pepsi-Cola Bottling Group..........G....... 914 767-6000
White Plains *(G-17178)*
Pepsi-Cola Metro Btlg Co Inc..........G....... 914 767-6000
White Plains *(G-17179)*
Pepsi-Cola Metro Btlg Co Inc..........E....... 914 253-2000
Purchase *(G-13979)*
Pepsi-Cola Metro Btlg Co Inc..........D....... 607 795-1399
Horseheads *(G-6615)*
Pepsi-Cola Newburgh Btlg Inc..........C....... 845 562-5400
Newburgh *(G-12797)*
Pepsico..........F....... 419 252-0247
Hawthorne *(G-6276)*
Pepsico..........E....... 914 801-1500
Valhalla *(G-16395)*
Pepsico Inc..........B....... 914 742-4500
Valhalla *(G-16396)*
Pepsico Inc..........A....... 914 253-2000
Purchase *(G-13982)*
Pepsico Inc..........E....... 914 253-3474
White Plains *(G-17182)*
Pepsico Inc..........F....... 914 253-2713
Purchase *(G-13983)*
Pepsico World Trading Co Inc..........G....... 914 767-6000
White Plains *(G-17184)*

BEVERAGES, NONALCOHOLIC: Carbonated, Canned & Bottled, Etc

Beverage Works Incorporated..........G....... 718 834-0500
Brooklyn *(G-1689)*
Blue Star Beverages Corp..........G....... 718 381-3535
Brooklyn *(G-1703)*
Bottling Group LLC..........B....... 800 789-2626
White Plains *(G-17113)*
Brave Chefs Incorporated..........G....... 347 956-5905
Little Neck *(G-7530)*
Chohehco LLC..........G....... 315 420-4624
Skaneateles *(G-15478)*
Green Zone Food Service Inc..........G....... 917 709-1728
Corona *(G-4020)*
Hmo Beverage Corp..........G....... 917 371-6100
Brooklyn *(G-2078)*
Hydrive Energy..........G....... 914 925-9100
Rye *(G-15086)*
Juices Enterprises Inc..........G....... 718 953-1860
Brooklyn *(G-2157)*
Liquid Management Partners LLC..........F....... 516 775-5050
New Hyde Park *(G-8892)*
Nexbev Industries LLC..........F....... 917 626-5255
Pearl River *(G-13486)*
Save More Beverage Corp..........G....... 518 371-2520
Halfmoon *(G-5938)*
Switch Beverage Company LLC..........F....... 203 202-7383
Port Washington *(G-13885)*
Treo Brands LLC..........G....... 914 341-1850
Harrison *(G-6011)*

BEVERAGES, NONALCOHOLIC: Cider

Beak & Skiff Cider Mill Inc..........G....... 315 677-5105
La Fayette *(G-7265)*
Lakeside Cider Mill Farm Inc..........G....... 518 399-8359
Ballston Lake *(G-581)*
Mullers Cider House LLC..........G....... 585 287-5875
Rochester *(G-14544)*
Nine Pin Ciderworks LLC..........F....... 518 449-9999
Albany *(G-109)*
Schutt Cider Mill..........F....... 585 872-2924
Webster *(G-16760)*

BEVERAGES, NONALCOHOLIC: Flavoring extracts & syrups, nec

Baldwin Richardson Foods Co..........C....... 315 986-2727
Macedon *(G-8010)*
Citrus and Allied Essences Ltd..........E....... 516 354-1200
Floral Park *(G-5207)*
Danisco US Inc..........D....... 585 277-4300
Rochester *(G-14322)*
Delbia Do Company Inc..........G....... 718 585-2226
Bronx *(G-1315)*
Delbia Do Company Inc..........F....... 718 585-2226
Bronx *(G-1316)*
Dr Pepper Snapple Group Inc..........C....... 315 589-4911
Williamson *(G-17251)*
DSM Nutritional Products LLC..........C....... 518 372-5155
Schenectady *(G-15276)*
DSM Nutritional Products LLC..........C....... 518 372-5155
Glenville *(G-5716)*
Interntnl Flvors Frgrnces Inc..........C....... 212 765-5500
New York *(G-10681)*
Natural Organics Laboratories..........B....... 631 957-5600
Amityville *(G-314)*
Pepsico Inc..........A....... 914 253-2000
Purchase *(G-13981)*
Star Kay White Inc..........D....... 845 268-2600
Congers *(G-3885)*

PRODUCT SECTION

BINDING SVC: Books & Manuals

Synergy Flavors NY Company LLC ....G....... 585 232-6648
  Rochester *(G-14735)*
Torre Products Co Inc ....G....... 212 925-8989
  New York *(G-12396)*
Virginia Dare Extract Co Inc ....C....... 718 788-6320
  Brooklyn *(G-2747)*
Wynn Starr Flavors Inc ....E....... 845 584-3080
  Congers *(G-3888)*

BEVERAGES, NONALCOHOLIC: Fruit Drnks, Under 100% Juice, Can

A Health Obsession LLC ....E....... 347 850-4587
  Brooklyn *(G-1534)*
Ba Sports Nutrition LLC ....C....... 718 357-7402
  Whitestone *(G-17230)*
Cheribundi Inc ....E....... 800 699-0460
  Geneva *(G-5585)*
Mnm Service Distributors Inc ....G....... 914 337-5268
  Bronxville *(G-1501)*
Nantucket Allserve Inc ....B....... 914 612-4000
  Elmsford *(G-4778)*
Purely Maple LLC ....F....... 203 997-9309
  New York *(G-11777)*

BEVERAGES, NONALCOHOLIC: Lemonade, Bottled & Canned, Etc

Dirty Lemon Beverages LLC ....G....... 877 897-7784
  New York *(G-9935)*

BEVERAGES, NONALCOHOLIC: Soft Drinks, Canned & Bottled, Etc

Austin Nichols & Co Inc ....F....... 519 561-5225
  New York *(G-9319)*
Boylan Bottling Co Inc ....G....... 800 289-7978
  New York *(G-9499)*
Cornell Beverages Inc ....F....... 718 381-3000
  Brooklyn *(G-1803)*
Dr Pepper Snapple Group Inc ....C....... 315 589-4911
  Williamson *(G-17251)*
Energy Brands Inc ....D....... 212 545-6000
  New York *(G-10089)*
General Cinema Bevs of Ohio ....A....... 914 767-6000
  Somers *(G-15531)*
Johnnie Ryan Co Inc ....F....... 716 282-1606
  Niagara Falls *(G-12856)*
La Cola 1 Inc ....F....... 917 509-6669
  New York *(G-10944)*
Load/N/Go Beverage Corp ....F....... 585 218-4019
  Rochester *(G-14502)*
Manhattan Special Bottling ....F....... 718 388-4144
  Brooklyn *(G-2262)*
Monfefo LLC ....G....... 347 779-2600
  Brooklyn *(G-2336)*
New York Bottling Co Inc ....F....... 718 963-3232
  Bronx *(G-1410)*
Pepsi-Cola Bottling Co NY Inc ....F....... 718 649-2465
  College Point *(G-3826)*
Pepsi-Cola Bottling Co NY Inc ....B....... 914 699-2600
  Mount Vernon *(G-8760)*
Pepsi-Cola Bottling Co NY Inc ....G....... 718 786-8550
  Maspeth *(G-8195)*
Pepsi-Cola Bottling Co NY Inc ....D....... 718 892-1570
  Bronx *(G-1425)*
Pepsi-Cola Sales and Dist Inc ....G....... 914 253-2000
  Purchase *(G-13980)*
Pepsico Sales Inc ....G....... 914 253-2000
  Purchase *(G-13985)*
Scotia Beverages Inc ....A....... 518 370-3621
  Schenectady *(G-15318)*
Stewarts Processing Corp ....D....... 518 581-1200
  Ballston Spa *(G-609)*

BEVERAGES, NONALCOHOLIC: Tea, Iced, Bottled & Canned, Etc

East Coast Cultures LLC ....F....... 917 261-3010
  Kingston *(G-7217)*

BEVERAGES, WINE & DISTILLED ALCOHOLIC, WHOLESALE: Liquor

Austin Nichols & Co Inc ....F....... 519 561-5225
  New York *(G-9319)*
Cruzin Management Inc ....E....... 212 641-8700
  New York *(G-9818)*
Marnier-Lapostolle Inc ....D....... 212 207-4350
  New York *(G-11187)*

BEVERAGES, WINE & DISTILLED ALCOHOLIC, WHOLESALE: Neutral Sp

Spanish Artisan Wine Group LLC ....G....... 914 414-6982
  Patterson *(G-13468)*

BEVERAGES, WINE & DISTILLED ALCOHOLIC, WHOLESALE: Wine

Coyote Moon LLC ....F....... 315 686-5600
  Clayton *(G-3711)*
Royal Wine Corporation ....F....... 845 236-4000
  Marlboro *(G-8136)*

BEVERAGES, WINE WHOLESALE : Wine Coolers

Hoptron Brewtique ....G....... 631 438-0296
  Patchogue *(G-13448)*

BICYCLE SHOPS

Bignay Inc ....G....... 786 346-1673
  New York *(G-9446)*
Worksman Trading Corp ....E....... 718 322-2000
  Ozone Park *(G-13413)*

BICYCLES WHOLESALERS

East Coast Cycle LLC ....G....... 631 780-5360
  Farmingdale *(G-4992)*

BICYCLES, PARTS & ACCESS

Bignay Inc ....G....... 786 346-1673
  New York *(G-9446)*
East Coast Cycle LLC ....G....... 631 780-5360
  Farmingdale *(G-4992)*
Evelo Inc ....G....... 917 251-8743
  Rockaway Park *(G-14813)*
Great American Bicycle LLC ....E....... 518 584-8100
  Saratoga Springs *(G-15184)*
Social Bicycles Inc ....E....... 917 746-7624
  Brooklyn *(G-2602)*

BILLETS: Steel

Homogeneous Metals Inc ....D....... 315 839-5421
  Clayville *(G-3715)*

BILLFOLD INSERTS: Plastic

Quality Lineals Usa Inc ....G....... 516 378-6577
  Merrick *(G-8427)*

BILLIARD & POOL TABLES & SPLYS

A Hyatt Ball Co Ltd ....G....... 518 747-0272
  Fort Edward *(G-5347)*
International Leisure Pdts Inc ....E....... 631 254-2155
  Edgewood *(G-4615)*

BINDING SVC: Books & Manuals

514 Adams Corporation ....G....... 516 352-6948
  Franklin Square *(G-5369)*
A-Quick Bindery LLC ....G....... 631 491-1110
  West Babylon *(G-16788)*
Agrecolor Inc ....F....... 516 741-8700
  Mineola *(G-8525)*
Argo Lithographers Inc ....E....... 718 729-2700
  Long Island City *(G-7702)*
Arista Innovations Inc ....E....... 516 746-2262
  Mineola *(G-8529)*
Baum Christine and John Corp ....G....... 585 621-8910
  Rochester *(G-14241)*
Beastons Budget Printing ....G....... 585 244-2721
  Rochester *(G-14244)*
Benchemark Printing Inc ....D....... 518 393-1361
  Schenectady *(G-15262)*
Bernard Hall ....G....... 585 425-3340
  Fairport *(G-4853)*
Beyer Graphics Inc ....D....... 631 543-3900
  Commack *(G-3850)*
Bg Bindery Inc ....G....... 631 767-4242
  Maspeth *(G-8150)*
Boncraft Inc ....D....... 716 662-9720
  Tonawanda *(G-16167)*
Bondy Printing Corp ....G....... 631 242-1510
  Bay Shore *(G-677)*
Brodock Press Inc ....D....... 315 735-9577
  Utica *(G-16333)*
Brooks Litho Digital Group Inc ....G....... 631 789-4500
  Deer Park *(G-4136)*
C & C Bindery Co Inc ....E....... 631 752-7078
  Farmingdale *(G-4963)*
Carlara Group Ltd ....G....... 914 769-2020
  Pleasantville *(G-13744)*
Carnels Printing Inc ....G....... 516 883-3355
  Port Washington *(G-13826)*
Castlereagh Printcraft Inc ....D....... 516 623-1728
  Freeport *(G-5402)*
Chakra Communications Inc ....E....... 607 748-7491
  Endicott *(G-4806)*
Challenge Graphics Svcs Inc ....E....... 631 586-0171
  Deer Park *(G-4138)*
Classic Album ....E....... 718 388-2818
  Brooklyn *(G-1785)*
Cohber Press Inc ....D....... 585 475-9100
  West Henrietta *(G-16906)*
Copy Corner Inc ....G....... 718 388-4545
  Brooklyn *(G-1802)*
Cosmos Communications Inc ....C....... 718 482-1800
  Long Island City *(G-7734)*
D G M Graphics Inc ....E....... 516 223-2220
  Merrick *(G-8416)*
Dalee Bookbinding Co Inc ....F....... 914 965-1660
  Yonkers *(G-17449)*
David Helsing ....G....... 607 796-2681
  Horseheads *(G-6601)*
Dependable Lithographers Inc ....F....... 718 472-4200
  Long Island City *(G-7741)*
Dispatch Graphics Inc ....F....... 212 307-5943
  New York *(G-9938)*
Division Den-Bar Enterprises ....G....... 914 381-2220
  Mamaroneck *(G-8065)*
Dowd - Witbeck Printing Corp ....F....... 518 274-2421
  Troy *(G-16256)*
DP Murphy Co Inc ....D....... 631 673-9400
  Deer Park *(G-4154)*
E B B Graphics Inc ....E....... 516 750-5510
  Westbury *(G-17006)*
E L Smith Printing Co Inc ....E....... 201 373-0111
  New City *(G-8831)*
Eastside Printers ....F....... 315 437-6515
  East Syracuse *(G-4540)*
Eastwood Litho Inc ....E....... 315 437-2626
  Syracuse *(G-15950)*
Erhard & Gilcher Inc ....E....... 315 474-1072
  Syracuse *(G-15958)*
Flare Multicopy Corp ....E....... 718 258-8860
  Brooklyn *(G-1983)*
Flp Group LLC ....F....... 315 252-7583
  Auburn *(G-495)*
Foster - Gordon Manufacturing ....G....... 631 589-6776
  Bohemia *(G-1064)*
Fulton Newspapers Inc ....E....... 315 598-6397
  Fulton *(G-5471)*
Gateway Prtg & Graphics Inc ....E....... 716 823-3873
  Hamburg *(G-5949)*
Gazette Press Inc ....E....... 914 963-8300
  Rye *(G-15082)*
Graphicomm Inc ....G....... 716 283-0830
  Niagara Falls *(G-12845)*
Haig Press Inc ....E....... 631 582-5800
  Hauppauge *(G-6111)*
Hudson Printing Co Inc ....E....... 718 937-8600
  New York *(G-10572)*
In-House Inc ....F....... 718 445-9007
  College Point *(G-3812)*
Interstate Litho Corp ....G....... 631 232-6025
  Brentwood *(G-1182)*
Jack J Florio Jr ....G....... 716 434-9123
  Lockport *(G-7625)*
James Conolly Printing Co ....E....... 585 426-4150
  Rochester *(G-14480)*
Jane Lewis ....G....... 607 722-0584
  Binghamton *(G-925)*
Johnnys Ideal Printing Co ....G....... 518 828-6666
  Hudson *(G-6651)*
Jon Lyn Ink Inc ....G....... 516 546-2312
  Merrick *(G-8420)*
Kader Lithograph Company Inc ....C....... 917 664-4380
  Long Island City *(G-7804)*
Kaufman Brothers Printing ....E....... 212 563-1854
  New York *(G-10858)*
King Lithographers Inc ....E....... 914 667-4200
  Mount Vernon *(G-8743)*
Louis Heindl & Son Inc ....E....... 585 454-5080
  Rochester *(G-14504)*
Loy L Press Inc ....G....... 716 634-5966
  Buffalo *(G-3069)*

Employee Codes: A=Over 500 employees, B=251-500
C=101-250, D=51-100, E=20-50, F=10-19, G=5-9

BINDING SVC: Books & Manuals

Melcher Media Inc ....F 212 727-2322
  New York *(G-11249)*
Mercury Print Productions Inc ....C 585 458-7900
  Rochester *(G-14525)*
Midgley Printing Corp ....G 315 475-1864
  Syracuse *(G-16009)*
Moneast Inc ....G 845 298-8898
  Wappingers Falls *(G-16595)*
Multiple Imprssons of Rchester ....G 585 546-1160
  Rochester *(G-14545)*
Newport Graphics Inc ....E 212 924-2600
  New York *(G-11433)*
Ozipko Enterprises Inc ....G 585 424-6740
  Rochester *(G-14581)*
Prestige Envelope & Lithograph ....F 631 521-7043
  Merrick *(G-8426)*
Printing Resources Inc ....E 518 482-2470
  Albany *(G-124)*
Pro Printing ....G 516 561-9700
  Lynbrook *(G-7983)*
Progressive Graphics & Prtg ....G 315 331-3635
  Newark *(G-12762)*
Prompt Bindery Co Inc ....E 212 675-5181
  New York *(G-11754)*
Psychonomic Society Inc ....E 512 381-1494
  New York *(G-11764)*
Quad/Graphics Inc ....A 518 581-4000
  Saratoga Springs *(G-15198)*
Reynolds Book Bindery LLC ....F 607 772-8937
  Binghamton *(G-941)*
Richard Ruffner ....F 631 234-4600
  Central Islip *(G-3536)*
Riverside Mfg Acquisition LLC ....C 585 458-2090
  Rochester *(G-14650)*
Rmd Holding Inc ....G 845 628-0030
  Mahopac *(G-8031)*
Roger Michael Press Inc ....F 732 752-0800
  Brooklyn *(G-2523)*
Rosemont Press Incorporated ....E 212 239-4770
  New York *(G-11935)*
Rosen Mandell & Immerman Inc ....E 212 691-2277
  New York *(G-11936)*
Sentinel Printing Inc ....F 516 334-7400
  Westbury *(G-17054)*
Shipman Printing Inds Inc ....E 716 504-7700
  Niagara Falls *(G-12893)*
Spectrum Prtg Lithography Inc ....F 212 255-3131
  New York *(G-12182)*
Thomas Group Inc ....F 212 947-6400
  New York *(G-12340)*
Tobay Printing Co Inc ....E 631 842-3300
  Copiague *(G-3957)*
Tom & Jerry Printcraft Forms ....E 914 777-7468
  Mamaroneck *(G-8081)*
Tri-Lon Clor Lithographers Ltd ....E 212 255-6140
  New York *(G-12421)*
Vicks Lithograph & Prtg Corp ....C 315 272-2401
  Yorkville *(G-17544)*
Vin-Clair Inc ....F 845 429-4998
  West Haverstraw *(G-16878)*
Webster Printing Corporation ....F 585 671-1533
  Webster *(G-16768)*
Welsh Gold Stampers Inc ....E 718 984-5031
  Staten Island *(G-15776)*
Westchester Mailing Service ....E 914 948-1116
  White Plains *(G-17212)*
William Charles Prtg Co Inc ....F 516 349-0900
  Plainview *(G-13674)*
Wilson Press LLC ....E 315 568-9693
  Seneca Falls *(G-15395)*
Won & Lee Inc ....E 516 222-0712
  Garden City *(G-5552)*
Wynco Press One Inc ....G 516 354-6145
  Glen Oaks *(G-5656)*
X Myles Mar Inc ....E 212 683-2015
  New York *(G-12699)*
Zan Optics Products Inc ....E 718 435-0533
  Brooklyn *(G-2794)*
Zenger Partners LLC ....E 716 876-2284
  Kenmore *(G-7181)*

BINDING SVC: Magazines

Copy Room Inc ....F 212 371-8600
  New York *(G-9781)*

BINDING SVC: Pamphlets

Mid-Island Bindery Inc ....E 631 293-0180
  Farmingdale *(G-5064)*

BINDING SVC: Trade

Gold Pride Press Inc ....E 585 224-8800
  Rochester *(G-14431)*
Piroke Trade Inc ....G 646 515-1537
  Brooklyn *(G-2436)*
Quality Bindery Service Inc ....E 716 883-5185
  Buffalo *(G-3173)*
Whitford Development Inc ....F 631 471-7711
  Port Jefferson *(G-13802)*

BINDINGS: Bias, Made From Purchased Materials

Empire Bias Binding Co Inc ....F 718 545-0300
  Long Island City *(G-7759)*

BINS: Prefabricated, Sheet Metal

Golden Group International Ltd ....G 845 440-1025
  Patterson *(G-13464)*
H & M Leasing Corp ....G 631 225-5246
  Copiague *(G-3930)*

BIOLOGICAL PRDTS: Bacterial Vaccines

Ip Med Inc ....G 516 766-3800
  Oceanside *(G-13102)*

BIOLOGICAL PRDTS: Blood Derivatives

Instrumentation Laboratory Co ....C 845 680-0028
  Orangeburg *(G-13253)*

BIOLOGICAL PRDTS: Exc Diagnostic

Acorda Therapeutics Inc ....C 914 347-4300
  Ardsley *(G-402)*
Advance Biofactures Corp ....E 516 593-7000
  Lynbrook *(G-7972)*
AG Biotech Inc ....G 585 346-0020
  Livonia *(G-7590)*
Albany Molecular Research Inc ....G 518 512-2234
  Albany *(G-38)*
Albany Molecular Research Inc ....B 518 512-2000
  Albany *(G-39)*
Bioreclamationivt LLC ....D 516 483-1196
  Westbury *(G-16999)*
Cypress Bioscience Inc ....C 858 452-2323
  New York *(G-9836)*
Ecological Laboratories Inc ....D 516 823-3441
  Lynbrook *(G-7978)*
Kadmon Holdings Inc ....D 212 308-6000
  New York *(G-10836)*
Life Technologies Corporation ....D 716 774-6700
  Grand Island *(G-5775)*
Nanoprobes Inc ....F 631 205-9490
  Yaphank *(G-17414)*
Nxxi Inc ....F 914 701-4500
  Purchase *(G-13978)*
Oligomerix Inc ....G 914 997-8877
  New York *(G-11514)*
Omrix Biopharmaceuticals Inc ....C 908 218-0707
  New York *(G-11517)*
Rentschler Biotechnologie GMBH ....F 631 656-7137
  Hauppauge *(G-6203)*
Roar Biomedical Inc ....G 631 591-2749
  Calverton *(G-3325)*
Stemcultures LLC ....E 518 621-0848
  Rensselaer *(G-14062)*
Synergy Pharmaceuticals Inc ....G 212 227-8611
  New York *(G-12283)*
Vyera Pharmaceuticals LLC ....E 646 356-5577
  New York *(G-12600)*
Wyeth Holdings LLC ....D 845 602-5000
  Pearl River *(G-13493)*
Wyeth LLC ....A 973 660-5000
  New York *(G-12697)*
Zeptometrix Corporation ....D 716 882-0920
  Buffalo *(G-3288)*

BIOLOGICAL PRDTS: Extracts

Akshar Extracts Inc ....G 631 588-9727
  Ronkonkoma *(G-14885)*

BIOLOGICAL PRDTS: Vaccines

AV Therapeutics Inc ....E 917 497-5523
  New York *(G-9323)*
International Aids Vaccine Ini ....C 212 847-1111
  New York *(G-10672)*
International Aids Vaccine Ini ....F 646 381-8066
  Brooklyn *(G-2109)*

BIOLOGICAL PRDTS: Vaccines & Immunizing

Siga Technologies Inc ....E 212 672-9100
  New York *(G-12088)*

BLADES: Saw, Chain Type

Quality Saw & Knife Inc ....F 631 491-4747
  West Babylon *(G-16850)*

BLADES: Saw, Hand Or Power

Niabraze LLC ....F 716 447-1082
  Tonawanda *(G-16203)*

BLANKBOOKS

Dalee Bookbinding Co Inc ....F 914 965-1660
  Yonkers *(G-17449)*

BLANKBOOKS & LOOSELEAF BINDERS

Classic Album ....E 718 388-2818
  Brooklyn *(G-1785)*
Colad Group LLC ....D 716 961-1776
  Buffalo *(G-2900)*
Datamax International Inc ....E 212 693-0933
  New York *(G-9870)*
Foster - Gordon Manufacturing ....G 631 589-6776
  Bohemia *(G-1064)*
GPM Associates LLC ....E 585 335-3940
  Dansville *(G-4103)*
Graphic Image Incorporated ....C 631 249-9600
  Melville *(G-8353)*
Leather Indexes Corp ....D 516 827-1900
  Hicksville *(G-6391)*
Roger Michael Press Inc ....F 732 752-0800
  Brooklyn *(G-2523)*

BLANKBOOKS: Albums

Albumx Corp ....D 914 939-6878
  Port Chester *(G-13766)*
Art Leather Mfg Co Inc ....A 516 867-4716
  Oyster Bay *(G-13392)*
Classic Album LLC ....D 718 388-2818
  Brooklyn *(G-1786)*
Dorose Novelty Co Inc ....F 718 451-3088
  East Elmhurst *(G-4413)*
King Album Inc ....E 631 253-9500
  West Babylon *(G-16833)*
Lanwood Industries Inc ....E 718 786-3000
  Bay Shore *(G-709)*
Leather Craftsmen Inc ....C 631 752-9000
  Farmingdale *(G-5041)*
Leather Craftsmen Inc ....E 714 429-9763
  Farmingdale *(G-5042)*
Mypublisher Inc ....F 914 773-4312
  Elmsford *(G-4776)*

BLANKBOOKS: Albums, Record

Brookvale Records Inc ....F 631 587-7722
  West Babylon *(G-16801)*
Motema Music LLC ....G 212 860-6969
  New York *(G-11335)*
Renegade Nation Ltd ....F 212 868-9000
  New York *(G-11865)*
Simon & Simon LLC ....G 202 419-0490
  New York *(G-12103)*
Tm Music Inc ....F 212 471-4000
  New York *(G-12376)*
Tommy Boy Entertainment LLC ....F 212 388-8300
  New York *(G-12386)*
Wmg Acquisition Corp ....F 212 275-2000
  New York *(G-12676)*

BLANKBOOKS: Checkbooks & Passbooks, Bank

ABC Check Printing Corp ....F 718 855-4702
  Brooklyn *(G-1546)*

BLANKBOOKS: Diaries

Quo Vadis Editions Inc ....E 716 648-2602
  Hamburg *(G-5963)*

PRODUCT SECTION

BLANKBOOKS: Memorandum, Printed

General Diaries Corporation .... F 516 371-2244
  Inwood *(G-6797)*
Quotable Cards Inc .... G 212 420-7552
  New York *(G-11802)*

BLANKETS & BLANKETING, COTTON

Northwest Textile Holding Inc .... D 516 484-6996
  Roslyn *(G-15046)*

BLASTING SVC: Sand, Metal Parts

Carpenter Industries Inc .... F 315 463-4284
  Syracuse *(G-15905)*
Thomas Foundry LLC .... G 315 361-9048
  Oneida *(G-13190)*
Tropical Driftwood Originals .... G 516 623-0980
  Roosevelt *(G-15033)*

BLINDS & SHADES: Vertical

Blindtek Designer Systems Inc .... F 914 347-7100
  Elmsford *(G-4746)*
Designers Touch Inc .... G 718 641-3718
  Long Beach *(G-7669)*
J Gimbel Inc .... E 718 296-5200
  West Hempstead *(G-16888)*
KPP Ltd .... G 516 338-5201
  Westbury *(G-17031)*
Vertical Research Partners LLC .... F 212 257-6499
  New York *(G-12554)*

BLINDS : Window

Comfortex Corporation .... C 518 273-3333
  Watervliet *(G-16707)*
D & D Window Tech Inc .... G 212 308-2822
  New York *(G-9838)*
Drapery Industries Inc .... F 585 232-2992
  Rochester *(G-14338)*
Fabric Quilters Unlimited Inc .... E 516 333-2866
  Westbury *(G-17011)*
Hunter Douglas Inc .... D 845 664-7000
  Pearl River *(G-13482)*
Hunter Douglas Inc .... C 212 588-0564
  New York *(G-10580)*
Instant Verticals Inc .... G 631 501-0001
  Farmingdale *(G-5019)*
Levolor Window Furnishings Inc .... B 845 664-7000
  Pearl River *(G-13485)*
Nu Ways Inc .... G 585 254-7510
  Rochester *(G-14567)*
Tentina Window Fashions Inc .... C 631 957-9585
  Lindenhurst *(G-7513)*
TLC Vision (usa) Corporation .... G 914 395-3949
  Hartsdale *(G-6021)*

BLOCK & BRICK: Sand Lime

Everblock Systems LLC .... G 844 422-5625
  New York *(G-10143)*

BLOCKS & BRICKS: Concrete

All American Concrete Corp .... G 718 497-3301
  Brooklyn *(G-1583)*
All County Block & Supply Corp .... G 631 589-3675
  Bohemia *(G-1008)*
Barrasso & Sons Trucking Inc .... E 631 581-0360
  Islip Terrace *(G-6854)*
Chenango Concrete Corp .... F 607 334-2545
  Norwich *(G-13039)*
Cossitt Concrete Products Inc .... F 315 824-2700
  Hamilton *(G-5970)*
Crest Haven Precast Inc .... G 518 483-4750
  Burke *(G-3292)*
Dicks Concrete Co Inc .... E 845 374-5966
  New Hampton *(G-8844)*
Edgewood Industries Inc .... G 516 227-2447
  Garden City *(G-5514)*
Fort Miller Service Corp .... F 518 695-5000
  Greenwich *(G-5907)*
Grace Associates Inc .... G 718 767-9000
  Harrison *(G-6005)*
Hanson Aggregates New York LLC ... G 607 276-5881
  Almond *(G-206)*
Imperia Masonry Supply Corp .... E 914 738-0900
  Pelham *(G-13517)*
Jenna Concrete Corporation .... E 718 842-5250
  Bronx *(G-1369)*
Jenna Harlem River Inc .... G 718 842-5997
  Bronx *(G-1370)*
Modern Block LLC .... G 315 923-7443
  Clyde *(G-3754)*
Palumbo Block Co Inc .... E 845 832-6100
  Dover Plains *(G-4340)*
Phelps Cement Products Inc .... E 315 548-9415
  Phelps *(G-13558)*
Smithtown Concrete Products .... F 631 265-1815
  Saint James *(G-15117)*
Superior Block Corp .... F 718 421-0900
  Brooklyn *(G-2647)*
Unilock New York Inc .... G 845 278-6700
  Brewster *(G-1227)*

BLOCKS: Chimney Or Fireplace, Concrete

Ace Cntracting Consulting Corp .... G 631 567-4752
  Bohemia *(G-1001)*
Chimney Doctors Americas Corp ...... G 631 868-3586
  Bayport *(G-751)*
Great American Awning & Patio .... F 518 899-2300
  Ballston Spa *(G-596)*

BLOCKS: Landscape Or Retaining Wall, Concrete

Creative Yard Designs Inc .... G 315 706-6143
  Manlius *(G-8103)*
Everblock Systems LLC .... G 844 422-5625
  New York *(G-10143)*
Northeast Mesa LLC .... G 845 878-9344
  Carmel *(G-3430)*
Troys Landscape Supply Co Inc .... F 518 785-1526
  Cohoes *(G-3784)*

BLOCKS: Paving, Concrete

Nicolia Concrete Products Inc .... D 631 669-0700
  Lindenhurst *(G-7500)*
Unilock Ltd .... E 716 822-6074
  Buffalo *(G-3260)*

BLOCKS: Paving, Cut Stone

Unilock New York Inc .... G 845 278-6700
  Brewster *(G-1227)*

BLOCKS: Radiation-Proof, Concrete

Radiation Shielding Systems .... F 888 631-2278
  Suffern *(G-15819)*

BLOCKS: Standard, Concrete Or Cinder

Colonie Block and Supply Co .... G 518 869-8411
  Colonie *(G-3845)*
Cranesville Block Co Inc .... E 518 684-6154
  Amsterdam *(G-341)*
Cranesville Block Co Inc .... E 315 773-2296
  Felts Mills *(G-5175)*
Duke Concrete Products Inc .... E 518 793-7743
  Queensbury *(G-14008)*
Felicetti Concrete Products .... G 716 284-5740
  Niagara Falls *(G-12839)*
Gone South Concrete Block Inc .... E 315 598-2141
  Fulton *(G-5473)*
Grandview Block & Supply Co .... E 518 346-7981
  Schenectady *(G-15292)*
Lafarge North America Inc .... E 518 756-5000
  Ravena *(G-14036)*
Lage Industries Corporation .... E 718 342-3400
  Brooklyn *(G-2190)*
Montfort Brothers Inc .... E 845 896-6694
  Fishkill *(G-5194)*
Morningstar Concrete Products .... F 716 693-4020
  Tonawanda *(G-16201)*
New York Ready Mix Inc .... G 516 338-6969
  Westbury *(G-17042)*
Riefler Concrete Products LLC .... C 716 649-3260
  Hamburg *(G-5964)*
Suffolk Cement Products Inc .... E 631 727-2317
  Calverton *(G-3328)*
Taylor Concrete Products Inc .... E 315 788-2191
  Watertown *(G-16696)*

BLOWERS & FANS

Air Crafters Inc .... C 631 471-7788
  Ronkonkoma *(G-14883)*
American Filtration Tech Inc .... E 585 359-4130
  West Henrietta *(G-16900)*

BOAT BUILDING & REPAIRING: Motorized

Applied Safety LLC .... G 718 608-6292
  Long Island City *(G-7697)*
Buffalo Filter LLC .... D 716 835-7000
  Lancaster *(G-7331)*
Camfil USA Inc .... G 518 456-6085
  Syracuse *(G-15903)*
Daikin Applied Americas Inc .... D 315 253-2771
  Auburn *(G-490)*
Delphi Automotive Systems LLC ..... A 585 359-6000
  West Henrietta *(G-16909)*
Ducon Technologies Inc .... E 631 420-4900
  Farmingdale *(G-4988)*
Ducon Technologies Inc .... F 631 694-1700
  New York *(G-9988)*
Dundas-Jafine Inc .... E 716 681-9690
  Alden *(G-180)*
Filtros Ltd .... E 585 586-8770
  East Rochester *(G-4478)*
Healthway Products Company .... E 315 207-1410
  Oswego *(G-13357)*
Moffitt Fan Corporation .... E 585 768-7010
  Le Roy *(G-7439)*
North American Filter Corp .... D 800 265-8943
  Newark *(G-12760)*
Parker-Hannifin Corporation .... D 248 628-6017
  Lancaster *(G-7355)*
Standard Motor Products Inc .... B 718 392-0200
  Long Island City *(G-7912)*

BLOWERS & FANS

Ametek Technical & Indus Pdts .... E 845 246-3401
  Saugerties *(G-15208)*
Rotron Incorporated .... B 845 679-2401
  Woodstock *(G-17381)*
Rotron Incorporated .... G 845 679-2401
  Woodstock *(G-17382)*

BLUEPRINTING SVCS

A Esteban & Company Inc .... E 212 989-7000
  New York *(G-9031)*

BOAT BUILDING & REPAIR

American Metalcraft Marine .... G 315 686-9891
  Clayton *(G-3710)*
Cayuga Wooden Boatworks Inc .... E 315 253-7447
  Ithaca *(G-6868)*
Coecles Hbr Marina & Boat Yard ..... F 631 749-0856
  Shelter Island *(G-15408)*
Eastern Welding Inc .... G 631 727-0306
  Riverhead *(G-14154)*
Gar Wood Custom Boats .... G 518 494-2966
  Brant Lake *(G-1170)*
Global Marine Power Inc .... E 631 208-2933
  Calverton *(G-3319)*
Hacker Boat Company Inc .... E 518 543-6731
  Silver Bay *(G-15468)*
Hampton Shipyards Inc .... F 631 653-6777
  East Quogue *(G-4470)*
Jag Manufacturing Inc .... E 518 762-9558
  Johnstown *(G-7147)*
Katherine Blizniak .... G 716 674-8545
  West Seneca *(G-16978)*
May Ship Repair Contg Corp .... E 718 442-9700
  Staten Island *(G-15726)*
Metalcraft Marine Us Inc .... F 315 501-4015
  Cape Vincent *(G-3410)*
Mokai Manufacturing Inc .... G 845 566-8287
  Newburgh *(G-12789)*
Robert E Derecktor Inc .... D 914 698-0962
  Mamaroneck *(G-8078)*
Scarano Boatbuilding Inc .... E 518 463-3401
  Albany *(G-133)*
Tumblehome Boatshop .... G 518 623-5050
  Warrensburg *(G-16603)*
Wooden Boatworks .... G 631 477-6507
  Greenport *(G-5896)*

BOAT BUILDING & REPAIRING: Fiberglass

Fantasy Glass Compan .... G 845 786-5818
  Stony Point *(G-15794)*
Superboats Inc .... G 631 226-1761
  Lindenhurst *(G-7510)*

BOAT BUILDING & REPAIRING: Motorized

Marathon Boat Group Inc .... F 607 849-3211
  Marathon *(G-8116)*

Employee Codes: A=Over 500 employees, B=251-500
C=101-250, D=51-100, E=20-50, F=10-19, G=5-9

BOAT BUILDING & REPAIRING: Non-Motorized

PRODUCT SECTION

BOAT BUILDING & REPAIRING: Non-Motorized
Rocking The Boat Inc ....F 718 466-5799
  Bronx *(G-1441)*

BOAT BUILDING & RPRG: Fishing, Small, Lobster, Crab, Oyster
AVS Laminates Inc ....E 631 286-2136
  Bellport *(G-821)*

BOAT DEALERS
Global Marine Power Inc ....E 631 208-2933
  Calverton *(G-3319)*
Marathon Boat Group Inc ....F 607 849-3211
  Marathon *(G-8116)*
Marina Holding Corp ....F 718 646-9283
  Brooklyn *(G-2270)*
Superboats Inc ....G 631 226-1761
  Lindenhurst *(G-7510)*

BOAT DEALERS: Canoe & Kayak
Johnson Outdoors Inc ....C 607 779-2200
  Binghamton *(G-926)*

BOAT LIFTS
Kleinfelder John ....G 716 753-3163
  Mayville *(G-8247)*

BOAT REPAIR SVCS
Cayuga Wooden Boatworks Inc ....E 315 253-7447
  Ithaca *(G-6868)*
Nochem Paint Stripping Inc ....G 631 563-2750
  Blue Point *(G-994)*
Robert E Derecktor Inc ....D 914 698-0962
  Mamaroneck *(G-8078)*
Superboats Inc ....G 631 226-1761
  Lindenhurst *(G-7510)*

BOAT YARD: Boat yards, storage & incidental repair
Robert E Derecktor Inc ....D 914 698-0962
  Mamaroneck *(G-8078)*

BOATS & OTHER MARINE EQPT: Plastic
Global Marine Power Inc ....E 631 208-2933
  Calverton *(G-3319)*

BODIES: Truck & Bus
Able Weldbuilt Industries Inc ....F 631 643-9700
  Deer Park *(G-4110)*
Conti Auto Body Corp ....G 516 921-6435
  Syosset *(G-15837)*
Daimler Buses North Amer Inc ....A 315 768-8101
  Oriskany *(G-13332)*
Donver Incorporated ....F 716 945-1910
  Kill Buck *(G-7195)*
Premium Bldg Components Inc ....E 518 885-0194
  Ballston Spa *(G-606)*
Unicell Body Company Inc ....F 585 424-2660
  Rochester *(G-14767)*

BODY PARTS: Automobile, Stamped Metal
Albert Kemperle Inc ....E 718 629-1084
  Brooklyn *(G-1574)*
Automotive LLC ....F 248 728-8642
  Batavia *(G-624)*
Ford Motor Company ....B 716 821-4000
  Buffalo *(G-2967)*
Kustom Korner ....F 716 646-0173
  Hamburg *(G-5956)*
M & W Aluminum Products Inc ....F 315 414-0005
  Syracuse *(G-16003)*
Racing Industries Inc ....E 631 905-0100
  Calverton *(G-3324)*
Sage Parts Plus ....G 718 651-1898
  Flushing *(G-5297)*

BOILER REPAIR SHOP
A L Eastmond & Sons Inc ....D 718 378-3000
  Bronx *(G-1254)*
Empire Industrial Systems Corp ....F 631 242-4619
  Bay Shore *(G-697)*

Flushing Boiler & Welding Co ....G 718 463-1266
  Brooklyn *(G-1988)*
Troy Boiler Works Inc ....E 518 274-2650
  Troy *(G-16282)*

BOILERS & BOILER SHOP WORK
Marine Boiler & Welding Inc ....F 718 378-1900
  Bronx *(G-1390)*
Supreme Boilers Inc ....G 718 342-2220
  Brooklyn *(G-2651)*

BOILERS: Low-Pressure Heating, Steam Or Hot Water
Best Boilers Inc ....F 718 372-4210
  Brooklyn *(G-1685)*
ECR International Inc ....D 315 797-1310
  Utica *(G-16351)*
ECR International Inc ....C 716 366-5500
  Dunkirk *(G-4365)*
Rockmills Steel Products Corp ....F 718 366-8300
  Maspeth *(G-8199)*

BOLTS: Metal
Baco Enterprises Inc ....D 718 589-6225
  Bronx *(G-1278)*
Jem Threading Specialties Inc ....G 718 665-3341
  Bronx *(G-1368)*
Simon Defense Inc ....G 516 217-6000
  Middle Island *(G-8441)*
Supply Technologies (ny) ....F 212 966-3310
  Albany *(G-139)*

BONDERIZING: Bonderizing, Metal Or Metal Prdts
Clad Metal Specialties Inc ....F 631 666-7750
  Bay Shore *(G-682)*

BOOK STORES
Barrons Educational Series Inc ....D 631 434-3311
  Hauppauge *(G-6051)*
Penguin Random House LLC ....A 212 572-6162
  New York *(G-11623)*
Penguin Random House LLC ....C 212 366-2377
  Albany *(G-117)*
Rizzoli Intl Publications Inc ....E 212 387-3400
  New York *(G-11903)*
Romantic Times Inc ....F 718 237-1097
  Brooklyn *(G-2524)*
Royal Fireworks Printing Co ....F 845 726-3333
  Unionville *(G-16326)*
Samuel French Inc ....E 212 206-8990
  New York *(G-11980)*
Second Chance Press Inc ....G 631 725-1101
  Sag Harbor *(G-15108)*
Sharedbook Inc ....E 646 442-8840
  New York *(G-12066)*
Society For The Study ....E 212 822-8806
  New York *(G-12144)*
Soho Press Inc ....G 212 260-1900
  New York *(G-12147)*
Thornwillow Press Ltd ....D 212 980-0738
  New York *(G-12350)*
William S Hein & Co Inc ....D 716 882-2600
  Getzville *(G-5619)*

BOOKS, WHOLESALE
Anthroposophic Press Inc ....G 518 851-2054
  Clifton Park *(G-3721)*
Columbia University Press ....E 212 459-0600
  New York *(G-9740)*
Kensington Publishing Corp ....D 212 407-1500
  New York *(G-10876)*
Kodansha USA Inc ....F 917 322-6200
  New York *(G-10906)*
Living Well Innovations Inc ....G 646 517-3200
  Hauppauge *(G-6138)*
Macmillan Publishers Inc ....A 646 307-5151
  New York *(G-11115)*
Macmillan Publishing Group LLC ....B 212 674-5151
  New York *(G-11116)*
Moznaim Publishing Co Inc ....G 718 853-0525
  Brooklyn *(G-2342)*
North Country Books Inc ....G 315 735-4877
  Utica *(G-16376)*
North-South Books Inc ....E 212 706-4545
  New York *(G-11476)*

Rizzoli Intl Publications Inc ....E 212 387-3400
  New York *(G-11903)*
S P Books Inc ....G 212 431-5011
  New York *(G-11963)*
Samuel French Inc ....E 212 206-8990
  New York *(G-11980)*
Scholium International Inc ....G 516 883-8032
  Port Washington *(G-13880)*
Swift Fulfillment Services ....G 516 593-1198
  Lynbrook *(G-7990)*
Te Neues Publishing Company ....F 212 627-9090
  New York *(G-12310)*
W W Norton & Company Inc ....C 212 354-5500
  New York *(G-12602)*

BOOTHS: Spray, Sheet Metal, Prefabricated
Auto Body Services LLC ....F 631 431-4640
  Lindenhurst *(G-7477)*

BOOTS: Women's
Lsil & Co Inc ....G 914 761-0998
  White Plains *(G-17160)*
S & W Ladies Wear ....G 718 431-2800
  Brooklyn *(G-2546)*

BOTTLE CAPS & RESEALERS: Plastic
Berry Global Inc ....C 315 986-2161
  Macedon *(G-8011)*
Captive Plastics LLC ....D 716 366-2112
  Dunkirk *(G-4358)*

BOTTLED GAS DEALERS: Propane
Blue Rhino Global Sourcing Inc ....E 516 752-0670
  Melville *(G-8329)*

BOTTLED WATER DELIVERY
Mayer Bros Apple Products Inc ....D 716 668-1787
  West Seneca *(G-16980)*

BOTTLES: Plastic
Alphamed Bottles Inc ....F 631 275-5042
  Hauppauge *(G-6036)*
Capitol Plastic Products Inc ....C 518 627-0051
  Amsterdam *(G-339)*
Chapin International Inc ....C 585 343-3140
  Batavia *(G-628)*
Chapin Manufacturing Inc ....C 585 343-3140
  Batavia *(G-629)*
Cortland Plastics Intl LLC ....E 607 662-0120
  Cortland *(G-4043)*
David Johnson ....F 315 493-4735
  Carthage *(G-3441)*
Intrapac International Corp ....C 518 561-2030
  Plattsburgh *(G-13697)*
Kybod Group LLC ....G 408 306-1657
  New York *(G-10936)*
Nalge Nunc International Corp ....A 585 498-2661
  Rochester *(G-14547)*
Pvc Container Corporation ....C 518 672-7721
  Philmont *(G-13566)*
Samco Scientific Corporation ....C 800 522-3359
  Rochester *(G-14687)*
Schless Bottles Inc ....F 718 236-2790
  Brooklyn *(G-2561)*
Vista Packaging Inc ....E 718 854-9200
  Brooklyn *(G-2750)*
Weber Intl Packg Co LLC ....D 518 561-8282
  Plattsburgh *(G-13738)*

BOTTLES: Vacuum
Cant Live Without It LLC ....D 844 517-9355
  New York *(G-9569)*

BOUTIQUE STORES
Elab Smokers Boutique ....G 585 865-4513
  Rochester *(G-14362)*

BOWLING EQPT & SPLYS
Joe Moro ....G 607 272-0591
  Ithaca *(G-6890)*
Mac Swed Inc ....F 212 684-7730
  New York *(G-11110)*

PRODUCT SECTION

BOX & CARTON MANUFACTURING EQPT

Standard Paper Box Machine Co .... E 718 328-3300
  Bronx *(G-1461)*

BOXES & CRATES: Rectangular, Wood

J & M Packaging Inc .... F 631 608-3069
  Hauppauge *(G-6124)*
Northeast Pallet & Cont Co Inc .... F 518 271-0535
  Troy *(G-16267)*
R D A Container Corporation .... E 585 247-2323
  Gates *(G-5578)*

BOXES & SHOOK: Nailed Wood

Great Lakes Specialties .... E 716 672-4622
  Fredonia *(G-5383)*
McGraw Wood Products LLC .... E 607 836-6465
  Mc Graw *(G-8254)*
McIntosh Box & Pallet Co Inc .... D 315 675-8511
  Bernhards Bay *(G-857)*
McIntosh Box & Pallet Co Inc .... E 315 446-9350
  Rome *(G-14848)*
Philpac Corporation .... E 716 875-8005
  Buffalo *(G-3147)*
Quality Woodworking Corp .... F 718 875-3437
  Brooklyn *(G-2483)*
Reuter Pallet Pkg Sys Inc .... G 845 457-9937
  Montgomery *(G-8638)*

BOXES: Corrugated

Arma Container Corp .... E 631 254-1200
  Deer Park *(G-4125)*
Buckeye Corrugated Inc .... D 585 924-1600
  Victor *(G-16489)*
Cattaraugus Containers Inc .... E 716 676-2000
  Franklinville *(G-5379)*
Georgia-Pacific LLC .... C 518 346-6151
  Schenectady *(G-15290)*
Inner-Pak Container Inc .... F 631 289-9700
  Patchogue *(G-13449)*
International Paper Company .... C 585 663-1000
  Rochester *(G-14473)*
International Paper Company .... C 607 775-1550
  Conklin *(G-3894)*
Island Container Corp .... D 631 253-4400
  Wyandanch *(G-17391)*
J & M Packaging Inc .... F 631 608-3069
  Hauppauge *(G-6124)*
Kapstone Container Corporation .... C 518 842-2450
  Amsterdam *(G-352)*
Lakeside Container Corp .... F 518 561-6150
  Plattsburgh *(G-13701)*
Norampac New England Inc .... C 860 923-9563
  Schenectady *(G-15308)*
Norampac New York City Inc .... C 718 340-2100
  Maspeth *(G-8189)*
Packaging Corporation America .... F 315 785-9083
  Watertown *(G-16692)*
Pactiv LLC .... C 315 457-6780
  Liverpool *(G-7565)*
Philpac Corporation .... E 716 875-8005
  Buffalo *(G-3147)*
Prestige Box Corporation .... E 516 773-3115
  Great Neck *(G-5850)*
Professional Packg Svcs Inc .... E 518 677-5100
  Eagle Bridge *(G-4381)*
R D A Container Corporation .... E 585 247-2323
  Gates *(G-5578)*
Seneca FLS Spc & Logistics Co .... D 315 568-4139
  Seneca Falls *(G-15393)*
Star Corrugated Box Co Inc .... G 718 386-3200
  Flushing *(G-5301)*
Syracuse Corrugated Box Corp .... F 315 437-9901
  East Syracuse *(G-4582)*
Westrock - Southern Cont LLC .... C 315 487-6111
  Camillus *(G-3355)*
Westrock CP LLC .... C 716 694-1000
  North Tonawanda *(G-13023)*
Westrock Rkt Company .... C 330 296-5155
  Deer Park *(G-4251)*

BOXES: Filing, Paperboard Made From Purchased Materials

Paul T Freund Corporation .... D 315 597-4873
  Palmyra *(G-13438)*

BOXES: Mail Or Post Office, Collection/Storage, Sheet Metal

Maloya Laser Inc .... E 631 543-2327
  Commack *(G-3863)*

BOXES: Packing & Shipping, Metal

Alpine Paper Box Co Inc .... E 718 345-4040
  Brooklyn *(G-1592)*

BOXES: Paperboard, Folding

Abbot & Abbot Box Corp .... F 888 930-5972
  Long Island City *(G-7678)*
Alpha Packaging Industries Inc .... E 718 267-4115
  Long Island City *(G-7687)*
Arkay Packaging Corporation .... E 631 273-2000
  Hauppauge *(G-6043)*
Burt Rigid Box Inc .... D 607 433-2510
  Oneonta *(G-13198)*
Cattaraugus Containers Inc .... E 716 676-2000
  Franklinville *(G-5379)*
Climax Packaging Inc .... C 315 376-8000
  Lowville *(G-7963)*
Color Carton Corp .... D 718 665-0840
  Bronx *(G-1303)*
Designers Folding Box Corp .... E 716 853-5141
  Buffalo *(G-2929)*
Disc Graphics Inc .... C 631 300-1129
  Hauppauge *(G-6085)*
Disc Graphics Inc .... E 631 234-1400
  Hauppauge *(G-6086)*
F M Howell & Company .... D 607 734-6291
  Elmira *(G-4697)*
Flower City Printing Inc .... C 585 663-9000
  Rochester *(G-14396)*
Gavin Mfg Corp .... E 631 467-0040
  Farmingdale *(G-5005)*
Gaylord Bros Inc .... D 315 457-5070
  North Syracuse *(G-12961)*
HSM Packaging Corporation .... D 315 476-7996
  Liverpool *(G-7546)*
Knoll Printing & Packaging Inc .... E 516 621-0100
  Syosset *(G-15846)*
M C Packaging Corporation .... E 631 643-3763
  Babylon *(G-547)*
Multi Packg Solutions Intl Ltd .... F 646 885-0005
  New York *(G-11348)*
Novel Box Company Ltd .... E 718 965-2222
  Brooklyn *(G-2388)*
Paper Box Corp .... D 212 226-7490
  New York *(G-11576)*
Premier Packaging Corporation .... E 585 924-8460
  Victor *(G-16520)*
Prestige Box Corporation .... E 516 773-3115
  Great Neck *(G-5850)*
Specialized Packg Group Inc .... G 315 638-4355
  Baldwinsville *(G-574)*
Specialized Packg Radisson LLC .... C 315 638-4355
  Baldwinsville *(G-575)*
Standard Group .... E 718 335-5500
  Great Neck *(G-5859)*
Standard Group LLC .... C 718 507-6430
  Great Neck *(G-5860)*
Viking Industries Inc .... D 845 883-6325
  New Paltz *(G-8927)*
Visitainer Corp .... E 718 636-0300
  Brooklyn *(G-2749)*

BOXES: Paperboard, Set-Up

A Fleisig Paper Box Corp .... F 212 226-7490
  New York *(G-9033)*
American Package Company Inc .... E 718 389-4444
  Brooklyn *(G-1603)*
Brick & Ballerstein Inc .... D 718 497-1400
  Ridgewood *(G-14116)*
Burt Rigid Box Inc .... D 607 433-2510
  Oneonta *(G-13198)*
Cascades New York Inc .... D 718 340-2100
  Maspeth *(G-8152)*
Clarke-Boxit Corporation .... G 716 487-1950
  Jamestown *(G-7015)*
Drescher Paper Box Inc .... D 716 854-0288
  Buffalo *(G-2934)*
Earlville Paper Box Co Inc .... E 315 691-2131
  Earlville *(G-4385)*
F M Howell & Company .... D 607 734-6291
  Elmira *(G-4697)*
Fairview Paper Box Corp .... E 585 786-5230
  Warsaw *(G-16604)*

Friedel Paper Box & Converting .... G 315 437-3325
  Baldwinsville *(G-568)*
Jordon Box Company Inc .... E 315 422-3419
  Syracuse *(G-15989)*
Ketchum Manufacturing Co Inc .... F 518 696-3331
  Lake Luzerne *(G-7296)*
Lionel Habas Associates Inc .... F 212 860-8454
  New York *(G-11033)*
Parlor City Paper Box Co Inc .... D 607 772-0600
  Binghamton *(G-937)*
Prestige Box Corporation .... E 516 773-3115
  Great Neck *(G-5850)*
Propak Inc .... E 518 677-5100
  Eagle Bridge *(G-4382)*
Pure Trade Us Inc .... E 212 256-1600
  New York *(G-11774)*
Seneca FLS Spc & Logistics Co .... D 315 568-4139
  Seneca Falls *(G-15393)*

BOXES: Plastic

American Package Company Inc .... E 718 389-4444
  Brooklyn *(G-1603)*
Hornet Group Inc .... D 845 858-6400
  Port Jervis *(G-13808)*
Novel Box Company Ltd .... E 718 965-2222
  Brooklyn *(G-2388)*
Philcom Ltd .... C 716 875-8005
  Buffalo *(G-3146)*
Printex Packaging Corporation .... D 631 234-4300
  Islandia *(G-6840)*
R P M Industries Inc .... E 315 255-1105
  Auburn *(G-512)*
Rui Xing International Trdg Co .... G 516 298-2667
  Hicksville *(G-6417)*

BOXES: Solid Fiber

Burt Rigid Box Inc .... D 607 433-2510
  Oneonta *(G-13198)*
Specialized Packg Radisson LLC .... C 315 638-4355
  Baldwinsville *(G-575)*

BOXES: Stamped Metal

Novel Box Company Ltd .... E 718 965-2222
  Brooklyn *(G-2388)*

BOXES: Switch, Electric

Cables and Chips Inc .... E 212 619-3132
  New York *(G-9544)*

BOXES: Wooden

Abbot & Abbot Box Corp .... F 888 930-5972
  Long Island City *(G-7678)*
M &L Industry of NY Inc .... G 845 827-6255
  Highland Mills *(G-6439)*
Norjac Boxes Inc .... E 631 842-1300
  Copiague *(G-3940)*

BRAKES & BRAKE PARTS

Interparts International Inc .... E 516 576-2000
  Plainview *(G-13639)*
Rpb Distributors LLC .... G 914 244-3600
  Mount Kisco *(G-8687)*

BRAKES: Electromagnetic

Magtrol Inc .... E 716 668-5555
  Buffalo *(G-3075)*

BRASS FOUNDRY, NEC

Eastern Finding Corp .... F 516 747-6640
  New Hyde Park *(G-8874)*

BRAZING SVCS

Parfuse Corp .... E 516 997-1795
  Westbury *(G-17046)*
W R P Welding Ltd .... F 631 249-8859
  Farmingdale *(G-5149)*

BRAZING: Metal

Captech Industries LLC .... G 347 374-1182
  Rome *(G-14836)*
Hi-Temp Brazing Inc .... E 631 491-4917
  Deer Park *(G-4170)*
Milgo Industrial Inc .... D 718 388-6476
  Brooklyn *(G-2317)*

BRAZING: Metal

Milgo Industrial Inc ....G....... 718 387-0406
  Brooklyn **(G-2318)**

BRIC-A-BRAC

Five Star Creations Inc ....E....... 845 783-1187
  Monroe **(G-8589)**

BRICK, STONE & RELATED PRDTS WHOLESALERS

Barrasso & Sons Trucking Inc ....E....... 631 581-0360
  Islip Terrace **(G-6854)**
Clemente Latham Concrete Corp ....D....... 518 374-2222
  Schenectady **(G-15271)**
East Coast Mines Ltd ....E....... 631 653-5445
  East Quogue **(G-4469)**
Hampton Sand Corp ....G....... 631 325-5533
  Westhampton **(G-17086)**
Hanson Aggregates PA LLC ....E....... 585 624-3800
  Honeoye Falls **(G-6557)**
Imperia Masonry Supply Corp ....E....... 914 738-0900
  Pelham **(G-13517)**
Peckham Materials Corp ....F....... 518 494-2313
  Chestertown **(G-3650)**
Phelps Cement Products Inc ....E....... 315 548-9415
  Phelps **(G-13558)**

BRICKS & BLOCKS: Structural

Everblock Systems LLC ....G....... 844 422-5625
  New York **(G-10143)**
Semco Ceramics Inc ....G....... 315 782-3000
  Watertown **(G-16694)**

BRICKS: Concrete

Brickit ....E....... 631 727-8977
  Hauppauge **(G-6056)**

BRIDAL SHOPS

Vera Wang Group LLC ....C....... 212 575-6400
  New York **(G-12542)**

BRIDGE COMPONENTS: Bridge sections, prefabricated, highway

Apollo Steel Corporation ....F....... 716 283-8758
  Niagara Falls **(G-12820)**
Port Authority of NY & NJ ....D....... 718 390-2534
  Staten Island **(G-15744)**

BRIEFCASES

Coach Stores Inc ....A....... 212 643-9727
  New York **(G-9717)**

BROADCASTING & COMMS EQPT: Antennas, Transmitting/Comms

Century Metal Parts Corp ....E....... 631 667-0800
  Bay Shore **(G-680)**
Edo LLC ....G....... 631 630-4000
  Amityville **(G-284)**
Fei-Zyfer Inc ....G....... 714 933-4045
  Uniondale **(G-16316)**
John Mezzalingua Assoc LLC ....C....... 315 431-7100
  Liverpool **(G-7551)**
Millennium Antenna Corp ....F....... 315 798-9374
  Utica **(G-16372)**
Sinclair Technologies Inc ....E....... 716 874-3682
  Hamburg **(G-5966)**

BROADCASTING & COMMS EQPT: Rcvr-Transmitter Unt, Transceiver

Magnet-Ndctive Systems Ltd USA ....E....... 585 924-4000
  Victor **(G-16514)**

BROADCASTING & COMMUNICATION EQPT: Transmit-Receiver, Radio

Columbia Telecom Group ....G....... 631 501-5000
  New York **(G-9737)**

BROADCASTING & COMMUNICATIONS EQPT: Cellular Radio Telephone

Advanced Comm Solutions ....G....... 914 693-5076
  Ardsley **(G-403)**

Bullitt Mobile LLC ....D....... 631 424-1749
  Bohemia **(G-1024)**
Nycom Business Solutions Inc ....G....... 516 345-6000
  Franklin Square **(G-5376)**
Parrys Incorporated ....F....... 315 824-0002
  Hamilton **(G-5972)**

BROADCASTING & COMMUNICATIONS EQPT: Studio Eqpt, Radio & TV

Bet Networks Incorporated ....E....... 212 846-8111
  New York **(G-9422)**
Big Fish Entertainment LLC ....C....... 646 797-4955
  New York **(G-9443)**
Hopewell Precision Inc ....E....... 845 221-2737
  Hopewell Junction **(G-6579)**
Times Square Studios Ltd ....C....... 212 930-7720
  New York **(G-12371)**

BROADCASTING & COMMUNICATIONS EQPT: Transmitting, Radio/TV

Armstrong Transmitter Corp ....F....... 315 673-1269
  Marcellus **(G-8117)**

BROKERS' SVCS

Remsen Graphics Corp ....G....... 718 643-7500
  Brooklyn **(G-2510)**

BROKERS: Automotive

Monroe County Auto Svcs Inc ....E....... 585 764-3741
  Rochester **(G-14540)**

BROKERS: Business

Spanish Artisan Wine Group LLC ....G....... 914 414-6982
  Patterson **(G-13468)**

BROKERS: Food

Quinn and Co of NY Ltd ....D....... 212 868-1900
  New York **(G-11800)**

BROKERS: Loan

Mml Software Ltd ....E....... 631 941-1313
  East Setauket **(G-4506)**

BROKERS: Printing

Alabaster Group Inc ....G....... 516 867-8223
  Freeport **(G-5391)**
C & C Duplicators Inc ....E....... 631 244-0800
  Bohemia **(G-1025)**
Melmont Fine Pringng/Graphics ....G....... 516 939-2253
  Bethpage **(G-872)**
Prestige Envelope & Lithograph ....F....... 631 521-7043
  Merrick **(G-8426)**

BRONZE FOUNDRY, NEC

American Blade Mfg LLC ....G....... 607 656-4204
  Greene **(G-5880)**
American Blade Mfg LLC ....F....... 607 432-4518
  Oneonta **(G-13193)**
Argos Inc ....E....... 845 528-0576
  Putnam Valley **(G-13989)**
Excalbur Brnze Sculpture Fndry ....E....... 718 366-3444
  Brooklyn **(G-1947)**

BROOMS & BRUSHES

Braun Industries Inc ....E....... 516 741-6000
  Albertson **(G-155)**
Cpac Inc ....E....... 585 382-3223
  Leicester **(G-7442)**
Full Circle Home LLC ....G....... 212 432-0001
  New York **(G-10270)**
K & R Allied Inc ....F....... 718 625-6610
  Brooklyn **(G-2161)**
Perfex Corporation ....F....... 315 826-3600
  Poland **(G-13757)**

BROOMS & BRUSHES: Hair Pencils Or Artists' Brushes

Teka Fine Line Brushes Inc ....E....... 718 692-2928
  Brooklyn **(G-2673)**

BROOMS & BRUSHES: Household Or Indl

Abtex Corporation ....E....... 315 536-7403
  Dresden **(G-4342)**
Braun Bros Brushes Inc ....G....... 631 667-2179
  Valley Stream **(G-16427)**
Brushtech (disc) Inc ....F....... 518 563-8420
  Plattsburgh **(G-13684)**
Culicover & Shapiro Inc ....G....... 516 597-4888
  Hicksville **(G-6364)**
FM Brush Co Inc ....C....... 718 821-5939
  Glendale **(G-5667)**
Rossiter & Schmitt Co Inc ....G....... 516 937-3610
  Bay Shore **(G-734)**
Volckening Inc ....E....... 718 748-0294
  Brooklyn **(G-2754)**
Young & Swartz Inc ....F....... 716 852-2171
  Buffalo **(G-3286)**

BROOMS & BRUSHES: Paint & Varnish

Linzer Products Corp ....C....... 631 253-3333
  West Babylon **(G-16836)**

BROOMS & BRUSHES: Paint Rollers

131-11 Atlantic RE Inc ....D....... 718 441-7700
  Richmond Hill **(G-14077)**
Pan American Roller Inc ....F....... 914 762-8700
  Ossining **(G-13350)**
Premier Paint Roller Co LLC ....F....... 718 441-7700
  Richmond Hill **(G-14090)**
Royal Paint Roller Corp ....E....... 516 367-4370
  Woodbury **(G-17319)**

BROOMS & BRUSHES: Paintbrushes

E & W Manufacturing Co Inc ....E....... 516 367-4370
  Woodbury **(G-17307)**
Kirschner Brush LLC ....F....... 718 292-1809
  Bronx **(G-1377)**

BRUSH BLOCKS: Carbon Or Molded Graphite

Lifestyle Design Usa Ltd ....G....... 212 279-9400
  New York **(G-11021)**

BRUSHES

Walter R Tucker Entps Ltd ....E....... 607 467-2866
  Deposit **(G-4305)**

BUCKLES & PARTS

Maxine Denker Inc ....G....... 212 689-1440
  Staten Island **(G-15725)**

BUILDING & OFFICE CLEANING SVCS

Rumsey Corp ....G....... 914 751-3640
  Yonkers **(G-17501)**

BUILDING & STRUCTURAL WOOD MBRS: Timbers, Struct, Lam Lumber

Empire Building Products Inc ....G....... 518 695-6094
  Schuylerville **(G-15340)**
New England Barns Inc ....E....... 631 445-1461
  Southold **(G-15584)**

BUILDING & STRUCTURAL WOOD MEMBERS

Architctral Mllwk Installation ....E....... 631 499-0755
  East Northport **(G-4453)**
Faulkner Truss Company Inc ....G....... 315 536-8894
  Dresden **(G-4343)**
Harvest Homes Inc ....E....... 518 895-2341
  Delanson **(G-4259)**
Railtech Composites Inc ....F....... 518 324-6190
  Plattsburgh **(G-13721)**
Structural Wood Corporation ....E....... 315 388-4442
  Waddington **(G-16542)**
Timber Frames Inc ....G....... 585 374-6405
  Canandaigua **(G-3388)**
Ufp New York LLC ....E....... 607 563-1556
  Sidney **(G-15465)**
Unadilla Silo Company Inc ....D....... 607 369-9341
  Sidney **(G-15466)**

PRODUCT SECTION

BUILDING & STRUCTURAL WOOD MEMBERS: Arches, Laminated Lumber
Stephenson Lumber Company Inc........G....... 518 548-7521
  Speculator *(G-15587)*

BUILDING BOARD & WALLBOARD, EXC GYPSUM
Continental Buchanan LLC................D....... 703 480-3800
  Buchanan *(G-2799)*

BUILDING BOARD: Gypsum
Continental Buchanan LLC................D....... 703 480-3800
  Buchanan *(G-2799)*

BUILDING CLEANING & MAINTENANCE SVCS
Broadway National Group LLC............D....... 800 797-4467
  Ronkonkoma *(G-14909)*
JM Murray Center Inc......................C....... 607 756-9913
  Cortland *(G-4055)*
JM Murray Center Inc......................C....... 607 756-0246
  Cortland *(G-4056)*
Richard Ruffner...............................F....... 631 234-4600
  Central Islip *(G-3536)*

BUILDING COMPONENTS: Structural Steel
International Metals Trdg LLC............G....... 866 923-0182
  Melville *(G-8361)*
Kuno Steel Products Corp.................F....... 516 938-8500
  Hicksville *(G-6389)*
Leray Homes Inc.............................G....... 315 788-6087
  Watertown *(G-16685)*
Marovato Industries Inc....................F....... 718 389-0800
  Brooklyn *(G-2277)*
Stone Bridge Iron and Stl Inc.............D....... 518 695-3752
  Gansevoort *(G-5504)*
Torino Indus Fabrication Inc...............G....... 631 509-1640
  Bellport *(G-839)*
Wilston Enterprises Inc.....................F....... 716 483-1411
  Jamestown *(G-7076)*

BUILDING ITEM REPAIR SVCS, MISCELLANEOUS
Aireactor Inc...................................F....... 718 326-2433
  Woodside *(G-17335)*
ER Butler & Co Inc..........................E....... 212 925-3565
  New York *(G-10107)*
Manuf Appld Renova Sys..................G....... 518 654-9084
  Corinth *(G-3981)*
Otis Elevator Company....................E....... 917 339-9600
  New York *(G-11547)*

BUILDING PRDTS & MATERIALS DEALERS
Arnan Development Corp..................D....... 607 432-8391
  Oneonta *(G-13194)*
Cossitt Concrete Products Inc............F....... 315 824-2700
  Hamilton *(G-5970)*
Delocon Wholesale Inc.....................F....... 716 592-2711
  Springville *(G-15630)*
Gone South Concrete Block Inc.........E....... 315 598-2141
  Fulton *(G-5473)*
Imperia Masonry Supply Corp............E....... 914 738-0900
  Pelham *(G-13517)*
Norandex Inc Vestal........................G....... 607 786-0778
  Vestal *(G-16475)*
Phelps Cement Products Inc.............G....... 315 548-9415
  Phelps *(G-13558)*
Structural Wood Corporation.............E....... 315 388-4442
  Waddington *(G-16542)*

BUILDING PRDTS: Concrete
Access Products Inc........................G....... 800 679-4022
  Buffalo *(G-2809)*
Duke Company...............................G....... 607 347-4455
  Ithaca *(G-6874)*
Hanson Aggregates East LLC............G....... 716 372-1574
  Allegany *(G-203)*
Oneida Sales & Service Inc...............F....... 716 270-0433
  Lackawanna *(G-7271)*

BUILDING PRDTS: Stone
Icestone LLC..................................E....... 718 624-4900
  Brooklyn *(G-2093)*

Roto Salt Company Inc.....................E....... 315 536-3742
  Penn Yan *(G-13542)*

BUILDING STONE, ARTIFICIAL: Concrete
Crown Hill Stone Inc........................E....... 716 326-4601
  Westfield *(G-17076)*

BUILDINGS & COMPONENTS: Prefabricated Metal
All American Building.......................G....... 607 797-7123
  Binghamton *(G-882)*
Austin Mohawk and Company LLC....E....... 315 793-3000
  Utica *(G-16331)*
Birdair Inc......................................D....... 716 633-9500
  Amherst *(G-231)*
Deraffele Mfg Co Inc........................E....... 914 636-6850
  New Rochelle *(G-8939)*
Framing Technology Inc...................E....... 585 464-8470
  Rochester *(G-14402)*
Man Products Inc............................E....... 631 789-6500
  Farmingdale *(G-5049)*
Metals Building Products..................E....... 844 638-2527
  Holbrook *(G-6491)*
Mobile Mini Inc................................F....... 315 732-4555
  Utica *(G-16373)*
Morton Buildings Inc........................E....... 585 786-8191
  Warsaw *(G-16605)*
Overhead Door Corporation..............D....... 518 828-7652
  Hudson *(G-6659)*
Walpole Woodworkers Inc.................G....... 631 726-2859
  Water Mill *(G-16628)*

BUILDINGS, PREFABRICATED: Wholesalers
Shafer & Sons.................................G....... 315 853-5285
  Westmoreland *(G-17094)*

BUILDINGS: Portable
Mobile Mini Inc................................E....... 631 543-4900
  Commack *(G-3864)*
Qub9 Inc...G....... 585 484-1808
  Rochester *(G-14641)*
Universal Shielding Corp...................E....... 631 667-7900
  Deer Park *(G-4244)*
Veerhouse Voda Haiti LLC.................E....... 917 353-5944
  New York *(G-12537)*

BUILDINGS: Prefabricated, Metal
Energy Panel Structures Inc.............G....... 315 923-7777
  Clyde *(G-3750)*
Energy Panel Structures Inc.............G....... 585 343-1777
  Clyde *(G-3751)*
Energy Panel Structures Inc.............E....... 518 355-6708
  Schenectady *(G-15278)*
Metadure Defense & SEC LLC..........F....... 631 249-2141
  Farmingdale *(G-5058)*
Nci Group Inc..................................D....... 315 339-1245
  Rome *(G-14852)*

BUILDINGS: Prefabricated, Plastic
Euro Woodworking Inc.....................G....... 718 246-9172
  Brooklyn *(G-1944)*

BUILDINGS: Prefabricated, Wood
Cort Contracting.............................F....... 845 758-1190
  Red Hook *(G-14041)*
Duro-Shed Inc.................................E....... 585 344-0800
  Buffalo *(G-2936)*
Eastern Exterior Wall.......................E....... 631 589-3880
  Bohemia *(G-1057)*
Energy Panel Structures Inc.............G....... 315 923-7777
  Clyde *(G-3750)*
Energy Panel Structures Inc.............G....... 585 343-1777
  Clyde *(G-3751)*
Energy Panel Structures Inc.............E....... 518 355-6708
  Schenectady *(G-15278)*
Historcal Soc of Mddltown Walk........G....... 845 342-0941
  Middletown *(G-8478)*
Northern Design & Bldg Assoc..........E....... 518 747-2200
  Queensbury *(G-14019)*
Walpole Woodworkers Inc.................G....... 631 726-2859
  Water Mill *(G-16628)*
Wood Tex Products LLC....................D....... 607 243-5141
  Himrod *(G-6449)*

BUILDINGS: Prefabricated, Wood
Lapp Management Corp..................G....... 607 243-5141
  Himrod *(G-6448)*
Roscoe Brothers Inc........................F....... 607 844-3750
  Dryden *(G-4347)*
Shafer & Sons.................................G....... 315 853-5285
  Westmoreland *(G-17094)*
Shelter Enterprises Inc....................D....... 518 237-4100
  Cohoes *(G-3783)*

BULLETIN BOARDS: Wood
Aarco Products Inc..........................F....... 631 924-5461
  Yaphank *(G-17400)*
Bulletin Boards & Dirctry Pdts............F....... 914 248-8008
  Yorktown Heights *(G-17523)*

BUMPERS: Motor Vehicle
4bumpers Llc..................................F....... 212 721-9600
  New York *(G-9021)*

BURIAL VAULTS: Concrete Or Precast Terrazzo
Beck Vault Company........................G....... 315 337-7590
  Rome *(G-14835)*
Doric Vault of Wny Inc......................F....... 716 828-1776
  Buffalo *(G-2933)*
Ideal Burial Vault Company...............G....... 585 599-2242
  Corfu *(G-3977)*
Robert M Vault................................G....... 315 243-1447
  Bridgeport *(G-1235)*
Suhor Industries Inc........................F....... 585 377-5100
  Fairport *(G-4890)*

BURLAP & BURLAP PRDTS
James Thompson & Company Inc....G....... 212 686-4242
  New York *(G-10738)*

BURNERS: Gas, Indl
Dyson-Kissner-Moran Corp................E....... 212 661-4600
  Poughkeepsie *(G-13915)*
Flynn Burner Corporation..................E....... 914 636-1320
  New Rochelle *(G-8944)*
Frederick Cowan & Company Inc.......F....... 631 369-0360
  Riverhead *(G-14155)*

BUSES: Wholesalers
Leonard Bus Sales Inc.....................G....... 607 467-3100
  Rome *(G-14847)*

BUSHINGS & BEARINGS: Copper, Exc Machined
Amt Incorporated............................E....... 518 284-2910
  Sharon Springs *(G-15405)*

BUSHINGS: Cast Steel, Exc Investment
Pcore Electric Company Inc..............D....... 585 768-1200
  Le Roy *(G-7440)*

BUSINESS ACTIVITIES: Non-Commercial Site
Adirondack Leather Pdts Inc............F....... 607 547-5798
  Fly Creek *(G-5317)*
Ajmadison Corp..............................D....... 718 532-1800
  Brooklyn *(G-1572)*
Aka Sport Inc..................................F....... 631 858-9888
  Dix Hills *(G-4312)*
American Comfort Direct LLC............E....... 201 364-8309
  New York *(G-9165)*
Anne Taintor Inc..............................G....... 718 483-9312
  Brooklyn *(G-1613)*
Appliedea Inc..................................G....... 212 920-6822
  New York *(G-9234)*
Arm Construction Company Inc........G....... 646 235-6520
  East Elmhurst *(G-4410)*
Aureonic...G....... 518 791-9331
  Gansevoort *(G-5499)*
Buperiod PBC.................................G....... 917 406-9804
  Brooklyn *(G-1740)*
Catch Ventures Inc.........................F....... 347 620-4351
  New York *(G-9601)*
Cfp Purchasing Inc..........................G....... 705 806-0383
  Flushing *(G-5238)*

Employee Codes: A=Over 500 employees, B=251-500
C=101-250, D=51-100, E=20-50, F=10-19, G=5-9

BUSINESS ACTIVITIES: Non-Commercial Site
PRODUCT SECTION

Cloud Rock Group LLC ....G.... 516 967-6023
Roslyn *(G-15041)*
Dapper Dads Inc ....G.... 917 903-8045
Brooklyn *(G-1840)*
Darmiyan LLC ....G.... 917 689-0389
New York *(G-9864)*
Dezawy LLC ....G.... 917 436-8820
New York *(G-9918)*
Do It Different Inc ....G.... 917 842-0230
New York *(G-9945)*
Eccella Corporation ....G.... 855 879-3223
New York *(G-10026)*
Envent Systems Inc ....G.... 646 294-6980
Pelham *(G-13516)*
Excell Print & Promotions Inc ....G.... 914 437-8668
White Plains *(G-17133)*
Fresh Prints LLC ....E.... 917 826-2752
New York *(G-10259)*
Garrett J Cronin ....G.... 914 761-9299
White Plains *(G-17137)*
Gorga Fehren Fine Jewelry LLC ....G.... 646 861-3595
New York *(G-10379)*
Greene Brass & Alum Fndry LLC ....G.... 607 656-4204
Bloomville *(G-990)*
Hair Ventures LLC ....F.... 718 664-7689
Irvington *(G-6813)*
HHS Pharmaceuticals Inc ....F.... 347 674-1670
New York *(G-10516)*
Hovee Inc ....F.... 646 249-6200
New York *(G-10565)*
Hs Homeworx LLC ....G.... 646 870-0406
New York *(G-10568)*
Hum Limited Liability Corp ....G.... 631 525-2174
Nesconset *(G-8822)*
Inscape (new York) Inc ....D.... 716 665-6210
Falconer *(G-4909)*
Intelligent Ctrl Systems LLC ....G.... 516 340-1011
Huntington *(G-6697)*
Joel Zelcer ....F.... 917 525-6790
Brooklyn *(G-2143)*
L VII Resilient LLC ....F.... 631 987-5819
Medford *(G-8284)*
Labrador Stone Inc ....G.... 570 465-2120
Binghamton *(G-928)*
Latchable Inc ....E.... 646 833-0604
New York *(G-10969)*
Lotus Apparel Designs Inc ....G.... 646 236-9363
Westbury *(G-17034)*
Magcrest Packaging Inc ....G.... 845 425-0451
Monsey *(G-8609)*
New York Qrtrly Foundation Inc ....F.... 917 843-8825
Brooklyn *(G-2377)*
On Line Power Technologies ....G.... 914 968-4440
Yonkers *(G-17489)*
Pap Chat Inc ....G.... 516 350-1888
Brooklyn *(G-2417)*
Patrick Rohan ....G.... 718 781-2573
Monticello *(G-8646)*
Patuga LLC ....G.... 716 204-7220
Williamsville *(G-17276)*
Phoenix Usa LLC ....G.... 646 351-6598
New York *(G-11671)*
Pilot Inc ....G.... 212 951-1133
New York *(G-11681)*
Pilot Inc ....G.... 212 951-1133
New York *(G-11682)*
Pink Box Accessories LLC ....G.... 716 777-4477
Brooklyn *(G-2435)*
Plain Digital Inc ....G.... 914 310-0280
Scarsdale *(G-15252)*
Playfitness Corp ....G.... 917 497-5443
Staten Island *(G-15743)*
Playground NY Inc ....F.... 505 920-7236
Brooklyn *(G-2439)*
Playlife LLC ....G.... 646 207-9082
New York *(G-11696)*
Qub9 Inc ....G.... 585 484-1808
Rochester *(G-14641)*
Ready Check Glo Inc ....G.... 516 547-1849
East Northport *(G-4463)*
Ready To Assemble Company Inc ....E.... 516 825-4397
Valley Stream *(G-16448)*
Rision Inc ....G.... 212 987-2628
New York *(G-11900)*
Roscoe Brothers Inc ....F.... 607 844-3750
Dryden *(G-4347)*
Scan-A-Chrome Color Inc ....G.... 631 532-6146
Copiague *(G-3948)*
Sensor & Decontamination Inc ....F.... 301 526-8389
Binghamton *(G-944)*
Slyde Inc ....F.... 917 331-2114
Long Island City *(G-7908)*
Smn Medical PC ....F.... 844 362-2428
Rye *(G-15094)*
South Central Boyz ....G.... 718 496-7270
Brooklyn *(G-2611)*
Special Circle Inc ....F.... 516 595-9988
New Hyde Park *(G-8909)*
Treauu Inc ....G.... 703 731-0196
New York *(G-12417)*
Trovvit Inc ....G.... 718 908-5376
Brooklyn *(G-2704)*
Urthworx Inc ....G.... 646 373-7535
New York *(G-12503)*
Verris Inc ....G.... 201 565-1648
New York *(G-12548)*
Vertical Lax Inc ....G.... 518 669-3699
Albany *(G-149)*
Viewsport International Inc ....G.... 585 259-1562
Penfield *(G-13528)*
Virtuvent Inc ....G.... 646 845-0387
New York *(G-12579)*
Vortex Ventures Inc ....G.... 516 946-8345
North Baldwin *(G-12929)*
Wrkbook LLC ....F.... 914 355-1293
White Plains *(G-17215)*
Zinerva Pharmaceuticals LLC ....G.... 630 729-4184
Clarence Center *(G-3708)*

BUSINESS FORMS WHOLESALERS

American Print Solutions Inc ....G.... 718 208-2309
Brooklyn *(G-1605)*
Chem-Puter Friendly Inc ....E.... 631 331-2259
Mount Sinai *(G-8696)*
Composite Forms Inc ....F.... 914 937-1808
Port Chester *(G-13768)*
Empire Business Forms Inc ....F.... 845 471-5666
Poughkeepsie *(G-13917)*

BUSINESS FORMS: Printed, Continuous

Five Boro Holding LLC ....F.... 718 431-9500
Brooklyn *(G-1980)*
Idc Printing & Sty Co Inc ....G.... 516 599-0400
Lynbrook *(G-7979)*
Linden Forms & Systems Inc ....E.... 212 219-1100
Brooklyn *(G-2229)*
Syracuse Computer Forms Inc ....E.... 315 478-0108
Syracuse *(G-16075)*

BUSINESS FORMS: Printed, Manifold

Abra-Ka-Data Systems Ltd ....E.... 631 667-5550
Deer Park *(G-4111)*
Amsterdam Printing & Litho Inc ....F.... 518 842-6000
Amsterdam *(G-333)*
Amsterdam Printing & Litho Inc ....E.... 518 842-6000
Amsterdam *(G-334)*
Bmg Printing and Promotion LLC ....G.... 631 231-9200
Bohemia *(G-1022)*
Gateway Prtg & Graphics Inc ....E.... 716 823-3873
Hamburg *(G-5949)*
Maggio Data Forms Printing Ltd ....C.... 631 348-0343
Hauppauge *(G-6150)*
Marcy Business Forms Inc ....G.... 718 935-9100
Brooklyn *(G-2268)*
P P I Business Forms Inc ....G.... 716 825-1241
Buffalo *(G-3129)*
Resonant Legal Media LLC ....D.... 800 781-3591
New York *(G-11873)*
Richard Ruffner ....F.... 631 234-4600
Central Islip *(G-3536)*
Rmf Printing Technologies Inc ....E.... 716 683-7500
Lancaster *(G-7364)*
RR Donnelley & Sons Company ....D.... 716 773-0647
Grand Island *(G-5781)*
RR Donnelley & Sons Company ....D.... 716 773-0300
Grand Island *(G-5782)*
Select-A-Form Inc ....D.... 631 981-3076
Holbrook *(G-6499)*
Taylor Communications Inc ....F.... 937 221-1303
Melville *(G-8388)*
Taylor Communications Inc ....F.... 718 352-0220
Westbury *(G-17058)*
Williamson Law Book Co ....F.... 585 924-3400
Victor *(G-16537)*

BUSINESS MACHINE REPAIR, ELECTRIC

National Time Recording Eqp Co ....F.... 212 227-3310
New York *(G-11375)*
Neopost USA Inc ....E.... 631 435-9100
Hauppauge *(G-6172)*
Xerox Corporation ....C.... 585 427-4500
Rochester *(G-14797)*
Yellow E House Inc ....G.... 718 888-2000
Flushing *(G-5315)*

BUSINESS SUPPORT SVCS

Cabezon Design Group Inc ....G.... 718 488-9868
Brooklyn *(G-1748)*
Diamond Inscription Tech ....F.... 646 366-7944
New York *(G-9926)*

BUTADIENE: Indl, Organic, Chemical

Unified Solutions For Clg Inc ....F.... 718 782-8800
Brooklyn *(G-2716)*

BUTTONS

Buttons & Trimcom Inc ....F.... 212 868-1971
New York *(G-9537)*
E-Won Industrial Co Inc ....E.... 212 750-9610
New York *(G-10008)*
Empire State Metal Pdts Inc ....E.... 718 847-1617
Richmond Hill *(G-14085)*
Emsig Manufacturing Corp ....F.... 718 784-7717
New York *(G-10077)*
Emsig Manufacturing Corp ....F.... 518 828-7301
Hudson *(G-6643)*
Emsig Manufacturing Corp ....E.... 718 784-7717
New York *(G-10078)*
Eu Design LLC ....G.... 212 420-7788
New York *(G-10135)*
Joyce Trimming Inc ....G.... 212 719-3110
New York *(G-10811)*
Kraus & Sons Inc ....F.... 212 620-0408
New York *(G-10926)*
Mona Slide Fasteners Inc ....E.... 718 325-7700
Bronx *(G-1404)*
National Die & Button Mould Co ....E.... 201 939-7800
Brooklyn *(G-2357)*
Shimada Shoji (hk) Limited ....G.... 212 268-0465
New York *(G-12073)*

CABINETS & CASES: Show, Display & Storage, Exc Wood

260 Oak Street Inc ....G.... 877 852-4676
Buffalo *(G-2802)*
Able Steel Equipment Co Inc ....F.... 718 361-9240
Long Island City *(G-7679)*
S & K Counter Tops Inc ....G.... 716 662-7986
Orchard Park *(G-13321)*

CABINETS: Bathroom Vanities, Wood

Nagad Cabinets Inc ....G.... 718 382-7200
Brooklyn *(G-2353)*
New York Vanity and Mfg Co ....E.... 718 417-1010
Freeport *(G-5425)*
Tristate Contract Sales LLC ....G.... 845 782-2614
Chester *(G-3648)*

CABINETS: Entertainment

Dbs Interiors Corp ....F.... 631 491-3013
West Babylon *(G-16813)*
Loffreno Cstm Interiors Contg ....E.... 718 981-0319
Staten Island *(G-15721)*
Time Base Corporation ....E.... 631 293-4068
Edgewood *(G-4630)*
W Designe Inc ....E.... 914 736-1058
Peekskill *(G-13509)*

CABINETS: Entertainment Units, Household, Wood

Cleary Custom Cabinets Inc ....F.... 516 939-2475
Hicksville *(G-6357)*
Handcraft Cabinetry Inc ....G.... 914 681-9437
White Plains *(G-17144)*

CABINETS: Factory

Creative Stone & Cabinets ....G.... 631 772-6548
Selden *(G-15371)*
T O Gronlund Company Inc ....F.... 212 679-3535
New York *(G-12291)*
Thornwood Products Ltd ....E.... 914 769-9161
Thornwood *(G-16144)*

Wood Etc Inc ......F 315 484-9663
Syracuse *(G-16099)*

CABINETS: Filing, Metal

Schwab Corp ......E 585 381-4900
Rochester *(G-14696)*

CABINETS: Filing, Wood

Red White & Blue Entps Corp ......G 718 565-8080
Woodside *(G-17366)*

CABINETS: Kitchen, Metal

American Best Cabinets Inc ......E 845 369-6666
Suffern *(G-15807)*
Hellas Stone Inc ......G 718 545-4716
Astoria *(G-442)*
Majestic Home Imprvs Distr ......G 718 853-5079
Brooklyn *(G-2256)*
Manhattan Cabinets Inc ......G 212 548-2436
New York *(G-11152)*
Methods Tooling & Mfg Inc ......E 845 246-7100
Mount Marion *(G-8693)*

CABINETS: Kitchen, Wood

Able Kitchen ......F 877 268-1264
Cedarhurst *(G-3482)*
Acme Kitchenettes Corp ......E 518 828-4191
Hudson *(G-6632)*
Aka Enterprises ......E 716 474-4579
Wyoming *(G-17395)*
Aki Cabinets Inc ......E 718 721-2541
Astoria *(G-429)*
Amoroso Wood Products Co Inc ......G 631 249-4998
Melville *(G-8327)*
Andike Millwork Inc ......G 718 894-1796
Maspeth *(G-8146)*
Artone LLC ......D 716 664-2232
Jamestown *(G-7008)*
Atlantic States Distributing ......G 518 427-6364
Menands *(G-8400)*
Auburn-Watson Corp ......F 716 876-8000
Depew *(G-4272)*
Bauerschmidt & Sons Inc ......D 718 528-3500
Jamaica *(G-6934)*
Bloch Industries LLC ......D 585 334-9600
Rochester *(G-14253)*
Cabinet Shapes Corp ......F 718 784-6255
Long Island City *(G-7722)*
Cabinetry By Tbr Inc ......G 516 365-8500
Manhasset *(G-8088)*
Cabinets By Stanley Inc ......G 718 222-5861
Brooklyn *(G-1749)*
Cambridge Kitchens Mfg Inc ......F 516 935-5100
Hicksville *(G-6353)*
Candlelight Cabinetry Inc ......C 716 434-2114
Lockport *(G-7603)*
Capital Kit Cab & Door Mfrs ......G 718 886-0303
College Point *(G-3805)*
Carefree Kitchens Inc ......G 631 567-2120
Holbrook *(G-6464)*
Carlos & Alex Atelier Inc ......E 718 441-8911
Richmond Hill *(G-14083)*
Casa Collection Inc ......G 718 694-0272
Brooklyn *(G-1764)*
Catskill Craftsmen Inc ......D 607 652-7321
Stamford *(G-15644)*
Central Kitchen Corp ......F 631 283-1029
Southampton *(G-15564)*
Chicone Builders LLC ......G 607 535-6540
Montour Falls *(G-8648)*
Classic Cabinets ......F 845 357-4331
Suffern *(G-15809)*
Clearwood Custom Carpentry and ......E 315 432-8422
East Syracuse *(G-4533)*
Columbia Cabinets LLC ......G 212 972-7550
Mount Kisco *(G-8665)*
Columbia Cabinets LLC ......F 518 283-1700
Saratoga Springs *(G-15178)*
Commercial Millworks Inc ......G 315 475-7479
Syracuse *(G-15921)*
Cosmopolitan Cabinet Company ......G 631 467-4960
Ronkonkoma *(G-14918)*
Craft Custom Woodwork Co Inc ......F 718 821-2162
Maspeth *(G-8155)*
Creative Cabinet Corp America ......E 631 751-5768
Stony Brook *(G-15790)*
Custom CAS Inc ......E 718 726-3575
Long Island City *(G-7736)*
Custom Woodcraft LLC ......F 315 843-4234
Munnsville *(G-8796)*
D & M Custom Cabinets Inc ......F 516 678-2818
Oceanside *(G-13095)*
Dak Mica and Wood Products ......G 631 467-0749
Ronkonkoma *(G-14920)*
Dbs Interiors Corp ......F 631 491-3013
West Babylon *(G-16813)*
Deakon Homes and Interiors ......F 518 271-0342
Troy *(G-16255)*
Di Fiore and Sons Custom Wdwkg ......G 718 278-1663
Long Island City *(G-7744)*
EC Wood & Company Inc ......F 718 388-2287
Deer Park *(G-4157)*
EM Pfaff & Son Inc ......F 607 739-3691
Horseheads *(G-6604)*
Enterprise Wood Products Inc ......F 718 853-9243
Brooklyn *(G-1930)*
Fantasy Home Improvement Corp ......G 718 277-4021
Brooklyn *(G-1962)*
Fina Cabinet Corp ......G 718 409-2900
Mount Vernon *(G-8726)*
Fra-Rik Formica Fabg Co Inc ......G 718 597-3335
Bronx *(G-1339)*
Garrison Woodworking Inc ......F 845 726-3525
Westtown *(G-17098)*
Glissade New York LLC ......E 631 756-4800
Farmingdale *(G-5007)*
Greenway Cabinetry Inc ......F 516 877-0009
Williston Park *(G-17285)*
Hearth Cabinets and More Ltd ......G 315 641-1197
Liverpool *(G-7545)*
Hendrickson Custom Cabinetry ......F 718 401-0137
Bronx *(G-1358)*
Hollywood Cabinets Co ......G 516 354-0857
Elmont *(G-4733)*
Home Ideal Inc ......G 718 762-8998
Flushing *(G-5259)*
Ignelzi Interiors Inc ......E 718 464-0279
Queens Village *(G-13995)*
J Percoco Industries Inc ......G 631 312-4572
Bohemia *(G-1075)*
Jordache Woodworking Corp ......F 718 349-3373
Brooklyn *(G-2146)*
K-Binet Inc ......G 845 348-1149
Blauvelt *(G-966)*
Kalnitz Kitchens Inc ......F 716 684-1700
Buffalo *(G-3043)*
Kw Distributors Group Inc ......F 718 843-3500
Ozone Park *(G-13408)*
Longo Commercial Cabinets Inc ......E 631 225-4290
Lindenhurst *(G-7491)*
Lyn Jo Kitchens Inc ......G 718 336-6060
Brooklyn *(G-2242)*
Material Process Systems Inc ......F 718 302-3081
Brooklyn *(G-2286)*
Matteo & Antonio Bartolotta ......F 315 252-2220
Auburn *(G-506)*
McGraw Wood Products LLC ......E 607 836-6465
Mc Graw *(G-8254)*
Mega Cabinets Inc ......E 631 789-4112
Amityville *(G-311)*
Methods Tooling & Mfg Inc ......E 845 246-7100
Mount Marion *(G-8693)*
Metro Kitchens Corp ......F 718 434-1166
Brooklyn *(G-2310)*
Michael Bernstein Design Assoc ......E 718 456-9277
Brooklyn *(G-2313)*
Michael P Mmarr ......G 315 623-9380
Constantia *(G-3907)*
Millco Woodworking LLC ......F 585 526-6844
Hall *(G-5940)*
Modern Cabinet Company Inc ......E 845 473-4900
Poughkeepsie *(G-13936)*
N Y Elli Design Corp ......F 718 228-0014
Maspeth *(G-8184)*
Neo Cabinetry LLC ......F 718 403-0456
Brooklyn *(G-2364)*
NY Cabinet Factory Inc ......F 718 256-6541
Brooklyn *(G-2392)*
Pgs Millwork Inc ......D 212 244-6610
New York *(G-11663)*
Piccini Industries Ltd ......E 845 365-0614
Orangeburg *(G-13262)*
Precision Dental Cabinets Inc ......F 631 543-3870
Smithtown *(G-15518)*
Premier Woodcraft Ltd ......E 610 383-6624
White Plains *(G-17188)*
Premium Woodworking LLC ......G 631 485-3133
West Babylon *(G-16849)*
R & M Thermofoil Doors Inc ......G 718 206-4991
Jamaica *(G-6980)*
Ralph Payne ......G 718 222-4200
Brooklyn *(G-2496)*
Red White & Blue Entps Corp ......G 718 565-8080
Woodside *(G-17366)*
Ribble Lumber Inc ......G 315 536-6221
Penn Yan *(G-13541)*
Royal Custom Cabinets ......G 315 376-6042
Lowville *(G-7970)*
S & V Custom Furniture Mfg ......F 516 746-8299
Mineola *(G-8569)*
S Donadic Woodworking Inc ......D 718 361-9888
Sunnyside *(G-15830)*
Salko Kitchens Inc ......F 845 565-4420
New Windsor *(G-8998)*
Salmon Crek Cabinetry Inc ......E 315 589-5419
Williamson *(G-17254)*
Serway Bros Inc ......E 315 337-0601
Rome *(G-14864)*
Sherry-Mica Products Inc ......G 631 471-7513
Ronkonkoma *(G-15009)*
Silva Cabinetry Inc ......E 914 737-7697
Buchanan *(G-2801)*
Skyline Custom Cabinetry Inc ......G 631 393-2983
Farmingdale *(G-5120)*
Stone Expo & Cabinetry LLC ......F 516 292-2988
West Hempstead *(G-16895)*
Upstate Cabinet Co Inc ......F 585 429-5090
Rochester *(G-14773)*
Viola Cabinet Corporation ......G 716 284-6327
Niagara Falls *(G-12905)*
W Designe Inc ......E 914 736-1058
Peekskill *(G-13509)*
White House Cabinet Shop LLC ......G 607 674-9358
Sherburne *(G-15421)*
William Brooks Woodworking ......F 718 495-9767
Brooklyn *(G-2768)*
Win Wood Cabinetry Inc ......G 516 304-2216
Greenvale *(G-5901)*
Wood Etc Inc ......F 315 484-9663
Syracuse *(G-16099)*
Yonkers Cabinets Inc ......G 914 668-2133
Yonkers *(G-17518)*
Your Furniture Designers Inc ......G 845 947-3046
West Haverstraw *(G-16879)*
Your Way Custom Cabinets Inc ......G 914 371-1870
Mount Vernon *(G-8792)*

CABINETS: Office, Metal

Creative Cabinetry Corporation ......G 914 963-6061
Yonkers *(G-17447)*
Natural Stone & Cabinet Inc ......G 718 388-2988
Brooklyn *(G-2360)*
Riverfront Costume Design ......G 716 693-2501
North Tonawanda *(G-13008)*

CABINETS: Office, Wood

Chicone Builders LLC ......G 607 535-6540
Montour Falls *(G-8648)*
Commercial Display Design LLC ......F 607 336-7353
Norwich *(G-13044)*
Concepts In Wood of CNY ......E 315 463-8084
Syracuse *(G-15923)*
Craft Custom Woodwork Co Inc ......F 718 821-2162
Maspeth *(G-8155)*
Creative Cabinetry Corporation ......G 914 963-6061
Yonkers *(G-17447)*
Fina Cabinet Corp ......G 718 409-2900
Mount Vernon *(G-8726)*
Loffreno Cstm Interiors Contg ......E 718 981-0319
Staten Island *(G-15721)*
N Y Elli Design Corp ......F 718 228-0014
Maspeth *(G-8184)*
Poppin Inc ......D 212 391-7200
New York *(G-11707)*
Riverfront Costume Design ......G 716 693-2501
North Tonawanda *(G-13008)*
Stylecraft Interiors Inc ......F 516 487-2133
Great Neck *(G-5862)*
Three R Enterprises Inc ......E 585 254-5050
Rochester *(G-14752)*
Wood Etc Inc ......F 315 484-9663
Syracuse *(G-16099)*

CABINETS: Radio & Television, Metal

CIDC Corp ......F 718 342-5820
Brooklyn *(G-1779)*

Employee Codes: A=Over 500 employees, B=251-500
C=101-250, D=51-100, E=20-50, F=10-19, G=5-9
2018 Harris
New York Manufacturers Directory
1147

CABINETS: Show, Display, Etc, Wood, Exc Refrigerated

Custom Design Kitchens Inc ....F....... 518 355-4446
Duanesburg *(G-4350)*
E F Thresh Inc ....G....... 315 437-7301
East Syracuse *(G-4539)*
Fleetwood Cabinet Co Inc ....G....... 516 379-2139
Brooklyn *(G-1986)*
Johnny Mica Inc ....G....... 631 225-5213
Lindenhurst *(G-7488)*
Rasjada Enterprises Ltd ....F....... 631 242-1055
Bay Shore *(G-728)*
Telesca-Heyman Inc ....F....... 212 534-3442
New York *(G-12319)*

CABLE TELEVISION

Hearst Holdings Inc ....F....... 212 649-2000
New York *(G-10493)*
Historic TW Inc ....E....... 212 484-8000
New York *(G-10530)*
Time Warner Companies Inc ....D....... 212 484-8000
New York *(G-12369)*

CABLE TELEVISION PRDTS

Arcom Automatics LLC ....G....... 315 422-1230
Syracuse *(G-15876)*
Arrow-Communication Labs Inc ....B....... 315 422-1230
Syracuse *(G-15879)*
Belden Inc ....B....... 607 796-5600
Horseheads *(G-6597)*
Eagle Comtronics Inc ....C....... 315 451-3313
Liverpool *(G-7543)*
Eeg Enterprises Inc ....F....... 516 293-7472
Farmingdale *(G-4995)*

CABLE: Coaxial

Hyperline Systems Inc ....G....... 613 736-8500
Brooklyn *(G-2090)*

CABLE: Fiber

Cables and Chips Inc ....E....... 212 619-3132
New York *(G-9544)*
Fiber Instrument Sales Inc ....C....... 315 736-2206
Oriskany *(G-13333)*
Fiberone LLC ....F....... 315 434-8877
East Syracuse *(G-4543)*
Triad Network Technologies ....E....... 585 924-8505
Victor *(G-16533)*

CABLE: Fiber Optic

Cable Your World Inc ....G....... 631 509-1180
Port Jeff STA *(G-13787)*
Complete Fiber Solutions Inc ....G....... 718 828-8900
Bronx *(G-1305)*
Corning Incorporated ....G....... 607 974-6729
Painted Post *(G-13417)*
Corning Incorporated ....A....... 607 974-9000
Corning *(G-3983)*
Corning Incorporated ....E....... 607 248-1200
Corning *(G-3986)*
Corning Specialty Mtls Inc ....G....... 607 974-9000
Corning *(G-3991)*
Fiberdyne Labs Inc ....D....... 315 895-8470
Frankfort *(G-5362)*
TLC-The Light Connection Inc ....D....... 315 736-7384
Oriskany *(G-13341)*

CABLE: Nonferrous, Shipboard

Monroe Cable Company Inc ....C....... 845 692-2800
Middletown *(G-8487)*

CABLE: Noninsulated

Cortland Cable Company Inc ....E....... 607 753-8275
Cortland *(G-4039)*
J Davis Manufacturing Co Inc ....E....... 315 337-7574
Rome *(G-14844)*
Nexans Energy USA Inc ....C....... 845 469-2141
Chester *(G-3637)*
Reelcology Inc ....F....... 845 258-1880
Pine Island *(G-13580)*
Ultra Clarity Corp ....G....... 719 470-1010
Spring Valley *(G-15625)*
Weico Wire & Cable Inc ....E....... 631 254-2970
Edgewood *(G-4634)*

CABLE: Ropes & Fiber

Cortland Company Inc ....D....... 607 753-8276
Cortland *(G-4040)*

CABLE: Steel, Insulated Or Armored

Dragon Trading Inc ....G....... 212 717-1496
New York *(G-9974)*
Dsr International Corp ....G....... 631 427-2600
Great Neck *(G-5820)*
Northeast Wire and Cable Co ....G....... 716 297-8483
Niagara Falls *(G-12870)*

CAGES: Wire

Renco Group Inc ....G....... 212 541-6000
New York *(G-11864)*

CALCULATING & ACCOUNTING EQPT

Hand Held Products Inc ....B....... 315 554-6000
Skaneateles Falls *(G-15490)*
Merchant Service Pymnt Access ....G....... 212 561-5516
Uniondale *(G-16321)*

CALIBRATING SVCS, NEC

Phymetrix Inc ....G....... 631 627-3950
Medford *(G-8291)*
Quality Vision Services Inc ....D....... 585 544-0450
Rochester *(G-14638)*

CAMERA & PHOTOGRAPHIC SPLYS STORES

Eastchester Photo Services ....G....... 914 961-6596
Eastchester *(G-4594)*

CAMERAS & RELATED EQPT: Photographic

Bescor Video Accessories Ltd ....F....... 631 420-1717
Farmingdale *(G-4960)*
Columbia Telecom Group ....G....... 631 501-5000
New York *(G-9737)*
Fanvision Entertainment LLC ....G....... 917 297-7428
New York *(G-10191)*
Focus Camera Inc ....F....... 718 437-8800
Brooklyn *(G-1990)*
Lake Image Systems Inc ....F....... 585 321-3630
Henrietta *(G-6319)*
Rear View Safety Inc ....F....... 855 815-3842
Brooklyn *(G-2502)*
Watec America Corporation ....E....... 702 434-6111
Middletown *(G-8506)*

CANDLE SHOPS

Candles By Foster ....G....... 914 739-9226
Peekskill *(G-13499)*
Northern Lights Entps Inc ....G....... 585 593-1200
Wellsville *(G-16781)*

CANDLES

A & L Asset Management Ltd ....C....... 718 566-1500
Brooklyn *(G-1525)*
Astron Candle Manufacturing Co ....G....... 718 728-3330
Long Island City *(G-7705)*
Betterbee Inc ....F....... 518 314-0575
Greenwich *(G-5905)*
Candle In The Window Inc ....F....... 718 852-5743
Brooklyn *(G-1755)*
Candles By Foster ....G....... 914 739-9226
Peekskill *(G-13499)*
Cathedral Candle Co ....D....... 315 422-9119
Syracuse *(G-15909)*
Crusader Candle Co Inc ....E....... 718 625-0005
Brooklyn *(G-1820)*
Hs Homeworx LLC ....G....... 646 870-0406
New York *(G-10568)*
International Design Assoc Ltd ....G....... 212 687-0333
New York *(G-10675)*
Joya LLC ....F....... 718 852-6979
Brooklyn *(G-2152)*
Kkw Corp ....E....... 631 589-5454
Sayville *(G-15240)*
Lux Mundi Corp ....G....... 631 244-4596
Ronkonkoma *(G-14962)*
Muench-Kreuzer Candle Company ....D....... 315 471-4515
Syracuse *(G-16014)*
Northern Lights Entps Inc ....G....... 585 593-1200
Wellsville *(G-16781)*
Old Williamsburgh Candle Corp ....C....... 718 566-1500
Brooklyn *(G-2401)*
Quality Candle Mfg Co Inc ....F....... 631 842-8475
Copiague *(G-3945)*
Simcha Candle Co Inc ....G....... 845 783-0406
New Windsor *(G-9001)*
Thompson Ferrier LLC ....G....... 212 244-2212
New York *(G-12347)*
TV Guilfoil & Associates Inc ....G....... 315 453-0920
Syracuse *(G-16086)*

CANDLES: Wholesalers

Candle In The Window Inc ....F....... 718 852-5743
Brooklyn *(G-1755)*

CANDY & CONFECTIONS: Cake Ornaments

Naples Vly Mrgers Acqstons LLC ....G....... 585 490-1339
Naples *(G-8813)*
OH How Cute Inc ....G....... 347 838-6031
Staten Island *(G-15739)*
Pfeil & Holing Inc ....D....... 718 545-4600
Woodside *(G-17362)*

CANDY & CONFECTIONS: Candy Bars, Including Chocolate Covered

Chocomaker Inc ....G....... 716 877-3146
Buffalo *(G-2893)*
Eatingevolved LLC ....F....... 631 675-2440
Setauket *(G-15400)*
Fine and Raw Chocolate ....G....... 718 366-3633
Brooklyn *(G-1975)*
N Make Mold Inc ....E....... 716 877-3146
Buffalo *(G-3101)*
Nycjbs LLC ....F....... 212 533-1888
New York *(G-11496)*
Vigneri Chocolate Inc ....G....... 585 254-6160
Rochester *(G-14782)*

CANDY & CONFECTIONS: Chocolate Candy, Exc Solid Chocolate

Aigner Chocolates Inc ....G....... 718 544-1850
Forest Hills *(G-5325)*
Amiram Dror Inc ....F....... 212 979-9505
Brooklyn *(G-1609)*
Chocolate Pizza Company Inc ....F....... 315 673-4098
Marcellus *(G-8118)*
Robert Pikcilingis ....F....... 518 355-1860
Altamont *(G-215)*

CANDY & CONFECTIONS: Fudge

Alrajs Inc ....E....... 631 225-0300
Lindenhurst *(G-7474)*

CANDY, NUT & CONFECTIONERY STORES: Candy

5th Avenue Chocolatiere Ltd ....F....... 516 561-1570
Valley Stream *(G-16423)*
5th Avenue Chocolatiere Ltd ....G....... 212 935-5454
Freeport *(G-5388)*
Adirondack Chocolate Co Ltd ....F....... 518 946-7270
Wilmington *(G-17290)*
Amiram Dror Inc ....F....... 212 979-9505
Brooklyn *(G-1609)*
Commodore Chocolatier USA Inc ....F....... 845 561-3960
Newburgh *(G-12774)*
Ford Gum & Machine Company Inc ....D....... 716 542-4561
Akron *(G-19)*
Godiva Chocolatier Inc ....E....... 212 984-5900
New York *(G-10368)*
Hercules Candy Co ....F....... 315 463-4339
East Syracuse *(G-4551)*
Hudson Valley Chocolatier Inc ....F....... 845 831-8240
Beacon *(G-781)*
Jo-Mart Candies Corp ....F....... 718 375-1277
Brooklyn *(G-2142)*
Lady-N-Th-wndow Chocolates Inc ....F....... 631 549-1059
Huntington *(G-6702)*
Noras Candy Shop ....F....... 315 337-4530
Rome *(G-14853)*
Parkside Candy Co Inc ....F....... 716 833-7540
Buffalo *(G-3137)*
Roger L Urban Inc ....E....... 716 693-5391
North Tonawanda *(G-13010)*
Seaward Candies ....G....... 585 638-6761
Holley *(G-6518)*

PRODUCT SECTION

CARDS: Greeting

The Chocolate Shop ....G....... 716 882-5055
Buffalo *(G-3241)*

CANDY, NUT & CONFECTIONERY STORES: Confectionery

Noaspence Inc...G....... 516 433-7848
Hicksville *(G-6401)*

CANDY: Chocolate From Cacao Beans

Adirondack Chocolate Co Ltd ....F....... 518 946-7270
Wilmington *(G-17290)*
Aigner Chocolates Inc ....G....... 718 544-1850
Forest Hills *(G-5325)*
Chocolate Pizza Company Inc ....F....... 315 673-4098
Marcellus *(G-8118)*
Encore Chocolates Inc ....G....... 585 266-2970
Rochester *(G-14370)*
Godiva Chocolatier Inc ....E....... 212 984-5900
New York *(G-10368)*
Godiva Chocolatier Inc ....E....... 718 271-3603
Elmhurst *(G-4675)*
Landies Candies Co Inc ....F....... 716 834-8212
Buffalo *(G-3062)*
Madelaine Chocolate Novlt Inc ....D....... 718 945-1500
Rockaway Beach *(G-14810)*
Roger L Urban Inc ....E....... 716 693-5391
North Tonawanda *(G-13010)*
Superior Confections Inc ....D....... 718 698-3300
Staten Island *(G-15766)*

CANNED SPECIALTIES

Global Food Source & Co Inc ....G....... 914 320-9615
Tuckahoe *(G-16294)*
Goya Foods Inc ....D....... 716 549-0076
Angola *(G-380)*
Grandma Browns Beans Inc ....F....... 315 963-7221
Mexico *(G-8430)*
Kawasho Foods USA Inc ....F....... 212 841-7400
New York *(G-10859)*

CANOPIES: Sheet Metal

Austin Mohawk and Company LLC.......E....... 315 793-3000
Utica *(G-16331)*

CANS: Aluminum

Anheuser-Busch Companies LLC........G....... 718 589-2610
Bronx *(G-1275)*
Ball Metal Beverage Cont Corp ....C....... 845 692-3800
Middletown *(G-8461)*
Reynolds Metals Company LLC ....G....... 212 518-5400
New York *(G-11882)*

CANS: Metal

Ardagh Metal Packaging USA Inc ....C....... 607 584-3300
Conklin *(G-3889)*
Ball Metal Beverage Cont Corp ....C....... 518 587-6030
Saratoga Springs *(G-15172)*
Brakewell Stl Fabricators Inc.................E....... 845 469-9131
Chester *(G-3628)*
Erie Engineered Products Inc ....E....... 716 206-0204
Lancaster *(G-7338)*
Hornet Group Inc ....D....... 845 858-6400
Port Jervis *(G-13808)*
J C Industries Inc ....E....... 631 420-1920
West Babylon *(G-16826)*
Metal Container Corporation ....C....... 845 567-1500
New Windsor *(G-8989)*
Seneca Foods Corporation ....D....... 315 926-0531
Marion *(G-8130)*
Silgan Containers Mfg Corp ....C....... 315 946-4826
Lyons *(G-8002)*

CANVAS PRDTS

Ace Canvas & Tent Corp ....F....... 631 648-0614
Ronkonkoma *(G-14876)*
Anchor Canvas LLC...............................G....... 631 265-5602
Smithtown *(G-15505)*
Breton Industries Inc ....D....... 518 842-3030
Amsterdam *(G-337)*
Broadway Neon Sign Corp ....F....... 908 241-4177
Ronkonkoma *(G-14910)*
Brock Awnings Ltd ....F....... 631 765-5200
Hampton Bays *(G-5982)*
Custom European Imports Inc ....E....... 845 357-5718
Sloatsburg *(G-15502)*

Dor-A-Mar Canvas Products Co ....F....... 631 750-9202
West Sayville *(G-16963)*
Jag Manufacturing Inc ....E....... 518 762-9558
Johnstown *(G-7147)*
Kragel Co Inc ....G....... 716 648-1344
Hamburg *(G-5955)*
M & M Canvas & Awnings Inc ....G....... 631 424-5370
Islandia *(G-6838)*
Nationwide Tarps Incorporated ....D....... 518 843-1545
Amsterdam *(G-362)*
Northern Awning & Sign Company ......G....... 315 782-8515
Watertown *(G-16690)*
Point Canvas Company Inc...................G....... 607 692-4381
Whitney Point *(G-17249)*
Service Canvas Co Inc ....F....... 716 853-0558
Buffalo *(G-3211)*
Utility Canvas Inc ....G....... 845 255-9290
Gardiner *(G-5565)*
Y & A Trading Inc ....F....... 718 436-6333
Brooklyn *(G-2785)*

CANVAS PRDTS, WHOLESALE

Awning Mart Inc ....G....... 315 699-5928
Cicero *(G-3671)*
Brock Awnings Ltd ....F....... 631 765-5200
Hampton Bays *(G-5982)*
Point Canvas Company Inc...................G....... 607 692-4381
Whitney Point *(G-17249)*

CANVAS PRDTS: Convertible Tops, Car/Boat, Fm Purchased Mtrl

Automtve Uphl Cnvertible Tops ....G....... 914 961-4242
Tuckahoe *(G-16293)*
Mc Coy Tops and Interiors Inc ....G....... 718 458-5800
Woodside *(G-17353)*
Quantum Sails Rochester LLC ....G....... 585 342-5200
Rochester *(G-14640)*

CANVAS PRDTS: Shades, Made From Purchased Materials

Jo-Vin Decorators Inc ....E....... 718 441-9350
Woodhaven *(G-17324)*
Laminated Window Products Inc ....F....... 631 242-6883
Bay Shore *(G-708)*

CAPACITORS: Fixed Or Variable

General Electric Company ....B....... 518 746-5750
Hudson Falls *(G-6673)*

CAPACITORS: NEC

American Tchncal Ceramics Corp ....B....... 631 622-4700
Huntington Station *(G-6732)*
American Technical Ceramics ....G....... 631 622-4758
Huntington Station *(G-6733)*
American Technical Ceramics ....E....... 631 622-4700
Huntington Station *(G-6734)*
AVX Corporation ....D....... 716 372-6611
Olean *(G-13155)*
Custom Electronics Inc ....D....... 607 432-3880
Oneonta *(G-13207)*
Electron Coil Inc ....D....... 607 336-7414
Norwich *(G-13046)*
Ems Development Corporation ....D....... 631 345-6200
Yaphank *(G-17407)*
Hipotronics Inc ....C....... 845 279-8091
Brewster *(G-1217)*
Integer Holdings Corporation ....E....... 716 937-5100
Alden *(G-183)*
Kemet Properties LLC ....G....... 718 654-8079
Bronx *(G-1374)*
Knowles Cazenovia Inc ....C....... 315 655-8710
Cazenovia *(G-3473)*
MTK Electronics Inc...............................E....... 631 924-7666
Medford *(G-8290)*
Passive-Plus Inc.....................................F....... 631 425-0938
Huntington *(G-6708)*
Stk Electronics Inc ....E....... 315 655-8476
Cazenovia *(G-3479)*
Strux Corp ....E....... 516 768-3969
Lindenhurst *(G-7508)*
Tronser Inc..G....... 315 655-9528
Cazenovia *(G-3480)*
Viking Technologies Ltd ....E....... 631 957-8000
Lindenhurst *(G-7516)*
Virtue Paintball LLC ....E....... 631 617-5560
Hauppauge *(G-6251)*

Voltronics LLC..E....... 410 749-2424
Cazenovia *(G-3481)*

CAPS & PLUGS: Electric, Attachment

Delfingen Us-New York Inc ....E....... 716 215-0300
Niagara Falls *(G-12832)*

CAR WASH EQPT

Econocraft Worldwide Mfg Inc ....G....... 914 966-2280
Yonkers *(G-17455)*
Hercules International Inc ....E....... 631 423-6900
Huntington Station *(G-6746)*
I A S National Inc ....E....... 631 423-6900
Huntington Station *(G-6748)*
Klee Corp ....G....... 585 272-0320
Rochester *(G-14492)*
Liquid Industries Inc ....G....... 716 628-2999
Niagara Falls *(G-12860)*
Metro Lube ....G....... 718 947-1167
Rego Park *(G-14047)*
Wetlook Detailing Inc.............................G....... 212 390-8877
Brooklyn *(G-2762)*

CARBIDES

Carbide-Usa LLC....................................G....... 607 331-9353
Elmira *(G-4687)*
Lakeshore Carbide Inc ....G....... 716 462-4349
Lake View *(G-7304)*
Transport National Dev Inc ....E....... 716 662-0270
Orchard Park *(G-13325)*

CARBON & GRAPHITE PRDTS, NEC

Carbon Graphite Materials Inc..............G....... 716 792-7979
Brocton *(G-1248)*
Carbonfree Chemicals Spe I LLC ....E....... 914 421-4900
White Plains *(G-17120)*
Ceramaterials LLC ....E....... 518 701-6722
Port Jervis *(G-13803)*
Go Blue Technologies Ltd ....G....... 631 404-6285
North Babylon *(G-12918)*
Graphite Metallizing Corp ....D....... 914 968-8400
Yonkers *(G-17466)*
Hh Liquidating Corp ....A....... 646 282-2500
New York *(G-10515)*
Kureha Advanced Materials Inc ....F....... 724 295-3352
New York *(G-10933)*
Mwi Inc ....D....... 585 424-4200
Rochester *(G-14546)*
Pyrotek Incorporated ....E....... 716 731-3221
Sanborn *(G-15153)*

CARBONS: Electric

Metallized Carbon Corporation ....C....... 914 941-3738
Ossining *(G-13347)*

CARDBOARD PRDTS, EXC DIE-CUT

M C Packaging Corporation ....E....... 631 694-3012
Farmingdale *(G-5047)*
M C Packaging Corporation ....E....... 631 643-3763
Babylon *(G-547)*

CARDBOARD: Waterproof, Made From Purchased Materials

Ums Manufacturing LLC ....F....... 518 562-2410
Plattsburgh *(G-13734)*

CARDIOVASCULAR SYSTEM DRUGS, EXC DIAGNOSTIC

Mesoblast Inc ....G....... 212 880-2060
New York *(G-11265)*

CARDS: Color

Mooney-Keehley Inc ....G....... 585 271-1573
Rochester *(G-14541)*
Tele-Pak Inc ....E....... 845 426-2300
Monsey *(G-8620)*

CARDS: Greeting

1/2 Off Cards Wantagh Inc ....G....... 516 809-9832
Wantagh *(G-16576)*
Anne Taintor Inc ....G....... 718 483-9312
Brooklyn *(G-1613)*
Avanti Press Inc ....E....... 212 414-1025
New York *(G-9326)*

Employee Codes: A=Over 500 employees, B=251-500
C=101-250, D=51-100, E=20-50, F=10-19, G=5-9

CARDS: Greeting

Company	Loc	Phone
Massimo Friedman Inc	E	716 836-0408
Buffalo (G-3078)		
Paper House Productions Inc	E	845 246-7261
Saugerties (G-15219)		
Paper Magic Group Inc	B	631 521-3682
New York (G-11577)		
Quotable Cards Inc	G	212 420-7552
New York (G-11802)		
Schurman Fine Papers	C	212 206-0067
New York (G-12020)		

CARDS: Identification

Company	Loc	Phone
Allsafe Technologies Inc	D	716 691-0400
Amherst (G-225)		
Alpha Incorporated	G	718 765-1614
Brooklyn (G-1590)		
Global Security Tech LLC	F	917 838-4507
New York (G-10363)		
Iadc Inc	F	718 238-0623
Staten Island (G-15707)		
Metropltan Data Sltons MGT Inc	F	516 586-5520
Farmingdale (G-5060)		
Multi Packaging Solutions Inc	E	646 885-0005
New York (G-11347)		

CARDS: Playing

Company	Loc	Phone
Marketshare LLC	G	631 273-0598
Brentwood (G-1188)		

CARPET DYEING & FINISHING

Company	Loc	Phone
Eskayel Inc	G	347 703-8084
Brooklyn (G-1940)		

CARPETS & RUGS: Tufted

Company	Loc	Phone
Interfaceflor LLC	E	212 686-8284
New York (G-10670)		

CARPETS, RUGS & FLOOR COVERING

Company	Loc	Phone
Aladdin Manufacturing Corp	C	212 561-8715
New York (G-9121)		
Bloomsburg Carpet Inds Inc	G	212 688-7447
New York (G-9468)		
Carpet Fabrications Intl	E	914 381-6060
Mamaroneck (G-8058)		
Edward Fields Incorporated	F	212 310-0400
New York (G-10038)		
Excellent Art Mfg Corp	F	718 388-7075
Inwood (G-6795)		
Jbl Trading LLC	G	347 394-5592
New York (G-10749)		
Kalati Company Inc	G	516 423-9132
Great Neck (G-5834)		
Lanes Flr Cvrngs Intriors Inc	E	212 532-5200
New York (G-10962)		
Loom Concepts LLC	G	212 813-9586
New York (G-11059)		
Lorena Canals USA Inc	G	844 567-3622
Hastings On Hudson (G-6025)		
Michaelian & Kohlberg Inc	G	212 431-9009
New York (G-11278)		
Northpoint Trading Inc	F	212 481-8001
New York (G-11478)		
Odegard Inc	F	212 545-0069
Long Island City (G-7860)		
Pawling Corporation	D	845 373-9300
Wassaic (G-16622)		
Quality Carpet One Floor & HM	G	718 941-4200
Brooklyn (G-2478)		
Rosecore Division	F	516 504-4530
Great Neck (G-5852)		
Shaw Contract Flrg Svcs Inc	G	212 953-7429
New York (G-12067)		
Shyam Ahuja Limited	G	212 644-5910
New York (G-12080)		
Sunrise Tile Inc	G	718 939-0538
Flushing (G-5303)		
Tandus Centiva Inc	C	212 206-7170
New York (G-12302)		
Tdg Operations LLC	G	212 779-4300
New York (G-12309)		
Tiger 21 LLC	G	212 360-1700
New York (G-12356)		
Wells Rugs Inc	G	516 676-2056
Glen Cove (G-5644)		

CARPETS: Hand & Machine Made

Company	Loc	Phone
Elizabeth Eakins Inc	F	212 628-1950
New York (G-10062)		
Tsar USA LLC	F	646 415-7968
New York (G-12438)		

CARPETS: Textile Fiber

Company	Loc	Phone
Scalamandre Silks Inc	D	212 980-3888
New York (G-12002)		

CARRIAGES: Horse Drawn

Company	Loc	Phone
Tectran Inc	G	800 776-5549
Cheektowaga (G-3619)		

CARRYING CASES, WHOLESALE

Company	Loc	Phone
Bristol Boarding Inc	G	585 271-7860
Rochester (G-14265)		
Coach Stores Inc	A	212 643-9727
New York (G-9717)		
Sigma Worldwide LLC	G	646 217-0629
New York (G-12089)		

CASEMENTS: Aluminum

Company	Loc	Phone
Rohlfs Stined Leaded GL Studio	E	914 699-4848
Mount Vernon (G-8773)		

CASES, WOOD

Company	Loc	Phone
Bragley Mfg Co Inc	E	718 622-7469
Brooklyn (G-1711)		

CASES: Attache'

Company	Loc	Phone
Dlx Industries Inc	D	718 272-9420
Brooklyn (G-1870)		
Randa Accessories Lea Gds LLC	D	212 354-5100
New York (G-11825)		
Trafalgar Company LLC	G	212 768-8800
New York (G-12411)		

CASES: Carrying

Company	Loc	Phone
Ead Cases	F	845 343-2111
Middletown (G-8471)		
Fieldtex Products Inc	C	585 427-2940
Rochester (G-14391)		
Merzon Leather Co Inc	C	718 782-6260
Brooklyn (G-2306)		
Sigma Worldwide LLC	G	646 217-0629
New York (G-12089)		
Three Point Ventures LLC	F	585 697-3444
Rochester (G-14751)		

CASES: Carrying, Clothing & Apparel

Company	Loc	Phone
212 Biz LLC	G	212 391-4444
New York (G-9010)		
Calvin Klein Inc	E	212 292-9000
New York (G-9556)		
Donna Morgan LLC	G	212 575-2550
New York (G-9956)		

CASES: Jewelry

Company	Loc	Phone
Ada Gems Corp	G	212 719-0100
New York (G-9070)		
Astucci US Ltd	G	212 725-3171
New York (G-9295)		
Bauble Bar Inc	D	646 664-4803
New York (G-9383)		
K Displays	F	718 854-6045
Brooklyn (G-2163)		
Unique Packaging Corporation	G	514 341-5872
Champlain (G-3576)		

CASES: Nonrefrigerated, Exc Wood

Company	Loc	Phone
R H Guest Incorporated	G	718 675-7600
Brooklyn (G-2490)		

CASES: Packing, Nailed Or Lock Corner, Wood

Company	Loc	Phone
Falvo Manufacturing Co Inc	F	315 738-7682
Utica (G-16353)		
Technical Packaging Inc	F	516 223-2300
Baldwin (G-561)		

CASES: Plastic

Company	Loc	Phone
Bragley Mfg Co Inc	E	718 622-7469
Brooklyn (G-1711)		
Displays By Rioux Inc	G	315 458-3639
North Syracuse (G-12958)		
Hamlet Products Inc	F	914 665-0307
Mount Vernon (G-8734)		
Sigma Worldwide LLC	G	646 217-0629
New York (G-12089)		

CASES: Sample Cases

Company	Loc	Phone
Fibre Case & Novelty Co Inc	G	212 254-6060
New York (G-10210)		
Progressive Fibre Products Co	E	212 566-2720
New York (G-11751)		

CASES: Shipping, Nailed Or Lock Corner, Wood

Company	Loc	Phone
Bristol Boarding Inc	G	585 271-7860
Rochester (G-14265)		
McIntosh Box & Pallet Co Inc	F	315 789-8750
Geneva (G-5594)		

CASH REGISTER REPAIR SVCS

Company	Loc	Phone
SPX Flow Us LLC	G	585 436-5550
Rochester (G-14722)		

CASING-HEAD BUTANE & PROPANE PRODUCTION

Company	Loc	Phone
Blue Rhino Global Sourcing Inc	E	516 752-0670
Melville (G-8329)		

CASINGS: Sheet Metal

Company	Loc	Phone
Craft-Tech Mfg Corp	G	631 563-4949
Bohemia (G-1038)		

CASKETS & ACCESS

Company	Loc	Phone
Milso Industries Inc	F	631 234-1133
Hauppauge (G-6164)		
North Hudson Woodcraft Corp	E	315 429-3105
Dolgeville (G-4330)		

CASKETS WHOLESALERS

Company	Loc	Phone
Milso Industries Inc	F	631 234-1133
Hauppauge (G-6164)		

CAST STONE: Concrete

Company	Loc	Phone
Steindl Cast Stone Co Inc	G	718 296-8530
Woodhaven (G-17326)		

CASTERS

Company	Loc	Phone
Dimanco Inc	G	315 797-0470
Utica (G-16347)		
Workshop Art Fabrication	F	845 331-0385
Kingston (G-7252)		

CASTINGS GRINDING: For The Trade

Company	Loc	Phone
Grind	G	646 558-3250
New York (G-10407)		
Herbert Wolf Corp		212 242-0300
New York (G-10504)		
Precision Disc Grinding Corp	F	516 747-5450
Mineola (G-8564)		

CASTINGS: Aerospace Investment, Ferrous

Company	Loc	Phone
Brinkman Precision Inc	D	585 429-5001
West Henrietta (G-16905)		
Cpp-Syracuse Inc	E	315 687-0014
Chittenango (G-3662)		
Worldwide Resources Inc	F	718 760-5000
Brooklyn (G-2783)		

CASTINGS: Aerospace, Aluminum

Company	Loc	Phone
Broetje Automation-Usa Inc	C	716 204-8640
Williamsville (G-17264)		
E M T Manufacturing Inc	F	516 333-1917
East Meadow (G-4442)		
Eastern Strategic Materials	E	212 332-1619
New York (G-10018)		
Mpi Consulting Incorporated		631 253-2377
West Babylon (G-16844)		

PRODUCT SECTION

CERAMIC FIBER

CASTINGS: Aerospace, Nonferrous, Exc Aluminum

Summit Aerospace Inc .... G 718 433-1326
  Long Island City (G-7922)

CASTINGS: Aluminum

Airflex Industrial Inc .... E 631 752-1234
  Farmingdale (G-4940)
Armstrong Mold Corporation .... E 315 437-1517
  East Syracuse (G-4521)
Armstrong Mold Corporation .... D 315 437-1517
  East Syracuse (G-4522)
Eastern Castings Co .... F 518 677-5610
  Cambridge (G-3335)
Hitachi Metals America Ltd .... E 914 694-9200
  Purchase (G-13975)
J & J Bronze & Aluminum Cast .... E 718 383-2111
  Brooklyn (G-2120)
Milward Alloys Inc .... E 716 434-5536
  Lockport (G-7631)
Taylor Metalworks Inc .... C 716 662-3113
  Orchard Park (G-13323)

CASTINGS: Brass, Bronze & Copper

Rodeo of NY Inc .... E 212 730-0744
  New York (G-11923)

CASTINGS: Brass, NEC, Exc Die

Discover Casting Inc .... F 212 302-5060
  New York (G-9936)

CASTINGS: Bronze, NEC, Exc Die

Art Bedi-Makky Foundry Corp .... G 718 383-4191
  Brooklyn (G-1634)
J & J Bronze & Aluminum Cast .... E 718 383-2111
  Brooklyn (G-2120)
Modern Art Foundry Inc .... E 718 728-2030
  Astoria (G-448)

CASTINGS: Commercial Investment, Ferrous

Cs Manufacturing Limited .... E 607 587-8154
  Alfred (G-196)

CASTINGS: Die, Aluminum

Albest Metal Stamping Corp .... D 718 388-6000
  Brooklyn (G-1575)
Crown Die Casting Corp .... E 914 667-5400
  Mount Vernon (G-8720)
Greene Brass & Alum Fndry LLC .... G 607 656-4204
  Bloomville (G-990)
Greenfield Industries Inc .... D 516 623-9230
  Freeport (G-5415)
ITT Corporation .... D 315 568-2811
  Seneca Falls (G-15383)
ITT LLC .... D 914 641-2000
  Seneca Falls (G-15387)
Jamestown Bronze Works Inc .... G 716 665-2302
  Jamestown (G-7039)
Louis Iannettoni .... D 315 454-3231
  Syracuse (G-16002)
Pinnacle Manufacturing Co Inc .... E 585 343-5664
  Batavia (G-646)
Tpi Arcade Inc .... D 585 492-0122
  Arcade (G-400)

CASTINGS: Die, Lead

American Casting and Mfg Corp .... D 800 342-0333
  Plainview (G-13611)
American Casting and Mfg Corp .... G 516 349-7010
  Plainview (G-13612)

CASTINGS: Die, Nonferrous

Albest Metal Stamping Corp .... D 718 388-6000
  Brooklyn (G-1575)
Crown Die Casting Corp .... E 914 667-5400
  Mount Vernon (G-8720)
Crown Novelty Works Inc .... G 631 253-0949
  Melville (G-8338)
Mar-A-Thon Filters Inc .... E 631 957-4774
  Lindenhurst (G-7492)
Thomas Foundry LLC .... G 315 361-9048
  Oneida (G-13190)

CASTINGS: Die, Zinc

Cast-All Corporation .... E 516 741-4025
  Mineola (G-8536)
Cast-All Corporation .... E 516 741-4025
  Mineola (G-8535)
Greenfield Die Casting Corp .... E 516 623-9230
  Freeport (G-5414)
Pinnacle Manufacturing Co Inc .... E 585 343-5664
  Batavia (G-646)

CASTINGS: Ductile

Hitachi Metals America Ltd .... E 914 694-9200
  Purchase (G-13975)
Jamestown Iron Works Inc .... F 716 665-2818
  Falconer (G-4913)
Noresco Industrial Group Inc .... E 516 759-3355
  Glen Cove (G-5635)

CASTINGS: Gray Iron

Oneida Foundries Inc .... E 315 363-4570
  Oneida (G-13181)

CASTINGS: Machinery, Aluminum

Auto-Mate Technologies LLC .... F 631 727-8886
  Riverhead (G-14149)
Corbett Stves Pttern Works Inc .... E 585 546-7109
  Rochester (G-14310)

CASTINGS: Machinery, Nonferrous, Exc Die or Aluminum Copper

Plattco Corporation .... E 518 563-4640
  Plattsburgh (G-13715)
Zierick Manufacturing Corp .... D 800 882-8020
  Mount Kisco (G-8690)

CASTINGS: Precision

Buffalo Metal Casting Co Inc .... E 716 874-6211
  Buffalo (G-2877)
Controlled Castings Corp .... E 516 349-1718
  Plainview (G-13621)
General Motors LLC .... B 315 764-2000
  Massena (G-8226)
Lamothermic Corp .... D 845 278-6118
  Brewster (G-1219)
Miller Technology Inc .... G 631 694-2224
  Farmingdale (G-5065)
Quality Castings Inc .... E 732 409-3203
  Long Island City (G-7883)

CASTINGS: Steel

A & V Castings Inc .... G 212 997-0042
  New York (G-9029)

CATALOG & MAIL-ORDER HOUSES

Avcom of Virginia Inc .... D 585 924-4560
  Victor (G-16485)
Iac/Interactivecorp .... A 212 314-7300
  New York (G-10590)
Kate Spade & Company .... B 212 354-4900
  New York (G-10854)
Lechler Laboratories Inc .... E 845 426-6800
  Spring Valley (G-15613)
Rda Holding Co .... F 914 238-1000
  New York (G-11837)
Valmont Inc .... F 212 685-1653
  New York (G-12519)

CATALOG SHOWROOMS

Studio 21 LA Inc .... E 718 965-6579
  Brooklyn (G-2634)

CATALYSTS: Chemical

Ames Goldsmith Corp .... F 518 792-7435
  Glens Falls (G-5685)
Next Potential LLC .... G 401 742-5190
  New York (G-11441)
Signa Chemistry Inc .... F 212 933-4101
  New York (G-12092)
UOP LLC .... E 716 879-7600
  Tonawanda (G-16232)

CATAPULTS

Catapult .... G 323 839-6204
  New York (G-9600)
Laser & Electron Beam Inc .... G 603 626-6080
  New York (G-10967)

CATERERS

Delicious Foods Inc .... F 718 446-9352
  Corona (G-4019)
Life Corp .... G 516 426-5737
  Port Washington (G-13859)
Soutine Inc .... G 212 496-1450
  New York (G-12170)

CEILING SYSTEMS: Luminous, Commercial

Green Beam Led Inc .... G 718 439-6262
  Brooklyn (G-2051)

CEMENT & CONCRETE RELATED PRDTS & EQPT: Bituminous

Presti Ready Mix Concrete Inc .... G 516 378-6006
  Freeport (G-5430)

CEMENT ROCK: Crushed & Broken

Schaefer Entps of Deposit .... E 607 467-4990
  Deposit (G-4303)

CEMENT: Heat Resistant

Roccera LLC .... F 585 426-0887
  Rochester (G-14654)

CEMENT: Hydraulic

Lafarge North America Inc .... E 716 651-9235
  Lancaster (G-7346)
Lafarge North America Inc .... G 716 854-5791
  Buffalo (G-3061)
Lafarge North America Inc .... E 716 772-2621
  Lockport (G-7626)
Lafarge North America Inc .... D 914 930-3027
  Buchanan (G-2800)
Lafarge North America Inc .... E 518 756-5000
  Ravena (G-14036)
Upstone Materials Inc .... G 518 873-2275
  Lewis (G-7452)

CEMENT: Masonry

Ciment St-Laurent Inc .... C 518 943-4040
  Catskill (G-3454)
Lafarge Building Materials Inc .... F 518 756-5000
  Ravena (G-14035)

CEMENT: Natural

Euro Gear (usa) Inc .... G 518 578-1775
  Plattsburgh (G-13690)
Hanson Aggregates New York LLC .... F 716 665-4620
  Jamesville (G-7081)

CEMENT: Portland

Lehigh Cement Company .... C 518 792-1137
  Glens Falls (G-5703)
Pallette Stone Corporation .... E 518 584-2421
  Gansevoort (G-5501)

CEMETERY MEMORIAL DEALERS

Glen Plaza Marble & Gran Inc .... G 516 671-1100
  Glen Cove (G-5630)
North Shore Monuments Inc .... G 516 759-2156
  Glen Head (G-5653)

CERAMIC FIBER

Argosy Composite Advanced Mate .... F 212 268-0003
  New York (G-9251)
Cetek Inc .... E 845 452-3510
  Poughkeepsie (G-13911)
Enrg Inc .... F 716 873-2939
  Buffalo (G-2954)
Heany Industries Inc .... D 585 889-2700
  Scottsville (G-15358)
Starfire Systems Inc .... E 518 899-9336
  Schenectady (G-15323)
Ufx Holding I Corporation .... G 212 644-5900
  New York (G-12462)

Employee Codes: A=Over 500 employees, B=251-500
C=101-250, D=51-100, E=20-50, F=10-19, G=5-9

CERAMIC FIBER

Ufx Holding II Corporation ....G....... 212 644-5900
 New York *(G-12463)*
Unifrax Holding Co ....G....... 212 644-5900
 New York *(G-12473)*
Unifrax I LLC ....C....... 716 768-6500
 Tonawanda *(G-16231)*
Unifrax I LLC ....C....... 716 696-3000
 Tonawanda *(G-16230)*

CERAMIC FLOOR & WALL TILE WHOLESALERS

Dal-Tile Corporation ....G....... 718 894-9574
 Maspeth *(G-8159)*
Dal-Tile Corporation ....G....... 914 835-1801
 Harrison *(G-6003)*

CHAIN: Welded, Made From Purchased Wire

Columbus McKinnon Corporation ....C....... 716 689-5400
 Getzville *(G-5607)*
Columbus McKinnon Corporation ....C....... 716 689-5400
 Getzville *(G-5608)*
Columbus McKinnon Corporation ....C....... 716 689-5400
 Getzville *(G-5609)*

CHAMBERS & CAISSONS

Hyperbaric Technologies Inc ....G....... 518 842-3030
 Amsterdam *(G-350)*

CHANDELIERS: Commercial

Global Lighting Inc ....G....... 914 591-4095
 Yonkers *(G-17463)*

CHANDELIERS: Residential

Swarovski Lighting Ltd ....B....... 518 324-6378
 Plattsburgh *(G-13732)*

CHARCOAL: Activated

Calgon Carbon Corporation ....G....... 716 531-9113
 North Tonawanda *(G-12982)*
Carbon Activated Corporation ....G....... 716 662-2005
 Orchard Park *(G-13281)*

CHASSIS: Motor Vehicle

Wendys Auto Express Inc ....G....... 845 624-6100
 Nanuet *(G-8808)*

CHEESE WHOLESALERS

Alps Provision Co Inc ....E....... 718 721-4477
 Astoria *(G-430)*

CHEMICAL ELEMENTS

2 Elements Real Est LLC ....G....... 315 635-4662
 Baldwinsville *(G-563)*

CHEMICAL INDICATORS

LTS (chemical) Inc ....F....... 845 494-2940
 Orangeburg *(G-13256)*

CHEMICAL PROCESSING MACHINERY & EQPT

Charles Ross & Son Company ....D....... 631 234-0500
 Hauppauge *(G-6064)*
Maharlika Holdings LLC ....F....... 631 319-6203
 Ronkonkoma *(G-14963)*
National Equipment Corporation ....F....... 718 585-0200
 Harrison *(G-6006)*
National Equipment Corporation ....E....... 718 585-0200
 Bronx *(G-1408)*
Spectrum Catalysts Inc ....G....... 631 560-3683
 Central Islip *(G-3537)*
Stainless Design Concepts Ltd ....E....... 845 246-3631
 Saugerties *(G-15224)*
Surepure Inc ....G....... 917 368-8480
 New York *(G-12267)*
West Metal Works Inc ....E....... 716 895-4900
 Buffalo *(G-3278)*

CHEMICAL: Sodm Compnds/Salts, Inorg, Exc Rfnd Sodm Chloride

Chemtrade Chemicals US LLC ....G....... 315 478-2323
 Syracuse *(G-15913)*

CHEMICALS & ALLIED PRDTS WHOLESALERS, NEC

Aithaca Chemical Corp ....F....... 516 229-2330
 Uniondale *(G-16311)*
Alumiseal Corp ....E....... 518 329-2820
 Copake Falls *(G-3914)*
Caswell Inc ....F....... 315 946-1213
 Lyons *(G-7997)*
Chemlube International LLC ....F....... 914 381-5800
 Harrison *(G-6000)*
Chemlube Marketing Inc ....F....... 914 381-5800
 Harrison *(G-6001)*
Cytec Olean Inc ....D....... 716 372-9650
 Olean *(G-13163)*
Ecological Laboratories Inc ....D....... 516 823-3441
 Lynbrook *(G-7978)*
FBC Chemical Corporation ....G....... 716 681-1581
 Lancaster *(G-7339)*
Finger Lakes Chemicals Inc ....E....... 585 454-4760
 Rochester *(G-14392)*
Island Pyrochemical Inds Corp ....F....... 516 746-2100
 Mineola *(G-8551)*
Jad Corp of America ....E....... 718 762-8900
 College Point *(G-3816)*
Nalco Company LLC ....E....... 518 796-1985
 Saratoga Springs *(G-15193)*
Poly Scientific R&D Corp ....E....... 631 586-0400
 Bay Shore *(G-721)*
Tattersall Industries LLC ....E....... 518 381-4270
 Schenectady *(G-15327)*
Thatcher Company New York Inc ....E....... 315 589-9330
 Williamson *(G-17255)*
Water Wise of America Inc ....G....... 585 232-1210
 Rochester *(G-14785)*

CHEMICALS & ALLIED PRDTS, WHOLESALE: Alkalines & Chlorine

Arcadia Chem Preservative LLC ....G....... 516 466-5258
 Great Neck *(G-5806)*

CHEMICALS & ALLIED PRDTS, WHOLESALE: Anti-Corrosion Prdts

Engineering Maint Pdts Inc ....F....... 516 624-9774
 Oyster Bay *(G-13395)*

CHEMICALS & ALLIED PRDTS, WHOLESALE: Aromatic

Classic Flavors Fragrances Inc ....G....... 212 777-0004
 New York *(G-9691)*

CHEMICALS & ALLIED PRDTS, WHOLESALE: Chemical Additives

Mitsui Chemicals America Inc ....E....... 914 253-0777
 Rye Brook *(G-15098)*
Specialty Minerals Inc ....E....... 212 878-1800
 New York *(G-12178)*

CHEMICALS & ALLIED PRDTS, WHOLESALE: Chemicals, Indl

Dynasty Chemical Corp ....E....... 518 463-1146
 Menands *(G-8402)*
Umicore USA Inc ....E....... 919 874-7171
 Glens Falls *(G-5714)*

CHEMICALS & ALLIED PRDTS, WHOLESALE: Dry Ice

South Shore Ice Co Inc ....F....... 516 379-2056
 Roosevelt *(G-15032)*

CHEMICALS & ALLIED PRDTS, WHOLESALE: Essential Oils

Flavormatic Industries Inc ....E....... 845 297-9100
 Wappingers Falls *(G-16587)*

CHEMICALS & ALLIED PRDTS, WHOLESALE: Oxygen

Praxair Distribution Inc ....G....... 315 457-5821
 Liverpool *(G-7569)*

CHEMICALS & ALLIED PRDTS, WHOLESALE: Plastics Materials, NEC

Ampac Paper LLC ....B....... 845 778-5511
 Walden *(G-16549)*
Josh Packaging Inc ....E....... 631 822-1660
 Hauppauge *(G-6127)*
Marval Industries Inc ....D....... 914 381-2400
 Mamaroneck *(G-8071)*

CHEMICALS & ALLIED PRDTS, WHOLESALE: Plastics Prdts, NEC

Albea Cosmetics America Inc ....E....... 212 371-5100
 New York *(G-9124)*
Autronic Plastics Inc ....D....... 516 333-7577
 Central Islip *(G-3510)*
Broder Mfg Inc ....G....... 718 366-1667
 Brooklyn *(G-1717)*
Vinyl Materials Inc ....E....... 631 586-9444
 Deer Park *(G-4249)*

CHEMICALS & ALLIED PRDTS, WHOLESALE: Plastics Sheets & Rods

Astra Products Inc ....G....... 631 464-4747
 Copiague *(G-3921)*

CHEMICALS & ALLIED PRDTS, WHOLESALE: Polyurethane Prdts

Vincent Manufacturing Co Inc ....F....... 315 823-0280
 Little Falls *(G-7528)*

CHEMICALS & ALLIED PRDTS, WHOLESALE: Salts & Polishes, Indl

R Schleider Contracting Corp ....G....... 631 269-4249
 Kings Park *(G-7204)*

CHEMICALS & ALLIED PRDTS, WHOLESALE: Syn Resin, Rub/Plastic

Clarence Resins and Chemicals ....G....... 716 406-9804
 Clarence Center *(G-3699)*

CHEMICALS & ALLIED PRDTS, WHOLESALE: Waxes, Exc Petroleum

Collinite Corporation ....G....... 315 732-2282
 Utica *(G-16336)*

CHEMICALS/ALLIED PRDTS, WHOL: Coal Tar Prdts, Prim/Intermdt

Castoleum Corporation ....F....... 914 664-5877
 Mount Vernon *(G-8715)*

CHEMICALS: Agricultural

Agrochem Inc ....E....... 518 226-4850
 Saratoga Springs *(G-15171)*
BASF Corporation ....B....... 914 785-2000
 Tarrytown *(G-16111)*
E I Du Pont De Nemours & Co ....C....... 718 761-0043
 Staten Island *(G-15688)*
FMC Corporation ....E....... 716 735-3761
 Middleport *(G-8455)*
G & S Farm & Home Inc ....G....... 716 542-9922
 Akron *(G-20)*

CHEMICALS: Alcohols

Full Motion Beverage Inc ....G....... 631 585-1100
 Plainview *(G-13632)*

CHEMICALS: Aluminum Chloride

Vanchlor Company Inc ....F....... 716 434-2624
 Lockport *(G-7656)*
Vanchlor Company Inc ....F....... 716 434-2624
 Lockport *(G-7657)*

CHEMICALS: Aluminum Compounds

Benzsay & Harrison Inc ....G....... 518 895-2311
 Delanson *(G-4257)*
Somerville Acquisitions Co Inc ....F....... 845 856-5261
 Huguenot *(G-6682)*
Somerville Tech Group Inc ....D....... 908 782-9500
 Huguenot *(G-6683)*

CHEMICALS: NEC

CHEMICALS: Aluminum Oxide
Meliorum Technologies Inc .... G 585 313-0616
Rochester *(G-14524)*

CHEMICALS: Brine
Texas Brine Company LLC .... G 585 495-6228
Wyoming *(G-17398)*

CHEMICALS: Calcium & Calcium Compounds
Minerals Technologies Inc .... E 212 878-1800
New York *(G-11302)*

CHEMICALS: Compounds Or Salts, Iron, Ferric Or Ferrous
North American Hoganas Inc .... E 716 285-3451
Niagara Falls *(G-12869)*

CHEMICALS: Fire Retardant
Flame Control Coatings LLC .... E 716 282-1399
Niagara Falls *(G-12842)*
Gordon Fire Equipment LLC .... G 845 691-5700
Highland *(G-6431)*
International Fire-Shield Inc .... F 315 255-1006
Auburn *(G-499)*
Kent Chemical Corporation .... E 212 521-1700
New York *(G-10878)*
Safeguard Inc .... F 631 929-3273
Wading River *(G-16545)*
Supresta US LLC .... E 914 674-9434
Ardsley *(G-405)*

CHEMICALS: Formaldehyde
Hexion Inc .... E 518 792-8040
South Glens Falls *(G-15548)*

CHEMICALS: High Purity Grade, Organic
Molecular Glasses Inc .... G 585 210-2861
Rochester *(G-14539)*

CHEMICALS: High Purity, Refined From Technical Grade
Aithaca Chemical Corp .... F 516 229-2330
Uniondale *(G-16311)*
Germanium Corp America Inc .... F 315 853-4900
Clinton *(G-3744)*
Incitec Pivot Limited .... G 212 238-3010
New York *(G-10625)*

CHEMICALS: Hydrogen Peroxide
US Peroxide .... G 716 775-5585
Grand Island *(G-5788)*

CHEMICALS: Inorganic, NEC
Akzo Nobel Chemicals LLC .... C 914 674-5008
Dobbs Ferry *(G-4324)*
Anchor Commerce Trading Corp .... G 516 881-3485
Atlantic Beach *(G-467)*
Arkema Inc .... C 585 243-6359
Piffard *(G-13573)*
Auterra Inc .... G 518 382-9600
Schenectady *(G-15260)*
BASF Corporation .... G 973 245-6000
Tarrytown *(G-16112)*
BASF Corporation .... B 914 788-1627
Peekskill *(G-13498)*
BASF Corporation .... B 212 450-8280
New York *(G-9379)*
BASF Corporation .... C 631 689-0200
East Setauket *(G-4497)*
BASF Corporation .... B 914 785-2000
Tarrytown *(G-16111)*
Byk USA Inc .... E 845 469-5800
Chester *(G-3629)*
Cerion Energy Inc .... E 585 271-5630
Rochester *(G-14289)*
Cerion LLC .... E 585 271-5630
Rochester *(G-14290)*
Chemours Company Fc LLC .... E 716 278-5100
Niagara Falls *(G-12826)*
Chemtrade Chemicals US LLC .... E 315 430-7650
Syracuse *(G-15912)*

Danisco US Inc .... D 585 277-4300
Rochester *(G-14322)*
Dynasty Chemical Corp .... E 518 463-1146
Menands *(G-8402)*
E I Du Pont De Nemours & Co .... E 585 339-4200
Rochester *(G-14342)*
Emco Chemical (usa) Corp .... E 718 797-3652
Brooklyn *(G-1920)*
Esm Group Inc .... F 716 446-8914
Amherst *(G-239)*
Esm Special Metals & Tech Inc .... E 716 446-8914
Amherst *(G-241)*
Ferro Corporation .... E 585 586-8770
East Rochester *(G-4477)*
Ferro Corporation .... C 315 536-3357
Penn Yan *(G-13532)*
Ferro Electronics Materials .... E 716 278-9400
Niagara Falls *(G-12841)*
FMC Corporation .... E 716 735-3761
Middleport *(G-8455)*
Hampshire Chemical Corp .... D 315 539-9221
Waterloo *(G-16651)*
Innovative Municipal Pdts US .... E 800 387-5777
Glenmont *(G-5684)*
Interstate Chemical Co Inc .... F 585 344-2822
Batavia *(G-641)*
Kowa American Corporation .... E 212 303-7800
New York *(G-10920)*
Lawn Elements Inc .... F 631 656-9711
Holbrook *(G-6485)*
Moog Inc .... D 716 731-6300
Niagara Falls *(G-12865)*
Multisorb Tech Intl LLC .... G 716 824-8900
Buffalo *(G-3099)*
Multisorb Technologies Inc .... E 716 668-4191
Cheektowaga *(G-3609)*
Multisorb Technologies Inc .... E 716 656-1402
Buffalo *(G-3100)*
Poly Scientific R&D Corp .... E 631 586-0400
Bay Shore *(G-721)*
Polyset Company Inc .... E 518 664-6000
Mechanicville *(G-8260)*
Praxair Inc .... F 716 879-2000
Tonawanda *(G-16212)*
S E A Supplies Ltd .... F 516 694-6677
Plainview *(G-13661)*
Scientific Polymer Products .... G 585 265-0413
Ontario *(G-13236)*
Specialty Minerals Inc .... G 518 585-7982
Ticonderoga *(G-16150)*
Specialty Minerals Inc .... E 212 878-1800
New York *(G-12178)*
Summit Research Labs Inc .... C 845 856-5261
Huguenot *(G-6684)*
Tangram Company LLC .... E 631 758-0460
Holtsville *(G-6538)*
Thatcher Company New York Inc .... E 315 589-9330
Williamson *(G-17255)*
Van De Mark Chemical Co Inc .... D 716 433-6764
Lockport *(G-7655)*
VWR Chemicals LLC .... E 518 297-4444
Rouses Point *(G-15069)*
Washingtom Mills Elec Mnrls .... D 716 278-6600
Niagara Falls *(G-12907)*

CHEMICALS: Isotopes, Radioactive
Isonics Corporation .... G 212 356-7400
New York *(G-10710)*

CHEMICALS: Lithium Compounds, Inorganic
Alpha-En Corporation .... F 914 418-2000
Yonkers *(G-17428)*

CHEMICALS: Medicinal
Biotemper .... G 516 302-7985
Carle Place *(G-3413)*
Proper Chemical Ltd .... G 631 420-8000
Farmingdale *(G-5101)*

CHEMICALS: Medicinal, Organic, Uncompounded, Bulk
Asept Pak Inc .... E 518 651-2026
Malone *(G-8038)*
Good Earth Inc .... G 716 684-8111
Lancaster *(G-7341)*

CHEMICALS: Metal Salts/Compounds, Exc Sodium, Potassium/Alum
PVS Technologies Inc .... E 716 825-5762
Buffalo *(G-3169)*

CHEMICALS: NEC
Akzo Nobel Chemicals LLC .... G 716 778-8554
Burt *(G-3294)*
Akzo Nobel Chemicals LLC .... C 914 674-5008
Dobbs Ferry *(G-4324)*
Anabec Inc .... G 716 759-1674
Clarence *(G-3683)*
Balchem Corporation .... B 845 326-5600
New Hampton *(G-8842)*
Barson Composites Corporation .... E 516 752-7882
Old Bethpage *(G-13147)*
Bcp Ingredients Inc .... D 845 326-5600
New Hampton *(G-8843)*
Bonide Products Inc .... C 315 736-8231
Oriskany *(G-13329)*
C & A Service Inc .... G 516 354-1200
Floral Park *(G-5205)*
Calfonex Company .... F 845 778-2212
Walden *(G-16551)*
Citrus and Allied Essences Ltd .... E 516 354-1200
Floral Park *(G-5207)*
Classic Flavors Fragrances Inc .... G 212 777-0004
New York *(G-9691)*
Danisco US Inc .... D 585 256-5200
Rochester *(G-14321)*
E I Du Pont De Nemours & Co .... E 585 339-4200
Rochester *(G-14342)*
Fitzsimmons Systems Inc .... F 315 214-7010
Cazenovia *(G-3472)*
Hampshire Chemical Corp .... D 315 539-9221
Waterloo *(G-16651)*
Heterochemical Corporation .... F 516 561-8225
Valley Stream *(G-16435)*
I A S National Inc .... E 631 423-6900
Huntington Station *(G-6748)*
Indium Corporation of America .... E 315 793-8200
Utica *(G-16366)*
Instrumentation Laboratory Co .... C 845 680-0028
Orangeburg *(G-13253)*
Kemper System America Inc .... E 716 558-2971
West Seneca *(G-16979)*
Mdi Holdings LLC .... A 212 559-1127
New York *(G-11228)*
Micro Powders Inc .... E 914 332-6400
Tarrytown *(G-16120)*
Momentive Performance .... G 281 325-3536
Waterford *(G-16636)*
Momentive Performance Mtls Inc .... D 914 784-4807
Tarrytown *(G-16121)*
Monroe Fluid Technology Inc .... E 585 392-3434
Hilton *(G-6444)*
Nalco Company LLC .... E 518 796-1985
Saratoga Springs *(G-15193)*
New Fine Chemicals Inc .... G 631 321-8151
Lindenhurst *(G-7498)*
Octagon Process LLC .... G 845 680-8800
Orangeburg *(G-13259)*
Pure Kemika LLC .... G 718 745-2200
Flushing *(G-5293)*
PVS Chemical Solutions Inc .... D 716 825-5762
Buffalo *(G-3168)*
Reddi Car Corp .... E 631 589-3141
Sayville *(G-15243)*
Rochester Midland Corporation .... C 585 336-2200
Rochester *(G-14665)*
Royce Associates A Ltd Partnr .... G 516 367-6298
Jericho *(G-7115)*
Specialty Minerals Inc .... E 212 878-1800
New York *(G-12178)*
Tam Ceramics LLC .... D 716 278-9480
Niagara Falls *(G-12898)*
Tangram Company LLC .... E 631 758-0460
Holtsville *(G-6538)*
Utility Manufacturing Co Inc .... E 516 997-6300
Westbury *(G-17068)*
Venue Graphics Supply Inc .... F 718 361-1690
Long Island City *(G-7942)*
Wyeth Holdings LLC .... D 845 602-5000
Pearl River *(G-13493)*
Yiwen Usa Inc .... F 212 370-0828
New York *(G-12715)*

CHEMICALS: Organic, NEC

CHEMICALS: Organic, NEC

Akzo Nobel Chemicals LLC ....G....... 716 778-8554
  Burt *(G-3294)*
Akzo Nobel Functional Chem LLC ....D...... 845 276-8200
  Brewster *(G-1205)*
Akzo Nobel Inc ....G....... 914 674-5181
  Dobbs Ferry *(G-4325)*
Ames Goldsmith Corp ....F....... 518 792-7435
  Glens Falls *(G-5685)*
Arcadia Chem Preservative LLC ....G....... 516 466-5258
  Great Neck *(G-5806)*
Arkema Inc ....C....... 585 243-6359
  Piffard *(G-13573)*
Balchem Corporation ....B....... 845 326-5600
  New Hampton *(G-8842)*
Bamboo Global Industries ....G....... 973 943-1878
  New York *(G-9365)*
BASF Corporation ....B....... 518 465-6534
  Rensselaer *(G-14056)*
BASF Corporation ....B....... 914 785-2000
  Tarrytown *(G-16111)*
Brockyn Corporation ....F....... 631 244-2770
  Bohemia *(G-1023)*
Caltex International Ltd ....E....... 315 425-1040
  Syracuse *(G-15902)*
China Ruitai Intl Holdings Ltd ....G....... 718 740-2278
  Hollis *(G-6521)*
Collaborative Laboratories ....D....... 631 689-0200
  East Setauket *(G-4498)*
Dancker Sellew & Douglas Inc ....G....... 908 231-1600
  East Syracuse *(G-4536)*
Danisco US Inc ....D....... 585 256-5200
  Rochester *(G-14321)*
Eastman Chemical Company ....D....... 585 722-2905
  Rochester *(G-14346)*
Enviro Service & Supply Corp ....F....... 347 838-6500
  Staten Island *(G-15692)*
Evonik Corporation ....E....... 518 233-7090
  Waterford *(G-16632)*
FMC Corporation ....C....... 716 879-0400
  Tonawanda *(G-16181)*
Hampshire Chemical Corp ....D....... 315 539-9221
  Waterloo *(G-16651)*
Henpecked Husband Farms Corp ....G....... 631 728-2800
  Speonk *(G-15599)*
International Mtls & Sups Inc ....G....... 518 834-9899
  Keeseville *(G-7167)*
Islechem LLC ....E....... 716 773-8401
  Grand Island *(G-5774)*
Jos H Lowenstein and Sons Inc ....D....... 718 218-8013
  Brooklyn *(G-2147)*
Marval Industries Inc ....D....... 914 381-2400
  Mamaroneck *(G-8071)*
Oak-Bark Corporation ....G....... 518 372-5691
  Scotia *(G-15352)*
Poly Scientific R&D Corp ....E....... 631 586-0400
  Bay Shore *(G-721)*
Polymer Slutions Group Fin LLC ....G....... 212 771-1717
  New York *(G-11704)*
Rose Solomon Co ....E....... 718 855-1788
  Brooklyn *(G-2527)*
Royce Associates A Ltd Partnr ....G....... 516 367-6298
  Jericho *(G-7115)*
Solvents Company Inc ....F....... 631 595-9300
  Kingston *(G-7238)*
Telechemische Inc ....G....... 845 561-3237
  Newburgh *(G-12805)*
Twin Lake Chemical Inc ....F....... 716 433-3824
  Lockport *(G-7653)*
United Biochemicals LLC ....E....... 716 731-5161
  Sanborn *(G-15156)*

CHEMICALS: Phenol

Si Group Inc ....C....... 518 347-4200
  Schenectady *(G-15319)*
Si Group Inc ....C....... 518 347-4200
  Rotterdam Junction *(G-15059)*

CHEMICALS: Silica Compounds

Precision Elctro Mnrl Pmco Inc ....E....... 716 284-2484
  Niagara Falls *(G-12881)*

CHEMICALS: Sodium Bicarbonate

Church & Dwight Co Inc ....F....... 518 887-5109
  Schenectady *(G-15270)*

CHEMICALS: Sodium/Potassium Cmpnds,Exc Bleach,Alkalies/Alum

Tibro Water Technologies Ltd ....F....... 647 426-3415
  Sherrill *(G-15432)*

CHEMICALS: Sulfur Chloride

PVS Chemical Solutions Inc ....D....... 716 825-5762
  Buffalo *(G-3168)*
Sabre Energy Services LLC ....F....... 518 514-1572
  Slingerlands *(G-15500)*

CHEMICALS: Water Treatment

Crystal Fusion Tech Inc ....F....... 631 253-9800
  Lindenhurst *(G-7482)*
Cytec Industries Inc ....D....... 716 372-9650
  Olean *(G-13162)*
Ecological Laboratories Inc ....D....... 516 823-3441
  Lynbrook *(G-7978)*
Halfmoon Town Water Department ....G....... 518 233-7489
  Waterford *(G-16633)*
Water Wise of America Inc ....G....... 585 232-1210
  Rochester *(G-14784)*
Water Wise of America Inc ....G....... 585 232-1210
  Rochester *(G-14785)*

CHEWING GUM

Ford Gum & Machine Company Inc ....D....... 716 542-4561
  Akron *(G-19)*
Simply Gum Inc ....E....... 917 721-8032
  New York *(G-12106)*
Sweetworks Inc ....C....... 716 634-4545
  Buffalo *(G-3230)*

CHILD DAY CARE SVCS

Parents Guide Network Corp ....E....... 212 213-8840
  New York *(G-11584)*

CHILDREN'S & INFANTS' CLOTHING STORES

Slims Bagels Unlimited Inc ....E....... 718 229-1140
  Oakland Gardens *(G-13086)*

CHILDREN'S WEAR STORES

JM Originals Inc ....C....... 845 647-3003
  Ellenville *(G-4648)*
S & C Bridals LLC ....E....... 212 789-7000
  New York *(G-11960)*

CHIMES: Electric

Analog Digital Technology LLC ....G....... 585 698-1845
  Rochester *(G-14219)*
Ingham Industries Inc ....G....... 631 242-2493
  Holbrook *(G-6480)*

CHIMNEY CAPS: Concrete

American Chimney Supplies Inc ....G....... 631 434-2020
  Hauppauge *(G-6039)*

CHIMNEYS & FITTINGS

American Chimney Supplies Inc ....G....... 631 434-2020
  Hauppauge *(G-6039)*
Chimney Doctors Americas Corp ....G....... 631 868-3586
  Bayport *(G-751)*

CHINA COOKWARE

Swissmar Inc ....G....... 905 764-1121
  Niagara Falls *(G-12896)*

CHLORINE

Indian Springs Mfg Co Inc ....F....... 315 635-6101
  Baldwinsville *(G-570)*

CHOCOLATE, EXC CANDY FROM BEANS: Chips, Powder, Block, Syrup

5th Avenue Chocolatiere Ltd ....G....... 212 935-5454
  Freeport *(G-5388)*
5th Avenue Chocolatiere Ltd ....F....... 516 561-1570
  Valley Stream *(G-16423)*
Associated Brands Inc ....B....... 585 798-3475
  New York *(G-9291)*
Big Heart Pet Brands ....E....... 716 891-6566
  Buffalo *(G-2864)*
Chocolate By Design Inc ....G....... 631 737-0082
  Bohemia *(G-1029)*
Eating Evolved Inc ....G....... 516 510-2601
  East Setauket *(G-4499)*
Gnosis Chocolate Inc ....G....... 646 688-5549
  Long Island City *(G-7780)*
Hershey Kiss 203 Inc ....G....... 516 503-3740
  Wantagh *(G-16579)*
Jo-Mart Candies Corp ....F....... 718 375-1277
  Brooklyn *(G-2142)*
Joyva Corp ....D....... 718 497-0170
  Brooklyn *(G-2153)*
Lanco Corporation ....C....... 631 231-2300
  Ronkonkoma *(G-14957)*
Le Chocolat LLC ....G....... 845 352-8301
  Monsey *(G-8608)*
Mast Brothers Inc ....E....... 718 388-2625
  Brooklyn *(G-2283)*
Momn Pops Inc ....E....... 845 567-0640
  Cornwall *(G-4009)*
Noras Candy Shop ....F....... 315 337-4530
  Rome *(G-14853)*
Robert Pikcilingis ....F....... 518 355-1860
  Altamont *(G-215)*
Settons Intl Foods Inc ....E....... 631 543-8090
  Commack *(G-3868)*
Simply Natural Foods LLC ....E....... 631 543-9600
  Commack *(G-3869)*
Sweetriot Inc ....G....... 212 431-7468
  New York *(G-12277)*
The Chocolate Shop ....G....... 716 882-5055
  Buffalo *(G-3241)*

CHOCOLATE, EXC CANDY FROM PURCH CHOC: Chips, Powder, Block

Aletheas Chocolates Inc ....E....... 716 633-8620
  Williamsville *(G-17259)*
Commodore Chocolatier USA Inc ....F....... 845 561-3960
  Newburgh *(G-12774)*
Ctac Holdings LLC ....E....... 212 924-2280
  Brooklyn *(G-1822)*
Dilese International Inc ....F....... 716 855-3500
  Buffalo *(G-2931)*
Dolce Vite International LLC ....G....... 713 962-5767
  Brooklyn *(G-1871)*
Doma Marketing Inc ....G....... 516 684-1111
  Port Washington *(G-13833)*
Emvi Inc ....G....... 518 883-5111
  Broadalbin *(G-1240)*
Ernex Corporation Inc ....E....... 718 951-2251
  Brooklyn *(G-1938)*
Godiva Chocolatier Inc ....E....... 718 677-1452
  Brooklyn *(G-2036)*
Godiva Chocolatier Inc ....G....... 212 809-8990
  New York *(G-10369)*
Greenwood Winery LLC ....E....... 315 432-8132
  East Syracuse *(G-4547)*
Jacques Torres Chocolate LLC ....E....... 212 414-2462
  New York *(G-10733)*
Lady-N-Th-wndow Chocolates Inc ......F....... 631 549-1059
  Huntington *(G-6702)*
Le Chocolate of Rockland LLC ....E....... 845 533-4125
  Suffern *(G-15816)*
Madisons Delight LLC ....F....... 718 720-8900
  Staten Island *(G-15724)*
Nibmor Project LLC ....F....... 718 374-5091
  Great Neck *(G-5840)*
Reserve Confections Inc ....F....... 845 371-7744
  Spring Valley *(G-15622)*
Rip Van Wafels Inc ....E....... 415 529-5403
  Brooklyn *(G-2516)*
Sweetworks Inc ....C....... 716 634-4545
  Buffalo *(G-3230)*
Yes Were Nuts Ltd ....G....... 516 374-1940
  Hewlett *(G-6341)*

CHRISTMAS TREE LIGHTING SETS: Electric

Rbw Studio LLC ....E....... 212 388-1621
  Brooklyn *(G-2501)*

CHUCKS

Northfeld Precision Instr Corp ....E....... 516 431-1112
  Island Park *(G-6822)*

PRODUCT SECTION

CLEANING EQPT: Commercial

CHURCHES
Christian Press Inc ....G...... 718 886-4400
  Flushing (G-5240)

CHUTES & TROUGHS
Sargent Manufacturing Inc ....G...... 212 722-7000
  New York (G-11991)

CIGAR & CIGARETTE HOLDERS
Beast Vapes Nyc ....G...... 718 714-8139
  Brooklyn (G-1673)
Beyond Vape ....G...... 917 909-1113
  Brooklyn (G-1691)
Bridge City Vape Co LLC ....G...... 845 625-7962
  Poughkeepsie (G-13910)
Brooklyn Vape ....G...... 917 336-7363
  Brooklyn (G-1735)
Cortlandt Smoke and Vape ....G...... 914 930-7592
  Montrose (G-8652)
Creative Vape ....G...... 347 927-0982
  Brooklyn (G-1815)
Dragon Vapes Nyc ....G...... 718 801-7855
  Flushing (G-5246)
Empire City Vape LLC ....G...... 718 676-6166
  Brooklyn (G-1925)
Gottavape ....G...... 518 945-8273
  Schenectady (G-15291)
High Times Vape ....G...... 631 569-5322
  Patchogue (G-13447)
Molly Vapes Inc ....G...... 718 743-0120
  Brooklyn (G-2335)
Mr Vape Guru ....G...... 845 796-2274
  Monticello (G-8645)
Sector4vapes ....G...... 607 377-2224
  Corning (G-4001)
Smoke N Vape ....G...... 212 390-1654
  New York (G-12137)
Time2vape LLC ....G...... 718 335-0401
  Jackson Heights (G-6924)
Vape Flavorium ....G...... 607 346-7276
  Horseheads (G-6623)
Vape Paradise Inc ....G...... 845 467-4517
  Middletown (G-8504)
Vape4style Inc ....G...... 718 395-0406
  Brooklyn (G-2738)
Z Vape Station/Atlantic Smoke ....G...... 516 442-0548
  Freeport (G-5446)

CIGAR LIGHTERS EXC PRECIOUS METAL
Arcadia Mfg Group Inc ....E...... 518 434-6213
  Green Island (G-5871)
Arcadia Mfg Group Inc ....G...... 518 434-6213
  Menands (G-8399)

CIGARETTE & CIGAR PRDTS & ACCESS
Iquit Cig LLC ....G...... 718 475-1422
  Brooklyn (G-2113)
Saakshi Inc ....G...... 315 475-3988
  Syracuse (G-16050)

CIRCUIT BOARDS, PRINTED: Television & Radio
Kendall Circuits Inc ....E...... 631 473-3636
  Mount Sinai (G-8697)
TCS Electronics Inc ....E...... 585 337-4301
  Farmington (G-5165)

CIRCUIT BOARDS: Wiring
Coast To Coast Circuits Inc ....E...... 585 254-2980
  Rochester (G-14302)
Nationwide Circuits Inc ....E...... 585 328-0791
  Rochester (G-14548)
Stever-Locke Industries Inc ....G...... 585 624-3450
  Honeoye Falls (G-6565)

CIRCUIT BREAKERS
Real Industry Inc ....F...... 805 435-1255
  New York (G-11842)

CIRCUITS, INTEGRATED: Hybrid
Emtron Hybrids Inc ....E...... 631 924-9668
  Yaphank (G-17408)
General Microwave Corporation ....F...... 516 802-0900
  Syosset (G-15844)

CIRCUITS: Electronic
A K Allen Co Inc ....C...... 516 747-5450
  Mineola (G-8522)
A R V Precision Mfg Inc ....G...... 631 293-9643
  Farmingdale (G-4934)
AAR Allen Services Inc ....E...... 516 222-9000
  Garden City (G-5507)
Accessories For Electronics ....E...... 516 847-0158
  South Hempstead (G-15553)
Advance Circuit Technology Inc ....E...... 585 328-2000
  Rochester (G-14191)
Aeroflex Plainview Inc ....B...... 516 694-6700
  Plainview (G-13609)
Aeroflex Plainview Inc ....G...... 631 231-9100
  Hauppauge (G-6030)
All Shore Industries Inc ....F...... 718 720-0018
  Staten Island (G-15655)
Alloy Machine & Tool Co Inc ....G...... 516 593-3445
  Lynbrook (G-7974)
American Quality Technology ....F...... 607 777-9488
  Binghamton (G-884)
Anaren Inc ....A...... 315 432-8909
  East Syracuse (G-4519)
B H M Metal Products Co ....G...... 845 292-5297
  Kauneonga Lake (G-7165)
Canfield Electronics Inc ....F...... 631 585-4100
  Lindenhurst (G-7480)
Chiplogic Inc ....F...... 631 617-6317
  Yaphank (G-17404)
Cloud Toronto Inc ....F...... 408 569-4542
  Williamsville (G-17267)
Communications & Energy Corp ....F...... 315 446-5723
  Syracuse (G-15922)
Dynamic Hybirds Inc ....G...... 315 426-8110
  Syracuse (G-15947)
Eastland Electronics Co Inc ....G...... 631 580-3800
  Ronkonkoma (G-14926)
Fei Communications Inc ....C...... 516 794-4500
  Uniondale (G-16315)
Hypres Inc ....E...... 914 592-1190
  Elmsford (G-4764)
IEC Electronics Corp ....A...... 315 331-7742
  Newark (G-12752)
Imrex LLC ....B...... 516 479-3675
  Oyster Bay (G-13396)
Island Circuits International ....G...... 516 625-5555
  College Point (G-3815)
Island Research and Dev Corp ....D...... 631 471-7100
  Ronkonkoma (G-14943)
Jaguar Industries Inc ....F...... 845 947-1800
  Haverstraw (G-6261)
Jenlor Ltd ....G...... 315 637-9080
  Fayetteville (G-5173)
Jet Components Inc ....G...... 631 436-7300
  Islandia (G-6835)
Keltron Electronics (de Corp) ....F...... 631 567-6300
  Ronkonkoma (G-14949)
Logitek Inc ....D...... 631 567-1100
  Bohemia (G-1089)
Mekatronics Incorporated ....E...... 516 883-6805
  Port Washington (G-13865)
Meridian Technologies Inc ....E...... 516 285-1000
  Elmont (G-4735)
Merit Electronic Design Co Inc ....C...... 631 667-9699
  Edgewood (G-4619)
Mid Hdson Wkshp For The Dsbled ....E...... 845 471-3820
  Poughkeepsie (G-13935)
Mirion Technologies Ist Corp ....D...... 607 562-4300
  Horseheads (G-6612)
Nelson Holdings Ltd ....G...... 607 772-1794
  Binghamton (G-935)
Oakdale Industrial Elec Corp ....F...... 631 737-4090
  Ronkonkoma (G-14982)
Opus Technology Corporation ....F...... 631 271-1883
  Melville (G-8374)
Pcb Piezotronics Inc ....B...... 716 684-0003
  Depew (G-4294)
Photonamics Inc ....F...... 585 426-3774
  Rochester (G-14602)
Polycast Industries Inc ....G...... 631 595-2530
  Bay Shore (G-722)
Precision Assembly Tech Inc ....E...... 631 699-9400
  Bohemia (G-1115)
Premier Systems LLC ....G...... 631 587-9700
  Babylon (G-550)
Quality Contract Assemblies ....F...... 585 663-9030
  Rochester (G-14636)
R L C Electronics Inc ....D...... 914 241-1334
  Mount Kisco (G-8684)
Rdi Inc ....F...... 914 773-1000
  Mount Kisco (G-8686)
Rem-Tronics Inc ....D...... 716 934-2697
  Dunkirk (G-4372)
Rochester Industrial Ctrl Inc ....D...... 315 524-4555
  Ontario (G-13235)
Rochester Industrial Ctrl Inc ....D...... 315 524-4555
  Ontario (G-13234)
Safe Circuits Inc ....G...... 631 586-3682
  Dix Hills (G-4320)
Scientific Components Corp ....B...... 718 368-2060
  Brooklyn (G-2564)
Sendec Corp ....C...... 585 425-3390
  Fairport (G-4883)
Sonaer Inc ....G...... 631 756-4780
  West Babylon (G-16860)
Sopark Corp ....C...... 716 822-0434
  Buffalo (G-3219)
Stetron International Inc ....F...... 716 854-3443
  Buffalo (G-3225)
Surmotech Inc ....D...... 585 742-1220
  Victor (G-16527)
T-S-K Electronics Inc ....G...... 716 693-3916
  North Tonawanda (G-13017)
Te Connectivity Corporation ....E...... 585 785-2500
  Rochester (G-14743)
Telephonics Corporation ....E...... 631 549-6000
  Huntington (G-6722)
Telephonics Corporation ....A...... 631 755-7000
  Farmingdale (G-5137)
Tlsi Incorporated ....D...... 631 470-8880
  Huntington (G-6726)
Torotron Corporation ....G...... 718 428-6992
  Fresh Meadows (G-5460)
Trading Services International ....F...... 212 501-0142
  New York (G-12410)
Unison Industries LLC ....B...... 607 335-5000
  Norwich (G-13057)
Vestal Electronic Devices LLC ....F...... 607 773-8461
  Endicott (G-4838)
Werlatone Inc ....E...... 845 278-2220
  Patterson (G-13470)
Xedit Corp ....G...... 718 380-1592
  Queens Village (G-14000)

CIRCULAR KNIT FABRICS DYEING & FINISHING
A-One Moving & Storage Inc ....E...... 718 266-6002
  Brooklyn (G-1542)
Gehring Tricot Corporation ....C...... 315 429-8551
  Dolgeville (G-4329)
Lifestyle Design Usa Ltd ....G...... 212 279-9400
  New York (G-11021)

CLAMPS & COUPLINGS: Hose
United Metal Industries Inc ....G...... 516 354-6800
  New Hyde Park (G-8913)

CLAY PRDTS: Architectural
Jq Woodworking Inc ....G...... 516 766-3424
  Oceanside (G-13104)
Lenon Models Inc ....G...... 212 229-1581
  New York (G-11001)

CLAYS, EXC KAOLIN & BALL
Applied Minerals Inc ....E...... 212 226-4265
  Brooklyn (G-1620)

CLEANING EQPT: Blast, Dustless
Cleaning Tech Group LLC ....E...... 716 665-2340
  Jamestown (G-7016)
Guyson Corporation of USa ....E...... 518 587-7894
  Saratoga Springs (G-15186)

CLEANING EQPT: Carpet Sweepers, Exc Household Elec Vacuum
American Comfort Direct LLC ....E...... 201 364-8309
  New York (G-9165)

CLEANING EQPT: Commercial
Oxford Cleaners ....G...... 212 734-0006
  New York (G-11552)

Employee Codes: A=Over 500 employees, B=251-500
C=101-250, D=51-100, E=20-50, F=10-19, G=5-9

CLEANING EQPT: High Pressure

Arpa USA	G	212 965-4099
New York (G-9255)		
Custom Klean Corp	F	315 865-8101
Holland Patent (G-6513)		
Heliojet Cleaning Tech Inc	F	585 768-8710
Le Roy (G-7433)		
Power Scrub It Inc	F	516 997-2500
Westbury (G-17048)		

CLEANING OR POLISHING PREPARATIONS, NEC

Arrow Chemical Corp	F	516 377-7770
Freeport (G-5398)		
Clean All of Syracuse LLC	G	315 472-9189
Syracuse (G-15916)		
Collinite Corporation	G	315 732-2282
Utica (G-16336)		
FBC Chemical Corporation	G	716 681-1581
Lancaster (G-7339)		
George Basch Co Inc	F	516 378-8100
North Bellmore (G-12937)		
Grillbot LLC	G	646 258-5639
New York (G-10406)		
Mdi Holdings LLC	A	212 559-1127
New York (G-11228)		
Progressive Products LLC	G	914 417-6022
Rye Brook (G-15100)		
Spic and Span Company	F	914 524-6823
Tarrytown (G-16132)		
Topps-All Products of Yonkers	F	914 968-4226
Yonkers (G-17508)		
U S Plychmical Overseas Corp	E	845 356-5530
Chestnut Ridge (G-3657)		
US Polychemical Holding Corp	E	845 356-5530
Spring Valley (G-15628)		

CLEANING PRDTS: Degreasing Solvent

Solvents Company Inc	F	631 595-9300
Kingston (G-7238)		

CLEANING PRDTS: Deodorants, Nonpersonal

Car-Freshner Corporation	C	315 788-6250
Watertown (G-16663)		

CLEANING PRDTS: Disinfectants, Household Or Indl Plant

Castoleum Corporation	F	914 664-5877
Mount Vernon (G-8715)		
King Research Inc	E	718 788-0122
Brooklyn (G-2171)		
Noble Pine Products Co Inc	F	914 664-5877
Mount Vernon (G-8756)		
Spongebath LLC	G	917 475-1347
Astoria (G-457)		

CLEANING PRDTS: Drycleaning Preparations

Connie French Cleaners Inc	G	516 487-1343
Great Neck (G-5818)		
Wedding Gown Preservation Co	D	607 748-7999
Endicott (G-4839)		

CLEANING PRDTS: Indl Plant Disinfectants Or Deodorants

Mirandy Products Ltd	E	516 489-6800
South Hempstead (G-15554)		

CLEANING PRDTS: Laundry Preparations

Connies Laundry	G	716 822-2800
Buffalo (G-2906)		
Laundress Inc	F	212 209-0074
New York (G-10973)		
Lb Laundry Inc	G	347 399-8030
Flushing (G-5271)		

CLEANING PRDTS: Metal Polish

Conrad Blasius Equipment Co	G	516 753-1200
Plainview (G-13620)		

CLEANING PRDTS: Polishing Preparations & Related Prdts

Royce Associates A Ltd Partnr	G	516 367-6298
Jericho (G-7115)		

CLEANING PRDTS: Rug, Upholstery/Dry Clng Detergents/Spotters

Greenmaker Industries LLC	F	866 684-7800
Farmingdale (G-5009)		

CLEANING PRDTS: Sanitation Preparations

Adirondack Waste MGT Inc	G	518 585-2224
Ticonderoga (G-16147)		
City of New York	C	718 236-2693
Brooklyn (G-1782)		
County Waste Management Inc	G	914 592-5007
Harrison (G-6002)		
Simply Amazing Enterprises Inc	G	631 503-6452
Melville (G-8383)		
TWI-Laq Industries Inc	F	718 638-5860
Bronx (G-1481)		

CLEANING PRDTS: Sanitation Preps, Disinfectants/Deodorants

Scully Sanitation	G	315 899-8996
West Edmeston (G-16875)		
Walter G Legge Company Inc	G	914 737-5040
Peekskill (G-13510)		

CLEANING PRDTS: Shoe Polish Or Cleaner

Premier Brands of America Inc	E	718 325-3000
Mount Vernon (G-8764)		
Premier Brands of America Inc	C	914 667-6200
Mount Vernon (G-8763)		

CLEANING PRDTS: Specialty

Caltex International Ltd	E	315 425-1040
Syracuse (G-15902)		
Chem-Puter Friendly Inc	E	631 331-2259
Mount Sinai (G-8696)		
Chemclean Corporation	E	718 525-4500
Jamaica (G-6937)		
Enviro Service & Supply Corp	F	347 838-6500
Staten Island (G-15692)		
Finger Lakes Chemicals Inc	E	585 454-4760
Rochester (G-14392)		
Four Sasons Multi-Services Inc	G	347 843-6262
Bronx (G-1338)		
Gliptone Manufacturing Inc	F	631 285-7250
Ronkonkoma (G-14933)		
Griffin Chemical Company LLC	G	716 693-2465
North Tonawanda (G-12993)		
HFC Prestige Intl US LLC	A	212 389-7800
New York (G-10514)		
Nuvite Chemical Compounds Corp	F	718 383-8351
Brooklyn (G-2391)		
Sensor & Decontamination Inc	F	301 526-8389
Binghamton (G-944)		
Spray Nine Corporation	D	800 477-7299
Johnstown (G-7157)		

CLEANING PRDTS: Window Cleaning Preparations

Tjb Sunshine Enterprises	F	518 384-6483
Ballston Lake (G-587)		

CLEANING SVCS: Industrial Or Commercial

Wellspring Omni Holdings Corp	A	212 318-9800
New York (G-12638)		

CLIPPERS: Fingernail & Toenail

Revlon Consumer Products Corp	B	212 527-4000
New York (G-11879)		

CLIPS & FASTENERS, MADE FROM PURCHASED WIRE

Hohmann & Barnard Inc	E	631 234-0600
Hauppauge (G-6118)		
Hohmann & Barnard Inc	E	518 357-9757
Schenectady (G-15295)		

CLOSURES: Closures, Stamped Metal

Van Blarcom Closures Inc	C	718 855-3810
Brooklyn (G-2735)		

CLOSURES: Plastic

Hlp Klearfold Packaging Pdts	F	718 554-3271
New York (G-10534)		
Industrial Paper Tube Inc	F	718 893-5000
Bronx (G-1363)		
Van Blarcom Closures Inc	C	718 855-3810
Brooklyn (G-2735)		

CLOTHING & ACCESS, WOMEN, CHILD & INFANT, WHOL: Diapers

First Quality Hygienic Inc	F	516 829-3030
Great Neck (G-5827)		

CLOTHING & ACCESS, WOMEN, CHILD & INFANT, WHOL: Scarves

Gce International Inc	D	212 704-4800
New York (G-10304)		
Lr Paris LLC	G	703 652-1132
New York (G-11084)		

CLOTHING & ACCESS, WOMEN, CHILD & INFANT, WHOLESALE: Under

Apparel Partnership Group LLC	G	212 302-7722
New York (G-9230)		
Mrt Textile Inc		800 674-1073
New York (G-11341)		

CLOTHING & ACCESS, WOMEN, CHILD & INFANT, WHSLE: Sportswear

Bandit International Ltd	F	718 402-2100
Bronx (G-1279)		
Kidz Concepts LLC	D	212 398-1110
New York (G-10882)		
Sensational Collection Inc	G	212 840-7388
New York (G-12047)		

CLOTHING & ACCESS, WOMEN, CHILDREN & INFANT, WHOL: Access

Embassy Apparel Inc	F	212 768-8330
New York (G-10071)		
Fad Inc	E	631 385-2460
Huntington (G-6694)		

CLOTHING & ACCESS, WOMEN, CHILDREN & INFANT, WHOL: Gloves

Fownes Brothers & Co Inc	E	212 683-0150
New York (G-10244)		
Fownes Brothers & Co Inc	E	518 752-4411
Gloversville (G-5726)		

CLOTHING & ACCESS, WOMEN, CHILDREN & INFANT, WHOL: Handbags

Coach Stores Inc	A	212 643-9727
New York (G-9717)		
Goyard Inc	G	212 813-0005
New York (G-10383)		
Goyard Miami LLC	G	212 813-0005
New York (G-10384)		
Graphic Image Incorporated	C	631 249-9600
Melville (G-8353)		
Quilted Koala Ltd	F	800 223-5678
New York (G-11799)		
Street Smart Designs Inc	G	646 865-0056
New York (G-12236)		

CLOTHING & ACCESS, WOMEN, CHILDREN & INFANT, WHOL: Sweaters

B & B Sweater Mills Inc	F	718 456-8693
Brooklyn (G-1656)		
Keryakos Inc	F	518 344-7092
Schenectady (G-15300)		

CLOTHING & ACCESS, WOMEN, CHILDREN & INFANTS, WHOL: Purses

Formart Corp	F	212 819-1819
New York (G-10238)		

PRODUCT SECTION

CLOTHING & FURNISHINGS, MENS & BOYS, WHOLESALE: Apprl Belts

CLOTHING & ACCESS, WOMEN, CHILDREN/INFANT, WHOL: Baby Goods

Sunwin Global Industry Inc .... G 646 370-6196
  New York *(G-12261)*

CLOTHING & ACCESS, WOMEN, CHILDREN/INFANT, WHOL: Nightwear

Komar Luxury Brands .... G 646 472-0060
  New York *(G-10913)*

CLOTHING & ACCESS, WOMEN, CHILDREN/INFANT, WHOL: Outerwear

Outerstuff LLC .... E 212 594-9700
  New York *(G-11548)*

CLOTHING & ACCESS, WOMEN, CHILDREN/INFANT, WHOL: Swimsuits

Christina Sales Inc .... F 212 391-0710
  New York *(G-9664)*

CLOTHING & ACCESS, WOMENS, CHILDRE'S & INFANTS, WHOL: Suits

Tiger Fashion Inc .... E 212 244-1175
  New York *(G-12357)*
Travis Ayers Inc .... E 212 921-5165
  New York *(G-12416)*

CLOTHING & ACCESS, WOMENS, CHILDREN & INFANTS, WHOL: Hats

Mega Power Sports Corporation .... G 212 627-3380
  New York *(G-11246)*

CLOTHING & ACCESS: Costumes, Masquerade

Lr Paris LLC .... G 703 652-1132
  New York *(G-11084)*
Rubies Masquerade Company LLC .... G 718 846-1008
  Richmond Hill *(G-14096)*

CLOTHING & ACCESS: Costumes, Theatrical

Barbara Matera Ltd .... D 212 475-5006
  New York *(G-9367)*
Costume Armour Inc .... F 845 534-9120
  Cornwall *(G-4008)*
D-C Theatricks .... G 716 847-0180
  Buffalo *(G-2919)*
Euroco Costumes Inc .... G 212 629-9665
  New York *(G-10139)*
Izquierdo Studios Ltd .... F 212 807-9757
  New York *(G-10712)*
Parsons-Meares Ltd .... D 212 242-3378
  Long Island City *(G-7866)*
Schneeman Studio Limited .... G 212 244-3330
  New York *(G-12008)*

CLOTHING & ACCESS: Cummerbunds

J M C Bow Co Inc .... F 718 686-8110
  Brooklyn *(G-2124)*
Lakeview Innovations Inc .... F 212 502-6702
  New York *(G-10956)*
Westchester Wine Warehouse LLC .... F 914 824-1400
  White Plains *(G-17213)*

CLOTHING & ACCESS: Footlets

Jersey Express Inc .... F 716 834-6151
  Buffalo *(G-3035)*

CLOTHING & ACCESS: Handicapped

Brooklyn Denim Co .... F 718 782-2600
  Brooklyn *(G-1724)*
Crosswinds Sourcing LLC .... G 646 438-6904
  New York *(G-9814)*
Danny R Couture Corp .... G 212 594-1095
  New York *(G-9861)*
Eb Couture Ltd .... E 212 912-0190
  New York *(G-10023)*
Kww Productions Corp .... F 212 398-8181
  New York *(G-10935)*
M2 Fashion Group Holdings Inc .... G 917 208-2948
  New York *(G-11108)*

Ribz LLC .... G 212 764-9595
  New York *(G-11887)*
Timeless Fashions LLC .... G 212 730-9328
  New York *(G-12370)*

CLOTHING & ACCESS: Handkerchiefs, Exc Paper

Gce International Inc .... D 212 704-4800
  New York *(G-10304)*
My Hanky Inc .... F 646 321-0869
  Brooklyn *(G-2350)*

CLOTHING & ACCESS: Hospital Gowns

New York Hospital Disposable .... E 718 384-1620
  Brooklyn *(G-2373)*
Shamron Mills Ltd .... G 212 354-0430
  New York *(G-12062)*

CLOTHING & ACCESS: Men's Miscellaneous Access

Accessries Direct Intl USA Inc .... F 646 448-8200
  New York *(G-9060)*
Adf Accessories Inc .... G 516 450-5755
  Lynbrook *(G-7971)*
Apollo Apparel Group LLC .... F 212 398-6585
  New York *(G-9226)*
Bh Brand Inc .... E 212 239-1635
  New York *(G-9433)*
Carter Enterprises LLC .... E 718 853-5052
  Brooklyn *(G-1762)*
Dreamwave LLC .... E 212 594-4250
  New York *(G-9976)*
Foot Locker Retail Inc .... F 516 827-5306
  Hicksville *(G-6374)*
Hoehn Inc .... F 518 463-8900
  Albany *(G-87)*
Hudson Dying & Finishing LLC .... E 518 752-4389
  Gloversville *(G-5731)*
Intercotton Company Inc .... G 212 265-3809
  New York *(G-10669)*
Jimeale Incorporated .... G 917 686-5383
  New York *(G-10774)*
Jolibe Atelier LLC .... F 347 882-6617
  New York *(G-10795)*
Jonathan Meizler LLC .... G 212 213-2977
  New York *(G-10797)*
Joseph Industries Inc .... G 212 764-0010
  New York *(G-10804)*
Linder New York LLC .... F 646 678-5819
  New York *(G-11029)*
Meryl Diamond Ltd .... D 212 730-0333
  New York *(G-11262)*
New York Accessory Group Inc .... E 212 532-7911
  New York *(G-11416)*
New York Popular Inc .... D 718 499-2020
  Brooklyn *(G-2376)*
Nmny Group LLC .... E 212 944-6500
  New York *(G-11462)*
NY 1 Art Gallery Inc .... G 917 698-0626
  New Hyde Park *(G-8898)*
Ppr Direct Marketing LLC .... F 718 965-8600
  Brooklyn *(G-2447)*
Rjm2 Ltd .... G 212 944-1660
  New York *(G-11906)*
Robert Miller Associates LLC .... F 718 392-1640
  Long Island City *(G-7892)*
Rosetti Handbags and ACC .... E 212 273-3765
  New York *(G-11939)*
Swank Inc .... B 212 867-2600
  New York *(G-12270)*
Trash and Vaudeville Inc .... G 212 777-1727
  New York *(G-12415)*
Ufo Contemporary Inc .... F 212 226-5400
  New York *(G-12461)*
Unified Inc led .... F 646 370-4650
  New York *(G-12470)*
Zam Barrett Dialogue Inc .... G 646 649-0140
  Brooklyn *(G-2793)*

CLOTHING & ACCESS: Suspenders

Perry Ellis Menswear LLC .... C 212 221-7500
  New York *(G-11643)*
Randa Accessories Lea Gds LLC .... D 212 354-5100
  New York *(G-11825)*
Trafalgar Company LLC .... F 212 768-8800
  New York *(G-12411)*

CLOTHING & APPAREL STORES: Custom

Knucklehead Embroidery Inc .... G 607 797-2725
  Johnson City *(G-7129)*
Peter Papastrat .... G 607 723-8112
  Binghamton *(G-938)*

CLOTHING & FURNISHINGS, MEN & BOY, WHOLESALE: Suits/Trousers

Hugo Boss Usa Inc .... D 212 940-0600
  New York *(G-10574)*

CLOTHING & FURNISHINGS, MEN'S & BOYS', WHOLESALE: Fur

Georgy Creative Fashions Inc .... G 212 279-4885
  New York *(G-10328)*

CLOTHING & FURNISHINGS, MEN'S & BOYS', WHOLESALE: Gloves

Fownes Brothers & Co Inc .... E 212 683-0150
  New York *(G-10244)*
Fownes Brothers & Co Inc .... E 518 752-4411
  Gloversville *(G-5726)*

CLOTHING & FURNISHINGS, MEN'S & BOYS', WHOLESALE: Hats

Ideal Creations Inc .... E 212 563-5928
  New York *(G-10600)*
Mega Power Sports Corporation .... G 212 627-3380
  New York *(G-11246)*

CLOTHING & FURNISHINGS, MEN'S & BOYS', WHOLESALE: Neckwear

Mongru Neckwear Inc .... E 718 706-0406
  Long Island City *(G-7847)*
Roffe Accessories Inc .... F 212 213-1440
  New York *(G-11924)*

CLOTHING & FURNISHINGS, MEN'S & BOYS', WHOLESALE: Scarves

Gce International Inc .... D 212 704-4800
  New York *(G-10304)*

CLOTHING & FURNISHINGS, MEN'S & BOYS', WHOLESALE: Shirts

Hard Ten Clothing Inc .... G 212 302-1321
  New York *(G-10457)*
Just Brass Inc .... G 212 724-5447
  New York *(G-10826)*

CLOTHING & FURNISHINGS, MEN'S & BOYS', WHOLESALE: Trousers

Texwood Inc (u S A) .... G 212 262-8383
  New York *(G-12327)*

CLOTHING & FURNISHINGS, MEN'S & BOYS', WHOLESALE: Umbrellas

Adam Scott Designs Inc .... E 212 420-8866
  New York *(G-9071)*

CLOTHING & FURNISHINGS, MEN'S & BOYS', WHOLESALE: Uniforms

Custom Sportswear Corp .... G 914 666-9200
  Bedford Hills *(G-797)*

CLOTHING & FURNISHINGS, MENS & BOYS, WHOL: Sportswear/Work

Bilco Industries Inc .... F 917 783-5008
  New York *(G-9447)*
John Varvatos Company .... E 212 812-8000
  New York *(G-10793)*

CLOTHING & FURNISHINGS, MENS & BOYS, WHOLESALE: Apprl Belts

Dynasty Belts Inc .... E 516 625-6280
  New Hyde Park *(G-8873)*
New Classic Inc .... F 718 609-1100
  Long Island City *(G-7855)*

Employee Codes: A=Over 500 employees, B=251-500
C=101-250, D=51-100, E=20-50, F=10-19, G=5-9

CLOTHING ACCESS STORES: Umbrellas

PRODUCT SECTION

CLOTHING ACCESS STORES: Umbrellas
Zip-Jack Industries Ltd .... E 914 592-2000
  Tarrytown *(G-16136)*

CLOTHING STORES, NEC
1 Atelier LLC .... G 917 916-2968
  New York *(G-9004)*
Fad Inc .... E 631 385-2460
  Huntington *(G-6694)*
Kcp Holdco Inc .... F 212 265-1500
  New York *(G-10866)*
Kenneth Cole Productions Inc .... B 212 265-1500
  New York *(G-10873)*
Marsha Fleisher .... F 845 679-6500
  Woodstock *(G-17380)*

CLOTHING STORES: Dancewear
Shirl-Lynn of New York .... F 315 363-5898
  Oneida *(G-13189)*

CLOTHING STORES: Designer Apparel
Randall Loeffler Inc .... E 212 226-8787
  New York *(G-11826)*

CLOTHING STORES: Jeans
Brooklyn Denim Co .... F 718 782-2600
  Brooklyn *(G-1724)*
Gbg Denim Usa LLC .... F 646 839-7000
  New York *(G-10298)*
Joseph (uk) Inc .... G 212 570-0077
  New York *(G-10802)*

CLOTHING STORES: Leather
Leather Artisan .... G 518 359-3102
  Childwold *(G-3658)*
Lost Worlds Inc .... G 212 923-3423
  New York *(G-11073)*

CLOTHING STORES: T-Shirts, Printed, Custom
JP Signs .... G 518 569-3907
  Chazy *(G-3589)*
Randy Sixberry .... G 315 265-6211
  Potsdam *(G-13901)*

CLOTHING STORES: Uniforms & Work
All American Awards Inc .... F 631 567-2025
  Bohemia *(G-1007)*
Vans Inc .... F 631 724-1011
  Lake Grove *(G-7293)*

CLOTHING STORES: Unisex
David Peyser Sportswear Inc .... E 212 695-7716
  New York *(G-9877)*

CLOTHING STORES: Work
Protech (llc) .... E 518 725-7785
  Gloversville *(G-5734)*

CLOTHING, WOMEN & CHILD, WHLSE: Dress, Suit, Skirt & Blouse
Billy Beez Usa LLC .... G 315 741-5099
  Syracuse *(G-15889)*
Billy Beez Usa LLC .... F 646 606-2249
  New York *(G-9451)*
Billy Beez Usa LLC .... G 845 915-4709
  West Nyack *(G-16943)*

CLOTHING/ACCESS, WOMEN, CHILDREN/INFANT, WHOL: Apparel Belt
New Classic Inc .... F 718 609-1100
  Long Island City *(G-7855)*

CLOTHING/FURNISHINGS, MEN/BOY, WHOL: Furnishings, Exc Shoes
Embassy Apparel Inc .... F 212 768-8330
  New York *(G-10071)*

CLOTHING: Academic Vestments
Tr Apparel LLC .... E 310 595-4337
  New York *(G-12406)*
Tr Apparel LLC .... G 646 358-3888
  New York *(G-12407)*

CLOTHING: Access
David & Young Co Inc 212 594-6034
  New York *(G-9873)*
J & C Finishing .... E 718 456-1087
  Ridgewood *(G-14123)*
Jmk Enterprises LLC 845 634-8100
  New City *(G-8833)*
Patient-Wear LLC 914 740-7770
  Bronx *(G-1423)*
S & B Fashion Inc 718 482-1386
  Long Island City *(G-7898)*
Twcc Product and Sales 212 614-9364
  New York *(G-12450)*

CLOTHING: Access, Women's & Misses'
1 Atelier LLC .... G 917 916-2968
  New York *(G-9004)*
Accessries Direct Intl USA Inc ...... F 646 448-8200
  New York *(G-9060)*
Bag Bazaar Ltd .... E 212 689-3508
  New York *(G-9357)*
Bh Brand Inc 212 239-1635
  New York *(G-9433)*
Botkier Ny LLC .... G 212 343-2782
  New York *(G-9493)*
Carolina Amato Inc 212 768-9095
  New York *(G-9587)*
Collection Xiix Ltd .... C 212 686-8990
  New York *(G-9729)*
DFA New York LLC 212 523-0021
  New York *(G-9919)*
Fad Inc .... E 631 385-2460
  Huntington *(G-6694)*
Four Dee Inc .... D 718 615-1695
  Brooklyn *(G-1999)*
Giulietta LLC .... G 212 334-1859
  Brooklyn *(G-2025)*
Hoehn Inc .... F 518 463-8900
  Albany *(G-87)*
Krasner Group Inc 212 268-4100
  New York *(G-10925)*
Ksk International Inc 212 354-7770
  New York *(G-10930)*
New Concepts of New York LLC ... E 212 695-4999
  Brooklyn *(G-2368)*
New York Accessory Group Inc .... E 212 532-7911
  New York *(G-11416)*
ODY Accessories Inc 212 239-0580
  New York *(G-11510)*
Popnyc 1 LLC 646 684-4600
  New York *(G-11706)*
Uspa Accessories LLC 212 868-2590
  New York *(G-12513)*
White Gate Holdings Inc .... E 212 564-3266
  New York *(G-12652)*

CLOTHING: Aprons, Exc Rubber/Plastic, Women, Misses, Junior
Elizabeth Wilson 516 486-2157
  Uniondale *(G-16314)*
Republic Clothing Group Inc .... C 212 719-3000
  New York *(G-11869)*
Richard Manufacturing Co Inc 718 254-0958
  Brooklyn *(G-2513)*

CLOTHING: Aprons, Harness
Breton Industries Inc .... D 518 842-3030
  Amsterdam *(G-337)*
Mama Luca Production Inc 212 582-9700
  New York *(G-11148)*

CLOTHING: Aprons, Work, Exc Rubberized & Plastic, Men's
Richard Manufacturing Co Inc ...... G 718 254-0958
  Brooklyn *(G-2513)*

CLOTHING: Athletic & Sportswear, Men's & Boys'
Adpro Sports LLC .... D 716 854-5116
  Buffalo *(G-2815)*
Bandit International Ltd .... F 718 402-2100
  Bronx *(G-1279)*
Beluga Inc .... E 212 594-5511
  New York *(G-9400)*
Benetton Trading Usa Inc .... G 212 593-0290
  New York *(G-9406)*
Bilco Industries Inc .... F 917 783-5008
  New York *(G-9447)*
Billion Tower USA LLC .... G 212 220-0608
  New York *(G-9450)*
Broken Threads Inc .... G 212 730-4351
  New York *(G-9519)*
Caps Teamwear Inc .... G 585 663-1750
  Rochester *(G-14277)*
Central Mills Inc .... C 212 221-0748
  New York *(G-9617)*
City Jeans Inc .... G 718 239-5353
  Bronx *(G-1301)*
Columbia Sportswear Company ... C 631 274-6091
  Deer Park *(G-4141)*
Continental Knitting Mills .... G 631 242-5330
  Deer Park *(G-4142)*
Cougar Sport Inc .... E 212 947-3054
  New York *(G-9792)*
David Peyser Sportswear Inc ...... B 631 231-7788
  Bay Shore *(G-689)*
David Peyser Sportswear Inc ...... E 212 695-7716
  New York *(G-9877)*
Endurance LLC .... E 212 719-2500
  New York *(G-10086)*
Eternal Fortune Fashion LLC .... F 212 965-5322
  New York *(G-10131)*
Ferris USA LLC .... G 617 895-8102
  New York *(G-10207)*
Feyem USA Inc .... G 845 363-6253
  Brewster *(G-1216)*
Gametime Sportswear Plus LLC .. G 315 724-5893
  Utica *(G-16358)*
General Sportwear Company Inc . G 212 764-5820
  New York *(G-10317)*
Groupe 16sur20 LLC .... F 212 625-1620
  New York *(G-10415)*
Haculla Nyc Inc .... F 718 886-3163
  Fresh Meadows *(G-5455)*
Hansae Co Ltd .... G 212 354-6690
  New York *(G-10455)*
Hf Mfg Corp 212 594-9142
  New York *(G-10513)*
Jacob Hidary Foundation Inc .... F 212 736-6540
  New York *(G-10731)*
John Varvatos Company .... E 212 812-8000
  New York *(G-10793)*
Joseph (uk) Inc .... G 212 570-0077
  New York *(G-10802)*
Kicks Closet Sportswear Inc .... G 347 577-0857
  Bronx *(G-1376)*
Kidz World Inc .... F 212 563-4949
  New York *(G-10883)*
Lakeview Sportswear Corp .... G 800 965-6550
  Brooklyn *(G-2192)*
London Paris Ltd .... G 718 564-4793
  Brooklyn *(G-2237)*
Luxe Imagine Consulting LLC ..... G 212 273-9770
  New York *(G-11095)*
M Hidary & Co Inc .... D 212 736-6540
  New York *(G-11102)*
Mann Consultants LLC .... E 914 763-0512
  Waccabuc *(G-16541)*
Mee Accessories LLC .... C 917 262-1000
  New York *(G-11244)*
Miss Group .... G 212 391-2535
  New York *(G-11307)*
Nautica International Inc .... G 212 541-5757
  New York *(G-11381)*
Nine West Holdings Inc .... G 212 575-2571
  New York *(G-11455)*
North American Mills Inc .... F 212 695-6146
  New York *(G-11473)*
On The Double Inc .... G 518 431-3571
  Germantown *(G-5603)*
One Step Up Ltd .... D 212 398-1110
  New York *(G-11521)*
P & I Sportswear Inc 718 934-4587
  New York *(G-11559)*
Ps38 LLC .... F 212 819-1123
  New York *(G-11763)*

PRODUCT SECTION

CLOTHING: Blouses, Women's & Girls'

Pvh Corp .... G 212 381-3800
  New York *(G-11781)*
Ralph Lauren Corporation .... B 212 318-7000
  New York *(G-11819)*
Ramsbury Property Us Inc .... F 212 223-6250
  New York *(G-11823)*
Rp55 Inc .... G 212 840-4035
  New York *(G-11947)*
Ruleville Manufacturing Co Inc .... G 212 695-1620
  New York *(G-11953)*
S & S Fashions Inc .... G 718 328-0001
  Bronx *(G-1442)*
Sandy Dalal Ltd .... G 212 532-5822
  New York *(G-11985)*
Sb Corporation .... G 212 822-3166
  New York *(G-11999)*
Sister Sister Inc .... G 212 629-9600
  New York *(G-12110)*
Sport Athleisure Ltd .... F 212 868-6505
  New York *(G-12189)*
Sterling Possessions Ltd .... G 212 594-0418
  New York *(G-12221)*
Tbhl International LLC .... F 212 799-2007
  New York *(G-12307)*
Tibana Finishing Inc .... E 718 417-5375
  Ridgewood *(G-14140)*
Tillsonburg Company USA Inc .... E 267 994-8096
  New York *(G-12360)*
Under Armour Inc .... E 518 761-6787
  Lake George *(G-7289)*
Warnaco Group Inc .... E 212 287-8000
  New York *(G-12614)*
Warnaco Inc .... B 212 287-8000
  New York *(G-12615)*

CLOTHING: Athletic & Sportswear, Women's & Girls'

Adpro Sports LLC .... D 716 854-5116
  Buffalo *(G-2815)*
Alpha 6 Distributions LLC .... F 516 801-8290
  Locust Valley *(G-7659)*
Amber Bever Inc .... G 212 391-4911
  Brooklyn *(G-1594)*
Anna Sui Corp .... E 212 768-1951
  New York *(G-9214)*
Avalin LLC .... F 212 842-2286
  New York *(G-9325)*
B Tween LLC .... F 212 819-9040
  New York *(G-9347)*
Bam Sales LLC .... G 212 781-3000
  New York *(G-9364)*
Bandier Corp .... G 212 242-5400
  New York *(G-9366)*
Bilco Industries Inc .... F 917 783-5008
  New York *(G-9447)*
Casuals Etc Inc .... D 212 838-1319
  New York *(G-9598)*
Continental Knitting Mills .... G 631 242-5350
  Deer Park *(G-4142)*
Dianos Kathryn Designs .... G 212 267-1584
  New York *(G-9927)*
Doral Apparel Group Inc .... G 917 208-5652
  New York *(G-9959)*
Dr Jayscom .... G 888 437-5297
  New York *(G-9973)*
First Love Fashions LLC .... F 212 256-1089
  New York *(G-10221)*
Hearts of Palm LLC .... E 212 944-6660
  New York *(G-10495)*
Hearts of Palm LLC .... D 212 944-6660
  New York *(G-10496)*
Hot Shot Hk LLC .... E 212 921-1111
  New York *(G-10556)*
Jaya Apparel Group LLC .... F 212 764-4980
  New York *(G-10746)*
Joseph Abboud Manufacturing .... G 212 586-9140
  New York *(G-10803)*
Katz Martell Fashion Trdg Intl .... G 212 840-0070
  New York *(G-10857)*
Kicks Closet Sportswear Inc .... G 347 577-0857
  Bronx *(G-1376)*
Koral Industries .... F 212 719-0392
  New York *(G-10914)*
Lai Apparel Design Inc .... E 212 382-1075
  New York *(G-10954)*
Leslie Stuart Co Inc .... F 212 629-4551
  New York *(G-11011)*
Liquid Knits Inc .... F 718 706-6600
  Long Island City *(G-7819)*

Mango Usa Inc .... E 718 998-6050
  Brooklyn *(G-2260)*
Mars Fashions Inc .... E 718 402-2200
  Bronx *(G-1391)*
MISS Sportswear Inc .... F 212 391-2535
  Brooklyn *(G-2324)*
MISS Sportswear Inc .... G 212 391-2535
  Brooklyn *(G-2325)*
MISS Sportswear Inc .... F 718 369-6012
  Brooklyn *(G-2326)*
Nine West Holdings Inc .... G 212 221-6376
  New York *(G-11454)*
Nine West Holdings Inc .... E 215 785-4000
  New York *(G-11457)*
Nine West Holdings Inc .... G 212 575-2571
  New York *(G-11455)*
On The Double Inc .... G 518 431-3571
  Germantown *(G-5603)*
One Step Up Ltd .... D 212 398-1110
  New York *(G-11521)*
P & I Sportswear Inc .... G 718 934-4587
  New York *(G-11559)*
Penfli Industries Inc .... F 212 947-6080
  Great Neck *(G-5848)*
Richard Leeds Intl Inc .... E 212 532-4546
  New York *(G-11888)*
Robespierre Inc .... G 212 764-8810
  New York *(G-11913)*
Senneth LLC .... G 347 232-3170
  Monsey *(G-8617)*
Sensational Collection Inc .... G 212 840-7388
  New York *(G-12047)*
Shirl-Lynn of New York .... F 315 363-5898
  Oneida *(G-13189)*
Sport Athleisure Ltd .... F 212 868-6505
  New York *(G-12189)*
Stony Apparel Corp .... G 212 391-0022
  New York *(G-12232)*
Swatfame Inc .... G 212 944-8022
  New York *(G-12273)*
Tillsonburg Company USA Inc .... E 267 994-8096
  New York *(G-12360)*
Z-Ply Corp .... E 212 398-7011
  New York *(G-12721)*
Zg Apparel Group LLC .... E 212 944-2510
  New York *(G-12730)*

CLOTHING: Baker, Barber, Lab/Svc Ind Apparel, Washable, Men

Bespoke Apparel Inc .... G 212 382-0330
  New York *(G-9419)*
HC Contracting Inc .... D 212 643-9292
  New York *(G-10477)*

CLOTHING: Bathing Suits & Beachwear, Children's

Warnaco Group Inc .... E 212 287-8000
  New York *(G-12614)*

CLOTHING: Bathing Suits & Swimwear, Girls, Children & Infant

Baby Uv/Kids Uv Inc .... F 917 301-9020
  Stony Brook *(G-15787)*
Candlesticks Inc .... F 212 947-8900
  New York *(G-9566)*
In Mocean Group LLC .... D 212 944-0317
  New York *(G-10622)*
Oxygen Inc .... G 516 433-1144
  Hicksville *(G-6405)*

CLOTHING: Bathing Suits & Swimwear, Knit

IaMmaliamills LLC .... G 805 845-2137
  Brooklyn *(G-2091)*
Tomas Maier .... G 212 988-8686
  New York *(G-12384)*

CLOTHING: Bathrobes, Mens & Womens, From Purchased Materials

Natori Company Incorporated .... D 212 532-7796
  New York *(G-11378)*
Richard Leeds Intl Inc .... E 212 532-4546
  New York *(G-11888)*
Sketch Studio Trading Inc .... G 212 244-2875
  New York *(G-12114)*

CLOTHING: Beachwear, Knit

Beachbuttons LLC .... G 917 306-9369
  New York *(G-9387)*

CLOTHING: Belts

Barrera Jose & Maria Co Ltd .... E 212 239-1994
  New York *(G-9376)*
Coach Inc .... B 212 594-1850
  New York *(G-9714)*
Coach Stores Inc .... A 212 643-9727
  New York *(G-9717)*
Courtlandt Boot Jack Co Inc .... E 718 445-6200
  Flushing *(G-5242)*
Daniel M Friedman & Assoc Inc .... E 212 695-5545
  New York *(G-9859)*
Dynasty Belts Inc .... E 516 625-6280
  New Hyde Park *(G-8873)*
Gbg USA Inc .... D 646 839-7083
  New York *(G-10301)*
Gbg USA Inc .... E 212 615-3400
  New York *(G-10302)*
Nassau Suffolk Brd of Womens .... E 631 666-8835
  Bay Shore *(G-718)*
New Classic Inc .... F 718 609-1100
  Long Island City *(G-7855)*
P M Belts Usa Inc .... E 800 762-3580
  Brooklyn *(G-2413)*
Perry Ellis Menswear LLC .... E 212 221-7500
  New York *(G-11643)*
Queue Solutions LLC .... F 631 750-6440
  Bohemia *(G-1121)*
Randa Accessories Lea Gds LLC .... D 212 354-5100
  New York *(G-11825)*
Sandy Duftler Designs Ltd .... F 516 379-3084
  North Baldwin *(G-12925)*
Sh Leather Novelty Company .... G 718 387-7742
  Brooklyn *(G-2574)*
Trafalgar Company LLC .... E 212 768-8800
  New York *(G-12411)*
Universal Elliot Corp .... G 212 736-8877
  New York *(G-12491)*
Walco Leather Co Inc .... E 212 243-2244
  Bedford *(G-795)*
Xinya International Trading Co .... G 212 216-9681
  New York *(G-12704)*

CLOTHING: Blouses & Shirts, Girls' & Children's

Cheri Mon Baby LLC .... G 212 354-5511
  New York *(G-9640)*
Gw Acquisition LLC .... E 212 736-4848
  New York *(G-10430)*

CLOTHING: Blouses, Boys', From Purchased Materials

Jacks and Jokers 52 LLC .... G 917 740-2595
  New York *(G-10727)*
Nat Nast Company Inc .... G 212 575-1186
  New York *(G-11365)*

CLOTHING: Blouses, Women's & Girls'

18 Rocks LLC .... E 631 465-9990
  Melville *(G-8320)*
Accessries Direct Intl USA Inc .... F 646 448-8200
  New York *(G-9060)*
Apparel Group Ltd .... E 212 328-1200
  New York *(G-9229)*
August Silk Inc .... E 212 643-2400
  New York *(G-9315)*
August Silk Inc .... E 212 643-2400
  New York *(G-9316)*
Ben Wachter Associates Inc .... G 212 736-4064
  New York *(G-9401)*
Bernard Chaus Inc .... D 212 354-1280
  New York *(G-9411)*
Bernard Chaus Inc .... C 646 562-4700
  New York *(G-9412)*
Cyberlimit Inc .... F 212 840-9597
  New York *(G-9833)*
Cynthia Rowley Inc .... F 212 242-3803
  New York *(G-9835)*
Embassy Apparel Inc .... F 212 768-8330
  New York *(G-10071)*
Fetherston Design Group LLC .... E 212 643-7537
  New York *(G-10208)*
Feyem USA Inc .... G 845 363-6253
  Brewster *(G-1216)*

Employee Codes: A=Over 500 employees, B=251-500
C=101-250, D=51-100, E=20-50, F=10-19, G=5-9

2018 Harris
New York Manufacturers Directory

1159

CLOTHING: Blouses, Women's & Girls'

Fourtys Ny Inc .... F 212 382-0301
  New York *(G-10243)*
Gildan Apparel USA Inc .... D 212 476-0341
  New York *(G-10336)*
Glamourpuss Nyc LLC .... G 212 722-1370
  New York *(G-10346)*
Grey State Apparel LLC .... E 212 255-4216
  New York *(G-10403)*
Hansae Co Ltd .... G 212 354-6690
  New York *(G-10455)*
Ind Rev LLC .... F 212 221-4700
  New York *(G-10628)*
Kate Spade & Company .... B 212 354-4900
  New York *(G-10854)*
Krasner Group Inc .... G 212 268-4100
  New York *(G-10925)*
Ksk International Inc .... E 212 354-7770
  New York *(G-10930)*
Lea & Viola Inc .... G 646 918-6866
  New York *(G-10981)*
Liberty Apparel Company Inc .... E 718 625-4000
  New York *(G-11017)*
Lt2 LLC .... E 212 684-1510
  New York *(G-11086)*
M S B International Ltd .... F 212 302-5551
  New York *(G-11105)*
Maggy London International Ltd .... D 212 944-7199
  New York *(G-11129)*
Mega Sourcing Inc .... G 646 682-0304
  Merrick *(G-8424)*
Melwood Partners Inc .... G 516 307-8030
  Garden City *(G-5533)*
Mulitex Usa Inc .... G 212 398-0440
  New York *(G-11346)*
Nyc Knitwear Inc .... E 212 840-1313
  New York *(G-11495)*
Orchid Manufacturing Co Inc .... F 212 840-5700
  New York *(G-11536)*
Plugg LLC .... F 212 840-6655
  New York *(G-11700)*
Ramy Brook LLC .... E 212 744-2789
  New York *(G-11824)*
Raven New York LLC .... G 212 584-9690
  New York *(G-11829)*
Rio Apparel USA Inc .... G 212 869-9150
  New York *(G-11898)*
Robert Danes Danes Inc .... G 212 226-1351
  New York *(G-11910)*
Saad Collection Inc .... G 212 937-0341
  New York *(G-11966)*
Soho Apparel Ltd .... G 212 840-1109
  New York *(G-12146)*
Spencer AB Inc .... G 646 831-3728
  New York *(G-12184)*
Style Partners Inc .... F 212 904-1499
  New York *(G-12245)*
Sweet Apparel Inc .... G 212 221-3321
  New York *(G-12275)*
Tibana Finishing Inc .... E 718 417-5375
  Ridgewood *(G-14140)*
Triumph Apparel Corporation .... E 212 302-2606
  New York *(G-12429)*
Turn On Products Inc .... D 212 764-2121
  New York *(G-12446)*
Ursula of Switzerland Inc .... E 518 237-2580
  Waterford *(G-16645)*
Vanity Room Inc .... F 212 921-7154
  New York *(G-12526)*
Ventura Enterprise Co Inc .... E 212 391-0170
  New York *(G-12541)*
Westside Clothing Co Inc .... G 212 273-9898
  New York *(G-12646)*
Yeohlee Inc .... F 212 631-8099
  New York *(G-12712)*

CLOTHING: Blouses, Womens & Juniors, From Purchased Mtrls

79 Metro Ltd .... G 212 944-4030
  New York *(G-9025)*
Agi Brooks Production Co Inc .... F 212 268-1533
  New York *(G-9107)*
Alexander Wang Incorporated .... D 212 532-3103
  New York *(G-9133)*
Amerex Corporation .... G 212 221-3151
  New York *(G-9160)*
Anna Sui Corp .... E 212 768-1951
  New York *(G-9214)*
Brooke Leigh Ltd .... F 212 736-9098
  New York *(G-9520)*

Donna Karan Company LLC .... C 212 789-1500
  New York *(G-9952)*
Donna Karan Company LLC .... B 212 789-1500
  New York *(G-9953)*
Donna Karan International Inc .... F 212 789-1500
  New York *(G-9954)*
Donna Karan International Inc .... E 212 768-5800
  New York *(G-9955)*
Elie Tahari Ltd .... G 212 398-2622
  New York *(G-10054)*
Elie Tahari Ltd .... D 212 763-2000
  New York *(G-10056)*
Fuller Sportswear Co Inc .... G 516 773-3353
  Great Neck *(G-5830)*
Gabrielle Andra .... G 212 366-9624
  New York *(G-10287)*
Geoffrey Beene Inc .... E 212 371-5570
  New York *(G-10323)*
International Direct Group Inc .... E 212 921-9036
  New York *(G-10676)*
Jeanjer LLC .... A 212 944-1330
  New York *(G-10756)*
Land n Sea Inc .... D 212 703-2980
  New York *(G-10959)*
Necessary Objects Ltd .... E 212 334-9888
  Long Island City *(G-7854)*
Orchard Apparel Group Ltd .... G 212 268-8701
  New York *(G-11535)*
Paddy Lee Fashions Inc .... F 718 786-6020
  Long Island City *(G-7865)*
Pat & Rose Dress Inc .... D 212 279-1357
  New York *(G-11593)*
Permit Fashion Group Inc .... E 212 912-0988
  New York *(G-11639)*
Phillips-Van Heusen Europe .... F 212 381-3500
  New York *(G-11668)*
Pvh Corp .... D 212 381-3500
  New York *(G-11780)*
Pvh Corp .... F 212 719-2600
  New York *(G-11783)*
Rhoda Lee Inc .... D 212 840-5700
  New York *(G-11886)*
S & S Manufacturing Co Inc .... D 212 444-6000
  New York *(G-11961)*
Stitch & Couture Inc .... E 212 947-9204
  New York *(G-12229)*
Tahari ASL LLC .... B 212 763-2800
  New York *(G-12295)*
Turn On Products Inc .... F 212 764-4545
  New York *(G-12447)*

CLOTHING: Brassieres

Cupid Foundations Inc .... D 212 686-6224
  New York *(G-9824)*
East Coast Molders Inc .... C 516 240-6000
  Oceanside *(G-13098)*
Edith Lances Corp .... E 212 683-1990
  New York *(G-10034)*
New York Elegance Entps Inc .... F 212 685-3088
  New York *(G-11420)*
Valmont Inc .... F 212 685-1653
  New York *(G-12519)*
Wacoal America Inc .... C 718 794-1032
  Bronx *(G-1491)*

CLOTHING: Bridal Gowns

Anna B Inc .... G 516 680-6609
  Syosset *(G-15834)*
B S J Limited .... E 212 764-4600
  New York *(G-9344)*
B S J Limited .... G 212 221-8403
  New York *(G-9345)*
Bms Designs Inc .... E 718 828-5792
  Bronx *(G-1284)*
Brides Inc .... G 718 435-6092
  Brooklyn *(G-1713)*
Lovely Bride LLC .... G 212 924-2050
  New York *(G-11082)*
Shane Tex Inc .... F 516 486-7522
  Hempstead *(G-6309)*
Stitch & Couture Inc .... E 212 947-9204
  New York *(G-12229)*
Thread LLC .... G 212 414-8844
  New York *(G-12351)*
Vera Wang Group LLC .... C 212 575-6400
  New York *(G-12542)*

CLOTHING: Burial

Rose Solomon Co .... E 718 855-1788
  Brooklyn *(G-2527)*

CLOTHING: Capes & Jackets, Women's & Misses'

Uniqlo USA LLC .... F 877 486-4756
  New York *(G-12479)*

CLOTHING: Capes, Exc Fur/Rubber, Womens, Misses & Juniors

Adrienne Landau Designs Inc .... F 212 695-8362
  New York *(G-9080)*

CLOTHING: Chemises, Camisoles/Teddies, Women, Misses/Junior

Mrt Textile Inc .... G 800 674-1073
  New York *(G-11341)*

CLOTHING: Children & Infants'

Andy & Evan Industries Inc .... G 212 967-7908
  New York *(G-9204)*
Carters Inc .... G 585 387-9043
  Rochester *(G-14281)*
Carters Inc .... G 315 637-3128
  Fayetteville *(G-5171)*
Carters Inc .... G 631 549-6781
  Huntington Station *(G-6737)*
Consolidated Childrens AP Inc .... G 212 239-8615
  New York *(G-9764)*
Gce International Inc .... F 212 868-0500
  New York *(G-10305)*
Grand Knitting Mills Inc .... E 631 226-5000
  Amityville *(G-289)*
Great Universal Corp .... F 917 302-0065
  New York *(G-10400)*
Haddad Bros Inc .... E 718 377-7505
  Brooklyn *(G-2060)*
Haddad Bros Inc .... F 212 563-2117
  New York *(G-10437)*
JM Originals Inc .... C 845 647-3003
  Ellenville *(G-4648)*
Manchu New York Inc .... G 212 921-5050
  New York *(G-11150)*
Michael Stuart Inc .... E 718 821-0704
  Brooklyn *(G-2314)*
S & C Bridals LLC .... F 212 789-7000
  New York *(G-11960)*
Silly Phillie Creations Inc .... E 718 492-6300
  Brooklyn *(G-2583)*
Skip Hop Inc .... E 646 902-9874
  New York *(G-12118)*
Skip Hop Holdings Inc .... G 212 868-9850
  New York *(G-12119)*
Sports Products America LLC .... E 212 594-5511
  New York *(G-12192)*
Thats My Girl Inc .... G 212 695-0020
  Brooklyn *(G-2675)*

CLOTHING: Children's, Girls'

Aerobic Wear Inc .... G 631 673-1830
  Huntington Station *(G-6730)*
Amerimade Coat Inc .... G 212 216-0925
  New York *(G-9184)*
Devil Dog Manufacturing Co Inc .... G 845 647-4411
  Ellenville *(G-4647)*
Domani Fashions Corp .... G 718 797-0505
  Brooklyn *(G-1872)*
Franco Apparel Group Inc .... D 212 967-7272
  New York *(G-10249)*
Gerson & Gerson Inc .... D 212 244-6775
  New York *(G-10330)*
Gw Acquisition LLC .... E 212 736-4848
  New York *(G-10430)*
Haddad Bros Inc .... E 718 377-7505
  Brooklyn *(G-2060)*
Isfel Co Inc .... G 212 736-6216
  New York *(G-10708)*
Jeanjer LLC .... A 212 944-1330
  New York *(G-10756)*
JM Originals Inc .... C 845 647-3003
  Ellenville *(G-4648)*
Jomat New York Inc .... E 718 369-7641
  Brooklyn *(G-2145)*
Kahn-Lucas-Lancaster Inc .... D 212 239-2407
  New York *(G-10837)*

PRODUCT SECTION

CLOTHING: Dresses

Land n Sea Inc .... D 212 703-2980
  New York *(G-10959)*
Liberty Apparel Company Inc .... E 718 625-4000
  New York *(G-11017)*
Lollytogs Ltd .... D 212 502-6000
  New York *(G-11053)*
M Hidary & Co Inc .... D 212 736-6540
  New York *(G-11102)*
Michael Stuart Inc .... E 718 821-0704
  Brooklyn *(G-2314)*
Miltons of New York Inc .... G 212 997-3359
  New York *(G-11298)*
Outerstuff LLC .... E 212 594-9700
  New York *(G-11548)*
Pink Crush LLC .... G 718 788-6978
  New York *(G-11686)*
Pti-Pacific Inc .... G 212 414-8495
  New York *(G-11765)*
Rogers Group Inc .... E 212 643-9292
  New York *(G-11928)*
S Rothschild & Co Inc .... C 212 354-8550
  New York *(G-11964)*
Sch Dpx Corporation .... G 917 405-5377
  New York *(G-12003)*
Silly Phillie Creations Inc .... E 718 492-6300
  Brooklyn *(G-2583)*
Swatfame Inc .... G 212 944-8022
  New York *(G-12273)*
Therese The Childrens Collectn .... G 518 346-2315
  Schenectady *(G-15328)*
Yigal-Azrouel Inc .... E 212 302-1194
  New York *(G-12713)*
Z-Ply Corp .... E 212 398-7011
  New York *(G-12721)*
ZIC Sportswear Inc .... E 718 361-9022
  Long Island City *(G-7962)*

CLOTHING: Clergy Vestments

Davis .... G 716 833-4678
  Buffalo *(G-2922)*
Roth Clothing Co Inc .... G 718 384-4927
  Brooklyn *(G-2528)*
Warner .... G 716 446-0663
  Buffalo *(G-3274)*

CLOTHING: Coats & Jackets, Leather & Sheep-Lined

Andrew M Schwartz LLC .... G 212 391-7070
  New York *(G-9203)*
Cockpit Usa Inc .... F 212 575-1616
  New York *(G-9719)*
Cockpit Usa Inc .... F 212 575-1616
  New York *(G-9720)*
Excelled Sheepskin & Lea Coat .... F 212 594-5843
  New York *(G-10157)*
Gloria Apparel Inc .... F 212 947-0869
  New York *(G-10364)*
J Percy For Mrvin Rchards Ltd .... E 212 944-5300
  New York *(G-10721)*
Lost Worlds Inc .... G 212 923-3423
  New York *(G-11073)*

CLOTHING: Coats & Suits, Men's & Boys'

Adrian Jules Ltd .... D 585 342-5886
  Rochester *(G-14190)*
Advance Apparel Intl Inc .... G 212 944-0984
  New York *(G-9083)*
Allytex LLC .... G 518 376-7539
  Ballston Spa *(G-590)*
Amerimade Coat Inc .... G 212 216-0925
  New York *(G-9184)*
Check Group LLC .... D 212 221-4700
  New York *(G-9637)*
Christian Casey LLC .... E 212 500-2200
  New York *(G-9660)*
Christian Casey LLC .... E 212 500-2200
  New York *(G-9661)*
Concorde Apparel Company LLC .... G 212 307-7848
  New York *(G-9756)*
Excelled Sheepskin & Lea Coat .... F 212 594-5843
  New York *(G-10157)*
G-III Apparel Group Ltd .... B 212 403-0500
  New York *(G-10282)*
Giliberto Designs Inc .... E 212 695-0216
  New York *(G-10337)*
Great 4 Image Inc .... E 518 424-2058
  Rensselaer *(G-14058)*
Hana Sportswear Inc .... G 315 639-6332
  Dexter *(G-4308)*
Hickey Freeman Tailored CL Inc .... B 585 467-7240
  Rochester *(G-14453)*
Hugo Boss Usa Inc .... D 212 940-0600
  New York *(G-10574)*
J & X Production Inc .... F 718 200-1228
  New York *(G-10716)*
L F Fashion Orient Intl Co Ltd .... G 917 667-3398
  New York *(G-10939)*
M Hidary & Co Inc .... D 212 736-6540
  New York *(G-11102)*
Manchu New York Inc .... G 212 921-5050
  New York *(G-11150)*
Mv Corp Inc .... G 631 273-8020
  Bay Shore *(G-717)*
Opposuits USA Inc .... E 917 438-8878
  New York *(G-11530)*
Pat & Rose Dress Inc .... D 212 279-1357
  New York *(G-11593)*
Proper Cloth LLC .... G 646 964-4221
  New York *(G-11758)*
Public School .... G 212 302-1108
  New York *(G-11768)*
Therese The Childrens Collectn .... G 518 346-2315
  Schenectady *(G-15328)*
Vinci Enterprise Corp .... F 212 768-7888
  New York *(G-12570)*
Woodmere Fabrics Inc .... G 212 695-0144
  New York *(G-12684)*
Wp Lavori USA Inc .... G 212 244-6074
  New York *(G-12694)*
Yong Ji Productions Inc .... E 917 559-4616
  Corona *(G-4032)*

CLOTHING: Coats, Leatherette, Oiled Fabric, Etc, Mens & Boys

House Pearl Fashions (us) Ltd .... F 212 840-3183
  New York *(G-10564)*

CLOTHING: Coats, Tailored, Mens/Boys, From Purchased Mtls

Blueduck Trading Ltd .... G 212 268-3122
  New York *(G-9475)*

CLOTHING: Cold Weather Knit Outerwear, Including Ski Wear

Kc Collections LLC .... G 212 302-4412
  New York *(G-10865)*

CLOTHING: Corset Access, Clasps & Stays

Higgins Supply Company Inc .... D 607 836-6474
  Mc Graw *(G-8253)*

CLOTHING: Costumes

Costume Culture By Franco LLC .... G 718 821-7100
  Glendale *(G-5664)*
Creative Costume Co .... G 212 564-5552
  Liverpool *(G-7542)*
Cygnet Studio Inc .... F 646 450-4550
  New York *(G-9834)*
Eric Winterling Inc .... E 212 629-7686
  New York *(G-10108)*
John Kristiansen New York Inc .... F 212 388-1097
  New York *(G-10789)*
Kidz Concepts LLC .... D 212 398-1110
  New York *(G-10882)*
Kiton Building Corp .... E 212 486-3224
  New York *(G-10893)*
Koon Enterprises LLC .... G 718 886-3163
  Fresh Meadows *(G-5456)*
Moresca Clothing and Costume .... F 845 331-6012
  Ulster Park *(G-16309)*
Prolink Industries Inc .... F 212 354-5690
  New York *(G-11752)*
Rubies Costume Company Inc .... B 718 846-1008
  Richmond Hill *(G-14093)*
Rubies Costume Company Inc .... D 631 777-3300
  Bay Shore *(G-736)*
Rubies Costume Company Inc .... C 718 441-0834
  Richmond Hill *(G-14094)*
Rubies Costume Company Inc .... C 631 951-3688
  Bay Shore *(G-737)*
Rubies Costume Company Inc .... E 516 326-1500
  Melville *(G-8382)*
Rubies Costume Company Inc .... C 718 846-1008
  Richmond Hill *(G-14095)*
South Central Boyz .... G 718 496-7270
  Brooklyn *(G-2611)*

CLOTHING: Diaper Covers, Waterproof, From Purchased Material

Hercules Group Inc .... E 212 813-8000
  Port Washington *(G-13842)*

CLOTHING: Disposable

A Lunt Design Inc .... F 716 662-0781
  Orchard Park *(G-13272)*
Cortland Industries Inc .... F 212 575-2710
  New York *(G-9788)*
Dvf Studio LLC .... D 212 741-6607
  New York *(G-9993)*
Dvf Studio LLC .... G 646 576-8009
  New York *(G-9994)*
HB Athletic Inc .... F 914 560-8422
  New Rochelle *(G-8955)*
Hpk Industries LLC .... F 315 724-0196
  Utica *(G-16362)*
Lakeland Industries Inc .... C 631 981-9700
  Ronkonkoma *(G-14956)*
Rainforest Apparel LLC .... G 212 840-0880
  New York *(G-11817)*

CLOTHING: Down-Filled, Men's & Boys'

Nyc Idol Apparel Inc .... G 212 997-9797
  New York *(G-11494)*

CLOTHING: Dresses

18 Rocks LLC .... E 631 465-9990
  Melville *(G-8320)*
A & M Rosenthal Entps Inc .... E 646 638-9600
  New York *(G-9028)*
Agi Brooks Production Co Inc .... F 212 268-1533
  New York *(G-9107)*
Allison Che Fashion Inc .... E 212 391-1433
  New York *(G-9141)*
Amj DOT LLC .... G 718 775-3288
  Brooklyn *(G-1610)*
Anna Sui Corp .... E 212 768-1951
  New York *(G-9214)*
Arteast LLC .... G 212 965-8787
  New York *(G-9267)*
August Silk Inc .... E 212 643-2400
  New York *(G-9315)*
August Silk Inc .... E 212 643-2400
  New York *(G-9316)*
Cachet Industries Inc .... E 212 944-2188
  New York *(G-9546)*
Christian Siriano Holdings LLC .... E 212 695-5494
  New York *(G-9663)*
Csco LLC .... E 212 221-5100
  New York *(G-9819)*
CTS LLC .... E 212 278-0058
  New York *(G-9820)*
Cynthia Rowley Inc .... F 212 242-3803
  New York *(G-9835)*
Dalma Dress Mfg Co Inc .... E 212 391-8296
  Greenvale *(G-5898)*
Damianou Sportswear Inc .... D 718 204-5600
  Woodside *(G-17342)*
Dave & Johnny Ltd .... E 212 302-9050
  New York *(G-9871)*
Donna Karan Company LLC .... C 212 789-1500
  New York *(G-9952)*
Donna Karan Company LLC .... C 716 297-0752
  Niagara Falls *(G-12833)*
Donna Karan Company LLC .... B 212 789-1500
  New York *(G-9953)*
Donna Karan International Inc .... F 212 789-1500
  New York *(G-9954)*
Donna Karan International Inc .... E 212 768-5800
  New York *(G-9955)*
Elana Laderos Ltd .... F 212 764-0840
  New York *(G-10047)*
Faviana International Inc .... E 212 594-4422
  New York *(G-10200)*
Four Seasons Fashion Mfg Inc .... E 212 947-6820
  New York *(G-10242)*
G-III Apparel Group Ltd .... E 212 403-0500
  New York *(G-10283)*
Geoffrey Beene Inc .... E 212 371-5570
  New York *(G-10323)*
Haddad Bros Inc .... E 718 377-5505
  Brooklyn *(G-2060)*

Employee Codes: A=Over 500 employees, B=251-500
C=101-250, D=51-100, E=20-50, F=10-19, G=5-9

2018 Harris
New York Manufacturers Directory

CLOTHING: Dresses

Halmode Apparel Inc .... A 212 819-9114
  New York *(G-10442)*
Haute By Blair Stanley LLC .... G 212 557-7868
  New York *(G-10472)*
I S C A Corp .... F 212 719-5123
  New York *(G-10587)*
Icer Scrubs LLC .... F 212 221-4700
  New York *(G-10597)*
Infinity Sourcing Services LLC .... G 212 868-2900
  New York *(G-10636)*
J R Nites .... G 212 354-9670
  New York *(G-10723)*
Jiranimo Industries Ltd .... F 212 921-5106
  New York *(G-10776)*
Jon Teri Sports Inc .... E 212 398-0657
  New York *(G-10796)*
Jovani Fashion Ltd .... E 212 279-0222
  New York *(G-10810)*
Judys Group Inc .... E 212 921-0515
  New York *(G-10815)*
Jump Design Group Inc .... C 212 869-3300
  New York *(G-10820)*
Kasper Group LLC .... C 212 354-4311
  New York *(G-10853)*
Kelly Grace Corp .... D 212 704-9603
  New York *(G-10870)*
Krasner Group Inc .... G 212 268-4100
  New York *(G-10925)*
L F Fashion Orient Intl Co Ltd .... G 917 667-3398
  New York *(G-10939)*
Lm Mignon LLC .... F 212 730-9221
  New York *(G-11044)*
Lmr Group Inc .... G 212 730-9221
  New York *(G-11045)*
Lou Sally Fashions Corp .... E 212 354-9670
  New York *(G-11075)*
Lou Sally Fashions Corp .... E 212 354-1283
  New York *(G-11076)*
Melwood Partners Inc .... G 516 307-8030
  Garden City *(G-5533)*
Milliore Fashion Inc .... G 212 302-0001
  New York *(G-11296)*
Necessary Objects Ltd .... E 212 334-9888
  Long Island City *(G-7854)*
Pat & Rose Dress Inc .... D 212 279-1357
  New York *(G-11593)*
Patra Ltd .... F 212 764-6575
  New York *(G-11596)*
Phoebe Company LLC .... D 212 302-5556
  New York *(G-11669)*
Plugg LLC .... F 212 840-6655
  New York *(G-11700)*
Post Modern Productions Inc .... G 212 719-3916
  New York *(G-11711)*
Product Development Intl LLC .... G 212 279-6170
  New York *(G-11748)*
Quality Patterns Inc .... D 212 704-0355
  New York *(G-11794)*
R & M Richards Inc .... D 212 921-8820
  New York *(G-11808)*
Ralph Lauren Corporation .... F 212 221-7751
  New York *(G-11822)*
Raven New York LLC .... G 212 584-9690
  New York *(G-11829)*
Rogan LLC .... G 212 680-1407
  New York *(G-11925)*
Rogan LLC .... E 646 496-9339
  New York *(G-11926)*
Ronni Nicole Group LLC .... E 212 764-1000
  New York *(G-11933)*
Sg Nyc LLC .... E 310 210-1837
  New York *(G-12053)*
Skinz Inc .... E 516 593-3139
  Lynbrook *(G-7988)*
Spencer AB Inc .... G 646 831-3728
  New York *(G-12184)*
SSG Fashions Ltd .... G 212 221-0933
  New York *(G-12203)*
Studio Krp LLC .... F 310 589-5777
  New York *(G-12242)*
Style Partners Inc .... F 212 904-1499
  New York *(G-12245)*
Tabrisse Collections Inc .... F 212 921-1014
  New York *(G-12293)*
Tahari ASL LLC .... B 212 763-2800
  New York *(G-12295)*
Texport Fabrics Corp .... F 212 226-6066
  New York *(G-12326)*
Therese The Childrens Collectn .... G 518 346-2315
  Schenectady *(G-15328)*
Tom & Linda Platt Inc .... F 212 221-7208
  New York *(G-12379)*
Turn On Products Inc .... F 212 764-4545
  New York *(G-12447)*
Vanity Room Inc .... F 212 921-7154
  New York *(G-12526)*
Wear Abouts Apparel Inc .... F 212 827-0888
  New York *(G-12630)*
Worth Collection Ltd .... E 212 268-0312
  New York *(G-12691)*
Yeohlee Inc .... F 212 631-8099
  New York *(G-12712)*

CLOTHING: Dresses & Skirts

Betsy & Adam Ltd .... E 212 302-3750
  New York *(G-9425)*

CLOTHING: Dresses, Knit

Summit Apparel Inc .... E 631 213-8299
  Hauppauge *(G-6226)*
Winter Water Factory .... G 646 387-3247
  Brooklyn *(G-2777)*

CLOTHING: Dressing Gowns, Mens/Womens, From Purchased Matls

Jisan Trading Corporation .... E 212 244-1269
  New York *(G-10777)*
Mata Fashions LLC .... G 917 716-7894
  New York *(G-11199)*

CLOTHING: Foundation Garments, Women's

Deunall Corporation .... C 516 667-8875
  Levittown *(G-7449)*
E P Sewing Pleating Inc .... E 212 967-2575
  New York *(G-10003)*
Rago Foundations LLC .... D 718 728-8436
  Astoria *(G-453)*

CLOTHING: Furs

Anastasia Furs International .... E 212 868-9241
  New York *(G-9198)*
Avante .... G 516 782-4888
  Great Neck *(G-5810)*
B Smith Furs Inc .... F 212 967-5290
  New York *(G-9346)*
Dennis Basso Couture Inc .... F 212 794-4500
  New York *(G-9899)*
Georgy Creative Fashions Inc .... G 212 279-4885
  New York *(G-10328)*
Miller & Berkowitz Ltd .... F 212 244-5459
  New York *(G-11294)*
Sekas International Ltd .... F 212 629-6095
  New York *(G-12040)*
Stefan Furs Inc .... F 212 594-2788
  New York *(G-12214)*
Tom Moriber Furs Inc .... F 212 244-2180
  New York *(G-12383)*

CLOTHING: Garments, Indl, Men's & Boys

Beardslee Realty .... G 516 747-5557
  Mineola *(G-8530)*
Classic Designer Workshop Inc .... G 212 730-8480
  New York *(G-9690)*
Kse Sportsman Media Inc .... D 212 852-6600
  New York *(G-10929)*
Stealth Inc .... F 718 252-7900
  Brooklyn *(G-2623)*

CLOTHING: Girdles & Other Foundation Garments, Knit

Maidenform LLC .... F 201 436-9200
  New York *(G-11137)*

CLOTHING: Girdles & Panty Girdles

Burlen Corp .... F 212 684-0052
  New York *(G-9532)*

CLOTHING: Gloves, Knit, Exc Dress & Semidress

Hawkins Fabrics Inc .... E 518 773-9550
  Gloversville *(G-5729)*

CLOTHING: Gowns & Dresses, Wedding

Alvina Vlenta Couture Collectn .... F 212 921-7058
  New York *(G-9156)*
Alvina Vlenta Couture Collectn .... G 212 921-7058
  New York *(G-9157)*
Arcangel Inc .... G 347 771-0789
  New York *(G-9244)*
Bernard Chaus Inc .... D 212 354-1280
  New York *(G-9411)*
Birnbaum & Bullock Ltd .... G 212 242-2914
  New York *(G-9455)*
Christos Inc .... E 212 921-0025
  New York *(G-9666)*
Couture Inc .... G 212 921-1166
  New York *(G-9798)*
Diamond Bridal Collection Ltd .... E 212 302-0210
  New York *(G-9923)*
Everlasting Memories .... G 716 833-1111
  Blasdell *(G-956)*
Jlm Couture Inc .... D 212 921-7058
  New York *(G-10780)*
Paris Wedding Center Corp .... F 347 368-4085
  Flushing *(G-5286)*
Paris Wedding Center Corp .... E 212 267-8088
  New York *(G-11586)*
Parsley Apparel Corp .... E 631 981-7181
  Ronkonkoma *(G-14989)*
Paula Varsalona Ltd .... F 212 570-9100
  New York *(G-11601)*

CLOTHING: Gowns, Formal

Amsale Aberra LLC .... E 212 695-5936
  New York *(G-9191)*
Bari-Jay Fashions Inc .... E 212 921-1551
  New York *(G-9373)*
Crisada Inc .... G 718 729-9730
  Long Island City *(G-7735)*
D J Night Ltd .... E 212 302-9050
  New York *(G-9839)*
Elizabeth Fillmore LLC .... G 212 647-0863
  New York *(G-10063)*
Lily & Taylor Inc .... F 212 564-5459
  New York *(G-11028)*
Patra Ltd .... F 212 764-6575
  New York *(G-11595)*
Patra Ltd .... E 212 764-6575
  New York *(G-11597)*
Pronovias USA Inc .... E 212 897-6393
  New York *(G-11755)*
Ursula of Switzerland Inc .... E 518 237-2580
  Waterford *(G-16645)*

CLOTHING: Hats & Caps, Leather

J Lowy Co .... G 718 338-7324
  Brooklyn *(G-2123)*

CLOTHING: Hats & Caps, NEC

A-1 Skull Cap Corp .... E 718 633-9333
  Brooklyn *(G-1540)*
Athletic Cap Co Inc .... E 718 398-1300
  Staten Island *(G-15661)*
Genesco Inc .... G 585 227-3080
  Rochester *(G-14414)*
Lids Corporation .... E 718 338-7790
  Brooklyn *(G-2219)*
Paletot Ltd .... F 212 268-3774
  New York *(G-11569)*

CLOTHING: Hats & Caps, Uniform

Bonk Sam Uniforms Civilian Cap .... E 718 585-0665
  Bronx *(G-1285)*
Hankin Brothers Cap Co .... F 716 892-8840
  Buffalo *(G-3004)*
Kays Caps Inc .... G 518 273-6079
  Troy *(G-16242)*
Kingform Cap Company Inc .... D 516 822-2501
  Hicksville *(G-6386)*
New ERA Cap Co Inc .... B 716 604-9000
  Buffalo *(G-3106)*
New ERA Cap Co Inc .... C 716 604-9000
  Buffalo *(G-3107)*
New ERA Cap Co Inc .... F 716 549-0445
  Derby *(G-4307)*
Tanen Cap Co .... F 212 254-7100
  Brooklyn *(G-2667)*

CLOTHING: Hats & Headwear, Knit

Gce International Inc ....D...... 212 704-4800
  New York *(G-10304)*
Lids Corporation ....G...... 518 459-7060
  Albany *(G-98)*

CLOTHING: Hosiery, Men's & Boys'

Etc Hosiery & Underwear Ltd ....G...... 212 947-5151
  New York *(G-10130)*
Gina Group LLC ....E...... 212 947-2445
  New York *(G-10339)*
Haddad Hosiery LLC ....G...... 212 251-0022
  New York *(G-10438)*
High Point Design LLC ....F...... 212 354-2400
  New York *(G-10517)*
Lr Acquisition LLC ....F...... 212 301-8765
  New York *(G-11083)*
New Hampton Creations Inc ....G...... 212 244-7474
  New York *(G-11410)*
Richard Edelson ....G...... 914 428-7573
  Hartsdale *(G-6018)*
Spartan Brands Inc ....F...... 212 340-0320
  New York *(G-12175)*
You and ME Legwear LLC ....F...... 212 279-9292
  New York *(G-12718)*

CLOTHING: Hosiery, Pantyhose & Knee Length, Sheer

Classic Hosiery Inc ....E...... 845 342-6661
  Middletown *(G-8465)*
Ellis Products Corp ....G...... 516 791-3732
  Valley Stream *(G-16431)*
Gina Group LLC ....E...... 212 947-2445
  New York *(G-10339)*
Hot Sox Company Incorporated ....E...... 212 957-2000
  New York *(G-10557)*

CLOTHING: Hospital, Men's

Adar Medical Uniform LLC ....F...... 718 935-1197
  Brooklyn *(G-1559)*
Eighteen Liana Trading Inc ....E...... 718 369-4247
  New York *(G-10043)*
Norcorp Inc ....E...... 914 666-1310
  Mount Kisco *(G-8680)*

CLOTHING: Housedresses

Millennium Productions Inc ....F...... 212 944-6203
  New York *(G-11293)*

CLOTHING: Jackets & Vests, Exc Fur & Leather, Women's

Amerimade Coat Inc ....G...... 212 216-0925
  New York *(G-9184)*
Donna Karan International Inc ......F...... 212 789-1500
  New York *(G-9954)*
Donna Karan International Inc ......G...... 212 768-5800
  New York *(G-9955)*
Standard Manufacturing Co Inc ....D...... 518 235-2200
  Troy *(G-16280)*
Tiger J LLC ....E...... 212 465-9300
  New York *(G-12358)*

CLOTHING: Jackets, Knit

Freedom Rains Inc ....G...... 646 710-4512
  New York *(G-10255)*

CLOTHING: Jeans, Men's & Boys'

Guess Inc ....E...... 845 928-3930
  Central Valley *(G-3552)*
Guess Inc ....E...... 315 539-5634
  Waterloo *(G-16650)*
Guess Inc ....E...... 212 286-9856
  New York *(G-10422)*
Guess Inc ....E...... 716 298-3561
  Niagara Falls *(G-12849)*
Messex Group Inc ....G...... 646 229-2582
  New York *(G-11266)*
One Jeanswear Group Inc ....B...... 212 835-3500
  New York *(G-11520)*

CLOTHING: Knit Underwear & Nightwear

In Toon Amkor Fashions Inc ....E...... 718 937-4546
  Long Island City *(G-7793)*

Jockey International Inc ....E...... 212 840-4900
  New York *(G-10785)*
Maidenform LLC ....F...... 201 436-9200
  New York *(G-11137)*
Native Textiles Inc ....G...... 212 951-5100
  New York *(G-11377)*
Spartan Brands Inc ....F...... 212 340-0320
  New York *(G-12175)*

CLOTHING: Leather

Avanti U S A Ltd ....F...... 716 695-5800
  Tonawanda *(G-16162)*
Dada Group US Inc ....G...... 631 888-0818
  Bayside *(G-764)*
G-III Apparel Group Ltd ....B...... 212 403-0500
  New York *(G-10282)*
Georgy Creative Fashions Inc ......G...... 212 279-4885
  New York *(G-10328)*
Louis Schwartz ....G...... 845 356-6624
  Spring Valley *(G-15615)*
Studio One Leather Design Inc ....F...... 212 760-1701
  New York *(G-12243)*

CLOTHING: Leather & sheep-lined clothing

Cockpit Usa Inc ....F...... 908 558-9704
  New York *(G-9721)*
G-III Leather Fashions Inc ....E...... 212 403-0500
  New York *(G-10284)*

CLOTHING: Leg Warmers

Z Best Printing Inc ....F...... 631 595-1400
  Deer Park *(G-4255)*

CLOTHING: Maternity

Medi-Tech International Corp ....E...... 800 333-0109
  Brooklyn *(G-2295)*
Zoomers Inc ....E...... 718 369-2656
  Brooklyn *(G-2796)*

CLOTHING: Men's & boy's clothing, nec

Apogee Retail NY ....G...... 516 731-1727
  Levittown *(G-7445)*
By Robert James ....E...... 212 253-2121
  New York *(G-9538)*
Eon Collections ....E...... 212 695-1263
  New York *(G-10101)*
Nevaeh Jeans Company ....G...... 845 641-4255
  New York *(G-11400)*
Piaget ....F...... 212 355-6444
  New York *(G-11675)*

CLOTHING: Men's & boy's underwear & nightwear

Apparel Partnership Group LLC ....G...... 212 302-7722
  New York *(G-9230)*
Candlesticks Inc ....F...... 212 947-8900
  New York *(G-9566)*
Christian Casey LLC ....E...... 212 500-2200
  New York *(G-9660)*
Christian Casey LLC ....E...... 212 500-2200
  New York *(G-9661)*
Revolutionwear Inc ....G...... 617 669-9191
  New York *(G-11881)*
Solo Licensing Corp ....G...... 212 244-5505
  New York *(G-12150)*
Tommy John Inc ....E...... 800 708-3490
  New York *(G-12387)*
Waterbury Garment LLC ....E...... 212 725-1500
  New York *(G-12625)*

CLOTHING: Mens & Boys Jackets, Sport, Suede, Leatherette

Broadway Knitting Mills Inc ....G...... 716 692-4421
  North Tonawanda *(G-12979)*
G-III Apparel Group Ltd ....B...... 212 403-0500
  New York *(G-10282)*
Standard Manufacturing Co Inc ....D...... 518 235-2200
  Troy *(G-16280)*

CLOTHING: Millinery

Albrizio Inc ....G...... 212 719-5290
  Brooklyn *(G-1576)*
Lenore Marshall Inc ....G...... 212 947-5945
  New York *(G-11002)*

CLOTHING: Outerwear, Knit

Lloyds Fashions Inc ....D...... 631 435-3353
  Brentwood *(G-1187)*

CLOTHING: Neckties, Knit

Mongru Neckwear Inc ....E...... 718 706-0406
  Long Island City *(G-7847)*

CLOTHING: Neckwear

Emunas Sales Inc ....F...... 718 621-3138
  Brooklyn *(G-1928)*
Fogel Neckwear Corp ....D...... 212 686-7673
  New York *(G-10236)*
JS Blank & Co Inc ....E...... 212 689-4835
  New York *(G-10813)*
MANE Enterprises Inc ....D...... 718 472-4955
  Long Island City *(G-7830)*
Mongru Neckwear Inc ....E...... 718 706-0406
  Long Island City *(G-7847)*
Roffe Accessories Inc ....F...... 212 213-1440
  New York *(G-11924)*
S Broome and Co Inc ....D...... 718 663-6800
  Long Island City *(G-7899)*
Selini Neckwear Inc ....G...... 212 268-5488
  New York *(G-12044)*
Tie View Neckwear Co Inc ....G...... 718 853-4156
  Brooklyn *(G-2680)*
Valenti Neckwear Co Inc ....G...... 914 969-0700
  Yonkers *(G-17511)*
W B Bow Tie Corp ....F...... 212 683-6130
  New York *(G-12601)*
Warnaco Inc ....B...... 212 287-8000
  New York *(G-12615)*
Wetherall Contracting NY Inc ......G...... 718 894-7011
  Middle Village *(G-8451)*

CLOTHING: Outerwear, Knit

Alpha Knitting Mills Inc ....F...... 718 628-6300
  Brooklyn *(G-1591)*
Andrea Strongwater ....G...... 212 873-0905
  New York *(G-9202)*
Asian Global Trading Corp ....G...... 718 786-0998
  Long Island City *(G-7704)*
Binghamton Knitting Co Inc ....E...... 607 722-6941
  Binghamton *(G-889)*
Dressy Tessy Inc ....G...... 212 869-0750
  New York *(G-9978)*
E I Du Pont De Nemours & Co ....E...... 716 876-4420
  Buffalo *(G-2938)*
Elegant Headwear Co Inc ....G...... 212 695-8520
  New York *(G-10051)*
Emerald Holdings Inc ....G...... 718 797-4404
  Brooklyn *(G-1921)*
Fashion Avenue Knits Inc ....F...... 718 456-9000
  New York *(G-10196)*
Fast-Trac Entertainment Ltd ....G...... 888 758-8886
  New York *(G-10199)*
Gabani Inc ....G...... 631 283-4930
  Southampton *(G-15567)*
GAME Sportswear Ltd ....E...... 914 962-1701
  Yorktown Heights *(G-17527)*
Gildan Apparel USA Inc ....D...... 212 476-0341
  New York *(G-10336)*
Hamil America Inc ....F...... 212 244-2645
  New York *(G-10444)*
Hania By Anya Cole LLC ....G...... 212 302-3550
  New York *(G-10453)*
Lynch Knitting Mills Inc ....E...... 718 821-3436
  Brooklyn *(G-2243)*
Machinit Inc ....G...... 631 454-9297
  Farmingdale *(G-5048)*
Mars Fashions Inc ....E...... 718 402-2200
  Bronx *(G-1391)*
Mdj Sales Associates Inc ....G...... 914 420-5897
  Mamaroneck *(G-8072)*
Metro Knitting Corp ....F...... 718 894-0765
  Middle Village *(G-8449)*
Native Textiles Inc ....G...... 212 951-5100
  New York *(G-11377)*
North Star Knitting Mills Inc ....G...... 718 894-4848
  Glendale *(G-5675)*
S & V Knits Inc ....E...... 631 752-1595
  Farmingdale *(G-5116)*
T & R Knitting Mills Inc ....F...... 212 840-8665
  New York *(G-12287)*

Employee Codes: A=Over 500 employees, B=251-500
C=101-250, D=51-100, E=20-50, F=10-19, G=5-9

CLOTHING: Outerwear, Lthr, Wool/Down-Filled, Men, Youth/Boy

Brigantine Inc ....G 212 354-8550
New York *(G-9511)*
Herman Kay Company Ltd ....C 212 239-2025
New York *(G-10505)*
I Spiewak & Sons Inc ....E 212 695-1620
New York *(G-10588)*
Maiyet Inc ....G 212 343-9999
New York *(G-11139)*
Vf Outdoor Inc ....E 718 698-6215
Staten Island *(G-15775)*
Vf Outdoor LLC ....E 845 928-4900
Central Valley *(G-3556)*

CLOTHING: Outerwear, Women's & Misses' NEC

525 America LLC ....G 212 921-5688
New York *(G-9023)*
5th & Ocean Clothing Inc ....C 716 604-9000
Buffalo *(G-2804)*
6th Avenue Showcase Inc ....G 212 382-0400
New York *(G-9024)*
A & B Finishing Inc ....E 718 522-4702
Brooklyn *(G-1524)*
Accessory Street LLC ....F 212 686-8990
New York *(G-9059)*
Alleson of Rochester Inc ....D 800 641-0041
Rochester *(G-14202)*
Ally Nyc Corp ....G 212 447-7277
New York *(G-9145)*
Angel-Made In Heaven Inc ....G 718 832-4778
Brooklyn *(G-1611)*
Aura International Mfg Inc ....G 212 719-1418
New York *(G-9317)*
Bagznyc Corp ....F 212 643-8202
New York *(G-9358)*
Bank-Miller Co Inc ....E 914 227-9357
Pelham *(G-13514)*
Big Bang Clothing Inc ....G 212 221-0379
New York *(G-9442)*
Canada Goose Inc ....G 888 276-6297
New York *(G-9561)*
Canada Goose Us Inc ....G 888 276-6297
Williamsville *(G-17266)*
Candlesticks Inc ....F 212 947-8900
New York *(G-9566)*
Carolina Herrera Ltd ....E 212 944-5757
New York *(G-9588)*
Central Mills Inc ....C 212 221-0748
New York *(G-9617)*
China Ting Fashion Group (usa) ....G 212 716-1600
New York *(G-9653)*
Comint Apparel Group LLC ....E 212 947-7474
New York *(G-9743)*
Consolidated Fashion Corp ....G 212 719-3000
New York *(G-9766)*
Cynthia Rowley Inc ....F 212 242-3803
New York *(G-9835)*
Dalma Dress Mfg Co Inc ....E 212 391-8296
Greenvale *(G-5898)*
Dana Michele LLC ....G 917 757-7777
New York *(G-9853)*
Dani II Inc ....F 212 869-5999
New York *(G-9857)*
Design For All LLC ....E 212 523-0021
New York *(G-9905)*
Donna Karan International Inc ....F 212 789-1500
New York *(G-9954)*
Donna Karan International Inc ....G 212 768-5800
New York *(G-9955)*
Elie Tahari Ltd ....D 212 398-2622
New York *(G-10055)*
Emerald Holdings Inc ....G 718 797-4404
Brooklyn *(G-1921)*
Emerson & Oliver LLC ....G 585 775-9929
Rochester *(G-14365)*
Falls Manufacturing Inc ....G 518 672-7189
Philmont *(G-13565)*
Four Seasons Fashion Mfg Inc ....E 212 947-6820
New York *(G-10242)*
G-III Apparel Group Ltd ....B 212 403-0500
New York *(G-10282)*
G-III Leather Fashions Inc ....B 212 403-0500
New York *(G-10284)*
GAME Sportswear Ltd ....E 914 962-1701
Yorktown Heights *(G-17527)*
Golden Leaves Knitwear Inc ....E 718 875-8235
Brooklyn *(G-2038)*
Hana Sportswear Inc ....E 315 639-6332
Dexter *(G-4308)*
Herman Kay Company Ltd ....C 212 239-2025
New York *(G-10505)*
Hot Line Industries Inc ....F 516 764-0400
Plainview *(G-13634)*
House Pearl Fashions (us) Ltd ....F 212 840-3183
New York *(G-10564)*
Idra Alta Moda LLC ....E 914 644-8202
New York *(G-10604)*
Int Trading USA LLC ....C 212 760-2338
New York *(G-10657)*
Isabel Toledo Enterprises Inc ....E 212 685-0948
New York *(G-10707)*
J Percy For Mrvin Rchards Ltd ....E 212 944-5300
New York *(G-10721)*
Jesse Joeckel ....G 631 668-2772
Montauk *(G-8623)*
Jomat New York Inc ....E 718 369-7641
Brooklyn *(G-2145)*
Just Bottoms & Tops Inc ....F 212 564-3202
New York *(G-10825)*
Karen Kane Inc ....E 212 827-0980
New York *(G-10847)*
Kasper Group LLC ....F 212 354-4311
New York *(G-10852)*
Lahoya Enterprise Inc ....E 718 886-8799
College Point *(G-3818)*
Land n Sea Inc ....D 212 703-2980
New York *(G-10959)*
Lemral Knitwear Inc ....D 718 210-0175
Brooklyn *(G-2211)*
Lgb Inc ....E 212 278-8280
New York *(G-11016)*
Liberty Apparel Company Inc ....E 718 625-4000
New York *(G-11017)*
Light Inc ....G 212 629-3255
New York *(G-11025)*
Lily & Taylor Inc ....E 212 564-5459
New York *(G-11028)*
Luxe Imagine Consulting LLC ....G 212 273-9770
New York *(G-11095)*
M A M Knitting Mills Corp ....E 800 570-0093
Brooklyn *(G-2248)*
Maggy Boutique Ltd ....E 212 997-5222
New York *(G-11128)*
Maiyet Inc ....G 212 343-9999
New York *(G-11139)*
Manchu New York Inc ....E 212 921-5050
New York *(G-11150)*
Manchu Times Fashion Inc ....G 212 921-5050
New York *(G-11151)*
Marconi Intl USA Co Ltd ....E 212 391-2626
New York *(G-11170)*
Marina Holding Corp ....F 718 646-9283
Brooklyn *(G-2270)*
Meskita Lifestyle Brands LLC ....E 212 695-5054
New York *(G-11264)*
Miguelina Inc ....F 212 925-0320
New York *(G-11288)*
Miltons of New York Inc ....G 212 997-3359
New York *(G-11298)*
Moes Wear Apparel Inc ....F 718 940-1597
Brooklyn *(G-2333)*
Mv Corp Inc ....C 631 273-8020
Bay Shore *(G-717)*
Mystic Inc ....B 212 239-2025
New York *(G-11358)*
Only Hearts Ltd ....E 718 783-3218
New York *(G-11523)*
Outerstuff LLC ....E 212 594-9700
New York *(G-11548)*
Pacific Alliance Usa Inc ....E 336 500-8184
New York *(G-11564)*
Pacific Alliance Usa Inc ....E 646 839-7000
New York *(G-11565)*
Pat & Rose Dress Inc ....D 212 279-1357
New York *(G-11593)*
Petrunia LLC ....F 607 277-1930
Ithaca *(G-6905)*
Primo Coat Corp ....E 718 349-2070
Long Island City *(G-7877)*
Pti-Pacific Inc ....E 212 414-8495
New York *(G-11765)*
Pvh Corp ....D 212 502-6300
New York *(G-11782)*
Ralph Lauren Corporation ....E 917 934-4200
New York *(G-11821)*
RD Intrntnl Style ....E 212 382-2360
New York *(G-11836)*
Republic Clothing Corporation ....E 212 719-3000
New York *(G-11868)*
Rogers Group Inc ....E 212 643-9292
New York *(G-11928)*
Rvc Enterprises LLC ....E 212 391-4600
New York *(G-11957)*
S & V Knits Inc ....E 631 752-1595
Farmingdale *(G-5116)*
S & W Knitting Mills Inc ....E 718 237-2416
Brooklyn *(G-2545)*
Sentimental Inc ....G 212 221-0282
New York *(G-12049)*
Smooth Industries Incorporated ....E 212 869-1080
New York *(G-12138)*
SRP Apparel Group Inc ....G 212 764-4810
New York *(G-12201)*
Standard Manufacturing Co Inc ....D 518 235-2200
Troy *(G-16280)*
Sunynams Fashions Ltd ....E 212 268-5200
New York *(G-12262)*
Survival Inc ....G 631 385-5060
Centerport *(G-3506)*
Tbhl International LLC ....F 212 799-2007
New York *(G-12307)*
THE Design Group Inc ....F 212 681-1548
New York *(G-12330)*
Tiger J LLC ....E 212 465-9300
New York *(G-12358)*
Vf Imagewear Inc ....E 718 352-2363
Bayside *(G-772)*
Vf Outdoor LLC ....E 845 928-4900
Central Valley *(G-3556)*
Warnaco Group Inc ....E 212 287-8000
New York *(G-12614)*
Yigal-Azrouel Inc ....E 212 302-1194
New York *(G-12713)*
Zar Group LLC ....G 212 944-2510
New York *(G-12723)*
Zia Power Inc ....E 845 661-8388
New York *(G-12731)*

CLOTHING: Overcoats & Topcoats, Men/Boy, Purchased Materials

Ralph Lauren Corporation ....B 212 318-7000
New York *(G-11819)*

CLOTHING: Pants, Work, Men's, Youths' & Boys'

Ace Drop Cloth Canvas Pdts Inc ....E 718 731-1550
Bronx *(G-1261)*

CLOTHING: Panty Hose

Brach Knitting Mills Inc ....F 845 651-4450
Florida *(G-5217)*
Fine Sheer Industries Inc ....F 212 594-4224
New York *(G-10216)*

CLOTHING: Raincoats, Exc Vulcanized Rubber, Purchased Matls

Levy Group Inc ....C 212 398-0707
New York *(G-11014)*
Mycra Pac Designer Wear Inc ....G 925 631-6878
New York *(G-11355)*

CLOTHING: Robes & Dressing Gowns

Komar Luxury Brands ....G 646 472-0060
New York *(G-10913)*
Lady Ester Lingerie Corp ....E 212 689-1729
New York *(G-10951)*
Palmbay Ltd ....G 718 424-3388
Flushing *(G-5285)*

CLOTHING: Robes & Housecoats, Children's

Waterbury Garment LLC ....E 212 725-1500
New York *(G-12625)*

CLOTHING: Scarves & Mufflers, Knit

180s LLC ....E 410 534-6320
New York *(G-9007)*

CLOTHING: Service Apparel, Women's

Bestec Concept Inc ....G 718 937-5848
Long Island City *(G-7715)*

PRODUCT SECTION

CLOTHING: Sportswear, Women's

Chloe International Inc .... F 212 730-6661
New York *(G-9655)*
Fashion Ave Sweater Knits LLC .... D 212 302-8282
New York *(G-10195)*
GMC Mercantile Corp .... F 212 498-9488
New York *(G-10366)*
HC Contracting Inc .... D 212 643-9292
New York *(G-10477)*
Jsc Designs Ltd .... E 212 302-1001
New York *(G-10814)*
Lotus Apparel Designs Inc .... G 646 236-9363
Westbury *(G-17034)*
Mag Brands LLC .... D 212 629-9600
New York *(G-11124)*
RAK Finishing Corp .... E 718 416-4242
Howard Beach *(G-6626)*

CLOTHING: Shawls, Knit

Lloyds Fashions Inc .... D 631 435-3353
Brentwood *(G-1187)*

CLOTHING: Sheep-Lined

US Authentic LLC .... G 914 767-0295
Katonah *(G-7163)*

CLOTHING: Shirts

Andy & Evan Industries Inc .... G 212 967-7908
New York *(G-9204)*
August Silk Inc .... E 212 643-2400
New York *(G-9315)*
August Silk Inc .... G 212 643-2400
New York *(G-9316)*
Ben Wachter Associates Inc .... G 212 736-4064
New York *(G-9401)*
Bowe Industries Inc .... D 718 441-6464
Glendale *(G-5661)*
Bowe Industries Inc .... D 718 441-6464
Glendale *(G-5662)*
Check Group LLC .... D 212 221-4700
New York *(G-9637)*
Christian Casey LLC .... E 212 500-2200
New York *(G-9660)*
Christian Casey LLC .... E 212 500-2200
New York *(G-9661)*
Colony Holdings Intl LLC .... F 212 868-2800
New York *(G-9730)*
Cyberlimit Inc .... F 212 840-9597
New York *(G-9833)*
Donna Karan International Inc .... F 212 789-1500
New York *(G-9954)*
Donna Karan International Inc .... G 212 768-5800
New York *(G-9955)*
Garan Incorporated .... C 212 563-1292
New York *(G-10294)*
Garan Manufacturing Corp .... G 212 563-2000
New York *(G-10295)*
Gbg National Brands Group LLC .... G 646 839-7000
New York *(G-10299)*
Groupe 16sur20 LLC .... F 212 625-1620
New York *(G-10415)*
Haddad Bros Inc .... F 212 563-2117
New York *(G-10437)*
Interbrand LLC .... G 212 840-9595
New York *(G-10667)*
Jordache Enterprises Inc .... D 212 944-1330
New York *(G-10799)*
Jordache Enterprises Inc .... C 212 643-8400
New York *(G-10800)*
Just Brass Inc .... G 212 724-5447
New York *(G-10826)*
Lt2 LLC .... E 212 684-1510
New York *(G-11086)*
M S B International Ltd .... F 212 302-5551
New York *(G-11105)*
Mega Sourcing Inc .... G 646 682-0304
Merrick *(G-8424)*
Miltons of New York Inc .... G 212 997-3359
New York *(G-11298)*
Mulitex Usa Inc .... G 212 398-0440
New York *(G-11346)*
Oxford Industries Inc .... F 212 840-2288
New York *(G-11554)*
Perry Ellis Menswear LLC .... C 212 221-7500
New York *(G-11643)*
Ralph Lauren Corporation .... G 212 421-1570
New York *(G-11820)*
Roffe Accessories Inc .... F 212 213-1440
New York *(G-11924)*

Saad Collection Inc .... G 212 937-0341
New York *(G-11966)*
Schwartz Textile Converting Co .... E 718 499-8243
Brooklyn *(G-2562)*
Sifonya Inc .... G 212 620-4512
New York *(G-12087)*
Whittall & Shon .... G 212 594-2626
New York *(G-12656)*
Yale Trouser Corporation .... F 516 255-0700
Oceanside *(G-13128)*

CLOTHING: Shirts, Dress, Men's & Boys'

Americo Group Inc .... E 212 563-2700
New York *(G-9181)*
Americo Group Inc .... E 212 563-2700
New York *(G-9182)*
Arthur Gluck Shirtmakers Inc .... F 212 755-8165
Brooklyn *(G-1638)*
Ferris USA LLC .... G 617 895-8102
New York *(G-10207)*
Gce International Inc .... D 773 263-1210
New York *(G-10306)*
Great Universal Corp .... F 917 302-0065
New York *(G-10400)*
Phillips-Van Heusen Europe .... F 212 381-3500
New York *(G-11668)*
Pvh Corp .... G 212 381-3500
New York *(G-11780)*
Pvh Corp .... G 845 561-0233
New Windsor *(G-8995)*
Pvh Corp .... G 631 254-8200
Deer Park *(G-4220)*
Pvh Corp .... G 212 719-2600
New York *(G-11783)*
Ralph Lauren Corporation .... B 212 318-7000
New York *(G-11819)*
Warnaco Inc .... E 212 287-8000
New York *(G-12615)*
Warnaco Inc .... F 718 722-3000
Brooklyn *(G-2760)*

CLOTHING: Shirts, Knit

KD Dids Inc .... G 718 402-2012
Bronx *(G-1373)*
Ralph Lauren Corporation .... B 212 318-7000
New York *(G-11819)*
Warnaco Inc .... F 718 722-3000
Brooklyn *(G-2760)*

CLOTHING: Shirts, Sports & Polo, Men & Boy, Purchased Mtrl

Ibrands International LLC .... F 212 354-1330
New York *(G-10593)*
Sue & Sam Co Inc .... E 718 436-1672
Brooklyn *(G-2640)*

CLOTHING: Shirts, Sports & Polo, Men's & Boys'

Perry Ellis International Inc .... F 212 536-5400
New York *(G-11641)*
Perry Ellis International Inc .... G 212 536-5499
New York *(G-11642)*

CLOTHING: Shirts, Women's & Juniors', From Purchased Mtrls

Brach Knitting Mills Inc .... F 845 651-4450
Florida *(G-5217)*
Jordache Enterprises Inc .... D 212 944-1330
New York *(G-10799)*
Jordache Enterprises Inc .... C 212 643-8400
New York *(G-10800)*

CLOTHING: Skirts

Alfred Dunner Inc .... D 212 478-4300
New York *(G-9134)*
Anna Sui Corp .... E 212 768-1951
New York *(G-9214)*
Brooke Leigh Ltd .... F 212 736-9098
New York *(G-9520)*
Bruno & Canio Ltd .... E 845 624-3060
Nanuet *(G-8799)*
Carolina Herrera Ltd .... F 212 944-4757
New York *(G-9588)*
Geoffrey Beene Inc .... F 212 371-5570
New York *(G-10323)*

Hampshire Sub II Inc .... D 631 321-0923
New York *(G-10446)*
Kayo of California .... G 212 354-6336
New York *(G-10862)*
Nyc Idol Apparel Inc .... G 212 997-9797
New York *(G-11494)*
Pat & Rose Dress Inc .... D 212 279-1357
New York *(G-11593)*
Permit Fashion Group Inc .... G 212 912-0988
New York *(G-11639)*
Rhoda Lee Inc .... C 212 840-5700
New York *(G-11886)*
Tenby LLC .... C 646 863-5890
New York *(G-12322)*
Turn On Products Inc .... F 212 764-4545
New York *(G-12447)*

CLOTHING: Slacks & Shorts, Dress, Men's, Youths' & Boys'

Montero International Inc .... G 212 695-1787
Westbury *(G-17041)*

CLOTHING: Slacks, Girls' & Children's

Garan Incorporated .... C 212 563-1292
New York *(G-10294)*
Garan Manufacturing Corp .... G 212 563-2000
New York *(G-10295)*
Jordache Enterprises Inc .... D 212 944-1330
New York *(G-10799)*
Jordache Enterprises Inc .... C 212 643-8400
New York *(G-10800)*

CLOTHING: Sleeping Garments, Men's & Boys'

Sleepwear Holdings Inc .... C 516 466-4738
New York *(G-12126)*

CLOTHING: Sleeping Garments, Women's & Children's

Allure Fashions Inc .... G 516 829-2470
Great Neck *(G-5804)*
Candlesticks Inc .... F 212 947-8900
New York *(G-9566)*
Kokin Inc .... E 212 643-8225
New York *(G-10908)*
Komar Luxury Brands .... G 646 472-0060
New York *(G-10913)*
Natori Company Incorporated .... D 212 532-7796
New York *(G-11378)*
Richard Leeds Intl Inc .... E 212 532-4546
New York *(G-11888)*
Waterbury Garment LLC .... E 212 725-1500
New York *(G-12625)*

CLOTHING: Slipper Socks

Palmbay Ltd .... G 718 424-3388
Flushing *(G-5285)*

CLOTHING: Socks

Ace Drop Cloth Canvas Pdts Inc .... E 718 731-1550
Bronx *(G-1261)*
Ashko Group LLC .... F 212 594-6050
New York *(G-9283)*
Customize Elite Socks LLC .... G 212 533-8551
New York *(G-9829)*
Fine Sheer Industries Inc .... F 212 594-4224
New York *(G-10216)*
Galiva Inc .... G 903 600-5755
Brooklyn *(G-2013)*
Gbg Socks LLC .... E 646 839-7000
New York *(G-10300)*
La Strada Dance Footwear Inc .... G 631 242-1401
Deer Park *(G-4187)*
Socks and More of NY Inc .... G 718 769-1785
Brooklyn *(G-2603)*
Sticky Socks LLC .... E 212 541-5927
New York *(G-12228)*
Strassburg Medical LLC .... G 716 433-9368
North Tonawanda *(G-13016)*
United Retail II .... G 212 966-9692
New York *(G-12485)*

CLOTHING: Sportswear, Women's

31 Phillip Lim LLC .... E 212 354-6540
New York *(G-9018)*

Employee Codes: A=Over 500 employees, B=251-500
C=101-250, D=51-100, E=20-50, F=10-19, G=5-9

American Apparel Trading Corp	G	212 764-5990	New York (G-9163)
Angel-Made In Heaven Inc	G	212 869-5678	New York (G-9206)
Argee America Inc	G	212 768-9840	New York (G-9250)
AZ Yashir Bapaz Inc	G	212 947-7357	New York (G-9338)
Bandit International Ltd	F	718 402-2100	Bronx (G-1279)
Bernard Chaus Inc	D	212 354-1280	New York (G-9411)
Bernard Chaus Inc	C	646 562-4700	New York (G-9412)
Cai Design Inc	F	212 401-9973	New York (G-9548)
Cathy Daniels Ltd	E	212 354-8000	New York (G-9604)
Central Apparel Group Ltd	F	212 868-6505	New York (G-9614)
City Sites Sportswear Inc	E	718 375-2990	Brooklyn (G-1784)
Daily Wear Sportswear Corp	G	718 972-0533	Brooklyn (G-1835)
Danice Stores Inc	F	212 665-0389	New York (G-9858)
Double Take Fashions Inc	G	718 832-9000	New York (G-9962)
Drew Philips Corp	G	212 354-0095	New York (G-9979)
Eileen Fisher Inc	C	914 591-5700	Irvington (G-6810)
El-La Design Inc	G	212 382-1080	New York (G-10046)
F & J Designs Inc	G	212 302-8755	New York (G-10167)
French Atmosphere Inc	F	516 371-9100	New York (G-10257)
Halmode Apparel Inc	A	212 819-9114	New York (G-10442)
Ikeddi Enterprises Inc	F	212 302-7644	New York (G-10611)
Ikeddi Enterprises Inc	G	212 302-7644	New York (G-10612)
In Moda com Inc	E	718 788-4466	New York (G-10623)
Intriguing Threads Apparel Inc	F	212 768-8733	New York (G-10689)
J & E Talit Inc	G	718 850-1333	Richmond Hill (G-14088)
Jaxis Inc	G	212 302-7611	Brooklyn (G-2134)
JEnvie Sport Inc	G	212 967-2322	New York (G-10760)
Joe Benbasset Inc	E	212 268-4920	New York (G-10786)
Jonden Manufacturing Co Inc	F	516 442-4895	Oceanside (G-13103)
Kayo of California	G	212 354-6336	New York (G-10862)
Lea Apparel Inc	G	718 418-2800	Glendale (G-5672)
Leggiadro International Inc	E	212 997-8766	New York (G-10996)
Life Style Design Group	E	212 391-8666	New York (G-11020)
Marcasiano Inc	G	212 614-9412	New York (G-11168)
Max Leon Inc	F	845 928-8201	Central Valley (G-3553)
Meryl Diamond Ltd	D	212 730-0333	New York (G-11262)
Millennium Productions Inc	F	212 944-6203	New York (G-11293)
Morelle Products Ltd	F	212 391-8070	New York (G-11329)
Nine West Holdings Inc	G	212 642-3860	New York (G-11453)
Nine West Holdings Inc	E	212 642-3860	New York (G-11459)
Nlhe LLC	E	212 594-0012	New York (G-11460)
Noah Enterprises Ltd	G	212 736-2888	New York (G-11464)
Park Avenue Sportswear Ltd	F	718 369-0520	Brooklyn (G-2422)
Pride & Joys Inc	F	212 594-9820	New York (G-11729)
Pvh Corp	G	212 381-3800	New York (G-11781)
Ramsbury Property Us Inc	F	212 223-6250	New York (G-11823)
Rene Portier Inc	G	718 853-7896	Brooklyn (G-2511)
Ritchie Corp	F	212 768-0083	New York (G-11902)
Robespierre Inc	C	212 594-0012	New York (G-11914)
S & S Manufacturing Co Inc	D	212 444-6000	New York (G-11961)
S2 Sportswear Inc	F	347 335-0713	Brooklyn (G-2550)
Salisbury Sportswear Inc	E	516 221-9519	Bellmore (G-817)
Snowman	G	212 239-8818	New York (G-12142)
Ssa Trading Ltd	F	646 465-9500	New York (G-12202)
SSG Fashions Ltd	G	212 221-0933	New York (G-12203)
St John	G	718 720-8367	Staten Island (G-15760)
St John	G	718 771-4541	Brooklyn (G-2616)
Steilmann European Selections	D	914 997-0015	Port Chester (G-13783)
Sterling Possessions Ltd	G	212 594-0418	New York (G-12221)
Street Beat Sportswear Inc	F	718 302-1500	Brooklyn (G-2632)
TR Designs Inc	E	212 398-9300	New York (G-12408)
Turn On Products Inc	D	212 764-2121	New York (G-12446)
Urban Apparel Group Inc	E	212 947-7009	New York (G-12498)
Warrior Sports Inc	G	315 536-0937	Penn Yan (G-13544)
West Pacific Enterprises Corp	G	212 564-6800	New York (G-12641)

CLOTHING: Suits & Skirts, Women's & Misses'

Bindle and Keep	G	917 740-5002	Brooklyn (G-1698)
Opposuits USA Inc	E	917 438-8878	New York (G-11530)
R & M Richards Inc	D	212 921-8820	New York (G-11808)
Tiger Fashion Inc	E	212 244-1175	New York (G-12357)
Zaralo LLC	G	212 764-4590	New York (G-12724)

CLOTHING: Suits, Men's & Boys', From Purchased Materials

Bindle and Keep	G	917 740-5002	Brooklyn (G-1698)
Canali USA Inc	E	212 767-0205	New York (G-9562)
Donna Karan Company LLC	C	212 789-1500	New York (G-9952)
Donna Karan Company LLC	B	212 789-1500	New York (G-9953)
Kozinn+sons Merchant Tailors	E	212 643-1916	New York (G-10921)
Martin Greenfield Clothiers	C	718 497-5480	Brooklyn (G-2279)
Michael Andrews LLC	F	212 677-1755	New York (G-11275)
Primo Coat Corp	E	718 349-2070	Long Island City (G-7877)
Roth Clothing Co Inc	G	718 384-4927	Brooklyn (G-2528)
Royal Clothing Corp	G	718 436-5841	Brooklyn (G-2530)
Tom James Company	F	212 581-6968	New York (G-12381)
Tom James Company	F	212 593-0204	New York (G-12382)
Xmh-Hfi Inc	A	585 467-7240	Rochester (G-14801)

CLOTHING: Sweaters & Sweater Coats, Knit

79 Metro Ltd	G	212 944-4030	New York (G-9025)
A & B Finishing Inc	E	718 522-4702	Brooklyn (G-1524)
Accurate Knitting Corp	G	646 552-2216	Brooklyn (G-1550)
B & B Sweater Mills Inc	F	718 456-8693	Brooklyn (G-1656)
Blueberry Knitting Inc	G	718 599-6520	Brooklyn (G-1704)
Charter Ventures LLC	F	212 868-0222	New York (G-9636)
Domani Fashions Corp	G	718 797-0505	Brooklyn (G-1872)
Endres Knitwear Co Inc	G	718 933-8687	Bronx (G-1330)
Golden Leaves Knitwear Inc	E	718 875-8235	Brooklyn (G-2038)
Great Adirondack Yarn Company	F	518 843-3381	Amsterdam (G-349)
Imperial Sweater Mills Inc	G	718 871-4414	Brooklyn (G-2098)
Jeric Knit Wear	G	631 979-8827	Smithtown (G-15513)
Jj Basics LLC	E	212 768-4779	New York (G-10778)
Julia Knit Inc	G	718 848-1900	Ozone Park (G-13407)
K & S Childrens Wear Inc	E	718 624-0006	Brooklyn (G-2162)
Keryakos Inc	F	518 344-7092	Schenectady (G-15300)
Knit Illustrated Inc	E	212 268-9054	New York (G-10900)
Knit Resource Center Ltd	G	212 221-1990	New York (G-10901)
M A M Knitting Mills Corp	E	800 570-0093	Brooklyn (G-2248)
M B M Manufacturing Inc	F	718 769-4148	Brooklyn (G-2250)
Manrico Usa Inc	G	212 794-4200	New York (G-11163)
Marble Knits Inc	E	718 237-7990	Brooklyn (G-2267)
Matchables Inc	F	718 389-9318	Brooklyn (G-2285)
New York Sweater Company Inc	E	845 629-9533	New York (G-11428)
Phillips-Van Heusen Europe	F	212 381-3500	New York (G-11668)
Premier Knits Ltd	F	718 323-8264	Ozone Park (G-13410)
Pvh Corp	D	212 381-3500	New York (G-11780)
Rags Knitwear Ltd	F	718 782-8417	Brooklyn (G-2492)
S & T Knitting Co Inc	E	607 722-7558	Conklin (G-3900)
S & W Knitting Mills Inc	E	718 237-2416	Brooklyn (G-2545)
Sage Knitwear Inc	G	718 628-7902	West Babylon (G-16856)
Sares International Inc	E	718 366-8412	Brooklyn (G-2557)
Sarug Inc	D	718 339-2791	Brooklyn (G-2558)
Sarug Inc	G	718 381-7300	Ridgewood (G-14135)
Sweater Brand Inc	G	718 797-0505	Brooklyn (G-2655)
T & R Knitting Mills Inc	E	718 497-4017	Glendale (G-5681)
United Knitwear International	G	212 354-2920	New York (G-12484)
WR Design Corp	E	212 354-9000	New York (G-12695)

CLOTHING: Sweaters, Men's & Boys'

Bernette Apparel LLC	F	212 279-5526	New York (G-9413)
Cotton Emporium Inc	G	718 894-3365	Glendale (G-5665)
Just Bottoms & Tops Inc	F	212 564-3202	New York (G-10825)
Komar Luxury Brands	G	646 472-0060	New York (G-10913)
M A M Knitting Mills Corp	E	800 570-0093	Brooklyn (G-2248)
S & W Knitting Mills Inc	E	718 237-2416	Brooklyn (G-2545)
Scharf and Breit Inc	E	516 282-0287	Williston Park (G-17286)
Schwartz Textile Converting Co	E	718 499-8243	Brooklyn (G-2562)

PRODUCT SECTION

CLOTHING: Uniforms, Policemen's, From Purchased Materials

Uniqlo USA LLC ....F 877 486-4756
New York *(G-12479)*

CLOTHING: Sweatshirts & T-Shirts, Men's & Boys'

Kt Group Inc ....G 212 760-2500
New York *(G-10931)*

CLOTHING: Swimwear, Men's & Boys'

Comme-Ci Comme-CA AP Group ....E 631 300-1035
Hauppauge *(G-6070)*
Swimwear Anywhere Inc ....E 845 858-4141
Port Jervis *(G-13817)*

CLOTHING: Swimwear, Women's & Misses'

A H Schreiber Co Inc ....D 212 594-7234
New York *(G-9036)*
Christina Sales Inc ....F 212 391-0710
New York *(G-9664)*
Comme-Ci Comme-CA AP Group ....E 631 300-1035
Hauppauge *(G-6070)*
Feldman Manufacturing Corp ....D 718 433-1700
Long Island City *(G-7768)*
I ABC Corporation ....E 315 639-3100
Dexter *(G-4309)*
Malia Mills Inc ....F 212 354-4200
Brooklyn *(G-2258)*
Michael Feldman Inc ....D 718 433-1700
Long Island City *(G-7842)*
Ocean Waves Swim LLC ....G 212 967-4481
New York *(G-11508)*
Sea Waves Inc ....G 516 766-4201
Oceanside *(G-13118)*
Swimwear Anywhere Inc ....D 631 420-1400
Farmingdale *(G-5131)*
Swimwear Anywhere Inc ....E 845 858-4141
Port Jervis *(G-13817)*
Venus Manufacturing Co Inc ....D 315 639-3100
Dexter *(G-4310)*

CLOTHING: T-Shirts & Tops, Knit

American T Shirts Inc ....G 212 563-7125
New York *(G-9180)*
Central Mills Inc ....C 212 221-0748
New York *(G-9617)*
Hanesbrands Inc ....F 646 472-4117
New York *(G-10451)*
J & E Talit Inc ....G 718 850-1333
Richmond Hill *(G-14088)*
Jfs Inc ....F 646 264-1200
New York *(G-10769)*
Mann Consultants LLC ....E 914 763-0512
Waccabuc *(G-16541)*

CLOTHING: T-Shirts & Tops, Women's & Girls'

Alfred Dunner Inc ....D 212 478-4300
New York *(G-9134)*
Bowe Industries Inc ....D 718 441-6464
Glendale *(G-5661)*
Courage Clothing Co Inc ....F 212 354-5690
New York *(G-9796)*
Garan Incorporated ....C 212 563-1292
New York *(G-10294)*
Garan Manufacturing Corp ....G 212 563-2000
New York *(G-10295)*
Gce International Inc ....D 212 704-4800
New York *(G-10304)*
Golden Horse Enterprise NY Inc ....G 212 594-3339
New York *(G-10373)*
T Rj Shirts Inc ....G 347 642-3071
East Elmhurst *(G-4418)*

CLOTHING: Tailored Suits & Formal Jackets

Crisada Inc ....G 718 729-9730
Long Island City *(G-7735)*
John Kochis Custom Designs ....G 212 244-6046
New York *(G-10788)*
Shane Tex Inc ....F 516 486-7522
Hempstead *(G-6309)*

CLOTHING: Ties, Bow, Men's & Boys', From Purchased Materials

J M C Bow Co Inc ....F 718 686-8110
Brooklyn *(G-2124)*

CLOTHING: Ties, Handsewn, From Purchased Materials

Ralph Lauren Corporation ....B 212 318-7000
New York *(G-11819)*
Tie King Inc ....G 212 714-9611
New York *(G-12355)*

CLOTHING: Ties, Neck & Bow, Men's & Boys'

Tie King Inc ....E 718 768-8484
Brooklyn *(G-2679)*

CLOTHING: Ties, Neck, Men's & Boys', From Purchased Material

Countess Mara Inc ....G 212 768-7300
New York *(G-9795)*
Mallory & Church LLC ....G 212 868-7888
New York *(G-11146)*
Perry Ellis Menswear LLC ....C 212 221-7500
New York *(G-11643)*
Randa Accessories Lea Gds LLC ....D 212 354-5100
New York *(G-11825)*

CLOTHING: Tights & Leg Warmers

Look By M Inc ....G 212 213-4019
New York *(G-11057)*

CLOTHING: Trousers & Slacks, Men's & Boys'

Adrian Jules Ltd ....D 585 342-5886
Rochester *(G-14190)*
Check Group LLC ....D 212 221-4700
New York *(G-9637)*
Christian Casey LLC ....E 212 500-2200
New York *(G-9660)*
Christian Casey LLC ....E 212 500-2200
New York *(G-9661)*
Groupe 16sur20 LLC ....F 212 625-1620
New York *(G-10415)*
Hertling Trousers Inc ....E 718 784-6100
Brooklyn *(G-2077)*
Hugo Boss Usa Inc ....D 212 940-0600
New York *(G-10574)*
Int Trading USA LLC ....C 212 760-2338
New York *(G-10657)*
Jordache Enterprises Inc ....D 212 944-1330
New York *(G-10799)*
Jordache Enterprises Inc ....C 212 643-8400
New York *(G-10800)*
Lucky Brand Dungarees LLC ....E 631 350-7358
Huntington Station *(G-6752)*
M Hidary & Co Inc ....D 212 736-6540
New York *(G-11102)*
M S B International Ltd ....F 212 302-5551
New York *(G-11105)*
Miltons of New York Inc ....G 212 997-3359
New York *(G-11298)*
Mulitex Usa Inc ....G 212 398-0440
New York *(G-11346)*
Pat & Rose Dress Inc ....D 212 279-1357
New York *(G-11593)*
Perry Ellis International Inc ....F 212 536-5400
New York *(G-11641)*
Primo Coat Corp ....E 718 349-2070
Long Island City *(G-7877)*
Ralph Lauren Corporation ....B 212 318-7000
New York *(G-11819)*
Sean John Clothing Inc ....E 212 500-2200
New York *(G-12029)*
Sean John Clothing Inc ....E 212 500-2200
New York *(G-12030)*

CLOTHING: Underwear, Knit

Balanced Tech Corp ....E 212 768-8330
New York *(G-9362)*
Jockey International Inc ....E 518 761-0965
Lake George *(G-7286)*

CLOTHING: Underwear, Men's & Boys'

Becks Classic Mfg Inc ....D 631 435-3800
Brentwood *(G-1175)*
Check Group LLC ....D 212 221-4700
New York *(G-9637)*
Comme-Ci Comme-CA AP Group ....E 631 300-1035
Hauppauge *(G-6070)*

Twist Intimate Group LLC ....G 212 695-5990
New York *(G-12451)*
Warnaco Group LLC ....E 212 287-8000
New York *(G-12614)*
Warnaco Inc ....B 212 287-8000
New York *(G-12615)*
Warnaco Inc ....F 718 722-3000
Brooklyn *(G-2760)*
Wickers Sportswear Inc ....G 631 543-1700
Commack *(G-3872)*

CLOTHING: Underwear, Women's & Children's

Enticing Lingerie Inc ....E 718 998-8625
Brooklyn *(G-1931)*
Intimateco LLC ....G 212 239-4411
New York *(G-10686)*
Lady Ester Lingerie Corp ....E 212 689-1729
New York *(G-10951)*
Luxerdame Co Inc ....E 718 752-9800
Long Island City *(G-7825)*
Natori Company Incorporated ....E 212 532-7796
New York *(G-11379)*
Only Hearts Ltd ....E 718 783-3218
New York *(G-11523)*
Solo Licensing Corp ....G 212 244-5505
New York *(G-12150)*
Wickers Sportswear Inc ....G 631 543-1700
Commack *(G-3872)*

CLOTHING: Uniforms & Vestments

Craft Clerical Clothes Inc ....E 212 764-6122
New York *(G-9803)*
JM Studio Inc ....F 646 546-5514
New York *(G-10782)*
NY Orthopedic Usa Inc ....D 718 852-5330
Brooklyn *(G-2393)*
RA Newhouse Inc ....D 516 248-6670
Mineola *(G-8565)*

CLOTHING: Uniforms, Ex Athletic, Women's, Misses' & Juniors'

Adar Medical Uniform LLC ....F 718 935-1197
Brooklyn *(G-1559)*
Bestec Concept Inc ....G 718 937-5848
Long Island City *(G-7715)*
Elie Tahari Ltd ....D 212 763-2000
New York *(G-10056)*
Lady Brass Co Inc ....G 516 887-8040
Hewlett *(G-6332)*
Marlou Garments Inc ....F 516 739-7100
New Hyde Park *(G-8893)*
Shane Tex Inc ....F 516 486-7522
Hempstead *(G-6309)*
Uniforms By Park Coats Inc ....E 718 499-1182
Brooklyn *(G-2717)*

CLOTHING: Uniforms, Men's & Boys'

Bestec Concept Inc ....G 718 937-5848
Long Island City *(G-7715)*
Elite Uniforms Ltd ....G 516 487-5481
Great Neck *(G-5821)*
Occunomix International LLC ....E 631 741-1940
Port Jeff STA *(G-13792)*
Otex Protective Inc ....G 585 232-7160
Rochester *(G-14580)*
Uniforms By Park Coats Inc ....E 718 499-1182
Brooklyn *(G-2717)*
Urban Textiles Inc ....F 212 777-1900
New York *(G-12501)*
Vf Imagewear Inc ....E 718 352-2363
Bayside *(G-772)*

CLOTHING: Uniforms, Military, Men/Youth, Purchased Materials

Med-Eng LLC ....E 315 713-0103
Ogdensburg *(G-13140)*

CLOTHING: Uniforms, Policemen's, From Purchased Materials

Strong Group Inc ....G 516 766-6300
Oceanside *(G-13119)*

Employee Codes: A=Over 500 employees, B=251-500
C=101-250, D=51-100, E=20-50, F=10-19, G=5-9

CLOTHING: Uniforms, Team Athletic

American Challenge Enterprises...........G		631 595-7171
New Hyde Park (G-8860)		
Mayberry Shoe Company Inc..............G		315 692-4086
Manlius (G-8107)		
Nepenthes America Inc.....................G		212 343-4262
New York (G-11389)		
Pti-Pacific Inc...................................G		212 414-8495
New York (G-11765)		
R J Liebe Athletic Company ....D		585 237-6111
Perry (G-13548)		
Tamka Sport LLC.............................G		718 224-7820
Douglaston (G-4337)		
Warrior Sports Inc..........................G		315 536-0937
Penn Yan (G-13544)		

CLOTHING: Uniforms, Work

Best Medical Wear Ltd......................G		718 858-5544
Brooklyn (G-1686)		
Bestec Concept Inc..........................G		718 937-5848
Long Island City (G-7715)		
David Christy...................................G		607 863-4610
Cincinnatus (G-3681)		
Lady Brass Co Inc...........................G		516 887-8040
Hewlett (G-6332)		
Vf Imagewear Inc.............................E		718 352-2363
Bayside (G-772)		

CLOTHING: Warm Weather Knit Outerwear, Including Beachwear

Warm...G		212 925-1200
New York (G-12613)		

CLOTHING: Waterproof Outerwear

A W R Group Inc..............................F		718 729-0412
Long Island City (G-7676)		
Essex Manufacturing Inc..................D		212 239-0080
New York (G-10119)		
Float Tech Inc..................................G		518 266-0964
Troy (G-16257)		
Top Fortune Usa Ltd........................G		516 608-2694
Lynbrook (G-7991)		

CLOTHING: Work Apparel, Exc Uniforms

Enzo Manzoni LLC............................G		212 464-7000
Brooklyn (G-1932)		
Ferris USA LLC................................G		617 895-8102
New York (G-10207)		

CLOTHING: Work, Men's

5 Star Apparel LLC...........................G		212 563-1233
New York (G-9022)		
AKOS Group Ltd..............................E		212 683-4747
New York (G-9119)		
American Apparel Ltd.......................G		516 504-4559
Great Neck (G-5805)		
Badgley Mischka Licensing LLC........E		212 921-1585
New York (G-9354)		
Billion Tower Intl LLC.......................F		212 220-0608
New York (G-9449)		
Broadway Knitting Mills Inc..............G		716 692-4421
North Tonawanda (G-12979)		
Courage Clothing Co Inc...................F		212 354-5690
New York (G-9796)		
Dalcom USA Ltd...............................F		516 466-7733
Great Neck (G-5819)		
Doral Apparel Group Inc...................G		917 208-5652
New York (G-9959)		
Du Monde Trading Inc......................E		212 944-1306
New York (G-9984)		
E J Manufacturing Inc......................G		516 313-9380
Merrick (G-8417)		
Far East Industries Inc.....................G		718 687-2482
New Hyde Park (G-8878)		
Hillary Merchant Inc.........................G		646 575-9242
New York (G-10521)		
Joseph Abboud Manufacturing.........G		212 586-9140
New York (G-10803)		
Kollage Work Too Ltd.......................G		212 695-1821
New York (G-10910)		
Medline Industries Inc......................B		845 344-3301
Middletown (G-8484)		
Mesh LLC...G		646 839-7000
New York (G-11263)		
New York Hospital Disposable..........E		718 384-1620
Brooklyn (G-2373)		
Occunomix International LLC...........E		631 741-1940
Port Jeff STA (G-13792)		
Penfli Industries Inc.........................F		212 947-6080
Great Neck (G-5848)		
Rag & Bone Industries LLC..............E		212 249-3331
New York (G-11814)		
Rag & Bone Industries LLC..............D		212 278-8214
New York (G-11815)		
Ruleville Manufacturing Co Inc.........E		212 695-1620
New York (G-11953)		
S & H Uniform Corp.........................G		914 937-6800
White Plains (G-17191)		
Sarar Usa Inc...................................G		845 928-8874
Central Valley (G-3554)		
Untuckit LLC....................................E		201 214-9054
New York (G-12494)		
Ventura Enterprise Co Inc................E		212 391-0170
New York (G-12541)		

CLUTCHES OR BRAKES: Electromagnetic

American Precision Inds Inc..............C		716 691-9100
Amherst (G-227)		
Fortitude Industries..........................D		607 324-1500
Hornell (G-6589)		

CLUTCHES, EXC VEHICULAR

Machine Components Corp...............E		516 694-7222
Plainview (G-13644)		
Magtrol Inc......................................G		716 668-5555
Buffalo (G-3075)		

COAL MINING SERVICES

Desku Group Inc..............................G		646 436-1464
Brooklyn (G-1857)		
Dowa International Corp..................F		212 697-3217
New York (G-9968)		
Randgold Resources Ltd...................E		212 815-2129
New York (G-11827)		
Starfuels Inc....................................G		914 289-4800
White Plains (G-17197)		
Trimet Coal LLC..............................E		718 951-3654
Brooklyn (G-2699)		

COAL MINING SVCS: Bituminous, Contract Basis

Lessoilcom.......................................G		516 319-5052
Franklin Square (G-5374)		

COAL MINING: Anthracite

Acrs Inc...F		914 288-8100
White Plains (G-17101)		

COATING COMPOUNDS: Tar

Aremco Products Inc........................F		845 268-0039
Valley Cottage (G-16402)		
Polyset Company Inc.......................E		518 664-6000
Mechanicville (G-8260)		
Spray-Tech Finishing Inc..................F		716 664-6317
Jamestown (G-7062)		

COATING OR WRAPPING SVC: Steel Pipe

Specialty Bldg Solutions Inc.............G		631 393-6918
West Babylon (G-16863)		

COATING SVC

Cnv Architectural Coatings Inc.........G		718 418-9584
Brooklyn (G-1788)		
Kwong CHI Metal Fabrication...........G		718 369-6429
Brooklyn (G-2184)		

COATING SVC: Electrodes

Chepaume Industries LLC.................G		315 829-6400
Vernon (G-16456)		
Hilord Chemical Corporation............E		631 234-7373
Hauppauge (G-6117)		

COATING SVC: Hot Dip, Metals Or Formed Prdts

Paradigm Group LLC........................G		718 860-1538
Bronx (G-1421)		

COATING SVC: Metals & Formed Prdts

Applause Coating LLC......................F		631 231-5223
Brentwood (G-1173)		
Deloka LLC......................................G		315 946-6910
Lyons (G-7999)		
Dynocoat Inc...................................F		631 244-9344
Holbrook (G-6472)		
Electronic Coating Tech Inc..............F		518 688-2048
Cohoes (G-3771)		
Future Spray Finishing Co................G		631 242-6252
Deer Park (G-4168)		
Greene Technologies Inc..................D		607 656-4166
Greene (G-5884)		
Master Craft Finishers Inc................G		631 586-0540
Deer Park (G-4195)		
Modern Coating and Research..........F		315 597-3517
Palmyra (G-13437)		
NC Industries Inc.............................F		248 528-5200
Buffalo (G-3103)		
Oerlikon Blzers Cating USA Inc........E		716 270-2228
Amherst (G-254)		
Oerlikon Blzers Cating USA Inc........E		716 270-2228
Amherst (G-255)		
Oerlikon Blzers Cating USA Inc........E		716 564-8557
Buffalo (G-3121)		
Qualicoat Inc...................................D		585 293-2650
Churchville (G-3669)		
Sentry Metal Blast Inc.....................E		716 285-5241
Lockport (G-7645)		
Sequa Corporation...........................E		201 343-1122
Orangeburg (G-13269)		
Solidus Industries Inc......................D		607 749-4540
Homer (G-6550)		
Swain Technology Inc......................F		585 889-2786
Scottsville (G-15362)		
Trojan Metal Fabrication Inc............E		631 968-5040
Bay Shore (G-745)		
W W Custom Clad Inc.....................D		518 673-3322
Canajoharie (G-3362)		

COATING SVC: Metals, With Plastic Or Resins

Heany Industries Inc........................D		585 889-2700
Scottsville (G-15358)		
Hudson Valley Coatings LLC............G		845 398-1778
Congers (G-3882)		
Metal Cladding Inc..........................D		716 434-5513
Lockport (G-7629)		
Piper Plastics Corp..........................E		631 842-6889
Copiague (G-3942)		
Pro-Teck Coating Inc.......................F		716 537-2619
Holland (G-6510)		
Tj Powder Coaters LLC....................G		607 724-4779
Binghamton (G-949)		

COATING SVC: Rust Preventative

Hubbell Galvanizing Inc...................G		315 736-8311
Yorkville (G-17539)		
Monroe County Auto Svcs Inc..........E		585 764-3741
Rochester (G-14540)		

COATING SVC: Silicon

Momentive Performance Mtls Inc......E		518 237-3330
Waterford (G-16638)		
Momentive Prfmce Mtls Holdings.....A		518 533-4600
Albany (G-102)		
Mpm Holdings Inc............................G		518 237-3330
Waterford (G-16639)		
Mpm Intermediate Holdings Inc........G		518 237-3330
Waterford (G-16640)		

COATINGS: Air Curing

Enecon Corporation..........................D		516 349-0022
Medford (G-8274)		

COATINGS: Epoxy

Delta Polymers Inc...........................G		631 254-6240
Bay Shore (G-693)		
Designer Epoxy Finishes Inc.............G		646 943-6044
Melville (G-8340)		
Robert Greenburg.............................G		845 586-2226
Margaretville (G-8123)		

COATINGS: Polyurethane

Absolute Coatings Inc......................E		914 636-0700
New Rochelle (G-8929)		

PRODUCT SECTION

Gabriela Systems Ltd .... G 631 225-7952
  Lindenhurst (G-7487)
Paint Over Rust Products Inc .... E 914 636-0700
  New Rochelle (G-8964)

COFFEE SVCS

Adirondack Ice & Air Inc .... F 518 483-4340
  Malone (G-8036)

COILS & TRANSFORMERS

Aeroflex Incorporated .... B 516 694-6700
  Plainview (G-13608)
All Shore Industries Inc .... F 718 720-0018
  Staten Island (G-15655)
American Trans-Coil Corp .... F 516 922-9640
  Oyster Bay (G-13390)
Bel Transformer Inc .... D 516 239-5777
  Inwood (G-6792)
Electron Coil Inc .... D 607 336-7414
  Norwich (G-13046)
Ems Development Corporation .... D 631 345-6200
  Yaphank (G-17407)
Ems Development Corporation .... D 631 924-4736
  Yaphank (G-17406)
Eni Technology Inc .... B 585 427-8300
  Rochester (G-14374)
Es Beta Inc .... E 631 582-6740
  Ronkonkoma (G-14927)
Frequency Selective Networks .... F 718 424-7500
  Valley Stream (G-16433)
Fuse Electronics Inc .... G 607 352-3222
  Kirkwood (G-7260)
Gowanda - Bti LLC .... D 716 492-4081
  Arcade (G-394)
Hipotronics Inc .... C 845 279-8091
  Brewster (G-1217)
M F L B Inc .... F 631 254-8300
  Bay Shore (G-712)
Mini-Circuits Fort Wayne LLC .... B 718 934-4500
  Brooklyn (G-2322)
Misonix Inc .... D 631 694-9555
  Farmingdale (G-5067)
Mitchell Electronics Corp .... E 914 699-3800
  Mount Vernon (G-8753)
New York Fan Coil LLC .... G 646 580-1344
  Coram (G-3970)
Rdi Inc .... F 914 773-1000
  Mount Kisco (G-8686)
Sag Harbor Industries Inc .... E 631 725-0440
  Sag Harbor (G-15107)

COILS: Electric Motors Or Generators

Electron Coil Inc .... D 607 336-7414
  Norwich (G-13046)
Sag Harbor Industries Inc .... E 631 725-0440
  Sag Harbor (G-15107)

COILS: Pipe

Falcon Perspectives Inc .... G 718 706-9168
  Long Island City (G-7766)

COIN OPERATED LAUNDRIES & DRYCLEANERS

Oxford Cleaners .... G 212 734-0006
  New York (G-11552)

COIN-OPERATED LAUNDRY

Reynolds Drapery Service Inc .... F 315 845-8632
  Newport (G-12816)
Sky Laundromat Inc .... E 718 639-7070
  Jamaica (G-6986)

COKE: Calcined Petroleum, Made From Purchased Materials

Hh Liquidating Corp .... A 646 282-2500
  New York (G-10515)

COKE: Produced In Chemical Recovery Coke Ovens

Tonawanda Coke Corporation .... D 716 876-6222
  Tonawanda (G-16226)

COLLECTION AGENCY, EXC REAL ESTATE

Debt Resolve Inc .... G 914 949-5500
  White Plains (G-17128)
Nyt Capital LLC .... F 212 556-1234
  New York (G-11503)

COLLEGES, UNIVERSITIES & PROFESSIONAL SCHOOLS

Stony Brook University .... E 631 632-6434
  Stony Brook (G-15793)

COLLETS

Hardinge Inc .... B 607 734-2281
  Elmira (G-4701)

COLOR SEPARATION: Photographic & Movie Film

Applied Image Inc .... E 585 482-0300
  Rochester (G-14225)
Eastern Color Stripping Inc .... F 631 563-3700
  Bohemia (G-1056)

COLORS: Pigments, Inorganic

BASF Beauty Care Solutions LLC .... G 631 689-0200
  Stony Brook (G-15788)
BASF Corporation .... B 914 737-2554
  Peekskill (G-13497)
Heany Industries Inc .... D 585 889-2700
  Scottsville (G-15358)

COLORS: Pigments, Organic

Sml Brothers Holding Corp .... D 718 402-2000
  Bronx (G-1455)

COMFORTERS & QUILTS, FROM MANMADE FIBER OR SILK

Ess Bee Industries Inc .... E 718 894-5202
  Brooklyn (G-1942)

COMMERCIAL & INDL SHELVING WHOLESALERS

Tri-Boro Shlving Prtition Corp .... F 718 782-8527
  Ridgewood (G-14142)

COMMERCIAL & OFFICE BUILDINGS RENOVATION & REPAIR

Kng Construction Co Inc .... F 212 595-1451
  Warwick (G-16615)

COMMERCIAL ART & GRAPHIC DESIGN SVCS

Art Digital Technologies LLC .... F 646 649-4820
  Brooklyn (G-1636)
Artscroll Printing Corp .... E 212 929-2413
  New York (G-9275)
Avalon Copy Centers Amer Inc .... D 315 471-3333
  Syracuse (G-15883)
Avalon Copy Centers Amer Inc .... E 716 995-7777
  Buffalo (G-2847)
Clinton Signs Inc .... E 585 482-1620
  Webster (G-16743)
David Helsing .... G 607 796-2681
  Horseheads (G-6601)
Dowd - Witbeck Printing Corp .... F 518 274-2421
  Troy (G-16256)
Dynamic Photography Inc .... G 516 381-2951
  Roslyn (G-15043)
Eye Graphics & Printing Inc .... F 718 488-0606
  Brooklyn (G-1953)
F X Graphix Inc .... G 716 871-1511
  Buffalo (G-2957)
Fred Weidner & Son Printers .... G 212 964-8676
  New York (G-10254)
Hunt Graphics Inc .... G 631 751-5349
  Coram (G-3967)
Jay Turoff .... F 718 856-7300
  Brooklyn (G-2135)
Kader Lithograph Company Inc .... C 917 664-4380
  Long Island City (G-7804)
Kjckd Inc .... G 518 435-9696
  Latham (G-7395)
Lane Park Graphics Inc .... G 914 273-5898
  Patterson (G-13466)
Messenger Press .... G 518 885-9231
  Ballston Spa (G-603)
Patrick Rohan .... G 718 781-2573
  Monticello (G-8646)
Resonant Legal Media LLC .... E 212 687-7100
  New York (G-11872)
Riverwood Signs By Dandev Desi .... G 845 229-0282
  Hyde Park (G-6776)
Scan-A-Chrome Color Inc .... G 631 532-6146
  Copiague (G-3948)
Zacmel Graphics LLC .... G 631 944-6031
  Deer Park (G-4256)

COMMERCIAL EQPT WHOLESALERS, NEC

Hamlet Products Inc .... F 914 665-0307
  Mount Vernon (G-8734)

COMMERCIAL EQPT, WHOLESALE: Bakery Eqpt & Splys

Pfeil & Holing Inc .... D 718 545-4600
  Woodside (G-17362)

COMMERCIAL EQPT, WHOLESALE: Comm Cooking & Food Svc Eqpt

A and K Machine and Welding .... G 631 231-2552
  Bay Shore (G-663)
Genpak LLC .... C 845 343-7971
  Middletown (G-8476)
Mar-A-Thon Filters Inc .... G 631 957-4774
  Lindenhurst (G-7492)
Meades Welding and Fabricating .... G 631 581-1555
  Islip (G-6849)
Modern Craft Bar Rest Equip .... G 631 226-5647
  Lindenhurst (G-7496)
S & D Welding Corp .... G 631 454-0383
  West Babylon (G-16855)

COMMERCIAL EQPT, WHOLESALE: Display Eqpt, Exc Refrigerated

Bfma Holding Corporation .... G 607 753-6746
  Cortland (G-4036)

COMMERCIAL EQPT, WHOLESALE: Mannequins

Lifestyle-Trimco .... E 718 257-9101
  Brooklyn (G-2220)
R P M Industries Inc .... E 315 255-1105
  Auburn (G-512)

COMMERCIAL EQPT, WHOLESALE: Restaurant, NEC

Bari Engineering Corp .... E 212 966-2080
  New York (G-9372)
R-S Restaurant Eqp Mfg Corp .... F 212 925-0335
  New York (G-11811)
Roger & Sons Inc .... G 212 226-4734
  New York (G-11927)

COMMERCIAL EQPT, WHOLESALE: Scales, Exc Laboratory

A & K Equipment Incorporated .... G 705 428-3573
  Watertown (G-16655)
Itin Scale Co Inc .... E 718 336-5900
  Brooklyn (G-2118)

COMMERCIAL EQPT, WHOLESALE: Store Fixtures & Display Eqpt

Manhattan Display Inc .... G 718 392-1365
  Long Island City (G-7832)

COMMERCIAL LAUNDRY EQPT

Fowler Route Co Inc .... F 917 653-4640
  Yonkers (G-17461)

COMMERCIAL PHOTOGRAPHIC STUDIO

Falconer Printing & Design Inc .... F 716 665-2121
  Falconer (G-4906)

Employee Codes: A=Over 500 employees, B=251-500
C=101-250, D=51-100, E=20-50, F=10-19, G=5-9

COMMERCIAL PRINTING & NEWSPAPER PUBLISHING COMBINED

COMMERCIAL PRINTING & NEWSPAPER PUBLISHING COMBINED

Company	Code	Phone
Amnewyork — New York (G-9188)	D	212 239-5555
Aspect Printing Inc — Brooklyn (G-1642)	E	347 789-4284
Bleezarde Publishing Inc — Ravena (G-14033)	G	518 756-2030
Buffalo Standard Printing Corp — Buffalo (G-2882)	F	716 835-9454
Catskill Delaware Publications — Callicoon (G-3312)	F	845 887-5200
Community News Group LLC — Brooklyn (G-1795)	C	718 260-2500
Daily News LP — New York (G-9845)	A	212 210-2100
Denton Publications Inc — Elizabethtown (G-4640)	D	518 873-6368
Denton Publications Inc — Plattsburgh (G-13689)	E	518 561-9680
E W Smith Publishing Co — New Windsor (G-8983)	F	845 562-1218
Eagle Media Partners LP — Syracuse (G-15949)	E	315 434-8889
Gatehuse Media PA Holdings Inc — Pittsford (G-13591)	E	585 598-0030
Holdens Screen Supply Corp — New York (G-10539)	G	212 627-2727
Huersch Marketing Group LLC — Green Island (G-5875)	F	518 874-1045
Ithaca Journal News Co Inc — Ithaca (G-6889)	E	607 272-2321
Local Media Group Inc — Middletown (G-8482)	D	845 341-1100
New Berlin Gazette — Norwich (G-13050)	E	607 847-6131
Nyc Trade Printers Corp — Woodside (G-17359)	F	718 606-0610
Nyp Holdings Inc — New York (G-11500)	A	212 997-9272
Ogden Newspapers Inc — Jamestown (G-7055)	C	716 487-1111
Prometheus International Inc — Long Island City (G-7878)	F	718 472-0700
Richner Communications Inc — Garden City (G-5543)	C	516 569-4000
Ubm LLC — New York (G-12459)	F	516 562-5000
William Boyd Printing Co Inc — Latham (G-7411)	C	518 339-5832
Wolfe Publications Inc — Canandaigua (G-3389)	C	585 394-0770
Zenith Color Comm Group Inc — Long Island City (G-7961)	E	212 989-4400

COMMON SAND MINING

Company	Code	Phone
E F Lippert Co Inc — Allegany (G-202)	F	716 373-1100
Hanson Aggregates East LLC — Penn Yan (G-13536)	G	315 536-9391
Hanson Aggregates PA Inc — Jordanville (G-7160)	E	315 858-1100
Hanson Aggregates PA Inc — Saint Johnsville (G-15120)	F	518 568-2444
Hanson Aggregates PA LLC — Jamesville (G-7083)	E	315 469-5501
Hanson Aggregates PA LLC — Skaneateles (G-15485)	E	315 685-3321
Hanson Aggregates PA LLC — Oriskany Falls (G-13342)	F	315 821-7222
Sagaponack Sand & Gravel Corp — Bridgehampton (G-1233)	E	631 537-2424

COMMUNICATION HEADGEAR: Telephone

Company	Code	Phone
Astrocom Electronics Inc — Oneonta (G-13195)	D	607 432-1930
Prager Metis Cpas LLC — New York (G-11715)	F	212 972-7555
Rus Industries Inc — Niagara Falls (G-12887)	E	716 284-7828

COMMUNICATIONS CARRIER: Wired

Company	Code	Phone
Comsec Ventures International — Lake Placid (G-7297)	G	518 523-1600
Fiberdyne Labs Inc — Frankfort (G-5362)	D	315 895-8470

COMMUNICATIONS EQPT & SYSTEMS, NEC

Company	Code	Phone
All Products Designs — Smithtown (G-15504)	G	631 748-6901
Light Phone Inc — Brooklyn (G-2222)	G	415 595-0044
Lik LLC — Northport (G-13033)	F	516 848-5135

COMMUNICATIONS EQPT REPAIR & MAINTENANCE

Company	Code	Phone
Unitone Communication Systems — New York (G-12488)		212 777-9090
Zetek Corporation — New York (G-12729)	F	212 668-1485

COMMUNICATIONS EQPT WHOLESALERS

Company	Code	Phone
AES Electronics Inc — New York (G-9101)	G	212 371-8120
Caravan International Corp — New York (G-9578)	G	212 223-7190
Communication Power Corp — Hauppauge (G-6071)		631 434-7306
Sinclair Technologies Inc — Hamburg (G-5966)	E	716 874-3682

COMMUNICATIONS EQPT: Microwave

Company	Code	Phone
Amplitech Inc — Bohemia (G-1010)		631 521-7738
Amplitech Group Inc — Bohemia (G-1011)		631 521-7831
Comtech PST Corp — Melville (G-8336)	C	631 777-8900
Comtech Telecom Corp — Melville (G-8337)	C	631 962-7000
Specialty Microwave Corp — Ronkonkoma (G-15011)	F	631 737-2175
United Satcom Inc — Flushing (G-5310)		718 359-4100

COMMUNICATIONS EQPT: Radio, Marine

Company	Code	Phone
Maritime Broadband Inc — Long Island City (G-7833)	E	347 404-6041

COMMUNICATIONS SVCS

Company	Code	Phone
Aspire One Communications LLC — Cornwall (G-4007)	F	201 281-2998
Forerunner Technologies Inc — Bohemia (G-1063)	E	631 337-2100

COMMUNICATIONS SVCS: Cellular

Company	Code	Phone
Bayside Beepers & Cellular — Glen Oaks (G-5654)	G	718 343-3888
Squond Inc — Brooklyn (G-2615)	E	718 778-6630

COMMUNICATIONS SVCS: Data

Company	Code	Phone
Forerunner Technologies Inc — Bohemia (G-1063)	E	631 337-2100

COMMUNICATIONS SVCS: Facsimile Transmission

Company	Code	Phone
Alternative Technology Corp — Hastings On Hudson (G-6022)	G	914 478-5900
Key Computer Svcs of Chelsea — New York (G-10880)	D	212 206-8060

COMMUNICATIONS SVCS: Internet Host Svcs

Company	Code	Phone
Nyemac Inc — Montauk (G-8626)	G	631 668-1303

COMMUNICATIONS SVCS: Online Svc Providers

Company	Code	Phone
Beauty America LLC — Great Neck (G-5811)	E	917 744-1430
Martha Stewart Living — New York (G-11189)	C	212 827-8000

COMMUNICATIONS SVCS: Proprietary Online Svcs Networks

Company	Code	Phone
Working Mother Media Inc — New York (G-12686)	D	212 351-6400

COMMUNICATIONS SVCS: Satellite Earth Stations

Company	Code	Phone
Loral Space Communications Inc — New York (G-11062)	B	212 697-1105

COMMUNICATIONS SVCS: Signal Enhancement Network Svcs

Company	Code	Phone
Fiberdyne Labs Inc — Frankfort (G-5362)	D	315 895-8470

COMMUNICATIONS SVCS: Telephone, Data

Company	Code	Phone
Akoustis Inc — Canandaigua (G-3363)	E	585 919-3073

COMMUNICATIONS SVCS: Telephone, Local

Company	Code	Phone
Highcrest Investors LLC — New York (G-10519)	D	212 702-4323

COMMUNICATIONS SVCS: Telephone, Voice

Company	Code	Phone
ABS Talkx Inc — Bay Shore (G-664)	G	631 254-9100

COMMUNITY CHESTS

Company	Code	Phone
Heat and Frost Inslatrs & Asbs — Astoria (G-441)	G	718 784-3456

COMMUTATORS: Electronic

Company	Code	Phone
Amron Electronics Inc — Ronkonkoma (G-14898)	E	631 737-1234

COMPACT DISCS OR CD'S, WHOLESALE

Company	Code	Phone
Imago Recording Company — New York (G-10615)	G	212 751-3033

COMPACT LASER DISCS: Prerecorded

Company	Code	Phone
A To Z Media Inc — New York (G-9040)	F	212 260-0237
Atlantic Recording Corp — New York (G-9304)	B	212 707-2000
Bertelsmann Inc — New York (G-9417)	E	212 782-1000
Historic TW Inc — New York (G-10530)	E	212 484-8000
Media Technologies Ltd — Eastport (G-4596)	F	631 467-7900
Mmo Music Group Inc — Elmsford (G-4774)	G	914 592-1188
Optic Solution LLC — Saranac (G-15161)	F	518 293-4034
Sony Corporation of America — New York (G-12157)	C	212 833-8000
Time Warner Companies Inc — New York (G-12369)	E	212 484-8000
Vaire LLC — Huntington Station (G-6765)	G	631 271-4933

COMPACTORS: Trash & Garbage, Residential

Company	Code	Phone
A Gatty Products Inc — Elmsford (G-4741)	G	914 592-3903

COMPARATORS: Optical

Company	Code	Phone
Quality Vision Services Inc — Rochester (G-14638)	D	585 544-0450

COMPOSITION STONE: Plastic

Company	Code	Phone
Seaway Mats Inc — Malone (G-8047)	G	518 483-2560

COMPOST

Company	Code	Phone
Long Island Compost Corp — Westbury (G-17033)	C	516 334-6600
Scotts Company LLC — Yaphank (G-17416)	E	631 289-7444

PRODUCT SECTION
COMPUTER PERIPHERAL EQPT, NEC

COMPRESSORS, AIR CONDITIONING: Wholesalers

Toshiba America Inc ....E...... 212 596-0600
  New York (G-12398)

COMPRESSORS: Air & Gas

Buffalo Compressed Air Inc ....G...... 716 783-8673
  Cheektowaga (G-3591)
Chapin International Inc ....C...... 585 343-3140
  Batavia (G-628)
Chapin Manufacturing Inc ....C...... 585 343-3140
  Batavia (G-629)
Comairco Equipment Inc ....G...... 716 656-0211
  Cheektowaga (G-3592)
Cooper Turbocompressor Inc ......B...... 716 896-6600
  Buffalo (G-2910)
Crosman Corporation ....E...... 585 657-6161
  Bloomfield (G-980)
Crosman Corporation ....E...... 585 398-3920
  Farmington (G-5157)
Cyclone Air Power Inc ....G...... 718 447-3038
  Staten Island (G-15684)
Dresser-Rand Group Inc ....D...... 716 375-3000
  Olean (G-13164)
Gas Tchnlgy Enrgy Cncepts LLC ...G...... 716 831-9695
  Buffalo (G-2980)
GM Components Holdings LLC ....B...... 716 439-2463
  Lockport (G-7619)
GM Components Holdings LLC ....B...... 716 439-2011
  Lockport (G-7620)
Idex Corporation ....G...... 585 292-8121
  Rochester (G-14463)
Mahle Indstrbeteiligungen GMBH ...D...... 716 319-6700
  Amherst (G-248)
Screw Compressor Tech Inc ....F...... 716 827-6600
  Buffalo (G-3208)
Turbopro Inc ....G...... 716 681-8651
  Alden (G-187)

COMPRESSORS: Air & Gas, Including Vacuum Pumps

Air Techniques Inc ....B...... 516 433-7676
  Melville (G-8324)
Atlas Copco Comptec LLC ....B...... 518 765-3344
  Voorheesville (G-16538)
Eastern Air Products LLC ....F...... 716 391-1866
  Lancaster (G-7337)

COMPRESSORS: Refrigeration & Air Conditioning Eqpt

Graham Corporation ....B...... 585 343-2216
  Batavia (G-638)
Standard Motor Products Inc ......B...... 718 392-0200
  Long Island City (G-7912)

COMPUTER & COMPUTER SOFTWARE STORES

A I T Computers Inc ....G...... 518 266-9010
  Troy (G-16245)
Astrodyne Inc ....G...... 516 536-5755
  Oceanside (G-13092)
Biofeedback Instrument Corp .....G...... 212 222-5665
  New York (G-9453)
G S Communications USA Inc ....E...... 718 389-7371
  Brooklyn (G-2011)
J & N Computer Services Inc .....F...... 585 388-8780
  Fairport (G-4864)
Lasertech Crtridge RE-Builders ...G...... 518 373-1246
  Clifton Park (G-3725)
Maia Systems LLC ....G...... 718 206-0100
  Jamaica (G-6963)
Taste and See Entrmt Inc ....G...... 516 285-3010
  Valley Stream (G-16452)
Tpa Computer Corp ....F...... 877 866-6044
  Carmel (G-3434)

COMPUTER & COMPUTER SOFTWARE STORES: Peripheral Eqpt

Cables and Chips Inc ....E...... 212 619-3132
  New York (G-9544)

COMPUTER & COMPUTER SOFTWARE STORES: Software, Bus/Non-Game

Noetic Partners Inc ....F...... 212 836-4351
  New York (G-11466)
Pointman LLC ....G...... 716 842-1439
  Buffalo (G-3153)

COMPUTER & COMPUTER SOFTWARE STORES: Software, Computer Game

Sony Broadband Entertainment ....F...... 212 833-6800
  New York (G-12156)

COMPUTER & OFFICE MACHINE MAINTENANCE & REPAIR

Chem-Puter Friendly Inc ....E...... 631 331-2259
  Mount Sinai (G-8696)
Innovative Systems of New York ...G...... 516 541-7410
  Massapequa Park (G-8220)
Parrys Incorporated ....F...... 315 824-0002
  Hamilton (G-5972)

COMPUTER DISKETTES WHOLESALERS

Formats Unlimited Inc ....F...... 631 249-9200
  Deer Park (G-4166)

COMPUTER FORMS

Boces Business Office ....F...... 607 763-3300
  Binghamton (G-892)
Multi Packaging Solutions Inc .....E...... 646 885-0005
  New York (G-11347)
Specialized Printed Forms Inc .....E...... 585 538-2381
  Caledonia (G-3310)

COMPUTER GRAPHICS SVCS

Affluent Design Inc ....F...... 631 655-2556
  Mastic Beach (G-8236)
Belsito Communications Inc ....F...... 845 534-9700
  New Windsor (G-8978)
Beyer Graphics Inc ....D...... 631 543-3900
  Commack (G-3850)
Christian Bus Endeavors Inc ....E...... 315 788-8560
  Watertown (G-16665)

COMPUTER HARDWARE REQUIREMENTS ANALYSIS

Quality and Asrn Tech Corp ....G...... 646 450-6762
  Ridge (G-14106)

COMPUTER INTERFACE EQPT: Indl Process

Anchor Commerce Trading Corp ..G...... 516 881-3485
  Atlantic Beach (G-467)
Aspex Incorporated ....E...... 212 966-0410
  New York (G-9290)
ATI Trading Inc ....F...... 718 888-7918
  Flushing (G-5235)
Cal Blen Electronic Industries .....F...... 631 242-6243
  Huntington (G-6691)
Cosa Xentaur Corporation ....E...... 631 345-3434
  Yaphank (G-17405)
Industrial Machine Repair ....G...... 607 272-0717
  Ithaca (G-6885)
Macrolink Inc ....E...... 631 924-8200
  Medford (G-8288)
Sixnet LLC ....E...... 518 877-5173
  Ballston Lake (G-585)
Vetra Systems Corporation ....E...... 631 434-3185
  Hauppauge (G-6249)

COMPUTER PERIPHERAL EQPT REPAIR & MAINTENANCE

Xerox Corporation ....C...... 585 427-4500
  Rochester (G-14797)

COMPUTER PERIPHERAL EQPT, NEC

A I T Computers Inc ....G...... 518 266-9010
  Troy (G-16245)
Aalborg Instrs & Cntrls Inc ....D...... 845 398-3160
  Orangeburg (G-13238)
Aero-Vision Technologies Inc .....E...... 631 643-8349
  Melville (G-8322)
Aeroflex Plainview Inc ....C...... 631 231-9100
  Hauppauge (G-6030)
Andrea Electronics Corporation ...G...... 631 719-1800
  Bohemia (G-1012)
Anorod Corporation ....C...... 631 380-2100
  East Setauket (G-4495)
Aruba Networks Inc ....G...... 732 343-1305
  New York (G-9276)
Atlaz International Ltd ....F...... 516 239-1854
  Lawrence (G-7416)
Aventura Technologies Inc ....E...... 631 300-4000
  Commack (G-3848)
B V M Associates ....E...... 631 254-6220
  Shirley (G-15438)
Chem-Puter Friendly Inc ....E...... 631 331-2259
  Mount Sinai (G-8696)
Chemung Cnty Chpter Nysarc Inc ..C...... 607 734-6151
  Elmira (G-4688)
Clayton Dubilier & Rice Fun ....E...... 212 407-5200
  New York (G-9695)
Datatran Labs Inc ....G...... 845 856-4313
  Port Jervis (G-13805)
Digiorange Inc ....G...... 718 787-1500
  Brooklyn (G-1862)
Dynamic Decisions Inc ....F...... 908 755-5000
  Fresh Meadows (G-5453)
Eastman Kodak Company ....B...... 585 724-4000
  Rochester (G-14348)
Ems Development Corporation ...G...... 631 345-6200
  Yaphank (G-17407)
Gasoft Equipment Inc ....F...... 845 863-1010
  Newburgh (G-12777)
Glowa Manufacturing Inc ....E...... 607 770-0811
  Binghamton (G-913)
Hauppauge Computer Works Inc ..E...... 631 434-1600
  Hauppauge (G-6113)
Hauppauge Digital Inc ....E...... 631 434-1600
  Hauppauge (G-6114)
Hergo Ergonomic Support ....E...... 718 894-0639
  Maspeth (G-8175)
Hitachi Metals America Ltd ....E...... 914 694-9200
  Purchase (G-13975)
HP Inc ....D...... 212 835-1640
  New York (G-10566)
Humanscale Corporation ....B...... 212 725-4749
  New York (G-10578)
IBM World Trade Corporation .....G...... 914 765-1900
  Armonk (G-411)
Innovative Systems of New York ...G...... 516 541-7410
  Massapequa Park (G-8220)
Inpora Technologies LLC ....D...... 646 838-2474
  New York (G-10650)
Kantek Inc ....E...... 516 594-4600
  Oceanside (G-13105)
Lsc Peripherals Incorporated ......G...... 631 244-0707
  Bohemia (G-1092)
Luminescent Systems Inc ....B...... 716 655-0800
  East Aurora (G-4398)
Macrolink Inc ....E...... 631 924-8200
  Medford (G-8288)
Maia Systems LLC ....G...... 718 206-0100
  Jamaica (G-6963)
Marco Manufacturing Inc ....E...... 845 485-1571
  Poughkeepsie (G-13934)
Mirion Technologies Ist Corp ......D...... 607 562-4300
  Horseheads (G-6612)
NCR Corporation ....C...... 607 273-5310
  Ithaca (G-6901)
Norazza Inc ....G...... 716 706-1160
  Buffalo (G-3116)
O Rama Light Inc ....E...... 518 539-9000
  South Glens Falls (G-15552)
Orbit International Corp ....C...... 631 435-8300
  Hauppauge (G-6180)
Perceptive Pixel Inc ....E...... 701 367-5845
  New York (G-11631)
Performance Technologies Inc ....E...... 585 256-0200
  Rochester (G-14596)
Phoenix Venture Fund LLC ....E...... 212 759-1909
  New York (G-11672)
QED Technologies Intl Inc ....E...... 585 256-6540
  Rochester (G-14633)
Rdi Inc ....F...... 914 773-1000
  Mount Kisco (G-8686)
Reliable Elec Mt Vernon Inc ....E...... 914 668-4440
  Mount Vernon (G-8772)
Rodale Wireless Inc ....E...... 631 231-0044
  Hauppauge (G-6205)
Ruhle Companies Inc ....E...... 914 287-4000
  Valhalla (G-16398)
S G I ....G...... 917 386-0385
  New York (G-11962)

COMPUTER PERIPHERAL EQPT, NEC

Sima Technologies LLC ....G....... 412 828-9130
  Hauppauge (G-6215)
Sony Corporation of America ....C....... 212 833-8000
  New York (G-12157)
Symbol Technologies LLC ....F....... 631 738-2400
  Bohemia (G-1136)
Synaptics Incorporated ....F....... 585 899-4300
  Rochester (G-14734)
Technomag Inc ....G....... 631 246-6142
  East Setauket (G-4512)
Todd Enterprises Inc ....D....... 516 773-8087
  Great Neck (G-5863)
Torrent Ems LLC ....F....... 716 312-4099
  Lockport (G-7651)
Toshiba Amer Info Systems Inc ....B....... 949 583-3000
  New York (G-12397)
Vader Systems LLC ....F....... 716 688-1600
  Getzville (G-5618)
Vishay Thin Film LLC ....C....... 716 283-4025
  Niagara Falls (G-12906)
Vuzix Corporation ....E....... 585 359-5900
  West Henrietta (G-16928)
Wantagh Computer Center ....F....... 516 826-2189
  Wantagh (G-16584)
Welch Allyn Inc ....A....... 315 685-4100
  Skaneateles Falls (G-15493)
Wilson & Wilson Group ....G....... 212 729-4736
  Forest Hills (G-5337)
Xerox Corporation ....D....... 516 677-1500
  Melville (G-8393)
Xerox Corporation ....E....... 585 423-3538
  Rochester (G-14798)
Xerox Corporation ....C....... 585 427-4500
  Rochester (G-14797)
Z-Axis Inc ....D....... 315 548-5000
  Phelps (G-13563)
Zebra Technologies Entp Corp ....E....... 800 722-6234
  Holtsville (G-6542)

COMPUTER PERIPHERAL EQPT, WHOLESALE

Atlaz International Ltd ....F....... 516 239-1854
  Lawrence (G-7416)
Cbord Group Inc ....C....... 607 257-2410
  Ithaca (G-6869)
Chem-Puter Friendly Inc ....E....... 631 331-2259
  Mount Sinai (G-8696)
Digicom International Inc ....F....... 631 249-8999
  Farmingdale (G-4986)

COMPUTER PERIPHERAL EQPT: Encoders

Iweb Design Inc ....F....... 805 243-8305
  Bronx (G-1366)
Sequential Electronics Systems ......E....... 914 592-1345
  Elmsford (G-4791)

COMPUTER PERIPHERAL EQPT: Film Reader Devices

P C Rfrs Radiology ....G....... 212 586-5700
  Long Island City (G-7862)

COMPUTER PERIPHERAL EQPT: Graphic Displays, Exc Terminals

Binghamton Simulator Co Inc ....E....... 607 321-2980
  Binghamton (G-891)
Dia-Nielsen USA Incorporated ....G....... 856 642-9700
  Buffalo (G-2930)
Medsim-Eagle Simulation Inc ....F....... 607 658-9354
  Endicott (G-4824)
Mp Displays LLC ....G....... 845 268-4113
  Valley Cottage (G-16409)
Watson Productions LLC ....F....... 516 334-9766
  Hauppauge (G-6255)

COMPUTER PERIPHERAL EQPT: Input Or Output

Gunther Partners LLC ....G....... 212 521-2930
  New York (G-10428)
Pda Panache Corp ....G....... 631 776-0523
  Bohemia (G-1112)

COMPUTER PROGRAMMING SVCS

Actv Inc (del Corp) ....D....... 212 995-9500
  New York (G-9068)

Billing Blocks Inc ....F....... 718 442-5006
  Staten Island (G-15667)
BMC Software Inc ....E....... 212 402-1500
  New York (G-9479)
Cdml Computer Services Ltd ....G....... 718 428-9063
  Fresh Meadows (G-5452)
Data Key Communication LLC ......E....... 315 445-2347
  Fayetteville (G-5172)
Davis Ziff Publishing Inc ....G....... 212 503-3500
  New York (G-9885)
Defran Systems Inc ....E....... 212 727-8342
  New York (G-5892)
Digitronik Dev Labs Inc ....F....... 585 360-0043
  Rochester (G-14329)
Fidesa US Corporation ....B....... 212 269-9000
  New York (G-10212)
Fog Creek Software Inc ....G....... 866 364-2733
  New York (G-10235)
Fuel Data Systems Inc ....G....... 800 447-7870
  Middletown (G-8475)
Hauppauge Computer Works Inc ...E....... 631 434-1600
  Hauppauge (G-6113)
Hudson Software Corporation ....G....... 914 773-0400
  Elmsford (G-4763)
Infinity Augmented Reality Inc ....G....... 917 677-2084
  New York (G-10635)
Irv Inc ....E....... 212 334-4507
  New York (G-10705)
L3 Technologies Inc ....G....... 607 721-5465
  Kirkwood (G-7261)
Lockheed Martin Corporation ....D....... 315 793-5800
  New Hartford (G-8852)
Matrixcare Inc ....G....... 518 583-6400
  New York (G-11204)
Openfin Inc ....G....... 917 450-8822
  New York (G-11526)
PC Solutions & Consulting ....G....... 607 735-0466
  Elmira (G-4711)
Qlogix Entertainment LLC ....E....... 215 459-6315
  New York (G-11790)
Safe Passage International Inc .....F....... 585 292-4910
  Rochester (G-14686)
Suite Solutions Inc ....G....... 716 929-3050
  Amherst (G-263)
Syrasoft LLC ....G....... 315 708-0341
  Baldwinsville (G-577)
Wetpaintcom Inc ....E....... 206 859-6300
  New York (G-12647)
X Function Inc ....E....... 212 231-0092
  New York (G-12698)

COMPUTER PROGRAMMING SVCS: Custom

Endava Inc ....G....... 212 920-7240
  New York (G-10083)
Modern Farmer Media Inc ....F....... 518 828-7447
  Hudson (G-6658)
US Beverage Net Inc ....F....... 315 579-2025
  Syracuse (G-16089)

COMPUTER RELATED MAINTENANCE SVCS

Century Direct LLC ....C....... 212 763-0600
  Islandia (G-6827)
Global Applctions Solution LLC .....G....... 212 741-9595
  New York (G-10354)
IBM World Trade Corporation ....G....... 914 765-1900
  Armonk (G-411)
Laurus Development Inc ....F....... 716 823-1202
  Buffalo (G-3063)

COMPUTER SERVICE BUREAU

Datalink Computer Products ....F....... 914 666-2358
  Mount Kisco (G-8668)
Hudson Software Corporation ....E....... 914 773-0400
  Elmsford (G-4763)

COMPUTER SOFTWARE DEVELOPMENT

Advanced Barcode Tech Inc ....F....... 516 570-8100
  Great Neck (G-5799)
Evolve Guest Controls LLC ....F....... 855 750-9090
  Port Washington (G-13836)
Falconstor Software Inc ....C....... 631 777-5188
  Melville (G-8347)
Geoweb3d Inc ....F....... 607 323-1114
  Vestal (G-16471)
Lake Image Systems Inc ....F....... 585 321-3630
  Henrietta (G-6319)
Ontra Presentations LLC ....G....... 212 213-1315
  New York (G-11524)

Os33 Inc ....G....... 708 336-3466
  New York (G-11542)
Roomactually LLC ....G....... 646 388-1922
  New York (G-11934)
Sale 121 Corp ....D....... 240 855-8988
  New York (G-11972)
Standard Analytics Io Inc ....G....... 917 882-5422
  New York (G-12205)
Structuredweb Inc ....E....... 201 325-3110
  New York (G-12240)
Williamson Law Book Co ....F....... 585 924-3400
  Victor (G-16537)

COMPUTER SOFTWARE DEVELOPMENT & APPLICATIONS

Amcom Software Inc ....F....... 212 951-7600
  New York (G-9159)
Forerunner Technologies Inc ....E....... 631 337-2100
  Bohemia (G-1063)
Hearst Digital Studios Inc ....E....... 212 969-7552
  New York (G-10492)
Innovation In Motion Inc ....G....... 407 878-7551
  Long Beach (G-7672)
Ipsidy Inc ....D....... 407 951-8640
  Long Beach (G-7673)
Magsoft Corporation ....E....... 518 877-8390
  Ballston Spa (G-601)
Orpheo USA Corp ....G....... 212 464-8255
  New York (G-11540)
Pitney Bowes Software Inc ....F....... 518 272-0014
  Troy (G-16272)
Post Road ....F....... 203 545-2122
  New York (G-11712)
Randall Loeffler Inc ....E....... 212 226-8787
  New York (G-11826)
Vepo Solutions LLC ....G....... 914 384-2121
  Cross River (G-4086)

COMPUTER SOFTWARE SYSTEMS ANALYSIS & DESIGN: Custom

Complex Biosystems Inc ....G....... 315 464-8007
  Liverpool (G-7541)
Inprotopia Corporation ....F....... 917 338-7501
  New York (G-10651)
Laurus Development Inc ....G....... 716 823-1202
  Buffalo (G-3063)
Live Vote II Inc ....G....... 646 343-9053
  New York (G-11041)
Vizbee Inc ....G....... 650 787-1424
  New York (G-12586)
Vormittag Associates Inc ....G....... 800 824-7776
  Ronkonkoma (G-15023)

COMPUTER STORAGE DEVICES, NEC

Datalink Computer Products ....F....... 914 666-2358
  Mount Kisco (G-8668)
Emcs LLC ....G....... 716 523-2002
  Hamburg (G-5947)
Garland Technology LLC ....F....... 716 242-8500
  Buffalo (G-2979)
Gim Electronics Corp ....F....... 516 942-3382
  Hicksville (G-6377)
Quantum Asset Recovery ....G....... 716 393-2712
  Buffalo (G-3174)
Quantum Knowledge LLC ....G....... 631 727-6111
  Riverhead (G-14166)
Quantum Logic Corp ....G....... 516 746-1380
  New Hyde Park (G-8904)
Quantum Mechanics Ny LLC ....G....... 917 519-7077
  Huntington (G-6711)
Sony Corporation of America ....C....... 212 833-8000
  New York (G-12157)
Technologies Application LLC ......F....... 607 275-0345
  Cortland (G-4070)
Todd Enterprises Inc ....D....... 516 773-8087
  Great Neck (G-5863)
William S Hein & Co Inc ....F....... 716 882-2600
  Getzville (G-5619)

COMPUTER TERMINALS

AG Neovo Professional Inc ....F....... 212 647-9080
  New York (G-9106)
Clayton Dubilier & Rice Fun ....E....... 212 407-5200
  New York (G-9695)
Igt Global Solutions Corp ....D....... 518 382-2900
  Schenectady (G-15296)

PRODUCT SECTION

CONCRETE PRDTS

International Bus Mchs Corp ....A 845 433-1234
  Poughkeepsie *(G-13927)*
Nu - Communitek LLC ....F 516 433-3553
  Hicksville *(G-6402)*
Orbit International Corp ....C 631 435-8300
  Hauppauge *(G-6180)*
Symbio Technologies LLC ....G 914 576-1205
  White Plains *(G-17200)*

COMPUTER TERMINALS: CRT

Cine Design Group LLC ....G 646 747-0734
  New York *(G-9670)*

COMPUTER-AIDED DESIGN SYSTEMS SVCS

Circuits & Systems Inc ....E 516 593-4301
  East Rockaway *(G-4488)*
Trident Precision Mfg Inc ....D 585 265-2010
  Webster *(G-16764)*

COMPUTER-AIDED ENGINEERING SYSTEMS SVCS

Complex Biosystems Inc ....G 315 464-8007
  Liverpool *(G-7541)*

COMPUTERS, NEC

Alliance Magnetic LLC ....G 914 944-1690
  Ossining *(G-13344)*
Argon Corp ....F 516 487-5314
  Great Neck *(G-5807)*
Arnouse Digital Devices Corp ....D 516 673-4444
  New Hyde Park *(G-8862)*
Binghamton Simulator Co Inc ....E 607 321-2980
  Binghamton *(G-891)*
Columbia Telecom Group ....G 631 501-5000
  New York *(G-9737)*
Computer Conversions Corp ....E 631 261-3300
  East Northport *(G-4454)*
Critical Link LLC ....E 315 425-4045
  Syracuse *(G-15932)*
Data-Pac Mailing Systems Corp ....F 585 671-0210
  Webster *(G-16744)*
Datacom Systems Inc ....E 315 463-9541
  East Syracuse *(G-4537)*
Dees Audio & Vision ....G 585 719-9256
  Rochester *(G-14326)*
Digicom International Inc ....F 631 249-8999
  Farmingdale *(G-4986)*
Dynamic Decisions Inc ....F 908 755-5000
  Fresh Meadows *(G-5453)*
E-Systems Group LLC ....E 607 775-1100
  Conklin *(G-3893)*
Ebc Technologies Inc ....D 631 729-8182
  Hauppauge *(G-6091)*
Electronic Systems Inc ....G 631 589-4389
  Holbrook *(G-6473)*
Envent Systems Inc ....G 646 294-6980
  Pelham *(G-13516)*
Flash Ventures Inc ....F 212 255-7070
  New York *(G-10230)*
H&L Computers Inc ....E 516 873-8088
  Flushing *(G-5255)*
Hand Held Products Inc ....B 315 554-6000
  Skaneateles Falls *(G-15490)*
Hi-Tech Advanced Solutions Inc ....F 718 926-3488
  Forest Hills *(G-5330)*
Human Electronics Inc ....G 315 724-9850
  Utica *(G-16363)*
IBM World Trade Corporation ....G 914 765-1900
  Armonk *(G-411)*
International Bus Mchs Corp ....A 607 754-9558
  Endicott *(G-4819)*
Irpenscom ....G 585 507-7997
  Penfield *(G-13523)*
J & N Computer Services Inc ....F 585 388-8780
  Fairport *(G-4864)*
Kemp Technologies Inc ....E 631 345-5292
  New York *(G-10871)*
Lockheed Martin Corporation ....C 516 228-2000
  Uniondale *(G-16320)*
M&C Associates LLC ....E 631 467-4760
  Hauppauge *(G-6148)*
Medsim-Eagle Simulation Inc ....F 607 658-9354
  Endicott *(G-4824)*
N & G of America Inc ....F 516 428-3414
  Plainview *(G-13650)*
N & L Instruments Inc ....F 631 471-4000
  Ronkonkoma *(G-14973)*

NCR Corporation ....C 516 876-7200
  Jericho *(G-7110)*
One Technologies LLC ....G 718 509-0704
  Brooklyn *(G-2405)*
Photon Vision Systems Inc ....F 607 749-2689
  Homer *(G-6549)*
Qualtronic Devices Inc ....F 631 360-0859
  Smithtown *(G-15520)*
Revivn Inc ....F 347 762-8193
  Brooklyn *(G-2512)*
Revonate Manufacturing LLC ....E 315 433-1160
  Syracuse *(G-16045)*
Todd Enterprises Inc ....D 516 773-8087
  Great Neck *(G-5863)*
Toshiba Amer Info Systems Inc ....B 949 583-3000
  New York *(G-12397)*
Transland Sourcing LLC ....G 718 596-5704
  Brooklyn *(G-2694)*
Wantagh Computer Center ....F 516 826-2189
  Wantagh *(G-16584)*
Yellow E House Inc ....G 718 888-2000
  Flushing *(G-5315)*

COMPUTERS, NEC, WHOLESALE

Todd Enterprises Inc ....D 516 773-8087
  Great Neck *(G-5863)*

COMPUTERS, PERIPHERALS & SOFTWARE, WHOLESALE: Disk Drives

Formats Unlimited Inc ....F 631 249-9200
  Deer Park *(G-4166)*

COMPUTERS, PERIPHERALS & SOFTWARE, WHOLESALE: Printers

Newport Business Solutions Inc ....F 631 319-6129
  Bohemia *(G-1105)*
Printer Components Inc ....G 585 924-5190
  Fairport *(G-4877)*

COMPUTERS, PERIPHERALS & SOFTWARE, WHOLESALE: Software

Base Systems Inc ....G 845 278-1991
  Brewster *(G-1208)*
Cgi Technologies Solutions Inc ....F 212 682-7411
  New York *(G-9624)*
Escholar LLC ....F 914 989-2900
  White Plains *(G-17131)*
Infinite Software Solutions ....F 718 982-1315
  Staten Island *(G-15708)*
Interntnl Publcatns Media Grup ....G 917 604-9602
  New York *(G-10682)*
Kse Sportsman Media Inc ....D 212 852-6600
  New York *(G-10929)*
Pointman LLC ....G 716 842-1439
  Buffalo *(G-3153)*
Visible Systems Corporation ....E 508 628-1510
  Oneida *(G-13192)*

COMPUTERS: Indl, Process, Gas Flow

Pneumercator Company Inc ....E 631 293-8450
  Hauppauge *(G-6192)*

COMPUTERS: Mainframe

Policy ADM Solutions Inc ....E 914 332-4320
  Tarrytown *(G-16125)*

COMPUTERS: Mini

Oracle America Inc ....D 518 427-9353
  Albany *(G-112)*
Oracle America Inc ....D 585 317-4648
  Fairport *(G-4873)*

COMPUTERS: Personal

Apple Bank For Savings ....G 718 486-7294
  Brooklyn *(G-1618)*
Apple Commuter Inc ....G 917 299-0066
  New Hyde Park *(G-8861)*
Apple Healing & Relaxation ....G 718 278-1089
  Long Island City *(G-7696)*
Apple Med Urgent Care PC ....G 914 523-5965
  Mount Vernon *(G-8707)*
G S Communications USA Inc ....E 718 389-7371
  Brooklyn *(G-2011)*

Go Go Apple Inc ....G 646 264-8909
  Elmhurst *(G-4674)*
Stargate Computer Corp ....G 516 474-4799
  Port Jeff STA *(G-13794)*
Telxon Corporation ....E 631 738-2400
  Holtsville *(G-6539)*
Toshiba America Inc ....E 212 596-0600
  New York *(G-12398)*
Wilcro Inc ....G 716 632-4204
  Buffalo *(G-3280)*

CONCENTRATES, DRINK

Constellation Brands Inc ....D 585 678-7100
  Victor *(G-16493)*
Mr Smoothie ....G 845 296-1686
  Poughkeepsie *(G-13938)*
Roar Beverages LLC ....E 631 683-5565
  Huntington *(G-6715)*

CONCENTRATES, FLAVORING, EXC DRINK

Consumer Flavoring Extract Co ....F 718 435-0201
  Brooklyn *(G-1797)*

CONCRETE CURING & HARDENING COMPOUNDS

Hanson Aggregates PA LLC ....F 585 436-3250
  Rochester *(G-14440)*
Watson Bowman Acme Corp ....D 716 691-8162
  Amherst *(G-271)*

CONCRETE MIXERS

Minimax Concrete Corp ....G 716 444-8908
  Grand Island *(G-5777)*
X-Treme Ready Mix Inc ....G 718 739-3384
  Jamaica *(G-7001)*

CONCRETE PLANTS

Oneida Sales & Service Inc ....E 716 822-8205
  Buffalo *(G-3123)*
Oneida Sales & Service Inc ....F 716 270-0433
  Lackawanna *(G-7271)*
Seville Central Mix Corp ....D 516 293-6190
  Old Bethpage *(G-13151)*

CONCRETE PRDTS

A & R Concrete Products LLC ....E 845 562-0640
  New Windsor *(G-8975)*
Alpine Building Supply Inc ....G 718 456-2522
  Ridgewood *(G-14112)*
Arnan Development Corp ....D 607 432-8391
  Oneonta *(G-13194)*
Baliva Concrete Products Inc ....G 585 328-8442
  Rochester *(G-14240)*
Barrett Paving Materials Inc ....F 315 737-9471
  Clayville *(G-3712)*
Buffalo Crushed Stone Inc ....E 716 826-7310
  Buffalo *(G-2872)*
City Mason Corp ....F 718 658-3796
  Jamaica *(G-6939)*
Diamond Precast Products Inc ....F 631 874-3777
  Center Moriches *(G-3489)*
East Main Associates ....D 585 624-1990
  Lima *(G-7466)*
Elderlee Incorporated ....C 315 789-6670
  Oaks Corners *(G-13088)*
Express Concrete Inc ....G 631 273-4224
  Brentwood *(G-1180)*
Get Real Surfaces Inc ....F 845 337-4483
  Poughkeepsie *(G-13921)*
Grace Associates Inc ....G 718 767-9000
  Harrison *(G-6005)*
Great ATL Pr-Cast Con Statuary ....G 718 948-5677
  Staten Island *(G-15703)*
Jab Concrete Supply Corp ....E 718 842-5250
  Bronx *(G-1367)*
Jenna Concrete Corporation ....E 718 842-5250
  Bronx *(G-1369)*
Jenna Harlem River Inc ....G 718 842-5997
  Bronx *(G-1370)*
John E Potente & Sons Inc ....G 516 935-8585
  Hicksville *(G-6385)*
Lafarge North America Inc ....E 518 756-5000
  Ravena *(G-14036)*
Long Island Geotech ....G 631 473-1044
  Port Jefferson *(G-13798)*
M K Ulrich Construction Inc ....F 716 893-5777
  Buffalo *(G-3071)*

Employee Codes: A=Over 500 employees, B=251-500
C=101-250, D=51-100, E=20-50, F=10-19, G=5-9

Mid-Hudson Concrete Pdts Inc..........G....... 845 265-3141
Cold Spring *(G-3788)*
Nicolia Concrete Products Inc..........D....... 631 669-0700
Lindenhurst *(G-7500)*
NY Tempering LLC..........G....... 718 326-8989
Maspeth *(G-8190)*
Quikrete Companies Inc..........E....... 716 213-2027
Lackawanna *(G-7273)*
Riefler Concrete Products LLC..........C....... 716 649-3260
Hamburg *(G-5964)*
Stag Brothers Cast Stone Co..........G....... 718 629-0975
Brooklyn *(G-2617)*
Suhor Industries Inc..........G....... 716 483-6818
Jamestown *(G-7064)*
Taylor Concrete Products Inc..........E....... 315 788-2191
Watertown *(G-16696)*
Towne House Restorations Inc..........G....... 718 497-9200
Long Island City *(G-7932)*
Unilock New York Inc..........G....... 845 278-6700
Brewster *(G-1227)*
Upstone Materials Inc..........G....... 518 483-2671
Malone *(G-8050)*
Upstone Materials Inc..........G....... 518 873-2275
Lewis *(G-7452)*
Woodards Concrete Products Inc..........E....... 845 361-3471
Bullville *(G-3289)*

CONCRETE PRDTS, PRECAST, NEC

Afco Precast Sales Corp..........D....... 631 924-7114
Middle Island *(G-8438)*
Callanan Industries Inc..........E....... 315 697-9569
Canastota *(G-3393)*
Callanan Industries Inc..........C....... 518 374-2222
Albany *(G-57)*
Callanan Industries Inc..........E....... 845 331-6868
Kingston *(G-7211)*
Callanan Industries Inc..........G....... 518 785-5666
Latham *(G-7385)*
Castek Inc..........G....... 914 636-1000
New Rochelle *(G-8936)*
David Kucera Inc..........E....... 845 255-1044
Gardiner *(G-5562)*
Dillner Precast Inc..........G....... 631 421-9130
Lloyd Harbor *(G-7593)*
Dillner Precast Inc..........G....... 631 421-9130
Huntington Station *(G-6741)*
Dynasty Metal Works Inc..........G....... 631 284-3719
Riverhead *(G-14153)*
Fort Miller Group Inc..........B....... 518 695-5000
Greenwich *(G-5906)*
Fort Miller Service Corp..........F....... 518 695-5000
Greenwich *(G-5907)*
Gamble & Gamble Inc..........G....... 716 731-3239
Sanborn *(G-15147)*
Glens Falls Ready Mix Inc..........F....... 518 793-1695
Queensbury *(G-14010)*
Glenwood Cast Stone Inc..........G....... 718 859-6500
Brooklyn *(G-2028)*
Guardian Concrete Inc..........F....... 518 372-0080
Schenectady *(G-15294)*
Island Ready Mix Inc..........E....... 631 874-3777
Center Moriches *(G-3492)*
Lakelands Concrete Pdts Inc..........E....... 585 624-1990
Lima *(G-7467)*
Lhv Precast Inc..........E....... 845 336-8880
Kingston *(G-7225)*
Long Island Precast Inc..........E....... 631 286-0240
Brookhaven *(G-1508)*
Oldcastle Precast Inc..........F....... 518 767-2116
South Bethlehem *(G-15536)*
Oldcastle Precast Inc..........E....... 518 767-2112
Selkirk *(G-15378)*
P J R Industries Inc..........E....... 716 825-9300
Buffalo *(G-3128)*
Pelkowski Precast Corp..........F....... 631 269-5727
Kings Park *(G-7203)*
Robinson Concrete Inc..........E....... 315 253-6666
Auburn *(G-513)*
Sunnycrest Inc..........E....... 315 252-7214
Auburn *(G-518)*
Transpo Industries Inc..........E....... 914 636-1000
New Rochelle *(G-8972)*
Wel Made Enterprises Inc..........F....... 631 752-1238
Farmingdale *(G-5151)*

CONCRETE: Asphaltic, Not From Refineries

Monticello Black Top Corp..........G....... 845 434-7280
Thompsonville *(G-16138)*
Peckham Industries Inc..........E....... 914 949-2000
White Plains *(G-17175)*
Peckham Industries Inc..........F....... 518 943-0155
Catskill *(G-3461)*
Peckham Industries Inc..........F....... 518 893-2176
Greenfield Center *(G-5889)*
PSI Transit Mix Corp..........G....... 631 382-7930
Smithtown *(G-15519)*
Seabreeze Pavement of Ny LLC..........G....... 585 338-2333
Rochester *(G-14699)*
Swift River Associates Inc..........G....... 716 875-0902
Tonawanda *(G-16225)*

CONCRETE: Bituminous

Barrett Paving Materials Inc..........E....... 315 353-6611
Norwood *(G-13058)*
Pallette Stone Corporation..........E....... 518 584-2421
Gansevoort *(G-5501)*

CONCRETE: Ready-Mixed

A-1 Transitmix Inc..........F....... 718 292-3200
Bronx *(G-1256)*
Advanced Ready Mix Corp..........F....... 718 497-5020
Brooklyn *(G-1565)*
All American Transit Mix Corp..........G....... 718 417-3654
Brooklyn *(G-1584)*
Atlas Concrete Batching Corp..........D....... 718 523-3000
Jamaica *(G-6931)*
Atlas Transit Mix Corp..........C....... 718 523-3000
Jamaica *(G-6932)*
Barney & Dickenson Inc..........E....... 607 729-1536
Vestal *(G-16462)*
Barrett Paving Materials Inc..........F....... 315 788-2037
Watertown *(G-16658)*
Best Concrete Mix Corp..........E....... 718 463-5500
Flushing *(G-5236)*
Bonded Concrete Inc..........E....... 518 273-5800
Watervliet *(G-16704)*
Bonded Concrete Inc..........F....... 518 674-2854
West Sand Lake *(G-16960)*
Brewster Transit Mix Corp..........E....... 845 279-3738
Brewster *(G-1210)*
Brewster Transit Mix Corp..........E....... 845 279-3738
Brewster *(G-1211)*
Byram Concrete & Supply LLC..........F....... 914 682-4477
White Plains *(G-17117)*
C & C Ready-Mix Corporation..........E....... 607 797-5108
Vestal *(G-16465)*
C & C Ready-Mix Corporation..........F....... 607 687-1690
Owego *(G-13376)*
Capital Concrete Inc..........G....... 716 648-8001
Hamburg *(G-5942)*
Casa Redimix Concrete Corp..........F....... 718 589-1555
Bronx *(G-1291)*
Ccz Ready Mix Concrete Corp..........G....... 516 579-7352
Levittown *(G-7448)*
Cemex Cement Inc..........D....... 212 317-6000
New York *(G-9610)*
Century Ready Mix Inc..........G....... 631 888-2200
West Babylon *(G-16806)*
Champion Materials Inc..........G....... 315 493-2654
Carthage *(G-3439)*
Champion Materials Inc..........E....... 315 493-2654
Carthage *(G-3440)*
Chenango Concrete Corp..........F....... 518 294-9964
Richmondville *(G-14101)*
Clark Concrete Co Inc..........G....... 315 478-4101
Syracuse *(G-15915)*
Classic Concrete Corp..........F....... 516 822-1800
Hicksville *(G-6356)*
Clemente Latham Concrete Corp..........D....... 518 374-2222
Schenectady *(G-15271)*
Cobleskill Red E Mix & Supply..........F....... 518 234-2015
Amsterdam *(G-340)*
Corona Ready Mix Inc..........F....... 718 271-5940
Corona *(G-4017)*
Cortland Ready Mix Inc..........F....... 607 753-3063
Cortland *(G-4044)*
Cossitt Concrete Products Inc..........F....... 315 824-2700
Hamilton *(G-5970)*
Costanza Ready Mix Inc..........G....... 516 783-4444
North Bellmore *(G-12934)*
Cranesville Block Co Inc..........E....... 315 732-2135
Utica *(G-16340)*
Cranesville Block Co Inc..........F....... 845 292-1585
Liberty *(G-7458)*
Cranesville Block Co Inc..........E....... 845 896-5687
Fishkill *(G-5189)*
Cranesville Block Co Inc..........E....... 845 331-1775
Kingston *(G-7214)*
Cranesville Block Co Inc..........G....... 315 384-4000
Norfolk *(G-12915)*
Cranesville Block Co Inc..........E....... 518 684-6154
Amsterdam *(G-341)*
Cranesville Block Co Inc..........E....... 315 773-2296
Felts Mills *(G-5175)*
Custom Mix Inc..........G....... 516 797-7090
Massapequa Park *(G-8218)*
Dalrymple Grav & Contg Co Inc..........F....... 607 739-0391
Pine City *(G-13577)*
Dalrymple Holding Corp..........E....... 607 737-6200
Pine City *(G-13578)*
Deer Park Sand & Gravel Corp..........E....... 631 586-2323
Bay Shore *(G-691)*
Dicks Concrete Co Inc..........E....... 845 374-5966
New Hampton *(G-8844)*
Dunkirk Construction Products..........G....... 716 366-5220
Dunkirk *(G-4362)*
E Tetz & Sons Inc..........D....... 845 692-4486
Middletown *(G-8470)*
East Coast Spring Mix Inc..........G....... 845 355-1215
New Hampton *(G-8845)*
Electric City Concrete Co Inc..........E....... 518 887-5560
Amsterdam *(G-343)*
Empire Transit Mix Inc..........E....... 718 384-3000
Brooklyn *(G-1927)*
F H Stickles & Son Inc..........F....... 518 851-9048
Livingston *(G-7587)*
Ferrara Bros LLC..........E....... 718 939-3030
Flushing *(G-5248)*
Fulmont Ready-Mix Company Inc..........E....... 518 887-5560
Amsterdam *(G-347)*
G & J Rdymx & Masnry Sup Inc..........F....... 718 454-0800
Hollis *(G-6523)*
Glens Falls Ready Mix Inc..........G....... 518 793-1695
Amsterdam *(G-348)*
Glens Falls Ready Mix Inc..........F....... 518 793-1695
Queensbury *(G-14010)*
Grandview Concrete Corp..........E....... 518 346-7981
Schenectady *(G-15293)*
Greco Bros Rdymx Con Co Inc..........G....... 718 855-6271
Brooklyn *(G-2050)*
Haley Concrete Inc..........F....... 716 492-0849
Delevan *(G-4260)*
Hanson Aggregates East LLC..........F....... 585 798-0762
Medina *(G-8307)*
Hanson Aggregates East LLC..........F....... 716 372-1574
Falconer *(G-4907)*
Hanson Aggregates East LLC..........E....... 315 548-2911
Phelps *(G-13556)*
Hanson Aggregates New York LLC..........F....... 716 665-4620
Jamestown *(G-7032)*
Hanson Aggregates New York LLC..........F....... 585 638-5841
Pavilion *(G-13472)*
Hanson Aggregates New York LLC..........C....... 315 469-5501
Jamesville *(G-7082)*
Inwood Material..........F....... 516 371-1842
Inwood *(G-6799)*
Iroquois Rock Products Inc..........F....... 585 381-7010
Rochester *(G-14476)*
Island Ready Mix Inc..........E....... 631 874-3777
Center Moriches *(G-3492)*
James Town Macadam Inc..........D....... 716 665-4504
Falconer *(G-4911)*
Jenna Concrete Corporation..........E....... 718 842-5250
Bronx *(G-1369)*
Jenna Harlem River Inc..........G....... 718 842-5997
Bronx *(G-1370)*
Jet Redi Mix Concrete Inc..........F....... 631 580-3640
Ronkonkoma *(G-14947)*
King Road Materials Inc..........F....... 518 382-5354
Albany *(G-95)*
Kings Park Ready Mix Corp..........F....... 631 269-4330
Kings Park *(G-7202)*
Lafarge North America Inc..........E....... 518 756-5000
Ravena *(G-14036)*
Lazarek Inc..........G....... 315 343-1242
Oswego *(G-13359)*
Lehigh Cement Company..........E....... 518 943-5940
Catskill *(G-3458)*
Lewbro Ready Mix Inc..........G....... 315 497-0498
Groton *(G-5921)*
Manitou Concrete..........D....... 585 424-6040
Rochester *(G-14513)*
Manzione Ready Mix Corp..........G....... 718 628-3837
Brooklyn *(G-2265)*
Mastro Concrete Inc..........G....... 718 528-6788
Rosedale *(G-15038)*
Mix N Mac LLC..........G....... 845 381-5536
Middletown *(G-8486)*
N Y Western Concrete Corp..........G....... 585 343-6850
Batavia *(G-644)*

New Atlantic Ready Mix Corp ....G....... 718 812-0739
Hollis *(G-6524)*
Nex-Gen Ready Mix Corp ....G....... 347 231-0073
Bronx *(G-1412)*
Nicolia Ready Mix Inc ....E....... 631 669-7000
Lindenhurst *(G-7501)*
Northern Ready-Mix Inc.......................E....... 315 598-2141
Fulton *(G-5487)*
Oldcastle Precast Inc.........................F....... 518 767-2116
South Bethlehem *(G-15536)*
Oneida Sales & Service Inc.................F....... 716 270-0433
Lackawanna *(G-7271)*
Otsego Ready Mix Inc..........................F....... 607 432-3400
Oneonta *(G-13213)*
Precision Ready Mix Inc.......................G....... 718 658-5600
Jamaica *(G-6977)*
Presti Ready Mix Concrete Inc ....G....... 516 378-6006
Freeport *(G-5430)*
Quality Ready Mix Inc..........................F....... 516 437-0100
New Hyde Park *(G-8903)*
Queens Ready Mix Inc..........................G....... 718 526-4919
Jamaica *(G-6979)*
Quikrete Companies Inc.......................E....... 315 673-2020
Marcellus *(G-8119)*
Residential Fences Corp......................E....... 631 205-9758
Ridge *(G-14107)*
Richmond Ready Mix Corp ....G....... 917 731-8400
Staten Island *(G-15755)*
Riefler Concrete Products LLC.............C....... 716 649-3260
Hamburg *(G-5964)*
Robinson Concrete Inc.........................E....... 315 253-6666
Auburn *(G-513)*
Robinson Concrete Inc.........................F....... 315 492-6200
Jamesville *(G-7085)*
Robinson Concrete Inc.........................F....... 315 676-4662
Brewerton *(G-1202)*
Rochester Asphalt Materials.................D....... 585 924-7360
Farmington *(G-5163)*
Rochester Asphalt Materials.................G....... 585 381-7010
Rochester *(G-14656)*
Rural Hill Sand and Grav Corp ....F....... 315 846-5212
Woodville *(G-17383)*
Russian Mix Inc....................................G....... 347 385-7198
Brooklyn *(G-2537)*
Saunders Concrete Co Inc....................F....... 607 756-7905
Cortland *(G-4067)*
Scara-Mix Inc.......................................E....... 718 442-7357
Staten Island *(G-15756)*
Seville Central Mix Corp.......................D....... 516 868-3000
Freeport *(G-5438)*
Seville Central Mix Corp.......................D....... 516 293-6190
Old Bethpage *(G-13151)*
Seville Central Mix Corp.......................E....... 516 239-8333
Lawrence *(G-7425)*
South Shore Ready Mix Inc...................G....... 516 872-3049
Valley Stream *(G-16451)*
Star Ready Mix East Inc ....F....... 631 289-8787
East Hampton *(G-4436)*
Star Ready Mix Inc ....F....... 631 289-8787
Medford *(G-8294)*
Stephen Miller Gen Contrs Inc..............E....... 518 661-5601
Gloversville *(G-5738)*
Suffolk Cement Products Inc................E....... 631 727-2317
Calverton *(G-3328)*
Sullivan Concrete Inc ....F....... 845 888-2235
Cochecton *(G-3769)*
T Mix Inc...G....... 646 379-6814
Brooklyn *(G-2660)*
TEC - Crete Transit Mix Corp ....E....... 718 657-6880
Ridgewood *(G-14139)*
Thousand Island Ready Mix Con..........G....... 315 686-3203
La Fargeville *(G-7264)*
Torrington Industries Inc.......................G....... 315 676-4662
Central Square *(G-3545)*
United Materials LLC ....D....... 716 683-1432
North Tonawanda *(G-13022)*
United Materials LLC ....E....... 716 731-2332
Sanborn *(G-15157)*
United Materials LLC ....G....... 716 662-0564
Orchard Park *(G-13326)*
United Transit Mix Inc ....F....... 718 416-3400
Brooklyn *(G-2723)*
Upstone Materials Inc...........................F....... 315 265-8036
Plattsburgh *(G-13736)*
Upstone Materials Inc...........................G....... 315 764-0251
Massena *(G-8233)*
Upstone Materials Inc...........................G....... 518 873-2275
Lewis *(G-7452)*
Upstone Materials Inc...........................D....... 518 561-5321
Plattsburgh *(G-13735)*
US Concrete Inc ....E....... 718 853-4644
Roslyn Heights *(G-15058)*
US Concrete Inc ....E....... 718 438-6800
Brooklyn *(G-2731)*
W F Saunders & Sons Inc ....F....... 315 469-3217
Nedrow *(G-8819)*
Watertown Concrete Inc ....F....... 315 788-1040
Watertown *(G-16698)*

CONDENSERS & CONDENSING UNITS: Air Conditioner

Cold Point Corporation ....E....... 315 339-2331
Rome *(G-14838)*
Motivair Corporation.............................E....... 716 691-9222
Amherst *(G-250)*

CONDENSERS: Fixed Or Variable

Viking Technologies Ltd........................E....... 631 957-8000
Lindenhurst *(G-7516)*

CONDENSERS: Heat Transfer Eqpt, Evaporative

Alstrom Corporation..............................E....... 718 824-4901
Bronx *(G-1271)*
Roemac Industrial Sales Inc ....G....... 716 692-7332
North Tonawanda *(G-13009)*
Rubicon Industries Corp.......................E....... 718 434-4700
Brooklyn *(G-2535)*

CONDENSERS: Motors Or Generators

GM Components Holdings LLC.............B....... 716 439-2463
Lockport *(G-7619)*
GM Components Holdings LLC.............B....... 716 439-2011
Lockport *(G-7620)*

CONDUITS & FITTINGS: Electric

Highland Valley Supply Inc ....F....... 845 849-2863
Wappingers Falls *(G-16592)*
Producto Electric Corp..........................E....... 845 359-4900
Orangeburg *(G-13265)*
Quadristi LLC ....F....... 585 279-3318
Rochester *(G-14635)*
Superflex Ltd ....E....... 718 768-1400
Brooklyn *(G-2646)*

CONDUITS: Pressed Pulp Fiber, Made From Purchased Materials

Stanley Paper Co Inc ....F....... 518 489-1131
Albany *(G-136)*

CONFECTIONERY PRDTS WHOLESALERS

Mrchocolatecom LLC ....F....... 718 875-9772
Brooklyn *(G-2347)*
Roger L Urban Inc.................................E....... 716 693-5391
North Tonawanda *(G-13010)*

CONFECTIONS & CANDY

5th Avenue Chocolatiere Ltd ....F....... 516 561-1570
Valley Stream *(G-16423)*
5th Avenue Chocolatiere Ltd ....G....... 212 935-5454
Freeport *(G-5388)*
C Howard Company Inc........................G....... 631 286-7940
Bellport *(G-822)*
Calico Cottage Inc.................................E....... 631 841-2100
Amityville *(G-277)*
Chocolat Moderne LLC..........................G....... 212 229-4797
New York *(G-9657)*
Chocolations LLC ....G....... 914 777-3600
Mamaroneck *(G-8060)*
Custom Candy Concepts Inc ....G....... 516 824-3228
Inwood *(G-6793)*
Demets Candy Company LLC..............G....... 607 562-8600
Horseheads *(G-6602)*
Dilese International Inc.........................F....... 716 855-3500
Buffalo *(G-2931)*
Dylans Candy Bar Inc ....F....... 646 735-0078
New York *(G-9998)*
Fairbanks Mfg LLC................................C....... 845 341-0002
Middletown *(G-8474)*
Gertrude Hawk Chocolates Inc.............E.....
Watertown *(G-16673)*
Godiva Chocolatier Inc ....E....... 212 984-5900
New York *(G-10368)*
Gravymaster Inc....................................E....... 203 453-1893
Canajoharie *(G-3360)*
Handsome Dans LLC.............................G....... 917 965-2499
New York *(G-10449)*
Hedonist Artisan Chocolates.................F....... 585 461-2815
Rochester *(G-14452)*
Hercules Candy Co ....F....... 315 463-4339
East Syracuse *(G-4551)*
Hudson Valley Chocolatier Inc ....F....... 845 831-8240
Beacon *(G-781)*
In Room Plus Inc...................................E....... 716 838-9433
Buffalo *(G-3023)*
Jo-Mart Candies Corp...........................F....... 718 375-1277
Brooklyn *(G-2142)*
Joyva Corp ....D....... 718 497-0170
Brooklyn *(G-2153)*
Lady-N-Th-wndow Chocolates Inc ....F....... 631 549-1059
Huntington *(G-6702)*
Lanco Corporation.................................C....... 631 231-2300
Ronkonkoma *(G-14957)*
Little Bird Chocolates Inc......................G....... 646 620-6395
Massapequa *(G-8211)*
Momn Pops Inc ....E....... 845 567-0640
Cornwall *(G-4009)*
Mrchocolatecom LLC ....F....... 718 875-9772
Brooklyn *(G-2347)*
Noras Candy Shop.................................F....... 315 337-4530
Rome *(G-14853)*
Papa Bubble ....G....... 212 966-2599
New York *(G-11575)*
Premium Sweets USA Inc ....G....... 718 739-6000
Jamaica *(G-6978)*
Rajbhog Foods Inc................................E....... 718 358-5105
Flushing *(G-5294)*
Richardson Brands Company ....C....... 800 839-8938
Canajoharie *(G-3361)*
Roger L Urban Inc.................................E....... 716 693-5391
North Tonawanda *(G-13010)*
Salty Road Inc ....G....... 347 673-3925
Brooklyn *(G-2555)*
Satin Fine Foods Inc.............................D....... 845 469-1034
Chester *(G-3642)*
Scaccianoce Inc....................................F....... 718 991-4462
Bronx *(G-1449)*
Seaward Candies ....G....... 585 638-6761
Holley *(G-6518)*
Settons Intl Foods Inc ....E....... 631 543-8090
Commack *(G-3868)*
Simply Natural Foods LLC....................E....... 631 543-9600
Commack *(G-3869)*
Steve & Andys Organics Inc.................G....... 718 499-7933
Brooklyn *(G-2629)*
Stones Homemade Candies Inc ....G....... 315 343-8401
Oswego *(G-13367)*
Sweetworks Inc ....C....... 716 634-4545
Buffalo *(G-3230)*
Tomric Systems Inc ....G....... 716 854-6050
Buffalo *(G-3247)*
Valenti Distributing...............................G....... 716 824-2304
Blasdell *(G-962)*
Vidal Candies USA Inc..........................G....... 609 781-8169
New York *(G-12565)*
Wellspring Corp ....G....... 212 529-5454
New York *(G-12637)*
Worlds Finest Chocolate Inc.................C....... 718 332-2442
Brooklyn *(G-2782)*

CONFINEMENT SURVEILLANCE SYS MAINTENANCE & MONITORING SVCS

Par Technology Corporation.................D....... 315 738-0600
New Hartford *(G-8853)*

CONNECTORS & TERMINALS: Electrical Device Uses

Fiber Instrument Sales Inc ....C....... 315 736-2206
Oriskany *(G-13333)*
International Key Supply LLC...............F....... 631 983-6096
Farmingdale *(G-5020)*
Zierick Manufacturing Corp ....D....... 800 882-8020
Mount Kisco *(G-8690)*

CONNECTORS: Cord, Electric

Crown Die Casting Corp........................E....... 914 667-5400
Mount Vernon *(G-8720)*
EB Acquisitions LLC ....D....... 212 355-3310
New York *(G-10022)*

CONNECTORS: Electrical

CONNECTORS: Electrical

- Automatic Connector Inc .... F 631 543-5000
  Hauppauge *(G-6048)*
- Command Components Corporation ...G 631 666-4411
  Bay Shore *(G-686)*
- Pei/Genesis Inc .... G 631 256-1747
  Farmingville *(G-5169)*
- SL Industries Inc .... D 212 520-2300
  New York *(G-12124)*

CONNECTORS: Electronic

- Accessories For Electronics .... E 631 847-0158
  South Hempstead *(G-15553)*
- Amphenol Corporation .... B 607 563-5364
  Sidney *(G-15458)*
- Amphenol Corporation .... A 607 563-5011
  Sidney *(G-15459)*
- Automatic Connector Inc .... F 631 543-5000
  Hauppauge *(G-6048)*
- Belden Inc .... B 607 796-5600
  Horseheads *(G-6597)*
- Casa Innovations Inc .... G 718 965-6600
  Brooklyn *(G-1765)*
- EBY Electro Inc .... E 516 576-7777
  Plainview *(G-13628)*
- Executive Machines Inc .... E 718 965-6600
  Brooklyn *(G-1950)*
- Felchar Manufacturing Corp .... A 607 723-3106
  Binghamton *(G-909)*
- I Trade Technology Ltd .... G 615 348-7233
  Suffern *(G-15814)*
- Ieh Corporation .... C 718 492-4440
  Brooklyn *(G-2094)*
- Keystone Electronics Corp .... C 718 956-8900
  Astoria *(G-444)*
- Kirtas Inc .... G 585 924-5999
  Victor *(G-16510)*
- Kirtas Inc .... E 585 924-2420
  Victor *(G-16511)*
- Leviton Manufacturing Co Inc .... B 631 812-6000
  Melville *(G-8363)*
- Mason Industries Inc .... B 631 348-0282
  Hauppauge *(G-6152)*
- Mill-Max Mfg Corp .... C 516 922-6000
  Oyster Bay *(G-13397)*
- Mini-Circuits Fort Wayne LLC .... B 718 934-4500
  Brooklyn *(G-2322)*
- NEa Manufacturing Corp .... E 516 371-4200
  Inwood *(G-6803)*
- Power Connector Inc .... E 631 563-7878
  Bohemia *(G-1114)*
- Ppc Broadband Inc .... B 315 431-7200
  East Syracuse *(G-4569)*
- Princetel Inc .... F 914 579-2410
  Hawthorne *(G-6277)*
- Rdi Inc .... F 914 773-1000
  Mount Kisco *(G-8686)*
- Resonance Technologies Inc .... E 631 237-4901
  Ronkonkoma *(G-15002)*
- Sitewatch Technology LLC .... G 207 778-3246
  East Quogue *(G-4471)*
- Supplynet Inc .... G 800 826-0279
  Valley Cottage *(G-16418)*
- Sureseal Corporation .... G 607 336-6676
  Norwich *(G-13056)*
- Taro Manufacturing Company Inc .... F 315 252-9430
  Auburn *(G-520)*
- Universal Remote Control Inc .... D 914 630-4343
  Harrison *(G-6012)*
- Virtue Paintball LLC .... G 631 617-5560
  Hauppauge *(G-6251)*
- Whirlwind Music Distrs Inc .... D 800 733-9473
  Rochester *(G-14790)*

CONNECTORS: Solderless, Electric-Wiring Devices

- Andros Manufacturing Corp .... F 585 663-5700
  Rochester *(G-14221)*

CONSTRUCTION & MINING MACHINERY WHOLESALERS

- American Material Processing .... F 315 695-6204
  Phoenix *(G-13568)*
- Gone South Concrete Block Inc .... E 315 598-2141
  Fulton *(G-5473)*

CONSTRUCTION & ROAD MAINTENANCE EQPT: Drags, Road

- Drillco National Group Inc .... E 718 726-9801
  Long Island City *(G-7747)*
- Highway Garage .... G 518 568-2837
  Saint Johnsville *(G-15122)*

CONSTRUCTION EQPT: Attachments

- Hansteel (usa) Inc .... G 212 226-0105
  New York *(G-10456)*
- Primoplast Inc .... F 631 750-0680
  Bohemia *(G-1117)*

CONSTRUCTION EQPT: Attachments, Snow Plow

- Cives Corporation .... D 315 543-2321
  Harrisville *(G-6014)*
- Pro-Tech Wldg Fabrication Inc .... E 585 436-9855
  Rochester *(G-14626)*
- Town of Ohio 315 392-2055
  Forestport *(G-5339)*

CONSTRUCTION EQPT: Crane Carriers

- Crane Equipment & Service Inc .... G 716 689-5400
  Amherst *(G-236)*

CONSTRUCTION EQPT: Cranes

- Dave Sandel Cranes Inc .... G 631 325-5588
  Westhampton *(G-17085)*
- Industrial Handling Svcs Inc .... G 518 399-0488
  Alplaus *(G-207)*
- Kinedyne Inc .... F 716 667-6833
  Orchard Park *(G-13303)*
- Sierson Crane & Welding Inc .... G 315 723-6914
  Westmoreland *(G-17095)*

CONSTRUCTION EQPT: Dozers, Tractor Mounted, Material Moving

- Rapistak Corporation .... G 716 822-2804
  Blasdell *(G-957)*

CONSTRUCTION EQPT: Hammer Mills, Port, Incl Rock/Ore Crush

- Schutte-Buffalo Hammermill LLC .... E 716 855-1202
  Buffalo *(G-3207)*

CONSTRUCTION EQPT: Rakes, Land Clearing, Mechanical

- Got Wood LLC .... G 315 440-8857
  Cleveland *(G-3718)*

CONSTRUCTION EQPT: Rollers, Sheepsfoot & Vibratory

- S R & R Industries Inc .... G 845 692-8329
  Middletown *(G-8496)*

CONSTRUCTION EQPT: SCRAPERS, GRADERS, ROLLERS & SIMILAR EQPT

- Gei International Inc .... F 315 463-9261
  East Syracuse *(G-4546)*

CONSTRUCTION EQPT: Wrecker Hoists, Automobile

- Pauls Rods & Restos Inc 631 665-7637
  Deer Park *(G-4211)*
- Vanhouten Motorsports .... G 315 387-6312
  Lacona *(G-7277)*

CONSTRUCTION MATERIALS, WHOLESALE: Aggregate

- Twin County Recycling Corp .... F 516 827-6900
  Westbury *(G-17067)*

CONSTRUCTION MATERIALS, WHOLESALE: Awnings

- Acme Awning Co Inc .... F 718 409-1881
  Bronx *(G-1263)*

- Kassis Superior Sign Co Inc .... F 315 463-7446
  Syracuse *(G-15992)*

CONSTRUCTION MATERIALS, WHOLESALE: Block, Concrete & Cinder

- Lazarek Inc .... G 315 343-1242
  Oswego *(G-13359)*
- Taylor Concrete Products Inc .... E 315 788-2191
  Watertown *(G-16696)*

CONSTRUCTION MATERIALS, WHOLESALE: Blocks, Building, NEC

- Sg Blocks Inc .... G 615 585-2639
  Brooklyn *(G-2573)*

CONSTRUCTION MATERIALS, WHOLESALE: Building Stone, Granite

- Glen Plaza Marble & Gran Inc .... G 516 671-1100
  Glen Cove *(G-5630)*
- MCM Natural Stone Inc .... F 585 586-6510
  Rochester *(G-14523)*

CONSTRUCTION MATERIALS, WHOLESALE: Building Stone, Marble

- Stone & Terrazzo World Inc .... G 718 361-6899
  Long Island City *(G-7920)*

CONSTRUCTION MATERIALS, WHOLESALE: Building, Exterior

- Bestway Enterprises Inc .... E 607 753-8261
  Cortland *(G-4034)*
- Bob Murphy Inc .... F 607 729-3553
  Vestal *(G-16464)*
- Dolomite Products Company Inc .... E 315 524-1998
  Rochester *(G-14337)*
- Tri-State Brick & Stone NY Inc .... D 212 366-0300
  New York *(G-12423)*

CONSTRUCTION MATERIALS, WHOLESALE: Building, Interior

- Great American Industries Inc .... G 607 729-9331
  Vestal *(G-16472)*
- Nanz Custom Hardware Inc .... E 212 367-7000
  New York *(G-11364)*
- Nanz Custom Hardware Inc .... E 212 367-7000
  Deer Park *(G-4200)*

CONSTRUCTION MATERIALS, WHOLESALE: Cement

- Dicks Concrete Co Inc .... E 845 374-5966
  New Hampton *(G-8844)*
- Lehigh Cement Company .... E 518 943-5940
  Catskill *(G-3458)*

CONSTRUCTION MATERIALS, WHOLESALE: Clay, Exc Refractory

- Walsh & Hughes Inc .... G 631 427-5904
  Huntington Station *(G-6766)*

CONSTRUCTION MATERIALS, WHOLESALE: Concrete Mixtures

- Barney & Dickenson Inc .... E 607 729-1536
  Vestal *(G-16462)*

CONSTRUCTION MATERIALS, WHOLESALE: Door Frames

- Lif Industries Inc .... D 516 390-6800
  Port Washington *(G-13858)*
- Lif Industries Inc .... E 718 767-8800
  Whitestone *(G-17240)*
- Milanese Commercial Door LLC .... F 518 658-0398
  Berlin *(G-856)*

CONSTRUCTION MATERIALS, WHOLESALE: Glass

- Twin Pane Insulated GL Co Inc .... F 631 924-1060
  Yaphank *(G-17423)*

PRODUCT SECTION

CONSTRUCTION: Single-family Housing, New

CONSTRUCTION MATERIALS, WHOLESALE: Gravel

Brewster Transit Mix Corp .... E 845 279-3738
  Brewster *(G-1210)*
Deer Park Sand & Gravel Corp .... E 631 586-2323
  Bay Shore *(G-691)*
Jamestown Macadam Inc .... F 716 664-5108
  Jamestown *(G-7042)*

CONSTRUCTION MATERIALS, WHOLESALE: Lime Building Prdts

Specialty Minerals Inc .... E 212 878-1800
  New York *(G-12178)*

CONSTRUCTION MATERIALS, WHOLESALE: Limestone

Minerals Technologies Inc .... E 212 878-1800
  New York *(G-11302)*

CONSTRUCTION MATERIALS, WHOLESALE: Masons' Materials

Colonie Block and Supply Co .... G 518 869-8411
  Colonie *(G-3845)*
Grandview Block & Supply Co .... E 518 346-7981
  Schenectady *(G-15292)*

CONSTRUCTION MATERIALS, WHOLESALE: Millwork

I Meglio Corp .... E 631 617-6900
  Brentwood *(G-1181)*

CONSTRUCTION MATERIALS, WHOLESALE: Molding, All Materials

Globmarble LLC .... G 347 717-4088
  Brooklyn *(G-2031)*
Jaxson Rollforming Inc .... E 631 842-7775
  Amityville *(G-298)*

CONSTRUCTION MATERIALS, WHOLESALE: Paving Materials

Barrett Paving Materials Inc .... E 315 353-6611
  Norwood *(G-13058)*
Classic Concrete Corp .... F 516 822-1800
  Hicksville *(G-6356)*

CONSTRUCTION MATERIALS, WHOLESALE: Paving Mixtures

Peckham Materials Corp .... D 914 686-2045
  White Plains *(G-17176)*

CONSTRUCTION MATERIALS, WHOLESALE: Prefabricated Structures

Morton Buildings Inc .... E 585 786-8191
  Warsaw *(G-16605)*

CONSTRUCTION MATERIALS, WHOLESALE: Roof, Asphalt/Sheet Metal

Jordan Panel Systems Corp .... E 631 754-4900
  East Northport *(G-4459)*

CONSTRUCTION MATERIALS, WHOLESALE: Roofing & Siding Material

Marathon Roofing Products Inc .... F 716 685-3340
  Orchard Park *(G-13307)*
Park Ave Bldg & Roofg Sups LLC .... E 718 403-0100
  Brooklyn *(G-2421)*
S & J Sheet Metal Supply .... G 718 384-0800
  Brooklyn *(G-2540)*

CONSTRUCTION MATERIALS, WHOLESALE: Sand

F H Stickles & Son Inc .... F 518 851-9048
  Livingston *(G-7587)*
Monticello Black Top Corp .... G 845 434-7280
  Thompsonville *(G-16138)*

CONSTRUCTION MATERIALS, WHOLESALE: Septic Tanks

Guardian Concrete Inc .... F 518 372-0080
  Schenectady *(G-15294)*

CONSTRUCTION MATERIALS, WHOLESALE: Siding, Exc Wood

Pal Aluminum Inc .... G 516 937-1990
  Hicksville *(G-6408)*

CONSTRUCTION MATERIALS, WHOLESALE: Stone, Crushed Or Broken

Buffalo Crushed Stone Inc .... F 716 566-9636
  Franklinville *(G-5378)*
Callahan & Nannini Quarry Inc .... G 845 496-4323
  Salisbury Mills *(G-15139)*
Callanan Industries Inc .... E 845 457-3158
  Montgomery *(G-8628)*
Dalrymple Grav & Contg Co Inc .... E 607 529-3235
  Chemung *(G-3621)*
Grosso Enterprises Inc .... F 845 361-5211
  Montgomery *(G-8631)*
Hanson Aggregates PA LLC .... F 315 782-2300
  Watertown *(G-16674)*
Pallette Stone Corporation .... E 518 584-2421
  Gansevoort *(G-5501)*
Seneca Stone Corporation .... F 315 549-8253
  Fayette *(G-5170)*
Troy Sand & Gravel Co Inc .... F 518 674-2854
  West Sand Lake *(G-16961)*

CONSTRUCTION MATERIALS, WHOLESALE: Tile, Clay/Other Ceramic

Foro Marble Co Inc .... E 718 852-2322
  Brooklyn *(G-1995)*
Kowa American Corporation .... E 212 303-7800
  New York *(G-10920)*

CONSTRUCTION MATERIALS, WHOLESALE: Windows

Excel Aluminum Products Inc .... G 315 471-0925
  Syracuse *(G-15960)*
Express Building Supply Inc .... E 516 608-0379
  Oceanside *(G-13099)*
New Bgnnngs Win Door Dstrs LLC .... F 845 214-0698
  Poughkeepsie *(G-13939)*
Norandex Inc Vestal .... G 607 786-0778
  Vestal *(G-16475)*

CONSTRUCTION MATLS, WHOL: Lumber, Rough, Dressed/Finished

Berry Industrial Group Inc .... G 845 353-8338
  Nyack *(G-13062)*

CONSTRUCTION SAND MINING

Buffalo Crushed Stone Inc .... G 607 587-8102
  Alfred Station *(G-199)*
Country Side Sand & Gravel .... F 716 988-3271
  South Dayton *(G-15541)*
Eagle Harbor Sand & Gravel Inc .... G 585 798-4501
  Albion *(G-167)*
Elam Sand & Gravel Corp .... E 585 657-8000
  Bloomfield *(G-981)*
John Vespa Inc .... F 315 788-6330
  Watertown *(G-16678)*
Lazarek Inc .... G 315 343-1242
  Oswego *(G-13359)*
Little Valley Sand & Gravel .... G 716 938-6676
  Little Valley *(G-7534)*
Palumbo Sand & Gravel Company .... E 845 832-3356
  Dover Plains *(G-4341)*
Ruby Engineering LLC .... F 646 391-4600
  Brooklyn *(G-2536)*
Rural Hill Sand and Grav Corp .... F 315 846-5212
  Woodville *(G-17383)*
Syracusa Sand and Gravel Inc .... F 585 924-7146
  Victor *(G-16529)*

CONSTRUCTION SITE PREPARATION SVCS

Kevin Regan Logging Ltd .... G 315 245-3890
  Camden *(G-3345)*

CONSTRUCTION: Bridge

Dalrymple Holding Corp .... E 607 737-6200
  Pine City *(G-13578)*
Tiki Industries Inc .... G 516 779-3629
  Riverhead *(G-14171)*

CONSTRUCTION: Commercial & Institutional Building

Dynasty Stainless Steel & Meta .... E 718 205-6623
  Maspeth *(G-8164)*
Stephen Miller Gen Contrs Inc .... E 518 661-5601
  Gloversville *(G-5738)*

CONSTRUCTION: Dry Cleaning Plant

Genco John .... G 716 483-5446
  Jamestown *(G-7028)*

CONSTRUCTION: Food Prdts Manufacturing or Packing Plant

Patla Enterprises Inc .... G 315 790-0143
  Sherrill *(G-15429)*
Sidco Food Distribution Corp .... F 718 733-3939
  Bronx *(G-1451)*

CONSTRUCTION: Guardrails, Highway

Elderlee Incorporated .... E 315 789-6670
  Oaks Corners *(G-13088)*

CONSTRUCTION: Heavy Highway & Street

A Colarusso and Son Inc .... E 518 828-3218
  Hudson *(G-6631)*
Barrett Paving Materials Inc .... F 315 788-2037
  Watertown *(G-16658)*
Dalrymple Holding Corp .... E 607 737-6200
  Pine City *(G-13578)*
Peckham Materials Corp .... E 518 747-3353
  Hudson Falls *(G-6680)*
Suit-Kote Corporation .... E 607 535-2743
  Watkins Glen *(G-16722)*

CONSTRUCTION: Indl Building & Warehouse

Siemens Industry Inc .... E 716 568-0983
  Buffalo *(G-3214)*

CONSTRUCTION: Indl Building, Prefabricated

Zebra Technologies Entp Corp .... E 800 722-6234
  Holtsville *(G-6542)*

CONSTRUCTION: Indl Buildings, New, NEC

Orange County Ironworks LLC .... E 845 769-3000
  Montgomery *(G-8636)*
Stephen Miller Gen Contrs Inc .... E 518 661-5601
  Gloversville *(G-5738)*

CONSTRUCTION: Pharmaceutical Manufacturing Plant

Knf Clean Room Products Corp .... E 631 588-7000
  Ronkonkoma *(G-14951)*

CONSTRUCTION: Religious Building

Makarenko Studios Inc .... G 914 968-7673
  Yorktown Heights *(G-17528)*

CONSTRUCTION: Single-Family Housing

Fantasy Home Improvement Corp .... G 718 277-4021
  Brooklyn *(G-1962)*
Frost Publications Inc .... G 845 726-3232
  Westtown *(G-17097)*
Kasson & Keller Inc .... A 518 853-3421
  Fonda *(G-5320)*

CONSTRUCTION: Single-family Housing, New

Capitol Restoration Corp .... G 516 783-1425
  North Bellmore *(G-12932)*

Employee Codes: A=Over 500 employees, B=251-500
C=101-250, D=51-100, E=20-50, F=10-19, G=5-9

CONSTRUCTION: Steel Buildings

CONSTRUCTION: Steel Buildings
Steele Truss Company Inc .... E 518 562-4663
  Plattsburgh *(G-13727)*

CONSTRUCTION: Street Surfacing & Paving
Barrett Paving Materials Inc .... E 315 353-6611
  Norwood *(G-13058)*
Cofire Paving Corporation .... E 718 463-1403
  Flushing *(G-5241)*
John T Montecalvo Inc .... G 631 325-1492
  Speonk *(G-15600)*
Lomin Construction Company .... G 516 759-5734
  Glen Head *(G-5650)*

CONSTRUCTION: Tennis Court
Lomin Construction Company .... G 516 759-5734
  Glen Head *(G-5650)*

CONSTRUCTION: Warehouse
Tech Park Food Services LLC .... G 585 295-1250
  Rochester *(G-14745)*

CONSTRUCTION: Waste Water & Sewage Treatment Plant
Richard R Cain Inc .... F 845 229-7410
  Hyde Park *(G-6775)*

CONSULTING SVC: Business, NEC
Batavia Precision Glass LLC .... G 585 343-6050
  Buffalo *(G-2854)*
Cambridge Whos Who Pubg Inc .... E 516 833-8440
  Uniondale *(G-16312)*
Ceramaterials LLC .... G 518 701-6722
  Port Jervis *(G-13803)*
Chromagraphics Press Inc .... E 631 367-6160
  Melville *(G-8332)*
Integrated Graphics Inc .... G 212 592-5600
  New York *(G-10659)*
Marketplace Slutions Group LLC .... E 631 868-0111
  Holbrook *(G-6490)*
Milmar Food Group II LLC .... C 845 294-5400
  Goshen *(G-5752)*
Next Step Publishing Inc .... F 585 742-1260
  Victor *(G-16518)*
Resonant Legal Media LLC .... E 212 687-7100
  New York *(G-11872)*
Seed Media Group LLC .... E 646 502-7050
  New York *(G-12035)*
Slosson Edctl Publications Inc .... F 716 652-0930
  East Aurora *(G-4403)*
Trendsformers Ltd Liability Co .... G 888 700-2423
  New York *(G-12419)*
UI Information & Insights Inc .... E 518 640-9200
  Latham *(G-7409)*

CONSULTING SVC: Computer
Caminus Corporation .... D 212 515-3600
  New York *(G-9559)*
Cgi Technologies Solutions Inc .... E 212 682-7411
  New York *(G-9624)*
Classroom Inc .... E 212 545-8400
  New York *(G-9694)*
Dohnsco Inc .... G 516 773-4800
  Manhasset *(G-8092)*
Lynx Analytics Inc .... G 475 227-7347
  New York *(G-11096)*
Pegasystems Inc .... E 212 626-6550
  New York *(G-11619)*

CONSULTING SVC: Educational
National Rding Styles Inst Inc .... F 516 921-5500
  Syosset *(G-15851)*

CONSULTING SVC: Engineering
Complex Biosystems Inc .... G 315 464-8007
  Liverpool *(G-7541)*
Exergy LLC .... E 516 832-9300
  Garden City *(G-5518)*
General Composites Inc .... E 518 963-7333
  Willsboro *(G-17289)*
Glasgow Products Inc .... E 516 374-5937
  Woodmere *(G-17331)*
Innovation Associates Inc .... C 607 798-9376
  Johnson City *(G-7126)*

Laser & Electron Beam Inc .... G 603 626-6080
  New York *(G-10967)*
Mdek Inc .... G 347 569-7318
  Brooklyn *(G-2292)*
Procomponents Inc .... E 516 683-0909
  Westbury *(G-17051)*
Select Controls Inc .... E 631 567-9010
  Bohemia *(G-1127)*
Skae Power Solutions LLC .... E 845 365-9103
  Palisades *(G-13427)*

CONSULTING SVC: Financial Management
Principia Partners LLC .... D 212 480-2270
  New York *(G-11735)*

CONSULTING SVC: Human Resource
Chequedcom Inc .... E 888 412-0699
  Saratoga Springs *(G-15177)*

CONSULTING SVC: Management
Altius Aviation LLC .... G 315 455-7555
  Syracuse *(G-15873)*
Barker Steel LLC .... E 518 465-6221
  Albany *(G-49)*
Beer Marketers Insights Inc .... G 845 507-0040
  Suffern *(G-15808)*
Ca Inc .... A 800 225-5224
  New York *(G-9543)*
Gary Roth & Associates Ltd .... E 516 333-1000
  Westbury *(G-17017)*
Marketplace Slutions Group LLC .... E 631 868-0111
  Holbrook *(G-6490)*
Res Media Group Inc .... F 212 320-3750
  New York *(G-11870)*

CONSULTING SVC: Marketing Management
In-Step Marketing Inc .... F 212 797-3450
  New York *(G-10624)*
Maven Marketing LLC .... F 615 510-3248
  New York *(G-11207)*
Ramsbury Property Us Inc .... F 212 223-6250
  New York *(G-11823)*
Rfn Inc .... F 516 764-5100
  Bay Shore *(G-729)*
Tri-Force Sales LLC .... E 732 261-5507
  New York *(G-12420)*
Zacks Enterprises Inc .... E 800 366-4924
  Orangeburg *(G-13270)*

CONSULTING SVC: Online Technology
Orthstar Enterprises Inc .... D 607 562-2100
  Horseheads *(G-6614)*

CONSULTING SVC: Sales Management
Island Marketing Corp .... G 516 739-0500
  Mineola *(G-8549)*
Karp Overseas Corporation .... E 718 784-2105
  Maspeth *(G-8179)*

CONSULTING SVCS, BUSINESS: Communications
L3 Technologies Inc .... D 631 231-1700
  Hauppauge *(G-6134)*
Redcom Laboratories Inc .... C 585 924-6567
  Victor *(G-16524)*

CONSULTING SVCS, BUSINESS: Energy Conservation
Gotham Energy 360 LLC .... F 917 338-1023
  New York *(G-10380)*
Project Energy Savers LLC .... F 718 596-4231
  Brooklyn *(G-2470)*
Western Oil and Gas JV Inc .... G 914 967-4758
  Rye *(G-15095)*

CONSULTING SVCS, BUSINESS: Publishing
Mnn Holding Company LLC .... F 404 558-5251
  Brooklyn *(G-2331)*

CONSULTING SVCS, BUSINESS: Safety Training Svcs
Bullex Inc .... E 518 689-2023
  Albany *(G-55)*

CONSULTING SVCS, BUSINESS: Sys Engnrg, Exc Computer/Prof
Laurus Development Inc .... F 716 823-1202
  Buffalo *(G-3063)*
Parlor Labs Inc .... G 866 801-7323
  New York *(G-11590)*
Sale 121 Corp .... D 240 855-8988
  New York *(G-11972)*

CONSULTING SVCS, BUSINESS: Systems Analysis & Engineering
Syntel Inc .... F 212 785-9810
  New York *(G-12285)*

CONSULTING SVCS, BUSINESS: Systems Analysis Or Design
Relx Inc .... E 212 309-8100
  New York *(G-11858)*
Visible Systems Corporation .... E 508 628-1510
  Oneida *(G-13192)*

CONSULTING SVCS, BUSINESS: Test Development & Evaluation
Micro Semicdtr Researches LLC .... G 646 863-6070
  New York *(G-11281)*

CONSULTING SVCS, BUSINESS: Testing, Educational Or Personnel
Bright Kids Nyc Inc .... E 917 539-4575
  New York *(G-9512)*

CONSULTING SVCS: Oil
Gotham Energy 360 LLC .... F 917 338-1023
  New York *(G-10380)*

CONSULTING SVCS: Scientific
Cognigen Corporation .... D 716 633-3463
  Buffalo *(G-2898)*
Guosa Life Sciences Inc .... F 718 813-7806
  North Baldwin *(G-12923)*

CONTACT LENSES
Acuity Polymers Inc .... G 585 458-8409
  Rochester *(G-14187)*
Alden Optical Laboratory Inc .... F 716 937-9181
  Lancaster *(G-7326)*
Coopervision Inc .... A 585 385-6810
  West Henrietta *(G-16907)*
Coopervision Inc .... A 585 889-3301
  Scottsville *(G-15357)*
Coopervision Inc .... C 585 385-6810
  Victor *(G-16494)*
Coopervision Inc .... D 585 385-6810
  Victor *(G-16495)*
Corneal Design Corporation .... F 301 670-7076
  Lima *(G-7465)*
J I Intrntnal Contact Lens Lab .... G 718 997-1212
  Rego Park *(G-14045)*

CONTACTS: Electrical
Micro Contacts Inc .... E 516 433-4830
  Hicksville *(G-6397)*

CONTAINERS, GLASS: Cosmetic Jars
Baralan Usa Inc .... E 718 849-5768
  Richmond Hill *(G-14080)*

CONTAINERS, GLASS: Food
Pennsauken Packing Company LLC .... G 585 377-7700
  Fairport *(G-4875)*

CONTAINERS, GLASS: Medicine Bottles
Velvet Healing By Alma Corp .... G 347 271-4220
  Bronx *(G-1488)*

CONTAINERS: Cargo, Wood & Metal Combination
219 South West .... G 315 474-2065
  Syracuse *(G-15864)*

PRODUCT SECTION

Sg Blocks Inc .... G 615 585-2639
  Brooklyn *(G-2573)*

CONTAINERS: Cargo, Wood & Wood With Metal

Airline Container Services .... G 516 371-4125
  Lido Beach *(G-7461)*
Concord Express Cargo Inc .... G 718 276-7200
  Jamaica *(G-6942)*

CONTAINERS: Corrugated

Action Rack Display Mfg .... F 718 257-7111
  Brooklyn *(G-1557)*
Ares Printing and Packg Corp .... C 718 858-8760
  Brooklyn *(G-1627)*
Bellotti Packaging Inc .... F 315 433-0131
  East Syracuse *(G-4527)*
Brand Box USA LLC .... G 607 584-7682
  Binghamton *(G-894)*
Cascades New York Inc .... C 518 346-6151
  Schenectady *(G-15268)*
Color Carton Corp .... D 718 665-0840
  Bronx *(G-1303)*
Fennell Industries LLC .... E 607 733-6693
  Elmira *(G-4698)*
Fiber USA Corp .... G 718 888-1512
  Flushing *(G-5249)*
Gavin Mfg Corp .... E 631 467-0040
  Farmingdale *(G-5005)*
International Paper Company .... F 716 852-2144
  Buffalo *(G-3029)*
International Paper Company .... D 518 372-6461
  Glenville *(G-5717)*
Jamestown Cont of Rochester .... D 585 254-9190
  Rochester *(G-14481)*
Jamestown Container Corp .... C 716 665-4623
  Falconer *(G-4912)*
Key Container Corp .... G 631 582-3847
  East Islip *(G-4437)*
Lee Philips Packaging Inc .... F 631 580-3306
  Ronkonkoma *(G-14959)*
M C Packaging Corporation .... E 631 643-3763
  Babylon *(G-547)*
Mazel Supply .... G 212 947-2213
  Brooklyn *(G-2290)*
Mkt329 Inc .... F 631 249-5500
  Farmingdale *(G-5068)*
Packaging Corporation America ...... C 315 457-6780
  Liverpool *(G-7564)*
Pactiv LLC .... E 585 248-1213
  Pittsford *(G-13601)*
Parlor City Paper Box Co Inc .... D 607 772-0600
  Binghamton *(G-937)*
Specialized Packg Group Inc .... G 315 638-4355
  Baldwinsville *(G-574)*
Technical Packaging Inc .... F 516 223-2300
  Baldwin *(G-561)*
Track 7 Inc .... G 845 544-1810
  Warwick *(G-16618)*

CONTAINERS: Foil, Bakery Goods & Frozen Foods

De Luxe Packaging Corp .... E 416 754-4633
  Saugerties *(G-15212)*
Tri-State Food Jobbers Inc .... G 718 921-1211
  Brooklyn *(G-2696)*

CONTAINERS: Food & Beverage

Cmc-Kuhnke Inc .... F 518 694-3310
  Albany *(G-65)*
Marley Spoon Inc .... C 646 934-6970
  New York *(G-11186)*
Tio Foods LLC .... F 305 672-6645
  New York *(G-12373)*

CONTAINERS: Food, Folding, Made From Purchased Materials

Diamond Packaging Holdings LLC ... G 585 334-8030
  Rochester *(G-14327)*
Mod-Pac Corp .... C 716 898-8480
  Buffalo *(G-3091)*
Pactiv LLC .... C 518 562-6101
  Plattsburgh *(G-13712)*

CONTAINERS: Food, Liquid Tight, Including Milk

International Paper Company .... C 607 775-1550
  Conklin *(G-3894)*

CONTAINERS: Glass

Anchor Glass Container Corp .... B 607 737-1933
  Elmira Heights *(G-4721)*
Certainteed Corporation .... C 716 823-3684
  Lackawanna *(G-7269)*
Intrapac International Corp .... C 518 561-2030
  Plattsburgh *(G-13697)*
Owens-Brockway Glass Cont Inc .... C 315 258-3211
  Auburn *(G-510)*
Rocco Bormioli Glass Co Inc .... E 212 719-0606
  New York *(G-11917)*
Saint Gobain Grains & Powders ...... A 716 731-8200
  Niagara Falls *(G-12888)*
Schott Corporation .... D 914 831-2200
  Elmsford *(G-4786)*
SGD North America .... E 212 753-4200
  New York *(G-12054)*
SGD Pharma Packaging Inc .... G 212 223-7100
  New York *(G-12055)*

CONTAINERS: Laminated Phenolic & Vulcanized Fiber

Diemolding Corporation .... G 315 363-4710
  Wampsville *(G-16574)*
Skydyne Company .... D 845 858-6400
  Port Jervis *(G-13816)*

CONTAINERS: Liquid Tight Fiber, From Purchased Materials

Acran Spill Containment Inc .... G 631 841-2300
  Amityville *(G-274)*
Custom Manufacturing Inc .... G 607 569-2738
  Hammondsport *(G-5976)*

CONTAINERS: Metal

Abbot & Abbot Box Corp .... F 888 930-5972
  Long Island City *(G-7678)*
Erie Engineered Products Inc .... E 716 206-0204
  Lancaster *(G-7338)*
Hornet Group Inc .... D 845 858-6400
  Port Jervis *(G-13808)*
Medi-Ray Inc .... D 877 898-3003
  Tuckahoe *(G-16295)*
Mobile Mini Inc .... F 315 732-4555
  Utica *(G-16373)*
Westrock - Southern Cont LLC .... C 315 487-6111
  Camillus *(G-3355)*
Westrock CP LLC .... C 716 694-1000
  North Tonawanda *(G-13023)*

CONTAINERS: Plastic

A R Arena Products Inc .... E 585 277-1680
  Rochester *(G-14176)*
Albea Cosmetics America Inc .... E 212 371-5100
  New York *(G-9124)*
Amcor Rigid Plastics Usa LLC .... E 716 366-2440
  Dunkirk *(G-4356)*
Baralan Usa Inc .... F 718 849-5768
  Richmond Hill *(G-14080)*
Berry Global Inc .... C 315 484-0397
  Solvay *(G-15528)*
Berry Global Group Inc .... F 315 986-6270
  Macedon *(G-8012)*
Billie-Ann Plastics Pkg Corp .... E 718 497-3409
  Brooklyn *(G-1695)*
Chem-Tainer Industries Inc .... E 631 422-8300
  West Babylon *(G-16808)*
Consolidated Container Co LLC ...... F 585 343-9351
  Batavia *(G-630)*
Form A Rockland Plastics Inc .... G 315 848-3300
  Cranberry Lake *(G-4083)*
Forteq North America Inc .... D 585 427-9410
  West Henrietta *(G-16911)*
Gary Plastic Packaging Corp .... B 718 893-2200
  Bronx *(G-1343)*
Great Pacific Entps US Inc .... E 518 761-2593
  Glens Falls *(G-5698)*
GSE Composites Inc .... F 631 389-1300
  Hauppauge *(G-6110)*
Ingenious Designs LLC .... C 631 254-3376
  Ronkonkoma *(G-14941)*
Iridium Industries Inc .... E 516 504-9700
  Great Neck *(G-5833)*
Jamestown Plastics Inc .... E 716 792-4144
  Brocton *(G-1249)*
Kenney Manufacturing Displays ...... F 631 231-5563
  Brentwood *(G-1185)*
Kernow North America .... F 585 586-3590
  Pittsford *(G-13594)*
M I T Poly-Cart Corp .... G 212 724-7290
  New York *(G-11103)*
Micromold Products Inc .... E 914 969-2850
  Yonkers *(G-17485)*
Oneida Molded Plastics LLC .... D 315 363-7990
  Oneida *(G-13184)*
Ontario Plastics Inc .... E 585 663-2644
  Rochester *(G-14572)*
Pactiv LLC .... G 847 482-2000
  Canandaigua *(G-3382)*
Pactiv LLC .... C 518 562-6120
  Plattsburgh *(G-13713)*
Pactiv LLC .... C 518 793-2524
  Glens Falls *(G-5710)*
Plastic Solutions Inc .... E 631 234-9013
  Bayport *(G-754)*
Plastic Sys/Gr Bflo Inc .... G 716 835-7555
  Buffalo *(G-3152)*
Plasticware LLC .... E 845 267-0790
  Monsey *(G-8612)*
Powertex Inc .... E 518 297-4000
  Rouses Point *(G-15067)*
Quoin LLC .... A 914 967-9400
  Rye *(G-15092)*
Rynone Manufacturing Corp .... F 607 565-8187
  Waverly *(G-16730)*
Silgan Plastics LLC .... C 315 536-5690
  Penn Yan *(G-13543)*
Summit Manufacturing LLC .... G 631 952-1570
  Bay Shore *(G-741)*
Visitainer Corp .... E 718 636-0300
  Brooklyn *(G-2749)*

CONTAINERS: Sanitary, Food

Consolidated Container Co LLC ...... C 585 262-6470
  Rochester *(G-14309)*

CONTAINERS: Shipping & Mailing, Fiber

American Intrmdal Cont Mfg LLC ..... G 631 774-6790
  Hauppauge *(G-6041)*

CONTAINERS: Shipping, Bombs, Metal Plate

828 Express Inc .... G 917 577-9019
  Staten Island *(G-15649)*
Erie Engineered Products Inc .... E 716 206-0204
  Lancaster *(G-7338)*
Vship Co .... F 718 706-8566
  Astoria *(G-459)*
Wayne Integrated Tech Corp .... E 631 242-0213
  Edgewood *(G-4633)*

CONTAINERS: Shipping, Wood

Hood Industries Inc .... F 716 836-0301
  Buffalo *(G-3014)*

CONTAINERS: Wood

Abbot & Abbot Box Corp .... F 888 930-5972
  Long Island City *(G-7678)*
David Isseks & Sons Inc .... E 212 966-8694
  New York *(G-9875)*
Essex Box & Pallet Co Inc .... E 518 834-7279
  Keeseville *(G-7166)*
Great Lakes Specialties .... E 716 672-4622
  Fredonia *(G-5383)*
Pluribus Products Inc .... E 718 852-1614
  Bayville *(G-775)*

CONTRACT FOOD SVCS

Herris Gourmet Inc .... G 917 578-2308
  Brooklyn *(G-2076)*

CONTRACTOR: Framing

Timber Frames Inc .... G 585 374-6405
  Canandaigua *(G-3388)*

CONTRACTOR: Rigging & Scaffolding

Safespan Platform Systems Inc ...... D 716 694-3332
  Tonawanda *(G-16218)*

Employee Codes: A=Over 500 employees, B=251-500
C=101-250, D=51-100, E=20-50, F=10-19, G=5-9

CONTRACTORS: Acoustical & Ceiling Work

Newmat Northeast Corp .... F 631 253-9277
West Babylon *(G-16846)*

CONTRACTORS: Acoustical & Insulation Work

New York State Foam Enrgy LLC .... G 845 534-4656
Cornwall *(G-4010)*

CONTRACTORS: Antenna Installation

Fred A Nudd Corporation .... E 315 524-2531
Ontario *(G-13223)*

CONTRACTORS: Awning Installation

Awning Mart Inc .... G 315 699-5928
Cicero *(G-3671)*
Awnings Plus Inc .... F 716 693-3690
Tonawanda *(G-16163)*
Space Sign .... F 718 961-1112
College Point *(G-3834)*

CONTRACTORS: Boiler & Furnace

Empire Industrial Systems Corp .... F 631 242-4619
Bay Shore *(G-697)*

CONTRACTORS: Boiler Maintenance Contractor

Empire Industrial Burner Svc .... F 631 242-4619
Deer Park *(G-4161)*

CONTRACTORS: Building Eqpt & Machinery Installation

Advanced Door Solutions Inc .... G 631 773-6100
Holbrook *(G-6457)*
Assa Abloy Entrance Systems US .... E 315 492-6600
East Syracuse *(G-4524)*
Bargold Storage Systems LLC .... E 718 247-7000
Long Island City *(G-7713)*
Otis Elevator Company .... E 917 339-9600
New York *(G-11547)*
Schindler Elevator Corporation .... C 212 708-1000
New York *(G-12005)*
Windowman Inc (usa) .... G 718 246-2626
Brooklyn *(G-2774)*

CONTRACTORS: Building Sign Installation & Mntnce

Alley Cat Signs Inc .... F 631 924-7446
Middle Island *(G-8439)*
Clinton Signs Inc .... G 585 482-1620
Webster *(G-16743)*
Flexlume Sign Corporation .... G 716 884-2020
Buffalo *(G-2965)*
Gloede Neon Signs Ltd Inc .... F 845 471-4366
Poughkeepsie *(G-13922)*
Jem Sign Corp .... G 516 867-4466
Hempstead *(G-6299)*
Lanza Corp .... G 914 937-6360
Port Chester *(G-13778)*
North Shore Neon Sign Co Inc .... E 718 937-4848
Flushing *(G-5282)*
Rapp Signs Inc .... F 607 656-8167
Greene *(G-5885)*
Ray Sign Inc .... F 518 377-1371
Schenectady *(G-15313)*
Rgm Signs Inc .... G 718 442-0598
Staten Island *(G-15754)*
Sign Works Incorporated .... E 914 592-0700
Elmsford *(G-4792)*
T J Signs Unlimited LLC .... G 631 273-4800
Islip *(G-6852)*

CONTRACTORS: Carpentry Work

EZ Lift Operator Corp .... F 845 356-1676
Spring Valley *(G-15606)*
Innova Interiors Inc .... E 718 401-2122
Bronx *(G-1365)*
Mestel Brothers Stairs & Rails .... C 516 496-4127
Syosset *(G-15848)*

CONTRACTORS: Carpentry, Cabinet & Finish Work

Cabinet Shapes Corp .... F 718 784-6255
Long Island City *(G-7722)*
Capital Kit Cab & Door Mfrs .... G 718 886-0303
College Point *(G-3805)*
Central Kitchen Corp .... F 631 283-1029
Southampton *(G-15564)*
Dak Mica and Wood Products .... G 631 467-0749
Ronkonkoma *(G-14920)*
Eugenia Selective Living Inc .... F 631 277-1461
Islip *(G-6847)*
Hennig Custom Woodwork Corp .... G 516 536-3460
Oceanside *(G-13101)*
Johnny Mica Inc .... G 631 225-5213
Lindenhurst *(G-7488)*
Jq Woodworking Inc .... G 516 766-3424
Oceanside *(G-13104)*
M & C Furniture .... G 718 422-2136
Brooklyn *(G-2244)*
Metro Kitchens Corp .... F 718 434-1166
Brooklyn *(G-2310)*
Ralph Payne .... G 718 222-4200
Brooklyn *(G-2496)*

CONTRACTORS: Carpentry, Cabinet Building & Installation

Auburn-Watson Corp .... F 716 876-8000
Depew *(G-4272)*
Daniel Demarco and Assoc Inc .... E 631 598-7000
Amityville *(G-283)*
Fontrick Door Inc .... E 585 345-6032
Batavia *(G-634)*
Home Ideal Inc .... G 718 762-8998
Flushing *(G-5259)*
Koeppels Kustom Kitchens Inc .... G 518 489-0092
Albany *(G-96)*
Manhattan Cabinets Inc .... G 212 548-2436
New York *(G-11152)*
Precision Dental Cabinets Inc .... F 631 543-3870
Smithtown *(G-15518)*
Yost Neon Displays Inc .... G 716 674-6780
West Seneca *(G-16985)*

CONTRACTORS: Carpentry, Finish & Trim Work

Millwright Wdwrk Installetion .... E 631 587-2635
West Babylon *(G-16842)*

CONTRACTORS: Ceramic Floor Tile Installation

Icestone LLC .... E 718 624-4900
Brooklyn *(G-2093)*

CONTRACTORS: Closed Circuit Television Installation

Sartek Industries Inc .... E 631 473-3555
Port Jefferson *(G-13801)*

CONTRACTORS: Commercial & Office Building

United Steel Products Inc .... D 718 478-5330
Corona *(G-4031)*

CONTRACTORS: Communications Svcs

Professional Technology Inc .... G 315 337-4156
Rome *(G-14858)*

CONTRACTORS: Concrete

A Colarusso and Son Inc .... E 518 828-3218
Hudson *(G-6631)*
Geneva Granite Co Inc .... F 315 789-8142
Geneva *(G-5590)*
Seneca Stone Corporation .... G 607 737-6200
Pine City *(G-13579)*

CONTRACTORS: Concrete Pumping

Barney & Dickenson Inc .... E 607 729-1536
Vestal *(G-16462)*

CONTRACTORS: Concrete Repair

Capitol Restoration Corp .... G 516 783-1425
North Bellmore *(G-12932)*

CONTRACTORS: Construction Site Cleanup

Darrell Mitchell .... G 646 659-7075
Arverne *(G-422)*

CONTRACTORS: Countertop Installation

Contempra Design Inc .... G 718 984-8586
Staten Island *(G-15681)*
Countertops & Cabinets Inc .... G 315 433-1038
Syracuse *(G-15930)*
FX INC .... F 212 244-2240
New York *(G-10277)*
Johnny Mica Inc .... G 631 225-5213
Lindenhurst *(G-7488)*
Joseph Fedele .... G 718 448-3658
Staten Island *(G-15716)*
Rochester Countertop Inc .... F 585 338-2260
Rochester *(G-14662)*
Thornwood Products Ltd .... E 914 769-9161
Thornwood *(G-16144)*

CONTRACTORS: Demountable Partition Installation

Able Steel Equipment Co Inc .... F 718 361-9240
Long Island City *(G-7679)*

CONTRACTORS: Directional Oil & Gas Well Drilling Svc

Turner Undgrd Instllations Inc .... F 585 739-0238
Henrietta *(G-6323)*

CONTRACTORS: Drywall

L & J Interiors Inc .... G 631 218-0838
Bohemia *(G-1084)*
Nordic Interior Inc .... C 718 456-7000
College Point *(G-3824)*

CONTRACTORS: Electrical

331 Holding Inc .... E 585 924-1740
Victor *(G-16482)*
A & S Electric .... G 212 228-2030
Brooklyn *(G-1528)*
B J S Electric .... G 845 774-8166
Chester *(G-3627)*
C & G Video Systems Inc .... G 315 452-1490
Liverpool *(G-7536)*
Cooperfriedman Elc Sup Co Inc .... G 718 269-4906
Long Island City *(G-7733)*
Mitsubishi Elc Pwr Pdts Inc .... G 516 962-2813
Melville *(G-8367)*
Schuler-Haas Electric Corp .... G 607 936-3514
Painted Post *(G-13419)*
Siemens Industry Inc .... E 585 797-2300
Rochester *(G-14707)*
Spectrum Cable Corporation .... G 585 235-7714
Rochester *(G-14719)*

CONTRACTORS: Electronic Controls Installation

Emco Electric Services LLC .... G 212 420-9766
New York *(G-10073)*
Evolve Guest Controls LLC .... F 855 750-9090
Port Washington *(G-13836)*
Qsf Inc .... G 585 247-6200
Gates *(G-5577)*
Zeppelin Electric Company Inc .... G 631 928-9467
East Setauket *(G-4516)*

CONTRACTORS: Energy Management Control

Ihi Inc .... E 212 599-8100
New York *(G-10610)*
T S B A Group Inc .... E 718 565-6000
Sunnyside *(G-15831)*

CONTRACTORS: Excavating

Ribble Lumber Inc .... G 315 536-6221
Penn Yan *(G-13541)*

PRODUCT SECTION

CONTRACTORS: Oil & Gas Well Drilling Svc

CONTRACTORS: Excavating Slush Pits & Cellars Svcs

Alice Perkins ....G....... 716 378-5100
Salamanca *(G-15125)*

CONTRACTORS: Exterior Wall System Installation

Plant-Tech2o Inc ....G....... 516 483-7845
Hempstead *(G-6307)*

CONTRACTORS: Fence Construction

City Store Gates Mfg Corp ....E....... 718 939-9700
College Point *(G-3806)*
Dart Awning Inc ....F....... 718 945-4224
Freeport *(G-5404)*
Fence Plaza Corp ....G....... 718 469-2200
Brooklyn *(G-1970)*
Fort Miller Service Corp ....F....... 518 695-5000
Greenwich *(G-5907)*
Interstate Wood Products Inc ....E....... 631 842-4488
Amityville *(G-296)*
Master-Halco Inc ....F....... 631 585-8150
Ronkonkoma *(G-14966)*
Metro Door Inc ....D....... 800 669-3667
Islandia *(G-6839)*
Oneida Sales & Service Inc ....E....... 716 822-8205
Buffalo *(G-3123)*
Ourem Iron Works Inc ....F....... 914 476-4856
Yonkers *(G-17492)*
Universal Steel Fabricators ....F....... 718 342-0782
Brooklyn *(G-2729)*
Wood Innovations of Suffolk ....G....... 631 698-2345
Medford *(G-8297)*

CONTRACTORS: Fiber Optic Cable Installation

Complete Fiber Solutions Inc ....G....... 718 828-8900
Bronx *(G-1305)*

CONTRACTORS: Fiberglass Work

Primary Plastics Inc ....F....... 607 785-4865
Endwell *(G-4843)*

CONTRACTORS: Fire Detection & Burglar Alarm Systems

Detekion Security Systems Inc ....F....... 607 729-7179
Vestal *(G-16469)*
Sentry Devices Corp ....G....... 631 491-3191
Dix Hills *(G-4321)*
Simplexgrinnell LP ....G....... 845 774-4120
Harriman *(G-5996)*

CONTRACTORS: Fire Escape Installation

Firecom Inc ....C....... 718 899-6100
Woodside *(G-17345)*
Triboro Iron Works Inc ....G....... 718 361-9600
Long Island City *(G-7934)*

CONTRACTORS: Fire Sprinkler System Installation Svcs

Simplexgrinnell LP ....G....... 845 774-4120
Harriman *(G-5996)*

CONTRACTORS: Floor Laying & Other Floor Work

Delta Polymers Inc ....G....... 631 254-6240
Bay Shore *(G-693)*
Designer Epoxy Finishes Inc ....G....... 646 943-6044
Melville *(G-8340)*

CONTRACTORS: Garage Doors

Griffon Corporation ....E....... 212 957-5000
New York *(G-10405)*

CONTRACTORS: Gas Field Svcs, NEC

Empire State Pipeline ....G....... 585 321-1560
Rush *(G-15071)*
Petro Inc ....G....... 516 686-1717
Plainview *(G-13657)*
Schmitt Sales Inc ....G....... 716 632-8595
Williamsville *(G-17277)*

Speedway LLC ....F....... 718 815-6897
Staten Island *(G-15759)*
T A S Sales Service LLC ....G....... 518 234-4919
Cobleskill *(G-3764)*

CONTRACTORS: Gasoline Condensation Removal Svcs

Gas Recovery Systems LLC ....F....... 914 421-4903
White Plains *(G-17138)*

CONTRACTORS: Glass, Glazing & Tinting

A&B McKeon Glass Inc ....G....... 718 525-2152
Staten Island *(G-15651)*
Advanced Door Solutions Inc ....G....... 631 773-6100
Holbrook *(G-6457)*
Benson Industries Inc ....F....... 212 779-3230
New York *(G-9407)*
Chapman Stained Glass Studio ....G....... 518 449-5552
Albany *(G-61)*
Global Glass Corp ....G....... 516 681-2309
Hicksville *(G-6378)*
Jordan Panel Systems Corp ....E....... 631 754-4900
East Northport *(G-4459)*
Lafayette Mirror & Glass Co ....G....... 718 768-0660
New Hyde Park *(G-8891)*
Upstate Insulated Glass Inc ....G....... 315 475-4960
Central Square *(G-3546)*

CONTRACTORS: Heating & Air Conditioning

Automated Control Logic Inc ....F....... 914 769-8880
Thornwood *(G-16139)*
City Cooling Enterprises Inc ....G....... 718 331-7400
Brooklyn *(G-1780)*
Fedders Islandaire Inc ....D....... 631 471-2900
East Setauket *(G-4500)*
Heat-Timer Corporation ....E....... 212 481-2020
Bronx *(G-1356)*
Layton Manufacturing Corp ....F....... 718 498-6000
Brooklyn *(G-2197)*
Nelson Air Device Corporation ....C....... 718 729-3801
Maspeth *(G-8186)*
Prokosch and Sonn Sheet Metal ....E....... 845 562-4211
Newburgh *(G-12799)*
Robin Industries Ltd ....F....... 718 218-9616
Brooklyn *(G-2522)*
Vincent Genovese ....G....... 631 281-8170
Mastic Beach *(G-8237)*

CONTRACTORS: Highway & Street Construction, General

Tiki Industries Inc ....G....... 516 779-3629
Riverhead *(G-14171)*

CONTRACTORS: Highway & Street Paving

Pavco Asphalt Inc ....E....... 631 289-3223
Holtsville *(G-6532)*
Peckham Materials Corp ....D....... 914 686-2045
White Plains *(G-17176)*
Suit-Kote Corporation ....C....... 607 753-1100
Cortland *(G-4069)*
Suit-Kote Corporation ....E....... 716 664-3750
Jamestown *(G-7065)*

CONTRACTORS: Home & Office Intrs Finish, Furnish/Remodel

Drapery Industries Inc ....F....... 585 232-2992
Rochester *(G-14338)*
Griffon Corporation ....E....... 212 957-5000
New York *(G-10405)*

CONTRACTORS: Hydraulic Eqpt Installation & Svcs

A Gatty Products Inc ....G....... 914 592-3903
Elmsford *(G-4741)*

CONTRACTORS: Hydronics Heating

Corona Plumbing & Htg Sup Inc ....G....... 718 424-4133
Corona *(G-4016)*

CONTRACTORS: Insulation Installation, Building

Advanced Comfort Systems Inc ....F....... 518 884-8444
Ballston Spa *(G-588)*

CONTRACTORS: Kitchen & Bathroom Remodeling

Di Fiore and Sons Custom Wdwkg ....G....... 718 278-1663
Long Island City *(G-7744)*
Triad Counter Corp ....E....... 631 750-0615
Bohemia *(G-1143)*

CONTRACTORS: Lighting Syst

Light Blue USA LLC ....G....... 718 475-2515
Brooklyn *(G-2221)*
Vincent Conigliaro ....F....... 845 340-0489
Kingston *(G-7251)*

CONTRACTORS: Machinery Installation

Finger Lakes Conveyors Inc ....G....... 315 539-9246
Waterloo *(G-16647)*
Re-Al Industrial Corp ....G....... 716 542-4556
Akron *(G-25)*

CONTRACTORS: Marble Installation, Interior

Aurora Stone Group LLC ....F....... 315 471-6869
East Syracuse *(G-4525)*
Marble Doctors LLC ....E....... 203 628-8339
New York *(G-11167)*

CONTRACTORS: Masonry & Stonework

Premier Group NY ....F....... 212 229-1200
New York *(G-11720)*
Tiki Industries Inc ....G....... 516 779-3629
Riverhead *(G-14171)*

CONTRACTORS: Mechanical

All-City Metal Inc ....E....... 718 937-3975
Maspeth *(G-8142)*
Joy Edward Company ....E....... 315 474-3360
East Syracuse *(G-4561)*
Metro Duct Systems Inc ....F....... 718 278-4294
Long Island City *(G-7840)*

CONTRACTORS: Multi-Family Home Remodeling

Rob Herschenfeld Design Inc ....F....... 718 456-6801
Brooklyn *(G-2520)*

CONTRACTORS: Office Furniture Installation

Evans & Paul LLC ....E....... 516 576-0800
Plainview *(G-13629)*

CONTRACTORS: Oil & Gas Building, Repairing & Dismantling Svc

Cotton Well Drilling Co Inc ....G....... 716 672-2788
Sheridan *(G-15422)*
Steel Excel Inc ....G....... 914 461-1300
White Plains *(G-17198)*

CONTRACTORS: Oil & Gas Field Geological Exploration Svcs

Aquifer Drilling & Testing Inc ....C....... 516 616-6026
Mineola *(G-8528)*

CONTRACTORS: Oil & Gas Field Geophysical Exploration Svcs

Schlumberger Technology Corp ....C....... 607 378-0105
Horseheads *(G-6621)*
Smith International Inc ....D....... 212 350-9400
New York *(G-12133)*

CONTRACTORS: Oil & Gas Well Casing Cement Svcs

Sabre Energy Services LLC ....F....... 518 514-1572
Slingerlands *(G-15500)*

CONTRACTORS: Oil & Gas Well Drilling Svc

Alden Aurora Gas Company Inc ....G....... 716 937-9484
Alden *(G-177)*
Barber & Deline Enrgy Svcs LLC ....F....... 315 696-8961
Tully *(G-16298)*
Barber & Deline LLC ....F....... 607 749-2619
Tully *(G-16299)*

CONTRACTORS: Oil & Gas Well Drilling Svc

Copper Ridge Oil Inc .... G 716 372-4021
  Jamestown *(G-7019)*
Geotechnical Drilling Inc .... D 516 616-6055
  Mineola *(G-8546)*
Lenape Energy Inc .... G 585 344-1200
  Alexander *(G-190)*
Lukoil North America LLC .... E 212 421-4141
  New York *(G-11091)*
Schneider Amalco Inc .... F 917 470-9674
  New York *(G-12009)*
Steel Partners Holdings LP .... E 212 520-2300
  New York *(G-12212)*
U S Energy Development Corp .... D 716 636-0401
  Getzville *(G-5617)*
Western Oil and Gas JV Inc .... G 914 967-4758
  Rye *(G-15095)*

CONTRACTORS: Oil & Gas Well Flow Rate Measurement Svcs

Five Star Field Services .... G 347 446-6816
  Long Beach *(G-7671)*

CONTRACTORS: Oil & Gas Wells Svcs

I & S of NY Inc .... F 716 373-7001
  Allegany *(G-204)*
Superior Energy Services Inc .... G 716 483-0100
  Jamestown *(G-7067)*

CONTRACTORS: Oil Field Haulage Svcs

Lenape Energy Inc .... G 585 344-1200
  Alexander *(G-190)*

CONTRACTORS: Oil Field Lease Tanks: Erectg, Clng/Rprg Svcs

Wellspring Omni Holdings Corp .... A 212 318-9800
  New York *(G-12638)*

CONTRACTORS: Oil Sampling Svcs

P & C Gas Measurements Service ..... F 716 257-3412
  Cattaraugus *(G-3466)*

CONTRACTORS: Oil/Gas Well Construction, Rpr/Dismantling Svcs

A & Mt Realty Group LLC .... F 718 974-5871
  Brooklyn *(G-1527)*
Arm Construction Company Inc .... G 646 235-6520
  East Elmhurst *(G-4410)*
Babula Construction Inc .... G 716 681-0886
  Lancaster *(G-7329)*
Barber & Deline Enrgy Svcs LLC ..... F 315 696-8961
  Tully *(G-16298)*
Darrell Mitchell .... G 646 659-7075
  Arverne *(G-422)*
Fame Construction Inc .... E 718 626-1000
  Astoria *(G-440)*
Iron Eagle Group Inc .... E 888 481-4445
  New York *(G-10704)*
Mep Alaska LLC .... G 646 535-9005
  Brooklyn *(G-2302)*
Occhioerosso John .... F 718 541-7025
  Staten Island *(G-15738)*
Prefab Construction Inc .... F 631 821-9613
  Sound Beach *(G-15535)*
Professional Remodelers Inc .... G 516 565-9300
  West Hempstead *(G-16894)*

CONTRACTORS: On-Site Welding

303 Contracting Inc .... E 716 896-2122
  Orchard Park *(G-13271)*
A and K Machine and Welding .... G 631 231-2552
  Bay Shore *(G-663)*
Abdo Shtmtl & Fabrication Inc ...... G 315 894-4664
  Frankfort *(G-5358)*
AG Tech Welding Corp .... G 845 398-0005
  Tappan *(G-16102)*
Bridgehampton Steel & Wldg Inc .... F 631 537-2486
  Bridgehampton *(G-1230)*
Dorgan Welding Service .... G 315 462-9030
  Phelps *(G-13554)*
Flushing Boiler & Welding Co .... G 718 463-1266
  Brooklyn *(G-1988)*
G & C Welding Co Inc .... G 516 883-3228
  Port Washington *(G-13839)*
Glenridge Fabricators Inc .... F 718 456-2297
  Glendale *(G-5670)*

Hadfield Inc .... F 631 981-4314
  Ronkonkoma *(G-14938)*
Hagner Industries Inc .... G 716 873-5720
  Buffalo *(G-3003)*
Hallock Fabricating Corp .... G 631 727-2441
  Riverhead *(G-14156)*
Jacksons Welding LLC .... G 607 756-2725
  Cortland *(G-4054)*
Kleinfelder John .... G 716 753-3163
  Mayville *(G-8247)*
Marine Boiler & Welding Inc .... F 718 378-1900
  Bronx *(G-1390)*
Reliable Welding & Fabrication ..... G 631 758-2637
  Patchogue *(G-13459)*
S & D Welding Corp .... G 631 454-0383
  West Babylon *(G-16855)*
Tioga Tool Inc .... F 607 785-6005
  Endicott *(G-4835)*

CONTRACTORS: Ornamental Metal Work

Bonura and Sons Iron Works .... F 718 381-4100
  Franklin Square *(G-5371)*
E F Iron Works & Construction ...... G 631 242-4766
  Bay Shore *(G-696)*
GCM Metal Industries Inc .... G 718 386-4059
  Brooklyn *(G-2016)*
Irony Limited Inc .... G 631 329-4065
  East Hampton *(G-4431)*
M K Ulrich Construction Inc .... F 716 893-5777
  Buffalo *(G-3071)*

CONTRACTORS: Paint & Wallpaper Stripping

Nochem Paint Stripping Inc .... G 631 563-2750
  Blue Point *(G-994)*

CONTRACTORS: Painting & Wall Covering

Abdo Shtmtl & Fabrication Inc ...... G 315 894-4664
  Frankfort *(G-5358)*
D & I Finishing Inc .... G 631 471-3034
  Bohemia *(G-1044)*

CONTRACTORS: Pipe Laying

AAA Welding and Fabrication of .... G 585 254-2830
  Rochester *(G-14177)*

CONTRACTORS: Plastering, Plain or Ornamental

Foster Reeve & Associates Inc ...... G 718 609-0090
  Brooklyn *(G-1997)*

CONTRACTORS: Plumbing

Aquifer Drilling & Testing Inc .... C 516 616-6026
  Mineola *(G-8528)*
Metro City Group Inc .... G 516 781-2500
  Bellmore *(G-814)*

CONTRACTORS: Power Generating Eqpt Installation

Ls Power Equity Partners LP .... A 212 615-3456
  New York *(G-11085)*

CONTRACTORS: Prefabricated Fireplace Installation

Chimney Doctors Americas Corp .... G 631 868-3586
  Bayport *(G-751)*

CONTRACTORS: Prefabricated Window & Door Installation

Europrojects Intl Inc .... G 917 262-0795
  New York *(G-10140)*
Pace Window and Door Corp .... E 585 924-8350
  Victor *(G-16519)*
Pella Corporation .... C 631 208-0710
  Calverton *(G-3322)*
Proof Industries Inc .... G 631 694-7663
  Farmingdale *(G-5100)*
Royal Windows Mfg Corp .... E 631 435-8888
  Bay Shore *(G-735)*
Tri-State Window Factory Corp ..... D 631 667-8600
  Deer Park *(G-4242)*

CONTRACTORS: Refrigeration

Alumiseal Corp .... E 518 329-2820
  Copake Falls *(G-3914)*

CONTRACTORS: Roofing

Tiedemann Waldemar Inc .... F 716 875-5665
  Buffalo *(G-3244)*

CONTRACTORS: Roustabout Svcs

Jemcap Servicing LLC .... G 212 213-9353
  New York *(G-10758)*
Legal Servicing LLC .... G 716 565-9300
  Williamsville *(G-17273)*
Sovereign Servicing System LLC .... F 914 779-1400
  Bronxville *(G-1503)*

CONTRACTORS: Safety & Security Eqpt

Napco Security Tech Inc .... A 631 842-9400
  Amityville *(G-313)*
Windowman Inc (usa) .... G 718 246-2626
  Brooklyn *(G-2774)*

CONTRACTORS: Sandblasting Svc, Building Exteriors

Bruce Pierce .... G 716 731-9310
  Sanborn *(G-15142)*
Miller Metal Fabricating Inc .... G 585 359-3400
  Rochester *(G-14534)*
North Shore Monuments Inc .... G 516 759-2156
  Glen Head *(G-5653)*

CONTRACTORS: Seismograph Survey Svcs

Wellspring Omni Holdings Corp ..... A 212 318-9800
  New York *(G-12638)*

CONTRACTORS: Sheet Metal Work, NEC

Aabco Sheet Metal Co Inc .... D 718 821-1166
  Ridgewood *(G-14110)*
B & R Sheet .... G 718 558-5544
  Jamaica *(G-6933)*
Berjen Metal Industries Ltd .... G 631 673-7979
  Huntington *(G-6688)*
Broadalbin Manufacturing Corp ..... E 518 883-5313
  Broadalbin *(G-1239)*
Goergen-Mackwirth Co Inc .... E 716 874-4800
  Buffalo *(G-2993)*
Lodolce Machine Co Inc .... E 845 246-7017
  Saugerties *(G-15216)*
Pro Metal of NY Corp .... G 516 285-0440
  Valley Stream *(G-16445)*

CONTRACTORS: Sheet metal Work, Architectural

A&B McKeon Glass Inc .... E 718 525-2152
  Staten Island *(G-15651)*
Morgik Metal Designs .... F 212 463-0304
  New York *(G-11330)*

CONTRACTORS: Siding

Tri-State Window Factory Corp ..... D 631 667-8600
  Deer Park *(G-4242)*

CONTRACTORS: Single-family Home General Remodeling

Bator Bintor Inc .... F 347 546-6503
  Brooklyn *(G-1670)*
Deakon Homes and Interiors .... F 518 271-0342
  Troy *(G-16255)*
Kng Construction Co Inc .... F 212 595-1451
  Warwick *(G-16615)*
Texas Home Security Inc .... E 516 747-2100
  New Hyde Park *(G-8910)*

CONTRACTORS: Solar Energy Eqpt

Solar Energy Systems LLC .... F 718 389-1545
  Brooklyn *(G-2606)*

CONTRACTORS: Sound Eqpt Installation

L A R Electronics Corp .... G 716 285-0555
  Niagara Falls *(G-12858)*
Telephone Sales & Service Co .... E 212 233-8505
  New York *(G-12318)*

PRODUCT SECTION

CONTRACTORS: Stone Masonry
Stuart-Dean Co Inc ..... F 718 472-1326
  Long Island City *(G-7921)*

CONTRACTORS: Store Fixture Installation
Mass Mdsg Self Selection Eqp ..... E 631 234-3300
  Bohemia *(G-1097)*

CONTRACTORS: Store Front Construction
A&B McKeon Glass Inc ..... G 718 525-2152
  Staten Island *(G-15651)*
Brooklyn Store Front Co Inc ..... G 718 384-4372
  Brooklyn *(G-1733)*

CONTRACTORS: Structural Iron Work, Structural
M & L Steel & Ornamental Iron ..... F 718 816-8660
  Staten Island *(G-15723)*
Miscellnous Ir Fabricators Inc ..... F 518 355-1822
  Schenectady *(G-15306)*
Moon Gates Company ..... G 718 426-0023
  East Elmhurst *(G-4417)*
Triboro Iron Works Inc ..... G 718 361-9600
  Long Island City *(G-7934)*

CONTRACTORS: Structural Steel Erection
Barry Steel Fabrication Inc ..... E 716 433-2144
  Lockport *(G-7599)*
Cives Corporation ..... C 315 287-2200
  Gouverneur *(G-5758)*
GCM Metal Industries Inc ..... F 718 386-4059
  Brooklyn *(G-2016)*
Irv Schroder & Sons Inc ..... E 518 828-0194
  Stottville *(G-15803)*
Rochester Structural LLC ..... E 585 436-1250
  Rochester *(G-14674)*
Roth Design & Consulting Inc ..... G 718 209-0193
  Brooklyn *(G-2529)*

CONTRACTORS: Svc Station Eqpt Installation, Maint & Repair
North American Svcs Group LLC ..... F 518 885-1820
  Ballston Spa *(G-604)*

CONTRACTORS: Textile Warping
Tli Import Inc ..... G 917 578-4568
  Brooklyn *(G-2681)*

CONTRACTORS: Tile Installation, Ceramic
Alp Stone Inc ..... F 718 706-6166
  Long Island City *(G-7686)*
Quality Carpet One Floor & HM ..... G 718 941-4200
  Brooklyn *(G-2478)*

CONTRACTORS: Ventilation & Duct Work
Aabco Sheet Metal Co Inc ..... D 718 821-1166
  Ridgewood *(G-14110)*
Aeroduct Inc ..... E 516 248-9550
  Mineola *(G-8524)*
Liffey Sheet Metal Corp ..... F 347 381-1134
  Long Island City *(G-7816)*
Merz Metal & Machine Corp ..... E 716 893-7786
  Buffalo *(G-3083)*

CONTRACTORS: Water Intake Well Drilling Svc
US Pump Corp ..... G 516 303-7799
  West Hempstead *(G-16896)*

CONTRACTORS: Water Well Drilling
Barber & Deline LLC ..... F 607 749-2619
  Tully *(G-16299)*

CONTRACTORS: Water Well Servicing
Yr Blanc & Co LLC ..... G 716 800-3999
  Buffalo *(G-3287)*

CONTRACTORS: Waterproofing
Tiki Industries Inc ..... G 516 779-3629
  Riverhead *(G-14171)*

CONTRACTORS: Well Chemical Treating Svcs
Metro Group Inc ..... D 718 392-3616
  Long Island City *(G-7841)*

CONTRACTORS: Well Logging Svcs
Jay Little Oil Well Servi ..... G 716 925-8905
  Limestone *(G-7473)*
Schlumberger Technology Corp ..... C 607 378-0105
  Horseheads *(G-6621)*
Smith International Inc ..... D 212 350-9400
  New York *(G-12133)*

CONTRACTORS: Window Treatment Installation
Instant Verticals Inc ..... F 631 501-0001
  Farmingdale *(G-5019)*
Majestic Curtains LLC ..... G 718 898-0774
  Elmhurst *(G-4678)*

CONTRACTORS: Windows & Doors
Advanced Door Solutions Inc ..... G 631 773-6100
  Holbrook *(G-6457)*
D Best Service Co Inc ..... G 718 972-6133
  Brooklyn *(G-1829)*
Ecker Window Corp ..... D 914 776-0000
  Yonkers *(G-17454)*
Triple H Construction Inc ..... E 516 280-8252
  East Meadow *(G-4448)*
Window-Fix Inc ..... E 718 854-3475
  Brooklyn *(G-2773)*
Windowman Inc (usa) ..... G 718 246-2626
  Brooklyn *(G-2774)*

CONTRACTORS: Wood Floor Installation & Refinishing
Stuart-Dean Co Inc ..... F 718 472-1326
  Long Island City *(G-7921)*
Sunrise Tile Inc ..... G 718 939-0538
  Flushing *(G-5303)*
Zahk Sales Inc ..... G 631 348-9300
  Islandia *(G-6844)*

CONTROL CIRCUIT DEVICES
Inertia Switch Inc ..... E 845 359-8300
  Orangeburg *(G-13251)*

CONTROL EQPT: Electric
Addex Inc ..... G 315 331-7700
  Newark *(G-12748)*
Altronix Corp ..... D 718 567-8181
  Brooklyn *(G-1593)*
Calia Technical Inc ..... G 718 447-3928
  Staten Island *(G-15675)*
Conic Systems Inc ..... F 845 856-4053
  Port Jervis *(G-13804)*
Continental Instruments LLC ..... E 631 842-9400
  Amityville *(G-280)*
Edo LLC ..... C 631 630-4000
  Amityville *(G-286)*
Electronic Machine Parts LLC ..... F 631 434-3700
  Hauppauge *(G-6093)*
Goddard Design Co ..... G 718 599-0170
  Brooklyn *(G-2035)*
ITT Corporation ..... E 585 269-7109
  Hemlock *(G-6287)*
ITT Corporation ..... D 315 568-2811
  Seneca Falls *(G-15383)*
ITT Inc ..... F 914 641-2000
  White Plains *(G-17152)*
ITT LLC ..... D 315 258-4904
  Auburn *(G-500)*
ITT LLC ..... D 914 641-2000
  Seneca Falls *(G-15387)*
ITT LLC ..... B 914 641-2000
  White Plains *(G-17154)*
Kussmaul Electronics Co Inc ..... E 631 218-0298
  West Sayville *(G-16965)*
N E Controls LLC ..... F 315 626-2480
  Syracuse *(G-16016)*
Nitram Energy Inc ..... E 716 662-6540
  Orchard Park *(G-13310)*
Peraton Inc ..... E 315 838-7000
  Rome *(G-14857)*
Ruhle Companies Inc ..... E 914 287-4000
  Valhalla *(G-16398)*
Weldcomputer Corporation ..... F 518 283-2897
  Troy *(G-16289)*

CONTROL EQPT: Noise
Burgess-Manning Inc ..... D 716 662-6540
  Orchard Park *(G-13280)*
I D E Processes Corporation ..... F 718 544-1177
  Kew Gardens *(G-7190)*
Mason Industries Inc ..... B 631 348-0282
  Hauppauge *(G-6152)*
Mason Industries Inc ..... G 631 348-0282
  Hauppauge *(G-6153)*
Soundcoat Company Inc ..... D 631 242-2200
  Deer Park *(G-4236)*
Vibration & Noise Engrg Corp ..... G 716 827-4959
  Orchard Park *(G-13327)*
Vibration Eliminator Co Inc ..... E 631 841-4000
  Copiague *(G-3959)*

CONTROL PANELS: Electrical
Abasco Inc ..... E 716 649-4790
  Hamburg *(G-5941)*
Avanti Control Systems Inc ..... E 518 921-4368
  Gloversville *(G-5722)*
Benfield Control Systems Inc ..... F 914 948-6660
  White Plains *(G-17112)*
Boulay Fabrication Inc ..... F 315 677-5247
  La Fayette *(G-7266)*
Custom Controls ..... G 315 253-4785
  Scipio Center *(G-15343)*
Link Control Systems Inc ..... F 631 471-3950
  Ronkonkoma *(G-14960)*
Micro Instrument Corp ..... D 585 458-3150
  Rochester *(G-14528)*
Odyssey Controls Inc ..... E 585 548-9800
  Bergen *(G-850)*
Se-Mar Electric Co Inc ..... E 716 674-7404
  West Seneca *(G-16982)*
Smith Control Systems Inc ..... F 518 828-7646
  Hudson *(G-6666)*
Transit Air Inc ..... E 607 324-0216
  Hornell *(G-6595)*

CONTROLS & ACCESS: Indl, Electric
Bomac Inc ..... E 315 433-9181
  Syracuse *(G-15892)*
Entertron Industries Inc ..... E 716 772-7216
  Lockport *(G-7613)*
Fics Inc ..... E 607 359-4474
  Addison *(G-6)*
Gemtrol Inc ..... G 716 894-0716
  Buffalo *(G-2983)*
General Oil Equipment Co Inc ..... E 716 691-7012
  Amherst *(G-242)*
ICM Controls Corp ..... F 315 233-5266
  North Syracuse *(G-12964)*
Interntnal Cntrls Msrmnts Corp ..... C 315 233-5266
  North Syracuse *(G-12965)*
Morris Products Inc ..... F 518 743-0523
  Queensbury *(G-14018)*
Soft-Noze Usa Inc ..... G 315 732-2726
  Frankfort *(G-5367)*

CONTROLS & ACCESS: Motor
Designatronics Incorporated ..... B 516 328-3300
  Hicksville *(G-6367)*
Eaton Corporation ..... C 212 319-2100
  New York *(G-10021)*
Eaton Corporation ..... C 585 394-1780
  Canandaigua *(G-3373)*
Eaton Corporation ..... C 516 353-3017
  East Meadow *(G-4443)*
Eaton Hydraulics LLC ..... G 716 375-7132
  Olean *(G-13168)*
Eatons Crouse Hinds Business ..... F 315 477-7000
  Syracuse *(G-15953)*
Electro-Kinetics Inc ..... F 845 887-4930
  Callicoon *(G-3313)*
ITT Aerospace Controls LLC ..... G 914 641-2000
  White Plains *(G-17151)*
Powr-UPS Corp ..... E 631 345-5700
  Shirley *(G-15451)*
Teknic Inc ..... E 585 784-7454
  Victor *(G-16530)*

CONTROLS: Access, Motor

CONTROLS: Access, Motor

Bakery Innovative Tech Corp .... F 631 758-3081
  Patchogue *(G-13440)*
Bemco of Western Ny Inc .... G 716 823-8400
  Buffalo *(G-2860)*
Schmersal Inc .... E 914 347-4775
  Hawthorne *(G-6279)*

CONTROLS: Automatic Temperature

Advantex Solutions Inc .... G 718 278-2290
  Bellerose *(G-805)*
Automated Bldg MGT Systems Inc ..... E 516 216-5603
  Floral Park *(G-5202)*
Day Automation Systems Inc .... D 585 924-4630
  Victor *(G-16496)*
Intellidyne LLC .... F 516 676-0777
  Plainview *(G-13637)*
Intrepid Control Service Inc .... G 718 886-8771
  Flushing *(G-5262)*
Johnson Controls Inc .... E 585 924-9346
  Victor *(G-16508)*
Logical Control Solutions Inc .... F 585 424-5340
  Victor *(G-16513)*
Pii Holdings Inc .... G 716 876-9951
  Buffalo *(G-3149)*
Protective Industries Inc .... D 716 876-9951
  Buffalo *(G-3167)*
Protective Industries Inc .... C 716 876-9951
  Buffalo *(G-3165)*
Siemens Industry Inc .... E 585 797-2300
  Rochester *(G-14707)*
T S B A Group Inc .... E 718 565-6000
  Sunnyside *(G-15831)*
Use Acquisition LLC .... F 516 812-6800
  New Hyde Park *(G-8916)*

CONTROLS: Electric Motor

Dyson-Kissner-Moran Corp .... E 212 661-4600
  Poughkeepsie *(G-13915)*
US Drives Inc .... D 716 731-1606
  Niagara Falls *(G-12904)*

CONTROLS: Environmental

Anderson Instrument Co Inc .... D 518 922-5315
  Fultonville *(G-5491)*
Automated Building Controls .... G 914 381-2860
  Mamaroneck *(G-8055)*
Cascade Technical Services LLC .... F 516 596-6300
  Lynbrook *(G-7977)*
Cascade Technical Services LLC .... G 518 355-2201
  Schenectady *(G-15267)*
Clean Room Depot Inc .... F 631 589-3033
  Holbrook *(G-6466)*
Cox & Company Inc .... C 212 366-0200
  Plainview *(G-13623)*
Daikin Applied Americas Inc .... D 315 253-2771
  Auburn *(G-490)*
E Global Solutions Inc .... G 516 767-5138
  Port Washington *(G-13834)*
East Hudson Watershed Corp .... G 845 319-6349
  Patterson *(G-13463)*
Evolve Guest Controls LLC .... F 855 750-9090
  Port Washington *(G-13836)*
Fedders Islandaire Inc .... D 631 471-2900
  East Setauket *(G-4500)*
Fuel Watchman Sales & Service .... F 718 665-6100
  Bronx *(G-1340)*
Grillmaster Inc .... E 718 272-9191
  Howard Beach *(G-6625)*
Heating & Burner Supply Inc .... G 718 665-0006
  Bronx *(G-1357)*
Infitec Inc .... D 315 433-1150
  East Syracuse *(G-4557)*
Johnson Controls Inc .... E 716 688-7340
  Buffalo *(G-3037)*
Leo Schultz .... G 716 969-0945
  Cheektowaga *(G-3606)*
Long Island Analytical Labs .... F 631 472-3400
  Holbrook *(G-6487)*
Microb Phase Services .... F 518 877-8948
  Clifton Park *(G-3728)*
Pulsafeeder Inc .... C 585 292-8000
  Rochester *(G-14632)*
RE Hansen Industries Inc .... C 631 471-2900
  East Setauket *(G-4510)*
Transit Air Inc .... E 607 324-0216
  Hornell *(G-6595)*

Zebra Environmental Corp .... F 516 596-6300
  Lynbrook *(G-7993)*

CONTROLS: Marine & Navy, Auxiliary

L-3 Cmmnctons Ntronix Holdings .... D 212 697-1111
  New York *(G-10942)*

CONTROLS: Numerical

Teale Machine Company Inc .... D 585 244-6700
  Rochester *(G-14744)*

CONTROLS: Positioning, Electric

Sequential Electronics Systems .... E 914 592-1345
  Elmsford *(G-4791)*

CONTROLS: Relay & Ind

Afi Cybernetics Corporation .... E 607 732-3244
  Elmira *(G-4682)*
Air Crafters Inc .... C 631 471-7788
  Ronkonkoma *(G-14883)*
Anderson Instrument Co Inc .... D 518 922-5315
  Fultonville *(G-5491)*
Con Rel Auto Electric Inc .... E 518 356-1646
  Schenectady *(G-15273)*
Cox & Company Inc .... C 212 366-0200
  Plainview *(G-13623)*
Designatronics Incorporated .... G 516 328-3300
  Hicksville *(G-6366)*
Deutsch Relays .... F 631 342-1700
  Hauppauge *(G-6084)*
Digital Instruments Inc .... F 716 874-5848
  Tonawanda *(G-16176)*
Eaton Corporation .... G 716 691-0008
  Buffalo *(G-2944)*
Elevator Systems Inc .... E 516 239-4044
  Garden City *(G-5515)*
Enetics Inc .... E 585 924-5010
  Victor *(G-16499)*
Exfo Burleigh Pdts Group Inc .... D 585 301-1530
  Canandaigua *(G-3374)*
G C Controls Inc .... E 607 656-4117
  Greene *(G-5883)*
I E D Corp .... F 631 348-0424
  Islandia *(G-6832)*
Industrial Indxing Systems Inc .... E 585 924-9181
  Victor *(G-16506)*
JE Miller Inc .... E 315 437-6811
  East Syracuse *(G-4560)*
Kaman Automation Inc .... D 585 254-8840
  Rochester *(G-14490)*
Kearney-National Inc .... F 212 661-4600
  New York *(G-10868)*
Linde LLC .... D 716 773-7552
  Grand Island *(G-5776)*
Logitek Inc .... D 631 567-1100
  Bohemia *(G-1089)*
Magnus Precision Mfg Inc .... D 315 548-8032
  Phelps *(G-13557)*
Moog Inc .... C 716 805-8100
  East Aurora *(G-4401)*
Moog Inc .... A 716 652-2000
  Elma *(G-4664)*
Nas-Tra Automotive Inds Inc .... C 631 225-1225
  Lindenhurst *(G-7497)*
National Time Recording Eqp Co .... F 212 227-3310
  New York *(G-11375)*
North Point Technology LLC .... F 866 885-3377
  Endicott *(G-4828)*
Nsi Industries LLC .... C 800 841-2505
  Mount Vernon *(G-8757)*
Omntec Mfg Inc .... E 631 981-2001
  Ronkonkoma *(G-14985)*
Panelogic Inc .... F 607 962-6319
  Corning *(G-3998)*
Peerless Instrument Co Inc .... C 631 396-6500
  Farmingdale *(G-5086)*
Precision Mechanisms Corp .... F 516 333-5955
  Westbury *(G-17049)*
Pulsafeeder Inc .... C 585 292-8000
  Rochester *(G-14632)*
Rochester Industrial Ctrl Inc .... D 315 524-4555
  Ontario *(G-13234)*
Rockwell Automation Inc .... E 585 487-2700
  Pittsford *(G-13602)*
Service Mfg Group Inc .... F 716 893-1482
  Buffalo *(G-3212)*
Ssac Inc .... E 800 843-8848
  Baldwinsville *(G-576)*

Stetron International Inc .... F 716 854-3443
  Buffalo *(G-3225)*
Techniflo Corporation .... G 716 741-3500
  Clarence Center *(G-3706)*
Tork Inc .... D 914 664-3542
  Mount Vernon *(G-8784)*
Unimar Inc .... F 315 699-4400
  Syracuse *(G-16087)*
Zeppelin Electric Company Inc .... G 631 928-9467
  East Setauket *(G-4516)*

CONTROLS: Thermostats, Exc Built-in

Bilbee Controls Inc .... F 518 622-3033
  Cairo *(G-3297)*

CONTROLS: Voice

Voices For All LLC .... G 518 261-1664
  Mechanicville *(G-8263)*

CONVENIENCE STORES

Schaefer Logging Inc .... F 607 467-4990
  Deposit *(G-4304)*

CONVENTION & TRADE SHOW SVCS

Mechanical Displays Inc .... G 718 258-5588
  Brooklyn *(G-2294)*

CONVERTERS: Data

Annese & Associates Inc .... G 716 972-0076
  Buffalo *(G-2831)*
Cisco Systems Inc .... C 212 714-4000
  New York *(G-9675)*
Data Device Corporation .... B 631 567-5600
  Bohemia *(G-1045)*
Lockheed Martin .... E 315 456-3333
  Syracuse *(G-16000)*
Scroll Media Inc .... E 617 395-8904
  New York *(G-12027)*

CONVERTERS: Frequency

Applied Power Systems Inc .... E 516 935-2230
  Hicksville *(G-6346)*

CONVERTERS: Phase Or Rotary, Electrical

Automation Source Technologies .... F 631 643-1678
  West Babylon *(G-16797)*

CONVERTERS: Power, AC to DC

Curtis/Palmer Hydroelectric LP .... G 518 654-6297
  Corinth *(G-3979)*
Endicott Research Group Inc .... D 607 754-9187
  Endicott *(G-4812)*
G B International Trdg Co Ltd .... C 607 785-0938
  Endicott *(G-4817)*

CONVERTERS: Torque, Exc Auto

American Torque Inc .... F 718 526-2433
  Jamaica *(G-6929)*

CONVEYOR SYSTEMS: Belt, General Indl Use

American Material Processing .... F 315 318-0017
  Phoenix *(G-13567)*
Desmi-Afti Inc .... E 716 662-0632
  Orchard Park *(G-13292)*
Greenbelt Industries Inc .... E 800 668-1114
  Buffalo *(G-3000)*

CONVEYOR SYSTEMS: Bulk Handling

Ward Industrial Equipment Inc .... G 716 856-6966
  Buffalo *(G-3273)*

CONVEYOR SYSTEMS: Pneumatic Tube

Shako Inc .... G 315 437-1294
  East Syracuse *(G-4577)*

CONVEYOR SYSTEMS: Robotic

International Robotics Inc .... F 914 630-1060
  Larchmont *(G-7375)*
United Rbotic Integrations LLC .... G 716 683-8334
  Alden *(G-188)*

CONVEYORS & CONVEYING EQPT

[...]5 Main Street Snyder Inc .... G 716 833-3270
  [Bu]ffalo (G-2803)
[...]mprene Inc .... C 845 831-2800
  [B]eacon (G-777)
[...]mprene Holding Inc .... C 845 831-2800
  [B]eacon (G-778)
[...]umbus McKinnon Corporation ..... C 716 689-5400
  [G]etzville (G-5607)
[...]umbus McKinnon Corporation ..... C 716 689-5400
  [G]etzville (G-5608)
[...]umbus McKinnon Corporation ..... C 716 689-5400
  [G]etzville (G-5609)
[...]iry Conveyor Corp .... D 845 278-7878
  [B]rewster (G-1212)
[...]eneral Splice Corporation .... G 914 271-5131
  [C]roton On Hudson (G-4089)
[...]lasgow Products Inc .... E 516 374-5937
  Woodmere (G-17331)
[...]aines Equipment Inc .... E 607 566-8531
  Avoca (G-534)
[...]ohl Machine & Conveyor Co Inc ... E 716 882-7210
  Buffalo (G-3013)
J White Corporation .... D 631 293-3788
  Farmingdale (G-5016)
J D Handling Systems Inc .... F 518 828-9676
  Ghent (G-5620)
Joldeson One Aerospace Inds .... D 718 848-7396
  Ozone Park (G-13406)
Northeast Conveyors Inc .... F 585 768-8912
  Lima (G-7468)
Noto Industrial Corp .... G 631 736-7600
  Coram (G-3971)
Raymond Corporation .... E 315 643-5000
  East Syracuse (G-4572)
Raymond Corporation .... A 800 235-7200
  Greene (G-5887)
Re-Al Industrial Corp .... F 716 542-4556
  Akron (G-25)
Renold Inc .... D 716 326-3121
  Westfield (G-17080)
Rlp Holdings Inc .... F 716 852-0832
  Buffalo (G-3187)
Rota Pack Inc .... F 631 274-1037
  Farmingdale (G-5113)
Speedways Conveyors Inc .... E 716 893-2222
  Buffalo (G-3223)
Troy Belting and Supply Co .... D 518 272-4920
  Watervliet (G-16715)

COOKING & FOOD WARMING EQPT: Commercial

Advance Tabco Inc .... D 631 242-8270
  Edgewood (G-4605)
Attias Oven Corp .... G 718 499-0145
  Brooklyn (G-1651)
Bakers Pride Oven Co Inc .... C 914 576-0200
  New Rochelle (G-8932)
Carts Mobile Food Eqp Corp .... E 718 788-5540
  Brooklyn (G-1763)
IMC Teddy Food Service .... E 631 789-8881
  Amityville (G-294)
Kinplex Corp .... E 631 242-4800
  Edgewood (G-4617)
Kinplex Corp .... E 631 242-4800
  Edgewood (G-4618)
Korin Japanese Trading Corp .... E 212 587-7021
  New York (G-10916)
R-S Restaurant Eqp Mfg Corp .... F 212 925-0335
  New York (G-11811)
Roger & Sons Inc .... E 212 226-4734
  New York (G-11927)
Toga Manufacturing Inc .... G 631 242-4800
  Edgewood (G-4631)
Wilder Manufacturing Co Inc .... D 516 222-0433
  Garden City (G-5550)

COOKING & FOODWARMING EQPT: Coffee Brewing

Arista Coffee Inc .... G 347 531-0813
  Maspeth (G-8148)

COOKING & FOODWARMING EQPT: Commercial

Advance Food Service Co Inc .... C 631 242-4800
  Edgewood (G-4604)

COOKING WARE, EXC PORCELAIN ENAMELED

Allied Metal Spinning Corp .... D 718 893-3300
  Bronx (G-1269)

COOKING WARE: Cooking Ware, Porcelain Enameled

Schiller Stores Inc .... G 631 208-9400
  Riverhead (G-14168)
Wilmax Usa LLC .... F 917 388-2790
  New York (G-12666)

COOKWARE, STONEWARE: Coarse Earthenware & Pottery

Schiller Stores Inc .... G 845 928-4316
  Central Valley (G-3555)

COOKWARE: Fine Earthenware

Lifetime Stainless Steel Corp .... G 585 924-9393
  Victor (G-16512)
Mackenzie-Childs LLC .... C 315 364-6118
  Aurora (G-528)
Williams-Sonoma Stores Inc .... F 212 633-2203
  New York (G-12664)

COOLING TOWERS: Metal

Manhattan Cooling Towers Inc .... F 212 279-1045
  Long Island City (G-7831)
SPX Corporation .... B 585 436-5550
  Rochester (G-14721)

COPPER ORES

Global Gold Corporation .... F 914 925-0020
  Rye (G-15084)

COPPER PRDTS: Refined, Primary

Hengyuan Copper USA Inc .... G 718 357-6666
  Whitestone (G-17237)

COPPER: Rolling & Drawing

Aurubis Buffalo Inc .... F 716 879-6700
  Buffalo (G-2844)
Aurubis Buffalo Inc .... B 716 879-6700
  Buffalo (G-2845)
Continental Cordage Corp .... D 315 655-9800
  Cazenovia (G-3470)

COPYRIGHT BUYING & LICENSING

Abkco Music & Records Inc .... D 212 399-0300
  New York (G-9050)
Penhouse Media Group Inc .... C 212 702-6000
  New York (G-11625)
Scholastic Corporation .... G 212 343-6100
  New York (G-12015)

CORD & TWINE

Albany International Corp .... C 607 749-7226
  Homer (G-6543)
Sampo Inc .... E 315 896-2606
  Barneveld (G-617)
Simplicity Creative Group Inc .... A 212 686-7676
  New York (G-12105)

CORE WASH OR WAX

Beyond Beauty Basics LLC .... F 516 731-7100
  Levittown (G-7447)

CORES: Magnetic

Fair-Rite Products Corp .... C 845 895-2055
  Wallkill (G-16563)

CORK & CORK PRDTS: Tiles

Globus Cork Inc .... F 347 963-4059
  Bronx (G-1346)

CORRESPONDENCE SCHOOLS

Boardman Simons Publishing .... E 212 620-7200
  New York (G-9482)
Simmons-Boardman Pubg Corp .... G 212 620-7200
  New York (G-12101)

CORRUGATED PRDTS: Boxes, Partition, Display Items, Sheet/Pad

Dory Enterprises Inc .... F 607 565-7079
  Waverly (G-16726)
Enterprise Container LLC .... E 631 253-4400
  Wyandanch (G-17390)
General Fibre Products Corp .... D 516 358-7500
  New Hyde Park (G-8880)
Land Packaging Corp .... F 914 472-5976
  Scarsdale (G-15249)
Mechtronics Corporation .... E 845 831-9300
  Beacon (G-783)
Niagara Sheets LLC .... D 716 692-1129
  North Tonawanda (G-13001)
President Cont Group II LLC .... B 845 516-1600
  Middletown (G-8492)
Technical Library Service Inc .... F 212 219-0770
  Brooklyn (G-2670)
Westrock Cp LLC .... C 770 448-2193
  New Hartford (G-8858)
Westrock CP LLC .... F 716 692-6510
  North Tonawanda (G-13024)

COSMETIC PREPARATIONS

Abbe Laboratories Inc .... F 631 756-2223
  Farmingdale (G-4936)
Albion Cosmetics Inc .... F 212 869-1052
  New York (G-9125)
Ardex Cosmetics of America .... E 518 283-6700
  Troy (G-16248)
Becca Inc .... F 646 568-6250
  New York (G-9390)
Brucci Ltd .... E 914 965-0707
  Yonkers (G-17438)
Bycmac Corp .... E 845 255-0884
  Gardiner (G-5561)
Clark Botanicals Inc .... F 914 826-4319
  Bronxville (G-1500)
Clinique Laboratories LLC .... G 212 572-4200
  New York (G-9698)
Dermatech Labs Inc .... F 631 225-1700
  Lindenhurst (G-7484)
Drt Laboratories LLC .... G 845 547-2034
  Airmont (G-12)
Estee Lauder Inc .... C 631 454-7000
  Melville (G-8346)
Estee Lauder Inc .... D 212 756-4800
  New York (G-10127)
Ex-It Medical Devices Inc .... G 212 653-0637
  New York (G-10153)
Forsythe Cosmetic Group Ltd .... F 516 239-4200
  Freeport (G-5411)
Fusion Brands America Inc .... E 212 269-1387
  New York (G-10273)
Gurwitch Products LLC .... D 281 275-7000
  New York (G-10429)
Jackel Inc .... D 908 359-2039
  New York (G-10726)
June Jacobs Labs LLC .... D 212 471-4830
  New York (G-10823)
Kantian Skincare LLC .... G 631 780-4711
  Smithtown (G-15514)
Lady Burd Exclusive Cosmt Inc .... C 631 454-0444
  Farmingdale (G-5040)
Lechler Laboratories Inc .... E 845 426-6800
  Spring Valley (G-15613)
Liddell Corporation .... F 716 297-8557
  Niagara Falls (G-12859)
Malin + Goetz Inc .... F 212 244-7771
  New York (G-11145)
Mana Products Inc .... B 718 361-2550
  Long Island City (G-7828)
Marietta Corporation .... B 607 753-6746
  Cortland (G-4057)
Mehron Inc .... E 845 426-1700
  Chestnut Ridge (G-3652)
Nature Only Inc .... G 917 922-6539
  Forest Hills (G-5333)
Naturpathica Holistic Hlth Inc .... D 631 329-8792
  East Hampton (G-4434)
Newburgh Distribution Corp .... G 845 561-6330
  New Windsor (G-8991)
Oasis Cosmetic Labs Inc .... F 631 758-0038
  Holtsville (G-6531)
Olan Laboratories Inc .... D 631 582-2082
  Hauppauge (G-6177)
Peppermints Salon Inc .... F 718 357-6304
  Whitestone (G-17242)

Employee Codes: A=Over 500 employees, B=251-500
C=101-250, D=51-100, E=20-50, F=10-19, G=5-9

COSMETIC PREPARATIONS

Peter Thomas Roth Labs LLC.............E....... 212 581-5800
  New York (G-11653)
Plastic & Reconstructive Svcs.............G....... 914 584-5605
  Mount Kisco (G-8683)
Redken 5th Avenue Nyc LLC.............G....... 212 984-5113
  New York (G-11846)
Scientific Solutions Globl LLC.............F....... 516 543-3376
  Carle Place (G-3423)
Shiseido Americas Corporation.............G....... 212 805-2300
  New York (G-12077)
Skin Nutrition Intl Inc.............E....... 212 231-8355
  New York (G-12116)
Solabia USA Inc.............G....... 212 847-2397
  New York (G-12148)
Stamapro Inc.............G....... 888 623-5003
  Carle Place (G-3424)
Temptu Inc.............G....... 718 937-9503
  Long Island City (G-7926)
Topiderm Inc.............C....... 631 226-7979
  Amityville (G-330)
Universal Packg Systems Inc.............A....... 631 543-2277
  Hauppauge (G-6245)
Victoria Albi Intl Inc.............F....... 212 689-2600
  New York (G-12563)
Xania Labs Inc.............G....... 718 361-2550
  Long Island City (G-7957)
Yoyo Lip Gloss Inc.............F....... 718 357-6304
  Astoria (G-462)

COSMETICS & TOILETRIES

AEP Environmental LLC.............F....... 716 446-0739
  Buffalo (G-2818)
Alexandria Professional LLC.............G....... 716 242-8514
  Williamsville (G-17260)
Allan John Company.............F....... 212 940-2210
  New York (G-9136)
Antimony New York LLC.............G....... 917 232-1836
  New York (G-9219)
Art of Shaving - FI LLC.............G....... 212 362-1493
  New York (G-9262)
Bare Escentuals Inc.............G....... 646 537-0070
  New York (G-9371)
Bellarno International Ltd.............G....... 212 302-4107
  New York (G-9397)
Bio-Botanica Inc.............D....... 631 231-0987
  Hauppauge (G-6053)
Bobbi Brown Prof Cosmt Inc.............E....... 646 613-6500
  New York (G-9483)
Borghese Inc.............E....... 212 659-5318
  New York (G-9491)
Butterfly Beauty LLC.............G....... 646 604-4289
  New York (G-9536)
California Fragrance Company.............E....... 631 424-4023
  Huntington Station (G-6736)
China Huaren Organic Pdts Inc.............G....... 212 232-0120
  New York (G-9647)
Clinique Services Inc.............G....... 212 572-4200
  New York (G-9699)
Collaborative Laboratories.............D....... 631 689-0200
  East Setauket (G-4498)
Common Sense Natural Soap.............E....... 518 677-0224
  Cambridge (G-3334)
Conopco Inc.............E....... 585 647-8322
  Rochester (G-14308)
Coty Inc.............C....... 212 389-7000
  New York (G-9789)
Coty Inc.............D....... 212 389-7300
  New York (G-9790)
Delbia Do Company Inc.............F....... 718 585-2226
  Bronx (G-1316)
Elite Parfums Ltd.............D....... 212 983-2640
  New York (G-10060)
Estee Lauder Companies Inc.............A....... 917 606-3240
  New York (G-10121)
Estee Lauder Companies Inc.............G....... 212 756-4800
  New York (G-10122)
Estee Lauder Companies Inc.............A....... 212 572-4200
  New York (G-10123)
Estee Lauder Companies Inc.............A....... 212 572-4200
  New York (G-10124)
Estee Lauder Companies Inc.............A....... 646 602-7590
  New York (G-10125)
Estee Lauder Inc.............A....... 212 572-4200
  New York (G-10126)
Estee Lauder International Inc.............G....... 212 572-4200
  New York (G-10128)
Eternal Love Parfums Corp.............G....... 516 921-6100
  Syosset (G-15841)
FMC International Ltd.............G....... 914 935-0918
  Purchase (G-13972)
Four Paws Products Ltd.............D....... 631 436-7421
  Ronkonkoma (G-14931)
Good Home Co Inc.............G....... 212 352-1509
  New York (G-10377)
Hain Celestial Group Inc.............C....... 516 587-5000
  New Hyde Park (G-8882)
HFC Prestige Intl US LLC.............A....... 212 389-7800
  New York (G-10514)
Inter Parfums Inc.............D....... 212 983-2640
  New York (G-10664)
Intercos America Inc.............G....... 845 732-3910
  West Nyack (G-16948)
Interntnal Flvors Frgrnces Inc.............C....... 212 765-5500
  New York (G-10681)
Jean Philippe Fragrances LLC.............D....... 212 983-2640
  New York (G-10755)
Judith N Graham Inc.............G....... 914 921-5446
  Rye (G-15087)
Kind Group LLC.............C....... 212 645-0800
  New York (G-10888)
Klg Usa LLC.............A....... 845 856-5311
  Port Jervis (G-13811)
LOreal Usa Inc.............G....... 917 606-9554
  New York (G-11065)
Lornamead Inc.............F....... 716 874-7190
  New York (G-11072)
Mana Products Inc.............B....... 718 361-5204
  Long Island City (G-7829)
Marvellissima Intl Ltd.............G....... 212 682-7306
  New York (G-11194)
Maybelline Inc.............A....... 212 885-1310
  New York (G-11214)
Mentholatum Company.............E....... 716 677-2500
  Orchard Park (G-13309)
New Avon LLC.............F....... 716 572-4842
  Buffalo (G-3104)
New Avon LLC.............A....... 212 282-8500
  New York (G-11403)
Paula Dorf Cosmetics Inc.............E....... 212 582-0073
  New York (G-11600)
Pdk Labs Inc.............D....... 631 273-2630
  Hauppauge (G-6184)
Procter & Gamble Company.............C....... 646 885-4201
  New York (G-11747)
Professional Buty Holdings Inc.............F....... 631 787-8576
  Hauppauge (G-6199)
Puig Usa Inc.............E....... 212 271-5940
  New York (G-11771)
Quality King Distributors Inc.............C....... 631 439-2027
  Ronkonkoma (G-14998)
Revlon Inc.............B....... 212 527-4000
  New York (G-11878)
Revlon Consumer Products Corp.............B....... 212 527-4000
  New York (G-11879)
Robert Racine.............E....... 518 677-0224
  Cambridge (G-3338)
Sally Beauty Supply LLC.............G....... 716 831-3286
  West Seneca (G-16981)
Scent-A-Vision Inc.............E....... 631 424-4905
  Huntington Station (G-6759)
Skin Atelier Inc.............F....... 845 294-1202
  Goshen (G-5753)
Sml Acquisition LLC.............C....... 914 592-3130
  Elmsford (G-4793)
Sundial Brands LLC.............C....... 631 842-8800
  Amityville (G-327)
Sundial Group LLC.............E....... 631 842-8800
  Amityville (G-329)
Symrise Inc.............E....... 845 469-7675
  Chester (G-3645)
Tomia Beauty Brands LLC.............G....... 917 301-0125
  New York (G-12385)
Tula Life LLC.............G....... 201 895-3309
  New York (G-12443)
Unilever United States Inc.............F....... 212 546-0200
  New York (G-12474)
Unilever United States Inc.............C....... 212 546-0200
  New York (G-12475)
United-Guardian Inc.............E....... 631 273-0900
  Hauppauge (G-6244)
Verla International Ltd.............B....... 845 561-2440
  New Windsor (G-9003)
Zela International Co.............E....... 518 436-1833
  Albany (G-154)

COSMETICS WHOLESALERS

Abbe Laboratories Inc.............F....... 631 756-2223
  Farmingdale (G-4936)
Borghese Inc.............E....... 212 659-5318
  New York (G-9491)
Clinique Laboratories LLC.............G....... 212 572-4
  New York (G-9698)
Dermatech Labs Inc.............F....... 631 225-1
  Lindenhurst (G-7484)
Essie Cosmetics Ltd.............D....... 212 818-1
  New York (G-10120)
Fusion Brands America Inc.............E....... 212 269-1
  New York (G-10273)
Lotta Luv Beauty LLC.............F....... 646 786-28
  New York (G-11074)
Mana Products Inc.............B....... 718 361-25
  Long Island City (G-7828)
Marvellissima Intl Ltd.............G....... 212 682-73
  New York (G-11194)
New Avon LLC.............A....... 212 282-850
  New York (G-11403)
Shiseido Americas Corporation.............G....... 212 805-230
  New York (G-12077)
Xania Labs Inc.............G....... 718 361-255
  Long Island City (G-7957)
Zela International Co.............E....... 518 436-183
  Albany (G-154)

COSTUME JEWELRY & NOVELTIES: Apparel, Exc Precious Metals

Jj Fantasia Inc.............G....... 212 868-1198
  New York (G-10779)
Kenneth J Lane Inc.............F....... 212 868-1780
  New York (G-10874)
Von Musulin Patricia.............G....... 212 206-8345
  New York (G-12593)

COSTUME JEWELRY & NOVELTIES: Bracelets, Exc Precious Metals

Aniiwe Inc.............G....... 347 683-1891
  Brooklyn (G-1612)
Vitafede.............F....... 213 488-0136
  New York (G-12582)

COSTUME JEWELRY & NOVELTIES: Costume Novelties

Jay Turoff.............F....... 718 856-7300
  Brooklyn (G-2135)

COSTUME JEWELRY & NOVELTIES: Earrings, Exc Precious Metals

Fashion Accents LLC.............F....... 401 331-6626
  New York (G-10194)

COSTUME JEWELRY & NOVELTIES: Exc Semi & Precious

Accessory Plays LLC.............E....... 212 564-7301
  New York (G-9058)
Barrera Jose & Maria Co Ltd.............E....... 212 239-1994
  New York (G-9376)
Ben-Amun Co Inc.............E....... 212 944-6480
  New York (G-9402)
Carol For Eva Graham Inc.............F....... 212 889-8686
  New York (G-9585)
Catherine Stein Designs Inc.............E....... 212 840-1188
  New York (G-9603)
Ciner Manufacturing Co Inc.............E....... 212 947-3770
  New York (G-9672)
Dabby-Reid Ltd.............F....... 212 356-0040
  New York (G-9842)
Erickson Beamon Ltd.............F....... 212 643-4810
  New York (G-10109)
Fantasia Jewelry Inc.............F....... 212 921-9590
  New York (G-10189)
Horly Novelty Co Inc.............G....... 212 226-4800
  New York (G-10550)
J & H Creations Inc.............E....... 212 465-0962
  New York (G-10714)
Jaymar Jewelry Co Inc.............G....... 212 564-4788
  New York (G-10748)
Lesilu Productions Inc.............G....... 212 947-6419
  New York (G-11010)
Magic Novelty Co Inc.............E....... 212 304-2777
  New York (G-11131)
Marlborough Jewels Inc.............G....... 718 768-2000
  Brooklyn (G-2274)
Mwsi Inc.............D....... 914 347-4200
  Hawthorne (G-6275)
Salmco Jewelry Corp.............F....... 212 695-8792
  New York (G-11975)

PRODUCT SECTION

CULTURE MEDIA

Steezys LLC .... G 646 276-5333
  New York *(G-12213)*
Stephan & Company ACC Ltd .... E 212 481-3888
  New York *(G-12218)*
Top Shelf Jewelry Inc .... F 845 647-4661
  Ellenville *(G-4653)*

COSTUME JEWELRY & NOVELTIES: Pins, Exc Precious Metals

Custom Pins Inc .... G 914 690-9378
  Elmsford *(G-4755)*

COUGH MEDICINES

Purine Pharma LLC .... E 315 705-4030
  Mount Vernon *(G-8768)*

COUNTER & SINK TOPS

Arcy Plastic Laminates Inc .... E 518 235-0753
  Albany *(G-45)*
Auratic Inc .... G 914 413-8154
  New York *(G-9318)*
Countertops & Cabinets Inc .... G 315 433-1038
  Syracuse *(G-15930)*
Delocon Wholesale Inc .... F 716 592-2711
  Springville *(G-15630)*
Empire Fabricators Inc .... G 585 235-3050
  Rochester *(G-14366)*
Frank J Martello .... G 585 235-2780
  Rochester *(G-14403)*
Icestone LLC .... E 718 624-4900
  Brooklyn *(G-2093)*
Joseph Fedele .... G 718 448-3658
  Staten Island *(G-15716)*
Koeppels Kustom Kitchens Inc .... G 518 489-0092
  Albany *(G-96)*
Metropolitan Granite & MBL Inc .... G 585 342-7020
  Rochester *(G-14526)*
Nlr Counter Tops LLC .... G 347 295-0410
  New York *(G-11461)*
Pine Hill Fabricators .... G 716 823-2474
  Buffalo *(G-3150)*
Precision Built Tops LLC .... G 607 336-5417
  Norwich *(G-13053)*
Ridge Cabinet & Showcase Inc .... E 585 663-0560
  Rochester *(G-14649)*
Rochester Countertop Inc .... F 585 338-2260
  Rochester *(G-14662)*
Solid Surfaces Inc .... D 585 292-5340
  Rochester *(G-14716)*
Triad Counter Corp .... E 631 750-0615
  Bohemia *(G-1143)*
Wilbedone Inc .... E 607 756-8813
  Cortland *(G-4071)*
Wolak Inc .... G 315 839-5366
  Clayville *(G-3717)*

COUNTERS & COUNTING DEVICES

Cmp Advnced Mech Sltons NY LLC .... G 607 352-1712
  Binghamton *(G-898)*
Designatronics Incorporated .... G 516 328-3300
  Hicksville *(G-6366)*
Designatronics Incorporated .... G 516 328-3970
  Hicksville *(G-6368)*
Encore Electronics Inc .... E 518 584-5354
  Saratoga Springs *(G-15179)*
Environment-One Corporation .... C 518 346-6161
  Schenectady *(G-15279)*

COUNTERS OR COUNTER DISPLAY CASES, EXC WOOD

Gerald Frd Packg Display LLC .... F 716 692-2705
  Tonawanda *(G-16182)*
Glasbau Hahn America LLC .... G 845 566-3331
  Newburgh *(G-12780)*
Stone Expo & Cabinetry LLC .... F 516 292-2988
  West Hempstead *(G-16895)*

COUNTERS OR COUNTER DISPLAY CASES, WOOD

Bloch Industries LLC .... D 585 334-9600
  Rochester *(G-14253)*
Creative Counter Tops Inc .... F 845 471-6480
  Poughkeepsie *(G-13913)*
Serway Bros Inc .... E 315 337-0601
  Rome *(G-14864)*

COUNTERS: Mechanical

Melland Gear Instr of Huppauge .... E 631 234-0100
  Hauppauge *(G-6156)*

COUNTING DEVICES: Controls, Revolution & Timing

Heat-Timer Corporation .... E 212 481-2020
  Bronx *(G-1356)*
Schlumberger Technology Corp .... C 607 378-0105
  Horseheads *(G-6621)*

COUNTING DEVICES: Electromechanical

K-Technologies Inc .... E 716 828-4444
  Buffalo *(G-3042)*
Vantage Mfg & Assembly LLC .... E 845 471-5290
  Poughkeepsie *(G-13954)*

COUNTING DEVICES: Speed Indicators & Recorders, Vehicle

Curtis Instruments Inc .... C 914 666-2971
  Mount Kisco *(G-8666)*

COUPLINGS: Shaft

Cobham Management Services Inc .... A 716 662-0006
  Orchard Park *(G-13287)*
Howden North America Inc .... D 803 741-2700
  Depew *(G-4283)*
Kinemotive Corporation .... E 631 249-6440
  Farmingdale *(G-5035)*

COUPON REDEMPTION SVCS

Syracuse Letter Company Inc .... F 315 476-8328
  Bridgeport *(G-1236)*

COURIER SVCS, AIR: Package Delivery, Private

Miller Enterprises CNY Inc .... G 315 682-4999
  Manlius *(G-8108)*

COURIER SVCS: Ground

Comsec Ventures International .... G 518 523-1600
  Lake Placid *(G-7297)*

COVERS: Automobile Seat

Mc Coy Tops and Interiors Inc .... G 718 458-5800
  Woodside *(G-17353)*

COVERS: Automotive, Exc Seat & Tire

Automtive Uphl Cnvertible Tops .... G 914 961-4242
  Tuckahoe *(G-16293)*
Kamali Group Inc .... G 516 627-4000
  Great Neck *(G-5836)*

COVERS: Canvas

Covergrip Corporation .... G 855 268-3747
  Bohemia *(G-1037)*
Custom Canvas Manufacturing Co .... E 716 852-6372
  Buffalo *(G-2917)*

COVERS: Hot Tub & Spa

Commercial Fabrics Inc .... F 716 694-0641
  North Tonawanda *(G-12984)*

COVERS: Slip Made Of Fabric, Plastic, Etc.

Superior Decorators Inc .... F 718 381-4793
  Glendale *(G-5680)*

CRANE & AERIAL LIFT SVCS

Snyders Neon Displays Inc .... G 518 857-4100
  Colonie *(G-3847)*

CRANES & MONORAIL SYSTEMS

Debrucque Cleveland Tramrail S .... G 315 697-5160
  Canastota *(G-3395)*

CRANES: Indl Plant

Konecranes Inc .... F 585 359-4450
  Henrietta *(G-6318)*

CRANKSHAFTS & CAMSHAFTS: Machining

Peko Precision Products Inc .... F 585 301-1386
  Rochester *(G-14594)*
Westchstr Crnkshft Grndng .... G 718 651-3900
  East Elmhurst *(G-4419)*

CRATES: Fruit, Wood Wirebound

Wolfe Lumber Mill Inc .... G 716 772-7750
  Gasport *(G-5575)*

CREDIT BUREAUS

Nyt Capital LLC .... F 212 556-1234
  New York *(G-11503)*

CROWNS & CLOSURES

Protocase Incorporated .... C 866 849-3911
  Lewiston *(G-7456)*
Reynolds Packaging McHy Inc .... D 716 358-6451
  Falconer *(G-4918)*

CRUDE PETROLEUM & NATURAL GAS PRODUCTION

Hess Energy Exploration Ltd .... G 732 750-6500
  New York *(G-10508)*
Hess Explrtion Prod Hldngs Ltd .... G 732 750-6000
  New York *(G-10509)*

CRUDE PETROLEUM & NATURAL GAS PRODUCTION

Dlh Energy Service LLC .... G 716 410-0028
  Lakewood *(G-7315)*
Lukoil Americas Corporation .... E 212 421-4141
  New York *(G-11090)*
MRC Global (us) Inc .... F 607 739-8575
  Horseheads *(G-6613)*
Rocket Tech Fuel Corp .... F 516 810-8947
  Bay Shore *(G-732)*

CRUDE PETROLEUM PRODUCTION

Chanse Petroleum Corporation .... G 212 682-3789
  New York *(G-9629)*
China N E Petro Holdings Ltd .... A 212 307-3568
  New York *(G-9650)*
Hess Corporation .... B 212 997-8500
  New York *(G-10507)*
Hess Pipeline Corporation .... C 212 997-8500
  New York *(G-10511)*
Hess Tioga Gas Plant LLC .... C 212 997-8500
  New York *(G-10512)*
Resource PTRlm&ptrochmcl Intl .... E 212 537-3856
  New York *(G-11874)*
Speedway LLC .... F 631 738-2536
  Lake Grove *(G-7291)*
Stedman Energy Inc .... G 716 789-3018
  Mayville *(G-8250)*

CRUDES: Cyclic, Organic

Magic Tank LLC .... G 877 646-2442
  New York *(G-11133)*

CRYOGENIC COOLING DEVICES: Infrared Detectors, Masers

Philips Medical Systems Mr .... B 518 782-1122
  Latham *(G-7403)*

CRYSTALS

Crystal Is Inc .... E 518 271-7375
  Troy *(G-16240)*
Edo LLC .... G 631 630-4000
  Amityville *(G-284)*
Momentive Performance Mtls Inc .... E 518 237-3330
  Waterford *(G-16638)*
Mpm Holdings Inc .... E 518 237-3330
  Waterford *(G-16639)*
Mpm Intermediate Holdings Inc .... E 518 237-3330
  Waterford *(G-16640)*

CULTURE MEDIA

Angus Chemical Company .... E 716 283-1434
  Niagara Falls *(G-12819)*
Debmar-Mercury .... G 212 669-5025
  New York *(G-9890)*

Employee Codes: A=Over 500 employees, B=251-500
C=101-250, D=51-100, E=20-50, F=10-19, G=5-9

CULTURE MEDIA

Man of World ....G....... 212 915-0017
  New York *(G-11149)*

CULVERTS: Metal Plate

Lane Enterprises Inc ....F....... 607 776-3366
  Bath *(G-660)*

CUPS: Plastic Exc Polystyrene Foam

Capitol Cups Inc ....E....... 518 627-0051
  Amsterdam *(G-338)*

CURBING: Granite Or Stone

Granite Works LLC ....E....... 607 565-7012
  Waverly *(G-16727)*
Stone & Terrazzo World Inc ....G....... 718 361-6899
  Long Island City *(G-7920)*

CURTAIN & DRAPERY FIXTURES: Poles, Rods & Rollers

Abalene Decorating Services ....E....... 718 782-2000
  New York *(G-9046)*
Blinds To Go (us) Inc ....E....... 718 477-9523
  Staten Island *(G-15668)*
McCarroll Uphl Designs LLC ....G....... 518 828-0500
  Hudson *(G-6655)*
P E Guerin ....D....... 212 243-5270
  New York *(G-11561)*
Pj Decorators Inc ....E....... 516 735-9693
  East Meadow *(G-4447)*
Wcd Window Coverings Inc ....E....... 845 336-4511
  Lake Katrine *(G-7295)*

CURTAIN WALLS: Building, Steel

AM Architectural Metal & Glass ....E....... 845 942-8848
  Garnerville *(G-5567)*

CURTAINS & BEDDING: Knit

Commonwealth Home Fashion Inc ....D....... 514 384-8290
  Willsboro *(G-17288)*

CURTAINS & CURTAIN FABRICS: Lace

Creative Window Fashions Inc ....D....... 718 746-5817
  Whitestone *(G-17233)*
Mary Bright Inc ....G....... 212 677-1970
  New York *(G-11195)*

CURTAINS: Cottage Sets, From Purchased Materials

Northast Coml Win Trtments Inc ....D....... 845 331-0148
  Kingston *(G-7232)*

CURTAINS: Shower

Catalina Products Corp ....E....... 718 336-8288
  Brooklyn *(G-1766)*
Showeray Co ....D....... 718 965-3633
  Brooklyn *(G-2578)*

CURTAINS: Window, From Purchased Materials

Belle Maison USA Ltd ....E....... 718 805-0200
  Richmond Hill *(G-14081)*
Drapery Industries Inc ....F....... 585 232-2992
  Rochester *(G-14338)*

CUSHIONS & PILLOWS

Alexandra Ferguson LLC ....G....... 718 788-7768
  Brooklyn *(G-1580)*
Anhui Skyworth LLC ....D....... 917 940-6903
  Hempstead *(G-6288)*
Franks Cushions Inc ....F....... 718 848-1216
  Maspeth *(G-8172)*
Hollander Sleep Products LLC ....D....... 212 575-0400
  New York *(G-10542)*
Prime Feather Industries Ltd ....F....... 718 326-8701
  Suffern *(G-15818)*
Soft-Tex International Inc ....D....... 800 366-2324
  Waterford *(G-16642)*

CUSHIONS & PILLOWS: Bed, From Purchased Materials

Arlee Home Fashions Inc ....D....... 212 689-0020
  New York *(G-9253)*
Hollander HM Fshons Hldngs LLC ....F....... 212 575-0400
  New York *(G-10541)*
Home Fashions Intl LLC ....E....... 212 689-3579
  New York *(G-10544)*
Home Fashions Intl LLC ....F....... 212 684-0091
  New York *(G-10545)*
R & M Industries Inc ....F....... 212 366-6414
  New York *(G-11807)*

CUSHIONS: Textile, Exc Spring & Carpet

Advanced Medical Mfg Corp ....E....... 845 369-7535
  Suffern *(G-15806)*
Jakes Sneakers Inc ....G....... 718 233-1132
  Brooklyn *(G-2133)*
Wayne Decorators Inc ....G....... 718 529-4200
  Jamaica *(G-6999)*

CUSTOM COMPOUNDING OF RUBBER MATERIALS

Pawling Corporation ....C....... 845 855-1000
  Pawling *(G-13474)*
Tire Conversion Tech Inc ....E....... 518 372-1600
  Latham *(G-7406)*

CUT STONE & STONE PRODUCTS

Adirondack Precision Cut Stone ....F....... 518 681-3060
  Queensbury *(G-14001)*
Alart Inc ....G....... 212 840-1508
  New York *(G-9122)*
American Bluestone LLC ....F....... 607 369-2235
  Sidney *(G-15457)*
Barra & Trumbore Inc ....G....... 845 626-5442
  Kerhonkson *(G-7183)*
Busch Products Inc ....E....... 315 474-8422
  Syracuse *(G-15897)*
Crown Hill Stone Inc ....E....... 716 326-4601
  Westfield *(G-17076)*
Denton Stoneworks Inc ....E....... 516 746-1500
  Garden City Park *(G-5553)*
Devonian Stone New York Inc ....E....... 607 655-2600
  Windsor *(G-17294)*
European Marble Works Co Inc ....E....... 718 387-9778
  Garden City *(G-5517)*
First Presbyterian Church ....G....... 315 252-3861
  Auburn *(G-494)*
Fordham Marble Co Inc ....F....... 914 682-6699
  White Plains *(G-17136)*
Granite Tops Inc ....E....... 914 699-2909
  Mount Vernon *(G-8732)*
Masonville Stone Incorporated ....G....... 607 265-3597
  Masonville *(G-8138)*
New York Quarries Inc ....F....... 518 756-3138
  Alcove *(G-175)*
North American Stone Inc ....G....... 585 266-4020
  Rochester *(G-14561)*
North Shore Monuments Inc ....G....... 516 759-2156
  Glen Head *(G-5653)*
Pallette Stone Corporation ....E....... 518 584-2421
  Gansevoort *(G-5501)*
Rivera ....G....... 718 458-1488
  Flushing *(G-5295)*
Sanford Stone LLC ....E....... 607 467-1313
  Deposit *(G-4302)*
Seneca Stone Corporation ....F....... 315 549-8253
  Fayette *(G-5170)*
Seneca Stone Corporation ....G....... 607 737-6200
  Pine City *(G-13579)*
Vermont Structural Slate Co ....F....... 518 499-1912
  Whitehall *(G-17219)*
W F Saunders & Sons Inc ....F....... 315 469-3217
  Nedrow *(G-8819)*

CUTLERY

Advanced Machine Design Co Inc ....E....... 716 826-2000
  Buffalo *(G-2817)*
Cutco Cutlery Corporation ....B....... 716 372-3111
  Olean *(G-13161)*
Korin Japanese Trading Corp ....E....... 212 587-7021
  New York *(G-10916)*
Lifetime Brands Inc ....B....... 516 683-6000
  Garden City *(G-5526)*
Niabraze LLC ....F....... 716 447-1082
  Tonawanda *(G-16203)*
Novelty Crystal Corp ....E....... 718 458-6700
  Long Island City *(G-7858)*
Oneida International Inc ....G....... 315 361-3000
  Oneida *(G-13182)*
Oneida Silversmiths Inc ....G....... 315 361-3000
  Oneida *(G-13186)*
Ontario Knife Company ....D....... 716 676-5527
  Franklinville *(G-5380)*
Schilling Forge Inc ....E....... 315 454-4421
  Syracuse *(G-16055)*
Servotronics Inc ....C....... 716 655-5990
  Elma *(G-4668)*
Sherrill Manufacturing Inc ....C....... 315 280-0727
  Sherrill *(G-15430)*
Warren Cutlery Corp ....F....... 845 876-3444
  Rhinebeck *(G-14072)*
Woods Knife Corporation ....E....... 516 798-4972
  Massapequa *(G-8217)*

CUTLERY WHOLESALERS

Utica Cutlery Company ....D....... 315 733-4663
  Utica *(G-16387)*
Warren Cutlery Corp ....F....... 845 876-3444
  Rhinebeck *(G-14072)*

CUTOUTS: Cardboard, Die-Cut, Made From Purchased Materials

Lion Die-Cutting Co Inc ....E....... 718 383-8841
  Brooklyn *(G-2231)*

CUTOUTS: Distribution

Junior Achevement of Eastrn NY ....G....... 518 783-4336
  Latham *(G-7393)*
Product Station Inc ....F....... 516 942-4220
  Jericho *(G-7114)*

CUTTING SVC: Paper, Exc Die-Cut

A-1 Products Inc ....G....... 718 789-1818
  Brooklyn *(G-1539)*
J Mackenzie Ltd ....E....... 585 321-1770
  Rochester *(G-14477)*

CYCLIC CRUDES & INTERMEDIATES

Chemours Company Fc LLC ....E....... 716 278-5100
  Niagara Falls *(G-12826)*
Durez Corporation ....F....... 716 286-0100
  Niagara Falls *(G-12834)*
Micro Powders Inc ....E....... 914 332-6400
  Tarrytown *(G-16120)*
Mitsui Chemicals America Inc ....E....... 914 253-0777
  Rye Brook *(G-15098)*
Premier Brands of America Inc ....E....... 718 325-3000
  Mount Vernon *(G-8764)*

CYLINDER & ACTUATORS: Fluid Power

A K Allen Co Inc ....E....... 516 747-5450
  Mineola *(G-8522)*
Ameritool Mfg Inc ....E....... 315 668-2172
  Central Square *(G-3543)*
ITT Enidine Inc ....B....... 716 662-1900
  Orchard Park *(G-13299)*
Precision Mechanisms Corp ....E....... 516 333-5955
  Westbury *(G-17049)*
Triumph Actuation Systems LLC ....D....... 516 378-0162
  Freeport *(G-5443)*
Young & Franklin Inc ....D....... 315 457-3110
  Liverpool *(G-7586)*

CYLINDERS: Pressure

A K Allen Co Inc ....C....... 516 747-5450
  Mineola *(G-8522)*

DAIRY EQPT

Richard Stewart ....G....... 518 632-5363
  Hartford *(G-6015)*

DAIRY PRDTS STORE: Cheese

Artisanal Brands Inc ....E....... 914 441-3591
  Bronxville *(G-1499)*

DAIRY PRDTS STORE: Ice Cream, Packaged

Bleecker Pastry Tartufo Inc ....G....... 718 937-9830
  Long Island City *(G-7720)*

PRODUCT SECTION

DAIRY PRDTS: Frozen Desserts & Novelties

Clinton Creamery Inc .... F 917 324-9699
  Laurelton *(G-7412)*
Delicioso Coco Helado Inc .... F 718 292-1930
  Bronx *(G-1317)*
Marvel Dairy Whip Inc .... G 516 889-4232
  Lido Beach *(G-7463)*

DAIRY PRDTS STORES

Crosswinds Farm & Creamery .... G 607 327-0363
  Ovid *(G-13370)*

DAIRY PRDTS WHOLESALERS: Fresh

HP Hood LLC .... C 315 363-3870
  Oneida *(G-13179)*
Upstate Niagara Coop Inc .... E 716 484-7178
  Jamestown *(G-7073)*

DAIRY PRDTS: Bakers' Cheese

P & F Bakers Inc .... G 516 931-6821
  Hicksville *(G-6407)*

DAIRY PRDTS: Bottled Baby Formula

Infant Formula Laboratory Svc .... F 718 257-3000
  Brooklyn *(G-2103)*

DAIRY PRDTS: Butter

Canalside Creamery Inc .... G 716 695-2876
  North Tonawanda *(G-12983)*
O-At-Ka Milk Products Coop Inc .... B 585 343-0536
  Batavia *(G-645)*
Pure Ghee Inc .... G 718 224-7399
  Flushing *(G-5292)*

DAIRY PRDTS: Canned Baby Formula

Danone Nutricia Early .... E 914 872-8556
  White Plains *(G-17126)*

DAIRY PRDTS: Cheese

Agri-Mark Inc .... D 518 497-6644
  Chateaugay *(G-3584)*
Artisanal Brands Inc .... E 914 441-3591
  Bronxville *(G-1499)*
Castelli America LLC .... D 716 782-2101
  Ashville *(G-423)*
Emkay Trading Corp .... G 914 592-9000
  Elmsford *(G-4757)*
Emkay Trading Corp .... E 585 492-3800
  Arcade *(G-392)*
Empire Cheese Inc .... E 585 968-1552
  Cuba *(G-4095)*
Euphrates Inc .... D 518 762-3488
  Johnstown *(G-7142)*
F Cappiello Dairy Pdts Inc .... E 518 374-5064
  Schenectady *(G-15281)*
Fly Creek Cder Mill Orchrd Inc .... G 607 547-9692
  Fly Creek *(G-5319)*
Friendship Dairies LLC .... C 585 973-3031
  Friendship *(G-5466)*
Gharana Industries LLC .... G 315 651-4004
  Waterloo *(G-16649)*
Great Lakes Cheese NY Inc .... D 315 232-4511
  Adams *(G-3)*
HP Hood LLC .... D 607 295-8134
  Arkport *(G-408)*
Hudson Valley Creamery LLC .... F 518 851-2570
  Hudson *(G-6648)*
Instantwhip of Buffalo Inc .... E 716 892-7031
  Buffalo *(G-3027)*
Kraft Heinz Foods Company .... B 315 376-6575
  Lowville *(G-7965)*
Kraft Heinz Foods Company .... B 607 527-4584
  Campbell *(G-3358)*
Kraft Heinz Foods Company .... C 607 865-7131
  Walton *(G-16569)*
Lactalis American Group Inc .... B 716 827-2622
  Buffalo *(G-3059)*
Lactalis American Group Inc .... B 716 823-6262
  Buffalo *(G-3060)*
Leprino Foods Company .... C 570 888-9658
  Waverly *(G-16729)*
Mondelez Global LLC .... G 845 567-4701
  Newburgh *(G-12790)*
Mozzarella Fresca Incorporated .... G 559 752-4823
  Buffalo *(G-3096)*
Original Hrkmer Cnty Chese Inc .... D 315 895-7428
  Ilion *(G-6782)*

Rainbeau Ridge Farm .... G 914 234-2197
  Bedford Hills *(G-803)*
Sorrento Lactalis Inc .... G 716 823-6262
  Buffalo *(G-3221)*
Taam Tov Foods Inc .... G 718 788-8880
  Brooklyn *(G-2662)*
World Cheese Co Inc .... F 718 965-1700
  Brooklyn *(G-2780)*

DAIRY PRDTS: Cheese, Cottage

Garelick Farms LLC .... C 518 283-0820
  East Greenbush *(G-4422)*
HP Hood LLC .... D 607 295-8134
  Arkport *(G-408)*

DAIRY PRDTS: Concentrated Skim Milk

O-At-Ka Milk Products Coop Inc .... B 585 343-0536
  Batavia *(G-645)*

DAIRY PRDTS: Cream Substitutes

Sugar Foods Corporation .... E 212 753-6900
  New York *(G-12249)*

DAIRY PRDTS: Cream, Sweet

Emkay Trading Corp .... E 585 492-3800
  Arcade *(G-392)*

DAIRY PRDTS: Dairy Based Desserts, Frozen

Chobani Idaho LLC .... G 208 432-2248
  Norwich *(G-13043)*
Sweet Melodys LLC .... E 716 580-3227
  East Amherst *(G-4389)*

DAIRY PRDTS: Dietary Supplements, Dairy & Non-Dairy Based

Century Tom Inc .... G 347 654-3179
  Flushing *(G-5237)*
Dynatabs LLC .... F 718 376-6084
  Brooklyn *(G-1889)*
El-Gen LLC .... G 631 218-3400
  Bohemia *(G-1060)*
GNI Commerce Inc .... G 347 275-1155
  Brooklyn *(G-2034)*
Makers Nutrition LLC .... E 631 456-5397
  Hauppauge *(G-6151)*
Physiologics LLC .... F 800 765-6775
  Ronkonkoma *(G-14993)*
Vitakem Nutraceutical Inc .... C 631 956-8343
  Smithtown *(G-15524)*
Vitamin Power Incororated .... G 631 676-5790
  Hauppauge *(G-6253)*

DAIRY PRDTS: Dips & Spreads, Cheese Based

Cheese Experts USA Ltd Lblty .... G 908 275-3889
  Staten Island *(G-15678)*
East Hill Creamery LLC .... G 585 237-3622
  Perry *(G-13546)*
Lumazu LLC .... G 518 623-3372
  Warrensburg *(G-16600)*
Lumazu LLC .... F 518 623-3372
  Warrensburg *(G-16601)*

DAIRY PRDTS: Dried & Powdered Milk & Milk Prdts

Dairy Farmers America Inc .... C 585 409-2200
  Batavia *(G-632)*
Hain Celestial Group Inc .... C 516 587-5000
  New Hyde Park *(G-8882)*

DAIRY PRDTS: Evaporated Milk

Nestle Usa Inc .... C 914 272-4021
  White Plains *(G-17167)*

DAIRY PRDTS: Farmers' Cheese

Dwyer Farm LLC .... G 914 456-2742
  Walden *(G-16552)*

DAIRY PRDTS: Fermented & Cultured Milk Prdts

Kong Kee Food Corp .... E 718 937-2746
  Long Island City *(G-7809)*

Kraft Heinz Foods Company .... C 607 865-7131
  Walton *(G-16569)*
Upstate Niagara Coop Inc .... A 716 892-3156
  Buffalo *(G-3263)*

DAIRY PRDTS: Frozen Desserts & Novelties

Blue Pig Ice Cream Factory .... G 914 271-3850
  Croton On Hudson *(G-4088)*
Carols Polar Parlor .... G 315 468-3404
  Syracuse *(G-15904)*
Clinton Creamery Inc .... F 917 324-9699
  Laurelton *(G-7412)*
Crepini LLC .... E 347 422-0829
  Brooklyn *(G-1816)*
Crowley Foods Inc .... E 800 637-0019
  Binghamton *(G-900)*
Df Mavens Inc .... E 347 813-4705
  Astoria *(G-434)*
Ffc Holding Corp Subsidiaries .... F 716 366-5400
  Dunkirk *(G-4366)*
Fieldbrook Foods Corporation .... C 716 366-5400
  Dunkirk *(G-4367)*
Fresh Ice Cream Company LLC .... F 347 603-6021
  Brooklyn *(G-2006)*
G Pesso & Sons Inc .... G 718 224-9130
  Bayside *(G-766)*
GM Ice Cream Inc .... G 646 236-7383
  Queens Village *(G-13993)*
HP Hood LLC .... D 315 829-3339
  Vernon *(G-16458)*
HP Hood LLC .... A 607 772-6580
  Binghamton *(G-916)*
Jones Humdinger .... F 607 771-6501
  Binghamton *(G-927)*
Kozy Shack Enterprises LLC .... C 516 870-3000
  Hicksville *(G-6388)*
LArte Del Gelato Gruppo Inc .... F 718 383-6600
  Long Island City *(G-7815)*
Lickity Splits .... G 585 345-6091
  Batavia *(G-642)*
Macadoodles .... G 607 652-9019
  Stamford *(G-15645)*
Macedonia Ltd .... F 718 462-3596
  Brooklyn *(G-2253)*
Main Street Sweets .... G 914 332-5757
  Tarrytown *(G-16117)*
Marina Ice Cream .... G 718 235-3000
  Brooklyn *(G-2271)*
Moonlight Creamery .... G 585 223-0880
  Fairport *(G-4870)*
MSQ Corporation .... G 718 465-0900
  Queens Village *(G-13998)*
Ninas Custard .... E 716 636-0345
  Getzville *(G-5613)*
Nutrifast Inc .... F 347 671-3181
  New York *(G-11490)*
Olympic Ice Cream Co Inc .... E 718 849-6200
  Richmond Hill *(G-14089)*
Original Fowlers Choclat Inc .... G 716 668-2113
  Cheektowaga *(G-3612)*
Perrys Ice Cream Company Inc .... B 716 542-5492
  Akron *(G-24)*
Phyljohn Distributors Inc .... F 518 459-2775
  Albany *(G-120)*
Piazzas Ice Cream Ice Hse Inc .... G 718 818-8811
  Staten Island *(G-15742)*
Pop Bar LLC .... G 212 255-4874
  New York *(G-11705)*
Quaker Bonnet Inc .... G 716 885-7208
  Buffalo *(G-3172)*
Quality Dairy Farms Inc .... E 315 942-2611
  Boonville *(G-1166)*
Spatula LLC .... F 917 582-8684
  New York *(G-12176)*
Tia Lattrell .... G 845 373-9494
  Amenia *(G-220)*
Twisters .... G 585 346-3730
  Livonia *(G-7592)*
Unilever United States Inc .... F 212 546-0200
  New York *(G-12474)*
Unilever United States Inc .... C 212 546-0200
  New York *(G-12475)*
Van Alphen & Doran Corp .... G 518 782-9242
  Schenectady *(G-15332)*
Van Leeuwen Artisan Ice Cream .... G 718 701-1630
  Brooklyn *(G-2736)*
Wicked Spoon Inc .... F 646 335-2890
  New York *(G-12657)*

Employee Codes: A=Over 500 employees, B=251-500
C=101-250, D=51-100, E=20-50, F=10-19, G=5-9

DAIRY PRDTS: Ice Cream & Ice Milk

DAIRY PRDTS: Ice Cream & Ice Milk

Purity Ice Cream Co Inc .... F 607 272-1545
  Ithaca *(G-6908)*
Stewarts Processing Corp .... D 518 581-1200
  Ballston Spa *(G-609)*
TLC-Lc Inc .... E 212 756-8900
  New York *(G-12375)*
Washburns Dairy Inc .... E 518 725-0629
  Gloversville *(G-5743)*

DAIRY PRDTS: Ice Cream, Bulk

Bleecker Pastry Tartufo Inc .... G 718 937-9830
  Long Island City *(G-7720)*
Blue Marble Ice Cream .... F 718 858-5551
  Brooklyn *(G-1700)*
Byrne Dairy Inc .... E 315 475-2111
  Syracuse *(G-15898)*
Delicioso Coco Helado Inc .... F 718 292-1930
  Bronx *(G-1317)*
Grom Columbus LLC .... G 212 974-3444
  New York *(G-10412)*
Ice Cream Man Inc .... E 518 692-8382
  Greenwich *(G-5909)*
La Cremeria .... G 212 226-6758
  New York *(G-10945)*
Mamas .... G 518 399-2828
  Burnt Hills *(G-3293)*
Marvel Dairy Whip Inc .... G 516 889-4232
  Lido Beach *(G-7463)*
Paleteria Fernandez Inc .... E 914 315-1598
  Mamaroneck *(G-8074)*
Scoops R US Incorporated .... G 212 730-7959
  New York *(G-12024)*
Smartys Corner .... G 607 239-5276
  Endicott *(G-4834)*
Victory Garden .... G 212 206-7273
  New York *(G-12564)*

DAIRY PRDTS: Ice Cream, Packaged, Molded, On Sticks, Etc.

Byrne Dairy Inc .... B 315 475-2121
  La Fayette *(G-7267)*

DAIRY PRDTS: Milk, Condensed & Evaporated

Alpina Foods Inc .... F 855 886-1914
  Batavia *(G-622)*
Friendship Dairies LLC .... C 585 973-3031
  Friendship *(G-5466)*
FriesIndcmpina Ingrdnts N Amer .... E 607 746-0196
  Delhi *(G-4264)*
Kerry Bfnctnal Ingredients Inc .... D 607 334-1700
  Norwich *(G-13048)*
Nationwide Dairy Inc .... G 347 689-8148
  Brooklyn *(G-2359)*
Rich Products Corporation .... A 716 878-8000
  Buffalo *(G-3185)*
Solivaira Specialties Inc .... D 716 693-4009
  North Tonawanda *(G-13014)*

DAIRY PRDTS: Milk, Fluid

Crowley Foods Inc .... E 800 637-0019
  Binghamton *(G-900)*
Dairy Farmers America Inc .... E 816 801-6440
  East Syracuse *(G-4535)*
Dean Foods Company .... D 315 452-5001
  East Syracuse *(G-4538)*
Finger Lakes Cheese Trail .... F 607 857-5726
  Odessa *(G-13129)*
HP Hood LLC .... C 315 363-3870
  Oneida *(G-13179)*
HP Hood LLC .... B 315 658-2132
  La Fargeville *(G-7262)*
HP Hood LLC .... B 518 218-9097
  Albany *(G-88)*
HP Hood LLC .... D 315 829-3339
  Vernon *(G-16458)*
HP Hood LLC .... A 607 772-6580
  Binghamton *(G-916)*
Instantwhip of Buffalo Inc .... E 716 892-7031
  Buffalo *(G-3027)*
Kesso Foods Inc .... G 718 777-5303
  East Elmhurst *(G-4415)*
Kraft Heinz Foods Company .... B 607 527-4584
  Campbell *(G-3358)*
O-At-Ka Milk Products Coop Inc ..... B 585 343-0536
  Batavia *(G-645)*

Purity Ice Cream Co Inc .... F 607 272-1545
  Ithaca *(G-6908)*
Saputo Dairy Foods Usa LLC .... D 607 746-2141
  Delhi *(G-4267)*
Stewarts Processing Corp .... D 518 581-1200
  Ballston Spa *(G-609)*
Upstate Niagara Coop Inc .... D 315 389-5111
  North Lawrence *(G-12951)*
Upstate Niagara Coop Inc .... C 716 892-2121
  Buffalo *(G-3264)*

DAIRY PRDTS: Milk, Processed, Pasteurized, Homogenized/Btld

Byrne Dairy Inc .... B 315 475-2121
  La Fayette *(G-7267)*
Elmhurst Dairy Inc .... C 718 526-3442
  Jamaica *(G-6946)*
Midland Farms Inc .... D 518 436-7038
  Menands *(G-8408)*
Mountain Side Farms Inc .... E 718 526-3442
  Jamaica *(G-6971)*
Steuben Foods Incorporated .... C 716 655-4000
  Elma *(G-4669)*
Upstate Niagara Coop Inc .... C 585 458-1880
  Rochester *(G-14775)*
Upstate Niagara Coop Inc .... E 716 484-7178
  Jamestown *(G-7073)*

DAIRY PRDTS: Natural Cheese

Cemac Foods Corp .... F 914 835-0526
  Harrison *(G-5999)*
Crosswinds Farm & Creamery .... G 607 327-0363
  Ovid *(G-13370)*
Four Fat Fowl Inc .... G 518 733-5230
  Stephentown *(G-15779)*
Kutters Cheese Factory Inc .... E 585 599-3693
  Corfu *(G-3978)*
Mongiello Sales Inc .... E 845 436-4200
  Hurleyville *(G-6769)*
Mongiellos Itln Cheese Spc LLC ..... C 845 436-4200
  Hurleyville *(G-6770)*
Pecoraro Dairy Products Inc .... E 718 388-2379
  Brooklyn *(G-2424)*
Red Creek Cold Storage LLC .... G 315 576-2069
  Red Creek *(G-14038)*
Sandvoss Farms LLC .... G 585 297-7044
  East Bethany *(G-4406)*
Sargento Foods Inc .... G 920 893-8484
  New York *(G-11992)*

DAIRY PRDTS: Processed Cheese

Habco Corp .... E 631 789-1400
  Amityville *(G-290)*
HP Hood LLC .... D 315 829-3339
  Vernon *(G-16458)*

DAIRY PRDTS: Pudding Pops, Frozen

Allied Food Products Inc .... F 718 230-4227
  Brooklyn *(G-1588)*

DAIRY PRDTS: Sherbets, Dairy Based

Lumazu LLC .... G 518 623-3372
  Warrensburg *(G-16600)*
Lumazu LLC .... E 518 623-3372
  Warrensburg *(G-16601)*

DAIRY PRDTS: Spreads, Cheese

Noga Dairies Inc .... F 516 293-5448
  Farmingdale *(G-5076)*

DAIRY PRDTS: Whipped Topping, Exc Frozen Or Dry Mix

Hanan Products Company Inc .... E 516 938-1000
  Hicksville *(G-6382)*

DAIRY PRDTS: Yogurt, Exc Frozen

Bliss Foods Inc .... G 212 732-8888
  New York *(G-9465)*
Bliss Foods Inc .... F 212 732-8888
  New York *(G-9466)*
Chobani LLC .... C 607 337-1246
  Norwich *(G-13042)*
Chobani LLC .... G 607 847-6181
  New Berlin *(G-8826)*

Currant Company LLC .... G 845 266-8999
  Staatsburg *(G-15637)*
Dannon Company Inc .... G 914 872-8400
  White Plains *(G-17125)*
Fage USA Dairy Industry Inc .... B 518 762-5912
  Johnstown *(G-7143)*
Fage USA Holdings .... G 518 762-5912
  Johnstown *(G-7144)*
Maple Hill Creamery LLC .... E 518 758-7777
  Stuyvesant *(G-15804)*
Maple Hill Creamery LLC .... G 518 758-7777
  Kinderhook *(G-7197)*
Mualema LLC .... G 609 820-6098
  New York *(G-11344)*
Noga Dairies Inc .... F 516 293-5448
  Farmingdale *(G-5076)*
Steuben Foods Incorporated .... F 718 291-3333
  Jamaica *(G-6989)*
Twist It Top It .... G 718 793-8947
  Forest Hills *(G-5336)*
Whitney Foods Inc .... F 718 291-3333
  Jamaica *(G-7000)*
Yo Fresh Inc .... E 845 634-1616
  New City *(G-8841)*
Yo Fresh Inc .... G 518 982-0659
  Clifton Park *(G-3738)*

DAIRY PRDTS: Yogurt, Frozen

Berrywild .... G 212 686-5848
  New York *(G-9415)*
NY Froyo LLC .... G 516 312-4588
  Deer Park *(G-4208)*
Swirl Bliss LLC .... G 516 867-9475
  North Baldwin *(G-12927)*
Yog N Go Inc .... G 585 319-8110
  East Rochester *(G-4486)*

DATA PROCESSING & PREPARATION SVCS

Data Palette Info Svcs LLC .... D 718 433-1060
  Port Washington *(G-13830)*
Informa Solutions Inc .... E 516 543-3733
  New York *(G-10640)*
Rational Retention LLC .... E 518 489-3000
  Albany *(G-128)*
Relx Inc .... E 212 309-8100
  New York *(G-11858)*
Standard Analytics Io Inc .... G 917 882-5422
  New York *(G-12205)*

DATA PROCESSING SVCS

DP Murphy Co Inc .... D 631 673-9400
  Deer Park *(G-4154)*
Infinitlink Corporation .... G 934 777-0180
  West Babylon *(G-16822)*
Thomas Publishing Company LLC .. B 212 695-0500
  New York *(G-12342)*

DECORATIVE WOOD & WOODWORK

A Van Hoek Woodworking Limited .. G 718 599-4388
  Brooklyn *(G-1536)*
Aces Over Eights Inc .... G 585 292-9690
  Rochester *(G-14184)*
Adams Interior Fabrications .... F 631 249-8282
  Massapequa *(G-8207)*
Andike Millwork Inc .... G 718 894-1796
  Maspeth *(G-8146)*
Architectural Enhancements Inc ..... F 845 343-9663
  Middletown *(G-8460)*
Art Essentials of New York .... G 845 368-1100
  Airmont *(G-11)*
Atelier Viollet Corp .... G 718 782-1727
  Brooklyn *(G-1646)*
Brooks Woodworking Inc .... F 914 666-2029
  Mount Kisco *(G-8664)*
Budd Woodwork Inc .... F 718 389-1110
  Brooklyn *(G-1738)*
Cabinet Shapes Corp .... F 718 784-6255
  Long Island City *(G-7722)*
Craz Woodworking Assoc Inc .... F 631 205-1890
  Bellport *(G-823)*
Daniel Demarco and Assoc Inc .... E 631 598-7000
  Amityville *(G-283)*
Di Fiore and Sons Custom Wdwkg .. G 718 278-1663
  Long Island City *(G-7744)*
Digital Fabrication Wkshp Inc .... G 518 249-6500
  Hudson *(G-6641)*
Ed Negron Fine Woodworking .... G 718 246-1016
  Brooklyn *(G-1904)*

PRODUCT SECTION

DESIGN SVCS, NEC

Elephants Custom Furniture Inc .... D 917 509-3581
  Brooklyn (G-1918)
Furniture Dsign By Knossos Inc .... E 718 729-0404
  Woodside (G-17347)
Hennig Custom Woodwork Corp .... G 516 536-3460
  Oceanside (G-13101)
Innova Interiors Inc .... E 718 401-2122
  Bronx (G-1365)
James King Woodworking Inc .... G 518 761-6091
  Queensbury (G-14013)
Jeffrey John .... G 631 842-2850
  Amityville (G-299)
Jordache Woodworking Corp .... F 718 349-3373
  Brooklyn (G-2146)
K & B Woodworking Inc .... G 518 634-7253
  Cairo (G-3300)
M & R Woodworking & Finishing .... G 718 486-5480
  Brooklyn (G-2247)
McGraw Wood Products LLC .... E 607 836-6465
  Mc Graw (G-8254)
N Sketch Build Inc .... G 800 975-0597
  Fishkill (G-5195)
Northern Forest Pdts Co Inc .... G 315 942-6955
  Boonville (G-1164)
Pdj Components Inc .... E 845 469-9191
  Chester (G-3638)
Pella Corporation .... C 631 208-0710
  Calverton (G-3322)
Pgs Millwork Inc .... D 212 244-6610
  New York (G-11663)
Piccini Mnm Inc .... G 845 741-6770
  West Nyack (G-16953)
Prime Wood Products .... G 518 792-1407
  Queensbury (G-14021)
Richard Rothbard Inc .... G 845 355-2300
  Slate Hill (G-15496)
Windsor United Industries LLC .... E 607 655-3300
  Windsor (G-17295)
Wood Innovations of Suffolk .... G 631 698-2345
  Medford (G-8297)
Woodmotif Inc .... F 516 564-8325
  Hempstead (G-6312)
Woodtronics Inc .... G 914 962-5205
  Yorktown Heights (G-17537)

DEFENSE SYSTEMS & EQPT

Eastern Strategic Materials .... E 212 332-1619
  New York (G-10018)
UNI Source Technology .... F 514 748-8888
  Champlain (G-3575)

DEGREASING MACHINES

Cleaning Tech Group LLC .... E 716 665-2340
  Jamestown (G-7016)

DEHYDRATION EQPT

Purvi Enterprises Incorporated .... G 347 808-9448
  Maspeth (G-8196)

DELAY LINES

Allen Avionics Inc .... E 516 248-8080
  Mineola (G-8526)
Esc Control Electronics LLC .... E 631 467-5328
  Sayville (G-15236)

DENTAL EQPT

Boehm Surgical Instrument .... F 585 436-6584
  Rochester (G-14259)
Brandt Equipment LLC .... G 718 994-0800
  Bronx (G-1287)
J H M Engineering .... E 718 871-1810
  Brooklyn (G-2122)
Kay See Dental Mfg Co .... F 816 842-2817
  New York (G-10860)
Lucas Dental Equipment Co Inc .... F 631 244-2807
  Bohemia (G-1093)

DENTAL EQPT & SPLYS

Air Techniques Inc .... B 516 433-7676
  Melville (G-8324)
Art Dental Laboratory Inc .... G 516 437-1882
  Floral Park (G-5201)
Avalonbay Communities Inc .... E 516 484-7766
  Glen Cove (G-5624)
Buffalo Dental Mfg Co Inc .... E 516 496-7200
  Syosset (G-15836)

Cmp Industries LLC .... E 518 434-3147
  Albany (G-66)
Columbia Dentoform Corporation .... E 718 482-1569
  Long Island City (G-7732)
Crosstex International Inc .... D 631 582-6777
  Hauppauge (G-6079)
Crosstex International Inc .... F 631 582-6777
  Hauppauge (G-6080)
Cynosure Inc .... G 516 594-3333
  Hicksville (G-6365)
Darby Dental Supply .... G 516 688-6421
  Jericho (G-7099)
Dedeco International Sales Inc .... E 845 887-4840
  Long Eddy (G-7674)
Dentek Oral Care Inc .... D 865 983-1300
  Tarrytown (G-16114)
Glaxosmithkline LLC .... D 518 239-6901
  East Durham (G-4409)
Henry Schein Inc .... E 315 431-0340
  East Syracuse (G-4550)
Henry Schein Fincl Svcs LLC .... G 631 843-5500
  Melville (G-8356)
Impladent Ltd .... G 718 465-1810
  Jamaica (G-6957)
JM Murray Center Inc .... C 607 756-9913
  Cortland (G-4055)
JM Murray Center Inc .... C 607 756-0246
  Cortland (G-4056)
Lelab Dental Laboratory Inc .... G 516 561-5050
  Valley Stream (G-16439)
Light Dental Labs Inc .... G 516 785-7730
  Massapequa (G-8210)
Luitpold Pharmaceuticals Inc .... E 631 924-4000
  Shirley (G-15447)
Mini-Max Dntl Repr Eqpmnts Inc .... G 631 242-0322
  Deer Park (G-4198)
Oramaax Dental Products Inc .... F 516 771-8514
  Freeport (G-5428)
Precision Dental Ceramics of B .... F 716 681-4133
  Bowmansville (G-1168)
Professional Manufacturers .... F 631 586-2440
  Deer Park (G-4219)
Sabra Dental Products .... G 914 945-0836
  Ossining (G-13352)
Schilling Forge Inc .... E 315 454-4421
  Syracuse (G-16055)
Temrex Corporation .... E 516 868-6221
  Freeport (G-5441)
Tiger Supply Inc .... G 631 293-2700
  Farmingdale (G-5140)
Total Dntl Implant Sltions LLC .... G 212 877-3777
  Valley Stream (G-16453)
Valplast International Corp .... F 516 442-3923
  Westbury (G-17069)

DENTAL EQPT & SPLYS WHOLESALERS

Impladent Ltd .... G 718 465-1810
  Jamaica (G-6957)
Oramaax Dental Products Inc .... F 516 771-8514
  Freeport (G-5428)

DENTAL EQPT & SPLYS: Cabinets

Precision Dental Cabinets Inc .... F 631 543-3870
  Smithtown (G-15518)
Stylecraft Interiors Inc .... F 516 487-2133
  Great Neck (G-5862)

DENTAL EQPT & SPLYS: Compounds

Lornamead Inc .... D 716 874-7190
  New York (G-11072)

DENTAL EQPT & SPLYS: Cutting Instruments

Smile Specialists .... G 877 337-6135
  New York (G-12131)

DENTAL EQPT & SPLYS: Dental Materials

Grasers Dental Ceramics .... G 716 649-5100
  Orchard Park (G-13297)
Marotta Dental Studio Inc .... E 631 249-7520
  Farmingdale (G-5051)
Safe-Dent Enterprises LLC .... G 845 362-0141
  Monsey (G-8615)

DENTAL EQPT & SPLYS: Enamels

Gallery 57 Dental .... E 212 246-8700
  New York (G-10289)

Gan Kavod Inc .... G 315 797-3114
  New Hartford (G-8850)
Jeffrey D Menoff .... G 716 665-1468
  Jamestown (G-7046)

DENTAL EQPT & SPLYS: Laboratory

A D K Dental Lab .... G 518 563-6093
  Plattsburgh (G-13677)
Cmp Industries LLC .... G 518 434-3147
  Albany (G-67)
Nu Life Restorations of L I .... D 516 489-5200
  Old Westbury (G-13154)
Sentage Corporation .... E 914 664-2200
  Mount Vernon (G-8779)

DENTAL EQPT & SPLYS: Orthodontic Appliances

Cettel Studio of New York Inc .... G 518 494-3622
  Chestertown (G-3649)
Ortho Dent Laboratory Inc .... F 716 839-1900
  Williamsville (G-17274)
Vincent Martino Dental Lab .... F 716 674-7800
  Buffalo (G-3269)

DENTAL EQPT & SPLYS: Sterilizers

Cpac Equipment Inc .... F 585 382-3223
  Leicester (G-7443)

DENTAL EQPT & SPLYS: Teeth, Artificial, Exc In Dental Labs

A-Implant Dental Lab Corp .... E 212 582-4720
  New York (G-9041)
Martins Dental Studio .... G 315 788-0800
  Watertown (G-16686)
Yes Dental Laboratory Inc .... E 914 333-7550
  Tarrytown (G-16135)

DENTAL EQPT & SPLYS: Wax

Corning Rubber Company Inc .... F 631 738-0041
  Ronkonkoma (G-14917)

DENTISTS' OFFICES & CLINICS

Comprehensive Dental Tech .... G 607 467-4456
  Hancock (G-5985)
Marotta Dental Studio Inc .... E 631 249-7520
  Farmingdale (G-5051)

DEPILATORIES, COSMETIC

LOreal Usa Inc .... E 212 389-4201
  New York (G-11066)

DERMATOLOGICALS

Intellicell Biosciences Inc .... G 646 576-8700
  New York (G-10660)
Skincare Products Inc .... G 917 837-5255
  New York (G-12117)

DERRICKS: Oil & Gas Field

Derrick Corporation .... C 716 685-4892
  Cheektowaga (G-3595)

DESALTER KITS: Sea Water

Luxfer Magtech Inc .... D 631 727-8600
  Riverhead (G-14162)

DESIGN SVCS, NEC

1 Atelier LLC .... G 917 916-2968
  New York (G-9004)
A To Z Media Inc .... F 212 260-0237
  New York (G-9040)
Acad Design Corp .... F 585 254-6960
  Rochester (G-14179)
Holland & Sherry Inc .... E 212 542-8410
  New York (G-10540)
International Direct Group Inc .... E 212 921-9036
  New York (G-10676)
Internodal International Inc .... E 631 765-0037
  Southold (G-15583)
Jinglebell Inc .... G 914 219-5395
  Armonk (G-414)
Leo D Bernstein & Sons Inc .... E 212 337-9578
  New York (G-11003)

Employee Codes: A=Over 500 employees, B=251-500
C=101-250, D=51-100, E=20-50, F=10-19, G=5-9

DESIGN SVCS, NEC

Linita Design & Mfg Corp .... E 716 566-7753
  Lackawanna *(G-7270)*
Northern Design & Bldg Assoc .... E 518 747-2200
  Queensbury *(G-14019)*
Peerless Instrument Co Inc .... C 631 396-6500
  Farmingdale *(G-5086)*
Polymag Tek Inc .... F 585 235-8390
  Rochester *(G-14606)*
Skincare Products Inc .... G 917 837-5255
  New York *(G-12117)*
Twcc Product and Sales .... E 212 614-9364
  New York *(G-12450)*

DESIGN SVCS: Commercial & Indl

New Dimensions Research Corp .... C 631 694-1356
  Melville *(G-8369)*
Precision Systems Mfg Inc .... E 315 451-3480
  Liverpool *(G-7570)*
Prim Hall Enterprises Inc .... F 518 561-7408
  Plattsburgh *(G-13719)*
Riverwood Signs By Dandev Desi .... G 845 229-0282
  Hyde Park *(G-6776)*
Voss Manufacturing Inc .... D 716 731-5062
  Sanborn *(G-15158)*

DESIGN SVCS: Computer Integrated Systems

331 Holding Inc .... E 585 924-1740
  Victor *(G-16482)*
Cisco Systems Inc .... C 212 714-4000
  New York *(G-9675)*
Informa Solutions Inc .... E 516 543-3733
  New York *(G-10640)*
Innovative Systems of New York .... G 516 541-7410
  Massapequa Park *(G-8220)*
Kld Labs Inc .... E 631 549-4222
  Hauppauge *(G-6131)*
Performance Technologies Inc .... E 585 256-0200
  Rochester *(G-14596)*
Siemens Industry Inc .... E 716 568-0983
  Buffalo *(G-3214)*

DESIGN SVCS: Shoe

Soludos LLC .... F 212 219-1101
  New York *(G-12153)*

DETECTION APPARATUS: Electronic/Magnetic Field, Light/Heat

Sensormatic Electronics LLC .... F 845 365-3125
  Orangeburg *(G-13268)*
Sentry Technology Corporation .... E 631 739-2000
  Ronkonkoma *(G-15006)*
Sentry Technology Corporation .... F 800 645-4224
  Ronkonkoma *(G-15007)*

DIAGNOSTIC SUBSTANCES

Bella International Inc .... G 716 484-0102
  Jamestown *(G-7009)*
Biochemical Diagnostics Inc .... E 631 595-9200
  Edgewood *(G-4609)*
Biopool Us Inc .... E 716 483-3851
  Jamestown *(G-7010)*
Chembio Diagnostic Systems Inc .... C 631 924-1135
  Medford *(G-8269)*
Chembio Diagnostics Inc .... C 631 924-1135
  Medford *(G-8270)*
Clark Laboratories Inc .... F 716 483-3851
  Jamestown *(G-7014)*
Danisco US Inc .... D 585 256-5200
  Rochester *(G-14321)*
E-Z-Em Inc .... E 609 524-2864
  Melville *(G-8343)*
Eagle International LLC .... G 917 282-2536
  Nanuet *(G-8802)*
Enzo Life Sciences Inc .... E 631 694-7070
  Farmingdale *(G-4997)*
Immco Diagnostics Inc .... D 716 691-6911
  Buffalo *(G-3022)*
Kannalife Sciences Inc .... G 516 669-3219
  Lloyd Harbor *(G-7594)*
Lesanne Life Sciences LLC .... G 914 234-0860
  Bedford *(G-793)*
Lifelink Monitoring Corp .... F 845 336-2098
  Bearsville *(G-787)*
Siemens Hlthcare Dgnostics Inc .... E 914 631-0475
  Tarrytown *(G-16130)*
US Diagnostics Inc .... E 866 216-5308
  New York *(G-12506)*
Welch Allyn Inc .... A 315 685-4100
  Skaneateles Falls *(G-15494)*

DIAGNOSTIC SUBSTANCES OR AGENTS: Blood Derivative

Lifescan Inc .... B 516 557-2693
  Wantagh *(G-16580)*
Ortho-Clinical Diagnostics Inc .... E 716 631-1281
  Williamsville *(G-17275)*
Ortho-Clinical Diagnostics Inc .... E 585 453-3000
  Rochester *(G-14577)*

DIAGNOSTIC SUBSTANCES OR AGENTS: In Vivo

Darmiyan LLC .... G 917 689-0389
  New York *(G-9864)*
Ken-Ton Open Mri PC .... G 716 876-7000
  Kenmore *(G-7179)*

DIAGNOSTIC SUBSTANCES OR AGENTS: Microbiology & Virology

Ufc Biotechnology .... G 716 777-3776
  Amherst *(G-269)*

DIAGNOSTIC SUBSTANCES OR AGENTS: Veterinary

Gotham Veterinary Center PC .... E 212 222-1900
  New York *(G-10381)*

DIAMOND MINING SVCS: Indl

Dynamic Design Group Inc .... G 212 840-9400
  New York *(G-9999)*
Romance & Co Inc .... E 212 382-0337
  New York *(G-11932)*
Signature Diamond Entps LLC .... E 212 869-5115
  New York *(G-12093)*

DIAMOND SETTER SVCS

Crystal Ceres Industries Inc .... D 716 283-0445
  Niagara Falls *(G-12830)*

DIAMONDS, GEMS, WHOLESALE

Antwerp Diamond Distributors .... F 212 319-3300
  New York *(G-9220)*
David Weisz & Sons Inc .... E 212 840-4747
  New York *(G-9881)*
Diamex Inc .... G 212 575-8145
  New York *(G-9922)*
Diamond Constellation Corp .... G 212 819-0324
  New York *(G-9924)*
E Schreiber Inc .... E 212 382-0280
  New York *(G-10004)*
Fine Cut Diamonds Corporation .... G 212 575-8780
  New York *(G-10215)*
Fischler Diamonds Inc .... G 212 921-8196
  New York *(G-10224)*
Global Gem Corporation .... G 212 350-9936
  New York *(G-10358)*
Gold & Diamonds Wholesale Outl .... G 718 438-7888
  Brooklyn *(G-2037)*
Herkimer Diamond Mines Inc .... E 315 891-7355
  Herkimer *(G-6327)*
J Klagsbrun Inc .... G 212 712-9388
  New York *(G-10720)*
Leo Schachter & Co Inc .... E 212 688-2000
  New York *(G-11006)*
Miller & Veit Inc .... F 212 247-2275
  New York *(G-11295)*
Romance & Co Inc .... E 212 382-0337
  New York *(G-11932)*
Steven Galapo Diamonds LLC .... G 212 221-3000
  New York *(G-12223)*
T M W Diamonds Mfg Co .... E 212 869-8444
  New York *(G-12289)*
United Gemdiam Inc .... E 718 851-5083
  Brooklyn *(G-2720)*
Waldman Alexander M Diamond Co .... E 212 921-8098
  New York *(G-12606)*

DIAMONDS: Cutting & Polishing

Ace Diamond Corp .... G 212 730-8231
  New York *(G-9063)*
Antwerp Diamond Distributors .... F 212 319-3300
  New York *(G-9220)*
Antwerp Sales Intl Inc .... F 212 354-6515
  New York *(G-9221)*
Baroka Creations Inc .... G 212 768-0527
  New York *(G-9374)*
Dialase Inc .... G 212 575-8833
  New York *(G-9921)*
Diamex Inc .... G 212 575-8145
  New York *(G-9922)*
Diamond Constellation Corp .... G 212 819-0324
  New York *(G-9924)*
Dresdiam Inc .... E 212 819-2217
  New York *(G-9977)*
E Schreiber Inc .... E 212 382-0280
  New York *(G-10004)*
Fine Cut Diamonds Corporation .... G 212 575-8780
  New York *(G-10215)*
Fischler Diamonds Inc .... G 212 921-8196
  New York *(G-10224)*
Guild Diamond Products Inc .... F 212 871-0007
  New York *(G-10424)*
Hershel Horowitz Corp .... G 212 719-1710
  New York *(G-10506)*
Ideal Brilliant Co Inc .... F 212 840-2044
  New York *(G-10599)*
J A G Diamond Manufacturers .... G 212 575-0660
  New York *(G-10717)*
J Klagsbrun Inc .... G 212 712-9388
  New York *(G-10720)*
Julius Klein Group .... E 212 719-1811
  New York *(G-10818)*
Kaleko Bros .... G 212 819-0100
  New York *(G-10839)*
Lazare Kaplan Intl Inc .... D 212 972-9700
  New York *(G-10975)*
Miller & Veit Inc .... F 212 247-2275
  New York *(G-11295)*
Precision Diamond Cutters Inc .... G 212 719-4438
  New York *(G-11718)*
Shah Diamonds Inc .... E 212 888-9393
  New York *(G-12059)*
Steven Galapo Diamonds LLC .... G 212 221-3000
  New York *(G-12223)*
T M W Diamonds Mfg Co .... E 212 869-8444
  New York *(G-12289)*
United Gemdiam Inc .... E 718 851-5083
  Brooklyn *(G-2720)*
Waldman Alexander M Diamond Co .... E 212 921-8098
  New York *(G-12606)*
William Goldberg Diamond Corp .... E 212 980-4343
  New York *(G-12660)*
Windiam Usa Inc .... G 212 542-0949
  New York *(G-12667)*

DIAPERS: Cloth

Becks Classic Mfg Inc .... D 631 435-3800
  Brentwood *(G-1175)*

DIAPERS: Disposable

Bentley Manufacturing Inc .... G 212 714-1800
  New York *(G-9408)*
Mr Disposable Inc .... F 718 388-8574
  Brooklyn *(G-2344)*

DIE CUTTING SVC: Paper

Able National Corp .... E 718 386-8801
  Brooklyn *(G-1549)*

DIE SETS: Presses, Metal Stamping

Gay Sheet Metal Dies Inc .... G 716 877-0208
  Buffalo *(G-2981)*

DIES & TOOLS: Special

Ace Specialty Co Inc .... G 716 874-3670
  Tonawanda *(G-16156)*
All Out Die Cutting Inc .... E 718 346-6666
  Brooklyn *(G-1586)*
Amada Tool America Inc .... D 585 344-3900
  Batavia *(G-623)*
Anka Tool & Die Inc .... E 845 268-4116
  Congers *(G-3875)*
Arro Tool & Die Inc .... F 716 763-6203
  Lakewood *(G-7311)*
Art Precision Metal Products .... F 631 842-8889
  Copiague *(G-3920)*
Barron Metal Products Inc .... E 914 965-1232
  Yonkers *(G-17434)*

PRODUCT SECTION

DISPLAY FIXTURES: Wood

Bennett Die & Tool Inc .... E 607 739-5629
 Horseheads (G-6598)
Bennett Die & Tool Inc .... F 607 273-2836
 Ithaca (G-6860)
Brighton Tool & Die Designers .... F 716 876-0879
 Tonawanda (G-16169)
Carbaugh Tool Company Inc .... E 607 739-3293
 Elmira (G-4686)
Charles A Rogers Entps Inc .... E 585 924-6400
 Victor (G-16490)
Coil Stamping Inc .... F 631 588-3040
 Holbrook (G-6467)
Cuddeback Machining Inc .... G 585 392-5889
 Hilton (G-6443)
Diemax of Rochester Inc .... G 585 288-3912
 Rochester (G-14328)
Diemolding Corporation .... F 315 363-4710
 Wampsville (G-16575)
Dixon Tool and Manufacturing .... G 585 235-1352
 Rochester (G-14334)
Eden Tool & Die Inc .... G 716 992-4240
 Eden (G-4599)
Electro Form Corp .... F 607 722-6404
 Binghamton (G-906)
Enhanced Tool Inc .... E 716 691-5200
 Amherst (G-238)
Etna Tool & Die Corporation .... F 212 475-4350
 New York (G-10133)
Hytech Tool & Die Inc .... G 716 488-2796
 Jamestown (G-7035)
Intri-Cut Inc .... F 716 691-5200
 Amherst (G-246)
James Wire Die Co .... G 315 894-3233
 Ilion (G-6781)
K D M Die Company Inc .... F 716 828-9000
 Buffalo (G-3041)
Keyes Machine Works Inc .... G 585 426-5059
 Gates (G-5576)
Long Island Tool & Die Inc .... G 631 225-0600
 Copiague (G-3935)
M J M Tooling Corp .... G 718 292-3590
 Bronx (G-1388)
Machine Tool Specialty .... G 315 699-5287
 Cicero (G-3677)
Machinecraft Inc .... E 585 436-1070
 Rochester (G-14507)
Magnus Precision Mfg Inc .... D 315 548-8032
 Phelps (G-13557)
Mantel & Mantel Stamping Corp ...... G 631 467-1916
 Ronkonkoma (G-14964)
May Tool & Die Inc .... G 716 695-1033
 Tonawanda (G-16198)
Micron Inds Rochester Inc .... G 585 247-6130
 Rochester (G-14533)
Ms Machining Inc .... G 607 723-1105
 Binghamton (G-934)
Multifold Die Ctng Finshg Corp .... G 631 232-1235
 Hauppauge (G-6170)
Mustang-Major Tool & Die Co .... G 716 992-9200
 Eden (G-4601)
Niagara Punch & Die Corp .... G 716 896-7619
 Buffalo (G-3112)
Nijon Tool Co Inc .... F 631 242-3434
 Deer Park (G-4204)
P & R Industries Inc .... F 585 544-1811
 Rochester (G-14584)
Pacific Die Cast Inc .... F 845 778-6374
 Walden (G-16553)
Palma Tool & Die Company Inc ...... E 716 681-4685
 Lancaster (G-7353)
Phelinger Tool & Die Corp .... G 716 685-1780
 Alden (G-184)
Precision Grinding & Mfg Corp .... C 585 458-4300
 Rochester (G-14615)
Precision Machining and Mfg .... G 845 647-5380
 Wawarsing (G-16732)
Precision Tl Die & Stamping Co ...... F 516 561-0041
 Valley Stream (G-16444)
Pronto Tool & Die Co Inc .... E 631 981-8920
 Ronkonkoma (G-14997)
Prototype Manufacturing Corp .... F 716 695-1700
 North Tonawanda (G-13005)
Raloid Tool Co Inc .... F 518 664-4261
 Mechanicville (G-8261)
Ram Precision Tool Inc .... G 716 759-8722
 Lancaster (G-7362)
Rid Lom Precision Mfg .... E 585 594-8600
 Rochester (G-14648)
Rochester Stampings Inc .... F 585 467-5241
 Rochester (G-14672)
S B Whistler & Sons Inc .... E 585 798-3000
 Medina (G-8313)
Sharon Metal Stamping Corp .... G 718 828-4510
 Bronx (G-1450)
Stamp Rite Tool & Die Inc .... G 718 752-0334
 Long Island City (G-7911)
Thayer Tool & Die Inc .... F 716 782-4841
 Ashville (G-427)
Tips & Dies Inc .... F 315 337-4161
 Rome (G-14865)
Tools & Stamping Corp .... G 718 392-4040
 Brooklyn (G-2683)
Trinity Tools Inc .... E 716 694-1111
 North Tonawanda (G-13021)
Ultimate Prcision Met Pdts Inc .... C 631 249-9441
 Farmingdale (G-5146)

DIES: Cutting, Exc Metal

Royal Molds Inc .... F 718 382-7686
 Brooklyn (G-2532)

DIES: Extrusion

D Maldari & Sons Inc .... E 718 499-3555
 Brooklyn (G-1830)

DIES: Paper Cutting

Evergreen Corp Central NY .... F 315 454-4175
 Syracuse (G-15959)

DIES: Plastic Forming

Alliance Precision Plas Corp .... C 585 426-5310
 Rochester (G-14204)
Alliance Precision Plas Corp .... E 585 426-5310
 Rochester (G-14205)
Quality Lineals Usa Inc .... E 516 378-6577
 Freeport (G-5432)

DIES: Steel Rule

Dynamic Dies Inc .... F 585 247-4010
 Rochester (G-14341)
Great Lakes Pressed Steel Corp .... E 716 885-4037
 Buffalo (G-2998)
National Steel Rule Die Inc .... F 718 402-1396
 Bronx (G-1409)
Paragon Steel Rule Dies Inc .... F 585 254-3395
 Rochester (G-14592)

DIODES: Light Emitting

Acolyte Technologies Corp .... F 212 629-3239
 New York (G-9066)
Data Display USA Inc .... C 631 218-2130
 Holbrook (G-6471)
Emagin Corporation .... D 845 838-7900
 Hopewell Junction (G-6575)
Hisun Optoelectronics Co Ltd .... F 718 886-6966
 Flushing (G-5258)
Ic Technologies LLC .... G 212 966-7895
 New York (G-10595)
Light Blue USA LLC .... G 718 475-2515
 Brooklyn (G-2221)
Oledworks LLC .... E 585 287-6802
 Rochester (G-14568)
S3j Electronics LLC .... E 716 206-1309
 Lancaster (G-7366)
Tarsier Ltd .... C 212 401-6181
 New York (G-12305)
Veriled Inc .... G 877 521-5520
 New York (G-12546)

DIODES: Solid State, Germanium, Silicon, Etc

Leviton Manufacturing Co Inc .... B 631 812-6000
 Melville (G-8363)

DIRECT SELLING ESTABLISHMENTS: Beverage Svcs

Tao Group LLC .... G 646 625-4818
 New York (G-12303)

DIRECT SELLING ESTABLISHMENTS: Encyclopedias & Publications

Economist Newspaper Group Inc .... C 212 541-0500
 New York (G-10032)

DIRECT SELLING ESTABLISHMENTS: Food Svcs

New Dynamics Corporation .... E 845 692-0022
 Middletown (G-8488)

DISCOUNT DEPARTMENT STORES

First Choice News Inc .... G 212 477-2044
 New York (G-10218)

DISCS & TAPE: Optical, Blank

L & M Optical Disc LLC .... D 718 649-3500
 New York (G-10938)
Sony Corporation of America .... C 212 833-8000
 New York (G-12157)
Sony Dadc US Inc .... B 212 833-8800
 New York (G-12158)

DISHWASHING EQPT: Commercial

Hobart Corporation .... E 585 427-9000
 Rochester (G-14458)
Strategies North America Inc .... G 716 945-6053
 Salamanca (G-15135)

DISINFECTING SVCS

Vital Vio Inc .... F 914 245-6048
 Troy (G-16286)

DISK & DRUM DRIVES & COMPONENTS: Computers

Globalfoundries US Inc .... C 518 305-9013
 Malta (G-8051)

DISK DRIVES: Computer

Formats Unlimited Inc .... F 631 249-9200
 Deer Park (G-4166)
Sale 121 Corp .... D 240 855-8988
 New York (G-11972)
Toshiba Amer Info Systems Inc ...... B 949 583-3000
 New York (G-12397)

DISPENSING EQPT & PARTS, BEVERAGE: Beer

Niagara Dispensing Tech Inc .... F 716 636-9827
 Buffalo (G-3108)

DISPENSING EQPT & PARTS, BEVERAGE: Cold, Exc Coin-Operated

Lightron Corporation .... G 516 938-5544
 Jericho (G-7107)

DISPENSING EQPT & PARTS, BEVERAGE: Fountain/Other Beverage

Chudnow Manufacturing Co Inc ...... E 516 593-4222
 Oceanside (G-13094)
Klearbar Inc .... G 516 684-9892
 Port Washington (G-13855)

DISPENSING EQPT & SYSTEMS, BEVERAGE: Liquor

Oyster Bay Pump Works Inc .... F 516 933-4500
 Hicksville (G-6406)

DISPLAY CASES: Refrigerated

Mohawk Cabinet Company Inc .... F 518 725-0645
 Gloversville (G-5733)

DISPLAY FIXTURES: Showcases, Wood, Exc Refrigerated

R H Guest Incorporated .... G 718 675-7600
 Brooklyn (G-2490)

DISPLAY FIXTURES: Wood

16 Tons Inc .... E 718 418-8446
 Brooklyn (G-1511)
All Merchandise Display Corp .... G 718 257-2221
 Highland Mills (G-6438)
David Flatt Furniture Ltd .... F 718 937-7944
 Long Island City (G-7739)

DISPLAY FIXTURES: Wood

Hunter Metal Industries Inc ....D....... 631 475-5900
  East Patchogue (G-4467)
J M P Display Fixture Co Inc ....G....... 718 649-0333
  Brooklyn (G-2126)
Marplex Furniture Corporation ....G....... 914 969-7755
  Yonkers (G-17484)
Specialty Services ....G....... 585 728-5650
  Wayland (G-16735)

DISPLAY ITEMS: Corrugated, Made From Purchased Materials

Calpac Incorporated ....F....... 631 789-0502
  Amityville (G-278)
Displays & Beyond Inc ....F....... 718 805-7786
  Glendale (G-5666)
General Die and Die Cutng Inc ....D....... 516 665-3584
  Roosevelt (G-15028)
Mp Displays LLC ....G....... 845 268-4113
  Valley Cottage (G-16409)
Spaeth Design Inc ....E....... 718 606-9685
  Woodside (G-17369)

DISPLAY STANDS: Merchandise, Exc Wood

Exclusive Designs ....F....... 516 378-5258
  Freeport (G-5407)
Trylon Wire & Metal Works Inc ....E....... 718 542-4472
  Bronx (G-1480)

DISTILLATES: Hardwood

Tioga Hardwoods Inc ....G....... 607 657-8686
  Berkshire (G-852)

DOCK OPERATION SVCS, INCL BLDGS, FACILITIES, OPERS & MAINT

Kleinfelder John ....G....... 716 753-3163
  Mayville (G-8247)

DOCKS: Floating, Wood

Meeco Sullivan LLC ....C....... 800 232-3625
  Warwick (G-16617)

DOCKS: Prefabricated Metal

Guardian Booth LLC ....F....... 844 992-6684
  Spring Valley (G-15610)
Metallic Ladder Mfg Corp ....F....... 716 358-6201
  Randolph (G-14029)
T Shore Products Ltd ....G....... 315 252-9174
  Auburn (G-519)

DOCUMENT EMBOSSING SVCS

Batavia Press LLC ....E....... 585 343-4429
  Batavia (G-625)

DOLLIES: Mechanics'

Durall Dolly LLC ....F....... 802 728-7122
  Brooklyn (G-1884)

DOLOMITE: Crushed & Broken

Dolomite Products Company Inc ....E....... 315 524-1998
  Rochester (G-14337)

DOLOMITIC MARBLE: Crushed & Broken

Rock Iroquois Products Inc ....E....... 585 637-6834
  Brockport (G-1247)
Tilcon New York Inc ....D....... 845 480-3249
  Flushing (G-5306)
Tilcon New York Inc ....D....... 845 615-0216
  Goshen (G-5754)
Tilcon New York Inc ....D....... 845 457-3158
  Montgomery (G-8639)

DOMESTIC HELP SVCS

Custom Klean Corp ....F....... 315 865-8101
  Holland Patent (G-6513)

DOOR & WINDOW REPAIR SVCS

Lif Industries Inc ....E....... 718 767-8800
  Whitestone (G-17240)
United Steel Products Inc ....D....... 718 478-5330
  Corona (G-4031)

DOOR OPERATING SYSTEMS: Electric

Assa Abloy Entrance Systems US ....E....... 315 492-6600
  East Syracuse (G-4524)
EZ Lift Operator Corp ....F....... 845 356-1676
  Spring Valley (G-15606)
V E Power Door Co Inc ....E....... 631 231-4500
  Brentwood (G-1198)
Windowman (usa) ....G....... 718 246-2626
  Brooklyn (G-2774)

DOORS & WINDOWS WHOLESALERS: All Materials

Pella Corporation ....C....... 631 208-0710
  Calverton (G-3322)
Royal Windows Mfg Corp ....E....... 631 435-8888
  Bay Shore (G-735)
Structural Wood Corporation ....E....... 315 388-4442
  Waddington (G-16542)

DOORS & WINDOWS: Screen & Storm

I Fix Screen ....G....... 631 421-1938
  Centereach (G-3497)
Optimum Window Mfg Corp ....E....... 845 647-1900
  Ellenville (G-4650)
Pal Manufacturing Corp ....E....... 516 937-1990
  Hicksville (G-6409)

DOORS & WINDOWS: Storm, Metal

A & S Window Associates Inc ....E....... 718 275-7900
  Glendale (G-5657)
Air Tite Manufacturing Inc ....C....... 516 897-0295
  Long Beach (G-7667)
All United Window Corp ....E....... 718 624-0490
  Brooklyn (G-1587)
Corkhill Manufacturing Co Inc ....E....... 718 528-7413
  Jamaica (G-6943)
Excel Aluminum Products Inc ....E....... 315 471-0925
  Syracuse (G-15960)
Karey Kassl Corp ....E....... 516 349-8484
  Plainview (G-13641)
Pioneer Window Holdings Inc ....F....... 516 822-7000
  Hicksville (G-6414)
Pioneer Window Holdings Inc ....E....... 518 762-5526
  Johnstown (G-7152)
Texas Home Security Inc ....E....... 516 747-2100
  New Hyde Park (G-8910)

DOORS: Dormers, Wood

Dorm Company Corporation ....G....... 502 551-6195
  Cheektowaga (G-3596)

DOORS: Fiberglass

Europrojects Intl Inc ....G....... 917 262-0795
  New York (G-10140)

DOORS: Fire, Metal

Ace Fire Door Corp ....E....... 718 901-0001
  Bronx (G-1262)
Altype Fire Door Corp ....G....... 718 292-3500
  Bronx (G-1272)
General Fire-Proof Door Corp ....E....... 718 893-5500
  Bronx (G-1344)
Interntional Fireprof Door Inc ....F....... 718 783-1310
  Brooklyn (G-2111)
Lif Industries Inc ....E....... 718 767-8800
  Whitestone (G-17240)
M & D Installers Inc ....D....... 718 782-6978
  Brooklyn (G-2245)
Mercury Lock and Door Service ....E....... 718 542-7048
  Bronx (G-1395)
Metalline Fire Door Co Inc ....E....... 718 583-2320
  Bronx (G-1396)
Schwab Corp ....E....... 585 381-4900
  Rochester (G-14696)
Statewide Fireproof Door Co ....F....... 845 268-6043
  Valley Cottage (G-16416)
Supreme Fire-Proof Door Co Inc ....F....... 718 665-4224
  Bronx (G-1466)
Universal Fire Proof Door ....E....... 718 455-8442
  Brooklyn (G-2726)

DOORS: Folding, Plastic Or Plastic Coated Fabric

Custom Door & Mirror Inc ....E....... 631 414-7725
  Farmingdale (G-4980)

Perma Tech Inc

Perma Tech Inc ....E....... 716 854-0707
  Buffalo (G-3145)

DOORS: Garage, Overhead, Metal

Amarr Company ....F....... 585 426-8290
  Rochester (G-14210)
American Rolling Door Ltd ....G....... 718 273-0485
  Staten Island (G-15658)
Griffon Corporation ....E....... 212 957-5000
  New York (G-10405)
L & L Overhead Garage Doors ....G....... 718 721-2518
  Long Island City (G-7813)
Overhead Door Corporation ....D....... 518 828-7652
  Hudson (G-6659)
Roly Door Sales Inc ....G....... 716 877-1515
  Hamburg (G-5965)

DOORS: Garage, Overhead, Wood

Griffon Corporation ....E....... 212 957-5000
  New York (G-10405)

DOORS: Glass

Executive Mirror Doors Inc ....G....... 631 234-1090
  Ronkonkoma (G-14928)
Hecht & Sohn Glass Co Inc ....G....... 718 782-8295
  Brooklyn (G-2070)
Unico Inc ....F....... 845 562-9255
  Newburgh (G-12806)

DOORS: Rolling, Indl Building Or Warehouse, Metal

American Steel Gate Corp ....G....... 718 291-4050
  Jamaica (G-6928)
Robert-Masters Corp ....G....... 718 545-1030
  Woodside (G-17367)
Steelmasters Inc ....E....... 718 498-2854
  Brooklyn (G-2626)
Thompson Overhead Door Co Inc ....F....... 718 788-2470
  Brooklyn (G-2678)
United Steel Products Inc ....D....... 914 968-7782
  Flushing (G-5311)

DOORS: Wooden

Ace Fire Door Corp ....E....... 718 901-0001
  Bronx (G-1262)
Burt Millwork Corporation ....E....... 718 257-4601
  Albertson (G-156)
Capital Kit Cab & Door Mfrs ....G....... 718 886-0303
  College Point (G-3805)
Chautauqua Woods Corp ....E....... 716 366-3808
  Dunkirk (G-4360)
D R Cornue Woodworks ....G....... 315 655-9463
  Cazenovia (G-3471)
Living Doors Inc ....F....... 631 924-5393
  Medford (G-8285)
Overhead Door Corporation ....D....... 518 828-7652
  Hudson (G-6659)
Quality Millwork Corp ....E....... 718 892-2250
  Bronx (G-1437)
Rochester Lumber Company ....E....... 585 924-7171
  Farmington (G-5164)
Select Interior Door Ltd ....E....... 585 535-9900
  North Java (G-12950)
Yesteryears Vintage Doors LLC ....G....... 315 324-5250
  Hammond (G-5974)

DOWN FEATHERS

Eastern Feather & Down Corp ....G....... 718 387-4100
  Brooklyn (G-1899)

DRAPERIES & CURTAINS

Abalene Decorating Services ....E....... 718 782-2000
  New York (G-9046)
Associated Drapery & Equipment ....F....... 516 671-5245
  Monroe (G-8583)
Baby Signature Inc ....G....... 212 686-1700
  New York (G-9351)
Bettertex Inc ....F....... 212 431-3373
  New York (G-9426)
Bramson House Inc ....C....... 516 764-5006
  Freeport (G-5400)
C & G of Kingston Inc ....D....... 845 331-0148
  Kingston (G-7209)
Cabriole Designs Inc ....G....... 212 593-4528
  New York (G-9545)

PRODUCT SECTION

DRUGS/DRUG PROPRIETARIES, WHOL: Proprietary/Patent Medicines

Decorative Novelty Co Inc.............................F......718 965-8600
  Brooklyn (G-1848)
J Edlin Interiors Ltd......................................F......212 243-2111
  New York (G-10718)
Jo-Vin Decorators Inc..................................E......718 441-9350
  Woodhaven (G-17324)
Laregence Inc..E......212 736-2548
  New York (G-10964)
Louis Hornick & Co Inc.................................G......212 679-2448
  New York (G-11077)
Majestic Curtains LLC..................................G......718 898-0774
  Elmhurst (G-4678)
Mason Contract Products LLC....................D......516 328-6900
  New Hyde Park (G-8894)
McCarroll Uphl Designs LLC........................G......518 828-0500
  Hudson (G-6655)
Mistdoda Inc...E......919 735-7111
  New York (G-11309)
Mutual Sales Corp..E......718 361-8373
  Long Island City (G-7848)
Richloom Fabrics Corp.................................F......212 685-5400
  New York (G-11894)
Richloom Fabrics Group Inc........................F......212 685-5400
  New York (G-11895)
Richloom Home Fashions Corp...................F......212 685-5400
  New York (G-11896)
Royal Home Fashions Inc............................G......212 689-7222
  New York (G-11942)
Seaway Mats Inc..G......518 483-2560
  Malone (G-8047)
Showeray Co..D......718 965-3633
  Brooklyn (G-2578)
Shyam Ahuja Limited...................................G......212 644-5910
  New York (G-12080)
Terbo Ltd..G......718 847-2860
  Richmond Hill (G-14099)
White Plains Drapery Uphl Inc.....................E......914 381-0908
  Mamaroneck (G-8083)
White Workroom Inc....................................G......212 941-5910
  New York (G-12654)

DRAPERIES & DRAPERY FABRICS, COTTON

Designway Ltd..G......212 254-2220
  New York (G-9911)
Richloom Home Fashions Corp...................F......212 685-5400
  New York (G-11896)
Star Draperies Inc..F......631 756-7121
  Farmingdale (G-5125)
Versailles Drapery Upholstery.....................F......212 533-2059
  Long Island City (G-7944)
Wallace Home Design Ctr...........................G......631 765-3890
  Southold (G-15585)

DRAPERIES: Plastic & Textile, From Purchased Materials

Anthony Lawrence of New York..................E......212 206-8820
  Long Island City (G-7694)
County Draperies Inc...................................E......845 342-9009
  Middletown (G-8467)
Deangelis Ltd...E......212 348-8225
  Glen Head (G-5645)
Delta Upholsterers Inc.................................E......212 489-3308
  New York (G-9896)
Fabric Quilters Unlimited Inc.......................E......516 333-2866
  Westbury (G-17011)
Henry B Urban Inc.......................................E......212 489-3308
  New York (G-10500)
Laminated Window Products Inc.................F......631 242-6883
  Bay Shore (G-708)
Revman International Inc............................E......212 894-3100
  New York (G-11880)
Reynolds Drapery Service Inc....................F......315 845-8632
  Newport (G-12816)
Wayne Decorators Inc.................................G......718 529-4200
  Jamaica (G-6999)
Wcd Window Coverings Inc........................F......845 336-4511
  Lake Katrine (G-7295)

DRAPERY & UPHOLSTERY STORES: Draperies

Albert Menin Interiors Ltd............................F......212 876-3041
  Bronx (G-1268)
Reynolds Drapery Service Inc....................F......315 845-8632
  Newport (G-12816)
Versailles Drapery Upholstery.....................F......212 533-2059
  Long Island City (G-7944)
White Plains Drapery Uphl Inc.....................E......914 381-0908
  Mamaroneck (G-8083)

DRAPERY & UPHOLSTERY STORES: Slip Covers

McCarroll Uphl Designs LLC........................G......518 828-0500
  Hudson (G-6655)

DRAPES & DRAPERY FABRICS, FROM MANMADE FIBER

Pierce Arrow Drapery Mfg...........................G......716 876-3023
  Buffalo (G-3148)
Richloom Home Fashions Corp...................F......212 685-5400
  New York (G-11896)
Unique Quality Fabrics Inc..........................G......845 343-3070
  Middletown (G-8503)

DRIED FRUITS WHOLESALERS

Sahadi Fine Foods Inc.................................E......718 369-0100
  Brooklyn (G-2554)

DRILL BITS

Mibro Group..D......716 631-5713
  Buffalo (G-3084)

DRILLING MACHINERY & EQPT: Water Well

Blue Tee Corp..A......212 598-0880
  New York (G-9473)

DRINK MIXES, NONALCOHOLIC: Cocktail

American Juice Company LLC....................G......347 620-0252
  New York (G-9173)
Motts LLP...C......972 673-8088
  Elmsford (G-4775)

DRINKING PLACES: Alcoholic Beverages

Kurrier Inc..G......718 389-3018
  Brooklyn (G-2180)
Lafayette Pub Inc..E......212 925-4242
  New York (G-10952)

DRINKING PLACES: Night Clubs

Flushing Pharmacy Inc................................C......718 260-8999
  Brooklyn (G-1989)

DRINKING PLACES: Tavern

Club 1100..G......585 235-3478
  Rochester (G-14301)

DRINKING PLACES: Wine Bar

Wolffer Estate Vineyard Inc........................E......631 537-5106
  Sagaponack (G-15109)

DRINKING WATER COOLERS WHOLESALERS: Mechanical

Yr Blanc & Co LLC......................................G......716 800-3999
  Buffalo (G-3287)

DRIVE SHAFTS

Deer Park Driveshaft & Hose......................G......631 667-4091
  Deer Park (G-4149)
Dennys Drive Shaft Service........................G......716 875-6640
  Kenmore (G-7174)
Drive Shaft Shop Inc...................................F......631 348-1818
  Hauppauge (G-6090)
K M Drive Line Inc.......................................G......718 599-0628
  Brooklyn (G-2164)

DRIVES: High Speed Indl, Exc Hydrostatic

Magna Products Corp.................................E......585 647-2280
  Rochester (G-14510)
Nidec Indus Automtn USA LLC..................E......716 774-1193
  Grand Island (G-5778)

DRONES: Target, Used By Ships, Metal

Dz9 Power LLC..G......877 533-5530
  Olean (G-13167)

DROP CLOTHS: Fabric

Ace Drop Cloth Canvas Pdts Inc................E......718 731-1550
  Bronx (G-1261)

DRUG TESTING KITS: Blood & Urine

Healthcare Consulting Svcs Inc..................F......860 740-8660
  West Babylon (G-16821)
Yr Blanc & Co LLC......................................G......716 800-3999
  Buffalo (G-3287)

DRUGS & DRUG PROPRIETARIES, WHOL: Biologicals/Allied Prdts

Roar Biomedical Inc....................................G......631 591-2749
  Calverton (G-3325)

DRUGS & DRUG PROPRIETARIES, WHOLESALE

Alo Acquisition LLC....................................G......518 464-0279
  Albany (G-43)
Ip Med Inc...G......516 766-3800
  Oceanside (G-13102)

DRUGS & DRUG PROPRIETARIES, WHOLESALE: Blood Plasma

C T M Industries Ltd...................................E......718 479-3300
  Jamaica (G-6935)

DRUGS & DRUG PROPRIETARIES, WHOLESALE: Pharmaceuticals

Amneal Pharmaceuticals LLC....................E......631 952-0214
  Brookhaven (G-1505)
Amneal Pharmaceuticals LLC....................E......908 947-3120
  Brookhaven (G-1506)
Derm/Buro Inc...G......516 694-8300
  Plainview (G-13626)
Forest Laboratories LLC............................C......212 421-7850
  New York (G-10237)
G C Hanford Manufacturing Co..................C......315 476-7418
  Syracuse (G-15967)
Generics Bidco I LLC.................................G......256 859-4011
  Chestnut Ridge (G-3651)
Invagen Pharmaceuticals Inc.....................B......631 231-3233
  Hauppauge (G-6123)
Nutra-Scientifics LLC.................................G......917 238-8510
  Pomona (G-13759)
Polygen Pharmaceuticals Inc.....................E......631 392-4044
  Edgewood (G-4621)
Tocare LLC..G......718 767-0618
  Whitestone (G-17244)
Ucb Pharma Inc..B......919 767-2555
  Rochester (G-14765)
Vyera Pharmaceuticals LLC......................E......646 356-5577
  New York (G-12600)

DRUGS & DRUG PROPRIETARIES, WHOLESALE: Vitamins & Minerals

Healthy N Fit Intl Inc...................................F......914 271-6040
  Croton On Hudson (G-4090)
Natures Bounty Co......................................D......631 244-2021
  Ronkonkoma (G-14977)
Natures Bounty Co......................................A......631 200-2000
  Ronkonkoma (G-14978)
Nbty Manufacturing LLC.............................E......631 567-9500
  Ronkonkoma (G-14980)
Unipharm Inc...E......212 564-3634
  New York (G-12478)
Wellquest International Inc.........................G......212 689-9094
  New York (G-12636)

DRUGS ACTING ON THE CENTRAL NERVOUS SYSTEM & SENSE ORGANS

Acorda Therapeutics Inc............................C......914 347-4300
  Ardsley (G-402)

DRUGS AFFECTING NEOPLASMS & ENDOCRINE SYSTEMS

OSI Pharmaceuticals LLC..........................D......631 847-0175
  Farmingdale (G-5083)
OSI Pharmaceuticals LLC..........................G......631 962-2000
  Farmingdale (G-5084)

DRUGS/DRUG PROPRIETARIES, WHOL: Proprietary/Patent Medicines

Apothecus Pharmaceutical Corp................F......516 624-8200
  Oyster Bay (G-13391)

DRUGS: Parasitic & Infective Disease Affecting

Safetec of America Inc .... D 716 895-1822
  Buffalo *(G-3202)*

DRUMS: Fiber

Greif Inc .... D 716 836-4200
  Tonawanda *(G-16186)*

DRYCLEANING EQPT & SPLYS: Commercial

Q Omni Inc .... G 914 962-2726
  Yorktown Heights *(G-17533)*
Thermopatch Corporation .... D 315 446-8110
  Syracuse *(G-16082)*

DRYCLEANING SVC: Drapery & Curtain

Abalene Decorating Services .... E 718 782-2000
  New York *(G-9046)*
Reynolds Drapery Service Inc .... F 315 845-8632
  Newport *(G-12816)*

DUCTS: Sheet Metal

Aabco Sheet Metal Co Inc .... D 718 821-1166
  Ridgewood *(G-14110)*
Accurate Specialty Metal Fabri .... E 718 418-6895
  Middle Village *(G-8442)*
D and D Sheet Metal Corp .... F 718 465-7585
  Jamaica *(G-6945)*
Delta Sheet Metal Corp .... C 718 429-5805
  Long Island City *(G-7740)*
Karo Sheet Metal Inc .... E 718 542-8420
  Brooklyn *(G-2168)*
Liffey Sheet Metal Corp .... F 347 381-1134
  Long Island City *(G-7816)*
Nelson Air Device Corporation .... C 718 729-3801
  Maspeth *(G-8186)*
United Sheet Metal Corp .... E 718 482-1197
  Long Island City *(G-7937)*

DUMPSTERS: Garbage

Mount Kisco Transfer Stn Inc .... G 914 666-6350
  Mount Kisco *(G-8678)*

DYES & PIGMENTS: Organic

Deep Dyeing Inc .... F 718 418-7187
  Manhasset *(G-8091)*
East Cast Clor Compounding Inc .... G 631 491-9000
  West Babylon *(G-16815)*
F M Group Inc .... F 845 589-0102
  Congers *(G-3881)*
Rand Machine Products Inc .... G 716 985-4681
  Sinclairville *(G-15475)*

DYES & TINTS: Household

Chromananotech LLC .... G 607 239-9626
  Vestal *(G-16467)*

DYES: Synthetic Organic

Jos H Lowenstein and Sons Inc .... D 718 218-8013
  Brooklyn *(G-2147)*

EATING PLACES

A T A Bagel Shoppe Inc .... G 718 352-4948
  Bayside *(G-759)*
Capco Marketing .... F 315 699-1687
  Baldwinsville *(G-567)*
Cascade Mountain Winery & Rest .... F 845 373-9021
  Amenia *(G-218)*
Food Gems Ltd .... E 718 296-7788
  Ozone Park *(G-13405)*
Gilded Otter Brewing Co .... D 845 256-1700
  New Paltz *(G-8919)*
Heron Hill Vineyards Inc .... E 607 868-4241
  Hammondsport *(G-5978)*
Hyde Park Brewing Co Inc .... E 845 229-8277
  Hyde Park *(G-6773)*
Lakeside Cider Mill Farm Inc .... G 518 399-8359
  Ballston Lake *(G-581)*
Malina Management Company Inc .... E 607 535-9614
  Montour Falls *(G-8649)*
Piemonte Home Made Ravioli Co .... F 718 429-1972
  Woodside *(G-17363)*
Rawpothecary Inc .... G 917 783-7770
  Brooklyn *(G-2498)*
Rosina Food Products Inc .... C 716 668-0123
  Buffalo *(G-3193)*
Sign Company .... G 212 967-2113
  New York *(G-12091)*

EDUCATIONAL PROGRAM ADMINISTRATION, GOVERNMENT: State

University At Albany .... E 518 437-8686
  Albany *(G-147)*

EDUCATIONAL PROGRAMS ADMINISTRATION SVCS

Stony Brook University .... E 631 632-6434
  Stony Brook *(G-15793)*
Suny At Binghamton .... D 607 777-2316
  Binghamton *(G-946)*

EDUCATIONAL SVCS

Rainbeau Ridge Farm .... G 914 234-2197
  Bedford Hills *(G-803)*
Social Science Electronic Pubg .... F 585 442-8170
  Rochester *(G-14714)*

EDUCATIONAL SVCS, NONDEGREE GRANTING: Continuing Education

Conference Board Inc .... C 212 759-0900
  New York *(G-9760)*

ELASTOMERS

Elastomers Inc .... G 716 633-4883
  Williamsville *(G-17269)*
Everfab Inc .... D 716 655-1550
  East Aurora *(G-4395)*
Hutchinson Industries Inc .... E 716 852-1435
  Buffalo *(G-3016)*
Rodgard Corporation .... E 716 852-1435
  Buffalo *(G-3191)*

ELECTRIC MOTOR & GENERATOR AUXILIARY PARTS

International Control Products .... F 716 558-4400
  West Seneca *(G-16977)*

ELECTRIC MOTOR REPAIR SVCS

A & C/Furia Electric Motors .... F 914 949-0585
  White Plains *(G-17100)*
Alpha DC Motors Inc .... F 315 432-9039
  Syracuse *(G-15871)*
B & R Electric Motor Inc .... G 631 752-7533
  Farmingdale *(G-4958)*
B J S Electric .... G 845 774-8166
  Chester *(G-3627)*
Bayshore Electric Motors .... G 631 475-1397
  Patchogue *(G-13441)*
Daves Electric Motors & Pumps .... G 212 982-2930
  New York *(G-9872)*
Electric Motor Specialty Inc .... G 716 487-1458
  Jamestown *(G-7026)*
General Electric Company .... E 315 456-3304
  Syracuse *(G-15971)*
General Electric Company .... E 518 459-4110
  Albany *(G-82)*
Genesis Electrical Motors .... G 718 274-7030
  Woodside *(G-17348)*
Lawtons Electric Motor Service .... G 315 393-2728
  Ogdensburg *(G-13138)*
Longo New York Inc .... F 212 929-7128
  New York *(G-11055)*
Northeastern Electric Motors .... G 518 793-5939
  Hadley *(G-5926)*
Prime Electric Motors Inc .... G 718 784-1124
  Long Island City *(G-7876)*
Troy Belting and Supply Co .... D 518 272-4920
  Watervliet *(G-16715)*
United Richter Electrical Mtrs .... F 716 855-1945
  Buffalo *(G-3261)*

ELECTRIC SERVICES

Besicorp Ltd .... F 845 336-7700
  Kingston *(G-7208)*
County Energy Corp .... G 718 626-7000
  Brooklyn *(G-1807)*

ELECTRIC SVCS, NEC Power Transmission

Hess Corporation .... B 212 997-8500
  New York *(G-10507)*

ELECTRIC SVCS, NEC: Power Generation

Caithness Equities Corporation .... E 212 599-2112
  New York *(G-9549)*

ELECTRICAL APPARATUS & EQPT WHOLESALERS

Aerospace Lighting Corporation .... D 631 563-6400
  Bohemia *(G-1004)*
Amertac Holdings Inc .... G 610 336-1330
  Monsey *(G-8602)*
Bombardier Trnsp Holdings USA .... D 607 776-4791
  Bath *(G-654)*
Edison Price Lighting Inc .... D 718 685-0700
  Long Island City *(G-7753)*
Ener-G-Rotors Inc .... G 518 372-2608
  Schenectady *(G-15277)*
Hammond Manufacturing Co Inc .... F 716 630-7030
  Cheektowaga *(G-3602)*
Linear Lighting Corporation .... C 718 361-7552
  Long Island City *(G-7818)*
LSI Lightron Inc .... A 845 562-5500
  New Windsor *(G-8988)*
Medi-Ray Inc .... D 877 898-3003
  Tuckahoe *(G-16295)*
On Line Power Technologies .... G 914 968-4440
  Yonkers *(G-17489)*
Pcb Piezotronics Inc .... B 716 684-0003
  Depew *(G-4294)*
Pompian Manufacturing Co Inc .... G 914 476-7076
  Yonkers *(G-17497)*
Powr-UPS Corp .... E 631 345-5700
  Shirley *(G-15451)*
S & J Trading Inc .... G 718 347-1323
  Floral Park *(G-5216)*
Stk Electronics Inc .... E 315 655-8476
  Cazenovia *(G-3479)*

ELECTRICAL APPLIANCES, TELEVISIONS & RADIOS WHOLESALERS

AVI-Spl Employee .... B 212 840-4801
  New York *(G-9330)*
Sony Music Entertainment .... A 212 833-8500
  New York *(G-12159)*

ELECTRICAL CONSTRUCTION MATERIALS WHOLESALERS

All-Lifts Incorporated .... E 518 465-3461
  Albany *(G-42)*
Morris Products Inc .... F 518 743-0523
  Queensbury *(G-14018)*

ELECTRICAL CURRENT CARRYING WIRING DEVICES

Alstom Signaling Inc .... E 585 274-8700
  Schenectady *(G-15258)*
Atc Plastics LLC .... E 212 375-2515
  New York *(G-9297)*
Belden Inc .... B 607 796-5600
  Horseheads *(G-6597)*
C A M Graphics Co Inc .... E 631 842-3400
  Farmingdale *(G-4964)*
Charlton Precision Pdts Inc .... G 845 338-2351
  Kingston *(G-7212)*
Cooper Power Systems LLC .... B 716 375-7100
  Olean *(G-13160)*
Cox & Company Inc .... C 212 366-0200
  Plainview *(G-13623)*
Exxelia-Raf Tabtronics LLC .... E 585 243-4331
  Piffard *(G-13574)*
Inertia Switch Inc .... E 845 359-8300
  Orangeburg *(G-13251)*
Jaguar Industries Inc .... F 845 947-1800
  Haverstraw *(G-6261)*
Joldeson One Aerospace Inds .... D 718 848-7396
  Ozone Park *(G-13406)*
Kelta Inc .... E 631 789-5000
  Edgewood *(G-4616)*
L3 Technologies Inc .... A 631 436-7400
  Hauppauge *(G-6133)*
Leviton Manufacturing Co Inc .... B 631 812-6000
  Melville *(G-8363)*

PRODUCT SECTION

ELECTRICAL EQPT: Automotive, NEC

Company	Code	Phone
Lighting Holdings Intl LLC, Purchase (G-13976)	A	845 306-1850
Lite Brite Manufacturing Inc, Brooklyn (G-2233)	F	718 855-9797
Lourdes Industries Inc, Hauppauge (G-6146)	D	631 234-6600
MD Electronics Corporation, Jamestown (G-7052)	D	716 488-0300
Mini-Circuits Fort Wayne LLC, Brooklyn (G-2322)	B	718 934-4500
Mono-Systems Inc, Buffalo (G-3094)	E	716 821-1344
NEa Manufacturing Corp, Inwood (G-6803)	E	516 371-4200
Orbit International Corp, Hauppauge (G-6180)	C	631 435-8300
Pass & Seymour Inc, Syracuse (G-16032)	B	315 468-6211
Reynolds Packaging McHy Inc, Falconer (G-4918)	D	716 358-6451
Rodale Wireless Inc, Hauppauge (G-6205)	E	631 231-0044
Russell Industries Inc, Lynbrook (G-7986)	F	516 536-5000
Saturn Industries Inc, Hudson (G-6663)	E	518 828-9956
Sinclair Technologies Inc, Hamburg (G-5966)	E	716 874-3682
Stever-Locke Industries Inc, Honeoye Falls (G-6565)	G	585 624-3450
Superpower Inc, Schenectady (G-15325)	E	518 346-1414
Switching Power Inc, Ronkonkoma (G-15013)	D	631 981-7231
Swivelier Company Inc, Blauvelt (G-970)	D	845 353-1455
Tappan Wire & Cable Inc, Blauvelt (G-971)	C	845 353-9000
Utility Systems Tech Inc, Watervliet (G-16716)	F	518 326-4142
Whirlwind Music Distrs Inc, Rochester (G-14790)	D	800 733-9473

ELECTRICAL DISCHARGE MACHINING, EDM

Company	Code	Phone
Fermer Precision Inc, Ilion (G-6779)	D	315 822-6371
Hoercher Industries Inc, East Rochester (G-4480)	G	585 398-2982
K & H Industries Inc, Hamburg (G-5953)	F	716 312-0088

ELECTRICAL EQPT & SPLYS

Company	Code	Phone
303 Contracting Inc, Orchard Park (G-13271)	E	716 896-2122
331 Holding Inc, Victor (G-16482)	E	585 924-1740
A & S Electric, Brooklyn (G-1528)	G	212 228-2030
Advanced Mfg Techniques, Clifton Park (G-3720)	G	518 877-8560
Allcom Electric Corp, Yonkers (G-17427)	G	914 803-0433
Altaquip LLC, Ronkonkoma (G-14893)	G	631 580-4740
American Avionic Tech Corp, Medford (G-8266)	G	631 924-8200
Amertac Holdings Inc, Monsey (G-8602)	G	610 336-1330
Ametek Inc, Rochester (G-14218)	D	585 263-7700
Atlas Switch Co Inc, Garden City (G-5509)	E	516 222-6280
B & H Electronics Corp, Monroe (G-8584)	E	845 782-5000
Binghamton Simulator Co Inc, Binghamton (G-891)	E	607 321-2980
Bombardier Trnsp Holdings USA, Bath (G-654)	D	607 776-4791
Bren-Tronics Inc, Commack (G-3853)	C	631 499-5155
Buffalo Filter LLC, Lancaster (G-7331)	D	716 835-7000
Castle Power Solutions LLC, South Glens Falls (G-15547)	F	518 743-1600
Cathay Global Co Inc, Bayside Hills (G-774)	G	718 229-0920
Cooper Industries LLC, Syracuse (G-15928)	E	315 477-4500
Cooper Power Systems LLC, Olean (G-13160)	B	716 375-7100
Cooperfriedman Elc Sup Co Inc, Long Island City (G-7733)	G	718 269-4906
Da Electric, Bronx (G-1312)	E	347 270-3422
Dahill Distributors Inc, Brooklyn (G-1834)	G	347 371-9453
Denmar Electric, Nanuet (G-8801)	F	845 624-4430
Dorsey Metrology Intl Inc, Poughkeepsie (G-13914)	E	845 229-2929
Eastco Manufacturing Corp, Pelham (G-13515)	F	914 738-5667
Eaton Crouse-Hinds, Syracuse (G-15952)	C	315 477-7000
Edo LLC, Amityville (G-285)	A	631 630-4200
Emco Electric Services LLC, New York (G-10073)	E	212 420-9766
Emcom Inc, Auburn (G-492)	D	315 255-5300
Euchner USA Inc, East Syracuse (G-4541)	F	315 701-0315
Flanagan Electric Corp, Holbrook (G-6476)	E	631 567-2976
G X Electric Corporation, New York (G-10281)	E	212 921-0400
General Electric Company, Skaneateles (G-15482)	G	315 554-2000
Gerome Technologies Inc, Menands (G-8404)	D	518 463-1324
Green Island Power Authority, Green Island (G-5874)	F	518 273-0661
Gsa Upstate NY, Oakdale (G-13076)	G	631 244-5744
Guardian Systems Tech Inc, East Aurora (G-4397)	F	716 481-5597
Hergo Ergonomic Support, Maspeth (G-8175)	E	718 894-0639
Home Depot USA Inc, Newburgh (G-12782)	C	845 561-6540
Htf Components Inc, White Plains (G-17149)	G	914 703-6795
Iconix Inc, Hauppauge (G-6120)	F	516 513-1420
Intelligent Ctrl Systems LLC, Huntington (G-6697)	G	516 340-1011
Itin Scale Co Inc, Brooklyn (G-2118)	E	718 336-5900
J H M Engineering, Brooklyn (G-2122)	E	718 871-1810
Knf Clean Room Products Corp, Ronkonkoma (G-14951)	E	631 588-7000
Koregon Enterprises Inc, Champlain (G-3571)	G	450 218-6836
Kyle R Lawrence Electric Inc, Palmyra (G-13435)	G	315 502-4181
L3 Technologies Inc, Kirkwood (G-7261)	C	607 721-5465
Lucas Electric, Seaford (G-15367)	G	516 809-8619
Madison Electric, Cambria Heights (G-3331)	F	718 358-4121
Manhattan Scientifics Inc, New York (G-11156)	E	212 541-2405
Manor Electric Supply Corp, Brooklyn (G-2264)	F	718 648-8003
Manufacturing Solutions Inc, Rochester (G-14515)	E	585 235-3320
Marzullo Electric LLC, Syracuse (G-16004)	G	315 455-1050
Mitsubishi Elc Pwr Pdts Inc, Melville (G-8367)	G	516 962-2813
Multi Tech Electric, Woodside (G-17356)	F	718 606-2695
Nash Electric Services Inc, Yonkers (G-17487)	F	914 226-8375
Nbn Technologies LLC, Rochester (G-14551)	G	585 355-5556
Nk Electric LLC, Croton On Hudson (G-4091)	G	914 271-0222
OEM Solutions Inc, Clarence (G-3694)	G	716 864-9324
Optimum Applied Systems Inc, Poughkeepsie (G-13942)	F	845 471-3333
Piller Power Systems Inc, Middletown (G-8491)	E	845 695-6658
Pinpoint Systems Intl Inc, Bellport (G-835)	D	631 775-2100
Promptus Electronic Hdwr Inc, Mount Vernon (G-8767)	E	914 699-4700
Rodale Wireless Inc, Hauppauge (G-6205)	E	631 231-0044
Ross Electronics Ltd, Haverstraw (G-6264)	E	718 569-6643
Schuler-Haas Electric Corp, Painted Post (G-13419)	G	607 936-3514
Sima Technologies LLC, Hauppauge (G-6215)	F	412 828-9130
Simulaids Inc, Saugerties (G-15223)	D	845 679-2475
Skae Power Solutions LLC, Palisades (G-13427)	E	845 365-9103
Smithers Tools & Mch Pdts Inc, Rhinebeck (G-14070)	D	845 876-3063
Striano Electric Co Inc, Garden City Park (G-5556)	E	516 408-4969
Sunwire Electric Corp, Brooklyn (G-2644)	G	718 456-7500
T Jn Electric, Mahopac (G-8033)	F	917 560-0981
T Jn Electric Inc, Mahopac (G-8034)	F	845 628-6970
Tory Electric, Bedford (G-794)	G	914 292-5036
Triborough Electric, Whitestone (G-17246)	G	718 321-2144
U E Systems Incorporated, Elmsford (G-4797)	E	914 592-1220
United Technologies Corp, Pittsford (G-13603)	B	866 788-5095
Werner Brothers Electric Inc, Rexford (G-14066)	G	518 377-3056
Z-Axis Inc, Phelps (G-13563)	D	315 548-5000

ELECTRICAL EQPT FOR ENGINES

Company	Code	Phone
Cummins Inc, Jamestown (G-7021)	B	812 377-5000
Delphi Automotive Systems LLC, West Henrietta (G-16909)	A	585 359-6000
Kearney-National Inc, New York (G-10868)	F	212 661-4600
Leviton Manufacturing Co Inc, Melville (G-8363)	B	631 812-6000
Nas-Tra Automotive Inds Inc, Lindenhurst (G-7497)	C	631 225-1225
Sopark Corp, Buffalo (G-3219)	C	716 822-0434

ELECTRICAL EQPT REPAIR & MAINTENANCE

Company	Code	Phone
A L Eastmond & Sons Inc, Bronx (G-1254)	D	718 378-3000
Alstom Transportation Inc, New York (G-9155)	E	212 692-5353
Alstom Transportation Inc, West Henrietta (G-16899)	E	800 717-4477
Hobart Corporation, Commack (G-3861)	E	631 864-3440
Strecks Inc, Watervliet (G-16714)	E	518 273-4410

ELECTRICAL EQPT REPAIR SVCS

Company	Code	Phone
B & R Electric Motor Inc, Farmingdale (G-4958)	G	631 752-7533
Siemens Industry Inc, Rochester (G-14707)	E	585 797-2300
Zetek Corporation, New York (G-12729)	F	212 668-1485

ELECTRICAL EQPT REPAIR SVCS: High Voltage

Company	Code	Phone
Evergreen High Voltage LLC, Lake Placid (G-7298)	G	281 814-9973
Safeworks LLC, Woodside (G-17368)	G	800 696-5577

ELECTRICAL EQPT: Automotive, NEC

Company	Code	Phone
Autel US Inc, Farmingdale (G-4956)	G	631 923-2620
Ev-Box North America Inc, New York (G-10141)	G	646 930-6305
International Key Supply LLC, Farmingdale (G-5020)	F	631 983-6096

Employee Codes: A=Over 500 employees, B=251-500
C=101-250, D=51-100, E=20-50, F=10-19, G=5-9

ELECTRICAL EQPT: Household

East Side Development Corp ....G....... 585 242-9219
  Rochester *(G-14345)*
Kinetic Marketing Inc ....G....... 212 620-0500
  New York *(G-10890)*
World Trading Center Inc ....G....... 631 273-3330
  Hauppauge *(G-6260)*

ELECTRICAL GOODS, WHOLESALE: Batteries, Dry Cell

Lyntronics Inc ....E....... 631 205-1061
  Yaphank *(G-17412)*

ELECTRICAL GOODS, WHOLESALE: Burglar Alarm Systems

Altronix Corp ....D....... 718 567-8181
  Brooklyn *(G-1593)*
Detekion Security Systems Inc..........F....... 607 729-7179
  Vestal *(G-16469)*

ELECTRICAL GOODS, WHOLESALE: Capacitors

AVX Corporation ....D....... 716 372-6611
  Olean *(G-13155)*

ELECTRICAL GOODS, WHOLESALE: Connectors

Cables and Chips Inc........................E....... 212 619-3132
  New York *(G-9544)*
I Trade Technology Ltd ....G....... 615 348-7233
  Suffern *(G-15814)*

ELECTRICAL GOODS, WHOLESALE: Electronic Parts

Falconer Electronics Inc ....D....... 716 665-4176
  Falconer *(G-4905)*
Intex Company Inc ....D....... 516 223-0200
  Freeport *(G-5417)*
Oakdale Industrial Elec Corp ....F....... 631 737-4090
  Ronkonkoma *(G-14982)*
Sj Associates Inc ....E....... 516 942-3232
  Jericho *(G-7119)*
Veja Electronics Inc ....D....... 631 321-6086
  Deer Park *(G-4247)*

ELECTRICAL GOODS, WHOLESALE: Facsimile Or Fax Eqpt

Alternative Technology Corp ....G....... 914 478-5900
  Hastings On Hudson *(G-6022)*

ELECTRICAL GOODS, WHOLESALE: Fans, Household

Canarm Ltd ....G....... 800 267-4427
  Ogdensburg *(G-13134)*

ELECTRICAL GOODS, WHOLESALE: Fittings & Construction Mat

Veja Electronics Inc ....D....... 631 321-6086
  Deer Park *(G-4247)*

ELECTRICAL GOODS, WHOLESALE: Household Appliances, NEC

East Side Development Corp ....G....... 585 242-9219
  Rochester *(G-14345)*

ELECTRICAL GOODS, WHOLESALE: Intercommunication Eqpt

Apple Core Electronics Inc ....F....... 718 628-4068
  Brooklyn *(G-1619)*
Elite Cellular Accessories Inc ....E....... 877 390-2502
  Deer Park *(G-4158)*
Ingham Industries Inc ....G....... 631 242-2493
  Holbrook *(G-6480)*

ELECTRICAL GOODS, WHOLESALE: Light Bulbs & Related Splys

Led Waves Inc ....F....... 347 416-6182
  Brooklyn *(G-2205)*
Olive Led Lighting Inc ....G....... 718 746-0830
  College Point *(G-3825)*
Sir Industries Inc..............................G....... 631 234-2444
  Hauppauge *(G-6216)*

ELECTRICAL GOODS, WHOLESALE: Lighting Fittings & Access

Gagne Associates Inc......................E....... 800 800-5954
  Johnson City *(G-7123)*
Jed Lights Inc ....F....... 516 812-5001
  Deer Park *(G-4180)*

ELECTRICAL GOODS, WHOLESALE: Lighting Fixtures, Comm & Indl

Canarm Ltd..G....... 800 267-4427
  Ogdensburg *(G-13134)*
Creative Stage Lighting Co Inc ....E....... 518 251-3302
  North Creek *(G-12949)*
Unimar Inc ....F....... 315 699-4400
  Syracuse *(G-16087)*

ELECTRICAL GOODS, WHOLESALE: Lighting Fixtures, Residential

Prestigeline Inc ....D....... 631 273-3636
  Bay Shore *(G-724)*
Rapid-Lite Fixture Corporation ....F....... 347 599-2600
  Brooklyn *(G-2497)*

ELECTRICAL GOODS, WHOLESALE: Mobile telephone Eqpt

5yz Logistics LLC ....A....... 516 813-9500
  Plainview *(G-13605)*

ELECTRICAL GOODS, WHOLESALE: Motors

Electric Motor Specialty Inc..............G....... 716 487-1458
  Jamestown *(G-7026)*
Empire Division Inc...........................D....... 315 476-6273
  Syracuse *(G-15957)*
Heating & Burner Supply Inc ....G....... 718 665-0006
  Bronx *(G-1357)*
Northeastern Electric Motors ....E....... 518 793-5939
  Hadley *(G-5926)*

ELECTRICAL GOODS, WHOLESALE: Semiconductor Devices

Enplas America Inc ....G....... 646 892-7811
  New York *(G-10095)*
Lakestar Semi Inc ....F....... 212 974-6254
  New York *(G-10955)*

ELECTRICAL GOODS, WHOLESALE: Signaling, Eqpt

BNo Intl Trdg Co Inc ....G....... 716 487-1900
  Jamestown *(G-7012)*

ELECTRICAL GOODS, WHOLESALE: Sound Eqpt

L A R Electronics Corp ....G....... 716 285-0555
  Niagara Falls *(G-12858)*
Magic Tech Co Ltd ....G....... 516 539-7944
  West Hempstead *(G-16891)*
Samson Technologies Corp ....D....... 631 784-2200
  Hicksville *(G-6418)*

ELECTRICAL GOODS, WHOLESALE: Telephone Eqpt

Columbia Telecom Group ....G....... 631 501-5000
  New York *(G-9737)*
Harris Corporation ....F....... 718 767-1100
  Whitestone *(G-17236)*

ELECTRICAL GOODS, WHOLESALE: Transformers

Buffalo Power Elec Ctr De ....E....... 716 651-1600
  Depew *(G-4275)*

ELECTRICAL GOODS, WHOLESALE: VCR & Access

Toshiba America Inc ....E....... 212 596-0600
  New York *(G-12398)*

ELECTRICAL GOODS, WHOLESALE: Vacuum Cleaners, Household

Empire Division Inc...........................D....... 315 476-6273
  Syracuse *(G-15957)*

ELECTRICAL GOODS, WHOLESALE: Video Eqpt

Bescor Video Accessories Ltd ....F....... 631 420-1717
  Farmingdale *(G-4960)*
Russell Industries Inc ....F....... 516 536-5000
  Lynbrook *(G-7986)*

ELECTRICAL GOODS, WHOLESALE: Wire & Cable

Cortland Company Inc......................D....... 607 753-8276
  Cortland *(G-4040)*
Cygnus Automation Inc....................E....... 631 981-0909
  Bohemia *(G-1043)*
Hyperline Systems Inc.....................G....... 613 736-8500
  Brooklyn *(G-2090)*

ELECTRICAL GOODS, WHOLESALE: Wire & Cable, Electronic

Cables and Chips Inc........................E....... 212 619-3132
  New York *(G-9544)*
Cables Unlimited Inc........................E....... 631 563-6363
  Yaphank *(G-17403)*
Dsr International Corp ....G....... 631 427-2600
  Great Neck *(G-5820)*

ELECTRICAL HOUSEHOLD APPLIANCE REPAIR

East Side Development Corp ....G....... 585 242-9219
  Rochester *(G-14345)*

ELECTRICAL INDL APPARATUS, NEC

Calibration Technologies Inc ....G....... 631 676-6133
  Centereach *(G-3495)*
Energy Harvesters LLC ....G....... 617 325-9852
  Rochester *(G-14371)*
Key Signals ....G....... 631 433-2962
  East Moriches *(G-4449)*

ELECTRICAL SPLYS

Cooper Industries LLC ....E....... 315 477-7000
  Syracuse *(G-15928)*
Rwb Controls Inc ....G....... 716 897-4341
  Buffalo *(G-3198)*
Tudor Electrical Supply Co Inc ....G....... 212 867-7550
  New York *(G-12442)*

ELECTRICAL SUPPLIES: Porcelain

Cetek Inc ....E....... 845 452-3510
  Poughkeepsie *(G-13911)*
Corning Incorporated ....E....... 607 974-1274
  Painted Post *(G-13416)*
Ferro Electronics Materials ....C....... 716 278-9400
  Niagara Falls *(G-12841)*
Ferro Electronics Materials ....G....... 315 536-3357
  Penn Yan *(G-13533)*
Ferro Electronics Materials ....C....... 315 536-3357
  Penn Yan *(G-13534)*
Filtros Ltd ....E....... 585 586-8770
  East Rochester *(G-4478)*

ELECTROCARS: Golfer Transportation

Mdek Inc ....G....... 347 569-7318
  Brooklyn *(G-2292)*

ELECTRODES: Fluorescent Lamps

Preston Glass Industries Inc ....E....... 718 997-8888
  Forest Hills *(G-5335)*

PRODUCT SECTION

ELECTRODES: Thermal & Electrolytic

J V Precision Inc .... G 518 851-3200
  Hudson *(G-6649)*
Saturn Industries Inc .... E 518 828-9956
  Hudson *(G-6663)*

ELECTROMEDICAL EQPT

Argon Medical Devices Inc .... G 585 321-1130
  Henrietta *(G-6316)*
C R Bard Inc .... A 518 793-2531
  Glens Falls *(G-5690)*
Caliber Imging Diagnostics Inc .... E 585 239-9800
  Rochester *(G-14273)*
Cardiac Life Products Inc .... G 585 267-7775
  East Rochester *(G-4473)*
Conmed Corporation .... D 315 797-8375
  Utica *(G-16338)*
Excel Technology Inc .... F 212 355-3400
  New York *(G-10156)*
Fonar Corporation .... C 631 694-2929
  Melville *(G-8349)*
Forest Medical LLC .... G 315 434-9000
  East Syracuse *(G-4545)*
Infimed Inc .... D 315 453-4545
  Liverpool *(G-7547)*
Infimed Inc .... G 585 383-1710
  Pittsford *(G-13593)*
J H M Engineering .... E 718 871-1810
  Brooklyn *(G-2122)*
Jaracz Jr Joseph Paul .... G 716 533-1377
  Orchard Park *(G-13301)*
Kal Manufacturing Corporation .... E 585 265-4310
  Webster *(G-16751)*
Med Services Inc .... D 631 218-6450
  Bohemia *(G-1099)*
Misonix Inc .... D 631 694-9555
  Farmingdale *(G-5067)*
Natus Medical Incorporated .... G 631 457-4430
  Hauppauge *(G-6171)*
Netech Corporation .... F 631 531-0100
  Farmingdale *(G-5075)*
New York Marine Elec Inc .... G 631 734-6050
  Hampton Bays *(G-5983)*
Pharmadva LLC .... G 585 469-1410
  West Henrietta *(G-16922)*
Philips Medical Systems Mr .... B 518 782-1122
  Latham *(G-7403)*
Radiancy Inc .... F 845 398-1647
  Orangeburg *(G-13267)*
Ray Medica Inc .... E 952 885-0500
  New York *(G-11832)*
Sonomed Inc .... E 516 354-0900
  New Hyde Park *(G-8908)*
Soterix Medical Inc .... F 888 990-8327
  New York *(G-12167)*
Stand Up Mri of Lynbrook PC .... G 516 256-1558
  Lynbrook *(G-7989)*
Sun Scientific Inc .... G 914 479-5108
  Dobbs Ferry *(G-4327)*
Ultradian Diagnostics LLC .... G 518 618-0046
  Rensselaer *(G-14063)*
Vasomedical Inc .... B 516 997-4600
  Plainview *(G-13668)*
Vermed Inc .... D 800 669-6905
  Buffalo *(G-3267)*
Visiplex Instruments Corp .... D 845 365-0190
  Elmsford *(G-4798)*
Z-Axis Inc .... D 315 548-5000
  Phelps *(G-13563)*

ELECTRON TUBES

Harris Corporation .... E 585 244-5830
  Rochester *(G-14446)*
Y & Z Precision Inc .... F 516 349-8243
  Plainview *(G-13676)*

ELECTRON TUBES: Cathode Ray

Passur Aerospace Inc .... G 631 589-6800
  Bohemia *(G-1111)*
Thomas Electronics Inc .... C 315 923-2051
  Clyde *(G-3757)*

ELECTRONIC COMPONENTS

Bud Barger Assoc Inc .... G 631 696-6703
  Farmingville *(G-5167)*
Haynes Roberts Inc .... F 212 989-1901
  New York *(G-10476)*
Lighthouse Components .... E 917 993-6820
  New York *(G-11027)*
Marcon Electronic Systems LLC .... G 516 633-6396
  Freeport *(G-5420)*
Mezmeriz Inc .... G 607 216-8140
  Ithaca *(G-6897)*
MLS Sales .... G 516 681-2736
  Bethpage *(G-873)*
Sln Group Inc .... G 718 677-5969
  Brooklyn *(G-2598)*
Space Coast Semiconductor Inc .... F 631 414-7131
  Farmingdale *(G-5123)*

ELECTRONIC DETECTION SYSTEMS: Aeronautical

Accutrak Inc .... F 212 925-5330
  New York *(G-9061)*

ELECTRONIC DEVICES: Solid State, NEC

Autodyne Manufacturing Co Inc .... F 631 957-5858
  Lindenhurst *(G-7478)*
Automated Control Logic Inc .... F 914 769-8880
  Thornwood *(G-16139)*
Bharat Electronics Limited .... G 516 248-4021
  Garden City *(G-5510)*
DJS Nyc Inc .... G 845 445-8618
  Monsey *(G-8606)*
Enrg Inc .... F 716 873-2939
  Buffalo *(G-2954)*
Orbit International Corp .... C 631 435-8300
  Hauppauge *(G-6180)*
Piezo Electronics Research .... F 845 735-9349
  Pearl River *(G-13487)*
Sonotec US Inc .... C 631 415-4758
  Islandia *(G-6842)*
Thermo Cidtec Inc .... E 315 451-9410
  Liverpool *(G-7580)*

ELECTRONIC EQPT REPAIR SVCS

Ah Elctronic Test Eqp Repr Ctr .... F 631 234-8979
  Central Islip *(G-3509)*
Alexy Associates Inc .... E 845 482-3000
  Bethel *(G-858)*
Custom Sound and Video .... E 585 424-5000
  Rochester *(G-14317)*

ELECTRONIC LOADS & POWER SPLYS

Berkshire Transformer .... G 631 467-5328
  Central Islip *(G-3512)*
D & S Supplies Inc .... F 718 721-5256
  Astoria *(G-432)*
Engagement Technology LLC .... F 914 591-7600
  Elmsford *(G-4759)*
Eni Technology Inc .... B 585 427-8300
  Rochester *(G-14374)*
Mechanical Pwr Conversion LLC .... F 607 766-9620
  Binghamton *(G-930)*
New York Digital Corporation .... F 631 630-9798
  Huntington Station *(G-6755)*
Prime Electronic Components .... F 631 254-0101
  Deer Park *(G-4217)*
Pvi Solar Inc .... G 212 280-2100
  New York *(G-11784)*
SC Textiles Inc .... F 631 944-6262
  Huntington *(G-6718)*
Superior Motion Controls Inc .... F 516 420-2921
  Farmingdale *(G-5130)*
Three Five III-V Materials Inc .... F 212 213-8290
  New York *(G-12352)*
Ultralife Corporation .... A 315 332-7100
  Newark *(G-12766)*

ELECTRONIC PARTS & EQPT WHOLESALERS

Apex Signal Corporation .... D 631 567-1100
  Bohemia *(G-1013)*
Apollo Display Tech Corp .... E 631 580-4360
  Ronkonkoma *(G-14899)*
Becker Electronics Inc .... D 631 619-9100
  Ronkonkoma *(G-14907)*
Canfield Electronics Inc .... F 631 585-4100
  Lindenhurst *(G-7480)*
Claddagh Electronics Ltd .... F 718 784-0571
  Long Island City *(G-7728)*
Cypress Semiconductor Corp .... F 631 261-1358
  Northport *(G-13028)*
Electronic Devices Inc .... E 914 965-4400
  Yonkers *(G-17456)*
Forerunner Technologies Inc .... E 631 337-2100
  Bohemia *(G-1063)*
G B International Trdg Co Ltd .... C 607 785-0938
  Endicott *(G-4817)*
General Microwave Corporation .... F 516 802-0900
  Syosset *(G-15844)*
High Frequency Tech Co Inc .... G 631 242-3020
  Deer Park *(G-4171)*
Htf Components Inc .... G 914 703-6795
  White Plains *(G-17149)*
Hudson Xinde Energy Inc .... G 212 220-7112
  New York *(G-10573)*
Iba Industrial Inc .... E 631 254-6800
  Edgewood *(G-4614)*
Iconix Inc .... F 516 513-1420
  Hauppauge *(G-6120)*
Jaguar Industries Inc .... G 845 947-1800
  Haverstraw *(G-6261)*
Kinetic Marketing Inc .... G 212 620-0600
  New York *(G-10890)*
L K Manufacturing Corp .... E 631 243-6910
  West Babylon *(G-16834)*
Mill-Max Mfg Corp .... C 516 922-6000
  Oyster Bay *(G-13397)*
New Sensor Corporation .... D 718 937-8300
  Long Island City *(G-7856)*
Omntec Mfg Inc .... E 631 981-2001
  Ronkonkoma *(G-14985)*
Ramsey Electronics LLC .... E 585 924-4560
  Victor *(G-16522)*
Sag Harbor Industries Inc .... E 631 725-0440
  Sag Harbor *(G-15107)*
Semitronics Corp .... E 516 223-0200
  Freeport *(G-5437)*
Switching Power Inc .... D 631 981-7231
  Ronkonkoma *(G-15013)*
Ultravolt Inc .... D 631 471-4444
  Ronkonkoma *(G-15020)*
Ying Ke Youth Age Group Inc .... F 929 402-8458
  Dix Hills *(G-4323)*

ELECTRONIC SHOPPING

Scientifics Direct Inc .... F 716 773-7500
  Tonawanda *(G-16220)*

ELECTRONIC TRAINING DEVICES

Ces Industries Inc .... E 631 782-7088
  Islandia *(G-6828)*
Full Circle Studios LLC .... G 716 875-7740
  Buffalo *(G-2975)*
Rockwell Collins Simulation .... D 607 352-1298
  Binghamton *(G-942)*
Telephonics Corporation .... D 631 755-7000
  Farmingdale *(G-5138)*
Telephonics Corporation .... D 631 470-8800
  Huntington *(G-6724)*

ELECTROPLATING & PLATING SVC

G J C Ltd Inc .... E 607 770-4500
  Binghamton *(G-912)*
General Galvanizing Sup Co Inc .... E 718 589-4300
  Bronx *(G-1345)*
Metal Man Restoration .... F 914 662-4218
  Mount Vernon *(G-8750)*
Psb Ltd .... F 585 654-7078
  Rochester *(G-14630)*

ELEVATORS & EQPT

A & D Entrances LLC .... F 718 989-2441
  Wyandanch *(G-17384)*
An Excelsior Elevator Corp .... F 516 408-3070
  Westbury *(G-16995)*
Bhi Elevator Cabs Inc .... F 516 431-5665
  Island Park *(G-6818)*
CEC Elevator Cab Corp .... D 718 328-3632
  Bronx *(G-1292)*
Dural Door Company Inc .... F 718 729-1333
  Long Island City *(G-7749)*
E Z Entry Doors Inc .... F 716 434-3440
  Lockport *(G-7611)*
Elevator Accessories Mfg .... F 914 739-7004
  Peekskill *(G-13501)*
Herbert Wolf Corp .... G 212 242-0300
  New York *(G-10504)*
Interface Products Co Inc .... G 631 242-4605
  Bay Shore *(G-705)*

Employee Codes: A=Over 500 employees, B=251-500
C=101-250, D=51-100, E=20-50, F=10-19, G=5-9

ELEVATORS & EQPT

Keystone Iron & Wire Works Inc .... G 844 258-7986
 East Rockaway *(G-4490)*
Monitor Elevator Products LLC .... D 631 543-4334
 Hauppauge *(G-6169)*
National Elev Cab & Door Corp .... E 718 478-5900
 Woodside *(G-17357)*
Otis Elevator Company .... F 315 736-0167
 Yorkville *(G-17543)*
Otis Elevator Company .... E 917 339-9600
 New York *(G-11547)*
Otis Elevator Company .... G 914 375-7800
 Yonkers *(G-17491)*
Otis Elevator Company .... E 518 426-4006
 Albany *(G-113)*
Schindler Elevator Corporation .... C 718 417-3131
 Glendale *(G-5678)*
Schindler Elevator Corporation .... D 516 860-1321
 Hicksville *(G-6419)*
Schindler Elevator Corporation .... E 800 225-3123
 New York *(G-12006)*

ELEVATORS WHOLESALERS

An Excelsior Elevator Corp .... F 516 408-3070
 Westbury *(G-16995)*
EZ Lift Operator Corp .... F 845 356-1676
 Spring Valley *(G-15606)*

ELEVATORS: Installation & Conversion

Schindler Elevator Corporation .... E 800 225-3123
 New York *(G-12006)*

ELEVATORS: Stair, Motor Powered

S & H Enterprises Inc .... G 888 323-8755
 Queensbury *(G-14023)*

EMBLEMS: Embroidered

A Garys Treasures .... F 518 383-1171
 Clifton Park *(G-3719)*
Eagle Regalia Co Inc .... F 845 425-2245
 Spring Valley *(G-15604)*
Glenda Inc .... G 718 442-8981
 Staten Island *(G-15699)*
Quist Industries Ltd .... F 718 243-2800
 Brooklyn *(G-2487)*
Voyager Emblems Inc .... C 416 255-3421
 Buffalo *(G-3271)*

EMBOSSING SVC: Paper

Welsh Gold Stampers Inc .... E 718 984-5031
 Staten Island *(G-15776)*

EMBROIDERING & ART NEEDLEWORK FOR THE TRADE

Active World Solutions Inc .... G 718 922-9404
 Brooklyn *(G-1558)*
Aditiany Inc .... G 212 997-8440
 New York *(G-9076)*
All American Awards Inc .... F 631 567-2025
 Bohemia *(G-1007)*
Clinton Clrs & EMB Shoppe Inc .... G 315 853-8421
 Clinton *(G-3743)*
Control Research Inc .... G 631 225-1111
 Amityville *(G-281)*
Design Archives Inc .... G 212 768-0617
 New York *(G-9904)*
Eiseman-Ludmar Co Inc .... F 516 932-6990
 Hicksville *(G-6372)*
Expressions Punching & Digitiz .... G 718 291-1177
 Jamaica *(G-6947)*
Holland & Sherry Inc .... E 212 542-8410
 New York *(G-10540)*
Instant Monogramming Inc .... G 585 654-5550
 Rochester *(G-14471)*
Kabrics .... G 607 962-6344
 Corning *(G-3996)*
Karishma Fashions Inc .... G 718 565-5404
 Jackson Heights *(G-6923)*
Kevin J Kassman .... G 585 529-4245
 Rochester *(G-14491)*
Loremanss Embroidery Engrav .... F 518 834-9205
 Keeseville *(G-7168)*
Mrinalini Inc .... G 646 510-2747
 New York *(G-11339)*
Northeast Stitches & Ink Inc .... E 518 798-5549
 South Glens Falls *(G-15551)*
Planet Embroidery .... F 718 381-4827
 Ridgewood *(G-14130)*
Point Canvas Company Inc .... G 607 692-4381
 Whitney Point *(G-17249)*
River Rat Design .... F 315 393-4770
 Ogdensburg *(G-13142)*
Ross L Sports Screening Inc .... F 716 824-5350
 Buffalo *(G-3195)*
Round Top Knit & Screening .... G 518 622-3600
 Round Top *(G-15064)*
Royal Tees Inc .... G 845 357-9448
 Suffern *(G-15820)*
Sand Hill Industries Inc .... G 518 885-7991
 Ballston Spa *(G-607)*
Sciane Enterprises Inc .... G 845 452-2400
 Poughkeepsie *(G-13949)*
Screen Gems Inc .... G 845 561-0036
 New Windsor *(G-8999)*
Shykat Promotions .... G 866 574-2757
 Forestville *(G-5343)*
Stephen M Kiernan .... G 716 836-6300
 Buffalo *(G-3224)*
U All Inc .... E 518 438-2558
 Albany *(G-144)*
U S Embroidery Inc .... G 718 585-9662
 Bronx *(G-1482)*
Uniform Namemakers Inc .... G 716 626-5474
 Buffalo *(G-3259)*
Wicked Smart LLC .... G 518 459-2855
 Watervliet *(G-16717)*

EMBROIDERING SVC

All About Art Inc .... F 718 321-0755
 Flushing *(G-5232)*
American Quality Embroidery .... G 631 467-3200
 Ronkonkoma *(G-14895)*
Arena Graphics Inc .... G 516 767-5108
 Port Washington *(G-13823)*
East Coast Embroidery Ltd .... G 631 254-3878
 Deer Park *(G-4155)*
F X Graphix Inc .... G 716 871-1511
 Buffalo *(G-2957)*
Hosel & Ackerson Inc .... G 212 575-1490
 New York *(G-10552)*
Human Technologies Corporation .... F 315 735-3532
 Utica *(G-16364)*
Mainly Monograms Inc .... E 845 624-4923
 West Nyack *(G-16949)*
Monte Goldman Embroidery Co .... F 212 874-5397
 New York *(G-11327)*
NY Embroidery Inc .... G 516 822-6456
 Hicksville *(G-6403)*
On The Job Embroidery & AP .... G 914 381-3556
 Mamaroneck *(G-8073)*
Penn & Fletcher Inc .... F 212 239-6868
 Long Island City *(G-7870)*
Rescuestuff Inc .... G 718 318-7570
 Peekskill *(G-13505)*

EMBROIDERING SVC: Schiffli Machine

American Images Inc .... F 716 825-8888
 Buffalo *(G-2825)*
Rmb Embroidery Service .... G 585 271-5560
 Rochester *(G-14652)*

EMBROIDERING: Swiss Loom

Stucki Embroidery Works Inc .... F 845 657-2308
 Boiceville *(G-1155)*

EMBROIDERY ADVERTISING SVCS

Dray Enterprises Inc .... F 585 768-2201
 Le Roy *(G-7431)*
Northeast Promotional Group In .... G 518 793-1024
 South Glens Falls *(G-15550)*

EMERGENCY ALARMS

All Metro Emrgncy Response Sys .... G 516 750-9100
 Lynbrook *(G-7973)*
Lifewatch Inc .... F 800 716-1433
 Hewlett *(G-6333)*
Napco Security Tech Inc .... A 631 842-9400
 Amityville *(G-313)*
Octopus Advanced Systems Inc .... G 914 771-6110
 Yonkers *(G-17488)*
Personal Alarm SEC Systems .... F 212 448-1944
 New York *(G-11647)*
Simplexgrinnell LP .... D 585 288-6200
 Rochester *(G-14711)*
Simplexgrinnell LP .... E 518 952-6040
 Clifton Park *(G-3734)*
Simplexgrinnell LP .... G 845 774-4120
 Harriman *(G-5996)*
Simplexgrinnell LP .... E 315 437-4660
 East Syracuse *(G-4578)*
Simplexgrinnell LP .... F 607 338-5100
 East Syracuse *(G-4579)*
Synergx Systems Inc .... D 516 433-4700
 Woodside *(G-17374)*
Telemergency Ltd .... G 914 629-4222
 White Plains *(G-17202)*
Telephonics Corporation .... F 631 755-7000
 Huntington *(G-6723)*

EMPLOYMENT AGENCY SVCS

Equal Opprtnity Pblcations Inc .... F 631 421-9421
 Melville *(G-8344)*
Symphony Talent LLC .... D 212 999-9000
 New York *(G-12279)*
Vaultcom Inc .... E 212 366-4212
 New York *(G-12535)*

ENAMELING SVC: Metal Prdts, Including Porcelain

F & H Metal Finishing Co Inc .... F 585 798-2151
 Medina *(G-8304)*

ENAMELS

Si Group Inc .... C 518 347-4200
 Schenectady *(G-15319)*

ENCLOSURES: Electronic

Compac Development Corporation .... D 631 881-4903
 Hauppauge *(G-6072)*
Fabrication Specialties Corp .... G 631 242-0326
 Deer Park *(G-4163)*
Kerns Manufacturing Corp .... C 718 784-4044
 Long Island City *(G-7807)*
National Computer & Electronic .... G 631 242-7222
 Deer Park *(G-4201)*

ENERGY MEASUREMENT EQPT

New York Enrgy Synthetics Inc .... G 212 634-4787
 New York *(G-11421)*
Performance Systems Contg Inc .... E 607 277-6240
 Ithaca *(G-6904)*
Urban Green Energy Inc .... E 917 720-5681
 New York *(G-12499)*

ENGINE REBUILDING: Diesel

D & W Diesel Inc .... F 518 437-1300
 Latham *(G-7387)*
Jack W Miller .... G 585 538-2399
 Scottsville *(G-15359)*

ENGINE REBUILDING: Gas

Washer Solutions Inc .... F 585 742-6388
 Victor *(G-16536)*

ENGINEERING SVCS

901 D LLC .... E 845 369-1111
 Airmont *(G-10)*
Acad Design Corp .... F 585 254-6960
 Rochester *(G-14179)*
Acme Engineering Products Inc .... E 518 236-5659
 Mooers *(G-8654)*
Alstom Transportation Inc .... E 212 692-5353
 New York *(G-9155)*
Alstom Transportation Inc .... E 800 717-4477
 West Henrietta *(G-16899)*
American Avionic Tech Corp .... D 631 924-8200
 Medford *(G-8266)*
Atlantic Industrial Tech Inc .... E 631 234-3131
 Shirley *(G-15437)*
Avanti Control Systems Inc .... G 518 921-4368
 Gloversville *(G-5722)*
Beltran Technologies Inc .... E 718 338-3311
 Brooklyn *(G-1678)*
Benfield Control Systems Inc .... E 914 948-6660
 White Plains *(G-17112)*
Bombardier Trnsp Holdings USA .... D 607 776-4791
 Bath *(G-654)*
Bsu Inc .... E 607 272-8100
 Ithaca *(G-6867)*
Critical Link LLC .... E 315 425-4045
 Syracuse *(G-15932)*

PRODUCT SECTION

ETCHING & ENGRAVING SVC

Dayton T Brown Inc ....B....... 631 589-6300
  Bohemia *(G-1048)*
Della Systems Inc ....F....... 631 580-0010
  Ronkonkoma *(G-14921)*
Digitronik Dev Labs Inc ....F....... 585 360-0043
  Rochester *(G-14329)*
Excalbur Brnze Sculpture Fndry ....E....... 718 366-3444
  Brooklyn *(G-1947)*
H S Assembly Inc ....G....... 585 266-4287
  Rochester *(G-14436)*
Howden North America Inc ....D....... 716 817-6900
  Depew *(G-4284)*
Interntnal Elctronic Mchs Corp ...E....... 518 268-1636
  Troy *(G-16263)*
Linita Design & Mfg Corp ....E....... 716 566-7753
  Lackawanna *(G-7270)*
Lourdes Industries Inc ....D....... 631 234-6600
  Hauppauge *(G-6146)*
Millennium Antenna Corp ....F....... 315 798-9374
  Utica *(G-16372)*
Optics Technology Inc ....G....... 585 586-0950
  Pittsford *(G-13599)*
Photon Gear Inc ....F....... 585 265-3360
  Ontario *(G-13231)*
Remington Arms Company LLC ....A....... 315 895-3482
  Ilion *(G-6783)*
Rt Solutions LLC ....G....... 585 245-3456
  Rochester *(G-14683)*
Sg Blocks Inc ....G....... 615 585-2639
  Brooklyn *(G-2573)*
SOS International LLC ....C....... 212 742-2410
  New York *(G-12166)*
Stone Well Bodies & Mch Inc ....E....... 315 497-3512
  Genoa *(G-5602)*

ENGINEERING SVCS: Building Construction

Roth Design & Consulting Inc ....E....... 718 209-0193
  Brooklyn *(G-2529)*

ENGINEERING SVCS: Electrical Or Electronic

C Speed LLC ....E....... 315 453-1043
  Liverpool *(G-7537)*
Nervve Technologies Inc ....E....... 716 800-2250
  New York *(G-11391)*
Tkm Technologies Inc ....G....... 631 474-4700
  Port Jeff STA *(G-13796)*

ENGINEERING SVCS: Heating & Ventilation

Vincent Genovese ....G....... 631 281-8170
  Mastic Beach *(G-8237)*

ENGINEERING SVCS: Industrial

Advanced Machine Design Co Inc ....E....... 716 826-2000
  Buffalo *(G-2817)*

ENGINEERING SVCS: Marine

L-3 Cmmnctons Ntronix Holdings ....D....... 212 697-1111
  New York *(G-10942)*

ENGINEERING SVCS: Mechanical

Calvary Design Team Inc ....C....... 585 347-6127
  Webster *(G-16738)*

ENGINEERING SVCS: Petroleum

Amincor Inc ....C....... 347 821-3452
  New York *(G-9186)*

ENGINEERING SVCS: Pollution Control

Clean Gas Systems Inc ....E....... 631 467-1600
  Hauppauge *(G-6066)*

ENGINEERING SVCS: Professional

Nasiff Associates Inc ....G....... 315 676-2346
  Central Square *(G-3544)*

ENGINEERING SVCS: Sanitary

Nes Bearing Company Inc ....E....... 716 372-6532
  Olean *(G-13173)*

ENGINEERING SVCS: Structural

Marovato Industries Inc ....F....... 718 389-0800
  Brooklyn *(G-2277)*

Tebbens Steel LLC ....F....... 631 208-8330
  Calverton *(G-3329)*

ENGINES: Internal Combustion, NEC

AB Engine ....G....... 518 557-3510
  Latham *(G-7377)*
Briggs & Stratton Corporation ....F....... 315 495-0100
  Sherrill *(G-15426)*
Briggs & Stratton Corporation ....C....... 315 495-0100
  Munnsville *(G-8795)*
Cummins - Allison Corp ....D....... 718 263-2482
  Kew Gardens *(G-7188)*
Cummins Inc ....D....... 716 456-2676
  Lakewood *(G-7313)*
Cummins Inc ....A....... 716 456-2111
  Lakewood *(G-7314)*
Cummins Inc ....B....... 812 377-5000
  Jamestown *(G-7021)*
Cummins Inc ....B....... 718 892-2400
  Bronx *(G-1308)*
Cummins Northeast LLC ....E....... 315 437-2296
  Syracuse *(G-15935)*
Mannesmann Corporation ....D....... 212 258-4000
  New York *(G-11160)*
Perkins International Inc ....G....... 309 675-1000
  Buffalo *(G-3144)*

ENGINES: Jet Propulsion

Omega Industries & Development ....E....... 516 349-8010
  Plainview *(G-13654)*

ENGRAVING SVC, NEC

Aldine Inc (ny) ....D....... 212 226-2870
  New York *(G-9129)*
Bates Jackson Engraving Co Inc ....E....... 716 854-3000
  Buffalo *(G-2855)*
Tripi Engraving Co Inc ....E....... 718 383-6500
  Brooklyn *(G-2700)*
Zan Optics Products Inc ....E....... 718 435-0533
  Brooklyn *(G-2794)*

ENGRAVING SVC: Jewelry & Personal Goods

Ashburns Inc ....G....... 212 227-5692
  New York *(G-9281)*
Eastern Silver of Boro Park ....G....... 718 854-5600
  Brooklyn *(G-1900)*
Rayana Designs Inc ....E....... 718 786-2040
  Long Island City *(G-7889)*

ENGRAVING SVCS

Loremanss Embroidery Engrav ..F....... 518 834-9205
  Keeseville *(G-7168)*
Mooney-Keehley Inc ....G....... 585 271-1573
  Rochester *(G-14541)*

ENGRAVING: Steel line, For The Printing Trade

Lgn Materials & Solutions ....F....... 888 414-0005
  Mount Vernon *(G-8747)*

ENGRAVINGS: Plastic

Custom House Engravers Inc .....G....... 631 567-3004
  Bohemia *(G-1042)*

ENTERTAINERS & ENTERTAINMENT GROUPS

Comsec Ventures International ....E....... 518 523-1600
  Lake Placid *(G-7297)*
G Schirmer Inc ....G....... 212 254-2100
  New York *(G-10280)*
Tele-Pak Inc ....E....... 845 426-2300
  Monsey *(G-8620)*

ENTERTAINMENT SVCS

Marvel Entertainment LLC ....C....... 212 576-4000
  New York *(G-11193)*

ENVELOPES

Apec Paper Industries Ltd ....G....... 212 730-0088
  New York *(G-9222)*
Buffalo Envelope Inc ....F....... 716 686-0100
  Depew *(G-4274)*
Cambridge-Pacific Inc ....E....... 518 677-5988
  Cambridge *(G-3333)*

Cenveo Inc ....D....... 716 662-2800
  Orchard Park *(G-13283)*
Conformer Products Inc ....F....... 516 504-6300
  Great Neck *(G-5817)*
CPW Direct Mail Group LLC ......E....... 631 588-6565
  Farmingdale *(G-4975)*
East Cast Envlepe Graphics LLC ....E....... 718 326-2424
  Maspeth *(G-8165)*
Jacmax Industries LLC ....G....... 718 439-3743
  Brooklyn *(G-2129)*
Kleer-Fax Inc ....D....... 631 225-1100
  Amityville *(G-303)*
Mercury Envelope Co Inc ....E....... 516 678-6744
  Rockville Centre *(G-14824)*
Old Ue LLC ....B....... 718 707-0700
  Long Island City *(G-7861)*
Poly-Pak Industries Inc ....B....... 631 293-6767
  Melville *(G-8377)*
Premier Packaging Corporation ....E....... 585 924-8460
  Victor *(G-16520)*
Rochester 100 Inc ....C....... 585 475-0200
  Rochester *(G-14655)*
Westrock Mwv LLC ....C....... 212 688-5000
  New York *(G-12645)*
X-L Envelope and Printing Inc ....F....... 716 852-2135
  Buffalo *(G-3284)*

ENVELOPES WHOLESALERS

A C Envelope Inc ....G....... 516 420-0646
  Farmingdale *(G-4933)*
Apec Paper Industries Ltd ....G....... 212 730-0088
  New York *(G-9222)*
Buffalo Envelope Inc ....F....... 716 686-0100
  Depew *(G-4274)*
Diversified Envelope Ltd ....F....... 585 615-4697
  Rochester *(G-14333)*
Matt Industries Inc ....E....... 315 472-1316
  Syracuse *(G-16005)*
Prestige Envelope & Lithograph ....F....... 631 521-7043
  Merrick *(G-8426)*

ENVIRONMENTAL QUALITY PROGS ADMIN, GOVT: Waste Management

City of New York ....C....... 718 236-2693
  Brooklyn *(G-1782)*

ENZYMES

D-Best Equipment Corp ....E....... 516 358-0965
  West Hempstead *(G-16883)*
Zymtrnix Catalytic Systems Inc ....G....... 918 694-8206
  Ithaca *(G-6920)*

EPOXY RESINS

American Epoxy and Metal Inc ....G....... 718 828-7828
  Scarsdale *(G-15245)*
Astro Chemical Company Inc ....E....... 518 399-5338
  Ballston Lake *(G-578)*
John C Dolph Company Inc ....E....... 732 329-2333
  Schenectady *(G-15298)*

EQUIPMENT: Pedestrian Traffic Control

Cq Traffic Control Devices LLC ....G....... 518 767-0057
  Selkirk *(G-15376)*

EQUIPMENT: Rental & Leasing, NEC

Beck Vault Company ....G....... 315 337-7590
  Rome *(G-14835)*
G E Inspection Technologies LP ....C....... 315 554-2000
  Skaneateles *(G-15481)*
Millennium Stl Rack Rntals Inc ....G....... 718 965-4736
  Brooklyn *(G-2320)*
Mobile Mini Inc ....F....... 315 732-4555
  Utica *(G-16373)*
Raymond Corporation ....A....... 800 235-7200
  Greene *(G-5887)*
Raymond Corporation ....E....... 315 643-5000
  East Syracuse *(G-4572)*

ESCALATORS: Passenger & Freight

Allround Logistics Inc ....G....... 718 544-8945
  Forest Hills *(G-5326)*

ETCHING & ENGRAVING SVC

Accurate Pnt Powdr Coating Inc ....F....... 585 235-1650
  Rochester *(G-14182)*

Employee Codes: A=Over 500 employees, B=251-500
C=101-250, D=51-100, E=20-50, F=10-19, G=5-9

ETCHING & ENGRAVING SVC

Advanced Coating Service LLC..........G....... 585 247-3970
　Rochester *(G-14192)*
Ascribe Inc..E....... 585 413-0298
　Rochester *(G-14234)*
Custom House Engravers Inc..........G....... 631 567-3004
　Bohemia *(G-1042)*
Custom Laser Inc..............................E....... 716 434-8600
　Lockport *(G-7606)*
Everlasting Images............................E....... 607 785-8743
　Endicott *(G-4814)*
Precision Laser Technology LLC.....F....... 585 458-6208
　Rochester *(G-14616)*
Steel Partners Holdings LP..............E....... 212 520-2300
　New York *(G-12212)*
Stuart-Dean Co Inc............................F....... 718 472-1326
　Long Island City *(G-7921)*

ETCHING SVC: Metal

Jamestown Bronze Works Inc..........G....... 716 665-2302
　Jamestown *(G-7039)*

ETCHING SVC: Photochemical

Newchem Inc.....................................E....... 315 331-7680
　Newark *(G-12759)*

ETHANOLAMINES

Western New York Energy LLC........E....... 585 798-9693
　Medina *(G-8317)*

ETHYLENE-PROPYLENE RUBBERS: EPDM Polymers

Hilord Chemical Corporation............E....... 631 234-7373
　Hauppauge *(G-6117)*

EXCAVATING EQPT

Kinshofer Usa Inc..............................E....... 716 731-4333
　Sanborn *(G-15150)*

EXPANSION JOINTS: Rubber

Mercer Rubber Co..............................C....... 631 348-0282
　Hauppauge *(G-6158)*

EXPLOSIVES

Dyno Nobel Inc..................................D....... 845 338-2144
　Ulster Park *(G-16308)*
Maxam North America Inc...............G....... 313 322-8651
　Ogdensburg *(G-13139)*

EXPLOSIVES, EXC AMMO & FIREWORKS WHOLESALERS

Island Ordnance Systems LLC.......F....... 516 746-2100
　Mineola *(G-8550)*
Maxam North America Inc...............G....... 313 322-8651
　Ogdensburg *(G-13139)*

EXTENSION CORDS

Ncc Ny LLC..E....... 718 943-7000
　Brooklyn *(G-2363)*

EXTRACTS, FLAVORING

Craftmaster Flavor Technology........F....... 631 789-8607
　Amityville *(G-282)*

EXTRACTS: Dying Or Tanning, Natural

Prismatic Dyeing & Finshg Inc........D....... 845 561-1800
　Newburgh *(G-12798)*

EYEGLASS CASES

Montana Global LLC..........................G....... 212 213-1572
　Jamaica *(G-6970)*

EYEGLASSES

Colors In Optics Ltd..........................D....... 718 845-0300
　New Hyde Park *(G-8867)*
Corinne McCormack Inc...................F....... 212 868-7919
　New York *(G-9785)*
Essilor Laboratories Amer Inc..........E....... 845 365-6700
　Orangeburg *(G-13248)*
Frame Works America Inc................E....... 631 288-1300
　Westhampton Beach *(G-17087)*
Hirsch Optical Corp............................D....... 516 752-2211
　Farmingdale *(G-5013)*
Humanware USA Inc.........................E....... 800 722-3393
　Champlain *(G-3570)*
M Factory USA Inc............................G....... 917 410-7878
　Brooklyn *(G-2251)*
Optogenics of Syracuse Inc.............D....... 315 446-3000
　Syracuse *(G-16026)*
Parker Warby Retail Inc....................E....... 646 517-5223
　New York *(G-11589)*

EYEGLASSES: Sunglasses

Xinya International Trading Co........G....... 212 216-9681
　New York *(G-12704)*

EYES: Artificial

Mager & Gougelman Inc...................G....... 212 661-3939
　New York *(G-11127)*
Mager & Gougelman Inc...................G....... 212 661-3939
　Hempstead *(G-6302)*
Mager & Gougelman Inc...................G....... 516 489-0202
　Hempstead *(G-6303)*
Mark F Rosenhaft N A O..................G....... 516 374-1010
　Cedarhurst *(G-3485)*
Strauss Eye Prosthetics Inc.............G....... 585 424-1350
　Rochester *(G-14729)*

FABRIC FINISHING: Mending, Wool

Woolmark Americas Inc...................G....... 347 767-3160
　New York *(G-12685)*

FABRIC STORES

Creation Baumann USA Inc.............E....... 516 764-7431
　Rockville Centre *(G-14818)*
Lifestyle Design Usa Ltd..................G....... 212 279-9400
　New York *(G-11021)*
Missiontex Inc...................................F....... 718 532-9053
　Brooklyn *(G-2327)*

FABRICATED METAL PRODUCTS, NEC

Albany Mtal Fbrcation Holdings......G....... 518 463-5161
　Albany *(G-40)*
Atech-Seh Metal Fabricator..............E....... 716 895-8888
　Buffalo *(G-2841)*
Brooklyn Cstm Met Fbrction Inc......G....... 718 499-1573
　Brooklyn *(G-1723)*
Factory East.......................................E....... 718 280-1558
　Brooklyn *(G-1957)*
James D Rubino Inc..........................G....... 631 244-8730
　Bohemia *(G-1076)*
Kwong CHI Metal Fabrication..........G....... 718 369-6429
　Brooklyn *(G-2184)*
PBL Industries Corp..........................F....... 631 979-4266
　Smithtown *(G-15516)*
Range Repair Warehouse.................G....... 585 235-0980
　Penfield *(G-13525)*
Total Metal Resource........................F....... 718 384-7818
　Brooklyn *(G-2688)*

FABRICS & CLOTH: Quilted

American Country Quilts & Lin........G....... 631 283-5466
　Southampton *(G-15562)*
Pink Inc..E....... 212 352-8282
　New York *(G-11685)*

FABRICS: Alpacas, Mohair, Woven

Alicia Adams Alpaca Inc...................G....... 845 868-3366
　Millbrook *(G-8510)*

FABRICS: Apparel & Outerwear, Broadwoven

Equissentials LLC.............................F....... 607 432-2856
　Oneonta *(G-13208)*
Interaxissourcingcom Inc.................E....... 212 905-6001
　New York *(G-10666)*
Light House Hill Marketing...............F....... 212 354-1338
　New York *(G-11024)*
Nazim Izzak Inc.................................G....... 212 920-5546
　Long Island City *(G-7852)*
Oakhurst Partners LLC.....................G....... 212 502-3220
　New York *(G-11505)*
Pinder International Inc....................G....... 631 273-0324
　Hauppauge *(G-6190)*
Yarnz International Inc.....................G....... 212 868-5883
　New York *(G-12711)*

FABRICS: Apparel & Outerwear, Cotton

A and J Apparel Corp........................G....... 212 398-8899
　New York *(G-9030)*
A3 Apparel LLC..................................G....... 888 403-9669
　New York *(G-9043)*
Accolade USA Inc..............................C....... 866 423-5071
　Cheektowaga *(G-3590)*
Advanced Fashions Technology.....G....... 212 221-0606
　New York *(G-9092)*
Alliance Exports LLC.........................G....... 347 208-3547
　New York *(G-9138)*
Bandier Corp.....................................G....... 212 242-5400
　New York *(G-9366)*
Basileus Company LLC....................F....... 315 963-3516
　Manlius *(G-8101)*
Benartex Inc......................................E....... 212 840-3250
　New York *(G-9404)*
Bill Blass Group LLC........................F....... 212 689-8957
　New York *(G-9448)*
Charming Fashion Inc......................G....... 212 730-2872
　New York *(G-9635)*
Creation Baumann USA Inc.............E....... 516 764-7431
　Rockville Centre *(G-14818)*
Cy Fashion Corp................................G....... 212 730-8600
　New York *(G-9832)*
Equipment Apparel LLC...................D....... 212 502-1890
　New York *(G-10105)*
Gw Acquisition LLC...........................E....... 212 736-4848
　New York *(G-10430)*
Hanesbrands Inc...............................G....... 212 576-9300
　New York *(G-10452)*
Harley Robert D Company Ltd........G....... 212 947-1872
　New York *(G-10458)*
Horizon Apparel Mfg Inc..................G....... 516 361-4878
　Atlantic Beach *(G-468)*
Internationl Studios Inc....................G....... 212 819-1616
　New York *(G-10680)*
Knightly Endeavors...........................F....... 845 340-0949
　Kingston *(G-7223)*
Magic Brands International LLC......F....... 212 563-4999
　New York *(G-11130)*
Pacific City International..................F....... 646 309-1250
　New York *(G-11566)*
Phoenix Usa LLC..............................G....... 646 351-6598
　New York *(G-11671)*
Premium 5 Kids LLC.........................F....... 212 563-4999
　New York *(G-11721)*
Refuel Inc..G....... 917 645-2974
　New York *(G-11850)*
Shahin Designs Ltd...........................G....... 212 737-7225
　New York *(G-12060)*
Success Apparel LLC.......................G....... 212 502-1890
　New York *(G-12248)*
US Design Group Ltd.......................G....... 212 354-4070
　New York *(G-12505)*

FABRICS: Apparel & Outerwear, From Manmade Fiber Or Silk

Concepts Nyc Inc..............................E....... 212 244-1033
　New York *(G-9754)*
JM Manufacturer Inc.........................G....... 212 869-0626
　New York *(G-10781)*
New York Poplin LLC........................G....... 718 768-3296
　Brooklyn *(G-2375)*

FABRICS: Automotive, From Manmade Fiber

Maharam Fabric Corporation...........G....... 631 582-3434
　Yaphank *(G-17413)*

FABRICS: Bags & Bagging, Cotton

Nochairs Inc......................................G....... 917 748-8731
　New York *(G-11465)*

FABRICS: Bonded-Fiber, Exc Felt

Imperial Laminators Co Inc..............F....... 718 272-9500
　Brooklyn *(G-2096)*

FABRICS: Broad Woven, Goods, Cotton

Beyond Loom Inc..............................G....... 212 575-3100
　New York *(G-9429)*
Gerli & Co Inc....................................E....... 212 213-1919
　New York *(G-10329)*
Lydall Performance Mtl Inc..............C....... 518 273-6320
　Green Island *(G-5877)*

PRODUCT SECTION

FABRICS: Broadwoven, Cotton

Company	Code	Phone
Ann Gish Inc	G	212 969-9200
New York *(G-9213)*		
Joy of Learning	G	718 443-6463
Brooklyn *(G-2151)*		
Marsha Fleisher	F	845 679-6500
Woodstock *(G-17380)*		
Meder Textile Co Inc	G	516 883-0409
Port Washington *(G-13861)*		
Scalamandre Wallpaper Inc	B	631 467-8800
Hauppauge *(G-6210)*		
Schneider Mills Inc	C	828 632-0801
New York *(G-12013)*		
Westpoint Home LLC	A	212 930-2074
New York *(G-12643)*		
Westpoint International Inc	F	212 930-2044
New York *(G-12644)*		

FABRICS: Broadwoven, Synthetic Manmade Fiber & Silk

Company	Code	Phone
Apex Texicon Inc	E	516 239-4400
New York *(G-9223)*		
Creation Baumann USA Inc	E	516 764-7431
Rockville Centre *(G-14818)*		
Eastern Silk Mills Inc	G	212 730-1300
New York *(G-10017)*		
Fabric Resources Intl Ltd	F	516 829-4550
Great Neck *(G-5825)*		
Fibrix LLC	E	716 683-4100
Depew *(G-4281)*		
Gerli & Co Inc	E	212 213-1919
New York *(G-10329)*		
Ivi Services Inc	D	607 729-5111
Binghamton *(G-924)*		
Jag Manufacturing Inc	E	518 762-9558
Johnstown *(G-7147)*		
Jakob Schlaepfer Inc	G	212 221-2323
New York *(G-10736)*		
Scalamandre Wallpaper Inc	B	631 467-8800
Hauppauge *(G-6210)*		
Schneider Mills Inc	C	828 632-0801
New York *(G-12013)*		
Superior Fiber Mills Inc	E	718 782-7500
Brooklyn *(G-2649)*		
Toltec Fabrics Inc	C	212 706-9310
New York *(G-12378)*		
Toray Industries Inc	G	212 697-8150
New York *(G-12394)*		

FABRICS: Broadwoven, Wool

Company	Code	Phone
Acker & LI Mills Corporation	G	212 307-7247
New York *(G-9065)*		
Citisource Industries Inc	E	212 683-1033
New York *(G-9678)*		
Fabric Resources Intl Ltd	F	516 829-4550
Great Neck *(G-5825)*		
Hawkins Fabrics Inc	E	518 773-9550
Gloversville *(G-5729)*		
Scalamandre Wallpaper Inc	B	631 467-8800
Hauppauge *(G-6210)*		

FABRICS: Brocade, Cotton

Company	Code	Phone
La Lame Inc	G	212 921-9770
New York *(G-10947)*		

FABRICS: Canvas

Company	Code	Phone
Geordie Magee Uphl & Canvas	G	315 676-7679
Brewerton *(G-1200)*		
Sita Finishing Inc	F	718 417-5295
Brooklyn *(G-2594)*		
Taikoh USA Inc	F	646 556-6652
New York *(G-12296)*		

FABRICS: Chemically Coated & Treated

Company	Code	Phone
Kiltronx Enviro Systems LLC	E	917 971-7177
Hauppauge *(G-6129)*		
Perry Plastics Inc	F	718 747-5600
Flushing *(G-5288)*		

FABRICS: Coated Or Treated

Company	Code	Phone
Breton Industries Inc	D	518 842-3030
Amsterdam *(G-337)*		
Chemprene Inc	C	845 831-2800
Beacon *(G-777)*		
Chemprene Holding Inc	C	845 831-2800
Beacon *(G-778)*		
Comfort Care Textiles Inc	E	631 543-0531
Commack *(G-3854)*		
Eurotex Inc	F	716 205-8861
Niagara Falls *(G-12837)*		
Fabric Resources Intl Ltd	F	516 829-4550
Great Neck *(G-5825)*		
Newtex Industries Inc	E	585 924-9135
Victor *(G-16517)*		
Precision Custom Coatings LLC	C	212 868-5770
New York *(G-11717)*		

FABRICS: Cords

Company	Code	Phone
Schoen Trimming & Cord Co Inc	F	212 255-3949
New York *(G-12014)*		

FABRICS: Corduroys, Cotton

Company	Code	Phone
Paramount Cord & Brackets	G	212 325-9100
White Plains *(G-17171)*		

FABRICS: Denims

Company	Code	Phone
AV Denim Inc	E	212 764-6668
New York *(G-9322)*		
Axis Na LLC	F	212 840-4005
New York *(G-9337)*		
Brooklyn Denim Co	F	718 782-2600
Brooklyn *(G-1724)*		
Jrg Apparel Group Company Ltd	E	212 997-0900
New York *(G-10812)*		
SD Eagle Global Inc	G	516 822-1778
Jericho *(G-7118)*		
Xing Lin USA Intl Corp	G	212 947-4846
New York *(G-12703)*		

FABRICS: Elastic, From Manmade Fiber Or Silk

Company	Code	Phone
A B C Elastic Corp	G	718 388-2953
Brooklyn *(G-1530)*		

FABRICS: Fiberglass, Broadwoven

Company	Code	Phone
Fiber Glass Industries Inc	D	518 842-4000
Amsterdam *(G-345)*		
Fiber Glass Industries Inc	D	518 843-3533
Amsterdam *(G-346)*		
Newtex Industries Inc	E	585 924-9135
Victor *(G-16517)*		
Polytex Inc	D	716 549-5100
Angola *(G-381)*		

FABRICS: Glass, Narrow

Company	Code	Phone
Mergence Studios Ltd	F	212 288-5616
Hauppauge *(G-6159)*		

FABRICS: Glove, Lining

Company	Code	Phone
J & M Textile Co Inc	F	212 268-8000
New York *(G-10715)*		

FABRICS: Hand Woven

Company	Code	Phone
Thistle Hill Weavers	G	518 284-2729
Cherry Valley *(G-3624)*		

FABRICS: Handkerchief, Cotton

Company	Code	Phone
Northpoint Trading Inc	F	212 481-8001
New York *(G-11478)*		

FABRICS: Jacquard Woven, From Manmade Fiber Or Silk

Company	Code	Phone
Simplicity Creative Group Inc	A	212 686-7676
New York *(G-12105)*		

FABRICS: Jean

Company	Code	Phone
Apollo Apparel Group LLC	F	212 398-6585
New York *(G-9226)*		

FABRICS: Jersey Cloth

Company	Code	Phone
Cap USA Jerseyman Harlem Inc	G	212 222-7942
New York *(G-9572)*		

FABRICS: Lace & Decorative Trim, Narrow

Company	Code	Phone
Eiseman-Ludmar Co Inc	F	516 932-6990
Hicksville *(G-6372)*		

FABRICS: Lace & Lace Prdts

Company	Code	Phone
Orbit Industries LLC	F	914 244-1500
Mount Kisco *(G-8681)*		
Solstiss Inc	G	212 719-9194
New York *(G-12152)*		
Super-Trim Inc	E	212 255-2370
New York *(G-12263)*		

FABRICS: Lace, Knit, NEC

Company	Code	Phone
Hosel & Ackerson Inc	G	212 575-1490
New York *(G-10552)*		
Klauber Brothers Inc	D	212 686-2531
New York *(G-10897)*		

FABRICS: Laminated

Company	Code	Phone
A-One Laminating Corp	G	718 266-6002
Brooklyn *(G-1541)*		
A-One Moving & Storage Inc	E	718 266-6002
Brooklyn *(G-1542)*		
Co2 Textiles LLC	G	212 269-2222
New York *(G-9707)*		
Imperial Laminators Co Inc	E	718 272-9500
Brooklyn *(G-2096)*		
New York Cutting & Gumming Co	E	212 563-4146
Middletown *(G-8489)*		
Tpi Industries LLC	E	845 692-2820
Middletown *(G-8500)*		

FABRICS: Linings & Interlinings, Cotton

Company	Code	Phone
Navas Designs Inc	E	818 988-9050
New York *(G-11382)*		

FABRICS: Long Cloth, Cotton

Company	Code	Phone
Haleys Comet Seafood Corp	E	212 571-1828
New York *(G-10441)*		

FABRICS: Nonwoven

Company	Code	Phone
Albany International Corp	C	518 445-2200
Rensselaer *(G-14053)*		
Fabrication Enterprises Inc	E	914 591-9300
Elmsford *(G-4761)*		
Legendary Auto Interiors Ltd	E	315 331-1212
Newark *(G-12754)*		
Mgk Group Inc	E	212 989-2732
New York *(G-11273)*		
Saint-Gobain Adfors Amer Inc	D	716 775-3900
Grand Island *(G-5783)*		
Saint-Gobain Adfors Amer Inc	D	585 589-4401
Albion *(G-173)*		

FABRICS: Nylon, Broadwoven

Company	Code	Phone
Kragel Co Inc	G	716 648-1344
Hamburg *(G-5955)*		

FABRICS: Paper, Broadwoven

Company	Code	Phone
Albany International Corp	C	518 445-2200
Rensselaer *(G-14053)*		

FABRICS: Pile Warp or Flat Knit

Company	Code	Phone
George Knitting Mills Corp	G	212 242-3300
New York *(G-10326)*		

FABRICS: Pile, Circular Knit

Company	Code	Phone
Hill Knitting Mills Inc	E	718 846-5000
Richmond Hill *(G-14087)*		

FABRICS: Pocketing Twill, Cotton

Company	Code	Phone
Cai Inc	E	212 819-0008
New York *(G-9547)*		

FABRICS: Polyester, Broadwoven

Company	Code	Phone
Marly Home Industries USA Inc	G	718 388-3030
Brooklyn *(G-2276)*		

FABRICS: Print, Cotton

Company	Code	Phone
Neilson International Inc	G	631 454-0400
Farmingdale *(G-5073)*		
Perfect Print Inc	E	718 832-5280
Brooklyn *(G-2430)*		

Employee Codes: A=Over 500 employees, B=251-500
C=101-250, D=51-100, E=20-50, F=10-19, G=5-9

FABRICS: Resin Or Plastic Coated

FABRICS: Resin Or Plastic Coated
GE Polymershapes ....F 516 433-4092
  Hicksville *(G-6376)*
Piedmont Plastics Inc ....G 518 724-0563
  Albany *(G-121)*
Tonoga Inc ....C 518 658-3202
  Petersburg *(G-13551)*

FABRICS: Rubberized
Chemprene Inc ....C 845 831-2800
  Beacon *(G-777)*
Chemprene Holding Inc ....C 845 831-2800
  Beacon *(G-778)*
Kelson Products Inc ....G 716 825-2585
  Orchard Park *(G-13302)*

FABRICS: Shirting, Cotton
Gotham T-Shirt Corp ....G 516 676-0900
  Sea Cliff *(G-15363)*

FABRICS: Shoe
Avitto Leather Goods Inc ....G 212 219-7501
  New York *(G-9332)*

FABRICS: Silk, Broadwoven
Beyond Loom Inc ....G 212 575-3100
  New York *(G-9429)*
Himatsingka America Inc ....E 212 252-0802
  New York *(G-10524)*
Himatsingka Holdings NA Inc ....G 212 545-8929
  New York *(G-10525)*

FABRICS: Silk, Narrow
Solstiss Inc ....G 212 719-9194
  New York *(G-12152)*

FABRICS: Spandex, Broadwoven
La Lame Inc ....G 212 921-9770
  New York *(G-10947)*

FABRICS: Specialty Including Twisted Weaves, Broadwoven
Intertex USA Inc ....F 212 279-3601
  New York *(G-10683)*

FABRICS: Stretch, Cotton
Shindo Usa Inc ....G 212 868-9311
  New York *(G-12074)*

FABRICS: Surgical Fabrics, Cotton
Medline Industries Inc ....B 845 344-3301
  Middletown *(G-8484)*

FABRICS: Tapestry, Cotton
Renaissnce Crpt Tapestries Inc ....F 212 696-0080
  New York *(G-11863)*

FABRICS: Tricot
Hudson Fabrics LLC ....F 518 671-6100
  Hudson *(G-6647)*
Litchfield Fabrics of NC ....G 518 773-9500
  Gloversville *(G-5732)*
Veratex Inc ....F 212 683-9300
  New York *(G-12544)*

FABRICS: Trimmings
Albert Siy ....G 718 359-0389
  Flushing *(G-5231)*
American Spray-On Corp ....E 212 929-2100
  New York *(G-9179)*
Angel Textiles Inc ....G 212 532-0900
  New York *(G-9205)*
Athletic Cap Co Inc ....E 718 398-1300
  Staten Island *(G-15661)*
Barnaby Prints Inc ....F 845 477-2501
  Greenwood Lake *(G-5917)*
Bondy Printing Corp ....G 631 242-1510
  Bay Shore *(G-677)*
C H Thompson Company Inc ....D 607 724-1094
  Binghamton *(G-897)*
Coe Displays Inc ....G 718 937-5658
  Long Island City *(G-7730)*
Cooper & Clement Inc ....E 315 454-8135
  Syracuse *(G-15926)*
D & R Silk Screening Ltd ....F 631 234-7464
  Central Islip *(G-3520)*
Decal Makers Inc ....G 516 221-7200
  Bellmore *(G-813)*
Eagle Lace Dyeing Corp ....F 212 947-2712
  New York *(G-10010)*
Emtron Hybrids Inc ....G 631 924-9668
  Yaphank *(G-17408)*
Flp Group LLC ....F 315 252-7583
  Auburn *(G-495)*
Freeport Screen & Stamping ....G 516 379-0330
  Freeport *(G-5412)*
Ihd Motorsports LLC ....F 979 690-1669
  Binghamton *(G-920)*
Jack J Florio Jr ....G 716 434-9123
  Lockport *(G-7625)*
Kenmar Shirts Inc ....E 718 824-3880
  Bronx *(G-1375)*
L I C Screen Printing Inc ....E 516 546-7289
  Merrick *(G-8421)*
Loremanss Embroidery Engrav ....F 518 834-9205
  Keeseville *(G-7168)*
Master Craft Finishers Inc ....E 631 586-0540
  Deer Park *(G-4195)*
Master Image Printing Inc ....G 914 347-4400
  Elmsford *(G-4772)*
New York Binding Co Inc ....E 718 729-2454
  Long Island City *(G-7857)*
Northeast Stitches & Ink Inc ....E 518 798-5549
  South Glens Falls *(G-15551)*
Round Top Knit & Screening ....G 518 622-3600
  Round Top *(G-15064)*
Sellco Industries Inc ....E 607 756-7594
  Cortland *(G-4068)*
Simplicity Creative Group Inc ....A 212 686-7676
  New York *(G-12105)*
Solidus Industries Inc ....D 607 749-4540
  Homer *(G-6550)*
Todd Walbridge ....G 585 254-3018
  Rochester *(G-14755)*
U All Inc ....E 518 438-2558
  Albany *(G-144)*
Zan Optics Products Inc ....E 718 435-0533
  Brooklyn *(G-2794)*

FABRICS: Trimmings, Textile
American Trim Mfg Inc ....E 518 239-8151
  Durham *(G-4379)*
Bardwil Industries Inc ....E 212 944-1870
  New York *(G-9369)*
Champion Zipper Corp ....G 212 239-0414
  New York *(G-9627)*
Danray Textiles Corp ....F 212 354-5213
  New York *(G-9862)*
Jakob Schlaepfer Inc ....E 212 221-2323
  New York *(G-10736)*
Marketing Action Xecutives Inc ....G 212 971-9155
  New York *(G-11183)*
New Classic Trade Inc ....E 347 822-9052
  Jamaica *(G-6972)*
Scalamandre Silks Inc ....D 212 980-3888
  New York *(G-12002)*
Tamber Knits Inc ....E 212 730-1121
  New York *(G-12298)*

FABRICS: Upholstery, Cotton
Mgk Group Inc ....E 212 989-2732
  New York *(G-11273)*
N Y Contract Seating Inc ....E 718 417-9298
  Maspeth *(G-8183)*

FABRICS: Varnished Glass & Coated Fiberglass
Architectural Fiberglass Corp ....E 631 842-4772
  Copiague *(G-3918)*

FABRICS: Wall Covering, From Manmade Fiber Or Silk
Art People Inc ....G 212 431-4865
  New York *(G-9263)*
Judscott Handprints Ltd ....F 914 347-5515
  Elmsford *(G-4768)*
Mgk Group Inc ....E 212 989-2732
  New York *(G-11273)*
National Contract Industries ....G 212 249-0045
  New York *(G-11370)*

FABRICS: Warp & Flat Knit Prdts
Fab Industries Corp ....E 516 498-3200
  Great Neck *(G-5824)*
Gehring Tricot Corporation ....C 315 429-8551
  Dolgeville *(G-4329)*
Ssjjj Manufacturing LLC ....G 516 498-3200
  Great Neck *(G-5858)*

FABRICS: Warp Knit, Lace & Netting
Apex Aridyne Corp ....G 516 239-4400
  Inwood *(G-6789)*
Binghamton Knitting Co Inc ....E 607 722-6941
  Binghamton *(G-889)*
Helmont Mills Inc ....G 518 568-7913
  Saint Johnsville *(G-15121)*
Ipm US Inc ....G 212 481-7967
  New York *(G-10696)*
Mohawk Fabric Company Inc ....F 518 842-3090
  Amsterdam *(G-359)*
Somerset Industries Inc ....E 518 773-7383
  Gloversville *(G-5737)*
Sunwin Global Industry Inc ....G 646 370-6196
  New York *(G-12261)*

FABRICS: Weft Or Circular Knit
Apex Aridyne Corp ....G 516 239-4400
  Inwood *(G-6789)*
Apex Texicon Inc ....E 516 239-4400
  New York *(G-9223)*
Lemral Knitwear Inc ....D 718 210-0175
  Brooklyn *(G-2211)*
S & W Knitting Mills Inc ....E 718 237-2416
  Brooklyn *(G-2545)*

FABRICS: Woven, Narrow Cotton, Wool, Silk
Albany International Corp ....C 518 445-2200
  Rensselaer *(G-14053)*
American Canvas Binders Corp ....G 914 969-0300
  Yonkers *(G-17430)*
Breton Industries Inc ....D 518 842-3030
  Amsterdam *(G-337)*
Depot Label Company Inc ....G 631 467-2952
  Patchogue *(G-13443)*
Labeltex Mills Inc ....G 212 279-6165
  New York *(G-10950)*
Newtex Industries Inc ....E 585 924-9135
  Victor *(G-16517)*
Simplicity Creative Group Inc ....A 212 686-7676
  New York *(G-12105)*
Skil-Care Corporation ....G 914 963-2040
  Yonkers *(G-17502)*
Valley Industrial Products Inc ....E 631 385-9300
  Huntington *(G-6727)*

FACILITIES SUPPORT SVCS
Johnson Controls Inc ....C 585 724-2232
  Rochester *(G-14485)*

FACSIMILE COMMUNICATION EQPT
Alternative Technology Corp ....G 914 478-5900
  Hastings On Hudson *(G-6022)*

FAMILY CLOTHING STORES
Kate Spade & Company ....B 212 354-4900
  New York *(G-10854)*
Land n Sea Inc ....D 212 703-2980
  New York *(G-10959)*
Missiontex Inc ....G 718 532-9053
  Brooklyn *(G-2327)*
Ramsbury Property Us Inc ....F 212 223-6250
  New York *(G-11823)*
Round Top Knit & Screening ....G 518 622-3600
  Round Top *(G-15064)*
S & T Knitting Co Inc ....E 607 722-7558
  Conklin *(G-3900)*

FANS, BLOWING: Indl Or Commercial
Apgn Inc ....E 518 324-4150
  Plattsburgh *(G-13679)*
Canarm Ltd ....G 800 267-4427
  Ogdensburg *(G-13134)*
Oestreich Metal Works Inc ....G 315 463-4268
  Syracuse *(G-16022)*

PRODUCT SECTION

FIBER & FIBER PRDTS: Protein

Rapid Fan & Blower Inc .... F 718 786-2060
 Long Island City *(G-7887)*

FANS, EXHAUST: Indl Or Commercial

Howden North America Inc .... D 803 741-2700
 Depew *(G-4283)*

FANS, VENTILATING: Indl Or Commercial

Howden North America Inc .... D 716 817-6900
 Depew *(G-4284)*

FARM & GARDEN MACHINERY WHOLESALERS

Oxbo International Corporation .... D 585 548-2665
 Byron *(G-3295)*
Saxby Implement Corp .... F 585 624-2938
 Mendon *(G-8414)*

FARM PRDTS, RAW MATERIALS, WHOLESALE: Bristles

Cenibra Inc .... G 212 818-8242
 New York *(G-9612)*

FARM PRDTS, RAW MATERIALS, WHOLESALE: Hides

Hastings Hide Inc .... G 516 295-2400
 Inwood *(G-6798)*

FARM SPLY STORES

Bailey Boonville Mills Inc .... G 315 942-2131
 Boonville *(G-1159)*
Gramco Inc .... G 716 592-2845
 Springville *(G-15632)*
Lowville Farmers Coop Inc .... E 315 376-6587
 Lowville *(G-7966)*

FARM SPLYS, WHOLESALE: Beekeeping Splys, Nondurable

Northast Ctr For Bekeeping LLC .... F 800 632-3379
 Greenwich *(G-5910)*

FASTENERS: Metal

John Hassall LLC .... D 516 334-6200
 Westbury *(G-17025)*
Pmb Precision Products Inc .... F 631 491-6753
 North Babylon *(G-12919)*
Universal Metals Inc .... G 516 829-0896
 Great Neck *(G-5866)*

FASTENERS: Metal

D Best Service Co Inc .... G 718 972-6133
 Brooklyn *(G-1829)*
Southco Inc .... B 585 624-2545
 Honeoye Falls *(G-6564)*

FASTENERS: Notions, NEC

American Pride Fasteners LLC .... E 631 940-8292
 Bay Shore *(G-669)*
CPI of Falconer Inc .... E 716 664-4444
 Falconer *(G-4901)*
Cw Fasteners & Zippers Corp .... F 212 594-3203
 New York *(G-9831)*
Fasteners Depot LLC .... F 718 622-4222
 Brooklyn *(G-1963)*
Hardware Specialty Co Inc .... F 315 434-9093
 East Syracuse *(G-4549)*
Jem Threading Specialties Inc .... G 718 665-3341
 Bronx *(G-1368)*
Kenwin Sales Corp .... G 516 933-7553
 Westbury *(G-17030)*

FASTENERS: Notions, Snaps

M H Stryke Co Inc .... F 631 242-2660
 Deer Park *(G-4193)*
Rings Wire Inc .... F 212 741-9779
 New York *(G-11897)*

FASTENERS: Notions, Zippers

Champion Zipper Corp .... G 212 239-0414
 New York *(G-9627)*

Riri USA Inc .... G 212 268-3866
 New York *(G-11899)*

FAUCETS & SPIGOTS: Metal & Plastic

Giagni Enterprises LLC .... G 914 699-6500
 Mount Vernon *(G-8729)*
Giagni International Corp .... G 914 699-6500
 Mount Vernon *(G-8730)*
Hanco Metal Products Inc .... F 212 787-5992
 Brooklyn *(G-2065)*
I W Industries Inc .... C 631 293-9494
 Melville *(G-8359)*

FEATHERS: Renovating

Eser Realty Corp .... E 718 383-0565
 Brooklyn *(G-1939)*

FELT: Acoustic

Ghani Textiles Inc .... G 718 859-4561
 Brooklyn *(G-2023)*
Soundcoat Company Inc .... D 631 242-2200
 Deer Park *(G-4236)*

FENCE POSTS: Iron & Steel

Bonura and Sons Iron Works .... F 718 381-4100
 Franklin Square *(G-5371)*

FENCES & FENCING MATERIALS

Rose Fence Inc .... E 516 223-0777
 Freeport *(G-5434)*
Rose Fence Inc .... D 516 790-2308
 Halesite *(G-5929)*
Sunward Electronics Inc .... F 518 687-0030
 Troy *(G-16281)*

FENCES OR POSTS: Ornamental Iron Or Steel

786 Iron Works Corp .... G 718 418-4808
 Brooklyn *(G-1521)*
Fence Plaza Corp .... G 718 469-2200
 Brooklyn *(G-1970)*
Jamaica Iron Works Inc .... F 718 657-4849
 Jamaica *(G-6959)*
McAllisters Precision Wldg Inc .... F 518 221-3455
 Menands *(G-8406)*
Ourem Iron Works Inc .... F 914 476-4856
 Yonkers *(G-17492)*
Tee Pee Fence and Railing .... F 718 658-8323
 Jamaica *(G-6993)*
Triple H Construction Inc .... E 516 280-8252
 East Meadow *(G-4448)*

FENCING DEALERS

A & T Iron Works Inc .... E 914 632-8992
 New Rochelle *(G-8928)*
Fence Plaza Corp .... G 718 469-2200
 Brooklyn *(G-1970)*
Long Lumber and Supply Corp .... F 518 439-1661
 Slingerlands *(G-15499)*
Rose Fence Inc .... F 516 223-0777
 Baldwin *(G-560)*
Walpole Woodworkers Inc .... G 631 726-2859
 Water Mill *(G-16628)*

FENCING MATERIALS: Docks & Other Outdoor Prdts, Wood

Atlas Fence & Railing Co Inc .... E 718 767-2200
 Whitestone *(G-17229)*
Cffco USA Inc .... G 718 747-1118
 Jericho *(G-7095)*
Di Vico Craft Products Ltd .... G 845 265-9390
 Cold Spring *(G-3787)*

FENCING MATERIALS: Plastic

Amadeo Serrano .... G 516 608-8359
 Freeport *(G-5395)*
Atlas Fence & Railing Co Inc .... E 718 767-2200
 Whitestone *(G-17229)*
Benners Gardens LLC .... G 518 828-1055
 Hudson *(G-6638)*
Oneonta Fence .... G 607 433-6707
 Oneonta *(G-13212)*

FENCING MATERIALS: Wood

Interstate Wood Products Inc .... E 631 842-4488
 Amityville *(G-296)*
Long Lumber and Supply Corp .... F 518 439-1661
 Slingerlands *(G-15499)*
Rose Fence Inc .... F 516 223-0777
 Baldwin *(G-560)*
Walpole Woodworkers Inc .... G 631 726-2859
 Water Mill *(G-16628)*

FENCING: Chain Link

Master-Halco Inc .... F 631 585-8150
 Ronkonkoma *(G-14966)*

FERRITES

Hoosier Magnetics Inc .... E 315 323-5832
 Ogdensburg *(G-13137)*

FERROALLOYS

CCA Holding Inc .... C 716 446-8800
 Amherst *(G-232)*
Medima LLC .... C 716 741-0400
 Clarence *(G-3693)*
Thyssenkrupp Materials NA Inc .... F 212 972-8800
 New York *(G-12354)*

FERROMANGANESE, NOT MADE IN BLAST FURNACES

Globe Metallurgical Inc .... D 716 804-0862
 Niagara Falls *(G-12844)*

FERTILIZERS: NEC

Carolina Eastern-Vail Inc .... E 518 854-9785
 Salem *(G-15137)*
Commodity Resource Corporation .... F 585 538-9500
 Caledonia *(G-3305)*
Growmark Fs LLC .... F 585 538-2186
 Caledonia *(G-3306)*

FERTILIZERS: Nitrogenous

Agrium Advanced Tech US Inc .... F 631 286-0598
 Bohemia *(G-1005)*
Growth Products Ltd .... F 914 428-1316
 White Plains *(G-17142)*
Rt Solutions LLC .... G 585 245-3456
 Rochester *(G-14683)*

FERTILIZERS: Phosphatic

Occidental Chemical Corp .... G 716 694-3827
 North Tonawanda *(G-13002)*
Occidental Chemical Corp .... C 716 278-7794
 Niagara Falls *(G-12874)*

FIBER & FIBER PRDTS: Acrylic

Solid Surface Acrylics LLC .... F 716 743-1870
 North Tonawanda *(G-13013)*

FIBER & FIBER PRDTS: Fluorocarbon

Dynax Corporation .... G 914 764-0202
 Pound Ridge *(G-13959)*

FIBER & FIBER PRDTS: Organic, Noncellulose

Dal-Tile Corporation .... G 718 894-9574
 Maspeth *(G-8159)*
Fibrix LLC .... E 716 683-4100
 Depew *(G-4281)*
Solutia Business Entps Inc .... F 314 674-1000
 New York *(G-12154)*

FIBER & FIBER PRDTS: Polyester

Marly Home Industries USA Inc .... G 718 388-3030
 Brooklyn *(G-2276)*
Stein Fibers Ltd .... F 518 489-5700
 Albany *(G-137)*

FIBER & FIBER PRDTS: Protein

Vybion Inc .... F 607 266-0860
 Ithaca *(G-6918)*

Employee Codes: A=Over 500 employees, B=251-500
C=101-250, D=51-100, E=20-50, F=10-19, G=5-9

FIBER & FIBER PRDTS: Synthetic Cellulosic

FIBER & FIBER PRDTS: Synthetic Cellulosic

3M Company .... B 716 876-1596
  Tonawanda *(G-16154)*
Cortland Cable Company Inc .... E 607 753-8276
  Cortland *(G-4039)*
Cytec Industries Inc .... D 716 372-9650
  Olean *(G-13162)*
E I Du Pont De Nemours & Co .... E 716 876-4420
  Buffalo *(G-2938)*
International Fiber Corp .... F 716 693-4040
  North Tonawanda *(G-12995)*
Solivaira Specialties Inc .... D 716 693-4009
  North Tonawanda *(G-13014)*
Solvaira Specialties Inc .... C 716 693-4040
  North Tonawanda *(G-13015)*

FIBER OPTICS

Biolitec Inc .... E 413 525-0600
  New York *(G-9454)*
Complete Fiber Solutions Inc .... G 718 828-8900
  Bronx *(G-1305)*
Photonic Controls LLC .... F 607 562-4585
  Horseheads *(G-6616)*

FIBERS: Carbon & Graphite

Metal Coated Fibers Inc .... E 518 280-8514
  Schenectady *(G-15304)*

FILLERS & SEALERS: Wood

Uc Coatings Corporation .... E 716 833-9366
  Buffalo *(G-3257)*

FILM & SHEET: Unsuppported Plastic

American Acrylic Corporation .... E 631 422-2200
  West Babylon *(G-16795)*
API Industries Inc .... B 845 365-2200
  Orangeburg *(G-13239)*
API Industries Inc .... C 845 365-2200
  Orangeburg *(G-13240)*
Berry Global Inc .... C 315 986-2161
  Macedon *(G-8011)*
Berry Plastics Corporation .... B 315 986-6270
  Macedon *(G-8013)*
Comco Plastics Inc .... E 718 849-9000
  Huntington Station *(G-6738)*
D Bag Lady Inc .... G 585 425-8095
  Fairport *(G-4858)*
Ecoplast & Packaging LLC .... E 718 996-0800
  Brooklyn *(G-1902)*
Excellent Poly Inc .... F 718 768-6555
  Brooklyn *(G-1948)*
Franklin Poly Film Inc .... E 718 492-3523
  Brooklyn *(G-2002)*
Great Lakes Plastics Co Inc .... E 716 896-3100
  Buffalo *(G-2997)*
Integument Technologies Inc .... F 716 873-1199
  Tonawanda *(G-16193)*
Kent Chemical Corporation .... E 212 521-1700
  New York *(G-10878)*
Knf Clean Room Products Corp .... E 631 588-7000
  Ronkonkoma *(G-14951)*
Msi Inc .... F 845 639-6683
  New City *(G-8834)*
Nova Packaging Ltd Inc .... E 914 232-8406
  Katonah *(G-7161)*
Oaklee International Inc .... D 631 436-7900
  Ronkonkoma *(G-14983)*
Pace Polyethylene Mfg Co Inc .... E 914 381-3000
  Harrison *(G-6007)*
Pliant LLC .... B 315 986-6286
  Macedon *(G-8020)*
R & F Boards & Dividers Inc .... G 718 331-1529
  Brooklyn *(G-2488)*
Rainbow Poly Bag Co Inc .... E 718 386-3500
  Brooklyn *(G-2495)*
Sand Hill Industries Inc .... G 518 885-7991
  Ballston Spa *(G-607)*
Scapa North America .... E 315 413-1111
  Liverpool *(G-7573)*
Swimline Corp .... E 631 254-2155
  Edgewood *(G-4626)*
Top Quality Products Inc .... G 212 213-1988
  New York *(G-12390)*
Toray Industries Inc .... G 212 697-8150
  New York *(G-12394)*
Trinity Packaging Corporation .... E 716 668-3111
  Buffalo *(G-3251)*

Turner Bellows Inc .... E 585 235-4456
  Rochester *(G-14763)*

FILM BASE: Cellulose Acetate Or Nitrocellulose Plastics

Bfgg Investors Group LLC .... G 585 424-3456
  Rochester *(G-14248)*
Island Pyrochemical Inds Corp .... F 516 746-2100
  Mineola *(G-8551)*

FILM PROCESSING & FINISHING LABORATORY

Toppan Printing Co Amer Inc .... E 212 596-7747
  New York *(G-12391)*

FILM: Motion Picture

Big Indie - Beautiful Boy LLC .... G 917 464-5599
  Woodstock *(G-17377)*
Dolby Laboratories Inc .... F 212 767-1700
  New York *(G-9948)*

FILTERS

American Filtration Tech Inc .... F 585 359-4130
  West Henrietta *(G-16900)*
Burnett Process Inc .... E 585 277-1623
  Rochester *(G-14270)*
Drasgow Inc .... E 585 786-3603
  Gainesville *(G-5497)*
Foseco Inc .... F 914 345-4760
  Tarrytown *(G-16115)*
Hilliard Corporation .... B 607 733-7121
  Elmira *(G-4703)*
Hilliard Corporation .... E 607 733-7121
  Elmira *(G-4704)*
Lydall Performance Mtls Inc .... F 518 273-6320
  Green Island *(G-5878)*
Pall Corporation .... A 516 484-5400
  Port Washington *(G-13870)*
Pall Corporation .... A 607 753-6041
  Cortland *(G-4059)*
Parker-Hannifin Corporation .... D 248 628-6017
  Lancaster *(G-7355)*
Peregrine Industries Inc .... E 631 838-2870
  New York *(G-11632)*
Pyrotek Incorporated .... E 716 731-3221
  Sanborn *(G-15153)*
SC Supply Chain Management LLC ...... G 212 344-3322
  New York *(G-12001)*
Sidco Filter Corporation .... F 585 289-3100
  Manchester *(G-8086)*
Sinclair International Company .... E 518 798-2361
  Queensbury *(G-14025)*
Stavo Industries Inc .... E 845 331-5389
  Kingston *(G-7242)*

FILTERS & SOFTENERS: Water, Household

H2o Solutions Inc .... F 518 527-0915
  Stillwater *(G-15782)*
Menpin Supply Corp .... F 718 415-4168
  Brooklyn *(G-2300)*
Pure Planet Waters LLC .... F 718 676-7900
  Brooklyn *(G-2475)*
Royal Prestige Lasting Co .... F 516 280-5148
  Hempstead *(G-6308)*
Water Technologies Inc .... G 315 986-0000
  Macedon *(G-8022)*

FILTERS: Air

Air Engineering Filters Inc .... G 914 238-5945
  Chappaqua *(G-3578)*
Air Export Mechanical .... G 917 709-5310
  Flushing *(G-5230)*
Air Wave Air Conditioning Co .... E 212 545-1122
  Bronx *(G-1266)*
Automotive Filters Mfg Inc .... F 631 435-1010
  Bohemia *(G-1016)*
Filta Clean Co Inc .... E 718 495-3800
  Brooklyn *(G-1974)*
Healthway Home Products Inc .... E 315 298-2904
  Pulaski *(G-13968)*
Isolation Systems Inc .... F 716 694-6390
  North Tonawanda *(G-12997)*
Nexstar Holding Corp .... G 716 929-9000
  Amherst *(G-251)*
Northland Filter Intl LLC .... E 315 207-1410
  Oswego *(G-13361)*

Pliotron Company America LLC .... G 716 298-4457
  Niagara Falls *(G-12878)*
R P Fedder Corp .... E 585 288-1600
  Rochester *(G-14643)*
Roome Technologies Inc .... G 585 229-4437
  Honeoye *(G-6552)*

FILTERS: Air Intake, Internal Combustion Engine, Exc Auto

Modern-TEC Manufacturing Inc .... G 716 625-8700
  Lockport *(G-7632)*
Pall Corporation .... A 516 484-5400
  Port Washington *(G-13870)*
Pall Corporation .... A 607 753-6041
  Cortland *(G-4059)*

FILTERS: General Line, Indl

Adams Sfc Inc .... E 716 877-2608
  Tonawanda *(G-16157)*
American Felt & Filter Co Inc .... D 845 561-3560
  New Windsor *(G-8977)*
Cross Filtration Ltd Lblty Co .... G 315 412-1539
  Moravia *(G-8657)*
Filter Tech Inc .... D 315 682-8815
  Manlius *(G-8104)*
Graver Technologies LLC .... E 585 624-1330
  Honeoye Falls *(G-6556)*
North American Filter Corp .... D 800 265-8943
  Newark *(G-12760)*
Service Filtration Corp .... E 716 877-2608
  Tonawanda *(G-16221)*
Stavo Industries Inc .... F 845 331-4552
  Kingston *(G-7241)*

FILTERS: Motor Vehicle

Automotive Filters Mfg Inc .... F 631 435-1010
  Bohemia *(G-1016)*
P & F Industries Inc .... E 631 694-9800
  Melville *(G-8375)*
Pall Corporation .... A 516 484-5400
  Port Washington *(G-13870)*
Pall Corporation .... A 607 753-6041
  Cortland *(G-4059)*

FILTRATION DEVICES: Electronic

Allen Avionics Inc .... E 516 248-8080
  Mineola *(G-8526)*
Fil-Coil (fc) Corp .... E 631 467-5328
  Sayville *(G-15237)*
Microwave Filter Company Inc .... E 315 438-4700
  East Syracuse *(G-4564)*
MTK Electronics Inc .... E 631 924-7666
  Medford *(G-8290)*
Prms Inc .... G 631 851-7945
  Shirley *(G-15452)*
Service Filtration Corp .... E 716 877-2608
  Tonawanda *(G-16221)*
Tte Filters LLC .... G 716 532-2234
  Gowanda *(G-5763)*

FINANCIAL INVESTMENT ACTIVITIES, NEC: Financial Reporting

Dow Jones & Company Inc .... E 212 597-5983
  New York *(G-9966)*
Ruby Newco LLC .... G 212 852-7000
  New York *(G-11951)*

FINANCIAL INVESTMENT ADVICE

Bernhard Arnold & Company Inc .... G 212 907-1500
  New York *(G-9414)*
Envy Publishing Group Inc .... G 212 253-9874
  New York *(G-10100)*
Investors Business Daily Inc .... F 212 626-7676
  New York *(G-10693)*
Moneypaper Inc .... F 914 925-0022
  Rye *(G-15090)*
Swaps Monitor Publications Inc .... F 212 742-8550
  New York *(G-12271)*

FINANCIAL SVCS

Sixteen Markets Inc .... F 347 759-1024
  New York *(G-12113)*

PRODUCT SECTION

FLAT GLASS: Antique

FINDINGS & TRIMMINGS Fabric, NEC
Lending Trimming Co Inc..........D...... 212 242-7502
New York *(G-10999)*

FINDINGS & TRIMMINGS Waistbands, Trouser
Cai Inc..........E...... 212 819-0008
New York *(G-9547)*

FINDINGS & TRIMMINGS: Apparel
Eagle Finishing..........E...... 718 497-7875
Brooklyn *(G-1897)*
Mas Cutting Inc..........G...... 212 869-0826
New York *(G-11196)*

FINDINGS & TRIMMINGS: Fabric
Legendary Auto Interiors Ltd..........E...... 315 331-1212
Newark *(G-12754)*

FINGERNAILS, ARTIFICIAL
Ivy Enterprises Inc..........B...... 516 621-9779
Port Washington *(G-13848)*
Uptown Nails LLC..........C...... 800 748-1881
New York *(G-12497)*

FINGERPRINT EQPT
Fingerprint America Inc..........G...... 518 435-1609
Albany *(G-80)*

FINISHING AGENTS: Leather
Androme Leather Inc..........F...... 518 773-7945
Gloversville *(G-5721)*

FIRE ARMS, SMALL: Guns Or Gun Parts, 30 mm & Below
Magpump LLC..........G...... 585 444-9812
Henrietta *(G-6320)*
Oriskany Arms Inc..........F...... 315 737-2196
Oriskany *(G-13336)*

FIRE ARMS, SMALL: Pellet & BB guns
Crosman Corporation..........E...... 585 657-6161
Bloomfield *(G-980)*
Crosman Corporation..........E...... 585 398-3920
Farmington *(G-5157)*

FIRE ARMS, SMALL: Rifles Or Rifle Parts, 30 mm & below
Hart Rifle Barrel Inc..........G...... 315 677-9841
Syracuse *(G-15978)*
Kyntec Corporation..........G...... 716 810-6956
Buffalo *(G-3056)*

FIRE CONTROL OR BOMBING EQPT: Electronic
Cooper Crouse-Hinds LLC..........B...... 866 764-5454
Syracuse *(G-15927)*

FIRE DETECTION SYSTEMS
Firecom Inc..........C...... 718 899-6100
Woodside *(G-17345)*
Firetronics Inc..........G...... 516 997-5151
Jericho *(G-7102)*
Zetek Corporation..........F...... 212 668-1485
New York *(G-12729)*

FIRE ESCAPES
Jamestown Fab Stl & Sup Inc..........G...... 716 665-2227
Jamestown *(G-7040)*

FIRE EXTINGUISHERS: Portable
Bullex Inc..........E...... 518 689-2023
Albany *(G-56)*
Nubian Heritage..........G...... 631 265-3551
Hauppauge *(G-6176)*
Trove Inc..........F...... 212 268-2046
Brooklyn *(G-2703)*

FIRE OR BURGLARY RESISTIVE PRDTS
Clad Industries LLC..........G...... 585 413-4359
Macedon *(G-8014)*
Crystalizations Systems Inc..........F...... 631 467-0090
Holbrook *(G-6469)*
Empire Metal Finishing Inc..........E...... 718 545-6700
Astoria *(G-438)*
Finger Lakes Conveyors Inc..........G...... 315 539-9246
Waterloo *(G-16647)*
Maximum Security Products Corp..........E...... 518 233-1800
Waterford *(G-16634)*
Nrd LLC..........E...... 716 773-7634
Grand Island *(G-5779)*
Thyssenkrupp Materials NA Inc..........F...... 212 972-8800
New York *(G-12354)*

FIRE PROTECTION EQPT
First Due Fire Equipment Inc..........F...... 845 222-1329
Garnerville *(G-5568)*
Lifc Corp..........G...... 516 426-5737
Port Washington *(G-13859)*

FIREARMS & AMMUNITION, EXC SPORTING, WHOLESALE
Island Ordnance Systems LLC..........F...... 516 746-2100
Mineola *(G-8550)*

FIREARMS: Small, 30mm or Less
Benjamin Sheridan Corporation..........G...... 585 657-6161
Bloomfield *(G-975)*
Dan Wesson Corp..........F...... 607 336-1174
Norwich *(G-13045)*
Redding-Hunter Inc..........E...... 607 753-3331
Cortland *(G-4066)*
Remington Arms Company LLC..........A...... 315 895-3482
Ilion *(G-6783)*
Sycamore Hill Designs Inc..........G...... 585 820-7322
Victor *(G-16528)*
Tri-Technologies Inc..........E...... 914 699-2001
Mount Vernon *(G-8787)*

FIREFIGHTING APPARATUS
Bullex Inc..........F...... 518 689-2023
Albany *(G-55)*
Eastern Precision Mfg..........G...... 845 358-1951
Nyack *(G-13066)*
Firematic Supply Co Inc..........G...... 631 924-3181
East Yaphank *(G-4593)*
Fountainhead Group Inc..........C...... 315 736-0037
New York Mills *(G-12742)*
William R Shoemaker Inc..........G...... 716 649-0511
Hamburg *(G-5968)*

FIREPLACE & CHIMNEY MATERIAL: Concrete
Chim-Cap Corp..........E...... 800 262-9622
Farmingdale *(G-4968)*
Chimney Doctors Americas Corp..........G...... 631 868-3586
Bayport *(G-751)*

FIREPLACE EQPT & ACCESS
William H Jackson Company..........G...... 718 784-4482
Long Island City *(G-7952)*

FIREWORKS
Alonzo Fire Works Display Inc..........G...... 518 664-9994
Mechanicville *(G-8256)*
Fantasy Fireworks Display..........G...... 518 664-1809
Stillwater *(G-15781)*
Young Explosives Corp..........D...... 585 394-1783
Canandaigua *(G-3390)*

FIREWORKS DISPLAY SVCS
Alonzo Fire Works Display Inc..........G...... 518 664-9994
Mechanicville *(G-8256)*
Young Explosives Corp..........D...... 585 394-1783
Canandaigua *(G-3390)*

FISH & SEAFOOD PROCESSORS: Canned Or Cured
Blue Ocean Food Trading LLC..........G...... 718 689-4291
Brooklyn *(G-1701)*

Deelka Vision Corp..........E...... 718 937-4121
Sunnyside *(G-15827)*
Sangster Foods Inc..........F...... 212 993-9129
Brooklyn *(G-2556)*

FISH & SEAFOOD PROCESSORS: Fresh Or Frozen
6th Ave Gourmet Inc..........G...... 845 782-9067
Monroe *(G-8582)*
Foo Yuan Food Products Co Inc..........G...... 212 925-2840
Long Island City *(G-7773)*
Rich Products Corporation..........A...... 716 878-8000
Buffalo *(G-3185)*

FISHING EQPT: Lures
Bruynswick Sales Inc..........F...... 845 789-2049
New Paltz *(G-8918)*
Heads & Tails Lure Co..........F...... 607 739-7900
Horseheads *(G-6609)*
Northern King Lures Inc..........G...... 585 865-3373
Rochester *(G-14566)*

FITTINGS & ASSEMBLIES: Hose & Tube, Hydraulic Or Pneumatic
KSA Manufacturing LLC..........F...... 315 488-0809
Camillus *(G-3351)*
Power Drives Inc..........D...... 716 822-3600
Buffalo *(G-3155)*

FITTINGS: Pipe
Legacy Valve LLC..........F...... 914 403-5075
Valhalla *(G-16394)*
Martin Brass Works Inc..........G...... 718 523-3146
Jamaica *(G-6964)*
Total Piping Solutions Inc..........F...... 716 372-0160
Olean *(G-13176)*
United Pipe Nipple Co Inc..........F...... 516 295-2468
Hewlett *(G-6338)*

FITTINGS: Pipe, Fabricated
D & G Welding Inc..........G...... 716 873-3088
Buffalo *(G-2918)*

FIXTURES & EQPT: Kitchen, Metal, Exc Cast Aluminum
Acme Kitchenettes Corp..........E...... 518 828-4191
Hudson *(G-6632)*
Vanity Fair Bathmart Inc..........F...... 718 584-6700
Bronx *(G-1487)*

FIXTURES: Bank, Metal, Ornamental
Jonathan Metal & Glass Ltd..........D...... 718 846-8000
Jamaica *(G-6960)*

FIXTURES: Cut Stone
Jamestown Kitchen & Bath Inc..........G...... 716 665-2299
Jamestown *(G-7041)*

FLAGPOLES
Flagpoles Incorporated..........D...... 631 751-5500
East Setauket *(G-4501)*
Pole-Tech Co Inc..........F...... 631 689-5525
East Setauket *(G-4508)*

FLAGS: Fabric
AAa Amercn Flag Dctg Co Inc..........G...... 212 279-3524
New York *(G-9044)*
Art Flag Company Inc..........F...... 212 334-1890
New York *(G-9259)*
City Signs Inc..........G...... 718 375-5933
Brooklyn *(G-1783)*
Eagle Regalia Co Inc..........F...... 845 425-2245
Spring Valley *(G-15604)*
National Flag & Display Co Inc..........E...... 212 228-6600
New York *(G-11371)*

FLAT GLASS: Antique
Munn Works LLC..........E...... 914 665-6100
Mount Vernon *(G-8755)*

Employee Codes: A=Over 500 employees, B=251-500
C=101-250, D=51-100, E=20-50, F=10-19, G=5-9

FLAT GLASS: Building

FLAT GLASS: Building
Lazer Marble & Granite Corp ....G....... 718 859-9644
  Brooklyn *(G-2198)*
Tempco Glass Fabrication LLC ....G....... 718 461-6888
  Flushing *(G-5305)*

FLAT GLASS: Construction
RG Glass Creations Inc ....E....... 212 675-0030
  New York *(G-11885)*
Twin Pane Insulated GL Co Inc.................F....... 631 924-1060
  Yaphank *(G-17423)*

FLAT GLASS: Laminated
Glass Apps LLC ....F....... 310 987-1536
  New York *(G-10347)*

FLAT GLASS: Plate, Polished & Rough
Lafayette Mirror & Glass Co ....G....... 718 768-0660
  New Hyde Park *(G-8891)*
Zered Inc ....F....... 718 353-7464
  College Point *(G-3838)*

FLAT GLASS: Strengthened Or Reinforced
Saxon Glass Technologies Inc ....F....... 607 587-9630
  Alfred *(G-197)*

FLAT GLASS: Tempered
Strong Tempering GL Indust LLC ....F....... 718 765-0007
  Brooklyn *(G-2633)*

FLAT GLASS: Window, Clear & Colored
Express Building Supply Inc ....E....... 516 608-0379
  Oceanside *(G-13099)*
Manhattan Shade & Glass Co Inc.................D....... 212 288-5616
  New York *(G-11157)*
South Seneca Vinyl LLC ....G....... 315 585-6050
  Romulus *(G-14871)*
Window-Fix Inc ....E....... 718 854-3475
  Brooklyn *(G-2773)*

FLATWARE, STAINLESS STEEL
Utica Cutlery Company ....D....... 315 733-4663
  Utica *(G-16387)*

FLAVORS OR FLAVORING MATERIALS: Synthetic
Classic Flavors Fragrances Inc ....G....... 212 777-0004
  New York *(G-9691)*
Comax Aromatics Corporation ....E....... 631 249-0505
  Melville *(G-8334)*
Comax Manufacturing Corp ....D....... 631 249-0505
  Melville *(G-8335)*
Craftmaster Flavor Technology ....F....... 631 789-8607
  Amityville *(G-282)*
Interntnal Flvors Frgrnces Inc ....C....... 212 765-5500
  New York *(G-10681)*
Kent Chemical Corporation ....E....... 212 521-1700
  New York *(G-10878)*
Mafco Consolidated Group Inc.................F....... 212 572-8600
  New York *(G-11123)*

FLOOR COMPOSITION: Magnesite
Vescom Structural Systems Inc ....F....... 516 876-8100
  Westbury *(G-17070)*

FLOOR COVERING STORES
North Sunshine LLC ....F....... 307 027-1634
  Valley Cottage *(G-16410)*

FLOOR COVERING STORES: Carpets
Albert Menin Interiors Ltd ....F....... 212 876-3041
  Bronx *(G-1268)*
Elizabeth Eakins Inc ....F....... 212 628-1950
  New York *(G-10062)*
Wallace Home Design Ctr ....G....... 631 765-3890
  Southold *(G-15585)*

FLOOR COVERING: Plastic
Engineered Composites Inc.................E....... 716 362-0295
  Buffalo *(G-2953)*
H Risch Inc ....D....... 585 442-0110
  Rochester *(G-14435)*

FLOOR COVERINGS WHOLESALERS
Carpet Fabrications Intl.................E....... 914 381-6060
  Mamaroneck *(G-8058)*
Quality Carpet One Floor & HM ....G....... 718 941-4200
  Brooklyn *(G-2478)*

FLOOR COVERINGS: Textile Fiber
Mannington Mills Inc ....G....... 212 251-0290
  New York *(G-11161)*

FLOOR COVERINGS: Tile, Support Plastic
Engineered Plastics Inc.................E....... 800 682-2525
  Williamsville *(G-17270)*

FLOORING & GRATINGS: Open, Construction Applications
Oldcastle Precast Inc.................F....... 518 767-2116
  South Bethlehem *(G-15536)*

FLOORING: Hard Surface
East To West Architectural Pdts ....G....... 631 433-9690
  East Northport *(G-4455)*
Heritage Contract Flooring LLC ....F....... 716 853-1555
  Buffalo *(G-3011)*
Signature Systems Group LLC ....F....... 800 569-2751
  New York *(G-12094)*

FLOORING: Hardwood
Custom Woodwork Ltd.................F....... 631 727-5260
  Riverhead *(G-14151)*
Designer Hardwood Flrg CNY Inc ....F....... 315 207-0044
  Oswego *(G-13354)*
Fountain Tile Outlet Inc ....G....... 718 927-4555
  Brooklyn *(G-1998)*
Legno Veneto USA ....G....... 716 651-9169
  Depew *(G-4285)*
Madison & Dunn ....G....... 585 563-7760
  Rochester *(G-14509)*
MP Caroll Inc ....F....... 716 683-8520
  Cheektowaga *(G-3607)*
Mullican Flooring LP ....G....... 716 537-2642
  Holland *(G-6509)*
Tectonic Flooring USA LLC.................G....... 212 686-2700
  New York *(G-12316)*
Wood Floor Expo Inc ....G....... 212 472-0671
  New York *(G-12683)*

FLOORING: Tile
Tile Shop Inc ....G....... 585 424-2180
  Rochester *(G-14754)*

FLORISTS
M & S Schmalberg Inc ....F....... 212 244-2090
  New York *(G-11098)*

FLOWER ARRANGEMENTS: Artificial
Nsj Group Ltd ....F....... 631 893-9300
  Babylon *(G-548)*

FLOWER POTS Plastic
TVI Imports LLC ....G....... 631 793-3077
  Massapequa Park *(G-8223)*

FLOWERS: Artificial & Preserved
Faster-Form Corp.................D....... 800 327-3676
  New Hartford *(G-8849)*
M & S Schmalberg Inc ....F....... 212 244-2090
  New York *(G-11098)*

FLUID METERS & COUNTING DEVICES
Aalborg Instrs & Contrls Inc ....D....... 845 398-3160
  Orangeburg *(G-13238)*
Computer Instruments Corp ....E....... 516 876-8400
  Westbury *(G-17003)*
East Hills Instrument Inc ....F....... 516 621-8686
  Westbury *(G-17007)*
G & O Equipment Corp.................G....... 718 218-7844
  Bronx *(G-1341)*

FLUID POWER PUMPS & MOTORS
Atlantic Industrial Tech Inc ....E....... 631 234-3131
  Shirley *(G-15437)*
Huck International Inc ....C....... 845 331-7300
  Kingston *(G-7220)*
Hydroacoustics Inc ....F....... 585 359-1000
  Henrietta *(G-6317)*
ITT Corporation ....D....... 315 568-2811
  Seneca Falls *(G-15383)*
ITT Inc ....F....... 914 641-2000
  White Plains *(G-17152)*
ITT LLC ....B....... 914 641-2000
  White Plains *(G-17154)*
Parker-Hannifin Corporation ....C....... 585 425-7000
  Fairport *(G-4874)*
Trench & Marine Pump Co Inc ....C....... 212 423-9098
  Bronx *(G-1473)*
Triumph Actuation Systems LLC ....D....... 516 378-0162
  Freeport *(G-5443)*

FLUID POWER VALVES & HOSE FITTINGS
A K Allen Co Inc ....C....... 516 747-5450
  Mineola *(G-8522)*
Aalborg Instrs & Contrls Inc ....D....... 845 398-3160
  Orangeburg *(G-13238)*
Eastport Operating Partners LP ....G....... 212 387-8791
  New York *(G-10020)*
Key High Vacuum Products Inc ....E....... 631 584-5959
  Nesconset *(G-8823)*
Kinemotive Corporation ....E....... 631 249-6440
  Farmingdale *(G-5035)*
Lourdes Industries Inc ....D....... 631 234-6600
  Hauppauge *(G-6146)*
Moog Inc ....B....... 716 687-4954
  East Aurora *(G-4400)*
Own Instrument Inc ....F....... 914 668-6546
  Mount Vernon *(G-8758)*
Servotronics Inc ....C....... 716 655-5990
  Elma *(G-4668)*
Steel & Obrien Mfg Inc ....D....... 585 492-5800
  Arcade *(G-399)*
Upstate Tube Inc ....G....... 315 488-5636
  Camillus *(G-3354)*

FLUORO RUBBERS
Dynax Corporation ....G....... 914 764-0202
  Pound Ridge *(G-13959)*

FLUXES
Aufhauser Corporation ....F....... 516 694-8696
  Plainview *(G-13614)*
Carpet Beaters LLC ....G....... 877 375-9336
  Rosedale *(G-15036)*
Johnson Manufacturing Company ....F....... 716 881-3030
  Buffalo *(G-3038)*

FOAM CHARGE MIXTURES
C P Chemical Co Inc ....G....... 914 428-2517
  White Plains *(G-17118)*
Icynene US Acquisition Corp ....G....... 800 758-7325
  Buffalo *(G-3020)*

FOAM RUBBER
Foam Products Inc.................E....... 718 292-4830
  Bronx *(G-1337)*
Mhxco Foam Company LLC ....F....... 518 843-8400
  Amsterdam *(G-356)*
Par-Foam Products Inc ....C....... 716 855-2066
  Buffalo *(G-3135)*
Turner Bellows Inc ....E....... 585 235-4456
  Rochester *(G-14763)*

FOIL & LEAF: Metal
American Packaging Corporation ....G....... 585 254-2002
  Rochester *(G-14213)*
American Packaging Corporation ....C....... 585 254-9500
  Rochester *(G-14214)*
Pactiv LLC ....C....... 518 793-2524
  Glens Falls *(G-5710)*
Quick Roll Leaf Mfg Co Inc ....E....... 845 457-1500
  Montgomery *(G-8637)*
Thermal Process Cnstr Co ....E....... 631 293-6400
  Farmingdale *(G-5139)*

FOIL OR LEAF: Gold
Genesis One Unlimited ....G....... 516 208-5863
  West Hempstead *(G-16885)*

PRODUCT SECTION

FOOD PRDTS, CONFECTIONERY, WHOLESALE: Nuts, Salted/Roasted

FOIL: Aluminum
Alufoil Products Co Inc ....F 631 231-4141
  Hauppauge *(G-6037)*

FOIL: Copper
Oak-Mitsui Inc ....D 518 686-8060
  Hoosick Falls *(G-6569)*
Oak-Mitsui Technologies LLC ....E 518 686-4961
  Hoosick Falls *(G-6570)*
Steel Partners Holdings LP ....E 212 520-2300
  New York *(G-12212)*

FOIL: Laminated To Paper Or Other Materials
Alufoil Products Co Inc ....F 631 231-4141
  Hauppauge *(G-6037)*

FOOD CASINGS: Plastic
Pactiv LLC ....C 585 394-5125
  Canandaigua *(G-3381)*

FOOD PRDTS, BREAKFAST: Cereal, Infants' Food
Group International LLC ....G 718 475-8805
  Flushing *(G-5253)*
Sangster Foods Inc ....F 212 993-9129
  Brooklyn *(G-2556)*

FOOD PRDTS, BREAKFAST: Cereal, Wheat Flakes
General Mills Inc ....D 716 856-6060
  Buffalo *(G-2985)*

FOOD PRDTS, CANNED OR FRESH PACK: Fruit Juices
Apple & Eve LLC ....D 516 621-1122
  Port Washington *(G-13822)*
Mizkan America Inc ....D 585 765-9171
  Lyndonville *(G-7995)*
Motts LLP ....C 972 673-8088
  Elmsford *(G-4775)*
National Grape Coop Assn Inc ....E 716 326-5200
  Westfield *(G-17077)*
US Juice Partners LLC ....G 516 621-1122
  Port Washington *(G-13888)*
Welch Foods Inc A Cooperative ....C 716 326-5252
  Westfield *(G-17082)*

FOOD PRDTS, CANNED OR FRESH PACK: Vegetable Juices
Life Juice Brands LLC ....G 585 944-7982
  Pittsford *(G-13595)*

FOOD PRDTS, CANNED, NEC
Phillip Juan ....G 800 834-4543
  Staten Island *(G-15740)*

FOOD PRDTS, CANNED: Baby Food
Beech-Nut Nutrition Company ....B 518 839-0300
  Amsterdam *(G-336)*

FOOD PRDTS, CANNED: Barbecue Sauce
Jets Lefrois Corp ....G 585 637-5003
  Brockport *(G-1245)*

FOOD PRDTS, CANNED: Beans & Bean Sprouts
Sahadi Fine Foods Inc ....E 718 369-0100
  Brooklyn *(G-2554)*

FOOD PRDTS, CANNED: Catsup
Kensington & Sons LLC ....E 646 430-8298
  New York *(G-10875)*

FOOD PRDTS, CANNED: Ethnic
Delicious Foods Inc ....F 718 446-9352
  Corona *(G-4019)*
Iberia Foods Corp ....D 718 272-8900
  Brooklyn *(G-2092)*

Sangster Foods Inc ....F 212 993-9129
  Brooklyn *(G-2556)*

FOOD PRDTS, CANNED: Fruit Juices, Concentrated
Old Dutch Mustard Co Inc ....G 516 466-0522
  Great Neck *(G-5843)*

FOOD PRDTS, CANNED: Fruit Juices, Fresh
Cahoon Farms Inc ....E 315 594-8081
  Wolcott *(G-17298)*
Central Island Juice Corp ....F 516 338-8301
  Westbury *(G-17002)*
Cheribundi Inc ....E 800 699-0460
  Geneva *(G-5585)*
Cliffstar LLC ....A 716 366-6100
  Dunkirk *(G-4361)*
Club 1100 ....G 585 235-3478
  Rochester *(G-14301)*
Fresh Fanatic Inc ....F 516 521-6574
  Brooklyn *(G-2005)*
Mayer Bros Apple Products Inc ....D 716 668-1787
  West Seneca *(G-16980)*

FOOD PRDTS, CANNED: Fruit Purees
Global Natural Foods Inc ....E 845 439-3292
  Livingston Manor *(G-7589)*

FOOD PRDTS, CANNED: Fruits
Andros Bowman Products LLC ....G 540 217-4100
  Lyndonville *(G-7994)*
Fruitcrown Products Corp ....E 631 694-5800
  Farmingdale *(G-5003)*
Lagoner Farms Inc ....G 315 589-4899
  Williamson *(G-17253)*

FOOD PRDTS, CANNED: Fruits
Brooklyn Btlg Milton NY Inc ....C 845 795-2171
  Milton *(G-8516)*
Fly Creek Cder Mill Orchrd Inc ....G 607 547-9692
  Fly Creek *(G-5319)*
Goya Foods Inc ....D 716 549-0076
  Angola *(G-380)*
Hc Brill Co Inc ....G 716 685-4000
  Lancaster *(G-7343)*
Lidestri Foods Inc ....B 585 377-7700
  Fairport *(G-4867)*
Victoria Fine Foods LLC ....D 718 649-1635
  Brooklyn *(G-2742)*
Welch Foods Inc A Cooperative ....E 716 326-3131
  Westfield *(G-17083)*

FOOD PRDTS, CANNED: Fruits & Fruit Prdts
Amiram Dror Inc ....F 212 979-9505
  Brooklyn *(G-1609)*
Birds Eye Holdings Inc ....A 585 383-1850
  Rochester *(G-14250)*
Spf Holdings II LLC ....G 212 750-8300
  New York *(G-12185)*

FOOD PRDTS, CANNED: Italian
A & G Food Distributors LLC ....G 917 939-3457
  Bayside *(G-757)*
Antico Casale Usa LLC ....G 914 760-1100
  Whitestone *(G-17227)*
Indira Foods Inc ....F 718 343-1500
  Floral Park *(G-5215)*
Marketplace Slutions Group LLC ....E 631 868-0111
  Holbrook *(G-6490)*

FOOD PRDTS, CANNED: Jams, Including Imitation
Sbk Preserves Inc ....E 800 773-7378
  Bronx *(G-1448)*

FOOD PRDTS, CANNED: Jams, Jellies & Preserves
Beths Farm Kitchen ....G 518 799-3414
  Stuyvesant Falls *(G-15805)*
Eleanors Best ....F 845 809-5621
  Garrison *(G-5569)*
Sarabeths Kitchen LLC ....G 718 589-2900
  Bronx *(G-1447)*

FOOD PRDTS, CANNED: Maraschino Cherries
Dells Cherries LLC ....E 718 624-4380
  Brooklyn *(G-1850)*
Dells Cherries LLC ....E 718 624-4380
  Brooklyn *(G-1851)*

FOOD PRDTS, CANNED: Mexican, NEC
Eve Sales Corp ....F 718 589-6800
  Bronx *(G-1331)*

FOOD PRDTS, CANNED: Olives
L and S Packing Co ....D 631 845-1717
  Farmingdale *(G-5037)*

FOOD PRDTS, CANNED: Puddings, Exc Meat
Steuben Foods Incorporated ....F 718 291-3333
  Jamaica *(G-6989)*

FOOD PRDTS, CANNED: Ravioli
Borgattis Ravioli Egg Noodles ....G 718 367-3799
  Bronx *(G-1286)*

FOOD PRDTS, CANNED: Sauerkraut
Glk Foods LLC ....E 585 289-4414
  Shortsville *(G-15456)*
Seneca Foods Corporation ....C 315 781-8733
  Geneva *(G-5597)*

FOOD PRDTS, CANNED: Soup, Chicken
Morris Kitchen Inc ....F 646 413-5186
  Brooklyn *(G-2339)*

FOOD PRDTS, CANNED: Spaghetti & Other Pasta Sauce
Kaltech Food Packaging Inc ....E 845 856-1210
  Port Jervis *(G-13810)*
New York Pasta Authority Inc ....F 347 787-2130
  Brooklyn *(G-2374)*
Sneaky Chef Foods LLC ....F 914 301-3277
  Tarrytown *(G-16131)*
Wolfgang B Gourmet Foods Inc ....F 518 719-1727
  Catskill *(G-3463)*

FOOD PRDTS, CANNED: Tomato Sauce.
Vincents Food Corp ....F 516 481-3544
  Carle Place *(G-3425)*

FOOD PRDTS, CANNED: Tomatoes
Giovanni Food Co Inc ....D 315 457-2373
  Baldwinsville *(G-569)*
Morris Kitchen Inc ....F 646 413-5186
  Brooklyn *(G-2339)*
Private Lbel Fods Rchester Inc ....E 585 254-9205
  Rochester *(G-14625)*

FOOD PRDTS, CANNED: Vegetables
Green Valley Foods LLC ....G 315 926-4280
  Marion *(G-8124)*
Seneca Foods Corporation ....E 315 926-8100
  Marion *(G-8129)*
Seneca Foods Corporation ....G 315 926-4277
  Marion *(G-8131)*
Seneca Foods Corporation ....E 585 658-2211
  Leicester *(G-7444)*

FOOD PRDTS, CONFECTIONERY, WHOLESALE: Candy
Chocolat Moderne LLC ....G 212 229-4797
  New York *(G-9657)*
Chocolate Delivery Systems Inc ....D 716 854-6050
  Buffalo *(G-2892)*
OH How Cute Inc ....G 347 838-6031
  Staten Island *(G-15739)*
Premium Sweets USA Inc ....G 718 739-6000
  Jamaica *(G-6978)*

FOOD PRDTS, CONFECTIONERY, WHOLESALE: Nuts, Salted/Roasted
Sahadi Fine Foods Inc ....E 718 369-0100
  Brooklyn *(G-2554)*

Employee Codes: A=Over 500 employees, B=251-500
C=101-250, D=51-100, E=20-50, F=10-19, G=5-9

FOOD PRDTS, CONFECTIONERY, WHOLESALE: Snack Foods

FOOD PRDTS, CONFECTIONERY, WHOLESALE: Snack Foods

Materne North America Corp ....B...... 212 675-7881
  New York *(G-11202)*
Perrys Ice Cream Company Inc ....B...... 716 542-5492
  Akron *(G-24)*

FOOD PRDTS, DAIRY, WHOLESALE: Milk & Cream, Fluid

Elmhurst Dairy Inc ....C...... 718 526-3442
  Jamaica *(G-6946)*

FOOD PRDTS, FISH & SEAFOOD, WHOLESALE: Fresh

Fresh Fanatic Inc ....G...... 516 521-6574
  Brooklyn *(G-2005)*
Montauk Inlet Seafood Inc ....G...... 631 668-3419
  Montauk *(G-8625)*

FOOD PRDTS, FISH & SEAFOOD: Canned & Jarred, Etc

Harbors Maine Lobster LLC ....E...... 516 775-2400
  New Hyde Park *(G-8884)*
Premium Ocean LLC ....F...... 917 231-1061
  Bronx *(G-1434)*

FOOD PRDTS, FISH & SEAFOOD: Fish, Fresh, Prepared

Montauk Inlet Seafood Inc ....G...... 631 668-3419
  Montauk *(G-8625)*
Prince of The Sea Ltd ....E...... 516 333-6344
  Westbury *(G-17050)*

FOOD PRDTS, FISH & SEAFOOD: Fish, Smoked

Acme Smoked Fish Corp ....D...... 954 942-5598
  Brooklyn *(G-1556)*
Banner Smoked Fish Inc ....D...... 718 449-1992
  Brooklyn *(G-1663)*
Samaki Inc ....G...... 845 858-1012
  Port Jervis *(G-13815)*

FOOD PRDTS, FISH & SEAFOOD: Fresh, Prepared

Fish To Dish Inc ....F...... 718 972-7600
  Brooklyn *(G-1979)*

FOOD PRDTS, FISH & SEAFOOD: Fresh/Frozen Chowder, Soup/Stew

Shine Foods USA Inc ....G...... 516 784-9674
  Glen Oaks *(G-5655)*

FOOD PRDTS, FISH & SEAFOOD: Salmon, Smoked

Catsmo LLC ....F...... 845 895-2296
  Wallkill *(G-16562)*

FOOD PRDTS, FISH & SEAFOOD: Seafood, Frozen, Prepared

Oceans Cuisine Ltd ....F...... 631 209-9200
  Ridge *(G-14105)*

FOOD PRDTS, FROZEN: Breakfasts, Packaged

Juno Chefs ....D...... 845 294-5400
  Goshen *(G-5750)*

FOOD PRDTS, FROZEN: Dinners, Packaged

Alle Processing Corp ....C...... 718 894-2000
  Maspeth *(G-8143)*

FOOD PRDTS, FROZEN: Ethnic Foods, NEC

America NY RI Wang Fd Group Co ......E...... 718 628-8999
  Maspeth *(G-8145)*
Delicious Foods Inc ....F...... 718 446-9352
  Corona *(G-4019)*

FOOD PRDTS, FROZEN: Fruits & Vegetables

Atlantic Farm & Food Inc ....F...... 718 441-3152
  Richmond Hill *(G-14079)*
Metzger Speciality Brands ....G...... 212 957-0055
  New York *(G-11271)*

FOOD PRDTS, FROZEN: Fruits, Juices & Vegetables

Blend Smoothie Bar ....G...... 845 568-7366
  New Windsor *(G-8979)*
Cahoon Farms Inc ....E...... 315 594-8081
  Wolcott *(G-17298)*
Copra ....G...... 917 224-1727
  New York *(G-9780)*
Fly Creek Cder Mill Orchrd Inc ....G...... 607 547-9692
  Fly Creek *(G-5319)*
H&F Products Inc ....G...... 845 651-6100
  Monroe *(G-8591)*
National Grape Coop Assn Inc ....E...... 716 326-5200
  Westfield *(G-17077)*
T & Smoothie Inc ....G...... 631 804-6653
  Patchogue *(G-13461)*

FOOD PRDTS, FROZEN: NEC

Codinos Limited Inc ....E...... 518 372-3308
  Schenectady *(G-15272)*
Dufour Pastry Kitchens Inc ....E...... 718 402-8800
  Bronx *(G-1322)*
Dvash Foods Inc ....F...... 845 578-1959
  Monsey *(G-8607)*
Finger Food Products Inc ....E...... 716 297-4888
  Sanborn *(G-15146)*
Freeze-Dry Foods Inc ....E...... 585 589-6399
  Albion *(G-168)*
Julians Recipe LLC ....E...... 888 640-8880
  Brooklyn *(G-2158)*
Milmar Food Group II LLC ....C...... 845 294-5400
  Goshen *(G-5752)*
Seviroli Foods Inc ....E...... 516 222-6220
  Garden City *(G-5546)*
Tami Great Food Corp ....G...... 845 352-7901
  Monsey *(G-8619)*
Tuv Taam Corp ....E...... 718 855-2207
  Brooklyn *(G-2708)*
Unilever United States Inc ....F...... 212 546-0200
  New York *(G-12474)*
Unilever United States Inc ....E...... 212 546-0200
  New York *(G-12475)*

FOOD PRDTS, FROZEN: Pizza

D R M Management Inc ....E...... 716 668-0333
  Depew *(G-4278)*
F & R Enterprises Inc ....G...... 315 841-8189
  Waterville *(G-16701)*
Salarinos Italian Foods Inc ....F...... 315 697-9766
  Canastota *(G-3398)*

FOOD PRDTS, FROZEN: Snack Items

Hong Hop Co Inc ....E...... 212 962-1735
  New York *(G-10546)*
Les Chateaux De France Inc ....E...... 516 239-6795
  Inwood *(G-6800)*

FOOD PRDTS, FROZEN: Soups

Classic Cooking LLC ....D...... 718 439-0200
  Jamaica *(G-6941)*

FOOD PRDTS, FROZEN: Vegetables, Exc Potato Prdts

Birds Eye Foods Inc ....G...... 716 988-3218
  South Dayton *(G-15539)*
Classic Cooking LLC ....D...... 718 439-0200
  Jamaica *(G-6941)*
Prime Food Processing Corp ....D...... 718 963-2323
  Brooklyn *(G-2455)*
Seneca Foods Corporation ....E...... 315 926-8100
  Marion *(G-8129)*
Tami Great Food Corp ....G...... 845 352-7901
  Monsey *(G-8619)*

FOOD PRDTS, FROZEN: Whipped Topping

Kraft Heinz Foods Company ....B...... 585 226-4400
  Avon *(G-537)*

FOOD PRDTS, MEAT & MEAT PRDTS, WHOLESALE: Fresh

Alps Provision Co Inc ....E...... 718 721-4477
  Astoria *(G-430)*
Camellia General Provision Co ....E...... 716 893-5352
  Buffalo *(G-2887)*
Kamerys Wholesale Meats Inc ....G...... 716 372-6756
  Olean *(G-13170)*
Reliable Brothers Inc ....E...... 518 273-6732
  Green Island *(G-5879)*

FOOD PRDTS, WHOL: Canned Goods, Fruit, Veg, Seafood/Meats

Frank Wardynski & Sons Inc ....E...... 716 854-6083
  Buffalo *(G-2970)*
Spf Holdings II LLC ....G...... 212 750-8300
  New York *(G-12185)*
Wonton Food Inc ....C...... 718 628-6868
  Brooklyn *(G-2778)*

FOOD PRDTS, WHOLESALE: Beverage Concentrates

Motts LLP ....C...... 972 673-8088
  Elmsford *(G-4775)*

FOOD PRDTS, WHOLESALE: Beverages, Exc Coffee & Tea

A Health Obsession LLC ....E...... 347 850-4587
  Brooklyn *(G-1534)*
Pepsi-Cola Sales and Dist Inc ....G...... 914 253-2000
  Purchase *(G-13980)*
Pepsico Sales Inc ....G...... 914 253-2000
  Purchase *(G-13985)*
TLC-Lc Inc ....E...... 212 756-8900
  New York *(G-12375)*

FOOD PRDTS, WHOLESALE: Chocolate

Amiram Dror Inc ....F...... 212 979-9505
  Brooklyn *(G-1609)*
Chocolate Pizza Company Inc ....F...... 315 673-4098
  Marcellus *(G-8118)*
Commodore Chocolatier USA Inc ....F...... 845 561-3960
  Newburgh *(G-12774)*
Godiva Chocolatier Inc ....E...... 212 984-5900
  New York *(G-10368)*
Lanco Corporation ....C...... 631 231-2300
  Ronkonkoma *(G-14957)*

FOOD PRDTS, WHOLESALE: Coffee, Green Or Roasted

Coffee Holding Co Inc ....D...... 718 832-0800
  Staten Island *(G-15680)*
Elite Roasters Inc ....F...... 716 626-0307
  East Amherst *(G-4386)*
Orens Daily Roast Inc ....G...... 212 348-5400
  New York *(G-11538)*
Paul De Lima Company Inc ....D...... 315 457-3725
  Liverpool *(G-7566)*

FOOD PRDTS, WHOLESALE: Condiments

Kensington & Sons LLC ....E...... 646 430-8298
  New York *(G-10875)*

FOOD PRDTS, WHOLESALE: Cookies

212kiddish Inc ....G...... 718 705-7227
  Brooklyn *(G-1512)*

FOOD PRDTS, WHOLESALE: Flour

Archer-Daniels-Midland Company ....D...... 518 828-4691
  Hudson *(G-6635)*

FOOD PRDTS, WHOLESALE: Grains

Chia Usa LLC ....F...... 212 226-7512
  New York *(G-9643)*

FOOD PRDTS, WHOLESALE: Health

Sangster Foods Inc ....F...... 212 993-9129
  Brooklyn *(G-2556)*

PRODUCT SECTION

FOOD PRDTS: Doughs & Batters

FOOD PRDTS, WHOLESALE: Juices

Brooklyn Btlg Milton NY Inc .... C 845 795-2171
  Milton *(G-8516)*
Schutt Cider Mill .... F 585 872-2924
  Webster *(G-16760)*

FOOD PRDTS, WHOLESALE: Organic & Diet

Natural Lab Inc .... G 718 321-8848
  Flushing *(G-5277)*

FOOD PRDTS, WHOLESALE: Pasta & Rice

Deer Park Macaroni Co Inc .... F 631 667-4600
  Deer Park *(G-4151)*
Great Eastern Pasta Works LLC .... E 631 956-0889
  West Babylon *(G-16820)*
New York Ravioli Pasta Co Inc .... E 516 270-2852
  New Hyde Park *(G-8897)*
Steinway Pasta & Gelati Inc .... F 718 246-5414
  Brooklyn *(G-2628)*
Victoria Fine Foods LLC .... D 718 649-1635
  Brooklyn *(G-2742)*

FOOD PRDTS, WHOLESALE: Sandwiches

Fresh Fanatic Inc .... G 516 521-6574
  Brooklyn *(G-2005)*

FOOD PRDTS, WHOLESALE: Sausage Casings

DRG New York Holdings Corp .... D 914 668-9000
  Mount Vernon *(G-8723)*

FOOD PRDTS, WHOLESALE: Specialty

Castella Imports Inc .... C 631 231-5500
  Hauppauge *(G-6060)*
Fanshawe Foods LLC .... F 212 757-3130
  New York *(G-10188)*

FOOD PRDTS, WHOLESALE: Tea

White Coffee Corp .... D 718 204-7900
  Astoria *(G-461)*

FOOD PRDTS: Almond Pastes

American Almond Pdts Co Inc .... D 718 875-8310
  Brooklyn *(G-1597)*

FOOD PRDTS: Bran, Rice

Gassho Body & Mind Inc .... G 518 695-9991
  Schuylerville *(G-15341)*

FOOD PRDTS: Bread Crumbs, Exc Made In Bakeries

Gourmet Toast Corp .... G 718 852-4536
  Brooklyn *(G-2045)*
H & S Edible Products Corp .... E 914 413-3489
  Mount Vernon *(G-8733)*

FOOD PRDTS: Breakfast Bars

Glennys Inc .... G 516 377-1400
  Brooklyn *(G-2027)*
Keep Healthy Inc .... F 631 651-9090
  Northport *(G-13031)*

FOOD PRDTS: Cane Syrup, From Purchased Raw Sugar

Cane Sugar LLC .... G 212 329-2695
  New York *(G-9567)*

FOOD PRDTS: Cereals

Associated Brands Inc .... B 585 798-3475
  New York *(G-9291)*
Chia Usa LLC .... F 212 226-7512
  New York *(G-9643)*
Gabila Food Products Inc .... E 631 789-2220
  Copiague *(G-3928)*
Kellogg Company .... E 315 452-0310
  North Syracuse *(G-12968)*
Kellogg Company .... A 845 365-5284
  Orangeburg *(G-13255)*
Kraft Heinz Foods Company .... A 914 335-2500
  Tarrytown *(G-16116)*

Pepsico Inc .... A 914 253-2000
  Purchase *(G-13981)*
Sanzdranz LLC .... G 518 894-8625
  Delmar *(G-4271)*
Sanzdranz LLC .... G 518 894-8625
  Schenectady *(G-15316)*

FOOD PRDTS: Cheese Curls & Puffs

Emmi USA Inc .... F 845 268-9990
  Orangeburg *(G-13247)*

FOOD PRDTS: Chicken, Processed, Frozen

K&Ns Foods Usa LLC .... E 315 598-8080
  Fulton *(G-5479)*

FOOD PRDTS: Chocolate Bars, Solid

Amiram Dror Inc .... F 212 979-9505
  Brooklyn *(G-1609)*
Cemoi Inc .... G 212 583-4920
  New York *(G-9611)*
Max Brenner Union Square LLC .... G 646 467-8803
  New York *(G-11210)*
Mbny LLC .... F 646 467-8810
  New York *(G-11216)*
Micosta Enterprises Inc .... F 518 822-9708
  Hudson *(G-6657)*
Parkside Candy Co Inc .... F 716 833-7540
  Buffalo *(G-3137)*

FOOD PRDTS: Chocolate Coatings & Syrup

Fox 416 Corp .... E 718 385-4600
  Brooklyn *(G-2001)*

FOOD PRDTS: Coconut Oil

Jax Coco USA LLC .... G 347 688-8198
  New York *(G-10744)*

FOOD PRDTS: Coconut, Desiccated & Shredded

Far Eastern Coconut Company .... F 631 851-8800
  Central Islip *(G-3522)*

FOOD PRDTS: Coffee

Birch Guys LLC .... G 917 763-0751
  Long Island City *(G-7717)*
Cafe Kubal .... F 315 278-2812
  Syracuse *(G-15901)*
Caranda Emporium LLC .... F 212 866-7100
  New York *(G-9577)*
Coffee Holding Co Inc .... D 718 832-0800
  Staten Island *(G-15680)*
Elite Roasters Inc .... F 716 626-0307
  East Amherst *(G-4386)*
Fal Coffee Inc .... F 718 305-4255
  Brooklyn *(G-1959)*
Irving Farm Coffee Co Inc .... F 212 206-0707
  New York *(G-10706)*
Joseph H Navaie .... F 607 936-9030
  Corning *(G-3995)*
Kraft Heinz Foods Company .... A 914 335-2500
  Tarrytown *(G-16116)*
Maidstone Coffee Co .... E 585 272-1040
  Rochester *(G-14512)*
New York Gourmet Coffee Inc .... F 631 254-0076
  Bay Shore *(G-719)*
P Pascal Inc .... F 914 969-7933
  Yonkers *(G-17493)*
Paul De Lima Company Inc .... D 315 457-3725
  Liverpool *(G-7566)*
Paul De Lima Company Inc .... F 315 457-3725
  Cicero *(G-3678)*
Paul Delima Coffee Company .... G 315 457-3725
  Cicero *(G-3679)*
S J McCullagh Inc .... E 716 856-3473
  Buffalo *(G-3201)*
Star Mountain JFK Inc .... G 718 553-6787
  Jamaica *(G-6988)*
Vega Coffee Inc .... G 415 881-7969
  New York *(G-12538)*

FOOD PRDTS: Coffee Extracts

Brooklyn Roasting Works LLC .... G 718 855-1000
  Brooklyn *(G-1731)*
Death Wish Coffee Company LLC ...... F 518 400-1050
  Round Lake *(G-15061)*

Eldorado Coffee Roasters Ltd .... D 718 418-4100
  Maspeth *(G-8167)*

FOOD PRDTS: Coffee Roasting, Exc Wholesale Grocers

Bh Coffee Company LLC .... D 914 377-2500
  Elmsford *(G-4745)*
BK Associates Intl Inc .... F 607 432-1499
  Oneonta *(G-13196)*
Empire Coffee Company Inc .... E 914 934-1100
  Port Chester *(G-13773)*
Gillies Coffee Company .... E 718 499-7766
  Brooklyn *(G-2024)*
Gorilla Coffee Inc .... G 917 297-8947
  Brooklyn *(G-2041)*
Gorilla Coffee Inc .... G 718 230-3244
  Brooklyn *(G-2042)*
John A Vassilaros & Son Inc .... E 718 886-4140
  Flushing *(G-5264)*
Monkey Joe Roasting Company .... G 845 331-4598
  Kingston *(G-7231)*
Peaks Coffee Company .... F 315 565-1900
  Cazenovia *(G-3477)*
Regal Trading Inc .... E 914 694-6100
  Purchase *(G-13986)*
Where Is Utica Cof Rasting Inc .... F 315 269-8898
  Utica *(G-16389)*
White Coffee Corp .... D 718 204-7900
  Astoria *(G-461)*

FOOD PRDTS: Cooking Oils, Refined Vegetable, Exc Corn

C B S Food Products Corp .... F 718 452-2500
  Brooklyn *(G-1745)*
Healthy Brand Oil Corp .... F 718 937-0806
  Long Island City *(G-7786)*

FOOD PRDTS: Corn Chips & Other Corn-Based Snacks

Frito-Lay North America Inc .... D 716 631-2360
  Williamsville *(G-17271)*
Glennys Inc .... G 516 377-1400
  Brooklyn *(G-2027)*

FOOD PRDTS: Corn Sugars & Syrups

Archer-Daniels-Midland Company ..... G 585 346-2311
  Lakeville *(G-7305)*

FOOD PRDTS: Cottonseed Lecithin

Perimondo LLC .... G 212 749-0721
  New York *(G-11637)*

FOOD PRDTS: Dessert Mixes & Fillings

Deedee Desserts LLC .... G 716 627-2330
  Lake View *(G-7303)*
Noaspence Inc .... G 516 433-7848
  Hicksville *(G-6401)*
Rich Products Corporation .... A 716 878-8000
  Buffalo *(G-3185)*
VIP Foods Inc .... E 718 821-5330
  Ridgewood *(G-14143)*

FOOD PRDTS: Desserts, Ready-To-Mix

Butterwood Desserts Inc .... E 716 652-0131
  West Falls *(G-16876)*
Kozy Shack Enterprises LLC .... C 516 870-3000
  Hicksville *(G-6387)*
Kozy Shack Enterprises LLC .... C 516 870-3000
  Hicksville *(G-6388)*
Omg Desserts Inc .... F 585 698-1561
  Rochester *(G-14569)*

FOOD PRDTS: Dough, Pizza, Prepared

Ohio Baking Company Inc .... E 315 724-2033
  Utica *(G-16378)*

FOOD PRDTS: Doughs & Batters

Losurdo Foods Inc .... E 518 842-1500
  Amsterdam *(G-355)*

Employee Codes: A=Over 500 employees, B=251-500
C=101-250, D=51-100, E=20-50, F=10-19, G=5-9

FOOD PRDTS: Doughs & Batters From Purchased Flour

FOOD PRDTS: Doughs & Batters From Purchased Flour
Cohens Bakery Inc .... E 716 892-8149
  Buffalo *(G-2899)*

FOOD PRDTS: Dressings, Salad, Raw & Cooked Exc Dry Mixes
Mizkan America Inc .... F 585 798-5720
  Medina *(G-8311)*
Sum Sum LLC .... G 516 812-3959
  Oceanside *(G-13121)*

FOOD PRDTS: Dried & Dehydrated Fruits, Vegetables & Soup Mix
Goya Foods Inc .... D 716 549-0076
  Angola *(G-380)*
Shoreline Fruit LLC .... D 585 765-2639
  Lyndonville *(G-7996)*

FOOD PRDTS: Ducks, Processed, Fresh
Crescent Duck Farm Inc .... E 631 722-8700
  Aquebogue *(G-384)*

FOOD PRDTS: Ducks, Processed, NEC
Hudson Valley Foie Gras LLC .... F 845 292-2500
  Ferndale *(G-5179)*

FOOD PRDTS: Edible Oil Prdts, Exc Corn Oil
Consumer Flavoring Extract Co .... F 718 435-0201
  Brooklyn *(G-1797)*

FOOD PRDTS: Edible fats & oils
Bunge Limited Finance Corp .... C 914 684-2800
  White Plains *(G-17116)*
Kerry Bfnctnal Ingredients Inc .... D 607 334-1700
  Norwich *(G-13048)*

FOOD PRDTS: Egg Substitutes, Made From Eggs
Egg Low Farms Inc .... F 607 674-4653
  Sherburne *(G-15413)*

FOOD PRDTS: Eggs, Processed
Ready Egg Farms Inc .... G 607 674-4653
  Sherburne *(G-15416)*

FOOD PRDTS: Emulsifiers
Broome County .... E 607 785-9567
  Endicott *(G-4805)*
Chemicolloid Laboratories Inc .... F 516 747-2666
  New Hyde Park *(G-8866)*
Momentive Performance Mtls Inc .... D 914 784-4807
  Tarrytown *(G-16121)*
Redland Foods Corp .... F 716 288-9061
  Cheektowaga *(G-3616)*

FOOD PRDTS: Flavored Ices, Frozen
Elegant Desserts By Metro Inc .... F 718 388-1323
  Brooklyn *(G-1914)*
Four Brothers Italian Bakery .... G 914 741-5434
  Hawthorne *(G-6269)*
JMS Ices Inc .... F 718 448-0853
  Staten Island *(G-15714)*
My Most Favorite Food .... G 212 580-5130
  New York *(G-11353)*
Olympic Ice Cream Co Inc .... E 718 849-6200
  Jamaica *(G-6974)*
Primo Frozen Desserts Inc .... G 718 252-2312
  Brooklyn *(G-2456)*

FOOD PRDTS: Flour & Other Grain Mill Products
ADM Milling Co .... D 716 849-7333
  Buffalo *(G-2814)*
Ardent Mills LLC .... D 518 447-1700
  Albany *(G-46)*
Birkett Mills .... G 315 536-3311
  Penn Yan *(G-13529)*
Birkett Mills .... E 315 536-4112
  Penn Yan *(G-13530)*

Champlain Valley Mil Corp Inc .... G 518 962-4711
  Westport *(G-17096)*
Cochecton Mills Inc .... E 845 932-8282
  Cochecton *(G-3765)*
Sheppard Grain Enterprises LLC .... E 315 548-9271
  Phelps *(G-13560)*

FOOD PRDTS: Flour Mixes & Doughs
Aryzta LLC .... D 310 417-4700
  Rochester *(G-14232)*
Bektrom Foods Inc .... E 516 802-3800
  Syosset *(G-15835)*
Lollipop Tree Inc .... E 845 471-8733
  Auburn *(G-504)*

FOOD PRDTS: Fruit Juices
Cheribundi Inc .... E 800 699-0460
  Geneva *(G-5585)*
Dynamic Health Labs Inc .... E 718 858-0100
  Brooklyn *(G-1887)*
Global Natural Foods Inc .... E 845 439-3292
  Livingston Manor *(G-7589)*
Hain Blueprint Inc .... E 212 414-5741
  New Hyde Park *(G-8881)*
Pepsico Inc .... A 914 253-2000
  Purchase *(G-13981)*
Pura Fruta LLC .... F 415 279-5727
  Long Island City *(G-7880)*
Purely Maple Inc .... F 646 524-7135
  New York *(G-11776)*
Zoe Sakoutis LLC .... F 212 414-5741
  New York *(G-12736)*

FOOD PRDTS: Fruits & Vegetables, Pickled
United Farm Processing Corp .... C 718 933-6060
  Bronx *(G-1484)*

FOOD PRDTS: Fruits, Dehydrated Or Dried
Peeled Inc .... F 212 706-2001
  Brooklyn *(G-2425)*
Settons Intl Foods Inc .... E 631 543-8090
  Commack *(G-3868)*

FOOD PRDTS: Fruits, Dried Or Dehydrated, Exc Freeze-Dried
Associated Brands Inc .... B 585 798-3475
  New York *(G-9291)*
Marshall Ingredients LLC .... G 800 796-9353
  Wolcott *(G-17301)*

FOOD PRDTS: Gelatin Dessert Preparations
Original Hrkmr Cnty Chese Inc .... D 315 895-7428
  Ilion *(G-6782)*

FOOD PRDTS: Gluten Meal
Anthony Gigi Inc .... G 860 984-1943
  Shirley *(G-15435)*

FOOD PRDTS: Horseradish, Exc Sauce
Whalens Horseradish Products .... G 518 587-6404
  Galway *(G-5498)*

FOOD PRDTS: Ice, Blocks
Arctic Glacier Texas Inc .... E 215 283-0326
  Fairport *(G-4851)*
Clayville Ice Co Inc .... G 315 839-5405
  Clayville *(G-3713)*
Huntington Ice & Cube Corp .... F 718 456-2013
  Brooklyn *(G-2087)*

FOOD PRDTS: Ice, Cubes
Arctic Glacier USA .... E 215 283-0326
  Fairport *(G-4852)*
Henry Newman LLC .... F 607 273-8512
  Ithaca *(G-6883)*
Ice Cube Inc .... G 613 254-0071
  Deer Park *(G-4174)*

FOOD PRDTS: Instant Coffee
Altaro Corp .... F 855 674-2455
  Tarrytown *(G-16109)*
Orens Daily Roast Inc .... G 212 348-5400
  New York *(G-11538)*

Sangster Foods Inc .... F 212 993-9129
  Brooklyn *(G-2556)*

FOOD PRDTS: Jelly, Corncob
Larte Del Gelato Inc .... G 212 366-0570
  New York *(G-10966)*

FOOD PRDTS: Juice Pops, Frozen
Zings Company LLC .... G 631 454-0339
  Farmingdale *(G-5154)*

FOOD PRDTS: Macaroni Prdts, Dry, Alphabet, Rings Or Shells
Piemonte Home Made Ravioli Co .... F 718 429-1972
  Woodside *(G-17363)*
Queen Ann Macaroni Mfg Co Inc .... G 718 256-1061
  Brooklyn *(G-2485)*
Wing Kei Noodle Inc .... F 212 226-1644
  New York *(G-12671)*

FOOD PRDTS: Macaroni, Noodles, Spaghetti, Pasta, Etc
Cassinelli Food Products Inc .... G 718 274-4881
  Long Island City *(G-7724)*
Dairy Maid Raviolo Mfg .... F 718 449-2620
  Brooklyn *(G-1836)*
Deer Park Macaroni Co Inc .... G 631 667-4600
  Deer Park *(G-4150)*
Deer Park Macaroni Co Inc .... F 631 667-4600
  Deer Park *(G-4151)*
Piemonte Home Made Ravioli Co .... G 212 226-0475
  New York *(G-11680)*
Raffettos Corp .... E 212 777-1261
  New York *(G-11813)*
Ravioli Store Inc .... G 718 729-9300
  Long Island City *(G-7888)*
Twin Marquis Inc .... D 718 386-6868
  Brooklyn *(G-2710)*

FOOD PRDTS: Malt
Great Western Malting Co .... G 800 496-7732
  Champlain *(G-3569)*
Queen City Malting LLC .... G 716 481-1313
  Buffalo *(G-3175)*

FOOD PRDTS: Mayonnaise & Dressings, Exc Tomato Based
Kensington & Sons LLC .... E 646 430-8298
  New York *(G-10875)*

FOOD PRDTS: Mixes, Bread & Bread-Type Roll
Archer-Daniels-Midland Company .... E 518 828-4691
  Hudson *(G-6634)*

FOOD PRDTS: Mixes, Bread & Roll From Purchased Flour
Elis Bread (eli Zabar) Inc .... F 212 772-2011
  New York *(G-10058)*

FOOD PRDTS: Mixes, Doughnut From Purchased Flour
Dawn Food Products Inc .... C 716 830-8214
  Williamsville *(G-17268)*

FOOD PRDTS: Mixes, Pancake From Purchased Flour
New Hope Mills Inc .... F 315 252-2676
  Auburn *(G-507)*

FOOD PRDTS: Molasses, Mixed/Blended, Purchased Ingredients
Amalfi Ingredients LLC .... G 631 392-1526
  Deer Park *(G-4118)*

FOOD PRDTS: Mustard, Prepared
Old Dutch Mustard Co Inc .... G 516 466-0522
  Great Neck *(G-5843)*

FOOD PRDTS: Nuts & Seeds

American Almond Pdts Co Inc .... D 718 875-8310
  Brooklyn *(G-1597)*
Our Daily Eats LLC .... F 518 810-8412
  Albany *(G-114)*
Scaccianoce Inc .... F 718 991-4462
  Bronx *(G-1449)*
Sugar Foods Corporation .... E 212 753-6900
  New York *(G-12249)*
Whitsons Food Svc Bronx Corp ...... B 631 424-2700
  Islandia *(G-6843)*

FOOD PRDTS: Olive Oil

Bonelli Foods LLC .... G 212 346-0942
  New York *(G-9486)*
F Olivers LLC .... G 585 244-2585
  Rochester *(G-14389)*
L LLC .... E 716 885-3918
  Buffalo *(G-3057)*
Pietro Demarco Importers Inc .... F 914 969-3201
  Yonkers *(G-17496)*
Pinos Press Inc .... G 315 935-0110
  Syracuse *(G-16034)*

FOOD PRDTS: Oriental Noodles

Lams Foods Inc .... F 718 217-0476
  Queens Village *(G-13997)*
Twin Marquis Inc .... D 718 386-6868
  Brooklyn *(G-2710)*
Wonton Food Inc .... E 718 784-8178
  Long Island City *(G-7955)*
Wonton Food Inc .... C 718 628-6868
  Brooklyn *(G-2778)*
Wonton Food Inc .... F 212 677-8865
  New York *(G-12682)*

FOOD PRDTS: Pasta, Rice/Potatoes, Uncooked, Pkgd

Barilla America Ny Inc .... C 585 226-5600
  Avon *(G-536)*
Bektrom Foods Inc .... G 516 802-3800
  Syosset *(G-15835)*
New York Ravioli Pasta Co Inc .... E 516 270-2852
  New Hyde Park *(G-8897)*
Steinway Pasta & Gelati Inc .... F 718 246-5414
  Brooklyn *(G-2628)*

FOOD PRDTS: Pasta, Uncooked, Packaged With Other Ingredients

Great Eastern Pasta Works LLC ..... E 631 956-0889
  West Babylon *(G-16820)*
Hong Hop Co Inc .... E 212 962-1735
  New York *(G-10546)*
Johns Ravioli Company Inc .... F 914 576-7030
  New Rochelle *(G-8960)*
Labella Pasta Inc .... G 845 331-9130
  Kingston *(G-7224)*
Sfoglini LLC .... F 646 872-1035
  Brooklyn *(G-2572)*

FOOD PRDTS: Peanut Butter

ABC Peanut Butter LLC .... B 212 661-6886
  New York *(G-9048)*
Capitol City Specialties Co .... G 518 486-8935
  Albany *(G-59)*
Once Again Nut Butter Collectv ...... D 585 468-2535
  Nunda *(G-13059)*
Peanut Butter & Co Inc .... E 212 757-3130
  New York *(G-11604)*
Sneaky Chef Foods LLC .... F 914 301-3277
  Tarrytown *(G-16131)*
Wonder Natural Foods Corp .... G 631 726-4400
  Water Mill *(G-16629)*

FOOD PRDTS: Pickles, Vinegar

Allen Pickle Works Inc .... F 516 676-0640
  Glen Cove *(G-5622)*
Batampte Pickle Products Inc .... D 718 251-2100
  Brooklyn *(G-1669)*
Birds Eye Holdings Inc .... A 585 383-1850
  Rochester *(G-14250)*
French Associates Inc .... F 718 387-9880
  Fresh Meadows *(G-5454)*
Heintz & Weber Co Inc .... G 716 852-7171
  Buffalo *(G-3010)*
Moldova Pickles & Salads Inc .... G 718 284-2220
  Brooklyn *(G-2334)*

FOOD PRDTS: Pizza Doughs From Purchased Flour

Tosca Brick Oven Pizza Real .... G 718 430-0026
  Bronx *(G-1471)*

FOOD PRDTS: Pizza, Refrigerated

Ultra Thin Ready To Bake Pizza ..... E 516 679-6655
  Deer Park *(G-4243)*

FOOD PRDTS: Potato & Corn Chips & Similar Prdts

BSD Top Direct Inc .... G 646 468-0156
  West Babylon *(G-16802)*
Frito-Lay North America Inc .... E 585 343-5456
  Batavia *(G-635)*
Hain Celestial Group Inc .... C 516 587-5000
  New Hyde Park *(G-8882)*
Ideal Snacks Corporation .... C 845 292-7000
  Liberty *(G-7459)*
Pepsico Inc .... A 914 253-2000
  Purchase *(G-13981)*
Pepsico Inc .... B 914 253-2000
  White Plains *(G-17181)*
Pepsico Inc .... D 914 767-6976
  White Plains *(G-17183)*
Proformance Foods Inc .... G 703 869-3413
  Brooklyn *(G-2469)*
Robs Really Good LLC .... F 516 671-4411
  Sea Cliff *(G-15364)*
Saratoga Chips LLC .... G 877 901-6950
  Saratoga Springs *(G-15201)*
Switch Beverage Company LLC .... F 203 202-7383
  Port Washington *(G-13885)*
TLC-Lc Inc .... E 212 756-8900
  New York *(G-12375)*

FOOD PRDTS: Potato Chips & Other Potato-Based Snacks

Birds Eye Holdings Inc .... A 585 383-1850
  Rochester *(G-14250)*
Frito-Lay North America Inc .... D 607 775-7000
  Binghamton *(G-911)*
Terrells Potato Chip Co Inc .... D 315 437-2786
  Syracuse *(G-16081)*

FOOD PRDTS: Potato Sticks

Pupellos Organic Chips Inc .... F 718 710-9154
  Oakdale *(G-13079)*

FOOD PRDTS: Potatoes, Dried, Packaged With Other Ingredients

Martens Country Kit Pdts LLC .... F 315 776-8821
  Port Byron *(G-13762)*

FOOD PRDTS: Poultry, Processed, NEC

Wendels Poultry Farm .... G 716 592-2299
  East Concord *(G-4408)*

FOOD PRDTS: Poultry, Slaughtered & Dressed

Sing Ah Poultry .... G 718 625-7253
  Brooklyn *(G-2591)*

FOOD PRDTS: Preparations

212kiddish Inc .... G 718 705-7227
  Brooklyn *(G-1512)*
3v Company Inc .... E 718 858-7333
  Brooklyn *(G-1516)*
Ahhmigo LLC .... F 212 315-1818
  New York *(G-9111)*
Andros Bowman Products LLC ...... G 540 217-4100
  Lyndonville *(G-7994)*
Armour Bearer Group Inc .... G 646 812-4487
  Arverne *(G-421)*
Aryzta LLC .... D 310 417-4700
  Brooklyn *(G-14232)*
Associated Brands Inc .... B 585 798-3475
  New York *(G-9291)*
Bainbridge & Knight LLC .... E 212 986-5100
  New York *(G-9360)*
Baldwin Richardson Foods Co .... C 315 986-2727
  Macedon *(G-8010)*
Bombay Kitchen Foods Inc .... F 516 767-7401
  Port Washington *(G-13825)*
Brightline Ventures I LLC .... E 212 626-6829
  New York *(G-9513)*
Bylada Foods LLC .... D 845 623-1300
  West Nyack *(G-16944)*
Castella Imports Inc .... C 631 231-5500
  Hauppauge *(G-6060)*
Chan & Chan (usa) Corp .... G 718 388-9633
  Brooklyn *(G-1773)*
Child Nutrition Prog Dept Ed .... D 212 371-1000
  New York *(G-9644)*
China Huaren Organic Pdts Inc ...... G 212 232-0120
  New York *(G-9647)*
Conagra Brands Inc .... F 212 461-2410
  New York *(G-9753)*
Cookiebaker LLC .... G 716 878-8000
  Buffalo *(G-2909)*
D R M Management Inc .... E 716 668-0333
  Depew *(G-4278)*
Dundee Foods LLC .... F 585 377-7700
  Fairport *(G-4860)*
Event Services Corporation .... G 315 488-9357
  Solvay *(G-15530)*
Fanshawe Foods LLC .... F 212 757-3130
  New York *(G-10188)*
Flik International/Compass .... E 212 450-4750
  New York *(G-10232)*
Frito-Lay North America Inc .... D 607 775-7000
  Binghamton *(G-911)*
Glenn Foods Inc .... F 516 377-1400
  Freeport *(G-5413)*
Gold Pure Food Products Co Inc ... D 516 483-5600
  Hempstead *(G-6296)*
Gourmet Boutique LLC .... C 718 977-1200
  Jamaica *(G-6952)*
Gourmet Crafts Inc .... F 718 372-0505
  Brooklyn *(G-2044)*
Gourmet Guru Inc .... E 718 842-2828
  Bronx *(G-1349)*
Gravymaster Inc .... E 203 453-1893
  Canajoharie *(G-3360)*
HP Hood LLC .... D 607 295-8134
  Arkport *(G-408)*
Instantwhip of Buffalo Inc .... E 716 892-7031
  Buffalo *(G-3027)*
Joyva Corp .... D 718 497-0170
  Brooklyn *(G-2153)*
Kale Factory Inc .... G 917 363-6361
  Brooklyn *(G-2166)*
Kerry Bfnctnal Ingredients Inc .... D 607 334-1700
  Norwich *(G-13048)*
Kerry Inc .... G 845 584-3081
  Congers *(G-3883)*
Kraft Heinz Foods Company .... A 914 335-2500
  Tarrytown *(G-16116)*
Kraft Heinz Foods Company .... B 585 226-4400
  Avon *(G-537)*
Land OLakes Inc .... G 516 681-2980
  Hicksville *(G-6390)*
Lollipop Tree Inc .... E 845 471-8733
  Auburn *(G-504)*
Lugo Nutrition Inc .... G 302 573-2503
  Nyack *(G-13069)*
Mandalay Food Products Inc .... G 718 230-3370
  Brooklyn *(G-2259)*
Mediterrean Dyro Company .... E 718 786-4888
  Long Island City *(G-7839)*
Merb LLC .... F 631 393-3621
  Farmingdale *(G-5057)*
Meta-Therm Corp .... F 914 697-4840
  White Plains *(G-17164)*
Mighty Quinns Barbeque LLC .... C 973 777-8340
  New York *(G-11287)*
Milnot Holding Corporation .... G 518 839-0300
  Amsterdam *(G-358)*
Mizkan America Inc .... D 585 765-9171
  Lyndonville *(G-7995)*
Moira New Hope Food Pantry .... E 518 529-6524
  Moira *(G-8581)*
Mondelez Global LLC .... G 585 345-3300
  Batavia *(G-643)*
Morris Kitchen Inc .... F 646 413-5186
  Brooklyn *(G-2339)*
Natural Lab Inc .... G 718 321-8848
  Flushing *(G-5277)*
Naturally Free Food Inc .... G 631 361-9710
  Smithtown *(G-15515)*

Employee Codes: A=Over 500 employees, B=251-500
C=101-250, D=51-100, E=20-50, F=10-19, G=5-9

FOOD PRDTS: Preparations

Nestle Healthcare Ntrtn Inc .... G 516 249-5085
  Farmingdale *(G-5074)*
North Shore Farms Two Ltd .... G 516 280-6880
  Mineola *(G-8560)*
P-Hgh 2 Co Inc .... G 954 534-6058
  Buffalo *(G-3131)*
Parnasa International Inc .... G 516 394-0400
  Valley Stream *(G-16442)*
Pelican Bay Ltd .... F 718 729-9300
  Long Island City *(G-7869)*
Pellicano Specialty Foods Inc .... F 716 822-2366
  Buffalo *(G-3140)*
Pennant Ingredients Inc .... D 585 235-8160
  Rochester *(G-14595)*
Ponti Rossi Inc .... G 347 506-9616
  Brooklyn *(G-2441)*
Raw Indulgence Ltd .... F 866 498-4671
  Hawthorne *(G-6278)*
Rob Salamida Company Inc .... F 607 729-4868
  Johnson City *(G-7136)*
Sabra Dipping Company LLC .... F 516 249-0151
  Farmingdale *(G-5117)*
Salvador Colletti Blank .... G 718 217-6725
  Douglaston *(G-4334)*
Sapienza Pastry Inc .... E 516 352-5232
  Elmont *(G-4739)*
Settons Intl Foods Inc .... E 631 543-8090
  Commack *(G-3868)*
Terrace Management Inc .... E 914 737-0400
  Cortlandt Manor *(G-4080)*
Tuv Taam Corp .... E 718 855-2207
  Brooklyn *(G-2708)*
UFS Industries Inc .... D 718 822-1100
  Mount Vernon *(G-8790)*
Whitsons Food Svc Bronx Corp .... B 631 424-2700
  Islandia *(G-6843)*
Win-Holt Equipment Corp .... E 516 222-0335
  Woodbury *(G-17322)*

FOOD PRDTS: Prepared Meat Sauces Exc Tomato & Dry

American Specialty Mfg Co .... F 585 544-5600
  Rochester *(G-14215)*

FOOD PRDTS: Prepared Sauces, Exc Tomato Based

Bushwick Kitchen LLC .... G 917 297-1045
  Brooklyn *(G-1741)*
Elwood International Inc .... F 631 842-6600
  Copiague *(G-3925)*
Gold Pure Food Products Co Inc .... D 516 483-5600
  Hempstead *(G-6296)*
Gravymaster Inc .... E 203 453-1893
  Canajoharie *(G-3360)*
Mandarin Soy Sauce Inc .... E 845 343-1505
  Middletown *(G-8483)*
Rob Salamida Company Inc .... F 607 729-4868
  Johnson City *(G-7136)*
Sassy Sauce Inc .... G 585 621-1050
  Rochester *(G-14690)*
T R S Great American Rest .... F 516 294-1680
  Williston Park *(G-17287)*

FOOD PRDTS: Raw cane sugar

Supreme Chocolatier LLC .... E 718 761-9600
  Staten Island *(G-15767)*

FOOD PRDTS: Relishes, Vinegar

Jets Lefrois Corp .... G 585 637-5003
  Brockport *(G-1245)*

FOOD PRDTS: Rice, Milled

Real Co Inc .... G 347 433-8549
  Valley Cottage *(G-16412)*

FOOD PRDTS: Salads

Golden Taste Inc .... E 845 356-4133
  Spring Valley *(G-15609)*
M & M Food Products Inc .... F 718 821-1970
  Brooklyn *(G-2246)*
Radicle Farm LLC .... G 315 226-3294
  New York *(G-11812)*

FOOD PRDTS: Sauerkraut, Bulk

Glk Foods LLC .... E 585 289-4414
  Shortsville *(G-15456)*

FOOD PRDTS: Seasonings & Spices

Aromasong Usa Inc .... F 718 838-9669
  Brooklyn *(G-1632)*
Diva Farms Ltd .... G 315 735-4397
  Utica *(G-16349)*
La Flor Products Company Inc .... E 631 851-9601
  Hauppauge *(G-6136)*
Purespice LLC .... G 617 549-8400
  Hopewell Junction *(G-6584)*
SOS Chefs of New York Inc .... E 212 505-5813
  New York *(G-12164)*

FOOD PRDTS: Soup Mixes, Dried

Allied Food Products Inc .... E 718 230-4227
  Brooklyn *(G-1588)*
Interntional Gourmet Soups Inc .... E 212 768-7687
  Staten Island *(G-15709)*

FOOD PRDTS: Soy Sauce

Wanjashan International LLC .... F 845 343-1505
  Middletown *(G-8505)*

FOOD PRDTS: Spices, Including Ground

Extreme Spices Inc .... G 917 496-4081
  Maspeth *(G-8168)*
Manhattan Milling & Drying Co .... E 516 496-1041
  Woodbury *(G-17314)*
Victoria Fine Foods LLC .... D 718 649-1635
  Brooklyn *(G-2742)*
Wm E Martin and Sons Co Inc .... E 516 605-2444
  Roslyn *(G-15048)*

FOOD PRDTS: Spreads, Sandwich, Salad Dressing Base

Sabra Dipping Company LLC .... D 914 372-3900
  White Plains *(G-17193)*

FOOD PRDTS: Starches

Machoonjdgroup .... G 856 345-4689
  Medford *(G-8287)*

FOOD PRDTS: Sugar

Real Co Inc .... G 347 433-8549
  Valley Cottage *(G-16412)*
Sugar Foods Corporation .... E 212 753-6900
  New York *(G-12249)*
Sugar Shack Desert Company Inc .... E 518 523-7540
  Lake Placid *(G-7300)*
U S Sugar Co Inc .... E 716 828-1170
  Buffalo *(G-3256)*

FOOD PRDTS: Sugar, Beet

Beets Love Production LLC .... E 585 270-2471
  Rochester *(G-14245)*

FOOD PRDTS: Sugar, Cane

Asr Group International Inc .... C 914 963-2400
  Yonkers *(G-17433)*
Sweeteners Plus Inc .... D 585 728-3770
  Lakeville *(G-7309)*

FOOD PRDTS: Sugar, Corn

Sweetwater Energy Inc .... G 585 647-5760
  Rochester *(G-14732)*

FOOD PRDTS: Sugar, Granulated Cane, Purchd Raw Sugar/Syrup

Domino Foods Inc .... F 800 729-4840
  Yonkers *(G-17453)*

FOOD PRDTS: Syrup, Maple

Peaceful Valley Maple Farm .... G 518 762-0491
  Johnstown *(G-7150)*

FOOD PRDTS: Syrups

Casablanca Foods LLC .... G 212 317-1111
  New York *(G-9593)*

FOOD PRDTS: Tea

Bel Americas Inc .... G 646 454-8220
  New York *(G-9396)*
Farmers Hub LLC .... G 914 380-2945
  White Plains *(G-17135)*
Gillies Coffee Company .... E 718 499-7766
  Brooklyn *(G-2024)*
Tea Life LLC .... G 516 365-7711
  Manhasset *(G-8100)*

FOOD PRDTS: Tofu Desserts, Frozen

Pulmuone Foods Usa Inc .... E 845 365-3300
  Tappan *(G-16106)*

FOOD PRDTS: Tofu, Exc Frozen Desserts

Chan Kee Dried Bean Curd Inc .... G 718 622-0820
  Brooklyn *(G-1774)*
Seasons Soyfood Inc .... E 718 797-9896
  Brooklyn *(G-2567)*

FOOD PRDTS: Tortilla Chips

Tortilleria Chinantla Inc .... G 718 302-0101
  Brooklyn *(G-2687)*

FOOD PRDTS: Tortillas

Blue Tortilla LLC .... G 631 451-0100
  Selden *(G-15369)*
Buna Besta Tortillas .... G 347 987-3995
  Brooklyn *(G-1739)*
Fresh Tortillas Si Inc .... G 718 979-6666
  Staten Island *(G-15696)*
La Escondida Inc .... G 845 562-1387
  Newburgh *(G-12786)*
Maizteca Foods Inc .... E 718 641-3933
  South Richmond Hill *(G-15558)*
Tortilla Heaven Inc .... G 845 339-1550
  Kingston *(G-7245)*

FOOD PRDTS: Vegetables, Dried or Dehydrated Exc Freeze-Dried

Wm E Martin and Sons Co Inc .... E 516 605-2444
  Roslyn *(G-15048)*

FOOD PRDTS: Vegetables, Pickled

United Pickle Products Corp .... E 718 933-6060
  Bronx *(G-1485)*

FOOD PRDTS: Vinegar

Fleischmanns Vinegar Co Inc .... E 315 587-4414
  North Rose *(G-12952)*
Mizkan America Inc .... F 585 798-5720
  Medina *(G-8311)*
Mizkan Americas Inc .... F 315 483-6944
  Sodus *(G-15525)*
Old Dutch Mustard Co Inc .... E 516 466-0522
  Great Neck *(G-5843)*
Vinegar Hill Asset LLC .... G 718 469-0342
  Brooklyn *(G-2745)*

FOOD PRODUCTS MACHINERY

Ag-Pak Inc .... F 716 772-2651
  Gasport *(G-5570)*
Bakers Pride Oven Co Inc .... C 914 576-0200
  New Rochelle *(G-8932)*
Bari Engineering Corp .... E 212 966-2080
  New York *(G-9372)*
Buflovak LLC .... E 716 895-2100
  Buffalo *(G-2883)*
C-Flex Bearing Co Inc .... F 315 895-7454
  Frankfort *(G-5359)*
Carts Mobile Food Eqp Corp .... E 718 788-5540
  Brooklyn *(G-1763)*
Chester-Jensen Company .... E 610 876-6276
  Cattaraugus *(G-3465)*
Delsur Parts .... G 631 630-1606
  Brentwood *(G-1178)*
Elmar Industries Inc .... D 716 681-5650
  Depew *(G-4280)*
Esquire Mechanical Corp .... G 718 625-4006
  Brooklyn *(G-1941)*
G J Olney Inc .... E 315 827-4208
  Westernville *(G-17072)*

PRODUCT SECTION

FOUNDRIES: Nonferrous

Company	Code	Phone
Haines Equipment Inc	E	607 566-8531
Avoca *(G-534)*		
I J White Corporation	D	631 293-3788
Farmingdale *(G-5016)*		
Kinplex Inc	E	631 242-4800
Edgewood *(G-4618)*		
Ludwig Holdings Corp	D	845 340-9727
Kingston *(G-7227)*		
Lyophilization Systems Inc	G	845 338-0456
New Paltz *(G-8921)*		
M & E Mfg Co Inc	D	845 331-7890
Kingston *(G-7229)*		
National Equipment Corporation	F	718 585-0200
Harrison *(G-6006)*		
National Equipment Corporation	E	718 585-0200
Bronx *(G-1408)*		
Olmstead Products Corp	F	516 681-3700
Hicksville *(G-6404)*		
P & M LLC	E	631 842-2200
Amityville *(G-319)*		
Sidco Food Distribution Corp	F	718 733-3939
Bronx *(G-1451)*		
Simply Natural Foods LLC	E	631 543-9600
Commack *(G-3869)*		
SPX Flow Tech Systems Inc	D	716 692-3000
Getzville *(G-5616)*		
Vr Food Equipment Inc	F	315 531-8133
Farmington *(G-5166)*		
Wilder Manufacturing Co Inc	D	516 222-0433
Garden City *(G-5550)*		
Win-Holt Equipment Corp	C	516 222-0433
Garden City *(G-5551)*		

FOOD STORES: Delicatessen

Company	Code	Phone
Cassinelli Food Products Inc	G	718 274-4881
Long Island City *(G-7724)*		
Jim Romas Bakery Inc	E	607 748-7425
Endicott *(G-4823)*		
Mds Hot Bagels Deli Inc	G	718 438-5650
Brooklyn *(G-2293)*		
Sam A Lupo & Sons Inc	G	800 388-5452
Endicott *(G-4833)*		

FOOD STORES: Grocery, Independent

Company	Code	Phone
Mandalay Food Products Inc	G	718 230-3370
Brooklyn *(G-2259)*		

FOOD STORES: Supermarkets

Company	Code	Phone
Hana Pastries Inc	G	718 369-7593
Brooklyn *(G-2064)*		
Reisman Bros Bakery Inc	F	718 331-1975
Brooklyn *(G-2507)*		

FOOTWEAR, WHOLESALE: Athletic

Company	Code	Phone
Air Skate & Air Jump Corp	G	212 967-1201
New York *(G-9116)*		
Air Skate & Air Jump Corp	F	212 967-1201
Brooklyn *(G-1571)*		

FOOTWEAR, WHOLESALE: Shoe Access

Company	Code	Phone
Aniiwe Inc	G	347 683-1891
Brooklyn *(G-1612)*		
Bfma Holding Corporation	G	607 753-6746
Cortland *(G-4036)*		

FOOTWEAR, WHOLESALE: Shoes

Company	Code	Phone
Anthony L & S LLC	G	212 386-7245
New York *(G-9218)*		

FOOTWEAR: Cut Stock

Company	Code	Phone
Age Manufacturers Inc	D	718 927-0048
Brooklyn *(G-1569)*		
Golden Pacific Lxj Inc	G	267 975-6537
New York *(G-10375)*		
Premier Brands of America Inc	E	914 667-6200
Mount Vernon *(G-8763)*		

FORGINGS

Company	Code	Phone
Biltron Automotive Products	E	631 928-8613
Port Jeff STA *(G-13786)*		
Borgwarner Ithaca LLC	B	607 257-6700
Ithaca *(G-6864)*		
Borgwarner Morse TEC LLC	C	607 257-6700
Ithaca *(G-6866)*		
Burke Frging Heat Treating Inc	E	585 235-6060
Rochester *(G-14268)*		
Columbus McKinnon Corporation	D	716 689-5400
Getzville *(G-5610)*		
Delaware Valley Forge Inc	E	716 447-9140
Buffalo *(G-2924)*		
Designatronics Incorporated	G	516 328-3300
Hicksville *(G-6366)*		
Dragon Trading Inc	D	212 717-1496
New York *(G-9974)*		
Firth Rixson Inc	D	585 328-1383
Rochester *(G-14393)*		
Hohmann & Barnard Inc	E	631 234-0600
Hauppauge *(G-6118)*		
Hohmann & Barnard Inc	E	518 357-9757
Schenectady *(G-15295)*		
Jrlon Inc	D	315 597-4067
Palmyra *(G-13434)*		
Mattessich Iron LLC	G	315 409-8496
Memphis *(G-8394)*		
Peck & Hale LLC	E	631 589-2510
West Sayville *(G-16966)*		
Schilling Forge Inc	E	315 454-4421
Syracuse *(G-16055)*		
Special Metals Corporation	D	716 366-5663
Dunkirk *(G-4375)*		
Stoffel Polygon Systems Inc	F	914 961-2000
Tuckahoe *(G-16296)*		
Superior Motion Controls Inc	E	516 420-2921
Farmingdale *(G-5130)*		
Viking Iron Works Inc	F	845 471-5010
Poughkeepsie *(G-13956)*		
Vulcan Steam Forging Co	E	716 875-3680
Buffalo *(G-3272)*		
W J Albro Machine Works Inc	G	631 345-0657
Yaphank *(G-17424)*		
York Industries Inc	E	516 746-3736
Garden City Park *(G-5559)*		

FORGINGS: Aluminum

Company	Code	Phone
Arconic Inc	D	212 836-2758
New York *(G-9248)*		

FORGINGS: Armor Plate, Iron Or Steel

Company	Code	Phone
Trojan Steel	G	518 686-7426
Hoosick Falls *(G-6573)*		

FORGINGS: Automotive & Internal Combustion Engine

Company	Code	Phone
General Motors LLC	A	716 879-5000
Buffalo *(G-2986)*		

FORGINGS: Gear & Chain

Company	Code	Phone
Ball Chain Mfg Co Inc	D	914 664-7500
Mount Vernon *(G-8709)*		
Crown Industrial	G	607 745-8709
Cortland *(G-4047)*		
Kurz and Zobel Inc	G	585 254-9060
Rochester *(G-14494)*		

FORGINGS: Machinery, Ferrous

Company	Code	Phone
Alry Tool and Die Co Inc	E	716 693-2419
Tonawanda *(G-16159)*		

FORGINGS: Nonferrous

Company	Code	Phone
Hammond & Irving Inc	D	315 253-6265
Auburn *(G-498)*		
Nak International Corp	D	516 997-4212
Jericho *(G-7109)*		
Special Metals Corporation	D	716 366-5663
Dunkirk *(G-4375)*		

FORGINGS: Pump & compressor, Nonferrous

Company	Code	Phone
Penn State Metal Fabri	G	718 786-8814
Brooklyn *(G-2428)*		

FORMS: Concrete, Sheet Metal

Company	Code	Phone
Gt Innovations LLC	G	585 739-7659
Bergen *(G-844)*		

FOUNDRIES: Aluminum

Company	Code	Phone
American Blade Mfg LLC	F	607 432-4518
Oneonta *(G-13193)*		
American Blade Mfg LLC	G	607 656-4204
Greene *(G-5880)*		
Amt Incorporated	E	518 284-2910
Sharon Springs *(G-15405)*		
Carter Precision Metals LLC	G	516 333-1917
Westbury *(G-17001)*		
Consoldted Precision Pdts Corp	B	315 687-0014
Chittenango *(G-3660)*		
Crown Die Casting Corp	E	914 667-5400
Mount Vernon *(G-8720)*		
East Pattern & Model Corp	E	585 461-3240
Fairport *(G-4861)*		
Massena Metals Inc	F	315 769-3846
Massena *(G-8229)*		
Meloon Foundries LLC	E	315 454-3231
Syracuse *(G-16006)*		
Micro Instrument Corp	D	585 458-3150
Rochester *(G-14528)*		
Pyrotek Incorporated	D	607 756-3050
Cortland *(G-4064)*		
WGB Industries Inc	F	716 693-5527
Tonawanda *(G-16235)*		
Wolff & Dungey Inc	E	315 475-2105
Syracuse *(G-16098)*		

FOUNDRIES: Brass, Bronze & Copper

Company	Code	Phone
David Fehlman	G	315 455-8888
Syracuse *(G-15942)*		
Meloon Foundries LLC	E	315 454-3231
Syracuse *(G-16006)*		
Omega Wire Inc	E	315 337-4300
Rome *(G-14856)*		
Omega Wire Inc	D	315 689-7115
Jordan *(G-7158)*		

FOUNDRIES: Gray & Ductile Iron

Company	Code	Phone
Auburn Foundry Inc	F	315 253-4441
Auburn *(G-478)*		
En Tech Corp	F	845 398-0776
Tappan *(G-16104)*		
Matrix Steel Company Inc	E	718 381-6800
Brooklyn *(G-2287)*		
McWane Inc	B	607 734-2211
Elmira *(G-4708)*		

FOUNDRIES: Iron

Company	Code	Phone
Eastern Company	D	315 468-6251
Solvay *(G-15529)*		
Emcom Industries Inc	G	716 852-3711
Buffalo *(G-2950)*		
Noresco Industrial Group Inc	E	516 759-3355
Glen Cove *(G-5635)*		
Plattco Corporation	E	518 563-4640
Plattsburgh *(G-13715)*		

FOUNDRIES: Nonferrous

Company	Code	Phone
Allstar Casting Corporation	E	212 563-0909
New York *(G-9142)*		
Argos Inc	G	845 528-0576
Putnam Valley *(G-13989)*		
Carrera Casting Corp	C	212 382-3296
New York *(G-9589)*		
Cast-All Corporation	E	516 741-4025
Mineola *(G-8535)*		
Cpp-Syracuse Inc	E	315 687-0014
Chittenango *(G-3662)*		
Crown Die Casting Corp	E	914 667-5400
Mount Vernon *(G-8720)*		
Globalfoundries US Inc	E	518 305-9013
Malta *(G-8051)*		
Globalfoundries US Inc	F	408 462-3900
Ballston Spa *(G-595)*		
Greenfield Die Casting Corp	E	516 623-9230
Freeport *(G-5414)*		
J & J Bronze & Aluminum Cast	E	718 383-2111
Brooklyn *(G-2120)*		
Jamestown Bronze Works Inc	G	716 665-2302
Jamestown *(G-7039)*		
K & H Precision Products Inc	E	585 624-4894
Honeoye Falls *(G-6560)*		
Karbra Company	C	212 736-9300
New York *(G-10846)*		
Kelly Foundry & Machine Co	E	315 732-8313
Utica *(G-16370)*		
Medi-Ray Inc	D	877 898-3003
Tuckahoe *(G-16295)*		
Polich Tallix Inc	G	845 567-9464
Walden *(G-16554)*		
Wemco Casting LLC	D	631 563-8050
Bohemia *(G-1153)*		

Employee Codes: A=Over 500 employees, B=251-500
C=101-250, D=51-100, E=20-50, F=10-19, G=5-9

FOUNDRIES: Steel

Amt Incorporated	E	518 284-2910
Sharon Springs (G-15405)		
Brinkman Intl Group Inc	G	585 429-5000
Rochester (G-14263)		
C J Winter Machine Tech	E	585 429-5000
Rochester (G-14271)		
Eastern Industrial Steel Corp	G	845 639-9749
New City (G-8832)		
Frazer & Jones Co	D	315 468-6251
Syracuse (G-15964)		
Steel Craft Rolling Door	F	631 608-8662
Copiague (G-3952)		

FOUNDRIES: Steel Investment

Consoldted Precision Pdts Corp	B	315 687-0014
Chittenango (G-3660)		
Jbf Stainless LLC	E	315 569-2800
Frankfort (G-5363)		
Quality Castings Inc	E	732 409-3203
Long Island City (G-7883)		

FRAMES & FRAMING WHOLESALE

AC Moore Incorporated	G	516 796-5831
Bethpage (G-862)		
Framerica Corporation	D	631 650-1000
Yaphank (G-17409)		
Galas Framing Services	F	718 706-0007
Long Island City (G-7776)		
General Art Company Inc	F	212 255-1298
New York (G-10315)		
Inter Pacific Consulting Corp	G	718 460-2787
Flushing (G-5260)		

FRANCHISES, SELLING OR LICENSING

Hugo Boss Usa Inc	D	212 940-0600
New York (G-10574)		
John Varvatos Company	E	212 812-8000
New York (G-10793)		
Perry Ellis International Inc	F	212 536-5400
New York (G-11641)		

FREIGHT CONSOLIDATION SVCS

ITT Industries Holdings Inc	G	914 641-2000
White Plains (G-17153)		

FREIGHT FORWARDING ARRANGEMENTS

Marken LLP	G	631 396-7454
Farmingdale (G-5050)		

FRICTION MATERIAL, MADE FROM POWDERED METAL

Materion Brewster LLC	D	845 279-0900
Brewster (G-1221)		
Raytech Corp Asbestos Personal	G	516 747-0300
Mineola (G-8566)		
Raytech Corporation	G	718 259-7388
Woodbury (G-17317)		

FRUITS & VEGETABLES WHOLESALERS: Fresh

Sabra Dipping Company LLC	F	516 249-0151
Farmingdale (G-5117)		

FUEL ADDITIVES

E-Zoil Products Inc	E	716 213-0103
Tonawanda (G-16177)		
Enertech Labs Inc	G	716 332-9074
Buffalo (G-2952)		
Fppf Chemical Co Inc	G	716 856-9607
Buffalo (G-2969)		
Green Global Energy Inc	G	716 501-9770
Niagara Falls (G-12847)		
Kinetic Fuel Technology Inc	G	716 745-1461
Youngstown (G-17548)		

FUEL BRIQUETTES & WAXES

Costello Bros Petroleum Corp	G	914 237-3189
Yonkers (G-17446)		

FUEL BRIQUETTES OR BOULETS, MADE WITH PETROLEUM BINDER

Cooks Intl Ltd Lblty Co	G	212 741-4407
New York (G-9777)		

FUEL CELL FORMS: Cardboard, Made From Purchased Materials

Emergent Power Inc	G	201 441-3590
Latham (G-7389)		
Plug Power Inc	B	518 782-7700
Latham (G-7404)		

FUEL CELLS: Solid State

American Fuel Cell LLC	G	585 474-3993
Rochester (G-14212)		

FUEL DEALERS: Wood

B & J Lumber Co Inc	G	518 677-3845
Cambridge (G-3332)		

FUEL OIL DEALERS

Bluebar Oil Co Inc	F	315 245-4328
Blossvale (G-991)		
Costello Bros Petroleum Corp	G	914 237-3189
Yonkers (G-17446)		
Montauk Inlet Seafood Inc	G	631 668-3419
Montauk (G-8625)		

FUELS: Diesel

Algafuel America	G	516 295-2257
Hewlett (G-6331)		
Northern Biodiesel Inc	G	585 545-4534
Ontario (G-13228)		
Performance Diesel Service LLC	F	315 854-5269
Plattsburgh (G-13714)		
Tri-State Biodiesel LLC	D	718 860-6600
Bronx (G-1474)		

FUELS: Ethanol

A and L Home Fuel LLC	G	607 638-1994
Schenevus (G-15336)		
Avstar Fuel Systems Inc	G	315 255-1955
Auburn (G-482)		
Buell Fuel LLC	F	315 841-3000
Deansboro (G-4109)		
CAM Fuel Inc	G	718 246-4306
Brooklyn (G-1752)		
Castle Fuels Corporation	E	914 381-6600
Harrison (G-5998)		
Centar Fuel Co Inc	G	516 538-2424
West Hempstead (G-16882)		
Consolidated Edison Co NY Inc	F	914 933-2936
Rye (G-15081)		
Degennaro Fuel Service LLC	G	518 239-6350
Medusa (G-8318)		
Dib Managmnt Inc	F	718 439-8190
Brooklyn (G-1860)		
Economy Energy LLC	G	845 222-3384
Peekskill (G-13500)		
Fire Island Fuel	G	631 772-1482
Shirley (G-15441)		
Friendly Fuel Incorporated	G	518 581-7036
Saratoga Springs (G-15182)		
Friendly Star Fuel Inc	G	718 369-8801
Brooklyn (G-2007)		
Fuel Energy Services USA Ltd	E	607 846-2650
Horseheads (G-6607)		
Fuel Soul	G	516 379-0810
Merrick (G-8419)		
Fuel Tank Envmtl Svcs Corp	E	631 374-9083
Centerport (G-3502)		
Golden Renewable Energy LLC	G	914 920-9800
Yonkers (G-17464)		
Highrange Fuels Inc	G	914 930-8300
Cortlandt Manor (G-4076)		
J&R Fuel of LI Inc	G	631 234-1959
Central Islip (G-3528)		
Jmg Fuel Inc	G	631 579-4319
Ronkonkoma (G-14948)		
JRs Fuels Inc	G	518 622-9939
Cairo (G-3299)		
Kore Infrastructure LLC	G	646 532-9060
Glen Cove (G-5633)		
Leroux Fuels	F	518 563-3653
Plattsburgh (G-13702)		
Liberty Food and Fuel	G	315 299-4039
Syracuse (G-15997)		
Lift Safe - Fuel Safe Inc	F	315 423-7702
Syracuse (G-15998)		
Lo-Co Fuel Corp	G	631 929-5086
Wading River (G-16544)		
Logo	G	212 846-2568
New York (G-11050)		
Maio Fuel Company LP	G	914 683-1154
White Plains (G-17162)		
MNS Fuel Corp	F	516 735-3835
Ronkonkoma (G-14971)		
Morgan Fuel & Heating Co Inc	E	845 856-7831
Port Jervis (G-13812)		
Morgan Fuel & Heating Co Inc	E	845 246-4931
Saugerties (G-15217)		
Morgan Fuel & Heating Co Inc	E	845 626-7766
Kerhonkson (G-7185)		
Mt Fuel Corp	G	631 445-2047
Setauket (G-15403)		
N & L Fuel Corp	G	718 863-3538
Bronx (G-1407)		
Nagle Fuel Corporation	G	212 304-4618
New York (G-11362)		
North East Fuel Group Inc	G	718 984-6774
Staten Island (G-15735)		
Northeastern Fuel Corp	G	917 560-6241
Staten Island (G-15736)		
Patdan Fuel Corporation	G	718 326-3668
Middle Village (G-8450)		
Provident Fuel Inc	G	516 224-4427
Woodbury (G-17316)		
Quality Fuel 1 Corporation	G	631 392-4090
North Babylon (G-12920)		
RE Fuel	G	631 909-3316
Moriches (G-8659)		
Remsen Fuel Inc	G	718 984-9551
Staten Island (G-15752)		
S&B Alternative Fuels Inc	G	631 585-6637
Lake Grove (G-7290)		
Smith & Sons Fuels Inc	G	518 661-6112
Mayfield (G-8245)		
Southbay Fuel Injectors	G	516 442-4707
Rockville Centre (G-14829)		
Yankee Fuel Inc	G	631 880-8810
West Babylon (G-16873)		
York Fuel Incorporated	G	718 951-0202
Brooklyn (G-2790)		

FUELS: Jet

Regulus Energy LLC	F	716 200-7417
Tonawanda (G-16215)		

FUELS: Oil

209 Discount Oil	E	845 386-2090
Middletown (G-8458)		
Ergun Inc	G	631 721-0049
Roslyn Heights (G-15050)		
Fuel Energy Services USA Ltd	E	607 846-2650
Horseheads (G-6607)		
Heat USA II LLC	F	212 254-4328
College Point (G-3811)		
Heat USA II LLC	E	212 564-4328
New York (G-10497)		
Hygrade Fuel Inc	G	516 741-0723
Mineola (G-8547)		
Ringhoff Fuel Inc	G	631 878-0663
East Moriches (G-4450)		
Starfuels Inc	G	914 289-4800
White Plains (G-17197)		

FUNDRAISING SVCS

Consumer Reports Inc	B	914 378-2000
Yonkers (G-17445)		

FUNERAL HOMES & SVCS

Sunnycrest Inc	E	315 252-7214
Auburn (G-518)		

FUNGICIDES OR HERBICIDES

Bioworks Inc	G	585 924-4362
Victor (G-16487)		

FUR APPAREL STORES

Missiontex Inc	G	718 532-9053
Brooklyn (G-2327)		

FUR CLOTHING WHOLESALERS

Blum & Fink Inc ....F 212 695-2606
  New York *(G-9477)*
Georgy Creative Fashions Inc ....G 212 279-4885
  New York *(G-10328)*

FUR FINISHING & LINING: For The Fur Goods Trade

Steves Original Furs Inc ....E 212 967-8007
  New York *(G-12227)*

FUR: Apparel

Arbeit Bros Inc ....G 212 736-9761
  New York *(G-9241)*
CPT Usa LLC ....E 212 575-1616
  New York *(G-9801)*
Fox Unlimited Inc ....G 212 736-3071
  New York *(G-10245)*
Jerry Sorbara Furs Inc ....F 212 594-3897
  New York *(G-10761)*
Mink Mart Inc ....G 212 868-2785
  New York *(G-11304)*
Superior Furs Inc ....F 516 365-4123
  Manhasset *(G-8099)*
Xanadu ....G 212 465-0580
  New York *(G-12700)*

FUR: Coats

Stallion Inc ....E 718 706-0111
  Long Island City *(G-7910)*

FUR: Coats & Other Apparel

Blum & Fink Inc ....F 212 695-2606
  New York *(G-9477)*
J Percy For Mrvin Rchards Ltd ....E 212 944-5300
  New York *(G-10721)*
Moschos Furs Inc ....G 212 244-0255
  New York *(G-11333)*
N Pologeorgis Furs Inc ....F 212 563-2250
  New York *(G-11359)*
Samuel Schulman Furs Inc ....E 212 736-5550
  New York *(G-11981)*
USA Furs By George Inc ....G 212 643-1415
  New York *(G-12511)*

FUR: Hats

Best Brands Consumer Pdts Inc ....G 212 684-7456
  New York *(G-9420)*
Kaitery Furs Ltd ....G 718 204-1396
  Long Island City *(G-7805)*

FUR: Jackets

Anage Inc ....F 212 944-6533
  New York *(G-9195)*

FURNACES & OVENS: Indl

Buflovak LLC ....E 716 895-2100
  Buffalo *(G-2883)*
Cosmos Electronic Machine Corp ....E 631 249-2535
  Farmingdale *(G-4974)*
Embassy Industries Inc ....C 631 435-0209
  Hauppauge *(G-6095)*
Harper International Corp ....D 716 276-9900
  Buffalo *(G-3008)*
Hpi Co Inc ....G 718 851-2753
  Brooklyn *(G-2085)*
J H Buhrmaster Company Inc ....G 518 843-1700
  Amsterdam *(G-351)*
Linde LLC ....D 716 773-7552
  Grand Island *(G-5776)*
Parker-Hannifin Corporation ....D 716 685-4040
  Lancaster *(G-7356)*
Vincent Genovese ....G 631 281-8170
  Mastic Beach *(G-8237)*

FURNACES: Indl, Electric

Cooks Intl Ltd Lblty Co ....G 212 741-4407
  New York *(G-9777)*

FURNACES: Warm Air, Electric

Marathon Heater Co Inc ....G 607 657-8113
  Richford *(G-14076)*

FURNITURE & CABINET STORES: Cabinets, Custom Work

A Van Hoek Woodworking Limited ....G 718 599-4388
  Brooklyn *(G-1536)*
Central Kitchen Corp ....F 631 283-1029
  Southampton *(G-15564)*
Custom Woodcraft LLC ....F 315 843-4234
  Munnsville *(G-8796)*
Di Fiore and Sons Custom Wdwkg ....G 718 278-1663
  Long Island City *(G-7744)*
Jamestown Kitchen & Bath Inc ....G 716 665-2299
  Jamestown *(G-7041)*
Time Base Corporation ....E 631 293-4068
  Edgewood *(G-4630)*
Ultimate Styles of America ....F 631 254-0219
  Bay Shore *(G-746)*

FURNITURE & CABINET STORES: Custom

Red White & Blue Entps Corp ....G 718 565-8080
  Woodside *(G-17366)*

FURNITURE & FIXTURES Factory

Adirondack Scenic Inc ....D 518 638-8000
  Argyle *(G-407)*
Arper USA Inc ....G 212 647-8900
  New York *(G-9256)*
Artistry In Wood of Syracuse ....F 315 431-4022
  East Syracuse *(G-4523)*
Futon City Discounters Inc ....F 315 437-1328
  Syracuse *(G-15965)*
Interiors-Pft Inc ....G 212 244-9600
  Long Island City *(G-7795)*
J P Installations Warehouse ....F 914 576-3188
  New Rochelle *(G-8959)*
Modu-Craft Inc ....G 716 694-0709
  North Tonawanda *(G-13000)*
Modu-Craft Inc ....G 716 694-0709
  Tonawanda *(G-16200)*
T-Company LLC ....G 646 290-6365
  Smithtown *(G-15522)*

FURNITURE PARTS: Metal

Dimar Manufacturing Corp ....C 716 759-0351
  Clarence *(G-3685)*
Icestone LLC ....E 718 624-4900
  Brooklyn *(G-2093)*
Noll Reynolds Met Fabrication ....G 315 422-3333
  Syracuse *(G-16019)*
Protocase Incorporated ....C 866 849-3911
  Lewiston *(G-7456)*
Seetin Design Group Inc ....F 718 486-5610
  Brooklyn *(G-2568)*

FURNITURE REFINISHING SVCS

FX INC ....F 212 244-2240
  New York *(G-10277)*
Telesca-Heyman Inc ....F 212 534-3442
  New York *(G-12319)*

FURNITURE STOCK & PARTS: Carvings, Wood

Jim Quinn ....F 518 356-0398
  Schenectady *(G-15297)*
Mason Carvings Inc ....G 716 484-7884
  Jamestown *(G-7050)*

FURNITURE STOCK & PARTS: Dimension Stock, Hardwood

North Hudson Woodcraft Corp ....E 315 429-3105
  Dolgeville *(G-4330)*
Randolph Dimension Corporation ....F 716 358-6901
  Randolph *(G-14030)*

FURNITURE STOCK & PARTS: Frames, Upholstered Furniture, Wood

Artistic Frame Corp ....C 212 289-2100
  New York *(G-9270)*
Cassadaga Designs Inc ....G 716 595-3030
  Cassadaga *(G-3442)*
Empire Exhibits & Displays Inc ....F 518 266-9362
  Mechanicville *(G-8258)*
Vitobob Furniture Inc ....G 516 676-1696
  Long Island City *(G-7945)*

FURNITURE STOCK & PARTS: Hardwood

Guldenschuh Logging & Lbr LLC ....G 585 538-4750
  Caledonia *(G-3307)*

FURNITURE STORES

Chair Factory ....E 718 363-2383
  Brooklyn *(G-1771)*
Classic Sofa Ltd ....D 212 620-0485
  New York *(G-9692)*
D & W Design Inc ....E 845 343-3366
  Middletown *(G-8468)*
French & Itln Furn Craftsmen ....G 718 599-5000
  Brooklyn *(G-2004)*
Furniture Doctor Inc ....G 585 657-6941
  Bloomfield *(G-982)*
Futon City Discounters Inc ....F 315 437-1328
  Syracuse *(G-15965)*
Little Wolf Cabinet Shop Inc ....E 212 734-1116
  New York *(G-11039)*
Long Lumber and Supply Corp ....F 518 439-1661
  Slingerlands *(G-15499)*
Omega Furniture Manufacturing ....F 315 463-7428
  Syracuse *(G-16023)*
Pillow Perfections Ltd Inc ....G 718 383-2259
  Brooklyn *(G-2434)*
Recycled Brooklyn Group LLC ....F 917 902-0662
  Brooklyn *(G-2504)*
Safavieh Inc ....A 516 945-1900
  Port Washington *(G-13877)*
Smart Space Products LLC ....G 877 777-2441
  New York *(G-12130)*
Studio 21 LA Inc ....E 718 965-6579
  Brooklyn *(G-2634)*
Yepes Fine Furniture ....F 718 383-0221
  Brooklyn *(G-2787)*

FURNITURE STORES: Cabinets, Kitchen, Exc Custom Made

Home Ideal Inc ....G 718 762-8998
  Flushing *(G-5259)*

FURNITURE STORES: Custom Made, Exc Cabinets

Atelier Viollet Corp ....G 718 782-1727
  Brooklyn *(G-1646)*
Designway Ltd ....G 212 254-2220
  New York *(G-9911)*
John Langenbacher Co Inc ....E 718 328-0141
  Bronx *(G-1371)*

FURNITURE STORES: Juvenile

Casa Collection Inc ....G 718 694-0272
  Brooklyn *(G-1764)*

FURNITURE STORES: Office

FX INC ....F 212 244-2240
  New York *(G-10277)*

FURNITURE STORES: Outdoor & Garden

Walpole Woodworkers Inc ....G 631 726-2859
  Water Mill *(G-16628)*
Wood Innovations of Suffolk ....G 631 698-2345
  Medford *(G-8297)*

FURNITURE STORES: Unfinished

Universal Designs Inc ....G 718 721-1111
  Long Island City *(G-7938)*

FURNITURE UPHOLSTERY REPAIR SVCS

Sofa Doctor Inc ....G 718 292-6300
  Bronx *(G-1456)*

FURNITURE WHOLESALERS

Etna Products Co Inc ....F 212 989-7591
  New York *(G-10132)*
Furniture Doctor Inc ....G 585 657-6941
  Bloomfield *(G-982)*
Harden Furniture LLC ....C 315 675-3600
  Mc Connellsville *(G-8251)*
Holland & Sherry Inc ....E 212 542-8410
  New York *(G-10540)*

FURNITURE, HOUSEHOLD: Wholesalers

FURNITURE, HOUSEHOLD: Wholesalers

Steinbock-Braff Inc .... E 718 972-6500
Brooklyn *(G-2627)*

FURNITURE, OFFICE: Wholesalers

Artistic Frame Corp .... C 212 289-2100
New York *(G-9270)*
Kas-Ray Industries Inc .... F 212 620-3144
New York *(G-10849)*
Workplace Interiors LLC .... F 585 425-7420
Fairport *(G-4894)*

FURNITURE, WHOLESALE: Beds & Bedding

Jdt International LLC .... G 212 400-7570
New York *(G-10753)*
Wcd Window Coverings Inc .... E 845 336-4511
Lake Katrine *(G-7295)*

FURNITURE, WHOLESALE: Racks

ASAP Rack Rental Inc .... G 718 499-4495
Brooklyn *(G-1640)*
Reliable Welding & Fabrication .... G 631 758-2637
Patchogue *(G-13459)*

FURNITURE, WHOLESALE: Tables, Occasional

Vaughan Designs Inc .... G 212 319-7070
New York *(G-12534)*

FURNITURE: Bed Frames & Headboards, Wood

Inova LLC .... E 866 528-2804
Altamont *(G-211)*

FURNITURE: Bedroom, Wood

Fiber-Seal of New York Inc .... G 212 888-5580
New York *(G-10209)*

FURNITURE: Beds, Household, Incl Folding & Cabinet, Metal

Charles P Rogers Brass Beds .... F 212 675-4400
New York *(G-9633)*

FURNITURE: Bookcases, Office, Wood

F E Hale Mfg Co .... D 315 894-5490
Frankfort *(G-5361)*

FURNITURE: Box Springs, Assembled

Charles H Beckley Inc .... F 718 665-2218
Bronx *(G-1297)*

FURNITURE: Cabinets & Filing Drawers, Office, Exc Wood

Falvo Manufacturing Co Inc .... F 315 738-7682
Utica *(G-16353)*
Ulrich Planfiling Eqp Corp .... E 716 763-1815
Lakewood *(G-7319)*

FURNITURE: Cabinets & Vanities, Medicine, Metal

Glissade New York LLC .... E 631 756-4800
Farmingdale *(G-5007)*

FURNITURE: Chairs & Couches, Wood, Upholstered

Jackson Dakota Inc .... F 718 786-8600
Long Island City *(G-7797)*
Sleepable Sofas Ltd .... D 973 546-4502
New York *(G-12125)*

FURNITURE: Chairs, Household Upholstered

Avanti Furniture Corp .... F 516 293-8220
Farmingdale *(G-4957)*

FURNITURE: Chairs, Household Wood

Cassadaga Designs Inc .... G 716 595-3030
Cassadaga *(G-3442)*

Custom Display Manufacture .... G 516 783-6491
North Bellmore *(G-12936)*
Hunt Country Furniture Inc .... D 845 832-6601
Wingdale *(G-17296)*

FURNITURE: Chairs, Office Exc Wood

Keilhauer .... F 646 742-0192
New York *(G-10869)*
Poppin Inc .... D 212 391-7200
New York *(G-11707)*
Vitra Inc .... F 212 463-5700
New York *(G-12585)*

FURNITURE: Chairs, Office Wood

Interior Solutions of Wny LLC .... G 716 332-0372
Buffalo *(G-3028)*

FURNITURE: China Closets

Raff Enterprises .... G 518 218-7883
Albany *(G-127)*

FURNITURE: Church

American Bptst Chrches Mtro NY .... G 212 870-3195
New York *(G-9164)*

FURNITURE: Console Tables, Wood

Forecast Consoles Inc .... E 631 253-9000
Hauppauge *(G-6102)*

FURNITURE: Couches, Sofa/Davenport, Upholstered Wood Frames

Classic Sofa Ltd .... D 212 620-0485
New York *(G-9692)*

FURNITURE: Cribs, Metal

Hard Manufacturing Co Inc .... F 716 893-1800
Buffalo *(G-3005)*
NK Medical Products Inc .... G 716 759-7200
Amherst *(G-252)*
Novum Medical Products Inc .... F 716 759-7200
Amherst *(G-253)*

FURNITURE: Cut Stone

Puccio Design International .... F 516 248-6426
Garden City *(G-5542)*

FURNITURE: Desks & Tables, Office, Exc Wood

Kimball Office Inc .... E 212 753-6161
New York *(G-10886)*

FURNITURE: Desks & Tables, Office, Wood

Centre Interiors Wdwkg Co Inc .... E 718 323-1343
Ozone Park *(G-13402)*

FURNITURE: Desks, Wood

Bush Industries Inc .... C 716 665-2000
Jamestown *(G-7013)*

FURNITURE: Dinette Sets, Metal

Embassy Dinettes Inc .... G 631 253-2292
Deer Park *(G-4160)*

FURNITURE: Dining Room, Wood

Falcon Chair and Table Inc .... E 716 664-7136
Falconer *(G-4904)*

FURNITURE: Foundations & Platforms

Ideal Manufacturing Inc .... E 585 872-7190
East Rochester *(G-4481)*

FURNITURE: Garden, Exc Wood, Metal, Stone Or Concrete

Anandamali Inc .... F 212 343-8964
New York *(G-9197)*
Holland & Sherry Inc .... E 212 542-8410
New York *(G-10540)*

FURNITURE: Hospital

AFC Industries Inc .... D 718 747-0237
College Point *(G-3802)*
Brandt Equipment LLC .... G 718 994-0800
Bronx *(G-1287)*
Evans & Paul LLC .... E 516 576-0800
Plainview *(G-13629)*

FURNITURE: Hotel

Inova LLC .... E 866 528-2804
Altamont *(G-211)*
N3a Corporation .... D 516 284-6799
Inwood *(G-6802)*
Ramler International Ltd .... E 516 353-3106
Syosset *(G-15857)*
Smart Space Products LLC .... G 877 777-2441
New York *(G-12130)*
Timeless Decor LLC .... C 315 782-5759
Watertown *(G-16697)*

FURNITURE: Household, Metal

Brueton Industries Inc .... D 516 379-3400
Freeport *(G-5401)*
D & W Design Inc .... E 845 343-3366
Middletown *(G-8468)*
F&M Ornamental Designs LLC .... G 212 353-2600
New York *(G-10170)*
F&M Ornamental Designs LLC .... F 908 241-7776
New York *(G-10171)*
Furniture Doctor Inc .... G 585 657-6941
Bloomfield *(G-982)*
La Forge Francaise Ltd Inc .... G 631 591-0572
Riverhead *(G-14158)*
Meeker Sales Corp .... G 718 384-5400
Brooklyn *(G-2297)*
Royal Metal Products Inc .... E 518 966-4442
Surprise *(G-15832)*
Slava Industries Incorporated .... G 718 499-4850
Brooklyn *(G-2595)*
Steelcraft Manufacturing Co .... F 718 277-2404
Brooklyn *(G-2624)*

FURNITURE: Household, NEC

Matthew Shively LLC .... G 914 937-3531
Port Chester *(G-13779)*
Safcore LLC .... F 917 627-5263
Brooklyn *(G-2552)*

FURNITURE: Household, Upholstered On Metal Frames

Precision Orna Ir Works Inc .... G 718 379-5200
Bronx *(G-1433)*

FURNITURE: Household, Upholstered, Exc Wood Or Metal

3phase Industries LLC .... G 347 763-2942
Brooklyn *(G-1514)*
Albert Menin Interiors Ltd .... F 212 876-3041
Bronx *(G-1268)*
Culin/Colella Inc .... G 914 698-7727
Mamaroneck *(G-8063)*
Harome Designs LLC .... E 631 864-1900
Commack *(G-3860)*
L& JG Stickley Incorporated .... A 315 682-5500
Manlius *(G-8106)*
Mbh Furniture Innovations Inc .... G 845 354-8202
Spring Valley *(G-15617)*
Olollo Inc .... G 877 701-0110
Brooklyn *(G-2402)*
Ready To Assemble Company Inc .... E 516 825-4397
Valley Stream *(G-16448)*
Spancraft Ltd .... F 516 295-0055
Woodmere *(G-17332)*

FURNITURE: Household, Wood

A & S Woodworking Inc .... G 518 821-0832
Hudson *(G-6630)*
A-1 Manhattan Custom Furn Inc .... G 212 750-9800
Island Park *(G-6817)*
Anthony Lawrence of New York .... E 212 206-8820
Long Island City *(G-7694)*
Arthur Brown W Mfg Co .... F 631 243-5594
Deer Park *(G-4126)*
Arthur Lauer Inc .... E 845 255-7871
Gardiner *(G-5560)*

PRODUCT SECTION

FURNITURE: Mattresses, Innerspring Or Box Spring

Artisan Woodworking Ltd ....G...... 516 486-0818
  West Hempstead *(G-16880)*
Atelier Viollet Corp ....G...... 718 782-1727
  Brooklyn *(G-1646)*
Bel Art International ....E...... 718 402-2100
  Bronx *(G-1281)*
Benchmark Furniture Mfg ....D...... 718 257-4707
  Brooklyn *(G-1679)*
Black River Woodworking LLC ....G...... 315 376-8405
  Castorland *(G-3450)*
Brueton Industries Inc ....D...... 516 379-3400
  Freeport *(G-5401)*
Bush Industries Inc ....C...... 716 665-2000
  Jamestown *(G-7013)*
Carlos & Alex Atelier Inc ....E...... 718 441-8911
  Richmond Hill *(G-14083)*
Carver Creek Enterprises Inc ....E...... 585 657-7511
  Bloomfield *(G-977)*
Charles H Beckley Inc ....F...... 718 665-2218
  Bronx *(G-1297)*
Comerford Hennessy At Home Inc ....G...... 631 537-6200
  Bridgehampton *(G-1231)*
Concepts In Wood of CNY ....E...... 315 463-8084
  Syracuse *(G-15923)*
Conesus Lake Association Inc ....E...... 585 346-6864
  Lakeville *(G-7306)*
Cousins Furniture & Hm Imprvs ....G...... 631 254-3752
  Deer Park *(G-4143)*
Crawford Furniture Mfg Corp ....G...... 716 483-2102
  Jamestown *(G-7020)*
Custom Woodcraft LLC ....F...... 315 843-4234
  Munnsville *(G-8796)*
D & W Design Inc ....E...... 845 343-3366
  Middletown *(G-8468)*
David Sutherland Showrooms - N ......G...... 212 871-9717
  New York *(G-9879)*
Dbs Interiors Corp ....F...... 631 491-3013
  West Babylon *(G-16813)*
Dcl Furniture Manufacturing ....E...... 516 248-2683
  Mineola *(G-8538)*
Deakon Homes and Interiors ....G...... 518 271-0342
  Troy *(G-16255)*
Designs By Robert Scott Inc ....E...... 718 609-2535
  Brooklyn *(G-1856)*
Dessin/Fournir Inc ....G...... 212 758-0844
  New York *(G-9912)*
Dune Inc ....G...... 212 925-6171
  New York *(G-9989)*
Eclectic Cntract Furn Inds Inc ....F...... 212 967-5504
  New York *(G-10029)*
El Greco Woodworking Inc ....E...... 716 483-0315
  Jamestown *(G-7025)*
Emilia Interiors Inc ....F...... 718 629-4202
  Brooklyn *(G-1923)*
Eugenia Selective Living Inc ....F...... 631 277-1461
  Islip *(G-6847)*
Eurocraft Custom Furniture ....G...... 718 956-0600
  Long Island City *(G-7761)*
Fenix Furniture Co ....G...... 631 273-3500
  Bay Shore *(G-698)*
Final Dimension Inc ....G...... 718 786-0100
  Maspeth *(G-8171)*
Fine Arts Furniture Inc ....E...... 212 744-9139
  Long Island City *(G-7769)*
Franz Fischer Inc ....F...... 718 821-1300
  Brooklyn *(G-2003)*
Fred Schulz Inc ....G...... 845 724-3409
  Poughquag *(G-13957)*
French & Itln Furn Craftsmen ....G...... 718 599-5000
  Brooklyn *(G-2004)*
Furniture Doctor Inc ....G...... 585 657-6941
  Bloomfield *(G-982)*
Glendale Architectural WD Pdts ....E...... 718 326-2700
  Glendale *(G-5669)*
Hard Manufacturing Co Inc ....D...... 716 893-1800
  Buffalo *(G-3005)*
Harden Furniture LLC ....C...... 315 675-3600
  Mc Connellsville *(G-8251)*
Hayman-Chaffey Designs Inc ....F...... 212 889-7771
  New York *(G-10473)*
Henry B Urban Inc ....E...... 212 489-3308
  New York *(G-10500)*
Icon Design LLC ....E...... 585 768-6040
  Le Roy *(G-7434)*
Inter Craft Custom Furniture ....G...... 718 278-2573
  Astoria *(G-443)*
J Percoco Industries Inc ....G...... 631 312-4572
  Bohemia *(G-1075)*
K & B Woodworking Inc ....G...... 518 634-7253
  Cairo *(G-3300)*

Kazac Inc ....G...... 631 249-7299
  Farmingdale *(G-5031)*
Kittinger Company Inc ....E...... 716 876-1000
  Buffalo *(G-3050)*
Knoll Inc ....D...... 212 343-4124
  New York *(G-10902)*
L& JG Stickley Incorporated ....A...... 315 682-5500
  Manlius *(G-8106)*
Lanoves Inc ....G...... 718 384-1880
  Brooklyn *(G-2195)*
Little Wolf Cabinet Shop Inc ....E...... 212 734-1116
  New York *(G-11039)*
M & C Furniture ....G...... 718 422-2136
  Brooklyn *(G-2244)*
M T D Corporation ....F...... 631 491-3905
  West Babylon *(G-16837)*
Mackenzie-Childs LLC ....C...... 315 364-6118
  Aurora *(G-528)*
Manchester Wood Inc ....C...... 518 642-9518
  Granville *(G-5792)*
Mica International Ltd ....F...... 516 378-3400
  Freeport *(G-5423)*
New Day Woodwork Inc ....E...... 718 275-1721
  Glendale *(G-5674)*
Nicholas Dfine Furn Decorators ....F...... 914 245-8982
  Bronx *(G-1413)*
Patrick Mackin Custom Furn ....F...... 718 237-2592
  Brooklyn *(G-2423)*
Piccini Industries Ltd ....G...... 845 365-0614
  Orangeburg *(G-13262)*
Pillow Perfections Ltd Inc ....G...... 718 383-2259
  Brooklyn *(G-2434)*
Premier Woodcraft Ltd ....E...... 610 383-6624
  White Plains *(G-17188)*
Recycled Brooklyn Group LLC ....F...... 917 902-0662
  Brooklyn *(G-2504)*
Reis D Furniture Mfg ....E...... 516 248-5676
  Mineola *(G-8567)*
Renco Group Inc ....G...... 212 541-6000
  New York *(G-11864)*
Stillwater Wood & Iron ....G...... 518 664-4501
  Stillwater *(G-15783)*
Triple J Bedding LLC ....G...... 718 643-8005
  Brooklyn *(G-2701)*
Universal Designs Inc ....G...... 718 721-1111
  Long Island City *(G-7938)*
Wallace Home Design Ctr ....G...... 631 765-3890
  Southold *(G-15585)*
Walpole Woodworkers Inc ....G...... 631 726-2859
  Water Mill *(G-16628)*
Walter P Sauer LLC ....E...... 718 937-0600
  Brooklyn *(G-2759)*
William Somerville Maintenance ....D...... 212 534-4600
  New York *(G-12663)*
Woodmotif Inc ....F...... 516 564-8325
  Hempstead *(G-6312)*
World Trading Center Inc ....G...... 631 273-3330
  Hauppauge *(G-6260)*
Your Furniture Designers Inc ....G...... 845 947-3046
  West Haverstraw *(G-16879)*

FURNITURE: Hydraulic Barber & Beauty Shop Chairs

Pyrotek Incorporated ....E...... 716 731-3221
  Sanborn *(G-15153)*
Zebrowski Industries Inc ....G...... 716 532-3911
  Collins *(G-3844)*

FURNITURE: Institutional, Exc Wood

Able Steel Equipment Co Inc ....F...... 718 361-9240
  Long Island City *(G-7679)*
Artistry In Wood of Syracuse ....F...... 315 431-4022
  East Syracuse *(G-4523)*
Artone LLC ....D...... 716 664-2232
  Jamestown *(G-7008)*
Forecast Consoles Inc ....E...... 631 253-9000
  Hauppauge *(G-6102)*
Maximum Security Products Corp .....E...... 518 233-1800
  Waterford *(G-16634)*
Maxsecure Systems Inc ....G...... 800 657-4336
  Buffalo *(G-3080)*
N Y Elli Design Corp ....F...... 718 228-0014
  Maspeth *(G-8184)*
Pluribus Products Inc ....E...... 718 852-1614
  Bayville *(G-775)*
Rosenwach Tank Co Inc ....E...... 212 972-4411
  Astoria *(G-454)*
Seating Inc ....E...... 800 468-2475
  Nunda *(G-13060)*

Testori Interiors Inc ....E...... 518 298-4400
  Champlain *(G-3574)*
Unifor Inc ....F...... 212 673-3434
  New York *(G-12472)*

FURNITURE: Juvenile, Wood

Community Products LLC ....C...... 845 658-8799
  Rifton *(G-14144)*
Ducduc Inc ....F...... 212 226-1868
  New York *(G-9986)*

FURNITURE: Kitchen & Dining Room

Cab-Network Inc ....G...... 516 334-8666
  Westbury *(G-17000)*
Catskill Craftsmen Inc ....D...... 607 652-7321
  Stamford *(G-15644)*
Dinette Depot Ltd ....G...... 516 515-9623
  Brooklyn *(G-1865)*
East End Country Kitchens Inc ....F...... 631 727-2258
  Calverton *(G-3318)*
Innovant Inc ....G...... 212 929-4883
  New York *(G-10645)*
Lemode Concepts Inc ....G...... 631 841-0796
  Amityville *(G-305)*
Professional Cab Detailing Co ....F...... 845 436-7282
  Woodridge *(G-17333)*

FURNITURE: Kitchen & Dining Room, Metal

Renco Group Inc ....G...... 212 541-6000
  New York *(G-11864)*

FURNITURE: Laboratory

J H C Fabrications Inc ....E...... 718 649-0065
  Brooklyn *(G-2121)*
Modu-Craft Inc ....G...... 716 694-0709
  Tonawanda *(G-16200)*
Modu-Craft Inc ....G...... 716 694-0709
  North Tonawanda *(G-13000)*

FURNITURE: Living Room, Upholstered On Wood Frames

Hallagan Manufacturing Co Inc ....D...... 315 331-4640
  Newark *(G-12751)*

FURNITURE: Mattresses & Foundations

E & G Bedding Corp ....E...... 718 369-1092
  Brooklyn *(G-1890)*
M R C Industries Inc ....C...... 516 328-6900
  Port Washington *(G-13860)*
Steinbock-Braff Inc ....E...... 718 972-6500
  Brooklyn *(G-2627)*
VSM Investors LLC ....G...... 212 351-1600
  New York *(G-12597)*

FURNITURE: Mattresses, Box & Bedsprings

Brook North Farms Inc ....F...... 315 834-9390
  Auburn *(G-486)*
Comfort Bedding Inc ....E...... 718 485-7662
  Brooklyn *(G-1793)*
Duxiana Dux Bed ....G...... 212 755-2600
  New York *(G-9992)*
Hard Manufacturing Co Inc ....D...... 716 893-1800
  Buffalo *(G-3005)*
Jamestown Mattress Co ....E...... 716 665-2247
  Jamestown *(G-7043)*
Metro Mattress Corp ....E...... 716 205-2300
  Niagara Falls *(G-12864)*
Natural Dreams LLC ....G...... 718 760-4202
  Corona *(G-4027)*
Otis Bedding Mfg Co Inc ....E...... 716 825-2599
  Buffalo *(G-3127)*
Zzz Mattress Manufacturing ....E...... 718 454-1468
  Saint Albans *(G-15112)*

FURNITURE: Mattresses, Innerspring Or Box Spring

KKR Millennium GP LLC ....A...... 212 750-8300
  New York *(G-10894)*
Royal Bedding Co Buffalo Inc ....E...... 716 895-1414
  Buffalo *(G-3197)*
Sealy Mattress Co Albany Inc ....B...... 518 880-1600
  Troy *(G-16244)*

Employee Codes: A=Over 500 employees, B=251-500
C=101-250, D=51-100, E=20-50, F=10-19, G=5-9

FURNITURE: NEC

FURNITURE: NEC

Dellet Industries Inc ....F 718 965-0101
  Brooklyn *(G-1849)*
Inova LLC ....F 518 861-3400
  Altamont *(G-212)*
Porta Decor ....G 516 826-6900
  Hicksville *(G-6415)*

FURNITURE: Novelty, Wood

Feinkind Inc ....G 800 289-6136
  Irvington *(G-6811)*

FURNITURE: Office Panel Systems, Exc Wood

Afco Systems Inc ....C 631 249-9441
  Farmingdale *(G-4938)*
Aztec Industries Inc ....G 631 585-1331
  Ronkonkoma *(G-14903)*
Knoll Inc ....D 212 343-4124
  New York *(G-10902)*

FURNITURE: Office, Exc Wood

3phase Industries LLC ....G 347 763-2942
  Brooklyn *(G-1514)*
Able Steel Equipment Co Inc ....F 718 361-9240
  Long Island City *(G-7679)*
Allcraft Fabricators Inc ....D 631 951-4100
  Hauppauge *(G-6034)*
Aronowitz Metal Works ....G 845 356-1660
  Monsey *(G-8603)*
Artone LLC ....D 716 664-2232
  Jamestown *(G-7008)*
Brueton Industries Inc ....D 516 379-3400
  Freeport *(G-5401)*
Davies Office Refurbishing Inc ....C 518 426-7188
  Albany *(G-72)*
Davinci Designs Inc ....F 631 595-1095
  Deer Park *(G-4148)*
Dcl Furniture Manufacturing ....E 516 248-2683
  Mineola *(G-8538)*
Deakon Homes and Interiors ....F 518 271-0342
  Troy *(G-16255)*
E-Systems Group LLC ....E 607 775-1100
  Conklin *(G-3893)*
Eugenia Selective Living Inc ....F 631 277-1461
  Islip *(G-6847)*
Exhibit Corporation America ....E 718 937-2600
  Long Island City *(G-7763)*
Forecast Consoles Inc ....E 631 253-9000
  Hauppauge *(G-6102)*
FX INC ....F 212 244-2240
  New York *(G-10277)*
Hergo Ergonomic Support ....E 718 894-0639
  Maspeth *(G-8175)*
Hudson Valley Office Furn Inc ....G 845 565-6673
  Newburgh *(G-12784)*
Inscape Inc ....E 716 665-6210
  Falconer *(G-4910)*
Integrated Tech Support Svcs ....G 718 454-2497
  Saint Albans *(G-15111)*
Larson Metal Manufacturing Co ....E 716 665-6807
  Jamestown *(G-7049)*
Lucia Group Inc ....G 631 392-4900
  Deer Park *(G-4192)*
Modern Metal Fabricators Inc ....G 518 966-4142
  Hannacroix *(G-5991)*
New Dimensions Office Group ....D 718 387-0995
  Brooklyn *(G-2370)*
Piccini Industries Ltd ....E 845 365-0614
  Orangeburg *(G-13262)*
Premier Woodcraft Ltd ....E 610 383-6624
  White Plains *(G-17188)*
Roberts Office Furn Cncpts Inc ....E 315 451-9185
  Liverpool *(G-7572)*
Royal Metal Products Inc ....E 518 966-4442
  Surprise *(G-15832)*
Saturn Sales Inc ....E 519 658-5125
  Niagara Falls *(G-12892)*
Workplace Interiors LLC ....F 585 425-7420
  Fairport *(G-4894)*
Zographos Designs Ltd ....G 212 545-0227
  New York *(G-12737)*

FURNITURE: Office, Wood

A G Master Crafts Ltd ....F 516 745-6262
  Garden City *(G-5506)*
Artistic Products LLC ....E 631 435-0200
  Hauppauge *(G-6045)*
Artone LLC ....D 716 664-2232
  Jamestown *(G-7008)*
B D B Typewriter Supply Works ....E 718 232-4800
  Brooklyn *(G-1659)*
Bauerschmidt & Sons Inc ....D 718 528-3500
  Jamaica *(G-6934)*
Bloch Industries LLC ....D 585 334-9600
  Rochester *(G-14253)*
Brueton Industries Inc ....D 516 379-3400
  Freeport *(G-5401)*
Ccn International Inc ....G 315 789-4400
  Geneva *(G-5584)*
Culin/Colella Inc ....G 914 698-7727
  Mamaroneck *(G-8063)*
DAF Office Networks Inc ....G 315 699-7070
  Cicero *(G-3673)*
Dates Weiser Furniture Corp ....D 716 891-1700
  Buffalo *(G-2921)*
Davinci Designs Inc ....F 631 595-1095
  Deer Park *(G-4148)*
Dcl Furniture Manufacturing ....E 516 248-2683
  Mineola *(G-8538)*
Deakon Homes and Interiors ....F 518 271-0342
  Troy *(G-16255)*
Designs By Robert Scott Inc ....E 718 609-2535
  Brooklyn *(G-1856)*
Dimaio Millwork Corporation ....E 914 476-1937
  Yonkers *(G-17451)*
Divine Art Furniture Inc ....G 718 834-0111
  Brooklyn *(G-1867)*
E-Systems Group LLC ....E 607 775-1100
  Conklin *(G-3893)*
Eugenia Selective Living Inc ....F 631 277-1461
  Islip *(G-6847)*
Exhibit Corporation America ....E 718 937-2600
  Long Island City *(G-7763)*
Forecast Consoles Inc ....E 631 253-9000
  Hauppauge *(G-6102)*
Furniture By Craftmaster Ltd ....E 631 750-0658
  Bohemia *(G-1065)*
Glendale Architectural WD Pdts ....E 718 326-2700
  Glendale *(G-5669)*
Gunlocke Company LLC ....C 585 728-5111
  Wayland *(G-16734)*
H Freund Woodworking Co Inc ....E 516 334-3774
  Westbury *(G-17019)*
Harden Furniture LLC ....C 315 675-3600
  Mc Connellsville *(G-8251)*
Heartwood Specialties Inc ....G 607 654-0102
  Hammondsport *(G-5977)*
Hni Corporation ....C 212 683-2232
  New York *(G-10536)*
Humanscale Corporation ....B 212 725-4749
  New York *(G-10578)*
Innovant Inc ....C 631 348-1900
  Islandia *(G-6834)*
Innovant Inc ....D 212 929-4883
  New York *(G-10644)*
Kazac Inc ....G 631 249-7299
  Farmingdale *(G-5031)*
Kittinger Company Inc ....E 716 876-1000
  Buffalo *(G-3050)*
Knoll Inc ....D 716 891-1700
  Buffalo *(G-3051)*
Knoll Inc ....D 212 343-4124
  New York *(G-10902)*
Krefab Corporation ....E 631 842-5151
  Huntington *(G-6701)*
Lake Country Woodworkers Ltd ....E 585 374-6353
  Naples *(G-8812)*
Longo Commercial Cabinets Inc ....E 631 225-4290
  Lindenhurst *(G-7491)*
M T D Corporation ....F 631 491-3905
  West Babylon *(G-16837)*
Materials Design Workshop ....F 718 893-1954
  Bronx *(G-1393)*
Matteo & Antonio Bartolotta ....F 315 252-2220
  Auburn *(G-506)*
Miller Blaker Inc ....D 718 665-3930
  Bronx *(G-1401)*
Millers Millworks Inc ....E 585 494-1420
  Bergen *(G-849)*
New Dimensions Office Group ....D 718 387-0995
  Brooklyn *(G-2370)*
Nicholas Dfine Furn Decorators ....F 914 245-8982
  Bronx *(G-1413)*
Omega Furniture Manufacturing ....F 315 463-7428
  Syracuse *(G-16023)*
Pheonix Custom Furniture Ltd ....E 212 727-2648
  Long Island City *(G-7872)*
Piccini Industries Ltd ....E 845 365-0614
  Orangeburg *(G-13262)*
Premier Woodcraft Ltd ....E 610 383-6624
  White Plains *(G-17188)*
Princeton Upholstery Co Inc ....D 845 343-2196
  Middletown *(G-8493)*
Saraval Industries ....G 516 768-9033
  Nyack *(G-13070)*
Technology Desking Inc ....E 212 257-6998
  New York *(G-12315)*
Universal Designs Inc ....G 718 721-1111
  Long Island City *(G-7938)*
Upstate Office Liquidators Inc ....F 607 722-9234
  Johnson City *(G-7137)*
Woodmotif Inc ....F 516 564-8325
  Hempstead *(G-6312)*
Your Furniture Designers Inc ....G 845 947-3046
  West Haverstraw *(G-16879)*
Zographos Designs Ltd ....G 212 545-0227
  New York *(G-12737)*

FURNITURE: Outdoor, Wood

Long Lumber and Supply Corp ....F 518 439-1661
  Slingerlands *(G-15499)*
Sitecraft Inc ....G 718 729-4900
  Astoria *(G-456)*
Sundown Ski & Sport Shop Inc ....E 631 737-8600
  Lake Grove *(G-7292)*

FURNITURE: Pews, Church

Keck Group Inc ....F 845 988-5757
  Warwick *(G-16613)*

FURNITURE: Picnic Tables Or Benches, Park

Hartford Hwy Dept ....G 315 724-0654
  New Hartford *(G-8851)*
Studio 21 LA Inc ....E 718 965-6579
  Brooklyn *(G-2634)*
Town of Amherst ....E 716 631-7113
  Williamsville *(G-17283)*
Tymor Park ....G 845 724-5691
  Lagrangeville *(G-7285)*

FURNITURE: Rattan

Bielecky Bros Inc ....E 718 424-4764
  Woodside *(G-17337)*

FURNITURE: Restaurant

Dine Rite Seating Products Inc ....E 631 226-8899
  Lindenhurst *(G-7485)*
Excel Commercial Seating ....E 828 428-8338
  West Babylon *(G-16816)*
Hunt Country Furniture Inc ....D 845 832-6601
  Wingdale *(G-17296)*
L & D Manufacturing Corp ....G 718 665-5226
  Bronx *(G-1379)*
Lb Furniture Industries LLC ....C 518 828-1501
  Hudson *(G-6654)*
Maxsun Corporation ....F 718 418-6800
  Maspeth *(G-8182)*
Rollhaus Seating Products Inc ....F 718 729-9111
  Long Island City *(G-7893)*

FURNITURE: School

Inova LLC ....E 866 528-2804
  Altamont *(G-211)*

FURNITURE: Ship

Starliner Shipping & Travel ....G 718 385-1515
  Brooklyn *(G-2621)*

FURNITURE: Silverware Chests, Wood

McGraw Wood Products LLC ....E 607 836-6465
  Mc Graw *(G-8254)*

FURNITURE: Sleep

Sleep Improvement Center Inc ....F 516 536-5799
  Rockville Centre *(G-14827)*

PRODUCT SECTION

FURNITURE: Sofa Beds Or Convertible Sofas)

Sleepable Sofas Ltd .... D 973 546-4502
New York *(G-12125)*

FURNITURE: Storage Chests, Household, Wood

Premiere Living Products LLC .... F 631 873-4337
Dix Hills *(G-4318)*

FURNITURE: Tables & Table Tops, Wood

Ercole Nyc Inc .... F 212 675-2218
Brooklyn *(G-1937)*

FURNITURE: Tables, Office, Exc Wood

Prince Seating Corp .... E 718 363-2300
Brooklyn *(G-2458)*

FURNITURE: Tables, Office, Wood

Prince Seating Corp .... E 718 363-2300
Brooklyn *(G-2458)*

FURNITURE: Theater

Steeldeck Ny Inc .... F 718 599-3700
Brooklyn *(G-2625)*

FURNITURE: Upholstered

Arthur Lauer Inc .... E 845 255-7871
Gardiner *(G-5560)*
Artone LLC .... D 716 664-2232
Jamestown *(G-7008)*
August Studios .... G 718 706-6487
Long Island City *(G-7709)*
Deangelis Ltd .... G 212 348-8225
Glen Head *(G-5645)*
Delta Upholsterers Inc .... E 212 489-3308
New York *(G-9896)*
Doreen Interiors Ltd .... E 212 255-9008
New Hyde Park *(G-8872)*
Elan Upholstery Inc .... F 631 563-0650
Bohemia *(G-1061)*
Falvo Manufacturing Co Inc .... F 315 738-7682
Utica *(G-16353)*
Fiber-Seal of New York Inc .... E 212 888-5580
New York *(G-10209)*
Furniture By Craftmaster Ltd .... G 631 750-0658
Bohemia *(G-1065)*
H & H Furniture Inc .... G 718 850-5252
Jamaica *(G-6953)*
Harden Furniture LLC .... C 315 675-3600
Mc Connellsville *(G-8251)*
Henry B Urban Inc .... E 212 489-3308
New York *(G-10500)*
Jackson Dakota Inc .... G 212 838-9444
New York *(G-10728)*
Jays Furniture Products Inc .... E 716 876-8854
Buffalo *(G-3031)*
Kittinger Company Inc .... E 716 876-1000
Buffalo *(G-3050)*
Mackenzie-Childs LLC .... C 315 364-6118
Aurora *(G-528)*
Matteo & Antonio Bartolotta .... F 315 252-2220
Auburn *(G-506)*
Mazza Classics Incorporated .... G 631 390-9060
Farmingdale *(G-5055)*
McCarroll Uphl Designs LLC .... G 518 828-0500
Hudson *(G-6655)*
Mitchell Gold Co .... D 516 627-3525
Manhasset *(G-8096)*
Nicholas Dfine Furn Decorators .... F 914 245-8982
Bronx *(G-1413)*
Pheonix Custom Furniture Ltd .... E 212 727-2648
Long Island City *(G-7872)*
Princeton Upholstery Co Inc .... D 845 343-2196
Middletown *(G-8493)*
Rob Herschenfeld Design Inc .... F 718 456-6801
Brooklyn *(G-2520)*
Simon S Decorating Inc .... G 718 339-2931
Brooklyn *(G-2588)*
Slava Industries Incorporated .... G 718 499-8450
Brooklyn *(G-2595)*
Smith & Watson .... E 212 686-6444
New York *(G-12132)*
Sofa Doctor Inc .... G 718 292-6300
Bronx *(G-1456)*

Two Worlds Arts Ltd .... G 212 929-2210
Brooklyn *(G-2713)*
Versailles Drapery Upholstery .... F 212 533-2059
Long Island City *(G-7944)*
Walco Leather Co Inc .... E 212 243-2244
Bedford *(G-795)*
Wallace Home Design Ctr .... G 631 765-3890
Southold *(G-15585)*
Yepes Fine Furniture .... E 718 383-0221
Brooklyn *(G-2787)*

FURNITURE: Vehicle

Stidd Systems Inc .... E 631 477-2400
Greenport *(G-5895)*

FURRIERS

Anastasia Furs International .... G 212 868-9241
New York *(G-9198)*
Superior Furs Inc .... F 516 365-4123
Manhasset *(G-8099)*

FUSES: Electric

Leviton Manufacturing Co Inc .... B 631 812-6000
Melville *(G-8363)*
Soc America Inc .... F 631 472-6666
Ronkonkoma *(G-15010)*

GAMES & TOYS: Baby Carriages & Restraint Seats

Babysafe Usa LLC .... G 877 367-4141
Afton *(G-8)*

GAMES & TOYS: Banks

E C C Corp .... G 518 873-6494
Elizabethtown *(G-4641)*

GAMES & TOYS: Child Restraint Seats, Automotive

Pidyon Controls Inc .... G 212 683-9523
New York *(G-11679)*

GAMES & TOYS: Craft & Hobby Kits & Sets

Design Works Craft Inc .... G 631 244-5749
Bohemia *(G-1054)*
Innovative Designs LLC .... G 212 695-0892
New York *(G-10646)*
Master Art Corp .... G 845 362-6430
Spring Valley *(G-15616)*
R F Giardina Co .... F 516 922-1364
Oyster Bay *(G-13400)*
Spectrum Crafts Inc .... E 631 244-5749
Bohemia *(G-1133)*

GAMES & TOYS: Doll Hats

Beila Group Inc .... F 212 260-1948
New York *(G-9395)*

GAMES & TOYS: Dolls & Doll Clothing

Goldberger Company LLC .... F 212 924-1194
New York *(G-10371)*

GAMES & TOYS: Dolls, Exc Stuffed Toy Animals

ADC Dolls Inc .... C 212 244-4500
New York *(G-9073)*
Lovee Doll & Toy Co Inc .... G 212 242-1545
New York *(G-11081)*
Mattel Inc .... F 716 714-8514
East Aurora *(G-4399)*
Toy Admiration Co Inc .... E 914 963-9400
Yonkers *(G-17509)*

GAMES & TOYS: Electronic

212 Db Corp .... F 212 652-5600
New York *(G-9011)*
Barron Games Intl Co LLC .... F 716 630-0054
Buffalo *(G-2853)*
Marvel Entertainment LLC .... F 212 576-4000
New York *(G-11193)*

GAMES & TOYS: Game Machines, Exc Coin-Operated

Ellis Products Corp .... G 516 791-3732
Valley Stream *(G-16431)*

GAMES & TOYS: Miniature Dolls, Collectors'

Tonner Doll Company Inc .... E 845 339-9537
Kingston *(G-7244)*

GAMES & TOYS: Puzzles

Buffalo Games Inc .... D 716 827-8393
Buffalo *(G-2874)*
Compoz A Puzzle Inc .... G 516 883-2311
Port Washington *(G-13829)*
Tucker Jones House Inc .... E 631 642-9092
East Setauket *(G-4514)*

GAMES & TOYS: Scooters, Children's

Dakott LLC .... G 888 805-6795
New York *(G-9850)*
Famous Box Scooter Co .... G 631 943-2013
West Babylon *(G-16817)*

GAMES & TOYS: Trains & Eqpt, Electric & Mechanical

ATI Model Products Inc .... E 631 694-7022
Farmingdale *(G-4954)*
Gargraves Trackage Corporation .... G 315 483-6577
North Rose *(G-12953)*
Mechanical Displays Inc .... E 718 258-5588
Brooklyn *(G-2294)*
Pride Lines Ltd .... G 631 225-0033
Lindenhurst *(G-7503)*

GARBAGE CONTAINERS: Plastic

CT Industrial Supply Co Inc .... F 718 417-3226
Brooklyn *(G-1821)*
Rainbow Plastics Inc .... F 718 218-7288
Brooklyn *(G-2494)*
Think Green Junk Removal Inc .... F 845 297-7771
Wappingers Falls *(G-16597)*

GARBAGE DISPOSALS: Household

Platinum Carting Corp .... F 631 649-4322
Bay Shore *(G-720)*

GARBAGE DISPOSERS & COMPACTORS: Commercial

240 Michigan Street Inc .... F 716 434-6010
Lockport *(G-7596)*
Blue Tee Corp .... A 212 598-0880
New York *(G-9473)*

GARNET MINING SVCS

Barton Mines Company LLC .... C 518 798-5462
Glens Falls *(G-5688)*

GAS & OIL FIELD EXPLORATION SVCS

Able Environmental Services .... G 631 567-6585
Bohemia *(G-998)*
Aegis Oil Limited Ventures LLC .... F 646 233-4900
New York *(G-9099)*
America Capital Energy Corp .... G 212 983-8316
New York *(G-9161)*
Aterra Exploration LLC .... E 212 315-0030
New York *(G-9300)*
Bistate Oil Management Corp .... F 212 935-4110
New York *(G-9456)*
FT Seismic Support Inc .... C 607 527-8595
Campbell *(G-3357)*
Hess Energy Exploration Ltd .... G 732 750-6500
New York *(G-10508)*
Hess Explrtion Prod Hldngs Ltd .... G 732 750-6000
New York *(G-10509)*
JP Oil Group Inc .... G 607 563-1360
Sidney *(G-15462)*
KKR Ntrl Rsources Fund I-A LP .... F 212 750-8300
New York *(G-10895)*
Lenape Energy Inc .... G 585 344-1200
Alexander *(G-190)*
Lenape Resources Inc .... F 585 344-1200
Alexander *(G-191)*

Employee Codes: A=Over 500 employees, B=251-500
C=101-250, D=51-100, E=20-50, F=10-19, G=5-9

GAS & OIL FIELD EXPLORATION SVCS

Madoff Energy III LLC .... G ... 212 744-1918
  New York (G-11122)
Mep Alaska LLC .... G ... 646 535-9005
  Brooklyn (G-2302)
Native Amercn Enrgy Group Inc .... G ... 718 408-2323
  Forest Hills (G-5332)
Norse Energy Corp USA .... G ... 716 568-2048
  Buffalo (G-3117)
Occidental Energy Mktg Inc .... G ... 212 632-4950
  New York (G-11507)
Range Rsurces - Appalachia LLC .... E ... 716 753-3385
  Mayville (G-8249)
Sanguine Gas Exploration LLC .... E ... 212 582-8555
  New York (G-11986)
Seneca Resources Corporation .... F ... 716 630-6750
  Williamsville (G-17278)
Somerset Production Co LLC .... G ... 716 932-6480
  Buffalo (G-3217)
Springfield Oil Services Inc .... F ... 914 315-6812
  Harrison (G-6009)
Springfield Oil Services Inc .... G ... 516 482-5995
  Great Neck (G-5857)
U S Energy Development Corp .... D ... 716 636-0401
  Getzville (G-5617)
Unco United Oil Holdings LLC .... F ... 212 481-1003
  New York (G-12466)
Waffenbauch USA .... E ... 716 326-4508
  Westfield (G-17081)
Warren Energy Services LLC .... F ... 212 697-9660
  New York (G-12619)

GAS & OIL FIELD SVCS, NEC

Bass Oil & Chemical Llc .... F ... 718 628-4444
  Brooklyn (G-1667)
Case Brothers Inc .... G ... 716 925-7172
  Limestone (G-7472)
Essar Americas .... E ... 212 292-2600
  New York (G-10114)

GAS STATIONS

Marina Holding Corp .... F ... 718 646-9283
  Brooklyn (G-2270)

GASES & LIQUIFIED PETROLEUM GASES

Hudson Energy Services LLC .... G ... 630 300-0013
  Suffern (G-15813)
Osaka Gas Energy America Corp .... F ... 914 253-5500
  White Plains (G-17170)

GASES: Carbon Dioxide

Linde Merchant Production Inc .... G ... 315 593-1360
  Fulton (G-5483)

GASES: Flourinated Hydrocarbon

Hudson Technologies Company .... E ... 845 735-6000
  Pearl River (G-13481)

GASES: Indl

Airgas Inc .... E ... 585 436-7780
  Rochester (G-14197)
Airgas Usa LLC .... F ... 585 436-7781
  Rochester (G-14198)
Airgas USA LLC .... E ... 315 433-1295
  Syracuse (G-15867)
Matheson Tri-Gas Inc .... G ... 518 203-5003
  Cohoes (G-3774)
Matheson Tri-Gas Inc .... F ... 518 439-0362
  Feura Bush (G-5181)
Praxair Inc .... E ... 845 267-2337
  Valley Cottage (G-16411)
Praxair Inc .... E ... 716 649-1600
  Hamburg (G-5961)
Praxair Inc .... E ... 518 482-4360
  Albany (G-123)
Praxair Inc .... E ... 716 286-4600
  Niagara Falls (G-12879)
Praxair Inc .... C ... 845 359-4200
  Orangeburg (G-13263)
Praxair Inc .... E ... 716 879-4000
  Tonawanda (G-16213)

GASES: Neon

Neon .... F ... 212 727-5628
  New York (G-11388)

GASES: Nitrogen

Linde Gas North America LLC .... E ... 518 713-2015
  Cohoes (G-3773)
Linde Gas North America LLC .... F ... 315 431-4081
  Syracuse (G-15999)
Linde LLC .... E ... 716 847-0748
  Buffalo (G-3065)
Linde LLC .... D ... 518 439-8187
  Feura Bush (G-5180)

GASES: Oxygen

Air Products and Chemicals Inc .... D ... 518 463-4273
  Glenmont (G-5682)
Airgas Inc .... F ... 518 690-0068
  Albany (G-33)
Oxair Ltd .... E ... 716 298-8288
  Niagara Falls (G-12876)
Praxair Distribution Inc .... G ... 315 457-5821
  Liverpool (G-7569)
Praxair Distribution Inc .... F ... 315 735-6153
  Marcy (G-8122)

GASKET MATERIALS

Hollingsworth & Vose Company .... C ... 518 695-8000
  Greenwich (G-5908)
Jed Lights Inc .... F ... 516 812-5001
  Deer Park (G-4180)
Noroc Enterprises Inc .... F ... 718 585-3230
  Bronx (G-1414)

GASKETS

Allstate Gasket & Packing Inc .... F ... 631 254-4050
  Deer Park (G-4116)
Frank Lowe Rbr & Gasket Co Inc .... E ... 631 777-2707
  Shirley (G-15442)
Quick Cut Gasket & Rubber .... F ... 716 684-8628
  Lancaster (G-7361)
S A S Industries Inc .... F ... 631 727-1441
  Manorville (G-8112)

GASKETS & SEALING DEVICES

A L Sealing .... G ... 315 699-6900
  Chittenango (G-3659)
Apex Packing & Rubber Co Inc .... F ... 631 420-8150
  Farmingdale (G-4951)
Boonville Manufacturing Corp .... G ... 315 942-4368
  Boonville (G-1162)
Everlast Seals and Supply LLC .... F ... 718 388-7373
  Brooklyn (G-1946)
GM Components Holdings LLC .... D ... 716 439-2402
  Lockport (G-7621)
John Crane Inc .... D ... 315 593-6237
  Fulton (G-5478)
Schlegel Electronic Mtls Inc .... F ... 585 295-2030
  Rochester (G-14694)
Seal & Design Inc .... G ... 315 432-8021
  Syracuse (G-16058)
SKF USA Inc .... D ... 716 661-2600
  Jamestown (G-7060)
Temper Corporation .... E ... 518 853-3467
  Fonda (G-5322)
USA Sealing Inc .... E ... 716 288-9952
  Cheektowaga (G-3620)
Web Seal Inc .... E ... 585 546-1320
  Rochester (G-14786)
Xto Incorporated .... G ... 315 451-7807
  Liverpool (G-7585)

GASOLINE FILLING STATIONS

Hess Corporation .... B ... 212 997-8500
  New York (G-10507)
Lukoil North America LLC .... F ... 212 421-4141
  New York (G-11091)

GASOLINE WHOLESALERS

Bluebar Oil Co Inc .... F ... 315 245-4328
  Blossvale (G-991)
Seneca Nation Enterprise .... F ... 716 934-7430
  Irving (G-6807)

GATES: Dam, Metal Plate

Linita Design & Mfg Corp .... E ... 716 566-7753
  Lackawanna (G-7270)
Riverside Iron LLC .... F ... 315 535-4864
  Gouverneur (G-5762)

GATES: Ornamental Metal

City Store Gates Mfg Corp .... E ... 718 939-9700
  College Point (G-3806)
Inter-Fence Co Inc .... E ... 718 939-9700
  College Point (G-3814)
Moon Gates Company .... G ... 718 426-0023
  East Elmhurst (G-4417)
United Steel Products Inc .... D ... 914 968-7782
  Flushing (G-5311)
Vr Containment LLC .... G ... 917 972-3441
  Fresh Meadows (G-5461)

GAUGES

Dorsey Metrology Intl Inc .... E ... 845 229-2929
  Poughkeepsie (G-13914)
Trinity Tools Inc .... E ... 716 694-1111
  North Tonawanda (G-13021)

GEARS

Gear Motions Incorporated .... E ... 716 885-1080
  Buffalo (G-2982)
Gear Motions Incorporated .... E ... 315 488-0100
  Syracuse (G-15970)
Great Lakes Gear Co Inc .... G ... 716 694-0715
  Tonawanda (G-16183)
Perfect Gear & Instrument .... F ... 516 328-3330
  New Hyde Park (G-8902)
Perfect Gear & Instrument .... E ... 516 873-6122
  Garden City Park (G-5554)
Pro-Gear Co Inc .... G ... 716 684-3811
  Buffalo (G-3164)
Riley Gear Corporation .... E ... 716 694-0900
  North Tonawanda (G-13007)
S R & R Industries Inc .... G ... 845 692-8329
  Middletown (G-8496)
Secs Inc .... E ... 914 667-5600
  Mount Vernon (G-8777)
Secs Inc .... E ... 914 667-5600
  Mount Vernon (G-8778)
Superite Gear Instr of Hppauge .... G ... 631 234-0100
  Hauppauge (G-6228)

GEARS & GEAR UNITS: Reduction, Exc Auto

Perfection Gear Inc .... C ... 716 592-9310
  Springville (G-15635)

GEARS: Power Transmission, Exc Auto

Gleason Works .... A ... 585 473-1000
  Rochester (G-14429)
Jrlon Inc .... D ... 315 597-4067
  Palmyra (G-13434)
Khk Usa Inc .... G ... 516 248-3850
  Mineola (G-8552)
McGuigan Inc .... E ... 631 750-6222
  Bohemia (G-1098)
Niagara Gear Corporation .... E ... 716 874-3131
  Buffalo (G-3110)

GELATIN

Geliko LLC .... E ... 212 876-5620
  New York (G-10309)

GEM STONES MINING, NEC: Natural

Gemfields USA Incorporated .... G ... 212 398-5400
  New York (G-10311)
Ray Griffiths Inc .... G ... 212 689-7209
  New York (G-11831)

GEMSTONE & INDL DIAMOND MINING SVCS

Avs Gem Stone Corp .... G ... 212 944-6380
  New York (G-9334)
Didco Inc .... F ... 212 997-5022
  Rego Park (G-14044)
Double Star USA Inc .... G ... 212 929-2210
  Brooklyn (G-1876)
Herkimer Diamond Mines Inc .... E ... 315 891-7355
  Herkimer (G-6327)
Kotel Importers Inc .... F ... 212 245-6200
  New York (G-10919)

GENERAL & INDUSTRIAL LOAN INSTITUTIONS

Mitsui Chemicals America Inc .... E ... 914 253-0777
  Rye Brook (G-15098)

PRODUCT SECTION

GLASS PRDTS, PRESSED OR BLOWN: Chimneys, Lamp

GENERAL MERCHANDISE, NONDURABLE, WHOLESALE

Benson Sales Co Inc .... F 718 236-6743
  Brooklyn *(G-1683)*
Dahill Distributors Inc .... G 347 371-9453
  Brooklyn *(G-1834)*
French Associates Inc .... F 718 387-9880
  Fresh Meadows *(G-5454)*
Lokai Holdings LLC .... F 646 979-3474
  New York *(G-11052)*

GENERATING APPARATUS & PARTS: Electrical

Industrial Test Eqp Co Inc .... E 516 883-6423
  Port Washington *(G-13846)*
Mks Medical Electronics .... C 585 292-7400
  Rochester *(G-14538)*

GENERATION EQPT: Electronic

Alliance Control Systems Inc .... G 845 279-4430
  Brewster *(G-1206)*
C & M Circuits Inc .... E 631 589-0208
  Bohemia *(G-1027)*
Cellular Empire Inc .... D 800 778-3513
  Brooklyn *(G-1768)*
Curtis Instruments Inc .... C 914 666-2971
  Mount Kisco *(G-8666)*
Cygnus Automation Inc .... E 631 981-0909
  Bohemia *(G-1043)*
Donald R Husband Inc .... G 607 770-1990
  Johnson City *(G-7122)*
Ems Technologies Inc .... E 607 723-3676
  Binghamton *(G-907)*
General Electric Company .... E 518 459-4110
  Albany *(G-82)*
GW Lisk Company Inc .... E 315 548-2165
  Phelps *(G-13555)*
Tonoga Inc .... C 518 658-3202
  Petersburg *(G-13551)*

GENERATORS: Electric

Cellgen Inc .... E 516 889-9300
  Freeport *(G-5403)*
Getec Inc .... F 845 292-0800
  Ferndale *(G-5178)*

GENERATORS: Electrochemical, Fuel Cell

American Fuel Cell LLC .... G 585 474-3993
  Rochester *(G-14212)*

GENERATORS: Gas

Better Power Inc .... G 585 475-1321
  Rochester *(G-14247)*

GENERATORS: Ultrasonic

Uncharted Play Inc .... E 646 675-7783
  New York *(G-12465)*

GIFT SHOP

Csi International Inc .... E 800 441-2895
  Niagara Falls *(G-12831)*
Exotic Print and Paper Inc .... F 212 807-0465
  New York *(G-10160)*
Fly Creek Cder Mill Orchrd Inc .... G 607 547-9692
  Fly Creek *(G-5319)*
Frame Shoppe & Art Gallery .... G 516 365-6014
  Manhasset *(G-8093)*

GIFT, NOVELTY & SOUVENIR STORES: Artcraft & carvings

Kleinfelder John .... G 716 753-3163
  Mayville *(G-8247)*

GIFT, NOVELTY & SOUVENIR STORES: Gifts & Novelties

Issacs Yisroel .... G 718 851-7430
  Brooklyn *(G-2115)*
Mainly Monograms Inc .... E 845 624-4923
  West Nyack *(G-16949)*
Rip Van Wafels Inc .... E 415 529-5403
  Brooklyn *(G-2516)*

GIFT, NOVELTY & SOUVENIR STORES: Party Favors

Decorative Novelty Co Inc .... F 718 965-8600
  Brooklyn *(G-1848)*

GIFTS & NOVELTIES: Wholesalers

Cannizzaro Seal & Engraving Co .... G 718 513-6125
  Brooklyn *(G-1756)*
Full Circle Home LLC .... G 212 432-0001
  New York *(G-10270)*
Justa Company .... G 718 932-6139
  Long Island City *(G-7802)*
Mountain T-Shirts Inc .... G 518 943-4533
  Catskill *(G-3460)*
Nubian Heritage .... G 631 265-3551
  Hauppauge *(G-6176)*
OH How Cute Inc .... G 347 838-6031
  Staten Island *(G-15739)*
Studio Silversmiths Inc .... E 718 418-6785
  Ridgewood *(G-14138)*
Trove Inc .... F 212 268-2046
  Brooklyn *(G-2703)*

GIFTWARE: Brass

Lr Paris LLC .... G 703 652-1132
  New York *(G-11084)*

GLASS FABRICATORS

Benson Industries Inc .... F 212 779-3230
  New York *(G-9407)*
Glassfab Inc .... E 585 262-4000
  Rochester *(G-14425)*
Global Glass Corp .... G 516 681-2309
  Hicksville *(G-6378)*
Granville Glass & Granite .... E 518 812-0492
  Hudson Falls *(G-6676)*
Gray Glass Inc .... E 718 217-2943
  Queens Village *(G-13994)*
Kasson & Keller Inc .... A 518 853-3421
  Fonda *(G-5320)*
Michbi Doors Inc .... D 631 231-9050
  Brentwood *(G-1189)*
Oldcastle Building Envelope .... G 212 957-5400
  New York *(G-11513)*
Pal Manufacturing Corp .... E 516 937-1990
  Hicksville *(G-6409)*
Quality Enclosures Inc .... E 631 234-0115
  Central Islip *(G-3535)*
Royal Metal Products Inc .... E 518 966-4442
  Surprise *(G-15832)*
Safelite Glass Corp .... G 716 685-1358
  Depew *(G-4298)*
Select Interior Door Ltd .... E 585 535-9900
  North Java *(G-12950)*
Stark Aquarium Products Co Inc .... E 718 445-5357
  Flushing *(G-5302)*
Swift Glass Co Inc .... D 607 733-7166
  Elmira Heights *(G-4727)*
Vitarose Corp of America .... G 718 951-9700
  Brooklyn *(G-2751)*
Vitrix Inc .... G 607 936-8707
  Corning *(G-4005)*

GLASS PRDTS, FROM PURCHASED GLASS: Art

Carvart Glass Inc .... F 212 675-0030
  New York *(G-9591)*

GLASS PRDTS, FROM PURCHASED GLASS: Glass Beads, Reflecting

Potters Industries LLC .... E 315 265-4920
  Potsdam *(G-13900)*

GLASS PRDTS, FROM PURCHASED GLASS: Glassware

Exquisite Glass & Stone Inc .... G 718 937-9266
  Astoria *(G-439)*
Gmd Industries Inc .... G 718 445-8779
  College Point *(G-3810)*

GLASS PRDTS, FROM PURCHASED GLASS: Insulating

Dunlea Whl GL & Mirror Inc .... G 914 664-5277
  Mount Vernon *(G-8725)*
Rochester Insulated Glass Inc .... D 585 289-3611
  Manchester *(G-8085)*

GLASS PRDTS, FROM PURCHASED GLASS: Mirrored

Ad Notam LLC .... F 631 951-2020
  Hauppauge *(G-6028)*
Depp Glass Inc .... F 718 784-8500
  Long Island City *(G-7742)*
Dundy Glass & Mirror Corp .... E 718 723-5800
  Springfield Gardens *(G-15629)*
G & M Clearview Inc .... G 845 781-4877
  Monroe *(G-8590)*
Lafayette Mirror & Glass Co .... G 718 768-0660
  New Hyde Park *(G-8891)*
Mirror-Tech Manufacturing Co .... F 914 965-1232
  Yonkers *(G-17486)*

GLASS PRDTS, FROM PURCHASED GLASS: Mirrors, Framed

Apf Management Company LLC .... C 914 665-5400
  Yonkers *(G-17431)*
Apf Manufacturing Company LLC .... E 914 963-6300
  Yonkers *(G-17432)*
Munn Works LLC .... E 914 665-6100
  Mount Vernon *(G-8755)*
Timeless Decor LLC .... C 315 782-5759
  Watertown *(G-16697)*

GLASS PRDTS, FROM PURCHASED GLASS: Ornaments, Christmas Tree

Jinglebell Inc .... G 914 219-5395
  Armonk *(G-414)*
Rauch Industries Inc .... E 704 867-5333
  Tarrytown *(G-16127)*

GLASS PRDTS, FROM PURCHASED GLASS: Sheet, Bent

Flickinger Glassworks Inc .... G 718 875-1531
  Brooklyn *(G-1987)*

GLASS PRDTS, FROM PURCHASED GLASS: Watch Crystals

Jimmy Crystal New York Co Ltd .... E 212 594-0858
  New York *(G-10775)*
Lalique North America Inc .... E 212 355-6550
  New York *(G-10958)*

GLASS PRDTS, FROM PURCHASED GLASS: Windshields

Taylor Made Group LLC .... E 518 725-0681
  Gloversville *(G-5739)*

GLASS PRDTS, FROM PURCHD GLASS: Strengthened Or Reinforced

Campus Crafts Inc .... G 585 328-6780
  Rochester *(G-14274)*
Rochester Colonial Mfg Corp .... D 585 254-8191
  Rochester *(G-14661)*

GLASS PRDTS, PRESSED OR BLOWN: Bulbs, Electric Lights

Daylight Technology USA Inc .... G 973 255-8100
  Maspeth *(G-8160)*
Led Lumina USA LLC .... G 631 750-4433
  Bohemia *(G-1086)*

GLASS PRDTS, PRESSED OR BLOWN: Chimneys, Lamp

Sleepy Hollow Chimney Sup Ltd .... F 631 231-2333
  Brentwood *(G-1191)*

Employee Codes: A=Over 500 employees, B=251-500
C=101-250, D=51-100, E=20-50, F=10-19, G=5-9

GLASS PRDTS, PRESSED OR BLOWN: Glassware, Art Or Decorative

GLASS PRDTS, PRESSED OR BLOWN: Glassware, Art Or Decorative
- Architectural Glass Inc .... F 845 831-3116
  Beacon *(G-776)*
- Bedford Downing Glass .... G 718 418-6409
  Brooklyn *(G-1675)*
- Jay Strongwater Holdings LLC .... A 646 657-0558
  New York *(G-10745)*
- King Research Inc .... E 718 788-0122
  Brooklyn *(G-2171)*

GLASS PRDTS, PRESSED OR BLOWN: Lens Blanks, Optical
- Ion Optics Inc .... F 518 339-6853
  Albany *(G-89)*

GLASS PRDTS, PRESSED OR BLOWN: Optical
- Match Eyewear LLC .... E 516 877-0170
  Westbury *(G-17036)*
- Semrok Inc .... D 585 594-7050
  Rochester *(G-14702)*

GLASS PRDTS, PRESSED OR BLOWN: Ornaments, Christmas Tree
- Formcraft Display Products .... G 914 632-1410
  New Rochelle *(G-8945)*
- Jinglebell Inc .... G 914 219-5495
  Armonk *(G-414)*

GLASS PRDTS, PRESSED OR BLOWN: Scientific Glassware
- Scientifics Direct Inc .... F 716 773-7500
  Tonawanda *(G-16220)*

GLASS PRDTS, PRESSED/BLOWN: Glassware, Art, Decor/Novelty
- Bronx Wstchester Tempering Inc .... E 914 663-9400
  Mount Vernon *(G-8713)*
- Mata Ig .... G 212 979-7921
  New York *(G-11200)*
- Pasabahce USA .... G 212 683-1600
  New York *(G-11591)*

GLASS PRDTS, PURCHASED GLASS: Glassware, Scientific/Tech
- Community Glass Inc .... G 607 737-8860
  Elmira *(G-4689)*

GLASS PRDTS, PURCHASED GLASS: Insulating, Multiple-Glazed
- Upstate Insulated Glass Inc .... G 315 475-4960
  Central Square *(G-3546)*

GLASS PRDTS, PURCHD GLASS: Furniture Top, Cut, Beveld/Polshd
- Our Terms Fabricators Inc .... E 631 752-1517
  West Babylon *(G-16847)*
- Rn Furniture Corp .... G 347 960-9622
  Richmond Hill *(G-14092)*

GLASS PRDTS, PURCHSD GLASS: Ornamental, Cut, Engraved/D- cor
- Oneida International Inc .... G 315 361-3000
  Oneida *(G-13182)*
- Oneida Silversmiths Inc .... G 315 361-3000
  Oneida *(G-13186)*

GLASS STORE: Leaded Or Stained
- Flickinger Glassworks Inc .... G 718 875-1531
  Brooklyn *(G-1987)*

GLASS STORES
- Global Glass Corp .... G 516 681-2309
  Hicksville *(G-6378)*
- Oldcastle Buildingenvelope Inc .... C 631 234-2200
  Hauppauge *(G-6178)*
- Upstate Insulated Glass Inc .... G 315 475-4960
  Central Square *(G-3546)*

GLASS: Fiber
- Corning Incorporated .... A 607 974-9000
  Corning *(G-3983)*
- Corning Incorporated .... E 607 248-1200
  Corning *(G-3986)*
- Corning Specialty Mtls Inc .... G 607 974-9000
  Corning *(G-3991)*
- New York Enrgy Synthetics Inc .... G 212 634-4787
  New York *(G-11421)*
- Schott Corporation .... D 914 831-2200
  Elmsford *(G-4786)*
- Volpi Manufacturing USA Co Inc .... E 315 255-1737
  Auburn *(G-525)*

GLASS: Flat
- A Sunshine Glass & Aluminum .... E 718 932-8080
  Woodside *(G-17334)*
- Corning Incorporated .... E 607 974-8496
  Corning *(G-3988)*
- Corning Incorporated .... D 315 379-3200
  Canton *(G-3408)*
- Corning Incorporated .... E 607 974-6729
  Painted Post *(G-13417)*
- Global Glass Corp .... G 516 681-2309
  Hicksville *(G-6378)*
- Guardian Industries LLC .... B 315 787-7000
  Geneva *(G-5592)*
- Hecht & Sohn Glass Co Inc .... G 718 782-8295
  Brooklyn *(G-2070)*
- Pilkington North America Inc .... C 315 438-3341
  Syracuse *(G-16033)*
- Schott Corporation .... D 914 831-2200
  Elmsford *(G-4786)*
- Schott Gemtron Corporation .... C 423 337-3522
  Elmsford *(G-4787)*
- Schott Government Services LLC .... G 703 418-1409
  Elmsford *(G-4788)*
- Schott Solar Pv Inc .... G 888 457-6527
  Elmsford *(G-4790)*
- Stefan Sydor Optics Inc .... E 585 271-7300
  Rochester *(G-14726)*

GLASS: Insulating
- Tower Insulating Glass LLC .... E 516 887-3300
  North Bellmore *(G-12939)*

GLASS: Leaded
- Batavia Precision Glass LLC .... G 585 343-6050
  Buffalo *(G-2854)*

GLASS: Pressed & Blown, NEC
- Co-Optics America Lab Inc .... E 607 432-0557
  Oneonta *(G-13201)*
- Corning Incorporated .... D 607 974-9000
  Corning *(G-3984)*
- Corning Incorporated .... E 607 974-1274
  Painted Post *(G-13416)*
- Corning Incorporated .... E 607 974-9000
  Corning *(G-3985)*
- Corning Incorporated .... D 315 379-3200
  Canton *(G-3408)*
- Corning Incorporated .... E 607 433-3100
  Oneonta *(G-13205)*
- Corning Incorporated .... G 607 974-4488
  Corning *(G-3987)*
- Corning Incorporated .... E 607 974-6729
  Painted Post *(G-13417)*
- Corning International Corp .... G 607 974-9000
  Corning *(G-3989)*
- Corning Tropel Corporation .... C 585 377-3200
  Fairport *(G-4857)*
- Corning Vitro Corporation .... A 607 974-8605
  Corning *(G-3992)*
- Eye Deal Eyewear Inc .... G 716 297-1500
  Niagara Falls *(G-12838)*
- Germanow-Simon Corporation .... E 585 232-1440
  Rochester *(G-14420)*
- Gillinder Brothers Inc .... D 845 856-5375
  Port Jervis *(G-13807)*
- Glasteel Parts & Services Inc .... E 585 235-1010
  Rochester *(G-14426)*
- Lighting Holdings Intl LLC .... A 845 306-1850
  Purchase *(G-13976)*
- Navitar Inc .... D 585 359-4000
  Rochester *(G-14550)*
- Owens Corning Sales LLC .... B 518 475-3600
  Feura Bush *(G-5182)*
- Saint-Gobain Prfmce Plas Corp .... C 518 686-7301
  Hoosick Falls *(G-6571)*
- Schott Corporation .... D 315 255-2791
  Auburn *(G-514)*
- Stefan Sydor Optics Inc .... E 585 271-7300
  Rochester *(G-14726)*

GLASS: Stained
- Adirondack Stained Glass Works .... G 518 725-0387
  Gloversville *(G-5719)*
- Chapman Stained Glass Studio .... G 518 449-5552
  Albany *(G-61)*
- Makarenko Studios Inc .... G 914 968-7673
  Yorktown Heights *(G-17528)*
- Rohlfs Stined Leaded GL Studio .... E 914 699-4848
  Mount Vernon *(G-8773)*
- Somers Stain Glass Inc .... F 631 586-7772
  Deer Park *(G-4235)*
- Sunburst Studios Inc .... G 718 768-6360
  Brooklyn *(G-2642)*

GLASS: Structural
- Europrojects Intl Inc .... G 917 262-0795
  New York *(G-10140)*

GLASS: Tempered
- Oldcastle Buildingenvelope Inc .... C 631 234-2200
  Hauppauge *(G-6178)*
- Taylor Products Inc .... G 518 773-9312
  Gloversville *(G-5740)*

GLASSWARE STORES
- Benton Announcements Inc .... F 716 836-4100
  Buffalo *(G-2861)*
- Vitrix Inc .... G 607 936-8707
  Corning *(G-4005)*

GLASSWARE WHOLESALERS
- A Sunshine Glass & Aluminum .... E 718 932-8080
  Woodside *(G-17334)*

GLASSWARE: Laboratory
- TEC Glass & Inst LLC .... G 315 926-7639
  Marion *(G-8132)*

GLASSWARE: Laboratory & Medical
- Immco Diagnostics Inc .... D 716 691-6911
  Buffalo *(G-3022)*
- Mri Northtowns Group PC .... F 716 836-4646
  Buffalo *(G-3097)*

GLOBAL POSITIONING SYSTEMS & EQPT
- Evado Filip .... F 917 774-8666
  New York *(G-10142)*
- Intelibs Inc .... G 877 213-2640
  Stony Brook *(G-15791)*
- Rehabilitation International .... G 212 420-1500
  Jamaica *(G-6983)*

GLOVE MENDING, FACTORY BASIS
- Radio Circle Realty Inc .... E 914 241-8742
  Mount Kisco *(G-8685)*
- Valeo .... G 800 634-2704
  Yonkers *(G-17512)*

GLOVES: Fabric
- Falls Manufacturing Inc .... G 518 672-7189
  Philmont *(G-13565)*
- Gce International Inc .... F 212 868-0500
  New York *(G-10305)*

GLOVES: Leather
- American Target Marketing Inc .... E 518 725-4369
  Gloversville *(G-5720)*
- Fieldtex Products Inc .... C 585 427-2940
  Rochester *(G-14391)*
- Samco LLC .... E 518 725-4705
  Gloversville *(G-5735)*
- USA Sewing Inc .... E 315 792-8017
  Utica *(G-16386)*

PRODUCT SECTION

GREETING CARDS WHOLESALERS

GLOVES: Leather, Dress Or Semidress
Fownes Brothers & Co Inc ....E...... 212 683-0150
  New York (G-10244)
Fownes Brothers & Co Inc ....E...... 518 752-4411
  Gloversville (G-5726)

GLOVES: Leather, Work
Protech (llc) ....E...... 518 725-7785
  Gloversville (G-5734)
Worldwide Protective Pdts LLC ....C...... 877 678-4568
  Hamburg (G-5969)

GLOVES: Plastic
Elara Fdsrvice Disposables LLC ....G...... 877 893-3244
  Jericho (G-7100)

GLOVES: Safety
Hand Care Inc ....G...... 516 747-5649
  Roslyn (G-15044)

GLOVES: Work
Manzella Knitting ....G...... 716 825-0808
  Orchard Park (G-13306)

GLOVES: Woven Or Knit, From Purchased Materials
Fownes Brothers & Co Inc ....E...... 212 683-0150
  New York (G-10244)
Fownes Brothers & Co Inc ....E...... 518 752-4411
  Gloversville (G-5726)

GLUE
Hudson Industries Corporation ....E...... 518 762-4638
  Johnstown (G-7146)

GOLD ORE MINING
Andes Gold Corporation ....D...... 212 541-2495
  New York (G-9200)
Capital Gold Corporation ....G...... 212 668-0842
  New York (G-9575)

GOLD ORES
Global Gold Corporation ....F...... 914 925-0020
  Rye (G-15084)
Gncc Capital Inc ....G...... 702 951-9793
  New York (G-10367)

GOLD RECOVERY FROM TAILINGS
Fuda Group (usa) Corporation ....G...... 646 751-7488
  New York (G-10268)

GOLD STAMPING, EXC BOOKS
John Gailer Inc ....E...... 212 243-5662
  Long Island City (G-7799)
Welsh Gold Stampers Inc ....E...... 718 984-5031
  Staten Island (G-15776)

GOLF CARTS: Powered
Club Protector Inc ....G...... 716 652-4787
  Elma (G-4659)

GOLF EQPT
Morris Golf Ventures ....E...... 631 283-0559
  Southampton (G-15571)

GOURMET FOOD STORES
Dairy Maid Raviolo Mfg ....F...... 718 449-2620
  Brooklyn (G-1836)
Herris Gourmet Inc ....G...... 917 578-2308
  Brooklyn (G-2076)
Interntional Gourmet Soups Inc ....E...... 212 768-7687
  Staten Island (G-15709)
Johns Ravioli Company Inc ....F...... 914 576-7030
  New Rochelle (G-8960)
New York Ravioli Pasta Co Inc ....E...... 516 270-2852
  New Hyde Park (G-8897)
Queen Ann Macaroni Mfg Co Inc ....G...... 718 256-1061
  Brooklyn (G-2485)
Raffettos Corp ....E...... 212 777-1261
  New York (G-11813)

GOVERNMENT, EXECUTIVE OFFICES: Mayors'
City of Olean ....G...... 716 376-5694
  Olean (G-13158)
City of Oneonta ....G...... 607 433-3470
  Oneonta (G-13200)
Hartford Hwy Dept ....G...... 315 724-0654
  New Hartford (G-8851)
Town of Amherst ....E...... 716 631-7113
  Williamsville (G-17283)

GOVERNMENT, GENERAL: Administration
City of New York ....E...... 718 965-8787
  Brooklyn (G-1781)

GRANITE: Crushed & Broken
MCM Natural Stone Inc ....F...... 585 586-6510
  Rochester (G-14523)
Suffolk Granite Manufacturing ....E...... 631 226-4774
  Lindenhurst (G-7509)
Tilcon New York Inc ....D...... 845 358-3100
  West Nyack (G-16958)

GRANITE: Cut & Shaped
Amendola MBL & Stone Ctr Inc ....D...... 914 997-7968
  White Plains (G-17104)
Aurora Stone Group LLC ....F...... 315 471-6869
  East Syracuse (G-4525)
Capital Stone LLC ....G...... 518 382-7588
  Schenectady (G-15266)
Capital Stone Saratoga LLC ....G...... 518 226-8677
  Saratoga Springs (G-15175)
Glen Plaza Marble & Gran Inc ....G...... 516 671-1100
  Glen Cove (G-5630)
Granite & Marble Works Inc ....E...... 518 584-2800
  Gansevoort (G-5500)
House of Stone Inc ....G...... 845 782-7271
  Monroe (G-8592)
Marble Works Inc ....E...... 914 376-3653
  Yonkers (G-17483)
MCM Natural Stone Inc ....F...... 585 586-6510
  Rochester (G-14523)
PR & Stone & Tile Inc ....G...... 718 383-1115
  Brooklyn (G-2448)
Royal Marble & Granite Inc ....G...... 516 536-5900
  Oceanside (G-13116)

GRANITE: Dimension
Adirondack Natural Stone LLC ....E...... 518 499-0602
  Whitehall (G-17217)
Cold Spring Granite Company ....G...... 518 647-8191
  Au Sable Forks (G-474)
Imerys Usa Inc ....F...... 315 287-0780
  Gouverneur (G-5761)

GRANITE: Dimension
Alice Perkins ....G...... 716 378-5100
  Salamanca (G-15125)

GRAPHIC ARTS & RELATED DESIGN SVCS
Accent Label & Tag Co Inc ....G...... 631 244-7066
  Ronkonkoma (G-14875)
Adcomm Graphics Inc ....E...... 212 645-1298
  West Babylon (G-16790)
Advantage Printing Inc ....F...... 718 820-0688
  Kew Gardens (G-7187)
Alabaster Group Inc ....G...... 516 867-8223
  Freeport (G-5391)
Beebie Printing & Art Agcy Inc ....E...... 518 725-4528
  Gloversville (G-5723)
Desktop Publishing Concepts ....F...... 631 752-1934
  Farmingdale (G-4985)
Digital Evolution Inc ....E...... 212 732-2722
  New York (G-9929)
Eastern Metal of Elmira Inc ....D...... 607 734-2295
  Elmira (G-4692)
Gg Design and Printing ....G...... 718 321-3220
  New York (G-10332)
Greenwood Graphics Inc ....F...... 516 822-4856
  Hicksville (G-6381)
Horne Organization Inc ....F...... 914 572-1330
  Yonkers (G-17471)
Merlin Printing Inc ....E...... 631 842-6666
  Amityville (G-312)
Middletown Press ....G...... 845 343-1895
  Middletown (G-8485)
North American Graphics Inc ....F...... 212 725-2200
  New York (G-11472)
Pic A Poc Enterprises Inc ....G...... 631 981-2094
  Ronkonkoma (G-14994)
Play-It Productions Inc ....F...... 212 695-6530
  Port Washington (G-13873)
Proof 7 Ltd ....F...... 212 680-1843
  New York (G-11757)
Resonant Legal Media LLC ....D...... 800 781-3591
  New York (G-11873)
Tri Kolor Printing & Sty ....F...... 315 474-6753
  Syracuse (G-16085)
Vital Signs & Graphics Co Inc ....G...... 518 237-8372
  Cohoes (G-3785)

GRAPHIC LAYOUT SVCS: Printed Circuitry
J N White Associates Inc ....D...... 585 237-5191
  Perry (G-13547)

GRASSES: Artificial & Preserved
Techgrass ....F...... 646 719-2000
  New York (G-12314)

GRATINGS: Tread, Fabricated Metal
Fjs Industries Inc ....F...... 917 428-3797
  Brooklyn (G-1982)

GRAVE MARKERS: Concrete
Woodside Granite Industries ....G...... 585 589-6500
  Albion (G-174)

GRAVEL MINING
Buffalo Crushed Stone Inc ....F...... 716 566-9636
  Franklinville (G-5378)
Central Dover Development ....G...... 917 709-3266
  Dover Plains (G-4338)
Dalrymple Grav & Contg Co Inc ....E...... 607 529-3235
  Chemung (G-3621)
Diehl Development Inc ....G...... 585 494-2920
  Bergen (G-843)
Hanson Aggregates PA LLC ....E...... 585 624-1220
  Honeoye Falls (G-6558)
Hanson Aggregates PA LLC ....F...... 315 782-2300
  Watertown (G-16674)
Hanson Aggregates PA LLC ....E...... 315 789-6202
  Oaks Corners (G-13089)
Hanson Aggregates PA LLC ....E...... 585 624-3800
  Honeoye Falls (G-6557)
Hanson Aggregates PA LLC ....F...... 585 436-3250
  Rochester (G-14440)
IA Construction Corporation ....G...... 716 933-8787
  Portville (G-13893)
Knight Sttlement Sand Grav LLC ......E...... 607 776-2048
  Bath (G-659)
Rock Mountain Farms Inc ....G...... 845 647-9084
  Ellenville (G-4652)
Seven Springs Gravel Pdts LLC ....G...... 585 343-4336
  Batavia (G-647)
Shelby Crushed Stone Inc ....F...... 585 798-4501
  Medina (G-8314)

GREASE CUPS: Metal
Blue Manufacturing Co Inc ....G...... 607 796-2463
  Millport (G-8515)

GREASE TRAPS: Concrete
Long Island Green Guys ....G...... 631 664-4306
  Riverhead (G-14161)

GREASES: Lubricating
Summit Lubricants Inc ....E...... 585 815-0798
  Batavia (G-649)

GREENHOUSES: Prefabricated Metal
Fillmore Greenhouses Inc ....E...... 585 567-2678
  Portageville (G-13890)

GREETING CARDS WHOLESALERS
Paper House Productions Inc ....E...... 845 246-7261
  Saugerties (G-15219)

GRILLS & GRILLWORK: Woven Wire, Made From Purchased Wire

Nyc Fireplaces & Kitchens...............G....... 718 326-4328
  Maspeth *(G-8191)*

GRINDING BALLS: Ceramic

Malyn Industrial Ceramics Inc ....G....... 716 741-1510
  Clarence Center *(G-3705)*

GRINDING SVC: Precision, Commercial Or Indl

Acme Industries of W Babylon...........F....... 631 737-5231
  Ronkonkoma *(G-14877)*
Aip Mc Holdings LLC ....A....... 212 627-2360
  New York *(G-9115)*
Ascribe Inc..E....... 585 413-0298
  Rochester *(G-14234)*
Dean Manufacturing Inc ....F....... 607 770-1300
  Vestal *(G-16468)*
Micro Instrument Corp ....D....... 585 458-3150
  Rochester *(G-14528)*
Temrick Inc..G....... 631 567-8860
  Bohemia *(G-1139)*

GRINDING SVCS: Ophthalmic Lens, Exc Prescription

Empire Optical Inc ....F....... 585 454-4470
  Rochester *(G-14368)*

GRIT: Steel

Smm - North America Trade Corp ......G....... 212 604-0710
  New York *(G-12136)*

GRITS: Crushed & Broken

Hanson Aggregates PA LLC ....F....... 315 393-3743
  Ogdensburg *(G-13136)*
Hanson Aggregates PA LLC ....F....... 315 821-7222
  Oriskany Falls *(G-13342)*
Masten Enterprises LLC.......................C....... 845 932-8206
  Cochecton *(G-3767)*
Upstone Materials Inc..........................D....... 518 561-5321
  Plattsburgh *(G-13735)*

GROCERIES WHOLESALERS, NEC

Bimbo Bakeries Usa Inc ....C....... 718 463-6300
  Maspeth *(G-8151)*
Bimbo Bakeries Usa Inc ....E....... 800 856-8544
  Vestal *(G-16463)*
Bimbo Bakeries Usa Inc ....F....... 845 294-5282
  Goshen *(G-5746)*
Coca-Cola Bottling Co of NY ....F....... 518 459-2010
  Albany *(G-69)*
Coca-Cola Refreshments USA Inc .....E....... 718 401-5200
  Bronx *(G-1302)*
Cohens Bakery Inc..............................E....... 716 892-8149
  Buffalo *(G-2899)*
French Associates Inc..........................F....... 718 387-9880
  Fresh Meadows *(G-5454)*
Infant Formula Laboratory Svc............F....... 718 257-3000
  Brooklyn *(G-2103)*
Kozy Shack Enterprises LLC ....C....... 516 870-3000
  Hicksville *(G-6387)*
Kozy Shack Enterprises LLC ....C....... 516 870-3000
  Hicksville *(G-6388)*
Luxfer Magtech Inc ....D....... 631 727-8600
  Riverhead *(G-14162)*
Mandarin Soy Sauce Inc.....................C....... 845 343-1505
  Middletown *(G-8483)*
Rochester Coca Cola Bottling ....D....... 585 546-3900
  Rochester *(G-14660)*
S J McCullagh Inc ....E....... 716 856-3473
  Buffalo *(G-3201)*
Shine Foods USA Inc ....G....... 516 784-9674
  Glen Oaks *(G-5655)*
Wellspring Corp ....G....... 212 529-5454
  New York *(G-12637)*

GROCERIES, GENERAL LINE WHOLESALERS

Kong Kee Food Corp ....E....... 718 937-2746
  Long Island City *(G-7809)*
Mondelez Global LLC..........................G....... 585 345-3300
  Batavia *(G-643)*

GUARDRAILS

Elderlee Incorporated ....C....... 315 789-6670
  Oaks Corners *(G-13088)*

GUIDANCE SYSTEMS & EQPT: Space Vehicle

Harris Corporation ....A....... 585 269-6600
  Rochester *(G-14442)*
Harris Corporation ....B....... 585 269-5001
  Rochester *(G-14443)*
Harris Corporation ....C....... 585 269-5000
  Rochester *(G-14445)*

GUIDED MISSILES & SPACE VEHICLES

Edo LLC ....A....... 631 630-4200
  Amityville *(G-285)*
Lockheed Martin Corporation ....A....... 607 751-2000
  Owego *(G-13379)*
Lockheed Martin Corporation ....D....... 607 751-7434
  Owego *(G-13380)*

GUM & WOOD CHEMICALS

Metro Products & Services LLC ....F....... 866 846-8486
  Brooklyn *(G-2311)*
Westrock Mwv LLC ....C....... 212 688-5000
  New York *(G-12645)*

GUN STOCKS: Wood

Revival Industries Inc ....F....... 315 868-1085
  Ilion *(G-6784)*

GUNSMITHS

Michael Britt Inc ....G....... 516 248-2010
  Mineola *(G-8558)*
Precision Arms Inc ....G....... 845 225-1130
  Carmel *(G-3432)*

GUTTERS: Sheet Metal

Alfred B Parella ....G....... 518 872-1238
  Altamont *(G-208)*
Genesee Building Products LLC ....G....... 585 548-2726
  Stafford *(G-15640)*

GYPSUM PRDTS

East Pattern & Model Corp ....E....... 585 461-3240
  Fairport *(G-4861)*
Empire Gypsum Pdts & Sup Corp ......G....... 914 592-8141
  Elmsford *(G-4758)*
Lafarge North America Inc ....D....... 914 930-3027
  Buchanan *(G-2800)*
United States Gypsum Company ....C....... 585 948-5221
  Oakfield *(G-13085)*

HAIR & HAIR BASED PRDTS

Age Manufacturers Inc ....D....... 718 927-0048
  Brooklyn *(G-1569)*
American Culture Hair Inc....................E....... 631 242-3142
  Huntington Station *(G-6731)*
Blandi Products LLC ....F....... 908 377-2885
  New York *(G-9464)*
De Meo Brothers Inc ....G....... 212 268-1400
  New York *(G-9889)*
Hair Color Research Group Inc ....E....... 718 445-6026
  Flushing *(G-5256)*
Jason & Jean Products Inc ....F....... 718 271-8300
  Corona *(G-4022)*
Malouf Colette Inc ....F....... 212 941-9588
  New York *(G-11147)*
Mgd Brands Inc ....E....... 516 545-0150
  Plainview *(G-13648)*
Miss Jessies LLC ....F....... 718 643-9016
  New York *(G-11308)*
Premium Assure Inc ....G....... 605 252-9999
  Brooklyn *(G-2452)*
Spartan Brands Inc ....F....... 212 340-0320
  New York *(G-12174)*
Tactica International Inc ....F....... 212 575-0500
  New York *(G-12294)*

HAIR ACCESS WHOLESALERS

Mgd Brands Inc ....E....... 516 545-0150
  Plainview *(G-13648)*

HAIR CARE PRDTS

All Cultures Inc....................................E....... 631 293-3143
  Greenlawn *(G-5890)*
Belmay Holding Corporation ....E....... 914 376-1515
  Yonkers *(G-17436)*
Hair Ventures LLC ....F....... 718 664-7689
  Irvington *(G-6813)*
LOreal Usa Inc ....B....... 212 818-1500
  New York *(G-11064)*
LOreal Usa Inc ....G....... 212 984-4704
  New York *(G-11067)*
LOreal Usa Inc ....B....... 646 658-5477
  New York *(G-11068)*
Lornamead Inc ....D....... 716 874-7190
  Tonawanda *(G-16196)*
Pureology Research LLC....................F....... 212 984-4360
  New York *(G-11778)*
Zotos International Inc ....B....... 315 781-3207
  Geneva *(G-5601)*

HAIR CARE PRDTS: Hair Coloring Preparations

LOreal USA Products Inc ....G....... 212 818-1500
  New York *(G-11069)*
Salonclick LLC ....F....... 718 643-6793
  New York *(G-11976)*

HAIRPIN MOUNTINGS

Lemetric Hair Centers Inc ....F....... 212 986-5620
  New York *(G-10998)*
Shake-N-Go Fashion Inc ....E....... 516 944-7777
  Port Washington *(G-13881)*
Shake-N-Go Fashion Inc ....D....... 516 944-7777
  Port Washington *(G-13882)*

HANDBAG STORES

Graphic Image Incorporated ....C....... 631 249-9600
  Melville *(G-8353)*
Quilted Koala Ltd ....F....... 800 223-5678
  New York *(G-11799)*
Steven Madden Ltd ....B....... 718 446-1800
  Long Island City *(G-7919)*

HANDBAGS

Affordable Luxury Group Inc ....G....... 631 523-9266
  New York *(G-9103)*
Ahq LLC ....E....... 212 328-1560
  New York *(G-9112)*
Akh Group LLC ....G....... 646 320-8720
  New York *(G-9118)*
Bagznyc Corp ....F....... 212 643-8202
  New York *(G-9358)*
Coach Inc ....B....... 212 594-1850
  New York *(G-9714)*
Coach Inc ....G....... 518 456-5657
  Albany *(G-68)*
Essex Manufacturing Inc ....D....... 212 239-0080
  New York *(G-10119)*
McM Products USA Inc ....E....... 646 756-4090
  New York *(G-11226)*
Nine West Footwear Corporation ....B....... 800 999-1877
  New York *(G-11452)*
Pure Trade Us Inc ....E....... 212 256-1600
  New York *(G-11774)*
Quilted Koala Ltd ....F....... 800 223-5678
  New York *(G-11799)*
Rodem Incorporated ....F....... 212 779-7122
  New York *(G-11922)*

HANDBAGS: Women's

Atalla Handbags Inc............................G....... 718 965-5500
  Brooklyn *(G-1645)*
Baikal Inc ....D....... 212 239-4650
  New York *(G-9359)*
Coach Inc ....G....... 212 615-2082
  New York *(G-9708)*
Coach Inc ....F....... 212 581-4115
  New York *(G-9709)*
Coach Inc ....F....... 718 760-0624
  Elmhurst *(G-4672)*
Coach Inc ....F....... 585 425-7720
  Victor *(G-16492)*
Coach Inc ....F....... 212 245-4148
  New York *(G-9710)*
Coach Inc ....E....... 212 473-6925
  New York *(G-9711)*

PRODUCT SECTION

HARDWARE: Cabinet

Coach Inc .... F 212 754-0041
  New York *(G-9712)*
Coach Inc .... F 212 675-6403
  New York *(G-9713)*
Coach Leatherware Intl .... G 212 594-1850
  New York *(G-9715)*
Coach Services Inc .... G 212 594-1850
  New York *(G-9716)*
Coach Stores Inc .... A 212 643-9727
  New York *(G-9717)*
Dani Accessories Inc .... E 631 692-4505
  Cold Spring Harbor *(G-3793)*
Deux Lux Inc .... G 212 620-0801
  New York *(G-9915)*
Frenz Group LLC .... G 212 465-0908
  Whitestone *(G-17235)*
Kcp Holdco Inc .... F 212 265-1500
  New York *(G-10866)*
Kenneth Cole Productions Inc .... B 212 265-1500
  New York *(G-10873)*
Renco Group Inc .... G 212 541-6000
  New York *(G-11864)*
Roadie Products Inc .... E 631 567-8588
  Holbrook *(G-6497)*

HANDCUFFS & LEG IRONS

Boa Security Technologies Corp .... G 516 576-0295
  Huntington *(G-6690)*

HANDLES: Brush Or Tool, Plastic

Allen Field Co Inc .... F 631 665-2782
  Brightwaters *(G-1237)*

HANDLES: Wood

Fibron Products Inc .... E 716 886-2378
  Buffalo *(G-2961)*

HANGERS: Garment, Plastic

American Intl Trimming .... G 718 369-9643
  Brooklyn *(G-1600)*
Capco Wai Shing LLC .... G 212 268-1976
  New York *(G-9573)*
Prestige Hangers Str Fixs Corp .... G 718 522-6777
  Brooklyn *(G-2454)*

HANGERS: Garment, Wire

Styles Manufacturing Corp .... G 516 763-5303
  Oceanside *(G-13120)*

HANGERS: Garment, Wire

American Intl Trimming .... G 718 369-9643
  Brooklyn *(G-1600)*

HARDBOARD & FIBERBOARD PRDTS

Hi-Temp Fabrication Inc .... F 716 852-5655
  Buffalo *(G-3012)*

HARDWARE

Advantage Wholesale Supply LLC .... D 718 284-5346
  Brooklyn *(G-1566)*
American Casting and Mfg Corp .... G 516 349-7010
  Plainview *(G-13612)*
Amertac Holdings Inc .... G 610 336-1330
  Monsey *(G-8602)*
Barry Industries Inc .... F 212 242-5200
  New York *(G-9377)*
Cast-All Corporation .... E 516 741-4025
  Mineola *(G-8535)*
City Store Gates Mfg Corp .... E 718 939-9700
  College Point *(G-3806)*
Designatronics Incorporated .... B 516 328-3300
  Hicksville *(G-6367)*
Dico Products Corporation .... F 315 797-0470
  Utica *(G-16346)*
ER Butler & Co Inc .... E 212 925-3565
  New York *(G-10107)*
Excelco Developments Inc .... E 716 934-2651
  Silver Creek *(G-15470)*
H A Guden Company Inc .... E 631 737-2900
  Ronkonkoma *(G-14937)*
Industrial Electronic Hardware .... D 718 492-4440
  Brooklyn *(G-2101)*
Ingham Industries Inc .... G 631 242-2493
  Holbrook *(G-6480)*
ITR Industries Inc .... E 914 964-7063
  Yonkers *(G-17473)*

Jaquith Industries Inc .... E 315 478-5700
  Syracuse *(G-15985)*
Key High Vacuum Products Inc .... E 631 584-5959
  Nesconset *(G-8823)*
Kilian Manufacturing Corp .... D 315 432-0700
  Syracuse *(G-15993)*
Legendary Auto Interiors Ltd .... E 315 331-1212
  Newark *(G-12754)*
Liberty Brass Turning Co Inc .... E 718 784-2911
  Westbury *(G-17032)*
Lif Industries Inc .... E 718 767-8800
  Whitestone *(G-17240)*
Lightron Corporation .... G 516 938-5544
  Jericho *(G-7107)*
Magnetic Aids Inc .... G 845 863-1400
  Newburgh *(G-12787)*
Nielsen Hardware Corporation .... E 607 821-1475
  Binghamton *(G-936)*
Orbital Holdings Inc .... E 951 360-7100
  Buffalo *(G-3126)*
P & F Industries Inc .... E 631 694-9800
  Melville *(G-8375)*
Rosco Inc .... C 718 526-2601
  Jamaica *(G-6985)*
Syraco Products Inc .... E 315 476-5306
  Syracuse *(G-16072)*
Tattersall Industries LLC .... E 518 381-4270
  Schenectady *(G-15327)*
Yaloz Mould & Die Co Inc .... E 718 389-1131
  Brooklyn *(G-2786)*
York Industries Inc .... E 516 746-3736
  Garden City Park *(G-5559)*

HARDWARE & BUILDING PRDTS: Plastic

Abbott Industries Inc .... E 718 291-0800
  Jamaica *(G-6926)*
Associated Materials LLC .... F 631 467-4535
  Ronkonkoma *(G-14901)*
Cementex Latex Corp .... F 212 741-1770
  New York *(G-9609)*
Dortronics Systems Inc .... E 631 725-0505
  Sag Harbor *(G-15105)*
Gagne Associates Inc .... E 800 800-5954
  Johnson City *(G-7123)*
Hall Construction Pdts & Svcs .... G 518 747-7047
  Hudson Falls *(G-6678)*
Kelta Inc .... E 631 789-5000
  Edgewood *(G-4616)*
Markwik Corp .... F 516 470-1990
  Hicksville *(G-6396)*
Metal Cladding Inc .... D 716 434-5513
  Lockport *(G-7629)*
Pace Window and Door Corp .... E 585 924-8350
  Victor *(G-16519)*
Performance Advantage Co Inc .... F 716 683-7413
  Lancaster *(G-7357)*
Schlegel Systems Inc .... E 585 427-7200
  Rochester *(G-14695)*
Space Age Plstic Fbrcators Inc .... F 718 324-4062
  Bronx *(G-1457)*
Tii Technologies Inc .... E 516 364-9300
  Edgewood *(G-4629)*
Transpo Industries Inc .... E 914 636-1000
  New Rochelle *(G-8972)*

HARDWARE & EQPT: Stage, Exc Lighting

Martin Chafkin .... G 718 383-1155
  Brooklyn *(G-2278)*
Props Displays & Interiors .... F 212 620-3840
  New York *(G-11759)*
Steeldeck Ny Inc .... F 718 599-3700
  Brooklyn *(G-2625)*

HARDWARE CLOTH: Woven Wire, Made From Purchased Wire

Dico Products Corporation .... F 315 797-0470
  Utica *(G-16346)*

HARDWARE STORES

Lowville Farmers Coop Inc .... E 315 376-6587
  Lowville *(G-7966)*
Syracuse Industrial Sls Co Ltd .... F 315 478-5751
  Syracuse *(G-16077)*

HARDWARE STORES: Builders'

Ingham Industries Inc .... G 631 242-2493
  Holbrook *(G-6480)*

HARDWARE STORES: Pumps & Pumping Eqpt

A & C/Furia Electric Motors .... F 914 949-0585
  White Plains *(G-17100)*

HARDWARE STORES: Tools

Boro Park Cutting Tool Corp .... E 718 720-0610
  Staten Island *(G-15670)*
Parker Machine Company Inc .... F 518 747-0675
  Fort Edward *(G-9377)*
Zak Jewelry Tools Inc .... F 212 768-8122
  New York *(G-12722)*

HARDWARE WHOLESALERS

Amertac Holdings Inc .... G 610 336-1330
  Monsey *(G-8602)*
Barry Industries Inc .... F 212 242-5200
  New York *(G-9377)*
Best Way Tools By Anderson Inc .... E 631 586-4702
  Deer Park *(G-4130)*
Expo Furniture Designs Inc .... F 516 674-1420
  Glen Cove *(G-5352)*
Globe Electronic Hardware Inc .... F 718 457-0303
  Woodside *(G-17349)*
H A Guden Company Inc .... E 631 737-2900
  Ronkonkoma *(G-14937)*
Metalline Fire Door Co Inc .... E 718 583-2320
  Bronx *(G-1396)*
Steel-Brite Ltd .... F 631 589-4044
  Oakdale *(G-13082)*
Sure Flow Equipment Inc .... E 800 263-8251
  Tonawanda *(G-16224)*

HARDWARE, WHOLESALE: Bolts

Supply Technologies (ny) .... F 212 966-3310
  Albany *(G-139)*

HARDWARE, WHOLESALE: Builders', NEC

ER Butler & Co Inc .... E 212 925-3565
  New York *(G-10107)*
P E Guerin .... D 212 243-5270
  New York *(G-11561)*
S A Baxter LLC .... G 845 469-7995
  Chester *(G-3641)*

HARDWARE, WHOLESALE: Screws

Sg-TEC LLC .... G 631 750-6161
  Bohemia *(G-1128)*

HARDWARE, WHOLESALE: Security Devices, Locks

Shield Security Doors Ltd .... G 202 468-3308
  New York *(G-12072)*

HARDWARE: Aircraft

Fastener Dimensions Inc .... E 718 847-6321
  Ozone Park *(G-13404)*
Kyntec Corporation .... G 716 810-6956
  Buffalo *(G-3056)*
Magellan Aerospace Processing .... G 631 694-1818
  West Babylon *(G-16838)*
Mpi Consulting Incorporated .... F 631 253-2377
  West Babylon *(G-16843)*

HARDWARE: Builders'

Kelley Bros Hardware Corp .... G 315 852-3302
  De Ruyter *(G-4106)*
Northknight Logistics Inc .... F 716 283-3090
  Niagara Falls *(G-12871)*
Pk30 System LLC .... F 212 473-8050
  Stone Ridge *(G-15786)*
Progressive Hardware Co Inc .... G 631 445-1826
  East Northport *(G-4462)*
RKI Building Spc Co Inc .... G 718 728-7788
  College Point *(G-3830)*

HARDWARE: Cabinet

Daniel Demarco and Assoc Inc .... E 631 598-7000
  Amityville *(G-283)*
Darman Manufacturing Coinc .... F 315 724-9632
  Utica *(G-16344)*
Kenstan Lock & Hardware Co Inc .... E 631 423-1977
  Plainview *(G-13642)*

HARDWARE: Door Opening & Closing Devices, Exc Electrical

HARDWARE: Door Opening & Closing Devices, Exc Electrical

Nanz Custom Hardware Inc ....E...... 212 367-7000
New York (G-11364)
Nanz Custom Hardware Inc ....C...... 212 367-7000
Deer Park (G-4200)

HARDWARE: Furniture

Dreamseats LLC ....E...... 631 656-1066
Commack (G-3856)
Real Design Inc ....F...... 315 429-3071
Dolgeville (G-4332)
Water Street Brass Corporation ....E...... 716 763-0059
Lakewood (G-7320)
Weber-Knapp Company ....C...... 716 484-9135
Jamestown (G-7075)

HARDWARE: Furniture, Builders' & Other Household

Classic Brass Inc ....D...... 716 763-1400
Lakewood (G-7312)
Decorative Hardeware ....F...... 914 238-5251
Chappaqua (G-3579)
Morgik Metal Designs ....F...... 212 463-0304
New York (G-11330)

HARDWARE: Luggage

Crest Lock Co Inc ....F...... 718 345-9898
Brooklyn (G-1817)
Tools & Stamping Corp ....G...... 718 392-4040
Brooklyn (G-2683)

HARDWARE: Piano

Samscreen Inc....................................E...... 607 722-3979
Conklin (G-3901)

HARNESS ASSEMBLIES: Cable & Wire

Advanced Interconnect Mfg Inc............D...... 585 742-2220
Victor (G-16483)
Altec Datacom LLC ....G...... 631 242-2417
Bay Shore (G-668)
Amphenol Intrconnect Pdts Corp..........E...... 607 754-4444
Endicott (G-4803)
Apx Technologies Inc ....E...... 516 433-1313
Hicksville (G-6347)
Arnold-Davis LLC ....C...... 607 772-1201
Binghamton (G-886)
B3cg Interconnect Usa Inc....................F...... 450 491-4040
Plattsburgh (G-13681)
Badger Technologies Inc ....E...... 585 869-7101
Farmington (G-5155)
Badger Technologies Inc ....D...... 585 869-7101
Farmington (G-5156)
Becker Electronics Inc ....D...... 631 619-9100
Ronkonkoma (G-14907)
Bryit Group LLC ....F...... 631 563-6603
Holbrook (G-6461)
Cables Unlimited Inc ....E...... 631 563-6363
Yaphank (G-17403)
Condor Electronics Corp ....E...... 585 235-1500
Rochester (G-14305)
Hazlow Electronics Inc ....E...... 585 325-5323
Rochester (G-14450)
I3 Assembly LLC ....D...... 607 238-7077
Binghamton (G-918)
Lyntronics Inc ....E...... 631 205-1061
Yaphank (G-17412)
North Hills Signal Proc Corp ....G...... 516 682-7700
Syosset (G-15853)
Paal Technologies Inc ....G...... 631 319-6262
Ronkonkoma (G-14987)
Phoenix Cables Corporation ....C...... 845 691-6253
Highland (G-6433)
Sayeda Manufacturing Corp ....F...... 631 345-2525
Medford (G-8193)
Sturges Elec Pdts Co Inc ....E...... 607 844-8604
Dryden (G-4348)
TCS Electronics Inc ....E...... 585 337-4301
Farmington (G-5165)
Tony Baird Electronics Inc...................G...... 315 422-4430
Syracuse (G-16084)

HARNESSES, HALTERS, SADDLERY & STRAPS

Equicenter Inc ....E...... 585 742-2522
Honeoye Falls (G-6555)
Fiorentina LLC....................................G...... 516 208-5448
Merrick (G-8418)
Import-Export Corporation....................F...... 718 707-0880
Long Island City (G-7792)
Unique Overseas Inc ....G...... 516 466-9792
Great Neck (G-5865)

HAT BOXES

Tumi Inc ....C...... 212 447-8747
New York (G-12444)

HEADPHONES: Radio

Gotenna Inc ....F...... 415 894-2616
Brooklyn (G-2043)

HEALTH AIDS: Exercise Eqpt

D Squared Technologies Inc ....G...... 516 932-7319
Jericho (G-7098)
Gym Store Inc....................................E...... 718 366-7804
Maspeth (G-8174)
Hypoxico Inc ....E...... 212 972-1009
New York (G-10584)
Physicalmind Institute ....F...... 212 343-2150
New York (G-11674)

HEALTH SCREENING SVCS

Pharma-Smart International Inc...........E...... 585 427-0730
Rochester (G-14600)

HEARING AIDS

Benway-Haworth-Lwlr-Iacosta He ....F...... 518 432-4070
Albany (G-51)
Buffalo Hearg & Speech ....E...... 716 558-1105
West Seneca (G-16969)
Family Hearing Center ....G...... 845 897-3059
Fishkill (G-5191)
Hal-Hen Company Inc ....E...... 516 294-3200
New Hyde Park (G-8883)
Hearing Spech Ctr of Rochester ....E...... 585 286-9373
Webster (G-16749)
Roner Inc ....G...... 718 392-6020
Long Island City (G-7895)
Roner Inc ....E...... 718 392-6020
Long Island City (G-7896)
Todt Hill Audiological Svcs ....G...... 718 816-1952
Staten Island (G-15771)
Widex Usa Inc ....D...... 718 360-1000
Hauppauge (G-6257)
William H Shapiro ....G...... 212 263-7037
New York (G-12662)

HEAT EMISSION OPERATING APPARATUS

Zappone Chrysler Jeep Ddge Inc ....F...... 518 982-0610
Halfmoon (G-5939)

HEAT EXCHANGERS

Aerco International Inc ....C...... 845 580-8000
Blauvelt (G-963)
Costanzos Welding Inc ....E...... 716 282-0845
Niagara Falls (G-12829)
Fross Industries Inc ....E...... 716 297-0652
Niagara Falls (G-12843)
Inex Inc ....E...... 716 537-2270
Holland (G-6508)
Schwabel Fabricating Co Inc...............E...... 716 876-2086
Tonawanda (G-16219)
Yula Corporation ....F...... 718 991-0900
Bronx (G-1497)

HEAT EXCHANGERS: After Or Inter Coolers Or Condensers, Etc

American Precision Inds Inc................C...... 716 691-9100
Amherst (G-227)
API Heat Transf Thermasys Corp ....A...... 716 684-6700
Buffalo (G-2834)
API Heat Transfer Company ....F...... 716 684-6700
Buffalo (G-2835)
API Heat Transfer Inc.........................E...... 585 496-5755
Arcade (G-387)

PRODUCT SECTION

Nitram Energy Inc ....E...... 716 662-6540
Orchard Park (G-13310)
Slantco Manufacturing Inc ....G...... 516 484-2600
Greenvale (G-5900)

HEAT TREATING: Metal

A1 International Heat Treating ....G...... 718 863-5552
Bronx (G-1257)
Aterian Investment Partners LP ....E...... 212 547-2806
New York (G-9299)
B & W Heat Treating Company ....G...... 716 876-8184
Tonawanda (G-16164)
Bodycote Syracuse Heat Treatin ....E...... 315 451-0000
Syracuse (G-15891)
Bodycote Thermal Proc Inc ....E...... 585 436-7876
Rochester (G-14258)
Bsv Metal Finishers Inc ....E...... 585 349-7072
Spencerport (G-15591)
Buffalo Armory LLC ....G...... 716 935-6346
Buffalo (G-2870)
Burke Frging Heat Treating Inc...........E...... 585 235-6060
Rochester (G-14268)
Burton Industries Inc ....E...... 631 643-6660
West Babylon (G-16803)
Cpp - Steel Treaters ....E...... 315 736-3081
Oriskany (G-13331)
Expedient Heat Treating Corp.............G...... 716 433-1177
North Tonawanda (G-12988)
Gibraltar Industries Inc ....D...... 716 826-6500
Buffalo (G-2989)
Graywood Companies Inc..................E...... 585 254-7000
Rochester (G-14433)
Great Lakes Metal Treating ....F...... 716 694-1240
Tonawanda (G-16184)
Hercules Heat Treating Corp ....E...... 718 625-1266
Brooklyn (G-2073)
International Ord Tech Inc ....D...... 716 664-1100
Jamestown (G-7036)
Jasco Heat Treating Inc ....E...... 585 388-0071
Fairport (G-4865)
Modern Heat Trting Forging Inc ....F...... 716 884-2176
Buffalo (G-3093)
Parfuse Corp ....E...... 516 997-1795
Westbury (G-17046)
Rochester Steel Treating Works ....F...... 585 546-3348
Rochester (G-14673)
Rough Brothers Holding Co ....G...... 716 826-6500
Buffalo (G-3196)

HEATERS: Space, Exc Electric

American Comfort Direct LLC ....E...... 201 364-8309
New York (G-9165)

HEATERS: Swimming Pool, Oil Or Gas

Jus-Sar Fuel Inc ....G...... 845 791-8900
Harris (G-5997)
O C P Inc ....E...... 516 679-2000
Farmingdale (G-5079)

HEATERS: Unit, Domestic

Roberts-Gordon LLC ....D...... 716 852-4400
Buffalo (G-3188)

HEATING & AIR CONDITIONING EQPT & SPLYS WHOLESALERS

Siemens Industry Inc ....E...... 585 797-2300
Rochester (G-14707)
Split Systems Corp ....G...... 516 223-5511
North Baldwin (G-12926)

HEATING & AIR CONDITIONING UNITS, COMBINATION

Colburns AC Rfrgn ....F...... 716 569-3695
Frewsburg (G-5463)
Daikin Applied Americas Inc ....D...... 315 253-2771
Auburn (G-490)
Enviromaster International LLC ....D...... 315 336-3716
Rome (G-14839)
John F Krell Jr ....G...... 315 492-3201
Syracuse (G-15987)
Keeler Services ....G...... 607 776-5757
Bath (G-658)
Northern Air Systems Inc ....E...... 585 594-5050
Rochester (G-14564)
Pro Metal of NY Corp ....G...... 516 285-0440
Valley Stream (G-16445)

PRODUCT SECTION

HOMEFURNISHINGS & SPLYS, WHOLESALE: Decorative

HEATING EQPT & SPLYS

Company	Code	Phone
A Nuclimate Qulty Systems Inc	F	315 431-0226
Syracuse (G-15865)		
Carrier Corporation	B	315 432-6000
Syracuse (G-15907)		
Chentronics Corporation	E	607 334-5531
Norwich (G-13041)		
CIDC Corp	F	718 342-5820
Brooklyn (G-1779)		
Economy Pump & Motor Repair	G	718 433-2600
Astoria (G-436)		
Embassy Industries Inc	C	631 435-0209
Hauppauge (G-6095)		
Fedders Islandaire Inc	D	631 471-2900
East Setauket (G-4500)		
Fisonic Corp	G	212 732-3777
Long Island City (G-7772)		
Fisonic Corp	F	716 763-0295
New York (G-10227)		
Fulton Volcanic Inc	D	315 298-5121
Pulaski (G-13967)		
Juniper Elbow Co Inc	C	718 326-2546
Middle Village (G-8447)		
North Pk Innovations Group Inc	G	716 699-2031
Ellicottville (G-4657)		
Omega Heater Company Inc	D	631 588-8820
Ronkonkoma (G-14984)		
RE Hansen Industries Inc	C	631 471-2900
East Setauket (G-4510)		
Real Goods Solar Inc	C	845 708-0800
New City (G-8837)		
Slant/Fin Corporation	B	516 484-2600
Greenvale (G-5899)		
Unilux Advanced Mfg LLC	E	518 344-7490
Schenectady (G-15331)		
Vincent Genovese	G	631 281-8170
Mastic Beach (G-8237)		

HEATING EQPT: Complete

Company	Code	Phone
A Nuclimate Qulty Systems Inc	F	315 431-0226
Syracuse (G-15865)		
Dundas-Jafine Inc	E	716 681-9690
Alden (G-180)		
Siemens Industry Inc	E	716 568-0983
Buffalo (G-3214)		
Thomson Industries Inc	F	716 691-9100
Amherst (G-266)		

HEATING EQPT: Induction

Company	Code	Phone
Ambrell Corporation	F	585 889-0236
Scottsville (G-15356)		
Ultraflex Power Technologies	G	631 467-6814
Ronkonkoma (G-15019)		

HEATING SYSTEMS: Radiant, Indl Process

Company	Code	Phone
Radiant Pro Ltd	G	516 763-5678
Oceanside (G-13114)		

HEATING UNITS & DEVICES: Indl, Electric

Company	Code	Phone
Cvd Equipment Corporation	F	631 582-4365
Central Islip (G-3519)		
Easco Boiler Corp	E	718 378-3000
Bronx (G-1326)		
Fulton Volcanic Inc	D	315 298-5121
Pulaski (G-13967)		
Igniter Systems Inc	E	716 542-5511
Akron (G-21)		

HELICOPTERS

Company	Code	Phone
CIC International Ltd	D	212 213-0089
Brooklyn (G-1778)		

HELMETS: Athletic

Company	Code	Phone
Cascade Helmets Holdings Inc	G	315 453-3073
Liverpool (G-7539)		
Performance Lacrosse Group Inc	G	315 453-3073
Liverpool (G-7567)		

HIDES & SKINS

Company	Code	Phone
Adirondack Meat Company Inc	F	518 585-2333
Ticonderoga (G-16146)		

HIGH ENERGY PARTICLE PHYSICS EQPT

Company	Code	Phone
Advance Energy Systems NY LLC	G	315 735-5125
Utica (G-16329)		

Company	Code	Phone
Spirent Inc	G	631 208-0680
Riverhead (G-14170)		

HIGHWAY SIGNALS: Electric

Company	Code	Phone
BNo Intl Trdg Co Inc	G	716 487-1900
Jamestown (G-7012)		
Kentronics Inc	G	631 567-5994
Bohemia (G-1083)		
Traffic Lane Closures LLC	G	845 228-6100
Brewster (G-1226)		

HOBBY & CRAFT SPLY STORES

Company	Code	Phone
Paper House Productions Inc	E	845 246-7261
Saugerties (G-15219)		

HOBBY, TOY & GAME STORES: Ceramics Splys

Company	Code	Phone
Ceramaterials LLC	G	518 701-6722
Port Jervis (G-13803)		
Corning International Corp	G	607 974-9000
Corning (G-3989)		

HOBBY, TOY & GAME STORES: Toys & Games

Company	Code	Phone
Minted Green Inc	G	845 458-1845
Airmont (G-15)		

HOISTS

Company	Code	Phone
Columbus McKinnon Corporation	C	716 689-5400
Getzville (G-5607)		
Columbus McKinnon Corporation	C	716 689-5400
Getzville (G-5608)		
Columbus McKinnon Corporation	C	716 689-5400
Getzville (G-5609)		
Mannesmann Corporation	D	212 258-4000
New York (G-11160)		
Marros Equipment & Trucks	F	315 539-8702
Waterloo (G-16652)		
Mohawk Resources Ltd	D	518 842-1431
Amsterdam (G-360)		
Reimann & Georger Corporation	E	716 895-1156
Buffalo (G-3182)		
T Shore Products Ltd	G	315 252-9174
Auburn (G-519)		
Thego Corporation	G	631 776-2472
Bellport (G-838)		

HOLDING COMPANIES: Banks

Company	Code	Phone
Flavors Holdings Inc	G	212 572-8677
New York (G-10231)		

HOLDING COMPANIES: Investment, Exc Banks

Company	Code	Phone
Chemprene Inc	C	845 831-2800
Beacon (G-777)		
Geritrex Holdings Inc	G	914 668-4003
Mount Vernon (G-8728)		
Global Video LLC	D	516 222-2600
Woodbury (G-17310)		
Graphic Controls Holdings Inc	F	716 853-7500
Buffalo (G-2995)		
Hw Holdings Inc	G	212 399-1000
New York (G-10581)		
Noco Incorporated	G	716 833-6626
Tonawanda (G-16205)		
Pii Holdings Inc	G	716 876-9951
Buffalo (G-3149)		
Skip Hop Holdings Inc	G	212 868-9850
New York (G-12119)		

HOLDING COMPANIES: Personal, Exc Banks

Company	Code	Phone
Spf Holdings II LLC	G	212 750-8300
New York (G-12185)		

HOME DELIVERY NEWSPAPER ROUTES

Company	Code	Phone
Nyt Capital LLC	F	212 556-1234
New York (G-11503)		

HOME ENTERTAINMENT EQPT: Electronic, NEC

Company	Code	Phone
A and K Global Inc	D	718 412-1876
Bayside (G-758)		

Company	Code	Phone
Globa Phoni Compu Techn Solut	E	607 257-7279
Ithaca (G-6879)		
Request Inc	E	518 899-1254
Halfmoon (G-5936)		
Request Serious Play LLC	E	518 899-1254
Halfmoon (G-5937)		
Shyk International Corp	G	212 663-3302
New York (G-12081)		
Sing Trix	F	212 352-1500
New York (G-12108)		

HOME FOR THE MENTALLY RETARDED

Company	Code	Phone
Chemung Cnty Chpter Nysarc Inc	C	607 734-6151
Elmira (G-4688)		

HOME FURNISHINGS WHOLESALERS

Company	Code	Phone
Feldman Company Inc	F	212 966-1303
New York (G-10203)		
Lifetime Brands Inc	B	516 683-6000
Garden City (G-5526)		
Madison Industries Inc	F	212 679-5110
New York (G-11121)		

HOME HEALTH CARE SVCS

Company	Code	Phone
Curemdcom Inc	A	212 509-6200
New York (G-9826)		

HOMEBUILDERS & OTHER OPERATIVE BUILDERS

Company	Code	Phone
Hope International Productions	F	212 247-3188
New York (G-10548)		

HOMEFURNISHING STORES: Beddings & Linens

Company	Code	Phone
Duxiana Dux Bed	G	212 755-2600
New York (G-9992)		
Geneva Home Fashion LLC	F	212 213-8323
New York (G-10319)		
Metro Mattress Corp	E	716 205-2300
Niagara Falls (G-12864)		
Zzz Mattress Manufacturing	G	718 454-1468
Saint Albans (G-15112)		

HOMEFURNISHING STORES: Lighting Fixtures

Company	Code	Phone
David Weeks Studio	F	212 966-3433
New York (G-9880)		
Edison Power & Light Co Inc	F	718 522-0002
Brooklyn (G-1906)		
Maxsun Corporation	F	718 418-6800
Maspeth (G-8182)		
Rapid-Lite Fixture Corporation	F	347 599-2600
Brooklyn (G-2497)		
Serway Bros Inc	E	315 337-0601
Rome (G-14864)		
Sir Industries Inc	G	631 234-2444
Hauppauge (G-6216)		

HOMEFURNISHING STORES: Mirrors

Company	Code	Phone
Global Glass Corp	G	516 681-2309
Hicksville (G-6378)		

HOMEFURNISHING STORES: Vertical Blinds

Company	Code	Phone
Designers Touch Inc	G	718 641-3718
Long Beach (G-7669)		
Pj Decorators Inc	E	516 735-9693
East Meadow (G-4447)		

HOMEFURNISHING STORES: Window Furnishings

Company	Code	Phone
Blinds To Go (us) Inc	E	718 477-9523
Staten Island (G-15668)		
Wallace Home Design Ctr	G	631 765-3890
Southold (G-15585)		
White Plains Drapery Uphl Inc	E	914 381-0908
Mamaroneck (G-8083)		

HOMEFURNISHINGS & SPLYS, WHOLESALE: Decorative

Company	Code	Phone
Enchante Accessories Inc	C	212 689-6008
New York (G-10080)		

Employee Codes: A=Over 500 employees, B=251-500
C=101-250, D=51-100, E=20-50, F=10-19, G=5-9

HOMEFURNISHINGS & SPLYS, WHOLESALE: Decorative

PRODUCT SECTION

K Pat Incorporated .... G 212 688-5728
  New York *(G-10830)*
Mistdoda Inc .... E 919 735-7111
  New York *(G-11309)*
Secret Celebrity Licensing LLC .... G 212 812-9277
  New York *(G-12031)*

HOMEFURNISHINGS, WHOLESALE: Bedspreads

Ess Bee Industries Inc .... E 718 894-5202
  Brooklyn *(G-1942)*

HOMEFURNISHINGS, WHOLESALE: Blinds, Venetian

D & D Window Tech Inc .... G 212 308-2822
  New York *(G-9838)*

HOMEFURNISHINGS, WHOLESALE: Blinds, Vertical

Pj Decorators Inc .... E 516 735-9693
  East Meadow *(G-4447)*

HOMEFURNISHINGS, WHOLESALE: Carpets

Albert Menin Interiors Ltd .... F 212 876-3041
  Bronx *(G-1268)*
Elizabeth Eakins Inc .... F 212 628-1950
  New York *(G-10062)*

HOMEFURNISHINGS, WHOLESALE: Curtains

Baby Signature Inc .... G 212 686-1700
  New York *(G-9351)*
Louis Hornick & Co Inc .... G 212 679-2448
  New York *(G-11077)*

HOMEFURNISHINGS, WHOLESALE: Draperies

Reynolds Drapery Service Inc .... F 315 845-8632
  Newport *(G-12816)*
Star Draperies Inc .... F 631 756-7121
  Farmingdale *(G-5125)*
White Plains Drapery Uphl Inc .... E 914 381-0908
  Mamaroneck *(G-8083)*

HOMEFURNISHINGS, WHOLESALE: Kitchenware

Lifetime Chimney Supply LLC .... G 516 576-8144
  Plainview *(G-13643)*
Vanity Fair Bathmart Inc .... F 718 584-6700
  Bronx *(G-1487)*

HOMEFURNISHINGS, WHOLESALE: Linens, Table

Benson Sales Co Inc .... F 718 236-6743
  Brooklyn *(G-1683)*
Lintex Linens Inc .... B 212 679-8046
  New York *(G-11032)*

HOMEFURNISHINGS, WHOLESALE: Mirrors/Pictures, Framed/Unframd

Ad Notam LLC .... F 631 951-2020
  Hauppauge *(G-6028)*

HOMEFURNISHINGS, WHOLESALE: Pillowcases

Anhui Skyworth LLC .... D 917 940-6903
  Hempstead *(G-6288)*

HOMEFURNISHINGS, WHOLESALE: Rugs

Lorena Canals USA Inc .... G 844 567-3622
  Hastings On Hudson *(G-6025)*

HOMEFURNISHINGS, WHOLESALE: Sheets, Textile

Alok Inc .... G 212 643-4360
  New York *(G-9148)*

HOMEFURNISHINGS, WHOLESALE: Stainless Steel Flatware

Utica Cutlery Company .... D 315 733-4663
  Utica *(G-16387)*

HOMEFURNISHINGS, WHOLESALE: Window Covering Parts & Access

McCarroll Uphl Designs LLC .... G 518 828-0500
  Hudson *(G-6655)*
P E Guerin .... D 212 243-5270
  New York *(G-11561)*

HOMEFURNISHINGS, WHOLESALE: Wood Flooring

Wego International Floors LLC .... F 516 487-3510
  Great Neck *(G-5868)*

HOMES, MODULAR: Wooden

Best Mdlr HMS Afrbe P Q& S In .... F 631 204-0049
  Southampton *(G-15563)*
Bill Lake Homes Construction .... D 518 673-2424
  Sprakers *(G-15601)*
Westchester Modular Homes Inc .... C 845 832-9400
  Wingdale *(G-17297)*
Whitley East LLC .... D 718 403-0050
  Brooklyn *(G-2764)*

HOMES: Log Cabins

Alta Industries Ltd .... F 845 586-3336
  Halcottsville *(G-5927)*

HONES

09 Fishy Bll/Dsert Sunrise LLC .... G 518 583-6638
  Saratoga Springs *(G-15168)*
Charles A Hones Inc .... G 607 273-5720
  Ithaca *(G-6870)*

HORMONE PREPARATIONS

American Hormones Inc .... F 845 471-7272
  Poughkeepsie *(G-13904)*
Erika T Schwartz MD PC .... G 212 873-3420
  New York *(G-10110)*

HORSE & PET ACCESSORIES: Textile

Saratoga Horseworks Ltd .... E 518 843-6756
  Amsterdam *(G-368)*
Triple E Manufacturing .... F 716 761-6996
  Sherman *(G-15425)*

HORSE ACCESS: Harnesses & Riding Crops, Etc, Exc Leather

Hampton Transport Inc .... F 631 716-4445
  Coram *(G-3966)*
Stonegate Stabless .... G 518 746-7133
  Fort Edward *(G-5355)*

HOSE: Air Line Or Air Brake, Rubber Or Rubberized Fabric

Honeywell International Inc .... D 518 270-0200
  Troy *(G-16241)*

HOSE: Automobile, Plastic

Deer Park Driveshaft & Hose .... G 631 667-4091
  Deer Park *(G-4149)*

HOSE: Fire, Rubber

Cataract Hose Co .... E 914 941-9019
  Ossining *(G-13345)*

HOSE: Flexible Metal

Flex-Hose Company Inc .... E 315 437-1903
  East Syracuse *(G-4544)*
TI Group Auto Systems LLC .... G 315 568-7042
  Seneca Falls *(G-15394)*

HOSE: Plastic

Jain Irrigation Inc .... D 315 755-4400
  Watertown *(G-16676)*

Superflex Ltd .... E 718 768-1400
  Brooklyn *(G-2646)*
TI Group Auto Systems LLC .... G 315 568-7042
  Seneca Falls *(G-15394)*

HOSE: Pneumatic, Rubber Or Rubberized Fabric, NEC

Moreland Hose & Belting Corp .... G 631 563-7071
  Oakdale *(G-13078)*

HOSE: Rubber

Mason Industries Inc .... B 631 348-0282
  Hauppauge *(G-6152)*
Mercer Rubber Co .... C 631 348-0282
  Hauppauge *(G-6158)*

HOSE: Vacuum Cleaner, Rubber

Anchor Tech Products Corp .... E 914 592-0240
  Elmsford *(G-4742)*

HOSES & BELTING: Rubber & Plastic

Flex Enterprises Inc .... E 585 742-1000
  Victor *(G-16501)*
Habasit America Inc .... D 716 824-8484
  Buffalo *(G-3001)*
Hitachi Cable America Inc .... F 914 694-9200
  Purchase *(G-13973)*
Index Incorporated .... F 440 632-5400
  Bronx *(G-1362)*
Jed Lights Inc .... F 516 812-5001
  Deer Park *(G-4180)*
Peraflex Hose Inc .... F 716 876-8806
  Buffalo *(G-3143)*
Standard Motor Products Inc .... B 718 392-0200
  Long Island City *(G-7912)*
Troy Belting and Supply Co .... D 518 272-4920
  Watervliet *(G-16715)*
WF Lake Corp .... E 518 798-9934
  Queensbury *(G-14027)*

HOSPITALS: Cancer

Actinium Pharmaceuticals Inc .... E 646 677-3870
  New York *(G-9067)*

HOSPITALS: Medical & Surgical

Norcorp Inc .... E 914 666-1310
  Mount Kisco *(G-8680)*

HOT TUBS

D & M Enterprises Incorporated .... G 914 937-6430
  Port Chester *(G-13769)*

HOT TUBS: Plastic & Fiberglass

D & M Enterprises Incorporated .... G 914 937-6430
  Port Chester *(G-13769)*
Independent Home Products LLC .... E 718 541-1256
  West Hempstead *(G-16886)*

HOUSEHOLD APPLIANCE STORES: Air Cond Rm Units, Self-Contnd

Fedders Islandaire Inc .... D 631 471-2900
  East Setauket *(G-4500)*
RE Hansen Industries Inc .... C 631 471-2900
  East Setauket *(G-4510)*

HOUSEHOLD APPLIANCE STORES: Electric Household Appliance, Sm

Heaven Fresh USA Inc .... G 800 642-0367
  Niagara Falls *(G-12850)*

HOUSEHOLD APPLIANCE STORES: Fans, Electric

A & C/Furia Electric Motors .... F 914 949-0585
  White Plains *(G-17100)*

HOUSEHOLD APPLIANCE STORES: Garbage Disposals

Mount Kisco Transfer Stn Inc .... G 914 666-6350
  Mount Kisco *(G-8678)*

PRODUCT SECTION

HOUSEHOLD ARTICLES: Metal

Di Highway Sign Structure Corp .... E 315 736-8312
New York Mills *(G-12741)*
Gcm Steel Products Inc .... F 718 386-3346
Brooklyn *(G-2017)*
Hatfield Metal Fab Inc .... E 845 454-9078
Poughkeepsie *(G-13926)*
L D Flecken Inc .... F 631 777-4881
Yaphank *(G-17411)*
New York Manufactured Products .... F 585 254-9353
Rochester *(G-14552)*
Ulster County Iron Works LLC .... G 845 255-0003
New Paltz *(G-8925)*

HOUSEHOLD FURNISHINGS, NEC

AEP Environmental LLC .... F 716 446-0739
Buffalo *(G-2818)*
Ann Gish Inc .... G 212 969-9200
New York *(G-9213)*
Area Inc .... G 212 924-7084
New York *(G-9249)*
August Silk Inc .... E 212 643-2400
New York *(G-9315)*
August Silk Inc .... G 212 643-2400
New York *(G-9316)*
Caddy Concepts Inc .... F 516 570-6279
Great Neck *(G-5812)*
Creative Home Furnishings .... G 631 582-8000
Central Islip *(G-3517)*
Creative Scents USA Inc .... G 718 522-5901
Brooklyn *(G-1814)*
Dico Products Corporation .... F 315 797-0470
Utica *(G-16346)*
Elegant Linen Inc .... G 718 492-0297
Brooklyn *(G-1915)*
Ess Bee Industries Inc .... E 718 894-5202
Brooklyn *(G-1942)*
Excellent Art Mfg Corp .... F 718 388-7075
Inwood *(G-6795)*
Geneva Home Fashion LLC .... F 212 213-8323
New York *(G-10319)*
Henry B Urban Inc .... E 212 489-3308
New York *(G-10500)*
Kartell Us Inc .... G 212 966-6665
New York *(G-10848)*
Kim Seybert Inc .... E 212 564-7850
New York *(G-10885)*
Madison Industries Inc .... F 212 679-5110
New York *(G-11121)*
McCarroll Uphl Designs LLC .... G 518 828-0500
Hudson *(G-6655)*
Medline Industries Inc .... B 845 344-3301
Middletown *(G-8484)*
Mgk Group Inc .... E 212 989-2732
New York *(G-11273)*
MMS H & F Inc .... G 718 785-6663
Jamaica *(G-6969)*
Nationwide Tarps Incorporated .... D 518 843-1545
Amsterdam *(G-362)*
Nbets Corporation .... G 516 785-1259
Wantagh *(G-16582)*
Paramount Textiles Inc .... F 212 966-1040
New York *(G-11583)*
Performance Sourcing Group Inc .... E 914 636-2100
Scarsdale *(G-15251)*
Place Vendome Holding Co Inc .... C 212 696-0765
New York *(G-11693)*
Q Squared Design LLC .... E 212 686-8860
New York *(G-11788)*
Richloom Fabrics Corp .... F 212 685-5400
New York *(G-11894)*
Silly Phillie Creations Inc .... E 718 492-6300
Brooklyn *(G-2583)*
Skil-Care Corporation .... F 914 963-2040
Yonkers *(G-17502)*
Sleepable Sofas Ltd .... D 973 546-4502
New York *(G-12125)*
Sleeping Partners Intl Inc .... F 212 254-1515
Brooklyn *(G-2596)*
Sure Fit Inc .... E 212 395-9340
New York *(G-12266)*
Terbo Ltd .... G 718 847-2860
Richmond Hill *(G-14099)*
William Harvey Studio Inc .... G 718 599-4343
Brooklyn *(G-2769)*

HOUSEWARE STORES

Swissmar Inc .... G 905 764-1121
Niagara Falls *(G-12896)*

HOUSEWARES, ELECTRIC, EXC COOKING APPLIANCES & UTENSILS

World Trading Center Inc .... G 631 273-3330
Hauppauge *(G-6260)*

HOUSEWARES, ELECTRIC: Air Purifiers, Portable

Heaven Fresh USA Inc .... G 800 642-0367
Niagara Falls *(G-12850)*

HOUSEWARES, ELECTRIC: Cooking Appliances

Hrg Group Inc .... E 212 906-8555
New York *(G-10567)*
Peek A Boo USA Inc .... G 201 533-8700
New York *(G-11612)*

HOUSEWARES, ELECTRIC: Extractors, Juice

Goodnature Products Inc .... F 716 855-3325
Orchard Park *(G-13296)*
Sundance Industries Inc .... G 845 795-5809
Milton *(G-8519)*

HOUSEWARES, ELECTRIC: Fryers

Abbott Industries Inc .... E 718 291-0800
Jamaica *(G-6926)*

HOUSEWARES, ELECTRIC: Heaters, Sauna

US Health Equipment Company .... E 845 658-7576
Kingston *(G-7249)*

HOUSEWARES, ELECTRIC: Heaters, Space

Valad Electric Heating Corp .... F 888 509-4927
Montgomery *(G-8640)*
Valid Electric Corp .... E 914 631-9436
Montgomery *(G-8641)*

HOUSEWARES, ELECTRIC: Heating, Bsbrd/Wall, Radiant Heat

Vincent Genovese .... G 631 281-8170
Mastic Beach *(G-8237)*

HOUSEWARES, ELECTRIC: Humidifiers, Household

Dampits International Inc .... G 212 581-3047
New York *(G-9851)*
Remedies Surgical Supplies .... G 718 599-5301
Brooklyn *(G-2509)*

HOUSEWARES, ELECTRIC: Massage Machines, Exc Beauty/Barber

Advanced Response Corporation .... G 212 459-0887
New York *(G-9094)*
Quality Life Inc .... F 718 939-5787
College Point *(G-3828)*

HOUSEWARES: Dishes, China

Jill Fagin Enterprises Inc .... G 212 674-9383
New York *(G-10771)*
Korin Japanese Trading Corp .... E 212 587-7021
New York *(G-10916)*
Oneida International Inc .... G 315 361-3000
Oneida *(G-13182)*
Oneida Silversmiths Inc .... G 315 361-3000
Oneida *(G-13186)*

HOUSEWARES: Dishes, Earthenware

Ceramica Varm .... G 914 381-6215
New Rochelle *(G-8937)*

HOUSEWARES: Dishes, Plastic

Digitac Inc .... F 732 215-4020
Brooklyn *(G-1863)*
E-Z Ware Dishes Inc .... G 718 376-3244
Brooklyn *(G-1896)*
Etna Products Co Inc .... F 212 989-7591
New York *(G-10132)*
Howard Charles Inc .... G 917 902-6934
Woodbury *(G-17311)*

ICE CREAM & ICES WHOLESALERS

J M R Plastics Corporation .... G 718 898-9825
Middle Village *(G-8445)*
Novelty Crystal Corp .... E 718 458-6700
Long Island City *(G-7858)*
Ocala Group LLC .... F 516 233-2750
New Hyde Park *(G-8899)*
Peek A Boo USA Inc .... G 201 533-8700
New York *(G-11612)*
Robinson Knife .... F 716 685-6300
Buffalo *(G-3189)*
Villeroy & Boch Usa Inc .... E 212 213-8149
New York *(G-12569)*
Waddington North America Inc .... F 585 638-8200
Holley *(G-6519)*

HOUSEWARES: Kettles & Skillets, Cast Iron

Field Wares LLC .... G 508 380-6545
High Falls *(G-6428)*
S M S C Inc .... G 315 942-4394
Boonville *(G-1167)*
Staub Usa Inc .... G 914 747-0300
Pleasantville *(G-13751)*

HOUSEWARES: Pots & Pans, Glass

Art and Cook Inc .... F 718 567-7778
Brooklyn *(G-1633)*

HUMIDIFIERS & DEHUMIDIFIERS

Alfa Laval Kathabar Inc .... G 716 875-2000
Tonawanda *(G-16158)*
Heaven Fresh USA Inc .... G 800 642-0367
Niagara Falls *(G-12850)*
MSP Technologycom LLC .... G 631 424-7542
Centerport *(G-3505)*

HYDRAULIC EQPT REPAIR SVC

Mooradian Hydraulics & Eqp Co .... F 518 766-3866
Castleton On Hudson *(G-3448)*

Hard Rubber & Molded Rubber Prdts

Apple Rubber Products Inc .... E 716 684-6560
Lancaster *(G-7327)*
Apple Rubber Products Inc .... C 716 684-7649
Lancaster *(G-7328)*
Mason Industries Inc .... B 631 348-0282
Hauppauge *(G-6152)*
Prince Rubber & Plas Co Inc .... E 225 272-1653
Buffalo *(G-3161)*
Triangle Rubber Co Inc .... E 631 589-9400
Bohemia *(G-1144)*

ICE

Adirondack Ice & Air Inc .... F 518 483-4340
Malone *(G-8036)*
Annies Ice .... G 585 593-5605
Wellsville *(G-16774)*
Arctic Glacier Minnesota Inc .... E 585 388-0080
Fairport *(G-4849)*
Arctic Glacier Newburgh Inc .... G 718 456-2013
Brooklyn *(G-1625)*
Arctic Glacier Newburgh Inc .... F 845 561-0549
Newburgh *(G-12771)*
Arctic Glacier PA Inc .... E 610 494-8200
Fairport *(G-4850)*
Mamitas Ices Ltd .... F 718 738-3238
Ozone Park *(G-13409)*
Maplewood Ice Co Inc .... E 518 499-2345
Whitehall *(G-17218)*
South Shore Ice Co Inc .... F 516 379-2056
Roosevelt *(G-15032)*

ICE CREAM & ICES WHOLESALERS

Four Brothers Italian Bakery .... G 914 741-5434
Hawthorne *(G-6269)*
Fresh Ice Cream Company LLC .... F 347 603-6021
Brooklyn *(G-2006)*
Macedonia Ltd .... F 718 462-3596
Brooklyn *(G-2253)*
Marina Ice Cream .... G 718 235-3000
Brooklyn *(G-2271)*
Purity Ice Cream Co Inc .... F 607 272-1545
Ithaca *(G-6908)*
Washburns Dairy Inc .... E 518 725-0629
Gloversville *(G-5743)*

IDENTIFICATION TAGS, EXC PAPER

PRODUCT SECTION

IDENTIFICATION TAGS, EXC PAPER
Ketchum Manufacturing Co Inc ....F 518 696-3331
  Lake Luzerne *(G-7296)*

IGNEOUS ROCK: Crushed & Broken
Barrett Paving Materials Inc ....F 315 737-9471
  Clayville *(G-3712)*
Cayuga Crushed Stone Inc ....E 607 533-4273
  Lansing *(G-7373)*
Peckham Materials Corp ....E 518 747-3353
  Hudson Falls *(G-6680)*

IGNITION APPARATUS & DISTRIBUTORS
Magnum Shielding Corporation ....E 585 381-9957
  Pittsford *(G-13596)*
Martinez Specialties Inc ....G 607 898-3053
  Groton *(G-5922)*
Taro Manufacturing Company Inc ....F 315 252-9430
  Auburn *(G-520)*

IGNITION SYSTEMS: High Frequency
Standard Motor Products Inc ....B 718 392-0200
  Long Island City *(G-7912)*
Zenith Autoparts Corp ....E 845 344-1382
  Middletown *(G-8507)*

IGNITION SYSTEMS: Internal Combustion Engine
Zierick Manufacturing Corp ....D 800 882-8020
  Mount Kisco *(G-8690)*

INCINERATORS
Thermal Process Cnstr Co ....E 631 293-6400
  Farmingdale *(G-5139)*

INDICATORS: Cabin Environment
Excelsior Mlt-Cltural Inst Inc ....F 706 627-4285
  Flushing *(G-5247)*

INDL & PERSONAL SVC PAPER WHOLESALERS
Felix Schoeller North Amer Inc ....D 315 298-8425
  Pulaski *(G-13962)*
Josh Packaging Inc ....E 631 822-1660
  Hauppauge *(G-6127)*
Stanley Paper Co Inc ....F 518 489-1131
  Albany *(G-136)*

INDL & PERSONAL SVC PAPER, WHOL: Bags, Paper/Disp Plastic
Dawn Paper Co Inc ....F 516 596-9110
  East Rockaway *(G-4489)*
Dory Enterprises Inc ....F 607 565-7079
  Waverly *(G-16726)*
Dynamic Packaging Inc ....F 718 388-0800
  Brooklyn *(G-1888)*
Elara Fdsrvice Disposables LLC ....G 877 893-3244
  Jericho *(G-7100)*
Garb-O-Liner Inc ....G 914 235-1585
  New Rochelle *(G-8949)*
Golden Group International Ltd ....G 845 440-1025
  Patterson *(G-13464)*
M C Packaging Corporation ....E 631 643-3763
  Babylon *(G-547)*
Paramount Equipment Inc ....E 631 981-4422
  Ronkonkoma *(G-14988)*
Poly Craft Industries Corp ....E 631 630-6751
  Hauppauge *(G-6193)*
Primo Plastics Inc ....E 718 349-1000
  Brooklyn *(G-2457)*
Westrock Rkt Company ....C 330 296-5155
  Deer Park *(G-4251)*

INDL & PERSONAL SVC PAPER, WHOL: Boxes, Corrugtd/Solid Fiber
Cattaraugus Containers Inc ....E 716 676-2000
  Franklinville *(G-5379)*
Inner-Pak Container Inc ....F 631 289-9700
  Patchogue *(G-13449)*
Technical Packaging Inc ....F 516 223-2300
  Baldwin *(G-561)*

INDL & PERSONAL SVC PAPER, WHOL: Container, Paper/Plastic
Pactiv LLC ....C 585 394-5125
  Canandaigua *(G-3381)*

INDL & PERSONAL SVC PAPER, WHOL: Cups, Disp, Plastic/Paper
S J McCullagh Inc ....E 716 856-3473
  Buffalo *(G-3201)*

INDL & PERSONAL SVC PAPER, WHOLESALE: Boxes & Containers
Base Container Inc ....F 718 636-2004
  Brooklyn *(G-1666)*

INDL & PERSONAL SVC PAPER, WHOLESALE: Press Sensitive Tape
Edco Supply Corporation ....D 718 788-8108
  Brooklyn *(G-1905)*
Tape-It Inc ....E 631 243-4100
  Bay Shore *(G-743)*

INDL EQPT SVCS
Burnett Process Inc ....G 585 254-8080
  Rochester *(G-14269)*
Eis Inc ....D 585 426-5330
  Rochester *(G-14361)*
Keyes Machine Works Inc ....E 585 426-5059
  Gates *(G-5576)*
Oliver Gear Inc ....E 716 885-1080
  Buffalo *(G-3122)*

INDL GASES WHOLESALERS
Haun Welding Supply Inc ....F 607 846-2289
  Elmira *(G-4702)*

INDL MACHINERY & EQPT WHOLESALERS
Accurate Industrial Machining ....E 631 242-0566
  Holbrook *(G-6456)*
Advanced Photonics Inc ....F 631 471-3693
  Ronkonkoma *(G-14881)*
Analog Digital Technology LLC ....G 585 698-1845
  Rochester *(G-14219)*
Anderson Instrument Co Inc ....D 518 922-5315
  Fultonville *(G-5491)*
Anthony Manufacturing Inc ....G 631 957-9424
  Lindenhurst *(G-7476)*
Arbe Machinery Inc ....F 631 756-2477
  Farmingdale *(G-4953)*
Brinkman Products Inc ....B 585 235-4545
  Rochester *(G-14264)*
Brooklyn Brew Shop LLC ....F 718 874-0119
  Brooklyn *(G-1720)*
Buflovak LLC ....E 716 895-2100
  Buffalo *(G-2883)*
Charles Ross & Son Company ....D 631 234-0500
  Hauppauge *(G-6064)*
Conrad Blasius Equipment Co ....G 516 753-1200
  Plainview *(G-13620)*
DI Manufacturing Inc ....G 315 432-8977
  North Syracuse *(G-12959)*
Dorsey Metrology Intl Inc ....E 845 229-2929
  Poughkeepsie *(G-13914)*
Filling Equipment Co Inc ....F 718 445-2111
  College Point *(G-3808)*
Genesee Manufacturing Co Inc ....G 585 266-3201
  Rochester *(G-14415)*
Goulds Pumps Incorporated ....B 315 258-4949
  Auburn *(G-497)*
Goulds Pumps LLC ....A 315 568-2811
  Seneca Falls *(G-15382)*
Hades Manufacturing Corp ....F 631 249-4244
  Farmingdale *(G-5011)*
Halpern Tool Corp ....G 914 633-0038
  New Rochelle *(G-8953)*
Hunter Douglas Inc ....D 845 664-7000
  Pearl River *(G-13482)*
Innotech Graphic Eqp Corp ....G 845 268-6900
  Valley Cottage *(G-16405)*
ITT Goulds Pumps Inc ....F 914 641-2129
  Seneca Falls *(G-15385)*
John N Fehlinger Co Inc ....F 212 233-5656
  New York *(G-10791)*
Khk Usa Inc ....G 516 248-3850
  Mineola *(G-8552)*
Kinequip Inc ....F 716 694-5000
  Buffalo *(G-3049)*
Kps Capital Partners LP ....E 212 338-5100
  New York *(G-10922)*
Lubow Machine Corp ....F 631 226-1700
  Copiague *(G-3936)*
Makerbot Industries LLC ....C 347 334-6800
  Brooklyn *(G-2257)*
Mark - 10 Corporation ....E 631 842-9200
  Copiague *(G-3938)*
Micro Centric Corporation ....E 800 573-1139
  Plainview *(G-13649)*
N E Controls LLC ....F 315 626-2480
  Syracuse *(G-16016)*
Noresco Industrial Group Inc ....E 516 759-3355
  Glen Cove *(G-5635)*
Rapid Fan & Blower Inc ....F 718 786-2060
  Long Island City *(G-7887)*
Riverside Machinery Company ....E 718 492-7400
  Brooklyn *(G-2519)*
Rs Automation ....F 585 589-0199
  Albion *(G-172)*
Simmons Machine Tool Corp ....C 518 462-5431
  Menands *(G-8410)*
Specialty Steel Fabg Corp ....F 718 893-6326
  Bronx *(G-1459)*
Speedways Conveyors Inc ....E 716 893-2222
  Buffalo *(G-3223)*
Thread Check Inc ....D 631 231-1515
  Hauppauge *(G-6238)*
Troy Belting and Supply Co ....D 518 272-4920
  Watervliet *(G-16715)*
Uneeda Enterprizes Inc ....C 800 431-2494
  Spring Valley *(G-15626)*
Unicell Body Company Inc ....F 716 853-8628
  Schenectady *(G-15330)*
Viatran Corporation ....E 716 564-7813
  Tonawanda *(G-16233)*
Vibration & Noise Engrg Corp ....G 716 827-4959
  Orchard Park *(G-13327)*
Ward Industrial Equipment Inc ....G 716 856-6966
  Buffalo *(G-3273)*

INDL MACHINERY REPAIR & MAINTENANCE
4695 Main Street Snyder Inc ....G 716 833-3270
  Buffalo *(G-2803)*
Alternative Service Inc ....F 631 345-9500
  Yaphank *(G-17401)*
Atlantic Industrial Tech Inc ....E 631 234-3131
  Shirley *(G-15437)*
Dairy Conveyor Corp ....D 845 278-7878
  Brewster *(G-1212)*
Demartini Oil Equipment Svc ....G 518 463-5752
  Glenmont *(G-5683)*
General Oil Equipment Co Inc ....E 716 691-7012
  Amherst *(G-242)*
Konecranes Inc ....F 585 359-4450
  Henrietta *(G-6318)*
Locker Masters Inc ....F 518 288-3203
  Granville *(G-5790)*
Prim Hall Enterprises Inc ....F 518 561-7408
  Plattsburgh *(G-13719)*
Tchnologies N MRC Ameerica LLC .....G 716 822-4300
  Buffalo *(G-3235)*

INDL PATTERNS: Foundry Patternmaking
G Haynes Holdings Inc ....G 607 538-1160
  Bloomville *(G-989)*

INDL PROCESS INSTRUMENTS: Analyzers
Enerac Inc ....F 516 997-1554
  Holbrook *(G-6475)*
Vibro-Laser Instrs Corp LLC ....G 518 874-2700
  Glens Falls *(G-5715)*

INDL PROCESS INSTRUMENTS: Control
Conax Technologies LLC ....C 716 684-4500
  Buffalo *(G-2905)*
Electrcal Instrumentation Ctrl ....F 518 861-5789
  Delanson *(G-4258)*
Inficon Inc ....C 315 434-1149
  East Syracuse *(G-4555)*
Micromod Automtn & Contrls Inc ....F 585 321-9209
  Rochester *(G-14532)*
Nidec Indus Automtn USA LLC ....E 716 774-1193
  Grand Island *(G-5778)*

PRODUCT SECTION

INFRARED OBJECT DETECTION EQPT

Partlow Corporation .... C 518 922-5315
  Fultonville (G-5495)
Rwb Controls Inc .... G 716 897-4341
  Buffalo (G-3198)

INDL PROCESS INSTRUMENTS: Controllers, Process Variables

Anderson Instrument Co Inc .... D 518 922-5315
  Fultonville (G-5491)
Applied Power Systems Inc .... E 516 935-2230
  Hicksville (G-6346)
Classic Automation LLC .... E 585 241-6010
  Webster (G-16742)
Digitronik Dev Labs Inc .... F 585 360-0043
  Rochester (G-14329)
New Scale Technologies Inc .... E 585 924-4450
  Victor (G-16516)
Ormec Systems Corp .... E 585 385-3520
  Rochester (G-14573)

INDL PROCESS INSTRUMENTS: Digital Display, Process Variables

B Live LLC .... G 212 489-0721
  New York (G-9343)
Bae Systems Info & Elec Sys .... G 631 912-1525
  Greenlawn (G-5891)
Display Logic USA Inc .... G 631 406-1922
  Hauppauge (G-6087)

INDL PROCESS INSTRUMENTS: Elements, Primary

Aalborg Instrs & Cntrls Inc .... D 845 398-3160
  Orangeburg (G-13238)

INDL PROCESS INSTRUMENTS: Fluidic Devices, Circuit & Systems

ITT Corporation .... D 315 568-2811
  Seneca Falls (G-15383)
ITT Inc .... F 914 641-2000
  White Plains (G-17152)
ITT LLC .... D 914 641-2000
  Seneca Falls (G-15387)
ITT LLC .... B 914 641-2000
  White Plains (G-17154)
Swagelok Western NY .... G 585 359-8470
  West Henrietta (G-16927)

INDL PROCESS INSTRUMENTS: Indl Flow & Measuring

Computer Instruments Corp .... E 516 876-8400
  Westbury (G-17003)
Select Controls Inc .... E 631 567-9010
  Bohemia (G-1127)

INDL PROCESS INSTRUMENTS: Level & Bulk Measuring

Gizmo Products Inc .... G 585 301-0970
  Rochester (G-14424)

INDL PROCESS INSTRUMENTS: On-Stream Gas Or Liquid Analysis

Calibrated Instruments Inc .... F 914 741-5700
  Manhasset (G-8089)

INDL PROCESS INSTRUMENTS: Temperature

Norwich Aero Products Inc .... D 607 336-7636
  Norwich (G-13051)
Weiss Instruments Inc .... D 631 207-1200
  Holtsville (G-6541)

INDL PROCESS INSTRUMENTS: Water Quality Monitoring/Cntrl Sys

A C T Associates .... F 716 759-8348
  Clarence (G-3682)
Blue Tee Corp .... A 212 598-0880
  New York (G-9473)
Danaher Corporation .... C 516 443-9432
  New York (G-9854)
Ewt Holdings III Corp .... F 212 644-5900
  New York (G-10151)

Roessel & Co Inc .... G 585 458-5560
  Rochester (G-14678)

INDL SALTS WHOLESALERS

American Rock Salt Company LLC ...... E 585 991-6878
  Retsof (G-14064)

INDL SPLYS WHOLESALERS

Allstate Gasket & Packing Inc .... F 631 254-4050
  Deer Park (G-4116)
Applince Installation Svc Corp .... E 716 884-7425
  Buffalo (G-2837)
Bfg Marine Inc .... F 631 586-5500
  Bay Shore (G-674)
D K Machine Inc .... F 518 747-0626
  Fort Edward (G-5349)
Dura-Mill Inc .... F 518 899-2255
  Ballston Spa (G-594)
Executive Mirror Doors Inc .... G 631 234-1090
  Ronkonkoma (G-14928)
Flex Enterprises Inc .... E 585 742-1000
  Victor (G-16501)
Ford Regulator Valve Corp .... G 718 497-3255
  Brooklyn (G-1994)
Jar Metals Inc .... F 845 425-8901
  Nanuet (G-8804)
Macinnes Tool Corporation .... E 585 467-1920
  Rochester (G-14508)
Marks Corpex Banknote Co .... G 631 968-0277
  Bay Shore (G-713)
Peraflex Hose Inc .... F 716 876-8806
  Buffalo (G-3143)
Rollers Inc .... G 716 837-0700
  Buffalo (G-3192)
S A S Industries Inc .... F 631 727-1441
  Manorville (G-8112)
Troy Belting and Supply Co .... D 518 272-4920
  Watervliet (G-16715)

INDL SPLYS, WHOL: Fasteners, Incl Nuts, Bolts, Screws, Etc

Fastener Dimensions Inc .... E 718 847-6321
  Ozone Park (G-13404)
Reddi Car Corp .... G 631 589-3141
  Sayville (G-15243)
SD Christie Associates Inc .... G 914 734-1800
  Peekskill (G-13507)

INDL SPLYS, WHOLESALE: Abrasives

Barton Mines Company LLC .... C 518 798-5462
  Glens Falls (G-5688)
Sunbelt Industries Inc .... F 315 823-2947
  Little Falls (G-7526)
Uneeda Enterprizes Inc .... C 800 431-2494
  Spring Valley (G-15626)
Warren Cutlery Corp .... F 845 876-3444
  Rhinebeck (G-14072)

INDL SPLYS, WHOLESALE: Adhesives, Tape & Plasters

Xto Incorporated .... D 315 451-7807
  Liverpool (G-7585)

INDL SPLYS, WHOLESALE: Bearings

Raydon Precision Bearing Co .... G 516 887-2582
  Lynbrook (G-7984)

INDL SPLYS, WHOLESALE: Bins & Containers, Storage

McIntosh Box & Pallet Co Inc .... E 315 446-9350
  Rome (G-14848)

INDL SPLYS, WHOLESALE: Brushes, Indl

Braun Bros Brushes Inc .... G 631 667-2179
  Valley Stream (G-16427)

INDL SPLYS, WHOLESALE: Clean Room Splys

Air Crafters Inc .... C 631 471-7788
  Ronkonkoma (G-14883)
Knf Clean Room Products Corp .... E 631 588-7000
  Ronkonkoma (G-14951)

INDL SPLYS, WHOLESALE: Fasteners & Fastening Eqpt

American Pride Fasteners LLC ...... E 631 940-8292
  Bay Shore (G-669)
General Galvanizing Sup Co Inc .... E 718 589-4300
  Bronx (G-1345)

INDL SPLYS, WHOLESALE: Gears

Khk Usa Inc .... G 516 248-3850
  Mineola (G-8552)

INDL SPLYS, WHOLESALE: Knives, Indl

Save O Seal Corporation Inc .... G 914 592-3031
  Elmsford (G-4785)

INDL SPLYS, WHOLESALE: Power Transmission, Eqpt & Apparatus

Renold Holdings Inc .... G 716 326-3121
  Westfield (G-17079)

INDL SPLYS, WHOLESALE: Rubber Goods, Mechanical

Tattersall Industries LLC .... E 518 381-4270
  Schenectady (G-15327)
Triangle Rubber Co Inc .... E 631 589-9400
  Bohemia (G-1144)

INDL SPLYS, WHOLESALE: Seals

American Casting and Mfg Corp .... D 800 342-0333
  Plainview (G-13611)
Web Seal Inc .... E 585 546-1320
  Rochester (G-14786)

INDL SPLYS, WHOLESALE: Springs

Lee Spring Company LLC .... C 718 362-5183
  Brooklyn (G-2207)

INDL SPLYS, WHOLESALE: Tools

Dinosaw Inc .... E 518 828-9942
  Hudson (G-6642)

INDL SPLYS, WHOLESALE: Valves & Fittings

John N Fehlinger Co Inc .... F 212 233-5656
  New York (G-10791)
McWane Inc .... B 607 734-2211
  Elmira (G-4708)
Trident Valve Actuator Co .... F 914 698-2650
  Mamaroneck (G-8082)

INDUCTORS

Island Audio Engineering .... G 631 543-2372
  Commack (G-3862)

INFORMATION RETRIEVAL SERVICES

Alternative Technology Corp .... G 914 478-5900
  Hastings On Hudson (G-6022)
Aquifer Drilling & Testing Inc .... C 516 616-6026
  Mineola (G-8528)
Avalon Copy Centers Amer Inc ..... D 315 471-3333
  Syracuse (G-15883)
Avalon Copy Centers Amer Inc ..... E 716 995-7777
  Buffalo (G-2847)
Chakra Communications Inc .... E 716 505-7300
  Lancaster (G-7333)
Data Key Communication LLC ...... F 315 445-2347
  Fayetteville (G-5172)
IAC Search LLC .... E 212 314-7300
  New York (G-10589)
Iac/Interactivecorp .... A 212 314-7300
  New York (G-10590)
Meethappy Inc .... F 917 903-0591
  Seaford (G-15368)
New York Times Company .... B 212 556-1234
  New York (G-11429)
Realtimetraderscom .... E 716 632-6600
  Buffalo (G-3181)

INFRARED OBJECT DETECTION EQPT

Infrared Components Corp .... E 315 732-1544
  Utica (G-16368)

Employee Codes: A=Over 500 employees, B=251-500
C=101-250, D=51-100, E=20-50, F=10-19, G=5-9

INK OR WRITING FLUIDS

INK OR WRITING FLUIDS

American Electronic Products .... F 631 924-1299
 Yaphank *(G-17402)*
F M Group Inc .... F 845 589-0102
 Congers *(G-3881)*
Specialty Ink Co Inc .... F 631 586-3666
 Blue Point *(G-995)*

INK: Letterpress Or Offset

Bishop Print Shop Inc .... G 607 965-8155
 Edmeston *(G-4635)*

INK: Printing

Atlas Coatings Corp .... D 718 402-2000
 Bronx *(G-1276)*
Calchem Corporation .... G 631 423-5696
 Ronkonkoma *(G-14912)*
Flint Group Incorporated .... E 585 458-1223
 Rochester *(G-14395)*
Gotham Ink & Color Co Inc .... E 845 947-4000
 Stony Point *(G-15795)*
Image Specialists Inc .... F 631 475-0867
 Saint James *(G-15116)*
Inglis Co Inc .... G 315 475-1315
 Syracuse *(G-15982)*
Intrinsiq Materials Inc .... G 585 301-4432
 Rochester *(G-14475)*
Micro Powders Inc .... E 914 332-6400
 Tarrytown *(G-16120)*
Millennium Rmnfctred Toner Inc .... F 718 585-9887
 Bronx *(G-1400)*
Mitsubishi Chemical Amer Inc .... E 212 223-3043
 New York *(G-11310)*
Specialty Ink Co Inc .... F 631 586-3666
 Blue Point *(G-995)*
Superior Printing Ink Co Inc .... G 716 685-6763
 Cheektowaga *(G-3618)*
Wikoff Color Corporation .... F 585 458-0653
 Rochester *(G-14791)*

INK: Screen process

Standard Screen Supply Corp .... F 212 627-2727
 New York *(G-12206)*

INSECTICIDES

Island Marketing Corp .... G 516 739-0500
 Mineola *(G-8549)*
Noble Pine Products Co Inc .... F 914 664-5877
 Mount Vernon *(G-8756)*

INSPECTION & TESTING SVCS

Cs Automation Inc .... F 315 524-5123
 Ontario *(G-13220)*

INSTR, MEASURE & CONTROL: Gauge, Oil Pressure & Water Temp

Make-Waves Instrument Corp .... E 716 681-7524
 Buffalo *(G-3076)*

INSTRUMENTS & METERS: Measuring, Electric

Herman H Sticht Company Inc .... G 718 852-7602
 Brooklyn *(G-2074)*
Pulsafeeder Inc .... C 585 292-8000
 Rochester *(G-14632)*
S R Instruments Inc .... E 716 693-5977
 Tonawanda *(G-16216)*
Schlumberger Technology Corp .... C 607 378-0105
 Horseheads *(G-6621)*

INSTRUMENTS, LABORATORY: Differential Thermal Analysis

East Coast Envmtl Group Inc .... G 516 352-1946
 Farmingdale *(G-4993)*

INSTRUMENTS, LABORATORY: Magnetic/Elec Properties Measuring

CTB Enterprise LLC .... F 631 563-0088
 Holbrook *(G-6470)*
MMC Enterprises Corp .... G 800 435-1048
 Hauppauge *(G-6166)*

INSTRUMENTS, LABORATORY: Spectrometers

Spectra Vista Corporation .... G 845 471-7007
 Poughkeepsie *(G-13950)*

INSTRUMENTS, MEASURING & CNTRL: Gauges, Auto, Computer

Parker-Hannifin Corporation .... B 631 231-3737
 Hauppauge *(G-6183)*

INSTRUMENTS, MEASURING & CNTRL: Radiation & Testing, Nuclear

L N D Incorporated .... E 516 678-6141
 Oceanside *(G-13106)*
Mirion Tech Conax Nuclear Inc .... E 716 681-1973
 Buffalo *(G-3088)*
Mirion Technologies Ist Corp .... D 607 562-4300
 Horseheads *(G-6612)*
VJ Technologies Inc .... E 631 589-8800
 Bohemia *(G-1151)*

INSTRUMENTS, MEASURING & CNTRL: Testing, Abrasion, Etc

Magnetic Analysis Corporation .... D 914 530-2000
 Elmsford *(G-4771)*
Nis Manufacturing Inc .... G 518 456-2566
 Cohoes *(G-3777)*

INSTRUMENTS, MEASURING & CNTRLG: Aircraft & Motor Vehicle

James A Staley Co Inc .... F 845 878-3344
 Carmel *(G-3429)*

INSTRUMENTS, MEASURING & CNTRLG: Stress, Strain & Measure

Mechanical Technology Inc .... E 518 218-2550
 Albany *(G-101)*
MTI Instruments Inc .... E 518 218-2550
 Albany *(G-104)*

INSTRUMENTS, MEASURING & CNTRLG: Tensile Strength Testing

Andor Design Corp .... G 516 364-1619
 Syosset *(G-15833)*

INSTRUMENTS, MEASURING & CNTRLG: Thermometers/Temp Sensors

Qhi Group Incorporated .... G 646 512-5727
 New York *(G-11789)*

INSTRUMENTS, MEASURING & CONTROLLING: Gas Detectors

Industrial Test Eqp Co Inc .... E 516 883-6423
 Port Washington *(G-13846)*

INSTRUMENTS, MEASURING & CONTROLLING: Magnetometers

Vector Magnetics LLC .... E 607 273-8351
 Ithaca *(G-6917)*

INSTRUMENTS, MEASURING & CONTROLLING: Photogrammetrical

Elsag North America LLC .... G 877 773-5724
 Brewster *(G-1215)*

INSTRUMENTS, MEASURING & CONTROLLING: Toll Booths, Automatic

Highway Toll ADM LLC .... F 516 684-9584
 Roslyn Heights *(G-15051)*

INSTRUMENTS, MEASURING & CONTROLLING: Ultrasonic Testing

Aurora Technical Services Ltd .... G 716 652-1463
 East Aurora *(G-4392)*
U E Systems Incorporated .... E 914 592-1220
 Elmsford *(G-4797)*

INSTRUMENTS, MEASURING/CNTRL: Hydrometers, Exc Indl Process

Mobius Labs Inc .... G 518 961-2600
 Rexford *(G-14065)*
Peyser Instrument Corporation .... E 631 841-3600
 West Babylon *(G-16848)*

INSTRUMENTS, MEASURING/CNTRLG: Fare Registers, St Cars/Buses

Cubic Trnsp Systems Inc .... F 212 255-1810
 New York *(G-9821)*

INSTRUMENTS, MEASURING/CNTRLNG: Med Diagnostic Sys, Nuclear

Eastern Niagra Radiology .... E 716 882-6544
 Buffalo *(G-2942)*
H D M Labs Inc .... G 516 431-8357
 Island Park *(G-6820)*
Nuclear Diagnostic Pdts NY Inc .... G 516 575-4201
 Plainview *(G-13653)*
Oyster Bay Pump Works Inc .... F 516 933-4500
 Hicksville *(G-6406)*

INSTRUMENTS, OPTICAL: Borescopes

Machida Incorporated .... G 845 365-0600
 Orangeburg *(G-13257)*

INSTRUMENTS, OPTICAL: Elements & Assemblies, Exc Ophthalmic

Applied Coatings Holding Corp .... G 585 482-0300
 Rochester *(G-14224)*
Metavac LLC .... E 631 207-2344
 Holtsville *(G-6530)*
Photon Gear Inc .... F 585 265-3360
 Ontario *(G-13231)*

INSTRUMENTS, OPTICAL: Gratings, Diffraction

Newport Rochester Inc .... D 585 262-1325
 Rochester *(G-14556)*

INSTRUMENTS, OPTICAL: Lenses, All Types Exc Ophthalmic

Advanced Glass Industries Inc .... D 585 458-8040
 Rochester *(G-14193)*
Claude Tribastone Inc .... G 585 265-3776
 Ontario *(G-13219)*
Enplas America Inc .... G 646 892-7811
 New York *(G-10095)*
Jml Optical Industries LLC .... D 585 248-8900
 Rochester *(G-14484)*
Lens Triptar Co Inc .... G 585 473-4470
 Rochester *(G-14498)*
Meopta USA Inc .... C 631 436-5900
 Hauppauge *(G-6157)*
Optics Technology Inc .... G 585 586-0950
 Pittsford *(G-13599)*
Optimax Systems Inc .... C 585 265-1020
 Ontario *(G-13229)*
Rochester Precision Optics LLC .... C 585 292-5450
 West Henrietta *(G-16924)*
Spectrum Thin Films Inc .... E 631 901-1010
 Hauppauge *(G-6221)*

INSTRUMENTS, OPTICAL: Mirrors

Hudson Mirror LLC .... E 914 930-8906
 Peekskill *(G-13504)*
North American Enclosures Inc .... E 631 234-9500
 Central Islip *(G-3534)*

INSTRUMENTS, OPTICAL: Prisms

Ariel Optics Inc .... G 585 265-4820
 Ontario *(G-13217)*

INSTRUMENTS, OPTICAL: Sights, Telescopic

Evergreen Bleachers Inc .... G 518 654-9084
 Corinth *(G-3980)*

INSTRUMENTS, OPTICAL: Spyglasses

Digitac Inc .... F 732 215-4020
 Brooklyn *(G-1863)*

PRODUCT SECTION

INSTRUMENTS, OPTICAL: Test & Inspection

Quality Vision Intl Inc .... G 585 544-0400
  Rochester (G-14637)
Videk Inc .... E 585 377-0377
  Fairport (G-4892)

INSTRUMENTS, SURGICAL & MEDICAL: Blood & Bone Work

Accumed Corp .... G 716 853-1800
  Buffalo (G-2810)
East Coast Orthoic & Pros Cor .... D 516 248-5566
  Deer Park (G-4156)
Elite Medical Supply of NY .... G 716 712-0881
  West Seneca (G-16972)
Future Diagnostics LLC .... E 347 434-6700
  Brooklyn (G-2008)
Manhattan Eastside Dev Corp .... F 212 305-3275
  New York (G-11153)

INSTRUMENTS, SURGICAL & MEDICAL: Blood Pressure

American Diagnostic Corp .... D 631 273-6155
  Hauppauge (G-6040)
N Y B P Inc .... G 585 624-2541
  Mendon (G-8413)
W A Baum Co Inc .... D 631 226-3940
  Copiague (G-3961)

INSTRUMENTS, SURGICAL & MEDICAL: Catheters

Nasco Enterprises Inc .... G 516 921-9696
  Syosset (G-15849)
Novamed-Usa Inc .... E 914 789-2100
  Elmsford (G-4779)
Vante Inc .... F 716 778-7691
  Newfane (G-12813)

INSTRUMENTS, SURGICAL & MEDICAL: IV Transfusion

Sigma Intl Gen Med Apprtus LLC .... B 585 798-3901
  Medina (G-8315)

INSTRUMENTS, SURGICAL & MEDICAL: Inhalation Therapy

Beacon Spch Lnge Pthlgy Phys .... F 516 626-1635
  Roslyn (G-15040)

INSTRUMENTS, SURGICAL & MEDICAL: Inhalators

Ip Med Inc .... G 516 766-3800
  Oceanside (G-13102)

INSTRUMENTS, SURGICAL & MEDICAL: Knives

Huron TI Cutter Grinding Inc .... E 631 420-7000
  Farmingdale (G-5015)

INSTRUMENTS, SURGICAL & MEDICAL: Lasers, Surgical

Aerolase Corporation .... D 914 345-8300
  Tarrytown (G-16108)
Clerio Vision Inc .... F 617 216-7881
  Rochester (G-14300)

INSTRUMENTS, SURGICAL & MEDICAL: Muscle Exercise, Ophthalmic

Biodex Medical Systems Inc .... C 631 924-9000
  Shirley (G-15439)
Biodex Medical Systems Inc .... E 631 924-3146
  Shirley (G-15440)

INSTRUMENTS, SURGICAL & MEDICAL: Ophthalmic

Bausch & Lomb Incorporated .... B 585 338-6000
  Rochester (G-14242)
Corning Tropel Corporation .... C 585 377-3200
  Fairport (G-4857)
Sonomed Inc .... E 516 354-0900
  New Hyde Park (G-8908)

INSTRUMENTS, SURGICAL & MEDICAL: Physiotherapy, Electrical

Fabrication Enterprises Inc .... E 914 591-9300
  Elmsford (G-4761)

INSTRUMENTS, SURGICAL & MEDICAL: Skin Grafting

Skyler Brand Ventures LLC .... G 646 979-5904
  New York (G-12122)

INSTRUMENTS, SURGICAL & MEDICAL: Suction Therapy

Njr Medical Devices .... E 440 258-8204
  Cedarhurst (G-3487)

INSTRUMENTS: Analytical

A S A Precision Co Inc .... G 845 482-4870
  Jeffersonville (G-7092)
Advanced Mtl Analytics LLC .... G 321 684-0528
  Vestal (G-16461)
Advion Inc .... E 607 266-9162
  Ithaca (G-6857)
Bristol Instruments Inc .... G 585 924-2620
  Victor (G-16488)
Brookhaven Instruments Corp .... E 631 758-3200
  Holtsville (G-6526)
Carl Zeiss Inc .... C 914 747-1800
  Thornwood (G-16140)
Ceres Technologies Inc .... D 845 247-4701
  Saugerties (G-15210)
Chromosense LLC .... G 347 770-5421
  Brooklyn (G-1777)
Corning Incorporated .... E 607 974-6729
  Painted Post (G-13417)
East Hills Instrument Inc .... F 516 621-8686
  Westbury (G-17007)
EMD Millipore Corporation .... G 845 621-6560
  Mahopac (G-8025)
General Microwave Corporation .... F 516 802-0900
  Syosset (G-15844)
High Voltage Inc .... E 518 329-3275
  Copake (G-3913)
Multiwire Laboratories Ltd .... G 607 257-3378
  Ithaca (G-6900)
Nanotronics Imaging Inc .... E 212 401-6209
  Brooklyn (G-2354)
Novartis Pharmaceuticals Corp .... G 888 669-6682
  New York (G-11480)
Rheonix Inc .... D 607 257-1242
  Ithaca (G-6909)
Smartpill Corporation .... E 716 882-0701
  Buffalo (G-3216)
Thermo Fisher Scientific Inc .... G 716 774-6700
  Grand Island (G-5786)
Thermo Fisher Scientific Inc .... B 585 458-8008
  Rochester (G-14749)
Thermo Fisher Scientific Inc .... A 585 899-7610
  Rochester (G-14750)
Veeco Instruments Inc .... C 516 677-0200
  Woodbury (G-17321)

INSTRUMENTS: Colonoscopes, Electromedical

Gravity East Village Inc .... G 212 388-9788
  New York (G-10397)

INSTRUMENTS: Combustion Control, Indl

Aureonic .... G 518 791-9331
  Gansevoort (G-5499)

INSTRUMENTS: Electrocardiographs

Integrated Medical Devices .... G 315 457-4200
  Liverpool (G-7549)

INSTRUMENTS: Electrolytic Conductivity, Indl

Mark - 10 Corporation .... E 631 842-9200
  Copiague (G-3938)

INSTRUMENTS: Electrolytic Conductivity, Laboratory

Tokyo Electron America Inc .... G 518 292-4200
  Albany (G-143)

INSTRUMENTS: Endoscopic Eqpt, Electromedical

Elizabeth Wood .... G 315 492-5470
  Syracuse (G-15954)

INSTRUMENTS: Function Generators

Allied Motion Technologies Inc .... C 716 242-8634
  Amherst (G-224)

INSTRUMENTS: Generators Tachometer

Make-Waves Instrument Corp .... E 716 681-7524
  Buffalo (G-3076)

INSTRUMENTS: Indl Process Control

Ametek Inc .... D 585 263-7700
  Rochester (G-14218)
Cemtrex Inc .... C 631 756-9116
  Farmingdale (G-4967)
Ceres Technologies Inc .... D 845 247-4701
  Saugerties (G-15210)
Defelsko Corporation .... D 315 393-4450
  Ogdensburg (G-13135)
Digital Analysis Corporation .... F 315 685-0760
  Skaneateles (G-15479)
Dyna-Empire Inc .... C 516 222-2700
  Garden City (G-5513)
East Hills Instrument Inc .... F 516 621-8686
  Westbury (G-17007)
Electronic Machine Parts LLC .... F 631 434-3700
  Hauppauge (G-6093)
Emerson Electric Co .... E 212 244-2490
  New York (G-10074)
Fts Systems Inc .... D 845 687-5300
  Stone Ridge (G-15785)
Gurley Precision Instrs Inc .... C 518 272-6300
  Troy (G-16259)
Hades Manufacturing Corp .... F 631 249-4244
  Farmingdale (G-5011)
Harris Corporation .... C 703 668-6239
  Rome (G-14841)
Heidenhain International Inc .... C 716 661-1700
  Jamestown (G-7033)
Herman H Sticht Company Inc .... G 718 852-7602
  Brooklyn (G-2074)
Hilliard Corporation .... B 607 733-7121
  Elmira (G-4703)
Hilliard Corporation .... F 607 733-7121
  Elmira (G-4704)
Inficon Holding AG .... G 315 434-1100
  East Syracuse (G-4556)
Integrated Control Corp .... E 631 673-5100
  Huntington (G-6696)
Koehler Instrument Company Inc ..... D 631 589-3800
  Holtsville (G-6529)
Magtrol Inc .... E 716 668-5555
  Buffalo (G-3075)
Mausner Equipment Co Inc .... C 631 689-7358
  Setauket (G-15402)
Miller & Weber Inc .... E 718 821-7110
  Westbury (G-17039)
Mks Instruments Inc .... E 585 292-7472
  Rochester (G-14537)
Nutec Components Inc .... F 631 242-1224
  Deer Park (G-4206)
Orthstar Enterprises Inc .... D 607 562-2100
  Horseheads (G-6614)
Pcb Group Inc .... E 716 684-0001
  Depew (G-4292)
Poseidon Systems LLC .... F 585 239-6025
  Rochester (G-14608)
Pulsafeeder Inc .... C 585 292-8000
  Rochester (G-14632)
R K B Opto-Electronics Inc .... F 315 455-6636
  Syracuse (G-16038)
Schneider Elc Systems USA Inc ..... F 214 527-3099
  New York (G-12010)
Sequential Electronics Systems ...... E 914 592-1345
  Elmsford (G-4791)
Sixnet Holdings LLC .... G 518 877-5173
  Ballston Lake (G-586)
Solar Metrology LLC .... G 845 247-4701
  Holbrook (G-6500)

Telog Instruments Inc............E...... 585 742-3000
Victor *(G-16531)*
Thread Check Inc............D...... 631 231-1515
Hauppauge *(G-6238)*
Transtech Systems Inc............E...... 518 370-5558
Latham *(G-7408)*
Vacuum Instrument Corporation............D...... 631 737-0900
Ronkonkoma *(G-15021)*
Veeco Instruments Inc............C...... 516 677-0200
Woodbury *(G-17321)*
Vertiv Services Inc............G...... 516 349-8500
Plainview *(G-13673)*
Winters Instruments Inc............E...... 281 880-8607
Buffalo *(G-3283)*
Xentaur Corporation............E...... 631 345-3434
Yaphank *(G-17425)*

INSTRUMENTS: Laser, Scientific & Engineering

Applied Biophysics Inc............G...... 518 880-6860
Troy *(G-16246)*
Cambridge Manufacturing LLC............G...... 516 326-1350
New Hyde Park *(G-8865)*
Gemprint Corporation............E...... 212 997-0007
New York *(G-10313)*
Micro Photo Acoustics Inc............G...... 631 750-6035
Ronkonkoma *(G-14968)*
Porous Materials Inc............E...... 607 257-5544
Ithaca *(G-6906)*
Uptek Solutions Corp............F...... 631 256-5565
Bohemia *(G-1150)*

INSTRUMENTS: Measurement, Indl Process

Riverhawk Company LP............E...... 315 624-7171
New Hartford *(G-8854)*
Robat Inc............G...... 518 812-6244
Clifton Park *(G-3731)*

INSTRUMENTS: Measuring & Controlling

Aspex Incorporated............E...... 212 966-0410
New York *(G-9290)*
Biodesign Inc of New York............F...... 845 454-6610
Carmel *(G-3426)*
Carl Zeiss Inc............C...... 914 747-1800
Thornwood *(G-16140)*
Circor Aerospace Inc............D...... 631 737-1900
Hauppauge *(G-6065)*
Computer Instruments Corp............E...... 516 876-8400
Westbury *(G-17003)*
Cosense Inc............E...... 516 364-9161
Syosset *(G-15838)*
Dayton T Brown Inc............B...... 631 589-6300
Bohemia *(G-1048)*
Defelsko Corporation............D...... 315 393-4450
Ogdensburg *(G-13135)*
Dispersion Technology Inc............G...... 914 241-4777
Bedford Hills *(G-799)*
Dyna-Empire Inc............C...... 516 222-2700
Garden City *(G-5513)*
Dynamic Systems Inc............E...... 518 283-5350
Poestenkill *(G-13753)*
East Hills Instrument Inc............F...... 516 621-8686
Westbury *(G-17007)*
Electrical Controls Link............E...... 585 924-7010
Victor *(G-16498)*
Electro-Optical Products Corp............G...... 718 456-6000
Ridgewood *(G-14118)*
Enerac Inc............F...... 516 997-1554
Holbrook *(G-6475)*
Erbessd Reliability LLC............E...... 518 874-2700
Glens Falls *(G-5694)*
Fougera Pharmaceuticals Inc............C...... 631 454-7677
Melville *(G-8350)*
Freeman Technology Inc............E...... 732 829-8345
Bayside *(G-765)*
Gei International Inc............F...... 315 463-9261
East Syracuse *(G-4546)*
Hci Engineering............G...... 315 336-3450
Rome *(G-14842)*
Helmel Engineering Pdts Inc............E...... 716 297-8644
Niagara Falls *(G-12851)*
Herman H Sticht Company Inc............G...... 718 852-7602
Brooklyn *(G-2074)*
Hipotronics Inc............C...... 845 279-8091
Brewster *(G-1217)*
Imaginant Inc............E...... 585 264-0480
Pittsford *(G-13592)*
Itin Scale Co Inc............E...... 718 336-5900
Brooklyn *(G-2118)*
Kem Medical Products Corp............G...... 631 454-6565
Farmingdale *(G-5034)*
Kld Labs Inc............E...... 631 549-4222
Hauppauge *(G-6131)*
Liberty Controls Inc............G...... 718 461-0600
College Point *(G-3819)*
Machine Technology Inc............G...... 845 454-4030
Poughkeepsie *(G-13933)*
Magtrol Inc............E...... 716 668-5555
Buffalo *(G-3075)*
Mason Industries Inc............B...... 631 348-0282
Hauppauge *(G-6152)*
Miller & Weber Inc............E...... 718 821-7110
Westbury *(G-17039)*
MTS Systems Corporation............C...... 518 899-2140
Ballston Lake *(G-583)*
Norwich Aero Products Inc............D...... 607 336-7636
Norwich *(G-13051)*
Orolia Usa Inc............D...... 585 321-5800
Rochester *(G-14574)*
Pcb Piezotronics Inc............G...... 716 684-0001
Depew *(G-4293)*
Peerless Instrument Co Inc............C...... 631 396-6500
Farmingdale *(G-5086)*
Poseidon Systems LLC............F...... 585 239-6025
Rochester *(G-14608)*
Precision Design Systems Inc............E...... 585 426-4500
Rochester *(G-14614)*
Research Frontiers Inc............F...... 516 364-1902
Woodbury *(G-17318)*
Riverhawk Company LP............E...... 315 624-7171
New Hartford *(G-8854)*
RJ Harvey Instrument Corp............F...... 845 359-3943
Tappan *(G-16107)*
S P Industries Inc............D...... 845 255-5000
Gardiner *(G-5563)*
Schenck Corporation............D...... 631 242-4010
Deer Park *(G-4229)*
Schenck Trebel Corp............D...... 631 242-4397
Deer Park *(G-4230)*
Schott Corporation............D...... 914 831-2200
Elmsford *(G-4786)*
Teledyne Lecroy Inc............C...... 845 425-2000
Chestnut Ridge *(G-3656)*
Telog Instruments Inc............E...... 585 742-3000
Victor *(G-16531)*
Vacuum Instrument Corporation............D...... 631 737-0900
Ronkonkoma *(G-15021)*
Videk Inc............E...... 585 377-0377
Fairport *(G-4892)*
Weiss Instruments Inc............D...... 631 207-1200
Holtsville *(G-6541)*
Xeku Corporation............F...... 607 761-1447
Vestal *(G-16481)*
York Industries Inc............E...... 516 746-3736
Garden City Park *(G-5559)*
Zomega Terahertz Corporation............F...... 585 347-4337
Webster *(G-16771)*

INSTRUMENTS: Measuring Electricity

Agilent Technologies Inc............A...... 877 424-4536
New York *(G-9108)*
American Quality Technology............F...... 607 777-9488
Binghamton *(G-884)*
Ametek Inc............D...... 585 263-7700
Rochester *(G-14218)*
C Speed LLC............E...... 315 453-1043
Liverpool *(G-7537)*
C-Flex Bearing Co Inc............F...... 315 895-7454
Frankfort *(G-5359)*
Cetek Inc............E...... 845 452-3510
Poughkeepsie *(G-13911)*
East Hills Instrument Inc............F...... 516 621-8686
Westbury *(G-17007)*
Edo LLC............F...... 631 218-1413
Bohemia *(G-1058)*
Edo LLC............A...... 631 630-4200
Amityville *(G-285)*
Ems Development Corporation............D...... 631 924-4736
Yaphank *(G-17406)*
Enertiv Inc............G...... 646 350-3525
New York *(G-10091)*
Hipotronics Inc............C...... 845 279-8091
Brewster *(G-1217)*
Interntnal Elctronic Mchs Corp............E...... 518 268-1636
Troy *(G-16263)*
John Ramsey Elec Svcs LLC............G...... 585 298-9596
Victor *(G-16507)*
Larry Kings Corporation............G...... 718 481-8741
Rosedale *(G-15037)*
Linde LLC............D...... 716 773-7552
Grand Island *(G-5776)*
Logitek Inc............D...... 631 567-1100
Bohemia *(G-1089)*
Ludl Electronic Products Ltd............E...... 914 769-6111
Hawthorne *(G-6274)*
Magnetic Analysis Corporation............D...... 914 530-2000
Elmsford *(G-4771)*
Magtrol Inc............E...... 716 668-5555
Buffalo *(G-3075)*
North Atlantic Industries Inc............C...... 631 567-1100
Bohemia *(G-1106)*
Optimized Devices Inc............F...... 914 769-6100
Pleasantville *(G-13747)*
Peerless Instrument Co Inc............C...... 631 396-6500
Farmingdale *(G-5086)*
Practical Instrument Elec Inc............F...... 585 872-9350
Webster *(G-16755)*
R K B Opto-Electronics Inc............F...... 315 455-6636
Syracuse *(G-16038)*
Rodale Wireless Inc............E...... 631 231-0044
Hauppauge *(G-6205)*
Scientific Components Corp............E...... 631 243-4901
Deer Park *(G-4231)*
Trek Inc............F...... 716 438-7555
Lockport *(G-7652)*
Viatran Corporation............E...... 716 564-7813
Tonawanda *(G-16233)*
W & W Manufacturing Co............F...... 516 942-0011
West Islip *(G-16939)*
Zumbach Electronics Corp............D...... 914 241-7080
Mount Kisco *(G-8691)*

INSTRUMENTS: Measuring, Electrical Energy

Apogee Power Usa Inc............F...... 202 746-2890
Hartsdale *(G-6016)*
Quadlogic Controls Corporation............D...... 212 930-9300
Long Island City *(G-7882)*

INSTRUMENTS: Measuring, Electrical Power

Allied Motion Systems Corp............F...... 716 691-5868
Amherst *(G-223)*
Primesouth Inc............F...... 585 567-4191
Fillmore *(G-5184)*

INSTRUMENTS: Measuring, Electrical Quantities

Qualitrol Company LLC............C...... 586 643-3717
Fairport *(G-4879)*
Vermed Inc............D...... 800 669-6905
Buffalo *(G-3267)*

INSTRUMENTS: Medical & Surgical

Advanced Placement LLC............E...... 949 281-9086
Holbrook *(G-6458)*
Ala Scientific Instruments Inc............F...... 631 393-6401
Farmingdale *(G-4942)*
AM Bickford Inc............F...... 716 652-1590
Wales Center *(G-16559)*
American Healthcare Supply Inc............F...... 212 674-3636
New York *(G-9168)*
Angiodynamics Inc............B...... 518 975-1400
Queensbury *(G-14004)*
Angiodynamics Inc............B...... 518 792-4112
Glens Falls *(G-5687)*
Angiodynamics Inc............B...... 518 742-4430
Queensbury *(G-14005)*
Angiodynamics Inc............B...... 518 795-1400
Latham *(G-7380)*
Argon Medical Devices Inc............G...... 585 321-1130
Henrietta *(G-6316)*
Astra Tool & Instr Mfg Corp............E...... 914 747-3863
Hawthorne *(G-6266)*
Baxter Healthcare Corporation............B...... 800 356-3454
Medina *(G-8299)*
Becton Dickinson and Company............B...... 845 353-3371
Nyack *(G-13061)*
Bioresearch Inc............G...... 212 734-5315
Pound Ridge *(G-13958)*
Boehm Surgical Instrument............F...... 585 436-6584
Rochester *(G-14259)*
Bovie Medical Corporation............C...... 914 468-4009
Purchase *(G-13970)*
Buffalo Filter LLC............D...... 716 835-7000
Lancaster *(G-7331)*
Buxton Medical Equipment Corp............E...... 631 957-4500
Lindenhurst *(G-7479)*

PRODUCT SECTION

INSTRUMENTS: Test, Electronic & Electrical Circuits

Company	Code	Phone
C R Bard Inc Queensbury *(G-14007)*	B	518 793-2531
C R Bard Inc Glens Falls *(G-5690)*	A	518 793-2531
Caliber Imging Diagnostics Inc Rochester *(G-14273)*	E	585 239-9800
CN Group Incorporated White Plains *(G-17122)*	A	914 358-5690
Cognitiveflow Sensor Tech Stony Brook *(G-15789)*	G	631 513-9369
Conmed Corporation Utica *(G-16338)*	D	315 797-8375
Cynosure Inc Hicksville *(G-6365)*	G	516 594-3333
Daxor Corporation New York *(G-9888)*	E	212 244-0555
Delcath Systems Inc New York *(G-9893)*	E	212 489-2100
Derm/Buro Inc Plainview *(G-13626)*	G	516 694-8300
Designs For Vision Inc Ronkonkoma *(G-14922)*	C	631 585-3300
Elliquence LLC Baldwin *(G-557)*	F	516 277-9000
Endovor Inc New York *(G-10084)*	G	214 679-7385
Endovor LLC New York *(G-10085)*	G	214 679-7385
Esc Control Electronics LLC Sayville *(G-15236)*	G	631 467-5328
Extek Inc Rush *(G-15072)*	E	585 533-1672
Eyeglass Service Industries Bedford Hills *(G-800)*	G	914 666-3150
Flexbar Machine Corporation Islandia *(G-6831)*	E	631 582-8440
Fluorologic Inc Pittsford *(G-13588)*	G	585 248-2796
Ftt Medical Inc Rochester *(G-14406)*	G	585 444-0980
Gaymar Industries Inc Orchard Park *(G-13294)*	B	800 828-7341
Getinge Usa Inc Rochester *(G-14422)*	C	800 475-9040
Hanger Inc Rockville Centre *(G-14820)*	E	516 678-3650
Harmac Medical Products Inc Buffalo *(G-3006)*	C	716 897-4500
Hogil Pharmaceutical Corp White Plains *(G-17147)*	F	914 681-1800
Hurryworks LLC Port Washington *(G-13843)*	D	516 998-4600
Incredible Scents Inc Glen Head *(G-5648)*	G	516 656-3300
Integer Holdings Corporation Clarence *(G-3690)*	D	716 759-5200
Intersurgical Incorporated East Syracuse *(G-4558)*	F	315 451-2900
J H M Engineering Brooklyn *(G-2122)*	E	718 871-1810
Jaracz Jr Joseph Paul Orchard Park *(G-13301)*	G	716 533-1377
Liberty Install Inc Centerport *(G-3504)*	F	631 651-5655
Mdi East Inc South Glens Falls *(G-15549)*	E	518 747-8730
Medical Depot Inc Port Washington *(G-13862)*	B	516 998-4600
Medical Technology Products Greenlawn *(G-5893)*	G	631 285-6640
Medipoint Inc Mineola *(G-8557)*	F	516 294-8822
Medline Industries Inc Middletown *(G-8484)*	B	845 344-3301
Medsource Technologies LLC Orchard Park *(G-13308)*	D	716 662-5025
Mick Radio Nuclear Instrument Mount Vernon *(G-8752)*	F	718 597-3999
Misonix Inc Farmingdale *(G-5067)*	D	631 694-9555
Modular Medical Corp Bronx *(G-1403)*	E	718 829-2626
Monaghan Medical Corporation Plattsburgh *(G-13705)*	D	518 561-7330
Moog Inc Elma *(G-4664)*	A	716 652-2000
Nano Vibronix Inc Cedarhurst *(G-3486)*	F	516 374-8330
Nasiff Associates Inc Central Square *(G-3544)*	G	315 676-2346
Navilyst Medical Inc Glens Falls *(G-5707)*	A	800 833-9973
Ocala Group LLC New Hyde Park *(G-8899)*	F	516 233-2750
Orics Industries Inc Farmingdale *(G-5080)*	E	718 461-8613
Ortho Medical Products New York *(G-11541)*	F	212 879-3700
Orthocon Inc Irvington *(G-6815)*	E	914 357-2600
P Ryton Corp Long Island City *(G-7863)*	F	718 937-7052
Pall Corporation Cortland *(G-4059)*	A	607 753-6041
Pall Corporation Port Washington *(G-13870)*	A	516 484-5400
Parace Bionics LLC Yorktown Heights *(G-17531)*	G	877 727-2231
Parkchester Dps LLC Bronx *(G-1422)*	C	718 823-4411
Pavmed Inc New York *(G-11603)*	G	212 401-1951
Peter Digioia Plainview *(G-13656)*	G	516 644-5517
Praxis Powder Technology Inc Queensbury *(G-14020)*	E	518 812-0112
Precimed Inc Clarence *(G-3696)*	E	716 759-5600
Professional Medical Devices Harrison *(G-6008)*	F	914 835-0614
Progressive Orthotics Ltd Selden *(G-15375)*	G	631 732-5556
Rdd Pharma Inc New York *(G-11838)*	G	302 319-9970
Reichert Inc Depew *(G-4296)*	C	716 686-4500
Repro Med Systems Inc Chester *(G-3639)*	D	845 469-2042
Responselink Inc Latham *(G-7405)*	G	518 424-7776
Robert Bosch LLC Utica *(G-16381)*	E	315 733-3312
Seedings Lf Scnce Ventures LLC New York *(G-12036)*	G	917 913-8511
Seneca TEC Inc Fairport *(G-4885)*	G	585 381-2645
Simulaids Inc Saugerties *(G-15223)*	D	845 679-2475
Solid-Look Corporation Douglaston *(G-4335)*	G	917 683-1780
St Silicones Corporation Clifton Park *(G-3735)*	F	518 406-3208
Stj Enterprises Cedarhurst *(G-3488)*	D	516 612-0110
Tril Inc Copiague *(G-3958)*	G	631 645-7989
Vasomedical Inc Plainview *(G-13668)*	B	516 997-4600
Viterion Corporation Elmsford *(G-4799)*	F	914 333-6033
Vizio Medical Devices LLC New York *(G-12587)*	F	646 845-7382
Wyeth Holdings LLC Pearl River *(G-13493)*	D	845 602-5000

INSTRUMENTS: Meteorological

Company	Code	Phone
Climatronics Corp Bohemia *(G-1030)*	F	541 471-7111

INSTRUMENTS: Microwave Test

Company	Code	Phone
Hamilton Marketing Corporation Brockport *(G-1243)*	G	585 395-0678

INSTRUMENTS: Nautical

Company	Code	Phone
Moor Electronics Inc Buffalo *(G-3095)*	G	716 821-5304
New York Nautical Inc New York *(G-11424)*	G	212 962-4522

INSTRUMENTS: Optical, Analytical

Company	Code	Phone
Applied Image Inc Rochester *(G-14225)*	E	585 482-0300
Exfo Burleigh Pdts Group Inc Canandaigua *(G-3374)*	D	585 301-1530
Qioptiq Inc Fairport *(G-4878)*	E	585 223-2370

INSTRUMENTS: Oscillographs & Oscilloscopes

Company	Code	Phone
Teledyne Lecroy Inc Chestnut Ridge *(G-3656)*	C	845 425-2000

INSTRUMENTS: Pressure Measurement, Indl

Company	Code	Phone
Taber Acquisition Corp North Tonawanda *(G-13018)*	D	716 694-4000
Viatran Corporation Tonawanda *(G-16233)*	E	716 564-7813

INSTRUMENTS: Radar Testing, Electric

Company	Code	Phone
Anmar Acquisition LLC Rochester *(G-14222)*	G	585 352-7777

INSTRUMENTS: Radio Frequency Measuring

Company	Code	Phone
Omni-ID Usa Inc Rochester *(G-14570)*	E	585 697-9913
T & C Power Conversion Inc Rochester *(G-14738)*	F	585 482-5551
W D Technology Inc Eastchester *(G-4595)*	G	914 779-8738

INSTRUMENTS: Signal Generators & Averagers

Company	Code	Phone
Macrodyne Inc Clifton Park *(G-3727)*	F	518 383-3800

INSTRUMENTS: Standards & Calibration, Electrical Measuring

Company	Code	Phone
Ah Elctronic Test Eqp Repr Ctr Central Islip *(G-3509)*	F	631 234-8979

INSTRUMENTS: Telemetering, Indl Process

Company	Code	Phone
Medsafe Systems Inc Port Washington *(G-13864)*	G	516 883-8222

INSTRUMENTS: Temperature Measurement, Indl

Company	Code	Phone
Rotronic Instrument Corp Hauppauge *(G-6206)*	F	631 348-6844
Siemens Industry Inc Bohemia *(G-1131)*	C	631 218-1000
Springfield Control Systems Douglaston *(G-4336)*	G	718 631-0870
Tel-Tru Inc Rochester *(G-14746)*	D	585 295-0225

INSTRUMENTS: Test, Electronic & Electric Measurement

Company	Code	Phone
Avanel Industries Inc Westbury *(G-16998)*	F	516 333-0990
Clayton Dubilier & Rice Fun New York *(G-9695)*	E	212 407-5200
Comtech PST Corp Melville *(G-8336)*	C	631 777-8900
Evergreen High Voltage LLC Lake Placid *(G-7298)*	G	281 814-9973
Jre Test LLC Victor *(G-16509)*	G	585 298-9736
Millivac Instruments Inc Schenectady *(G-15305)*	E	518 355-8300
Nas CP Corp College Point *(G-3823)*	E	718 961-6757
Northeast Metrology Corp Depew *(G-4290)*	F	716 827-3770
Photonix Technologies Inc Endicott *(G-4832)*	F	607 786-4600
Precision Filters Inc Ithaca *(G-6907)*	E	607 277-3550
Ramsey Electronics LLC Victor *(G-16522)*	E	585 924-4560
Scj Associates Inc Rochester *(G-14697)*	E	585 359-0600

INSTRUMENTS: Test, Electronic & Electrical Circuits

Company	Code	Phone
Automated Control Logic Inc Thornwood *(G-16139)*	F	914 769-8880
Automation Correct LLC Syracuse *(G-15881)*	G	315 299-3589

Employee Codes: A=Over 500 employees, B=251-500
C=101-250, D=51-100, E=20-50, F=10-19, G=5-9

INSTRUMENTS: Test, Electronic & Electrical Circuits

Avcom of Virginia Inc ....D...... 585 924-4560
　Victor (G-16485)
Clarke Hess Communication RES ......G...... 631 698-3350
　Medford (G-8272)
General Microwave Corporation ....F...... 516 802-0900
　Syosset (G-15844)
Iet Labs Inc ....F...... 516 334-5959
　Roslyn Heights (G-15052)
Lexan Industries Inc ....F...... 631 434-7586
　Bay Shore (G-711)
Pulsar Technology Systems Inc ....G...... 718 361-9292
　Long Island City (G-7879)

INSTRUMENTS: Testing, Semiconductor

Pragmatics Technology Inc ....G...... 845 795-5071
　Milton (G-8517)

INSTRUMENTS: Thermal Conductive, Indl

Dau Thrmal Slutions N Amer Inc ....E...... 585 678-9025
　Macedon (G-8015)

INSTRUMENTS: Vibration

SKF USA Inc ....D...... 716 661-2600
　Jamestown (G-7060)
Voice Analysis Clinic ....G...... 212 245-3803
　New York (G-12592)

INSTRUMENTS: Viscometer, Indl Process

Beauty America LLC ....E...... 917 744-1430
　Great Neck (G-5811)

INSULATING COMPOUNDS

Zircar Ceramics Inc ....E...... 845 651-6600
　Florida (G-5223)

INSULATION & CUSHIONING FOAM: Polystyrene

C P Chemical Co Inc ....G...... 914 428-2517
　White Plains (G-17118)
Carlisle Construction Mtls LLC ....D...... 386 753-0786
　Montgomery (G-8629)
Foam Products Inc ....E...... 718 292-4830
　Bronx (G-1337)
New York State Foam Enrgy LLC ....G...... 845 534-4656
　Cornwall (G-4010)
Shelter Enterprises Inc ....D...... 518 237-4100
　Cohoes (G-3783)
Soundcoat Company Inc ....D...... 631 242-2200
　Deer Park (G-4236)
Thermal Foams/Syracuse Inc ....G...... 716 874-6474
　Buffalo (G-3242)

INSULATION MATERIALS WHOLESALERS

Regional MGT & Consulting Inc ....F...... 718 599-3718
　Brooklyn (G-2506)

INSULATION: Felt

Shannon Entps Wstn NY Inc ....D...... 716 693-7954
　North Tonawanda (G-13011)

INSULATION: Fiberglass

Burnett Process Inc ....G...... 585 254-8080
　Rochester (G-14269)
Elliot Industries Inc ....G...... 716 287-3100
　Ellington (G-4658)
Fbm Galaxy Inc ....F...... 315 463-5144
　East Syracuse (G-4542)
Primary Plastics Inc ....F...... 607 785-4865
　Endwell (G-4843)
Richlar Industries Inc ....F...... 315 463-5144
　East Syracuse (G-4574)

INSULATORS & INSULATION MATERIALS: Electrical

Alumiseal Corp ....E...... 518 329-2820
　Copake Falls (G-3914)
Gerome Technologies Inc ....D...... 518 463-1324
　Menands (G-8404)
Heat and Frost Inslatrs & Asbs ....G...... 718 784-3456
　Astoria (G-441)
J H C Fabrications Inc ....E...... 718 649-0065
　Brooklyn (G-2121)
Jpmorgan Chase Bank Nat Assn ....F...... 845 298-2461
　Wappingers Falls (G-16594)
Varflex Corporation ....C...... 315 336-4400
　Rome (G-14867)
Volt Tek Inc ....F...... 585 377-2050
　Fairport (G-4893)
Von Roll Usa Inc ....C...... 518 344-7100
　Schenectady (G-15334)

INSULATORS, PORCELAIN: Electrical

Lapp Insulators LLC ....C...... 585 768-6221
　Le Roy (G-7436)
Victor Insulators Inc ....C...... 585 924-2127
　Victor (G-16534)

INSULIN PREPARATIONS

Zinerva Pharmaceuticals LLC ....G...... 630 729-4184
　Clarence Center (G-3708)

INSURANCE CARRIERS: Life

Hrg Group Inc ....E...... 212 906-8555
　New York (G-10567)

INTEGRATED CIRCUITS, SEMICONDUCTOR NETWORKS, ETC

Akoustis Inc ....E...... 585 919-3073
　Canandaigua (G-3363)
Aljo-Gefa Precision Mfg LLC ....E...... 516 420-4419
　Old Bethpage (G-13146)
Artemis Inc ....G...... 631 232-2424
　Hauppauge (G-6044)
Globalfoundries US Inc ....F...... 408 462-3900
　Ballston Spa (G-595)
LSI Computer Systems ....G...... 631 271-0400
　Melville (G-8364)
Philips Medical Systems Mr ....B...... 518 782-1122
　Latham (G-7403)
Plures Technologies Inc ....G...... 585 905-0554
　Canandaigua (G-3385)
Pvi Solar Inc ....G...... 212 280-2100
　New York (G-11784)
Standard Microsystems Corp ....D...... 631 435-6000
　Hauppauge (G-6223)

INTERCOMMUNICATIONS SYSTEMS: Electric

Andrea Systems LLC ....E...... 631 390-3140
　Farmingdale (G-4950)
Apple Core Electronics Inc ....F...... 718 628-4068
　Brooklyn (G-1619)
AVI-Spl Employee ....B...... 212 840-4801
　New York (G-9330)
Capstream Technologies LLC ....G...... 716 945-7100
　Salamanca (G-15126)
Curbell Medical Products Inc ....F...... 716 667-2520
　Orchard Park (G-13289)
Curbell Medical Products Inc ....C...... 716 667-2520
　Orchard Park (G-13290)
Frequency Electronics Inc ....B...... 516 794-4500
　Uniondale (G-16317)
Goddard Design Co ....G...... 718 599-0170
　Brooklyn (G-2035)
Intercall Systems Inc ....E...... 516 294-4524
　Mineola (G-8548)
McDowell Research Co Inc ....D...... 315 332-7100
　Newark (G-12756)
Nu2 Systems LLC ....F...... 914 719-7272
　White Plains (G-17169)
Response Care Inc ....G...... 585 671-4144
　Webster (G-16759)
Roanwell Corporation ....E...... 718 401-0288
　Bronx (G-1440)
Simrex Corporation ....G...... 716 206-0174
　Buffalo (G-3215)
Telebyte Inc ....E...... 631 423-3232
　Hauppauge (G-6236)
Telephonics Corporation ....A...... 631 755-7000
　Farmingdale (G-5137)
Telesite USA Inc ....E...... 631 952-2288
　Hauppauge (G-6237)
TX Rx Systems Inc ....C...... 716 549-4700
　Angola (G-382)
Visiontron Corp ....E...... 631 582-8600
　Hauppauge (G-6252)

INTERIOR DECORATING SVCS

Furniture Doctor Inc ....G...... 585 657-6941
　Bloomfield (G-982)

INTERIOR DESIGN SVCS, NEC

Ann Gish Inc ....G...... 212 969-9200
　New York (G-9213)
Lulu DK LLC ....G...... 212 223-4234
　New York (G-11092)

INTERIOR DESIGNING SVCS

Exhibit Corporation America ....E...... 718 937-2600
　Long Island City (G-7763)

INTERIOR REPAIR SVCS

Auto-Mat Company Inc ....E...... 516 938-7373
　Hicksville (G-6349)

INTRAVENOUS SOLUTIONS

Mercer Milling Co ....E...... 315 701-1334
　Liverpool (G-7559)
Zenith Solutions ....G...... 718 575-8570
　Flushing (G-5316)

INVERTERS: Nonrotating Electrical

Applied Power Systems Inc ....E...... 516 935-2230
　Hicksville (G-6346)

INVERTERS: Rotating Electrical

IEC Holden Corporation ....F...... 518 213-3991
　Plattsburgh (G-13696)

INVESTMENT ADVISORY SVCS

Nsgv Inc ....E...... 212 367-3167
　New York (G-11483)
Value Line Inc ....D...... 212 907-1500
　New York (G-12520)

INVESTMENT FUNDS: Open-Ended

Altius Aviation LLC ....G...... 315 455-7555
　Syracuse (G-15873)
Kps Capital Partners LP ....E...... 212 338-5100
　New York (G-10922)

INVESTORS, NEC

Ascent Aerospace Holdings LLC ....G...... 212 916-8142
　New York (G-9279)

INVESTORS: Real Estate, Exc Property Operators

Hudson Xinde Energy Inc ....G...... 212 220-7112
　New York (G-10573)
Radio Circle Realty Inc ....E...... 914 241-8742
　Mount Kisco (G-8685)

INVESTORS: Security Speculators For Own Account

Acf Industries Holding LLC ....G...... 212 702-4363
　New York (G-9064)

IRON & STEEL PRDTS: Hot-Rolled

A-1 Iron Works Inc ....G...... 718 927-4766
　Brooklyn (G-1538)
Image Iron Works Inc ....G...... 718 592-8276
　Corona (G-4021)
N C Iron Works Inc ....G...... 718 633-4660
　Brooklyn (G-2352)
Niagara Specialty Metals Inc ....E...... 716 542-5552
　Akron (G-23)

IRON & STEEL: Corrugating, Cold-Rolled

Renco Group Inc ....G...... 212 541-6000
　New York (G-11864)

IRON ORE MINING

Essar Steel Minnesota LLC ....G...... 212 292-2600
　New York (G-10115)

IRON OXIDES

Applied Minerals Inc ....E...... 212 226-4265
　Brooklyn (G-1620)

PRODUCT SECTION

JEWELRY STORES: Precious Stones & Precious Metals

IRONING BOARDS
Garment Care Systems LLC .... G 518 674-1826
  Averill Park *(G-532)*

JANITORIAL & CUSTODIAL SVCS
New Dynamics Corporation .... E 845 692-0022
  Middletown *(G-8488)*
R H Crown Co Inc .... E 518 762-4589
  Johnstown *(G-7153)*

JANITORIAL EQPT & SPLYS WHOLESALERS
Collinite Corporation .... G 315 732-2282
  Utica *(G-16336)*
Emulso Corp .... G 716 854-2889
  Tonawanda *(G-16178)*
Nationwide Sales and Service .... F 631 491-6625
  Farmingdale *(G-5071)*

JEWELERS' FINDINGS & MATERIALS
Goldmark Inc .... E 718 438-0295
  Brooklyn *(G-2039)*
Nathan Berrie & Sons Inc .... G 516 432-8500
  Island Park *(G-6821)*
New York Findings Corp .... F 212 925-5745
  New York *(G-11422)*
Renco Manufacturing Inc .... E 718 392-8877
  Long Island City *(G-7891)*

JEWELERS' FINDINGS & MATERIALS: Castings
A J M Enterprises .... F 716 626-7294
  Buffalo *(G-2806)*
Allstar Casting Corporation .... E 212 563-0909
  New York *(G-9142)*
Ampex Casting Corporation .... F 212 719-1318
  New York *(G-9190)*
Asco Castings Inc .... G 212 719-9800
  Long Island City *(G-7703)*
Asur Jewelry Inc .... G 718 472-1687
  Long Island City *(G-7707)*
Carrera Casting Corp .... C 212 382-3296
  New York *(G-9589)*
D M J Casting Inc .... G 212 719-1951
  New York *(G-9840)*
Frank Billanti Casting Co Inc .... F 212 221-0440
  New York *(G-10250)*
Jaguar Casting Co Inc .... E 212 869-0197
  New York *(G-10734)*
Jewelry Arts Manufacturing .... E 212 382-3583
  New York *(G-10763)*
Karbra Company .... C 212 736-9300
  New York *(G-10846)*
Satco Castings Service Inc .... E 516 354-1500
  New Hyde Park *(G-8905)*

JEWELERS' FINDINGS & MATERIALS: Parts, Unassembled
Asa Manufacturing Inc .... E 718 853-3033
  Brooklyn *(G-1639)*
Kemp Metal Products Inc .... E 516 997-8860
  Westbury *(G-17029)*

JEWELERS' FINDINGS & MTLS: Jewel Prep, Instr, Tools, Watches
A J C Jewelry Contracting Inc .... G 212 594-3703
  New York *(G-9037)*
D R S Watch Materials .... E 212 819-0470
  New York *(G-9841)*
Zak Jewelry Tools Inc .... F 212 768-8122
  New York *(G-12722)*

JEWELERS' FINDINGS/MTRLS: Gem Prep, Settings, Real/Imitation
Jim Wachtler Inc .... G 212 755-4367
  New York *(G-10773)*
Nyman Jewelry Inc .... G 212 944-1976
  New York *(G-11499)*

JEWELRY & PRECIOUS STONES WHOLESALERS
Ace Diamond Corp .... G 212 730-8231
  New York *(G-9063)*
Carol Dauplaise Ltd .... E 212 997-5290
  New York *(G-9584)*
Clyde Duneier Inc .... D 212 398-1122
  New York *(G-9705)*
Dabby-Reid Ltd .... F 212 356-0040
  New York *(G-9842)*
Gemoro Inc .... G 212 768-8844
  New York *(G-10312)*
Jayden Star LLC .... E 212 686-0400
  New York *(G-10747)*
Justperfectmsp Ltd .... E 877 201-0005
  New York *(G-10827)*
Leo Schachter Diamonds LLC .... D 212 688-2000
  New York *(G-11007)*
Mark King Jewelry Inc .... G 212 921-0746
  New York *(G-11177)*
Michael Anthony Jewelers LLC .... C 914 699-0000
  Mount Vernon *(G-8751)*
Midura Jewels Inc .... G 213 265-8090
  New York *(G-11286)*
Neil Savalia Inc .... F 212 869-0123
  New York *(G-11386)*
Precision International Co Inc .... E 212 268-9090
  New York *(G-11719)*
William Goldberg Diamond Corp .... E 212 980-4343
  New York *(G-12660)*

JEWELRY APPAREL
All The Rage Inc .... G 516 605-2001
  Hicksville *(G-6344)*
Asher Jewelry Company Inc .... D 212 302-6233
  Great Neck *(G-5808)*
CJ Jewelry Inc .... F 212 719-2464
  New York *(G-9687)*
E Chabot Ltd .... E 212 575-1026
  Brooklyn *(G-1891)*
Eastern Jewelry Mfg Co Inc .... E 212 840-0001
  New York *(G-10016)*
Efron Designs Ltd .... G 718 482-8440
  Long Island City *(G-7757)*
Fam Creations .... E 212 869-4833
  New York *(G-10185)*
First Image Design Corp .... E 212 221-8282
  New York *(G-10220)*
H C Kionka & Co Inc .... F 212 227-3155
  New York *(G-10433)*
Jaguar Jewelry Casting NY Inc .... E 212 768-4848
  New York *(G-10735)*
Jayden Star LLC .... E 212 686-0400
  New York *(G-10747)*
JC Crystal Inc .... E 212 594-0858
  New York *(G-10750)*
Jean & Alex Jewelry Mfg & Cons .... F 212 935-7621
  New York *(G-10754)*
Le Hook Rouge LLC .... E 212 947-6272
  Brooklyn *(G-2201)*
Leo Schachter & Co Inc .... D 212 688-2000
  New York *(G-11006)*
Les Ateliers Tamalet .... E 929 325-7976
  New York *(G-11008)*
Love Bright Jewelry Inc .... E 516 620-2509
  Oceanside *(G-13107)*
MB Plastics Inc .... F 718 523-1180
  Greenlawn *(G-5892)*
Park West Jewelery Inc .... E 646 329-6145
  New York *(G-11588)*
R & R Grosbard Inc .... E 212 575-0077
  New York *(G-11809)*
Riva Jewelry Manufacturing Inc .... C 718 361-3100
  Brooklyn *(G-2517)*
Sterling Possessions Ltd .... E 212 594-0418
  New York *(G-12221)*
Thomas Sasson Co Inc .... E 212 697-4998
  New York *(G-12346)*
Verragio Ltd .... E 212 868-8181
  New York *(G-12547)*
Whitney Boin Studio Inc .... G 914 377-4385
  Yonkers *(G-17515)*

JEWELRY FINDINGS & LAPIDARY WORK
Alex and Ani LLC .... G 914 481-1506
  Rye *(G-15079)*
Boucheron Joaillerie USA Inc .... E 212 715-7330
  New York *(G-9494)*
Christopher Designs Inc .... E 212 382-1013
  New York *(G-9665)*
Creative Tools & Supply Inc .... G 212 279-7077
  New York *(G-9810)*
Danhier Co LLC .... F 212 563-7683
  New York *(G-9856)*
Gemini Manufactures .... F 716 633-0306
  Cheektowaga *(G-3601)*
Kaprielian Enterprises Inc .... D 212 645-6623
  New York *(G-10845)*
Leo Schachter Diamonds LLC .... D 212 688-2000
  New York *(G-11007)*
Loremi Jewelry Inc .... E 212 840-3429
  New York *(G-11071)*
Magic Novelty Co Inc .... E 212 304-2777
  New York *(G-11131)*
Mavito Fine Jewelry Ltd Inc .... F 212 398-9384
  New York *(G-11209)*
Max Kahan Inc .... F 212 575-4646
  New York *(G-11211)*
ME & Ro Inc .... G 212 431-8744
  New York *(G-11229)*
R G Flair Co Inc .... E 631 586-7311
  Bay Shore *(G-726)*
Touch Adjust Clip Co Inc .... G 631 589-3077
  Bohemia *(G-1141)*
Townley Inc .... E 212 779-0544
  New York *(G-12404)*
Via America Fine Jewelry Inc .... G 212 302-1218
  New York *(G-12560)*
Zirconia Creations Intl .... G 212 239-3730
  New York *(G-12733)*

JEWELRY FINDINGS WHOLESALERS
Cardona Industries USA Ltd .... G 516 466-5200
  Great Neck *(G-5813)*
New York Findings Corp .... F 212 925-5745
  New York *(G-11422)*

JEWELRY REPAIR SVCS
Burke & Bannayan .... G 585 723-1010
  Rochester *(G-14267)*
Carr Manufacturing Jewelers .... G 518 783-6093
  Latham *(G-7386)*
Richards & West Inc .... D 585 461-4088
  East Rochester *(G-4485)*

JEWELRY STORES
Burke & Bannayan .... G 585 723-1010
  Rochester *(G-14267)*
Carr Manufacturing Jewelers .... G 518 783-6093
  Latham *(G-7386)*
Charles Perrella Inc .... E 845 348-4777
  Nyack *(G-13063)*
Diamond Boutique .... G 516 444-3373
  Port Washington *(G-13831)*
Golden Integrity Inc .... E 212 764-6753
  New York *(G-10374)*
Henry Dunay Designs Inc .... E 212 768-9700
  New York *(G-10501)*
Iriniri Designs Ltd .... F 845 469-7934
  Sugar Loaf *(G-15824)*
Joan Boyce Ltd .... G 212 867-7474
  New York *(G-10783)*
Julius Cohen Jewelers Inc .... G 212 371-3050
  Brooklyn *(G-2159)*
Leonore Doskow Inc .... E 914 737-1335
  Cortlandt Manor *(G-4077)*
Love Bright Jewelry Inc .... E 516 620-2509
  Oceanside *(G-13107)*
Michael Anthony Jewelers LLC .... C 914 699-0000
  Mount Vernon *(G-8751)*
Mimi So International LLC .... E 212 300-8600
  New York *(G-11300)*
Neil Savalia Inc .... F 212 869-0123
  New York *(G-11386)*
Nyman Jewelry Inc .... G 212 944-1976
  New York *(G-11499)*
Royal Jewelry Mfg Inc .... E 212 302-2500
  Great Neck *(G-5853)*
Scott Kay Inc .... C 201 287-0100
  New York *(G-12025)*
Stanmark Jewelry Inc .... G 212 730-2557
  New York *(G-12207)*
Suna Bros Inc .... E 212 869-5670
  New York *(G-12257)*

JEWELRY STORES: Precious Stones & Precious Metals
Aaron Group LLC .... D 718 392-5454
  Mount Vernon *(G-8701)*
Atr Jewelry Inc .... F 212 819-0075
  New York *(G-9310)*

Employee Codes: A=Over 500 employees, B=251-500
C=101-250, D=51-100, E=20-50, F=10-19, G=5-9

2018 Harris
New York Manufacturers Directory

JEWELRY STORES: Precious Stones & Precious Metals

PRODUCT SECTION

Bourghol Brothers Inc .... G 845 268-9752
  Congers *(G-3878)*
David S Diamonds Inc .... F 212 921-8029
  New York *(G-9878)*
Harry Winston Inc .... C 212 399-1000
  New York *(G-10465)*
Hw Holdings Inc .... G 212 399-1000
  New York *(G-10581)*
Jim Wachtler Inc .... G 212 755-4367
  New York *(G-10773)*
Mellem Corporation .... F 607 723-0001
  Binghamton *(G-931)*
Midura Jewels Inc .... G 213 265-8090
  New York *(G-11286)*
Nicolo Raineri .... G 212 925-6128
  New York *(G-11447)*
O C Tanner Company .... G 914 921-2025
  Rye *(G-15091)*
Peter Atman Inc .... G 212 644-8882
  New York *(G-11650)*
Reinhold Brothers Inc .... E 212 867-8310
  New York *(G-11854)*
Richards & West Inc .... D 585 461-4088
  East Rochester *(G-4485)*
Shining Creations Inc .... G 845 358-4911
  New City *(G-8838)*

JEWELRY STORES: Silverware

Benton Announcements Inc .... F 716 836-4100
  Buffalo *(G-2861)*

JEWELRY, PREC METAL: Mountings, Pens, Lthr, Etc, Gold/Silver

Leo Ingwer Inc .... E 212 719-1342
  New York *(G-11004)*

JEWELRY, PRECIOUS METAL: Bracelets

Hammerman Bros Inc .... G 212 956-2800
  New York *(G-10445)*
Innovative Jewelry Inc .... G 718 408-8950
  Bay Shore *(G-703)*
Jacoby Enterprises LLC .... G 718 435-0289
  Brooklyn *(G-2132)*
Julius Cohen Jewelers Inc .... G 212 371-3050
  Brooklyn *(G-2159)*
Lokai Holdings LLC .... F 646 979-3474
  New York *(G-11052)*

JEWELRY, PRECIOUS METAL: Cases

Albea Cosmetics America Inc .... E 212 371-5100
  New York *(G-9124)*

JEWELRY, PRECIOUS METAL: Cigar & Cigarette Access

Cigar Oasis Inc .... G 516 520-5258
  Farmingdale *(G-4969)*

JEWELRY, PRECIOUS METAL: Earrings

Indonesian Imports Inc .... E 888 800-5899
  New York *(G-10633)*
Richline Group Inc .... E 212 643-2908
  New York *(G-11890)*
Unimax Supply Co Inc .... E 212 925-1051
  New York *(G-12476)*

JEWELRY, PRECIOUS METAL: Medals, Precious Or Semiprecious

Eagle Regalia Co Inc .... F 845 425-2245
  Spring Valley *(G-15604)*
Jacmel Jewelry Inc .... C 718 349-4300
  New York *(G-10730)*
North American Mint Inc .... G 585 654-8500
  Rochester *(G-14560)*
Sarkisians Jewelry Co .... G 212 869-1060
  New York *(G-11994)*

JEWELRY, PRECIOUS METAL: Mountings & Trimmings

Shining Creations Inc .... G 845 358-4911
  New City *(G-8838)*

JEWELRY, PRECIOUS METAL: Necklaces

Feldman Jewelry Creations Inc .... G 718 438-8895
  Brooklyn *(G-1968)*
Iridesse Inc .... F 718 230-6000
  New York *(G-10700)*

JEWELRY, PRECIOUS METAL: Pearl, Natural Or Cultured

Ashi Diamonds LLC .... E 212 319-8291
  New York *(G-9282)*
Clyde Duneier Inc .... D 212 398-1122
  New York *(G-9705)*
Dweck Industries Inc .... G 718 615-1695
  Brooklyn *(G-1885)*
Robin Stanley Inc .... G 212 871-0007
  New York *(G-11915)*

JEWELRY, PRECIOUS METAL: Pins

M H Manufacturing Incorporated .... F 212 461-6900
  New York *(G-11100)*
O C Tanner Company .... G 914 921-2025
  Rye *(G-15091)*

JEWELRY, PRECIOUS METAL: Rings, Finger

Alfred Butler Inc .... F 516 829-7460
  Great Neck *(G-5801)*
Grandeur Creations Inc .... G 212 643-1277
  New York *(G-10390)*
Hjn Inc .... F 212 398-9564
  New York *(G-10531)*
Standard Wedding Band Co .... G 516 294-0954
  Garden City *(G-5547)*

JEWELRY, PRECIOUS METAL: Rosaries/Other Sm Religious Article

Rand & Paseka Mfg Co Inc .... E 516 867-1500
  Freeport *(G-5433)*
Yofah Religious Articles Inc .... F 718 435-3288
  Brooklyn *(G-2788)*

JEWELRY, PRECIOUS METAL: Settings & Mountings

AF Design Inc .... G 347 548-5273
  New York *(G-9102)*
Gold & Diamonds Wholesale Outl .... G 718 438-7888
  Brooklyn *(G-2037)*
Golden Integrity Inc .... E 212 764-6753
  New York *(G-10374)*
Kaprielian Enterprises Inc .... F 212 645-6623
  New York *(G-10845)*
Kurt Gaum Inc .... F 212 719-2836
  New York *(G-10934)*
Mavito Fine Jewelry Ltd Inc .... F 212 398-9384
  New York *(G-11209)*
Reinhold Brothers Inc .... E 212 867-8310
  New York *(G-11854)*

JEWELRY, PRECIOUS METAL: Trimmings, Canes, Umbrellas, Etc

Houles USA Inc .... G 212 935-3900
  New York *(G-10559)*

JEWELRY, WHOLESALE

Aaron Group LLC .... D 718 392-5454
  Mount Vernon *(G-8701)*
AF Design Inc .... G 347 548-5273
  New York *(G-9102)*
American Originals Corporation .... G 212 836-4155
  New York *(G-9177)*
Anatoli Inc .... F 845 334-9000
  West Hurley *(G-16931)*
Classic Medallics Inc .... E 718 392-5410
  Mount Vernon *(G-8717)*
Crown Jewelers Intl Inc .... G 212 420-7800
  New York *(G-9816)*
Dasan Inc .... E 212 244-5410
  New York *(G-9865)*
Diana Kane Incorporated .... G 718 638-6520
  Brooklyn *(G-1858)*
E Chabot Ltd .... E 212 575-1026
  Brooklyn *(G-1891)*
Formart Corp .... F 212 819-1819
  New York *(G-10238)*
J & H Creations Inc .... E 212 465-0962
  New York *(G-10714)*
J R Gold Designs Ltd .... F 212 922-9292
  New York *(G-10722)*
Keith Lewis Studio Inc .... G 845 339-5629
  Rifton *(G-14146)*
Love Bright Jewelry Inc .... E 516 620-2509
  Oceanside *(G-13107)*
Magic Novelty Co Inc .... E 212 304-2777
  New York *(G-11131)*
Marlborough Jewels Inc .... G 718 768-2000
  Brooklyn *(G-2274)*
Mgd Brands Inc .... E 516 545-0150
  Plainview *(G-13648)*
Michael Bondanza Inc .... E 212 869-0043
  New York *(G-11276)*
Mimi So International LLC .... E 212 300-8600
  New York *(G-11300)*
Mwsi Inc .... G 914 347-4200
  Hawthorne *(G-6275)*
Pesselnik & Cohen Inc .... G 212 925-0287
  New York *(G-11648)*
Q Ed Creations .... G 212 391-1155
  New York *(G-11787)*
R M Reynolds .... G 315 789-7365
  Geneva *(G-5596)*
Richline Group Inc .... C 212 764-8454
  New York *(G-11891)*
Royal Jewelry Mfg Inc .... E 212 302-2500
  Great Neck *(G-5853)*
Select Jewelry Inc .... D 718 784-3626
  Long Island City *(G-7903)*
Shah Diamonds Inc .... F 212 888-9393
  New York *(G-12059)*
Shanu Gems Inc .... F 212 921-4470
  New York *(G-12063)*
Sterling Possessions Ltd .... G 212 594-0418
  New York *(G-12221)*
UNI Jewelry Inc .... G 212 398-1818
  New York *(G-12468)*

JEWELRY: Decorative, Fashion & Costume

Alexis Bittar LLC .... C 718 422-7580
  Brooklyn *(G-1581)*
Allure Jewelry and ACC LLC .... E 646 226-8057
  New York *(G-9143)*
Anatoli Inc .... F 845 334-9000
  West Hurley *(G-16931)*
Beth Ward Studios LLC .... F 646 922-7575
  New York *(G-9424)*
Bnns Co Inc .... G 212 302-1844
  New York *(G-9481)*
Carvin French Jewelers Inc .... E 212 755-6474
  New York *(G-9592)*
Columbus Trading Corp .... F 212 564-1780
  New York *(G-9741)*
Designs On Fifth Ltd .... G 212 921-4162
  New York *(G-9910)*
Ema Jewelry Inc .... D 212 575-8989
  New York *(G-10070)*
Eu Design LLC .... G 212 420-7788
  New York *(G-10135)*
Five Star Creations Inc .... G 845 783-1187
  Monroe *(G-8589)*
Formart Corp .... F 212 819-1819
  New York *(G-10238)*
Greenbeads Llc .... G 212 327-2765
  New York *(G-10402)*
Grinnell Designs Ltd .... E 212 391-5277
  New York *(G-10408)*
Holbrooke Inc .... G 646 397-4674
  New York *(G-10538)*
I Love Accessories Inc .... G 212 239-1875
  New York *(G-10585)*
International Inspirations Ltd .... E 212 465-8500
  New York *(G-10677)*
J J Creations Inc .... E 718 392-2828
  Long Island City *(G-7796)*
Jewelry Arts Manufacturing .... E 212 382-3583
  New York *(G-10763)*
Jill Fagin Enterprises Inc .... G 212 674-9383
  New York *(G-10771)*
K2 International Corp .... G 212 947-1734
  New York *(G-10834)*
Krainz Creations Inc .... E 212 583-1555
  New York *(G-10923)*
Leonore Doskow Inc .... E 914 737-1335
  Cortlandt Manor *(G-4077)*
Masterpiece Diamonds LLC .... F 212 986-1515
  New York *(G-11198)*

Mataci Inc D 212 502-1899
New York *(G-11201)*
Maurice Max Inc E 212 334-6573
New York *(G-11206)*
Nes Jewelry Inc D 212 502-0025
New York *(G-11392)*
Noir Jewelry LLC G 212 465-8500
New York *(G-11468)*
Orion Fashions Holdings LLC E 212 764-3332
New York *(G-11539)*
Pearl Erwin Inc E 212 889-7410
New York *(G-11605)*
Pearl Erwin Inc E 212 883-0650
New York *(G-11606)*
Pepe Creations Inc F 212 391-1514
New York *(G-11629)*
Pincharming Inc F 516 663-5115
Garden City *(G-5539)*
Reino Manufacturing Co Inc F 914 636-8990
New Rochelle *(G-8968)*
Rush Gold Manufacturing Ltd D 516 781-3155
Bellmore *(G-816)*
Sanoy Inc E 212 695-6384
New York *(G-11987)*
Sarina Accessories LLC F 212 239-8106
New York *(G-11993)*
Shira Accessories Ltd F 212 594-4455
New York *(G-12075)*
Swarovski North America Ltd G 914 423-4132
Yonkers *(G-17505)*
Swarovski North America Ltd G 212 695-1502
New York *(G-12272)*
Talbots Inc G 914 328-1034
White Plains *(G-17201)*
Toho Shoji (new York) Inc F 212 868-7466
New York *(G-12377)*
Tycoon International Inc G 212 563-7107
New York *(G-12454)*
Vetta Jewelry Inc E 212 564-8250
New York *(G-12556)*
Yacoubian Jewelers Inc E 212 302-6729
New York *(G-12708)*
Ziva Gem LLC F 646 416-5828
New York *(G-12735)*

JEWELRY: Precious Metal

A & V Castings Inc G 212 997-0042
New York *(G-9029)*
A Jaffe Inc C 212 843-7464
New York *(G-9038)*
Aaron Group LLC D 718 392-5454
Mount Vernon *(G-8701)*
Abraham Jwly Designers & Mfrs F 212 944-1149
New York *(G-9052)*
Abrimian Bros Corp F 212 382-1106
New York *(G-9053)*
Adamor Inc G 212 688-8885
New York *(G-9072)*
Alart Inc G 212 840-1508
New York *(G-9122)*
Alchemy Simya Inc E 646 230-1122
New York *(G-9126)*
Alex Sepkus Inc F 212 391-8466
New York *(G-9131)*
Alexander Primak Jewelry Inc D 212 398-0287
New York *(G-9132)*
Almond Jewelers Inc F 516 933-6000
Port Washington *(G-13821)*
Alpine Creations Ltd G 212 308-9353
New York *(G-9154)*
Ambras Fine Jewelry Inc E 718 784-5252
Long Island City *(G-7688)*
American Craft Jewelers Inc G 718 972-0945
Brooklyn *(G-1598)*
American Originals Corporation G 212 836-4155
New York *(G-9177)*
Anatoli Inc F 845 334-9000
West Hurley *(G-16931)*
Ancient Modern Art LLC F 212 302-0080
New York *(G-9199)*
Anima Group LLC G 917 913-2053
New York *(G-9211)*
Apicella Jewelers Inc E 212 840-2024
New York *(G-9224)*
AR & AR Jewelry Inc E 212 764-7916
New York *(G-9237)*
Arringement International Inc G 347 323-7974
Flushing *(G-5234)*
Art-TEC Jewelry Designs Ltd E 212 719-2941
New York *(G-9266)*
Ateret LLC G 212 819-0777
New York *(G-9298)*
Atlantic Precious Metal Cast G 718 937-7100
Long Island City *(G-7708)*
Atr Jewelry Inc F 212 819-0075
New York *(G-9310)*
B K Jewelry Contractor Inc E 212 398-9093
New York *(G-9342)*
Barber Brothers Jewelry Mfg F 212 819-0666
New York *(G-9368)*
Baroka Creations Inc G 212 768-0527
New York *(G-9374)*
Bartholomew Mazza Ltd Inc E 212 935-4530
New York *(G-9378)*
Bellataire Diamonds Inc F 212 687-8881
New York *(G-9398)*
Benlee Enterprises LLC F 212 730-7330
Long Island City *(G-7714)*
BH Multi Com Corp E 212 944-0020
New York *(G-9434)*
Bielka Inc G 212 980-6841
New York *(G-9439)*
Billanti Casting Co Inc E 516 775-4800
New Hyde Park *(G-8864)*
BJG Services LLC E 516 592-5692
New York *(G-9459)*
Bourghol Brothers Inc G 845 268-9752
Congers *(G-3878)*
Bral Nader Fine Jewelry Inc G 800 493-1222
New York *(G-9503)*
Brannkey Inc D 212 371-1515
New York *(G-9504)*
Brilliant Jewelers/Mjj Inc C 212 353-2326
New York *(G-9514)*
Bristol Seamless Ring Corp F 212 874-2645
New York *(G-9515)*
Burke & Bannayan G 585 723-1010
Rochester *(G-14267)*
Carlo Monte Designs Inc G 212 935-5611
New York *(G-9581)*
Carol Dauplaise Ltd E 212 997-5290
New York *(G-9584)*
Carr Manufacturing Jewelers G 518 783-6093
Latham *(G-7386)*
Carvin French Jewelers Inc E 212 755-6474
New York *(G-9592)*
Chaindom Enterprises Inc G 212 719-4778
New York *(G-9626)*
Chameleon Gems Inc F 516 829-3333
Great Neck *(G-5814)*
Charis & Mae Inc G 212 641-0816
New York *(G-9631)*
Charles Perrella Inc E 845 348-4777
Nyack *(G-13063)*
Charles Vaillant Inc G 212 752-4832
New York *(G-9634)*
Christopher Designs Inc E 212 382-1013
New York *(G-9665)*
Concord Jewelry Mfg Co LLC E 212 719-4030
New York *(G-9755)*
Creative Gold LLC E 718 686-2225
Brooklyn *(G-1813)*
Crescent Wedding Rings Inc G 212 869-8296
New York *(G-9813)*
Crown Jewelers Intl Inc G 212 420-7800
New York *(G-9816)*
Csi International Inc E 800 441-2895
Niagara Falls *(G-12831)*
D Oro Onofrio Inc G 718 491-2961
Brooklyn *(G-1831)*
Dasan Inc E 212 244-5410
New York *(G-9865)*
David Friedman Chain Co Inc F 212 684-1760
New York *(G-9874)*
David Howell Product Design E 914 666-4080
Bedford Hills *(G-798)*
David S Diamonds Inc F 212 921-8029
New York *(G-9878)*
David Weisz & Sons Inc G 212 840-4747
New York *(G-9881)*
David Yurman Enterprises LLC G 914 539-4444
White Plains *(G-17127)*
David Yurman Enterprises LLC B 212 896-1550
New York *(G-9882)*
David Yurman Enterprises LLC G 516 627-1700
Manhasset *(G-8090)*
David Yurman Enterprises LLC G 845 928-8660
Central Valley *(G-3550)*
David Yurman Retail LLC G 877 226-1400
New York *(G-9883)*
Diamond Distributors Inc G 212 921-9188
New York *(G-9925)*
Diana Kane Incorporated G 718 638-6520
Brooklyn *(G-1858)*
Dimoda Designs Inc E 212 355-8166
New York *(G-9932)*
Donna Distefano Ltd G 212 594-3757
New York *(G-9950)*
Doris Panos Designs Ltd G 631 245-0580
Melville *(G-8342)*
Duran Jewelry Inc G 212 431-1959
New York *(G-9990)*
E M G Creations Inc F 212 643-0960
New York *(G-10002)*
Earring King Jewelry Mfg Inc G 718 544-7947
New York *(G-10013)*
Echo Group Inc F 917 608-7440
New York *(G-10028)*
Eclipse Collection Jewelers F 212 764-6883
New York *(G-10030)*
Ed Levin Inc E 518 677-8595
Cambridge *(G-3336)*
Elegant Jewelers Mfg Co Inc F 212 869-4951
New York *(G-10052)*
Ema Jewelry Inc D 212 575-8989
New York *(G-10070)*
Emsaru USA Corp G 212 459-9355
New York *(G-10076)*
Eshel Jewelry Mfg Co Inc F 212 588-8800
New York *(G-10112)*
Eternal Line G 845 856-1999
Sparrow Bush *(G-15586)*
Euro Bands Inc F 212 719-9777
New York *(G-10137)*
F M Abdulky Inc F 607 272-7373
Ithaca *(G-6875)*
F M Abdulky Inc G 607 272-7373
Ithaca *(G-6876)*
Fantasia Jewelry Inc E 212 921-9590
New York *(G-10189)*
Five Star Creations Inc E 845 783-1187
Monroe *(G-8589)*
Frank Blancato Inc F 212 768-1495
New York *(G-10251)*
Gem Mine Corp G 516 367-1075
Woodbury *(G-17309)*
Gem-Bar Setting Inc G 212 869-9238
New York *(G-10310)*
Gemoro Inc G 212 768-8844
New York *(G-10312)*
Gemveto Jewelry Company Inc E 212 755-2522
New York *(G-10314)*
George Lederman Inc G 212 753-4556
New York *(G-10327)*
Giovane Ltd E 212 332-7373
New York *(G-10340)*
Global Gem Corporation G 212 350-9936
New York *(G-10358)*
Goldarama Company Inc G 212 730-7299
New York *(G-10370)*
Goldmark Products Inc E 631 777-3343
Farmingdale *(G-5008)*
Gorga Fehren Fine Jewelry LLC G 646 861-3595
New York *(G-10379)*
Gottlieb & Sons Inc E 212 575-1907
New York *(G-10382)*
Gramercy Jewelry Mfg Corp E 212 268-0461
New York *(G-10387)*
Guild Diamond Products Inc F 212 871-0007
New York *(G-10424)*
Gumuchian Fils Ltd F 212 593-3118
New York *(G-10427)*
H & T Goldman Corporation G 800 822-0272
New York *(G-10431)*
Hanna Altinis Co Inc E 718 706-1134
Long Island City *(G-7785)*
Hansa Usa LLC E 646 412-6407
New York *(G-10454)*
Harry Winston Inc C 212 399-1000
New York *(G-10465)*
Haskell Jewels Ltd E 212 764-3332
New York *(G-10471)*
Henry Design Studios Inc G 516 801-2760
Locust Valley *(G-7662)*
Henry Dunay Designs Inc E 212 768-9700
New York *(G-10501)*
Horo Creations LLC G 212 719-4818
New York *(G-10551)*
Hw Holdings Inc G 212 399-1000
New York *(G-10581)*

Employee Codes: A=Over 500 employees, B=251-500
C=101-250, D=51-100, E=20-50, F=10-19, G=5-9
2018 Harris
New York Manufacturers Directory
1241

JEWELRY: Precious Metal

Company	Section	Phone
Hy Gold Jewelers Inc, New York *(G-10582)*	G	212 744-3202
Ilico Jewelry Inc, Great Neck *(G-5831)*	G	516 482-0201
Imena Jewelry Manufacturer Inc, New York *(G-10617)*	F	212 827-0073
Incon Gems Inc, New York *(G-10626)*	F	212 221-8560
Inori Jewels, New York *(G-10649)*	F	347 703-5078
Intentions Jewelry Co LLC, Lagrangeville *(G-7279)*	G	845 226-4650
Iradj Moini Couture Ltd, New York *(G-10698)*	F	212 594-9242
Iriniri Designs Ltd, Sugar Loaf *(G-15824)*	F	845 469-7934
J H Jewelry Co Inc, New York *(G-10719)*	F	212 239-1330
J J Creations Inc, Long Island City *(G-7796)*	E	718 392-2828
J R Gold Designs Ltd, New York *(G-10722)*	F	212 922-9292
Jacobs & Cohen Inc, New York *(G-10732)*	E	212 714-2702
Jaguar Casting Co Inc, New York *(G-10734)*	E	212 869-0197
Jane Bohan Inc, New York *(G-10739)*	G	212 529-6090
Jasani Designs Usa Inc, New York *(G-10743)*	F	212 257-6465
Jay Strongwater Holdings LLC, New York *(G-10745)*	A	646 657-0558
Jay-Aimee Designs Inc, Hicksville *(G-6384)*	C	718 609-0333
Jeff Cooper Inc, Carle Place *(G-3417)*	F	516 333-8200
Jewelmak Inc, New York *(G-10762)*	E	212 398-2999
Jewelry Arts Manufacturing, New York *(G-10763)*	E	212 382-3583
Jewels By Star Ltd, New York *(G-10764)*	E	212 308-3490
Jeweltex Mfg Corp, New York *(G-10765)*	F	212 921-8188
Jimmy Crystal New York Co Ltd, New York *(G-10775)*	E	212 594-0858
JK Jewelry Inc, Rochester *(G-14483)*	D	585 292-0770
JK Manufacturing Inc, Locust Valley *(G-7663)*	G	212 683-3535
Joan Boyce Ltd, New York *(G-10783)*	G	212 867-7474
Jordan Scott Designs Ltd, New York *(G-10801)*	E	212 947-4250
Jotaly Inc, New York *(G-10808)*	A	212 886-6000
Justin Ashley Designs Inc, Long Island City *(G-7803)*	G	718 707-0200
Justperfectmsp Ltd, New York *(G-10827)*	E	877 201-0005
Justyna Kaminska NY Inc, New York *(G-10828)*	G	917 423-5527
Karbra Company, New York *(G-10846)*	C	212 736-9300
Keith Lewis Studio Inc, Rifton *(G-14146)*	G	845 339-5629
Krasner Group Inc, New York *(G-10925)*	G	212 268-4100
La Fina Design Inc, New York *(G-10946)*	G	212 689-6725
Lali Jewelry Inc, New York *(G-10957)*	G	212 944-2277
Le Paveh Ltd, New York *(G-10979)*	F	212 736-6110
Le Roi Inc, Fulton *(G-5482)*	F	315 342-3681
Le Vian Corp, Great Neck *(G-5837)*	D	516 466-7200
Le Vian Corp, New York *(G-10980)*	E	516 466-7200
Leser Enterprises Ltd, New York *(G-11009)*	F	212 644-8921
Lindsay-Hoenig Ltd, New York *(G-11030)*	G	212 575-9711
Loremi Jewelry Inc, New York *(G-11071)*	E	212 840-3429
Louis Tamis & Sons Inc, New York *(G-11078)*	E	212 684-1760
M & S Quality Co Ltd, New York *(G-11097)*	F	212 302-8757
M A R A Metals Ltd, Long Island City *(G-7826)*	G	718 786-7868
M Heskia Company Inc, New York *(G-11101)*	G	212 768-1845
Magnum Creation Inc, New York *(G-11136)*	F	212 642-0993
Manny Grunberg Inc, New York *(G-11162)*	E	212 302-6173
Marco Moore Inc, Great Neck *(G-5839)*	D	212 575-2090
Marina Jewelry Co Inc, New York *(G-11175)*	G	212 354-5027
Mark King Jewelry Inc, New York *(G-11177)*	G	212 921-0746
Mark Robinson Inc, New York *(G-11180)*	G	212 223-3515
Markowitz Jewelry Co Inc, Monroe *(G-8596)*	E	845 774-1175
Marlborough Jewels Inc, Brooklyn *(G-2274)*	G	718 768-2000
Martin Flyer Incorporated, New York *(G-11191)*	G	212 840-8899
Master Craft Jewelry Co Inc, Lynbrook *(G-7981)*	D	516 599-1012
Masterpiece Color LLC, New York *(G-11197)*	G	917 279-6056
Maxine Denker Inc, Staten Island *(G-15725)*	G	212 689-1440
ME & Ro Inc, New York *(G-11229)*	G	212 431-8744
Mellem Corporation, Binghamton *(G-931)*	F	607 723-0001
Mer Gems Corp, New York *(G-11252)*	G	212 714-9129
Mgd Brands Inc, Plainview *(G-13648)*	G	516 545-0150
Michael Anthony Jewelers LLC, Mount Vernon *(G-8751)*	C	914 699-0000
Michael Bondanza Inc, New York *(G-11276)*	E	212 869-0043
Midura Jewels Inc, New York *(G-11286)*	G	213 265-8090
Milla Global Inc, Brooklyn *(G-2319)*	G	516 488-3601
Mimi So International LLC, New York *(G-11300)*	E	212 300-8600
Min Ho Designs Inc, New York *(G-11301)*	G	212 838-3667
MJM Jewelry Corp, New York *(G-11311)*	G	212 354-5014
MJM Jewelry Corp, Brooklyn *(G-2330)*	D	718 596-1600
Monelle Jewelry, New York *(G-11325)*	G	212 977-9535
Mwsi Inc, Hawthorne *(G-6275)*	D	914 347-4200
N Y Bijoux Corp, New York *(G-11360)*	G	212 244-9585
Neil Savalia Inc, New York *(G-11386)*	F	212 869-0123
Nicolo Raineri, New York *(G-11447)*	E	212 925-6128
NP Roniet Creations Inc, New York *(G-11482)*	G	212 302-1847
Oscar Heyman & Bros Inc, New York *(G-11543)*	E	212 593-0400
Osnat Gad Inc, New York *(G-11544)*	G	212 957-0535
Overnight Mountings Inc, New Hyde Park *(G-8900)*	D	516 865-3000
Paragon Corporation, Port Washington *(G-13872)*	F	516 484-6090
Patuga LLC, Williamsville *(G-17276)*	G	716 204-7220
Pearl Erwin Inc, New York *(G-11605)*	E	212 889-7410
Pesselnik & Cohen Inc, New York *(G-11648)*	G	212 925-0287
Peter Atman Inc, New York *(G-11650)*	F	212 644-8882
PHC Restoration Holdings LLC, New York *(G-11665)*	F	212 643-0517
Photograve Corporation, Staten Island *(G-15741)*	E	718 667-4825
Pink Box Accessories LLC, Brooklyn *(G-2435)*	G	716 777-4477
Pronto Jewelry Inc, New York *(G-11756)*	E	212 719-9455
Punch Fashions LLC, New York *(G-11773)*	G	646 519-7333
Q Ed Creations, New York *(G-11787)*	G	212 391-1155
R Klein Jewelry Co Inc, Massapequa *(G-8214)*	D	516 482-3260
R M Reynolds, Geneva *(G-5596)*	G	315 789-7365
Regal Jewelry Inc, New York *(G-11852)*	G	212 382-1695
Renaissance Bijou Ltd, New York *(G-11862)*	G	212 869-1969
Richards & West Inc, East Rochester *(G-4485)*	D	585 461-4088
Richline Group Inc, New York *(G-11891)*	C	212 764-8454
Richline Group Inc, New York *(G-11892)*	C	914 699-0000
Robert Bartholomew Ltd, Port Washington *(G-13876)*	E	516 767-2970
Roberto Coin Inc, New York *(G-11912)*	F	212 486-4545
Royal Jewelry Mfg Inc, Great Neck *(G-5853)*	E	212 302-2500
Royal Miracle Corp, New York *(G-11943)*	E	212 921-5797
Rubinstein Jewelry Mfg Co, Long Island City *(G-7897)*	F	718 784-8650
Rudolf Friedman Inc, New York *(G-11952)*	F	212 869-5070
Rumson Acquisition LLC, New York *(G-11954)*	F	718 349-4300
Ryan Gems Inc, New York *(G-11958)*	E	212 697-0149
S & M Ring Corp, Hewlett *(G-6336)*	F	212 382-0900
S Kashi & Sons Inc, Great Neck *(G-5854)*	F	212 869-9393
S Scharf Inc, Massapequa *(G-8215)*	F	516 541-9552
Samuel B Collection Inc, Great Neck *(G-5855)*	G	516 466-1826
Sanoy Inc, New York *(G-11987)*	E	212 695-6384
Satco Castings Service Inc, New Hyde Park *(G-8905)*	E	516 354-1500
Satellite Incorporated, New York *(G-11996)*	G	212 221-6687
Scott Kay Inc, New York *(G-12025)*	C	201 287-0100
Select Jewelry Inc, Long Island City *(G-7903)*	D	718 784-3626
Shah Diamonds Inc, New York *(G-12059)*	F	212 888-9393
Shanu Gems Inc, New York *(G-12063)*	F	212 921-4470
Sharodine Inc, Port Washington *(G-13883)*	G	516 767-3548
Shiro Limited, New York *(G-12076)*	G	212 780-0007
Simco Manufacturing Jewelers, New York *(G-12098)*	F	212 575-8390
Simka Diamond Corp, New York *(G-12100)*	F	212 921-4420
Somerset Manufacturers Inc, Roslyn Heights *(G-15057)*	E	516 626-3832
Spark Creations Inc, New York *(G-12172)*	F	212 575-8385
Stanley Creations Inc, Long Island City *(G-7913)*	C	718 361-6100
Stanmark Jewelry Inc, New York *(G-12207)*	G	212 730-2557
Stone House Associates Inc, New York *(G-12230)*	G	212 221-7447
Sulphur Creations Inc, New York *(G-12251)*	G	212 719-2223
Sumer Gold Ltd, New York *(G-12253)*	G	212 354-8677
Suna Bros Inc, New York *(G-12257)*	E	212 869-5670
Sunrise Jewelers of NY Inc, Massapequa *(G-8216)*	G	516 541-1302
Tambetti Inc, New York *(G-12299)*	G	212 751-9584
Tamsen Z LLC, New York *(G-12300)*	G	212 292-6412
Tanagro Jewelry Corp, New York *(G-12301)*	F	212 753-2817
Technical Service Industries, Jamaica *(G-6992)*	E	212 719-9800
Teena Creations Inc, Freeport *(G-5440)*	G	516 867-1500

PRODUCT SECTION

Temple St Clair LLC .... E 212 219-8664
　New York *(G-12321)*
Tiga Holdings Inc .... E 845 838-3000
　Beacon *(G-786)*
Trianon Collection Inc .... E 212 921-9450
　New York *(G-12424)*
Ultra Fine Jewelry Mfg .... E 516 349-2848
　Plainview *(G-13667)*
UNI Jewelry Inc .... G 212 398-1818
　New York *(G-12468)*
Unique Designs Inc .... F 212 575-7701
　New York *(G-12480)*
United Brothers Jewelry Inc .... E 212 921-2558
　New York *(G-12483)*
Valentin & Kalich Jwly Mfg Ltd .... E 212 575-9044
　New York *(G-12516)*
Valentine Jewelry Mfg Co Inc .... E 212 382-0606
　New York *(G-12517)*
Variety Gem Co Inc .... F 212 921-1820
　Great Neck *(G-5867)*
Viktor Gold Enterprise Corp .... G 212 768-8885
　New York *(G-12568)*
Von Musulin Patricia .... G 212 206-8345
　New York *(G-12593)*
W & B Mazza & Sons Inc .... E 516 379-4130
　North Baldwin *(G-12930)*
Walter Edbril Inc .... E 212 532-3253
　New York *(G-12612)*
Weisco Inc .... F 212 575-8989
　New York *(G-12633)*
William Goldberg Diamond Corp .... E 212 980-4343
　New York *(G-12660)*
Xomox Jewelry Inc .... G 212 944-8428
　New York *(G-12706)*
Yurman Retail Inc 888 398-7626
　New York *(G-12720)*
Zeeba Jewelry Mfg Inc .... G 212 997-1009
　New York *(G-12728)*
Zelman & Friedman Jwly Mfg Co .... E 718 349-3400
　Long Island City *(G-7960)*

JIGS & FIXTURES

Amsco Inc .... F 716 823-4213
　Buffalo *(G-2829)*
Knise & Krick Inc .... E 315 422-3516
　Syracuse *(G-15995)*
Manhasset Tool & Die Co Inc .... F 716 684-6066
　Lancaster *(G-7349)*
Prime Tool & Die LLC .... G 607 334-5435
　Norwich *(G-13054)*

JOB PRINTING & NEWSPAPER PUBLISHING COMBINED

Adirondack Publishing Co Inc .... E 518 891-2600
　Saranac Lake *(G-15162)*
Albion-Holley Pennysaver Inc .... E 585 589-5641
　Albion *(G-164)*
Empire State Weeklies Inc .... E 585 671-1533
　Webster *(G-16747)*
Mexico Independent Inc .... E 315 963-3763
　Watertown *(G-16687)*
Thousand Islands Printing Co .... G 315 482-2581
　Alexandria Bay *(G-194)*

JOB TRAINING & VOCATIONAL REHABILITATION SVCS

Avcom of Virginia Inc .... D 585 924-4560
　Victor *(G-16485)*
Chemung Cnty Chpter Nysarc Inc .... C 607 734-6151
　Elmira *(G-4688)*

JOINTS: Ball Except aircraft & Auto

Advanced Thermal Systems Inc .... E 716 681-1800
　Lancaster *(G-7322)*
York Industries Inc .... E 516 746-3736
　Garden City Park *(G-5559)*

JOINTS: Expansion

Adsco Manufacturing Corp .... D 716 827-5450
　Buffalo *(G-2816)*
Mageba USA LLC .... E 212 317-1991
　New York *(G-11126)*
Mount Vernon Iron Works Inc .... G 914 668-7064
　Mount Vernon *(G-8754)*
Vulcraft of New York Inc .... C 607 529-9000
　Chemung *(G-3622)*

Watson Bowman Acme Corp .... D 716 691-8162
　Amherst *(G-271)*

JOINTS: Expansion, Pipe

Advanced Thermal Systems Inc .... E 716 681-1800
　Lancaster *(G-7322)*

KEYBOARDS: Computer Or Office Machine

Wey Inc .... G 212 532-3299
　New York *(G-12648)*

KEYS, KEY BLANKS

International Key Supply LLC .... F 631 983-6096
　Farmingdale *(G-5020)*

KILNS

Vent-A-Kiln Corporation .... G 716 876-2023
　Buffalo *(G-3266)*

KITCHEN CABINET STORES, EXC CUSTOM

Carefree Kitchens Inc .... G 631 567-2120
　Holbrook *(G-6464)*
Creative Cabinet Corp America .... E 631 751-5768
　Stony Brook *(G-15790)*
Custom Design Kitchens Inc .... F 518 355-4446
　Duanesburg *(G-4350)*
Joseph Fedele .... G 718 448-3658
　Staten Island *(G-15716)*
Michael P Mmarr .... G 315 623-9380
　Constantia *(G-3907)*
Mind Designs Inc .... G 631 563-3644
　Farmingville *(G-5168)*
S & K Counter Tops Inc .... G 716 662-7986
　Orchard Park *(G-13321)*
Serway Bros Inc .... E 315 337-0601
　Rome *(G-14864)*

KITCHEN CABINETS WHOLESALERS

Capital Kit Cab & Door Mfrs .... G 718 886-0303
　College Point *(G-3805)*
Carefree Kitchens Inc .... G 631 567-2120
　Holbrook *(G-6464)*
Central Kitchen Corp .... F 631 283-1029
　Southampton *(G-15564)*
Creative Cabinet Corp America .... E 631 751-5768
　Stony Brook *(G-15790)*
Custom Design Kitchens Inc .... F 518 355-4446
　Duanesburg *(G-4350)*
Dak Mica and Wood Products .... G 631 467-0749
　Ronkonkoma *(G-14920)*
Deer Pk Stair Bldg Mllwk Inc .... E 631 363-5000
　Blue Point *(G-993)*
Di Fiore and Sons Custom Wdwkg .... G 718 278-1663
　Long Island City *(G-7744)*
Eurocraft Custom Furniture .... G 718 956-0600
　Long Island City *(G-7761)*
Hennig Custom Woodwork Corp .... G 516 536-3460
　Oceanside *(G-13101)*
Johnny Mica Inc .... G 631 225-5213
　Lindenhurst *(G-7488)*
Joseph Fedele .... G 718 448-3658
　Staten Island *(G-15716)*
M & C Furniture .... G 718 422-2136
　Brooklyn *(G-2244)*
Mega Cabinets Inc .... E 631 789-4112
　Amityville *(G-311)*
Metro Kitchens Corp .... F 718 434-1166
　Brooklyn *(G-2310)*
Sherry-Mica Products Inc .... G 631 471-7513
　Ronkonkoma *(G-15009)*
Triad Counter Corp .... E 631 750-0615
　Bohemia *(G-1143)*

KITCHEN UTENSILS: Bakers' Eqpt, Wood

Charles Freihofer Baking Co .... G 518 463-2221
　Albany *(G-62)*
Unisource Food Eqp Systems Inc .... G 516 681-0537
　Holbrook *(G-6506)*

KITCHEN UTENSILS: Food Handling & Processing Prdts, Wood

Channel Manufacturing Inc .... E 516 944-6271
　Port Washington *(G-13827)*

KITCHEN UTENSILS: Wooden

Abbott Industries Inc .... E 718 291-0800
　Jamaica *(G-6926)*
Catskill Craftsmen Inc .... D 607 652-7321
　Stamford *(G-15644)*
Imperial Frames & Albums LLC .... G 718 832-9793
　Brooklyn *(G-2095)*
Thomas Matthews Wdwkg Ltd .... F 631 287-3657
　Southampton *(G-15578)*
Thomas Matthews Wdwkg Ltd .... F 631 287-2023
　Southampton *(G-15579)*

KITCHENWARE STORES

Lalique North America Inc .... E 212 355-6550
　New York *(G-10958)*
Lifetime Brands Inc .... B 516 683-6000
　Garden City *(G-5526)*
Nash Metalware Co Inc .... G 315 339-5794
　Rome *(G-14851)*
Roger & Sons Inc .... E 212 226-4734
　New York *(G-11927)*

KITCHENWARE: Plastic

L K Manufacturing Corp .... G 631 243-6910
　West Babylon *(G-16834)*
Mystic Apparel LLC .... E 212 279-2466
　New York *(G-11357)*

KNIT GOODS, WHOLESALE

A & B Finishing Inc .... E 718 522-4702
　Brooklyn *(G-1524)*
North Star Knitting Mills Inc .... G 718 894-4848
　Glendale *(G-5675)*
Premier Knits Ltd .... F 718 323-8264
　Ozone Park *(G-13410)*

KNIT OUTERWEAR DYEING & FINISHING, EXC HOSIERY & GLOVE

Grand Processing Inc .... E 718 388-0600
　Brooklyn *(G-2049)*

KNIVES: Agricultural Or indl

Lancaster Knives Inc .... E 716 683-5050
　Lancaster *(G-7347)*
Woods Knife Corporation .... E 516 798-4972
　Massapequa *(G-8217)*

LABELS: Cotton, Printed

Paxar Corporation .... E 845 398-3229
　Orangeburg *(G-13260)*
Sml USA Inc .... E 212 736-8800
　New York *(G-12135)*

LABELS: Paper, Made From Purchased Materials

Accent Label & Tag Co Inc .... G 631 244-7066
　Ronkonkoma *(G-14875)*
Apexx Omni-Graphics Inc .... D 718 326-3330
　Maspeth *(G-8147)*
Master Image Printing Inc .... G 914 347-4400
　Elmsford *(G-4772)*
Precision Label Corporation .... F 631 270-4490
　Farmingdale *(G-5097)*
Quadra Flex Corp .... G 607 758-7066
　Cortland *(G-4065)*
Quality Circle Products Inc .... D 914 736-6600
　Montrose *(G-8653)*
Stoney Croft Converters Inc .... F 718 608-9800
　Staten Island *(G-15764)*
Tri-Flex Label Corp .... E 631 293-0411
　Farmingdale *(G-5143)*

LABELS: Woven

Colonial Tag & Label Co Inc .... F 516 482-0508
　Great Neck *(G-5816)*
Imperial-Harvard Label Co .... F 212 736-8420
　New York *(G-10620)*
Itc Mfg Group Inc .... F 212 684-3696
　New York *(G-10711)*
Label Source Inc .... G 212 244-1403
　New York *(G-10948)*
Labels Inter-Global Inc .... F 212 398-0006
　New York *(G-10949)*

Employee Codes: A=Over 500 employees, B=251-500
C=101-250, D=51-100, E=20-50, F=10-19, G=5-9

LABELS: Woven — PRODUCT SECTION

R-Pac International Corp .... E 212 465-1818
New York *(G-11810)*
Sml USA Inc .... E 212 736-8800
New York *(G-12135)*
Triangle Label Tag Inc .... G 718 875-3030
Brooklyn *(G-2697)*

LABORATORIES, TESTING: Forensic

Siemens Hlthcare Dgnostics Inc .... E 914 631-0475
Tarrytown *(G-16130)*

LABORATORIES, TESTING: Pollution

Amincor Inc .... C 347 821-3452
New York *(G-9186)*

LABORATORIES, TESTING: Product Testing, Safety/Performance

Custom Sports Lab Inc .... G 212 832-1648
New York *(G-9828)*

LABORATORIES: Biological Research

Advance Biofactures Corp .... E 516 593-7000
Lynbrook *(G-7972)*
Cleveland Biolabs Inc .... E 716 849-6810
Buffalo *(G-2896)*
Neurotrope Inc 973 242-0005
New York *(G-11399)*
Synergy Pharmaceuticals Inc .... G 212 227-8611
New York *(G-12283)*

LABORATORIES: Biotechnology

Acorda Therapeutics Inc .... C 914 347-4300
Ardsley *(G-402)*
Albany Molecular Research Inc .... B 518 512-2000
Albany *(G-39)*
Collaborative Laboratories .... D 631 689-0200
East Setauket *(G-4498)*

LABORATORIES: Commercial Nonphysical Research

Ubm Inc .... A 212 600-3000
New York *(G-12458)*

LABORATORIES: Dental

Marotta Dental Studio Inc .... E 631 249-7520
Farmingdale *(G-5051)*
Martins Dental Studio .... G 315 788-0800
Watertown *(G-16686)*

LABORATORIES: Dental Orthodontic Appliance Production

Vincent Martino Dental Lab .... F 716 674-7800
Buffalo *(G-3269)*

LABORATORIES: Electronic Research

C & D Assembly Inc .... E 607 898-4275
Groton *(G-5919)*
Intrinsiq Materials Inc .... G 585 301-4432
Rochester *(G-14475)*
Mark - 10 Corporation .... E 631 842-9200
Copiague *(G-3938)*
Millennium Antenna Corp .... F 315 798-9374
Utica *(G-16372)*
Terahertz Technologies Inc .... G 315 736-3642
Oriskany *(G-13340)*

LABORATORIES: Medical

Immco Diagnostics Inc .... D 716 691-6911
Buffalo *(G-3022)*

LABORATORIES: Noncommercial Research

American Institute Physics Inc .... C 516 576-2410
Melville *(G-8326)*
Human Life Foundation Inc .... G 212 685-5210
New York *(G-10576)*

LABORATORIES: Physical Research, Commercial

Akzo Nobel Chemicals LLC .... C 914 674-5008
Dobbs Ferry *(G-4324)*

Albany Molecular Research Inc .... G 518 512-2234
Albany *(G-38)*
Amherst Systems Inc .... C 716 631-0610
Buffalo *(G-2828)*
Conmed Corporation 315 797-8375
Utica *(G-16338)*
Danisco US Inc .... D 585 256-5200
Rochester *(G-14321)*
Delphi Automotive Systems LLC .... A 585 359-6000
West Henrietta *(G-16909)*
Durata Therapeutics Inc .... G 646 871-6400
New York *(G-9991)*
Easton Pharmaceuticals Inc 347 284-0192
Lewiston *(G-7454)*
Fujitsu Ntwrk Cmmnications Inc ...... F 845 731-2000
Pearl River *(G-13479)*
Grumman Field Support Services ..... D 516 575-0574
Bethpage *(G-867)*
Interdgital Communications LLC ...... C 631 622-4000
Melville *(G-8360)*
International Aids Vaccine Ini 212 847-1111
New York *(G-10672)*
International Aids Vaccine Ini .... F 646 381-8066
Brooklyn *(G-2109)*
International Paper Company .... C 845 986-6409
Tuxedo Park *(G-16307)*
Islechem LLC 716 773-8401
Grand Island *(G-5774)*
Macrochem Corporation 212 514-8094
New York *(G-11117)*
Momentive Performance Mtls Inc .... D 914 784-4807
Tarrytown *(G-16121)*
Northrop Grumman Systems Corp .... A 516 575-0574
Bethpage *(G-875)*
OSI Pharmaceuticals LLC 631 962-2000
Farmingdale *(G-5084)*
Starfire Systems Inc .... F 518 899-9336
Schenectady *(G-15323)*
Transtech Systems Inc .... E 518 370-5558
Latham *(G-7408)*

LABORATORIES: Testing

Ken-Ton Open Mri PC .... G 716 876-7000
Kenmore *(G-7179)*

LABORATORIES: Testing

A & Z Pharmaceutical Inc .... D 631 952-3802
Hauppauge *(G-6026)*
B & H Electronics Corp .... E 845 782-5000
Monroe *(G-8584)*
Bga Technology LLC .... F 631 750-4600
Bohemia *(G-1021)*
Dayton T Brown Inc .... B 631 589-6300
Bohemia *(G-1048)*
G E Inspection Technologies LP .... C 315 554-2000
Skaneateles *(G-15481)*
Kyra Communications Corp .... F 516 783-6244
Seaford *(G-15366)*
Laser & Electron Beam Inc .... G 603 626-6080
New York *(G-10967)*
Miller & Weber Inc .... E 718 821-7110
Westbury *(G-17039)*
Northeast Metrology Corp .... F 716 827-3770
Depew *(G-4290)*
Stetron International Inc .... F 716 854-3443
Buffalo *(G-3225)*

LABORATORY APPARATUS & FURNITURE

Adirondack Machine Corporation ..... G 518 792-2258
Hudson Falls *(G-6669)*
Biodesign Inc of New York .... F 845 454-6610
Carmel *(G-3426)*
Bioins Inc .... F 646 398-3718
Yonkers *(G-17437)*
Dynamica Inc .... G 212 818-1900
New York *(G-10000)*
Fungilab Inc .... G 631 750-6361
Hauppauge *(G-6104)*
Healthalliance Hospital .... G 845 338-2500
Kingston *(G-7219)*
Hyman Podrusnick Co Inc .... G 718 853-4502
Brooklyn *(G-2089)*
Instrumentation Laboratory Co .... C 845 680-0028
Orangeburg *(G-13253)*
Integrted Work Envronments LLC .... G 716 725-5088
East Amherst *(G-4387)*
Itin Scale Co Inc .... E 718 336-5900
Brooklyn *(G-2118)*

Jamestown Metal Products LLC .... C 716 665-5313
Jamestown *(G-7044)*
Lab Crafters Inc .... E 631 471-7755
Ronkonkoma *(G-14954)*
Maripharm Laboratories .... F 716 984-6520
Niagara Falls *(G-12862)*
Nalge Nunc International Corp .... A 585 498-2661
Rochester *(G-14547)*
Newport Corporation .... E 585 248-4246
Rochester *(G-14555)*
Radon Testing Corp of America .... F 914 345-3380
Elmsford *(G-4782)*
S P Industries Inc .... D 845 255-5000
Gardiner *(G-5563)*
Staplex Company Inc .... E 718 768-3333
Brooklyn *(G-2619)*
Theta Industries Inc .... F 516 883-4088
Port Washington *(G-13887)*
VWR Education LLC .... C 585 359-2502
West Henrietta *(G-16929)*

LABORATORY APPARATUS: Furnaces

Crystal Linton Technologies .... F 585 444-8784
Rochester *(G-14314)*

LABORATORY APPARATUS: Pipettes, Hemocytometer

Vistalab Technologies Inc .... E 914 244-6226
Brewster *(G-1228)*

LABORATORY APPARATUS: Shakers & Stirrers

Scientific Industries Inc .... E 631 567-4700
Bohemia *(G-1125)*

LABORATORY EQPT, EXC MEDICAL: Wholesalers

Ankom Technology Corp .... E 315 986-8090
Macedon *(G-8008)*
Enzo Life Sciences Inc .... E 631 694-7070
Farmingdale *(G-4997)*
Eugenia Selective Living Inc .... F 631 277-1461
Islip *(G-6847)*
Integrted Work Envronments LLC ... G 716 725-5088
East Amherst *(G-4387)*
Lab Crafters Inc 631 471-7755
Ronkonkoma *(G-14954)*
Magic Touch Icewares Intl 212 794-2852
New York *(G-11134)*
TEC Glass & Inst LLC .... G 315 926-7639
Marion *(G-8132)*

LABORATORY EQPT: Chemical

Integrated Liner Tech Inc .... E 518 621-7422
Rensselaer *(G-14059)*

LABORATORY EQPT: Clinical Instruments Exc Medical

Next Advance Inc .... F 518 674-3510
Troy *(G-16265)*

LABORATORY EQPT: Measuring

East Hills Instrument Inc .... F 516 621-8686
Westbury *(G-17007)*

LABORATORY EQPT: Sterilizers

Steriliz LLC .... G 585 415-5411
Rochester *(G-14727)*

LABORATORY INSTRUMENT REPAIR SVCS

Theta Industries Inc .... F 516 883-4088
Port Washington *(G-13887)*

LACE GOODS & WARP KNIT FABRIC DYEING & FINISHING

Eagle Lace Dyeing Corp .... F 212 947-2712
New York *(G-10010)*
Gehring Tricot Corporation .... D 315 429-8551
Garden City *(G-5520)*
Somerset Dyeing & Finishing .... E 518 773-7383
Gloversville *(G-5736)*

PRODUCT SECTION

LAUNDRY & GARMENT SVCS, NEC: Reweaving, Textiles

LACQUERING SVC: Metal Prdts
Berkman Bros Inc .... E 718 782-1827
  Brooklyn *(G-1684)*

LADDERS: Metal
Brakewell Stl Fabricators Inc .... E 845 469-9131
  Chester *(G-3628)*
Trine Rolled Moulding Corp .... E 718 828-5200
  Bronx *(G-1477)*

LADDERS: Portable, Metal
Metallic Ladder Mfg Corp .... F 716 358-6201
  Randolph *(G-14029)*

LADDERS: Wood
Babcock Co Inc .... E 607 776-3341
  Bath *(G-653)*
Putnam Rolling Ladder Co Inc .... F 212 226-5147
  New York *(G-11779)*
Putnam Rolling Ladder Co Inc .... F 718 381-8219
  Brooklyn *(G-2476)*

LAMINATED PLASTICS: Plate, Sheet, Rod & Tubes
Allred & Associates Inc .... E 315 252-2559
  Elbridge *(G-4637)*
American Acrylic Corporation .... E 631 422-2200
  West Babylon *(G-16795)*
Architctral Dsign Elements LLC .... G 718 218-7800
  Brooklyn *(G-1623)*
Clear Cast Technologies Inc .... E 914 945-0848
  Ossining *(G-13346)*
Displays By Rioux Inc .... G 315 458-3639
  North Syracuse *(G-12958)*
Favorite Plastic Corp .... C 718 253-7000
  Brooklyn *(G-1964)*
Griffon Corporation .... E 212 957-5000
  New York *(G-10405)*
Inland Paper Products Corp .... E 718 827-8150
  Brooklyn *(G-2106)*
Iridium Industries Inc .... E 516 504-9700
  Great Neck *(G-5833)*
Jaguar Industries Inc .... F 845 947-1800
  Haverstraw *(G-6261)*
Nalge Nunc International Corp .... A 585 498-2661
  Rochester *(G-14547)*
Norton Performance Plas Corp .... G 518 642-2200
  Granville *(G-5795)*
Strux Corp .... E 516 768-3969
  Lindenhurst *(G-7508)*

LAMINATING SVCS
A & D Offset Printers Ltd .... G 516 746-2476
  Mineola *(G-8520)*
Copy Room Inc .... F 212 371-8600
  New York *(G-9781)*
Hennig Custom Woodwork Corp .... G 516 536-3460
  Oceanside *(G-13101)*

LAMP & LIGHT BULBS & TUBES
Foscarini Inc .... G 212 257-4412
  New York *(G-10240)*
Kreon Inc .... G 516 470-9522
  Bethpage *(G-869)*
La Mar Lighting Co Inc .... D 631 777-7700
  Farmingdale *(G-5039)*
Led Waves Inc .... F 347 416-6182
  Brooklyn *(G-2205)*
Lowel-Light Manufacturing Inc .... E 718 921-0600
  Brooklyn *(G-2241)*
Lumia Energy Solutions LLC .... G 516 478-5795
  Jericho *(G-7108)*
Make-Waves Instrument Corp .... E 716 681-7524
  Buffalo *(G-3076)*
Oledworks LLC .... E 585 287-6802
  Rochester *(G-14568)*
Philips Elec N Amer Corp .... C 607 776-3692
  Bath *(G-661)*
Ric-Lo Productions Ltd .... E 845 469-2285
  Chester *(G-3640)*
Satco Products Inc .... D 631 243-2022
  Edgewood *(G-4624)*
Siemens Corporation .... F 202 434-7800
  New York *(G-12084)*
Siemens USA Holdings Inc .... B 212 258-4000
  New York *(G-12086)*

Welch Allyn Inc .... A 315 685-4347
  Skaneateles Falls *(G-15495)*
Westron Corporation .... E 516 678-2300
  Oceanside *(G-13127)*

LAMP BULBS & TUBES, ELECTRIC: For Specialized Applications
Boehm Surgical Instrument .... F 585 436-6584
  Rochester *(G-14259)*

LAMP BULBS & TUBES, ELECTRIC: Light, Complete
Emitled Inc .... G 516 531-3533
  Westbury *(G-17009)*
Goldstar Lighting LLC .... F 646 543-6811
  New York *(G-10376)*

LAMP BULBS & TUBES/PARTS, ELECTRIC: Generalized Applications
General Electric Company .... A 518 385-4022
  Schenectady *(G-15283)*
Lighting Holdings Intl LLC .... A 845 306-1850
  Purchase *(G-13976)*
Saratoga Lighting Holdings LLC .... G 212 906-7800
  New York *(G-11990)*

LAMP FRAMES: Wire
Lyn Jo Enterprises Ltd .... G 716 753-2776
  Mayville *(G-8248)*

LAMP SHADES: Glass
Depp Glass Inc .... F 718 784-8500
  Long Island City *(G-7742)*
Somers Stain Glass Inc .... G 631 586-7772
  Deer Park *(G-4235)*

LAMP SHADES: Metal
Judis Lampshades Inc .... G 917 561-3921
  Brooklyn *(G-2156)*

LAMP STORES
Custom Lampshades Inc .... F 718 254-0500
  Brooklyn *(G-1826)*
Lighting Holdings Intl LLC .... A 845 306-1850
  Purchase *(G-13976)*

LAMPS: Floor, Residential
Adesso Inc .... E 212 736-4440
  New York *(G-9074)*

LAMPS: Fluorescent
K & H Industries Inc .... F 716 312-0088
  Hamburg *(G-5953)*
K & H Industries Inc .... E 716 312-0088
  Hamburg *(G-5954)*

LAMPS: Ultraviolet
Atlantic Ultraviolet Corp .... E 631 234-3275
  Hauppauge *(G-6047)*

LAND SUBDIVIDERS & DEVELOPERS: Commercial
Micro Instrument Corp .... D 585 458-3150
  Rochester *(G-14528)*

LAND SUBDIVISION & DEVELOPMENT
Nsgv Inc .... E 212 367-3167
  New York *(G-11483)*

LANGUAGE SCHOOLS
Japan America Learning Ctr Inc .... F 914 723-7600
  Scarsdale *(G-15248)*

LANTERNS
Mjk Enterprises LLC .... G 917 653-9042
  Brooklyn *(G-2329)*

LAPIDARY WORK & DIAMOND CUTTING & POLISHING
Engelack Gem Corporation .... G 212 719-3094
  New York *(G-10092)*
Fischer Diamonds Inc .... F 212 869-1990
  New York *(G-10223)*
Igc New York Inc .... G 212 764-0949
  New York *(G-10607)*
Sunshine Diamond Cutter Inc .... G 212 221-1028
  New York *(G-12260)*

LAPIDARY WORK: Contract Or Other
Dweck Industries Inc .... E 718 615-1695
  Brooklyn *(G-1886)*

LAPIDARY WORK: Jewel Cut, Drill, Polish, Recut/Setting
Classic Creations Inc .... G 516 498-1991
  Great Neck *(G-5815)*
Diamond Boutique .... G 516 444-3373
  Port Washington *(G-13831)*
Perma Glow Ltd Inc .... F 212 575-9677
  New York *(G-11638)*
Stephen J Lipkins Inc .... G 631 249-8866
  Farmingdale *(G-5127)*

LARD: From Slaughtering Plants
Bliss-Poston The Second Wind .... G 212 481-1055
  New York *(G-9467)*

LASER SYSTEMS & EQPT
Advanced Photonics Inc .... F 631 471-3693
  Ronkonkoma *(G-14881)*
Bare Beauty Laser Hair Removal .... G 718 278-2273
  New York *(G-9370)*
CVI Laser LLC .... D 585 244-7220
  Rochester *(G-14318)*
Exfo Burleigh Pdts Group Inc .... D 585 301-1530
  Canandaigua *(G-3374)*
Gb Group Inc .... G 212 594-3748
  New York *(G-10297)*
Lasermax Inc .... D 585 272-5420
  Rochester *(G-14496)*
Navitar Inc .... D 585 359-4000
  Rochester *(G-14550)*
Photomedex Inc .... E 888 966-1010
  Orangeburg *(G-13261)*
Teledyne Optech Inc .... F 585 427-8310
  Rochester *(G-14747)*
Uptek Solutions Corp .... F 631 256-5565
  Bohemia *(G-1150)*

LASERS: Welding, Drilling & Cutting Eqpt
Crysta-Lyn Chemical Company .... G 607 296-4721
  Binghamton *(G-901)*
Empire Plastics Inc .... E 607 754-9132
  Endwell *(G-4840)*
Trident Precision Mfg Inc .... D 585 265-2010
  Webster *(G-16764)*

LAUNDRY & DRYCLEANER AGENTS
Clinton Clrs & EMB Shoppe Inc .... G 315 853-8421
  Clinton *(G-3743)*

LAUNDRY & GARMENT SVCS, NEC: Fur Cleaning, Repairing/Storage
Anastasia Furs International .... G 212 868-9241
  New York *(G-9198)*

LAUNDRY & GARMENT SVCS, NEC: Garment Alteration & Repair
Connie French Cleaners Inc .... G 516 487-1343
  Great Neck *(G-5818)*

LAUNDRY & GARMENT SVCS, NEC: Reweaving, Textiles
Thistle Hill Weavers .... G 518 284-2729
  Cherry Valley *(G-3624)*

LAUNDRY & GARMENT SVCS: Dressmaking, Matl Owned By Customer

IBlt Inc .... E 212 768-0292
  New York *(G-10592)*

LAUNDRY EQPT: Commercial

G A Braun Inc .... E 315 475-3123
  Syracuse *(G-15966)*
Lb Laundry Inc .... G 347 399-8030
  Flushing *(G-5271)*

LAUNDRY EQPT: Household

AES Electronics Inc .... G 212 371-8120
  New York *(G-9101)*
Coinmach Service Corp .... A 516 349-8555
  Plainview *(G-13618)*
CSC Serviceworks Inc .... D 516 349-8555
  Plainview *(G-13624)*
CSC Serviceworks Holdings .... E 516 349-8555
  Plainview *(G-13625)*
Penn Enterprises Inc .... F 845 446-0765
  West Point *(G-16959)*
Pluslux LLC .... G 516 371-4400
  Inwood *(G-6805)*
Spin Holdco Inc .... G 516 349-8555
  Plainview *(G-13662)*

LAUNDRY SVC: Wiping Towel Sply

Hygrade .... G 718 488-9000
  Brooklyn *(G-2088)*
Yankee Corp .... F 718 589-1377
  Bronx *(G-1496)*

LAWN & GARDEN EQPT

Briggs & Stratton Corporation .... C 315 495-0100
  Munnsville *(G-8795)*
Cazenovia Equipment Co Inc .... G 315 736-0898
  Clinton *(G-3742)*
Chapin International Inc .... C 585 343-3140
  Batavia *(G-628)*
Chapin Manufacturing Inc .... C 585 343-3140
  Batavia *(G-629)*
Clopay Ames True Tmper Hldng .... F 516 938-5544
  Jericho *(G-7096)*
Fradan Manufacturing Corp .... F 914 632-3653
  New Rochelle *(G-8947)*
Real Bark Mulch LLC .... G 518 747-3650
  Fort Edward *(G-5353)*
Rhett M Clark Inc .... G 585 538-9570
  Caledonia *(G-3309)*

LAWN & GARDEN EQPT STORES

Nelson Holdings Ltd .... G 607 772-1794
  Binghamton *(G-935)*

LAWN & GARDEN EQPT: Carts Or Wagons

Kadco Usa Inc .... G 518 661-6068
  Mayfield *(G-8244)*

LAWN & GARDEN EQPT: Tractors & Eqpt

Eaton Brothers Corp .... G 716 649-8250
  Hamburg *(G-5945)*
Saxby Implement Corp .... F 585 624-2938
  Mendon *(G-8414)*

LAWN & GARDEN EQPT: Trimmers

Capital E Financial Group .... F 212 319-6550
  New York *(G-9574)*

LAWN MOWER REPAIR SHOP

Nelson Holdings Ltd .... G 607 772-1794
  Binghamton *(G-935)*

LEAD & ZINC

Hh Liquidating Corp .... A 646 282-2500
  New York *(G-10515)*
T L Diamond & Company Inc .... F 212 249-6660
  New York *(G-12288)*

LEAD PENCILS & ART GOODS

Aakron Rule Corp .... C 716 542-5483
  Akron *(G-17)*

Effanjay Pens Inc .... E 212 316-9565
  Long Island City *(G-7755)*
R & F Handmade Paints Inc .... F 845 331-3112
  Kingston *(G-7236)*
Utrecht Manufacturing Corp .... G 212 675-8699
  New York *(G-12515)*

LEASING & RENTAL SVCS: Earth Moving Eqpt

Duke Company .... G 607 347-4455
  Ithaca *(G-6874)*

LEASING & RENTAL: Computers & Eqpt

IBM World Trade Corporation .... G 914 765-1900
  Armonk *(G-411)*
Key Computer Svcs of Chelsea .... D 212 206-8060
  New York *(G-10880)*
Systems Trading Inc .... G 718 261-8900
  Melville *(G-8387)*

LEASING & RENTAL: Construction & Mining Eqpt

Christian Fabrication LLC .... G 315 822-0135
  West Winfield *(G-16986)*
Safeworks LLC .... F 800 696-5577
  Woodside *(G-17368)*

LEASING & RENTAL: Other Real Estate Property

Beardslee Realty .... G 516 747-5557
  Mineola *(G-8530)*

LEASING: Laundry Eqpt

Thermopatch Corporation .... D 315 446-8110
  Syracuse *(G-16082)*

LEASING: Shipping Container

A R Arena Products Inc .... E 585 277-1680
  Rochester *(G-14176)*
Shiprite Software Inc .... G 315 733-6191
  Utica *(G-16383)*

LEATHER GOODS, EXC FOOTWEAR, GLOVES, LUGGAGE/BELTING, WHOL

Pan American Leathers Inc .... G 978 741-4150
  New York *(G-11572)*

LEATHER GOODS: Belt Laces

McM Products USA Inc .... E 646 756-4090
  New York *(G-11226)*

LEATHER GOODS: Belting & Strapping

Fahrenheit NY Inc .... G 212 354-6554
  New York *(G-10180)*
Walco Leather Co Inc .... E 212 243-2244
  Bedford *(G-795)*

LEATHER GOODS: Boxes

Kamali Leather Corp .... G 518 762-2522
  Johnstown *(G-7148)*

LEATHER GOODS: Cases

Slim Line Case Co Inc .... F 585 546-3639
  Rochester *(G-14713)*

LEATHER GOODS: Corners, Luggage

Deluxe Travel Store Inc .... G 718 435-8111
  Brooklyn *(G-1853)*

LEATHER GOODS: Cosmetic Bags

Baker Products Inc .... G 212 459-2323
  White Plains *(G-17109)*
M G New York Inc .... F 212 371-5566
  New York *(G-11099)*
Penthouse Manufacturing Co Inc .... B 516 379-1300
  Freeport *(G-5429)*

LEATHER GOODS: Desk Sets

Star Desk Pad Co Inc .... E 914 963-9400
  Yonkers *(G-17504)*

LEATHER GOODS: Garments

Art Craft Leather Goods Inc .... F 718 257-7401
  Brooklyn *(G-1635)*
Dvf Studio LLC .... D 212 741-6607
  New York *(G-9993)*
Dvf Studio LLC .... G 646 576-8009
  New York *(G-9994)*
East West Global Sourcing Inc .... G 917 887-2286
  Brooklyn *(G-1898)*
Leather Outlet .... G 518 668-0328
  Lake George *(G-7287)*
Perrone Leather LLC .... D 518 853-4300
  Fultonville *(G-5496)*
Tucano Usa Inc .... G 212 966-9211
  New York *(G-12441)*

LEATHER GOODS: Holsters

Adirondack Leather Pdts Inc .... F 607 547-5798
  Fly Creek *(G-5317)*
Courtlandt Boot Jack Co Inc .... E 718 445-6200
  Flushing *(G-5242)*
Helgen Industries Inc .... C 631 841-6300
  Amityville *(G-292)*

LEATHER GOODS: Key Cases

Form A Rockland Plastics Inc .... G 315 848-3300
  Cranberry Lake *(G-4083)*

LEATHER GOODS: Personal

American Puff Corp .... D 516 379-1300
  Freeport *(G-5396)*
Art Leather Mfg Co Inc .... A 516 867-4716
  Oyster Bay *(G-13392)*
Astucci US Ltd .... F 718 752-9700
  Long Island City *(G-7706)*
Atlantic Specialty Co Inc .... E 845 356-2502
  Monsey *(G-8604)*
Coach Inc .... B 212 594-1850
  New York *(G-9714)*
Coach Stores Inc .... A 212 643-9727
  New York *(G-9717)*
Datamax International Inc .... E 212 693-0933
  New York *(G-9870)*
Elco Manufacturing Co Inc .... F 516 767-3577
  Port Washington *(G-13835)*
Excelled Sheepskin & Lea Coat .... F 212 594-5843
  New York *(G-10157)*
Fahrenheit NY Inc .... G 212 354-6554
  New York *(G-10180)*
Grownbeans Inc .... G 212 989-3486
  New York *(G-10416)*
Helgen Industries Inc .... C 631 841-6300
  Amityville *(G-292)*
Hemisphere Novelties Inc .... E 914 378-4100
  Yonkers *(G-17469)*
House of Portfolios Co Inc .... G 212 206-7323
  New York *(G-10562)*
House of Portfolios Co Inc .... F 212 206-7323
  New York *(G-10563)*
Just Brass Inc .... G 212 724-5447
  New York *(G-10826)*
Leather Artisan .... G 518 359-3102
  Childwold *(G-3658)*
Leather Impact Inc .... G 212 382-2788
  New York *(G-10985)*
Merzon Leather Co Inc .... C 718 782-6260
  Brooklyn *(G-2306)*
Neumann Jutta New York Inc .... F 212 982-7048
  New York *(G-11398)*
Walco Leather Co Inc .... E 212 243-2244
  Bedford *(G-795)*

LEATHER GOODS: Transmission Belting

Sampla Belting North Amer LLC .... E 716 667-7450
  Lackawanna *(G-7275)*

LEATHER GOODS: Wallets

L Y Z Creations Ltd Inc .... E 718 768-2977
  Brooklyn *(G-2187)*
Randa Accessories Lea Gds LLC .... D 212 354-5100
  New York *(G-11825)*
Trafalgar Company LLC .... G 212 768-8800
  New York *(G-12411)*

PRODUCT SECTION

LIGHTING FIXTURES, NEC

LEATHER TANNING & FINISHING
Aston Leather Inc		G	212 481-2760
New York *(G-9294)*			
Corium Corporation		F	914 381-0100
Mamaroneck *(G-8062)*			
Edsim Leather Co Inc		E	212 695-8500
New York *(G-10037)*			
Hastings Hide Inc		G	516 295-2400
Inwood *(G-6798)*			
Legendary Auto Interiors Ltd		E	315 331-1212
Newark *(G-12754)*			
Pearl Leather Finishers Inc		D	518 762-4543
Johnstown *(G-7151)*			

LEATHER, LEATHER GOODS & FURS, WHOLESALE
Leather Artisan		G	518 359-3102
Childwold *(G-3658)*			
Leather Impact Inc		G	212 382-2788
New York *(G-10985)*			
Tandy Leather Factory Inc		G	845 480-3588
Nyack *(G-13071)*			

LEATHER: Accessory Prdts
Adam Scott Designs Inc		E	212 420-8866
New York *(G-9071)*			
Ariel Tian LLC		G	212 457-1266
Forest Hills *(G-5327)*			
Automotive Leather Group LLC		F	516 627-4000
Great Neck *(G-5809)*			
Justin Gregory Inc		G	631 249-5187
Deer Park *(G-4182)*			
Kamali Group Inc		G	516 627-4000
Great Neck *(G-5836)*			
Pacific Worldwide Inc		F	212 502-3360
New York *(G-11567)*			
Tandy Leather Factory Inc		G	845 480-3588
Nyack *(G-13071)*			
Vic Demayos Inc		G	845 626-4343
Accord *(G-1)*			

LEATHER: Artificial
Beckmann Converting Inc		E	518 842-0073
Amsterdam *(G-335)*			

LEATHER: Bag
Givi Inc		F	212 586-5029
New York *(G-10343)*			
Hat Attack Inc		E	718 994-1000
Bronx *(G-1353)*			

LEATHER: Bookbinders'
Graphic Image Associates LLC		D	631 249-9600
Melville *(G-8352)*			
System of AME Binding		F	631 390-8560
Central Islip *(G-3539)*			

LEATHER: Case
Baker Products Inc		G	212 459-2323
White Plains *(G-17109)*			

LEATHER: Colored
Mohawk River Leather Works		F	518 853-3900
Fultonville *(G-5494)*			

LEATHER: Cut
A-1 Products Inc		G	718 789-1818
Brooklyn *(G-1539)*			
Hohenforst Splitting Co Inc		G	518 725-0012
Gloversville *(G-5730)*			

LEATHER: Die-cut
John Gailer Inc		E	212 243-5662
Long Island City *(G-7799)*			

LEATHER: Embossed
Rainbow Leather Inc		F	718 939-4762
College Point *(G-3829)*			

LEATHER: Finished
Androme Leather Inc		F	518 773-7945
Gloversville *(G-5721)*			

Arrow Leather Finishing Inc		E	518 762-3121
Johnstown *(G-7138)*			
Pan American Leathers Inc		G	978 741-4150
New York *(G-11572)*			

LEATHER: Glove
Shadal LLC		G	212 319-5946
New York *(G-12057)*			

LEATHER: Handbag
Graphic Image Incorporated		C	631 249-9600
Melville *(G-8353)*			
Street Smart Designs Inc		G	646 865-0056
New York *(G-12236)*			
Trebbianno LLC		E	212 868-2770
New York *(G-12418)*			

LEATHER: Processed
Pearl Leather Group LLC		E	516 627-4047
Great Neck *(G-5847)*			

LEATHER: Specialty, NEC
Walco Leather Co Inc		E	212 243-2244
Bedford *(G-795)*			

LEATHER: Upholstery
Kamali Automotive Group Inc		F	516 627-4000
Great Neck *(G-5835)*			

LEGAL & TAX SVCS
Westchester Law Journal Inc		G	914 948-0715
White Plains *(G-17211)*			

LEGAL OFFICES & SVCS
Dick Bailey Service Inc		F	718 522-4363
Brooklyn *(G-1861)*			
Thomson Reuters Corporation		A	646 223-4000
New York *(G-12349)*			
Wave Publishing Co Inc		F	718 634-4000
Rockaway Beach *(G-14811)*			

LEGITIMATE LIVE THEATER PRODUCERS
Abkco Music & Records Inc		D	212 399-0300
New York *(G-9050)*			

LENS COATING: Ophthalmic
Equicheck LLC		G	631 987-6356
Patchogue *(G-13444)*			
Optisource International Inc		E	631 924-8360
Bellport *(G-832)*			

LESSORS: Landholding Office
Rock Mountain Farms Inc		G	845 647-9084
Ellenville *(G-4652)*			

LIFESAVING & SURVIVAL EQPT, EXC MEDICAL, WHOLESALE
Aero Healthcare (us) LLC		G	855 225-2376
Valley Cottage *(G-16401)*			

LIGHT SENSITIVE DEVICES
Nsi Industries LLC		C	800 841-2505
Mount Vernon *(G-8757)*			
Tork Inc		D	914 664-3542
Mount Vernon *(G-8784)*			

LIGHTING EQPT: Flashlights
Psg Innovations Inc		F	917 299-8986
Valley Stream *(G-16446)*			

LIGHTING EQPT: Motor Vehicle, Headlights
Licenders		G	212 759-5200
New York *(G-11019)*			

LIGHTING EQPT: Motor Vehicle, NEC
Mobile Fleet Inc		G	631 206-2920
Hauppauge *(G-6168)*			

LIGHTING EQPT: Outdoor
AI Energy Solutions Led Llc		E	646 380-6670
New York *(G-9120)*			
Northern Air Technology Inc		G	585 594-5050
Rochester *(G-14565)*			
Outdoor Lightning Perspectives		G	631 266-6200
Huntington *(G-6707)*			

LIGHTING EQPT: Reflectors, Metal, For Lighting Eqpt
Island Lite Louvers Inc		E	631 608-4250
Amityville *(G-297)*			
Projector Lamp Services LLC		F	631 244-0051
Bohemia *(G-1119)*			

LIGHTING EQPT: Streetcar Fixtures
Power and Cnstr Group Inc		E	585 889-6020
Scottsville *(G-15360)*			

LIGHTING EQPT: Strobe Lighting Systems
Star Headlight Lantern Co Inc		C	585 226-9500
Avon *(G-540)*			

LIGHTING FIXTURES WHOLESALERS
Expo Furniture Designs Inc		F	516 674-1420
Glen Cove *(G-5627)*			
Global Lighting Inc		G	914 591-4095
Yonkers *(G-17463)*			
Lighting Holdings Intl LLC		A	845 306-1850
Purchase *(G-13976)*			
Matov Industries Inc		E	718 392-5060
Long Island City *(G-7836)*			
Quality HM Brands Holdings LLC		A	718 292-2024
Bronx *(G-1436)*			
Quoizel Inc		E	631 436-4402
Hauppauge *(G-6202)*			
Satco Products Inc		D	631 243-2022
Edgewood *(G-4624)*			
Solarwaterway Inc		E	888 998-5337
Brooklyn *(G-2607)*			
Visual Effects Inc		F	718 324-0011
Jamaica *(G-6998)*			

LIGHTING FIXTURES, NEC
Broadway National Group LLC		D	800 797-4467
Ronkonkoma *(G-14909)*			
Coldstream Group Inc		F	914 698-5959
Mamaroneck *(G-8061)*			
Cooper Industries LLC		E	315 477-7000
Syracuse *(G-15928)*			
Creative Stage Lighting Co Inc		E	518 251-3302
North Creek *(G-12949)*			
Edison Power & Light Co Inc		F	718 522-0002
Brooklyn *(G-1906)*			
Fabbian USA Corp		E	973 882-3824
New York *(G-10176)*			
General Led Corp		G	516 280-2854
Mineola *(G-8545)*			
Goddard Design Co		G	718 599-0170
Brooklyn *(G-2035)*			
Gordon S Anderson Mfg Co		G	845 677-3304
Millbrook *(G-8511)*			
Gti Graphic Technology Inc		E	845 562-7066
Newburgh *(G-12781)*			
HB Architectural Lighting Inc		E	347 851-4123
Bronx *(G-1354)*			
Illumination Technologies Inc		F	315 463-4673
East Syracuse *(G-4552)*			
J M Canty Inc		E	716 625-4227
Lockport *(G-7624)*			
Jaquith Industries Inc		E	315 478-5700
Syracuse *(G-15985)*			
Jed Lights Inc		F	516 812-5001
Deer Park *(G-4180)*			
Jt Roselle Lighting & Sup Inc		F	914 666-3700
Mount Kisco *(G-8674)*			
Julian A McDermott Corporation		E	718 456-3606
Ridgewood *(G-14124)*			
La Mar Lighting Co Inc		D	631 777-7700
Farmingdale *(G-5039)*			
Lamparts Co Inc		F	914 723-8986
Mount Vernon *(G-8745)*			
Lbg Acquisition LLC		E	212 226-1276
New York *(G-10976)*			
Light Blue USA LLC		G	718 475-2515
Brooklyn *(G-2221)*			

Employee Codes: A=Over 500 employees, B=251-500
C=101-250, D=51-100, E=20-50, F=10-19, G=5-9

2018 Harris
New York Manufacturers Directory

LIGHTING FIXTURES, NEC

Company	Sec	Phone
Lighting N Beyond LLC	G	718 669-9142
Blauvelt *(G-967)*		
Lighting Sculptures Inc	F	631 242-3387
Deer Park *(G-4190)*		
Luminescent Systems Inc	B	716 655-0800
East Aurora *(G-4398)*		
Olive Led Lighting Inc	G	718 746-0830
College Point *(G-3825)*		
Rodac USA Corp	E	716 741-3931
Clarence *(G-3698)*		
Saratoga Lighting Holdings LLC	G	212 906-7800
New York *(G-11990)*		
Sensio America	F	877 501-5337
Clifton Park *(G-3732)*		
Shakuff LLC	G	212 675-0383
Brooklyn *(G-2575)*		
Siemens Electro Industrial Sa	A	212 258-4000
New York *(G-12085)*		
Strider Global LLC	G	212 726-1302
New York *(G-12238)*		
Tarsier Ltd	C	212 401-6181
New York *(G-12305)*		
Tecnolux Incorporated	G	718 369-3900
Brooklyn *(G-2672)*		
Times Square Stage Ltg Co Inc	E	845 947-3034
Stony Point *(G-15800)*		
Truck-Lite Co LLC	E	716 665-2614
Falconer *(G-4923)*		
Vertex Innovative Solutions In	F	315 437-6711
Syracuse *(G-16091)*		
Vincent Conigliaro	F	845 340-0489
Kingston *(G-7251)*		
Visual Effects Inc	F	718 324-0011
Jamaica *(G-6998)*		
Vivid Rgb Lighting LLC	G	718 635-0817
Peekskill *(G-13508)*		

LIGHTING FIXTURES: Decorative Area

Company	Sec	Phone
Enchante Lites LLC	G	212 602-1818
New York *(G-10081)*		
Lindsey Adelman	E	718 623-3013
Brooklyn *(G-2230)*		
Secret Celebrity Licensing LLC	G	212 812-9277
New York *(G-12031)*		

LIGHTING FIXTURES: Fluorescent, Commercial

Company	Sec	Phone
A & L Lighting Ltd	F	718 821-1188
Medford *(G-8264)*		
La Mar Lighting Co Inc	D	631 777-7700
Farmingdale *(G-5039)*		
Legion Lighting Co Inc	E	718 498-1770
Brooklyn *(G-2209)*		
Lite Brite Manufacturing Inc	F	718 855-9797
Brooklyn *(G-2233)*		
Spectronics Corporation	C	516 333-4840
Westbury *(G-17055)*		

LIGHTING FIXTURES: Fluorescent, Residential

Company	Sec	Phone
Cooper Lighting LLC	E	315 579-2873
Syracuse *(G-15929)*		
Eaton Corporation	E	315 579-2872
Syracuse *(G-15951)*		

LIGHTING FIXTURES: Indl & Commercial

Company	Sec	Phone
A-1 Stamping & Spinning Corp	F	718 388-2626
Rockaway Park *(G-14812)*		
AEP Environmental LLC	F	716 446-0739
Buffalo *(G-2818)*		
Aesthonics Inc	D	646 723-2463
Brooklyn *(G-1567)*		
Al Energy Solutions Led Llc	E	646 380-6670
New York *(G-9120)*		
Altman Stage Lighting Co Inc	C	914 476-7987
Yonkers *(G-17429)*		
American Scientific Ltg Corp	E	718 369-1100
Brooklyn *(G-1606)*		
Apogee Translite Inc	E	631 254-6975
Deer Park *(G-4124)*		
Apparatus LLC	E	646 527-9732
New York *(G-9228)*		
Aquarii Inc	G	315 672-8807
Camillus *(G-3349)*		
Aristocrat Lighting Inc	F	718 522-0003
Brooklyn *(G-1630)*		
Arlee Lighting Corp	G	516 595-8558
Inwood *(G-6790)*		
Awaken Led Company	F	802 338-5971
Champlain *(G-3565)*		
Big Shine Worldwide Inc	G	845 444-5255
Newburgh *(G-12772)*		
Canarm Ltd	G	800 267-4427
Ogdensburg *(G-13134)*		
Cooper Industries LLC	E	315 477-7000
Syracuse *(G-15928)*		
Cooper Lighting LLC	E	516 470-1000
Hicksville *(G-6358)*		
Crownlite Mfg Corp	E	631 589-9100
Bohemia *(G-1040)*		
DAc Lighting Inc	E	914 698-5959
Mamaroneck *(G-8064)*		
Dreyfus Ashby Inc	E	212 818-0770
New York *(G-9980)*		
E-Ffinergy Group LLC	G	845 547-2424
Suffern *(G-15811)*		
Ecs Global	F	718 855-5888
Brooklyn *(G-1903)*		
Edison Price Lighting Inc	E	718 685-0700
Long Island City *(G-7752)*		
Edison Price Lighting Inc	E	718 685-0700
Long Island City *(G-7753)*		
Electric Lighting Agencies	E	212 645-4580
New York *(G-10049)*		
Elegance Lighting Ltd	F	631 509-0640
Centereach *(G-3496)*		
Green Energy Concepts Inc	G	845 238-2574
Chester *(G-3635)*		
Hudson Valley Lighting Inc	D	845 561-0300
Wappingers Falls *(G-16593)*		
Ideoli Group Inc	E	212 705-8769
Port Washington *(G-13845)*		
Jesco Lighting Inc	E	718 366-3211
Port Washington *(G-13850)*		
Jesco Lighting Group LLC	D	718 366-3211
Port Washington *(G-13851)*		
LDI Lighting Inc	G	718 384-4490
Brooklyn *(G-2200)*		
Light Waves Concept Inc	F	212 677-6400
Brooklyn *(G-2223)*		
Lighting By Dom Yonkers Inc	G	914 968-8700
Yonkers *(G-17480)*		
Lighting Services Inc	D	845 942-2800
Stony Point *(G-15797)*		
Linear Lighting Corporation	C	718 361-7552
Long Island City *(G-7818)*		
Lite-Makers Inc	E	718 739-9300
Jamaica *(G-6961)*		
Litelab Corp	G	718 361-6829
Long Island City *(G-7820)*		
Litelab Corp	C	716 856-4300
Buffalo *(G-3067)*		
LSI Lightron Inc	A	845 562-5500
New Windsor *(G-8988)*		
Lukas Lighting Inc	E	800 841-4011
Long Island City *(G-7824)*		
Luminatta Inc	G	914 664-3600
Mount Vernon *(G-8748)*		
Luminescent Systems Inc	B	716 655-0800
East Aurora *(G-4398)*		
Luxo Corporation	E	914 345-0067
Elmsford *(G-4770)*		
Magniflood Inc	E	631 226-1000
Amityville *(G-309)*		
Matov Industries Inc	E	718 392-5060
Long Island City *(G-7836)*		
Modulightor Inc	F	212 371-0336
New York *(G-11318)*		
North American Mfg Entps Inc	E	718 524-4370
Staten Island *(G-15733)*		
North American Mfg Entps Inc	E	718 524-4370
Staten Island *(G-15734)*		
Nulux Inc	E	718 383-1112
Ridgewood *(G-14128)*		
Oledworks LLC	E	585 287-6802
Rochester *(G-14568)*		
Philips Lighting N Amer Corp	C	646 265-7170
New York *(G-11667)*		
Preciseled Inc	E	516 418-5337
Valley Stream *(G-16443)*		
Primelite Manufacturing Corp	G	516 868-4411
Freeport *(G-5431)*		
Rapid-Lite Fixture Corporation	F	347 599-2600
Brooklyn *(G-2497)*		
Remains Lighting	E	212 675-8051
New York *(G-11861)*		
S E A Supplies Ltd	F	516 694-6677
Plainview *(G-13661)*		
Sandy Littman Inc	G	845 562-1112
Newburgh *(G-12802)*		
Saratoga Lighting Holdings LLC	G	212 906-7800
New York *(G-11990)*		
Savenergy Inc	G	516 239-1958
Garden City *(G-5545)*		
Savwatt Usa Inc	E	646 478-2676
New York *(G-11998)*		
Selux Corporation	C	845 691-7723
Highland *(G-6435)*		
Solarpath Inc	G	201 490-4499
New York *(G-12149)*		
Solarwaterway Inc	E	888 998-5337
Brooklyn *(G-2607)*		
Sonneman-A Way of Light	G	845 926-5469
Wappingers Falls *(G-16596)*		
Swivelier Company Inc	D	845 353-1455
Blauvelt *(G-970)*		
Twinkle Lighting Inc	G	718 225-0939
Flushing *(G-5309)*		
Versaponents Inc	F	631 242-3387
Deer Park *(G-4248)*		
Vision Quest Lighting Inc	E	631 737-4800
Ronkonkoma *(G-15022)*		
Vital Vio Inc	F	914 245-6048
Troy *(G-16286)*		
Vonn LLC	F	888 604-8666
Long Island City *(G-7946)*		
Xeleum Lighting LLC	F	954 617-8170
Mount Kisco *(G-8689)*		
Zumtobel Lighting Inc	C	845 691-6262
Highland *(G-6436)*		

LIGHTING FIXTURES: Motor Vehicle

Company	Sec	Phone
Copy Cat	G	718 934-2192
Brooklyn *(G-1801)*		
Truck-Lite Co LLC	E	716 665-2614
Falconer *(G-4923)*		
Truck-Lite Co LLC	C	716 665-6214
Falconer *(G-4924)*		
Wolo Mfg Corp	E	631 242-0333
Deer Park *(G-4253)*		

LIGHTING FIXTURES: Ornamental, Commercial

Company	Sec	Phone
LDI Lighting Inc	G	718 384-4490
Brooklyn *(G-2199)*		

LIGHTING FIXTURES: Public

Company	Sec	Phone
CEIT Corp	F	518 825-0649
Plattsburgh *(G-13686)*		
USA Illumination Inc	E	845 565-8500
New Windsor *(G-9002)*		

LIGHTING FIXTURES: Residential

Company	Sec	Phone
A-1 Stamping & Spinning Corp	F	718 388-2626
Rockaway Park *(G-14812)*		
Aesthonics Inc	D	646 723-2463
Brooklyn *(G-1567)*		
Artemis Studios Inc	D	718 788-6022
Brooklyn *(G-1637)*		
Canarm Ltd	G	800 267-4427
Ogdensburg *(G-13134)*		
Cooper Lighting LLC	E	516 470-1000
Hicksville *(G-6358)*		
Crownlite Mfg Corp	E	631 589-9100
Bohemia *(G-1040)*		
David Weeks Studio	F	212 966-3433
New York *(G-9880)*		
Decor By Dene Inc	F	718 376-5566
Brooklyn *(G-1847)*		
Dreyfus Ashby Inc	E	212 818-0770
New York *(G-9980)*		
ER Butler & Co Inc	E	212 925-3565
New York *(G-10107)*		
Excalbur Brnze Sculpture Fndry	E	718 366-3444
Brooklyn *(G-1947)*		
Hudson Valley Lighting Inc	D	845 561-0300
Wappingers Falls *(G-16593)*		
Jamaica Lamp Corp	E	718 776-5039
Queens Village *(G-13996)*		
Jimco Lamp & Manufacturing Co	G	631 218-2152
Islip *(G-6848)*		
Lasvit Inc	G	212 219-3043
New York *(G-10968)*		

PRODUCT SECTION

LOCKERS

Lexstar Inc ....E 845 947-1415
  Haverstraw *(G-6262)*
Litelab Corp ....C 716 856-4300
  Buffalo *(G-3067)*
Lyric Lighting Ltd Inc ....G 718 497-0109
  Ridgewood *(G-14127)*
Matov Industries Inc ....E 718 392-5060
  Long Island City *(G-7836)*
Modulightor Inc ....F 212 371-0336
  New York *(G-11318)*
New Generation Lighting Inc ....F 212 966-0328
  New York *(G-11408)*
Nulux Inc ....E 718 383-1112
  Ridgewood *(G-14128)*
Philips Elec N Amer Corp ....C 607 776-3692
  Bath *(G-661)*
Pompian Manufacturing Co Inc ....G 914 476-7076
  Yonkers *(G-17497)*
Preciseled Inc ....F 516 418-5337
  Valley Stream *(G-16443)*
Prestigeline Inc ....D 631 273-3636
  Bay Shore *(G-724)*
Quality HM Brands Holdings LLC ....A 718 292-2024
  Bronx *(G-1436)*
Quoizel Inc ....E 631 436-4402
  Hauppauge *(G-6202)*
Rapid-Lite Fixture Corporation ....F 347 599-2600
  Brooklyn *(G-2497)*
Remains Lighting ....E 212 675-8051
  New York *(G-11861)*
Sandy Littman Designs ....G 845 562-1112
  Newburgh *(G-12802)*
Saratoga Lighting Holdings LLC ....G 212 906-7800
  New York *(G-11990)*
Satco Products Inc ....D 631 243-2022
  Edgewood *(G-4624)*
Savwatt Usa Inc ....G 646 478-2676
  New York *(G-11998)*
Solarwaterway Inc ....E 888 998-5337
  Brooklyn *(G-2607)*
Swarovski Lighting Ltd ....B 518 563-7500
  Plattsburgh *(G-13731)*
Swivelier Company Inc ....D 845 353-1455
  Blauvelt *(G-970)*
Tarsier Ltd ....C 212 401-6181
  New York *(G-12305)*
Tudor Electrical Supply Co Inc ....F 212 867-7550
  New York *(G-12442)*
Ulster Precision Inc ....F 845 338-0995
  Kingston *(G-7246)*
Vaughan Designs Inc ....G 212 319-7070
  New York *(G-12534)*
Vision Quest Lighting Inc ....E 631 737-4800
  Ronkonkoma *(G-15022)*
Vonn LLC ....F 888 604-8666
  Long Island City *(G-7946)*
Wainland Inc ....E 718 626-2233
  Astoria *(G-460)*

LIGHTING FIXTURES: Residential, Electric

Expo Furniture Designs Inc ....F 516 674-1420
  Glen Cove *(G-5627)*
Lighting Collaborative Inc ....G 212 253-7220
  Brooklyn *(G-2224)*
Serway Bros Inc ....E 315 337-0601
  Rome *(G-14864)*

LIGHTING FIXTURES: Street

Eluminocity US Inc ....G 651 528-1165
  New York *(G-10068)*
Power and Cnstr Group Inc ....E 585 889-6020
  Scottsville *(G-15360)*

LIGHTS: Trouble lights

Lyn Jo Enterprises Ltd ....G 716 753-2776
  Mayville *(G-8248)*

LIME

Lime Energy Co ....G 704 892-4424
  Buffalo *(G-3064)*

LIME: Agricultural

Masick Soil Conservation Co ....F 518 827-5354
  Schoharie *(G-15339)*

LIMESTONE & MARBLE: Dimension

Domoteck Interiors Inc ....G 718 433-4300
  Woodside *(G-17343)*
Minerals Technologies Inc ....E 212 878-1800
  New York *(G-11302)*

LIMESTONE: Crushed & Broken

Barrett Paving Materials Inc ....F 315 737-9471
  Clayville *(G-3712)*
Cobleskill Stone Products Inc ....E 518 299-3066
  Prattsville *(G-13961)*
Cobleskill Stone Products Inc ....F 518 295-7121
  Schoharie *(G-15338)*
Cobleskill Stone Products Inc ....F 518 234-0221
  Cobleskill *(G-3760)*
Cobleskill Stone Products Inc ....F 607 637-4271
  Hancock *(G-5984)*
Hanson Aggregates PA Inc ....E 315 858-1100
  Jordanville *(G-7160)*
Hanson Aggregates PA LLC ....E 315 469-5501
  Jamesville *(G-7083)*
Hanson Aggregates PA LLC ....E 315 685-3321
  Skaneateles *(G-15485)*
Hanson Aggregates PA LLC ....E 585 624-1220
  Honeoye Falls *(G-6558)*
Hanson Aggregates PA LLC ....E 315 821-7222
  Oriskany Falls *(G-13342)*
Hanson Aggregates PA LLC ....E 315 789-6202
  Oaks Corners *(G-13089)*
Jml Quarries Inc ....E 845 932-8206
  Cochecton *(G-3766)*
John Vespa Inc ....F 315 788-6330
  Watertown *(G-16678)*
Lafarge North America Inc ....F 716 876-8788
  Tonawanda *(G-16195)*
Lilac Quarries   LLC ....G 607 867-4016
  Mount Upton *(G-8700)*
Patterson Materials Corp ....E 845 832-6000
  New Windsor *(G-8993)*
Shelby Crushed Stone Inc ....F 585 798-4501
  Medina *(G-8314)*
Specialty Minerals Inc ....E 212 878-1800
  New York *(G-12178)*
Upstone Materials Inc.............................E 518 891-0236
  Saranac Lake *(G-15167)*

LIMESTONE: Cut & Shaped

Hanson Aggregates East LLC ....F 315 493-3721
  Great Bend *(G-5798)*
Minerals Technologies Inc ....E 212 878-1800
  New York *(G-11302)*

LIMESTONE: Dimension

New York Quarries Inc ....F 518 756-3138
  Alcove *(G-175)*

LIMESTONE: Ground

Hanson Aggregates PA Inc ....F 518 568-2444
  Saint Johnsville *(G-15120)*
Hanson Aggregates PA LLC ....F 315 393-3743
  Ogdensburg *(G-13136)*

LINEN SPLY SVC: Coat

Maple Grove Corp ....E 585 492-5286
  Arcade *(G-396)*

LINENS & TOWELS WHOLESALERS

American Country Quilts & Lin ....G 631 283-5466
  Southampton *(G-15562)*
David King Linen Inc ....F 718 241-7298
  New York *(G-9876)*
Paramount Textiles Inc ....F 212 966-1040
  New York *(G-11583)*

LINENS: Napkins, Fabric & Nonwoven, From Purchased Materials

Bardwil Industries Inc ....E 212 944-1870
  New York *(G-9369)*

LINENS: Tablecloths, From Purchased Materials

Benson Sales Co Inc ....F 718 236-6743
  Brooklyn *(G-1683)*

Josie Accessories Inc ....D 212 889-6376
  New York *(G-10807)*
Michael Stuart Inc ....E 718 821-0704
  Brooklyn *(G-2314)*
Premier Skirting Products Inc ....F 516 239-6581
  Lawrence *(G-7422)*
Repellem Consumer Pdts Corp ....F 631 273-3992
  Bohemia *(G-1122)*
Tablecloths For Granted Ltd ....F 518 370-5481
  Schenectady *(G-15326)*
University Table Cloth Company ....F 845 371-3876
  Spring Valley *(G-15627)*

LINERS & COVERS: Fabric

Meyco Products Inc ....E 631 421-9800
  Melville *(G-8366)*
Vinyl Works Inc ....E 518 786-1200
  Latham *(G-7410)*

LINERS & LINING

Joshua Liner Gallery LLC ....F 212 244-7415
  New York *(G-10806)*
Themis Chimney Inc ....F 718 937-4716
  Brooklyn *(G-2677)*

LINERS: Indl, Metal Plate

Lifetime Chimney Supply LLC ....G 516 576-8144
  Plainview *(G-13643)*

LININGS: Apparel, Made From Purchased Materials

Bpe Studio Inc ....G 212 868-9896
  New York *(G-9500)*

LININGS: Fabric, Apparel & Other, Exc Millinery

Amoseastern Apparel Inc ....F 212 921-1859
  New York *(G-9189)*
Pangea Brands LLC ....G 617 638-0001
  New York *(G-11573)*
Pangea Brands LLC ....G 617 638-0001
  New York *(G-11574)*
Polkadot Usa Inc ....G 914 835-3697
  Mamaroneck *(G-8076)*

LIP BALMS

Lotta Luv Beauty LLC ....F 646 786-2847
  New York *(G-11074)*

LIPSTICK

Precision Cosmetics Mfg Co ....G 914 667-1200
  Mount Vernon *(G-8762)*

LIQUEFIED PETROLEUM GAS DEALERS

Praxair Distribution Inc ....G 315 457-5821
  Liverpool *(G-7569)*

LIQUID CRYSTAL DISPLAYS

Apollo Display Tech Corp ....E 631 580-4360
  Ronkonkoma *(G-14899)*
Dimension Technologies Inc ....G 585 436-3530
  Rochester *(G-14330)*
Orthogonal 585 254-2775
  Rochester *(G-14578)*
Plura Broadcast Inc ....F 516 997-5675
  Massapequa *(G-8212)*
W D Technology Inc ....F 914 779-8738
  Eastchester *(G-4595)*

LITHOGRAPHIC PLATES

Chakra Communications Inc ....E 716 505-7300
  Lancaster *(G-7333)*

LOCK & KEY SVCS

Advanced Door Solutions Inc ....G 631 773-6100
  Holbrook *(G-6457)*

LOCKERS

Locker Masters Inc ....F 518 288-3203
  Granville *(G-5790)*

LOCKERS: Refrigerated

Carrier Corporation .... B 315 432-3844
  East Syracuse *(G-4532)*
Storflex Holdings Inc .... C 607 962-2137
  Corning *(G-4003)*

LOCKS

A & L Doors & Hardware LLC .... F 718 585-8400
  Bronx *(G-1252)*
Delta Lock Company LLC .... F 631 238-7035
  Bohemia *(G-1051)*
Dortronics Systems Inc .... E 631 725-0505
  Sag Harbor *(G-15105)*
Eazy Locks LLC .... G 718 327-7770
  Far Rockaway *(G-4927)*
G Marks Hdwr Liquidating Corp ...... D 631 225-5400
  Amityville *(G-287)*
Safe Skies LLC .... G 888 632-5027
  New York *(G-11970)*

LOCKS: Coin-Operated

American Lckr SEC Systems Inc ...... E 716 699-2773
  Ellicottville *(G-4654)*

LOCKS: Safe & Vault, Metal

Secureit Tactical Inc .... F 800 651-8835
  Syracuse *(G-16059)*

LOCKSMITHS

A & L Doors & Hardware LLC .... F 718 585-8400
  Bronx *(G-1252)*

LOG LOADING & UNLOADING SVCS

Seaway Timber Harvesting Inc .... D 315 769-5970
  Massena *(G-8231)*

LOGGING

Attica Package Company Inc .... F 585 591-0510
  Attica *(G-471)*
B & B Forest Products Ltd .... F 518 622-0811
  Cairo *(G-3296)*
Central Timber Co Inc .... G 518 638-6338
  Granville *(G-5789)*
Chad Pierson .... G 518 251-0186
  Bakers Mills *(G-556)*
Clearlake Land Co Inc .... G 315 848-2427
  Star Lake *(G-15648)*
Dan Beers .... G 607 316-8895
  Earlville *(G-4384)*
Daniel & Lois Lyndaker Logging ...... G 315 346-6527
  Castorland *(G-3451)*
Davis Logging & Lumber .... G 315 245-1040
  Camden *(G-3342)*
Donald Snyder Jr .... F 315 265-4485
  Potsdam *(G-13896)*
Ed Beach Forest Management .... G 607 538-1745
  Bloomville *(G-988)*
Finger Lakes Timber Co Inc .... G 585 346-2990
  Livonia *(G-7591)*
Garland Logging LLC .... G 518 483-1170
  Malone *(G-8041)*
George Chilson Logging .... G 607 732-1558
  Elmira *(G-4699)*
GL & RL Logging Inc .... F 518 883-3936
  Broadalbin *(G-1241)*
Guldenschuh Logging & Lbr LLC ..... G 585 538-4750
  Caledonia *(G-3307)*
Harris Logging Inc .... E 518 792-1083
  Queensbury *(G-14011)*
Kevin Regan Logging Ltd .... G 315 245-3890
  Camden *(G-3345)*
Mountain Forest Products Inc .... G 518 597-3674
  Crown Point *(G-4093)*
Murray Logging LLC .... G 518 834-7372
  Keeseville *(G-7169)*
Northern Timber Harvesting LLC ...... F 585 233-7330
  Alfred Station *(G-200)*
Oak Valley Logging Inc .... G 518 622-8249
  Cairo *(G-3301)*
Peters LLC .... G 607 637-5470
  Hancock *(G-5988)*
Robert W Still .... F 315 942-5594
  Ava *(G-529)*
Russell Bass .... F 607 637-5253
  Hancock *(G-5989)*

Schaefer Logging Inc .... F 607 467-4990
  Deposit *(G-4304)*
Seaway Timber Harvesting Inc .... D 315 769-5970
  Massena *(G-8231)*
Tim Cretin Logging & Sawmill .... F 315 946-4476
  Lyons *(G-8003)*
Timothy L Simpson .... G 518 234-1401
  Sharon Springs *(G-15407)*
Van Cpeters Logging Inc .... G 607 637-3574
  Hancock *(G-5990)*
William Ward Logging .... F 518 946-7826
  Jay *(G-7089)*

LOGGING CAMPS & CONTRACTORS

Baker Logging & Firewood .... G 585 374-5733
  Naples *(G-8810)*
Couture Logging Inc .... G 607 753-6445
  Cortland *(G-4046)*
Couture Timber Harvesting .... G 607 836-4719
  Mc Graw *(G-8252)*
Decker Forest Products Inc .... G 607 563-2345
  Sidney *(G-15460)*
Homer Logging Contractor .... G 607 753-8553
  Homer *(G-6548)*
J & S Logging Inc .... E 315 262-2112
  South Colton *(G-15537)*
Klein & Sons Logging Inc .... F 845 292-6682
  Wht Sphr Spgs *(G-17250)*
Lizotte Logging Inc .... F 518 359-2200
  Tupper Lake *(G-16300)*
Matteson Logging Inc .... G 585 593-3037
  Wellsville *(G-16780)*
Paul J Mitchell Logging Inc .... E 518 359-7029
  Tupper Lake *(G-16302)*
Richard Bauer Logging .... G 585 343-4149
  Alexander *(G-193)*
Richards Logging LLC .... F 518 359-2775
  Tupper Lake *(G-16303)*
Robert W Butts Logging Co .... G 518 643-2897
  Peru *(G-13550)*
Smoothbore International Inc .... G 315 754-8124
  Red Creek *(G-14039)*
Snyder Logging .... G 315 265-1462
  Potsdam *(G-13902)*
Wadsworth Logging Inc .... G 518 863-6870
  Gloversville *(G-5742)*

LOGGING: Timber, Cut At Logging Camp

Got Wood LLC .... G 315 440-8857
  Cleveland *(G-3718)*
Lyndaker Timber Harvesting LLC ..... F 315 346-1328
  Castorland *(G-3452)*
Tonche Timber LLC .... G 845 389-3489
  Amsterdam *(G-370)*

LOGGING: Wood Chips, Produced In The Field

Chip It All Ltd .... G 631 473-2040
  Port Jefferson *(G-13797)*

LOGGING: Wooden Logs

Kapstone Container Corporation ..... D 518 842-2450
  Amsterdam *(G-352)*

LOOSELEAF BINDERS

Acco Brands USA LLC .... C 847 541-9500
  Ogdensburg *(G-13130)*
Brewer-Cantelmo Co Inc .... E 212 244-4600
  New York *(G-9510)*
Consolidated Loose Leaf Inc .... E 212 924-5800
  New York *(G-9767)*
Sellco Industries Inc .... E 607 756-7594
  Cortland *(G-4068)*

LOTIONS OR CREAMS: Face

3lab Inc .... F 201 567-9100
  New York *(G-9020)*
Distribio USA LLC .... G 212 989-6077
  New York *(G-9941)*
EL Erman International Ltd .... G 212 444-9440
  Brooklyn *(G-1911)*
Fsr Beauty Ltd .... G 212 447-0036
  New York *(G-10265)*
Gassho Body & Mind Inc .... G 518 695-9991
  Schuylerville *(G-15341)*

LOTIONS: SHAVING

Glacee Skincare LLC .... G 212 690-7632
  New York *(G-10344)*

LOUDSPEAKERS

Global Market Development Inc ...... E 631 667-1002
  Edgewood *(G-4613)*
Speaqua Corp .... E 858 334-9042
  Deer Park *(G-4237)*

LOUVERS: Ventilating

Airflex Industrial Inc .... E 631 752-1234
  Farmingdale *(G-4940)*
Airflex Industrial Inc .... E 631 752-1234
  Farmingdale *(G-4941)*
Imperial Damper & Louver Co .... E 718 731-3800
  Bronx *(G-1361)*

LOZENGES: Pharmaceutical

HHS Pharmaceuticals Inc .... F 347 674-1670
  New York *(G-10516)*

LUBRICANTS: Corrosion Preventive

Engineering Maint Pdts Inc .... F 516 624-9774
  Oyster Bay *(G-13395)*
Reliance Fluid Tech LLC .... E 716 332-0988
  Niagara Falls *(G-12885)*

LUBRICATING EQPT: Indl

Advanced Tchncal Solutions Inc ..... F 914 214-8230
  Yorktown Heights *(G-17522)*
Innovative Pdts of Amer Inc .... E 845 679-4500
  Woodstock *(G-17379)*

LUBRICATING OIL & GREASE WHOLESALERS

Chemlube International LLC .... F 914 381-5800
  Harrison *(G-6000)*
Chemlube Marketing Inc .... F 914 381-5800
  Harrison *(G-6001)*

LUBRICATION SYSTEMS & EQPT

Bowen Products Corporation .... G 315 498-4481
  Nedrow *(G-8818)*

LUGGAGE & BRIEFCASES

Adam Scott Designs Inc .... E 212 420-8866
  New York *(G-9071)*
Atlantic Specialty Co Inc .... E 845 356-2502
  Monsey *(G-8604)*
Bragley Mfg Co Inc .... E 718 622-7469
  Brooklyn *(G-1711)*
Deluxe Travel Store Inc .... G 718 435-8111
  Brooklyn *(G-1853)*
Fish & Crown Ltd .... D 212 707-9603
  New York *(G-10226)*
Golden Bridge Group Inc .... G 718 335-8882
  Elmhurst *(G-4676)*
Hornet Group Inc .... D 845 858-6400
  Port Jervis *(G-13808)*
Prepac Designs Inc .... G 914 524-7800
  Yonkers *(G-17498)*
Rhino Trunk & Case Inc .... E 585 244-4553
  Rochester *(G-14647)*
Rose Trunk Mfg Co Inc .... F 516 766-6686
  Oceanside *(G-13115)*
Royal Industries Inc .... E 718 369-3046
  Brooklyn *(G-2531)*
Trunk & Trolley LLC .... E 212 947-9001
  New York *(G-12433)*

LUGGAGE & LEATHER GOODS STORES: Leather, Exc Luggage & Shoes

House of Portfolios Co Inc .... G 212 206-7323
  New York *(G-10562)*
Tandy Leather Factory Inc .... G 845 480-3588
  Nyack *(G-13071)*

LUGGAGE WHOLESALERS

Deluxe Travel Store Inc .... G 718 435-8111
  Brooklyn *(G-1853)*

PRODUCT SECTION

LUGGAGE: Traveling Bags

Aka Sport Inc .... F 631 858-9888
  Dix Hills *(G-4312)*
Carry-All Canvas Bag Co Inc .... G 718 375-4230
  Brooklyn *(G-1761)*
Lo & Sons Inc .... F 917 775-4025
  Brooklyn *(G-2236)*
Tumi Inc .... C 212 742-8020
  New York *(G-12445)*

LUGGAGE: Wardrobe Bags

Goyard Inc .... G 212 813-0005
  New York *(G-10383)*
Goyard Miami LLC .... G 212 813-0005
  New York *(G-10384)*

LUMBER & BLDG MATLS DEALER, RET: Garage Doors, Sell/Install

Amarr Company .... F 585 426-8290
  Rochester *(G-14210)*
EZ Lift Operator Corp .... F 845 356-1676
  Spring Valley *(G-15606)*
L & L Overhead Garage Doors .... G 718 721-2518
  Long Island City *(G-7813)*

LUMBER & BLDG MATRLS DEALERS, RET: Bath Fixtures, Eqpt/Sply

Vaire LLC .... G 631 271-4933
  Huntington Station *(G-6765)*

LUMBER & BLDG MTRLS DEALERS, RET: Closets, Interiors/Access

Cubbies Unlimited Corporation .... F 631 586-8572
  Deer Park *(G-4146)*

LUMBER & BLDG MTRLS DEALERS, RET: Doors, Storm, Wood/Metal

Finger Lakes Trellis Supply .... G 315 904-4007
  Williamson *(G-17252)*

LUMBER & BLDG MTRLS DEALERS, RET: Windows, Storm, Wood/Metal

All United Window Corp .... E 718 624-0490
  Brooklyn *(G-1587)*
Express Building Supply Inc .... E 516 608-0379
  Oceanside *(G-13099)*

LUMBER & BUILDING MATERIALS DEALER, RET: Door & Window Prdts

City Store Gates Mfg Corp .... E 718 939-9700
  College Point *(G-3806)*
D D & L Inc .... F 607 729-9131
  Binghamton *(G-902)*
Executive Mirror Doors Inc .... G 631 234-1090
  Ronkonkoma *(G-14928)*
Lif Industries Inc .... E 718 767-8800
  Whitestone *(G-17240)*
M & D Installers Inc .... D 718 782-6978
  Brooklyn *(G-2245)*
Thompson Overhead Door Co Inc .... F 718 788-2470
  Brooklyn *(G-2678)*

LUMBER & BUILDING MATERIALS DEALER, RET: Masonry Matls/Splys

Afco Precast Sales Corp .... D 631 924-7114
  Middle Island *(G-8438)*
Cranesville Block Co Inc .... G 315 384-4000
  Norfolk *(G-12915)*
Ferrara Bros LLC .... E 718 939-3030
  Flushing *(G-5248)*
Guardian Concrete Inc .... F 518 372-0080
  Schenectady *(G-15294)*
Nicolia Concrete Products Inc .... D 631 669-0700
  Lindenhurst *(G-7500)*
Palumbo Block Co Inc .... G 845 832-6100
  Dover Plains *(G-4340)*

LUMBER & BUILDING MATERIALS DEALERS, RETAIL: Brick

Barrasso & Sons Trucking Inc .... E 631 581-0360
  Islip Terrace *(G-6854)*

LUMBER & BUILDING MATERIALS DEALERS, RETAIL: Countertops

Nlr Counter Tops LLC .... G 347 295-0410
  New York *(G-11461)*
NY Cabinet Factory Inc .... F 718 256-6541
  Brooklyn *(G-2392)*

LUMBER & BUILDING MATERIALS DEALERS, RETAIL: Paving Stones

Pallette Stone Corporation .... E 518 584-2421
  Gansevoort *(G-5501)*
Unilock New York Inc .... G 845 278-6700
  Brewster *(G-1227)*

LUMBER & BUILDING MATERIALS DEALERS, RETAIL: Sand & Gravel

Champion Materials Inc .... G 315 493-2654
  Carthage *(G-3439)*
Champion Materials Inc .... E 315 493-2654
  Carthage *(G-3440)*

LUMBER & BUILDING MATERIALS DEALERS, RETAIL: Tile, Ceramic

Amendola MBL & Stone Ctr Inc .... D 914 997-7968
  White Plains *(G-17104)*
Glen Plaza Marble & Gran Inc .... G 516 671-1100
  Glen Cove *(G-5630)*

LUMBER & BUILDING MATERIALS RET DEALERS: Millwork & Lumber

Andike Millwork Inc .... G 718 894-1796
  Maspeth *(G-8146)*
Attica Package Company Inc .... F 585 591-0510
  Attica *(G-471)*
Island Street Lumber Co Inc .... G 716 692-4127
  North Tonawanda *(G-12996)*
Meltz Lumber Co of Mellenville .... E 518 672-7021
  Hudson *(G-6656)*
Pella Corporation .... C 631 208-0710
  Calverton *(G-3322)*
Pgs Millwork Inc .... D 212 244-6610
  New York *(G-11663)*
Stephenson Lumber Company Inc .... E 518 548-7521
  Speculator *(G-15587)*

LUMBER & BUILDING MATLS DEALERS, RET: Concrete/Cinder Block

Cranesville Block Co Inc .... E 518 684-6154
  Amsterdam *(G-341)*
Duke Concrete Products Inc .... E 518 793-7743
  Queensbury *(G-14008)*
Fort Miller Service Corp .... F 518 695-5000
  Greenwich *(G-5907)*
Taylor Concrete Products Inc .... E 315 788-2191
  Watertown *(G-16696)*

LUMBER: Dimension, Hardwood

Norton-Smith Hardwoods Inc .... G 716 945-0346
  Salamanca *(G-15130)*
Wrights Hardwoods Inc .... G 716 595-2345
  Cassadaga *(G-3443)*

LUMBER: Fiberboard

Niagara Fiberboard Inc .... E 716 434-8881
  Lockport *(G-7635)*

LUMBER: Fuelwood, From Mill Waste

GM Palmer Inc .... F 585 492-2990
  Arcade *(G-393)*
PA Pellets LLC .... F 814 848-9970
  Pittsford *(G-13600)*

LUMBER: Furniture Dimension Stock, Softwood

Hennig Custom Woodwork Corp .... G 516 536-3460
  Oceanside *(G-13101)*

LUMBER: Hardwood Dimension

A D Bowman & Son Lumber Co .... E 607 692-2595
  Castle Creek *(G-3445)*

Carlson Wood Products Inc .... G 716 287-2923
  Sinclairville *(G-15473)*
Gutchess Lumber Co Inc .... C 607 753-3393
  Cortland *(G-4052)*
Potter Lumber Co LLC .... D 814 438-7888
  Hamburg *(G-5960)*
Sirianni Hardwoods Inc .... E 607 962-4688
  Painted Post *(G-13420)*

LUMBER: Hardwood Dimension & Flooring Mills

B & B Lumber Company Inc .... D 866 282-0582
  Jamesville *(G-7077)*
Clements Burrville Sawmill .... G 315 782-4549
  Watertown *(G-16666)*
Donver Incorporated .... F 716 945-1910
  Kill Buck *(G-7195)*
Fibron Products Inc .... E 716 886-2378
  Buffalo *(G-2961)*
Fitzpatrick and Weller Inc .... G 716 699-2393
  Ellicottville *(G-4655)*
H B Millwork Inc .... F 631 289-8086
  Medford *(G-8277)*
Horizon Floors I LLC .... F 212 509-9686
  New York *(G-10549)*
J & J Log & Lumber Corp .... D 845 832-6535
  Dover Plains *(G-4339)*
J A Yansick Lumber Co Inc .... G 585 492-4312
  Arcade *(G-395)*
Mm of East Aurora LLC .... F 716 651-9663
  Buffalo *(G-3089)*
Petteys Lumber 518 792-5943
  Fort Ann *(G-5344)*
Potter Lumber Co Inc .... G 716 373-1260
  Allegany *(G-205)*
Premier Hardwood Products Inc .... E 315 492-1786
  Jamesville *(G-7084)*
S Donadic Woodworking Inc .... D 718 361-9888
  Sunnyside *(G-15830)*
Tupper Lake Hardwoods Inc .... E 518 359-8248
  Tupper Lake *(G-16305)*
Wagner Hardwoods LLC .... E 607 594-3321
  Cayuta *(G-3467)*
Wagner Hardwoods LLC .... C 607 594-3321
  Cayuta *(G-3468)*
Wagner Millwork Inc .... D 607 687-5362
  Owego *(G-13386)*

LUMBER: Kiln Dried

Carlson Wood Products Inc .... G 716 287-2923
  Sinclairville *(G-15473)*
Mallery Lumber LLC .... G 607 637-2236
  Hancock *(G-5987)*
Salamanca Lumber Company Inc .... E 716 945-4810
  Salamanca *(G-15131)*

LUMBER: Plywood, Hardwood

Sure-Lock Industries LLC .... F 315 207-0044
  Oswego *(G-13368)*
Veneer One Inc .... E 516 536-6480
  Oceanside *(G-13125)*

LUMBER: Plywood, Hardwood or Hardwood Faced

Kings Quartet Corp .... G 845 986-9090
  Warwick *(G-16614)*

LUMBER: Plywood, Prefinished, Hardwood

Geonex International Corp .... G 212 473-4555
  New York *(G-10324)*

LUMBER: Plywood, Softwood

H B Millwork Inc .... F 631 289-8086
  Medford *(G-8277)*

LUMBER: Poles, Wood, Untreated

3b Timber Company Inc .... F 315 942-6580
  Boonville *(G-1158)*

LUMBER: Siding, Dressed

Weather Tight Exteriors .... G 631 375-5108
  Ridge *(G-14108)*

LUMBER: Silo Stock, Sawn

Machina Deus Lex Inc .... G 917 577-0972
Jamaica *(G-6962)*

LUMBER: Treated

Donver Incorporated .... F 716 945-1910
Kill Buck *(G-7195)*
Northeast Treaters Inc .... E 518 945-2660
Athens *(G-463)*
Northeast Treaters NY LLC .... E 518 945-2660
Athens *(G-464)*

LUNCHROOMS & CAFETERIAS

Wired Coffee and Bagel Inc .... F 518 506-3194
Malta *(G-8054)*

MACHINE PARTS: Stamped Or Pressed Metal

Action Machined Products Inc .... F 631 842-2333
Copiague *(G-3916)*
Allen Machine Products Inc .... E 631 630-8800
Hauppauge *(G-6035)*
Belrix Industries Inc .... G 716 821-5964
Buffalo *(G-2859)*
Brach Machine Inc .... F 585 343-9134
Batavia *(G-627)*
Bryant Machine Co Inc .... F 716 894-8282
Buffalo *(G-2868)*
Cgs Fabrication LLC .... F 585 347-6127
Webster *(G-16740)*
Cnc Manufacturing Corp .... E 718 728-6800
Long Island City *(G-7729)*
Colonial Precision Machinery .... G 631 249-0738
Farmingdale *(G-4971)*
Creative Design and Mch Inc .... E 845 778-9001
Rock Tavern *(G-14809)*
Custom Metal Incorporated .... F 631 643-4075
West Babylon *(G-16812)*
Electric Motors and Pumps Inc .... G 718 935-9118
Brooklyn *(G-1912)*
Forkey Construction & Fabg Inc .... E 607 849-4879
Cortland *(G-4048)*
G A Richards & Co Inc .... F 516 334-5412
Westbury *(G-17015)*
German Machine & Assembly Inc .... E 585 546-4200
Rochester *(G-14419)*
J P Machine Products Inc .... F 631 249-9229
Farmingdale *(G-5022)*
K Tooling LLC .... E 607 637-3781
Hancock *(G-5986)*
Lancaster Knives Inc .... E 716 683-5050
Lancaster *(G-7347)*
M F Manufacturing Enterprises .... G 516 822-5135
Hicksville *(G-6392)*
Maehr Industries Inc .... G 631 924-1661
Bellport *(G-829)*
Mega Tool & Mfg Corp .... E 607 734-8398
Elmira *(G-4709)*
Pervi Precision Company Inc .... G 631 589-5557
Bohemia *(G-1113)*
Rayco Manufacturing Co Inc .... F 516 431-2006
Jamaica *(G-6981)*
Reynolds Manufacturing Inc .... F 607 562-8936
Big Flats *(G-879)*
Sharon Manufacturing Co Inc .... G 631 242-8870
Deer Park *(G-4234)*
Solidus Industries Inc .... D 607 749-4540
Homer *(G-6550)*
Twinco Mfg Co Inc .... E 631 231-0022
Hauppauge *(G-6243)*
Vosky Precision Machining Corp .... F 631 737-3200
Ronkonkoma *(G-15024)*
Wessie Machine Inc .... G 315 926-4060
Marion *(G-8134)*
Zeta Machine Corp .... G 631 471-8832
Ronkonkoma *(G-15026)*

MACHINE SHOPS

A and K Machine and Welding .... G 631 231-2552
Bay Shore *(G-663)*
Acad Design Corp .... F 585 254-6960
Rochester *(G-14179)*
Addison Precision Mfg Corp .... D 585 254-1386
Rochester *(G-14188)*
Allied Industrial Products Co .... G 716 664-3893
Jamestown *(G-7006)*
Applied Technology Mfg Corp .... E 607 687-2200
Owego *(G-13375)*
Architectural Coatings Inc .... F 718 418-9584
Brooklyn *(G-1624)*
B & R Industries Inc .... F 631 736-2275
Medford *(G-8267)*
Birch Machine & Tool Inc .... G 716 735-9802
Middleport *(G-8454)*
Bms Manufacturing Co Inc .... E 607 535-2426
Watkins Glen *(G-16718)*
Carballo Contract Machining .... G 315 594-2511
Wolcott *(G-17299)*
Carbaugh Tool Company Inc .... E 607 739-3293
Elmira *(G-4686)*
Carter Precision Metals LLC .... F 516 333-1917
Westbury *(G-17001)*
Conesus Lake Association Inc .... E 585 346-6864
Lakeville *(G-7306)*
Courser Inc .... E 607 739-3861
Elmira *(G-4690)*
David Fehlman .... G 315 455-8888
Syracuse *(G-15942)*
DMD Machining Technology Inc .... G 585 659-8180
Kendall *(G-7171)*
Elite Precise Manufacturer LLC .... E 518 993-3040
Fort Plain *(G-5356)*
Engineering Mfg Tech LLC .... D 607 754-7111
Endicott *(G-4813)*
Euro Gear (usa) Inc .... E 518 578-1775
Plattsburgh *(G-13690)*
Everfab Inc .... D 716 655-1550
East Aurora *(G-4395)*
G & G C Machine & Tool Co Inc .... E 516 873-0999
Westbury *(G-17014)*
Genesis Machining Corp .... F 516 377-1197
North Baldwin *(G-12922)*
Gentner Precision Components .... G 315 597-5734
Palmyra *(G-13433)*
Gpp Post-Closing Inc .... E 585 334-4640
Rush *(G-15075)*
Harwitt Industries Inc .... F 516 623-9787
Freeport *(G-5416)*
Hohl Machine & Conveyor Co Inc .... E 716 882-7210
Buffalo *(G-3013)*
Hunter Machine Inc .... F 585 924-7480
Victor *(G-16505)*
Indian Springs Mfg Co Inc .... F 315 635-6101
Baldwinsville *(G-570)*
Industrial Precision Pdts Inc .... E 315 343-4421
Oswego *(G-13358)*
Industrial Services of Wny .... G 716 799-7788
Niagara Falls *(G-12854)*
Island Machine Inc .... G 518 562-1232
Plattsburgh *(G-13698)*
ISO Plastics Corp .... D 914 663-8300
Mount Vernon *(G-8739)*
J & J TI Die Mfg & Stampg Corp .... G 845 228-0242
Carmel *(G-3428)*
Jam Industries Inc .... E 585 458-9830
Rochester *(G-14479)*
Johnnys Machine Shop .... G 631 338-9733
West Babylon *(G-16831)*
Johnston Precision Inc .... E 315 253-4181
Auburn *(G-503)*
Jordan Machine Inc .... F 585 647-3585
Rochester *(G-14486)*
Kal Manufacturing Corporation .... E 585 265-4310
Webster *(G-16751)*
KMA Corporation .... G 518 743-1330
Glens Falls *(G-5701)*
M & S Precision Machine Co LLC .... F 518 747-1193
Queensbury *(G-14017)*
Magellan Aerospace Bethel Inc .... E 203 798-9373
Corona *(G-4024)*
Mar-A-Thon Filters Inc .... F 631 957-4774
Lindenhurst *(G-7492)*
Micro Instrument Corp .... D 585 458-3150
Rochester *(G-14528)*
Mitchell Machine Tool LLC .... E 585 254-7520
Rochester *(G-14536)*
Mount Vernon Machine Inc .... E 845 268-9400
Valley Cottage *(G-16408)*
Ms Spares LLC .... F 607 223-3024
Clay *(G-3709)*
Neptune Machine Inc .... F 718 852-4100
Brooklyn *(G-2365)*
New Age Precision Tech Inc .... E 631 471-4000
Ronkonkoma *(G-14981)*
Nitro Manufacturing LLC .... G 716 646-9900
North Collins *(G-12945)*
Optics Technology Inc .... E 585 586-0950
Pittsford *(G-13599)*
Precision Metals Corp .... E 631 586-5032
Bay Shore *(G-723)*
Precision Systems Mfg Inc .... E 315 451-3480
Liverpool *(G-7570)*
Progressive Mch & Design LLC .... C 585 924-5250
Victor *(G-16521)*
Pronto Tool & Die Co Inc .... E 631 981-8920
Ronkonkoma *(G-14997)*
Prz Technologies Inc .... F 716 683-1300
Lancaster *(G-7360)*
Roccera LLC .... F 585 426-0887
Rochester *(G-14654)*
Rochester Atomated Systems Inc .... E 585 594-3222
Rochester *(G-14657)*
Saturn Industries Inc .... E 518 828-9956
Hudson *(G-6663)*
Sick Inc .... E 585 347-2000
Webster *(G-16761)*
Source Technologies .... F 718 708-0305
Brooklyn *(G-2610)*
T R P Machine Inc .... E 631 567-9620
Bohemia *(G-1138)*
Tioga Tool Inc .... F 607 785-6005
Endicott *(G-4835)*
Tobeyco Manufacturing Co Inc .... F 607 962-2446
Corning *(G-4004)*
Triple Point Manufacturing .... G 631 218-4988
Bohemia *(G-1146)*
Triplett Machine Inc .... D 315 548-3198
Phelps *(G-13561)*
Twinco Mfg Co Inc .... E 631 231-0022
Hauppauge *(G-6243)*
Ultra Tool and Manufacturing .... F 585 467-3700
Rochester *(G-14766)*
V Lake Industries Inc .... G 716 885-9141
Buffalo *(G-3265)*
Vader Systems LLC .... F 716 688-1600
Getzville *(G-5618)*
Van Thomas Inc .... E 585 426-1414
Rochester *(G-14780)*
Verns Machine Co Inc .... E 315 926-4223
Marion *(G-8133)*
Village Decoration Ltd .... E 315 437-2522
East Syracuse *(G-4591)*
Wordingham Machine Co Inc .... E 585 924-2294
Rochester *(G-14794)*
Zip Products Inc .... F 585 482-0044
Rochester *(G-14805)*

MACHINE TOOL ACCESS: Balancing Machines

Schenck Corporation .... D 631 242-4010
Deer Park *(G-4229)*
Schenck Trebel Corp .... D 631 242-4397
Deer Park *(G-4230)*

MACHINE TOOL ACCESS: Cams

Designatronics Incorporated .... G 516 328-3300
Hicksville *(G-6366)*

MACHINE TOOL ACCESS: Cutting

Ameri-Cut Tool Grinding Inc .... G 716 692-3900
North Tonawanda *(G-12971)*
Boro Park Cutting Tool Corp .... F 718 720-0610
Staten Island *(G-15670)*
Champion Cutting Tool Corp .... E 516 536-8200
Rockville Centre *(G-14817)*
Drill America Inc .... G 516 764-5700
Oceanside *(G-13097)*
Dura-Mill Inc .... E 518 899-2255
Ballston Spa *(G-594)*
Genesee Manufacturing Co Inc .... G 585 266-3201
Rochester *(G-14415)*
Macinnes Tool Corporation .... E 585 467-1920
Rochester *(G-14508)*
Morgood Tools Inc .... D 585 436-8828
Rochester *(G-14542)*
NC Industries Inc .... F 248 528-5200
Buffalo *(G-3103)*
Northeastern Water Jet Inc .... F 518 843-4988
Amsterdam *(G-364)*
Rota File Corporation .... E 516 496-7200
Syosset *(G-15859)*
Steiner Technologies Inc .... F 585 425-5910
Fairport *(G-4887)*

MACHINE TOOL ACCESS: Diamond Cutting, For Turning, Etc

Advance D Tech Inc .... F 845 534-8248
  Cornwall *(G-4006)*

MACHINE TOOL ACCESS: Dies, Thread Cutting

Brinkman Intl Group Inc .... G 585 429-5000
  Rochester *(G-14263)*
C J Winter Machine Tech .... E 585 429-5000
  Rochester *(G-14271)*

MACHINE TOOL ACCESS: Dressing/Wheel Crushing Attach, Diamond

Scomac Inc .... F 585 494-2200
  Bergen *(G-851)*

MACHINE TOOL ACCESS: Drills

Truebite Inc .... F 607 786-3184
  Endicott *(G-4837)*

MACHINE TOOL ACCESS: Knives, Shear

Lancaster Knives Inc .... E 716 683-5050
  Lancaster *(G-7347)*

MACHINE TOOL ACCESS: Milling Machine Attachments

Innex Industries Inc .... E 585 247-3575
  Rochester *(G-14469)*

MACHINE TOOL ACCESS: Sockets

Socket Products Mfg Corp .... G 631 232-9870
  Islandia *(G-6841)*

MACHINE TOOL ACCESS: Tool Holders

New Market Products Co Inc .... F 607 292-6226
  Wayne *(G-16736)*
Robert J Faraone .... G 585 232-7160
  Rochester *(G-14653)*

MACHINE TOOL ACCESS: Tools & Access

Atwood Tool & Machine Inc .... E 607 648-6543
  Chenango Bridge *(G-3623)*
Fred M Velepec Co Inc .... F 718 821-6636
  Glendale *(G-5668)*
Fronhofer Tool Company Inc .... E 518 692-2496
  Cossayuna *(G-4081)*
Genius Tools Americas Corp .... F 716 662-6872
  Orchard Park *(G-13295)*
Huron TI Cutter Grinding Inc .... E 631 420-7000
  Farmingdale *(G-5015)*
JD Tool Inc .... G 607 786-3129
  Endicott *(G-4822)*
Methods Tooling & Mfg Inc .... E 845 246-7100
  Mount Marion *(G-8693)*
Rochling Advent Tool & Mold LP .... D 585 254-2000
  Rochester *(G-14677)*

MACHINE TOOL ATTACHMENTS & ACCESS

Curran Manufacturing Corp .... E 631 273-1010
  Hauppauge *(G-6081)*
Curran Manufacturing Corp .... E 631 273-1010
  Hauppauge *(G-6082)*
Flexbar Machine Corporation .... E 631 582-8440
  Islandia *(G-6831)*
Innovative Automation Inc .... F 631 439-3300
  Farmingdale *(G-5018)*
Jem Tool & Die Corp .... F 631 539-8734
  West Islip *(G-16934)*
Thuro Metal Products Inc .... E 631 435-0444
  Brentwood *(G-1194)*
Velmex Inc .... E 585 657-6151
  Bloomfield *(G-986)*
Willemin Macodel Incorporated .... F 914 345-3504
  Hawthorne *(G-6281)*

MACHINE TOOLS & ACCESS

Ale-Techniques Inc .... F 845 687-7200
  High Falls *(G-6426)*
American Linear Manufacturers .... F 516 333-1351
  Westbury *(G-16993)*

Baldwin Machine Works Inc .... G 631 842-9110
  Copiague *(G-3922)*
Bdp Industries Inc .... E 518 695-6851
  Greenwich *(G-5904)*
Bnm Product Service .... G 631 750-1586
  Holbrook *(G-6460)*
Circo File Corp .... G 516 922-1848
  Oyster Bay *(G-13393)*
Custom Service Solutions Inc .... G 585 637-3760
  Brockport *(G-1242)*
Dinosaw Inc .... E 518 828-9942
  Hudson *(G-6642)*
Dock Hardware Incorporated .... F 585 266-7920
  Rochester *(G-14335)*
Everfab Inc .... D 716 655-1550
  East Aurora *(G-4395)*
F W Roberts Mfg Co Inc .... F 716 434-3555
  Lockport *(G-7614)*
Flashflo Manufacturing Inc .... F 716 826-9500
  Buffalo *(G-2962)*
Gardei Industries LLC .... F 716 693-7100
  North Tonawanda *(G-12991)*
Germanow-Simon Corporation .... E 585 232-1440
  Rochester *(G-14420)*
Graywood Companies Inc .... E 585 254-7000
  Rochester *(G-14433)*
Griffin Manufacturing Company .... F 585 265-1991
  Webster *(G-16748)*
Heidenhain International Inc .... C 716 661-1700
  Jamestown *(G-7033)*
J H Robotics Inc .... E 607 729-3758
  Johnson City *(G-7127)*
JW Burg Machine & Tool Inc .... G 716 434-0015
  Clarence Center *(G-3704)*
Kps Capital Partners LP .... E 212 338-5100
  New York *(G-10922)*
Linde LLC .... D 716 773-7552
  Grand Island *(G-5776)*
M & S Precision Machine Co LLC .... F 518 747-1193
  Queensbury *(G-14017)*
Make-Waves Instrument Corp .... E 716 681-7524
  Buffalo *(G-3076)*
Michael Fiore Ltd .... G 516 561-8238
  Valley Stream *(G-16440)*
Micro Centric Corporation 800 573-1139
  Plainview *(G-13649)*
Myles Tool Company Inc .... E 716 731-1300
  Sanborn *(G-15151)*
Omega Tool Measuring Mchs Inc .... E 585 598-7800
  Fairport *(G-4872)*
Precision Mechanisms Corp .... E 516 333-5955
  Westbury *(G-17049)*
Production Metal Cutting Inc .... F 585 458-7136
  Rochester *(G-14629)*
Ross JC Inc .... G 716 439-1161
  Lockport *(G-7642)*
S & S Machinery Corp .... E 718 492-7400
  Brooklyn *(G-2541)*
S S Precision Gear & Instr .... E 718 457-7474
  Corona *(G-4029)*
Seneca Falls Machine Tool Co .... D 315 568-5804
  Seneca Falls *(G-15392)*
Sinn- Tech Industries Inc .... F 631 643-1171
  West Babylon *(G-16858)*
Streamline Precision Inc .... G 585 421-9050
  Fairport *(G-4889)*
Strippit Inc .... C 716 542-5500
  Akron *(G-26)*
Transport National Dev Inc .... E 716 662-0270
  Orchard Park *(G-13325)*
Trident Precision Mfg Inc .... D 585 265-2010
  Webster *(G-16764)*
Universal Tooling Corporation .... F 716 985-4691
  Gerry *(G-5606)*
Vandilay Industries Inc .... E 631 226-3064
  West Babylon *(G-16870)*

MACHINE TOOLS, METAL CUTTING: Centering

Rush Machinery Inc .... G 585 554-3070
  Rushville *(G-15078)*

MACHINE TOOLS, METAL CUTTING: Exotic, Including Explosive

High Speed Hammer Company Inc .... F 585 266-4287
  Rochester *(G-14456)*

MACHINE TOOLS, METAL CUTTING: Grind, Polish, Buff, Lapp

Elmira Grinding Works Inc .... F 607 734-1579
  Wellsburg *(G-16773)*
Hartchrom Inc .... F 518 880-0411
  Watervliet *(G-16710)*
Mortech Industries Inc .... G 845 628-6138
  Mahopac *(G-8028)*

MACHINE TOOLS, METAL CUTTING: Lathes

Zyp Precision LLC .... G 315 539-3667
  Waterloo *(G-16654)*

MACHINE TOOLS, METAL CUTTING: Numerically Controlled

Omega Tool Measuring Mchs Inc .... E 585 598-7800
  Fairport *(G-4872)*
Ppi Corp .... E 585 880-7277
  Rochester *(G-14611)*
Precise Tool & Mfg Inc .... D 585 247-0700
  Rochester *(G-14613)*

MACHINE TOOLS, METAL CUTTING: Tool Replacement & Rpr Parts

Adria Machine & Tool Inc .... E 585 889-3360
  Scottsville *(G-15355)*
Welch Machine Inc .... G 585 647-3578
  Rochester *(G-14787)*

MACHINE TOOLS, METAL FORMING: Die Casting & Extruding

Raloid Tool Co Inc .... F 518 664-4261
  Mechanicville *(G-8261)*

MACHINE TOOLS, METAL FORMING: Electroforming

Precision Eforming LLC .... F 607 753-7730
  Cortland *(G-4063)*

MACHINE TOOLS, METAL FORMING: Forging Machinery & Hammers

Special Metals Corporation .... D 716 366-5663
  Dunkirk *(G-4375)*
Trueforge Global McHy Corp .... G 516 825-7040
  Rockville Centre *(G-14830)*

MACHINE TOOLS, METAL FORMING: Forming, Metal Deposit

Vader Systems LLC .... F 716 688-1600
  Getzville *(G-5618)*

MACHINE TOOLS, METAL FORMING: Headers

American Racing Headers Inc .... E 631 608-1427
  Deer Park *(G-4120)*

MACHINE TOOLS, METAL FORMING: High Energy Rate

Arconic Inc .... G 716 358-6451
  Falconer *(G-4898)*
Smart High Voltage Solutions .... F 631 563-6724
  Bohemia *(G-1132)*

MACHINE TOOLS, METAL FORMING: Presses, Hyd & Pneumatic

Servotec Usa LLC .... G 518 671-6120
  Hudson *(G-6665)*

MACHINE TOOLS, METAL FORMING: Pressing

Mpi Incorporated .... D 845 471-7630
  Poughkeepsie *(G-13937)*

MACHINE TOOLS, METAL FORMING: Punching & Shearing

Manhasset Tool & Die Co Inc .... F 716 684-6066
  Lancaster *(G-7349)*

MACHINE TOOLS, METAL FORMING: Rebuilt

Uhmac Inc .... F 716 537-2343
  Holland (G-6512)

MACHINE TOOLS, METAL FORMING: Spinning, Spline Rollg/Windg

Gemcor Automation LLC .... D 716 674-9300
  West Seneca (G-16974)

MACHINE TOOLS: Metal Cutting

Abtex Corporation .... E 315 536-7403
  Dresden (G-4342)
Advanced Machine Design Co Inc ..... E 716 826-2000
  Buffalo (G-2817)
Alpine Machine Inc .... F 607 272-1344
  Ithaca (G-6858)
Alternative Service Inc .... F 631 345-9500
  Yaphank (G-17401)
Alton Manufacturing Inc .... D 585 458-2600
  Rochester (G-14209)
Ascension Industries Inc .... D 716 693-9381
  North Tonawanda (G-12974)
Aztec Mfg of Rochester .... G 585 352-8152
  Spencerport (G-15589)
Brinkman Products Inc .... B 585 235-4545
  Rochester (G-14264)
Bystronic Inc .... G 631 231-3677
  Hauppauge (G-6058)
Coastel Cable Tools Inc .... E 315 471-5361
  Syracuse (G-15918)
Crowley Fabg Machining Co Inc .... G 607 484-0299
  Endicott (G-4807)
Dinosaw Inc .... E 518 828-9942
  Hudson (G-6642)
East Coast Tool & Mfg .... G 716 826-5183
  Buffalo (G-2941)
Gb Aero Engine LLC .... B 914 925-9600
  Rye (G-15083)
Genco John .... G 716 483-5446
  Jamestown (G-7028)
Gleason Corporation .... A 585 473-1000
  Rochester (G-14428)
Graywood Companies Inc .... E 585 254-7000
  Rochester (G-14433)
H S Assembly Inc .... G 585 266-4287
  Rochester (G-14436)
Halpern Tool Corp .... G 914 633-0038
  New Rochelle (G-8953)
Hardinge Inc .... B 607 734-2281
  Elmira (G-4701)
IPC/Razor LLC .... D 212 551-4500
  New York (G-10695)
Ish Precision Machine Corp .... F 718 436-8858
  Brooklyn (G-2114)
J Vogler Enterprise LLC .... F 585 247-1625
  Rochester (G-14478)
Jalex Industries Ltd .... F 631 491-5072
  West Babylon (G-16828)
Kps Capital Partners LP .... E 212 338-5100
  New York (G-10922)
Kyocera Precision Tools Inc .... F 607 687-0012
  Owego (G-13378)
Lancaster Knives Inc .... E 716 683-5050
  Lancaster (G-7347)
Lk Industries Inc .... G 716 941-9202
  Glenwood (G-5718)
Lubow Machine Corp .... F 631 226-1700
  Copiague (G-3936)
Montrose Equipment Sales Inc .... F 718 388-7446
  Brooklyn (G-2337)
Multimatic Products Inc .... D 800 767-7633
  Ronkonkoma (G-14972)
Munson Machinery Company Inc .... E 315 797-0090
  Utica (G-16374)
Myles Tool Company Inc .... E 716 731-1300
  Sanborn (G-15151)
Nifty Bar Grinding & Cutting .... E 585 381-0450
  Penfield (G-13524)
Omega Consolidated Corporation ..... E 585 392-9262
  Hilton (G-6445)
P & R Industries Inc .... E 585 266-6725
  Rochester (G-14583)
Producto Corporation .... C 716 484-7131
  Jamestown (G-7057)
R Steiner Technologies Inc .... E 585 425-5912
  Fairport (G-4881)
Rapid Precision Machining Inc .... D 585 467-0780
  Rochester (G-14645)
S & S Machinery Corp .... E 718 492-7400
  Brooklyn (G-2541)
S & S Machinery Corp .... E 718 492-7400
  Brooklyn (G-2542)
Selflock Screw Products Co Inc .... E 315 541-4464
  Syracuse (G-16060)
Seneca Falls Capital Inc .... G 315 568-5804
  Seneca Falls (G-15391)
Seneca Falls Machine Tool Co .... D 315 568-5804
  Seneca Falls (G-15392)
Simmons Machine Tool Corp .... C 518 462-5431
  Menands (G-8410)
Teka Precision Inc .... G 845 753-1900
  Nyack (G-13072)
Transport National Dev Inc .... G 716 662-0270
  Orchard Park (G-13324)
Truemade Products Inc .... G 631 981-4755
  Ronkonkoma (G-15016)
Verns Machine Co Inc .... E 315 926-4223
  Marion (G-8133)
World LLC .... F 631 940-9121
  Deer Park (G-4254)
Zwack Incorporated .... E 518 733-5135
  Stephentown (G-15780)

MACHINE TOOLS: Metal Forming

Adaptive Mfg Tech Inc .... E 631 580-5400
  Ronkonkoma (G-14878)
Advanced Machine Design Co Inc ..... E 716 826-2000
  Buffalo (G-2817)
Advantage Metalwork Finshg LLC .... D 585 454-0160
  Rochester (G-14195)
Austin Industries Inc .... E 585 589-1353
  Albion (G-165)
Bdp Industries Inc .... E 518 695-6851
  Greenwich (G-5904)
Brinkman Intl Group Inc .... G 585 429-5000
  Rochester (G-14263)
Buffalo Machine Tls of Niagara .... F 716 201-1310
  Lockport (G-7602)
C & T Tool & Instrument Co .... E 718 429-1253
  Woodside (G-17338)
C J Winter Machine Tech .... E 585 429-5000
  Rochester (G-14271)
Commodore Manufacutring Corp ...... E 718 788-2600
  Brooklyn (G-1794)
Dover Global Holdings Inc .... F 212 922-1640
  New York (G-9964)
Ecko Fin & Tooling Inc .... F 716 487-0200
  Jamestown (G-7024)
Gh Induction Atmospheres LLC .... E 585 368-2120
  Rochester (G-14423)
Hydramec Inc .... E 585 593-5190
  Scio (G-15342)
Lourdes Systems Inc .... E 631 234-7077
  Hauppauge (G-6147)
Lubow Machine Corp .... F 631 226-1700
  Copiague (G-3936)
Miller Mechanical Services Inc .... E 518 792-0430
  Glens Falls (G-5705)
Prim Hall Enterprises Inc .... F 518 561-7408
  Plattsburgh (G-13719)
Producto Corporation .... C 716 484-7131
  Jamestown (G-7057)
Schaefer Machine Co Inc .... E 516 248-6880
  Mineola (G-8570)
Standard Paper Box Machine Co ..... G 718 328-3300
  Bronx (G-1461)
Strippit Inc .... C 716 542-5500
  Akron (G-26)
Taumel Metalforming Corp .... G 845 878-3100
  Patterson (G-13469)

MACHINERY & EQPT, AGRICULTURAL, WHOLESALE: Dairy

Brook North Farms Inc .... F 315 834-9390
  Auburn (G-486)

MACHINERY & EQPT, AGRICULTURAL, WHOLESALE: Landscaping Eqpt

Scotts Company LLC .... E 631 289-7444
  Yaphank (G-17416)
Upstone Materials Inc .... F 315 265-8036
  Plattsburgh (G-13736)

MACHINERY & EQPT, AGRICULTURAL, WHOLESALE: Lawn & Garden

Rhett M Clark Inc .... G 585 538-9570
  Caledonia (G-3309)

MACHINERY & EQPT, INDL, WHOL: Controlling Instruments/Access

Unimar Inc .... F 315 699-4400
  Syracuse (G-16087)

MACHINERY & EQPT, INDL, WHOL: Recording Instruments/Access

His Productions USA Inc .... G 212 594-3737
  New York (G-10528)

MACHINERY & EQPT, INDL, WHOLESALE: Conveyor Systems

Vetra Systems Corporation .... G 631 434-3185
  Hauppauge (G-6249)

MACHINERY & EQPT, INDL, WHOLESALE: Countersinks

Empire Fabricators Inc .... G 585 235-3050
  Rochester (G-14366)
Nlr Counter Tops LLC .... G 347 295-0410
  New York (G-11461)

MACHINERY & EQPT, INDL, WHOLESALE: Fans

Canarm Ltd .... G 800 267-4427
  Ogdensburg (G-13134)

MACHINERY & EQPT, INDL, WHOLESALE: Food Manufacturing

Vr Food Equipment Inc .... F 315 531-8133
  Farmington (G-5166)

MACHINERY & EQPT, INDL, WHOLESALE: Food Product Manufacturng

Crepini LLC .... E 347 422-0829
  Brooklyn (G-1816)
ET Oakes Corporation .... E 631 232-0002
  Hauppauge (G-6096)
Hobart Corporation .... E 631 864-3440
  Commack (G-3861)

MACHINERY & EQPT, INDL, WHOLESALE: Heat Exchange

Aavid Niagara LLC .... E 716 297-0652
  Niagara Falls (G-12817)

MACHINERY & EQPT, INDL, WHOLESALE: Hydraulic Systems

Ener-G-Rotors Inc .... G 518 372-2608
  Schenectady (G-15277)
Triumph Actuation Systems LLC ..... D 516 378-0162
  Freeport (G-5443)

MACHINERY & EQPT, INDL, WHOLESALE: Indl Machine Parts

Alternative Service Inc .... F 631 345-9500
  Yaphank (G-17401)
Rpb Distributors LLC .... G 914 244-3600
  Mount Kisco (G-8687)

MACHINERY & EQPT, INDL, WHOLESALE: Instruments & Cntrl Eqpt

Carl Zeiss Inc .... C 914 747-1800
  Thornwood (G-16140)
Winters Instruments Inc .... E 281 880-8607
  Buffalo (G-3283)

MACHINERY & EQPT, INDL, WHOLESALE: Machine Tools & Access

Cementex Latex Corp .... F 212 741-1770
  New York (G-9609)

PRODUCT SECTION

MACHINERY, FOOD PRDTS: Oilseed Crushing & Extracting

Curran Manufacturing Corp .... E 631 273-1010
  Hauppauge (G-6081)
NC Industries Inc .... F 248 528-5200
  Buffalo (G-3103)
S & S Machinery Corp .... E 718 492-7400
  Brooklyn (G-2542)

MACHINERY & EQPT, INDL, WHOLESALE: Measure/Test, Electric

Mausner Equipment Co Inc .... C 631 689-7358
  Setauket (G-15402)

MACHINERY & EQPT, INDL, WHOLESALE: Packaging

Millwood Inc .... F 518 233-1475
  Waterford (G-16635)
Modern Packaging Inc .... D 631 595-2437
  Deer Park (G-4199)

MACHINERY & EQPT, INDL, WHOLESALE: Paint Spray

Inglis Co Inc .... G 315 475-1315
  Syracuse (G-15982)

MACHINERY & EQPT, INDL, WHOLESALE: Pneumatic Tools

U S Air Tool Co Inc .... F 631 471-3300
  Ronkonkoma (G-15017)

MACHINERY & EQPT, INDL, WHOLESALE: Power Plant Machinery

Ultravolt Inc .... D 631 471-4444
  Ronkonkoma (G-15020)

MACHINERY & EQPT, INDL, WHOLESALE: Processing & Packaging

National Equipment Corporation .... F 718 585-0200
  Harrison (G-6006)
National Equipment Corporation .... E 718 585-0200
  Bronx (G-1408)

MACHINERY & EQPT, INDL, WHOLESALE: Robots

Automated Cells & Eqp Inc .... E 607 936-1341
  Painted Post (G-13415)

MACHINERY & EQPT, INDL, WHOLESALE: Safety Eqpt

Traffic Logix Corporation .... G 866 915-6449
  Spring Valley (G-15624)

MACHINERY & EQPT, INDL, WHOLESALE: Textile

John A Eberly Inc .... G 315 449-3034
  Syracuse (G-15986)
Sml USA Inc .... E 212 736-8800
  New York (G-12135)

MACHINERY & EQPT, INDL, WHOLESALE: Water Pumps

Air Flow Pump Corp .... G 718 241-2800
  Brooklyn (G-1570)

MACHINERY & EQPT, INDL, WHOLESALE: Woodworking

Putnam Rolling Ladder Co Inc .... F 212 226-5147
  New York (G-11779)

MACHINERY & EQPT, WHOLESALE: Construction, General

Zwack Incorporated .... E 518 733-5135
  Stephentown (G-15780)

MACHINERY & EQPT, WHOLESALE: Contractors Materials

Gny Equipment LLC .... F 631 667-1010
  Bay Shore (G-701)

MACHINERY & EQPT, WHOLESALE: Crushing, Pulverizng & Screeng

American Material Processing .... F 315 318-0017
  Phoenix (G-13567)

MACHINERY & EQPT, WHOLESALE: Masonry

Arman Development Corp .... D 607 432-8391
  Oneonta (G-13194)
Duke Concrete Products Inc .... E 518 793-7743
  Queensbury (G-14008)
Inwood Material .... F 516 371-1842
  Inwood (G-6799)
Palumbo Block Co Inc .... E 845 832-6100
  Dover Plains (G-4340)

MACHINERY & EQPT: Electroplating

Caswell Inc .... F 315 946-1213
  Lyons (G-7997)
Digital Matrix Corp .... E 516 481-7990
  Farmingdale (G-4987)
Precision Process Inc .... D 716 731-1587
  Niagara Falls (G-12882)
Sonicor Inc .... F 631 920-6555
  West Babylon (G-16861)
Technic Inc .... F 516 349-0700
  Plainview (G-13665)

MACHINERY & EQPT: Farm

Don Beck Inc .... G 585 493-3040
  Castile (G-3444)
Eastern Welding Inc .... G 631 727-0306
  Riverhead (G-14154)
Haines Equipment Inc .... E 607 566-8531
  Avoca (G-534)
House of The Foaming Case Inc .... G 718 454-0101
  Saint Albans (G-15110)
Landpro Equipment LLC .... B 716 665-3110
  Falconer (G-4914)
Oxbo International Corporation .... D 585 548-2665
  Byron (G-3295)
Plant-Tech2o Inc .... G 516 483-7845
  Hempstead (G-6307)
Road Cases USA Inc .... E 631 563-0633
  Bohemia (G-1123)
Zappala Farms AG Systems Inc .... E 315 626-6293
  Cato (G-3453)

MACHINERY & EQPT: Gas Producers, Generators/Other Rltd Eqpt

Audubon Machinery Corporation .... D 716 564-5165
  North Tonawanda (G-12975)
Mep Alaska LLC .... G 646 535-9005
  Brooklyn (G-2302)

MACHINERY & EQPT: Liquid Automation

Crandall Filling Machinery Inc .... G 716 897-3486
  Buffalo (G-2912)
Javlyn Process Systems LLC .... E 585 424-5580
  Rochester (G-14482)

MACHINERY & EQPT: Metal Finishing, Plating Etc

Cameo Metal Products Inc .... E 718 788-1106
  Brooklyn (G-1753)
P K G Equipment Incorporated .... E 585 436-4650
  Rochester (G-14585)
Qes Solutions Inc .... D 585 783-1455
  Rochester (G-14634)
R & B Machinery Corp .... G 716 894-3332
  Buffalo (G-3178)
Tompkins Metal Finishing Inc .... D 585 344-2600
  Batavia (G-650)

MACHINERY BASES

American Standard Mfg Inc .... E 518 868-2512
  Central Bridge (G-3507)
Brzozka Industries Inc .... F 631 588-8164
  Holbrook (G-6462)
Cleveland Polymer Tech LLC .... G 518 326-9146
  Watervliet (G-16706)
Kefa Industries Group Inc .... F 718 568-9297
  Rego Park (G-14046)
Machinery Mountings Inc .... F 631 851-0480
  Hauppauge (G-6149)

Win-Holt Equipment Corp .... C 516 222-0433
  Garden City (G-5551)

MACHINERY, COMMERCIAL LAUNDRY: Dryers, Incl Coin-Operated

Maxi Companies Inc .... G 315 446-1002
  De Witt (G-4108)

MACHINERY, COMMERCIAL LAUNDRY: Washing, Incl Coin-Operated

G A Braun Inc .... D 315 475-3123
  North Syracuse (G-12960)
Lynx Product Group LLC .... E 716 751-3100
  Wilson (G-17291)
Pressure Washing Services Inc .... G 607 286-7458
  Milford (G-8509)

MACHINERY, EQPT & SUPPLIES: Parking Facility

Automotion Parking Systems LLC ...... G 516 565-5600
  West Hempstead (G-16881)
Park Assist LLC .... D 646 666-7525
  New York (G-11587)

MACHINERY, FOOD PRDTS: Beverage

Brooklyn Brew Shop LLC .... F 718 874-0119
  Brooklyn (G-1720)
Kedco Inc .... F 516 454-7800
  Farmingdale (G-5032)
US Beverage Net Inc .... F 315 579-2025
  Syracuse (G-16089)

MACHINERY, FOOD PRDTS: Choppers, Commercial

Mary F Morse .... G 315 866-2741
  Mohawk (G-8575)

MACHINERY, FOOD PRDTS: Cutting, Chopping, Grinding, Mixing

ET Oakes Corporation .... E 631 232-0002
  Hauppauge (G-6096)

MACHINERY, FOOD PRDTS: Dairy & Milk

Chemicolloid Laboratories Inc .... F 516 747-2666
  New Hyde Park (G-8866)

MACHINERY, FOOD PRDTS: Dairy, Pasteurizing

Goodnature Products Inc .... F 716 855-3325
  Orchard Park (G-13296)

MACHINERY, FOOD PRDTS: Food Processing, Smokers

Bonduelle USA Inc .... E 585 948-5252
  Oakfield (G-13083)
Los Olivos Ltd .... C 631 773-6439
  Farmingdale (G-5046)

MACHINERY, FOOD PRDTS: Juice Extractors, Fruit & Veg, Comm

Juice Press LLC .... G 212 777-0034
  New York (G-10816)

MACHINERY, FOOD PRDTS: Milk Processing, NEC

Delaval Inc .... F 585 599-4696
  Corfu (G-3976)

MACHINERY, FOOD PRDTS: Mixers, Commercial

Expert Industries Inc .... E 718 434-6060
  Brooklyn (G-1951)

MACHINERY, FOOD PRDTS: Oilseed Crushing & Extracting

Caravella Food Corp .... F 646 552-0455
  Whitestone (G-17232)

Employee Codes: A=Over 500 employees, B=251-500
C=101-250, D=51-100, E=20-50, F=10-19, G=5-9

MACHINERY, FOOD PRDTS: Ovens, Bakery

PRODUCT SECTION

MACHINERY, FOOD PRDTS: Ovens, Bakery

- Home Maide Inc .... F 845 837-1700
  Harriman *(G-5994)*
- Mohawk Valley Manufacturing .... G 315 797-0851
  Frankfort *(G-5365)*
- Zaro Bake Shop Inc .... D 212 292-0175
  New York *(G-12725)*

MACHINERY, FOOD PRDTS: Packing House

- Desu Machinery Corporation .... D 716 681-5798
  Depew *(G-4279)*

MACHINERY, FOOD PRDTS: Presses, Cheese, Beet, Cider & Sugar

- Blue Toad Hard Cider .... E 585 424-5508
  Rochester *(G-14255)*

MACHINERY, FOOD PRDTS: Roasting, Coffee, Peanut, Etc.

- Wired Coffee and Bagel Inc .... F 518 506-3194
  Malta *(G-8054)*

MACHINERY, MAILING: Canceling

- Action Technologies Inc .... G 718 278-1000
  Long Island City *(G-7680)*

MACHINERY, MAILING: Mailing

- Pitney Bowes Inc .... C 518 283-0345
  Troy *(G-16271)*

MACHINERY, MAILING: Postage Meters

- Neopost USA Inc .... E 631 435-9100
  Hauppauge *(G-6172)*
- Pitney Bowes Inc .... E 212 564-7548
  New York *(G-11688)*
- Pitney Bowes Inc .... E 203 356-5000
  New York *(G-11689)*
- Pitney Bowes Inc .... E 516 822-0900
  Jericho *(G-7113)*

MACHINERY, METALWORKING: Assembly, Including Robotic

- Alliance Automation Systems .... C 585 426-2700
  Rochester *(G-14203)*
- Hover-Davis Inc .... C 585 352-9590
  Rochester *(G-14459)*
- Manufacturing Resources Inc .... E 631 481-0041
  Rochester *(G-14514)*
- Mold-A-Matic Corporation .... E 607 433-2121
  Oneonta *(G-13211)*
- Tessy Plastics Corp .... B 315 689-3924
  Skaneateles *(G-15488)*
- Unidex Corporation Western NY .... F 585 786-3170
  Warsaw *(G-16606)*
- Van Blarcom Closures Inc .... C 718 855-3810
  Brooklyn *(G-2735)*

MACHINERY, METALWORKING: Cutting & Slitting

- Expert Metal Slitters Corp .... G 718 361-2735
  Long Island City *(G-7765)*

MACHINERY, OFFICE: Perforators

- Cummins - Allison Corp .... D 718 263-2482
  Kew Gardens *(G-7188)*

MACHINERY, OFFICE: Stapling, Hand Or Power

- Staplex Company Inc .... E 718 768-3333
  Brooklyn *(G-2619)*

MACHINERY, OFFICE: Time Clocks &Time Recording Devices

- Central Time Clock Inc .... F 718 784-4900
  Long Island City *(G-7725)*
- Widmer Time Recorder Company .... F 212 227-0405
  New York *(G-12658)*

MACHINERY, OFFICE: Typing & Word Processing

- Magnetic Technologies Corp .... D 585 385-9010
  Rochester *(G-14511)*

MACHINERY, PACKAGING: Canning, Food

- Reynolds Packaging McHy Inc .... D 716 358-6451
  Falconer *(G-4918)*

MACHINERY, PACKAGING: Carton Packing

- Niagara Scientific Inc .... D 315 437-0821
  East Syracuse *(G-4566)*

MACHINERY, PACKAGING: Packing & Wrapping

- Fourteen Arnold Ave Corp .... F 315 272-1700
  Utica *(G-16356)*
- Turbofil Packaging Mchs LLC .... G 914 239-3878
  Mount Vernon *(G-8789)*
- Vetroelite Inc .... G 925 724-7900
  New York *(G-12555)*

MACHINERY, PAPER INDUSTRY: Converting, Die Cutting & Stampng

- Fbm Galaxy Inc .... F 315 463-5144
  East Syracuse *(G-4542)*
- Friedel Paper Box & Converting .... G 315 437-3325
  Baldwinsville *(G-568)*
- Richlar Industries Inc .... G 315 463-5144
  East Syracuse *(G-4574)*
- Rsb Associates Inc .... F 518 281-5067
  Altamont *(G-216)*

MACHINERY, PAPER INDUSTRY: Paper Mill, Plating, Etc

- F W Roberts Mfg Co Inc .... F 716 434-3555
  Lockport *(G-7614)*
- Sonicor Inc .... F 631 920-6555
  West Babylon *(G-16861)*

MACHINERY, PRINTING TRADES: Copy Holders

- Copy4les Inc .... F 212 487-9778
  New York *(G-9782)*
- Exacta LLC .... G 716 406-2303
  Clarence Center *(G-3701)*

MACHINERY, PRINTING TRADES: Plates

- C M E Corp .... F 315 451-7101
  Syracuse *(G-15900)*
- Csw Inc .... F 585 247-4010
  Rochester *(G-14315)*
- Impressions International Inc .... G 585 442-5240
  Rochester *(G-14467)*
- Rubber Stamps Inc .... E 212 675-1180
  Mineola *(G-8568)*

MACHINERY, PRINTING TRADES: Plates, Offset

- Apexx Omni-Graphics Inc .... D 718 326-3330
  Maspeth *(G-8147)*
- Total Offset Inc .... F 212 966-4482
  New York *(G-12400)*

MACHINERY, PRINTING TRADES: Presses, Envelope

- A C Envelope Inc .... G 516 420-0646
  Farmingdale *(G-4933)*

MACHINERY, PRINTING TRADES: Printing Trade Parts & Attchts

- Lexar Global LLC .... G 845 352-9700
  Valley Cottage *(G-16407)*
- Rollers Inc .... G 716 837-0700
  Buffalo *(G-3192)*

MACHINERY, PRINTING TRADES: Sticks

- Bmp America Inc .... G 585 798-0950
  Medina *(G-8300)*

MACHINERY, SEWING: Sewing & Hat & Zipper Making

- Cvd Equipment Corporation .... E 845 246-3631
  Saugerties *(G-15211)*

MACHINERY, TEXTILE: Card Cutting, Jacquard

- Mjk Cutting Inc .... F 718 384-7613
  Brooklyn *(G-2328)*

MACHINERY, TEXTILE: Embroidery

- Herrmann Group LLC .... G 716 876-9798
  Kenmore *(G-7176)*

MACHINERY, TEXTILE: Silk Screens

- Angel Textiles Inc .... G 212 532-0900
  New York *(G-9205)*
- Big Apple Sign Corp .... E 631 342-0303
  Islandia *(G-6826)*
- Screen Team Inc .... F 718 786-2424
  Long Island City *(G-7902)*

MACHINERY, TEXTILE: Thread Making Or Spinning

- Thread Check Inc .... D 631 231-1515
  Hauppauge *(G-6238)*

MACHINERY, WOODWORKING: Bandsaws

- Phoenix Wood Wrights Ltd .... F 631 727-9691
  Riverhead *(G-14165)*

MACHINERY, WOODWORKING: Cabinet Makers'

- Hat Factory Furniture Co .... G 914 788-6288
  Peekskill *(G-13503)*

MACHINERY, WOODWORKING: Furniture Makers

- Casa Nueva Custom Furnishing .... G 914 476-2272
  Yonkers *(G-17441)*
- Downtown Interiors Inc .... F 212 337-0230
  New York *(G-9969)*

MACHINERY, WOODWORKING: Lathes, Wood Turning Includes Access

- Hardinge Inc .... B 607 734-2281
  Elmira *(G-4701)*

MACHINERY, WOODWORKING: Pattern Makers'

- Corbett Stves Pttern Works Inc .... E 585 546-7109
  Rochester *(G-14310)*

MACHINERY, WOODWORKING: Sanding, Exc Portable Floor Sanders

- US Sander LLC .... G 518 875-9157
  Esperance *(G-4846)*

MACHINERY: Ammunition & Explosives Loading

- Eastend Enforcement Products .... G 631 878-8424
  Center Moriches *(G-3490)*

MACHINERY: Assembly, Exc Metalworking

- Alliance Automation Systems .... C 585 426-2700
  Rochester *(G-14203)*
- Distech Systems Inc .... G 585 254-7020
  Rochester *(G-14332)*
- Dynamasters Inc .... G 585 458-9970
  Rochester *(G-14340)*
- Griffin Automation Inc .... E 716 674-2300
  West Seneca *(G-16976)*
- Hubco Inc .... G 716 683-5940
  Alden *(G-182)*
- Lubow Machine Corp .... F 631 226-1700
  Copiague *(G-3936)*
- Machine Tool Repair & Sales .... G 631 580-2550
  Holbrook *(G-6489)*

PRODUCT SECTION

MACHINERY: Logging Eqpt

New Vision Industries Inc .... F 607 687-7700
  Endicott *(G-4827)*
Quality Manufacturing Sys LLC............ G 716 763-0988
  Lakewood *(G-7316)*
Rfb Associates Inc .... F 518 271-0551
  Fort Edward *(G-5354)*
Trident Precision Mfg Inc .... D 585 265-2010
  Webster *(G-16764)*
Veeco Process Equipment Inc .... C 516 677-0200
  Plainview *(G-13672)*

MACHINERY: Automotive Maintenance

Blue Star Products Inc .... F 631 952-3204
  Hauppauge *(G-6055)*
Glass Star America Inc .... F 631 291-9432
  Center Moriches *(G-3491)*
T-Rex Supply Corporation .... F 516 308-0505
  Hempstead *(G-6310)*

MACHINERY: Automotive Related

B&K Precision Corporation .... G 631 369-2665
  Manorville *(G-8110)*
Eltee Tool & Die Co .... F 607 748-4301
  Endicott *(G-4809)*
Hitachi Metals America Ltd .... E 914 694-9200
  Purchase *(G-13975)*
Reefer Tek Llc .... F 347 590-1067
  Bronx *(G-1439)*
Rfb Associates Inc .... F 518 271-0551
  Fort Edward *(G-5354)*
Riverview Associates Inc .... F 585 235-5980
  Rochester *(G-14651)*

MACHINERY: Billing

Gary Roth & Associates Ltd .... E 516 333-1000
  Westbury *(G-17017)*

MACHINERY: Brewery & Malting

Singlecut Beersmiths LLC .... F 718 606-0788
  Astoria *(G-455)*

MACHINERY: Bridge Or Gate, Hydraulic

Island Automated Gate Co LLC .... G 631 425-0196
  Huntington Station *(G-6749)*

MACHINERY: Concrete Prdts

Northrock Industries Inc .... E 631 924-6130
  Bohemia *(G-1107)*
Nycon Diamond & Tools Corp .... G 855 937-6922
  Bohemia *(G-1108)*

MACHINERY: Construction

AAAA York Inc .... F 718 784-6666
  Long Island City *(G-7677)*
Air-Flo Mfg Co Inc .... D 607 733-8284
  Elmira *(G-4684)*
Anderson Equipment Company .... D 716 877-1992
  Tonawanda *(G-16160)*
BW Elliott Mfg Co LLC .... B 607 772-0404
  Binghamton *(G-896)*
Capitol Eq 2 LLC .... G 518 886-8341
  Saratoga Springs *(G-15176)*
CCS Machinery Inc .... F 631 968-0900
  Bay Shore *(G-679)*
Ceno Technologies Inc .... G 716 885-5050
  Buffalo *(G-2890)*
Cooper Industries LLC .... E 315 477-7000
  Syracuse *(G-15928)*
Diamond Coring & Cutting Inc.............. G 718 381-4545
  Maspeth *(G-8161)*
Dover Global Holdings Inc .... F 212 922-1640
  New York *(G-9964)*
ET Oakes Corporation .... E 631 232-0002
  Hauppauge *(G-6096)*
Line Ward Corporation .... F 716 675-7373
  Buffalo *(G-3066)*
Mettle Concept Inc .... G 888 501-0680
  New York *(G-11270)*
Oswald Manufacturing Co Inc .... E 516 883-8850
  Port Washington *(G-13867)*
Penn State Metal Fabri .... G 718 786-8814
  Brooklyn *(G-2428)*
Pier-Tech Inc .... E 516 442-5420
  Oceanside *(G-13111)*
Precision Product Inc .... G 718 852-7127
  Brooklyn *(G-2450)*

Ziegler Truck & Diesl Repr Inc .... G 315 782-7278
  Watertown *(G-16699)*

MACHINERY: Cryogenic, Industrial

Cryomech Inc .... D 315 455-2555
  Syracuse *(G-15934)*
General Cryogenic Tech LLC .... F 516 334-8200
  Westbury *(G-17018)*

MACHINERY: Custom

Accede Mold & Tool Co Inc .... D 585 254-6490
  Rochester *(G-14180)*
Adaptive Mfg Tech Inc .... E 631 580-5400
  Ronkonkoma *(G-14878)*
Advanced Aerospace Machining .... G 631 694-7745
  Farmingdale *(G-4937)*
Aloi Solutions LLC .... E 585 292-0920
  Rochester *(G-14207)*
American Linear Manufacturers .... F 516 333-1351
  Westbury *(G-16993)*
Armstrong Mold Corporation .... D 315 437-1517
  East Syracuse *(G-4522)*
Auburn Bearing & Mfg Inc.................... G 315 986-7600
  Macedon *(G-8009)*
Calvary Design Team Inc .... E 585 347-6127
  Webster *(G-16738)*
Chart Inc .... F 518 272-3565
  Troy *(G-16252)*
Chocovision Corporation .... F 845 473-4970
  Poughkeepsie *(G-13912)*
Converter Design Inc............................ E 518 745-7138
  Glens Falls *(G-5691)*
Duetto Integrated Systems Inc .... F 631 851-0102
  Islandia *(G-6830)*
Dynak Inc .... F 585 271-2255
  Churchville *(G-3666)*
Endicott Precision Inc .... C 607 754-7076
  Endicott *(G-4811)*
Finesse Creations Inc .... F 718 692-2100
  Brooklyn *(G-1977)*
Hebeler LLC .... C 716 873-9300
  Tonawanda *(G-16188)*
Hebeler Process Solutions LLC .... E 716 873-9300
  Tonawanda *(G-16189)*
Interactive Instruments Inc .... F 518 347-0955
  Scotia *(G-15349)*
International Climbing Mchs .... G 607 288-4001
  Ithaca *(G-6887)*
J Soehner Corporation .... F 516 599-2534
  Rockville Centre *(G-14821)*
Jet Sew Corporation .... F 315 896-2683
  Barneveld *(G-613)*
Keller Technology Corporation .... C 716 693-3840
  Tonawanda *(G-16194)*
Keyes Machine Works Inc .... E 585 426-5059
  Gates *(G-5576)*
McGuigan Inc .... E 631 750-6222
  Bohemia *(G-1098)*
Modern Packaging Inc .... D 631 595-2437
  Deer Park *(G-4199)*
Ms Machining Inc .... G 607 723-1105
  Binghamton *(G-934)*
Northern Tier Cnc Inc .... G 518 236-4702
  Mooers Forks *(G-8655)*
R E F Precision Products .... F 631 242-4471
  Deer Park *(G-4221)*
Rand Machine Products Inc .... D 716 665-5217
  Falconer *(G-4916)*
Roboshop Inc .... G 315 437-6454
  Syracuse *(G-16046)*
Tricon Machine LLC .... G 585 671-0679
  Webster *(G-16763)*
Voss Manufacturing Inc .... D 716 731-5062
  Sanborn *(G-15158)*
W H Jones & Son Inc .... F 716 875-8233
  Kenmore *(G-7180)*
W J Albro Machine Works Inc .... G 631 345-0657
  Yaphank *(G-17424)*
Washburn Manufacturing Tech .... G 607 387-3991
  Trumansburg *(G-16292)*
Wendt Corporation .... G 716 391-1200
  Buffalo *(G-3277)*

MACHINERY: Drill Presses

Baldwin Machine Works Inc .... G 631 842-9110
  Copiague *(G-3922)*

MACHINERY: Electronic Component Making

CBA Group LLC .... A 607 779-7522
  Conklin *(G-3891)*
Designatronics Incorporated .... G 516 328-3300
  Hicksville *(G-6366)*
James Morris .... E 315 824-8519
  Hamilton *(G-5971)*
Sj Associates Inc .... E 516 942-3232
  Jericho *(G-7119)*
Ui Acquisition Holding Co .... G 607 779-7522
  Conklin *(G-3903)*
Ui Holding Company .... G 607 779-7522
  Conklin *(G-3904)*
Universal Instruments Corp .... C 800 842-9732
  Conklin *(G-3905)*

MACHINERY: Extruding

Kobe Steel USA Holdings Inc .... G 212 751-9400
  New York *(G-10904)*

MACHINERY: Fiber Optics Strand Coating

Accurate McHning Incorporation .... F 315 689-1428
  Elbridge *(G-4636)*

MACHINERY: Gear Cutting & Finishing

Gleason Works .... A 585 473-1000
  Rochester *(G-14429)*

MACHINERY: General, Industrial, NEC

Markpericom .... G 516 208-6824
  Oceanside *(G-13109)*

MACHINERY: Glassmaking

Emhart Glass Manufacturing Inc .... C 607 734-3671
  Horseheads *(G-6605)*
Wilt Industries Inc .... F 518 548-4961
  Lake Pleasant *(G-7301)*

MACHINERY: Grinding

Aip Mc Holdings LLC .... A 212 627-2360
  New York *(G-9115)*
Connex Grinding & Machining .... G 315 946-4340
  Lyons *(G-7998)*
Stephen Bader Company Inc .... F 518 753-4456
  Valley Falls *(G-16422)*

MACHINERY: Ice Cream

Pic Nic LLC .... G 914 245-6500
  Yorktown Heights *(G-17532)*

MACHINERY: Ice Crushers

American Material Processing .... F 315 318-0017
  Phoenix *(G-13567)*

MACHINERY: Ice Making

Hoshizaki Nrtheastern Dist Ctr .... G 516 605-1411
  Plainview *(G-13633)*

MACHINERY: Industrial, NEC

A P Manufacturing .... G 909 228-3049
  Bohemia *(G-996)*
Bay Horse Innovations Nyinc .... G 607 898-3337
  Groton *(G-5918)*
Elg Utica Alloys Holdings Inc .... G 315 733-0475
  Utica *(G-16352)*
Exigo Precision Inc .... G 585 254-5818
  Rochester *(G-14386)*
Kimber Mfg .... G 914 721-8417
  Yonkers *(G-17477)*
Northeast Hardware Specialties .... F 516 487-6868
  Mineola *(G-8561)*
Semi-Linear Inc .... G 212 243-2108
  New York *(G-12045)*

MACHINERY: Jewelers

Arbe Machinery Inc............................... F 631 756-2477
  Farmingdale *(G-4953)*

MACHINERY: Logging Eqpt

C J Logging Equipment Inc .... E 315 942-5431
  Boonville *(G-1163)*

Employee Codes: A=Over 500 employees, B=251-500
C=101-250, D=51-100, E=20-50, F=10-19, G=5-9

MACHINERY: Marking, Metalworking

Autostat Corporation ....F 516 379-9447
  Roosevelt (G-15027)

MACHINERY: Metalworking

Advanced Machine Design Co Inc ......E 716 826-2000
  Buffalo (G-2817)
Bartell Machinery Systems LLC ....C 315 336-7600
  Rome (G-14833)
Charles A Rogers Entps Inc ....E 585 924-6400
  Victor (G-16490)
Duall Finishing Inc ....G 716 827-1707
  Buffalo (G-2935)
Esm II Inc ....E 716 446-8888
  Amherst (G-240)
Hardinge Inc ....B 607 734-2281
  Elmira (G-4701)
Hje Company Inc ....G 518 792-8733
  Queensbury (G-14012)
Mono-Systems Inc ....E 716 821-1344
  Buffalo (G-3094)
Mtwli Precision Corp ....G 631 244-3767
  Bohemia (G-1102)
Munson Machinery Company Inc ....E 315 797-0090
  Utica (G-16374)
Pems Tool & Machine Inc ....E 315 823-3595
  Little Falls (G-7523)
Precision Systems Mfg Inc ....E 315 451-3480
  Liverpool (G-7570)
Reelex Packaging Solutions Inc ......E 845 878-7878
  Patterson (G-13467)
Riverside Machinery Company ....E 718 492-7400
  Brooklyn (G-2519)
S & S Machinery Corp ....E 718 492-7400
  Brooklyn (G-2541)
S & S Machinery Corp ....E 718 492-7400
  Brooklyn (G-2542)
Serge Duct Designs Inc ....E 718 783-7799
  Brooklyn (G-2570)
Strippit Inc ....C 716 542-5500
  Akron (G-26)
Vader Systems LLC ....F 716 688-1600
  Getzville (G-5618)
Voss Manufacturing Inc ....D 716 731-5062
  Sanborn (G-15158)
Xto Incorporated ....D 315 451-7807
  Liverpool (G-7585)

MACHINERY: Milling

Five Star Tool Co Inc ....E 585 328-9580
  Rochester (G-14394)

MACHINERY: Mining

Flatcut LLC ....G 212 542-5732
  Brooklyn (G-1984)
Lawson M Whiting Inc ....G 315 986-3064
  Macedon (G-8018)
Universal Metal Fabricators ....F 845 331-8248
  Kingston (G-7248)

MACHINERY: Optical Lens

Optipro Systems LLC ....D 585 265-0160
  Ontario (G-13230)
Universal Thin Film Lab Corp ....G 845 562-0601
  Newburgh (G-12808)

MACHINERY: Ozone

Queenaire Technologies Inc ....G 315 393-5454
  Ogdensburg (G-13141)

MACHINERY: Packaging

A & G Heat Sealing ....G 631 724-7764
  Smithtown (G-15503)
All Packaging McHy & Sups Corp ......F 631 588-7310
  Ronkonkoma (G-14888)
Automecha International Ltd ....E 607 843-2235
  Oxford (G-13388)
Dover Global Holdings Inc ....F 212 922-1640
  New York (G-9964)
Haines Equipment Inc ....E 607 566-8531
  Avoca (G-534)
Hypres Inc ....E 914 592-1190
  Elmsford (G-4764)
K C Technical Services Inc ....G 631 589-7170
  Bohemia (G-1082)
Kabar Manufacturing Corp ....E 631 694-6857
  Farmingdale (G-5029)
Millwood Inc ....F 518 233-1475
  Waterford (G-16635)
Modern Packaging Inc ....D 631 595-2437
  Deer Park (G-4199)
National Equipment Corporation ......E 718 585-0200
  Bronx (G-1408)
Orics Industries Inc ....E 718 461-8613
  Farmingdale (G-5080)
Overhead Door Corporation ....D 518 828-7652
  Hudson (G-6659)
Pacemaker Packaging Corp ....F 718 458-1188
  Woodside (G-17361)
Packaging Dynamics Ltd ....F 631 563-4499
  Bohemia (G-1110)
Rfb Associates Inc ....F 518 271-0551
  Fort Edward (G-5354)
Rota Pack Inc ....F 631 274-1037
  Farmingdale (G-5113)
Save O Seal Corporation Inc ....G 914 592-3031
  Elmsford (G-4785)
Sharon Manufacturing Co Inc ....E 631 242-8870
  Deer Park (G-4234)
Softpack International Inc ....E 631 544-7014
  Kings Park (G-7205)
Utleys Incorporated ....E 718 956-1661
  Woodside (G-17375)
Volckening Inc ....E 718 748-0294
  Brooklyn (G-2754)

MACHINERY: Paper Industry Miscellaneous

Automecha International Ltd ....E 607 843-2235
  Oxford (G-13388)
Cyclotherm of Watertown Inc ....E 315 782-1100
  Watertown (G-16670)
GL&v USA Inc ....D 518 747-2444
  Hudson Falls (G-6674)
GL&v USA Inc ....E 518 747-2444
  Hudson Falls (G-6675)
Haanen Packard Machinery Inc ....G 518 747-2330
  Hudson Falls (G-6677)
Interntnal Strpping Diecutting ......G 718 383-7720
  Brooklyn (G-2112)
Jacob Inc ....E 646 450-3067
  Brooklyn (G-2130)
Johnston Dandy Company ....G 315 455-5773
  Syracuse (G-15988)
Kadant Inc ....F 518 793-8801
  Glens Falls (G-5700)
Lake Image Systems Inc ....F 585 321-3630
  Henrietta (G-6319)
Sinclair International Company ......E 518 798-2361
  Queensbury (G-14025)
Verso Corporation ....B 212 599-2700
  New York (G-12550)

MACHINERY: Pharmaciutical

George Ponte Inc ....G 914 243-4202
  Jefferson Valley (G-7090)
Gordon S Anderson Mfg Co ....E 845 677-3304
  Millbrook (G-8511)
Innovation Associates Inc ....C 607 798-9376
  Johnson City (G-7126)
Michael Benalt Inc ....E 845 628-1008
  Mahopac (G-8027)

MACHINERY: Photographic Reproduction

Qls Solutions Group Inc ....E 716 852-2203
  Buffalo (G-3170)
Xerox Corporation ....A 585 422-4564
  Webster (G-16769)

MACHINERY: Plastic Working

Addex Inc ....G 781 344-5800
  Newark (G-12749)
Byfusion Inc ....G 347 563-5286
  Brooklyn (G-1744)
Century-Tech Inc ....G 516 493-9800
  Hempstead (G-6292)
Germanow-Simon Corporation ....E 585 232-1440
  Rochester (G-14420)
Haanen Packard Machinery Inc ....G 518 747-2330
  Hudson Falls (G-6677)
High Frequency Tech Co Inc ....F 631 242-3020
  Deer Park (G-4171)
Illinois Tool Works Inc ....C 716 681-8222
  Lancaster (G-7344)
Kabar Manufacturing Corp ....E 631 694-1036
  Farmingdale (G-5030)
Kabar Manufacturing Corp ....E 631 694-6857
  Farmingdale (G-5029)
Pearl Technologies Inc ....E 315 365-2632
  Savannah (G-15231)
Quality Strapping Inc ....D 718 418-1111
  Brooklyn (G-2482)
Ultrepet LLC ....D 781 275-6400
  Albany (G-146)
Valplast International Corp ....F 516 442-3923
  Westbury (G-17069)

MACHINERY: Printing Presses

Advance Grafix Equipment Inc ....G 917 202-4593
  Wyandanch (G-17386)

MACHINERY: Recycling

Adirondack Plas & Recycl Inc ....E 518 746-9212
  Argyle (G-406)
Andela Tool & Machine Inc ....G 315 858-0055
  Richfield Springs (G-14074)
Ben Weitsman of Albany LLC ....E 518 462-4444
  Albany (G-50)
Crumbrubber Technology Inc ....F 718 468-3988
  Hollis (G-6522)
Materials Recovery Company ....F 518 274-3681
  Troy (G-16264)

MACHINERY: Riveting

High Speed Hammer Company Inc ....F 585 266-4287
  Rochester (G-14456)

MACHINERY: Road Construction & Maintenance

Cimline Inc ....G 518 880-4073
  Albany (G-63)
Professional Pavers Corp ....E 718 784-7853
  Rego Park (G-14050)

MACHINERY: Rubber Working

Curtin-Hebert Co Inc ....F 518 725-7157
  Gloversville (G-5725)

MACHINERY: Screening Eqpt, Electric

Innovation In Motion Inc ....G 407 878-7561
  Long Beach (G-7672)

MACHINERY: Semiconductor Manufacturing

Cvd Equipment Corporation ....C 631 981-7081
  Central Islip (G-3518)
Cvd Equipment Corporation ....F 631 582-4365
  Central Islip (G-3519)
Globalfoundries US Inc ....F 512 457-3900
  Hopewell Junction (G-6578)
Lam Research Corporation ....E 845 896-0606
  Fishkill (G-5192)
Tokyo Electron America Inc ....G 518 289-3100
  Malta (G-8053)
Veeco Instruments Inc ....B 516 677-0200
  Plainview (G-13671)

MACHINERY: Separation Eqpt, Magnetic

Innovative Cleaning Solutions ....G 716 731-4408
  Sanborn (G-15148)

MACHINERY: Sheet Metal Working

U S Air Tool Co Inc ....F 631 471-3300
  Ronkonkoma (G-15017)

MACHINERY: Specialty

Force Dynamics Inc ....F 607 546-5023
  Trumansburg (G-16291)

MACHINERY: Textile

Aglika Trade LLC ....F 727 424-1944
  Middle Village (G-8443)
Corbertex LLC ....G 212 971-0008
  New York (G-9783)
Eastman Machine Company ....C 716 856-2200
  Buffalo (G-2943)
Herr Manufacturing Co Inc ....E 716 754-4341
  Tonawanda (G-16190)

PRODUCT SECTION

Mohawk Valley Knt McHy Co Inc .... F 315 736-3038
  New York Mills *(G-12745)*
Rfb Associates Inc .... F 518 271-0551
  Fort Edward *(G-5354)*
Schwabel Fabricating Co Inc .... E 716 876-2086
  Tonawanda *(G-16219)*
Simtec Industries Corporation .... G 631 293-0080
  Farmingdale *(G-5119)*

MACHINERY: Tire Shredding

Northeast Data .... G 845 331-5554
  Kingston *(G-7233)*
Shred Center .... G 716 664-3052
  Jamestown *(G-7059)*

MACHINERY: Voting

Dominion Voting Systems Inc .... F 404 955-9799
  Jamestown *(G-7023)*

MACHINERY: Wire Drawing

Carpenter Manufacturing Co .... E 315 682-9176
  Manlius *(G-8102)*
MGS Manufacturing Inc .... E 315 337-3350
  Rome *(G-14849)*

MACHINERY: Woodworking

Cem Machine Inc .... E 315 493-4258
  Carthage *(G-3438)*
James L Taylor Mfg Co .... E 845 452-3780
  Poughkeepsie *(G-13929)*
James L Taylor Mfg Co .... G 845 452-3780
  Poughkeepsie *(G-13930)*
Merritt Machinery LLC .... E 716 434-5558
  Lockport *(G-7628)*
Oneida Air Systems Inc .... E 315 476-5151
  Syracuse *(G-16025)*
Paratus Industries Inc .... E 716 826-2000
  Orchard Park *(G-13313)*

MACHINES: Forming, Sheet Metal

Cetek Inc .... E 845 452-3510
  Poughkeepsie *(G-13911)*

MACHINISTS' TOOLS: Measuring, Precision

B & B Precision Mfg Inc .... E 585 226-6226
  Avon *(G-535)*
Mausner Equipment Co Inc .... C 631 689-7358
  Setauket *(G-15402)*

MACHINISTS' TOOLS: Precision

East Side Machine Inc .... E 585 265-4560
  Webster *(G-16746)*
Egli Machine Company Inc .... E 607 563-3663
  Sidney *(G-15461)*
Hubbard Tool and Die Corp .... E 315 337-7840
  Rome *(G-14843)*
Lovejoy Chaplet Corporation .... E 518 686-5232
  Hoosick Falls *(G-6568)*
Melland Gear Instr of Huppauge .... E 631 234-0100
  Hauppauge *(G-6156)*
Miller Metal Fabricating Inc .... E 585 359-3400
  Rochester *(G-14534)*
Novatech Inc .... E 716 892-6682
  Cheektowaga *(G-3611)*
Park Enterprises Rochester Inc .... C 585 546-4200
  Rochester *(G-14593)*
Ppi Corp .... D 585 243-0300
  Rochester *(G-14612)*
Precision Grinding & Mfg Corp .... C 585 458-4300
  Rochester *(G-14615)*
Ptc Precision LLC .... E 607 748-8294
  Endwell *(G-4845)*
S & R Tool Inc .... G 585 346-2029
  Lakeville *(G-7308)*
Streamline Precision Inc .... G 585 421-9050
  Fairport *(G-4888)*
Townline Machine Co Inc .... F 315 462-3413
  Clifton Springs *(G-3741)*
Trimaster/Htech Holding LLC .... G 212 257-6772
  New York *(G-12427)*
Xactra Technologies Inc .... D 585 426-2030
  Rochester *(G-14795)*

MAGAZINES, WHOLESALE

Economist Newspaper NA Inc .... E 212 554-0676
  New York *(G-10033)*

Global Finance Media Inc .... F 212 447-7900
  New York *(G-10356)*

MAGNETIC INK & OPTICAL SCANNING EQPT

Capture Globa Integ Solut Inc .... G 718 352-0579
  Bayside Hills *(G-773)*
Hand Held Products Inc .... B 315 554-6000
  Skaneateles Falls *(G-15490)*
Hand Held Products Inc .... G 315 554-6000
  Skaneateles Falls *(G-15491)*
Peoples Choice M R I .... F 716 681-7377
  Buffalo *(G-3142)*
Symbol Technologies LLC .... G 631 738-3346
  Holtsville *(G-6537)*
Symbol Technologies LLC .... F 631 218-3907
  Holbrook *(G-6504)*

MAGNETIC RESONANCE IMAGING DEVICES: Nonmedical

Finger Lakes Radiology LLC .... G 315 787-5399
  Geneva *(G-5589)*
Islandia Mri Associates PC .... F 631 234-2828
  Central Islip *(G-3527)*

MAGNETIC TAPE, AUDIO: Prerecorded

C & C Duplicators Inc .... E 631 244-0800
  Bohemia *(G-1025)*

MAGNETOHYDRODYNAMIC DEVICES OR MHD

Passive-Plus Inc .... F 631 425-0938
  Huntington *(G-6708)*

MAGNETS: Ceramic

Arnold Magnetic Tech Corp .... C 585 385-9010
  Rochester *(G-14228)*
Eneflux Armtek Magnetics Inc .... G 516 576-3434
  Medford *(G-8275)*
Hitachi Metals America Ltd .... E 914 694-9200
  Purchase *(G-13975)*

MAGNETS: Permanent

Arnold Magnetic Tech Corp .... C 585 385-9010
  Rochester *(G-14228)*
Carpentier Industries LLC .... F 585 385-5550
  East Rochester *(G-4474)*
Magnaworks Technology Inc .... G 631 218-3431
  Bohemia *(G-1095)*
Magnetic Aids Inc .... G 845 863-1400
  Newburgh *(G-12787)*
MMC Magnetics Corp .... F 631 435-9888
  Hauppauge *(G-6167)*
Polymag Inc .... E 631 286-4111
  Bellport *(G-836)*
Precision Magnetics LLC .... E 585 385-9010
  Rochester *(G-14618)*
Technomag Inc .... G 631 246-6142
  East Setauket *(G-4512)*
Truebite Inc .... E 607 785-7664
  Vestal *(G-16479)*
Wtbi Inc .... G 631 547-1993
  Huntington Station *(G-6767)*

MAGNIFIERS

Edroy Products Co Inc .... G 845 358-6600
  Nyack *(G-13067)*

MAIL-ORDER BOOK CLUBS

Global Video LLC .... D 516 222-2600
  Woodbury *(G-17310)*
Station Hill of Barrytown .... G 845 758-5293
  Barrytown *(G-619)*

MAIL-ORDER HOUSE, NEC

American Country Quilts & Lin .... G 631 283-5466
  Southampton *(G-15562)*
Chocolat Moderne LLC .... G 212 229-4797
  New York *(G-9657)*
Collinite Corporation .... G 315 732-2282
  Utica *(G-16336)*
Hamtronics Inc .... G 585 392-9430
  Rochester *(G-14438)*

Hubray Inc .... F 800 645-2855
  North Baldwin *(G-12924)*
Quaker Boy Inc .... E 716 662-3979
  Orchard Park *(G-13317)*
TRM Linen Inc .... G 718 686-6075
  Brooklyn *(G-2702)*

MAIL-ORDER HOUSES: Book & Record Clubs

Oxford University Press LLC .... B 212 726-6000
  New York *(G-11555)*
Oxford University Press LLC .... B 212 726-6000
  New York *(G-11556)*

MAIL-ORDER HOUSES: Books, Exc Book Clubs

Anthroposophic Press Inc .... G 518 851-2054
  Clifton Park *(G-3721)*
Looseleaf Law Publications Inc .... F 718 359-5559
  Flushing *(G-5275)*
Profits Direct Inc .... G 631 851-4083
  Ronkonkoma *(G-14996)*
Rizzoli Intl Publications Inc .... E 212 387-3400
  New York *(G-11903)*
Syracuse Cultural Workers Prj .... F 315 474-1132
  Syracuse *(G-16076)*
Trusted Media Brands Inc .... A 914 238-1000
  New York *(G-12435)*
Trusted Media Brands Inc .... F 914 244-5244
  White Plains *(G-17204)*

MAIL-ORDER HOUSES: Cards

Color Card LLC .... F 631 232-1300
  Central Islip *(G-3516)*

MAIL-ORDER HOUSES: Clothing, Exc Women's

Cockpit Usa Inc .... F 212 575-1616
  New York *(G-9719)*
Cockpit Usa Inc .... F 212 575-1616
  New York *(G-9720)*

MAIL-ORDER HOUSES: Computer Eqpt & Electronics

Gim Electronics Corp .... F 516 942-3382
  Hicksville *(G-6377)*

MAIL-ORDER HOUSES: Cosmetics & Perfumes

Borghese Inc .... E 212 659-5318
  New York *(G-9491)*

MAIL-ORDER HOUSES: Fitness & Sporting Goods

KD Dids Inc .... G 718 402-2012
  Bronx *(G-1373)*

MAIL-ORDER HOUSES: Food

Sbk Preserves Inc .... E 800 773-7378
  Bronx *(G-1448)*

MAIL-ORDER HOUSES: Furniture & Furnishings

Charles P Rogers Brass Beds .... F 212 675-4400
  New York *(G-9633)*
Wink Inc .... E 212 389-1382
  New York *(G-12672)*

MAIL-ORDER HOUSES: Gift Items

Jomar Industries Inc .... E 845 357-5773
  Airmont *(G-14)*

MAIL-ORDER HOUSES: Jewelry

Indonesian Imports Inc .... E 888 800-5899
  New York *(G-10633)*

MAIL-ORDER HOUSES: Magazines

Dlc Comprehensive Medical PC .... F 718 857-1200
  Brooklyn *(G-1869)*

Employee Codes: A=Over 500 employees, B=251-500
C=101-250, D=51-100, E=20-50, F=10-19, G=5-9

MAILING LIST: Brokers

MAILING LIST: Brokers
Luria Communications Inc...............G....... 631 329-4922
  East Hampton (G-4433)

MAILING LIST: Compilers
Select Information Exchange.............F....... 212 496-6435
  New York (G-12042)

MAILING SVCS, NEC
Data Palette Info Svcs LLC...............D....... 718 433-1060
  Port Washington (G-13830)
Dispatch Graphics Inc...................F....... 212 307-5943
  New York (G-9938)
DP Murphy Co Inc.......................D....... 631 673-9400
  Deer Park (G-4154)
Five Star Prtg & Mailing Svcs...........F....... 212 929-0300
  New York (G-10229)
Garden City Printers & Mailers..........F....... 516 485-1600
  West Hempstead (G-16884)
Hart Reproduction Services.............G....... 212 704-0556
  New York (G-10468)
Mason & Gore Inc.......................E....... 914 921-1025
  Rye (G-15089)
PDQ Shipping Services..................G....... 845 255-5500
  New Paltz (G-8922)
The Nugent Organization Inc............F....... 212 645-6600
  Oceanside (G-13123)
Westchester Mailing Service............E....... 914 948-1116
  White Plains (G-17212)

MANAGEMENT CONSULTING SVCS: Automation & Robotics
Cs Automation Inc......................F....... 315 524-5123
  Ontario (G-13220)
Javlyn Process Systems LLC.............E....... 585 424-5580
  Rochester (G-14482)

MANAGEMENT CONSULTING SVCS: Business
Hargrave Development...................F....... 716 877-7880
  Kenmore (G-7175)
Security Letter........................G....... 212 348-1553
  New York (G-12034)
Yale Robbins Inc.......................D....... 212 683-5700
  New York (G-12709)

MANAGEMENT CONSULTING SVCS: Construction Project
Darrell Mitchell.......................G....... 646 659-7075
  Arverne (G-422)

MANAGEMENT CONSULTING SVCS: Distribution Channels
Standard Analytics Io Inc..............G....... 917 882-5422
  New York (G-12205)

MANAGEMENT CONSULTING SVCS: Food & Beverage
Marley Spoon Inc.......................C....... 646 934-6970
  New York (G-11186)
SPX Flow Tech Systems Inc..............D....... 716 692-3000
  Getzville (G-5616)

MANAGEMENT CONSULTING SVCS: Foreign Trade
Communications & Energy Corp...........F....... 315 446-5723
  Syracuse (G-15922)

MANAGEMENT CONSULTING SVCS: Industrial
GE Global Research.....................G....... 518 387-5000
  Niskayuna (G-12911)

MANAGEMENT CONSULTING SVCS: Industrial & Labor
Terahertz Technologies Inc.............G....... 315 736-3642
  Oriskany (G-13340)

MANAGEMENT CONSULTING SVCS: Industry Specialist
ER Butler & Co Inc.....................E....... 212 925-3565
  New York (G-10107)
Ludwig Holdings Corp...................D....... 845 340-9727
  Kingston (G-7227)

MANAGEMENT CONSULTING SVCS: Real Estate
Visual Listing Systems Inc.............G....... 631 689-7222
  East Setauket (G-4515)

MANAGEMENT CONSULTING SVCS: Training & Development
Calia Technical Inc....................G....... 718 447-3928
  Staten Island (G-15675)
Serendipity Consulting Corp............F....... 914 763-8251
  South Salem (G-15560)

MANAGEMENT SERVICES
A & Mt Realty Group LLC................F....... 718 974-5871
  Brooklyn (G-1527)
Arnan Development Corp.................D....... 607 432-8391
  Oneonta (G-13194)
Elie Tahari Ltd........................D....... 212 398-2622
  New York (G-10055)
Fonar Corporation......................C....... 631 694-2929
  Melville (G-8349)
International Center For Postg.........G....... 607 257-5860
  Ithaca (G-6886)
Precision Disc Grinding Corp...........F....... 516 747-5450
  Mineola (G-8564)
Quoizel Inc............................E....... 631 436-4402
  Hauppauge (G-6202)

MANAGEMENT SVCS: Administrative
Supermedia LLC.........................D....... 212 513-9700
  New York (G-12265)
Tdk USA Corporation....................D....... 516 535-2600
  Uniondale (G-16323)

MANAGEMENT SVCS: Circuit, Motion Picture Theaters
Dolomite Products Company Inc..........E....... 315 524-1998
  Rochester (G-14337)

MANAGEMENT SVCS: Construction
Darrell Mitchell.......................G....... 646 659-7075
  Arverne (G-422)
Sg Blocks Inc..........................G....... 615 585-2639
  Brooklyn (G-2573)

MANAGEMENT SVCS: Restaurant
D R M Management Inc...................E....... 716 668-0333
  Depew (G-4278)

MANDRELS
Safina Center..........................G....... 808 888-9440
  Stony Brook (G-15792)

MANHOLES COVERS: Concrete
Jefferson Concrete Corp................D....... 315 788-4171
  Watertown (G-16677)

MANICURE PREPARATIONS
Angel Tips Nail Salon..................G....... 718 225-8300
  Little Neck (G-7529)
Essie Cosmetics Ltd....................D....... 212 818-1500
  New York (G-10120)

MANIFOLDS: Pipe, Fabricated From Purchased Pipe
M Manastrip-M Corporation..............G....... 518 664-2089
  Clifton Park (G-3726)

MANNEQUINS
Adel Rootstein (usa) Inc...............E....... 718 499-5650
  Brooklyn (G-1560)
Columbia Dentoform Corporation.........E....... 718 482-1569
  Long Island City (G-7732)
Genesis Mannequins USA II Inc..........G....... 212 505-6600
  New York (G-10318)
Lifestyle-Trimco.......................E....... 718 257-9101
  Brooklyn (G-2220)
Siegel & Stockman Inc..................G....... 212 633-1508
  New York (G-12083)

MANUFACTURING INDUSTRIES, NEC
141 Industries LLC.....................F....... 978 273-8831
  New York (G-9005)
A & W Metal Works Inc..................F....... 845 352-2346
  Garnerville (G-5566)
A&M Model Makers LLC...................G....... 626 813-9661
  Macedon (G-8006)
Accessible Bath Tech LLC...............F....... 518 937-1518
  Albany (G-30)
AFP Manufacturing Corp.................F....... 516 466-6464
  Great Neck (G-5800)
Air Flow Manufacturing.................F....... 607 733-8284
  Elmira (G-4683)
Atlas Metal Industries Inc.............G....... 607 776-2048
  Hammondsport (G-5975)
B F G Elcpltg and Mfg Co...............E....... 716 362-0888
  Blasdell (G-954)
Bee Green Industries Inc...............G....... 516 334-3525
  Carle Place (G-3412)
Dj Pirrone Industries Inc..............G....... 518 864-5496
  Pattersonville (G-13471)
Dolmen.................................F....... 912 596-1537
  Conklin (G-3892)
E-Z Global Wholesale Inc...............G....... 888 769-7888
  Brooklyn (G-1895)
EDM Mfg................................G....... 631 669-1966
  Babylon (G-545)
Essex Industries.......................G....... 518 942-6671
  Mineville (G-8573)
Falk Industries Inc....................F....... 518 725-2777
  Johnstown (G-7145)
Feraco Industries......................G....... 631 547-8120
  Huntington Station (G-6742)
Freedom Mfg LLC........................F....... 518 584-0441
  Saratoga Springs (G-15181)
Fun Industries of NY...................F....... 631 845-3805
  Farmingdale (G-5004)
Hudson Eastern Industries Inc..........G....... 917 295-5818
  Whitestone (G-17238)
J & R Unique Giftware..................E....... 718 821-0398
  Maspeth (G-8177)
John Prior.............................G....... 516 520-9801
  East Meadow (G-4446)
Just Right Carbines LLC................G....... 585 261-5331
  Canandaigua (G-3377)
Kafko (us) Corp........................G....... 877 721-7665
  Latham (G-7394)
Lois Kitchen LLC.......................G....... 216 308-9335
  New York (G-11051)
Martec Industries......................F....... 585 458-3940
  Rochester (G-14519)
Mitco Manufacturing....................G....... 800 338-8908
  Garden City (G-5535)
My Industries Inc......................G....... 845 638-2257
  New City (G-8835)
O Brien Gere Mfg Inc...................G....... 315 437-6100
  Liverpool (G-7563)
Ogd V-Hvac Inc.........................E....... 315 858-1002
  Van Hornesville (G-16455)
Ohserase Manufacturing LLC.............G....... 518 358-9309
  Hogansburg (G-6454)
Omicron Technologies Inc...............E....... 631 434-7697
  Holbrook (G-6494)
Oriskany Manufacturing LLC.............F....... 315 732-4962
  Yorkville (G-17541)
Oso Industries Inc.....................G....... 917 709-2050
  Brooklyn (G-2410)
Performance Precision Mfg LLC..........G....... 518 993-3033
  Fort Plain (G-5357)
Quest Manufacturing Inc................E....... 716 312-8000
  Hamburg (G-5962)
Remus Industries.......................G....... 914 906-1544
  Ossining (G-13351)
Rockwell Video Solutions LLC...........F....... 631 745-0582
  Southampton (G-15574)
Rutcarele Inc..........................G....... 347 830-5353
  Corona (G-4028)
Select Industries New York Inc.........F....... 800 723-5333
  New York (G-12041)
Sonaal Industries Inc..................G....... 718 383-3860
  Brooklyn (G-2609)
Tii Industries Inc.....................F....... 631 789-5000
  Copiague (G-3956)

PRODUCT SECTION

MEAT & MEAT PRDTS WHOLESALERS

Tiki Industries Inc ....G....... 516 779-3629
  Riverhead (G-14171)
Topoo Industries Incorporated ....G....... 718 331-3755
  Brooklyn (G-2685)
Unistel LLC ....D....... 585 341-4600
  Webster (G-16766)
Unither Manufacturing LLC ....F....... 585 274-5430
  Rochester (G-14770)
Unlimited Industries Inc ....G....... 631 666-9483
  Brightwaters (G-1238)
Water Splash Inc ....G....... 800 936-3430
  Champlain (G-3577)
Woodfalls Industries ....F....... 518 236-7201
  Plattsburgh (G-13740)
Zmz Mfg Inc ....G....... 518 234-4336
  Warnerville (G-16599)

MAPS

Mapeasy Inc ....F....... 631 537-6213
  Wainscott (G-16548)

MARBLE BOARD

Amendola MBL & Stone Ctr Inc ....D....... 914 997-7968
  White Plains (G-17104)

MARBLE, BUILDING: Cut & Shaped

Dicamillo Marble and Granite ....E....... 845 878-0078
  Patterson (G-13462)
International Stone Accessrs ....G....... 718 522-5399
  Brooklyn (G-2110)
Italian Marble & Granite Inc ....F....... 716 741-1800
  Clarence Center (G-3702)
Lace Marble & Granite Inc ....G....... 347 425-1645
  Brooklyn (G-2188)
Marble Doctors LLC ....E....... 203 628-8339
  New York (G-11167)
Monroe Industries Inc ....G....... 585 226-8230
  Avon (G-538)
Premier Group NY ....F....... 212 229-1200
  New York (G-11720)
Salsburg Dimensional Stone ....F....... 631 653-6790
  Brookhaven (G-1509)
Unique MBL Gran Orgnztion Corp ....G....... 718 482-0440
  Long Island City (G-7935)
White Plains Marble Inc ....G....... 914 347-6000
  Elmsford (G-4801)

MARBLE: Crushed & Broken

Sparclean MBL Refinishing Inc ....G....... 718 445-2351
  Ridgewood (G-14137)

MARINAS

Meeco Sullivan LLC ....C....... 800 232-3625
  Warwick (G-16617)

MARINE HARDWARE

Bfg Marine Inc ....F....... 631 586-5500
  Bay Shore (G-674)
Dover Marine Mfg & Sup Co Inc ....G....... 631 667-4300
  Deer Park (G-4153)
Rollson Inc ....E....... 631 423-9578
  Huntington (G-6717)
Taylor Made Group LLC ....E....... 518 725-0681
  Gloversville (G-5739)

MARINE RELATED EQPT

Kyntec Corporation ....G....... 716 810-6956
  Buffalo (G-3056)

MARINE SVC STATIONS

Accurate Marine Specialties ....G....... 631 589-5502
  Bohemia (G-1000)

MARKERS

Mark Dri Products Inc ....C....... 516 484-6200
  Bethpage (G-871)

MARKETS: Meat & fish

Schaller Manufacturing Corp ....D....... 718 721-5480
  New York (G-12004)

MARKING DEVICES

Bianca Group Ltd ....G....... 212 768-3011
  New York (G-9435)

C M E Corp ....F....... 315 451-7101
  Syracuse (G-15900)
East Coast Thermographers Inc ....E....... 718 321-3211
  College Point (G-3807)
Effanjay Pens Inc ....E....... 212 316-9565
  Long Island City (G-7755)
Hampton Art LLC ....E....... 631 924-1335
  Medford (G-8278)
Heidenhain International Inc ....C....... 716 661-1700
  Jamestown (G-7033)
Hodgins Engraving Co Inc ....D....... 585 343-4444
  Batavia (G-640)
Joseph Treu Successors Inc ....E....... 212 691-7026
  New York (G-10805)
Kelly Foundry & Machine Co ....E....... 315 732-8313
  Utica (G-16370)
Krengel Manufacturing Co Inc ....F....... 212 227-1901
  Fulton (G-5481)
New York Marking Devices Corp ....E....... 585 454-5188
  Rochester (G-14554)
New York Marking Devices Corp ....G....... 315 463-8641
  Syracuse (G-16018)
Tech Products Inc ....E....... 718 442-4900
  Staten Island (G-15770)
UI Corp ....G....... 201 203-4453
  Bayside (G-770)
United Sttes Brnze Sign of Fla ....E....... 516 352-5155
  New Hyde Park (G-8914)

MARKING DEVICES: Date Stamps, Hand, Rubber Or Metal

Koehlr-Gibson Mkg Graphics Inc ....E....... 716 838-5960
  Buffalo (G-3053)
Long Island Stamp & Seal Co ....F....... 718 628-8550
  Ridgewood (G-14126)

MARKING DEVICES: Embossing Seals & Hand Stamps

A & M Steel Stamps Inc ....G....... 516 741-6223
  Mineola (G-8521)
Cannizzaro Seal & Engraving Co ....F....... 718 513-6125
  Brooklyn (G-1756)
Rubber Stamp X Press ....F....... 631 423-1322
  Huntington Station (G-6758)

MARKING DEVICES: Embossing Seals, Corporate & Official

Sales Tax Asset Rceivable Corp ....G....... 212 788-5874
  New York (G-11974)

MARKING DEVICES: Figures, Metal

Thermopatch Corporation ....D....... 315 446-8110
  Syracuse (G-16082)

MARKING DEVICES: Irons, Marking Or Branding

Name Base Inc ....G....... 212 545-1400
  New York (G-11363)

MARKING DEVICES: Letters, Metal

I & I Systems ....G....... 845 753-9126
  Tuxedo Park (G-16306)

MARKING DEVICES: Numbering Machines

National Time Recording Eqp Co ....F....... 212 227-3310
  New York (G-11375)

MARKING DEVICES: Pads, Inking & Stamping

Dab-O-Matic Corp ....D....... 914 699-7070
  Mount Vernon (G-8722)
Specialty Ink Co Inc ....F....... 631 586-3666
  Blue Point (G-995)
United Silicone Inc ....D....... 716 681-8222
  Lancaster (G-7370)

MARKING DEVICES: Postmark Stamps, Hand, Rubber Or Metal

Rubber Stamps Inc ....E....... 212 675-1180
  Mineola (G-8568)

MARKING DEVICES: Screens, Textile Printing

Michael Todd Stevens ....G....... 585 436-9957
  Rochester (G-14527)
Ulano Product Inc ....C....... 718 622-5200
  Brooklyn (G-2714)
Ward Sales Co Inc ....G....... 315 476-5276
  Syracuse (G-16093)

MASKS: Gas

Go Blue Technologies Ltd ....G....... 631 404-6285
  North Babylon (G-12918)

MASQUERADE OR THEATRICAL COSTUMES STORES

D-C Theatricks ....G....... 716 847-0180
  Buffalo (G-2919)
Moresca Clothing and Costume ....F....... 845 331-6012
  Ulster Park (G-16309)

MASTIC ROOFING COMPOSITION

Savage & Son Installations LLC ....E....... 585 342-7533
  Rochester (G-14692)

MATERIALS HANDLING EQPT WHOLESALERS

Four-Way Pallet Corp ....E....... 631 351-3401
  Huntington Station (G-6744)
George Ponte Inc ....G....... 914 243-4202
  Jefferson Valley (G-7090)
High Frequency Tech Co Inc ....F....... 631 242-3020
  Deer Park (G-4171)
Koke Inc ....E....... 800 535-5303
  Queensbury (G-14016)
Overhead Door Corporation ....D....... 518 828-7652
  Hudson (G-6659)
Raymond Sales Corporation ....G....... 607 656-2311
  Greene (G-5888)
Tri-Boro Shlving Prtition Corp ....F....... 718 782-8527
  Ridgewood (G-14142)

MATS & MATTING, MADE FROM PURCHASED WIRE

Brook North Farms Inc ....F....... 315 834-9390
  Auburn (G-486)

MATS OR MATTING, NEC: Rubber

Seaway Mats Inc ....G....... 518 483-2560
  Malone (G-8047)

MATS, MATTING & PADS: Auto, Floor, Exc Rubber Or Plastic

Auto-Mat Company Inc ....E....... 516 938-7373
  Hicksville (G-6349)

MATS, MATTING & PADS: Nonwoven

North Sunshine LLC ....F....... 307 027-1634
  Valley Cottage (G-16410)

MATS: Blasting, Rope

T M International LLC ....G....... 718 842-0949
  Bronx (G-1469)

MATTRESS RENOVATING & REPAIR SHOP

E & G Bedding Corp ....E....... 718 369-1092
  Brooklyn (G-1890)

MATTRESS STORES

Otis Bedding Mfg Co Inc ....E....... 716 825-2599
  Buffalo (G-3127)

MEAT & MEAT PRDTS WHOLESALERS

Brooklyn Bangers LLC ....F....... 718 875-3535
  Brooklyn (G-1719)
Elmgang Enterprises I Inc ....F....... 212 868-4142
  New York (G-10065)
Tri-Town Packing Corp ....F....... 315 389-5101
  Brasher Falls (G-1171)

Employee Codes: A=Over 500 employees, B=251-500
C=101-250, D=51-100, E=20-50, F=10-19, G=5-9

2018 Harris
New York Manufacturers Directory

MEAT CUTTING & PACKING

MEAT CUTTING & PACKING

A To Z Kosher Meat Products Co .... E		718 384-7400
Brooklyn *(G-1535)*		
Caribbean Foods Delight Inc .... D		845 398-3000
Tappan *(G-16103)*		
Chefs Delight Packing Co .... F		718 388-8581
Brooklyn *(G-1776)*		
Crescent Duck Farm Inc .... E		631 722-8700
Aquebogue *(G-384)*		
Domestic Casing Co .... G		718 522-1902
Brooklyn *(G-1873)*		
DRG New York Holdings Corp .... D		914 668-9000
Mount Vernon *(G-8723)*		
Fairbank Reconstruction Corp .... D		800 628-3276
Ashville *(G-426)*		
Frank Wardynski & Sons Inc .... E		716 854-6083
Buffalo *(G-2970)*		
Globex Kosher Foods Inc .... E		718 630-5555
Brooklyn *(G-2030)*		
Gold Medal Packing Inc .... D		315 337-1911
Oriskany *(G-13334)*		
Ives Farm Market .... G		315 592-4880
Fulton *(G-5477)*		
Kamerys Wholesale Meats Inc .... G		716 372-6756
Olean *(G-13170)*		
Old World Provisions Inc .... D		518 465-7307
Troy *(G-16268)*		
Orleans Custom Packing Inc .... G		585 314-8227
Holley *(G-6516)*		
Side Hill Farmers Coop Inc .... G		315 447-4693
Canastota *(G-3399)*		
The Smoke House of Catskills .... G		845 246-8767
Saugerties *(G-15226)*		
Tri-Town Packing Corp .... F		315 389-5101
Brasher Falls *(G-1171)*		
We Work .... G		877 673-6628
New York *(G-12628)*		

MEAT MARKETS

Ives Farm Market .... G		315 592-4880
Fulton *(G-5477)*		
Mineo & Sapio Meats Inc .... G		716 884-2398
Buffalo *(G-3087)*		
The Smoke House of Catskills .... G		845 246-8767
Saugerties *(G-15226)*		

MEAT PRDTS: Bologna, From Purchased Meat

Atlantic Pork & Provisions Inc .... E		718 272-9550
Jamaica *(G-6930)*		

MEAT PRDTS: Boneless Meat, From Purchased Meat

Tower Isles Frozen Foods Ltd .... D		718 495-2626
Brooklyn *(G-2690)*		

MEAT PRDTS: Canned

Birds Eye Holdings Inc .... A		585 383-1850
Rochester *(G-14250)*		

MEAT PRDTS: Dried Beef, From Purchased Meat

Patla Enterprises Inc .... G		315 790-0143
Sherrill *(G-15429)*		

MEAT PRDTS: Frankfurters, From Purchased Meat

Marathon Enterprises Inc .... D		718 665-2560
Bronx *(G-1389)*		

MEAT PRDTS: Frozen

Caribbean Foods Delight Inc .... D		845 398-3000
Tappan *(G-16103)*		
Original Crunch Roll Fctry LLC .... G		716 402-5030
Amherst *(G-258)*		
Prime Food Processing Corp .... D		718 963-2323
Brooklyn *(G-2455)*		

MEAT PRDTS: Meat By-Prdts, From Slaughtered Meat

Cni Meat & Produce Inc .... G		516 599-5929
Valley Stream *(G-16430)*		

Huda Kawshai LLC .... G		929 255-7009
Jamaica *(G-6956)*		
Joel Kiryas Meat Market Corp .... F		845 782-9194
Monroe *(G-8593)*		
Robert & William Inc .... G		631 727-5780
Riverhead *(G-14167)*		
Sam A Lupo & Sons Inc .... G		800 388-5352
Endicott *(G-4833)*		
USA Halal Foods Inc .... G		718 291-9111
Long Island City *(G-7939)*		

MEAT PRDTS: Meat Extracts, From Purchased Meat

Reliable Brothers Inc .... E		518 273-6732
Green Island *(G-5879)*		

MEAT PRDTS: Pork, From Slaughtered Meat

Hilltown Pork Inc .... E		518 781-4050
Canaan *(G-3359)*		

MEAT PRDTS: Prepared Beef Prdts From Purchased Beef

Bianca Burgers LLC .... F		516 764-9591
Rockville Centre *(G-14816)*		
Freirich Julian Co Inc .... E		718 361-9111
Long Island City *(G-7775)*		

MEAT PRDTS: Prepared Pork Prdts, From Purchased Meat

Hansel n Gretel Brand Inc C		718 326-0041
Glendale *(G-5671)*		
Lancaster Quality Pork Inc .... F		718 439-8822
Brooklyn *(G-2194)*		
Schaller Manufacturing Corp .... D		718 721-5480
New York *(G-12004)*		

MEAT PRDTS: Sausage Casings, Natural

Brooklyn Casing Co Inc .... G		718 522-0866
Brooklyn *(G-1721)*		
Camellia General Provision Co .... G		716 893-5352
Buffalo *(G-2887)*		
Domestic Casing Co .... G		718 522-1902
Brooklyn *(G-1873)*		
Frank Wardynski & Sons Inc .... E		716 854-6083
Buffalo *(G-2970)*		
Niagara Tying Service Inc .... E		716 825-0066
Buffalo *(G-3114)*		
Rapa Independent North America .... G		518 561-0513
Plattsburgh *(G-13723)*		

MEAT PRDTS: Sausages & Related Prdts, From Purchased Meat

Elmgang Enterprises I Inc .... F		212 868-4142
New York *(G-10065)*		
Schonwetter Enterprises Inc .... E		518 237-0171
Cohoes *(G-3782)*		

MEAT PRDTS: Sausages, From Purchased Meat

Arnolds Meat Food Products .... E		718 384-8071
Brooklyn *(G-1631)*		
Buffalo Provisions Co Inc .... F		718 292-4300
Elmhurst *(G-4671)*		
Cibao Meat Products Inc .... D		718 993-5072
Bronx *(G-1299)*		
De Ans Pork Products Inc .... E		718 788-2464
Brooklyn *(G-1845)*		
Hanzlian Sausage Incorporated .... G		716 891-5247
Cheektowaga *(G-3603)*		
Salarinos Italian Foods Inc .... F		315 697-9766
Canastota *(G-3398)*		

MEAT PRDTS: Sausages, From Slaughtered Meat

Sahlen Packing Company Inc .... D		716 852-8677
Buffalo *(G-3204)*		

MEAT PRDTS: Snack Sticks, Incl Jerky, From Purchased Meat

Big Johns Adirondack Inc .... E		518 587-3680
Saratoga Springs *(G-15173)*		

Holy Cow Kosher LLC .... G		347 788-8620
Spring Valley *(G-15611)*		
Provisionaire & Co LLC .... E		646 681-8600
Brooklyn *(G-2473)*		

MEAT PRDTS: Variety, Fresh Edible Organs

Martin D Whitbeck .... G		607 746-7642
Delhi *(G-4265)*		

MEAT PRDTS: Veal, From Slaughtered Meat

Delft Blue LLC C		315 768-7100
New York Mills *(G-12740)*		

MEAT PROCESSED FROM PURCHASED CARCASSES

Adirondack Meat Company Inc .... F		518 585-2333
Ticonderoga *(G-16146)*		
Alle Processing Corp C		718 894-2000
Maspeth *(G-8143)*		
Alps Provision Co Inc .... E		718 721-4477
Astoria *(G-430)*		
Brooklyn Bangers LLC .... F		718 875-3535
Brooklyn *(G-1719)*		
Cni Meat & Produce Inc .... G		516 599-5929
Valley Stream *(G-16430)*		
Dinos Sausage & Meat Co Inc .... F		315 732-2661
Utica *(G-16348)*		
Fairbank Reconstruction Corp .... D		800 628-3276
Ashville *(G-426)*		
Hilltown Pork Inc .... E		518 781-4050
Canaan *(G-3359)*		
Jacks Gourmet LLC .... F		718 954-4681
Brooklyn *(G-2128)*		
Milan Provision Co Inc .... E		718 899-7678
Corona *(G-4026)*		
Mineo & Sapio Meats Inc .... G		716 884-2398
Buffalo *(G-3087)*		
Mr Pierogi LLC .... F		718 499-7821
Brooklyn *(G-2345)*		
Picone Meat Specialties Ltd .... G		914 381-3002
Mamaroneck *(G-8075)*		
Pork King Sausage Inc .... E		718 542-2810
Bronx *(G-1432)*		
Rosina Food Products Inc C		716 668-0123
Buffalo *(G-3193)*		
Rosina Holding Inc .... G		716 668-0123
Buffalo *(G-3194)*		
Schrader Meat Market .... F		607 869-6328
Romulus *(G-14870)*		
Sun Ming Jan Inc .... F		718 418-8221
Brooklyn *(G-2641)*		
Syracuse Casing Co Inc .... F		315 475-0309
Syracuse *(G-16073)*		
Tyson Deli Inc .... B		716 826-6400
Buffalo *(G-3255)*		
White Eagle Packing Co Inc .... F		518 374-4366
Schenectady *(G-15335)*		
Zweigles Inc .... D		585 546-1740
Rochester *(G-14806)*		

MED, DENTAL & HOSPITAL EQPT, WHOL: Incontinent Prdts/Splys

Koregon Enterprises Inc .... G		450 218-6836
Champlain *(G-3571)*		

MEDIA BUYING AGENCIES

Selby Marketing Associates Inc .... F		585 377-0750
Fairport *(G-4882)*		
Ubm LLC .... D		516 562-7800
New Hyde Park *(G-8912)*		

MEDIA: Magnetic & Optical Recording

Aarfid LLC .... G		716 992-3999
Eden *(G-4597)*		
BMA Media Services Inc .... E		585 385-2060
Rochester *(G-14256)*		
Dm2 Media LLC .... E		646 419-4357
New York *(G-9943)*		
Next Big Sound Inc .... G		646 657-9837
New York *(G-11440)*		
Stamper Technology Inc .... G		585 247-8370
Rochester *(G-14724)*		

PRODUCT SECTION

MEDICAL & SURGICAL SPLYS: Technical Aids, Handicapped

MEDICAL & HOSPITAL EQPT WHOLESALERS

AEP Environmental LLC .... F 716 446-0739
  Buffalo *(G-2818)*
Allied Pharmacy Products Inc .... G 516 374-8862
  Woodmere *(G-17328)*
Hogil Pharmaceutical Corp .... F 914 681-1800
  White Plains *(G-17147)*
Nova Health Systems Inc .... G 315 798-9018
  Utica *(G-16377)*
Occunomix International LLC .... E 631 741-1940
  Port Jeff STA *(G-13792)*
Precimed Inc .... E 716 759-5600
  Clarence *(G-3696)*
Progressive Orthotics Ltd .... G 631 732-5556
  Selden *(G-15375)*
Roner Inc .... G 718 392-6020
  Long Island City *(G-7895)*
TSS Foam Industries Corp .... F 585 538-2321
  Caledonia *(G-3311)*

MEDICAL & HOSPITAL SPLYS: Radiation Shielding Garments

Biodex Medical Systems Inc .... C 631 924-9000
  Shirley *(G-15439)*
Biodex Medical Systems Inc .... E 631 924-3146
  Shirley *(G-15440)*
Xylon Industries Inc .... G 631 293-4717
  Farmingdale *(G-5153)*

MEDICAL & SURGICAL SPLYS: Bandages & Dressings

Aero Healthcare (us) LLC .... G 855 225-2376
  Valley Cottage *(G-16401)*
Euromed Inc .... D 845 359-4039
  Orangeburg *(G-13249)*

MEDICAL & SURGICAL SPLYS: Braces, Orthopedic

Arimed Orthotics Prosthetics P ..... F 718 979-6155
  Staten Island *(G-15660)*
Complete Orthopedic Svcs Inc ..... E 516 357-9113
  East Meadow *(G-4440)*
Eschen Prosthetic & Orthotic L .... E 212 606-1262
  New York *(G-10111)*
Hanger Prsthetcs & Ortho Inc ...... D 607 795-1220
  Elmira *(G-4700)*
Lorelei Orthotics Prosthetics .... G 212 727-2011
  New York *(G-11070)*

MEDICAL & SURGICAL SPLYS: Clothing, Fire Resistant & Protect

Elwood Specialty Products Inc ...... F 716 877-6622
  Buffalo *(G-2948)*

MEDICAL & SURGICAL SPLYS: Cosmetic Restorations

Northwell Health Inc .... B 888 387-5811
  New York *(G-11479)*

MEDICAL & SURGICAL SPLYS: Cotton & Cotton Applicators

Advanced Enterprises Inc .... F 845 342-1009
  Middletown *(G-8459)*

MEDICAL & SURGICAL SPLYS: Ear Plugs

Cirrus Healthcare Products LLC ... E 631 692-7600
  Cold Spring Harbor *(G-3792)*
New Dynamics Corporation .... E 845 692-0022
  Middletown *(G-8488)*

MEDICAL & SURGICAL SPLYS: Foot Appliances, Orthopedic

Brannock Device Co Inc .... E 315 475-9862
  Liverpool *(G-7535)*
Fiber Foot Appliances Inc .... G 631 465-9199
  Farmingdale *(G-5002)*
Schuster & Richard Labortories ... G 718 358-8607
  College Point *(G-3831)*

MEDICAL & SURGICAL SPLYS: Gynecological Splys & Appliances

Cityscape Ob/Gyn PLLC .... F 212 683-3595
  New York *(G-9686)*
Womens Health Care PC .... G 718 850-0009
  Richmond Hill *(G-14100)*

MEDICAL & SURGICAL SPLYS: Limbs, Artificial

Aaaaar Orthopedics Inc .... G 845 278-4938
  Brewster *(G-1203)*
Creative Orthotics & Prosthet .... F 607 734-7215
  Elmira *(G-4691)*
Creative Orthotics Prosthetics ...... G 607 771-4672
  Binghamton *(G-899)*
Gfh Orthotic & Prosthetic Labs .... G 631 467-3725
  Bohemia *(G-1068)*
Goldberg Prosthetic & Orthotic .... F 631 689-6606
  East Setauket *(G-4502)*
Green Prosthetics & Orthotics ..... G 716 484-1088
  Jamestown *(G-7030)*
Hanger Prsthetcs & Ortho Inc ...... G 607 771-4672
  Binghamton *(G-915)*
Hanger Prsthetcs & Ortho Inc ...... G 315 472-5200
  Syracuse *(G-15976)*
Hanger Prsthetcs & Ortho Inc ...... G 315 789-4810
  Geneva *(G-5593)*
Lehneis Orthotics Prosthetic .... G 631 369-3115
  Riverhead *(G-14159)*
National Prosthetic Orthot .... G 718 767-8400
  Bayside *(G-768)*
North Shore Orthtics Prsthtics ..... G 631 928-3040
  Port Jeff STA *(G-13791)*
Orthopedic Treatment Facility ...... G 718 898-7326
  Woodside *(G-17360)*
Progressive Orthotics Ltd .... G 631 732-5556
  Selden *(G-15375)*
Prosthetic Rehabilitation Ctr .... G 845 565-8255
  Newburgh *(G-12800)*
Robert Cohen .... G 718 789-0996
  Ozone Park *(G-13411)*
Rochester Orthopedic Labs .... G 585 272-1060
  Rochester *(G-14666)*

MEDICAL & SURGICAL SPLYS: Models, Anatomical

Columbia Dentoform Corporation ... E 718 482-1569
  Long Island City *(G-7732)*

MEDICAL & SURGICAL SPLYS: Orthopedic Appliances

Advantage Orthotics Inc .... G 631 368-1754
  East Northport *(G-4452)*
Apollo Orthotics Corp .... G 516 333-3223
  Carle Place *(G-3411)*
Church Communities NY Inc .... E 518 589-5103
  Elka Park *(G-4643)*
Church Communities NY Inc .... E 518 589-5103
  Elka Park *(G-4644)*
Community Products LLC .... C 845 658-8799
  Rifton *(G-14144)*
Community Products LLC .... E 845 572-3433
  Chester *(G-3631)*
Cranial Technologies Inc .... F 914 472-0975
  Scarsdale *(G-15246)*
Custom Sports Lab Inc .... G 212 832-1648
  New York *(G-9828)*
East Cast Orthtics Prosthetics ..... F 716 856-5192
  Buffalo *(G-2940)*
East Coast Orthoic & Pros Cor ..... F 212 923-2161
  New York *(G-10014)*
Hanger Prsthetcs & Ortho Inc ...... G 607 776-8013
  Bath *(G-657)*
Higgins Supply Company Inc .... D 607 836-6474
  Mc Graw *(G-8253)*
Klemmt Orthotics & Prosthetics ... G 607 770-4400
  Johnson City *(G-7128)*
Langer Biomechanics Inc .... G 800 645-5520
  Ronkonkoma *(G-14958)*
Latorre Orthopedic Laboratory ..... F 518 786-8655
  Latham *(G-7400)*
M H Mandelbaum Orthotic .... F 631 473-8668
  Port Jefferson *(G-13799)*
Medi-Ray Inc .... D 877 898-3003
  Tuckahoe *(G-16295)*
Ortho Medical Products .... F 212 879-3700
  New York *(G-11541)*
Orthotics & Prosthetics Dept .... F 585 341-9299
  Rochester *(G-14579)*
Profoot Inc .... E 718 965-8600
  Brooklyn *(G-2468)*
Progressive Orthotics Ltd .... F 631 447-3860
  East Patchogue *(G-4468)*
Rehabilitation Tech of Syracuse ... G 315 426-9920
  Syracuse *(G-16044)*
Stj Orthotic Services Inc .... F 631 956-0181
  Lindenhurst *(G-7507)*

MEDICAL & SURGICAL SPLYS: Personal Safety Eqpt

Aramsco Inc .... F 718 361-7540
  Ridgewood *(G-14113)*
Bio-Chem Barrier Systems LLC ... G 631 261-2682
  Northport *(G-13025)*
Hygrade .... G 718 488-9000
  Brooklyn *(G-2088)*
Kem Medical Products Corp .... G 631 454-6565
  Farmingdale *(G-5034)*
Lakeland Industries Inc .... C 631 981-9700
  Ronkonkoma *(G-14956)*
NY Orthopedic Usa Inc .... D 718 852-5330
  Brooklyn *(G-2393)*
Occunomix International LLC ...... E 631 741-1940
  Port Jeff STA *(G-13792)*

MEDICAL & SURGICAL SPLYS: Prosthetic Appliances

Advanced Prosthetics Orthotics .... F 516 365-7225
  Manhasset *(G-8087)*
Flo-Tech Orthotic & Prosthetic .... G 607 387-3070
  Trumansburg *(G-16290)*
Great Lakes Orthopedic Labs ...... G 716 878-7307
  Buffalo *(G-2996)*
J-K Prosthetics & Orthotics .... E 914 699-2077
  Mount Vernon *(G-8740)*
New England Orthotic & Prost ..... G 212 682-9313
  New York *(G-11407)*
New York Rhbilitative Svcs LLC ... F 516 239-0990
  Lawrence *(G-7421)*
Orthocraft Inc .... G 718 951-1700
  Brooklyn *(G-2408)*
Orthopedic Arts Laboratory Inc ... G 718 858-2400
  Brooklyn *(G-2409)*
Prosthetics By Nelson Inc .... G 716 894-6666
  Cheektowaga *(G-3614)*
Sampsons Prsthtic Orthotic Lab ... E 518 374-6011
  Schenectady *(G-15315)*
Stafford Labs Orthotics/Prosth ..... F 845 692-5227
  Middletown *(G-8497)*
Tonawanda Limb & Brace Inc ...... G 716 695-1131
  Tonawanda *(G-16227)*

MEDICAL & SURGICAL SPLYS: Respiratory Protect Eqpt, Personal

Monaghan Medical Corporation ... G 315 472-2136
  Syracuse *(G-16013)*
Sontek Industries Inc .... G 781 749-3055
  New York *(G-12155)*
Venture Respiratory Inc .... F 718 437-3633
  Brooklyn *(G-2739)*

MEDICAL & SURGICAL SPLYS: Sponges

54321 Us Inc .... G 716 695-0258
  Tonawanda *(G-16155)*
Medical Action Industries Inc .... C 631 231-4600
  Hauppauge *(G-6155)*

MEDICAL & SURGICAL SPLYS: Suspensories

Ortho Rite Inc .... E 914 235-9100
  New Rochelle *(G-8963)*

MEDICAL & SURGICAL SPLYS: Technical Aids, Handicapped

Orcam Inc .... F 800 713-3741
  New York *(G-11534)*

Employee Codes: A=Over 500 employees, B=251-500
C=101-250, D=51-100, E=20-50, F=10-19, G=5-9

MEDICAL EQPT REPAIR SVCS, NON-ELECTRIC

Med Services Inc.................................D.....631 218-6450
  Bohemia (G-1099)

MEDICAL EQPT: Diagnostic

Advantage Plus Diagnostics Inc............G.....631 393-5044
  Melville (G-8321)
American Bio Medica Corp...................D.....518 758-8158
  Kinderhook (G-7196)
Biochemical Diagnostics Inc..................E.....631 595-9200
  Edgewood (G-4609)
E-Z-Em Inc...E.....609 524-2864
  Melville (G-8343)
Ken-Ton Open Mri PC..........................G.....716 876-7000
  Kenmore (G-7179)
Lydia H Soifer & Assoc Inc....................F.....914 683-5401
  White Plains (G-17161)
Memory Md Inc....................................G.....917 318-0215
  New York (G-11250)
Nanobionovum LLC...............................F.....518 581-1171
  Saratoga Springs (G-15194)
Ortho-Clinical Diagnostics Inc................B.....585 453-4771
  Rochester (G-14575)
Ortho-Clinical Diagnostics Inc................F.....585 453-5200
  Rochester (G-14576)
Ovitz Corporation.................................G.....585 474-4695
  West Henrietta (G-16920)
Pharma-Smart International Inc..............E.....585 427-0730
  Rochester (G-14600)
Proactive Medical Products LLC............G.....845 205-6004
  Mount Vernon (G-8766)
RJ Harvey Instrument Corp...................F.....845 359-3943
  Tappan (G-16107)
Vasomedical Solutions Inc.....................D.....516 997-4600
  Plainview (G-13669)
Welch Allyn Inc....................................A.....315 685-4100
  Skaneateles Falls (G-15493)
Welch Allyn Inc....................................A.....315 685-4100
  Skaneateles Falls (G-15494)
Welch Allyn Inc....................................A.....315 685-4347
  Skaneateles Falls (G-15495)

MEDICAL EQPT: Electromedical Apparatus

Biofeedback Instrument Corp.................G.....212 222-5665
  New York (G-9453)
Conmed Andover Medical Inc.................F.....315 797-8375
  Utica (G-16337)
Conmed Corporation.............................B.....315 797-8375
  Utica (G-16339)
Health Care Originals Inc......................G.....585 471-8215
  Rochester (G-14451)

MEDICAL EQPT: Electrotherapeutic Apparatus

Complex Biosystems Inc......................G.....315 464-8007
  Liverpool (G-7541)

MEDICAL EQPT: Heart-Lung Machines, Exc Iron Lungs

Advd Heart Phys & Surgs......................F.....212 434-3000
  New York (G-9096)
Gary Gelbfish MD.................................G.....718 258-3004
  Brooklyn (G-2015)
Jarvik Heart Inc...................................E.....212 397-3911
  New York (G-10742)

MEDICAL EQPT: Laser Systems

Buffalo Filter LLC.................................D.....716 835-7000
  Lancaster (G-7331)
Ddc Technologies Inc...........................G.....516 594-1533
  Oceanside (G-13096)
Juvly Aesthetics Inc.............................D.....614 686-3627
  New York (G-10829)
Laser and Varicose Vein Trtmnt.............G.....718 667-1777
  Staten Island (G-15720)
New Primecare....................................G.....516 822-4031
  Hewlett (G-6334)
New York Laser & Aestheticks...............G.....516 627-7777
  Roslyn (G-15045)
Photomedex Inc...................................E.....888 966-1010
  Orangeburg (G-13261)
Photonics Industries Intl Inc..................D.....631 218-2240
  Ronkonkoma (G-14992)
Teledyne Optech Inc............................F.....585 427-8310
  Rochester (G-14747)

University of Rochester.........................B.....585 275-3483
  Rochester (G-14772)

MEDICAL EQPT: MRI/Magnetic Resonance Imaging Devs, Nuclear

City Sports Imaging Inc........................E.....212 481-3600
  New York (G-9684)

MEDICAL EQPT: PET Or Position Emission Tomography Scanners

Nirx Medical Technologies LLC..............F.....516 676-6479
  Glen Head (G-5652)

MEDICAL EQPT: Patient Monitoring

Equivital Inc.......................................E.....646 513-4169
  New York (G-10106)
Novamed-Usa Inc...............................E.....914 789-2100
  Elmsford (G-4779)
Ocean Cardiac Monitoring....................G.....631 777-3700
  Deer Park (G-4209)
Quadrant Biosciences Inc....................F.....315 614-2325
  Syracuse (G-16037)

MEDICAL EQPT: Sterilizers

Getinge Sourcing LLC..........................C.....585 475-1400
  Rochester (G-14421)
Getinge Usa Inc..................................C.....800 475-9040
  Rochester (G-14422)
SPS Medical Supply Corp.....................F.....585 968-2377
  Cuba (G-4096)
Steriliz LLC..G.....585 415-5411
  Rochester (G-14727)

MEDICAL EQPT: Ultrasonic Scanning Devices

Empire Open Mri.................................G.....914 961-1777
  Yonkers (G-17457)
Global Instrumentation LLC..................F.....315 682-0272
  Manlius (G-8105)
Imacor Inc..E.....516 393-0970
  Garden City (G-5523)
Jadak LLC..F.....315 701-0678
  North Syracuse (G-12966)

MEDICAL EQPT: Ultrasonic, Exc Cleaning

Nanovibronix Inc.................................F.....914 233-3004
  Elmsford (G-4777)
Stj Enterprises....................................D.....516 612-0110
  Cedarhurst (G-3488)

MEDICAL EQPT: X-Ray Apparatus & Tubes, Radiographic

Genesis Digital Imaging Inc..................G.....310 305-7358
  Rochester (G-14417)
Quantum Medical Imaging LLC.............D.....631 567-5800
  Rochester (G-14639)
Siemens Corporation...........................F.....202 434-7800
  New York (G-12084)
Siemens USA Holdings Inc...................B.....212 258-4000
  New York (G-12086)

MEDICAL EQPT: X-Ray Apparatus & Tubes, Therapeutic

Community Products LLC.....................C.....845 658-8799
  Rifton (G-14144)

MEDICAL PHOTOGRAPHY & ART SVCS

Burns Archive Photographic Dis............G.....212 889-1938
  New York (G-9533)

MEDICAL, DENTAL & HOSPITAL EQPT, WHOL: Dentists' Prof Splys

Crosstex International Inc....................D.....631 582-6777
  Hauppauge (G-6079)

MEDICAL, DENTAL & HOSPITAL EQPT, WHOL: Hosptl Eqpt/Furniture

Creative Orthotics & Prosthet................F.....607 734-7215
  Elmira (G-4691)
Medical Action Industries Inc................C.....631 231-4600
  Hauppauge (G-6155)

MEDICAL, DENTAL & HOSPITAL EQPT, WHOL: Surgical Eqpt & Splys

Medline Industries Inc..........................B.....845 344-3301
  Middletown (G-8484)
Paramount Textiles Inc.........................F.....212 966-1040
  New York (G-11583)

MEDICAL, DENTAL & HOSPITAL EQPT, WHOLESALE: Diagnostic, Med

Memory Md Inc....................................G.....917 318-0215
  New York (G-11250)
Pharma-Smart International Inc.............E.....585 427-0730
  Rochester (G-14600)

MEDICAL, DENTAL & HOSPITAL EQPT, WHOLESALE: Med Eqpt & Splys

Ala Scientific Instruments Inc...............F.....631 393-6401
  Farmingdale (G-4942)
American Healthcare Supply Inc............F.....212 674-3636
  New York (G-9168)
Basil S Kadhim....................................G.....888 520-5192
  New York (G-9380)
Brinkman Precision Inc........................D.....585 429-5001
  West Henrietta (G-16905)
Lehneis Orthotics Prosthetic................G.....631 369-3115
  Riverhead (G-14159)
Peter Digioia.......................................G.....516 644-5517
  Plainview (G-13656)
Quantum Medical Imaging LLC.............D.....631 567-5800
  Rochester (G-14639)
Sontek Industries Inc..........................G.....781 749-3055
  New York (G-12155)

MEDICAL, DENTAL & HOSPITAL EQPT, WHOLESALE: Medical Lab

Integrted Work Envronments LLC.........G.....716 725-5088
  East Amherst (G-4387)

MELAMINE RESINS: Melamine-Formaldehyde

Hexion Inc..E.....518 792-8040
  South Glens Falls (G-15548)
Queen City Manufacturing Inc..............G.....716 877-1102
  Buffalo (G-3176)

MEMBERSHIP ORGANIZATIONS, PROFESSIONAL: Health Association

Curemdcom Inc...................................A.....212 509-6200
  New York (G-9826)

MEMBERSHIP ORGS, BUSINESS: Growers' Marketing Advisory Svc

Atlantic Farm & Food Inc......................F.....718 441-3152
  Richmond Hill (G-14079)

MEMBERSHIP ORGS, CIVIC, SOCIAL/FRAT: Educator's Assoc

Modern Language Assn Amer Inc..........C.....646 576-5000
  New York (G-11315)

MEMORIALS, MONUMENTS & MARKERS

Domenick Denigris Inc.........................E.....718 823-2264
  Bronx (G-1318)

MEMORY DEVICES: Magnetic Bubble

Dynamic Photography Inc....................G.....516 381-2951
  Roslyn (G-15043)

MEN'S & BOYS' CLOTHING ACCESS STORES

Broadway Knitting Mills Inc..................G.....716 692-4421
  North Tonawanda (G-12979)
Giliberto Designs Inc............................E.....212 695-0216
  New York (G-10337)
Swank Inc...B.....212 867-2600
  New York (G-12270)

PRODUCT SECTION

METAL FABRICATORS: Architechtural

MEN'S & BOYS' CLOTHING STORES

By Robert James .... G 212 253-2121
  New York *(G-9538)*
Elie Tahari Ltd .... G 212 398-2622
  New York *(G-10054)*
Hugo Boss Usa Inc .... D 212 940-0600
  New York *(G-10574)*
Kcp Holdco Inc .... F 212 265-1500
  New York *(G-10866)*
Kenneth Cole Productions Inc .... B 212 265-1500
  New York *(G-10873)*
Mee Accessories LLC .... C 917 262-1000
  New York *(G-11244)*
Mega Sourcing Inc .... G 646 682-0304
  Merrick *(G-8424)*
Michael Andrews LLC .... F 212 677-1755
  New York *(G-11275)*
Perrone Leather LLC .... D 518 853-4300
  Fultonville *(G-5496)*
Perry Ellis Menswear LLC .... C 212 221-7500
  New York *(G-11643)*
Phillips-Van Heusen Europe .... F 212 381-3500
  New York *(G-11668)*
Pvh Corp .... D 212 381-3500
  New York *(G-11780)*
Sanctuary Brands LLC .... G 212 704-4014
  New York *(G-11982)*

MEN'S & BOYS' CLOTHING WHOLESALERS, NEC

All Net Ltd .... F 516 504-4559
  Great Neck *(G-5803)*
Billion Tower Intl LLC .... F 212 220-0608
  New York *(G-9449)*
D-C Theatricks .... G 716 847-0180
  Buffalo *(G-2919)*
Enzo Manzoni LLC .... G 212 464-7000
  Brooklyn *(G-1932)*
G-III Apparel Group Ltd .... B 212 403-0500
  New York *(G-10282)*
Herrmann Group LLC .... G 716 876-9798
  Kenmore *(G-7176)*
Jeans Inc .... G 646 223-1122
  New York *(G-10757)*
Kate Spade & Company .... B 212 354-4900
  New York *(G-10854)*
Kenmar Shirts Inc .... E 718 824-3880
  Bronx *(G-1375)*
M Hidary & Co Inc .... D 212 736-6540
  New York *(G-11102)*
Moresca Clothing and Costume .... F 845 331-6012
  Ulster Park *(G-16309)*
Mountain T-Shirts Inc .... G 518 943-4533
  Catskill *(G-3460)*
New York Popular Inc .... D 718 499-2020
  Brooklyn *(G-2376)*
Penfli Industries Inc .... F 212 947-6080
  Great Neck *(G-5848)*
Ryba General Merchandise Inc .... G 718 522-2028
  Brooklyn *(G-2539)*
Sanctuary Brands LLC .... G 212 704-4014
  New York *(G-11982)*
United Knitwear International .... G 212 354-2920
  New York *(G-12484)*
Wp Lavori USA Inc .... G 212 244-6074
  New York *(G-12694)*

MEN'S & BOYS' SPORTSWEAR CLOTHING STORES

Cockpit Usa Inc .... F 212 575-1616
  New York *(G-9719)*
Cockpit Usa Inc .... F 212 575-1616
  New York *(G-9720)*
Foot Locker Retail Inc .... F 516 827-5306
  Hicksville *(G-6374)*
Herrmann Group LLC .... G 716 876-9798
  Kenmore *(G-7176)*
John Varvatos Company .... E 212 812-8000
  New York *(G-10793)*
Mainly Monograms Inc .... E 845 624-4923
  West Nyack *(G-16949)*
Royal Tees Inc .... G 845 357-9448
  Suffern *(G-15820)*

MEN'S & BOYS' SPORTSWEAR WHOLESALERS

Bandit International Ltd .... F 718 402-2100
  Bronx *(G-1279)*
Cockpit Usa Inc .... F 212 575-1616
  New York *(G-9719)*
Cockpit Usa Inc .... F 212 575-1616
  New York *(G-9720)*
Mee Accessories LLC .... C 917 262-1000
  New York *(G-11244)*
Sterling Possessions Ltd .... G 212 594-0418
  New York *(G-12221)*

MEN'S & BOYS' UNDERWEAR WHOLESALERS

Apparel Partnership Group LLC .... G 212 302-7722
  New York *(G-9230)*

MEN'S SUITS STORES

Kozinn+sons Merchant Tailors .... E 212 643-1916
  New York *(G-10921)*
Royal Clothing Corp .... G 718 436-5841
  Brooklyn *(G-2530)*

MERCHANDISING MACHINE OPERATORS: Vending

Worksman Trading Corp .... E 718 322-2000
  Ozone Park *(G-13413)*

METAL & STEEL PRDTS: Abrasive

Datum Alloys Inc .... G 607 239-6274
  Endicott *(G-4808)*
Pellets LLC .... G 716 693-1750
  North Tonawanda *(G-13003)*
Raulli and Sons Inc .... E 315 479-2515
  Syracuse *(G-16042)*

METAL COMPONENTS: Prefabricated

Precision Fabrication LLC .... G 585 591-3449
  Attica *(G-473)*

METAL CUTTING SVCS

Elmsford Sheet Metal Works Inc .... D 914 739-6300
  Cortlandt Manor *(G-4074)*
S & S Prtg Die-Cutting Co Inc .... F 718 388-8990
  Brooklyn *(G-2543)*

METAL DETECTORS

Detector Pro .... G 845 635-3488
  Pleasant Valley *(G-13742)*

METAL FABRICATORS: Architechtural

A & T Iron Works Inc .... E 914 632-8992
  New Rochelle *(G-8928)*
A1 Ornamental Iron Works Inc .... G 718 265-3055
  Brooklyn *(G-1544)*
Accurate Welding Service Inc .... G 516 333-1730
  Westbury *(G-16988)*
Aero-Data Metal Crafters Inc .... C 631 471-7733
  Ronkonkoma *(G-14882)*
Aldo Frustacci Iron Works Inc .... F 718 768-0707
  Brooklyn *(G-1577)*
Aldos Iron Works Inc .... G 718 834-0408
  Brooklyn *(G-1578)*
All American Metal Corporation .... E 516 623-0222
  Freeport *(G-5393)*
All Metal Specialties Inc .... G 716 664-6009
  Jamestown *(G-7005)*
Allied Bronze Corp (del Corp) .... E 646 421-6400
  New York *(G-9139)*
Alpha Iron Works LLC .... F 585 424-7260
  Rochester *(G-14208)*
Armento Incorporated .... G 716 875-2423
  Kenmore *(G-7173)*
Babylon Iron Works Inc .... G 631 643-3311
  West Babylon *(G-16798)*
Bobrick Washroom Equipment Corp .... F 518 877-7444
  Clifton Park *(G-3723)*
Cabezon Design Group Inc .... G 718 488-9868
  Brooklyn *(G-1748)*
Caliper Architecture PC .... G 718 302-2427
  Brooklyn *(G-1750)*
Caliperstudio Co .... G 718 302-2427
  Brooklyn *(G-1751)*
Creative Metal Fabricators .... G 631 567-2266
  Bohemia *(G-1039)*
D V S Iron & Aluminum Works .... G 718 768-7961
  Brooklyn *(G-1832)*
E & J Iron Works Inc .... E 718 665-6040
  Bronx *(G-1324)*
E F Iron Works & Construction .... G 631 242-4766
  Bay Shore *(G-696)*
Ej Group Inc .... G 315 699-2601
  Cicero *(G-3674)*
Elevator Accessories Mfg .... F 914 739-7004
  Peekskill *(G-13501)*
Flushing Iron Weld Inc .... E 718 359-2208
  Flushing *(G-5250)*
Forest Iron Works Inc .... G 516 671-4229
  Locust Valley *(G-7661)*
Giumenta Corp .... E 718 832-1200
  Brooklyn *(G-2026)*
Global Steel Products Corp .... C 631 586-3455
  Deer Park *(G-4169)*
Grillmaster Inc .... E 718 272-9191
  Howard Beach *(G-6625)*
Hi-Tech Metals Inc .... E 718 894-1212
  Maspeth *(G-8176)*
International Creative Met Inc .... F 718 424-8179
  Woodside *(G-17350)*
ITR Industries Inc .... E 914 964-7063
  Yonkers *(G-17473)*
Jerry Cardullo Iron Works Inc .... F 631 242-8881
  Bay Shore *(G-707)*
Kammetal Inc .... F 718 722-9991
  Brooklyn *(G-2167)*
Kenal Services Corp .... G 315 788-9226
  Watertown *(G-16679)*
Keuka Studios Inc .... G 585 624-5960
  Rush *(G-15076)*
Kms Contracting Inc .... F 718 495-6500
  Brooklyn *(G-2175)*
Lopopolo Iron Works Inc .... G 718 339-0572
  Brooklyn *(G-2239)*
M B C Metal Inc .... F 718 384-6713
  Brooklyn *(G-2249)*
Martin Chafkin .... G 718 383-1155
  Brooklyn *(G-2278)*
Martin Orna Ir Works II Inc .... G 516 354-3923
  Elmont *(G-4734)*
Material Process Systems Inc .... F 718 302-3081
  Brooklyn *(G-2286)*
Maximum Security Products Corp .... E 518 233-1800
  Waterford *(G-16634)*
Melto Metal Products Co Inc .... E 516 546-8866
  Freeport *(G-5422)*
Mestel Brothers Stairs & Rails .... C 516 496-4127
  Syosset *(G-15848)*
Metalworks Inc .... E 718 319-0011
  Bronx *(G-1397)*
Milgo Industrial Inc .... D 718 388-6476
  Brooklyn *(G-2317)*
Milgo Industrial Inc .... G 718 387-0406
  Brooklyn *(G-2318)*
Mison Concepts Inc .... G 516 933-8000
  Hicksville *(G-6398)*
Modern Art Foundry Inc .... E 718 728-2030
  Astoria *(G-448)*
Morgik Metal Designs .... F 212 463-0304
  New York *(G-11330)*
Moro Corporation .... E 607 724-4241
  Binghamton *(G-933)*
New Dimensions Office Group .... G 718 387-0995
  Brooklyn *(G-2370)*
New England Tool Co Ltd .... G 845 651-7550
  Florida *(G-5221)*
Old Dutchmans Wrough Iron Inc .... G 716 688-2034
  Getzville *(G-5614)*
Paley Studios Ltd .... F 585 232-5260
  Rochester *(G-14588)*
Pawling Corporation .... D 845 373-9300
  Wassaic *(G-16622)*
Peconic Ironworks Ltd .... F 631 204-0323
  Southampton *(G-15573)*
Phoenix Metal Designs Inc .... G 516 597-4100
  Hicksville *(G-6413)*
Pk30 System LLC .... F 212 473-8050
  Stone Ridge *(G-15786)*
Railings By New Star Brass .... E 516 358-1153
  Brooklyn *(G-2493)*
Raulli and Sons Inc .... D 315 479-6693
  Syracuse *(G-16040)*
Raulli Iron Works Inc .... F 315 337-8070
  Rome *(G-14860)*

Employee Codes: A=Over 500 employees, B=251-500
C=101-250, D=51-100, E=20-50, F=10-19, G=5-9

Riverside Iron LLC ....F 315 535-4864
Gouverneur *(G-5762)*
Rollson Inc ....E 631 423-9578
Huntington *(G-6717)*
Royal Metal Products Inc ....E 518 966-4442
Surprise *(G-15832)*
S A Baxter LLC ....G 845 469-7995
Chester *(G-3641)*
Safespan Platform Systems Inc ....D 716 694-3332
Tonawanda *(G-16218)*
Steel Sales Inc ....E 607 674-6363
Sherburne *(G-15419)*
Steel Work Inc ....G 585 232-1555
Rochester *(G-14725)*
Steps Plus Inc ....D 315 432-0885
Syracuse *(G-16068)*
Studio 40 Inc ....G 212 420-8631
Brooklyn *(G-2635)*
Studio Dellarte ....G 718 599-3715
Brooklyn *(G-2636)*
Superior Metal & Woodwork Inc ....E 631 465-9004
Farmingdale *(G-5129)*
Tonys Ornamental Ir Works Inc ....E 315 337-3730
Rome *(G-14866)*
Tropical Driftwood Originals ....G 516 623-0980
Roosevelt *(G-15033)*
United Iron Inc ....E 914 667-5700
Mount Vernon *(G-8791)*
Universal Steel Fabricators ....F 718 342-0782
Brooklyn *(G-2729)*
Village Wrought Iron Inc ....F 315 683-5589
Fabius *(G-4848)*
Waverly Iron Corp ....E 631 732-2800
Medford *(G-8296)*
West End Iron Works Inc ....G 518 456-1105
Albany *(G-150)*
Z-Studios Dsign Fbrication LLC ....G 347 512-4210
Brooklyn *(G-2792)*

METAL FABRICATORS: Plate

Acro Industries Inc ....C 585 254-3661
Rochester *(G-14186)*
Aero-Data Metal Crafters Inc ....C 631 471-7733
Ronkonkoma *(G-14882)*
Allstate Gasket & Packing Inc ....F 631 254-4050
Deer Park *(G-4116)*
American Boiler Tank Wldg Inc ....E 518 463-5012
Albany *(G-44)*
Ametek Inc ....C 516 832-7710
Garden City *(G-5508)*
Arvos Inc ....B 585 593-2700
Wellsville *(G-16775)*
Atlantic Industrial Tech Inc ....E 631 234-3131
Shirley *(G-15437)*
Bellmore Steel Products Corp ....F 516 785-9667
Bellmore *(G-811)*
Blackstone Advanced Tech LLC ....C 716 665-5410
Jamestown *(G-7011)*
Breton Industries Inc ....D 518 842-3030
Amsterdam *(G-337)*
Bridgehampton Steel & Wldg Inc ....F 631 537-2486
Bridgehampton *(G-1230)*
Bruce Pierce ....G 716 731-9310
Sanborn *(G-15142)*
Buflovak LLC ....E 716 895-2100
Buffalo *(G-2883)*
C & F Fabricators & Erectors ....G 607 432-3520
Colliersville *(G-3839)*
Charles Ross & Son Company ....D 631 234-0500
Hauppauge *(G-6064)*
Cigar Box Studios Inc ....F 845 236-9283
Marlboro *(G-8135)*
Contech Engnered Solutions LLC ....F 716 870-9091
Orchard Park *(G-13288)*
Direkt Force LLC ....E 716 652-3022
East Aurora *(G-4394)*
ECR International Inc ....D 315 797-1310
Utica *(G-16351)*
ECR International Inc ....C 716 366-5500
Dunkirk *(G-4365)*
Endicott Precision Inc ....C 607 754-7076
Endicott *(G-4811)*
Expert Industries Inc ....E 718 434-6060
Brooklyn *(G-1951)*
Feldmeier Equipment Inc ....D 315 823-2000
Syracuse *(G-15963)*
Fulton Boiler Works Inc ....C 315 298-5121
Pulaski *(G-13965)*
Global Steel Products Corp ....C 631 586-3455
Deer Park *(G-4169)*
Jaquith Industries Inc ....E 315 478-5700
Syracuse *(G-15985)*
Marex Aquisition Corp ....C 585 458-3940
Rochester *(G-14518)*
Methods Tooling & Mfg Inc ....E 845 246-7100
Mount Marion *(G-8693)*
Mitsubishi Chemical Amer Inc ....E 212 223-3043
New York *(G-11310)*
Pfaudler US Inc ....C 585 235-1000
Rochester *(G-14599)*
Roemac Industrial Sales Inc ....G 716 692-7332
North Tonawanda *(G-13009)*
Rosenwach Tank Co Inc ....E 212 972-4411
Astoria *(G-454)*
Seibel Modern Mfg & Wldg Corp ....D 716 683-1536
Lancaster *(G-7367)*
Slant/Fin Corporation ....B 516 484-2600
Greenvale *(G-5899)*

METAL FABRICATORS: Sheet

303 Contracting Inc ....E 716 896-2122
Orchard Park *(G-13271)*
A & L Shtmtl Fabrications Corp ....E 718 842-1600
Bronx *(G-1253)*
Abdo Shtmtl & Fabrication Inc ....G 315 894-4664
Frankfort *(G-5358)*
Aberdeen Blower & Shtmtl Works ....G 631 661-6100
West Babylon *(G-16789)*
Accra Sheetmetal LLC ....G 631 920-2087
Wyandanch *(G-17385)*
Acme Architectural Pdts Inc ....D 718 384-7800
Brooklyn *(G-1554)*
Acro-Fab Ltd ....E 315 564-6688
Hannibal *(G-5992)*
Advanced Precision Technology ....F 845 279-3540
Brewster *(G-1204)*
Advantech Industries Inc ....C 585 247-0701
Rochester *(G-14196)*
Aero Trades Mfg Corp ....E 516 746-3360
Mineola *(G-8523)*
Aeroduct Inc ....E 516 248-9550
Mineola *(G-8524)*
Afco Systems Inc ....C 631 249-9441
Farmingdale *(G-4938)*
Aj Genco Mch Sp McHy Rdout Svc ....F 716 664-4925
Falconer *(G-4896)*
Aldo Frustacci Iron Works Inc ....F 718 768-0707
Brooklyn *(G-1577)*
Aleta Industries Inc ....F 718 349-0040
Brooklyn *(G-1579)*
Alkemy Machine LLC ....G 585 436-8730
Rochester *(G-14201)*
All Around Spiral Inc ....G 631 588-0220
Ronkonkoma *(G-14887)*
All Island Blower & Shtmtl ....F 631 567-7070
Bohemia *(G-1009)*
All Star Carts & Vehicles Inc ....D 631 666-5581
Bay Shore *(G-667)*
Allen Machine Products Inc ....E 631 630-8800
Hauppauge *(G-6035)*
Alliance Welding & Steel Fabg ....F 516 775-7600
Floral Park *(G-5199)*
Allure Metal Works Inc ....F 631 588-0220
Ronkonkoma *(G-14891)*
Alnik Service Corporation ....G 516 873-7300
New Hyde Park *(G-8859)*
Alpine Machine Inc ....F 607 272-1344
Ithaca *(G-6858)*
Alternative Service Inc ....F 631 345-9500
Yaphank *(G-17401)*
Amsco Inc ....F 716 823-4213
Buffalo *(G-2829)*
Apparatus Mfg Inc ....G 845 471-5116
Poughkeepsie *(G-13905)*
Arcadia Mfg Group Inc ....E 518 434-6213
Green Island *(G-5871)*
Arcadia Mfg Group Inc ....G 518 434-6213
Menands *(G-8399)*
Architctral Shetmetal Pdts Inc ....G 518 381-6144
Scotia *(G-15345)*
Arlan Damper Corporation ....E 631 589-7431
Bohemia *(G-1015)*
Art Precision Metal Products ....F 631 842-8889
Copiague *(G-3920)*
Ascension Industries Inc ....D 716 693-9381
North Tonawanda *(G-12974)*
Asp Industries Inc ....E 585 254-9130
Rochester *(G-14235)*
Atlantis Equipment Corporation ....F 518 733-5910
Stephentown *(G-15778)*
Auburn Tank & Manufacturing Co ....F 315 255-2788
Auburn *(G-480)*
Avalanche Fabrication Inc ....F 585 545-4000
Ontario *(G-13218)*
B & B Sheet Metal Inc ....E 718 433-2501
Long Island City *(G-7710)*
B & H Precision Fabricators ....F 631 563-9620
Bohemia *(G-1017)*
B & R Sheet ....G 718 558-5544
Jamaica *(G-6933)*
Banner Metalcraft Inc ....D 631 563-7303
Ronkonkoma *(G-14906)*
Bargold Storage Systems LLC ....E 718 247-7000
Long Island City *(G-7713)*
Batavia Enclosures Inc ....G 585 344-1797
Arcade *(G-388)*
Berjen Metal Industries Ltd ....G 631 673-7979
Huntington *(G-6688)*
Best Tinsmith Supply Inc ....G 518 863-2541
Northville *(G-13036)*
Blackstone Advanced Tech LLC ....C 716 665-5410
Jamestown *(G-7011)*
Boss Precision Ltd ....D 585 352-7070
Spencerport *(G-15590)*
Broadway Neon Sign Corp ....F 908 241-4177
Ronkonkoma *(G-14910)*
C & T Tool & Instrument Co ....E 718 429-1253
Woodside *(G-17338)*
C J & C Sheet Metal Corp ....F 631 376-9425
West Babylon *(G-16805)*
Cannon Industries Inc ....D 585 254-8080
Rochester *(G-14276)*
CBM Fabrications Inc ....E 518 399-8023
Ballston Lake *(G-580)*
Center Sheet Metal Inc ....C 718 378-4476
Bronx *(G-1293)*
Chamtek Mfg Inc ....E 585 328-4900
Rochester *(G-14293)*
Cherry Holding Ltd ....G 516 679-3748
North Bellmore *(G-12933)*
City Cooling Enterprises Inc ....G 718 331-7400
Brooklyn *(G-1780)*
Clark Specialty Co Inc ....E 607 776-3193
Bath *(G-655)*
CPI Industries Inc ....D 631 909-3434
Manorville *(G-8111)*
Crown Die Casting Corp ....E 914 667-5400
Mount Vernon *(G-8720)*
Cutting Edge Metal Works ....E 631 981-8333
Holtsville *(G-6528)*
Cw Metals Inc ....E 917 416-7906
Long Island City *(G-7737)*
D & G Sheet Metal Co Inc ....F 718 326-9111
Maspeth *(G-8158)*
Dawson Metal Company Inc ....C 716 664-3811
Jamestown *(G-7022)*
Dimar Manufacturing Corp ....C 716 759-0351
Clarence *(G-3685)*
Dj Acquisition Management Corp ....D 585 265-3000
Ontario *(G-13222)*
Doortec Archtctural Met GL LLC ....E 718 567-2730
Brooklyn *(G-1875)*
DOT Tool Co Inc ....G 607 724-7001
Binghamton *(G-904)*
Dundas-Jafine Inc ....E 716 681-9690
Alden *(G-180)*
Dynasty Stainless Steel & Meta ....E 718 205-6623
Maspeth *(G-8164)*
Elevator Accessories Mfg ....F 914 739-7004
Peekskill *(G-13501)*
Elmsford Sheet Metal Works Inc ....D 914 739-6300
Cortlandt Manor *(G-4074)*
Empire Air Specialties Inc ....E 518 689-4440
Albany *(G-77)*
Endicott Precision Inc ....C 607 754-7076
Endicott *(G-4811)*
Engineering Mfg Tech LLC ....D 607 754-7111
Endicott *(G-4813)*
Expert Industries Inc ....E 718 434-6060
Brooklyn *(G-1951)*
F M L Industries Inc ....G 607 749-7273
Homer *(G-6545)*
Federal Sheet Metal Works Inc ....F 315 735-4730
Utica *(G-16355)*
Five Star Industries Inc ....E 716 674-2589
West Seneca *(G-16973)*
Fred A Nudd Corporation ....E 315 524-2531
Ontario *(G-13223)*
Goergen-Mackwirth Co Inc ....E 716 874-4800
Buffalo *(G-2993)*

PRODUCT SECTION

METAL RESHAPING & REPLATING SVCS

Greene Technologies Inc ....D...... 607 656-4166
  Greene *(G-5884)*
Hana Sheet Metal Inc ....G...... 914 377-0773
  Yonkers *(G-17468)*
Hansen Steel ....E...... 585 398-2020
  Farmington *(G-5161)*
Hatfield Metal Fab Inc ....E...... 845 454-9078
  Poughkeepsie *(G-13926)*
Hergo Ergonomic Support ....E...... 718 894-0639
  Maspeth *(G-8175)*
Hermann Gerdens Inc ....G...... 631 841-3132
  Copiague *(G-3931)*
Hi-Tech Industries NY Inc ....E...... 607 217-7361
  Johnson City *(G-7125)*
Hrd Metal Products Inc ....G...... 631 243-6700
  Deer Park *(G-4173)*
Hunter Douglas Inc ....D...... 845 664-7000
  Pearl River *(G-13482)*
I Rauchs Sons Inc ....E...... 718 507-8844
  East Elmhurst *(G-4414)*
IEC Electronics Corp ....C...... 585 647-1760
  Rochester *(G-14464)*
Incodema Inc ....E...... 607 277-7070
  Ithaca *(G-6884)*
Industrial Fabricating Corp ....E...... 315 437-3353
  East Syracuse *(G-4553)*
Intellimetal Inc ....D...... 585 424-3260
  Rochester *(G-14472)*
Jamestown Advanced Pdts Corp ...E...... 716 483-3406
  Jamestown *(G-7037)*
Jaquith Industries Inc ....E...... 315 478-5700
  Syracuse *(G-15985)*
Jar Metals Inc ....F...... 845 425-8901
  Nanuet *(G-8804)*
Joe P Industries Inc ....F...... 631 293-7889
  Farmingdale *(G-5026)*
K Barthelmes Mfg Co Inc ....F...... 585 328-8140
  Rochester *(G-14489)*
Kal Manufacturing Corporation ......E...... 585 265-4310
  Webster *(G-16751)*
Kassis Superior Sign Co Inc ....F...... 315 463-7446
  Syracuse *(G-15992)*
Ksm Group Ltd ....G...... 716 751-6006
  Newfane *(G-12811)*
Leader Sheet Metal Inc ....F...... 347 271-4961
  Bronx *(G-1382)*
Manufacturing Resources Inc ....E...... 631 481-0041
  Rochester *(G-14514)*
Marex Aquisition Corp ....C...... 585 458-3940
  Rochester *(G-14518)*
Mariah Metal Products Inc ....G...... 516 938-9783
  Hicksville *(G-6394)*
Mason Scott Industries LLC ....F...... 516 349-1800
  Roslyn Heights *(G-15054)*
McAlpin Industries Inc ....C...... 585 266-3060
  Rochester *(G-14521)*
McHone Industries Inc ....D...... 716 945-3380
  Salamanca *(G-15128)*
MD International Industries ....E...... 631 254-3100
  Deer Park *(G-4197)*
Mega Vision Inc ....E...... 718 228-1065
  Brooklyn *(G-2298)*
Merz Metal & Machine Corp ....E...... 716 893-7786
  Buffalo *(G-3083)*
Metal Solutions Inc ....E...... 315 732-6271
  Utica *(G-16371)*
Metalsmith Inc ....G...... 631 467-1500
  Holbrook *(G-6492)*
Methods Tooling & Mfg Inc ....E...... 845 246-7100
  Mount Marion *(G-8693)*
Metro Duct Systems Inc ....F...... 718 278-4294
  Long Island City *(G-7840)*
Middleby Corporation ....E...... 631 226-6688
  Lindenhurst *(G-7495)*
Mitsubishi Chemical Amer Inc ....E...... 212 223-3043
  New York *(G-11310)*
Monarch Metal Fabrication Inc ......G...... 631 563-8967
  Bohemia *(G-1100)*
Ms Spares LLC ....G...... 607 223-3024
  Clay *(G-3709)*
N & L Instruments Inc ....F...... 631 471-4000
  Ronkonkoma *(G-14973)*
Nci Group Inc ....D...... 315 339-1245
  Rome *(G-14852)*
North Coast Outfitters Ltd ....E...... 631 727-5580
  Riverhead *(G-14164)*
Northeast Fabricators LLC ....D...... 607 865-4031
  Walton *(G-16570)*
Northern Awning & Sign Company ...G...... 315 782-8515
  Watertown *(G-16690)*

Olympic Manufacturing Inc ....E...... 631 231-8900
  Hauppauge *(G-6179)*
Omc Inc ....C...... 718 731-5001
  Bronx *(G-1417)*
Pathfinder Industries Inc ....E...... 315 593-2483
  Fulton *(G-5488)*
PDQ Manufacturing Co Inc ....E...... 845 889-3123
  Rhinebeck *(G-14069)*
Pirnat Precise Metals Inc ....E...... 631 293-9169
  Farmingdale *(G-5090)*
Plattsburgh Sheet Metal Inc ....G...... 518 561-4930
  Plattsburgh *(G-13716)*
Precision Fabrication LLC ....E...... 585 591-3449
  Attica *(G-473)*
Precision Metals Corp ....E...... 631 586-5032
  Bay Shore *(G-723)*
Precision Mtal Fabricators Inc ....E...... 718 832-9805
  Brooklyn *(G-2449)*
Precision Systems Mfg Inc ....E...... 315 451-3480
  Liverpool *(G-7570)*
Product Integration & Mfg Inc ....E...... 585 436-6260
  Rochester *(G-14628)*
Prokosch and Sonn Sheet Metal ...E...... 845 562-4211
  Newburgh *(G-12799)*
Protofast Holding Corp ....G...... 631 753-2549
  Copiague *(G-3944)*
R D R Industries Inc ....F...... 315 866-5020
  Mohawk *(G-8576)*
Rami Sheet Metal Inc ....G...... 845 426-2948
  Spring Valley *(G-15620)*
Rayco Manufacturing Co Inc ....F...... 516 431-2006
  Jamaica *(G-6981)*
Read Manufacturing Company Inc ...E...... 631 567-4487
  Holbrook *(G-6496)*
Reynolds Manufacturing Inc ....F...... 607 562-8936
  Big Flats *(G-879)*
Rigidized Metals Corporation ....E...... 716 849-4703
  Buffalo *(G-3186)*
Robert E Derecktor Inc ....D...... 914 698-0962
  Mamaroneck *(G-8078)*
Rochester Colonial Mfg Corp ....D...... 585 254-8191
  Rochester *(G-14661)*
Rollson Inc ....E...... 631 423-9578
  Huntington *(G-6717)*
Royal Metal Products Inc ....E...... 518 966-4442
  Surprise *(G-15832)*
S & B Machine Works Inc ....E...... 516 997-2666
  Westbury *(G-17053)*
S & J Sheet Metal Supply ....G...... 718 384-0800
  Brooklyn *(G-2540)*
S & T Machine Inc ....F...... 718 272-2484
  Brooklyn *(G-2544)*
Savaco Inc ....G...... 716 751-9455
  Newfane *(G-12812)*
Service Mfg Group Inc ....E...... 716 893-1482
  Buffalo *(G-3213)*
Simmons Fabricating Svc Inc ....E...... 845 635-3755
  Pleasant Valley *(G-13743)*
Solidus Industries Inc ....D...... 607 749-4540
  Homer *(G-6550)*
Standard Industrial Works Inc ....F...... 631 888-0130
  Bay Shore *(G-739)*
Steel Sales Inc ....E...... 607 674-6363
  Sherburne *(G-15419)*
Steel Work Inc ....G...... 585 232-1555
  Rochester *(G-14725)*
Sterling Industries Inc ....E...... 631 753-3070
  Farmingdale *(G-5128)*
T Lemme Mechanical Inc ....E...... 518 436-4136
  Menands *(G-8411)*
Tatra Mfg Corporation ....F...... 631 691-1184
  Copiague *(G-3955)*
TCS Industries Inc ....D...... 585 426-1160
  Rochester *(G-14742)*
Technimetal Precision Inds ....E...... 631 231-8900
  Hauppauge *(G-6234)*
Themis Chimney Inc ....F...... 718 937-4716
  Brooklyn *(G-2677)*
Tri-Metal Industries Inc ....E...... 716 691-3323
  Amherst *(G-268)*
Tri-Technologies Inc ....E...... 914 699-2001
  Mount Vernon *(G-8787)*
Trident Precision Mfg Inc ....E...... 585 265-2010
  Webster *(G-16764)*
Tripar Manufacturing Co Inc ....G...... 631 563-0855
  Bohemia *(G-1145)*
Truform Manufacturing Corp ....E...... 585 458-1090
  Rochester *(G-14762)*
Trylon Wire & Metal Works Inc ......E...... 718 542-4472
  Bronx *(G-1480)*

Ucr Steel Group LLC ....F...... 718 764-3414
  Uniondale *(G-16324)*
Ucr Steel Group LLC ....F...... 718 764-3414
  Ronkonkoma *(G-15018)*
Ulster Precision Inc ....E...... 845 338-0995
  Kingston *(G-7246)*
Ultimate Prcision Met Pdts Inc ......C...... 631 249-9441
  Farmingdale *(G-5146)*
Unadilla Silo Company Inc ....D...... 607 369-9341
  Sidney *(G-15466)*
Universal Precision Corp ....E...... 585 321-9760
  Rochester *(G-14771)*
Universal Shielding Corp ....E...... 631 667-7900
  Deer Park *(G-4244)*
Vance Metal Fabricators Inc ....D...... 315 789-5626
  Geneva *(G-5600)*
Vin Mar Precision Metal Inc ....F...... 631 563-6608
  Copiague *(G-3960)*
Voss Manufacturing Inc ....D...... 716 731-5062
  Sanborn *(G-15158)*
Wainland Inc ....E...... 718 626-2233
  Astoria *(G-460)*
Wenig Corporation ....E...... 718 542-3600
  Bronx *(G-1494)*
Wg Sheet Metal Corp ....G...... 718 235-3093
  Brooklyn *(G-2763)*
William Kanes Mfg Corp ....G...... 718 346-1515
  Brooklyn *(G-2770)*
Zahk Sales Inc ....E...... 631 348-9300
  Islandia *(G-6844)*

METAL FABRICATORS: Structural, Ship

Cameron Bridge Works LLC ....E...... 607 734-9456
  Elmira *(G-4685)*
Miller Metal Fabricating Inc ....G...... 585 359-3400
  Rochester *(G-14534)*

METAL FINISHING SVCS

21st Century Finishes Inc ....F...... 516 221-7000
  North Bellmore *(G-12931)*
ABS Metal Corp ....G...... 646 302-9018
  Hewlett *(G-6330)*
Anthony River Inc ....F...... 315 475-1315
  Syracuse *(G-15875)*
D & I Finishing Inc ....G...... 631 471-3034
  Bohemia *(G-1044)*
D & W Enterprises LLC ....E...... 585 590-6727
  Medina *(G-8303)*
Eastside Oxide Co ....E...... 607 734-1253
  Elmira *(G-4693)*
Ever-Nu-Metal Products Inc ....F...... 646 423-5833
  Brooklyn *(G-1945)*
First Impressions Finishing ....G...... 631 467-2244
  Ronkonkoma *(G-14929)*
General Plating LLC ....E...... 585 423-0830
  Rochester *(G-14412)*
Halmark Architectural Finshg ....E...... 718 272-1831
  Brooklyn *(G-2062)*
I W Industries Inc ....C...... 631 293-9494
  Melville *(G-8359)*
L W S Inc ....F...... 631 580-0472
  Ronkonkoma *(G-14953)*
Maracle Industrial Finshg Co ....E...... 585 387-9077
  Rochester *(G-14516)*
Master Craft Finishers Inc ....E...... 631 586-0540
  Deer Park *(G-4195)*
Multitone Finishing Co Inc ....G...... 516 485-1043
  West Hempstead *(G-16892)*
Oerlikon Blzers Cating USA Inc .....E...... 716 564-8557
  Buffalo *(G-3121)*
Paradigm Group LLC ....G...... 718 860-1538
  Bronx *(G-1421)*
Products Superb Inc ....G...... 315 923-7057
  Clyde *(G-3756)*
Rainbow Powder Coating Corp ......G...... 631 586-4019
  Deer Park *(G-4223)*
Saccomize Inc ....G...... 818 287-3000
  Bronx *(G-1445)*
Surface Finish Technology ....F...... 607 732-2909
  Elmira *(G-4716)*
Vibra Tech Industries Inc ....F...... 914 946-1916
  White Plains *(G-17208)*

METAL RESHAPING & REPLATING SVCS

Elmsford Sheet Metal Works Inc ...D...... 914 739-6300
  Cortlandt Manor *(G-4074)*
Miscellnous Ir Fabricators Inc ....E...... 518 355-1822
  Schenectady *(G-15306)*

Employee Codes: A=Over 500 employees, B=251-500
C=101-250, D=51-100, E=20-50, F=10-19, G=5-9

METAL SERVICE CENTERS & OFFICES

METAL SERVICE CENTERS & OFFICES

Albea Cosmetics America Inc .... E 212 371-5100
New York *(G-9124)*
Aufhauser Corporation .... F 516 694-8696
Plainview *(G-13614)*
Cannon Industries Inc .... D 585 254-8080
Rochester *(G-14276)*
Specialty Steel Fabg Corp .... F 718 893-6326
Bronx *(G-1459)*
Steel Sales Inc .... E 607 674-6363
Sherburne *(G-15419)*

METAL SPINNING FOR THE TRADE

Acme Architectural Products .... B 718 360-0700
Brooklyn *(G-1553)*
American Metal Spinning Pdts .... G 631 454-6276
West Babylon *(G-16796)*
Art Precision Metal Products .... F 631 842-8889
Copiague *(G-3920)*
Bridgeport Metalcraft Inc .... G 315 623-9597
Constantia *(G-3906)*
Gem Metal Spinning & Stamping .... G 718 729-7014
Long Island City *(G-7778)*
Hy-Grade Metal Products Corp .... G 315 475-4221
Syracuse *(G-15980)*
Koch Metal Spinning Co Inc .... E 716 835-3631
Buffalo *(G-3052)*
Long Island Metalform Inc .... F 631 242-9088
Deer Park *(G-4191)*
Russco Metal Spinning Co Inc .... F 516 872-6055
Oceanside *(G-13117)*
S D Z Metal Spinning Stamping .... F 718 778-3600
Brooklyn *(G-2548)*
Toronto Metal Spinning and Ltg .... E 905 793-1174
Niagara Falls *(G-12900)*

METAL STAMPING, FOR THE TRADE

A-1 Stamping & Spinning Corp .... F 718 388-2626
Rockaway Park *(G-14812)*
Ajl Manufacturing Inc .... C 585 254-1128
Rochester *(G-14199)*
Albest Metal Stamping Corp .... D 718 388-6000
Brooklyn *(G-1575)*
Alton Manufacturing Inc .... D 585 458-2600
Rochester *(G-14209)*
American Mtal Stmping Spinning .... F 718 384-1500
Brooklyn *(G-1602)*
Belmet Products Inc .... E 718 542-8220
Bronx *(G-1282)*
Charles A Rogers Entps Inc .... E 585 924-6400
Victor *(G-16490)*
D-K Manufacturing Corp .... E 315 592-4327
Fulton *(G-5469)*
Dayton Industries Inc .... E 718 542-8144
Bronx *(G-1314)*
Die-Matic Products LLC .... E 516 433-7900
Plainview *(G-13627)*
Feldware Inc .... E 718 372-0486
Brooklyn *(G-1969)*
Gay Sheet Metal Dies Inc .... G 716 877-0208
Buffalo *(G-2981)*
Genesee Metal Stampings Inc .... G 585 475-0450
West Henrietta *(G-16912)*
Rolite Mfg Inc .... E 716 683-0259
Lancaster *(G-7365)*
S & S Prtg Die-Cutting Co Inc .... F 718 388-8990
Brooklyn *(G-2543)*
Smithers Tools & Mch Pdts Inc .... D 845 876-3063
Rhinebeck *(G-14070)*
Square Stamping Mfg Corp .... E 315 896-2641
Barneveld *(G-618)*
Tools & Stamping Corp .... G 718 392-4040
Brooklyn *(G-2683)*
Trident Precision Mfg Inc .... D 585 265-2010
Webster *(G-16764)*
Ultimate Prcision Met Pdts Inc .... C 631 249-9441
Farmingdale *(G-5146)*
Volkert Precision Tech Inc .... E 718 464-9500
Queens Village *(G-13999)*

METAL STAMPINGS: Patterned

Corbett Stves Pttern Works Inc .... E 585 546-7109
Rochester *(G-14310)*

METAL STAMPINGS: Perforated

Erdle Perforating Holdings Inc .... D 585 247-4700
Rochester *(G-14376)*

National Wire & Metal Tech Inc .... E 716 661-9180
Jamestown *(G-7054)*
Pall Corporation .... A 607 753-6041
Cortland *(G-4059)*

METAL STAMPINGS: Rigidized

Rigidized Metals Corporation .... E 716 849-4703
Buffalo *(G-3186)*

METAL TREATING COMPOUNDS

Foseco Inc .... F 914 345-4760
Tarrytown *(G-16115)*
Technic Inc .... F 516 349-0700
Plainview *(G-13665)*

METAL, TITANIUM: Sponge & Granules

Saes Smart Materials Inc .... E 315 266-2026
New Hartford *(G-8855)*

METAL: Heavy, Perforated

Perforated Screen Surfaces .... E 866 866-8690
Conklin *(G-3898)*

METALLIC ORES WHOLESALERS

Umicore USA Inc .... E 919 874-7171
Glens Falls *(G-5714)*

METALS SVC CENTERS & WHOL: Structural Shapes, Iron Or Steel

Alp Steel Corp .... E 716 854-3030
Buffalo *(G-2821)*
Blue Tee Corp .... A 212 598-0880
New York *(G-9473)*
GCM Metal Industries Inc .... F 718 386-4059
Brooklyn *(G-2016)*
Reliable Welding & Fabrication .... G 631 758-2637
Patchogue *(G-13459)*
Supreme Steel Inc .... F 631 884-1320
Lindenhurst *(G-7512)*
Universal Steel Fabricators .... F 718 342-0782
Brooklyn *(G-2729)*

METALS SVC CENTERS & WHOLESALERS: Cable, Wire

Ultra Clarity Corp .... G 719 470-1010
Spring Valley *(G-15625)*

METALS SVC CENTERS & WHOLESALERS: Iron & Steel Prdt, Ferrous

Ewt Holdings III Corp .... F 212 644-5900
New York *(G-10151)*

METALS SVC CENTERS & WHOLESALERS: Misc Nonferrous Prdts

Amt Incorporated .... E 518 284-2910
Sharon Springs *(G-15405)*

METALS SVC CENTERS & WHOLESALERS: Nonferrous Sheets, Etc

Umicore USA Inc .... E 919 874-7171
Glens Falls *(G-5714)*

METALS SVC CENTERS & WHOLESALERS: Pipe & Tubing, Steel

Accord Pipe Fabricators Inc .... E 718 657-3900
Jamaica *(G-6927)*
ASAP Rack Rental Inc .... G 718 499-4495
Brooklyn *(G-1640)*

METALS SVC CENTERS & WHOLESALERS: Sheets, Metal

Hatfield Metal Fab Inc .... E 845 454-9078
Poughkeepsie *(G-13926)*

METALS SVC CENTERS & WHOLESALERS: Steel

Asm USA Inc .... F 212 925-2906
New York *(G-9287)*

Hitachi Metals America Ltd .... E 914 694-9200
Purchase *(G-13975)*
Massena Metals Inc .... F 315 769-3846
Massena *(G-8229)*
Nathan Steel Corp .... F 315 797-1335
Utica *(G-16375)*
R & S Machine Center Inc .... E 518 563-4016
Plattsburgh *(G-13720)*

METALS SVC CENTERS & WHOLESALERS: Tin & Tin Base Metals

Tin Box Company of America Inc .... E 631 845-1600
Farmingdale *(G-5142)*

METALS SVC CENTERS & WHOLESALERS: Tubing, Metal

Tube Fabrication Company Inc .... F 716 673-1871
Fredonia *(G-5384)*

METALS: Precious NEC

American Material Processing .... F 315 695-6204
Phoenix *(G-13568)*
Doral Refining Corp .... E 516 223-3684
Freeport *(G-5405)*
Eco-Bat America LLC .... C 845 692-4414
Middletown *(G-8472)*
Euro Pacific Precious Metals .... G 212 481-0310
New York *(G-10138)*
Handy & Harman Ltd .... A 212 520-2300
New York *(G-10450)*
Sph Group Holdings LLC .... F 212 520-2300
New York *(G-12186)*
Starfuels Inc .... G 914 289-4800
White Plains *(G-17197)*
Wallace Refiners Inc .... G 212 391-2649
New York *(G-12610)*

METALS: Precious, Secondary

Encore Refining and Recycling .... G 631 319-1910
Holbrook *(G-6474)*
Handy & Harman .... E 914 461-1300
White Plains *(G-17145)*
Sabin Metal Corporation .... F 631 329-1695
East Hampton *(G-4435)*
Sabin Metal Corporation .... C 585 538-2194
Scottsville *(G-15361)*

METALS: Primary Nonferrous, NEC

Ames Goldsmith Corp .... F 518 792-7435
Glens Falls *(G-5685)*
Billanti Casting Co Inc .... E 516 775-4800
New Hyde Park *(G-8864)*
Goldmark Products Inc .... E 631 777-3343
Farmingdale *(G-5008)*
Marina Jewelry Co Inc .... G 212 354-5027
New York *(G-11175)*
Materion Advanced Materials .... C 800 327-1355
Buffalo *(G-3079)*
Materion Advanced Materials 800 327-1355
Brewster *(G-1220)*
RS Precision Industries Inc .... E 631 420-0424
Farmingdale *(G-5115)*
S & W Metal Trading Corp .... G 212 719-5070
Brooklyn *(G-2547)*
Sabin Metal Corporation .... C 585 538-2194
Scottsville *(G-15361)*
Sigmund Cohn Corp .... D 914 664-5300
Mount Vernon *(G-8780)*
Tdy Industries LLC .... E 716 433-4411
Lockport *(G-7648)*

METALWORK: Miscellaneous

Abasco Inc .... E 716 649-4790
Hamburg *(G-5941)*
Accurate Metal Weather Strip .... G 914 668-6042
Mount Vernon *(G-8704)*
Coral Management Corp .... G 718 893-9286
Bronx *(G-1306)*
Designs By Novello Inc .... G 914 934-7711
Port Chester *(G-13770)*
Empire Metal Finishing Inc .... E 718 545-6700
Astoria *(G-438)*
Fala Technologies Inc .... E 845 336-4000
Kingston *(G-7218)*
Genesee Metal Products Inc .... E 585 968-6000
Wellsville *(G-16779)*

PRODUCT SECTION

MILLWORK

Halmark Architectural Finshg ....E 718 272-1831
  Brooklyn *(G-2062)*
Hornet Group Inc ....D 845 858-6400
  Port Jervis *(G-13808)*
Integrity Tool Incorporated ....F 315 524-4409
  Ontario *(G-13226)*
Janed Enterprises ....F 631 694-4494
  Farmingdale *(G-5025)*
Kraman Iron Works Inc ....F 212 460-8400
  New York *(G-10924)*
Lane Enterprises Inc ....E 518 885-4385
  Ballston Spa *(G-599)*
Longstem Organizers Inc ....G 914 777-2174
  Jefferson Valley *(G-7091)*
Metal Products Intl LLC ....G 716 215-1930
  Niagara Falls *(G-12863)*
Northern Metalworks Corp ....G 646 523-1689
  Selden *(G-15374)*
Orange County Ironworks LLC ....E 845 769-3000
  Montgomery *(G-8636)*
Orbital Holdings Inc ....E 951 360-7100
  Buffalo *(G-3126)*
Paragon Aquatics ....E 845 452-5500
  Lagrangeville *(G-7282)*
Ppi Corp ....E 585 880-7277
  Rochester *(G-14611)*
Risa Management Corp ....E 718 361-2606
  Maspeth *(G-8197)*
Riverside Iron LLC ....E 315 535-4864
  Gouverneur *(G-5762)*
Rollform of Jamestown Inc ....F 716 665-5310
  Jamestown *(G-7058)*
Semans Enterprises Inc ....F 585 444-0097
  West Henrietta *(G-16925)*
Signature Metal MBL Maint LLC ......D 718 292-8280
  Bronx *(G-1453)*
Sims Steel Corporation ....E 631 587-8670
  Lindenhurst *(G-7505)*
Sinn-Tech Industries Inc ....G 631 643-1171
  West Babylon *(G-16859)*
Tebbens Steel LLC ....F 631 208-8330
  Calverton *(G-3329)*
Tonys Ornamental Ir Works Inc ....E 315 337-3730
  Rome *(G-14866)*
United Iron Inc ....E 914 667-5700
  Mount Vernon *(G-8791)*
West Metal Works Inc ....E 716 895-4900
  Buffalo *(G-3278)*

METALWORK: Ornamental

Arcadia Mfg Group Inc ....E 518 434-6213
  Green Island *(G-5871)*
Arcadia Mfg Group Inc ....G 518 434-6213
  Menands *(G-8399)*
Duke of Iron Inc ....G 631 543-3600
  Smithtown *(G-15508)*
Iron Art Inc ....G 914 592-7977
  Elmsford *(G-4765)*
Kendi Iron Works Inc ....E 718 821-2722
  Brooklyn *(G-2169)*
Kleinfelder John ....G 716 753-3163
  Mayville *(G-8247)*
Koenig Iron Works Inc ....E 718 433-0900
  Long Island City *(G-7808)*
Kryten Iron Works Inc ....G 914 345-0990
  Hawthorne *(G-6272)*
Shanker Industries Inc ....G 631 940-9889
  Deer Park *(G-4233)*
Tensator Inc ....D 631 666-0300
  Bay Shore *(G-744)*

METALWORKING MACHINERY WHOLESALERS

S & S Machinery Corp ....E 718 492-7400
  Brooklyn *(G-2541)*

METER READERS: Remote

Quadlogic Controls Corporation ......D 212 930-9300
  Long Island City *(G-7882)*

METERING DEVICES: Flow Meters, Impeller & Counter Driven

Flexim Americas Corporation ....F 631 492-2300
  Edgewood *(G-4612)*
SPX Flow Us LLC ....G 585 436-5550
  Rochester *(G-14722)*

Turbo Machined Products LLC ....E 315 895-3010
  Frankfort *(G-5368)*

METERING DEVICES: Totalizing, Consumption

Siemens Industry Inc ....C 631 231-3600
  Hauppauge *(G-6213)*

METERING DEVICES: Water Quality Monitoring & Control Systems

Gurley Precision Instrs Inc ....C 518 272-6300
  Troy *(G-16259)*
Vepo Solutions LLC ....G 914 384-2121
  Cross River *(G-4086)*

METERS: Elasped Time

Curtis Instruments Inc ....C 914 666-2971
  Mount Kisco *(G-8666)*
Frequency Electronics Inc ....B 516 794-4500
  Uniondale *(G-16317)*

METERS: Liquid

Walter R Tucker Entps Ltd ....E 607 467-2866
  Deposit *(G-4305)*

METHANOL: Natural

Ocip Holding LLC ....G 646 589-6180
  New York *(G-11509)*

MICA PRDTS

Fra-Rik Formica Fabg Co Inc ....G 718 597-3335
  Bronx *(G-1339)*
Reliance Mica Co Inc ....G 718 788-0282
  Rockaway Park *(G-14815)*
S & J Trading Inc ....G 718 347-1323
  Floral Park *(G-5216)*

MICROCIRCUITS, INTEGRATED: Semiconductor

Aeroflex Incorporated ....B 516 694-6700
  Plainview *(G-13608)*
Aeroflex Plainview Inc ....B 516 694-6700
  Plainview *(G-13609)*
Microchip Technology Inc ....G 631 233-3280
  Hauppauge *(G-6162)*
Park Electrochemical Corp ....E 631 465-3600
  Melville *(G-8376)*
Telephonics Tlsi Corp ....C 631 470-8854
  Huntington *(G-6725)*

MICROFILM EQPT

Mekatronics Incorporated ....E 516 883-6805
  Port Washington *(G-13865)*

MICROMANIPULATOR

Anaren Microwave Inc ....G 315 432-8909
  East Syracuse *(G-4520)*

MICROPHONES

Andrea Electronics Corporation .....G 631 719-1800
  Bohemia *(G-1012)*
Theodore A Rapp Associates ....G 845 469-2100
  Chester *(G-3647)*

MICROPROCESSORS

Eversan Inc ....F 315 736-3967
  Whitesboro *(G-17221)*
I E D Corp ....F 631 348-0424
  Islandia *(G-6832)*
INTEL Corporation ....D 408 765-8080
  Getzville *(G-5611)*

MICROWAVE COMPONENTS

Antenna & Radome Res Assoc .....E 631 231-8400
  Bay Shore *(G-670)*
Cobham Holdings (us) Inc ....A 716 662-0006
  Orchard Park *(G-13285)*
Cobham Holdings Inc ....E 716 662-0006
  Orchard Park *(G-13286)*
Frequency Electronics Inc ....B 516 794-4500
  Uniondale *(G-16317)*

General Microwave Corporation ....F 516 802-0900
  Syosset *(G-15844)*
L-3 Cmmnctns Fgn Holdings Inc ...E 212 697-1111
  New York *(G-10941)*
L3 Technologies Inc ....E 631 289-0363
  Patchogue *(G-13453)*
L3 Technologies Inc ....B 212 697-1111
  New York *(G-10943)*
Lexan Industries Inc ....F 631 434-7586
  Bay Shore *(G-711)*
Microwave Circuit Tech Inc ....E 631 845-1041
  Farmingdale *(G-5061)*
Microwave Filter Company Inc ......E 315 438-4700
  East Syracuse *(G-4564)*
Passive-Plus Inc ....F 631 425-0938
  Huntington *(G-6708)*
Sendec Corp ....E 585 425-5965
  Fairport *(G-4884)*
Spectrum Microwave Inc ....E 315 253-6241
  Auburn *(G-517)*

MICROWAVE OVENS: Household

Toshiba America Inc ....E 212 596-0600
  New York *(G-12398)*

MILITARY INSIGNIA

Baldwin Ribbon & Stamping Corp ...F 718 335-6700
  Woodside *(G-17336)*

MILITARY INSIGNIA, TEXTILE

Skd Tactical Inc ....G 845 897-2889
  Highland Falls *(G-6437)*

MILL PRDTS: Structural & Rail

Matrix Steel Company Inc ....G 718 381-6800
  Brooklyn *(G-2287)*

MILLINERY SUPPLIES: Veils & Veiling, Bridal, Funeral, Etc

Paula Varsalona Ltd ....F 212 570-9100
  New York *(G-11601)*

MILLING: Grain Cereals, Cracked

Cargill Incorporated ....G 716 665-6570
  Kennedy *(G-7182)*

MILLWORK

Adams Interior Fabrications ....F 631 249-8282
  Massapequa *(G-8207)*
Amstutze Woodworking ....G 518 946-8206
  Upper Jay *(G-16327)*
Architctral Mllwk Installation ....E 631 499-0755
  East Northport *(G-4453)*
Auburn Custom Millwork Inc ....G 315 253-3843
  Auburn *(G-477)*
Bloch Industries LLC ....D 585 334-9600
  Rochester *(G-14253)*
BNC Innovative Woodworking ....F 718 277-2800
  Brooklyn *(G-1705)*
Braga Woodworks ....G 845 342-4636
  Middletown *(G-8462)*
Broadway Neon Sign Corp ....F 908 241-4177
  Ronkonkoma *(G-14910)*
Carob Industries Inc ....F 631 225-0900
  Lindenhurst *(G-7481)*
Christiana Millwork Inc ....E 315 492-9099
  Jamesville *(G-7079)*
City Store Gates Mfg Corp ....E 718 939-9700
  College Point *(G-3806)*
Clearwood Custom Carpentry and ...E 315 432-8422
  East Syracuse *(G-4533)*
Columbus Woodworking Inc ....G 607 674-4546
  Sherburne *(G-15412)*
Concepts In Wood of CNY ....E 315 463-8084
  Syracuse *(G-15923)*
Cousins Furniture & Hm Imprvs .....E 631 254-3752
  Deer Park *(G-4143)*
Craftsmen Woodworkers Ltd ....E 718 326-3350
  Maspeth *(G-8156)*
Creative Laminates Inc ....F 315 463-7580
  Syracuse *(G-15931)*
Crown Mill Work Corp ....G 845 371-2200
  Monsey *(G-8605)*
Crown Woodworking Corp ....E 718 974-6415
  Brooklyn *(G-1819)*

Employee Codes: A=Over 500 employees, B=251-500
C=101-250, D=51-100, E=20-50, F=10-19, G=5-9

MILLWORK   PRODUCT SECTION

Cuccio-Zanetti Inc .... G 518 587-1363
  Middle Grove *(G-8437)*
Custom Door & Mirror Inc .... E 631 414-7725
  Farmingdale *(G-4980)*
Custom Stair & Millwork Co .... G 315 839-5793
  Sauquoit *(G-15228)*
Dbs Interiors Corp .... F 631 491-3013
  West Babylon *(G-16813)*
Deerfield Millwork Inc .... F 631 726-9663
  Water Mill *(G-16626)*
Duncan & Son Carpentry Inc .... E 914 664-4311
  Mount Vernon *(G-8724)*
Dune Woodworking .... G 631 996-2482
  Riverhead *(G-14152)*
Ed Negron Fine Woodworking .... G 718 246-1016
  Brooklyn *(G-1904)*
Efj Inc .... D 518 234-4799
  Cobleskill *(G-3762)*
EM Pfaff & Son Inc .... F 607 739-3691
  Horseheads *(G-6604)*
Five Star Millwork LLC .... F 845 920-0247
  Pearl River *(G-13478)*
Garrison Woodworking Inc .... F 845 726-3525
  Westtown *(G-17098)*
Grace Ryan & Magnus Mllwk LLC .... D 914 665-0902
  Mount Vernon *(G-8731)*
Gw Manufacturing .... E 718 386-8078
  Ridgewood *(G-14122)*
H B Millwork Inc .... F 631 289-8086
  Medford *(G-8277)*
H B Millwork Inc .... G 631 924-4195
  Yaphank *(G-17410)*
Highland Organization Corp .... E 631 991-3240
  Deer Park *(G-4172)*
Hulley Holding Company Inc .... F 716 332-3982
  Kenmore *(G-7178)*
I Meglio Corp .... E 631 617-6900
  Brentwood *(G-1181)*
Island Street Lumber Co Inc .... G 716 692-4127
  North Tonawanda *(G-12996)*
J Percoco Industries Inc .... G 631 312-4572
  Bohemia *(G-1075)*
Jacobs Woodworking LLC .... G 315 427-8999
  Syracuse *(G-15984)*
Jays Furniture Products Inc .... E 716 876-8854
  Buffalo *(G-3031)*
JEm Wdwkg & Cabinets Inc .... F 518 828-5361
  Hudson *(G-6650)*
John Langenbacher Co Inc .... E 718 328-0141
  Bronx *(G-1371)*
KB Millwork Inc .... G 516 280-2183
  Levittown *(G-7451)*
Krefab Corporation .... F 631 842-5151
  Huntington *(G-6701)*
M & D Millwork LLC .... F 631 789-1439
  Amityville *(G-307)*
Mack Wood Working .... G 845 657-6625
  Shokan *(G-15455)*
Mason Woodworks LLC .... G 917 363-7052
  Brooklyn *(G-2281)*
Medina Millworks LLC .... G 585 798-2969
  Medina *(G-8309)*
Metropolitan Fine Mllwk Corp .... F 914 669-4900
  North Salem *(G-12955)*
Michbi Doors Inc .... D 631 231-9050
  Brentwood *(G-1189)*
Millco Woodworking LLC .... F 585 526-6844
  Hall *(G-5940)*
Millwright Wdwrk Installetion .... E 631 587-2635
  West Babylon *(G-16842)*
North Fork Wood Works Inc .... G 631 255-4028
  Mattituck *(G-8240)*
Northern Forest Pdts Co Inc .... G 315 942-6955
  Boonville *(G-1164)*
Pella Corporation .... C 631 208-0710
  Calverton *(G-3322)*
Peter Productions Devivi Inc .... F 315 568-8484
  Waterloo *(G-16653)*
Pgs Millwork Inc .... D 212 244-6610
  New York *(G-11663)*
Piccini Industries Ltd .... E 845 365-0614
  Orangeburg *(G-13262)*
Professional Cab Detailing Co .... F 845 436-7282
  Woodridge *(G-17333)*
Quaker Millwork & Lumber Inc .... E 716 662-3388
  Orchard Park *(G-13318)*
Randolph Dimension Corporation .... F 716 358-6901
  Randolph *(G-14030)*
RB Woodcraft Inc .... G 315 474-2429
  Syracuse *(G-16043)*

Richard Anthony Corp .... E 914 922-7141
  Yorktown Heights *(G-17534)*
Rj Millworkers Inc .... E 607 433-0525
  Oneonta *(G-13215)*
Roode Hoek & Co Inc .... F 718 522-5921
  Brooklyn *(G-2525)*
Russin Lumber Corp .... F 845 457-4000
  Newburgh *(G-12801)*
S Donadic Woodworking Inc .... D 718 361-9888
  Sunnyside *(G-15830)*
Shawmut Woodworking & Sup Inc .... G 212 920-8900
  New York *(G-12068)*
Specialty Services .... G 585 728-5650
  Wayland *(G-16735)*
Syracuse Industrial Sls Co Ltd .... F 315 478-5751
  Syracuse *(G-16077)*
TDS Woodworking Inc .... F 718 442-5298
  Staten Island *(G-15768)*
Three R Enterprises Inc .... E 585 254-5050
  Rochester *(G-14752)*
Tiedemann Waldemar Inc .... F 716 875-5665
  Buffalo *(G-3244)*
Unicenter Millwork Inc .... G 716 741-8201
  Clarence Center *(G-3707)*
Universal Custom Millwork Inc .... D 518 330-6622
  Amsterdam *(G-372)*
Urban Woodworks Ltd .... G 718 827-1570
  Brooklyn *(G-2730)*
Wagner Millwork Inc .... D 607 687-5362
  Owego *(G-13386)*
Wolfe Lumber Mill Inc .... G 716 772-7750
  Gasport *(G-5575)*
Xylon Industries Inc .... G 631 293-4717
  Farmingdale *(G-5153)*
Zanzano Woodworking Inc .... G 914 725-6025
  Scarsdale *(G-15255)*

MINE DEVELOPMENT SVCS: Nonmetallic Minerals

Resource Capital Funds LP .... G 631 692-9111
  Huntington *(G-6713)*

MINERAL ABRASIVES MINING SVCS

Capital Gold Corporation .... G 212 668-0842
  New York *(G-9575)*

MINERAL MINING: Nonmetallic

Hargrave Development .... F 716 877-7880
  Kenmore *(G-7175)*

MINERAL PRODUCTS

American Crmic Process RES LLC .... G 315 828-6268
  Phelps *(G-13552)*

MINERAL WOOL

Owens Corning Sales LLC .... B 518 475-3600
  Feura Bush *(G-5182)*
Soundcoat Company Inc .... D 631 242-2200
  Deer Park *(G-4236)*
Unifrax I LLC .... C 716 696-3000
  Tonawanda *(G-16230)*

MINERAL WOOL INSULATION PRDTS

Unifrax Corporation .... E 716 278-3800
  Niagara Falls *(G-12903)*

MINERALS: Ground or Treated

Allied Aero Services Inc .... G 631 277-9368
  Brentwood *(G-1172)*
DSM Nutritional Products LLC .... C 518 372-5155
  Schenectady *(G-15276)*
DSM Nutritional Products LLC .... E 518 372-5155
  Glenville *(G-5716)*
Mineralbious Corp .... F 516 498-9715
  Westbury *(G-17040)*
Minerals Technologies Inc .... E 212 878-1800
  New York *(G-11302)*
Northeast Solite Corporation .... E 845 246-2646
  Saugerties *(G-15218)*
Northeast Solite Corporation .... E 845 246-2177
  Mount Marion *(G-8694)*
Oro Avanti Inc .... G 516 487-5185
  Great Neck *(G-5844)*

MINIATURES

Islip Miniture Golf .... G 631 940-8900
  Bay Shore *(G-706)*

MINING EXPLORATION & DEVELOPMENT SVCS

Coremet Trading Inc .... G 212 964-3600
  New York *(G-9784)*

MINING SVCS, NEC: Lignite

US Pump Corp .... G 516 303-7799
  West Hempstead *(G-16896)*

MINING: Sand & Shale Oil

Kimmeridge Energy MGT Co LLC .... F 646 517-7252
  New York *(G-10887)*

MIRROR REPAIR SHOP

D Best Service Co Inc .... G 718 972-6133
  Brooklyn *(G-1829)*

MIRRORS: Motor Vehicle

Prisma Glass & Mirror Inc .... G 718 366-7191
  Ridgewood *(G-14132)*
Rosco Inc .... C 718 526-2601
  Jamaica *(G-6985)*

MIXING EQPT

Munson Machinery Company Inc .... E 315 797-0090
  Utica *(G-16374)*

MIXTURES & BLOCKS: Asphalt Paving

Albany Asp & Aggregates Corp .... E 518 436-8916
  Albany *(G-34)*
All Phases Asp & Ldscpg Dsgn .... F 631 588-1372
  Ronkonkoma *(G-14889)*
Barrett Paving Materials Inc .... E 607 723-5367
  Binghamton *(G-887)*
Barrett Paving Materials Inc .... E 315 788-2037
  Watertown *(G-16658)*
Bross Quality Paving .... G 845 532-7116
  Ellenville *(G-4646)*
C & C Ready-Mix Corporation .... E 607 687-1690
  Owego *(G-13376)*
Callanan Industries Inc .... C 518 374-2222
  Albany *(G-57)*
Callanan Industries Inc .... E 845 331-6868
  Kingston *(G-7211)*
Canal Asphalt Inc .... E 914 667-8500
  Mount Vernon *(G-8714)*
Cofire Paving Corporation .... E 718 463-1403
  Flushing *(G-5241)*
Cold Mix Manufacturing Corp .... F 718 463-1444
  Mount Vernon *(G-8718)*
Deans Paving Inc .... G 315 736-7601
  Marcy *(G-8121)*
Doctor Pavers .... G 516 342-6016
  Bethpage *(G-865)*
Dolomite Products Company Inc .... F 585 352-0460
  Spencerport *(G-15593)*
G&G Sealcoating and Paving Inc .... E 585 787-1500
  Ontario *(G-13224)*
Gernatt Asphalt Products Inc .... E 716 532-3371
  Collins *(G-3842)*
Gernatt Asphalt Products Inc .... G 716 496-5111
  Springville *(G-15631)*
Grace Associates Inc .... E 718 767-9000
  Harrison *(G-6005)*
Graymont Materials Inc .... E 518 561-5200
  Plattsburgh *(G-13693)*
Hanson Aggregates East LLC .... E 585 343-1787
  Stafford *(G-15641)*
J Pahura Contractors .... E 585 589-5793
  Albion *(G-169)*
Jamestown Macadam Inc .... F 716 664-5108
  Jamestown *(G-7042)*
Jet-Black Sealers Inc .... G 716 891-4197
  Buffalo *(G-3036)*
John T Montecalvo Inc .... G 631 325-1492
  Speonk *(G-15600)*
Kal-Harbour Inc .... F 518 266-0690
  Albany *(G-93)*
Kings Park Asphalt Corporation .... G 631 269-9774
  Hauppauge *(G-6130)*

PRODUCT SECTION

Lafarge North America Inc .... E 518 756-5000
  Ravena *(G-14036)*
Morlyn Asphalt Corp .... G 845 888-2695
  Cochecton *(G-3768)*
Narde Paving Company Inc .... E 607 737-7177
  Elmira *(G-4710)*
Nicolia Concrete Products Inc .... D 631 669-0700
  Lindenhurst *(G-7500)*
Northeastern Sealcoat Inc .... F 585 544-4372
  Rochester *(G-14563)*
Package Pavement Company Inc ...... D 845 221-2224
  Stormville *(G-15802)*
Patterson Blacktop Corp .... E 914 949-2000
  White Plains *(G-17172)*
Patterson Materials Corp .... E 914 949-2000
  White Plains *(G-17173)*
Pavco Asphalt Inc .... E 631 289-3223
  Holtsville *(G-6532)*
Peckham Industries Inc .... G 518 945-1120
  Athens *(G-465)*
Peckham Materials Corp .... E 518 945-1120
  Athens *(G-466)*
Peckham Materials Corp .... E 518 494-2313
  Chestertown *(G-3650)*
Peckham Materials Corp .... E 518 747-3353
  Hudson Falls *(G-6680)*
Prima Asphalt and Concrete .... F 631 289-3223
  Holtsville *(G-6533)*
Rason Asphalt Inc .... G 631 293-6210
  Farmingdale *(G-5107)*
Rason Asphalt Inc .... G 516 671-1500
  Glen Cove *(G-5639)*
Rochester Seal Pro LLC .... G 585 594-3818
  Rochester *(G-14669)*
Sheldon Slate Products Co Inc .... E 518 642-1280
  Middle Granville *(G-8434)*
Suit-Kote Corporation .... F 315 735-8501
  Oriskany *(G-13338)*
Suit-Kote Corporation .... E 607 535-2743
  Watkins Glen *(G-16722)*
Thalle Industries Inc .... E 914 762-3415
  Briarcliff Manor *(G-1229)*
Tri City Highway Products Inc .... E 607 722-2967
  Binghamton *(G-951)*
Tri-City Highway Products Inc .... E 518 294-9964
  Richmondville *(G-14102)*
Twin County Recycling Corp .... F 516 827-6900
  Westbury *(G-17067)*
Ultimate Pavers Corp .... E 917 417-2652
  Staten Island *(G-15772)*
Unilock New York Inc .... G 845 278-6700
  Brewster *(G-1227)*
Universal Ready Mix Inc .... G 516 746-4535
  New Hyde Park *(G-8915)*
Upstone Materials Inc .... G 518 873-2275
  Lewis *(G-7452)*
Zielinskis Asphalt Inc .... F 315 306-4057
  Oriskany Falls *(G-13343)*

MOBILE COMMUNICATIONS EQPT

2p Agency Usa Inc .... G 212 203-5586
  Brooklyn *(G-1513)*
Andrea Electronics Corporation .... G 631 719-1800
  Bohemia *(G-1012)*
AT&T Corp .... G 716 639-0673
  Williamsville *(G-17262)*
Cmb Wireless Group LLC .... B 631 750-4700
  Bohemia *(G-1032)*
Elite Cellular Accessories Inc .... E 877 390-2502
  Deer Park *(G-4158)*
Flycell Inc .... D 212 400-1212
  New York *(G-10233)*
Icell Inc .... C 516 590-0007
  Hempstead *(G-6298)*
Igo Inc .... E 408 596-0061
  New York *(G-10608)*
Imobile of Ny LLC .... G 212 505-3355
  New York *(G-10619)*
Innovation In Motion Inc .... G 407 878-7561
  Long Beach *(G-7672)*
M&S Accessory Network Corp .... F 347 492-7790
  New York *(G-11107)*
Toura LLC .... F 646 652-8668
  Brooklyn *(G-2689)*

MOBILE HOMES

All Star Carts & Vehicles Inc .... D 631 666-5581
  Bay Shore *(G-667)*
Champion Home Builders Inc .... C 315 841-4122
  Sangerfield *(G-15160)*

Leatherstocking Mobile Home PA ...... G 315 839-5691
  Sauquoit *(G-15229)*

MOBILE HOMES WHOLESALERS

Century Ready Mix Inc .... G 631 888-2200
  West Babylon *(G-16806)*

MODELS

Copesetic Inc .... F 315 684-7780
  Morrisville *(G-8662)*
Creative Models & Prototypes .... G 516 433-6828
  Hicksville *(G-6362)*
Marilyn Model Management Inc .... F 646 556-7587
  New York *(G-11174)*
Tri-Force Sales LLC .... E 732 261-5507
  New York *(G-12420)*

MODELS: General, Exc Toy

Active Manufacturing Inc .... F 607 775-3162
  Kirkwood *(G-7257)*
J T Systematic .... G 607 754-0929
  Endwell *(G-4841)*

MODULES: Computer Logic

Intech 21 Inc .... F 516 626-7221
  Port Washington *(G-13847)*
International Bus Mchs Corp .... E 212 324-5000
  New York *(G-10673)*

MODULES: Solid State

Data Device Corporation .... B 631 567-5600
  Bohemia *(G-1045)*

MOLDED RUBBER PRDTS

Buffalo Lining & Fabricating .... G 716 883-6500
  Buffalo *(G-2876)*
Enviroform Recycled Pdts Inc .... G 315 789-1810
  Geneva *(G-5586)*
Moldtech Inc .... E 716 685-3344
  Lancaster *(G-7351)*
SD Christie Associates Inc .... G 914 734-1800
  Peekskill *(G-13507)*
Short Jj Associates Inc .... F 315 986-3511
  Macedon *(G-8021)*
Traffic Logix Corporation .... G 866 915-6449
  Spring Valley *(G-15624)*

MOLDING COMPOUNDS

Coda Resources Ltd .... D 718 649-1666
  Brooklyn *(G-1789)*
Craftech .... D 518 828-5011
  Chatham *(G-3585)*
Hanet Plastics Usa Inc .... G 518 324-5850
  Plattsburgh *(G-13694)*
Imperial Polymers Inc .... G 718 387-4741
  Brooklyn *(G-2097)*
Jrlon Inc .... D 315 597-4067
  Palmyra *(G-13434)*
Majestic Mold & Tool Inc .... F 315 695-2079
  Phoenix *(G-13569)*
Plaslok Corp .... G 716 681-7755
  Buffalo *(G-3151)*

MOLDINGS, ARCHITECTURAL: Plaster Of Paris

Foster Reeve & Associates Inc .... G 718 609-0090
  Brooklyn *(G-1997)*

MOLDINGS: Picture Frame

AC Moore Incorporated .... G 516 796-5831
  Bethpage *(G-862)*
Frame Shoppe & Art Gallery .... G 516 365-6014
  Manhasset *(G-8093)*
Framerica Corporation .... D 631 650-1000
  Yaphank *(G-17409)*
General Art Company Inc .... F 212 255-1298
  New York *(G-10315)*
Julius Lowy Frame Restoring Co .... E 212 861-8585
  New York *(G-10819)*
P B & H Moulding Corporation .... E 315 455-1756
  Fayetteville *(G-5174)*
Quattro Frameworks Inc .... F 718 361-2620
  Long Island City *(G-7885)*
Quebracho Inc .... G 718 326-3605
  Brooklyn *(G-2484)*

MONORAIL SYSTEMS

Sky Frame & Art Inc .... E 212 925-7856
  New York *(G-12120)*

MOLDS: Indl

Aaron Tool & Mold Inc .... G 585 426-5100
  Rochester *(G-14178)*
All American Precision TI Mold .... F 585 436-3080
  West Henrietta *(G-16897)*
Allmetal Chocolate Mold Co Inc .... F 631 752-2888
  West Babylon *(G-16793)*
American Orthotic Lab Co Inc .... G 718 961-6487
  College Point *(G-3803)*
Blue Chip Mold Inc .... F 585 647-1790
  Rochester *(G-14254)*
Century Mold Company Inc .... D 585 352-8600
  Rochester *(G-14287)*
Chenango Valley Tech Inc .... E 607 674-4115
  Sherburne *(G-15411)*
Custom Molding Solutions Inc .... E 585 293-1702
  Churchville *(G-3665)*
East Pattern & Model Corp .... E 585 461-3240
  Fairport *(G-4861)*
G N R Plastics Inc .... G 631 724-8758
  Smithtown *(G-15509)*
Gatti Tool & Mold Inc .... F 585 328-1350
  Rochester *(G-14409)*
Globmarble LLC .... G 347 717-4088
  Brooklyn *(G-2031)*
HNST Mold Inspections LLC .... G 845 215-9258
  Nanuet *(G-8803)*
Hy-Tech Mold Inc .... F 585 247-2450
  Rochester *(G-14461)*
J T Systematic .... G 607 754-0929
  Endwell *(G-4841)*
James B Crowell & Sons Inc .... G 845 895-3464
  Wallkill *(G-16564)*
Mold-Rite Plastics LLC .... G 518 561-1812
  Plattsburgh *(G-13704)*
Nicoform Inc .... G 585 454-5530
  Rochester *(G-14557)*
Nordon Inc .... G 585 546-6200
  Rochester *(G-14558)*
PMI Industries LLC .... F 585 464-8050
  Rochester *(G-14605)*
Rochester Tool and Mold Inc .... F 585 464-9336
  Rochester *(G-14675)*
Rochling Advent Tool & Mold LP .... D 585 254-2000
  Rochester *(G-14677)*
Romold Inc .... F 585 529-4440
  Rochester *(G-14679)*
Royal Molds Inc .... F 718 382-7686
  Brooklyn *(G-2532)*
Sb Molds LLC .... D 845 352-3700
  Monsey *(G-8616)*
Star Mold Co Inc .... G 631 694-2283
  Farmingdale *(G-5126)*
Stuart Tool & Die Inc .... E 716 488-1975
  Falconer *(G-4922)*
Syntec Technologies Inc .... F 585 464-9336
  Rochester *(G-14737)*
T A Tool & Molding Inc .... G 631 293-0172
  Farmingdale *(G-5133)*
W N R Pattern & Tool Inc .... G 716 681-9334
  Lancaster *(G-7371)*

MOLDS: Plastic Working & Foundry

A & D Tool Inc .... G 631 243-4339
  Dix Hills *(G-4311)*
Accede Mold & Tool Co Inc .... D 585 254-6490
  Rochester *(G-14180)*
Clifford H Jones Inc .... F 716 693-2444
  Tonawanda *(G-16174)*
Inter Molds Inc .... G 631 667-8580
  Bay Shore *(G-704)*
Moldcraft Inc .... E 716 684-1126
  Depew *(G-4288)*
Northern Design Inc .... G 716 652-7071
  East Aurora *(G-4402)*
Universal Tooling Corporation .... F 716 985-4691
  Gerry *(G-5606)*

MONORAIL SYSTEMS

American Material Processing .... F 315 695-6204
  Phoenix *(G-13568)*

Employee Codes: A=Over 500 employees, B=251-500
C=101-250, D=51-100, E=20-50, F=10-19, G=5-9

MONUMENTS & GRAVE MARKERS, EXC TERRAZZO

Galle & Zinter Inc .... G 716 833-4212
  Buffalo (G-2978)

MONUMENTS: Concrete

Eastern Granite Inc .... G 718 356-9139
  Staten Island (G-15691)
Presbrey-Leland Inc .... G 914 949-2264
  Valhalla (G-16397)
St Raymond Monument Co .... G 718 824-3600
  Bronx (G-1460)

MONUMENTS: Cut Stone, Exc Finishing Or Lettering Only

Dominic De Nigris Inc .... E 718 597-4460
  Bronx (G-1319)
Suffolk Granite Manufacturing .... E 631 226-4774
  Lindenhurst (G-7509)

MOPS: Floor & Dust

Cpac Inc .... E 585 382-3223
  Leicester (G-7442)
Ingenious Designs LLC .... C 631 254-3376
  Ronkonkoma (G-14941)
National Wire & Metal Tech Inc .... E 716 661-9180
  Jamestown (G-7054)
Perfex Corporation .... F 315 826-3600
  Poland (G-13757)

MORTGAGE BANKERS

Caithness Equities Corporation .... E 212 599-2112
  New York (G-9549)

MOTION PICTURE & VIDEO PRODUCTION SVCS

Chakra Communications Inc .... E 716 505-7300
  Lancaster (G-7333)
Crain Communications Inc .... C 212 210-0100
  New York (G-9805)
Entertainment Weekly Inc .... C 212 522-5600
  New York (G-10097)
Laird Telemedia .... C 845 339-9555
  Mount Marion (G-8692)
North Six Inc .... F 212 463-7227
  New York (G-11475)
Taste and See Entrmt Inc .... G 516 285-3010
  Valley Stream (G-16452)

MOTION PICTURE & VIDEO PRODUCTION SVCS: Non-Theatrical, TV

Scholastic Corporation .... G 212 343-6100
  New York (G-12015)

MOTION PICTURE PRODUCTION & DISTRIBUTION

21st Century Fox America Inc .... D 212 852-7000
  New York (G-9013)
Historic TW Inc .... E 212 484-8000
  New York (G-10530)
Sony Broadband Entertainment .... F 212 833-6800
  New York (G-12156)
Time Warner Companies Inc .... D 212 484-8000
  New York (G-12369)

MOTION PICTURE PRODUCTION & DISTRIBUTION: Television

Martha Stewart Living .... C 212 827-8000
  New York (G-11189)

MOTION PICTURE PRODUCTION ALLIED SVCS

Yam TV LLC .... G 917 932-5418
  New York (G-12710)

MOTION PICTURE PRODUCTION SVCS

Abkco Music & Records Inc .... D 212 399-0300
  New York (G-9050)

MOTOR & GENERATOR PARTS: Electric

Allied Motion Technologies Inc .... C 315 782-5910
  Watertown (G-16656)
Chart Inc .... F 518 272-3565
  Troy (G-16252)
Chemark International USA Inc .... G 631 593-4566
  Deer Park (G-4140)
Ems Development Corporation .... D 631 924-4736
  Yaphank (G-17406)
Hes Inc .... G 607 359-2974
  Addison (G-7)
Moley Magnetics Inc .... G 716 434-4023
  Lockport (G-7633)
Power and Composite Tech LLC .... D 518 843-6825
  Amsterdam (G-366)
Stature Electric Inc .... B 315 782-5910
  Watertown (G-16695)

MOTOR HOMES

Authority Transportation Inc .... F 888 933-1268
  Dix Hills (G-4314)

MOTOR REPAIR SVCS

Aai Acquisition LLC .... D 800 333-0519
  Auburn (G-476)
Accurate Marine Specialties .... G 631 589-5502
  Bohemia (G-1000)
Premco Inc .... F 914 636-7095
  New Rochelle (G-8966)
RC Entps Bus & Trck Inc .... G 518 568-5753
  Saint Johnsville (G-15123)

MOTOR SCOOTERS & PARTS

Piaggio Group Americas Inc .... E 212 380-4400
  New York (G-11676)
Ying Ke Youth Age Group Inc .... F 929 402-8458
  Dix Hills (G-4323)

MOTOR VEHICLE ASSEMBLY, COMPLETE: Autos, Incl Specialty

Auto Sport Designs Inc .... F 631 425-1555
  Huntington Station (G-6735)
Cabot Coach Builders Inc .... G 516 625-4000
  Roslyn Heights (G-15049)
Marcovicci-Wenz Engineering .... G 631 467-9040
  Ronkonkoma (G-14965)
Medical Coaches Incorporated .... E 607 432-1333
  Oneonta (G-13210)
Pcb Coach Builders Corp .... G 718 897-7606
  Rego Park (G-14049)

MOTOR VEHICLE ASSEMBLY, COMPLETE: Buses, All Types

JP Bus & Truck Repair Ltd .... F 914 592-2872
  Elmsford (G-4767)
Leonard Bus Sales Inc .... G 607 467-3100
  Rome (G-14847)
Prevost Car US Inc .... C 518 957-2052
  Plattsburgh (G-13717)

MOTOR VEHICLE ASSEMBLY, COMPLETE: Cars, Armored

Armor Dynamics Inc .... F 845 658-9200
  Kingston (G-7207)

MOTOR VEHICLE ASSEMBLY, COMPLETE: Fire Department Vehicles

AB Fire Inc .... G 917 416-6444
  Brooklyn (G-1545)
Global Fire Corporation .... E 888 320-1799
  New York (G-10357)
Madrid Fire District .... G 315 322-4346
  Madrid (G-8024)
Scehenvus Fire Dist .... D 607 638-9017
  Schenevus (G-15337)

MOTOR VEHICLE ASSEMBLY, COMPLETE: Military Motor Vehicle

CIC International Ltd .... D 212 213-0089
  Brooklyn (G-1778)

MOTOR VEHICLE ASSEMBLY, COMPLETE: Motor Buses

Daimler Buses North Amer Inc .... A 315 768-8101
  Oriskany (G-13332)

MOTOR VEHICLE ASSEMBLY, COMPLETE: Snow Plows

Brothers-In-Lawn Property .... G 716 279-6191
  Tonawanda (G-16170)
Sabre Enterprises Inc .... G 315 430-3127
  Syracuse (G-16051)
Smart Systems Inc .... E 607 776-5380
  Bath (G-662)

MOTOR VEHICLE ASSEMBLY, COMPLETE: Truck & Tractor Trucks

Air Flow Manufacturing .... F 607 733-8284
  Elmira (G-4683)
Dejana Trck Utility Eqp Co LLC .... C 631 544-9000
  Kings Park (G-7200)
Tee Pee Auto Sales Corp .... F 516 338-9333
  Westbury (G-17059)

MOTOR VEHICLE ASSEMBLY, COMPLETE: Trucks, Pickup

Dejana Trck Utility Eqp Co LLC .... E 631 549-0944
  Huntington (G-6693)

MOTOR VEHICLE DEALERS: Automobiles, New & Used

Cabot Coach Builders Inc .... G 516 625-4000
  Roslyn Heights (G-15049)
Split Rock Trading Co Inc .... G 631 929-3261
  Wading River (G-16546)

MOTOR VEHICLE DEALERS: Cars, Used Only

Secor Marketing Group Inc .... G 914 381-3600
  Mamaroneck (G-8079)

MOTOR VEHICLE PARTS & ACCESS: Acceleration Eqpt

Lemans Corporation .... G 518 885-7500
  Ballston Spa (G-600)

MOTOR VEHICLE PARTS & ACCESS: Air Conditioner Parts

GM Components Holdings LLC .... C 716 439-2237
  Lockport (G-7618)
Titanx Engine Cooling Inc .... B 716 665-7129
  Jamestown (G-7071)
Transcedar Industries Ltd .... G 716 731-6442
  Niagara Falls (G-12901)

MOTOR VEHICLE PARTS & ACCESS: Bearings

Fcmp Inc .... F 716 692-4623
  Tonawanda (G-16179)

MOTOR VEHICLE PARTS & ACCESS: Body Components & Frames

Johnson Controls Inc .... C 585 724-2232
  Rochester (G-14485)

MOTOR VEHICLE PARTS & ACCESS: Cylinder Heads

M2 Race Systems Inc .... G 607 882-9078
  Ithaca (G-6892)

MOTOR VEHICLE PARTS & ACCESS: Electrical Eqpt

Katikati Inc .... G 585 678-1764
  West Henrietta (G-16915)
Nassau Auto Remanufacturer .... G 516 485-4500
  Hempstead (G-6305)

PRODUCT SECTION

MOTORS: Generators

MOTOR VEHICLE PARTS & ACCESS: Engines & Parts

- ARC Remanufacturing Inc ....D...... 718 728-0701
  Long Island City (G-7698)
- Curtis L Maclean L C ....B...... 716 898-7800
  Buffalo (G-2915)
- Jt Precision Inc ....E...... 716 795-3860
  Barker (G-612)
- Marcovicci-Wenz Engineering ....G...... 631 467-9040
  Ronkonkoma (G-14965)
- Standard Motor Products Inc ....B...... 718 392-0200
  Long Island City (G-7912)

MOTOR VEHICLE PARTS & ACCESS: Fuel Systems & Parts

- Kearney-National Inc ....F...... 212 661-4600
  New York (G-10868)
- TI Group Auto Systems LLC ....G...... 315 568-7042
  Seneca Falls (G-15394)

MOTOR VEHICLE PARTS & ACCESS: Gears

- Enplas America Inc ....G...... 646 892-7811
  New York (G-10095)
- Gleason Works ....A...... 585 473-1000
  Rochester (G-14429)

MOTOR VEHICLE PARTS & ACCESS: Power Steering Eqpt

- CRS Remanufacturing Co Inc ....F...... 718 739-1720
  Jamaica (G-6944)

MOTOR VEHICLE PARTS & ACCESS: Propane Conversion Eqpt

- Kurtz Truck Equipment Inc ....F...... 607 849-3468
  Marathon (G-8115)

MOTOR VEHICLE PARTS & ACCESS: Sanders, Safety

- Smith Metal Works Newark Inc ....E...... 315 331-1651
  Newark (G-12763)
- Vehicle Safety Dept ....F...... 315 458-6683
  Syracuse (G-16090)
- Zwack Incorporated ....E...... 518 733-5435
  Stephentown (G-15780)

MOTOR VEHICLE PARTS & ACCESS: Tops

- Electron Top Mfg Co Inc ....E...... 718 846-7400
  Richmond Hill (G-14084)

MOTOR VEHICLE PARTS & ACCESS: Transmission Housings Or Parts

- Northeastern Transports Inc ....F...... 716 833-0792
  Hamburg (G-5958)

MOTOR VEHICLE PARTS & ACCESS: Transmissions

- Banner Transmission & Eng Co ....F...... 516 221-9459
  Bellmore (G-810)

MOTOR VEHICLE PARTS & ACCESS: Wheel rims

- Extreme Auto Accessories Corp ....F...... 718 978-6722
  South Ozone Park (G-15557)

MOTOR VEHICLE PARTS & ACCESS: Wiring Harness Sets

- Agri Services Co ....G...... 716 937-6618
  Alden (G-176)

MOTOR VEHICLE SPLYS & PARTS WHOLESALERS: New

- American Auto ACC Incrporation ....E...... 718 886-6600
  Flushing (G-5233)
- K M Drive Line Inc ....G...... 718 599-0628
  Brooklyn (G-2164)
- Knorr Brake Holding Corp ....G...... 315 786-5356
  Watertown (G-16681)
- Trading Services International ....F...... 212 501-0142
  New York (G-12410)
- Walter R Tucker Entps Ltd ....E...... 607 467-2866
  Deposit (G-4305)

MOTOR VEHICLE: Hardware

- Fuccillo Ford Nelliston Inc ....G...... 518 993-5555
  Nelliston (G-8820)
- Wolo Mfg Corp ....E...... 631 242-0333
  Deer Park (G-4253)

MOTOR VEHICLE: Radiators

- API Heat Transf Thermasys Corp ....A...... 716 684-6700
  Buffalo (G-2834)

MOTOR VEHICLE: Steering Mechanisms

- Biltron Automotive Products ....E...... 631 928-8613
  Port Jeff STA (G-13786)
- Steering Columns Galore Inc ....G...... 845 278-5762
  Mahopac (G-8032)

MOTOR VEHICLES & CAR BODIES

- Antonicelli Vito Race Car ....G...... 716 684-2205
  Buffalo (G-2833)
- Fiberglass Replacement Parts ....F...... 716 893-6471
  Buffalo (G-2960)
- Jtekt Torsen North America ....F...... 585 464-5000
  Rochester (G-14487)
- Ranger Design Us Inc ....E...... 800 565-5321
  Ontario (G-13233)
- Roberts Nichols Fire Apparatus ....G...... 518 431-1945
  Cohoes (G-3781)
- Tesla Motors Inc ....A...... 212 206-1204
  New York (G-12325)
- Transprttion Collaborative Inc ....E...... 845 988-2333
  Warwick (G-16619)
- Troyer Inc ....F...... 585 352-5590
  Rochester (G-14760)

MOTOR VEHICLES, WHOLESALE: Recreational, All-Terrain

- Adirondack Power Sports ....G...... 518 481-6269
  Malone (G-8037)

MOTOR VEHICLES, WHOLESALE: Truck bodies

- Smart Systems Inc ....E...... 607 776-5380
  Bath (G-662)

MOTORCYCLE & BICYCLE PARTS: Gears

- Pidyon Controls Inc ....G...... 212 683-9523
  New York (G-11679)

MOTORCYCLE DEALERS

- Se-Mar Electric Co Inc ....E...... 716 674-7404
  West Seneca (G-16982)
- Split Rock Trading Co Inc ....G...... 631 929-3261
  Wading River (G-16546)

MOTORCYCLE DEALERS: Bicycles, Motorized

- Bignay Inc ....G...... 786 346-1673
  New York (G-9446)

MOTORCYCLES & RELATED PARTS

- Golub Corporation ....D...... 518 943-3903
  Catskill (G-3456)
- Golub Corporation ....D...... 518 899-6063
  Malta (G-8052)
- Golub Corporation ....D...... 315 363-0679
  Oneida (G-13177)
- Golub Corporation ....D...... 607 336-2588
  Norwich (G-13047)
- Golub Corporation ....D...... 518 583-3697
  Saratoga Springs (G-15183)
- Golub Corporation ....D...... 518 822-0076
  Hudson (G-6645)
- Golub Corporation ....D...... 607 235-7240
  Binghamton (G-914)
- Golub Corporation ....D...... 845 344-0327
  Middletown (G-8477)
- Ihd Motorsports LLC ....F...... 979 690-1669
  Binghamton (G-920)
- Indian Larry Legacy ....G...... 718 609-9184
  Brooklyn (G-2100)
- Orange County Choppers Inc ....G...... 845 522-5200
  Newburgh (G-12793)
- Price Chopper Operating Co ....F...... 518 562-3565
  Plattsburgh (G-13718)
- Price Chopper Operating Co ....F...... 518 456-5115
  Guilderland (G-5925)
- Robs Cycle Supply ....G...... 315 292-6878
  Syracuse (G-16047)
- Sumax Cycle Products Inc ....F...... 315 768-1058
  Oriskany (G-13339)
- Super Price Chopper Inc ....F...... 716 893-3323
  Buffalo (G-3228)

MOTORS: Electric

- Aeroflex Plainview Inc ....B...... 516 694-6700
  Plainview (G-13609)
- Current Applications Inc ....E...... 315 788-4689
  Watertown (G-16669)
- Elton El Mantle Inc ....G...... 315 432-9067
  Syracuse (G-15955)
- Empire Division Inc ....D...... 315 476-6273
  Syracuse (G-15957)
- Franklin Electric Co Inc ....A...... 718 244-7744
  Jamaica (G-6950)
- John G Rubino Inc ....E...... 315 253-7396
  Auburn (G-502)
- R M S Motor Corporation ....F...... 607 723-2323
  Binghamton (G-939)
- Sopark Corp ....C...... 716 822-0434
  Buffalo (G-3219)

MOTORS: Generators

- Aeroflex Plainview Inc ....C...... 631 231-9100
  Hauppauge (G-6030)
- Allied Motion Technologies Inc ....C...... 716 242-8634
  Amherst (G-224)
- American Precision Inds Inc ....C...... 716 691-9100
  Amherst (G-227)
- Ametek Inc ....G...... 631 467-8400
  Ronkonkoma (G-14896)
- Ametek Inc ....C...... 607 763-4700
  Binghamton (G-885)
- Ametek Inc ....D...... 585 263-7700
  Rochester (G-14218)
- ARC Systems Inc ....E...... 631 582-8020
  Hauppauge (G-6042)
- D & D Motor Systems Inc ....E...... 315 701-0861
  Syracuse (G-15938)
- Designatronics Incorporated ....B...... 516 328-3300
  Hicksville (G-6367)
- Emes Motor Inc ....G...... 718 387-2445
  Brooklyn (G-1922)
- Ener-G-Rotors Inc ....F...... 518 372-2608
  Schenectady (G-15277)
- Eni Technology Inc ....B...... 585 427-8300
  Rochester (G-14374)
- Faradyne Motors LLC ....F...... 315 331-5985
  Palmyra (G-13430)
- Felchar Manufacturing Corp ....A...... 607 723-3106
  Binghamton (G-909)
- Gaffney Kroese Supply Corp ....F...... 516 228-5091
  Garden City (G-5519)
- General Electric Company ....B...... 518 385-2211
  Schenectady (G-15287)
- Generation Power LLC ....G...... 315 234-2451
  Syracuse (G-15972)
- Got Power Inc ....G...... 631 767-9493
  Ronkonkoma (G-14935)
- Island Components Group Inc ....F...... 631 563-4224
  Holbrook (G-6482)
- Kaddis Manufacturing Corp ....G...... 585 624-3070
  Honeoye Falls (G-6561)
- Lcdrives Corp ....F...... 860 712-8926
  Potsdam (G-13897)
- Makerbot Industries LLC ....C...... 347 334-6800
  Brooklyn (G-2257)
- Modular Devices Inc ....D...... 631 345-3100
  Shirley (G-15449)
- Nidec Motor Corporation ....F...... 315 434-9303
  East Syracuse (G-4567)
- Powercomplete LLC ....G...... 212 228-4129
  New York (G-11714)
- Premco Inc ....F...... 914 636-7095
  New Rochelle (G-8966)
- Protective Power Systms & Cntr ....F...... 845 773-9016
  Poughkeepsie (G-13944)
- Ruhle Companies Inc ....E...... 914 287-4000
  Valhalla (G-16398)
- Sima Technologies LLC ....G...... 412 828-9130
  Hauppauge (G-6215)

Employee Codes: A=Over 500 employees, B=251-500
C=101-250, D=51-100, E=20-50, F=10-19, G=5-9

MOTORS: Generators

Supergen Products LLC .... G 315 573-7887
  Newark (G-12765)
Troy Belting and Supply Co .... D 518 272-4920
  Watervliet (G-16715)
W J Albro Machine Works Inc .... G 631 345-0657
  Yaphank (G-17424)

MOTORS: Torque

Aeroflex Incorporated .... B 516 694-6700
  Plainview (G-13608)

MOVIE THEATERS, EXC DRIVE-IN

Sony Broadband Entertainment ...... F 212 833-6800
  New York (G-12156)
Taste and See Entrmt Inc .... G 516 285-3010
  Valley Stream (G-16452)

MOWERS & ACCESSORIES

Benishty Brothers Corp .... G 646 339-9991
  Woodmere (G-17329)

MULTIPLEXERS: Telephone & Telegraph

Fiberall Corp .... E 516 371-5200
  Inwood (G-6796)
Toshiba America Inc .... E 212 596-0600
  New York (G-12398)

MUSEUMS

Historcal Soc of Mddltown Walk .... G 845 342-0941
  Middletown (G-8478)

MUSEUMS & ART GALLERIES

Njf Publishing Corp .... G 631 345-5200
  Shirley (G-15450)
Paley Studios Ltd .... F 585 232-5260
  Rochester (G-14588)

MUSIC BROADCASTING SVCS

Michael Karp Music Inc .... G 212 840-3285
  New York (G-11277)

MUSIC COPYING SVCS

Boosey & Hawkes Inc .... E 212 358-5300
  New York (G-9490)

MUSIC DISTRIBUTION APPARATUS

Nykon Inc .... G 315 483-0504
  Sodus (G-15526)
Tunecore Inc .... E 646 651-1060
  Brooklyn (G-2706)

MUSIC LICENSING & ROYALTIES

Warner Music Group Corp .... B 212 275-2000
  New York (G-12616)

MUSIC LICENSING TO RADIO STATIONS

Historic TW Inc .... E 212 484-8000
  New York (G-10530)
Time Warner Companies Inc .... D 212 484-8000
  New York (G-12369)

MUSIC RECORDING PRODUCER

Euphorbia Productions Ltd .... G 212 533-1700
  New York (G-10136)

MUSICAL ENTERTAINERS

Wmg Acquisition Corp .... F 212 275-2000
  New York (G-12676)

MUSICAL INSTRUMENT PARTS & ACCESS, WHOLESALE

Carl Fischer LLC .... E 212 777-0900
  New York (G-9580)
Musicskins LLC .... F 646 827-4271
  Brooklyn (G-2349)

MUSICAL INSTRUMENT REPAIR

Fodera Guitars Inc .... F 718 832-3455
  Brooklyn (G-1991)
Guitar Specialist Inc .... G 914 533-5589
  South Salem (G-15559)

Sadowsky Guitars Ltd .... F 718 433-1990
  Long Island City (G-7900)

MUSICAL INSTRUMENTS & ACCESS: Carrying Cases

Roadie Products Inc .... E 631 567-8588
  Holbrook (G-6497)
Xstatic Pro Inc .... F 718 237-2299
  Brooklyn (G-2784)

MUSICAL INSTRUMENTS & ACCESS: NEC

DAddario & Company Inc .... E 718 599-6660
  Brooklyn (G-1833)
DAndrea Inc .... E 516 496-2200
  Syosset (G-15839)
Evans Manufacturing LLC .... D 631 439-3300
  Farmingdale (G-4999)
Fodera Guitars Inc .... F 718 832-3455
  Brooklyn (G-1991)
J D Calato Manufacturing Co .... G 716 285-3546
  Niagara Falls (G-12855)
Muzet Inc .... F 315 452-0050
  Syracuse (G-16015)
Nathan Love LLC .... F 212 925-7111
  New York (G-11366)
Roli USA Inc .... F 412 600-4840
  New York (G-11929)
Samson Technologies Corp .... D 631 784-2200
  Hicksville (G-6418)
Sound Source Inc .... G 585 271-5370
  Rochester (G-14717)
Steinway Musical Instrs Inc .... E 781 894-9770
  New York (G-12215)

MUSICAL INSTRUMENTS & ACCESS: Pianos

Steinway Inc .... A 718 721-2600
  Long Island City (G-7916)
Steinway and Sons .... C 718 721-2600
  Long Island City (G-7917)

MUSICAL INSTRUMENTS & ACCESS: Pipe Organs

Kerner and Merchant .... G 315 463-8023
  East Syracuse (G-4562)

MUSICAL INSTRUMENTS & PARTS: Brass

Siegfrieds Call Inc .... G 845 765-2275
  Beacon (G-785)

MUSICAL INSTRUMENTS & PARTS: String

Barbera Transduser Systems .... F 718 816-3025
  Staten Island (G-15664)
DAddario & Company Inc .... D 631 439-3300
  Melville (G-8339)
DAddario & Company Inc .... A 631 439-3300
  Farmingdale (G-4982)
Sadowsky Guitars Ltd .... F 718 433-1990
  Long Island City (G-7900)

MUSICAL INSTRUMENTS & SPLYS STORES

Albert Augustine Ltd .... D 718 913-9635
  Mount Vernon (G-8706)
Barbera Transduser Systems .... F 718 816-3025
  Staten Island (G-15664)
Carl Fischer LLC .... E 212 777-0900
  New York (G-9580)
DAndrea Inc .... E 516 496-2200
  Syosset (G-15839)
Fodera Guitars Inc .... F 718 832-3455
  Brooklyn (G-1991)
Hipshot Products Inc .... F 607 532-9404
  Interlaken (G-6786)

MUSICAL INSTRUMENTS & SPLYS STORES: Pianos

Steinway Inc .... A 718 721-2600
  Long Island City (G-7916)
Steinway and Sons .... C 718 721-2600
  Long Island City (G-7917)

MUSICAL INSTRUMENTS WHOLESALERS

Samson Technologies Corp .... D 631 784-2200
  Hicksville (G-6418)

MUSICAL INSTRUMENTS: Blowers, Pipe Organ

Elsener Organ Works Inc .... G 631 254-2744
  Deer Park (G-4159)

MUSICAL INSTRUMENTS: Electric & Electronic

New Sensor Corporation .... D 718 937-8300
  Long Island City (G-7856)

MUSICAL INSTRUMENTS: Guitars & Parts, Electric & Acoustic

DAngelico Guitars of America ...... G 732 380-0995
  New York (G-9855)
Dimarzio Inc .... E 718 442-6655
  Staten Island (G-15686)
Guitar Specialist Inc .... G 914 533-5589
  South Salem (G-15559)
Hipshot Products Inc .... F 607 532-9404
  Interlaken (G-6786)
Luthier Musical Corp .... G 212 397-6038
  New York (G-11094)
Stuart Spector Designs Ltd .... G 845 246-6124
  Saugerties (G-15225)

MUSICAL INSTRUMENTS: Harmonicas

Jason Ladanye Guitar Piano & H ... E 518 527-3973
  Albany (G-91)

MUSICAL INSTRUMENTS: Organs

Gluck Orgelbau Inc .... G 212 233-2684
  New York (G-10365)
Leonard Carlson .... G 518 477-4710
  East Greenbush (G-4423)

MUSICAL INSTRUMENTS: Reeds

Rico International .... G 818 767-7711
  Farmingdale (G-5109)

MUSICAL INSTRUMENTS: Strings, Instrument

Albert Augustine Ltd .... D 718 913-9635
  Mount Vernon (G-8706)
E & O Mari Inc .... D 845 562-4400
  Newburgh (G-12775)
Mari Strings Inc .... F 212 799-6781
  New York (G-11172)

NAIL SALONS

Angel Tips Nail Salon .... G 718 225-8300
  Little Neck (G-7529)

NAME PLATES: Engraved Or Etched

Advanced Graphics Company ...... F 607 692-7875
  Whitney Point (G-17248)
C & M Products Inc .... G 315 471-3303
  Syracuse (G-15899)
Harold Wood Co Inc .... G 716 873-1535
  Buffalo (G-3007)
Nameplate Mfrs of Amer .... E 631 752-0055
  Farmingdale (G-5070)
Precision Design Systems Inc ...... E 585 426-4500
  Rochester (G-14614)
The Gramecy Group .... G 518 348-1325
  Clifton Park (G-3736)

NAMEPLATES

Decal Makers Inc .... E 516 221-7200
  Bellmore (G-813)
Island Nameplate Inc .... G 845 651-4005
  Florida (G-5220)
Modern Decal Co .... G 315 622-2778
  Liverpool (G-7561)
Signature Name Plate Co Inc ...... G 585 321-9960
  Rochester (G-14709)

NATIONAL SECURITY FORCES

Metadure Defense & SEC LLC ..... F 631 249-2141
  Farmingdale (G-5058)

NATURAL BUTANE PRODUCTION
Center State Propane LLC ....G........ 315 841-4044
  Waterville *(G-16700)*
Green Buffalo Fuel LLC ....F 716 768-0600
  Tonawanda *(G-16185)*

NATURAL GAS DISTRIBUTION TO CONSUMERS
Noco Incorporated ....G........ 716 833-6626
  Tonawanda *(G-16205)*

NATURAL GAS LIQUIDS PRODUCTION
Nfe Management LLC ....F 212 798-6100
  New York *(G-11442)*
Western Oil and Gas JV Inc ....G........ 914 967-4758
  Rye *(G-15095)*

NATURAL GAS PRODUCTION
County Energy Corp ....G........ 718 626-7000
  Brooklyn *(G-1807)*
Flownet LLC ....G........ 716 685-4036
  Lancaster *(G-7340)*
Green Buffalo Fuel LLC ....F 716 768-0600
  Tonawanda *(G-16185)*
Ipp Energy LLC ....G........ 607 773-3307
  Binghamton *(G-923)*
Repsol Oil & Gas Usa LLC ....G........ 607 562-4000
  Horseheads *(G-6618)*
Reserve Gas Company Inc ....G........ 716 937-9484
  Alden *(G-185)*

NATURAL GAS TRANSMISSION & DISTRIBUTION
Lenape Energy Inc ....G........ 585 344-1200
  Alexander *(G-190)*
Lenape Resources Inc ....F 585 344-1200
  Alexander *(G-191)*

NATURAL GASOLINE PRODUCTION
20 Bliss St Inc ....G........ 716 326-2790
  Westfield *(G-17073)*

NATURAL PROPANE PRODUCTION
Paraco Gas Corporation ....G........ 845 279-8414
  Brewster *(G-1223)*
Paraco Gas Corporation ....E 800 647-4427
  Rye Brook *(G-15099)*

NAUTICAL & NAVIGATIONAL INSTRUMENT REPAIR SVCS
Moor Electronics Inc ....G........ 716 821-5304
  Buffalo *(G-3095)*

NAVIGATIONAL SYSTEMS & INSTRUMENTS
Lockheed Martin Corporation ....A 315 456-0123
  Liverpool *(G-7554)*

NET & NETTING PRDTS
Apex Texicon Inc ....E 516 239-4400
  New York *(G-9223)*

NETS: Laundry
Sky Laundromat Inc ....E 718 639-7070
  Jamaica *(G-6986)*

NEW & USED CAR DEALERS
Auto Sport Designs Inc ....F 631 425-1555
  Huntington Station *(G-6735)*
Fuccillo Ford Nelliston Inc ....G........ 518 993-5555
  Nelliston *(G-8820)*
Zappone Chrysler Jeep Ddge Inc ....F 518 982-0610
  Halfmoon *(G-5939)*

NEWS DEALERS & NEWSSTANDS
Chronicle Express ....F 315 536-4422
  Penn Yan *(G-13531)*

NEWS FEATURE SYNDICATES
Hearst Business Media Corp ....F 631 650-4441
  Great River *(G-5870)*

Hearst Corporation ....A 212 649-2000
  New York *(G-10482)*
New York Times Company ....B 212 556-1234
  New York *(G-11429)*

NEWS PICTURES GATHERING & DISTRIBUTING SVCS
Kraus Organization Limited ....G........ 212 686-5411
  New York *(G-10927)*

NEWS SYNDICATES
Thomson Reuters Corporation ....A 646 223-4000
  New York *(G-12349)*

NEWSPAPERS & PERIODICALS NEWS REPORTING SVCS
Dow Jones & Company Inc ....E 212 597-5983
  New York *(G-9966)*

NEWSPAPERS, WHOLESALE
Best Line Inc ....G........ 917 670-6210
  Staten Island *(G-15666)*
Nyt Capital LLC ....F 212 556-1234
  New York *(G-11503)*

NEWSSTAND
Division Street News Corp ....F 518 234-2515
  Cobleskill *(G-3761)*

NICKEL ALLOY
Nickel City Studios Photo Jour ....G........ 716 200-0956
  Buffalo *(G-3115)*
Nickel Group LLC ....G........ 212 706-7906
  Rockaway Park *(G-14814)*

NONCURRENT CARRYING WIRING DEVICES
Chase Corporation ....F 631 827-0476
  Northport *(G-13027)*
Complete SEC & Cntrls Inc ....F 631 421-7200
  Huntington Station *(G-6739)*
Delta Metal Products Co Inc ....E 718 855-4200
  Brooklyn *(G-1852)*
Lapp Insulators LLC ....C 585 768-6221
  Le Roy *(G-7436)*
Zierick Manufacturing Corp ....D 800 882-8020
  Mount Kisco *(G-8690)*

NONFERROUS: Rolling & Drawing, NEC
Continental Cordage Corp ....D 315 655-9800
  Cazenovia *(G-3470)*
Cpp-Syracuse Inc ....E 315 687-0014
  Chittenango *(G-3662)*
Eco-Bat America LLC ....C 845 692-4414
  Middletown *(G-8472)*
Medi-Ray Inc ....D 877 898-3003
  Tuckahoe *(G-16295)*
Nationwide Precision Pdts Corp ....B 585 272-7100
  Rochester *(G-14549)*
Selectrode Industries Inc ....G........ 631 547-5470
  Huntington Station *(G-6760)*
Sigmund Cohn Corp ....D 914 664-5300
  Mount Vernon *(G-8780)*

NONMETALLIC MINERALS: Support Activities, Exc Fuels
Crystal Ceres Industries Inc ....D 716 283-0445
  Niagara Falls *(G-12830)*

NOTARIES PUBLIC
Chesu Inc ....F 239 564-2803
  East Hampton *(G-4427)*

NOTEBOOKS, MADE FROM PURCHASED MATERIALS
Anne Taintor Inc ....G........ 718 483-9312
  Brooklyn *(G-1613)*

NOTIONS: Button Blanks & Molds
Connection Mold Inc ....G........ 585 458-6463
  Rochester *(G-14307)*

NOTIONS: Pins, Straight, Steel Or Brass
Karp Overseas Corporation ....E 718 784-2105
  Maspeth *(G-8179)*

NOTIONS: Studs, Shirt, Exc Precious/Semi Metal/Stone
Columbia Button Nailhead Corp ....F 718 386-3414
  Brooklyn *(G-1791)*

NOVELTIES
Best Priced Products Inc ....G........ 914 345-3800
  Elmsford *(G-4744)*
Fish & Crown Ltd ....D 212 707-9603
  New York *(G-10226)*
Jacobs Juice Corp ....G........ 646 255-2860
  Brooklyn *(G-2131)*
Jpm Fine Woodworking LLC ....G........ 516 236-7605
  Jericho *(G-7106)*
Orlandi Inc ....D 631 756-0110
  Farmingdale *(G-5081)*
Orlandi Inc ....E 631 756-0110
  Farmingdale *(G-5082)*

NOVELTIES & SPECIALTIES: Metal
Buttons & Trimcom Inc ....F 212 868-1971
  New York *(G-9537)*
Criterion Bell & Specialty ....E 718 788-2600
  Brooklyn *(G-1818)*
Polich Tallix Inc ....D 845 567-9464
  Walden *(G-16554)*
Split Rock Trading Co Inc ....G........ 631 929-3261
  Wading River *(G-16546)*
Stylebuilt Accessories Inc ....F 917 439-0578
  East Rockaway *(G-4493)*

NOVELTIES: Leather
Art Leather Mfg Co Inc ....A 516 867-4716
  Oyster Bay *(G-13392)*

NOVELTIES: Paper, Made From Purchased Materials
National Advertising & Prtg ....G........ 212 629-7650
  New York *(G-11369)*
P C I Paper Conversions Inc ....F 315 437-1641
  Syracuse *(G-16030)*

NOVELTIES: Plastic
Buttons & Trimcom Inc ....F 212 868-1971
  New York *(G-9537)*
Frisch Plastics Corp ....G........ 973 685-5936
  Hartsdale *(G-6017)*
GPM Associates LLC ....E 585 335-3940
  Dansville *(G-4103)*
Kling Magnetics Inc ....E 518 392-4000
  Chatham *(G-3586)*
Pelican Products Co Inc ....E 718 860-3220
  Bronx *(G-1424)*
Pleasure Chest Sales Ltd ....E 212 242-4185
  New York *(G-11697)*
Ppr Direct Inc ....F 718 965-8600
  Brooklyn *(G-2446)*
Royal Industries Inc ....E 718 369-3046
  Brooklyn *(G-2531)*
Skd Distribution Corp ....E 718 525-6000
  Jericho *(G-7120)*

NOVELTY SHOPS
Mgd Brands Inc ....E 516 545-0150
  Plainview *(G-13648)*

NOZZLES & SPRINKLERS Lawn Hose
Artys Sprnklr Svc Instllation ....F 516 538-4371
  East Meadow *(G-4438)*

NOZZLES: Spray, Aerosol, Paint Or Insecticide
Sono-Tek Corporation ....D 845 795-2020
  Milton *(G-8518)*

NUCLEAR REACTORS: Military Or Indl
Energy Nuclear Operations ....E 315 342-0055
  Oswego *(G-13356)*

NURSERIES & LAWN & GARDEN SPLY STORES, RETAIL: Fertilizer

Scotts Company LLC .... E 631 289-7444
  Yaphank (G-17416)

NURSERIES & LAWN & GARDEN SPLY STORES, RETAIL: Sod

E F Lippert Co Inc .... F 716 373-1100
  Allegany (G-202)

NURSERIES & LAWN & GARDEN SPLY STORES, RETAIL: Top Soil

East Coast Mines Ltd .... E 631 653-5445
  East Quogue (G-4469)
Grosso Materials Inc .... F 845 361-5211
  Montgomery (G-8631)
Hampton Sand Corp .... G 631 325-5533
  Westhampton (G-17086)

NURSERIES & LAWN/GARDEN SPLY STORE, RET: Lawnmowers/Tractors

Kelley Farm & Garden Inc .... E 518 234-2332
  Cobleskill (G-3763)

NURSERY & GARDEN CENTERS

Birkett Mills .... G 315 536-3311
  Penn Yan (G-13529)
G & S Farm & Home Inc .... G 716 542-9922
  Akron (G-20)

NUTS: Metal

Buckley Qc Fasteners Inc .... E 716 662-1490
  Orchard Park (G-13278)
Dependable Acme Threaded Pdts . G 516 338-4700
  Westbury (G-17004)
Zierick Manufacturing Corp .... D 800 882-8020
  Mount Kisco (G-8690)

OFFICE EQPT WHOLESALERS

Artistic Products LLC .... E 631 435-0200
  Hauppauge (G-6045)
Automecha International Ltd .... E 607 843-2235
  Oxford (G-13388)
DAF Office Networks Inc .... G 315 699-7070
  Cicero (G-3673)
Finesse Creations Inc .... F 718 692-2100
  Brooklyn (G-1977)

OFFICE EQPT, WHOLESALE: Duplicating Machines

Media Technologies Ltd .... F 631 467-7900
  Eastport (G-4596)

OFFICE FIXTURES: Exc Wood

Air Crafters Inc .... C 631 471-7788
  Ronkonkoma (G-14883)
Evans & Paul LLC .... E 516 576-0800
  Plainview (G-13629)

OFFICE FIXTURES: Wood

Bauerschmidt & Sons Inc .... D 718 528-3500
  Jamaica (G-6934)

OFFICE FURNITURE REPAIR & MAINTENANCE SVCS

Davies Office Refurbishing Inc ...... C 518 426-7188
  Albany (G-72)
Jim Quinn .... F 518 356-0398
  Schenectady (G-15297)
Roberts Office Furn Cncpts Inc ..... E 315 451-9185
  Liverpool (G-7572)

OFFICE SPLY & STATIONERY STORES

American Office Supply Inc .... F 516 294-9444
  Westbury (G-16994)
Flynns Inc .... F 212 339-8700
  New York (G-10234)
Tripi Engraving Co Inc .... E 718 383-6500
  Brooklyn (G-2700)

OFFICE SPLY & STATIONERY STORES: Office Forms & Splys

A & D Offset Printers Ltd .... G 516 746-2476
  Mineola (G-8520)
Datagraphic Business Systems ..... G 516 485-9069
  Brentwood (G-1177)
Grant Hamilton .... F 716 652-0320
  East Aurora (G-4396)
Idc Printing & Sty Co Inc .... G 516 599-0400
  Lynbrook (G-7979)
J P Printing Inc .... G 516 293-6110
  Farmingdale (G-5023)
Kleer-Fax Inc .... D 631 225-1100
  Amityville (G-303)
Richard Ruffner .... F 631 234-4600
  Central Islip (G-3536)
Rmd Holding Inc .... G 845 628-0030
  Mahopac (G-8031)
Short Run Forms Inc .... D 631 567-7171
  Bohemia (G-1130)

OFFICE SPLY & STATIONERY STORES: Writing Splys

Tefft Publishers Inc .... G 518 692-9290
  Greenwich (G-5914)

OFFICE SPLYS, NEC, WHOLESALE

DAF Office Networks Inc .... G 315 699-7070
  Cicero (G-3673)
Falconer Printing & Design Inc ..... F 716 665-2121
  Falconer (G-4906)
Rike Enterprises Inc .... F 631 277-8338
  Islip (G-6851)
Robert Tabatznik Assoc Inc .... F 845 336-4555
  Kingston (G-7237)

OFFICES & CLINICS OF DENTISTS: Prosthodontist

Goldberg Prosthetic & Orthotic ... F 631 689-6606
  East Setauket (G-4502)

OFFICES & CLINICS OF DRS, MED: Specialized Practitioners

Erika T Schwartz MD PC .... G 212 873-3420
  New York (G-10110)

OFFICES & CLINICS OF HEALTH PRACTITIONERS: Nutritionist

Everlast Worldwide Inc .... E 212 239-0990
  New York (G-10147)

OIL & GAS FIELD MACHINERY

Basin Holdings US LLC .... E 212 695-7376
  New York (G-9382)
Derrick Corporation .... C 716 683-9010
  Buffalo (G-2928)
Schlumberger Technology Corp 607 378-0105
  Horseheads (G-6621)
Smith International Inc .... F 585 265-2330
  Ontario (G-13237)

OIL FIELD MACHINERY & EQPT

Anchor Commerce Trading Corp .. G 516 881-3485
  Atlantic Beach (G-467)
Desmi-Afti Inc .... E 716 662-0632
  Orchard Park (G-13292)

OIL FIELD SVCS, NEC

Alba Fuel Corp .... G 718 931-1700
  Bronx (G-1267)
Bluebar Oil Co Inc .... F 315 245-4328
  Blossvale (G-991)
Fuel Energy Services USA Ltd 607 846-2650
  Horseheads (G-6607)
Gas Field Specialists Inc .... D 716 378-6422
  Horseheads (G-6608)
Grit Energy Services Inc 212 701-4500
  New York (G-10409)
Marcellus Energy Services LLC .... E 607 236-0038
  Candor (G-3404)
Petro Inc 516 686-1900
  Hicksville (G-6412)

Rpc Inc .... E 347 873-3935
  Elmont (G-4738)
Schneider Amalco Inc .... F 917 470-9674
  New York (G-12009)
U S Energy Development Corp .... D 716 636-0401
  Getzville (G-5617)

OIL ROYALTY TRADERS

Schneider Amalco Inc .... F 917 470-9674
  New York (G-12009)

OILS & GREASES: Blended & Compounded

Battenfeld-American Inc .... E 716 822-8410
  Buffalo (G-2856)
Valvoline Inc .... G 914 684-0170
  White Plains (G-17205)

OILS & GREASES: Lubricating

Battenfeld Grease Oil Corp NY ..... E 716 695-2100
  North Tonawanda (G-12978)
Baums Castorine Company Inc ... G 315 336-8154
  Rome (G-14834)
Beka World LP .... G 905 821-1050
  Buffalo (G-2858)
Bestline International RES Inc ..... G 518 631-2177
  Schenectady (G-15263)
Black Bear Company Inc .... E 718 784-7330
  Long Island City (G-7718)
Blaser Swisslube Holding Corp .... F 845 294-3200
  Goshen (G-5748)
Castoleum Corporation .... F 914 664-5877
  Mount Vernon (G-8715)
Chemlube International LLC .... F 914 381-5800
  Harrison (G-6000)
Chemlube Marketing Inc .... F 914 381-5800
  Harrison (G-6001)
Finish Line Technologies Inc .... E 631 666-7300
  Hauppauge (G-6099)
Inland Vacuum Industries Inc ..... F 585 293-3330
  Churchville (G-3667)
Interdynamics .... F 914 241-1423
  Mount Kisco (G-8672)
Loobrica International Corp .... F 347 997-0296
  Staten Island (G-15722)
Noco Incorporated .... G 716 833-6626
  Tonawanda (G-16205)
Oil and Lubricant Depot LLC .... F 718 258-9220
  Amityville (G-317)
Ore-Lube Corporation .... F 631 205-0030
  Bellport (G-833)
Polycast Industries Inc .... G 631 595-2530
  Bay Shore (G-722)
Specialty Silicone Pdts Inc .... E 518 885-8826
  Ballston Spa (G-608)
Tribology Inc .... E 631 345-3000
  Yaphank (G-17421)

OILS: Essential

Natures Warehouse .... F 800 215-4372
  Philadelphia (G-13564)
Torre Products Co Inc .... F 212 925-8989
  New York (G-12396)

OILS: Lubricating

Oil Solutions Intl Inc .... G 631 608-8889
  Amityville (G-318)
R H Crown Co Inc .... E 518 762-4589
  Johnstown (G-7153)

OILS: Lubricating

Blaser Production Inc .... F 845 294-3200
  Goshen (G-5747)
Mdi Holdings LLC .... A 212 559-1127
  New York (G-11228)
Monroe Fluid Technology Inc ...... E 585 392-3434
  Hilton (G-6444)
Tallmans Express Lube .... G 315 266-1033
  New Hartford (G-8857)

OILS: Orange

Solvents Company Inc .... F 631 595-9300
  Kingston (G-7238)

OILS: Still

E and V Energy Corporation .... F 315 786-2067
  Watertown (G-16672)

PRODUCT SECTION

OINTMENTS

Easton Pharmaceuticals Inc ....G...... 347 284-0192
  Lewiston *(G-7454)*
Slv Labs LLC ....G...... 631 901-1170
  Hauppauge *(G-6217)*

ON-LINE DATABASE INFORMATION RETRIEVAL SVCS

Endava Inc ....G...... 212 920-7240
  New York *(G-10083)*
News Corporation ....C...... 212 416-3400
  New York *(G-11435)*
Optionline LLC ....E...... 516 218-3225
  Garden City *(G-5538)*
Penton Media Inc ....B...... 212 204-4200
  New York *(G-11627)*

OPERATOR: Apartment Buildings

Gallagher Printing Inc ....E...... 716 873-2434
  Buffalo *(G-2977)*
Hospitality Inc ....E...... 212 268-1930
  New York *(G-10554)*

OPERATOR: Nonresidential Buildings

Omega Industries & Development ....E...... 516 349-8010
  Plainview *(G-13654)*

OPHTHALMIC GOODS

21st Century Optics Inc ....E...... 347 527-1079
  Long Island City *(G-7675)*
Accu Coat Inc ....G...... 585 288-2330
  Rochester *(G-14181)*
Bausch & Lomb Holdings Inc ....G...... 585 338-6000
  New York *(G-9384)*
Bausch & Lomb Incorporated ....B...... 585 338-6000
  Rochester *(G-14242)*
Bausch & Lomb Incorporated ....B...... 585 338-6000
  Rochester *(G-14243)*
Designs For Vision Inc ....C...... 631 585-3300
  Ronkonkoma *(G-14922)*
Doug Lambertson Od ....G...... 718 698-9300
  Staten Island *(G-15687)*
Esc Control Electronics LLC ....E...... 631 467-5328
  Sayville *(G-15236)*
Eyeworks Inc ....G...... 585 454-4470
  Rochester *(G-14388)*
Glasses USA LLC ....F...... 212 784-6094
  New York *(G-10349)*
Lens Lab ....G...... 718 379-2020
  Bronx *(G-1385)*
Lens Lab Express ....G...... 718 921-5488
  Brooklyn *(G-2212)*
Lens Lab Express of Graham Ave ......G...... 718 486-0117
  Brooklyn *(G-2213)*
Lens Lab Express Southern Blvd ....G...... 718 626-5184
  Astoria *(G-446)*
North Bronx Retinal & Ophthlmi ....G...... 347 535-4932
  Bronx *(G-1415)*
Oakley Inc ....D...... 212 575-0960
  New York *(G-11506)*
Surgical Design Corp ....F...... 914 273-2445
  Armonk *(G-418)*
Wyeth Holdings LLC ....D...... 845 602-5000
  Pearl River *(G-13493)*

OPHTHALMIC GOODS WHOLESALERS

21st Century Optics Inc ....E...... 347 527-1079
  Long Island City *(G-7675)*
Lens Lab Express Southern Blvd ....G...... 718 626-5184
  Astoria *(G-446)*
Winchester Optical Company ....E...... 607 734-4251
  Elmira *(G-4718)*

OPHTHALMIC GOODS: Frames & Parts, Eyeglass & Spectacle

Art-Craft Optical Company Inc ....E...... 585 546-6640
  Rochester *(G-14231)*
His Vision Inc ....E...... 585 254-0022
  Rochester *(G-14457)*
Zyloware Corporation ....D...... 914 708-1200
  Port Chester *(G-13785)*

OPHTHALMIC GOODS: Frames, Lenses & Parts, Eyeglasses

Eye Deal Eyewear Inc ....G...... 716 297-1500
  Niagara Falls *(G-12838)*
Moscot Wholesale Corp ....G...... 212 647-1550
  New York *(G-11334)*
Optika Eyes Ltd ....G...... 631 567-8852
  Sayville *(G-15242)*
Winchester Optical Company ....E...... 607 734-4251
  Elmira *(G-4718)*

OPHTHALMIC GOODS: Lenses, Ophthalmic

Co-Optics America Lab Inc ....E...... 607 432-0557
  Oneonta *(G-13201)*
Tri-Supreme Optical LLC ....D...... 631 249-2020
  Farmingdale *(G-5144)*

OPHTHALMIC GOODS: Spectacles

Modo Retail LLC ....E...... 212 965-4900
  New York *(G-11316)*
Spectacle Optical Inc ....G...... 646 706-1015
  Rego Park *(G-14051)*

OPHTHALMIC GOODS: Temples & Fronts, Ophthalmic

Kathmando Valley Preservation ....F...... 212 727-0074
  New York *(G-10856)*

OPTICAL GOODS STORES

Hart Specialties Inc ....D...... 631 226-5600
  Amityville *(G-291)*
Match Eyewear LLC ....E...... 516 877-0170
  Westbury *(G-17036)*
Optika Eyes Ltd ....G...... 631 567-8852
  Sayville *(G-15242)*
Parker Warby Retail Inc ....G...... 646 517-5223
  New York *(G-11589)*

OPTICAL GOODS STORES: Opticians

Eyeglass Service Industries ....G...... 914 666-3150
  Bedford Hills *(G-800)*
Lens Lab Express ....G...... 718 921-5488
  Brooklyn *(G-2212)*

OPTICAL INSTRUMENTS & APPARATUS

Aeroflex Incorporated ....B...... 516 694-6700
  Plainview *(G-13608)*
Applied Image Inc ....E...... 585 482-0300
  Rochester *(G-14225)*
Carl Zeiss Inc ....C...... 914 747-1800
  Thornwood *(G-16140)*
Halo Optical Products Inc ....D...... 518 773-4256
  Gloversville *(G-5728)*
Hart Specialties Inc ....D...... 631 226-5600
  Amityville *(G-291)*
Kevin Freeman ....G...... 631 447-5321
  Patchogue *(G-13452)*
Leica Microsystems Inc ....G...... 716 686-3000
  Depew *(G-4286)*
Lumetrics Inc ....F...... 585 214-2455
  Rochester *(G-14505)*
Plx Inc ....E...... 631 586-4190
  Deer Park *(G-4214)*
Westchester Technologies Inc ....E...... 914 736-1034
  Peekskill *(G-13511)*

OPTICAL INSTRUMENTS & LENSES

21st Century Optics Inc ....E...... 347 527-1079
  Long Island City *(G-7675)*
Aeroflex Plainview Inc ....B...... 516 694-6700
  Plainview *(G-13609)*
Anorad Corporation ....C...... 631 380-2100
  East Setauket *(G-4495)*
Apollo Optical Systems Inc ....E...... 585 272-6170
  West Henrietta *(G-16901)*
Binoptics LLC ....E...... 607 257-3200
  Ithaca *(G-6862)*
Caliber Imging Diagnostics Inc ....E...... 585 239-9800
  Rochester *(G-14273)*
CK Coatings ....G...... 585 502-0425
  Le Roy *(G-7429)*
Corning Tropel Corporation ....C...... 585 377-3200
  Fairport *(G-4857)*
CVI Laser LLC ....D...... 585 244-7220
  Rochester *(G-14318)*
Dorsey Metrology Intl Inc ....E...... 845 229-2929
  Poughkeepsie *(G-13914)*
Dynamic Laboratories Inc ....E...... 631 231-7474
  Ronkonkoma *(G-14923)*
Eele Laboratories LLC ....F...... 631 244-0051
  Bohemia *(G-1059)*
Exfo Burleigh Pdts Group Inc ....D...... 585 301-1530
  Canandaigua *(G-3374)*
Genesis Vision Inc ....E...... 585 254-0193
  Rochester *(G-14418)*
Gradient Lens Corporation ....E...... 585 235-2620
  Rochester *(G-14432)*
Gurley Precision Instrs Inc ....C...... 518 272-6300
  Troy *(G-16259)*
Isp Optics Corporation ....D...... 914 591-3070
  Irvington *(G-6814)*
Keon Optics Inc ....F...... 845 429-7103
  Stony Point *(G-15796)*
Match Eyewear LLC ....E...... 516 877-0170
  Westbury *(G-17036)*
Micatu Inc ....G...... 888 705-8836
  Horseheads *(G-6610)*
Navitar Inc ....D...... 585 359-4000
  Rochester *(G-14550)*
Nikon Instruments Inc ....D...... 631 547-4200
  Melville *(G-8372)*
Novanta Inc ....E...... 818 341-5151
  Syracuse *(G-16020)*
Optics Plus Inc ....G...... 716 744-2636
  Tonawanda *(G-16208)*
Optipro Systems LLC ....D...... 585 265-0160
  Ontario *(G-13230)*
Orafol Americas Inc ....F...... 585 272-0290
  West Henrietta *(G-16918)*
Planar Optics Inc ....G...... 585 671-0100
  Webster *(G-16754)*
Qioptiq Inc ....E...... 585 223-2370
  Fairport *(G-4878)*
Rochester Photonics Corp ....D...... 585 387-0674
  Rochester *(G-14668)*
RPC Photonics Inc ....F...... 585 272-2840
  Rochester *(G-14682)*
Santa Fe Manufacturing Corp ....G...... 631 234-0100
  Hauppauge *(G-6208)*
Schott Corporation ....D...... 315 255-2791
  Auburn *(G-514)*
Spectral Systems LLC ....E...... 845 896-2200
  Hopewell Junction *(G-6585)*
Stefan Sydor Optics Inc ....E...... 585 271-7300
  Rochester *(G-14726)*
Steven John Opticians ....G...... 718 543-3336
  Bronx *(G-1463)*
Surgical Design Corp ....F...... 914 273-2445
  Armonk *(G-418)*
Synergy Intrntnal Optrnics LLC ....E...... 631 277-0500
  Ronkonkoma *(G-15014)*
Tele-Vue Optics Inc ....E...... 845 469-4551
  Chester *(G-3646)*
Unimed Optical ....G...... 718 384-3600
  Brooklyn *(G-2718)*
US Optical LLC ....E...... 315 463-4800
  East Syracuse *(G-4590)*
Va Inc ....E...... 585 385-5930
  Rochester *(G-14777)*
Victory Vision Care Inc ....G...... 718 622-2020
  Brooklyn *(G-2743)*
Welch Allyn Inc ....A...... 315 685-4100
  Skaneateles Falls *(G-15494)*

OPTICAL SCANNING SVCS

Kjckd Inc ....G...... 518 435-9696
  Latham *(G-7395)*
Printech Business Systems Inc ....F...... 212 290-2542
  New York *(G-11740)*

OPTOMETRIC EQPT & SPLYS WHOLESALERS

Orafol Americas Inc ....F...... 585 272-0290
  West Henrietta *(G-16918)*

ORAL PREPARATIONS

Robell Research Inc ....G...... 212 755-6577
  New York *(G-11909)*

ORDNANCE

Dyno Nobel Inc ....D...... 845 338-2144
  Ulster Park *(G-16308)*

ORDNANCE

Island Ordnance Systems LLC .... F 516 746-2100
  Mineola *(G-8550)*
Magellan Aerospace NY Inc .... C 718 699-4000
  Corona *(G-4025)*
Mil-Spec Industries Corp .... G 516 625-5787
  Glen Cove *(G-5634)*

ORGAN TUNING & REPAIR SVCS

Kerner and Merchant .... G 315 463-8023
  East Syracuse *(G-4562)*

ORGANIZATIONS: Medical Research

Encysive Pharmaceuticals Inc .... E 212 733-2323
  New York *(G-10082)*

ORGANIZATIONS: Noncommercial Biological Research

Nxxi Inc .... F 914 701-4500
  Purchase *(G-13978)*

ORGANIZATIONS: Professional

Physicalmind Institute .... F 212 343-2150
  New York *(G-11674)*
Public Relations Soc Amer Inc .... E 212 460-1400
  New York *(G-11767)*

ORGANIZATIONS: Religious

Albany Catholic Press Assoc .... G 518 453-6688
  Albany *(G-35)*
American Jewish Congress Inc .... E 212 879-4500
  New York *(G-9172)*
Nationwide Custom Services .... G 845 365-0414
  Tappan *(G-16105)*
Seneca Media Inc .... D 607 324-1425
  Hornell *(G-6593)*
United Synggue Cnsrvtive Jdism .... E 212 533-7800
  New York *(G-12487)*

ORGANIZATIONS: Research Institute

Alo Acquisition LLC .... G 518 464-0279
  Albany *(G-43)*
Katikati Inc .... G 585 678-1764
  West Henrietta *(G-16915)*

ORGANIZATIONS: Scientific Research Agency

Loobrica International Corp .... G 347 997-0296
  Staten Island *(G-15722)*

ORGANIZERS, CLOSET & DRAWER Plastic

Cubbies Unlimited Corporation .... F 631 586-8572
  Deer Park *(G-4146)*
Plascoline Inc .... F 917 410-5754
  New York *(G-11694)*

ORNAMENTS: Christmas Tree, Exc Electrical & Glass

Criterion Bell & Specialty .... E 718 788-2600
  Brooklyn *(G-1818)*
Patience Brewster Inc .... F 315 685-8336
  Skaneateles *(G-15486)*

ORTHOPEDIC SUNDRIES: Molded Rubber

Advanced Back Technologies .... G 631 231-0076
  Hauppauge *(G-6029)*
Certified Health Products Inc .... E 718 339-7498
  Brooklyn *(G-1770)*
Newyork Pedorthic Associates .... G 718 236-7700
  Brooklyn *(G-2380)*

OSCILLATORS

Centroid Inc .... E 516 349-0070
  Plainview *(G-13616)*

OUTLETS: Electric, Convenience

99cent World and Variety Corp .... G 212 740-0010
  New York *(G-9026)*
Another 99 Cent Paradise .... G 718 786-4578
  Sunnyside *(G-15825)*
Bronx New Way Corp .... G 347 431-1385
  Bronx *(G-1288)*
Dollar Popular Inc .... G 914 375-0361
  Yonkers *(G-17452)*
RE 99 Cents Inc .... G 718 639-2325
  Woodside *(G-17365)*

PACKAGE DESIGN SVCS

Force Digital Media Inc .... G 631 243-0243
  Deer Park *(G-4165)*
Hornet Group Inc .... D 845 858-6400
  Port Jervis *(G-13808)*
Maxworld Inc .... G 212 242-7588
  New York *(G-11213)*
Titherington Design & Mfg .... F 518 324-2205
  Plattsburgh *(G-13733)*

PACKAGED FROZEN FOODS WHOLESALERS, NEC

Bagelovers Inc .... F 607 844-3683
  Dryden *(G-4345)*

PACKAGING & LABELING SVCS

Atlantic Essential Pdts Inc .... D 631 434-8333
  Hauppauge *(G-6046)*
Bfma Holding Corporation .... E 607 753-6746
  Cortland *(G-4036)*
Ccmi Inc .... G 315 781-3270
  Geneva *(G-5583)*
Elite Roasters Inc .... F 716 626-0307
  East Amherst *(G-4386)*
F M Howell & Company .... D 607 734-6291
  Elmira *(G-4697)*
Klg Usa LLC .... A 845 856-5311
  Port Jervis *(G-13811)*
Marietta Corporation .... B 607 753-0982
  Cortland *(G-4058)*
Nice-Pak Products Inc .... B 845 365-2772
  Orangeburg *(G-13258)*
Nutra Solutions USA Inc .... E 631 392-1900
  Deer Park *(G-4207)*
Orlandi Inc .... D 631 756-0110
  Farmingdale *(G-5081)*
Orlandi Inc .... E 631 756-0110
  Farmingdale *(G-5082)*
Paul Michael Group Inc .... G 631 585-5700
  Ronkonkoma *(G-14990)*
Piezo Electronics Research .... F 845 735-9349
  Pearl River *(G-13487)*
Princeton Label & Packaging .... E 609 490-0800
  Patchogue *(G-13458)*
Products Superb Inc .... G 315 923-7057
  Clyde *(G-3756)*
Professional Disposables Inc .... A 845 365-1700
  Orangeburg *(G-13266)*
Sugar Foods Corporation .... E 212 753-6900
  New York *(G-12249)*
Universal Packg Systems Inc .... A 631 543-2277
  Hauppauge *(G-6245)*
Valentine Packaging Corp .... F 718 418-6000
  Maspeth *(G-8205)*
Weather Products Corporation .... G 315 474-8593
  Syracuse *(G-16094)*

PACKAGING MATERIALS, INDL: Wholesalers

Philpac Corporation .... E 716 875-8005
  Buffalo *(G-3147)*

PACKAGING MATERIALS, WHOLESALE

Patco Tapes Inc .... G 718 497-1527
  Maspeth *(G-8194)*
Technical Library Service Inc .... F 212 219-0770
  Brooklyn *(G-2670)*
Technical Packaging Inc .... F 516 223-2300
  Baldwin *(G-561)*
Terphane Holdings LLC .... G 585 657-5800
  Bloomfield *(G-984)*
W N Vanalstine & Sons Inc .... G 518 237-1436
  Cohoes *(G-3786)*

PACKAGING MATERIALS: Paper

Allen-Bailey Tag & Label Inc .... D 585 538-2324
  Caledonia *(G-3303)*
Anasia Inc .... G 718 588-1407
  Bronx *(G-1274)*
Apexx Omni-Graphics Inc .... F 718 326-3330
  Maspeth *(G-8147)*
Ares Box LLC .... D 718 858-8760
  Brooklyn *(G-1626)*
Bemis Company Inc .... C 631 794-2900
  Edgewood *(G-4608)*
Berry Plastics Corporation .... B 315 986-6270
  Macedon *(G-8013)*
CCL Label Inc .... C 716 852-2155
  Buffalo *(G-2889)*
Classic Labels Inc .... E 631 467-2300
  Patchogue *(G-13442)*
Colad Group LLC .... D 716 961-1776
  Buffalo *(G-2900)*
Craft Packaging Inc .... G 718 633-4045
  Brooklyn *(G-1810)*
De Luxe Packaging Corp .... E 416 754-4633
  Saugerties *(G-15212)*
Depot Label Company Inc .... G 631 467-2952
  Patchogue *(G-13443)*
General Fibre Products Corp .... D 516 358-7500
  New Hyde Park *(G-8880)*
General Trade Mark La .... E 718 979-7261
  Staten Island *(G-15698)*
Idesco Corp .... F 212 889-2530
  New York *(G-10602)*
International Paper Company .... C 585 663-1000
  Rochester *(G-14473)*
K Sidrane Inc .... E 631 393-6974
  Farmingdale *(G-5028)*
Multi Packaging Solutions Inc .... C 516 488-2000
  Hicksville *(G-6400)*
Multi Packaging Solutions Inc .... E 646 885-0005
  New York *(G-11347)*
Nameplate Mfrs of Amer .... E 631 752-0055
  Farmingdale *(G-5070)*
Nova Packaging Ltd Inc .... E 914 232-8406
  Katonah *(G-7161)*
Pactech Packaging LLC .... D 585 458-8008
  Rochester *(G-14587)*
Pactiv LLC .... B 518 562-6101
  Plattsburgh *(G-13712)*
Paperworks Industries Inc .... F 913 621-0922
  Baldwinsville *(G-572)*
Penta-Tech Coated Products LLC .... F 315 986-4098
  Macedon *(G-8019)*
Pliant LLC .... B 315 986-6286
  Macedon *(G-8020)*
Print Pack Inc .... C 404 460-7000
  Farmingdale *(G-5098)*
Printex Packaging Corporation .... D 631 234-4300
  Islandia *(G-6840)*
Quality Circle Products Inc .... D 914 736-6600
  Montrose *(G-8653)*
Rynone Packaging Corp .... G 607 565-8173
  Waverly *(G-16731)*
Saint-Gobain Prfmce Plas Corp .... C 518 642-2200
  Granville *(G-5796)*
Shaant Industries Inc .... E 716 366-3654
  Dunkirk *(G-4374)*
Time Release Sciences Inc .... E 716 823-4580
  Buffalo *(G-3245)*
Transcntinental Ultra Flex Inc .... B 718 272-9100
  Brooklyn *(G-2693)*
Valley Industrial Products Inc .... E 631 385-9300
  Huntington *(G-6727)*
Westrock Mwv LLC .... C 212 688-5000
  New York *(G-12645)*

PACKAGING MATERIALS: Paper, Coated Or Laminated

American Packaging Corporation .... G 585 254-2002
  Rochester *(G-14213)*
American Packaging Corporation .... C 585 254-9500
  Rochester *(G-14214)*
Cove Point Holdings LLC .... F 212 599-3388
  New York *(G-9800)*
Patco Tapes Inc .... G 718 497-1527
  Maspeth *(G-8194)*
Tri-Plex Packaging Corporation .... E 212 481-6070
  New York *(G-12422)*

PACKAGING MATERIALS: Paper, Thermoplastic Coated

F M Howell & Company .... D 607 734-6291
  Elmira *(G-4697)*
Smart USA Inc .... E 718 416-4400
  Glendale *(G-5679)*

PRODUCT SECTION

PAINTS, VARNISHES & SPLYS WHOLESALERS

PACKAGING MATERIALS: Plastic Film, Coated Or Laminated

Allied Converters Inc .... E 914 235-1585
  New Rochelle **(G-8931)**
Arm Global Solutions Inc .... G 844 276-4525
  Rochester **(G-14226)**
Ecoplast & Packaging LLC .... G 718 996-0800
  Brooklyn **(G-1902)**
Folene Packaging LLC .... G 917 626-6740
  Brooklyn **(G-1992)**
Kal Pac Corp .... F 845 457-7013
  Montgomery **(G-8633)**
Mason Transparent Package Inc .... E 718 792-6000
  Bronx **(G-1392)**
Packstar Group Inc .... D 716 853-1688
  Buffalo **(G-3133)**
Pregis LLC .... D 518 743-3100
  Glens Falls **(G-5712)**
RMS Packaging Inc .... F 914 205-2070
  Peekskill **(G-13506)**
Universal Packg Systems Inc .... A 631 543-2277
  Hauppauge **(G-6245)**
W E W Container Corporation .... E 718 827-8150
  Brooklyn **(G-2757)**

PACKAGING MATERIALS: Polystyrene Foam

24 Seven Enterprises Inc .... G 845 563-9033
  New Windsor **(G-8974)**
Barclay Brown Corp .... F 718 376-7166
  Brooklyn **(G-1665)**
Calpac Incorporated .... F 631 789-0502
  Amityville **(G-278)**
Cellect LLC .... C 508 744-6906
  Saint Johnsville **(G-15118)**
Chesu Inc .... F 239 564-2803
  East Hampton **(G-4427)**
Chocolate Delivery Systems Inc .... D 716 854-6050
  Buffalo **(G-2892)**
Fedex Ground Package Sys Inc .... G 800 463-3339
  Plattsburgh **(G-13691)**
First Qlty Packg Solutions LLC .... F 516 829-3030
  Great Neck **(G-5826)**
Interntnal Bus Cmmncations Inc .... E 516 352-4505
  New Hyde Park **(G-8887)**
Jamestown Container Corp .... C 716 665-4623
  Falconer **(G-4912)**
Jem Container Corp .... F 800 521-0145
  Plainview **(G-13640)**
Knoll Printing & Packaging Inc .... E 516 621-0100
  Syosset **(G-15846)**
Lamar Plastics Packaging Ltd .... G 516 378-2500
  Freeport **(G-5419)**
Printex Packaging Corporation .... D 631 234-4300
  Islandia **(G-6840)**
R D A Container Corporation .... E 585 247-2323
  Gates **(G-5578)**
Shell Containers Inc (ny) .... E 516 352-4505
  New Hyde Park **(G-8906)**
Snow Craft Co Inc .... F 516 739-1399
  New Hyde Park **(G-8907)**
Stephen Gould Corporation .... F 212 497-8180
  New York **(G-12219)**
Technical Packaging Inc .... F 516 223-2300
  Baldwin **(G-561)**
W Stuart Smith Inc .... E 585 742-3310
  Victor **(G-16535)**
Walnut Packaging Inc .... E 631 293-3836
  Farmingdale **(G-5150)**

PACKAGING MATERIALS: Resinous Impregnated Paper

Cameo Process Corp .... G 914 948-0082
  White Plains **(G-17119)**

PACKAGING: Blister Or Bubble Formed, Plastic

Di Domenico Packaging Co Inc .... G 718 727-5454
  Staten Island **(G-15685)**
Formatix Corp .... E 631 467-3399
  Ronkonkoma **(G-14930)**

PACKING & CRATING SVC

Precision Techniques Inc .... D 718 991-1440
  Stony Point **(G-15798)**

PACKING MATERIALS: Mechanical

Bag Arts Ltd .... G 212 684-7020
  New York **(G-9355)**
Gaddis Industrial Equipment .... F 516 759-3100
  Glen Cove **(G-5629)**
Technical Packaging Inc .... F 516 223-2300
  Baldwin **(G-561)**
Thermal Foams/Syracuse Inc .... E 315 699-8734
  Cicero **(G-3680)**
Unique Packaging Corporation .... G 514 341-5872
  Champlain **(G-3576)**

PACKING SVCS: Shipping

Miller Enterprises CNY Inc .... G 315 682-4999
  Manlius **(G-8108)**

PACKING: Metallic

Commercial Gaskets New York .... F 212 244-8130
  New York **(G-9745)**

PADDING: Foamed Plastics

Arm Rochester Inc .... F 585 354-5077
  Rochester **(G-14227)**
Philpac Corporation .... E 716 875-8005
  Buffalo **(G-3147)**

PADS: Desk, Exc Paper

Star Desk Pad Co Inc .... E 914 963-9400
  Yonkers **(G-17504)**

PADS: Desk, Paper, Made From Purchased Materials

General Diaries Corporation .... F 516 371-2244
  Inwood **(G-6797)**

PADS: Mattress

Continental Quilting Co Inc .... E 718 499-9100
  New Hyde Park **(G-8869)**

PAGERS: One-way

Bayside Beepers & Cellular .... G 718 343-3888
  Glen Oaks **(G-5654)**

PAINT STORE

Atlas Coatings Group Corp .... D 718 469-8787
  Brooklyn **(G-1650)**
Mercury Paint Corporation .... D 718 469-8787
  Brooklyn **(G-2303)**
Nautical Marine Paint Corp .... E 718 462-7000
  Brooklyn **(G-2361)**
Starlite Pnt & Varnish Co Inc .... G 718 292-6420
  Bronx **(G-1462)**

PAINTING SVC: Metal Prdts

Aircraft Finishing Corp .... F 631 422-5000
  West Babylon **(G-16792)**
Buffalo Finishing Works Inc .... G 716 893-5266
  Buffalo **(G-2873)**
Buffalo Metal Finishing Co .... G 716 883-2751
  Buffalo **(G-2878)**
Color Craft Finishing Corp .... F 631 563-3230
  Bohemia **(G-1034)**
D & I Finishing Inc .... G 631 471-3034
  Bohemia **(G-1044)**
Duzmor Painting Inc .... G 585 768-4760
  Le Roy **(G-7432)**
Industrial Paint Services Corp .... F 607 687-0107
  Owego **(G-13377)**
Keymark Corporation .... A 518 853-3421
  Fonda **(G-5321)**
Mac Artspray Finishing Corp .... F 718 649-3800
  Brooklyn **(G-2252)**
McHugh Painting Co Inc .... F 716 741-8077
  Clarence **(G-3692)**
Rims Like New Inc .... F 845 537-0396
  Middletown **(G-8495)**
Tailored Coatings Inc .... E 716 893-4869
  Buffalo **(G-3234)**

PAINTS & ADDITIVES

Atlas Coatings Group Corp .... D 718 469-8787
  Brooklyn **(G-1650)**

Farrow and Ball Inc .... F 212 752-5544
  New York **(G-10193)**
Fougera Pharmaceuticals Inc .... C 631 454-7677
  Melville **(G-8350)**
General Coatings Tech Inc .... E 718 821-1232
  Ridgewood **(G-14120)**
Inglis Co Inc .... G 315 475-1315
  Syracuse **(G-15982)**
Liberty Panel Center Inc .... F 718 647-2763
  Brooklyn **(G-2217)**
Mercury Paint Corporation .... D 718 469-8787
  Brooklyn **(G-2303)**
Reddi Car Corp .... G 631 589-3141
  Sayville **(G-15243)**
Sml Brothers Holding Corp .... D 718 402-2000
  Bronx **(G-1455)**
Starlite Pnt & Varnish Co Inc .... G 718 292-6420
  Bronx **(G-1462)**
T J Ronan Paint Corp .... E 718 292-1100
  Bronx **(G-1468)**
Talyarps Corporation .... D 914 699-3030
  Pelham **(G-13520)**
Talyarps Corporation .... E 914 699-3030
  Mount Vernon **(G-8781)**

PAINTS & ALLIED PRODUCTS

A & B Color Corp (del) .... G 718 441-5482
  Kew Gardens **(G-7186)**
Akzo Nobel Coatings Inc .... E 610 603-7589
  Long Island City **(G-7682)**
Angiotech Biocoatings Corp .... E 585 321-1130
  Henrietta **(G-6315)**
Anthony River Inc .... F 315 475-1315
  Syracuse **(G-15875)**
Atc Plastics LLC .... E 212 375-2515
  New York **(G-9297)**
B & F Architectural Support Gr .... E 212 279-6488
  New York **(G-9340)**
Barson Composites Corporation .... E 516 752-7882
  Old Bethpage **(G-13147)**
Benjamin Moore & Co .... E 518 736-1723
  Johnstown **(G-7139)**
Cytec Industries Inc .... D 716 372-9650
  Olean **(G-13162)**
Eric S Turner & Company Inc .... F 914 235-7114
  New Rochelle **(G-8943)**
Excel Paint Applicators Inc .... E 347 221-1968
  Inwood **(G-6794)**
Fayette Street Coatings Inc .... G 315 488-5401
  Syracuse **(G-15962)**
Fayette Street Coatings Inc .... F 315 488-5401
  Liverpool **(G-7544)**
Garco Manufacturing Corp Inc .... G 718 287-3330
  Brooklyn **(G-2014)**
Heany Industries Inc .... E 585 889-2700
  Scottsville **(G-15358)**
Inhance Technologies LLC .... E 716 825-9031
  Buffalo **(G-3026)**
Insulating Coatings Corp .... F 607 723-1727
  Binghamton **(G-922)**
Jrlon Inc .... D 315 597-4067
  Palmyra **(G-13434)**
Nautical Marine Paint Corp .... E 718 462-7000
  Brooklyn **(G-2361)**
Nortek Powder Coating LLC .... F 315 337-2339
  Rome **(G-14854)**
Peter Kwasny Inc .... G 727 641-1462
  Hauppauge **(G-6187)**
Regent Paints Inc .... G 917 966-6011
  Glendale **(G-5676)**
T C Dunham Paint Company Inc .... E 914 969-4202
  Yonkers **(G-17506)**
Yewtree Millworks Corp .... G 914 320-5851
  Yonkers **(G-17517)**

PAINTS & VARNISHES: Plastics Based

Industrial Finishing Products .... F 718 342-4871
  Brooklyn **(G-2102)**

PAINTS, VARNISHES & SPLYS WHOLESALERS

Regent Paints Inc .... G 917 966-6011
  Glendale **(G-5676)**

Employee Codes: A=Over 500 employees, B=251-500
C=101-250, D=51-100, E=20-50, F=10-19, G=5-9

PAINTS, VARNISHES & SPLYS, WHOLESALE: Paints

A & B Color Corp (del)............G....... 718 441-5482
Kew Gardens *(G-7186)*
Benjamin Moore & Co............E....... 518 736-1723
Johnstown *(G-7139)*

PALLET REPAIR SVCS

Four-Way Pallet Corp............E....... 631 351-3401
Huntington Station *(G-6744)*

PALLETIZERS & DEPALLETIZERS

Arpac LLC............F....... 315 471-5103
Syracuse *(G-15878)*

PALLETS

A D Bowman & Son Lumber Co............E....... 607 692-2595
Castle Creek *(G-3445)*
Dwa Pallet Inc............G....... 518 746-1047
Hudson Falls *(G-6672)*
Just Wood Pallets Inc............G....... 718 644-7013
New Windsor *(G-8986)*
North Shore Pallet Inc............G....... 631 673-4700
Huntington Station *(G-6756)*
Pooran Pallet Inc............G....... 718 938-7970
Bronx *(G-1431)*
Sanjay Pallets Inc............G....... 347 590-2485
Bronx *(G-1446)*
Steven Coffey Pallet S Inc............G....... 585 261-6783
Rochester *(G-14728)*

PALLETS & SKIDS: Wood

Berry Industrial Group Inc............G....... 845 353-8338
Nyack *(G-13062)*
Best Pallet & Crate LLC............G....... 518 438-2945
Albany *(G-52)*
Chemung Cnty Chpter Nysarc Inc............C....... 607 734-6151
Elmira *(G-4688)*
Dimensional Mills Inc............G....... 518 746-1047
Hudson Falls *(G-6671)*
Four-Way Pallet Corp............E....... 631 351-3401
Huntington Station *(G-6744)*
McIntosh Box & Pallet Co Inc............F....... 315 789-8750
Geneva *(G-5594)*
McIntosh Box & Pallet Co Inc............E....... 315 446-9350
Rome *(G-14848)*
Nefab Packaging North East LLC............E....... 518 346-9105
Scotia *(G-15351)*
Ongweoweh Corp............D....... 607 266-7070
Ithaca *(G-6903)*
Pallet Services Inc............E....... 585 647-4020
Rochester *(G-14590)*
Reuter Pallet Pkg Sys Inc............G....... 845 457-9937
Montgomery *(G-8638)*

PALLETS: Wood & Metal Combination

Pallet Division Inc............G....... 585 328-3780
Rochester *(G-14589)*

PALLETS: Wooden

Abbot & Abbot Box Corp............F....... 888 930-5972
Long Island City *(G-7678)*
B & B Lumber Company Inc............D....... 866 282-0582
Jamesville *(G-7077)*
B&B Albany Pallet Company LLC............E....... 315 492-1786
Jamesville *(G-7078)*
Clements Burrville Sawmill............G....... 315 782-4549
Watertown *(G-16666)*
Crawford Furniture Mfg Corp............C....... 716 483-2102
Jamestown *(G-7020)*
Custom Shipping Products Inc............F....... 716 355-4437
Clymer *(G-3758)*
D & F Pallet Inc............F....... 716 672-2984
Fredonia *(G-5381)*
Essex Box & Pallet Co Inc............E....... 518 834-7279
Keeseville *(G-7166)*
G & H Wood Products LLC............F....... 716 372-5510
Olean *(G-13169)*
Great Lakes Specialites............E....... 716 672-4622
Fredonia *(G-5383)*
Lindley Wood Works Inc............F....... 607 523-7786
Lindley *(G-7519)*
McIntosh Box & Pallet Co Inc............D....... 315 675-8511
Bernhards Bay *(G-857)*
Neville Mfg Svc & Dist Inc............F....... 716 834-3038
Cheektowaga *(G-3610)*
Northeast Pallet & Cont Co Inc............F....... 518 271-0535
Troy *(G-16267)*
Orleans Pallet Company Inc............F....... 585 589-0781
Albion *(G-170)*
Pallets Inc............E....... 518 747-4177
Fort Edward *(G-5351)*
Pallets R US Inc............E....... 631 758-2360
Bellport *(G-834)*
Paul Bunyan Products Inc............E....... 315 696-6164
Cortland *(G-4062)*
Peco Pallet Inc............E....... 914 376-5444
Irvington *(G-6816)*
Peter C Herman Inc............E....... 315 926-4100
Marion *(G-8128)*
Vansantis Development Inc............E....... 315 461-0113
Liverpool *(G-7581)*
Wolfe Lumber Mill Inc............G....... 716 772-7750
Gasport *(G-5575)*

PANEL & DISTRIBUTION BOARDS: Electric

Allied Circuits LLC............E....... 716 551-0285
Buffalo *(G-2820)*
Claddagh Electronics Ltd............E....... 718 784-0571
Long Island City *(G-7728)*

PANELS: Building, Wood

Harvest Homes Inc............E....... 518 895-2341
Delanson *(G-4259)*

PANELS: Cardboard, Die-Cut, Made From Purchased Materials

Hubray Inc............F....... 800 645-2855
North Baldwin *(G-12924)*

PANELS: Wood

Northeast Panel & Truss LLC............E....... 845 339-3656
Kingston *(G-7234)*

PAPER & BOARD: Die-cut

All Out Die Cutting Inc............E....... 718 346-6666
Brooklyn *(G-1586)*
American Dsplay Die Ctters Inc............E....... 212 645-1274
New York *(G-9166)*
Art Industries of New York............E....... 212 633-9200
New York *(G-9260)*
Borden & Riley Paper Co Inc............E....... 718 454-9494
Hollis *(G-6520)*
Dia............G....... 212 675-4097
New York *(G-9920)*
General Die and Die Cutng Inc............D....... 516 665-3584
Roosevelt *(G-15028)*
General Fibre Products Corp............D....... 516 358-7500
New Hyde Park *(G-8880)*
Glens Falls Business Forms Inc............F....... 518 798-6643
Queensbury *(G-14009)*
Kleer-Fax Inc............D....... 631 225-1100
Amityville *(G-303)*
Leather Indexes Corp............D....... 516 827-1900
Hicksville *(G-6391)*
Manufacturers Indexing Pdts............G....... 631 271-0956
Halesite *(G-5928)*
Mid Island Die Cutting Corp............C....... 631 293-0180
Farmingdale *(G-5062)*
Miken Companies Inc............D....... 716 668-6311
Buffalo *(G-3085)*
New York Cutting & Gumming Co............E....... 212 563-4146
Middletown *(G-8489)*
Norampac New York City Inc............C....... 718 340-2100
Maspeth *(G-8189)*
Orange Die Cutting Corp............C....... 845 562-0900
Newburgh *(G-12794)*
Paperworld Inc............E....... 516 221-2702
Bellmore *(G-815)*
Precision Diecutting Inc............G....... 315 776-8465
Port Byron *(G-13764)*
Premier Packaging Corporation............E....... 585 924-8460
Victor *(G-16520)*
S & S Prtg Die-Cutting Co Inc............F....... 718 388-8990
Brooklyn *(G-2543)*
Spectrum Prtg Lithography Inc............F....... 212 255-3131
New York *(G-12182)*
Welsh Gold Stampers Inc............E....... 718 984-5031
Staten Island *(G-15776)*

PAPER CONVERTING

Aigner Label Holder Corp............F....... 845 562-4510
New Windsor *(G-8976)*
Beetins Wholesale Inc............F....... 718 524-0899
Staten Island *(G-15665)*
Best Time Processor LLC............G....... 917 455-4126
Richmond Hill *(G-14082)*
Eagles Nest Holdings LLC............E....... 513 874-5270
New York *(G-10011)*
Felix Schoeller North Amer Inc............C....... 315 298-5133
Pulaski *(G-13963)*
Gardei Industries LLC............F....... 716 693-7100
North Tonawanda *(G-12991)*
Gavin Mfg Corp............E....... 631 467-0040
Farmingdale *(G-5005)*
Global Tissue Group Inc............E....... 631 924-3019
Medford *(G-8276)*
Graphic Cntrls Acqisition Corp............B....... 716 853-7500
Buffalo *(G-2994)*
Graphic Controls Holdings Inc............F....... 716 853-7500
Buffalo *(G-2995)*
Interface Performance Mtls............F....... 315 346-3100
Beaver Falls *(G-789)*
Katz Group Americas Inc............E....... 716 995-3059
Sanborn *(G-15149)*
Marketing Group International............G....... 631 754-8095
Northport *(G-13034)*
Millcraft Paper Company............E....... 716 856-5135
Buffalo *(G-3086)*
Northeastern Paper Corp............G....... 631 659-3634
Huntington *(G-6705)*
Noteworthy Industries Inc............C....... 518 842-2662
Amsterdam *(G-365)*
P C I Paper Conversions Inc............C....... 315 437-1641
Syracuse *(G-16027)*
Pack America Corp............G....... 212 508-6666
New York *(G-11568)*
Paradigm Mktg Consortium Inc............E....... 516 677-6012
Syosset *(G-15855)*
RB Converting Inc............G....... 607 777-1325
Binghamton *(G-940)*
S D Warren Company............D....... 914 696-5544
White Plains *(G-17192)*
Trinity Packaging Corporation............F....... 914 273-4111
Armonk *(G-419)*
VIP Paper Trading Inc............E....... 212 382-4642
New York *(G-12573)*
Waymor1 Inc............E....... 518 677-8511
Cambridge *(G-3339)*

PAPER MANUFACTURERS: Exc Newsprint

Albany International Corp............C....... 518 445-2230
Menands *(G-8397)*
Ampac Paper LLC............B....... 845 778-5511
Walden *(G-16549)*
Atlas Recycling LLC............G....... 212 925-3280
New York *(G-9309)*
Burrows Paper Corporation............D....... 315 823-2300
Little Falls *(G-7520)*
Carta Usa LLC............E....... 585 436-3012
Rochester *(G-14279)*
Clearwater Paper Corporation............D....... 315 287-1200
Gouverneur *(G-5759)*
Dunmore Corporation............D....... 845 279-5061
Brewster *(G-1214)*
Euro Fine Paper Inc............G....... 516 238-5253
Garden City *(G-5516)*
Freeport Paper Industries Inc............D....... 631 851-1555
Central Islip *(G-3523)*
Georgia-Pacific LLC............A....... 518 561-3500
Plattsburgh *(G-13692)*
International Paper Company............A....... 518 585-6761
Ticonderoga *(G-16148)*
International Paper Company............C....... 845 986-6409
Tuxedo Park *(G-16307)*
International Paper Company............C....... 607 775-1550
Conklin *(G-3894)*
International Paper Company............C....... 315 797-5120
Utica *(G-16369)*
Lenaro Paper Co Inc............F....... 631 439-8800
Central Islip *(G-3529)*
Minimill Technologies Inc............F....... 315 692-4557
Syracuse *(G-16011)*
Mohawk Fine Papers Inc............E....... 518 237-1741
Cohoes *(G-3776)*
Mohawk Fine Papers Inc............B....... 518 237-1740
Cohoes *(G-3775)*
Omniafiltra LLC............E....... 315 346-7300
Beaver Falls *(G-790)*
Paper Solutions Inc............F....... 718 499-4226
Brooklyn *(G-2418)*
Sca Tissue North America LLC............E....... 518 692-8434
Greenwich *(G-5912)*

PRODUCT SECTION

PAPER: Corrugated

Sca Tissue North America LLC............C...... 518 583-2785
 Saratoga Springs *(G-15203)*
Twin Rivers Paper Company LLC..........C...... 315 823-2300
 Little Falls *(G-7527)*
Verso Corporation................................B...... 212 599-2700
 New York *(G-12550)*
Verso Paper Management LP..................A...... 781 320-8660
 New York *(G-12551)*
Verso Paper Management LP..................G...... 212 599-2700
 New York *(G-12552)*

PAPER PRDTS

Bigname Commerce LLC........................D...... 631 693-1070
 Amityville *(G-276)*

PAPER PRDTS: Feminine Hygiene Prdts

Corman USA Inc....................................G...... 718 727-7455
 Staten Island *(G-15682)*
Maxim Hygiene Products Inc..................F...... 516 621-3323
 Mineola *(G-8556)*
Rochester Midland Corporation.............C...... 585 336-2200
 Rochester *(G-14665)*

PAPER PRDTS: Infant & Baby Prdts

Kas Direct LLC....................................E...... 516 934-0541
 Westbury *(G-17028)*
Nuk USA LLC..G...... 914 366-2820
 Tarrytown *(G-16123)*
Skip Hop Inc..E...... 646 902-9874
 New York *(G-12118)*
Skip Hop Holdings Inc..........................G...... 212 868-9850
 New York *(G-12119)*

PAPER PRDTS: Molded Pulp Prdts

Fibercel Packaging LLC........................E...... 716 933-8703
 Portville *(G-13892)*

PAPER PRDTS: Napkins, Sanitary, Made From Purchased Material

Precare Corp..G...... 631 667-1055
 Hauppauge *(G-6195)*

PAPER PRDTS: Pattern Tissue

Stephen Singer Pattern Co Inc.............F...... 212 947-2902
 New York *(G-12220)*

PAPER PRDTS: Pressed & Molded Pulp & Fiber Prdts

Pactiv LLC..G...... 585 394-1525
 Canandaigua *(G-3380)*

PAPER PRDTS: Pressed Pulp Prdts

Huhtamaki Inc.....................................A...... 315 593-5311
 Fulton *(G-5475)*

PAPER PRDTS: Sanitary

Attends Healthcare Inc........................A...... 212 338-5100
 New York *(G-9311)*
Becks Classic Mfg Inc..........................D...... 631 435-3800
 Brentwood *(G-1175)*
Cellu Tissue - Long Island LLC.............C...... 631 232-2626
 Central Islip *(G-3514)*
Crosstex International Inc...................D...... 631 582-6777
 Hauppauge *(G-6079)*
First Quality Products Inc...................F...... 516 829-4949
 Great Neck *(G-5828)*
Georgia-Pacific LLC............................A...... 518 561-3500
 Plattsburgh *(G-13692)*
Monthly Gift Inc..................................G...... 888 444-9661
 New York *(G-11328)*
Nice-Pak Products Inc.........................B...... 845 365-2772
 Orangeburg *(G-13258)*
Nutek Disposables Inc........................G...... 516 829-3030
 Great Neck *(G-5841)*
Precare Corp......................................G...... 631 524-5171
 Hauppauge *(G-6194)*
Professional Disposables Inc..............A...... 845 365-1700
 Orangeburg *(G-13266)*
Sqp Inc...C...... 518 831-6800
 Schenectady *(G-15322)*
Waymor1 Inc......................................E...... 518 677-8511
 Cambridge *(G-3339)*

PAPER PRDTS: Tampons, Sanitary, Made From Purchased Material

Alyk Inc..F...... 917 968-2552
 New York *(G-9158)*
L VII Resilient LLC..............................F...... 631 987-5819
 Medford *(G-8284)*

PAPER PRDTS: Toilet Paper, Made From Purchased Materials

Deluxe Packaging Corp.......................F...... 845 246-6090
 Saugerties *(G-15213)*

PAPER PRDTS: Toweling Tissue

Crosstex International Inc...................D...... 631 582-6777
 Hauppauge *(G-6079)*

PAPER PRDTS: Towels, Napkins/Tissue Paper, From Purchd Mtrls

Cascades Tssue Group-Sales Inc.........D...... 518 238-1900
 Waterford *(G-16630)*
First Quality Hygienic Inc...................G...... 516 829-3030
 Great Neck *(G-5827)*
Florelle Tissue Corporation................E...... 647 997-7405
 Brownville *(G-2797)*
HFC Prestige Intl US LLC...................A...... 212 389-7800
 New York *(G-10514)*
N3a Corporation................................D...... 516 284-6799
 Inwood *(G-6802)*
Procter & Gamble Company..............C...... 646 885-4201
 New York *(G-11747)*
Select Products Holdings LLC............C...... 855 777-3532
 Huntington *(G-6720)*
US Alliance Paper Inc........................C...... 631 254-3030
 Edgewood *(G-4632)*

PAPER, WHOLESALE: Fine

Lenaro Paper Co Inc..........................F...... 631 439-8800
 Central Islip *(G-3529)*
Xerox Corporation..............................C...... 585 427-4500
 Rochester *(G-14797)*

PAPER, WHOLESALE: Printing

Chesu Inc...F...... 239 564-2803
 East Hampton *(G-4427)*
Malone Industrial Press Inc................G...... 518 483-5880
 Malone *(G-8044)*

PAPER: Absorbent

Cascades Tssue Group-Sales Inc........E...... 819 363-5100
 Waterford *(G-16631)*
National Paper Converting Inc............G...... 607 687-6049
 Owego *(G-13381)*

PAPER: Adding Machine Rolls, Made From Purchased Materials

Gaylord Bros Inc................................D...... 315 457-5070
 North Syracuse *(G-12961)*
Paperworld Inc..................................E...... 516 221-2702
 Bellmore *(G-815)*

PAPER: Adhesive

Avery Dennison Corporation..............C...... 845 680-3873
 Orangeburg *(G-13242)*
Cove Point Holdings LLC...................F...... 212 599-3388
 New York *(G-9800)*
Label Makers Inc...............................E...... 631 319-6329
 Bohemia *(G-1085)*
Oaklee International Inc...................D...... 631 436-7900
 Ronkonkoma *(G-14983)*
Rochester 100 Inc.............................C...... 585 475-0200
 Rochester *(G-14655)*
Stoney Croft Converters Inc..............F...... 718 608-9800
 Staten Island *(G-15764)*
Triangle Label Tag Inc......................C...... 718 875-3030
 Brooklyn *(G-2697)*

PAPER: Art

Donne Dieu..G...... 212 226-0573
 Brooklyn *(G-1874)*

PAPER: Bristols

Bristol Core Inc..................................F...... 585 919-0302
 Canandaigua *(G-3365)*
Bristol/White Plains............................G...... 914 681-1800
 White Plains *(G-17115)*

PAPER: Building, Insulating & Packaging

CCT (us) Inc.......................................F...... 716 297-7509
 Niagara Falls *(G-12825)*
Howard J Moore Company Inc...........E...... 631 351-8467
 Plainview *(G-13635)*

PAPER: Business Form

Bigrow Paper Mfg Corp......................F...... 718 624-4439
 Brooklyn *(G-1694)*
Chem-Puter Friendly Inc....................E...... 631 331-2259
 Mount Sinai *(G-8696)*
Datagraphic Business Systems..........E...... 516 485-9069
 Brentwood *(G-1177)*
United Data Forms Inc......................F...... 631 218-0104
 Bohemia *(G-1148)*

PAPER: Card

Lion Die-Cutting Co Inc.....................E...... 718 383-8841
 Brooklyn *(G-2231)*

PAPER: Chemically Treated, Made From Purchased Materials

Micro Essential Laboratory................E...... 718 338-3618
 Brooklyn *(G-2315)*

PAPER: Cigarette

Schweitzer-Mauduit Intl Inc...............C...... 518 329-4222
 Ancram *(G-375)*

PAPER: Cloth, Lined, Made From Purchased Materials

Albany International Corp..................D...... 518 447-6400
 Menands *(G-8398)*

PAPER: Coated & Laminated, NEC

A-One Laminating Corp......................G...... 718 266-6002
 Brooklyn *(G-1541)*
Adflex Corporation.............................E...... 585 454-2950
 Rochester *(G-14189)*
C & R De Santis Inc..........................E...... 718 447-5076
 Staten Island *(G-15673)*
CCL Label Inc....................................C...... 716 852-2155
 Buffalo *(G-2889)*
Classic Labels Inc..............................E...... 631 467-2300
 Patchogue *(G-13442)*
Dunmore Corporation........................D...... 845 279-5061
 Brewster *(G-1214)*
Felix Schoeller North Amer Inc..........D...... 315 298-8425
 Pulaski *(G-13962)*
Greenbush Tape & Label Inc.............E...... 518 465-2389
 Albany *(G-83)*
K Sidrane Inc....................................E...... 631 393-6974
 Farmingdale *(G-5028)*
Liberty Label Mfg Inc........................F...... 631 737-2365
 Holbrook *(G-6486)*
Miken Companies Inc........................D...... 716 668-6311
 Buffalo *(G-3085)*
Mohawk Fine Papers Inc...................B...... 518 237-1740
 Cohoes *(G-3775)*
Neenah Northeast LLC......................C...... 315 376-3571
 Lowville *(G-7968)*
New York Cutting & Gumming Co......E...... 212 563-4146
 Middletown *(G-8489)*
Overnight Labels Inc.........................E...... 631 242-4240
 Deer Park *(G-4210)*
P C I Paper Conversions Inc..............C...... 315 437-1641
 Syracuse *(G-16027)*
Princeton Label & Packaging............E...... 609 490-0800
 Patchogue *(G-13458)*
S & S Prtg Die-Cutting Co Inc..........F...... 718 388-8990
 Brooklyn *(G-2543)*

PAPER: Corrugated

General Fibre Products Corp..............D...... 516 358-7500
 New Hyde Park *(G-8880)*

Employee Codes: A=Over 500 employees, B=251-500
C=101-250, D=51-100, E=20-50, F=10-19, G=5-9

PAPER: Envelope — PRODUCT SECTION

PAPER: Envelope
- Tag Envelope Co Inc .... E 718 389-6844
  College Point **(G-3835)**

PAPER: Filter
- Andex Corp .... E 585 328-3790
  Rochester **(G-14220)**
- Hollingsworth & Vose Company .... C 518 695-8000
  Greenwich **(G-5908)**
- Knowlton Technologies LLC .... C 315 782-0600
  Watertown **(G-16683)**

PAPER: Kraft
- APC Paper Company Inc .... D 315 384-4225
  Norfolk **(G-12914)**
- Kapstone Container Corporation .... D 518 842-2450
  Amsterdam **(G-352)**
- Scalamandre Wallpaper Inc .... B 631 467-8800
  Hauppauge **(G-6210)**

PAPER: Parchment
- Palisades Paper Inc .... G 845 354-0333
  Spring Valley **(G-15619)**

PAPER: Printer
- Summit Fincl Disclosure LLC .... E 212 913-0510
  New York **(G-12255)**

PAPER: Specialty
- Cottrell Paper Company Inc .... E 518 885-1702
  Rock City Falls **(G-14807)**
- Dunn Paper - Natural Dam Inc .... D 315 287-1200
  Gouverneur **(G-5760)**
- Gratitude & Company Inc .... G 607 277-3188
  Ithaca **(G-6881)**
- Neenah Northeast LLC .... D 315 782-5800
  Brownville **(G-2798)**
- Potsdam Specialty Paper Inc .... D 315 265-4000
  Potsdam **(G-13899)**

PAPER: Tissue
- Burrows Paper Corporation .... D 315 823-2300
  Little Falls **(G-7521)**
- Morcon Inc .... C 518 677-8511
  Cambridge **(G-3337)**
- North End Paper Co Inc .... G 315 593-8100
  Fulton **(G-5485)**
- Precare Corp .... G 631 667-1055
  Hauppauge **(G-6195)**
- Twin Rivers Paper Company LLC .... E 315 348-8491
  Lyons Falls **(G-8005)**

PAPER: Wrapping
- Flower Cy Tissue Mills Co Inc .... E 585 458-9200
  Rochester **(G-14398)**

PAPER: Wrapping & Packaging
- Gooding Co Inc .... E 716 434-5501
  Lockport **(G-7622)**

PAPER: Writing
- Automation Papers Inc .... G 315 432-0565
  Syracuse **(G-15882)**

PAPERBOARD
- Alpine Paper Box Co Inc .... E 718 345-4040
  Brooklyn **(G-1592)**
- American Wire Tie Inc .... E 716 337-2412
  North Collins **(G-12942)**
- Carthage Specialty Pprbd Inc .... D 315 493-2120
  Carthage **(G-3437)**
- Interface Performance Mtls Inc .... D 518 686-3400
  Hoosick Falls **(G-6567)**
- Ms Paper Products Co Inc .... G 718 624-0248
  Brooklyn **(G-2348)**
- Niagara Fiberboard Inc .... E 716 434-8881
  Lockport **(G-7635)**
- Pactiv LLC .... E 585 248-1213
  Pittsford **(G-13601)**
- Professional Packg Svcs Inc .... E 518 677-5100
  Eagle Bridge **(G-4381)**

PAPERBOARD CONVERTING
- Allied Converters Inc .... E 914 235-1585
  New Rochelle **(G-8931)**
- Deltacraft Paper Company LLC .... C 716 856-5135
  Buffalo **(G-2925)**
- Mid-York Press Inc .... D 607 674-4491
  Sherburne **(G-15415)**
- Winghing 8 Ltd .... G 718 439-0021
  Brooklyn **(G-2776)**

PAPERBOARD PRDTS: Building Insulating & Packaging
- Greenfiber Albany Inc .... D 518 842-1470
  Gloversville **(G-5727)**
- Shell Containers Inc (ny) .... E 516 352-4505
  New Hyde Park **(G-8906)**

PAPERBOARD PRDTS: Container Board
- Kapstone Container Corporation .... D 518 842-2450
  Amsterdam **(G-352)**
- Westrock - Solvay Llc .... C 315 484-9050
  Syracuse **(G-16095)**
- Westrock CP LLC .... D 315 484-9050
  Syracuse **(G-16096)**

PAPERBOARD PRDTS: Folding Boxboard
- Burt Rigid Box Inc .... F 607 433-2510
  Oneonta **(G-13199)**
- Di Domenico Packaging Co Inc .... G 718 727-5454
  Staten Island **(G-15685)**
- Enterprise Folding Box Co Inc .... E 716 876-6421
  Buffalo **(G-2955)**
- Paper Box Corp .... D 212 226-7490
  New York **(G-11576)**

PAPERBOARD PRDTS: Kraft Linerboard
- Continental Kraft Corp .... G 516 681-9090
  Jericho **(G-7097)**

PAPERBOARD PRDTS: Packaging Board
- Farrington Packaging Corp .... E 315 733-4600
  Utica **(G-16354)**

PAPERBOARD PRDTS: Pressboard
- Neenah Northeast LLC .... D 315 782-5800
  Brownville **(G-2798)**

PAPERBOARD: Boxboard
- Prestige Box Corporation .... E 516 773-3115
  Great Neck **(G-5850)**

PAPERBOARD: Liner Board
- Cascades New York Inc .... C 716 285-3681
  Niagara Falls **(G-12824)**
- Greenpac Mill LLC .... C 716 299-0560
  Niagara Falls **(G-12848)**
- Westrock Mwv LLC .... C 212 688-5000
  New York **(G-12645)**

PAPIER-MACHE PRDTS, EXC STATUARY & ART GOODS
- Specialty Quality Packg LLC .... D 914 580-3200
  Scotia **(G-15354)**

PARACHUTES
- National Parachute Industries .... E 908 782-1646
  Palenville **(G-13423)**
- Yoland Corporation .... E 718 499-4803
  Brooklyn **(G-2789)**

PARKING LOTS
- Deans Paving Inc .... G 315 736-7601
  Marcy **(G-8121)**

PARTITIONS & FIXTURES: Except Wood
- All American Metal Corporation .... E 516 623-0222
  Freeport **(G-5393)**
- American Standard Mfg Inc .... E 518 868-2512
  Central Bridge **(G-3507)**
- Avf Inc .... F 951 360-7111
  Buffalo **(G-2849)**
- Bobrick Washroom Equipment Inc .... D 518 877-7444
  Clifton Park **(G-3723)**
- Bridge Metal Industries LLC .... C 914 663-9200
  Mount Vernon **(G-8712)**
- Core Group Displays Inc .... E 845 876-5109
  Rhinebeck **(G-14067)**
- Dakota Systems Mfg Corp .... G 631 249-5811
  Farmingdale **(G-4983)**
- E-Systems Group LLC .... E 607 775-1100
  Conklin **(G-3893)**
- Hergo Ergonomic Support .... E 718 894-0639
  Maspeth **(G-8175)**
- Inscape Inc .... E 716 665-6210
  Falconer **(G-4910)**
- Joldeson One Aerospace Inds .... D 718 848-7396
  Ozone Park **(G-13406)**
- La Mar Lighting Co Inc .... D 631 777-7700
  Farmingdale **(G-5039)**
- Mass Mdsg Self Selection Eqp .... E 631 234-3300
  Bohemia **(G-1097)**
- Maximum Security Products Corp .... E 518 233-1800
  Waterford **(G-16634)**
- Milton Merl & Associates Inc .... G 212 634-9292
  New York **(G-11297)**
- Mobile Media Inc .... E 845 744-8080
  Pine Bush **(G-13575)**
- Modu-Craft Inc .... G 716 694-0709
  Tonawanda **(G-16200)**
- Sturdy Store Displays Inc .... E 718 389-9919
  Brooklyn **(G-2638)**
- Traco Manufacturing Inc .... G 585 343-2434
  Batavia **(G-651)**

PARTITIONS WHOLESALERS
- CNA Specialties Inc .... G 631 567-7929
  Sayville **(G-15235)**

PARTITIONS: Nonwood, Floor Attached
- All American Metal Corporation .... G 516 223-1760
  Freeport **(G-5392)**
- Global Steel Products Corp .... C 631 586-3455
  Deer Park **(G-4169)**
- Inscape (new York) Inc .... D 716 665-6210
  Falconer **(G-4909)**
- Knickerbocker Partition Corp .... D 516 546-0550
  Freeport **(G-5418)**

PARTITIONS: Solid Fiber, Made From Purchased Materials
- Westrock Rkt Company .... C 770 448-2193
  Camillus **(G-3356)**

PARTITIONS: Wood & Fixtures
- Artone LLC .... D 716 664-2232
  Jamestown **(G-7008)**
- Champion Millwork Inc .... E 315 463-0711
  Syracuse **(G-15911)**
- Custom Countertops Inc .... G 716 685-2871
  Depew **(G-4277)**
- Dbs Interiors Corp .... F 631 491-3013
  West Babylon **(G-16813)**
- Deakon Homes and Interiors .... F 518 271-0342
  Troy **(G-16255)**
- Encore Retail Systems Inc .... F 718 385-3443
  Mamaroneck **(G-8066)**
- Farrington Packaging Corp .... E 315 733-4600
  Utica **(G-16354)**
- Fina Cabinet Corp .... G 718 409-2900
  Mount Vernon **(G-8726)**
- Gaughan Construction Corp .... G 718 850-9577
  Richmond Hill **(G-14086)**
- Gotham City Industries Inc .... E 914 713-0979
  Scarsdale **(G-15247)**
- Greenleaf Cabinet Makers LLC .... F 315 432-4600
  Syracuse **(G-15974)**
- Hamlet Products Inc .... F 914 665-0307
  Mount Vernon **(G-8734)**
- Heartwood Specialties Inc .... G 607 654-0102
  Hammondsport **(G-5977)**
- Home Ideal Inc .... F 718 762-8998
  Flushing **(G-5259)**
- Industrial Support Inc .... D 716 662-2954
  Buffalo **(G-3024)**
- Integrated Wood Components Inc .... E 607 467-1739
  Deposit **(G-4301)**
- Inter State Laminates Inc .... E 518 283-8355
  Poestenkill **(G-13754)**

PRODUCT SECTION

Michael P Mmarr .... G 315 623-9380
 Constantia *(G-3907)*
New Dimensions Office Group .... D 718 387-0995
 Brooklyn *(G-2370)*
Premier Woodworking Inc .... E 631 236-4100
 Hauppauge *(G-6197)*
Steelcraft Manufacturing Co .... F 718 277-2404
 Brooklyn *(G-2624)*
Stein Industries Inc .... E 631 789-2222
 Amityville *(G-325)*
Unico Inc .... F 845 562-9255
 Newburgh *(G-12806)*
Universal Designs Inc .... G 718 721-1111
 Long Island City *(G-7938)*
Winerackscom Inc .... E 845 658-7181
 Tillson *(G-16152)*

PARTITIONS: Wood, Floor Attached

Steeldeck Ny Inc .... F 718 599-3700
 Brooklyn *(G-2625)*

PARTS: Metal

All-State Diversified Pdts Inc .... E 315 472-4728
 Syracuse *(G-15869)*
Alliance Innovative Mfg Inc .... E 716 822-1626
 Lackawanna *(G-7268)*
Ross Metal Fabricators Inc .... E 631 586-7000
 Deer Park *(G-4227)*
Zone Fabricators Inc .... F 718 272-0200
 Ozone Park *(G-13414)*

PARTY & SPECIAL EVENT PLANNING SVCS

Proof 7 Ltd .... F 212 680-1843
 New York *(G-11757)*

PASTES, FLAVORING

American Almond Pdts Co Inc .... D 718 875-8310
 Brooklyn *(G-1597)*

PATENT OWNERS & LESSORS

Compositech Ltd .... C 516 835-1458
 Woodbury *(G-17305)*
Eagle Telephonics Inc .... F 631 471-3600
 Bohemia *(G-1055)*
General Microwave Corporation .... F 516 802-0900
 Syosset *(G-15844)*

PATTERNS: Indl

A & T Tooling LLC .... G 716 601-7299
 Lancaster *(G-7321)*
Armstrong Mold Corporation .... E 315 437-1517
 East Syracuse *(G-4521)*
Armstrong Mold Corporation .... D 315 437-1517
 East Syracuse *(G-4522)*
Bianca Group Ltd .... G 212 768-3011
 New York *(G-9435)*
City Pattern Shop Inc .... F 315 463-5239
 Syracuse *(G-15914)*
IBIt Inc .... E 212 768-0292
 New York *(G-10592)*
K & H Precision Products Inc .... E 585 624-4894
 Honeoye Falls *(G-6560)*
Studio One Leather Design Inc .... F 212 760-1701
 New York *(G-12243)*
W N R Pattern & Tool Inc .... G 716 681-9334
 Lancaster *(G-7371)*
Wolff & Dungey Inc .... E 315 475-2105
 Syracuse *(G-16098)*
Woodward Industries Inc .... F 716 692-2442
 Tonawanda *(G-16236)*

PAVERS

Lomin Construction Company .... G 516 759-5734
 Glen Head *(G-5650)*
Technopaving New York Inc .... G 631 351-6472
 Huntington Station *(G-6763)*

PAVING MATERIALS: Prefabricated, Concrete

Copeland Coating Company .... F 518 766-2932
 Nassau *(G-8817)*

PAVING MIXTURES

Dolomite Products Company Inc .... E 315 524-1998
 Rochester *(G-14337)*

Dolomite Products Company Inc .... F 607 324-3636
 Hornell *(G-6587)*
Dolomite Products Company Inc .... E 585 586-2568
 Penfield *(G-13522)*
Dolomite Products Company Inc .... F 585 768-7295
 Le Roy *(G-7430)*
Iroquois Rock Products Inc .... F 585 381-7010
 Rochester *(G-14476)*

PENCILS & PENS WHOLESALERS

Mark Dri Products Inc .... C 516 484-6200
 Bethpage *(G-871)*
Pda Panache Corp .... G 631 776-0523
 Bohemia *(G-1112)*

PENS & PARTS: Ball Point

Effanjay Pens Inc .... E 212 316-9565
 Long Island City *(G-7755)*
Gotham Pen Co Inc .... E 212 675-7904
 Yonkers *(G-17465)*
Mercury Pen Company Inc .... G 518 899-9653
 Ballston Lake *(G-582)*

PENS & PARTS: Cartridges, Refill, Ball Point

STS Refill America LLC .... G 516 934-8008
 Hicksville *(G-6422)*

PENS & PENCILS: Mechanical, NEC

A & L Pen Manufacturing Corp .... D 718 499-8966
 Brooklyn *(G-1526)*
Aakron Rule Corp .... C 716 542-5483
 Akron *(G-17)*
Harper Products Ltd .... C 516 997-2330
 Westbury *(G-17021)*
Henry Morgan .... F 718 317-5013
 Staten Island *(G-15704)*
Pelican Products Co Inc .... E 718 860-3220
 Bronx *(G-1424)*

PERFUME: Concentrated

Thompson Ferrier LLC .... G 212 244-2212
 New York *(G-12347)*

PERFUME: Perfumes, Natural Or Synthetic

Christian Dior Perfumes LLC .... C 212 931-2200
 New York *(G-9662)*
Delbia Do Company Inc .... G 718 585-2226
 Bronx *(G-1315)*
Elias Fragrances Inc .... F 718 693-6400
 Rye Brook *(G-15096)*
Flavormatic Industries Inc .... E 845 297-9100
 Wappingers Falls *(G-16587)*

PERFUMES

Alan F Bourguet .... F 516 883-4315
 Port Washington *(G-13820)*
Cassini Parfums Ltd .... G 212 753-7540
 New York *(G-9595)*
Coty US LLC .... C 212 389-7000
 New York *(G-9791)*
Coty US LLC .... B 212 389-7000
 Uniondale *(G-16313)*
Editions De Prfums Madison LLC .... F 646 666-0527
 New York *(G-10035)*
Estee Lauder Inc .... D 631 531-1000
 Melville *(G-8345)*
F L Demeter Inc .... E 516 487-5187
 Great Neck *(G-5823)*
Fragrance Acquisitions LLC .... D 845 534-9172
 Newburgh *(G-12776)*
Fragrance Outlet Inc .... F 845 928-1408
 Central Valley *(G-3551)*
Hogan Flavors & Fragrances .... E 212 598-4310
 New York *(G-10537)*
JP Filling Inc .... D 845 534-4793
 Mountainville *(G-8794)*
Laurice El Badry Rahme Ltd .... E 212 633-1641
 New York *(G-10974)*
Le Labo Holding LLC .... E 844 316-9319
 New York *(G-10978)*
Le Labo Holding LLC .... E 646 719-1740
 Brooklyn *(G-2202)*
Perfume Americana Inc .... G 212 683-8029
 New York *(G-11634)*
Perfume Amrcana Whlesalers Inc .... F 212 683-8029
 New York *(G-11635)*

Perfumers Workshop Intl Ltd .... G 212 644-8950
 New York *(G-11636)*
Selective Beauty Corporation .... F 585 336-7600
 New York *(G-12043)*
Value Fragrances Inc .... G 845 294-5726
 Goshen *(G-5756)*

PERLITE: Processed

Skyline LLC .... E 631 403-4131
 East Setauket *(G-4511)*

PERSONAL APPEARANCE SVCS

Womens Health Care PC .... G 718 850-0009
 Richmond Hill *(G-14100)*

PERSONAL CREDIT INSTITUTIONS: Consumer Finance Companies

Steel Partners Holdings LP .... E 212 520-2300
 New York *(G-12212)*

PET ACCESS: Collars, Leashes, Etc, Exc Leather

American Leather Specialties .... D 800 556-6488
 Brooklyn *(G-1601)*

PET COLLARS, LEASHES, MUZZLES & HARNESSES: Leather

Dog Good Products LLC .... G 212 789-7000
 New York *(G-9947)*
Finger Lakes Lea Crafters LLC .... F 315 252-4107
 Auburn *(G-493)*
Max 200 Performance Dog Eqp .... E 315 776-9588
 Port Byron *(G-13763)*

PET SPLYS

Clara Papa .... G 315 733-2660
 Utica *(G-16334)*
Four Paws Products Ltd .... D 631 436-7421
 Ronkonkoma *(G-14931)*
Grand Island Animal Hospital .... E 716 773-7645
 Grand Island *(G-5773)*
Hrg Group Inc .... E 212 906-8555
 New York *(G-10567)*
Image Tech .... F 716 635-0167
 Buffalo *(G-3021)*
Kittywalk Systems Inc .... G 516 627-8418
 Port Washington *(G-13854)*
Petland Discounts Inc .... E 516 821-3194
 Hewlett *(G-6335)*
Pets n People Inc .... G 631 232-1200
 Hauppauge *(G-6188)*
Soggy Doggy Productions LLC .... G 877 504-4811
 Larchmont *(G-7376)*
Spectrum Brands Inc .... B 631 232-1200
 Hauppauge *(G-6220)*
Unique Petz LLC .... E 212 714-1800
 New York *(G-12481)*

PET SPLYS WHOLESALERS

American Leather Specialties .... D 800 556-6488
 Brooklyn *(G-1601)*
Clara Papa .... G 315 733-2660
 Utica *(G-16334)*

PETROLEUM & PETROLEUM PRDTS, WHOLESALE Engine Fuels & Oils

Bass Oil Company Inc .... E 718 628-4444
 Brooklyn *(G-1668)*

PETROLEUM & PETROLEUM PRDTS, WHOLESALE: Bulk Stations

Hess Corporation .... B 212 997-8500
 New York *(G-10507)*

PETROLEUM PRDTS WHOLESALERS

Industrial Raw Materials LLC .... F 212 688-8080
 Plainview *(G-13636)*
Noco Incorporated .... G 716 833-6626
 Tonawanda *(G-16205)*
Tricon Des LLC .... G 619 227-0778
 Bronx *(G-1476)*

Employee Codes: A=Over 500 employees, B=251-500
C=101-250, D=51-100, E=20-50, F=10-19, G=5-9

PEWTER WARE

Quest Bead & Cast Inc ....G..... 212 354-1737
New York *(G-11797)*

Silver City Group Inc ....G..... 315 363-0344
Sherrill *(G-15431)*

PHARMACEUTICAL PREPARATIONS: Adrenal

Central Islip Pharmacy Inc ....G..... 631 234-6039
Central Islip *(G-3515)*

PHARMACEUTICAL PREPARATIONS: Barbituric Acid

872 Hunts Point Pharmacy Inc ....G..... 718 991-3519
Bronx *(G-1251)*

PHARMACEUTICAL PREPARATIONS: Digitalis

Intstrux LLC ....E..... 646 688-2782
New York *(G-10690)*

PHARMACEUTICAL PREPARATIONS: Druggists' Preparations

Akari Therapeutics PLC ....G..... 646 350-0702
New York *(G-9117)*

Asence Inc ....E..... 347 335-2606
New York *(G-9280)*

Biomed Pharmaceuticals Inc ....G..... 914 592-0525
Hawthorne *(G-6267)*

Bristol-Myers Squibb Company ....E..... 315 432-2000
East Syracuse *(G-4529)*

Century Grand Inc ....F..... 212 925-3838
New York *(G-9620)*

Cognigen Corporation ....D..... 716 633-3463
Buffalo *(G-2898)*

Drt Laboratories LLC ....G..... 845 547-2034
Airmont *(G-12)*

Flushing Pharmacy Inc ....C..... 718 260-8999
Brooklyn *(G-1989)*

Fougera Pharmaceuticals Inc ....C..... 631 454-7677
Hicksville *(G-6375)*

Global Alliance For Tb ....E..... 212 227-7540
New York *(G-10351)*

Ima Life North America Inc ....C..... 716 695-6354
Tonawanda *(G-16191)*

Kingston Pharma LLC ....G..... 315 705-4019
Massena *(G-8228)*

Marietta Corporation ....B..... 607 753-6746
Cortland *(G-4057)*

Ony Inc Baird Researchpark ....E..... 716 636-9096
Buffalo *(G-3124)*

Pace Up Pharmaceuticals LLC ....F..... 631 450-4495
Lindenhurst *(G-7502)*

Pharbest Pharmaceuticals Inc ....E..... 631 249-5130
Farmingdale *(G-5087)*

Pharmavantage LLC ....G..... 631 321-8171
Babylon *(G-549)*

Pine Pharmaceuticals LLC ....G..... 716 248-1025
Tonawanda *(G-16211)*

Triceutical Inc ....F..... 631 249-0003
Bronx *(G-1475)*

Wavodyne Therapeutics Inc ....G..... 954 632-6630
West Henrietta *(G-16930)*

PHARMACEUTICAL PREPARATIONS: Medicines, Capsule Or Ampule

Futurebiotics LLC ....E..... 631 273-6300
Hauppauge *(G-6105)*

Nanorx Inc ....G..... 914 671-0224
Chappaqua *(G-3581)*

PHARMACEUTICAL PREPARATIONS: Penicillin

G C Hanford Manufacturing Co ....C..... 315 476-7418
Syracuse *(G-15967)*

PHARMACEUTICAL PREPARATIONS: Pills

A & Z Pharmaceutical Inc ....D..... 631 952-3802
Hauppauge *(G-6026)*

PHARMACEUTICAL PREPARATIONS: Proprietary Drug PRDTS

Ip Med Inc ....G..... 516 766-3800
Oceanside *(G-13102)*

Time-Cap Laboratories Inc ....C..... 631 753-9090
Farmingdale *(G-5141)*

PHARMACEUTICAL PREPARATIONS: Solutions

Container Tstg Solutions LLC ....F..... 716 487-3300
Jamestown *(G-7018)*

Container Tstg Solutions LLC ....F..... 716 487-3300
Sinclairville *(G-15474)*

Guosa Life Sciences Inc ....F..... 718 813-7806
North Baldwin *(G-12923)*

Kent Chemical Corporation ....E..... 212 521-1700
New York *(G-10878)*

Medek Laboratories Inc ....E..... 845 943-4988
Monroe *(G-8597)*

Mskcc Rmipc ....F..... 212 639-6212
New York *(G-11342)*

Pall Corporation ....A..... 516 484-5400
Port Washington *(G-13870)*

Petnet Solutions Inc ....G..... 865 218-2000
New York *(G-11654)*

R J S Direct Marketing Inc ....F..... 631 667-5768
Deer Park *(G-4222)*

Sterrx LLC ....E..... 518 324-7879
Plattsburgh *(G-13728)*

Zitomer LLC ....G..... 212 737-5560
New York *(G-12734)*

PHARMACEUTICAL PREPARATIONS: Tablets

Aiping Pharmaceutical Inc ....G..... 631 952-3802
Hauppauge *(G-6031)*

Bli International Inc ....C..... 631 940-9000
Deer Park *(G-4133)*

Chartwell Pharma Nda B2 Holdin ....G..... 845 268-5000
Congers *(G-3879)*

Eckerson Drugs Inc ....G..... 845 352-1800
Spring Valley *(G-15605)*

Innovative Labs LLC ....D..... 631 231-5522
Hauppauge *(G-6121)*

Invagen Pharmaceuticals Inc ....C..... 631 949-6367
Central Islip *(G-3525)*

Marken LLP ....G..... 631 396-7454
Farmingdale *(G-5050)*

Satnam Distributors LLC ....G..... 516 802-0600
Jericho *(G-7116)*

PHARMACEUTICAL PREPARATIONS: Water, Sterile, For Injections

Sterrx LLC ....F..... 518 324-7879
Plattsburgh *(G-13729)*

PHARMACEUTICALS

3v Company Inc ....E..... 718 858-7333
Brooklyn *(G-1516)*

5th Avenue Pharmacy Inc ....G..... 718 439-8585
Brooklyn *(G-1519)*

888 Pharmacy Inc ....F..... 718 871-8833
Brooklyn *(G-1522)*

A & Z Pharmaceutical Inc ....C..... 631 952-3800
Hauppauge *(G-6027)*

Abh Pharma Inc ....D..... 631 392-4692
Edgewood *(G-4603)*

Abraxis Bioscience LLC ....G..... 716 773-0800
Grand Island *(G-5764)*

Actavis Laboratories Ny Inc ....D..... 631 693-8000
Copiague *(G-3915)*

Actinium Pharmaceuticals Inc ....E..... 646 677-3870
New York *(G-9067)*

Advance Pharmaceutical Inc ....E..... 631 981-4600
Holtsville *(G-6525)*

Affymax Inc ....G..... 650 812-8700
New York *(G-9104)*

Alfred Khalily Inc ....F..... 516 504-0059
Great Neck *(G-5802)*

Allied Pharmacy Products Inc ....G..... 516 374-8862
Woodmere *(G-17328)*

Altaire Pharmaceuticals Inc ....C..... 631 722-5988
Aquebogue *(G-383)*

American Bio Medica Corp ....D..... 518 758-8150
Kinderhook *(G-7196)*

American Regent Inc ....B..... 631 924-4000
Shirley *(G-15434)*

Amneal Pharmaceuticals LLC ....E..... 908 231-1911
Brookhaven *(G-1504)*

Amneal Pharmaceuticals LLC ....E..... 631 952-0214
Brookhaven *(G-1505)*

Amneal Pharmaceuticals LLC ....E..... 908 947-3120
Brookhaven *(G-1506)*

Anacor Pharmaceuticals Inc ....C..... 212 733-2323
New York *(G-9194)*

Angiogenex Inc ....G..... 347 468-6799
New York *(G-9207)*

Anterios Inc ....G..... 212 303-1683
New York *(G-9217)*

Apothecus Pharmaceutical Corp ....F..... 516 624-8200
Oyster Bay *(G-13391)*

Athenex Inc ....C..... 716 427-2950
Buffalo *(G-2842)*

Athenex Inc ....D..... 716 427-2950
Buffalo *(G-2843)*

Athenex Pharma Solutions LLC ....G..... 877 463-7823
Clarence *(G-3684)*

Atlantic Essential Pdts Inc ....D..... 631 434-8333
Hauppauge *(G-6046)*

Auven Therapeutics MGT LP ....F..... 212 616-4000
New York *(G-9321)*

Auxilium Pharmaceuticals Inc ....F..... 484 321-2022
Rye *(G-15080)*

Avenue Therapeutics Inc ....G..... 781 652-4500
New York *(G-9328)*

Axim Biotechnologies Inc ....G..... 212 751-0001
New York *(G-9336)*

Azurrx Biopharma Inc ....F..... 646 699-7855
Brooklyn *(G-1655)*

Barc Usa Inc ....E..... 516 719-1052
New Hyde Park *(G-8863)*

BASF Corporation ....B..... 914 785-2000
Tarrytown *(G-16111)*

Bausch & Lomb Holdings Inc ....G..... 585 338-6000
New York *(G-9384)*

Bausch & Lomb Incorporated ....B..... 585 338-6000
Rochester *(G-14242)*

Baxter International Inc ....G..... 845 457-9370
Montgomery *(G-8627)*

Beyondspring Inc ....E..... 646 305-6387
New York *(G-9431)*

Beyondspring Phrmceuticals Inc ....F..... 646 305-6387
New York *(G-9432)*

Bicon Pharmaceutical Inc ....F..... 631 593-4199
Deer Park *(G-4131)*

Biospecifics Technologies Corp ....G..... 516 593-7000
Lynbrook *(G-7976)*

Bristol-Myers Squibb Company ....A..... 212 546-4000
New York *(G-9516)*

Bristol-Myers Squibb Company ....C..... 516 832-2191
Garden City *(G-5511)*

Campbell Alliance Group Inc ....E..... 212 377-2740
New York *(G-9560)*

Cancer Targeting Systems ....G..... 212 965-4534
New York *(G-9564)*

Cellvation Inc ....G..... 212 554-4520
New York *(G-9608)*

Cerovene Inc ....F..... 845 359-1101
Orangeburg *(G-13243)*

Cerovene Inc ....F..... 845 267-2055
Valley Cottage *(G-16403)*

Chartwell Pharmaceuticals LLC ....D..... 845 268-5000
Congers *(G-3880)*

Cleveland Biolabs Inc ....E..... 716 849-6810
Buffalo *(G-2896)*

Combe Incorporated ....C..... 914 694-5454
White Plains *(G-17123)*

Contract Pharmacal Corp ....E..... 631 231-4610
Hauppauge *(G-6073)*

Contract Pharmacal Corp ....E..... 631 231-4610
Hauppauge *(G-6074)*

Contract Pharmacal Corp ....E..... 631 231-4610
Hauppauge *(G-6075)*

Contract Pharmacal Corp ....E..... 631 231-4610
Hauppauge *(G-6076)*

Contract Pharmacal Corp ....C..... 631 231-4610
Hauppauge *(G-6077)*

Contract Pharmacal Corp ....F..... 631 231-4610
Hauppauge *(G-6078)*

Contract Phrmctcals Ltd Nagara ....C..... 716 887-3400
Buffalo *(G-2908)*

Cortice Biosciences Inc ....F..... 646 747-9090
New York *(G-9787)*

CRS Nuclear Services LLC ....F..... 716 810-0688
Cheektowaga *(G-3593)*

Delcath Systems Inc ....E..... 212 489-2100
New York *(G-9893)*

Dr Reddys Laboratories NY Inc ..... E 518 827-7702
Middleburgh *(G-8452)*
Edlaw Pharmaceuticals Inc ..... E 631 454-6888
Farmingdale *(G-4994)*
Eli Lilly and Company ..... F 516 622-2244
New Hyde Park *(G-8876)*
Encysive Pharmaceuticals Inc ..... E 212 733-2323
New York *(G-10082)*
Enumeral Biomedical Corp ..... G 347 227-4787
New York *(G-10099)*
Enzo Life Sciences Inc ..... E 631 694-7070
Farmingdale *(G-4997)*
Enzo Life Sciences Intl Inc ..... E 610 941-0430
Farmingdale *(G-4998)*
Eon Labs Inc ..... F 516 478-9700
New Hyde Park *(G-8877)*
Epic Pharma LLC ..... C 718 276-8600
Laurelton *(G-7413)*
Forest Laboratories LLC ..... C 212 421-7850
New York *(G-10237)*
Forest Laboratories LLC ..... D 212 421-7850
Hauppauge *(G-6103)*
Forest Laboratories LLC ..... C 631 858-6010
Commack *(G-3857)*
Fortress Biotech Inc ..... F 781 652-4500
New York *(G-10239)*
Fougera Pharmaceuticals Inc ..... C 631 454-7677
Melville *(G-8350)*
Fresenius Kabi Usa LLC ..... B 716 773-0053
Grand Island *(G-5771)*
Fresenius Kabi USA LLC ..... E 716 773-0800
Grand Island *(G-5772)*
Generics Bidco I LLC ..... G 256 859-4011
Chestnut Ridge *(G-3651)*
Geritrex LLC ..... E 914 668-4003
Mount Vernon *(G-8727)*
Geritrex Holdings Inc ..... G 914 668-4003
Mount Vernon *(G-8728)*
Glaxosmithkline LLC ..... E 845 341-7590
Montgomery *(G-8630)*
Glaxosmithkline LLC ..... E 845 797-3259
Wappingers Falls *(G-16591)*
Glaxosmithkline LLC ..... E 585 738-9025
Rochester *(G-14427)*
Glaxosmithkline LLC ..... E 716 913-5679
Buffalo *(G-2990)*
Glaxosmithkline LLC ..... D 518 239-6901
East Durham *(G-4409)*
Glaxosmithkline LLC ..... E 518 852-9637
Mechanicville *(G-8259)*
Glycobia Inc ..... G 607 339-0051
Ithaca *(G-6880)*
Greenkissny Inc ..... G 914 304-4323
White Plains *(G-17141)*
Greentree Pharmacy Inc ..... F 718 768-2700
Brooklyn *(G-2055)*
Healthone Pharmacy Inc ..... F 718 495-9015
Brooklyn *(G-2068)*
Hi-Tech Pharmacal Co Inc ..... C 631 789-8228
Amityville *(G-293)*
Hogil Pharmaceutical Corp ..... F 914 681-1800
White Plains *(G-17147)*
Hospira Inc ..... C 716 684-9400
Buffalo *(G-3015)*
Ibio Inc ..... E 302 355-0650
New York *(G-10591)*
Innogenix Inc ..... F 631 450-4704
Amityville *(G-295)*
Intercept Pharmaceuticals Inc ..... D 646 747-1000
New York *(G-10668)*
International Life Science ..... G 631 549-0471
Huntington *(G-6698)*
Intra-Cellular Therapies Inc ..... E 212 923-3344
New York *(G-10687)*
Invagen Pharmaceuticals Inc ..... B 631 231-3233
Hauppauge *(G-6123)*
Izun Pharmaceuticals Corp ..... F 212 618-6357
New York *(G-10713)*
Jerome Stvens Phrmcuticals Inc ..... F 631 567-1113
Bohemia *(G-1078)*
JRS Pharma LP ..... E 845 878-8300
Patterson *(G-13465)*
Kadmon Corporation LLC ..... F 212 308-6000
New York *(G-10835)*
Kadmon Holdings Inc ..... D 212 308-6000
New York *(G-10836)*
Kannalife Sciences Inc ..... G 516 669-3219
Lloyd Harbor *(G-7594)*
Kbl Healthcare LP ..... G 212 319-5555
New York *(G-10863)*

Klg Usa LLC ..... A 845 856-5311
Port Jervis *(G-13811)*
Life Pill Laboratories LLC ..... G 914 682-2146
White Plains *(G-17159)*
Liptis Pharmaceuticals USA Inc ..... A 845 627-0260
Spring Valley *(G-15614)*
LNK International Inc ..... D 631 435-3500
Hauppauge *(G-6139)*
LNK International Inc ..... D 631 435-3500
Hauppauge *(G-6140)*
LNK International Inc ..... D 631 435-3500
Hauppauge *(G-6141)*
LNK International Inc ..... D 631 543-3787
Hauppauge *(G-6142)*
LNK International Inc ..... D 631 435-3500
Hauppauge *(G-6143)*
LNK International Inc ..... D 631 231-3415
Hauppauge *(G-6144)*
LNK International Inc ..... D 631 231-4020
Hauppauge *(G-6145)*
Luitpold Pharmaceuticals Inc ..... B 631 924-4000
Shirley *(G-15446)*
Macrochem Corporation ..... G 212 514-8094
New York *(G-11117)*
Mallinckrodt LLC ..... A 607 538-9124
Hobart *(G-6452)*
Maxus Pharmaceuticals Inc ..... F 631 249-0003
Farmingdale *(G-5054)*
Medtech Products Inc ..... F 914 524-6810
Tarrytown *(G-16119)*
Mentholatum Company ..... E 716 677-2500
Orchard Park *(G-13309)*
Mustang Bio Inc ..... G 781 652-4500
New York *(G-11351)*
Neurotrope Inc ..... G 973 242-0005
New York *(G-11399)*
Noho Health Inc ..... E 877 227-3631
New York *(G-11467)*
Norwich Pharmaceuticals Inc ..... B 607 335-3000
Norwich *(G-13052)*
Nostrand Pharmacy LLC ..... G 718 282-2956
Brooklyn *(G-2387)*
Novartis Corporation ..... E 914 592-7476
Tarrytown *(G-16122)*
Novartis Corporation ..... D 718 276-8600
Laurelton *(G-7414)*
Novartis Pharmaceuticals Corp ..... G 718 276-8600
Laurelton *(G-7415)*
Noven Pharmaceuticals Inc ..... E 212 682-4420
New York *(G-11481)*
Nutra-Scientifics LLC ..... G 917 238-8510
Pomona *(G-13759)*
Nutrascience Labs Inc ..... E 631 247-0660
Farmingdale *(G-5078)*
NV Prrcone MD Cosmeceuticals ..... G 212 734-2537
New York *(G-11491)*
NY Phrmacy Compounding Ctr Inc ..... G 201 403-5151
Astoria *(G-450)*
Ohr Pharmaceutical Inc ..... F 212 682-8452
New York *(G-11512)*
Oligomerix Inc ..... G 914 997-8877
New York *(G-11514)*
Ony Biotech Inc ..... E 716 636-9096
Amherst *(G-257)*
Ophthotech Corporation ..... C 212 845-8200
New York *(G-11529)*
Ovid Therapeutics Inc ..... E 646 661-7661
New York *(G-11550)*
P & L Development LLC ..... D 516 986-1700
Westbury *(G-17043)*
P & L Development LLC ..... D 516 986-1700
Westbury *(G-17044)*
P & L Development LLC ..... D 516 986-1700
Westbury *(G-17045)*
Par Pharmaceutical Inc ..... B 845 573-5500
Chestnut Ridge *(G-3653)*
Par Phrmceutical Companies Inc ..... E 845 573-5500
Chestnut Ridge *(G-3654)*
Par Sterile Products LLC ..... E 845 573-5500
Chestnut Ridge *(G-3655)*
Pdk Labs Inc ..... D 631 273-2630
Hauppauge *(G-6184)*
Perrigo Company ..... E 718 960-9900
Bronx *(G-1426)*
Perrigo New York Inc ..... F 718 901-2800
Bronx *(G-1427)*
Perrigo New York Inc ..... B 718 960-9900
Bronx *(G-1428)*
Pfizer HCP Corporation ..... F 212 733-2323
New York *(G-11656)*

Pfizer Inc ..... A 212 733-2323
New York *(G-11657)*
Pfizer Inc ..... B 518 297-6611
Rouses Point *(G-15066)*
Pfizer Inc ..... C 914 437-5868
White Plains *(G-17186)*
Pfizer Inc ..... C 937 746-3603
New York *(G-11658)*
Pfizer Inc ..... D 212 733-6276
New York *(G-11659)*
Pfizer Inc ..... C 804 257-2000
New York *(G-11660)*
Pfizer Inc ..... C 212 733-2323
New York *(G-11661)*
Pfizer Overseas LLC ..... G 212 733-2323
New York *(G-11662)*
Pharmaceutic Labs LLC ..... F 518 608-1060
Albany *(G-119)*
Photomedex Inc ..... E 888 966-1010
Orangeburg *(G-13261)*
Polygen Pharmaceuticals Inc ..... E 631 392-4044
Edgewood *(G-4621)*
Precision Pharma Services Inc ..... C 631 752-7314
Melville *(G-8378)*
Prestige Brands Intl LLC ..... F 914 524-6810
Tarrytown *(G-16126)*
Prime Pack LLC ..... F 732 253-7734
New York *(G-11732)*
Progenics Pharmaceuticals Inc ..... D 646 975-2500
New York *(G-11750)*
Purinepharma LLC ..... G 732 485-1400
Massena *(G-8230)*
Quogue Capital LLC ..... G 212 554-4475
New York *(G-11801)*
Quva Pharma Inc ..... G 973 224-7795
New York *(G-11804)*
Randob Labs Ltd ..... G 845 534-2197
Cornwall *(G-4012)*
Regeneron Pharmaceuticals Inc ..... B 914 847-7000
Tarrytown *(G-16128)*
Regenron Hlthcare Slutions Inc ..... A 914 847-7000
Tarrytown *(G-16129)*
Relmada Therapeutics Inc ..... F 646 677-3853
New York *(G-11857)*
Retrophin LLC ..... G 646 564-3680
New York *(G-11876)*
Rij Pharmaceutical Corporation ..... E 845 692-5799
Middletown *(G-8494)*
Rls Holdings Inc ..... G 716 418-7274
Clarence *(G-3697)*
Rohto USA Inc ..... G 716 677-2500
Orchard Park *(G-13320)*
Ropack USA Inc ..... F 631 482-7777
Commack *(G-3866)*
S1 Biopharma Inc ..... G 201 839-0941
New York *(G-11965)*
Salutem Group LLC ..... G 347 620-2640
New York *(G-11977)*
Saptalis Pharmaceuticals LLC ..... F 631 231-2751
Hauppauge *(G-6209)*
Scarguard Labs LLC ..... F 516 482-8050
Great Neck *(G-5856)*
Sciarra Laboratories Inc ..... G 516 933-7853
Hicksville *(G-6420)*
Sciegen Pharmaceuticals Inc ..... D 631 434-2723
Hauppauge *(G-6211)*
Scienta Pharmaceuticals LLC ..... G 845 589-0774
Valley Cottage *(G-16414)*
Seidlin Consulting ..... G 212 496-2043
New York *(G-12039)*
Shennong Pharmaceuticals Inc ..... E 347 422-2200
New York *(G-12070)*
Shrineeta Pharmacy ..... G 212 234-7959
New York *(G-12078)*
Shrineeta Pharmacy Inc ..... E 212 234-7959
New York *(G-12079)*
Siga Technologies Inc ..... E 212 672-9100
New York *(G-12088)*
Silarx Pharmaceuticals Inc ..... D 845 352-4020
Carmel *(G-3433)*
Silver Oak Pharmacy Inc ..... G 718 922-3400
Brooklyn *(G-2584)*
Sincerus LLC ..... G 800 419-2804
Brooklyn *(G-2590)*
Skills Alliance Inc ..... G 646 492-5300
New York *(G-12115)*
Stemline Therapeutics Inc ..... E 646 502-2311
New York *(G-12216)*
Steri-Pharma LLC ..... E 315 473-7180
Syracuse *(G-16069)*

Employee Codes: A=Over 500 employees, B=251-500
C=101-250, D=51-100, E=20-50, F=10-19, G=5-9
2018 Harris
New York Manufacturers Directory
1285

PHARMACEUTICALS

PRODUCT SECTION

Strategic Pharma Services Inc .... F 631 231-5424
 Brentwood (G-1192)
Strativa Pharmaceuticals Inc .... F 201 802-4000
 Spring Valley (G-15623)
Sunquest Pharmaceuticals Inc .... F 855 478-6779
 Hicksville (G-6424)
Synergy Pharmaceuticals Inc .... E 212 297-0020
 New York (G-12284)
Syntho Pharmaceuticals Inc .... G 631 755-9898
 Farmingdale (G-5132)
Tg Therapeutics Inc .... D 212 554-4484
 New York (G-12328)
Tishcon Corp .... C 516 333-3056
 Westbury (G-17062)
Tishcon Corp .... C 516 333-3050
 Westbury (G-17063)
Tmp Technologies Inc .... D 716 895-6100
 Buffalo (G-3246)
Tocare LLC .... G 718 767-0618
 Whitestone (G-17244)
Tongli Pharmaceuticals USA Inc .... F 212 842-8837
 Flushing (G-5307)
Tonix Phrmceuticals Holdg Corp .... E 212 980-9155
 New York (G-12388)
Topiderm Inc .... C 631 226-7979
 Amityville (G-330)
Topix Pharmaceuticals Inc .... B 631 226-7979
 Amityville (G-331)
Transparency Life Sciences LLC .... F 862 252-1216
 New York (G-12414)
Tyme Technologies Inc .... G 646 205-1603
 New York (G-12456)
Ucb Pharma Inc .... B 919 767-2555
 Rochester (G-14765)
United-Guardian Inc .... E 631 273-0900
 Hauppauge (G-6244)
Unither Manufacturing LLC .... C 585 475-9000
 Rochester (G-14769)
Venus Pharmaceuticals Intl Inc .... F 631 249-1140
 Hauppauge (G-6248)
Verona Pharma Inc .... F 914 797-5007
 White Plains (G-17207)
Viropro Inc .... E 650 300-5190
 New York (G-12576)
Vitalis LLC 646 831-7338
 New York (G-12583)
Vitane Pharmaceuticals Inc .... E 845 267-6700
 Congers (G-3887)
Vvs International Inc 212 302-5410
 New York (G-12599)
Wyeth Holdings LLC .... D 845 602-5000
 Pearl River (G-13293)
X-Gen Pharmaceuticals Inc .... E 607 562-2700
 Big Flats (G-880)
X-Gen Pharmaceuticals Inc .... E 631 261-8188
 Elmira (G-4720)
X-Gen Pharmaceuticals Inc .... E 607 562-2700
 Horseheads (G-6624)
Xstelos Holdings Inc .... G 212 729-4962
 New York (G-12707)
Ys Marketing Inc .... E 718 778-6080
 Brooklyn (G-2791)

PHARMACEUTICALS: Mail-Order Svc

Generics Bidco I LLC .... G 256 859-4011
 Chestnut Ridge (G-3651)
Greentree Pharmacy Inc .... F 718 768-2700
 Brooklyn (G-2055)
Natures Bounty Co .... D 631 244-2021
 Ronkonkoma (G-14977)
Natures Bounty Co .... A 631 200-2000
 Ronkonkoma (G-14978)

PHARMACEUTICALS: Medicinal & Botanical Prdts

Accredo Health Incorporated .... G 718 353-3012
 Flushing (G-5228)
Albany Molecular Research Inc .... F 518 433-7700
 Rensselaer (G-14054)
Albany Molecular Research Inc .... F 518 512-2000
 Rensselaer (G-14055)
Alo Acquisition LLC .... G 518 464-0279
 Albany (G-43)
Collaborative Laboratories .... D 631 689-0200
 East Setauket (G-4498)
GE Healthcare Inc .... F 516 626-2799
 Port Washington (G-13841)
Immudyne Inc .... F 914 244-1777
 Mount Kisco (G-8671)

Kannalife Sciences Inc .... G 516 669-3219
 Lloyd Harbor (G-7594)
Natures Bounty Co .... F 631 200-2000
 Bayport (G-753)
Regeneron Pharmaceuticals Inc .... E 518 488-6000
 Rensselaer (G-14061)
Setauket Manufacturing Co .... G 631 231-7272
 Ronkonkoma (G-15008)
Stauber California Inc .... F 845 651-4443
 Florida (G-5222)

PHARMACIES & DRUG STORES

Biomed Pharmaceuticals Inc .... G 914 592-0525
 Hawthorne (G-6267)
Far Rockaway Drugs Inc .... F 718 471-2500
 Far Rockaway (G-4929)
J P R Pharmacy Inc .... F 718 327-0600
 Far Rockaway (G-4930)
Nucare Pharmacy Inc .... F 212 426-9300
 New York (G-11485)
Nucare Pharmacy West LLC .... F 212 462-2525
 New York (G-11486)

PHONOGRAPH NEEDLES

Grado Laboratories Inc .... F 718 435-5340
 Brooklyn (G-2047)

PHONOGRAPH RECORDS WHOLESALERS

Hope International Productions .... F 212 247-3188
 New York (G-10548)
Sony Music Holdings Inc .... A 212 833-8000
 New York (G-12162)

PHONOGRAPH RECORDS: Prerecorded

Abkco Music & Records Inc .... D 212 399-0300
 New York (G-9050)
Eks Manufacturing Inc .... F 917 217-0784
 Brooklyn (G-1909)
Hope International Productions .... F 212 247-3188
 New York (G-10548)

PHOSPHATES

International Ord Tech Inc .... D 716 664-1100
 Jamestown (G-7036)
Mdi Holdings LLC .... A 212 559-1127
 New York (G-11228)

PHOTOCOPY MACHINES

Cannon Industries Inc .... D 585 254-8080
 Rochester (G-14276)
Facsimile Cmmncations Inds Inc .... D 212 741-6400
 New York (G-10178)
Xerox Corporation .... D 212 330-1386
 New York (G-12702)
Xerox Corporation .... C 585 427-4500
 Rochester (G-14797)

PHOTOCOPYING & DUPLICATING SVCS

A & D Offset Printers Ltd .... G 516 746-2476
 Mineola (G-8520)
A Q P Inc .... G 585 256-1690
 Rochester (G-14175)
Apple Press 914 723-6660
 White Plains (G-17106)
Avalon Copy Centers Amer Inc .... D 315 471-3333
 Syracuse (G-15883)
Avalon Copy Centers Amer Inc .... E 716 995-7777
 Buffalo (G-2847)
Capital Dst Print & Imaging .... D 518 456-6773
 Schenectady (G-15265)
Carges Entps of Canandaigua .... G 585 394-2600
 Canandaigua (G-3367)
Cds Productions Inc .... G 518 385-8255
 Schenectady (G-15269)
Chakra Communications Inc .... E 607 748-7491
 Endicott (G-4806)
Clarion Publications Inc .... F 585 243-3530
 Geneseo (G-5579)
Clarsons Corp .... F 585 235-8775
 Rochester (G-14299)
Constas Printing Corporation .... G 315 474-2176
 Syracuse (G-15924)
Dealer-Presscom Inc .... G 631 589-0434
 Bohemia (G-1049)
Evolution Impressions Inc .... D 585 473-6600
 Rochester (G-14382)

Fairmount Press .... G 212 255-2300
 New York (G-10183)
Fambus Inc .... G 607 785-3700
 Endicott (G-4815)
Fedex Office & Print Svcs Inc .... G 718 982-5223
 Staten Island (G-15694)
Graphic Fabrications Inc .... G 516 763-3222
 Rockville Centre (G-14819)
Graphicomm Inc .... G 716 283-0830
 Niagara Falls (G-12845)
Graphics of Utica .... G 315 797-4868
 Remsen (G-14052)
Jon Lyn Ink Inc .... G 516 546-2312
 Merrick (G-8420)
Kjckd Inc .... G 518 435-9696
 Latham (G-7395)
Leader Printing Inc .... F 516 546-1544
 Merrick (G-8422)
Mercury Print Productions Inc .... C 585 458-7900
 Rochester (G-14525)
Miller Enterprises CNY Inc .... G 315 682-4999
 Manlius (G-8108)
Multiple Imprssons of Rchester .... G 585 546-1160
 Rochester (G-14545)
National Reproductions Inc .... E 212 619-3800
 New York (G-11372)
North Delaware Printing Inc .... G 716 692-0576
 Tonawanda (G-16206)
Persch Service Print Inc .... G 716 366-2677
 Dunkirk (G-4371)
R & L Press of SI Inc .... G 718 667-3258
 Staten Island (G-15748)
Rapid Print and Marketing Inc .... G 585 924-1520
 Victor (G-16523)
Shipmtes/Printmates Holdg Corp .... D 518 370-1158
 Scotia (G-15353)
Shiprite Software Inc .... G 315 733-6191
 Utica (G-16383)
Silver Griffin Inc .... F 518 272-7771
 Troy (G-16279)
Twin Counties Pro Printers Inc .... F 518 828-3278
 Hudson (G-6667)
William J Ryan .... G 585 392-6200
 Hilton (G-6447)
Woodbury Printing Plus + Inc .... G 845 928-6610
 Central Valley (G-3557)

PHOTOELECTRIC DEVICES: Magnetic

MMC Magnetics Corp .... F 631 435-9888
 Hauppauge (G-6167)
Truebite Inc .... E 607 785-7664
 Vestal (G-16479)

PHOTOENGRAVING SVC

Atlas Graphics Inc .... G 516 997-5527
 Westbury (G-16997)
Koehlr-Gibson Mkg Graphics Inc .... E 716 838-5960
 Buffalo (G-3053)
Rapid Service Engraving Co .... G 716 896-4555
 Buffalo (G-3180)

PHOTOFINISHING LABORATORIES

Eastman Kodak Company .... B 585 724-4000
 Rochester (G-14348)

PHOTOGRAPH DEVELOPING & RETOUCHING SVCS

Digital Evolution Inc .... E 212 732-2722
 New York (G-9929)

PHOTOGRAPHIC EQPT & SPLY: Sound Recordg/Reprod Eqpt, Motion

Kelmar Systems Inc .... F 631 421-1230
 Huntington Station (G-6751)

PHOTOGRAPHIC EQPT & SPLYS

Astrodyne Inc 516 536-5755
 Oceanside (G-13092)
AVI-Spl Employee .... B 212 840-4801
 New York (G-9330)
Carestream Health Inc .... B 585 627-1800
 Rochester (G-14278)
Chemung Cnty Chpter Nysarc Inc .... C 607 734-6151
 Elmira (G-4688)
Cpac Inc .... E 585 382-3223
 Leicester (G-7442)

PRODUCT SECTION

PICTURE FRAMES: Metal

Creatron Services Inc .... E 516 437-5119
 Floral Park *(G-5208)*
Eastman Kodak Company .... E 585 724-4000
 Rochester *(G-14358)*
Ebsco Industries Inc .... G 585 398-2000
 Farmington *(G-5158)*
Emda Inc .... F 631 243-6363
 Edgewood *(G-4611)*
Garys Loft .... G 212 244-0970
 New York *(G-10296)*
Henrys Deals Inc .... E 347 821-4685
 Brooklyn *(G-2072)*
Kodak Alaris Inc .... B 585 290-2891
 Rochester *(G-14493)*
Kogeto Inc .... G 646 490-8169
 New York *(G-10907)*
Labgrafix Printing Inc .... G 516 280-8300
 Lynbrook *(G-7980)*
Lanel Inc .... F 516 437-5119
 Floral Park *(G-5212)*
Lowel-Light Manufacturing Inc .... E 718 921-0600
 Brooklyn *(G-2241)*
Mirion Technologies Ist Corp .... D 607 562-4300
 Horseheads *(G-6612)*
Norazza Inc .... G 716 706-1160
 Buffalo *(G-3116)*
Rockland Colloid Corp .... G 845 359-5559
 Piermont *(G-13572)*
Stallion Technologies Inc .... G 315 622-1176
 Liverpool *(G-7576)*
Thermo Cidtec Inc .... E 315 451-9410
 Liverpool *(G-7580)*
Tiffen Company LLC .... G 631 273-2500
 Hauppauge *(G-6239)*
Tiffen Company LLC .... D 631 273-2500
 Hauppauge *(G-6240)*
Vishay Thin Film LLC .... C 716 283-4025
 Niagara Falls *(G-12906)*
Xerox Corporation .... F 585 423-4711
 Rochester *(G-14796)*
Xerox Corporation .... B 212 716-4000
 New York *(G-12701)*
Xerox Corporation .... E 914 397-1319
 White Plains *(G-17216)*
Xerox Corporation .... D 585 425-6100
 Fairport *(G-4895)*
Xerox Corporation .... E 845 918-3147
 Suffern *(G-15823)*
Xerox Corporation .... E 518 434-6543
 Albany *(G-152)*
Xerox Corporation .... D 585 423-5090
 Webster *(G-16770)*
Xerox Corporation .... C 585 264-5584
 Rochester *(G-14799)*
Xerox Corporation .... D 716 831-3300
 Buffalo *(G-3285)*

PHOTOGRAPHIC EQPT & SPLYS WHOLESALERS

AVI-Spl Employee .... B 212 840-4801
 New York *(G-9330)*
Rockland Colloid Corp .... G 845 359-5559
 Piermont *(G-13572)*

PHOTOGRAPHIC EQPT & SPLYS: Cameras, Aerial

Fluxdata Incorporated .... G 800 425-0176
 Rochester *(G-14399)*
Geospatial Systems Inc .... F 585 427-8310
 West Henrietta *(G-16913)*

PHOTOGRAPHIC EQPT & SPLYS: Cameras, Still & Motion Pictures

Critical Imaging LLC .... E 315 732-5020
 Utica *(G-16341)*

PHOTOGRAPHIC EQPT & SPLYS: Developers, Not Chemical Plants

Eastchester Photo Services .... G 914 961-6596
 Eastchester *(G-4594)*

PHOTOGRAPHIC EQPT & SPLYS: Editing Eqpt, Motion Picture

Avid Technology Inc .... E 212 983-2424
 New York *(G-9331)*
Kyle Editing LLC .... G 212 675-3464
 New York *(G-10937)*

PHOTOGRAPHIC EQPT & SPLYS: Film, Sensitized

Eastman Kodak Company .... D 585 722-2187
 Rochester *(G-14347)*
Eastman Kodak Company .... B 585 724-4000
 Rochester *(G-14348)*
Eastman Kodak Company .... D 585 724-5600
 Rochester *(G-14349)*
Eastman Kodak Company .... D 585 722-9695
 Pittsford *(G-13587)*
Eastman Kodak Company .... D 585 726-6261
 Rochester *(G-14350)*
Eastman Kodak Company .... D 585 724-4000
 Rochester *(G-14351)*
Eastman Kodak Company .... F 800 698-3324
 Rochester *(G-14352)*
Eastman Kodak Company .... D 585 722-4385
 Rochester *(G-14353)*
Eastman Kodak Company .... D 585 588-5598
 Rochester *(G-14354)*
Eastman Kodak Company .... C 585 726-7000
 Rochester *(G-14355)*
Eastman Kodak Company .... D 585 722-4007
 Rochester *(G-14356)*
Eastman Kodak Company .... D 585 588-3896
 Rochester *(G-14357)*
Eastman Park Micrographics Inc .... E 866 934-4376
 Rochester *(G-14359)*
Truesense Imaging Inc .... C 585 784-5500
 Rochester *(G-14761)*

PHOTOGRAPHIC EQPT & SPLYS: Graphic Arts Plates, Sensitized

Gpc International Inc .... G 631 752-9600
 Melville *(G-8351)*

PHOTOGRAPHIC EQPT & SPLYS: Plates, Sensitized

Apexx Omni-Graphics Inc .... D 718 326-3330
 Maspeth *(G-8147)*

PHOTOGRAPHIC EQPT & SPLYS: Printing Eqpt

Jack L Popkin & Co Inc .... G 718 361-6700
 Kew Gardens *(G-7192)*
Printer Components Inc .... G 585 924-5190
 Fairport *(G-4877)*

PHOTOGRAPHIC EQPT & SPLYS: Processing Eqpt

All-Pro Imaging Corp .... E 516 433-7676
 Melville *(G-8325)*

PHOTOGRAPHIC EQPT & SPLYS: Shutters, Camera

Va Inc .... E 585 385-5930
 Rochester *(G-14777)*

PHOTOGRAPHIC EQPT & SPLYS: Toners, Prprd, Not Chem Plnts

Efam Enterprises LLC .... E 718 204-1760
 Long Island City *(G-7754)*
Hilord Chemical Corporation .... E 631 234-7373
 Hauppauge *(G-6117)*
Konica Mnolta Sups Mfg USA Inc ...... D 845 294-8400
 Goshen *(G-5751)*
Lasertech Crtridge RE-Builders .... G 518 373-1246
 Clifton Park *(G-3725)*
Toner-N-More Inc .... G 718 232-6200
 Brooklyn *(G-2682)*

PHOTOGRAPHIC EQPT/SPLYS, WHOL: Cameras/Projectors/Eqpt/Splys

Bescor Video Accessories Ltd .... F 631 420-1717
 Farmingdale *(G-4960)*

PHOTOGRAPHIC LIBRARY SVCS

Kraus Organization Limited .... G 212 686-5411
 New York *(G-10927)*

PHOTOGRAPHIC PEOCESSING CHEMICALS

Champion Photochemistry Inc .... D 585 760-6444
 Rochester *(G-14292)*

PHOTOGRAPHIC PROCESSING EQPT & CHEMICALS

Air Techniques Inc .... B 516 433-7676
 Melville *(G-8324)*
Seneca TEC Inc .... G 585 381-2645
 Fairport *(G-4885)*
Sima Technologies LLC .... G 412 828-9130
 Hauppauge *(G-6215)*

PHOTOGRAPHIC SENSITIZED GOODS, NEC

Turner Bellows Inc .... E 585 235-4456
 Rochester *(G-14763)*

PHOTOGRAPHIC SVCS

Labgrafix Printing Inc .... G 516 280-8300
 Lynbrook *(G-7980)*

PHOTOGRAPHY SVCS: Commercial

Folio Graphics Co Inc .... G 718 763-2076
 Brooklyn *(G-1993)*

PHOTOGRAPHY SVCS: Portrait Studios

Classic Album .... E 718 388-2818
 Brooklyn *(G-1785)*
Classic Album LLC .... D 718 388-2818
 Brooklyn *(G-1786)*

PHOTOGRAPHY SVCS: Still Or Video

Dynamic Photography Inc .... G 516 381-2951
 Roslyn *(G-15043)*

PHOTOTYPESETTING SVC

Digital Color Concepts Inc .... E 212 989-4888
 New York *(G-9928)*

PHOTOVOLTAIC Solid State

Besicorp Ltd .... F 845 336-7700
 Kingston *(G-7208)*
Onyx Solar Group LLC .... G 917 951-9732
 New York *(G-11525)*
Solar Thin Films Inc .... F 516 341-7787
 Uniondale *(G-16322)*

PHYSICAL FITNESS CENTERS

Womens Health Care PC .... G 718 850-0009
 Richmond Hill *(G-14100)*

PHYSICIANS' OFFICES & CLINICS: Medical doctors

M H Mandelbaum Orthotic .... F 631 473-8668
 Port Jefferson *(G-13799)*
Smn Medical PC .... F 844 362-2428
 Rye *(G-15094)*

PICTURE FRAMES: Metal

Access Display Group Inc .... F 516 678-7772
 Freeport *(G-5389)*
Bristol Gift Co Inc .... F 845 496-2821
 Washingtonville *(G-16620)*
Custom Frame & Molding Co .... F 631 491-9091
 West Babylon *(G-16811)*
Dobrin Industries Inc .... G 800 353-2229
 Lockport *(G-7609)*
Elias Artmetal Inc .... F 516 873-7501
 Mineola *(G-8540)*
Frame Shoppe & Art Gallery .... G 516 365-6014
 Manhasset *(G-8093)*
Inter Pacific Consulting Corp .... G 718 460-2787
 Flushing *(G-5260)*
Jay Strongwater Holdings LLC .... A 646 657-0558
 New York *(G-10745)*
Picture Perfect Framing .... G 718 851-1884
 Brooklyn *(G-2432)*
Structural Industries Inc .... C 631 471-5200
 Bohemia *(G-1134)*

PICTURE FRAMES: Wood

Amci Ltd	D	718 937-5858
Long Island City *(G-7689)*		
Apf Manufacturing Company LLC	E	914 963-6300
Yonkers *(G-17432)*		
Cdnv Wood Carving Frames Inc	F	914 375-3447
Yonkers *(G-17442)*		
Drummond Framing Inc	F	212 647-1701
New York *(G-9983)*		
FG Galassi Moulding Co Inc	G	845 258-2100
Goshen *(G-5749)*		
Fred M Lawrence Co Inc	E	718 786-7227
Bay Shore *(G-699)*		
Galas Framing Services	F	718 706-0007
Long Island City *(G-7776)*		
Grant-Noren	G	845 726-4281
Westtown *(G-17099)*		
House of Heydenryk Jr Inc	F	212 206-9611
New York *(G-10561)*		
Hubray Inc	F	800 645-2855
North Baldwin *(G-12924)*		
Interntonal Consmr Connections	F	516 481-3438
West Hempstead *(G-16887)*		
Lco Destiny LLC	B	315 782-3302
Watertown *(G-16684)*		
North American Enclosures Inc	E	631 234-9500
Central Islip *(G-3534)*		
Picture Perfect Framing	G	718 851-1884
Brooklyn *(G-2432)*		
Regence Picture Frames Inc	E	718 779-0888
Lynbrook *(G-7985)*		
Structural Industries Inc	C	631 471-5200
Bohemia *(G-1134)*		

PICTURE FRAMING SVCS, CUSTOM

Frame Shoppe & Art Gallery	G	516 365-6014
Manhasset *(G-8093)*		
Galas Framing Services	F	718 706-0007
Long Island City *(G-7776)*		
Interntonal Consmr Connections	F	516 481-3438
West Hempstead *(G-16887)*		
Timeless Decor LLC	C	315 782-5759
Watertown *(G-16697)*		

PICTURE PROJECTION EQPT

Just Lamps of New York Inc	F	716 626-2240
Buffalo *(G-3039)*		

PIECE GOODS & NOTIONS WHOLESALERS

Hpk Industries LLC	F	315 724-0196
Utica *(G-16362)*		
J & M Textile Co Inc	F	212 268-8000
New York *(G-10715)*		
Triangle Label Tag Inc	G	718 875-3030
Brooklyn *(G-2697)*		

PIECE GOODS, NOTIONS & DRY GOODS, WHOL: Textile Converters

Bank-Miller Co Inc	E	914 227-9357
Pelham *(G-13514)*		
Klauber Brothers Inc	D	212 686-2531
New York *(G-10897)*		
La Lame Inc	G	212 921-9770
New York *(G-10947)*		

PIECE GOODS, NOTIONS & DRY GOODS, WHOL: Textiles, Woven

Kowa American Corporation	E	212 303-7800
New York *(G-10920)*		
Mutual Sales Corp	E	718 361-8373
Long Island City *(G-7848)*		
Zorlu USA Inc	F	212 689-4622
New York *(G-12739)*		

PIECE GOODS, NOTIONS & DRY GOODS, WHOLESALE: Fabrics, Knit

Continental Knitting Mills	G	631 242-5330
Deer Park *(G-4142)*		

PIECE GOODS, NOTIONS & DRY GOODS, WHOLESALE: Fabrics, Lace

Empire Bias Binding Co Inc	F	718 545-0300
Long Island City *(G-7759)*		

PIECE GOODS, NOTIONS & DRY GOODS, WHOLESALE: Sewing Access

Penn & Fletcher Inc	F	212 239-6868
Long Island City *(G-7870)*		
Super-Trim Inc	E	212 255-2370
New York *(G-12263)*		
Bfma Holding Corporation	G	607 753-6746
Cortland *(G-4036)*		

PIECE GOODS, NOTIONS & OTHER DRY GOODS, WHOLESALE: Bridal

Alvina Vlenta Couture Collectn	G	212 921-7058
New York *(G-9157)*		

PIECE GOODS, NOTIONS & OTHER DRY GOODS, WHOLESALE: Buttons

Emsig Manufacturing Corp	F	518 828-7301
Hudson *(G-6643)*		
Hemisphere Novelties Inc	E	914 378-4100
Yonkers *(G-17469)*		

PIECE GOODS, NOTIONS & OTHER DRY GOODS, WHOLESALE: Fabrics

Creation Baumann USA Inc	E	516 764-7431
Rockville Centre *(G-14818)*		
Eu Design LLC	G	212 420-7788
New York *(G-10135)*		
Sifonya Inc	E	212 620-4512
New York *(G-12087)*		

PIECE GOODS, NOTIONS & OTHER DRY GOODS, WHOLESALE: Woven

Citisource Industries Inc	E	212 683-1033
New York *(G-9678)*		

PIECE GOODS, NOTIONS/DRY GOODS, WHOL: Drapery Mtrl, Woven

Richloom Fabrics Corp	F	212 685-5400
New York *(G-11894)*		
Scalamandre Silks Inc	D	212 980-3888
New York *(G-12002)*		

PIECE GOODS, NOTIONS/DRY GOODS, WHOL: Linen Piece, Woven

Simple Elegance New York Inc	F	718 360-1947
Brooklyn *(G-2589)*		

PIECE GOODS, NOTIONS/DRY GOODS, WHOL: Sewing Splys/Notions

Artistic Ribbon Novelty Co Inc	E	212 255-4224
New York *(G-9271)*		

PILLOW FILLING MTRLS: Curled Hair, Cotton Waste, Moss

American Home Mfg LLC	G	212 643-0680
New York *(G-9169)*		

PILLOWS: Sponge Rubber

Schlegel Systems Inc	C	585 427-7200
Rochester *(G-14695)*		

PINS

Jin Pin Market Inc	G	718 898-0788
Jackson Heights *(G-6922)*		
Pin Pharma Inc	G	212 543-2583
New York *(G-11683)*		
Pins N Needles	G	212 535-6222
New York *(G-11687)*		
Pni Capital Partners	G	516 466-7120
Westbury *(G-17047)*		

PIPE & FITTING: Fabrication

Accord Pipe Fabricators Inc	E	718 657-3900
Jamaica *(G-6927)*		
Advanced Thermal Systems Inc	E	716 681-1800
Lancaster *(G-7322)*		
Albany Nipple and Pipe Mfg	E	518 270-2162
Troy *(G-16239)*		
Arcadia Mfg Group Inc	E	518 434-6213
Green Island *(G-5871)*		
Arcadia Mfg Group Inc	G	518 434-6213
Menands *(G-8399)*		
Cobey Inc	C	716 362-9550
Buffalo *(G-2897)*		
Daikin Applied Americas Inc	D	315 253-2771
Auburn *(G-490)*		
Flatcut LLC	E	212 542-5732
Brooklyn *(G-1984)*		
H & H Metal Specialty Inc	E	716 665-2110
Jamestown *(G-7031)*		
J D Steward Inc	G	718 358-0169
Flushing *(G-5263)*		
James Woerner Inc	G	631 454-9330
Farmingdale *(G-5024)*		
Juniper Elbow Co Inc	C	718 326-2546
Middle Village *(G-8447)*		
Juniper Industries Florida Inc	G	718 326-2546
Middle Village *(G-8448)*		
Leo International Inc	E	718 290-8005
Brooklyn *(G-2214)*		
Leroy Plastics Inc	D	585 768-8158
Le Roy *(G-7437)*		
Long Island Pipe Supply Inc	G	718 456-7877
Flushing *(G-5274)*		
Long Island Pipe Supply Inc	G	518 270-2159
Troy *(G-16243)*		
Long Island Pipe Supply Inc	E	516 222-8008
Garden City *(G-5529)*		
Met Weld International LLC	D	518 765-2318
Altamont *(G-213)*		
Micromold Products Inc	E	914 969-2850
Yonkers *(G-17485)*		
Rochester Tube Fabricators	F	585 254-0290
Rochester *(G-14676)*		
Tag Flange & Machining Inc	G	516 536-1300
Oceanside *(G-13122)*		
Truly Tubular Fitting Corp	F	914 664-4686
Mount Vernon *(G-8788)*		
Wedco Fabrications Inc	G	718 852-6330
College Point *(G-3836)*		

PIPE & FITTINGS: Cast Iron

Cpp - Guaymas	C	315 687-0014
Chittenango *(G-3661)*		
Dragon Trading Inc	G	212 717-1496
New York *(G-9974)*		

PIPE & FITTINGS: Pressure, Cast Iron

Acme Nipple Mfg Co Inc	G	716 873-7491
Buffalo *(G-2811)*		
Penner Elbow Company Inc	F	718 526-9000
Elmhurst *(G-4679)*		

PIPE CLEANERS

R V Dow Enterprises Inc	F	585 454-5862
Rochester *(G-14644)*		

PIPE JOINT COMPOUNDS

Continental Buchanan LLC	D	703 480-3800
Buchanan *(G-2799)*		

PIPE: Concrete

Binghamton Precast & Sup Corp	E	607 722-0334
Binghamton *(G-890)*		
Roman Stone Construction Co	E	631 667-0566
Bay Shore *(G-733)*		

PIPE: Extruded, Aluminum

North American Pipe Corp	F	516 338-2863
Jericho *(G-7111)*		

PIPE: Plastic

Advanced Distribution System	D	845 848-2357
Palisades *(G-13425)*		
BMC LLC	E	716 681-7755
Buffalo *(G-2866)*		
Hancor Inc	D	607 565-3033
Waverly *(G-16728)*		
Micromold Products Inc	E	914 969-2850
Yonkers *(G-17485)*		
National Pipe & Plastics Inc	C	607 729-9381
Vestal *(G-16474)*		
North American Pipe Corp	F	516 338-2863
Jericho *(G-7111)*		

PRODUCT SECTION

PLASTICS MATERIAL & RESINS

Prince Rubber & Plas Co Inc .... E 225 272-1653
Buffalo (G-3161)

PIPE: Sheet Metal

Lane Enterprises Inc .... E 518 885-4385
Ballston Spa (G-599)

PIPES & TUBES: Steel

Coventry Manufacturing Co Inc .... E 914 668-2212
Mount Vernon (G-8719)
Handy & Harman .... E 914 461-1300
White Plains (G-17145)
Liberty Pipe Incorporated .... G 516 747-2472
Mineola (G-8554)
Markin Tubing LP .... F 585 495-6211
Buffalo (G-3077)
McHone Industries Inc .... D 716 945-3380
Salamanca (G-15128)
Micromold Products Inc .... E 914 969-2850
Yonkers (G-17485)
Ocean Steel Corporation .... E 607 584-7500
Conklin (G-3897)
Stony Brook Mfg Co Inc .... E 631 369-9530
Calverton (G-3326)
Super Steelworks Corporation .... G 718 386-4770
Deer Park (G-4239)
Tricon Piping Systems Inc .... F 315 655-4178
Canastota (G-3401)
Welded Tube Usa Inc .... D 716 828-1111
Lackawanna (G-7276)

PIPES & TUBES: Welded

Oriskany Mfg Tech LLC .... E 315 732-4962
Yorkville (G-17542)

PIPES: Steel & Iron

Cs Manufacturing Limited .... E 607 587-8154
Alfred (G-196)
Lino International Inc .... G 516 482-7100
Great Neck (G-5838)

PIPES: Tobacco

Ryers Creek Corp .... E 607 523-6617
Corning (G-4000)
S M Frank & Company Inc .... G 914 739-3100
New Windsor (G-8997)

PISTONS & PISTON RINGS

Fcmp Inc .... F 716 692-4623
Tonawanda (G-16179)

PLACEMATS: Plastic Or Textile

Baby Signature Inc .... G 212 686-1700
New York (G-9351)

PLANING MILLS: Independent, Exc Millwork

Embassy Millwork Inc .... F 518 839-0965
Amsterdam (G-344)

PLANING MILLS: Millwork

Mind Designs Inc .... G 631 563-3644
Farmingville (G-5168)

PLANT CARE SVCS

Plant-Tech2o Inc .... G 516 483-7845
Hempstead (G-6307)

PLAQUES: Clay, Plaster/Papier-Mache, Factory Production

B & R Promotional Products .... G 212 563-0040
New York (G-9341)

PLAQUES: Picture, Laminated

B & R Promotional Products .... G 212 563-0040
New York (G-9341)
Donorwall Inc .... F 212 766-9670
New York (G-9958)
Kelly Foundry & Machine Co .... E 315 732-8313
Utica (G-16370)

PLASMAS

C T M Industries Ltd .... E 718 479-3300
Jamaica (G-6935)
Coral Blood Service .... F 800 483-4888
Elmsford (G-4752)
D C I Plasma Center Inc .... G 914 241-1646
Mount Kisco (G-8667)
Lake Immunogenics Inc .... F 585 265-1973
Ontario (G-13227)

PLASTER WORK: Ornamental & Architectural

American Wood Column Corp .... G 718 782-3163
Brooklyn (G-1608)

PLASTIC COLORING & FINISHING

Color Craft Finishing Corp .... F 631 563-3230
Bohemia (G-1034)

PLASTIC PRDTS

Castino Corporation .... G 845 229-0341
Hyde Park (G-6772)
G and G Service .... G 518 785-9247
Latham (G-7390)
Kc Tag Co .... G 518 842-6666
Amsterdam (G-353)
Sabic Innovative Plastics .... E 713 448-7474
East Greenbush (G-4424)

PLASTIC PRDTS REPAIR SVCS

All Spec Finishing Inc .... E 607 770-9174
Binghamton (G-883)

PLASTICIZERS, ORGANIC: Cyclic & Acyclic

Wecare Organics LLC .... E 315 689-1937
Jordan (G-7159)

PLASTICS FILM & SHEET

Astra Products Inc .... G 631 464-4747
Copiague (G-3921)
Dunmore Corporation .... D 845 279-5061
Brewster (G-1214)
Farber Plastics Inc .... E 516 378-4860
Freeport (G-5408)
Farber Trucking Corp .... E 516 378-4860
Freeport (G-5409)
Favorite Plastic Corp .... C 718 253-7000
Brooklyn (G-1964)
Kings Film & Sheet Inc .... E 718 624-7510
Brooklyn (G-2174)
Maco Bag Corporation .... C 315 226-1000
Newark (G-12755)
Royal Plastics Corp .... E 718 647-7500
Brooklyn (G-2533)

PLASTICS FILM & SHEET: Polyethylene

Clear View Bag Company Inc .... C 518 458-7153
Albany (G-64)
Nationwide Tarps Incorporated .... D 518 843-1545
Amsterdam (G-362)
Potential Poly Bag Inc .... G 718 258-0800
Brooklyn (G-2443)
Sentinel Products Corp .... F 518 568-7036
Saint Johnsville (G-15124)

PLASTICS FILM & SHEET: Polyvinyl

Shaant Industries Inc .... E 716 366-3654
Dunkirk (G-4374)

PLASTICS FILM & SHEET: Vinyl

Ace Canvas & Tent Corp .... F 631 648-0614
Ronkonkoma (G-14876)
Latham International Inc .... F 518 346-5292
Schenectady (G-15302)
Latham International Inc .... G 518 783-7776
Latham (G-7396)
Nuhart & Co Inc .... D 718 383-8484
Brooklyn (G-2390)
Orafol Americas Inc .... E 585 272-0309
Henrietta (G-6321)
Plascal Corp .... G 516 249-2200
Farmingdale (G-5091)
Pocono Pool Products-North .... E 518 283-1023
Rensselaer (G-14060)

Robeco/Ascot Products Inc .... G 516 248-1521
Garden City (G-5544)
Vinyl Materials Inc .... E 631 586-9444
Deer Park (G-4249)

PLASTICS FINISHED PRDTS: Laminated

Advanced Assembly Services Inc .... G 716 217-8144
Angola (G-378)
Anthony River Inc .... F 315 475-1315
Syracuse (G-15875)
Blue Sky Plastic Production .... F 718 366-3966
Brooklyn (G-1702)
Inter State Laminates Inc .... E 518 283-8355
Poestenkill (G-13754)
Solid Surface Acrylics Inc .... E 716 743-1870
North Tonawanda (G-13012)
Synthetic Textiles Inc .... G 716 842-2598
Buffalo (G-3231)
Unico Special Products Inc .... E 845 562-9255
Newburgh (G-12807)

PLASTICS MATERIAL & RESINS

American Acrylic Corporation .... E 631 422-2200
West Babylon (G-16795)
Ashley Resin Corp .... G 718 851-8111
Brooklyn (G-1641)
Atc Plastics LLC .... E 212 375-2515
New York (G-9297)
Bairnco Corporation .... E 914 461-1300
White Plains (G-17108)
Barrett Bronze Inc .... E 914 699-6060
Mount Vernon (G-8710)
Ccmi Inc .... G 315 781-3270
Geneva (G-5583)
Clarence Resins and Chemicals .... G 716 406-9804
Clarence Center (G-3699)
CN Group Incorporated .... A 914 358-5690
White Plains (G-17122)
Cytec Industries Inc .... D 716 372-9650
Olean (G-13162)
Cytec Olean Inc .... D 716 372-9650
Olean (G-13163)
Dice America Inc 585 869-6200
Victor (G-16497)
Durez Corporation .... F 716 286-0100
Niagara Falls (G-12834)
E I Du Pont De Nemours & Co .... E 716 876-4420
Buffalo (G-2938)
Endurart Inc .... E 212 473-7000
New York (G-10087)
GE Plastics .... G 518 475-5011
Selkirk (G-15377)
General Vy-Coat LLC .... E 718 266-6002
Brooklyn (G-2019)
Global Plastics LP .... F 800 417-4605
New York (G-10361)
International Casein Corp Cal .... G 516 466-4363
Great Neck (G-5832)
Macneil Polymers Inc .... F 716 681-7755
Buffalo (G-3073)
Maviano Corp .... G 845 494-2598
Monsey (G-8610)
MB Plastics Inc .... F 718 523-1180
Greenlawn (G-5892)
Mitsui Chemicals America Inc .... E 914 253-0777
Rye Brook (G-15098)
Momentive Performance Mtls Inc .... D 914 784-4807
Tarrytown (G-16121)
Nationwide Tarps Incorporated .... D 518 843-1545
Amsterdam (G-362)
Parker-Hannifin Corporation .... E 315 926-4211
Marion (G-8127)
Polycast Industries Inc .... E 631 595-2530
Bay Shore (G-722)
Sabic Innovative Plas US LLC .... B 518 475-5011
Selkirk (G-15380)
Saga International Recycl LLC .... G 718 621-5900
Brooklyn (G-2553)
Saint-Gobain Prfmce Plas Corp .... C 518 642-2200
Granville (G-5796)
SC Medical Overseas Inc .... G 516 935-8500
Jericho (G-7117)
Solid Surfaces Inc .... E 585 292-5340
Rochester (G-14716)
Telechemische Inc .... G 845 561-3237
Newburgh (G-12805)
Terphane Holdings LLC .... E 585 657-5800
Bloomfield (G-984)
Tmp Technologies Inc .... D 716 895-6100
Buffalo (G-3246)

Employee Codes: A=Over 500 employees, B=251-500
C=101-250, D=51-100, E=20-50, F=10-19, G=5-9

PLASTICS MATERIAL & RESINS — PRODUCT SECTION

Toray Holding (usa) Inc .... E 212 697-8150
  New York (G-12393)
Toray Industries Inc 212 697-8150
  New York (G-12394)
Transpo Industries Inc .... E 914 636-1000
  New Rochelle (G-8972)
Tri-Seal Holdings Inc .... D 845 353-3300
  Blauvelt (G-972)
Unico Inc .... F 845 562-9255
  Newburgh (G-12806)
Wilsonart Intl Holdings LLC .... E 516 935-6980
  Bethpage (G-878)
WR Smith & Sons Inc .... G 845 620-9400
  Nanuet (G-8809)

PLASTICS MATERIALS, BASIC FORMS & SHAPES WHOLESALERS

Fibre Materials Corp .... E 516 349-1660
  Plainview (G-13631)
Plastic-Craft Products Corp .... E 845 358-3010
  West Nyack (G-16954)

PLASTICS PROCESSING

A & G Heat Sealing .... G 631 724-7764
  Smithtown (G-15503)
A-1 Products Inc .... G 718 789-1818
  Brooklyn (G-1539)
Adirondack Plas & Recycl Inc ..... E 518 746-9212
  Argyle (G-406)
All American Precision TI Mold ... F 585 436-3080
  West Henrietta (G-16897)
American Visuals Inc .... G 631 694-6104
  Farmingdale (G-4949)
Brandys Mold and Tool Ctr Ltd ... F 585 334-8333
  West Henrietta (G-16904)
Buffalo Polymer Processors Inc ... E 716 537-3153
  Holland (G-6507)
Cdj Stamping Inc .... G 585 224-8120
  Rochester (G-14283)
Centro Inc .... B 212 791-9450
  New York (G-9619)
Commodore Plastics LLC .... E 585 657-7777
  Bloomfield (G-979)
Continental Latex Corp .... F 718 783-7883
  Brooklyn (G-1798)
CSP Technologies Inc .... E 518 627-0051
  Amsterdam (G-342)
Custom Lucite Creations Inc ...... F 718 871-2000
  Brooklyn (G-1827)
Dacobe Enterprises LLC .... F 315 368-0093
  Utica (G-16343)
Dawnex Industries Inc .... F 718 384-0199
  Brooklyn (G-1843)
Eck Plastic Arts Inc .... E 607 722-3227
  Binghamton (G-905)
Fbm Galaxy Inc .... F 315 463-5144
  East Syracuse (G-4542)
Fei Products LLC .... E 716 693-6230
  North Tonawanda (G-12990)
Formed Plastics Inc .... D 516 334-2300
  Carle Place (G-3414)
Genpak LLC .... C 845 343-7971
  Middletown (G-8476)
Germanow-Simon Corporation .... E 585 232-1440
  Rochester (G-14420)
Gifford Group Inc .... F 212 569-8500
  New York (G-10334)
Imperial Polymers Inc .... G 718 387-4741
  Brooklyn (G-2097)
Inhance Technologies LLC .... E 716 825-9031
  Buffalo (G-3026)
Innovative Plastics Corp .... C 845 359-7500
  Orangeburg (G-13252)
Johnson Manufacturing Co .... G 631 472-1184
  Bayport (G-752)
L I C Screen Printing Inc .... E 516 546-7289
  Merrick (G-8421)
Major-IPC Inc .... G 845 292-2200
  Liberty (G-7460)
Md4 Holdings Inc .... F 315 434-1869
  East Syracuse (G-4563)
Mettowee Lumber & Plastics Co . E 518 642-1100
  Granville (G-5793)
Mold-A-Matic Corporation .... E 607 433-2121
  Oneonta (G-13211)
Nalge Nunc International Corp ... A 585 498-2661
  Rochester (G-14547)
P V C Molding Technologies ...... F 315 331-1212
  Newark (G-12761)

Patmian LLC .... B 212 758-0770
  New York (G-11594)
Plastic Works .... G 914 576-2050
  New Rochelle (G-8965)
Plastic-Craft Products Corp .... E 845 358-3010
  West Nyack (G-16954)
Plasticycle Corporation .... G 914 997-6882
  White Plains (G-17187)
Prince Rubber & Plas Co Inc 225 272-1653
  Buffalo (G-3161)
Richlar Industries Inc .... F 315 463-5144
  East Syracuse (G-4574)
Rimco Plastics Corp 607 739-3864
  Horseheads (G-6619)
Royce Associates A Ltd Partnr .. G 516 367-6298
  Jericho (G-7115)
Russell Plastics Tech Co Inc ...... C 631 963-8602
  Lindenhurst (G-7504)
Seal Reinforced Fiberglass Inc ... E 631 842-2230
  Copiague (G-3949)
Seal Reinforced Fiberglass Inc ... E 631 842-2230
  Copiague (G-3950)
Shamrock Plastic Corporation ..... G 585 328-6040
  Rochester (G-14704)
Shamrock Plastics & Tool Inc .... G 585 328-6040
  Rochester (G-14705)
Silvatrim Corp .... C 212 675-0933
  New York (G-12097)
Structural Industries Inc .... E 631 471-5200
  Bohemia (G-1134)
Teva Womens Health Inc .... F 716 693-6230
  North Tonawanda (G-13020)
Toray Industries Inc 212 697-8150
  New York (G-12394)
Tulip Molded Plastics Corp .... D 716 282-1261
  Niagara Falls (G-12902)
Unifab Inc 585 235-1760
  Rochester (G-14768)
Unifuse LLC .... F 845 889-4000
  Staatsburg (G-15639)
United Plastics Inc .... G 718 389-2255
  Brooklyn (G-2721)
Usheco Inc .... F 845 658-9200
  Kingston (G-7250)
Viele Manufacturing Corp .... B 718 893-2200
  Bronx (G-1490)
Vinyl Materials Inc 631 586-9444
  Deer Park (G-4249)
W Kintz Plastics Inc .... C 518 296-8513
  Howes Cave (G-6629)
Zan Optics Products Inc .... E 718 435-0533
  Brooklyn (G-2794)
Zone Fabricators Inc .... F 718 272-0200
  Ozone Park (G-13414)

PLASTICS SHEET: Packing Materials

Edco Supply Corporation .... D 718 788-8108
  Brooklyn (G-1905)
Knoll Printing & Packaging Inc ... 516 621-0100
  Syosset (G-15846)
Precision Packaging Pdts Inc ..... C 585 638-8200
  Holley (G-6517)
Tri-Seal Holdings Inc .... D 845 353-3300
  Blauvelt (G-972)

PLASTICS: Blow Molded

Bst United Corp .... F 631 777-2110
  Farmingdale (G-4962)
Confer Plastics Inc .... C 800 635-3213
  North Tonawanda (G-12985)

PLASTICS: Cast

Albest Metal Stamping Corp ...... D 718 388-6000
  Brooklyn (G-1575)
Discover Casting Inc .... F 212 302-5060
  New York (G-9936)
Miller Technology Inc .... G 631 694-2224
  Farmingdale (G-5065)

PLASTICS: Extruded

Albany International Corp .... C 607 749-7226
  Homer (G-6543)
Burnham Polymeric Inc .... E 518 792-3040
  Fort Edward (G-5348)
Certainteed Corporation 716 827-7560
  Buffalo (G-2891)
Christi Plastics Inc 585 436-8510
  Rochester (G-14296)

E & T Plastic Mfg Co Inc .... E 718 729-6226
  Long Island City (G-7751)
East Cast Clor Compounding Inc . G 631 491-9000
  West Babylon (G-16815)
Eastern Industrial Steel Corp ...... G 845 639-9749
  New City (G-8832)
Finger Lakes Extrusion Corp ...... E 585 905-0632
  Canandaigua (G-3375)
Kleer-Fax Inc .... D 631 225-1100
  Amityville (G-303)
Pawling Engineered Pdts Inc ...... C 845 855-1000
  Pawling (G-13475)
Phoenix Services Group LLC ..... E 518 828-6611
  Hudson (G-6661)
Streamline Plastics Co Inc .... E 718 401-4000
  Bronx (G-1464)

PLASTICS: Finished Injection Molded

A R V Precision Mfg Inc .... G 631 293-9643
  Farmingdale (G-4934)
Alliance Precision Plas Corp ...... C 585 426-5310
  Rochester (G-14204)
Alliance Precision Plas Corp ...... E 585 426-5310
  Rochester (G-14205)
Aluminum Injection Mold Co LLC .. G 585 502-6087
  Le Roy (G-7427)
Anna Young Assoc Ltd .... C 516 546-4400
  Freeport (G-5397)
Aztec Tool Co Inc .... E 631 243-1144
  Edgewood (G-4607)
Colonie Plastics Corp .... C 631 434-6969
  Bay Shore (G-684)
Epp Team Inc .... E 585 454-4995
  Rochester (G-14375)
Everblock Systems LLC .... G 844 422-5625
  New York (G-10143)
H & H Hulls Inc .... G 518 828-1339
  Hudson (G-6646)
Harbec Inc .... D 585 265-0010
  Ontario (G-13225)
J T Systematic .... G 607 754-0929
  Endwell (G-4841)
Joe Pietryka Incorporated .... E 845 855-1201
  Pawling (G-13473)
K & H Precision Products Inc .... E 585 624-4894
  Honeoye Falls (G-6560)
Leidel Corporation .... E 631 244-0900
  Bohemia (G-1088)
M & M Molding Corp .... C 631 582-1900
  Central Islip (G-3530)
PMI Industries LLC .... E 585 464-8050
  Rochester (G-14605)
Primoplast Inc .... F 631 750-0680
  Bohemia (G-1117)
Sterling Molded Products Inc ..... E 845 344-4546
  Middletown (G-8498)

PLASTICS: Injection Molded

American Casting and Mfg Corp . D 800 342-0333
  Plainview (G-13611)
American Casting and Mfg Corp . 516 349-7010
  Plainview (G-13612)
American Spacer Technologies 518 828-1339
  Hudson (G-6633)
Anka Tool & Die Inc .... E 845 268-4116
  Congers (G-3875)
Armstrong Mold Corporation .... E 315 437-1517
  East Syracuse (G-4521)
Armstrong Mold Corporation .... D 315 437-1517
  East Syracuse (G-4522)
Autronic Plastics Inc .... D 516 333-7577
  Central Islip (G-3510)
Avanti U S A Ltd .... F 716 695-5800
  Tonawanda (G-16162)
Barton Tool Inc .... G 716 665-2801
  Falconer (G-4899)
Cambridge Security Seals LLC ... E 845 520-4111
  Pomona (G-13758)
Carolina Precision Plas LLC .... D 631 981-0743
  Ronkonkoma (G-14914)
Cast-All Corporation .... E 516 741-4025
  Mineola (G-8535)
Cast-All Corporation .... E 516 741-4025
  Mineola (G-8536)
Century Mold Company Inc .... D 585 352-8600
  Rochester (G-14287)
Century Mold Mexico LLC 585 352-8600
  Rochester (G-14288)
Champlain Plastics Inc .... D 518 297-3700
  Rouses Point (G-15065)

Chenango Valley Tech Inc....E.... 607 674-4115
Sherburne (G-15411)
Clifford H Jones Inc....F.... 716 693-2444
Tonawanda (G-16174)
CPI of Falconer Inc....E.... 716 664-4444
Falconer (G-4901)
Craftech Industries Inc....D.... 518 828-5001
Hudson (G-6640)
Cs Manufacturing Limited....E.... 607 587-8154
Alfred (G-196)
Currier Plastics Inc....D.... 315 255-1779
Auburn (G-489)
Cy Plastics Works Inc....E.... 585 229-2555
Honeoye (G-6551)
East Pattern & Model Corp....E.... 585 461-3240
Fairport (G-4861)
Em-Kay Molds Inc....G.... 716 895-6180
Buffalo (G-2949)
Ernie Green Industries Inc....D.... 585 295-8951
Rochester (G-14377)
Ernie Green Industries Inc....C.... 585 647-2300
Rochester (G-14378)
Ernie Green Industries Inc....D.... 585 647-2300
Rochester (G-14379)
Extreme Molding LLC....E.... 518 326-9319
Watervliet (G-16708)
Faro Industries Inc....F.... 585 647-6000
Rochester (G-14390)
Felchar Manufacturing Corp....A.... 607 723-3106
Binghamton (G-909)
G N R Plastics Inc....G.... 631 724-8758
Smithtown (G-15509)
Galt Industries Inc....G.... 212 758-0770
New York (G-10290)
Gen-West Associates LLC....G.... 315 255-1779
Auburn (G-496)
Genesee Precision Inc....E.... 585 344-0385
Batavia (G-636)
Hansa Plastics Inc....F.... 631 269-9050
Kings Park (G-7201)
Highland Injection Molding....D.... 716 945-2424
Salamanca (G-15127)
Ilion Plastics Inc....F.... 315 894-4868
Ilion (G-6780)
Illinois Tool Works Inc....D.... 860 435-2574
Millerton (G-8514)
Imco Inc....E.... 585 352-7810
Spencerport (G-15594)
Inteva Products LLC....B.... 248 655-8886
New York (G-10685)
K & H Industries Inc....F.... 716 312-0088
Hamburg (G-5953)
K & H Industries Inc....E.... 716 312-0088
Hamburg (G-5954)
Kobe Steel USA Holdings Inc....G.... 212 751-9400
New York (G-10904)
Master Molding Inc....F.... 631 694-1444
Farmingdale (G-5053)
Midbury Industries Inc....F.... 516 868-0600
Freeport (G-5424)
Milne Mfg Inc....F.... 716 772-2536
Gasport (G-5574)
Minico Industries Inc....G.... 631 595-1455
Bay Shore (G-716)
Natech Plastics Inc....E.... 631 580-3506
Ronkonkoma (G-14974)
New York Manufactured Products....F.... 585 254-9353
Rochester (G-14552)
Nordon Inc....D.... 585 546-6200
Rochester (G-14558)
Oneida Molded Plastics LLC....C.... 315 363-7980
Oneida (G-13183)
P M Plastics Inc....E.... 716 662-1255
Orchard Park (G-13311)
Peninsula Plastics Ltd....D.... 716 854-3050
Buffalo (G-3141)
Polymer Engineered Pdts Inc....D.... 585 426-1811
Rochester (G-14607)
Precision Techniques Inc....D.... 718 991-1440
Stony Point (G-15798)
Pylantis New York LLC....G.... 310 429-5911
Groton (G-5923)
Rochling Advent Tool & Mold LP....D.... 585 254-2000
Rochester (G-14677)
Southern Tier Plastics Inc....D.... 607 723-2601
Binghamton (G-945)
Staroba Plastics Inc....C.... 716 537-3153
Holland (G-6511)
Stuart Mold & Manufacturing....F.... 716 488-9765
Falconer (G-4921)
Surprise Plastics Inc....C.... 718 492-6355
Brooklyn (G-2654)
Syntec Technologies Inc....E.... 585 768-2513
Rochester (G-14736)
Syracuse Plastics LLC....C.... 315 637-9881
Liverpool (G-7578)
T A Tool & Molding Inc....F.... 631 293-0172
Farmingdale (G-5133)
Tessy Plastics Corp....B.... 315 689-3924
Skaneateles (G-15488)
Tessy Plastics Corp....A.... 315 689-3924
Elbridge (G-4639)
Titherington Design & Mfg....F.... 518 324-2205
Plattsburgh (G-13733)
Toolroom Express Inc....D.... 607 723-5373
Conklin (G-3902)
Trimac Molding Services....G.... 607 967-2900
Bainbridge (G-554)
Turbo Plastics Corp Inc....F.... 631 345-9768
Yaphank (G-17422)

PLASTICS: Molded

Abr Molding Andy LLC....F.... 212 576-1821
Ridgewood (G-14111)
Ace Molding & Tool Inc....G.... 631 567-2355
Bohemia (G-1002)
Baird Mold Making Inc....G.... 631 667-0322
Bay Shore (G-673)
Chocolate Delivery Systems Inc....D.... 716 854-6050
Buffalo (G-2892)
Craftech....D.... 518 828-5011
Chatham (G-3585)
Dutchland Plastics LLC....C.... 315 280-0247
Sherrill (G-15428)
Egli Machine Company Inc....E.... 607 563-3663
Sidney (G-15461)
Engineered Molding Tech LLC....F.... 518 482-2004
Albany (G-78)
Form-Tec Inc....E.... 516 867-0200
Freeport (G-5410)
ISO Plastics Corp....D.... 914 663-8300
Mount Vernon (G-8739)
K2 Plastics Inc....G.... 585 494-2727
Bergen (G-846)
Mechanical Rubber Pdts Co Inc....F.... 845 986-2271
Warwick (G-16616)
Mercury Plastics Corp....E.... 718 498-5400
Brooklyn (G-2304)
Mirage Moulding Mfg Inc....F.... 631 843-6168
Farmingdale (G-5066)
Monarch Plastics Inc....E.... 716 569-2175
Frewsburg (G-5465)
Msi-Molding Solutions Inc....E.... 315 736-2412
Rome (G-14850)
Niagara Fiberglass Inc....E.... 716 822-3921
Buffalo (G-3109)
Pawling Corporation....C.... 845 855-1000
Pawling (G-13474)
Peconic Plastics Inc....F.... 631 653-3676
Quogue (G-14028)
Pii Holdings Inc....G.... 716 876-9951
Buffalo (G-3149)
Piper Plastics Corp....E.... 631 842-6889
Copiague (G-3942)
Polymer Conversions Inc....D.... 716 662-8550
Orchard Park (G-13315)
Protective Industries Inc....C.... 716 876-9951
Buffalo (G-3165)
Protective Industries Inc....C.... 716 876-9855
Buffalo (G-3166)
Pulse Plastics Products Inc....E.... 718 328-5224
Bronx (G-1435)
Pvc Container Corporation....C.... 518 672-7721
Philmont (G-13566)
Sonoco-Crellin Intl Inc....B.... 518 392-2000
Chatham (G-3588)
Sweet Tooth Enterprises LLC....E.... 631 752-2888
West Babylon (G-16867)
Termatec Molding Inc....F.... 315 483-4150
Sodus (G-15527)
Thermold Corporation....C.... 315 697-3924
Canastota (G-3400)

PLASTICS: Polystyrene Foam

ABI Packaging Inc....E.... 716 677-2900
West Seneca (G-16967)
Berry Plastics Corporation....B.... 315 986-6270
Macedon (G-8013)
Burnett Process Inc....G.... 585 254-8080
Rochester (G-14269)
Cellect Plastics LLC....D.... 518 568-7036
Saint Johnsville (G-15119)
China Xd Plastics Company Ltd....G.... 212 747-1118
New York (G-9654)
Dura Foam Inc....E.... 718 894-2488
Maspeth (G-8163)
General Vy-Coat LLC....E.... 718 266-6002
Brooklyn (G-2019)
Great American Industries Inc....G.... 607 729-9331
Vestal (G-16472)
Hopp Companies Inc....F.... 516 358-4170
New Hyde Park (G-8886)
J & M Packaging Inc....F.... 631 608-3069
Hauppauge (G-6124)
Latham International Inc....G.... 518 783-7776
Latham (G-7396)
Latham Pool Products Inc....E.... 260 432-8731
Latham (G-7398)
Lewis & Myers Inc....G.... 585 494-1410
Bergen (G-847)
Par-Foam Products Inc....C.... 716 855-2066
Buffalo (G-3135)
Pliant LLC....B.... 315 986-6286
Macedon (G-8020)
Professional Packg Svcs Inc....E.... 518 677-5100
Eagle Bridge (G-4381)
Rimco Plastics Corp....E.... 607 739-3864
Horseheads (G-6619)
Saint-Gobain Prfmce Plas Corp....C.... 518 642-2200
Granville (G-5796)
Skd Distribution Corp....E.... 718 525-6000
Jericho (G-7120)
Strux Corp....E.... 516 768-3969
Lindenhurst (G-7508)
Tmp Technologies Inc....D.... 716 895-6100
Buffalo (G-3246)
TSS Foam Industries Corp....F.... 585 538-2321
Caledonia (G-3311)

PLASTICS: Thermoformed

Bo-Mer Plastics LLC....E.... 315 252-7216
Auburn (G-485)
Cjk Manufacturing LLC....F.... 585 663-6370
Rochester (G-14298)
Marval Industries Inc....D.... 914 381-2400
Mamaroneck (G-8071)
Pactiv Corporation....C.... 518 743-3100
Glens Falls (G-5709)
Weather Products Corporation....G.... 315 474-8593
Syracuse (G-16094)

PLATE WORK: Metalworking Trade

West Metal Works Inc....E.... 716 895-4900
Buffalo (G-3278)

PLATEMAKING SVC: Color Separations, For The Printing Trade

Absolute Color Corporation....G.... 212 868-0404
New York (G-9054)
Eastern Color Stripping Inc....F.... 631 563-3700
Bohemia (G-1056)
Lane Park Litho Plate....E.... 212 255-9100
New York (G-10961)
Lazer Incorporated....E.... 336 744-8047
Rochester (G-14497)
Leo P Callahan Inc....F.... 607 797-7314
Binghamton (G-929)
Micro Publishing Inc....G.... 212 533-9180
New York (G-11280)
Torch Graphics Inc....E.... 212 679-4334
New York (G-12395)

PLATEMAKING SVC: Embossing, For The Printing Trade

Aldine Inc (ny)....D.... 212 226-2870
New York (G-9129)

PLATEMAKING SVC: Gravure, Plates Or Cylinders

Charles Henricks Inc....F.... 212 243-5800
New York (G-9632)
Miroddi Imaging Inc....G.... 516 624-6898
Oyster Bay (G-13398)

PRODUCT

Employee Codes: A=Over 500 employees, B=251-500
C=101-250, D=51-100, E=20-50, F=10-19, G=5-9

2018 Harris
New York Manufacturers Directory

1291

PLATES

PLATES

Adflex Corporation	E	585 454-2950	
Rochester *(G-14189)*			
Circle Press Inc	D	212 924-4277	
New York *(G-9674)*			
Csw Inc	F	585 247-4010	
Rochester *(G-14315)*			
David Fehlman	G	315 455-8888	
Syracuse *(G-15942)*			
Dowd - Witbeck Printing Corp	F	518 274-2421	
Troy *(G-16256)*			
Gallant Graphics Ltd	E	845 868-1166	
Stanfordville *(G-15647)*			
Gazette Press Inc	E	914 963-8300	
Rye *(G-15082)*			
Karr Graphics Corp	E	212 645-6000	
Long Island City *(G-7806)*			
Mutual Engraving Company Inc	D	516 489-0534	
West Hempstead *(G-16893)*			
P & H Thermotech Inc	G	585 624-1310	
Lima *(G-7469)*			
Rigidized Metals Corporation	E	716 849-4703	
Buffalo *(G-3186)*			
Rotation Dynamics Corporation	E	585 352-9023	
Spencerport *(G-15597)*			
Syracuse Computer Forms Inc	E	315 478-0108	
Syracuse *(G-16075)*			
Tobay Printing Co Inc	E	631 842-3300	
Copiague *(G-3957)*			
Tripi Engraving Co Inc	E	718 383-6500	
Brooklyn *(G-2700)*			
Welsh Gold Stampers Inc	E	718 984-5031	
Staten Island *(G-15776)*			

PLATES: Paper, Made From Purchased Materials

Amscan Inc	F	845 469-9116	
Chester *(G-3626)*			
Amscan Inc	D	845 782-0490	
Harriman *(G-5993)*			
Apexx Omni-Graphics Inc	D	718 326-3330	
Maspeth *(G-8147)*			
Hadp LLC	F	518 831-6824	
Scotia *(G-15348)*			
Pactiv LLC	C	518 562-6101	
Plattsburgh *(G-13712)*			

PLATES: Plastic Exc Polystyrene Foam

Apexx Omni-Graphics Inc	D	718 326-3330	
Maspeth *(G-8147)*			
Pactiv LLC	C	585 393-3229	
Canandaigua *(G-3383)*			

PLATING & FINISHING SVC: Decorative, Formed Prdts

Jay Strongwater Holdings LLC	A	646 657-0558	
New York *(G-10745)*			

PLATING & POLISHING SVC

Abetter Processing Corp	F	718 252-2223	
Brooklyn *(G-1547)*			
Epner Technology Incorporated	E	718 782-8722	
Brooklyn *(G-1934)*			
Hartchrom Inc	F	518 880-0411	
Watervliet *(G-16710)*			
McAlpin Industries Inc	E	585 544-5335	
Rochester *(G-14522)*			
North East Finishing Co Inc	F	631 789-8000	
Copiague *(G-3941)*			
Praxair Surface Tech Inc	C	845 398-8322	
Orangeburg *(G-13264)*			
Precious Plate Inc	D	716 283-0690	
Niagara Falls *(G-12880)*			
Tcmf Inc	D	607 724-1094	
Binghamton *(G-948)*			
Wilco Finishing Corp	E	718 417-6405	
Brooklyn *(G-2767)*			

PLATING SVC: Chromium, Metals Or Formed Prdts

West Falls Machine Co Inc	F	716 655-0440	
East Aurora *(G-4404)*			

PLATING SVC: Electro

Airmarine Electroplating Corp	G	516 623-4406	
Freeport *(G-5390)*			
Astro Electroplating Inc	E	631 968-0656	
Bay Shore *(G-672)*			
Berkman Bros Inc	F	718 782-1827	
Brooklyn *(G-1684)*			
Bfg Manufacturing Services Inc	E	716 362-0888	
Buffalo *(G-2863)*			
Dan Kane Plating Co Inc	F	212 675-4947	
New York *(G-9852)*			
Dura Spec Inc	F	718 526-3053	
North Baldwin *(G-12921)*			
Electro Plating Service Inc	F	914 948-3777	
White Plains *(G-17130)*			
Epner Technology Incorporated	E	718 782-5948	
Brooklyn *(G-1933)*			
Eric S Turner & Company Inc	E	914 235-7114	
New Rochelle *(G-8943)*			
Finest Cc Corp	G	917 574-4525	
Bronx *(G-1334)*			
Frontier Plating	G	716 896-2811	
Buffalo *(G-2974)*			
Genesee Vly Met Finshg Co Inc	G	585 232-4412	
Rochester *(G-14416)*			
Greene Technologies Inc	D	607 656-4166	
Greene *(G-5884)*			
John Larocca & Son Inc	G	631 423-5256	
Huntington Station *(G-6750)*			
Kent Electro-Plating Corp	F	718 358-9599	
Dix Hills *(G-4315)*			
Key Tech Finishing	E	716 832-1232	
Buffalo *(G-3046)*			
Keystone Corporation	E	716 832-1232	
Buffalo *(G-3048)*			
Rayco of Schenectady Inc	E	518 212-5113	
Amsterdam *(G-367)*			
Sandys Bumper Mart Inc	G	315 472-8149	
Syracuse *(G-16053)*			
T & M Plating Inc	E	212 967-1110	
New York *(G-12286)*			
Tripp Plating Works Inc	G	716 894-2424	
Buffalo *(G-3252)*			
Tronic Plating Co Inc	F	516 293-7883	
Farmingdale *(G-5145)*			
Vernon Plating Works Inc	F	718 639-1124	
Woodside *(G-17376)*			
Victoria Plating Co Inc	D	718 589-1550	
Bronx *(G-1489)*			

PLATING SVC: Gold

Empire Metal Finishing Inc	E	718 545-6700	
Astoria *(G-438)*			
Sherrill Manufacturing Inc	C	315 280-0727	
Sherrill *(G-15430)*			

PLATING SVC: NEC

Aircraft Finishing Corp	F	631 422-5000	
West Babylon *(G-16792)*			
Buffalo Metal Finishing Co	E	716 883-2751	
Buffalo *(G-2878)*			
Coating Technology Inc	E	585 546-7170	
Rochester *(G-14303)*			
Galmer Ltd	G	718 392-4609	
Long Island City *(G-7777)*			
Nas CP Corp	E	718 961-6757	
College Point *(G-3823)*			
Nassau Chromium Plating Co Inc	E	516 746-6666	
Mineola *(G-8559)*			
Reynolds Tech Fabricators Inc	E	315 437-0532	
East Syracuse *(G-4573)*			
Rochester Overnight Pltg LLC	D	585 328-4590	
Rochester *(G-14667)*			
Silverman & Gorf Inc	E	718 625-1309	
Brooklyn *(G-2585)*			
US Electroplating Corp	G	631 293-1998	
West Babylon *(G-16869)*			

PLAYGROUND EQPT

Bears Management Group Inc	G	585 624-5694	
Lima *(G-7464)*			
Billy Beez Usa LLC	G	315 741-5099	
Syracuse *(G-15889)*			
Billy Beez Usa LLC	F	646 606-2249	
New York *(G-9451)*			
Billy Beez Usa LLC	G	845 915-4709	
West Nyack *(G-16943)*			
Eastern Jungle Gym Inc	E	845 878-9800	
Carmel *(G-3427)*			
Imagination Playground LLC	G	212 463-0334	
New York *(G-10613)*			

PLEATING & STITCHING FOR THE TRADE: Decorative & Novelty

A Trusted Name Inc	F	716 326-7400	
Westfield *(G-17074)*			

PLEATING & STITCHING FOR TRADE: Permanent Pleating/Pressing

Stanley Pleating Stitching Co	E	718 392-2417	
Long Island City *(G-7914)*			
Stylist Pleating Corp	F	718 384-8181	
Brooklyn *(G-2639)*			

PLEATING & STITCHING SVC

Athletic Cap Co Inc	E	718 398-1300	
Staten Island *(G-15661)*			
Custom Patches Inc	E	845 679-6320	
Woodstock *(G-17378)*			
Milaaya Inc	E	212 764-6386	
New York *(G-11291)*			
Pass Em-Entries Inc	F	718 392-0100	
Long Island City *(G-7867)*			
Todd Walbridge	G	585 254-3018	
Rochester *(G-14755)*			

PLEATING & TUCKING FOR THE TRADE

Vogue Too Plting Stitching EMB	F	212 354-1022	
New York *(G-12591)*			

PLUGS: Electric

K & H Industries Inc	F	716 312-0088	
Hamburg *(G-5953)*			

PLUMBING & HEATING EQPT & SPLY, WHOL: Htg Eqpt/Panels, Solar

Vincent Genovese	G	631 281-8170	
Mastic Beach *(G-8237)*			

PLUMBING & HEATING EQPT & SPLY, WHOLESALE: Hydronic Htg Eqpt

Flushing Boiler & Welding Co	G	718 463-1266	
Brooklyn *(G-1988)*			

PLUMBING & HEATING EQPT & SPLYS WHOLESALERS

Bobrick Washroom Equipment Inc	D	518 877-7444	
Clifton Park *(G-3723)*			
Siemens Industry Inc	E	585 797-2300	
Rochester *(G-14707)*			

PLUMBING & HEATING EQPT & SPLYS, WHOL: Plumbing Fitting/Sply

Great American Industries Inc	G	607 729-9331	
Vestal *(G-16472)*			
Long Island Pipe Supply Inc	E	516 222-8008	
Garden City *(G-5529)*			
P E Guerin	D	212 243-5270	
New York *(G-11561)*			

PLUMBING & HEATING EQPT & SPLYS, WHOL: Plumbng/Heatng Valves

Flow-Safe Inc	E	716 662-2585	
Orchard Park *(G-13293)*			

PLUMBING & HEATING EQPT & SPLYS, WHOL: Water Purif Eqpt

Empire Division Inc	D	315 476-6273	
Syracuse *(G-15957)*			
Neptune Soft Water Inc	F	315 446-5151	
Syracuse *(G-16017)*			

PLUMBING & HEATING EQPT & SPLYS, WHOLESALE: Brass/Fittings

Coronet Parts Mfg Co Inc	E	718 649-1750	
Brooklyn *(G-1804)*			

PRODUCT SECTION

PLUMBING & HEATING EQPT & SPLYS, WHOLESALE: Sanitary Ware

Porcelain Refinishing Corp ....F 516 352-4841
  Flushing *(G-5290)*

PLUMBING FIXTURES

Corona Plumbing & Htg Sup Inc ....G 718 424-4133
  Corona *(G-4016)*
ER Butler & Co Inc ....E 212 925-3565
  New York *(G-10107)*
Ferguson ....G 718 937-9500
  Maspeth *(G-8170)*
G Sicuranza Ltd ....G 516 759-0259
  Glen Cove *(G-5628)*
L A S Replacement Parts Inc ....F 718 583-4700
  Bronx *(G-1380)*
Liberty Brass Turning Co Inc ....E 718 784-2911
  Westbury *(G-17032)*
Malyn Industrial Ceramics Inc ....G 716 741-1510
  Clarence Center *(G-3705)*
Martin Brass Works Inc ....G 718 523-3146
  Jamaica *(G-6964)*
P E Guerin ....D 212 243-5270
  New York *(G-11561)*
Roccera LLC ....F 585 426-0887
  Rochester *(G-14654)*
Toto USA Inc ....G 917 237-0665
  New York *(G-12401)*
Toto USA Inc ....G 770 282-8686
  New York *(G-12402)*
Watermark Designs Holdings Ltd ....D 718 257-2800
  Brooklyn *(G-2761)*

PLUMBING FIXTURES: Brass, Incl Drain Cocks, Faucets/Spigots

A B S Brass Products Inc ....F 718 497-2115
  Brooklyn *(G-1531)*
Acme Parts Inc ....E 718 649-1750
  Brooklyn *(G-1555)*
Coronet Parts Mfg Co Inc ....E 718 649-1750
  Brooklyn *(G-1804)*
Coronet Parts Mfg Co Inc ....E 718 649-1750
  Brooklyn *(G-1805)*
Holyoke Fittings Inc ....F 718 649-0710
  Brooklyn *(G-2080)*
Jacknob International Ltd ....D 631 546-6560
  Hauppauge *(G-6126)*

PLUMBING FIXTURES: Plastic

An-Cor Industrial Plastics Inc ....D 716 695-3141
  North Tonawanda *(G-12972)*
Bow Industrial Corporation ....D 518 561-0190
  Champlain *(G-3566)*
Gms Hicks Street Corporation ....E 718 858-1010
  Brooklyn *(G-2033)*
On Point Reps Inc ....G 518 258-2268
  Montgomery *(G-8635)*
Quality Enclosures Inc ....E 631 234-0115
  Central Islip *(G-3535)*

POINT OF SALE DEVICES

Hopp Companies Inc ....F 516 358-4170
  New Hyde Park *(G-8886)*
Kenney Manufacturing Displays ....F 631 231-5563
  Brentwood *(G-1185)*
Powa Technologies Inc ....E 347 344-7848
  New York *(G-11713)*

POLISHING SVC: Metals Or Formed Prdts

Barnes Metal Finishing Inc ....F 585 798-4817
  Medina *(G-8298)*
Control Electropolishing Corp ....F 718 858-6634
  Brooklyn *(G-1799)*

POLYESTERS

Perfect Poly Inc ....E 631 265-0539
  Nesconset *(G-8825)*
Terphane Inc ....D 585 657-5800
  Bloomfield *(G-985)*

POLYETHYLENE RESINS

APS American Polymers Svcs Inc ....G 212 362-7711
  New York *(G-9236)*

POLYPROPYLENE RESINS

Exxonmobil Chemical Company ....C 315 966-1000
  Macedon *(G-8016)*

POLYTETRAFLUOROETHYLENE RESINS

Saint-Gobain Prfmce Plas Corp ....C 518 686-7301
  Hoosick Falls *(G-6572)*

POLYVINYL CHLORIDE RESINS

Adam Scott Designs Inc ....E 212 420-8866
  New York *(G-9071)*
De Originals Ltd ....G 516 474-6544
  Old Westbury *(G-13153)*
Kent Chemical Corporation ....E 212 521-1700
  New York *(G-10878)*
Newmat Northeast Corp ....F 631 253-9277
  West Babylon *(G-16846)*

POPCORN & SUPPLIES WHOLESALERS

Terrells Potato Chip Co Inc ....D 315 437-2786
  Syracuse *(G-16081)*

PORCELAIN ENAMELED PRDTS & UTENSILS

Chamart Exclusives Inc ....G 914 345-3870
  Elmsford *(G-4749)*

POSTERS

Candid Worldwide LLC ....G 212 799-5300
  Farmingdale *(G-4966)*
Clear Channel Outdoor Inc ....F 212 812-0000
  New York *(G-9696)*

POTTERY: Laboratory & Indl

Saint Gobain Grains & Powders ....A 716 731-8200
  Niagara Falls *(G-12888)*
Saint-Gbain Advnced Crmics LLC ....C 716 278-6066
  Niagara Falls *(G-12889)*

POULTRY & POULTRY PRDTS WHOLESALERS

Vineland Kosher Poultry Inc ....F 718 921-1347
  Brooklyn *(G-2746)*

POULTRY & SMALL GAME SLAUGHTERING & PROCESSING

Advanced Frozen Foods Inc ....E 516 333-6344
  Westbury *(G-16989)*
Campanellis Poultry Farm Inc ....G 845 482-2222
  Bethel *(G-859)*
Goya Foods Inc ....D 716 549-0076
  Angola *(G-380)*
Hoskie Co Inc ....D 718 628-8672
  Brooklyn *(G-2084)*
JW Consulting Inc ....G 845 325-7070
  Monroe *(G-8594)*
MB Food Processing Inc ....B 845 436-5001
  South Fallsburg *(G-15543)*
Murray Bresky Consultants Ltd ....B 845 436-5001
  South Fallsburg *(G-15544)*
Vineland Kosher Poultry Inc ....F 718 921-1347
  Brooklyn *(G-2746)*

POULTRY SLAUGHTERING & PROCESSING

Alle Processing Corp ....C 718 894-2000
  Maspeth *(G-8143)*
Hlw Acres LLC ....G 585 591-0795
  Attica *(G-472)*

POWDER PUFFS & MITTS

American Puff Corp ....D 516 379-1300
  Freeport *(G-5396)*
Penthouse Manufacturing Co Inc ....B 516 379-1300
  Freeport *(G-5429)*

POWDER: Metal

Buffalo Tungsten Inc ....D 716 759-6353
  Depew *(G-4276)*
Cws Powder Coatings Company LP ....G 845 398-2911
  Blauvelt *(G-964)*
Handy & Harman ....E 914 461-1300
  White Plains *(G-17145)*

POWDER: Silver

Ames Advanced Materials Corp ....D 518 792-5808
  South Glens Falls *(G-15545)*
Ames Goldsmith Corp ....F 518 792-7435
  Glens Falls *(G-5685)*

POWER GENERATORS

Ener-G Cogen LLC ....G 718 551-7170
  New York *(G-10088)*
Independent Field Svc LLC ....G 315 559-9243
  Syracuse *(G-15981)*
Intelligen Power Systems LLC ....G 212 750-0373
  Old Bethpage *(G-13150)*
K Road Moapa Solar LLC ....F 212 351-0535
  New York *(G-10831)*
Power Gneration Indus Engs Inc ....F 315 633-9389
  Bridgeport *(G-1234)*

POWER SPLY CONVERTERS: Static, Electronic Applications

Albatros North America Inc ....E 518 381-7100
  Ballston Spa *(G-589)*
Orbit International Corp ....D 631 435-8300
  Hauppauge *(G-6181)*

POWER SUPPLIES: All Types, Static

3835 Lebron Rest Eqp & Sup Inc ....E 212 942-8258
  New York *(G-9019)*
Applied Concepts Inc ....E 315 696-6676
  Tully *(G-16297)*
Applied Power Systems Inc ....E 516 935-2230
  Hicksville *(G-6346)*
Arstan Products International ....F 516 433-1313
  Hicksville *(G-6348)*
BC Systems Inc ....E 631 751-9370
  Setauket *(G-15399)*
Behlman Electronics Inc ....E 631 435-0410
  Hauppauge *(G-6052)*
Espey Mfg & Electronics Corp ....C 518 584-4100
  Saratoga Springs *(G-15180)*
Hipotronics Inc ....C 845 279-8091
  Brewster *(G-1217)*
Orbit International Corp ....C 631 435-8300
  Hauppauge *(G-6180)*
SL Industries Inc ....D 212 520-2300
  New York *(G-12124)*
Ultravolt Inc ....D 631 471-4444
  Ronkonkoma *(G-15020)*
Walter G Legge Company Inc ....G 914 737-5040
  Peekskill *(G-13510)*

POWER SUPPLIES: Transformer, Electronic Type

Applied Power Systems Inc ....E 516 935-2230
  Hicksville *(G-6346)*
Bright Way Supply Inc ....F 718 833-2882
  Brooklyn *(G-1716)*
Fil-Coil International LLC ....F 631 467-5328
  Sayville *(G-15238)*
Hammond Manufacturing Co Inc ....F 716 630-7030
  Cheektowaga *(G-3602)*
Tdk-Lambda Americas Inc ....F 631 967-3000
  Hauppauge *(G-6231)*

POWER SWITCHING EQPT

Switching Power Inc ....D 631 981-7231
  Ronkonkoma *(G-15013)*

POWER TOOLS, HAND: Grinders, Portable, Electric Or Pneumatic

Dean Manufacturing Inc ....F 607 770-1300
  Vestal *(G-16468)*

POWER TOOLS, HAND: Grinders, Portable, Electric Or Pneumatic

Hje Company Inc ....G 518 792-8733
  Queensbury *(G-14012)*
Imerys Steelcasting Usa Inc ....D 716 278-1634
  Niagara Falls *(G-12853)*
Oerlikon Metco (us) Inc ....G 716 270-2228
  Amherst *(G-256)*
Reed Systems Ltd ....F 845 647-3660
  Ellenville *(G-4651)*
Tam Ceramics Group of Ny LLC ....D 716 278-9400
  Niagara Falls *(G-12897)*

POWER TOOLS, HAND: Hammers, Portable, Elec/Pneumatic, Chip

POWER TOOLS, HAND: Hammers, Portable, Elec/Pneumatic, Chip
Rbhammers Corp .... F 845 353-5042
  Blauvelt *(G-968)*

POWER TRANSMISSION EQPT WHOLESALERS
Peerless-Winsmith Inc .... C 716 592-9311
  Springville *(G-15634)*
United Richter Electrical Mtrs .... F 716 855-1945
  Buffalo *(G-3261)*

POWER TRANSMISSION EQPT: Aircraft
Precision Gear Incorporated .... C 718 321-7200
  College Point *(G-3827)*

POWER TRANSMISSION EQPT: Mechanical
Babbitt Bearings Incorporated .... D 315 479-6603
  Syracuse *(G-15885)*
Borgwarner Morse TEC LLC .... C 607 257-6700
  Ithaca *(G-6866)*
BW Elliott Mfg Co LLC .... B 607 772-0404
  Binghamton *(G-896)*
Champlain Hudson Power Ex Inc .... G 518 465-0710
  Albany *(G-60)*
Cierra Industries Inc .... F 315 252-6630
  Auburn *(G-487)*
Designatronics Incorporated .... F 516 328-3300
  Hicksville *(G-6369)*
Designatronics Incorporated .... B 516 328-3300
  Hicksville *(G-6367)*
Eaw Electronic Systems Inc .... G 845 471-5290
  Poughkeepsie *(G-13916)*
Fait Usa Inc .... G 215 674-5310
  New York *(G-10184)*
Hudson Power Transmission Co .... G 718 622-3869
  Brooklyn *(G-2086)*
Huron TI Cutter Grinding Inc .... E 631 420-7000
  Farmingdale *(G-5015)*
Kaddis Manufacturing Corp .... G 585 624-3070
  Honeoye Falls *(G-6561)*
Ls Power Equity Partners LP .... F 212 615-3456
  New York *(G-11085)*
Metallized Carbon Corporation .... C 914 941-3738
  Ossining *(G-13347)*
On Line Power Technologies .... G 914 968-4440
  Yonkers *(G-17489)*
Package One Inc .... D 518 344-5425
  Schenectady *(G-15310)*
Renold Holdings Inc .... G 716 326-3121
  Westfield *(G-17079)*
Renold Inc .... D 716 326-3121
  Westfield *(G-17080)*
Sepac Inc .... E 607 732-2030
  Elmira *(G-4714)*
Watson Bowman Acme Corp .... D 716 691-8162
  Amherst *(G-271)*

PRECAST TERRAZZO OR CONCRETE PRDTS
Accurate Precast .... F 718 345-2910
  Brooklyn *(G-1551)*
Coastal Pipeline Products Corp .... E 631 369-4000
  Calverton *(G-3316)*
Coral Cast LLC .... E 516 349-1300
  Plainview *(G-13622)*
Key Cast Stone Company Inc .... E 631 789-2145
  Amityville *(G-302)*
Northeast Concrete Pdts Inc .... F 518 563-0700
  Plattsburgh *(G-13708)*
Superior Aggregates Supply LLC .... E 516 333-2923
  Lindenhurst *(G-7511)*
Superior Walls Upstate NY Inc .... D 585 624-9390
  Lima *(G-7471)*
Superior Wlls of Hdson Vly Inc .... E 845 485-4033
  Poughkeepsie *(G-13953)*

PRECIOUS METALS
Handy & Harman .... E 914 461-1300
  White Plains *(G-17145)*

PRECIOUS METALS WHOLESALERS
Wallace Refiners Inc .... G 212 391-2649
  New York *(G-12610)*

PRECIOUS STONES & METALS, WHOLESALE
Jacoby Enterprises LLC .... G 718 435-0289
  Brooklyn *(G-2132)*
S Kashi & Sons Inc .... F 212 869-9393
  Great Neck *(G-5854)*

PRECIOUS STONES WHOLESALERS
Gumuchian Fils Ltd .... F 212 593-3118
  New York *(G-10427)*
Incon Gems Inc .... F 212 221-8560
  New York *(G-10626)*
Jim Wachtler Inc .... G 212 755-4367
  New York *(G-10773)*

PRECIPITATORS: Electrostatic
Beltran Technologies Inc .... E 718 338-3311
  Brooklyn *(G-1678)*

PRERECORDED TAPE, CD & RECORD STORES: Video Discs/Tapes
Sony Broadband Entertainment .... F 212 833-6800
  New York *(G-12156)*

PRERECORDED TAPE, CD/RECORD STORES: Video Tapes, Prerecorded
Society For The Study .... G 212 822-8806
  New York *(G-12144)*

PRERECORDED TAPE, COMPACT DISC & RECORD STORES
Taste and See Entrmt Inc .... G 516 285-3010
  Valley Stream *(G-16452)*

PRERECORDED TAPE, COMPACT DISC & RECORD STORES: Records
Motema Music LLC .... G 212 860-6969
  New York *(G-11335)*

PRESSED FIBER & MOLDED PULP PRDTS, EXC FOOD PRDTS
Avco Industries Inc .... F 631 851-1555
  Central Islip *(G-3511)*
Cascades New York Inc .... C 518 238-1900
  Wynantskill *(G-17394)*
Interntnal Bus Cmmncations Inc .... E 516 352-4505
  New Hyde Park *(G-8887)*

PRESSES
Bars Precision Inc .... F 585 742-6380
  Mendon *(G-8412)*
Win Set Technologies LLC .... F 631 234-7077
  Centereach *(G-3499)*

PRIMARY METAL PRODUCTS
Bridge Components Inc .... G 716 731-1184
  Sanborn *(G-15140)*
Cintube Ltd .... F 518 324-3333
  Plattsburgh *(G-13687)*
Specialty Fabricators .... F 631 256-6982
  Oakdale *(G-13080)*
Ys Metal .... G 518 512-5275
  Albany *(G-153)*

PRINT CARTRIDGES: Laser & Other Computer Printers
Guttz Corporation of America .... F 914 591-9600
  Irvington *(G-6812)*
Hf Technologies LLC .... E 585 254-5030
  Hamlin *(G-5973)*
Northeast Toner Inc .... G 518 899-5545
  Ballston Lake *(G-584)*
Printer Components Inc .... E 585 924-5190
  Fairport *(G-4877)*
Qls Solutions Group Inc .... E 716 852-2203
  Buffalo *(G-3170)*
Smartoners Inc .... G 718 975-0197
  Brooklyn *(G-2600)*
Summit Technologies LLC .... E 631 590-1040
  Holbrook *(G-6502)*

PRINTED CIRCUIT BOARDS
A A Technology Inc .... D 631 913-0400
  Ronkonkoma *(G-14873)*
Advance Circuit Technology Inc .... E 585 328-2000
  Rochester *(G-14191)*
Advance Micro Power Corp .... F 631 471-6157
  Ronkonkoma *(G-14879)*
Advanced Digital Info Corp .... E 607 266-4000
  Ithaca *(G-6856)*
Advanced Manufacturing Svc Inc .... E 631 676-5210
  Ronkonkoma *(G-14880)*
American Quality Technology .... F 607 777-9488
  Binghamton *(G-884)*
American Tchncal Ceramics Corp .... B 631 622-4700
  Huntington Station *(G-6732)*
Ansen Corporation .... G 315 393-3573
  Ogdensburg *(G-13132)*
Ansen Corporation .... C 315 393-3573
  Ogdensburg *(G-13133)*
Bryit Group LLC .... F 631 563-6603
  Holbrook *(G-6461)*
Bsu Inc .... E 607 272-8100
  Ithaca *(G-6867)*
Buffalo Circuits Inc .... G 716 662-2113
  Orchard Park *(G-13279)*
C & D Assembly Inc .... E 607 898-4275
  Groton *(G-5919)*
C A M Graphics Co Inc .... E 631 842-3400
  Farmingdale *(G-4964)*
Chautauqua Circuits Inc .... G 716 366-5771
  Dunkirk *(G-4359)*
Cygnus Automation Inc .... E 631 981-0909
  Bohemia *(G-1043)*
Della Systems Inc .... F 631 580-0010
  Ronkonkoma *(G-14921)*
Entertron Industries Inc .... E 716 772-7216
  Lockport *(G-7613)*
Falconer Electronics Inc .... D 716 665-4176
  Falconer *(G-4905)*
Geometric Circuits Inc .... D 631 249-0230
  Holbrook *(G-6477)*
Hazlow Electronics Inc .... E 585 325-5323
  Rochester *(G-14450)*
I 3 Manufacturing Services Inc .... G 607 238-7077
  Binghamton *(G-917)*
I3 Electronics Inc .... C 607 238-7077
  Binghamton *(G-919)*
IEC Electronics Corp .... A 315 331-7742
  Newark *(G-12752)*
IEC Electronics Wire Cable Inc .... D 585 924-9010
  Newark *(G-12753)*
Irtronics Instruments Inc .... F 914 693-6291
  Ardsley *(G-404)*
Isine Inc .... G 631 913-4400
  Ronkonkoma *(G-14942)*
Jabil Circuit Inc .... B 845 471-9237
  Poughkeepsie *(G-13928)*
Mpl Inc .... E 607 266-0480
  Ithaca *(G-6899)*
NEa Manufacturing Corp .... E 516 371-4200
  Inwood *(G-6803)*
Oakdale Industrial Elec Corp .... F 631 737-4090
  Ronkonkoma *(G-14982)*
Ormec Systems Corp .... E 585 385-3520
  Rochester *(G-14573)*
Park Electrochemical Corp .... C 631 465-3600
  Melville *(G-8376)*
Performance Technologies Inc .... E 585 256-0200
  Rochester *(G-14596)*
Procomponents Inc .... E 516 683-0909
  Westbury *(G-17051)*
Rce Manufacturing LLC .... G 631 856-9005
  Commack *(G-3865)*
Rochester Industrial Ctrl Inc .... D 315 524-4555
  Ontario *(G-13234)*
Rumsey Corp .... G 914 751-3640
  Yonkers *(G-17501)*
S K Circuits Inc .... F 703 376-8718
  Oneida *(G-13188)*
Sag Harbor Industries Inc .... E 631 725-0440
  Sag Harbor *(G-15107)*
Sanmina Corporation .... B 607 689-5000
  Owego *(G-13384)*
Sopark Corp .... C 716 822-0434
  Buffalo *(G-3219)*
Stetron International Inc .... F 716 854-3435
  Buffalo *(G-3225)*
Surf-Tech Manufacturing Corp .... F 631 589-1194
  Bohemia *(G-1135)*

PRODUCT SECTION

PRINTING, COMMERCIAL: Bags, Plastic, NEC

Transistor Devices Inc ....E 631 471-7492
 Ronkonkoma *(G-15015)*
Windsor Technology LLC ....F 585 461-2500
 Rochester *(G-14792)*

PRINTERS & PLOTTERS

Blue Skies ....G 631 392-1140
 Deer Park *(G-4134)*
CNy Business Solutions ....G 315 733-5031
 Utica *(G-16335)*
Mdi Holdings LLC ....A 212 559-1127
 New York *(G-11228)*
Mg Imaging ....G 212 704-4073
 New York *(G-11272)*
Secuprint Inc ....G 585 341-3100
 Rochester *(G-14700)*
X Brand Editions ....G 718 482-7646
 Long Island City *(G-7956)*

PRINTERS' SVCS: Folding, Collating, Etc

JP Signs ....G 518 569-3907
 Chazy *(G-3589)*
Shield Press Inc ....G 212 431-7489
 New York *(G-12071)*

PRINTERS: Computer

Control Logic Corporation ....G 607 965-6423
 West Burlington *(G-16874)*
Future Star Digatech ....F 718 666-0350
 Brooklyn *(G-2009)*
Hf Technologies LLC ....E 585 254-5030
 Hamlin *(G-5973)*
Transact Technologies Inc ....D 607 257-8901
 Ithaca *(G-6914)*

PRINTERS: Magnetic Ink, Bar Code

Advanced Barcode Tech Inc ....F 516 570-8100
 Great Neck *(G-5799)*
CPW Direct Mail Group LLC ....E 631 588-6565
 Farmingdale *(G-4975)*
Jadak Technologies Inc ....D 315 701-0678
 North Syracuse *(G-12967)*
Paxar Corporation ....E 845 398-3229
 Orangeburg *(G-13260)*

PRINTING & BINDING: Book Music

Bridge Enterprises Inc ....G 718 625-6622
 Brooklyn *(G-1714)*

PRINTING & BINDING: Books

Book1one LLC ....G 585 458-2101
 Rochester *(G-14260)*
Hamilton Printing Company Inc ....C 518 732-2161
 Troy *(G-16260)*
Logical Operations Inc ....C 585 350-7000
 Rochester *(G-14503)*
Syracuse Cultural Workers Prj ....G 315 474-1132
 Syracuse *(G-16076)*

PRINTING & BINDING: Pamphlets

Bmg Printing and Promotion LLC ....G 631 231-9200
 Bohemia *(G-1022)*

PRINTING & EMBOSSING: Plastic Fabric Articles

Acorn Products Corp ....F 315 894-4868
 Ilion *(G-6778)*
Mountain T-Shirts Inc ....G 518 943-4533
 Catskill *(G-3460)*
Patrick Rohan ....G 718 781-2573
 Monticello *(G-8646)*
Starline Usa Inc ....C 716 773-0100
 Grand Island *(G-5785)*

PRINTING & ENGRAVING: Card, Exc Greeting

Abigal Press Inc ....D 718 641-5350
 Ozone Park *(G-13401)*
New York Sample Card Co Inc ....E 212 242-1242
 New York *(G-11426)*
Printery ....G 516 922-3250
 Oyster Bay *(G-13399)*
Proof 7 Ltd ....F 212 680-1843
 New York *(G-11757)*

PRINTING & ENGRAVING: Financial Notes & Certificates

Doremus FP LLC ....E 212 366-3800
 New York *(G-9960)*
Merrill New York Company Inc ....C 212 229-6500
 New York *(G-11261)*
Superior Print On Demand ....G 607 240-5231
 Vestal *(G-16478)*
Table Tops Paper Corp ....G 718 831-6440
 Brooklyn *(G-2663)*

PRINTING & ENGRAVING: Invitation & Stationery

Batavia Press LLC ....E 585 343-4429
 Batavia *(G-625)*
Jon Lyn Ink Inc ....G 516 546-2312
 Merrick *(G-8420)*
Lion In The Sun Park Slope Ltd ....G 718 369-4006
 Brooklyn *(G-2232)*
Sammba Printing Inc ....G 516 944-4449
 Port Washington *(G-13879)*

PRINTING & ENGRAVING: Plateless

K & B Stamping Co Inc ....G 914 664-8555
 Mount Vernon *(G-8741)*

PRINTING & ENGRAVING: Poster & Decal

BDR Creative Concepts Inc ....F 516 942-7768
 Farmingdale *(G-4959)*
Stickershopcom Inc ....G 631 563-4323
 Bayport *(G-755)*

PRINTING & STAMPING: Fabric Articles

Casual Friday Inc ....F 585 544-9470
 Rochester *(G-14282)*
Hollywood Advertising Banners ....E 631 842-3000
 Copiague *(G-3932)*

PRINTING & WRITING PAPER WHOLESALERS

Argo Lithographers Inc ....E 718 729-2700
 Long Island City *(G-7702)*
Shipmtes/Printmates Holdg Corp ....D 518 370-1158
 Scotia *(G-15353)*
Table Tops Paper Corp ....G 718 831-6440
 Brooklyn *(G-2663)*

PRINTING EQPT & SUPPLIES: Illustration & Poster Woodcuts

Patrick Rohan ....G 718 781-2573
 Monticello *(G-8646)*

PRINTING INKS WHOLESALERS

I N K T Inc ....F 212 957-2700
 New York *(G-10586)*
Interntnl Publcatns Media Grup ....G 917 604-9602
 New York *(G-10682)*
Won & Lee Inc ....E 516 222-0712
 Garden City *(G-5552)*

PRINTING MACHINERY

A-Mark Machinery Corp ....F 631 643-6300
 West Babylon *(G-16787)*
Anand Printing Machinery Inc ....G 631 667-3079
 Deer Park *(G-4122)*
Awt Supply Corp ....G 516 437-9105
 Elmont *(G-4730)*
Bartizan Data Systems LLC ....E 914 965-7977
 Yonkers *(G-17435)*
Castlereagh Printcraft Inc ....D 516 623-1728
 Freeport *(G-5402)*
Daige Products Inc ....F 516 621-2100
 Albertson *(G-157)*
Davis International Inc ....G 585 421-8175
 Fairport *(G-4859)*
Halm Industries Co Inc ....D 516 676-6900
 Glen Head *(G-5646)*
Halm Instrument Co Inc ....D 516 676-6900
 Glen Head *(G-5647)*
Hodgins Engraving Co Inc ....D 585 343-4444
 Batavia *(G-640)*
Innotech Graphic Eqp Corp ....G 845 268-6900
 Valley Cottage *(G-16405)*
International Imaging Mtls Inc ....A 716 691-6333
 Amherst *(G-245)*
Mekatronics Incorporated ....E 516 883-6805
 Port Washington *(G-13865)*
Micro Powders Inc ....E 914 332-6400
 Tarrytown *(G-16120)*
Mount Vernon Machine Inc ....E 845 268-9400
 Valley Cottage *(G-16408)*
Newport Business Solutions Inc ....F 631 319-6129
 Bohemia *(G-1105)*
Package Print Technologies ....E 716 871-9905
 Buffalo *(G-3132)*
Paxar Corporation ....E 845 398-3229
 Orangeburg *(G-13260)*
Perretta Graphics Corp ....E 845 473-0550
 Poughkeepsie *(G-13943)*
Prim Hall Enterprises Inc ....F 518 561-7408
 Plattsburgh *(G-13719)*
Southern Graphic Systems LLC ....E 315 695-7079
 Phoenix *(G-13571)*
Specilty Bus Mchs Holdings LLC ....E 212 587-9600
 New York *(G-12180)*
Sterling Toggle Inc ....F 631 491-0500
 West Babylon *(G-16864)*
Super Web Inc ....E 631 643-9100
 West Babylon *(G-16866)*
Universal Metal Fabricators ....E 845 331-8248
 Kingston *(G-7248)*
Vits International Inc ....E 845 353-5000
 Blauvelt *(G-973)*
Voodoo Manufacturing Inc ....E 646 893-8366
 Brooklyn *(G-2755)*
Woerner Industries Inc ....E 585 436-1934
 Rochester *(G-14793)*

PRINTING MACHINERY, EQPT & SPLYS: Wholesalers

Boxcar Press Incorporated ....E 315 473-0930
 Syracuse *(G-15893)*
Davis International Inc ....G 585 421-8175
 Fairport *(G-4859)*
Info Label Inc ....F 518 664-0791
 Halfmoon *(G-5933)*
Super Web Inc ....E 631 643-9100
 West Babylon *(G-16866)*

PRINTING TRADES MACHINERY & EQPT REPAIR SVCS

Efam Enterprises LLC ....E 718 204-1760
 Long Island City *(G-7754)*
Interntnl Strpping Diecutting ....G 718 383-7720
 Brooklyn *(G-2112)*
Jack L Popkin & Co Inc ....G 718 361-6700
 Kew Gardens *(G-7192)*

PRINTING, COMMERCIAL Newspapers, NEC

Buffalo Newspress Inc ....C 716 852-1600
 Buffalo *(G-2880)*
Expedi-Printing Inc ....C 516 513-0919
 Great Neck *(G-5822)*
Kim Jae Printing Co Inc ....G 212 691-6289
 Roslyn Heights *(G-15053)*
Kurrier Inc ....G 718 389-3018
 Brooklyn *(G-2180)*
Republican Registrar Inc ....G 315 497-1551
 Moravia *(G-8658)*
Stellar Printing Inc ....D 718 361-1600
 Long Island City *(G-7918)*
Webster Printing Corporation ....F 585 671-1533
 Webster *(G-16768)*

PRINTING, COMMERCIAL: Announcements, NEC

Kates Paperie Ltd ....G 212 966-3904
 New York *(G-10855)*

PRINTING, COMMERCIAL: Bags, Plastic, NEC

Bags Unlimited Inc ....E 585 436-6282
 Rochester *(G-14238)*
Dynamic Packaging Inc ....F 718 388-0800
 Brooklyn *(G-1888)*
Flexo Transparent LLC ....C 716 825-7710
 Buffalo *(G-2966)*

Employee Codes: A=Over 500 employees, B=251-500
C=101-250, D=51-100, E=20-50, F=10-19, G=5-9

PRINTING, COMMERCIAL: Business Forms, NEC

PRINTING, COMMERCIAL: Business Forms, NEC

Bfc Print Network Inc .... G 716 838-4532
  Amherst (G-230)
Empire Business Forms Inc .... F 845 471-5666
  Poughkeepsie (G-13917)
Endeavor Printing LLC .... G 718 570-2720
  Long Island City (G-7760)
General Business Supply Inc .... D 518 720-3939
  Watervliet (G-16709)
Kinaneco Inc .... E 315 468-6201
  Syracuse (G-15994)
Lifeforms Printing .... G 716 685-4500
  Depew (G-4287)
McAuliffe Paper Inc .... E 315 453-2222
  Liverpool (G-7558)
Select-A-Form Inc .... D 631 981-3076
  Holbrook (G-6499)
Short Run Forms Inc .... D 631 567-7171
  Bohemia (G-1130)
United Print Group Inc .... F 718 392-4242
  Long Island City (G-7936)
Vez Inc .... G 718 273-7002
  Staten Island (G-15774)

PRINTING, COMMERCIAL: Calendars, NEC

Won & Lee Inc .... G 516 222-0712
  Garden City (G-5552)

PRINTING, COMMERCIAL: Cards, Visiting, Incl Business, NEC

Create-A-Card Inc .... G 631 584-2273
  Saint James (G-15114)

PRINTING, COMMERCIAL: Circulars, NEC

Linda Campbell .... G 718 994-4026
  Bronx (G-1386)

PRINTING, COMMERCIAL: Coupons, NEC

Ad Publications Inc .... F 585 248-2888
  Pittsford (G-13584)

PRINTING, COMMERCIAL: Decals, NEC

Love Unlimited NY Inc .... E 718 359-8500
  Westbury (G-17035)
Modern Decal Co .... G 315 622-2778
  Liverpool (G-7561)
Seri Systems Inc .... E 585 272-5515
  Rochester (G-14703)

PRINTING, COMMERCIAL: Envelopes, NEC

Argo Envelope Corp .... D 718 729-2700
  Long Island City (G-7700)
Design Distributors Inc .... D 631 242-2000
  Deer Park (G-4152)
Diversified Envelope Ltd .... F 585 615-4697
  Rochester (G-14333)
Dupli Graphics Corporation .... G 315 422-4732
  Syracuse (G-15946)
Ehs Group LLC .... G 914 937-6162
  Port Chester (G-13772)
Federal Envelope Inc .... F 212 243-8380
  New York (G-10201)
Hudson Envelope Corporation .... E 212 473-6666
  New York (G-10569)
Matt Industries Inc .... C 315 472-1316
  Syracuse (G-16005)
Poly-Flex Corp .... F 631 586-9500
  Edgewood (G-4620)
Precision Envelope Co Inc .... G 631 694-3990
  Farmingdale (G-5096)
Sentinel Printing Inc .... G 516 334-7400
  Westbury (G-17054)
Shipman Printing Inds Inc .... E 716 504-7700
  Niagara Falls (G-12893)

PRINTING, COMMERCIAL: Imprinting

Burr & Son Inc .... G 315 446-1550
  Syracuse (G-15896)
Casual Home Worldwide Inc .... G 631 789-2999
  Amityville (G-279)
Genesis One Unlimited .... G 516 208-5863
  West Hempstead (G-16885)
Issacs Yisroel .... G 718 851-7430
  Brooklyn (G-2115)

Total Solution Graphics Inc .... G 718 706-1540
  Long Island City (G-7930)

PRINTING, COMMERCIAL: Invitations, NEC

Alpine Business Group Inc .... G 212 989-4198
  New York (G-9153)
Color Card LLC .... F 631 232-1300
  Central Islip (G-3516)

PRINTING, COMMERCIAL: Labels & Seals, NEC

American Casting and Mfg Corp .... D 800 342-0333
  Plainview (G-13611)
Classic Labels Inc .... E 631 467-2300
  Patchogue (G-13442)
Crisray Printing Corp .... E 631 293-3770
  Farmingdale (G-4976)
General Trade Mark La .... E 718 979-7261
  Staten Island (G-15698)
Greenbush Tape & Label Inc .... E 518 465-2389
  Albany (G-83)
Hammer Packaging Corp .... B 585 424-3880
  West Henrietta (G-16914)
Info Label Inc .... F 518 664-0791
  Halfmoon (G-5933)
Janco Press Inc .... G 631 563-3003
  Bohemia (G-1077)
Kroger Packaging Inc .... E 631 249-6690
  Farmingdale (G-5036)
Labels Inter-Global Inc .... F 212 398-0006
  New York (G-10949)
Niagara Label Company Inc .... F 716 542-3000
  Akron (G-22)
Precision Label Corporation .... F 631 270-4490
  Farmingdale (G-5097)
Print Pack Inc .... C 404 460-7000
  Farmingdale (G-5098)
Tapemaker Sales Co Inc .... E 516 333-0592
  Westbury (G-17057)
Triangle Label Tag Inc .... G 718 875-3030
  Brooklyn (G-2697)

PRINTING, COMMERCIAL: Letterpress & Screen

Drns Corp .... F 718 369-4530
  Brooklyn (G-1883)
Farthing Press Inc .... G 716 852-4674
  Buffalo (G-2959)
L I C Screen Printing Inc .... E 516 546-7289
  Merrick (G-8421)
Quist Industries Ltd .... F 718 243-2800
  Brooklyn (G-2487)
Regal Screen Printing Intl .... G 845 356-8181
  Spring Valley (G-15621)

PRINTING, COMMERCIAL: Literature, Advertising, NEC

A M & J Digital .... G 518 434-2579
  Menands (G-8395)
Bizbash Media Inc .... E 646 638-3600
  New York (G-9457)
Grado Group Inc .... G 718 556-4200
  Staten Island (G-15701)
Landlord Guard Inc .... F 212 695-6505
  New York (G-10960)
Nomad Editions LLC .... F 212 918-0992
  Bronxville (G-1502)
North American DF Inc .... G 718 698-2500
  Staten Island (G-15732)

PRINTING, COMMERCIAL: Magazines, NEC

Aspect Printing Inc .... E 347 789-4284
  Brooklyn (G-1642)
Hearst Corporation .... B 212 767-5800
  New York (G-10485)
L & M Uniserv Corp .... G 718 854-3700
  Brooklyn (G-2185)

PRINTING, COMMERCIAL: Periodicals, NEC

Willis Mc Donald Co Inc .... F 212 366-1526
  New York (G-12665)

PRINTING, COMMERCIAL: Post Cards, Picture, NEC

4 Over 4com Inc .... G 718 932-2700
  Astoria (G-428)

PRINTING, COMMERCIAL: Promotional

A&P Master Images LLC .... F 315 793-1934
  Utica (G-16328)
Bobley-Harmann Corporation .... G 516 433-3800
  Ronkonkoma (G-14908)
Cooper & Clement Inc .... E 315 454-8135
  Syracuse (G-15926)
Excell Print & Promotions Inc .... G 914 437-8668
  White Plains (G-17133)
Fulcrum Promotions & Prtg LLC .... G 203 909-6362
  New York (G-10269)
Gary Stock Corporation .... G 914 276-2700
  Croton Falls (G-4087)
Medallion Associates Inc .... E 212 929-9130
  New York (G-11233)
PDQ Shipping Services .... G 845 255-5500
  New Paltz (G-8922)
Printech Business Systems Inc .... F 212 290-2542
  New York (G-11740)
Scancorp Inc .... F 315 454-5596
  Syracuse (G-16054)
Swift Multigraphics LLC .... G 585 442-8000
  Rochester (G-14733)
Syracuse Letter Company Inc .... F 315 476-8328
  Bridgeport (G-1236)
Xpress Printing Inc .... G 516 605-1000
  Plainview (G-13675)

PRINTING, COMMERCIAL: Publications

Advance Finance Group LLC .... D 212 630-5900
  New York (G-9084)
Beis Moshiach Inc .... E 718 778-8000
  Brooklyn (G-1676)
Check-O-Matic Inc .... G 845 781-7675
  Monroe (G-8587)
Dental Tribune America LLC .... F 212 244-7181
  New York (G-9901)
Graphic Printing .... G 718 701-4433
  Bronx (G-1350)
Graphics 247 Corp .... G 718 729-2470
  Long Island City (G-7782)
J T Printing 21 .... G 718 484-3939
  Staten Island (G-15712)
Merchandiser Inc .... G 315 462-6411
  Clifton Springs (G-3739)
New York Christan Times Inc .... G 718 638-6397
  Brooklyn (G-2371)
Nys Nyu-Cntr Intl Cooperation .... E 212 998-3680
  New York (G-11502)
Sephardic Yellow Pages .... E 718 998-0299
  Brooklyn (G-2569)

PRINTING, COMMERCIAL: Screen

A Tradition of Excellence Inc .... G 845 638-4595
  New City (G-8828)
Acme Screenprinting LLC .... G 716 565-1052
  Buffalo (G-2812)
Active World Solutions Inc .... G 718 922-9404
  Brooklyn (G-1558)
Adco Innvtive Prmtnal Pdts Inc .... G 716 805-1076
  Buffalo (G-2813)
Advanced Graphics Company .... F 607 692-7875
  Whitney Point (G-17248)
Albert Siy .... G 718 359-0389
  Flushing (G-5231)
Alicia F Herdlein .... G 585 344-4411
  Batavia (G-621)
Arca Ink LLC .... G 518 798-0100
  South Glens Falls (G-15546)
Arena Graphics Inc .... G 516 767-5108
  Port Washington (G-13823)
Barnaby Prints Inc .... F 845 477-2501
  Greenwood Lake (G-5917)
Bidpress LLC .... G 267 973-8876
  New York (G-9438)
C & C Athletic Inc .... G 845 713-4670
  Walden (G-16550)
Carib Prints Ltd .... F 646 210-2863
  Bronx (G-1290)
Control Research Inc .... G 631 225-1111
  Amityville (G-281)
Custom 101 Prints Inc .... F 718 708-4425
  Bronx (G-1309)

PRODUCT SECTION

PRINTING, LITHOGRAPHIC: Periodicals

Custom Sportswear Corp .... G 914 666-9200
Bedford Hills *(G-797)*
D B F Associates .... G 718 328-0005
Bronx *(G-1310)*
Dkm Sales LLC .... E 716 893-7777
Buffalo *(G-2932)*
Efs Designs .... G 718 852-9511
Brooklyn *(G-1908)*
Freeport Screen & Stamping .... E 516 379-0330
Freeport *(G-5412)*
Fresh Prints LLC .... E 917 826-2752
New York *(G-10259)*
Graph-Tex Inc .... F 607 756-7791
Cortland *(G-4049)*
Graph-Tex Inc .... G 607 756-1875
Cortland *(G-4050)*
Graphics For Industry Inc .... F 212 889-6202
New York *(G-10395)*
Graphics Plus Printing Inc .... E 607 299-0500
Cortland *(G-4051)*
Gruber Display Co Inc .... F 718 882-8220
Bronx *(G-1351)*
Handone Studios Inc .... G 585 421-8175
Fairport *(G-4862)*
Herrmann Group LLC .... G 716 876-9798
Kenmore *(G-7176)*
Human Technologies Corporation .... F 315 735-3532
Utica *(G-16364)*
Island Silkscreen Inc .... G 631 757-4567
East Northport *(G-4458)*
J Kendall LLC .... G 646 739-4956
Yonkers *(G-17474)*
J M L Productions Inc .... D 718 643-1674
Brooklyn *(G-2125)*
J N White Associates Inc .... D 585 237-5191
Perry *(G-13547)*
Kenmar Shirts Inc .... E 718 824-3880
Bronx *(G-1375)*
Knucklehead Embroidery Inc .... G 607 797-2725
Johnson City *(G-7129)*
Logomax Inc .... G 631 420-0484
Farmingdale *(G-5044)*
Loremanss Embroidery Engrav .... F 518 834-9205
Keeseville *(G-7168)*
Mastercraft Decorators Inc .... E 585 223-5150
Fairport *(G-4869)*
Mastro Graphic Arts Inc .... E 585 436-7570
Rochester *(G-14520)*
Matthew-Lee Corporation .... F 631 226-0100
Lindenhurst *(G-7494)*
Metro Creative Graphics Inc .... E 212 947-5100
New York *(G-11268)*
Mixture Screen Printing .... G 845 561-2857
Newburgh *(G-12788)*
Mv Corp Inc .... C 631 273-8020
Bay Shore *(G-717)*
New Art Signs Co Inc .... G 718 443-0900
Glen Head *(G-5651)*
New Buffalo Shirt Factory Inc .... G 716 436-5839
Buffalo *(G-3105)*
Northwind Graphics .... G 518 899-9651
Ballston Spa *(G-605)*
One In A Million Inc .... G 516 829-1111
Valley Stream *(G-16441)*
Paratore Signs Inc .... G 315 455-5551
Syracuse *(G-16031)*
PDM Studios Inc .... G 716 694-8337
Tonawanda *(G-16210)*
Personal Graphics Corporation .... G 315 853-3421
Westmoreland *(G-17092)*
Peter Papastrat .... G 607 723-8112
Binghamton *(G-938)*
Pierrepont Visual Graphics .... E 585 305-9672
Rochester *(G-14604)*
Print Shoppe .... G 315 792-9585
Utica *(G-16380)*
R R Donnelley & Sons Company .... D 518 438-4722
Albany *(G-126)*
Rainbow Lettering .... G 607 732-5751
Elmira *(G-4713)*
Richs Stitches EMB Screenprint .... G 845 621-2175
Mahopac *(G-8030)*
Round Top Knit & Screening .... G 518 622-3600
Round Top *(G-15064)*
Royal Tees Inc .... G 845 357-9448
Suffern *(G-15820)*
Sand Hill Industries Inc .... G 518 885-7991
Ballston Spa *(G-607)*
Screen The World Inc .... F 631 475-0023
Holtsville *(G-6534)*

Shore Line Monogramming Inc .... F 914 698-8000
Mamaroneck *(G-8080)*
Shykat Promotions .... G 866 574-2757
Forestville *(G-5343)*
Sign Shop Inc .... G 631 226-4145
Copiague *(G-3951)*
Silk Screen Art Inc .... F 518 762-8423
Johnstown *(G-7155)*
Spst Inc .... G 607 798-6952
Vestal *(G-16477)*
Stromberg Brand Corporation .... F 914 739-7410
Valley Cottage *(G-16417)*
T L F Graphics Inc .... D 585 272-5500
Rochester *(G-14740)*
Tara Rific Screen Printing Inc .... G 718 583-6864
Bronx *(G-1470)*
Todd Walbridge .... G 585 254-3018
Rochester *(G-14755)*
U All Inc .... E 518 438-2558
Albany *(G-144)*
Universal Screening Associates .... G 718 232-2744
Brooklyn *(G-2728)*
Unlimited Ink Inc .... E 631 582-0696
Hauppauge *(G-6246)*
Viking Athletics Ltd .... E 631 957-8000
Lindenhurst *(G-7515)*
Voss Signs LLC .... E 315 682-6418
Manlius *(G-8109)*
Zacks Enterprises Inc .... E 800 366-4924
Orangeburg *(G-13270)*

PRINTING, COMMERCIAL: Stamps, Trading, NEC

Ashton-Potter USA Ltd .... C 716 633-2000
Williamsville *(G-17261)*

PRINTING, COMMERCIAL: Stationery, NEC

Hart Reproduction Services .... G 212 704-0556
New York *(G-10468)*

PRINTING, COMMERCIAL: Tags, NEC

Actioncraft Products Inc .... G 516 883-6423
Port Washington *(G-13818)*
Industrial Test Eqp Co Inc .... E 516 883-6423
Port Washington *(G-13846)*
Itc Mfg Group Inc .... F 212 684-3696
New York *(G-10711)*

PRINTING, LITHOGRAPHIC: Advertising Posters

First Displays Inc .... F 347 642-5972
Long Island City *(G-7771)*
V C N Group Ltd Inc .... G 516 223-4812
North Baldwin *(G-12928)*

PRINTING, LITHOGRAPHIC: Calendars

Redi Records Payroll .... F 718 854-6990
Brooklyn *(G-2505)*

PRINTING, LITHOGRAPHIC: Color

ABC Check Printing Corp .... F 718 855-4702
Brooklyn *(G-1546)*
Chakra Communications Inc .... E 716 505-7300
Lancaster *(G-7333)*
Crawford Print Shop Inc .... G 607 359-4970
Addison *(G-5)*
Create-A-Card Inc .... G 631 584-2273
Saint James *(G-15114)*
Digital United Color Prtg Inc .... G 845 986-9846
Warwick *(G-16610)*
Raith America Inc .... E 518 874-3000
Troy *(G-16274)*
Select-A-Form Inc .... D 631 981-3076
Holbrook *(G-6499)*
Spectrum Prtg Lithography Inc .... F 212 255-3931
New York *(G-12182)*

PRINTING, LITHOGRAPHIC: Decals

Aro-Graph Corporation .... G 315 463-8693
Syracuse *(G-15877)*
Decal Makers Inc .... E 516 221-7200
Bellmore *(G-813)*
Decal Techniques Inc .... G 631 491-1800
Bay Shore *(G-690)*

Paper House Productions Inc .... E 845 246-7261
Saugerties *(G-15219)*

PRINTING, LITHOGRAPHIC: Fashion Plates

Chan Luu LLC .... E 212 398-3163
New York *(G-9628)*

PRINTING, LITHOGRAPHIC: Forms & Cards, Business

Batavia Press LLC .... E 585 343-4429
Batavia *(G-625)*
Color Card LLC .... F 631 232-1300
Central Islip *(G-3516)*
Perfect Forms and Systems Inc .... F 631 462-1100
Smithtown *(G-15517)*
Webb-Mason Inc .... E 716 276-8792
Buffalo *(G-3276)*

PRINTING, LITHOGRAPHIC: Forms, Business

Precision Envelope Co Inc .... G 631 694-3990
Farmingdale *(G-5096)*

PRINTING, LITHOGRAPHIC: Letters, Circular Or Form

Brooklyn Circus .... F 718 858-0919
Brooklyn *(G-1722)*
F & D Services Inc .... F 718 984-1635
Staten Island *(G-15693)*

PRINTING, LITHOGRAPHIC: Menus

Ready Check Glo Inc .... G 516 547-1849
East Northport *(G-4463)*

PRINTING, LITHOGRAPHIC: Offset & photolithographic printing

Ace Printing & Publishing Inc .... F 718 939-0040
Flushing *(G-5229)*
Distinctive Printing Inc .... G 212 727-3000
New York *(G-9940)*
G & P Printing Inc .... F 212 274-8092
New York *(G-10278)*
Iron Horse Graphics Ltd .... G 631 537-3400
Bridgehampton *(G-1232)*
Kaymil Printing Company Inc .... F 212 594-3718
New York *(G-10861)*
Mdi Holdings LLC .... A 212 559-1127
New York *(G-11228)*
Printing Sales Group Limited .... E 718 258-8860
Brooklyn *(G-2464)*
Progressive Color Graphics .... E 212 292-8787
Great Neck *(G-5851)*
Remsen Graphics Corp .... G 718 643-7500
Brooklyn *(G-2510)*
Rgm Signs Inc .... G 718 442-0598
Staten Island *(G-15754)*
Superior Print On Demand .... G 607 240-5231
Vestal *(G-16478)*

PRINTING, LITHOGRAPHIC: On Metal

A I P Printing & Stationers .... G 631 929-5529
Wading River *(G-16543)*
Avon Reproductions Inc .... E 631 273-2400
Hauppauge *(G-6050)*
Challenge Graphics Svcs Inc .... E 631 586-0171
Deer Park *(G-4138)*
Cherry Lane Lithographing Corp .... E 516 293-9294
Plainview *(G-13617)*
David Helsing .... G 607 796-2681
Horseheads *(G-6601)*
Denton Advertising Inc .... E 631 586-4333
Bohemia *(G-1052)*
Hks Printing Company Inc .... F 212 675-2529
New York *(G-10533)*
Mansfield Press Inc .... F 212 265-5411
New York *(G-11165)*
Messenger Press .... G 518 885-9231
Ballston Spa *(G-603)*
Seneca West Printing Inc .... E 716 675-8010
West Seneca *(G-16983)*

PRINTING, LITHOGRAPHIC: Periodicals

Quantum Color Inc .... E 716 283-8700
Niagara Falls *(G-12883)*

PRINTING, LITHOGRAPHIC: Post Cards, Picture — PRODUCT SECTION

PRINTING, LITHOGRAPHIC: Post Cards, Picture

- Anne Taintor Inc ....G 718 483-9312
  Brooklyn (G-1613)

PRINTING, LITHOGRAPHIC: Promotional

- 21st Century Fox America Inc ....D 212 852-7000
  New York (G-9013)
- China Imprint LLC ....G 585 563-3391
  Rochester (G-14295)
- Gmp LLC ....D 914 939-0571
  Port Chester (G-13774)
- In-Step Marketing Inc ....F 212 797-3450
  New York (G-10624)
- R & L Press Inc ....G 718 447-8557
  Staten Island (G-15747)
- Source One Promotional Product ......G 516 208-6996
  Merrick (G-8428)

PRINTING, LITHOGRAPHIC: Publications

- Canyon Publishing Inc ....F 212 334-0227
  New York (G-9571)
- Hudson Park Press Inc ....G 212 929-8898
  New York (G-10571)
- Post Road ....F 203 545-2122
  New York (G-11712)
- Print By Premier LLC ....G 212 947-1365
  New York (G-11736)

PRINTING, LITHOGRAPHIC: Tags

- Kwik Ticket Inc ....F 718 421-3800
  Brooklyn (G-2183)
- Paxar Corporation ....E 845 398-3229
  Orangeburg (G-13260)

PRINTING, LITHOGRAPHIC: Tickets

- Worldwide Ticket Craft ....D 516 538-6200
  Merrick (G-8429)

PRINTING, LITHOGRAPHIC: Transfers, Decalcomania Or Dry

- Royal Tees Inc ....G 845 357-9448
  Suffern (G-15820)

PRINTING: Books

- Cct Inc ....G 212 532-3355
  New York (G-9606)
- Kravitz Design Inc ....G 212 625-1644
  New York (G-10928)
- North Country Books Inc ....G 315 735-4877
  Utica (G-16376)
- Twp America Inc ....G 212 274-8090
  New York (G-12453)
- Vicks Lithograph & Prtg Corp ....C 315 272-2401
  Yorkville (G-17544)

PRINTING: Books

- 450 Ridge St Inc ....G 716 754-2789
  Lewiston (G-7453)
- B-Squared Inc ....E 212 777-2044
  New York (G-9349)
- Bedford Freeman & Worth ....C 212 576-9400
  New York (G-9391)
- Centrisource Inc ....G 716 871-1105
  Tonawanda (G-16173)
- E Graphics Corporation ....G 718 486-9767
  Brooklyn (G-1893)
- Electronic Printing Inc ....G 631 218-2200
  Hauppauge (G-6094)
- Experiment LLC ....G 212 889-1659
  New York (G-10161)
- Flare Multicopy Corp ....E 718 258-8860
  Brooklyn (G-1983)
- Hudson Valley Paper Works Inc ....F 845 569-8883
  Newburgh (G-12785)
- In-House Inc ....F 718 445-9007
  College Point (G-3812)
- Literary Classics of US ....F 212 308-3360
  New York (G-11036)
- Printing Factory LLC ....F 718 451-0500
  Brooklyn (G-2462)
- Promotional Sales Books LLC ....G 212 675-0364
  New York (G-11753)
- Royal Fireworks Printing Co ....F 845 726-3333
  Unionville (G-16326)

- Steffen Publishing Inc ....D 315 865-4100
  Holland Patent (G-6514)
- Sterling Pierce Company Inc ....E 516 593-1170
  East Rockaway (G-4492)
- Stop Entertainment Inc ....F 212 242-7867
  Monroe (G-8599)
- The Nugent Organization Inc ....G 212 645-6600
  Oceanside (G-13123)
- Tobay Printing Co Inc ....G 631 842-3300
  Copiague (G-3957)
- Vicks Lithograph & Prtg Corp ....C 315 736-9344
  Yorkville (G-17545)
- Worzalla Publishing Company ....G 212 967-7909
  New York (G-12693)

PRINTING: Broadwoven Fabrics. Cotton

- Mountain T-Shirts Inc ....E 518 943-4533
  Catskill (G-3460)

PRINTING: Checkbooks

- Deluxe Corporation ....B 845 362-4054
  Spring Valley (G-15603)
- Wood Designs Deluxe Corp ....G 917 414-4640
  Island Park (G-6823)

PRINTING: Commercial, NEC

- 2 1 2 Postcards Inc ....E 212 767-8227
  New York (G-9008)
- 461 New Lots Avenue LLC ....G 347 303-9305
  Brooklyn (G-1518)
- 5 Stars Printing Corp ....F 718 461-4612
  Flushing (G-5227)
- A & A Graphics Inc II ....G 516 735-0078
  Seaford (G-15365)
- A C Envelope Inc ....G 516 420-0646
  Farmingdale (G-4933)
- A Graphic Printing Inc ....G 212 233-9696
  New York (G-9034)
- Academy Printing Services Inc ....G 631 765-3346
  Southold (G-15581)
- Accel Printing & Graphics ....G 914 241-3369
  Mount Kisco (G-8663)
- Adflex Corporation ....E 585 454-2950
  Rochester (G-14189)
- Adirondack Pennysaver Inc ....E 518 563-0100
  Plattsburgh (G-13678)
- Allsafe Technologies Inc ....G 716 691-0400
  Amherst (G-225)
- Alpina Copyworld Inc ....F 212 683-3511
  New York (G-9152)
- Alvin J Bart & Sons Inc ....C 718 417-1300
  Glendale (G-5660)
- Always Printing ....G 914 481-5209
  Port Chester (G-13767)
- AMA Precision Screening Inc ....F 585 293-0820
  Churchville (G-3663)
- Amax Printing Inc ....F 718 384-8600
  Maspeth (G-8144)
- American Office Supply Inc ....F 516 294-9444
  Westbury (G-16994)
- Amerikom Group Inc ....D 212 675-1329
  New York (G-9183)
- Ansun Graphics Inc ....F 315 437-6869
  Syracuse (G-15874)
- Apple Enterprises Inc ....G 718 361-2200
  Long Island City (G-7695)
- April Printing Co Inc ....F 212 685-7455
  New York (G-9235)
- Argo Lithographers Inc ....E 718 729-2700
  Long Island City (G-7702)
- Arista Innovations Inc ....E 516 746-2262
  Mineola (G-8529)
- Artistic Typography Corp ....G 212 463-8880
  New York (G-9272)
- Artistics Printing Corp ....G 516 561-2121
  Franklin Square (G-5370)
- Artscroll Printing Corp ....G 212 929-2413
  New York (G-9275)
- Asn Inc ....E 718 894-0800
  Maspeth (G-8149)
- Balajee Enterprises Inc ....G 212 629-6150
  New York (G-9361)
- Bartolomeo Publishing Inc ....G 631 420-4949
  West Babylon (G-16799)
- Bedford Freeman & Worth ....C 212 576-9400
  New York (G-9391)
- Beebie Printing & Art Agcy Inc ....G 518 725-4528
  Gloversville (G-5723)

- Benchmark Printing Inc ....D 518 393-1361
  Schenectady (G-15262)
- Berkshire Business Forms Inc ....F 518 828-2600
  Hudson (G-6639)
- Bestype Digital Imaging LLC ....F 212 966-6886
  New York (G-9421)
- Big Apple Sign Corp ....E 212 629-3650
  New York (G-9441)
- Body Builders Inc ....G 718 492-7997
  Brooklyn (G-1707)
- Bondy Printing Corp ....G 631 242-1510
  Bay Shore (G-677)
- BP Beyond Printing Inc ....G 516 328-2700
  Hempstead (G-6290)
- Bradley Marketing Group Inc ....G 212 967-6100
  New York (G-9501)
- Bridge Fulfillment Inc ....G 718 625-6622
  Brooklyn (G-1715)
- Brooks Litho Digital Group Inc ....G 631 789-4500
  Deer Park (G-4136)
- C F Print Ltd Inc ....F 631 567-2110
  Deer Park (G-4137)
- Cama Graphics Inc ....F 718 707-9747
  Long Island City (G-7723)
- Century Direct LLC ....C 212 763-0600
  Islandia (G-6827)
- Chakra Communications Inc ....E 607 748-7491
  Endicott (G-4806)
- Christian Bus Endeavors Inc ....G 315 788-8560
  Watertown (G-16665)
- Chroma Communications Inc ....G 631 289-8871
  Medford (G-8271)
- CHv Printed Company ....F 516 997-1101
  East Meadow (G-4439)
- Citiforms Inc ....G 212 334-9671
  New York (G-9676)
- Classic Album ....E 718 388-2818
  Brooklyn (G-1785)
- Colad Group LLC ....D 716 961-1776
  Buffalo (G-2900)
- Colonial Label Systems Inc ....E 631 254-0111
  Bay Shore (G-683)
- Colonial Tag & Label Co Inc ....F 516 482-0508
  Great Neck (G-5816)
- Comgraph Sales Service ....G 716 601-7243
  Elma (G-4660)
- Commercial Press Inc ....G 315 274-0028
  Canton (G-3407)
- Copy Room Inc ....F 212 371-8600
  New York (G-9781)
- Copy X/Press Ltd ....D 631 585-2200
  Ronkonkoma (G-14916)
- Curtis Prtg Co The Del Press ....G 518 477-4820
  East Greenbush (G-4421)
- Custom Prtrs Guilderland Inc ....F 518 456-2811
  Guilderland (G-5924)
- D G M Graphics Inc ....F 516 223-2220
  Merrick (G-8416)
- D3 Repro Group ....G 347 507-1051
  Long Island City (G-7738)
- DArcy Printing and Lithog ....G 212 924-1554
  New York (G-9863)
- Dash Printing Inc ....G 212 643-8534
  New York (G-9866)
- Data Flow Inc ....G 631 436-9200
  Medford (G-8273)
- Delft Printing Inc ....G 716 683-1100
  Lancaster (G-7335)
- DEW Graphics Inc ....E 212 727-8820
  New York (G-9917)
- Digital Brewery LLC ....G 646 665-2106
  Astoria (G-435)
- Digital Evolution Inc ....E 212 732-2722
  New York (G-9929)
- Direct Print Inc ....F 212 987-6003
  New York (G-9934)
- Dit Prints Incorporated ....G 518 885-4400
  Ballston Spa (G-593)
- Division Den-Bar Enterprises ....G 914 381-2220
  Mamaroneck (G-8065)
- Donald Bruhnke ....F 212 600-1260
  New York (G-9949)
- Dupli Graphics Corporation ....C 315 234-7286
  Syracuse (G-15945)
- Dutchess Plumbing & Heating ....G 845 889-8255
  Staatsburg (G-15638)
- E&I Printing ....F 212 206-0506
  New York (G-10006)
- Eagle Envelope Company Inc ....G 607 387-3195
  Syracuse (G-15948)

Elm Graphics Inc....G.... 315 737-5984
New Hartford (G-8848)
Enterprise Press Inc....C.... 212 741-2111
New York (G-10096)
Evenhouse Printing....G.... 716 649-2666
Hamburg (G-5948)
Evergreen Corp Central NY....F.... 315 454-4175
Syracuse (G-15959)
Excellent Printing Inc....G.... 718 384-7272
Brooklyn (G-1949)
Excelsus Solutions LLC....E.... 585 533-0003
Rochester (G-14384)
Exotic Print and Paper Inc....F.... 212 807-0465
New York (G-10160)
Eye Graphics & Printing Inc....F.... 718 488-0606
Brooklyn (G-1953)
F A Printing....G.... 212 974-5982
New York (G-10168)
Falconer Printing & Design Inc....F.... 716 665-2121
Falconer (G-4906)
Fedex Office & Print Svcs Inc....G.... 718 982-5223
Staten Island (G-15694)
First2print Inc....G.... 212 868-6886
New York (G-10222)
Flp Group LLC....F.... 315 252-7583
Auburn (G-495)
Force Digital Media Inc....G.... 631 243-0243
Deer Park (G-4165)
Franklin Packaging Inc....G.... 631 582-8900
Northport (G-13029)
Fred Weidner & Son Printers....G.... 212 964-8676
New York (G-10254)
Freeville Publishing Co Inc....F.... 607 844-9119
Freeville (G-5447)
G&J Graphics Inc....G.... 718 409-9874
Bronx (G-1342)
Gallant Graphics Ltd....E.... 845 868-1166
Stanfordville (G-15647)
Garrett J Cronin....G.... 914 761-9299
White Plains (G-17137)
Gatehouse Media LLC....C.... 585 598-0030
Pittsford (G-13589)
GE Healthcare Fincl Svcs Inc....G.... 212 713-2000
New York (G-10308)
Gem Reproduction Services Corp....G.... 845 298-0172
Wappingers Falls (G-16590)
Gem West Inc....G.... 631 567-4228
Patchogue (G-13445)
Genie Instant Printing Co Inc....F.... 212 575-8258
New York (G-10321)
Grand Meridian Printing Inc....E.... 718 937-3888
Long Island City (G-7781)
Graphic Lab Inc....E.... 212 682-1815
New York (G-10394)
Haig Press Inc....E.... 631 582-5800
Hauppauge (G-6111)
Hi-Tech Packg World-Wide LLC....G.... 845 947-1912
New Windsor (G-8985)
Horace J Metz....G.... 716 873-9103
Kenmore (G-7177)
Hospitality Inc....E.... 212 268-1930
New York (G-10554)
I N K T Inc....F.... 212 957-2700
New York (G-10586)
Idc Printing & Sty Co Inc....G.... 516 599-0400
Lynbrook (G-7979)
Image Typography Inc....G.... 631 218-6932
Holbrook (G-6479)
Impress Graphic Technologies....F.... 516 781-0845
Westbury (G-17023)
Impressive Imprints....F.... 716 692-0905
North Tonawanda (G-12994)
Incodema3d LLC....E.... 607 269-4390
Freeville (G-5449)
Integrated Graphics Inc....G.... 212 592-5600
New York (G-10659)
Iron Horse Graphics Ltd....G.... 631 537-3400
Bridgehampton (G-1232)
Jack J Florio Jr....G.... 716 434-9123
Lockport (G-7625)
Japan Printing & Graphics Inc....G.... 212 406-2905
New York (G-10741)
Joed Press....G.... 212 243-3620
New York (G-10787)
John Auguliaro Printing Co....G.... 718 382-5283
Brooklyn (G-2144)
Jomar Industries Inc....E.... 845 357-5773
Airmont (G-14)
Jomart Associates Inc....E.... 212 627-2153
Islandia (G-6836)

Kallen Corp....G.... 212 242-1470
New York (G-10841)
Kenan International Trading....G.... 718 672-4922
Corona (G-4023)
Key Computer Svcs of Chelsea....D.... 212 206-8060
New York (G-10880)
Lake Placid Advertisers Wkshp....E.... 518 523-3359
Lake Placid (G-7299)
Lauricella Press Inc....E.... 516 931-5906
Brentwood (G-1186)
Lennons Litho Inc....F.... 315 866-3156
Herkimer (G-6329)
Leo Paper Inc....G.... 917 305-0708
New York (G-11005)
Levon Graphics Corp....D.... 631 753-2022
Farmingdale (G-5043)
Linden Forms & Systems Inc....E.... 212 219-1100
Brooklyn (G-2229)
Loy L Press Inc....G.... 716 634-5966
Buffalo (G-3069)
M C Packaging Corporation....E.... 631 643-3763
Babylon (G-547)
Magazines & Brochures Inc....G.... 716 875-9699
Buffalo (G-3074)
Makerbot Industries LLC....G.... 347 457-5758
New York (G-11142)
Mason Transparent Package Inc....E.... 718 792-6000
Bronx (G-1392)
Master Image Printing Inc....G.... 914 347-4400
Elmsford (G-4772)
Measurement Incorporated....F.... 914 682-1969
White Plains (G-17163)
Media Signs LLC....G.... 718 252-7575
Brooklyn (G-2296)
Mega Graphics Inc....G.... 914 962-1402
Yorktown Heights (G-17529)
Menu Solutions Inc....D.... 718 575-5160
Bronx (G-1394)
Merlin Printing Inc....E.... 631 842-6666
Amityville (G-312)
Merrill Communications LLC....G.... 212 620-5600
New York (G-11258)
Merrill Corporation....D.... 917 934-7300
New York (G-11259)
Middletown Press....G.... 845 343-1895
Middletown (G-8485)
Miken Companies Inc....D.... 716 668-6311
Buffalo (G-3085)
Mimeocom Inc....B.... 212 847-3000
New York (G-11299)
Mini Graphics Inc....D.... 516 223-6464
Hauppauge (G-6165)
Mpe Graphics Inc....F.... 631 582-8900
Bohemia (G-1101)
Multi Packaging Solutions Inc....E.... 646 885-0005
New York (G-11347)
Nathan Printing Express Inc....G.... 914 472-0914
Scarsdale (G-15250)
New Deal Printing Corp....G.... 718 729-5800
New York (G-11404)
New York Legal Publishing....G.... 518 459-1100
Menands (G-8409)
Newport Business Solutions Inc....F.... 631 319-6129
Bohemia (G-1105)
Niagara Sample Book Co Inc....F.... 716 284-6151
Niagara Falls (G-12867)
Noble Checks Inc....G.... 212 537-6241
Brooklyn (G-2383)
North American Graphics Inc....F.... 212 725-2200
New York (G-11472)
North Six Inc....F.... 212 463-7227
New York (G-11475)
Ontario Label Graphics Inc....F.... 716 434-8505
Lockport (G-7639)
Origin Press Inc....G.... 516 746-2262
Mineola (G-8563)
Pace Editions Inc....G.... 212 675-7431
New York (G-11563)
Paulin Investment Company....E.... 631 957-8500
Amityville (G-320)
Penny Lane Printing Inc....D.... 585 226-8111
Avon (G-539)
Photo Agents Ltd....G.... 631 421-0258
Huntington (G-6709)
Pony Farm Press & Graphics....G.... 607 432-9020
Oneonta (G-13214)
Premier Ink Systems Inc....E.... 845 782-5802
Harriman (G-5995)
Presstek Printing LLC....F.... 585 266-2770
Rochester (G-14622)

Print City Corp....F.... 212 487-9778
New York (G-11737)
Print House Inc....D.... 718 443-7500
Brooklyn (G-2459)
Print Mall....G.... 718 437-7700
Brooklyn (G-2460)
Printed Image....G.... 716 821-1880
Buffalo (G-3162)
Printfacility Inc....G.... 212 349-4009
New York (G-11741)
Printing Max New York Inc....G.... 718 692-1400
Brooklyn (G-2463)
Printing Prmtnal Solutions LLC....F.... 315 474-1110
Syracuse (G-16035)
Printing Resources Inc....E.... 518 482-2470
Albany (G-124)
Printout Copy Corp....E.... 718 855-4040
Brooklyn (G-2465)
Printworks Printing & Design....G.... 315 433-8587
Syracuse (G-16036)
Priority Printing Entps Inc....F.... 646 285-0684
New York (G-11743)
Publimax Printing Corp....G.... 718 366-7133
Ridgewood (G-14133)
Quadra Flex Corp....G.... 607 758-7066
Cortland (G-4065)
Quality Graphics West Seneca....G.... 716 668-4528
Cheektowaga (G-3615)
Quality Impressions Inc....G.... 646 613-0002
New York (G-11793)
Quality Offset LLC....G.... 347 342-4660
Long Island City (G-7884)
R & M Graphics of New York....F.... 212 929-0294
New York (G-11806)
R R Donnelley & Sons Company....F.... 716 763-2613
Lakewood (G-7317)
Rfn Inc....F.... 516 764-5100
Bay Shore (G-729)
Richard Ruffner....F.... 631 234-4600
Central Islip (G-3536)
Rike Enterprises Inc....F.... 631 277-8338
Islip (G-6851)
RIT Printing Corp....F.... 631 586-6220
Bay Shore (G-731)
Rose Graphics LLC....F.... 516 547-6142
West Babylon (G-16854)
RR Donnelley & Sons Company....G.... 646 755-8125
New York (G-11948)
S & S Graphics Inc....F.... 914 668-4230
Mount Vernon (G-8775)
S L C Industries Incorporated....F.... 607 775-2299
Binghamton (G-943)
Salamanca Press Penny Saver....E.... 716 945-1500
Salamanca (G-15132)
Scan-A-Chrome Color Inc....G.... 631 532-6146
Copiague (G-3948)
Scotti Graphics Inc....E.... 212 367-9602
Long Island City (G-7901)
SDS Business Cards Inc....F.... 516 747-3131
Syosset (G-15860)
Shapeways Inc....D.... 914 356-5816
New York (G-12064)
Sharp Printing Inc....G.... 716 731-3994
Sanborn (G-15154)
Silver Griffin Inc....F.... 518 272-7771
Troy (G-16279)
Sino Printing Inc....F.... 212 334-6896
New York (G-12109)
Soho Letterpress Inc....F.... 718 788-2518
Brooklyn (G-2604)
Solarz Bros Printing Corp....G.... 718 383-1330
Brooklyn (G-2608)
Spaulding Law Printing Inc....G.... 315 422-4805
Syracuse (G-16065)
Spectrum Prtg Lithography Inc....F.... 212 255-3131
New York (G-12182)
Speedy Enterprise of USA Corp....G.... 718 463-3000
Flushing (G-5300)
St James Printing Inc....G.... 631 981-2095
Ronkonkoma (G-15012)
Standwill Packaging Inc....E.... 631 752-1236
Farmingdale (G-5124)
Starcraft Press Inc....G.... 718 383-6700
Long Island City (G-7915)
Starfire Printing Inc....G.... 631 736-1495
Holtsville (G-6535)
Structured 3d Inc....G.... 346 704-2614
Amityville (G-326)
Syracuse Label Co Inc....D.... 315 422-1037
Syracuse (G-16078)

Employee Codes: A=Over 500 employees, B=251-500
C=101-250, D=51-100, E=20-50, F=10-19, G=5-9

2018 Harris
New York Manufacturers Directory

1299

PRINTING: Commercial, NEC

T S O General Corp .... E 631 952-5320
  Brentwood *(G-1193)*
T&K Printing Inc .... F 718 439-9454
  Brooklyn *(G-2661)*
T-Base Communications USA Inc ...... E 315 713-0013
  Ogdensburg *(G-13144)*
Tapemaker Supply Company LLC ...... G 914 693-3407
  Hartsdale *(G-6020)*
Tc Transcontinental USA Inc .... G 818 993-4767
  New York *(G-12308)*
Tcmf Inc .... D 607 724-1094
  Binghamton *(G-948)*
Tele-Pak Inc .... E 845 426-2300
  Monsey *(G-8620)*
The Gramecy Group .... G 518 348-1325
  Clifton Park *(G-3736)*
Thomson Press (India) Limited .... G 646 318-0369
  Long Island City *(G-7929)*
Top Copi Reproductions Inc .... F 212 571-4141
  New York *(G-12389)*
Toppan Vintage Inc .... D 212 596-7747
  New York *(G-12392)*
Toprint Ltd .... G 718 439-0469
  Brooklyn *(G-2686)*
Tri-Lon Clor Lithographers Ltd .... E 212 255-6140
  New York *(G-12421)*
USA Custom Pad Corp .... E 607 563-9550
  Sidney *(G-15467)*
Varick Street Litho Inc .... G 646 843-0800
  New York *(G-12529)*
Venus Printing Company .... F 212 967-8900
  Hewlett *(G-6339)*
Veterans Offset Printing Inc .... G 585 288-2900
  Rochester *(G-14781)*
Weicro Graphics Inc .... E 631 253-3360
  West Babylon *(G-16872)*
Were Forms Inc .... G 585 482-4400
  Rochester *(G-14789)*
Westypo Printers Inc .... G 914 737-7394
  Peekskill *(G-13512)*
Wheeler/Rinstar Ltd .... F 212 244-1130
  New York *(G-12649)*
Willco Fine Art Ltd .... F 718 935-9567
  New York *(G-12659)*
William J Ryan .... G 585 392-6200
  Hilton *(G-6447)*
Wilson Press LLC .... E 315 568-9693
  Seneca Falls *(G-15395)*
Worldwide Ticket Craft .... D 516 538-6200
  Merrick *(G-8429)*
X Myles Mar Inc .... E 212 683-2015
  New York *(G-12699)*
X Press Screen Printing .... G 716 679-7788
  Dunkirk *(G-4377)*
Xl Graphics Inc .... G 212 929-8700
  New York *(G-12705)*

PRINTING: Engraving & Plate

Allstate Sign & Plaque Corp .... F 631 242-2828
  Deer Park *(G-4117)*
Custom House Engravers Inc .... G 631 567-3004
  Bohemia *(G-1042)*
D & A Offset Services Inc .... F 212 924-0612
  New York *(G-9837)*

PRINTING: Flexographic

Astro Label & Tag Ltd .... G 718 435-4474
  Brooklyn *(G-1643)*
Gemson Graphics Inc .... G 516 873-8400
  Albertson *(G-158)*
Marlow Printing Co Inc .... E 718 625-4948
  Brooklyn *(G-2275)*
Transcntinental Ultra Flex Inc .... B 718 272-9100
  Brooklyn *(G-2693)*
W N Vanalstine & Sons Inc .... D 518 237-1436
  Cohoes *(G-3786)*

PRINTING: Gravure, Business Form & Card

Alamar Printing Inc .... F 914 993-9007
  White Plains *(G-17102)*
Alfa Card Inc .... G 718 326-7107
  Glendale *(G-5658)*

PRINTING: Gravure, Color

Clarion Publications Inc .... F 585 243-3530
  Geneseo *(G-5579)*
Kinaneco Inc .... E 315 468-6201
  Syracuse *(G-15994)*

PRINTING: Gravure, Forms, Business

American Print Solutions Inc .... G 718 208-2309
  Brooklyn *(G-1605)*

PRINTING: Gravure, Imprinting

C C Industries Inc .... F 518 581-7633
  Saratoga Springs *(G-15174)*

PRINTING: Gravure, Job

Leonardo Printing Corp .... G 914 664-7890
  Mount Vernon *(G-8746)*
Sommer and Sons Printing Inc .... F 716 822-4311
  Buffalo *(G-3218)*

PRINTING: Gravure, Labels

Adflex Corporation .... E 585 454-2950
  Rochester *(G-14189)*
Janco Press Inc .... F 631 563-3003
  Bohemia *(G-1077)*
Liberty Label Mfg Inc .... F 631 737-2365
  Holbrook *(G-6486)*
Niagara Label Company Inc .... F 716 542-3000
  Akron *(G-22)*
Trust of Colum Unive In The Ci .... F 212 854-2793
  New York *(G-12434)*

PRINTING: Gravure, Promotional

Gemini Manufacturing LLC .... C 914 375-0855
  White Plains *(G-17139)*

PRINTING: Gravure, Rotogravure

Advanced Printing New York Inc .... G 212 840-8108
  New York *(G-9093)*
Benton Announcements Inc .... F 716 836-4100
  Buffalo *(G-2861)*
Color Industries LLC .... G 718 392-8301
  Long Island City *(G-7731)*
Copy Corner Inc .... G 718 388-4545
  Brooklyn *(G-1802)*
Ecoplast & Packaging LLC .... F 718 996-0800
  Brooklyn *(G-1902)*
Gruner + Jahr USA Group Inc .... B 866 323-9336
  New York *(G-10419)*
Image Sales & Marketing Inc .... G 516 238-7023
  Massapequa Park *(G-8219)*
Jack J Florio Jr .... G 716 434-9123
  Lockport *(G-7625)*
Karr Graphics Corp .... E 212 645-6000
  Long Island City *(G-7806)*
Krepe Kraft Inc .... B 716 826-7086
  Buffalo *(G-3055)*
Lane Park Graphics Inc .... G 914 273-5898
  Patterson *(G-13466)*
McG Graphics Inc .... G 631 499-0730
  Dix Hills *(G-4317)*
Mod-Pac Corp .... D 716 447-9013
  Buffalo *(G-3092)*
Paya Printing of NY Inc .... G 516 625-8346
  Albertson *(G-160)*
SRC Liquidation Company .... G 716 631-3900
  Williamsville *(G-17280)*
Tele-Pak Inc .... E 845 426-2300
  Monsey *(G-8620)*

PRINTING: Gravure, Stamps, Trading

Ashton-Potter USA Ltd .... C 716 633-2000
  Williamsville *(G-17261)*

PRINTING: Gravure, Stationery

Mrs John L Strong & Co LLC .... F 212 838-3775
  New York *(G-11340)*
Mutual Engraving Company Inc .... D 516 489-0534
  West Hempstead *(G-16893)*

PRINTING: Laser

Amsterdam Printing & Litho Inc .... F 518 792-6501
  Queensbury *(G-14003)*
Batavia Legal Printing Inc .... F 585 768-2100
  Le Roy *(G-7428)*
CPW Direct Mail Group LLC .... E 631 588-6565
  Farmingdale *(G-4975)*
Data Palette Info Svcs LLC .... D 718 433-1060
  Port Washington *(G-13830)*
Diamond Inscription Tech .... F 646 366-7944
  New York *(G-9926)*
Doctor Print Inc .... E 631 873-4560
  Hauppauge *(G-6088)*
PBR Graphics Inc .... G 518 458-2909
  Albany *(G-116)*

PRINTING: Letterpress

6727 11th Ave Corp .... F 718 837-8787
  Brooklyn *(G-1520)*
Brodock Press Inc .... D 315 735-9577
  Utica *(G-16333)*
Chenango Union Printing Inc .... G 607 334-2112
  Norwich *(G-13040)*
Craig Envelope Corp .... E 718 786-4277
  Hicksville *(G-6361)*
Eastwood Litho Inc .... E 315 437-2626
  Syracuse *(G-15950)*
Edgian Press Inc .... G 516 931-2114
  Hicksville *(G-6371)*
Efficiency Printing Co Inc .... F 914 949-8611
  White Plains *(G-17129)*
F & B Photo Offset Co Inc .... G 516 431-5433
  Island Park *(G-6819)*
Fairmount Press .... G 212 255-2300
  New York *(G-10183)*
Forward Enterprises Inc .... F 585 235-7670
  Rochester *(G-14401)*
Frederick Coon Inc .... E 716 683-6812
  Elma *(G-4661)*
Gazette Press Inc .... E 914 963-8300
  Rye *(G-15082)*
Golos Printing Inc .... G 607 732-1896
  Elmira Heights *(G-4723)*
Grover Cleveland Press Inc .... F 716 564-2222
  Amherst *(G-243)*
H T L & S Ltd .... F 718 435-4474
  Brooklyn *(G-2059)*
Harmon and Castella Printing .... G 845 471-9163
  Poughkeepsie *(G-13925)*
HI Speed Envelope Co Inc .... F 718 617-1600
  Mount Vernon *(G-8735)*
Hill Crest Press .... G 518 943-0671
  Catskill *(G-3457)*
Johnnys Ideal Printing Co .... G 518 828-6666
  Hudson *(G-6651)*
Judith Lewis Printer Inc .... G 516 997-7777
  Westbury *(G-17027)*
Kaufman Brothers Printing .... F 212 563-1854
  New York *(G-10858)*
Kaymil Printing Company Inc .... G 212 594-3718
  New York *(G-10861)*
Linco Printing Inc .... E 718 937-5141
  Long Island City *(G-7817)*
Louis Heindl & Son Inc .... G 585 454-5080
  Rochester *(G-14504)*
M T M Printing Co Inc .... F 718 353-3297
  College Point *(G-3820)*
Malone Industrial Press Inc .... G 518 483-5880
  Malone *(G-8044)*
Mark T Westinghouse .... G 518 678-3262
  Catskill *(G-3459)*
Maspeth Press Inc .... G 718 429-2363
  Maspeth *(G-8180)*
Midgley Printing Corp .... G 315 475-1864
  Syracuse *(G-16009)*
Mines Press Inc .... C 914 788-1800
  Cortlandt Manor *(G-4078)*
Moore Printing Company Inc .... G 585 394-1533
  Canandaigua *(G-3378)*
P & W Press Inc .... E 646 486-3417
  New York *(G-11560)*
Patrick Ryans Modern Press .... F 518 434-2921
  Albany *(G-115)*
RBHM Incorporated .... F 609 259-4900
  Brooklyn *(G-2500)*
S & S Prtg Die-Cutting Co Inc .... F 718 388-8990
  Brooklyn *(G-2543)*
Seneca West Printing Inc .... G 716 675-8010
  West Seneca *(G-16983)*
Source Envelope Inc .... G 866 284-0707
  Farmingdale *(G-5122)*
Star Press Pearl River Inc .... G 845 268-2294
  Valley Cottage *(G-16415)*
Stony Point Graphics Ltd .... G 845 786-3322
  Stony Point *(G-15799)*
Tovie Asarese Royal Prtg Co .... G 716 885-7692
  Buffalo *(G-3249)*
Tri Kolor Printing & Sty .... F 315 474-6753
  Syracuse *(G-16085)*
Weeks & Reichel Printing Inc .... G 631 589-1443
  Sayville *(G-15244)*

William Charles Prtg Co Inc ... E ... 516 349-0900 — Plainview *(G-13674)*

PRINTING: Lithographic

12pt Printing LLC ... G ... 718 376-2120 — Brooklyn *(G-1510)*
2 1 2 Postcards Inc ... E ... 212 767-8227 — New York *(G-9008)*
2 X 4 Inc ... E ... 212 647-1170 — New York *(G-9009)*
3g Graphics LLC ... G ... 716 634-2585 — Amherst *(G-221)*
450 Ridge St Inc ... G ... 716 754-2789 — Lewiston *(G-7453)*
518 Prints LLC ... G ... 518 674-5346 — Averill Park *(G-530)*
6727 11th Ave Corp ... F ... 718 837-8787 — Brooklyn *(G-1520)*
A C Envelope Inc ... G ... 516 420-0646 — Farmingdale *(G-4933)*
A Esteban & Company Inc ... E ... 212 989-7000 — New York *(G-9031)*
A Esteban & Company Inc ... E ... 212 714-2227 — New York *(G-9032)*
Accuprint ... G ... 518 456-2431 — Albany *(G-31)*
Adirondack Publishing Co Inc ... E ... 518 891-2600 — Saranac Lake *(G-15162)*
Advance Publications Inc ... D ... 718 981-1234 — Staten Island *(G-15653)*
Advanced Business Group Inc ... F ... 212 398-1010 — New York *(G-9090)*
Advanced Digital Printing LLC ... E ... 718 649-1500 — New York *(G-9091)*
Advertising Lithographers ... F ... 212 966-7771 — New York *(G-9098)*
Albert Siy ... G ... 718 359-0389 — Flushing *(G-5231)*
Aldine Inc (ny) ... D ... 212 226-2870 — New York *(G-9129)*
Alexander Polakovich ... G ... 718 229-6200 — Bayside *(G-761)*
All Color Business Spc Ltd ... G ... 516 420-0649 — Deer Park *(G-4115)*
All Time Products Inc ... G ... 718 464-1400 — Queens Village *(G-13990)*
Alpina Copyworld Inc ... F ... 212 683-3511 — New York *(G-9152)*
Alpine Business Group Inc ... G ... 212 989-4198 — New York *(G-9153)*
Amax Printing Inc ... F ... 718 384-8600 — Maspeth *(G-8144)*
American Business Forms Inc ... E ... 716 836-5111 — Amherst *(G-226)*
American Icon Industries Inc ... G ... 845 561-1299 — Newburgh *(G-12770)*
American Print Solutions Inc ... E ... 718 246-7800 — Brooklyn *(G-1604)*
Amsterdam Printing & Litho Inc ... F ... 518 842-6000 — Amsterdam *(G-333)*
Amsterdam Printing & Litho Inc ... E ... 518 842-6000 — Amsterdam *(G-334)*
Answer Printing Inc ... F ... 212 922-2922 — New York *(G-9216)*
Arcade Inc ... A ... 212 541-2600 — New York *(G-9243)*
Argo Envelope Corp ... D ... 718 729-2700 — Long Island City *(G-7700)*
Argo Lithographers Inc ... E ... 718 729-2700 — Long Island City *(G-7702)*
Art Digital Technologies LLC ... F ... 646 649-4820 — Brooklyn *(G-1636)*
Art Scroll Printing Corp ... F ... 212 929-2413 — New York *(G-9265)*
Artina Group Inc ... E ... 914 592-1850 — Elmsford *(G-4743)*
Artscroll Printing Corp ... E ... 212 929-2413 — New York *(G-9275)*
Asn Inc ... E ... 718 894-0800 — Maspeth *(G-8149)*
Atlas Print Solutions Inc ... E ... 212 949-8775 — New York *(G-9308)*
Avm Printing Inc ... F ... 631 351-1331 — Hauppauge *(G-6049)*
B D B Typewriter Supply Works ... E ... 718 232-4800 — Brooklyn *(G-1659)*
Badoud Communications Inc ... C ... 315 472-7821 — Syracuse *(G-15886)*
Ballantrae Lithographers Inc ... G ... 914 592-3275 — White Plains *(G-17110)*
Baum Christine and John Corp ... G ... 585 621-8910 — Rochester *(G-14241)*
Beastons Budget Printing ... G ... 585 244-2721 — Rochester *(G-14244)*
Benchemark Printing Inc ... D ... 518 393-1361 — Schenectady *(G-15262)*
Benjamin Printing Inc ... F ... 315 788-7922 — Adams *(G-2)*
Bennett Multimedia Inc ... F ... 718 629-1454 — Brooklyn *(G-1680)*
Bennett Printing Corporation ... F ... 718 629-1454 — Brooklyn *(G-1681)*
Bernard Hall ... G ... 585 425-3340 — Fairport *(G-4853)*
Bevilacque Group LLC ... F ... 212 414-8858 — Port Washington *(G-13824)*
Billing Coding and Prtg Inc ... G ... 718 827-9409 — Brooklyn *(G-1696)*
Bittner Company LLC ... F ... 585 214-1790 — Rochester *(G-14251)*
Bk Printing Inc ... G ... 315 565-5396 — East Syracuse *(G-4528)*
Bluesoho ... F ... 646 805-2583 — New York *(G-9476)*
Boka Printing Inc ... G ... 607 725-3235 — Binghamton *(G-893)*
Boncraft Inc ... D ... 716 662-9720 — Tonawanda *(G-16167)*
Bondy Printing Corp ... G ... 631 242-1510 — Bay Shore *(G-677)*
Boulevard Printing ... G ... 716 837-3800 — Tonawanda *(G-16168)*
Boxcar Press Incorporated ... E ... 315 473-0930 — Syracuse *(G-15893)*
BP Beyond Printing Inc ... G ... 516 328-2700 — Hempstead *(G-6290)*
Brodock Press Inc ... D ... 315 735-9577 — Utica *(G-16333)*
Brooks Litho Digital Group Inc ... G ... 631 789-4500 — Deer Park *(G-4136)*
Brown Printing Company ... E ... 212 782-7800 — New York *(G-9522)*
Business Card Express Inc ... E ... 631 669-3400 — West Babylon *(G-16804)*
C & R De Santis Inc ... E ... 718 447-5076 — Staten Island *(G-15673)*
C K Printing ... G ... 718 965-0388 — Brooklyn *(G-1746)*
C To C Design & Print Inc ... F ... 631 885-4020 — Ronkonkoma *(G-14911)*
Caboodle Printing Inc ... G ... 716 693-6000 — Williamsville *(G-17265)*
Cadmus Journal Services Inc ... D ... 607 762-5365 — Conklin *(G-3890)*
Canandaigua Msgnr Incorporated ... D ... 585 394-0770 — Canandaigua *(G-3366)*
Candid Litho Printing Ltd ... D ... 212 431-3800 — Farmingdale *(G-4965)*
Carlara Group Ltd ... G ... 914 769-2020 — Pleasantville *(G-13744)*
Castlereagh Printcraft Inc ... D ... 516 623-1728 — Freeport *(G-5402)*
Cathedral Corporation ... C ... 315 338-0021 — Rome *(G-14837)*
Catskill Delaware Publications ... F ... 845 887-5200 — Callicoon *(G-3312)*
Cazar Printing & Advertising ... G ... 718 446-4606 — Corona *(G-4015)*
Cds Productions Inc ... F ... 518 385-8255 — Schenectady *(G-15269)*
Chromagraphics Press Inc ... G ... 631 367-6160 — Melville *(G-8332)*
Circle Press Inc ... D ... 212 924-4277 — New York *(G-9674)*
Classic Color Graphics Inc ... E ... 516 822-9090 — Hicksville *(G-6354)*
Classic Color Graphics Inc ... G ... 516 822-9090 — Hicksville *(G-6355)*
Cloud Printing ... G ... 212 775-0888 — New York *(G-9701)*
Cody Printing Corp ... G ... 718 651-8854 — Woodside *(G-17341)*
Coe Displays Inc ... G ... 718 937-5658 — Long Island City *(G-7730)*
Colad Group LLC ... D ... 716 961-1776 — Buffalo *(G-2900)*
Color-Aid Corporation ... G ... 212 673-5500 — Hudson Falls *(G-6670)*
Commercial Print & Imaging ... E ... 716 597-0100 — Buffalo *(G-2902)*
Community Media LLC ... E ... 212 229-1890 — New York *(G-9749)*
Community Newspaper Group LLC ... F ... 607 432-1000 — Oneonta *(G-13203)*
Compass Printing Plus ... F ... 518 891-7050 — Saranac Lake *(G-15163)*
Compass Printing Plus ... G ... 518 523-3308 — Saranac Lake *(G-15164)*
Compucolor Associates Inc ... E ... 516 358-0000 — New Hyde Park *(G-8868)*
Copy Stop Inc ... G ... 914 428-5188 — White Plains *(G-17124)*
Coral Color Process Ltd ... E ... 631 543-5200 — Commack *(G-3855)*
Coral Graphic Services Inc ... C ... 516 576-2100 — Hicksville *(G-6360)*
Cosmos Communications Inc ... C ... 718 482-1800 — Long Island City *(G-7734)*
Coughlin Printing Group ... G ... 315 788-8560 — Watertown *(G-16668)*
Courier Printing Corp ... E ... 607 467-2191 — Deposit *(G-4300)*
Cronin Enterprises Inc ... G ... 914 345-9600 — Elmsford *(G-4754)*
Daily Record ... F ... 585 232-2035 — Rochester *(G-14320)*
Dan Trent Company Inc ... G ... 716 822-1422 — Buffalo *(G-2920)*
Dark Star Lithograph Corp ... G ... 845 634-3780 — New City *(G-8829)*
Datorib Inc ... G ... 631 698-6222 — Selden *(G-15372)*
Dawn Paper Co Inc ... F ... 516 596-9110 — East Rockaway *(G-4489)*
Deanco Digital Printing LLC ... F ... 212 371-2025 — Sunnyside *(G-15826)*
Denton Publications Inc ... D ... 518 873-6368 — Elizabethtown *(G-4640)*
Dependable Lithographers Inc ... F ... 718 472-4200 — Long Island City *(G-7741)*
Design Distributors Inc ... D ... 631 242-2000 — Deer Park *(G-4152)*
Designlogocom Inc ... G ... 212 564-0200 — New York *(G-9909)*
Digital Color Concepts Inc ... E ... 212 989-4888 — New York *(G-9928)*
Digital Imaging Tech LLC ... G ... 518 885-4400 — Ballston Spa *(G-592)*
Diversified Envelope Ltd ... F ... 585 615-4697 — Rochester *(G-14333)*
Division Street News Corp ... F ... 518 234-2515 — Cobleskill *(G-3761)*
Donmar Printing Co ... F ... 516 280-2239 — Mineola *(G-8539)*
Donnelley Financial LLC ... B ... 212 425-0298 — New York *(G-9957)*
Dovelin Printing Company Inc ... F ... 718 302-3951 — Brooklyn *(G-1877)*
Dual Print & Mail LLC ... D ... 716 775-8001 — Grand Island *(G-5768)*
Dual Print & Mail LLC ... D ... 716 684-3825 — Cheektowaga *(G-3597)*
Dupli Graphics Corporation ... C ... 315 234-7286 — Syracuse *(G-15945)*
Dyenamix Inc ... G ... 212 941-6642 — New York *(G-9997)*
E B B Graphics Inc ... F ... 516 750-5510 — Westbury *(G-17006)*
E L Smith Printing Co Inc ... E ... 201 373-0111 — New City *(G-8831)*
E W Smith Publishing Co ... F ... 845 562-1218 — New Windsor *(G-8983)*
Eagle Graphics Inc ... G ... 585 244-5006 — Rochester *(G-14343)*
East Coast Thermographers Inc ... E ... 718 321-3211 — College Point *(G-3807)*
Eastwood Litho Inc ... E ... 315 437-2626 — Syracuse *(G-15950)*
Echo Appellate Press Inc ... G ... 516 432-3601 — Long Beach *(G-7670)*
Edwards Graphic Co Inc ... G ... 718 548-6858 — Bronx *(G-1329)*
Efficiency Printing Co Inc ... F ... 914 949-8611 — White Plains *(G-17129)*
Entermarket ... G ... 914 437-7268 — Mount Kisco *(G-8669)*
Enterprise Press Inc ... C ... 212 741-2111 — New York *(G-10096)*
Evolution Impressions Inc ... D ... 585 473-6600 — Rochester *(G-14382)*

PRODUCT

Employee Codes: A=Over 500 employees, B=251-500
C=101-250, D=51-100, E=20-50, F=10-19, G=5-9

2018 Harris
New York Manufacturers Directory

1301

PRINTING: Lithographic — PRODUCT SECTION

Company	Code	Phone
Execuprint Inc — Rochester (G-14385)	G	585 288-5570
Executive Prtg & Direct Mail — Elmsford (G-4760)	G	914 592-3200
F5 Networks Inc — New York (G-10175)	G	888 882-7535
Falconer Printing & Design Inc — Falconer (G-4906)	F	716 665-2121
Fasprint — Malone (G-8040)	G	518 483-4631
Final Touch Printing Inc — Spring Valley (G-15607)	F	845 352-2677
First Line Printing Inc — Woodside (G-17346)	F	718 606-0860
Flower City Printing Inc — Rochester (G-14397)	G	585 512-1235
Flynns Inc — New York (G-10234)	E	212 339-8700
G W Canfield & Son Inc — Utica (G-16357)	G	315 735-5522
Gannett Stllite Info Ntwrk LLC — West Nyack (G-16946)	E	845 578-2300
Garden City Printers & Mailers — West Hempstead (G-16884)	F	516 485-1600
Gatehouse Media LLC — Canandaigua (G-3376)	D	585 394-0770
Gazette Press Inc — Rye (G-15082)	E	914 963-8300
Global Graphics Inc — Flushing (G-5252)	F	718 939-4967
Gn Printing — Long Island City (G-7779)	E	718 784-1713
Gotham Ink Corp — Syosset (G-15845)	G	516 677-1969
Government Data Publication — Brooklyn (G-2046)	E	347 789-8719
GPM Associates LLC — Dansville (G-4103)	E	585 335-3940
Grand Prix Litho Inc — Holbrook (G-6478)	E	631 242-4182
Graphic Fabrications Inc — Rockville Centre (G-14819)	G	516 763-3222
Graphicomm Inc — Niagara Falls (G-12845)	G	716 283-0830
Great Eastern Color Lith — Poughkeepsie (G-13923)	D	845 454-7420
Green Girl Prtg & Msgnr Inc — New York (G-10401)	G	212 575-0357
Grover Cleveland Press Inc — Amherst (G-243)	F	716 564-2222
Guaranteed Printing Svc Co Inc — Long Island City (G-7784)	E	212 929-2410
Haig Press Inc — Hauppauge (G-6111)	E	631 582-5800
Hamptons Magazine — Southampton (G-15568)	E	631 283-7125
Hearst Corporation — Albany (G-85)	A	518 454-5694
Hempstead Sentinel Inc — Hempstead (G-6297)	F	516 486-5000
Hooek Produktion Inc — New York (G-10547)	G	212 367-9111
Horne Organization Inc — Yonkers (G-17471)	F	914 572-1330
Huckleberry Inc — Hauppauge (G-6119)	G	631 630-5450
Hugh F McPherson Inc — Cheektowaga (G-3604)	G	716 668-6107
Hunt Graphics Inc — Coram (G-3967)	G	631 751-5349
I 2 Print Inc — Long Island City (G-7791)	F	718 937-8800
Impala Press Ltd — Ronkonkoma (G-14940)	G	631 588-4262
Ink Well — Brooklyn (G-2105)	G	718 253-9736
Instant Again LLC — Rochester (G-14470)	E	585 436-8003
Instant Stream Inc — New York (G-10654)	E	917 438-7182
Interstate Litho Corp — Brentwood (G-1182)	D	631 232-6025
J A T Printing Inc — Huntington (G-6699)	G	631 427-1155
J F B & Sons Lithographers — Lake Ronkonkoma (G-7302)	D	631 467-1444
J P Printing Inc — Farmingdale (G-5023)	G	516 293-6110
J V Haring & Son — Staten Island (G-15713)	F	718 720-1947
Jack J Florio Jr — Lockport (G-7625)	G	716 434-9123
Jam Printing Publishing Inc — Elmsford (G-4766)	G	914 345-8400
Jane Lewis — Binghamton (G-925)	G	607 722-0584
Japan Printing & Graphics Inc — New York (G-10741)	E	212 406-2905
Jfb Print Solutions Inc — Lido Beach (G-7462)	E	631 694-8300
Jon Lyn Ink Inc — Merrick (G-8420)	G	516 546-2312
Joseph Paul — Brooklyn (G-2148)	G	718 693-4269
Jurist Company Inc — Long Island City (G-7801)	G	212 243-8008
Just Press Print LLC — Rochester (G-14488)	G	585 783-1300
Kader Lithograph Company Inc — Long Island City (G-7804)	G	917 664-4380
Kaleidoscope Imaging Inc — New York (G-10838)	E	212 631-9947
Karr Graphics Corp — Long Island City (G-7806)	E	212 645-6000
Keeners East End Litho Inc — East Hampton (G-4432)	E	631 324-8565
Keller Bros & Miller Inc — Buffalo (G-3045)	G	716 854-2374
Key Brand Entertainment Inc — New York (G-10879)	E	212 966-5400
Kim Jae Printing Co Inc — Roslyn Heights (G-15053)	G	212 691-6289
King Lithographers Inc — Mount Vernon (G-8743)	E	914 667-4200
Kling Magnetics Inc — Chatham (G-3586)	E	518 392-4000
Kolcorp Industries Ltd — New York (G-10909)	F	212 354-0400
L & K Graphics Inc — Deer Park (G-4185)	G	631 667-2269
Label Gallery Inc — Norwich (G-13049)	E	607 334-3244
Lake Placid Advertisers Wkshp — Lake Placid (G-7299)	E	518 523-3359
Laser Printer Checks Corp — Monroe (G-8595)	G	845 782-5837
Laumont Labs Inc — New York (G-10972)	E	212 664-0595
Lehmann Printing Company Inc — New York (G-10997)	E	212 929-2395
Leigh Scott Enterprises Inc — Bellerose (G-806)	G	718 343-5440
LI Script LLC — Woodbury (G-17313)	G	631 321-3850
Liberty Label Mfg Inc — Holbrook (G-6486)	F	631 737-2365
Litmor Publishing Corp — Garden City (G-5527)	F	516 931-0012
Lmg National Publishing Inc — Fairport (G-4868)	E	585 598-6874
Logo Print Company — Hornell (G-6592)	G	607 324-5403
Loudon Ltd — East Northport (G-4460)	G	631 757-4447
Love Unlimited NY Inc — Westbury (G-17035)	E	718 359-8500
Loy L Press Inc — Buffalo (G-3069)	G	716 634-5966
M3 Graphic Group Ltd — New York (G-11109)	G	212 366-0863
Magazines & Brochures Inc — Buffalo (G-3074)	G	716 875-9699
Mahin Impressions Inc — Riverhead (G-14163)	G	212 871-9777
Marks Corpex Banknote Co — Bay Shore (G-713)	G	631 968-0277
Marlow Printing Co Inc — Brooklyn (G-2275)	F	718 625-4948
Master Image Printing Inc — Elmsford (G-4772)	E	914 347-4400
Mc Squared Nyc Inc — New York (G-11217)	F	212 947-2260
McG Graphics Inc — Dix Hills (G-4317)	G	631 499-0730
Mdr Printing Corp — Manhasset (G-8095)	G	516 627-3221
Merrill New York Company Inc — New York (G-11261)	C	212 229-6500
Michael K Lennon Inc — Westhampton Beach (G-17088)	E	631 288-5200
Mickelberry Communications Inc — New York (G-11279)	G	212 832-0303
Microera Printers Inc — Rochester (G-14530)	E	585 783-1300
Middletown Press — Middletown (G-8485)	G	845 343-1895
Midgley Printing Corp — Syracuse (G-16009)	G	315 475-1864
Miken Companies Inc — Buffalo (G-3085)	G	716 668-6311
Miller Enterprises CNY Inc — Manlius (G-8108)	G	315 682-4999
Minuteman Press Inc — Nanuet (G-8805)	G	845 623-2277
Minuteman Press Intl Inc — Jamaica (G-6968)	G	718 343-5440
Mod-Pac Corp — Buffalo (G-3092)	D	716 447-9013
Monarch Graphics Inc — Central Islip (G-3531)	F	631 232-1300
Moneast Inc — Wappingers Falls (G-16595)	G	845 298-8898
Multimedia Services Inc — Corning (G-3997)	E	607 936-3186
Multiple Imprssons of Rchester — Rochester (G-14545)	G	585 546-1160
Mutual Engraving Company Inc — West Hempstead (G-16893)	D	516 489-0534
Nameplate Mfrs of Amer — Farmingdale (G-5070)	E	631 752-0055
Nash Printing Inc — Plainview (G-13651)	F	516 935-4567
NCR Corporation — Ithaca (G-6901)	C	607 273-5310
New Goldstar 1 Printing Corp — New York (G-11409)	G	212 343-3909
New York Digital Print Center — Whitestone (G-17241)	G	718 767-1953
New York Press & Graphics Inc — Albany (G-106)	G	518 489-7089
North Delaware Printing Inc — Tonawanda (G-16206)	G	716 692-0576
Northern NY Newspapers Corp — Watertown (G-16691)	C	315 782-1000
Observer Daily Sunday Newsppr — Dunkirk (G-4370)	D	716 366-3000
Office Grabs NY Inc — Brooklyn (G-2398)	E	212 444-1331
Old Ue LLC — Long Island City (G-7861)	B	718 707-0700
Orlandi Inc — Farmingdale (G-5081)	D	631 756-0110
Orlandi Inc — Farmingdale (G-5082)	E	631 756-0110
P D R Inc — Plainview (G-13655)	G	516 829-5300
Pace Editions Inc — New York (G-11563)	G	212 675-7431
Paladino Prtg & Graphics Inc — Flushing (G-5284)	G	718 279-6000
Pama Enterprises Inc — Great Neck (G-5846)	G	516 504-6300
Parkside Printing Co Inc — Jericho (G-7112)	F	516 933-5423
Parrinello Printing Inc — Buffalo (G-3138)	F	716 633-7780
Paya Printing of NY Inc — Albertson (G-160)	G	516 625-8346
Persch Service Print Inc — Dunkirk (G-4371)	G	716 366-2677
Phillip Tissicher — Brooklyn (G-2431)	F	718 282-3310
Phoenix Graphics Inc — Rochester (G-14601)	E	585 232-4040
Photo Agents Ltd — Huntington (G-6709)	G	631 421-0258
Pic A Poc Enterprises Inc — Ronkonkoma (G-14994)	G	631 981-2094
Pine Bush Printing Co Inc — Albany (G-122)	G	518 456-2431
Platinum Printing & Graphics — Farmingdale (G-5092)	G	631 249-3325
Play-It Productions Inc — Port Washington (G-13873)	G	212 695-6530
Pop Printing Incorporated — Brooklyn (G-2442)	F	212 808-7800
Pre Cycled Inc — Brewster (G-1225)	G	845 278-7611
Preebro Printing — Brooklyn (G-2451)	G	718 633-7300

2018 Harris New York Manufacturers Directory

(G-0000) Company's Geographic Section entry number

Presstek Printing LLC F 585 266-2770 Rochester *(G-14622)*
Prestige Envelope & Lithograph F 631 521-7043 Merrick *(G-8426)*
Prestone Press LLC C 347 468-7900 Long Island City *(G-7875)*
Pricet Printing G 315 655-0369 Cazenovia *(G-3478)*
Print & Graphics Group G 518 371-4649 Clifton Park *(G-3730)*
Print Better Inc G 347 348-1841 Ridgewood *(G-14131)*
Print Center Inc G 718 643-9559 Cold Spring Harbor *(G-3795)*
Print Cottage LLC F 516 369-1749 Massapequa Park *(G-8222)*
Print It Here G 516 308-7785 Massapequa *(G-8213)*
Print It Inc G 845 371-2227 Monsey *(G-8613)*
Print Management Group Inc G 212 213-1555 New York *(G-11738)*
Print Market Inc G 631 940-8181 Deer Park *(G-4218)*
Print Media Inc D 212 563-4040 New York *(G-11739)*
Print On Demand Initiative Inc F 585 239-6044 Rochester *(G-14623)*
Print Seforim Bzul Inc G 718 679-1011 Brooklyn *(G-2461)*
Print Shop G 607 734-4937 Horseheads *(G-6617)*
Print Solutions Plus Inc G 315 234-3801 Liverpool *(G-7571)*
Printcorp Inc F 631 696-0641 Ronkonkoma *(G-14995)*
Printech Business Systems Inc F 212 290-2542 New York *(G-11740)*
Printers 3 Inc F 631 351-1331 Hauppauge *(G-6198)*
Printing Prep Inc E 716 852-5071 Buffalo *(G-3163)*
Printing Resources Inc E 518 482-2470 Albany *(G-124)*
Printing Spectrum Inc F 631 689-1010 East Setauket *(G-4509)*
Printing X Press Ions G 631 242-1992 Dix Hills *(G-4319)*
Printinghouse Press Ltd G 212 719-0990 New York *(G-11742)*
Printutopia F 718 788-1545 Brooklyn *(G-2466)*
Printz and Patternz LLC G 518 944-6020 Schenectady *(G-15311)*
Professional Solutions Print G 631 231-9300 Hauppauge *(G-6200)*
Profile Printing & Graphics G 631 273-2727 Hauppauge *(G-6201)*
Psychonomic Society Inc E 512 381-1494 New York *(G-11764)*
Quad/Graphics Inc E 718 706-7600 Long Island City *(G-7881)*
Quad/Graphics Inc A 212 206-5535 New York *(G-11791)*
Quad/Graphics Inc A 212 741-1001 New York *(G-11792)*
Quality Graphics Tri State G 845 735-2523 Pearl River *(G-13489)*
R Hochman Papers Incorporated F 516 466-6414 Brooklyn *(G-2491)*
Rapid Print and Marketing Inc G 585 924-1520 Victor *(G-16523)*
Rapid Reproductions LLC G 607 843-2221 Oxford *(G-13389)*
Rapid Service Engraving Co G 716 896-4555 Buffalo *(G-3180)*
RBHM Incorporated F 609 259-4900 Brooklyn *(G-2500)*
REM Printing Inc G 518 438-7338 Albany *(G-130)*
Resonant Legal Media LLC E 212 687-7100 New York *(G-11872)*
Rheinwald Printing Co Inc F 585 637-5100 Brockport *(G-1246)*
Richard Ruffner F 631 234-4600 Central Islip *(G-3536)*
RIT Printing Corp F 631 586-6220 Bay Shore *(G-731)*
Rmf Print Management Group F 716 683-4351 Depew *(G-4297)*
Robert Portegello Graphics G 718 241-8118 Brooklyn *(G-2521)*
Robert Tabatznik Assoc Inc F 845 336-4555 Kingston *(G-7237)*
Rosen Mandell & Immerman Inc E 212 691-2277 New York *(G-11936)*
Rv Printing G 631 567-8658 Holbrook *(G-6498)*
Ry-Gan Printing Inc G 585 482-7770 Rochester *(G-14684)*
Ryan Printing Inc E 845 535-3235 Blauvelt *(G-969)*
Sammba Printing Inc G 516 944-4449 Port Washington *(G-13879)*
Sample News Group LLC D 315 343-3800 Oswego *(G-13365)*
SDS Business Cards Inc F 516 747-3131 Syosset *(G-15860)*
Seaboard Graphic Services LLC E 315 652-4200 Liverpool *(G-7574)*
Seifert Graphics Inc F 315 736-2744 Oriskany *(G-13337)*
Sentinel Printing Inc G 516 334-7400 Westbury *(G-17054)*
Shipman Printing Inds Inc G 716 504-7700 Sanborn *(G-15155)*
Shipmtes/Printmates Holdg Corp D 518 370-1158 Scotia *(G-15353)*
Sign World Inc E 212 619-9000 Brooklyn *(G-2581)*
Sizzal LLC E 212 354-6123 Long Island City *(G-7907)*
Sloane Design Inc G 212 539-0184 Brooklyn *(G-2599)*
Source Envelope Inc G 866 284-0707 Farmingdale *(G-5122)*
South Bridge Press Inc G 212 233-4047 New York *(G-12169)*
Speedcard Inc G 631 472-1904 Holbrook *(G-6501)*
Sputnick 84 LLC G 844 667-7468 New York *(G-12200)*
St James Printing Inc G 631 981-2095 Ronkonkoma *(G-15012)*
St Lawrence County Newspapers D 315 393-1003 Ogdensburg *(G-13143)*
Star Press Pearl River Inc G 845 268-2294 Valley Cottage *(G-16415)*
Steffen Publishing Inc D 315 865-4100 Holland Patent *(G-6514)*
Sterling North America Inc E 631 243-6933 Hauppauge *(G-6225)*
Sterling Pierce Company Inc E 516 593-1170 East Rockaway *(G-4492)*
Sterling United Inc G 716 835-9290 Amherst *(G-262)*
Stevens Bandes Graphics Corp F 212 675-1128 New York *(G-12226)*
Stony Brook University E 631 632-6434 Stony Brook *(G-15793)*
Studley Printing & Publishing F 518 563-1414 Plattsburgh *(G-13730)*
Summit Print & Mail LLC G 716 433-1014 Lockport *(G-7647)*
Sun Printing Incorporated E 607 337-3034 Norwich *(G-13055)*
Syracuse Computer Forms Inc E 315 478-0108 Syracuse *(G-16075)*
Sz - Design & Print Inc F 845 352-0395 Monsey *(G-8618)*
Taylor G 518 954-2832 Amsterdam *(G-369)*
Technipoly Manufacturing Inc E 718 383-0363 Brooklyn *(G-2671)*
Teller Printing Corp G 718 486-3662 Brooklyn *(G-2674)*
The Kingsbury Printing Co Inc G 518 747-6606 Hudson Falls *(G-6681)*
Tobay Printing Co Inc E 631 842-3300 Copiague *(G-3957)*
Tom & Jerry Printcraft Forms E 914 777-7468 Mamaroneck *(G-8081)*
Torsaf Printers Inc G 516 569-5577 Hewlett *(G-6337)*
Transaction Printer Group G 607 274-2500 Ithaca *(G-6915)*
Transcntinental Ultra Flex Inc B 718 272-9100 Brooklyn *(G-2693)*
Transcontinental Printing GP G 716 626-3078 Amherst *(G-267)*
Tri-Lon Clor Lithographers Ltd E 212 255-6140 New York *(G-12421)*
Tri-Star Offset Corp E 718 894-5555 Maspeth *(G-8203)*
Triad Printing Inc G 845 343-2722 Middletown *(G-8501)*
Tripi Engraving Co Inc E 718 383-6500 Brooklyn *(G-2700)*
Troy Sign & Printing G 718 994-4482 Bronx *(G-1478)*
Upstate Printing Inc F 315 475-6140 Syracuse *(G-16088)*
Vanguard Graphics LLC C 607 272-1212 Ithaca *(G-6916)*
Variable Graphics LLC G 212 691-2323 New York *(G-12528)*
Vectra Inc G 718 361-1000 Long Island City *(G-7940)*
Vic-Gina Printing Company Inc G 914 636-0200 New Rochelle *(G-8973)*
Vicks Lithograph & Prtg Corp C 315 736-9344 Yorkville *(G-17545)*
Vicks Lithograph & Prtg Corp C 315 272-2401 Yorkville *(G-17544)*
VIP Printing G 718 641-9361 Howard Beach *(G-6627)*
Virgil Mountain Inc G 212 378-0007 New York *(G-12574)*
Wallkill Valley Publications E 845 561-0170 Newburgh *(G-12810)*
Walnut Printing Inc G 718 707-0100 Long Island City *(G-7947)*
Wappingers Falls Shopper Inc E 845 297-3723 Wappingers Falls *(G-16598)*
Webster Printing Corporation F 585 671-1533 Webster *(G-16768)*
Westmore Litho Corp G 718 361-9403 Long Island City *(G-7950)*
William Boyd Printing Co Inc C 518 339-5832 Latham *(G-7411)*
William J Kline & Son Inc D 518 843-1100 Amsterdam *(G-374)*
William J Ryan G 585 392-6200 Hilton *(G-6447)*
Wilson Press LLC E 315 568-9693 Seneca Falls *(G-15395)*
Winner Press Inc E 718 937-7715 Long Island City *(G-7953)*
Won & Lee Inc E 516 222-0712 Garden City *(G-5552)*
Wynco Press One Inc G 516 354-6145 Glen Oaks *(G-5656)*
X Myles Mar Inc E 212 683-2015 New York *(G-12699)*
X-L Envelope and Printing Inc F 716 852-2135 Buffalo *(G-3284)*
Yorktown Printing Corp C 914 962-2526 Yorktown Heights *(G-17538)*
Zacmel Graphics LLC G 631 944-6031 Deer Park *(G-4256)*
Zenger Group Inc E 716 871-1058 Tonawanda *(G-16238)*

PRINTING: Offset

514 Adams Corporation G 516 352-6948 Franklin Square *(G-5369)*
A & D Offset Printers Ltd G 516 746-2476 Mineola *(G-8520)*
A & M Litho Inc E 516 342-9727 Bethpage *(G-860)*
A Q P Inc G 585 256-1690 Rochester *(G-14175)*
Act Communications Group Inc F 631 669-2403 West Islip *(G-16932)*
Ad Vantage Press G 212 941-8355 New York *(G-9069)*
Ads-N-Color Inc E 718 797-0900 Brooklyn *(G-1563)*
Advantage Press Inc F 518 584-3405 Saratoga Springs *(G-15170)*
Advantage Printing Inc F 718 820-0688 Kew Gardens *(G-7187)*
Advantage Quick Print Inc G 212 989-5644 New York *(G-9095)*
Agrecolor Inc F 516 741-8700 Mineola *(G-8525)*
Ahw Printing Corp F 516 536-3600 Oceanside *(G-13091)*
Alamar Printing Inc F 914 993-9007 White Plains *(G-17102)*

Employee Codes: A=Over 500 employees, B=251-500
C=101-250, D=51-100, E=20-50, F=10-19, G=5-9
2018 Harris
New York Manufacturers Directory
1303

PRINTING: Offset — PRODUCT SECTION

- Albany Letter Shop Inc .... G 518 434-1172
  Albany *(G-37)*
- All Color Offset Printers Inc .... G 516 420-0649
  Farmingdale *(G-4943)*
- Allen William & Company Inc .... C 212 675-6461
  Glendale *(G-5659)*
- Allstatebannerscom Corporation .... G 718 300-1256
  Long Island City *(G-7685)*
- Alpha Printing Corp .... F 315 454-5507
  Syracuse *(G-15872)*
- Alpina Color Graphics Inc .... G 212 285-2700
  New York *(G-9151)*
- Amsterdam Printing & Litho Inc .... F 518 792-6501
  Queensbury *(G-14002)*
- Apple Press .... G 914 723-6660
  White Plains *(G-17106)*
- Ares Printing and Packg Corp .... C 718 858-8760
  Brooklyn *(G-1627)*
- Arista Innovations Inc .... E 516 746-2262
  Mineola *(G-8529)*
- Arnold Printing Corp .... F 607 272-7800
  Ithaca *(G-6859)*
- Arnold Taylor Printing Inc .... G 516 781-0564
  Bellmore *(G-809)*
- Atlantic Color Corp .... E 631 345-3800
  Shirley *(G-15436)*
- B & P Jays Inc .... G 716 668-8408
  Buffalo *(G-2851)*
- Bajan Group Inc .... G 518 464-2884
  Latham *(G-7381)*
- Barone Offset Printing Corp .... G 212 989-5500
  Mohegan Lake *(G-8577)*
- Bartolomeo Publishing Inc .... G 631 420-4949
  West Babylon *(G-16799)*
- Bates Jackson Engraving Co Inc .... E 716 854-3000
  Buffalo *(G-2855)*
- Beacon Press Inc .... G 212 691-5050
  White Plains *(G-17111)*
- Beehive Press Inc .... G 718 654-1200
  Bronx *(G-1280)*
- Bel Aire Offset Corp .... G 718 539-8333
  College Point *(G-3804)*
- Benchmark Graphics Ltd .... F 212 683-1711
  New York *(G-9405)*
- Beyer Graphics Inc .... D 631 543-3900
  Commack *(G-3850)*
- Bishop Print Shop Inc .... G 607 965-8155
  Edmeston *(G-4635)*
- Bmg Printing and Promotion LLC .... G 631 231-9200
  Bohemia *(G-1022)*
- Brennans Quick Print Inc .... G 518 793-4999
  Glens Falls *(G-5689)*
- Bridge Printing Inc .... G 212 243-5390
  Long Island City *(G-7721)*
- Brown Printers of Troy Inc .... F 518 235-4080
  Troy *(G-16250)*
- Brownstone Capitl Partners LLC .... G 212 889-0069
  New York *(G-9524)*
- Canaan Printing Inc .... F 718 729-3100
  Bayside *(G-763)*
- Canastota Publishing Co Inc .... G 315 697-9010
  Canastota *(G-3394)*
- Canfield & Tack Inc .... D 585 235-7710
  Rochester *(G-14275)*
- Capital Dst Print & Imaging .... G 518 456-6773
  Schenectady *(G-15265)*
- Carges Entps of Canandaigua .... G 585 394-2600
  Canandaigua *(G-3367)*
- Carnels Printing Inc .... G 516 883-3355
  Port Washington *(G-13826)*
- Carr Communications Group LLC .... F 607 748-0481
  Vestal *(G-16466)*
- Cayuga Press Cortland Inc .... E 888 229-8421
  Liverpool *(G-7540)*
- Cedar West Inc .... G 631 467-1444
  Ronkonkoma *(G-14915)*
- Chakra Communications Inc .... E 607 748-7491
  Endicott *(G-4806)*
- Chenango Union Printing Inc .... G 607 334-2112
  Norwich *(G-13040)*
- Cilyox Inc .... F 716 853-3809
  Buffalo *(G-2894)*
- Clarsons Corp .... F 585 235-8775
  Rochester *(G-14299)*
- Cohber Press Inc .... D 585 475-9100
  West Henrietta *(G-16906)*
- Color Carton Corp .... D 718 665-0840
  Bronx *(G-1303)*
- Colorfast .... F 212 929-2440
  New York *(G-9732)*
- Colorfully Yours Inc .... F 631 242-8600
  Bay Shore *(G-685)*
- Combine Graphics Corp .... G 212 695-4044
  Forest Hills *(G-5328)*
- Commerce Offset Ltd .... G 914 769-6671
  Thornwood *(G-16141)*
- Commercial Press Inc .... G 315 274-0028
  Canton *(G-3407)*
- Complemar Print LLC .... F 716 875-7238
  Buffalo *(G-2904)*
- Composite Forms Inc .... F 914 937-1808
  Port Chester *(G-13768)*
- Concept Printing Inc .... F 845 353-4040
  Nyack *(G-13064)*
- Conkur Printing Co Inc .... E 212 541-5980
  New York *(G-9762)*
- Consolidated Color Press Inc .... F 212 929-8197
  New York *(G-9765)*
- Constas Printing Corporation .... G 315 474-2176
  Syracuse *(G-15924)*
- Coral Graphic Services Inc .... C 516 576-2100
  Hicksville *(G-6359)*
- Craig Envelope Corp .... F 718 786-4277
  Hicksville *(G-6361)*
- Creative Forms Inc .... F 212 431-7540
  New York *(G-9807)*
- Creative Printing Corp .... F 212 226-3870
  New York *(G-9808)*
- Dealer-Presscom Inc .... G 631 589-0434
  Bohemia *(G-1049)*
- Dejay Litho Inc .... F 631 319-6916
  Bohemia *(G-1050)*
- Dell Communications Inc .... G 212 989-3434
  New York *(G-9895)*
- Delta Press Inc .... E 212 989-3445
  High Falls *(G-6427)*
- Design Lithographers Inc .... F 212 645-8900
  New York *(G-9906)*
- Dick Bailey Service Inc .... F 718 522-4363
  Brooklyn *(G-1861)*
- Dispatch Graphics Inc .... F 212 307-5943
  New York *(G-9938)*
- Doco Quick Print Inc .... G 315 782-6623
  Watertown *(G-16671)*
- Dowd - Witbeck Printing Corp .... F 518 274-2421
  Troy *(G-16256)*
- DP Murphy Co Inc .... D 631 673-9400
  Deer Park *(G-4154)*
- Dupli Graphics Corporation .... G 315 422-4732
  Syracuse *(G-15946)*
- East Ridge Quick Print .... F 585 266-4911
  Rochester *(G-14344)*
- Eastern Hills Printing .... G 716 741-3300
  Clarence *(G-3687)*
- Eastside Printers .... G 315 437-6515
  East Syracuse *(G-4540)*
- Edgian Press Inc .... G 516 931-2114
  Hicksville *(G-6371)*
- Eleanor Ettinger Inc .... E 212 925-7474
  New York *(G-10048)*
- Elmat Quality Printing Ltd .... F 516 569-5722
  Cedarhurst *(G-3483)*
- Empire Press Co .... F 718 756-9500
  Brooklyn *(G-1926)*
- Engrav-O-Type Press Inc .... F 585 262-7590
  Rochester *(G-14372)*
- Excel Graphics Services Inc .... F 212 929-2183
  New York *(G-10155)*
- Excelsior Graphics Inc .... G 212 730-6200
  New York *(G-10158)*
- F & B Photo Offset Co Inc .... G 516 431-5433
  Island Park *(G-6819)*
- F & T Graphics Inc .... F 631 643-1000
  Hauppauge *(G-6097)*
- F J Remey Co Inc .... E 516 741-5112
  Mineola *(G-8544)*
- Fambus Inc .... G 607 785-3700
  Endicott *(G-4815)*
- Farthing Press Inc .... G 716 852-4674
  Buffalo *(G-2959)*
- Federal Envelope Inc .... F 212 243-8380
  New York *(G-10201)*
- Finer Touch Printing Corp .... F 516 944-8000
  Port Washington *(G-13837)*
- Fitch Graphics Ltd .... E 212 619-3800
  New York *(G-10228)*
- Five Star Prtg & Mailing Svcs .... F 212 929-0300
  New York *(G-10229)*
- Flare Multicopy Corp .... E 718 258-8860
  Brooklyn *(G-1983)*
- Flower City Printing Inc .... C 585 663-9000
  Rochester *(G-14396)*
- Flp Group LLC .... F 315 252-7583
  Auburn *(G-495)*
- Fort Orange Press Inc .... E 518 489-3233
  Albany *(G-81)*
- Forward Enterprises Inc .... F 585 235-7670
  Rochester *(G-14401)*
- Francis Emory Fitch Inc .... E 212 619-3800
  New York *(G-10248)*
- Frederick Coon Inc .... E 716 683-6812
  Elma *(G-4661)*
- Freeville Publishing Co Inc .... F 607 844-9119
  Freeville *(G-5447)*
- Fulton Newspapers Inc .... E 315 598-6397
  Fulton *(G-5471)*
- Gallagher Printing Inc .... E 716 873-2434
  Buffalo *(G-2977)*
- Gallant Graphics Ltd .... E 845 868-1166
  Stanfordville *(G-15647)*
- Gateway Prtg & Graphics Inc .... E 716 823-3873
  Hamburg *(G-5949)*
- Gbv Promotions Inc .... F 631 231-7300
  Bay Shore *(G-700)*
- Gem Reproduction Services Corp .... G 845 298-0172
  Wappingers Falls *(G-16590)*
- Gemson Graphics Inc .... E 516 873-8400
  Albertson *(G-158)*
- General Business Supply Inc .... D 518 720-3939
  Watervliet *(G-16709)*
- Geneva Printing Company Inc .... G 315 789-8191
  Geneva *(G-5591)*
- Glens Falls Printing LLC .... F 518 793-0555
  Glens Falls *(G-5697)*
- Golos Printing Inc .... G 607 732-1896
  Elmira Heights *(G-4723)*
- Gooding Co Inc .... E 716 434-5501
  Lockport *(G-7622)*
- Grand Meridian Printing Inc .... E 718 937-3888
  Long Island City *(G-7781)*
- Graphics of Utica .... G 315 797-4868
  Remsen *(G-14052)*
- Graphics Plus Printing Inc .... E 607 299-0500
  Cortland *(G-4051)*
- Greenwood Graphics Inc .... F 516 822-4856
  Hicksville *(G-6381)*
- H T L & S Ltd .... F 718 435-4474
  Brooklyn *(G-2059)*
- H&E Service Corp .... D 646 472-1936
  Garden City *(G-5522)*
- Harmon and Castella Printing .... F 845 471-9163
  Poughkeepsie *(G-13925)*
- Heritage Printing Center .... G 518 563-8240
  Plattsburgh *(G-13695)*
- HI Speed Envelope Co Inc .... F 718 617-1600
  Mount Vernon *(G-8735)*
- Hill Crest Press .... G 518 943-0671
  Catskill *(G-3457)*
- Hillside Printing Inc .... F 718 658-6719
  Jamaica *(G-6955)*
- Hospitality Graphics Inc .... G 212 643-6700
  New York *(G-10553)*
- Hudson Envelope Corporation .... E 212 473-6666
  New York *(G-10569)*
- Hudson Printing Co Inc .... E 718 937-8600
  New York *(G-10572)*
- In-House Inc .... F 718 445-9007
  College Point *(G-3812)*
- Ink-It Printing Inc .... F 718 229-5590
  College Point *(G-3813)*
- International Newsppr Prtg Co .... E 516 626-6095
  Glen Head *(G-5649)*
- Interstate Thermographers Corp .... G 914 948-1745
  White Plains *(G-17150)*
- Iver Printing Inc .... G 718 275-2070
  New Hyde Park *(G-8888)*
- J & J Printing Inc .... G 315 458-7411
  Syracuse *(G-15983)*
- Jacobs Press Inc .... F 315 252-4861
  Auburn *(G-501)*
- James Conolly Printing Co .... E 585 426-4150
  Rochester *(G-14480)*
- JDS Graphics Inc .... F 973 330-3300
  New York *(G-10752)*
- Johnnys Ideal Printing Co .... G 518 828-6666
  Hudson *(G-6651)*
- Judith Lewis Printer Inc .... G 516 997-7777
  Westbury *(G-17027)*
- Kas-Ray Industries Inc .... F 212 620-3144
  New York *(G-10849)*

PRINTING: Offset

Kaufman Brothers Printing ....G...... 212 563-1854
  New York (G-10858)
Kent Associates Inc ....G...... 212 675-0722
  New York (G-10877)
Kenyon Press Inc ....E...... 607 674-9066
  Sherburne (G-15414)
Kinaneco Inc ....E...... 315 468-6201
  Syracuse (G-15994)
Kingsbury Printing Co Inc ....G...... 518 747-6606
  Queensbury (G-14015)
Knickerbocker Graphics Svcs ....F...... 212 244-7485
  New York (G-10899)
L I F Publishing Corp ....E...... 631 345-5200
  Shirley (G-15445)
L K Printing Corp ....G...... 914 761-1944
  White Plains (G-17157)
L M N Printing Company Inc ....E...... 516 285-8526
  Valley Stream (G-16438)
Lee Printing Inc ....G...... 718 237-1651
  Brooklyn (G-2206)
Lennons Litho Inc ....F...... 315 866-3156
  Herkimer (G-6329)
Levon Graphics Corp ....D...... 631 753-2022
  Farmingdale (G-5043)
Litho Dynamics Inc ....G...... 914 769-1759
  Hawthorne (G-6273)
Lithomatic Business Forms Inc ....G...... 212 255-6700
  New York (G-11037)
Louis Heindl & Son Inc ....G...... 585 454-5080
  Rochester (G-14504)
Lynmar Printing Corp ....G...... 631 957-8500
  Amityville (G-306)
M L Design Inc ....G...... 212 233-0213
  New York (G-11104)
M T M Printing Co Inc ....F...... 718 353-3297
  College Point (G-3820)
Madison Printing Corp ....G...... 607 273-3535
  Ithaca (G-6893)
Malone Industrial Press Inc ....G...... 518 483-5880
  Malone (G-8044)
Manifestation-Glow Press Inc ....G...... 718 380-5259
  Fresh Meadows (G-5458)
Marcal Printing Inc ....G...... 516 942-9500
  Hicksville (G-6393)
Marcy Printing Inc ....G...... 718 935-9100
  Brooklyn (G-2269)
Mark T Westinghouse ....G...... 518 678-3262
  Catskill (G-3459)
Marsid Group Ltd ....G...... 516 334-1603
  Carle Place (G-3422)
Mason & Gore Inc ....E...... 914 921-1025
  Rye (G-15089)
Medallion Associates Inc ....E...... 212 929-9130
  New York (G-11233)
Mercury Print Productions Inc ....C...... 585 458-7900
  Rochester (G-14525)
Mid Atlantic Graphics Corp ....E...... 631 345-3800
  Shirley (G-15448)
Mid-York Press Inc ....D...... 607 674-4491
  Sherburne (G-15415)
Midstate Printing Corp ....E...... 315 475-4101
  Liverpool (G-7560)
Mikam Graphics LLC ....D...... 212 684-9393
  New York (G-11290)
Miller Printing & Litho Inc ....G...... 518 842-0001
  Amsterdam (G-357)
Mines Press Inc ....C...... 914 788-1800
  Cortlandt Manor (G-4078)
Mitchell Prtg & Mailing Inc ....F...... 315 343-3531
  Oswego (G-13360)
MJB Printing Corp ....G...... 631 581-0177
  Islip (G-6850)
Monte Press Inc ....G...... 718 325-4999
  Bronx (G-1406)
Moore Printing Company Inc ....G...... 585 394-1533
  Canandaigua (G-3378)
Nesher Printing Inc ....G...... 212 760-2521
  New York (G-11393)
New Horizon Graphics Inc ....G...... 631 231-8055
  Hauppauge (G-6173)
New York Typing & Printing Co ....G...... 718 268-7900
  Forest Hills (G-5334)
Newburgh Envelope Corp ....G...... 845 566-4211
  Newburgh (G-12792)
Newport Graphics Inc ....E...... 212 924-2600
  New York (G-11433)
Newsgraphics of Delmar Inc ....E...... 518 439-5363
  Delmar (G-4270)
Northeast Commercial Prtg Inc ....G...... 518 459-5047
  Albany (G-110)

Northeast Prtg & Dist Co Inc ....E...... 518 563-8214
  Plattsburgh (G-13711)
Official Offset Corporation ....E...... 631 957-8500
  Amityville (G-316)
Olympic Press Inc ....F...... 212 242-4934
  New York (G-11516)
Orbis Brynmore Lithographics ....G...... 212 987-2100
  New York (G-11533)
Orffeo Printing & Imaging Inc ....G...... 716 681-5757
  Lancaster (G-7352)
Ozipko Enterprises Inc ....G...... 585 424-6740
  Rochester (G-14581)
P & W Press Inc ....G...... 646 486-3417
  New York (G-11560)
Panther Graphics Inc ....E...... 585 546-7163
  Rochester (G-14591)
Patrick Ryans Modern Press ....F...... 518 434-2921
  Albany (G-115)
Paul Michael Group Inc ....G...... 631 585-5700
  Ronkonkoma (G-14990)
Peachtree Enterprises Inc ....E...... 212 989-3445
  Long Island City (G-7868)
Perception Imaging Inc ....F...... 631 676-5262
  Holbrook (G-6495)
Petcap Press Corporation ....F...... 718 609-0910
  Long Island City (G-7871)
Petit Printing Corp ....G...... 716 871-9490
  Getzville (G-5615)
Pioneer Printers Inc ....F...... 716 693-7100
  North Tonawanda (G-13004)
Pollack Graphics Inc ....G...... 212 727-8400
  New York (G-11703)
Positive Print Litho Offset ....G...... 212 431-4850
  New York (G-11710)
Press of Fremont Payne Inc ....G...... 212 966-6570
  New York (G-11724)
Presstek Printing LLC ....F...... 585 467-8140
  Rochester (G-14621)
Printroc Inc ....F...... 585 461-2556
  Rochester (G-14624)
Pro Printing ....G...... 516 561-9700
  Lynbrook (G-7983)
Progressive Graphics & Prtg ....G...... 315 331-3635
  Newark (G-12762)
Prompt Printing Inc ....G...... 631 454-6524
  Farmingdale (G-5099)
Quad/Graphics Inc ....A...... 518 581-4000
  Saratoga Springs (G-15198)
Quadrangle Quickprints Ltd ....G...... 631 694-4464
  Melville (G-8380)
Quicker Printer Inc ....G...... 607 734-8622
  Elmira (G-4712)
Quickprint ....G...... 585 394-2600
  Canandaigua (G-3386)
R & J Graphics Inc ....F...... 631 293-6611
  Farmingdale (G-5105)
R & L Press of SI Inc ....G...... 718 667-3258
  Staten Island (G-15748)
R D Printing Associates Inc ....F...... 631 390-5964
  Farmingdale (G-5106)
Rasco Graphics Inc ....G...... 212 206-0447
  New York (G-11828)
Reflex Offset Inc ....G...... 516 746-4142
  Deer Park (G-4224)
Register Graphics Inc ....E...... 716 358-2921
  Randolph (G-14031)
Resonant Legal Media LLC ....D...... 800 781-3591
  New York (G-11873)
Rmd Holding Inc ....G...... 845 628-0030
  Mahopac (G-8031)
Rosemont Press Incorporated ....E...... 212 239-4770
  New York (G-11935)
Sand Hill Industries Inc ....E...... 518 885-7991
  Ballston Spa (G-607)
Sanford Printing Inc ....G...... 718 461-1202
  Flushing (G-5298)
Scotti Graphics Inc ....E...... 212 367-9602
  Long Island City (G-7901)
Searles Graphics Inc ....E...... 631 345-2202
  Yaphank (G-17417)
Security Offset Services Inc ....G...... 631 944-6031
  Huntington (G-6719)
Shield Press Inc ....G...... 212 431-7489
  New York (G-12071)
Shipman Printing Inds Inc ....G...... 716 504-7700
  Niagara Falls (G-12893)
Shoreline Publishing Inc ....G...... 914 738-7869
  Pelham (G-13519)
Speedway Press Inc ....G...... 315 343-3531
  Oswego (G-13366)

St Gerard Enterprises Inc ....F...... 631 473-2003
  Port Jeff STA (G-13793)
St Vincent Press Inc ....F...... 585 325-5320
  Rochester (G-14723)
Standwill Packaging Inc ....E...... 631 752-1236
  Farmingdale (G-5124)
Star Quality Printing Inc ....F...... 631 273-1900
  Hauppauge (G-6224)
Steval Graphics Concepts Inc ....F...... 516 576-0220
  Plainview (G-13663)
Stevenson Printing Co Inc ....G...... 516 676-1233
  Glen Cove (G-5642)
Stony Point Graphics Ltd ....G...... 845 786-3322
  Stony Point (G-15799)
Stubbs Printing Inc ....G...... 315 769-8641
  Massena (G-8232)
Stylistic Press Inc ....F...... 212 675-0797
  New York (G-12247)
Suffolk Copy Center Inc ....G...... 631 665-0570
  Bay Shore (G-740)
Summit MSP LLC ....G...... 716 433-1014
  Lockport (G-7646)
T C Peters Printing Co Inc ....G...... 315 724-4149
  Utica (G-16385)
The Nugent Organization Inc ....F...... 212 645-6600
  Oceanside (G-13123)
Thomas Group Inc ....F...... 212 947-6400
  New York (G-12340)
Top Copi Reproductions Inc ....F...... 212 571-4141
  New York (G-12389)
Toppan Printing Co Amer Inc ....E...... 212 596-7747
  New York (G-12391)
Total Concept Graphic Inc ....G...... 212 229-2626
  New York (G-12399)
Tovie Asarese Royal Prtg Co ....G...... 716 885-7692
  Buffalo (G-3249)
Trade Mark Graphics Inc ....G...... 718 306-0001
  Brooklyn (G-2692)
Tremont Offset Inc ....G...... 718 892-7333
  Bronx (G-1472)
Tri Kolor Printing & Sty ....F...... 315 474-6753
  Syracuse (G-16085)
Tri-Town News Inc ....E...... 607 561-3515
  Sidney (G-15464)
Tropp Printing Corp ....G...... 212 233-4519
  New York (G-12431)
Tucker Printers Inc ....D...... 585 359-3030
  Henrietta (G-6322)
Twenty-First Century Press Inc ....F...... 716 837-0800
  Buffalo (G-3254)
Twin Counties Pro Printers Inc ....F...... 518 828-3278
  Hudson (G-6667)
Unicom Graphic Communications ..G...... 212 221-2456
  New York (G-12469)
V & J Graphics Inc ....G...... 315 363-1933
  Oneida (G-13191)
Valentine Printing Corp ....G...... 718 444-4400
  Brooklyn (G-2734)
Veterans Offset Printing Inc ....G...... 585 288-2900
  Rochester (G-14781)
Viatech Pubg Solutions Inc ....E...... 631 968-8500
  Bay Shore (G-747)
Vincys Printing Ltd ....F...... 518 355-4363
  Schenectady (G-15333)
Vivona Business Printers Inc ....G...... 516 496-3453
  Syosset (G-15862)
Wall Street Business Pdts Inc ....E...... 212 563-4014
  New York (G-12608)
Warren Printing Inc ....F...... 212 627-5000
  Long Island City (G-7948)
Wayne Printing Inc ....F...... 914 761-2400
  White Plains (G-17210)
Weeks & Reichel Printing Inc ....G...... 631 589-1443
  Sayville (G-15244)
Weicro Graphics Inc ....G...... 631 253-3360
  West Babylon (G-16872)
Westchester Mailing Service ....G...... 914 948-1116
  White Plains (G-17212)
Westypo Printers Inc ....G...... 914 737-7394
  Peekskill (G-13512)
William Charles Prtg Co Inc ....G...... 516 349-0900
  Plainview (G-13674)
Winson Surnamer Inc ....G...... 718 729-8787
  Long Island City (G-7954)
Woodbury Printing Plus + Inc ....G...... 845 928-6610
  Central Valley (G-3557)
Zenger Partners LLC ....E...... 716 876-2284
  Kenmore (G-7181)

Employee Codes: A=Over 500 employees, B=251-500
C=101-250, D=51-100, E=20-50, F=10-19, G=5-9

PRINTING: Pamphlets

PRINTING: Pamphlets
Willis Mc Donald Co Inc ....F...... 212 366-1526
New York *(G-12665)*

PRINTING: Photo-Offset
Academy Printing Services Inc ....G..... 631 765-3346
Southold *(G-15581)*
Allied Reproductions Inc ....E...... 212 255-2472
New York *(G-9140)*
D G M Graphics Inc ....F...... 516 223-2220
Merrick *(G-8416)*
Genie Instant Printing Co Inc ....F...... 212 575-8258
New York *(G-10321)*
Kjckd Inc ....G..... 518 435-9696
Latham *(G-7395)*
Leader Printing Inc ....F...... 516 546-1544
Merrick *(G-8422)*
National Reproductions Inc ....E...... 212 619-3800
New York *(G-11372)*
Pronto Printer ....G..... 914 737-0800
Cortlandt Manor *(G-4079)*
Rapid Rays Printing & Copying ....G...... 716 852-0550
Buffalo *(G-3179)*
Scriven Duplicating Service ....G...... 518 233-8180
Troy *(G-16277)*
Three Star Offset Printing ....F...... 516 867-8223
Freeport *(G-5442)*

PRINTING: Photogravure
Dijifi LLC ....F...... 646 519-2447
Brooklyn *(G-1864)*

PRINTING: Photolithographic
BP Digital Imaging LLC ....G..... 607 753-0022
Cortland *(G-4038)*

PRINTING: Rotary Photogravure
Mastro Graphic Arts Inc ....E...... 585 436-7570
Rochester *(G-14520)*

PRINTING: Rotogravure
American Packaging Corporation ....C...... 585 254-9500
Rochester *(G-14214)*

PRINTING: Screen, Broadwoven Fabrics, Cotton
D & R Silk Screening Ltd ....F...... 631 234-7464
Central Islip *(G-3520)*
Dynamic Screenprinting ....G...... 518 487-4256
Albany *(G-74)*
Judscott Handprints Ltd ....F...... 914 347-5515
Elmsford *(G-4768)*
Loremanss Embroidery Engrav ....F...... 518 834-9205
Keeseville *(G-7168)*
Printery ....G...... 315 253-7403
Auburn *(G-511)*
Sciane Enterprises Inc ....G...... 845 452-2400
Poughkeepsie *(G-13949)*
Steve Poli Sales ....G...... 315 487-0394
Camillus *(G-3352)*
Tramwell Inc ....G...... 315 789-2762
Geneva *(G-5599)*
Ward Sales Co Inc ....G...... 315 476-5276
Syracuse *(G-16093)*
Z Best Printing Inc ....F...... 631 595-1400
Deer Park *(G-4255)*

PRINTING: Screen, Fabric
Apple Imprints Apparel Inc ....E...... 716 893-1130
Buffalo *(G-2836)*
Apsco Sports Enterprises Inc ....D...... 718 965-9500
Brooklyn *(G-1622)*
Aro-Graph Corporation ....G...... 315 463-8693
Syracuse *(G-15877)*
Art Flag Company Inc ....F...... 212 334-1890
New York *(G-9259)*
Creative Images & Applique ....D...... 718 821-8700
Maspeth *(G-8157)*
Dirt T Shirts Inc ....E...... 845 336-4230
Kingston *(G-7216)*
Galli Shirts and Sports AP ....G...... 845 226-7305
Stormville *(G-15801)*
Human Technologies Corporation .....F...... 315 735-3532
Utica *(G-16364)*

Irene Cerone ....G...... 315 668-2899
Brewerton *(G-1201)*
J M L Productions Inc ....D...... 718 643-1674
Brooklyn *(G-2125)*
Kevin J Kassman ....G...... 585 529-4245
Rochester *(G-14491)*
Mart-Tex Athletics Inc ....E...... 631 454-9583
Farmingdale *(G-5052)*
Park Avenue Imprints LLC ....G...... 716 822-5737
Buffalo *(G-3136)*
Printz and Patternz LLC ....G...... 518 944-6020
Schenectady *(G-15311)*
Rainbow Lettering ....G...... 607 732-5751
Elmira *(G-4713)*
Randy Sixberry ....G...... 315 265-6211
Potsdam *(G-13901)*
Special Tees ....G...... 718 980-0987
Staten Island *(G-15758)*
Viewsport International Inc ....G...... 585 259-1562
Penfield *(G-13528)*
Wicked Smart LLC ....F...... 518 459-2855
Watervliet *(G-16717)*

PRINTING: Screen, Manmade Fiber & Silk, Broadwoven Fabric
Dyenamix Inc ....G...... 212 941-6642
New York *(G-9997)*
Efs Designs ....G...... 718 852-9511
Brooklyn *(G-1908)*
Intertex USA Inc ....F...... 212 279-3601
New York *(G-10683)*
Judscott Handprints Ltd ....F...... 914 347-5515
Elmsford *(G-4768)*
Mv Corp Inc ....C...... 631 273-8020
Bay Shore *(G-717)*
Rescuestuff Inc ....E...... 718 318-7570
Peekskill *(G-13505)*
Screen Gems Inc ....G...... 845 561-0036
New Windsor *(G-8999)*
Valley Stream Sporting Gds Inc ....E...... 516 593-7800
Lynbrook *(G-7992)*

PRINTING: Thermography
Bco Industries Western NY Inc ....E...... 716 877-2800
Tonawanda *(G-16165)*
Business Card Express Inc ....E...... 631 669-3400
West Babylon *(G-16804)*
East Coast Thermographers Inc ....E...... 718 321-3211
College Point *(G-3807)*
Fineline Thermographers Inc ....E...... 718 643-1100
Brooklyn *(G-1976)*
Interstate Thermographers Corp ....E...... 914 948-1745
White Plains *(G-17150)*
Karr Graphics Corp ....E...... 212 645-6000
Long Island City *(G-7806)*

PROFESSIONAL EQPT & SPLYS, WHOLESALE: Analytical Instruments
Peyser Instrument Corporation ....E...... 631 841-3600
West Babylon *(G-16848)*

PROFESSIONAL EQPT & SPLYS, WHOLESALE: Engineers', NEC
Advanced Tchncal Solutions Inc ....F...... 914 214-8230
Yorktown Heights *(G-17522)*

PROFESSIONAL EQPT & SPLYS, WHOLESALE: Optical Goods
Carl Zeiss Inc ....C...... 914 747-1800
Thornwood *(G-16140)*
Dynamic Laboratories Inc ....E...... 631 231-7474
Ronkonkoma *(G-14923)*
Lens Lab Express ....E...... 718 921-5488
Brooklyn *(G-2212)*
Moscot Wholesale Corp ....G...... 212 647-1550
New York *(G-11334)*
Spectrum Thin Films Inc ....E...... 631 901-1010
Hauppauge *(G-6221)*
Tri-Supreme Optical LLC ....D...... 631 249-2020
Farmingdale *(G-5144)*

PROFESSIONAL EQPT & SPLYS, WHOLESALE: Scientific & Engineerg
Avanel Industries Inc ....F...... 516 333-0990
Westbury *(G-16998)*

Scientifics Direct Inc ....F...... 716 773-7500
Tonawanda *(G-16220)*
VWR Education LLC ....C...... 585 359-2502
West Henrietta *(G-16929)*

PROFESSIONAL EQPT & SPLYS, WHOLESALE: Theatrical
Steeldeck Ny Inc ....F...... 718 599-3700
Brooklyn *(G-2625)*

PROFILE SHAPES: Unsupported Plastics
Chelsea Plastics Inc ....F...... 212 924-4530
New York *(G-9639)*
Franklin Poly Film Inc ....E...... 718 492-3523
Brooklyn *(G-2002)*
Howard J Moore Company Inc ....E...... 631 351-8467
Plainview *(G-13635)*
Mitsui Chemicals America Inc ....E...... 914 253-0777
Rye Brook *(G-15098)*
Ontario Plastics Inc ....E...... 585 663-2644
Rochester *(G-14572)*

PROGRAM ADMIN, GOVT: Air, Water & Solid Waste Mgmt, Local
City of Kingston ....F...... 845 331-2490
Kingston *(G-7213)*

PROMOTION SVCS
Drns Corp ....F...... 718 369-4530
Brooklyn *(G-1883)*
Shykat Promotions ....G...... 866 574-2757
Forestville *(G-5343)*

PROPERTY DAMAGE INSURANCE
Xerox Corporation ....C...... 585 427-4500
Rochester *(G-14797)*

PROTECTION EQPT: Lightning
Heary Bros Lghtning Protection ....E...... 716 941-6141
Springville *(G-15633)*
Tii Technologies Inc ....E...... 516 364-9300
Edgewood *(G-4629)*

PUBLIC RELATIONS & PUBLICITY SVCS
Studley Printing & Publishing ....F...... 518 563-1414
Plattsburgh *(G-13730)*

PUBLISHERS: Art Copy
Classic Collections Fine Art ....G...... 914 591-4500
White Plains *(G-17121)*

PUBLISHERS: Art Copy & Poster
Luminary Publishing Inc ....F...... 845 334-8600
Kingston *(G-7228)*
Pace Editions Inc ....E...... 212 421-3237
New York *(G-11562)*
Space 150 ....C...... 612 332-6458
Brooklyn *(G-2612)*

PUBLISHERS: Book
Advance Publications Inc ....D...... 718 981-1234
Staten Island *(G-15653)*
Alba House Publishers ....E...... 718 698-2759
Staten Island *(G-15654)*
Alm Media LLC ....B...... 212 457-9400
New York *(G-9146)*
Alm Media Holdings Inc ....B...... 212 457-9400
New York *(G-9147)*
American Inst Chem Engineers ....D...... 646 495-1355
New York *(G-9170)*
Arbor Books Inc ....E...... 201 236-9990
New York *(G-9242)*
Aspen Publishers Inc ....A...... 212 771-0600
New York *(G-9288)*
Assouline Publishing Inc ....F...... 212 989-6769
New York *(G-9293)*
Ateres Publishing & Bk Bindery ....F...... 718 935-9355
Brooklyn *(G-1647)*
Atlas & Company LLC ....G...... 212 234-3100
New York *(G-9306)*
Barrons Educational Series Inc ....D...... 631 434-3311
Hauppauge *(G-6051)*
Bear Port Publishing Company ....F...... 877 337-8577
New York *(G-9388)*

Beauty Fashion Inc ... E ... 212 840-8800
New York (G-9389)
Bedford Freeman & Worth ... C ... 212 576-9400
New York (G-9391)
Bedrock Communications ... G ... 212 532-4150
New York (G-9394)
Benchmark Education Co LLC ... D ... 914 637-7200
New Rochelle (G-8933)
Bicker Inc ... F ... 212 688-0085
New York (G-9437)
Bloomsbury Publishing Inc ... D ... 212 419-5300
New York (G-9469)
Bmg Rights Management (us) LLC ... E ... 212 561-3000
New York (G-9480)
Bobley-Harmann Corporation ... G ... 516 433-3800
Ronkonkoma (G-14908)
Burns Archive Photographic Dis ... G ... 212 889-1938
New York (G-9533)
Byliner Inc ... E ... 415 680-3608
New York (G-9541)
Canopy Books LLC ... G ... 516 354-4888
Massapequa (G-8208)
CCC Publications Inc ... G ... 718 306-1008
Brooklyn (G-1767)
Conde Nast ... E ... 212 630-3642
New York (G-9757)
Curriculum Associates LLC ... F ... 978 313-1355
Brooklyn (G-1824)
Davis Ziff Publishing Inc ... D ... 212 503-3500
New York (G-9885)
Divine Phoenix LLC ... A ... 585 737-1482
Skaneateles (G-15480)
Dorling Kindersley Publishing ... D ... 212 213-4800
New York (G-9961)
Eagle Art Publishing Inc ... G ... 212 685-7411
New York (G-10009)
Edwin Mellen Press Inc ... E ... 716 754-2796
Lewiston (G-7455)
Entertainment Weekly Inc ... C ... 212 522-5600
New York (G-10097)
F P H Communications ... G ... 212 528-1728
New York (G-10169)
Fairchild Publications Inc ... A ... 212 630-4000
New York (G-10181)
Family Publishing Group Inc ... E ... 914 381-7474
Mamaroneck (G-8067)
Feminist Press Inc ... G ... 212 817-7915
New York (G-10205)
Franklin Report LLC ... G ... 212 639-9100
New York (G-10253)
Future Us Inc ... D ... 844 779-2822
New York (G-10276)
Ggp Publishing Inc ... F ... 914 834-8896
Harrison (G-6004)
Gq Magazine ... G ... 212 286-2860
New York (G-10385)
Grey House Publishing Inc ... E ... 845 483-3535
Poughkeepsie (G-13924)
Grey House Publishing Inc ... E ... 518 789-8700
Amenia (G-219)
Grolier International Inc ... G ... 212 343-6100
New York (G-10411)
Guilford Publications Inc ... G ... 800 365-7006
New York (G-10426)
Haights Cross Cmmnications Inc ... E ... 212 209-0500
New York (G-10439)
Haights Cross Operating Co ... E ... 914 289-9400
White Plains (G-17143)
Harpercollins Publishers LLC ... E ... 212 553-4200
New York (G-10461)
Harvard University Press ... D ... 212 337-0280
New York (G-10470)
Infopro Digital Inc ... C ... 212 457-9400
New York (G-10638)
Jim Henson Company Inc ... E ... 212 794-2400
New York (G-10772)
Juris Publishing Inc ... F ... 631 351-5430
Huntington (G-6700)
Kensington Publishing Corp ... D ... 212 407-1500
New York (G-10876)
Kwesi Legesse LLC ... G ... 347 581-9872
Brooklyn (G-2182)
Learningexpress LLC ... E ... 646 274-6454
New York (G-10984)
Legal Strategies Inc ... G ... 516 377-3940
Merrick (G-8423)
Lexis Publishing ... C ... 518 487-3000
Menands (G-8405)
Lippincott Massie McQuilkin L ... F ... 212 352-2055
New York (G-11034)
Literary Classics of US ... F ... 212 308-3360
New York (G-11036)
Living Well Innovations Inc ... G ... 646 517-3200
Hauppauge (G-6138)
M&M Printing Inc ... F ... 516 796-3020
Carle Place (G-3420)
Macmillan College Pubg Co Inc ... F ... 212 702-2000
New York (G-11113)
Martha Stewart Living ... C ... 212 827-8000
New York (G-11189)
Mathisen Ventures Inc ... G ... 212 986-1025
New York (G-11203)
McBooks Press Inc ... G ... 607 272-2114
Ithaca (G-6895)
McGraw-Hill School Educatn LLC ... A ... 646 766-2060
New York (G-11225)
Mediaplanet Publishing Hse Inc ... E ... 646 922-1400
New York (G-11237)
Meegenius Inc ... G ... 212 283-7285
New York (G-11245)
Merkos Linyonei Chinuch Inc ... E ... 718 778-0226
Brooklyn (G-2305)
Micro Publishing Inc ... G ... 212 533-9180
New York (G-11280)
N A R Associates Inc ... G ... 845 557-8713
Barryville (G-620)
New Press ... E ... 212 629-8802
New York (G-11413)
New York Legal Publishing ... G ... 518 459-1100
Menands (G-8409)
New York Qrtrly Foundation Inc ... F ... 917 843-8825
Brooklyn (G-2377)
News Corporation ... C ... 212 416-3400
New York (G-11435)
Nova Science Publishers Inc ... F ... 631 231-7269
Hauppauge (G-6175)
Other Press LLC ... G ... 212 414-0054
New York (G-11546)
Oxford University Press LLC ... B ... 212 726-6000
New York (G-11555)
Oxford University Press LLC ... G ... 212 726-6000
New York (G-11556)
Ozmodyl Ltd ... G ... 212 226-0622
New York (G-11558)
Pace Walkers of America Inc ... F ... 631 444-2147
Port Jefferson (G-13800)
Palgrave Macmillan Ltd ... G ... 646 307-5028
New York (G-11570)
Papercutz Inc ... G ... 646 559-4681
New York (G-11579)
Pearson Education Inc ... E ... 845 340-8700
Kingston (G-7235)
Pearson Education Inc ... F ... 212 782-3337
New York (G-11607)
Pearson Education Inc ... E ... 212 366-2000
New York (G-11608)
Pearson Education Inc ... F ... 201 236-7000
West Nyack (G-16952)
Pegasus Books NY Ltd ... G ... 646 343-9502
New York (G-11618)
Penguin Random House LLC ... E ... 212 782-1000
New York (G-11621)
Penguin Random House LLC ... C ... 212 366-2377
Albany (G-117)
Penton Business Media Inc ... F ... 914 949-8500
White Plains (G-17177)
Perseus Fisher Books LLC ... D ... 212 340-8100
New York (G-11645)
Phaidon Press Inc ... E ... 212 652-5400
New York (G-11664)
Philipp Feldheim Inc ... G ... 845 356-2282
Nanuet (G-8806)
Picador USA ... F ... 646 307-5629
New York (G-11678)
Poetry Mailing List Marsh Hawk ... G ... 516 766-1891
Oceanside (G-13112)
Poets House Inc ... F ... 212 431-7920
New York (G-11702)
Powerhouse Cultural Entrmt Inc ... F ... 212 604-9074
Brooklyn (G-2444)
Preserving Chrstn Publications ... G ... 315 942-6617
Boonville (G-1165)
Princton Archtctural Press LLC ... F ... 518 671-6100
Hudson (G-6662)
Pro Publica Inc ... D ... 212 514-5250
New York (G-11746)
Profits Direct Inc ... G ... 631 851-4083
Ronkonkoma (G-14996)
Prometheus Books Inc ... E ... 716 691-2158
Amherst (G-259)
PSR Press Ltd ... F ... 716 754-2266
Lewiston (G-7457)
Rapid Intellect Group Inc ... F ... 518 929-3210
Chatham (G-3587)
Rda Holding Co ... F ... 914 238-1000
New York (G-11837)
Readers Dgest Yung Fmilies Inc ... E ... 914 238-1000
Pleasantville (G-13749)
Reading Room Inc ... G ... 212 463-1029
New York (G-11840)
Relx Inc ... C ... 607 772-2600
Conklin (G-3899)
Repertoire International De Ll ... E ... 212 817-1990
New York (G-11867)
Rizzoli Intl Publications Inc ... F ... 212 387-3572
New York (G-11904)
Rosen Publishing Group Inc ... C ... 212 777-3017
New York (G-11937)
S P Books Inc ... G ... 212 431-5011
New York (G-11963)
Scholastic Corporation ... G ... 212 343-6100
New York (G-12015)
Scholastic Inc ... E ... 212 343-6100
New York (G-12017)
Scholium International Inc ... G ... 516 883-8032
Port Washington (G-13880)
Seven Stories Press Inc ... G ... 212 226-8760
New York (G-12052)
Sheridan House Inc ... G ... 914 725-5431
Scarsdale (G-15254)
Simon & Schuster Inc ... D ... 212 698-7000
New York (G-12102)
Simon Schuster Digital Sls Inc ... D ... 212 698-4391
New York (G-12104)
Six Boro Publishing ... G ... 347 589-6756
New York (G-12112)
Skyhorse Publishing Inc ... E ... 212 643-6816
New York (G-12121)
Springer Customer Svc Ctr LLC ... B ... 212 460-1500
New York (G-12196)
Square One Publishers Inc ... F ... 516 535-2010
Garden City Park (G-5555)
Station Hill of Barrytown ... G ... 845 758-5293
Barrytown (G-619)
Steffen Publishing Inc ... D ... 315 865-4100
Holland Patent (G-6514)
Stonesong Press LLC ... G ... 212 929-4600
New York (G-12231)
Storybooks Forever ... F ... 716 822-7845
Buffalo (G-3226)
Studio Fun International Inc ... E ... 914 238-1000
White Plains (G-17199)
Sweet Mouth Inc ... E ... 800 433-7758
New York (G-12276)
Targum Press USA Inc ... G ... 248 355-2266
Brooklyn (G-2668)
Teachers College Columbia Univ ... E ... 212 678-3929
New York (G-12312)
Thornwillow Press Ltd ... G ... 212 980-0738
New York (G-12350)
Time Home Entertainment Inc ... E ... 212 522-1212
New York (G-12361)
Time Inc ... E ... 212 522-1212
New York (G-12362)
Verso Inc ... G ... 718 246-8160
Brooklyn (G-2740)
W W Norton & Company Inc ... G ... 212 354-5500
New York (G-12603)
William H Sadlier Inc ... C ... 212 233-3646
New York (G-12661)
Wolters Kluwer US Inc ... F ... 212 894-8920
New York (G-12680)
Woodward/White Inc ... F ... 718 509-6082
Brooklyn (G-2779)
YS Publishing Co Inc ... G ... 212 682-9360
New York (G-12719)
Zinepak LLC ... F ... 212 706-8621
New York (G-12732)
Zola Books Inc ... G ... 917 822-4950
New York (G-12738)

PUBLISHERS: Book Clubs, No Printing

Humana Press Inc ... E ... 212 460-1500
New York (G-10577)

PUBLISHERS: Books, No Printing

Abbeville Press Inc ... E ... 212 366-5585
New York (G-9047)
Aip Publishing LLC ... C ... 516 576-2200
Melville (G-8323)

Amereon Ltd G 631 298-5100
Mattituck *(G-8238)*

American Institute Physics Inc C 516 576-2410
Melville *(G-8326)*

Amherst Media Inc G 716 874-4450
Buffalo *(G-2827)*

Annuals Publishing Co Inc G 212 505-0950
New York *(G-9215)*

Anthroposophic Press Inc G 518 851-2054
Clifton Park *(G-3721)*

Bertelsmann Pubg Group Inc A 212 782-1000
New York *(G-9418)*

Boardman Simons Publishing E 212 620-7200
New York *(G-9482)*

Bonnier Publishing Usa Inc E 212 321-0237
New York *(G-9487)*

British American Publishing D 518 786-6000
Latham *(G-7382)*

Cambridge University Press D 212 337-5000
New York *(G-9558)*

Campus Course Paks Inc G 516 877-3967
Garden City *(G-5512)*

Castle Connolly Medical Ltd E 212 367-8400
New York *(G-9597)*

CB Publishing LLC G 516 354-4888
Floral Park *(G-5206)*

Central Cnfrnce of Amrcn Rbbis F 212 972-3636
New York *(G-9615)*

Chain Store Age Magazine G 212 756-5000
New York *(G-9625)*

Church Publishing Incorporated G 212 592-1800
New York *(G-9667)*

Cinderella Press Ltd G 212 431-3130
New York *(G-9669)*

Clarkson N Potter Inc F 212 782-9000
New York *(G-9689)*

Columbia University Press E 212 459-0600
New York *(G-9738)*

Columbia University Press E 212 459-0600
New York *(G-9739)*

Columbia University Press E 212 459-0600
New York *(G-9740)*

Confrtrnity of Prescious Blood G 718 436-1120
Brooklyn *(G-1796)*

Continuum Intl Pubg Group Inc F 646 649-4215
New York *(G-9773)*

Daheshist Publishing Co Ltd F 212 581-8360
New York *(G-9843)*

Definition Press Inc F 212 777-4490
New York *(G-9891)*

Delaney Books Inc F 516 921-8888
Syosset *(G-15840)*

Demos Medical Publishing LLC F 516 889-1791
New York *(G-9897)*

Egmont US Inc G 212 685-0102
New York *(G-10041)*

Eleanor Ettinger Inc E 212 925-7474
New York *(G-10048)*

Facts On File Inc D 212 967-8800
New York *(G-10179)*

Farrar Straus and Giroux LLC E 212 741-6900
New York *(G-10192)*

Folio Graphics Co Inc G 718 763-2076
Brooklyn *(G-1993)*

Foxhill Press Inc E 212 995-9620
New York *(G-10246)*

Frank Merriwell Inc F 516 921-8888
Syosset *(G-15843)*

Gildan Media Corp F 718 459-6299
Flushing *(G-5251)*

Government Data Publication E 347 789-8719
Brooklyn *(G-2046)*

Grand Central Publishing C 212 364-1200
New York *(G-10388)*

Graphis Inc F 212 532-9387
New York *(G-10396)*

Guilford Publications Inc D 212 431-9800
New York *(G-10425)*

Hachette Book Group Inc B 800 759-0190
New York *(G-10436)*

Harpercollins Publishers LLC A 212 207-7000
New York *(G-10460)*

Harry N Abrams Incorporated D 212 206-7715
New York *(G-10464)*

Hearst Business Media Corp F 631 650-4441
Great River *(G-5870)*

Hearst Corporation A 212 649-2000
New York *(G-10482)*

Hearst Corporation E 212 649-2275
New York *(G-10491)*

Helvetica Press Incorporated G 212 737-1857
New York *(G-10499)*

Henry Holt and Company LLC D 646 307-5095
New York *(G-10502)*

Highline Media LLC C 859 692-2100
New York *(G-10520)*

Hippocrene Books Inc G 212 685-4371
New York *(G-10527)*

Houghton Mifflin Harcourt Pubg E 212 420-5800
New York *(G-10558)*

Houghton Mifflin Harcourt Pubg C 914 747-2709
Thornwood *(G-16143)*

Hudson Park Press Inc G 212 929-8898
New York *(G-10571)*

Infobase Publishing Company G 212 967-8800
New York *(G-10637)*

Ir Media Group (usa) Inc E 212 425-9649
New York *(G-10697)*

Jonathan David Publishers Inc F 718 456-8611
Middle Village *(G-8446)*

Judaica Press Inc G 718 972-6202
Brooklyn *(G-2155)*

K T A V Publishing House Inc F 201 963-9524
Brooklyn *(G-2165)*

Kodansha USA Inc G 917 322-6200
New York *(G-10906)*

Le Book Publishing Inc G 212 334-5252
New York *(G-10977)*

Lee & Low Books Incorporated F 212 779-4400
New York *(G-10992)*

Liveright Publishing Corp G 212 354-5500
New York *(G-11042)*

Looseleaf Law Publications Inc F 718 359-5559
Flushing *(G-5275)*

Macmillan Publishers Inc A 646 307-5151
New York *(G-11115)*

Macmillan Publishing Group LLC B 212 674-5151
New York *(G-11116)*

Malhame Publs & Importers Inc E 631 694-8600
Bohemia *(G-1096)*

Marshall Cavendish Corp E 914 332-8888
Tarrytown *(G-16118)*

Mary Ann Liebert Inc D 914 740-2100
New Rochelle *(G-8962)*

McGraw-Hill Education Inc E 646 766-2000
New York *(G-11222)*

McGraw-Hill School Education H B 646 766-2000
New York *(G-11224)*

Medikidz Usa Inc G 646 895-9319
New York *(G-11242)*

Melcher Media Inc F 212 727-2322
New York *(G-11249)*

Meredith Corporation D 515 284-2157
New York *(G-11256)*

Mesorah Publications Ltd E 718 921-9000
Brooklyn *(G-2307)*

Modern Language Assn Amer Inc C 646 576-5000
New York *(G-11315)*

Monacelli Press LLC G 212 229-9925
New York *(G-11323)*

Mondo Publishing Inc E 212 268-3560
New York *(G-11324)*

Moznaim Publishing Co Inc G 718 853-0525
Brooklyn *(G-2342)*

Mud Puddle Books Inc G 212 647-9168
New York *(G-11345)*

NBM Publishing Inc G 212 643-5407
New York *(G-11384)*

New City Press Inc G 845 229-0335
Hyde Park *(G-6774)*

New Directions Publishing F 212 255-0230
New York *(G-11405)*

North Shore Home Improver F 631 474-2824
Port Jeff STA *(G-13790)*

North-South Books Inc E 212 706-4545
New York *(G-11476)*

P J D Publications Ltd G 516 626-0650
New Hyde Park *(G-8901)*

Parachute Publishing LLC E 212 337-6743
New York *(G-11580)*

Penguin Random House LLC B 212 782-9000
New York *(G-11622)*

Penguin Random House LLC A 212 572-6162
New York *(G-11623)*

Penguin Random House LLC A 212 782-9000
New York *(G-11624)*

Peter Mayer Publishers Inc F 212 673-2210
New York *(G-11652)*

Peter Pauper Press Inc E 914 681-0144
White Plains *(G-17185)*

Prestel Publishing LLC G 212 995-2720
New York *(G-11725)*

Pwxyz LLC G 212 377-5500
New York *(G-11785)*

Quarto Group Inc E 212 779-0700
New York *(G-11796)*

Relx Inc E 212 309-8100
New York *(G-11858)*

Research Centre of Kabbalah G 718 805-0380
Richmond Hill *(G-14091)*

Richard C Owen Publishers Inc F 914 232-3903
Somers *(G-15534)*

Rizzoli Intl Publications Inc E 212 387-3400
New York *(G-11903)*

Ryland Peters & Small Inc G 646 791-5410
New York *(G-11959)*

Scholastic Inc A 800 724-6527
New York *(G-12016)*

Second Chance Press Inc G 631 725-1101
Sag Harbor *(G-15108)*

Social Register Association F 646 612-7314
New York *(G-12143)*

Soho Press Inc G 212 260-1900
New York *(G-12147)*

Springer Adis Us LLC F 212 460-1500
New York *(G-12195)*

Springer Publishing Co LLC E 212 431-4370
New York *(G-12198)*

Springer Scnce + Bus Media LLC D 781 871-6600
New York *(G-12199)*

STf Services Inc E 315 463-8506
East Syracuse *(G-4581)*

Suny At Binghamton D 607 777-2316
Binghamton *(G-946)*

Syracuse University Press Inc E 315 443-5534
Syracuse *(G-16080)*

Tom Doherty Associates Inc E 212 388-0100
New York *(G-12380)*

Trusted Media Brands Inc A 914 238-1000
New York *(G-12435)*

Trusted Media Brands Inc F 646 293-6025
New York *(G-12436)*

Trusted Media Brands Inc F 914 244-5244
White Plains *(G-17204)*

Unisystems Inc E 212 826-0850
New York *(G-12482)*

United Synggue Cnsrvtive Jdism E 212 533-7800
New York *(G-12487)*

Vaad LHafotzas Sichoes F 718 778-5436
Brooklyn *(G-2733)*

Vandam Inc F 212 929-0416
New York *(G-12522)*

Vantage Press Inc E 212 736-1767
New York *(G-12527)*

Vaultcom Inc E 212 366-4212
New York *(G-12535)*

Waldman Publishing Corporation F 212 730-9590
New York *(G-12607)*

William S Hein & Co Inc D 716 882-2600
Getzville *(G-5619)*

William S Hein & Co Inc D 716 882-2600
Buffalo *(G-3282)*

Wolters Kluwer US Inc E 631 517-8060
Babylon *(G-552)*

Workman Publishing Co Inc C 212 254-5900
New York *(G-12687)*

Workman Publishing Co Inc C 212 254-5900
New York *(G-12688)*

PUBLISHERS: Catalogs

AR Media Inc E 212 352-0731
New York *(G-9238)*

Christopher Anthony Pubg Co F 516 826-9205
Wantagh *(G-16577)*

Select Information Exchange F 212 496-6435
New York *(G-12042)*

PUBLISHERS: Comic Books, No Printing

Archie Comic Publications Inc D 914 381-5155
Pelham *(G-13513)*

Clp Pb LLC E 212 340-8100
New York *(G-9704)*

Continuity Publishing Inc F 212 869-4170
New York *(G-9771)*

Interntnl Publcatns Media Grup G 917 604-9602
New York *(G-10682)*

Marvel Entertainment LLC C 212 576-4000
New York *(G-11193)*

NBM Publishing Inc G 212 643-5407
New York *(G-11384)*

PRODUCT SECTION

PUBLISHERS: Magazines, No Printing

Valiant Entertainment LLC .... E 212 972-0361
New York *(G-12518)*

PUBLISHERS: Directories, NEC

Black Book Photography Inc .... F 212 979-6700
New York *(G-9460)*
Catholic News Publishing Co .... F 914 632-7771
Mamaroneck *(G-8059)*
Easy Book Publishing Inc .... G 518 459-6281
Albany *(G-75)*
Foundation Center Inc .... C 212 620-4230
New York *(G-10241)*
Hearst Business Media .... D 516 227-1300
Uniondale *(G-16318)*
Highline Media LLC .... C 859 692-2100
New York *(G-10520)*
Supermedia LLC .... D 212 513-9700
New York *(G-12265)*
Thomas Publishing Company LLC .... B 212 695-0500
New York *(G-12342)*

PUBLISHERS: Directories, Telephone

Associated Publishing Company .... E 325 676-4032
Buffalo *(G-2840)*
Hola Publishing Co .... G 718 424-3129
Long Island City *(G-7790)*
Mac Innes Enterprises Inc .... E 325 676-4032
Buffalo *(G-3072)*

PUBLISHERS: Guides

Family Publications Ltd .... F 212 947-2177
New York *(G-10186)*
Fredonia Pennysaver Inc .... F 716 679-1509
Fredonia *(G-5382)*
Metro Group Inc .... G 716 434-4055
Lockport *(G-7630)*
Mt Morris Shopper Inc .... G 585 658-3520
Mount Morris *(G-8695)*
Network Journal Inc .... G 212 962-3791
New York *(G-11397)*

PUBLISHERS: Magazines, No Printing

21st Century Fox America Inc .... D 212 852-7000
New York *(G-9013)*
2600 Enterprises Inc .... F 631 474-2677
Saint James *(G-15113)*
Abp International Inc .... E 212 490-3999
New York *(G-9051)*
Adirondack Life Inc .... F 518 946-2191
Jay *(G-7088)*
Advance Magazine Publs Inc .... C 212 450-7000
New York *(G-9088)*
Advanced Research Media Inc .... F 631 751-9696
Setauket *(G-15398)*
Adventure Publishing Group .... E 212 575-4510
New York *(G-9097)*
Aeon America Inc .... G 914 584-0275
New York *(G-9100)*
Alm Media LLC .... B 212 457-9400
New York *(G-9146)*
Alm Media Holdings Inc .... B 212 457-9400
New York *(G-9147)*
America Press Inc .... E 212 581-4640
New York *(G-9162)*
American Inst Chem Engineers .... D 646 495-1355
New York *(G-9170)*
Analysts In Media (aim) Inc .... E 212 488-1777
New York *(G-9196)*
Animal Fair Media Inc .... F 212 629-0392
New York *(G-9212)*
Art & Understanding Inc .... G 518 426-9010
Albany *(G-47)*
Atlantic Monthly Group Inc .... E 202 266-7000
New York *(G-9303)*
Beauty Fashion Inc .... E 212 840-8800
New York *(G-9389)*
Bedford Communications Inc .... E 212 807-8220
New York *(G-9393)*
Bellerophon Publications Inc .... E 212 627-9977
New York *(G-9399)*
Bertelsmann Pubg Group Inc .... A 212 782-1000
New York *(G-9418)*
Beverage Media Group Inc .... F 212 571-3232
New York *(G-9427)*
Blue Horizon Media Inc .... F 212 661-7878
New York *(G-9472)*
Brant Art Publications Inc .... E 212 941-2800
New York *(G-9505)*

Brant Publications Inc .... E 212 941-2800
New York *(G-9506)*
Buffalo Spree Publishing Inc .... E 716 783-9119
Buffalo *(G-2881)*
C Q Communications Inc .... E 516 681-2922
Hicksville *(G-6352)*
Carol Group Ltd 212 505-2030
New York *(G-9586)*
Centennial Media LLC .... F 646 527-7320
New York *(G-9613)*
Center For Inquiry Inc .... F 716 636-4869
Amherst *(G-233)*
Cfo Publishing LLC .... E 212 459-3004
New York *(G-9623)*
Coda Media Inc .... G 917 478-2565
New York *(G-9722)*
Commonweal Foundation Inc .... F 212 662-4200
New York *(G-9747)*
Consumer Reports Inc .... B 914 378-2000
Yonkers *(G-17445)*
Crain Communications Inc .... C 212 210-0100
New York *(G-9805)*
Daily Beast Company LLC .... E 212 445-4600
New York *(G-9844)*
Data Key Communication LLC .... F 315 445-2347
Fayetteville *(G-5172)*
Dennis Publishing Inc .... D 646 717-9500
New York *(G-9900)*
Discover Media LLC .... E 212 624-4800
New York *(G-9937)*
Dj Publishing Inc .... E 516 767-2500
Port Washington *(G-13832)*
Doctorow Communications Inc .... F 845 708-5166
New City *(G-8830)*
Dotto Wagner .... G 315 342-8020
Oswego *(G-13355)*
Dow Jones & Company Inc .... E 212 597-5983
New York *(G-9966)*
E W Williams Publications .... G 212 661-1516
New York *(G-10005)*
Earl G Graves Pubg Co Inc .... D 212 242-8000
New York *(G-10012)*
Essence Communications Inc .... E 212 522-1212
New York *(G-10116)*
Et Publishing Intl LLC .... F 212 838-7220
New York *(G-10129)*
Executive Business Media Inc .... E 516 334-3030
Westbury *(G-17010)*
Faces Magazine Inc .... F 201 843-4004
Poughkeepsie *(G-13918)*
Family Publishing Group Inc .... E 914 381-7474
Mamaroneck *(G-8067)*
Fridge Magazine Inc .... F 212 997-7673
New York *(G-10260)*
Frozen Food Digest Inc .... G 212 557-8600
New York *(G-10262)*
Fun Media Inc .... E 646 472-0135
New York *(G-10271)*
Getting The Word Out Inc .... G 518 891-9352
Saranac Lake *(G-15165)*
Golfing Magazine .... G 516 822-5446
Hicksville *(G-6380)*
Graphis Inc .... F 212 532-9387
New York *(G-10396)*
Gruner + Jahr Prtg & Pubg Co .... C 212 463-1000
New York *(G-10418)*
Halcyon Business Publications .... F 800 735-2732
Westbury *(G-17020)*
Hamptons Magazine .... E 631 283-7125
Southampton *(G-15568)*
Harpers Magazine Foundation .... E 212 420-5720
New York *(G-10462)*
Hart Energy Publishing Lllp .... E 212 621-4621
New York *(G-10467)*
Haymarket Group Ltd .... F 212 239-0855
New York *(G-10474)*
Haymarket Media Inc 646 638-6000
New York *(G-10475)*
Hearst Bus Communications Inc .... G 212 649-2000
New York *(G-10478)*
Hearst Business Media .... D 516 227-1300
Uniondale *(G-16318)*
Hearst Business Media Corp .... G 631 650-6151
Great River *(G-5869)*
Hearst Business Media Corp .... F 631 650-4441
Great River *(G-5870)*
Hearst Corporation .... A 212 649-2000
New York *(G-10482)*
Hearst Corporation .... D 516 382-4580
New York *(G-10486)*

Hearst Corporation .... E 212 649-2275
New York *(G-10491)*
Hearst Holdings Inc .... F 212 649-2000
New York *(G-10493)*
Herman Hall Communications .... F 718 941-1879
Brooklyn *(G-2075)*
Historic TW Inc .... E 212 484-8000
New York *(G-10530)*
Icd Publications Inc .... E 631 246-9300
Islandia *(G-6833)*
Imek Media LLC .... E 212 422-9000
New York *(G-10616)*
Intellitravel Media Inc .... G 646 695-6700
New York *(G-10663)*
Interhellenic Publishing Inc .... G 212 967-5016
New York *(G-10671)*
Interview Inc .... E 212 941-2900
New York *(G-10684)*
Irish America Inc .... E 212 725-2993
New York *(G-10701)*
JSD Communications Inc .... F 914 588-1841
Bedford *(G-792)*
Keller International Pubg LLC .... E 516 829-9210
Port Washington *(G-13853)*
Lagardere North America Inc .... E 212 477-7373
New York *(G-10953)*
Lebhar-Friedman Inc .... E 212 756-5000
New York *(G-10986)*
Lebhar-Friedman Inc .... C 212 756-5000
New York *(G-10987)*
Locations Magazine .... G 212 288-4745
New York *(G-11047)*
Macfadden Cmmnctions Group LLC .... C 212 979-4800
New York *(G-11111)*
Macmillan Holdings LLC .... F 212 576-9428
New York *(G-11114)*
Mag Inc .... E 607 257-6970
Ithaca *(G-6894)*
Manhattan Media LLC .... E 212 268-8600
New York *(G-11154)*
Mann Publications .... E 212 840-6266
New York *(G-11159)*
Mansueto Ventures LLC .... E 212 389-5300
New York *(G-11166)*
Maritime Activity Reports .... E 212 477-6700
New York *(G-11176)*
Mark Levine .... F 212 677-4457
New York *(G-11178)*
Martha Stewart Living .... E 212 827-8000
New York *(G-11189)*
Martha Stewart Living Omni LLC .... B 212 827-8000
New York *(G-11190)*
Martinelli Holdings LLC .... E 302 504-1361
Rye *(G-15088)*
Mass Appeal Magazine .... G 718 858-0979
Brooklyn *(G-2282)*
Mergent Inc .... B 212 413-7700
New York *(G-11257)*
Miami Media LLC .... E 212 268-8600
New York *(G-11274)*
Music & Sound Retailer Inc .... E 516 767-2500
Port Washington *(G-13866)*
Nation Company LP .... G 212 209-5400
New York *(G-11367)*
National Review Inc .... E 212 679-7330
New York *(G-11373)*
Nature America Inc .... B 212 726-9200
New York *(G-11380)*
New Art Publications Inc .... F 718 636-9100
Brooklyn *(G-2367)*
Newsgraphics of Delmar Inc .... E 518 439-5363
Delmar *(G-4270)*
Nickelodeon Magazines Inc .... G 212 541-1949
New York *(G-11446)*
Nsgv Inc .... E 212 367-3167
New York *(G-11483)*
Nyemac Inc .... G 631 668-1303
Montauk *(G-8626)*
Nylon LLc .... E 212 226-6454
New York *(G-11497)*
Nyrev Inc .... E 212 757-8070
New York *(G-11501)*
Paper Publishing Company Inc .... E 212 226-4405
New York *(G-11578)*
Parents Guide Network Corp .... E 212 213-8840
New York *(G-11584)*
Penhouse Media Group Inc .... C 212 702-6000
New York *(G-11625)*
Photo Industry Inc .... F 516 364-0016
Woodbury *(G-17315)*

Preparatory Magazine Group........D....... 718 761-4800
Staten Island *(G-15745)*
Prescribing Reference Inc........D....... 646 638-6000
New York *(G-11723)*
Professnal Spt Pblications Inc........C....... 212 697-1460
New York *(G-11749)*
Q Communications Inc........G....... 212 594-6520
New York *(G-11786)*
Quest Media Llc........F....... 646 840-3404
New York *(G-11798)*
Ramholtz Publishing Inc........D....... 718 761-4800
Staten Island *(G-15749)*
Rd Publications Inc........C....... 914 238-1000
Pleasantville *(G-13748)*
Readers Digest Assn Incthe........F....... 414 423-0100
New York *(G-11839)*
Real Estate Media Inc........E....... 212 929-6976
New York *(G-11841)*
Relx Inc........E....... 212 463-6644
New York *(G-11859)*
Rfp LLC........E....... 212 838-7733
New York *(G-11883)*
Risk Society Management Pubg........E....... 212 286-9364
New York *(G-11901)*
Rsl Media LLC........G....... 212 307-6760
New York *(G-11949)*
Ruby Newco LLC........G....... 212 852-7000
New York *(G-11951)*
Sandow Media LLC........F....... 646 805-0200
New York *(G-11984)*
Scholastic Corporation........G....... 212 343-6100
New York *(G-12015)*
Scholastic Inc........A....... 800 724-6527
New York *(G-12016)*
Smart & Strong LLC........E....... 212 938-2051
New York *(G-12129)*
Society For The Study........G....... 212 822-8806
New York *(G-12144)*
Sound Communications Inc........E....... 516 767-2500
Port Washington *(G-13884)*
Sports Illustrated For Kids........E....... 212 522-1212
New York *(G-12190)*
Spotlight Publications LLC........G....... 914 345-9473
Elmsford *(G-4794)*
Suburban Publishing Inc........F....... 845 463-0542
Fishkill *(G-5196)*
Sussex Publishers LLC........E....... 212 260-7210
New York *(G-12269)*
Testa Communications Inc........E....... 516 767-2500
Port Washington *(G-13886)*
Thomas Publishing Company LLC........G....... 212 695-0500
New York *(G-12344)*
Time Inc........A....... 212 522-1212
New York *(G-12363)*
Time Inc........E....... 212 522-0361
New York *(G-12364)*
Time Inc Affluent Media Group........B....... 212 382-5600
New York *(G-12365)*
Time Inc Affluent Media Group........G....... 212 382-5600
New York *(G-12366)*
Time Warner Companies Inc........D....... 212 484-8000
New York *(G-12369)*
Trusted Media Brands Inc........A....... 914 238-1000
New York *(G-12435)*
Trusted Media Brands Inc........F....... 646 293-6025
New York *(G-12436)*
Trusted Media Brands Inc........F....... 914 244-5244
White Plains *(G-17204)*
TV Guide Magazine Group Inc........D....... 212 852-7500
New York *(G-12449)*
U S Japan Publication NY Inc........G....... 212 252-8833
New York *(G-12457)*
Ulster Publishing Co Inc........E....... 845 334-8205
Kingston *(G-7247)*
US Frontline News Inc........E....... 212 922-9090
New York *(G-12507)*
US Weekly LLC........D....... 212 484-1616
New York *(G-12510)*
Vending Times Inc........F....... 516 442-1850
Rockville Centre *(G-14831)*
Veranda Publications Inc........G....... 212 903-5206
New York *(G-12543)*
Visionaire Publishing LLC........E....... 646 434-6091
New York *(G-12581)*
Weider Publications LLC........C....... 212 545-4800
New York *(G-12632)*
Welcome Magazine Inc........F....... 716 839-3121
Amherst *(G-272)*
Western New York Family Mag........G....... 716 836-3486
Buffalo *(G-3279)*
Wine & Spirits Magazine Inc........G....... 212 695-4660
New York *(G-12669)*
Working Mother Media Inc........D....... 212 351-6400
New York *(G-12686)*
Wsn Inc........G....... 212 924-7620
New York *(G-12696)*

PUBLISHERS: Maps

Vandam Inc........F....... 212 929-0416
New York *(G-12522)*

PUBLISHERS: Miscellaneous

212 Media LLC........E....... 212 710-3092
New York *(G-9012)*
ABRA Media Inc........G....... 518 398-1010
Pine Plains *(G-13581)*
Absolute Color Corporation........G....... 212 868-0404
New York *(G-9054)*
Adcomm Graphics Inc........E....... 212 645-1298
West Babylon *(G-16790)*
Add Associates Inc........G....... 315 449-3474
Cicero *(G-3670)*
Affluent Design Inc........F....... 631 655-2556
Mastic Beach *(G-8236)*
Albany Student Press Inc........E....... 518 442-5665
Albany *(G-41)*
Albion-Holley Pennysaver Inc........E....... 585 589-5641
Albion *(G-164)*
Alfred Mainzer Inc........E....... 718 392-4200
Long Island City *(G-7683)*
All Times Publishing LLC........E....... 315 422-7011
Syracuse *(G-15868)*
American Hsptals Patient Guide........F....... 518 346-1099
Schenectady *(G-15259)*
American Media Inc........D....... 212 545-4800
New York *(G-9174)*
American Media Inc........C....... 212 545-4800
New York *(G-9175)*
Amy Pak Publishing Inc........G....... 585 964-8188
Holley *(G-6515)*
Art Asiapacific Publishing LLC........G....... 212 255-6003
New York *(G-9258)*
Atypon Systems Inc........F....... 212 524-7060
New York *(G-9313)*
Award Publishing Limited........G....... 212 246-0405
New York *(G-9335)*
Blood Moon Productions Ltd........G....... 718 556-9410
Staten Island *(G-15669)*
Brownstone Publishers Inc........E....... 212 473-8200
New York *(G-9525)*
Bucksense Inc........E....... 877 710-2825
New York *(G-9527)*
Bulkley Dunton........E....... 212 863-1800
New York *(G-9528)*
Burdick Publications Inc........G....... 315 685-9500
Skaneateles *(G-15477)*
Bys Publishing LLC........G....... 315 655-9431
Cazenovia *(G-3469)*
Cambridge Whos Who Pubg Inc........E....... 516 833-8440
Uniondale *(G-16312)*
Castle Connolly Medical Ltd........E....... 212 367-8400
New York *(G-9597)*
Cayuga Press Cortland Inc........E....... 888 229-8421
Liverpool *(G-7540)*
Cherry Lane Magazine LLC........D....... 212 561-3000
New York *(G-9641)*
China Press........G....... 212 683-8282
New York *(G-9652)*
City Post Express Inc........G....... 718 995-8690
Jamaica *(G-6940)*
Coastal Publications Inc........F....... 631 725-1700
Sag Harbor *(G-15104)*
Communications & Energy Corp........F....... 315 446-5723
Syracuse *(G-15922)*
Community Cpons Frnchising Inc........E....... 516 277-1968
Glen Cove *(G-5625)*
Community Newsppr Holdings Inc........D....... 716 282-2311
Niagara Falls *(G-12828)*
Complete Publishing Solutions........G....... 212 242-7321
New York *(G-9751)*
Comps Inc........F....... 516 676-0400
Glen Cove *(G-5626)*
Consumer Reports Inc........B....... 914 378-2000
Yonkers *(G-17445)*
Couture Press........F....... 310 734-4831
New York *(G-9799)*
Custom Publishing Group Ltd........G....... 212 840-8800
New York *(G-9827)*
D C I Technical Inc........F....... 516 355-0464
Franklin Square *(G-5372)*
Dailycandy Inc........E....... 646 230-8719
New York *(G-9849)*
Dapper Dads Inc........G....... 917 903-8045
Brooklyn *(G-1840)*
Desi Talk LLC........F....... 212 675-7515
New York *(G-9903)*
Dezawy LLC........G....... 917 436-8820
New York *(G-9918)*
DK Publishing........F....... 212 366-2000
New York *(G-9942)*
Dlc Comprehensive Medical PC........F....... 718 857-1200
Brooklyn *(G-1869)*
Draper Associates Incorporated........F....... 212 255-2727
New York *(G-9975)*
Dryve LLC........G....... 646 279-3648
Bronx *(G-1321)*
Dwell Life Inc........E....... 212 382-2010
New York *(G-9995)*
Economy 24/7 Inc........E....... 917 403-8876
Brooklyn *(G-1901)*
Enjoy City North Inc........D....... 607 584-5061
Binghamton *(G-908)*
Ethis Communications Inc........G....... 212 791-1440
White Plains *(G-17132)*
Experiment Publishing LLC........G....... 212 889-1273
New York *(G-10162)*
F+w Media Inc........G....... 212 447-1400
New York *(G-10172)*
Fantasy Sports Media Group Inc........E....... 416 917-6002
New York *(G-10190)*
Federated Media Publishing LLC........G....... 917 677-7976
New York *(G-10202)*
Fidazzel Inc........G....... 917 557-3860
Bronx *(G-1333)*
First Games Publr Netwrk Inc........D....... 212 983-0501
New York *(G-10219)*
Fitzgerald Publishing Co Inc........G....... 914 793-5016
Yonkers *(G-17459)*
Gannett Co Inc........D....... 607 352-2702
Johnson City *(G-7124)*
Gds Publishing Inc........F....... 212 796-2000
New York *(G-10307)*
Gen Publishing Inc........D....... 914 834-3880
New Rochelle *(G-8950)*
Genius Media Group Inc........F....... 509 670-7502
Brooklyn *(G-2020)*
Glassview LLC........E....... 646 844-4922
New York *(G-10350)*
Global Grind Digital........E....... 212 840-9399
New York *(G-10360)*
Government Data Publication........E....... 347 789-8719
Brooklyn *(G-2046)*
Grey House Publishing Inc........E....... 518 789-8700
Amenia *(G-219)*
Grey House Publishing Inc........E....... 845 483-3535
Poughkeepsie *(G-13924)*
Gruner & Jahr USA........F....... 212 782-7870
New York *(G-10417)*
Guest Informat LLC........F....... 212 557-3010
New York *(G-10423)*
Guilford Publications Inc........D....... 212 431-9800
New York *(G-10425)*
Guilford Publications Inc........G....... 800 365-7006
New York *(G-10426)*
Hampton Press Incorporated........G....... 646 638-3800
New York *(G-10447)*
Harborside Press........G....... 631 470-4967
Huntington *(G-6695)*
Harpercollins........G....... 212 207-7000
New York *(G-10459)*
Hearst Communications Inc........C....... 212 649-2000
New York *(G-10481)*
Hearst Corporation........E....... 212 830-2980
New York *(G-10487)*
Helium Media Inc........G....... 917 596-4081
New York *(G-10498)*
Hibert Publishing LLC........G....... 914 381-7474
Rye *(G-15085)*
Home Service Publications........G....... 914 238-1000
Pleasantville *(G-13746)*
Humor Rainbow Incorporated........E....... 646 402-9113
New York *(G-10579)*
Intuition Publishing Limited........G....... 212 838-7115
New York *(G-10691)*
Jewish Heritage For Blind........G....... 718 338-4999
Brooklyn *(G-2138)*
Jobson Medical Information LLC........C....... 212 274-7000
New York *(G-10784)*
John Szoke Graphics Inc........G....... 212 219-8300
New York *(G-10792)*

Kalel Partners LLC ....F 347 561-7804
Flushing *(G-5265)*
Korangy Publishing Inc ....D 212 260-1332
New York *(G-10915)*
Kraus Organization Limited ....G 212 686-5411
New York *(G-10927)*
Kyra Communications Corp ....F 516 783-6244
Seaford *(G-15366)*
L & L Trucking Inc ....E 315 339-2550
Rome *(G-14846)*
Language and Graphics Inc ....G 212 315-5266
New York *(G-10963)*
Leadership Directories Inc ....E 212 627-4140
New York *(G-10982)*
Ledes Group Inc ....F 212 840-8800
New York *(G-10991)*
Lightbulb Press Inc ....E 212 485-8800
New York *(G-11026)*
Lino Press Inc ....E 718 665-2625
Bronx *(G-1387)*
Llcs Publishing Corp ....F 718 569-2703
Brooklyn *(G-2235)*
Lucky Peach LLC ....G 212 228-0031
New York *(G-11088)*
Macmillan Academic Pubg Inc ....F 212 226-1476
New York *(G-11112)*
Mailers-Pblsher Wlfare Tr Fund ....G 212 869-5986
New York *(G-11138)*
Marketresearchcom Inc ....F 212 807-2600
New York *(G-11184)*
Mary Ann Liebert Inc ....D 914 740-2100
New Rochelle *(G-8962)*
Media Transcripts Inc ....E 212 362-1481
New York *(G-11235)*
Medical Information Systems ....G 516 621-7200
Port Washington *(G-13863)*
Mens Journal LLC ....A 212 484-1616
New York *(G-11251)*
Menucha Publishers Inc ....F 718 232-0856
Brooklyn *(G-2301)*
Merchant Publishing Inc ....F 212 691-6666
New York *(G-11253)*
Merrill Corporation Inc ....D 212 620-5600
New York *(G-11260)*
Millennium Medical Publishing ....F 212 995-2211
New York *(G-11292)*
Minyanville Media Inc ....E 212 991-6200
New York *(G-11306)*
Morey Publishing ....E 516 284-3300
Farmingdale *(G-5069)*
Mortgage Press Ltd ....E 516 409-1400
Wantagh *(G-16581)*
Mtm Publishing Inc ....G 212 242-6930
New York *(G-11343)*
Multi-Health Systems Inc ....D 800 456-3003
Cheektowaga *(G-3608)*
My Publisher Inc ....G 212 935-5215
New York *(G-11354)*
National Health Prom Assoc ....E 914 421-2525
White Plains *(G-17166)*
National Rding Styles Inst Inc ....F 516 921-5500
Syosset *(G-15851)*
New York Legal Publishing ....G 518 459-1100
Menands *(G-8409)*
O Val Nick Music Co Inc ....G 212 873-2179
New York *(G-11504)*
Oakwood Publishing Co ....G 516 482-7720
Great Neck *(G-5842)*
One Story Inc ....G 917 816-3659
Brooklyn *(G-2404)*
Openroad Integrated Media Inc ....E 212 691-0900
New York *(G-11527)*
Osprey Publishing Inc ....G 212 419-5300
New York *(G-11545)*
Outlook Newspaper ....E 845 356-6261
Suffern *(G-15817)*
Outreach Publishing Corp ....G 718 773-0525
Brooklyn *(G-2412)*
Pace Editions Inc ....G 212 675-7431
New York *(G-11563)*
Paragon Publishing Inc ....G 718 302-2093
Brooklyn *(G-2420)*
Per Annum Inc ....E 212 647-8700
New York *(G-11630)*
Petersons Nelnet LLC ....C 609 896-1800
Albany *(G-118)*
Press Express ....G 914 592-3790
Elmsford *(G-4781)*
Primary Wave Publishing LLC ....G 212 661-6990
New York *(G-11730)*
Professnal Spt Pblications Inc ....F 516 327-9500
Elmont *(G-4736)*
Publishers Clearing House LLC ....E 516 249-4063
Melville *(G-8379)*
Quality Patterns Inc ....D 212 704-0355
New York *(G-11794)*
R W Publications Div of Wtrhs ....E 716 714-5620
Elma *(G-4666)*
Rda Holding Co ....F 914 238-1000
New York *(G-11837)*
Refinery 29 Inc ....D 212 966-3112
New York *(G-11849)*
Regan Arts LLC ....F 646 488-6610
New York *(G-11853)*
Reliable Press II Inc ....F 718 840-5812
Brooklyn *(G-2508)*
Repertoire International De LI ....E 212 817-1990
New York *(G-11867)*
Rockefeller University ....G 212 327-8568
New York *(G-11918)*
Rolling Stone Magazine ....G 212 484-1616
New York *(G-11930)*
Rosemont Press Incorporated ....G 212 239-4770
Deer Park *(G-4226)*
Rough Guides US Ltd ....D 212 414-3635
New York *(G-11941)*
Rsl Media LLC ....G 212 307-6760
New York *(G-11949)*
Sacks and Company New York ....G 212 741-1000
New York *(G-11969)*
Sag Harbor Express ....G 631 725-1700
Sag Harbor *(G-15106)*
Scepter Publishers Inc ....G 212 354-0670
New Rochelle *(G-8970)*
Seabay Media Holdings LLC ....G 212 457-7790
New York *(G-12028)*
Selby Marketing Associates Inc ....F 585 377-0750
Fairport *(G-4882)*
Sephardic Yellow Pages ....E 718 998-0299
Brooklyn *(G-2569)*
Sharedbook Inc ....E 646 442-8840
New York *(G-12066)*
Sing Tao Newspapers NY Ltd ....E 212 699-3800
New York *(G-12107)*
Slosson Edctl Publications Inc ....F 716 652-0930
East Aurora *(G-4403)*
Social Science Electronic Pubg ....F 585 442-8170
Rochester *(G-14714)*
Sony Music Holdings Inc ....A 212 833-8000
New York *(G-12162)*
Southampton Town Newspapers ....E 631 283-4100
Southampton *(G-15576)*
Stephen Singer Pattern Co Inc ....F 212 947-2902
New York *(G-12220)*
STf Services Inc ....E 315 463-8506
East Syracuse *(G-4581)*
Straight Arrow Publishing Co ....C 212 484-1616
New York *(G-12233)*
Strathmore Directories Ltd ....E 516 997-2525
Westbury *(G-17056)*
Student Lifeline Inc ....E 516 327-0800
Franklin Square *(G-5377)*
Summit Communications ....G 914 273-5504
Armonk *(G-417)*
Super Express USA Pubg Corp ....F 212 227-5800
Richmond Hill *(G-14098)*
Tablet Publishing Company Inc ....E 718 965-7333
Brooklyn *(G-2664)*
Taylor & Francis Group LLC ....C 212 216-7800
New York *(G-12306)*
Te Neues Publishing Company ....F 212 627-9090
New York *(G-12310)*
Theskimm Inc ....F 212 228-4628
New York *(G-12336)*
Thomson Reuters Corporation ....F 212 393-9461
New York *(G-12348)*
Thomson Reuters Corporation ....A 646 223-4000
New York *(G-12349)*
Trader Interntnal Publications ....G 914 631-6856
Sleepy Hollow *(G-15497)*
Treiman Publications Corp ....G 607 657-8473
Berkshire *(G-853)*
Tribune Entertainment Co Del ....E 203 866-2204
New York *(G-12425)*
Tribune Media Services Inc ....B 518 792-9914
Queensbury *(G-14026)*
Triumph Learning LLC ....E 212 652-0200
New York *(G-12430)*
Trusted Media Brands Inc ....A 914 238-1000
New York *(G-12435)*
Trusted Media Brands Inc ....F 914 244-5244
White Plains *(G-17204)*
Turbo Express Inc ....G 718 723-3686
Jamaica *(G-6996)*
Two Palms Press Inc ....F 212 965-8598
New York *(G-12452)*
Ucc Guide Inc ....F 518 434-0909
Albany *(G-145)*
Underline Communications LLC ....F 212 994-4340
New York *(G-12467)*
USA Custom Pad Corp ....E 607 563-9550
Sidney *(G-15467)*
Value Line Inc ....D 212 907-1500
New York *(G-12520)*
Vending Times Inc ....F 516 442-1850
Rockville Centre *(G-14831)*
Vendome Group LLC ....D 646 795-3899
New York *(G-12540)*
Viamedia Corporation ....G 718 485-7792
Brooklyn *(G-2741)*
Viewfinder Inc ....G 212 831-0939
New York *(G-12567)*
Vincys Printing Ltd ....F 518 355-4363
Schenectady *(G-15333)*
VWR Education LLC ....C 585 359-2502
West Henrietta *(G-16929)*
Watchanish LLC ....F 917 558-0404
New York *(G-12622)*
Wayuga Community Newspapers ....E 315 754-6229
Red Creek *(G-14040)*
Welcome Rain Publishers LLC ....G 212 686-1909
New York *(G-12634)*
Won & Lee Inc ....E 516 222-0712
Garden City *(G-5552)*
Yam TV LLC ....G 917 932-5418
New York *(G-12710)*

PUBLISHERS: Music Book

Boydell & Brewer Inc ....F 585 275-0419
Rochester *(G-14261)*
Congress For Jewish Culture ....G 212 505-8040
New York *(G-9761)*
Simmons-Boardman Pubg Corp ....G 212 620-7200
New York *(G-12101)*

PUBLISHERS: Music Book & Sheet Music

Boosey & Hawkes Inc ....E 212 358-5300
New York *(G-9490)*
Bourne Music Publishers ....F 212 391-4300
New York *(G-9496)*
C F Peters Corp ....E 718 416-7800
Glendale *(G-5663)*
Carbert Music Inc ....E 212 725-9277
New York *(G-9579)*
Downtown Music LLC ....G 212 625-2980
New York *(G-9971)*
Franklin-Douglas Inc ....F 516 883-0121
Port Washington *(G-13838)*
Lagunatic Music & Filmworks ....F 212 353-9600
Brooklyn *(G-2191)*
Lefrak Entertainment Co Ltd ....G 212 586-3600
New York *(G-10995)*
Mpl Communications Inc ....G 212 246-5881
New York *(G-11338)*
Reservoir Media Management Inc ....F 212 675-0541
New York *(G-11871)*
Sony/Atv Music Publishing LLC ....E 212 833-7730
New York *(G-12163)*

PUBLISHERS: Music, Book

Euphorbia Productions Ltd ....G 212 533-1700
New York *(G-10136)*
G Schirmer Inc ....G 212 254-2100
New York *(G-10280)*
G Schirmer Inc ....E 845 469-4699
Chester *(G-3634)*
Largo Music Inc ....G 212 756-5080
New York *(G-10965)*
Music Sales Corporation ....G 212 254-2100
New York *(G-11350)*
Peer International Corp ....E 212 265-3910
New York *(G-11613)*
Peermusic III Ltd ....F 212 265-3910
New York *(G-11615)*
Peermusic Ltd ....F 212 265-3910
New York *(G-11616)*

PUBLISHERS: Music, Sheet

Company	Col	Phone
Abkco Music & Records Inc — New York (G-9050)	D	212 399-0300
Charing Cross Music Inc — New York (G-9630)	G	212 541-7571
Historic TW Inc — New York (G-10530)	E	212 484-8000
Integrated Copyright Group — New York (G-10658)	E	615 329-3999
Ludlow Music Inc — New York (G-11089)	F	212 594-9795
Michael Karp Music Inc — New York (G-11277)	G	212 840-3285
Mom Dad Publishing Inc — New York (G-11321)	E	646 476-9170
Screen Gems-EMI Music Inc — New York (G-12026)	D	212 786-8000
Shapiro Bernstein & Co Inc — New York (G-12065)	F	212 588-0878
Time Warner Companies Inc — New York (G-12369)	D	212 484-8000

PUBLISHERS: Newsletter

Company	Col	Phone
Alm Media LLC — New York (G-9146)	B	212 457-9400
Alm Media Holdings Inc — New York (G-9147)	B	212 457-9400
Aspen Publishers Inc — New York (G-9288)	A	212 771-0600
Energy Intelligence Group Inc — New York (G-10090)	E	212 532-1112
Fischler Hockey Service — New York (G-10225)	F	212 749-4152
Grant Hamilton — East Aurora (G-4396)	F	716 652-0320
Hart Energy Publishing Lllp — New York (G-10467)	G	212 621-4621
London Theater News Ltd — New York (G-11054)	F	212 517-8608
Mathisen Ventures Inc — New York (G-11203)	G	212 986-1025
Redspring Communications Inc — Saratoga Springs (G-15200)	E	518 587-0547

PUBLISHERS: Newspaper

Company	Col	Phone
50+ Lifestyle — Bellport (G-819)	G	631 286-0058
A Zimmer Ltd — Syracuse (G-15866)	D	315 422-7011
Advance Magazine Publs Inc — New York (G-9088)	C	212 450-7000
Advertiser Publications Inc — Chester (G-3625)	F	845 783-1111
Afro Times Newspaper — Brooklyn (G-1568)	F	718 636-9500
After 50 Inc — Lancaster (G-7323)	G	716 832-9300
Albany Student Press Inc — Albany (G-41)	E	518 442-5665
Algemeiner Journal Inc — Brooklyn (G-1582)	G	718 771-0400
American Media Inc — New York (G-9174)	D	212 545-4800
American Media Inc — New York (G-9175)	C	212 545-4800
Amnews Corporation — New York (G-9187)	E	212 932-7400
Angel Media and Publishing — West Nyack (G-16941)	G	845 727-4949
Artvoice — Buffalo (G-2839)	F	716 881-6604
Bangla Patrika Inc — Long Island City (G-7712)	G	718 482-9923
Best Line Inc — Staten Island (G-15666)	G	917 670-6210
Brooklyn Journal Publications — Brooklyn (G-1728)	E	718 422-7400
Brooklyn Rail Inc — Brooklyn (G-1729)	F	718 349-8427
Bureau of National Affairs Inc — New York (G-9531)	E	212 687-4530
Business Journals — New York (G-9535)	F	212 790-5100
Camden News Inc — Camden (G-3340)	G	315 245-1849
Canandaigua Msgnr Incorporated — Canandaigua (G-3366)	D	585 394-0770
Canarsie Courier Inc — Brooklyn (G-1754)	F	718 257-0600
Cdc Publishing LLC — Morrisville (G-8661)	E	215 579-1695
China Daily Distribution Corp — New York (G-9646)	E	212 537-8888
China Newsweek Corporation — New York (G-9651)	F	212 481-2510
Chinese Medical Report Inc — Flushing (G-5239)	G	718 359-5676
Chronicle — Bronx (G-1298)	G	347 969-7281
Chronicle Express — Penn Yan (G-13531)	F	315 536-4422
Citizen Publishing Corp — Nanuet (G-8800)	F	845 627-1414
CNY Business Review Inc — Syracuse (G-15917)	F	315 472-3104
Columbia Daily Spectator — New York (G-9735)	G	212 854-9550
Community Media Group LLC — Delmar (G-4269)	G	518 439-4949
Community Media LLC — New York (G-9749)	E	212 229-1890
Community Newsppr Holdings Inc — Niagara Falls (G-12828)	D	716 282-2311
Cortland Standard Printing Co — Cortland (G-4045)	D	607 756-5665
Country Folks — Batavia (G-631)	G	585 343-9721
CT Publications Co — Corona (G-4018)	F	718 592-2196
Daily Freeman — Kingston (G-7215)	F	845 331-5000
Delaware County Times Inc — Delhi (G-4262)	G	607 746-2176
Der Yid Inc — Brooklyn (G-1855)	E	718 797-3900
Digital One USA Inc — Flushing (G-5245)	F	718 396-4890
Division Street News Corp — Cobleskill (G-3761)	F	518 234-2515
Dow Jones & Company Inc — New York (G-9965)	B	609 627-2999
Dray Enterprises Inc — Le Roy (G-7431)	F	585 768-2201
East Hampton Ind News Inc — East Hampton (G-4428)	E	631 324-2500
Economist Newspaper NA Inc — New York (G-10033)	E	212 554-0676
Ecuador News Inc — Woodside (G-17344)	F	718 205-7014
El Diario LLC — Brooklyn (G-1910)	C	212 807-4600
Fairchild Publications Inc — New York (G-10181)	A	212 630-4000
Finger Lakes Media Inc — Dundee (G-4352)	F	607 243-7600
Finger Lakes Printing Co Inc — Geneva (G-5588)	E	315 789-3333
Fire Island Tide Publication — Sayville (G-15239)	F	631 567-7470
Five Islands Publishing Inc — Bronx (G-1335)	F	631 583-5345
Gallagher Printing Inc — Buffalo (G-2977)	E	716 873-2434
Gannett Co Inc — Farmington (G-5160)	G	585 924-3406
Gannett Co Inc — New Rochelle (G-8948)	F	914 278-9315
Gannett Co Inc — Vestal (G-16470)	D	607 798-1234
Gannett Co Inc — Lakeville (G-7307)	G	585 346-4150
Gannett Stllite Info Ntwrk Inc — Mamaroneck (G-8068)	F	914 381-3400
Gatehouse Media LLC — Utica (G-16359)	E	315 792-5000
Gatehouse Media LLC — Corning (G-3993)	D	607 936-4651
Gatehouse Media LLC — Canandaigua (G-3376)	D	585 394-0770
Gatehouse Media LLC — Hornell (G-6590)	C	607 324-1425
General Media Strategies Inc — New York (G-10316)	G	212 586-4141
Gleaner Company Ltd — Jamaica (G-6951)	G	718 657-0788
Great North Road Media Inc — New York (G-10399)	F	646 619-1355
Hagedorn Communications Inc — New Rochelle (G-8951)	D	914 636-7400
Haitian Times Inc — New Rochelle (G-8952)	G	718 230-8700
Hamodia Corp — Brooklyn (G-2063)	F	718 853-9094
Hearst Corporation — Albany (G-85)	A	518 454-5694
Irish Tribune Inc — New York (G-10703)	F	212 684-3366
Jewish Journal — Brooklyn (G-2139)	G	718 630-9350
Jobs Weekly Inc — Hamburg (G-5952)	F	716 648-5627
Korea Times New York Inc — Long Island City (G-7812)	G	718 729-5555
L & M Publications Inc — Garden City (G-5525)	E	516 378-3133
Lantern Hall LLC — Brooklyn (G-2196)	G	718 381-2122
Lee Newspapers Inc — Palatine Bridge (G-13421)	F	518 673-3237
Lmg National Publishing Inc — Fairport (G-4868)	E	585 598-6874
Long Island Business News — Ronkonkoma (G-14961)	E	631 737-1700
Long Island Catholic Newspaper — Rockville Centre (G-14822)	E	516 594-1212
Long Islander Newspapers LLC — Huntington (G-6704)	G	631 427-7000
Malone Newspapers Corp — Malone (G-8045)	F	518 483-2000
Manhattan Times Inc — New York (G-11158)	F	212 569-5800
Mark I Publications Inc — Glendale (G-5673)	E	718 205-8000
Market Place Publications — Carle Place (G-3421)	E	516 997-7909
Massapequa Post — Massapequa Park (G-8221)	E	516 798-5100
Merchandiser Inc — Clifton Springs (G-3739)	G	315 462-6411
Ming Pao (new York) Inc — Long Island City (G-7843)	E	718 786-2888
Mortgage Press Ltd — Wantagh (G-16581)	E	516 409-1400
Nassau County Publications — Hempstead (G-4306)	G	516 481-5400
New York IL Bo Inc — Flushing (G-5279)	F	718 961-1538
New York Times Company — New York (G-11430)	F	212 556-4300
News Corporation — New York (G-11435)	C	212 416-3400
Newspaper Delivery Solutions — Staten Island (G-15731)	G	718 370-1000
Nick Lugo Inc — New York (G-11445)	F	212 348-2100
North Country This Week — Potsdam (G-13898)	G	315 265-1000
Northern NY Newspapers Corp — Watertown (G-16691)	G	315 782-1000
Noticia Hispanoamericana Inc — Baldwin (G-559)	E	516 223-5678
Nyp Holdings Inc — Brooklyn (G-2396)	D	718 260-2500
Observer Daily Sunday Newsppr — Dunkirk (G-4370)	D	716 366-3000
Oneida Publications Inc — Oneida (G-13185)	E	315 363-5100
Ottaway Newspapers Inc — Middletown (G-8490)	F	845 343-2181
Panagraphics Inc — Orchard Park (G-13312)	G	716 312-8088
Peace Times Weekly Inc — Flushing (G-5287)	G	718 762-6500
Pearson Inc — New York (G-11610)	D	212 641-2400
Putnam Cnty News Recorder LLC — Cold Spring (G-3789)	F	845 265-2468
Quality Guides — Westfield (G-17078)	G	716 326-3163
Realtimetraderscom — Buffalo (G-3181)	E	716 632-6600
Record Advertiser — North Tonawanda (G-13006)	F	716 693-1000
Rheinwald Printing Co Inc — Brockport (G-1246)	F	585 637-5100
Rizzoli Intl Publications Inc — New York (G-11905)	F	212 308-2000
Rochester Democrat & Chronicle — Rochester (G-14663)	E	585 232-7100

(G-0000) Company's Geographic Section entry number

Rocket Communications Inc F 716 873-2594
Buffalo *(G-3190)*
Royal News Corp F 212 564-8972
New York *(G-11944)*
Russkaya Reklama Inc E 718 769-3000
Brooklyn *(G-2538)*
Sag Harbor Express G 631 725-1700
Sag Harbor *(G-15106)*
Salamanca Press Penny Saver E 716 945-1500
Salamanca *(G-15132)*
Sample News Group LLC D 315 343-3800
Oswego *(G-13365)*
Satellite Network Inc F 718 336-2698
Brooklyn *(G-2560)*
Sb New York Inc D 212 457-7790
New York *(G-12000)*
Schneps Publications Inc E 718 224-5863
Bayside *(G-769)*
Seabay Media Holdings LLC G 212 457-7790
New York *(G-12028)*
Seneca Media Inc D 607 324-1425
Hornell *(G-6593)*
Sing Tao Newspapers NY Ltd F 212 431-9030
Brooklyn *(G-2592)*
SM News Plus Incorporated G 212 888-0153
New York *(G-12128)*
Smithtown News Inc E 631 265-2100
Smithtown *(G-15521)*
Southampton Town Newspapers F 631 288-1100
Westhampton Beach *(G-17090)*
Spring Publishing Corporation G 718 782-0881
Brooklyn *(G-2614)*
Star Sports Corp E 516 773-4075
Great Neck *(G-5861)*
Star-Gazette Fund Inc C 607 734-5151
Elmira *(G-4715)*
Stratconglobal Inc G 212 989-2355
New York *(G-12234)*
Straus Newspapers Inc E 845 782-4000
Chester *(G-3644)*
Sun-Times Media Group Inc E 716 945-1644
Salamanca *(G-15136)*
Syracuse Catholic Press Assn G 315 422-8153
Syracuse *(G-16074)*
Tegna Inc C 716 849-2222
Buffalo *(G-3238)*
Tenney Media Group D 315 853-5569
Clinton *(G-3747)*
The Sandhar Corp G 718 523-0819
Jamaica *(G-6994)*
Tompkins Weekly Inc G 607 539-7100
Ithaca *(G-6913)*
Tri-Village Publishers Inc D 518 843-1100
Amsterdam *(G-371)*
Tryp Times Square G 212 246-8800
New York *(G-12437)*
Ubm Inc A 212 600-3000
New York *(G-12458)*
Ubm LLC D 516 562-7800
New Hyde Park *(G-8912)*
Urdu Times G 718 297-8700
Jamaica *(G-6997)*
USA Today International Corp G 703 854-3400
New York *(G-12512)*
W H White Publications Inc G 914 725-2500
Dobbs Ferry *(G-4328)*
Wallkill Lodge No 627 F&Am F 845 778-7148
Walden *(G-16558)*
Webster Ontrio Wlwrth Pnnysver F 585 265-3620
Webster *(G-16767)*
Weekly Ajkal F 718 565-2100
Jackson Heights *(G-6925)*
Weekly Business News Corp G 212 689-5888
New York *(G-12631)*
West Seneca Bee Inc D 716 632-4700
Williamsville *(G-17284)*
Westbury Times D 516 747-8282
Mineola *(G-8572)*
William J Kline & Son Inc D 518 843-1100
Amsterdam *(G-374)*
World Journal LLC G 212 879-3933
New York *(G-12690)*
Yated Neeman Inc F 845 369-1600
Monsey *(G-8621)*

PUBLISHERS: Newspapers, No Printing

21st Century Fox America Inc G 845 735-1116
Pearl River *(G-13476)*
A C J Communications Inc F 631 587-5612
Babylon *(G-541)*
Albany Catholic Press Assoc G 518 453-6688
Albany *(G-35)*
Alm Media LLC B 212 457-9400
New York *(G-9146)*
Alm Media Holdings Inc B 212 457-9400
New York *(G-9147)*
American City Bus Journals Inc E 716 541-1654
Buffalo *(G-2823)*
American Sports Media LLC G 585 377-9636
Rochester *(G-14216)*
Angola Pennysaver Inc F 716 549-1164
Angola *(G-379)*
Architects Newspaper LLC F 212 966-0630
New York *(G-9245)*
Auburn Publishing Co D 315 253-5311
Auburn *(G-479)*
Bee Publications Inc D 716 632-4700
Williamsville *(G-17263)*
Belsito Communications Inc F 845 534-9700
New Windsor *(G-8978)*
Blue and White Publishing Inc F 215 431-3339
New York *(G-9471)*
Boonville Herald Inc G 315 942-4449
Boonville *(G-1161)*
Buffalo Law Journal G 716 541-1600
Buffalo *(G-2875)*
Business First of New York E 716 854-5822
Buffalo *(G-2884)*
Business First of New York E 518 640-6800
Latham *(G-7384)*
Catskill Mountain Publishing F 845 586-2601
Arkville *(G-409)*
Chase Media Group F 914 962-3871
Yorktown Heights *(G-17525)*
Clarion Publications Inc F 585 243-3530
Geneseo *(G-5579)*
Community Newspaper Group LLC F 607 432-1000
Oneonta *(G-13203)*
Community Newspaper Group LLC E 518 565-4114
Plattsburgh *(G-13688)*
Community Newsppr Holdings Inc D 716 693-1000
Niagara Falls *(G-12827)*
Community Newsppr Holdings Inc E 716 439-9222
Lockport *(G-7605)*
Courier-Life Inc C 718 260-2500
Brooklyn *(G-1809)*
Daily Cornell Sun E 607 273-0746
Ithaca *(G-6873)*
Daily Orange Corporation E 315 443-2314
Syracuse *(G-15940)*
Dale Press Inc E 718 543-6200
Bronx *(G-1313)*
Danet Inc F 718 266-4444
Brooklyn *(G-1839)*
Dans Paper Inc D 631 537-0500
Southampton *(G-15565)*
Das Yidishe Licht Inc G 718 387-3166
Brooklyn *(G-1841)*
Dbg Media G 718 599-6828
Brooklyn *(G-1844)*
Ecclesiastical Communications F 212 688-2399
New York *(G-10027)*
Empire Publishing Inc F 516 829-4000
Far Rockaway *(G-4928)*
Expositor Newspapers Inc G 585 427-2468
Rochester *(G-14387)*
Four Directions Inc E 315 829-8388
Vernon *(G-16457)*
Freetime Magazine Inc G 585 473-2266
Rochester *(G-14404)*
French Morning LLC G 646 290-7463
New York *(G-10258)*
FT Publications Inc D 212 641-6500
New York *(G-10266)*
FT Publications Inc E 212 641-2420
New York *(G-10267)*
Fulton Newspapers Inc E 315 598-6397
Fulton *(G-5471)*
Gannett Stllite Info Ntwrk Inc E 914 965-5000
Yonkers *(G-17462)*
Gannett Stllite Info Ntwrk LLC E 845 578-2300
West Nyack *(G-16946)*
Gatehouse Media LLC G 607 776-2121
Bath *(G-656)*
Gateway Newspapers Inc G 845 628-8400
Mahopac *(G-8026)*
Good Health Healthcare Newsppr F 585 421-8109
Victor *(G-16503)*
Highline Media LLC C 859 692-2100
New York *(G-10520)*
Hudson Valley Black Press G 845 562-1313
Newburgh *(G-12783)*
Impremedia LLC D 212 807-4785
Brooklyn *(G-2099)*
India Abroad Publications Inc D 212 929-1727
New York *(G-10631)*
Irish Echo Newspaper Corp F 212 482-4818
New York *(G-10702)*
Jewish Press Inc C 718 330-1100
Brooklyn *(G-2140)*
Jewish Week Inc E 212 921-7822
New York *(G-10766)*
John Lor Publishing Ltd E 631 475-1000
Patchogue *(G-13451)*
Johnson Newspaper Corporation E 518 483-4700
Malone *(G-8042)*
Journal Register Company D 518 584-4242
Saratoga Springs *(G-15191)*
Korea Times New York Inc D 718 784-4526
Long Island City *(G-7811)*
Korea Times New York Inc G 718 961-7979
Flushing *(G-5269)*
Lebhar-Friedman Inc E 212 756-5000
New York *(G-10986)*
Lebhar-Friedman Inc C 212 756-5000
New York *(G-10987)*
Lee Enterprises Incorporated C 518 792-3131
Glens Falls *(G-5702)*
Local Media Group Inc E 845 341-1100
Middletown *(G-8481)*
Local Media Group Inc F 845 340-4910
Kingston *(G-7226)*
Manchester Newspaper Inc E 518 642-1234
Granville *(G-5791)*
Manhattan Media LLC E 212 268-8600
New York *(G-11154)*
Miami Media LLC F 212 268-8600
New York *(G-11274)*
Moneysaver Advertising Inc F 585 593-1275
Olean *(G-13172)*
National Herald Inc E 718 784-5255
Long Island City *(G-7851)*
Neighbor To Neighbor News Inc G 585 492-2525
Arcade *(G-397)*
New Ski Inc E 607 277-7000
Ithaca *(G-6902)*
New York Cvl Srvc Emplys Pblsh F 212 962-2690
New York *(G-11418)*
New York Daily Challenge Inc E 718 636-9500
Brooklyn *(G-2372)*
News Communications Inc F 212 689-2500
New York *(G-11434)*
News Report Inc E 718 851-6607
Brooklyn *(G-2379)*
Newspaper Publisher LLC F 607 775-0472
Conklin *(G-3896)*
Newsweek LLC G 646 867-7100
New York *(G-11439)*
Nordic Press Inc G 212 686-3356
New York *(G-11470)*
Northern Tier Publishing Corp F 914 962-4748
Yorktown Heights *(G-17530)*
Novoye Rsskoye Slovo Pubg Corp D 646 460-4566
Brooklyn *(G-2389)*
Nyc Community Media LLC F 212 229-1890
Brooklyn *(G-2395)*
Oak Lone Publishing Co Inc E 518 792-1126
Glens Falls *(G-5708)*
Page Front Group Inc G 716 823-8222
Lackawanna *(G-7272)*
Patchogue Advance Inc E 631 475-1000
Patchogue *(G-13456)*
Publishing Group America Inc F 646 658-0550
New York *(G-11769)*
Richner Communications Inc G 516 569-4000
Lawrence *(G-7424)*
Rochester Business Journal E 585 546-8303
Rochester *(G-14658)*
Rochester Catholic Press F 585 529-9530
Rochester *(G-14659)*
S I Communications Inc F 914 725-2500
Scarsdale *(G-15253)*
Seneca Media Inc F 585 593-5300
Wellsville *(G-16784)*
Sing Tao Newspapers NY Ltd E 212 699-3800
New York *(G-12107)*
Southampton Town Newspapers E 631 283-4100
Southampton *(G-15576)*
Spartacist Publishing Co E 212 732-7860
New York *(G-12173)*

Steffen Publishing Inc D 315 865-4100
Holland Patent (G-6514)
Stuart Communications Inc F 845 252-7414
Narrowsburg (G-8815)
Tablet Publishing Company Inc E 718 965-7333
Brooklyn (G-2664)
Tefft Publishers Inc G 518 692-9290
Greenwich (G-5914)
Thestreet Inc D 212 321-5000
New York (G-12337)
Times Beacon Record Newspapers F 631 331-1154
East Setauket (G-4513)
Times Review Newspaper Corp E 631 354-8031
Mattituck (G-8243)
Tioga County Courier G 607 687-0108
Owego (G-13385)
Tribco LLC E 718 357-7400
Whitestone (G-17245)
Tricycle Foundation Inc G 800 873-9871
New York (G-12426)
Ulster Publishing Co Inc E 845 334-8205
Kingston (G-7247)
Ulster Publishing Co Inc F 845 255-7005
New Paltz (G-8926)
US Hispanic Media Inc G 212 885-8000
Brooklyn (G-2732)
Wallkill Valley Publications E 845 561-0170
Newburgh (G-12810)
Wappingers Falls Shopper Inc E 845 297-3723
Wappingers Falls (G-16598)
Wave Publishing Co Inc F 718 634-4000
Rockaway Beach (G-14811)
Westfair Communications Inc E 914 694-3600
White Plains (G-17214)
Westside News Inc F 585 352-3411
Spencerport (G-15598)
World Journal LLC C 718 746-8889
Whitestone (G-17247)
World Journal LLC E 718 445-2277
Flushing (G-5314)
Yonkers Time Publishing Co F 914 965-4000
Yonkers (G-17519)

PUBLISHERS: Pamphlets, No Printing

Spartacist Publishing Co E 212 732-7860
New York (G-12173)

PUBLISHERS: Periodical, With Printing

Artifex Press LLC F 212 414-1482
New York (G-9269)
Economist Newspaper Group Inc C 212 541-0500
New York (G-10032)
Eidosmedia Inc E 646 795-2100
New York (G-10042)
Frost Publications Inc G 845 726-3232
Westtown (G-17097)
Gruner + Jahr USA Group Inc B 866 323-9336
New York (G-10419)
H W Wilson Company Inc B 718 588-8635
Bronx (G-1352)
Impact Journals LLC G 800 922-0957
Orchard Park (G-13298)
Nylon Media Inc F 212 226-6454
New York (G-11498)
Playbill Incorporated E 212 557-5757
New York (G-11695)
The PRS Group Inc F 315 431-0511
East Syracuse (G-4583)
Yale Robbins Inc D 212 683-5700
New York (G-12709)

PUBLISHERS: Periodicals, Magazines

21st Century Fox America Inc D 212 447-4600
New York (G-9014)
A Guideposts Church Corp C 212 251-8100
New York (G-9035)
Advance Magazine Publs Inc D 212 286-2860
New York (G-9087)
American Jewish Committee G 212 891-1400
New York (G-9171)
American Towman Network Inc F 845 986-4546
Warwick (G-16608)
Annointed Buty Ministries LLC G 646 867-3796
Brooklyn (G-1614)
Archaelogy Magazine E 718 472-3050
Long Island City (G-7699)
Backstage LLC E 212 493-4243
Brooklyn (G-1661)
Bedford Freeman & Worth C 212 576-9400
New York (G-9391)
Berger & Wild LLC G 646 415-8459
New York (G-9410)
Binah Magazines Corp G 718 305-5200
Brooklyn (G-1697)
BJ Magazines Inc G 212 367-9705
New York (G-9458)
Bnei Aram Soba Inc F 718 645-4460
Brooklyn (G-1706)
Bust Inc G 212 675-1707
Brooklyn (G-1743)
Cambridge University Press D 212 337-5000
New York (G-9558)
Canopy Canopy Canopy Inc G 347 529-5182
New York (G-9568)
Choice Magazine Listening Inc G 516 883-8280
Port Washington (G-13828)
CNY Business Review Inc F 315 472-3104
Syracuse (G-15917)
College Calendar Company F 315 768-8242
Whitesboro (G-17220)
Complex Media Inc E 917 793-5831
New York (G-9752)
Cornell University E 607 254-2473
Ithaca (G-6872)
Crains New York Business E 212 210-0250
New York (G-9806)
Davis Ziff Publishing Inc D 212 503-3500
New York (G-9885)
Delaware County Times Inc G 607 746-2176
Delhi (G-4262)
Denton Publications Inc E 518 561-9680
Plattsburgh (G-13689)
Departures Magazine E 212 382-5600
New York (G-9902)
Dissent Magazine F 212 316-3120
New York (G-9939)
Dow Jones Aer Company Inc A 212 416-2000
New York (G-9967)
Downtown Media Group LLC F 646 723-4510
New York (G-9970)
Envy Publishing Group Inc G 212 253-9874
New York (G-10100)
Fairchild Publications Inc A 212 630-4000
New York (G-10181)
Fairchild Publishing LLC G 212 286-3897
New York (G-10182)
Fashion Calendar International G 212 289-0420
New York (G-10197)
Frontiers Unlimited Inc G 631 283-4663
Southampton (G-15566)
Genomeweb LLC F 212 651-5636
New York (G-10322)
Glamour Magazine G 212 286-2860
New York (G-10345)
Global Finance Magazine G 212 524-3223
New York (G-10355)
Global Finance Media Inc F 212 447-7900
New York (G-10356)
Good Times Magazine G 516 280-2100
Carle Place (G-3416)
Guernica F 914 414-7318
Brooklyn (G-2056)
Hammer Communications Inc F 631 261-5806
Northport (G-13030)
Hamptons Media LLC G 631 283-6900
Southampton (G-15569)
Healthy Way of Life Magazine G 718 616-1681
Brooklyn (G-2069)
Hearst Business Publishing Inc F 212 969-7500
New York (G-10479)
Hearst Corporation D 212 649-4271
New York (G-10488)
Hearst Corporation D 212 204-4300
New York (G-10489)
Holmes Group The Inc G 212 333-2300
New York (G-10543)
I On Youth G 716 832-6509
Buffalo (G-3019)
Ink Publishing Corporation G 347 294-1220
Brooklyn (G-2104)
Institutional Invester G 212 224-3300
New York (G-10656)
Intellignc The Ftr Cmptng Nwsl F 212 222-1123
New York (G-10662)
Jerome Levy Forecasting Center G 914 244-8617
Mount Kisco (G-8673)
L F International Inc D 212 756-5000
New York (G-10940)
L I F Publishing Corp E 631 345-5200
Shirley (G-15445)
Latina Media Ventures LLC E 212 642-0200
New York (G-10970)
Laurtom Inc E 914 273-2233
Mount Kisco (G-8677)
Long Island Catholic Newspaper E 516 594-1212
Rockville Centre (G-14822)
Lucky Magazine F 212 286-6220
New York (G-11087)
Magazine I Spectrum E E 212 419-7555
New York (G-11125)
Magnificat Inc F 914 502-1820
Yonkers (G-17482)
Media Press Corp E 212 791-6347
New York (G-11234)
Meredith Corporation F 212 499-2000
New York (G-11255)
Nation Magazine E 212 209-5400
New York (G-11368)
National Marketing Services F 516 942-9595
Roslyn Heights (G-15055)
Nervecom Inc F 212 625-9914
New York (G-11390)
New York Media LLC C 212 508-0700
New York (G-11423)
Next Step Publishing Inc F 585 742-1260
Victor (G-16518)
Njf Publishing Corp G 631 345-5200
Shirley (G-15450)
Northeast Group D 518 563-8214
Plattsburgh (G-13709)
Northeast Prtg & Dist Co Inc G 514 577-3545
Plattsburgh (G-13710)
Nova Science Publishers Inc F 631 231-7269
Hauppauge (G-6175)
Nsgv Inc E 212 367-3100
New York (G-11484)
Pearson Education Inc F 201 236-7000
West Nyack (G-16952)
Penton Media Inc B 212 204-4200
New York (G-11627)
Periodical Services Co Inc F 518 822-9300
Hudson (G-6660)
Professnal Spt Pblications Inc D 516 327-9500
Elmont (G-4737)
Ralph Martinelli E 914 345-3055
Elmsford (G-4783)
Rda Holding Co F 914 238-1000
New York (G-11837)
Relx Inc B 212 633-3900
New York (G-11860)
Res Media Group Inc F 212 320-3750
New York (G-11870)
Rolling Stone Magazine G 212 484-1616
New York (G-11930)
Rough Draft Publishing LLC F 212 741-4773
New York (G-11940)
Rye Record G 914 713-3213
Rye (G-15093)
Saveur Magazine E 212 219-7400
New York (G-11997)
Shoreline Publishing Inc G 914 738-7869
Pelham (G-13519)
Small Business Advisors Inc F 516 374-1387
Atlantic Beach (G-469)
Smooth Magazine F 212 925-1150
New York (G-12139)
Spin Magazine Media G 212 231-7400
New York (G-12187)
Springer Healthcare LLC E 212 460-1500
New York (G-12197)
Standard Analytics Io Inc G 917 882-5422
New York (G-12205)
Staten Island Parent Magazine G 718 761-4800
Staten Island (G-15762)
Steffen Publishing Inc D 315 865-4100
Holland Patent (G-6514)
Surface Magazine E 646 805-0200
New York (G-12268)
Swaps Monitor Publications Inc F 212 742-8550
New York (G-12271)
Time Out New York Partners LP D 646 432-3000
New York (G-12367)
TMC Usa LLC G 518 587-8920
Saratoga Springs (G-15205)
Ubm Inc A 212 600-3000
New York (G-12458)
US China Magazine E 212 663-4333
New York (G-12504)

PRODUCT SECTION

PUBLISHERS: Trade journals, No Printing

Vibe Media Group LLC .... D 212 448-7300
New York *(G-12561)*
Vickers Stock Research Corp .... E 212 425-7500
New York *(G-12562)*
Vogue Magazine .... D 212 286-2860
New York *(G-12590)*
Wallkill Valley Publications .... E 845 561-0170
Newburgh *(G-12810)*
Westfair Communications Inc .... E 914 694-3600
White Plains *(G-17214)*
Winsight LLC .... G 646 708-7309
New York *(G-12674)*
Womens E News Inc .... G 212 244-1720
New York *(G-12681)*

PUBLISHERS: Periodicals, No Printing

Academy of Political Science .... G 212 870-2500
New York *(G-9055)*
Alcoholics Anonymous Grapevine ..... F 212 870-3400
New York *(G-9128)*
Association For Cmpt McHy Inc .... D 212 869-7440
New York *(G-9292)*
Athlon Spt Communications Inc .... E 212 478-1910
New York *(G-9302)*
Bernhard Arnold & Company Inc ...... G 212 907-1500
New York *(G-9414)*
Boardman Simons Publishing .... E 212 620-7200
New York *(G-9482)*
Brownstone Publishers Inc .... E 212 473-8200
New York *(G-9525)*
Buffalo Spree Publishing Inc .... G 585 413-0040
Rochester *(G-14266)*
Capital Reg Wkly Newsppr Group ..... F 518 674-2841
Averill Park *(G-531)*
Cdc Publishing LLC .... E 215 579-1695
Morrisville *(G-8661)*
Conde Nast .... E 212 630-3642
New York *(G-9757)*
Conference Board Inc .... C 212 759-0900
New York *(G-9760)*
Congress For Jewish Culture .... G 212 505-8040
New York *(G-9761)*
Creative Magazine Inc .... G 516 378-0800
Merrick *(G-8415)*
Economist Intelligence Unit NA .... D 212 554-0600
New York *(G-10031)*
Fahy-Williams Publishing Inc .... F 315 781-6820
Geneva *(G-5587)*
Francis Emory Fitch Inc .... E 212 619-3800
New York *(G-10248)*
Global Entity Media Inc .... G 631 580-7772
Ronkonkoma *(G-14934)*
Government Data Publication .... E 347 789-8719
Brooklyn *(G-2046)*
Grants Financial Publishing .... F 212 809-7994
New York *(G-10393)*
Hearst Corporation .... E 212 649-3100
New York *(G-10483)*
Hearst Corporation .... A 518 454-5694
Albany *(G-85)*
Highline Media LLC .... C 859 692-2100
New York *(G-10520)*
Human Life Foundation Inc .... G 212 685-5210
New York *(G-10576)*
Impressions Inc .... G 212 594-5954
New York *(G-10621)*
International Center For Postg .... G 607 257-5860
Ithaca *(G-6886)*
Leadership Directories Inc .... E 212 627-4140
New York *(G-10982)*
Mathisen Ventures Inc .... G 212 986-1025
New York *(G-11203)*
McCarthy LLC .... F 646 862-5354
New York *(G-11220)*
Modern Farmer Media Inc .... F 518 828-7447
Hudson *(G-6658)*
Optionline LLC .... E 516 218-3225
Garden City *(G-5538)*
Parade Publications Inc .... E 212 450-7000
New York *(G-11581)*
Pati Inc .... F 718 244-6788
Jamaica *(G-6976)*
Pointwise Information Service .... F 315 457-4111
Liverpool *(G-7568)*
Psychonomic Society Inc .... E 512 381-1494
New York *(G-11764)*
Real Est Book of Long Island .... F 516 364-5000
Syosset *(G-15858)*
Shugar Publishing .... G 631 288-4404
Westhampton Beach *(G-17089)*

Simmons-Boardman Pubg Corp .... G 212 620-7200
New York *(G-12101)*
Spc Marketing Company .... G 631 661-2727
West Islip *(G-16937)*
Suffolk Community Council Inc .... G 631 434-9277
Deer Park *(G-4238)*
Swift Fulfillment Services .... G 516 593-1198
Lynbrook *(G-7990)*
Thestreet Inc .... D 212 321-5000
New York *(G-12337)*
Trader Interntnal Publications .... G 914 631-6856
Sleepy Hollow *(G-15497)*
Ubm LLC .... D 516 562-7800
New Hyde Park *(G-8912)*
Urban Racercom .... G 718 279-2202
Bayside *(G-771)*
Value Line Inc .... D 212 907-1500
New York *(G-12520)*
Value Line Publishing LLC .... C 201 842-8054
New York *(G-12521)*
World Guide Publishing .... E 800 331-7840
New York *(G-12689)*

PUBLISHERS: Posters

History Publishing Company LLC ..... G 845 398-8161
Palisades *(G-13426)*

PUBLISHERS: Racing Forms & Programs

Daily Racing Form Inc .... C 212 366-7600
New York *(G-9846)*

PUBLISHERS: Sheet Music

Carl Fischer LLC .... E 212 777-0900
New York *(G-9580)*
Kendor Music Inc .... F 716 492-1254
Delevan *(G-4261)*
Warner Music Inc .... D 212 275-2000
New York *(G-12617)*

PUBLISHERS: Shopping News

Freeville Publishing Co Inc .... F 607 844-9119
Freeville *(G-5447)*
Greater Rchster Advertiser Inc .... E 585 385-1974
East Rochester *(G-4479)*
Service Advertising Group Inc .... F 718 361-6161
Long Island City *(G-7904)*
Skylark Publications Ltd .... G 607 535-9866
Watkins Glen *(G-16721)*
Sneaker News Inc .... G 347 687-1588
New York *(G-12140)*

PUBLISHERS: Technical Manuals

Dayton T Brown Inc .... B 631 589-6300
Bohemia *(G-1048)*
Elsevier Inc .... B 212 633-3773
New York *(G-10067)*
Mosby Holdings Corp .... G 212 309-8100
New York *(G-11332)*

PUBLISHERS: Technical Manuals & Papers

Cambridge Info Group Inc .... F 301 961-6700
New York *(G-9557)*
Clearstep Technologies LLC .... G 315 952-3628
Camillus *(G-3350)*

PUBLISHERS: Technical Papers

Humana Press Inc .... E 212 460-1500
New York *(G-10577)*

PUBLISHERS: Telephone & Other Directory

Auto Market Publications Inc .... G 631 667-0500
Deer Park *(G-4129)*
Business Directory Inc .... F 718 486-8099
Brooklyn *(G-1742)*
Fashiondex Inc .... G 914 271-6121
New York *(G-10198)*
Golf Directories USA Inc .... G 516 365-5351
Manhasset *(G-8094)*
Infoservices International .... F 631 549-1805
Cold Spring Harbor *(G-3794)*
Israeli Yellow Pages .... E 718 520-1000
Kew Gardens *(G-7191)*
Korean Yellow Pages .... F 718 461-0073
Flushing *(G-5270)*
Long Islands Best Inc .... G 855 542-3785
Bohemia *(G-1090)*

Maximillion Communications LLC ..... D 212 564-3945
New York *(G-11212)*
Yellow Pages Inc .... G 845 639-6060
New City *(G-8840)*

PUBLISHERS: Textbooks, No Printing

Allworth Communications Inc .... F 212 777-8395
New York *(G-9144)*
Amsco School Publications Inc .... D 212 886-6500
New York *(G-9192)*
Bedford Freeman & Worth .... D 212 375-7000
New York *(G-9392)*
Booklinks Publishing Svcs LLC .... G 718 852-2116
Brooklyn *(G-1708)*
Brown Publishing Network Inc .... G 212 682-3330
New York *(G-9523)*
Cornell University .... D 607 277-2338
Ithaca *(G-6871)*
E W Williams Publications .... E 212 661-1516
New York *(G-10005)*
John Wiley & Sons Inc .... D 845 457-6250
Montgomery *(G-8632)*
Oxford Book Company Inc .... C 212 227-2120
New York *(G-11551)*
Peter Lang Publishing Inc .... F 212 647-7700
New York *(G-11651)*
Project Energy Savers LLC .... F 718 596-4231
Brooklyn *(G-2470)*
Stanley M Indig .... G 718 692-0648
Brooklyn *(G-2618)*
W W Norton & Company Inc .... C 212 354-5500
New York *(G-12602)*
Wordwise Inc .... G 914 232-5366
Katonah *(G-7164)*
Worth Publishers Inc .... C 212 475-6000
New York *(G-12692)*

PUBLISHERS: Trade journals, No Printing

Access Intelligence LLC .... A 212 204-4269
New York *(G-9057)*
American Institute Physics Inc .... C 516 576-2410
Melville *(G-8326)*
American Physical Society .... D 631 591-4025
Ridge *(G-14104)*
Aspen Publishers Inc .... A 212 771-0600
New York *(G-9288)*
Demos Medical Publishing LLC .... F 516 889-1791
New York *(G-9897)*
Direct Mktg Edctl Fndation Inc .... G 212 790-1512
New York *(G-9933)*
Elmont North Little League .... G 516 775-8210
Elmont *(G-4731)*
Hatherleigh Company Ltd .... G 607 538-1092
Hobart *(G-6451)*
Humana Press Inc .... E 212 460-1500
New York *(G-10577)*
International Data Group Inc .... E 212 331-7883
New York *(G-10674)*
Japan America Learning Ctr Inc .... F 914 723-7600
Scarsdale *(G-15248)*
Luria Communications Inc .... G 631 329-4922
East Hampton *(G-4433)*
Mary Ann Liebert Inc .... D 914 740-2100
New Rochelle *(G-8962)*
McMahon Group LLC .... D 212 957-5300
New York *(G-11227)*
NCM Publishers Inc .... G 212 691-9100
New York *(G-11385)*
Public Relations Soc Amer Inc .... E 212 460-1400
New York *(G-11767)*
Pwxyz LLC .... G 212 377-5500
New York *(G-11785)*
Relx Inc .... E 212 309-8100
New York *(G-11858)*
Security Letter .... F 212 348-1553
New York *(G-12034)*
Springer Adis Us LLC .... F 212 460-1500
New York *(G-12195)*
Springer Publishing Co LLC .... E 212 431-4370
New York *(G-12198)*
Springer Scnce + Bus Media LLC .... D 781 871-6600
New York *(G-12199)*
Thomas International Pubg Co .... F 212 613-3441
New York *(G-12341)*
Thomas Publishing Company LLC ... B 212 695-0500
New York *(G-12342)*
Westchester Law Journal Inc .... G 914 948-0715
White Plains *(G-17211)*

Employee Codes: A=Over 500 employees, B=251-500
C=101-250, D=51-100, E=20-50, F=10-19, G=5-9

PUBLISHING & BROADCASTING: Internet Only

PUBLISHING & BROADCASTING: Internet Only

Ai Media Group Inc ....F....... 212 660-2400
  New York *(G-9114)*
Aleteia Usa Inc ....G....... 914 502-1855
  Yonkers *(G-17426)*
Bdg Media Inc ....E....... 917 951-9768
  New York *(G-9386)*
Bright Line Eting Slutions LLC ....E....... 585 245-2956
  Pittsford *(G-13585)*
Byliner Inc ....E....... 415 680-3608
  New York *(G-9541)*
Classpass Inc ....E....... 888 493-5953
  New York *(G-9693)*
East Meet East Inc ....G....... 646 481-0033
  New York *(G-10015)*
Elite Daily Inc ....B....... 212 402-9097
  New York *(G-10059)*
Entrainant Inc ....G....... 212 946-4724
  New York *(G-10098)*
Epost International Inc ....G....... 212 352-9390
  New York *(G-10103)*
Equityarcade LLC ....G....... 678 232-1301
  Brooklyn *(G-1936)*
Golden Eagle Marketing LLC ....G....... 212 726-1242
  New York *(G-10372)*
Hearst Digital Studios Inc ....E....... 212 969-7552
  New York *(G-10492)*
Ibt Media Inc ....E....... 646 867-7100
  New York *(G-10594)*
Infinitlink Corporation ....G....... 934 777-0180
  West Babylon *(G-16822)*
Media Trust LLC ....G....... 212 802-1162
  New York *(G-11236)*
Medical Daily Inc ....E....... 646 867-7100
  New York *(G-11239)*
Mindbodygreen LLC ....E....... 347 529-6952
  Brooklyn *(G-2321)*
Narratively Inc ....E....... 203 536-0332
  Brooklyn *(G-2356)*
Nimbletv Inc ....F....... 646 502-7010
  New York *(G-11451)*
Panoply Media LLC ....E....... 646 382-5423
  Brooklyn *(G-2416)*
Playlife LLC ....E....... 646 207-9082
  New York *(G-11696)*
Qworldstar Inc ....G....... 212 768-4500
  New York *(G-11805)*
Renegade Nation Online LLC ....G....... 212 868-9000
  New York *(G-11866)*
Riot New Media Group Inc ....G....... 604 700-4896
  Brooklyn *(G-2515)*
Sagelife Parenting LLC ....G....... 315 299-5713
  Syracuse *(G-16052)*
Standard Analytics Io Inc ....G....... 917 882-5422
  New York *(G-12205)*
Statebook LLC ....G....... 845 383-1991
  Kingston *(G-7240)*
Thehuffingtonpostcom Inc ....E....... 212 245-7844
  New York *(G-12332)*
Total Webcasting Inc ....G....... 845 883-0909
  New Paltz *(G-8924)*
Trading Edge Ltd ....G....... 347 699-7079
  Ridgewood *(G-14141)*
Vidbolt Inc ....G....... 716 560-8944
  Buffalo *(G-3268)*
Vinous Group LLC ....G....... 917 275-5184
  New York *(G-12571)*
Zazoom LLC ....F....... 212 321-2100
  New York *(G-12726)*

PUBLISHING & PRINTING: Art Copy

Avalon Copy Centers Amer Inc ....D....... 315 471-3333
  Syracuse *(G-15883)*
Avalon Copy Centers Amer Inc ....E....... 716 995-7777
  Buffalo *(G-2847)*
Color Unlimited Inc ....G....... 212 802-7547
  New York *(G-9731)*
Soho Editions Inc ....E....... 914 591-5100
  Mohegan Lake *(G-8580)*

PUBLISHING & PRINTING: Book Clubs

Christian Book Publishing ....E....... 646 559-2533
  New York *(G-9659)*
Dreams To Print ....G....... 718 483-8020
  Brooklyn *(G-1881)*
National Learning Corp ....F....... 516 921-8888
  Syosset *(G-15850)*

PUBLISHING & PRINTING: Book Music

Ai Entertainment Holdings LLC ....F....... 212 247-6400
  New York *(G-9113)*
Alfred Publishing Co Inc ....D....... 315 736-1572
  Oriskany *(G-13328)*
Faces Magazine Inc ....D....... 845 454-7420
  Poughkeepsie *(G-13919)*
Kobalt Music Pubg Amer Inc ....D....... 212 247-6204
  New York *(G-10903)*

PUBLISHING & PRINTING: Books

450 Ridge St Inc ....G....... 716 754-2789
  Lewiston *(G-7453)*
Adir Publishing Co ....F....... 718 633-9437
  Brooklyn *(G-1561)*
Apollo Investment Fund VII LP ....G....... 212 515-3200
  New York *(G-9227)*
Bertelsmann Inc ....E....... 212 782-1000
  New York *(G-9417)*
Booklyn Artists Alliance ....G....... 718 383-9621
  Brooklyn *(G-1709)*
Callaway Arts & Entrmt Inc ....F....... 646 465-4667
  New York *(G-9553)*
Crabtree Publishing Inc ....E....... 212 496-5040
  New York *(G-9802)*
D C I Technical Inc ....F....... 516 355-0464
  Franklin Square *(G-5372)*
H W Wilson Company Inc ....B....... 718 588-8635
  Bronx *(G-1352)*
Interntnl Publcatns Media Grup ....E....... 917 604-9602
  New York *(G-10682)*
James Morgan Publishing ....G....... 212 655-5470
  New York *(G-10737)*
Klutz ....E....... 650 687-2600
  New York *(G-10898)*
Library Tales Publishing Inc ....G....... 347 394-2629
  New York *(G-11018)*
Metro Creative Graphics Inc ....E....... 212 947-5100
  New York *(G-11268)*
Multi Packaging Solutions Inc ....G....... 646 885-0005
  New York *(G-11347)*
Nationwide Custom Services ....G....... 845 365-0414
  Tappan *(G-16105)*
Natural E Creative LLC ....F....... 516 488-1143
  New Hyde Park *(G-8895)*
News India USA Inc ....G....... 212 675-7515
  New York *(G-11437)*
Pearson Inc ....D....... 212 641-2400
  New York *(G-11610)*
Pearson Longman LLC ....C....... 917 981-2200
  New York *(G-11611)*
Pearson Longman LLC ....E....... 212 641-2400
  White Plains *(G-17174)*
Samuel French Inc ....E....... 212 206-8990
  New York *(G-11980)*
T G S Inc ....E....... 516 629-6905
  Locust Valley *(G-7664)*
Windows Media Publishing LLC ....E....... 917 732-7892
  Brooklyn *(G-2775)*

PUBLISHING & PRINTING: Catalogs

Global Video LLC ....D....... 516 222-2600
  Woodbury *(G-17310)*
Gooding & Associates Inc ....F....... 631 749-3313
  Shelter Island *(G-15409)*
Mexico Independent Inc ....G....... 315 963-3763
  Watertown *(G-16687)*
Sentinel Printing Services Inc ....D....... 845 562-1218
  New Windsor *(G-9000)*
Thomas Publishing Company LLC ....D....... 212 695-0500
  New York *(G-12343)*

PUBLISHING & PRINTING: Comic Books

Medikidz Usa Inc ....G....... 646 895-9319
  New York *(G-11242)*

PUBLISHING & PRINTING: Directories, NEC

Hibu Inc ....C....... 516 730-1900
  East Meadow *(G-4445)*
Want-Ad Digest Inc ....F....... 518 279-1181
  Troy *(G-16287)*

PUBLISHING & PRINTING: Guides

Gametime Media Inc ....G....... 212 860-2090
  New York *(G-10293)*
Open-Xchange Inc ....F....... 914 332-5720
  Tarrytown *(G-16124)*

PUBLISHING & PRINTING: Magazines: publishing & printing

Advance Magazine Publs Inc ....A....... 212 286-2860
  New York *(G-9085)*
Advance Magazine Publs Inc ....D....... 212 790-4422
  New York *(G-9086)*
Advance Magazine Publs Inc ....D....... 212 697-0126
  New York *(G-9089)*
Advance Publications Inc ....D....... 718 981-1234
  Staten Island *(G-15653)*
Alpha Media Group Inc ....B....... 212 302-2626
  New York *(G-9150)*
American Graphic Design Awards ......G....... 212 696-4380
  New York *(G-9167)*
American Intl Media LLC ....F....... 845 359-4225
  White Plains *(G-17105)*
American Jewish Congress Inc ....E....... 212 879-4500
  New York *(G-9172)*
Artnews Ltd ....F....... 212 398-1690
  New York *(G-9274)*
Aspire One Communications LLC ......F....... 201 281-2998
  Cornwall *(G-4007)*
Bazaar ....G....... 212 903-5497
  New York *(G-9385)*
Bertelsmann Inc ....E....... 212 782-1000
  New York *(G-9417)*
Blackbook Media Corp ....E....... 212 334-1800
  New York *(G-9461)*
Bondi Digital Publishing LLC ....G....... 212 405-1655
  New York *(G-9485)*
Boy Scouts of America ....G....... 212 532-0985
  New York *(G-9498)*
Bullett Media LLC ....F....... 212 242-2123
  New York *(G-9530)*
Bz Media LLC ....F....... 631 421-4158
  Melville *(G-8330)*
Capco Marketing ....F....... 315 699-1687
  Baldwinsville *(G-567)*
City and State Ny LLC ....E....... 212 268-0442
  New York *(G-9680)*
City Real Estate Book Inc ....G....... 516 593-2949
  Valley Stream *(G-16428)*
Civil Svc Rtred Employees Assn ....F....... 718 937-0290
  Long Island City *(G-7727)*
Clarion Publications Inc ....F....... 585 243-3530
  Geneseo *(G-5579)*
CMX Media LLC ....E....... 917 793-5831
  New York *(G-9706)*
Commentary Inc ....F....... 212 891-1400
  New York *(G-9744)*
Conde Nast International Inc ....D....... 212 286-2860
  New York *(G-9758)*
Convenience Store News ....G....... 214 217-7800
  New York *(G-9774)*
Credit Union Journal Inc ....G....... 212 803-8200
  New York *(G-9811)*
Davler Media Group LLC ....E....... 212 315-0800
  New York *(G-9886)*
Distinction Magazine Inc ....E....... 631 843-3522
  Melville *(G-8341)*
Dow Jones & Company Inc ....B....... 609 627-2999
  New York *(G-9965)*
Ebner Publishing International ....G....... 646 742-0740
  New York *(G-10025)*
Elite Traveler LLC ....F....... 646 430-7900
  New York *(G-10061)*
Equal Opprtnity Pblcations Inc ....F....... 631 421-9421
  Melville *(G-8344)*
Essential Publications US LLC ....G....... 646 707-0898
  New York *(G-10117)*
Excelsior Publications ....G....... 607 746-7600
  Delhi *(G-4263)*
Green Apple Courage Inc ....G....... 716 614-4673
  Buffalo *(G-2999)*
Hearst Corporation ....E....... 212 903-5366
  New York *(G-10484)*
Hearst Corporation ....D....... 212 903-5000
  New York *(G-10490)*
Hello and Hola Media Inc ....E....... 212 807-4795
  Brooklyn *(G-2071)*
Homesell Inc ....F....... 718 514-0346
  Staten Island *(G-15705)*
Icarus Enterprises Inc ....G....... 917 969-4461
  New York *(G-10596)*
Index Magazine ....G....... 212 243-1428
  New York *(G-10630)*
Intercultural Alliance Artists ....G....... 917 406-1202
  Flushing *(G-5261)*
Jobson Medical Information LLC ....C....... 212 274-7000
  New York *(G-10784)*

PRODUCT SECTION

PUBLISHING & PRINTING: Newspapers

Kbs Communications LLC ....F 212 765-7124
New York *(G-10864)*
L Magazine LLC ....F 212 807-1254
Brooklyn *(G-2186)*
Latino Show Magazine Inc ....G 718 709-1151
Woodhaven *(G-17325)*
Livid Magazine ....F 929 340-7123
Brooklyn *(G-2234)*
Ltb Media (usa) Inc ....D 212 447-9555
Southampton *(G-15570)*
Luminary Publishing Inc ....F 845 334-8600
Kingston *(G-7228)*
M Shanken Communications Inc .....C 212 684-4224
New York *(G-11106)*
Marie Claire USA ....D 212 841-8493
New York *(G-11173)*
Meredith Corporation ....C 212 557-6600
New York *(G-11254)*
Meredith Corporation ....D 515 284-2157
New York *(G-11256)*
Metrosource Publishing Inc ....F 212 691-5127
New York *(G-11269)*
Mishpacha Magazine Inc ....G 718 686-9339
Brooklyn *(G-2323)*
New Hope Media LLC ....G 646 366-0830
New York *(G-11411)*
Niche Media Holdings LLc ....E 702 990-2500
New York *(G-11443)*
Northside Media Group LLC ....F 917 318-6513
Brooklyn *(G-2385)*
Northside Media Group LLC ....E 917 318-6513
Brooklyn *(G-2386)*
Odyssey Mag Pubg Group Inc ....E 212 545-4800
New York *(G-11511)*
Pensions & Investments ....E 212 210-0763
New York *(G-11626)*
Penton Media Inc ....G 212 204-4200
New York *(G-11628)*
Ragozin Data ....E 212 674-3123
Long Island City *(G-7886)*
Redbook Magazine ....F 212 649-3331
New York *(G-11845)*
Rnd Enterprises Inc ....G 212 627-0165
New York *(G-11907)*
Rodale Inc ....B 212 697-2040
New York *(G-11921)*
Romantic Times Inc ....F 718 237-1097
Brooklyn *(G-2524)*
Ross Communications Associates ....F 631 393-5089
Melville *(G-8381)*
Securities Data Publishing Inc ....G 212 631-1411
New York *(G-12033)*
Source Media LLC ....C 212 803-8200
New York *(G-12168)*
Stuff Magazine ....G 212 302-2626
New York *(G-12244)*
Summit Professional Networks ....D 212 557-7480
New York *(G-12256)*
T V Trade Media Inc ....F 212 288-3933
New York *(G-12292)*
Thomas Publishing Company LLC ..G 212 695-0500
New York *(G-12345)*
Time Inc ....E 212 522-1212
New York *(G-12362)*
Towse Publishing Co ....F 914 235-3095
New Rochelle *(G-8971)*
Trans-High Corporation ....E 212 387-0500
New York *(G-12412)*
TV Guide Magazine LLC ....G 800 866-1400
New York *(G-12448)*
Ubm LLC ....F 516 562-5000
New York *(G-12459)*
Universal Cmmncations of Miami ....C 212 986-5100
New York *(G-12489)*
Uptown Media Group LLC ....E 212 360-5073
New York *(G-12496)*
Urbandaddy Inc ....F 212 929-7905
New York *(G-12502)*
US News & World Report Inc ....C 212 716-6800
New York *(G-12509)*
Valassis Communications Inc ....G 585 627-4456
Rochester *(G-14778)*
Vanity Fair ....F 212 286-6052
New York *(G-12524)*
Wall Street Reporter Magazine ....D 212 363-2600
New York *(G-12609)*
Watch Journal Inc ....G 212 229-1500
New York *(G-12621)*
Wenner Media LLC ....B 212 484-1616
New York *(G-12639)*

World Business Media LLC ....F 212 344-0759
Massapequa Park *(G-8224)*

PUBLISHING & PRINTING: Music, Book

Alley Music Corp ....E 212 779-7977
New York *(G-9137)*
Atlas Music Publishing LLC ....G 646 502-5170
New York *(G-9307)*
Finger Lakes Massage Group ....F 607 272-9024
Ithaca *(G-6877)*
Johnny Bienstock Music ....E 212 779-7977
New York *(G-10794)*
Princess Music Publishing Co ....E 212 586-0240
New York *(G-11734)*
Spirit Music Group Inc ....E 212 533-7672
New York *(G-12188)*
Universal Edition Inc ....D 917 213-2177
New York *(G-12490)*
Wmg Acquisition Corp ....F 212 275-2000
New York *(G-12676)*
Wmg Holding Company Inc ....A 212 275-2000
New York *(G-12677)*

PUBLISHING & PRINTING: Newsletters, Business Svc

An Group Inc ....G 631 549-4090
Melville *(G-8328)*
Answer Printing Inc ....F 212 922-2922
New York *(G-9216)*
Ceo Cast Inc ....F 212 732-4300
New York *(G-9621)*
Church Bulletin Inc ....F 631 249-4994
West Babylon *(G-16809)*
Froebe Group LLC ....G 646 649-2150
New York *(G-10261)*
Portfolio Media Inc ....C 646 783-7100
New York *(G-11708)*
Scholastic Inc ....D 212 343-7100
New York *(G-12018)*
Shop Smart Central Inc ....G 914 962-3871
Yorktown Heights *(G-17535)*
Ubm Inc ....A 212 600-3000
New York *(G-12458)*

PUBLISHING & PRINTING: Newspapers

Advance Publications Inc ....D 718 981-1234
Staten Island *(G-15653)*
All Island Media Inc ....C 631 698-8400
Edgewood *(G-4606)*
All Island Media Inc ....E 516 942-8400
Hicksville *(G-6343)*
American Sports Media ....G 585 924-4250
Victor *(G-16484)*
AR Publishing Company Inc ....F 212 482-0303
New York *(G-9239)*
Asahi Shimbun America Inc ....F 212 398-0257
New York *(G-9278)*
Beth Kobliner Company LLC ....G 212 501-8407
New York *(G-9423)*
Bornomala USA Inc ....G 347 753-2355
Jackson Heights *(G-6921)*
Bradford Publications Inc ....C 716 373-2500
Olean *(G-13157)*
Brasilans Press Pblcations Inc ....E 212 764-6161
New York *(G-9507)*
Buffalo News Inc ....A 716 849-4401
Buffalo *(G-2879)*
Capital Region Wkly Newspapers ...E 518 877-7160
Albany *(G-58)*
Chester West County Press ....G 914 684-0006
Mount Vernon *(G-8716)*
Christian Press Inc ....G 718 886-4400
Flushing *(G-5240)*
City Newspaper ....G 585 244-3329
Rochester *(G-14297)*
Colors Fashion Inc ....F 212 629-0401
New York *(G-9733)*
Community Newsppr Holdings Inc ..E 585 798-1400
Medina *(G-8302)*
Copia Interactive LLC ....F 212 481-0520
New York *(G-9779)*
Daily Gazette Company ....B 518 374-4141
Schenectady *(G-15274)*
Daily Gazette Company ....C 518 395-3060
Schenectady *(G-15275)*
Daily Mail & Greene Cnty News .....F 518 943-2100
Catskill *(G-3455)*
Daily Racing Form LLC ....F 212 514-2180
New York *(G-9847)*

Daily Record ....F 585 232-2035
Rochester *(G-14320)*
Daily World Press Inc ....F 212 922-9201
New York *(G-9848)*
Der Blatt Inc ....F 845 783-1148
Monroe *(G-8588)*
Document Journal Inc ....G 646 586-3099
New York *(G-9946)*
DOT Publishing ....F 315 593-2510
Fulton *(G-5470)*
Dow Jones & Company Inc ....E 212 597-5983
New York *(G-9966)*
East Hampton Star Inc ....E 631 324-0002
East Hampton *(G-4429)*
El Aguila ....G 212 410-2450
New York *(G-10045)*
Epoch Times International Inc ....G 212 239-2808
New York *(G-10102)*
Event Journal Inc ....G 516 470-1811
Bethpage *(G-866)*
Evercore Partners Svcs E LLC ....A 212 857-3100
New York *(G-10144)*
Exhibits & More ....G 585 924-4040
Victor *(G-16500)*
Firefighters Journal ....E 718 391-0283
Long Island City *(G-7770)*
First Choice News Inc ....G 212 477-2044
New York *(G-10218)*
Francepress LLC ....G 646 202-9828
New York *(G-10247)*
Fredonia Pennysaver Inc ....G 716 679-1509
Fredonia *(G-5382)*
Gannett Co Inc ....G 516 484-7510
Port Washington *(G-13840)*
Gannett Co Inc ....D 585 232-7100
Rochester *(G-14408)*
Gannett Stllite Info Ntwrk Inc ....D 585 798-1400
Medina *(G-8305)*
Gannett Stllite Info Ntwrk LLC ....C 845 454-2000
Poughkeepsie *(G-13920)*
Gatehouse Media LLC ....G 585 598-0030
Pittsford *(G-13589)*
Gatehouse Media LLC ....F 315 866-2220
Herkimer *(G-6325)*
Gatehouse Media MO Holdings .....G 530 846-3661
Pittsford *(G-13590)*
Glens Falls Newspapers Inc ....G 518 792-3131
Glens Falls *(G-5696)*
Guidance Group Inc ....F 631 756-4618
Melville *(G-8354)*
Hearst Business Media Corp ....F 631 650-4441
Great River *(G-5870)*
Hearst Communications Inc ....A 415 777-7825
New York *(G-10480)*
Hearst Corporation ....A 212 649-2000
New York *(G-10482)*
Hearst Corporation ....E 212 649-2275
New York *(G-10491)*
Herald Press Inc ....G 718 784-5255
Long Island City *(G-7787)*
Herald Publishing Company LLC ...G 315 470-2022
New York *(G-10503)*
High Ridge News LLC ....G 718 548-7412
Bronx *(G-1359)*
Home Reporter Inc ....E 718 238-6600
Brooklyn *(G-2081)*
Hudson News Inc ....G 212 971-6800
New York *(G-10570)*
IMG The Daily ....G 212 541-5640
New York *(G-10618)*
Investment News ....E 212 210-0100
New York *(G-10692)*
Investors Business Daily Inc ....G 212 626-7676
New York *(G-10693)*
Johnson Acquisition Corp ....F 518 828-1616
Hudson *(G-6652)*
Journal News ....G 914 694-5000
White Plains *(G-17155)*
Journal Register Company ....E 212 257-7212
New York *(G-10809)*
Kch Publications Inc ....E 516 671-2360
Glen Cove *(G-5632)*
Korea Central Daily News Inc ....D 718 361-7700
Long Island City *(G-7810)*
Lee Publications Inc ....D 518 673-3237
Palatine Bridge *(G-13422)*
LI Community Newspapers Inc .....G 516 747-8282
Mineola *(G-8553)*
Litmor Publishing Corp ....F 516 931-0012
Garden City *(G-5527)*

Employee Codes: A=Over 500 employees, B=251-500
C=101-250, D=51-100, E=20-50, F=10-19, G=5-9

PUBLISHING & PRINTING: Newspapers

Livingston County News .... G 585 243-1234
  Geneseo *(G-5581)*
Local Media Group Inc .... B 845 341-1100
  Middletown *(G-8480)*
Local Media Group Inc .... F 845 794-3712
  Monticello *(G-8643)*
Long Island Cmnty Nwsppers Inc ... D 516 482-4490
  Mineola *(G-8555)*
Long Island Cmnty Nwsppers Inc ... F 631 427-7000
  Huntington *(G-6703)*
Louis Vuitton North Amer Inc .... G 212 644-2574
  New York *(G-11079)*
Lowville Newspaper Corporation ..... G 315 376-3525
  Lowville *(G-7967)*
Made Fresh Daily .... G 212 285-2253
  New York *(G-11119)*
Main Street Connect LLC .... F 203 803-4110
  Armonk *(G-415)*
Markets Media LLC .... G 646 442-4646
  New York *(G-11185)*
Melmont Fine Pringng/Graphics ..... G 516 939-2253
  Bethpage *(G-872)*
Mid-York Press Inc .... D 607 674-4491
  Sherburne *(G-15415)*
Ming Pao (new York) Inc .... F 212 334-2220
  New York *(G-11303)*
Ming Pao (new York) Inc .... D 718 786-2888
  Long Island City *(G-7844)*
Minority Reporter Inc .... G 585 225-3628
  Rochester *(G-14535)*
Moneypaper Inc .... F 914 925-0022
  Rye *(G-15090)*
Neighbor Newspapers .... G 631 226-2636
  Farmingdale *(G-5072)*
New Living Inc .... G 631 751-8819
  Patchogue *(G-13454)*
New Media Investment Group Inc ... B 212 479-3160
  New York *(G-11412)*
New York Daily News .... G 212 248-2100
  New York *(G-11419)*
New York Press Inc .... E 212 268-8600
  New York *(G-11425)*
New York Times Company .... B 212 556-1234
  New York *(G-11429)*
New York Times Company .... F 718 281-7000
  Flushing *(G-5280)*
New York University .... E 212 998-4300
  New York *(G-11431)*
New York1 News Operations .... F 212 379-3311
  New York *(G-11432)*
News India Usa LLC .... G 212 675-7515
  New York *(G-11436)*
News India USA Inc .... F 212 675-7515
  New York *(G-11437)*
News of The Highlands Inc .... F 845 534-7771
  Cornwall *(G-4011)*
Newsday LLC .... B 631 843-4050
  Melville *(G-8370)*
Newsday LLC .... C 631 843-3135
  Melville *(G-8371)*
Newspaper Times Union .... F 518 454-5676
  Albany *(G-108)*
Nikkei America Inc .... E 212 261-6200
  New York *(G-11450)*
Nyt Capital LLC .... F 212 556-1234
  New York *(G-11503)*
Observer .... G 347 915-5638
  Brooklyn *(G-2397)*
Outlook Newspaper .... E 845 356-6261
  Suffern *(G-15817)*
Owego Pennysaver Press Inc .... F 607 687-2434
  Owego *(G-13383)*
Pearson Longman LLC .... E 212 641-2400
  White Plains *(G-17174)*
Pennysaver Group Inc .... F 914 966-1400
  Yonkers *(G-17495)*
Post Journal .... F 716 487-1111
  Jamestown *(G-7056)*
Prospect News .... F 212 374-2800
  New York *(G-11760)*
R W Publications Div of Wtrhs .... E 716 714-5620
  Elma *(G-4666)*
R W Publications Div of Wtrhs .... E 716 714-5620
  Elma *(G-4667)*
Record .... G 518 270-1200
  Saratoga Springs *(G-15199)*
Record Review LLC .... F 914 244-0533
  Katonah *(G-7162)*
Ridgewood Times Prtg & Pubg .... E 718 821-7500
  Ridgewood *(G-14134)*

Right World View .... E 914 406-2994
  Purchase *(G-13987)*
Ruby Newco LLC .... G 212 852-7000
  New York *(G-11951)*
S G New York LLC .... F 631 698-8400
  Edgewood *(G-4623)*
S G New York LLC .... E 631 665-4000
  Bohemia *(G-1124)*
Second Amendment Foundation ..... G 716 885-6408
  Buffalo *(G-3209)*
Seneca County Area Shopper .... G 607 532-4333
  Ovid *(G-13372)*
Service Advertising Group Inc .... F 718 361-6161
  Long Island City *(G-7904)*
Shelter Island Reporter Inc .... G 631 749-1000
  Shelter Island *(G-15410)*
Sing Tao Newspapers NY Ltd .... E 718 821-0123
  Brooklyn *(G-2593)*
Spartan Publishing Inc .... F 716 664-7373
  Jamestown *(G-7061)*
Sports Pblications Prod NY LLC ..... D 212 366-7700
  New York *(G-12191)*
Sports Reporter Inc .... E 212 737-2750
  New York *(G-12193)*
Ssrja LLC .... F 718 725-7020
  Jamaica *(G-6987)*
St Lawrence County Newspapers ... D 315 393-1003
  Ogdensburg *(G-13143)*
Star Community Publishing .... C 631 843-4050
  Melville *(G-8384)*
Straus Communications .... E 845 782-4000
  Chester *(G-3643)*
The Earth Times Foundation .... E 718 297-0488
  Brooklyn *(G-2676)*
Tri-Town News Inc .... E 607 561-3515
  Sidney *(G-15464)*
Tribune Entertainment Co Del .... E 203 866-2204
  New York *(G-12425)*
Trilake Three Press Corp .... G 518 359-2462
  Tupper Lake *(G-16304)*
Ulster County Press Office .... G 845 687-4480
  High Falls *(G-6429)*
Unified Media Inc .... F 917 595-2710
  New York *(G-12471)*
Vnovom Svete .... G 212 302-9480
  New York *(G-12588)*
Vpj Publication Inc .... E 718 845-3221
  Howard Beach *(G-6628)*
W M T Publications Inc .... F 585 244-3329
  Rochester *(G-14783)*
Wayuga Community Newspapers ... E 315 754-6229
  Red Creek *(G-14040)*
Wayuga Community Newspapers ... G 315 594-2506
  Wolcott *(G-17302)*
Weisbeck Publishing Printing .... G 716 937-9226
  Alden *(G-189)*
West Publishing Corporation .... E 212 922-1920
  New York *(G-12642)*
William B Collins Company .... D 518 773-8272
  Gloversville *(G-5744)*
Williamsburg Bulletin .... E 718 387-0123
  Brooklyn *(G-2771)*
World Journal LLC .... F 718 871-5000
  Brooklyn *(G-2781)*
Yoga In Daily Life - NY Inc .... G 718 539-8548
  College Point *(G-3837)*

PUBLISHING & PRINTING: Pamphlets

Newkirk Products Inc .... C 518 862-3200
  Albany *(G-107)*

PUBLISHING & PRINTING: Patterns, Paper

Anglo II Ltd .... G 212 563-4980
  New York *(G-9208)*
Royalty Network Inc .... G 212 967-4300
  New York *(G-11946)*

PUBLISHING & PRINTING: Periodical Statistical Reports

Infinitlink Corporation .... G 934 777-0180
  West Babylon *(G-16822)*

PUBLISHING & PRINTING: Posters

Enhance A Colour Corp .... E 212 490-3620
  New York *(G-10093)*
Kjckd Inc .... G 518 435-9696
  Latham *(G-7395)*

PUBLISHING & PRINTING: Shopping News

Adirondack Pennysaver Inc .... E 518 563-0100
  Plattsburgh *(G-13678)*
Badoud Communications Inc .... C 315 472-7821
  Syracuse *(G-15886)*
City of New York .... E 718 965-8787
  Brooklyn *(G-1781)*
Rheinwald Printing Co Inc .... F 585 637-5100
  Brockport *(G-1246)*
S G New York LLC .... E 631 665-4000
  Bohemia *(G-1124)*
Salamanca Press Penny Saver .... E 716 945-1500
  Salamanca *(G-15132)*
Tenney Media Group .... D 315 853-5569
  Clinton *(G-3747)*

PUBLISHING & PRINTING: Technical Manuals

Dohnsco Inc .... G 516 773-4800
  Manhasset *(G-8092)*
Service Education Incorporated ...... G 585 264-9240
  Victor *(G-16526)*

PUBLISHING & PRINTING: Textbooks

Bright Kids Nyc Inc .... E 917 539-4575
  New York *(G-9512)*
Codesters Inc .... G 646 232-1025
  New York *(G-9723)*
Iat Interactive LLC .... E 914 273-2233
  Mount Kisco *(G-8670)*
McGraw-Hill Glbl Edctn Hldngs ...... D 646 766-2000
  New York *(G-11223)*
Pearson Education Holdings Inc ..... A 201 236-6716
  New York *(G-11609)*
Peri-Facts Academy .... G 585 275-6037
  Rochester *(G-14597)*
Petersons Nelnet LLC .... C 609 896-1800
  Albany *(G-118)*
Warodean Corporation .... G 718 359-5559
  Flushing *(G-5312)*

PUBLISHING & PRINTING: Trade Journals

Beer Marketers Insights Inc .... G 845 507-0040
  Suffern *(G-15808)*
Forum Publishing Co .... G 631 754-5000
  Centerport *(G-3501)*
Guilford Publications Inc .... D 212 431-9800
  New York *(G-10425)*
H F W Communications Inc .... F 315 703-7979
  East Syracuse *(G-4548)*
Hotelinteractive Inc .... F 631 424-7755
  Smithtown *(G-15510)*
Institute of Electrical and El .... E 212 705-8900
  New York *(G-10655)*
Lockwood Trade Journal Co Inc .... E 212 391-2060
  Long Island City *(G-7821)*
Med Reviews LLC .... E 212 239-5860
  New York *(G-11232)*
Strathmore Directories Ltd .... E 516 997-2525
  Westbury *(G-17056)*

PUBLISHING & PRINTING: Yearbooks

Herff Jones LLC .... E 607 936-2366
  Corning *(G-3994)*
Visant Secondary Holdings Corp ... E 914 595-8200
  Armonk *(G-420)*

PULP MILLS

APC Paper Company Inc .... D 315 384-4225
  Norfolk *(G-12914)*
Cenibra Inc .... G 212 818-8242
  New York *(G-9612)*
Central Nat Pulp & Ppr Sls Inc .... A 914 696-9000
  Purchase *(G-13971)*
International Paper Company .... C 607 775-1550
  Conklin *(G-3894)*
ITT Engineered Valves LLC .... E 662 257-6982
  Seneca Falls *(G-15384)*
ITT Industries Holdings Inc .... G 914 641-2000
  White Plains *(G-17153)*
Parsons & Whittemore Inc .... E 914 937-9009
  Port Chester *(G-13780)*
Parsons Whittemore Entps Corp .... E 914 937-9009
  Port Chester *(G-13781)*

PRODUCT SECTION

PULP MILLS: Mech Pulp, Incl Groundwood & Thermomechanical

Norton Pulpstones Incorporated ....G...... 716 433-9400
  Lockport *(G-7638)*

PULP MILLS: Mechanical & Recycling Processing

Advanced Recovery & Recycl LLC ....F 315 450-3301
  Baldwinsville *(G-565)*
Hamlin Bottle & Can Return Inc.............G...... 585 259-1301
  Brockport *(G-1244)*
Suffolk Indus Recovery Corp................D...... 631 732-6403
  Coram *(G-3974)*

PULP MILLS: Soda Pulp

R D S Mountain View Trucking ....G...... 315 823-4265
  Little Falls *(G-7524)*

PUMICE

A&B Conservation LLC ....G...... 845 282-7272
  Monsey *(G-8601)*

PUMP GOVERNORS: Gas Machines

Dormitory Authority - State NY ....G...... 631 434-1487
  Brentwood *(G-1179)*

PUMPS

Air Flow Pump Corp ....G...... 718 241-2800
  Brooklyn *(G-1570)*
Air Techniques Inc ....B...... 516 433-7676
  Melville *(G-8324)*
American Ship Repairs Company ....F 718 435-5570
  Brooklyn *(G-1607)*
Armstrong Pumps Inc ....D...... 716 693-8813
  North Tonawanda *(G-12973)*
Buffalo Pumps Inc ....C...... 716 693-1850
  North Tonawanda *(G-12981)*
Curaegis Technologies Inc ....E...... 585 254-1100
  Rochester *(G-14316)*
Daikin Applied Americas Inc ....D...... 315 253-2771
  Auburn *(G-490)*
Federal Pump Corporation ....E...... 718 451-2000
  Brooklyn *(G-1967)*
Fisonic Corp ....F 716 763-0295
  New York *(G-10227)*
Fluid Handling LLC ....G...... 716 897-2800
  Cheektowaga *(G-3600)*
Gardner Dnver Oberdorfer Pumps ....E...... 315 437-0361
  Syracuse *(G-15969)*
Goulds Pumps Incorporated ....B...... 315 258-4949
  Auburn *(G-497)*
Goulds Pumps LLC ....A...... 315 568-2811
  Seneca Falls *(G-15382)*
ITT Corporation ....D...... 315 568-2811
  Seneca Falls *(G-15383)*
ITT Goulds Pumps Inc ....A...... 914 641-2129
  Seneca Falls *(G-15385)*
ITT Water Technology Inc....................B...... 315 568-2811
  Seneca Falls *(G-15388)*
John N Fehlinger Co Inc ....F 212 233-5656
  New York *(G-10791)*
Ketcham Pump Co Inc ....F 718 457-0800
  Woodside *(G-17351)*
Lanco Manufacturing Co ....G...... 516 292-8953
  West Hempstead *(G-16890)*
Linde LLC ....D...... 716 773-7552
  Grand Island *(G-5776)*
Mannesmann Corporation ....D...... 212 258-4000
  New York *(G-11160)*
McWane Inc ....B...... 607 734-2211
  Elmira *(G-4708)*
Oberdorfer Pumps Inc ....E...... 315 437-0361
  Syracuse *(G-16021)*
Oyster Bay Pump Works Inc ....F 516 933-4500
  Hicksville *(G-6406)*
Pulsafeeder Inc ....C...... 585 292-8000
  Rochester *(G-14632)*
Sihi Pumps Inc ....E...... 716 773-6450
  Grand Island *(G-5784)*
Voss Usa Inc ....C...... 212 995-2255
  New York *(G-12596)*
Wastecorp Pumps LLC ....F 888 829-2783
  New York *(G-12620)*
Westmoor Ltd ....F 315 363-1500
  Sherrill *(G-15433)*
Xylem Inc ....F 716 862-4123
  Seneca Falls *(G-15396)*
Xylem Inc ....C...... 315 258-4949
  Auburn *(G-527)*
Xylem Inc ....D...... 315 239-2499
  Seneca Falls *(G-15397)*
Xylem Inc ....B...... 914 323-5700
  Rye Brook *(G-15102)*

PUMPS & PARTS: Indl

Century-Tech Inc ....F 718 326-9400
  Hempstead *(G-6291)*
Fisonic Corp ....G...... 212 732-3777
  Long Island City *(G-7772)*
Stavo Industries Inc ....F 845 331-4552
  Kingston *(G-7241)*

PUMPS & PUMPING EQPT REPAIR SVCS

A & C/Furia Electric Motors ....F 914 949-0585
  White Plains *(G-17100)*
American Ship Repairs Company ....F 718 435-5570
  Brooklyn *(G-1607)*
Daves Electric Motors & Pumps ....G...... 212 982-2930
  New York *(G-9872)*
Fuel Energy Services USA Ltd ....E...... 607 846-2650
  Horseheads *(G-6607)*
Sunset Ridge Holdings Inc ....F 716 487-1458
  Jamestown *(G-7066)*

PUMPS & PUMPING EQPT WHOLESALERS

Electric Motors and Pumps Inc ....G...... 718 935-9118
  Brooklyn *(G-1912)*
Gny Equipment LLC ....F 631 667-1010
  Bay Shore *(G-701)*

PUMPS, HEAT: Electric

Economy Pump & Motor Repair ....G....... 718 433-2600
  Astoria *(G-436)*

PUMPS: Domestic, Water Or Sump

Flow Control LLC ....C...... 914 323-5700
  Rye Brook *(G-15097)*
Geopump Inc ....G...... 585 798-6666
  Medina *(G-8306)*
Liberty Pumps Inc ....C...... 800 543-2550
  Bergen *(G-848)*
Pentair Water Pool and Spa Inc ....E...... 845 452-5500
  Lagrangeville *(G-7283)*
Trench & Marine Pump Co Inc ....E...... 212 423-9098
  Bronx *(G-1473)*
Water Cooling Corp ....G...... 718 723-6500
  Rosedale *(G-15039)*

PUMPS: Fluid Power

Parker-Hannifin Corporation ....C...... 716 686-6400
  Lancaster *(G-7354)*

PUMPS: Measuring & Dispensing

Aptargroup Inc ....C...... 845 639-3700
  Congers *(G-3876)*
Charles Ross & Son Company ....D...... 631 234-0500
  Hauppauge *(G-6064)*
Economy Pump & Motor Repair ....G....... 718 433-2600
  Astoria *(G-436)*
Pulsafeeder Inc ....C...... 585 292-8000
  Rochester *(G-14632)*
Schlumberger Technology Corp ....C...... 607 378-0105
  Horseheads *(G-6621)*
Valois of America Inc ....C...... 845 639-3700
  Congers *(G-3886)*

PUMPS: Vacuum, Exc Laboratory

Graham Corporation ....B...... 585 343-2216
  Batavia *(G-638)*
Kinequip Inc ....F 716 694-5000
  Buffalo *(G-3049)*
Precision Plus Vacuum Parts ....D...... 716 297-2039
  Sanborn *(G-15152)*

PUNCHES: Forming & Stamping

Arro Manufacturing LLC ....F 716 763-6203
  Lakewood *(G-7310)*
Pivot Punch Corporation ....D...... 716 625-8000
  Lockport *(G-7640)*
Precise Punch Corporation ....F 716 625-8000
  Lockport *(G-7641)*

PURIFICATION & DUST COLLECTION EQPT

Buffalo Bioblower Tech LLC ....G...... 716 625-8618
  Lockport *(G-7601)*
Hilliard Corporation ....B...... 607 733-7121
  Elmira *(G-4703)*
Hilliard Corporation ....F 607 733-7121
  Elmira *(G-4704)*
Low-Cost Mfg Co Inc ....E...... 516 627-3282
  Carle Place *(G-3419)*
Oneida Air Systems Inc ....E...... 315 476-5151
  Syracuse *(G-16025)*

PURSES: Women's

Formart Corp ....F 212 819-1819
  New York *(G-10238)*

PUSHCARTS & WHEELBARROWS

Truxton Corp ....G...... 718 842-6000
  Bronx *(G-1479)*

QUICKLIME

Minerals Technologies Inc ....E...... 212 878-1800
  New York *(G-11302)*

RACE TRACK OPERATION

P S M Group Inc ....E...... 716 532-6686
  Forestville *(G-5342)*

RACEWAYS

Pole Position Raceway ....G...... 716 683-7223
  Cheektowaga *(G-3613)*
Speedzone Inc ....G...... 631 750-1973
  Oakdale *(G-13081)*

RACKS & SHELVING: Household, Wood

American Epoxy and Metal Inc ....G...... 718 828-7828
  Scarsdale *(G-15245)*

RACKS: Display

Eazy Movements ....G...... 716 837-2083
  Buffalo *(G-2945)*

RACKS: Garment, Exc Wood

All Racks Industries Inc ....G...... 212 244-1069
  New York *(G-9135)*
ASAP Rack Rental Inc ....G...... 718 499-4495
  Brooklyn *(G-1640)*
Lifestyle-Trimco ....E...... 718 257-9101
  Brooklyn *(G-2220)*
Millennium Stl Rack Rntals Inc ....G...... 718 965-4736
  Brooklyn *(G-2320)*
Ted-Steel Industries Ltd ....G...... 212 279-3878
  New York *(G-12317)*

RACKS: Garment, Wood

Lifestyle-Trimco ....E...... 718 257-9101
  Brooklyn *(G-2220)*

RACKS: Pallet, Exc Wood

Frazier Industrial Company ....D...... 315 539-9256
  Waterloo *(G-16648)*

RADAR SYSTEMS & EQPT

Artemis Inc ....G...... 631 232-2424
  Hauppauge *(G-6044)*
ITT Corporation ....D...... 315 568-2811
  Seneca Falls *(G-15383)*
ITT Inc ....F 914 641-2000
  White Plains *(G-17152)*
ITT LLC ....B...... 914 641-2000
  White Plains *(G-17154)*
ITT LLC ....A...... 914 641-2000
  Seneca Falls *(G-15387)*
Laufer Wind Group LLC ....F 212 792-3912
  New York *(G-10971)*
Penetradar Corporation ....F 716 731-2629
  Niagara Falls *(G-12877)*
Systems Drs C3 Inc ....B...... 716 631-6200
  Buffalo *(G-3232)*

Employee Codes: A=Over 500 employees, B=251-500
C=101-250, D=51-100, E=20-50, F=10-19, G=5-9

RADAR SYSTEMS & EQPT

Telephonics Corporation ....A....... 631 755-7000
 Farmingdale *(G-5137)*
Traffic Logix Corporation ....G....... 866 915-6459
 Spring Valley *(G-15624)*

RADIATORS, EXC ELECTRIC

Original Convector Specialist ....G....... 718 342-5820
 Brooklyn *(G-2406)*

RADIO & TELEVISION COMMUNICATIONS EQUIPMENT

Actv Inc (del Corp) ....D....... 212 995-9500
 New York *(G-9068)*
Airnet Communications Corp ....F....... 516 338-0008
 Westbury *(G-16991)*
Ashly Audio Inc ....E....... 585 872-0010
 Webster *(G-16737)*
AVI-Spl Employee ....B....... 212 840-4801
 New York *(G-9330)*
Benchmark Media Systems Inc ....F....... 315 437-6300
 Syracuse *(G-15888)*
Chyronhego Corporation ....D....... 631 845-2000
 Melville *(G-8333)*
CJ Component Products LLC ....G....... 631 567-3733
 Oakdale *(G-13074)*
Clever Devices Ltd ....E....... 516 433-6100
 Woodbury *(G-17304)*
Edo LLC ....A....... 631 630-4200
 Amityville *(G-285)*
Electro-Metrics Corporation ....E....... 518 762-2600
 Johnstown *(G-7140)*
Eni Technology Inc ....B....... 585 427-8300
 Rochester *(G-14374)*
Fujitsu Ntwrk Cmmnications Inc ....F....... 845 731-2000
 Pearl River *(G-13479)*
GE Mds LLC ....C....... 585 242-9600
 Rochester *(G-14410)*
Griffon Corporation ....E....... 212 957-5000
 New York *(G-10405)*
Gurley Precision Instrs Inc ....C....... 518 272-6300
 Troy *(G-16259)*
Hand Held Products Inc ....B....... 315 554-6000
 Skaneateles Falls *(G-15490)*
Harris Corporation ....A....... 585 244-5830
 Rochester *(G-14441)*
Harris Corporation ....B....... 585 244-5830
 Rochester *(G-14447)*
Harris Corporation ....F....... 718 767-1100
 Whitestone *(G-17236)*
Harris Corporation ....B....... 585 244-5830
 Rochester *(G-14448)*
Icon Enterprises Intl Inc ....E....... 718 752-9764
 Mohegan Lake *(G-8578)*
It Commodity Sourcing Inc ....G....... 718 677-1577
 Brooklyn *(G-2116)*
L3 Technologies Inc ....A....... 631 436-7400
 Hauppauge *(G-6133)*
Listec Video Corp ....G....... 631 273-3029
 Hauppauge *(G-6137)*
Mark Peri International ....F....... 516 208-6824
 Oceanside *(G-13108)*
Mini-Circuits Fort Wayne LLC ....B....... 718 934-4500
 Brooklyn *(G-2322)*
Mirion Tech Imaging LLC ....E....... 607 562-4300
 Horseheads *(G-6611)*
Motorola Solutions Inc ....C....... 718 330-2163
 Brooklyn *(G-2341)*
Motorola Solutions Inc ....C....... 518 869-9517
 Albany *(G-103)*
Movin On Sounds and SEC Inc ....E....... 516 489-2350
 Franklin Square *(G-5375)*
Navitar Inc ....D....... 585 359-4000
 Rochester *(G-14550)*
NBC Universal LLC ....E....... 718 482-8310
 Long Island City *(G-7853)*
Quanta Electronics Inc ....F....... 631 961-9953
 Centereach *(G-3498)*
Quintel Usa Inc ....E....... 585 420-8364
 Rochester *(G-14642)*
Rodale Wireless Inc ....E....... 631 231-0044
 Hauppauge *(G-6205)*
Ruhle Companies Inc ....E....... 914 287-4000
 Valhalla *(G-16398)*
Sdr Technology Inc ....G....... 716 583-1249
 Alden *(G-186)*
Sequential Electronics Systems ....E....... 914 592-1345
 Elmsford *(G-4791)*
Shoretel Inc ....G....... 877 654-3573
 Rochester *(G-14706)*

Spectracom Corporation ....E....... 585 321-5800
 Rochester *(G-14718)*
STI-Co Industries Inc ....E....... 716 662-2680
 Orchard Park *(G-13322)*
Telephonics Corporation ....A....... 631 755-7000
 Farmingdale *(G-5137)*
Telxon Corporation ....E....... 631 738-2400
 Holtsville *(G-6539)*
Vuum LLC ....G....... 212 868-3459
 New York *(G-12598)*
W & W Manufacturing Co ....F....... 516 942-0011
 West Islip *(G-16939)*
Whirlwind Music Distrs Inc ....D....... 800 733-9473
 Rochester *(G-14790)*
Zetek Corporation ....F....... 212 668-1485
 New York *(G-12729)*

RADIO & TELEVISION REPAIR

NCR Corporation ....C....... 516 876-7200
 Jericho *(G-7110)*

RADIO BROADCASTING & COMMUNICATIONS EQPT

Apex Airtronics Inc ....E....... 718 485-8560
 Brooklyn *(G-1615)*
Appairent Technologies Inc ....D....... 585 214-2460
 West Henrietta *(G-16902)*
Fleetcom Inc ....F....... 914 776-5582
 Yonkers *(G-17460)*
Hamtronics Inc ....G....... 585 392-9430
 Rochester *(G-14438)*
Imagine Communications Corp ....F....... 212 303-4200
 New York *(G-10614)*
L3 Technologies Inc ....D....... 631 436-7400
 Hauppauge *(G-6135)*
Motorola Solutions Inc ....C....... 518 348-0833
 Halfmoon *(G-5934)*
North American MBL Systems Inc ....E....... 718 898-8700
 Woodside *(G-17358)*
Persistent Systems LLC ....E....... 212 561-5895
 New York *(G-11646)*
Wireless Communications Inc ....G....... 845 353-5921
 Nyack *(G-13073)*

RADIO BROADCASTING STATIONS

Hearst Business Media Corp ....F....... 631 650-4441
 Great River *(G-5870)*
Hearst Corporation ....A....... 212 649-2000
 New York *(G-10482)*
Iheartcommunications Inc ....C....... 585 454-4884
 Rochester *(G-14465)*
New York Times Company ....B....... 212 556-1234
 New York *(G-11429)*

RADIO COMMUNICATIONS: Airborne Eqpt

Eni Mks Products Group ....F....... 585 427-8300
 Rochester *(G-14373)*

RADIO RECEIVER NETWORKS

Cntry Cross Communications LLC ....F....... 386 758-9696
 Jamestown *(G-7017)*
Iheartcommunications Inc ....C....... 585 454-4884
 Rochester *(G-14465)*
Iheartcommunications Inc ....E....... 212 603-4660
 New York *(G-10609)*

RADIO, TELEVISION & CONSUMER ELECTRONICS STORES: Eqpt, NEC

Electrotech Service Eqp Corp ....E....... 718 626-7700
 Astoria *(G-437)*
Parrys Incorporated ....F....... 315 824-0002
 Hamilton *(G-5972)*
Pass & Seymour Inc ....B....... 315 468-6211
 Syracuse *(G-16032)*
Sound Source Inc ....G....... 585 271-5370
 Rochester *(G-14717)*

RADIO, TV & CONSUMER ELECTRONICS: VCR & Access

Elite Cellular Accessories Inc ....E....... 877 390-2502
 Deer Park *(G-4158)*

PRODUCT SECTION

RADIO, TV/CONSUMER ELEC STORES: Antennas, Satellite Dish

L3 Technologies Inc ....D....... 631 231-1700
 Hauppauge *(G-6134)*

RAILINGS: Prefabricated, Metal

Paragon Aquatics ....E....... 845 452-5500
 Lagrangeville *(G-7282)*

RAILINGS: Wood

Blooming Grove Stair Co ....F....... 845 783-4245
 Monroe *(G-8585)*
Blooming Grove Stair Co ....G....... 845 791-4016
 Monticello *(G-8642)*
D K P Wood Railings & Stairs ....F....... 631 665-8656
 Bay Shore *(G-688)*
Deer Pk Stair Bldg Mllwk Inc ....E....... 631 363-5000
 Blue Point *(G-993)*
Rockaway Stairs Ltd ....G....... 718 945-0047
 Far Rockaway *(G-4931)*
Stairworld Inc ....G....... 718 441-9722
 Richmond Hill *(G-14097)*

RAILROAD CAR RENTING & LEASING SVCS

Acf Industries Holding LLC ....G....... 212 702-4363
 New York *(G-9064)*
Highcrest Investors LLC ....D....... 212 702-4323
 New York *(G-10519)*
Starfire Holding Corporation ....E....... 914 614-7000
 White Plains *(G-17196)*

RAILROAD CAR REPAIR SVCS

Acf Industries Holding LLC ....G....... 212 702-4363
 New York *(G-9064)*
Ebenezer Railcar Services Inc ....E....... 716 674-5650
 West Seneca *(G-16971)*
Highcrest Investors LLC ....D....... 212 702-4323
 New York *(G-10519)*
Starfire Holding Corporation ....E....... 914 614-7000
 White Plains *(G-17196)*

RAILROAD CARGO LOADING & UNLOADING SVCS

Packstar Group Inc ....D....... 716 853-1688
 Buffalo *(G-3133)*

RAILROAD EQPT

Alstom Signaling Inc ....E....... 585 274-8700
 Schenectady *(G-15258)*
Alstom Transportation Inc ....E....... 212 692-5353
 New York *(G-9155)*
Alstom Transportation Inc ....E....... 800 717-4477
 West Henrietta *(G-16899)*
Bombardier Mass Transit Corp ....B....... 518 566-0150
 Plattsburgh *(G-13683)*
CAF Usa Inc ....D....... 607 737-3004
 Elmira Heights *(G-4722)*
Cox & Company Inc ....C....... 212 366-0200
 Plainview *(G-13623)*
Eagle Bridge Machine & Tl Inc ....E....... 518 686-4541
 Eagle Bridge *(G-4380)*
Ebenezer Railcar Services Inc ....E....... 716 674-5650
 West Seneca *(G-16971)*
Gray Manufacturing Inds LLC ....F....... 607 281-1325
 Hornell *(G-6591)*
Horne Products Inc ....G....... 631 293-0773
 Farmingdale *(G-5014)*
Hudson Machine Works Inc ....C....... 845 279-1413
 Brewster *(G-1218)*
Knorr Brake Holding Corp ....G....... 315 786-5356
 Watertown *(G-16681)*
Peck & Hale LLC ....E....... 631 589-2510
 West Sayville *(G-16966)*
Semec Corp ....F....... 518 825-0160
 Plattsburgh *(G-13725)*
Strato Transit Components LLC ....G....... 518 686-4541
 Eagle Bridge *(G-4383)*
Twinco Mfg Co Inc ....E....... 631 231-0022
 Hauppauge *(G-6243)*
Westcode Incorporated ....E....... 607 766-9881
 Binghamton *(G-953)*

RAILROAD EQPT & SPLYS WHOLESALERS

Horne Products Inc ....G....... 631 293-0773
 Farmingdale *(G-5014)*

PRODUCT SECTION

RAILROAD EQPT, EXC LOCOMOTIVES
- Bombardier Transportation .... D 607 324-0216
  Hornell *(G-6586)*
- Kawasaki Rail Car Inc .... C 914 376-4700
  Yonkers *(G-17476)*
- Transco Railway Products Inc .... E 716 824-1219
  Blasdell *(G-961)*

RAILROAD EQPT: Brakes, Air & Vacuum
- Knorr Brake Company LLC .... G 518 561-1387
  Plattsburgh *(G-13700)*
- Knorr Brake Truck Systems Co ..... B 315 786-5200
  Watertown *(G-16682)*
- New York Air Brake LLC .... C 315 786-5219
  Watertown *(G-16688)*
- Westinghouse A Brake Tech Corp .. D 518 561-0044
  Plattsburgh *(G-13739)*

RAILROAD EQPT: Cars & Eqpt, Dining
- Acf Industries Holding LLC .... G 212 702-4363
  New York *(G-9064)*
- Highcrest Investors LLC .... D 212 702-4323
  New York *(G-10519)*
- Starfire Holding Corporation .... E 914 614-7000
  White Plains *(G-17196)*

RAILROAD EQPT: Cars & Eqpt, Rapid Transit
- Seisenbacher Inc .... F 585 730-4960
  Rochester *(G-14701)*
- Westinghouse A Brake Tech Corp .. F 914 347-8650
  Elmsford *(G-4800)*

RAILROAD EQPT: Cars & Eqpt, Train, Freight Or Passenger
- General Electric Company .... E 845 567-7410
  Newburgh *(G-12778)*

RAILROAD EQPT: Cars, Maintenance
- Koshii Maxelum America Inc .... E 845 471-0500
  Poughkeepsie *(G-13931)*

RAILROAD EQPT: Locomotives & Parts, Indl
- Higher Power Industries Inc .... G 914 709-9800
  Yonkers *(G-17470)*
- Niagara Cooler Inc .... G 716 434-1235
  Lockport *(G-7634)*
- Rand Machine Products Inc .... G 716 665-5217
  Falconer *(G-4916)*

RAILROAD EQPT: Lubrication Systems, Locomotive
- American Motive Power Inc .... E 585 335-3132
  Dansville *(G-4101)*

RAILROAD RELATED EQPT: Railway Track
- Applied Technology Mfg Corp .... E 607 687-2200
  Owego *(G-13375)*
- Railworks Transit Systems Inc ...... E 212 502-7900
  New York *(G-11816)*

RAILS: Steel Or Iron
- Artistic Ironworks Inc .... G 631 665-4285
  Bay Shore *(G-671)*

RAMPS: Prefabricated Metal
- Landmark Group Inc .... E 845 358-0350
  Valley Cottage *(G-16406)*

RAZORS, RAZOR BLADES
- HFC Prestige Intl US LLC .... A 212 389-7800
  New York *(G-10514)*

RAZORS: Electric
- Harrys Inc .... D 888 212-6855
  New York *(G-10466)*

REAL ESTATE AGENCIES & BROKERS
- Yale Robbins Inc .... D 212 683-5700
  New York *(G-12709)*

REAL ESTATE OPERATORS, EXC DEVELOPERS: Apartment Hotel
- Atlas Bituminous Co Inc .... F 315 457-2394
  Syracuse *(G-15880)*

REAL ESTATE OPERATORS, EXC DEVELOPERS: Commercial/Indl Bldg
- Bertelsmann Inc .... B 212 782-1000
  New York *(G-9417)*
- E F Thresh Inc .... G 315 437-7301
  East Syracuse *(G-4539)*
- Penhouse Media Group Inc .... C 212 702-6000
  New York *(G-11625)*

RECLAIMED RUBBER: Reworked By Manufacturing Process
- Hti Recycling LLC .... E 716 433-9294
  Lockport *(G-7623)*
- Rubberform Recycled Pdts LLC .... F 716 478-0404
  Lockport *(G-7644)*

RECORD BLANKS: Phonographic
- Chesky Records Inc .... F 212 586-7799
  New York *(G-9642)*
- Europadisk LLC .... E 718 407-7300
  Long Island City *(G-7762)*

RECORDERS: Sound
- Interaction Insight Corp .... G 800 285-2950
  New York *(G-10665)*

RECORDING HEADS: Speech & Musical Eqpt
- Felluss Recording .... G 212 727-8055
  New York *(G-10204)*
- Fine Sounds Group Inc .... F 212 364-0219
  New York *(G-10217)*

RECORDING TAPE: Video, Blank
- VDO Lab Inc .... G 914 949-1741
  White Plains *(G-17206)*

RECORDS & TAPES: Prerecorded
- Columbia Records Inc .... F 212 833-8000
  New York *(G-9736)*
- Cult Records LLC .... G 718 395-2077
  New York *(G-9822)*
- Dorling Kindersley Publishing .... D 212 213-4800
  New York *(G-9961)*
- Emusiccom Inc .... E 212 201-9240
  New York *(G-10079)*
- Extreme Group Holdings LLC .... F 212 833-8000
  New York *(G-10164)*
- High Quality Video Inc .... F 212 686-9534
  New York *(G-10518)*
- His Productions USA Inc .... G 212 594-3737
  New York *(G-10528)*
- Imago Recording Company .... G 212 751-3033
  New York *(G-10615)*
- Lefrak Entertainment Co Ltd .... G 212 586-3600
  New York *(G-10995)*
- Pete Levin Music Inc .... G 845 247-9211
  Saugerties *(G-15221)*
- Pivot Records LLC .... F 718 417-1213
  Brooklyn *(G-2437)*
- Recorded Anthology of Amrcn Mus .. F 212 290-1695
  Brooklyn *(G-2503)*
- Roadrunner Records Inc .... E 212 274-7500
  New York *(G-11908)*
- Side Hustle Music Group LLC .... F 800 219-4003
  New York *(G-12082)*
- Sony Broadband Entertainment .... F 212 833-6800
  New York *(G-12156)*
- Sony Music Entertainment .... A 212 833-8500
  New York *(G-12159)*
- Sony Music Entertainment Inc ...... A 212 833-8000
  New York *(G-12160)*
- Sony Music Entertainment Inc ...... E 212 833-5057
  New York *(G-12161)*
- Sony Music Holdings Inc .... A 212 833-8000
  New York *(G-12162)*
- Taste and See Entrmt Inc .... G 516 285-3010
  Valley Stream *(G-16452)*
- Universal Music Group Inc .... F 212 333-8277
  New York *(G-12492)*
- Warner Music Group Corp .... B 212 275-2000
  New York *(G-12616)*
- Warner Music Inc .... D 212 275-2000
  New York *(G-12617)*
- Wmg Holding Company Inc .... A 212 275-2000
  New York *(G-12677)*

RECORDS OR TAPES: Masters
- Bridge Records Inc .... G 914 654-9270
  New Rochelle *(G-8935)*
- John Marshall Sound Inc .... A 212 265-6066
  New York *(G-10790)*
- Masterdisk Corporation .... F 212 541-5022
  Elmsford *(G-4773)*
- Peer-Southern Productions Inc ..... E 212 265-3910
  New York *(G-11614)*
- Sterling Sound Inc .... E 212 604-9433
  New York *(G-12222)*
- Wea International Inc .... A 212 275-1300
  New York *(G-12629)*

RECOVERY SVCS: Metal
- Island Recycling Corp .... G 631 234-6688
  Central Islip *(G-3526)*

RECREATIONAL & SPORTING CAMPS
- Steel Excel Inc .... G 914 461-1300
  White Plains *(G-17198)*

RECTIFIERS: Electrical Apparatus
- Ems Development Corporation ..... D 631 924-4736
  Yaphank *(G-17406)*
- Solid Sealing Technology Inc .... E 518 266-6019
  Watervliet *(G-16713)*

RECTIFIERS: Solid State
- Electronic Devices Inc .... E 914 965-4400
  Yonkers *(G-17456)*

RECYCLABLE SCRAP & WASTE MATERIALS WHOLESALERS
- Metalico Aluminum Recovery Inc .. E 315 463-9500
  Syracuse *(G-16007)*

RECYCLING: Paper
- Andritz Inc .... E 518 745-2988
  Glens Falls *(G-5686)*
- Fcr LLC .... G 845 926-1071
  Beacon *(G-780)*
- Georgia-Pacific Corrugared LLC ... D 585 343-3800
  Batavia *(G-637)*
- Harvest Technologies Inc .... G 518 899-7124
  Ballston Spa *(G-597)*
- Repapers Corporation .... F 305 691-1635
  Hicksville *(G-6416)*
- Sierra Processing LLC .... F 518 433-0020
  Schenectady *(G-15320)*

REELS: Cable, Metal
- Hannay Reels Inc .... C 518 797-3791
  Westerlo *(G-17071)*
- Reelcology Inc .... F 845 258-1880
  Pine Island *(G-13580)*

REFINERS & SMELTERS: Aluminum
- Metalico Aluminum Recovery Inc .. E 315 463-9500
  Syracuse *(G-16007)*

REFINERS & SMELTERS: Antimony, Primary
- Zerovalent Nanometals Inc .... G 585 298-8592
  Rochester *(G-14804)*

REFINERS & SMELTERS: Cobalt, Primary
- Umicore USA Inc .... E 919 874-7171
  Glens Falls *(G-5714)*

REFINERS & SMELTERS: Copper
- Sherburne Metal Sales Inc .... F 607 674-4441
  Sherburne *(G-15417)*
- Tecnofil Chenango SAC .... E 607 674-4441
  Sherburne *(G-15420)*

REFINERS & SMELTERS: Copper, Secondary

Ben Weitsman of Albany LLC .... E 518 462-4444
Albany *(G-50)*

REFINERS & SMELTERS: Germanium, Primary

Germanium Corp America Inc .... G 315 732-3744
Utica *(G-16360)*

REFINERS & SMELTERS: Gold

Electro Alloy Recovery Inc .... G 631 879-7530
Bohemia *(G-1062)*
General Refining & Smelting .... G 516 538-4747
Hempstead *(G-6294)*
General Refining Corporation .... G 516 538-4747
Hempstead *(G-6295)*

REFINERS & SMELTERS: Lead, Secondary

Eco-Bat America LLC .... C 845 692-4414
Middletown *(G-8472)*

REFINERS & SMELTERS: Nonferrous Metal

Advanced Precision Technology .... F 845 279-3540
Brewster *(G-1204)*
Amt Incorporated .... E 518 284-2910
Sharon Springs *(G-15405)*
Cora Materials Corp .... F 516 488-6300
New Hyde Park *(G-8870)*
General Refining & Smelting .... G 516 538-4747
Hempstead *(G-6294)*
Germanium Corp America Inc .... F 315 853-4900
Clinton *(G-3744)*
Karbra Company .... C 212 736-9300
New York *(G-10846)*
Parfuse Corp .... E 516 997-1795
Westbury *(G-17046)*
Pluribus Products Inc .... E 718 852-1614
Bayville *(G-775)*
Real Industry Inc .... F 805 435-1255
New York *(G-11842)*
S & W Metal Trading Corp .... G 212 719-5070
Brooklyn *(G-2547)*
Scepter Inc .... E 315 568-4225
Seneca Falls *(G-15390)*
Sims Group USA Holdings Corp .... D 718 786-6031
Long Island City *(G-7906)*
Special Metals Corporation .... D 716 366-5663
Dunkirk *(G-4375)*

REFINERS & SMELTERS: Platinum Group Metal Refining, Primary

AAA Catalytic Recycling Inc .... F 631 920-7944
Farmingdale *(G-4935)*

REFINERS & SMELTERS: Silicon, Primary, Over 99% Pure

Globe Metallurgical Inc .... D 716 804-0862
Niagara Falls *(G-12844)*

REFINERS & SMELTERS: Silver

Rochester Silver Works LLC .... G 585 743-1610
Rochester *(G-14671)*
Umicore Technical Materials .... C 518 792-7700
Glens Falls *(G-5713)*

REFINERS & SMELTERS: Zinc, Primary, Including Slabs & Dust

Hh Liquidating Corp .... A 646 282-2500
New York *(G-10515)*

REFINING LUBRICATING OILS & GREASES, NEC

Industrial Oil Tank Service .... F 315 736-6080
Oriskany *(G-13335)*
Safety-Kleen Systems Inc .... F 716 855-2212
Buffalo *(G-3203)*

REFINING: Petroleum

California Petro Trnspt Corp .... G 212 302-5151
New York *(G-9551)*

Global Earth Energy .... G 716 332-7150
Buffalo *(G-2991)*
Hess Corporation .... B 212 997-8500
New York *(G-10507)*
Hess Oil Virgin Island Corp .... A 212 997-8500
New York *(G-10510)*
Hess Pipeline Corporation .... C 212 997-8500
New York *(G-10511)*
Koch Supply & Trading LP .... G 212 319-4895
New York *(G-10905)*
Petre Alii Petroleum .... G 315 785-1037
Watertown *(G-16693)*
Tricon Des LLC .... G 619 227-0778
Bronx *(G-1476)*

REFRACTORIES: Alumina Fused

Global Alumina Corporation .... G 212 351-0000
New York *(G-10352)*
Global Alumina Services Co .... B 212 309-8060
New York *(G-10353)*

REFRACTORIES: Brick

Capitol Restoration Corp .... G 516 783-1425
North Bellmore *(G-12932)*

REFRACTORIES: Brick

Saint-Gobain Strl Ceramics .... A 716 278-6233
Niagara Falls *(G-12891)*

REFRACTORIES: Clay

Filtros Ltd .... E 585 586-8770
East Rochester *(G-4478)*
Upstate Refractory Svcs Inc .... E 315 331-2955
Newark *(G-12767)*

REFRACTORIES: Graphite, Carbon Or Ceramic Bond

Blasch Precision Ceramics Inc .... D 518 436-1263
Menands *(G-8401)*
Surmet Ceramics Corporation .... F 716 875-4091
Buffalo *(G-3229)*

REFRACTORIES: Nonclay

Ask Chemicals Hi-Tech LLC .... D 607 587-9146
Alfred Station *(G-198)*
Ceramaterials LLC .... G 518 701-6722
Port Jervis *(G-13803)*
Filtros Ltd .... E 585 586-8770
East Rochester *(G-4478)*
Lucideon .... F 518 382-0082
Schenectady *(G-15303)*
Monofrax LLC .... C 716 483-7200
Falconer *(G-4915)*
Rembar Company LLC .... E 914 693-2620
Dobbs Ferry *(G-4326)*
Saint-Gobain Dynamics Inc .... F 716 278-6007
Niagara Falls *(G-12890)*
Silicon Carbide Products Inc .... E 607 562-8599
Horseheads *(G-6622)*
Unifrax I LLC .... C 716 696-3000
Tonawanda *(G-16230)*
Zircar Refr Composites Inc .... G 845 651-4481
Florida *(G-5225)*
Zircar Zirconia Inc .... G 845 651-3040
Florida *(G-5226)*

REFRACTORIES: Plastic

Hoffmans Trade Group LLC .... E 518 250-5556
Troy *(G-16261)*

REFRACTORY CASTABLES

Hanyan & Higgins Company Inc .... G 315 769-8838
Massena *(G-8227)*

REFRACTORY MATERIALS WHOLESALERS

Upstate Refractory Svcs Inc .... E 315 331-2955
Newark *(G-12767)*

REFRIGERATION & HEATING EQUIPMENT

A&S Refrigeration Equipment .... G 718 993-6030
Bronx *(G-1255)*
Besicorp Ltd .... F 845 336-7700
Kingston *(G-7208)*

Bombardier Trnsp Holdings USA .... D 607 776-4791
Bath *(G-654)*
Carrier Corporation .... A 315 432-6000
Syracuse *(G-15908)*
Carrier Corporation .... B 315 432-6000
Syracuse *(G-15907)*
Columbia Pool Accessories Inc .... G 718 993-0389
Bronx *(G-1304)*
Environmental Temp Systems LLC .... G 516 640-5818
Mineola *(G-8541)*
Fts Systems Inc .... D 845 687-5300
Stone Ridge *(G-15785)*
GM Components Holdings LLC .... B 716 439-2463
Lockport *(G-7619)*
GM Components Holdings LLC .... B 716 439-2011
Lockport *(G-7620)*
Healthway Products Company .... E 315 207-1410
Oswego *(G-13357)*
Hydro-Air Components Inc .... C 716 827-6510
Buffalo *(G-3018)*
Kedco Inc .... F 516 454-7800
Farmingdale *(G-5032)*
Manning Lewis Div Rubicon Inds .... E 908 687-2400
Brooklyn *(G-2263)*
Mgr Equipment Corp .... E 516 239-3030
Inwood *(G-6801)*
Nationwide Coils Inc .... G 914 277-7396
Mount Kisco *(G-8679)*
Niagara Blower Company .... C 800 426-5169
Tonawanda *(G-16204)*
Parker-Hannifin Corporation .... D 716 685-4040
Lancaster *(G-7356)*
Pfannenberg Manufacturing LLC .... D 716 685-6866
Lancaster *(G-7359)*
Solitec Incorporated .... F 315 298-4213
Pulaski *(G-13969)*
Supermarket Equipment Depo Inc .... G 718 665-6200
Bronx *(G-1465)*
Trane US Inc .... D 718 721-8844
Long Island City *(G-7933)*
Trane US Inc .... G 914 593-0303
Elmsford *(G-4795)*
Trane US Inc .... E 315 234-1500
East Syracuse *(G-4585)*
Trane US Inc .... E 518 785-1315
Latham *(G-7407)*
Trane US Inc .... E 585 256-2500
Rochester *(G-14757)*
Trane US Inc .... E 716 626-1260
Buffalo *(G-3250)*
Trane US Inc .... E 631 952-9477
Plainview *(G-13666)*
Universal Parent and Youth .... F 917 754-2426
Brooklyn *(G-2727)*
York International Corporation .... D 718 389-4152
Long Island City *(G-7958)*

REFRIGERATION EQPT & SPLYS WHOLESALERS

Maplewood Ice Co Inc .... E 518 499-2345
Whitehall *(G-17218)*

REFRIGERATION EQPT: Complete

American Refrigeration Inc .... G 212 699-4000
New York *(G-9178)*
Atmost Refrigeration Co Inc .... G 518 828-2180
Hudson *(G-6637)*
Cleanroom Systems Inc .... E 315 452-7400
North Syracuse *(G-12957)*
Foster Refrigerators Entp .... F 518 671-6036
Hudson *(G-6644)*
Millrock Technology Inc .... E 845 339-5700
Kingston *(G-7230)*
S & V Restaurant Eqp Mfrs Inc .... E 718 220-1140
Bronx *(G-1444)*

REFRIGERATION REPAIR SVCS

Colburns AC Rfrgn .... F 716 569-3695
Frewsburg *(G-5463)*

REFRIGERATION SVC & REPAIR

Foster Refrigerators Entp .... F 518 671-6036
Hudson *(G-6644)*
Heat-Timer Corporation .... E 212 481-2020
Bronx *(G-1356)*
Medi-Ray Inc .... D 877 898-3003
Tuckahoe *(G-16295)*

REFRIGERATORS & FREEZERS WHOLESALERS

Acme Kitchenettes Corp ....E....... 518 828-4191
  Hudson *(G-6632)*

REFUSE SYSTEMS

APC Paper Company Inc......................D....... 315 384-4225
  Norfolk *(G-12914)*

REGULATORS: Generator Voltage

Marvel Equipment Corp Inc ....G....... 718 383-6597
  Brooklyn *(G-2280)*

REGULATORS: Power

Trac Regulators Inc.................................E....... 914 699-9352
  Mount Vernon *(G-8785)*

REGULATORS: Transmission & Distribution Voltage

Telephone Sales & Service Co.................E....... 212 233-8505
  New York *(G-12318)*

REGULATORS: Transmission & Distribution Voltage

Precision Electronics Inc ....F....... 631 842-4900
  Copiague *(G-3943)*

RELAYS & SWITCHES: Indl, Electric

C D A Inc ....G....... 631 473-1595
  Nesconset *(G-8821)*
Select Controls Inc ....E....... 631 567-9010
  Bohemia *(G-1127)*

RELAYS: Electronic Usage

Dri Relays Inc ....D....... 631 342-1700
  Hauppauge *(G-6089)*
Hasco Componets ....E....... 516 328-9292
  New Hyde Park *(G-8885)*
Precision Electronics Inc ....F....... 631 842-4900
  Copiague *(G-3943)*

RELIGIOUS SPLYS WHOLESALERS

Cathedral Candle Co...............................D....... 315 422-9119
  Syracuse *(G-15909)*
Leiter Sukkahs Inc ....G....... 718 436-0303
  Brooklyn *(G-2210)*
Malhame Publs & Importers Inc ....E....... 631 694-8600
  Bohemia *(G-1096)*
Rose Solomon Co ....E....... 718 855-1788
  Brooklyn *(G-2527)*

REMOVERS & CLEANERS

G & M Dege Inc ....F....... 631 475-1450
  East Patchogue *(G-4466)*
Rapid Removal LLC ....F....... 716 665-4663
  Falconer *(G-4917)*

REMOVERS: Paint

Nochem Paint Stripping Inc....................G....... 631 563-2750
  Blue Point *(G-994)*

RENTAL CENTERS: General

Grayhawk Leasing LLC ....G....... 914 767-6000
  Somers *(G-15532)*

RENTAL SVCS: Business Machine & Electronic Eqpt

Neopost USA Inc ....E....... 631 435-9100
  Hauppauge *(G-6172)*
Pitney Bowes Inc ....E....... 212 564-7548
  New York *(G-11688)*
Pitney Bowes Inc ....E....... 203 356-5000
  New York *(G-11689)*
Pitney Bowes Inc ....E....... 516 822-0900
  Jericho *(G-7113)*

RENTAL SVCS: Costume

Rubies Costume Company Inc ....B....... 718 846-1008
  Richmond Hill *(G-14093)*

Rubies Costume Company Inc ....D....... 631 777-3300
  Bay Shore *(G-736)*
Rubies Costume Company Inc ....C....... 631 951-3688
  Bay Shore *(G-737)*
Rubies Costume Company Inc ....C....... 718 846-1008
  Richmond Hill *(G-14095)*
Rubies Costume Company Inc ....E....... 516 326-1500
  Melville *(G-8382)*

RENTAL SVCS: Electronic Eqpt, Exc Computers

Sentry Technology Corporation ....E....... 631 739-2000
  Ronkonkoma *(G-15006)*

RENTAL SVCS: Eqpt, Theatrical

Martin Chafkin ....G....... 718 383-1155
  Brooklyn *(G-2278)*
Mutual Sales Corp...................................E....... 718 361-8373
  Long Island City *(G-7848)*
Production Resource Group LLC ....D....... 877 774-7088
  Armonk *(G-416)*
Production Resource Group LLC ....E....... 845 567-5700
  New Windsor *(G-8994)*

RENTAL SVCS: Invalid Splys

Konrad Prosthetics & Orthotics ....E....... 516 485-9164
  West Hempstead *(G-16889)*

RENTAL SVCS: Live Plant

Plant-Tech2o Inc ....G....... 516 483-7845
  Hempstead *(G-6307)*

RENTAL SVCS: Pallet

Peco Pallet Inc...E....... 914 376-5444
  Irvington *(G-6816)*

RENTAL SVCS: Tent & Tarpaulin

Ace Canvas & Tent Corp ....F....... 631 648-0614
  Ronkonkoma *(G-14876)*
Classic Awnings Inc ....F....... 716 649-0390
  Hamburg *(G-5943)*

RENTAL: Video Tape & Disc

Simulaids Inc...D....... 845 679-2475
  Saugerties *(G-15223)*

REPEATERS: Passive

Innovative Power Products Inc.................E....... 631 563-0088
  Holbrook *(G-6481)*

REPRODUCTION SVCS: Video Tape Or Disk

Bertelsmann Inc......................................E....... 212 782-1000
  New York *(G-9417)*
Play-It Productions Inc............................F....... 212 695-6530
  Port Washington *(G-13873)*
Professional Tape Corporation................G....... 516 656-5519
  Glen Cove *(G-5638)*

RESEARCH, DEV & TESTING SVCS, COMM: Chem Lab, Exc Testing

Advanced Polymer Solutions LLC ....G....... 516 621-5800
  Port Washington *(G-13819)*

RESEARCH, DEVELOPMENT & TEST SVCS, COMM: Business Analysis

Economist Intelligence Unit NA ....D....... 212 554-0600
  New York *(G-10031)*

RESEARCH, DEVELOPMENT & TEST SVCS, COMM: Cmptr Hardware Dev

Argon Corp..F....... 516 487-5314
  Great Neck *(G-5807)*
Digitronik Dev Labs Inc ....F....... 585 360-0043
  Rochester *(G-14329)*
Mitsui Chemicals America Inc ....E....... 914 253-0777
  Rye Brook *(G-15098)*

RESEARCH, DEVELOPMENT & TEST SVCS, COMM: Research, Exc Lab

Dowa International Corp ....F....... 212 697-3217
  New York *(G-9968)*
Intra-Cellular Therapies Inc.....................E....... 212 923-3344
  New York *(G-10687)*

RESEARCH, DEVELOPMENT & TESTING SVCS, COMM: Research Lab

MTI Instruments Inc ....F....... 518 218-2550
  Albany *(G-104)*

RESEARCH, DEVELOPMENT & TESTING SVCS, COMMERCIAL: Medical

Athenex Inc...D....... 716 427-2950
  Buffalo *(G-2843)*
Health Care Originals Inc ....G....... 585 471-8215
  Rochester *(G-14451)*
Rohto USA Inc...G....... 716 677-2500
  Orchard Park *(G-13320)*

RESEARCH, DEVELOPMENT & TESTING SVCS, COMMERCIAL: Opinion

SOS International LLC ....C....... 212 742-2410
  New York *(G-12166)*

RESEARCH, DVLPMT & TESTING SVCS, COMM: Merger, Acq & Reorg

Toppan Vintage Inc ....D....... 212 596-7747
  New York *(G-12392)*

RESEARCH, DVLPT & TEST SVCS, COMM: Mkt Analysis or Research

International Data Group Inc...................E....... 212 331-7883
  New York *(G-10674)*

RESIDENTIAL REMODELERS

Andike Millwork Inc ....G....... 718 894-1796
  Maspeth *(G-8146)*
Di Fiore and Sons Custom Wdwkg ....G....... 718 278-1663
  Long Island City *(G-7744)*
Majestic Home Imprvs Distr ....G....... 718 853-5079
  Brooklyn *(G-2256)*

RESINS: Custom Compound Purchased

Advance Chemicals Usa Inc ....G....... 718 633-1030
  Brooklyn *(G-1564)*
Ampacet Corporation ....A....... 914 631-6600
  Tarrytown *(G-16110)*
Atc Plastics LLC......................................E....... 212 375-2515
  New York *(G-9297)*
Cryovac Inc..C....... 585 436-3211
  Rochester *(G-14313)*
Lahr Recycling & Resins Inc....................F....... 585 425-8608
  Fairport *(G-4866)*
Marval Industries Inc ....D....... 914 381-2400
  Mamaroneck *(G-8071)*
Polyset Company Inc..............................E....... 518 664-6000
  Mechanicville *(G-8260)*
Si Group Inc...C....... 518 347-4200
  Schenectady *(G-15319)*
Solepoxy Inc ....D....... 716 372-6300
  Olean *(G-13175)*

RESISTORS

Dahua Electronics Corporation ....E....... 718 886-2188
  Flushing *(G-5243)*
Hvr Advnced Pwr Components Inc ....F....... 716 693-4700
  Cheektowaga *(G-3605)*
Kionix Inc ....C....... 607 257-1080
  Ithaca *(G-6891)*
Microgen Systems Inc ....E....... 585 214-2426
  West Henrietta *(G-16916)*
Micropen Technologies Corp ....D....... 585 624-2610
  Honeoye Falls *(G-6562)*
Passive-Plus Inc ....F....... 631 425-0938
  Huntington *(G-6708)*
Stetron International Inc..........................F....... 716 854-3443
  Buffalo *(G-3225)*
Virtue Paintball LLC ....E....... 631 617-5560
  Hauppauge *(G-6251)*

RESISTORS

Vishay Americas Inc .... C 315 938-7575
  Henderson *(G-6313)*
Vishay Thin Film LLC .... C 716 283-4025
  Niagara Falls *(G-12906)*

RESISTORS & RESISTOR UNITS

Micropen Technologies Corp .... D 585 624-2610
  Honeoye Falls *(G-6562)*

RESORT HOTELS

Quinn and Co of NY Ltd .... D 212 868-1900
  New York *(G-11800)*

RESPIRATORS

Medical Acoustics LLC .... F 716 218-7353
  Buffalo *(G-3082)*

RESTAURANT EQPT REPAIR SVCS

Applince Installation Svc Corp .... E 716 884-7425
  Buffalo *(G-2837)*
Hobart Corporation .... E 631 864-3440
  Commack *(G-3861)*
Ronbar Laboratories Inc .... F 718 937-6755
  Long Island City *(G-7894)*

RESTAURANT EQPT: Carts

A-Plus Restaurant Equipment .... G 718 522-2656
  Brooklyn *(G-1543)*
All Star Carts & Vehicles Inc .... D 631 666-5581
  Bay Shore *(G-667)*

RESTAURANT EQPT: Food Wagons

Carts Mobile Food Eqp Corp .... E 718 788-5540
  Brooklyn *(G-1763)*
Kinplex Corp .... E 631 242-4800
  Edgewood *(G-4618)*
Restaurant 570 8th Avenue LLC .... F 646 722-8191
  New York *(G-11875)*
Tao Group LLC .... G 646 625-4818
  New York *(G-12303)*

RESTAURANT EQPT: Sheet Metal

E G M Restaurant Equipment Mfg .... G 718 782-9800
  Brooklyn *(G-1892)*
Shanghai Stove Inc .... F 718 599-4583
  Brooklyn *(G-2577)*

RESTAURANTS: Full Svc, American

Empire Brewing Company Inc .... D 315 925-9308
  Syracuse *(G-15956)*

RESTAURANTS: Full Svc, Mexican

Tortilla Heaven Inc .... E 845 339-1550
  Kingston *(G-7245)*

RESTAURANTS: Full Svc, Seafood

Fire Island Sea Clam Co Inc .... G 631 589-2199
  West Sayville *(G-16964)*

RESTAURANTS: Limited Svc, Coffee Shop

Aphrodites .... G 718 224-1774
  Whitestone *(G-17228)*

RESTAURANTS: Limited Svc, Ice Cream Stands Or Dairy Bars

Blue Pig Ice Cream Factory .... G 914 271-3850
  Croton On Hudson *(G-4088)*
Purity Ice Cream Co Inc .... F 607 272-1545
  Ithaca *(G-6908)*

RESTAURANTS: Limited Svc, Lunch Counter

Roslyn Bread Company Inc .... E 516 625-1470
  Roslyn Heights *(G-15056)*

RESTAURANTS: Ltd Svc, Ice Cream, Soft Drink/Fountain Stands

Nestle Healthcare Ntrtn Inc .... G 516 249-5085
  Farmingdale *(G-5074)*

RESUME WRITING SVCS

Key Computer Svcs of Chelsea 212 206-8060
  New York *(G-10880)*

RETAIL BAKERY: Bagels

999 Bagels Inc .... G 718 915-0742
  Brooklyn *(G-1523)*
A T A Bagel Shoppe Inc .... G 718 352-4948
  Bayside *(G-759)*
Bagel Grove Inc .... E 315 724-8015
  Utica *(G-16332)*
Bagel Lites LLC 855 813-7888
  Long Island City *(G-7711)*
M & M Bagel Corp 516 295-1222
  Cedarhurst *(G-3484)*
Mds Hot Bagels Deli Inc 718 438-5650
  Brooklyn *(G-2293)*

RETAIL BAKERY: Bread

Addeo Bakers Inc 718 367-8316
  Bronx *(G-1264)*
Giovanni Bakery Corp .... F 212 695-4296
  New York *(G-10341)*
Harrison Bakery West 315 422-1468
  Syracuse *(G-15977)*
Rock Hill Bakehouse Ltd .... E 518 743-1627
  Gansevoort *(G-5503)*
Roslyn Bread Company Inc 516 625-1470
  Roslyn Heights *(G-15056)*
Tosca Brick Oven Pizza Real 718 430-0026
  Bronx *(G-1471)*

RETAIL LUMBER YARDS

Axtell Bradtke Lumber Co .... G 607 265-3850
  Masonville *(G-8137)*
Deer Pk Stair Bldg Mllwk Inc 631 363-5000
  Blue Point *(G-993)*
Guldenschuh Logging & Lbr LLC 585 538-4750
  Caledonia *(G-3307)*
Lowville Farmers Coop Inc .... E 315 376-6587
  Lowville *(G-7966)*

RETAIL STORES, NEC

Exhibits & More 585 924-4040
  Victor *(G-16500)*
Mark F Rosenhaft N A O 516 374-1010
  Cedarhurst *(G-3485)*

RETAIL STORES: Alarm Signal Systems

Lifewatch Inc .... F 800 716-1433
  Hewlett *(G-6333)*
Personal Alarm SEC Systems .... F 212 448-1944
  New York *(G-11647)*
Table Tops Paper Corp .... G 718 831-6440
  Brooklyn *(G-2663)*

RETAIL STORES: Alcoholic Beverage Making Eqpt & Splys

Dutch Spirits LLC .... F 518 398-1022
  Pine Plains *(G-13582)*

RETAIL STORES: Aquarium Splys

C B Management Services Inc .... F 845 735-2300
  Pearl River *(G-13477)*

RETAIL STORES: Artificial Limbs

Creative Orthotics & Prosthet .... F 607 734-7215
  Elmira *(G-4691)*
Goldberg Prosthetic & Orthotic .... F 631 689-6606
  East Setauket *(G-4502)*
Green Prosthetics & Orthotics .... G 716 484-1088
  Jamestown *(G-7030)*
Hanger Inc 718 575-5504
  Forest Hills *(G-5329)*
Konrad Prosthetics & Orthotics 516 485-9164
  West Hempstead *(G-16889)*
Lehneis Orthotics Prosthetic .... G 631 369-3115
  Riverhead *(G-14159)*
M H Mandelbaum Orthotic .... F 631 473-8668
  Port Jefferson *(G-13799)*
North Shore Orthtics Prsthtics 631 928-3040
  Port Jeff STA *(G-13791)*
Prosthetic Rehabilitation Ctr .... G 845 565-8255
  Newburgh *(G-12800)*

Ultrapedics Ltd .... G 718 748-4806
  Brooklyn *(G-2715)*

RETAIL STORES: Audio-Visual Eqpt & Splys

Audio Video Invasion Inc .... F 516 345-2636
  Plainview *(G-13613)*
Tony Baird Electronics Inc .... G 315 422-4430
  Syracuse *(G-16084)*

RETAIL STORES: Awnings

A 3-D Signs & Awnings Inc .... G 718 252-7575
  Brooklyn *(G-1529)*
Acme Awning Co Inc .... F 718 409-1881
  Bronx *(G-1263)*
Alley Cat Signs Inc .... F 631 924-7446
  Middle Island *(G-8439)*
Awning Mart Inc .... G 315 699-5928
  Cicero *(G-3671)*
City Signs Inc .... G 718 375-5933
  Brooklyn *(G-1783)*
Dart Awning Inc .... F 718 945-4224
  Freeport *(G-5404)*
Di Sanos Creative Canvas Inc .... G 315 894-3137
  Frankfort *(G-5360)*
Graphic Signs & Awnings Ltd .... G 718 227-6000
  Staten Island *(G-15702)*
Kenan International Trading .... G 718 672-4922
  Corona *(G-4023)*
Lanza Corp 914 937-6360
  Port Chester *(G-13778)*
Lotus Awnings Enterprises Inc .... G 718 965-4824
  Brooklyn *(G-2240)*
Mauceri Sign Inc .... F 718 656-7700
  Jamaica *(G-6965)*
Proof Industries Inc .... G 631 694-7663
  Farmingdale *(G-5100)*
Rgm Signs Inc .... G 718 442-0598
  Staten Island *(G-15754)*
Space Sign .... F 718 961-1112
  College Point *(G-3834)*
Steinway Awning II LLC .... G 718 729-2965
  Astoria *(G-458)*

RETAIL STORES: Cake Decorating Splys

Pfeil & Holing Inc .... D 718 545-4600
  Woodside *(G-17362)*

RETAIL STORES: Canvas Prdts

Brock Awnings Ltd .... F 631 765-5200
  Hampton Bays *(G-5982)*
Geordie Magee Uphl & Canvas .... G 315 676-7679
  Brewerton *(G-1200)*

RETAIL STORES: Cleaning Eqpt & Splys

Collinite Corporation .... G 315 732-2282
  Utica *(G-16336)*
Empire Division Inc .... D 315 476-6273
  Syracuse *(G-15957)*
Mortech Industries Inc .... G 845 628-6138
  Mahopac *(G-8028)*

RETAIL STORES: Concrete Prdts, Precast

Riefler Concrete Products LLC .... C 716 649-3260
  Hamburg *(G-5964)*

RETAIL STORES: Cosmetics

Borghese Inc .... E 212 659-5318
  New York *(G-9491)*
Malin + Goetz Inc .... F 212 244-7771
  New York *(G-11145)*
New Avon LLC .... A 212 282-8500
  New York *(G-11403)*

RETAIL STORES: Electronic Parts & Eqpt

G B International Trdg Co Ltd .... C 607 785-0938
  Endicott *(G-4817)*
I Trade Technology Ltd .... G 615 348-7233
  Suffern *(G-15814)*
Industrial Support Inc .... D 716 662-2954
  Buffalo *(G-3024)*
Ross Electronics Ltd .... E 718 569-6643
  Haverstraw *(G-6264)*

PRODUCT SECTION

RETAIL STORES: Engine & Motor Eqpt & Splys
Electric Motors and Pumps Inc .... G 718 935-9118
Brooklyn *(G-1912)*

RETAIL STORES: Farm Eqpt & Splys
Birkett Mills .... G 315 536-3311
Penn Yan *(G-13529)*

RETAIL STORES: Fiberglass Materials, Exc Insulation
Architectural Fiberglass Corp .... E 631 842-4772
Copiague *(G-3918)*

RETAIL STORES: Fire Extinguishers
C E King & Sons Inc .... G 631 324-4944
East Hampton *(G-4426)*
Sausbiers Awning Shop Inc .... G 518 828-3748
Hudson *(G-6664)*

RETAIL STORES: Gravestones, Finished
Woodside Granite Industries .... G 585 589-6500
Albion *(G-174)*

RETAIL STORES: Hearing Aids
Benway-Haworth-Lwlr-Iacosta He .... F 518 432-4070
Albany *(G-51)*

RETAIL STORES: Ice
Henry Newman LLC .... F 607 273-8512
Ithaca *(G-6883)*
South Shore Ice Co Inc .... F 516 379-2056
Roosevelt *(G-15032)*

RETAIL STORES: Infant Furnishings & Eqpt
Mam USA Corporation .... F 914 269-2500
Purchase *(G-13977)*

RETAIL STORES: Medical Apparatus & Splys
Goodman Main Stopper Mfg Co .... F 718 875-5140
Brooklyn *(G-2040)*
Medical Action Industries Inc .... C 631 231-4600
Hauppauge *(G-6155)*
NY Orthopedic Usa Inc .... D 718 852-5330
Brooklyn *(G-2393)*

RETAIL STORES: Mobile Telephones & Eqpt
2p Agency Usa Inc .... G 212 203-5586
Brooklyn *(G-1513)*
Sima Technologies LLC .... G 412 828-9130
Hauppauge *(G-6215)*

RETAIL STORES: Monuments, Finished To Custom Order
Presbrey-Leland Inc .... G 914 949-2264
Valhalla *(G-16397)*
St Raymond Monument Co .... G 718 824-3600
Bronx *(G-1460)*

RETAIL STORES: Motors, Electric
A & C/Furia Electric Motors .... F 914 949-0585
White Plains *(G-17100)*
Economy Pump & Motor Repair .... G 718 433-2600
Astoria *(G-436)*
Emes Motor Inc .... G 718 387-2445
Brooklyn *(G-1922)*

RETAIL STORES: Orthopedic & Prosthesis Applications
Arimed Orthotics Prosthetics P .... F 718 875-8754
Brooklyn *(G-1628)*
Creative Orthotics Prosthetics .... G 607 771-4672
Binghamton *(G-899)*
Klemmt Orthotics & Prosthetics .... G 607 770-4400
Johnson City *(G-7128)*
Ortho Medical Products .... F 212 879-3700
New York *(G-11541)*
Orthocraft Inc .... G 718 951-1700
Brooklyn *(G-2408)*
Progressive Orthotics Ltd .... F 631 447-3860
East Patchogue *(G-4468)*

Progressive Orthotics Ltd .... G 631 732-5556
Selden *(G-15375)*
Prosthetics By Nelson Inc .... F 716 894-6666
Cheektowaga *(G-3614)*
Sampsons Prsthtic Orthotic Lab .... E 518 374-6011
Schenectady *(G-15315)*

RETAIL STORES: Pet Food
J & M Feed Corporation .... G 631 281-2152
Shirley *(G-15444)*

RETAIL STORES: Photocopy Machines
Printer Components Inc .... G 585 924-5190
Fairport *(G-4877)*

RETAIL STORES: Religious Goods
A-1 Skull Cap Corp .... E 718 633-9333
Brooklyn *(G-1540)*
J Lowy Co .... G 718 338-7324
Brooklyn *(G-2123)*
Moznaim Publishing Co Inc .... G 718 853-0525
Brooklyn *(G-2342)*
Y & A Trading Inc .... F 718 436-6333
Brooklyn *(G-2785)*

RETAIL STORES: Stones, Crystalline, Rough
Amendola MBL & Stone Ctr Inc .... D 914 997-7968
White Plains *(G-17104)*
Hanson Aggregates PA LLC .... E 585 624-1220
Honeoye Falls *(G-6558)*

RETAIL STORES: Telephone Eqpt & Systems
ABS Talkx Inc .... G 631 254-9100
Bay Shore *(G-664)*

RETAIL STORES: Tents
Leiter Sukkahs Inc .... G 718 436-0303
Brooklyn *(G-2210)*

RETAIL STORES: Water Purification Eqpt
Neptune Soft Water Inc .... F 315 446-5151
Syracuse *(G-16017)*

RETAIL STORES: Welding Splys
Haun Welding Supply Inc .... F 607 846-2289
Elmira *(G-4702)*

REUPHOLSTERY & FURNITURE REPAIR
Furniture Doctor Inc .... G 585 657-6941
Bloomfield *(G-982)*
Henry B Urban Inc .... E 212 489-3308
New York *(G-10500)*
KPP Ltd .... G 516 338-5201
Westbury *(G-17031)*
White Plains Drapery Uphl Inc .... E 914 381-0908
Mamaroneck *(G-8083)*

REUPHOLSTERY SVCS
Anthony Lawrence of New York .... E 212 206-8820
Long Island City *(G-7694)*

RIBBONS & BOWS
Artistic Ribbon Novelty Co Inc .... E 212 255-4224
New York *(G-9271)*
Phoenix Ribbon Co Inc .... G 212 239-0155
New York *(G-11670)*

RIBBONS, NEC
Essential Ribbons Inc .... G 212 967-4173
New York *(G-10118)*
Fashion Ribbon Co Inc .... E 718 482-0100
Long Island City *(G-7767)*

RIBBONS: Machine, Inked Or Carbon
International Imaging Mtls Inc .... A 716 691-6333
Amherst *(G-245)*

RIDING APPAREL STORES
Robert Viggiani .... G 914 423-4046
Yonkers *(G-17500)*

ROLLERS & FITTINGS: Window Shade

RIVETS: Metal
John Hassall LLC .... D 516 334-6200
Westbury *(G-17025)*

ROAD MATERIALS: Bituminous, Not From Refineries
Alliance Paving Materials Inc .... G 315 337-0795
Rome *(G-14832)*
R Schleider Contracting Corp .... G 631 269-4249
Kings Park *(G-7204)*
Rochester Asphalt Materials .... G 585 381-7010
Rochester *(G-14656)*

ROBOTS: Assembly Line
Automated Cells & Eqp Inc .... E 607 936-1341
Painted Post *(G-13415)*
Honeybee Robotics Ltd .... E 212 966-0661
Brooklyn *(G-2083)*
J H Robotics Inc .... E 607 729-3758
Johnson City *(G-7127)*
McHone Industries Inc .... D 716 945-3380
Salamanca *(G-15128)*
Uipath .... C 844 432-0455
New York *(G-12464)*

ROCK SALT MINING
American Rock Salt Company LLC .... E 585 991-6878
Retsof *(G-14064)*
Steel City Salt LLC .... G 716 532-0000
Collins *(G-3843)*

ROCKET LAUNCHERS
CIC International Ltd .... D 212 213-0089
Brooklyn *(G-1778)*

ROCKETS: Space & Military
Lockheed Martin Corporation .... A 315 456-0123
Liverpool *(G-7554)*

RODS: Extruded, Aluminum
Jem Threading Specialties Inc .... G 718 665-3341
Bronx *(G-1368)*

RODS: Plastic
Comco Plastics Inc .... E 718 849-9000
Huntington Station *(G-6738)*
Great Lakes Plastics Co Inc .... E 716 896-3100
Buffalo *(G-2997)*

RODS: Steel & Iron, Made In Steel Mills
Hitachi Metals America Ltd .... E 914 694-9200
Purchase *(G-13974)*
Mardek LLC .... G 585 735-9333
Pittsford *(G-13597)*

RODS: Welding
Aufhauser Corporation .... F 516 694-8696
Plainview *(G-13614)*
Aufhauser Manufacturing Corp .... E 516 694-8696
Plainview *(G-13615)*

ROLL COVERINGS: Rubber
Finzer Holding LLC .... E 315 597-1147
Palmyra *(G-13431)*

ROLL FORMED SHAPES: Custom
Inscape (new York) Inc .... D 716 665-6210
Falconer *(G-4909)*
Lakeside Capital Corporation .... E 716 664-2555
Jamestown *(G-7048)*
Rolite Mfg Inc .... E 716 683-0259
Lancaster *(G-7365)*

ROLLED OR DRAWN SHAPES, NEC: Copper & Copper Alloy
Sherburne Metal Sales Inc .... F 607 674-4441
Sherburne *(G-15417)*

ROLLERS & FITTINGS: Window Shade
Windowtex Inc .... F 877 294-3580
Garden City Park *(G-5558)*

ROLLING MILL MACHINERY

Anthony Manufacturing Inc .... G 631 957-9424
Lindenhurst *(G-7476)*
Ivy Classic Industries Inc .... E 914 632-8200
New Rochelle *(G-8958)*
Johnston Dandy Company .... G 315 455-5773
Syracuse *(G-15988)*
Mannesmann Corporation .... D 212 258-4000
New York *(G-11160)*
Polymag Tek Inc .... F 585 235-8390
Rochester *(G-14606)*

ROLLS & BLANKETS, PRINTERS': Rubber Or Rubberized Fabric

Enbi Indiana Inc .... E 585 647-1627
Rochester *(G-14369)*
Package Print Technologies .... E 716 871-9905
Buffalo *(G-3132)*

ROLLS: Rubber, Solid Or Covered

Idg LLC .... E 315 797-1000
Utica *(G-16365)*
Rotation Dynamics Corporation .... E 585 352-9023
Spencerport *(G-15597)*

ROOFING MATERIALS: Asphalt

Johns Manville Corporation .... E 518 565-3000
Plattsburgh *(G-13699)*
Marathon Roofing Products Inc .... F 716 685-3340
Orchard Park *(G-13307)*

ROOFING MATERIALS: Sheet Metal

Brothers Roofing Supplies Co .... E 718 779-0280
East Elmhurst *(G-4411)*
Pal Aluminum Inc .... G 516 937-1990
Hicksville *(G-6408)*
Pal Aluminum Inc .... E 718 262-0091
Jamaica *(G-6975)*

ROPE

Gladding Braided Products LLC .... E 315 653-7211
South Otselic *(G-15555)*

ROTORS: Motor

Taro Manufacturing Company Inc .... F 315 252-9430
Auburn *(G-520)*

RUBBER

David Fehlman .... G 315 455-8888
Syracuse *(G-15942)*
Integrated Liner Tech Inc .... E 518 621-7422
Rensselaer *(G-14059)*
Release Coatings New York Inc .... G 585 593-2335
Wellsville *(G-16782)*

RUBBER PRDTS: Automotive, Mechanical

Bridgestone APM Company .... D 419 423-9552
Sanborn *(G-15141)*

RUBBER PRDTS: Mechanical

Apple Rubber Products Inc .... C 716 684-7649
Lancaster *(G-7328)*
Delford Industries Inc .... D 845 342-3901
Middletown *(G-8469)*
Finzer Holding LLC .... E 315 597-1147
Palmyra *(G-13431)*
Mechanical Rubber Pdts Co Inc .... F 845 986-2271
Warwick *(G-16616)*
Moldtech Inc .... E 716 685-3344
Lancaster *(G-7351)*
Ms Spares LLC .... G 607 223-3024
Clay *(G-3709)*
Pawling Corporation .... C 845 855-1000
Pawling *(G-13474)*
Pawling Corporation .... D 845 373-9300
Wassaic *(G-16622)*
Pawling Engineered Pdts Inc .... C 845 855-1000
Pawling *(G-13475)*
Pilot Products Inc .... F 718 728-2141
Long Island City *(G-7873)*
R & A Industrial Products .... G 716 823-4300
Buffalo *(G-3177)*
The Centro Company Inc .... G 914 533-2200
South Salem *(G-15561)*

Triangle Rubber Co Inc .... E 631 589-9400
Bohemia *(G-1144)*

RUBBER PRDTS: Medical & Surgical Tubing, Extrudd & Lathe-Cut

Precision Extrusion Inc .... E 518 792-1199
Glens Falls *(G-5711)*

RUBBER PRDTS: Oil & Gas Field Machinery, Mechanical

Camso Manufacturing Usa Ltd .... D 518 561-7528
Plattsburgh *(G-13685)*

RUBBER PRDTS: Reclaimed

Cementex Latex Corp .... F 212 741-1770
New York *(G-9609)*
Zylon Corporation .... F 845 425-9469
Monsey *(G-8622)*

RUBBER PRDTS: Silicone

Canton Bio-Medical Inc .... E 518 283-5963
Poestenkill *(G-13752)*
Depco Inc .... F 631 582-1995
Hauppauge *(G-6083)*
Silicone Products & Technology .... C 716 684-1155
Lancaster *(G-7368)*
Specialty Silicone Pdts Inc .... E 518 885-8826
Ballston Spa *(G-608)*
Vasquez Tito .... F 212 944-0441
New York *(G-12533)*

RUBBER PRDTS: Sponge

Tmp Technologies Inc .... D 716 895-6100
Buffalo *(G-3246)*

RUBBER PRDTS: Wet Suits

Great American Industries Inc .... G 607 729-9331
Vestal *(G-16472)*

RUBBER STRUCTURES: Air-Supported

Continental Latex Corp .... F 718 783-7883
Brooklyn *(G-1798)*

RUGS: Hand & Machine Made

Mark Nelson Designs LLC .... F 646 422-7020
New York *(G-11179)*
Mgk Group Inc .... E 212 989-2732
New York *(G-11273)*
Renaissnce Crpt Tapestries Inc .... F 212 696-0080
New York *(G-11863)*
Safavieh Inc .... A 516 945-1900
Port Washington *(G-13877)*

RULERS: Metal

Gei International Inc .... F 315 463-9261
East Syracuse *(G-4546)*

SAFES & VAULTS: Metal

Gardall Safe Corporation .... E 315 432-9115
Syracuse *(G-15968)*
Schwab Corp .... E 585 381-4900
Rochester *(G-14696)*

SAFETY EQPT & SPLYS WHOLESALERS

Human Condition Safety Inc .... F 646 867-0644
New York *(G-10575)*
Valeo .... G 800 634-2704
Yonkers *(G-17512)*

SAILBOAT BUILDING & REPAIR

Allen Boat Co Inc .... G 716 842-0800
Buffalo *(G-2819)*

SAILS

Allen Boat Co Inc .... G 716 842-0800
Buffalo *(G-2819)*
Doyle-Hild Sailmakers .... G 718 885-2255
Bronx *(G-1320)*
Melbourne C Fisher Yacht Sails .... G 631 673-5055
Huntington Station *(G-6753)*
Ulmer Sales LLC .... F 718 885-1700
Bronx *(G-1483)*

SALES PROMOTION SVCS

Platinum Sales Promotion Inc .... G 718 361-0200
Long Island City *(G-7874)*

SALT

Cargill Incorporated .... D 607 535-6300
Watkins Glen *(G-16719)*
Real Co Inc .... G 347 433-8549
Valley Cottage *(G-16412)*
Roto Salt Company Inc .... E 315 536-3742
Penn Yan *(G-13542)*
Topaz Industries Inc .... F 631 207-0700
Holtsville *(G-6540)*
US Salt LLC .... D 607 535-2721
Watkins Glen *(G-16723)*

SALT & SULFUR MINING

Morton Salt Inc .... F 585 493-2511
Silver Springs *(G-15472)*

SAMPLE BOOKS

Federal Sample Card Corp .... D 718 458-1344
Elmhurst *(G-4673)*
New York Sample Card Co Inc .... E 212 242-1242
New York *(G-11426)*
Niagara Sample Book Co Inc .... F 716 284-6151
Niagara Falls *(G-12867)*

SAND & GRAVEL

110 Sand Company .... E 631 694-2822
Melville *(G-8319)*
110 Sand Company .... F 631 694-2822
West Babylon *(G-16786)*
A Colarusso and Son Inc .... E 518 828-3218
Hudson *(G-6631)*
Barrett Paving Materials Inc .... G 607 723-5367
Binghamton *(G-887)*
Belangers Gravel & Stone Inc .... G 585 728-3906
Wayland *(G-16733)*
Bonsal American Inc .... E 631 208-8073
Calverton *(G-3314)*
Callanan Industries Inc .... E 845 331-6868
Kingston *(G-7211)*
Chenango Asphalt Products .... F 607 334-3117
Norwich *(G-13038)*
Dalrymple Grav & Contg Co Inc .... F 607 739-0391
Pine City *(G-13577)*
Dalrymple Holding Corp .... E 607 737-6200
Pine City *(G-13578)*
E Tetz & Sons Inc .... D 845 692-4486
Middletown *(G-8470)*
East Coast Mines Ltd .... E 631 653-5445
East Quogue *(G-4469)*
Frew Run Gravel Products Inc .... G 716 569-4712
Frewsburg *(G-5464)*
Genoa Sand & Gravel Lnsg .... G 607 533-4551
Freeville *(G-5448)*
Greenebuild LLC .... F 917 562-0556
Brooklyn *(G-2054)*
Hanson Aggregates East LLC .... E 315 548-2911
Phelps *(G-13556)*
Johnson S Sand Gravel Inc .... G 315 771-1450
La Fargeville *(G-7263)*
Lafarge North America Inc .... E 716 651-9235
Lancaster *(G-7346)*
Lafarge North America Inc .... E 518 756-5000
Ravena *(G-14036)*
McEwan Trucking & Grav Produc .... G 716 609-1828
East Concord *(G-4407)*
Milestone Construction Corp .... G 718 459-8500
Rego Park *(G-14048)*
Mitchell Stone Products LLC .... G 518 359-7029
Tupper Lake *(G-16301)*
New York Sand & Stone LLC .... G 718 596-2897
Maspeth *(G-8188)*
Northeast Solite Corporation .... E 845 246-2177
Mount Marion *(G-8694)*
R G King General Construction .... G 315 583-3560
Adams Center *(G-4)*
R J Valente Gravel Inc .... E 518 279-1001
Cropseyville *(G-4085)*
Rd2 Construction & Dem LLC .... F 718 980-1650
Staten Island *(G-15750)*
Republic Construction Co Inc .... G 914 235-3654
New Rochelle *(G-8969)*
Robinson Concrete Inc .... E 315 253-6666
Auburn *(G-513)*

PRODUCT SECTION

SAWS & SAWING EQPT

Seneca Stone Corporation .... G 607 737-6200
 Pine City **(G-13579)**
Smith Sand & Gravel Inc .... G 315 673-4124
 Marcellus **(G-8120)**
Speyside Holdings LLC .... E 845 928-2221
 Highland Mills **(G-6440)**
Syracuse Sand & Gravel LLC .... G 315 548-8207
 Fulton **(G-5489)**
Tilcon New York Inc .... D 845 358-3100
 West Nyack **(G-16958)**
Titus Mountain Sand & Grav LLC .... G 518 483-3740
 Malone **(G-8049)**
Tri City Highway Products Inc .... E 607 722-2967
 Binghamton **(G-951)**
Tri-City Highway Products Inc .... E 518 294-9964
 Richmondville **(G-14102)**
Troy Sand & Gravel Co Inc .... F 518 674-2854
 West Sand Lake **(G-16961)**
United Materials LLC .... G 716 662-0564
 Orchard Park **(G-13326)**
US Allegro Inc .... E 347 408-6601
 Maspeth **(G-8204)**

SAND MINING

Country Side Sand & Gravel .... G 716 988-3271
 Collins **(G-3840)**
Dicks Concrete Co Inc .... E 845 374-5966
 New Hampton **(G-8844)**
H L Robinson Sand & Gravel .... F 607 659-5153
 Candor **(G-3403)**
Hampton Sand Corp .... G 631 325-5533
 Westhampton **(G-17086)**
Rush Gravel Corp .... G 585 533-1740
 Honeoye Falls **(G-6563)**
Sparrow Mining Co .... G 718 519-6600
 Bronx **(G-1458)**
Tilcon New York Inc .... E 845 942-0602
 Tomkins Cove **(G-16153)**

SAND: Hygrade

New Jersey Pulverizing Co Inc .... F 516 921-9595
 Syosset **(G-15852)**
Precision Elctro Mnrl Pmco Inc .... E 716 284-2484
 Niagara Falls **(G-12881)**

SANDSTONE: Crushed & Broken

County Line Stone Co Inc .... E 716 542-5435
 Akron **(G-18)**
Shelby Crushed Stone Inc .... F 585 798-4501
 Medina **(G-8314)**

SANITARY SVCS: Environmental Cleanup

Hygrade .... G 718 488-9000
 Brooklyn **(G-2088)**

SANITARY SVCS: Waste Materials, Recycling

Crumbrubber Technology Inc .... F 718 468-3988
 Hollis **(G-6522)**
Hampton Sand Corp .... G 631 325-5533
 Westhampton **(G-17086)**
Ivi Services Inc .... D 607 729-5111
 Binghamton **(G-924)**
Kore Infrastructure LLC .... E 646 532-9060
 Glen Cove **(G-5633)**
Twin County Recycling Corp .... F 516 827-6900
 Westbury **(G-17067)**

SANITARY WARE: Metal

Advance Tabco Inc .... D 631 242-8270
 Edgewood **(G-4605)**
Kenbenco Inc .... F 845 246-3066
 Saugerties **(G-15215)**
Metpar Corp .... D 516 333-2600
 Westbury **(G-17038)**
Unico Inc .... F 845 562-9255
 Newburgh **(G-12806)**

SANITATION CHEMICALS & CLEANING AGENTS

Aireactor Inc .... F 718 326-2433
 Woodside **(G-17335)**
American Wax Company Inc .... E 718 392-8080
 Long Island City **(G-7691)**
Bennett Manufacturing Co Inc .... C 716 937-9161
 Alden **(G-178)**

Car-Freshner Corporation .... D 315 788-6250
 Watertown **(G-16664)**
Cleanse TEC .... E 718 346-9111
 Brooklyn **(G-1787)**
Colgate-Palmolive Company .... A 212 310-2000
 New York **(G-9726)**
Cpac Inc .... E 585 382-3223
 Leicester **(G-7442)**
Crescent Marketing Inc .... E 716 337-0145
 North Collins **(G-12943)**
Crosstex International Inc .... D 631 582-6777
 Hauppauge **(G-6079)**
James Richard Specialty Chem .... E 914 478-7500
 Hastings On Hudson **(G-6024)**
Micro Powders Inc .... E 914 332-6400
 Tarrytown **(G-16120)**
Olin Chlor Alkali Logistics .... C 716 278-6411
 Niagara Falls **(G-12875)**
P S M Group Inc .... E 716 532-6686
 Forestville **(G-5342)**
Rochester Midland Corporation .... C 585 336-2200
 Rochester **(G-14665)**
Safetec of America Inc .... D 716 895-1822
 Buffalo **(G-3202)**
Synco Chemical Corporation .... E 631 567-5300
 Bohemia **(G-1137)**
Tribology Inc .... E 631 345-3000
 Yaphank **(G-17421)**
US Nonwovens Corp .... A 631 952-0100
 Brentwood **(G-1196)**

SASHES: Door Or Window, Metal

A G M Deco Inc .... F 718 624-6200
 Brooklyn **(G-1532)**
A G M Deco Inc .... F 718 624-6200
 Brooklyn **(G-1533)**
Hopes Windows Inc .... C 716 665-5124
 Jamestown **(G-7034)**
Thermal Tech Doors Inc .... E 516 745-0100
 Garden City **(G-5548)**

SATCHELS

Barclay Brown Corp .... F 718 376-7166
 Brooklyn **(G-1665)**

SATELLITES: Communications

Geosync Microwave Inc .... G 631 760-5567
 Hauppauge **(G-6107)**
Globecomm Systems Inc .... C 631 231-9800
 Hauppauge **(G-6109)**
Loral Space & Commnctns Holdng .... E 212 697-1105
 New York **(G-11061)**
Loral Space Communications Inc .... B 212 697-1105
 New York **(G-11062)**
Loral Spacecom Corporation .... E 212 697-1105
 New York **(G-11063)**
Orbcomm Inc .... F 703 433-6396
 Utica **(G-16379)**
Village Video Productions Inc .... G 631 752-9311
 West Babylon **(G-16871)**

SAW BLADES

Allway Tools Inc .... D 718 792-3636
 Bronx **(G-1270)**
Amana Tool Corp .... D 631 752-1300
 Farmingdale **(G-4947)**
Diamond Saw Works Inc .... E 716 496-7417
 Chaffee **(G-3560)**
Dinosaw Inc .... E 518 828-9942
 Hudson **(G-6642)**
Suffolk McHy & Pwr Tl Corp .... E 631 289-7153
 Patchogue **(G-13460)**

SAWDUST & SHAVINGS

Bono Sawdust Supply Co Inc .... G 718 446-1374
 Corona **(G-4014)**

SAWDUST, WHOLESALE

Attica Package Company Inc .... F 585 591-0510
 Attica **(G-471)**

SAWING & PLANING MILLS

A D Bowman & Son Lumber Co .... E 607 692-2595
 Castle Creek **(G-3445)**
Angelica Forest Products Inc .... G 585 466-3205
 Angelica **(G-376)**

Axtell Bradtke Lumber Co .... G 607 265-3850
 Masonville **(G-8137)**
B & J Lumber Co Inc .... G 518 677-3845
 Cambridge **(G-3332)**
Baillie Lumber Co LP .... E 315 942-5284
 Boonville **(G-1160)**
Bissel-Babcock Millwork Inc .... F 716 761-6976
 Sherman **(G-15423)**
Brookside Lumber Inc .... G 315 497-0937
 Moravia **(G-8656)**
Capital Sawmill Service .... G 518 479-0729
 Nassau **(G-8816)**
Casters Custom Sawing .... G 315 387-5104
 Sandy Creek **(G-15159)**
Clements Burrville Sawmill .... G 315 782-4549
 Watertown **(G-16666)**
Cote Hardwood Products Inc .... F 607 898-5737
 Locke **(G-7595)**
Crawford Furniture Mfg Corp .... C 716 483-2650
 Jamestown **(G-7020)**
Curran Renewable Energy LLC .... E 315 769-2000
 Massena **(G-8225)**
Dlr Enterprises LLC .... G 315 813-2911
 Sherrill **(G-15427)**
Donver Incorporated .... F 716 945-1910
 Kill Buck **(G-7195)**
Farney Lumber Corporation .... F 315 346-6013
 Lowville **(G-7964)**
Greene Lumber Co LP .... E 607 278-6101
 Davenport **(G-4105)**
Hawkeye Forest Products LP .... F 608 534-6156
 Hamburg **(G-5951)**
J & J Log & Lumber Corp .... D 845 832-6535
 Dover Plains **(G-4339)**
Lyons & Sullivan Inc .... G 518 584-1523
 Saratoga Springs **(G-15192)**
McDonough Hardwoods Ltd .... E 315 829-3449
 Vernon Center **(G-16460)**
Meltz Lumber Co of Mellenville .... E 518 672-7021
 Hudson **(G-6656)**
Mettowee Lumber & Plastics Co .... C 518 642-1100
 Granville **(G-5793)**
Owletts Saw Mills .... G 607 525-6340
 Woodhull **(G-17327)**
Pallets Inc .... F 518 747-4177
 Fort Edward **(G-5351)**
PDJ Inc .... G 315 655-8824
 Cazenovia **(G-3476)**
Piccini Industries Ltd .... E 845 365-0614
 Orangeburg **(G-13262)**
Potter Lumber Co Inc .... F 716 373-1260
 Allegany **(G-205)**
Rudy Stempel & Family Sawmill .... G 518 872-0431
 East Berne **(G-4405)**
Russell Bass .... F 607 637-5253
 Hancock **(G-5989)**
S Donadic Woodworking Inc .... D 718 361-9888
 Sunnyside **(G-15830)**
Saw Mill Pediatrics Pllc .... G 914 449-6064
 Pleasantville **(G-13750)**
Scotts Company LLC .... E 631 289-7444
 Yaphank **(G-17416)**
Simplicity Bandsaw Inc .... G 716 557-8805
 Hinsdale **(G-6450)**
Spiegel Woodworks Inc .... F 845 336-8090
 Kingston **(G-7239)**
St Lawrence Lumber Inc .... G 315 649-2990
 Three Mile Bay **(G-16145)**
Swanson Lumber .... G 716 499-1726
 Gerry **(G-5605)**
Tupper Lake Hardwoods Inc .... E 518 359-8248
 Tupper Lake **(G-16305)**
Urrey Lumber .... G 518 827-4851
 Middleburgh **(G-8453)**
Wagner Millwork Inc .... D 607 687-5362
 Owego **(G-13386)**

SAWING & PLANING MILLS: Custom

Gutchess Freedom Inc .... D 716 492-2824
 Freedom **(G-5387)**

SAWMILL MACHINES

Cannonsville Lumber Inc .... G 607 467-3380
 Deposit **(G-4299)**

SAWS & SAWING EQPT

Kelley Farm & Garden Inc .... E 518 234-2332
 Cobleskill **(G-3763)**

SCAFFOLDS: Mobile Or Stationary, Metal

Safeworks LLC .... F 800 696-5577
  Woodside (G-17368)

SCALES & BALANCES, EXC LABORATORY

A & K Equipment Incorporated .... G 705 428-3573
  Watertown (G-16655)
Circuits & Systems Inc .... E 516 593-4301
  East Rockaway (G-4488)
Itin Scale Co Inc .... E 718 336-5900
  Brooklyn (G-2118)

SCALES: Baby

Scale-Tronix Inc .... F 914 948-8117
  Skaneateles (G-15487)

SCALP TREATMENT SVCS

British Science Corporation .... G 212 980-8700
  Staten Island (G-15672)

SCANNING DEVICES: Optical

Broadnet Technologies Inc .... F 315 443-3694
  Syracuse (G-15895)
Cal Blen Electronic Industries .... F 631 242-6243
  Huntington (G-6691)
Jadak LLC .... F 315 701-0678
  North Syracuse (G-12966)
Symbol Technologies LLC .... A 631 737-6851
  Holtsville (G-6536)
T&K Printing Inc .... F 718 439-9454
  Brooklyn (G-2661)

SCISSORS: Hand

Klein Cutlery LLC .... D 585 928-2500
  Bolivar (G-1156)

SCRAP & WASTE MATERIALS, WHOLESALE: Ferrous Metal

Blue Tee Corp .... A 212 598-0880
  New York (G-9473)
Massena Metals Inc .... F 315 769-3846
  Massena (G-8229)

SCRAP & WASTE MATERIALS, WHOLESALE: Metal

Umicore USA Inc .... E 919 874-7171
  Glens Falls (G-5714)

SCRAP & WASTE MATERIALS, WHOLESALE: Plastics Scrap

Fiber USA Corp .... G 718 888-1512
  Flushing (G-5249)

SCRAP & WASTE MATERIALS, WHOLESALE: Rags

Yankee Corp .... F 718 589-1377
  Bronx (G-1496)

SCREENS: Projection

Dnp Electronics America LLC .... D 212 503-1060
  New York (G-9944)

SCREENS: Window, Metal

Alumil Fabrication Inc .... F 845 469-2874
  Newburgh (G-12769)
Bison Steel Incorporated .... G 716 683-0900
  Depew (G-4273)
Norandex Inc Vestal .... G 607 786-0778
  Vestal (G-16475)
Renewal By Andersen LLC .... E 631 843-1716
  Farmingdale (G-5108)
Window Tech Systems Inc .... E 518 899-9000
  Ballston Spa (G-610)

SCREENS: Woven Wire

Star Wire Mesh Fabricators .... G 212 831-4133
  New York (G-12209)

SCREW MACHINE PRDTS

Acme Precision Screw Pdts Inc .... F 585 328-2028
  Rochester (G-14185)
Albert Gates Inc .... D 585 594-9401
  North Chili (G-12940)
All Type Screw Machine Pdts .... G 516 334-5100
  Westbury (G-16992)
Anderson Precision Inc .... F 716 484-1148
  Jamestown (G-7007)
Andros Manufacturing Corp .... F 585 663-5700
  Rochester (G-14221)
Brinkman Intl Group Inc .... F 585 429-5000
  Rochester (G-14263)
Broda Machine Co Inc .... F 716 297-3221
  Niagara Falls (G-12822)
C R C Manufacturing Inc .... F 585 254-8820
  Rochester (G-14272)
C&C Automatics Inc .... G 315 331-1436
  Newark (G-12750)
Century Metal Parts Corp .... E 631 667-0800
  Bay Shore (G-680)
Craftech Industries Inc .... D 518 828-5001
  Hudson (G-6640)
Curtis Screw Co Inc .... E 716 898-7800
  Buffalo (G-2916)
Elmira Grinding Works Inc .... F 607 734-1579
  Wellsburg (G-16773)
Emory Machine & Tool Co Inc .... F 585 436-9610
  Farmington (G-5159)
Five Star Tool Co Inc .... E 585 328-9580
  Rochester (G-14394)
Globe Electronic Hardware Inc .... F 718 457-0303
  Woodside (G-17349)
Gsp Components Inc .... D 585 436-3377
  Rochester (G-14434)
Hanco Metal Products Inc .... F 212 787-5992
  Brooklyn (G-2065)
I W Industries Inc .... E 631 293-9494
  Melville (G-8359)
J & J Swiss Precision Inc .... E 631 243-5584
  Deer Park (G-4176)
Kaddis Manufacturing Corp .... G 585 624-3070
  Honeoye Falls (G-6561)
Kathleen B Mead .... G 585 247-0146
  Webster (G-16752)
Ktd Screw Machine Inc .... E 631 243-6861
  Deer Park (G-4184)
Lexington Machining LLC .... D 585 235-0880
  Rochester (G-14499)
Lexington Machining LLC .... C 585 235-0880
  Rochester (G-14500)
Liberty Brass Turning Co Inc .... E 718 784-2911
  Westbury (G-17032)
M Manastrip-M Corporation .... G 518 664-2089
  Clifton Park (G-3726)
Manacraft Precision Inc .... F 914 654-0967
  Pelham (G-13518)
Manth-Brownell Inc .... C 315 687-7263
  Kirkville (G-7254)
Marmach Machine Inc .... G 585 768-8800
  Le Roy (G-7438)
Micro Threaded Products Inc .... G 585 288-0080
  Rochester (G-14529)
Miggins Screw Products Inc .... G 845 279-2307
  Brewster (G-1222)
Muller Tool Inc .... E 716 895-3658
  Buffalo (G-3098)
Multimatic Products Inc .... D 800 767-7633
  Ronkonkoma (G-14972)
Murphy Manufacturing Co Inc .... G 585 223-0100
  Fairport (G-4871)
Norwood Screw Machine Parts .... F 516 481-6644
  Mineola (G-8562)
Precision Machine Tech LLC .... D 585 467-1840
  Rochester (G-14617)
R P M Machine Co .... G 585 671-3744
  Webster (G-16757)
Ranney Precision .... F 716 731-6418
  Niagara Falls (G-12884)
Selflock Screw Products Co Inc .... E 315 541-4464
  Syracuse (G-16060)
Supply Technologies (ny) .... F 212 966-3310
  Albany (G-139)
Supreme Screw Products Inc .... D 718 293-6600
  Plainview (G-13664)
T & L Automatics Inc .... C 585 647-3717
  Rochester (G-14739)
TAC Screw Products Inc .... F 585 663-5840
  Rochester (G-14741)
Taylor Metalworks Inc .... C 716 662-3113
  Orchard Park (G-13323)
Teale Machine Company Inc .... D 585 244-6700
  Rochester (G-14744)
Thuro Metal Products Inc .... E 631 435-0444
  Brentwood (G-1194)
Tri-Technologies Inc .... E 914 699-2001
  Mount Vernon (G-8787)
Trihex Manufacturing Inc .... G 315 589-9331
  Williamson (G-17256)
Triple Point Manufacturing .... G 631 218-4988
  Bohemia (G-1146)
Umbro Machine & Tool Co Inc .... F 845 876-4669
  Rhinebeck (G-14071)
Vanguard Metals Inc .... F 631 234-6500
  Central Islip (G-3541)
Verns Machine Co Inc .... G 315 926-4223
  Marion (G-8133)

SCREW MACHINES

Johnson Mch & Fibr Pdts Co Inc .... F 716 665-2003
  Jamestown (G-7047)
Swiss Specialties Inc .... F 631 567-8800
  Wading River (G-16547)

SCREWS: Metal

Anthony Manno & Co Inc .... G 631 445-1834
  Deer Park (G-4123)
John F Rafter Inc .... G 716 992-3425
  Eden (G-4600)
Kinemotive Corporation .... E 631 249-6440
  Farmingdale (G-5035)
Radax Industries Inc .... E 585 265-2055
  Webster (G-16758)
Socket Products Mfg Corp .... G 631 232-9870
  Islandia (G-6841)
Tamperproof Screw Company Inc .... F 516 931-1616
  Hicksville (G-6425)

SEALANTS

Deal International Inc .... E 585 288-4444
  Rochester (G-14325)
J M Canty Inc .... E 716 625-4227
  Lockport (G-7624)
R-Co Products Corporation .... F 800 854-7657
  Lakewood (G-7318)
Saint-Gobain Prfmce Plas Corp .... C 518 642-2200
  Granville (G-5796)
Walsh & Hughes Inc .... G 631 427-5904
  Huntington Station (G-6766)

SEARCH & DETECTION SYSTEMS, EXC RADAR

Frequency Electronics Inc .... B 516 794-4500
  Uniondale (G-16317)
Saab Defense and SEC USA LLC .... F 315 445-5009
  East Syracuse (G-4575)
U S Tech Corporation .... F 315 437-7207
  East Syracuse (G-4587)
Virtualapt Corp .... G 917 293-3173
  Brooklyn (G-2748)
VJ Technologies Inc .... E 631 589-8800
  Bohemia (G-1151)

SEARCH & NAVIGATION SYSTEMS

901 D LLC .... E 845 369-1111
  Airmont (G-10)
Accipiter Radar Corporation .... G 716 508-4432
  Orchard Park (G-13273)
Ametek Inc .... D 585 263-7700
  Rochester (G-14218)
Amherst Systems Inc .... C 716 631-0610
  Buffalo (G-2828)
Aventura Technologies Inc .... E 631 300-4000
  Commack (G-3848)
C Speed LLC .... E 315 453-1043
  Liverpool (G-7537)
C-Flex Bearing Co Inc .... F 315 895-7454
  Frankfort (G-5359)
Clayton Dubilier & Rice Fun .... E 212 407-5200
  New York (G-9695)
Computer Instruments Corp .... E 516 876-8400
  Westbury (G-17003)
Cox & Company Inc .... F 212 366-0200
  Plainview (G-13623)
Dyna-Empire Inc .... C 516 222-2700
  Garden City (G-5513)

PRODUCT SECTION

SEMICONDUCTORS & RELATED DEVICES

Edo LLC .... G 631 630-4000
  Amityville *(G-284)*
Edo LLC .... A 631 630-4200
  Amityville *(G-285)*
Emergency Beacon Corp .... F 914 576-2700
  New Rochelle *(G-8941)*
Flightline Electronics Inc .... D 585 742-5340
  Victor *(G-16502)*
Harris Corporation .... C 703 668-6239
  Rome *(G-14841)*
Inficon Inc .... C 315 434-1149
  East Syracuse *(G-4555)*
Joldeson One Aerospace Inds .... D 718 848-7396
  Ozone Park *(G-13406)*
Kerns Manufacturing Corp .... C 718 784-4044
  Long Island City *(G-7807)*
L-3 Cmmnctns Fgn Holdings Inc .... E 212 697-1111
  New York *(G-10941)*
L3 Technologies Inc .... B 212 697-1111
  New York *(G-10943)*
Lockheed Martin Corporation .... A 607 751-2000
  Owego *(G-13379)*
Lockheed Martin Corporation .... D 607 751-7434
  Owego *(G-13380)*
Lockheed Martin Corporation .... D 212 697-1105
  New York *(G-11049)*
Lockheed Martin Corporation .... E 716 297-1000
  Niagara Falls *(G-12861)*
Lockheed Martin Global Inc .... E 315 456-2982
  Liverpool *(G-7555)*
Logitek Inc .... D 631 567-1100
  Bohemia *(G-1089)*
Magellan Aerospace NY Inc .... C 718 699-4000
  Corona *(G-4025)*
Metro Dynmc Scntific Instr Lab .... F 631 842-4300
  West Babylon *(G-16841)*
Mirion Technologies Ist Corp .... D 607 562-4300
  Horseheads *(G-6612)*
Northrop Grumman Corporation .... A 703 280-2900
  Bethpage *(G-874)*
Norwich Aero Products Inc .... D 607 336-7636
  Norwich *(G-13051)*
Orthstar Enterprises Inc .... D 607 562-2100
  Horseheads *(G-6614)*
Rodale Wireless Inc .... E 631 231-0044
  Hauppauge *(G-6205)*
Transistor Devices Inc .... E 631 471-7492
  Ronkonkoma *(G-15015)*
Tusk Manufacturing Inc .... E 631 567-3449
  Bohemia *(G-1147)*
U E Systems Incorporated .... F 914 592-1220
  Elmsford *(G-4797)*
Vacuum Instrument Corporation .... D 631 737-0900
  Ronkonkoma *(G-15021)*
Worldwide Arntcal Cmpnents Inc .... F 631 842-3780
  Copiague *(G-3962)*
Worldwide Arntcal Cmpnents Inc .... G 631 842-3780
  Copiague *(G-3963)*

SEAT BELTS: Automobile & Aircraft

Davis Restraint Systems Inc .... F 631 563-1500
  Bohemia *(G-1047)*

SEATING: Bleacher, Portable

E & D Specialty Stands Inc .... E 716 337-0161
  North Collins *(G-12944)*

SEATING: Chairs, Table & Arm

Chair Factory .... E 718 363-2383
  Brooklyn *(G-1771)*

SECRETARIAL SVCS

New York Typing & Printing Co .... G 718 268-7900
  Forest Hills *(G-5334)*

SECURITY CONTROL EQPT & SYSTEMS

Aabacs Group Inc .... F 718 961-3577
  College Point *(G-3799)*
Albatros North America Inc .... E 518 381-7100
  Ballston Spa *(G-589)*
Altronix Corp .... D 718 567-8181
  Brooklyn *(G-1593)*
Ameta International Co Ltd .... G 416 992-8036
  Buffalo *(G-2826)*
Atlantic Electronic Tech LLC .... G 800 296-2177
  Brooklyn *(G-1648)*
BDB Technologies LLC .... G 800 921-4270
  Brooklyn *(G-1672)*
C & G Video Systems Inc .... G 315 452-1490
  Liverpool *(G-7536)*
Comsec Ventures International .... G 518 523-1600
  Lake Placid *(G-7297)*
Detekion Security Systems Inc .... F 607 729-7179
  Vestal *(G-16469)*
Eyelock Corporation .... G 855 393-5625
  New York *(G-10165)*
Eyelock LLC .... G 855 393-5625
  New York *(G-10166)*
Fire Fox Security Corp .... G 917 981-9280
  Brooklyn *(G-1978)*
Forte Network .... E 631 390-9050
  East Northport *(G-4457)*
Innovative Video Tech Inc .... F 631 388-5700
  Hauppauge *(G-6122)*
Issco Corporation .... F 212 732-8748
  Garden City *(G-5524)*
Mkj Communications Corp .... G 212 206-0072
  New York *(G-11312)*
Napco Security Tech Inc .... A 631 842-9400
  Amityville *(G-313)*
National Security Systems Inc .... E 516 627-2222
  Manhasset *(G-8097)*
Protex International Corp .... D 631 563-4250
  Bohemia *(G-1120)*
Shield Security Doors Ltd .... G 202 468-3308
  New York *(G-12072)*

SECURITY DEVICES

Avalonics Inc .... F 516 238-7074
  Levittown *(G-7446)*
Canary Connect Inc .... C 212 390-8576
  New York *(G-9563)*
Century Systems Ltd .... E 718 543-5991
  Bronx *(G-1294)*
Custom Sound and Video .... E 585 424-5000
  Rochester *(G-14317)*
Dyson-Kissner-Moran Corp .... E 212 661-4600
  Poughkeepsie *(G-13915)*
Fairview Bell and Intercom .... E 718 627-8621
  Brooklyn *(G-1958)*
Fiber Instrument Sales Inc .... C 315 736-2206
  Oriskany *(G-13333)*
Hampton Technologies LLC .... F 631 924-1335
  Medford *(G-8279)*
Hawk-I Security Inc .... G 631 656-1056
  Hauppauge *(G-6115)*
Highlander Realty Inc .... E 914 235-8073
  New Rochelle *(G-8956)*
Intellicheck Mobilisa Inc .... E 516 992-1900
  Jericho *(G-7104)*
Manhole Brrier SEC Systems Inc .... D 516 741-1032
  Kew Gardens *(G-7194)*
News/Sprts Microwave Rentl Inc .... E 619 670-0572
  New York *(G-11438)*
Parabit Systems Inc .... E 516 378-4800
  Roosevelt *(G-15031)*
Scorpion Security Products Inc .... G 607 724-9999
  Vestal *(G-16476)*
Securevue Inc .... G 631 587-5850
  West Islip *(G-16936)*
Security Defense System .... G 718 769-7900
  Whitestone *(G-17243)*
Security Dynamics Inc .... F 631 392-1701
  Bohemia *(G-1126)*
Triton Infosys Inc .... E 877 308-2388
  New York *(G-12428)*
Videotec Security Inc .... G 518 825-0020
  Plattsburgh *(G-13737)*

SECURITY EQPT STORES

Mod-Pac Corp .... C 716 898-8480
  Buffalo *(G-3091)*

SECURITY PROTECTIVE DEVICES MAINTENANCE & MONITORING SVCS

Basil S Kadhim .... G 888 520-5192
  New York *(G-9380)*
Security Defense System .... G 718 769-7900
  Whitestone *(G-17243)*

SECURITY SYSTEMS SERVICES

Indegy Inc .... E 866 801-5394
  New York *(G-10629)*
Intralinks Holdings Inc .... E 212 543-7700
  New York *(G-10688)*
Synergx Systems Inc .... D 516 433-4700
  Woodside *(G-17374)*
World Business Media LLC .... F 212 344-0759
  Massapequa Park *(G-8224)*

SEMICONDUCTOR & RELATED DEVICES: Read-Only Memory Or ROM

Monolithic Coatings Inc .... G 914 621-2765
  Sharon Springs *(G-15406)*

SEMICONDUCTOR CIRCUIT NETWORKS

Nanomas Technologies Inc .... F 607 821-4208
  Endicott *(G-4826)*

SEMICONDUCTOR DEVICES: Wafers

Thermoaura Inc .... F 518 813-4997
  Albany *(G-142)*

SEMICONDUCTORS & RELATED DEVICES

Able Electronics Inc .... F 631 924-5386
  Bellport *(G-820)*
Accumetrics Inc .... F 716 684-0002
  Latham *(G-7378)*
Accumetrics Associates Inc .... F 518 393-2200
  Latham *(G-7379)*
Advis .... G 585 568-0100
  Caledonia *(G-3302)*
Aeroflex Holding Corp .... A 516 694-6700
  Plainview *(G-13607)*
Aeroflex Plainview Inc .... C 631 231-9100
  Hauppauge *(G-6030)*
Atlantis Energy Systems Inc .... G 916 438-2930
  Poughkeepsie *(G-13908)*
Beech Grove Technology Inc .... G 845 223-6844
  Hopewell Junction *(G-6574)*
Bga Technology LLC .... F 631 750-4600
  Bohemia *(G-1021)*
Central Semiconductor Corp .... D 631 435-1110
  Hauppauge *(G-6061)*
Ceres Technologies Inc .... D 845 247-4701
  Saugerties *(G-15210)*
Cold Springs R & D Inc .... F 315 413-1237
  Syracuse *(G-15920)*
Compositech Ltd .... C 516 835-1458
  Woodbury *(G-17305)*
Convergent Med MGT Svcs LLC .... G 718 921-6159
  Brooklyn *(G-1800)*
Cooper Power Systems LLC .... B 716 375-7100
  Olean *(G-13160)*
Corning Incorporated .... C 607 248-1200
  Corning *(G-3986)*
Corning Incorporated .... A 607 974-9000
  Corning *(G-3983)*
Corning Incorporated .... G 607 974-6729
  Painted Post *(G-13417)*
Corning Specialty Mtls Inc .... G 607 974-9000
  Corning *(G-3991)*
Crystalonics Inc .... F 631 981-6140
  Ronkonkoma *(G-14919)*
Curtiss-Wright Controls .... C 631 756-4740
  Farmingdale *(G-4977)*
Cypress Semiconductor Corp .... F 631 261-1358
  Northport *(G-13028)*
Dionics-Usa Inc .... G 516 997-7474
  Westbury *(G-17005)*
Elite Semi Conductor Products .... G 631 884-8400
  Lindenhurst *(G-7486)*
Endicott Interconnect Tech Inc .... A 866 820-4820
  Endicott *(G-4810)*
General Semiconductor Inc .... G 631 300-3818
  Hauppauge *(G-6106)*
Globalfoundries US 2 LLC .... C 512 457-3900
  Hopewell Junction *(G-6577)*
Globalfoundries US Inc .... F 512 457-3900
  Hopewell Junction *(G-6578)*
Gs Direct LLC .... C 212 902-1000
  New York *(G-10420)*
Gurley Precision Instrs Inc .... C 518 272-6300
  Troy *(G-16259)*
H K Technologies Inc .... G 212 779-0100
  New York *(G-10435)*
Hi-Tron Semiconductor Corp .... E 631 231-1500
  Hauppauge *(G-6116)*
Hipotronics Inc .... C 845 279-8091
  Brewster *(G-1217)*
Ilc Holdings Inc .... G 631 567-5600
  Bohemia *(G-1072)*

Employee Codes: A=Over 500 employees, B=251-500
C=101-250, D=51-100, E=20-50, F=10-19, G=5-9

SEMICONDUCTORS & RELATED DEVICES

Ilc Industries LLC .... F 631 567-5600
  Bohemia *(G-1073)*
International Bus Mchs Corp .... C 800 426-4968
  Hopewell Junction *(G-6580)*
Intex Company Inc .... D 516 223-0200
  Freeport *(G-5417)*
Isine Inc .... G 631 913-4400
  Ronkonkoma *(G-14942)*
J H Rhodes Company Inc .... F 315 829-3600
  Vernon *(G-16459)*
Lakestar Semi Inc .... F 212 974-6254
  New York *(G-10955)*
Lasermax Inc .... D 585 272-5420
  Rochester *(G-14496)*
Lightspin Technologies Inc .... G 301 656-7600
  Endwell *(G-4842)*
Logitek Inc .... D 631 567-1100
  Bohemia *(G-1089)*
M C Products .... E 631 471-4070
  Holbrook *(G-6488)*
Marcon Services .... G 516 223-8019
  Freeport *(G-5421)*
Marktech International Corp .... E 518 956-2980
  Latham *(G-7401)*
Materion Brewster LLC .... D 845 279-0900
  Brewster *(G-1221)*
McG Electronics Inc .... E 631 586-5125
  Deer Park *(G-4196)*
Micro Contract Manufacturing .... G 631 738-7874
  Medford *(G-8289)*
Micro Semicdtr Researches LLC .... G 646 863-6070
  New York *(G-11281)*
Microchip Technology Inc .... C 607 785-5992
  Endicott *(G-4825)*
Micromem Technologies ....F 212 672-1806
  New York *(G-11282)*
Mini-Circuits Fort Wayne LLC .... B 718 934-4500
  Brooklyn *(G-2322)*
Navitar Inc .... D 585 359-4000
  Rochester *(G-14550)*
On Semiconductor Corporation .... G 585 784-5770
  Rochester *(G-14571)*
Procomponents Inc .... E 516 683-0909
  Westbury *(G-17051)*
Riverhawk Company LP .... E 315 624-7171
  New Hartford *(G-8854)*
RSM Electron Power Inc .... D 631 586-7600
  Deer Park *(G-4228)*
RSM Electron Power Inc .... D 631 586-7600
  Hauppauge *(G-6207)*
Ruhle Companies Inc .... E 914 287-4000
  Valhalla *(G-16398)*
Schott Corporation .... D 315 255-2791
  Auburn *(G-514)*
Schott Lithotec USA Corp .... D 845 463-5300
  Elmsford *(G-4789)*
Semitronics Corp .... E 516 223-0200
  Freeport *(G-5437)*
Sendyne Corp .... G 212 966-0663
  New York *(G-12046)*
Silicon Pulsed Power LLC .... G 610 407-4700
  Clifton Park *(G-3733)*
Sinclair Technologies Inc ....E 716 874-3682
  Hamburg *(G-5966)*
Solid Cell Inc .... G 585 426-5000
  Rochester *(G-14715)*
Spectron Glass & Electronics ....F 631 582-5600
  Hauppauge *(G-6218)*
Stetron International Inc ....F 716 854-3443
  Buffalo *(G-3225)*
Sumitomo Elc USA Holdings Inc .... G 212 490-6610
  New York *(G-12254)*
Super Conductor Materials Inc .... F 845 368-0240
  Suffern *(G-15821)*
Swissbit Na Inc .... G 914 935-1400
  Port Chester *(G-13784)*
Symwave Inc .... G 949 542-4400
  Hauppauge *(G-6229)*
Tel Technology Center Amer LLC .... E 512 424-4200
  Albany *(G-141)*
Telephonics Corporation .... E 631 549-6000
  Huntington *(G-6722)*
Thales Laser SA .... D 585 223-2370
  Fairport *(G-4891)*
Tlsi Incorporated .... D 631 470-8880
  Huntington *(G-6726)*
University At Albany .... E 518 437-8686
  Albany *(G-147)*
Vgg Holding LLC .... G 212 415-6500
  New York *(G-12558)*

Viking Technologies Ltd .... E 631 957-8000
  Lindenhurst *(G-7516)*
Vistec Lithography Inc ....F 518 874-3184
  Troy *(G-16284)*
Washington Foundries Inc .... G 516 374-8447
  Hewlett *(G-6340)*
Widetronix Inc .... G 607 330-4752
  Ithaca *(G-6919)*
Zastech Inc .... G 516 496-4777
  Syosset *(G-15863)*

SENSORS: Temperature For Motor Windings

Irtronics Instruments Inc .... F 914 693-6291
  Ardsley *(G-404)*

SENSORS: Temperature, Exc Indl Process

Titan Controls Inc 516 358-2407
  New York *(G-12374)*

SEPARATORS: Metal Plate

Motivair Corporation .... E 716 691-9222
  Amherst *(G-250)*

SEPTIC TANKS: Concrete

Bistrian Cement Corporation .... F 631 324-1123
  East Hampton *(G-4425)*
H F Cary & Sons .... G 607 598-2563
  Lockwood *(G-7658)*
Suffolk Cement Precast Inc .... G 631 727-4432
  Calverton *(G-3327)*

SEPTIC TANKS: Plastic

Roth Global Plastics Inc .... E 315 475-0100
  Syracuse *(G-16048)*

SERVICES, NEC

G and G Service .... G 518 785-9247
  Latham *(G-7390)*

SERVOMOTORS: Electric

Magna Products Corp .... E 585 647-2280
  Rochester *(G-14510)*

SEWAGE & WATER TREATMENT EQPT

City of Kingston .... F 845 331-2490
  Kingston *(G-7213)*
Clearcove Systems Inc ....F 585 734-3012
  Victor *(G-16491)*
Ewt Holdings III Corp .... F 212 644-5900
  New York *(G-10151)*
Ferguson Enterprises Inc .... E 800 437-1146
  New Hyde Park *(G-8879)*
Northeast Water Systems LLC .... G 585 943-9225
  Kendall *(G-7172)*
Yr Blanc & Co LLC .... G 716 800-3999
  Buffalo *(G-3287)*

SEWAGE TREATMENT SYSTEMS & EQPT

Environment-One Corporation .... C 518 346-6161
  Schenectady *(G-15279)*
Hudson Xinde Energy Inc .... G 212 220-7112
  New York *(G-10573)*
Orege North America Inc .... G 770 862-9388
  New York *(G-11537)*
Richard R Cain Inc .... F 845 229-7410
  Hyde Park *(G-6775)*

SEWER CLEANING EQPT: Power

Dyna-Vac Equipment Inc .... F 315 865-8084
  Stittville *(G-15784)*
Pathfinder 103 Inc .... G 315 363-4260
  Oneida *(G-13187)*

SEWING CONTRACTORS

TSS Foam Industries Corp .... F 585 538-2321
  Caledonia *(G-3311)*

SEWING MACHINES & PARTS: Indl

Herbert Jaffe Inc .... G 718 392-1956
  Long Island City *(G-7788)*
Tompkins Srm LLC .... G 315 422-8763
  Syracuse *(G-16083)*

SEWING, NEEDLEWORK & PIECE GOODS STORE: Needlework Gds/Sply

Viking Athletics Ltd .... E 631 957-8000
  Lindenhurst *(G-7515)*

SEWING, NEEDLEWORK & PIECE GOODS STORES: Sewing & Needlework

Great Adirondack Yarn Company .... F 518 843-3381
  Amsterdam *(G-349)*

SHADES: Lamp & Light, Residential

Custom Lampshades Inc .... F 718 254-0500
  Brooklyn *(G-1826)*

SHADES: Lamp Or Candle

Artemis Studios Inc .... D 718 788-6022
  Brooklyn *(G-1637)*
Blanche P Field LLC .... E 212 355-6616
  New York *(G-9463)*
Diane Studios Inc .... D 718 788-6007
  Brooklyn *(G-1859)*
Jamaica Lamp Corp .... E 718 776-5039
  Queens Village *(G-13996)*
Jimco Lamp & Manufacturing Co .... G 631 218-2152
  Islip *(G-6848)*
Our Own Candle Company Inc .... F 716 769-5000
  Findley Lake *(G-5185)*
Ray Gold Shade Inc .... F 718 377-8892
  Brooklyn *(G-2499)*

SHADES: Window

Mechoshade Systems Inc .... C 718 729-2020
  Long Island City *(G-7838)*
Solar Screen Co Inc .... G 718 592-8222
  Corona *(G-4030)*
Windowcraft Inc .... F 516 294-3580
  Garden City Park *(G-5557)*

SHALE MINING, COMMON

Callahan & Nannini Quarry Inc .... G 845 496-4323
  Salisbury Mills *(G-15139)*
Grosso Materials Inc .... F 845 361-5211
  Montgomery *(G-8631)*

SHALE: Expanded

Norlite LLC .... B 518 235-0030
  Cohoes *(G-3778)*

SHAPES & PILINGS, STRUCTURAL: Steel

Markin Tubing Inc .... C 585 495-6211
  Wyoming *(G-17397)*
Pecker Iron Works LLC .... G 914 665-0100
  Mount Kisco *(G-8682)*
Rochester Structural LLC .... E 585 436-1250
  Rochester *(G-14674)*

SHEATHING: Paper

Sabin Robbins Paper Company .... E 513 874-5270
  New York *(G-11967)*

SHEET METAL SPECIALTIES, EXC STAMPED

Aero-Data Metal Crafters Inc .... C 631 471-7733
  Ronkonkoma *(G-14882)*
Asm USA Inc .... F 212 925-2906
  New York *(G-9287)*
Choppy V M & Sons LLC .... E 518 266-1444
  Troy *(G-16253)*
Construction Parts Whse Inc .... G 315 445-1310
  East Syracuse *(G-4534)*
Custom Sheet Metal Corp .... G 315 463-9105
  Syracuse *(G-15936)*
Dayton T Brown Inc .... B 631 589-6300
  Bohemia *(G-1048)*
Franchet Metal Craft Inc .... G 718 658-6400
  Jamaica *(G-6949)*
Metal Tek Products .... G 516 586-4514
  Plainview *(G-13646)*
P R B Metal Products Inc .... F 631 467-1800
  Ronkonkoma *(G-14986)*
Penasack Machine Company Inc .... E 585 589-7044
  Albion *(G-171)*
Service Mfg Group Inc .... F 716 893-1482
  Buffalo *(G-3212)*

PRODUCT SECTION

SHEET MUSIC STORES
Golfing Magazine .... G 516 822-5446
  Hicksville *(G-6380)*

SHEET MUSIC, WHOLESALE
Carl Fischer LLC .... E 212 777-0900
  New York *(G-9580)*

SHEETING: Laminated Plastic
Advanced Structures Corp .... F 631 667-5000
  Deer Park *(G-4113)*

SHEETS & STRIPS: Aluminum
Alcoa Fastening Systems .... G 585 368-5049
  Rochester *(G-14200)*
Alcoa USA Corp .... F 212 518-5400
  New York *(G-9127)*
Arconic Inc .... D 212 836-2758
  New York *(G-9248)*

SHEETS: Fabric, From Purchased Materials
Elegant Linen Inc .... E 718 871-3535
  Brooklyn *(G-1916)*

SHELVES & SHELVING: Wood
Forecast Consoles Inc .... E 631 253-9000
  Hauppauge *(G-6102)*
Karp Associates Inc .... D 631 768-8300
  Melville *(G-8362)*

SHELVING: Office & Store, Exc Wood
Abaco Steel Products Inc .... G 631 589-1800
  Bohemia *(G-997)*
Jack Luckner Steel Shelving Co .... D 718 363-0500
  Maspeth *(G-8178)*
Lucia Group Inc .... G 631 392-4900
  Deer Park *(G-4192)*
Tri-Boro Shlving Prtition Corp .... F 718 782-8527
  Ridgewood *(G-14142)*
Your Furniture Designers Inc .... G 845 947-3046
  West Haverstraw *(G-16879)*

SHERARDIZING SVC: Metals Or Metal Prdts
Superior Metals & Processing .... G 718 545-7500
  Long Island City *(G-7923)*

SHIELDS OR ENCLOSURES: Radiator, Sheet Metal
Interior Metals .... E 718 439-7324
  Brooklyn *(G-2108)*
Radiation Shielding Systems .... F 888 631-2278
  Suffern *(G-15819)*
Rand Products Manufacturing Co .... G 518 374-9871
  Schenectady *(G-15312)*
Steelcraft Manufacturing Co .... F 718 277-2404
  Brooklyn *(G-2624)*

SHIMS: Metal
McD Metals LLC .... F 518 456-9694
  Albany *(G-100)*
Romac Electronics Inc .... G 516 349-7900
  Plainview *(G-13660)*

SHIP BLDG & RPRG: Drilling & Production Platforms, Oil/Gas
Cgsi Group LLC .... F 516 986-5503
  Bronx *(G-1296)*

SHIP BUILDING & REPAIRING: Cargo Vessels
Reynolds Shipyard Corporation .... F 718 981-2800
  Staten Island *(G-15753)*

SHIP BUILDING & REPAIRING: Cargo, Commercial
Steelways Inc .... E 845 562-0860
  Newburgh *(G-12804)*

SHIP BUILDING & REPAIRING: Ferryboats
Robert E Derecktor Inc .... D 914 698-0962
  Mamaroneck *(G-8078)*

SHIP BUILDING & REPAIRING: Lighthouse Tenders
Highland Museum & Lighthouse .... F 508 487-1121
  Cairo *(G-3298)*

SHIP BUILDING & REPAIRING: Offshore Sply Boats
Weldrite Closures Inc .... E 585 429-8790
  Rochester *(G-14788)*

SHIP BUILDING & REPAIRING: Rigging, Marine
Clark Rigging & Rental Corp .... F 585 265-2910
  Webster *(G-16741)*
Dragon Trading Inc .... G 212 717-1496
  New York *(G-9974)*

SHIP BUILDING & REPAIRING: Tankers
McQuilling Partners Inc .... E 516 227-5718
  Garden City *(G-5531)*

SHIPBUILDING & REPAIR
Alpha Marine Repair .... E 718 816-7150
  Staten Island *(G-15657)*
Caddell Dry Dock & Repr Co Inc .... C 718 442-2112
  Staten Island *(G-15674)*
Excelco Developments Inc .... E 716 934-2651
  Silver Creek *(G-15470)*
Excelco/Newbrook Inc .... D 716 934-2644
  Silver Creek *(G-15471)*
George G Sharp Inc .... E 212 732-2800
  New York *(G-10325)*
Huntington Ingalls Inc .... E 518 884-3834
  Saratoga Springs *(G-15188)*
May Ship Repair Contg Corp .... E 718 442-9700
  Staten Island *(G-15726)*
Metalcraft Marine Us Inc .... F 315 501-4015
  Cape Vincent *(G-3410)*
Moran Shipyard Corporation .... C 718 981-5600
  Staten Island *(G-15728)*
Moran Towing Corporation .... G 718 981-5600
  Staten Island *(G-15729)*
Port Everglades Machine Works .... F 516 367-2280
  Plainview *(G-13658)*
Scarano Boat Building Inc .... E 518 463-3401
  Albany *(G-132)*
United Ship Repair Inc .... F 718 237-2800
  Brooklyn *(G-2722)*
Viking Mar Wldg Ship Repr LLC .... F 718 758-4116
  Brooklyn *(G-2744)*

SHIPPING AGENTS
Hastings Hide Inc .... G 516 295-2400
  Inwood *(G-6798)*

SHOCK ABSORBERS: Indl
Kyntec Corporation .... G 716 810-6956
  Buffalo *(G-3056)*
Taylor Devices Inc .... C 716 694-0800
  North Tonawanda *(G-13019)*

SHOE & BOOT ACCESS
Randall Loeffler Inc .... E 212 226-8787
  New York *(G-11826)*

SHOE MATERIALS: Counters
Counter Evolution .... G 212 647-7505
  New York *(G-9793)*
Custom Countertops Inc .... G 716 646-1579
  Orchard Park *(G-13291)*
Custom Countertops Inc .... G 716 685-2871
  Depew *(G-4277)*
Custom Design Kitchens Inc .... F 518 355-4446
  Duanesburg *(G-4350)*

SHOE MATERIALS: Plastic
311 Industries Corp .... G 607 846-4520
  Endicott *(G-4802)*

SHOE MATERIALS: Quarters
Priscilla Quart Co Firts .... G 516 365-2755
  Manhasset *(G-8098)*
Tread Quarters .... G 800 876-6676
  Rochester *(G-14758)*
Wash Quarters LLC .... G 989 802-2017
  Wallkill *(G-16567)*

SHOE MATERIALS: Sole Parts
MBA Orthotics Inc .... G 631 392-4755
  Bay Shore *(G-714)*

SHOE MATERIALS: Uppers
Upper Ninty LLC .... G 646 863-3105
  New York *(G-12495)*

SHOE REPAIR SHOP
Arimed Orthotics Prosthetics P .... F 718 875-8754
  Brooklyn *(G-1628)*

SHOE STORES
GH Bass & Co .... E 646 768-4600
  New York *(G-10333)*
Givi Inc .... F 212 586-5029
  New York *(G-10343)*
Kcp Holdco Inc .... F 212 265-1500
  New York *(G-10866)*
Kenneth Cole Productions Inc .... B 212 265-1500
  New York *(G-10873)*
Nine West Footwear Corporation .... B 800 999-1877
  New York *(G-11452)*
Wallico Shoes Corp .... G 212 826-7171
  New York *(G-12611)*

SHOE STORES: Children's
Jakes Sneakers Inc .... G 718 233-1132
  Brooklyn *(G-2133)*

SHOE STORES: Custom
Bandier Corp .... G 212 242-5400
  New York *(G-9366)*

SHOE STORES: Orthopedic
Arimed Orthotics Prosthetics P .... F 718 875-8754
  Brooklyn *(G-1628)*

SHOE STORES: Women's
Lsil & Co Inc .... G 914 761-0998
  White Plains *(G-17160)*

SHOES & BOOTS WHOLESALERS
Ashko Group LLC .... F 212 594-6050
  New York *(G-9283)*
Nine West Footwear Corporation .... B 800 999-1877
  New York *(G-11452)*
Wallico Shoes Corp .... G 212 826-7171
  New York *(G-12611)*

SHOES: Athletic, Exc Rubber Or Plastic
Custom Sports Lab Inc .... G 212 832-1648
  New York *(G-9828)*
Kicks Closet Sportswear Inc .... G 347 577-0857
  Bronx *(G-1376)*
Mango Usa Inc .... E 718 998-6050
  Brooklyn *(G-2260)*
Mayberry Shoe Company Inc .... G 315 692-4086
  Manlius *(G-8107)*
McM Products USA Inc .... E 646 756-4090
  New York *(G-11226)*
Reebok International Ltd .... E 212 221-6375
  New York *(G-11847)*
Reebok International Ltd .... C 718 370-0471
  Staten Island *(G-15751)*
Vsg International LLC .... G 718 300-8171
  Brooklyn *(G-2756)*

SHOES: Ballet Slippers
La Strada Dance Footwear Inc .... G 631 242-1401
  Deer Park *(G-4187)*

SHOES: Canvas, Rubber Soled

Inkkas LLC .... G 646 845-9803
  New York *(G-10643)*
Little Eric Shoes On Madison .... G 212 717-1513
  New York *(G-11038)*
Mango Usa Inc .... E 718 998-6050
  Brooklyn *(G-2260)*
Vans Inc .... F 631 724-1011
  Lake Grove *(G-7293)*
Vans Inc .... F 718 349-2311
  Brooklyn *(G-2737)*

SHOES: Infants' & Children's

Everlast Worldwide Inc .... E 212 239-0990
  New York *(G-10147)*
GH Bass & Co. .... E 646 768-4600
  New York *(G-10333)*
Reebok International Ltd .... C 914 948-3719
  White Plains *(G-17190)*
Steven Madden Ltd .... B 718 446-1800
  Long Island City *(G-7919)*

SHOES: Men's

Air Skate & Air Jump Corp .... G 212 967-1201
  New York *(G-9116)*
Air Skate & Air Jump Corp .... F 212 967-1201
  Brooklyn *(G-1571)*
Bm America LLC .... E 201 438-7733
  New York *(G-9478)*
Coach Inc .... B 212 594-1850
  New York *(G-9714)*
Detny Footwear Inc .... G 212 423-1040
  New York *(G-9913)*
GH Bass & Co .... E 646 768-4600
  New York *(G-10333)*
Kcp Holdco Inc .... F 212 265-1500
  New York *(G-10866)*
Kcp Operating Company LLC .... D 212 265-1500
  New York *(G-10867)*
Kenneth Cole Productions LP .... E 212 265-1500
  New York *(G-10872)*
Kenneth Cole Productions Inc .... B 212 265-1500
  New York *(G-10873)*
Lake View Manufacturing LLC .... F 315 364-7892
  King Ferry *(G-7198)*
Nicholas Kirkwood LLC .... G 646 559-5239
  New York *(G-11444)*
Phillips-Van Heusen Europe .... F 212 381-3500
  New York *(G-11668)*
Pvh Corp .... D 212 381-3500
  New York *(G-11780)*
Rockport Company LLC .... D 631 243-0418
  Deer Park *(G-4225)*
Rockport Company LLC .... G 718 271-3627
  Elmhurst *(G-4680)*
Steven Madden Ltd .... D 845 348-7026
  West Nyack *(G-16956)*
Steven Madden Ltd .... E 212 736-3283
  New York *(G-12224)*
Steven Madden Ltd .... B 718 446-1800
  Long Island City *(G-7919)*
T O Dey Service Corp .... F 212 683-6300
  New York *(G-12290)*
Tic TAC Toes Mfg Corp .... D 518 773-8187
  Gloversville *(G-5741)*

SHOES: Men's, Sandals

Neumann Jutta New York Inc .... F 212 982-7048
  New York *(G-11398)*

SHOES: Orthopedic, Men's

Jerry Miller Molded Shoes Inc .... F 716 881-3920
  Buffalo *(G-3034)*
Pedifix Inc .... E 845 277-2850
  Brewster *(G-1224)*
Tru Mold Shoes Inc .... E 716 881-4484
  Buffalo *(G-3253)*

SHOES: Orthopedic, Women's

Jerry Miller Molded Shoes Inc .... F 716 881-3920
  Buffalo *(G-3034)*
Pedifix Inc .... E 845 277-2850
  Brewster *(G-1224)*
T O Dey Service Corp .... F 212 683-6300
  New York *(G-12290)*
Tru Mold Shoes Inc .... E 716 881-4484
  Buffalo *(G-3253)*

SHOES: Plastic Or Rubber

Anthony L & S LLC .... G 212 386-7245
  New York *(G-9218)*
Detny Footwear Inc .... G 212 423-1040
  New York *(G-9913)*
Homegrown For Good LLC .... F 857 540-6361
  New Rochelle *(G-8957)*
Nike Inc .... E 212 226-5433
  New York *(G-11449)*
Nike Inc .... E 631 242-3014
  Deer Park *(G-4205)*
Nike Inc .... E 631 960-0184
  Islip Terrace *(G-6855)*
Nike Inc .... G 716 298-5615
  Niagara Falls *(G-12868)*
Pro Line Manufacturing Co LLC .... G 973 692-9696
  New York *(G-11745)*
Skechers USA Inc .... F 718 585-3024
  Bronx *(G-1454)*
Timing Group LLC .... F 646 878-2600
  New York *(G-12372)*
Wallico Shoes Corp .... G 212 826-7171
  New York *(G-12611)*

SHOES: Plastic Or Rubber Soles With Fabric Uppers

Soludos LLC .... F 212 219-1101
  New York *(G-12153)*

SHOES: Rubber Or Rubber Soled Fabric Uppers

Crocs Inc .... F 845 928-3002
  Central Valley *(G-3549)*

SHOES: Women's

Akh Group LLC .... G 646 320-8720
  New York *(G-9118)*
Alpargatas Usa Inc .... E 646 277-7171
  New York *(G-9149)*
Coach Inc .... B 212 594-1850
  New York *(G-9714)*
Detny Footwear Inc .... G 212 423-1040
  New York *(G-9913)*
Everlast Worldwide Inc .... E 212 239-0990
  New York *(G-10147)*
GH Bass & Co. .... E 646 768-4600
  New York *(G-10333)*
Kcp Operating Company LLC .... D 212 265-1500
  New York *(G-10867)*
Kenneth Cole Productions Inc .... B 212 265-1500
  New York *(G-10873)*
Lake View Manufacturing LLC .... F 315 364-7892
  King Ferry *(G-7198)*
Nicholas Kirkwood LLC .... G 646 559-5239
  New York *(G-11444)*
Nine West Footwear Corporation .... B 800 999-1877
  New York *(G-11452)*
Steven Madden Ltd .... D 212 695-5545
  New York *(G-12225)*
Steven Madden Ltd .... B 718 446-1800
  Long Island City *(G-7919)*
Tic TAC Toes Mfg Corp .... D 518 773-8187
  Gloversville *(G-5741)*

SHOES: Women's, Dress

Adl Design Inc .... G 516 949-6658
  Huntington *(G-6685)*
Attitudes Footwear Inc .... G 212 754-9113
  New York *(G-9312)*
Mango Usa Inc .... E 718 998-6050
  Brooklyn *(G-2260)*

SHOES: Women's, Sandals

Neumann Jutta New York Inc .... F 212 982-7048
  New York *(G-11398)*

SHOPPING CENTERS & MALLS

Northpoint Trading Inc .... F 212 481-8001
  New York *(G-11478)*

SHOT PEENING SVC

Metal Improvement Company LLC .... D 607 533-7000
  Lansing *(G-7374)*

SHOWCASES & DISPLAY FIXTURES: Office & Store

Aarco Products Inc .... F 631 924-5461
  Yaphank *(G-17400)*
Abbott Industries Inc .... E 718 291-0800
  Jamaica *(G-6926)*
Dejah Associates Inc .... E 631 265-2185
  Bay Shore *(G-692)*
Four S Showcase Manufacturing .... G 718 649-4900
  Brooklyn *(G-2000)*
Glaro Inc .... D 631 234-1717
  Hauppauge *(G-6108)*
Ledan Inc .... E 631 239-1226
  Northport *(G-13032)*
Manhattan Display Inc .... G 718 392-1365
  Long Island City *(G-7832)*
Mega Vision Inc .... E 718 228-1065
  Brooklyn *(G-2298)*
Steven Kraus Associates Inc .... G 631 923-2033
  Huntington *(G-6721)*
Visual Millwork & Fix Mfg Inc .... D 718 267-7800
  Deer Park *(G-4250)*

SHOWER STALLS: Metal

CNA Specialties Inc .... G 631 567-7929
  Sayville *(G-15235)*
ITR Industries Inc .... E 914 964-7063
  Yonkers *(G-17473)*

SHOWER STALLS: Plastic & Fiberglass

ITR Industries Inc .... E 914 964-7063
  Yonkers *(G-17473)*

SHREDDERS: Indl & Commercial

Chester Shred-It/West .... E 914 407-2502
  Valhalla *(G-16391)*

SIDING & STRUCTURAL MATERIALS: Wood

Greater Niagara Bldg Ctr Inc .... F 716 299-0543
  Niagara Falls *(G-12846)*
Gutchess Lumber Co Inc .... C 607 753-3393
  Cortland *(G-4052)*
L J Valente Inc .... G 518 674-3750
  Averill Park *(G-533)*
Mohawk Metal Mfg & Sls .... G 315 853-7663
  Westmoreland *(G-17091)*
One Tree Dist .... G 315 701-2924
  Syracuse *(G-16024)*
Tri-State Brick & Stone NY Inc .... D 212 366-0300
  New York *(G-12423)*
Upstate Increte Incorporated .... G 585 254-2010
  Rochester *(G-14774)*

SIDING MATERIALS

Texture Plus Inc .... E 631 218-9200
  Bohemia *(G-1140)*

SIGN LETTERING & PAINTING SVCS

Sign Shop Inc .... G 631 226-4145
  Copiague *(G-3951)*

SIGN PAINTING & LETTERING SHOP

Clinton Signs Inc .... G 585 482-1620
  Webster *(G-16743)*
Lanza Corp .... G 914 937-6360
  Port Chester *(G-13778)*
Paratore Signs Inc .... G 315 455-5551
  Syracuse *(G-16031)*
Ray Sign Inc .... F 518 377-1371
  Schenectady *(G-15313)*
Santoro Signs Inc .... G 716 895-8875
  Buffalo *(G-3205)*

SIGNALING APPARATUS: Electric

Intelligent Traffic Systems .... G 631 567-5994
  Bohemia *(G-1074)*
L-3 Cmmnctons Fgn Holdings Inc .... E 212 697-1111
  New York *(G-10941)*
L3 Technologies Inc .... B 212 697-1111
  New York *(G-10943)*
North Hills Signal Proc Corp .... F 516 682-7740
  Syosset *(G-15854)*
Werma (usa) Inc .... G 315 414-0200
  East Syracuse *(G-4592)*

PRODUCT SECTION

SIGNS & ADVERTISING SPECIALTIES

SIGNALING DEVICES: Sound, Electrical

Sensor Films Incorporated ....E 585 738-3500
  Victor *(G-16525)*

SIGNALS: Railroad, Electric

Alstom Signaling Inc ....B 585 783-2000
  Schenectady *(G-15257)*
Alstom Signaling Inc ....E 585 274-8700
  Schenectady *(G-15258)*
Star Headlight Lantern Co Inc ....C 585 226-9500
  Avon *(G-540)*
Twinco Mfg Co Inc ....E 631 231-0022
  Hauppauge *(G-6243)*

SIGNALS: Traffic Control, Electric

Apex Signal Corporation ....D 631 567-1100
  Bohemia *(G-1013)*
Comet Flasher Inc ....G 716 821-9595
  Buffalo *(G-2901)*
General Traffic Equipment Corp ......F 845 569-9000
  Newburgh *(G-12779)*
Power Line Constructors Inc ....E 315 853-6183
  Clinton *(G-3746)*

SIGNALS: Transportation

Alstom Signaling Inc ....G 800 717-4477
  West Henrietta *(G-16898)*

SIGNS & ADVERTISING SPECIALTIES

A 3-D Signs & Awnings Inc ....G 718 252-7575
  Brooklyn *(G-1529)*
A B C Mc Cleary Sign Co Inc ....F 315 493-3550
  Carthage *(G-3435)*
A M S Sign Designs ....G 631 467-7722
  Centereach *(G-3494)*
Aakron Rule Corp ....C 716 542-5483
  Akron *(G-17)*
ABC Windows and Signs Corp ....F 718 353-6210
  College Point *(G-3800)*
Accurate Signs & Awnings Inc ....F 718 788-0302
  Brooklyn *(G-1552)*
Acme Signs of Baldwinsville ....G 315 638-4865
  Baldwinsville *(G-564)*
Ad Makers Long Island Inc ....F 631 595-9100
  Deer Park *(G-4112)*
Adirondack Sign Perfect Inc ....E 518 409-7446
  Saratoga Springs *(G-15169)*
All Signs ....G 973 736-2113
  Staten Island *(G-15656)*
Alley Cat Signs Inc ....F 631 924-7446
  Middle Island *(G-8439)*
Allied Decorations Co Inc ....F 315 637-0273
  Syracuse *(G-15870)*
American Car Signs Inc ....G 518 227-1173
  Duanesburg *(G-4349)*
Architectural Sign Group Inc ....G 516 326-1800
  Elmont *(G-4729)*
Artscroll Printing Corp ....E 212 929-2413
  New York *(G-9275)*
Asi Sign Systems Inc ....G 646 742-1320
  New York *(G-9284)*
Asi Sign Systems Inc ....G 716 775-0104
  Grand Island *(G-5765)*
Atomic Signworks ....G 315 779-7446
  Watertown *(G-16657)*
Bedford Precision Parts Corp ....E 914 241-2211
  Bedford Hills *(G-796)*
Bmg Printing and Promotion LLC ...G 631 231-9200
  Bohemia *(G-1022)*
Broadway National Group LLC ....D 800 797-4467
  Ronkonkoma *(G-14909)*
Buckeye Corrugated Inc ....D 585 924-1600
  Victor *(G-16489)*
Bulow & Associates Inc ....G 716 838-0298
  Tonawanda *(G-16171)*
Cab Signs Inc ....E 718 479-2424
  Brooklyn *(G-1747)*
Central Rede Sign Co Inc ....G 716 213-0797
  Tonawanda *(G-16172)*
Chautauqua Sign Co Inc ....G 716 665-2222
  Falconer *(G-4900)*
City Signs Inc ....G 718 375-5933
  Brooklyn *(G-1783)*
Climax Packaging Inc ....C 315 376-8000
  Lowville *(G-7963)*
Coe Displays Inc ....G 718 937-5658
  Long Island City *(G-7730)*

Colad Group LLC ....D 716 961-1776
  Buffalo *(G-2900)*
Colonial Redi Record Corp ....E 718 972-7433
  Brooklyn *(G-1790)*
Community Products LLC ....E 845 658-8351
  Rifton *(G-14145)*
Crown Sign Systems Inc ....F 914 375-2118
  Mount Vernon *(G-8721)*
Custom Display Manufacture ....G 516 783-6491
  North Bellmore *(G-12936)*
Decree Signs & Graphics Inc ....F 973 278-3603
  Floral Park *(G-5209)*
Design A Sign of Putnam Inc ....G 845 279-5328
  Brewster *(G-1213)*
Designplex LLC ....G 845 358-6647
  Nyack *(G-13065)*
Display Producers Inc ....C 718 904-1200
  New Rochelle *(G-8940)*
Displays & Beyond Inc ....F 718 805-7786
  Glendale *(G-5666)*
East End Sign Design Inc ....G 631 399-2574
  Mastic *(G-8234)*
Eastern Concepts Ltd ....F 718 472-3377
  Sunnyside *(G-15828)*
Eastern Metal of Elmira Inc ....D 607 734-2295
  Elmira *(G-4692)*
Elderlee Incorporated ....E 315 789-6670
  Oaks Corners *(G-13088)*
Executive Sign Corp ....G 212 397-4050
  Cornwall On Hudson *(G-4013)*
Exhibit Corporation America ....E 718 937-2600
  Long Island City *(G-7763)*
Fastsigns ....F 518 456-7446
  Albany *(G-79)*
Flado Enterprises Inc ....G 716 668-6400
  Depew *(G-4282)*
Flair Display Inc ....F 718 324-9330
  Bronx *(G-1336)*
Fletcher Enterprises Inc ....F 716 837-7446
  Buffalo *(G-2963)*
Forrest Engraving Co Inc ....F 845 228-0200
  New Rochelle *(G-8946)*
Fortune Sign ....E 646 383-8682
  Brooklyn *(G-1996)*
Fossil Industries Inc ....E 631 254-9200
  Deer Park *(G-4167)*
G I Certified Inc ....E 212 397-1945
  New York *(G-10279)*
Graphic Signs & Awnings Ltd ....F 718 227-6000
  Staten Island *(G-15702)*
Graphitek Inc ....F 518 686-5966
  Hoosick Falls *(G-6566)*
Greyline Signs Inc ....G 716 947-4526
  Derby *(G-4306)*
HI Tech Signs of NY Inc ....G 516 794-7880
  East Meadow *(G-4444)*
Hollywood Signs Inc ....F 917 577-7333
  Brooklyn *(G-2079)*
ID Signsystems Inc ....E 585 266-5750
  Rochester *(G-14462)*
Ideal Signs Inc ....G 718 292-9196
  Bronx *(G-1360)*
Image360 ....G 585 272-1234
  Rochester *(G-14466)*
Impressive Imprints Inc ....G 631 293-6161
  Farmingdale *(G-5017)*
International Patterns Inc ....D 631 952-2000
  Plainview *(G-13638)*
Jaf Converters Inc ....E 631 842-3131
  Copiague *(G-3934)*
Jal Signs Inc ....F 516 536-7280
  Baldwin *(G-558)*
Jax Signs and Neon Inc ....G 607 727-3420
  Endicott *(G-4821)*
Jay Turoff ....F 718 856-7300
  Brooklyn *(G-2135)*
Jem Sign Corp ....G 516 867-4466
  Hempstead *(G-6299)*
JP Signs ....G 518 569-3907
  Chazy *(G-3589)*
Kenan International Trading ....G 718 672-4922
  Corona *(G-4023)*
KP Industries Inc ....F 516 679-3161
  North Bellmore *(G-12938)*
Kraus & Sons Inc ....F 212 620-0408
  New York *(G-10926)*
L I C Screen Printing Inc ....E 516 546-7289
  Merrick *(G-8421)*
L Miller Design Inc ....G 631 242-1163
  Deer Park *(G-4186)*

L Y Z Creations Ltd Inc ....E 718 768-2977
  Brooklyn *(G-2187)*
Lanco Corporation ....C 631 231-2300
  Ronkonkoma *(G-14957)*
Lanza Corp ....G 914 937-6360
  Port Chester *(G-13778)*
Letterama Inc ....G 516 349-0800
  West Babylon *(G-16835)*
Lifestyle-Trimco ....E 718 257-9101
  Brooklyn *(G-2220)*
Linear Signs Inc ....F 631 532-5330
  Lindenhurst *(G-7490)*
M Santoliquido Corp ....F 914 375-6674
  Yonkers *(G-17481)*
Marigold Signs Inc ....F 516 433-7446
  Hicksville *(G-6395)*
Maxworld Inc ....E 212 242-7588
  New York *(G-11213)*
Mekanism Inc ....E 212 226-2772
  New York *(G-11248)*
Metropolitan Sign & Riggin ....G 718 231-0010
  Bronx *(G-1398)*
Metropolitan Signs Inc ....G 315 638-1448
  Baldwinsville *(G-571)*
Midwood Signs & Design Inc ....G 718 499-9041
  Brooklyn *(G-2316)*
Millennium Signs & Display Inc ......E 516 292-8000
  Hempstead *(G-6304)*
Miller Mohr Display Inc ....G 631 941-2769
  East Setauket *(G-4505)*
Mixture Screen Printing ....G 845 561-2857
  Newburgh *(G-12788)*
Modulex New York Inc ....E 646 742-1320
  New York *(G-11317)*
Monasani Signs Inc ....G 631 266-2635
  East Northport *(G-4461)*
Morris Brothers Sign Svc Inc ....G 212 675-9130
  New York *(G-11331)*
Movinads & Signs LLC ....G 518 378-3000
  Halfmoon *(G-5935)*
Mr Sign Usa Inc ....F 718 218-3321
  Brooklyn *(G-2346)*
Nameplate Mfrs of Amer ....E 631 752-0055
  Farmingdale *(G-5070)*
New Art Signs Co Inc ....G 718 443-0900
  Glen Head *(G-5651)*
New Dimensions Research Corp ...C 631 694-1356
  Melville *(G-8369)*
New Kit On The Block ....C 631 757-5655
  Bohemia *(G-1104)*
Noel Assoc ....G 516 371-5420
  Inwood *(G-6804)*
Norampac New York City Inc ....C 718 340-2100
  Maspeth *(G-8189)*
North Shore Neon Sign Co Inc ....E 718 937-4848
  Flushing *(G-5282)*
Northeastern Sign Corp ....G 315 265-6657
  South Colton *(G-15538)*
Northern Awning & Sign Company ...G 315 782-8515
  Watertown *(G-16690)*
Nysco Products LLC ....D 718 792-9000
  Bronx *(G-1416)*
On The Mark Digital Printing & ....G 716 823-3373
  Hamburg *(G-5959)*
Orlandi Inc ....D 631 756-0110
  Farmingdale *(G-5081)*
Orlandi Inc ....E 631 756-0110
  Farmingdale *(G-5082)*
Penn Signs Inc ....E 718 797-1112
  Brooklyn *(G-2427)*
Precision Signscom Inc ....D 631 842-5060
  Amityville *(G-323)*
Premier Sign Systems LLC ....E 585 235-0390
  Rochester *(G-14620)*
Promotional Development Inc ....D 718 485-8550
  Brooklyn *(G-2471)*
Qcr Express Corp ....G 888 924-5888
  Astoria *(G-452)*
Quick Sign F X ....F 516 249-6531
  Farmingdale *(G-5104)*
Resonant Legal Media LLC ....D 800 781-3591
  New York *(G-11873)*
Rgm Signs Inc ....G 718 442-0598
  Staten Island *(G-15754)*
Riverwood Signs By Dandev Desi ...G 845 229-0282
  Hyde Park *(G-6776)*
Royal Promotion Group Inc ....D 212 246-3780
  New York *(G-11945)*
Rpf Associates Inc ....G 631 462-7446
  Commack *(G-3867)*

Employee Codes: A=Over 500 employees, B=251-500
C=101-250, D=51-100, E=20-50, F=10-19, G=5-9

Rsquared Ny Inc ....D 631 521-8700
Edgewood *(G-4622)*
Santoro Signs Inc ....G 716 895-8875
Buffalo *(G-3205)*
Saxton Corporation ....E 518 732-7705
Castleton On Hudson *(G-3449)*
Sellco Industries Inc ....E 607 756-7594
Cortland *(G-4068)*
Seneca Signs LLC ....G 315 446-9420
Syracuse *(G-16061)*
Sign & Signs ....G 718 941-6200
Brooklyn *(G-2579)*
Sign A Rama Inc ....G 631 952-3324
Hauppauge *(G-6214)*
Sign A Rama of Syracuse ....G 315 446-9420
Syracuse *(G-16064)*
Sign City of New York Inc ....G 718 661-1118
College Point *(G-3833)*
Sign Company ....G 212 967-2113
New York *(G-12091)*
Sign Design Group New York Inc ....F 718 392-0779
Long Island City *(G-7905)*
Sign Group Inc ....E 718 438-7103
Brooklyn *(G-2580)*
Sign Guys LLC ....G 315 253-4276
Auburn *(G-515)*
Sign Here Enterprises LLC ....G 914 328-3111
Hartsdale *(G-6019)*
Sign Studio Inc ....F 518 266-0877
Troy *(G-16278)*
Sign Works Incorporated ....E 914 592-0700
Elmsford *(G-4792)*
Sign World Inc ....E 212 619-9000
Brooklyn *(G-2581)*
Signature Industries Inc ....F 516 679-5177
Freeport *(G-5439)*
Signexpo Enterprises Inc ....F 212 925-8585
New York *(G-12095)*
Signs Inc ....G 518 483-4759
Malone *(G-8048)*
Signs Ink Ltd ....F 914 739-9059
Yorktown Heights *(G-17536)*
Signs of Success Ltd ....F 516 295-6000
Lynbrook *(G-7987)*
Smith Graphics Inc ....G 631 420-4180
Farmingdale *(G-5121)*
Snyders Neon Displays Inc ....G 518 857-4100
Colonie *(G-3847)*
Space Sign ....F 718 961-1112
College Point *(G-3834)*
Spanjer Corp ....G 347 448-8033
Long Island City *(G-7909)*
Specialty Signs Co Inc ....F 212 243-8521
New York *(G-12179)*
Spectrum On Broadway ....F 718 932-5388
Woodside *(G-17370)*
Speedy Sign A Rama USA Inc ....G 516 783-1075
Bellmore *(G-818)*
Starlite Media LLC ....G 212 909-7700
New York *(G-12211)*
Stepping Stones One Day Signs ....G 518 237-5774
Waterford *(G-16643)*
Strategic Signage Sourcing LLC ....F 518 450-1093
Saratoga Springs *(G-15204)*
Tech Products Inc ....E 718 442-4900
Staten Island *(G-15770)*
Three Gems Inc ....G 516 248-0388
New Hyde Park *(G-8911)*
Timely Signs of Kingston Inc ....F 845 331-8710
Kingston *(G-7243)*
Tj Signs Unlimited LLC ....C 631 273-4800
Islip *(G-6853)*
Todd Walbridge ....G 585 254-3018
Rochester *(G-14755)*
Tru-Art Sign Co Inc ....F 718 658-5068
Jamaica *(G-6995)*
Ultimate Signs & Designs Inc ....E 516 481-0800
Hempstead *(G-6311)*
United Sttes Brnze Sign of Fla ....E 516 352-5155
New Hyde Park *(G-8914)*
Universal Signs and Svc Inc ....E 631 446-1121
Deer Park *(G-4245)*
USA Signs of America Inc ....D 631 254-6900
Deer Park *(G-4246)*
Valle Signs and Awnings ....F 516 408-3440
Uniondale *(G-16325)*
Valley Creek Side Inc ....G 315 839-5526
Clayville *(G-3716)*
Vez Inc ....G 718 273-7002
Staten Island *(G-15774)*
Viana Signs Corp ....F 516 887-2000
Oceanside *(G-13126)*
Victory Signs Inc ....G 315 762-0220
Canastota *(G-3402)*
Visual ID Source Inc ....F 516 307-9759
Mineola *(G-8571)*
Visual Impact Graphics Inc ....G 585 548-7118
Batavia *(G-652)*
Vital Signs & Graphics Co Inc ....G 518 237-8372
Cohoes *(G-3785)*
Voss Signs LLC ....E 315 682-6418
Manlius *(G-8109)*
Wedel Sign Company Inc ....G 631 727-4577
Riverhead *(G-14173)*
Westchester Signs Inc ....G 914 666-7446
Mount Kisco *(G-8688)*
Wizard Equipment Inc ....G 315 414-9999
Syracuse *(G-16097)*
Wl Concepts & Production Inc ....G 516 538-5300
Freeport *(G-5445)*
Woodbury Printing Plus + Inc ....G 845 928-6610
Central Valley *(G-3557)*
X Press Signs Inc ....G 716 892-3000
West Seneca *(G-16984)*
Yellowpagecitycom ....F 585 410-6688
Rochester *(G-14802)*
Yong Xin Kitchen Supplies Inc ....F 212 995-8908
New York *(G-12717)*
Z-Car-D Corp ....E 631 424-2077
Huntington Station *(G-6768)*

SIGNS & ADVERTISING SPECIALTIES: Artwork, Advertising

Adstream America LLC ....E 212 804-8498
New York *(G-9081)*
Liberty Awnings & Signs Inc ....G 347 203-1470
East Elmhurst *(G-4416)*
National Prfmce Solutions Inc ....D 718 833-4767
Brooklyn *(G-2358)*
Pereira & ODell LLC ....E 212 897-1000
New York *(G-11633)*
Pyx Inc ....G 718 469-4253
Brooklyn *(G-2477)*
Rocket Fuel Inc ....F 212 594-8888
New York *(G-11919)*
United Print Group Inc ....F 718 392-4242
Long Island City *(G-7936)*
Whispr Group Inc ....F 212 924-3979
New York *(G-12651)*

SIGNS & ADVERTISING SPECIALTIES: Displays, Paint Process

Chameleon Color Cards Ltd ....D 716 625-9452
Lockport *(G-7604)*
Faster-Form Corp ....D 800 327-3676
New Hartford *(G-8849)*
Mechtronics Corporation ....C 845 231-1400
Beacon *(G-782)*
Mechtronics Corporation ....E 845 831-9300
Beacon *(G-783)*
Props Displays & Interiors ....F 212 620-3840
New York *(G-11759)*

SIGNS & ADVERTISING SPECIALTIES: Letters For Signs, Metal

Brooklyn Signs LLC ....G 718 252-7575
Brooklyn *(G-1732)*
Stickershopcom Inc ....G 631 563-4323
Bayport *(G-755)*

SIGNS & ADVERTISING SPECIALTIES: Novelties

Amsterdam Printing & Litho Inc ....F 518 842-6000
Amsterdam *(G-333)*
Amsterdam Printing & Litho Inc ....E 518 842-6000
Amsterdam *(G-334)*
Dkm Sales LLC ....E 716 893-7777
Buffalo *(G-2932)*
Jomar Industries Inc ....E 845 357-5773
Airmont *(G-14)*
Keep America Beautiful Inc ....G 518 842-4388
Amsterdam *(G-354)*
Kling Magnetics Inc ....E 518 392-4000
Chatham *(G-3586)*
Mastercraft Manufacturing Co ....G 718 729-5620
Long Island City *(G-7835)*
National Advertising & Prtg ....G 212 629-7650
New York *(G-11369)*
Northeast Promotional Group In ....G 518 793-1024
South Glens Falls *(G-15550)*
Pama Enterprises Inc ....G 516 504-6300
Great Neck *(G-5846)*
Tempo Industries Inc ....G 516 334-6900
Westbury *(G-17060)*
Von Pok & Chang New York Inc ....G 212 599-0556
New York *(G-12594)*

SIGNS & ADVERTISING SPECIALTIES: Scoreboards, Electric

Eversan Inc ....F 315 736-3967
Whitesboro *(G-17221)*

SIGNS & ADVERTISING SPECIALTIES: Signs

Allstate Sign & Plaque Corp ....F 631 242-2828
Deer Park *(G-4117)*
Art Parts Signs Inc ....G 585 381-2134
East Rochester *(G-4472)*
Big Apple Sign Corp ....E 631 342-0303
Islandia *(G-6826)*
Big Apple Sign Corp ....E 212 629-3650
New York *(G-9441)*
Checklist Boards Corporation ....G 585 586-0152
Rochester *(G-14294)*
Dura Engraving Corporation ....E 718 706-6400
Long Island City *(G-7748)*
Executive Sign Corporation ....G 212 397-4050
New York *(G-10159)*
Hanson Sign Screen Prcess Corp ....E 716 661-3900
Falconer *(G-4908)*
Hermosa Corp ....E 315 768-4320
New York Mills *(G-12744)*
L S Sign Co Inc ....F 718 469-8600
Ridgewood *(G-14125)*
Mauceri Sign Inc ....F 718 656-7700
Jamaica *(G-6965)*
Mohawk Sign Systems Inc ....E 518 842-5303
Amsterdam *(G-361)*
Nas Quick Sign Inc ....G 716 876-7599
Buffalo *(G-3102)*
Poncio Signs ....G 718 543-4851
Bronx *(G-1430)*
Quorum Group LLC ....D 585 798-8888
Medina *(G-8312)*
Rapp Signs Inc ....F 607 656-8167
Greene *(G-5885)*
Rome Sign & Display Co ....G 315 336-0550
Rome *(G-14861)*
Sign Center Inc ....F 212 967-2113
New York *(G-12090)*
Sign Impressions Inc ....G 585 723-0420
Rochester *(G-14708)*
Sign Language Inc ....G 585 237-2620
Perry *(G-13549)*
Suma Industries Inc ....G 646 436-5202
New York *(G-12252)*
Universal 3d Innovation Inc ....F 516 837-9423
Valley Stream *(G-16454)*

SIGNS & ADVERTSG SPECIALTIES: Displays/Cutouts Window/Lobby

American Visuals Inc ....G 631 694-6104
Farmingdale *(G-4949)*
Azar International Inc ....E 845 624-8808
Nanuet *(G-8797)*
Creative Solutions Group Inc ....B 914 771-4200
Yonkers *(G-17448)*
Display Marketing Group Inc ....E 631 348-4450
Islandia *(G-6829)*
Display Presentations Ltd ....D 631 951-4050
Brooklyn *(G-1866)*
DSI Group Inc ....C 800 553-2202
Maspeth *(G-8162)*
Edge Display Group Entp Inc ....F 631 498-1373
Bellport *(G-825)*
Hadley Exhibits Inc ....D 716 874-3666
Buffalo *(G-3002)*
Joseph Struhl Co Inc ....F 516 741-3660
New Hyde Park *(G-8889)*
King Displays Inc ....F 212 629-8455
New York *(G-10891)*
Lamar Plastics Packaging Ltd ....D 516 378-2500
Freeport *(G-5419)*
Mystic Display Co Inc ....G 718 485-2651
Brooklyn *(G-2351)*

PRODUCT SECTION

SOAPS & DETERGENTS

Nationwide Exhibitor Svcs Inc ....F 631 467-2034
 Central Islip *(G-3532)*
New Style Signs Limited Inc ....F 212 242-7848
 New York *(G-11414)*
Newline Products Inc ....C 972 881-3318
 New Windsor *(G-8992)*
Plasti-Vue Corp ....G 718 463-2300
 Flushing *(G-5289)*
Platinum Sales Promotion Inc ....G 718 361-0200
 Long Island City *(G-7874)*
Polyplastic Forms Inc ....E 631 249-5011
 Farmingdale *(G-5093)*
R & J Displays Inc ....E 631 491-3500
 West Babylon *(G-16851)*
Signs & Decal Corp ....E 718 486-6400
 Brooklyn *(G-2582)*
Steel-Brite Ltd ....F 631 589-4044
 Oakdale *(G-13082)*
Timely Signs Inc ....G 516 285-5339
 Elmont *(G-4740)*
Unique Display Mfg Corp ....G 516 546-3800
 Freeport *(G-5444)*
Visual Citi Inc ....C 631 482-3030
 Lindenhurst *(G-7518)*

SIGNS, EXC ELECTRIC, WHOLESALE

Fedex Office & Print Svcs Inc ....G 718 982-5223
 Staten Island *(G-15694)*
Mixture Screen Printing ....G 845 561-2857
 Newburgh *(G-12788)*
New Kit On The Block ....G 631 757-5655
 Bohemia *(G-1104)*

SIGNS: Electrical

Artkraft Strauss LLC ....E 212 265-5155
 New York *(G-9273)*
Clinton Signs Inc ....G 585 482-1620
 Webster *(G-16743)*
Flexlume Sign Corporation ....G 716 884-2020
 Buffalo *(G-2965)*
Gloede Neon Signs Ltd Inc ....F 845 471-4366
 Poughkeepsie *(G-13922)*
Motion Message Inc ....F 631 924-9500
 Bellport *(G-831)*
Olson Sign Company Inc ....G 518 370-2118
 Schenectady *(G-15309)*
Ray Sign Inc ....F 518 377-1371
 Schenectady *(G-15313)*
Spectrum Signs Inc ....E 631 756-1010
 Woodside *(G-17371)*
T J Signs Unlimited LLC ....E 631 273-4800
 Islip *(G-6852)*
Trans-Lux Corporation ....D 800 243-5544
 New York *(G-12413)*
Visual Effects Inc ....F 718 324-0011
 Jamaica *(G-6998)*

SIGNS: Neon

Broadway Neon Sign Corp ....F 908 241-4177
 Ronkonkoma *(G-14910)*
Frank Torrone & Sons Inc ....F 718 273-7600
 Staten Island *(G-15695)*
K & B Stamping Co Inc ....G 914 664-8555
 Mount Vernon *(G-8741)*
Manhattan Neon Sign Corp ....F 212 714-0430
 New York *(G-11155)*
Mds USA Inc ....E 718 358-5588
 Flushing *(G-5276)*
Super Neon Light Co Inc ....G 718 236-5667
 Brooklyn *(G-2645)*
Turoff Tower Graphics Inc ....F 718 856-7300
 Brooklyn *(G-2707)*
Ulrich Sign Co Inc ....E 716 434-0167
 Lockport *(G-7654)*
Yost Neon Displays Inc ....G 716 674-6780
 West Seneca *(G-16985)*

SILICA MINING

American Minerals Inc ....F 646 747-4222
 New York *(G-9176)*
St Silicones Inc ....G 518 664-0745
 Mechanicville *(G-8262)*

SILICON & CHROMIUM

Medima LLC ....C 716 741-0400
 Clarence *(G-3693)*

SILICON WAFERS: Chemically Doped

Isonics Corporation ....G 212 356-7400
 New York *(G-10710)*

SILICONE RESINS

George M Dujack ....G 518 279-1303
 Troy *(G-16258)*
Meliorum Technologies Inc ....G 585 313-0616
 Rochester *(G-14524)*
Pawling Corporation ....C 845 855-1000
 Pawling *(G-13474)*

SILICONES

Crown Delta Corporation ....E 914 245-8910
 Yorktown Heights *(G-17526)*
Momentive Performance Mtls Inc ....A 614 986-2495
 Waterford *(G-16637)*
Momentive Performance Mtls Inc ....E 518 237-3330
 Waterford *(G-16638)*
Momentive Prfmce Mtls Holdings ....A 518 533-4600
 Albany *(G-102)*
Mpm Holdings Inc ....E 518 237-3330
 Waterford *(G-16639)*
Mpm Intermediate Holdings Inc ....E 518 237-3330
 Waterford *(G-16640)*
Mpm Silicones LLC ....A 518 233-3330
 Waterford *(G-16641)*
Specialty Silicone Pdts Inc ....E 518 885-8826
 Ballston Spa *(G-608)*

SILK SCREEN DESIGN SVCS

Buffalo Circuits Inc ....G 716 662-2113
 Orchard Park *(G-13279)*
Mainly Monograms Inc ....E 845 624-4923
 West Nyack *(G-16949)*

SILVER ORES

Global Gold Corporation ....F 914 925-0020
 Rye *(G-15084)*

SILVER ORES PROCESSING

Rochester Silver Works LLC ....E 585 477-9501
 Rochester *(G-14670)*

SILVERSMITHS

D W Haber & Son Inc ....E 718 993-6405
 Bronx *(G-1311)*
Denvin Inc ....E 718 232-3389
 Brooklyn *(G-1854)*
R Goldsmith ....F 718 239-1396
 Bronx *(G-1438)*
Swed Masters Workshop LLC ....F 212 644-8822
 New York *(G-12274)*

SILVERWARE

Studio Silversmiths Inc ....E 718 418-6785
 Ridgewood *(G-14138)*

SILVERWARE & PLATED WARE

Oneida International Inc ....G 315 361-3000
 Oneida *(G-13182)*
Oneida Silversmiths Inc ....G 315 361-3000
 Oneida *(G-13186)*

SILVERWARE, SILVER PLATED

Sherrill Manufacturing Inc ....C 315 280-0727
 Sherrill *(G-15430)*

SIMULATORS: Flight

BSC Associates LLC ....F 607 321-2980
 Binghamton *(G-895)*
Northrop Grumman Intl Trdg Inc ....G 716 626-7233
 Buffalo *(G-3118)*

SINKS: Vitreous China

Kraus USA Inc ....F 800 775-0703
 Port Washington *(G-13856)*

SKIN CARE PRDTS: Suntan Lotions & Oils

St Tropez Inc ....G 800 366-6383
 New York *(G-12204)*

SKYLIGHTS

Citros Building Materials Co ....E 718 779-0727
 East Elmhurst *(G-4412)*
Gottlieb Schwartz Family ....E 718 761-2010
 Staten Island *(G-15700)*

SLAB & TILE: Precast Concrete, Floor

Duranm Inc ....G 914 774-3367
 Cortlandt Manor *(G-4073)*
Rain Catchers Seamless Gutters ....G 516 520-1956
 Bethpage *(G-877)*

SLABS: Steel

Safespan Platform Systems Inc ....E 716 694-1100
 Tonawanda *(G-16217)*

SLATE PRDTS

Evergreen Slate Company Inc ....D 518 642-2530
 Middle Granville *(G-8431)*
North American Slate Inc ....G 518 642-1702
 Granville *(G-5794)*
Northeast Solite Corporation ....E 845 246-2177
 Mount Marion *(G-8694)*
Sheldon Slate Products Co Inc ....E 518 642-1280
 Middle Granville *(G-8434)*
Vermont Natural Stoneworks ....E 518 642-2460
 Middle Granville *(G-8436)*

SLATE: Dimension

Hadeka Stone Corp ....E 518 282-9605
 Hampton *(G-5981)*
Hilltop Slate Inc ....E 518 642-1453
 Middle Granville *(G-8432)*
Vermont Multicolor Slate ....G 518 642-2400
 Middle Granville *(G-8435)*

SLINGS: Rope

All-Lifts Incorporated ....E 518 465-3461
 Albany *(G-42)*

SLIP RINGS

Princetel Inc ....F 914 579-2410
 Hawthorne *(G-6277)*

SLIPPERS: House

RG Barry Corporation ....F 212 244-3145
 New York *(G-11884)*

SMOKE DETECTORS

Fuel Watchman Sales & Service ....F 718 665-6100
 Bronx *(G-1340)*
Nrd LLC ....E 716 773-7634
 Grand Island *(G-5779)*

SNOW PLOWING SVCS

Northeastern Sealcoat Inc ....F 585 544-4372
 Rochester *(G-14563)*

SOAPS & DETERGENTS

Aura Detergent LLC ....F 718 824-2162
 Bronx *(G-1277)*
Baums Castorine Company Inc ....G 315 336-8154
 Rome *(G-14834)*
Chemite Inc ....G 607 529-3218
 Waverly *(G-16725)*
Colgate-Palmolive Company ....A 212 310-2000
 New York *(G-9726)*
Colgate-Palmolive Nj Inc ....E 212 310-2000
 New York *(G-9728)*
Combe Incorporated ....C 914 694-5454
 White Plains *(G-17123)*
Cosco Enterprises Inc ....G 718 383-4488
 Ridgewood *(G-14117)*
Cpac Inc ....E 585 382-3223
 Leicester *(G-7442)*
Crosstex International Inc ....D 631 582-6777
 Hauppauge *(G-6079)*
Dr Jacobs Naturals LLC ....E 718 265-1522
 Brooklyn *(G-1878)*
Ecolab Inc ....F 716 683-6298
 Cheektowaga *(G-3598)*
Enviro Service & Supply Corp ....F 347 838-6500
 Staten Island *(G-15692)*

Gfl USA Inc ....G.... 917 297-8701
Brooklyn (G-2022)
Greenmaker Industries LLC ....F.... 866 684-7800
Farmingdale (G-5009)
H & H Laboratories Inc ....F.... 718 624-8041
Brooklyn (G-2057)
H & H Laboratories Inc ....G.... 718 624-8041
Brooklyn (G-2058)
Medtech Products Inc ....F.... 914 524-6810
Tarrytown (G-16119)
Monroe Fluid Technology Inc ....E.... 585 392-3434
Hilton (G-6444)
Natures Warehouse ....F.... 800 215-4372
Philadelphia (G-13564)
Pro-Line Solutions Inc ....G.... 914 664-0002
Mount Vernon (G-8765)
Robert Racine ....E.... 518 677-0224
Cambridge (G-3338)
Sabon Management LLC ....F.... 212 982-0968
New York (G-11968)
Sunfeather Natural Soap Co Inc ....G.... 315 265-1776
Potsdam (G-13903)

SOAPS & DETERGENTS: Textile

T S Pink Corp ....F.... 607 432-1100
Oneonta (G-13216)

SOCIAL SERVICES INFORMATION EXCHANGE

Human Life Foundation Inc ....G.... 212 685-5210
New York (G-10576)

SOCIAL SVCS, HANDICAPPED

Choice Magazine Listening Inc ....G.... 516 883-8280
Port Washington (G-13828)

SOCIAL SVCS: Individual & Family

Maramont Corporation ....B.... 718 439-8900
Brooklyn (G-2266)
Suffolk Community Council Inc ....G.... 631 434-9277
Deer Park (G-4238)

SOFT DRINKS WHOLESALERS

Load/N/Go Beverage Corp ....F.... 585 218-4019
Rochester (G-14502)
Save More Beverage Corp ....G.... 518 371-2520
Halfmoon (G-5938)

SOFTWARE PUBLISHERS: Application

Advanced Comfort Systems Inc ....F.... 518 884-8444
Ballston Spa (G-588)
Amcom Software Inc ....F.... 212 951-7600
New York (G-9159)
Apogy LLC ....E.... 866 766-1723
New York (G-9225)
Appliedea Inc ....G.... 212 920-6822
New York (G-9234)
Automated & MGT Solutions LLC ....G.... 518 283-5352
East Greenbush (G-4420)
Big White Wall Holding Inc ....F.... 917 281-2649
New York (G-9445)
Braze ....E.... 504 327-7269
New York (G-9508)
Bull Street LLC ....G.... 212 495-9855
New York (G-9529)
C S I G Inc ....G.... 845 383-3800
Kingston (G-7210)
Callaway Digital Arts Inc ....E.... 212 675-3050
New York (G-9554)
Capital Programs Inc ....G.... 212 842-4640
New York (G-9576)
Catalyst Group Inc ....G.... 212 243-7777
New York (G-9599)
Catch Ventures Inc ....F.... 347 620-4351
New York (G-9601)
Cbord Group Inc ....C.... 607 257-2410
Ithaca (G-6869)
Cloud Rock Group LLC ....G.... 516 967-6023
Roslyn (G-15041)
Contactive Inc ....E.... 646 476-9059
New York (G-9770)
Customshow Inc ....G.... 800 255-5303
New York (G-9830)
Dbase LLC ....G.... 607 729-0234
Binghamton (G-903)
Do It Different Inc ....G.... 917 842-0230
New York (G-9945)
Document Strategies LLC ....F.... 585 506-9000
Rochester (G-14336)
Dwnld Inc ....E.... 484 483-6572
New York (G-9996)
Eft Analytics Inc ....G.... 212 290-2300
New York (G-10040)
Elepath Inc ....G.... 347 417-4975
Brooklyn (G-1917)
Empire Innovation Group LLC ....F.... 716 852-5000
Buffalo (G-2951)
Epicor Software Corporation ....E.... 805 496-6789
Schenectady (G-15280)
Evidon Inc ....D.... 917 262-2530
New York (G-10148)
Exchange My Mail Inc ....F.... 516 605-1835
Jericho (G-7101)
Express Checkout LLC ....G.... 646 512-2068
New York (G-10163)
Freshop Inc ....E.... 585 738-6035
Rochester (G-14405)
Galaxy Software LLC ....G.... 631 244-8405
Oakdale (G-13075)
Grantoo LLC ....G.... 646 356-0460
New York (G-10392)
Identifycom Inc ....G.... 212 235-0000
New York (G-10601)
Incentivate Health LLC ....G.... 518 469-8491
Saratoga Springs (G-15189)
INTEL Corporation ....D.... 408 765-8080
Getzville (G-5611)
Jpm and Associates ....F.... 516 483-4699
Uniondale (G-16319)
Jump Ramp Games Inc ....E.... 212 500-1456
New York (G-10821)
Knight Life Entertainment ....G.... 646 733-8911
Brooklyn (G-2176)
Live Vote II Inc ....G.... 646 343-9053
New York (G-11041)
Lookbooks Media Inc ....F.... 646 737-3360
New York (G-11058)
Lovingly LLC ....E.... 845 977-0775
Fishkill (G-5193)
Luluvise Inc ....E.... 914 309-7812
New York (G-11093)
Madhat Inc ....G.... 518 947-0732
New York (G-11120)
Mdamerica Wellness Inc ....F.... 631 396-0991
Melville (G-8365)
Meethappy Inc ....F.... 917 903-0591
Seaford (G-15368)
Mej Beats LLC ....G.... 516 707-6655
New York (G-11247)
Microstrategy Incorporated ....F.... 888 537-8135
New York (G-11284)
Molabs Inc ....G.... 310 721-6828
New York (G-11319)
Mpr Magazine App Inc ....E.... 718 403-0303
Brooklyn (G-2343)
Nervve Technologies Inc ....E.... 716 800-2250
New York (G-11391)
Nitel Inc ....G.... 347 731-1558
Brooklyn (G-2382)
Omx (us) Inc ....A.... 646 428-2800
New York (G-11518)
One-Blue LLC ....G.... 212 223-4380
New York (G-11522)
P8h Inc ....E.... 212 343-1142
Brooklyn (G-2414)
Pefin Technologies LLC ....F.... 917 715-3720
New York (G-11617)
Pexip Inc ....E.... 703 338-3544
New York (G-11655)
Piano Software Inc ....D.... 646 350-1999
New York (G-11677)
Pingmd Inc ....G.... 212 632-2665
New York (G-11684)
Piwik Pro LLC ....E.... 888 444-0049
New York (G-11690)
Playground NY Inc ....F.... 505 920-7236
Brooklyn (G-2439)
Plectica LLC ....G.... 917 304-7052
New York (G-11698)
Preplay Inc ....G.... 917 297-7428
New York (G-11722)
Proginet Corporation ....E.... 516 535-3600
Garden City (G-5541)
Prospector Network ....E.... 212 601-2781
New York (G-11761)
Pts Financial Technology LLC ....E.... 844 825-7634
New York (G-11766)
Quovo Inc ....E.... 646 216-9437
New York (G-11803)
Raleigh and Drake Pbc ....F.... 212 625-8212
New York (G-11818)
Revivn Inc ....F.... 347 762-8193
Brooklyn (G-2512)
Robert Ehrlich ....G.... 516 353-4617
New York (G-11911)
Robot Fruit Inc ....F.... 631 423-7250
Huntington (G-6716)
Seed Media Group LLC ....E.... 646 502-7050
New York (G-12035)
Serendipity Consulting Corp ....F.... 914 763-8251
South Salem (G-15560)
Signpost Inc ....C.... 877 334-2837
New York (G-12096)
Sitecompli LLC ....E.... 800 564-1152
New York (G-12111)
Smn Medical PC ....F.... 844 362-2428
Rye (G-15094)
Spring Inc ....G.... 646 732-0323
New York (G-12194)
Striata Inc ....D.... 212 918-4677
New York (G-12237)
Superchat LLC ....G.... 212 352-8581
New York (G-12264)
Synced Inc ....G.... 917 565-5591
New York (G-12281)
Tabi Inc ....G.... 347 701-1051
Flushing (G-5304)
Theirapp LLC ....E.... 212 896-1255
New York (G-12333)
Thing Daemon Inc ....E.... 917 746-9895
New York (G-12338)
Tootter Inc ....E.... 212 204-7937
Brooklyn (G-2684)
Tpa Computer Corp ....F.... 877 866-6044
Carmel (G-3434)
Trac Medical Solutions Inc ....G.... 518 346-7799
Schenectady (G-15329)
Treauu Inc ....G.... 703 731-0196
New York (G-12417)
True Erp New York ....E.... 631 582-7210
Hauppauge (G-6241)
Usq Group LLC ....G.... 212 777-7751
New York (G-12514)
Virtual Frameworks Inc ....F.... 646 690-8207
New York (G-12577)
West Internet Trading Company ....G.... 415 484-5848
New York (G-12640)
White Label Partners LLC ....G.... 917 445-6650
New York (G-12653)
Whiteboard Ventures Inc ....F.... 855 972-6346
New York (G-12655)
Winesoft International Corp ....G.... 914 400-6247
Yonkers (G-17516)
Wink Inc ....E.... 212 389-1382
New York (G-12672)
Wink Labs Inc ....E.... 916 717-0437
New York (G-12673)
Xborder Entertainment LLC ....G.... 518 726-7036
Plattsburgh (G-13741)
Zipari Inc ....E.... 855 558-7884
Brooklyn (G-2795)

SOFTWARE PUBLISHERS: Business & Professional

Aarfid LLC ....G.... 716 992-3999
Eden (G-4597)
Abel Noser Solutions LLC ....E.... 646 432-4000
New York (G-9049)
Adgorithmics LLC ....G.... 646 277-8728
New York (G-9075)
Agrinetix Cmpt Systems LLC ....F.... 877 978-5477
Henrietta (G-6314)
Appfigures Inc ....F.... 212 343-7900
New York (G-9232)
Aspen Research Group Ltd ....G.... 212 425-9588
New York (G-9289)
Augury Inc ....F.... 347 699-5011
New York (G-9314)
Automated Office Systems Inc ....F.... 516 396-5555
Valley Stream (G-16426)
Aycan Medical Systems LLC ....F.... 585 271-3078
Rochester (G-14236)
B601 V2 Inc ....G.... 646 391-6431
New York (G-9350)
Beyondly Inc ....F.... 646 658-3665
New York (G-9430)

PRODUCT SECTION

SOFTWARE PUBLISHERS: Education

Big Data Bizviz LLC .... G 716 803-2367
  West Seneca *(G-16968)*
Botify Corporation .... G 617 576-2005
  New York *(G-9492)*
Boundless Spatial Inc .... E 646 831-5531
  New York *(G-9495)*
Boxbee Inc .... G 646 612-7839
  New York *(G-9497)*
Broadway Technology LLC .... E 646 912-6450
  New York *(G-9518)*
Business Integrity Inc .... G 718 238-2008
  New York *(G-9534)*
Ca Inc .... A 800 225-5224
  New York *(G-9543)*
Caminus Corporation .... D 212 515-3600
  New York *(G-9559)*
Careconnector .... G 919 360-2987
  Brooklyn *(G-1760)*
Checkm8 Inc .... F 212 268-0048
  New York *(G-9638)*
Chequedcom Inc .... E 888 412-0699
  Saratoga Springs *(G-15177)*
Clarityad Inc .... G 646 397-4198
  New York *(G-9688)*
Clearview Social Inc .... G 801 414-7675
  Buffalo *(G-2895)*
Conversant LLC .... G 212 471-9570
  New York *(G-9775)*
Creditiq Inc .... F 888 988-4223
  New York *(G-9812)*
Cross Border Transactions LLC ... E 646 767-7342
  Tarrytown *(G-16113)*
Crunched Inc .... G 415 484-9909
  New York *(G-9817)*
Curaegis Technologies Inc ...... E 585 254-1100
  Rochester *(G-14316)*
Cureatr Inc .... E 212 203-3927
  New York *(G-9825)*
Dartcom Incorporated .... G 315 790-5456
  New Hartford *(G-8847)*
Dow Jones & Company Inc ..... E 212 597-5983
  New York *(G-9966)*
Dropcar Inc .... G 646 342-1595
  New York *(G-9982)*
EBM Care Inc .... G 212 500-5000
  New York *(G-10024)*
Eccella Corporation .... G 855 879-3223
  New York *(G-10026)*
Efront Financial Solutions Inc ... E 212 220-0660
  New York *(G-10039)*
Elodina Inc .... G 646 402-5202
  New York *(G-10066)*
Endava Inc .... G 212 920-7240
  New York *(G-10083)*
Equilend Holdings LLC .... E 212 901-2200
  New York *(G-10104)*
EZ Systems US Inc .... C 212 634-6899
  Brooklyn *(G-1955)*
Findmine Inc .... F 925 787-6181
  New York *(G-10214)*
Fusion Telecom Intl Inc .... C 212 201-2400
  New York *(G-10275)*
Gifts Software Inc .... E 904 438-6000
  New York *(G-10335)*
Globalquest Solutions Inc .... F 716 601-3524
  Buffalo *(G-2992)*
Heartland Commerce Inc .... E 845 920-0800
  Pearl River *(G-13480)*
Hovee Inc .... F 646 249-6200
  New York *(G-10565)*
Igambit Inc .... E 631 670-6777
  Smithtown *(G-15511)*
Inprotopia Corporation .... F 917 338-7501
  New York *(G-10651)*
Intelligize Incorporated .... F 571 612-8580
  New York *(G-10661)*
Ivalua Inc .... F 650 930-9710
  Brooklyn *(G-2119)*
Kasisto Inc .... F 917 734-4750
  New York *(G-10851)*
Kindling Inc .... F 212 400-6296
  New York *(G-10889)*
Klara Technologies Inc .... F 844 215-5272
  New York *(G-10896)*
Latchable Inc .... E 646 833-0604
  New York *(G-10969)*
Laurus Development Inc .... F 716 823-1202
  Buffalo *(G-3063)*
Liftforward Inc .... E 917 693-4993
  New York *(G-11023)*

Livetiles Corp .... F 917 472-7887
  New York *(G-11043)*
Loyaltyplant Inc .... F 551 221-2701
  Forest Hills *(G-5331)*
Market Factory Inc .... F 212 625-9988
  New York *(G-11181)*
Micro Systems Specialists Inc ... G 845 677-6150
  Millbrook *(G-8512)*
Mobo Systems Inc .... D 212 260-0895
  New York *(G-11314)*
Network Infrstructure Tech Inc .... E 212 404-7340
  New York *(G-11396)*
Nift Group Inc .... G 504 505-1144
  Brooklyn *(G-2381)*
Noetic Partners Inc .... F 212 836-4351
  New York *(G-11466)*
Numerix LLC .... D 212 302-2220
  New York *(G-11487)*
Oracle Corporation .... C 212 508-7700
  New York *(G-11531)*
Orangenius Inc .... F 631 742-0648
  New York *(G-11532)*
Orthstar Enterprises Inc .... E 607 562-2100
  Horseheads *(G-6614)*
Pb Mapinfo Corporation .... A 518 285-6000
  Troy *(G-11269)*
Pegasystems Inc .... E 212 626-6550
  New York *(G-11619)*
Pilot Inc .... G 212 951-1133
  New York *(G-11681)*
Pilot Inc .... G 212 951-1133
  New York *(G-11682)*
Pitney Bowes Software Inc ...... F 518 272-0014
  Troy *(G-16272)*
Pointman LLC .... G 716 842-1439
  Buffalo *(G-3153)*
Powa Technologies Inc .... E 347 344-7848
  New York *(G-11713)*
Pricing Engine Inc .... F 917 549-3289
  New York *(G-11728)*
Principia Partners LLC .... D 212 480-2270
  New York *(G-11735)*
Pulse Insights LLC .... F 888 718-6860
  New York *(G-11772)*
Purebase Networks Inc .... G 646 670-8964
  New York *(G-11775)*
Quality and Asrn Tech Corp ..... G 646 450-6762
  Ridge *(G-14106)*
Reality Analytics Inc .... G 347 363-2200
  New York *(G-11843)*
Relavis Corporation .... E 212 995-2900
  New York *(G-11855)*
Ringlead Inc .... G 310 906-0545
  Huntington *(G-6714)*
Rision Inc .... G 212 987-2628
  New York *(G-11900)*
Ritnoa Inc .... E 212 660-2148
  Bellerose *(G-807)*
RPS Holdings Inc .... E 607 257-7778
  Ithaca *(G-6910)*
Sapphire Systems Inc .... F 212 905-0100
  New York *(G-11989)*
Sefaira Inc .... G 855 733-2472
  New York *(G-12037)*
Serraview America Inc .... D 800 903-3716
  New York *(G-12050)*
Shake Inc .... F 650 544-5479
  New York *(G-12061)*
Siemens Product Life Mgmt Sftw ... E 585 389-8699
  Fairport *(G-4886)*
Sixteen Markets Inc .... F 347 759-1024
  New York *(G-12113)*
Solve Advisors Inc .... G 646 699-5041
  Rockville Centre *(G-14828)*
Squond Inc .... E 718 778-6630
  Brooklyn *(G-2615)*
Stop N Shop LLC .... G 518 512-9657
  Albany *(G-138)*
Structuredweb Inc .... E 201 325-3110
  New York *(G-12240)*
Styleclick Inc .... D 212 329-0300
  New York *(G-12246)*
Super Company Inc .... G 315 569-5153
  Syracuse *(G-16071)*
Symphony Talent LLC .... D 212 999-9000
  New York *(G-12279)*
Synergy Resources Inc .... E 631 665-2050
  Central Islip *(G-3538)*
Talaera .... G 206 229-0631
  Brooklyn *(G-2666)*

Team Builders Inc .... F 718 979-1005
  Staten Island *(G-15769)*
Telmar Information Services .... E 212 725-3000
  New York *(G-12320)*
Thinktrek Inc .... F 212 884-8399
  New York *(G-12339)*
Tika Mobile Inc .... G 646 650-5545
  New York *(G-12359)*
Transportgistics Inc .... F 631 567-4100
  Mount Sinai *(G-8699)*
Trueex LLC .... E 646 786-8526
  New York *(G-12432)*
Tyme Global Technologies LLC ... E 212 796-1950
  New York *(G-12455)*
UI Information & Insights Inc ... E 518 640-9200
  Latham *(G-7409)*
Varsity Monitor LLC .... E 212 691-6292
  New York *(G-12532)*
Velocity Outsourcing LLC .... E 212 891-4043
  New York *(G-12539)*
Virtuvent Inc .... G 646 845-0387
  New York *(G-12579)*
Vita Rara Inc .... E 518 369-7356
  Troy *(G-16285)*
Whentech LLC .... F 212 571-0042
  New York *(G-12650)*
Wochit Inc .... G 212 979-8343
  New York *(G-12679)*
Ypis of Staten Island Inc .... G 718 815-4557
  Staten Island *(G-15777)*

SOFTWARE PUBLISHERS: Computer Utilities

BMC Software Inc .... E 212 402-1500
  New York *(G-9479)*
Vline Inc .... G 512 222-5464
  Brooklyn *(G-2753)*
Wagner Technical Services Inc ... F 845 566-4018
  Newburgh *(G-12809)*

SOFTWARE PUBLISHERS: Education

Accelify Solutions LLC .... E 888 922-2354
  New York *(G-9056)*
Brainpop LLC .... E 212 574-6017
  New York *(G-9502)*
Childrens Progress Inc .... E 212 730-0905
  New York *(G-9645)*
Classroom Inc .... E 212 545-8400
  New York *(G-9694)*
Coalition On Positive Health ..... F 212 633-2500
  New York *(G-9718)*
Cognotion Inc .... G 347 692-0640
  New York *(G-9724)*
Comet Informatics LLC .... G 585 385-2310
  Pittsford *(G-13586)*
Health Care Compliance .... F 516 478-4100
  Jericho *(G-7103)*
Isimulate LLC .... G 877 947-2831
  Albany *(G-90)*
Jumprope Inc .... G 347 927-5867
  New York *(G-10822)*
Learningateway LLC .... F 212 920-7969
  Brooklyn *(G-2204)*
Maven Marketing LLC .... F 615 510-3248
  New York *(G-11207)*
Multimedia Plus Inc .... F 212 982-3229
  New York *(G-11349)*
Nemaris Inc .... E 646 794-8648
  New York *(G-11387)*
Parlor Labs Inc .... G 866 801-7323
  New York *(G-11590)*
Playfitness Corp .... G 917 497-5443
  Staten Island *(G-15743)*
Prime Research Solutions LLC ... G 917 836-7941
  Flushing *(G-5291)*
Qlogix Entertainment LLC .... G 215 459-6315
  New York *(G-11790)*
San Jae Educational Resou ..... G 845 364-5458
  Pomona *(G-13761)*
Scholastic Corporation .... G 212 343-6100
  New York *(G-12015)*
Scholastic Inc .... A 800 724-6527
  New York *(G-12016)*
Schoolnet Inc .... C 646 496-9000
  New York *(G-12019)*
Sciterra LLC .... G 646 883-3724
  New York *(G-12023)*
Skillsoft Corporation .... G 585 240-7500
  Rochester *(G-14712)*

Employee Codes: A=Over 500 employees, B=251-500
C=101-250, D=51-100, E=20-50, F=10-19, G=5-9

Special Circle Inc .... F 516 595-9988
New Hyde Park *(G-8909)*
Teachergaming LLC .... F 866 644-9323
New York *(G-12311)*
Teachley LLC .... G 347 552-1272
New York *(G-12313)*
Tequipment Inc .... D 516 922-3508
Huntington Station *(G-6764)*
Time To Know Inc .... F 212 230-1210
New York *(G-12368)*
Trovvit Inc .... G 718 908-5376
Brooklyn *(G-2704)*
Virtusphere Inc .... F 607 760-2207
Binghamton *(G-952)*

SOFTWARE PUBLISHERS: Home Entertainment

Avalanche Studios New York Inc .... D 212 993-6447
New York *(G-9324)*
Clever Goats Media LLC .... G 917 512-0340
New York *(G-9697)*
E H Hurwitz & Associates .... G 718 884-3766
Bronx *(G-1325)*
Magic Numbers Inc .... G 646 839-8578
New York *(G-11132)*
Mdcare911 LLC .... G 917 640-4869
Brooklyn *(G-2291)*
Reentry Games Inc .... G 646 421-0080
New York *(G-11848)*
Udisense Inc .... G 858 442-9875
New York *(G-12460)*
Urthworx Inc .... G 646 373-7535
New York *(G-12503)*
Vizbee Inc .... G 650 787-1424
New York *(G-12586)*

SOFTWARE PUBLISHERS: NEC

2k Inc .... G 646 536-3007
New York *(G-9015)*
30dc Inc .... G 212 962-4400
New York *(G-9016)*
30dc Inc .... F 212 962-4400
New York *(G-9017)*
A K A Computer Consulting Inc .... G 718 351-5200
Staten Island *(G-15650)*
A2ia Corp .... G 917 237-0390
New York *(G-9042)*
Accela Inc .... F 631 563-5005
Ronkonkoma *(G-14874)*
Adl Data Systems Inc .... E 914 591-1800
Hawthorne *(G-6265)*
Adobe Systems Inc .... E 212 471-0904
New York *(G-9077)*
Adobe Systems Incorporated .... C 212 592-1400
New York *(G-9078)*
Adobe Systems Incorporated .... E 212 471-0904
New York *(G-9079)*
Adtech Us Inc .... C 212 402-4840
New York *(G-9082)*
Advanced Cmpt Sftwr Consulting .... G 718 300-3577
Bronx *(G-1265)*
Advanced Cyber Security Corp .... E 866 417-9155
Bohemia *(G-1003)*
Andigo New Media Inc .... G 212 727-8445
New York *(G-9201)*
Ansa Systems of USA Inc .... G 718 835-3743
Valley Stream *(G-16425)*
Application Security Inc .... D 212 912-4100
New York *(G-9233)*
Apprenda Inc .... D 518 383-2130
Troy *(G-16247)*
Appsbidder Inc .... G 917 880-4269
Brooklyn *(G-1621)*
APS Enterprise Software Inc .... E 631 784-7720
Huntington *(G-6686)*
Archive360 Inc .... E 212 731-2438
New York *(G-9247)*
Articulate Global Inc .... C 800 861-4880
New York *(G-9268)*
Arumai Technologies Inc .... F 914 217-0038
Armonk *(G-410)*
Asite LLC .... D 203 545-3089
New York *(G-9286)*
AT&T Corp .... F 212 317-7048
New York *(G-9296)*
Base Systems Inc .... G 845 278-1991
Brewster *(G-1208)*
Bigwood Systems Inc .... G 607 257-0915
Ithaca *(G-6861)*
Billing Blocks Inc .... F 718 442-5006
Staten Island *(G-15667)*
Blue Wolf Group LLC .... D 866 455-9653
New York *(G-9474)*
Brigadoon Software Inc .... G 845 624-0909
Nanuet *(G-8798)*
Buncee LLC .... F 631 591-1390
Calverton *(G-3315)*
Business Management Systems .... F 914 245-8558
Yorktown Heights *(G-17524)*
Byte Consulting Inc .... G 646 500-8606
New York *(G-9542)*
California US Holdings Inc .... A 212 726-6500
New York *(G-9552)*
Callidus Software Inc .... F 212 554-7300
New York *(G-9555)*
Candex Solutions Inc .... G 215 650-3214
New York *(G-9565)*
Carnival Inc .... G 415 781-9815
New York *(G-9582)*
Cavalry Solutions .... G 315 422-1699
Syracuse *(G-15910)*
Cdml Computer Services Ltd .... G 718 428-9063
Fresh Meadows *(G-5452)*
Ceipal LLC .... G 585 351-2934
Rochester *(G-14284)*
Ceipal LLC .... G 585 584-1316
Rochester *(G-14285)*
Celonis Inc .... G 941 615-9670
Brooklyn *(G-1769)*
Cgi Technologies Solutions Inc .... F 212 682-7411
New York *(G-9624)*
Cinch Technologies Inc .... G 212 266-0022
New York *(G-9668)*
Cinedigm Software .... G 212 206-9001
New York *(G-9671)*
Citixsys Technologies Inc .... G 212 745-1365
New York *(G-9679)*
Clayton Dubilier & Rice Fun .... E 212 407-5200
New York *(G-9695)*
Cloudparc Inc .... G 954 665-5962
New York *(G-9702)*
Cloudsense Inc .... G 917 880-6195
New York *(G-9703)*
Commercehub Inc .... G 518 810-0700
Albany *(G-71)*
Commify Technology .... F 917 603-1822
New York *(G-9746)*
Comprehensive Dental Tech .... G 607 467-4456
Hancock *(G-5985)*
Condeco Software Inc .... E 917 677-7600
New York *(G-9759)*
Construction Technology Inc .... G 914 747-8900
Valhalla *(G-16392)*
Coocoo SMS Inc .... F 646 459-4260
Huntington *(G-6692)*
CTI Software Inc .... F 631 253-3550
Deer Park *(G-4145)*
Cuffs Planning & Models Ltd .... G 914 632-1883
New Rochelle *(G-8938)*
Cultureiq Inc .... G 212 755-8633
New York *(G-9823)*
Curemdcom Inc .... A 212 509-6200
New York *(G-9826)*
Cyandia Inc .... F 315 679-4268
Syracuse *(G-15937)*
Cybersports Inc .... G 315 737-7150
Utica *(G-16342)*
Dashlane Inc .... E 212 596-7510
New York *(G-9867)*
Data Implementation Inc .... G 212 979-2015
New York *(G-9868)*
Davel Systems Inc .... G 718 382-6024
Brooklyn *(G-1842)*
Debt Resolve Inc .... G 914 949-5500
White Plains *(G-17128)*
Defran Systems Inc .... E 212 727-8342
New York *(G-9892)*
Delivery Systems Inc .... F 212 221-7007
New York *(G-9894)*
Deniz Information Systems .... G 212 750-5199
New York *(G-9898)*
Digital Brewery LLC .... G 646 665-2106
Astoria *(G-435)*
Diligent Board Member Svcs LLC .... E 212 741-8181
New York *(G-9930)*
Diligent Corporation .... B 212 741-8181
New York *(G-9931)*
Dynamo Development Inc .... G 212 385-1552
New York *(G-10001)*
Eastnets Americas Corp .... F 212 631-0666
New York *(G-10019)*
Ebeling Associates Inc .... F 518 688-8700
Halfmoon *(G-5932)*
Electronic Arts Inc .... G 212 672-0722
New York *(G-10050)*
Elevondata Labs Inc .... E 470 222-5438
New York *(G-10053)*
Emblaze Systems Inc .... C 212 371-1100
New York *(G-10072)*
Empowrx LLC .... G 212 755-3577
New York *(G-10075)*
Enterprise Tech Group Inc .... F 914 588-0327
New Rochelle *(G-8942)*
Ert Software Inc .... G 845 358-5721
Blauvelt *(G-965)*
Ex El Enterprises Ltd .... F 212 489-4500
New York *(G-10152)*
Exact Solutions Inc .... F 212 707-8627
New York *(G-10154)*
EZ Newsletter LLC .... F 412 943-7777
Brooklyn *(G-1954)*
F R A M Technologies Inc .... G 718 338-6230
Brooklyn *(G-1956)*
F-O-R Software LLC .... F 212 231-9506
New York *(G-10173)*
F-O-R Software LLC .... E 914 220-8800
White Plains *(G-17134)*
F-O-R Software LLC .... G 212 724-3920
New York *(G-10174)*
Facts On File Inc .... D 212 967-8800
New York *(G-10179)*
Falconstor Software Inc .... C 631 777-5188
Melville *(G-8347)*
Fastnet Software Intl Inc .... F 888 740-7790
East Northport *(G-4456)*
Femtech Women Powered Software .... D 516 328-2631
Franklin Square *(G-5373)*
Fidelus Technologies LLC .... D 212 616-7800
New York *(G-10211)*
Fidesa US Corporation .... B 212 269-9000
New York *(G-10212)*
Filestream Inc .... F 516 759-4100
Locust Valley *(G-7660)*
Flextrade Systems Inc .... C 516 627-8993
Great Neck *(G-5829)*
Flogic Inc .... F 914 478-1352
Hastings On Hudson *(G-6023)*
Fog Creek Software Inc .... G 866 364-2733
New York *(G-10235)*
Formats Unlimited Inc .... F 631 249-9200
Deer Park *(G-4166)*
Frazer Computing Inc .... E 315 379-3500
Canton *(G-3409)*
Fruit St Hlth Pub Beneft Corp .... G 347 960-6400
New York *(G-10264)*
Fuel Data Systems Inc .... G 800 447-7870
Middletown *(G-8475)*
Games For Change Inc .... G 212 242-4922
New York *(G-10292)*
Geoweb3d Inc .... F 607 323-1114
Vestal *(G-16471)*
Glassbox US Inc .... D 917 378-2933
New York *(G-10348)*
Glitnir Ticketing Inc .... G 516 390-5168
Levittown *(G-7450)*
Global Applctions Solution LLC .... G 212 741-9595
New York *(G-10354)*
Group Commerce Inc .... F 646 346-0598
New York *(G-10413)*
Hailo Network Usa Inc .... G 646 561-8552
New York *(G-10440)*
Happy Software Inc .... G 518 584-4668
Saratoga Springs *(G-15187)*
Heineck Associates Inc .... G 631 207-2347
Bellport *(G-827)*
High Performance Sftwr USA Inc .... E 866 616-4958
Valley Stream *(G-16436)*
Hinge Inc .... F 502 445-3111
New York *(G-10526)*
Hudson Software Corporation .... E 914 773-0400
Elmsford *(G-4763)*
Human Condition Safety Inc .... F 646 867-0644
New York *(G-10575)*
Huntington Services Inc .... G 516 795-8500
Massapequa *(G-8209)*
IAC Search LLC .... E 212 314-7300
New York *(G-10589)*
Iac/Interactivecorp .... A 212 314-7300
New York *(G-10590)*

Idoc Software Inc	G	516 680-9090	New York (G-10603)
Incycle Software Corp	G	212 626-2608	New York (G-10627)
Indegy Inc	E	866 801-5394	New York (G-10629)
Infinity Augmented Reality Inc	G	917 677-2084	New York (G-10635)
Info Quick Solutions	E	315 463-1400	Liverpool (G-7548)
Infobase Publishing Company	G	212 967-8800	New York (G-10637)
Infor Global Solutions Inc	D	646 336-1700	New York (G-10639)
Informa Solutions Inc	E	516 543-3733	New York (G-10640)
Informatica LLC	F	212 845-7650	New York (G-10641)
Informerly Inc	G	646 238-7137	New York (G-10642)
Innovation MGT Group Inc	F	800 889-0987	Shirley (G-15443)
Insight Unlimited Inc	G	914 861-2090	Chappaqua (G-3580)
Insight Venture Partners IV	C	212 230-9200	New York (G-10652)
Inspired Entertainment Inc	G	646 565-3861	New York (G-10653)
Instrumental Software Tech	G	518 602-0001	Saratoga Springs (G-15190)
International Bus Mchs Corp	E	914 345-5219	Armonk (G-412)
International Bus Mchs Corp	E	914 499-2000	Armonk (G-413)
International MGT Netwrk	F	646 401-0032	New York (G-10679)
Internodal International Inc	E	631 765-0037	Southold (G-15583)
Intralinks Holdings Inc	E	212 543-7700	New York (G-10688)
Invision Inc	G	212 557-5554	New York (G-10694)
Ipsidy Inc	D	407 951-8640	Long Beach (G-7673)
Irv Inc	E	212 334-4507	New York (G-10705)
Isisnet LLC	G	212 239-1205	New York (G-10709)
Joseph A Filippazzo Software	G	718 987-1626	Staten Island (G-15715)
Kaseya US Sales LLC	D	415 694-5700	New York (G-10850)
Kastor Consulting Inc	G	718 224-9109	Bayside (G-767)
Key Computer Svcs of Chelsea	D	212 206-8060	New York (G-10880)
Keynote Systems Corporation	G	716 564-1332	Buffalo (G-3047)
Kronos Incorporated	E	518 459-5545	Albany (G-97)
Latham Software Sciences Inc	F	518 785-1100	Latham (G-7399)
Lincdoc LLC	G	585 563-1669	East Rochester (G-4484)
Lmt Technology Solutions	F	585 784-7470	Rochester (G-14501)
Lynx Analytics Inc	G	475 227-7347	New York (G-11096)
Magsoft Corporation	G	518 877-8390	Ballston Spa (G-601)
Maler Technologies Inc	G	212 391-2070	New York (G-11144)
Marcus Goldman Inc	F	212 431-0707	New York (G-11171)
Market Logic Software Inc	F	646 405-1041	New York (G-11182)
Matrixcare Inc	G	518 583-6400	New York (G-11204)
McAfee LLC	G	646 728-1440	New York (G-11218)
Mealplan Corp	G	909 706-8398	New York (G-11231)
Medical Transcription Billing	A	631 863-1198	New York (G-11240)
Medidata Solutions Inc	B	212 918-1800	New York (G-11241)
Medius Software Inc	F	877 295-0058	New York (G-11243)
Meta Pharmacy Systems Inc	E	516 488-6189	Garden City (G-5534)
Microcad Trning Consulting Inc	G	617 923-0500	Lagrangeville (G-7281)
Microcad Trning Consulting Inc	G	631 291-9484	Hauppauge (G-6161)
Microsoft Corporation	A	914 323-2150	White Plains (G-17165)
Microsoft Corporation	G	631 760-2340	Huntington Station (G-6754)
Microsoft Corporation	F	212 245-2100	New York (G-11283)
Microsoft Corporation	D	516 380-1531	Hauppauge (G-6163)
Midas Mdici Group Holdings Inc	G	212 792-0920	New York (G-11285)
Mml Software Ltd	E	631 941-1313	East Setauket (G-4506)
Mobile Data Systems Inc	G	631 360-3400	Nesconset (G-8824)
Mobile Hatch Inc	G	212 314-7300	New York (G-11313)
Mobileapp Systems LLC	G	716 667-2780	Buffalo (G-3090)
Mongodb Inc	A	646 727-4092	New York (G-11326)
Nastel Technologies Inc	C	631 761-9100	Plainview (G-13652)
Navatar Group Inc	E	212 863-9655	New York (G-11383)
Netegrity Inc	C	631 342-6000	Central Islip (G-3533)
Netologic Inc	E	212 269-3796	New York (G-11394)
Netsuite Inc	G	646 652-5700	New York (G-11395)
Neverware Inc	F	516 302-3223	New York (G-11401)
New Triad For Collaborative	E	212 873-9610	New York (G-11415)
Nikish Software Corp	G	631 754-1618	Hauppauge (G-6174)
Olympic Software & Consulting	G	631 351-0655	Melville (G-8373)
Ontra Presentations LLC	G	212 213-1315	New York (G-11524)
Openfin Inc	G	917 450-8822	New York (G-11526)
Operative Media Inc	C	212 994-8930	New York (G-11528)
Os33 Inc	G	708 336-3466	New York (G-11542)
Overture Media Inc	G	917 446-7455	New York (G-11549)
Pap Chat Inc	G	516 350-1888	Brooklyn (G-2417)
Par Technology Corporation	D	315 738-0600	New Hartford (G-8853)
Pareteum Corporation	D	212 984-1096	New York (G-11585)
Patient Portal Tech Inc	F	315 638-2030	Baldwinsville (G-573)
Patron Technology Inc	G	212 271-4328	New York (G-11598)
Peer Software Incorporated	G	631 979-1770	Hauppauge (G-6186)
Perry Street Software Inc	G	415 935-1429	New York (G-11644)
Plain Digital Inc	G	914 310-0280	Scarsdale (G-15252)
Platform Experts Inc	G	646 843-7100	Brooklyn (G-2438)
Poly Software International	G	845 735-9301	Pearl River (G-13488)
Portable Tech Solutions LLC	F	631 727-8084	Calverton (G-3323)
Portware LLC	D	212 425-5233	New York (G-11709)
Practicepro Software Systems	G	516 222-0010	Garden City (G-5540)
Pretlist	G	646 368-1849	New York (G-11727)
Professional Access LLC	G	212 432-2844	Chappaqua (G-3582)
Pupa Tek Inc	G	631 664-7817	Huntington (G-6710)
Quartet Financial Systems Inc	F	845 358-6071	New York (G-11795)
Radnor-Wallace	G	516 767-2131	Port Washington (G-13875)
Rational Retention LLC	E	518 489-3000	Albany (G-128)
Rational Retention LLC	G	518 489-3000	Albany (G-129)
Razorfish LLC	F	212 798-6600	New York (G-11834)
Red Oak Software Inc	G	585 454-3170	Rochester (G-14646)
Reliant Security	E	917 338-2200	New York (G-11856)
Robly Digital Marketing LLC	E	917 238-0730	New York (G-11916)
Robocom Us LLC	F	631 861-2045	Farmingdale (G-5111)
Rockport Pa LLC	F	212 482-8580	New York (G-11920)
Roomactually LLC	G	646 388-1922	New York (G-11934)
Ryba Software Inc	G	718 264-9352	Fresh Meadows (G-5459)
S C T	F	585 467-7740	Rochester (G-14685)
Safe Passage International Inc	F	585 292-4910	Rochester (G-14686)
Sakonnet Technology LLC	E	212 849-9267	New York (G-11971)
Salentica Systems Inc	E	212 672-1777	New York (G-11973)
Sas Institute Inc	F	212 757-3826	New York (G-11995)
Sculptgraphicz Inc	G	646 837-7302	Brooklyn (G-2565)
Secured Services Inc	G	866 419-3900	New York (G-12032)
Segovia Technology Co	F	212 868-4412	New York (G-12038)
Servicenow Inc	F	914 318-1168	New York (G-12051)
Shiprite Software Inc	G	315 733-6191	Utica (G-16383)
Shoretel Inc	G	877 654-3573	Rochester (G-14706)
Shritec Consultants Inc	G	516 621-7072	Albertson (G-163)
Similarweb Inc	F	347 685-5422	New York (G-12099)
Skystem LLC	G	877 778-3320	New York (G-12123)
Slidebean Incorporated	F	866 365-0588	New York (G-12127)
Slyde Inc	F	917 331-2114	Long Island City (G-7908)
Sneakers Software Inc	F	800 877-9221	New York (G-12141)
Social Bicycles Inc	E	917 746-7624	Brooklyn (G-2602)
Softlink International	E	914 574-8197	White Plains (G-17195)
Software & General Services Co	G	315 986-4184	Walworth (G-16573)
Somml Health LLC	G	518 880-2170	Albany (G-135)
Soroc Technology Corp	G	716 849-5913	Buffalo (G-3220)
SS&c Financial Services LLC	C	914 670-3600	Harrison (G-6010)
Stensul Inc	E	212 380-8620	New York (G-12217)
Strada Soft Inc	G	718 556-6940	Staten Island (G-15765)
Structured Retail Products	G	212 224-3692	New York (G-12239)
Successware Inc	F	716 565-2338	Williamsville (G-17281)
Suite Solutions Inc	E	716 929-3050	Amherst (G-263)
Super Software	G	845 735-0000	New City (G-8839)
Sutton Place Software Inc	G	631 421-1737	Melville (G-8386)
Symantec Corporation	D	646 487-6000	New York (G-12278)
Synco Technologies Inc	G	212 255-2031	New York (G-12282)
Syntel Inc	F	212 785-9810	New York (G-12285)
Syrasoft LLC	F	315 708-0341	Baldwinsville (G-577)
Systems Trading Inc	G	718 261-8900	Melville (G-8387)
Tap2play LLC	G	914 960-6232	New York (G-12304)

PRODUCT

Employee Codes: A=Over 500 employees, B=251-500
C=101-250, D=51-100, E=20-50, F=10-19, G=5-9
2018 Harris
New York Manufacturers Directory
1339

SOFTWARE PUBLISHERS: NEC

Targetprocess Inc .... F 877 718-2617
 Amherst *(G-265)*
Tech Software LLC .... G 516 986-3050
 Melville *(G-8389)*
Tel Tech International .... E 516 393-5174
 Melville *(G-8390)*
Tensa Software .... F 914 686-5376
 White Plains *(G-17203)*
Terranua US Corp .... F 212 852-9028
 New York *(G-12324)*
Thomson Reuters Corporation .... A 646 223-4000
 New York *(G-12349)*
Tradepaq Corporation .... F 914 332-9174
 Tarrytown *(G-16134)*
Tss-Transport Snltn Sstms .... G 917 267-8534
 New York *(G-12439)*
Ttg LLC .... G 917 777-0959
 New York *(G-12440)*
Tunaverse Media Inc .... G 631 778-8350
 Hauppauge *(G-6242)*
Two Rivers Computing Inc .... G 914 968-9239
 Yonkers *(G-17510)*
U X World Inc .... G 914 375-6167
 Hawthorne *(G-6280)*
Upstate Records Management LLC .. G 518 834-1144
 Keeseville *(G-7170)*
Value Spring Technology Inc .... F 917 705-4658
 Harrison *(G-6013)*
Varnish Software Inc .... G 201 857-2832
 New York *(G-12530)*
Varonis Systems Inc .... A 877 292-8767
 New York *(G-12531)*
Vehicle Tracking Solutions LLC .... E 631 586-7400
 Commack *(G-3870)*
Verris Inc .... G 201 565-1648
 New York *(G-12548)*
Vertana Group LLC .... G 646 430-8226
 New York *(G-12553)*
Vhx Corporation .... F 347 689-1446
 New York *(G-12559)*
Vicarious Visions Inc .... D 518 283-4090
 Troy *(G-16283)*
Viridis Learning Inc .... G 347 420-9181
 New York *(G-12575)*
Visible Systems Corporation .... E 508 628-1510
 Oneida *(G-13192)*
Visual Listing Systems Inc .... G 631 689-7222
 East Setauket *(G-4515)*
Vormittag Associates Inc .... G 800 824-7776
 Ronkonkoma *(G-15023)*
Watchitoo Inc .... G 212 354-5888
 New York *(G-12623)*
Water Oracle .... G 845 876-8327
 Rhinebeck *(G-14073)*
Wetpaintcom Inc .... E 206 859-6300
 New York *(G-12647)*
Wizq Inc .... F 586 381-9048
 New York *(G-12675)*
Woodbury Systems Group Inc .... G 516 364-2653
 Woodbury *(G-17323)*
Wrkbook LLC .... F 914 355-1293
 White Plains *(G-17215)*
X Function Inc .... E 212 231-0092
 New York *(G-12698)*
Zedge Inc .... D 330 577-3424
 New York *(G-12727)*

SOFTWARE PUBLISHERS: Operating Systems

Enterprise Network NY Inc .... F 516 263-0641
 Brooklyn *(G-1929)*
J9 Technologies Inc .... E 412 586-5038
 New York *(G-10724)*
Northrop Grumman Systems Corp .. E 315 336-0500
 Rome *(G-14855)*
Reason Software Company Inc .... F 646 664-1038
 New York *(G-11844)*

SOFTWARE PUBLISHERS: Publisher's

Avocode Inc .... F 646 934-8410
 New York *(G-9333)*
Brainworks Software Dev Corp .... G 631 563-5000
 Sayville *(G-15233)*
Catholic News Publishing Co .... F 914 632-4771
 Mamaroneck *(G-8059)*
Ceros Inc .... E 347 744-9250
 New York *(G-9622)*
Datadog Inc .... E 866 329-4466
 New York *(G-9869)*

Digital Associates LLC .... G 631 983-6075
 Smithtown *(G-15507)*
Hyperlaw Inc .... F 212 873-6982
 New York *(G-10583)*
Irene Goodman Literary Agency ..... G 212 604-0330
 New York *(G-10699)*
Maz Digital Inc .... E 646 692-9799
 New York *(G-11215)*
Mediapost Communications LLC .... E 212 204-2000
 New York *(G-11238)*
Mnn Holding Company LLC .... F 404 558-5251
 Brooklyn *(G-2331)*
On Demand Books LLC .... G 212 966-2222
 New York *(G-11519)*
Spektrix Inc .... G 646 741-5110
 New York *(G-12183)*
Tradewins Publishing Corp .... G 631 361-6916
 Smithtown *(G-15523)*
Vortex Ventures Inc .... G 516 946-8345
 North Baldwin *(G-12929)*

SOFTWARE PUBLISHERS: Word Processing

Cegid Corporation .... F 212 757-9038
 New York *(G-9607)*

SOFTWARE TRAINING, COMPUTER

Microcad Trning Consulting Inc ...... G 617 923-0500
 Lagrangeville *(G-7281)*

SOLAR CELLS

Atlantis Energy Systems Inc .... F 845 486-4052
 Poughkeepsie *(G-13907)*
Ely Beach Solar LLC .... G 718 796-9400
 New York *(G-10069)*
Idalia Solar Technologies LLC .... G 212 792-3913
 New York *(G-10598)*
Nationwide Tarps Incorporated ...... D 518 843-1545
 Amsterdam *(G-362)*
Panasonic Corp North America ...... D 888 765-2489
 Buffalo *(G-3134)*
Renewable Energy Inc .... G 718 690-2691
 Little Neck *(G-7533)*
Schott Solar Pv Inc .... E 888 457-6527
 Elmsford *(G-4790)*
Warner Energy LLC .... G 315 457-3828
 Liverpool *(G-7583)*
Yingli Green Enrgy Amricas Inc ...... E 888 686-8820
 New York *(G-12714)*

SOLAR HEATING EQPT

Atlantis Energy Systems Inc .... G 916 438-2930
 Poughkeepsie *(G-13908)*
Atlantis Solar Inc .... F 916 226-9183
 Potsdam *(G-13895)*
I-Evolve Techonology Services .... E 801 566-5268
 Amherst *(G-244)*
Integrated Solar Tech LLC .... G 914 249-9364
 Port Chester *(G-13776)*
Mx Solar USA LLC .... E 732 356-7300
 New York *(G-11352)*
Nanopv Corporation .... C 609 851-3666
 Liverpool *(G-7562)*
New Energy Systems Group .... C 917 573-0302
 New York *(G-11406)*
Prism Solar Technologies Inc .... E 845 883-4200
 Highland *(G-6434)*
Solar Energy Systems LLC .... F 718 389-1545
 Brooklyn *(G-2606)*

SOLDERS

Braze Alloy Inc .... E 718 815-5757
 Staten Island *(G-15671)*
Indium Corporation of America ...... E 800 446-3486
 Clinton *(G-3745)*
Indium Corporation of America ...... E 315 793-8200
 Utica *(G-16366)*
Indium Corporation of America ...... E 315 381-2330
 Utica *(G-16367)*
Jewelers Solder Supply Inc .... F 718 637-1256
 Brooklyn *(G-2137)*

SOLID CONTAINING UNITS: Concrete

Heidenhain International Inc .... C 716 661-1700
 Jamestown *(G-7033)*

SOLVENTS

Solvents Company Inc .... F 631 595-9300
 Kingston *(G-7238)*

SONAR SYSTEMS & EQPT

Lockheed Martin Corporation .... E 315 456-6604
 Syracuse *(G-16001)*
Lockheed Martin Overseas .... F 315 456-0123
 Liverpool *(G-7556)*

SOUND EQPT: Electric

Audible Difference Inc .... E 212 662-4848
 Brooklyn *(G-1652)*
Audible Difference Inc .... G 212 662-4848
 Brooklyn *(G-1653)*
Isolation Technology Inc .... G 631 253-3314
 West Babylon *(G-16824)*
Magic Tech Co Ltd .... G 516 539-7944
 West Hempstead *(G-16891)*

SOUND EQPT: Underwater

L-3 Cmmnctons Ntronix Holdings ... D 212 697-1111
 New York *(G-10942)*

SOUND REPRODUCING EQPT

Citation Manufacturing Co Inc .... G 845 425-6868
 Spring Valley *(G-15602)*
Samson Technologies Corp .... D 631 784-2200
 Hicksville *(G-6418)*
Vtb Holdings Inc .... G 914 345-2255
 Valhalla *(G-16399)*

SPACE VEHICLE EQPT

Gb Aero Engine LLC .... B 914 925-9600
 Rye *(G-15083)*
GKN Aerospace Monitor Inc .... B 562 619-8558
 Amityville *(G-288)*
L-3 Cmmnctons Fgn Holdings Inc .. E 212 697-1111
 New York *(G-10941)*
L3 Technologies Inc .... A 631 436-7400
 Hauppauge *(G-6133)*
L3 Technologies Inc .... B 212 697-1111
 New York *(G-10943)*
Lockheed Martin Corporation .... E 716 297-1000
 Niagara Falls *(G-12861)*
Magellan Aerospace NY Inc .... C 718 699-4000
 Corona *(G-4025)*
Moog Inc .... A 716 652-2000
 Elma *(G-4664)*
Saturn Industries Inc .... E 518 828-9956
 Hudson *(G-6663)*
Servotronics Inc .... C 716 655-5990
 Elma *(G-4668)*
SKF USA Inc .... D 716 661-2869
 Falconer *(G-4919)*
SKF USA Inc .... D 716 661-2600
 Falconer *(G-4920)*
Turbine Engine Comp Utica .... A 315 768-8070
 Whitesboro *(G-17225)*
Unison Industries LLC .... B 607 335-5000
 Norwich *(G-13057)*

SPACE VEHICLES

Lockheed Martin Overseas LLC ...... D 301 897-6923
 Liverpool *(G-7557)*

SPARK PLUGS: Internal Combustion Engines

Karlyn Industries Inc .... F 845 351-2249
 Southfields *(G-15580)*

SPAS

461 New Lots Avenue LLC .... G 347 303-9305
 Brooklyn *(G-1518)*
Skincare Products Inc .... G 917 837-5255
 New York *(G-12117)*

SPEAKER SYSTEMS

Covington Sound .... G 646 256-7486
 Bronx *(G-1307)*
L A R Electronics Corp .... G 716 285-0555
 Niagara Falls *(G-12858)*
Professional Technology Inc .... G 315 337-4156
 Rome *(G-14858)*

PRODUCT SECTION

SPORTING & RECREATIONAL GOODS & SPLYS WHOLESALERS

Pure Acoustics Inc .... G 718 788-4411
  Brooklyn *(G-2474)*

SPECIAL EVENTS DECORATION SVCS
Allied Decorations Co Inc .... F 315 637-0273
  Syracuse *(G-15870)*
Hotelinteractive Inc .... F 631 424-7755
  Smithtown *(G-15510)*
Ubm LLC .... D 516 562-7800
  New Hyde Park *(G-8912)*

SPECIALTY FOOD STORES: Coffee
Coffee Holding Co Inc .... D 718 832-0800
  Staten Island *(G-15680)*
Death Wish Coffee Company LLC .... F 518 400-1050
  Round Lake *(G-15061)*
Orens Daily Roast Inc .... G 212 348-5400
  New York *(G-11538)*

SPECIALTY FOOD STORES: Health & Dietetic Food
Ajes Pharmaceuticals LLC .... E 631 608-1728
  Copiague *(G-3917)*
Cosmic Enterprise .... G 718 342-6257
  Brooklyn *(G-1806)*
Natures Bounty Co .... D 631 244-2021
  Ronkonkoma *(G-14977)*
Natures Bounty Co .... A 631 200-2000
  Ronkonkoma *(G-14978)*
Only Natural Inc .... F 516 897-7001
  Oceanside *(G-13110)*
Setauket Manufacturing Co .... G 631 231-7272
  Ronkonkoma *(G-15008)*

SPECIALTY FOOD STORES: Juices, Fruit Or Vegetable
Mayer Bros Apple Products Inc .... D 716 668-1787
  West Seneca *(G-16980)*
Nantucket Allserve Inc .... B 914 612-4000
  Elmsford *(G-4778)*
Schutt Cider Mill .... F 585 872-2924
  Webster *(G-16760)*

SPECIALTY FOOD STORES: Vitamin
Natures Warehouse .... F 800 215-4372
  Philadelphia *(G-13564)*

SPERM BANK
Daxor Corporation .... E 212 244-0555
  New York *(G-9888)*

SPONGES: Plastic
3M Company .... B 716 876-1596
  Tonawanda *(G-16154)*

SPOOLS: Fiber, Made From Purchased Materials
Syraco Products Inc .... F 315 476-5306
  Syracuse *(G-16072)*

SPOOLS: Indl
McIntosh Box & Pallet Co Inc .... E 315 446-9350
  Rome *(G-14848)*

SPORTING & ATHLETIC GOODS: Bags, Golf
Athalon Sportgear Inc .... G 212 268-8070
  New York *(G-9301)*

SPORTING & ATHLETIC GOODS: Bowling Alleys & Access
Hootz Family Bowling Inc .... F 518 756-4668
  Ravena *(G-14034)*

SPORTING & ATHLETIC GOODS: Bowling Pins
Qubicaamf Worldwide LLC .... C 315 376-6541
  Lowville *(G-7969)*

SPORTING & ATHLETIC GOODS: Bows, Archery
Perfect Form Manufacturing LLC .... G 585 500-5923
  West Henrietta *(G-16921)*

SPORTING & ATHLETIC GOODS: Boxing Eqpt & Splys, NEC
Everlast Worldwide Inc .... E 212 239-0990
  New York *(G-10147)*

SPORTING & ATHLETIC GOODS: Camping Eqpt & Splys
Adirondack Outdoor Center LLC .... G 315 369-2300
  Old Forge *(G-13152)*
J R Products Inc .... G 716 633-7565
  Clarence Center *(G-3703)*
Recreational Equipment Inc .... G 914 410-9500
  Yonkers *(G-17499)*

SPORTING & ATHLETIC GOODS: Cartridge Belts
Car Doctor Motor Sports LLC .... G 631 537-1548
  Water Mill *(G-16625)*

SPORTING & ATHLETIC GOODS: Driving Ranges, Golf, Electronic
Paddock Chevrolet Golf Dome .... E 716 504-4059
  Tonawanda *(G-16209)*

SPORTING & ATHLETIC GOODS: Dumbbells & Other Weight Eqpt
TDS Fitness Equipment .... E 607 733-6789
  Elmira *(G-4717)*

SPORTING & ATHLETIC GOODS: Fishing Bait, Artificial
Fishing Valley LLC .... G 716 523-6158
  Lockport *(G-7615)*
Makiplastic .... G 716 772-2222
  Gasport *(G-5573)*

SPORTING & ATHLETIC GOODS: Fishing Eqpt
Cortland Line Mfg LLC .... E 607 756-2851
  Cortland *(G-4041)*
Fly-Tyers Carry-All LLC .... G 607 821-1460
  Charlotteville *(G-3583)*
Rome Specialty Company Inc .... E 315 337-8200
  Rome *(G-14862)*
Sampo Inc .... E 315 896-2606
  Barneveld *(G-617)*

SPORTING & ATHLETIC GOODS: Fishing Tackle, General
Sea Isle Custom Rod Builders .... G 516 868-8855
  Freeport *(G-5436)*

SPORTING & ATHLETIC GOODS: Game Calls
Quaker Boy Inc .... E 716 662-3979
  Orchard Park *(G-13317)*

SPORTING & ATHLETIC GOODS: Gymnasium Eqpt
Peloton Interactive Inc .... E 866 650-1996
  New York *(G-11620)*

SPORTING & ATHLETIC GOODS: Hockey Eqpt & Splys, NEC
Hart Sports Inc .... G 631 385-1805
  Huntington Station *(G-6745)*
Kohlberg Sports Group Inc .... G 914 241-7430
  Mount Kisco *(G-8676)*

SPORTING & ATHLETIC GOODS: Lacrosse Eqpt & Splys, NEC
Maverik Lacrosse LLC .... A 516 213-3050
  New York *(G-11208)*

Tosch Products Ltd .... G 315 672-3040
  Camillus *(G-3353)*

SPORTING & ATHLETIC GOODS: Pools, Swimming, Exc Plastic
Asia Connection LLC .... F 212 369-4644
  New York *(G-9285)*
Charm Mfg Co Inc .... E 607 565-8161
  Waverly *(G-16724)*
Imperial Pools Inc .... C 518 786-1200
  Latham *(G-7392)*
Latham Pool Products Inc .... C 518 951-1000
  Latham *(G-7397)*
Polytech Pool Mfg Inc .... F 718 492-8991
  Brooklyn *(G-2440)*

SPORTING & ATHLETIC GOODS: Pools, Swimming, Plastic
Florida North Inc .... F 518 868-2888
  Sloansville *(G-15501)*
Hinspergers Poly Industries .... E 585 798-6625
  Medina *(G-8308)*
Swimline Corp .... E 631 254-2155
  Edgewood *(G-4626)*
Wilbar International Inc .... D 631 951-9800
  Hauppauge *(G-6258)*

SPORTING & ATHLETIC GOODS: Shafts, Golf Club
Elmira Country Club Inc .... G 607 734-6251
  Elmira *(G-4694)*

SPORTING & ATHLETIC GOODS: Shooting Eqpt & Splys, General
Otis Products Inc .... C 315 348-4300
  Lyons Falls *(G-8004)*

SPORTING & ATHLETIC GOODS: Skateboards
Blades .... F 212 477-1059
  New York *(G-9462)*

SPORTING & ATHLETIC GOODS: Skates & Parts, Roller
Chapman Skateboard Co Inc .... G 631 321-4773
  Deer Park *(G-4139)*

SPORTING & ATHLETIC GOODS: Target Shooting Eqpt
Devin Mfg Inc .... F 585 496-5770
  Arcade *(G-391)*

SPORTING & ATHLETIC GOODS: Team Sports Eqpt
Adpro Sports LLC .... D 716 854-5116
  Buffalo *(G-2815)*
Warrior Sports Inc .... G 315 536-0937
  Penn Yan *(G-13544)*

SPORTING & ATHLETIC GOODS: Tennis Eqpt & Splys
Rottkamp Tennis Inc .... E 631 421-0040
  Huntington Station *(G-6757)*

SPORTING & REC GOODS, WHOLESALE: Camping Eqpt & Splys
Adirondack Outdoor Center LLC .... G 315 369-2300
  Old Forge *(G-13152)*
Johnson Outdoors Inc .... C 607 779-2200
  Binghamton *(G-926)*

SPORTING & RECREATIONAL GOODS & SPLYS WHOLESALERS
Everlast Sports Mfg Corp .... E 212 239-0990
  New York *(G-10146)*
Graph-Tex Inc .... G 607 756-1875
  Cortland *(G-4050)*
Refuel Inc .... G 917 645-2974
  New York *(G-11850)*

Employee Codes: A=Over 500 employees, B=251-500
C=101-250, D=51-100, E=20-50, F=10-19, G=5-9

SPORTING & RECREATIONAL GOODS & SPLYS WHOLESALERS — PRODUCT SECTION

Walsh & Hughes Inc .... G 631 427-5904
  Huntington Station (G-6766)

SPORTING & RECREATIONAL GOODS, WHOL: Sharpeners, Sporting

Dead Ringer LLC .... G 585 355-4685
  Rochester (G-14324)

SPORTING & RECREATIONAL GOODS, WHOLESALE: Bicycle

Worksman Trading Corp .... E 718 322-2000
  Ozone Park (G-13413)

SPORTING & RECREATIONAL GOODS, WHOLESALE: Boat Access & Part

Brock Awnings Ltd .... F 631 765-5200
  Hampton Bays (G-5982)
Di Sanos Creative Canvas Inc .... G 315 894-3137
  Frankfort (G-5360)
Katherine Blizniak .... G 716 674-8545
  West Seneca (G-16978)

SPORTING & RECREATIONAL GOODS, WHOLESALE: Fishing

Fly-Tyers Carry-All LLC .... G 607 821-1460
  Charlotteville (G-3583)

SPORTING & RECREATIONAL GOODS, WHOLESALE: Fishing Tackle

Hemisphere Novelties Inc .... E 914 378-4100
  Yonkers (G-17469)

SPORTING & RECREATIONAL GOODS, WHOLESALE: Fitness

Valeo .... G 800 634-2704
  Yonkers (G-17512)

SPORTING & RECREATIONAL GOODS, WHOLESALE: Hot Tubs

Charm Mfg Co Inc .... E 607 565-8161
  Waverly (G-16724)

SPORTING & RECREATIONAL GOODS, WHOLESALE: Skiing

Sundown Ski & Sport Shop Inc .... E 631 737-8600
  Lake Grove (G-7292)

SPORTING & RECREATIONAL GOODS, WHOLESALE: Watersports

Great American Industries Inc .... G 607 729-9331
  Vestal (G-16472)

SPORTING GOODS

Absolute Fitness US Corp .... D 732 979-8582
  Bayside (G-760)
Apparel Production Inc .... E 212 278-8362
  New York (G-9231)
Azibi Ltd .... F 212 869-6550
  New York (G-9339)
Bob Perani Sport Shops Inc .... G 585 427-2930
  Rochester (G-14257)
Buffalo Sports Inc .... G 716 826-7700
  Blasdell (G-955)
Burnt Mill Smithing .... G 585 293-2380
  Churchville (G-3664)
Burton Corporation .... D 802 862-4500
  Champlain (G-3567)
City Sports Inc .... G 212 730-2009
  New York (G-9683)
Cooperstown Bat Co Inc .... F 607 547-2415
  Fly Creek (G-5318)
Cooperstown Bat Co Inc .... G 607 547-2415
  Cooperstown (G-3910)
Cy Plastics Works Inc .... E 585 229-2555
  Honeoye (G-6551)
Everlast Sports Mfg Corp .... E 212 239-0990
  New York (G-10146)
Excellent Art Mfg Corp .... F 718 388-7075
  Inwood (G-6795)

Good Show Sportwear Inc .... F 212 334-8751
  New York (G-10378)
Grand Slam Safety LLC .... G 315 766-7008
  Croghan (G-4084)
Hana Sportswear Inc .... E 315 639-6332
  Dexter (G-4308)
Hector Pt Sr Rehab Svc Pllc .... G 518 371-5554
  Clifton Park (G-3724)
Herrmann Group LLC .... E 716 876-9798
  Kenmore (G-7176)
Jag Manufacturing Inc .... E 518 762-9558
  Johnstown (G-7147)
Johnson Outdoors Inc .... C 607 779-2200
  Binghamton (G-926)
Mattel Inc .... F 716 714-8514
  East Aurora (G-4399)
Michael Britt Inc .... G 516 248-2010
  Mineola (G-8558)
Nalge Nunc International Corp .... A 585 498-2661
  Rochester (G-14547)
North Coast Outfitters Ltd .... G 631 727-5580
  Riverhead (G-14164)
PNC Sports .... G 516 665-2244
  Deer Park (G-4215)
Pocono Pool Products-North .... E 518 283-1023
  Rensselaer (G-14060)
PRC Liquidating Company .... G 212 823-9626
  New York (G-11716)
Promats Athletics LLC .... E 607 746-8911
  Delhi (G-4266)
Radar Sports LLC .... G 516 678-1919
  Oceanside (G-13113)
Rawlings Sporting Goods Co Inc .... D 315 429-8511
  Dolgeville (G-4331)
Rising Stars Soccer Club CNY .... E 315 381-3096
  Westmoreland (G-17093)
Roscoe Little Store Inc .... G 607 498-5553
  Roscoe (G-15035)
Sportsfield Specialties Inc .... E 607 746-8911
  Delhi (G-4268)
Stephenson Custom Case Company .... E 905 542-8762
  Niagara Falls (G-12895)
Vertical Lax Inc .... G 518 669-3699
  Albany (G-149)
Viking Athletics Ltd .... E 631 957-8000
  Lindenhurst (G-7515)
Watson Adventures LLC .... G 212 564-8293
  New York (G-12626)

SPORTING GOODS STORES, NEC

A Trusted Name Inc .... F 716 326-7400
  Westfield (G-17074)
Arena Graphics Inc .... G 516 767-5108
  Port Washington (G-13823)
Burnt Mill Smithing .... G 585 293-2380
  Churchville (G-3664)
Cooperstown Bat Co Inc .... F 607 547-2415
  Fly Creek (G-5318)
Cooperstown Bat Co Inc .... G 607 547-2415
  Cooperstown (G-3910)
Glenda Inc .... G 718 442-8981
  Staten Island (G-15699)
Graph-Tex Inc .... G 607 756-1875
  Cortland (G-4050)
Great American Bicycle LLC .... E 518 584-8100
  Saratoga Springs (G-15184)
Pda Panache Corp .... G 631 776-0523
  Bohemia (G-1112)
Shore Line Monogramming Inc .... F 914 698-8000
  Mamaroneck (G-8080)
Vic Demayos Inc .... G 845 626-4343
  Accord (G-1)

SPORTING GOODS STORES: Camping Eqpt

Johnson Outdoors Inc .... C 607 779-2200
  Binghamton (G-926)

SPORTING GOODS STORES: Fishing Eqpt

Sea Isle Custom Rod Builders .... G 516 868-8855
  Freeport (G-5436)

SPORTING GOODS STORES: Playground Eqpt

Eastern Jungle Gym Inc .... E 845 878-9800
  Carmel (G-3427)

SPORTING GOODS STORES: Skateboarding Eqpt

Chapman Skateboard Co Inc .... G 631 321-4773
  Deer Park (G-4139)

SPORTING GOODS STORES: Tennis Goods & Eqpt

Walsh & Hughes Inc .... G 631 427-5904
  Huntington Station (G-6766)

SPORTING GOODS: Archery

Copper John Corporation .... F 315 258-9269
  Auburn (G-488)
Outdoor Group LLC .... C 585 201-5358
  West Henrietta (G-16919)
Shehawken Archery Co Inc .... F 607 967-8333
  Bainbridge (G-553)

SPORTING GOODS: Fishing Nets

Koring Bros Inc .... G 888 233-1292
  New Rochelle (G-8961)
Osprey Boat .... G 631 331-4153
  Mount Sinai (G-8698)

SPORTING GOODS: Sailboards

Alternatives For Children .... E 631 271-0777
  Dix Hills (G-4313)

SPORTING GOODS: Skin Diving Eqpt

Sunny Scuba Inc .... G 212 333-4915
  New York (G-12259)

SPORTING GOODS: Surfboards

Bungers Surf Shop .... G 631 244-3646
  Sayville (G-15234)
Pilgrim Surf & Supply .... G 718 218-7456
  Brooklyn (G-2433)

SPORTING/ATHLETIC GOODS: Gloves, Boxing, Handball, Etc

Fownes Brothers & Co Inc .... E 212 683-0150
  New York (G-10244)
Fownes Brothers & Co Inc .... E 518 752-4411
  Gloversville (G-5726)
Olympia Sports Company Inc .... F 914 347-4737
  Elmsford (G-4780)

SPORTS APPAREL STORES

Gametime Sportswear Plus LLC .... G 315 724-5893
  Utica (G-16358)
Hanesbrands Inc .... G 212 576-9300
  New York (G-10452)
JM Studio Inc .... F 646 546-5514
  New York (G-10782)
Refuel Inc .... G 917 645-2974
  New York (G-11850)
Unlimited Ink Inc .... E 631 582-0696
  Hauppauge (G-6246)

SPORTS PROMOTION SVCS

Professnl Spt Pblications Inc .... C 212 697-1460
  New York (G-11749)

SPOUTING: Plastic & Fiberglass Reinforced

Saint-Gobain Prfmce Plas Corp .... E 518 283-5963
  Poestenkill (G-13755)

SPRAYING & DUSTING EQPT

Spfm Corp .... G 718 788-6800
  Brooklyn (G-2613)

SPRAYING EQPT: Agricultural

Fountainhead Group Inc .... C 315 736-0037
  New York Mills (G-12742)

SPRAYS: Artificial & Preserved

Jenray Products Inc .... E 914 375-5596
  Yonkers (G-17475)

PRODUCT SECTION

STAMPINGS: Metal

SPRINGS: Coiled Flat

Angelica Spring Company Inc ....F 585 466-7892
  Angelica *(G-377)*
Newport Magnetics Inc ....G 315 845-8878
  Newport *(G-12815)*
Whiting Door Mfg Corp ....D 716 542-3070
  Akron *(G-28)*

SPRINGS: Leaf, Automobile, Locomotive, Etc

Red Onyx Industrial Pdts LLC ....G 516 459-6035
  Huntington *(G-6712)*
Whitesboro Spring & Alignment ....F 315 736-4441
  Whitesboro *(G-17226)*

SPRINGS: Mechanical, Precision

Lee Spring Company LLC ....C 718 362-5183
  Brooklyn *(G-2207)*
Unimex Corporation ....C 718 236-2222
  Brooklyn *(G-2719)*

SPRINGS: Precision

Fennell Spring Company LLC ....D 607 739-3541
  Horseheads *(G-6606)*
Kinemotive Corporation ....E 631 249-6440
  Farmingdale *(G-5035)*

SPRINGS: Sash Balances

Pullman Mfg Corporation ....G 585 334-1350
  Rochester *(G-14631)*

SPRINGS: Steel

Chet Kruszkas Service Inc ....F 716 662-7450
  Orchard Park *(G-13284)*
Isolation Dynamics Corp ....E 631 491-5670
  West Babylon *(G-16823)*
Lee Spring Company LLC ....C 718 362-5183
  Brooklyn *(G-2207)*
Midstate Spring Inc ....E 315 437-2623
  Syracuse *(G-16010)*
Temper Corporation ....E 518 853-3467
  Fonda *(G-5322)*

SPRINGS: Wire

Ajax Wire Specialty Co Inc ....F 516 935-2333
  Hicksville *(G-6342)*
Barnes Group Inc ....G 315 457-9200
  Syracuse *(G-15887)*
Commerce Spring Corp ....F 631 293-4844
  Farmingdale *(G-4972)*
Commercial Communications LLC ....G 845 343-9078
  Middletown *(G-8466)*
Lee Spring LLC ....E 718 236-2222
  Brooklyn *(G-2208)*
Midstate Spring Inc ....E 315 437-2623
  Syracuse *(G-16010)*
Teka Precision Inc ....G 845 753-1900
  Nyack *(G-13072)*
The Caldwell Manufacturing Co ....D 585 352-3790
  Rochester *(G-14748)*
The Caldwell Manufacturing Co ....E 585 352-2803
  Victor *(G-16532)*
Unimex Corporation ....D 212 755-8800
  New York *(G-12477)*

SPRINKLING SYSTEMS: Fire Control

Allied Inspection Services LLC ....F 716 489-3199
  Falconer *(G-4897)*
Gem Fabrication of NC ....G 704 278-6713
  Garden City *(G-5521)*
Long Island Pipe Supply Inc ....E 516 222-8008
  Garden City *(G-5528)*
Reliable Autmtc Sprnklr Co Inc ....B 800 431-1588
  Elmsford *(G-4784)*
Sentry Automatic Sprinkler ....F 631 723-3095
  Riverhead *(G-14169)*
Tyco Simplexgrinnell ....E 315 437-9664
  East Syracuse *(G-4586)*
Tyco Simplexgrinnell ....E 716 483-0079
  Jamestown *(G-7072)*
Tyco Simplexgrinnell ....D 315 337-6353
  Taberg *(G-16100)*

STAGE LIGHTING SYSTEMS

Altman Stage Lighting Co Inc ....C 914 476-7987
  Yonkers *(G-17429)*

Methods Tooling & Mfg Inc ....E 845 246-7100
  Mount Marion *(G-8693)*
Ric-Lo Productions Ltd ....E 845 469-2285
  Chester *(G-3640)*
Sir Industries Inc ....G 631 234-2444
  Hauppauge *(G-6216)*

STAINLESS STEEL

American Chimney Supplies Inc ....G 631 434-2020
  Hauppauge *(G-6039)*
Bryant Manufacturing Wny Inc ....G 716 894-8282
  Buffalo *(G-2869)*
Dakota Systems Mfg Corp ....G 631 249-5811
  Farmingdale *(G-4983)*
Hallock Fabricating Corp ....G 631 727-2441
  Riverhead *(G-14156)*
Qsf Inc ....E 585 247-6200
  Gates *(G-5577)*
Quality Stainless Steel NY Inc ....F 718 748-1785
  Brooklyn *(G-2481)*
Recon Construction Corp ....E 718 939-1305
  Little Neck *(G-7532)*
Sims Group USA Holdings Corp ....D 718 786-6031
  Long Island City *(G-7906)*
Tdy Industries LLC ....E 716 433-4411
  Lockport *(G-7648)*
Viraj - USA Inc ....E 516 280-8380
  Garden City *(G-5549)*

STAIRCASES & STAIRS, WOOD

A W Hamel Stair Mfg Inc ....F 518 346-3031
  Schenectady *(G-15256)*
Adirondack Stairs Inc ....F 845 246-2525
  Saugerties *(G-15207)*
Capital District Stairs Inc ....E 518 383-2449
  Halfmoon *(G-5931)*
Island Stairs Corp ....G 347 645-0560
  Staten Island *(G-15710)*
Mestel Brothers Stairs & Rails ....C 516 496-4127
  Syosset *(G-15848)*
Monroe Stair Products Inc ....E 845 783-4245
  Monroe *(G-8598)*
Monroe Stair Products Inc ....E 845 791-4016
  Monticello *(G-8644)*
Quality Stair Builders Inc ....E 631 694-0711
  Farmingdale *(G-5103)*
S R Sloan Inc ....D 315 736-7730
  Whitesboro *(G-17223)*
Stated Island Stair Inc ....G 718 317-9276
  Staten Island *(G-15761)*
Staten Island Stair Inc ....G 718 317-9276
  Staten Island *(G-15763)*
United Rockland Holding Co Inc ....E 845 357-1900
  Suffern *(G-15822)*

STAMPED ART GOODS FOR EMBROIDERING

Dirt T Shirts Inc ....E 845 336-4230
  Kingston *(G-7216)*

STAMPING SVC: Book, Gold

Mines Press Inc ....C 914 788-1800
  Cortlandt Manor *(G-4078)*

STAMPINGS: Automotive

P R B Metal Products Inc ....F 631 467-1800
  Ronkonkoma *(G-14986)*
Thyssenkrupp Materials NA Inc ....G 585 279-0000
  Rochester *(G-14753)*
Utica Metal Products Inc ....D 315 732-6163
  Utica *(G-16388)*

STAMPINGS: Metal

4m Precision Industries Inc ....E 315 252-8415
  Auburn *(G-475)*
Able National Corp ....E 718 386-8801
  Brooklyn *(G-1549)*
Acro Industries Inc ....C 585 254-3661
  Rochester *(G-14186)*
Advanced Structures Corp ....E 631 667-5000
  Deer Park *(G-4113)*
Afco Systems Inc ....C 631 249-9441
  Farmingdale *(G-4938)*
All Out Die Cutting Inc ....E 718 346-6666
  Brooklyn *(G-1586)*
Arnell Inc ....G 516 486-7098
  Hempstead *(G-6289)*

Arro Manufacturing LLC ....F 716 763-6203
  Lakewood *(G-7310)*
Arro Tool & Die Inc ....F 716 763-6203
  Lakewood *(G-7311)*
B & R Tool Inc ....G 718 948-2729
  Staten Island *(G-15662)*
B H M Metal Products Co ....G 845 292-5297
  Kauneonga Lake *(G-7165)*
Bailey Manufacturing Co LLC ....E 716 965-2731
  Forestville *(G-5340)*
Barnes Group Inc ....G 315 457-9200
  Syracuse *(G-15887)*
Barron Metal Products Inc ....E 914 965-1232
  Yonkers *(G-17434)*
Bel-Bee Products Incorporated ....F 845 353-0300
  West Nyack *(G-16942)*
Bowen Products Corporation ....G 315 498-4481
  Nedrow *(G-8818)*
C & H Precision Tools Inc ....E 631 758-3806
  Holtsville *(G-6527)*
Cameo Metal Products Inc ....E 718 788-1106
  Brooklyn *(G-1753)*
Cannon Industries Inc ....D 585 254-8080
  Rochester *(G-14276)*
Cep Technologies Corporation ....E 914 968-4100
  Yonkers *(G-17443)*
Check-Mate Industries Inc ....E 631 491-1777
  West Babylon *(G-16807)*
Chivvis Enterprises Inc ....E 631 842-9055
  Copiague *(G-3923)*
Cobbe Industries Inc ....E 716 287-2661
  Gerry *(G-5604)*
Coda Resources Ltd ....D 718 649-1666
  Brooklyn *(G-1789)*
Compar Manufacturing Corp ....E 212 304-2777
  New York *(G-9750)*
Crosby Company ....E 716 852-3522
  Buffalo *(G-2913)*
Dayton Rogers New York LLC ....D 585 349-4040
  Rochester *(G-14323)*
Dunkirk Metal Products Wny LLC ....E 716 366-2555
  Dunkirk *(G-4363)*
Endicott Precision Inc ....C 607 754-7076
  Endicott *(G-4811)*
Engineering Mfg Tech LLC ....D 607 754-7111
  Endicott *(G-4813)*
Falso Industries Inc ....E 315 463-0266
  Syracuse *(G-15961)*
Forsyth Industries Inc ....E 716 652-1070
  Buffalo *(G-2968)*
Freeport Screen & Stamping ....E 516 379-0330
  Freeport *(G-5412)*
Gasser & Sons Inc ....C 631 543-6600
  Commack *(G-3858)*
Gleason Works ....A 585 473-1000
  Rochester *(G-14429)*
Great Lakes Pressed Steel Corp ....E 716 885-4037
  Buffalo *(G-2998)*
Greene Technologies Inc ....E 607 656-4166
  Greene *(G-5884)*
International Ord Tech Inc ....D 716 664-1100
  Jamestown *(G-7036)*
Johnson & Hoffman LLC ....D 516 742-3333
  Carle Place *(G-3418)*
Lamparts Co Inc ....F 914 723-8986
  Mount Vernon *(G-8745)*
Magic Novelty Co Inc ....E 212 304-2777
  New York *(G-11131)*
Mantel & Mantel Stamping Corp ....G 631 467-1916
  Ronkonkoma *(G-14964)*
Marex Aquisition Corp ....C 585 458-3940
  Rochester *(G-14518)*
Matov Industries Inc ....E 718 392-5060
  Long Island City *(G-7836)*
McHone Industries Inc ....D 716 945-3380
  Salamanca *(G-15128)*
National Die & Button Mould Co ....E 201 939-7800
  Brooklyn *(G-2357)*
OEM Solutions Inc ....G 716 864-9324
  Clarence *(G-3694)*
P R B Metal Products Inc ....F 631 467-1800
  Ronkonkoma *(G-14986)*
P&G Metal Components Corp ....D 716 896-7900
  Buffalo *(G-3130)*
Precision Photo-Fab Inc ....D 716 821-9393
  Buffalo *(G-3158)*
Precision TI Die & Stamping Co ....F 516 561-0041
  Valley Stream *(G-16444)*
Premier Metals Group ....E 585 436-4020
  Rochester *(G-14619)*

Employee Codes: A=Over 500 employees, B=251-500
C=101-250, D=51-100, E=20-50, F=10-19, G=5-9

STAMPINGS: Metal

Pronto Tool & Die Co Inc .... E 631 981-8920
 Ronkonkoma *(G-14997)*
Quality Metal Stamping LLC .... G 516 255-9000
 Rockville Centre *(G-14826)*
R G Flair Co Inc .... E 631 586-7311
 Bay Shore *(G-726)*
Richter Metalcraft Corporation .... E 845 895-2025
 Wallkill *(G-16565)*
Rochester Stampings Inc .... F 585 467-5241
 Rochester *(G-14672)*
Sharon Metal Stamping Corp .... G 718 828-4510
 Bronx *(G-1450)*
Simplex Manufacturing Co Inc .... F 315 252-7524
 Auburn *(G-516)*
Stampcrete International Ltd .... E 315 451-2837
 Liverpool *(G-7577)*
Stamped Fittings Inc .... E 607 733-9988
 Elmira Heights *(G-4726)*
Stever-Locke Industries Inc .... G 585 624-3450
 Honeoye Falls *(G-6565)*
Tooling Enterprises Inc .... F 716 842-0445
 Buffalo *(G-3248)*
Tri-Technologies Inc .... E 914 699-2001
 Mount Vernon *(G-8787)*
TRW Automotive Inc .... B 315 255-3311
 Auburn *(G-522)*
TRW Automotive US LLC .... C 315 255-3311
 Auburn *(G-523)*
Universal Shielding Corp .... E 631 667-7900
 Deer Park *(G-4244)*
Van Reenen Tool & Die Inc .... F 585 288-6000
 Rochester *(G-14779)*
W & H Stampings Inc .... E 631 234-6161
 Hauppauge *(G-6254)*
Web Associates Inc .... G 716 883-3377
 Buffalo *(G-3275)*
WR Smith & Sons Inc .... G 845 620-9400
 Nanuet *(G-8809)*

STANDS & RACKS: Engine, Metal

Devin Mfg Inc .... F 585 496-5770
 Arcade *(G-391)*

STARTERS: Motor

Con Rel Auto Electric Inc .... E 518 356-1646
 Schenectady *(G-15273)*

STATIC ELIMINATORS: Ind

Nrd LLC .... E 716 773-7634
 Grand Island *(G-5779)*

STATIONARY & OFFICE SPLYS, WHOLESALE: Laser Printer Splys

Interntnl Publcatns Media Grup .... G 917 604-9602
 New York *(G-10682)*
Printer Components Inc .... E 585 924-5190
 Fairport *(G-4877)*

STATIONARY & OFFICE SPLYS, WHOLESALE: Stationery

F J Remey Co Inc .... E 516 741-5112
 Mineola *(G-8544)*
One In A Million Inc .... G 516 829-1111
 Valley Stream *(G-16441)*
Tripi Engraving Co Inc .... E 718 383-6500
 Brooklyn *(G-2700)*

STATIONER'S SUNDRIES: Rubber

Hampton Art LLC .... E 631 924-1335
 Medford *(G-8278)*
Rubber Stamps Inc .... E 212 675-1180
 Mineola *(G-8568)*

STATIONERY & OFFICE SPLYS WHOLESALERS

Argo Lithographers Inc .... E 718 729-2700
 Long Island City *(G-7702)*
Atlaz International Ltd .... F 516 239-1854
 Lawrence *(G-7416)*
Kas-Ray Industries Inc .... F 212 620-3144
 New York *(G-10849)*
Labels Inter-Global Inc .... F 212 398-0006
 New York *(G-10949)*

STATIONERY PRDTS

Bak USA Technologies Corp .... E 716 248-2704
 Buffalo *(G-2852)*
Cos TEC Manufacturing Corp .... G 631 589-7170
 Bohemia *(G-1035)*
Dynamic Intl Mfrs & Distrs Inc .... F 347 993-1914
 Suffern *(G-15810)*
Innovative Designs LLC .... E 212 695-0892
 New York *(G-10646)*
International Design Assoc Ltd .... G 212 687-0333
 New York *(G-10675)*
Kleer-Fax Inc .... D 631 225-1100
 Amityville *(G-303)*
Leather Indexes Corp .... D 516 827-1900
 Hicksville *(G-6391)*
P C I Paper Conversions Inc .... C 315 437-1641
 Syracuse *(G-16027)*
Paper Magic Group Inc .... B 631 521-3682
 New York *(G-11577)*
Princton Archtctural Press LLC .... E 518 671-6100
 Hudson *(G-6662)*
Westrock Mwv LLC .... C 212 688-5000
 New York *(G-12645)*

STATIONERY: Made From Purchased Materials

Allen William & Company Inc .... C 212 675-6461
 Glendale *(G-5659)*

STATUARY & OTHER DECORATIVE PRDTS: Nonmetallic

Design Research Ltd .... C 212 228-7675
 New York *(G-9907)*

STATUES: Nonmetal

Barrett Bronze Inc .... E 914 699-6060
 Mount Vernon *(G-8710)*
Dream Statuary Inc .... E 718 647-2024
 Brooklyn *(G-1880)*
Jonas Louis Paul Studios Inc .... G 518 851-2211
 Hudson *(G-6653)*

STEAM SPLY SYSTEMS SVCS INCLUDING GEOTHERMAL

Caithness Equities Corporation .... E 212 599-2112
 New York *(G-9549)*

STEAM, HEAT & AIR CONDITIONING DISTRIBUTION SVC

P&G Metal Components Corp .... D 716 896-7900
 Buffalo *(G-3130)*

STEEL & ALLOYS: Tool & Die

B H M Metal Products Co .... G 845 292-5297
 Kauneonga Lake *(G-7165)*
Fuller Tool Incorporated .... F 315 891-3183
 Newport *(G-12814)*
Spin-Rite Corporation .... F 585 266-5200
 Rochester *(G-14720)*

STEEL FABRICATORS

760 NI Holdings .... E 716 821-1391
 Buffalo *(G-2805)*
A & T Iron Works Inc .... G 914 632-8992
 New Rochelle *(G-8928)*
A-Fab Initiatives Inc .... G 716 877-5257
 Buffalo *(G-2807)*
A/C Design & Fabrication Corp .... G 718 227-8100
 Staten Island *(G-15652)*
AAA Welding and Fabrication of .... G 585 254-2830
 Rochester *(G-14177)*
Abalon Precision Mfg Corp .... F 914 665-7700
 Mount Vernon *(G-8702)*
Abalon Precision Mfg Corp .... F 718 589-5682
 Mount Vernon *(G-8703)*
Acadia Stairs 845 765-8600
 Fishkill *(G-5187)*
Accucut Inc 631 567-2868
 West Sayville *(G-16962)*
Achilles Construction Co Inc .... F 718 389-4717
 Mount Vernon *(G-8705)*
Ackroyd Metal Fabricators Inc .... F 518 434-1281
 Menands *(G-8396)*

Advanced Thermal Systems Inc .... E 716 681-1800
 Lancaster *(G-7322)*
Advantage Machining Inc .... F 716 731-6418
 Niagara Falls *(G-12818)*
Aero-Data Metal Crafters Inc .... C 631 471-7733
 Ronkonkoma *(G-14882)*
Airflex Corp .... D 631 752-1219
 Farmingdale *(G-4939)*
Aldo Frustacci Iron Works Inc .... F 718 768-0707
 Brooklyn *(G-1577)*
All-City Metal Inc .... E 718 937-3975
 Maspeth *(G-8142)*
Alp Steel Corp .... E 716 854-3030
 Buffalo *(G-2821)*
American Aerogel Corporation .... E 585 328-2140
 Rochester *(G-14211)*
Asp Industries Inc .... E 585 254-9130
 Rochester *(G-14235)*
Atlantis Equipment Corporation .... F 518 733-5910
 Stephentown *(G-15778)*
B H M Metal Products Co .... G 845 292-5297
 Kauneonga Lake *(G-7165)*
B P Nash Co Inc .... E 315 445-1310
 East Syracuse *(G-4526)*
Barber Welding Inc .... E 315 834-6645
 Weedsport *(G-16772)*
Barker Steel LLC .... E 518 465-6221
 Albany *(G-49)*
Barry Steel Fabrication Inc .... E 716 433-2144
 Lockport *(G-7599)*
Bear Metal Works Inc .... F 716 824-4350
 Buffalo *(G-2857)*
Bennett Manufacturing Co Inc .... C 716 937-9161
 Alden *(G-178)*
Bereza Iron Works Inc .... E 585 254-6311
 Rochester *(G-14246)*
Blackstone Advanced Tech LLC .... C 716 665-5410
 Jamestown *(G-7011)*
Bms Manufacturing Co Inc .... E 607 535-2426
 Watkins Glen *(G-16718)*
Bob Murphy Inc .... F 607 729-3553
 Vestal *(G-16464)*
Bombardier Transportation .... D 607 324-0216
 Hornell *(G-6586)*
Bombardier Trnsp Holdings USA .... D 607 776-4791
 Bath *(G-654)*
Bristol Metals Inc .... F 585 657-7665
 Bloomfield *(G-976)*
Burnt Hills Fabricators Inc .... F 518 885-1115
 Ballston Spa *(G-591)*
C & C Custom Metal Fabricators .... G 631 235-9646
 Hauppauge *(G-6059)*
C & C Metal Fabrications Inc .... F 315 598-7607
 Fulton *(G-5467)*
C & T Tool & Instrument Co .... E 718 429-1253
 Woodside *(G-17338)*
Cameron Mfg & Design Inc .... C 607 739-3606
 Horseheads *(G-6599)*
Carpenter Industries Inc .... F 315 463-4284
 Syracuse *(G-15905)*
Castle Harvester Co Inc .... G 585 526-5884
 Seneca Castle *(G-15381)*
CBM Fabrications Inc .... E 518 399-8023
 Ballston Lake *(G-580)*
Chautauqua Machine Spc LLC .... F 716 782-3276
 Ashville *(G-424)*
Christian Fabrication LLC .... G 315 822-0135
 West Winfield *(G-16986)*
Cives Corporation .... C 315 287-2200
 Gouverneur *(G-5758)*
Cobbe Industries Inc .... E 716 287-2661
 Gerry *(G-5604)*
Cobra Operating Industries LLC .... G 607 639-1700
 Afton *(G-9)*
Coco Architectureal Grilles .... G 631 482-9449
 Farmingdale *(G-4970)*
Columbia Metal Fabricators .... G 631 476-7527
 Port Jeff STA *(G-13788)*
Computerized Metal Bending Ser .... F 631 249-1177
 West Babylon *(G-16810)*
Cottonwood Metals Inc .... E 646 807-8674
 Bohemia *(G-1036)*
County Fabricators .... F 914 741-0219
 Pleasantville *(G-13745)*
Cyncal Steel Fabricators Inc .... F 631 254-5600
 Bay Shore *(G-687)*
D N Gannon Fabricating Inc .... G 315 463-7466
 Syracuse *(G-15939)*
Dennies Manufacturing Inc .... E 585 393-4646
 Canandaigua *(G-3371)*

PRODUCT SECTION

STEEL MILLS

Company	Code	Phone
Diversified Manufacturing Inc	F	716 681-7670
Lancaster *(G-7336)*		
Donald Stefan	G	716 492-1110
Chaffee *(G-3561)*		
Dynasty Metal Works Inc	G	631 284-3719
Riverhead *(G-14153)*		
E B Atlas Steel Corp	F	716 876-0900
Buffalo *(G-2937)*		
Eastern Manufacturing Inc	F	716 741-4572
Clarence Center *(G-3700)*		
Eastern Welding Inc	G	631 727-0306
Riverhead *(G-14154)*		
Elevator Accessories Mfg	F	914 739-7004
Peekskill *(G-13501)*		
Elmira Metal Works Inc	G	607 734-9813
Elmira *(G-4696)*		
Empire Industrial Systems Corp	F	631 242-4619
Bay Shore *(G-697)*		
Empire Metal Fabricators Inc	G	585 288-2140
Rochester *(G-14367)*		
Eps Iron Works Inc	G	516 294-5840
Mineola *(G-8542)*		
Erie Engineered Products Inc	E	716 206-0204
Lancaster *(G-7338)*		
Everfab Inc	D	716 655-1550
East Aurora *(G-4395)*		
Excel Industries Inc	E	716 542-5468
Clarence *(G-3689)*		
Farmingdale Iron Works Inc	G	631 249-5995
Farmingdale *(G-5000)*		
Feinstein Iron Works Inc	E	516 997-8300
Westbury *(G-17012)*		
Fence Plaza Corp	G	718 469-2200
Brooklyn *(G-1970)*		
Five Corners Repair Inc	F	585 322-7369
Bliss *(G-974)*		
Flagpoles Incorporated	D	631 751-5500
East Setauket *(G-4501)*		
Fort Miller Group Inc	B	518 695-5000
Greenwich *(G-5906)*		
Frazier Industrial Company	D	315 539-9256
Waterloo *(G-16648)*		
Gasport Welding & Fabg Inc	F	716 772-7205
Gasport *(G-5572)*		
George Industries LLC	C	607 748-3371
Endicott *(G-4818)*		
Gibraltar Industries Inc	D	716 826-6500
Buffalo *(G-2989)*		
Glenridge Fabricators Inc	F	718 456-2297
Glendale *(G-5670)*		
Hallock Fabricating Corp	G	631 727-2441
Riverhead *(G-14156)*		
Hansen Steel	E	585 398-2020
Farmington *(G-5161)*		
Homer Iron Works LLC	G	607 749-3963
Homer *(G-6547)*		
Hudson Steel Fabricators	E	585 454-3923
Rochester *(G-14460)*		
Industrial Fabricating Corp	E	315 437-3353
East Syracuse *(G-4553)*		
Industrial Support Inc	D	716 662-2954
Buffalo *(G-3024)*		
Inscape (new York) Inc	D	716 665-6210
Falconer *(G-4909)*		
Irony Limited Inc	G	631 329-4065
East Hampton *(G-4431)*		
Irv Schroder & Sons Inc	E	518 828-0194
Stottville *(G-15803)*		
Irving Woodlands LLC	E	607 723-4862
Conklin *(G-3895)*		
J F M Sheet Metal Inc	G	631 737-8494
Ronkonkoma *(G-14944)*		
J M Haley Corp	C	631 845-5200
Farmingdale *(G-5021)*		
Jaab Precision Inc	G	631 218-3725
Ronkonkoma *(G-14946)*		
James Woerner Inc	G	631 454-9330
Farmingdale *(G-5024)*		
Jbs LLC	E	518 346-0001
Scotia *(G-15350)*		
Jentsch & Co Inc	G	716 852-4111
Buffalo *(G-3033)*		
Joy Edward Company	E	315 474-3360
East Syracuse *(G-4561)*		
Jpw Structural Contracting Inc	E	315 432-1111
Syracuse *(G-15990)*		
K & E Fabricating Company Inc	F	716 829-1829
Buffalo *(G-3040)*		
Kal Manufacturing Corporation	E	585 265-4310
Webster *(G-16751)*		
KDO Industries Inc	G	631 608-4612
Amityville *(G-301)*		
King Steel Iron Work Corp	F	718 384-7500
Brooklyn *(G-2173)*		
Kleinfelder John	G	716 753-3163
Mayville *(G-8247)*		
Knj Fabricators LLC	F	347 234-6985
Bronx *(G-1378)*		
Koenig Iron Works Inc	E	718 433-0900
Long Island City *(G-7808)*		
Kryten Iron Works Inc	G	914 345-0990
Hawthorne *(G-6272)*		
Leading Edge Fabrication	G	631 274-9797
Deer Park *(G-4188)*		
Lindenhurst Fabricators Inc	G	631 226-3737
Lindenhurst *(G-7489)*		
M & L Steel & Ornamental Iron	F	718 816-8660
Staten Island *(G-15723)*		
Major-IPC Inc	G	845 292-2200
Liberty *(G-7460)*		
Marex Aquisition Corp	C	585 458-3940
Rochester *(G-14518)*		
Mason Industries Inc	B	631 348-0282
Hauppauge *(G-6152)*		
Maspeth Steel Fabricators Inc	G	718 361-9192
Long Island City *(G-7834)*		
Maspeth Welding Inc	F	718 497-5430
Maspeth *(G-8181)*		
Metal Concepts	G	845 592-1863
Beacon *(G-784)*		
Metal Crafts Inc	G	718 443-3333
Brooklyn *(G-2308)*		
Metal Fab LLC	G	607 775-3200
Binghamton *(G-932)*		
Metal Works of NY Inc	G	718 525-9440
Jamaica *(G-6966)*		
Miscellnous Ir Fabricators Inc	E	518 355-1822
Schenectady *(G-15306)*		
Mobile Mini Inc	F	315 732-4555
Utica *(G-16373)*		
Monarch Metal Fabrication Inc	G	631 563-8967
Bohemia *(G-1100)*		
Nathan Steel Corp	F	315 797-1335
Utica *(G-16375)*		
Nb Elctrcal Enclsures Mfrs Inc	E	718 272-8792
Brooklyn *(G-2362)*		
Nci Group Inc	D	315 339-1245
Rome *(G-14852)*		
New Vision Industries Inc	F	607 687-7700
Endicott *(G-4827)*		
New York Manufactured Products	F	585 254-9353
Rochester *(G-14552)*		
North E Rggers Erectors NY Inc	E	518 842-6377
Amsterdam *(G-363)*		
North Eastern Fabricators Inc	E	718 542-0450
New York *(G-11474)*		
Northeast Fabricators LLC	D	607 865-4031
Walton *(G-16570)*		
Oehlers Wldg & Fabrication Inc	F	716 821-1800
Buffalo *(G-3120)*		
Orange County Ironworks LLC	E	845 769-3000
Montgomery *(G-8636)*		
Oriskany Mfg Tech LLC	E	315 732-4962
Yorkville *(G-17542)*		
P K G Equipment Incorporated	E	585 436-4650
Rochester *(G-14585)*		
Patsy Strocchia & Sons Iron Wo	F	516 625-8800
Albertson *(G-159)*		
Pcx Aerostructures LLC	E	631 249-7901
Ronkonkoma *(G-14991)*		
Pcx Aerostructures LLC	E	631 467-2632
Farmingdale *(G-5085)*		
Peralta Metal Works Inc	G	718 649-8661
Brooklyn *(G-2429)*		
Perma Tech Inc	E	716 854-0707
Buffalo *(G-3145)*		
Pierce Industries LLC	E	585 458-0888
Rochester *(G-14603)*		
Pirod Inc	G	631 231-7660
Hauppauge *(G-6191)*		
Portfab LLC	F	718 542-3600
Amityville *(G-322)*		
Precision Metals Corp	F	631 586-5032
Bay Shore *(G-723)*		
Precision Polish LLC	E	315 894-3792
Frankfort *(G-5366)*		
Prime Materials Recovery Inc	G	315 697-5251
Canastota *(G-3397)*		
Productand Design Inc	F	718 858-2440
Brooklyn *(G-2467)*		
R & J Sheet Metal Distrs Inc	G	518 433-1525
Albany *(G-125)*		
R&S Steel LLC	E	315 281-0123
Rome *(G-14859)*		
Raulli and Sons Inc	D	315 479-6693
Syracuse *(G-16040)*		
REO Welding Inc	F	518 238-1022
Cohoes *(G-3780)*		
Risa Management Corp	E	718 361-2606
Maspeth *(G-8197)*		
RJ Precision LLC	G	585 768-8030
Stafford *(G-15642)*		
Robert E Derecktor Inc	D	914 698-0962
Mamaroneck *(G-8078)*		
Romar Contracting Inc	G	845 778-2737
Walden *(G-16555)*		
Roth Design & Consulting Inc	E	718 209-0193
Brooklyn *(G-2529)*		
Rothe Welding Inc	G	845 246-3051
Saugerties *(G-15222)*		
Rough Brothers Holding Co	G	716 826-6500
Buffalo *(G-3196)*		
Rs Automation	F	585 589-0199
Albion *(G-172)*		
Rus Industries Inc	E	716 284-7828
Niagara Falls *(G-12887)*		
Schenectady Steel Co Inc	E	518 355-3220
Schenectady *(G-15317)*		
Schneider Brothers Corporation	E	315 458-8369
Syracuse *(G-16056)*		
Schuler-Subra Inc	G	716 893-3100
Buffalo *(G-3206)*		
Seibel Modern Mfg & Wldg Corp	D	716 683-1536
Lancaster *(G-7367)*		
Sentry Metal Blast Inc	E	716 285-5241
Lockport *(G-7645)*		
Silverstone Shtmtl Fbrications	G	718 422-0380
Brooklyn *(G-2586)*		
Specialty Steel Fabg Corp	F	718 893-6326
Bronx *(G-1459)*		
Specialty Wldg & Fabg NY Inc	D	315 426-1807
Syracuse *(G-16066)*		
Standard Steel Fabricators	F	518 765-4820
Voorheesville *(G-16540)*		
Steel Tech SA LLC	G	845 786-3691
Thiells *(G-16137)*		
Stone Well Bodies & Mch Inc	E	315 497-3512
Genoa *(G-5602)*		
STS Steel Inc	D	518 370-2693
Schenectady *(G-15324)*		
Supreme Steel Inc	F	631 884-1320
Lindenhurst *(G-7512)*		
Team Fabrication Inc	G	716 655-4038
West Falls *(G-16877)*		
Titan Steel Corp	E	315 656-7046
Kirkville *(G-7256)*		
Triboro Iron Works Inc	G	718 361-9600
Long Island City *(G-7934)*		
Triton Builders Inc	E	631 841-2534
Amityville *(G-332)*		
Tropical Driftwood Originals	G	516 623-0980
Roosevelt *(G-15033)*		
Tymetal Corp	E	518 692-9930
Greenwich *(G-5915)*		
Ulster Precision Inc	E	845 338-0995
Kingston *(G-7246)*		
United Iron Inc	E	914 667-5700
Mount Vernon *(G-8791)*		
United Structure Solution Inc	F	347 227-7526
New York *(G-12486)*		
Universal Metal Works LLC	F	315 598-7607
Fulton *(G-5490)*		
Vance Metal Fabricators Inc	D	315 789-5626
Geneva *(G-5600)*		
Vulcan Iron Works Inc	G	631 395-6846
Manorville *(G-8114)*		
Ward Steel Company Inc	E	315 451-4566
Liverpool *(G-7582)*		
Welding Metallurgy Inc	G	631 253-0500
Hauppauge *(G-6256)*		
Whitacre Engineering Company	G	315 622-1075
Liverpool *(G-7584)*		
Winters Railroad Service Inc	G	716 337-2668
North Collins *(G-12948)*		

STEEL MILLS

Company	Code	Phone
Albaluz Films LLC	G	347 613-2321
New York *(G-9123)*		
Allvac	F	716 433-4411
Lockport *(G-7597)*		

Employee Codes: A=Over 500 employees, B=251-500
C=101-250, D=51-100, E=20-50, F=10-19, G=5-9

STEEL MILLS

Baker Tool & Die ....G....... 716 694-2025
North Tonawanda *(G-12976)*
Belmet Products Inc ....E....... 718 542-8220
Bronx *(G-1282)*
China Industrial Steel Inc ....G....... 646 328-1502
New York *(G-9648)*
Coventry Manufacturing Co Inc.......E....... 914 668-2212
Mount Vernon *(G-8719)*
DAgostino Iron Works Inc...........G....... 585 235-8850
Rochester *(G-14319)*
David Fehlman ....G....... 315 455-8888
Syracuse *(G-15942)*
Dunkirk Specialty Steel LLC ....C....... 716 366-1000
Dunkirk *(G-4364)*
Hmi Metal Powders ....C....... 315 839-5421
Clayville *(G-3714)*
Jaquith Industries Inc..................E....... 315 478-5700
Syracuse *(G-15985)*
Juniper Elbow Co Inc ....C....... 718 326-2546
Middle Village *(G-8447)*
Kenbenco Inc ....F....... 845 246-3066
Saugerties *(G-15215)*
Nucor Steel Auburn Inc ....B....... 315 253-4561
Auburn *(G-509)*
Republic Steel Inc ....B....... 716 827-2800
Blasdell *(G-958)*
Samuel Son & Co Inc....................G....... 716 856-6500
Blasdell *(G-959)*
Universal Stainless & Alloy ....D....... 716 366-1000
Dunkirk *(G-4376)*

STEEL, COLD-ROLLED: Sheet Or Strip, From Own Hot-Rolled

Renco Group Inc............................G....... 212 541-6000
New York *(G-11864)*

STEEL, COLD-ROLLED: Strip NEC, From Purchased Hot-Rolled

Worthington Industries Inc ....D....... 315 336-5500
Rome *(G-14868)*

STEEL, HOT-ROLLED: Sheet Or Strip

Jfe Engineering Corporation ....F....... 212 310-9320
New York *(G-10767)*
Jfe Steel America Inc...................G....... 212 310-9320
New York *(G-10768)*

STEEL: Cold-Rolled

Aero-Data Metal Crafters Inc.......C....... 631 471-7733
Ronkonkoma *(G-14882)*
Clover Wire Forming Co Inc ....E....... 914 375-0400
Yonkers *(G-17444)*
Gibraltar Industries Inc...............D....... 716 826-6500
Buffalo *(G-2989)*
Hitachi Metals America Ltd ....E....... 914 694-9200
Purchase *(G-13974)*
Northeast Cnstr Inds Inc..............F....... 845 565-1000
Montgomery *(G-8634)*
Rough Brothers Holding Co ....G....... 716 826-6500
Buffalo *(G-3196)*

STEEL: Galvanized

Elderlee Incorporated ....C....... 315 789-6670
Oaks Corners *(G-13088)*

STEEL: Laminated

Advantech Industries Inc ....C....... 585 247-0701
Rochester *(G-14196)*

STENCILS

Crafters Workshop Inc ....G....... 914 345-2838
Elmsford *(G-4753)*

STONE: Cast Concrete

Alp Stone Inc.................................F....... 718 706-6166
Long Island City *(G-7686)*
Corinthian Cast Stone Inc ....E....... 631 920-2340
Wyandanch *(G-17389)*

STONE: Crushed & Broken, NEC

Labrador Stone Inc ....G....... 570 465-2120
Binghamton *(G-928)*

STONE: Dimension, NEC

Dominic De Nigris Inc ....E....... 718 597-4460
Bronx *(G-1319)*
Finger Lakes Stone Co Inc..........F....... 607 273-4646
Ithaca *(G-6878)*
Hillburn Granite Company Inc ....G....... 845 357-8900
Hillburn *(G-6441)*
Suffolk Granite Manufacturing ...E....... 631 226-4774
Lindenhurst *(G-7509)*

STONE: Quarrying & Processing, Own Stone Prdts

Callanan Industries Inc................E....... 845 331-6868
Kingston *(G-7211)*
Dalrymple Holding Corp ....E....... 607 737-6200
Pine City *(G-13578)*
Graymont Materials Inc ....E....... 518 561-5200
Plattsburgh *(G-13693)*
Hanson Aggregates PA LLC ....E....... 315 789-6202
Oaks Corners *(G-13089)*
Iroquois Rock Products Inc ....F....... 585 381-7010
Rochester *(G-14476)*
New York Marble and Stone Corp .F....... 718 729-7272
Maspeth *(G-8187)*
Thalle Industries Inc....................E....... 914 762-3415
Briarcliff Manor *(G-1229)*

STONEWARE CLAY MINING

Devonian Stone New York Inc .....E....... 607 655-2600
Windsor *(G-17294)*

STORE FIXTURES, EXC REFRIGERATED: Wholesalers

Action Rack Display Mfg..............F....... 718 257-7111
Brooklyn *(G-1557)*
Alrod Associates Inc ....F....... 631 981-2193
Ronkonkoma *(G-14892)*
Artistry In Wood of Syracuse ......F....... 315 431-4022
East Syracuse *(G-4523)*
Leo D Bernstein & Sons Inc........E....... 212 337-9578
New York *(G-11003)*

STORE FIXTURES: Exc Wood

Alrod Associates Inc ....F....... 631 981-2193
Ronkonkoma *(G-14892)*
Fixtures 2000 Inc..........................B....... 631 236-4100
Hauppauge *(G-6100)*
Hamlet Products Inc.....................F....... 914 665-0307
Mount Vernon *(G-8734)*
Yaloz Mould & Die Co Inc............E....... 718 389-1131
Brooklyn *(G-2786)*

STORE FIXTURES: Wood

Abbott Industries Inc ....E....... 718 291-0800
Jamaica *(G-6926)*
Alrod Associates Inc ....F....... 631 981-2193
Ronkonkoma *(G-14892)*
Custom Wood Inc..........................G....... 718 927-4700
Brooklyn *(G-1828)*
Falvo Manufacturing Co Inc........F....... 315 738-7682
Utica *(G-16353)*
L & J Interiors Inc........................G....... 631 218-0838
Bohemia *(G-1084)*
Longo Commercial Cabinets Inc .E....... 631 225-4290
Lindenhurst *(G-7491)*
Madjek Inc......................................D....... 631 842-4475
Amityville *(G-308)*
Three R Enterprises Inc...............E....... 585 254-5050
Rochester *(G-14752)*

STORE FRONTS: Prefabricated, Metal

Eastern Storefronts & Mtls Inc....F....... 631 471-7065
Ronkonkoma *(G-14925)*
Empire Archtctural Systems Inc..E....... 518 773-5109
Johnstown *(G-7141)*
Gamma North Corporation ....E....... 716 902-5100
Alden *(G-181)*
Pk30 System LLC..........................E....... 212 473-8050
Stone Ridge *(G-15786)*

STORE FRONTS: Prefabricated, Wood

Empire Archtctural Systems Inc..E....... 518 773-5109
Johnstown *(G-7141)*

PRODUCT SECTION

STRAPPING

Gibraltar Industries Inc...............D....... 716 826-6500
Buffalo *(G-2989)*
Precision Spclty Fbrctions LLC...E....... 716 824-2108
Buffalo *(G-3159)*
Rough Brothers Holding Co ....G....... 716 826-6500
Buffalo *(G-3196)*

STRAPS: Apparel Webbing

H Group Inc....................................F....... 212 719-5500
New York *(G-10434)*

STRAPS: Bindings, Textile

Ambind Corp ....G....... 716 836-4365
Buffalo *(G-2822)*
New York Binding Co Inc ....E....... 718 729-2454
Long Island City *(G-7857)*

STRAPS: Braids, Textile

La Lame Inc....................................G....... 212 921-9770
New York *(G-10947)*

STRAPS: Cotton Webbing

Sturges Manufacturing Co Inc.....D....... 315 732-6159
Utica *(G-16384)*

STRAWS: Drinking, Made From Purchased Materials

Last Straw Inc................................E....... 516 371-2727
Lawrence *(G-7418)*
Plastirun Corporation ....E....... 631 273-2626
Brentwood *(G-1190)*
Sqp Inc..C....... 518 831-6800
Schenectady *(G-15322)*

STRUCTURAL SUPPORT & BUILDING MATERIAL: Concrete

Cossitt Concrete Products Inc ....F....... 315 824-2700
Hamilton *(G-5970)*
Geotech Associates Ltd ....G....... 631 286-0251
Brookhaven *(G-1507)*

STUDIOS: Artist's

Donne Dieu.....................................G....... 212 226-0573
Brooklyn *(G-1874)*
Eskayel Inc ....G....... 347 703-8084
Brooklyn *(G-1940)*

STUDIOS: Sculptor's

Surving Studios ....F....... 845 355-1430
Middletown *(G-8499)*

STUDS & JOISTS: Sheet Metal

Studco Building Systems US LLC.E....... 585 545-3000
Webster *(G-16762)*

SUBSCRIPTION FULFILLMENT SVCS: Magazine, Newspaper, Etc

Time Inc Affluent Media Group....G....... 212 382-5600
New York *(G-12366)*
Viatech Pubg Solutions Inc..........E....... 631 968-8500
Bay Shore *(G-747)*

SUGAR SUBSTITUTES: Organic

Cumberland Packing Corp............B....... 718 858-4200
Brooklyn *(G-1823)*
Flavors Holdings Inc.....................G....... 212 572-8677
New York *(G-10231)*
Sugar Foods Corporation ....E....... 212 753-6900
New York *(G-12249)*

SUNDRIES & RELATED PRDTS: Medical & Laboratory, Rubber

Geri-Gentle Corporation ....G....... 917 804-7807
Brooklyn *(G-2021)*
Impladent Ltd ....G....... 718 465-1810
Jamaica *(G-6957)*
Jamestown Scientific Inds LLC....F....... 716 665-3224
Jamestown *(G-7045)*
Life Medical Technologies LLC ...F....... 845 894-2121
Hopewell Junction *(G-6582)*

PRODUCT SECTION

Remedies Surgical Supplies .... G ... 718 599-5301
  Brooklyn *(G-2509)*
Tmp Technologies Inc .... D ... 585 495-6231
  Wyoming *(G-17399)*

SUNROOMS: Prefabricated Metal

Latium USA Trading LLC .... D ... 631 563-4000
  Holbrook *(G-6484)*
Sunbilt Solar Pdts By Sussman .... D ... 718 297-0228
  Jamaica *(G-6991)*

SUPERMARKETS & OTHER GROCERY STORES

Ives Farm Market .... G ... 315 592-4880
  Fulton *(G-5477)*
Melita Corp .... C ... 718 392-7280
  Astoria *(G-447)*
Ravioli Store Inc .... G ... 718 729-9300
  Long Island City *(G-7888)*
TLC-Lc Inc .... E ... 212 756-8900
  New York *(G-12375)*

SURFACE ACTIVE AGENTS

BASF Corporation .... B ... 914 785-2000
  Tarrytown *(G-16111)*
Bigsky Technologies LLC .... G ... 585 218-9499
  Rochester *(G-14249)*
Halmark Architectural Finshg .... E ... 718 272-1831
  Brooklyn *(G-2062)*
Momentive Performance Mtls Inc .... D ... 914 784-4807
  Tarrytown *(G-16121)*
Suit-Kote Corporation .... F ... 716 683-8850
  Buffalo *(G-3227)*

SURFACE ACTIVE AGENTS: Oils & Greases

Comander Terminals LLC .... F ... 516 922-7600
  Oyster Bay *(G-13394)*

SURGICAL & MEDICAL INSTRUMENTS WHOLESALERS

Derm/Buro Inc .... G ... 516 694-8300
  Plainview *(G-13626)*

SURGICAL APPLIANCES & SPLYS

Proficient Surgical Eqp Inc .... G ... 516 487-1175
  Port Washington *(G-13874)*
Steris Corporation .... G ... 877 887-1788
  Melville *(G-8385)*

SURGICAL APPLIANCES & SPLYS

Argon Medical Devices Inc .... G ... 585 321-1130
  Henrietta *(G-6316)*
Arimed Orthotics Prosthetics P .... F ... 718 875-8754
  Brooklyn *(G-1628)*
Avanti U S A Ltd .... F ... 716 695-5800
  Tonawanda *(G-16162)*
Backtech Inc .... G ... 973 279-0838
  New York *(G-9353)*
Byer California .... G ... 212 944-8989
  New York *(G-9540)*
Community Products LLC .... E ... 845 658-7720
  Chester *(G-3630)*
Community Products LLC .... E ... 518 589-5103
  Elka Park *(G-4645)*
Creative Orthotics Prosthetics .... G ... 607 431-2526
  Oneonta *(G-13206)*
Cy Plastics Works Inc .... E ... 585 229-2555
  Honeoye *(G-6551)*
Depuy Synthes Inc .... C ... 607 271-2500
  Horseheads *(G-6603)*
Derm/Buro Inc .... G ... 516 694-8300
  Plainview *(G-13626)*
Far Rockaway Drugs Inc .... F ... 718 471-2500
  Far Rockaway *(G-4929)*
Flexible Lifeline Systems Inc .... E ... 716 896-4949
  Buffalo *(G-2964)*
Grand Slam Holdings LLC .... E ... 212 583-5000
  New York *(G-10389)*
Hanger Inc .... G ... 718 575-5504
  Forest Hills *(G-5329)*
Hanger Prsthetcs & Ortho Inc .... F ... 607 277-6620
  Ithaca *(G-6882)*
Hanger Prsthetcs & Ortho Inc .... G ... 585 292-9510
  Rochester *(G-14439)*

Harvy Surgical Supply Corp .... E ... 718 939-1122
  Flushing *(G-5257)*
Hersco-Orthotic Labs Corp .... E ... 718 391-0416
  Long Island City *(G-7789)*
Howmedica Osteonics Corp .... G ... 518 783-1880
  Latham *(G-7391)*
Instrumentation Laboratory Co .... C ... 845 680-0028
  Orangeburg *(G-13253)*
Integer Holdings Corporation .... D ... 716 759-5200
  Clarence *(G-3690)*
J P R Pharmacy Inc .... F ... 718 327-0600
  Far Rockaway *(G-4930)*
Konrad Prosthetics & Orthotics .... G ... 516 485-9164
  West Hempstead *(G-16889)*
Mayflower Splint Co .... E ... 631 549-5131
  Dix Hills *(G-4316)*
Medline Industries Inc .... B ... 845 344-3301
  Middletown *(G-8484)*
Nortech Laboratories Inc .... F ... 631 501-1452
  Farmingdale *(G-5077)*
Nova Health Systems Inc .... G ... 315 798-9018
  Utica *(G-16377)*
Nucare Pharmacy Inc .... F ... 212 426-9300
  New York *(G-11485)*
Nucare Pharmacy West LLC .... F ... 212 462-2525
  New York *(G-11486)*
Overhead Door Corporation .... D ... 518 828-7652
  Hudson *(G-6659)*
Pall Biomedical Inc .... C ... 516 484-3600
  Port Washington *(G-13869)*
Pall Corporation .... A ... 607 753-6041
  Cortland *(G-4059)*
Pall Corporation .... A ... 607 753-6041
  Cortland *(G-4060)*
Pall Corporation .... A ... 516 484-2818
  Port Washington *(G-13871)*
Pall Corporation .... A ... 607 753-6041
  Cortland *(G-4061)*
Premier Brands of America Inc .... C ... 914 667-6200
  Mount Vernon *(G-8763)*
Robert Busse & Co Inc .... B ... 631 435-4711
  Hauppauge *(G-6204)*
Scientific Plastics Inc .... F ... 212 967-1199
  New York *(G-12022)*
Silipos Holding LLC .... E ... 716 283-0700
  Niagara Falls *(G-12894)*
SPS Medical Supply Corp .... D ... 585 359-0130
  Rush *(G-15077)*
Syracuse Prosthetic Center Inc .... G ... 315 476-9697
  Syracuse *(G-16079)*
TDS Fitness Equipment .... E ... 607 733-6789
  Elmira *(G-4717)*
Tumble Forms Inc .... E ... 315 429-3101
  Dolgeville *(G-4333)*
Turbine Engine Comp Utica .... A ... 315 768-8070
  Whitesboro *(G-17225)*
Ultrapedics Ltd .... G ... 718 748-4806
  Brooklyn *(G-2715)*
Upstate Medical Solutions Inc .... G ... 716 799-3782
  Buffalo *(G-3262)*
Wyeth Holdings LLC .... D ... 845 602-5000
  Pearl River *(G-13493)*

SURGICAL EQPT: See Also Instruments

Abyrx Inc .... F ... 914 357-2600
  Irvington *(G-6808)*
Avery Biomedical Devices Inc .... F ... 631 864-1600
  Commack *(G-3849)*
Conmed Corporation .... B ... 315 797-8375
  Utica *(G-16339)*
Lake Region Medical Inc .... C ... 716 662-5025
  Orchard Park *(G-13304)*
Schilling Forge Inc .... G ... 315 454-4421
  Syracuse *(G-16055)*
Surgical Design Corp .... F ... 914 273-2445
  Armonk *(G-418)*
T G M Products Inc .... G ... 631 491-0515
  Wyandanch *(G-17392)*

SURGICAL IMPLANTS

Agnovos Healthcare LLC .... G ... 646 502-5860
  New York *(G-9109)*
Bionic Eye Technologies Inc .... G ... 845 505-5254
  Fishkill *(G-5188)*
Paradigm Spine LLC 888 273-9897
  New York *(G-11582)*
Prosthodontic & Implant Den .... E ... 212 319-6363
  New York *(G-11762)*

SURVEYING SVCS: Aerial Digital Imaging

Systems Drs C3 Inc .... B ... 716 631-6200
  Buffalo *(G-3232)*

SVC ESTABLISHMENT EQPT & SPLYS WHOLESALERS

Architectural Textiles USA Inc .... E ... 212 213-6972
  New York *(G-9246)*
Licenders .... G ... 212 759-5200
  New York *(G-11019)*
Mirandy Products Ltd .... E ... 516 489-6800
  South Hempstead *(G-15554)*

SVC ESTABLISHMENT EQPT, WHOL: Cleaning & Maint Eqpt & Splys

Jad Corp of America .... E ... 718 762-8900
  College Point *(G-3816)*
Paradigm Mktg Consortium Inc .... E ... 516 677-6012
  Syosset *(G-15855)*

SVC ESTABLISHMENT EQPT, WHOLESALE: Beauty Parlor Eqpt & Sply

Ivy Enterprises Inc .... B ... 516 621-9779
  Port Washington *(G-13848)*
Ralph Payne .... G ... 718 222-4200
  Brooklyn *(G-2496)*

SVC ESTABLISHMENT EQPT, WHOLESALE: Firefighting Eqpt

Simplexgrinnell LP .... G ... 845 774-4120
  Harriman *(G-5996)*

SVC ESTABLISHMENT EQPT, WHOLESALE: Laundry Eqpt & Splys

Coinmach Service Corp .... A ... 516 349-8555
  Plainview *(G-13618)*
CSC Serviceworks Inc .... D ... 516 349-8555
  Plainview *(G-13624)*
CSC Serviceworks Holdings .... E ... 516 349-8555
  Plainview *(G-13625)*
G A Braun Inc .... D ... 315 475-3123
  North Syracuse *(G-12960)*
Low-Cost Mfg Co Inc .... G ... 516 627-3282
  Carle Place *(G-3419)*
Spin Holdco Inc .... G ... 516 349-8555
  Plainview *(G-13662)*

SWEEPING COMPOUNDS

Bono Sawdust Supply Co Inc .... G ... 718 446-1374
  Corona *(G-4014)*

SWIMMING POOL ACCESS: Leaf Skimmers Or Pool Rakes

Swimline International Corp .... C ... 631 254-2155
  Edgewood *(G-4627)*

SWIMMING POOL EQPT: Filters & Water Conditioning Systems

Abe Pool Service .... G ... 845 473-7730
  Hyde Park *(G-6771)*
Pentair Water Pool and Spa Inc .... E ... 845 452-5500
  Lagrangeville *(G-7283)*
Pleatco LLC .... D ... 516 609-0200
  Glen Cove *(G-5637)*

SWIMMING POOL SPLY STORES

Clean All of Syracuse LLC .... G ... 315 472-9189
  Syracuse *(G-15916)*

SWIMMING POOLS, EQPT & SPLYS: Wholesalers

Asia Connection LLC .... F ... 212 369-4644
  New York *(G-9285)*
Imperial Pools Inc .... C ... 518 786-1200
  Latham *(G-7392)*

SWITCHBOARDS & PARTS: Power

Electric Swtchbard Sltions LLC .... G ... 718 643-1105
  New Hyde Park *(G-8875)*

Employee Codes: A=Over 500 employees, B=251-500
C=101-250, D=51-100, E=20-50, F=10-19, G=5-9

2018 Harris
New York Manufacturers Directory

1347

SWITCHES

SWITCHES
Bassin Technical Sales Co .... E 914 698-9358
  Mamaroneck *(G-8056)*
Delta Metal Products Co Inc .... E 718 855-4200
  Brooklyn *(G-1852)*
Sector Microwave Inds Inc .... D 631 242-2245
  Deer Park *(G-4232)*

SWITCHES: Electric Power
Adeptronics Incorporated .... G 631 667-0659
  Bay Shore *(G-665)*
Marquardt Switches Inc .... C 315 655-8050
  Cazenovia *(G-3475)*
Transistor Devices Inc .... E 631 471-7492
  Ronkonkoma *(G-15015)*

SWITCHES: Electric Power, Exc Snap, Push Button, Etc
Atlas Switch Co Inc .... E 516 222-6280
  Garden City *(G-5509)*

SWITCHES: Electronic
C A M Graphics Co Inc .... E 631 842-3400
  Farmingdale *(G-4964)*
Dortronics Systems Inc .... E 631 725-0505
  Sag Harbor *(G-15105)*
Kearney-National Inc .... F 212 661-4600
  New York *(G-10868)*
NEa Manufacturing Corp .... E 516 371-4200
  Inwood *(G-6803)*
Scientific Components Corp .... B 718 934-4500
  Brooklyn *(G-2563)*
Secs Inc .... E 914 667-5600
  Mount Vernon *(G-8778)*
Spectron Glass & Electronics .... F 631 582-5600
  Hauppauge *(G-6218)*
Spectron Systems Technology .... F 631 582-5600
  Hauppauge *(G-6219)*

SWITCHES: Electronic Applications
Dortronics Systems Inc .... E 631 725-0505
  Sag Harbor *(G-15105)*
Machine Components Corp .... E 516 694-7222
  Plainview *(G-13644)*
Switches and Sensors Inc .... F 631 924-2167
  Yaphank *(G-17420)*

SWITCHES: Silicon Control
Senera Co Inc .... F 516 639-3774
  Valley Stream *(G-16450)*

SWITCHES: Starting, Fluorescent
Monarch Electric Products Inc .... G 718 583-7996
  Bronx *(G-1405)*

SWITCHES: Time, Electrical Switchgear Apparatus
Ems Development Corporation .... D 631 924-4736
  Yaphank *(G-17406)*

SWITCHGEAR & SWITCHBOARD APPARATUS
All City Switchboard Corp .... E 718 956-7244
  Long Island City *(G-7684)*
C A M Graphics Co Inc .... E 631 842-3400
  Farmingdale *(G-4964)*
Cooper Power Systems LLC .... B 716 375-7100
  Olean *(G-13160)*
Inertia Switch Inc .... E 845 359-8300
  Orangeburg *(G-13251)*
Marquardt Switches Inc .... C 315 655-8050
  Cazenovia *(G-3475)*
Pacs Switchgear LLC .... G 516 465-7100
  Bethpage *(G-876)*
Schneider Electric Usa Inc .... C 646 335-0220
  New York *(G-12012)*
Select Controls Inc .... E 631 567-9010
  Bohemia *(G-1127)*
Sinclair Technologies Inc .... E 716 874-3682
  Hamburg *(G-5966)*

SWITCHGEAR & SWITCHGEAR ACCESS, NEC
Cooper Industries LLC .... E 315 477-7000
  Syracuse *(G-15928)*
Electrotech Service Eqp Corp .... E 718 626-7700
  Astoria *(G-437)*

SWORDS
Starfire Swords Ltd Inc .... E 607 589-7244
  Spencer *(G-15588)*

SYNTHETIC RESIN FINISHED PRDTS, NEC
General Composites Inc .... E 518 963-7333
  Willsboro *(G-17289)*

SYRUPS, DRINK
Pepsi-Cola Metro Btlg Co Inc .... G 914 767-6000
  White Plains *(G-17179)*

SYRUPS, FLAVORING, EXC DRINK
3v Company Inc .... E 718 858-7333
  Brooklyn *(G-1516)*
Fox 416 Corp .... E 718 385-4600
  Brooklyn *(G-2001)*
Mapleland Farms LLC .... E 518 854-7669
  Salem *(G-15138)*

SYSTEMS INTEGRATION SVCS
Binghamton Simulator Co Inc .... E 607 321-2980
  Binghamton *(G-891)*
Medsim-Eagle Simulation Inc .... F 607 658-9354
  Endicott *(G-4824)*
New Media Investment Group Inc .... B 212 479-3160
  New York *(G-11412)*
Telxon Corporation .... E 631 738-2400
  Holtsville *(G-6539)*

SYSTEMS INTEGRATION SVCS: Local Area Network
Cables and Chips Inc .... E 212 619-3132
  New York *(G-9544)*

SYSTEMS SOFTWARE DEVELOPMENT SVCS
Ex El Enterprises Ltd .... F 212 489-4500
  New York *(G-10152)*
Inprotopia Corporation .... F 917 338-7501
  New York *(G-10651)*
Napco Security Tech Inc .... A 631 842-9400
  Amityville *(G-313)*
Roomactually LLC .... G 646 388-1922
  New York *(G-11934)*
Sale 121 Corp .... D 240 855-8988
  New York *(G-11972)*
Schoolnet Inc .... C 646 496-9000
  New York *(G-12019)*

TABLE OR COUNTERTOPS, PLASTIC LAMINATED
Allegany Laminating and Supply .... G 716 372-2424
  Allegany *(G-201)*
Contempra Design Inc .... G 718 984-8586
  Staten Island *(G-15681)*
Kitchen Specialty Craftsmen .... G 607 739-0833
  Elmira *(G-4707)*
Lif Distributing Inc .... F 631 630-6900
  Islandia *(G-6837)*
Red White & Blue Entps Corp .... G 718 565-8080
  Woodside *(G-17366)*
Wilsonart Intl Holdings LLC .... E 516 935-6980
  Bethpage *(G-878)*

TABLECLOTHS & SETTINGS
Broder Mfg Inc .... G 718 366-1667
  Brooklyn *(G-1717)*
Royal Copenhagen Inc .... F 845 454-4442
  Poughkeepsie *(G-13947)*

TABLES: Lift, Hydraulic
Columbus McKinnon Corporation .... C 716 689-5400
  Getzville *(G-5607)*

Columbus McKinnon Corporation .... C 716 689-5400
  Getzville *(G-5608)*
Columbus McKinnon Corporation .... C 716 689-5400
  Getzville *(G-5609)*

TABLETS & PADS: Book & Writing, Made From Purchased Material
Duck Flats Pharma .... G 315 689-3407
  Elbridge *(G-4638)*
USA Custom Pad Corp .... E 607 563-9550
  Sidney *(G-15467)*

TABLEWARE OR KITCHEN ARTICLES: Commercial, Fine Earthenware
Green Wave International Inc .... G 718 499-3371
  Brooklyn *(G-2052)*
Korin Japanese Trading Corp .... E 212 587-7021
  New York *(G-10916)*
Lifestyle International LLC .... G 917 757-0067
  New York *(G-11022)*

TABLEWARE: Household & Commercial, Semivitreous
Jill Fenichell Inc .... G 718 237-2490
  Brooklyn *(G-2141)*

TABLEWARE: Plastic
Pactiv LLC .... A 585 393-3149
  Canandaigua *(G-3384)*
Q Squared Design LLC .... E 212 686-8860
  New York *(G-11788)*
Supreme Poultry Inc .... G 718 472-0300
  Long Island City *(G-7924)*

TABLEWARE: Vitreous China
Carmona Nyc LLC .... G 718 227-6662
  Rego Park *(G-14043)*

TAGS & LABELS: Paper
Auto Data Systems Inc .... E 631 667-2382
  Deer Park *(G-4128)*
Depot Label Company Inc .... G 631 467-2952
  Patchogue *(G-13443)*
Gooding Co Inc .... E 716 434-5501
  Lockport *(G-7622)*
K Sidrane Inc .... E 631 393-6974
  Farmingdale *(G-5028)*
Sml USA Inc .... E 212 736-8800
  New York *(G-12135)*
Stickershopcom Inc .... G 631 563-4323
  Bayport *(G-755)*
Web-Tech Packaging Inc .... F 716 684-4520
  Lancaster *(G-7372)*

TAGS: Paper, Blank, Made From Purchased Paper
Allen-Bailey Tag & Label Inc .... D 585 538-2324
  Caledonia *(G-3303)*
Jerry Tomaselli .... F 718 965-1400
  Brooklyn *(G-2136)*
Tag Envelope Co Inc .... E 718 389-6844
  College Point *(G-3835)*

TAILORS: Custom
Adrian Jules Ltd .... D 585 342-5886
  Rochester *(G-14190)*

TALLOW: Animal
Baker Commodities Inc .... E 585 482-1880
  Rochester *(G-14239)*

TANK REPAIR SVCS
David Isseks & Sons Inc .... E 212 966-8694
  New York *(G-9875)*

TANKS & OTHER TRACKED VEHICLE CMPNTS
Lourdes Industries Inc .... D 631 234-6600
  Hauppauge *(G-6146)*
Tecmotiv (usa) Inc .... E 905 669-5911
  Niagara Falls *(G-12899)*

PRODUCT SECTION

TANKS: Concrete
Preload Concrete Structures ....E....... 631 231-8100
  Hauppauge *(G-6196)*

TANKS: Cryogenic, Metal
North American Svcs Group LLC ....F....... 518 885-1820
  Ballston Spa *(G-604)*

TANKS: Fuel, Including Oil & Gas, Metal Plate
Cardinal Tank Corp ....E....... 718 625-4350
  Brooklyn *(G-1759)*
Crown Tank Company LLC ....G....... 855 276-9682
  Horseheads *(G-6600)*
Stutzman Management Corp ....F....... 800 735-2013
  Lancaster *(G-7369)*

TANKS: Lined, Metal
Amherst Stnless Fbrication LLC ....E....... 716 691-7012
  Amherst *(G-228)*
General Oil Equipment Co Inc ....E....... 716 691-7012
  Amherst *(G-242)*
Modutank Inc ....F....... 718 392-1112
  Long Island City *(G-7846)*

TANKS: Military, Including Factory Rebuilding
Federal Prison Industries ....C....... 845 386-6819
  Otisville *(G-13369)*

TANKS: Plastic & Fiberglass
An-Cor Industrial Plastics Inc ....D....... 716 695-3141
  North Tonawanda *(G-12972)*
Chem-Tek Systems Inc ....F....... 631 253-3010
  Bay Shore *(G-681)*
Norwesco Inc ....F....... 607 687-8081
  Owego *(G-13382)*

TANKS: Standard Or Custom Fabricated, Metal Plate
Gasport Welding & Fabg Inc ....F....... 716 772-7205
  Gasport *(G-5572)*
K Industries Inc ....G....... 631 897-2125
  Bellport *(G-828)*
Stainless Metals Inc ....F....... 718 784-1454
  Woodside *(G-17372)*
Stavo Industries Inc ....F....... 845 331-4552
  Kingston *(G-7241)*
Steelways Inc ....E....... 845 562-0860
  Newburgh *(G-12804)*
Taylor Tank Company Inc ....E....... 718 434-1300
  Brooklyn *(G-2669)*

TANKS: Storage, Farm, Metal Plate
Bigbee Steel and Tank Company ....E....... 518 273-0801
  Watervliet *(G-16703)*

TANKS: Water, Metal Plate
David Isseks & Sons Inc ....E....... 212 966-8694
  New York *(G-9875)*
Jbren Corp ....F....... 716 332-5928
  Buffalo *(G-3032)*
Water Cooling Corp ....G....... 718 723-6500
  Rosedale *(G-15039)*

TANKS: Wood
Rosenwach Tank Co Inc ....E....... 212 972-4411
  Astoria *(G-454)*

TANNERIES: Leather
Colonial Tanning Corporation ....G....... 518 725-7171
  Gloversville *(G-5724)*
Myers Group LLC ....G....... 973 761-6414
  New York *(G-11356)*
Simco Leather Corporation ....E....... 518 762-7100
  Johnstown *(G-7156)*
Wood & Hyde Leather Co Inc ....E....... 518 725-7105
  Gloversville *(G-5745)*

TAPE DRIVES
Matrox Graphics Inc ....G....... 518 561-4417
  Plattsburgh *(G-13703)*

TAPES, ADHESIVE: MedicaL
Eis Inc ....D....... 585 426-5330
  Rochester *(G-14361)*
Tape Systems Inc ....F....... 914 668-3700
  Mount Vernon *(G-8782)*

TAPES: Audio Range, Blank
Orpheo USA Corp ....G....... 212 464-8255
  New York *(G-11540)*
West African Movies 718 731-2190
  Bronx *(G-1495)*

TAPES: Coated Fiberglass, Pipe Sealing Or Insulating
GM Insulation Corp ....F....... 516 354-6000
  Elmont *(G-4732)*

TAPES: Gummed, Cloth Or Paper Based, From Purchased Matls
Patco Tapes Inc ....G....... 718 497-1527
  Maspeth *(G-8194)*

TAPES: Magnetic
Professional Tape Corporation ....G....... 516 656-5519
  Glen Cove *(G-5638)*

TAPES: Pressure Sensitive
Berry Specialty Tapes LLC ....C....... 631 727-6000
  Riverhead *(G-14150)*
Kleen Stik Industries Inc ....F....... 718 984-5031
  Staten Island *(G-15718)*
Merco Hackensack Inc ....G....... 845 357-3699
  Hillburn *(G-6442)*
T L F Graphics Inc ....D....... 585 272-5500
  Rochester *(G-14740)*
Tape-It Inc ....E....... 631 243-4100
  Bay Shore *(G-743)*
Tri Star Label Inc ....E....... 914 237-4800
  Mount Vernon *(G-8786)*
Valley Industrial Products Inc ....E....... 631 385-9300
  Huntington *(G-6727)*

TARGET DRONES
Enlighten Air Inc ....G....... 917 656-1248
  New York *(G-10094)*

TELECOMMUNICATION SYSTEMS & EQPT
Aines Manufacturing Corp ....E....... 631 471-3900
  Islip *(G-6845)*
Alcatel-Lucent USA Inc ....D....... 516 349-4900
  Plainview *(G-13610)*
Clayton Dubilier & Rice Fun ....E....... 212 407-5200
  New York *(G-9695)*
Corning Incorporated ....E....... 607 248-1200
  Corning *(G-3986)*
Corning Incorporated ....G....... 607 974-6729
  Painted Post *(G-13417)*
Corning Incorporated ....A....... 607 974-9000
  Corning *(G-3983)*
ESi Cases & Accessories Inc ....E....... 212 883-8838
  New York *(G-10113)*
Forerunner Technologies Inc ....E....... 631 337-2100
  Bohemia *(G-1063)*
Harris Corporation ....E....... 585 244-5830
  Rochester *(G-14446)*
Interdgital Communications LLC ....C....... 631 622-4000
  Melville *(G-8360)*
Kelta Inc ....E....... 631 789-5000
  Edgewood *(G-4616)*
L3 Technologies Inc ....A....... 631 436-7400
  Hauppauge *(G-6133)*
Parabit Systems Inc ....E....... 516 378-4800
  Roosevelt *(G-15031)*
Performance Technologies Inc ....E....... 585 256-0200
  Rochester *(G-14596)*
Shoretel Inc ....G....... 877 654-3573
  Rochester *(G-14706)*
Telephonics Corporation ....D....... 631 755-7659
  Farmingdale *(G-5136)*
Telephonics Corporation ....A....... 631 755-7000
  Farmingdale *(G-5137)*
Tii Technologies Inc ....E....... 516 364-9300
  Edgewood *(G-4629)*

TELECOMMUNICATIONS CARRIERS & SVCS: Wired
Forerunner Technologies Inc ....E....... 631 337-2100
  Bohemia *(G-1063)*
Fusion Telecom Intl Inc ....C....... 212 201-2400
  New York *(G-10275)*
Globecomm Systems Inc ....C....... 631 231-9800
  Hauppauge *(G-6109)*
Human Electronics Inc 315 724-9850
  Utica *(G-16363)*
Key Computer Svcs of Chelsea ....D....... 212 206-8060
  New York *(G-10880)*

TELEMARKETING BUREAUS
S & H Uniform Corp 914 937-6800
  White Plains *(G-17191)*

TELEMETERING EQPT
L-3 Cmmnctons Fgn Holdings Inc ....E....... 212 697-1111
  New York *(G-10941)*
L3 Technologies Inc ....B....... 631 231-1700
  Hauppauge *(G-6132)*
L3 Technologies Inc ....D....... 607 721-5465
  Kirkwood *(G-7261)*
L3 Technologies Inc ....D....... 631 231-1700
  Hauppauge *(G-6134)*
L3 Technologies Inc ....B....... 212 697-1111
  New York *(G-10943)*

TELEPHONE ANSWERING SVCS
Milne Mfg Inc ....F....... 716 772-2536
  Gasport *(G-5574)*

TELEPHONE BOOTHS, EXC WOOD
Clark Specialty Co Inc ....E....... 607 776-3193
  Bath *(G-655)*
Parabit Systems Inc ....E....... 516 378-4800
  Roosevelt *(G-15031)*

TELEPHONE EQPT INSTALLATION
Telecommunication Concepts ....G....... 315 736-8523
  Whitesboro *(G-17224)*

TELEPHONE EQPT: Modems
Simrex Corporation ....G....... 716 206-0174
  Buffalo *(G-3215)*

TELEPHONE EQPT: NEC
ABS Talkx Inc ....G....... 631 254-9100
  Bay Shore *(G-664)*
Access 24 ....G....... 845 358-5397
  Valley Cottage *(G-16400)*
Audio-Sears Corp ....D....... 607 652-7305
  Stamford *(G-15643)*
Avaya Services Inc ....G....... 866 462-8292
  New York *(G-9327)*
Call Forwarding Technologies ....G....... 516 621-3600
  Greenvale *(G-5897)*
Columbia Telecom Group ....G....... 631 501-5000
  New York *(G-9737)*
Eagle Telephonics Inc ....F....... 631 471-3600
  Bohemia *(G-1055)*
I D Tel Corp ....F....... 718 876-6000
  Staten Island *(G-15706)*
R I R Communications Systems ....G....... 718 706-9957
  Mount Vernon *(G-8769)*
R I R Communications Systems ....E....... 718 706-9957
  Mount Vernon *(G-8770)*
Siemens Corporation ....F....... 202 434-7800
  New York *(G-12084)*
Siemens Industry Inc ....G....... 607 936-9512
  Corning *(G-4002)*
Siemens USA Holdings Inc ....B....... 212 258-4000
  New York *(G-12086)*
Telecommunication Concepts ....G....... 315 736-8523
  Whitesboro *(G-17224)*
Toshiba Amer Info Systems Inc ....B....... 949 583-3000
  New York *(G-12397)*

TELEPHONE SVCS
Tempo Industries Inc ....G....... 516 334-6900
  Westbury *(G-17060)*

TELEPHONE SWITCHING EQPT — PRODUCT SECTION

TELEPHONE SWITCHING EQPT
Redcom Laboratories Inc .... C 585 924-6567
 Victor (G-16524)

TELEPHONE: Fiber Optic Systems
Fiber Instrument Sales Inc .... C 315 736-2206
 Oriskany (G-13333)
Fiberwave Corporation .... C 718 802-9011
 Brooklyn (G-1972)
Fujitsu Ntwrk Cmmnications Inc .... F 845 731-2000
 Pearl River (G-13479)
Kent Optronics Inc .... F 845 897-0138
 Hopewell Junction (G-6581)
Sandstone Technologies Corp .... G 585 785-5537
 Rochester (G-14688)
Sandstone Technologies Corp .... G 585 785-5537
 Rochester (G-14689)
Splice Technologies Inc .... G 631 924-8108
 Manorville (G-8113)
Terahertz Technologies Inc .... G 315 736-3642
 Oriskany (G-13340)

TELEPHONE: Headsets
5yz Logistics LLC .... A 516 813-9500
 Plainview (G-13605)
Quality One Wireless LLC .... C 631 233-3337
 Ronkonkoma (G-14999)

TELEPHONE: Sets, Exc Cellular Radio
Afh Industries Incorporated .... F 646 351-1700
 New York (G-9105)
Maia Systems LLC .... G 718 206-0100
 Jamaica (G-6963)
Powermate Cellular .... G 718 833-9400
 Brooklyn (G-2445)

TELEVISION BROADCASTING & COMMUNICATIONS EQPT
Basil S Kadhim .... G 888 520-5192
 New York (G-9380)
Prime View USA Inc .... G 212 730-4905
 New York (G-11733)

TELEVISION BROADCASTING STATIONS
21st Century Fox America Inc .... D 212 852-7000
 New York (G-9013)
General Electric Company .... A 518 385-4022
 Schenectady (G-15283)
Hearst Business Media Corp .... F 631 650-4441
 Great River (G-5870)
Hearst Corporation .... A 212 649-2000
 New York (G-10482)
New York Times Company .... B 212 556-1234
 New York (G-11429)
Tegna Inc .... C 716 849-2222
 Buffalo (G-3238)
Tribune Entertainment Co Del .... E 203 866-2204
 New York (G-12425)

TELEVISION SETS
Jwin Electronics Corp .... D 516 626-7188
 Port Washington (G-13852)
Toshiba America Inc .... E 212 596-0600
 New York (G-12398)

TELEVISION: Cameras
Silicon Imaging Inc .... G 518 374-3367
 Niskayuna (G-12913)

TELEVISION: Closed Circuit Eqpt
AG Adriano Goldschmied Inc .... G 845 928-8616
 Central Valley (G-3547)
Click It Inc .... D 631 686-2900
 Hauppauge (G-6067)
Sartek Industries Inc .... G 631 473-3555
 Port Jefferson (G-13801)
Sentry Technology Corporation .... F 800 645-4224
 Ronkonkoma (G-15007)
Vicon Industries Inc .... C 631 952-2288
 Hauppauge (G-6250)

TEMPERING: Metal
Elmira Heat Treating Inc .... E 607 734-1577
 Elmira (G-4695)

TENT REPAIR SHOP
Custom Canvas Manufacturing Co .... E 716 852-6372
 Buffalo (G-2917)

TENTS: All Materials
Air Structures Amercn Tech Inc .... E 914 937-4500
 Port Chester (G-13765)
Dhs Systems LLC .... F 845 359-6066
 Orangeburg (G-13246)
Johnson Outdoors Inc .... C 607 779-2200
 Binghamton (G-926)
Kraus & Sons Inc .... C 212 620-0408
 New York (G-10926)
Leiter Sukkahs Inc .... C 718 436-0303
 Brooklyn (G-2210)
Select Fabricators Inc .... F 585 393-0650
 Canandaigua (G-3387)
Toptec Products LLC .... F 631 421-9800
 Melville (G-8391)

TERMINAL BOARDS
Veja Electronics Inc .... D 631 321-6086
 Deer Park (G-4247)

TERRA COTTA: Architectural
Boston Valley Pottery Inc .... D 716 649-7490
 Orchard Park (G-13277)

TEST KITS: Pregnancy
Inolife Technologies Inc .... G 212 348-5600
 New York (G-10648)
Ithaca Pregancy Center .... G 607 753-3909
 Cortland (G-4053)
Northeast Doulas 845 621-0654
 Mahopac (G-8029)
Working Family Solutions Inc 845 802-6182
 Saugerties (G-15227)

TESTERS: Battery
Sorfin Yoshimura Ltd .... G 516 802-4600
 Woodbury (G-17320)
Walter R Tucker Entps Ltd .... E 607 467-2866
 Deposit (G-4305)

TESTERS: Environmental
Caltex International Ltd .... F 315 425-1040
 Syracuse (G-15902)
Nexgen Enviro Systems Inc .... G 631 226-2930
 Lindenhurst (G-7499)
Niagara Scientific Inc .... D 315 437-0821
 East Syracuse (G-4566)

TESTERS: Integrated Circuit
Epoch Microelectronics Inc .... G 914 332-8570
 Valhalla (G-16393)
Xelic Incorporated .... F 585 415-2764
 Pittsford (G-13604)

TESTERS: Physical Property
G E Inspection Technologies LP .... C 315 554-2000
 Skaneateles (G-15481)
Gleason Corporation .... A 585 473-1000
 Rochester (G-14428)
Gleason Works .... A 585 473-1000
 Rochester (G-14429)
Gurley Precision Instrs Inc .... C 518 272-6300
 Troy (G-16259)

TESTERS: Water, Exc Indl Process
Ewt Holdings III Corp .... F 212 644-5900
 New York (G-10151)

TEXTILE & APPAREL SVCS
Newcastle Fabrics Corp .... G 718 388-6600
 Brooklyn (G-2378)
RAK Finishing Corp .... E 718 416-4242
 Howard Beach (G-6626)

TEXTILE BAGS WHOLESALERS
Adam Scott Designs Inc .... E 212 420-8866
 New York (G-9071)
Nochairs Inc .... G 917 748-8731
 New York (G-11465)

TEXTILE CONVERTERS: Knit Goods
Bank-Miller Co Inc .... E 914 227-9357
 Pelham (G-13514)
Sextet Fabrics Inc .... F 516 593-0608
 East Rockaway (G-4491)

TEXTILE FABRICATORS
Dream Green Productions .... G 917 267-8920
 Warwick (G-16611)

TEXTILE FINISH: Chem Coat/Treat, Fire Resist, Manmade
American Spray-On Corp .... E 212 929-2100
 New York (G-9179)
Beckmann Converting Inc .... E 518 842-0073
 Amsterdam (G-335)

TEXTILE FINISHING: Chemical Coating Or Treating
Reynolds Drapery Service Inc .... F 315 845-8632
 Newport (G-12816)

TEXTILE FINISHING: Chemical Coating Or Treating, Narrow
Albany Engnered Composites Inc .... F 518 445-2200
 Albany (G-36)

TEXTILE FINISHING: Dyeing, Broadwoven, Cotton
B & K Dye Cutting Inc .... G 718 497-5216
 Brooklyn (G-1657)
Dyenamix Inc .... G 212 941-6642
 New York (G-9997)

TEXTILE FINISHING: Dyeing, Finishing & Printng, Linen Fabric
American Country Quilts & Lin .... G 631 283-5466
 Southampton (G-15562)
China Ting Fashion Group (usa) .... G 212 716-1600
 New York (G-9653)
Duck River Textiles Inc .... G 212 679-2980
 New York (G-9987)

TEXTILE FINISHING: Dyeing, Manmade Fiber & Silk, Broadwoven
Eastern Silk Mills Inc .... G 212 730-1300
 New York (G-10017)

TEXTILE FINISHING: Embossing, Cotton, Broadwoven
Lee Dyeing Company NC Inc .... F 518 736-5232
 Johnstown (G-7149)

TEXTILE FINISHING: Embossing, Man Fiber & Silk, Broadwoven
Knucklehead Embroidery Inc .... G 607 797-2725
 Johnson City (G-7129)

TEXTILE FINISHING: Silk, Broadwoven
Raxon Fabrics Corp .... F 212 532-6816
 New York (G-11830)

TEXTILE FINISHING: Sponging, Cotton, Broadwoven, Trade
Basiloff LLC .... G 646 671-0353
 New York (G-9381)

TEXTILE PRDTS: Hand Woven & Crocheted
HMS Productions Inc .... D 212 719-9190
 New York (G-10535)

TEXTILE: Finishing, Cotton Broadwoven
All About Art Inc .... F 718 321-0755
 Flushing (G-5232)
Carolyn Ray Inc .... G 914 476-0619
 Yonkers (G-17440)
Central Textiles Inc .... F 212 213-8740
 New York (G-9618)

PRODUCT SECTION

TIRE INFLATORS: Hand Or Compressor Operated

Marcel Finishing Corp ....E 718 381-2889
  Plainview (G-13645)
Prismatic Dyeing & Finshg Inc ....D 845 561-1800
  Newburgh (G-12798)
Santee Print Works ....F 212 997-1570
  New York (G-11988)

TEXTILE: Finishing, Raw Stock NEC

Ben-Sak Textile Inc ....G 212 279-5122
  New York (G-9403)
Flexene Corp ....E 631 491-0580
  West Babylon (G-16818)
Hosel & Ackerson Inc ....G 212 575-1490
  New York (G-10552)
Majestic Rayon Corporation ....E 212 929-6443
  New York (G-11140)
Marcel Finishing Corp ....E 718 381-2889
  Plainview (G-13645)
National Spinning Co Inc ....E 212 382-6400
  New York (G-11374)
Newcastle Fabrics Corp ....G 718 388-6600
  Brooklyn (G-2378)
Prismatic Dyeing & Finshg Inc ....D 845 561-1800
  Newburgh (G-12798)
Skin Prints Inc ....G 845 920-8756
  Pearl River (G-13490)

TEXTILE: Goods, NEC

Alok Inc ....G 212 643-4360
  New York (G-9148)
Southern Adrndck Fbr Prdcrs CP ....G 518 692-2700
  Greenwich (G-5913)

TEXTILES

Stern & Stern Industries Inc ....D 607 324-4485
  Hornell (G-6594)

TEXTILES: Bagging, Jute

Ivi Services Inc ....D 607 729-5111
  Binghamton (G-924)

TEXTILES: Fibers, Textile, Rcvrd From Mill Waste/Rags

Ace Drop Cloth Canvas Pdts Inc ....E 718 731-1550
  Bronx (G-1261)

TEXTILES: Flock

Solivaira Specialties Inc ....D 716 693-4009
  North Tonawanda (G-13014)
Solvaira Specialties Inc ....C 716 693-4040
  North Tonawanda (G-13015)

TEXTILES: Linen Fabrics

David King Linen Inc ....F 718 241-7298
  New York (G-9876)
Novita Fabrics Furnishing Corp ....F 516 299-4500
  Glen Cove (G-5636)
Sabbsons International Inc ....F 718 360-1947
  Brooklyn (G-2551)
Sam Salem & Son LLC ....F 212 695-6020
  New York (G-11979)
Simple Elegance New York Inc ....F 718 360-1947
  Brooklyn (G-2589)
TRM Linen Inc ....G 718 686-6075
  Brooklyn (G-2702)

TEXTILES: Linings, Carpet, Exc Felt

G Fried Carpert Service ....E 516 333-3900
  Westbury (G-17016)

TEXTILES: Mill Waste & Remnant

Dean Trading Corp ....F 718 485-0600
  Brooklyn (G-1846)
Federal Prison Industries ....D 518 897-4000
  Ray Brook (G-14037)
S Hellerman Inc ....F 718 622-2995
  Brooklyn (G-2549)

TEXTILES: Tops & Top Processing, Manmade Or Other Fiber

Jo-Vin Decorators Inc ....E 718 441-9350
  Woodhaven (G-17324)

THEATRICAL LIGHTING SVCS

Creative Stage Lighting Co Inc ....E 518 251-3302
  North Creek (G-12949)

THEATRICAL PRODUCERS & SVCS

Congress For Jewish Culture ....G 212 505-8040
  New York (G-9761)
Peermusic Ltd ....F 212 265-3910
  New York (G-11616)

THEATRICAL SCENERY

Center Line Studios Inc ....F 845 534-7143
  New Windsor (G-8980)
Costume Armour Inc ....F 845 534-9120
  Cornwall (G-4008)
Hudson Scenic Studio Inc ....C 914 375-0900
  Yonkers (G-17472)
King Displays Inc ....F 212 629-8455
  New York (G-10891)
Production Resource Group LLC ....D 877 774-7088
  Armonk (G-416)
Production Resource Group LLC ....E 845 567-5700
  New Windsor (G-8994)
Stiegelbauer Associates Inc ....E 718 624-0835
  Brooklyn (G-2630)

THERMOMETERS: Indl

Kessler Thermometer Corp ....G 631 841-5500
  West Babylon (G-16832)
Oden Machinery Inc ....E 716 874-3000
  Tonawanda (G-16207)

THERMOMETERS: Liquid-In-Glass & Bimetal

Germanow-Simon Corporation ....E 585 232-1440
  Rochester (G-14420)

THERMOMETERS: Medical, Digital

Accuvein Inc ....D 816 997-9400
  Medford (G-8265)

THERMOPLASTIC MATERIALS

Bso Energy Corp ....F 212 520-1827
  New York (G-9526)
Plexi Craft Quality Products ....F 212 924-3244
  New York (G-11699)

THERMOPLASTICS

ADC Acquisition Company ....E 518 377-6471
  Niskayuna (G-12910)
On Time Plastics Inc ....G 516 442-4280
  Freeport (G-5426)

THERMOSETTING MATERIALS

Empire Plastics Inc ....E 607 754-9132
  Endwell (G-4840)

THIN FILM CIRCUITS

CAM Touchview Products Inc ....F 631 842-3400
  Sag Harbor (G-15103)

THREAD: All Fibers

Albany International Corp ....C 607 749-7226
  Homer (G-6543)
United Thread Mills Corp ....G 516 536-3900
  Oceanside (G-13124)

THREAD: Embroidery

American Quality Embroidery ....G 631 467-3200
  Ronkonkoma (G-14895)
One In A Million Inc ....G 516 829-1111
  Valley Stream (G-16441)

TICKET OFFICES & AGENCIES: Theatrical

London Theater News Ltd ....F 212 517-8608
  New York (G-11054)

TIES, FORM: Metal

American Wire Tie Inc ....E 716 337-2412
  North Collins (G-12942)

TILE: Asphalt, Floor

Shenfield Studio LLC ....F 315 436-8869
  Syracuse (G-16063)

TILE: Brick & Structural, Clay

Stone and Bath Gallery ....F 718 438-4500
  Brooklyn (G-2631)

TILE: Drain, Clay

Bistrian Cement Corporation ....F 631 324-1123
  East Hampton (G-4425)

TILE: Fireproofing, Clay

Certified Flameproofing Corp ....G 631 265-4824
  Smithtown (G-15506)
Noroc Enterprises Inc ....C 718 585-3230
  Bronx (G-1414)

TILE: Mosaic, Ceramic

Artsaics Studios Inc ....G 631 254-2558
  Deer Park (G-4127)

TILE: Stamped Metal, Floor Or Wall

Surving Studios ....F 845 355-1430
  Middletown (G-8499)

TILE: Terrazzo Or Concrete, Precast

Foro Marble Co Inc ....E 718 852-2322
  Brooklyn (G-1995)
Walter G Legge Company Inc ....G 914 737-5040
  Peekskill (G-13510)

TILE: Wall & Floor, Ceramic

Aremco Products Inc ....F 845 268-0039
  Valley Cottage (G-16402)
Dal-Tile Corporation ....G 914 835-1801
  Harrison (G-6003)
Lazer Marble & Granite Corp ....G 718 859-9644
  Brooklyn (G-2198)

TILE: Wall & Floor, clay

Quality Components Framing Sys ....F 315 768-1167
  Whitesboro (G-17222)

TIMBER PRDTS WHOLESALERS

Guldenschuh Logging & Lbr LLC ....G 585 538-4750
  Caledonia (G-3307)

TIMING DEVICES: Electronic

Eversan Inc ....F 315 736-3967
  Whitesboro (G-17221)
Infitec Inc ....D 315 433-1150
  East Syracuse (G-4557)

TIRE & INNER TUBE MATERIALS & RELATED PRDTS

Handy & Harman Ltd ....A 212 520-2300
  New York (G-10450)
Roli Retreads Inc ....E 631 694-7670
  Farmingdale (G-5112)
Sph Group Holdings LLC ....F 212 520-2300
  New York (G-12186)

TIRE CORD & FABRIC

Albany International Corp ....C 518 445-2230
  Menands (G-8397)
Designatronics Incorporated ....B 516 328-3300
  Hicksville (G-6367)
Haines Equipment Inc ....E 607 566-8531
  Avoca (G-534)
York Industries Inc ....E 516 746-3736
  Garden City Park (G-5559)

TIRE INFLATORS: Hand Or Compressor Operated

Vac Air Service Inc ....F 716 665-2206
  Jamestown (G-7074)

Employee Codes: A=Over 500 employees, B=251-500
C=101-250, D=51-100, E=20-50, F=10-19, G=5-9

TIRES & INNER TUBES

TIRES & INNER TUBES
- East Coast Intl Tire Inc .... F 718 386-9088
  Maspeth *(G-8166)*
- New York CT Loc246 Seiu Wel BF .... G 212 233-0616
  New York *(G-11417)*
- Sumitomo Rubber Usa LLC .... A 716 879-8200
  Tonawanda *(G-16223)*

TIRES: Auto
- McCarthy Tire Svc Co NY Inc .... F 518 449-5185
  Menands *(G-8407)*

TITANIUM MILL PRDTS
- NY Titanium Inc .... G 718 227-4244
  Staten Island *(G-15737)*
- Titanium Dem Remediation Group .... F 716 433-4100
  Lockport *(G-7650)*

TOBACCO LEAF PROCESSING
- Schweitzer-Mauduit Intl Inc .... C 518 329-4222
  Ancram *(G-375)*

TOBACCO: Chewing
- National Tobacco Company LP .... F 212 253-8185
  New York *(G-11376)*

TOBACCO: Chewing & Snuff
- Elab Smokers Boutique .... G 585 865-4513
  Rochester *(G-14362)*

TOBACCO: Cigarettes
- East End .... F 716 532-2622
  Collins *(G-3841)*
- Epuffer Inc .... G 718 374-6030
  Brooklyn *(G-1935)*
- Jacobs Tobacco Company .... E 518 358-4948
  Hogansburg *(G-6453)*
- Philip Morris Intl Inc .... D 917 663-2000
  New York *(G-11666)*
- PMI Global Services Inc .... E 917 663-2000
  New York *(G-11701)*
- R J Reynolds Tobacco Company .... C 716 871-1553
  Tonawanda *(G-16214)*
- Schweitzer-Mauduit Intl Inc .... C 518 329-4222
  Ancram *(G-375)*
- Seneca Manufacturing Company .... G 716 945-4400
  Salamanca *(G-15133)*
- Seneca Nation Enterprise .... F 716 934-7430
  Irving *(G-6807)*
- Vector Group Ltd .... B 212 409-2800
  New York *(G-12536)*

TOBACCO: Cigars
- American Cigar 718 969-0008
  Fresh Meadows *(G-5451)*
- Davidoff Gneva Madison Ave Inc .... G 212 751-9060
  New York *(G-9884)*
- Mafco Consolidated Group Inc .... F 212 572-8600
  New York *(G-11123)*
- Martinez Hand Made Cigars .... G 212 239-4049
  New York *(G-11192)*

TOBACCO: Smoking
- Mafco Consolidated Group Inc .... F 212 572-8600
  New York *(G-11123)*

TOILET FIXTURES: Plastic
- Metpar Corp .... D 516 333-2600
  Westbury *(G-17038)*

TOILET PREPARATIONS
- H & H Laboratories Inc .... F 718 624-8041
  Brooklyn *(G-2057)*
- H & H Laboratories Inc .... G 718 624-8041
  Brooklyn *(G-2058)*
- King Research Inc .... E 718 788-0122
  Brooklyn *(G-2171)*
- MZB Accessories LLC .... D 718 472-7500
  Long Island City *(G-7849)*

TOILET SEATS: Wood
- Swiss Madison LLC .... F 434 623-4766
  Brooklyn *(G-2656)*

TOILETRIES, COSMETICS & PERFUME STORES
- Estee Lauder Companies Inc .... A 212 572-4200
  New York *(G-10123)*
- Estee Lauder Inc .... A 212 572-4200
  New York *(G-10126)*
- Estee Lauder Inc .... D 631 531-1000
  Melville *(G-8345)*
- International Design Assoc Ltd .... G 212 687-0333
  New York *(G-10675)*

TOILETRIES, WHOLESALE: Hair Preparations
- EL Erman International Ltd .... G 212 444-9440
  Brooklyn *(G-1911)*

TOILETRIES, WHOLESALE: Perfumes
- Elias Fragrances Inc .... F 718 693-6400
  Rye Brook *(G-15096)*
- Elite Parfums Ltd .... D 212 983-2640
  New York *(G-10060)*
- Eternal Love Parfums Corp 516 921-6100
  Syosset *(G-15841)*
- Scent-A-Vision Inc .... E 631 424-4905
  Huntington Station *(G-6759)*
- Sundial Fragrances & Flavors 631 842-8800
  Amityville *(G-328)*
- Symrise Inc .... E 845 469-7675
  Chester *(G-3645)*
- Value Fragrances Inc .... G 845 294-5726
  Goshen *(G-5756)*

TOILETRIES, WHOLESALE: Toilet Preparations
- Bare Escentuals Inc 646 537-0070
  New York *(G-9371)*
- Quality King Distributors Inc .... C 631 439-2027
  Ronkonkoma *(G-14998)*

TOILETRIES, WHOLESALE: Toiletries
- Bfma Holding Corporation .... G 607 753-6746
  Cortland *(G-4036)*
- Gassho Body & Mind Inc 518 695-9991
  Schuylerville *(G-15341)*
- Robell Research Inc .... G 212 755-6577
  New York *(G-11909)*

TOMBSTONES: Terrazzo Or Concrete, Precast
- Eaton Brothers Corp 716 649-8250
  Hamburg *(G-5945)*

TOOL & DIE STEEL
- Baker Tool & Die & Die .... G 716 694-2025
  North Tonawanda *(G-12977)*

TOOLS: Carpenters', Including Levels & Chisels, Exc Saws
- Nyc District Council Ubcja .... G 212 366-7500
  New York *(G-11493)*

TOOLS: Hand
- Allway Tools Inc .... D 718 792-3636
  Bronx *(G-1270)*
- Ames Companies Inc .... E 607 739-4544
  Pine Valley *(G-13583)*
- Best Way Tools By Anderson Inc .... G 631 586-4702
  Deer Park *(G-4130)*
- Circo File Corp .... G 516 922-1848
  Oyster Bay *(G-13393)*
- Coastel Cable Tools Inc .... E 315 471-5361
  Syracuse *(G-15918)*
- Dead Ringer LLC 585 355-4685
  Rochester *(G-14324)*
- Dresser-Argus Inc .... G 718 643-1540
  Brooklyn *(G-1882)*
- Huron TI Cutter Grinding Inc .... E 631 420-7000
  Farmingdale *(G-5015)*
- Hydramec Inc .... E 585 593-5190
  Scio *(G-15342)*
- Ivy Classic Industries Inc .... E 914 632-8200
  New Rochelle *(G-8958)*
- Robinson Tools LLC .... G 585 586-5432
  Penfield *(G-13526)*
- Schilling Forge Inc .... E 315 454-4421
  Syracuse *(G-16055)*
- Snyder Manufacturing Inc .... E 716 945-0354
  Salamanca *(G-15134)*
- U S Air Tool Co Inc .... F 631 471-3300
  Ronkonkoma *(G-15017)*
- Winters Railroad Service Inc .... G 716 337-2668
  North Collins *(G-12948)*
- York Industries Inc .... E 516 746-3736
  Garden City Park *(G-5559)*

TOOLS: Hand, Engravers'
- Edward C Lyons Company Inc .... G 718 515-5361
  Bronx *(G-1327)*
- Edward C Muller Corp .... F 718 881-7270
  Bronx *(G-1328)*

TOOLS: Hand, Jewelers'
- Boucheron Joaillerie USA Inc .... G 212 715-7330
  New York *(G-9494)*
- Empire Devleopment .... G 716 789-2097
  Mayville *(G-8246)*
- The Swatch Group U S Inc .... G 212 297-9192
  New York *(G-12331)*

TOOLS: Hand, Mechanics
- Classic Tool Design Inc .... E 845 562-8700
  New Windsor *(G-8981)*

TOOLS: Hand, Plumbers'
- Design Source By Lg Inc .... E 212 274-0022
  New York *(G-9908)*
- Metro City Group Inc .... G 516 781-2500
  Bellmore *(G-814)*

TOOLS: Hand, Power
- Allied Motion Technologies Inc .... C 315 782-5910
  Watertown *(G-16656)*
- Awt Supply Corp .... G 516 437-9105
  Elmont *(G-4730)*
- Black & Decker (us) Inc .... B 914 235-6300
  Brewster *(G-1209)*
- Black & Decker (us) Inc .... G 716 884-6220
  Buffalo *(G-2865)*
- Black & Decker (us) Inc .... G 631 952-2008
  Hauppauge *(G-6054)*
- Dynabrade Inc .... C 716 631-0100
  Clarence *(G-3686)*
- Great American Tool Co Inc .... G 716 646-5700
  Hamburg *(G-5950)*
- Huck International Inc .... C 845 331-7300
  Kingston *(G-7220)*
- Ivy Classic Industries Inc .... E 914 632-8200
  New Rochelle *(G-8958)*
- Meritool LLC .... F 716 699-6005
  Ellicottville *(G-4656)*
- New York Industrial Works Inc .... G 718 292-0615
  Bronx *(G-1411)*
- P & F Industries Inc .... E 631 694-9800
  Melville *(G-8375)*
- Reimann & Georger Corporation .... E 716 895-1156
  Buffalo *(G-3182)*
- Stature Electric Inc .... B 315 782-5910
  Watertown *(G-16695)*
- Thomas C Wilson LLC .... E 718 729-3360
  Long Island City *(G-7928)*

TOOTHBRUSHES: Electric
- Quip Nyc Inc .... G 703 615-1076
  Brooklyn *(G-2486)*

TOOTHBRUSHES: Exc Electric
- Colgate-Palmolive Company .... A 212 310-2000
  New York *(G-9726)*
- Marketshare LLC .... G 631 273-0598
  Brentwood *(G-1188)*
- Violife LLC .... G 914 207-1820
  New York *(G-12572)*

TOOTHPASTES, GELS & TOOTHPOWDERS
- Colgat-Plmolive Centl Amer Inc .... G 212 310-2000
  New York *(G-9725)*
- Colgate-Palmolive Company .... A 212 310-2000
  New York *(G-9726)*

PRODUCT SECTION

TRANSFORMERS: Ignition, Domestic Fuel Burners

Colgate-Palmolive Company ....B 718 506-3961
  Queens Village *(G-13991)*
Colgate-Palmolive Globl Trdg ....G 212 310-2000
  New York *(G-9727)*
Quip Nyc Inc ....G 703 615-1076
  Brooklyn *(G-2486)*

TOWELS: Indl

Blu Sand LLC ....G 212 564-1147
  New York *(G-9470)*

TOWELS: Linen & Linen & Cotton Mixtures

Blc Textiles Inc ....E 844 500-7900
  Mineola *(G-8532)*

TOWERS, SECTIONS: Transmission, Radio & Television

Fred A Nudd Corporation ....E 315 524-2531
  Ontario *(G-13223)*

TOYS

Church Communities NY Inc ....E 518 589-5103
  Elka Park *(G-4643)*
Church Communities NY Inc ....E 518 589-5103
  Elka Park *(G-4644)*
Dana Michele LLC ....G 917 757-7777
  New York *(G-9853)*
Drescher Paper Box Inc ....F 716 854-0288
  Buffalo *(G-2934)*
Haba USA ....G 800 468-6873
  Skaneateles *(G-15483)*
Habermaass Corporation ....F 315 685-8919
  Skaneateles *(G-15484)*
Jim Henson Company Inc ....E 212 794-2400
  New York *(G-10772)*
Joel Zelcer ....F 917 525-6790
  Brooklyn *(G-2143)*
Jupiter Creations Inc ....G 917 493-9393
  New York *(G-10824)*
Kidtellect Inc ....G 617 803-1456
  New York *(G-10881)*
Kidz Toyz Inc ....G 914 261-4453
  Mount Kisco *(G-8675)*
Kling Magnetics Inc ....E 518 392-4000
  Chatham *(G-3586)*
Master Juvenile Products Inc ....F 845 647-8400
  Ellenville *(G-4649)*
Mattel Inc ....F 716 714-8514
  East Aurora *(G-4399)*
Ogosport LLC ....G 718 554-0777
  Brooklyn *(G-2399)*
Readent Inc ....F 212 710-3004
  White Plains *(G-17189)*
Sandbox Brands Inc ....G 212 647-8877
  New York *(G-11983)*
Toymax Inc ....G 212 633-6611
  New York *(G-12405)*
Vogel Applied Technologies ....G 212 677-3136
  New York *(G-12589)*
Way Out Toys Inc ....G 212 689-9094
  New York *(G-12627)*
Whats Next Manufacturing Inc ....E 585 492-1014
  Arcade *(G-401)*

TOYS & HOBBY GOODS & SPLYS, WHOLESALE: Arts/Crafts Eqpt/Sply

Multi Packaging Solutions Inc ....E 646 885-0005
  New York *(G-11347)*

TOYS & HOBBY GOODS & SPLYS, WHOLESALE: Balloons, Novelty

OH How Cute Inc ....G 347 838-6031
  Staten Island *(G-15739)*

TOYS & HOBBY GOODS & SPLYS, WHOLESALE: Educational Toys

Global Video LLC ....D 516 222-2600
  Woodbury *(G-17310)*

TOYS & HOBBY GOODS & SPLYS, WHOLESALE: Toys & Games

Last Straw Inc ....E 516 371-2727
  Lawrence *(G-7418)*

Minted Green Inc ....G 845 458-1845
  Airmont *(G-15)*
Way Out Toys Inc ....G 212 689-9094
  New York *(G-12627)*

TOYS & HOBBY GOODS & SPLYS, WHOLESALE: Toys, NEC

Toymax Inc ....G 212 633-6611
  New York *(G-12405)*

TOYS & HOBBY GOODS & SPLYS, WHOLESALE: Video Games

Barron Games Intl Co LLC ....F 716 630-0054
  Buffalo *(G-2853)*

TOYS, HOBBY GOODS & SPLYS WHOLESALERS

Fierce Fun Toys LLC ....G 646 322-7172
  New York *(G-10213)*
Habermaass Corporation ....F 315 685-8919
  Skaneateles *(G-15484)*

TOYS: Dolls, Stuffed Animals & Parts

Community Products LLC ....E 518 589-5103
  Elka Park *(G-4645)*
Cosmetics Plus Ltd ....G 516 768-7250
  Amagansett *(G-217)*
Dana Michele LLC ....G 917 757-7777
  New York *(G-9853)*
Jim Henson Company Inc ....E 212 794-2400
  New York *(G-10772)*
Jupiter Creations Inc ....G 917 493-9393
  New York *(G-10824)*
Madame Alexander Doll Co LLC ....D 212 244-4500
  New York *(G-11118)*
Minted Green Inc ....G 845 458-1845
  Airmont *(G-15)*

TOYS: Electronic

Littlebits Electronics Inc ....D 917 464-4577
  New York *(G-11040)*
Wobbleworks Inc ....F 718 618-9904
  New York *(G-12678)*

TOYS: Video Game Machines

C T A Digital Inc ....G 845 513-0433
  Monroe *(G-8586)*

TRADE SHOW ARRANGEMENT SVCS

Alm Media LLC ....B 212 457-9400
  New York *(G-9146)*
Alm Media Holdings Inc ....B 212 457-9400
  New York *(G-9147)*
International Data Group Inc ....E 212 331-7883
  New York *(G-10674)*
Relx Inc ....E 212 309-8100
  New York *(G-11858)*

TRADERS: Commodity, Contracts

De Meo Brothers Inc ....G 212 268-1400
  New York *(G-9889)*

TRAILERS & PARTS: Boat

Performance Custom Trailer ....G 518 504-4021
  Lake George *(G-7288)*

TRAILERS & PARTS: Truck & Semi's

Cross Country Mfg Inc ....F 607 656-4103
  Greene *(G-5881)*
Cross Country Mfg Inc ....F 607 656-4103
  Greene *(G-5882)*
Davis Trailer World LLC ....F 585 538-6640
  York *(G-17521)*
G L 7 Sales Plus Ltd ....G 631 696-8290
  Coram *(G-3965)*
General Welding & Fabg Inc ....G 716 652-0033
  Elma *(G-4662)*
Seneca Truck & Trailer Inc ....G 315 781-1100
  Geneva *(G-5598)*
Stone Well Bodies & Mch Inc ....E 315 497-3512
  Genoa *(G-5602)*

TRAILERS & TRAILER EQPT

Rolling Star Manufacturing Inc ....E 315 896-4767
  Barneveld *(G-616)*

TRAILERS: Bus, Tractor Type

Full Service Auto Body Inc ....F 718 831-9300
  Floral Park *(G-5211)*

TRAILERS: Semitrailers, Truck Tractors

Blue Tee Corp ....A 212 598-0880
  New York *(G-9473)*

TRANSDUCERS: Electrical Properties

American Aerospace Contrls Inc ....E 631 694-5100
  Farmingdale *(G-4948)*
Pcb Group Inc ....E 716 684-0001
  Depew *(G-4292)*
Ruhle Companies Inc ....E 914 287-4000
  Valhalla *(G-16398)*

TRANSDUCERS: Pressure

Dylix Corporation ....E 719 773-2985
  Grand Island *(G-5769)*
Kinemotive Corporation ....E 631 249-6440
  Farmingdale *(G-5035)*

TRANSFORMERS: Control

Current Controls Inc ....C 585 593-1544
  Wellsville *(G-16776)*

TRANSFORMERS: Distribution

Electron Coil Inc ....D 607 336-7414
  Norwich *(G-13046)*
Ems Development Corporation ....D 631 345-6200
  Yaphank *(G-17407)*
Kepco Inc ....E 718 461-7000
  Flushing *(G-5266)*
Kepco Inc ....D 718 461-7000
  Flushing *(G-5267)*
Kepco Inc ....E 718 461-7000
  Flushing *(G-5268)*
Schneider Electric It Corp ....F 646 335-0216
  New York *(G-12011)*

TRANSFORMERS: Distribution, Electric

Hale Electrical Dist Svcs Inc ....G 716 818-7595
  Wales Center *(G-16560)*
Siemens Corporation ....F 202 434-7800
  New York *(G-12084)*
Siemens USA Holdings Inc ....B 212 258-4000
  New York *(G-12086)*

TRANSFORMERS: Electric

Niagara Transformer Corp ....D 716 896-6500
  Buffalo *(G-3113)*
Transistor Devices Inc ....E 631 471-7492
  Ronkonkoma *(G-15015)*

TRANSFORMERS: Electronic

Atlantic Transformer Inc ....F 716 795-3258
  Barker *(G-611)*
Beta Transformer Tech Corp ....E 631 244-7393
  Bohemia *(G-1020)*
Data Device Corporation ....B 631 567-5600
  Bohemia *(G-1045)*
Esc Control Electronics LLC ....E 631 467-5328
  Sayville *(G-15236)*
Exxelia-Raf Tabtronics LLC ....E 585 243-4331
  Piffard *(G-13574)*
NEa Manufacturing Corp ....E 516 371-4200
  Inwood *(G-6803)*
Todd Systems Inc ....D 914 963-3400
  Yonkers *(G-17507)*
Urban Technologies Inc ....G 716 672-2709
  Fredonia *(G-5385)*

TRANSFORMERS: Ignition, Domestic Fuel Burners

Frederick Cowan & Company Inc ....F 631 369-0360
  Riverhead *(G-14155)*

Employee Codes: A=Over 500 employees, B=251-500
C=101-250, D=51-100, E=20-50, F=10-19, G=5-9

TRANSFORMERS: Power Related

TRANSFORMERS: Power Related

- Arstan Products International .... F 516 433-1313
  Hicksville *(G-6348)*
- Berkshire Transformer .... G 631 467-5328
  Central Islip *(G-3512)*
- Buffalo Power Elec Ctr De .... E 716 651-1600
  Depew *(G-4275)*
- Caddell Burns Manufacturing Co .... G 631 757-1772
  Northport *(G-13026)*
- Cooper Power Systems LLC .... B 716 375-7100
  Olean *(G-13160)*
- Exxelia-Raf Tabtronics LLC .... E 585 243-4331
  Piffard *(G-13574)*
- K Road Power Management LLC .... F 212 351-0535
  New York *(G-10832)*
- Piller Power Systems Inc .... E 845 695-6658
  Middletown *(G-8491)*
- Ram Transformer Technologies .... F 914 632-3988
  New Rochelle *(G-8967)*
- Reenergy Black River LLC .... E 315 773-2314
  Fort Drum *(G-5346)*
- Sag Harbor Industries Inc .... G 631 725-0440
  Sag Harbor *(G-15107)*
- Schneider Electric Usa Inc .... F 585 377-1313
  Penfield *(G-13527)*
- Spellman High Vltage Elec Corp .... B 631 630-3000
  Hauppauge *(G-6222)*
- Spence Engineering Company Inc .... C 845 778-5566
  Walden *(G-16556)*
- Sunward Electronics Inc .... F 518 687-0030
  Troy *(G-16281)*
- Switching Power Inc .... D 631 981-7231
  Ronkonkoma *(G-15013)*
- Veeco Instruments Inc .... C 516 349-8300
  Plainview *(G-13670)*

TRANSFORMERS: Specialty

- Allanson Inc .... G 631 293-3880
  Farmingdale *(G-4944)*
- Dyco Electronics Inc .... D 607 324-2030
  Hornell *(G-6588)*
- Mitchell Electronics Corp .... E 914 699-3800
  Mount Vernon *(G-8753)*

TRANSLATION & INTERPRETATION SVCS

- Language and Graphics Inc .... G 212 315-5266
  New York *(G-10963)*
- SOS International LLC .... C 212 742-2410
  New York *(G-12166)*

TRANSMISSIONS: Motor Vehicle

- A-Line Technologies Inc .... F 607 772-2439
  Binghamton *(G-881)*
- Auburn Bearing & Mfg Inc .... G 315 986-7600
  Macedon *(G-8009)*
- Pro Torque .... G 631 218-8700
  Bohemia *(G-1118)*
- Terrys Transmission .... G 315 458-4333
  North Syracuse *(G-12969)*

TRANSPORTATION EPQT & SPLYS, WHOLESALE: Acft/Space Vehicle

- Nell-Joy Industries Inc .... E 631 842-8989
  Copiague *(G-3939)*

TRANSPORTATION EQPT & SPLYS WHOLESALERS, NEC

- Worldwide Arntcal Cmpnents Inc .... G 631 842-3780
  Copiague *(G-3963)*
- Zebra Technologies Entp Corp .... E 800 722-6234
  Holtsville *(G-6542)*

TRANSPORTATION EQUIPMENT, NEC

- Truck-Lite Sub Inc .... G 800 888-7095
  Falconer *(G-4925)*

TRANSPORTATION: Local Passenger, NEC

- Hampton Transport Inc .... F 631 716-4445
  Coram *(G-3966)*

TRAP ROCK: Crushed & Broken

- Dolomite Products Company Inc .... E 585 586-2568
  Penfield *(G-13522)*

- Tilcon New York Inc .... B 845 358-4500
  West Nyack *(G-16957)*
- Tilcon New York Inc .... E 845 778-5591
  Walden *(G-16557)*
- Tilcon New York Inc .... D 845 358-3100
  West Nyack *(G-16958)*

TRAPS: Animal & Fish, Wire

- Cuba Specialty Mfg Co Inc .... F 585 567-4176
  Fillmore *(G-5183)*

TRAPS: Stem

- John N Fehlinger Co Inc .... F 212 233-5656
  New York *(G-10791)*

TRAVEL AGENCIES

- Mapeasy Inc .... F 631 537-6213
  Wainscott *(G-16548)*
- Quinn and Co of NY Ltd .... D 212 868-1900
  New York *(G-11800)*
- Rfp LLC .... E 212 838-7733
  New York *(G-11883)*

TRAVEL TRAILERS & CAMPERS

- All Star Carts & Vehicles Inc .... D 631 666-5581
  Bay Shore *(G-667)*

TRAYS: Cable, Metal Plate

- Mono-Systems Inc .... E 716 821-1344
  Buffalo *(G-3094)*

TRAYS: Plastic

- Commodore Machine Co Inc .... F 585 657-6916
  Bloomfield *(G-978)*
- SAV Thermo Inc .... F 631 249-9444
  West Babylon *(G-16857)*
- Tully Products Inc .... G 716 773-3166
  Grand Island *(G-5787)*

TROPHIES, NEC

- All American Awards Inc .... F 631 567-2025
  Bohemia *(G-1007)*
- Dwm International Inc .... F 646 290-7448
  Long Island City *(G-7750)*
- Endurart Inc .... E 212 473-7000
  New York *(G-10087)*

TROPHIES, PEWTER

- Valerie Bohigian .... G 914 631-8866
  Sleepy Hollow *(G-15498)*

TROPHIES, PLATED, ALL METALS

- Csi International Inc .... E 800 441-2895
  Niagara Falls *(G-12831)*

TROPHIES, SILVER

- Atlantic Trophy Co Inc 212 684-6020
  New York *(G-9305)*

TROPHIES: Metal, Exc Silver

- A D Mfg Corp .... F 516 352-6161
  Floral Park *(G-5197)*
- C & M Products Inc 315 471-3303
  Syracuse *(G-15899)*
- Classic Medallics Inc .... E 718 392-5410
  Mount Vernon *(G-8717)*
- New Dimension Awards Inc 718 236-8200
  Brooklyn *(G-2369)*

TROPHY & PLAQUE STORES

- Displays & Beyond Inc .... F 718 805-7786
  Glendale *(G-5666)*
- Jem Sign Corp .... G 516 867-4466
  Hempstead *(G-6299)*

TRUCK & BUS BODIES: Ambulance

- Jeffersonville Volunteer .... E 845 482-3110
  Jeffersonville *(G-7093)*

TRUCK & BUS BODIES: Motor Vehicle, Specialty

- Kurtz Truck Equipment Inc .... F 607 849-3468
  Marathon *(G-8115)*
- Rexford Services Inc .... G 716 366-6671
  Dunkirk *(G-4373)*

TRUCK & BUS BODIES: Truck, Motor Vehicle

- Demartini Oil Equipment Svc .... G 518 463-5752
  Glenmont *(G-5683)*
- Eastern Welding Inc .... G 631 727-0306
  Riverhead *(G-14154)*
- Marros Equipment & Trucks 315 539-8702
  Waterloo *(G-16652)*
- Renaldos Sales and Service Ctr .... G 716 337-3760
  North Collins *(G-12947)*
- Unicell Body Company Inc .... E 716 853-8628
  Buffalo *(G-3258)*
- USA Body Inc 315 852-6123
  De Ruyter *(G-4107)*
- Weld-Built Body Co Inc .... E 631 643-9700
  Wyandanch *(G-17393)*

TRUCK BODIES: Body Parts

- Brunner International Inc .... C 585 798-6000
  Medina *(G-8301)*
- Concrete Mixer Supplycom Inc .... G 716 375-5565
  Olean *(G-13159)*
- Ekostinger Inc .... F 585 739-0450
  East Rochester *(G-4476)*
- Fiberglass Replacement Parts .... F 716 893-6471
  Buffalo *(G-2960)*
- General Welding & Fabg Inc .... G 585 697-7660
  Rochester *(G-14413)*
- Tectran Mfg Inc .... D 800 776-5549
  Buffalo *(G-3237)*
- Unicell Body Company Inc .... F 716 853-8628
  Schenectady *(G-15330)*

TRUCK GENERAL REPAIR SVC

- Chet Kruszkas Service Inc .... F 716 662-7450
  Orchard Park *(G-13284)*
- Riverview Industries Inc .... G 845 265-5284
  Cold Spring *(G-3790)*

TRUCK PAINTING & LETTERING SVCS

- Jem Sign Corp .... G 516 867-4466
  Hempstead *(G-6299)*
- Monasani Signs Inc .... G 631 266-2635
  East Northport *(G-4461)*

TRUCK PARTS & ACCESSORIES: Wholesalers

- Chet Kruszkas Service Inc .... F 716 662-7450
  Orchard Park *(G-13284)*
- Unicell Body Company Inc .... E 716 853-8628
  Buffalo *(G-3258)*

TRUCKING & HAULING SVCS: Garbage, Collect/Transport Only

- Suffolk Indus Recovery Corp .... D 631 732-6403
  Coram *(G-3974)*

TRUCKING, DUMP

- Alice Perkins .... G 716 378-5100
  Salamanca *(G-15125)*
- Ribble Lumber Inc .... G 315 536-6221
  Penn Yan *(G-13541)*

TRUCKING: Except Local

- Platinum Sales Promotion Inc .... G 718 361-0200
  Long Island City *(G-7874)*

TRUCKING: Local, Without Storage

- Clark Concrete Co Inc .... G 315 478-4101
  Syracuse *(G-15915)*
- Haley Concrete Inc .... F 716 492-0849
  Delevan *(G-4260)*
- J & S Logging Inc .... E 315 262-2112
  South Colton *(G-15537)*
- Little Valley Sand & Gravel .... G 716 938-6676
  Little Valley *(G-7534)*

PRODUCT SECTION

TRUCKS & TRACTORS: Industrial

- Arlington Equipment Corp .... G 518 798-5867
  Queensbury (G-14006)
- ASAP Rack Rental Inc .... G 718 499-4495
  Brooklyn (G-1640)
- B & J Delivers Inc .... G 631 524-5550
  Brentwood (G-1174)
- Channel Manufacturing Inc .... E 516 944-6271
  Port Washington (G-13827)
- Ducon Technologies Inc .... F 631 694-1700
  New York (G-9988)
- Ducon Technologies Inc .... E 631 420-4900
  Farmingdale (G-4988)
- E-One Inc .... D 716 646-6790
  Hamburg (G-5944)
- Mettler-Toledo Inc .... C 607 257-6000
  Ithaca (G-6896)
- Raymond Consolidated Corp .... C 800 235-7200
  Greene (G-5886)
- Raymond Corporation .... A 800 235-7200
  Greene (G-5887)
- Raymond Corporation .... E 315 643-5000
  East Syracuse (G-4572)
- Speedways Conveyors Inc .... E 716 893-2222
  Buffalo (G-3223)
- Win-Holt Equipment Corp .... C 516 222-0433
  Garden City (G-5551)

TRUCKS: Forklift

- Continental Lift Truck Inc .... F 718 738-4738
  South Ozone Park (G-15556)
- Raymond Corporation .... C 607 656-2311
  East Syracuse (G-4570)
- Raymond Corporation .... B 315 463-5000
  East Syracuse (G-4571)
- Raymond Sales Corporation .... G 607 656-2311
  Greene (G-5888)
- Stanley Industrial Eqp LLC .... G 315 656-8733
  Kirkville (G-7255)

TRUCKS: Indl

- Meteor Express Inc .... F 718 551-9177
  Jamaica (G-6967)
- Pb08 Inc .... G 347 866-7353
  Hicksville (G-6410)
- Ward Lafrance Truck Corp .... F 518 893-1865
  Saratoga Springs (G-15206)

TRUNKS

- nk In My Trunk Inc .... G 631 420-5865
  armingdale (G-5027)

ISSES: Wood, Floor

- Truss & Pallet LLC .... F 716 433-5400
  rt (G-7637)

S: Wood, Roof

- No   nel & Truss LLC .... E 845 339-3656
  K   -7234)
- P &   .... E 716 496-5484
  Cha   563)
- Pdj Co   s Inc .... E 845 469-9191
  Ches   8)
- Proof In   c .... G 631 694-7663
  Farmin   100)
- Rocheste   Company .... E 585 924-7171
  Farming   4)
- S R Sloan   .... D 315 736-7730
  Whitesbor   223)
- Steele Truss   any Inc .... E 518 562-4663
  Plattsbur   3727)
- Ufp Nev   C .... E 716 496-5484
  Cha   4)
-          K LLC .... E 518 828-2888
        n (G-6668)
-   p New York LLC .... E 315 253-2758
  Auburn (G-524)

TUBE & TUBING FABRICATORS

- Coventry Manufacturing Co Inc .... E 914 668-2212
  Mount Vernon (G-8719)
- Ram Fabricating LLC .... E 315 437-6654
  Syracuse (G-16039)
- Spinco Metal Products Inc .... D 315 331-6285
  Newark (G-12764)

- Star Tubing Corp .... G 716 483-1703
  Jamestown (G-7063)
- Tube Fabrication Company Inc .... F 716 673-1871
  Fredonia (G-5384)

TUBES: Finned, For Heat Transfer

- CMS Heat Transfer Division Inc .... E 631 968-0084
  Bohemia (G-1033)

TUBES: Generator, Electron Beam, Beta Ray

- E-Beam Services Inc .... G 516 622-1422
  Hicksville (G-6370)

TUBES: Paper

- Caraustar Industries Inc .... G 716 874-0393
  Buffalo (G-2888)

TUBES: Paper Or Fiber, Chemical Or Electrical Uses

- Industrial Paper Tube Inc .... F 718 893-5000
  Bronx (G-1363)

TUBES: Steel & Iron

- Markin Tubing LP .... F 585 495-6211
  Buffalo (G-3077)
- TI Group Auto Systems LLC .... G 315 568-7042
  Seneca Falls (G-15394)

TUBES: Vacuum

- New Sensor Corporation .... D 718 937-8300
  Long Island City (G-7856)

TUBES: Wrought, Welded Or Lock Joint

- Markin Tubing LP .... D 585 495-6211
  Wyoming (G-17396)
- Markin Tubing Inc .... C 585 495-6211
  Wyoming (G-17397)
- Thyssenkrupp Materials NA Inc .... G 585 279-0000
  Rochester (G-14753)

TUBING: Flexible, Metallic

- Conrad Blasius Equipment Co .... G 516 753-1200
  Plainview (G-13620)

TUBING: Glass

- Gray Glass Inc .... E 718 217-2943
  Queens Village (G-13994)

TUBING: Plastic

- Finger Lakes Extrusion Corp .... E 585 905-0632
  Canandaigua (G-3375)
- Hancor Inc .... D 607 565-3033
  Waverly (G-16728)

TUBING: Seamless

- TI Group Auto Systems LLC .... G 315 568-7042
  Seneca Falls (G-15394)

TUNGSTEN CARBIDE

- Buffalo Tungsten Inc .... D 716 759-6353
  Depew (G-4276)
- Niagara Refining LLC .... E 716 706-1400
  Depew (G-4289)

TUNGSTEN CARBIDE POWDER

- Golden Egret LLC .... G 516 922-2839
  East Norwich (G-4465)

TURBINE GENERATOR SET UNITS: Hydraulic, Complete

- Hdm Hydraulics LLC .... D 716 694-8004
  Tonawanda (G-16187)
- Signa Chemistry Inc .... F 212 933-4101
  New York (G-12092)

TURBINES & TURBINE GENERATOR SET UNITS, COMPLETE

- Ingersoll-Rand Company .... E 716 896-6600
  Buffalo (G-3025)

TURBINES & TURBINE GENERATOR SET UNITS: Gas, Complete

- General Electric Company .... B 518 385-3716
  Schenectady (G-15286)
- General Electric Company .... B 518 385-2211
  Schenectady (G-15287)

TURBINES & TURBINE GENERATOR SETS

- Awr Energy Inc .... F 585 469-7750
  Plattsburgh (G-13680)
- Beowawe Binary LLC .... E 646 829-3900
  New York (G-9409)
- Cooper Turbocompressor Inc .... B 716 896-6600
  Buffalo (G-2910)
- Dresser-Rand Company .... A 585 596-3100
  Wellsville (G-16777)
- Dresser-Rand Group Inc .... D 716 375-3000
  Olean (G-13164)
- Gas Turbine Controls Corp .... E 914 693-0830
  Hawthorne (G-6270)
- GE Global Research .... B 518 387-5000
  Niskayuna (G-12911)
- GE Transportation Eng Systems .... G 518 258-9276
  Schenectady (G-15282)
- General Electric Company .... B 518 385-2211
  Schenectady (G-15284)
- General Electric Company .... B 203 373-2756
  Schenectady (G-15285)
- General Electric Company .... B 518 387-5000
  Schenectady (G-15288)
- General Electric Company .... B 518 385-3439
  Schenectady (G-15289)
- Mission Critical Energy Inc .... G 716 276-8465
  Getzville (G-5612)
- Prime Turbine Parts LLC .... G 518 306-7306
  Saratoga Springs (G-15197)
- Siemens Government Tech Inc .... B 585 593-1234
  Wellsville (G-16785)
- Stork H & E Turbo Blading Inc .... C 607 277-4968
  Ithaca (G-6911)
- Tgp Flying Cloud Holdings LLC .... E 646 829-3900
  New York (G-12329)
- Tuthill Corporation .... B 631 727-1097
  Riverhead (G-14172)
- Weaver Wind Energy LLC .... G 607 379-9463
  Freeville (G-5450)
- Wind Products Inc .... G 212 292-3135
  Brooklyn (G-2772)
- Worldwide Gas Turbine Pdts Inc .... G 518 877-7200
  Clifton Park (G-3737)

TURBINES & TURBINE GENERATOR SETS & PARTS

- Turbine Engine Comp Utica .... A 315 768-8070
  Whitesboro (G-17225)
- Turbo Machined Products LLC .... E 315 895-3010
  Frankfort (G-5368)

TURBINES: Gas, Mechanical Drive

- Omega Industries & Development .... E 516 349-8010
  Plainview (G-13654)

TURBINES: Hydraulic, Complete

- Atlantic Projects Company Inc .... F 518 878-2065
  Clifton Park (G-3722)
- Corfu Machine Inc .... E 585 418-4083
  Corfu (G-3975)
- Frontier Hydraulics Corp .... F 716 694-2070
  Buffalo (G-2973)

TURBINES: Steam

- General Electric Company .... A 518 385-4022
  Schenectady (G-15283)
- General Electric Company .... E 518 385-7620
  Niskayuna (G-12912)

TURBO-GENERATORS

- Mannesmann Corporation .... D 212 258-4000
  New York (G-11160)

TURKEY PROCESSING & SLAUGHTERING

- Hansel n Gretel Brand Inc .... C 718 326-0041
  Glendale (G-5671)

TWINE PRDTS

A & A Line & Wire Corp F 718 456-2657
Maspeth *(G-8139)*

TYPESETTING SVC

514 Adams Corporation G 516 352-6948
Franklin Square *(G-5369)*

Act Communications Group Inc F 631 669-2403
West Islip *(G-16932)*

Advance Publications Inc D 718 981-1234
Staten Island *(G-15653)*

Agrecolor Inc F 516 741-8700
Mineola *(G-8525)*

Alabaster Group Inc G 516 867-8223
Freeport *(G-5391)*

Albion-Holley Pennysaver Inc E 585 589-5641
Albion *(G-164)*

Arista Innovations Inc E 516 746-2262
Mineola *(G-8529)*

Art Resources Transfer Inc G 212 255-2919
New York *(G-9264)*

Artscroll Printing Corp E 212 929-2413
New York *(G-9275)*

Bates Jackson Engraving Co Inc E 716 854-3000
Buffalo *(G-2855)*

Baum Christine and John Corp G 585 621-8910
Rochester *(G-14241)*

Bco Industries Western NY Inc E 716 877-2800
Tonawanda *(G-16165)*

Beastons Budget Printing G 585 244-2721
Rochester *(G-14244)*

Beehive Press Inc G 718 654-1200
Bronx *(G-1280)*

Benchemark Printing Inc D 518 393-1361
Schenectady *(G-15262)*

Bernard Hall G 585 425-3340
Fairport *(G-4853)*

Beyer Graphics Inc D 631 543-3900
Commack *(G-3850)*

Boncraft Inc D 716 662-9720
Tonawanda *(G-16167)*

Bondy Printing Corp G 631 242-1510
Bay Shore *(G-677)*

Brodock Press Inc D 315 735-9577
Utica *(G-16333)*

Brooks Litho Digital Group Inc G 631 789-4500
Deer Park *(G-4136)*

Bytheway Publishing Services F 607 334-8365
Norwich *(G-13037)*

Carlara Group Ltd G 914 769-2020
Pleasantville *(G-13744)*

Carnels Printing Inc G 516 883-3355
Port Washington *(G-13826)*

Castlereagh Printcraft Inc D 516 623-1728
Freeport *(G-5402)*

Chakra Communications Inc E 716 505-7300
Lancaster *(G-7333)*

Chakra Communications Inc E 607 748-7491
Endicott *(G-4806)*

Challenge Graphics Svcs Inc E 631 586-0171
Deer Park *(G-4138)*

Clarsons Corp F 585 235-8775
Rochester *(G-14299)*

Cohber Press Inc D 585 475-9100
West Henrietta *(G-16906)*

Consolidated Color Press Inc F 212 929-8197
New York *(G-9765)*

Cortland Standard Printing Co D 607 756-5665
Cortland *(G-4045)*

Cosmos Communications Inc C 718 482-1800
Long Island City *(G-7734)*

Csw Inc F 585 247-4010
Rochester *(G-14315)*

D G M Graphics Inc F 516 223-2220
Merrick *(G-8416)*

Desktop Publishing Concepts F 631 752-1934
Farmingdale *(G-4985)*

Digital Page LLC F 518 446-9129
Albany *(G-73)*

Dispatch Graphics Inc F 212 307-5943
New York *(G-9938)*

Dowd - Witbeck Printing Corp F 518 274-2421
Troy *(G-16256)*

DP Murphy Co Inc D 631 673-9400
Deer Park *(G-4154)*

Draper Associates Incorporated F 212 255-2727
New York *(G-9975)*

E B B Graphics Inc F 516 750-5510
Westbury *(G-17006)*

Eastwood Litho Inc E 315 437-2626
Syracuse *(G-15950)*

Empire Press Co G 718 756-9500
Brooklyn *(G-1926)*

Falconer Printing & Design Inc F 716 665-2121
Falconer *(G-4906)*

Flare Multicopy Corp E 718 258-8860
Brooklyn *(G-1983)*

Flp Group LLC F 315 252-7583
Auburn *(G-495)*

Fort Orange Press Inc E 518 489-3233
Albany *(G-81)*

Fulton Newspapers Inc E 315 598-6397
Fulton *(G-5471)*

Gallant Graphics Ltd E 845 868-1166
Stanfordville *(G-15647)*

Gateway Prtg & Graphics Inc E 716 823-3873
Hamburg *(G-5949)*

Gazette Press Inc E 914 963-8300
Rye *(G-15082)*

Gg Design and Printing G 718 321-3220
New York *(G-10332)*

Graphic Fabrications Inc G 516 763-3222
Rockville Centre *(G-14819)*

Graphicomm Inc G 716 283-0830
Niagara Falls *(G-12845)*

Grid Typographic Services Inc F 212 627-0303
New York *(G-10404)*

Hamptons Magazine E 631 283-7125
Southampton *(G-15568)*

Hks Printing Company Inc F 212 675-2529
New York *(G-10533)*

Hugh F McPherson Inc G 716 668-6107
Cheektowaga *(G-3604)*

In-House Inc F 718 445-9007
College Point *(G-3812)*

Interstate Litho Corp D 631 232-6025
Brentwood *(G-1182)*

Jack J Florio Jr G 716 434-9123
Lockport *(G-7625)*

James Conolly Printing Co E 585 426-4150
Rochester *(G-14480)*

Jane Lewis G 607 722-0584
Binghamton *(G-925)*

Johnnys Ideal Printing Co G 518 828-6666
Hudson *(G-6651)*

Jon Lyn Ink Inc G 516 546-2312
Merrick *(G-8420)*

L M N Printing Company Inc E 516 285-8526
Valley Stream *(G-16438)*

Lake Placid Advertisers Wkshp E 518 523-3359
Lake Placid *(G-7299)*

Leigh Scott Enterprises Inc G 718 343-5440
Bellerose *(G-806)*

Litmor Publishing Corp F 516 931-0012
Garden City *(G-5527)*

Loudon Ltd G 631 757-4447
East Northport *(G-4460)*

Louis Heindl & Son Inc G 585 454-5080
Rochester *(G-14504)*

Loy L Press Inc G 716 634-5966
Buffalo *(G-3069)*

Medallion Associates Inc E 212 929-9130
New York *(G-11233)*

Mercury Print Productions Inc C 585 458-7900
Rochester *(G-14525)*

Midgley Printing Corp G 315 475-1864
Syracuse *(G-16009)*

Mines Press Inc C 914 788-1800
Cortlandt Manor *(G-4078)*

Moneast Inc G 845 298-8898
Wappingers Falls *(G-16595)*

Multiple Imprssons of Rchester G 585 546-1160
Rochester *(G-14545)*

Mutual Engraving Company Inc D 516 489-0534
West Hempstead *(G-16893)*

News India USA Inc F 212 675-7515
New York *(G-11437)*

Newspaper Publisher LLC F 607 775-0472
Conklin *(G-3896)*

Official Offset Corporation E 631 957-8500
Amityville *(G-316)*

Ozipko Enterprises Inc G 585 424-6740
Rochester *(G-14581)*

P D R Inc G 516 829-5300
Plainview *(G-13655)*

Panagraphics Inc G 716 312-8088
Orchard Park *(G-13312)*

Patrick Ryans Modern Press F 518 434-2921
Albany *(G-115)*

Presstek Printing LLC F 585 467-8140
Rochester *(G-14621)*

Prestige Envelope & Lithograph F 631 521-7043
Merrick *(G-8426)*

Printery G 516 922-3250
Oyster Bay *(G-13399)*

Printing Resources Inc E 518 482-2470
Albany *(G-124)*

Pro Printing G 516 561-9700
Lynbrook *(G-7983)*

Progressive Graphics & Prtg G 315 331-3635
Newark *(G-12762)*

Publishing Synthesis Ltd G 212 219-0135
New York *(G-11770)*

Quad/Graphics Inc A 518 581-4000
Saratoga Springs *(G-15198)*

Quicker Printer Inc G 607 734-8622
Elmira *(G-4712)*

Rmd Holding Inc G 845 628-0030
Mahopac *(G-8031)*

Scotti Graphics Inc E 212 367-9602
Long Island City *(G-7901)*

Sentinel Printing Inc G 516 334-7400
Westbury *(G-17054)*

Stone Crest Industries Inc G 607 652-2665
Stamford *(G-15646)*

Syracuse Computer Forms Inc E 315 478-0108
Syracuse *(G-16075)*

Thomas Group Inc F 212 947-6400
New York *(G-12340)*

Times Review Newspaper Corp E 631 354-8031
Mattituck *(G-8243)*

Tobay Printing Co Inc E 631 842-3300
Copiague *(G-3957)*

Tom & Jerry Printcraft Forms E 914 777-7468
Mamaroneck *(G-8081)*

Torsaf Printers Inc G 516 569-5577
Hewlett *(G-6337)*

Tri Kolor Printing & Sty F 315 474-6753
Syracuse *(G-16085)*

Tri-Lon Clor Lithographers Ltd E 212 255-6140
New York *(G-12421)*

Tripi Engraving Co Inc E 718 383-6500
Brooklyn *(G-2700)*

Voss Signs LLC E 315 682-6418
Manlius *(G-8109)*

Wallkill Valley Publications E 845 561-0170
Newburgh *(G-12810)*

Webster Printing Corporation F 585 671-1533
Webster *(G-16768)*

Westchester Mailing Service E 914 948-1116
White Plains *(G-17212)*

Wilson Press LLC E 315 568-9693
Seneca Falls *(G-15395)*

Woodbury Printing Plus + Inc G 845 928-6610
Central Valley *(G-3557)*

Worldwide Ticket Craft D 516 538-6200
Merrick *(G-8429)*

Wynco Press One Inc G 516 354-6145
Glen Oaks *(G-5656)*

X Myles Mar Inc E 212 683-2015
New York *(G-12699)*

Zenger Partners LLC E 716 876-2284
Kenmore *(G-7181)*

TYPESETTING SVC: Computer

Cds Productions Inc F 518 385-8255
Schenectady *(G-15269)*

TYPOGRAPHY

Artistic Typography Corp G 212 463-8880
New York *(G-9272)*

Rubber Stamps Inc E 212 675-1180
Mineola *(G-8568)*

ULTRASONIC EQPT: Cleaning, Exc Med & Dental

Alexy Associates Inc E 845 482-3000
Bethel *(G-858)*

Tectran Inc G 800 776-5549
Cheektowaga *(G-3619)*

UMBRELLAS & CANES

Essex Manufacturing Inc D 212 239-0080
New York *(G-10119)*

Gustbuster Ltd G 631 391-9000
Farmingdale *(G-5010)*

PRODUCT SECTION

VALVES: Fluid Power, Control, Hydraulic & pneumatic

UMBRELLAS: Garden Or Wagon
Zip-Jack Industries Ltd...............................E...... 914 592-2000
  Tarrytown *(G-16136)*

UNIFORM STORES
Craft Clerical Clothes Inc..........................G...... 212 764-6122
  New York *(G-9803)*

UNIVERSITY
Cornell University....................................D...... 607 277-2338
  Ithaca *(G-6871)*
Cornell University....................................E...... 607 254-2473
  Ithaca *(G-6872)*
New York University.................................E...... 212 998-4300
  New York *(G-11431)*
Suny At Binghamton................................D...... 607 777-2316
  Binghamton *(G-946)*
Trust of Colum Unive In The Ci................F...... 212 854-2793
  New York *(G-12434)*
University of Rochester...........................B...... 585 275-3483
  Rochester *(G-14772)*

UNSUPPORTED PLASTICS: Floor Or Wall Covering
Pacific Designs Intl Inc.............................G...... 718 364-2867
  Bronx *(G-1420)*

UPHOLSTERY FILLING MATERIALS
Global Resources Sg Inc..........................F...... 212 686-1411
  New York *(G-10362)*
Manrico Usa Inc......................................G...... 212 794-4200
  New York *(G-11164)*

UPHOLSTERY MATERIALS, BROADWOVEN
Scalamandre Silks Inc.............................D...... 212 980-3888
  New York *(G-12002)*
Stark Scalamandre Fabric LLC................D...... 212 376-2900
  New York *(G-12210)*

UPHOLSTERY WORK SVCS
August Studios..G...... 718 706-6487
  Long Island City *(G-7709)*
Bettertex Inc..F...... 212 431-3373
  New York *(G-9426)*
Dine Rite Seating Products Inc................E...... 631 226-8899
  Lindenhurst *(G-7485)*
Elan Upholstery Inc..................................F...... 631 563-0650
  Bohemia *(G-1061)*
Terbo Ltd...G...... 718 847-2860
  Richmond Hill *(G-14099)*

URANIUM ORE MINING, NEC
Global Gold Corporation...........................F...... 914 925-0020
  Rye *(G-15084)*

USED CAR DEALERS
A Zimmer Ltd...D...... 315 422-7011
  Syracuse *(G-15866)*
Want-Ad Digest Inc..................................F...... 518 279-1181
  Troy *(G-16287)*

USED MERCHANDISE STORES: Building Materials
Veeco Instruments Inc.............................C...... 516 349-8300
  Plainview *(G-13670)*

UTENSILS: Cast Aluminum, Cooking Or Kitchen
August Thomsen Corp..............................E...... 516 676-7100
  Glen Cove *(G-5623)*
Smart USA Inc...E...... 718 416-4500
  Glendale *(G-5679)*

UTENSILS: Household, Cooking & Kitchen, Metal
Corning Vitro Corporation.........................A...... 607 974-8605
  Corning *(G-3992)*
Lb Furniture Industries LLC......................C...... 518 828-1501
  Hudson *(G-6654)*
Nash Metalware Co Inc............................F...... 315 339-5794
  Rome *(G-14851)*

Oxo International Inc................................C...... 212 242-3333
  New York *(G-11557)*
Progressus Company Inc.........................F...... 516 255-0245
  Rockville Centre *(G-14825)*

UTENSILS: Household, Cooking & Kitchen, Porcelain Enameled
Hyman Podrusnick Co Inc........................G...... 718 853-4502
  Brooklyn *(G-2089)*

UTENSILS: Household, Metal, Exc Cast
Korin Japanese Trading Corp...................E...... 212 587-7021
  New York *(G-10916)*

UTENSILS: Household, Porcelain Enameled
Seneca Ceramics Corp............................G...... 315 781-0100
  Phelps *(G-13559)*

UTILITY TRAILER DEALERS
J D Handling Systems Inc........................F...... 518 828-9676
  Ghent *(G-5620)*

VACUUM CLEANER STORES
Nationwide Sales and Service..................F...... 631 491-6625
  Farmingdale *(G-5071)*

VACUUM CLEANERS: Household
American Comfort Direct LLC...................E...... 201 364-8309
  New York *(G-9165)*
D & C Cleaning Inc..................................F...... 631 789-5659
  Copiague *(G-3924)*
Global Resources Sg Inc..........................F...... 212 686-1411
  New York *(G-10362)*
Nationwide Sales and Service..................F...... 631 491-6625
  Farmingdale *(G-5071)*
Tri County Custom Vacuum......................G...... 845 774-7595
  Monroe *(G-8600)*

VACUUM CLEANERS: Indl Type
Empire Division Inc..................................D...... 315 476-6273
  Syracuse *(G-15957)*
Key High Vacuum Products Inc...............E...... 631 584-5959
  Nesconset *(G-8823)*
National Vac Envmtl Svcs Corp................F...... 518 743-0563
  Glens Falls *(G-5706)*

VACUUM SYSTEMS: Air Extraction, Indl
Adams Sfc Inc...E...... 716 877-2608
  Tonawanda *(G-16157)*
Auburn Vacuum Forming Co Inc..............F...... 315 253-2440
  Auburn *(G-481)*
Edwards Vacuum LLC.............................D...... 800 848-9800
  Sanborn *(G-15145)*

VALUE-ADDED RESELLERS: Computer Systems
Amherst Systems Inc...............................C...... 716 631-0610
  Buffalo *(G-2828)*
Graphics Slution Providers Inc.................G...... 845 677-5088
  Lagrangeville *(G-7278)*

VALVES & PIPE FITTINGS
A K Allen Co Inc......................................C...... 516 747-5450
  Mineola *(G-8522)*
Aalborg Instrs & Contrls Inc.....................D...... 845 398-3160
  Orangeburg *(G-13238)*
Anderson Precision Inc............................D...... 716 484-1148
  Jamestown *(G-7007)*
Curtiss-Wright Flow Ctrl Corp...................C...... 631 293-3800
  Farmingdale *(G-4978)*
Delaware Mfg Inds Corp...........................D...... 716 743-4360
  North Tonawanda *(G-12986)*
Devin Mfg Inc...F...... 585 496-5770
  Arcade *(G-391)*
Flomatic Corporation................................E...... 518 761-9797
  Glens Falls *(G-5695)*
Ford Regulator Valve Corp.......................G...... 718 497-3255
  Brooklyn *(G-1994)*
Goodman Main Stopper Mfg Co...............F...... 718 875-5140
  Brooklyn *(G-2040)*
J H Robotics Inc......................................E...... 607 729-3758
  Johnson City *(G-7127)*
Key High Vacuum Products Inc...............E...... 631 584-5959
  Nesconset *(G-8823)*

Kingston Hoops Summer..........................G...... 845 401-6830
  Kingston *(G-7222)*
Lance Valves..G...... 716 681-5825
  Lancaster *(G-7348)*
M Manastrip-M Corporation.....................G...... 518 664-2089
  Clifton Park *(G-3726)*
Make-Waves Instrument Corp..................E...... 716 681-7524
  Buffalo *(G-3076)*
Micromold Products Inc...........................E...... 914 969-2850
  Yonkers *(G-17485)*
Rand Machine Products Inc.....................D...... 716 665-5217
  Falconer *(G-4916)*
Ross Valve Mfg..G...... 518 274-0961
  Troy *(G-16275)*
Sigmamotor Inc.......................................E...... 716 735-3115
  Middleport *(G-8457)*
Spence Engineering Company Inc...........C...... 845 778-5566
  Walden *(G-16556)*
Steel & Obrien Mfg Inc.............................D...... 585 492-5800
  Arcade *(G-399)*
Sure Flow Equipment Inc........................E...... 800 263-8251
  Tonawanda *(G-16224)*
William E Williams Valve Corp..................E...... 718 392-1660
  Long Island City *(G-7951)*

VALVES & REGULATORS: Pressure, Indl
Doyle & Roth Mfg Co Inc.........................F...... 212 269-7840
  New York *(G-9972)*
Spence Engineering Company Inc...........C...... 845 778-5566
  Walden *(G-16556)*
Total Energy Fabrication Corp.................G...... 580 363-1500
  North Salem *(G-12956)*

VALVES: Aerosol, Metal
901 D LLC..E...... 845 369-1111
  Airmont *(G-10)*
Chapin International Inc...........................C...... 585 343-3140
  Batavia *(G-628)*
Chapin Manufacturing Inc.........................C...... 585 343-3140
  Batavia *(G-629)*
Fabritex Inc..G...... 706 376-6584
  New York *(G-10177)*
Jordan Panel Systems Corp.....................E...... 631 754-4900
  East Northport *(G-4459)*
Peak Motion Inc.......................................G...... 716 534-4925
  Clarence *(G-3695)*
Peelle Company.......................................G...... 631 231-6000
  Hauppauge *(G-6185)*

VALVES: Aircraft
Valvetech Inc...E...... 315 548-4551
  Phelps *(G-13562)*

VALVES: Aircraft, Control, Hydraulic & Pneumatic
Young & Franklin Inc................................D...... 315 457-3110
  Liverpool *(G-7586)*

VALVES: Aircraft, Fluid Power
Dmic Inc...F...... 716 743-4360
  North Tonawanda *(G-12987)*
Moog Inc..A...... 716 652-2000
  Elma *(G-4664)*
Tactair Fluid Controls Inc.........................C...... 315 451-3928
  Liverpool *(G-7579)*

VALVES: Control, Automatic
ADC Industries Inc...................................E...... 516 596-1304
  Valley Stream *(G-16424)*

VALVES: Fluid Power, Control, Hydraulic & pneumatic
Aerco International Inc.............................C...... 845 580-8000
  Blauvelt *(G-963)*
BW Elliott Mfg Co LLC..............................B...... 607 772-0404
  Binghamton *(G-896)*
Direkt Force LLC......................................E...... 716 652-3022
  East Aurora *(G-4394)*
Dsti Inc..G...... 716 557-2362
  Olean *(G-13165)*
Dynamic Sealing Tech Inc........................G...... 716 376-0708
  Olean *(G-13166)*

Employee Codes: A=Over 500 employees, B=251-500
C=101-250, D=51-100, E=20-50, F=10-19, G=5-9

2018 Harris
New York Manufacturers Directory

VALVES: Gas Cylinder, Compressed

Caithness Equities Corporation .... E 212 599-2112
New York *(G-9549)*

VALVES: Hard Rubber

Inflation Systems Inc .... E 914 381-8070
Mamaroneck *(G-8069)*

VALVES: Indl

Air System Products Inc .... F 716 683-0435
Lancaster *(G-7324)*
Byelocorp Scientific Inc .... E 212 785-2580
New York *(G-9539)*
Curtiss-Wright Flow Ctrl Corp .... C 631 293-3800
Farmingdale *(G-4978)*
Curtiss-Wright Flow Ctrl Corp .... C 631 293-3800
Farmingdale *(G-4979)*
Dresser-Rand Company .... A 585 596-3100
Wellsville *(G-16777)*
Flow-Safe Inc .... E 716 662-2585
Orchard Park *(G-13293)*
J H Buscher Inc .... G 716 667-2003
Orchard Park *(G-13300)*
McWane Inc .... B 607 734-2211
Elmira *(G-4708)*
Murphy Manufacturing Co Inc .... G 585 223-0100
Fairport *(G-4871)*
Plattco Corporation .... E 518 563-4640
Plattsburgh *(G-13715)*
Precision Valve & Automtn Inc .... C 518 371-2684
Cohoes *(G-3779)*
Syraco Products Inc .... F 315 476-5306
Syracuse *(G-16072)*
Town Food Service Eqp Co Inc .... F 718 388-5650
Brooklyn *(G-2691)*
Trac Regulators Inc .... E 914 699-9352
Mount Vernon *(G-8785)*
William E Williams Valve Corp .... E 718 392-1660
Long Island City *(G-7951)*

VALVES: Plumbing & Heating

Lemode Plumbing & Heating .... E 718 545-3336
Astoria *(G-445)*
Smiths Gas Service Inc .... G 518 438-0400
Albany *(G-134)*
Venco Sales Inc .... E 631 754-0782
Huntington *(G-6729)*

VALVES: Regulating & Control, Automatic

Digital Home Creations Inc .... G 585 576-7070
Webster *(G-16745)*
ITT LLC .... G 315 568-4733
Seneca Falls *(G-15386)*
Tyco Simplexgrinnell .... E 315 437-9664
East Syracuse *(G-4586)*

VALVES: Water Works

Flomatic Corporation .... E 518 761-9797
Glens Falls *(G-5695)*

VARNISHES, NEC

John C Dolph Company Inc .... E 732 329-2333
Schenectady *(G-15298)*
Royce Associates A Ltd Partnr .... G 516 367-6298
Jericho *(G-7115)*
Si Group Inc .... C 518 347-4200
Rotterdam Junction *(G-15060)*

VEGETABLE STANDS OR MARKETS

Lakeside Cider Mill Farm Inc .... G 518 399-8359
Ballston Lake *(G-581)*

VEHICLES: All Terrain

Kens Service & Sales Inc .... F 716 683-1155
Elma *(G-4663)*

VEHICLES: Recreational

Adirondack Power Sports .... G 518 481-6269
Malone *(G-8037)*
Bullet Industries Inc .... G 585 352-0835
Spencerport *(G-15592)*

VENDING MACHINES & PARTS

Cubic Trnsp Systems Inc .... F 212 255-1810
New York *(G-9821)*
Vengo Inc .... G 866 526-7054
Long Island City *(G-7941)*

VENTILATING EQPT: Metal

Air Louver & Damper Inc .... E 718 392-3232
Maspeth *(G-8141)*
Air Louver & Damper Inc .... F 718 392-3232
Long Island City *(G-7681)*
GM Sheet Metal Inc .... F 718 349-2830
Brooklyn *(G-2032)*
Imperial Damper & Louver Co .... E 718 731-3800
Bronx *(G-1361)*
M&G Duravent Inc .... F 518 463-7284
Albany *(G-99)*
Spence Engineering Company Inc ...... C 845 778-5566
Walden *(G-16556)*

VENTILATING EQPT: Sheet Metal

Empire Ventilation Eqp Co Inc .... F 718 728-2143
Florida *(G-5219)*
Lambro Industries Inc .... D 631 842-8088
Amityville *(G-304)*

VENTURE CAPITAL COMPANIES

Capital E Financial Group .... F 212 319-6550
New York *(G-9574)*
Circle Peak Capital MGT LLC .... E 646 230-8812
New York *(G-9673)*

VETERINARY PHARMACEUTICAL PREPARATIONS

Ark Sciences Inc .... G 646 943-1520
Islandia *(G-6825)*
H W Naylor Co Inc .... F 607 263-5145
Morris *(G-8660)*
Inolife Technologies Inc .... G 212 348-5600
New York *(G-10648)*

VIBRATORS: Concrete Construction

Ozteck Industries Inc .... E 516 883-8857
Port Washington *(G-13868)*

VIDEO & AUDIO EQPT, WHOLESALE

Lanel Inc .... F 516 437-5119
Floral Park *(G-5212)*
Listec Video Corp .... G 631 273-3029
Hauppauge *(G-6137)*
Professional Tape Corporation .... G 516 656-5519
Glen Cove *(G-5638)*
Video Technology Services Inc .... F 516 937-9700
Syosset *(G-15861)*

VIDEO CAMERA-AUDIO RECORDERS: Household Use

Digitac Inc .... F 732 215-4020
Brooklyn *(G-1863)*

VIDEO EQPT

Video Technology Services Inc .... F 516 937-9700
Syosset *(G-15861)*

VIDEO PRODUCTION SVCS

Amherst Media Inc .... G 716 874-4450
Buffalo *(G-2827)*
Scholastic Inc .... A 800 724-6527
New York *(G-12016)*
Wochit Inc .... G 212 979-8343
New York *(G-12679)*

VIDEO REPAIR SVCS

Video Technology Services Inc .... F 516 937-9700
Syosset *(G-15861)*

VIDEO TAPE PRODUCTION SVCS

NCM Publishers Inc .... G 212 691-9100
New York *(G-11385)*
Physicalmind Institute .... F 212 343-2150
New York *(G-11674)*

VINYL RESINS, NEC

Manufacturers Indexing Pdts .... G 631 271-0956
Halesite *(G-5928)*

VISUAL COMMUNICATIONS SYSTEMS

Vicon Industries Inc .... C 631 952-2288
Hauppauge *(G-6250)*

VITAMINS: Natural Or Synthetic, Uncompounded, Bulk

Abh Natures Products Inc .... E 631 249-5783
Edgewood *(G-4602)*
Ajes Pharmaceuticals LLC .... E 631 608-1728
Copiague *(G-3917)*
Gemini Pharmaceuticals Inc .... C 631 543-3334
Commack *(G-3859)*
Healthee Endeavors Inc .... G 718 653-5499
Bronx *(G-1355)*
Healthy N Fit Intl Inc .... F 914 271-6040
Croton On Hudson *(G-4090)*
Natural Organics Inc .... C 631 293-0030
Melville *(G-8368)*
Natures Bounty Co .... F 631 244-2065
Ronkonkoma *(G-14976)*
Natures Bounty Co .... F 518 452-5813
Albany *(G-105)*
Natures Bounty Co .... D 631 244-2021
Ronkonkoma *(G-14977)*
Natures Bounty Co .... A 631 200-2000
Ronkonkoma *(G-14978)*
Natures Bounty Co .... D 631 200-7338
Ronkonkoma *(G-14979)*
Natures Bounty Co .... F 631 588-3492
Holbrook *(G-6493)*
Nbty Manufacturing LLC .... E 631 567-9500
Ronkonkoma *(G-14980)*
Nutra Solutions USA Inc .... E 631 392-1900
Deer Park *(G-4207)*
Nutraqueen LLC .... F 347 368-6568
New York *(G-11489)*
Only Natural Inc .... F 516 897-7001
Oceanside *(G-13110)*
Princeton Sciences .... G 845 368-1214
Airmont *(G-16)*
Vitalize Labs LLC .... G 212 966-6130
New York *(G-12584)*
Vitamix Laboratories Inc .... E 631 465-9245
Commack *(G-3871)*
Wellquest International Inc .... G 212 689-9094
New York *(G-12636)*

VITAMINS: Pharmaceutical Preparations

Bi Nutraceuticals Inc .... D 631 232-1105
Central Islip *(G-3513)*
Bronson Nutritionals LLC .... E 631 750-0000
Hauppauge *(G-6057)*
Danbury Pharma LLC .... E 631 393-6333
Farmingdale *(G-4984)*
FB Laboratories Inc .... E 631 750-0000
Hauppauge *(G-6098)*
Kabco Pharmaceuticals Inc .... G 631 842-3600
Amityville *(G-300)*
Natural Organics Laboratories .... B 631 957-5600
Amityville *(G-314)*
Natures Bounty (ny) Inc .... F 631 567-9500
Bohemia *(G-1103)*
Natures Bounty (ny) Inc .... A 631 580-6137
Ronkonkoma *(G-14975)*
Natures Value Inc .... C 631 846-2500
Coram *(G-3969)*
Nutraceutical Wellness LLC .... G 888 454-3320
New York *(G-11488)*
Premium Processing Corp .... D 631 232-1105
Babylon *(G-551)*
Tishcon Corp .... C 516 333-3056
Westbury *(G-17061)*
Tishcon Corp .... C 516 333-3050
Westbury *(G-17064)*
Unipharm Inc .... E 212 564-3634
New York *(G-12478)*
Very Best Irtj .... F 914 271-6585
Croton On Hudson *(G-4092)*
Wellmill LLC .... F 631 465-9245
Farmingdale *(G-5152)*

PRODUCT SECTION

WEDDING CHAPEL: Privately Operated

WALL COVERINGS WHOLESALERS

Scalamandre Wallpaper Inc .... B 631 467-8800
  Hauppauge *(G-6210)*

WALLBOARD: Decorated, Made From Purchased Materials

Aniiwe Inc .... G 347 683-1891
  Brooklyn *(G-1612)*

WALLPAPER & WALL COVERINGS

Adelphi Paper Hangings .... G 518 284-9066
  Sharon Springs *(G-15404)*
Eskayel Inc .... G 347 703-8084
  Brooklyn *(G-1940)*
Flavor Paper Ltd .... F 718 422-0230
  Brooklyn *(G-1985)*
Gerald McGlone .... G 518 482-2613
  Colonie *(G-3846)*
Larkin Anya Ltd .... G 718 361-1827
  Long Island City *(G-7814)*
Sunnyside Decorative Prints Co ...... G 516 671-1935
  Glen Cove *(G-5643)*

WALLPAPER: Made From Purchased Paper

Lulu DK LLC .... G 212 223-4234
  New York *(G-11092)*

WALLS: Curtain, Metal

A&B McKeon Glass Inc .... G 718 525-2152
  Staten Island *(G-15651)*
Metalsigma Usa Inc .... G 212 731-4346
  New York *(G-11267)*
Pierce Steel Fabricators .... F 716 372-7652
  Olean *(G-13174)*

WAREHOUSE CLUBS STORES

Brucci Ltd .... E 914 965-0707
  Yonkers *(G-17438)*

WAREHOUSING & STORAGE FACILITIES, NEC

Acme Signs of Baldwinsville .... G 315 638-4865
  Baldwinsville *(G-564)*
Cambridge University Press .... D 212 337-5000
  New York *(G-9558)*
Eastern Welding Inc .... G 631 727-0306
  Riverhead *(G-14154)*
Medical Action Industries Inc .... C 631 231-4600
  Hauppauge *(G-6155)*

WAREHOUSING & STORAGE, REFRIGERATED: Frozen Or Refrig Goods

Adirondack Ice & Air Inc .... F 518 483-4340
  Malone *(G-8036)*

WAREHOUSING & STORAGE: General

George G Sharp Inc .... E 212 732-2800
  New York *(G-10325)*
Ivi Services Inc .... D 607 729-5111
  Binghamton *(G-924)*
Lighting Holdings Intl LLC .... A 845 306-1850
  Purchase *(G-13976)*
Platinum Sales Promotion Inc .... G 718 361-0200
  Long Island City *(G-7874)*
Wayuga Community Newspapers ... G 315 594-2506
  Wolcott *(G-17302)*

WAREHOUSING & STORAGE: General

Canfield & Tack Inc .... D 585 235-7710
  Rochester *(G-14275)*
Dayleen Intimates Inc .... E 914 969-5900
  Yonkers *(G-17450)*

WAREHOUSING & STORAGE: Refrigerated

Crescent Duck Farm Inc .... E 631 722-8700
  Aquebogue *(G-384)*

WARM AIR HEATING & AC EQPT & SPLYS, WHOLESALE Air Filters

R P Fedder Corp .... E 585 288-1600
  Rochester *(G-14643)*

WARM AIR HEATING/AC EQPT/SPLYS, WHOL Dehumidifiers, Exc Port

MSP Technologycom LLC .... G 631 424-7542
  Centerport *(G-3505)*

WARM AIR HEATING/AC EQPT/SPLYS, WHOL: Ventilating Eqpt/Sply

DI Manufacturing Inc .... E 315 432-8977
  North Syracuse *(G-12959)*

WASHCLOTHS

1510 Associates LLC .... G 212 828-8720
  New York *(G-9006)*

WASHERS: Metal

Superior Washer & Gasket Corp .... D 631 273-8282
  Hauppauge *(G-6227)*

WASHERS: Plastic

Fibre Materials Corp .... E 516 349-1660
  Plainview *(G-13631)*

WASHERS: Spring, Metal

J T D Stamping Co Inc .... E 631 643-4144
  West Babylon *(G-16827)*

WATCH STRAPS, EXC METAL

International Time Products .... G 516 931-0005
  Jericho *(G-7105)*
Roma Industries LLC .... G 212 268-0723
  New York *(G-11931)*

WATCHCASES

American Time Mfg Ltd .... F 585 266-5120
  Rochester *(G-14217)*

WATCHES

Croton Watch Co Inc .... E 800 443-7639
  West Nyack *(G-16945)*
E Gluck Corporation .... C 718 784-0700
  Little Neck *(G-7531)*
First Sbf Holding Inc .... F 845 425-9882
  Valley Cottage *(G-16404)*
Geneva Watch Company Inc .... E 212 221-1177
  New York *(G-10320)*
Life Watch Technology Inc .... D 917 669-2428
  Flushing *(G-5273)*
Visage Swiss Watch LLC .... G 212 594-7991
  New York *(G-12580)*

WATCHES & PARTS, WHOLESALE

E Gluck Corporation .... C 718 784-0700
  Little Neck *(G-7531)*

WATER PURIFICATION EQPT: Household

Airgle Corporation .... E 866 501-7750
  Ronkonkoma *(G-14884)*
Atlantic Ultraviolet Corp .... E 631 234-3275
  Hauppauge *(G-6047)*
Water Energy Systems LLC .... G 844 822-7665
  New York *(G-12624)*

WATER SUPPLY

Ewt Holdings III Corp .... F 212 644-5900
  New York *(G-10151)*

WATER TREATMENT EQPT: Indl

Business Advisory Services .... G 718 337-3740
  Far Rockaway *(G-4926)*
City of Olean .... G 716 376-5694
  Olean *(G-13158)*
City of Oneonta .... G 607 433-3470
  Oneonta *(G-13200)*
Integrated Water Management ...... G 607 844-4276
  Dryden *(G-4346)*
Metro Group Inc .... D 718 392-3616
  Long Island City *(G-7841)*
Neptune Soft Water Inc .... F 315 446-5151
  Syracuse *(G-16017)*
New Windsor Waste Water Plant ... F 845 561-2550
  New Windsor *(G-8990)*
Ossining Village of Inc .... G 914 202-9668
  Ossining *(G-13349)*
R C Kolstad Water Corp .... G 585 216-2230
  Ontario *(G-13232)*
Water Treatment Services Inc .... G 914 241-2261
  Bedford Hills *(G-804)*

WATER: Mineral, Carbonated, Canned & Bottled, Etc

Global Brands Inc .... G 845 358-1212
  Nyack *(G-13068)*
Just Beverages LLC .... F 480 388-1133
  Glens Falls *(G-5699)*
New York Spring Water Inc .... E 212 777-4649
  New York *(G-11427)*
Nirvana Inc .... C 315 942-4900
  Forestport *(G-5338)*
Saratoga Spring Water Company ... E 518 584-6363
  Saratoga Springs *(G-15202)*

WATER: Pasteurized & Mineral, Bottled & Canned

Ariesun Inc .... E 866 274-3049
  Mount Vernon *(G-8708)*
Mayer Bros Apple Products Inc ..... D 716 668-1787
  West Seneca *(G-16980)*
Water Resources Group LLC .... G 631 824-9088
  Cold Spring Harbor *(G-3796)*

WATER: Pasteurized, Canned & Bottled, Etc

Crystal Rock LLC .... E 716 626-7460
  Buffalo *(G-2914)*
Let Water Be Water LLC .... G 212 627-2630
  New York *(G-11012)*
Superleaf LLC .... G 888 887-4318
  Brooklyn *(G-2650)*

WATERPROOFING COMPOUNDS

Penetron International Ltd .... F 631 941-9700
  East Setauket *(G-4507)*

WAVEGUIDES & FITTINGS

M W Microwave Corp .... F 516 295-1814
  Lawrence *(G-7419)*

WAX REMOVERS

Comfort Wax Incorporated .... F 718 204-7028
  Astoria *(G-431)*

WAXES: Mineral, Natural

Koster Keunen Waxes Ltd .... F 631 589-0400
  Sayville *(G-15241)*

WAXES: Paraffin

Industrial Raw Materials LLC .... F 212 688-8080
  Plainview *(G-13636)*
Kent Chemical Corporation .... E 212 521-1700
  New York *(G-10878)*

WAXES: Petroleum, Not Produced In Petroleum Refineries

Industrial Raw Materials LLC .... G 212 688-8080
  New York *(G-10634)*
Premier Ingridients Inc .... G 516 641-6763
  Great Neck *(G-5849)*

WEATHER STRIPS: Metal

Accurate Metal Weather Strip .... G 914 668-6042
  Mount Vernon *(G-8704)*

WEAVING MILL, BROADWOVEN FABRICS: Wool Or Similar Fabric

Loomstate LLC .... E 212 219-2300
  New York *(G-11060)*

WEDDING CHAPEL: Privately Operated

Silver Griffin Inc .... E 518 272-7771
  Troy *(G-16279)*

Employee Codes: A=Over 500 employees, B=251-500
C=101-250, D=51-100, E=20-50, F=10-19, G=5-9

WEIGHING MACHINERY & APPARATUS

WEIGHING MACHINERY & APPARATUS

Measupro Inc .... F 845 425-8777
  Spring Valley *(G-15618)*
Mettler-Toledo Inc .... C 607 257-6000
  Ithaca *(G-6896)*
S R Instruments Inc .... E 716 693-5977
  Tonawanda *(G-16216)*
Weighing & Systems Tech Inc .... G 518 274-2797
  Troy *(G-16288)*

WELDING & CUTTING APPARATUS & ACCESS, NEC

McAllisters Precision Wldg Inc .... F 518 221-3455
  Menands *(G-8406)*

WELDING EQPT

Apogee Translite Inc .... E 631 254-6975
  Deer Park *(G-4124)*
Lubow Machine Corp .... F 631 226-1700
  Copiague *(G-3936)*
Riverview Industries Inc .... G 845 265-5284
  Cold Spring *(G-3790)*
Vante Inc .... F 716 778-7691
  Newfane *(G-12813)*

WELDING EQPT & SPLYS WHOLESALERS

Haun Welding Supply Inc .... G 315 592-5012
  Fulton *(G-5474)*
Jacksons Welding LLC .... G 607 756-2725
  Cortland *(G-4054)*
Matheson Tri-Gas Inc .... F 518 439-0362
  Feura Bush *(G-5181)*

WELDING EQPT: Electrical

3krf LLC .... G 516 208-6824
  Oceanside *(G-13090)*
FWC Networks Inc .... F 718 408-1558
  Brooklyn *(G-2010)*

WELDING MACHINES & EQPT: Ultrasonic

Branson Ultrasonics Corp .... E 585 624-8000
  Honeoye Falls *(G-6553)*
Sonicor Inc .... F 631 920-6555
  West Babylon *(G-16861)*

WELDING REPAIR SVC

303 Contracting Inc .... E 716 896-2122
  Orchard Park *(G-13271)*
A & J Machine & Welding Inc .... F 631 845-7586
  Farmingdale *(G-4932)*
AAA Welding and Fabrication of .... G 585 254-2830
  Rochester *(G-14177)*
Accurate Welding Service Inc .... G 516 333-1730
  Westbury *(G-16988)*
Acro-Fab Ltd .... E 315 564-6688
  Hannibal *(G-5992)*
Airweld Inc .... G 631 924-6366
  Ridge *(G-14103)*
Aj Genco Mch Sp McHy Rdout Svc ...... F 716 664-4925
  Falconer *(G-4896)*
Allen Tool Phoenix Inc .... E 315 463-7533
  East Syracuse *(G-4518)*
Alliance Services Corp .... F 516 775-7600
  Floral Park *(G-5198)*
Alliance Welding & Steel Fabg .... F 516 775-7600
  Floral Park *(G-5199)*
Alloy Metal Works Inc .... G 631 694-8163
  Farmingdale *(G-4945)*
Alpine Machine Inc .... F 607 272-1344
  Ithaca *(G-6858)*
ARC TEC Wldg & Fabrication Inc .... G 718 982-9274
  Staten Island *(G-15659)*
Atlantis Equipment Corporation .... F 518 733-5910
  Stephentown *(G-15778)*
Barber Welding Inc .... E 315 834-6645
  Weedsport *(G-16772)*
Benemy Welding & Fabrication .... G 315 548-8500
  Phelps *(G-13553)*
Bms Manufacturing Co Inc .... E 607 535-2426
  Watkins Glen *(G-16718)*
Bracci Ironworks Inc .... F 718 629-2374
  Brooklyn *(G-1710)*
Brenseke George Wldg Ir Works .... G 631 271-4870
  Deer Park *(G-4135)*
Broadalbin Manufacturing Corp .... E 518 883-5313
  Broadalbin *(G-1239)*

Bruce Pierce .... G 716 731-9310
  Sanborn *(G-15142)*
C G & Son Machining Inc .... G 315 964-2430
  Williamstown *(G-17257)*
CBM Fabrications Inc .... E 518 399-8023
  Ballston Lake *(G-580)*
Certified Fabrications Inc .... F 716 731-8123
  Sanborn *(G-15144)*
Competicion Mower Repair .... G 516 280-6584
  Mineola *(G-8537)*
Cs Automation Inc .... E 315 524-5123
  Ontario *(G-13220)*
Custom Laser Inc .... E 716 434-8600
  Lockport *(G-7606)*
D & G Welding Inc .... G 716 873-3088
  Buffalo *(G-2918)*
Deck Bros Inc .... E 716 852-0262
  Buffalo *(G-2923)*
Dennies Manufacturing Inc .... E 585 393-4646
  Canandaigua *(G-3371)*
Donald Stefan .... G 716 492-1110
  Chaffee *(G-3561)*
Dorgan Welding Service .... G 315 462-9030
  Phelps *(G-13554)*
E B Industries LLC .... E 631 293-8565
  Farmingdale *(G-4991)*
Eagle Welding Machine .... G 315 594-1845
  Wolcott *(G-17300)*
Etna Tool & Die Corporation .... F 212 475-4350
  New York *(G-10133)*
Excelco/Newbrook Inc .... D 716 934-2644
  Silver Creek *(G-15471)*
F M L Industries Inc .... G 607 749-7273
  Homer *(G-6545)*
Flushing Boiler & Welding Co .... G 718 463-1266
  Brooklyn *(G-1988)*
Formac Welding Inc .... E 631 421-5525
  Huntington Station *(G-6743)*
Fuller Fabrications .... G 315 469-7415
  Jamesville *(G-7080)*
G & C Welding Co Inc .... E 516 883-3228
  Port Washington *(G-13839)*
Gasport Welding & Fabg Inc .... F 716 772-7205
  Gasport *(G-5572)*
Gc Mobile Services Inc .... G 914 736-9730
  Cortlandt Manor *(G-4075)*
Genco John .... G 716 483-5446
  Jamestown *(G-7028)*
General Welding & Fabg Inc .... G 716 652-0033
  Elma *(G-4662)*
General Welding & Fabg Inc .... G 716 681-8200
  Buffalo *(G-2987)*
Guthrie Heli-ARC Inc .... E 585 548-5053
  Bergen *(G-845)*
Hadfield Inc .... F 631 981-4314
  Ronkonkoma *(G-14938)*
Hadleys Fab-Weld Inc .... G 315 926-5101
  Marion *(G-8125)*
Hansen Steel .... E 585 398-2020
  Farmington *(G-5161)*
Hartman Enterprises Inc .... D 315 363-7300
  Oneida *(G-13178)*
Haskell Machine & Tool Inc .... F 607 749-2421
  Homer *(G-6546)*
Haun Welding Supply Inc .... F 607 846-2289
  Elmira *(G-4702)*
Haun Welding Supply Inc .... G 315 592-5012
  Fulton *(G-5474)*
Homer Iron Works LLC .... G 607 749-3963
  Homer *(G-6547)*
Huntington Welding & Iron .... G 631 423-3331
  Huntington Station *(G-6747)*
Ingleside Machine Co Inc .... D 585 924-3046
  Farmington *(G-5162)*
Jacksons Welding LLC .... G 607 756-2725
  Cortland *(G-4054)*
Kon Tat Group Corporation .... G 718 207-5022
  Brooklyn *(G-2179)*
L & S Metals Inc .... G 716 692-6865
  North Tonawanda *(G-12998)*
Lagasse Works Inc .... G 315 946-9202
  Lyons *(G-8000)*
Lagoe-Oswego Corp .... G 315 343-3160
  Rochester *(G-14495)*
Linita Design & Mfg Corp .... E 716 566-7753
  Lackawanna *(G-7270)*
M and M Industrial Welding .... G 631 451-6044
  Medford *(G-8286)*
M M Welding .... E 315 363-3980
  Oneida *(G-13180)*

Maple Grove Corp .... E 585 492-5286
  Arcade *(G-396)*
Maria Dionisio Welding Inc .... G 631 956-0815
  Lindenhurst *(G-7493)*
Maspeth Welding Inc .... E 718 497-5430
  Maspeth *(G-8181)*
Meades Welding and Fabricating .... G 631 581-1555
  Islip *(G-6849)*
Mega Tool & Mfg Corp .... E 607 734-8398
  Elmira *(G-4709)*
Miller Metal Fabricating Inc .... F 585 359-3400
  Rochester *(G-14534)*
Modern Mechanical Fab Inc .... G 518 298-5177
  Champlain *(G-3572)*
Mooradian Hydraulics & Eqp Co .... F 518 766-3866
  Castleton On Hudson *(G-3448)*
Ms Spares LLC .... G 607 223-3024
  Clay *(G-3709)*
New Age Ironworks Inc .... F 718 277-1895
  Brooklyn *(G-2366)*
New York Manufacturing Corp .... F 585 254-9353
  Rochester *(G-14553)*
North Country Welding Inc .... G 315 788-9718
  Watertown *(G-16689)*
NY Iron Inc .... F 718 302-9000
  Long Island City *(G-7859)*
Phillip J Ortiz Manufacturing .... G 845 226-7030
  Hopewell Junction *(G-6583)*
Phoenix Welding & Fabg Inc .... G 315 695-2223
  Phoenix *(G-13570)*
Pro-Tech Wldg Fabrication Inc .... E 585 436-9855
  Rochester *(G-14626)*
Qsf Inc .... G 585 247-6200
  Gates *(G-5577)*
Quality Industrial Services .... F 716 667-7703
  Orchard Park *(G-13319)*
Reliable Welding & Fabrication .... G 631 758-2637
  Patchogue *(G-13459)*
REO Welding Inc .... F 518 238-1022
  Cohoes *(G-3780)*
Rini Tank & Truck Service .... F 718 384-6606
  Brooklyn *(G-2514)*
Rj Welding & Fabricating Inc .... G 315 523-1288
  Clifton Springs *(G-3740)*
Robert M Brown .... F 607 426-6250
  Montour Falls *(G-8650)*
Rothe Welding Inc .... G 845 246-3051
  Saugerties *(G-15222)*
S & D Welding Corp .... G 631 454-0383
  West Babylon *(G-16855)*
S J B Fabrication .... F 716 895-0281
  Buffalo *(G-3200)*
Smithers Tools & Mch Pdts Inc .... D 845 876-3063
  Rhinebeck *(G-14070)*
Strecks Inc .... E 518 273-4410
  Watervliet *(G-16714)*
Tangent Machine & Tool Corp .... F 631 249-3088
  Farmingdale *(G-5134)*
Technapulse LLC .... F 631 234-8700
  Hauppauge *(G-6233)*
Tek Weld .... F 631 694-5503
  Hauppauge *(G-6235)*
Tracey Welding Co Inc .... G 518 756-6309
  Coeymans *(G-3770)*
Walters & Walters Inc .... F 347 202-8535
  Bronx *(G-1493)*
Watkins Welding and Mch Sp Inc .... G 914 949-6168
  White Plains *(G-17209)*
Waynes Welding Inc .... E 315 768-6146
  Yorkville *(G-17547)*
Welding and Brazing Svcs Inc .... G 607 397-1009
  Richfield Springs *(G-14075)*
Welding Chapter of New York 212 481-1496
  New York *(G-12635)*
West Metal Works Inc .... E 716 895-4900
  Buffalo *(G-3278)*

WELDING SPLYS, EXC GASES: Wholesalers

Austin Industries Inc .... G 585 589-1353
  Albion *(G-165)*

WELDING TIPS: Heat Resistant, Metal

JE Monahan Fabrications LLC .... F 518 761-0414
  Queensbury *(G-14014)*
National Maint Contg Corp .... D 716 285-1583
  Niagara Falls *(G-12866)*

PRODUCT SECTION

WELDMENTS

Glenridge Fabricators Inc .... F 718 456-2297
  Glendale *(G-5670)*
Industrial Fabricating Corp .... E 315 437-8234
  East Syracuse *(G-4554)*
Miller Metal Fabricating Inc .... G 585 359-3400
  Rochester *(G-14534)*

WHEELBARROWS

Clopay Ames True Tmper Hldng .... F 516 938-5544
  Jericho *(G-7096)*

WHEELCHAIR LIFTS

S & H Enterprises Inc .... G 888 323-8755
  Queensbury *(G-14023)*

WHEELCHAIRS

Crosley Medical Products Inc .... F 631 595-2547
  Deer Park *(G-4144)*
Future Mobility Products Inc .... E 716 783-9130
  Buffalo *(G-2976)*
Gadabout USA Wheelchairs Inc .... F 585 338-2110
  Rochester *(G-14407)*
Palmer Industries Inc .... G 607 754-8741
  Endicott *(G-4829)*
Palmer Industries Inc .... G 607 754-2957
  Endicott *(G-4830)*
Palmer Industries Inc .... G 607 754-1954
  Endicott *(G-4831)*
Skil-Care Corporation .... C 914 963-2040
  Yonkers *(G-17502)*
Vcp Mobility Inc .... B 718 356-7827
  Staten Island *(G-15773)*
VSM Investors LLC .... G 212 351-1600
  New York *(G-12597)*

WHEELS

Wheel & Tire Depot Ex Corp .... G 914 375-2100
  Yonkers *(G-17514)*

WHEELS & PARTS

Bam Enterprises Inc .... G 716 773-7634
  Grand Island *(G-5767)*
Factory Wheel Warehouse Inc .... G 516 605-2131
  Plainview *(G-13630)*
Motor Components LLC .... D 607 737-8011
  Elmira Heights *(G-4724)*

WHEELS: Abrasive

Jta USA Inc .... G 718 722-0902
  Brooklyn *(G-2154)*

WHEELS: Buffing & Polishing

Barker Brothers Incorporated .... D 718 456-6400
  Ridgewood *(G-14114)*
Dimanco Inc .... G 315 797-0470
  Utica *(G-16347)*
Divine Brothers Company .... C 315 797-0470
  Utica *(G-16350)*

WHEELS: Iron & Steel, Locomotive & Car

Nitro Wheels Inc .... F 716 337-0709
  North Collins *(G-12946)*

WHEELS: Rolled, Locomotive

Higher Power Industries Inc .... G 914 709-9800
  Yonkers *(G-17470)*

WIGS & HAIRPIECES

M and J Hair Center Inc .... F 516 872-1010
  Garden City *(G-5530)*
Moti Inc .... F 718 436-4280
  Brooklyn *(G-2340)*

WIND TUNNELS

United Wind Inc .... F 800 268-9896
  Brooklyn *(G-2724)*

WINDINGS: Coil, Electronic

American Precision Inds Inc .... C 716 691-9100
  Amherst *(G-227)*

American Precision Inds Inc .... D 716 652-3600
  East Aurora *(G-4390)*
American Precision Inds Inc .... D 585 496-5755
  Arcade *(G-386)*
Caddell Burns Manufacturing Co .... E 631 757-1772
  Northport *(G-13026)*
Mohawk Electro Techniques Inc .... D 315 896-2661
  Barneveld *(G-615)*
Precision Electronics Inc .... F 631 842-4900
  Copiague *(G-3943)*

WINDMILLS: Electric Power Generation

EDP Renewables North Amer LLC .... G 518 426-1650
  Albany *(G-76)*
Wind Solutions LLC .... G 518 813-8029
  Esperance *(G-4847)*

WINDOW & DOOR FRAMES

Action Bullet Resistant .... F 631 422-0888
  West Islip *(G-16933)*
D D & L Inc .... F 607 729-9131
  Binghamton *(G-902)*
Deronde Doors and Frames Inc .... F 716 895-8888
  Buffalo *(G-2927)*
J Sussman Inc .... E 718 297-0228
  Jamaica *(G-6958)*
Jaidan Industries Inc .... F 516 944-3650
  Port Washington *(G-13849)*
Kasson & Keller Inc .... A 518 853-3421
  Fonda *(G-5320)*
Master Window & Door Corp .... F 718 782-5407
  Brooklyn *(G-2284)*
New Bgnnngs Win Door Dstrs LLC .... F 845 214-0698
  Poughkeepsie *(G-13939)*
Sunrise Door Solutions .... G 631 464-4139
  Copiague *(G-3953)*
Window Rama Enterprises Inc .... G 631 462-9054
  Commack *(G-3873)*

WINDOW BLIND REPAIR SVCS

Window-Fix Inc .... E 718 854-3475
  Brooklyn *(G-2773)*

WINDOW FRAMES & SASHES: Plastic

Hart To Hart Industries Inc .... G 716 492-2709
  Chaffee *(G-3562)*
JSM Vinyl Products Inc .... F 516 775-4520
  New Hyde Park *(G-8890)*
Northeast Windows Usa Inc .... E 516 378-6577
  Merrick *(G-8425)*

WINDOW FRAMES, MOLDING & TRIM: Vinyl

Eastern Enterprise Corp .... F 718 727-8600
  Staten Island *(G-15690)*
Kasson & Keller Inc .... A 518 853-3421
  Fonda *(G-5320)*
Tri-State Window Factory Corp .... D 631 667-8600
  Deer Park *(G-4242)*
Vinyline Window and Door Inc .... F 914 476-3500
  Yonkers *(G-17513)*
Window Tech Systems Inc .... E 518 899-9000
  Ballston Spa *(G-610)*

WINDOW TRIMMING SVCS

New Business Solutions Inc .... F 631 789-1500
  Amityville *(G-315)*

WINDOWS, LOUVER: Metal

Grover Aluminum Products Inc .... E 631 475-3500
  Patchogue *(G-13446)*

WINDOWS: Wood

J Zeluck Inc .... E 718 251-8060
  Brooklyn *(G-2127)*
Kelly Window Systems Inc .... E 631 420-8500
  Farmingdale *(G-5033)*
Pella Corporation .... B 607 223-2023
  Johnson City *(G-7131)*
Pella Corporation .... B 607 231-8550
  Johnson City *(G-7132)*
Pella Corporation .... B 607 238-2812
  Johnson City *(G-7133)*
Pella Corporation .... B 516 385-3622
  Albertson *(G-161)*
Pella Corporation .... B 607 238-2812
  Johnson City *(G-7134)*

WIRE & WIRE PRDTS

Pella Corporation .... B 516 385-3622
  Albertson *(G-162)*
Pella Corporation .... B 607 231-8550
  Johnson City *(G-7135)*
Royal Windows Mfg Corp .... E 631 435-8888
  Bay Shore *(G-735)*
Stealth Archtctral Windows Inc .... F 718 821-6666
  Brooklyn *(G-2622)*
Window Technologies LLC .... G 402 464-0202
  New York *(G-12668)*

WINE & DISTILLED ALCOHOLIC BEVERAGES WHOLESALERS

Constellation Brands Inc .... D 585 678-7100
  Victor *(G-16493)*
Liquid Management Partners LLC .... F 516 775-5050
  New Hyde Park *(G-8892)*

WINE CELLARS, BONDED: Wine, Blended

Hickory Road Land Co LLC .... G 607 243-9114
  Dundee *(G-4355)*
Solstars Inc .... G 212 605-0430
  New York *(G-12151)*
Tickle Hill Winery .... G 607 546-7740
  Hector *(G-6286)*
Wine Services Inc .... G 631 722-3800
  Riverhead *(G-14174)*

WIRE

Bekaert Corporation .... E 716 830-1321
  Amherst *(G-229)*
CFS Enterprises Inc .... E 718 585-0500
  Bronx *(G-1295)*
EB Acquisitions LLC .... D 212 355-3310
  New York *(G-10022)*
Hanes Supply Inc .... E 518 438-0139
  Albany *(G-84)*
Island Industries Corp .... G 631 451-8825
  Coram *(G-3968)*
Lee Spring Company LLC .... C 718 362-5183
  Brooklyn *(G-2207)*
Liberty Fabrication Inc .... G 718 495-5735
  Brooklyn *(G-2216)*
Nupro Technologies LLC .... F 412 422-5922
  Canandaigua *(G-3379)*
Owl Wire & Cable LLC .... G 315 697-2011
  Canastota *(G-3396)*
Spectrum Cable Corporation .... G 585 235-7714
  Rochester *(G-14719)*
Tappan Wire & Cable Inc .... C 845 353-9000
  Blauvelt *(G-971)*
Web Associates Inc .... G 716 883-3377
  Buffalo *(G-3275)*

WIRE & CABLE: Aluminum

Irtronics Instruments Inc .... F 914 693-6291
  Ardsley *(G-404)*
SI Partners Inc .... G 516 433-1415
  Hicksville *(G-6421)*

WIRE & WIRE PRDTS

369 River Road Inc .... E 716 694-5001
  North Tonawanda *(G-12970)*
Abbott Industries Inc .... E 718 291-0800
  Jamaica *(G-6926)*
Albest Metal Stamping Corp .... D 718 388-6000
  Brooklyn *(G-1575)*
All-Lifts Incorporated .... E 518 465-3461
  Albany *(G-42)*
American Wire Tie Inc .... E 716 337-2412
  North Collins *(G-12942)*
Angelica Spring Company Inc .... F 585 466-7892
  Angelica *(G-377)*
Bayshore Wire Products Corp .... F 631 451-8825
  Coram *(G-3964)*
Better Wire Products Inc .... E 716 883-3377
  Buffalo *(G-2862)*
Cable Management Solutions Inc .... E 631 674-0004
  Bay Shore *(G-678)*
Clover Wire Forming Co Inc .... E 914 375-0400
  Yonkers *(G-17444)*
Compar Manufacturing Corp .... E 212 304-2777
  New York *(G-9750)*
Continental Cordage Corp .... D 315 655-9800
  Cazenovia *(G-3470)*
Cuddeback Machining Inc .... G 585 392-5889
  Hilton *(G-6443)*

Employee Codes: A=Over 500 employees, B=251-500
C=101-250, D=51-100, E=20-50, F=10-19, G=5-9

WIRE & WIRE PRDTS

Engineering Mfg Tech LLC ....D 607 754-7111
Endicott *(G-4813)*

Flanagans Creative Disp Inc ....E 845 858-2542
Port Jervis *(G-13806)*

Flatcut LLC ....G 212 542-5732
Brooklyn *(G-1984)*

Hitachi Metals America Ltd ....E 914 694-9200
Purchase *(G-13974)*

Interstate Wood Products Inc ....E 631 842-4488
Amityville *(G-296)*

Kehr-Buffalo Wire Frame Co Inc ....E 716 897-2288
Buffalo *(G-3044)*

Lubow Machine Corp ....F 631 226-1700
Copiague *(G-3936)*

Magic Novelty Co Inc ....E 212 304-2777
New York *(G-11131)*

Oneida Sales & Service Inc ....E 716 822-8205
Buffalo *(G-3123)*

Peck & Hale LLC ....E 631 589-2510
West Sayville *(G-16966)*

Quality Industrial Services ....F 716 667-7703
Orchard Park *(G-13319)*

Rose Fence Inc ....F 516 223-0777
Baldwin *(G-560)*

SCI Bore Inc ....G 212 674-7128
New York *(G-12021)*

Selectrode Industries Inc ....G 631 547-5470
Huntington Station *(G-6760)*

Sigmund Cohn Corp ....D 914 664-5300
Mount Vernon *(G-8780)*

Teka Precision Inc ....G 845 753-1900
Nyack *(G-13072)*

Trylon Wire & Metal Works Inc ....E 718 542-4472
Bronx *(G-1480)*

Utility Engineering Co ....F 845 735-8900
Pearl River *(G-13492)*

WIRE CLOTH & WOVEN WIRE PRDTS, MADE FROM PURCHASED WIRE

G Bopp USA Inc ....G 845 296-1065
Wappingers Falls *(G-16589)*

Sinclair International Company ....E 518 798-2361
Queensbury *(G-14025)*

WIRE FABRIC: Welded Steel

Technical Wldg Fabricators LLC ....F 518 463-2229
Albany *(G-140)*

WIRE FENCING & ACCESS WHOLESALERS

Master-Halco Inc ....F 631 585-8150
Ronkonkoma *(G-14966)*

WIRE MATERIALS: Copper

Camden Wire Co Inc ....A 315 245-3800
Camden *(G-3341)*

International Wire Group ....F 315 245-3800
Camden *(G-3343)*

Omega Wire Inc ....D 315 689-7115
Jordan *(G-7158)*

Omega Wire Inc ....B 315 245-3800
Camden *(G-3346)*

Owi Corporation ....G 315 245-4305
Camden *(G-3347)*

Performance Wire & Cable Inc ....F 315 245-2594
Camden *(G-3348)*

WIRE MATERIALS: Steel

American Wire Tie Inc ....E 716 337-2412
North Collins *(G-12942)*

Continental Cordage Corp ....D 315 655-9800
Cazenovia *(G-3470)*

Hitachi Metals America Ltd ....E 914 694-9200
Purchase *(G-13974)*

Hohmann & Barnard Inc ....E 631 234-0600
Hauppauge *(G-6118)*

Omega Wire Inc ....D 315 689-7115
Jordan *(G-7158)*

Rolling Gate Supply Corp ....G 718 366-5258
Glendale *(G-5677)*

Rose Fence Inc ....F 516 223-0777
Baldwin *(G-560)*

Sigmund Cohn Corp ....D 914 664-5300
Mount Vernon *(G-8780)*

WIRE PRDTS: Ferrous Or Iron, Made In Wiredrawing Plants

Forsyth Industries Inc ....E 716 652-1070
Buffalo *(G-2968)*

Handy & Harman ....E 914 461-1300
White Plains *(G-17145)*

WIRE PRDTS: Steel & Iron

Handy & Harman Ltd ....A 212 520-2300
New York *(G-10450)*

Sph Group Holdings LLC ....F 212 520-2300
New York *(G-12186)*

WIRE WHOLESALERS

Awt Supply Corp ....G 516 437-9105
Elmont *(G-4730)*

WIRE: Barbed

Cobra Systems Inc ....F 845 338-6675
Bloomington *(G-987)*

WIRE: Barbed & Twisted

Cobra Manufacturing Corp ....G 845 514-2505
Lake Katrine *(G-7294)*

WIRE: Communication

Caldwell Bennett Inc ....E 315 337-8540
Oriskany *(G-13330)*

Corning Optcal Cmmncations LLC ....F 607 974-7543
Corning *(G-3990)*

WIRE: Mesh

Aeroflex Incorporated ....B 516 694-6700
Plainview *(G-13608)*

WIRE: Nonferrous

Camden Wire Co Inc ....A 315 245-3800
Camden *(G-3341)*

Colonial Wire & Cable Co Inc ....D 631 234-8500
Hauppauge *(G-6069)*

Continental Cordage Corp ....D 315 655-9800
Cazenovia *(G-3470)*

Convergent Cnnctivity Tech Inc ....G 845 651-5250
Florida *(G-5218)*

Corning Cable Systems Cr Un ....G 607 974-9000
Corning *(G-3982)*

Corning Incorporated ....G 646 521-9600
New York *(G-9786)*

Cortland Cable Company Inc ....E 607 753-8276
Cortland *(G-4039)*

International Wire Group Inc ....B 315 245-2000
Camden *(G-3344)*

Jaguar Industries Inc ....F 845 947-1800
Haverstraw *(G-6261)*

Kris-Tech Wire Company Inc ....E 315 339-5268
Rome *(G-14845)*

Leviton Manufacturing Co Inc ....B 631 812-6000
Melville *(G-8363)*

Rdi Inc ....F 914 773-1000
Mount Kisco *(G-8686)*

Rockland Insulated Wire Cable ....G 845 429-3103
Haverstraw *(G-6263)*

Siemens Corporation ....F 202 434-7800
New York *(G-12084)*

Siemens USA Holdings Inc ....B 212 258-4000
New York *(G-12086)*

Sinclair Technologies Inc ....E 716 874-3682
Hamburg *(G-5966)*

Steelflex Electro Corp ....D 516 226-4466
Lindenhurst *(G-7506)*

Tappan Wire & Cable Inc ....C 845 353-9000
Blauvelt *(G-971)*

United Wire Technologies Inc ....F 315 623-7203
Constantia *(G-3908)*

Universal Builders Supply Inc ....F 845 758-8801
Red Hook *(G-14042)*

Whirlwind Music Distrs Inc ....D 800 733-9473
Rochester *(G-14790)*

WIRE: Nonferrous, Appliance Fixture

County WD Applnc & TV Srvc of ....F 585 328-7417
Rochester *(G-14311)*

WIRE: Steel, Insulated Or Armored

Able Industries Inc ....F 914 739-5685
Cortlandt Manor *(G-4072)*

Aerospace Wire & Cable Inc ....E 718 358-2345
College Point *(G-3801)*

WOMEN'S & CHILDREN'S CLOTHING WHOLESALERS, NEC

Alpha 6 Distributions LLC ....F 516 801-8290
Locust Valley *(G-7659)*

Arteast LLC ....G 212 965-8787
New York *(G-9267)*

Bilco Industries Inc ....F 917 783-5008
New York *(G-9447)*

D-C Theatricks ....G 716 847-0180
Buffalo *(G-2919)*

Design Archives Inc ....G 212 768-0617
New York *(G-9904)*

Eb Couture Ltd ....E 212 912-0190
New York *(G-10023)*

Grand Knitting Mills Inc ....E 631 226-5000
Amityville *(G-289)*

Halmode Apparel Inc ....A 212 819-9114
New York *(G-10442)*

Hampshire Sub II Inc ....D 631 321-0923
New York *(G-10446)*

JM Originals Inc ....C 845 647-3003
Ellenville *(G-4648)*

Kate Spade & Company ....B 212 354-4900
New York *(G-10854)*

Kenmar Shirts Inc ....E 718 824-3880
Bronx *(G-1375)*

Lloyds Fashions Inc ....G 631 435-3353
Brentwood *(G-1187)*

M Hidary & Co Inc ....D 212 736-6540
New York *(G-11102)*

Maggy Boutique Ltd ....E 212 997-5222
New York *(G-11128)*

Mango Usa Inc ....E 718 998-6050
Brooklyn *(G-2260)*

Moresca Clothing and Costume ....F 845 331-6012
Ulster Park *(G-16309)*

Mystic Apparel LLC ....E 212 279-2466
New York *(G-11357)*

New York Popular Inc ....D 718 499-2020
Brooklyn *(G-2376)*

Only Hearts Ltd ....E 718 783-3218
New York *(G-11523)*

Penfli Industries Inc ....F 212 947-6080
Great Neck *(G-5848)*

Soho Apparel Ltd ....G 212 840-1109
New York *(G-12146)*

Therese The Childrens Collectn ....G 518 346-2315
Schenectady *(G-15328)*

United Knitwear International ....G 212 354-2920
New York *(G-12484)*

Ying Ke Youth Age Group Inc ....F 929 402-8458
Dix Hills *(G-4323)*

WOMEN'S & GIRLS' SPORTSWEAR WHOLESALERS

Argee America Inc ....G 212 768-9840
New York *(G-9250)*

Casuals Etc Inc ....D 212 838-1319
New York *(G-9598)*

Danice Stores Inc ....F 212 665-0389
New York *(G-9858)*

F & J Designs Inc ....G 212 302-8755
New York *(G-10167)*

Jaxis Inc ....G 212 302-7611
Brooklyn *(G-2134)*

Lollytogs Ltd ....D 212 502-6000
New York *(G-11053)*

Morelle Products Ltd ....F 212 391-8070
New York *(G-11329)*

Noah Enterprises Ltd ....G 212 736-2888
New York *(G-11464)*

S2 Sportswear Inc ....F 347 335-0713
Brooklyn *(G-2550)*

Sterling Possessions Ltd ....G 212 594-0418
New York *(G-12221)*

WOMEN'S CLOTHING STORES

Amj DOT LLC ....G 718 775-3288
Brooklyn *(G-1610)*

Elie Tahari Ltd ....G 212 398-2622
New York *(G-10054)*

PRODUCT SECTION

WOODWORK: Interior & Ornamental, NEC

Joseph (uk) Inc ....G 212 570-0077
  New York (G-10802)
Kozinn+sons Merchant Tailors ....E 212 643-1916
  New York (G-10921)
Mee Accessories LLC ....C 917 262-1000
  New York (G-11244)
Mega Sourcing Inc ....G 646 682-0304
  Merrick (G-8424)
Uniqlo USA LLC ....F 877 486-4756
  New York (G-12479)

WOMEN'S CLOTHING STORES: Ready-To-Wear

Hillary Merchant Inc ....G 646 575-9242
  New York (G-10521)
Phillips-Van Heusen Europe ....F 212 381-3500
  New York (G-11668)
Pvh Corp ....D 212 381-3500
  New York (G-11780)
Stallion Inc ....F 718 706-0111
  Long Island City (G-7910)

WOMEN'S SPECIALTY CLOTHING STORES

Dvf Studio LLC ....D 212 741-6607
  New York (G-9993)
Dvf Studio LLC ....G 646 576-8009
  New York (G-9994)

WOMEN'S SPORTSWEAR STORES

A H Schreiber Co Inc ....D 212 594-7234
  New York (G-9036)
Central Apparel Group Ltd ....F 212 868-6505
  New York (G-9614)
Mainly Monograms Inc ....E 845 624-4923
  West Nyack (G-16949)
Royal Tees Inc ....G 845 357-9448
  Suffern (G-15820)

WOOD FENCING WHOLESALERS

Interstate Wood Products Inc ....E 631 842-4488
  Amityville (G-296)
Master-Halco Inc ....F 631 585-8150
  Ronkonkoma (G-14966)

WOOD PRDTS

Aid Wood Working ....F 631 244-7768
  Bohemia (G-1006)
Meadowwood NY LLC ....G 212 729-5400
  New York (G-11230)

WOOD PRDTS: Beekeeping Splys

Betterbee Inc ....F 518 314-0575
  Greenwich (G-5905)
Northast Ctr For Bekeeping LLC ....F 800 632-3379
  Greenwich (G-5910)

WOOD PRDTS: Clothespins

Green Renewable Inc ....E 518 658-2233
  Berlin (G-855)

WOOD PRDTS: Display Forms, Boot & Shoe

Encore Retail Systems Inc ....F 718 385-3443
  Mamaroneck (G-8066)

WOOD PRDTS: Engraved

Lanwood Industries Inc ....E 718 786-3000
  Bay Shore (G-709)

WOOD PRDTS: Furniture Inlays, Veneers

American Woods & Veneers Works ....E 718 937-2195
  Long Island City (G-7692)

WOOD PRDTS: Jalousies, Glass, Wood Framed

Paul David Enterprises Inc ....G 646 667-5530
  New York (G-11599)

WOOD PRDTS: Ladders & Stepladders

York Ladder Inc ....F 718 784-6666
  Long Island City (G-7959)

WOOD PRDTS: Laundry

American Casino Equipment Mfg ....F 631 242-2440
  Deer Park (G-4119)
Grohe America Inc ....G 212 206-8820
  New York (G-10410)

WOOD PRDTS: Mantels

Funda-Mantels LLC ....G 631 924-1404
  Mastic (G-8235)

WOOD PRDTS: Moldings, Unfinished & Prefinished

Adriatic Wood Products Inc ....E 718 922-4621
  Brooklyn (G-1562)
Attica Millwork Inc ....F 585 591-2333
  Attica (G-470)
Fire Island Sea Clam Co Inc ....G 631 589-2199
  West Sayville (G-16964)
Old World Mouldings Inc ....G 631 563-8660
  Bohemia (G-1109)
Scanga Woodworking Corp ....E 845 265-9115
  Cold Spring (G-3791)
Spiegel Woodworks Inc ....F 845 336-8090
  Kingston (G-7239)

WOOD PRDTS: Mulch Or Sawdust

Premium Mulch & Materials Inc ....F 631 320-3666
  Coram (G-3972)
Wholesale Mulch & Sawdust Inc ....G 607 687-2637
  Owego (G-13387)

WOOD PRDTS: Novelties, Fiber

Cowee Forest Products Inc ....E 518 658-2233
  Berlin (G-854)
Graphics Slution Providers Inc ....G 845 677-5088
  Lagrangeville (G-7278)
Ryers Creek Corp ....E 607 523-6617
  Corning (G-4000)

WOOD PRDTS: Outdoor, Structural

Amish Structure ....G 607 257-1070
  Dryden (G-4344)
Wolski Wood Works Inc ....G 718 577-9816
  Flushing (G-5313)

WOOD PRDTS: Panel Work

Empire Building Products Inc ....G 518 695-6094
  Schuylerville (G-15340)

WOOD PRDTS: Rulers & Rules

Aakron Rule Corp ....C 716 542-5483
  Akron (G-17)

WOOD PRDTS: Shavings & Packaging, Excelsior

RWS Manufacturing Inc ....G 518 361-1657
  Queensbury (G-14022)

WOOD PRDTS: Shoe Trees

R P M Industries Inc ....E 315 255-1105
  Auburn (G-512)

WOOD PRDTS: Signboards

Paramount Graphix ....G 845 367-5003
  Port Jervis (G-13813)

WOOD PRDTS: Silo Staves

Unadilla Silo Company Inc ....D 607 369-9341
  Sidney (G-15466)

WOOD PRDTS: Survey Stakes

T Eason Land Surveyor ....G 631 474-2200
  Port Jeff STA (G-13795)

WOOD PRDTS: Trellises

Finger Lakes Trellis Supply ....G 315 904-4007
  Williamson (G-17252)

WOOD PRDTS: Trophy Bases

Cherry Creek Woodcraft Inc ....E 716 988-3211
  South Dayton (G-15540)
M A Moslow & Bros Inc ....E 716 896-2950
  Buffalo (G-3070)

WOOD PRDTS: Window Backs, Store Or Lunchroom, Prefabricated

Vitarose Corp of America ....G 718 951-9700
  Brooklyn (G-2751)

WOOD PRDTS: Yard Sticks

Cfp Purchasing Inc ....G 705 806-0383
  Flushing (G-5238)

WOOD PRODUCTS: Reconstituted

Bedford Wdwrk Instllations Inc ....G 914 764-9434
  Bedford (G-791)
Northeastern Products Corp ....E 518 623-3161
  Warrensburg (G-16602)
Zircar Refr Composites Inc ....F 845 651-2200
  Florida (G-5224)

WOOD TREATING: Creosoting

Colorspec Coatings Intl Inc ....F 631 472-8251
  Holbrook (G-6468)
Osmose Holdings Inc ....A 716 882-5905
  Depew (G-4291)

WOOD TREATING: Flooring, Block

Wego International Floors LLC ....F 516 487-3510
  Great Neck (G-5868)

WOOD TREATING: Structural Lumber & Timber

Bestway Enterprises Inc ....E 607 753-8261
  Cortland (G-4034)
Bestway of New York Inc ....E 607 753-8261
  Cortland (G-4035)
Genesee Reserve Buffalo LLC ....E 716 824-3116
  Buffalo (G-2988)

WOODWORK & TRIM: Interior & Ornamental

Beaver Creek Industries Inc ....G 607 545-6382
  Canaseraga (G-3391)
Inform Studio Inc ....F 718 401-6149
  Bronx (G-1364)
Miller Blaker Inc ....D 718 665-3930
  Bronx (G-1401)
P H Custom Woodworking Corp ....E 917 801-1444
  Bronx (G-1419)
Props Displays & Interiors ....F 212 620-3840
  New York (G-11759)
Upstate Door Inc ....D 585 786-3880
  Warsaw (G-16607)
Vander Heyden Woodworking ....G 212 242-0525
  New York (G-12523)
Wood Innovations of Suffolk ....G 631 698-2345
  Medford (G-8297)

WOODWORK: Carved & Turned

Architectural Dctg Co LLC ....E 845 483-1340
  Poughkeepsie (G-13906)
Lanza Corp ....G 914 937-6360
  Port Chester (G-13778)
Superior Wood Turnings ....F 716 483-1254
  Jamestown (G-7069)

WOODWORK: Interior & Ornamental, NEC

A Losee & Sons ....G 516 676-3060
  Glen Cove (G-5621)
American Wood Column Corp ....G 718 782-3163
  Brooklyn (G-1608)
Bauerschmidt & Sons Inc ....D 718 528-3500
  Jamaica (G-6934)
Brauen Construction ....G 585 492-0042
  Arcade (G-390)
Custom Wood Inc ....G 718 927-4700
  Brooklyn (G-1828)
DAngelo Home Collections Inc ....G 917 267-8920
  Warwick (G-16609)
DC Contracting & Building Corp ....F 631 385-1117
  Huntington Station (G-6740)

Employee Codes: A=Over 500 employees, B=251-500
C=101-250, D=51-100, E=20-50, F=10-19, G=5-9

WOODWORK: Interior & Ornamental, NEC

Ignelzi Interiors Inc ....E....... 718 464-0279
  Queens Village (G-13995)
Kng Construction Co Inc ....F....... 212 595-1451
  Warwick (G-16615)
Michael Bernstein Design Assoc ....E....... 718 456-9277
  Brooklyn (G-2313)
Nordic Interior Inc ....C....... 718 456-7000
  College Point (G-3824)
Zeller Woodworks LLC ....F....... 585 254-7607
  Rochester (G-14803)

WOOL: Grease

Sivko Furs Inc ....G....... 607 698-4827
  Canisteo (G-3405)

WOVEN WIRE PRDTS, NEC

Joldeson One Aerospace Inds ....D....... 718 848-7396
  Ozone Park (G-13406)

WRITING FOR PUBLICATION SVCS

Mosby Holdings Corp ....G....... 212 309-8100
  New York (G-11332)

X-RAY EQPT & TUBES

Air Techniques Inc ....B....... 516 433-7676
  Melville (G-8324)
American Access Care LLC ....F....... 631 582-9729
  Hauppauge (G-6038)
Biodex Medical Systems Inc ....C....... 631 924-9000
  Shirley (G-15439)
Dra Imaging PC ....E....... 845 296-1057
  Wappingers Falls (G-16586)
Flow X Ray Corporation ....D....... 631 242-9729
  Deer Park (G-4164)
Mitegen LLC ....G....... 607 266-8877
  Ithaca (G-6898)

Multiwire Laboratories Ltd ....G....... 607 257-3378
  Ithaca (G-6900)
New York Imaging Service Inc ....F....... 716 834-8022
  Tonawanda (G-16202)
Phantom Laboratory Inc ....F....... 518 692-1190
  Greenwich (G-5911)
Photo Medic Equipment Inc ....D....... 631 242-6600
  Deer Park (G-4213)
R M F Health Management L L C ....E....... 718 854-5400
  Wantagh (G-16583)
RC Imaging Inc ....G....... 585 392-4336
  Hilton (G-6446)
Surescan Corporation ....E....... 607 321-0042
  Binghamton (G-947)
VJ Technologies Inc ....E....... 631 589-8800
  Bohemia (G-1151)
Wolf X-Ray Corporation ....D....... 631 242-9729
  Deer Park (G-4252)

X-RAY EQPT REPAIR SVCS

RC Imaging Inc ....G....... 585 392-4336
  Hilton (G-6446)

YARN & YARN SPINNING

Advanced Yarn Technologies Inc ....E....... 518 239-6600
  Durham (G-4378)
Colortex Inc ....G....... 212 564-2000
  New York (G-9734)
Missiontex Inc ....G....... 718 532-9053
  Brooklyn (G-2327)
National Spinning Co Inc ....E....... 212 382-6400
  New York (G-11374)
United Thread Mills Corp ....G....... 516 536-3900
  Oceanside (G-13124)

YARN MILLS: Twisting

Majestic Rayon Corporation ....E....... 212 929-6443
  New York (G-11140)

YARN WHOLESALERS

Colortex Inc ....G....... 212 564-2000
  New York (G-9734)
Great Adirondack Yarn Company ....F....... 518 843-3381
  Amsterdam (G-349)
National Spinning Co Inc ....E....... 212 382-6400
  New York (G-11374)

YARN: Embroidery, Spun

Printz and Patternz LLC ....G....... 518 944-6020
  Schenectady (G-15311)

YARN: Natural & Animal Fiber, Spun

Great Adirondack Yarn Company ....F....... 518 843-3381
  Amsterdam (G-349)

YARN: Specialty & Novelty

A Thousand Cranes Inc ....F....... 212 724-9596
  New York (G-9039)
K F I Inc ....G....... 516 546-2904
  Roosevelt (G-15030)
La Lame Inc ....G....... 212 921-9770
  New York (G-10947)

YARN: Weaving, Twisting, Winding Or Spooling

Marsha Fleisher ....F....... 845 679-6500
  Woodstock (G-17380)

YOGURT WHOLESALERS

Fage USA Holdings ....G....... 518 762-5912
  Johnstown (G-7144)
Kesso Foods Inc ....G....... 718 777-5303
  East Elmhurst (G-4415)